To Margaret, my very dear
and favorite friend.
Happy Birthday!

With my love
for always,
Margy

The Concise Baker's Biographical Dictionary of Musicians

The Concise Baker's Biographical Dictionary of Musicians

Nicolas Slonimsky

SCHIRMER BOOKS
A Division of Macmillan, Inc.
NEW YORK

Schirmer Books
A Division of Macmillan, Inc.
866 Third Avenue, New York, N.Y. 10022

Collier Macmillan Canada, Inc.

Library of Congress Catalog Card Number: **87-32328**

Printed in the United States of America

printing number
  2 3 4 5 6 7 8 9 10

Library of Congress Cataloging-in-Publication Data

Baker, Theodore, 1851-1934.
  The concise Baker's biographical dictionary of
musicians.

  Abridged version of: Baker's Biographical dictionary
of musicians, 7th ed.
  Includes bibliographies.
  1. Music—Bio-bibliography. I. Slonimsky,
Nicolas, 1894-   . II. Title.
ML105.B16 1988   780'.92'2 [B]   87-32328
ISBN 0-02-872411-9

Preface

Baker's is a household name for me. I have been associated with *Baker's Biographical Dictionary of Musicians* since 1949, when I was asked by its publisher, G. Schirmer, to prepare a supplement to its Fourth Edition. I applied to my job conscientiously, adding a number of entries on modern European and American composers and performers, with a generous infusion of new Soviet musicians. I made good, and as a result, I was entrusted with compiling an entirely new Fifth Edition. Published in 1958 in a large single volume of 1,855 pages, it proceeded from a medieval abbot named Aaron to the Swiss composer Zwyssig. The book was greeted with rousing plaudits in the press. TIME magazine called me a Musical Supersleuth. A New York classical music radio station put out a special program entitled "Slonimsky's Lexicographical Discoveries."

But soon I began discovering chinks in my escutcheon. I had no business calling the English pianist Harriet Cohen a Dame. She was a Dame only in Spain, where she had received the order of Merit of Honor. The violinist Charles de Bériot did not procreate a son in 1883, for he died in 1870, and posthumous insemination was not practiced in his time. His son was born in 1833. The German musician known as "der alte Ries" did not become a father at the age of nine in 1784 but at the age of twenty-nine, for he was born not in 1775 as I had it in *Baker's*, but in 1755. So apologetic corrigenda had to be published in a supplement in 1965. Another supplement, bringing biographies up to date and sadly listing the inevitable necrology, came out in 1971. In 1978 a completely revised Sixth Edition of *Baker's* was published, an impressive tome numbering 1,955 pages. It was greeted by a veritable eruption of bravos in the press. I liked best of all what the critic of the *Los Angeles Times* had to say about it. "Run, do not walk, to the nearest music store," he urged, to buy the newly furbished *Baker's*. Apparently, many people, and not only in California, followed his call, for the Sixth Edition sold even faster than the previous ones, so that I had to plunge headlong into the Seventh Edition. It came out in 1984, a hefty volume of 2,577 pages, weighing in at eight and a half pounds.

Dr. Johnson described the typical lexicographer (of whom he was, of course, a shining example) as "a harmless drudge." I beg to differ. The drudgery is, at least in my experience, often a source of joy, akin to the famous, although astronomically unlikely, elevation of soul when a new planet swims into a stargazer's ken, as Keats imagined such a discovery. I experienced such a joy when a British composer named Edward Maryon swam into my ken. His publishers had written me that he was long dead—yet I could never get his obit from the British sources. I even wrote to the owner of the house he occupied in London, but my letter was returned to me with the notification that the building had been destroyed during the blitz. I then inquired at Scotland Yard. Was there a suspicion of crime? the inspector queried. No. Well, in that case, it was out of their jurisdiction. And then all of a sudden, Maryon himself, very much alive, somehow discovered that there was a person in America who was eager to get in touch with him. We engaged in lively correspondence. Then Maryon really died. Some months after his death, a trunk arrived from Maryon's estate in England at my address in Boston. He had instructed the executors of his will to send it to me, for I was apparently the only person who had taken interest in his works. The trunk contained a number of his manuscripts and also personal documents dating back to the reign of Henry VIII, among them a parchment proclaiming him Duke d'Aulby. I donated the materials to the Boston Public Library, and there was a nice story in local papers about this extraordinary case.

My curiosity was not always rewarded by such response. A Russian woman living in Italy asked me to find out whether her father, the violinist Vasili Bezekirsky, who had emigrated to America early in the century, was still alive. It took me quite a few months to track him down in a small town in upstate New York. Yes, he was alive, I wrote to his daughter. I expected to receive from both

Preface

father and daughter an appreciation of my effort. Instead, I got a rather sour postcard from Bezekirsky: "Dear Sir, Your mission was successful, if you call unpleasant and demanding letters from my daughter a success. I am in no position to help her in any way." Bezekirsky died a few years later. I never heard from his daughter.

On the other side of the ledger, I was really pleased to receive an acknowledgment from an American composer named Walter Stockhoff (whom Busoni once praised as "a fresh voice from the New World that could revitalize the tired art of Europe"): "As pure, cool, crystal-clear water revives one thirsting in the desert, so intelligence, understanding, sympathy and sense of values come to brighten one's pathway. There is a noble generosity in your giving thought to my work. Through the greatness of your nature you strengthen others."

And now I have to say a few words about the purpose of the present, abridged, edition of *Baker's*. The previous seven editions kept growing and growing. This edition, on the other hand, has been reduced to about one-half the size of the preceding Seventh Edition. Major surgery was required to accomplish this aim. Its methodology was governed by its purpose: to prepare a music dictionary for quick reference, giving prominence to great figures of music but eliminating the secondary entries. Thus, music critics, church organists, librarians, editors, theorists, and commentators, all of whose honorable names fill the pages of dictionaries, will be cast aside without prejudice. Minor composers of all lands whose works cease to be performed after they die will also be allowed to enter the realm of dignified shades. Who wants to know the facts of life of a musical savant who spent his life compiling catalogues? Who wants to know what happened to an obscure tenor who sang in a provincial Italian opera house until his voice cracked? Who is interested in finding out why a once-ambitious violin virtuoso eventually had to earn a living in the last stand of the second violin section of a third-rate orchestra? And who would examine the mass of musical manuscripts of a perfectly honorable composer whose works nobody wants to perform? But enough of these dark visions of forgotten self-styled geniuses! A reference work must deal with viable productions.

In the Seventh Edition of *Baker's* I included hundreds of pop musicians, passing idols of the hour—in fact, as I put it in that book's preface, practically all performers with an operable larynx, short of singing whales. I was accused by some critics of treating such momentary celebrities with "genial contempt." Not so. Some performers who have a natural power of fascination for multitudes are legitimate movers of musical culture. But others are mere followers of the public taste. The problem in the present abridged edition is to separate true artists of the people from imitators and crown followers. So the Beatles are to remain in their venerable place; and so are many singers and instrumentalists who, for better or for worse (time will decide which), have colored our century. Yes, Frank Sinatra; yes, Elvis Presley; yes, Benny Goodman; yes, even Liberace. Being celebrated is not necessarily a mark of Cain.

This slenderized edition of *Baker's* is taken from the Seventh Edition without any revisions. A list of death dates which were accumulated since the publication of the Seventh Edition is included as a memorial to all the worthy musicians who made *Baker's Biographical Dictionary* the fine reference work that it is.

Nicolas Slonimsky
Los Angeles, September 1, 1987

Memorial Necrology

This Concise Edition was made possible by the fact that the original Seventh Edition was on a computerized data base. We have been able to delete from that data base but no additions or updating were allowed. This list includes dates of death for musicians in the present Concise Dictionary as well as those in the Seventh Edition (1984) of *Baker's Biographical Dictionary of Musicians*.

ABRAMSKY, ALEXANDER, ? 29 AUG 1985
ALWYN, WILLIAM, Southwold, Suffolk 11 SEP 1985
AMFITEATROV, DANIELE, Rome 7 JUN 1983
AMMANN, BENNO, Rome 14 MAR 1986
ANTILL, JOHN, Sydney 29 DEC 1986
ARLEN, HAROLD, NYC 23 APR 1986
ARNOLD, BYRON, Oscoda, MI 25 DEC 1971
ARNOLD, DENIS, Budapest 28 APR 1986
ASKENASE, STEFAN, Cologne 18 OCT 1985
AZMAYPARASHVILI, SHALVA, Tbilisi 17 MAY 1957

BAMBERGER, CARL, NYC 18 JUL 1987
BARDOS, LAJOS, Budapest 18 NOV 1986
BELY, VICTOR, ? 1983
BENEDITO Y VIVES, RAFAEL, Madrid 1963
BERNIER, RENÉ, Brussels 8 SEP 1984
BERTOUILLE, GÉRARD, Brussels 12 DEC 1981
BILT, PETER VAN DER, Amsterdam 25 SEP 1983
BLACHUT, BENO, Prague 10 JAN 1985
BLATNÝ, JOSEF, Brno 18 JUL 1980
BOVY, VINA, Ghent 16 MAY 1983
BOYDEN, DAVID DODGE, Berkeley 18 SEP 1986
BRAVNIČAR, MATIJIA, Ljubljana 25 NOV 1977
BRKANOVIĆ, IVAN, Zagreb 20 FEB 1987
BRUCKNER-RÜGGEBERG, WILHELM, Hamburg 1 APR 1985

BUNIN, REVOL, Moscow SEP 1976
CACIOPPO, GEORGE, Ann Arbor, MI 4 APR 1984
CAILLIET, LUCIEN, Woodland Hills, CA 3 JAN 1985
CARNER, MOSCO, Cornwall 3 AUG 1985
CASTON, SAUL, Winston-Salem, NC 28 JUL 1970
CEHANOVSKY, GEORGE, Yorktown Hts, NY 25 MAR 1986
CHAJES, JULIUS, Royal Oak, MI 24 FEB 1985
CHASINS, ABRAM, NYC 21 JUN 1987
CIORTEA, TUDOR, Bucharest 13 OCT 1982
CIPRA, MILO, Zagreb 9 JUL 1985
CLARKE, KENNY, Montreuil-Sous-Bois, nr Paris 26 JAN 1985
CLERCX, SUZANNE, Liège 27 SEP 1985
COELHO, RUY, Lisbon 5 MAY 1986
COOPER, MARTIN, Richmond, Surrey 15 MAR 1986
CORENA, FERNANDO, Lugano 26 NOV 1984
CRESTON, PAUL, San Diego 24 AUG 1985
CRUZ, IVO, Lisbon 8 SEP 1985
CUMBERWORTH, STARLING, Cleveland 8 AUG 1985
CURTISS, MINA, Bridgeport, CT 1 NOV 1985

DANKEVICH, KONSTANTIN, Kiev 26 FEB 1984
DARVAS, GABOR, Budapest 18 FEB 1985
DAVIS, EDDIE "LOCKJAW," Culver City, CA 3 NOV 1986

Memorial Necrology

DESARZENS, VICTOR,
  Lausanne 13 FEB 1986
DICKENSON, VICTOR, NYC 16 NOV 1984
DIETHER, JACK, NYC 22 JAN 1987
DOUGHERTY, CELIUS,
  Effort, PA 22 DEC 1986
DUCKLES, VINCENT,
  Berkeley, CA 1 JUL 1985
DUKE, JOHN, Northampton,
  MA 26 OCT 1984
DURUFLÉ, MAURICE, Paris 16 JUN 1986

EDMUNDS, JOHN, Berkeley 9 DEC 1986
ELKAN, HENRI, Philadelphia 12 JUN 1980
ELMORE, ROBERT HALL,
  Ardmore, PA 22 SEP 1985
EWEN, DAVID, Miami Beach 28 DEC 1985

FARNADI, EDITH, Graz 14 DEC 1973
FELDMAN, MORTON, Buffalo,
  NY 3 SEP 1987
FERGUSON, DONALD,
  Minneapolis 11 MAY 1985
FERNÁNDES, ARMONDO
  JOSÉ, Lisbon 3 MAY 1983
FERRARA, FRANCO,
  Florence 6 SEP 1985
FINNEY, THEODORE,
  Pittsburgh 19 MAY 1978
FORREST, HAMILTON,
  London 26 DEC 1963
FOURNIER, PIERRE, Geneva 8 JAN 1985
FRANCI, BENVENUTO,
  Rome 27 FEB 1985
FREY, WALTER, Zurich 28 MAY 1985
FRIEMANN, WITOLD, Laski,
  Poland 22 MAR 1977
FULTON, R. NORMAN,
  Birmingham 5 AUG 1980

GARANT, SERGE, Sherbrooke,
  Quebec 1 NOV 1986
GIANNINI, DUSOLINA,
  Florence 26 JUN 1986
GILELS, EMIL, Moscow 14 OCT 1985
GOODMAN, BENNY, NYC 13 JUN 1986
GORODNITZKI, SASCHA,
  NYC 4 APR 1986

GROUT, DONALD JAY,
  Skaneateles, NY 9 MAR 1987
GROVEN, EIVIND, Oslo 8 FEB 1977
GRUMIAUX, ARTHUR,
  Brussels 16 OCT 1986
GRÜMMER, ELISABETH,
  Berlin 6 NOV 1986

HAGGIN, BERNARD H.,
  NYC 29 MAY 1987
HALLNÄS, HILDING,
  Stockholm 11 SEP 1984
HANDFORD, MAURICE,
  Warminster 16 DEC 1986
HARRISON, GUY FRASER,
  San Miguel de Allende, MX 20 FEB 1986
HENNING, ERVIN ARTHUR,
  Boston 27 JUL 1982
HERMAN, REINHOLD
  LUDWIG, Berlin 2 NOV 1922
HERMAN, WOODY, Los
  Angeles 29 OCT 1987
HERZOG, GEORGE,
  Indianapolis 4 NOV 1983
HIRT, FRANZ-JOSEF, Bern 20 MAY 1985
HLOBIL, EMIL, Prague 25 JAN 1987
HOÉRÉE, ARTHUR, Paris 3 JAN 1986
HÖLLER, KARL, Hausham 14 APR 1987
HULL, ANNE, Westport, CT 31 JAN 1984
HÜSCH, GERHARD, Munich 21 NOV 1984
HUSMANN, HEINRICH,
  Brussels 8 NOV 1983

IVANOV, KONSTANTIN, ? 1984
IVANOVS, JANIS, Riga 27 MAR 1983

JANKÉLÉVITCH,
  VLADIMIR, Paris 6 JUN 1985
JAROFF, SERGE, Lakewood,
  NJ 5 OCT 1985
JEANNERET, ALBERT, ? 25 APR 1973
JOCHUM, EUGEN, Munich 26 MAR 1987
JONES, JO (NATHAN), NYC 3 SEP 1985
JONES, "PHILLY JOE,"
  Philadelphia 30 AUG 1985
JONES, THAD, Copenhagen 20 AUG 1986
JONG, MARINUS DE, Ekeren 13 JUN 1984

KABALEVSKY, DMITRI,
Moscow   16 FEB 1987
KARJALAINEN, AHTI,
Jyväskylä   2 OCT 1986
KELLER, HANS, London   6 NOV 1985
KETTING, PIET, Rotterdam   25 MAY 1984
KIELLAND, OLAV, Bø,
Telemark   5 AUG 1985
KING, HAROLD CHARLES,
Amsterdam   12 JUN 1984
KOLINSKI, MIECZYSLAW,
Toronto   7 MAY 1981
KÓRODI, ANDRÁS, Venice   17 SEP 1986
KOSAKOFF, REUVEN, NYC   6 MAY 1987
KOUGUELL, ARKADIE, Glen
Head, L.I., NY   20 NOV 1985
KRAUS, LILI, Asheville, NC   6 NOV 1986
KRESÁNEK, JOZEF, Bratislava   14 MAR 1986
KRIPS, HENRY, Adelaide   25 JAN 1987
KRUL, ELI, NYC (?)   1970
KUNZ, ERNST, Olten   7 FEB 1980

LAKS, SIMON, Paris   11 DEC 1983
LARSSON, LARS-ERIK,
Halsingborg   27 DEC 1986
LÁSZLO, ALEXANDER, Los
Angeles   17 NOV 1970
LAURO, ANTONIO, Caracas   1 APR 1986
LE CAINE, HUGH, Ottawa   3 JUL 1977
LEFÉBURE, YVONNE, Paris   23 JAN 1986
LE FLEM, PAUL, Trégastel
(Côtes-du-Nord)   31 JUL 1984
LE FLEMING,
CHRISTOPHER, Woodbury,
Devon.   19 JUN 1985
LEIVISKA, HELVI, Helsinki   12 AUG 1982
LHOTKA-KALINSKI, IVO,
Zagreb   29 JAN 1987
LIBERACE, WALTER, Palm
Springs   4 FEB 1987
LINDEMAN, OSMO, Helsinki   15 FEB 1987
LINSTEAD, GEORGE,
Sheffield   29 DEC 1974
LIST, EUGENE, NYC   28 FEB 1985
LITINSKY, GENRIK, Moscow   26 JUL 1985
LONDON, GEORGE, Armonk,
NY   23 MAR 1985

LOWINSKY, EDWARD,
Chicago   12 OCT 1985
LUKÁCS, MIKLÓS, Budapest   1 NOV 1986

MACRAE, GORDON, Lincoln,
NE   24 JAN 1986
MAGNE, MICHEL, Cergy-
Pontoise (Val d'Oise)   19 DEC 1984
MAHRENHOLZ,
CHRISTHARD, Hannover   15 MAR 1980
MAKEDONSKI, KIRIL,
Skopje, Yugo.   2 JUN 1980
MARCHAL, ANDRÉ, St.-Jean-
de-Luz   27 AUG 1980
MAREK, CZESLAW, Zurich   17 JUL 1985
MARTUCCI, PAOLO, NYC   18 OCT 1980
MARX, KARL, Stuttgart   8 MAY 1985
MATAČIĆ, LOVRO VON,
Zagreb   4 JAN 1985
McDOWELL, JOHN, Scarsdale,
NY   3 SEP 1985
McHOSE, ALLEN,
Canandaigua, NY   14 SEP 1986
MENGELBERG, KAREL,
Amsterdam   11 JUL 1984
MICHALAK, THOMAS,
Newark, NJ   10 JUL 1986
MIGNONE, FRANCISCO, Rio
de Janeiro   20 FEB 1986
MIHALOVICI, MARCEL, Paris   12 AUG 1985
MILES, MAURICE, Hereford   26 JUN 1985
MOESCHINGER, ALBERT,
Thun, Switz.   25 SEP 1985
MOKRANJAC, VASILIJE,
Belgrade   27 MAY 1984
MOLDOVAN, MIHAI,
Bucharest   11 SEP 1981
MOLNÁR, ANTAL, Budapest   7 DEC 1983
MOMPOU, FEDERICO,
Barcelona   30 JUN 1987
MONTGOMERY, MERLE,
Arlington, VA   25 AUG 1986
MOORE, GERALD, Penn,
Buckinghamshire   13 MAR 1987
MOYSE, MARCEL,
Brattleboro, VT   1 NOV 1984

Memorial Necrology

MOYZES, ALEXANDER, Bratislava — 20 NOV 1984

MÜNCH, HANS, Basel — 7 SEP 1983

MUNCLINGER MILAN, Prague — 30 MAR 1986

MURPHY, TURK, San Francisco — 30 MAY 1987

MYERS, ROLLO, Chichester — 1 JAN 1985

NASTASIJEVIČ, SVETOMIR, Belgrade — 17 AUG 1979

NAYLOR, BERNARD, Victoria — 19 MAY 1986

NIYAZI, ? — SEP 1984

NOVÁK, JAN, Ulm — 17 NOV 1984

NOVIKOV, ANATOLY, ? — 1984

NYIREGYHÁZI, ERWIN, Los Angeles — 13 APR 1987

OLEVSKY, JULIAN, Amherst, MA — 25 MAY 1985

OLSEN, SPARRE, Oslo — 8 NOV 1984

ORMANDY, EUGENE, Philadelphia — 12 MAY 1985

ORTHEL, LÉON, The Hague — 6 SEP 1985

PALKOVSKÝ, OLDŘICH, Gottwaldov — 13 MAY 1983

PEARS, SIR PETER, Aldeburgh — 3 APR 1986

PEERCE, JAN, NYC — 15 DEC 1984

PEETERS, FLOR, Antwerp — 4 JUL 1986

PERSICHETTI, VINCENT, Philadelphia — 14 AUG 1987

POKRASS, DMITRI, Moscow — 20 DEC 1978

POSTON, ELIZABETH, Highfield, Hertfordshire — 18 MAR 1987

PREVITALI, FERNANDO, Rome — 1 AUG 1985

PROHASKA, FELIX, Vienna — 29 MAR 1987

QUINET, MARCEL, Woluwé-St. Lambert — 16 DEC 1986

RABINOVICH, DAVID, Moscow — 23 JUL 1978

RAINIER, PRIAULX, Besse-en-Chandesse (Auvergne) — 10 OCT 1986

RANCZAK, HILDEGARDE, Munich — FEB 1987

RASKIN, JUDITH, NYC — 21 DEC 1984

RAUTIO, MATTI, Tampere — 22 JUN 1986

REUTTER, HERMANN, Heidenheim an der Brenz — 1 JAN 1985

REY, CEMAL RESHID, Istanbul — 7 OCT 1985

RICH, BUDDY, Los Angeles — 2 APR 1987

RIDDLE, NELSON, Los Angeles — 6 OCT 1985

RIDOUT, GODFREY, Toronto — 24 NOV 1984

RISTIĆ, MILAN, Belgrade — 20 DEC 1982

ROBINSON, FORBES, London — 13 MAY 1987

ROBINSON, STANFORD, Brighton — 25 OCT 1984

ROCCA, LODOVICO, Turin — 25 JUN 1986

ROSE, LEONARD, White Plains, NY — 16 NOV 1984

ROSENBERG, HILDING, Stockholm — 19 MAY 1985

ROSENSTOCK, JOSEPH, NYC — 17 OCT 1985

ROSENTHAL, HAROLD, London — 19 MAY 1987

RUBBRA, EDMUND, Gerrards Cross — 13 FEB 1986

RUDHYAR, DANE, San Francisoco — 13 SEP 1985

RUFER, JOSEF, Berlin — 7 NOV 1985

SAINT-MARCOUX, MICHELINE COULOMBE, Montreal — 2 FEB 1985

SAKAČ, BRANIMIR, Zagreb — 29 DEC 1979

SALZER, FELIX, NYC — 12 AUG 1986

SANROMÁ, JÉSUS MARÍA, San Juan, PR — 12 OCT 1984

SANTA CRUZ, DOMINGO, Santiago, Chile — 7 JAN 1987

SARGEANT, WINTRHOP, Salisbury, CT — 15 AUG 1986

SCHIBLER, ARMIN, Zürich — 7 SEP 1986

SCHICK, GEORGE, NYC — 7 MAR 1985

SCHMITT-WALTER, KARL, Kreuth, Oberbayern — 14 JAN 1985

SCHREIBER, FREDERICK, NYC — 15 JAN 1985

SCHUH, WILLI, Zürich — 4 OCT 1986

SEGOVIA, ANDRÉS, Madrid — 2 JUN 1987

SESSIONS, ROGER, Princeton, NJ — 16 MAR 1985

SIMS, "ZOOT," NYC	23 MAR	1985
SIOHAN, ROBERT, Paris	16 JUL	1985
SMETÁČEK, VÁCLAV, Prague	18 FEB	1986
SMITH, KATE, Raleigh, NC	17 JUN	1986
SOCOR, MATEI, Bucharest	30 MAY	1980
SONNINEN, AHTI, Helsinki	27 AUG	1984
ŠROM, KAREL, Prague	21 OCT	1981
STEINPRESS, BORIS,?	21 MAY	1986
STREICH, RITA, Vienna	20 MAR	1987
ŠULEK, STJEPAN, Zagreb	16 JAN	1986
SUTHERLAND, MARGARET, Melbourne	12 AUG	1984
SYKES, JAMES, Hanover, NH	26 JUL	1985
TAGLIAFERRO, MAGDA, Rio de Janeiro	9 SEP	1986
TAJČEVIĆ, MARKO, Belgrade	19 JUL	1984
TANSMAN, ALEXANDRE, Paris	15 NOV	1986
TATE, PHYLLIS, London	27 MAY	1987
TIJARDOVIĆ, IVO, Zagreb	19 MAR	1976
TOLONEN, JOUKO, Turku	23 JUL	1986
TRIMBLE, LESTER, NYC	31 DEC	1986
TURNER, JOSEPH VERNON "BIG JOE," Inglewood, CA	24 NOV	1985
URSULEAC, VIORICA, Ehrwald, Tirol	22 OCT	1985
VAČKÁŘ, DALIBOR, Prague	21 OCT	1984
VASCONCELOS, JORGE CRONER DE, Lisbon	9 DEC	1974
VOSTŘÁK, ZBYNĚK, Strakonice	4 AUG	1985
VOTTO, ANTONINO, Milan	9 SEP	1985
VUKRAGOVIĆ, MIHAILO, Belgrade	14 MAR	1986
WAESBERGHE, J. SMITS VAN, Amsterdam	9 OCT	1986
WATSON, CLAIRE, Utting, Ger.	16 JUL	1986
WHITE, ERIC WALTER, London	13 SEP	1985
WHITNEY, ROBERT, Louisville, KY	22 NOV	1986
WIJDEVELD, WOLFGANG, Laren	12 DEC	1985
WILLIAMS, CHARLES "COOTIE," Long Island, NY	15 SEP	1985
WILSON, TEDDY, New Britain, CT	31 JUL	1986
WIREN, DAG, Danderyd	19 APR	1986
WÜHRER, FRIEDRICH, Mannheim	27 DEC	1975
YANSONS, ARVID, Manchester	21 NOV	1984
YARDUMIAN, RICHARD, Bryn Athyn, PA	15 AUG	1985
YASSER, JOSEPH, NYC	6 SEP	1981
ZECCHI, CARLO, Salzburg	31 AUG	1984
ZEIDMAN, BORIS, ?	30 DEC	1981
ZIMBALIST, EFREM, SR., Reno, NV	22 FEB	1985
ZNOVSKY-BOROVSKY, ALEXANDER, ?	8 MAR	1983

CORRECTIONS AND ADDITIONS FOR
BAKER'S SEVENTH:

FREITAS, FREDERICO, DE,	12 JAN	1980
GLEASON, HAROLD, La Jolla (not Claremont)	28 JUN	1980
HANSON, HOWARD,	26 FEB	1981
ROLLIN, JEAN, Bayeux (Calvados)		

A

Aaron, Pietro, Italian theorist; b. Florence, 1489; d. Venice, 1545. He was cantor at the Cathedral of Imola in 1521; at the Rimini Cathedral in 1523. In 1525 he was "maestro di casa" in a Venetian house; in 1536 entered the Order of Jerusalem. He publ. *Libri tres de institutione harmonica* (Bologna, 1516); *Thoscanello de la musica* (Venice, 1523; 4 reprints, 1525–62); *Trattato della natura et cognitione di tutti gli tuoni di canto figurato* (Venice, 1525; reproduced in part, in an Eng. trans., in O. Strunk's *Source Readings in Music History,* N.Y., 1950); *Lucidario in musica di alcune opinione antiche e moderne* (Venice, 1545); *Compendiolo di molti dubbi, segreti, et sentenze intorno al canto fermo et figurato* (Milan, posthumous; title page bears the inscription: "In memoria eterna erit Aron").

Abaco, Evaristo Felice dall', Italian composer; b. Verona, July 12, 1675; d. Munich, July 12, 1742. He came from a well-placed family in Verona, and studied violin and cello there. He was in Modena from 1696–1701. In 1704 he was at the Bavarian court in Munich; then he followed the Duke of Bavaria to Belgium and France, where he became acquainted with French music, which left some influence on his later works. In 1715 he returned to Munich, and was active as leader of the court orch. He wrote 12 violin sonatas, with Cello or Cembalo, op. 1 (1706); *Concerti da chiesa* for 4 String Instruments, op. 2 (1714); *6 Sonate da chiesa* and *6 Sonate da camera* for 3 String Instruments, op. 3 (1715); *12 Sonate da camera* for Violin and Cello, op. 4 (1716; arranged by Chédeville for Musette, Flute, Oboe, and Continuo); *6 Concerti* for 7 Instruments (4 Violins, Viola, Bassoon or Cello, and Bass), op. 5 (1717); Concerto for Violin Solo with Instruments, op. 6 (1730; his most important work). Sandberger publ. a biographical sketch and a selection from op. 1–4 in vol. 1 of Denkmäler der Tonkunst in Bayern, and a 2nd selection in vol. 16 (9.i); Riemann edited 3 trio sonatas.

Abbado, Claudio, outstanding Italian conductor, brother of **Marcello Abbado;** b. Milan, June 26, 1933. If the documentation of the genealogical record of his family is to be trusted, he was a direct descendant of a Moorish chieftain, Abdul Abbad, who was expelled from Spain in 1492. Abbado received his early training in music from his father, a professional violinist; then enrolled in the Milan Cons., graduating in 1955 in piano; later took piano lessons in Salzburg with Friedrich Gulda; from 1956 to 1958 he attended the conducting classes of Hans Swarowsky at the Vienna Academy of Music; also spent the summers of 1956 and 1957 working with Carlo Zecchi and Alceo Galliera at the Accademia Chigiana in Siena. In 1958 he won the Koussevitzky conducting prize at the Berkshire Music Center in Tanglewood; in 1963 he was one of the three winners of the Mitropoulos Competition in N.Y. He made his professional American debut as conductor with the N.Y. Phil. on April 7, 1963. In 1965 he appeared as a symph. conductor at La Scala in Milan; also in 1965 he began conducting the Vienna Phil., leading it in Salzburg, in Vienna, and on tour. He began to conduct opera at La Scala in 1967; became its principal conductor in 1968, its music director in 1972, and its artistic director in 1976. In 1972–73 he took the Vienna Phil. to Japan and China; in 1974 he conducted concerts in Russia with the La Scala company; in 1976 he led appearances in the U.S. with both the Vienna Phil. and the La Scala company, which had its American debut during the celebrations of the Bicentennial. In 1979 he was appointed principal conductor of the London Symph. In 1982 he was named principal guest conductor of the Chicago Symph. Orch. In all these varied positions he proved himself a leader of the finest distinction, as competent and congenial with operas by Verdi as with symphs. by Mahler.

Abbado, Marcello, Italian pianist and composer; brother of **Claudio Abbado;** b. Milan, Oct. 7, 1926. He studied at the Cons. in Milan with Gavazzeni (piano) and Ghedini (composition), graduating in 1947. In 1951 he was appointed instructor at the Cons. of Venice; from 1958 to 1966 he was director of the Liceo Musicale in Piacenza; in 1966 was appointed director of the Rossini Cons. in Pesaro; in 1972 became director of the Milan Cons. In 1979 he became principal conductor of the London Symph. Orch., and in 1983 was appointed its music director. He has written a cantata, *Ciapo* (1945); *Lento e Rondo* for Violin and Piano (1949); *Costruziono* for 5 Small Orchs. (1964); Double Concerto for Violin, Piano, and 2 Chamber Orchs. (1967); Quadruple Concerto for Piano, Violin, Viola, Cello, and Orch. (1969); 3 string quartets (1947, 1953, 1969); piano pieces.

Abbatini, Antonio Maria, Italian composer; b. Tiferno (Città di Castello), c.1597; d. there, c.1679. He served as maestro di cappella at the Lateran (1626–28) and other Roman churches; was at the church of Loreto from March to Oct. 1667. In 1672 he was employed at S. Maria Maggiore. He wrote 3 operas; the first, *Dal male al bene,* written in 1653, is of historical importance because it introduced a final ensemble; his other operas were *Ione* (Vienna, 1666) and *La comica del cielo* or *La Baltasara* (Rome, 1668); he also composed a dramatic cantata, *Il pianto di Rodomonte* (Orvieto, 1633). He publ. 3 books of masses, 4 books of psalms, various antiphons (1630, 1638, 1677), and 5 books of motets (1635).

Abbott, Emma, American soprano; b. Chicago, Dec. 9, 1850; d. Salt Lake City, Jan. 5, 1891. Her father was a singer and her brother a violinist; as a young woman she filled engagements with them in hotels and clubs. Her first regular employment was with Chapin's choir in N.Y. (1870–72) at a salary of $1,500 a year. In March 1872 she went to Europe, where she took voice lessons with Sangiovanni in Milan and with Marchesi, Wartel, and Delle Sedie in Paris. She made her professional debut as an opera singer in London on May 2, 1876, in the role of Maria in Donizetti's *La Fille du régiment;* returning to America, she sang the same role in N.Y. on Feb. 8, 1877. She was in many ways an American primitive, traveling with her own small opera company across the country; at her performances she was prone to interpolate her "specialties" in the opera scores, such as singing the hymn "Nearer My God to Thee" in *Faust.*

Abe, Komei, Japanese composer; b. Hiroshima, Sept. 1, 1911. He studied cello at the Tokyo Academy of Music, graduating in 1933; took postgraduate composition courses there with Klaus Pringsheim (1933–36) and conducting with Joseph Rosenstock (1935–39); then became a prof. at the Elizabeth Music College at Kyoto; was from 1969–74 a prof. at Kyoto Municipal Univ. of Arts.
    WORKS: *Theme and Variations* for Orch. (Tokyo, Feb. 8, 1936); *Kleine Suite* for Orch. (Tokyo, Feb. 27, 1937); Cello Concerto (Tokyo, March 31, 1942); Piano Concerto (1945; Tokyo, March 27, 1947); 2 symphs.: No. 1 (Tokyo, May 9, 1957) and No. 2 (Tokyo, Oct. 10, 1960); *Serenade* for Orch. (Tokyo, Oct. 7, 1963); Sinfonietta (Tokyo, Jan. 14, 1965); 9 string quartets (1935, 1937, 1939, 1943, 1946, 1948, 1950, 1952, 1955); 2 flute sonatas (1942, 1949); Clarinet Quintet (1942); *Divertimento* for Saxophone and Piano (1951; orchestrated 1953); *Divertimento* for 9 Instruments (1954); Sextet for Flute, Clarinet, Violin, Viola, Cello, and Piano (1964); *A Picture Book for Children* for Piano (1967); Piano Sonatina (1970); 3 piano sonatinas for children (1971); *Variation on a Subject by Grieg* for 4 Trumpets, 4 Horns, 3 Trombones, and Tuba (1972); choral music; songs; film music.

Abel, Carl Friedrich, German viola da gamba player and composer; b. Cöthen, Dec. 22, 1723; d. London, June 20, 1787. He studied with his father, a player on the gamba; then moved to Leipzig, where he enrolled in the Thomasschule; then lived for many years in Dresden, where he joined the Court Orch. (1743–58). In 1759 he went to London, making it his permanent home; in 1764 became court musician to Queen Charlotte, a position he held until his death. He also became associated with Bach's son, the "London Bach," John (Johann) Christian, and with him organized a series of concerts, which gained renown as as the Bach-Abel Concerts (1765–81). Abel composed a number of instrumental works, among them several symphs., a *Sinfonia concertante,* several piano concertos, string quartets, trio sonatas, piano sonatas, violin sonatas, and pieces for the viola da gamba. In his style of composition he followed the Mannheim School, emphasizing symmetric instrumental forms and diversified dynamics. His Symph. in E-flat major was erroneously ascribed to Mozart and even listed as K. 18; A51, which testifies, however obliquely, to the intrinsic worth of his music. Abel was the last great virtuoso on the viola da gamba of the Classical period, until the revival of Baroque instruments in the 20th century by Dolmetsch and others. Abel's compositions have been publ. in a collected edition by W. Knape, *K.F. Abel: Kompositionen* (Cuxhaven, 1958–74); Knape also prepared a *Bibliographisch-thematisches Verzeichnis der Kompositionen von Karl Friedrich Abel* (Cuxhaven, 1971).

Abendroth, Walter, noted German writer on music; b. Hannover, May 29, 1896. He studied music in Berlin and Munich; eventually established himself in Hamburg. He publ. valuable biographical monographs on Pfitzner (Munich, 1935), Brahms (Berlin, 1939), and Bruckner (Berlin, 1940); also *Kleine Geschichte der Musik* (Frankfurt, 1959) and an autobiographical pamphlet, *Ich warne Neugierige* (Munich, 1966). He was also a prolific composer; among his works are 5 symphs., a Viola Concerto, several violin sonatas, and numerous songs.

Abert, Hermann, eminent German musicologist; b. Stuttgart, March 25, 1871; d. there, Aug. 13, 1927. He studied with his father, a noted musician; then with Bellermann, Fleischer, and Friedlaender in Berlin; he received his Ph.D. from the Univ. of Berlin in 1897 with the dissertation *Die Lehre vom Ethos in der griechischen Musik* (publ. in Leipzig, 1899); completed his Habilitation in 1902 at the Univ. of Halle with *Die ästhetischen Grundsätze der mittelalterlichen Melodiebildung* (publ. in Halle, 1902); was named honorary prof. there in 1909 and lecturer in 1911. In 1920 he became prof. at the Univ. of Leipzig (succeeding Hugo Riemann) and in 1923, at the Univ. of Berlin (succeeding August Kretzschmar). He was one of the outstanding scholars of his time, noted for his wide-ranging musicological interests. Among his important writings, his exhaustively rewritten and revised edition of Jahn's biography of Mozart is still valuable; it was publ. as *Wolfgang Amadeus Mozart: Neu bearbeitete und erweitert Ausgabe von Otto Jahns "Mozart"* (2 vols., Leipzig, 1919–21; it was further revised by his daughter and publ. in 1955–56); other books include *Robert Schumann* (Berlin, 1903; 4th ed., 1920); *Die Musikanschauung des Mittelalters und ihre Grundlagen* (Halle, 1905); *Niccolo Jommelli als Opernkomponist* (Halle, 1908); *Goethe und die Musik* (Engelhorn, 1922); he also wrote a biography of his father (Leipzig, 1916). His collected writings were posthumously edited by F. Blume as *Gesammelte Schriften und Vorträge* (Halle, 1929).

Abraham, Gerald, eminent English writer on music; b. Newport, Isle of Wight, March 9, 1904. He studied piano; became interested in philology; mastered the Russian language and made a profound study of Russian music. He further extended his knowledge to embrace the development of Romantic and national music in the 19th century, and the modern trends of the 20th century. From 1935 to 1947 he was connected with the BBC in London; from 1947 to 1962 was a prof. of music at Liverpool Univ. (1947–62); then returned to work with the BBC (1962–67). In 1974 he was made a Commander of the Order of the British Empire.

Abraham, Paul, Hungarian composer of light operas; b. Apatin, Nov. 2, 1892; d. Hamburg, May 6, 1960. He studied in Budapest and wrote chamber music before turning to light opera. His most successful operetta was *Viktoria und ihr Husar* (Vienna, Dec. 23, 1930); his other popular productions were *Die Blume von Hawaii* (Leipzig, July 24, 1931) and *Ball im Savoy* (Berlin, Dec. 23, 1932). In 1938 Abraham went to the U.S., but suffered a mental breakdown and in 1955 was committed to a sanatorium in Hamburg, where he died.

Abravanel, Maurice, distinguished American conductor; b. Saloniki, Greece, Jan. 6, 1903, of Sephardic Jewish parents (an ancestor is reputed to have been chancellor to Ferdinand and Isabella of Spain). He was taken to Switzerland at the age of 6, and studied general subjects at the Univ. of Lausanne; in 1922 he went to Berlin, where he took composition lessons with Kurt Weill; with the advent of the Nazi regime in 1933, Abravanel moved to Paris, where he conducted ballet; in 1934–35 he toured Australia; in 1936 he received an offer to join the staff of the Metropolitan Opera in N.Y.; made his debut there on Dec. 26, 1936, conducting *Samson et Dalila;* generally adverse reviews compelled him to leave the Metropolitan in 1938. He turned to leading Broadway musicals; conducted a season with the Chicago Opera Co. (1940–41). In 1947 he became conductor of the Utah Symph. Orch. at Salt Lake City, and revealed a great talent for building up the orch.; in the 30 years of his conductorship it became one of the finest symph. orchs. in the U.S.; he also introduced many modern works into its repertoire. In 1976 he underwent open-heart surgery; in 1979 he retired as music director of the Utah Symph.

Absil, Jean, eminent Belgian composer; b. Bonsecours, Oct. 23, 1893; d. Brussels, Feb. 2, 1974. He studied organ and composition at the Brussels Cons.; later took lessons in advanced composition with Gilson. He won the Prix Agniez for his First Symph. (1921); in 1922 won a 2nd Prix de Rome for the cantata *La Guerre;* also received the Prix Rubens. His First Piano Concerto was commissioned by the 1938 Concours Ysaÿe in Brussels as the compulsory work for the 12 finalists in the contest eventually won by Emil Gilels. He was music director of the Academy of Etterbeek in Brussels (1922–64); taught at the Brussels Cons. (1930–59); was also one of the founders of the *Revue Internationale de Musique*. Absil evolved an individual style, characterized by rhythmic variety, free tonality, and compact counterpoint.

Abt, Franz, German songwriter and conductor; b. Eilenburg, Dec. 22, 1819; d. Wiesbaden, March 31, 1885. His father, a clergyman, sent him to Leipzig Thomasschule to study theology; he later obtained an excellent musical education both there and at the Univ. He became a choral conductor in Zürich (1841). In 1852 he was appointed 2nd conductor at the Brunswick Court; in 1855 became first conductor. In 1869 he traveled, as a choral conductor, to Paris, London, and Russia; in 1872 he made a highly successful tour in America. He retired on a pension from Brunswick in 1882. Abt wrote over 600 works, comprising more than 3,000 numbers; the largest are the 7 secular cantatas. His popularity as a songwriter is due chiefly to the flowing, easy, and elegant style of his vocal melodies, some of which (*Wenn die Schwalben heimwärts zieh'n, Gute Nacht, du mein herziges Kind, So viele Tausend Blumen,* etc.) have become so well-known as to be mistaken for genuine folk songs.

Achron, Isidor, Russian-American pianist, brother of **Joseph Achron;** b. Warsaw, Nov. 24, 1892; d. New York, May 12, 1948. He studied at the St. Petersburg Cons. with Anna Essipoff (piano) and with Liadov (composition). In 1922 he settled in the U.S.; naturalized in 1928. From 1922–33 he was accompanist to Jascha Heifetz; was also active as a piano teacher in N.Y. He was also a composer; played his Piano Concerto with the N.Y. Phil. Orch. on Dec. 9, 1937; his *Suite Grotesque* for Orch. was first performed in St. Louis, Jan. 30, 1942. He also wrote a number of piano pieces, all in a moderate Romantic manner in the prevalent tradition of the time.

Achron, Joseph, Russian-American violinist and composer, brother of **Isidor Achron;** b. Losdseje, near Suwalki, Poland, May 13, 1886; d. Hollywood, April 29, 1943. In 1890 the family moved to Warsaw. He studied violin there, and gave his first public concert at the age of 7. In 1898 he entered the St. Petersburg Cons. as a student of Leopold Auer in violin and with Liadov in music theory. Graduating in 1904, he went to Berlin, where he appeared as a soloist with orchs. In 1907 he returned to St. Petersburg to continue his studies in theory and orchestration at the conservatory there. In 1911 he organized, along with several Jewish musicians, a society for Jewish folklore. One of the products of his research was the popular *Hebrew Melody* for Violin and Piano (1911), based on a Hasidic theme. During World War I he was a member of the music corps of the Russian army. In 1919–21 he was active as composer for the Hebrew Chamber Theater in Petrograd; in 1922 he went again to Berlin; in 1924 he was in Palestine, and in 1925 emigrated to the U.S.; became a naturalized American citizen in 1930. He lived in N.Y. until 1934; then went to Hollywood, where he earned his living as a violinist in film studios, and continued to compose energetically. His early compositions are marked by characteristic Russian harmonies with a distinctly Romantic aura, but under the impact of modern techniques he developed a strong idiom based on purely structural principles employing atonal and polytonal devices. Schoenberg wrote about him in the program book of a memorial concert of Achron's compositions given in Los Angeles in 1945: "Joseph Achron is one of the most underestimated of modern composers, but the originality and profound elaboration of his ideas guarantee that his works will last." Achron's major compositions include a suite for Chamber Orch., *Golem* (1932), the last section of which is the exact retrograde movement of the first section, to symbolize the undoing of the monster Golem; 3 violin concertos in which he appeared as soloist: No. 1 (Boston, Jan. 24, 1927); No. 2 (Los Angeles, Dec. 19, 1936); No. 3 (Los Angeles, March 31, 1939); *4 tableaux fantastiques* for Violin and Piano (1907); *Chromatic String Quartet* (1907); 2 violin sonatas (1910, 1918); *Hazan* for Cello and Orch. (1912); *2 Hebrew Pieces* for Violin and Piano (1912); *Suite bizarre* for Violin and Piano (1916); *Scher* for Violin and Piano (1916); *Elegy* for String Quartet (1927); *Statuettes* for Piano (1929); *Sextet* for Flute, Oboe, Clarinet, Bassoon, Horn, and Trumpet (1938); Piano Concerto (1941); *Evening Service for the Sabbath* (1930); songs and choruses.

Ackté (real name, **Achté**), **Aïno,** Finnish dramatic soprano; b. Helsinki, April 23, 1876; d. Nummela, Aug. 8, 1944. She studied at the Paris Cons. and made her debut at the Paris Opéra as Marguerite (Oct. 8, 1897). She sang the same role at her first appearance in the U.S. at the Metropolitan Opera (Feb. 20, 1904). Her performance of Salomé in Strauss's opera at Covent Garden (Dec. 8, 1910) led to an invitation from Richard Strauss to sing the part in Dresden and Paris. Her other roles were Juliette, Ophélie, Gilda, Nedda, Elsa, Elisabeth, and Sieglinde. Her memoirs are publ. in Finnish, Swedish, and German.

Adam, Adolphe (-Charles), celebrated French opera composer; b. Paris, July 24, 1803; d. there, May 3, 1856. He studied piano with his father, a professional pianist, and with Lemoine; then went to the Paris Cons., where he became a student of Benoist in organ playing, of Reicha in counterpoint, and of Boieldieu in composition. Boieldieu exercised the greatest influence on Adam's development as an opera composer; another powerful influence was that of Hérold. Adam devoted his entire career exclusively to the music of the theater; he obtained his first success with a short comic opera, *Le Châlet,* produced at the Opéra-Comique on Sept. 25, 1834, which held the stage for 1,400 performances through the years; a far greater success was the production of *Le Postillon de Longjumeau* at the Opéra-Comique on Oct. 13, 1836, an opera that achieved permanence in the operatic repertoire all over the world. There followed a long series of stage works; at times Adam produced two or more operas in a single season. In the process of inevitable triage, most of them went by the board, but a considerable number remained in the repertoire; among these was the comic opera *Si j'étais roi* (Paris, Sept. 4, 1852). Adam wrote 53 operas in all, an astonishing example of fecundity, since his entire life comprised not quite 53 years. Perhaps his most durable work was not an opera but a ballet, *Giselle* (Paris Opéra, June 28, 1841), a perennial in choreographic history which continues to be performed with no sign of decline in popularity. His song *Cantique de Noël* also became popular. Unfortunately, Adam was a poor businessman; in 1847 he ventured into the field of management with an operatic enterprise, the Opéra-National, which failed miserably and brought him to the brink of financial ruin. In 1849 he was appointed prof. at the Paris Cons.; he also traveled widely in Europe, visiting London, Berlin, and St. Petersburg. As one of the creators of French opera, Adam ranks with Auber and Boieldieu in the expressive power of his melodic material and a sense of dramatic development. Adam's memoirs were published posthumously in 2 volumes, *Souvenirs d'un musicien* (1857) and *Derniers Souvenirs d'un musicien* (1859).

Adam (or **Adan**) **de la Halle** (or **Hale**), called "Le Bossu d'Arras" ("Hunchback of Arras"); b. Arras, c.1237; d. Naples, c.1287. A famous trouvère, many of whose works have been preserved, the most interesting is a dramatic pastoral, *Le Jeu de Robin et de Marion* (1285), written for the Anjou court at Naples and resembling an opéra comique in its plan. He was gifted in the dual capacity of poet and composer. Both monodic and polyphonic works of his survive. A facsimile reprint of one of the important MS sources of Adam's works is issued as *Le Chansonnier d'Arras,* introduction by A. Jeanroy (Paris, 1925). For transcriptions of most of the extant music, see E. de Coussemaker, *Œuvres complètes du trouvère Adam de la Halle* (1872); F. Gennrich, *Rondeaux, Virelais und Balladen* (Dresden; I, 1921; II, 1927); J. Chailley, *Adam de la Halle: Rondeaux* (Paris, 1942); F. Gennrich, *Le Jeu de Robin et de Marion,* in *Musikwissenschaftliche Studienbibliothek* (Langen, 1962); N. Wilkins, *The Lyric Works of Adam de la Halle: Chansons, Jeux-Partis, Rondeaux, Motets* (Dallas, 1967). Transcriptions of the texts only: R. Berger, *Canchons und Partures des altfranzösischen Trouvère Adan de la Halle le Bochu d'Arras* (1900); L. Nicod, *Les Partures Adan: Les Jeux-partis d'Adam de la Halle* (Paris, 1917); E. Langlois, *Le Jeu de la Feuillée* (Paris, 1923); id., *Le Jeu de Robin et de Marion* (Paris, 1924); A. Langfors, *Recueil général des jeux-partis français* (2 vols., Paris, 1926). A new edition of the complete works, using all known music and text sources, including those never before transcribed, is being prepared by a consortium of music and language specialists at City Univ. of N.Y.

Adam de St. Victor, French Augustine monk who developed the rhymed liturgical sequence; b. c.1110; d. (possibly) July 8, 1192. He was cantor at the St. Victor Cloister in Paris. His significance lies in his decisive introduction of rhymed "proses," or sequences, each consisting of 12 or more stanzas, in which the first half was given a new melody, while the 2nd half was set to the same melody. Adam de St. Victor wrote a great many such sequences, and influenced their further development.

Adams, John, American composer; b. Worcester, Mass., Feb. 15, 1947. He spent the tender years of his life in the healthy atmosphere of Vermont and New Hampshire; his father taught him clarinet, and he later took clarinet lessons with Felix Viscuglia, a member of the Boston Symph. Orch. He subsequently entered Harvard College, receiving his B.A. (magna cum laude) in 1969 and his M.A. in music composition in 1971. At Harvard his principal teacher was Leon Kirchner; he also worked in composition with David Del Tredici and had some sessions with Sessions. While still in college he conducted the Bach Society Orch. and was a substitute clarinetist with the Boston Symph. and the Boston Opera Co. In 1969 he played the solo part in Walter Piston's Clarinet Concerto at Carnegie Hall in N.Y. In 1971 he moved to San Francisco, where he found a congenial environment for his activities as a conductor and composer. He was appointed head of the composition dept. at the San Francisco Cons. (1971–81). In 1978 he began working with Edo de Waart, music director of the San Francisco Symph., as new music adviser and later as composer-in-residence. His own music covers a wide spectrum of media, including works for video, tape, and live electronics; he also wrote the musical film score for *Matter of Heart,* a psychological documentary dealing with the life and theories of Carl G. Jung. In 1982 he was awarded a Guggenheim fellowship. In his compositions he reveals himself as an apostle of the idea that a maximum effect can be achieved with a minimum of practical means, a notion usually described by the somewhat inaccurate term "minimalism," wherein a composer postulates harmonic and melodic austerity with audacious repetitiveness, withal electing to use the simplest time-honored units of the musical structure, to wit, major triads in the fundamental positions, with the tonic in the bass. John Adams is a modernist among minimalists, for he allows for a constant flow of divergent tonalities in his works, but he also succeeds in exploiting such elementary harmonic progressions as the serenely cadential alternations of the tonic and the dominant, achieving a desired effect. Typical of such works are his *Harmonium* for Chorus and Orch. and the grandiose popular score titled *Grand Pianola Music.*
  WORKS: For Orch., *Common Tones in Simple Time* (1979); *Harmonium* for Chorus and Orch., to verses by John Donne and Emily Dickinson (San Francisco, April 15, 1981); *Grand Pianola Music* for 2 Pianos, 2 Sopranos, and Contralto (San Francisco, Feb. 20, 1982, composer conducting); *Bridge of Dreams* for Orch. (1982–83); *Shaker Loops* for Strings (1978); for Piano: *Ragamarole* (1973); *China Gates* (1977); *Phrygian Gates* (1977).

Adderley, Julian Edwin ("Cannonball"), American jazz alto saxophone player; b. Tampa, Fla., Sept. 15, 1928; d. Gary, Ind., Aug. 8, 1975. He began his career as a member of a jazz group at a Greenwich Village club in N.Y.; in 1956 he formed his own combo with his brother **Nat Adderley** (b. Tampa, Nov. 25, 1931), who plays the cornet. He achieved fame mainly through his recordings, beginning with *African Waltz* in 1961. He received an academic education, graduating from Florida A. & M. with a B.A. in music. For 8 years (1948–56) he was a band director at Dillard High School in Fort Lauderdale. After leaving his school position, he lectured frequently in colleges on the subject of his "black experience in music." He owes his nickname, "Cannonball," to the mispronunciation of *cannibal*, a slurring reference to his voracious eating habits. He suffered a stroke during a concert engagement in Gary, Ind. Among his most successful recordings were *Dis Here; Sermonette; Work Song; Jive Samba; Mercy, Mercy, Mercy; Walk Tall.* He also wrote *Suite Cannon*, its title alluding both to his academic background and to his popular nickname.

Addinsell, Richard, English composer of theater and film music; b. London, Jan. 13, 1904; d. there, Nov. 14, 1977. He studied law at Oxford Univ. and music at the Royal College of Music in London. His first theater score was for Clemence Dane's play *Come of Age* (1928). In 1929 he went to Berlin and Vienna for further musical study. In 1933, Eva Le Gallienne commissioned him to write the music for her production of *Alice in Wonderland.* He then wrote a series of successful film scores, among them *A Tale of Two Cities, Blithe Spirit, Fire over England,* and *Dark Journey.* During World War II he wrote film music for several patriotic documentaries, among them *Siege of Tobruk* and *We Sail at Midnight.* He achieved fame with a score for the film *Dangerous Moonlight* (released in the U.S. as *Suicide Squadron*), containing a movement for piano and orch. which became immensely popular under the title *Warsaw Concerto.* While the music is a feeble imitation of Rachmaninoff's Second Piano Concerto, it possesses a popular flair that made it a classic of pop music.

Addison, John, English composer; b. Cobham, Surrey, March 16, 1920. He was educated at Wellington College, and in 1938 entered the Royal College of Music. His studies were interrupted by World War II, during which he served in a cavalry regiment. After the war he continued his musical education with Gordon Jacob in composition, Leon Goossens in oboe, and Frederick Thurston in clarinet. In 1951 he joined the staff of the Royal College of Music; there until 1958, when he decided to devote himself mainly to composition for films. He wrote music for more than 60 motion pictures, both in England and the U.S., including such popular productions as *Tom Jones* (1963), which won for him an Academy Award; *The Loved One* (1965); *Torn Curtain* (1966); *The Charge of the Light Brigade* (1968); *Sleuth* (1972); *The Seven Per Cent Solution,* a comedy involving Sherlock Holmes and Freud (1976). His film music is particularly effective in epical subjects with understated humor. Apart from film music, he

wrote *Variations* for Piano and Orch. (1948); Concerto for Trumpet, Strings, and Percussion (1949); Woodwind Sextet (1949); Trio for Oboe, Clarinet, and Bassoon (1950); Trio for Flute, Oboe, and Piano; *Serenade and Conversation Piece* for 2 Soprano Voices, Harpsichord, Organ, and Harp. He also wrote music for television documentaries. Since 1975 Addison has divided his time between Los Angeles and a small village in the French Alps, where he does some skiing and mountaineering.

Adler, Guido, eminent Austrian musicologist; b. Eibenschütz, Moravia, Nov. 1, 1855; d. Vienna, Feb. 15, 1941. He studied at the Vienna Cons. under Bruckner and Dessoff; entered Vienna Univ. in 1874 and founded, in cooperation with Felix Mottl and K. Wolf, the academical Wagner Society; took the degree of Dr.Jur. in 1878, and in 1880 that of Dr.Phil. (Dissertation, *Die historischen Grundklassen der christlich-abendländischen Musik bis 1600*), and in 1881 qualified as an instructor, lecturing on musical science (thesis, *Studie zur Geschichte der Harmonie*). With Chrysander and Spitta he founded, in 1884, the *Vierteljahrsschrift für Musikwissenschaft.* In 1885 he was appointed prof. of musicology at the German Univ. at Prague. In 1892 he was elected president of the Central Committee of the Internationale Ausstellung für Musik und Theater. In 1895 he succeeded Hanslick as prof. of music history at the Univ. of Vienna, retiring in 1927. Important books by Adler are *Methode der Musikgeschichte* (1919); *Der Stil in der Musik* (1911; 2nd ed., 1929); *Gustav Mahler* (1916); *Handbuch der Musikgeschichte* (one vol., 1924; 2nd ed. in 2 vols., 1930); *Wollen und Wirken,* memoirs (Vienna, 1935). He was also editor of the monumental collection Denkmäler der Tonkunst in Österreich from its inception (the first vol. appeared in 1894) until 1938 (83 vols. in all). He contributed many articles to music periodicals.

Adler, Kurt Herbert, noted Austrian-born American conductor and operatic administrator; b. Vienna, April 2, 1905. He studied at the Vienna Academy of Music and the Univ. of Vienna; made his debut as a conductor at the Max Reinhardt Theater there in 1925; subsequently conducted at the Volksoper, and also in Germany, Italy, and Czechoslovakia. He served as assistant to Toscanini at the Salzburg Festival in 1936. In 1938 he settled in the U.S.; from 1938–43 was guest conductor of the Chicago Opera. In 1943 he was appointed chorus master of the San Francisco Opera, and in 1953 became its artistic director; in 1956 he was named its general director. He retired in 1981 and was made its general director emeritus. Under his direction the San Francisco Opera prospered greatly, advancing to the foremost ranks of American opera theaters. In 1980 Adler was made an Honorary Knight Commander of the Order of the British Empire. He is not related to Kurt Adler.

Adlgasser, Anton Cajetan, German organist and composer; b. Inzell, Bavaria, Oct. 1, 1729; d. Salzburg, Dec. 22, 1777. He studied with Johann Eberlin in Salzburg; on Dec. 11, 1750, was appointed organist at Salzburg Cathedral and held this post until his death (he died of a stroke while playing the organ). Adlgasser enjoyed a great reputation as a musical scholar and was admired by the young Mozart. He wrote an opera, *La Nitteti* (Salzburg, 1766); several oratorios and sacred dramas; 7 symphs.; piano sonatas and church works.

Adorno (real name, **Wiesengrund**), **Theodor,** significant German musician and philosopher; b. Frankfurt, Sept. 11, 1903; d. Visp, Switzerland, Aug. 6, 1969. He studied music with Sekles in Frankfurt and with Alban Berg in Vienna; was for several years prof. at the Univ. of Frankfurt. Devoting himself mainly to music criticism, he was editor of the progressive music journal *Anbruch* in Vienna (1928–31). In 1934 he went to Oxford, and later emigrated to the U.S., where he became connected with radio research at Princeton Univ. (1938–41); subsequently lived in California. He returned to Germany in 1949 and became director of the Institut für Sozialforschung in Frankfurt. He publ. numerous essays dealing with the sociology of music, among them *Philosophie der neuen Musik* (Tübingen, 1949); *Dissonanzen: Musik in der verwalteten Welt* (Göttingen, 1956); *Arnold Schönberg* (Berlin, 1957); *Klangfiguren* (Berlin, 1959); *Einleitung in die Musiksoziologie* (Frankfurt, 1962); *Moments musicaux* (Frankfurt, 1964); *Form in der Neuen Musik* (Mainz, 1966); *Impromptus* (Frankfurt, 1968); *Alban Berg, der Meister des kleinsten Übergangs* (Vienna, 1968). Adorno advised Thomas Mann in the musical parts of his novel *Doktor Faustus*. He exercised a deep influence on the trends in musical philosophy and general esthetics, applying the sociological tenets of Karl Marx and the psychoanalytic techniques of Freud. In his speculative writings he introduced the concept of "cultural industry," embracing all types of musical techniques, from dodecaphony to jazz. A Festschrift was publ. in honor of his 60th birthday under the title *Zeugnisse* (Frankfurt, 1963). Numerous articles in several languages have been publ. on Adorno's theories in various music journals. In his early writings he used the hyphenated name **Wiesengrund-Adorno.**

Agay, Dénes, Hungarian-American pianist, composer, and arranger; b. Budapest, June 10, 1911. He studied at the Budapest Academy of Music, graduating in 1933. In 1939 he went to the U.S. and settled in N.Y. as a piano teacher. Since 1950 he has been active mainly as an editor of educational material for piano students; he compiled several collections of piano music adapted for beginners (*Easy Classics to Moderns, The Young Pianist's Library*, etc.).

Agazzari, Agostino, Italian composer; b. Siena, Dec. 2, 1578; d. there, April 10, 1640. He was maestro di cappella at the German College in Rome (1602–3), then at the church of St. Apollinaris and the "seminario romano"; he adopted Viadana's innovations in sacred vocal music (writing church concertos for one or 2 voices with instrumental harmonic support). In 1613–14 he was organist at the Siena Cathedral. His works, variously reprinted in Germany and the Netherlands, were in great favor and very numerous (madrigals, Psalms, motets, and other church music). His treatise *La musica ecclesiastica* (Siena, 1638) is a theoretical endeavor to bring the practice of church music into accord with the Resolution of the Council of Trent; he was also among the first to give written instructions for performing the basso continuo, presented in the tract *Del sonare sopra il basso con tutti gli strumenti e del loro uso nel concerto* (Siena, 1607; in Eng., O. Strunk, *Source Readings in Music History,* N.Y., 1950). His pastoral drama *Eumelio* (1606) is one of the earliest operas.

Ager, Milton, American composer of popular music; b. Chicago, Oct. 6, 1893; d. Inglewood, Calif., May 6, 1979. He began his career as a pianist in silent film theaters and accompanist to singers in vaudeville. He served in the U.S. Army Morale Division during World War I. His song *Happy Days Are Here Again* was selected by Franklin D. Roosevelt as his campaign song in 1932, and became an anthem of the Democratic Party in subsequent election campaigns. Ager also wrote the greatly popular ballads *Ain't She Sweet, Crazy Words, Crazy Tune,* and *Hard-Hearted Hannah.*

Agostini, Mezio, Italian composer; b. Fano, Aug. 12, 1875; d. there, April 22, 1944. He studied with his father and with Carlo Pedrotti at the Liceo Rossini in Pesaro (1885–92). He was a prof. of harmony there from 1900–9, when he was appointed as successor to Wolf-Ferrari in the position of director of the Liceo Benedetto Marcello in Venice (1909–40). He was active as an opera conductor in Venice and other Italian cities; also gave chamber music concerts as a pianist. His *Trio* won first prize at the international competition in Paris in 1904. He wrote the *Iovo e Maria* (1896); *Il Cavaliere del Sogno* (Fano, Feb. 24, 1897); *La penna d'Airone* (1896); *Alcibiade* (1902); *America* (also entitled *Hail Columbia,* after Longfellow, 1904); *L'ombra* (1907); *L'agnello del sogno* (1928); *La figlio del navarca* (Fano, Sept. 3, 1938). He also wrote a symph., 4 orch. suites, a piano concerto, 2 string quartets, 2 piano trios, a cello sonata, a violin sonata, the cantata *A Rossini,* numerous piano pieces and songs.

Agostini, Paolo, Italian organist and composer; b. Vallerano, 1583; d. Rome, Oct. 3, 1629. He studied with Giovanni Bernardino Nanino in Rome; was organist at S. Maria in Trastevere, in Rome, and at S. Lorenzo in Damaso. He succeeded Vincenzo Ugolini as maestro di cappella at the Vatican in 1626. Agostini's publ. works—7 books of Psalms (1619), 2 books of Magnificats and antiphons (1620), and 5 books of masses (1624–28)—are only a small portion of his total output. Most of his MSS are preserved in various Roman libraries. His music displays great ingenuity of contrapuntal structure; some of his choral works are written for 48 independent parts.

Agricola, Alexander, composer of the Netherlands school, sometimes said to have been of German extraction, but referred to as a Belgian in his epitaph; b. Flanders, c.1446; d. Valladolid, Spain, 1506. He entered the service of the Duke of Milan in 1471; then went to Cambrai; in 1476 he is mentioned as "petit vicaire" at Cambrai Cathedral. He later traveled in Italy; entered the service of Philip I of Burgundy in 1500 and followed him to Spain in 1502, returning to Belgium in 1505. He went to Spain again in January 1506 and died shortly afterward. Thirty-one of Agricola's songs and motets were printed by Petrucci (Venice, 1501–3), who also publ. a vol. of 5 masses based on chanson material: *Le Serviteur, Je ne demande, Malheur me bat, Primi toni, Secundi toni* (Venice, 1503).

Agricola, Johann Friedrich, German organist and composer; b. Dobitzschen, near Altenburg, Jan. 4, 1720; d. Berlin, Dec. 2, 1774. He entered the Univ. of Leipzig as a law student in 1738, studying music meanwhile with J.S. Bach, and later (1741) with Johann Quantz in Berlin. In 1751 Agricola was appointed court composer to Frederick the Great; in 1759 he succeeded Karl Graun as director of the Royal Chapel. Agricola wrote 11 operas (produced between 1750 and 1772 at Berlin and Potsdam) and church music; he also made arrangements of the King's compositions. He taught singing and in 1757 translated Pier Tosi's *Opinioni de' cantori.* Under the pseudonym **Flavio Amicio Olibrio** Agricola printed some polemical pamphlets directed against the theorist Friedrich Marpurg; he was also a collaborator with Jakob Adlung in the latter's *Musica mechanica organoedi* (1768).

Agricola, Martin, important German music theorist and writer; b. Schwiebus (Brandenburg), Jan. 6, 1486; d. Magdeburg, June 10, 1556. His real name was **Sore,** but he adopted the Latin name Agricola to indicate his peasant origin. Mattheson says that he was the first to abandon the old tablature for modern notation, but this is not quite accurate; Agricola merely proposed an improved system for lute tablature. From 1519 he was a private music teacher in Magdeburg; in 1525 was cantor at the first Lutheran church there. His friend and patron, Rhaw of Wittenberg, publ. most of Agricola's works, the magnum opus being *Musica instrumentalis deudsch* (i.e., "Set in German"; first ed., Wittenberg, 1529; 4th ed., considerably revised, 1545; modern reprint, Leipzig, 1896). This work, although derived from Virdung's *Musica getutscht,* contains much new material and is set in couplet verse in the German vernacular. Further works are: *Ein kurtz deudsche Musica* (1529; 3rd ed. as *Musica choralis deudsch,* l533); *Musica figuralis deudsch,* with the supplement *Büchlein von den proportionibus* (1532); *Scholia in musicam planam Venceslai Philomatis* (1538); *Rudimenta musices* (1539); *Quaestiones vulgatiores in musicam* (1543); *Duo libri musices* (posthumous; Wittenberg, 1561; includes reprints of

Musica choralis and *Musica figuralis;* and 54 *Instrumentische Gesänge* as a supplement). Compositions: *Ein Sangbüchlein aller Sonntags-Evangelien* (1541); *Neue deutsche geistliche Gesänge* (1544); *Hymni aliquot sacri* (1552); *Melodiae scholasticae* (1557).

Aguirre, Julián, Argentine composer; b. Buenos Aires, Jan. 28, 1868; d. there, Aug. 13, 1924. He was taken to Spain as a child; studied at the Madrid Cons., returning to Buenos Aires in 1887. His works are mostly miniatures for Piano in the form of stylized Argentine dances and songs. He wrote 61 opus numbers; *Gato* and *Huella* (op. 49), his most popular pieces, were orchestrated by Ansermet, who performed them in Buenos Aires (April 6, 1930); the *Huella* was also arranged for Violin and Piano by Jascha Heifetz. Other notable works are *Aires nacionales argentinos* (op. 17) and *Zamba* (op. 40).

Agujari, Lucrezia (known as **La Bastardina,** or **Bastardella**), being the natural daughter of a nobleman), a brilliant Italian singer; b. Ferrara, 1743; d. Parma, May 18, 1783. Her father entrusted her instruction to P. Lambertini; in 1764 she made a triumphant debut at Florence, followed by a succession of brilliant appearances in Milan and other Italian cities; also in London. Mozart wrote of her that she had "a lovely voice, a flexible throat, and an incredibly high range." In 1780 she married the Italian composer **Giuseppe Colla,** whose songs she constantly performed at her concerts. Her compass was phenomenal, embracing 3 octaves (C^1–C^4).

Ahle, Johann Rudolf, German composer; b. Mühlhausen, Dec. 24, 1625; d. there, July 9, 1673. From 1646 he was cantor in Erfurt, in 1654, and in 1661 was elected burgomaster of the town. Ahle was a diligent composer of church music and writer of theoretical works. His *Compendium pro tonellis* (1648) ran through 4 editions, 2nd as *Brevis et perspicua introductio in artem musicum* (1673), 3rd and 4th as *Kurze und deutliche Anleitung* (1690 and 1704). His principal compositions include: *Geistlich Dialoge,* songs in several parts (1648); *Thüringischer Lustgarten* (1657); *Geistliche Fest- und Communionandachten* (posthumous). Many of his songs are still popular in Thuringia. A selection from his works was publ. by J. Wolf in Denkmäler Deutscher Tonkunst (vol. V).

Ahlstrom, David, American composer; b. Lancaster, N.Y., Feb. 22, 1927. He studied composition with Henry Cowell and Bernard Rogers; became interested in Asian philosophy and took lessons with Haridas Chaudhuri. He obtained a Ph.D. in composition from the Eastman School of Music in Rochester, N.Y., in 1961; then taught music theory at Northwestern Univ. (1961–62), Southern Methodist Univ. in Dallas (1962–67), and Eastern Illinois Univ. in Charleston (1967–76). In 1976 he moved to San Francisco, and became active in the production of new American stage music. Among his own works, the most significant is his opera *America, I Love You,* to a libretto by e.e. cummings, first produced in its entirety, composer conducting, in San Francisco on June 25, 1983; other operas are *Doctor Faustus Lights the Lights,* after Gertrude Stein (San Francisco, Oct. 29, 1982), and *Three Sisters Who Are Not Sisters,* also derived from Gertrude Stein's text, produced under Ahlstrom's direction in San Francisco, Sept. 17, 1982. He also wrote several symphs. and clarinet sonatas, and a number of theater works employing electronic sound and dance.

Ahronovich, Yuri, Russian conductor; b. Leningrad, May 13, 1932. He studied conducting with Kurt Sanderling and Nathan Rachlin. He then appeared with leading opera houses and orchs. in the Soviet Union. In 1974 he conducted at the Cologne Opera and at Covent Garden in London. In 1975 he became chief conductor of the Gürzenich Orch. in Cologne; in 1982 he assumed the post of chief conductor of the Stockholm Phil., while retaining his position in Cologne.

Aiblinger, Johann Kaspar, German conductor and composer; b. Wasserburg, Bavaria, Feb. 23, 1779; d. Munich, May 6, 1867. He studied music in Munich, then at Bergamo under Simon Mayr (1802); lived at Vicenza (1803–11), then became 2nd maestro di cappella to the viceroy at Milan; founded the Odeon (a society for the cultivation of Classical vocal music) at Venice, in collaboration with Abbé Trentino; was engaged (1819) for the Italian opera in Munich as maestro al cembalo; returned in 1833 to Bergamo, and amassed a fine collection of ancient classical music, now in the Staatsbibliothek at Munich. He wrote many sacred compositions (masses, Requiems, liturgies, Psalms, etc.), which were very popular. He also wrote an opera, *Rodrigo e Ximene* (Munich, 1821), and 3 ballets.

Aichinger, Gregor, important German church composer; b. Regensburg, 1564; d. Augsburg, Jan. 21, 1628. At the age of 13 he went to Munich, where he was under the tutelage of Orlando Lasso; then entered the Univ. of Ingolstadt. He made 2 journeys to Rome; visited Venice, where he mastered the art of Venetian polyphony. He eventually settled in Augsburg as choirmaster and vicar of the Cathedral. He wrote almost exclusively for voices, to Latin texts; his sacred works are remarkable for their practical value and for the excellence of their musical content. Among his many publ. works are 3 books of *Sacrae cantiones* (Venice, 1590; Augsburg, 1595; Nuremberg, 1597); *Tricinia Mariana* (Innsbruck, 1598); *Divinae laudes* (Augsburg, 1602); etc. His publication *Cantiones ecclesiaticae cum basso generali et continuo* (Dillingen, 1607) is noteworthy as one of the earliest works in which the term "basso continuo" appears in the title. A selection of Aichinger's works is included in vol. 18 (formerly 10.i) of Denkmäler der Tonkunst in Bayern, prefaced with a biographical article by the editor, Th. Kroyer.

Aitken, Robert, noted Canadian flutist and com-

poser; b. Kentville, Nova Scotia, Aug. 28, 1939. He studied flute with Marcel Moyse, Julius Baker, and Jean-Pierre Rampal; took courses in composition with Barbara Pentland at the Univ. of British Columbia in Vancouver and with John Weinzweig at the Univ. of Toronto; also received instruction in electronic music from Myron Schaeffer. He then was principal flutist of several Canadian orchs. and taught flute playing at the Royal Cons. in Toronto; he held the degrees of B.M. in composition (1961) and M.M. (1964). In 1971 he organized the New Music Concerts in Toronto; in 1972 he was appointed to the faculty of the Univ. of Toronto. In his music he explores unusual instrumental combinations and spatial concepts of antiphonal groupings.

Akimenko (real name, **Yakimenko**), **Fyodor,** Russian composer; b. Kharkov, Feb. 20, 1876; d. Paris, Jan. 3, 1945. He studied with Balakirev at the Court Chapel in St. Petersburg (1886–90), then with Liadov and Rimsky-Korsakov at the St. Petersburg Cons. (1895–1900). He was the first composition teacher of Stravinsky, whom he taught privately. After the Russian Revolution he emigrated to Paris, where he remained until his death. He wrote mostly for piano in the manner of the Russian lyric school, and had the good fortune of having his pieces and songs publ. by Belaiev; some of them were included in anthologies of Russian music. He wrote an opera, *The Fairy of the Snows* (1914); a concert overture, which was conducted by Rimsky-Korsakov in St. Petersburg on Nov. 20, 1899; an orch. fantasy, conducted by Glazunov in St. Petersburg on Oct. 28, 1900; *Petite ballade* for Clarinet and Piano; *Pastorale* for Oboe and Piano; Piano Trio; Violin Sonata; Cello Sonata; 2 *Sonata-Fantasias* for Piano; numerous character pieces for piano, and songs.

Akiyama, Kazuyoshi, brilliant Japanese conductor; b. Tokyo, Jan. 2, 1941. He attended the Toho School of Music, studying conducting with Hideo Saito. In 1964 he became conductor of the Tokyo Symph. Orch. His other posts include: principal guest conductor, New Japan Phil., Tokyo; principal conductor, Osaka Phil.; resident conductor and music director, Vancouver Symph. Orch.; music director, American Symph. Orch., N.Y. (1973–78).

Alain, Jehan, French organist and composer; b. St. Germain-en-Laye, Feb. 3, 1911; killed in action at Petits-Puis, near Saumur, June 20, 1940. He received his earliest instruction in music from his father; composed a piece entitled *Etude sur un thème de quatre notes* at the age of 8; then studied organ with Marcel Dupré and composition with Paul Dukas and Roger-Ducasse. Altogether he wrote 127 opus numbers, most of them for organ. His death at the age of 29, while he was leading a motorcycle patrol during the last days of hostilities in France, was a great loss to French music.

Alain, Marie-Claire, noted French organist, sister of **Jehan Alain;** b. St. Germain-en-Laye, Aug. 10, 1926. She was educated at the Paris Cons., studying harmony with Duruflé, counterpoint and fugue with Plé-Caussade, and organ with Dupré. She made her debut in Paris in 1950; later gave successful organ recitals in Europe and the U.S.; she became particularly noted for her authoritative renditions of the organ music of the Baroque period.

Alain, Olivier, French pianist, musicologist, and composer, brother of **Jehan** and **Marie-Claire Alain;** b. St. Germain-en-Laye, Aug. 3, 1918. He studied organ and piano in his youth; then took courses in composition with Aubin and Messiaen at the Paris Cons. From 1950–64 he served as director of the Cons. in St. Germain-en-Laye; in 1961 he was appointed to the faculty of the Ecole César Franck in Paris. He composed an oratorio, *Chant funèbre sur les morts en montagne* (1950); also wrote motets and pieces for organ and piano. He publ. the manual *L'Harmoni* (Paris, 1965) and the monograph *Bach* (Paris, 1970).

Alaleona, Domenico, Italian theorist and composer; b. Montegiorgio, Nov. 16, 1881; d. there, Dec. 28, 1928. He studied organ and clarinet in his native town; in 1901 went to Rome, where he studied piano with Sgambati, organ with Renzi, and theory with De Sanctis at Santa Cecilia Academy; was then active as a choral conductor in Leghorn and Rome; in 1911 obtained the post of prof. of musical esthetics at Santa Cecilia. He wrote an opera, *Mirra* (1912; produced in Rome, March 31, 1920, with critical acclaim, but not revived); a Requiem; *Sinfonia italiana;* 12 *Canzoni italiane;* and 4 *Laudi italiane* for various Instrumental Groups; a cycle of 18 songs, *Melodie Pascoliane;* etc. However, his importance lies in his theoretical writings. His valuable book *Studi sulla storia dell' oratorio musicale in Italia* (Turin, 1908) was reprinted in Milan (1945) as *Storia dell'oratorio musicale in Italia* and is now a standard work. A believer in musical progress, he contributed several original ideas to the theory of modern music, notably in his article "L'armonia modernissima," *Rivista Musicale Italiana* (1911), and originated the term "dodecafonia." He also contributed articles on Italian composers to Eaglefield-Hull's *Dictionary of Modern Music and Musicians* (London, 1924). The entry on Alaleona in that dictionary contains a detailed list of his works and bibliography.

Alary, Jules (Giulio) Eugène Abraham, Italian-French composer; b. Mantua, March 16, 1814; d. Paris, April 17, 1891. He studied at the Cons. of Milan; then played the flute at La Scala. In 1838 he settled in Paris as a successful voice teacher and composer. He wrote numerous operas, among them *Rosamunda* (Florence, June 10, 1840); *Le tre nozze* (Paris, March 29, 1851; a polka-duet from it, sung by Henrietta Sontag and Lablache, was highly popular); and *Sardanapalo* (St. Petersburg, Feb. 16, 1852). His opera *La Voix humaine* had the curious distinction of being staged at the Paris Opéra (Dec. 30, 1861) with the sole purpose of making use of the scenery left over after the fiasco of *Tannhäuser* (the action

of Alary's opera takes place in Wartburg, as does that of *Tannhäuser*). It held the stage for 13 performances (*Tannhäuser* had 3). Alary also wrote a mystery play, *Redemption* (Paris, April 14, 1850), much sacred music, and some chamber works.

Albanese, Licia, noted Italian-American soprano; b. Bari, July 22, 1913. She studied with Emanuel De Rosa in Bari and with Giuseppina Baldassare-Tedeschi in Milan. She made her operatic debut under unusual circumstances at the Teatro Lirico in Milan when she was urgently summoned to sing the second part of *Madama Butterfly* as Cio-Cio-San to substitute for a soprano who was taken ill during the first act. In 1935 she won first prize for best singing in a national Italian contest, and made her official debut in Parma on Dec. 10, 1935, again as Cio-Cio-San. Her success was so great that she was offered a contract with the San Carlo Opera in Naples, and subsequently became a member of La Scala in Milan. She received a number of high honors, among them the Order of Merit in Italy and the award of the Lady Grand Cross of the Equestrian Order of the Holy Sepulchre, which was given to her by Pope Pius XI. On Feb. 9, 1940, she made a brilliant debut at the Metropolitan Opera in N.Y. in her favorite role as Cio-Cio-San; she continued to sing with the Metropolitan for 26 years; altogether she sang there 286 times in N.Y. and 115 times on tour, in 17 roles; besides Cio-Cio-San, which she performed 72 times, she sang Mimi in *La Bohème,* Marguerite in *Faust,* Violetta in *La Traviata,* Desdemona in *Otello,* and Tosca. She gave her final performance at the Metropolitan on April 16, 1966. She returned to the stage for a recital at Carnegie Hall on Feb. 22, 1970, in a program of operatic arias; she sang again at a benefit of the Puccini Foundation in Town Hall, N.Y., on Feb. 5, 1975. She married in 1945 an Italian-American businessman, Joseph Gimma.

Albani, Dame Emma (stage name of **Marie Louise Cécile Emma Lajeunesse**), Canadian dramatic soprano; b. Chambly, near Montreal, Nov. 1, 1847; d. London, April 3, 1930. She sang in a Catholic church in Albany, N.Y., in 1864; was then sent to Europe for study, first in Paris with Duprez, and then in Milan with Lamperti, who dedicated to her his treatise on the trill). She made her debut as Amina in *La Sonnambula* in Messina in 1870, under the name of Albani, taken from an old Italian family. After further appearances in Italy, she made her London debut, again as Amina (Covent Garden, April 2, 1872). In 1873 she sang in Moscow and St. Petersburg. Her American operatic debut was in the same role at the N.Y. Academy of Music, in Max Strakosch's company (Oct. 21, 1874). It paved the way for later successes with the Metropolitan Opera, where she made her first appearance as Gilda (Dec. 23, 1891). Her last important operatic engagement was as Isolde at Covent Garden (June 26, 1896). She sang in concerts, however, for several years longer. Her farewell concert took place at the Royal Albert Hall in London on Oct. 14, 1911. Her repertoire included the roles of Marguerite, Mignon, Ophelia, Elsa, Elisabeth, Lucia, and Desdemona. Albani married Ernest Gye, the lessee of Covent Garden, in 1878. In her singing, she combined high technical skill with profound feeling. She was equally successful on the operatic stage and in oratorio. In appreciation of her services to British art, she was made a Dame of the British Empire (1925). She publ. her memoirs, *Forty Years of Song* (London, 1911).

Albani, Mattia (real name, **Mathias Alban**), violin maker; b. S. Niccolo di Kaltern (Alto Adige), March (baptized, March 28) 1621; d. Bolzano, Feb. 7, 1712. He was a pupil of Jakob Stainer. Violins of Albani's are extant dating from as early as the end of 1644. His best examples date from 1680 onward. The great vogue his violins enjoyed spawned many forgeries; false Albani labels have been discovered on violins dating from as early as 1640; the original labels appeared from 1690. A son, **Giuseppe,** his pupil, worked from 1680–1722 at Bolzano, and another son, **Michele** (1677–1730), at Graz. Other violin makers named Albani, or at least using the name on their instruments (perhaps for its commercial value), are the following, none appearing to have been connected with the family of the original Mattia: Mattia (Rome, c.1650–1715); Nicola (worked at Mantua, c.1763); Filippo (active c.1773); Francesco (active at Graz, c.1724); Michele (at Palermo, 18th century); and Paolo (at Palermo and Cremona, 1630–70).

Albéniz, Isaac, eminent Spanish composer; b. Camprodón, May 29, 1860; d. Cambo-les-Bains (Pyrénées), May 18, 1909. Endowed with exceptionally precocious musical gifts, he was exhibited as a child pianist at a tender age; soon he began taking formal piano lessons with Narciso Oliveros in Barcelona. His sister **Clementine Albéniz** was also a precocious pianist, and they gave concerts together. When he was seven, his mother took him to Paris, where he was accepted as a private pupil by the famous prof. Marmontel, the teacher of Bizet and Debussy. Returning to Spain, he studied with Mendizábal at the Madrid Cons., but possessed by the spirit of adventure, he stowed away on a ship bound for Puerto Rico; from there he made his way to the southern states of the U.S., where he earned a living by playing at places of entertainment. He finally returned to Spain and, having acquired a considerable technique as a serious pianist, he traveled to Europe, and enrolled at the Leipzig Cons. as a student of Jadassohn and Reinecke. Once again in Spain, he was befriended by Count Guillermo Morphy, who sent him to the Brussels Cons., where he studied piano with Brassin and composition with Gevaert and Dupont; he won first prize in 1879; in 1880 he met Liszt in Budapest. After a trip to South America he settled in Barcelona in 1883; there he married Rosina Jordana; one of their daughters, Laura Albéniz, became a well-known painter. A meeting with the eminent musicologist and folk song collector Felipe Pedrell influenced Albéniz in the direction of national Spanish music. Still anxious to perfect his technique of composition, he went to Paris for studies with Paul Dukas and Vincent d'Indy. Abandoning his career as concert pianist, he spent several years in London (1890–93), and in 1893 settled in Paris; there he taught piano at the Schola Cantorum; from 1900 to 1902 he was in Barcelona, and then returned once more to Paris; in 1903 he moved to Nice; later he went to Cambo-les-Bains in the Pyrénées, where he died shortly before his 49th birthday.

Almost all of the works of Albéniz are written for piano, and all without exception are inspired by Spanish folklore. He thus established the modern school of Spanish piano literature, derived from original rhythms and melodic patterns, rather than imitating the imitations of national Spanish music by French and Russian composers. His piano suite *Iberia*, composed between 1906 and 1909, is a brilliant display of piano virtuosity.

Alberghi, Paolo Tommaso, Italian violinist, composer, and teacher; b. Faenza (baptized, Dec. 31), 1716; d. there, Oct. 11, 1785. He studied violin with Tartini; then was a violinist at the Faenza Cathedral, where his brother Don Francesco Alberghi was maestro di cappella; was named first violinist in 1755; upon the death of his brother in 1760, he was appointed maestro di cappella. He was highly esteemed as a violinist and a teacher; among his pupils was Giuseppe Sarti. He composed mostly instrumental works; wrote some 20 violin concertos, which are notable for their late Baroque virtuosity; also composed sonatas and trios; his sacred works include a Magnificat and a Mass.

d'Albert, Eugène (Francis Charles), British-born German pianist and composer; b. Glasgow, April 10, 1864; d. Riga, March 3, 1932. His father, **Charles Louis Napoléon d'Albert** (b. Nienstetten, near Hamburg, Feb. 25, 1809; d. London, May 26, 1886), was a dancing master who wrote popular music; it was from him that d'Albert received his early instruction in music. At the age of 10 he entered the New Music School in London, where he studied piano with Pauer and theory with Stainer, Prout, and Sir Arthur Sullivan. He made extraordinary progress as both a pianist and a composer, and after several appearances at the Popular Concerts, was the soloist in Schumann's concerto at the Crystal Palace in London (Feb. 5, 1881). On Oct. 24, 1881, when only 17, he played his own piano concerto at one of Hans Richter's concerts, arousing great enthusiasm; the press compared him to Mozart and Mendelssohn. He received a Mendelssohn fellowship and went to Vienna; later he studied with Liszt, who was greatly impressed by his technique and often referred to him as "the young Tausig." In 1895, d'Albert was appointed conductor at Weimar; in 1907, became director of the Hochschule für Musik in Berlin. In the wake of his success, he repudiated his English birth, adopting German citizenship, and made repeated statements derogatory to English culture and even to his former English teachers; he further changed his first name to a German form, **Eugen.** During the First World War, he was vocal in his enmity toward England, which led in turn to an understandable repugnance among British musicians to accept his music. Despite a brilliant beginning, Eugène d'Albert did not justify his early promise, and his operas and other works are rarely revived. His musical idiom oscillates between the Italian melodic style and German contrapuntal writing, and fails to achieve originality. A considerable corpus of his autograph music MSS, including 11 of his operas (though not *Tiefland*), was acquired in 1963 by the Library of Congress. Eugène d'Albert's personal life was a stormy one. He was married 6 times; his first wife (1892–95) was Teresa Carreño; his 2nd was the singer Hermine Finck.

WORKS: D'Albert composed industriously. He publ. 2 piano concertos (in B minor and E); Cello Concerto in C; 2 overtures: *Hyperion* and *Esther;* Symph. in F; Orch. Suite in 5 movements (1924); Piano Sonata; Piano Suite in 5 movements; 2 string quartets; *Der Mensch und das Leben* for 6-part Chorus and Orch. (op. 14); 4 piano pieces, op. 16 (Waltz, Scherzo, Intermezzo, Ballade); minor piano pieces and songs. However, his main interest was in the field of opera. Of his 20 operas, the most successful were *Tiefland,* first staged at the German opera in Prague (Nov. 15, 1903), and *Die toten Augen* (Dresden, March 5, 1916). His other operas include: *Der Rubin* (Karlsruhe, Oct. 12, 1893); *Ghismonda* (Dresden, Nov. 28, 1895); *Gernot* (Mannheim, April 11, 1897); *Die Abreise* (Frankfurt, Oct. 20, 1898); *Kain* (Berlin, Feb. 17, 1900); *Der Improvisator* (Berlin, Feb. 20, 1902); *Flauto solo* (Prague, Nov. 12, 1905); *Tragaldabas,* or *Der geborgte Ehemann* (Hamburg, Dec. 3, 1907); *Izeÿl* (Hamburg, Nov. 6, 1909); *Die verschenkte Frau* (Vienna, Feb. 6, 1912); *Liebesketten* (Vienna, Nov. 12, 1912); *Der Stier von Olivera* (Leipzig, March 10, 1918); *Revolutionshochzeit* (Leipzig, Oct. 26, 1919); *Scirocco* (Darmstadt, May 18, 1921); *Mareike von Nymwegen* (Hamburg, Oct. 31, 1923); *Der Golem* (Frankfurt, Nov. 14, 1926); *Die schwarze Orchidee* (Leipzig, Dec. 1, 1928); *Mister Wu* (unfinished; completed by Leo Blech; Dresden, Sept. 29, 1932).

Albert, Heinrich, German composer; b. Lobenstein, Saxony, July 8, 1604; d. Königsberg, Oct. 6, 1651. In 1622 he went to Dresden to study music with his cousin Heinrich Schütz; then studied law at the Univ. of Leipzig; traveled to Warsaw with a peace delegation in 1627, but was seized as a prisoner of war by the Swedes; upon his release in 1628, he settled in Königsberg; was appointed cathedral organist in 1631; took courses with Johann Stobäus. He publ. in Königsberg 8 books of arias (1638–50); a cantata, *Musikalische Kürbs-Hütte* (1645), consisting of a cycle of 12 terzets to Albert's own texts (a modern reprint was issued by J.M. Müller-Blattau in 1932). A selection of his songs is found in the *Neudrucke deutscher Litteraturwerke* (Halle, 1883); the arias in vols. XII and XIII of Denkmäler Deutscher Tonkunst.

Albert, Stephen, American composer; b. New York, Feb. 6, 1941. He played trumpet, French horn, and piano in the school band in Great Neck, N.Y.; also took private lessons in composition with Elie Siegmeister, who made his home there. In 1958 he enrolled in the Eastman School of Music in Rochester, N.Y., in the class of Bernard Rogers. In 1960 he went to Stockholm to study with Karl-Birger Blomdahl; returning to the U.S., he took courses at the Philadelphia Musical Academy with Roy Harris and Joseph Castaldo. In 1962 he studied counterpoint with George Rochberg at the Univ. of Pennsylvania in Philadelphia. In 1965–67 he lived in Rome on an American Prix de Rome grant. In 1968–69 he held a Guggenheim fellowship; in 1970–71 he was a lecturer at Stanford Univ.; in 1974–76 was on the faculty at Smith College in Northampton, Mass. Albert's style of composition reflects his geographical wanderings and intellectual wanderings, resulting in a pragmatic and unprejudiced selection of fitting idioms. Thus, while refusing to renounce tonality, he espouses the quaquaversality of modern moods and modes without blundering into the crepuscular regions of serialistic glossolalia. *Musicus sum; musicae nil a me alienum puto,* seems to be his motto: nothing that is of music is alien to him.

Alberti, Domenico, Venetian composer; b. Venice, 1710; d. Formio (or Rome), c.1740. He studied with Lotti, and won considerable renown as a singer and harpsichord player; wrote 3 operas, *Endimione, Galatea,* and *Olimpiade.* In 1737 he was a member of the Venetian Embassy in Rome, and made several appearances there as a singer and player. His fame in music history rests on his reputed invention of the arpeggio style of keyboard accompaniment, which became known as the "Alberti Bass." His set of 8 sonatas, publ. by Walsh in London, gives many illustrations of this device.

Alberti, Gasparo, Italian composer; b. Padua, c.1480; d. Bergamo, c.1560. He became a singer at Santa Maria Maggiore in Bergamo in 1508; periodically he served as its maestro di cappella (until 1554). He is regarded as one of the most significant composers of sacred polyphonic vocal music in Italy in the early Renaissance. His works include 2 8-voice Magnificat settings; Psalms; 5 masses; Lamentations; canticles.

Albicastro, Henricus (real name, **Heinrich Weissenburg**), Swiss violinist and composer; b. Switzerland at an uncertain date; d. c.1738 in the Netherlands, where he was a court musician. His works for string instruments were publ. in Amsterdam between 1700 and 1706; of these, 12 concertos *a* 4, a trio sonata, and several violin sonatas with basso continuo are available in modern editions.

Albinoni, Tomaso, Italian violinist and composer; b. Venice, June 8, 1671; d. there, Jan. 17, 1750. Between 1694 and 1740 he produced 53 operas, most of them in Venice. He rarely absented himself from Venice, but it is known that he attended the premiere of his opera *Griselda* in Florence (1703), serving as concertmaster in the orch.; in 1722 he was in Munich, where he presented his festive opera *I veri amici*. It is, however, as a composer of instrumental music that he is significant. Bach, his close contemporary, admired Albinoni's music; made arrangements of 2 fugues from Albinoni's trio sonatas.

Alboni, Marietta (real name, **Maria Anna Marzia Alboni**), famous Italian contralto; b. Città di Castello, March 6, 1823; d. Ville d'Avray, France, June 23, 1894. She studied in Bologna with Mombelli; in 1841 was introduced to Rossini, who agreed to give her lessons. She made her debut in Bologna, in Pacini's opera *Saffo* (Oct. 3, 1842); shortly afterward sang at La Scala in Rossini's *Assedio de Corinto* (*Le Siège de Corinthe;* Dec. 30, 1842). She then sang in Russia and obtained great success during the season of 1844–45 in St. Petersburg, appearing at the Italian opera with Tamburini, Rubini, and Mme. Viardot. After appearances in Prague, Berlin, and Hamburg, she appeared in the spring of 1847 in Rome and at Covent Garden, where she became a rival of Jenny Lind with the public. So successful were her London appearances that her fees were increased to 2,000 pounds a season. She gave 4 "concerts-spectacles" in Paris in Oct. 1847; made her Paris opera debut in Rossini's *Semiramide* (Dec. 2, 1847). Auber wrote the opera *Zéline ou La Corbeille d'oranges* for her and she sang at its premiere (May 16, 1851). She made an American tour from June 1852 till May 1853 in concert and opera, appearing in N.Y., Boston, and other cities. On July 21, 1853, Alboni married Count Pepoli, who died on Oct. 10, 1867; on Jan. 22, 1877, she married Charles Ziéger, a French officer, and settled in France. Suffering from excessive obesity, she gradually retired from the stage, but continued to appear occasionally in concert, singing while sitting in a large chair. Her vocal range was exceptional, from the contralto G to high soprano C, enabling her to sing soprano parts. She bequeathed a large sum of money to the city of Paris. In appreciation, the City Council, on Oct. 15, 1895, named a street in Passy after her. Arthur Pougin's monograph *Marietta Alboni* (Paris, 1912) quotes many of her autobiographical notes and presents a documented outline of her career.

Albrechtsberger, Johann Georg, famous Austrian theoretical writer, composer, and teacher; b. Klosterneuburg, near Vienna, Feb. 3, 1736; d. Vienna, March 7, 1809. After holding positions as organist and music master in smaller towns, especially in Melk (1759–65), where his fine playing attracted the Emperor Joseph's notice, in 1772 he was engaged in Vienna as regens chori to the Carmelites; was appointed court organist in the same year, and, in 1792, music director at St. Stephen's Cathedral. His important theoretical writings (complete ed. publ. by Seyfried) are: *Gründliche Anweisung zur Composition* (1790 and 1818; French ed., 1814); *Kurzgefasste Methode, den Generalbass zu erlernen* (1792; also in French); *Clavierschule für Anfänger* (1808); and some lesser essays. A selection from his instrumental works is publ. in Denkmäler der Tonkunst in Österreich, vol. 33 (formerly 16.ii); the MS scores (in the possession of Prince Esterhazy-Galantha) comprise 26 masses, 43 graduals, 34 offertories, 6 oratorios; 28 trios, 42 quartets, and 38 quintets for strings; besides a great variety of church music. He had many celebrated pupils, among whom was Beethoven (from Jan. 1794 to March 1795). Scholars regard the quality of instruction he gave to Beethoven as of a very high order.

Albrici (or **Alberici**), **Vincenzo,** Italian organist, harpsichordist, and composer; b. Rome, June 26, 1631; d. Prague, Aug. 8, 1696. He was born into a musical family; his father, Domenico, was an alto singer; his brother, Bartolomeo, was also a musician. Vincenzo Albrici was a boy soprano at the German College in Rome, where he studied with Carissimi (1641–46); he then accompanied his father and brother to Lombardy, Germany, Flanders, and Sweden; was in the service of Queen Christina of Sweden (1652–53); in 1654 he became a Kapellmeister at the Dresden court, where he served with Schütz and Bontempi; in 1660 he was once more in the service of Queen Christina; in 1662–63 he was again in Dresden. He subsequently went to England, where he entered the service of King Charles II. He returned to Dresden about 1668; was named director of the Italian musicians at the court in 1676; after the Italian musicians were dismissed in 1680, he became organist at the Thomaskirche in Leipzig in 1681 (he was briefly converted to the Protestant faith). In 1682 he became organist at St. Augustus in Prague, a post he held until his death. He composed about 40 Latin motets, Italian solo cantatas, and some other vocal works.

Albright, William (Hugh), American composer, pianist, and organist; b. Gary, Ind., Oct. 20, 1944. He studied piano with Rosetta Goodkind and music theory with Hugh Aitken at the Juilliard Preparatory Dept. in N.Y. (1959–62); then took courses in composition with Ross Lee Finney and Leslie Bassett at the Univ. of Michigan; also studied organ with Marilyn Mason there (1963–70). In 1968 he went to France and studied composition with Olivier Messiaen at the Paris Cons.; also took private lessons with Max Deutsch. In 1970 he joined the faculty of the Univ. of Michigan to teach composition; also served as associate director of its Electronic Music Studio. He received a Guggenheim fellowship in 1976; was composer-in-residence at the American Academy in Rome in 1979. In his compositions he pursues quaquaversal methods of experimental music, using varied techniques according to need. He has also made a concert career as a pianist in programs of ragtime and jazz.

Alcantara, Theo, Spanish conductor; b. Cuenca, April 16, 1941. He studied at the Madrid Cons.; then took courses in conducting at the Mozarteum in Salzburg. He began his career as a conductor with the Frankfurt Opera Orch. (1964–66); then came to the U.S., where he served as director of orchs. at the

Univ. of Michigan in Ann Arbor (1968–73), and then music director of the Grand Rapids Symph. Orch. (1973–78). In 1978 he became music director and principal conductor of the Phoenix Symph. Orch.; also artistic director of the Music Academy of the West in Santa Barbara, in 1981. He appeared as a conductor with the Metropolitan Opera, N.Y. City Opera, Washington, D.C., Opera, San Diego Opera, and others; also conducted the orchs. of Philadelphia, Pittsburgh, and Detroit, and in Europe.

Alda, Frances (real name, **Frances Davies**), lyric soprano; b. Christchurch, New Zealand, May 31, 1883; d. Venice, Sept. 18, 1952. She studied with Marchesi in Paris, and made her debut as Manon at the Opéra-Comique (April 15, 1904). She later sang in Brussels, London, Milan, Warsaw, and Buenos Aires. Her debut at the Metropolitan Opera was on Dec. 7, 1908 (opposite Caruso in *Rigoletto*); her farewell appearance there, on Dec. 28, 1929, in *Manon Lescaut.* She also made numerous recital tours in the U.S. Her principal roles included Louise, Mimi, Manon, Marguerite, Juliette, Gilda, Violetta, and Aida. She married Giulio Gatti-Casazza, manager of the Metropolitan Opera, on April 3, 1910; divorced, 1928; married Ray Vir Den in 1941. In 1939 she became an American citizen. She wrote an autobiography, *Men, Women and Tenors* (Boston, 1937).

Alderighi, Dante, Italian composer and pianist; b. Taranto, July 7, 1898; d. Rome, Dec. 12, 1968. He went to Rome as a child and studied with Giovanni Sgambati; from 1911–14 he was in Leipzig, studying piano with Teichmüller and theory with Krehl. Returning to Italy, he took lessons in composition with Malipiero; gave many recitals and began to write music criticism. In 1936 he was appointed prof. of piano at Santa Cecilia Academy in Rome.
   WORKS: 2 piano concertos; *Fantasia* for Piano and Chamber Orch. (1932); *Rococo Suite* for Band (1932; revised 1952); oratorio, *Maria a Nazareth* (1949); *Divertimento* for Piano and Strings (1952); many choral works.

Aldrich, Putnam (Calder), American harpsichord player and music scholar; b. South Swansea, Mass., July 14, 1904; d. Cannes, France, April 18, 1975. He studied at Yale Univ. (B.A., 1926); then went to Europe and took piano lessons with Tobias Matthay in London (1926–27) and harpsichord with Wanda Landowska in Paris (1929–33); later took his Ph.D. at Harvard Univ. (1942). From 1950 to 1969 he was on the faculty at Stanford Univ. in California. He publ. an important treatise, *Ornamentation in J.S. Bach's Organ Works* (N.Y., 1950), as part of a much larger and very valuable work on Baroque ornamentation, originally submitted as his doctoral dissertation at Harvard; the work still awaits publication. He also publ. *Rhythm in 17th-century Italian Monody* (London, 1965).

d'Alembert, Jean-le-Rond, French philosopher and encyclopedist; b. Paris, Nov. 16, 1717; d. there, Oct. 29, 1783. He was the illegitimate child of one Mme. de Tencin and an artillery officer named Destouches; his mother abandoned him on the steps of the church of St. Jean-le-Rond, which name was subsequently attached to him. Later his father acknowledged him, and enabled him to study. He was sent to the Mazarin College, and progressed rapidly in mathematics. He also was interested in theoretical musical subjects, and publ. several treatises on acoustics and on the theory of music: *Recherches sur la courbe, que forme une corde tendue mise en vibration* (1749); *Recherches sur les vibrations des cordes sonores* and *Recherches sur la vitesse du son* (both in *Opuscules mathématiques,* Paris, 1761–80); *Reflexions sur la musique en général et sur la musique française en particulier* (1754); *Reflexions sur la théorie de la musique* (1777). His best-known work on music was *Eléments de musique, théorique et pratique, suivant les principes de M. Rameau* (1752), which went into 6 editions. He contributed several articles on music to the famous *Encyclopédie,* which he edited with Diderot.

Alessandrescu, Alfred, eminent Rumanian composer and conductor; b. Bucharest, Aug. 14, 1893; d. there, Feb. 18, 1959. He studied piano and theory at the Bucharest Cons. with Kiriac and Castaldi (1903–11); then went to Paris, where he took composition courses with Vincent d'Indy at the Schola Cantorum and with Paul Vidal at the Paris Cons. (1913–14). Returning to Bucharest, he was active as a pianist. In 1921 he was appointed conductor of the Rumanian Opera in Bucharest, retaining this post until his death; also conducted the Budapest Phil. Orch. (1926–40) and was artistic director of the Bucharest Radio (1933–59); appeared as a conductor in Germany and France; was piano accompanist to Georges Enesco, Jacques Thibaud, and others.

Alessandri, Felice, Italian opera composer; b. Rome, Nov. 24, 1747; d. Casinalbo, Aug. 15, 1798. He studied music in Naples; then lived in Paris (1765–68) and in London (1768). From 1784–89 he was in Russia; then in Berlin as 2nd conductor at the Royal Opera (1789–92); finally returned to Italy. Alessandri wrote about 30 operas in all; 2 were produced in London: *La moglie fedele* (1768) and *Il re alla caccia* (1769); and 2 at La Scala in Milan: *Calliroe* (Dec. 26, 1778) and *Ezio* (first given in Verona for Carnevale, 1767; staged at La Scala Feb. 1, 1782). In Potsdam he produced *Il ritorno di Ulisse* (Jan. 25, 1790); *Dario* (1791); and the comic opera *La compagnia d'opera a Nanchino* (1790), which exhibited the colorful effects of pseudo-Chinese music. His opera *Virginia* was given in Venice (Dec. 26, 1793). He also wrote an oratorio, *Betulia liberata* (1781); *6 sinfonie* in 8 parts; 6 trio sonatas for 2 Violins and Basso Continuo; etc.; all in the then-prevalent Italian manner.

d'Alessandro, Raffaele, Swiss composer; b. Gallen, March 17, 1911; d. Lausanne, March 17, 1959 (on his 48th birthday). He studied music with Victor Schlatter and Willi Schuh in Zürich; then went to

Paris, where he studied composition with Nadia Boulanger and organ with Marcel Dupré. In 1940 he returned to Switzerland and settled in Lausanne, where he became active as a pianist, organist, and composer.

Alessandro, Victor, American conductor; b. Waco, Texas, Nov. 27, 1915; d. San Antonio, Nov. 27, 1976 (on his 61st birthday). He studied French horn with his father; then took composition courses with Howard Hanson and Bernard Rogers at the Eastman School of Music in Rochester, N.Y.; subsequently attended classes at the Santa Cecilia Academy in Rome; returning to the U.S., he was conductor of the Oklahoma Symph. Orch. (1938–51); in 1951 was appointed conductor of the San Antonio Orch., a position which he held until his death.

Alexandrov, Alexander, Russian composer; b. Plakhino (Riazan dist.), April 1, 1883; d. Berlin, July 8, 1946, during a concert tour. He studied with Rimsky-Korsakov and Glazunov at the St. Petersburg Cons. (1899–1901) and later at the Moscow Cons. with Vasilenko (1909–13). In 1928 he organized the Red Army Ensemble and conducted it on numerous tours in Russia and abroad. His song *Hymn of the Bolshevik Party,* with a new set of words, was proclaimed the Soviet national anthem on March 15, 1944.

Alexandrov, Anatoli, eminent Russian pianist and composer; b. Moscow, May 25, 1888; d. there, April 16, 1982. He studied with Taneyev at the Moscow Cons. (1907–10); also studied composition there with Vasilenko and piano with Igumnov, graduating in 1916. In 1923 he became a prof. at the Moscow Cons. He composed mainly for piano; wrote 14 piano sonatas (1914–71); in his style of composition he followed the main lines of Rachmaninoff and Scriabin. His other works include 2 operas, *Bela* (Moscow, Dec. 10, 1946) and *Wild Bara* (Moscow, March 2, 1957); 4 string quartets (1914–53); *Classical Suite* for Orch. (1926); *Dithyramb* for Double Bass and Piano (1959); several song cycles; and incidental music for theatrical plays.

Alfano, Franco, eminent Italian composer; b. Posilippo (Naples), March 8, 1875; d. San Remo, Oct. 27, 1954. He studied composition with Paolo Serrao in Naples, and with Jadassohn and Hans Sitt in Leipzig. From the beginning of his musical career, Alfano was interested in opera. His first stage work, *Miranda,* was produced in Leipzig when he was barely 20; another opera, *La fonte di Enchir,* followed (Breslau, Nov. 8, 1898). In 1899 he went to Paris and became fascinated by light theater music. While in Paris he wrote *Napoli,* a ballet in the folk manner, which was staged at the Folies-Bergères (Jan. 28, 1901), proving so successful that it ran for 160 successive performances. Returning to Italy, he began work on an opera based on Tolstoy's novel *Resurrection.* It was produced as *Risurrezione* in Turin (Nov. 4, 1904) with sensational acclaim; the American premiere (Chicago, Dec. 31, 1925) was

equally successful; there were also numerous performances in Germany and France. The opera was widely praised for its dramatic power and melodic richness in the best tradition of realistic Italian opera. Alfano continued to compose industriously for another half-century, but his later operas failed to equal the success of *Risurrezione.* They are: *Il Principe Zilah* (Genoa, Feb. 3, 1909); *L'ombra di Don Giovanni* (La Scala, April 3, 1914); *La leggenda di Sakuntala* (Bologna, Dec. 10, 1921); *Madonna Imperia,* lyric comedy (Turin, May 5, 1927; Metropolitan Opera, N.Y., Feb. 8, 1928); *L'Ultimo Lord* (Naples, April 19, 1930); *Cyrano de Bergerac* (Rome, Jan. 22, 1936); *Il Dottor Antonio* (Rome, April 30, 1949). Alfano also wrote 3 symphs. (1909, 1932, 1934), 3 string quartets, a violin sonata, a cello sonata, and a ballet, *Vesuvius* (1938; a symph. poem was drawn from it in 1946). One of Alfano's signal achievements was that he completed Puccini's last opera, *Turandot,* adding the last scene. His *Hymn to Bolivar* for Chorus and Orch., written for the centennial of Bolivar's death, was performed in Caracas, Venezuela, on Dec. 22, 1930. He was also active in the field of musical education; was successively director of the Liceo Musicale in Bologna (1918–23); director of the Turin Cons. (1923–39); superintendent of the Teatro Massimo in Palermo (1940–42); and (1947–50) acting director of the Rossini Cons. in Pesaro.

Alfarabi (or **Alpharabius,** properly **Al Farabi**), **Abu Nasr,** so named from his birthplace, Farab (now transoxine Othrâx), Arabian music theorist; b. c.870; d. Damascus, c.950. Of Turkish descent, he was a Greek scholar and attempted unsuccessfully to introduce the Greek musical system into his country. He was renowned for his writings on philosophy, political science, and the arts; his principal work is *Kitab al-Musiqi al-Kabir* (*Greater Book about Music;* reprint with commentary, Cairo, 1967), dealing with acoustics, intervals, scales, instruments, and rhythm. The 2nd vol. of this work was lost. Excerpts from this book are contained in Kosegarten's *Alii Ispahanis Liber Cantilenarum Magnus* (1840) and in J. Land's *Recherches sur l'histoire de la gamme arabe* (Leyden, 1884). Another treatise, *Kitab al-Iqua'at,* was trans. into German by E. Neubauer in *Oriens* (1968/69).

Alfieri, Pietro, Italian music scholar; b. Rome, June 29, 1801; d. there, June 12, 1863. He was a member of the Camaldolese Order; taught Gregorian music at the English College in Rome. His major work is *Raccolta di musica sacra* (1841–46), a collection of 16th-century church music in 7 vols., which includes virtually all representative works of Palestrina; other collections are *Excerpta ex celebrioribus de musica viris* (Rome, 1840), containing works by Palestrina, Victoria, and Allegri; *Raccolta di motetti* (1841); etc. His essays on Gregorian chant are very valuable: *Ristabilimento del canto e della musica ecclesiastica* (1843); *Saggio storico del canto gregoriano* (1855); *Prodromo sulla restaurazione de' libri di canto ecclesiastico detto* *gregoriano* (1857); etc. He also publ. a biography of N. Jommelli (1845) and contributed articles on musical subjects to Italian periodicals.

Alfvén, Hugo, outstanding Swedish composer; b. Stockholm, May 1, 1872; d. Falun, May 8, 1960. He studied violin at the Stockholm Cons. (1887–91); continued these studies with Lars Zetterquist until 1896 while taking composition lessons from Johan Lindegren. He was then sent by the government to Brussels to complete his violin studies with César Thomson (1896–99). Government scholarships in 1896, 1897, and 1899, as well as the Jenny Lind stipend (1900–03), enabled him to study composition in many European countries. In 1910 he became music director at the Univ. of Uppsala and conductor of the student chorus until his retirement in 1939; continued to conduct various mixed choruses.
WORKS: His best-known work is *Midsommarvaka (Midsummer Vigil;* Stockholm, May 10, 1904), the first of his 3 Swedish rhapsodies for Orch. It was produced as a ballet, *La Nuit de Saint-Jean,* by the Ballets Suédois in Paris, Oct. 25, 1920, and had over 250 perfs. in 4 years. His other works include the 2nd and 3rd Swedish rhapsodies: *Uppsala* (1907) and *Dalecarlian* (1937); 5 symphs.: No. 1 (1896–97; Stockholm, Feb. 9, 1897); No. 2 (1898–99; Stockholm, May 2, 1899); No. 3 (1905–06; Göteborg, Dec. 5, 1906); No. 4, with Soprano and Tenor (1918–19; Stockholm, Nov. 4, 1919); No. 5 (1942–52; first complete perf., Stockholm, April 30, 1952; Alfvén withdrew the work except for the first movement, which subsequently had frequent perfs. as a separate piece); 2 ballet pantomimes: *Bergakungen (The Mountain King;* 1923) and *Den förlorade sonen (The Prodigal Son;* 1957); *En skärgårdssägen (A Tale of the Skerries),* symph. poem (1905); *Festspiel (Festival Music)* for Orch. (1907); suite of incidental music to the play *Gustaf II Adolf* (1932); *Synnöve Solbakken,* suite for Small Orch. (1934); 10 cantatas, many contributed for various occasions, such as patriotic anniversaries, among them one celebrating the 450th year since the founding of Uppsala Univ. (1927) and another on the 500th jubilee of the Swedish Parliament (1935); Violin Sonata (1896); *Elegie* for Horn and Organ (1897); *Skärgårdsbilder (Pictures from the Skerries)* for Piano (1902); a ballad on Gustaf Vasa for Soloists, Mixed Chorus, and Organ (1920); numerous male choruses and folk-song arrangements. The music of Alfvén represents the best traits of Scandinavian national art, along the lines of Grieg and Sibelius. He publ. 4 vols. of memoirs: *Första satsen* (Stockholm, 1946); *Tempo furioso* (1948); *I dur och moll* (1949); *Finale* (1952).

Algarotti, Francesco, Italian musician and scholar; b. Venice, Dec. 11, 1712; d. Pisa, May 3, 1764. The fame of his great knowledge reached Frederick the Great, who invited him to Berlin in 1740 and gave him the title of Count, and, in 1747, that of "Chevalier de l'ordre pour le mérite." In 1753 Algarotti returned to Italy. His musical monument is the *Saggio sopra l'opera in musica,* publ. in 1755; also in many later eds., including German and French transla-

tions. The English text of the *Saggio . . .* is reproduced in part in O. Strunk's *Source Readings in Music History* (N.Y., 1950).

Aliabiev, Alexander, Russian song composer; b. Tobolsk, Siberia, Aug. 15, 1787; d. Moscow, March 6, 1851. His father was the governor of Tobolsk, and Aliabiev spent his childhood there. The family went to St. Petersburg in 1796, and in 1804 settled in Moscow. He studied music in Moscow and had his first songs publ. in 1810. During the War of 1812, he served in the Russian army, and participated in the entry of the Russian army into Dresden and Paris. Returning to Russia, he lived in St. Petersburg, in Voronezh, and in Moscow. In 1825 he was arrested on suspicion of murder after a card game, was sentenced to prison, and in 1828 was deported to his birthplace in Siberia. There he organized concerts of popular music and also composed. In 1831 he was allowed to return to European Russia and lived in the Caucasus and in Orenburg. In 1843 he returned to Moscow, but was still under police surveillance. He wrote more than 100 songs, of which *The Nightingale* became extremely popular; it is often used in the music lesson scene in Russian productions of Rossini's opera *The Barber of Seville;* Glinka and Liszt made piano arrangements of it. He also wrote a symph., 3 string quartets, 2 piano trios, a piano quintet, a violin sonata, a Quartet for 4 Flutes, a Quintet for Wind Instruments, a piano sonata, choruses. Among his works for the theater are scores of incidental music to *The Prisoner of the Caucasus* and to Shakespeare's plays; also stage ballads: *The Village Philosopher, The Moon Night,* and *Theatrical Combat* (with Verstovsky and Mauer).

Ali Akbar Khan, Indian instrumentalist; b. Shibpore, Bengal, April 14, 1922. He studied dhrupad, dhamar, khayal, and sarod with his father; pakhawaj and tabla with his uncle. He founded the Ali Akbar College of Music in Calcutta in 1956; toured widely in Europe, America, and Japan as a virtuoso; held the post of court musician in Jodhpur. He has written a number of new ragas. Several of his students achieved prominence as Indian instrumentalists in their own right.

Alkan (real name, **Morhange**), **Charles-Henri Valentin,** French pianist and composer of Jewish extraction; b. Paris, Nov. 30, 1813; d. there, March 29, 1888. His 4 brothers were also musicians; his father was the founder of a school for Jewish children. Alkan's talent was precocious, and he was accepted at the Paris Cons. at the age of 6 and studied piano with Zimmermann. In 1833 he visited London, then returned to Paris, where his main activities were playing concerts in the fashionable salons and teaching piano. He entered the brilliant circle of musicians and littérateurs, among whom were Chopin, George Sand, Hugo, and Liszt.
WORKS: Like Chopin, Alkan wrote almost exclusively for piano; the list of his works includes 76 opus numbers, in addition to many pieces not numbered by opus. His pieces are programmatic, bear-

ing such titles as *Désir;* a set of variations, *Les Omnibus; Le Vent* (op. 15); *Le Tambour bat aux champs* (op. 50); he was the first composer to write a piece descriptive of the railroad (*Le Chemin de fer,* op. 27). His 2 sets of études, in all major and minor keys (op. 35 and 39), of transcendent difficulty, present great interest as examples of modern piano technique. Other works are *3 études de bravoure* (op. 16); *Le Preux, Etude de concert* (op. 17); *3 pièces poétiques* (op. 18); *Bourrée d'Auvergne* (op. 29); Sonata (op. 33, subtitled *Les 4 Ages*); *Les Mois* (opp. 8, 74), comprising 12 pieces; etc. He also wrote 2 piano concertos, a Piano Trio, a Cello Sonata, and vocal music. César Franck arranged several of his pieces for organ. For a long time Alkan's music was completely forgotten, but his significance as an inventive composer became more evident in the 20th century.

Allegri, Domenico, Italian composer; b. Rome, 1585; d. there, Sept. 5, 1629. He was maestro di cappella at Santa Maria Maggiore from 1610–29, and was one of the first to provide vocal music with an independent instrumental accompaniment. A few of his motets are extant (a soprano solo, a tenor duet, and a bass solo, each accompanied by 2 violins).

Allegri, Gregorio, Italian composer; b. Rome, c.1582; d. there, Feb. 7, 1652. He was a choirboy in Rome from 1591–96; then studied with Giovanni Maria Nanino (1600–1607). He entered the Papal Chapel in 1630 after serving for some years as chorister and composer for the Cathedral at Fermo. He is chiefly known as the composer of the celebrated *Miserere* in 9 parts (i.e., for 2 Choirs, one singing 4 parts and one 5), regularly sung during Holy Week at the Sistine Chapel; Mozart wrote this out after hearing it twice, though surreptitiously, since its publication was forbidden on pain of excommunication; since then it has been frequently published. Many other works by Allegri are preserved in MS; one book of *concertini* and 2 books of *mottetti* have been printed; also a 4-part Sonata for Strings, which might be regarded as the prototype of the string quartet.

Allen, Betty, black American mezzo-soprano; b. Campbell, Ohio, March 17, 1930. She attended Wilberforce Univ. (1944–46); then studied at the Hartford School of Music (1950–53); among her teachers were Paul Ulanowsky and Zinka Milanov. She sang at the N.Y. City Opera in 1954; also sang opera in San Francisco, Houston, Boston, and Santa Fe. On Feb. 20, 1973, she made her Metropolitan Opera debut in N.Y. She taught at the Manhattan School of Music and the North Carolina School of the Arts. In 1979 she became executive director of the Harlem School of the Arts.

Allen, Sir Hugh Percy, eminent English organist and educator; b. Reading, Dec. 23, 1869; d. Oxford, Feb. 20, 1946. He studied with Dr. F. Read in Reading, and at Oxford Univ. (Mus.Doc., 1898). At the age of 11 he acted as church organist in Reading. Thereafter he was an organist at various churches and cathedrals until the turn of the century. He was appointed organist at New College, Oxford (1901–18), and later (1908–18) director of music at Univ. College in Reading. In 1918 he succeeded Sir Walter Parratt as prof. of music at Oxford, and in the same year became director of the Royal College of Music in London, from which he resigned in 1937 (succeeded by George Dyson). He was knighted in 1920. For many years he conducted the London and the Oxford Bach Choirs; he was an ardent promoter of British music.

Allen, Paul Hastings, American composer; b. Hyde Park, Mass., Nov. 28, 1883; d. Boston, Sept. 28, 1952. He studied at Harvard Univ. (A.B., 1903); then went to Italy. During World War I he was in the American diplomatic service in Italy; returning to the U.S. in 1920, he settled in Boston. He learned to play virtually all the orch. instruments as well as piano, and acquired fluent knowledge in Italian, German, and French, as well as a smattering of Russian. His music reflected the Italian techniques in operatic composition, while his instrumental works were written largely in a Romantic manner. He wrote much chamber music for unusual combinations, such as a Quartet for 2 Clarinets, Basset Horn, and Bass Clarinet.
WORKS: Operas: *Il filtro* (Genoa, Oct. 26, 1912); *Milda* (Venice, June 14, 1913); *L'ultimo dei Mohicani* (Florence, Feb. 24, 1916); *Cleopatra* (1921); *La piccola Figaro* (1931); *Pilgrim Symphony* (1910; received the Paderewski prize); piano pieces; choral works; songs.

Allen, Thomas, English baritone; b. Seaham, Sept. 10, 1944. He was educated at the Royal College of Music in London; after singing in the Glyndebourne Chorus, he made his debut with the Welsh National Opera in 1969; from 1971 he sang at Covent Garden; also at the Aldeburgh and Glyndebourne festivals, and in Paris, Florence, and Buenos Aires. He is generally regarded as one of the best European baritones, praised for both his lyric and dramatic abilities.

Allende (-Sarón), (Pedro) Humberto, eminent Chilean composer; b. Santiago, June 29, 1885; d. there, Aug. 16, 1959. He studied violin and music theory at the National Cons. in Santiago (1889–1908); then taught in public schools there. In 1918 he visited France and Spain; in 1928 served as Chilean delegate to the Congress of Popular Arts in Prague, under the auspices of the League of Nations; in 1929 he took part in the Festival of Ibero-American Music in Barcelona. Returning to Santiago, he taught composition at the National Cons. (1930–50). He received the National Arts Prize in appreciation of his work in musical ethnology. His music is marked with an exquisite sense of authentic Chilean folk song, while the purely formal structure follows the impressionistic manner akin to that of Debussy, Ravel, and Granados.

Almeida, Laurindo, Brazilian guitarist; b. São Paulo, Sept. 2, 1917. After mastering the guitar, he settled in Rio de Janeiro and made appearances on the radio; also led his own orch. at the Casino da Urca. In 1947 he moved to the U.S.; was a soloist with Stan Kenton's jazz band; subsequently gave numerous recitals and was a soloist with symph. orchs.; also appeared in recital with his wife, the soprano **Deltra Eamon.**

Almquist, Carl Jonas Love, Swedish composer; b. Stockholm, Nov. 28, 1793; d. Bremen, Nov. 26, 1866. He studied at Uppsala Univ., and composed songs to his own words, but refused to study music theory for fear that his instinct for simple melodic writing might be destroyed by learning. His life was an adventurous one; he was forced to leave Sweden after an accusation of murder was leveled against him. From 1851 to 1865 he lived in America; then went to Germany, where he died. His publications included the song collection *Törnrosens bok* (Stockholm, 1832–42); he also publ. *Fria Fantasier* for Piano (1847–49).

Alpaerts, Flor, Belgian composer; b. Antwerp, Sept. 12, 1876; d. there, Oct. 5, 1954. He studied composition with Benoit and Blockx and violin at the Flemish Cons. in Antwerp; in 1903 he joined its staff; was its director from 1934–41. He conducted the local orch. at the Zoological Gardens (1919–51); was in charge of the edition of works by Peter Benoit. His own music is marked by an intense feeling for the modalities of Flemish folk songs.

Altenburg, Johann Ernst, German trumpet player and composer; b. Weissenfels, June 15, 1734; d. Bitterfeld, May 14, 1801. He served as a field trumpeter during the Seven Years' War; returning to civilian life, he became an organist at Bitterfeld. He wrote the first specialized manual on playing the trumpet and kettledrums, *Versuch einer Anleitung zur heroisch-musikalischen Trompeter- und Paukerkunst* (Halle, 1795; reprinted, Dresden, 1911); also pieces for 2, 4, 6, and 8 trumpets, and a Concerto for 7 Trumpets and Kettledrums.

Althouse, Paul, American tenor; b. Reading, Pa., Dec. 2, 1889; d. New York, Feb. 6, 1954. He studied with Oscar Saenger; made his debut as Dimitri in the American premiere of *Boris Godunov* at the Metropolitan Opera on March 19, 1913; continued on its roster until 1920, and joined it again in 1923; sang Wagnerian roles as a Heldentenor at the Metropolitan from 1934 to 1940; was a soloist with Toscanini and the N.Y. Philharmonic in Beethoven's Ninth Symph.; also toured in Europe, Australia, and New Zealand as a concert singer; subsequently was chiefly active as a vocal teacher in N.Y. Among his most prominent students were Eleanor Steber and Richard Tucker.

Altnikol, Johann Christoph, German organist and composer; b. Berna, Silesia, Dec. 1719 (baptized, Jan. 1, 1720); d. Naumburg, July 25, 1759. He was a pupil of Bach during the period of 1744–48; then served as an organist at St. Wenzel's Church in Naumburg. On Jan. 20, 1749, Altnikol married Bach's daughter Elisabeth. In a letter of recommendation Bach described him as "quite skillful in composition." Furthermore, Altnikol acted as Bach's copyist and was instrumental in establishing authentic texts of several of Bach's works.

Altschuler, Modest, Russian cellist and conductor; b. Mogilev, Feb. 15, 1873; d. Los Angeles, Sept. 12, 1963. He studied cello at the Warsaw Cons. as a child; then went to Moscow, where he took courses in composition with Arensky and Taneyev and in piano and conducting with Safonov at the Moscow Cons., graduating in 1890. After touring Russia as a cellist, he emigrated to America, and in 1903 organized in N.Y. the Russian Symph. Society. He conducted its first concert on Jan. 7, 1904; for some 12 years the concerts of this organization became an important cultural medium for performances of Russian music in America. One of Altschuler's signal accomplishments was the world premiere of Scriabin's *Le Poème de l'extase,* which he gave in N.Y. on Dec. 10, 1908, in advance of its Russian performance. At the same concert Mischa Elman made his American debut as a concert violinist. Altschuler also conducted the first American performance of Scriabin's *Prométhée,* in N.Y. on March 20, 1915, at which he made an unsuccessful attempt to include the part of *Luce* (a color organ), prescribed by Scriabin in the score. Among other Russian composers whose works Altschuler presented for the first time in America were Rachmaninoff, Liadov, Vasilenko, and Ippolitov-Ivanov. Altschuler eventually retired to Los Angeles; he wrote an autobiography which remains unpublished.

Alvary (real name, **Achenbach**), **Max,** German tenor; b. Düsseldorf, May 3, 1856; d. near Gross-Tabarz, Thuringia, Nov. 7, 1898. His father was a noted painter. Alvary studied with Julius Stockhausen in Frankfurt; later took voice lessons with Lamperti in Milan. He made his debut in Weimar in 1879, and lived in Weimar until 1885. On Nov. 25, 1885, he made his American debut at the Metropolitan Opera in N.Y. as Don José in *Carmen,* singing the role in German; he remained with the Metropolitan until 1889; then made guest appearances in Munich, Hamburg, and Bayreuth. He was particularly noted for his Wagnerian roles.

Alwyn, William, English composer; b. Northampton, Nov. 7, 1905. He studied with McEwen at the Royal Academy of Music in London (1920–23) but failed to graduate; non obstante he was appointed to the faculty of the Royal Academy in 1927, and taught there for 28 years. In 1949 he organized the Composers' Guild of Great Britain. In 1978 he was made a Commander of the Order of the British Empire. As a composer he acquired a knack for writing effective film music; between 1936 and 1963 he wrote background scores for more than 60 films, including *Desert Victory* (1943), *Odd Man Out* (1947), *Fallen Idol* (1949), *The Magic Box* (1951), *The Silent Enemy* (1958), *Swiss Family Robinson* (1960), *The Naked Edge* (1961), *In Search of the Castaways* (1961), and *The Running Man* (1963). He also composed a great deal of instrumental and choral music; his early works were written in a straightforward neo-Classical manner, but eventually he began experimenting with continental atonality.

Alypios, Greek musical theorist, who flourished in the middle of the 4th century. His *Introduction to Music* is the chief source of specific information regarding ancient Greek notation; it contains a summary of Greek scales in all their transpositions, for both voices and instruments. This treatise was publ. by Meursius (Leyden, 1616); by Meibom in his *Antiquae musicae auctores septem* (Amsterdam, 1652); and reprinted by F. Bellermann in *Die Tonleitern und Musiknoten der Griechen* (Berlin, 1847). A new critical edition is found in Jan's *Musici scriptores graeci* (1895). A graphic explanation of the notation of Alypios is presented by A. Samoiloff in his article "Die Alypiusschen Reihen der altgriechischen Tonbezeichnung," *Archiv für Musikwissenschaft* (1924; pp. 383–400).

Amadei, Filippo, Italian opera composer; b. Reggio, c.1670; d. probably in Rome, c.1729. His claim to attention is that under the name of **Signor Pippo** (diminutive of Filippo) he wrote the first act of the opera *Muzio Scevola,* for which Bononcini wrote the 2nd act and Handel the 3rd, and which was produced at the Royal Academy of Music in London on April 15, 1721. His other works are the opera *Teodosio il Giovane* (Rome, 1711), the oratorio *Il trionfo di Tito* (Rome, 1709), and the cantata *Il pensiero* (Rome, 1709). Amadei's name was erroneously converted into **Filippo Mattei** by Mattheson in his *Critica musica,* and the mistake was carried into reference works and Handel's biographies.

Amalia Friederike, Princess of Saxony who wrote comedies under the name of **Amalie Heiter;** b. Dresden, Aug. 10, 1794; d. there, Sept. 18, 1870. She composed several light operas (*Una donna, Le tre cinture, Die Siegesfahne, Der Kanonenschuss,* etc.) and church music.

Amati, a renowned Italian family of violin makers working at Cremona. (1) **Andrea** (b. between 1500 and 1505; d. before 1580) was the first violin maker of the family. He established the prototype of Italian instruments, with characteristics found in modern violins. His sons were (2) **Antonio** (b. c.1538; d. c.1595), who built violins of varying sizes; and (3) **Girolamo** (b. c.1561; d. Nov. 2, 1630), who continued the tradition established by his father, and worked together with his brother, Antonio. (4) **Nicola,** or **Niccolò** (b. Dec. 3, 1596; d. April 12, 1684) was the most illustrious of the Amati family. He was the son of Girolamo Amati, and signed his labels "Nicolaus Amati Cremonens, Hieronimi filius Antonii nepos."

He built some of the "grand Amatis," large violins of powerful tone surpassing in clarity and purity those made by his father and his grandfather, Andrea. In Nicola's workshop both Andrea Guarneri and Antonio Stradivari received their training. (5) **Girolamo** (b. Feb. 26, 1649; d. Feb. 21, 1740), son of Nicola and the last of the family, produced violins inferior to those of his father, his grandfather, and his great-grandfather. In his work he departed from the family tradition in many respects and seemed to be influenced by Stradivari's method without equaling his superb workmanship.

Ambros, August Wilhelm, eminent musical historiographer; b. Mauth, near Prague, Nov. 17, 1816; d. Vienna, June 28, 1876. He studied law and music; rapidly rose in the legal profession; was appointed public prosecutor in Prague (1850), but continued to devote much time to music; publ. his *Die Grenzen der Musik und Poesie* (Leipzig, 1856; Eng. trans., N.Y., 1893) as a reply to Hanslick's views on esthetics; followed by a brilliant collection of essays under the title *Culturhistorische Bilder aus dem Musikleben der Gegenwart* (Leipzig, 1860); also publ. 2 collections of articles, *Bunte Blätter* (1872–74; 2nd ed. by E. Vogel, 1896). In 1869 Ambros was appointed prof. of music at Prague Univ. and Prague Cons.; in 1872 received a post in the Ministry of Justice in Vienna; he also taught at the Vienna Cons. His major work was the monumental *Geschichte der Musik* commissioned by the publisher Leuckart in 1860. Ambros spent many years of research in the libraries of Munich, Vienna, and several Italian cities for this work, but died before completing the 4th vol., which was edited from his notes by C.F. Becker and G. Nottebohm; a 5th vol. was publ. in 1882 by O. Kade from newly collected materials. W. Langhans wrote a sequel in a more popular style under the title *Die Geschichte der Musik des 17., 18. und 19. Jahrhunderts,* bringing the work up to date (2 vols., 1882–86). A list of names and a general index were issued by W. Bäumker (1882). A 2nd edition of the original 4 vols. (Leipzig, 1880) contains the following: Vol. I, *The Beginnings of Music;* Vol. II, *From the Christian Era to the First Flemish School;* Vol. III, *From the Netherlands Masters to Palestrina;* Vol. IV, *Palestrina, His Contemporaries and Immediate Successors.* Vol. I has been rewritten, not always for the better, by B. Sokolovsky; vol. II was reprinted in a new revision by Riemann (1892); vol. IV by Leichtentritt (1909); Vol. V was revised and enlarged by O. Kade (1911). Ambros was also an excellent practical musician, a proficient pianist, and a composer. He wrote an opera in Czech, *Bretislav a Jitka;* overtures to *Othello* and *Magico prodigioso;* numerous songs; and religious music.

Ambrose (Ambrosius), Christian saint and creator of "Ambrosian Chant"; b. Trier (Trèves), c.333; d. Milan, April 4, 397. He was elected Bishop of Milan in 374; canonized after his death. In 384 he became responsible for the regulation and development of singing in the Western Church by the introduction and cultivation of ritual song (antiphonal and congregational) as practiced at the time in the Eastern Church. His indisputable authorship of several sacred songs has earned him the title of "Father of Christian Hymnology," but his reputed composition of the Ambrosian Chant *Te Deum laudamus* (said to have been sung by St. Ambrose and St. Augustine at the baptism of the latter) is mythical.

Ameling, Elly, Dutch soprano; b. Rotterdam, Feb. 8, 1934. She studied in Rotterdam, The Hague, and Paris; then began a most successful career as a concert singer; won great acclaim for her appearances with the Concertgebouw Orch. and the Rotterdam Phil. In 1973 she made her operatic debut at the Netherlands Opera, but continued to concentrate upon the concert literature. As a recitalist, she sang in many of the major European music centers; also in N.Y.

Ameller, André (Charles Gabriel), French composer; b. Arnaville, Jan. 2, 1912. He studied composition with Roger-Ducasse and Gaubert at the Paris Cons.; also violin and double bass. He was taken prisoner of war in Germany in 1940; after the end of the war he returned to France, and in 1953 was appointed director of the Cons. in Dijon. He wrote operas: *La Lance de Fingal* (1947); *Sampiero Corso, Monsieur Personne* (1957); *Cyrnos* (Nancy, April 6, 1962); ballets: *La Coupe de sang* (1950) and *Oiseaux du vieux Paris* (1967); Cello Concerto (1946); *Jeux de table* for Saxophone and Piano (1955); *Terre secrète,* 6 poems for Voice and Orch. (1956); *Airs hétérogènes* for Wind Ensemble (1966); *Hétérodoxes* for 2 Flutes, 2 Trumpets, String Quartet, and String Orch. (1969).

Amfiteatrov, Daniele, Russian composer and conductor; b. St. Petersburg, Oct. 29, 1901. His father was a famous journalist. He studied composition with Wihtol in St. Petersburg and with Křička in Prague; later took lessons with Respighi in Rome. During the season of 1937–38 he was associate conductor of the Minneapolis Symph.; in 1941 he went to Hollywood and wrote film music; he became an American citizen in 1944. He eventually made his home in Venice. He composed *Poema del mare* for Orch. (1925); *American Panorama,* a symph. suite (1934); a Requiem (1960); and some chamber music.

Amiot, Père Jean Joseph Marie, French ecclesiastic; b. Toulon, Feb. 8, 1718; d. Peking, Oct. 9, 1793. He was a Jesuit missionary to China; while there, he translated Li Koang Ti's work on Chinese music: *Commentaire sur le livre classique touchant la musique des anciens;* also wrote *Mémoires sur la musique des Chinois, tant anciens que modernes* (vol. VI of *Mémoires concernant l'histoire, les sciences, les arts . . . des Chinois;* Paris, 1780, ed. by Abbé Roussier).

Amirkhanian, Charles, American avant-garde composer of Armenian extraction; b. Fresno, Calif., Jan. 19, 1945. He began experimenting in composition without outside help, probing the potentialities of sound phenomena independently of traditional musical content. His *Composition No. 1* was a solo for an acoustically amplified Ratchet (1965). His *Symphony I* (1965) is scored for 12 Players and 200-odd nonmusical objects, ranging from pitchpipes to pitchforks. In collaboration with the painter Ted Greer, Amirkhanian developed a radical system of notation in which visual images are transduced by performers into sound events. Representative of this intermedia genre are *Micah, the Prophet,* a cantata for 4 Intoning Males, 2 Accordions, 2 Drummers, and 2 Painters (1965); and particularly *Mooga Pook,* a tetraphallic action for Dancers, realistically notated on graph paper, which was produced in San Francisco, Dec. 12, 1967. He also evolved the art of "text-sound composition" for magnetic tape; to this category belong such pieces as *Words* (1969); *Oratora Konkurso Rezulto: Autoro de la Jaro,* an Esperanto recitation (1970); *If In Is* (1971); *Spoffy Nene* (1971); *Just* (1972); *Heavy Aspirations* (1973); *Seatbelt Seatbelt* (1973); *MUGIC* (1973); *Muchrooms* (1974); *Beemsterboer* (1975); *Mahogany Ballpark* (1976); *Dutiful Ducks* (1977). In 1969 Amirkhanian became "sound sensitivity information director" of radio station KPFA in Berkeley, Calif.; produced "Ode to Gravity," a weekly program of avant-garde music. In 1975 he organized, with the visual artists Carol Law and Jim Petrillo and poet Betsy Davids, a group called, with a deliberate letter substitution, Mugicians Union. In 1977 he was appointed to the faculty of the interdisciplinary creative arts dept. of San Francisco State Univ.

Amirov, Fikret Dzhamil, Azerbaijani composer; b. Kirovabad, Nov. 22, 1922; d. Baku, Feb. 20,1984. He received his early musical instruction from his father, who was a singer and guitarist; he then studied composition at the Cons. of Azerbaijan, graduating in 1948. His compositions reflect the melorhythmic patterns of popular Azerbaijani music, marked by characteristic oriental inflections, while retaining a classical format and development, particularly in variation form. Among his works are a symph. poem, *To the Memory of the Heroes of the Great National War* (1944); Double Concerto for Violin, Piano, and Orch. (1948); *The Pledge of the Korean Guerrilla Fighter* for Voice and Orch. (1951); several symph. suites based on the national modes ("mugamas"), of which *Shur* is the best known; and the opera *Sevil* (Baku, Dec. 25, 1953). He also wrote a piano concerto on Arab themes (1957; in collaboration with Nazirova). In 1959 he visited the U.S. as a member of the Soviet delegation of composers under the auspices of the State Dept.

Amram, David, American composer; b. Philadelphia, Nov. 17, 1930, of Jewish parents. He played a bugle in school; then studied trumpet at the Music Settlement School, and also played piano. When he was 12, the family moved to Washington, D.C.; soon he played trumpet in school bands; later switched to the French horn. In 1948 he enrolled at the Oberlin (Ohio) College Cons., and continued his practicing on the French horn; later shifted to George Washington Univ., graduating in 1952. He then enlisted in the U.S. Army, and played the French horn in the Seventh Army Symph. Orch., which was stationed in Germany. In 1955 he returned to the U.S. and studied composition with Vittorio Giannini at the Manhattan School of Music. He also studied privately with Charles Mills. Very soon he found his way into the inviting world of public theater. He wrote incidental music for off-Broadway productions of Shakespeare's plays, and finally landed lucrative jobs in the films; he composed sound tracks for such hits as *Splendor in the Grass* (1961), *The Manchurian Candidate* (1962), and *The Arrangement* (1969). He also wrote jazz music, sacred services for the Park Avenue Synagogue in N.Y., and straight concert pieces, braving somehow the danger of cross-pollination of these quaquaversal activities. On May 8, 1960, he gave an evening of his works in N.Y., among them a *Shakespearean Concerto,* and presented another pan-Amram concert in N.Y. on Feb. 20, 1962. There followed a cornucopia of cantatas, and in 1965, a radio opera, *The Final Ingredient.* In 1966–67 he received an exclusive appointment as composer-in-residence of the N.Y. Phil. As a sign of public recognition of his music, the National Education Television network broadcast on April 17, 1969, a documentary, proudly entitled "The World of David Amram." Amram was also the recipient of several grants by the State Dept. and U.S. Information Agency for travel abroad. He visited some 25 countries; he also joined a jazz group to play in Cuba in 1977. He eagerly absorbed the varicolored ethnic materials, which he used, in metamorphosis, in some of his own compositions. In 1979 he received an honorary doctorate from Moravian College, Bethlehem, Pa.

Amy, Gilbert, French composer and conductor; b. Paris, Aug. 29, 1936. He studied composition with Darius Milhaud and Olivier Messiaen at the Paris Cons., and counterpoint and fugue with Plé-Caussade. In 1962 he began making appearances as a conductor; served as director of Domaine Musical from 1967 to 1973. In his music he followed the Baroque precepts of antiphony and concertante, combining these forms with serialist procedures. WORKS: *Œil de fumée* for Soprano and Piano (1955); *Variations* for 4 Instruments (1956); *Cantate brève* to words by García Lorca (1957); *Mouvements* for 17 Instruments (1958); *Antiphonies* for 2 Orchs. (1963); *Triade* for Orch. (1964); *Trajectoires* for Violin and Orch. (1966); *Cycle* for 6 Percussion Players (1967); *Chant* for Orch. (Donaueschingen, Oct. 20, 1968); *Relais* for 5 Brass Instruments (1969); *Refrains* for Orch. (1972); *D'un espace déployé* for Solo Soprano, 2 Pianos, and 2 Orchs. (Paris, March 10, 1973); *Sonata pian' e forte* for 2 Voices and 12 Players (1974); *7 Sites* for 14 Players (1975).

Anchieta, Juan de, Spanish composer; b. probably in Urrestilla, near Azpeitia, 1462; d. Azpeitia, July 30, 1523. In 1489 he entered the service of Queen Isabella as a singer in the court chapel; upon the Queen's death in 1504, he entered the service of her daughter, Joanna, consort of Philip the Fair; he accompanied them to Flanders and England. In addition to his duties as Joanna's chaplain and singer, he was made a benefice-holder (in absentia) at Villarino in 1499; was also named rector of the parish church of S. Sebastian de Soreasu in Azpeitia in 1500; became Abbot of Arbos in 1518. He was pensioned by the court of Charles V in 1519. Anchieta composed sacred and secular vocal works, most of them for large choirs; several of these were publ. in modern editions in *Monumentos de la música española,* vols. I (1941), V (1947), and X (1951).

Ancina, Giovanni Giovenale, Italian composer of sacred music; b. Fossano, Oct. 19, 1545; d. Saluzzo, Aug. 31, 1604. He was a student of medicine and theology, but became deeply interested in sacred services in music after he met Filippo Neri, the creator of the oratorio. On Oct. 1, 1580, he joined the Congregazione dei Preti dell'Oratorio, founded by Neri. He began writing music for the church; publ. *Tempio armonico della beata Vergine* (Rome, 1599).

Ancot, a family of musicians at Bruges. (1) **Jean,** *père* (b. Bruges, Oct. 22, 1779; d. there, July 12, 1848), violin virtuoso, pianist, and composer. He studied (1799–1804) in Paris under Baillot, Kreutzer, and Catel; then settled in Bruges as a teacher; publ. 4 violin concertos, overtures, marches, sacred music, etc.; most of his works are still in MS. He taught his sons, Jean and Louis. (2) **Jean,** *fils* (b. Bruges, July 6, 1799; d. Boulogne, June 5, 1829). He finished his education at the Paris Cons. under Pradher and Berton; an accomplished pianist, he was successful in London (1823–25); eventually settled in Boulogne. Considering that he died short of his 30th birthday, he was an astonishingly prolific composer (225 works, among them a piano concerto, sonatas, études, 4-hand fantasias, and violin concertos). (3) **Louis** (b. Bruges, June 3, 1803; d. there, 1836). For a time, he was pianist to the Duke of Sussex in London; made extended continental tours, taught at Boulogne and Tours, and finally returned to Bruges. He wrote piano music in salon style.

Anda, Géza, eminent Hungarian pianist; b. Budapest, Nov. 19, 1921; d. Zürich, June 13, 1976. He studied with Dohnányi at the Royal Academy of Music in Budapest; won the Liszt Prize. During World War II he went to Switzerland; became a Swiss citizen in 1955. He made his American debut with the Philadelphia Orch. on Oct. 21, 1955. He was an ardent champion of the music of Béla Bartók, and performed all of Bartók's 3 piano concertos numerous times; he also was a congenial interpreter of the music of Brahms. Later on he made a specialty of Mozart, acting both as soloist and conductor in all of Mozart's piano concertos. He publ. a vol. of Mozart cadenzas (Berlin and Wiesbaden, 1973). Apart from his concerts he also held seminars in Switzerland.

Andersen, (Carl) Joachim, Danish flute player and composer, son and pupil of the flutist **Christian Joachim Andersen;** b. Copenhagen, April 29, 1847; d. there, May 7, 1909. From 1869–77, he was a member of the Royal Orch.; in 1881 he was in Berlin, where he was co-founder and, for 10 years, first flutist and assistant conductor of the Phil. Orch.; from 1893, was conductor of the Palace Orch. at Copenhagen. He wrote solo works for Flute; also pieces with Orch.: *Hungarian Fantasia; Ballade; Dance of the Sylphs;* 24 easy and 24 difficult études, etc. His brother, **Vigo** (b. Copenhagen, April 21, 1852; d. by suicide in Chicago, Jan. 28, 1895), was an eminent flute player; he was first flutist in the Thomas Orch. in Chicago.

Anderson, Laurie, seeded American composer of avant-garde persuasion; b. Chicago, June 5, 1947. Renouncing the tradition of conventional modernism, she set for herself a goal of uniting all arts as they were in ancient music, but co-opted the various techniques of new arts, from topical pop to electronics, playbacking with herself on magnetic tape and projecting images on a screen. In her performing techniques she combined speech, song, and facial mesmerization of the audience. The generic category of these exertions became known as "performance art." She uses a variety of instruments in her stage productions, including a homemade violin activated by a luminous bow made of electronic tape. She also changed her voice electronically, producing weird otherworldly effects. Her satirical piece *New York Social Life* was scored for voices and tamboura; another piece, *Time to Go,* for guitar, violin, and organ, repeated exhortations of a museum guard to visitors to leave at the closing time. Amazingly enough, her arcane art found enthusiastic response among young audiences commonly addicted to less subtle exhibitions, and she became a popular entertainer during her tours in the U.S. and in Europe. Her song *O, Superman* became a hit. In 1976 she gave a successful exhibition of her psychomusicurgy at the Berlin Akademie der Kunst. In 1983 she produced her multimedia epic, *United States,* on the themes of transportation, politics, money, and love.

Anderson, Leroy, American composer of light instrumental music; b. Cambridge, Mass., June 29, 1908; d. Woodbury, Conn., May 18, 1975. He received his first musical training from his mother, an organist, and studied double bass with Gaston Dufresne in Boston. He then took courses in theory of composition with Walter Spalding, Edward Ballantine, and Walter Piston at Harvard Univ., obtaining his B.A. magna cum laude in 1929 and his M.A. in 1930. From 1932–35 he was conductor of the Harvard Univ. Band. In 1935 he became an arranger for the Boston Pops. In 1942 he entered the U.S. Army and was stationed in Iceland. A linguist, he acted as translator, particularly in Scandinavian languages (Anderson was of Swedish extraction). In 1939 he wrote a piece for String Orch. called *Jazz Pizzicato,* which was played at the Boston Pops and became an immediate hit. This was followed by a number of similar inventive instrumental novelties, among them *Jazz Legato, The Syncopated Clock* (1950), *Fiddle Faddle, Sleigh Ride* (1950), *Serenata, A Trumpeter's Lullaby, China Doll, A Bugler's Holiday, Blue Tango* (his greatest success, 1952), *The Typewriter.* He also wrote a musical, *Goldilocks* (N.Y., Oct. 11, 1958).

Anderson (née **Philpot**), **Lucy,** English pianist; b. Bath, Dec. 12, 1797; d. London, Dec. 24, 1878. Her father, John Philpot, was a prof. of music; she settled in London; was the first woman to be engaged as piano soloist by the Phil. Society. She married George Frederick Anderson in 1820; he became Master of the Queen's Musick (1848–70); Lucy Anderson taught piano to Queen Victoria and her children.

Anderson, Marian, celebrated black American contralto; b. South Philadelphia, Feb. 17, 1902, into a poor family; her father sold ice and coal; her mother helped eke out the family income by taking in laundry. Marian Anderson sang in a choir at the Union Baptist Church in South Philadelphia. Funds were raised for her to study voice with Giuseppe Boghetti; in 1923 she won first prize at a singing contest in Philadelphia, and in 1925 she received first prize at a contest held by the N.Y. Phil. at Lewisohn Stadium, appearing as a soloist there on Aug. 27, 1925. In 1929 she gave a recital at Carnegie Hall. In 1930 she made her first European appearance in London; she soon extended her European tours to include Sweden, Norway, and Finland; she also gave successful concerts in Paris, Vienna, Brussels, Geneva, and Salzburg; also made a tour of Russia. Her singing of Negro spirituals produced a sensation wherever she sang in Europe. Returning to the U.S., she gave a concert in Town Hall, N.Y. (Nov. 30, 1935), and in Carnegie Hall (Jan. 30, 1936). In Feb. 1939, she became a center of national attention when the Daughters of the American Revolution refused to let her appear at Constitution Hall in Washington, D.C., citing the organization's rules of racial segregation. The resulting publicity only contributed to her success; Eleanor Roosevelt sent her resignation to the DAR, and the Secretary of the Interior, Harold L. Ickes, invited Marian Anderson to sing at the Lincoln Memorial on Easter Sunday, April 9, 1939: a huge audience attended; the concert was broadcast. She was given the prestigious Spingarn Award for the "highest and noblest achievement by an American Negro" during the year. Another landmark in the history of freedom was established when she sang the role of Ulrica in *Un ballo in maschera* at the Metropolitan Opera on Jan. 7, 1955, breaking the unspoken prohibition against black artists' singing there. In 1957 and 1958 she was designated by President Eisenhower to be a delegate to the General Assembly of the United Nations. Honors piled upon honors in her life. She was awarded honorary degrees from Princeton Univ. and N.Y. Univ., and received medals from the governments of Sweden, Finland, Japan, and other countries. President Johnson awarded her the American Freedom Medal. She sang at the inaugural ball for President Kennedy in 1961. On the occasion of her 75th birthday, a resolution was passed by the U.S. Congress to strike a gold medal in her honor. She publ. her autobiography, *My Lord, What a Morning* (N.Y., 1956).

Anderson, T.J. (Thomas Jefferson), black American composer; b. Coatesville, Pa., Aug. 17, 1928, a son of schoolteachers. He attended classes in Washington, D.C., and Cincinnati; played in a school orch.; then entered West Virginia State College; received his bachelor of music degree at Pa. State Univ.; then taught music at High Point, N.C. (1951–54). In 1954 he attended composition classes with Scott Huston at the Cincinnati Cons. of Music and with Philip Bezanson and Richard Hervig at the Univ. of Iowa in Iowa City, obtaining his Ph.D. in 1958. In 1964 he took a summer course in composition with Darius Milhaud at Aspen, Colorado. From 1958 to 1963 he was prof. of music at Langston Univ., Oklahoma; from 1963 to 1969 he taught at the Tennessee State Univ., Nashville; and from 1968 to 1971 he was composer-in-residence with the Atlanta Symph. Orch.; then taught at Morehouse College in Atlanta (1971–72), and in 1972 was appointed chairman of the Tufts Univ. music dept. in Medford, Mass., serving until 1980; and continued to teach there. He served as chairman of the Advisory Board of the Black Music Center at the Univ. of Indiana (1969–71). In 1976 he went to Brazil under the aegis of the Office of Cultural Relations of the U.S. Dept. of State. He played a major role in the revival of interest in the music of Scott Joplin, and arranged Joplin's opera *Treemonisha* for its production in Atlanta (Jan. 28, 1972). His own style of composition is audaciously modern, while preserving a deeply felt lyricism in melodic patterns; his harmonies are taut and intense without abandoning the basic tonal frame; his contrapuntal usages suggest folklike ensembles, but he freely varies his techniques according to the character of each particular piece. His resources are quaquaversal, and he excludes none in his creative process.

WORKS: FOR THE STAGE: Opera, *Soldier Boy, Soldier*, to a story of a Vietnam veteran (Bloomington, Oct. 23, 1982); operetta, *The Shell Fairy* (1977). FOR ORCH.: *Pyknon* (1958); *Introduction and Allegro* (1959); *New Dances* (1960); *Classical Symphony* (1961); *Symphony in Three Movements*, in memory of John F. Kennedy (1964; Oklahoma City, April 10, 1964); *Squares* (Chickasha, Oklahoma, Feb. 25, 1966); *Rotations* for Symphonic Band (1967); Chamber Symph. (Nashville, Nov. 24, 1969); *Transitions* for Chamber Orch. (Tanglewood Festival, Berkshire Music Center, Aug. 2, 1971); *Intervals*, 7 orch. sets (1970–71). FOR VOICES AND ORCH.: *Personals*, cantata in commemoration of the centennial of Fisk Univ. (Nashville, April 28, 1966); *Beyond Silence* for Tenor and Instruments (1973); *In Memoriam Malcolm X* (N.Y., April 7, 1974); *Horizons '76* for Soprano and Orch., a U.S. Bicentennial commission, for 3 Speakers, Dancer, and Instruments (Chicago, June 11, 1978); *Messages, a Creole Fantasy* for Voices and Orch. (1979). FOR CHAMBER GROUPS: *Pieces for Clarinet and Chamber Orchestra* (Oklahoma City, March 25, 1962); *5 Bagatelles* for Oboe, Violin, and Harpsichord (1963); *5 Etudes and a Fancy* for Woodwind Quintet (1964); *Connections* for String Quintet (1966); *Swing Set*, duo for Clarinet and Piano (1973); *5 Easy Pieces* for Violin, Piano, and Jew's Harp (1974); *Variations on a Theme by Alban Berg* for Viola and Piano (1977); also piano pieces, among them *5 Portraitures of 2 People* for Piano, 4-hands (1965), and *Watermelon* (1971).

André, (Johann) Anton, 3rd son of **Johann André;** b. Offenbach, Oct. 6, 1775; d. there, April 6, 1842. A precocious talent, he studied with Karl Vollweiler in Mannheim (1792–93); was a fine pianist, violinist, and composer before entering the Univ. of Jena; after completing his studies, he made extensive travels; on his father's death, took charge of the business, adding particular luster to its good name by the purchase, in 1799, of Mozart's entire musical remains. He publ. Mozart's autograph thematic catalogue, and supplemented it by a list of the works so acquired. By accepting the application of the lithographic process to music engraving (1799), he took another long stride toward placing his firm in the front rank. He was also a composer (2 operas, symphs., songs, etc.), a successful teacher, and a noteworthy theorist. He wrote 2 vols. on harmony, counterpoint, canon, and fugue (1832–42; new revised ed., abridged, 1974–78); and *Anleitung zum Violinspiele*. His sons were: (1) **Carl August** (b. Offenbach, June 15, 1806; d. Frankfurt, Feb. 15, 1887), head (from 1835) of the Frankfurt branch opened in 1828, and founder of a piano factory ("Mozartflügel"); author of *Der Klavierbau und seine Geschichte* (1855). (2) **Julius** (b. Offenbach, June 4, 1808; d. there, April 17, 1880), a fine organist and pianist, pupil of Aloys Schmitt (his grandfather's pupil), author of a *Praktische Orgelschule*, composer of several interesting organ compositions, and arranger of Mozart's works for piano, 4-hands. (3) **Johann August** (b. Offenbach, March 2, 1817; d. there, Oct. 29, 1887), his father's successor (1839) in the publishing establishment. His 2 sons, **Karl** (b. Aug. 24, 1853; d. June 29, 1914) and **Adolf** (b. April 10, 1855; d. Sept 10, 1910), succeeded to the business. (4) **Jean Baptiste** (de St.-Gilles; b. Offenbach, March 7, 1823; d. Frankfurt, Dec. 9, 1882), pianist and composer of various pieces for piano and voice, a pupil of A. Schmitt, Taubert (piano), and Kessler and Dehn (harmony); lived for years in Berlin; had the honorary title of "Herzoglich Bernbergischer Hofkapellmeister."

André, Johann, German composer, publisher, and father of a musical family; b. Offenbach, March 28, 1741; d. there, June 18, 1799. He founded (Sept. 1, 1774) at Offenbach a music publishing house under his name and had publ. 1,200 compositions by the time of his death. For 7 years (1777–84) he was Kapellmeister of Döbbelin's Theater in Berlin. He was a prolific composer, author of 19 singspiels and 14 miscellaneous scores for the stage, among them *Der Töpfer* (Hanau, Jan. 22, 1773) and *Der Liebhaber als Automat* (Berlin, Sept. 11, 1782). Bretzner wrote the libretto of *Die Entführung aus dem Serail,* or *Belmont und Constanze,* for him; the opera was produced in Berlin, May 25, 1781. The same text was used the following year by Mozart for his celebrated work, which elicited Bretzner's haughty protest against "a certain man named Mozart" for the unauthorized use of his libretto. Among André's songs, the *Rheinweinlied* ("Bekränzt mit Laub") was widely performed. André is credited with being the composer of the first "durchkomponierte Ballade," *Die Weiber von Weinsberg* (1783).

André, Maurice, French trumpet virtuoso; b. Alès, near Nîmes, May 24, 1933. He was apprenticed as a coal miner, the trade he plied from his 14th through his 18th year; his father was also a coal miner, but he played the trumpet in his free hours; André practiced on the trumpet, too, and enrolled in the class of Barthélémy; received the Prix d'Honneur and joined the Paris Radio Orch.; was later the first trumpet in the Lamoureux Orch.; also played in jazz groups. In 1956 he won an international competition in Geneva, and in 1963 won the International Music Competition of the German Radio; then played in chamber orchs. In 1974 he made his American debut as a soloist with the Württemberg Chamber Orch. on tour. Soon he became well-known as a proponent of the Baroque repertoire; he also performed modern trumpet concertos, some written especially for him; he made some 260 recordings, including 30 different trumpet concertos. An ardent collector, he owns 80 trumpets of different types and national origins; as a trumpet virtuoso, he tours all over the world; in 1983 he made one of his frequent visits to America.

Andreae, Volkmar, eminent Swiss conductor and accomplished composer; b. Bern, July 5, 1879; d. Zürich, June 18, 1962. He studied music with Karl Munzinger in Bern and later with Wüllner at the Cologne Cons.; was then répétiteur at the Royal Opera in Munich; in 1902 he became conductor of the municipal chorus of Zürich, and in 1904 of the male chorus there; in 1906 was appointed to lead the Tonhalle Orch. of Zürich, a post he held until 1949; during his long tenure there, he championed the music of Bruckner, Strauss, Mahler, and Debussy. From 1914 until 1941 he served as director of the Zürich Cons. In his own compositions, Andreae reflected the post-Romantic tendencies of German music.

Andrée, Elfrida, Swedish organist and composer; b. Visby, Feb. 19, 1841; d. Göteborg, Jan. 11, 1929. She studied at the Stockholm Cons., and later took lessons with Niels Gade in Copenhagen; at the same time she also studied telegraphy and was the first woman telegraph operator in Sweden. In 1867 she was appointed organist at the Göteborg Cathedral. She established a series of popular concerts and presented about 800 programs. In consideration of her achievements, she was elected a member of the Swedish Academy of Music. She was a pioneer among Swedish women as an organist and composer. She wrote 4 symphs., and a Swedish Mass, which had frequent performances.

Andreis, Josip, eminent Croatian musicographer; b. Split, March 19, 1909; d. Zagreb, Jan. 16, 1982. He studied philology in Zagreb and Rome; also took courses in composition. In 1945 he was appointed to the faculty of the Music Academy in Zagreb, retiring in 1972. He publ. an encyclopedia of music in the Croatian language, issued in Zagreb in 2 vols. (1958, 1963); another work of importance was a 3-vol. edition, also in the Croatian language, on music history (Zagreb, 1951–54; 2nd ed., 1966). Other publications were *Yugoslav Music* (in English; Belgrade, 1959) and a monograph on the Yugoslav composer Gotovac (Split, 1957).

Andrevi, Francisco, prominent Spanish church music composer; b. Sanahuja, near Lérida, Nov. 16, 1786; d. Barcelona, Nov. 23, 1853. He started as a choirboy, and from his earliest years devoted himself to the study of church music. At the age of 22 he became music director at the Cathedral of Segorbe; then held similar posts at the churches at Barcelona, Valencia, and Seville. During the civil war in Spain he was in Bordeaux (1832–42); later (1845–49) in Paris, where he publ. his *Traité d'Harmonie et de Composition* (1848; in the same year it was also publ. in Spanish). Andrevi returned to Barcelona in 1849. He wrote a sacred drama, *Juicio universal;* also much choral music, most of which is in MS; 2 of his sacred choruses (*Nunc dimittis* and *Salve regina*) are included in Eslava's *Lira Sacra-Hispana.*

Andriessen, Hendrik, eminent Dutch organist and composer, brother of **Willem Andriessen;** b. Haarlem, Sept. 17, 1892; d. Heemstede, April 12, 1981. He studied music with his brother; then took piano and organ lessons with Louis Robert and J.B. de Pauw; studied composition with Bernard Zweers at the Amsterdam Cons. (1914–16); subsequently taught harmony there (1928–34). He succeeded his father as organist at St. Joseph's Church in Haarlem (1916–34); was then organist at Utrecht Cathedral (1934–49). He was director of the Royal Cons. in The Hague (1949–57) and special prof. at the Catholic Univ. in Nijmegen (1952–63). His own music is Romantically inspired; some of his instrumental works make use of modern devices, including melodic atonality and triadic polytonality. He was particularly esteemed for his ability to revive the authentic modalities of Gregorian chant; his choral works present a remarkable confluence of old usages with modern technical procedures.

WORKS: OPERAS: *Philomela* (Holland Festival, June 23, 1950) and *De Spiegel uit Venetië* (*The Mirror from Venice;* 1964; Dutch Television, Oct. 5, 1967). FOR ORCH.: 4 symphs. (1930, 1937, 1946, 1954); *Variations and Fugue on a Theme of Kuhnau* for String Orch. (1935); *Capriccio* (1941); *Variations on a Theme of Couperin* for Flute, Harp, and Strings

(1944); *Ballet Suite* (1947); *Ricercare* (1949); *Wilhemus van Nassouwe,* rhapsody (1950); Organ Concerto (1950); *Symphonic Étude* (1952; The Hague, Oct. 15, 1952); *Libertas venit,* rhapsody (1954); *Mascherata,* fantasy (1962); *Symphonie concertante* (1962); Violin Concerto (1968–69); Concertino for Oboe and String Orch. (1969–70); Concertino for Cello and Orch. (1970); *Chromatic Variations* for Flute, Oboe, Violin, Cello, and Strings (1970); *Canzone* (1971); *Chantecler,* overture (1972).

Andriessen, Louis, Dutch composer, son of **Hendrik Andriessen;** b. Utrecht, June 6, 1939. He first studied with his father and with Kees van Baaren at the Royal Cons. in The Hague (1957–62); also took lessons with Luciano Berio in Milan (1962–63). He was a co-founder of a Charles Ives Society in Amsterdam. His works are conceived in an advanced idiom.

WORKS: Flute Sonata (1956); *Séries* for 2 Pianos (1958); *Percosse* for Flute, Trumpet, Bassoon, and Percussion (1958); Nocturnes for Soprano and Chamber Orch. (1959); *Aanloop en sprongen* for Flute, Oboe, and Clarinet (1961); *Ittrospezione I* for 2 Pianos (1961), *II* for Orch. (1963), and *III* for 2 Pianos, and Chamber Ensemble or Saxophone (1964); *A Flower Song I* for Solo Violin (1963), *II* for Solo Oboe (1963), and *III* for Solo Cello (1964); *Sweet* for Recorder or Flute (1964); *Double* for Clarinet and Piano (1965); *Paintings* for Recorder or Flute, and Piano (1965); *Souvenirs d'enfance* for Piano and Tape (1966); *Anachronie,* to the memory of Charles Ives, *I* for Orch. (1965–66; Rotterdam, Jan. 18, 1968) and *II* for Solo Oboe, 4 Horns, Piano, Harp, and String Orch. (1969); *Contra-tempus* for 23 Musicians (1968); the anti-imperialist collective opera *Reconstructie* (1968–69; Holland Festival, June 29, 1969; in collaboration with Reinbert de Leeuw, Misha Mengelberg, Peter Schat, and Jan van Vlijmen); *Hoe het is (What It's Like)* for Live-Electronic Improvisers and 52 Strings (Rotterdam, Sept. 14, 1970); *Spektakel (Uproar)* for 16 Winds, 6 Percussionists, and Electronic Instruments (1970); *The 9 Symphonies of Beethoven* for Promenade Orch. and Ice Cream Bell (1970); *De Volharding (The Persistence)* for Piano and Winds (1972); *On Jimmy Yancey* for Chamber Ensemble (1973); *Il Principe,* after Machiavelli, for 2 Choirs, Winds, Piano, and Bass Guitar (1974); *Symphonieën der Nederlanden* for Brass Band (1974); *De Statt (The State)* for 4 Women's Voices and 27 Instruments (1972–76); *Workers' Union,* symph. movement for any loud-speaking group of Instruments (1975); *Hoketus* for 2 Panpipes, 2 Pianos, and Electronics (1977); *Orpheus,* for theater (1977); Symph. for Open Strings (1978).

Andriessen, Willem, Dutch pianist and composer, brother of **Hendrik Andriessen;** b. Haarlem, Oct. 25, 1887; d. Amsterdam, March 29, 1964. He studied piano and composition at the Amsterdam Cons. (1903–8); taught piano at The Hague Cons. (1910–17) and at the Rotterdam Cons.; from 1937–53 was director of the Amsterdam Cons. He was a professional pianist of a high caliber. He wrote a Piano Concerto (1908); *3 Songs* for Voice and Orch. (1911); *Hei, 't was de Mei,* scherzo for Orch. (1912); Piano Sonata (1938); Piano Sonatina (1945).

Anerio, Felice, Italian composer, brother of **Giovanni Francesco Anerio;** b. Rome, c.1560; d. there, Sept. 27, 1614. He studied with G.M. Manni; was a chorister at Santa Maria Maggiore in Rome (1568–75); then sang at St. Peter's under Palestrina (from May 1575 to March 1579). In 1584 he became maestro di cappella of the English College in Rome. After Palestrina's death, Anerio was appointed by Clement VIII to succeed him as composer to the Papal Chapel (April 3, 1594). His eminence as a composer is best attested by the fact that several of his compositions were for a long time supposed to be Palestrina's own. Besides MSS in Roman libraries, many of Anerio's works are extant in printed collections. They include: *Madrigali spirituali a 5* (1585; reprinted 1598); *Canzonette a 4* (1586; reprinted 1603, 1607); *Madrigali a 5* (1587); *Madrigali a 6,* book I (1590; reprinted 1599); *Concerti spirituali a 4* (1593); *Sacri hymni e cantica a 8,* book I (1596); *Madrigali a 3* (1598); *Madrigali a 6,* book II (1602); *Responsorii per la Settimana Santa a 4* (1602); *Sacri hymni e cantica a 8,* book II (1602); *Responsoria a 4* (1606).

Anerio, Giovanni Francesco, Italian composer, younger brother of **Felice Anerio;** b. Rome, c.1567; d. on his way from Poland to Italy in June 1630 (buried in Graz, June 12, 1630). He served as a chorister at St. Peter's from 1575 to 1579, and sang, with his brother, under Palestrina. From 1600 to 1603 he was maestro di cappella at the Lateran church. In 1607 he was at the court of King Sigismund III of Poland in Cracow; in 1608 he returned to Rome; then became choirmaster at the Cathedral of Verona, and later held similar positions at the Seminario Romano (1611–12) and at the Jesuit Church of S. Maria dei Monti in Rome (1613–20). In 1616 he was ordained a priest. In 1624 he visited Treviso, near Venice; then became choirmaster at the Polish Court in Warsaw. He was a prolific composer; several of his works were printed in Italy. He also arranged Palestrina's 6-part *Missa Papae Marcelli* for 4 voices (Rome, 1600).

Anet, Baptiste, (actually **Jean-Baptiste**), French violinist, son of **Jean-Baptiste Anet,** *père;* b. Paris, and was baptized on Jan. 2, 1676; d. Lunéville, Aug. 14, 1755. He was a pupil of Corelli in Rome; upon returning to France, he was a member of the Royal Chapel in Paris; in 1737 he went to Lunéville as a court musician to the former Polish King Stanislas Leszczynski. He publ. 3 sets of sonatas for violin with basso continuo (1729) and 3 collections of duets for musettes (1726, 1730, 1734).

Anet, Jean-Baptiste, père, French violinist; b. Paris, June 20, 1650; d. there, April 28, 1710. He was active as a teacher in Paris; in 1699 he became a member of the 24 Violons du Roi. He was the father of another **Jean-Baptiste Anet,** who was known simply as Baptiste Anet.

Anfossi, Pasquale, Italian opera composer; b. Taggia, near Naples, April 5, 1727; d. Rome, Feb. 1797. He studied composition with Piccinni, and began writing operas in the prevalent Italian manner. His third opera, *L'Incognita perseguitata,* produced in Rome in 1773, won popular approval; its subject was the same as Piccinni's previously staged opera, but if contemporary reports are to be trusted, Anfossi's opera was more successful than that of his erstwhile master. Encouraged by his success, Anfossi proceeded to write one opera after another; according to some accounts, he wrote 76 operas; a more plausible computation credits him with no fewer than 60, but no more than 70 operas. In 1779 he was in Paris; from Dec. 1782 to 1786 he was at the King's Theater in London as director of the Italian opera there. He then traveled in Germany; returning to Italy, he was appointed maestro di cappella at the Lateran church in 1791, and turned his attention to sacred compositions; he composed at least 12 oratorios, and a number of masses and Psalms. Mozart wrote two arias for use in Anfossi's opera *Il Curioso indiscreto* (Vienna, 1783) and for *Le Gelosie fortunate* (Vienna, 1788).

Angeles, Victoria de Los (real name, **Victoria Gómez Cima**), famous Spanish soprano; b. Barcelona, Nov. 1, 1923. She studied at the Barcelona Cons., and made her concert debut there in 1944. In 1946 she made her first operatic appearance at the Teatro Lírico in Barcelona. In 1947 she won first prize at the International Singing Contest in Geneva. Returning to Barcelona, she sang Elsa in *Lohengrin,* Marguerite in *Faust,* and other important roles. In 1949 she performed at the Paris Opéra as Marguerite; in 1950 she appeared at Covent Garden in London as Mimi in *La Bohème.* Her American debut took place in a recital at Carnegie Hall in N.Y., on Oct. 24, 1950. On March 17, 1951, she appeared at the Metropolitan Opera in N.Y. as Marguerite in *Faust.* She continued to sing at the Metropolitan during the years 1955–59 and in 1961. In 1953 she gave concerts in South Africa, and in 1956, in Australia. In 1957 she sang at the Vienna State Opera; in 1961–62 she was a guest artist at the Bayreuth Festival. She retired from the stage in 1969 but continued to give occasional recitals; she excelled particularly in Spanish and French songs. On Nov. 28, 1948, she married Enrique Magriñá Mir; they lived mostly in Barcelona.

Angelini, Bontempi Giovanni Andrea. See **Bontempi, Giovanni Andrea.**

d'Anglebert, Jean-Henri, French clavecin player; b. Paris, probably in 1628; d. there, April 23, 1691. He studied with Champion de Chambonnières; in 1662 he succeeded his teacher as clavecinist to Louis XIV. In 1689 he publ. a collection, *Pièces de clavecin avec la manière de les jouer,* containing original suites, arrangements of airs from Lully's operas, and 22 variations on *Folies d'Espagne* (the theme later used by Corelli); the same vol. contains instruction on figured bass. D'Anglebert contributed greatly to the establishment of the French method of performance on the clavecin. His extant compositions were publ. in 1934 by Marguerite Roesgen-Champion in *Publications de la Société Française de Musicologie,* also containing biographical information. His son **Jean-Baptiste Henri d'Anglebert** (b. Paris, Sept. 5, 1661; d. there, Nov. 1735) succeeded him as court musician.

Anglès, Higini (Catalan form; in Spanish, **Higinio Anglès**), distinguished musicologist; b. Maspujols, Catalonia, Jan. 1, 1888; d. Rome, Dec. 8, 1969. He studied philosophy at Tarragona (1900–13); musicology with Felipe Pedrell and composition with V.M. Gibert in Barcelona (1913–19). In 1917 he became head of the music dept. of the Barcelona library. In 1923 he went to Germany and studied with W. Gurlitt at Freiburg and F. Ludwig at Göttingen. In 1924 he returned to Barcelona, and in 1927 became prof. of music history at the Cons. With the outbreak of the Spanish Civil War in 1936, he went to Munich; returned to Barcelona in 1939. In 1943 he was appointed director of the Instituto Español de Musicologia; in 1947 he became director of the Pontifical Inst. of Sacred Music in Rome. His most important publication is *El Códex Musical de Las Huelgas* (3 vols., 1928–31), containing facsimiles and transcriptions of Spanish music of the 13th and 14th centuries. Part of the text of this edition was publ. in the *Musical Quarterly* (Oct. 1940). He publ. the following books: *Cantigas del Rei N'Anfos el Savi* (Barcelona, 1927); *Historia de la música española* (Barcelona, 1935); *La música a Catalunya fins al segle XIII* (Barcelona, 1935); *La música española desde la edad media hasta nuestros dias* (Barcelona, 1941); and many smaller works. He edited the collected works of J. Pujol (1925); the organ works of Cabanilles (1926); *La música en la corte de los reyes católicos* (2 vols.; Madrid, 1941; Barcelona, 1947); *Recopilación de sonetos,* etc. by Juan Vásquez (Barcelona, 1946); *El cancionero musical de Palacio* (Barcelona, 1947). Anglès contributed to many music journals and wrote articles on Spanish music for *Die Musik in Geschichte und Gegenwart.* He was regarded as an outstanding expert on Spanish music of the Middle Ages.

Animuccia, Giovanni, Italian composer of sacred music; b. Florence, c.1514; d. Rome, March 25, 1571. In 1555 he was appointed maestro di cappella at St. Peter's as successor to Palestrina (who returned to that post after Animuccia's death in 1571). He worked with Filippo Neri, for whom he composed his *Laudi spirituali* (2 vols.; 1563 and 1570), which were performed by Neri in his "oratorium." These are contrapuntal hymnlike songs of praise, rather than forerunners of true oratorio. Other publ. works are 4 books of madrigals (1547, 1551, 1554, 1565), a book of masses (1567), and a book of Magnificats (1568). Animuccia's compositions mark a gradual emancipation from the involved formalism of the Flemish School in the direction of a more practical style, which approached that of Palestrina. Animuccia possessed a great skill in polyphony, demonstrated especially in his ingenious canonic writing.

Annibale (**Il Padovano,** from his birthplace, Padua), Italian organist and composer; b. Padua, c.1527; d. Graz, March 15, 1575. He was organist at San Marco (1552–64); in 1567 was appointed "Obrister Musicus" to the Archduke Carl at Graz; in 1570 named Kapellmeister.
WORKS: A book of *ricercari a* 4 (1556; modern ed. by N. Pierront and J.P. Hennebains, 1934); a book of madrigals *a* 5 (1564); a book of motets *a* 5–6 (1567); a book of masses *a* 5 (1573); a book of *Toccate e Ricercari* for Organ (1604). Two ricercari for Organ are reprinted in vol. III of Torchi's *L'Arte musicale in Italia.*

Anrooy (properly, **Anrooij**), **Peter van,** Dutch conductor and composer; b. Zalt-Boomel, Oct. 13, 1879; d. The Hague, Dec. 31, 1954. He studied with Johan Wagenaar in Utrecht; in 1899 he went to Moscow, where he studied violin and conducting with Willem Kes and Taneyev. He played the violin in the orchs. of Glasgow and Zürich (1902); then was active as a conductor in Groningen (1905) and Arnhem (1910); in 1917 became conductor of the Residentie Orch. in The Hague, retiring in 1935. He wrote an orch. rhapsody on Dutch themes, *Piet Hein* (1901); Ballade for Violin and Orch. (1902); several pieces of chamber music.

Ansermet, Ernest, celebrated Swiss conductor; b. Vevey, Nov. 11, 1883; d. Geneva, Feb. 20, 1969. He studied mathematics with his father, who was a schoolteacher, and received his musical training from his mother. He became himself a mathematics teacher, and taught school in Lausanne (1906–10). At the same time he took courses in music with Denéréaz, Barblan, and Ernest Bloch; he also studied conducting with Mottl in Munich and with Nikisch in Berlin. From then on he devoted himself mainly to conducting. He led the summer concerts in Montreux (1912–14), and from 1915–18 was conductor of the regular symph. concerts in Geneva. In 1918 he organized the prestigious Orchestre de la Suisse Romande in Geneva, at which he performed a great deal of modern French and Russian music; he retired from conducting in 1967. He met Stravinsky, who introduced him to Diaghilev, and subsequently conducted Diaghilev's Ballets Russes. On Sept. 28, 1918, he presented in Lausanne the first performance of Stravinsky's *L'Histoire du soldat.* He made numerous guest appearances as conductor with the Ballets Russes in Paris, London, Italy, Spain, South America, and the U.S., and also conducted performances with major American symph. orchs., attaining the reputation of a scholarly and progressive musician capable of fine interpretations of both Classical and modern works. He himself composed a symph. poem, *Feuilles de printemps;* orchestrated Debussy's *6 épigraphes antiques,* and 2 Argentinian dances by Julian Aguirre.

He publ. *Le Geste du chef d'orchestre* (Lausanne, 1943) and *Les Fondements de la musique dans la conscience humaine* (2 vols.; Neuchâtel, 1961), making use of mathematical formulations to demonstrate the lack of validity in 12-tone technique and other advanced methods of composition.

Ansorge, Conrad (Eduard Reinhold), German pianist; b. Buchwald, near Löbau, Silesia, Oct. 15, 1862; d. Berlin, Feb. 13, 1930. He studied at the Leipzig Cons. (1880–82) and was one of the last pupils of Liszt in Weimar (1885). He toured in Russia and America; then lived in Weimar (1893–95) and in Berlin (from 1895). From 1898 he taught at the Klindworth-Scharwenka Cons. In 1920 he gave courses at the German Cons. in Prague. Ansorge excelled as an interpreter of Romantic compositions; he was called "a metaphysician among pianists" for his insight into the inner meaning of the music of Beethoven, Schubert, and Schumann. He wrote a piano concerto, a string sextet, 2 string quartets, and a cello sonata; *Ballade, Traumbilder, Polish Dances,* and 3 sonatas for piano; and a Requiem.

Antes, John, American Moravian (*Unitas Fratrum*) minister; b. Frederickstownship, Pa., March 24, 1740; d. Bristol, England, Dec. 17, 1811. He left America in 1764, and was a missionary in Egypt, where he was beaten and crippled by order of a bey who tried to extort money from him. He spent the rest of his life in England. A watchmaker by trade, he was an inventive artisan. He constructed several string instruments; one violin made by him in Bethlehem, Pa., in 1759 is preserved in the Museum of the Moravian Historical Society at Nazareth, Pa. A contribution by Antes to the *Allgemeine musikalische Zeitung* in 1806 describes a device for better violin tuning, as well as improvements of the violin bow and of the keyboard hammer. Antes also invented a machine with which one could turn pages while playing. He wrote about 25 melodious short anthems to German or English words for Chorus, Winds, Strings, and Organ. All of his MS compositions are in the Archives of the Moravian Church at Bethlehem, and at Winston-Salem, N.C.; compositions in MS are also found in the Archiv der Brüder-Unität in Herrnhut, Germany. His 3 string trios were discovered in 1949. They are the earliest known chamber works by a native American. His interesting autobiography was publ. in *Nachrichten aus der Brüder-Gemeine* (1845).

Antheil, George, remarkable American composer who cut a powerful swath in the world of modern music by composing dissonant and loud pieces glorifying the age of the machine; b. Trenton, N.J., July 8, 1900; d. New York, Feb. 12, 1959. He studied music theory with Constantine von Sternberg in Philadelphia; then went to N.Y. to take lessons in composition with Ernest Bloch. Defying the norms of flickering musical conservatism, Antheil wrote piano pieces under such provocative titles as *Sonate sauvage, Mechanisms,* and *Airplane Sonata.* In 1922 he went to Europe and gave a number of concerts featuring his own compositions as well as some impressionist music. He spent a year in Berlin and then went to Paris, which had become his domicile for several years; he was one of the first American students of the legendary Nadia Boulanger, who was to be the *nourrice* of a whole generation of modernistically minded Americans. In Paris he also made contact with such great literary figures as James Joyce and Ezra Pound; in the natural course of events, Antheil became the self-styled *enfant terrible* of modern music. Naively infatuated with the new world of the modern machine, he composed a *Ballet mécanique* with the avowed intention to "épater les bourgeois." The culmination of Antheil's Paris period was marked by the performance of an orchestral suite from his *Ballet mécanique* (June 19, 1926), with musical material taken from a score he wrote for a film by Fernand Léger. He then returned to America as a sort of conquering hero of modern music, and staged a spectacular production of the *Ballet mécanique* at Carnegie Hall in N.Y. on April 10, 1927, employing a set of airplane propellers, 8 pianos, and a large battery of drums, creating an uproar in the audience and much publicity in the newspapers. A revival of the *Ballet mécanique* took place in N.Y. on Feb. 20, 1954, with a recording of the noise of a jet plane replacing the obsolescent propellers, but the piece was received by the public and press as merely a curiosity of the past.

Abandoning all attempts to shock the public by extravaganza, Antheil turned to composition of operas. His first complete opera, *Transatlantic*, to his own libretto, portraying the turmoil attendant on the presidential election, and employing jazz rhythms, was staged on May 25, 1930, in Frankfurt, Germany, arousing a modicum of interest. Another opera, *Mr. Bloom and the Cyclops*, based on James Joyce's novel *Ulysses*, never progressed beyond fragmentary sketches. A second opera, *Helen Retires*, with a libretto by John Erskine, was produced in N.Y. on Feb. 28, 1934. In 1936, Antheil moved to Hollywood, where he wrote some film music and ran a syndicated column of advice to perplexed lovers; another of his whimsical diversions was working on a torpedo device, in collaboration with the motion picture actress Hedy Lamarr; they actually filed a patent, No. 2,292,387, dated June 10, 1941, for an invention relating to a "secret communication system involving the use of carrier waves of different frequencies, especially useful in the remote control of dirigible craft, such as torpedoes." It is not known whether the Antheil-Lamarr device was ever used in naval warfare. He continued to write symphs., operas, and other works, but in the spirit of the times, reduced his musical idiom to accessible masses of sound. These works were rarely performed, and in the light of musical history, Antheil remains a herald of the avant-garde of yesterday. He publ. an autobiography, *Bad Boy of Music* (N.Y., 1945). He was married to Elizabeth ("Böski") Markus, a niece of the Austrian novelist Arthur Schnitzler; she died in 1978. Antheil was the subject of a monograph by Ezra Pound entitled *Antheil and the Treatise on Harmony, with Supplementary Notes* (Chicago, 1927), which,

however, had little bearing on Antheil and even less on harmony.

WORKS: OPERAS: *Transatlantic* (Frankfurt, May 25, 1930); *Helen Retires* (N.Y., Feb. 28, 1934); *Volpone*, after Ben Jonson (Los Angeles, Jan. 9, 1953); *The Brothers* (Denver, July 28, 1954); *The Wish* (Louisville, Ky., April 2, 1955); *Cabeza de vaca*, opera cantata (produced posthumously on CBS Television, June 10, 1962). BALLETS: *Ballet mécanique* (Paris, June 19, 1926; N.Y., April 10, 1927); *The Capital of the World* (N.Y., Dec. 27, 1953). FOR ORCH.: *Zingareska* (Berlin, Nov. 21, 1922); a "symphony" for 5 Instruments, also referred to as "Quintet" (1923); Symph. No. 1, in F major (1926; N.Y., April 10, 1927; a finale from it was originally labeled *Jazz Symphonietta*, and later rescored and renamed *Jazz Symphony*); Symph. No. 2, subtitled *American Symphony* (1937); Symph. No. 3 (1942); Symph. No. 4 (NBC Symph. Orch., N.Y., Stokowski conducting, Feb. 13, 1944); Symph. No. 5, subtitled *The Joyous* (Philadelphia, Dec. 21, 1948); Symph. No. 6 (San Francisco, Feb. 10, 1949); Piano Concerto (1926); *McKonkey's Ferry*, orchestral overture (1948); *Over the Plains* (1948); *Serenade* for String Orch. (1948); *Tom Sawyer: A Mark Twain Overture* (1950). CHAMBER MUSIC: 3 string quartets (1924, 1928, 1948); 4 violin sonatas (1923–48); Piano Trio (1950); 5 piano sonatas (1922–50); a group of pieces for Piano Solo under the title *La Femme: 100 têtes*, inspired by Max Ernst's book of collages of that title (1933); *Eight Fragments* from Shelley, for Chorus (1951); *Songs of Experience* for Voice and Piano (1948). FOR FILMS: *The Plainsman* (1937); *Specter of the Rose* (1946); *Knock on Any Door* (1949); *The Juggler* (1953); *Not as a Stranger* (1955); *The Pride and the Passion* (1957).

Apel, Willi, eminent music scholar; b. Konitz, Germany, Oct. 10, 1893. He studied mathematics at the univs. of Bonn (1912), Munich (1913), and Berlin (1918–21). He received his Ph.D. from the Univ. of Berlin in 1932; concurrently he studied music and took piano lessons. He taught mathematics and music in Germany until 1936, when he emigrated to the U.S. He gave lecture courses at Harvard Univ. (1938–42); in 1950 was engaged as prof. of musicology at Indiana Univ., Bloomington; retired in 1964 as prof. emeritus. While in Germany, he edited 2 volumes of early piano music, *Musik aus früher Zeit für Klavier* (Mainz, 1934). His other German publications were *Die Fuge* (1932) and his doctoral dissertation, *Accidentien und Tonalität in den Musikdenkmälern des 15. und 16. Jahrhunderts;* it was publ. as vol. 24 in the *Collection d'études musicologiques* (Strasbourg, 1937); a second augmented ed. appeared in Baden-Baden in 1972. In America he publ. the extremely valuable treatises and compilations *The Notation of Polyphonic Music, 900–1600* (Cambridge, Mass., 1942; 5th revised ed., 1961); *The Harvard Dictionary of Music*, a prime reference work of musical terminology (Cambridge, Mass., 1944; 2nd ed., revised and enlarged, Cambridge, 1969); *Historical Anthology of Music*, 2 vols. (with A.T. Davison; Cambridge, Mass.,

1946 and 1949); *Masters of the Keyboard* (Cambridge, Mass., 1947); *Gregorian Chant* (Bloomington, Ind., 1958). A Festschrift in Apel's honor, *Essays in Musicology*, ed. by H. Tischler (Bloomington, Ind., 1968), contains a bibliography of his writings.

Apostel, Hans Erich, Austrian composer; b. Karlsruhe, Jan. 22, 1901; d. Vienna, Nov. 30, 1972. After early studies in Karlsruhe he went to Vienna in 1921, and became a pupil in composition of Schoenberg and Alban Berg. He served as an editor at Universal Edition and in that capacity prepared for publication the posthumous works of Berg. He was also active as a teacher. Apostel received numerous prizes for his own works, among them the Grand Prize of the City of Vienna (1948) and the Grand Prize of the Republic of Austria (1957). In 1951 he adopted the method of composition with 12 tones according to Schoenberg's precepts, without, however, avoiding tonal combinations. He experimented in Klangfarben effects, and applied audible overtones in his piano pieces by holding down the keys without striking them. His music was often performed at international festivals, but it never penetrated beyond the confines of Central Europe.

Appenzeller (Appencellers, Appenzelder, Appenzelders), Benedictus, Franco-Flemish composer of the first half of the 16th century. Possibly a pupil of Josquin, he served Mary of Hungary as court musician and master of choirboys at her chapel in Brussels (1537–c.1554) and probably accompanied her on her visit to Germany (1551). Appenzeller's works were formerly attributed to Benedictus Ducis, a German composer whose identity was confused with his. Among Appenzeller's extant compositions are a book of chansons (1542; 2 of the chansons from this collection had been publ. by Attaingnant in 1529 without being ascribed to Appenzeller); a lament on the death of Josquin (1521), which uses half of the *Musae Jovis* text; and a double canon on *Sancta Maria* embroidered on a tablecloth for Mary of Hungary (1548). Pieces by him are included in the 2nd *Musyckboexken* of Susato; the *Hortus Musarum,* part I (1552), publ. by Phalese, contains a transcription for 2 lutes of a piece by Appenzeller.

Applebaum, Edward, American composer; b. Los Angeles, Sept. 28, 1937. He studied piano as a youth; later studied with Henri Lazarof and Lukas Foss at the Univ. of Calif. at Los Angeles (Ph.D., 1966). In 1969 he was composer-in-residence of the Oakland Symph. Orch.; in 1971 became a prof. of theory and composition at the Univ. of Calif. at Santa Barbara.
WORKS: Piano Sonata (1965); String Trio (1966); Variations for Orch. (1966); Concerto for Viola and Chamber Orch. (1967); *Montages* for Clarinet, Cello, and Piano (1968); *Shantih* for Cello and Piano (1969); Symph. No. 1 (1970); *Foci* for Viola and Piano (1971); . . . *When Dreams Do Show Thee Me* . . . , triple concerto for Clarinet, Cello, Piano, Chamber Orch., and 9 Vocal Soloists (1972); Piano Trio (1972); *Reflections for Piano Trio* (1972); *The Face in the Cameo* for Clarinet and Piano (1973); *The Frieze of Life,* one-act chamber opera (1974); *To Remember,* trio for Clarinet, Cello, and Piano (1976); *The Garden* for Soprano, Chamber Ensemble, and Tape (1979); Piano Sonata No. 2 (1980); Symph. No. 2 (St. Louis, Oct. 6, 1983).

Aprile, Giuseppe, Italian male contralto; b. Martina Franca, Apulia, Oct. 28, 1731; d. there, Jan. 11, 1813. He studied voice with his father, and since he showed signs of excellence, his father had him evirated at the age of 11. He then studied singing in Naples and appeared as a soprano at the Naples Royal Chapel in 1751. He made his professional debut as a singer at the Teatro San Carlo in Naples in 1753; he subsequently sang at the Court of Württemberg in Stuttgart (1756), and remained in that service for 10 years. He later was active as a teacher in Naples; among his pupils was Cimarosa. Aprile's vocal treatise *The Modern Italian Method of Singing, with 36 Solfeggi* was publ. by Broderip in London in 1791 and was reprinted in several editions and translated into several languages.

Apthorp, William Foster, American music critic; b. Boston, Mass., Oct. 24, 1848; d. Vevey, Switzerland, Feb. 19, 1913. A graduate of Harvard Univ. (1869), he studied music with Paine. He taught music at the New England Cons. and lectured on music history at Boston Univ. He wrote music criticism for the *Atlantic Monthly* (1872–77); was music and drama critic on the *Boston Evening Transcript* (1881–1903). In his criticisms Apthorp violently opposed new Russian, French, and German music (his intemperate attacks on Tchaikovsky elicited protests from his readers). Apthorp was also the annotator of the Boston Symph. programs (1892–1901). He publ. several books: *Musicians and Music Lovers* (N.Y., 1894); *By the Way,* a collection of short essays in 2 vols.: I, *About Music,* and II, *About Musicians* (Boston, 1898); *The Opera, Past and Present* (N.Y., 1901). He was co-editor of *Scribner's Cyclopedia of Music and Musicians* (N.Y., 1888–90).

Araja, Francesco, Italian composer; b. Naples, June 25, 1709; d. Bologna, 1770. He produced his first opera, *Lo matremmonejo pe' mennetta,* in the Neapolitan dialect (Naples, 1729); his subsequent operas were *Berenice* (Florence, 1730); *La forza dell'amore e dell'odio* (Milan, 1734); *Lucio Vero* (Venice, Jan. 4, 1735). In 1735 he was engaged as music director and court composer in St. Petersburg. There he wrote annual pieces for court occasions, beginning with the cantata *La gara dell'amore e del zelo* (April 28, 1736). Among his operas given at the Russian court were *La Semiramide riconosciuta* (Feb. 9, 1737); *Artaserse* (1738); *Seleuco* (1744); *Scipione* (1745); *Mitridate* (1747); *L'asilo della pace* (1748); *Bellerofonte* (1750); *Eudossa incoronata* (1751). He wrote 17 operas; *La clemenza di Tito,* attributed to him by some, was the work of Hasse. On Feb. 27, 1755, Araja presented in St. Petersburg the first opera ever composed to a libretto in the Russian language, on the story of Cephalus and Procris, written by the famous Russian dramatist Sumarokov. Araja was in Italy from 1740–42, and again from 1759–62; in 1762 he revisited Russia briefly at the summons of Peter III, his great admirer, returning to Italy after the Czar's death. Nothing is known of Araja's last years.

Arakishvili, Dmitri, Georgian composer; b. Vladikavkaz, Feb. 23, 1873; d. Tiflis, Aug. 13, 1953. He studied composition at the Moscow Phil. Inst. with Ilyinsky and also took private lessons with Gretchaninov. At the same time he studied archaeology and ethnic sciences; in 1901 he became a member of the Musical Ethnographic Commission at the Univ. of Moscow. In 1906 he took part in the organization of the Moscow People's Cons., which offered free music lessons to impecunious students. He was editor of the Moscow publication *Music and Life* (1908–12). In 1918 he moved to Tiflis, where he was active as a teacher and conductor. He composed one of the earliest national Georgian operas, *The Legend of Shota Rustaveli* (Tiflis, Feb. 5, 1919); a comic opera, *Dinara* (1926); 3 symphs. (1934, 1942, 1951); *Hymn of the New East* for Orch. (1933); and film music. But his best compositions are some 80 art songs in a lyrico-dramatic manner reflecting the Georgian modalities.

d'Aranyi, Jelly, Hungarian violinist, grandniece of **Joachim** and sister of the violinist **Adila Fachiri;** b. Budapest, May 30, 1893; d. Florence, March 30, 1966. She studied violin with Hubay in Budapest; after some concerts in Europe, she went to America and made her debut in a solo recital in N.Y. on Nov. 26, 1927; made her 2nd American tour in 1932. She frequently appeared in joint recitals with Myra Hess. A pioneer in modern music, she gave first performances of many new works. Béla Bartók's First Violin Sonata, Ravel's *Tzigane,* and the *Concerto Accademico* for Violin and Orch. by Vaughan Williams are dedicated to her. She attracted considerable attention in 1937 when she proclaimed that Schumann's spirit appeared to her during a séance and revealed the secret of his unpublished Violin Concerto; but Schumann's ghost spoke ungrammatical German, which aroused suspicion concerning the authenticity of the phenomenon; besides, it had long been known that the MS of the concerto was preserved at the Berlin State Library; the first performance of the piece was eventually given in Germany by another violinist. Jelly d'Aranyi was given a chance, however, to perform it with the BBC Orch. in London on Feb. 16, 1938.

Arapov, Boris, eminent Russian composer and pedagogue; b. St. Petersburg, Sept. 12, 1905. He was a scion of an intellectual family; his grandfather was a lawyer; his father was a naturalist. He spent his childhood in Poltava, where he received his early musical training; in 1921 the family returned to St. Petersburg (now renamed Petrograd); he studied composition with Shcherbachev at the Cons. there, graduating in 1930; was then appointed to its faculty as an instructor (1930) and later prof. (1940).

Among his pupils were many Soviet composers of stature, including Dmitri Tolstoy, Falik, Uspensky, Banshchikov, Knaifel, and Sergei Slonimsky. The years 1941–44 Arapov spent in Tashkent, in Uzbekistan, where the entire faculty of the Leningrad Cons. was evacuated during the siege of Leningrad. There he studied indigenous folklore, and wrote an Uzbeki opera, *Khodji Nasreddin.* After the siege was lifted, Arapov returned to Leningrad, resumed his pedagogical duties, and continued to compose. In 1955–56 he was in China, where he wrote several works on Chinese themes. In 1959 he visited Korea, and composed a symph. using the pentatonic Korean modes. During the years 1950–73 he also traveled in Europe. Arapov's compositions represent to perfection the evolutionary character of Soviet music, taking their source in the Russian traditions of the previous centuries, making ample use of ethnic materials of the constituent regions of the immense territory of the U.S.S.R., and integrating the native homophonic melorhythms in an increasingly complex tapestry of colorful fabrics, richly ornamented with occasional application of such modern devices as dodecaphonic melodic structures. But Arapov was also able to produce a virtuoso display of instrumental techniques for piano and other instruments.

Arauxo (or **Arauxo**), **(Francisco).** See **Correa de Araujo, (Francisco).**

Arban, (Joseph) Jean-Baptiste (Laurent), renowned French cornet player and pedagogue; b. Lyons, Feb. 28, 1825; d. Paris, April 9, 1889. He studied trumpet at the Paris Cons. with Dauverné (1841–45); then was engaged as a leader of Parisian salon orchs. In 1857 he became a prof. of saxhorn at the Ecole Militaire in Paris; in 1869 he joined the faculty of the Paris Cons. as a teacher of cornet; then traveled to Russia as a conductor; returning to Paris in 1880, he resumed his post as a teacher. Arban is acknowledged as the founder of the modern school of trumpet playing. He publ. the standard manual *Grande méthode complète pour cornet à pistons et de saxhorn* (Paris, 1864); also made arrangements for cornet.

Arbeau, Thoinot (anagram of real name, **Jehan Tabourot**), French writer; b. Dijon, March 17, 1520; d. Langres, July 23, 1595. He owes his fame to his didactic treatise in dialogue form, *Orchésographie, et traité en forme de dialogue par lequel toutes personnes peuvent facilement apprendre et pratiquer l'honnête exercise des danses* (Langres, 1588; 2nd ed., 1589), which contains not only instructions for dancing (indicating dance steps by a simple system of initial letters), but also valuable observations on the dance music of his time. It was publ. in Eng. trans. by C.W. Beaumont (London, 1925) and M. Evans (N.Y., 1948).

Arbós, Enrique Fernández, Spanish violinist and conductor; b. Madrid, Dec. 24, 1863; d. San Sebastian, June 2, 1939. He studied violin with Monasterio in Madrid, with Vieuxtemps in Brussels, and with Joachim in Berlin. After successful tours in Europe, he returned to Spain in 1888; taught violin at the Madrid Cons. In 1889 he was concertmaster of the Glasgow Symph. Orch.; from 1894–1916 he held the post of honorary prof. at the Royal College of Music in London. He was appointed conductor of the new Madrid Symph. Orch. in 1904; conducted in the U.S. (1928–31), then in Europe. At the outbreak of the Spanish Civil War in 1936 he retired to San Sebastian. Arbós was the author of a comic opera, *El centro de la tierra* (Madrid, Dec. 22, 1895). He was a brilliant orchestrator; his arrangement of the music from *Iberia* by Albéniz is very popular.

Arcadelt, Jacob (or **Jachet Arkadelt, Archadet, Arcadet, Harcadelt**), great Flemish composer; b. probably in Liège, c.1505; d. Paris, Oct. 14, 1568. He was "magister puerorum" to the Papal Chapel (1539), and choirmaster (1540). In 1544 he held the office of "camerlingo." He went to France in 1546; returned to Rome in May 1547. In 1555 he again went to France, this time with the Duc de Guise. Arcadelt is mentioned in Paris as "Regis musicus" in 1557. In the domain of secular music, his Roman period was, in the main, devoted to the madrigal; his Paris period, to the French chanson.
WORKS: He wrote 20 motets, about 120 French chansons, and 200 madrigals. Of his extant works, the most important are 6 books of 5-part madrigals (Venice, 1538–56; his finest and most characteristic compositions) and 3 books of masses in 3–7 parts (Paris, 1557).

Archer, Violet, prolific Canadian pianist and composer; b. Montreal, April 24, 1913. She studied composition with Champagne, and piano at the McGill Cons. in Montreal (1932–36); took private lessons with Bartók in N.Y. (1942) and attended courses in composition with Hindemith at Yale Univ. (1948–49). She taught at McGill (1944–47), at North Texas State College (1950–53), and at the Univ. of Oklahoma (1953–61), and served, since 1962, as chairman of the composition dept. at the Univ. of Alberta, Edmonton. Her music is structurally strong, polyphonically disciplined, and generally kept within organized tonality, with occasional dodecaphonic episodes.

Ardévol, José, Cuban composer; b. Barcelona, March 13, 1911; d. Havana, Jan. 7, 1981. He studied with his father, conductor of an orch. in Barcelona; at the age of 19 he went to Havana, where he organized a chamber group; he also edited the magazine *La Música.* He became active in musical politics after the revolution of 1959, and served in various capacities in Cuba and elsewhere; was appointed national director for music, a post which he held until 1965. Several of his works have distinct revolutionary connotations.

Arditi, Luigi, Italian composer and conductor; b. Crescentino, Piedmont, July 16, 1822; d. Hove, near Brighton, England, May 1, 1903. He studied violin, piano, and composition at the Milan Cons., where

he also produced his first opera, *I Briganti* (1841). He then embarked on a career as an operatic conductor. From 1846 he traveled in Cuba, where he produced his opera *Il Corsaro* (Havana, 1846); also visited N.Y. and Philadelphia. In N.Y. he produced his opera *La Spia* (March 24, 1856). He finally settled in London (1858) as a conductor and vocal teacher, while making annual tours with the Italian Opera in Germany and Austria. He conducted in St. Petersburg in 1871 and 1873. His operas and other works were never revived, but he created a perennial success with his vocal waltz *Il bacio.* He wrote his autobiography, *My Reminiscences* (N.Y., 1896).

Arensky, Anton, Russian composer; b. Novgorod, July 12, 1861; d. Terijoki, Finland, Feb. 25, 1906. He studied at the St. Petersburg Cons. with Johanssen and Rimsky-Korsakov (1879–82); then taught harmony at the Moscow Cons. (1882–94). Returning to St. Petersburg, he conducted the choir of the Imperial Chapel (1895–1901); a victim of tuberculosis, he spent his last years in a sanatorium in Finland. In his music he followed Tchaikovsky's lyric style.
WORKS: 3 operas: *A Dream on the Volga* (Moscow, Jan. 2, 1891); *Raphael* (Moscow, May 6, 1894); *Nal and Damayanti* (Moscow, Jan. 22, 1904); 2 symphs. (he conducted the first perfs. of both in Moscow, Nov. 24, 1883, and Dec. 21, 1889). He was more successful in his works for smaller forms; his *Variations* for String Orch. on Tchaikovsky's song *The Christ Child Had a Garden* (originally the *Variations* formed the slow movement of Arensky's Quartet, op. 35, in A minor for Violin, Viola, and 2 Cellos) became a standard work. His Piano Trio also retains its popularity. His 4 suites for 2 pianos, expertly written, are often heard; he also arranged these suites for orch. Some of his songs are included in vocal anthologies. Other works are: music to Pushkin's poem *The Fountain of Bakhtchissaray;* ballet, *Egyptian Nights* (St. Petersburg, 1900); *The Diver,* ballad for Voices and Orch.; *Coronation Cantata; Marche solennelle* for Orch.; *Intermezzo* for String Orch.; Piano Concerto; Violin Concerto in A minor; a Fantasy on epic Russian songs, for Piano and Orch.; Piano Quintet in D; String Quartet in G, op. 11; pieces for cello; works for violin; many pieces for piano solo. He publ. *Manual of Harmony* (translated into German) and *Handbook of Musical Forms.*

d'Arezzo, Guido. See **Guido d'Arezzo.**

Argenta, Ataulfo, Spanish conductor; b. Castro Urdiales, Santander, Nov. 19, 1913; d. in an automobile accident at Los Molinos, near Madrid, Jan. 21, 1958. He studied at the Madrid Cons.; then went to Germany, where he took lessons in conducting with Carl Schuricht. Returning to Spain in 1939, he conducted various small groups; in 1945 he was appointed director of the National Orch. in Madrid.

Argento, Dominick, greatly talented American composer excelling especially in opera; b. York, Pa., Oct. 27, 1927. He played the piano, but had no formal instruction in music theory; after high school he enlisted in the U.S. Army as a cryptographer (1945–47). In 1947 he enrolled at the Peabody Cons. of Music in Baltimore, where he took courses with Nicolas Nabokov and Hugo Weisgall, graduating in 1951 with a B.A. degree. He then went to Italy on a Fulbright fellowship and studied piano with Pietro Scarpini and composition with Luigi Dallapiccola at the Conservatorio Cherubini in Florence. Upon returning to the U.S., he attended classes of Henry Cowell in composition at the Peabody Cons. in Baltimore; eager to pursue his studies further, he entered the Eastman School of Music in Rochester, N.Y., where his teachers were Howard Hanson and Bernard Rogers; in 1957 he received his doctorate in music there. In 1957 he was awarded a Guggenheim fellowship, which enabled him to go once more to Florence and work on his opera *Colonel Jonathan the Saint;* in 1964 he obtained his second Guggenheim fellowship. In 1958 he was appointed to the music faculty of the Univ. of Minnesota in Minneapolis; also in 1964 he became a founder of the Center Opera in Minnesota, later renamed the Minnesota Opera. The connection gave Argento an opportunity to present his operas under his own supervision. In 1980 he was elected a member of the American Academy and Institute of Arts and Letters. In the pantheon of American composers Argento occupies a distinct individual category, outside any certifiable modernistic trend or technical idiom. He writes melodious music in a harmonious treatment, so deliberate in intent that even his apologists profess embarrassment at its unimpeded flow; there is also a perceptible ancestral strain in the bel canto style of his Italianate opera scores; most important, audiences, and an increasing number of sophisticated critics, profess their admiration for his unusual songfulness. Yet an analysis of Argento's productions reveals the presence of acerb harmonies and artfully acidulated melismas.

WORKS: OPERAS: *Sicilian Limes* (N.Y., Oct. 1, 1954); *The Boor,* after Chekhov's short comedy (Rochester, May 6, 1957); *Colonel Jonathan the Saint* (1958–61; Denver, Dec. 31, 1971); *Christopher Sly,* a scene from Shakespeare's play *The Taming of the Shrew* (Minneapolis, May 31, 1963); *The Masque of Angels* (Minneapolis, Jan. 9, 1964); *Shoemaker's Holiday* (Minneapolis, June 1, 1967); *Postcard from Morocco* (Minneapolis, Oct. 14, 1971); *The Voyage of Edgar Allan Poe* (Minneapolis, April 24, 1976; achieved great critical acclaim); *Miss Havisham's Fire* (1978). OTHER VOCAL WORKS: Oratorio, *Jonah and the Whale* (Minneapolis, March 9, 1974); *Song about Spring,* song cycle for Soprano and Orch. (1950; revised in 1954 and 1960); *Ode to the West Wind,* Concerto for Soprano and Orch. (1956); *6 Elizabethan Songs* for Voice and Piano (1962); *The Revelation of St. John the Divine,* rhapsody for Tenor, Men's Chorus, Brass, and Percussion (1966); *A Nation of Cowslips* for Chorus (1968); *Letters from Composers,* song cycle for Tenor and Guitar (1968); *Tria Carmina Paschalia,* 3 songs to Latin verses for Women's Voices, Harp, and Guitar (1970); *To Be Sung upon the Water* for Voice, Clarinet, and Piano (1973); *A Waterbird Talks,* monodrama (1974); *From the Diary of Virginia Woolf* for Voice and Piano (1974; awarded the Pulitzer Prize); *In Praise of Music,* 7 songs for Orch. (1977). BALLET: *Resurrection of Don Juan* (Rochester, May 5, 1936). CHAMBER MUSIC: *Divertimento* for Piano and Strings (Rochester, July 2, 1958); String Quartet (1956); *Royal Invitation (or Homage to the Queen of Tonga)* for Chamber Orch. (St. Paul, Minn., March 22, 1964); *Variations (The Mask of Night)* for Orch. with Soprano Solo in the final variations (Minneapolis, Jan. 26, 1966); *Bravo Mozart!,* concerto for Oboe, Violin, Horn, and Orch. (1969); *A Ring of Time,* preludes and pageants for Instruments (1972).

Argerich, Martha, pianist; b. Buenos Aires, June 5, 1941. She studied with Gulda, Magaloff, and Madeleine Lipatti; made her debut in Buenos Aires in 1949. After taking part in several piano competitions, she became successful as a soloist, both in Europe and America. She was married for some years to the Swiss conductor **Charles Dutoit.**

Aribon (Aribo Scholasticus, Aribon de Liège, Aribon de Freising, and **Aribon d'Orléans),** medieval scholar; b. probably in Liège, c.1000; d. Orléans, c.1078. In 1024 he was chancellor to the Bishop of Liège; after a short period of service he went to Italy, where he acquired a knowledge of the methods of Guido d'Arezzo. From 1060–70 he was again in Liège as preceptor at the Cathedral school; then went to Orléans. Aribon was the author of the important treatise *De musica,* written in Liège c.1065. It is reproduced in Gerbert's *Scriptores* (vol. II, pp. 197–230) and in J. Smits van Waesberghe's *Corpus scriptorum de musica* (vol. II, Rome, 1951).

d'Arienzo, Nicola, Italian composer; b. Naples, Dec. 22, 1842; d. there, April 25, 1915. He composed an opera in the Neapolitan dialect at the age of 18; a series of Italian operas followed: *I due mariti* (Naples, Feb. 1, 1866); *Il cacciatore delle Alpi* (Naples, June 23, 1870); *Il cuoco* (Naples, June 11, 1873); *I Viaggi* (Milan, June 28, 1875); *La figlia del diavolo* (Naples, Nov. 16, 1879; his most successful opera, which aroused considerable controversy for its realistic tendencies); *I tre coscritti* (Naples, Feb. 10, 1880); etc. He also wrote 2 symphs. and much choral music. He publ. a treatise, *Introduzione del sistema tetracordale nella moderna musica,* favoring pure intonation; a historical essay, *Dell' opera comica dalle origini a Pergolesi* (1887; German trans., 1902); several monographs on Italian composers and numerous articles in periodicals.

Ariosti, Attilio, Italian opera composer; b. Bologna, Nov. 5, 1666; d. c.1729. He joined the Servite Order in 1688, but later abandoned it. He served as organist in Bologna in 1693; in 1697 he was in Berlin as court musician. From 1703–11 he was in Vienna, then returned to Bologna. He was in London in 1716 and again from 1723–27. A vol. of his cantatas and "lessons" for viola d'amore, on which he was an accomplished performer, was publ. in London in 1724. Ariosti then disappeared, the most probable conjecture being that he returned to Italy and died there in obscurity. Burney's attribution to Ariosti of one act of the opera *Muzio Scevola* (produced in London on April 15, 1721) is an anachronism, for Ariosti was not in London at the time.

Aristakesian, Emin, Armenian composer; b. Erevan, Nov. 19, 1936. He studied composition with Yegiazarian at the Erevan Cons., graduating in 1961; then taught in various Armenian institutes. Much of his music is, in its melorhythmic structure, derived from Armenian folk songs.
WORKS: Ballet, *Prometheus* (Erevan, 1967); *Armenia*, oratorio (1961); 2 symphs. (1962, 1975); Viola Concerto (1963); Sinfonietta for Strings, Piano, and Xylophone (1969); *Suite* for String Quintet (1955); *Poem* for Piano Quintet (1959); *Polyphonic Variations* for String Quartet (1960); *Fantastic Variations* for Piano (1964); *Capriccio* for Piano (1965); *Poem about Lenin* for Chorus and Piano (1970); Piano Sonata (1971); *5 Sharageans of Saak Parteva* for Voice and Piano (1972); other songs.

Aristides Quintilianus, Greek writer on music; lived A.D. c.200 in Smyrna. His treatise *De musica libri VII* was printed in Meibom's *Antiquae musicae auctores septem* (1652) and by A. Jahn (1882); R. Schäfke publ. it in German (1937) with a commentary. Despite the dubious authenticity of some of his descriptions of Greek scales, the work is one of the basic sources of our knowledge of ancient Greek music.

Aristotle, famous Greek philosopher, pupil of Plato; b. Stagira, 384 B.C.; d. Chalcis, 322 B.C. The 19th section of the *Problems,* once ascribed to him, is the product of a much later follower of his theories; the English translation, by E.S. Forster, is found in *The Works of Aristotle,* vol. 7 (Oxford, 1927); the Greek text with French translation and commentary by F.A. Gevaert and C. Vollgraff is publ. in *Les Problèmes musicaux d'Aristote* (3 vols., 1899–1902). Aristotle's actual writings on music are reproduced by K. von Jan in his *Musici scriptores Graeci* (1895). The name Aristotle was also used by a writer on mensurable music of the 12th–13th centuries, whose treatise is publ. by E. de Coussemaker in his *Scriptores,* vol. I.

Aristoxenos, one of the earliest Greek writers on music; b. Tarentum, 354 B.C. His *Harmonic Elements* (complete) and *Rhythmical Elements* (fragmentary) are among the most important treatises on Greek music theory that have come down to us. They have been publ. by R. Westphal and F. Saran (2 vols.; 1883, 1893); also by H.S. Macran, with English and Greek text and a commentary (1902). The *Harmonic Elements* are included, in an English translation, in O. Strunk's *Source Readings in Music History* (N.Y., 1950). See also L. Laloy, *Aristoxène de Tarente* (1904); C.F.A. Williams, *The Aristoxenian Theory of Musical Rhythm* (Cambridge, 1911).

Arlen, Harold (real name, **Hyman Arluck**), American composer of popular music; b. Buffalo, Feb. 15, 1905. He studied music privately with Simon Bucharoff. As a small child he joined the choir of a synagogue where his father was cantor. At 15 he began to earn a living as a pianist on lake steamboats and in nightclubs. Then he went to N.Y., where he became engaged in a variety of professions, as a singer with jazz bands, a pianist, an arranger, and finally a composer. Possessing a natural gift for melody, he created numerous song hits, of which *Stormy Weather* (1932) became a classic of American popular music. He wrote several successful musicals for Broadway, among them *Bloomer Girl* (1944); *St. Louis Woman* (1946); *House of Flowers* (1954); *Jamaica* (1957). He also wrote music for films, among them the score for *The Wizard of Oz* (1939).

Armstrong, Louis, famous black American jazz trumpeter, familiarly known as "Satchmo" (for "Satchel Mouth," with reference to his spacious and resonant oral cavity); b. New Orleans, July 4, 1900; d. New York, July 6, 1971. At age 13 he was arrested for firing his stepfather's gun during a New Year's Eve celebration, and was placed in the black Waifs Home for Boys; there he learned to read music and play several instruments, excelling on the cornet. After his release he worked as a musician, mostly in Storyville, the red-light district of New Orleans; in 1921 he went to Chicago, where he played cornet in King Oliver's Creole Jazz Band until 1924; in 1925 he organized his own band—the Hot 5, later the Hot 7— and rapidly earned fame; set an endurance record when he sounded high C on the trumpet 280 times in succession. His style of improvisation revolutionized jazz performance in the 1920s, and he won admirers all over the world; some critics hailed him as "the Einstein of Jazz." He continued to play at jazz festivals in the 1960s, and his recording of the song *Hello Dolly* was a best-seller in 1964. His wife during the years 1924–31 was **Lil(lian) Hardin** (b. Memphis, Tenn., Feb. 3, 1898; d. Chicago, Aug. 7, 1971), who served as pianist for King Oliver's group from 1920–23, and then with the Hot 5 and Hot 7 combos; they were divorced in 1938. Armstrong wrote an autobiography, *Satchmo, My Life in New Orleans* (N.Y., 1954).

Arne, Michael, English opera composer; b. London, 1741; d. there, Jan. 14, 1786. He was a natural son of **Thomas Augustine Arne.** He was trained as an actor and a singer, and made his debut in a concert in London on Feb. 20, 1750. He also acquired considerable skill as a harpsichord player. In 1771–72 he traveled in Germany as a conductor of stage music; from 1776 he was in Dublin; at some time prior to 1784 he returned to London. He was known for his eccentricities; among his vagaries was an earnest preoccupation with alchemy in search of the philosopher's stone to convert base metals into gold, a quest which proved a disappointment.

WORKS: 9 operas (all perf. in London), including *Hymen* (Jan. 23, 1764); *Cymon* (Jan. 2, 1767); *The Artifice* (April 14, 1780); *The Choice of Harlequin* (Dec. 26, 1781); *Vertumnus and Pomona* (Feb. 21, 1782); also collaborations with other composers in about 14 productions.

Arne, Thomas Augustine, famous English dramatic composer; b. London, March 12, 1710; d. there, March 5, 1778. His father, an upholsterer, sent him to Eton; he then spent 3 years in a solicitor's office. He studied music on the side, much against his father's wishes, and acquired considerable skill on the violin. He soon began to write musical settings, "after the Italian manner," to various plays. His first production was Addison's *Rosamond* (March 7, 1733). He renamed Fielding's *Tragedy of Tragedies* as *Opera of Operas,* and produced it at the Haymarket Theatre (Oct. 29, 1733); a masque, *Dido and Aeneas,* followed (Jan. 12, 1734). His most important work was the score of *Comus* (Drury Lane, March 4, 1738). On Aug. 1, 1740, he produced at Clivedon, Buckinghamshire, the masque *Alfred,* the finale of which contains the celebrated song *Rule Britannia,* which became a national patriotic song of Great Britain. In the meantime, on March 15, 1737, Arne married Cecilia Young, daughter of the organist Charles Young, and herself a fine singer. In 1742 he went with her to Dublin, where he also stayed in 1755 and 1758. Of his many dramatic productions the following were performed at Drury Lane in London: *The Temple of Dullness* (Jan. 17, 1745); *Harlequin Incendiary* (March 3, 1746); *The Triumph of Peace* (Feb. 21, 1748); *Britannia* (May 9, 1755); *Beauty and Virtue* (Feb. 26, 1762); *The Rose* (Dec. 2, 1772). The following were staged at Covent Garden: *Harlequin Sorcerer* (Feb. 11, 1752); *The Prophetess* (Feb. 1, 1758); *Thomas and Sally* (Nov. 28, 1760); *Love in a Village* (Dec. 8, 1762); *The Fairy Prince* (Nov. 12, 1771). He further contributed separate numbers to 28 theatrical productions, among them songs to Shakespeare's *As You Like It;* "Where the Bee Sucks" in *The Tempest;* etc. He wrote 2 oratorios: *The Death of Abel* (Dublin, Feb. 18, 1744) and *Judith* (Drury Lane, Feb. 27, 1761), the latter remarkable for the introduction of female voices into the choral parts. He also wrote numerous glees and catches, and miscellaneous instrumental music. He received the honorary degree of D.Mus. from Oxford Univ. (July 6, 1759), which accounts for his familiar appellation of "Dr. Arne."

d'Arneiro, (José Augusto) Ferreira Veiga, Viscount, distinguished Portuguese composer; b. Macao, China, Nov. 22, 1838; d. San Remo, July 7, 1903. He studied with Botelho, Schira, and Soarcs in Lisbon. The production of his ballet *Gina* (Lisbon, 1866) attracted attention; he then produced an opera, *L'Elisire di Giovinezza* (Lisbon, March 31, 1876), followed by *La Derelitta* (Lisbon, 1885). *Te Deum,* performed in Lisbon and in London in 1871, was very successful; it was later given in Paris under the somewhat affected title of "Symphonie-Cantate."

Arnell, Richard, English composer; b. London, Sept. 15, 1917. He studied with John Ireland at the Royal College of Music in London (1935–38). In 1939 he went to America; when Winston Churchill had a reception at Columbia Univ. in 1946, Arnell wrote *Prelude and Flourish* for Brass Instruments, performed at the occasion. In 1948 Arnell returned to London. His music may be described as festive without pomposity, and very English.

WORKS: Operas: *Love in Transit* (London, Feb. 27, 1958); *The Petrified Princess* (London, May 5, 1959); *Moonflowers* (Kent, July 23, 1959); *Combat Zone* (Hempstead, N.Y., Hofstra College, April 27, 1969). Ballets: *Harlequin in April,* suggested by T.S. Eliot's *The Waste Land* (London, May 8, 1951); *The Great Detective,* about Sherlock Holmes (1953). Also 5 symphs. (1941–68); Overture, *The New Age* (N.Y., Jan. 13, 1941); *Quasi variazioni* (N.Y., March 15, 1942); Violin Concerto (N.Y., April 22, 1946); 2 piano concertos (1946; 1966); *Abstract Forms,* Suite for Strings (Bath, June 2, 1951); *Lord Byron,* a symph. portrait (London, Nov. 19, 1952); 5 string quartets; other chamber music; piano pieces.

Arnold, Byron, American composer; b. Vancouver, Wash., Aug. 15, 1901. He studied at Willamette Univ. (B.A., 1924) and later at the Eastman School of Music in Rochester, N.Y., with Bernard Rogers and Howard Hanson. From 1938–48 he was on the faculty of the Univ. of Alabama. One of his most original pieces is a symph. suite entitled *5 Incapacitated Preludes,* each portraying a serious incapacitation (deafness, blindness, paralysis, etc.; the deaf prelude instructs the players to pretend they are playing music, but without producing any sounds); it was performed in Rochester on April 19, 1937. He also wrote *3 Fantasticisms* for Orch.; piano pieces; songs. He publ. *Folk Songs of Alabama* (1950).

Arnold, Denis, English musicologist; b. Sheffield, Dec. 15, 1926. He was educated at Sheffield Univ. (B.A., 1947; B.Mus., 1948; M.A., 1950). In 1951 he became a lecturer at Queen's Univ., Belfast; in 1964 he was made senior lecturer at the Univ. of Hull; in 1969 became a prof. of music at the Univ. of Nottingham; from 1975 was a prof. of music at Oxford Univ. In 1976 he became joint editor of *Music & Letters.* He is regarded as one of the foremost authorities on Italian music of the Renaissance and the early Baroque period.

WRITINGS: *Monteverdi* (London, 1963); *Marenzio* (London, 1965); *Monteverdi Madrigals* (London, 1967); *The Monteverdi Companion,* with N. Fortune (London, 1968); *Giovanni Gabrieli* (London, 1974); *Giovanni Gabrieli and the Music of the Venetian High Renaissance* (Oxford, 1979).

Arnold, Malcolm, prolific and versatile British composer; b. Northampton, Oct. 21, 1921. He studied trumpet, conducting, and composition at the Royal College of Music in London (1938–40); played first trumpet with the London Phil. (1942–44, 1946–48). He then devoted himself chiefly to composition, developing a melodious and harmonious style of writing that possessed the quality of immediate appeal to the general public while avoiding obvious banality; many of his works reveal modalities common to English folk songs, often invested in acridly pleasing harmonies. His experience as a trumpeter and conductor of popular concerts provided a secure feeling for propulsive rhythms and brilliant sonorities. He had a knack for composing effective background music for films. In his sound track for *The Bridge on the River Kwai* he popularized the rollicking march *Colonel Bogey,* originally composed by Kenneth Alford in 1914. In 1970 Arnold was made a Commander of the Order of the British Empire.

WORKS: OPERAS: *The Dancing Master* (1951) and *The Open Window* (London, Dec. 14, 1956). BALLETS: *Homage to the Queen* (produced at Covent Garden, London, in the presence of Queen Elizabeth II, on June 2, 1953); *Rinaldo and Armida* (1954); *Sweeney Todd* (1958); and *Electra* (1963). OTHER STAGE WORKS: Nativity play, *Song of Simeon* (1958); a children's spectacle, *The Turtle Drum* (1967). FOR ORCH.: Symph. for Strings (1946); 8 numbered symphs.: No. 1 (Cheltenham Festival, July 6, 1951); No. 2 (Bournemouth, May 25, 1953); No. 3 (1954–57; London, Dec. 2, 1957); No. 4 (London, Nov. 2, 1960); No. 5 (Cheltenham Festival, 1961); No. 6 (Sheffield, June 28, 1968, Arnold conducting); No. 7 (London, May 1974, Arnold conducting); No. 8 (N.Y., May 5, 1979); 15 solo concertos: 2 for Horn (1945, 1956); 2 for Clarinet (1948, 1974); one for Piano Duet (1951); one for Oboe (1952); 2 for Flute (1954, 1972); one for Harmonica (1954; London, Aug. 14, 1954, Larry Adler, soloist); one for Organ (1954); one for Guitar (1958); one for 2 Violins (1962); one for 2 Pianos, 3-hands (1969); one for Viola (1970); one for Trumpet (1981); 10 overtures: *Beckus the Dandipratt* (1943); *Festival Overture* (1946); *The Smoke* (1948); *A Sussex Overture* (1951); *Tam O'Shanter* (1955); *A Grand, Grand Overture* for 3 Vacuum Cleaners, One Floor Polisher, 4 Rifles, and Orch. (1956; London, Nov. 13, 1956); *Commonwealth Christmas Overture* (1957); *Peterloo* (1968); *Anniversary Overture* (1968); *The Fair Field* (1972); tone poem, *Larch Trees* (1943); Serenade for Small Orch. (1950); *8 English Dances* in 2 sets (1950–51); *The Sound Barrier,* rhapsody (1952); 3 sinfoniettas (1954, 1958, 1964); *2 Little Suites* (1955, 1962); Serenade for Guitar and Strings (1955); *4 Scottish Dances* (1957); *4 Cornish Dances* (1966); Concerto for 28 Players (1970); *Fantasy for Audience and Orch.* (1970); *A Flourish for Orchestra* (1973); *Fantasy* for Brass Band (1974); *Philharmonic Concerto* (1977); Symph. for Brass Instruments (1979).

Arnold, Samuel, celebrated English composer, organist, and music scholar; b. London, Aug. 10, 1740; d. there, Oct. 22, 1802. He received his musical training from Gates and Nares as a chorister of the Chapel Royal. He showed a gift for composition early on, and was commissioned to arrange the music for the play *The Maid of the Mill;* for this he selected songs by some 20 composers, including Bach, and added several numbers of his own; the resulting pasticcio was produced with success at Covent Garden (Jan. 31, 1765). This was the first of his annual productions for Covent Garden and other theaters in London, of which the following were composed mainly by Arnold: *Harlequin Dr. Faustus* (Nov. 18, 1766); *The Royal Garland* (Oct. 10, 1768); *The Magnet* (June 27, 1771); *A Beggar on Horseback* (June 16, 1785); *The Gnome* (Aug. 5, 1788); *New Spain, or Love in Mexico* (July 16, 1790); *The Surrender of Calais* (July 30, 1791); *The Enchanted Wood* (July 25, 1792); *The 63rd Letter* (July 18, 1802). He also wrote several oratorios, among them *The Cure of Saul* (1767); *Abimelech; The Resurrection; The Prodigal Son;* and *Elisha* (1795; his last oratorio). On the occasion of a performance of *The Prodigal Son* at Oxford Univ. in 1773, Arnold was given the degree of D.Mus. In 1783, he became the successor of Nares as composer to the Chapel Royal, for which he wrote several odes and anthems. In 1789 Arnold was engaged as conductor of the Academy of Ancient Music; in 1793 he became organist of Westminster Abbey. He was buried in Westminster Abbey, near Purcell and Blow. Arnold's edition of Handel's works, begun in 1786, was carried out by him in 36 vols., embracing about 180 numbers; it is, however, incomplete and inaccurate in many respects. His principal work is *Cathedral Music* (4 vols.; 1790); its subtitle describes its contents: "A collection in score of the most valuable and useful compositions for that Service by the several English Masters of the last 200 years." It forms a sequel to Boyce's work of the same name. A new edition of Arnold's *Cathedral Music* was issued by Rimbault (1847).

Arnould, (Madeleine) Sophie, French operatic soprano; b. Paris, Feb. 13, 1740; d. there, Oct. 22, 1802. She studied singing with Mme. Fel and acting with Mlle. Clairon; made her debut at the Paris Opéra on Dec. 15, 1757. She created the title role in Gluck's *Iphigénie en Aulide* (April 19, 1774), and after a highly successful career, retired in 1778 with a pension of 2,000 livres. Gabriel Pierné wrote a one-act "lyric comedy," *Sophie Arnould* (1926), based on incidents of her life.

Arrau, Claudio, eminent Chilean pianist; b. Chillán, Feb. 6, 1903. He received his early training from his mother, an amateur pianist, and as a child played a program of pieces by Mozart, Beethoven, and Chopin at a public performance in Santiago. In 1911 he was sent by the Chilean government to Berlin, where he took lessons with Martin Krause. In 1914–15 he gave piano recitals in Germany and Scandinavia, attracting attention by his precocious talent. In 1921 he returned to Chile, making his first professional appearances there and elsewhere in South America. In 1924 he made his first American tour as a soloist with the Boston Symph. Orch. and the Chicago Symph. In 1925 he was appointed to the faculty of the Stern Cons. in Berlin. He won the Grand Prix International des Pianistes at Geneva in 1927; in 1929 he made a tour of Russia, returning for a 2nd tour the following year. During the season 1935–36 he presented in Berlin the complete keyboard works of Bach in 12 recitals; in 1936 he performed all keyboard works of Mozart in 5 recitals in Berlin. In 1938 he played all 32 piano sonatas and all 5 piano concertos of Beethoven in Mexico City, and in 1939 repeated this series in Buenos Aires and Santiago. In 1941 he settled permanently in N.Y., devoting himself to concert appearances and teaching. In 1947 he made a tour of Australia, and in 1949 gave a series of concerts in South Africa; in 1951 toured in Israel; in 1956 played in India; in 1958 gave concerts in Prague and Bucharest; in 1965 made his first tour in Japan. In 1962–69 he made a complete recording of Beethoven's sonatas. He also supervised the edition of the Urtext of Beethoven's piano sonatas. In his playing, Arrau combines a Classical purity and precision of style with a rhapsodic éclat.

Arriaga, Juan Crisóstomo, precocious Spanish composer; b. Rigoitia, near Bilbao, Jan. 27, 1806; d. Paris, Jan. 17, 1826 (10 days before his 20th birthday). At the age of 11, he wrote an Octet for French Horn, Strings, Guitar, and Piano, subtitled *Nada y mucho;* at 13, a 2-act opera, *Los esclavos felices.* On the strength of these works he was accepted at the Paris. Cons., where he studied with Baillot and Fétis. In Paris he wrote a Symph.; a biblical scene, *Agar;* 3 string quartets; several fugues; piano pieces; songs. On Aug. 13, 1933, a memorial to him was unveiled in Bilbao and a Comisión Permanente Arriaga was formed to publish his works. Under its auspices, the vocal score of the opera and the full scores of his Symph. and Octet were printed. A bibliographical pamphlet, *Resurgimiento de las obras de Arriaga,* by Juan de Eresalde was also publ. (Bilbao, 1953).

Arrieta y Corera, Pascual Juan Emilio, Spanish composer; b. Puente la Reina, Oct. 21, 1823; d. Madrid, Feb. 11, 1894. He studied at the Milan Cons. (1839–45) with Vaccai; returned to Spain in 1846; was a prof. at the Madrid Cons. in 1857; became its director in 1868. He wrote more than 50 zarzuelas and several grand operas in Italian. Of these productions the most important is *La conquista de Granada,* produced in Madrid (Oct. 10, 1850) with Arrieta himself conducting, and revived 5 years later under the title *Isabel la Católica* (Madrid, Dec. 18, 1855). Other successful zarzuelas and operas are *Ildegonda* (Milan, Feb. 28, 1845); *El Domino Azul* (Madrid, Feb. 19, 1853); *El Grumete* (Madrid, June 17, 1853; its sequel, *La Vuelta del Corsario,* was perf. in Madrid, Feb. 18, 1863); *Marina* (Madrid, Sept. 21, 1855; revised and produced as a grand opera, Madrid, Oct. 4, 1871); *S. Francesco da Siena* (Madrid, Oct. 27, 1883).

Arrigoni, Carlo, Italian composer; b. Florence, Dec. 5, 1697; d. there, Aug. 19, 1744. He left Italy as a young man; in 1728 he was in Brussels. In 1732 he was invited to London by a group favorable to Italian composers in opposition to Handel; there he produced an opera, *Fernando* (London, Feb. 5, 1734). Arrigoni then went back to Italy through Vienna, where he produced an oratorio, *Esther* (1738); re-

turning to Florence, he staged his new operas *Sirbace* and *Scipione nelle Spagne* (1739). His 10 *Cantate da camera* were publ. in London (1732). Several airs from his opera *Fernando* are preserved in the British Museum; Burney mistakenly attributed the music of this opera to Porpora.

Arroyo, Martina, American soprano; b. Harlem, N.Y., Feb. 2, 1936. She is of partly Hispanic, partly black origin. Her voice teacher was Marinka Gurewich, who remained her principal mentor throughout her professional career. After graduation from Hunter College (B.A., 1956), she sang in the American premiere of Pizzetti's *Assassinio nella cattedrale* at Carnegie Hall in N.Y., on Sept. 17, 1958. In 1959 she married an Italian viola player, Emilio Poggioni, but their marriage ended in divorce. On March 14, 1959, she made her debut with the Metropolitan Opera as the Celestial Voice in *Don Carlos;* then sang incidental parts in Wagner's tetralogy. In 1963 she toured Europe; made appearances with the Vienna State Opera, at the Berlin State Opera, and in Zürich. Returning to the U.S., she was a soloist with the N.Y. Phil. and other orchs. She demonstrated her professional mettle when on Feb. 6, 1965, she was suddenly called to substitute for Birgit Nilsson as Aida at the Metropolitan Opera, a challenge she carried off brilliantly; after that she was given major roles at the Metropolitan; she sang Elvira in *Ernani,* Leonora in *Il Trovatore,* Elsa in *Lohengrin,* Donna Anna in *Don Giovanni,* and Aida, all with excellent success. What is even more remarkable, she proved herself technically equal to the complex soprano parts in the works of such avant-garde composers as Varèse, Dallapiccola, and Stockhausen, which she selflessly performed at special concerts.

Artaria, music publishing house in Vienna, founded by the cousins **Carlo** (1747–1808) and **Francesco Artaria** (1744–1808). They opened a music shop on Kohlmarkt in 1769, and in 1778 began printing music; they introduced the method of zinc plating for the first time in Vienna. In 1779 the firm acquired some of Haydn's works, which brought them fame; music of Clementi, Salieri, and Boccherini was publ. later. Artaria publ. Mozart's 6 violin sonatas (K. 296, 376–80), the *Haffner-Sinfonie,* and 6 string quartets dedicated to Haydn, among other works, thus becoming Mozart's most important publisher in his lifetime. Other first editions in Artaria's catalogue were several songs by Schubert; Beethoven's C major Quintet, op. 29, and string quartets, opp. 130 and 133. The last owners were **Carl August** (d. 1919), **Dominik** (d. 1936), and **Franz Artaria** (d. 1942). After 1932, the old house became an art gallery and an auction bureau, preserving the name Artaria.

Arteaga, Esteban de, Spanish writer on music; b. Moraleja de Coca, Segovia, Dec. 26, 1747; d. Paris, Oct. 30, 1799. He joined the Jesuit Order at 16, and was banished to Corsica when the Jesuits were proscribed in Spain. He left the Order in 1769; from 1773–78 he studied philosophy at the Univ. of Bologna; there he formed a friendship with Padre Martini, and at his behest undertook a history of the musical theater in Italy. The resulting work, *Le rivoluzioni del teatro musicale italiano dalla sua origine fino al presente*, was publ. in 3 vols. in Bologna and Venice (1783–86; the materials in the Bologna ed. partly overlap, partly supplement those in the Venice ed.); it was brought out in German by J. Forkel (2 vols., Leipzig, 1789); a summary was publ. in French (1802). Arteaga's strong and often critical opinions expressed in this work antagonized many Italian writers who resented the intrusion of a foreigner into their own field. A polemical exchange of considerable acrimony followed; Arteaga's views were attacked by Matteo Borsa in the tract *Del gusto presente in letteratura italiana ...* and by Vincenzo Manfredini in *Difesa della musica moderna ...* (Bologna, 1786). After a sojourn in Venice (1785), Arteaga lived in Rome (1786–87); in 1796 he went to Florence and later to Paris. In addition to his magnum opus, he publ. a book on esthetics, *Investigaciones filosóficas sobre la belleza ideal ...* (Madrid, 1789; new ed., Madrid, 1943). A book of essays, *Lettere musico-filologiche*, and the treatise *Del ritmo sonoro e del ritmo muto nella musica degli antichi* (long regarded as lost) were publ. in Madrid in 1944, with an extensive biographical account by the editor Miguel Batllori, who also gives the bibliographical synopsis of the Bologna and Venice editions of *Rivoluzioni*.

Artôt, Alexandre-Joseph Montagney, Belgian violinist; b. Brussels, Jan. 25, 1815; d. Ville-d'Avray, July 20, 1845. He studied with his father, **Maurice Artôt,** and with Snel; then took lessons from Rodolphe and Auguste Kreutzer at the Paris Cons., obtaining first prize (1828). He then played concerts on the Continent; made his debut in London (June 3, 1839) in his own *Fantaisie* for Violin and Orch. In 1843 he embarked on an American concert tour. He wrote a violin concerto, several sets of variations for violin, and some chamber music.

Artôt, Désirée (baptismal name, **Marguerite-Joséphine Désiré Montagney**), Belgian mezzo-soprano, daughter of **Jean-Désiré Artôt**; b. Paris, July 21, 1835; d. Berlin, April 3, 1907. She studied with Mme. Viardot-Garcia; sang in Belgium, the Netherlands, and England (1857). Meyerbeer engaged her to sing in *Le Prophète* at the Paris Opéra (Feb. 5, 1858); she was greatly praised by Berlioz and other Paris musicians and critics. In 1858 she went to Italy; then made appearances in London. In 1868 she was in Russia, where she was briefly engaged to Tchaikovsky; however, this engagement was quickly disrupted by her marriage (on Sept. 15, 1869) to the Spanish singer **Padilla y Ramos** (1842–1906). Their daughter was **Lola Artôt de Padilla.**

Artôt, Jean-Désiré, Belgian horn player and composer; b. Paris, Sept. 23, 1803; d. Brussels, March 25, 1887. He was a pupil and successor of his father, **Maurice Artôt.** From 1843 he taught at the Brussels Cons.; also played in the court orch. He publ. fantasias and études for horn, and quartets for cornets à pistons.

Artôt, Maurice Montagney, ancestor of a celebrated line of musicians (the true family name being Montagney); b. Gray (Haute-Saône), Feb. 3, 1772; d. Brussels, Jan. 8, 1829. He was a bandmaster in the French army; then went to Brussels, where he became first horn player at the Théâtre de la Monnaie. A versatile musician, he also played the guitar and taught singing.

Artusi, Giovanni Maria, Italian contrapuntist and writer on music; b. Bologna, c.1540; d. there, Aug. 18, 1613. He became canon-in-ordinary at S. Salvatore in Bologna in Feb. 1562. A capable musician and writer who studied with Zarlino, Artusi was reactionary in his musical philosophy. His first publication, *L'arte del contrappunto* (in 2 parts; Venice, 1586 and 1598), has considerable theoretical value. He then publ. several polemical essays directed mainly against the innovations of Monteverdi and others: the characteristically named vol. *L'Artusi, ovvero Delle imperfettioni della moderna musica* (Venice, 1600; reproduced in part in Eng. by O. Strunk in *Source Readings in Music History*, N.Y., 1950); a posthumous attack on his teacher Zarlino in *Impresa del R.P. Gioseffo Zarlino* (Bologna, 1604); *Considerazioni musicali* (1603; as part II of *L'Artusi*, etc.); *Discorso musicale ...* (1606) and *Discorso secondo musicale* (both attacking Monteverdi); and further polemical essays against Bottrigari and Vincenzo Galileo. Monteverdi replied to Artusi in a leaflet entitled *Ottuso accademico* and in the preface to his 5th book of madrigals; this reply is reproduced in Strunk's *Source Readings in Music History*. Bottrigari replied in a pamphlet entitled *Ant' Artusi*. As a composer, Artusi followed the old school; he publ. a set of 4-part *Canzonette* (1598) and an 8-part motet, *Cantate Domino* (1599).

Artzibushev, Nicolai, Russian composer, music editor, and pedagogue; b. Tsarskoe-Selo, March 7, 1858; d. Paris, April 15, 1937. He studied with Rimsky-Korsakov and Soloviev; in 1908 was elected president of the St. Petersburg Royal Music Society. After the Revolution he went to Paris, where he was in charge of the Belaiev publishing house. As a composer, he is chiefly known for his melodious piano pieces and songs in a distinct style of the Russian national school; he also wrote a *Valse Fantasia* for Orch. and was one of the group of composers who contributed to the collection *Variations on a Russian Theme* for String Quartet; other variations were by Rimsky-Korsakov, Glazunov, Liadov, and Scriabin.

Asafiev, Boris, Russian composer and writer on music; b. St. Petersburg, July 29, 1884; d. Moscow, Jan. 27, 1949. He studied with Kalafati and Liadov at the St. Petersburg Cons., graduating in 1910; at the same time he studied philology and history at St. Petersburg Univ. He then became a ballet coach at the Opera. In 1914 he began writing music criticism under the pseudonym **Igor Glebov.** Subsequently he publ. his literary writings under that name, sometimes indicating his real name as well. He always signed his musical works, however, with the name Asafiev. In 1920 he was appointed dean of the dept. of music of the Inst. of History of Arts in Petrograd. He was also an editor of the journal *Novaya Muzyka* (1924–28); within a few years he publ. brief monographs on Mussorgsky, Scriabin, Rimsky-Korsakov, Liszt, Chopin, etc.; translated articles from German, French, and Italian. He was a prof. of history, theory, and composition at the Leningrad Cons. (1925–43); then was director of the research section at the Moscow Cons.; at the same time he continued to compose, mostly for the stage. The following ballets by him were performed in Leningrad: *Flames of Paris* (Nov. 7, 1932); *The Fountain of Bakhtchisaray*, after Pushkin (Sept. 28, 1934; very popular); *The Partisan Days* (May 16, 1937); *The Prisoner of the Caucasus* (April 14, 1938). Altogether he wrote 9 operas, 27 ballets, works for orch., and chamber music. But it was as a historian of Russian music that Asafiev-Glebov was especially important. He continued the tradition of Vladimir Stasov in his ardent advocacy of the national Russian style. He publ. *The Russian Poets in Russian Music* (with a valuable catalogue of Russian vocal works; 1921); *Symphonic Etudes*, an account of the evolution of the Russian operatic style (1922); *Stravinsky*, a comprehensive analysis of Stravinsky's works (Leningrad, 1929; later he repudiated the favorable view of Stravinsky expressed in this book); *Russian Music from the Beginning of the Nineteenth Century* (1930; Eng. trans. by A. Swan; American Council of Learned Societies, 1953); *Musical Form as a Process* (2 vols.; 1930 and 1947); *Glinka* (Moscow, 1947; the only book on music to receive the Stalin Prize). A 7-vol. edition of Asafiev's collected writings was begun in Moscow in 1952.

Ascone, Vicente, Uruguayan composer of Italian extraction; b. Siderno, Aug. 16, 1897; d. Montevideo, March 5, 1979. He was brought to Uruguay as a child; studied trumpet and composition. Most of his music is rooted in Uruguayan folk songs, while stylistically he followed the traditional Italian formulas. He wrote 5 operas, of which *Paraná Gauzú*, based on an Indian subject, was produced in Montevideo on July 25, 1931. He further wrote 3 symphs. (1945, 1955, 1959); *Politonal* for Piano and Orch. (1967); a Trumpet Concerto (1969); a Violin Concerto (1970); a symph. poem, *Sobre el Rio Uruguay* (1946); and numerous songs.

Ashkenazy, Vladimir, greatly gifted Russian pianist and conductor; b. Gorkey, July 6, 1937. His parents were professional pianists and taught him to play at an early age; subsequently he took regular lessons with Anaida Sumbatian at the Central Music School in Moscow, and in 1955 entered the class of Lev Oborin at the Moscow Cons. In 1955 he won 2nd prize at the International Chopin Competition in Warsaw. A great turning point in his career was reached when in 1956, at the age of 19, he won first prize in the Queen Elisabeth of Belgium International Competition in Brussels; in 1958 he made his first tour of the U.S.; in 1962 he and John Ogdon were both awarded first prizes in Moscow in the Tchaikovsky International Competition in Moscow. In 1961 he married a young pianist, Sofia Johannsdottir of Iceland, who was studying in Moscow at the time. In 1963 they went to England while retaining their common Soviet citizenship. In 1968 they moved to Reykjavik, and in 1972 Ashkenazy became a citizen of Iceland; their 4 children speak English and Icelandic. As a pianist, he proved himself a statistical maximalist with a desire for completeness; thus he played all of Beethoven's 5 piano concertos and all of Rachmaninoff's 4 piano concertos; he also performed works by Scriabin and other early modern composers. Like the best of prizewinning Russians, he possesses a formidable but well-controlled and intelligent virtuoso technique. He was also drawn into conducting, and in 1981 was appointed principal guest conductor of the Phil. Orch. of London.

Ashley, Robert, American composer; b. Ann Arbor, Mich., March 28, 1930. He studied music at the Univ. of Michigan (B.Mus., 1952) and The Manhattan School of Music (M.Mus., 1954); took postgraduate courses in psychoacoustics at the Univ. of Michigan (1957–60). In his independent composition he pursues the ideal of "total musical events," which absorbs gesticulation, natural human noises, and the entire planetary environment. In 1961 he became co-founder of the ONCE group, dedicated to such actions, in Ann Arbor; from 1958–66 he operated an electronic music studio in association with the composer Gordon Mumma; in 1970 was appointed co-director of the Center of Contemporary Music at Mills College in Oakland, California.

WORKS: Most of his works utilize electronic sounds; of these the following are notable for the totality of their envergure: *The 4th of July* (1960); *Something* for Clarinet, Piano, and Tape (1961); *Detroit Divided* (1962); *Complete with Heat* (1962); *Kitty Hawk*, an "anti-gravity piece" (1964); *Untitled Mixes* (1965); *Night Train* (1966); *The Trial of Anne Opie Wehrer and Unknown Accomplices for Crimes against Humanity* (1968); *Purposeful Lady Slow Afternoon* (1968); *Illusion Models* for Hypothetical Computer (1970); *In Memoriam Crazy Horse*, symph. (1964); the episodic operas *Perfect Lives* (1977–81) and *Atalanta* (1982); several film scores: *The Image in Time* (1957); *The Bottleman* (1960); *Jenny and the Poet* (1964); *My May* (1965); *Overdrive* (1968); *Portraits, Self-portraits and Still Lifes* (1969); *Battery Davis* (1970). He also composes music performable on traditional instruments, among them *Maneuvers for Small Hands* for Piano (1961), Quartet for any number of Instruments (1965), and organ pieces.

Ashton, Algernon (Bennet Langton), English composer; b. Durham, Dec. 9, 1859; d. London, April 10, 1937. His family moved to Leipzig, and he studied at the Leipzig Cons. with Reinecke and Jadassohn (1875–79); later took lessons with Raff in Frankfurt (1880). Returning to England, he obtained the post of piano teacher at the Royal College of Music (1885–1910). He was a prolific composer, having written more than 160 opus numbers, mostly in a conventional German style: 5 symphs.; 3 overtures; a piano concerto; a violin concerto; 3 piano quintets; 3 piano quartets; 3 piano trios; Trio for Clarinet, Viola, and Bassoon; Trio for Piano, Horn, and Viola; 5 violin sonatas; 5 cello sonatas; a viola sonata; and more than 200 piano works (among them a sonata, 3 fantasias, and various picturesque pieces such as *Idyls* and *Roses and Thorns*); also more than 200 songs, choral pieces, and organ works. Many of his chamber music compositions were publ., but he was never given recognition as a composer; however, he acquired notoriety by his curious letters in the English press dealing with a variety of subjects. Many of these letters he collected in his vols. *Truth, Wit and Wisdom* (London, 1904) and *More Truth, Wit and Wisdom* (London, 1905).

Asioli, Bonifazio, Italian composer; b. Correggio, Aug. 30, 1769; d. there, May 18, 1832. He began writing music at a very early age. He studied with Angelo Morighi in Parma (1780–82); then lived in Bologna and Venice as a harpsichord player. His first opera, *La Volubile,* was produced in Correggio (1785) with marked success; it was followed by *Le nozze in villa* (Correggio, 1786); *Cinna* (Milan, 1793); and *Gustavo al Malabar* (Turin, 1802). In 1787 he was private maestro to the Marquis Gherardini in Turin; then in Venice (1796–99); subsequently he went to Milan and taught at the Cons. (1808–14). Asioli wrote 7 operas; an oratorio, *Giacobbe in Galaad;* many cantatas; instrumental music; sacred choral works; etc. He was the author of several textbooks: *Principi elementari di musica* (Milan, 1809; also in English, German, and French); *Trattato d'armonia e d'accompagnamento* (1813); also manuals for Harpsichord, Voice, and Double Bass. His theoretical book *Il maestro di composizione* was publ. posthumously (1836).

Asola, Giammateo, Italian composer; b. Verona, c. 1532; d. Venice, Oct. 1, 1609. He entered the congregation of secular canons at S. Giorgio in Alga in 1546; held benefices at S. Stefano in Verona from 1566; subsequently served as a secular priest. He became maestro di cappella at Treviso Cathedral in 1577; then served in a similar capacity at Vicenza Cathedral in 1578. In 1588 he became one of the chaplains at S. Severo in Venice. He was active as a teacher; among his pupils was Leone Leoni. He wrote much sacred music in the style of Palestrina. The *Opera omnia,* edited by G. Vecchi, began to appear in 1963.

Asow, Erich H. Müller von. See **Mueller von Asow, Erich H.**

Aspestrand, Sigwart, Norwegian opera composer; b. Fredrikshald, Nov. 13, 1856; d. Oslo, Dec. 31, 1941. He studied at Leipzig and Berlin and spent 30 years of his life (1885–1915) in Germany. Of his 7 operas, *Die Seemansbraut,* produced in Gotha (March 29, 1894) and later in Oslo (March 18, 1907), was the most successful. His other operas, all in German, are: *Der Recke von Lyrskovsheid, Freyas Alter, Die Wette, Der Kuss auf Sicht, Robin Hood,* and *Pervonte.*

Asplmayr, Franz, Austrian composer; b. Linz (baptized, April 2) 1728; d. Vienna, July 29, 1786. He studied with his father; wrote ballets for the Austrian court. Historically, Asplmayr was important as one of the earliest Austrian composers to adopt the instrumental style, rich in dynamics, as established by the Mannheim school.
WORKS: Ballets: *Agamemnon, Iphigenie en Tauride, Acis et Galathée;* a Singspiel, *Die Kinder der Natur;* music for Shakespeare's *Macbeth* (1777) and *The Tempest* (1781); chamber music: *6 Serenate,* op. 1; *6 Quatuors concertants,* op. 2; *6 Trios,* op. 5; *6 Quatours,* op. 6.

Assmayer, Ignaz, Austrian composer; b. Salzburg, Feb. 11, 1790; d. Vienna, Aug. 31, 1862. He studied piano, organ, and theory with A. Brunmayrs in Salzburg and later with T. Gerls. In 1815 he moved to Vienna, where he took lessons with Salieri. In 1846 he was appointed first Kapellmeister in Vienna, succeeding Eybler. He wrote several oratorios, among them *Saul und David, Sauls Tod,* and *Das Gelübde,* which he performed with the Vienna Tonkünstler Society. He further wrote 21 masses, 2 requiems, and other sacred works, as well as some 60 instrumental compositions, many of which were publ.

Aston, Hugh, English composer; b. c.1480; d. York, Dec. 9, 1522. These dates apply to the son of a certain Richard Aston of Mawdesley in Lancashire. After obtaining his B.A. (1505–6) and M.A. (Oct. 30, 1507) from Oxford, he moved to Cambridge to study canon law; he was throughout his life associated with St. John's College, Cambridge. On May 27, 1509, he became Prebend of St. Stephen's, Westminster, and in 1515, Archdeacon of York. Among Aston's authentic works are 2 masses (*Te Deum* for 5 Voices and *Videte manus meas* for 6 Voices); 2 other vocal works for 5 Voices (*Gaude Virgo Mater Christi* and *Te Deum laudamus*); and 3 fragments publ. in *Tudor Church Music* (vol. X). More unusual for the time is Aston's *Hornpipe* for Virginal, which is preserved in a MS at the British Museum; it is the earliest-known piece for the instrument. Of the 10 other dances in this MS, some, notably *My Lady Carey's Dompe,* may also be Aston's work.

d'Astorga, Emanuele (Gioacchino Cesare Rincón), Italian composer of operas; b. Augusta, Sicily, March 20, 1680; d. probably in Madrid, after 1757. Of a noble Spanish family which had settled in Augusta early in the 17th century, he was a baron in his own right, from his estate Ogliastro, nearby. Later in life he moved to Palermo; during the revolution of 1708 he was an officer in the municipal guard. In 1712 he went to Vienna, and was in Znaim in 1713; he left Vienna in 1714 and returned to Palermo, where he became a senator. It is known that he sold his Sicilian estate in 1744 and went to Spain, where he was in the service of the king. D'Astorga was widely known as a versatile and highly educated person; he was also adept as a singer and a cembalo player, but never regarded music as his primary profession. He composed at least 3 operas; the first, *La moglie nemica,* was produced at Palermo in 1698; the 2nd and most notable, *Dafni,* was staged at Genoa on April 21, 1709, and was probably also heard in Barcelona (1709) and in Breslau (1726); the 3rd, *Amor tirannico,* was given in Venice in 1710. He also wrote numerous chamber cantatas and himself publ. 12 of them in one vol. (Lisbon, 1726). His best-known work is *Stabat Mater* for 4 Voices; it was first heard in Oxford in 1752; a new edition of it was publ. by R. Franz in 1878. In his 2-vol. biography of d'Astorga (Leipzig, 1911 and 1919), Hans Volkmann refutes the unsupported statement of R. Pohl in the first edition of *Grove's Dictionary* that d'Astorga died at Raudnitz on Aug. 21, 1736; Volkmann also exposes the romantic account of d'Astorga's life publ. by Rochlitz in vol. II of *Für Freunde der Tonkunst* (1825) as a fanciful invention. *Astorga,* an opera based on his life, was written by J.J. Abert (1866). See also O. Tiby, "E. D'Astorga," *Acta Musicologica* (1953).

Atanasov, Georgi, Bulgarian composer; b. Plovdiv, May 18, 1881; d. Fasano, Italy, Nov. 17, 1931. He went to Italy in 1901, and took lessons in composition with Mascagni at the Pesaro Cons. Returning to Bulgaria, he became active as a military bandleader, as well as a composer. He wrote two of the earliest operas on national Bulgarian subjects, *Borislav* (Sofia, March 4, 1911) and *Gergana* (Stara Zagora, July 1, 1925); other operas were *Zapustialata vodenitza (The Abandoned Mill), Altzek,* and *Tzveta;* he also wrote two children's operas, *The Sick Teacher* and *About Birds.*

Attaignant (also **Attaingnant, Atteignant**), **Pierre,** French printer of music who lived during the first half of the 16th century; d. Paris, 1552. He was probably the earliest printer in France to employ movable type in music printing. His first publication was a *Breviarium Noviomense* (1525). He continued to publ. a great many works, including 18 dances in tablature for the Lute (1529); 25 pavans (1530); a folio edition of 7 books of masses (1532); 13 books of motets (1534–35); and a series of 35 books of chansons (1539–49) containing 927 part-songs by French and Flemish composers. Reprints: E. Bernoulli, facsimile edition of 4 books under the title *Chansons und Tänze* (Munich, 1914); 31 chansons in Henry Expert's *Les Maîtres Musiciens de la Renaissance française* (1894–1908); D. Heartz, *Preludes, Chansons, Dances for Lute (1529–30)* (1964); *Danseries à 4 parties,* in Le Pupitre, 9 (Paris, 1969).

Atterberg, Kurt, eminent Swedish composer; b. Göteborg, Dec. 12, 1887; d. Stockholm, Feb. 15, 1974. He studied engineering and was employed in the wireless service; then took courses in composition at the Stockholm Cons. with Hallén, and in Berlin with Schillings (1910–12). In 1913 he was appointed conductor at the Drama Theater in Stockholm, holding this post until 1922; in 1919 he began writing music criticism and continued to contribute to Stockholm newspapers until 1957; concurrently he was also employed at the Swedish patent office (1912–68) and served as secretary of the Royal Academy of Music in Stockholm (1940–53). He was one of the founders of the Society of Swedish Composers in 1924, and was on its board until 1947. During all this time he continued to compose with inexhaustible energy, producing works in all genres: operas, ballets, symphs., concertos, choruses, and chamber music, all with preordained precision of form and technique. It is ironic that his music remained hermetically sealed within the confines of Sweden, rarely if ever performed beyond its borders. Atterberg's name attracted unexpected attention when he was declared winner of the ill-conceived Schubert Centennial Contest organized in 1928 by the Columbia Phonograph Co., with the declared intention to finish Schubert's Unfinished Symphony. The entire venture was severely criticized in musical circles as an attempt to derive commercial advantage under the guise of an homage to a great composer. Rumors spread that Atterberg had deliberately imitated the style of composition of some members of the jury (Glazunov, Alfano, Nielsen) in order to ingratiate himself with them so as to secure the prize, but Atterberg denied any such suggestion, pointing out that he knew the names only of those in the jury from the Nordic zone, whereas the international membership comprised 10 national zones. Furthermore, the symph. he had submitted was written in a far more advanced style than Atterberg's previous symph. works and was certainly much more modern than any music by the jury members, using as it did such procedures as polytonality. There can be no doubt, however, that Atterberg was a master technician of his craft, and that his music had a powerful appeal. That it never gained a wider audience can be ascribed only to an unfathomable accident of world culture.

WORKS: OPERAS (all produced in Stockholm): *Härvard Harpolekare (Harvard the Potter,* 1915–17; Sept. 29, 1919; revised as *Härvard der Harfner* and produced in German at Chemnitz, 1936; a later version with new 3rd act produced in Linz, Austria, June 14, 1952); *Bäckahästen* (1923–24; Jan. 23, 1925); *Fanal* (1929–32; Jan. 27, 1934); *Aladdin* (1936–41; March 18, 1941); *Stormen,* after Shakespeare's *Tempest* (1946–47; Sept. 19, 1948). BALLETS: *Per Svinaherde (Peter the Swineherd,* 1914–15); ballet-pantomime, *De fävitska jungfrurna (The Wise and Foolish Virgins,* 1920; Paris, Nov. 18, 1920). SYMPHS.: No. 1 (1909–11; Stockholm, Jan. 10, 1912); No. 2 (1911–13; Stockholm, Feb. 11, 1912); No. 3 (1914–16; Stockholm, Nov. 28, 1916); No. 4, *Sinfonia piccola* (1918; Stockholm, March 27, 1919); No. 5, Sinfonia funèbre (1919–22; Stockholm, Jan. 6, 1923); No. 6 (1927–28; won the Schubert Centennial Prize; Stockholm, Oct. 15, 1928); No. 7, *Sinfonia romantica* (1942; Frankfurt, Feb. 14, 1943); No. 8 (1944; Helsinki, Feb. 9, 1945); No. 9, *Sinfonia visionaria*, with Mezzo-soprano, Baritone, and Chorus (1955–56; Helsinki, Feb. 26, 1957); also a *Sinfonia* for Strings (1952–53); *Varmlandsrhapsodi* on northern Swedish folk tunes, written in honor of Selma Lagerlöf's 75th birthday (broadcast over the Swedish radio Nov. 20, 1933).

Attwood, Thomas, English organist and composer; b. London, Nov. 23, 1765; d. there, March 24, 1838. He was a chorister at the Chapel Royal under Nares and Ayrton from the age of 9. Following a performance before the Prince of Wales (afterward George IV), he was sent to Italy for further study; there he received instruction in Naples from Filippo Cinque and Gaetano Latilla. He then went to Vienna, where Mozart accepted him as a pupil; his notes from these theory and composition lessons are printed in the *Neue Mozart Ausgabe*, X/30/1. In 1787 he returned to London and held various posts as an organist. He was also music tutor to the Duchess of York (1791) and to the Princess of Wales (1795). A founder of the London Phil. Society (1813), he conducted some of its concerts. He occupied an important position in the English music world; when Mendelssohn came to London as a young man, Attwood lent him enthusiastic support. Attwood was a prolific composer of operas, of which many were produced in London, including *The Prisoner* (Oct. 18, 1792); *The Mariners* (May 10, 1793); *The Packet Boat* (May 13, 1794); *The Smugglers* (April 13, 1796); *The Fairy Festival* (May 13, 1797); *The Irish Tar* (Aug. 24, 1797); *The Devil of a Lover* (March 17, 1798); *The Magic Oak* (Jan. 29, 1799); *True Friends* (Feb. 19, 1800); *The Sea-Side Story* (May 12, 1801). In all, Attwood wrote 28 operas, in some of which he used material from other composers (he included music by Mozart in *The Prisoner* and *The Mariners*). He also wrote church music, piano sonatas, songs, and glees.

Auber, Daniel-François-Esprit, prolific French composer of comic operas; b. Caen (Normandy), Jan. 29, 1782; d. Paris, May 12, 1871. His father, an art dealer in Paris, sent him to London to acquire knowledge of business. Auber learned music as well as trade and wrote several songs for social entertainment in London. Political tension between France and England, however, forced him to return to Paris in 1803; there he devoted himself exclusively to music. His pasticcio *L'Erreur d'un moment,* a resetting of an old libretto, was produced by an amateur group in Paris in 1806; his next theatrical work was *Julie,* performed privately, with an accompaniment of 6 string instruments, in 1811. Cherubini, who was in the audience, was attracted by Auber's talent and subsequently gave him some professional advice. Auber's first opera to be given publicly in Paris was *Le Séjour militaire* (1813); 6 years later the Opéra-Comique produced his new work *Le Testament et les billets-doux* (1819). These operas passed without favorable notice, but his next production, *La Bergère châtelaine* (1820), was a definite success. From that time until nearly the end of his life, hardly a year elapsed without the production of a new opera. Not counting amateur performances, 45 operas from Auber's pen were staged in Paris between 1813 and 1869. He was fortunate in having the collaboration of the best librettist of the time, Scribe, who wrote (alone, or with other writers) no fewer than 37 libretti for Auber's operas. Auber's fame reached its height with *Masaniello, ou La Muette de Portici,* produced at the Opéra, Feb. 29, 1828. Its success was enormous. Historically, it laid the foundation of French grand opera with Meyerbeer's *Robert le Diable* and Rossini's *Guillaume Tell.* Its vivid portrayal of popular fury stirred French and Belgian audiences; revolutionary riots followed its performance in Brussels (Aug. 25, 1830). Another popular success was achieved by him with his Romantic opera *Fra Diavolo* (Opéra-Comique, Jan. 28, 1830), which became a standard work. Despite these successes with grand opera, Auber may be rightfully regarded as a founder of the French comic opera, a worthy successor of Boieldieu and at least an equal of Adam and Hérold. The influence of Rossini was noted by contemporary critics, but on the whole, Auber's music preserves a distinctive quality of its own. Rossini himself remarked that although Auber's music is light, his art is profound. Auber was greatly appreciated by the successive regimes in France; in 1829 he succeeded Gossec at the Academy; in 1842 he was appointed director of the Paris Cons. by Louis Philippe, and retained this post until his death. In 1852 Napoleon III made him imperial maître de chapelle. At the age of 87 he produced his last opera, *Rêve d'amour.* Auber lived virtually all his life in Paris, remaining there even during the siege by the Germans. He died, during the days of the Paris Commune, at the age of 89. His memory was honored by the Academy. Among his operas (most of which were produced at the Opéra-Comique) are also the following: *Le Cheval de bronze* (March 23, 1835); *Le Domino noir* (Dec. 2, 1837); *Les Diamants de la couronne* (March 6, 1841); *Manon Lescaut* (Feb. 23, 1856); *Le Premier Jour de bonheur* (Feb. 15, 1868).

Aubert, Jacques (called **"le vieux"**), celebrated French violinist; b. Paris, Sept. 30, 1689; d. Belleville, near Paris, May (buried, May 19) 1753. He was a pupil of Senaillé; in 1719 he became bandleader to the Duke of Bourbon; in 1727 was one of the King's 24 violinists; he played in the orch. of the Grand Opéra as first violinist from 1728–52, and took part in the Concert Spirituel (1729–40). He publ. 33 separate instrumental works; was also the first in France to write instrumental concertos (scored for 4 violins and a bass). His music, distinguished by elegance, contributed to the formation of the French "style galant."

Aubert, Louis-François-Marie, French composer;

b. Paramé, Ille-et-Vilaine, Feb. 19, 1877; d. Paris, Jan. 9, 1968. Of precocious talent, he entered the Paris Cons. as a child, and studied piano with Diémer, theory with Lavignac, and advanced composition with Gabriel Fauré; he also sang in church choirs. His song *Rimes tendres* was publ. when he was 19. His *Fantaisie* for Piano and Orch. was performed in Paris by the Colonne Orch. with his teacher Diémer as soloist (Nov. 17, 1901). His *Suite brève* for 2 Pianos was presented at the Paris Exposition in 1900; an orch. version was performed for the first time in Paris on April 27, 1916. Aubert's major work is an operatic fairy tale, *La Forêt bleue* (Geneva, Jan. 7, 1913); an American production was staged in Boston on March 8, 1913, attracting considerable attention. The Paris production of *La Forêt bleue,* delayed by the war, took place on June 10, 1924, at the Opéra-Comique. Aubert's style is largely determined by the impressionistic currents of the early 20th century; like Debussy and Ravel, he was attracted by the music of Spain and wrote several pieces in the Spanish idiom, of which the symph. poem *Habanera* (Paris, March 22, 1919) was particularly successful.

WORKS: The list of Aubert's works further includes: *La Légende du sang* for Narrator, Chorus, and Orch. (1902); 3 ballets: *La Momie* (1903); *Chrysothémis* (1904); *La Nuit ensorcélée* (1922); *6 poèmes arabes* for Voice and Orch. (1907); a song cycle, *Crépuscules d'automne* (Paris, Feb. 20, 1909); *Nuit mauresque* for Voice and Orch. (1911); *Dryade* for Orch. (1921); *Caprice* for Violin and Orch. (1925); *Feuilles d'images,* symph. suite (Paris, March 7, 1931); *Saisons* for Chorus and Orch. (1937); *Offrande aux victimes de la guerre* for Orch. (1947); *Le Tombeau de Châteaubriand* for Orch. (1948); *Cinéma,* ballet (1953); *Improvisation* for 2 Guitars (1960); a set of 3 piano pieces, *Sillages* (1913); a piano quintet; songs; etc.

Aubéry du Boulley, Prudent-Louis, French composer; b. Verneuil, Eure, Dec. 9, 1796; d. there, Jan. 28, 1870. He studied at the Paris Cons. with Momigny, Méhul, and Cherubini. He wrote much chamber music, in which he used the guitar; publ. a guitar method and a textbook, *Grammaire musicale* (Paris, 1830). He was an active teacher in his native province, and contributed much to the cultivation of music there.

Aubin, Tony, French composer and pedagogue; b. Paris, Dec. 8, 1907; d. there, Sept. 21, 1981. He studied at the Paris Cons. with Samuel-Rousseau, Noël Gallon, and Paul Dukas; in 1930 he won the first Grand Prix de Rome. Upon return to Paris from Rome, he studied conducting with Philippe Gaubert, and later was in charge of the music division at the Paris Radio until the collapse of France in 1940; from 1945 to 1960 he served as conductor with the French Radio; concurrently he taught at the Paris Cons. In 1968 he was elected member of the Académie des Beaux-Arts. A pragmatic composer, Aubin cultivated an eclectic idiom calculated to impress professionals and please common music-lovers.

Aubry, Pierre, French music scholar; b. Paris, Feb. 14, 1874; d. (following a fencing accident) Dieppe, Aug. 31, 1910. He began his education as a philologist; studied oriental languages, and traveled to Turkestan on a research project. He then became interested in medieval music; was, for a time, lecturer on music history at the Ecole des Hautes Etudes Sociales. His theories of notation are based on a plausible interpretation of medieval writers.

Audran, Edmond, French composer of light opera, son of **Marius-Pierre Audran;** b. Lyons, April 12, 1840; d. Tierceville, Aug. 17, 1901. He studied at the Ecole Niedermayer in Paris (graduated in 1859). In 1861 he was appointed organist at St. Joseph's Church in Marseilles, where he produced his first operetta, *L'Ours et le Pacha* (1862). He wrote a funeral march on Meyerbeer's death (1864). After the production of *Le Grand Mogol* (Marseilles, Feb. 24, 1877), he returned to Paris, and staged *Les Noces d'Olivette* (Nov. 13, 1879). With the production of *La Mascotte* (Bouffes-Parisiens, Dec. 28, 1880), Audran achieved fame; this operetta became immensely popular; thousands of performances were given in Paris and all over the world. He continued to produce new operettas almost annually; of these, the following were successful: *Gillette de Narbonne* (1882); *La Cigale et la fourmi* (1886); *Miss Hélyett* (1890); *Sainte Freya* (1892); *Madame Suzette* (1893); *Mon Prince* (1893); *La Duchesse de Ferrare* (1895); *Photis* (1896); *La Poupée* (1896); *Monsieur Lohengrin* (1896); *Les Petites Femmes* (1897).

Auer, Leopold, celebrated Hungarian violinist and pedagogue; b. Veszprém, June 7, 1845; d. Loschwitz, near Dresden, July 15, 1930. He studied with Ridley Kohné in Budapest and with Dont in Vienna; later took lessons with Joachim. From 1864–66 he was in Düsseldorf as concertmaster of the orch.; in 1866 in Hamburg. In 1868 he was called to St. Petersburg as soloist in the Imperial Orch., and prof. of violin at the newly founded Cons. He became one of the most famous violin teachers in Russia; among his pupils were Elman, Zimbalist, Heifetz, and many other virtuosos. Tchaikovsky originally dedicated his Violin Concerto to him, but was offended when Auer suggested some revisions, and changed the dedication to Brodsky. Nevertheless, the Concerto became Auer's favorite work, and he made it a *pièce de résistance* for all his pupils. After the Revolution he left Russia. On March 23, 1918, he played a concert in N.Y.; settling permanently in America, he devoted himself exclusively to teaching. He publ. the manuals *Violin Playing as I Teach It* (N.Y., 1921) and *Violin Master Works and Their Interpretation* (1925); and an autobiography, *My Long Life in Music* (1923).

Auger, Arleen, American soprano; b. Los Angeles, Sept. 13, 1939. She was educated at Calif. State Univ. in Long Beach; also studied with Ralph Errolle in Chicago; then went to Europe, where she made her debut in 1967 as the Queen of the Night in Mozart's *Die Zauberflöte* at the Vienna State Opera; was a member there until 1974; in 1969 she sang at the N.Y. City Opera; also sang in Munich, Hamburg, London, Paris, and other cities; in addition, made numerous concert appearances and gave lieder recitals. She made her Metropolitan Opera debut on Oct. 2, 1978, as Marzelline in *Fidelio.*

Aulin, Tor, Swedish violinist and composer; b. Stockholm, Sept. 10, 1866; d. Saltsjobaden, March 1, 1914. He studied with C.J. Lindberg in Stockholm (1877–83) and with Sauret and P. Scharwenka in Berlin (1884–86). In 1887 he established the Aulin String Quartet, and traveled with it in Germany and Russia. He was concertmaster at the Stockholm Opera from 1889–1902, but continued his concert career, and was considered the greatest Scandinavian violinist since Ole Bull. Aulin was appointed conductor of the Stockholm Phil. Society in 1902; was leader of the Göteborg Orch. from 1909–12. As a conductor and violinist, he made determined propaganda for Swedish composers. He wrote incidental music to Strindberg's *Mäster Olof,* 3 violin concertos, several suites of Swedish dances for Orch., a violin sonata, a violin method, and songs. His sister, **Laura Aulin** (b. Gävle, Jan. 9, 1860; d. Örebro, Jan. 11, 1928), was a well-known pianist; she also composed chamber and piano music.

Auric, Georges, notable French composer; b. Lodève (Hérault), Feb. 15, 1899; d. Paris, July 23, 1983. He first studied music at the Cons. of Montpellier; then went to Paris, where he was a student of Caussade at the Paris Cons. and of Vincent d'Indy and Albert Roussel at the Schola Cantorum. While still in his early youth (1911–15) he wrote something like 300 songs and piano pieces; at 18 he composed a ballet, *Les Noces de Gamache.* At 20 he completed a comic opera, *La Reine de cœur;* however, he was dissatisfied with this early effort and destroyed the manuscript. In the aftermath of continental disillusion following World War I he became a proponent of the anti-Romantic movement in France, with the apostles of this age of disenchantment, Erik Satie and Jean Cocteau, preaching the new values of urban culture, with modern America as a model. Satie urged young composers to produce "auditory pleasure without demanding disproportionate attention from the listener," while Cocteau elevated artistic ugliness to an aesthetic ideal. Under Satie's aegis, Auric joined several French composers of his generation in a group described as "Les Nouveaux Jeunes," which later became known as "Les Six" (the other five were Milhaud, Honegger, Poulenc, Durey, and Germaine Tailleferre). Auric soon established an important connection with the impresario Serge Diaghilev, who commissioned him to write a number of ballets for his Paris company; Auric's facile yet felicitous manner of composing, with mock-romantic connotations, fitted perfectly into Diaghilev's scheme; particularly successful were Auric's early ballets, *Les Fâcheux* (1924) and *Les Matelots* (1925). He also wrote music for the movies, of which *A nous la liberté* (1932) achieved popular success as a symph. suite. Auric's familiari-

ty with the theater earned him important administrative posts; from 1962 to 1968 he acted as general administrator of both the Grand Opéra and Opéra-Comique in Paris. From 1954 to 1977 he served as president of the French Union of Composers and Authors. In 1962 he was elected to the membership of the Académie des Beaux-Arts.

WORKS: BALLETS: *Les Fâcheux* (Monte Carlo, Jan. 19, 1924); *Les Matelots* (Paris, June 17, 1925); *La Pastorale* (Paris, May 26, 1926); *Les Enchantements d'Alcine* (Paris, May 21, 1929); *Les Imaginaires* (Paris, May 31, 1934); *Le Peintre et son modèle* (Paris, Nov. 16, 1949); *Phèdre* (Paris, May 23, 1950); *La Pierre enchantée* (Paris, June 23, 1950); *Chemin de lumière* (Munich, March 27, 1952); *Coup de feu* (Paris, May 7, 1952); *La Chambre* (Paris, 1955); *Le Bal des voleurs* (Paris, 1960); also (in collaboration with Milhaud and others), *Les Mariés de la Tour Eiffel,* to the scenario of Jean Cocteau (Paris, June 15, 1921). FILM MUSIC: *Le Sang d'un poète* (1930); *A nous la liberté* (1932); *Les Mystères de Paris* (1936); *La Belle et la bête* (1946); *Symphonie pastorale* (1946); *Les Parents terribles* (1949); *Orphée* (1950); *Moulin Rouge* (1952); *Gervaise* (1956); *Bonjour, tristesse* (1957). INSTRUMENTAL MUSIC: Piano Sonata (1932); Violin Sonata (1937); Partita for 2 Pianos (1958); *Suite Symphonique* (1960); Flute Sonata (1964).

Aus der Ohe, Adele, German pianist; b. Hannover, Dec. 11, 1864; d. Berlin, Dec. 7, 1937. She studied as a child with Kullak in Berlin; at the age of 12 became a pupil of Liszt for 7 years. She then played concerts in Europe; made her American debut with Liszt's First Piano Concerto in N.Y. (Dec. 23, 1886) and continued her American tours for 17 consecutive years. She played 51 times with the Boston Symph. Orch. between 1887 and 1906. One of the highlights of her career was her appearance as soloist in Tchaikovsky's First Piano Concerto under Tchaikovsky's own direction at his last concert (St. Petersburg, Oct. 28, 1893). Because of a crippling illness, she was forced to abandon her concert career; she lost her accumulated earnings in the German currency inflation in the 1920s, and from 1928 till her death, subsisted on a pension from the Bagby Music Lovers Foundation of N.Y.

Austin, Larry, American avant-garde composer; b. Duncan, Okla., Sept. 12, 1930. He studied music with Violet Archer at the North Texas State Univ., Denton (B.M., 1951; M.M., 1952); with Darius Milhaud at Mills College; and with Andrew Imbrie and Seymour Shifrin at the Univ. of Calif., Berkeley (1955–58). In 1969 he took a special course in computer-generated music systems at Stanford Univ. From 1958 to 1972 he served as prof. of music at the Univ. of Calif., Davis; this sojourn was especially significant, since it was on the Davis campus that Austin became a co-founder of a unique modern music unperiodical, *Source,* which counted among its contributors the *crème de la crème* of the world's most intransigent modernists, who were given total freedom to express their innermost personalities in graphic notation and in verbal annotations. (Alas, *Source* dried out at its 13th issue, and became a collector's item.) In 1963, Austin and his colleagues at Davis formed the New Music Ensemble, exploring free group improvisation. This period was followed by further experimentation in synthetic arts in so-called "event/complexes," combining a quad-rastereophonic tape with various instruments and voices. In the meantime, Austin was active as a lecturer and conductor. He made 3 European concert and lecture tours (1964–65, 1967, 1973), 2 in South America (1969, 1973), and several in the U.S. and Canada. In 1972 he was appointed chairman of the dept. of music, Univ. of South Florida, Tampa; also served as director of systems complex for the Studio of Performing Arts at the univ. there. In 1978 he received a professorship at his alma mater, North Texas State Univ. He was a recipient of numerous grants and several commissions from various prestigious organizations. Most of Austin's compositions are cast for mixed media, in which theatrical, acoustical, and dynamic elements are integrated into manifestations of universal vitality. In order to attain a maximum impact with a minimum of anarchy, he introduced the concept of coordinated improvisation, which he termed "open styles." His research projects include the development of software for hybrid computer systems for electronic music.

Austral (real name, **Wilson**), **Florence,** Australian soprano; b. Richmond, near Melbourne, April 26, 1892; d. Newcastle, New South Wales, May 15, 1968. She studied at the Melbourne Cons. (1914–18); made her operatic debut as Brünnhilde at Covent Garden in London, under the auspices of the newly formed British National Opera Co. (May 16, 1922); later she sang the roles of Isolde and Aida. She toured the U.S. between 1925 and 1931 with her husband, the flutist **John Amadeo;** eventually returned to Australia.

Aventinus (real name, **Turmair**), **Johannes,** German theorist; b. Abensberg (whence Aventinus), July 4, 1477; d. Regensburg, Jan. 9, 1534. His treatise *Annales Boiorum* (1554) contains considerable information (not always trustworthy) about musical matters. He also edited Nicolaus Faber's *Musica rudimenta admodum brevia* (1516).

Avison, Charles, English organist and composer; b. Newcastle-upon-Tyne, 1709 (old style; baptized, Feb. 16); d. there, May 9, 1770. He acquired the rudiments of music at home; was appointed organist at St. John's church in Newcastle on Oct. 13, 1735; took up his post in 1736. An enterprising musician, he organized in Newcastle a series of subscription concerts, one of the earliest musical presentations of its kind in Great Britain; was music director of the Newcastle Musical Society in 1738; held this post until his death. He wrote a large number of concertos employing various combinations of strings with harpsichord continuo, and sonatas in which the keyboard instrument is given a predominant func-

tion. These works were publ. between 1740 and 1769; in 1758 Avison collected 26 concertos in 4 books, arranged in score, for strings *a* 7 (4 violins, viola, cello, bass), with harpsichord; other works were 12 keyboard concertos with string quartet, 18 quartets for keyboard with 2 violins and cello, and 3 vols. of trio sonatas for keyboard with 2 violins. His *Essay on Musical Expression* (London, 1752) is historically important as an early exposition of relative musical values by an English musician. His views were opposed by an anonymous pamphlet, *Remarks on Mr. Avison's Essay...in a Letter from a Gentleman in London,* which was probably written by Prof. William Hayes of Oxford (London, 1753). Not to be thus thwarted, Avison publ. a rebuttal that same year, reinforced by a statement of worth contributed by a Dr. Jortin. He renewed his demurrer by publishing in 1775 another edition of the polemical exchange. Among his scholarly publications is Marcello's *Psalm-Paraphrases* with an English text, containing a biography of Marcello (jointly with John Garth, 1757).

Avshalomov, Aaron, Russian-American composer; b. Nikolayevsk, Siberia, Nov. 11, 1894; d. New York, April 26, 1965. He studied at the Zürich Cons.; in 1914 he went to China, where he wrote a number of works on Chinese subjects, making use of authentic Chinese themes. On April 24, 1925, he conducted the first performance in Peking of his first opera on a Chinese subject, *Kuan Yin;* his 2nd opera, also on a Chinese subject, *The Great Wall,* was staged in Shanghai on Nov. 26, 1945, and also was presented in Nanking under the sponsorship of Madame Chiang Kai-Shek, the wife of the powerful generalissimo. His other works composed in China were also performed for the first time in Shanghai, among them: *Peiping Hutungs,* symph. sketch (Feb. 7, 1933; also given by Stokowski with the Philadelphia Orch., Nov. 8, 1935); *The Soul of the Ch'in,* ballet (May 21, 1933); *Incense Shadows,* pantomime (March 13, 1935); Piano Concerto (Jan. 19, 1936); Violin Concerto (Jan. 16, 1938); First Symph. (March 17, 1940, composer conducting); *Buddha and the 5 Planetary Deities,* choreographic tableau (April 18, 1942). In 1947 Avshalomov came to America, where he continued to compose works in large forms, among them his 2nd Symph. (Cincinnati, Dec. 30, 1949); 3rd Symph. (1950); 4th Symph. (1951).

Avshalomov, Jacob, American composer, son of **Aaron Avshalomov;** b. Tsingtao, China, March 28, 1919. His mother was American; his father, Russian. He studied music in Peking; in 1936 he was in Shanghai, where material circumstances forced him to work for a time in a slaughterhouse. In 1937 he came to the U.S.; studied with Ernst Toch in Los Angeles; then with Bernard Rogers in Rochester, N.Y. From 1943–45 he was in the U.S. Army as an interpreter. From 1947–54 he was an instructor at Columbia Univ.; received a Guggenheim fellowship in 1952; in 1954 he was appointed permanent conductor of the Portland (Oreg.) Junior Symph. His music reflects the many cultures with which he was in contact; while the form is cohesive, the materials are multifarious, with tense chromatic harmonies and quasi-oriental inflections.

Ax, Emanuel, outstanding Polish-born American pianist; b. Lwow, June 8, 1949. He began to play the violin at age 6; soon took up the piano and studied with his father, who was a coach at the Lwow Opera House. The family moved to Warsaw when he was 8, and then to Winnipeg, Canada, when he was 10; in 1961 settled in N.Y., where he enrolled at the Juilliard School of Music as a student of Mieczyslaw Munz; he also received a bachelor's degree in French from Columbia Univ., in 1970. He made a concert tour of South America in 1969; became a U.S. citizen in 1970. He competed at the Chopin (1970) and Queen Elisabeth (1972) competitions; in both placed only 7th; in 1971 won 3rd place in the Vianna da Motta Competition in Lisbon; then made his N.Y. debut at Alice Tully Hall on March 12, 1973. A long-awaited victory came in 1974, when he won first place in the Artur Rubinstein International Piano Master Competition in Tel Aviv; among its awards was a contract for an American concert tour; there followed numerous appearances throughout the U.S. and Europe. He was awarded the Avery Fisher Prize in 1979. In addition to his fine interpretations of the standard repertoire, he has also distinguished himself as a champion of contemporary music.

Ayrton, Edmund, English organist and composer, father of **William Ayrton;** b. Ripon, Yorkshire, baptized on Nov. 19, 1734, probably born the day before; d. London, May 22, 1808. He studied organ with Nares; from 1755 was organist in various churches; in 1764 was appointed Gentleman of the Chapel Royal, and in 1780 was appointed lay vicar at Westminster Abbey. He was in charge of the Chapel Royal from 1780–1805. In 1784, he was given the degree of D.Mus. at Trinity College in Cambridge, and in 1788, D.Mus. at Oxford. He wrote a number of anthems, of which *Begin unto My God with Timbrels,* scored for 4 vocal soloists, mixed choir, 2 oboes, 2 bassoons, 2 trumpets, timpani, and strings, obtained great success at its performance on June 29, 1784, in St. Paul's Cathedral in London. His glee *An Ode to Harmony* (1799) was also popular. He was admittedly a faithful imitator of Handel, but the judgment of Wesley, who described Ayrton as "one of the most egregious blockheads under the sun," seems unduly severe.

Ayrton, William, English organist, son of **Edmund Ayrton;** b. London, Feb. 24, 1777; d. there, March 8, 1858. He received a fine education; was one of the original founders of the London Phil. Society in 1813; wrote music criticism for the *Morning Chronicle* (1813–26) and for the *Examiner* (1837–51). In 1823 he started the publication of the historically important London music periodical *Harmonicon,* and was its editor; from 1834–37 edited *The Musical Library,* which publ. vocal and instrumental music. He also compiled a practical collection, *Sacred Minstrelsy* (2 vols.; 1835).

Azevedo, Alexis-Jacob, French writer on music; b. Bordeaux, March 18, 1813; d. Paris, Dec. 21, 1875. He was a prolific contributor to *Le Ménestrel* and other French music magazines; publ. monographs on Félicien David (1863) and Rossini (1864); a pamphlet, *La Verité sur Rouget de Lisle et la Marseillaise* (Dieppe, 1864); *La Transposition par les nombres* (Paris, 1874); a collection of articles, *Les Doubles-croches malades* (1874); etc.

B

Babbi, (Pietro Giovanni) Cristoforo (Bartolomeo Gasparre), Italian violinist and composer, son of **Gregorio Babbi;** b. Cesena, May 6, 1745; d. Dresden, Nov. 19, 1814. He studied violin, counterpoint, and composition with Paolo Alberghi in Faenza; subsequently was primo violino at the festas there (1766, 1769, 1770, 1772); also played in the orch. of the Rimini Opera (1773). In 1774 he was elected a member of the Accademia Filarmonica of Bologna; then was maestro di cappella at the Teatro Comunale there (1775–78); in 1779 he became primo violino and direttore d'orchestra in Forlì. He was called to Dresden in 1781 as provisional Konzertmeister; received a permanent appointment in 1782, and proceeded to reorganize the Kapelle; he held an equal place with J.G. Naumann, the Dresden Kapellmeister. He composed symphs., operas, concertos, and other works.

Babbitt, Milton Byron, American composer and theorist; b. Philadelphia, May 10, 1916. He received his early musical training in Jackson, Mississippi; at the same time he revealed an acute flair for mathematical reasoning; this double faculty determined the formulation of his musical theories, in which he promulgated a system of melodic and rhythmic sets ultimately leading to integral serialism. His academic studies included courses with Philip James and Marion Bauer at N.Y.Univ. (B.A. 1935) and at Princeton Univ. (M.A. 1942); he also had private sessions with Sessions. From 1943 to 1945 he taught both music theory and mathematics at Princeton Univ.; in 1960 was named prof. of music there. He held a Guggenheim grant in 1961; was elected a member of the National Institute of Arts and Letters in 1965. At Princeton and Columbia univs. he inaugurated an experimental program of electronic music, with the aid of a newly constructed synthesizer. Taking as the point of departure the Schoenbergian method of composition with 12 different tones, Babbitt extended the serial principle to embrace 12 different note values, 12 different time intervals between instrumental entries, 12 different dynamic levels, and 12 different instrumental timbres. In order to describe the potential combinations of the basic 4 aspects of the tone-row, he introduced the term "combinatoriality," with symmetric parts of a tone-row designated as "derivations." His paper "Twelve-Tone Invariants as Compositional Determinants," published in *The Musical Quarterly* of April 1960, gives a résumé of his system of total serialism. The serial application of rhythmic values is expounded in Babbitt's paper "Twelve-Tone Rhythmic Structure and the Electronic Medium," published in *Perspectives of New Music* (Fall 1962).

Babbitt's scientific-sounding theories have profoundly influenced the musical thinking of young American composers; a considerable literature, both intelligible and unintelligible, arose in special publications to penetrate and, if at all possible, to illuminate Babbitt's mind-boggling speculations. His original music, some of it aurallly beguiling, can be fully understood only after a preliminary study of its underlying compositional plan. In 1982 he won a special citation of the Pulitzer Committee for "his life's work as a distinguished and seminal American composer."

WORKS: *Three Compositions for Piano* (1947); *Composition for 4 Instruments* (1948); *Composition* for 12 Instruments (1948); *Composition* for Viola and Piano (1950); *The Widow's Lament in Springtime* for Voice and Piano (1950); *Du,* a song cycle (1951); Quartet for Flute, Oboe, Clarinet, and Bassoon (1953); String Quartet No. 1 (1954); String Quartet No. 2 (1954); *Two Sonnets* for Voice and 3 Instruments (1955); *Semisimple Variations* for Piano (1956); *All Set* for Jazz Ensemble (1957); *Sounds and Words,* to a text of disparate syllables for Voice and Piano (1958); *Composition* for Voice and 6 Instruments (1960); *Composition* for Synthesizer (1961); *Vision and Prayer,* song for Soprano and Synthesized Magnetic Tape (1961); *Philomel* for Voice and Magnetic Tape (1964); *Ensemble* for Synthesizer (1964); *Relata I* for Orch. (1965); *Post-Partitions* for Piano (1966); *Sextets* for Violin and Piano (the title refers to the sextuple parameters of the work, 1966); *Correspondences* for String Orch. and Synthesized Magnetic Tape (1967); *Relata II* for Orch. (1968); *Occasional Variations,* a compost collated by Synthesizer (1969); String Quartet No. 3 (1970); *Phonemena* for Soprano and Piano (1970); *Arie da Capo* for 5 Players, "models of similar, interval-preserving, registrally uninterpreted pitch-class and metrically-durationally uninterpreted time-point aggregate arrays" (1974); *Reflections* for Piano and Synthesized Tape (1975); Concerti for Violin, Small Orch., and Synthesized Tape (N.Y., March 13, 1976); *Paraphrases* for 9 Wind Instruments and Piano (1979); *A Solo Requiem* for Soprano and 2 Pianists (N.Y., Feb. 10, 1979); *Dual* for Cello and Piano (1980); *Elizabethan Sextette,* 6 poems for 6 Unaccompanied Voices (1981).

Babini, Matteo, famous Italian tenor; b. Bologna, Feb. 19, 1754; d. there, Sept. 22, 1816. He studied with Cortoni; made his debut in 1780; then toured England, Russia, Germany, and Austria with great acclaim. He settled in Paris as a court favorite until the Revolution forced him to leave France; he was in Berlin in 1792 and in Trieste in 1796. Brighenti publ. an "Elogio" in his memory (Bologna, 1821).

Bacarisse, Salvador, Spanish composer; b. Madrid, Sept. 12, 1898; d. Paris, Aug. 7, 1963. He studied at the Cons. of Madrid with Conrado del Campo; received the Premio Nacional de Música 3 times, in 1923, 1930, and 1934. During the Spanish Civil War he was active in the music section of the loyalist army, and after its defeat in 1939 went to Paris, where he remained until his death. He wrote music in all genres; among his works are an opera, *Charlot* (1933); the symph. poem *La tragedia de Doña Ajada* (1929); *Corrida de feria,* a ballet (1930); Piano Concerto (1933); *Tres movimientos concertantes* for String Trio and Orch. (1934); a cantata, *Por la paz y felicidad de las naciones* (1950); Concerto for Guitar and Orch. (Paris, Oct. 22, 1953); 2 string quartets; piano pieces; songs.

Bacchius, Greek theorist who flourished A.D. c.350. His treatise, *Isagoge musicae artis,* was publ. by Mersenne (1623); with Latin trans. and commentary by Morellus (1623); also by Meibom (1652) and Carl von Jan (with German trans. and analysis in the Program of the Strasbourg Lyceum, 1890; Greek text alone in Jan's "Scriptores," 1895). French translations were publ. by Mersenne (in Book I of his *Harmonie universelle,* 1627) and Ruelle (1896). The work is a musical catechism in dialogue form. Another treatise, having no dialogue, attributed to Bacchius and edited by Bellermann (in German, 1841) and Vincent (in French, 1847) is not by Bacchius but by his contemporary Dionysios.

Baccusi, Ippolito, Italian composer; b. Mantua, 1530; d. Verona, Sept. 2, 1608. He served as maestro di cappella at San Marco in Venice. In 1570 he was in Ravenna as an organist and in 1572 in Verona; from 1584 to 1587 he was maestro di cappella in Mantua; in 1591 went to Verona. He publ. 5 books of masses (1570–96); 7 books of madrigals (1570–1605); also numerous other choral works. His music shows the influence of the Venetian school; his motets have considerable expressive power.

Bacewicz, Grażyna, significant Polish composer; b. Lodz, Feb. 5, 1909; d. Warsaw, Jan. 17, 1969. She studied composition and violin at the Warsaw Cons., graduating in 1932; continued her study of composition with Nadia Boulanger in Paris (1933–34); upon her return to Poland, she taught at the Lodz Cons.; in 1966 she was appointed prof. at the State Academy of Music in Warsaw. A prolific composer, she adopted a neo-Classical style, characterized by a firm rhythmic pulse and crisp dissonant harmonies.

WORKS: Comic radio opera, *Przygody króla Artura (The Adventures of King Arthur,* 1959); 3 ballets: *Z chlopa Król (A Peasant Becomes King,* 1953); *Esik in Ostende* (1964); *Pożądanie (Desire,* 1968); Sinfonietta (1937); 7 violin concertos (1938, 1946, 1948, 1952, 1954, 1957, 1965); Overture (1943); 4 numbered symphs. (1942–45, 1950, 1952, 1953); an unnumbered Symph. for String Orch. (1943–46); *Olympic Cantata* (1948); Concerto for String Orch. (1948); Piano Concerto (1949); 2 cello concertos (1951, 1963); *Polish Overture* (1954); Partita for Orch. (1955); Variations for Orch. (1957); *Muzyka* for Strings, 5 Trumpets, and Percussion (Warsaw, Sept. 14, 1959); *Pensieri notturni* for Chamber Orch. (1961); Concerto for Orch. (1962); *Cantata,* after Wyspiański's "Acropolis" (1964); *Musica Sinfonica* (1965); Divertimento for String Orch. (1965); *Incrustations* for Horn and Chamber Ensemble (1965); *Contradizione* for Chamber Orch. (1966; Dartmouth College, Hanover, N.H., Aug. 2, 1967); 2-Piano Concerto (1966); *In una parte* for Orch. (1967); Viola Concerto (1967–68); Wind Quintet (1932); Trio for Oboe, Violin, and Cello (1935); 7 string quartets (1938, 1942, 1947, 1950, 1955, 1960, 1965); 5 violin sonatas (1945, 1946, 1947, 1951, 1955); Quartet for 4 Violins (1949); 2 piano quintets (1952, 1965); solo Violin Sonata (1958); Quartet for 4 Cellos (1964); Trio for Oboe, Harp, and Percussion (1965); *4 Caprices* for Solo Violin (1968); 3 piano sonatas (1935, 1949, 1952); *10 Concert Studies* for Piano (1957); *Esquisse* for Organ (1966).

Bach is the name of the illustrious family which, during 2 centuries, gave to the world a number of musicians and composers of distinction. History possesses few records of such remarkable examples of hereditary art, which culminated in the genius of Johann Sebastian Bach. In the Bach genealogy, the primal member was Johannes or Hans Bach, who is mentioned in 1561 as a guardian of the municipality of Wechmar, a town near Gotha. Also residing in Wechmar was his relative **Veit Bach;** a baker by trade, he was also skillful in playing on a small cittern. Another relative, **Caspar Bach,** who lived from 1570 to 1640, was a Stadtpfeifer in Gotha who later served as a town musician in Arnstadt. His 5 sons, **Caspar, Johannes, Melchior, Nicolaus,** and **Heinrich,** were all town musicians. Another Bach, **Johannes Bach** (1550–1626), was known as "der Spielmann," that is, "minstrel," and thus was definitely described as primarily a musician by vocation. His 3 sons, **Johannes, Christoph,** and **Heinrich,** were also musicians. J.S. Bach took great interest in his family history, and in 1735 prepared a genealogy under the title *Ursprung der musicalisch-Bachischen Familie. The Bach Reader,* compiled by H. David and A. Mendel (N.Y., 1945; revised ed., 1966), contains extensive quotations from this compendium. Karl Geiringer's books *The Bach Family: Seven Generations of Creative Genius* (N.Y., 1954) and *Music of the Bach Family: An Anthology* (Cambridge, Mass., 1955) give useful genealogical tables of Bach's family. Bach's father, **Johann Ambrosius,** was a twin brother of Bach's uncle; the twins bore such an extraordinary physical resemblance that, according to the testimony of Carl Philipp Emanuel Bach, their own wives had difficulty telling them apart after dark. To avoid confusion, they had them wear vests of different colors. A vulgar suggestion that because of this similarity Bach may have been begotten by his uncle is too gross to require a refutation.

When the family became numerous and widely dispersed, its members agreed to assemble on a fixed date each year. Erfurt, Eisenach, and Arnstadt were the places chosen for these meetings, which are said to have continued until the middle of the 18th century, as many as 120 persons of the name of Bach then assembling. At these meetings, a cher-

ished pastime was the singing of "quodlibets," comic polyphonic potpourris of popular songs. An amusing example attributed to J.S. Bach is publ. in *Veröffentlichungen der Neuen Bach-Gesellschaft* (vol. XXXII, 2).

Bach, Carl Philipp Emanuel (the "Berlin" or "Hamburg" Bach), 3rd (and 2nd surviving) son of **Johann Sebastian;** b. Weimar, March 8, 1714; d. Hamburg, Dec. 14, 1788. He was educated under his father's tuition at the Thomasschule in Leipzig; then studied jurisprudence at the Univ. of Leipzig and at the Univ. of Frankfurt-an-der-Oder. Turning to music as his chief vocation, he went to Berlin in 1738; in 1740 he was confirmed as chamber musician to Frederick the Great of Prussia. In that capacity he arranged his father's visit to Potsdam. In March 1768 he assumed the post of cantor at the Johanneum (the Lateinschule) in Hamburg, and also served as music director for the 5 major churches. He held these posts until his death. Abandoning the strict polyphonic style of composition of his great father, he became an adept of the new school of piano writing, a master of "Empfindsamkeit" ("intimate expressiveness"), the North German counterpart of the French Rococo. His *Versuch über die wahre Art das Clavier zu spielen . . .* (2 parts, 1753–62; re-edited by Schelling in 1857; new, but incomplete, ed. by W. Niemann, 1906) became a very influential work which yielded much authentic information about musical practices of the 2nd half of the 18th century. An Eng. trans. of the *Versuch . . .*, entitled *Essay on the True Art of Playing Keyboard Instruments,* was publ. by W. Mitchell (N.Y., 1949). His autobiography was reprinted by W. Kahl in *Selbstbiographien deutscher Musiker des XVIII. Jahrhunderts* (Cologne, 1948); an Eng. trans. was made by W. Newman, "Emanuel Bach's Autobiography," *Musical Quarterly* (April 1965). His compositions are voluminous (a complete catalogue by E. Helm, *A New Thematic Catalog of the Works of Carl Philipp Emanuel Bach,* is in preparation).

WORKS: For clavier, numerous solo pieces, concertos with orch.; quartets; trios; duets; 20 orch. symphs.; many miscellaneous pieces for wind instruments; trios for flute, violin, and double bass; flute, oboe, and cello concertos; soli for flute, viola da gamba, oboe, cello, and harp; duets for flute and violin and for 2 violins; also pieces for clarinet. Vocal music: 2 oratorios: *Die Israeliten in der Wüste* and *Die Auferstehung und Himmelfahrt Jesu;* 22 Passions; cantatas; about 300 songs; etc. Editions of his various works include the following: C. Krebs, ed., *Die Sechs Sammlungen von Sonaten, freien Fantasien und Rondos für Kenner und Liebhaber* (Leipzig, 1895; revised ed. by L. Hoffmann, Erbrecht, 1953); O. Vrieslander, *Kleine Stücke für Klavier* (Hannover, 1930); O. Vrieslander, *Vier leichte Sonaten* (Hannover, 1932); K. Herrman, ed., *Sonaten und Stücke* (Leipzig, 1938); V. Luithlen and H. Kraus, eds., *Klavierstücke* (Vienna, 1938); K. Herrman, ed., *Leichte Tänze und Stücke für Klavier* (Hamburg, 1949); P. Friedheim, ed., *Six Sonatas for Keyboard* (N.Y., 1967); H. Ferguson, ed., *Keyboard*

Works of C.P.E. Bach (4 vols., London, 1983).

Bach, Christoph, 2nd son of **Johann(es Hans)** "der Spielmann" and grandfather of **Johann Sebastian;** b. Wechmar, April 19, 1613; d. Arnstadt, Sept. 12, 1661. He was a court musician in Weimar; from 1642 he was a town musician in Erfurt; from 1654, court and town musician in Arnstadt. The only known musical item by him is publ. in the *Bach-Jahrbuch* (1928).

Bach, Georg Christoph, eldest son of **Christoph;** b. Erfurt, Sept. 6, 1642; d. Schweinfurt, April 24, 1697. He was cantor in Themar from 1668; in Schweinfurt from 1684. A cantata of his is publ. in *Das Erbe deutscher Musik* (vol. II, Leipzig, 1935).

Bach, Heinrich, 3rd son of **Johann(es Hans)** "der Spielmann"; b. Wechmar, Sept. 16, 1615; d. Arnstadt, July 10, 1692. He was a town musician in Schweinfurt from 1629, in Erfurt fron 1635, and in Arnstadt from 1641; from 1641, was also organist at the Liebfrauenkirche in Arnstadt, a post he held for 51 years, until his death. M. Schneider publ. a thematic index of his works in the *Bach-Jahrbuch* (1907, pp. 105–9). A cantata of his is found in *Das Erbe deutscher Musik* (vol. II, Leipzig, 1935); also 3 organ chorales in D. Hellmann, ed., *Orgelwerke der Familie Bach* (Leipzig, 1967).

Bach, Johann Aegidius, 2nd son of **Johann(es Hans);** b. Erfurt, Feb. 9, 1645; d. there (buried, Nov. 22), 1716. He succeeded his father as municipal music director in Erfurt in 1682; was also organist at the Michaeliskirche there from 1690, succeeding Pachelbel.

Bach, Johann Ambrosius, 2nd son of **Christoph,** twin brother of **Johann Christoph,** and father of **Johann Sebastian;** b. Erfurt, Feb. 22, 1645; d. Eisenach, Feb. 20, 1695. As a boy, he went to Arnstadt; was trained as a Stadtpfeifer. In 1667 he became a member of the town band in Erfurt; from 1671 was court trumpeter and director of the town band in Eisenach. He was married twice: on April 8, 1668, to Maria Elisabeth Lämmerhirt (b. Erfurt, Feb. 24, 1644; d. Eisenach, May 3, 1694), the mother of Johann Sebastian; and on Nov. 27, 1694, to the widow of his cousin Johann Günther Bach.

Bach, Johann Bernhard, son of **Johann Aegidius,** one of the best organists and composers of his generation; b. Erfurt, Nov. 23, 1676; d. Eisenach, June 11, 1749. He was an organist at Erfurt and Magdeburg, and the successor to **Johann Christoph** as organist at Eisenach (1703); also served the Duke of Saxe-Eisenach. He wrote harpsichord pieces; also a number of organ chorales: 2 of these have been publ. in *Das Erbe deutscher Musik* (vol. IX, Leipzig, 1937); 2 more in D. Hellmann, ed., *Orgelwerke der Familie Bach* (Leipzig, 1967). He also wrote 4 orch. suites; one was publ. by A. Fareanu (Leipzig, 1920); another by K. Geiringer, *Music of the Bach Family: An An-*

thology (Cambridge, Mass., 1955).

Bach, Johann (John) Christian (the "London" Bach), 11th and youngest surviving son of **Johann Sebastian Bach;** b. Leipzig, Sept. 5, 1735; d. London, Jan. 1, 1782. He received early instruction in music from his father, after whose death in 1750 he went to Berlin to study with his brother **Carl Philipp Emanuel.** In 1754 he went to Italy, where he continued his studies with Padre Martini; he also found a patron in Count Agostino Litta of Milan. He converted to the Roman Catholic faith in order to be able to obtain work, and became one of the organists at the Cathedral in Milan (1760–62); he also traveled throughout the country and composed several successful operas during his stay in Italy. In 1762 he went to England; his highly acclaimed opera *Orione* was given its premiere in London on Feb. 19, 1763; in 1764 he was appointed music master to the Queen. From 1764 to 1781 he gave, together with C.F. Abel, a series of London concerts. When child Mozart was taken to London in 1764, J.C. Bach took great interest in him and improvised with him at the keyboard; Mozart retained a lifelong affection for him; he used 3 of J.C. Bach's piano sonatas as thematic material for his piano concertos. J.C. Bach was a highly prolific composer; he wrote about 90 symphs., several piano concertos, 6 quintets, a Piano Sextet, violin sonatas, and numerous piano sonatas. In his music he adopted the *style galant* of the 2nd half of the 18th century, with an emphasis on expressive "affects" and brilliance of instrumental display. He thus totally departed from the ideals of his father, and became historically a precursor of the Classical era as exemplified by the works of Mozart.

WORKS: Although he was known mainly as an instrumental composer, J.C. Bach also wrote successful operas, most of them to Italian librettos, for production in London; among them were: *Artaserse* (Turin, Dec. 26, 1760); *Catone in Utica* (Naples, Nov. 4, 1761); *Alessandro nell' Indie* (Naples, Jan. 20, 1762); *Orione, ossia Diana vendicata* (London, Feb. 19, 1763); *Zanaida* (London, May 7, 1763); *Adriano in Siria* (London, Jan. 26, 1765); *Carattaco* (London, Feb. 14, 1767); *Temistocle* (Mannheim, Nov. 4, 1772); *Lucio Silla* (Mannheim, Nov. 4, 1774); *La clemenza di Scipione* (London, April 4, 1778); *Amadis de Gaule* (Paris, Dec. 14, 1779).

Bach, Johann Christoph, eldest son of **Heinrich,** organist and composer of the highest distinction among the earlier Bachs; b. Arnstadt, Dec. 3, 1642; d. Eisenach, March 31, 1703. From 1663 to 1665 he was an organist in Arnstadt; from 1665, in Eisenach; from 1700, was court musician there. A thematic catalogue of his compositions was publ. by M. Schneider in the *Bach-Jahrbuch* (1907, pp. 132–77). C.P.E. Bach described him as a "great and expressive composer"; his works are printed in *Das Erbe deutscher Musik* (vols. I and II, Leipzig, 1935); several of his motets were publ. by V. Junk (Leipzig, 1922); 44 chorales with preludes for Organ were edited by M. Fischer (Kassel, 1936); his *Praeludium* *und Fuge* for Organ is in D. Hellman, ed., *Orgelwerke der Familie Bach* (Leipzig, 1967).

Bach, Johann Christoph, twin brother of **Johann Ambrosius;** b. Erfurt, Feb. 22, 1645; d. Arnstadt, Aug. 25, 1693. He was a Stadtpfeifer in Erfurt from 1666; in Arnstadt, from 1671. The physical resemblance between him and his twin brother (father of **Johann Sebastian**) was such that, according to the testimony of C.P.E. Bach, even their wives had difficulty distinguishing between them.

Bach, Johann Christoph, brother of **Johann Sebastian** and eldest son of **Johann Ambrosius;** b. Erfurt, June 16, 1671; d. Ohrdruf, Feb. 22, 1721. He was a pupil of Pachelbel; served as organist at the Thomaskirche in Erfurt and for a short time at Arnstadt; from 1690 he was organist at the Michaeliskirche in Ohrdruf, where Johann Sebastian stayed with him for almost 5 years.

Bach, Johann Christoph Friedrich (the "Bückeburg" Bach), 9th son of **Johann Sebastian;** b. Leipzig, June 21, 1732; d. Bückeburg, Jan. 26, 1795. He studied music with his father; then attended the Univ. of Leipzig, where he took courses in jurisprudence. Adopting music as his principal vocation, he became a chamber musician in Bückeburg, a post he held until his death. Although less known as a composer than his brothers, he was a fine musician. A selected edition of his works was edited by G. Schünemann and sponsored by the Fürstliches Institut für Musikwissenschaftliche Forschung (1920–22). Schünemann also edited several oratorios in the Denkmäler deutscher Tonkunst (vol. 56, 1917). G. Walter edited the cantata *Die Amerikanerin* (Berlin, 1919), and L. Duttenhofer, a set of 6 quartets (Paris, 1922); several other chamber works may be found in K. Geiringer, *Music of the Bach Family: An Anthology* (Cambridge, Mass., 1955); 3 symphs. have been edited in facsimile by H. Wohlfarth (Bückeburg, 1966).

Bach, Johann Ernst, only son of **Johann Bernhard;** b. Eisenach, Jan. 28, 1722; d. there, Sept. 1, 1777. He was a pupil of his uncle, **Johann Sebastian.** After studying law at the Univ. of Leipzig, he returned to Eisenach and practiced as an advocate. In 1748 he became assistant organist to his father at the Georgenkirche; succeeded him as organist in 1749. In 1756 he became Court Kapellmeister to the fused courts of Weimar, Gotha, and Eisenach. When this arrangement was dissolved in 1758, he retained his position and worked in the administration of the ducal finances in Eisenach. He publ. *Sammlung auserlesener Fabeln mit Melodeyen* (ed. by H. Kretzschmar in Denkmäler Deutscher Tonkunst, vol. 42, 1910) and other works. Only a small part of his works has been publ.; his Passion oratorio, *O Seele, deren Sehen,* is in Denkmäler Deutscher Tonkunst, vol. 48, 1914. A sonata is in K. Geiringer, *Music of the Bach Family: An Anthology* (Cambridge, Mass., 1955). Two fantasies and fugues for organ are found in D. Hellmann, ed., *Orgelwerke der Familie Bach* (Leipzig, 1967).

Bach, Johann(es Hans), eldest son of **Johann(es Hans)** "der Spielmann"; b. Wechmar, Nov. 26, 1604; d. Erfurt, May 13, 1673. He was apprenticed to Christoph Hoffman, Stadtpfeifer in Suhl; was a town musician in Erfurt; from 1636, was organist at the Predigerkirche there. Several of his compositions are extant.

Bach, Johann Ludwig, son of **Johann Jacob** and a great-grandson of Lips Bach (d. Oct. 10, 1620); b. Thal, Feb. 4, 1677; d. Meiningen (buried, March 1), 1731. In 1699 he became a court musician in Meiningen; was appointed cantor in 1703, and Court Kapellmeister in 1711. He wrote numerous vocal compositions; also orch. works, but few have been preserved.

Bach, Johann Michael, brother of **Johann Christoph** and father of Maria Barbara, first wife of **Johann Sebastian;** b. Arnstadt, Aug. 9, 1648; d. Gehren, May 17, 1694. From 1673 he was organist and town clerk of Gehren; also worked as a maker of instruments. His works are listed in the *Bach-Jahrbuch* (1907, pp. 109–32); many of them are included in *Das Erbe deutscher Musik* (vol. I, Leipzig, 1935); motets of his are publ. in Denkmäler Deutscher Tonkunst (vols. 49 and 50, 1915). Some of his organ compositions are found in *Das Erbe deutscher Musik* (vol. IX, Leipzig, 1937); 72 organ chorales are included in D. Hellman, ed., *Orgelwerke der Familie Bach* (Leipzig, 1967).

Bach, Johann Nicolaus, eldest son of **Johann Christoph;** b. Eisenach, Oct. 10, 1669; d. Jena, Nov. 4, 1753. He was educated at the Univ. of Jena; in 1694 he became organist at Jena, and in 1719 was also at the Univ. He was an expert on organ building and also made keyboard instruments. He wrote a fine *Missa* (Kyrie and Gloria; ed. by A. Fareanu and V. Junk, Leipzig, 1920); a comic cantata, *Der Jenaische Wein- und Bierrufer,* a scene from Jena Univ. life (ed. by F. Stein, Leipzig, 1921); suites for keyboard, which are not preserved, and organ chorales, of which only one is known.

Bach, Johann Sebastian, supreme arbiter and lawgiver of music, a master comparable in greatness of stature with Aristotle in philosophy and Leonardo da Vinci in art; b. Eisenach, March 21 (baptized, March 23), 1685; d. Leipzig, July 28, 1750. He was a member of an illustrious family of musicians who were active in various capacities as performing artists, composers, and teachers. That so many Bachs were musicians lends support to the notion that music is a hereditary faculty, that some subliminal cellular unit may be the nucleus of musicality. The word "Bach" itself means "stream" in the German language; the rhetorical phrase that Johann Sebastian Bach was not a mere stream but a whole ocean of music ("Nicht Bach aber Meer haben wir hier") epitomizes Bach's encompassing magnitude. Yet despite the grandeur of the phenomenon of Bach, he was not an isolated figure dwelling in the splendor of his genius apart from the zeitgeist, the spirit of his time. Just as Aristotle was not only an abstract philosopher but also an educator (Alexander the Great was his pupil), just as Leonardo da Vinci was not only a painter of portraits but also a practical man of useful inventions, so Bach was a mentor to young students, a master organist and instructor who spent his life within the confines of his native Thuringia as a teacher and composer of works designed for immediate performance in church and in the schoolroom. Indeed, the text of the dedication of his epoch-making work *Das wohltemperierte Clavier oder Praeludia und Fugen* emphasizes its pedagogical aspect: "The Well-tempered Clavier, or Preludes and Fugues in all tones and semitones, both with the major third of Ut Re Mi, and the minor third of Re Mi Fa, composed and notated for the benefit and exercise of musical young people eager to learn, as well as for a special practice for those who have already achieved proficiency and skill in this study." The MS is dated 1722. Bach's system of "equal temperament" (which is the meaning of "well-tempered" in the title *Well-tempered Clavier*) postulated the division of the octave into 12 equal semitones, making it possible to transpose and to effect a modulation into any key, a process unworkable in the chaotic tuning of keyboard instruments before Bach's time. Bach was not the first to attempt the tempered division, however. J.K.F. Fischer anticipated him in his collection *Ariadne musica* (with the allusion to the thread of Ariadne that allowed Theseus to find his way out of the Cretan labyrinth); publ. in 1700, it contained 20 preludes and fugues in 19 different keys. Undoubtedly Bach was aware of this edition; actually, the subjects of several of Bach's preludes and fugues are similar to the point of identity to the themes of Fischer's work. These coincidences do not detract from the significance of Bach's accomplishment, for it is the beauty and totality of development that makes Bach's work vastly superior to those of any of his putative predecessors.

It is interesting to note that Bach shared the belief in numerical symbolism held by many poets and artists of his time. By summing up the cardinal numbers corresponding to the alphabetical order of the letters of his last name, he arrived at the conclusion that the number 14 had a special significance in his life (B = 2, A = 1, C = 3, H = 8; $2 + 1 + 3 + 8 = 14$). That the number of buttons on his waistcoat in one of his portraits is 14 may be an indication of the significance he attached to this number. The theme of Bach's chorale *Von deinen Thron tret' ich hiermit,* which he wrote shortly before his death, contains 14 notes, while the notes in the entire melody number 43, comprising the sum total of the alphabetical index of letters in J.S. Bach ($10 + 19 + 2 + 1 + 3 + 8 = 43$). In Bach's chorale prelude *Wenn wir in Höchsten Nöten sein,* the principal melody contains 166 notes, which represents the alphabetical sum of the full name JOHANN SEBASTIAN BACH ($10 + 15 + 8 + 1 + 14 + 14 + 19 + 5 + 2 +$

$1 + 19 + 20 + 9 + 1 + 14 + 2 + 1 + 3 + 8 = 166$). The symbolism of melodies and harmonies in Baroque music, expressing various states of mind, joy or sadness has been accepted as a valid "doctrine of affects" by musical philosophers, among them Albert Schweitzer. Indeed, there seems to be little doubt that a natural connection exists between such a line as "Geh' auf! Geh' auf!" and an ascending major arpeggio in a Bach cantata, or that, generally speaking, major modes represent joy and exhilaration, and minor keys suggest melancholy and sadness. We find numerous instances in the choral works of Baroque composers of the use of a broken diminished-seventh-chord in a precipitous downward movement to depict the fall from grace and regression to Hell. The chromatic weaving around a thematic tone often represents in Bach's cantatas and Passions the thorny crown around the head of Jesus Christ. An ascending scale of several octaves, sung by basses, tenors, altos, and sopranos in succession, is found to accompany the words "We follow you." A hypothesis may be advanced that such tonal patterns were used by Baroque composers to facilitate the comprehension of the meaning of the text by the congregation in church performances. Indeed, such word painting has become an accepted procedure in the last 2 or 3 centuries; composers equated major keys with joy and virtue, and minor keys with melancholy and sin. Similarly, fast tempos and duple time are commonly used by composers to express joy, while slow movements are reserved for scenes of sadness.

The term "Baroque" had a humble origin; it was probably derived from *barroco,* the Portuguese word for a deformed pearl; originally it had a decidedly negative meaning, and was often applied in the 17th century to describe a corrupt style of Renaissance architecture. Through the centuries the word underwent a change of meaning toward lofty excellence. In this elevated sense, "Baroque" came to designate an artistic development between the years 1600 and 1800. The advent of Bach marked the greatest flowering of Baroque music; his name became a synonym of perfection. Max Reger was told by Hugo Riemann that he could be the 2nd Bach, and his skill in composition almost justified his aspiration; Ferruccio Busoni was described by his admirers as the Bach of the modern era; a similar honor was claimed for Hindemith by his disciples. Yet the art of Bach remains unconquerable. Although he wrote most of his contrapuntal works as a didactic exercise, there are in his music extraordinary visions into the remote future; consider, for instance, the A minor Fugue of the first book of the *Well-tempered Clavier,* in which the inversion of the subject seems to violate all the rules of proper voice-leading in its bold leap from the tonic upward to the 7th of the scale and then up a third. The answer to the subject of the F minor Fugue of the first book suggests the chromatic usages of later centuries. In the art of variations, Bach was supreme. A superb example is his set of keyboard pieces known as the *Goldberg Variations,* so named because it was commissioned by the Russian diplomat Kayserling through the mediation of Bach's

Bach

pupil Johann Gottlieb Goldberg, who was in Kayserling's service as a harpsichord player. These variations are listed by Bach as the 4th part of the *Clavier-Übung;* the didactic title of this division is characteristic of Bach's intention to write music for utilitarian purposes, be it for keyboard exercises, for church services, or for chamber music. A different type of Bach's great musical projections is exemplified by his *Concerts à plusieurs instruments,* known popularly as the *Brandenburg Concertos,* for they were written for Christian Ludwig, margrave of Brandenburg. They represent the crowning achievement of the Baroque; each concerto is set in a balanced form of 3 movements, with the fast sections in the outer movements and the slow movement in the middle. Nos. 2, 4, and 5 of the *Brandenburg Concertos* are essentially concerti grossi, in which a group of solo instruments—the concertino—is contrasted with the accompanying string orch. Finally, *Die Kunst der Fuge,* Bach's last composition, which he wrote in 1749, represents an encyclopedia of fugues, canons, and various counterpoints based on the same theme. Here Bach's art of purely technical devices, such as inversion, canon, augmentation, diminution, double fugue, triple fugue, at times appearing in fantastic optical symmetry so that the written music itself forms a balanced design, is calculated to instruct the musical mind as well as delight the aural sense. Of these constructions, the most extraordinary is represented by *Das Musikalisches Opfer (A Musical Offering),* composed by Bach for Frederick the Great of Prussia. Bach's 2nd son, **Carl Philipp Emanuel,** who served as chamber musician to the court of Prussia, arranged for Bach to visit Frederick's palace in Potsdam; Bach arrived there, accompanied by his son **Wilhelm Friedemann,** on May 7, 1747. The ostensible purpose of Bach's visit was to test the Silbermann pianos installed in the palace. The King, who liked to flaunt his love for the arts and sciences, gave Bach a musical theme of his own invention and asked him to compose a fugue upon it. Bach also presented an organ recital at the Heiliggeistkirche in Potsdam and attended a chamber music concert held by the King; on that occasion he improvised a fugue in 6 parts on a theme of his own. Upon his return to Leipzig, Bach set to work on the King's theme. Gallantly, elegantly, he inscribed the work, in scholastic Latin, "Regis Iussu Cantio et Reliqua Canonica Arte Resoluta" ("At the King's command, the cantus and supplements are in a canonic manner resolved"). The initials of the Latin words form the acronym RICERCAR a technical term etymologically related to the word "research" and applied to any study that is instructive in nature. The work is subdivided into 13 sections; it includes a puzzle canon in 2 parts, marked "quaerendo invenietis" ("you will find it by seeking"). Bach had the score engraved, and sent it to the King on July 7, 1747. Intellectually independent as Bach was, he never questioned the immanent rights of established authority. He was proud of the title Royal Polish and Electoral Saxon Court Composer to the King of Poland and Elector of Saxony, bestowed upon him in 1736 while he was in the service of Duke Christian

of Weissenfels, and he even regarded the position of cantor of the Thomasschule in Leipzig as inferior to it. In his dedications to royal personages he adhered to the customary humble style, which was extended even to the typography of his dedicatory prefaces. In such dedications the name of the exalted commissioner was usually printed in large letters, with conspicuous indentation, while Bach's own signature, preceded by elaborate verbal genuflection, appeared in the smallest type of the typographer's box.

Bach's biography is singularly lacking in dramatic events. He attended the Latin school in Eisenach, and apparently was a good student, as demonstrated by his skill in the Latin language. His mother died in 1694; his father remarried and died soon afterward. Bach's school years were passed at the Lyceum in the town of Ohrdruf; his older brother **Johann Christoph** lived there; he helped Bach in his musical studies; stories that he treated Bach cruelly must be dismissed as melodramatic inventions. Through the good offices of Elias Herda, cantor of the Ohrdruf school, Bach received an opportunity to move, for further education, to Lüneburg; there he was admitted to the Mettenchor of the Michaeliskirche. In March of 1703 he obtained employment as an attendant to Johann Ernst, Duke of Weimar; he was commissioned to make tests on the new organ of the Neukirche in Arnstadt; on Aug. 9, 1703, he was appointed organist there. In Oct. 1705 he obtained a leave of absence to travel to Lübeck to hear the famous organist Dietrich Buxtehude. The physical mode of Bach's travel there leaves much to be explained. The common versions found in most biographies tell that Bach made that journey on foot. But the distance between Arnstadt and Lübeck is 212 miles (335 km) and the route lies through the forbidding Harz Mountain chain, with its legendary peak Brocken, which, according to common superstition, was the site of the midnight gathering of a coven of witches. Assuming that Bach had about a month to spend in Lübeck to attend Buxtehude's concerts (or else the journey would not have been worthwhile), he had about 45 days to cover 424 miles (670 km) for a round trip: he would have had to travel on the average of 20 miles a day. The actual travel time between Arnstadt and Lübeck, considering the absence of good roads, must have been much longer. Not only would it have been exhausting in the extreme, even for a young man of 19 (Bach's age at the time), but it would have necessitated a change of 3 or 4 pairs of heavy boots that would wear out in the generally inclement weather during the months of Nov. and Dec. A query for information from the office of the Oberbürgermeister of Arnstadt elicited the suggestion that Bach (and Handel, who made a similar journey before) must have hired himself out as a valet to a coach passenger, a not uncommon practice among young men of the time. The impetus of Bach's trip was presumably the hope of obtaining Buxtehude's position as organist upon his retirement, but there was a peculiar clause attached to the contract for such a candidate: Buxtehude had 5 unmarried daughters; his successor was expected to marry the eldest of them. Buxtehude himself obtained his post through such an expedient, but Bach apparently was not prepared for matrimony under such circumstances.

On June 15, 1707, Bach became organist at the Blasiuskirche in Mühlhausen. On Oct. 17, 1707, he married his cousin Maria Barbara Bach, who was the daughter of **Johann Michael Bach.** On Feb. 4, 1708, Bach composed his cantata *Gott ist mein König* for the ocassion of the installation of a new Mühlhausen town council. This was the first work of Bach's that was publ. Although the circumstances of his employment in Mühlhausen were seemingly favorable, Bach resigned his position on June 25, 1708, and accepted the post of court organist to Duke Wilhelm Ernst of Weimar. In Dec. 1713 Bach visited Halle, the birthplace of Handel; despite its proximity to Bach's own place of birth in Eisenach, the 2 great composers never met. On March 2, 1714, Duke Wilhelm Ernst offered Bach the position of Konzertmeister. In Sept. 1717 Bach went to Dresden to hear the famous French organist Louis Marchand, who resided there at the time. It was arranged that Bach and Marchand would hold a contest as virtuosos, but Marchand left Dresden before the scheduled event. This anecdote should not be interpreted frivolously as Marchand's fear of competing; other factors may have intervened to prevent the meeting. Johann Samuel Drese, the Weimar music director, died on Dec. 1, 1716; Bach expected to succeed him in that prestigious position, but the Duke gave the post to Drese's son. Again, this episode should not be interpreted as the Duke's lack of appreciation for Bach's superior abilities; the appointment may have merely followed the custom of letting such administrative posts remain in the family. In 1717 Bach accepted the position of Kapellmeister and music director to Prince Leopold of Anhalt in Cöthen, but a curious contretemps developed when the Duke of Weimar refused to release Bach from his obligation, and even had him held under arrest from Nov. 6 to Dec. 2, 1717, before Bach was finally allowed to proceed to Cöthen. The Cöthen period was one of the most productive in Bach's life; there he wrote his great set of *Brandenburg Concertos*, the *Clavierbüchlein für Wilhelm Friedemann Bach*, and the first book of *Das Wohltemperierte Clavier*. In Oct. 1719 Bach was in Halle once more, but again missed meeting Handel, who had already gone to England. In 1720 Bach accompanied Prince Leopold to Karlsbad. A tragedy supervened when Bach's devoted wife was taken ill and died before Bach could be called to her side; she was buried on July 7, 1720, leaving Bach to take care of their 7 children. In 1720 Bach made a long journey to Hamburg, where he again met the aged Reinken, who was then 97 years old. It is a part of the Bach legend that Reinken was greatly impressed with Bach's virtuosity and exclaimed, "I believed that the art of organ playing was dead, but it lives in you!" Bach remained a widower for nearly a year and a half before he married his 2nd wife, Anna Magdalena Wilcken, a daughter of a court trumpeter at Weissenfels, on Dec. 3, 1721. They had 13 children during their happy marital life. New avenues were opened to Bach when Johann Kuh-

nau, the cantor of Leipzig, died, on June 5, 1722. Although Bach applied for his post, the Leipzig authorities offered it first to Telemann of Hamburg, and when he declined, to Christoph Graupner of Darmstadt; only when Graupner was unable to obtain a release from his current position was Bach given the post. He traveled to Leipzig on Feb. 7, 1723, for a trial performance, earning a favorable reception. On April 22, 1723, Bach was elected to the post of cantor of the city of Leipzig and was officially installed on May 31, 1723. As director of church music, Bach's duties included the care of musicians for the Thomaskirche, Nicolaikirche, Matthaeikirche, and Petrikirche, and he was also responsible for the provision of the music to be performed at the Thomaskirche and Nicolaikirche. There were more mundane obligations that Bach was expected to discharge, such as gathering firewood for the Thomasschule, about which Bach had recurrent disputes with the rector; eventually he sought the intervention of the Elector of Saxony in the affair. It was in Leipzig that Bach created his greatest sacred works: the *St. John Passion,* the Mass in B minor, and the *Christmas Oratorio.* In 1729 he organized at the Thomasschule the famous Collegium Musicum, composed of professional musicians and univ. students with whom he gave regular weekly concerts; he led this group until 1737, and again from 1739 to 1741. He made several visits to Dresden, where his eldest son, Wilhelm Friedemann, served as organist at the Sophienkirche. In June 1747 Bach joined the Societät der Musikalischen Wissenschaften, a scholarly organization founded by a former member of the Collegium Musicum, Lorenz C. Mizler, a learned musician, Latinist, and mathematician who spent his life confounding his contemporaries and denouncing them as charlatans and ignorant pretenders to knowledge. The rules of the society required an applicant to submit a sample of his works; Bach contributed a triple canon in 6 parts and presented it, along with the canonic variations *Vom Himmel hoch da komm' ich her.* This was one of Bach's last works. He suffered from a cataract that was gradually darkening his vision. A British optician named John Taylor, who plied his trade in Saxony, operated on Bach's eyes in the spring of 1749; the operation, performed with the crude instruments of the time, left Bach almost totally blind. The same specialist operated also on Handel, with no better results. The etiology of Bach's last illness is unclear. It is said that on July 18, 1750, his vision suddenly returned (possibly when the cataract receded spontaneously), but a cerebral hemorrhage supervened, and a few days later Bach was dead. Bach's great contrapuntal work, *Die Kunst der Fuge,* remained unfinished. The final page bears this inscription by C.P.E. Bach: "Upon this Fugue, in which the name B-A-C-H is applied as a countersubject, the author died." Bach's widow, Anna Magdalena, survived him by nearly 10 years; she died on Feb. 27, 1760. In 1895 Wilhelm His, an anatomy prof. at the Univ. of Leipzig, performed an exhumation of Bach's body, made necessary because of the deterioration of the wooden coffin, and took remarkable photographs of Bach's skeleton, which he publ. under the title *J.S. Bach, Forschungen über dessen Grabstätte, Gebeine und Antlitz* (Leipzig, 1895). On July 28, 1949, on the 199th anniversary of Bach's death, his coffin was transferred to the choir room of the Thomaskirche.

Of Bach's 20 children, 10 reached maturity. His sons Wilhelm Friedemann, Carl Philipp Emanuel, **Johann Christoph Friedrich**, and **Johann (John) Christian** (the "London" Bach) made their mark as independent composers. Among Bach's notable pupils were Johann Friedrich Agricola, Johann Christoph Altnikol, Heinrich Nilolaus Gerber, Johann Theophilus Goldberg, Gottfried August Homilius, Johann Philipp Kirnberger, Johann Christian Kettel, Johann Tobias Krebs, and Johann Ludwig Krebs. It is historically incorrect to maintain that Bach was not appreciated by his contemporaries; Bach's sons Carl Philipp Emanuel and the "London" Bach kept his legacy alive for a generation after Bach's death. True, they parted from Bach's art of contrapuntal writing; Carl Philipp Emanuel turned to the fashionable *style galant*, and wrote keyboard works of purely harmonic content. The first important biography of Bach was publ. in 1802, by J.N. Forkel.

Dramatic accounts of music history are often inflated. It is conventional to say that Bach's music was rescued from oblivion by Mendelssohn, who conducted the *St. Matthew Passion* in Berlin in 1829, but Mozart and Beethoven had practiced Bach's preludes and fugues. Bach's genius was never dimmed; he was never a prophet without a world. The centennial of Bach's death in 1850 was observed by the inception of the Leipzig Bach-Gesellschaft, a society founded by Carl Becker, Moritz Hauptmann, Otto Jahn, and Robert Schumann. Concurrently, the publishing firm of Breitkopf & Härtel inaugurated the publication of the complete edition of Bach's works; a Neue Bach-Gesellschaft was founded in 1900; it supervised the publication of the important *Bach-Jahrbuch*, a scholarly journal begun in 1904. The bicentennial of Bach's death, in 1950, brought about a new series of memorials and celebrations. With the development of the electric phonograph record, and later of the digital method of recording with high fidelity, Bach's works were made available to large masses of the public. Modern composers, even those who champion the total abandonment of all conventional methods of composition and the abolition of musical notation, are irresistibly drawn to Bach as a precursor; suffice it to mention Alban Berg's use of Bach's chorale *Es ist genug* in the concluding section of his Violin Concerto dedicated to the memory of Alma Mahler's young daughter. It is interesting to note also that Bach's famous acronym B-A-C-H consists of 4 different notes in a chromatic alternation, thus making it possible to use it as an element of a 12-tone row. Bach's images have been imblazoned on popular T-shirts; postage stamps with his portrait have been issued by a number of nations in Europe, Asia, and Africa. The slogan "Back to Bach," adopted by composers of the early 20th century, seems to hold true for every musical era.

In the list of Bach's works given below, each composition is identified by the BWV (Bach-Werke-Verzeichnis) number established by W. Schmieder in his *Thematisch-systematisches Verzeichnis der musikalischen Werke von Johann Sebastian Bach. Bach-Werke-Verzeichnis* (Leipzig, 1950; 3rd ed., 1961).

WORKS: CHURCH CANTATAS: About 200 are extant. The following list gives the BWV number, title, and date of first performance: 1, *Wie schön leuchtet der Morgenstern* (March 25, 1725); 2, *Ach Gott, vom Himmel sieh darein* (June 18, 1724); 3, *Ach Gott, wie manches, Herzeleid* (Jan. 14, 1725); 4, *Christ lag in Todesbanden* (c.1707–8); 5, *Wo soll ich fliehen hin* (Oct. 15, 1724); 6, *Bleib bei uns, denn es will Abend werden* (April 2, 1725); 7, *Christ unser Herr zum Jordan kam* (June 24, 1724); 8, *Liebster Gott, wann werd ich sterben?* (Sept. 24, 1724); 9, *Es ist das Heil uns kommen her* (c.1732–35); 10, *Meine Seel erhebt den Herren* (July 2, 1724); 11, *Lobet Gott in seinen Reichen* (Ascension oratorio; May 19, 1735); 12, *Weinen, Klagen, Sorgen, Zagen* (April 22, 1714); 13, *Meine Seufzer, meine Tränen* (Jan. 20, 1726); 14, *Wär Gott nicht mit uns diese Zeit* (Jan. 30, 1735); 16, *Herr Gott, dich Loben wir* (Jan. 1, 1726); 17, *Wer Dank opfert, der preiset mich* (Sept. 22, 1726); 18, *Gleichwie der Regen und Schnee vom Himmel fällt* (c.1714); 19, *Es erhub sich ein Streit* (Sept. 29, 1726); 20, *O Ewigkeit, du Donnerwort* (June 11, 1724); 21, *Ich hatte viel Bekummernis* (c.1714); 22, *Jesus nahm zu sich die Zwölfe* (Feb. 7, 1723); 23, *Du wahrer Gott und Davids Sohn* (Feb. 7, 1723); 24, *Ein ungefärbt Gemüte* (June 20, 1723); 25, *Es ist nichts Gesundes an meinem Leibe* (Aug. 29, 1723); 26, *Ach wie flüchtig, ach wie nichtig* (Nov. 19, 1724); 27, *Wer weiss, wie nahe mir mein Ende!* (Oct. 6, 1726); 28, *Gottlob! nun geht das Jahr zu Ende* (Dec. 30, 1725); 29, *Wir danken dir, Gott, wir danken dir* (Aug. 27, 1731); 30, *Freue dich, erlöste Schar* (c.1738); 31, *Der Himmel lacht! die Erde jubilieret* (April 21, 1715); 32, *Liebster Jesu, mein Verlangen* (Jan. 13, 1726); 33, *Allein zu dir, Herr Jesu Christ* (Sept. 3, 1724); 34, *O ewiges Feuer, O Ursprung der Liebe* (based upon 34a; early 1740s); 34a, *O ewiges Feuer, O Ursprung der Liebe* (part of score not extant; 1726); 35, *Geist und Seele wird verwirret* (Sept. 8, 1726); 36, *Schwingt freudig euch empor* (based upon secular cantata 36c; Dec. 2, 1731); 37, *Wer da gläubet und getauft wird* (May 18, 1724); 38, *Aus tiefer Not schrei ich zu dir* (Oct. 29, 1724); 39, *Brich dem Hungrigen dein Brot* (June 23, 1726); 40, *Dazu ist erschienen der Sohn Gottes* (Dec. 26, 1723); 41, *Jesu, nun sei gepreiset* (Jan. 1, 1725); 42, *Am Abend aber desselbigen Sabbats* (April 8, 1725); 43, *Gott fähret auf mit Jauchzen* (May 30, 1726); 44, *Sie werden euch in die Bann tun* (May 21, 1724); 45, *Es ist dir gesagt, Mensch, was gut ist* (Aug. 11, 1726); 46, *Schauet doch und sehet* (Aug. 1, 1723); 47, *Wer sich selbst erhöhet* (Oct. 13, 1726); 48, *Ich elender Mensch, wer wird mich erlösen* (Oct. 3, 1723); 49, *Ich geh und suche mit Verlangen* (Nov. 3, 1726); 50, *Nun ist das Heil und die Kraft* (date unknown); 51, *Jauchzet Gott in allen Landen!* (Sept. 17, 1730); 52, *Falsche Welt, dir trau ich nicht* (Nov. 24, 1726); 54, *Widerstehe doch der Sünde* (July 15, 1714); 55, *Ich armer Mensch, ich Sündenknecht* (Nov. 17, 1726);

56, *Ich will den Kreuzstab gerne tragen* (Oct. 27, 1726); 57, *Selig ist der Mann* (Dec. 26, 1725); 58, *Ach Gott, wie manches Herzeleid* (Jan. 5, 1727); 59, *Wer mich liebet, der wird mein Wort halten* (c.1723–24); 60, *O Ewigkeit, du Donnerwort* (Nov. 7, 1723); 61, *Nun komm, der Heiden Heiland* (1714); 62, *Nun komm, der Heiden Heiland* (Dec. 3, 1724); 63, *Christen, ätzet diesen Tag* (c.1716); 64, *Sehet, welch eine Liebe* (Dec. 27, 1723); 65, *Sie werden aus Saba alle kommen* (Jan. 6, 1724); 66, *Erfreut euch, ihr Herzen* (based upon lost secular cantata 66a; April 10, 1724); 67, *Halt im Gedächtnis Jesum Christ* (April 16, 1724); 68, *Also hat Gott die Welt geliebt* (May 21, 1725); 69, *Lobe den Herrn, meine Seele* (based upon 69a; 1740s); 69a, *Lobe den Herrn, meine Seele* (Aug. 15, 1723); 70, *Wachet! betet! betet! wachet!* (based upon 70a; Nov. 21, 1723); 70a, *Wachet! betet! betet! wachet!* (music not extant; Dec. 6, 1716); 71, *Gott ist mein König* (Feb. 4, 1708); 72, *Alles nur nach Gottes Willen* (Jan. 27, 1726); 73, *Herr, wie du willt, so schicks mit mir* (Jan. 23, 1724); 74, *Wer mich liebet, der wird mein Wort halten* (based partly upon 59; May 20, 1725); 75, *Die Elenden sollen essen* (May 30, 1723); 76, *Die Himmel erzählen die Ehre Gottes* (June 6, 1723); 77, *Du sollt Gott, deinen Herren, lieben* (Aug. 22, 1723); 78, *Jesu, der du meine Seele* (Sept. 10, 1724); 79, *Gott der Herr ist Sonn und Schild* (Oct. 31, 1725); 80, *Ein feste Burg ist unser Gott* (based upon 80a; Oct. 31, 1724); 80a, *Alles, was von Gott geboren* (music not extant; 1715); 80b, *Ein feste Burg ist unser Gott* (Oct. 31, 1723); 81, *Jesus schläft, was soll ich hoffen?* (Jan. 30, 1724); 82, *Ich habe genug* (Feb. 2, 1727); 83, *Erfreute Zeit im neuen Bunde* (Feb. 2, 1724); 84, *Ich bin vergnügt mit meinem Glücke* (Feb. 9, 1727); 85, *Ich bin ein guter Hirt* (April 15, 1725); 86, *Wahrlich, wahrlich, ich sage euch* (May 14, 1724); 87, *Bisher habt ihr nichts gebeten* (May 6, 1725); 88, *Siehe, ich will viel Fischer aussenden* (July 21, 1726); 89, *Was soll ich aus dir machen, Ephraim?* (Oct. 24, 1723); 90, *Es reisset euch ein schrecklich Ende* (Nov. 14, 1723); 91, *Gelobet seist du, Jesu Christ* (Dec. 25, 1724); 92, *Ich hab in Gottes Herz und Sinn* (Jan. 28, 1725); 93, *Wer nur den lieben Gott lässt walten* (July 9, 1724); 94, *Was frag ich nach der Welt* (Aug. 6, 1724); 95, *Christus, der ist mein Leben* (Sept. 12, 1723); 96, *Herr Christ, der einge Gottessohn* (Oct. 8, 1724); 97, *In allen meinen Taten* (1734); 98, *Was Gott tut, das ist wohlgetan* (Nov. 10, 1726); 99, *Was Gott tut, das ist wohlgetan* (Sept. 17, 1724); 100, *Was Gott tut, das ist wohlgetan* (c.1732–35); 101, *Nimm von uns, Herr, du treuer Gott* (Aug. 13, 1724); 102, *Herr, deine Augen sehen nach dem Glauben* (Aug. 25, 1726); 103, *Ihr werdet weinen und heulen* (April 22, 1725); 104, *Du Hirte Israel* (April 23, 1724); 105, *Herr, gehe nicht ins Gericht* (July 25, 1723); 106, *Gottes Ziet ist die allerbeste Zeit* (c.1707); 107, *Was willst du dich betrüben* (July 23, 1724); 108, *Es ist euch gut, dass ich hingehe* (April 29, 1725); 109, *Ich glaube, lieber Herr, hilf meinem Unglauben!* (Oct. 17, 1723); 110, *Unser Mund sei voll Lachens* (Dec. 25, 1725); 111, *Was mein Gott will, das g'scheh allzeit* (Jan. 21, 1725); 112, *Der Herr ist mein getreuer Hirt* (April 8, 1731); 113, *Herr Jesu Christ, du höchstes Gut* (Aug. 20, 1724); 114, *Ach, lieben Christen, seid getrost* (Oct. 1, 1724); 115, *Mache dich, mein Geist, bereit* (Nov. 5, 1724); 116, *Du Friedefürst, Herr Jesu Christ* (Nov. 26, 1724); 117, *Sei Lob und Ehr dem höchsten Gut* (c.1728–31); 119, *Preise, Jerusalem, den Herrn* (Aug. 30, 1723); 120, *Gott, man lobet dich in der Stille* (c.1728–29); 120a, *Herr Gott, Beherrscher aller Dinge* (based upon 120; part of score not extant; c.1729); 120b, *Gott, man lobet dich in der Stille* (based upon 120; music not extant; 1730); 121, *Christum wir sollen loben schon* (Dec. 26, 1724); 122, *Das neugeborne Kindelein* (Dec. 31, 1724); 123, *Liebster Immanuel, Herzog der Frommen* (Jan. 6, 1725); 124, *Meinen Jesum lass ich nicht* (Jan. 7, 1725); 125, *Mit Fried und Freud ich fahr dahin* (Feb. 2, 1725); 126, *Erhalt uns, Herr, bei deinem Wort* (Feb. 4, 1725); 127, *Herr Jesu Christ, wahr' Mensch und Gott* (Feb. 11, 1725); 128, *Auf Christi Himmelfahrt allein* (May 10, 1725); 129, *Gelobet sei der Herr, mein Gott* (c.1726–27); 130, *Herr Gott, dich loben alle wir* (Sept. 29, 1724); 131, *Aus der Tiefen rufe ich, Herr, zu dir* (1707); 132, *Bereitet die Wege, bereitet die Bahn!* (1715); 133, *Ich freue mich in dir* (Dec. 27, 1724); 134, *Ein Herz, das seinen Jesum lebend weiss* (based upon secular contata 134a; April 11, 1724); 135, *Ach Herr, mich armen Sünder* (June 25, 1724); 136, *Erforsche mich, Gott, und erfahre mein Herz* (July 18, 1723); 137, *Lobe den Herren, den mächtigen König der Ehren* (Aug. 19, 1725); 138, *Warum betrübst du dich, mein Herz?* (Sept. 5, 1723); 139, *Wohl dem, der sich auf seinen Gott* (Nov. 12, 1724); 140, *Wachet auf, ruft uns die Stimme* (Nov. 25, 1731); 144, *Nimm, was dein ist, und gehe hin* (Feb. 6, 1724); 145, *Ich lebe, mein Herze, zu deinem Ergötzen* (c. 1729); 146, *Wir müssen durch viel Trübsal* (c.1726–28); 147, *Herz und Mund und Tat und Leben* (based upon 147a; July 2, 1723); 147a, *Herz und Mund und Tat und Leben* (not extant; Dec. 20, 1716); 148, *Bringet dem Herrn Ehre seines Namens* (Sept. 19, 1723); 149, *Man singet mit Freuden vom Sieg* (c.1728–29); 150, *Nach dir, Herr, verlanget mich* (c.1708–9); 151, *Süsser Trost, mein Jesus kommt* (Dec. 27, 1725); 152, *Tritt auf die Glaubensbahn* (Dec. 30, 1714); 153, *Schau, lieber Gott, wie meine Feind* (Jan. 2, 1724); 154, *Mein liebster Jesus ist verloren* (Jan. 9, 1724); 155, *Mein Gott, wie lang, ach lange* (Jan. 19, 1716); 156, *Ich steh mit einem Fuss im Grabe* (Jan. 23, 1729); 157, *Ich lasse dich nicht, du segnest mich denn* (Feb. 6, 1727); 158, *Der Friede sei mit dir* (date unknown); 159, *Sehet, wir gehn hinauf gen Jerusalem* (Feb. 27, 1729); 161, *Komm, du süsse Todesstunde* (Oct. 6, 1715); 162, *Ach! ich sehe, jetzt, da ich zur Hochzeit gehe* (Nov. 3, 1715); 163, *Nur jedem das Seine* (Nov. 24, 1715); 164, *Ihr, die ihr euch von Christo nennet* (Aug. 26, 1725); 165, *O heilges Geist- und Wasserbad* (June 16, 1715); 166, *Wo gehest du hin?* (May 7, 1724); 167, *Ihr Menschen, rühmet Gottes Liebe* (June 24, 1723); 168, *Tue Rechnung! Donnerwort* (July 29, 1725); 169, *Gott soll allein mein Herze haben* (Oct. 20, 1726); 170, *Vergnügte Ruh', beliebte Seelenlust* (July 28, 1726); 171, *Gott, wie dein Name, so ist auch dein Ruhm* (c.1729); 172, *Erschallet, ihr Lieder* (May 20, 1714); 173, *Erhöhtes Fleisch und Blut* (based upon secular contata 173a; May 29, 1724); 174, *Ich liebe den Höchsten von ganzem Gemüte* (June 6, 1729);

175, *Er rufet seinen Schafen mit Namen* (May 22, 1725); 176, *Es ist ein trotzig, und versagt Ding* (May 27, 1725); 177, *Ich ruf zu dir, Herr Jesu Christ* (July 6, 1732); 178, *Wo Gott der Herr nicht bei uns hält* (July 30, 1724); 179, *Siehe zu, dass deine Gottesfurcht* (Aug. 8, 1723); 180, *Schmücke dich, o liebe Seele* (Oct. 22, 1724); 181, *Leichtgesinnte Flattergeister* (Feb. 13, 1724); 182, *Himmelskönig, sei willkommen* (1714); 183, *Sie werden euch in den Bann tun* (May 13, 1725); 184, *Erwünschtes Freudenlicht* (based upon lost secular cantata 184a; May 30, 1724); 185, *Barmherziges Herze der ewigen Liebe* (July 14, 1715); 186, *Ärgre dich, o Seele, nicht* (based upon 186a; July 11, 1723); 186a, *Ärgre dich o Seele, nicht* (not extant; Dec. 13, 1716); 187, *Es wartet alles auf dich* (Aug. 4, 1726); 188, *Ich habe meine Zuversicht* (c.1728); 190, *Singet dem Herrn ein neues Lied!* (part of score not extant; Jan. 1, 1724); 190a, *Singet dem Herrn ein neues Lied!* (based upon 190; not extant; 1730); 191, *Gloria in excelsis Deo* (based upon 232, Mass in B minor; c.1740); 192, *Nun danket alle Gott* (part of score not extant; 1730); 193, *Ihr Tore zu Zion* (c.1727); 194, *Höchsterwünschtes Freudenfest* (based upon lost secular cantata 194a; Nov. 2, 1723); 195, *Dem Gerechten muss das Licht* (c.1737); 196, *Der Herr denket an uns* (c.1708); 197, *Gott ist unsre Zuversicht* (c.1742); 197a, *Ehre sie Gott in der Höhe* (part of score not extant, c.1728); 199, *Mein Herze schwimmt im Blut* (Aug. 12, 1714); 200, *Bekennen will ich seinen Namen* (fragment only extant; c.1742). BWV numbers have been assigned to the following lost or incomplete cantatas: 223, *Meine Seele soll Gott loben* (not extant; date unknown); 224a, *Klagt, Kinder, klagt es aller Welt* (music not extant; March 24, 1729); Anh., 1, *Gesegnet ist die Zuversicht* (not extant; date unknown); Anh. 2, fragment only; Anh. 3, *Gott, gib dein Gerichte dem Könige* (music not extant; 1730) Anh. 4, *Wünschet Jerusalem Glück* (music not extant; c.1727); Anh. 4a, *Wünschet Jerusalem Glück* (music not extant; 1730); Anh. 5, *Lobet den Herrn, alle seine Heerscharen* (music not extant; Dec. 10, 1718); Anh. 14, *Sein Segen fliesst daher wie ein Strom* (music not extant; Feb. 12, 1725); Anh. 15, *Siehe, der Hüter Israel* (not extant; April 27, 1724); Anh. 17, *Mein Gott, nimm die gerechte Seele* (not extant; date unknown); 1,045, title unknown (autograph fragment only extant; c.1742); also the following without BWV numbers: *Herrscher des Himmels, König der Ehren* (final chorus only, based upon secular cantata 208, extant; Aug. 29, 1740); *Ich bin ein Pilgrim auf der Welt* (fragment of 4th movement only extant; April 18, 1729); *Ihr wallenden Wolken* (not extant; date unknown); *Leb ich oder leb ich nicht* (music not extant; May 19, 1715); *Sie werden euch in den Bann tun* (6-bar sketch only); etc. BWV numbers have been assigned to the following doubtful and spurious cantatas: 15, *Denn du wirst meine Seele* (by J.L. Bach); 53, *Schlage doch, gewünschte Stunde* (by G.M. Hoffmann); 141, *Das ist je gewisslich wahr* (by Telemann); 142, *Uns ist ein Kind geboren* (doubtful); 143, *Lobe den Herrn, meine Seele* (doubtful); 160, *Ich weiss, dass mein Erlöser lebt* (by Telemann); 189, *Meine Seele rühmt und preist* (doubtful); 217, *Gedenke, Herr, wie es uns gehet* (spuri-

ous); 218, *Gott der Hoffnung erfülle euch* (by Telemann); 219, *Siehe, es hat überwunden der Löwe* (by Telemann); 220, *Lobt ihn mit Herz und Munde* (spurious); 221, *Wer sucht die Pracht, wer wünscht den Glanz* (spurious); 222, *Mein Odem ist schwach* (by J.E. Bach); Anh. 16, *Schliesset die Gruft! ihr Trauerglocken* (not extant; doubtful); also without BWV number, *Siehe, eine Jungfrau ist schwanger* (doubtful).

SECULAR CANTATAS: 22 are extant in full: 30a, *Angenehmes Wiederau, freue dich* (Sept. 28, 1737); 36b, *Die Freude reget sich* (c.1735); 36c, *Schwingt freudig euch empor* (1725); 134a, *Die Zeit, die Tag und Jahre macht* (Jan. 1, 1719); 173a, Durchlauchster Leopold (c.1722); 198, *Trauer Ode: Lass, Fürstin, lass noch einen Strahl* (Oct. 17, 1727); 201, *Der Streit zwischen Phoebus und Pan: Geschwinde, ihr wirbeln der Winde* (c.1729); 202, *Weichet nur, betrübte Schatten* (c.1718–23); 203, *Amore traditore* (date unknown); 204, *Ich bin in mir vergnügt* (c.1726–27); 205, *Der zufriedengestellte Äolus: Zerreisset, zerspringet, zertrümmert die Gruft* (Aug. 3, 1725); 206, *Schleicht, spielende Wellen* (Oct. 7, 1736); 207, *Vereinigte Zwietracht der wechselnden Saiten* (Dec. 11, 1726); 207a, *Auf, schmetternde Töne* (Aug. 3, 1735); 208, *Was mir behagt, ist nur die muntre Jagd!* (c.1713); 209, *Non sa che sia dolore* (c.1734); 210, *O holder Tag, erwünschte Zeit* (c.1740); 211, *Schweigt stille, plaudert nicht* (Coffee Cantata; c.1734–35); 212, *Mer hahn en neue Oberkeet* (Peasant Cantata; Aug. 30, 1742); 213, *Hercules auf dem Scheidewege: Lasst uns sorgen, lasst uns wachen* (Sept. 5, 1733); 214, *Tönet, ihr Pauken! Erschallet, Trompeten!* (Dec. 8, 1733); 215, *Preise dein Glücke, gesegnetes Sachsen* (Oct. 5, 1734). BWV numbers have been assigned to the following lost or incomplete cantatas: 36a, *Steigt freudig in die Luft* (music not extant; Nov. 30, 1726); 66a, *Der Himmel dacht auf Anhalts Ruhm und Glück* (music not extant; Dec. 10, 1718); 184a, title unknown (not extant; Dec. 10, 1718); 193a, *Ihr Häuser des Himmels, ihr scheinenden Lichter* (music not extant; Aug. 3, 1727); 194a, title unknown (not extant); 205a, *Blast Lärmen, ihr Feinde!* (based upon 205; music not extant; Feb. 19, 1734); 208a, *Was mir behagt, ist nur die muntre Jagd!* (music not extant; c.1740–42); 210a, *O angenehme Melodei!* (music not extant; c.1738–40); 216, *Vergnügte Pleissenstadt* (only partially extant; Feb. 5, 1728); 216a, *Erwählte Pleissenstadt* (music not extant; c.1728); 249a, *Entfliehet, verschwindet, entweichet, ihr Sorgen* (music not extant; Feb. 23, 1725); 249b, *Die Feier des Genius: Verjaget, zerstreuet, zerrüttet, ihr Sterne* (music not extant; Aug. 25, 1726); Anh. 6, *Dich loben die lieblichen Strahlen* (music not extant; Jan. 1, 1720); Anh. 7, *Heut ist gewiss ein guter Tag* (music not extant; Dec. 10, 1720); Anh. 8, title unknown (not extant); Anh. 9, *Entfernet euch, ihr heitern Sterne* (music not extant; May 12, 1727); Anh. 10, *So kämpfet nur, ihr muntern Töne* (music not extant; Aug. 25, 1731); Anh. 11, *Es lebe der König, der Vater im Lande* (music not extant; Aug. 3, 1732); Anh. 12, *Frohes Volk, vergnügte Sachsen* (based upon Anh. 18; music not extant; Aug. 3, 1733); Anh. 13, *Willkommen! Ihr herrschenden Götter* (music not extant; April 28,

1738); Anh. 18, *Froher Tag, verlangte Stunden* (music not extant; June 5, 1732); Anh. 19, *Thomana sass annoch betrübt* (music not extant; Nov. 21, 1734); Anh. 20, title unknown (not extant); also, without BWV number, *Auf! süss entzückende Gewalt* (music not extant; Nov. 27, 1725).

OTHER CHURCH MUSIC: 232, Mass in B minor (assembled c.1747–49 from music previously composed by Bach); 233, 233a, 234–36, 4 *missae breves:* F major (Kyrie in F major), A major, G minor, G major (late 1730s); 237–41, 5 settings of the Sanctus: C major, D major, D minor, G major, D major (although preserved in Bach's own hand, these appear to be arrangements of works by other composers, 238 excepted); 243a, Magnificat in E-flat major (including 4 Christmas texts: *Vom Himmel hoch, Freut euch und jubiliert, Gloria in excelsis, Virga Jesse floruit;* Dec. 25, 1723); 243, a revision of the preceding, without Christmas texts, as Magnificat in D major (c.1728–31); 244, *Matthäuspassion* (*St. Matthew Passion;* first perf. April 11, 1727, or April 15, 1729); 245, *Johannespassion* (*St. John Passion;* April 7, 1724; later revised); 248, *Weihnachtsoratorium* (*Christmas Oratorio*), 6 cantatas for Christmas to Epiphany: *Jauchzet, frohlocket, auf preiset die Tage* (Dec. 25, 1734), *Und es waren Hirten in derselben Gegend* (Dec. 26, 1734), *Herrscher des Himmels, erhöre das Lallen* (Dec. 27, 1734), *Fallt mit Danken, fallt mit Loben* (Jan. 1, 1735), *Ehre sei dir, Gott, gesungen* (Jan. 2, 1735), *Herr, wenn die stolzen Feinde schnauben* (Jan. 6, 1735); 249, *Easter Oratorio* (first perf. as a cantata, April 1, 1725; revised as an oratorio 1732–35); motets, including 225, *Singet dem Herrn ein Neues Lied* (May 12, 1727), 226, *Der Geist hilft unser Schwachheit auf* (Oct. 24, 1729), 227, *Jesu, meine Freude* (July 18, 1723), 228, *Fürchte dich nicht* (Feb. 4, 1726), 229, *Komm, Jesu, komm!* (March 26, 1730), 230, *Lobet den Herrn alle Heiden* (date unknown). Also 247, *St. Mark Passion* (score and parts not extant; March 23, 1731; partial reconstruction from other works made by D. Hellmann, Stuttgart, 1964); 246, *St. Luke Passion* (spurious).

CHORALES: 3 wedding chorales for 4 Voices: 250, *Was Gott tut das ist wohlgetan;* 251, *Sei Lob und Ehr' dem höchsten Gut;* 252, *Nun danket alle Gott.* Also, 186 arrangements for 4 Voices: 253, *Ach bleib bei uns, Herr Jesu Christ;* 254, *Ach Gott, erhör' mein Seufzen;* 255, *Ach Gott und Herr;* 256, *Ach lieben Christen, seid getrost;* 259, *Ach, was soll ich Sünder machen;* 260, *Allein Gott in der Höh' sei Ehr';* 261, *Allein zu dir, Herr Jesu Christ;* 262, *Alle Menschen müssen sterben;* 263, *Alles ist an Gottes Segen;* 264, *Als der gütige Gott;* 265, *Als Jesus Christus in der Nacht;* 266, *Als vierzig Tag nach Ostern;* 267, *An Wasserflüssen Babylon;* 268, *Auf, auf, mein Herz, und du mein ganzer Sinn;* 269, *Aus meines Herzens Grunde;* 270, *Befiehl du deine Wege;* 271, *Befiehl du deine Wege;* 272, *Befiehl du deine Wege;* 273, *Christ, der du bist der helle Tag;* 274, *Christe, der du bist Tag und Licht;* 275, *Christe, du Beistand deiner Kreuzgemeinde;* 276, *Christ ist erstanden;* 277, *Christ lag in Todesbanden;* 278, *Christ lag in Todesbanden;* 279, *Christ lag in Todesbanden;* 280, *Christ, unser Herr, zum Jordan kam;* 281, *Christus,*

der ist mein Leben; 282, *Christus, der ist mein Leben;* 283, *Christus, der uns selig macht;* 284, *Christus ist erstanden, hat überwunden;* 285, *Da der Herr Christ zu Tische sass;* 286, *Danket dem Herren;* 287, *Dank sei Gott in der Höhe;* 288, *Das alte Jahr vergangen ist;* 289, *Das alte Jahr vergangen ist;* 290, *Das walt' Gott Vater und Gott Sohn;* 291, *Das walt' mein Gott, Vater, Sohn und heiliger Geist;* 292, *Den Vater dort oben;* 293, *Der du bist drei in Einigkeit;* 294, *Der Tag, der ist so freudenreich;* 295, *Das heil'gen Geistes reiche Gnad';* 296, *Die Nacht ist kommen;* 297, *Die Sonn' hat sich mit ihrem Glanz;* 298, *Dies sind die heil'gen zehn Gebot';* 299, *Dir, dir, Jehova, will ich singen;* 300, *Du grosser Schmerzensmann;* 301, *Du, o schönes Weltgebäude;* 302, *Ein' feste Burg ist unser Gott;* 303, *Ein' feste Burg ist unser Gott;* 304, *Eins ist Not! ach Herr, dies Eine;* 305, *Erbarm' dich mein, o, Herre Gott;* 306, *Erstanden ist der heil'ge Christ;* 307, *Es ist gewisslich an der Zeit;* 308, *Es spricht der Unweisen Mund wohl;* 309, *Es stehn vor Gottes Throne;* 310, *Es wird schier der letzte Tag herkommen;* 311, *Es woll' uns Gott genädig sein;* 312, *Es woll' uns Gott genädig sein;* 327, *Für deinen Thron tret' ich hiermit;* 313, *Für Freuden lasst uns springen;* 314, *Gelobet seist du, Jesu Christ;* 315, *Gib dich zufrieden und sei stille;* 316, *Gott, der du selber bist das Licht;* 317, *Gott, der Vater, wohn' uns bei;* 318, *Gottes Sohn ist kommen;* 319, *Gott hat das Evangelium;* 320, *Gott lebet noch;* 321, *Gottlob, es geht nunmehr zu Ende;* 322, *Gott sei gelobet und gebenedeiet;* 323, *Gott sei uns gnädig;* 325, *Heilig, heilig, heilig;* 326, *Herr Gott, dich loben alle wir;* 328, *Herr, Gott, dich loben wir;* 329, *Herr, ich denk' an jene Zeit;* 330, *Herr, ich habe missgehandelt;* 331, *Herr, ich habe missgehandelt;* 332, *Herr Jesu Christ, dich zu uns wend';* 333, *Herr Jesu Christ, du hast bereit't;* 334, *Herr Jesu Christ, du höchstes Gut;* 335, *Herr Jesu Christ, mein's Lebens Licht;* 336, *Herr Jesu Christ, wahr'r Mensch und Gott;* 337, *Herr, nun lass in Frieden;* 338, *Herr, straf mich nicht in deinem Zorn;* 339, *Herr, wie du willst, so schick's mit mir;* 340, *Herzlich lieb hab ich dich, o Herr;* 341, *Heut' ist, o Mensch, ein grosser Trauertag;* 342, *Heut' triumphieret Gottes Sohn;* 343, *Hilf, Gott, dass mir's gelinge;* 344, *Hilf, Herr Jesu, lass gelingen;* 345, *Ich bin ja, Herr, in deiner Macht;* 346, *Ich dank' dir, Gott, für all' Wohltat;* 347, *Ich dank' dir, lieber Herre;* 348, *Ich dank' dir, lieber Herre;* 349, *Ich dank' dis schon durch deinen Sohn;* 350, *Ich danke dir, o Gott, in deinem Throne;* 351, *Ich hab' mein' Sach' Gott heimgestellt;* 352, *Jesu, der du meine Seele;* 353, *Jesu, der du meine Seele;* 354, *Jesu, der du meine Seele;* 355, *Jesu, der du selbst so wohl;* 356, *Jesu, du mein liebstes Leben;* 357, *Jesu, Jesu, du bist mein;* 358, *Jesu, meine Freude;* 359, *Jesu meiner Seelen Wonne;* 360, *Jesu meiner Seelen Wonne;* 361, *Jesu, meines Herzens Freud';* 362, *Jesu, nun sei gepreiset;* 363, *Jesus Christus, unser Heiland;* 364, *Jesus Christus, unser Heiland;* 365, *Jesus, meine Zuversicht;* 366, *Ihr Gestirn', ihr hohlen Lüfte;* 367, *In allen meinen Taten;* 368, *In dulci jubilo;* 369, *Keinen hat Gott verlassen;* 370, *Komm, Gott Schöpfer, heiliger Geist;* 371, *Kyrie, Gott Vater in Ewigkeit;* 372, *Lass, o Herr, dein Ohr sich neigen;* 373, *Liebster Jesu, wir sind hier;*

374, *Lobet den Herren, denn er ist freundlich;* 375, *Lobt Gott, ihr Christen, allzugleich;* 376, *Lobt Gott, ihr Christen, allzugleich;* 377, *Mach's mit mir, Gott, nach deiner Güt';* 378, *Meine Augen schliess' ich jetzt;* 379, *Meinen Jesum lass' ich nicht, Jesus;* 380, *Meinen Jesum lass' ich nicht, weil;* 322, *Meine Seele erhebet den Herrn;* 381, *Meines Lebens letzte Zeit;* 382, *Mit Fried' und Freud' ich fahr' dahin;* 383, *Mitten wir im Leben sind;* 384, *Nicht so traurig, nicht so sehr;* 385, *Nun bitten wir den heiligen Geist;* 386, *Nun danket alle Gott;* 387, *Nun freut euch, Gottes Kinder all';* 388, *Nun freut euch, lieben Christen, g'mein;* 389, *Nun lob', mein' Seel', den Herren;* 390, *Nun lob', mein' Seel', den Herren;* 391, *Nun preiset alle Gottes Barmherzigkeit;* 392, *Nun ruhen alle Wälder;* 393, *O Welt, sieh hier dein Leben;* 394, *O Welt, sieh dein Leben;* 395, *O Welt, sieh hier dein Leben;* 396, *Nun sich der Tag geendet hat;* 397, *O Ewigkeit, du Donnerwort;* 398, *O Gott, du frommer Gott;* 399, *O Gott, du frommer Gott;* 400, *O Herzensangst, o Bangigkeit;* 401, *O Lamm Gottes, unschuldig;* 402, *O Mensch, bewein' dein' Sünde gross;* 403, *O Mensch, schau Jesum Christum an;* 404, *O Traurigkeit, o Herzeleid;* 405, *O wie selig seid ihr doch, ihr Frommen;* 406, *O wie selig seid ihr doch, ihr Frommen;* 407, *O wir armen Sünder;* 408, *Schaut, ihr Sünder;* 409, *Seelen-Bräutigam;* 410, *Sei gegrüsset, Jesu gütig;* 411, *Singet dem Herrn ein neues Lied;* 412, *So gibst du nun, mein Jesu, gute Nacht;* 413, *Sollt' ich meinem Gott nicht singen;* 414, *Uns ist ein Kindlein heut' gebor'n;* 415, *Valet will ich dir geben;* 416, *Vater unser im Himmelreich;* 417, *Von Gott will ich nicht lassen;* 418, *Von Gott will ich nicht lassen;* 419, *Von Gott will ich nicht lassen;* 257, *Wär' Gott nicht mit uns diese Zeit;* 420, *Warum betrübst du dich, mein Herz;* 421, *Warum betrübst du dich, mein Herz;* 422, *Warum sollt' ich mich denn grämen;* 423, *Was betrübst du dich, mein Herze;* 424, *Was bist du doch, o Seele, so betrübet;* 425, *Was willst du dich, o meine Seele;* 426, *Weltlich Ehr' und zeitlich Gut;* 427, *Wenn ich in Angst und Not;* 428, *Wenn mein Stündlein vorhanden ist;* 429, *Wenn mein Stündlein vorhanden ist;* 430, *Wenn mein Stündlein vorhanden ist;* 431, *Wenn wir in höchsten Nöten sein;* 432, *Wenn wir in höchsten Nöten sein;* 433, *Wer Gott vertraut, hat wohl gebaut;* 434, *Wer nur den lieben Gott lässt walten;* 435, *Wie bist du, Seele, in mir so gar betrübt;* 436, *Wie schön leuchtet der Morgenstern;* 437, *Wir glauben all' an einen Gott;* 258, *Wo Gott der Herr nicht bei uns hält;* 438, *Wo Gott zum Haus nicht gibt sein' Gunst.*

SACRED SONGS: 69 for One Voice with Basso Continuo only: 439, *Ach, dass nicht die letzte Stunde;* 440, *Auf, auf! die rechte Zeit ist hier;* 441, *Auf, auf! mein Herz, mit Freuden;* 422, *Beglückter Stand getreuer Seelen;* 443, *Beschränkt, ihr Weisen dieser Welt;* 444, *Brich entzwei, mein armes Herze;* 445, *Brunnquell aller Güter;* 446, *Der lieben Sonnen Licht und Pracht;* 447, *Der Tag ist hin, die Sonne gehet nieder;* 448, *Der Tag mit seinem Lichte;* 449, *Dich bet' ich an, mein höchster Gott;* 450, *Die bittre Leidenszeit beginnet abermal;* 451, *Die goldne Sonne, voll Freud' und Wonne;* 452, *Dir, dir Jehovah, will ich singen* (melody by Bach); 453, *Eins ist*

Not! ach Herr, dies Eine; 454, *Ermuntre dich, mein schwacher Geist;* 455, *Erwürgtes Lamm, das die verwahrten Siegel;* 456, *Es glänzet der Christen;* 457, *Es ist nun aus mit meinem Leben;* 458, *Es ist vollbracht! vergiss ja nicht;* 459, *Es kostet viel, ein Christ zu sein;* 460, *Gieb dich zufrieden und sei stille;* 461, *Gott lebet noch;* *Seele, was verzagst du doch?;* 462, *Gott, wie gross ist deine Güte;* 463, *Herr, nicht schicke deine Rache;* 464, *Ich bin ja, Herr, in deiner Macht;* 465, *Ich freue mich in der;* 466, *Ich halte treulich still und liebe;* 467, *Ich lass' dich nicht;* 468, *Ich liebe Jesum alle Stund';* 469, *Ich steh' an deiner Krippen hier;* 476, *Ihr Gestirn', ihr hohen Lüfte;* 471, *Jesu, deine Liebeswunden;* 470, *Jesu, Jesu, du bist mein;* 472, *Jesu, meines Glaubens Zier;* 473, *Jesu, meines Herzens Freud';* 474, *Jesus ist das schönste Licht;* 475, *Jesus, unser Trost und Leben;* 477, *Kein Stündlein geht dahin;* 478, *Komm, süsser Tod, komm, sel'ge Ruh'!* (melody by Bach); 479, *Kommt, Seelen, dieser Tag;* 480, *Kommt wieder aus der finstern Gruft;* 481, *Lasset uns mit Jesu ziehen;* 482, *Liebes Herz, bedenke doch;* 483, *Liebster Gott, wann werd' ich sterben?;* 484, *Liebster Herr Jesu! wo bleibest du so lange?;* 485, *Liebster Immanuel, Herzog der Frommen;* 488, *Meines Lebens letzte Zeit;* 486, *Mein Jesu, dem die Seraphinen;* 487, *Mein Jesu! was für Seelenweh;* 489, *Nicht so traurig, nicht so sehr;* 490, *Nur mein Jesus ist mein Leben;* 491, *O du Liebe meine Liebe;* 492, *O finstre Nacht;* 493, *O Jesulein süss, o Jesulein mild;* 494, *O liebe Seele, zieh' die Sinnen;* 495, *O wie selig seid ihr doch, ihr Frommen;* 496, *Sellen-Bräutigam, Jesu, Gottes Lamm!;* 497, *Seelenweide, meine Freude;* 499, *Sei gegrüsset, Jesu gütig;* 498, *Selig, wer an Jesum denkt;* 500, *So gehst du nun, mein Jesu, hin;* 501, *So giebst du nun, mein Jesu, gute Nacht;* 502, *So wünsch' ich mir zu guter Letzt;* 503, *Steh' ich bei meinem Gott;* 504, *Vergiss mein nicht, dass ich dein nicht;* 505, *Vergiss mein nicht, vergiss mein nicht* (melody by Bach); 506, *Was bist du doch, o Seele, so betrübet;* 507, *Wo ist mein Schäflein, das ich liebe.* BWV numbers have been assigned to the following sacred songs, which are most likely spurious: 519, *Hier lieg' ich nun;* 520, *Das walt' mein Gott;* 521, *Gott mein Herz dir Dank;* 522, *Meine Seele, lass es gehen;* 523, *Ich gnüge mich an meinem Stande.*

FOR ORGAN: 525-30, 6 trio sonatas: E-flat major, C minor, D minor, E minor, C major, G major; 531, Prelude and Fugue in C major; 532, Prelude and Fugue in D major; 533, Prelude and Fugue in E minor; 534, Prelude and Fugue in F minor; 535, Prelude and Fugue in G minor; 536, Prelude and Fugue in A major; 537, Fantasia and Fugue in C minor; 538, Toccata and Fugue in D minor, "Dorian"; 539, Prelude and Fugue in D minor; 540, Toccata and Fugue in F major; 541, Prelude and Fugue in G major; 542, Fantasia and Fugue in G minor; 543, Prelude and Fugue in A minor; 544, Prelude and Fugue in B minor; 545, Prelude and Fugue in C major; 546, Prelude and Fugue in C minor; 547, Prelude and Fugue in C major; 548, Prelude and Fugue in E minor; 549, Prelude and Fugue in C minor; 550, Prelude and Fugue in G major; 551, Prelude and Fugue in A minor; 552, Prelude and Fugue in E-flat major, "St. Anne"; 562,

Fantasia and Fugue in C minor; 563, Fantasia in B minor; 564, Toccata, Adagio, and Fugue in C major; 565, Toccata and Fugue in D minor; 566, Prelude and Fugue in E major; 568, Prelude in G major; 569, Prelude in A minor; 570, Fantasia in C major; 572, Fantasia in G major; 573, Fantasia in C major; 574, Fugue in C minor (on a theme by Legrenzi); 575, Fugue in C minor; 578, Fugue in G minor; 579, Fugue in B minor (on a theme by Corelli); 582, Passacaglia in C minor; 583, Trio in D minor; 586, Trio in G major (Bach's organ transcription of a work by Telemann); 587, Aria in F major (transcription from Couperin); 588, Canzona in D minor; 590, Pastorale in F major; 592–97, 6 concertos: G major (arrangement of a concerto by Duke Johann Ernst of Saxe-Weimar), A minor (arrangement of Vivaldi's op. 3, no. 8), C major (arrangement of Vivaldi's op. 7, no. 5), C major (arrangement of a concerto by Duke Johann Ernst of Saxe-Weimar), D minor (arrangement of Vivaldi's op. 3, no. 11), E-flat major (arrangement of a concerto by an unknown composer); 598, Pedal-Exercitium; 802–5, 4 duettos: E minor, F major, G major, A minor; 1,027a, Trio in G major (transcription from final movement of sonata 1,027). BWV numbers have been assigned to the following doubtful and spurious works: 131a, Fugue in G minor (spurious); 561, Fantasia and Fugue in A minor (spurious); 567, Prelude in C major (spurious); 571 Fantasia in G major (spurious); 576, Fugue in G major (spurious); 577, Fugue in G major (spurious); 580, Fugue in D major (spurious); 581, Fugue in G major (spurious); 584, Trio in G minor (doubtful); 585, Trio in C minor (by J.F. Fasch); 589, Allabreve in D major (doubtful); 591, Kleines harmonisches Labyrinth (doubtful); also 8 brief preludes and fugues: C major, D minor, E minor, F major, G major, G minor, A minor, B-flat major (doubtful).

OTHER ORGAN MUSIC: 45 Chorales in Das Orgel-Büchlein: 599, *Nun komm, der Heiden Heiland;* 600, *Gott, durch deine Güte;* 601, *Herr Christ, der ein'ge Gottes-Sohn;* 602, *Lob sei dem allmächtigen Gott;* 603, *Puer natus in Bethelhem;* 604, *Gelobet seist du, Jesu Christ;* 605, *Der Tag, der ist so freudenreich;* 606, *Vom Himmel hoch, da komm' ich her;* 607, *Vom Himmel kam der Engel Schar;* 608, *In dulci jubilo;* 609, *Lobt Gott, ihr Christen, allzugleich;* 610, *Jesu, meine Freude;* 611, *Christum wir sollen loben schon;* 612, *Wir Christenleut';* 613, *Helft mir Gottes Güte preisen;* 614, *Das alte Jahr vergangen ist;* 615, *In dir ist Freude;* 616, *Mit Fried' und Freud' ich fahr dahin;* 617, *Herr Gott, nun schleuss den Himmel auf;* 618, *O Lamm Gottes unschuldig;* 619, *Christe, du Lamm Gottes;* 620, *Christus, der uns selig macht;* 621, *Da Jesus an dem Kreuze stund';* 622, *O Mensch, bewein' dein' Sünde gross;* 623, *Wir danken dir, Herr Jesu Christ;* 624, *Hilf Gott, dass mir's gelinge;* 625, *Christ lag in Todesbanden;* 626, *Jesus Christus, unser Heiland;* 627, *Christ ist erstanden;* 628, *Erstanden ist der heil'ge Christ;* 629, *Erschienen ist der herrliche Tag;* 630, *Heut' triumphieret Gottes Sohn;* 631, *Komm, Gott Schöpfer, heiliger Geist;* 632, *Herr Jesu Christ, dich zu uns wend';* 633, *Liebster Jesu, wir sind hier;* 635, *Dies sind die heil'gen zehn Gebot';* 636, *Vater unser im Himmelreich;* 637, *Durch*

Adam's Fall ist ganz verderbt; 638, *Es ist das Heil uns Kommen her;* 639, *Ich ruf' zu dir, Herr Jesu Christ;* 640, *In dich hab' ich gehoffet, Herr;* 641, *Wenn wir in höchsten Nöten sein;* 642, *Wer nur den lieben Gott lässt walten;* 643, *Alle Menschen müssen sterben;* 644, *Ach wie nichtig, ach wie flüchtig;* 6 chorales publ. by J.G. Schübler, hence the name Schübler-Chorales: 645, *Wachet auf, ruft uns die Stimme* (based upon Cantata 140, 4th movement), 646, *Wo soll ich fliehen hin* (source unknown), 647, *Wer nur den lieben Gott lässt walten* (based upon Cantata 93, 4th movement), 648, *Meine Seele erhebet den Herren* (based upon Cantata 10, 5th movement), 649, *Ach bleib' bei uns, Herr Jesu Christ* (based upon Cantata 6, 3rd movement), 650, *Kommst du nun, Jesu, vom Himmel herunter* (based upon Cantata 137, 2nd movement); 651, *Fantasia super Komm, Heiliger Geist;* 652, *Komm, Heiliger Geist;* 653, *An Wasserflüssen Babylon;* 654, *Schmücke, dich, o liebe Seele;* 655, *Trio super Herr Jesu Christ, dich zu uns wend;* 656, *O Lamm Gottes, unschuldig;* 657, *Nun danket alle Gott;* 658, *Von Gott will ich nicht lassen;* 659, *Nun komm, der Heiden Heiland;* 660, *Trio super Nun komm, der Heiden Heiland;* 661, *Nun komm, der Heiden Heiland;* 662, *Allein Gott in der Höh sei Ehr;* 663, *Allein Gott in der Höh sei Ehr;* 664, *Trio super Allein Gott in der Höh sei Ehr;* 665, *Jesus Christus, unser Heiland;* 666, *Jesus Christus, unser Heiland;* 667, *Komm, Gott Schöpfer, Heiliger Geist;* 668, *Wenn wir in höchsten Nöten sein (Vor deinen Thron tret ich).* Chorale preludes in the 3rd part of the *Clavier-Übung:* 669, *Kyrie, Gott Vater in Ewigkeit;* 670, *Christe, aller Welt Trost;* 671, *Kyrie, Gott heiliger Geist;* 672, *Kyrie, Gott Vater in Ewigkeit;* 673, *Christe, aller Welt Trost;* 674, *Kyrie, Gott heiliger Geist;* 675, *Allein Gott in der Höh sei Ehr;* 676, *Allein Gott in der Höh sei Ehr;* 677, *Fughetta super Allein Gott in der Höh sei Ehr;* 678, *Dies sind die heiligen zehen Gebot;* 679, *Fughetta super Dies sind die heiligen zehen Gebot;* 680, *Wir glauben all an einen Gott;* 681, *Fughetta super Wir glauben all an einen Gott;* 682, *Vater unser im Himmelreich;* 683, *Vater unser im Himmelreich;* 684, *Christ, unser Herr, zum Jordan kam;* 685, *Christ, unser Herr, zum Jordan kam;* 686, *Aus tiefer Not schrei ich zu dir;* 687, *Aus tiefer Not schrei ich zu dir;* 688, *Jesus Christus, unser Heiland, der von uns den Zorn Gottes wandt;* 689, *Fuga super Jesus Christus unser Heiland.* Further chorales: 690, *Wer nur den lieben Gott lässt walten;* 691, *Wer nur den lieben Gott lässt walten;* 694, *Wo soll ich fliehen hin;* 695, *Fantasia super Christ lag in Todesbanden;* 696, *Christum wir sollen loben schon;* 697, *Gelobet seist du, Jesu Christ;* 698, *Herr Christ, der einig Gottes Sohn;* 699, *Nun komm, der Heiden Heiland;* 700, *Vom Himmel hoch, da komm ich her;* 701, *Vom Himmel hoch, da komm ich her;* 703, *Gottes Sohn ist kommen;* 704, *Lob sei dem allmächtigen Gott;* 706, *Liebster Jesu, wir sind hier;* 709, *Herr Jesu Christ, dich zu uns wend;* 710, *Wir Christenleut' haben jetzt Freud;* 711, *Allein Gott in der Höh sei Ehr;* 712, *In dich hab ich gehoffet, Herr;* 713, *Fantasia super Jesu, meine Freude;* 714, *Ach Gott und Herr;* 715, *Allein Gott in der Höh sei Ehr;* 717, *Allein Gott in* der Höh sei Ehr; 718, *Christ lag in Todesbanden;* 720, *Ein feste Burg ist unser Gott;* 721, *Erbarm dich mein, o Herre Gott;* 722, *Gelobet seist du, Jesu Christ;* 724, *Gott, durch deine Güte (Gottes Sohn ist kommen);* 725, *Herr Gott, dich loben wir;* 726, *Herr Jesu Christ, dich zu uns wend;* 727, *Herzlich tut mich verlangen;* 728, *Jesus, meine Zuversicht;* 729, *In dulci jubilo;* 730, *Liebster Jesu, wir sind hier;* 731, *Liebster Jesu, wir sind hier;* 732, *Lobt Gott, ihr Christen, allzugleich;* 733, *Meine Seele erhebet den Herren (Fuge über das Magnificat);* 734a, *Nun freut euch, lieben Christen gmein; O Lamm Gottes, unschuldig;* 735, *Fantasia super Valet will ich dir geben;* 736, *Valet will ich dir geben;* 737, *Vater unser im Himmelreich;* 738, *Vom Himmel hoch, da komm ich her;* 739, *Wie schön leucht't uns der Morgenstern;* 741, *Ach Gott vom Himmel sieh darein;* 753, *Jesu, meine Freude;* 764, *Wie schön leuchtet uns der Morgenstern;* 766, *Christ, der du bist der helle Tag;* 767, *O Gott, du frommer Gott;* 768, *Sei gegrüsset, Jesu gütig.* BWV numbers have been assigned to the following doubtful and spurious works: 691a, *Wer nur den lieben Gott lässt walten* (doubtful); 692, *Ach Gott und Herr* (by J.G. Walther); 693, *Ach Gott und Herr* (by J.G. Walther); 695a, *Fantasia super Christ lag in Todesbanden* (doubtful); 702, *Das Jesulein soll doch mein Trost* (doubtful); 705, *Durch Adam's Fall ist ganz verderbt* (doubtful); 707, *Ich hab' mein' Sach' Gott heimgestellt* (doubtful); 708, *Ich hab' mein' Sach' Gott heimgestellt* (doubtful); 713a, *Fantasia super Jesu, meine Freude* (doubtful); 716, *Fuga super Allein Gott in der Höh sei Ehr* (doubtful); 719, *Der Tag, der ist so freudenreich* (doubtful); 723, *Gelobet seist du, Jesu Christ* (doubtful); 734, *Nun freut euch, lieben Christen gmein* (doubtful); 740, *Wir glauben all' an einen Gott, Vater* (doubtful); 742, *Ach Herr, mich armen Sünder* (spurious); 743, *Ach, was ist doch unser Leben* (spurious); 744, *Auf meinen lieben Gott* (doubtful); 745, *Aus der Tiefe rufe ich* (doubtful); 746, *Christ ist erstanden* (doubtful); 747, *Christus, der uns selig macht* (spurious); 748, *Gott der Vater wohn' uns bei* (doubtful); 749, *Herr Jesu Christ, dich zu uns wend'* (spurious); 750, *Herr Jesu Christ, mein's Lebens Licht* (spurious); 751, *In dulci jubilo* (spurious); 752, *Jesu, der du meine Seele* (spurious); 754, *Liebster Jesu, wir sind hier* (spurious); 755, *Nun freut euch, lieben Christen* (spurious); 756, *Nun ruhen alle Wälder* (spurious); 757, *O Herre Gott, dein göttlich's Wort* (spurious); 758, *O Vater, allmächtiger Gott* (doubtful); 759, *Schmücke dich, o liebe Seele* (by G.A. Homilius); 760, *Vater unser im Himmelreich* (doubtful); 761, *Vater unser im Himmelreich* (doubtful); 762, *Vater user im Himmelreich* (spurious); 763, *Wie schön leuchtet der Morgenstern* (spurious); 765, *Wir glauben all' an einen Gott* (spurious); 770, *Ach, was soll ich Sünder machen?* (doubtful); 771, *Allein Gott in der Höh sei Ehr'* (nos. 3 and 8 by A.N. Vetter).

OTHER KEYBOARD MUSIC: 772–86, 15 2-part inventions in the *Clavier-Büchlein für Wilhelm Friedemann Bach:* C major, C minor, D major, D minor, E-flat major, E major, E minor, F major, F minor, G major, G minor, A major, A minor, B-flat major, B minor; 787–801, 15 3-part inventions, called sin-

fonias, in the *Clavier-Büchlein für Wilhelm Friedemann Bach:* C major, C minor, D major, D minor, E-flat major, E major, E minor, F major, F minor, G major, G minor, A major, A minor, B-flat major, B minor; 806–11, 6 English Suites: A major, A minor, G minor, F major, E minor, D minor; 812–17, 6 French Suites: D minor, C minor, B minor, E-flat major, G major, E major; 825–30, 6 partitas in part one of the *Clavier-Übung:* B-flat major, C minor, A minor, D major, G major, E minor; 831, *Ouvertüre nach französischer Art,* a partita in B minor in part 2 of the *Clavier-Übung;* 846–93, *Das wohltemperierte Clavier (The Well-Tempered Clavier),* in 2 parts: 24 Preludes and Fugues in each part in all the major and minor keys; 971, *Concerto nach Italiänischen Gusto (Concerto in the Italian Style)* in part 2 of the *Clavier-Übung;* 988, *Aria mit verschiedenen Veraenderungen* (the so-called *Goldberg Variations*), part 4 of the *Clavier-Übung.* Further keyboard works: 818, Suite in A minor; 819, Suite in E-flat major; 820, Ouverture in F major; 821, Suite in B-flat major; 822, Suite in G minor; 823, Suite in F minor; 832, Partie in A major; 833, Prelude and Partita in F major; 836 and 837, 2 allemandes in G minor (one unfinished); 841–43, 3 minuets: G major, G minor, G major; 894, Prelude and Fugue in A minor; 896, Prelude and Fugue in A major; 900, Prelude and Fughetta in E minor; 901, Prelude and Fughetta in F major; 902, Prelude and Fughetta in G major; 903, Chromatic Fantasia and Fugue in D minor; 904, Fantasia and Fugue in A minor; 906, Fantasia and Fugue in C minor; 910, Toccata in F-sharp minor; 911, Toccata in C minor; 912, Toccata in D major; 913, Toccata in D minor; 914, Toccata in E minor; 915, Toccata in G minor; 916, Toccata in G major; 944, Fugue in A minor; 946, Fugue in C major; 950, Fugue in A major (on a theme by Albinoni); 951, Fugue in B minor (on a theme by Albinoni); 953, Fugue in C major; 954, Fugue in B-flat major; 955, Fugue in B-flat major; 958, Fugue in A minor; 959, Fugue in A minor; 963, Sonata in D major; 965, Sonata in A minor (based upon a sonata by J.A. Reinken); 966, Sonata in C major (based upon part of a sonata by J.A. Reinken); 967, Sonata in A minor (based upon the first movement of a sonata by an unknown source); 989, Aria variata in A minor, 991, Air with variations in C minor (fragment); 992, *Capriccio sopra la lontananza del suo fratello dilettissimo (Capriccio on the Departure of His Most Beloved Brother),* in B-flat major; 993, Capriccio in E major; also 924–30, 6 works from the *Clavier-Büchlein für Wilhelm Friedemann Bach:* Praeambulum in C major, Prelude in D minor, Praeambulum in F major, Prelude in F major, Trio in G minor, Praeambulum in G minor; 933–38, 6 preludes: C major, C minor, D minor, D major, E major, E minor; 939-43, 5 Preludes: C major, D minor, E minor, A minor, C major; 994, Applicatio in C major, the first piece in the *Clavier-Büchlein für Wilhelm Friedemann Bach;* several pieces in the 2 parts of the *Clavier-Büchlein für Anna Magdalena Bach;* and 972–87, 16 concertos: D major (arrangement of Vivaldi's op. 3, no. 9), G major (arrangement of Vivaldi's op. 8/II, no. 2), D minor (arrangement of Oboe Concerto by A. Marcello), G minor (arrangement of Vivaldi's op.

4, no. 6), C major (arrangement of Vivaldi's op. 3, no. 12), C major (source unknown), F major (arrangement of Vivaldi's op. 3, no. 3), B minor (source unknown), G major (arrangement of Vivaldi's op. 4, no. 1), C minor (source unknown), B-flat major (arrangement of a concerto by Duke Johann Ernst of Saxe-Weimar), G minor (source unknown), C major (arrangement of a concerto by Duke Johann Ernst of Saxe-Weimar), G minor (arrangement of Violin Concerto by Telemann), G major (source unknown), D minor (arrangement of a concerto by Duke Johann Ernst of Saxe-Weimar). BWV numbers have been assigned to the following doubtful and spurious works: 824, Suite in A major (fragment; by Telemann); Allemande in C minor (spurious); 835, Allemande in A minor (by Kirnberger); 838, Allemande and Courante in A major (by C. Graupner); 839, Sarabande in G minor (spurious); 840, Courante in G major (by Telemann); 844, Scherzo in D minor (by W.F. Bach); 845, Gigue in F minor (spurious); 895, Prelude and Fugue in A minor (doubtful); 897, Prelude and Fugue in A minor (partly doubtful; prelude by C.H. Dretzel); 898, Prelude and Fugue in B-flat major (doubtful); 899, Prelude and Fughetta in D minor (doubtful); 905, Fantasia and Fugue in D minor (doubtful); 907, Fantasia and Fughetta in B-flat major (doubtful); 908, Fantasia and Fughetta in D major (doubtful); 909, Concerto and Fugue in C minor (doubtful); 917, Fantasia in G minor (doubtful); 918, Fantasia on a rondo in C minor (doubtful); 919, Fantasia in C minor (doubtful); 920, Fantasia in G minor (doubtful); 921, Prelude in C minor (doubtful); 922, Prelude in A minor (doubtful); 923, Prelude in B minor (doubtful); 945, Fugue in E minor (spurious); 947, Fugue in A minor (doubtful); 948, Fugue in D minor (doubtful); 949, Fugue in A major (doubtful); 952, Fugue in C major (doubtful); 956, Fugue in E minor (doubtful); 957, Fugue in G major (doubtful); 960, Fugue in E minor (unfinished; spurious); 961, Fughetta in C minor (doubtful); 962, Fugato in E minor (by Albrechtsberger); 964, Sonata in D minor (doubtful; arrangement of Violin Sonata 1,003); 968, Adagio in G major (doubtful; arrangement of first movement of Violin Sonata 1,005); 969, Andante in G minor (spurious); 970, Presto in D minor (by W.F. Bach); 990, Sarabande con partite in C major (spurious); etc.

FOR LUTE: 995, Suite in G minor; 996, Suite in E minor; 997, Partita in C minor; 998, Prelude, Fugue, and Allegro in E-flat major; 999, Prelude in C minor; 1,000, Fugue in G minor; 1,006a, Partita in E major (arrangement of 1,006).

CHAMBER MUSIC: 1,001–6, sonatas and partitas for Solo Violin: Sonata No. 1 in G minor, Partita No. 1 in B minor, Sonata No. 2 in A minor, Partita No. 2 in D minor, Sonata No. 3 in C major, Partita No. 3 in E major; 1,007–12, 6 suites for Solo Cello: G major, D minor, C major, E-flat major, C minor, D major; 1,013, Partita in A minor for flute; 1,014–19, 6 sonatas for Violin and Harpsichord: No. 1 in B minor, No. 2 in A major, No. 3 in E major, No. 4 in C minor, No. 5 in F minor, No. 6 in G major; 1,021, Sonata in G major for Violin and Basso Continuo; 1,023, Sonata in E minor for Violin and Basso Continuo; 1,027–29, 3 sonatas for Harpsichord and Viola da Gamba: G major, D major, G minor; 1,030, Sonata in B minor for Flute and Harpsichord; 1,032, Sonata in A major for Flute and Harpsichord; 1,034, Sonata in E minor for Flute and Basso Continuo; 1,035, Sonata in E major for Flute and Basso Continuo; 1,039, Sonata in G major for 2 Flutes and Basso Continuo; 1,040, Trio in F major for Violin, Oboe, and Basso Continuo. BWV numbers have been assigned to the following doubtful and spurious works: 1,020, Sonata in G minor for Violin and Harpsichord (doubtful); 1,022, Sonata in F major for Violin and Harpsichord (most likely spurious); 1,024, Sonata in C minor for Violin and Basso Continuo (doubtful); 1,025, Suite in A major for Violin and Harpsichord (doubtful); 1,026, Fugue in G minor for Violin and Harpsichord (doubtful); 1,037, Sonata in C major for 2 Violins and Harpsichord (most likely spurious); 1,031, Sonata in E-flat major for Flute and Harpsichord (doubtful); 1,033, Sonata in C major for Flute and Basso Continuo (doubtful); 1,036, Sonata in D minor for 2 Violins and Harpsichord (most likely spurious); 1,038, Sonata in G major for Flute, Violin, and Basso Continuo (most likely spurious).

FOR ORCH.: 1,041, Concerto in A minor for Violin; 1,042, Concerto in E major for Violin; 1,043, Concerto in D minor for 2 Violins; 1,044, Concerto in A minor for Flute, Violin, and Harpsichord; 1,046–51, 6 *Brandenburg Concertos:* No. 1 in F major, No. 2 in F major, No. 3 in G major, No. 4 in G major, No. 5 in D major, No. 6 in B-flat major; 1,052, Concerto in D minor for Harpsichord; 1053, Concerto in E major for Harpsichord; 1,054, Concerto in D major for Harpsichord; 1,055, Concerto in A major for Harpsichord; 1,056, Concerto in F minor for Harpsichord; 1,057, Concerto in F major for Harpsichord; 1,058, Concerto in G minor for Harpsichord; 1,059, Concerto in D minor for Harpsichord; 1,060, Concerto in C minor for 2 Harpsichords; 1,061, Concerto in C major for 2 Harpsichords; 1,062, Concerto in C minor for 2 Harpsichords; 1,063, Concerto in D minor for 3 Harpsichords; 1,064, Concerto in C major for 3 Harpsichords; 1,065, Concerto in A minor for 4 Harpsichords (arrangement of Vivaldi's op. 3, no. 10); 1,066–69, 4 suites or *ouvertures:* No. 1 in C major, No. 2 in B minor, No. 3 in D major, No. 4 in D major. Also 1,045, concerto movement in D major for Violin (fragment); 1,046a, Sinfonia in F major (early version of 1,046); 1,070, Overture in G minor (most likely spurious).

OTHER WORKS: 769, *Einige canonische Veränderungen über das Weynacht Lied, Vom Himmel hoch da komm' ich her* for Organ (composed for his membership in the Societät der Musikalischen Wissenschaften); 1,079, *Musikalisches Opfer (Musical Offering);* 1,080, *Die Kunst der Fuge (The Art of the Fugue).*

Bach, Wilhelm Friedemann (the "Halle" Bach), eldest son of **Johann Sebastian;** b. Weimar, Nov. 22, 1710; d. Berlin, July 1, 1784. He was a pupil of his father; studied at the Thomasschule in Leipzig (1723–29); also studied violin with J.G. Graun in Merseburg (1726); in 1729 he enrolled at the Univ. of Leipzig, where he took courses in in mathematics, philosophy, and law. In 1733 he became organist of the Sophienkirche in Dresden; in 1746 he was appointed organist of the Liebfrauenkirche in Halle, a post he held until 1764. In 1774 he went to Berlin. As a composer, he was highly gifted; his music reflects the influences of the Baroque and Rococo styles. An edition of his selected works was begun by the Abteilung für Musik Preussischen Akademie der Kunste; vol. I contains 4 trios (Leipzig, 1935). His Sinfonias opp. 64 and 65 have been edited by W. Lebermann (Mainz, 1971); opp. 67–71 by M. Schneider (Leipzig, 1914); his piano compositions have been edited by W. Rehberg in *Die Söhne Bachs* (1933); 3 excerpts are in K. Geiringer, *Music of the Bach Family: An Anthology* (Cambridge, Mass., 1955). His organ works are printed in E. Power Biggs and G. Weston, eds., *W.F. Bach: Complete Works for Organ* (N.Y., 1947).

Bach, Wilhelm Friedrich Ernst, son of **Johann Christoph Friedrich,** and grandson and last male descendant of **Johann Sebastian;** b. Bückeburg, May 23, 1759; d. Berlin, Dec. 25, 1845. He studied with his father and with his uncle **Johann Christoph** in London. In 1787 he became music director at Minden; in 1788 he was named Kapellmeister and harpsichordist to Queen Friedrike of Prussia; in 1797 he was appointed to a similar position to Queen Luise; also served as music master to the royal princes. He attended the dedication of the J.S. Bach monument in Leipzig on April 23, 1843. See K. Geiringer, *Music of the Bach Family: An Anthology* (Cambridge, Mass., 1955).

Bachauer, Gina, eminent Greek pianist; b. Athens, May 21, 1913; d. there, Aug. 22, 1976. Her father was of Austrian descent; her mother, Italian. She showed her aptitude as a pianist at the age of 5; entered the Athens Cons., where her teacher was Waldemar Freeman. She then went to Paris, where she took lessons with Alfred Cortot at the Ecole Normale de Musique. In 1933 she won the Medal of Honor at the International Contest for Pianists in Vienna; between 1933 and 1935 she received occasional instructions from Rachmaninoff in France and Switzerland; in 1935 she made her professional début with the Athens Symph. Orch. under the direction of Mitropoulos; she was also piano soloist in Paris in 1937 with Monteux. During World War II she lived in Alexandria, Egypt, and played several hundred concerts for the Allied Forces in the Middle East. On Jan. 21, 1946, she made her London debut with the New London Orch. under the direction of Alec Sherman, who became her second husband. Her first American appearance took place in N.Y. on Oct. 15, 1950. Only 35 people attended this concert, but she received unanimous acclaim from the critics, and her career was assured. The uncommon vigor of her technique suggested comparisons with Teresa Carreño; her repertoire ranged from Mozart to Stravinsky; in both classical and modern works she displayed impeccable taste. She died suddenly of a heart attack in Athens on the day she was to appear as soloist with the National Symph. Orch.

of Washington at the Athens Festival.

Bachelet, Alfred, French composer; b. Paris, Feb. 26, 1864; d. Nancy, Feb. 10, 1944. He studied at the Paris Cons.; received the Grand Prix de Rome for his cantata, *Cléopatre* (1890). From his earliest works, Bachelet devoted himself mainly to opera. In his youth, he was influenced by Wagnerian ideas, but later adopted a more national French style. During World War I he conducted at the Paris Opéra; in 1919 became director of the Nancy Cons.; in 1939 was elected a member of the Académie des Beaux Arts.

WORKS: Lyric dramas: *Scémo* (Paris Opéra, May 6, 1914) and *Un jardin sur l'Oronte* (Paris Opéra, Nov. 3, 1932); *Quand la cloche sonnera,* one-act music drama, his most successful work (Opéra-Comique, Nov.6, 1922); ballets: *La Fête chez la Pouplinière* and *Castor et Pollux* by Rameau (adapted and rewritten); orchestral works with voices: *L'Amour des Ondines, Joie, Le Songe de la Sulamith, Noël; Surya* for Tenor, Chorus, and Orch. (1940); *Ballade* for Violin and Orch.; songs.

Bäck, Sven-Erik, significant Swedish composer; b. Stockholm, Sept. 16, 1919. He studied violin at the Royal Academy of Music in Stockholm (1938–43); composition with Hilding Rosenberg (1940–45); then went to Switzerland and took courses in medieval music at the Schola Cantorum in Basel (1948–50); later studied advanced composition with Petrassi in Rome (1951). Returning to Sweden, he played violin and also viola in two local string quartets and conducted the "Chamber Orchestra 1953" until 1957. In 1959 he was appointed director of the Swedish Radio music school at Edsberg Castle outside Stockholm. As a composer, he at first embraced the Scandinavian romantic manner, but soon began experimentation in serial procedures, later annexing electronic sound.

WORKS: His first important work which attracted merited praise was the radio opera *Tranfjädrarna (The Crane Feathers),* a symbolist subject from Japanese Noh drama (1956; Swedish Radio, Feb. 28, 1957; first stage performance, Stockholm, Feb. 19, 1958). His other works are: a scenic oratorio, *Ett spel om Maria, Jesu Moder (A Play about Mary, Mother of Jesus;* Swedish Radio, April 4, 1958); a chamber opera, *Gästabudet (The Feast;* Stockholm, Nov. 12, 1958); a radio opera, *Fågeln (The Birds;* Swedish Radio, Feb. 14, 1961; later versions for stage and commercial recording, 1969); a ballet, *Ikaros* (Stockholm, May, 1963); a television ballet, *Movements* (Swedish Television, Feb. 27, 1966); a ballet, *Kattresan (Cat's Journey;* 1969; original version was a "concerto per bambini" for Children's Chorus, 2 Recorders, Violin, and Percussion, 1952); 2 electronic ballets, *Mur och port (Wall and Gate;* Stockholm, Jan. 17, 1971) and *Genom Jorden genom havet (Through the Earth, Through the Sea;* 1971; Stockholm, June 1972); also, 3 string quartets (1945, 1947, 1962); string quintet, *Exercises* (1948); Solo Flute Sonata (1949); *Expansive Preludes* for Piano (1949); *Sonata alla ricercare* for Piano (1950); *Sinfonia per*

archi (1951); *Sinfonia Sacra* for Chorus and Orch.
· (1953); Trio for Viola, Cello, and Double Bass (1953);
Sinfonia da camera (1954); Sonata for 2 Cellos
(1957); Violin Concerto (1957); *Impromptu* for
Piano (1957); *A Game around a Game* for Strings
and Percussion (Donaueschingen, Oct. 17, 1959); *Ar-
kitektur* for 2 Wind Orchs. and Percussion (1960);
Favola for Clarinet and Percussion (1962); *Intrada*
for Orch. (Stockholm, April 26, 1964); Cello Concerto (1965); *O Altitudo I* for Organ (1966; orch. version, *O Altitudo II*, 1966); *5 Preludes* for Clarinet
and Percussion (1966); *Humlan* for Chorus, Cello,
Piano, and Percussion (1968); *...in principio...* for
Tape (1969); String Trio (1970); *For Eliza* for Organ
or Tape ad lib. (1971); *Aperio* for 3 Orch. Groups,
each including Electronic Sound (1973); *Decet* for
Wind Quintet, String Quartet, and Double Bass
(1973); *Där fanns en brunn* for Chorus, Flute, Clarinet, Cello, Percussion, and Piano or Organ (1973);
Just da de langsta skuggorna... for 4 Singers and
10 Instruments (1974); *Tollo I* for Piano Duet (1974)
and *II* for 2 Pianos and Microphones (1975); *Time
Present* for 2 Violins, Echo Filter, and Feedback Systems (1975); many motets and religious cantatas;
short electronic pieces. A list of works is printed
in "Verkerförteckning 1945–1966," *Nutida Musik*
(1966/67).

Backer-Grøndahl, Agathe, Norwegian composer
and pianist; b. Holmestrand, Dec. 1, 1847; d. Ormöen,
near Oslo, June 16, 1907. She studied in Norway
with Kjerulf and Lindemann, in Florence with
Hans von Bülow, and in Weimar with Liszt; married
the singing teacher Grøndahl (1875). Among her
piano works, *Etudes de Concert, Romantische
Stücke,* and *Trois Morceaux* became well known
and have been frequently reprinted. She also wrote
a song cycle, *Des Kindes Frühlingstag.*

Backhaus, Wilhelm, eminent German-born Swiss
pianist and pedagogue; b. Leipzig, March 26, 1884; d.
Villach, Austria, July 5, 1969. He studied with Reck-
endorf in Leipzig (1891–99); made his debut there at
the age of 8. After studying briefly with Eugène
d'Albert in Frankfurt (1899), he began his career
with a major tour in 1900; soon acquired a fine reputation in Europe as both a pianist and a teacher. He
made his U.S. debut on Jan. 5, 1912, as soloist in
Beethoven's 5th Piano Concerto with Walter Damrosch and the N.Y. Symph. Orch. In 1930 he settled
in Lugano, where he continued to teach, and
became a Swiss citizen. Following World War II, he
resumed his concert tours; made his last appearance in the U.S. at a recital in N.Y. in 1962, at the age
of 78, displaying undiminished vigor as a virtuoso.
He died while visiting Austria for a concert engagement. He was particularly distinguished in his interpretations of the works of Beethoven and
Brahms.

Bacon, Ernst, remarkable American composer; b.
Chicago, May 26, 1898. He studied music theory at
Northwestern Univ. with P.C. Lutkin (1915–18), and
later at the Univ. of Chicago with Arne Oldberg and

T. Otterstroem; also took private piano lessons in
Chicago with Alexander Raab (1916–21). In 1924 he
went to Vienna, where he took private composition
lessons with Karl Weigl and Franz Schmidt. Returning to America, he studied composition with Ernest
Bloch in San Francisco, and conducting with Eugene Goossens in Rochester, N.Y. From 1934 to 1937
he was supervisor of the Federal Music Project in
San Francisco; simultaneously deployed numerous
related activities, as a conductor and a music critic.
He was on the faculty of Converse College in South
Carolina (1938–45) and Syracuse Univ. (1945–63). He
also engaged in literary pursuits—wrote poetry and
publ. a book of aphorisms—and espoused radical
politics. A musician of exceptional inventive powers, he published a brochure, *Our Musical Idiom*
(Chicago, 1917), when he was 19; in it he outlines the
new resources of musical composition. In some of
his piano works he evolved a beguiling technique of
mirror reflection between the right and the left
hand, exact as to the intervals, with white and black
keys in one hand reflected respectively by white
and black keys in the other hand. However, Ernst
Bacon is generally regarded as primarily a composer of lyric songs. In 1963 he went to California and
lived in Orinda, near San Francisco.
WORKS: Symph. No. 1 for Piano and Orch. (1932);
Symph. No. 2 (1937; Chicago, Feb. 5, 1940); Symph.
No. 3, *Great River,* for Narrator and Orch. (1956);
Symph. No. 4 (1963); a musical play, *A Tree on the
Plains* (Spartanburg, S.C., May 2, 1942); a folk opera,
A Drumlin Legend (N.Y., May 4, 1949); *By Blue On-
tario,* oratorio to words by Walt Whitman (1958);
The Last Invocation, a Requiem, to poems by Walt
Whitman, Emily Dickinson, and others (1968–71);
Nature, a cantata cycle (1968); ballets: *Jehovah and
the Ark* (1968–70) and *The Parliament of Fowls*
(1975); songs to words by Emily Dickinson and Walt
Whitman: *From Emily's Diary* for Soprano, Alto,
Women's Chorus, and Orch. (1945); *The Lord Star,*
cantata (1950); *Songs of Eternity* (1932); *Black and
White Songs* for Baritone and Orch. (1932); *Twilight,* 3 songs for Voice and Orch. (1932); *Midnight
Special,* 4 songs for Voice and Orch. (1932); Piano
Quintet (1946); Cello Sonata (1946); String Quintet
(1951); *Riolama* for Piano and Orch., in 10 short
movements (1964); *Spirits and Places,* a cycle with
geographical connotations for Organ (1966); *Saws,* a
suite of canons for Chorus and Piano (1971); *Dr.
Franklin,* music play for the bicentennial (1976), to
text by Cornel Lengyel. Among Bacon's publ. books
are *Words on Music* (1960) and *Notes on the Piano*
(1963). A collection of his songs, *Grass Roots* for
Soprano, Alto, and Piano, was publ. in 2 vols. in 1976.

Badarzewska, Thekla, Polish composer of salon
music; b. Warsaw, 1834; d. there, Sept. 29, 1861. At
the age of 17 she publ. in Warsaw a piano piece,
Molitwa dziewicy (A Maiden's Prayer), which was
republ. as a supplement to the Paris *Revue et Gazette Musicale* in 1859, and unaccountably seized
the imagination not only of inhibited virgins, but of
sentimental amateur pianists all over the world.
More than 100 editions of this unique piece of salon

pianism, dripping maudlin arpeggios, were publ. in the 19th century, and the thing was still widely sold even in the 20th century. Badarzewska wrote 34 more piano pieces in the salon style, but none of them matched *A Maiden's Prayer.* An ungentlemanly German critic opined in an obituary that "Badarzewska's early death saved the musical world from a veritable inundation of intolerable lachrymosity."

Badia, Conchita (Conxita), noted Spanish soprano; b. Barcelona, Nov. 14, 1897; d. there, May 2, 1975. She studied piano and voice with Granados; also had lessons with Casals and Manuel de Falla. She made her debut in Barcelona as a concert singer in 1913 in the first performance of *Canciónes amatorias* by Granados, with the composer as piano accompanist. She subsequently devoted herself to concert appearances, excelling as an interpreter of Spanish and Latin American music; often appeared in performances with Casals and his orch. in Barcelona. In later years she taught voice in Barcelona, where her most famous pupil was Montserrat Caballé.

Badings, Henk, eminent Dutch composer; b. Bandung, Indonesia, Jan. 17, 1907, of Dutch parents. He was orphaned at an early age and came to the Netherlands. He first studied mining engineering at the Delft Polytechnic Univ.; then began to compose without any formal study and produced a symph. which was performed in Amsterdam by Mengelberg with the Concertgebouw Orch. on July 6, 1930; however, he discarded the work, and wrote another symph. 2 years later to replace it. At the same time he began taking lessons in composition with Willem Pijper (1930–31); afterward taught music at the Rotterdam Cons. (1934–37), at the Lyceum in Amsterdam (1937–41), and at the Cons. of The Hague (1941–45). He was temporarily barred from professional activities after the end of World War II on charges of cultural collaboration with the Germans during the Netherlands' occupation, but regained his status in 1947. In 1961 he was appointed prof. of acoustics at the Univ. of Utrecht. In 1962 he was guest lecturer at the Univ. of Adelaide in Australia. From 1966 to 1972 he was prof. of composition at the Staatliche Hochschule für Musik in Stuttgart. His style of composition may be described as romantic modernism marked by intense dynamism. In melodic progressions he often employs the scale of alternating major and minor seconds known in the Netherlands as the "Pijper scale." After 1950 he began experimenting with electronic sound and microtonal divisions, especially the 31-tone scale devised by the Dutch physicist Adriaan Fokker.

Badura-Skoda, Paul, eminent Austrian pianist, music editor, and pedagogue; b. Vienna, Oct. 6, 1927. He was brought up by his stepfather, Skoda, whose name he adopted professionally. He studied science as well as music; graduated from the Vienna Cons. in 1948. A scholarly musician, he won several prizes for excellence. He had a successful career as a con-

cert pianist; gave recitals in Europe; made his N.Y. debut on Jan. 10, 1953. From 1966 until 1971 he was artist-in-residence at the Univ. of Wisconsin. On Sept. 19, 1951, he married **Eva Halfar** (b. Munich, Jan. 15, 1929), who collaborated with him on his various editions. He publ. *Mozart-Interpretation* (Vienna, 1957; in collaboration with Eva Badura-Skoda; in Eng. as *Interpreting Mozart on the Keyboard,* N.Y., 1962; also in Japanese, Tokyo, 1963) and *Die Klaviersonaten von Ludwig van Beethoven* (with J. Demus, Wiesbaden, 1970); also contributed valuable articles on Chopin, Schubert, and others to German music journals.

Baez, Joan, politically active American folksinger of English, Irish, and Mexican descent; b. Staten Island, N.Y., Jan. 9, 1941. She played the guitar by ear; then studied drama at Boston Univ. She made her first impact on American mass consciousness in 1959 when she appeared at the Newport Folk Festival. In 1965 she founded the Institute for the Study of Non-Violence; joined the struggle against the Vietnam War and supported the organizing fight of the United Farm Workers' Union. Accompanying herself on the guitar, she appeared at numerous concerts promoting topical humanitarian causes.

Baïf, Jean-Antoine de, French composer and poet; b. Venice, Feb. 19, 1532; d. Paris, Sept. 19, 1589. He was brought to Paris as a child, and formed a friendship with Ronsard and other eminent poets. In 1570 he founded the Académie de Poésie et de Musique, with the aim of reviving the music and poetry of ancient Greece. He developed a system of "musique mesurée," which he believed would possess a moral force similar to the Greek ideas of "ethos." Settings of his poems were composed by Jacques Maudit in *26 Chansonnettes mesurées* (1586) for 4 Voices; and by Claude Le Jeune, in *Le Printemps* (1603). Both of these collections have been reprinted in Henri Expert's *Maîtres musiciens* (1899–1901; vols. X, XII, XIII, and XIV). Baïf's musical works comprise 12 sacred songs and several works in lute tablature.

Bailey, Lillian. See **Henschel, Lillian June.**

Bailey, Pearl (Mae), black American singer of popular music; b. Newport News, Va., March 29, 1918. After winning an amateur contest in Philadelphia at 15, she quit school to pursue a career as an entertainer; worked as a dancer and a singer in various nightclubs in Washington, D.C., Baltimore, and N.Y. She made her Broadway debut in 1946 in *St. Louis Woman* and subsequently appeared in *Arms and the Girl* (1950), *Bless You All* (1950), and *House of Flowers* (1954); her greatest success came in 1967, when she starred in the all-black version of the hit musical *Hello, Dolly!* She also appeared in films, including *Carmen Jones* (1954), *St. Louis Blues* (1958), and *Porgy and Bess* (1959), and had her own television show (1970–71). She gained fame with her renditions of *Birth of the Blues; Toot Toot Tootsie, Goodbye; Takes Two to Tango,* and *Row, Row, Row.* She publ. 2 entertaining accounts of her life and career, *The Raw Pearl* (N.Y., 1968) and *Talking to Myself* (N.Y., 1971).

Baillie, Dame Isobel, Scottish soprano; b. Hawick, Roxburghshire, March 9, 1895; d. Manchester, Sept. 24, 1983. She was educated in Manchester; then went to Italy and began to take voice lessons in Milan. She made her concert debut in London in 1923, and through the years established herself as a successful singer, particularly in oratorio. It is said that she sang the *Messiah* more than 1,000 times. In 1978 Queen Elizabeth II made her a Dame Commander of the Order of the British Empire.

Baillot, Pierre-Marie-François de Sales, celebrated French violinist; b. Passy, near Paris, Oct. 1, 1771; d. Paris, Sept. 15, 1842. The son of a schoolmaster, he received an excellent education; at the age of 9 he became a pupil of the French violinist Sainte-Marie; he later was sent to Rome, where he studied under Pollani; returned to Paris in 1791. He met Viotti, who obtained for him a position in the orch. of the Théâtre Feydeau; later he served as a clerk in the Ministry of Finance. In 1795 he received the important appointment as violin teacher at the newly opened Paris Cons.; but continued to study composition with Cherubini, Reicha, and Catel. In 1802 he joined Napoleon's private instrumental ensemble; toured Russia with the cellist Lamarre (1805–8). Upon his return to Paris, he organized chamber music concerts, which enjoyed excellent success; also gave concerts in Belgium, the Netherlands, and England. In 1821 he became first violinist at the Paris Opéra; from 1825 he was also solo violinist in the Royal Orch. Baillot's musical compositions, rarely performed, comprise 9 violin concertos, 3 string quartets, 15 trios, a Symph. Concertante for 2 Violins with Orch., 6 violin duos, etc. Baillot's name is chiefly remembered through his manual *L'Art du violon* (1834); with Rode and Kreutzer he wrote a *Méthode de Violon,* adopted by the Paris Cons. and republished in numerous editions and languages; he also edited the *Méthode de violoncelle* by Levasseur, Catel, and Baudiot.

Bainbridge, Katharine, American composer; b. Basingstoke, England, June 30, 1863; d. Hollywood, Feb. 12, 1967 (at the age of 103!). She settled in the U.S. in 1898 and became active as a poetess and composer. She wrote the lyrics of numerous songs, with music by Charles Wakefield Chadman, Rudolf Friml, and others. One of her songs won the First Prize of the Women's International Assoc. of Aeronautics.

Baini, Giuseppe (also known as **Abbate Baini**), Italian writer on music and composer; b. Rome, Oct. 21, 1775; d. there, May 21, 1844. He received rudimentary training from his uncle, Lorenzo Baini; then entered the Seminario Romano, where his instructor, Stefano Silveyra, indoctrinated him with the spirit of Palestrina's music. In 1795 he became a member of the papal choir at St. Peter's; he continued his studies there with Bianchini; in 1802 he took courses with Jannaconi, whom he succeeded as maestro di cappella at St. Peter's (1818). In 1821 he wrote his masterpiece, a 10-part *Miserere,* which was accepted for singing at the Sistine Chapel during Holy Week, in alternation with the *Misereres* of Allegri and Bai. He also wrote many Psalms, hymns, masses, and motets. His great ambition was to publ. a complete edition of Palestrina's works, but he was able to prepare only two vols. for publication. The monument of his devotion to Palestrina was his exhaustive biography, *Memorie storicocritiche della vita e delle opere di Giovanni Pierluigi da Palestrina* (Rome, 1828; German trans. by Kandler, with notes by Kiesewetter, 1834), which remains extremely valuable despite its occasional inaccuracies. He also wrote a *Saggio sopra l'identità de' ritmi musicali e poetici* (1820). Haberl publ. an essay on Baini in the *Kirchenmusikalisches Jahrbuch* (1894).

Baird, Tadeusz, prominent Polish composer; b. Grodzisk Mazowiecki, July 26, 1928; d. Warsaw, Sept. 2, 1981. He studied music privately in Lodz with Sikorski and Woytowicz during the war years (1943–44); after the war he enrolled at the Warsaw Cons. and took courses with Rytel and Perkowski (1947–51); had piano lessons with Wituski (1948–51). He further studied musicology with Zofia Lissa at the Univ. of Warsaw (1948–52). In 1949, together with Jan Krenz and Kazimierz Serocki, he founded a progressive society of composers under the name Group 49. In 1956 he became active in initiating the First International Festival of Contemporary Music, during the "Warsaw Autumn." In 1977 he was appointed prof. of composition at the Chopin Academy of Music in Warsaw. As a composer, Baird won numerous awards, among them the Fitelberg Competition of 1958, 3 prizes of the Tribune Internationale des Compositeurs in Paris (1959, 1963, 1966), and the Polish State Awards for his 3 symphs. (1951, 1964, 1969). He also was awarded the Commander's Cross of the Order of Poland's Revival (1964) and the Order of the Banner of Labor, Second and First Class (1974, 1981). His early music followed the neo-Romantic modalities characteristic of Polish music; further evolution was marked by complex structures in the manner of dynamic expressionism, with occasional applications of serialism.

Baker, David, American composer and jazz musician; b. Indianapolis, Dec. 21, 1931. He graduated from Indiana Univ. in 1953; also studied music theory privately with Heiden, Schuller, Orrego-Salas, William Russo, and George Russell. He subsequently taught music in small colleges and public school; in 1966 became chairman of the dept. of jazz studies at Indiana Univ. As a jazz performer, he played the trombone with Stan Kenton, Lionel Hampton, and Quincy Jones. His own compositions fuse jazz improvisation with ultramodern devices, including serial procedures.

Baker, Dame Janet, celebrated English mezzo-soprano; b. Hatfield, Yorkshire, Aug. 21, 1933. Her parents were music-lovers and she grew up in an artistic atmosphere from her early childhood. She took academic courses at the College for Girls in York, and also began to take singing lessons in London, where her teachers were Helene Isepp and Meriel St. Clair. She won a prize in 1956 which made it possible for her to travel to Salzburg and attend singing classes at the Mozarteum there. Later she enrolled in a master class of Lotte Lehmann in London. She sang in the chorus at the Glyndebourne Festival (1956) and also filled engagements in opera productions in Oxford and London. In 1960 she gave a recital at the Edinburgh Festival. In 1961 she had a part in Bach's *St. John Passion* which made it Copenhagen, and later sang in Bach's B minor Mass in Zürich. A decisive turn in her career came with her membership in the English Opera Group directed by Benjamin Britten; on May 16, 1971, she appeared in the leading role in Britten's opera *Owen Wingrave* on television. She made her first American appearance in 1966 as soloist with the San Francisco Symph. in Mahler's *Das Lied von der Erde.* On Dec. 2, 1966, she presented a solo recital in N.Y., with excellent reviews. Her subsequent engagements took her all over Europe; her fame as an artist of intellectual brilliance grew. In 1970 she was named a Commander of the Order of the British Empire, and in 1976 Queen Elizabeth II made her a Dame of the British Empire. She gave her last operatic appearance in 1982. An account of her final operatic season was publ. in her book *Full Circle* (London, 1982).

Baker, Theodore, American writer on music, and the compiler of the original edition of the present dictionary bearing his name; b. New York, June 3, 1851; d. Dresden, Germany, Oct. 13, 1934. As a young man, he was trained for business pursuits; in 1874 he decided to devote himself to musical studies; he went to Leipzig, where he took courses with Oskar Paul; he received his Dr.Phil. there in 1882 for his dissertation *Über die Musik der nordamerikanischen Wilden,* the first serious study of American Indian music. He lived in Germany until 1890; then returned to the U.S., and became literary editor and translator for the publishing house of G. Schirmer, Inc. (1892); he retired in 1926 and went back to Germany. In 1895 he publ. *A Dictionary of Musical Terms,* which went through more than 25 printings and sold over a million copies; another valuable work was *A Pronouncing Pocket Manual of Musical Terms* (1905). He also issued *The Musician's Calendar and Birthday Book* (1915–17). In 1900 G. Schirmer, Inc., publ. *Baker's Biographical Dictionary of Musicians,* which became Baker's imperishable monument. The first edition included the names of many American musicians not represented in musical reference works at the time; a 2nd edition was publ. in 1905; the 3rd edition, revised and enlarged by Alfred Remy, was issued in 1919; the 4th edition appeared in 1940 under the general editorship of Carl Engel. A Supplement in 1949 was compiled by Nicolas Slonimsky, who undertook in

1958 a completely revised 5th edition of the Dictionary and compiled the Supplements of 1965 and 1971. In 1978 Slonimsky edited the 6th edition of *Baker's Biographical Dictionary of Musicians.* The present edition is also edited by him.

Bakfark, Valentin, celebrated Hungarian lutenist; b. Kronstadt, 1507; d. Padua, Aug. 15, 1576. He was brought up by the family of his brother's wife, **Greff** (or **Graew**), and used that name in conjunction with his own; the spelling **Bacfarc** or **Bekwark** is also encountered. As a youth he was in the service of the King of Hungary (1526–40) in Buda, where he studied lute. He was later attached to the court of Sigismund Augustus of Poland in Wilna (1549–66). He subsequently traveled in Germany, France, and Italy, eventually settling in Padua, where he died of the plague. He published works for the lute in tablature: *Intabulatura* (Lyons, 1552; reprinted as *Premier Livre de Tablature de Luth,* Paris, 1564). A 2nd book, *Harmonicarum Musicarum ... tomus primus,* appeared in Cracow in 1564, and was reprinted in Antwerp in 1569. Some of his works are included in Denkmäler der Tonkunst in Österreich (vol. XVIII, 2).

Balakirev, Mily (pronounced "Balákirev," with the stress on the second syllable, not the third), greatly significant Russian composer, protagonist of the Russian national school of composition; b. Nizhny-Novgorod, Jan. 2, 1837 (new style; Dec. 21, 1836, old style); d. St. Petersburg, May 29, 1910. His mother gave him his first piano lessons; he was then sent to Moscow, where he took piano lessons with Alexandre Dubuque, and studied music theory with a German musician named Karl Eisrich; he put Balakirev in touch with Oulibishev, author of a book on Mozart who owned an estate in Nizhny-Novgorod. Balakirev often took part in private musical evenings at Oulibishev's estate, playing piano. In 1853–54 he attended classes in mathematics at the Univ. of Kazan. In 1855 he went to St. Petersburg, where he was introduced to Glinka, who encouraged him to continue his musical studies. On Feb. 24, 1856, Balakirev made his first appearance as a composer in St. Petersburg, playing the solo part in the first movement of his Piano Concerto; his *Overture on the Theme of Three Russian Songs* was performed in Moscow on Jan. 2, 1859, and his overture *King Lear,* at a concert of the Univ. of St. Petersburg on Nov. 27, 1859. In 1860 he took a boat ride down the Volga River from his birthplace at Nizhny-Novgorod to the delta at the Caspian Sea; during this trip he collected, notated, and harmonized a number of Russian songs; his collection included the universally popular *Song of the Volga Boatmen,* also known as *Song of the Burlaks* (peasants who pulled large boats loaded with grain upstream on the Volga). In 1863 Balakirev organized in St. Petersburg a musical group which became known as the Balakirev Circle. Its avowed aim was to make national propaganda of Russian music to oppose the passive imitation of classical German compositions, which at the time exercised a commanding influence in Russia. Simultaneously, he founded the Free Music School in St. Petersburg, and gave concerts which included works by Russian musicians as well as those of recognized German masters. These activities coincided with the rise of a Slavophile movement among patriotic Russian writers and artists, based on the realization of a kinship of blood and the similarity of the Slavic languages (Czech, Serbian, Polish, Bulgarian) and further stimulated by a series of wars against Turkey, aimed at the liberation of Bulgaria; a dream of uniting all Slavic nations under the loving domination of Mother Russia animated Balakirev and other musicians. In 1866 he went to Prague with the intention of conducting Glinka's operas there, but the outbreak of the Austro-Prussian War forced the cancellation of these plans. He repeated his visit to Prague in 1867 and was able to conduct *Ruslan and Ludmila* there on Feb. 16, 17, and 19, 1867; then he conducted *A Life for the Czar,* on Feb. 22, 1867. He took this opportunity to invite several Czech musicians to take part in a concert of music by Russian and Czech composers conducted by Balakirev at his Free Music School on May 24, 1867; the program included, besides the works by the Czech guests, compositions by Borodin, Cui, Mussorgsky, Rimsky-Korsakov, and Balakirev himself. The occasion proved to be of historical importance, for it moved the critic Vladimir Stasov to write an article in which he proudly declared that Russia, too, had its "mighty little company" (*moguchaya kuchka*) of fine musicians; the phrase became a catchword of Russian musical nationalism; in general music histories it came to be known as "The Mighty Five." But the spiritual drive toward the union with the Western Slavic nations was not the only animating force in the music of "The Mighty Five." It combines, somehow, with the historical drive toward the exotic Moslem lands through the Caucasus to Persia in the South and to Central Asia in the East. Balakirev became fascinated with the quasi-oriental melodies and rhythms of the Caucasus during his several trips there. In 1869 he wrote a brilliant oriental fantasy for piano entitled *Islamey;* its technical difficulties rival the transcendental studies of Liszt. His associates, especially Rimsky-Korsakov and Borodin, also paid tribute to the colorful glories of the East, the first in his *Scheherazade,* and the second in his symphonic movement *In the Steppes of Central Asia.* Among his comrades, Balakirev was always a leader; when Rimsky-Korsakov went on a prolonged cruise as a midshipman in the Russian Imperial Navy, he maintained a remarkable correspondence with Balakirev, who gave him specific advice in composition. Unaccountably, Balakirev slackened the tempo of his work as a composer, conductor, and teacher; he seems to have had trouble completing his scores. In 1872 he discontinued his concerts at the Free Music School, and took a clerical job in the railroad transport administration; in 1873 he became music inspector in a women's educational inst. in St. Petersburg; in 1875 he took another administrative job in a women's school. In 1881 he returned to musical activities, and on March 29, 1882, he conducted at the Free

Music School the premiere of the first symph. by the 16-year-old Glazunov; he also began to work on the revision of his early scores. His *Second Overture on Russian Themes,* originally performed in St. Petersburg on April 18, 1864, and retitled *One Thousand Years* to commemorate the millennium of Russia observed in 1862, was revised by Balakirev in 1882 and renamed *Russia.* It took Balakirev many years to complete his symph. poem *Tamara,* which he conducted in St. Petersburg on March 19, 1883; the score, inspired by Lermontov's poem and permeated by Caucasian melodic inflections, was dedicated to Liszt. Balakirev spent 33 years (1864–97) working intermittently on his Symph. in C, which he conducted at a concert at the Free Music School on April 23, 1898; this was his last appearance as a conductor. He completed his 2nd Symph. in D minor between 1900 and 1908; it was performed in St. Petersburg on April 23, 1909. He worked on his First Piano Concerto in 1855 and began the composition of his 2nd Piano Concerto in 1861, but laid it aside until 1909; it was completed after his death by Liapunov. In 1883 he became director of music of the Imperial Chapel, resigning from this post in 1894. During his last years, Balakirev was increasingly unsociable and morose; he became estranged from Rimsky-Korsakov when the latter became chief adviser to Belayev, the wealthy publisher who ceased to support the Free School headed by Balakirev and instead sponsored a series of Russian Symphony Concerts in 1886, attracting a number of younger Russian composers, among them Glazunov, Liadov, Arensky, and Ippolitov-Ivanov. Their quarrel reached such lamentable extremes that they did not even greet each other at public places or at concerts. Still, Rimsky-Korsakov continued to perform Balakirev's music at his concerts. Balakirev made a tremendous impact on the destinies of Russian music, particularly because of his patriotic convictions that Russia could rival Germany and other nations in the art of music. But he left fewer works than his long life would have justified, and they are rarely performed. Among his lesser compositions are *Spanish Overture* (1886); *Czech Overture* (1867); Octet for Flute, Oboe, French Horn, Violin, Viola, Cello, Double Bass, and Piano (1850–56); 2 Piano Sonatas (1857, 1905); and a Piano Sonatina (1909). He made an effective piano transcription of Glinka's song *The Lark* and wrote about 35 original songs; he further publ. an important collection of Russian folk songs (1865). A complete edition of Balakirev's piano works was publ. in Moscow in 1952; a collection of all of his songs was publ. in Moscow in 1937.

Balanchivadze, Andrei, Georgian composer (brother of the choreographer **George Balanchine**); b. St. Petersburg, June 1, 1906. He studied with his father, the composer **Meliton Balanchivadze;** then entered the Tiflis Cons., where he took courses in piano, and in composition with Ippolitov-Ivanov. In 1935 he joined the staff of the Tiflis Cons., and in 1962 became chairman of the composition dept.; numerous Georgian composers are his students. In his music he makes use of Georgian folk motifs in a tasteful harmonic framework characteristic of the national Russian school of composition. Among his works is the first Georgian ballet, *The Heart of the Mountains* (1936); another ballet, *Mtsyri,* after Lermontov, was produced in Tiflis in 1964. His other works include 2 symphs. (1944, 1959); symph. poem, *The Ocean* (1952); 4 piano concertos (1944, 1946, 1952, 1968); choruses and songs.

Balanchivadze, Meliton, noted Russian composer; b. in the village of Banodzha, Dec. 24, 1862; d. Kutaisi, Nov. 21, 1937. He was educated in the ecclesiastical seminary in Tiflis, where he sang in a chorus. In 1880 he became a member of the local opera theater; in 1882 he organized a chorus and arranged Georgian folk songs. In 1889 he went to St. Petersburg, where he took vocal lessons, and in 1891 entered Rimsky-Korsakov's class in composition. In 1895 he organized a series of choral concerts of Georgian music. After the Revolution he returned to Georgia, where he continued his work of ethnic research. He composed a national Georgian opera, *Tamara the Treacherous* (1897), and a number of songs in the manner of Georgian folk music.

Bales, Richard, American conductor and composer; b. Alexandria, Va., Feb. 3, 1915. He studied at the Eastman School of Music in Rochester, N.Y., and took a course in conducting under Koussevitzky at the Berkshire Music Center in Tanglewood. In 1943 he was appointed conductor of the National Gallery Orch. in Washington; at this post he introduced numerous works by American composers, both old and new. His ingenious potpourri of Southern songs, *The Confederacy* (1954), became very popular. Other works include 2 orch. suites inspired by watercolors in the National Gallery in Washington, *American Design* (Washington, May 26, 1957) and *American Chronicle* (Washington, May 23, 1965).

Balfe, Michael William, notable Irish composer; b. Dublin, May 15, 1808; d. Rowney Abbey, Hertfordshire, Oct. 20, 1870. He was the son of a dancing master, and as a small child played the violin for his father's dancing classes. He subsequently took violin lessons with O'Rourke. After his father's death on Jan. 6, 1823, Balfe went to London, where he studied violin with Charles Edward Horn and composition with Carl Friedrich Horn. In 1824 he was engaged as a violinist at the Drury Lane Theatre; also sang in London and in the provinces. His patron, Count Mazzara, took him to Italy in 1825; there he took composition lessons with Federici in Milan and voice lessons with Pilippo Galli; there he produced his first ballet, *La Pérouse* (1826). He met Rossini, who advised him to continue singing lessons with Bordogni; in 1828 he was engaged as principal baritone at the Italian Opera in Paris. In Italy he married the Hungarian vocalist **Lina Rosa** (b. 1808; d. London, June 8, 1888). Returning to England in 1833, he devoted himself to the management of opera houses and to composition. He was manager of the Lyceum Theatre during the 1841–42 season. He

made London his principal residence, with occasional visits to Vienna (1846), Berlin (1848), St. Petersburg, and Trieste (1852–56). Apart from his administrative duties, he displayed great energy in composing operas, most of them to English librettos; of these, *The Bohemian Girl,* produced at the Drury Lane Theatre in London on Nov. 27, 1843, obtained an extraordinary success and became a perennial favorite on the English stage; it was also translated into French, German, and Italian. In 1864 he retired to his country seat at Rowney Abbey. His daughter, Victoire, made her debut as a singer at the Lyceum Theatre in London in 1857.

Ball, Ernest R., American composer of popular songs; b. Cleveland, July 21, 1878; d. Santa Ana, Calif., May 3, 1927. He studied at Cleveland Cons.; moved to N.Y., where he earned his living as a vaudeville pianist. His first success came with the song *Will You Love Me in December as You Do in May?* to the words of James J. Walker (later, mayor of N.Y.). No less successful were his sentimental songs *Mother Machree, When Irish Eyes Are Smiling, Little Bit of Heaven, Dear Little Boy of Mine, Till the Sands of the Desert Grow Cold, Love Me and the World Is Mine,* etc., sung by John McCormack and other famous artists. Ball was a charter member of ASCAP (1914).

Ballantine, Edward, American composer; b. Oberlin, Ohio, August 6, 1886; d. Oak Bluffs, Mass., July 2, 1971. He studied with Walter Spalding at Harvard Univ.; graduated with highest honors in 1907; took piano courses with Artur Schnabel and Rudolph Ganz in Berlin (1907–9). In 1912 he was appointed instructor at Harvard; became assistant prof. in 1926; associate prof. in 1932; retired in 1947. His first publ. work was a musical play, *The Lotos Eaters* (1907); 3 of his orch. pieces were performed by the Boston Symph. Orch.: *From the Garden of Hellas* (Feb. 9, 1923); *Prelude to The Delectable Forest* (Dec. 10, 1914); *The Eve of St. Agnes* (Jan. 19, 1917); and one, *By a Lake in Russia,* by the Boston Pops (June 27, 1922). He also wrote a Violin Sonata and songs. His most striking work is a set of piano variations on *Mary Had a Little Lamb* (1924) in the styles of 10 composers; a 2nd series of variations on the same tune (1943) includes stylizations of Stravinsky, Gershwin, and others.

Ballard, a family of French music printers. The establishment was founded on Aug. 14, 1551, by Robert Ballard, whose patent from Henri II made him "Seul imprimeur de la musique de la chambre, chapelle, et menus plaisirs du roy"; the patent was renewed to various members of the family until 1776, when it expired. The firm enjoyed a virtual monopoly on French music printing, and continued under the management of the Ballard family until 1788. Until c.1750, the movable types invented in 1540 by Guillaume le Bé were used; the Ballards printed Lully's operas in this style (from 1700); later printings were from engraved copper-plates.

Ballard, Louis W., American Indian composer of Quapaw-Cherokee extraction (his Indian name is **Hunka-No-Zhe,** which means Grand Eagle); b. Miami, Okla., July 8, 1931. He studied piano and composition at Oklahoma Univ. and Tulsa Univ.; obtained his B.A. in music in 1954, and M.M. in composition in 1962. He subsequently took private lessons with Darius Milhaud, Castelnuovo-Tedesco, and Carlos Surinach. In 1964 he traveled in Europe under the auspices of the State Dept.; was awarded a Ford Foundation grant in 1971. He was subsequently appointed program director at the Bureau of Indian Affairs in Washington, D.C. (1971–79). Virtually all his compositions are musical realizations of authentic Indian melodies and rhythms.

Ballif, Claude, French composer; b. Paris, May 22, 1924. He studied composition at the Paris Cons. with Tony Aubin, Noël Gallon, and Messiaen, and later in Berlin with Blacher and Rufer. For several years he was connected with various pedagogical institutes in Paris; in 1964 he was appointed to the staff of the Cons. of Reims. He has also written articles on subjects dealing with modern musical techniques.

Balsam, Artur, Polish-born American pianist and pedagogue; b. Warsaw, Feb. 8, 1906. He studied in Lodz; made his debut there at the age of 12; then went to Berlin and enrolled at the Berlin Hochschule für Musik; in 1930 obtained the prestigious Mendelssohn Prize; in 1932 he made a U.S. tour with Yehudi Menuhin. With the advent of the anti-Semitic Nazi regime in 1933, he settled in America, where he became a superlative accompanist to celebrated artists; also played much chamber music and gave occasional solo recitals. He served on the faculties of the Eastman School of Music, Boston Univ., and the Manhattan School of Music; also composed cadenzas for several piano concertos of Mozart.

Baltzar, Thomas, German violinist and composer; b. Lübeck, c.1630; d. London (buried, July 27), 1663. He was a member of a family of German musicians; in 1653 he was made a chamber violinist to Queen Christina of Sweden; about 1655 he went to England, where he established himself as a soloist at private musical gatherings. In 1661 he was named a musician-in-ordinary for the violin in the King's Private Musick. He also composed several works for violin.

Bampton, Rose, American operatic soprano; b. Lakewood, Ohio, Nov. 28, 1908. She studied with Queena Mario at the Curtis Inst. of Music in Philadelphia; then took academic courses at Drake Univ. in Des Moines, Iowa, where she obtained a doctorate of fine arts. She sang as contralto with the Philadelphia Opera (1929–32), then changed to mezzo-soprano and finally to soprano, so that she could sing the roles of both Amneris (mezzo-soprano) and Aida (soprano). She made her debut at the Metropolitan Opera in N.Y. on Nov. 28, 1932, as Laura in *La Gioconda,* and continued on its staff until 1945; she was again with the Metropolitan Opera from 1947 to 1950. She made annual appearances at the Teatro Colón in Buenos Aires from 1942 to 1948; then returned to N.Y. She was married to the conductor **Wilfrid Pelletier.**

Banchieri, Adriano, Italian organist and composer; b. Bologna, Sept. 3, 1568; d. there, 1634. He studied with Lucio Barbieri and Giuseppe Guami. On Sept. 8, 1589, he took Holy Orders and entered the monastery of Monte Oliveto. In 1592 he was at the monastery of S. Bartolomeo in Lucca; 1593, in Siena; was organist at Santa Maria in Regola di Imola in 1600. In 1608 he returned to Bologna, remaining there until his death. Despite his clerical rank (he became abbot in 1620), Banchieri never abandoned music, and was active at the Accademia Filarmonica in Bologna (where he was known as "Il dissonante"). He wrote numerous stage works, historically important in the evolution of early opera. Among these dramatic works were *La pazzia senile* (1598); *Il zabaione musicale* (1604); *La barca da Venezia per Padova* (1605); *La prudenza giovanile* (1607); *Tirsi, Filli e Clori* (1614). He wrote a number of masses for 3 to 8 Voices, and other sacred vocal works; also several groups of instrumental works: *I canzoni alla francese a 4 voci per sonar* (1595); *Dialoghi, concentus e sinfonie* (1625); *Il virtuoso ritrovato accademico* (1626); etc. As a theorist, he advocated the extension of the hexachord and proposed to name the 7th degree of the scale by the syllables *ba* and *bi* (corresponding to B-flat and B). Banchieri's theoretical work *L'organo suonarino* (Venice, 1605) gives instructions for accompaniment with figured bass; his *Moderna prattica musicale* (Venice, 1613) contains further elaborations of the subject. Banchieri was the first to use the signs *f* and *p* for loudness and softness (in his *Libro III di nuovi pensieri ecclesiastici,* 1613). He also wrote dramatic plays under the name of **Camillo Scaliggeri della Fratta.** A reprint of his *Sinfonia d'istromenti* (1607) is found in A. Schering's *Geschichte der Musik in Beispielen* (No. 151); the organ pieces from *L'organo suonarino* are reprinted in Torchi's *Arte musicale in Italia* (vol. III). Banchieri further publ. the treatises *Cartella musicale del canto figurato, fermo e contrappunto* (Venice, 1614); *Direttorio monastico di canto fermo* (Bologna, 1615); and *Lettere armoniche* (Bologna, 1628).

Bandrowski-Sas, Aleksander, noted Polish tenor; b. Lubaczów, April 22, 1860; d. Cracow, May 28, 1913. He made his stage debut as a baritone in an operetta production in Lwow in 1881, using the name **Barski;** then studied voice with Sangiovanni in Milan and Salvi in Vienna; subsequently pursued a successful career as a tenor, using the name **Brandt;** sang in Vienna (1890), in Berlin (1896, 1898), and in Dresden and Munich, and at La Scala in Milan (1896, 1899); was a member of the Frankfurt Opera (1889–1901); also filled engagements in N.Y., Philadelphia, Chicago, and Boston. He retired from the stage in 1904, and then taught voice in Cracow.

Banister, John, English violinist and composer; b. London, 1630; d. there, Oct. 3, 1679. After he had received some musical instruction from his father, his skill earned him the patronage of King Charles II, who sent him to France for further study; was later a member of Charles's band, until an outspoken preference for the English over the French musicians playing in it caused his expulsion. Banister was director of a music school, and established the first public concerts not associated with taverns or other gathering places in which music was of only incidental importance, in London (1672–78); was a prominent figure in the English musical life of his day. He wrote music for Davenant's *Circe* and Shakespeare's *The Tempest* (both 1676); composed *New Ayres and Dialogues* for Voices and Viols (London, 1678); contributed to Playford's *Courtly Masquing Ayres* (1662), and to Lock's *Melothesia* (1673); also wrote music for plays by Dryden, Shadwell, and Wycherley.

Banti-Giorgi, Brigida, famous Italian soprano; b. Monticelli d'Ongina (Piacenza), 1759; d. Bologna, Feb. 18, 1806. She sang in Paris cafés, where she attracted the attention of de Vismes, director of the Paris Opéra, who engaged her to sing there. She made her debut on Nov. 1, 1776, singing a song during the intermission. She then studied with Sacchini. In 1779 she went to London for a season; then sang in Vienna (1780), Venice (1782–83), Warsaw (1789), and Madrid (1793–94). Paisiello wrote for her his opera *Giuochi di Agrigento,* and she sang at its premiere (Venice, May 16, 1792). From 1794 to 1802 she sang at King's Theatre in London; then retired. She married the dancer Zaccaria Banti; her son wrote her biography.

Bantock, Sir Granville, eminent English composer; b. London, Aug. 7, 1868; d. there, Oct. 16, 1946. He studied at the Royal Academy of Music, graduating in 1892; was the first holder of the Macfarren Scholarship. His earliest works were presented at the Academy concerts: an Egyptian ballet suite, *Rameses II;* overture, *The Fire Worshippers;* and a short opera, *Caedmar,* which was later presented at the Crystal Palace (Oct. 18, 1893). He then developed varied activities; he was founder and editor of *New Quarterly Musical Review* (1893–96); toured as a musical comedy conductor (1894–95); organized and conducted concerts devoted to works by young British composers; conducted a military band and later a full orch. at New Brighton (1897–1901). At the same time he was engaged in teaching activities; in 1907 he succeeded Sir Edward Elgar as prof. of music at Birmingham Univ., a post he retained until 1934, when he became chairman of the board of Trinity College of Music. In 1938, at the age of 70, he undertook a journey to India and Australia, returning to England on the eve of World War II. He was married in 1898 to Helen von Schweitzer, daughter of the poet Hermann von Schweitzer. Bantock was knighted in 1930. As a composer, he was attracted to exotic subjects with mystical overtones; his interests were cosmopolitan and embraced all civilizations, with a particular predilection for the Celtic and oriental cultures; however, his music was set in Western terms. He was a strong believer in the programmatic significance of musical images, and most of his works bear titles relating to literature, mythology, or legend. Yet he was a typically British composer in the treatment of his materials. His works are brilliantly scored and effective in performance, but few of them have been retained in the repertoire of musical organizations.

Banwart, Jakob, German composer; b. Sigmaringen, May 19, 1609; d. Konstanz, c.1657. He studied with Daniel Bollius, the court organist in Sigmaringen; then (1629–31) continued his education at Dillingen Univ., where he received a master's degree; he was ordained in Konstanz in 1632, and subsequently was active as a musician at the court there; in 1641 he became Kapellmeister of the Cathedral. He composed mostly music for the church, but also took time off to write a collection of humorous dialogues, quodlibets, and other pieces which were publ. in his lifetime.

Baranović, Krešimir, eminent Croatian composer; b. Šibenik, July 25, 1894; d. Belgrade, Sept. 17, 1975. He studied piano and theory in Zagreb and in Vienna. He was subsequently a theater conductor in Zagreb (1915–27); then traveled with Anna Pavlova's ballet group (1927–28). Returning to Yugoslavia, he was music director of the Zagreb Opera (1929–40); then served as a prof. at the Belgrade Academy (1946–61); was also conductor of the Belgrade Phil. (1952–61). He retired in 1963. A prolific composer, he was successful mostly in music for the theater.

Barati, George, eminent Hungarian-American cellist, composer, and conductor; b. Györ, April 3, 1913. He studied cello and theory at the Budapest Cons., and was first cellist at the Budapest Opera (1936–38). In 1939 he emigrated to America; attended courses of Roger Sessions at Princeton Univ. (1939–43); served as bandleader with the U.S. Army (1943–46); from 1946 to 1950 he played cello with the San Francisco Symph. Orch. In 1950 he was appointed conductor of the Honolulu Symph. Orch. in Hawaii, a post he held until 1968; then was executive director of the Montalvo Center for the Arts in Saratoga, Calif. (1968–78); concurrently served as music director of the Santa Cruz County Symph. (1971–80). As a composer, he wrote fine music in a modern European tradition; during his stay in Hawaii he studied native melodic and rhythmic patterns of exotic South Sea islands, which found a reflection in some of his works of the period.

Barbaja, Domenico, successful Italian impresario; b. Milan, c.1775; d. Posillipo, near Naples, Oct. 19, 1841. Early in life he exhibited a talent for making money by concocting and selling food and sweets that satisfied popular tastes; he was reputed to be the inventor of whipped cream with coffee or chocolate, which became known as *barbajata,* or *granita di caffè*. In 1808 he obtained the lease of the gambling tables in Naples. On Oct. 7, 1809, he was appointed manager of all of the royal opera houses in Naples; so powerful did he become that he was nicknamed "Viceroy of Naples." Upon the advice of his mistress, the well-known singer Isabella Colbran, he entered the theatrical business, and in 1826 was appointed manager of La Scala in Milan; simultaneously he was impresario of San Carlo in Naples (1809–24) and two theaters in Vienna (1821–28). He continued the management of La Scala until 1832. A convivial character, he easily formed friendships with Rossini, Bellini, and Donizetti, and induced them to write operas for the theaters under his management. Emil Lucka wrote a novel, *Der Impresario* (Vienna, 1937), based on his life.

Barbeau, Marius, eminent French-Canadian musician and folklorist; b. Ste. Marie de Beauce, Quebec, March 5, 1883; d. Ottawa, Feb. 27, 1969. He studied at Oxford Univ., obtaining his diploma in anthropology as a Rhodes scholar in 1910; later took courses at the Sorbonne in Paris. In 1911 he was appointed anthropologist at the Victoria Memorial Museum in Ottawa; was pensioned in 1948. His main study was devoted to the codification of folkloric materials of Canadian Indians and the French population of Quebec. He collected more than 6,000 melodies and 13,000 texts of French-Canadian folk songs and many thousands of Indian melodies, making use of phonograph recordings. From 1927 to 1930 he was in charge of folk music festivals in Quebec. In 1956 he organized the Canadian Folk Music Society. He published 30 books and 10 anthologies of songs in collaboration with other Canadian folklorists. Among his most important publications are "Chants populaires du Canada," *Journal of American Folklore* (1919); *Folksongs of French Canada* (with E. Sapir; New Haven, 1925); *Jongleur Songs of Old Quebec* (Toronto, 1962). For a bibliography of Barbeau's writings, almost 100 books and 600 articles, see Israel Katz, "Marius Barbeau, 1883–1969," *Ethnomusicology* (Jan. 1970).

Barber, Samuel, American composer of superlative gifts; b. West Chester, Pa., March 9, 1910; d. New York, Jan. 23, 1981. His mother was a good pianist; her sister was the famous opera contralto **Louise Homer.** Barber began taking piano lessons as a child with William Hatton Green; he also improvised, and composed a piano piece, entitled *Sadness.* At the age of 10 he attempted to write an opera, *The Rose Tree.* He played piano at school functions, and had an occasional job as organist in a local church. At the age of 14 he enrolled at the newly founded Curtis Inst. of Music in Philadelphia; there he studied piano with Isabelle Vengerova, composition with Rosario Scalero, and conducting with Fritz Reiner. He also took singing lessons with Emilio de Gogorza. So successful was he as a voice student that he ventured to appear in public as a mellow baritone. However, it was free composition that became his absorbing labor. At the time when most American composers exerted their ingenuity writing sophisticated music laced with unresolvable dissonances, Barber kept aloof from facile and fashionable modernism. He adopted an idiom, lyrical and romantic in nature, which had a distinct originality in its melodic and harmonic aspects. His *Overture to the School for Scandal,* after Sheridan (1933), attracted favorable attention. It was closely followed by *Music for a Scene from Shelley,* which had numerous performances. In 1935 Barber received a Pulitzer traveling scholarship and the American Prix de Rome. His *Symphony No. 1,* in one movement, which he composed in Rome, became the first American work to be presented at the Salzburg Festival of Contemporary Music (July 25, 1937). On Nov. 5, 1938, Toscanini conducted the NBC Symph. Orch. in Barber's *Essay for Orchestra No. 1* and *Adagio for Strings* (arranged from Barber's String Quartet); the *Adagio* was destined to become one of the most popular American works of serious music, and through some lurid aberration of circumstance, it also became a favorite selection at state funerals. It formed the background music at Roosevelt's commemorative service in 1945; the passionate serenity of its modal strains moved the family and friends of Princess Grace of Monaco to tears when it was played at her funeral on Sept. 18, 1982. From 1939 to 1942, Barber intermittently taught orchestration at the Curtis Inst. In the autumn of 1942 he joined the Army Air Force, which commissioned him to write a symph., his second. The original score included an electronic instrument producing sound in imitation of radio signals; it was successfully performed by Koussevitzky with the Boston Symph. Orch. in 1944; but after the war Barber decided to eliminate such incidental intercalations; this demilitarized version was performed by the Philadelphia Orch. in 1949. Still dissatisfied with the resultant product, he discarded the work except for the 2nd movement, which he retitled as *Night Flight,* and had it performed in Cleveland in 1964. Barber was discharged from the air force in 1945 and settled in Mt. Kisco, N.Y., in a house (named "Capricorn") that he had purchased jointly with Gian Carlo Menotti in 1943. Barber was always devoted to the art of the theater. He wrote a ballet, *The Serpent Heart,* for Martha Graham (1946), which was later revised and produced by her group under the title *Cave of the Heart;* from it he drew an orchestral suite, *Medea;* a further version of the music was *Medea's Meditation and Dance of Vengeance.* In his *Prayers of Kierkegaard* for Soprano, Chorus, and Orch. (1954), Barber essayed the style of modern oratorio. But it was not until 1958 that he wrote his first opera, *Vanessa,* with a romantic libretto by his lifelong friend Gian Carlo Menotti; it was produced by the Metropolitan Opera in N.Y. on Jan. 15, 1958, and earned Barber his first of two Pulitzer Prizes in music; a revised version was produced in 1978 at the Spoleto Festival U.S.A. in Charleston, S.C., on May 27, 1978. A much more ambitious opera, commissioned by the Metropolitan Opera, was *Antony and Cleopatra,* in 3 acts, after Shakespeare, produced with a grand display of expectations at the opening of the new Metropolitan Opera House in N.Y. on Sept. 16, 1966. Unfortunately, the production was haunted by mechanical mishaps. A specially constructed revolving stage did not rotate properly, the acoustics were faulty, and the annoyed newspaper critics damned the music along with the staging. Barber attempted to recoup the work with a libretto revamped by Menotti, but the new version, performed at the Juilliard School of Music (1975), failed to justify his hopes. Disillusioned in his capacity to create a modern grand opera, Barber produced a light operatic sketch, *A Hand of Bridge,* to a libretto by Menotti (1959), but it passed without much notice. However, Barber was gloriously vindicated as an important composer by a succession of fine works of instrumental music; particularly notable was his Piano Concerto (1962), a striking work in an original modern idiom, spontaneously acclaimed in repeated performances in America and Europe, which won him his second Pulitzer Prize. No less remarkable was his Piano Sonata, introduced by Vladimir Horowitz in 1949; in it Barber made ample use of modernistic resources, including incidental applications of 12-tone writing. Another example of Barber's brilliant use of pianistic resources was his witty piano suite *Excursions* (1945). Barber excelled in new American music primarily as a melodist; perhaps the circumstance that he studied singing as a youth had contributed to his sensitive handling of vocally shaped patterns. Although the harmonic structures of his music remained fundamentally tonal, he made free use of chromatic techniques, verging on atonality and polytonality, while his mastery of modern counterpoint enabled him to write canons and fugues in effective neo-Baroque sequences. His orchestration was opulent without being turgid; his treatment of solo instruments was unfailingly congenial to their nature even though requiring a virtuoso technique. Barber held three Guggenheim fellowships (1945, 1947, 1949). In 1959 Harvard Univ. conferred upon him an honorary degree of Doctor of Fine Arts.

WORKS: OPERAS: *Vanessa,* to a libretto by Menotti (Metropolitan Opera, N.Y., Jan. 15, 1958; revised version, Spoleto Festival U.S.A., Charleston, S.C., May 27, 1978); *Antony and Cleopatra,* after Shakespeare (N.Y., Sept. 16, 1966; revised, and produced in a new version at the Juilliard School of Music, N.Y., Feb. 6, 1975); *A Hand of Bridge,* one-act opera, to a libretto by Menotti, for 4 Solo Voices and Chamber Orch. (1958; Festival of Two Worlds, Spoleto, Italy, June 17, 1959).

BALLETS: *The Serpent Heart* (performed by Martha Graham and her dance group, N.Y., May 10, 1946; revised and produced under the title *Cave of the Heart,* N.Y., Feb. 27, 1947).

FOR ORCH.: *Overture to the School for Scandal,* after Sheridan (Philadelphia, Aug. 30, 1933); *Music for a Scene from Shelley* (N.Y., March 24, 1935); *Symphony No. 1,* in one movement (Rome, Dec. 13, 1936); *Adagio for Strings,* arranged from the slow movement of the String Quartet (N.Y., NBC Symph. Orch., conducted by Toscanini, Nov. 5, 1938; *Barber's Essay No. 1* was performed at the same concert); *Essay No. 2* (N.Y. Philharmonic, Bruno Walter conducting, April 16, 1942); *Commando March,*

originally for military band (performed in its symphonic form, Boston Symph., Koussevitzky conducting, Oct. 29, 1943); *Symphony No. 2* (Boston, March 3, 1944; conducted by Koussevitzky; an antiseptic version, radically cleansed of instrumental irrelevancies, was performed by the Philadelphia Orch., Ormandy conducting, Jan. 21, 1949; in another surgical operation, the second movement was reworked, retitled *Night Flight,* and first performed in Cleveland, Oct. 8, 1964); *Capricorn Concerto* for Flute, Oboe, Trumpet, and Strings (N.Y., Oct. 8, 1944); *Medea,* suite from the ballet *The Serpent Heart* (Philadelphia, Dec. 5, 1947); *Souvenirs,* ballet suite, originally for Piano, 4-hands; for Orch. (Chicago, Nov. 13, 1953; stage production, N.Y., Nov. 15, 1955); *Medea's Meditation and Dance of Vengeance,* a revised version of the symph. suite *Medea* (N.Y., Feb. 2, 1956); *Toccata Festiva* for Organ and Orch. (Philadelphia, Sept. 30, 1960); *Die Natali,* choral prelude for Christmas (Boston Symph. Orch., Lincoln Center, N.Y., Dec. 22, 1960); *Fadograph from a Yestern Scene,* after a line in James Joyce's *Finnegans Wake* (Pittsburgh, Sept. 10, 1971); *Essay No. 3* for Orch. (N.Y., Sept. 14, 1978); *Canzonetta* for Oboe and String Orch. (1980; incomplete; orchestrated by Charles Turner, and first perf. by the N.Y. Phil., Dec. 17, 1981).

CONCERTOS: Violin Concerto (Philadelphia, Feb. 7, 1941, Albert Spalding, soloist; Ormandy conducting); Cello Concerto (Boston Symph., Raya Garbuzova, soloist; Koussevitzky conducting, April 5, 1946); Piano Concerto (Boston Symph., Lincoln Center, N.Y., Sept. 24, 1962, John Browning, soloist; Erich Leinsdorf conducting).

VOCAL WORKS: *Dover Beach,* after a poem by Matthew Arnold, for Voice and String Quartet (1931; N.Y., March 5, 1933); *A Stopwatch and an Ordnance Map* for Male Chorus, Brass, and Timpani (Philadelphia, April 23, 1940); *Sure on This Shining Night,* to words by James Agee, for Voice and Orch. (1938); *Knoxville: Summer of 1915* for Voice and Orch., to a text of James Agee from his novel *A Death in the Family* (Boston Symph., Koussevitzky conducting, April 9, 1948); *Prayers of Kierkegaard* for Soprano, Chorus, and Orch. (Boston Symph., Dec. 3, 1954); *Andromache's Farewell* for Voice and Orch. (N.Y., April 4, 1963); *The Lovers* for Baritone, Chorus, and Orch., to words by Pablo Neruda (Philadelphia, Sept. 22, 1971).

CHAMBER MUSIC: *Serenade* for String Quartet, or String Orch. (Philadelphia, May 5, 1930); Cello Sonata (1932); String Quartet (1936; 2nd movement, *Adagio,* extracted from it and arranged for String Orch., was widely perf.); *Summer Music* for Woodwind Quintet (Detroit, March 20, 1956); *Canzone* for Flute and Piano (1962; arranged from the 2nd movement of the Piano Concerto); *Mutations from Bach* for Brass and Timpani (1968).

SONGS: *The Daisies,* to words by James Stephens (1927); *With Rue My Heart Is Laden,* to words by A.E. Housman (1928); 3 Songs to poems from *Chamber Music* by James Joyce (1936); *A Nun Takes the Veil,* to words by G.M. Hopkins (1937); *The Secrets of the Old,* to words by W.B. Yeats (1938); *The Queen's Face on the Summery Coin,* to words by

Robert Horan (1942); *Monks and Raisins,* to words by J.G. Villa (1943); *Nuvoletta,* to words by James Joyce (1947); *Mélodies passagères,* 5 songs, to words by Rilke (1951); *Hermit Songs,* 10 songs after old Irish texts (Washington, D.C., Oct. 30, 1953, Leontyne Price, soloist); *Despite and Still,* 5 songs to words by Graves, Roethke, and Joyce (1969); *3 Songs* for Baritone and Piano (N.Y., April 30, 1974, Fischer-Dieskau, soloist).

FOR CHORUS: *The Virgin Martyrs* (1935); *Let Down the Bars, O Death* (1936); *Reincarnation,* 3 songs after poems by Stephens, for Mixed Chorus a cappella (1940).

FOR PIANO SOLO: *Excursions* (1944); Piano Sonata in E-flat minor (Havana, Cuba, Dec. 9, 1949, Horowitz, soloist; N.Y. performance, also by Horowitz, Jan. 23, 1950); *Souvenirs* for Piano, 4-hands, also for Orch. (1953); *Nocturne: Homage to John Field* (1959); *Ballade* (1977); also *Wonderous Love,* variations on a shape-note hymn, for Organ (1958).

Barbieri, Carlo Emmanuele, Italian conductor and composer; b. Genoa, Oct. 22, 1822; d. Budapest, Sept. 28, 1867. He was educated at the Naples Cons., where he studied voice with Crescenti and composition with Mercadante. In 1845 he embarked on a career as an opera conductor; eventually settled in Buda, where he conducted at the National Theater from 1862 until his death. He wrote 5 operas: *Cristoforo Colombo* (Berlin, 1848); *Nisida, la perla di Procida* (1851); *Carlo und Carlin* (1859); *Arabella* (Budapest, 1862); and *Perdita, Ein Wintermärchen* (Leipzig, 1865); church music, German and Italian songs.

Barbieri, Fedora, Italian mezzo-soprano; b. Trieste, June 4, 1920. She studied with local teachers; then moved to Milan, where her teacher was Giulia Tess. She made her professional debut at the Florence Opera in 1940; then filled engagements, in the midst of a raging war, in Germany, Belgium, and the Netherlands. After the end of hostilities she sang at La Scala in Milan, in Paris, and in London. She made her American debut in San Francisco; then sang in Chicago; from 1950 to 1953 and again in 1967 she appeared with the Metropolitan Opera in N.Y. Her best roles were Azucena in *Il Trovatore* and Amneris in *Aida;* she also sang the title role in *Carmen.*

Barbieri, Francisco Asenjo, Spanish composer; b. Madrid, Aug. 3, 1823; d. there, Feb. 19, 1894. He studied clarinet, voice, and composition at the Madrid Cons., then engaged in multifarious activities as a café pianist, music copyist, and choral conductor. He found his true vocation in writing zarzuelas, and composed 78 of them. The following, all produced in Madrid, were particularly successful: *Gloria y peluca* (March 9, 1850); *Jugar con fuego* (Oct. 6, 1851); *Los diamantes de la corona* (Sept. 15, 1854); *Pan y Toros* (Dec. 22, 1864); *El Barberillo de Lavapiés* (Dec. 18, 1874). Barbieri edited a valuable collection, *Cancionero musical de los siglos XV y XVI,* and publ. a number of essays on Spanish music.

Barbireau (or **Barbirau, Barbarieu, Barbyrianus, Barberau, Barbacola**), **Jacques** (**Jacobus**), Flemish composer; b. Mons, c.1408; d. Antwerp, Aug. 8, 1491. He was appointed Maître de Chapelle at Notre Dame Cathedral in Antwerp in 1448, and served there until his death. Okeghem was one of his pupils. Barbireau was greatly esteemed by his contemporaries; his opinions were copiously cited by Tinctoris. He wrote exclusively for the church; composed a Mass for 5 Voices, *Virgo parens Christi; Missa Pascale* for 4 Voices; antiphons; Psalms; anthems.

Barbirolli, Sir John, eminent English conductor; b. London, Dec. 2, 1899, of Italian-French parentage; d. there, July 29, 1970. His baptismal names were Giovanni Battista, given by his father, a professional violinist. He studied cello; received a scholarship to the Trinity College of Music in 1910 and another scholarship to the Royal Academy of Music, graduating in 1916; he made his first appearance as a cellist at the age of 12, on Dec. 16, 1911, at the Queen's Hall. In 1916 he became a member of the Queen's Hall Orch. In 1918–19 he served in the British Army; afterwards resumed his musical career. In 1923 he joined the International String Quartet and toured with it. In 1925 he organized a chamber orch. in Chelsea, which he conducted for several years; later was a conductor with the British National Opera Co. (1926–29). He gained recognition when on Dec. 12, 1927, he successfully substituted for Beecham at a concert of the London Symph. Orch. In 1928 he was a guest conductor at Covent Garden, and a regular conductor there from 1929 to 1933; in 1933 he was named conductor of the Scottish Orch., Glasgow, and the Leeds Symph. Orch. He made his American debut with the N.Y. Phil. on Nov. 5, 1936, and was engaged as its permanent conductor in 1937. However, he failed to impress the N.Y. critics, and in 1943 he returned to England, where he was named conductor of the Hallé Orch. of Manchester. In 1958 he was appointed its conductor-in-chief. Renewing his American career, he served as conductor of the Houston Symph. (1961–67), while continuing his tenancy of the Hallé Orch., from which he finally retired in 1968 with the title of Conductor Laureate for Life. He was knighted in 1949 and made a Companion of Honour in 1969. A commemorative postage stamp with his portrait was issued by the Post Office of Great Britain on Sept. 1, 1980. Barbirolli was distinguished primarily in the Romantic repertoire; his interpretations were marked by nobility, expressive power, and brilliance. He had a fine pragmatic sense of shaping the music according to its inward style, without projecting his own personality upon it. However, this very objectivity tempered his success with American audiences, accustomed to charismatic flamboyance in music-making. He had a special affinity for English music, and performed many works of Elgar, Delius, and Britten. He conducted the first performances of the 7th and 8th symphs. by Vaughan Williams; also made transcriptions for string orch. and French horns of 5 pieces from the Fitzwilliam

Virginal Book (perf. by him under the title *Elizabethan Suite* in Los Angeles, Dec. 4, 1941). He composed for his 2nd wife, the oboist Evelyn Rothwell, an Oboe Concerto on themes by Pergolesi.

Barblan, Otto, Swiss organist and composer; b. Scanfs, Switzerland, March 22, 1860; d. Geneva, Dec. 19, 1943. He studied at the Stuttgart Cons. (1878–84); made his debut as an organist at Augsburg (1885); taught at Chur (1885–87); then became organist at the Cathedral of Geneva, prof. at the Cons., and conductor of the "Société de Chant Sacré" (1887). He wrote an *Ode Patriotique* (1896); a *Festspiel* (Chur, May 28, 1899) commemorating the 400th anniversary of the battle of Calven, and containing the chorus *Terre des monts*, which has attained great popularity, placing it next to the national anthem as a patriotic song; *Post tenebras lux*, cantata for the Calvin jubilee (1909); String Quartet; Variations and Triple Fugue on B-A-C-H; Passion according to St. Luke (Geneva, April 9, 1919).

Bardi, Giovanni de', Count of Vernio, Italian nobleman, patron of music and art, and composer; b. Florence, Feb. 5, 1534; d. Rome, 1612. He was the founder of the Florentine Camerata, a group of musicians who met at his home (1576–c.1582) to discuss the music of Greek antiquity; this led to the beginnings of opera. Count Bardi was descended from an old Guelph banking family; he was a philologist, mathematician, neo-Platonic philosopher, and lover of Dante. He was a member of the Crusca Academy, a literary group founded in 1583 whose ideas had great influence on the Camerata. Bardi is known to have been in Rome in 1567; he lent support to Vincenzo Galilei, a member of the Camerata. In 1580 Bardi married Lucrezia Salvati. The masques of 1589, commemorating the marriage of Grand Duke Ferdinand, were conceived largely by Bardi. In 1592 he left for Rome to become chamberlain at the court of Pope Clement VIII. Caccini was his secretary in 1592. Bardi's writings are: *Discorso sopra il giuoco del calzio fiorentino* (Florence, 1580); *Ristretto delle grandezze di Roma* (Rome, 1600); *Discorso mandato a Caccini sopra la musica antica* in Doni's *Lyra Barberina* (Florence, 1763). Among his compositions are a madrigal in 4 Voices, *Misere habitator* in Malvezzi's *Intermedi e concerti* (Venice, 1591); the madrigal *Lauro ohime Lauro* in *Il Lauro secco, lib.* I (Ferrara, 1582). Among contemporary documents which refer to him are Vincenzo Galilei's *Dialogo della musica antica e della moderna* (translated in part in O. Strunk's *Source Readings in Music History*, N.Y., 1951; also included is a letter from Bardi's son to G.B. Doni commenting on Bardi's ideas).

Barenboim, Daniel, greatly talented pianist and conductor; b. Buenos Aires, Argentina, Nov. 15, 1942. He studied music with his parents; appeared in public as a child pianist in Buenos Aires at the age of 7; in 1952 the family settled in Israel. During the summers of 1954 and 1955 he was in Salzburg, where he studied piano with Edwin Fischer and took lessons in conducting with Igor Markevitch, and chamber music playing with Enrico Mainardi. In 1954–56 he studied music theory with Nadia Boulanger in Paris; also enrolled at the Santa Cecilia Academy in Rome, where he became one of the youngest students to receive a diploma in 1956. He also studied conducting with Carlo Zecchi at the Chigiana Academy in Siena. He gave piano recitals in Paris in 1955 and in London in 1956. On Jan. 20, 1957, he made his American debut at Carnegie Hall, N.Y., playing Prokofiev's First Piano Concerto with Leopold Stokowski conducting the Symph. of the Air. He gave his first U.S. solo recital in N.Y. on Jan. 17, 1958. He made his debut as a conductor in Haifa in 1957; in 1960 he played all 32 Beethoven sonatas in a series of concerts in Tel Aviv; he repeated this cycle in N.Y. As a pianist, he subordinated Romantic passion to Classical balance of form and thematic content. As a conductor he gave congenial performances of the masterpieces of Romantic music; became particularly engrossed in the music of Anton Bruckner, and was awarded the Bruckner Medal of the Bruckner Society of America. In 1967 he conducted the Israel Phil. on its tour of the U.S.; in 1968 he led the London Symph. Orch. at its appearance in N.Y.; he subsequently filled engagements with the Boston Symph., Chicago Symph., Philadelphia Orch., and N.Y. Phil. He made his first appearance as an opera conductor at the Edinburgh Festival in 1973. In 1975 he was named music director of the Orch. de Paris. On June 15, 1967, he married, in Jerusalem, the English cellist **Jacqueline DuPré,** who became converted to Judaism. They appeared in numerous sonata programs until, tragically, she was stricken in 1972 with multiple sclerosis and had to abandon her career.

Barere, Simon, Russian virtuoso pianist; b. Odessa, Sept. 1, 1896; d. suddenly, while performing Grieg's Piano Concerto in Carnegie Hall, N.Y., April 2, 1951. He studied with Anna Essipoff at the St. Petersburg Cons. and, after her death, with Felix Blumenfeld. After graduation, concertized in Germany, Sweden, and the U.S. He was praised for his extraordinary virtuosity, and was once described in the *New York Times* as "truly a giant of the keyboard." His death came to him unexpectedly during a concert of the Philadelphia Orch. in Carnegie Hall; he suddenly collapsed, fell on the floor, and died backstage; the rest of the program was cancelled.

Bargiel, Woldemar, German composer; b. Berlin, Oct. 3, 1828; d. there, Feb. 23, 1897. He was a half brother of **Clara Schumann.** As a boy he sang at the Berlin Cathedral and studied counterpoint with Dehn, and at the Leipzig Cons. (1846–50) with Hauptmann, Moscheles, Gade, and Rietz; became prof. at the Cologne Cons. in 1859. He was a teacher and conductor in Rotterdam (1865–75); in 1874 became prof. of composition at the Berlin Hochschule für Musik. He was greatly admired by Schumann and Brahms, and his works, in a Romantic vein, were frequently performed; almost all of his music was publ. during his lifetime. He wrote a

Symph.; 3 overtures; String Octet; 4 string quartets; 3 piano trios; violin sonatas; numerous piano pieces and songs.

Barili, Alfredo, Italian-American pianist, composer, and pedagogue; b. Florence, Aug. 2, 1854; d. Atlanta, Ga., Nov. 17, 1935, in an accident when he took a walk and was struck by a bus. He was a scion of an illustrious musical family; his father, **Ettore Barili,** an excellent musician in his own right, was a half-brother of the operatic diva **Adelina Patti.** Alfredo Barili was taken to America in his infancy and was taught piano by his father, making his public debut as a pianist in N.Y. on April 7, 1865. In 1868 the family relocated to Philadelphia, where he studied with Carl Wolfsohn, a German musician who claimed to be the first to perform all 32 piano sonatas of Beethoven in a series of concerts. In 1872 Barili went to Germany and enrolled at the Cologne Cons., studying piano with Friedrich Gernsheim and James Kwast, and composition with Ferdinand Hiller. Returning to the U.S. in 1880, he settled in Atlanta, taught for 6 years at the Atlanta Female Inst., and in 1886 founded his own "music academy," teaching piano at a fee of $1.50 per lesson. He maintained a cordial relationship with his famous aunt, Adelina Patti, and acted as her piano accompanist at a London concert in 1911. He also composed some perishable salon music in the approved manner of the time. His piano piece *Cradle Song* went into 26 editions; also popular among his pupils were his *Danse caprice, Miniature Gavotte,* and *Spanish Serenade.*

Barkauskas, Vytautas, outstanding Lithuanian composer; b. Kaunas, March 25, 1931. He studied music at the Tallat-Kelpša Music College in Vilna while also studying physics and mathematics at the State Pedagogical Inst. there (1949–53); then took composition with Račiunas and orchestration with Balsis at the Lithuanian State Cons. (1953–59); in 1961 joined its faculty. He wrote several cantatas in the style of socialist realism; in his instrumental compositions he makes use of advanced cosmopolitan techniques, including serialism and aleatory improvisation.

Barlow, Wayne (Brewster), American composer; b. Elyria, Ohio, Sept. 6, 1912. He studied with Bernard Rogers and Howard Hanson at the Eastman School of Music in Rochester, N.Y. (B.M., 1934; M.M., 1935; Ph.D., 1937); also took courses from Schoenberg at the Univ. of Southern Calif. in Los Angeles (1935). In 1937 he was appointed to the faculty of the Eastman School of Music; in 1968 became chairman of its composition dept. and director of its electronic music studio; retired in 1973 from the former post and continued to hold the latter until his retirement in 1978. He publ. *Foundations of Music* (N.Y., 1963).

Bärmann, Heinrich (Joseph), renowned German clarinetist; b. Potsdam, Feb. 14, 1784; d. Munich, June 11, 1847. He studied oboe at the School of Military Music in Potsdam, and as a youth served as

bandmaster in the Prussian Life Guards; then studied clarinet with Beer and Tausch. He was in the Prussian army at Jena, and was captured by the French, but made his escape and traveled to Munich, where he obtained the post of a court musician. Weber became his friend, and wrote a Clarinet Concertino and the 2 Clarinet Concertos for him; they appeared together at concerts in Prague and in Germany (1811–12); later Bärmann gave concerts in France, England, and Russia. He wrote a number of works for the clarinet, including concertos, fantasias, quintets, quartets, and sonatas; he also prepared teaching pieces and technical exercises for the clarinet, which are still in use in Germany. The Adagio from his Quintet No. 3 in E-flat major, op. 23, which he wrote in 1821, has been unaccountably attributed to Wagner, and so listed in numerous collections of clarinet pieces. It was republ. in 1971 by Breitkopf und Härtel under Bärmann's name.

Barnard, Charlotte (Mrs. Charles Barnard), English songwriter; b. Louth, Dec. 23, 1830; d. Dover, Jan. 30, 1869. In 1866 she publ. under the pen name of **Claribel** the ballad *Come Back to Erin,* which attained great popularity. She also wrote poetry.

Barnett, John, English composer; b. Bedford, July 15, 1802; d. Leckhampton, April 17, 1890. He was the son of a German jeweler named Bernhard Beer, but Anglicized his name when he moved to England. He wrote operettas and various other pieces of light music before producing his first full-fledged opera, *The Mountain Sylph* (London, Aug. 25, 1834); this was followed by 2 more operas, *Fair Rosamond* (London, Feb. 28, 1837) and *Farinelli* (London, Feb. 8, 1839). In 1841 he settled in Cheltenham as a voice teacher, but about 1870 moved to a country residence, Cotteswold in Leckhampton, where he remained until his death. Among his works are a symph., 3 string quartets, and songs numbering in the thousands. He also publ. two singing methods, *Systems and Singing Masters* (1842) and *School for the Voice* (1844).

Barnett, John Francis, English composer; nephew of **John Barnett;** b. London, Oct. 16, 1837; d. there, Nov. 24, 1916. He studied piano in London and in Leipzig. In 1883 he was appointed to the staff of the Royal College of Music in London. He wrote a Symph. (1864), several playable symphonic overtures and singable cantatas, several of them inspired by literary works. Among his oratorios, *The Raising of Lazarus,* first performed in London on June 18, 1873, was much performed in churches. He publ. an engaging vol., *Musical Reminiscences and Impressions* (London, 1906).

Baron, Samuel, American flutist and conductor; b. New York, April 27, 1925. He studied at Brooklyn College and the Juilliard School of Music; his flute teachers were Georges Barrère and Arthur Lora; he also took lessons in conducting with Edgar Schenkman; then played flute in several orchs. In 1949 he helped to found the N.Y. Woodwind Quintet, with which he played for 20 years; in 1948 he organized the N.Y. Brass Ensemble. He was also active as a teacher, serving on the faculties of the Mannes, Juilliard, and Yale schools of music; in 1966 he joined the faculty of the State Univ. of N.Y. at Stony Brook. He publ. *Chamber Music for Winds* (N.Y., 1969).

Baroni, Leonora, Italian singer, known as **"L'Adrianella"** and **"L'Adrianetta";** b. Mantua, Dec. 1611; d. Rome, April 6, 1670. She studied with her mother, the famous singer **Andreana Basile.** In 1633 she went to Rome; in 1644 she proceeded to Paris and appeared at the court of the Queen Regent of France, Anne of Austria. In 1645 she returned to Italy.

Barraine, Elsa, French composer; b. Paris, Feb. 13, 1910. Her father was a cellist, her mother a singer. She studied at the Paris Cons. with Paul Dukas, Jean Gallon, and Caussade; received the second Prix de Rome in 1928. She composed 3 symphs. (1931, 1938, 1947) and a curiously realistic symph. poem, *Pogromes* (*Pogroms;* referring to the Nazi persecutions of Jews; performed in Paris, March 11, 1939). Other works include *Suite astrologique* for Orch. (1947); *Atmosphère* for Oboe and 10 Instruments, on Hindu rhythms (1967); *Musique rituelle* for Organ, Gongs, and Xylorimba (1968).

Barraqué, Jean, French composer of advanced modern tendencies; b. Paris, Jan. 17, 1928; d. there, Aug. 17, 1973. He studied with Jean Langlais at the Paris Cons. and privately with Olivier Messiaen. From his early works, he devoted himself to experimentation, absorbing all resources of modern music, including dodecaphony and electronics. His most celebrated work is the Piano Sonata No. 1 (1950–52); another major work is *Séquence* (1950–55), scored for Soprano, Piano, Harp, Violin, Cello, and Assorted Percussion; other works are *Le temps restitué* for Voices and Orch. (1957); *Au-delà du hasard* for Voices and 4 Instrumental Groups (Paris, Jan. 26, 1960); *Chant après chant* for Voice, Percussion, and Piano (1966); Concerto for 6 Instrumental Groups, Vibraphone, and Clarinet (1968); and Piano Sonata No. 2 (1976). Barraqué planned the composition of an immense work in 13 parts which was to be the expression of his world philosophy, but the work remained in fragments at his death. A listing of his works is contained in "Propos impromptu. Jean Barraqué," *Courier Musical de France* 26 (1969). Despite the scarcity of his completed works, Barraqué impressed musicians as a potential genius. André Hodeir devotes an enthusiastic chapter to Barraqué in his book *La Musique depuis Debussy* (Paris, 1961; Eng. trans., *Since Debussy;* N.Y. and London, 1961).
WRITINGS: *Debussy* (Paris, 1962).

Barraud, Henry, French composer; b. Bordeaux, April 23, 1900. He studied music without a teacher, while engaged in the family wine business in Bordeaux. In 1926 he entered the Paris Cons. and stud-

ied with Louis Aubert; also studied composition with Dukas and fugue with Caussade. In 1937 Barraud was appointed director of music for the International Exposition in Paris. He served in the French army during World War II; after the demobilization he lived in Marseilles. After the liberation of Paris in 1944 he was appointed music director of Radiodiffusion Française; he retired in 1965. In 1969 he received the Grand Prix National de la Musique.
WORKS: *Finale dans le mode rustique* (Paris, 1932); *Poème* for Orch. (1934); *Concerto de camera* for 30 Instruments (1936); *Le Mystère des Saints Innocents,* oratorio (1942–44); *Le Diable à la Kermesse,* ballet (1943; a symph. suite from it was broadcast by Paris Radio, April 26, 1945); Piano Concerto (N.Y. Phil., Dec. 5, 1946); *Offrande à une ombre* (in memory of a brother killed by the Germans as a member of the Resistance; first U.S. performance, St. Louis, Jan. 10, 1947); *La Farce du Maître Pathelin* (Paris, June 24, 1948); *Symphonie de Numance* (Baden-Baden, Dec. 3, 1950); Concertino for Piano and 4 Winds (1953); *Numance,* opera (Paris, April 15, 1955); *Te Deum* for Chorus and 6 Instruments (1955); Symph. for String Orch. (1955); Symph. No. 3 (Boston, March 7, 1958); *Rapsodie cartésienne* for Orch. (1959); *Rapsodie dionysienne* for Orch. (1961); *Lavinia,* opera-buffa (Aix-en-Provence, July 20, 1961); Divertimento for Orch. (1962); Concerto for Flute and Strings (1963); *Symphonie concertante* for Trumpet and Orch. (1965); *3 études* for Orch.; *Une Saison en enfer,* symph. suite after Rimbaud (1969). Barraud also publ. books on Berlioz (Paris, 1955; 2nd ed., 1966), on the problems of modern music, *Pour comprendre les musiques d'aujourd'hui* (Paris, 1968), and on the analysis of selected operas, *Les Cinq Grands Opéras* (Paris, 1972).

Barrère, Georges, French flute virtuoso; b. Bordeaux, Oct. 31, 1876; d. Kingston, N.Y., June 14, 1944. He studied at the Paris Cons. (1889–95), graduating with first prize; was solo flutist at Colonne Concerts and at the Paris Opéra (1897–1905). He came to America in 1905; played flute with the N.Y. Symph. Orch. (1905–28); taught at the Inst. of Musical Art, N.Y., and at the Juilliard School of Music. He was the founder of the Barrère Little Symph. (1914); composed a *Nocturne* for Flute; *Chanson d'automne* for Voice; also edited classical works for flute.

Barrientos, Maria, Spanish coloratura soprano; b. Barcelona, March 10, 1884; d. Ciboure, France, Aug. 8, 1946. She studied at the Barcelona Cons.; made her operatic debut at the age of 15 in Barcelona, on March 4, 1899, and while still at a very young age made a successful tour of Europe. She made her American debut at the Metropolitan Opera House in N.Y. as Lucia on Jan. 31, 1916, and remained with it until 1920; then returned to Europe.

Barrière, Jean, French cellist and composer; b. c.1705; d. Paris, June 6, 1747. In 1730 he was appointed as a musician-in-ordinary at the Royal Academy of Music in Paris; then went to Rome, where he studied cello with Alborea; returned to Paris in 1739, and made a fine career as a virtuoso cellist at the Concert Spirituel. He publ. 6 books of cello sonatas (Paris, 1733–39).

Barrios Fernandez, Angel, Spanish composer; b. Granada, Jan. 4, 1882; d. Madrid, Nov. 27, 1964. Of a musical family (his father was a famous guitarist), he studied violin and played in bands as a child. He later studied theory with Conrado del Campo in Madrid and with Gédalge in Paris. At the same time, he perfected his guitar playing; formed a trio, Iberia, and traveled in Europe playing Spanish popular music. He spent his declining years in Madrid. In collaboration with his teacher Conrado del Campo, he wrote a successful operetta, *El Avapiés* (Madrid, 1919) and several zarzuelas: *La Suerte, La Romería, Seguidilla gitana, Castigo de Dios, En Nombre del Rey,* and *Lola se va a los puertos;* also numerous overtures and other orchestral pieces based on popular Spanish motifs.

Barsanti, Francesco, Italian flutist and composer; b. Lucca, c.1690; d. London, 1772. He studied at the Univ. of Padua; served as a flutist and oboist in the Italian opera in London; then spent some time in Scotland, returning to London in 1743. He wrote 9 overtures; 12 violin concertos; 6 flute solos with Bass; 6 sonatas for 12 Violins with Bass; 6 antiphons in Palestrina style; numerous pieces for various instruments. He publ. *A Collection of Old Scots Tunes* (Edinburgh, 1742).

Barshai, Rudolf, Russian conductor; b. Labinskaya, near Krasnodar, Sept. 28, 1924. He studied violin at the Moscow Cons. with Lev Zeitlin and viola with Borisovsky, graduating in 1948; also studied conducting with Ilya Musin in Leningrad; in 1955 he organized the Moscow Chamber Orch., which became extremely successful; many Soviet composers wrote works for it. In 1976 he emigrated to Israel, and led the Israel Chamber Orch. in Tel Aviv until 1981. He also appeared as a guest conductor in Europe, the U.S., and Japan. In 1982 he was named principal conductor and artistic adviser of the Bournemouth Symph. Orch.

Barstow, Josephine, English soprano; b. Sheffield, Sept. 27, 1940. She studied at the Univ. of Birmingham; then joined Opera for All in 1964; later studied at the London Opera Centre; was a member of the Sadler's Wells Opera (1967–68); from 1968 sang with the Welsh National Opera; from 1969 made many appearances at Covent Garden. She made her Metropolitan Opera debut on March 28, 1977, as Musetta in *La Bohème*. A versatile singer, her repertoire ranges from traditional to contemporary roles.

Barth, Hans, pianist and composer; b. Leipzig, June 25, 1897; d. Jacksonville, Fla., Dec. 9, 1956. When a small child, he won a scholarship at the Leipzig Cons. and studied under Carl Reinecke; came to the U.S. in 1907, but made frequent trips to Germany. His meeting with Busoni inspired him to experiment with new scales; with the aid of George L. Weitz, he perfected a portable quarter-tone piano (1928), on which he played in Carnegie Hall (Feb. 3, 1930); composed a Piano Concerto for this instrument, with a string orch. also tuned in quarter-tones (played by him with Stokowski and the Philadelphia Orch., March 28, 1930). Other works using quarter-tones: Suite for Strings, Brass, and Kettledrums; Piano Quintet; also a Piano Concerto for normal tuning (1928) and two piano sonatas; operetta, *Miragia* (1938); a piano manual, *Technic* (1935); various essays, etc.

Barthélémon, François-Hippolyte, French violinist and composer; b. Bordeaux, July 27, 1741; d. London, July 20, 1808. His father was French and his mother Irish. He held posts as violinist in various theater orchs. in London; became intimately acquainted with Haydn during Haydn's London visit in 1792. He was greatly praised as a violinist; Burney speaks of his tone as being "truly vocal." Barthélémon wrote mostly for the stage; among his operas, the most notable are *Pelopida* (London, May 24, 1766); *The Judgement of Paris* (London, Aug. 24, 1768); *Le Fleuve Scamandre* (Paris, Dec. 22, 1768); *The Maid of the Oaks* (The Oaks, near Epsom, June 1774); *Belphegor* (London, March 16, 1778). In addition, he wrote a Violin Concerto; 2 sets of duos for violins; 6 string quartets; catches and glees to English words (many of them publ.). He was married to Mary Young, a noted singer descended from Anthony Young; his daughter contributed a biographical edition (London, 1827) of selections from Barthélémon's oratorio *Jefte in Masfa.*

Bartók, Béla, great Hungarian composer; b. Nagyszentmiklós (now Sînnicolau Mare, Rumania), March 25, 1881; d. New York, Sept. 26, 1945. His father was a school headmaster; his mother was a proficient pianist, and he received his first piano lessons from her. He began playing the piano in public at the age of 11. In 1894 the family moved to Pressburg (Bratislava), where he took piano lessons with László Erkel, son of the famous Hungarian opera composer; he also studied harmony with Anton Hyrtl. In 1899 he enrolled at the Royal Academy of Music in Budapest, where he studied piano with István Thomán and composition with Hans Koessler; he graduated in 1903. His earliest compositions reveal the combined influence of Liszt, Brahms, and Richard Strauss; however, he soon became interested in exploring the resources of national folk music, which included not only Hungarian melorhythms but also elements of other ethnic strains in his native Transylvania , including Rumanian and Slovak. He formed a cultural friendship with Zoltán Kodály, and together they traveled through the land collecting folk songs, which they publ. in 1906. In 1907 Bartók succeeded István Thomán as professor of piano at the Royal Academy of Music. His interest in folk-song research led him to tour North Africa in 1913. In 1919 he served as a member of the musical directorate of the short-lived Hungarian Democratic Republic with Dohnányi and Kodály; was also deputy director of the Academy of Music. Although a brilliant pianist, he limited his concert programs mainly to his own compositions; he also gave concerts playing works for 2 pianos with his second wife, **Ditta Pásztory** (d. Budapest, Nov. 21, 1982, at the age of 80). In his own compositions he soon began to feel the fascination of tonal colors and impressionistic harmonies as cultivated by Debussy and other modern French composers. The basic texture of his music remained true to tonality, which he expanded to chromatic polymodal structures and unremittingly dissonant chordal combinations; in his piano works he exploited the extreme registers of the keyboard, often in the form of tone clusters to simulate pitchless drumbeats. He made use of strong asymmetrical rhythmic figures suggesting the modalities of Slavic folk music, a usage that imparted a somewhat acrid coloring to his music. The melodic line of his works sometimes veered toward atonality in its chromatic involutions; in some instances he employed melodic figures comprising the 12 different notes of the chromatic scale; however, he never adopted the integral techniques of the 12-tone method.

Bartók toured the U.S. as a pianist from Dec. 1927 to Feb. 1928; also gave concerts in the Soviet Union in 1929. He resigned his position at the Budapest Academy of Music in 1934, but continued his research work in ethnomusicology as a member of the Hungarian Academy of Sciences, where he was engaged in the preparation of the monumental *Corpus Musicae Popularis Hungaricae.* With the outbreak of World War II, Bartók decided to leave Europe; in the fall of 1940 he went to the U.S., where he remained until his death from polycythemia. In 1940 he received an honorary Ph.D. from Columbia Univ.; he also did folk-song research there as a visiting assistant in music (1941–42). His last completed score, the *Concerto for Orchestra,* commissioned by Koussevitzky, proved to be his most popular work. His Third Piano Concerto was virtually completed at the time of his death, except for the last 17 bars, which were arranged and orchestrated by his pupil Tibor Serly.

Throughout his life, and particularly during his last years in the U.S., Bartók experienced constant financial difficulties, and complained bitterly of his inability to support himself and his family. Actually, he was apt to exaggerate his pecuniary troubles, which were largely due to his uncompromising character. He arrived in America in favorable circumstances; his traveling expenses were paid by the American patroness Elizabeth Sprague Coolidge, who also engaged him to play at her festival at the Library of Congress for a generous fee. Bartók was offered the opportunity to give a summer course in composition at a midwestern college on advantageous terms, when he was still well enough to undertake such a task, but he proposed to teach piano instead, and the deal collapsed. Ironically, performances and recordings of his music increased enormously after his death, and the value of his estate reached a great sum of money. Posthu-

mous honors were not lacking: Hungary issued a series of stamps with Bartók's image; a street in Budapest was named Bartók Street; the centenary of his birth (1981) was celebrated throughout the world by concerts and festivals devoted to his works.

Far from being a cerebral purveyor of abstract musical designs, Bartók was an ardent student of folkways, seeking the roots of meters, rhythms, and modalities in the spontaneous songs and dances of the people. Indeed, he regarded his analytical studies of popular melodies as his most important contribution to music. Even during the last years of his life, already weakened by illness, he applied himself assiduously to the arrangement of Serbo-Croatian folk melodies of Yugoslavia from recordings placed in his possession. He was similarly interested in the natural musical expression of children; he firmly believed that children are capable of absorbing modalities and asymmetrical rhythmic structures with greater ease than adults trained in the rigid disciplines of established music schools. His remarkable collection of piano pieces entitled, significantly, *Mikrokosmos* was intended as a method to initiate beginners into the world of unfamiliar tonal and rhythmic combinations; in this he provided a parallel means of instruction to the Kodály method of schooling.

WORKS: FOR THE STAGE: *A kékszakállú herceg vará (Duke Bluebeard's Castle),* opera in one act, op. 11 (1911; revised 1912, 1918; Budapest, May 24, 1918, Egisto Tango conducting; U.S. premiere, N.Y. City Opera, Oct. 2, 1952); *A fából faragott királyfi (The Wooden Prince),* ballet in one act, op. 13 (1914–16; Budapest, May 12, 1917, Egisto Tango conducting; orch. suite, 1924; Budapest, Nov. 23, 1931; revised, 1932); *A czodálatos mandarin (The Miraculous Mandarin),* pantomime in one act, op. 19 (1918–19; Cologne, Nov. 27, 1926; orch. suite, 1924; revised, 1927; Budapest, Oct. 15, 1928, Ernst von Dohnányi conducting).

FOR ORCH.: *Scherzo* (only scored movement of a projected symph. in E-flat major, 1902; Budapest, Feb. 29, 1904); *Kossuth,* symph. poem (1903; Budapest, Jan. 13, 1904); *Rhapsody* for Piano and Orch., op. 1 (1904; Paris, Aug. 1905, Bartók, soloist); Scherzo for Piano and Orch., op. 2 (1904; posthumous, Budapest, Sept. 28, 1961); Suite No. 1, op. 3 (1905; movements 1, 3–5 performed in Vienna, Nov. 29, 1905; first complete performance, Budapest, March 1, 1909; revised, 1920); Suite No. 2, for Small Orch., op. 4 (1905–7; first performance of 2nd movement, Scherzo, only; Berlin, Jan. 2, 1909; first complete performance, Budapest, Nov. 22, 1909; revised, 1920, 1943; transcribed for 2 Pianos, 1941); *Two Portraits,* op. 5 (No. 1, 1907–8; No. 2, 1911; No. 1, Budapest, Feb. 12, 1911; first complete performance, Budapest, April 20, 1916); Violin Concerto No. 1 (1907–8; score discovered in 1958; posthumous, Basel, May 30, 1958, Schneeberger, soloist; Paul Sacher conducting); *Two Pictures (Deux Images),* op. 10 (1910; Budapest, Feb. 25, 1913); *Four Pieces,* op. 12 (1912, orchestrated, 1921; Budapest, Jan. 9, 1922); *Dance Suite* for Orch. (1923; Budapest, Nov. 19, 1923); 3 piano concertos: No. 1 (1926; Frankfurt, July 1, 1927, Bartók, soloist; Furtwängler conducting), No. 2 (1930–31; Frankfurt, Jan. 23, 1933, Bartók, soloist; Rosbaud conducting), and No. 3 (1945; last 17 measures composed by Tibor Serly; posthumous, Philadelphia, Feb. 8, 1946, Sándor, soloist; Ormandy conducting); *Rhapsody* No. 1 for Violin and Orch. (1928; also versions for Violin or Cello and Piano; Königsberg, Nov. 1, 1929, Szigeti, soloist; Scherchen conducting); *Rhapsody* No. 2 for Violin and Orch. (1928; also for Violin and Piano; Budapest, Nov. 25, 1929, Székely, soloist; E. Dohnányi conducting); *Music for Strings, Percussion, and Celesta*, one of Bartók's most often played works (1936; Basel, Jan. 21, 1937, Paul Sacher conducting); Violin Concerto No. 2 (1937–38; Amsterdam, March 23, 1939, Székely, soloist; Mengelberg conducting); *Divertimento* for String Orch. (1939; Basel, June 11, 1940); Concerto for 2 Pianos and Orch. (1940; orchestration of Sonata for 2 Pianos and Percussion; London, Nov. 14, 1942); Concerto for Orch. (commissioned by Koussevitzky, 1943; perf. under his direction, Boston, Dec. 1, 1944); Viola Concerto (1945; left unfinished in sketches; reconstructed and orchestrated by Tibor Serly, 1947–49; posthumous, Minneapolis, Dec. 2, 1949, Primrose, soloist; Dorati conducting; also arranged by Serly for Cello and Orch.); various orch. transcriptions of Rumanian and Hungarian folk and peasant dances, originally for piano.

CHAMBER MUSIC: 3 youthful, unnumbered violin sonatas: C minor, Op. 5 (1895), A major, Op. 17 (1897), and E minor (1903); Piano Quartet in C minor, op. 20 (1898); an unnumbered String Quartet in F major (1898); Duo for 2 Violins (1902); *Albumblatt* for Violin and Piano (1902); Piano Quintet (1904; Vienna, Nov. 21, 1904); 6 numbered string quartets: No. 1, op. 7 (1908; Budapest, March 19, 1910), No. 2, op. 17 (1915–17; Budapest, March 3, 1918), No. 3 (1927; London, Feb. 19, 1929), No. 4 (1928; Budapest, March 20, 1929), No. 5 (1934; Washington, D.C., April 8, 1935), No. 6 (1939; N.Y., Jan. 20, 1941); 2 numbered violin sonatas: No. 1 (1921; London, March 24, 1922), No. 2 (1922; London, May 7, 1923); *Rhapsody* No. 1 for Violin and Piano (1928; Budapest, Nov. 22, 1929, Szigeti, violinist; Bartók, pianist; also versions for Cello and Piano, and Violin and Orch.); *Rhapsody* No. 2 for Violin and Piano (1928; Amsterdam, Nov. 19, 1928; revised, 1944; also a version for Violin and Orch.); *44 Duos* for 2 Violins (1931); Sonata for 2 Pianos and Percussion (1937; Basel, Jan. 16, 1938, Bartók and his wife, Ditta Bartók, soloists; also for Orch. as Concerto for 2 Pianos and Orch.); *Contrasts* for Violin, Clarinet, and Piano (1938; N.Y., Jan. 9, 1939; a ballet, *Caprichos*, based on the music of *Contrasts* (N.Y., Jan. 29, 1950); Sonata for Solo Violin (1944; N.Y., Nov. 26, 1944, Menuhin, soloist).

FOR PIANO: *Rhapsody*, op. 1 (1904; Pressburg, Nov. 4, 1906, Bartók, soloist); *14 Bagatelles*, op. 6 (1908; Berlin, June 29, 1908); *10 Easy Pieces* (1908); *2 Elegies*, op. 8b (1908–9; Budapest, April 21, 1919, Bartók, soloist); *For Children* (originally 85 easy pieces in 4 vols., 1908–9; revised, 1945, reducing the number to 79, divided into 2 vols.); *7 Sketches*, op. 9 (1908–10; revised, 1945); *4 Dirges* (1910); *3 Burlesques* (1908–11); *Allegro barbaro* (1911); *6 Rumanian Folk Dances* (1909–15); *Rumanian Christmas Carols*, or *Colinde* (1915); Sonatina (1915); *Suite*, op. 14 (1916; Budapest, April 21, 1919, Bartók, soloist); *15 Hungarian Peasant Songs* (1914–18); *3 Etudes*, op. 18 (1918); *8 Improvisations on Hungarian Peasant Songs* (1920; Budapest, Feb. 27, 1921, Bartók, soloist); Sonata (1926; Budapest, Dec. 8, 1926, Bartók, soloist); *Out of Doors* (1926); *9 Little Pieces* (1926; Budapest, Dec. 8, 1926, Bartók, soloist); *3 Rondos on Folk Tunes* (No. 1, 1916, Nos. 2 and 3, 1927); *Petite Suite* (1936); *Mikrokosmos* (1926–39), 153 progressive pieces publ. in 6 vols.; a unique attempt to write a piano method in a modern idiom with varying meters, modes, and dissonant counterpoint; *7 Pieces from Mikrokosmos* for 2 Pianos (c.1939); Suite for 2 Pianos (1941; transcription from Suite No. 2, for Small Orch., Op. 4).

FOR VOICE: *20 Hungarian Folksongs* for Voice and Piano (first 10 by Bartók, second 10 by Kodály; 1906; revised, 1938); *8 Hungarian Folksongs* for Voice and Piano (1907–17); *3 Village Scenes* for Female Voices and Chamber Orch. (1926; N.Y., Feb. 1, 1927; this is a transcription of 3 of *5 Village Scenes* for Voice and Piano, 1924; Budapest, Dec. 8, 1926); *20 Hungarian Folksongs* for Voice and Piano (4 vols., 1929); *Cantata Profana* for Tenor, Baritone, Chorus, and Orch. (1930; BBC, London, May 25, 1934); 27 Choruses for Women's or Children's Voices a cappella (1935); numerous settings of various folk songs.

WRITINGS: *Cântece poporale românești din comitatul Bihor (Ungaria)/Chansons populaires roumaines du département Bihar (Hongrie)* (Bucharest, 1913; revised ed. in Eng. as incorporated in B. Suchoff, ed., *Rumanian Folk Music*, The Hague, vols. I–III, 1967); *Erdélyi magyarság népdalok* (Transylvanian Folk Songs; Budapest, 1923; with Kodály); "Die Volksmusik der Rumänen von Maramureş," *Sammelbände für vergleichende Musikwissenschaft*, IV (Munich, 1923; in Eng. as incorporated in B. Suchoff, ed., *Rumanian Folk Music*, The Hague, vol. V, 1975); *A magyar népdal* (Budapest, 1924; in German as *Das ungarische Volkslied*, Berlin, 1925; in Eng. as *Hungarian Folk Music*, London, 1931; enlarged ed., with valuable addenda, as *The Hungarian Folk Song*, ed. by B. Suchoff, Albany, N.Y., 1981); *Népzenénk és a szomszéd ńepek népzenéje* (Our Folk Music and the Folk Music of Neighboring Peoples; Budapest, 1934; in German as *Die Volksmusik der Magyaren und der benachbarten Völker*, Berlin, 1935; in French as "La Musique populaire des Hongrois et des peuples voisins," *Archivum Europae Centro Orientalis*, II; Budapest, 1936); *Die Melodien der rumänischen Colinde (Weihnachtslieder)* (Vienna, 1935; in Eng. in B. Suchoff, ed., *Rumanian Folk Music*, The Hague, vol. IV, 1975); *Miért és hogyan gyüjtsünk népzenét* (Why and How Do We Collect Folk Music? Budapest, 1936; in French as *Pourquoi et comment recueille-t-on la musique populaire?*, Geneva, 1948); *Serbo-Croatian Folk Songs* (N.Y., 1951; with A. Lord; reprinted in B. Suchoff, ed., *Yugoslav Folk Music*, vol. I, Albany, N.Y., 1978); also articles in various musical magazines, among them "Hungarian Peasant Music," *Musical Quarterly* (July 1933).

The New York Bartók Archive is publishing an edition of Bartók's writings in English translations in its Studies in Musicology series. The following vols., under the editorship of Benjamin Suchoff, have been publ.: *Rumanian Folk Music* (The Hague, vols. I–III, 1967; vols. IV–V, 1975); *Turkish Folk Music from Asia Minor* (Princeton, 1976); *Béla Bartók's Essays* (selected essays; London and N.Y., 1976); *Yugoslav Folk Music* (4 vols., Albany, N.Y., 1978); *The Hungarian Folk Song* (Albany, N.Y., 1981).

Bartoletti, Bruno, noted Italian conductor; b. Sesto Fiorentino, June 10, 1926. He studied flute at the Florence Cons.; then played flute at the Teatro Comunale in Florence; in 1949 he became an assistant conductor at the Teatro Comunale; later conducted at the Maggio Musicale Fiorentino and the Royal Theater in Copenhagen. In 1956 he made his U.S. debut with the Lyric Opera of Chicago; in 1964 became its co-artistic Director with Pino Donati, and sole artistic director in 1975; was also musical director of the Rome Opera (1965–69); made many guest appearances in Milan, Buenos Aires, San Francisco, and N.Y. In addition to his thorough knowledge of the Italian operatic repertoire, he also conducted French and Russian operas.

Bartolino da Padova (Magister **Frater Bartolinus** de Padua; **Frater carmelitus**), Italian composer; flourished in the 2nd half of the 14th century. He was a member of the Carmelite Order, active in Padua. Some 38 works have been attributed to him, consisting of ballads and madrigals in the style of Jacopo da Bologna. See J. Wolf, ed., *Der Squarcialupi-Codex Pal. 87 der Biblioteca Medicea Laurenziana zu Florenz* (Lippstadt, 1955); W. Marrocco, ed., *Italian Secular Music*, in *Polyphonic Music of the Fourteenth Century*, IX (1974).

Bartolomeo degli Organi (Baccio Fiorentino), Italian organist and composer; b. Florence, Dec. 24, 1474; d. there, Dec. 12, 1539. At the age of 13 he became a singer at Ss. Annunziata in Florence; subsequently served as organist at several Florentine churches; also was a singer in the service of Lorenzo de' Medici, Duke of Urbino. In 1509 he was appointed principal organist at the Cathedral in Florence. Among his extant compositions are 10 Italian secular pieces and several instrumental works. See F. D'Accone, ed., *Music of the Florentine Renaissance*, in Corpus Mensurabilis Musicae, XXXII/2 (1967).

Bartoš, Jan Zdeněk, Czech composer; b. Dvůr Králové nad-Labem, June 4, 1908; d. Prague, June 1, 1981. He played the violin as a youth; then took composition lessons with Otakar Šín and with Jaroslav Křička at the Prague Cons., graduating in 1943. He earned his living playing in dance orchs.; from 1945 to 1956 he was a member of the Music Section of the Ministry of Education and Culture; in 1958 was appointed teacher of composition at the Prague Cons. In his music he followed the national traditions of the Czech school.

Barvík, Miroslav, Czech composer; b. Luzice, Sept. 14, 1919. He studied with Kaprál at the Brno Cons. and with Novák in Prague. In 1948 he was appointed director of the Prague Cons.; in 1966 he was named director of the state theater in Brno. In his works he followed the prescriptions of socialist realism, advocating immediate accessibility and clear national reference. In this manner he wrote his politico-patriotic cantatas *Song of the Fatherland* (1944) and *Thanks to the Soviet Union* (1946). His choral work *Hands Off Korea* was directed against the participation of U.S. forces or other non-Korean combatants in the conflict. He publ. 3 books: *Music of the Revolutionaries* (Prague, 1964), *Jak poslouchat hudbu* (Prague, 1961; 2nd ed., 1962), and *Hovory o hudbe* (Prague, 1961).

Baryphonus, Henricus (real name, **Heinrich Pipegrop**), German music theorist and composer; b. Wernigerode, Harz, Sept. 17, 1581; d. Quedlinburg, Saxe-Anhalt, Jan. 13, 1655. He studied at the Lateinschule in his native town; continued his education at the Univ. of Helmstedt. In 1605 he went to Quedlinburg, where he became cantor at St. Benedicti and a teacher at the Gymnasium; from 1606 was Subkonrector there. He wrote some 17 treatises on music, but only his *Pleiades musicae, quae in certas sectiones distributae praecipuas quaestiones musicas discutiunt* (Halberstadt, 1615) is extant, and only 2 of his compositions survive.

Barzin, Leon, Belgian-American conductor; b. Brussels, Nov. 27, 1900. He was brought to the U.S. in 1902; his father played viola in the orch. of the Metropolitan Opera; his mother was a ballerina. He studied violin with his father and later in Belgium with Eugène Ysaÿe. In 1925 he was appointed first viola player of the N.Y. Phil., retaining his post until 1929, when he was engaged as assistant conductor of the American Orch. Society, which was reorganized in 1930 as the National Orch. Assoc., with Barzin as principal conductor and music director; he continued in this capacity until 1959, and again from 1970 till 1976. He was also music director of the Ballet Society and N.Y. City Ballet (1948–58); from 1958 until 1960 he conducted concerts of the Association des Concerts Pasdeloup in Paris, France; and was at the same time instructor at the Schola Cantorum there. He received the Order of the Légion d'Honneur in 1960. Barzin was particularly successful in training semi-professional and student orchs.; especially with the National Orch. Assoc., he attained remarkable results.

Barzun, Jacques, eminent French-American historian, educator, and author of books on music; b. Créteil (Seine), Nov. 30, 1907. He came to America in 1919; was educated at Columbia Univ. (A.B., 1927; Ph.D., 1932); became a lecturer in history there in 1927, and a full prof. in 1945; he became an American citizen in 1933. In 1955 he was made dean of the Columbia graduate faculties, then dean of faculties and provost in 1958; he also assumed the chair of Seth Low Prof. of History in 1960; he resigned these posts in 1967; continued to lecture there until 1975. He exercised considerable influence on American higher education by advocating broad reading in various fields rather than narrow specialization. His books concerned with music include *Darwin, Marx, Wagner; Critique of a Heritage* (Boston, 1941; revised ed., 1958); *Berlioz and the Romantic Century* (the outstanding modern study of his life and works, based upon exhaustive documentation; 2 vols., Boston, 1950; 3rd ed., revised, 1969); ed. *Pleasures of Music* (N.Y., 1951); ed. and trans. *Nouvelles lettres de Berlioz, 1830–1868; New Letters of Berlioz, 1830–1868* (N.Y., 1954); publ. a new trans. of Berlioz's *Evenings with the Orchestra* (N.Y., 1956; 2nd ed., 1973); also wrote a survey, *Music in American Life* (N.Y., 1956).

Bas, Giulio, Italian organist and music editor; b. Venice, April 21, 1874; d. Vobbia, near Genoa, July 27, 1929. He studied in Munich with Rheinberger and in Venice with Bossi; was organist in the churches of Venice and Rome; in 1915 became prof. of theory and history at the Milan Cons. He wrote several textbooks on music theory; was a department editor of *Musica d'oggi.* Among his textbooks are *Metodo per l'accompagnamento del canto gregoriano* (Turin, 1920); and *Manuale di canto gregoriano* (Dusseldorf, 1910).

Başelt, Fritz (Friedrich Gustav Otto), composer; b. Öls, Silesia, May 26, 1863; d. Frankfurt, Nov. 11, 1931. He studied with Emil Kohler in Breslau and with Ludwig Bussler in Berlin; was a musician, music dealer, composer, teacher, and conductor in Breslau, Essen, and Nuremberg; after 1894 he settled in Frankfurt am Main, where he conducted the Philharmonischer Verein and the Frankfurt Sängervereinigung. He wrote many light operas: *Der Fürst von Sevilla* (Nuremberg, 1888); *Don Alvaro* (Ansbach, 1892); *Der Sohn des Peliden* (Kassel, 1893); *Die Annaliese* (Kassel, 1896); *Die Musketiere im Damenstift* (Kassel, 1896); *Die Circusfee* (Berlin, 1897); also 2 ballets: *Die Altweibermühle* (Frankfurt, 1906), and *Rokoko* (Frankfurt, 1907); some 100 male choruses; many instrumental pieces; songs.

Basie, Count (real name, **William**), topmost American jazz pianist, exponent of the Big Band era of jazzification; b. Red Bank, N.J., Aug. 21, 1904; d. Hollywood, Fla., April 26, 1984. He received his early musical training from his mother, a professional pianist; then played with Bennie Moten's orch. After various peripeteia he became stranded in Kansas City in 1935, playing in a small band in a nightclub; it was there that he acquired the derisively nobiliary appellation Count. In 1936 he took his band to Chicago and then to N.Y. He attracted attention by his peculiar piano technique, emphasizing passages played by a single finger while directing his band with a glance, or a movement of the eyebrow. He met Fats Waller in Harlem and was fascinated by his discursive brilliance on the keys; he adopted Waller's manner but altered it in the direction of rich economy of means. He conducted big band engagements, but in 1950 decided to give up the large sound and formed an octet; however, in 1951 he organized a new big band, with which he made a highly successful tour of Europe; he played a command performance for the Queen of England during his British tour in 1957. In 1976 he suffered a heart attack, but after a period of recuperation, returned to an active career. In 1981 he received the Kennedy Center honors for achievement in the performing arts; at a White House reception that followed, President Ronald Reagan said that Count Basie had revolutionized jazz. Among his greatest hits were *One O'Clock Jump,* which became his theme song; *Jumpin' at the Woodside; Goin' to Chicago; Lester Leaps In; Broadway; April in Paris;* and *L'il Darlin'.* Roulette Records released a 2-record set, *The Count Basie Story* (1961), which includes a biographical booklet by Leonard Feather.

Basile, Andreana, famous Italian contralto and instrumentalist; b. Posillipo, c.1580; d. Rome, c.1640. She attracted the public by her extraordinary beauty and became known as "la bella Adriana." She often accompanied herself on the harp and guitar; in Naples she married Muzio Baroni, a Calabrian nobleman. In 1610 she was engaged by the court of Vincenzo Gonzaga, the Duke of Mantua; she remained a principal singer at his court until 1624, and was praised by Monteverdi for her musicianship. In 1633 she settled in Rome. Her daughter was **Leonora Baroni,** who became a famous singer in her own right.

Basili, Francesco, Italian composer; b. Loreto, Jan. 31, 1767; d. Rome, March 25, 1850. He studied with his father, **Andrea Basili,** and later with Giovanni Battista Borghi; then entered the Santa Cecilia Academy in Rome, where he took courses with Jannaconi. He served as conductor in various provincial Italian theaters; from 1827 to 1837 he was director of the Milan Cons. He wrote 13 operas and a number of dramatic oratorios. In 1837 he became conductor at St. Peter's Cathedral in Rome.

Bassani (Bassano), Giovanni, Italian composer, singer, and violinist; b. c.1558; d. Venice, 1617. He was a singer at San Marco in Venice in 1585; then served as singing teacher at the seminary there in 1595; in 1615 he was first violin soloist at the Chapel of the Basilica; remained there until his death. The following instrumental works by him are extant: *Fantasie a tre voci per cantar e sonar* (1585); *Il fiore dei capricci musicali a 4 voci* (1588); *Motetti, madrigali e canzioni francesi di diversi auttori ... diminuiti per sonar con ogni sorti de stromenti* (1591; reprinted in 1602 in an arrangement for one voice with organ ad lib.; containing works of Clemens non Papa, Créquillon, Palestrina, and others; the term *diminuiti* refers to ornamentation of the original vocal compositions); 2 vols. of *Motetti per concerti ecclesiastici* for 5–12 voices (1598–99); a vol. of *Canzonette* for 4 voices (1587), etc.

Bassani (Bassano, Bassiani), Giovanni Battista, Italian composer, organist, and violinist; b. Padua, c.1647; d. Bergamo, Oct. 1, 1716. He studied with Legrenzi and Castrovillari; in 1667 he became a member of the funereally named Accademia della Morte in Ferrara, serving as organist. On July 3, 1677, he became a member of the more cheerful Accademia Filarmonica in Bologna; also served as maestro di cappella and organist of the apocalyptic Confraternità del Finale in Modena. In 1680 he became maestro di cappella to the Duke of Mirandola; in 1682 he was appointed principe of the Accademia Filarmonica; in 1683 and 1684 he was maestro di cappella of the Accademia della Morte. In 1687 he was named maestro di cappella of the Ferrara Cathedral, and in 1712, maestro di cappella at S. Maria Maggiore in Bergamo; also taught at the music school of the Congregazione di Carità there. His extant works include the following: Operas, *Amorosa Preda di Paride* (Bologna, 1683); *Falaride tiranno d'Agrigento* (Venice, 1683); *Alarico re de Goti* (Ferrara, 1685); *Vitige* (Ferrara, 1686); *Il trionfo di Venere in Ida* (Ferrara, 1688); *Gli amori alla moda* (Ferrara, 1688); *Ginevra, infante di Scozia* (Ferrara, 1690); *Il coceio Nerva* (Ferrara, 1691); *Gli amori tra gl'odii* (Verona, 1693). Oratorios: *La morte delusa* (1686); *Giona* (1689); *Nella luna celestiale* (1687); *Il Conte de Bacheville* (1696); *Mose risorto dalle acque* (1698); *Gl'Impegni del divino amore* (1703); *Il trionfo della fede* (1707). He also wrote numerous masses, and other sacred music. Of his instrumental works, several suites and trio sonatas are reprinted in Torchi's *L'arte musicale in Italia* (vol. VII) and in J.W. Wasielewski's *Instrumentalsätze vom Ende des XVI. bis Ende des XVII. Jahrhunderts* (1874). A cantata is included in Riemann's *Kantaten-Frühling* (vol. II); some vocal works are publ. by G.F. Malipiero in *Classici della musica italiana.*

Bassett, Leslie, American composer; b. Hanford, Calif., Jan. 22, 1923. He studied piano; played the trombone in jazz combos; was a trombonist during his military service, playing in the 13th Armored Division Band. He then enrolled in Fresno (Calif.) State College (B.A., 1947); later studied composition with Ross Lee Finney at the Univ. of Michigan (M.M., 1949; D.M., 1956); also took private lessons with Arthur Honegger and Nadia Boulanger in Paris in 1950. In 1952 he was appointed to the faculty of the Univ. of Michigan; was made a prof. there in 1965 and became chairman of the composition dept. in 1970; in 1977 he became the Albert A. Stanley Distinguished Univ. Prof. of Music there. He held the American Prix de Rome in 1961–63, and received the National Inst. of Arts and Letters Award in 1964. In 1966 he received the Pulitzer Prize in music for his *Variations for Orchestra.* He held a Guggenheim fellowship in 1973–74 and again in 1980–81; in 1981 became a member of the American Academy and Inst. of Arts and Letters. In his music he pursues the ideal of structural logic within the judicial limits of the modern school of composition, with some serial elements discernible in his use of thematic rhythms and motivic periodicity.

Bassi, Luigi, Italian opera baritone; b. Pesaro, Sept. 4, 1766; d. Dresden, Sept. 13, 1825. He studied with Pietro Morandi of Bologna; made his debut in Pesaro at the age of thirteen; he then sang in Florence; went to Prague in 1784, where he soon became greatly appreciated. Mozart wrote the part of Don Giovanni for him and heeded his advice in matters of detail. Bassi was in Vienna from 1806–14; then briefly in Prague; in 1815 he joined an Italian opera company in Dresden.

Baston, Josquin, Flemish composer of the mid-16th century. It is known that from May 1552 to Oct. 1553 he was at the Polish Court of Sigismund Augustus at Cracow. Motets and chansons by Baston appeared between 1542 and 1559 in various collections: Susato's *Het ierste musyck boexken* (Antwerp, 1551); Salbinger's *Concertus* (Augsburg, 1545); also in Louvain (published by Phalèse). His *Lament* has 2 middle voices singing the *Requiem aeternam* in canon 6 times while the other voices have fresh parts. See R. van Maldeghem (ed.), *Trésor musical* (1865–93; vol. XII).

Bate, Stanley Richard, English composer; b. Plymouth, Dec. 12, 1911; d. London, Oct. 19, 1959. He studied composition with Vaughan Williams and piano with Arthur Benjamin at the Royal College of Music in London (1931–35); then took courses with Nadia Boulanger in Paris and with Hindemith in Berlin. During World War II he was in Australia; in 1942 he went to the U.S.; in 1945 he was in Brazil and in 1950 he returned to London. On Nov. 7, 1938, he married the Australian-born composer **Peggy Glanville-Hicks** (divorced 1948). He wrote music in a finely structured cosmopolitan manner, making use of modern devices but observing the classical forms and shunning doctrinaire systems. He wrote several ballets, among them *Goyescas* (1937), *Perseus* (1938), and *Cap over Mill* (1938). He composed 4 symphs.; of these, the 3rd (1940) was performed 14 years after its composition, at the Cheltenham Festival, July 14, 1954, with remarkable success. His 4th Symph. was given in London on Nov. 20, 1955. Other works are 3 piano concertos (he was the soloist in his 2nd Piano Concerto, which he performed with the N.Y. Phil., conducted by Thomas Beecham, on Feb. 8, 1942), 2 sinfoniettas, 3 violin concertos, Viola Concerto, Cello Concerto, Harpsichord Concerto, 2 string quartets, Sonata for Recorder and Piano, Violin Sonata, Flute Sonata, Oboe Sonata, 9 piano sonatinas, and other piano pieces.

Bates, Joah, British organist; b. Halifax (England), March (baptized, March 8) 1741; d. London, June 8, 1799. He studied organ with Hartley in Rochdale and Wainwright in Manchester; then went to Eton and Cambridge for further education. In 1760 became a tutor of King's College in Cambridge; received his B.A. in 1764 and M.A. in 1767. He then went to London, where he organized the series known as Concerts of Antient Music (1776); also acted as conductor of the famous Handel Commemoration Festivals (1784–87; 1791).

Bates (née **Harrop**), **Sarah,** English singer; b. c.1755; d. London, 1811. She was born into a poor family; worked in a Halifax factory to support herself; finally she made her way to London and studied with **Joah Bates,** whom she married in 1780; she also took lessons with Antonio Sacchini. She made her formal debut at Covent Garden in *Judas Maccabaeus* on Feb. 14, 1777. She made regular appearances at her husband's Concerts of Antient Music series.

Bates, William, English composer who flourished in the second half of the 18th century. He wrote popular English operas in the ballad-opera style. His most popular work was *Flora or Hob in the Well,* which he wrote and arranged in 1760 (Covent Garden, April 25, 1770), using 7 of John Hippisley's songs from the 1729 *Flora or Hob's Opera,* together with 8 new songs of his own and a new overture. Neither of his works is to be confused with Thomas Doggett's 1711 farce with songs, a forerunner of the true ballad opera, variously titled *The Country Wake or Hob* or *The Country Wake.* His other stage works are *The Jovial Crew* (1760, altered to *The Ladies Frolick* in 1770); *The Theatrical Candidates* (1775); *The Device, or The Marriage Officer* (1777); *Second Thought Is Best* (1778); also a grand opera, *Pharnaces* (London, Feb. 15, 1765).

Bateson, Thomas, English composer; b. Cheshire County; d. probably in Dublin, March 1630. He was organist at Chester Cathedral in 1599–1609. In 1609 he became vicar choral and organist of the Cathedral of the Holy Trinity in Dublin. He is said to have been the first music graduate of Trinity College, earning his Mus.B. in 1612 and his M.A. in 1622. As a composer, Bateson is especially noted for his madrigals, although they are regarded as inferior to those by Morley or Weelkes. In 1604 he publ. a collection of 29 madrigals for 3 to 6 voices; it included the madrigal *When Oriana walked to take the ayre,* originally intended for publication in Morley's *Triumphs of Oriana.* A second set of 30 madrigals was publ. in 1618. Both sets are reprinted in *The English Madrigal School* (vols. 21–22), edited by E.H. Fellowes.

Batistin. See **Stuck, Johann Baptist.**

Bataille, Charles-Aimable, French bass; b. Nantes, Sept. 30, 1822; d. Paris, May 2, 1872. He was originally a medical student; then turned to music and studied voice at the Paris Cons. He made his debut at the Opéra-Comique in *La Fille du régiment* (June 22, 1848). He created several roles in operas by Thomas, Adam, Halévy, and Meyerbeer. A throat disorder ended his stage career; he retired in 1863. He was on the staff of the Paris Cons. from 1861. He publ. an extensive method of singing in 2 vols.: 1. *Nouvelles recherches sur la phonation*

(1861); 2. *De la physiologie appliquée au mécanisme du chant* (1863).

Batten, Adrian, English organist and composer; b. Salisbury (baptized, March 1), 1591; d. London, 1637. He studied at Winchester with the Cathedral organist John Holmes; in 1614 went to London as vicar choral of Westminster Abbey. In 1626 he became vicar choral and organist at St. Paul's Cathedral. A prolific composer, he left 15 services and 47 anthems in manuscript. Some of his pieces are included in Boyce's *Cathedral Music.* A modern reprint of one of his services is included in *The Choir;* several anthems have been publ. by Novello. Batten also transcribed into organ score numerous sacred choral works, some of which have come down to us only through his transcriptions. His organ book is described in *Tudor Church Music* (1922, vol. II).

Battistini, Gaudenzio, Italian composer, grandson of **Giacomo Battistini;** b. Novara, June 30, 1722; d. there, Feb. 25, 1800. He succeeded his father, Giuseppe Battistini, in 1747 as organist of the chapel of San Gaudenzio in Novara, and served for more than 50 years until his death. He wrote numerous church works in a highly developed polyphonic style. A biographical sketch and examples of his music are found in Vito Fedeli, *Le cappelle musicali di Novara* in vol. III of *Istituzioni e monumenti dell' arte musicale italiana* (Milan, 1933).

Battistini, Giacomo, Italian composer; b. 1665; d. Novara, Feb. 5, 1719. He was organist at the Novara Cathedral (1694–1706); then at the church of San Gaudenzio. He is reputed to have been the first to introduce the violoncello into instrumental accompaniment. He composed several masses, motets, organ works; also contributed music to the third act of the drama *Antemio in Roma* (1695; with A. Besozzi and D. Erba). See Vito Fedeli, *Le cappelle musicali di Novara* in vol. III of *Istituzioni e monumenti dell' arte musicale italiana* (Milan, 1933), containing musical illustrations from Battistini's works.

Battistini, Mattia, celebrated Italian baritone; b. Rome, Feb. 27, 1856; d. Collebaccaro, near Rome, Nov. 7, 1928. He first studied medicine at the Univ. of Rome; then began taking singing lessons. He made his debut at the Teatro Argentino in Rome on Dec. 11, 1878, as Alfonso XI in Donizetti's *La Favorita;* subsequently appeared at Covent Garden in London (1883), at the San Carlo Opera in Naples (1886), at Drury Lane in London (1887), and at La Scala in Milan (1888). He then embarked on a worldwide tour, and acquired great popularity in South America, Spain, and Russia, and continued his active career until the last months of his life. He was a master of bel canto, with a remarkably expressive high register; was particularly successful in the parts of Rigoletto, Figaro in Rossini's *Barber of Seville,* and Valentin in Gounod's *Faust.*

Battle, Kathleen, black American soprano; b.

Portsmouth, Ohio, Aug. 13, 1948. She studied voice with Franklin Bens at the Univ. of Cincinnati College-Conservatory of Music (B.Mus., 1970; M.Mus., 1971); then made her debut at the Spoleto Festival in 1972 in the Brahms *Requiem;* subsequently sang with the N.Y. Phil., the Cleveland Orch., the Los Angeles Phil., and other leading American orchs. She made her Metropolitan Opera debut in N.Y. as the Shepherd in *Tannhäuser* on Sept. 18, 1978, and soon acquired a fine reputation among American singers. In 1983 she was awarded an honorary doctorate from her alma mater.

Baudrier, Yves, French composer; b. Paris, Feb. 11, 1906. He was primarily a law student; was mainly autodidact in music. In 1936 he, jointly with Messiaen, Jolivet, and Daniel-Lesur, formed the group La Jeune France, dedicated to the promotion of purely national French music, whether modern or traditional. In 1946 he made a lecture tour in the U.S. He wrote a symph. poem, *Eleonora,* after Edgar Allan Poe (1938); a symph. poem, *Le Grand Voiler* (1939); a Symphony (1945); and Suite for Trumpet (1966).

Bauer, Harold, distinguished pianist; b. Kingston on Thames, near London, of an English mother and a German father, April 28, 1873; d. Miami, March 12, 1951. He studied violin with his father and Adolf Politzer; made his debut as a violinist in London; in 1892 he went to Paris and studied piano for a year with Paderewski; in 1893 made his first tour as a pianist in Russia; gave piano recitals throughout Europe; in 1900 made his U.S. debut with the Boston Symph. Orch.; appeared as soloist with other U.S. orchs., with eminent chamber music groups, and as a recitalist. He founded the Beethoven Assoc. in N.Y. (1918); was president of the Friends of Music in the Library of Congress, Washington, D.C. Among his writings are: "Self-Portrait of the Artist as a Young Man," *Musical Quarterly* (April 1943); *Harold Bauer, His Book* (N.Y., 1948). He edited works by Schubert and Brahms, and Mussorgsky's *Pictures at an Exhibition.* A considerable corpus of his papers was acquired by the Music Division of the Library of Congress.

Bauer, Marion Eugenie, American composer and writer; b. Walla Walla, Wash., Aug. 15, 1887; d. South Hadley, Mass., Aug. 9, 1955. Her parents were of French extraction; she received her early education from her father, who was an amateur musician. She then went to Paris, where she took piano lessons with Pugno, and theory with André Gédalge and Nadia Boulanger; also took some lessons with Jean Paul Ertel in Berlin. Returning to America, she continued her studies with Henry Holden Huss and others. She taught at N.Y. Univ. (1926–51); was associate prof. there (1930–51); was annual lecturer at the summer Chautauqua Institute in 1928 and 1929; from 1933 through 1952 gave lecture recitals each summer; in 1940 joined the faculty at the Inst. of Musical Arts in N.Y.; taught at the Juilliard School of Music from 1940 to 1944. She was a mem-ber of the executive board of the League of Composers in N.Y., and had an active teaching career in music history and composition. Her own music oscillates pleasurably between Germanic Romanticism and Gallic Impressionism. Prudently, she wrote mostly in small forms, and was at her best in her piano pieces; among them were *From New Hampshire Woods* (1921); *Indian Pipes* (1928); *Sun Splendor* (1926; later orchestrated and performed by Stokowski with the N.Y. Phil., Oct. 25, 1947); *Dance Sonata* (1932). Her choral works include *Three Noëls* (1929); *A Garden Is a Lovesome Thing* (1938); *The Thinker* (1938); and *China* for Chorus with Orch. (Worcester Festival, Oct. 12, 1945). She also wrote quite a few pieces of chamber music: String Quartet (1928); *Fantasia quasi una sonata* for Violin and Piano (1928); Suite for Oboe and Clarinet (1932); Viola Sonata (1936); *Pan,* choreographic sketch for 7 Instruments and Piano (1937); Concertino for Oboe, Clarinet, and String Quartet (1940); Sonatina for Oboe and Piano (1940); Trio Sonata for Flute, Cello, and Piano; and *American Youth Concerto* for Piano and Orch. (1943). She was a successful popularizer of music history. Her publications include *How Music Grew* (1925; with Ethel Peyser), which had several printings; *Music through the Ages* (1932; also with Ethel Peyser; revised ed., 1967); *Twentieth Century Music* (1933, and still of use); and *How Opera Grew* (1955; once more with Ethel Peyser), which had, despite the clumsy title, several reprints.

Bauldewijn, Noël, also known as **Baudoin, Bauldewyn, Bauldeweyn, Balduin, Bauldoin,** or in Latin as **Natalis Balduinus;** Flemish composer; b. c.1480; d. Antwerp, 1529. From Aug. 31, 1509, to July 29, 1513, he served as choir director at the Church of St. Rombaut at Mechelen. On Nov. 16, 1513, he was appointed choir director at Notre Dame in Antwerp, where he remained until his death. His 2 motets were included by Petrucci in his collection *Motetti della Corona* (1519); 3 motets were publ. by Proske; a Chanson was included in Tylman Susato's *Le Sixième Livre contenant 31 chansons* (Antwerp, 1545); in addition, 10 motets and 6 masses by him are also known.

Baumann, Hermann, noted German horn player and pedagogue; b. Hamburg, Aug. 1, 1934. He studied in Hamburg; then played first horn in Dortmund (1957–61) and with the Stuttgart Radio Symph. Orch. (1961–67); won the International Music Competition in Munich in 1964, and made tours in Germany and abroad. In 1969 he was appointed a prof. at the Staatliche Folkwang Hochschule in Essen.

Baumgartner, Rudolf, Swiss violinist and conductor; b. Zürich, Sept. 14, 1917. He was educated at the Univ. of Zürich, and later went to Vienna and Paris for further study. He then began to appear as a violinist, both as a soloist and in chamber music ensembles. After World War II, he turned his energies to conducting. In 1956 he helped organize the Festival Strings at the Lucerne Music Festival, becoming its first music director. In 1960 he was appointed director of the Lucerne Cons.

Baumgartner, Wilhelm, Swiss pianist and composer, author of the popular Swiss song *O mein Heimatland;* b. Rorschach, Nov. 15, 1820; d. Zürich, March 17, 1867. He attended the Gymnasium in Zürich and the Univ. of Zürich; studied piano and music theory with Alexander Müller. In 1842 he moved to St. Gall; in 1844 he went to Berlin, where he continued his musical studies with Taubert. In 1845 he returned to Switzerland, where he taught piano and conducted choruses. He became greatly honored in Switzerland, when, in 1846, he wrote a patriotic male chorus in 4 parts, *O mein Heimatland,* which in time achieved the status of an unofficial national anthem.

Bausch, Ludwig Christian August, celebrated violin maker; b. Naumburg, Jan. 15, 1805; d. Leipzig, May 26, 1871. He established shops for making and repairing violins in Dresden (1826), Dessau (1828), Leipzig (1839), and Wiesbaden (1862). His son **Ludwig** (b. Dessau, Nov. 10, 1829; d. Leipzig, April 7, 1871) first lived in N.Y. and later established his own violin shop in Leipzig. **Otto,** a younger son (b. Leipzig, Aug. 6, 1841; d. there, Dec. 30, 1875), inherited the business, which then passed to A. Paulus at Markneukirchen.

Bausznern, Waldemar von, German composer; b. Berlin, Nov. 29, 1866; d. Potsdam, Aug. 20, 1931. He studied music with Kiel and Bargiel in Berlin; subsequently was active mainly as a choral conductor; also taught at the Cons. of Cologne (1903–8), at the Musikhochschule in Weimar (1908–16), where he also served as director, and at the Hoch Cons. in Frankfurt, where he was a teacher and director (1916–23). He also taught at the Academy of Arts and the Academy for Church and School Music in Berlin. He was a prolific composer; wrote the operas *Dichter und Welt* (Weimar, 1897); *Dürer in Venedig* (Weimar, 1901); *Herbort und Hilde* (Mannheim, 1902); *Der Bundschuh* (Frankfurt, 1904); 8 symphs., of which the 3rd and the 5th have choral finales; numerous sacred choral works; 4 string quartets; 2 piano quintets; 2 piano trios; 2 violin sonatas. He edited the score of the opera *Der Barbier von Bagdad* by Peter Cornelius and completed his unfinished opera *Gunlöd,* which was produced in this version in Cologne in 1906. His symphs., academically Romantic in their high-flown idiom, still retain a spark of vitality, to judge by their infrequent performances in Germany.

Bautista, Julián, Spanish composer; b. Madrid, April 21, 1901; d. Buenos Aires, July 8, 1961. He studied violin with Julio Francés, piano with Pilar Fernández de la Mora, and composition with Conrado del Campo at the Madrid Cons.; then taught there during the Spanish Civil War. After Madrid fell, Bautista fled to Argentina, where he was on the faculty of the National Cons. of Buenos Aires. His music, delicately colored and rhythmically robust, invariably reflected Spanish folk melodies.

Bax, Sir Arnold (Edward Trevor), outstanding English composer; b. London, Nov. 8, 1883; d. Cork, Ireland, Oct. 3, 1953. He entered the Royal Academy of Music in 1900; studied piano with Matthay and composition with Corder there; won its Gold Medal as a pianist in 1905, the year in which he completed his studies. After a visit to Dresden in 1905, he went to Ireland. Although not ethnically Irish, he became interested in ancient Irish folklore; wrote poetry and prose under the name of Dermot O'Byrne; also found inspiration in Celtic legends for his work as a composer. In 1910 he returned to England; that same year he visited Russia, and composed a series of piano pieces in a pseudo-Russian style: *May Night in the Ukraine; Gopak; In a Vodka Shop;* etc.; also wrote music to James M. Barrie's skit *The Truth about the Russian Dancers.* In 1931 he received the Gold Medal of the Royal Phil. Society of London; was awarded honorary degrees from the Univ. of Oxford in 1934 and Durham Univ. in 1935; was knighted at the Coronation of King George VI in 1937; was made Master of the King's Musick in 1941. He was an excellent pianist, but was reluctant to play in public; he never appeared as a conductor of his own works. Bax was an extremely prolific composer; his style is rooted in neo-Romanticism, but impressionistic elements are much in evidence in his instrumental compositions; his harmony is elaborate and rich in chromatic progressions; his contrapuntal fabric is free and emphasizes complete independence of component melodies. In his many settings of folk songs, he succeeded in adapting simple melodies to effective accompaniments in modern harmonies; in his adaptations of old English songs, he successfully re-created the archaic style of the epoch. He recorded the story of his life and travels in his candid autobiography, *Farewell, My Youth* (London, 1943).

WORKS: 7 symphs.: No. 1 (1921; London, Dec. 4, 1922); No. 2 (1924–25; Boston, Dec. 13, 1929); No. 3 (1929; London, March 14, 1930); No. 4 (1930; San Francisco, March 16, 1932); No. 5 (dedicated to Sibelius; 1931; London, Jan. 15, 1934); No. 6 (1934; London, Nov. 21, 1935); No. 7 (dedicated to the American people; 1939; N.Y., June 9, 1939).

BALLETS: *Between Dusk and Dawn* (1917); *The Truth about the Russian Dancers* (1920).

SYMPH. POEMS: *In the Faery Hills* (1909); *Christmas Eve on the Mountains* (1911–12); *Nympholept* (1912); *The Garden of Fand* (1913); *The Happy Forest* (1914; orchestrated 1921); *November Woods* (1917); *Tintagel* (1917); *Summer Music* (1920); *Mediterranean* (1920 version for Piano; orchestrated 1921).

OTHER ORCH. WORKS: 4 pieces: *Pensive Twilight; Dance in the Sun; From the Mountains of Home; Dance of Wild Irravel* (1912–13); *Scherzo sinfonico* (1913); *Romantic Overture* (1926); *Two Northern Ballads* (1927; 1933); *Overture to a Picaresque Comedy* (1930); *The Tale the Pine Trees Knew* (1931); *Overture to Adventure* (1935–36); *Rogue's Comedy Overture* (1935–36); *London Pageant* (1937–

38); *A Legend* (1944); *Coronation March* (1953).

INSTRUMENTAL WORKS WITH ORCH.: *Symphonic Variations* for Piano and Orch. (1917); *Phantasy* for Viola and Orch. (1920); Cello Concerto (1932); Violin Concerto (1937–38); Concertante for Piano, left-hand (1948–49).

Bayle, François, French composer; b. Tamatabe, Madagascar, April 27, 1932. He studied academic sciences and music in France; was a student in composition of Olivier Messiaen, and with Pierre Schaeffer, whose Groupe de Recherches Musicales he joined in 1966. His works are mostly montages, collages, and acoustical barrages. He constructed the following musical compositions: *Points critiques* for Horn, Piano, Cello, and Percussion (1960); *Pluriel* for 19 Instruments and Loudspeakers (1963); *L'Oiseau chanteur*, musique concrète (1963); *Espaces inevitables*, musique concrète (1967); *L'Experience acoustique*, musique concrète (1970–77).

Bazelon, Irwin (Allen), American composer; b. Evanston, Ill., June 4, 1922. He took piano lessons with Irving Harris and Magdalen Messmann; studied composition with Leon Stein. He received his B.A. degree from De Paul Univ. in Chicago in 1945 and his M.A. degree in 1946; then took composition lessons with Hindemith at Yale Univ., with Darius Milhaud at Mills College in Oakland, Calif. (1946–48), and with Ernest Bloch at the Univ. of Calif. in Berkeley (1947). In 1948 he settled in N.Y. and earned a living by writing commercial jingles; also contributed incidental music for Shakespeare plays produced at the American Shakespeare Theater in Stratford, Conn. In his compositions he makes use of quaquaversal techniques, ranging from rudimentary triadic progressions to complex dodecaphonic structures; rhythmically, he likes to inject jazz syncopation. He publ. *Knowing the Score: Notes on Film Music* in 1975.

Bazzini, Antonio, Italian violinist and composer; b. Brescia, March 11, 1818; d. Milan, Feb. 10, 1897. Encouraged by Paganini, before whom he played in 1836, Bazzini embarked upon a series of successful tours through Italy, France, Spain, Belgium, Poland, England, and Germany (1837–63); taught at the Milan Cons. from 1873, and in 1882 became its director.
WORKS: *Turanda,* opera after Gozzi's *Turandot* (La Scala, Milan, Jan. 13, 1867); *Francesca da Rimini,* symph. poem (1890); symph. overtures to Alfieri's *Saul* (1866) and to Shakespeare's *King Lear* (1868); numerous violin pieces, of which *Ronde des lutins* became extremely popular.

Beach, Mrs. H.H.A. (maiden name, **Amy Marcy Cheney**), American composer; b. Henniker, N.H., Sept. 5, 1867; d. New York, Dec. 27, 1944. She was descended of early New England colonists, and was a scion of a cultural family. She entered a private school in Boston; studied piano with Ernest Perabo and Carl Baermann; received instruction in harmony from Junius W. Hill. She made her debut as a pianist in Boston on Oct. 24, 1883, playing a piano concerto by Moscheles with an orchestra. On Dec. 3, 1885, at the age of 18, she married Dr. H.H.A. Beach, a Boston surgeon, a quarter of a century older than she was. The marriage was a happy one, and as a token of her loyalty to her husband, see used as her professional name Mrs. H.H.A. Beach. She began to compose modestly, mostly for piano, but soon embarked on an ambitious project, a Mass, which was performed by the Handel and Haydn Society in Boston on Feb. 18, 1892; she was the first woman to have a composition performed by that organization. On Oct. 30, 1896, her *Gaelic Symphony,* based on Irish folk tunes, was performed by the Boston Symph. with exceptional success. In 1897 she played her Violin Sonata with Franz Kneisel. On April 6, 1900, she appeared as the soloist with the Boston Symph. in the first performance of her Piano Concerto. She also wrote a great many songs in an endearing Romantic manner. Her husband died in 1910, and Mrs. Beach decided to go to Europe; she played her works in Berlin, Leipzig, and Hamburg, attracting considerable attention as the first of her sex and national origin to be able to compose music of a European quality of excellence. She returned to the U.S. in 1914 and lived in N.Y. Her music, unpretentious in its idiom and epigonic in its historical aspect, retained its importance as the work of a pioneer woman composer in America.
WORKS: Mass in E flat (Boston, Feb. 18, 1892); *Gaelic Symphony* (Boston, Oct. 30, 1896); Piano Concerto (Boston, April 6, 1900). Cantatas: *The Minstrel and the King; Festival Jubilate; The Chambered Nautilus; Canticles of the Sun; Christ in the Universe; The Rose of Avontown, Sylvania; The Sea Fairies.* Chamber music: Violin Sonata (1896); Piano Quintet (1908); String Quartet (1929); Piano Trio (1938). For Piano: *Valse-Caprice; Ballad; 4 Sketches; Hermit Thrush at Morn; Nocturne; 5 Improvisations; Variations on Balkan Themes* for 2 Pianos.

Beach, John Parsons, American composer; b. Gloversville, N.Y., Oct. 11, 1877; d. Pasadena, Calif., Nov. 6, 1953. He studied piano at the New England Cons. in Boston; then went to Europe, where he took lessons with Gédalge in Paris and Malipiero in Venice. Returning to Boston, he took additional lessons with Loeffler. He held various teaching jobs; finally settled in Pasadena. His opera *Pippa's Holiday* was performed in Paris in 1915, and his ballet *Phantom Satyr* was given in Asolo, Italy, July 6, 1925; another ballet, *Mardi Gras,* was staged in New Orleans (Feb. 15, 1926). His orch. works include *New Orleans Street Cries* (Philadelphia, April 22, 1927; Stokowski conducting); *Asolani* (Minneapolis, Nov. 12, 1926); *Angelo's Letter* for Tenor and Chamber Orch. (N.Y., Feb. 27, 1929). He also composed *Naïve Landscapes* for Piano, Flute, Oboe, and Clarinet (1917); *Poem* for String Quartet (1920); *Concert* for Violin, Viola, Cello, Flute, Oboe, and Clarinet (1929); many songs.

Beard, John, renowned English tenor; b. c.1717; d. Hampton, Feb. 5, 1791. He studied with Bernard Gates at the Chapel Royal; while still a youth, he sang in Handel's *Esther* in London (1732). He left the Chapel Royal in 1734; on Nov. 9, 1734, he made his debut as Silvio in Handel's *Il Pastor fido* at Covent Garden; he subsequently appeared in about 10 operas, many oratorios, masques, and odes by Handel. In 1761 he became manager of Covent Garden, but continued to make appearances as a singer; he retired in 1767 owing to increasing deafness.

Beardslee, Bethany, American soprano; b. Lansing, Mich., Dec. 25, 1927. She studied at Michigan State Univ.; then received a scholarship to the Juilliard School of Music in N.Y.; she soon became known as a specialist in modern music, evolving an extraordinary technique with a flutelike ability to sound impeccably precise intonation; she mastered the art of *Sprechstimme,* which enabled her to give fine renditions of such works as Schoenberg's *Pierrot Lunaire;* she also was a brilliant performer of vocal parts in scores by Alban Berg, Anton von Webern, and Stravinsky. In 1976 she joined the faculty of Westminster Choir College; in 1981–82 was a prof. of music at the Univ. of Texas in Austin. She married the composer **Godfrey Winham** in 1960.

Beaulieu (real name, **Martin-Beaulieu**), **Marie-Désiré,** French composer and author; b. Paris, April 11, 1791; d. Niort, Dec. 21, 1863. He studied violin with Kreutzer, composition with Benincori and Abbé Roze; then studied with Méhul at the Paris Cons.; won the Prix de Rome in 1810; wrote the operas *Anacréon* and *Philadelphie;* the oratorios *L'Hymne du matin, L'Hymne de la nuit,* etc.; also other sacred music, as well as secular songs. He publ. the essays: *Du rythme, des effets qu'il produit et de leurs causes* (1852); *Mémoire sur ce qui reste de la musique de l'ancienne Grèce dans les premiers chants de l'Eglise* (1852); *Mémoire sur le caractère que doit avoir la musique de l'Eglise* (1858); *Mémoire sur l'origine de la musique* (1859). His main contribution to French musical culture was his organizing of annual music festivals in provincial towns; founded the Association Musicale de l'Ouest in 1835, and the Societé des Concerts de Chant Classique in 1860, to which he bequeathed 100,000 francs.

Beauvarlet-Charpentier, Jean-Jacques, famous French organist; b. Abbeville, June 28, 1734; d. Paris, May 6, 1794. His father was organist of the Hospice de la Charité in Lyons; his mother was the singer **Marie Birol,** who appeared on the stage under the name Marie Beauvarlet-Charpentier. He succeeded his father as organist in Lyons; from 1763–71 he made appearances there at the Académie des Beaux Arts. He first played in Paris at a Concert Spirituel in 1759; in 1771 he was called to Paris as organist of the Royal Abbey of St. Victor; in 1772 he became organist at St. Paul, and also at St. Eloi des Orfèvres (from 1777) and Notre Dame (from 1783; with 3 other organists). He was also a composer, but his music attracted little notice. His son, **Jacques-Marie Beauvarlet-Charpentier** (b. Lyons, July 3, 1766; d. Paris, Sept. 7, 1834), was also an organist and composer.

Becerra Schmidt, Gustavo, Chilean composer; b. Temuco, Aug. 26, 1925. He studied at the Santiago Cons., first with Pedro Allende, and then with Domingo Santa Cruz; from 1953 to 1956 he traveled in Europe; from 1968 to 1970 he served as cultural attaché to the Chilean embassy in Bonn. In 1971 he received the Premio Nacional de Arte in music. His early works are set in the traditional manner of neo-Classical composition, but soon he adopted an extremely radical modern idiom, incorporating dodecaphonic and aleatory procedures and outlining a graphic system of notation, following the pictorial representation of musical sounds of the European avant-garde, but introducing some new elements, such as indication of relative loudness by increasing the size of the notes on a music staff with lines far apart. His works include the opera *La muerte de Don Rodrigo* (1958); 3 symphonies (1955, 1958, 1960); oratorios, *La Araucana* (1965) and *Lord Cochrane de Chile* (1967); Violin Concerto (1950); Flute Concerto (1957); Piano Concerto (1958); 4 guitar concertos (1964–70); Concerto for Oboe, Clarinet, and Bassoon, with String Orch. (1970); 7 string quartets; Saxophone Quartet; 3 violin sonatas; Viola Sonata; 3 cello sonatas; Sonata for Double Bass and Piano; pieces for solo oboe and solo trombone; numerous choral works. A special issue of *Revista Musical Chilena* (1972), dedicated to Becerra Schmidt, contains a complete catalogue of his works.

Becher, Alfred Julius, English composer and music critic, who became a martyr of the revolutionary movement in 1848; b. Manchester, April 27, 1803; d. Vienna (executed), Nov. 23, 1848. He studied in Germany; in 1841 went to Vienna; in 1848 he began issuing the revolutionary paper *Der Radikale,* and that same year was arrested for treason and shot. He published a monograph on Jenny Lind, in German (Vienna, 1846); he also wrote a Symph., some chamber music, and songs.

Bechet, Sidney, famous black American jazz clarinetist and soprano saxophonist; b. New Orleans, May 14, 1897; d. Garches, France, May 14, 1959. He took up the clarinet when he was 6 years old; learned to play blues and rags in black honky-tonks in Storyville, the brothel district of New Orleans; after playing with many of the leading jazz musicians in New Orleans and on tour, he went to Chicago in 1917; settled in N.Y. in 1919. He made tours to London and Paris; then led his own band in N.Y.; later worked with Noble Sissle, Duke Ellington, Tommy Ladnier, and Zutty Singleton. During the 1940s he led his own jazz groups in N.Y.; in 1947 he settled in Paris. He was one of the most important jazz musicians of his era, highly acclaimed as the master of the soprano saxophone. He publ. an autobiography, *Treat It Gentle* (N.Y., 1960).

Bechstein, (Friedrich Wilhelm) Carl, German piano manufacturer; b. Gotha, June 1, 1826; d. Berlin, March 6, 1900. He worked in German factories; also in London; in 1853 set up a modest shop in Berlin; constructed his first grand piano in 1856; established branches in France, Russia, and England. After World War I, the London branch continued under the direction of C. Bechstein, grandson of the founder; after his death (1931), it became an independent British firm, Bechstein Piano Co., Ltd. The Bechstein piano possesses a particularly harmonious tone, capable of producing a mellifluous cantilena; for many years it was a favorite instrument of pianists of the Romantic school.

Beck, Conrad, distinguished Swiss composer; b. Lohn, near Schaffhausen, June 16, 1901. He studied at the Zürich Cons. with Andreae, and in Paris with Ernst Lévy; lived in Paris and Berlin; settled in Basel in 1932 and became a radio conductor there. In 1939 he was appointed director of the music section of Radio Basel; resigned in 1966. A prolific composer, Beck adopted a neo-Classical style, rich in contrapuntal texture. Several of his works were featured at the festivals of the International Society for Contemporary Music, among them the overture *Innominata* (Vienna, June 16, 1932) and Chamber Cantata (Warsaw, April 15, 1939). He wrote 7 symphs. (1925–58; Symph. No. 7, subtitled *Aeneas-Silvius,* was first performed in Zürich, Feb. 25, 1958); *Lyric Cantata* (Munich, May 22, 1931); Piano Concerto (1933); *Konzertmusik* for Oboe and String Orch. (Basel, April 30, 1933); Chamber Concerto for Cembalo and String Orch. (Basel, Nov. 27, 1942); Viola Concerto (1949); oratorio *Der Tod zu Basel* (Basel, May 22, 1953); Concertino for Clarinet, Bassoon, and Orch. (1954); Christmas motet, *Es kommt ein Schiff geladen; Die Sonnenfinsternis,* cantata (Lucerne, Aug. 25, 1967); Clarinet Concerto (1968); *Fantasie* for Orch. (1969); *Sonata a quattro* for Violin, Flute, Oboe, and Bassoon (1970); 4 string quartets; 2 violin sonatas; 2 cello sonatas; 2 string trios; piano music; choral works.

Becker, Constantin Julius, German composer and author; b. Freiberg, Saxony, Feb. 3, 1811; d. Oberlössnitz, Feb. 26, 1859. He studied singing with Anacker and composition with Karl Becker; from 1837–46 edited the *Neue Zeitschrift für Musik,* in association with Schumann; in 1843 settled in Dresden; taught singing, composed, and wrote novels on musical subjects. In 1846 he went to Oberlössnitz, where he spent the remainder of his life. He wrote an opera, *Die Erstürmung von Belgrad* (Leipzig, May 21, 1848); a Symph.; various vocal works. However, he is best known for his manuals: *Männergesangschule* (1845), *Harmonielehre für Dilettanten* (1842), and *Kleine Harmonielehre* (1844). He also publ. the novel *Die Neuromantiker* (1840), trans. *Voyage musical* by Berlioz into German (1843).

Becker, Dietrich, German violinist, organist, and composer; b. Hamburg, 1623; d. there, 1679. He began his career as an organist in Ahrensburg, Holstein (1645); subsequently was active as a violinist in Hamburg. In 1658 he became violinist at the court chapel in Celle. In 1662 he was appointed court violinist in Hamburg; was named director of the court orch. in 1667 and appointed director of music at the Hamburg Cathedral in 1674. As a composer, he wrote a number of works of chamber music.

WORKS: *Musicalische Frühlings-Früchte* for 3 to 5 Instruments and Basso Continuo (Hamburg, 1668; 2nd ed., 1673); *Erster Theil ... Sonaten und Suiten* for 2 Violins and Basso Continuo (Hamburg, 1674); *Trauer- und Begrabnüss-Musik* for Soprano, Alto, Tenor, Bass, Violin, Bassoon, 3 Viole da Braccio, and Basso Continuo (Glückstadt, 1678); *Ander Theil ... Sonaten und Suiten* for 2 Violins and Basso Continuo (Hamburg, 1679); also sacred choral music and songs.

Becker, Gustave Louis, American pianist and teacher; b. Richmond, Texas, May 22, 1861; d. Epsom, Surrey, England, Feb. 25, 1959. He made his public debut at the age of 11; studied in N.Y. with Constantin von Sternberg and at the Hochschule für Musik, Berlin (1888–91). Returning to N.Y., he became Rafael Joseffy's assistant at the National Cons. He continued his teaching activities privately. On May 23, 1952, the 80th anniversary of his public appearance as a child prodigy, he gave a piano recital in Steinway Hall; on his 94th birthday, May 22, 1955, played at a concert in N.Y., arranged by his friends. He wrote 2 suites for String Quartet; *Herald of Freedom* for Chorus (1925); many vocal and piano pieces, about 200 numbers in all. He publ. several pedagogic works: *Exercise for Accuracy; Superior Graded Course for the Piano; Musical Syllable System for Vocal Sight Reading;* and many magazine articles.

Becker, Hugo, famous German cellist, son of **Jean Becker;** b. Strasbourg, Feb. 13, 1863; d. Geiselgasteig, July 30, 1941. He first studied with his father; later with Grützmacher, Kündinger, de Swert, and Piatti; was a cellist in the Frankfurt Opera orch. (1884–86); was a member of the Heermann quartet (1890–1906); taught at the Königliche Hochschule in Berlin (1909–29). He was not only one of the finest soloists, but also a remarkable ensemble player; was for many years a member of the Marteau-Dohnányi-Becker trio; also played with Ysaÿe and Busoni. Among his compositions are a Cello Concerto and smaller cello pieces. He publ. *Mechanik und Ästhetik des Violoncellspiels* (Vienna, 1929).

Becker, Jean, German violinist; b. Mannheim, May 11, 1833; d. there, Oct. 10, 1884. He studied with his father; then with Vincenz Lachner and Hugo Hildebrandt; his principal teacher was Aloys Kettenus. He was concertmaster of the Mannheim Orch. from 1855 to 1865. In 1865 he settled in Florence, and established the renowned Florentine Quartet (dissolved in 1880). The remaining years of his life were spent touring with his children: **Jeanne,** pianist, pupil of Reinecke and Bargiel (b. Mannheim, June 9, 1859; d. there, April 6, 1893); **Hans,** violist (b. Strasbourg, May 12, 1860; d. Leipzig, May 1, 1917); and the cellist **Hugo Becker.**

Becker, John J., remarkable American composer; b. Henderson, Ky., Jan. 22, 1886; d. Wilmette, Ill., Jan. 21, 1961. He studied at the Cincinnati Cons., then was at the Wisconsin Cons. in Milwaukee, where he was a pupil of Alexander von Fielitz, Carl Busch, and Wilhelm Middleschulte (Ph.D., 1923). From 1917 to 1927 he served as director of music at Notre Dame Univ.; was chairman of the fine arts dept. at the College of St. Thomas in St. Paul from 1929 to 1933. He was subsequently Minnesota State Director for the Federal Music Project (1935–41) and prof. of music at Barat College of the Sacred Heart at Lake Forest, Ill. (1943–57), and taught sporadically at the Chicago Musical College. His early works are characterized by romantic moods in a somewhat Germanic manner. About 1930 he was drawn into the circle of modern American music; was on the editorial board of *New Music Quarterly,* founded by Cowell, and became associated with Charles Ives. He conducted modern American works with various groups in St. Paul. Striving to form a style that would be both modern and recognizably American, he wrote a number of pieces for various instrumental groups under the title *Soundpiece.* He also developed a type of dramatic work connecting theatrical action with music. Becker's music is marked by sparse sonorities of an incisive rhythmic character contrasted with dissonant conglomerates of massive harmonies.

Beckwith, John, Canadian composer; b. Victoria, British Columbia, March 9, 1927. He studied music with Alberto Guerrero at the Univ. of Toronto (Mus.B., 1947); then went to Paris to study with Nadia Boulanger (1950–52). Returning to Toronto, he served as music critic of the Toronto *Star* (1959–65); in 1952 he was appointed to the music faculty of the Univ. of Toronto; served as its dean in 1970–77. His music is marked by pragmatic modernism, with ingenious application of urban folk tunes, occasionally venturing into the hazardous regions of structural collage.

Bedford, David, English composer; b. London, Aug. 4, 1937. He studied at the Royal Academy of Music in London with Lennox Berkeley (1958–61); then went to Italy, where he took lessons with Luigi Nono in Venice; also worked in the electronic music studios in Milan. Returning to England, he taught at Queen's College in London and played the organ in pop groups.

Bedos de Celles, Dom François, French organ theorist; b. Caux, near Béziers, Jan. 24, 1709; d. Saint-Denis, Nov. 25, 1779. He became a Benedictine monk at Toulouse in 1726; wrote an important treatise, *L'Art du facteur d'orgues* (3 vols.; Paris, 1766–78); a 4th volume, containing historical notes on the organ, appeared in German (1793); a modern edition was publ. in Kassel (1934–36; Eng. trans., 1977). He also wrote an account of a new organ at St. Martin de Tours in the *Mercure de France* (Jan. 1762; a German trans. is included in Adlung's *Musica mechanica organoedi*).

Beecham, Sir Thomas, celebrated English conductor; b. St. Helens, near Liverpool, April 29, 1879; d. London, March 8, 1961. His father, Sir Joseph Beecham, was a man of great wealth derived from the manufacture of the once-famous Beecham pills, which worked wonders on anemic people; thanks to them, young Beecham could engage in life's pleasures and the arts without troublesome regard for economic limitations. He had his first music lessons from a rural organist; from 1892 to 1897 he attended the Rossall School at Lancashire, and later went to Wadham College, Oxford. In 1899 he organized, mainly for his own delectation, an amateur ensemble, the St. Helen's Orch. Society; also in 1899 he had a chance to conduct a performance with the prestigious Hallé Orch. in Manchester. In 1902 he got a job as conductor of K. Trueman's traveling opera company, which gave him valuable practical experience in dealing with theater music. In 1905 he gave his first professional symph. concert in London, with members of the Queen's Hall Orch.; in 1906 he assembled the New Symph. Orch., which he led until 1908; then formed a group in his own name, the Beecham Symph. Orch., which presented its first concert in London on Feb. 22, 1909. In 1910, Beecham appeared in a new role, that of operatic impresario; from then until 1913 he worked at Covent Garden and at His Majesty's Theatre. During this period he made bold to invite Richard Strauss to Covent Garden to conduct his own operas. Next, Beecham conducted opera at the Theatre Royal at Drury Lane. In 1916 he became conductor of the Royal Phil. Society concerts; then gave operatic productions with the Beecham Opera Company. By that time his reputation as a forceful and charismatic conductor was securely established in England. His audiences grew; the critics, impressed by his imperious ways and his unquestioned ability to bring out spectacular operatic productions, sang his praise; however, some commentators found much to criticize in his somewhat cavalier treatment of the classics. In appreciation of his services to British music, Beecham was knighted in 1916; at the death of his father, he succeeded to the title of baronet. But all of his inherited money was not enough to pay for Beecham's exorbitant financial disbursements in his ambitious enterprises, and in 1919 he was declared bankrupt. He rebounded a few years later and continued his extraordinary career. In 1928 he made his American debut conducting the N.Y. Phil. In 1929 he organized and conducted the Delius Festival in London, to which Delius himself, racked by tertiary syphilitic affliction, paralyzed and blind, was brought from his residence in France to attend Beecham's musical homage to him. In 1932, Beecham organized the London Phil. Orch.; contemptuous of general distaste for the Nazi regime in Germany, he took the London Phil. to Berlin in 1936 for a concert which was attended by the Führer in person. Returning to England, he continued his activities, conducting opera and symphony. As the war situation deteriorated on the Continent, Beecham went to the U.S. in May 1940, and also toured Australia. In 1941 he was engaged as music director and conductor of the Seattle Symph. Orch., retaining this post until 1943;

he also filled guest engagements at the Metropolitan Opera in N.Y. from 1942 to 1944. In America he was not exempt from sharp criticism, which he haughtily dismissed as philistine complaints. On his part, he was outspoken in his snobbish disdain for the cultural inferiority of England's wartime allies, often spicing his comments with mild obscenities, usually of a scatological nature. Returning to England, he founded, in 1946, still another orch., the Royal Phil.; in 1951 he resumed his post as conductor at Covent Garden. In 1957 Queen Elizabeth II made him a Companion of Honour. Beecham was married three times: to Utica Celestia Wells, in 1903 (divorced in 1942); Betty Hamby (in 1943), who died in 1957; and to his young secretary, Shirley Hudson, in 1959. In 1960 he suffered a series of massive heart attacks and died. He publ. an autobiography, *A Mingled Chime* (London, 1943), and also an extensive biography of Delius (London, 1959). To mark his centennial, a commemorative postage stamp with Beecham's portrait was issued by the Post Office of Great Britain on Sept. 1, 1980.

Beecher, Carl Milton, American composer; b. Lafayette, Ind., Oct. 22, 1883; d. Portland, Oreg., Nov. 21, 1968. He graduated from Northwestern Univ. in 1908; then went to Berlin, where he took lessons in piano with Josef Lhévinne. Returning to America, he was on the faculty of his alma mater (1913–36); then spent 11 years in Tahiti. Returning finally to America in 1947, he became prof. at the Portland (Oreg.) School of Music. He wrote mainly for piano in miniature forms; among his piano pieces is a suite, *Remembrances of Times Past;* 9 *Musical Profiles;* and 5 *Aquatints.*

Beer, Jacob Liebmann. Original name of **Giacomo Meyerbeer.**

Beer, Johann, Austrian-born German music theorist and polemicist; b. St. Georg, Upper Austria, Feb. 28, 1655; d. (accidentally shot while watching a shooting contest) Weissenfels, Aug. 6, 1700. He studied music at the Benedictine monastery in Lambach; then attended classes at Reichersberg, Passau, and the Gymnasium Poeticum in Regensburg; in 1676 he became a student in theology at the Univ. of Leipzig; in 1685 he was appointed Konzertmeister of the court orch. in Weissenfels. His writings are of interest as a curiosity reflecting the musical mores of his time; he publ. polemical pamphlets directed against contemporary writers who deprecated music as dangerous for morals. In such pamphlets he used the pseudonym **Ursus,** Latin for the German *Bär,* which is a homonym of his real name, Beer, i.e., Bear, the ursine animal. One such publication opens with the words "Ursus murmurat" ("The Bear growls"), and another, "Ursus vulpinatur," i.e., "Bear leads a fox hunt." Both assail a certain Gottfried Vockerodt, who claimed that the depravity of Nero and Caligula was the result of their immoderate love of music. Beer also publ. *Bellum musicum (Musical War;* Nuremberg, 1719).

Beer, Joseph, Bohemian clarinetist; b. Grünwald, May 18, 1744; d. Berlin, Oct. 28, 1812. He was first a trumpet player; served in the Austro-Hungarian army, and later was in the service of France. He learned to play the clarinet in Paris; from 1780 to 1792 he was a chamber musician in St. Petersburg; upon his return he was attached to the court chapel in Potsdam. Beer's principal improvement of the clarinet was the attachment of a fifth key. He wrote many compositions for his instrument.

Beer-Walbrunn, Anton, German composer; b. Kohlberg, Bavaria, June 29, 1864; d. Munich, March 22, 1929. He was a pupil of Rheinberger, Bussmeyer, and Abel at the Akademie der Tonkunst in Munich; from 1901 was an instructor there; made prof. in 1908. He wrote the operas: *Die Sühne* (Lübeck, 1894); *Don Quixote* (Munich, 1908); *Das Ungeheuer* (Karlsruhe, 1914); *Der Sturm* (1914; after Shakespeare); incidental music to *Hamlet* (1909); 2 symphs.; *Mahomet's Gesang* for Chorus and Orch.; *Lustspielouvertüre;* Violin Concerto; Piano Quintet; church music; many compositions for various instruments. He also supervised new editions of works of Wilhelm Friedemann Bach.

Beeson, Jack Hamilton, American composer; b. Muncie, Ind., July 15, 1921. He studied at the Eastman School of Music in Rochester, N.Y., with Burrill Phillips, Bernard Rogers, and Howard Hanson; received his M.M. in 1943; later studied at Columbia Univ., and took private lessons with Béla Bartók during Bartók's stay in N.Y. in his last year of life. In 1945 Beeson joined the staff of Columbia Univ.; was made a prof. there in 1965; served as chairman of the music dept. from 1968 to 1972; was named MacDowell Prof. of Music in 1967. He held the American Prix de Rome in 1948–50; in 1958–59 received a Guggenheim fellowship; in 1976 was made a member of the American Academy and Inst. of Arts and Letters. His music is marked by enlightened utilitarianism; particularly forceful are his operatic compositions.

Beethoven, Ludwig van, the great German composer whose unsurpassed genius, expressed with supreme mastery in his symphs., chamber music, concertos, and piano sonatas, revealing an extraordinary power of invention, marked a historic turn in the art of composition; b. Bonn, Dec. 15 or 16 (baptized, Dec. 17), 1770; d. Vienna, March 26, 1827. (Beethoven himself maintained, against all evidence, that he was born in 1772, and that the 1770 date referred to his older brother, deceased in infancy, whose forename was also Ludwig.) The family was of Dutch extraction (the surname Beethoven meant "beet garden" in Dutch). Beethoven's grandfather, **Ludwig van Beethoven** (b. Malines, Belgium, Jan. 5, 1712; d. Bonn, Dec. 24, 1773), served as choir director of the church of St. Pierre in Louvain in 1731; in 1732 he went to Liège, where he sang bass in the cathedral choir of St. Lambert; in 1733 he became a member of the choir in Bonn; there he married Maria Poll. Prevalent infant mortality took its statistically predictable tribute; the couple's only surviving child was Johann van Beethoven; he married a young widow, Maria Magdalena Leym (born Keverich), daughter of the chief overseer of the kitchen at the palace in Ehrenbreitstein; they were the composer's parents. Beethoven firmly believed that the nobiliary particle "van" in the family name betokened a nobility; in his demeaning litigation with his brother's widow over the guardianship of Beethoven's nephew Karl, he argued before the Vienna magistrate that as a nobleman he should be given preference over his sister-in-law, a commoner, but the court rejected his Beethoven was Franz Ries. Beethoven also learned to elevated connotation of its German counterpart, "von." Beethoven could never provide a weightier claim of noble descent. In private, he even tolerated without forceful denial the fantastic rumor that he was a natural son of royalty, a love child of Friedrich Wilhelm II, or even of Frederick the Great.

Beethoven's father gave him rudimentary instruction in music; he learned to play both the violin and the piano; Tobias Friedrich Pfeiffer, a local musician, gave him formal piano lessons; the court organist in Bonn, Gilles van Eeden, instructed him in keyboard playing and in music theory; Franz Rovantini gave him violin lessons; another violinist who taught Beethoven was Franz Reis. Beethoven also learned to play the French horn, under the guidance of the professional musician Nikolaus Simrock. Beethoven's academic training was meager; he was, however, briefly enrolled at the Univ. of Bonn in 1789. His first important teacher of composition was Christian Gottlob Neefe, a thorough musician who seemed to understand his pupil's great potential even in his early youth. He guided Beethoven in the study of Bach and encouraged him in keyboard improvisation. At the age of 12, in 1782, Beethoven composed *9 Variations for Piano on a March of Dressler,* his first work to be publ. In 1783 he played the cembalo in the court orch. in Bonn; in 1784 the Elector Maximilian Franz officially appointed him to the post of deputy court organist, a position he retained until 1792; from 1788–92 Beethoven also served as a violist in theater orchs. In 1787 the Elector sent Beethoven to Vienna, where he stayed for a short time; the report that he played for Mozart and that Mozart pronounced him a future great composer seems to be a figment of somebody's eager imagination. After a few weeks in Vienna Beethoven went to Bonn when he received news that his mother was gravely ill; she died on July 17, 1787. Beethoven was obliged to provide sustenance for his 2 younger brothers; his father, who took to drink in excess, could not meet his obligations. Beethoven earned some money by giving piano lessons to the children of Helene von Breuning, the widow of a court councillor. He also met important wealthy admirers, among them Count Ferdinand von Waldstein, who was to be immortalized by Beethoven's dedication to him of a piano sonata bearing his name. Beethoven continued to compose; some of his works of the period were written in homage to royalty, as a cantata on the death of the Emperor Joseph II and a cantata on the accession of Emperor Leopold II; other pieces were designed for performance at aristocratic gatherings.

In 1790 an event of importance took place in Beethoven's life when Haydn was honored in Bonn by the Elector on his way to London; it is likely that Beethoven was introduced to him, and that Haydn encouraged him to come to Vienna to study with him. However that might be, Beethoven went to Vienna in November 1792, and began his studies with Haydn. Not very prudently, Beethoven approached the notable teacher Johann Schenk to help him write the mandatory exercises prior to delivering them to Haydn for final appraisal. In the meantime, Haydn had to go to London again, and Beethoven's lessons with him were discontinued. Instead, Beethoven began a formal study of counterpoint with Johann Georg Albrechtsberger, a learned musician and knowledgeable pedagogue; these studies continued for about a year, until 1795. Furthermore, Beethoven took lessons in vocal composition with the illustrious Italian composer Salieri, who served as Imperial Kappelmeister at the Austrian Court. Beethoven was fortunate to find a generous benefactor in Prince Karl Lichnowsky, who awarded him, beginning about 1800, an annual stipend of 600 florins; he was amply repaid for this bounty by entering the pantheon of music history through Beethoven's dedication to him of the *Sonate pathétique* and other works, as well as his first opus number, a piano trio. Among other aristocrats of Vienna who were introduced into the gates of permanence through Beethoven's dedications was Prince Franz Joseph Lobkowitz, whose name adorns the title pages of the 6 String Quartets, op. 18; the Eroica Symph. (after Beethoven unsuccessfully tried to dedicate it to Napoleon); the Triple Concerto, op. 56; and (in conjunction with Prince Razumovsky) the 5th and 6th symphs.—a glorious florilegium of great music. Prince Razumovsky, the Russian ambassador to Vienna, played an important role in Beethoven's life. From 1808–16 he maintained in his residence a string quartet in which he himself played the 2nd violin (the leader was Beethoven's friend Schuppanzigh). It was to Razumovsky that Beethoven dedicated his 3 string quartets that became known as the Razumovsky quartets, in which Beethoven made use of authentic Russian folk themes. Razumovsky also shared with Lobkowitz the dedications of Beethoven's 5th and 6th symphs. Another Russian patron was Prince Golitzyn, for whom Beethoven wrote his great string quartets opp. 127, 130, and 132.

Beethoven made his first public appearance in Vienna on March 29, 1795, as soloist in one of his piano concertos (probably the B-flat major Concerto, op. 19). In 1796 he played in Prague, Dresden, Leipzig, and Berlin. He also participated in "competitions," fashionable at the time, with other pianists, which were usually held in aristocratic salons. In 1799 he competed with Joseph Wölffl and in 1800 with Daniel Steibelt. On April 2, 1800, he presented a concert of his works in the Burgtheater in Vienna, at which his First Symph. in C major and the Septet in E-flat major were performed for the first time. Other compositions at the threshold of the century were the Piano Sonata in C minor, op. 13, the *Pathétique;* the C-major Piano Concerto, op. 15; "sonata quasi una fantasia" for Piano in C-sharp minor, op. 27, celebrated under the nickname *Moonlight Sonata* (so described by a romantically inclined critic but not specifically accepted by Beethoven); the D major Piano Sonata known as *Pastoral;* 8 violin sonatas; 4 piano trios; 4 string trios; 6 string quartets; Septet for Wind Instruments and Strings; several sets of variations; and a number of songs.

Wilhelm von Lenz, a Russian musician of German extraction who wrote books in the French language, publ. in St. Petersburg in 1852 a 2-vol. essay, *Beethoven et ses trois styles,* in which he separated Beethoven's list of compositions into 3 periods. Despite this arbitrary chronological division, the work became firmly established in Beethoven literature. According to Lenz, the first period embraced Beethoven's works from his early years to the end of the 18th century, marked by a style closely related to the formal methods of Haydn. The 2nd period, covering the years 1801–14, was signaled by a more personal, quasi-Romantic mood, beginning with the *Moonlight Sonata;* the last period, extending from 1814 to Beethoven's death in 1827, comprised the most individual, the most unconventional, the most innovative works, such as his last string quartets and the 9th Symph., with its extraordinary choral finale.

Beethoven's early career in Vienna was marked by fine success; he was popular not only as a virtuoso pianist and a composer, but also as a social figure who was welcome in the aristocratic circles of Vienna; Beethoven's students included society ladies and even royal personages, such as Archduke Rudolf of Austria, to whom Beethoven dedicated the so-called Archduke Trio, op. 97. But Beethoven's progress was fatefully affected by a mysteriously growing deafness, which reached a crisis in 1802. On Oct. 8 and 10, 1802, Beethoven wrote a poignant document known as the "Heiligenstadt Testament," for it was drawn in the village of Heiligenstadt, where Beethoven resided at the time. The document, not discovered until after Beethoven's death, voiced Beethoven's despair at the realization that the most important sense of his being, the sense of hearing, was inexorably failing. He implored his brothers, in case of his early death, to consult his physician, Dr. Schmidt, who knew the secret of his "lasting malady" contracted 6 years before he wrote the Testament, i.e., in 1796. The etiology of his illness leaves little doubt that the malady was the dreaded "lues," with symptoms including painful intestinal disturbances, enormous enlargement of the pancreas, cirrhosis of the liver, and, most ominously, the porous degeneration of the roof of the cranium, observable in the life mask of 1812 and clearly shown in the photograph of Beethoven's skull taken when his body was exhumed in 1863. However, the impairment of his hearing may have had an independent cause, an otosclerosis, resulting in the shriveling of the auditory nerves and concomitant dilation of the accompanying arteries. Externally, there were signs of tinnitus, a constant buzzing in the ears, about which Beethoven complained. Beethoven's reverential biographer A.W. Thayer states plainly in a letter dated Oct. 29, 1880, that it was known to several friends of Beethoven that the cause of his combined ailments was syphilis. A full account of Beethoven's illness is found in Dr. Dieter Kerner's book *Krankheiten grosser Musiker* (Stuttgart, 1973; vol. 1, pp. 89–140).

To the end of his life Beethoven hoped to find a remedy for his deafness among the latest "scientific" medications. His Konversationshefte bear a pathetic testimony to these hopes; in one, dated 1819, he notes down the address of a Dr. Mayer, who treated deafness by "sulphur vapor" and a vibrations machine. By tragic irony, Beethoven's deafness greatly contributed to the study of his personality, thanks to the existence of the "conversation books" in which his interlocutors wrote down their questions and Beethoven replied, also usually in writing, a method of communication which became a rule in Beethoven's life after 1818. Unfortunately, Beethoven's friend and amanuensis, Anton Schindler, altered or deleted many of these; it seems also likely that he destroyed Beethoven's correspondence with his doctors, as well as the recipes which apparently contained indications of treatment by mercury, the universal medication against venereal and other diseases at the time.

It is remarkable that under these conditions Beethoven was able to continue his creative work with his usual energy; there seem to be no periods of interruption in the chronology of his list of works, and similarly there is no apparent influence of his moods of depression on the content of his music; tragic and joyful musical passages had equal shares in his inexhaustible flow of varied works. On April 5, 1803, Beethoven presented a concert of his compositions in Vienna at which he was soloist in his 3rd Piano Concerto; the program also contained performances of his 2nd Symph. and of the oratorio *Christus am Oelberge.* On May 24, 1803, he played in Vienna the piano part of his Violin Sonata, op. 47, known as the *Kreutzer Sonata,* although Kreutzer himself did not introduce it; in his place the violin part was taken over by the mulatto artist George Bridgetower. During the years of 1803 and 1804 Beethoven composed his great Symph. No. 3 in E-flat major, op. 55, the *Eroica.* It has an interesting history. Beethoven's disciple Ferdinand Ries relates that Beethoven tore off the title page of the MS of the score originally dedicated to Napoleon, after learning of his proclamation as Emperor of France in 1804, and supposedly exclaimed, "So he is a tyrant like all the others after all!" Ries reported this story shortly before his death, some 34 years after the composition of the *Eroica,* which throws great doubt on its credibility. Indeed, in a letter to the publishing firm of Breitkopf & Härtel, dated Aug. 26, 1804, long after Napoleon's proclamation of Empire, Beethoven still refers to the title of the work as "really Bonaparte." His own copy of the score shows that he crossed out the designation "Inttitulata Bonaparte," but allowed the words written in pencil, in German, "Geschrieben auf Bonaparte" to stand. In October 1806, when the first edition of the orch. parts was publ. in Vienna, the symph. received the title "Sinfonia eroica composta per festeggiare il sovvenire d'un grand' uomo" ("heroic symphony, composed to celebrate the memory of a great man"). But who was the great man whose memory was being celebrated in Beethoven's masterpiece? Napoleon was very much alive and was still leading his Grand Armée to new conquests, so the title would not apply. Yet, the famous funeral march in the score expressed a sense of loss and mourning. The mystery remains. There is evidence that Beethoven continued to have admiration for Napoleon. He once remarked that had he been a military man he could have matched Napoleon's greatness on the battlefield. Beethoven and Napoleon were close contemporaries; Napoleon was a little more than a year older than Beethoven.

In 1803 Emanuel Schikaneder, manager of the Theater an der Wien, asked Beethoven to compose an opera to a libretto he had prepared under the title *Vestas Feuer (The Vestal Flame)*, but Beethoven showed no interest in such a project; instead he began work on another opera, based on J.N. Bouilly's *Léonore, ou L'Amour conjugal.* The completed opera was named *Fidelio,* which was the heroine's assumed name in her successful efforts to save her imprisoned husband. The opera was given at the Theater an der Wien on Nov. 20, 1805, under difficult circumstances, a few days after the French army entered Vienna. There were only 3 performances before the opera was rescheduled for March 29 and April 10, 1806; after another long hiatus a greatly revised version of *Fidelio* was produced on May 23, 1814. Beethoven wrote 3 versions of the Overture for *Léonore;* for another performance, on May 26, 1814, he revised the Overture once more, and this time it was performed under the title *Fidelio Overture.*

An extraordinary profusion of creative masterpieces marked the years 1802–8 in Beethoven's life. During these years he brought out the 3 String Quartets, op. 59, dedicated to Count Razumovsky; the 4th, 5th, and 6th symphs.; the Violin Concerto; the 4th Piano Concerto; the Triple Concerto; the *Coriolan* Overture; and a number of piano sonatas, including the D minor, op. 31; No. 2, the *Tempest;* the C major, op. 53, the *Waldstein;* and the F minor, op. 57, the *Appassionata.* On Dec. 22, 1808, Beethoven played in Vienna the solo part of his 4th Piano Concerto, and in the same concert the 5th and 6th symphs. were heard for the first time; the concert lasted some 4 hours. Still, financial difficulties beset Beethoven. The various annuities from patrons were uncertain, and the devaluation of the Austrian currency played havoc with his calculations. In Oct. 1808, King Jerome Bonaparte of Westphalia offered Beethoven the post of Kapellmeister of Kassel at a substantial salary, but Beethoven decided to remain in Vienna. Between 1809 and 1812, Beethoven wrote his 5th Piano Concerto; the String Quartet in E-flat major, op. 74; the incidental music to Goethe's drama *Egmont;* the 7th and 8th symphs.; and his Piano Sonata in E-flat major, op. 81a, whimsically subtitled "Das Lebewohl, Abwesenheit und Wiedersehn," also known by its French subtitle, "Les Adieux, l'absence, et le retour." He also added a specific description to the work, "Sonate caractéristique." This explicit characterization was rare with Beethoven; he usually avoided programmatic descriptions, preferring to have his music stand by itself. Even in his 6th Symph., the *Pastorale,* which bore specific subtitles for each movement and had the famous imitations of birds singing and the realistic portrayal of a storm, Beethoven decided to append a cautionary phrase: "More as an expression of one's feelings than a picture." Beethoven specifically denied that the famous introductory call in the 5th Symph. represented the knock of Fate at his door, but the symbolic association was too powerful to be removed from the legend; yet the characteristic iambic tetrameter was anticipated in several of Beethoven's works, among them the *Appassionata* and the 4th Piano Concerto. Czerny, who was close to Beethoven in Vienna, claimed that the theme was derived by Beethoven from the cry of the songbird Emberiza, or Emmerling, a species to which the common European goldfinch belongs, which Beethoven may have heard during his walks in the Vienna woods, a cry that is piercing enough to compensate for Beethoven's loss of aural acuity. However that may be, the 4-note motif became inexorably connected with the voice of doom for enemies and the exultation of the victor in battle. It was used as a victory call by the Allies in World War II; the circumstance that 3 short beats followed by one long beat spelled V for Victory in Morse code reinforced its effectiveness. The Germans could not very well jail people for whistling a Beethoven tune, so they took it over themselves as the first letter of the archaic German word Viktoria, and trumpeted it blithely over their radios. Another famous nicknamed work by Beethoven was the *Emperor Concerto,* a label attached to the 5th Piano Concerto, op. 73. Beethoven wrote it in 1809, when Napoleon's star was still high in the European firmament, and some publicist decided that the martial strains of the music, with its sonorous fanfares, must have been a tribute to the Emperor of the French. Patriotic reasons seemed to underlie Beethoven's designation of his Piano Sonata, op. 106, as the *Hammerklavier Sonata,* that is, a work written for a hammer keyboard, or fortepiano, as distinct from harpsichord. But all of Beethoven's piano sonatas were for fortepiano; moreover, Beethoven assigned the title *Hammerklavier* to each of the 4 sonatas, namely opp. 101, 106, 109, and 110, using the old German word for fortepiano; by so doing, Beethoven desired to express his patriotic consciousness of being a German.

Like many professional musicians, Beethoven was occasionally called upon to write a work glorifying an important event or a famous personage. Pieces of this kind seldom achieve validity, and usually produce bombast. Such a work was Beethoven's *Wellingtons Sieg oder Die Schlacht bei Vittoria,* celebrating the British victory over Joseph Bonaparte, Napoleon's brother who temporarily sat on the Spanish throne. In 1814, Beethoven wrote a cantata entitled *Der glorreiche Augenblick,* intended to mark the "glorious moment" of the fall of Bee-

Beethoven

thoven's erstwhile idol, Napoleon.

Personal misfortunes, chronic ailments, and intermittent quarrels with friends and relatives preoccupied Beethoven's entire life. He ardently called for peace among men, but he never achieved peace with himself. Yet he could afford to disdain the attacks in the press; on the margin of a critical but justified review of Beethoven's *Wellington's Victory*, he wrote, addressing the writer: "You wretched scoundrel! What I excrete [he used the vulgar German word *scheisse*] is better than anything you could ever think up!"

Beethoven was overly suspicious; he even accused the faithful Schindler of dishonestly mishandling the receipts from the sale of tickets at the first performance of the 9th Symph. He exaggerated his poverty; he possessed some shares and bonds which he kept in a secret drawer. He was untidy in personal habits: he often used preliminary drafts of his compositions to cover the soup and even the chamber pot, leaving telltale circles on the MS. He was strangely naive; he studiously examined the winning numbers of the Austrian government lottery, hoping to find a numerological clue to a fortune for himself. His handwriting was all but indecipherable. An earnest Beethoveniac spent time with a microscope trying to figure out what kind of soap Beethoven wanted his housekeeper to purchase for him; the scholar's efforts were crowned with triumphant success: the indecipherable word was *gelbe*—Beethoven wanted a piece of yellow soap. Q.E.D. The copying of his MSS presented difficulties; not only were the notes smudged, but sometimes Beethoven even failed to mark a crucial accidental. A copyist said that he would rather copy 20 pages of Rossini than a single page of Beethoven. On the other hand, Beethoven's sketchbooks, containing many alternative drafts, are extremely valuable, for they introduce a scholar into the inner sanctum of Beethoven's creative process.

Beethoven had many devoted friends and admirers in Vienna, but he spent most of his life in solitude. Carl Czerny reports in his diary that Beethoven once asked him to let him lodge in his house, but Czerny declined, explaining that his aged parents lived with him and he had no room for Beethoven. Deprived of the pleasures and comforts of family life, Beethoven sought to find a surrogate in his nephew Karl, son of Caspar Carl Beethoven, who died in 1815. Beethoven regarded his sister-in-law as an unfit mother; he went to court to gain sole guardianship over the boy; in his private letters, and even in his legal depositions, he poured torrents of vilification upon the woman, implying even that she was engaged in prostitution. In his letters to Karl he often signed himself as the true father of the boy. In 1826 Karl attempted suicide; it would be unfair to ascribe this act to Beethoven's stifling avuncular affection; Karl later went into the army and enjoyed a normal life.

Gallons of ink have been unnecessarily expended on the crucial question of Beethoven's relationship with women. That Beethoven dreamed of an ideal life companion is clear from his numerous utterances and candid letters to friends, in some of which he asked them to find a suitable bride for him. But there is no inkling that he kept company with any particular woman in Vienna. Beethoven lacked social graces; he could not dance; he was unable to carry on a light conversation about trivia; and behind it all there was the dreadful reality of his deafness. He could speak, but could not always understand when he was spoken to. With close friends he used an unwieldy ear trumpet; but such contrivances were obviously unsuitable in a social gathering. There were several objects of his secret passions, among his pupils or the society ladies to whom he dedicated his works. But somehow he never actually proposed marriage, and they usually married less hesitant suitors. It was inevitable that Beethoven should seek escape in fantasies. The greatest of these fantasies was the famous letter addressed to an "unsterbliche Geliebte," the "Immortal Beloved," couched in exuberant emotional tones characteristic of the sentimental romances of the time, and strangely reminiscent of Goethe's novel *The Sorrows of Young Werther*. The letter was never mailed; it was discovered in the secret compartment of Beethoven's writing desk after his death. The clues to the identity of the object of his passion were maddeningly few. He voiced his fervid anticipation of an impending meeting at some place indicated only by the initial letter "K."; he dated his letter as Monday, the 6th of July, without specifying the year. Eager Beethoveniacs readily established that the most likely year was 1812, when July 6 fell on a Monday. A complete inventory of ladies of Beethoven's acquaintance from 14 to 40 years of age was laid out, and the lengthy charade unfolded, lasting one and a half centuries. The most likely "Immortal Beloved" seemed to be Antoine Brentano, the wife of a merchant. But Beethoven was a frequent visitor at their house; his letters to her (sent by ordinary city post) and her replies expressed mutual devotion, but they could not be stylistically reconciled with the torrid protestation of undying love in the unmailed letter. And if indeed Frau Brentano was the "Immortal Beloved," why could not a tryst have been arranged in Vienna when her husband was away on business? There were other candidates; one researcher established, from consulting the town records of arrivals and departures, that Beethoven and a certain lady of his Vienna circle were in Prague on the same day, and that about 9 months later she bore a child who seemed to bear a remarkable resemblance to Beethoven. Another researcher, exploring the limits of the incredible, concluded that Beethoven had sexual relations with his sister-in-law and that his execration of her stemmed from this relationship. It was asserted also that a certain musician conversant with the lowlife of Vienna supplied Beethoven with *filles de joie* for pay. The nadir of monstrous speculation was reached by a pseudo-Freudian investigator who advanced the notion that Beethoven nurtured incestuous desires toward his nephew and that his demands drove the boy to his suicide attempt.

The so-called 3rd style of Beethoven was assigned by biographers to the last 10 or 15 years of his life.

It included the composition of his monumental 9th Symph., completed in 1824 and first performed in Vienna on May 7, 1824; the program also included excerpts from the *Missa Solemnis* and *Die Weihe des Hauses (The Consecration of the House)*. It was reported, on scant evidence, that Caroline Unger, the contralto soloist in the *Missa Solemnis,* had to pull Beethoven by the sleeve at the end of the performance so that he would acknowledge the applause he could not hear. With the 9th Symph., Beethoven completed the evolution of the symph. form as he envisioned it. Its choral finale was Beethoven's manifesto addressed to the world at large, to the text from Schiller's ode *An die Freude (To Joy)*. In it, Beethoven, through Schiller, appealed to all humanity to unite in universal love. Here a musical work, for the first time, served a political ideal. Rumors that Beethoven was planning to compose still another symph. were not substantiated; indeed, the number 9 became symbolic for future composers as the point of musical infinity; Mahler and Bruckner recoiled from exceeding the magic number. Beethoven's last string quartets, opp. 127, 130, 131, and 132, served as counterparts of Beethoven's last symph. in their striking innovations, dramatic pauses, and novel instrumental tone colors.

In Dec. 1826, on his way back to Vienna from a visit in Gneixendorf, Beethoven was stricken with a fever that developed into a mortal pleurisy; dropsy and jaundice supervened to this condition; surgery to relieve the accumulated fluid in his organism was unsuccessful, and he died on the afternoon of March 26, 1827. It was widely reported that an electric storm struck Vienna as Beethoven lay dying; its occurrence was indeed confirmed by the contemporary records in the Vienna weather bureau, but the story that Beethoven raised his clenched fist aloft as a gesture of defiance to an overbearing Heaven must be relegated to fantasy; he was far too feeble either to clench his fist or to raise his arm. The funeral of Beethoven was held in all solemnity.

Beethoven was memorialized in festive observations of the centennial and bicentennial of his birth, and of the centennial and sesquicentennial of his death. The house where he was born in Bonn was declared a museum. Monuments were erected to him in many cities. Commemorative postage stamps bearing his image were issued not only in Germany and Austria, but in Russia and other countries. Streets were named after him in many cities of the civilized world, including even Los Angeles.

Beethoven's music marks a division between the Classical period of the 18th century, exemplified by the great names of Mozart and Haydn, and the new spirit of Romantic music that characterized the entire course of the 19th century. There are certain purely external factors that distinguish these 2 periods of musical evolution; one of them pertains to sartorial matters. Music before Beethoven was *Zopfmusik,* pigtail music. Haydn and Mozart are familiar to us by portraits in which their heads are crowned by elaborate wigs; Beethoven's hair was by contrast luxuriant in its unkempt splendor. The music of the 18th century possessed the magnitude

of mass production. The accepted number of Haydn's symphs., according to his own count, is 104, but even in his own catalogue Haydn allowed a duplication of one of his symph. works. Mozart wrote about 40 symphs. during his short lifetime. Haydn's symphs. were constructed according to an easily defined formal structure; while Mozart's last symphs. show greater depth of penetration, they do not depart from the Classical convention. Besides, both Haydn and Mozart wrote instrumental works variously entitled cassations, serenades, divertimentos, and suites, which were basically synonymous with symphs. But Beethoven did not write serenades or other works in quasi-symph. form. And his symphs. were few in number and mutually different. The first and 2nd symphs. may still be classified as *Zopfmusik,* but with the 3rd Symph. he entered a new world of music. No symph. written before had contained a clearly defined funeral march. Although the 5th Symph. had no designated program, it lent itself easily to programmatic interpretation. Wagner attached a bombastic label, "Apotheosis of the Dance," to Beethoven's 7th Symph. The 8th escaped a sobriquet, and the 9th is usually known as the *Choral* symph. With the advent of Beethoven, the manufacture of symphs. en masse had ceased; Schumann, Brahms, Tchaikovsky, and their contemporaries wrote but a few symphs. each, and each had a distinctive physiognomy. Beethoven had forever destroyed *Zopfmusik,* and opened the floodgates of the Romantic era. Beethoven's music was individual; it was emotionally charged; his Kreutzer Sonata served as a symbol for Tolstoy's celebrated moralistic tale of that name, in which the last movement of the sonata leads the woman pianist into the receptive arms of the concupiscent violinist. But technically the sonata is very difficult for amateurs to master, and Tolstoy's sinners were an ordinary couple in old Russia.

Similarly novel were Beethoven's string quartets; a musical abyss separated his last string quartets from his early essays in the same form. Trios, violin sonatas, cello sonatas, and the 32 great piano sonatas also represent evolutionary concepts. Yet Beethoven's melody and harmony did not diverge from the sacrosanct laws of euphony and tonality. The famous dissonant chord introducing the last movement of the 9th Symph. resolves naturally into the tonic, giving only a moment's pause to the ear. Beethoven's favorite device of pairing the melody in the high treble with triadic chords in close harmony in the deep bass was a peculiarity of his style but not necessarily an infringement of the Classical rules. Yet contemporary critics found some of these practices repugnant and described Beethoven as an eccentric bent on creating unconventional sonorities. Equally strange to the untutored ear were pregnant pauses and sudden modulations in his instrumental works. Beethoven was not a contrapuntist by taste or skill. With the exception of his monumental *Grosse Fuge,* composed as the finale of the String Quartet, op. 133, his fugal movements were usually free canonic imitations. There is only a single instance in Beethoven's music of the crab movement, a variation achieved by running the theme in reverse. But Beethoven was a master of instrumental variation, deriving extraordinary transformations through melodic and rhythmic alterations of a given theme. Beethoven's op. 120, 33 variations for piano on a waltz theme by the Viennese publisher Diabelli, represents one of the greatest achievements in the art.

When Hans von Bülow was asked which was his favorite key signature, he replied that it was E-flat major, the tonality of the *Eroica*, for it had 3 flats: one for Bach, one for Beethoven, and one for Brahms. Beethoven became forever the 2nd B in popular music books.

The literature on Beethoven is immense. The basic catalogues are those by G. Kinsky and H. Halm, *Das Werk Beethovens. Thematisch-Bibliographisches Verzeichnis seiner sämtlichen vollendenten Kompositionen,* publ. in Munich and Duisburg in 1955, and by W. Hess, *Verzeichnis der Gesamtausgabe veröffentlichen Werke Ludwig van Beethovens,* publ. in Wiesbaden in 1957. Beethoven attached opus numbers to most of his works, and they are essential in a catalogue of his works.

WORKS: FOR ORCH.: 9 symphs.: No. 1, in C major, op. 21 (1800; Vienna, April 2, 1800); No. 2, in D major, op. 36 (1801–2; Vienna, April 5, 1803); No. 3, in E-flat major, op. 55, *Eroica* (1803–4; Vienna, April 7, 1805); No. 4, in B-flat major, op. 60 (1806; Vienna, March 5, 1807); No. 5, in C minor, op. 67 (sketches from 1803; 1807–8; Vienna, Dec. 22, 1808); No. 6, in F major, op. 68, *Pastoral* (sketches from 1803; 1808; Vienna, Dec. 22, 1808); No. 7, in A major, op. 92 (1811–12; Vienna, Dec. 8, 1813); No. 8, in F major, op. 93 (1812; Vienna, Feb. 27, 1814); No. 9, in D minor, op. 125, *Choral* (sketches from 1815–18; 1822–24; Vienna, May 7, 1824); also a fragment of a Symph. in C minor, Hess 298 from the Bonn period.—Incidental music: Overture to Collin's *Coriolan,* in C minor, op. 62 (1807; Vienna, March 1807); *Egmont,* op. 84, to Goethe's drama (with overture; 1809–10; Vienna, June 15, 1810); *Die Ruinen von Athen (The Ruins of Athens),* op. 113, to Kotzebue's drama (with overture; 1811; Pest, Feb. 10, 1812); *König Stephan (King Stephen),* op. 117, to Kotzebue's drama (with overture; 1811; Pest, Feb. 10, 1812); Triumphal March in C major for Kuffner's *Tarpeja* (1813; March 26, 1813); music to Duncker's drama *Leonore Prohaska* (1815); Overture in C major, op. 124, to Meisl's drama *Die Weihe des Hauses (The Consecration of the House;* 1822; Vienna, Oct. 3, 1822).—Further overtures: 4 overtures written for the opera *Leonore,* later named *Fidelio: Leonore* No. 1, in C major, op. 138 (1806–7; Feb. 7, 1828); *Leonore* No. 2, op. 72a (1804–5; Vienna, Nov. 20, 1805); *Leonore* No. 3, op. 72b (1805–6; Vienna, March 29, 1806); *Fidelio,* op. 72c (1814; Vienna, May 27, 1814); *Namensfeier (Nameday)* in C major, op. 115 (1814–15; Vienna, Dec. 25, 1815).—Other works for Orch. or Wind Band: 12 Minuets, WoO 7 (1795); 12 German Dances (1795); 12 Contredanses (1802?); March "für die bohmische Landwehr" in F major (1809); March in F major (1810); Polonaise in D major, WoO 21 (1810); Ecossaise in D major (1810); Ecossaise in G major (1810); *Wellingtons Sieg oder Die Schlacht bei Vittoria (Wellington's Victory or The Battle of Vit-* *toria;* also known as the *Battle* symph.), op. 91 (1813; Vienna, Dec. 8, 1813); March in D major (1816); *Gratulations-Menuet* in E-flat major, WoO 3 (1822; Nov. 3, 1822); March with Trio in C major (1822?).— Ballets: *Ritterballett (Knight's Ballet;* 1790–91; Bonn, March 6, 1791); *Die Geschöpfe des Prometheus (The Creatures of Prometheus),* op. 43 (overture, introduction, and 16 numbers; 1800–1; Vienna, March 28, 1801).—Works for Solo Instruments and Orch.: Piano Concerto in E-flat major (1784); *Romance* in E minor for Piano, Flute, Bassoon, and Orch., Hess 13 (1786; only a fragment extant); Violin Concerto in C major (1790–92; only a portion of the first movement is extant); Oboe Concerto in F major, Hess 12 (1792?–93?; not extant; only a few sketches survive); Rondo in B-flat major for Piano and Orch. (1793; solo part finished by Czerny); Piano Concerto No. 2, in B-flat major, op. 19 (probably begun during the Bonn period, perhaps as early as 1785; revised 1794–95 and 1798; Vienna, March 29, 1795; when publ. in Leipzig in 1801, it was listed as "No. 2"); Piano Concerto No. 1, in C major, op. 15 (1795; revised 1800; Vienna, Dec. 18, 1795; when publ. in Vienna in 1801, it was listed as "No. 1"); *Romance* in F major for Violin and Orch., op. 50 (1798?; Nov. 1798?); Piano Concerto No. 3, in C minor, op. 37 (1800?; Vienna, April 5, 1803); *Romance* in G major for Violin and Orch., op. 40 (1801?–2); Triple Concerto in C major for Piano, Violin, Cello, and Orch., op. 56 (1803–4; Vienna, May 1808); Piano Concerto No. 4, in G major, op. 58 (1805–6; Vienna, March 1807); Violin Concerto in D major, op. 61 (1806; Vienna, Dec. 23, 1806; cadenza for the first movement and 3 cadenzas for the finale; also arranged as a piano concerto in 1807); Fantasia in C minor for Piano, Chorus, and Orch., op. 80, *Choral Fantasy* (1808; Vienna, Dec. 22, 1808); Piano Concerto No. 5, in E-flat major, op. 73, *Emperor* (1809; Leipzig, 1810; first Vienna perf., Nov. 28, 1811); also 11 cadenzas for piano concertos nos. 1–4, and 2 for Mozart's Piano Concerto No. 20, in D minor, K. 466.

CHAMBER MUSIC: 3 String Quartets: E-flat major, D major, and C major (1785); Trio in G major for Piano, Flute, and Bassoon, WoO 37 (1786); Minuet in A-flat major for String Quartet, Hess 33 (1790); Piano Trio in E-flat major (1791); *Allegretto* in E-flat major for Piano Trio, Hess 48 (1790–92); Violin Sonata in A major, Hess 46 (1790–92; only a fragment is extant); *Allegro and Minuet* in G major for 2 Flutes (1792); Octet in E-flat major for 2 Oboes, 2 Clarinets, 2 Horns, and 2 Bassoons, op. 103 (1792–93); Variations in F major on Mozart's "Se vuol ballare" from *Le nozze di Figaro* for Piano and Violin (1792–93); *Rondino* in E-flat major for 2 Oboes, 2 Clarinets, 2 Horns, and 2 Bassoons (1793); Quintet in E-flat major for Oboe, 3 Horns, and Bassoon, Hess 19 (1793); *Rondo* in G major for Piano and Violin (1793–94); String Trio in E-flat major, op. 3 (1793); 3 Piano Trios: E-flat major, G major, and C minor, op. 1 (1794–95); Trio in C major for 2 Oboes and English Horn, op. 87 (1795); String Quintet in E-flat major, op. 4 (1795); Variations in C major on Mozart's "La ci darem la mano" from *Don Giovanni* for 2 Oboes and English Horn (1795); Sextet in E-flat major for 2 Horns, 2 Violins, Viola, and Cello, op. 81b (1795);

Sextet in E-flat major for 2 Clarinets, 2 Horns, and 2 Bassoons, op. 71 (1796); Sonatina in C minor for Piano and Mandolin (1796); *Adagio* in E-flat major for Piano and Mandolin (1796); Sonatina in C major for Piano and Mandolin (1796); *Andante and Variations* in D major for Piano and Mandolin (1796); 6 German Dances for Piano and Violin (1796); 2 Cello Sonatas: F major and G minor, op. 5 (1796); Variations in G major on Handel's "See the Conquering Hero Comes" from *Judas Maccabaeus* for Piano and Cello (1796); Variations in F major on Mozart's "Ein Mädchen oder Weibchen" from *Die Zauberflöte* for Piano and Cello, op. 66 (1796); Quintet in E-flat major for Piano, Oboe, Clarinet, Horn, and Bassoon, op. 16 (1796–97); Duet in E-flat major for Viola and Cello (1796–97); Serenade in D major for String Trio, op. 8 (1796–97); Trio in B-flat major for Piano, Clarinet or Violin, and Cello, op. 11 (1797); 3 String Trios: G major, D major, and C minor, op. 9 (1797–98); 3 Violin Sonatas: D major, A major, and E-flat major, op. 12 (1797–98); March in B-flat major for 2 Clarinets, 2 Horns, and 2 Bassoons (1798); 6 String Quartets: F major, G major, D major, C minor, A major, and B-flat major, op. 18 (1798–1800); Septet in E-flat major for Clarinet, Horn, Bassoon, Violin, Viola, Cello, and Double Bass, op. 20 (1799–1800); Horn (or Cello) Sonata in F major, op. 17 (1800; Vienna, April 18, 1800); Violin Sonata in A minor, op. 23 (1800–1); Violin Sonata in F major, op. 24, *Spring* (1800–1); Variations in E-flat major on Mozart's "Bei Männern, welche Liebe fühlen" from *Die Zauberflöte* for Piano and Cello (1801); Serenade in D major for Flute, Violin, and Viola, op. 25 (1801); String Quintet in C major, op. 29 (1801); String Quartet in F major, Hess 34 (an arrangement of the Piano Sonata No. 9, in E-flat major, op. 14, No. 1; 1801–2); 3 Violin Sonatas: A major, C minor, and G major, op. 30 (1801–2); 14 Variations in E-flat major for Piano, Violin, and Cello, op. 44 (sketches from 1792; 1802?); Violin Sonata in A minor, op. 47, *Kreutzer* (1802–3; Vienna, May 24, 1803); Trio in E-flat major for Piano, Clarinet or Violin, and Cello, op. 38 (an arrangement of the Septet, op. 20; 1803); Variations in G major on Müller's "Ich bin der Schneider Kakadu" for Piano, Violin, and Cello, op. 121a (1803?; revised 1816); Serenade in D major for Piano, and Flute or Violin, op. 41 (an arrangement of the Serenade in D major, op. 25; 1803); *Notturno* in D major for Piano and Viola, op. 42 (an arrangement of the Serenade in D major, op. 8; 1803); 3 String Quartets: F major, E minor, and C major, op. 59, *Razumovsky* (1805–6); Cello Sonata in A major, op. 69 (1807–8); 2 Piano Trios: D major and E-flat major, op. 70 (1808); String Quartet in E-flat major, op. 74, *Harp* (1809); String Quartet in F minor, op. 95, *Serioso* (1810); Piano Trio in B-flat major, op. 97, *Archduke* (1810–11); Violin Sonata in G major, op. 96 (1812); *Allegretto* in B-flat major for Piano Trio (1812); *3 equali* for 4 Trombones: D minor, D major, and B-flat major (1812); 2 Cello Sonatas: C major and D major, op. 102 (1815); String Quintet in C minor, op. 104 (an arrangement of the Piano Trio in C major, op. 1, No. 3; 1817); Prelude in D minor for String Quintet, Hess 40 (1817?); Fugue in D major for String Quintet, op. 137 (1817); 6 National Airs with Variations for Piano, and Flute or Violin, op. 105 (1818?); 10 National Airs with Variations for Piano, and Flute or Violin, op. 107 (1818); Duet in A major for 2 Violins (1822); String Quartet in E-flat major, op. 127 (1824–25); String Quartet in A minor, op. 132 (1825); String Quartet in B-flat major, op. 130 (with the *Grosse Fuge* as the finale, 1825; *Rondo finale,* 1826); *Grosse Fuge* in B-flat major for String Quartet, op. 133 (1825); String Quartet in C-sharp minor, op. 131 (1825–26); String Quartet in F major, op. 135 (1826); String Quintet in C major, Hess 41 (1826; extant in piano transcription only).

PIANO SONATAS: Three: in E-flat major, F minor, and D major, *Kurfürstensonaten* (1783); F major (1792); No. 1, in F minor, op. 2, No. 1 (1793–95); No. 2, in A major, op. 2, No. 2 (1794–95); No. 3, in C major, op. 2, No. 3 (1794–95); No. 19, in G minor, op. 49, No. 1 (1797); No. 20, in G major, op. 49, No. 2 (1795–96); No. 4, in E-flat major, op. 7 (1796–97); No. 5, in C minor, op. 10, No. 1 (1795–97); No. 6, in F major, op. 10, No. 2 (1796–97); No. 7, in D major, op. 10, No. 3 (1797–98); C major, WoO 51 (fragment; 1797–98); No. 8, in C minor, op. 13, *Pathétique* (1798–99); No. 9, in E major, op. 14, No. 1 (1798); No. 10, in G major, op. 14, No. 2 (1799); No. 11, in B-flat major, op. 22 (1800); No. 12, in A-flat major, op. 26, *Funeral March* (1800–1); No. 13, in E-flat major, op. 27, No. 1, "quasi una fantasia" (1800–1); No. 14, in C-sharp minor, op. 27, No. 2, "quasi una fantasia," *Moonlight* (1801); No. 15, in D major, op. 28, *Pastoral* (1801); No. 16, in G major, op. 31, No. 1 (1801–2); No. 17, in D minor, op. 31, No. 2, *Tempest* (1801–2); No. 18, in E-flat major, op. 31, No. 3 (1801–2); No. 21, in C major, op. 53, *Waldstein* (1803–4); No. 22, in F major, op. 54 (1803–4); No. 23, in F minor, op. 57, *Appassionata* (1804–5); No. 24, in F-sharp minor, op. 78 (1809); No. 25, in G major, op. 79 (1809); No. 26, in E-flat major, op. 81a, "Das Lebewohl, Abwesenheit und Wiedersehn"; also known by its French subtitle, "Les Adieux, l'absence, et le retour" (1809); No. 27, in E minor, op. 90 (1814); No. 28, in A major, op. 101 (1816); No. 29, in B-flat major, op. 106, *Hammerklavier* (1817–18); No. 30, in E major, op. 109 (1820); No. 31, in A-flat major, op. 110 (1821); No. 31, in C minor, op. 111 (1821–22).

VARIATIONS FOR PIANO: 9 Variations in C minor on a March by Dressler (1782); 24 Variations in D major on Righini's Arietta "Venni amore" (1790–91); 13 Variations in A major on the Arietta "Es war einmal ein alter Mann" from Dittersdorf's *Das rote Käppchen* (1792); 6 Variations in F major on a Swiss Song (1792?; also for Harp); 12 Variations on the "Menuet à la Viganò" from Haibel's *Le nozze disturbate* in C major (1795); 9 Variations in A major on the Aria "Quant' è più bello" from Paisiello's *La molinara* (1795); 6 Variations in G major on the Duet "Nel cor più non mi sento" from Paisiello's *Le molinara* (1795); 8 Variations in C major on the Romance "Un Fièvre brûlante" from Grétry's *Richard Cœur de Lion* (1795?); 12 Variations in A major on a Russian Dance from Wranitzky's *Das Waldmädchen* (1796–97); 10 Variations in B-flat major on the Duet "La stessa, le stessissima" from Salieri's *Falstaff* (1799); 7 Variations in F major on the Quartet "Kind, willst du ruhig schlafen" from Winter's

97

Das unterbrochene Opferfest (1799); 6 Variations in F major on the Trio "Tändeln und Scherzen" from Süssmayr's *Soliman II* (1799); 6 Variations in G major on an Original Theme (1800); 6 Variations in F major on an Original Theme, op. 34 (1802); 15 Variations and a Fugue in E-flat major on an Original Theme, op. 35, *Eroica* (1802); 7 Variations in C major on "God Save the King" (1803); 5 Variations in D major on "Rule Britannia" (1803); 32 Variations in C minor on an Original Theme (1806); 6 Variations in D major on an Original Theme, op. 76 (1809); 33 Variations in C major on a Waltz by Diabelli, op. 120 (1819; 1823).

OTHER WORKS FOR PIANO: Rondo in C major (1783); Rondo in A major (1783); 2 Preludes through All 12 Major Keys, op. 39 (1789; also for Organ); *Allemande* in A major (1793); *Rondo a capriccio* in G major, op. 129, "Rage over a Lost Penny" (1795); Fugue in C major, Hess 64 (1795); *Presto* in C minor (1795?); *Allegretto* in C minor (1796–97); *Allegretto* in C minor, Hess 69 (1796–97); Rondo in C major, op. 51, No. 1 (1796?–97?); Rondo in G major, op. 51, No. 2 (1798?); 7 Bagatelles: E-flat major, C major, F major, A major, C major, D major, and A-flat major, op. 33 (1801–2); Bagatelle "Lustig-Traurig" in C major, WoO 54 (1802); *Allegretto* in C major (1803); Andante in F major, "Andante favori" (1803); Prelude in F minor (1804); Minuet in E-flat major (1804); Fantasia in G minor/B-flat major, op. 77 (1809); Bagatelle "Für Elise" in A minor (1810); Polonaise in C major, op. 89 (1814); Bagatelle in B-flat major (1818); Concert Finale in C major, Hess 65 (1820–21); Allegretto in B minor (1821); 11 Bagatelles: G minor, C major, D major, A major, C minor, G major, C major, C major, A minor, A major, and B-flat major, op. 119 (1820–22); 6 Bagatelles: G major, G minor, E-flat major, B minor, G major, and E-flat major, op. 126 (1823–24); Waltz in E-flat major (1824); *Allegretto quasi andante* in G minor (1825); Waltz in D major (1825); Ecossaise in E-flat major (1825).—For Piano, 4-hands: 8 Variations in C major on a Theme by Count Waldstein (1792); Sonata in D major, op. 6 (1796–97); 6 Variations in D major on "Ich denke dein" (by Beethoven) (1799–1803); 3 Marches: C major, E-flat major, and D major, op. 45 (1803?); an arrangement of the *Grosse Fuge*, op. 133, as op. 134 (1826).

VOCAL MUSIC: Operas: *Fidelio*, op. 72 (first version, 1804–5; Theater an der Wien, Vienna, Nov. 20, 1805; 2nd version, 1805–6; Theater an der Wien, March 29, 1806; final version, 1814; Kärnthnertortheater, Vienna, May 23, 1814); also a fragment from the unfinished opera *Vestas Feuer (The Vestal Flame)*, Hess 115 (1803); singspiels: "Germania," the finale of the pasticcio *Die gute Nachricht* (1814; Kärnthnertortheater, April 11, 1814), and "Es ist vollbracht," the finale of the pasticcio *Die Ehrenpforten* (1815; Kärnthnertortheater, July 15, 1815).—Choral works with Orch.: *Cantate auf den Tod Kaiser Joseph des Zweiten (Cantata on the Death of the Emperor Joseph II;* 1790); *Cantate auf die Erhebung Leopold des Zweiten zur Kaiserwürde (Cantata on the Accession of Emperor Leopold II;* 1790); oratorio, *Christus am Oelberge (Christ on the Mount of Olives)*, op. 85 (1803; Vienna, April 5, 1803; revised 1804

and 1811); Mass in C major, op. 86 (1807; Eisenstadt, Sept. 13, 1807); *Chor auf die verbündeten Fürsten "Ihr weisen Gründer"* (1814); cantata, *Der glorreiche Augenblick (The Glorious Moment)*, op. 136 (1814; Vienna, Nov. 29, 1814); *Meeresstille und glückliche Fahrt (Calm Seas and Prosperous Voyage)*, op. 112, after Goethe (1814–15; Vienna, Dec. 25, 1815); Mass in D major, op. 123, *Missa Solemnis* (1819–23; Kyrie, Credo, and Agnus Dei only, Vienna, May 7, 1824); Opferlied, "Die Flamme lodert" (1822; 2nd version, op. 121b, 1823–24); Bundeslied, "In allen guten Stunden," op. 122, after Goethe (1823–24).—Additional choral works: Abschiedsgesang, "Die Stunde schlägt" (1814); Cantata campestre, "Un lieto brindisi" (1814); Gesang der Mönche, "Rasch tritt der Tod," from Schiller's *Wilhelm Tell* (1817); Hochzeitslied, "Auf Freunde, singt dem Gott der Ehen" (2 versions; 1819); Birthday Cantata for Prince Lobkowitz, "Es lebe unser theurer Fürst" (1823).—Works for Solo Voices and Orch.: Prüfung des Küssens "Meine weise Mutter spricht" for Bass (1790–92); "Mit Mädeln sich vertragen" from Goethe's *Claudine von Villa Bella* for Bass (1790?–92); *Primo amore*, scena and aria for Soprano (1790–92); 2 arias: "O welch' ein Leben" for Tenor and "Soll ein Schuh nicht drücken" for Soprano, for Umlauf's singspiel *Die schöne Schusterin* (1795–96); *Ah, perfido!*, scena and aria for Soprano from Metastasio's *Achille in Sciro*, op. 65 (1795–96); *No, non turbarti*, scena and aria for Soprano from Metastasio's *La tempesta* (1801–2); "Ne' giorni tuoi felici," duet for Soprano and Tenor from Metastasio's *Olimpiade* (1802–3); *Tremate, empi, tremate* for Soprano, Tenor, and Bass, op. 116 (1801–2; 1814); *Elegischer Gesang:* "Sanft wie du lebtest" for Soprano, Alto, Tenor, Bass, and String Quartet or Piano, op. 118 (1814).—Songs: More than 80, including the following: *O care selve* (1794); *Opferlied* (1794; revised 1801–2); *Adelaide*, op. 46 (1794–95); 6 Songs, op. 48, after Gellert (1802); 8 Songs, op. 52 (1790–96); *An die Hoffnung*, op. 32 (1805); 6 Songs, op. 75 (1809); 4 Ariettas and a Duet for Soprano and Tenor, op. 82 (1809); 3 Songs, op. 83, after Goethe (1810); *Merkenstein*, op. 100 (1814–15); *An die Hoffnung*, op. 94 (1815); 6 Songs: *An die ferne Geliebte*, op. 98 (1815–16); *Der Mann von Wort*, op. 99 (1816); *Der Kuss*, op. 128 (1822); arrangements of English, Scottish, Irish, Welsh, Italian, and other folk songs for voice, piano, violin, and cello; numerous canons; etc.

Beheim, Michel, German minnesinger; b. Sülzbach, near Weinsberg, Sept. 27, 1416; d. there (murdered), 1474. He was active as a soldier and singer in the service of various German, Danish, and Hungarian princes; was one of the earliest of the Meistersingers who still retained some of the characteristics of the Minnesinger; finally settled in Sülzbach as village major or magistrate. He composed many songs; 11 are preserved at Heidelberg and Munich.

Behr, Franz, German composer; b. Lübtheen, Mecklenburg, July 22, 1837; d. Dresden, Feb. 15, 1898. He published many salon pieces for the piano, some under the pseudonyms of **Georges Bachmann, William Cooper, Charles Morley,** and **Francesco d'Orso.** His waltz *Les Sylphes* became very popular.

Behrend, Jeanne, American pianist and teacher; b. Philadelphia, May 11, 1911. She studied piano with Josef Hofmann and composition with Rosario Scalero at the Curtis Inst. of Music in Philadelphia; subsequently taught piano at various institutions, including her alma mater and the Juilliard School of Music in N.Y. She particularly distinguished herself as a proponent of American music. She edited songs of Stephen Foster, piano music of Gottschalk, and early American choral music.

Behrens, Hildegard, noted German soprano; b. Varel, Oldenburg, Feb. 9, 1937. Of an intellectual bent, she entered the Univ. of Freiburg in the faculty of jurisprudence, astoundingly graduating as a junior barrister. Making a sudden decision to exploit her natural vocal talents, she began to study voice with Ines Leuwen at the Freiburg Academy of Music. In 1971 she became a member of the Opera Studio of the Deutsche Oper am Rhein in Düsseldorf; in 1972 became a member of the Deutsche Oper; also made guest appearances with the Frankfurt Opera, Zürich Opera, Vienna State Opera, Salzburg Festival, Bavarian State Opera in Munich, and Paris Opéra. She was particularly impressive in dramatic roles in modern operas, as *Salome* and *Fidelio*, as Marie in *Wozzeck*, and Kát'a Kabanová in Janáček's opera. On Oct. 15, 1976, she made her American debut at the Metropolitan Opera, N.Y., as Giorgetta in *Il Tabarro*.

Behrens, Jack, American composer; b. Lancaster, Pa., March 25, 1935. He studied composition at the Juilliard School of Music, N.Y., with Bergsma, Persichetti, and Mennin, graduating in 1959; then took courses at Harvard Univ. with Leon Kirchner and Roger Sessions, obtaining his Ph.D. in composition in 1973. He was subsequently on the faculty of the Univ. of Saskatchewan, Canada (1962–66), and of Calif. State College, Bakersfield (1970–76); in 1976 he was appointed chairman of the dept. of theory and composition at the Univ. of Western Ontario, London, Canada. In his music he adopts a sophisticated modern idiom without transgressing into the musically unfeasible.

Beiderbecke, Bix (real name, **Leon Bismarck Beiderbecke**), American jazz cornet player; b. Davenport, Iowa, March 10, 1903; d. New York, Aug. 6, 1931. His parents, German immigrants, were amateur musicians, and he began to play as a small child. As he grew he developed a flair for ragtime and jazz. He played cornet in various jazz groups in Chicago and St. Louis, and developed his distinctive style of rhythmic lyricism. In 1927 he joined the Paul Whiteman band. Although lacking a formal musical education, he wrote a number of beguilingly attractive piano pieces of which one, *In a Mist*, shows a curious impressionistic coloring. Addicted to alcohol, he succumbed at the age of 28. His musical legacy was preserved in recordings, and soon a cult was formed around his name, which was greatly enhanced by the publication of Dorothy Baker's semi-fictional biography, *Young Man with a Horn* (N.Y., 1938). Two factual biographies were publ. in 1974: R. Berton, *Remembering Bix: A Memoir of the Jazz Age*, and R. Sudhalter and P. Evans, *Bix: Man and Legend.*

Beinum, Eduard van, eminent Dutch conductor; b. Arnhem, Sept. 3, 1900; d. Amsterdam, April 13, 1959. He studied violin with his brother, and piano with J.B. de Pauw; also took lessons in composition from Sem Dresden. He made his first appearance as a pianist with the Concertgebouw Orch. in Amsterdam in 1920; then devoted himself to choral conducting. In 1931 he was appointed associate conductor of the Concertgebouw; in 1945 he succeeded Mengelberg (who had been disfranchised for his collaboration with the Germans during their occupation of the Netherlands) as principal conductor of the orch. He was also a guest conductor of various European orchs.: the Leningrad Phil. (1937), the London Phil. (1946, 1949, 1950); he made his American debut with the Philadelphia Orch. on Jan. 8, 1954; in the autumn of 1954 toured the U.S. with the Concertgebouw. From 1957 until shortly before his death he was the principal guest conductor with the Los Angeles Phil. Beinum was regarded by most critics as an intellectual conductor whose chief concern was the projection of the music itself rather than the expression of his own musical personality. He was equally capable in the Classical, Romantic, and modern works.

Beissel, Johann Conrad, German-American composer of religious music; founder of the sect of Solitary Brethren of the Community of Sabbatarians; b. Eberbach on the Neckar, Palatinate, March 1, 1690; d. Ephrata, Pa., July 6, 1768. He migrated to America in 1720 for religious reasons. His first attempt to build up a "solitary" residence failed, but in 1732 he started the community at Ephrata, which became a flourishing religious and artistic center. Beissel, who styled himself Bruder Friedsam (Brother Peaceful), was a prolific writer of hymns in fanciful German, publ. in various collections, some printed by Benjamin Franklin, some by the community at Ephrata. He composed tunes for his hymns and harmonized them according to his own rules. His compositions were collected in beautifully illuminated MSS, many of which are preserved at the Library of Congress and the Library of the Historical Society of Pa. Beissel was not a trained musician, but had original ideas; his religious fanaticism inspired him to write some startling music; in several of his hymns he made use of an antiphonal type of vocal composition with excellent effect. He left a tract explaining his harmonic theory and his method of singing. Beissel's hymns are collected chiefly in *Zionistischer Weyrauchs Hügel* (1739), *Das Gesang der einsamen und verlassenen Turtel Taube, das ist der christlichen Kirche* (1747), and *Paradisisches Wunder Spiel* (2 independent publications, 1754 and 1766). Only texts were printed in these volumes, but the 1754 issue was arranged so that the music could be inserted by hand. Beissel's life was first described in the *Chronicon Ephratense*, compiled by the brethren Lamech and Agrippa, publ. at Ephrata in a German edition in 1786, and in an Eng. trans. by J.M. Hark at Lancaster in 1889.

Bekker, Paul, eminent writer on music; b. Berlin, Sept. 11, 1882; d. New York, March 7, 1937. He studied violin with Rehfeld, piano with Sormann, and theory with Horwitz; began his career as a violinist with the Berlin Phil. In 1909 he devoted himself mainly to writing. He was music critic of *Berliner Neueste Nachrichten* (1906–9) and of *Berliner Allgemeine Zeitung* (1909–11); also served as chief music critic at *Frankfurter Zeitung* from 1911. Later he was Intendant of the Kassel Stadttheater (1925); then in Wiesbaden (1927). In 1933 he left Germany, being unable to cope with the inequities of the Nazi regime. He publ. biographies of Oskar Fried (1907) and Jacques Offenbach (1909); also *Das Musikdrama der Gegenwart* (1909); *Beethoven* (1911; in Eng., 1926); *Das deutsche Musikleben, Versuch einer soziologischen Musikbetrachtung* (1916); *Die Sinfonie von Beethoven bis Mahler* (1918; in Russian, 1926); *Franz Schreker* (1919); *Kunst und Revolution* (1919); *Die Weltgeltung der deutschen Musik* (1920); *Die Sinfonien G. Mahlers* (1921); *Richard Wagner* (1924; in Eng., 1931); *Von den Naturreichen des Klanges* (1924); *Musikgeschichte als Geschichte der musikalischen Formwandlungen* (1926; in French, 1929); *Das Operntheater* (1930); *Briefe an zeitgenössische Musiker* (1932); *Wandlungen der Oper* (Zürich, 1934; Eng. trans. by Arthur Mendel as *The Changing Opera*, N.Y., 1935); *The Story of the Orchestra* (his last book; written in Eng.; N.Y., 1936).

Belafonte, Harry (Harold George, Jr.), American folksinger; b. New York, March 1, 1927, of a Jamaican mother and a Martiniquan father. As a youth he lived partly in N.Y., partly in Jamaica; worked as a janitor and a cart pusher in Manhattan. When his voice was discovered, he got singing jobs in Greenwich Village restaurants; acted the role of Joe in the film *Carmen Jones* (1954). From 1948–57 he was married to the black child psychologist Frances Marguerite Byrd; his second marriage was to Julie Robinson. His greatest success came as an interpreter of Calypso songs, which he performed with great dramatic power. He made numerous tours abroad.

Belaiev (Belaieff), Mitrofan, renowned Russian music publisher; b. St. Petersburg, Feb. 22, 1836; d. there, Jan. 10, 1904. His father, a rich lumber dealer, gave him an excellent education. After his father's death in 1885, Belaiev decided to use part of the income from the business for a music publishing enterprise devoted exclusively to the publication of works by Russian composers (the printing was done in Leipzig); he also established concerts of Russian

music in St. Petersburg (10 symph. concerts and 4 concerts of chamber music each season) and provided funds for prizes awarded for the best compositions. He placed Rimsky-Korsakov, Glazunov, and Liadov on the jury for these multifarious activities. The "Belaiev Editions" became a vital factor in the development of Russian national music. Although a conservative, Belaiev was generous toward representatives of the modern school, such as Scriabin; early in Scriabin's career, Belaiev provided the financial means for him to travel in Europe. The catalogue of Belaiev's publications includes the greatest names in Russian music: Mussorgsky, Rimsky-Korsakov, Borodin, Balakirev, Cui, Scriabin, Glière, Glazunov, Gretchaninov, Liadov, Liapunov, Taneyev, and Nicolas Tcherepnin, as well as many lesser and even obscure composers, such as Akimenko, Alferaky, Amani, Antipov, Artzibushev, Blumenfeld, Kalafati, Kopylov, Sokolov, Steinberg, Wihtol, Zolotarev, and others. The complete list of Belaiev's editions is available in the *Verzeichnis der in Deutschland seit 1868 erschienenen Werke russischer Komponisten* (Leipzig, 1950).

Belcher, Supply, American hymn writer, dubbed "the Handel of Maine"; b. Stoughton, Mass., April 9, 1751; d. Farmington, Maine, June 9, 1836. He was a tavern keeper and original member (with Billings) of the Stoughton Musical Society, the earliest American performing group that held regular meetings. He served in the Revolutionary War under George Washington; subsequently lived in Farmington, Maine. He publ., in 1794, a collection of hymns, *Harmony of Maine.*

Bell, Joshua, precocious American violinist; b. Bloomington, Ind., Dec. 9, 1967. He first studied violin with Mimi Zweig; made his debut as a soloist with the Bloomington Symph. Orch. in 1975 at the age of 7; subsequently studied with Josef Gingold at the Indiana Univ. School of Music; also took summer courses with Ivan Galamian and a master class with Henryk Szeryng. He won the grand prize in the first annual *Seventeen Magazine*/General Motors National Concerto Competition in Rochester, N.Y., which led to his appearance as a soloist with the Philadelphia Orch. under Riccardo Muti on Sept. 24, 1982; he was the youngest soloist ever to appear with it at a subscription concert.

Bell, William Henry, English composer; b. St. Albans, Aug. 20, 1873; d. Gordon's Bay, Cape Province, South Africa, April 13, 1946. He studied at his hometown; won the Goss Scholarship for the Royal College of Music in London (1889); studied organ with Stegall, violin with Burnett, piano with Izard, and composition with Corder and Stanford. He taught harmony at his alma mater (1903–12); in 1912 was appointed director of the South African College of Music in Cape Town; retired in 1935. He was extremely critical of himself as a composer, and destroyed many of his manuscripts. Among his surviving works are the operas *Hippolytus* (after Euripides; 1914) and *Isabeau* (1924). Other works include *Walt Whitman Symphony* (1899); Symph. No. 2 (1917–18); Symph. No. 3 (1918–19); *South African Symphony* (1927); Symph. in F minor (1932); *A Vision of Delight* (1906); *Arcadian Suite* (1908); the symph. poems *Love among the Ruins* (1908); *The Shepherd* (1908); *La Fée des sources* (1912); and *Veldt Loneliness* (1921); Viola Concerto; Violin Sonata.

Bella, Ján Levoslav (Johann Leopold), Slovak composer; b. Lipto-Szentmiklós, Upper Hungary, Sept. 4, 1843; d. Bratislava, May 25, 1936. He studied theology in Banska Bystrica; then went to Vienna, where he studied composition with Sechter (1863–65). He was ordained a priest in 1866 and served as church music director at Kremnica (1869). In 1873 he received a scholarship to study in Germany and in Prague; in 1881 he relinquished his priesthood, and subsequently was organist at the Protestant church in Hermannstadt, Transylvania, and music director of the municipality there. He went to Vienna in 1921; in 1928 he returned to Bratislava. He wrote a great quantity of church music in the strict style; also composed an opera, *Wieland der Schmied* (Bratislava, April 28, 1926); a symph. poem, *Schicksal und Ideal* (Prague, March 19, 1876); some chamber music; songs; and piano pieces.

Belleville-Oury, Caroline de. See **Oury, Anna Caroline.**

Bell'Haver, Vincenzo, Italian organist; b. Venice, c.1530; d. there, Oct. 1587. He was a pupil of Andrea Gabrieli, and upon the latter's death, succeeded him as first organist of San Marco on Oct. 30, 1586; he himself died a year later, and his position was taken over by Gioseffo Guami. Bell'Haver publ. several books of madrigals (1567–75), of which only Book II, containing works for 5 Voices, is extant; single works survive in various collections.

Belli, Domenico, Italian composer; b. c.1590; d. (buried, May 5) 1627. He lived most of his life in Florence. On Sept. 19, 1619, he and his wife entered the service of the Medici court. As a composer, he was one of the earliest representatives of the new monodic style; Caccini praised his music. However, the claim that his short opera, *Il pianto d'Orfeo,* or *Orfeo Dolente* (Florence, 1616; reprinted Brussels, 1927, in Tirabassi's ed.), was the earliest opera ever written is questionable. Among his instrumental works is *Arie per sonarsi con il chitarrone* (Venice, 1616).

Belli, Girolamo, composer of the Venetian school; b. Argenta, near Ferrara, 1552; d. there, c.1618. He studied with L. Luzzaschi; was a singer at the Gonzaga court at Mantua. He publ. 3 books of madrigals *a* 6 (1583; 1584; 1593), 9 books of madrigals *a* 5 (1584; 1586; 9th ed., 1617); 2 books of canzonets *a* 4 (1584; 1593); *Sacrae cantiones a* 6 (1585), *a* 8 (1589), and *a* 10 (1594); 2 Magnificats (1610); and *Salmi a* 5; some 5-part madrigals in the collection *De'floridi virtuosi d'Italia* (1586).

Belli, Giulio, Italian composer; b. Longiano, c.1560; d. c.1621. He was a student of Cimello; joined the Franciscan order in 1789; held positions as maestro di cappella at Imola (1582), Carpi (1590), and Ferrara (1592–93). In 1594 he went to Venice, where he served at the church of the Cà Grande (1595), at Montagnana Cathedral (1596), and later at San Marco (1615). His interim posts included service at the court of Duke Alfonso II d'Este and at the Accademia della Morte in Ferrara (1597), at the Osimo Cathedral in Ferrara (1599), at the Ravenna Cathedral (1600), and at Forli (1603), San Antonio, Padua (1606–08), the Imola Cathedral (1611–13), the Cà Grande in Venice (1615–21), and again at Imola (1621). He was a prolific composer; publications of his works appeared between 1584 and 1615, some being reissued several times, among them madrigals and canzonets (1584; 1593); psalms and vespers (1596; 1604); masses (1586; 1595; 1599; 1608); *sacrae cantiones* (1600); motets (1605); *falsi bordoni* (1605, 1607); and *concerti ecclesiastici* (1613). Many of these works are provided with *basso continuo.*

Bellincioni, Gemma, Italian soprano who once enjoyed fame; b. Monza, Aug. 18, 1864; d. Naples, April 23, 1950. She studied singing with her father; made her operatic debut in Naples at the age of 15. In 1884 she made a concert tour of Spain; in 1885 she sang in Rome, and in 1886 made her debut at La Scala, Milan. She married the once-famous Italian tenor **Roberto Stagno,** and the marriage proved fortunate; they sang together in opera and in concert all over Europe and in Buenos Aires, but somehow she was never invited to the U.S. In 1906 she sang the title role in *Salome* in its Italian premiere; on May 17, 1890, she sang Santuzza in the first performance of *Cavalleria rusticana,* with her husband in the role of her operatic ex-lover. On Nov. 17, 1898, she sang at the Teatro Lirico in Milan the title role in *Fedora* by Giordano at its premiere, with Caruso in the role of her Russian paramour. Her husband died in 1897, but she continued to appear in opera and gave concert tours. From 1911 to 1915 she conducted an opera studio in Berlin; then lived in Rome and Naples; in 1933 she became a prof. of singing at the Cons. of Naples. She publ. an autobiography, *Io ed il palcoscenico* (Milan, 1920).

Bellini, Vincenzo, famous Italian opera composer and a master of operatic bel canto; b. Catania, Sicily, Nov. 3, 1801; d. Puteaux, near Paris, Sept. 23, 1835. He was a scion of a musical family; his grandfather was maestro di cappella to the Benedictines in Catania, and organist of the Sacro Collegio di Maria in Misterbianco; his father also served as maestro di cappella. Bellini received his first musical instruction from his father and grandfather, and soon revealed a fine gift of melody. The Duke and Duchess of San Martino e Montalbo took interest in him and in 1819 arranged to have him enter the Real Collegio di Musica di San Sebastiano in Naples, where he studied harmony and accompaniment with Giovanni Furno and counterpoint with Giacomo Tritto; Carlo Conti supervised him as a *maestrino* and tutor. He further studied the vocal arts with Girolamo Crescentini and composition with Nicola Zingarelli. Under their guidance he made a detailed study of the works of Pergolesi, Jommelli, Paisiello, and Cimarosa, as well as those of the German classics. While still in school he wrote several sinfonias, two masses, and the cantata *Ismene* (1824). His first opera, *Adelson e Salvini*, was given at the Collegio in 1825; it was followed by an important production on the stage of the Teatro San Carlo in Naples of his 2nd opera, *Bianca e Gernando* (1826), a score later revised as *Bianca e Fernando* (1828). In 1827 Bellini went to Milan, where he was commissioned by the impresario Barbaja to write an "opera seria" for the famous Teatro alla Scala; it was *Il Pirata*, which obtained fine success at its production in 1827; it was also given in Vienna in 1828. It was followed by another opera, *La Straniera*, produced at La Scala in 1829; also in 1829 Bellini had the opera *Zaira* produced in Parma. He was then commissioned to write a new opera for the Teatro La Fenice in Venice, on a Shakespearean libretto; it was *I Capuleti ed i Montecchi*; produced in 1830, it had a decisive success. Even more successful was his next opera, *La Sonnambula*, produced in Milan in 1831 with the celebrated prima donna Giuditta Pasta as Amina. Pasta also appeared in the title role of Bellini's most famous opera, *Norma*, produced at La Scala in Milan in 1831, which at its repeated productions established Bellini's reputation as a young master of the Italian operatic bel canto. His following opera, *Beatrice di Tenda*, produced in Venice in 1833, failed to sustain his series of successes. He then had an opportunity to go to London and Paris, and it was in Paris that he produced in 1835 his last opera, *I Puritani*, which fully justified the expectations of his admirers. Next to *Norma*, it proved to be one of the greatest masterpieces of Italian operatic art; its Paris production featured a superb cast which included Grisi, Rubini, Tamburini, and Lablache. Bellini was on his way to fame and universal artistic recognition when he was stricken with a fatal affliction of amebiasis, and died 6 weeks before his 34th birthday. His remains were reverently removed to his native Catania in 1876.

Bellini's music represents the Italian operatic school at its most glorious melodiousness, truly reflected by the term "bel canto." In his writing, the words, the rhythm, the melody, the harmony, and the instrumental accompaniment unite in mutual perfection. The lyric flow and dramatic expressiveness of his music provide a natural medium for singers in the Italian language, with the result that his greatest masterpieces, *La Sonnambula* and *Norma*, remain in the active repertoire of opera houses of the entire world, repeatedly performed by touring Italian opera companies and by native forces everywhere.

For the libretti of his operas Bellini selected melodramatic subjects possessing a natural appeal to the public, with romantic female figures in the center of the action. In *Il Pirata*, the heroine loses her reason when her lover is condemned to death for killing her unloved husband; in *La Sonnambula*, the sleepwalker innocently wanders into the bedroom of a lord and is suspected of infidelity by her lover but is exonerated when she is observed again walking in her sleep; in *Norma* a Druid priestess sacrifices herself when she ascends a funeral pyre with her Roman lover as a penalty for her betrayal of her sacred duty; in *I Puritani*, set in the period of the civil war in Britain, the heroine goes mad when she believes she has been betrayed by her beloved, but regains her reason when he accounts for his essentially noble actions.

WORKS: OPERAS: *Adelson e Salvini* (dramma semiserio, 1824–25; Real Collegio di Musica di San Sebastiano, Naples, between Feb. 10 and 15, 1825; 2nd version, 1826; not perf.); *Bianca e Gernando* (melodramma, 1825–26; Teatro San Carlo, Naples, May 30, 1826; revised version as *Bianca e Fernando*, 1828; Teatro Carlo Felice, Genoa, April 7, 1828); *Il Pirata* (opera seria, 1827; Teatro alla Scala, Milan, Oct. 27, 1827); *La Straniera* (opera seria, 1828–29; Teatro alla Scala, Milan, Feb. 14, 1829); *Zaira* (opera seria, 1829; Teatro Ducale, Parma, May 16, 1829); *I Capuleti ed i Montecchi* (tragedia lirica, 1830; Teatro La Fenice, Venice, March 11, 1830); *La Sonnambula* (melodramma, 1831; Teatro Carcano, Milan, March 6, 1831); *Norma* (opera seria, 1831; Teatro alla Scala, Milan, Dec. 26, 1831); *Beatrice di Tenda* (opera seria, 1833; Teatro La Fenice, Venice, March 16, 1833); *I Puritani* (melodramma serio, 1834–35; first perf. as *I Puritani e i cavalieri* at the Théâtre-Italien, Paris, Jan. 24, 1835).

Bellman, Carl Michael, Swedish poet and composer; b. Stockholm, Feb. 4, 1740; d. there, Feb. 11, 1795. He publ. an important collection of songs to his own words; however, most of the music in it was taken from other sources, including publ. works by known composers. He also published lyric ballads expressive of folk life, *Fredmans epistlar* (1790) and *Fredmans sanger* (1791).

Belza, Igor. See **Boelza, Igor.**

Bemberg, Herman, French dramatic composer; b. Paris, March 29, 1859; d. Bern, Switzerland, July 21, 1931. He studied at the Paris Cons. with Dubois, Franck, and Massenet; won the Rossini prize in 1885. Among his works are: cantata for Soprano and Orch., *La Mort de Jeanne d'Arc* (1886); short opera, *Le Baiser de Suzon* (Paris, 1888); grand opera, *Elaine* (Covent Garden, London, July 5, 1892; N.Y., Dec. 17, 1894). He also publ. numerous songs, of which *Chant hindou* became extremely popular.

Bembo, Antonia, composer; b. presumably in Venice, c. 1670; death date unknown. Between 1690 and 1695 she went to Paris; sang for Louis XIV, and received a pension from him enabling her to devote herself to composition. Extant works (in the Paris Bibliothèque Nationale): *Produzioni armoniche*, collection of 40 pieces (motets, duets, soli for soprano, etc., with figured bass or instrumental accompaniment, set to sacred Latin, French, and Italian texts); *Te Deum* for 3 Voices and String Orch.; *Divertimento* for 5-voiced Chorus with String Orch.; *Te Deum,* with Large Orch.; *Exaudiat* for 3 Voices, 2 "symphonie" parts, and Basso Continuo; an opera, *L'Ercole Amante* (1707); *Les Sept Psaumes de David* for various vocal combinations with instrumental accompaniment.

Ben-Haim, Paul, eminent Israeli composer; b. Munich, July 5, 1897; d. Tel Aviv, Jan. 14, 1984. His original name was **Frankenburger;** he changed it to the Hebrew name Ben-Haim after the capture of Germany by the anti-Semitic Hitlerites. He played the violin as a child; then entered the Munich Academy of Arts (1915–20); in 1920 he became an assistant conductor at the Munich Opera, and from 1924–31 conducted opera and a symph. orch. in Augsburg. He left Germany as soon as the country was taken over by the Nazis, and settled in Tel Aviv; there he engaged in a profound study of the folk music of the Middle East, and used it in many of his works, becoming a patriotic composer of his ancestral land. Still, he preserved his traditional learning of Baroque and Romantic European modalities, and contined to compose in the pragmatic forms of symphs. and concertos; several of his scores are fermented by Hebrew melos. He received the Israel State Prize in 1957 for his work inspired by King David, *The Sweet Psalmist of Israel,* which was performed widely in Israel, and was conducted by Leonard Bernstein with the N.Y. Phil. in 1959. His *Kabbalai Shabbat (Friday Evening Service)* was performed in N.Y. in 1968 to mark the 20th anniversary of the founding of the State of Israel. Also popular was his Sonata in G for Violin Solo, which was frequently included in concert programs of Yehudi Menuhin.

Benatzky, Ralph, Czech composer of light opera; b. Moravské-Budejovice, June 5, 1884; d. Zürich, Oct. 16, 1957. He studied in Prague with Veit and Klinger and in Munich with Mottl; then lived mostly in Vienna and Berlin. After the annexation of Austria by the Nazis in 1938, he went to America; after the war he settled in Switzerland. An exceptionally prolific composer, he wrote 92 stage works, about 250 motion picture scores, and perhaps 5,000 songs. His most successful operetta was *Im weissen Rössl,* first produced in Berlin, Nov. 8, 1930. His other operettas are: *Der lachende Dreibund* (Berlin, Oct. 31, 1913); *Yuschi tanzt* (Vienna, April 3, 1920); *Adieu Mimi* (Vienna, June 9, 1926); *Casanova* (Berlin, Sept. 1, 1928); *Bezauberndes Fräulein* (1935); *Kleinstadtzauber* (1947); *Ein Liebestraum* (on Liszt's themes; 1951); *Don Juans Wiederkehr* (1953).

Benda, Franz (František), famous Bohemian violinist and important composer; brother of **George Anton (Jiří Antonín) Benda;** b. Alt-Benatek, Bohemia, Nov. (baptized, Nov. 22) 1709; d. Neuendorf, near Potsdam, March 7, 1786. In 1718 he became a chorister at the Church of St. Nicolas in Prague; in 1720 he was taken to Dresden, where he sang at the

Hofkapelle. In 1723 he returned to Prague. It was not until much later that he began a serious study of music, with Löbel, Koniček, and J.S. Graun at Ruppin. In 1733 he joined the orch. of the Crown Prince (afterwards Friedrich II) as first violinist; in 1771 was named Konzertmeister. During his long years of service for Friedrich II he accompanied him at his flute concerts. Among his works are 17 violin concertos, 17 symphs., numerous solo sonatas, and various pieces of chamber music. His autobiography was publ. in the *Neue Berliner Musikzeitung* in 1856.

Benda, Friedrich (Wilhelm Heinrich), German violinist, son of **Franz Benda;** b. Potsdam, July 15, 1745; d. there, June 19, 1814. He studied violin with his father, and music theory with J.P. Kirnberger. From 1765 to 1810 he served as a royal chamber musician at Potsdam.

WORKS: *Orpheus* (Berlin, Jan. 16, 1785; concert performance); *Alceste* (1786); *Das Blumenmädchen* (Berlin, July 16, 1806); 2 cantatas, *Pygmalion* and *Die Grazien;* 2 oratorios, *Die Junger am Grabe des Auferstandenen* and *Das Lob des Höchsten;* 2 violin concertos; 2 flute concertos; numerous piano pieces.

Benda, Friedrich Ludwig, German violinist and composer, son of **George Benda;** b. Gotha, Sept. 4, 1752; d. Königsberg, March 20, 1792. In 1775 he joined the orch. of the Seyler troupe in Gotha; after 1779 was employed as a violinist in theaters in Berlin and Hamburg. In 1782 he was engaged as violinist and Cammer-Compositeur to the Duke of Mecklenburg-Schwerin. In 1788 he settled in Königsberg. He composed the music for G.F. Grossmann's *Der Barbier von Sevilla* (Leipzig, May 7, 1776); also wrote cantatas and a number of instrumental works.

Benda, George Anton (Jiří Antonín), important Bohemian composer, brother of **Franz Benda;** b. Alt-Benatek, June (baptized, June 30) 1722; d. Köstritz, Nov. 6, 1795. He was the third son of **Johann Georg Benda.** He studied at the Jesuit college in Jicin (1739–42); then went to Prussia. In May 1750 he was appointed Kapellmeister to Duke Friedrich III of Saxe-Gotha. In 1765 he received a ducal stipend to go to Italy for half a year. In 1778 he went to Hamburg; also traveled to Vienna; finally settled in Köstritz. His works were distinguished for their dramatic use of rapidly alternating moods (*"Affekte"*), which became a characteristic trait of the North German School of composition and exercised considerable influence on the development of opera and ballad forms in Germany; his effective use of melodrama (spoken recitative accompanied by orch.) was an important innovation.

WORKS: Operas: *Ariadne auf Naxos* (Gotha, Jan. 27, 1775); *Medea* (Leipzig, May 1, 1775); *Philon und Theone,* also known as *Almansor und Nadine* (Gotha, Sept. 20, 1779); the singspiels *Der Dorfjahrmarkt* (1775), *Romeo und Julia* (1776), and *Der Holzhauer* (1778); cantatas, 3 piano concertos; 8 symphs.; 16 piano sonatas; flute sonata.

Benda, Karl Hermann Heinrich, German violinist, son of **Franz Benda;** b. Potsdam, May 2, 1748; d. Berlin, March 15, 1836. He studied with his father; entered the service of the Prussian Court about 1766; in 1802 he was appointed Konzertmeister. He was the teacher of King Friedrich Wilhelm III. Of his works, only a Violin Sonata is extant.

Bender, Paul, German bass; b. Driedorf, July 28, 1875; d. Munich, Nov. 25, 1947. He studied with Luise Reuss-Belce and Baptist Hoffmann; made his operatic debut as Sarastro in *The Magic Flute* in Breslau (1900). He subsequently joined the Munich Opera Co. and was a member from 1903 to 1933. He made his American debut at the Metropolitan Opera in N.Y. on Nov. 17, 1922, and remained on its roster until 1927. He included both serious and comic roles in his repertoire; was particularly effective in the bass parts in Wagner's operas; in his concert recitals he performed a number of songs by Carl Loewe.

Bendinelli, Agostino, Italian composer and teacher; b. Lucca, April 26, 1635; d. there, c.1703. He was active as canon of St. John Lateran in Rome; also served as superintendent of the monastery of S. Frediano in Lucca and as prior of S. Agostino in Piacenza and S. Leonardo in Lucca. His most famous pupil was G.M. Bononcini. His only extant publ. in his *Psalmi vespertini ternis, quaternis, quinisque vocibus ad organum concinendi una cum litanis BVM,* op. 1 (Bologna, 1671).

Bendix, Max, American conductor and composer; b. Detroit, March 28, 1866; d. Chicago, Dec. 6, 1945. He studied in Germany; was concertmaster of the Metropolitan Opera House (1885), and the Thomas Orch. in N.Y. and Chicago (1886–96); later was an opera conductor in N.Y. He wrote a Violin Concerto; *Pavlova,* a valse-caprice for Orch.; also ballet scores for special productions.

Bendl, Karl (Karel), Czech composer and conductor; b. Prague, April 16, 1838; d. there, Sept. 20, 1897. He studied at the Prague Organ School with Blažek, Pietsch, and Zvonar. In 1864–65 he was active as a conductor in Brussels, Amsterdam, and Paris. Returning to Prague in 1865, he conducted the male choral society Hlahol for 12 years; also was briefly deputy conductor at the Provisional Theater in Prague. He subsequently served as an organist at the church of St. Nicholas in Prague. He was an ardent supporter of Dvořák and Smetana in the cause of creating a national school of Czech music.

Benedetti, Francesco Maria, Italian composer; b. Assisi, 1683; d. there, 1746. He was a Franciscan priest; served as maestro di cappella at S. Francesco in Turin (1710–13), at the Basilica in Assisi (1713–16), at the Turin Cathedral and the Cathedral of Aosta (1716–28); in 1729 he resumed his post in Assisi, where he remained until 1744. He was a prolific composer of sacred music.

Benedetti Michelangeli, Arturo. See **Michelangeli, Arturo Benedetti.**

Benedict, Sir Julius, German-English conductor and composer; b. Stuttgart, Nov. 27, 1804; d. London, June 5, 1885. He was the son of a Jewish banker; from his earliest childhood he showed a decisive musical talent. He took lessons with J.C.L. Abeille in Stuttgart; then had further instruction with Hummel at Weimar. Hummel introduced him to Weber, and he became Weber's private pupil. In 1823, Benedict was appointed conductor of the Kärnthnerthor Theater in Vienna; in 1825 he obtained a similar post at the Teatro San Carlo in Naples and also at the Fondo Theater there. He produced his first opera, *Giacinta ed Ernesto,* in Naples in 1827. His second opera was *I Portoghesi in Goa,* produced in Naples on June 28, 1830. In 1834 Benedict went to Paris, and in 1835 he proceeded to London, where he remained for the rest of his life. In 1836 he became music director at the Opera Buffa at the Lyceum Theatre. He conducted opera at the Drury Lane Theatre from 1838 to 1848. His first opera in English, *The Gypsy's Warning,* was produced at Drury Lane under his direction on April 19, 1838. He also conducted at Covent Garden; led the Monday Popular Concerts; served as music director of the Norwich Festivals (1845–78); and conducted the Liverpool Phil. Society (1876–80). In recognition of his services, he was knighted in 1871. In 1850–52 he accompanied Jenny Lind on her American tours. His reputation as conductor and composer was considerable, both in Europe and America. Among his operas the most successful was *The Lily of Killarney,* which was produced at Covent Garden on Feb. 8, 1862; it was also staged in America and Australia. His other operas are *The Brides of Venice* (Drury Lane, April 22, 1844); *The Crusaders* (Drury Lane, Feb. 26, 1846); *The Lake of Glenaston* (1862); *The Bride of Song* (Covent Garden, Dec. 3, 1864). He also wrote the cantatas *Undine* (1860); *Richard Cœur-de-Lion* (1863); *The Legend of St. Cecilia* (1866); *Graziella* (1882); an oratorio, *St. Peter* (1870); a symph.; 2 piano concertos; and other instrumental works. He publ. biographies of Mendelssohn (London, 1850) and Weber (London, 1881; 2nd ed., 1913); both contained information from his personal acquaintance with Mendelssohn and Weber.

Benedictus Appenzeller. See **Appenzeller, Benedictus.**

Benet, John, English composer who flourished in the 15th century. He wrote mostly church music. The following works are extant: 2 motets, *Lux fulget ex Anglia* and *Tellus purpureum;* an isorhythmic motet, *Gaude pia Magdalena;* and several numbers from incomplete masses. Stylistically he belonged to the school of John Dunstable and Lionel Power. His *Sanctus* and *Agnus* are found in H. Wooldrige's *Early English Harmony* (2 vols., 1897 and 1913); *Gaude pia Magdalena* was edited in *Early English Church Music,* VIII (1968); *Lux fulget ex*

Anglia and *Tellus purpureum* in B. Trowell's dissertation, *Music under the Plantagenets* (Univ. of Cambridge, 1960).

Benevoli, Orazio, Italian composer; b. Rome, April 19, 1605; d. there, June 17, 1672. He was the son of a French baker who Italianized his name when he settled in Rome. He studied with Vincenzo Ugolini and sang in the boys' choir in the school "dei francesi" in Rome (1617–23); also had some instruction from Lorenzo Ratti. After completion of his study period he had successive posts as maestro di cappella; served at Santa Maria in Trastevere (1624–30); at Santo Spirito, Sassia (1630–38); and at San Luigi dei Francesi (1638–44). In 1644 he went to Vienna, where he served at the Court until 1646; then returned to Rome as maestro di cappella at Santa Maria Maggiore; was also attached to the Vatican. His music shows influences of the Palestrina style combined with polychoral techniques of the Venetians; some of his sacred works call for 12 separate choirs. A considerable controversy arose when some music historians attributed to Benevoli the composition of the *Missa salisburgensis,* containing 53 separate parts, which was cited as an example of Benevoli's extraordinary contrapuntal skill. Such a Mass was indeed commissioned by Salzburg in 1628, but it was not composed by Benevoli; whoever wrote it, its performance did not take place until about 1682. This Mass and a hymn in 56 voices were reprinted in Denkmäler der Tonkunst in Österreich; another Mass, which was really composed by Benevoli and was performed at the Santa Maria sopra Minerva Church in Rome in 1650, is set for 12 choirs of 4 voices each.

Benjamin, Arthur, Australian composer and pianist; b. Sydney, Sept. 18, 1893; d. London, April 9, 1960. He received his musical training in Brisbane; then went to London, where he studied piano with Frederick Cliffe and composition with Charles Stanford at the Royal College of Music. After serving in the British army during World War I, he was a piano instructor at the Sydney Cons. in Australia (1919–21). Later he taught at the Royal College of Music in London; was engaged as conductor of the Vancouver Symph. Orch. in Canada (1941–46); eventually returned to London. WORKS: 5 operas: *The Devil Take Her* (London, Dec. 1, 1931); *Prima Donna* (1933; London, Feb. 23, 1949); *A Tale of Two Cities,* after Dickens (1949–50; BBC, London, April 17, 1953; prizewinner of Festival of Britain opera competition); *Mañana,* a television opera (1956); *Tartuffe,* after Molière (1960; completed by A. Boustead; performed posthumously, London, Nov. 30, 1964); *Orlando's Silver Wedding* (London, Festival of Britain, May 1951), ballet; Piano Concertino (1927); *Light Music,* suite (1928–33); Violin Concerto (1932); *Heritage,* ceremonial march (1935); *Romantic Fantasy* for Violin, Viola, and Orch. (London, March 24, 1938); *Overture to an Italian Comedy* (London, March 2, 1937); *Cotillon,* suite of 9 English dance tunes (1938); 2 *Jamaican Pieces* (1938; includes the highly popular *Jamaican Rum-*

ba; arranged also for One or 2 Pianos); *Prelude to Holiday* (Indianapolis, Jan. 17, 1941); Sonatina for Chamber Orch. (1940); Concerto for Oboe and Strings, transcribed from Cimarosa (1942); Symph. No. 1 (1944–45; Cheltenham Festival, June 30, 1948); Suite for Flute and Strings, transcribed from Scarlatti (1945); *Elegy, Waltz and Toccata,* concerto for Viola, and Orch. or Piano (1945); *From San Domingo* (1945); *Caribbean Dance* (1946); Ballade for Strings (1947); *Concerto quasi una fantasia* for Piano and Orch. (Sydney, Sept. 5, 1950, composer soloist); Harmonica Concerto (London, Aug. 15, 1953); *North American Square Dances* for 2 Pianos and Orch. (Pittsburgh, April 1, 1955); 3 *Pieces* for Violin and Piano (1919); 3 *Impressions* for Voice and String Quartet (1920); 2 string quartets: No. 1, *Pastorale Fantasia* (1924); No. 2 (1959); Violin Sonatina (1924); Suite for Piano (1927); Cello Sonatina (1938); 2 *Jamaican Songs* for 2 Pianos (1949); *Le Tombeau de Ravel: Valse Caprice* for Clarinet or Viola, and Piano (1949); Divertimento for Wind Quintet (1960); songs and choral music.

Bennet John, English composer; b. c.1570, probably in Lancashire. In 1599 he publ. *Madrigalls to Foure Voyces,* containing 17 compositions. He contributed a well-known madrigal, *All creatures now are merry minded,* to The Triumph of Oriana (1601) and composed 6 songs for Ravenscroft's *Briefe Discourse* (1914). Bennet's works have been reprinted by Fellowes in *The English Madrigal School.*

Bennett, Joseph, English critic and writer on music; b. Berkeley, Gloucestershire, Nov. 29, 1831; d. Purton, June 12, 1911. After serving in various musical positions in London, he wrote music criticism for *The Sunday Times, Pall Mall Gazette,* and *The Graphic;* was annotator of the programs of the Phil. Society (1885–1903) and of the Saturday Popular Concerts; also wrote libretti for several English composers.

Bennett, Richard Rodney, prolific and successful English composer; b. Broadstairs, Kent, March 29, 1936. He studied with Lennox Berkeley and Howard Ferguson at the Royal Academy of Music in London (1953–56); later took private lessons with Boulez in Paris (1957–58). Returning to London, he was engaged to teach at the Royal Academy of Music (1963–65); then went to the U.S. as a visiting prof. at the Peabody Cons. in Baltimore (1970–71). His music may be called "optimistic" in its facility of diatonic technique and felicity of songful expression; his instrumental works adhere to neo-Baroque forms. He is also adept in music for films, as illustrated in the atonal hippophilia of his background score for *Equus* (1977). WORKS: FOR THE STAGE: *The Ledge,* chamber opera (Sadler's Wells Theatre, London, Sept. 11, 1961); 3-act opera, *The Mines of Sulphur* (London, Feb. 24, 1965); comic opera, *Penny for a Song* (London, Oct. 31, 1967); a children's opera, *All the King's Men* (Coventry, March 28, 1969); 3-act opera, *Victory,* after the novel by Conrad (Covent Garden, London,

April 13, 1970); *Isadora,* ballet (Covent Garden, London, April 30, 1981).

FOR ORCH.: Horn Concerto (1956); *Journal* (1960); *Calendar* for Chamber Ensemble (London, Nov. 24, 1960); *Suite française* for Chamber Orch. (1961); *London Pastoral* for Chamber Ensemble (1961); *Nocturnes* for Chamber Orch. (1962); *A Jazz Calendar* for 12 Instruments (1963–64; produced as a ballet, Covent Garden, 1968); *Aubade* (London, Sept. 1, 1964); *Soliloquy* for Voice and Jazz Ensemble (1966); *Epithalamion* for Chorus and Orch. (1966); 2 symphs.: No. 1 (London, Feb. 10, 1966); No. 2 (N.Y., Jan. 18, 1968); Piano Concerto (Birmingham, Sept. 19, 1968); Concerto for Oboe and String Orch. (Aldeburgh Festival, June 6, 1971); Concerto for Guitar and Chamber Ensemble (London, Nov. 18, 1970); Viola Concerto (N.Y., July 3, 1973); Concerto for Orch. (Denver, Feb. 25, 1974); Violin Concerto (Birmingham, March 25, 1976); *Zodiac* (Washington, D.C., March 30, 1976); *Serenade* (London, April 24, 1977); *Acteon* for Horn and Orch. (London, Aug. 12, 1977); *Music for Strings* (Cheltenham, July 7, 1978); Double-bass Concerto (London, Oct. 15, 1978); *Sonnets to Orpheus* for Cello and Orch. (Edinburgh, Sept. 3, 1979); Harpsichord Concerto (St. Louis, Dec. 4, 1980); *Anniversaries* (London, Sept. 9, 1982); *Lamento* for Flute and Strings (1983).

FILM MUSIC: *The Nanny* (1965); *Billion Dollar Brain* (1967); *Nicholas and Alexandra* (about the last Imperial Romanovs; 1971); *Murder on the Orient Express* (1974); *Equus* (1977).

Bennett, Robert Russell, American composer and expert arranger and orchestrator; b. Kansas City, June 15, 1894; d. New York, Aug. 17, 1981. He was a member of a musical family; his father played in the Kansas City Phil. and his mother was a piano teacher. He studied music theory with Carl Busch, conductor of the Kansas City Symph. Orch.; in 1916 he moved to N.Y., where he earned a living copying music for G. Schirmer Co. He served in the U.S. Army in World War I; returning to civilian life, he began a career as orchestrator of musical comedy scores. Having earned enough money to travel, he went to Paris to study composition with Nadia Boulanger; in 1927 and 1928 he held a Guggenheim fellowship. He then undertook composition in earnest. Success haunted him. His music, which is distinguished by a facile flow of easily communicated melodies and rhythms in luscious harmonies and resplendent orchestration, found a receptive audience; he had no difficulties in having his works performed by top orchs. and celebrated conductors. However, his audience was limited to the U.S.; little of his music penetrated the cosmopolitan halls of Europe. He prospered mainly by his extraordinary expertise in arranging popular musical comedies in idiomatic instrumental colors. He provided arrangements for such successful shows as *Oklahoma!, Show Boat, South Pacific, The King and I, My Fair Lady,* and *The Sound of Music.* He received an Academy Award in 1955 for his scoring of the motion picture *Oklahoma!* He was also active as a conductor on the radio. His feats of organization and memory were extraordinary; he rarely had to revise his scoring, which he usually put down in calligraphic notation in the final copy.

WORKS: Operas, *Maria Malibran* (N.Y., April 8, 1935) and *The Enchanted Kiss* (N.Y., Dec. 30, 1945); operetta, *Endymion* (1927); for Orch.: *Charleston Rhapsody* (1926); *Paysage* (1928); *Sights and Sounds* (1929); March for 2 Pianos and Orch. (Los Angeles, July 18, 1930); *Abraham Lincoln Symphony* (Philadelphia, Oct. 24, 1931); *Adagio Eroico* (Philadelphia, April 25, 1935); Concerto Grosso for Band (Rochester, Dec. 9, 1932); *Hollywood Scherzo* (NBC, Nov. 15, 1936); 8 Etudes for Orch. (CBS, July 17, 1938); Symph. in D "for the Dodgers" (N.Y., Aug. 3, 1941); Violin Concerto (NBC, Dec. 26, 1941); *The Four Freedoms,* symph. sketch after 4 paintings by Norman Rockwell (Los Angeles, Dec. 16, 1943); Symph. (1946); *A Dry Weather Legend* (Knoxville, 1947); Piano Concerto (1948); Violin Sonata (1927); *Toy Symphony* for 5 Woodwinds (1928); Organ Sonata (1929); *Water Music* for String Quartet (1937); *Hexapoda* for Violin and Piano (1940); *Five Improvisations* for Trio (1946); *Sonatine* for Soprano and Harp (1947); *Six Souvenirs* for 2 Flutes and Piano (1948); Concerto for Violin, Piano, and Orch. (Portland, Oreg., March 18, 1963); Concerto for Guitar and Orch. (1970); *Suite on Old American Dances* for Band (1949); *Symphonic Songs* for Band (1958); Concerto for Wind Quintet and Wind Orch. (1958); Symph. (1963). He publ. a book on orchestration, *Instrumentally Speaking* (N.Y., 1975).

Bennett, Sir William Sterndale, distinguished English pianist, conductor, and composer; b. Sheffield, April 13, 1816; d. London, Feb. 1, 1875. His father, Robert Bennett, an organist, died when he was a child, and he was then placed in the care of his grandfather, John Bennett, who was also a musician. At the age of 8 he was admitted to the choir of King's College Chapel, Cambridge, and at 10 he became a pupil at the Royal Academy of Music in London, where he studied theory with Charles Lucas and piano with William Henry Holmes, and played violin in the academy orch. under Cipriani Potter; he later studied music theory there with William Crotch. Soon he began to compose; he was 16 years old when he was the soloist in the first performance of his Piano Concerto No. 1 in Cambridge on Nov. 28, 1832. In 1836 he made an extensive visit to Leipzig, where he became a close friend of Mendelssohn and Schumann; also appeared as a pianist and conductor of his own works with the Gewandhaus Orch. there. He continued to compose industriously, and played his Piano Concerto No. 4 with the Gewandhaus Orch. in Leipzig on Jan. 17, 1839. He visited Germany again in 1841–42. From 1843 to 1856 he gave a series of chamber music concerts in London; in 1849 he founded the Bach Society. From 1856 to 1866 he conducted the Phil. Society of London; concurrently he held the post of prof. of music at Cambridge Univ.; in 1866 he assumed the position of principal of the Royal Academy of Music. His reputation as a composer grew; Mendelssohn and Schumann were eloquent in praising his works. He amassed honors: in 1856 he received the honorary degree of D.Mus. from Cambridge Univ., which also conferred on him the degree of M.A. in 1867; he received the degree of D.C.L. from Oxford Univ. in 1870; in a culmination of these honors, he was knighted by Queen Victoria in 1871. The final honor was his burial in Westminster Abbey. His music seems to have been laid to posthumous immobility with his honored body; the great appreciation he enjoyed in Germany declined, and the desultory attempts to restore him to fame in England proved abortive; not a single work retained its erstwhile vitality. Yet at his best, Bennett could produce music not recognizably inferior to that of Schumann's lesser works. There is every reason and every chance for its natural resuscitation.

Benoit, Peter, foremost Flemish composer; b. Harlebeke, Belgium, Aug. 17, 1834; d. Antwerp, March 8, 1901. He studied at the Brussels Cons. with Fétis (1851–55); while there he earned his living by conducting theater orchs. He also wrote music for Flemish plays; at the age of 22 he produced his first opera in Flemish, *Het dorp in't gebergte (A Mountain Village),* staged in Brussels on Dec. 14, 1856. With his cantata *Le Meurtre d'Abel* Benoit obtained the Belgian Prix de Rome (1857); however, he did not go to Italy, but traveled instead in Germany. As part of his duties he submitted a short *Cantate de Noël* to Fétis, who praised Benoit's music; he also wrote the essay *L'Ecole de musique flamande et son avenir,* proclaiming his fervent faith in the future of a national Flemish school of composition, of which he was the most ardent supporter. His one-act opera *Roi des Aulnes* was presented in Brussels (Dec. 2, 1859); the Théâtre-Lyrique of Paris tentatively accepted it; Benoit spent many months in Paris awaiting its production, which never took place; in the meantime he acted as 2nd conductor at the Bouffes-Parisiens. In 1863 he returned to Belgium, where he produced his 2nd Flemish opera, *Isa* (Brussels, Feb. 24, 1867). In 1867 he founded the Flemish Music School in Antwerp; he militated for many years to obtain official status for it. In 1898 it was finally granted, and the school became the Royal Flemish Cons.; Benoit remained its director to the end of his life. In Belgium Benoit is regarded as the originator of the Flemish musical tradition in both composition and education; but although he cultivated the Flemish idiom in most of his works, his musical style owes much to French and German influences. Apart from his successful early operas, he wrote the opera *Pompeja* (1895), which was not produced; Flemish oratorios: *Lucifer* (Brussels, Sept. 30, 1866; highly successful; considered his masterpiece); *De Schelde* (1868); *De Oorlog (War;* 1873); dramatic musical score, *Charlotte Corday* (1876); historic music drama, *De Pacificatie van Ghent* (1876); *Rubens Cantata* (1877; greatly acclaimed); children's oratorio, *De Waereld in (In the World;* 1878); cantatas: *Hucbald* (1880) and *De Genius des Vaderlands* (1880); oratorio, *De Rhijn* (1889); etc. Of his church music, the most important is his *Quadrilogie religieuse* (Antwerp, April 24,

1864), of which the component parts had been separately performed in 1860, 1862, and 1863; also *Drama Christi* (1871). Benoit wrote relatively little instrumental music; his symph. poems for piano with orch. and for flute with orch. have been performed. He also composed many songs in French and in Flemish. In his propaganda for national Flemish music, Benoit contributed numerous papers and articles, among them *Considérations à propos d'un projet pour l'institution de festivals en Belgique* (1874); *Verhandeling over de nationale Toonkunde* (2 vols.; Antwerp, 1877–79); *De Vlaamsche Muziekschool van Antwerpen* (1889; a history of the Antwerp School of Music); *De Oorsprong van het Cosmopolitisme in de Muziek* (1876). In 1880 he was elected a corresponding member of the Belgian Royal Academy; in 1882, a full member.

Bentzon, Jørgen, Danish composer (cousin of **Niels Viggo Bentzon**); b. Copenhagen, Feb. 14, 1897; d. Hørsholm, July 9, 1951. He studied composition with Carl Nielsen (1915–18). At the same time he took courses in jurisprudence; subsequently he was attached to the Ministry of Justice in Denmark, and served as clerk of records of the Danish Supreme Court. He also taught piano and theory at a People's School of Music in Copenhagen. As a composer he followed the Romantic trends current in Scandinavia; an influence of his teacher Carl Nielsen pervades his music.

Bentzon, Niels Viggo, eminent Danish composer; b. Copenhagen, Aug. 24, 1919. He is a descendant of **Johann Ernst Hartmann** (1726–93), an early German-born Danish composer. The musical tradition of the family continued through many generations (his cousin was **Jørgen Bentzon**). He studied piano with his mother; took classes in music theory with Knud Jeppesen. In 1950 he was appointed to the faculty of the Royal Danish Cons. in Copenhagen. In his early compositions he assimilated a neo-Classical idiom, distinguished by compact contrapuntal writing and harmonic clarity without avoidance of justifiable dissonance; later he adopted a metamorphic technique, characterized by an evolution of varied shapes emanating from the basic musical subject, exemplified in his Symph. No. 4, subtitled *Metamorphoses;* this metamorphism naturally led to the personal formulation of serial techniques. After 1960 his works vary in style, consisting of "happenings," audiovisual scores, 3rd-stream technique, graphic notation, and the like.

Benzell, Mimi, American soprano; b. Bridgeport, Conn., April 6, 1922; d. Manhasset, Long Island, N.Y., Dec. 23, 1970. Her grandfather was a singer of Jewish folk songs in Russia before his emigration to America. She studied at the David Mannes Music School in N.Y.; appeared at the Metropolitan Opera on Jan. 5, 1945, in the role of the Queen of the Night in *The Magic Flute;* in the next 5 years she sang about 20 different roles with the Metropolitan, including Gilda in *Rigoletto* and Musetta in *La Bohème.* In 1949 she abandoned grand opera and became a popular singer in Broadway shows and in nightclubs.

Berberian, Cathy, versatile American mezzo-soprano; b. Attleboro, Mass., July 4, 1925; d. Rome, March 6, 1983. She was of Armenian parentage; she studied singing, dancing, and the art of pantomime; took courses at Columbia Univ. and N.Y. Univ.; then went to Italy; attracted wide attention in 1958, when she performed the ultrasurrealist *Fontana Mix* by John Cage, which demanded a fantastic variety of sound effects. Her vocal range extended to 3 octaves, causing one bewildered music critic to remark that she could sing both Tristan and Isolde. Thanks to her uncanny ability to produce ultrahuman (and subhuman) tones, and her willingness to incorporate into her professional vocalization a variety of animal noises, guttural sounds, grunts and growls, squeals, squeaks and squawks, clicks and clucks, shrieks and screeches, hisses, hoots, and hollers, she instantly became the darling of inventive composers of the avant-garde, who eagerly dedicated to her their otherwise unperformable cantatas. She married one of them, **Luciano Berio,** in 1950, but they were separated in 1966. She could also intone classical music, and made a favorable impression with her recording of works by Monteverdi. Shortly before her death she sang her own version of the *Internationale* for an Italian television program commemorating the centennial of the death of Karl Marx (1983). She was an avant-garde composer in her own right; she wrote multimedia works, such as *Stripsody,* an arresting soliloquy of labial and laryngeal sounds, and an eponymously titled piano piece, *Morsicat(h)y.* She resented being regarded as a "circus freak," and insisted that her objective was merely to meet the challenge of the new art of her time.

Berchem (or **Berghem**), **Jachet (de)** (also **Jaquet, Jacquet**), Flemish composer; b. Berchem, near Antwerp, early in the 16th century; d. Ferrara, 1580. He was in the service of the Duke of Ferrara from 1555. He has been confused with his contemporary Jachet de Mantua; also with Jachet Buus and Giaches de Wert. Berchem's 27 madrigals for 5 Voices appeared in 1546, and 24 madrigals for 4 Voices in 1555; 3 books containing settings of stanzas from *Orlando furioso* and dedicated to Duke Alfonso II of Ferrara were publ. in 1561. Modern reprints of Berchem's works are included in the following editions: R. van Maldeghem, *Trésor musical* (1865–93), vols. XI and XX (chansons); vols. XXVII and XXVIII (madrigals); R. Eitner, *Publikationen älterer praktischer und theoretischer Musikwerke* (1873–1905), vols. IX and XI (chansons).

Berezovsky, Maximus, Russian singer and composer; b. Glukhov, Oct. 27, 1740; d. St. Petersburg, April 2, 1777. He studied at the Kiev Ecclesiastic Academy; then was chorister at the Court Chapel in St. Petersburg. He attracted attention by his lyric voice, and in 1765 was sent by the Russian government to Bologna for further study. He became a

pupil of Padre Martini, and wrote an opera, *Demofoonte* (1773), which was produced in Bologna. Upon his return to Russia, he was unable to compete with Italian musicians who had acquired all the lucrative positions in the field of vocal teaching and opera; he became despondent and cut his throat. In addition to his opera, he left a *Credo* and 17 other sacred works; in these he made an attempt to follow the natural accents of the Russian text, which was an innovation at the time.

Berezowsky, Nicolai, talented Russian composer; b. St. Petersburg, May 17, 1900; d. New York, Aug. 27, 1953. He studied piano, violin, and voice at the Imperial Chapel in St. Petersburg; graduated in 1916, and obtained work as a violinist in the orch. of the provincial opera theater in Saratov, on the Volga River; there he played until 1919, when he joined the orch. of the Bolshoi Theater in Moscow. He crossed the border to Poland in 1920, managed to obtain an American visa, and arrived in N.Y. in 1922. He was engaged as a violinist in the orch. of the Capital Theater; in 1923 he joined the N.Y. Phil., remaining there until 1929. At the same time he took violin lessons with Paul Kochanski and studied composition with Rubin Goldmark. In 1928 he became an American citizen. He began to compose in larger forms; his clarinet sextet was performed at a chamber music festival in Washington, D.C., on Oct. 7, 1926. In 1929 his orchestral *Hebrew Suite* was conducted by Mengelberg with the N.Y. Philharmonic. Soon Berezowsky obtained other opportunities; Koussevitzky let him conduct the Boston Symph. in performances of his First Symph. in 1931 and his Fourth Symph. in 1943; Koussevitzky himself conducted Berezowsky's Second and Third Symphs. The famous German violinist Carl Flesch played the solo part of Berezowsky's Violin Concerto with the Dresden Phil. in 1930; Primrose played his Viola Concerto in 1942; and Piatigorsky performed his *Concerto lirico* with Koussevitzky and the Boston Symph. Berezowsky continued to play violin and conduct. From 1932 to 1936 and from 1941 to 1946 he was violinist and assistant conductor with the Columbia Broadcasting System, and from 1935 to 1940 was a member of the Coolidge String Quartet. He held a Guggenheim fellowship in 1948. His cantata *Gilgamesh* (1947) was favorably received, and his children's opera *Babar the Elephant* (1953) had numerous performances. His music possesses a Romantic quality, ingratiatingly Russian in color; in his later works he introduced fine impressionistic harmonies. He died of intestinal congestion apparently caused by a suicidal dose of powerful sedative drugs. His first wife (he was married twice) wrote a sweet little memoir, *Duet with Nicky,* describing his happier days.

Berg, Alban, greatly significant Austrian composer whose music combined classical clarity of design and highly original melodic and harmonic techniques that became historically associated with the New Viennese School; b. Vienna, Feb. 9, 1885; d. there, Dec. 24, 1935 (of an abscess that could have been cured by sulfa drugs overnight had such medication existed at his time). He played piano as a boy and composed songs without formal training. He worked as a clerk in a government office in Lower Austria; in 1904 he met Arnold Schoenberg, who became his teacher, mentor, and close friend; he remained Schoenberg's pupil for 6 years. A fellow classmate was Anton von Webern; together they initiated the radical movement known to history as the Second Vienna School of composition. In Nov. 1918 Schoenberg organized in Vienna the Society for Private Musical Performances (Verein für Musikalische Privataufführungen) with the purpose of performing works unacceptable to established musical society. So as to emphasize the independence of the new organization, music critics were excluded from attendance. The society was disbanded in 1923, having accomplished its purpose. In 1925 Alban Berg joined the membership of the newly created International Society for Contemporary Music, which continued in an open arena the promotion of fresh musical ideas.

Berg's early works reflected the Romantic style of Wagner, Hugo Wolf, and Mahler; typical of this period were his *3 Pieces for Orchestra* (1913–15). As early as 1917 Berg began work on his opera *Wozzeck* (after the romantic play by Büchner), which was to become his masterpiece. The score represents an ingenious synthesis of Classical forms and modern techniques; it is organized as a series of purely symph. sections in traditional Baroque forms, among them a passacaglia with 21 variations, a dance suite, and a rhapsody, in a setting marked by dissonant counterpoint. Its first production at the Berlin State Opera, on Dec. 14, 1925, precipitated a storm of protests and press reviews of extreme violence; a similarly critical reception was accorded to *Wozzeck* in Prague on Nov. 11, 1926. Undismayed, Berg and his friends responded by publishing a brochure incorporating the most vehement of these reviews so as to shame and denounce the critics. Leopold Stokowski, ever eager to defy convention, gave the first American performance of *Wozzeck* in Philadelphia on March 19, 1931; it aroused a great deal of interest and was received with cultured equanimity. Thereafter, performances of *Wozzeck* multiplied in Europe (including Russia), and in due time it became recognized as the modern masterpiece that it is. The original manuscript was acquired from the composer by the Library of Congress in Washington, D.C. Shortly after the completion of *Wozzeck*, Berg wrote a *Lyric Suite* for string quartet in 6 movements; it was first played in Vienna by the Kolisch Quartet on Jan. 8, 1927; in 1928 Berg arranged the 2nd, 3rd, and 4th movements for string orch., which were performed in Berlin on Jan. 21, 1929. Rumors of a suppressed vocal part for the 6th movement of the suite, bespeaking Berg's secret affection for a married woman, Hanna Fuchs-Robettin, impelled Douglas M. Greene to institute a search for the original score; he discovered it in 1976 and, with the help of the American scholar George Perle, decoded the vocal line in an annotated copy of the score that Berg's widow, understandably reluctant to perpetuate her husband's emotional aberrations, turned over to a Vienna library. The text proved to be Stefan Georg's rendition of Baudelaire's *De Profundis clamavi* from *Les Fleurs du mal.* Berg inserted in the score all kinds of semiotical and numerological clues to his affection in a sort of symbolical synthesis. The *Lyric Suite* with its vocal finale was played for the first time at Abraham Goodman House, N.Y., by the Columbia String Quartet and Katherine Ciesinski, mezzo-soprano, on Nov. 1, 1979.

Berg's second opera, *Lulu* (1929–35), to a libretto derived from 2 plays by Wedekind, was left unfinished at Berg's death; 2 acts and 2 fragments of the 3rd act were performed posthumously in Zürich on June 2, 1937. Again, Berg's widow intervened to forestall any attempt to have the work reconstituted by another musician. However, Berg's publishers, asserting their legal rights, commissioned the Viennese composer Friedrich Cerha to re-create the 3rd act from materials available in other authentic sources, or used by Berg elsewhere; the task required 12 years (1962–74) for its completion. After Berg's widow died, several opera houses openly competed for the Cerha version of the work; the premiere of the complete opera, incorporating this version, was first presented at the Paris Opéra on Feb. 24, 1979; the first American performance followed in Santa Fe, N.M., on July 28, 1979. As in *Wozzeck*, so in *Lulu*, Berg organized the score in a series of classical forms; but while *Wozzeck* was written before Schoenberg's formulation of the method of composition in 12 tones related solely to one another, *Lulu* was set in full-fledged dodecaphonic techniques; even so, Berg allowed himself frequent divagations, contrary to the dodecaphonic code, into triadic tonal harmonies.

Berg's last completed work was a violin concerto commissioned by the American violinist Louis Krasner, who gave its first performance at the Festival of the International Society for Contemporary Music in Barcelona, on April 19, 1936. The score bears the inscription "Dam Andenken eines Engels" ("To the memory of an angel"), the angel being the daughter of Alma Mahler and Walter Gropius who died of consumption at an early age. The work is couched in the 12-tone technique, with free and frequent interludes of passing tonality.

WORKS: OPERAS: *Wozzeck* after a play of Büchner (1917–21; Berlin, Dec. 14, 1925; Prague, Nov. 11, 1926; Philadelphia, March 19, 1931); *Lulu* (after Wedekind's plays, *Erdgeist* and *Die Büchse der Pandora*; incomplete; partial perf., Zürich, June 2, 1937; with a reconstructed and partially recomposed 3rd act by Friedrich Cerha, Paris, Feb. 24, 1979; Santa Fe, N.M., July 28, 1979). OTHER WORKS: Concerto for Violin and Orch. (Barcelona, April 19, 1936; Louis Krasner, soloist); *7 frühe Lieder* for Voice and Piano (1905–8; orchestrated in 1928); Piano Sonata, op. 1 (1908; revised 1920); *4 Lieder* for Medium Voice and Piano, op. 2 (1908–9; revised 1920); String Quartet, op. 3 (1910; revised 1924); *Altenberg Lieder*, "5 orch. songs" with Voice, op. 4 (1912); *3 Stücke* for Orch. (1913–15; revised 1929; first complete perf., Oldenburg, April 14, 1930; *4 Stücke* for Clarinet and Piano, op. 5 (1913); *Kammerkonzert* for Piano, Violin, and 13 Wind Instruments, (the thematic material based on letter-notes in the names of Arnold Schoenberg, Anton Webern, and Alban Berg; 1923–25; March 20, 1927; its *Adagio*, scored for Violin, Clarinet, and Piano, was arranged in 1934); *Lyrische Suite* for String Quartet (1925-26; first performed by the Kolisch Quartet in Vienna, Jan. 8, 1927); a version for String Orch. of 3 movements (Nos. 2, 3, and 4) was arranged in 1928 (first performed in Berlin, Jan. 21, 1929; the premiere of the *Lyrische Suite* with a newly discovered vocal finale took place at Abraham Goodman House, N.Y., with the Columbia String Quartet and Katherine Ciesinski, mezzo-soprano, on Nov.1, 1979); *Der Wein* for Soprano and Orch., after Baudelaire (Königsberg, June 4, 1930); piano arrangement of Schoenberg's *Gurre Lieder.*

Berg, Gunnar, Danish composer; b. St. Gall, Switzerland, to Danish parents, Jan. 11, 1909. He studied composition with Jeppesen and piano with Hermann Koppel in Copenhagen (1935–48); went to Paris in 1948 to study with Honegger and stayed there until 1957; returning to Copenhagen, he joined the avant-garde groups with the aim of liberating music from unnecessary academism. In his works he employs a sui generis serial technique in which each theme is a "cell" consisting of 5 to 10 notes, a model suggested to him by the experiments in cellular biology conducted by the bacteriologist Gaffky.

Berg, Josef, Czech composer; b. Brno, March 8, 1927; d. there, Feb. 26, 1971. He studied with Petrželka at the Brno Cons. (1946–50); was music editor of Brno Radio (1950–53); wrote simple music for the Folk Art ensemble. Later he began using 12-tone techniques. His most original works are the satirical chamber operas, to his own texts: *The Return of Odysseus* (1962); *European Tourism* (1963); *Euphrides in Front of the Gates of Tymenas* (1964); *Breakfast at Slankenwald Castle* (1966). He also wrote 3 symphs. (1950, 1952, 1955); Viola Sonata (1958); Fantasia for 2 Pianos (1958); Sextet for Piano, Harp, and String Quartet (1959); *Songs of the New Werther* for Bass-baritone and Piano (1962); Nonet for 2 Harps, Piano, Harpsichord, and Percussion (1962); *Sonata in Modo Classico* for Harpsichord and Piano (1963); *Organ Music on a Theme of Gilles Binchois* (1964); String Quartet (1966); 2 *Canti* for Baritone, Instrumental Ensemble, Organ, and Metronome (1966); *Ó Corino* for 4 Solo Voices and Classical Orch. (1967); *Oresteia* for Vocal Quartet, Narrator, and Instrumental Ensemble (1967).

Berg, (Carl) Natanaël, Swedish composer; b. Stockholm, Feb. 9, 1879; d. there, Oct. 14, 1957. He first studied surgery; then entered the Stockholm Cons., where he studied singing; later he went abroad and took courses in composition in Germany. His works are couched in a characteristically Scandinavian romantic manner.

WORKS: 5 operas, all produced in Stockholm: *Leila* (Feb. 29, 1912); *Engelbrekt* (Sept. 21, 1929); *Judith* (Feb. 22, 1936); *Brigitta* (Jan. 10, 1942); *Genoveva* (Oct. 25, 1947); ballets: *Älvorna* (1914); *Sensitiva* (1919); *Hertiginnans friare (The Duchess's Suitors* 1920); 5 symphs. with subtitles: No. 1, *Alles endet was entstehet* (1913); No. 2, *Årstiderna (The Tides;* 1916); No. 3, *Makter (Power;* 1917); No. 4, *Pezzo sinfonico* (1918); No. 5, *Trilogia delle passioni* (1922); symph. poems: *Traumgewalten* (1911); *Varde ljus* (1914); *Reverenza; Suite* for Orch. (1930); oratorios: *Mannen och kvinnan (Man and Woman;* 1911); *Israels lovsång (Israel's Hymns;* 1915); *Das Hohelied* (1925); Violin Concerto (1918); Serenade for Violin and Orch. (1923); Piano Concerto (1931); Piano Quintet (1917); 2 string quartets (1917, 1919); songs.

Bergamo, Petar, Serbian composer; b. Split, Feb. 27, 1930. He studied composition at the Belgrade Academy of Music with Rajičič; in 1966 joined its faculty as assistant prof. His overture *Navigare necesse est* (Belgrade, Feb. 27, 1962) typifies his style and manner, with a reference to the necessity of navigating in finding one's way in the modern method of composition; his *Musica concertante* for Orch. (Belgrade, Feb. 18, 1963) points to a neo-Baroque formalism. He further wrote 2 symphs. (1957 and 1963); *Concerto abbreviato* for Clarinet Solo (1966); *Ritrovari per tre* for Piano Trio (1967); *I colori d'argento* for Flute, Harpsichord, and a Chamber Group (1968); a String Quartet (1958); and a ballet, *Steps* (1970).

Berger, Arthur, American composer and writer on music; b. New York, May 15, 1912. After a preliminary study with Vincent Jones at N.Y. Univ., he moved to Boston. From 1934 to 1937 he studied at the Longy School of Music in Cambridge, Mass., and later attended the Harvard Graduate School, where he took courses in composition with Walter Piston, and academic musical subjects with Archibald T. Davidson and Hugo Leichtentritt. Subsequently he went to Paris to study composition with Nadia Boulanger. Returning to the U.S. in 1939, he entered Mills College in Oakland, Calif., to study composition with Darius Milhaud. In 1942–43 he was on the staff of Brooklyn College; in 1953 he was appointed prof. of music at Brandeis Univ.; in 1973–74 he was visiting prof. of music at Harvard Univ.; in 1975–76 he was the recipient of a Guggenheim fellowship. His musical idiom reveals the influence of divergent schools of composition, including a sui generis serialism and the neo-Classical pragmatism of Stravinsky. His works, in whatever idiom, are characterized by a strong formal structure; the title of one of his most cogent scores, *Ideas of Order*, is a declaration of principles. Arthur Berger was also an able music critic; he covered concerts in N.Y. for the *New York Sun* (1943–46) and for the *New York Herald-Tribune* (1946–53). He also wrote a monograph on Aaron Copland (N.Y., 1953).

Berger, Erna, German soprano; b. Cossebaude, near Dresden, Oct. 19, 1900. She studied voice in Dresden with Melita Hirzel; made her operatic debut with the Dresden State Opera in 1925; sang there until 1930. On Nov. 21, 1949, she appeared at the Metropolitan Opera in N.Y. as Sophie in *Der Rosenkavalier;* remained on its roster until 1951; retired from the stage in 1955; returned to Germany and settled in Hamburg as a voice teacher. She gave her last solo recital in Munich on Feb. 15, 1968, at the age of 67. Her best operatic parts were Gilda in *Rigoletto* and Rosina in *Il Barbiere di Siviglia.*

Berger, Francesco, English pianist and composer; b. London, June 10, 1834; d. there (at the age of 98), April 25, 1933. He studied harmony with Luigi Ricci in Trieste, piano with Karl Lickl in Vienna; later studied with Hauptmann and Plaidy at Leipzig; returned to London, where he was a prof. of piano at the Royal Academy of Music and at the Guildhall School of Music; made frequent concert tours through Great Britain and Ireland; was for some years director and, from 1884–1911, honorary secretary of the Phil. Society. He composed an opera, *Il Lazzarone,* and a Mass; overtures and incidental music to Wilkie Collins's *The Frozen Deep* and *The Lighthouse;* many songs and piano pieces. He publ. *First Steps at the Pianoforte; Reminiscences, Impressions and Anecdotes; Musical Expressions, Phrases and Sentences;* and a *Musical Vocabulary in 4 Languages* (1922); in 1931 he publ. his memoirs, entitled (with reference to his age) *97.*

Berger, Ludwig, German composer and pianist; b. Berlin, April 18, 1777; d. there, Feb. 16, 1839. He studied flute and piano; went to Berlin in 1799; there he received instruction in harmony and counterpoint with Gürrlich. In 1804 he went to Russia, but fled in the face of Napoleon's invasion in 1812; in 1815 he returned to Berlin and was active mainly as a teacher; his students included Mendelssohn, Henselt, and Taubert. He wrote a Piano Concerto, 7 piano sonatas, songs, and numerous piano works.

Berger, Rudolf, Czech opera singer; b. Brno, April 17, 1874; d. New York, Feb. 27, 1915. He began his career as a baritone with the Berlin Opera (1904–7); then went to N.Y. and studied with Oscar Saenger; changed his voice to tenor; and returned to Germany. He made his American debut at the Metropolitan Opera in N.Y. on Feb. 5, 1914, as Siegmund in *Die Walküre;* was on its roster until his death. His repertoire consisted of 96 baritone and 18 tenor roles; he sang Jokanaan in *Salome* 79 times. He was married to the soprano **Marie Rappold.**

Berger, Theodor, Austrian composer; b. Traismauer, May 18, 1905. He studied in Vienna with Franz Schmidt; evolved under Schmidt's influence a strong Romantic idiom within the framework of Classical forms. His music acquired many important supporters in Austria and Germany, but rarely penetrates beyond Central Europe.

Berghem, Jachet de. See **Berchem, Jachet (de).**

Bergiron de Briou, Nicolas-Antoine, Seigneur du Fort Michon, French composer; b. Lyons, Dec. 12, 1690; d. there, before April 27, 1768. He studied classical literature and law at the Univ. of Paris; with J.P. Christin, he established in 1713 the Académie des Beaux-Arts in Lyons, and remained associated with it in various capacities until 1764. He composed a number of cantatas and motets; other works include divertissements and several operas.

Berglund, Joel, Swedish bass-baritone; b. Torsaker, June 4, 1903. He was educated at the Cons. in Stockholm; made his debut there in 1928. He then appeared in Zürich, Vienna, and Buenos Aires; also sang in Chicago. He sang at Bayreuth in 1942; after World War II, he returned to America, appearing at the Metropolitan Opera (1945–49). He then was director of the Royal Opera in Stockholm (1949–56); he retired from the stage in 1970. He was regarded as one of the leading Wagnerian singers of his generation.

Berglund, Paavo, Finnish conductor; b. Helsinki, April 14, 1929. He studied at the Sibelius Academy. In 1956 he became associate conductor of the Finnish Radio Symph. Orch. in 1962 became its principal conductor. From 1972 to 1979 he served as music director of the Bournemouth Symph. Orch.; synchronously he conducted the Helsinki Phil. Orch. (1975–79). In 1981 he was appointed principal guest conductor of the Scottish National Orch. in Glasgow. He was named an Officer of the Order of the British Empire in 1977.

Bergman, Erik, Finnish composer; b. Uusikaarlepyy (Nykarleby), Nov. 24, 1911. He studied composition with Erik Furuhjelm at the Helsinki Cons. (1931–38); then with Heinz Tiessen at the Hochschule für Musik in Berlin, Joseph Marx in Vienna, and Wladimir Vogel in Switzerland. In 1963 he joined the staff of his Finnish alma mater, (renamed the Sibelius Academy); retired in 1976. Stylistically, Bergman cultivates varied techniques, ranging from medieval modality to dodecaphony. His predilection is for polyphonic vocal music.

Bergmann, Carl, German cellist and conductor; b. Ebersbach, Saxony, April 12, 1821; d. New York, Aug. 10, 1876. He was a pupil of Zimmermann in Zittau and of Hesse in Breslau; in consequence of his involvement in the revolutionary events of 1848–49, he left Germany and went to America. In 1850 he joined the traveling Germania Orch. as a cellist; later became its conductor; also led the Handel and Haydn Society of Boston (1852–54). In 1854 he went to N.Y. and became conductor of the German men's chorus "Arion." On April 21, 1855, he made an impressive debut as a guest conductor of the N.Y. Phil., and was named its sole conductor for the 1855–56 season; from 1856 to 1866 he shared the conductorship with Theodore Eisfeld. In 1866 he became permanent conductor of the N.Y. Phil., a position he held until his death. He continued to perform as a cellist, taking part in the Mason-Thomas chamber music concerts; furthermore, he led a series of Sacred Concerts, in programs of both choral and orch. music. He was a progressive musician, and presented works of Berlioz, Liszt, and Wagner at the time when their music did not suit the tastes of the American public.

Bergonzi, Carlo, noted Italian tenor; b. Polisene, near Parma, July 13, 1924. He studied voice in Parma with Grandini; made his operatic debut as a baritone in Lecce in 1948, singing Figaro in *Il Barbiere di Siviglia;* then established himself as a tenor; in 1951 sang the role of Andrea Chénier in Bari; in 1953 he appeared at La Scala in Milan with much success; from 1953 sang in London. He made his U.S. debut with the Chicago Lyric Opera in 1955; on Nov. 13, 1956, he made his first appearance at the Metropolitan Opera in N.Y. as Radames in *Aida,* and continued to be on its roster in subsequent seasons. He was particularly distinguished in the lyrico-dramatic roles in Italian operas.

Bergonzi, Carlo, Italian violin maker; b. Cremona, c. 1683; d. there, 1747. He began manufacturing violins about 1720, working independently of Stradivarius and other violin makers of his time. His son, **Michael Angelo Bergonzi,** continued the trade, as did his grandsons, **Carlo, Nicola,** and **Zosimo Bergonzi.**

Bergsma, William Laurence, notable American composer; b. Oakland, Calif., April 1, 1921. His mother, a former opera singer, gave him piano lessons; he also practiced the violin. After the family moved to Redwood City, Bergsma entered Burlingame High School, where he had some music theory lessons. In 1937 he began to take lessons in composition with Howard Hanson, who was at that time teaching a course at the Univ. of Southern Calif. in Los Angeles. He composed a ballet, *Paul Bunyan,* and Hanson conducted a suite from it with the Rochester Civic Orch. in Rochester, N.Y., on April 29, 1939. Bergsma also took courses at Stanford Univ.; from 1940 to 1944 he attended the Eastman School of Music in Rochester, studying general composition with Howard Hanson and orchestration with Bernard Rogers. He graduated in 1942, and received his M.M. degree in 1944. In 1944 Bergsma became an instructor in music at Drake Univ. in Des Moines. In 1946 and in 1951 he held Guggenheim fellowships. In 1946 he was appointed to the faculty of the Juilliard School of Music, N.Y., where he taught until 1963. From 1963 to 1971, Bergsma served as director of the School of Music of the Univ. of Washington in Seattle. During his teaching activities he continued to compose, receiving constant encouragement from an increasing number of performances of his works. His style of composition is that of classical Romanticism having a strong formal structure without lapsing into modernistic formalism. The Romantic side of his music is reflected in his melodious lyricism. He never subscribed to fashionable theories of doctrinaire modernity.

WORKS: OPERAS: *The Wife of Martin Guerre* (N.Y., Feb. 15, 1956); *The Murder of Comrade Sharik* (1973). Ballets: *Paul Bunyan* (San Francisco, June 22, 1939); *Senor Commandante* (Rochester, May 1, 1942).

FOR ORCH.: Symphony for Chamber Orch. (Rochester, April 14, 1943); *Music on a Quiet Theme* (Rochester, April 22, 1943); Symphony No. 1 (1946–49; CBS Radio, May 20, 1950); *A Carol on Twelfth Night,* symph. poem (1953); *Chameleon Variations* (1960); *In Celebration: Toccata for the Sixth Day,* commissioned for the inaugural week concert of the Juilliard Orch. during the week of dedication of Phil. Hall at Lincoln Center for the Performing Arts (N.Y., Sept. 28, 1962); *Documentary One* (1963; suite from a film score); *Serenade, To Await the Moon* for Chamber Orch. (La Jolla, Calif., Aug. 22, 1965); Violin Concerto (Tacoma, Wash., May 18, 1966); *Documentary Two* (1967); Symphony No. 2, *Voyages* (Great Falls, Mont., May 11, 1976).

Berio, Luciano, Italian composer of extreme musicoscientific tendencies; b. Oneglia, Oct. 24, 1925. He studied music with his father, an organist, then entered the Cons. of Milan, where he took courses in composition with Ghedini and in conducting with Giulini. In 1951 he went to the U.S. and attended a seminar given by Luigi Dallapiccola at Tanglewood. In America he married an extraordinary singer named **Cathy Berberian,** who was willing and able to sing his most excruciating soprano parts; they were divorced in 1966, but magnanimously she continued to sing his music after their separation. Back in Italy, he joined the staff of the Italian Radio; founded the Studio di Fonologia Musicale for experimental work on acoustics; edited the progressive magazine *Incontri Musicali*; later on he joined the Institut de Recherche et de Coordination Acoustique/Musique (IRCAM) in Paris, working in close cooperation with its director, Pierre Boulez. From 1965 to 1972 he was on the faculty of the Juilliard School of Music in N.Y., and subsequently maintained a tenuous connection with America. Perhaps the most unusual characteristic of his creative philosophy is his impartial eclecticism, by which he permits himself to use the widest variety of resources, from Croatian folk songs to *objets trouvés.* He is equally liberal in his use of graphic notation; some of his scores look like expressionist drawings. He is one of the few contemporary composers who can touch the nerve endings of sensitive listeners and music critics, one of whom described his *Sinfonia* with ultimate brevity: "It stinks." (The last traceable use of the word was applied by Hanslick in 1875 to Tchaikovsky's Violin Concerto.) But if *Sinfonia* stank, then so did, by implication, the ample quotes from Mahler, Ravel, and Richard Strauss used as *objets trouvés* in this work. Apart from pure (or impure, depending on perception) music, Berio uses in his works all the artifacts and artifices of popular pageants, including mimodrama choreodrama, concrete noises, acrobats, clowns, jugglers, and organ grinders.

WORKS: *Concertino* for Clarinet, Violin, Harp, Celesta, and String Orch. (1949); *Opus No. Zoo* for

Woodwind Quintet (1951); *2 Pezzi* for Violin and Piano (1951); *5 Variazioni* for Piano (1952); *Chamber Music,* to poems by James Joyce, for Voice, Clarinet, Cello, and Harp (1952); *Variazioni* for Chamber Orch. (1953); *Mimomusique,* ballet (1953); *Nones* for Orch. (1954); String Quartet (1955); *Allelujah I* for Orch. (1956); *Allelujah II* for 5 Instrumental Groups (1956–58); *Serenata* for Flute and 14 Instruments (1957); *Sequenze I* for Flute and 14 Instruments (1957); *Tempi concertati* for Chamber Orch. (1959); *Differences* for 5 Instruments and Stereophonic Tape (1959); *Circles,* to poems by e.e. cummings, for Voice, Harp, and Percussion (1960); *Quaderni* for Orch. (1960); *Sequenze II* for Harp (1963); *Traces,* for Voices and Orch. (1964); *Sincronie* for String Quartet (1964); *Epifanie* for Female Voices with Orch. (1959–63); *Chemins I* for Harp and Orch. (1965); *Chemins II* for Viola and 9 Instruments (1967); *Chemins II b* for Orch. (1969); *Chemins II c* for Orch. (1972); *Chemins III* for Viola, 9 Instruments, and Orch. (1968); *Chemins IV* for Oboe and Strings (1975); *Sequenze III* for Female Voice (1966); *Sequenze IV* for Piano (1966); *Sequenze V* for Trombone Solo (1966); *Sequenze VI* for Viola (1967); *Sequenze VII* for Oboe (1969); *Sequenze VIII* for Percussion (1975); *Sequenze IX* for Violin (1975); multifarious agglutinations and sonoristic amalgamations for electronic instruments (*Mutazioni, Perspectives, Omaggio a Joyce, Momento,* etc.); *Sinfonia,* containing a movement based on remembered fragments of works by Mahler, Ravel, Richard Strauss, etc. (N.Y., Oct. 10, 1968); *Air* for Soprano and Orch. (1969); *Bewegung* for Orch. (1970); *Opera,* spectacle for Mixed Media (Santa Fe, N.Mex., Aug. 12, 1970; completely revised 1976); *Memory* for Electronic Piano and Electronic Harpsichord (N.Y., March 12, 1971); *Prayer,* a speech sound event with Magnetic Tape Accompaniment (N.Y., April 5, 1971); *Recital* for Soprano and 17 Instruments (1971); *Amores* for 16 Vocal Soloists and 14 Instruments (1971–72); *Still* for Orch. (1973); Concerto for 2 pianos and Orch. (1973); *Eindrücke* for Orch. (1973–74); *Linea* for 2 Pianos, Marimba, and Vibraphone (1974); *Points on the Curve to Find ...* for Piano and 22 Instruments (1974); *Per la dolce memoria de quel giorno,* ballet (1974); *Après vidage* for Orch. (1974); *Coro* for 40 Voices and 40 Instruments (1974–76); *Il malato immaginario* for String Orch. (1975); Cello Concerto (1976); *Ritorno degli snovidenia (Return of Dreams;* "snovidenia" is a Russian word for "dream visions") for Cello and Orch. (Los Angeles, Jan. 25, 1979, composer conducting); *Mille Musiciens pour la paix* for 12 Wind Instruments (Lille, France, Nov. 22, 1981; composer conducting); *La vera storia,* opera to a highly diversified action, including Acrobats and featuring a Wordless Soprano (La Scala, Milan, March 9, 1982).

Bériot, Charles-Auguste de, celebrated Belgian violinist; b. Louvain, Feb. 20, 1802; d. Brussels, April 8, 1870. A precocious virtuoso, he played in Paris in 1821, and later toured in England. The famous singer **Maria Malibran** was often a joint artist at his recitals; they became intimate in 1830, and were married in 1836, but she died as a result of a riding mishap a few months after their marriage. Bériot himself developed various ailments and had to retire from a concert career because of a paralysis of his left arm. He taught violin at the Brussels Cons. from 1843 to 1852. He wrote 10 violin concertos and 11 sets of variations for Violin, as well as numerous minor pieces of chamber music. His violin methods, *Premier guide des violinistes* and *Méthode de violon* (Paris, 1858), were popular pedagogical works.

Bériot, Charles-Wilfride de, French pianist; b. Paris, Feb. 21, 1833; d. Sceaux du Gâtinais, Oct. 22, 1914. He was a natural son of *Charles-Auguste de Bériot* and *Maria Malibran,* born before their marriage (which took place in 1836). He studied piano with Thalberg, and later became a prof. of piano, playing at the Paris Cons. He composed a symph. poem, *Fernand Cortez;* 3 piano concertos; and a collection of pieces for violin and piano entitled *Opéras sans paroles.* With his father he compiled a *Méthode d'accompagnement.*

Berkeley, Sir Lennox, significant English composer; b. Boar's Hill, near Oxford, May 12, 1903. He studied French and philosophy at Merton College, Oxford (1922–26); then took lessons in composition with Nadia Boulanger in Paris (1927–32). Returning to London in 1935, he was on the staff of the music dept. of the BBC (1942–45); then was a prof. of composition at the Royal Academy of Music in London (1946–68). He was attracted from the beginning by the spirit of neo-Classical music, and his early works bear the imprint of the Paris manner as exemplified by the neo-Baroque formulas of Ravel and Stravinsky; but soon he formed an individual idiom which may be termed "modern English," broadly melodious, richly harmonious, and translucidly polyphonic. He was knighted in 1974.
WORKS: 4 operas: *Nelson,* in 3 acts (1951; preview with Piano accompaniment, London, Feb. 14, 1953; first complete perf., London Sept. 22, 1954; an orch. *Suite: Nelson* was drawn from it in 1955); *A Dinner Engagement,* in one act (1954; Aldeburgh Festival, June 17, 1954); *Ruth,* in one act (1956; London, Oct. 2, 1956); *Castaway* (Aldeburgh Festival, June 3, 1967); ballet, *The Judgement of Paris* (1938); oratorio, *Jonah* (1935); Overture (Barcelona, April 23, 1936); *Domini est Terra* for Chorus and Orch. (1937; International Society for Contemporary Music Festival, London, June 17, 1938); *Introduction and Allegro* for 2 Pianos and Orch. (1938); *Serenade* for String Orch. (1939); 4 symphs.: No. 1 (1940; London, July 8, 1943); No. 2 (1956–58; Birmingham, Feb. 24, 1959; revised 1976); No. 3, in one movement (1968–69; Cheltenham, July 9, 1969); No. 4 (1976–77); *Divertimento* for Orch. (1943); *Nocturne* for Orch. (1946); *4 Poems of St. Teresa* for Contralto and Strings (1947); *Stabat Mater* for 6 Solo Voices and 12 Instruments (1947); Concerto for Piano and Orch. (1947); 2-Piano Concerto (1948); *Colonus' Praise* for Chorus and Orch. (1949); Sinfonietta (1950); *Gibbons Variations* for Tenor, Chorus, Strings, and Or-

gan (1951); Flute Concerto (1952; London, July 29, 1953); Suite for Orch. (1953); Concerto for Piano and Double String Orch. (1958; London, Feb. 11, 1959); *An Overture* for Light Orch. (1959); *Suite: A Winter's Tale* for Orch. (1960); *5 Pieces* for Violin and Orch. (1961; London, July 3, 1962); Concerto for Violin and Chamber Orch. (1961); *Batter My Heart* for Soprano, Chorus, Organ, and Chamber Orch. (1962); *4 Ronsard Sonnets* (Set 2) for Tenor and Orch. (1963; London, Aug. 9, 1963; version with Chamber Orch., Set 1, for 2 Tenors and Piano, 1952); *Partita* for Chamber Orch. (1965); *Signs in the Dark* for Chorus and Strings (1967); *Magnificat* for Chorus and Orch. (1968; London, July 8, 1968); *Windsor Variations* for Chamber Orch. (1969); *Dialogue* for Cello and Chamber Orch. (1970); *Sinfonia Concertante* for Oboe and Chamber Orch. (1973; London, Aug. 3, 1973); *Antiphon* for String Orch. (1973); *Voices of the Night* for Orch. (1973; Birmingham, Aug. 22, 1973); Suite for Strings (1974); Guitar Concerto (1974; London, July 4, 1974); 3 string quartets (1935, 1942, 1970); Violin Sonatina (1942); String Trio (1943); Viola Sonata (1945); *Introduction and Allegro* for Solo Violin (1946); *Theme and Variations* and *Elegy* and *Toccata*, all for Violin and Piano (all 1950); Trio for Violin, Horn, and Piano (1954); Sextet for Clarinet, Horn, and String Quartet (1955); Concerto for Flute, Violin, Cello, and Harpsichord or Piano (1955); Sonatina for Solo Guitar (1957); Oboe Sonatina (1962); *Diversions* for 8 Instruments (1964); *Nocturne* for Harp (1967); Quartet for Oboe and String Trio (1967); *Theme and Variations* for Solo Guitar (1970); *Introduction and Allegro* for Double Bass and Piano (1971); Duo for Cello and Piano (1971); *In memoriam Igor Stravinsky* for String Quartet (1971); Quintet for Piano and Winds (1975); *Concert Studies* for Piano, sets 1 and 2 (1940, 1972); Sonata for Piano (1945); Sonatina for 2 Pianos (1959); Theme and Variations for 2 Pianos (1968); *3 Pieces* for Organ (1966–68); *Fantasia* for Organ (1976); numerous other pieces for piano; several songs, with piano, organ, harp, or guitar accompaniment; choruses.

Berlin, Irving (real name, **Israel Balin**), famous American composer of popular music; b. Tyumen, Russia, May 11, 1888. He was brought to the U.S. in 1893. He never had any formal music training and never learned to read or write music, yet he succeeded in producing songs, most of them to his own lyrics, that are remarkable for their natural melodic patterns and rhythmic prosody, making a perfect blend of words and melodies. One of his songs, *God Bless America*, which he wrote in 1918 while serving in the American Expeditionary Force, acquired the informal status of a national anthem and is often performed at patriotic occasions; according to sales records compiled in 1978, it brought in $673,939.46 in royalties, all of which Berlin donated to the Boy Scouts and Girl Scouts of America. Another great song, *White Christmas*, which Berlin wrote for the motion picture *Holiday Inn*, became a sentimental hit among American troops stationed in tropical bases in the Pacific during World War II;

113,067,354 records of this song and 5,566,845 copies of sheet music for it were sold in America between 1942 and 1978. In July 1954, Berlin received a Congressional Medal for his patriotic songs, particularly *God Bless America*. In 1973 he presented his upright piano to the Smithsonian Inst. in Washington, D.C.; this was an instrument fitted with a special mechanism which shifts the keyboard automatically to effect a modulation; according to his own statement, Berlin composed most of his songs in the key of F-sharp major, covering mainly the black keys, and then transposed the melody by ear. A man of exceptional modesty, Berlin rarely participated in public events in his honor. He celebrated his 90th birthday in 1978 at home with his wife of 52 years, 3 daughters, and 9 grandchildren. His financial interests were taken care of by his publishing enterprise, Irving Berlin Music, Inc., founded in 1919, and also by ASCAP, of which he was a member since its early years. His first copyrighted song was *Marie from Sunny Italy*, registered on May 8, 1907, for which he wrote only the lyrics.

WORKS: SONGS: *Marie from Sunny Italy* (1907; lyrics only); *Alexander's Ragtime Band* (1911; enormously popular); *Everybody's Doing It* (1911); *Ragtime Violin* (1911); *International Rag* (1913); *When that midnight choo-choo leaves for Alabam* (1912); *When I lost you* (1912); *I want to go back to Michigan* (1914); *When I leave the world behind* (1915); *What'll I Do?* (1924); *All Alone* (1924); *Remember* (1925); *Always* (1925); *The Song Is Ended but the Melody Lingers On* (1927); *Russian Lullaby* (1927); *Blue Skies* (1927; very popular); *White Christmas* (1942; enormously popular); *Mr. President* (1962). MUSICAL REVUES: *Watch Your Step* (1914); *Yip, Yip Yaphank*, containing the song *O how I hate to get up in the morning* (1918); 3 *Ziegfeld Follies* (1918, 1919, 1920; includes the celebrated songs *A pretty girl is like a melody* and *Mandy*); *Music Box Revues* (1921, 1922, 1923, 1925); *Face the Music* (1932); *As Thousands Cheer* (1933; includes the songs *Easter Parade* and *Heat Wave*); *Louisiana Purchase* (1940); *This Is the Army* (1942); *Annie Get Your Gun* (1946); *Miss Liberty* (1949); *Call Me Madam* (1950). FILM SCORES: *Top Hat* (1935); *Follow the Fleet* (1936); *On the Avenue* (1937); *Carefree* (1938); *Second Fiddle* (1939); *Holiday Inn* (1942); *Blue Skies* (1946); *Easter Parade* (1948).

Berlioz, Gabriel Pierre, French composer (not related to Hector Berlioz); b. Paris, June 25, 1916. He studied in Paris with Roussel and d'Indy. He wrote Viola Concerto (1935); *Francezaïc*, comic opera (1939); *Symphonie parisienne* (1942); *Jardin hanté*, ballet (1943); Piano Trio (1944); *Divertissement* for Violin, Cello, Piano, and String Orch. (1945); Concerto for Kettledrums and Orch. (1951; Paris, Jan. 25, 1953); Bassoon Concerto (1952); Symph. No. 2 (1953); pieces for tuba and piano, saxophone and piano, flute and piano, etc.

Berlioz, (Louis-) Hector, great French composer who exercised profound influence on the course of modern music in the direction of sonorous grandiosity, and propagated the Romantic ideal of program music, unifying it with literature; b. La Côte-Saint-André, Isère, Dec. 11, 1803; d. Paris, March 8, 1869. His father was a medical doctor who possessed musical inclinations; under his guidance Berlioz learned to play the flute, and later took up the guitar; however, he never became an experienced performer on any instrument. Following his father's desire that he study medicine, he went to Paris, where he entered the Ecole de Médecine; at the same time he began taking private lessons in composition from Jean François Lesueur. In 1824, he abandoned his medical studies to dedicate himself entirely to composition; his first important work was a *Messe solennelle,* which was performed at a Paris church on July 10, 1825; he then wrote an instrumental work entitled *La Révolution grecque,* inspired by the revolutionary uprising in Greece against the Ottoman domination. He was 22 years old when he entered the Paris Cons. as a pupil of his first music teacher, Lesueur, in composition, and of Anton Reicha in counterpoint and fugue. In 1826, Berlioz wrote an opera, *Les Francs-juges,* which never came to a complete performance. In 1827 he submitted his cantata *La Mort d'Orphée* for the Prix de Rome, but it was rejected. On May 26, 1828, he presented a concert of his works at the Paris Cons., including the *Resurrexit* from the *Messe solennelle, La Révolution grecque,* and the overtures *Les Francs-juges* and *Waverley.* Also in 1828 he obtained second prize for the Prix de Rome with his cantata *Herminie.* In 1828–29 he wrote *Huit scènes de Faust,* after Goethe; this was the score that was eventually revised and produced as *La Damnation de Faust.* In 1829, he applied for the Prix de Rome once more with the score of *La Mort de Cléopâtre,* but no awards were given that year. He finally succeeded in winning the first Prix de Rome with *La Mort de Sardanapale;* it was performed in Paris on Oct. 30, 1830. In the meantime, Berlioz allowed himself to be passionately infatuated with the Irish actress Harriet Smithson after he attended her performance as Ophelia in Shakespeare's *Hamlet,* given by a British drama troupe in Paris on Sept. 11, 1827. He knew no English and Miss Smithson spoke no French; he made no effort to engage her attention personally; conveniently, he found a surrogate for his passion in the person of Camille Moke, a young pianist. Romantically absorbed in the ideal of love through music, Berlioz began to write his most ambitious and, as time and history proved, his most enduring work, which he titled *Symphonie fantastique;* it was to be an offering of adoration and devotion to Miss Smithson. Rather than follow the formal subdivisions of a symphony, Berlioz decided to integrate the music through a recurring unifying theme, which he called *idée fixe,* appearing in various guises through the movements of the *Symphonie fantastique.* To point out the personal nature of the work he subtitled it "Episode de la vie d'un artiste." The artist of the title was Berlioz himself, so that in a way the symphony became a musical autobiography. The five divisions of the score are: I. *Reveries, Passions;* II. *A Ball;* III. *Scene in the Fields;* IV.

March to the Scaffold; V. *Dream of a Witches' Sabbath.* Berlioz supplied a literary program to the music: a "young musician of morbid sensibilities" takes opium to find surcease from amorous madness. Berlioz himself, be it noted, never smoked opium, but this hallucinogenic substance was in vogue at the time, and was the subject of several mystic novels and pseudo-scientific essays. In the *Symphonie fantastique* the object of the hero's passion haunts him through the device of the *idée fixe;* she appears first as an entrancing, but unattainable, vision; as an enticing dancer at a ball; then as a deceptive pastoral image. He penetrates her disguise and kills her, a crime for which he is led to the gallows. At the end she reveals herself as a wicked witch at a Sabbath orgy. The fantastic program design does not interfere, however, with an orderly organization of the score, and the wild fervor of the music is astutely subordinated to the symphonic form. The *idée fixe* itself serves merely as a recurring motif, not unlike similar musical reminiscences in Classical symphonies. Interestingly enough, in the *March to the Scaffold* Berlioz makes use of a section from his earlier score *Les Francs-juges,* and merely inserts a few bars of the *idée fixe* in it to justify the incorporation of unrelated musical material. No matter; *Symphonie fantastique* with or without Miss Smithson, with or without *idée fixe,* emerges as a magnificent tapestry of sound; its unflagging popularity for a century and a half since its composition testifies to its evocative power. The *Symphonie fantastique* was first performed at the Paris Cons. on Dec. 5, 1830, with considerable success, although the conservatory director, the strict perfectionist Cherubini, who failed to attend the performance, spoke disdainfully of it from a cursory examination of the score. Nor did Miss Smithson herself grace the occasion by her physical presence. Incongruously, the published score of the *Symphonie fantastique* is dedicated to the stern Russian czar Nicholas I. That this apotheosis of passionate love should have been inscribed to one of Russia's most unpleasant czars is explained by the fact that Berlioz had been well received in Russia in 1847. Berlioz followed the *Symphonie fantastique* with a sequel entitled *Lélio, ou Le Retour à la vie,* purported to signalize the hero's renunciation of his morbid obsessions. Both works were performed at a single concert in Paris on Dec. 9, 1832, and this time La Smithson made her appearance. A most remarkable encounter followed between them; as if to prove the romantic notion of the potency of music as an aid to courtship, Berlioz and Smithson soon became emotionally involved and they were married on Oct. 3, 1833. Alas, their marriage proved less enduring than the music that fostered their romance. Smithson broke a leg (on March 16, 1833) even before the marriage ceremony; and throughout their life together she was beset by debilitating illnesses. They had a son, who died young. Berlioz found for himself a more convenient woman companion, one Maria Recio, whom he married shortly after Smithson's death in 1854. Berlioz survived his second wife, too; she died in 1862.

Whatever the peripeteia of his personal life,

Berlioz

Berlioz never lost the lust for music. During his stay in Italy, following his reception of the Prix de Rome, he produced the overtures *Le Roi Lear* (1831) and *Rob Roy* (1832). His next important work was *Harold en Italie,* for the very unusual setting of a solo viola with orch.; it was commissioned by Paganini (although never performed by him), and was inspired by Lord Byron's poem *Childe Harold.* It was first performed in Paris on Nov. 23, 1834. Berlioz followed it with an opera, *Benvenuto Cellini* (1834–37), which had its first performance at the Paris Opéra on Sept. 10, 1838. It was not successful, and Berlioz revised the score; the new version had its first performance in Weimar in 1852, conducted by Liszt. About the same time, Berlioz became engaged in writing musical essays; from 1833 to 1863 he served as music critic for the *Journal des Débats;* in 1834 he began to write for the *Gazette Musicale.* In 1835 he entered a career as conductor. In 1837 he received a government commission to compose the *Grande messe des morts (Requiem),* for which he demanded a huge chorus. It was first performed at a dress rehearsal in Paris on Dec. 4, 1837, with the public performance following the next day. On Dec. 16, 1838, Berlioz conducted a successful concert of his works in Paris; the legend has it that Paganini came forth after the concert and knelt in homage to Berlioz; if sources (including Berlioz himself) are to be trusted, Paganini subsequently gave Berlioz the sum of 20,000 francs. In 1839, Berlioz was named assistant librarian of the Paris Cons. and was awarded the Order of the Légion d'Honneur. On Nov. 24, 1839, Berlioz conducted, in Paris, the first performance of his dramatic symphony *Roméo et Juliette,* after Shakespeare; the work is regarded as one of the most moving lyrical invocations of Shakespeare's tragedy, rich in melodic invention and instrumental interplay. In 1840, Berlioz received another government commission to write a *Grande symphonie funèbre et triomphale.* This work gave Berlioz a clear imperative to build a sonorous edifice of what he imagined to be an architecture of sounds. The work was to commemorate the soldiers fallen in the fight for Algeria, and if contemporary reports can be taken literally, he conducted it with a drawn sword through the streets of Paris, accompanying the ashes of the military heroes to their interment in the Bastille column. The spirit of grandiosity took possession of Berlioz. At a concert after the Exhibition of Industrial Products in 1844 in Paris he conducted Beethoven's Fifth Symphony with 36 double basses, Weber's *Freischütz Overture* with 24 French horns, and the *Prayer of Moses* from Rossini's opera with 25 harps. He boasted that his 1,022 performers achieved an ensemble worthy of the finest string quartet. For his grandiose *L'Impériale,* written to celebrate the distribution of prizes by Napoleon III at the Paris Exhibition of Industrial Products in 1855, Berlioz had 1,200 performers, augmented by huge choruses and a military band. As if anticipating the modus operandi of a century thence, Berlioz installed 5 subconductors and, to keep them in line, activated an "electric metronome" with his left hand while holding the conducting baton in his right. And it was probably at Berlioz's suggestion that Vuillaume constructed a monstrous Octo-bass, a double bass 10 feet high, for use in a huge orch.; it was, however, never actually employed. Such indulgences generated a chorus of derision on the part of classical musicians and skeptical music critics; caricatures represented Berlioz as a madman commanding a heterogeneous mass of instrumentalists and singers driven to distraction by the music. Berlioz deeply resented these attacks and bitterly complained to friends about the lack of a congenial artistic environment in Paris.

But whatever obloquy he suffered, he also found satisfaction in the pervading influence he had on his contemporaries, among them Wagner, Liszt, and the Russian school of composers. Indeed, his grandiosity had gradually attained true grandeur; he no longer needed huge ensembles to exercise the magic of his music. In 1844 he wrote the overture *Le Carnaval romain,* partially based on music from his unsuccessful opera *Benvenuto Cellini.* There followed the overture *La Tour de Nice* (later revised under the title *Le Corsaire*). In 1845 he undertook the revision of his early score after Goethe, which now assumed the form of a dramatic legend entitled *La Damnation de Faust.* The score included the *Marche hongroise,* in which Berlioz took the liberty of conveying Goethe's Faust to Hungary. The march became extremely popular as a separate concert number. In 1847, Berlioz undertook a highly successful tour to Russia, and in the following year he traveled to England. In 1849 he composed his grand *Te Deum;* he conducted its first performance in Paris on April 28, 1855, at a dress rehearsal; it was given a public performance two days later with excellent success. In 1852 he traveled to Weimar at the invitation of Liszt, who organized a festival of his music. Between 1850 and 1854 he wrote the oratorio *L'Enfance du Christ;* he conducted it in Paris on Dec. 10, 1854. Although Berlioz was never able to achieve popular success with his operatic productions, he turned to composing stage music once more between 1856 and 1860. For the subject he selected the great epic of Virgil relating to the Trojan War; the title was to be *Les Troyens.* He encountered difficulties in producing this opera in its entirety, and in 1863 divided the score into two sections: *La Prise de Troie* and *Les Troyens à Carthage.* Only the second part was produced in his lifetime; it received its premiere at the Théâtre-Lyrique in Paris on Nov. 4, 1863; the opera had 22 performances and the financial returns made it possible for Berlioz to abandon his occupation as a newspaper music critic. His next operatic project was *Béatrice et Bénédict,* after Shakespeare's play *Much Ado about Nothing.* He conducted its first performance in Baden-Baden on Aug. 9, 1862. Despite frail health and a state of depression generated by his imaginary failure as composer and conductor in France, he achieved a series of successes abroad. He conducted *La Damnation de Faust* in Vienna in 1866, and he went to Russia during the season 1867–68. There he had a most enthusiastic reception among Russian musicians, who welcomed him as a true prophet of the new era in music.

Posthumous recognition came slowly to Berlioz; long after his death some conservative critics still referred to his music as bizarre and willfully dissonant. No cult comparable to the one around the names of Wagner and Liszt was formed to glorify Berlioz's legacy. Of his works only the overtures and the *Symphonie fantastique* became regular items on symphony programs. Performances of his operas were still rare events. Since Berlioz never wrote solo works for piano or any other instrument, concert recitals had no opportunity to include his name in the program. However, a whole literature was published about Berlioz in all European languages, securing his rightful place in music history.

WRITINGS: *Grand Traité d'instrumentation et d'orchestration modernes* (Paris, 1843; numerous subsequent eds.; in Eng., 1858; eds. covering modern usages were published in German by Felix Weingartner, Leipzig, 1904, and Richard Strauss, Leipzig, 1905); *Le Chef d'orchestre, Théorie de son art* (Paris, 1855; in Eng. as *The Orchestral Conductor, Theory of His Art,* N.Y., 1902); *Voyage musical en Allemagne et en Italie, Etudes sur Beethoven, Gluck, et Weber. Mélanges et nouvelles* (2 vols., Paris, 1844); *Les Soirées de l'orchestre* (Paris, 1852; in Eng. as *Evenings in the Orchestra,* trans. by C. Roche, with introduction by Ernest Newman, N.Y., 1929; new Eng. trans. as *Evenings with the Orchestra* by J. Barzun, N.Y., 1956; 2nd ed., 1973); *Les Grotesques de la musique* (Paris, 1859); *A travers chants: Etudes musicales, adorations, boutades, et critiques* (Paris, 1862); *Les Musiciens et la musique* (a series of articles collected from the *Journal des Débats;* with introduction by A. Hallays, Paris, 1903); *Mémoires de Hector Berlioz* (Paris, 1870; 2nd ed. in 2 vols., Paris, 1878; in English, London, 1884; new trans. by R. and E. Holmes, with annotation by Ernest Newman, N.Y., 1932; another Eng. trans. by D. Cairns, N.Y., 1969; corrected ed., 1975). An incomplete edition of literary works of Berlioz was publ. in German by Breitkopf and Härtel: *Literarische Werke* (10 vols. in 5, Leipzig, 1903–4) and *Gesammelte Schriften* (4 vols., Leipzig, 1864).

WORKS: OPERAS: *Estelle et Némorin* (1823; not performed; score destroyed); *Les Francs-juges* (1826; not performed; revised, 1829 and 1833; overture and 5 movements extant); *Benvenuto Cellini* (1834–37; Paris Opéra, Sept. 10, 1838; revised, 1852; Weimar, Nov. 17, 1852); *La Nonne sanglante* (1841–47; score unfinished); *Les Troyens* (1856–58; revised, 1859–60; divided into 2 parts, 1863: I, *La Prise de Troie* [first performed in German under Mottl, Karlsruhe, Dec. 6, 1890]; II, *Les Troyens à Carthage* [first performed under Deloffre, Théâtre-Lyrique, Paris, Nov. 4, 1863]; first performance of both parts in French, with major cuts, Brussels, Dec. 26–27, 1906; first complete performance, *sans* cuts, alterations, etc., in Eng. under Alexander Gibson, Glasgow, May 3, 1969; in French, under Colin Davis, Royal Opera House, Covent Garden, London Sept. 17, 1969); *Béatrice et Bénédict* (1860–62; Baden-Baden, Aug. 9, 1862).

SYMPHONIES: *Symphonie fantastique: Episode de la vie d'un artiste,* op. 14a (1830; Paris, Dec. 5, 1830; revised, 1831); *Harold en Italie,* for Solo Viola and Orch., op. 16 (1834; Paris, Nov. 23, 1834); *Roméo et Juliette,* for Solo Voices, Chorus, and Orch., op. 17 (1839; Paris, Nov. 24, 1839); *Grande symphonie funèbre et triomphale,* op. 15 (1840; Paris, July 28, 1840).

OTHER WORKS FOR ORCH.: *Waverley,* overture, op.1 (1827–28; Paris, May 26, 1828); *Rob Roy,* full title *Intrata di Rob Roy Macgregor,* overture (1831: Paris, April 14, 1833); *Le Roi Lear,* overture, op. 4 (1831; Paris, Dec. 22, 1833); *Rêverie et caprice,* romance for Violin and Orch., op. 8 (1841); *Le Carnaval romain,* overture, op. 9 (1844; Paris, Feb. 3, 1844); *La Tour de Nice,* overture (1844; Paris, Jan. 19, 1845; revised 1851–52 as *Le Corsaire,* op. 21; Braunschweig, April 8, 1854); *Marche troyenne* (arranged from Act I of *Les Troyens;* 1864).

MAJOR CHORAL WORKS: *Mass* (1824; Saint-Roch, July 10, 1825; only Resurrexit extant); *La Révolution grecque,* scène héroïque (1825–26; Paris, May 26, 1828); *La Mort d'Orphée,* monologue et bacchanale (1827; first performed under Cortot, Paris, Oct. 16, 1932); *Huit scènes de Faust* (1828–29; one movement only performed, Paris, Nov. 29, 1829); *La Mort de Sardanapale* (1830; Paris, Oct. 30, 1830); *Fantaisie sur la Tempête de Shakespeare* (1830; performed as *Ouverture pour la Tempête de Shakespeare,* Paris, Nov. 7, 1830); *Le Retour à la vie,* op. 14b, monodrame lyrique (1831–32; Paris, Dec. 9, 1832; revised, 1854, as *Lélio, ou Le retour à la vie*); *Grande messe des morts (Requiem),* op. 5 (1837; Paris, Dec. 4 [dress rehearsal], Dec. 5 [public performance], 1837; revised, 1852 and 1867); *La damnation de Faust,* légende dramatique, op. 24 (1845–46; Paris, Dec. 6, 1846); *Te Deum,* op. 22 (1849; Paris, April 28 [dress rehearsal], April 30 [public performance], 1855); *L'Enfance du Christ,* trilogie sacrée, op. 25 (1850–54; Paris, Dec. 10, 1854).

WORKS FOR SOLO VOICE AND ORCH.: *Herminie,* scène lyrique (1828); *La Mort de Cléopâtre,* scène lyrique (1829). Also more than 40 songs, including 9 songs after Thomas Moore (1829; 3 orchestrated); *La Captive,* op. 12 (1832; orchestrated, 1834 and 1848); *Les Nuits d'été,* 6 songs, op. 7 (1840–41; orchestrated, 1843–56); *La Mort d'Ophélie* (1842; orchestrated, 1848; published as *Tristia,* no. 2, 1849).

Berman, Lazar, brilliant Soviet pianist; b. Leningrad, Feb. 26, 1930. He studied with Goldenweiser at the Moscow Cons., graduating in 1953. In 1956 he obtained the fifth prize at the Brussels International Contest under the sponsorship of Queen Elisabeth of Belgium, and in the same year obtained the third prize at the Budapest Liszt contest. These were the modest beginnings of a brilliant career as a virtuoso pianist. In 1970 he made a highly successful tour of Italy; in 1976 he toured the U.S. with tremendous acclaim. In his repertoire he showed a distinct predilection for the Romantic period of piano music; among modern composers his favorites were Scriabin and Prokofiev. His titanic technique, astounding in the facility of bravura passages, did not preclude the excellence of his poetic evocation of lyric moods.

Bermudo, Juan, Spanish music theorist; b. Ecija, Seville, c.1510; d. Andalusia, after 1555. He first studied theology and devoted himself to preaching; later turned to music and studied at the Univ. of Alcalá de Henares. He spent 15 years as a Franciscan monk in Andalusia; in 1550 he entered the service of the Archbishop of Andalusia, where Cristóbal de Morales was choir director. The writings of Bermudo constitute an important source of information on Spanish instrumental music of the 16th century. His most comprehensive work is the *Declaración de instrumentos musicales* (Osuna, 1549 and 1555). It deals with theory, in which his authorities were Gafurius, Glareanus, and Ornithoparchus; instruments, including problems of tuning, technique of performance, and repertoire; and critical evaluation of contemporary composers, showing familiarity with the works of Josquin, Willaert, and Gombert. Bermudo also wrote *El Arte tripharia* (Osuna, 1550). Thirteen organ pieces by him are included in F. Pedrell, *Salterio Sacro-Hispano.*

Bernac, Pierre, French baritone; b. Paris, Jan. 12, 1899; d. Villeneuve-les-Avignon, Oct. 17, 1979. His real name was **Pierre Bertin,** which he changed in order to avoid confusion with another Pierre Bertin, an actor. He started on his career as a singer rather late in life, and was first engaged in finance as a member of his father's brokerage house in Paris. His musical tastes were decidedly in the domain of modern French songs; on May 2, 1926, he gave a recital in Paris with a program of songs by Francis Poulenc and Georges Auric; at other concerts he sang works by Debussy, Ravel, Honegger, and Milhaud. Eager to learn the art of German lieder, he went to Salzburg to study with Reinhold von Warlich. Returning to Paris, he devoted himself to concerts and teaching. He became a lifelong friend to Francis Poulenc, who wrote many songs for him and acted as his piano accompanist in many of their tours through Europe and America. He also conducted master classes in the U.S. and was on the faculty of the American Cons. at Fontainebleau. He publ. a valuable manual, *The Interpretation of French Songs* (N.Y., 1970; 2nd ed., 1976) and a monograph, *Francis Poulenc: The Man and His Songs* (N.Y., 1977).

Bernacchi, Antonio Maria, celebrated Italian singer; b. Bologna, June (baptized, June 23) 1685; d. there, March 13, 1756. He was a castrato; studied voice with Pistocchi and G.A. Ricieri. In 1700 he was sopranist at the church of S. Petronio in Bologna; made his operatic debut in Genoa in 1703; between 1709 and 1735 had a number of engagements in Venice, and between 1712 and 1731 made several appearances in Bologna. He also sang in Munich (1720–27). In 1716–17 he sang in London, and in 1729 he was engaged by Handel as a substitute for Senesino for the London seasons of the Italian Opera; however, he failed to please the British operagoers and returned to his native town of Bologna, where he opened a singing school. In his singing he cultivated the style of vocal embellishments in the manner of the French *roulades.* He composed some worthwhile pieces, among them *Grave et Fuga a 4; Kyrie a 5;* and *Justus ut palma a 5.*

Bernard, Moritz (Matvey), Russian music publisher and pianist; b. Mitau, 1794; d. St. Petersburg, May 9, 1871. He studied piano with John Field in Moscow, and later was active as a piano teacher; in 1822 he moved to St. Petersburg, where he purchased a music store of Dalmas, and began publishing music. Bernard's printing press publ. songs by Glinka and Dargomyzhsky, and piano pieces by Anton Rubinstein and other important Russian composers. In 1840 he began publishing a musical monthly, *Nouvelliste,* which continued publication until 1914, many years after his death. Bernard's son took charge of the music store until 1885, when the stock was purchased by Jurgenson. Bernard composed an opera, *Olga,* which was performed in St. Petersburg in 1845; also publ. a valuable collection, *Songs of the Russian People* (St. Petersburg, 1847); a collection of children's pieces, *L'Enfant-pianiste;* and some original piano pieces and songs, some of which were printed in the Soviet Union.

Bernardi, Bartolomeo, Italian violinist and composer; b. Bologna, c.1660; d. Copenhagen, May 23, 1732. He received an invitation from the Danish Court to serve as a violinist and composer, and began his work there on Jan. 1, 1703; after an absence of several years (1705–10), he returned to Copenhagen and was appointed director of court music. In Copenhagen he produced 2 operas, *Il Gige fortunato* and *Diana e la Fortuna;* he also wrote an opera, *La Libussa,* for a production in Prague in 1703; the music of these operas is lost. His trio sonatas were published in Bologna (1692, 1696).

Bernardi, Francesco. See **Senesino, Francesco.**

Bernart de Ventadorn, Troubadour poet and composer; flourished in the 2nd half of the 12th century. His vita states that he was born in the castle of Ventadorn in the province of Limousin, and later was in the service of the Duchess of Normandy, Eleanor of Aquitaine, and of Raimon V, Count of Toulouse. He is believed to have entered a monastery in Dordogne, where he lived until his death. Some 45 poems are attributed to him, and 18 survive with complete melodies.

Berners, Lord (originally **Gerald Tyrwhitt**), eccentric British composer; b. Arley Park, Bridgnorth (Shropshire), Sept. 18, 1883; d. London, April 19, 1950. A scion of nobility and wealth, he was educated at Eton; lived many years in France, Italy, and Germany; studied music and art in Dresden and Vienna; then served as honorary attaché to the British diplomatic service in Constantinople (1909–11) and in Rome (1911–20). Returning to England, he joined the artistic smart set in London; was on intimate terms with George Bernard Shaw and H.G. Wells; took lessons in composition with Vaughan

Williams; also had some friendly advice on orchestration from Casella and Stravinsky. As a composer, he was influenced by Satie's musical nihilism and affected bizarre social behavior; he was fond of practical jokes and elaborate spoofs; characteristic of his musical humor was a set of *3 Funeral Marches* for Piano (*For a Statesman, For a Canary, For a Rich Aunt,* the last in raucous dissonances). Possessing a facile literary gift, he publ. half a dozen novels and 2 autobiographical books written in an ironic and self-deprecatory vein, *First Childhood* (London, 1934) and *A Distant Prospect* (London, 1945). Overflowing with talents, he was also an amateur chef de cuisine and a passable painter; his oils were exhibited in London, in 1931 and 1936. He succeeded to the barony of Berners in 1918.

WORKS: Comic opera, *Le Carrosse du Saint-Sacrement,* after Mérimée (1923; Paris, April 24, 1924; revised 1926); 5 ballets: *The Triumph of Neptune* (1926; Diaghilev's Ballets Russes production, London, Dec. 3, 1926); *Luna Park* (1930; London Pavilion, 1930); *A Wedding Bouquet,* with Chorus, to a libretto by Gertrude Stein (1936; London, April 27, 1937); *Cupid and Psyche* (1938; London, April 27, 1939); *Les Sirènes* (1946; London, Nov. 12, 1946); *3 Pieces* (*Chinoiseries, Valse sentimentale,* and *Kasatchok*) for Orch. (1916; Manchester, March 8, 1919); *Fantaisie espagnole* for Orch. (1918–19); Fugue in C minor for Orch. (1924); *Adagio, Variations and Hornpipe* for String Orch. (arranged from *The Triumph of Neptune,* 1926); piano pieces: *3 Short Funeral Marches* (1914); *Le Poisson d'or* (1914); *3 fragments psychologiques* (1915); *Valses bourgeoises* for 2 Pianos (1919); scores for 3 films: *Halfway House* (1943), *Champagne Charlie* (1944), and *Nicholas Nickleby* (1946); songs.

Bernhard, Christoph, German composer; b. Kolberg, Jan. 1, 1628; d. Dresden, Nov. 14, 1692. He studied with Paul Siefert in Danzig and with Schütz in Dresden. The Elector sent him to study singing in Italy (1649); in 1655 he became 2nd Kapellmeister in Dresden, but was forced to resign through the disaffection of his Italian associates. He then went to Hamburg, where he served as a cantor (1664–74); was recalled by the Elector to Dresden and was appointed first Kapellmeister, as successor to Schütz. He enjoyed great respect as a composer, particularly for his mastery of counterpoint. He publ. *Geistliche Harmonien* (Dresden, 1665; new ed., Kassel, 1972) and *Prudentia prudentiana* (Hamburg, 1669); a treatise on composition and another on counterpoint are in MS. Three major treatises in translation with annotation by W. Hilse are publ. in "The Treatises of Christoph Bernhard," *Music Forum,* III (1973). Some of his cantatas were publ. by M. Seiffert in vol. VI of Denkmäler Deutscher Tonkunst.

Bernheimer, Martin, American music critic; b. Munich, Sept. 28, 1936. He was taken to the U.S. as a child in 1940; studied music at Brown Univ. (B.A., 1958) and N.Y. Univ. (M.A., 1962); in the interim, took courses in music at the Munich Cons. (1958–59). Returning to the U.S., he was a member of the music faculty at N.Y. Univ. (1960–62); served as contributing critic for the *N.Y. Herald Tribune* (1959–62) and assistant music editor of *Saturday Review* (1962–65). In 1965 he was appointed music editor of the *Los Angeles Times;* in 1966 became instructor in the Rockefeller programs for training music critics at the Univ. of Southern Calif., Los Angeles; also was a member of the faculty of the Univ. of Calif., Los Angeles (since 1969). As a critic, he possesses a natural facility and not infrequently a beguiling felicity of literary style; he espouses noble musical causes with crusading fervor, but he can be aggressively opinionated and ruthlessly devastating to composers, performers, or administrators whom he dislikes; as a polemicist he is a *rara avis* among contemporary critics, who seldom rise to the pitch of moral or musical indignation; Bernheimer also possesses a surprising knowledge of music in all its ramifications, which usually protects him from perilous pratfalls. In 1981 he received the Pulitzer Prize for distinguished classical music criticism.

Bernier, Nicolas, French composer; b. Mantes, Seine-et-Oise, June 5, 1665; d. Paris, July 6, 1734. He held the post of organist at Chartres Cathedral (1694–98); in 1698 he was appointed maître de musique at St. Germain l'Auxerrois in Paris; then served at Sainte-Chapelle in Paris (1704–26). He publ. 8 books of "cantates profanes," of which *Les Nuits de Sceaux* is an important example of French secular cantatas. He also wrote a Te Deum. His *Principes de composition de M. Bernier* was trans. into Eng. by P. Nelson and publ. as *Nicolas Bernier: Principles of Composition* (Brooklyn, 1964).

Berno von Reichenau, German theorist of the 11th century; b. c.970; d. in Cloister of Reichenau, June 7, 1048. In 1008 he was installed as Abbot of the Cloister of Reichenau; accompanied Emperor Henry II to Rome for coronation in 1014, and in 1027 attended the coronation in Rome of Emperor Conrad II. He wrote learned treatises on music, which can be found in J.P. Migne's *Patrologiae cursus completus* (vol. 142) and in Gerbert's *Scriptores* (vol. 2). A monograph on his system of music was publ. by W. Brambach (Leipzig, 1881).

Bernstein, Elmer, talented American composer of film music; b. New York, April 4, 1922. He studied with Roger Sessions and Stefan Wolpe at the Juilliard School of Music in N.Y.; served in the U.S. Air Force during World War II; after the end of the war he settled in Hollywood and became a highly successful composer of background scores, particularly in dramatic films; of these the most effective were *The Man with the Golden Arm; The Ten Commandments; Desire under the Elms; The Magnificent Seven; To Kill a Mockingbird; Walk on the Wild Side; The Great Escape; The Carpetbaggers; Hawaii.* He has also composed chamber music.

Bernstein, Leonard, greatly gifted American conductor and composer, equally successful in writing symph. music of profound content and strikingly

Bernstein

effective Broadway shows, and, in the field of performance, a conductor of magnetic powers, exercising a charismatic spell on audiences in America and the world at large; b. Lawrence, Mass., Aug. 25, 1918, of a family of Russian-Jewish immigrants. His given first name was Louis, which at the age of 16 he had legally changed to Leonard to avoid confusion with other, pre-existent, Louis Bernsteins in the family. He studied piano with Helen Coates and Heinrich Gebhard in Boston. In 1935 he entered Harvard Univ. and took courses in music theory with Tillman Merritt, counterpoint and fugue with Walter Piston, and orchestration with Edward Burlingame Hill; he graduated in 1939. He then went to Philadelphia, where he studied piano with Isabelle Vengerova, conducting with Fritz Reiner, and orchestration with Randall Thompson at the Curtis Inst. of Music. During the summers of 1940 and 1941 he attended the Berkshire Music Center at Tanglewood, where he received instruction in conducting with Koussevitzky, who took great interest in his talent and made every effort to promote his career as a professional conductor. He also did some work for publishers, arranging music for band under the interlingual pseudonym **Lenny Amber** (Bernstein is the German word for "amber"). He conducted occasional concerts with local groups in Boston; in 1943 he obtained the job of assistant conductor to Arthur Rodzinski, then conductor of the N.Y. Phil.; his great chance to show his capacities came on Nov. 14, 1943, when he was called upon on short notice to conduct a difficult program in substitution for Bruno Walter, who was to lead that particular concert but happened to be indisposed, while Rodzinski was out of town. He acquitted himself brilliantly and was roundly praised for his courage in facing a trying situation with exemplary professional confidence. This was the beginning of one of the most brilliant conducting careers in American history. Bernstein became the first native-born American musician to become conductor of the N.Y. Phil., the post to which he acceded in 1958. He also filled other engagements, among them conducting the N.Y. City Center Orch. (1945–48), and was guest conductor of the International Music Festival in Prague in 1946. In 1958 he made a tour with the N.Y. Phil. in South America; in 1959 he took the orch. on a grand tour of Russia and 17 other countries in Europe and the Near East; in 1960 he toured Japan, Alaska, and Canada; on July 9, 1967, he led a memorable concert with the Israel Phil. in Jerusalem, at the conclusion of Israel's devastating Six Day War, in a program of works by Mendelssohn and Mahler. He was the first American conductor to lead a regular performance at La Scala in Milan, where he conducted Cherubini's opera *Medea* in 1953. In 1969 he resigned as permanent conductor of the N.Y. Phil. in order to have more time for composition and other projects; the orch. bestowed upon him the unprecedented honorific title of "laureate conductor," enabling him to give special performances with the orch. from time to time. In the summer of 1976 he took the orch. on a Bicentennial tour of 13 concerts in 11 European cities during a period of 17 days, in programs emphasizing American music. Ebullient with communicative talents, Bernstein initiated in 1958 a televised series of Young People's Concerts with the N.Y. Phil. in which he served as an astute commentator; these concerts were greatly popular with audiences extending beyond the eponymous youth. His eagerness to impart his wide knowledge in various fields to a willing audience found its expression in the classes he conducted at Brandeis Univ. (1951–55), and concurrently in the summer sessions at the Berkshire Music Center at Tanglewood. In 1972–73 he was a lecturer at the prestigious Norton series at Harvard Univ.; in 1974 he lectured at the Massachusetts Inst. of Technology. He was the recipient of many honors: the Order of Merit from Chile (1964); the Order of the Lion Commander from Finland (1965); that of Chevalier of the French Legion of Honor (1968); that of Cavaliere from Italy (1969); the Austrian Honorary Distinction in Science and Art (1976); the Albert Einstein Commemorative Award in the Arts from the Einstein College of Medicine; an International Education Award, presented to him by President Nixon, and the George Foster Peabody Award for his television programs. He also held an honorary doctorate of letters from the Univ. of Warwick in England (1974). An excellent pianist in his own right, Bernstein often appeared as a soloist in classical or modern concertos, playing and conducting the orch. from the keyboard. An intellectual by nature, and a litterateur by avocation, as well as an occasional poet, he took pride in publishing some excellent sonnets and other poems. An inevitable overflow of his spiritual and animal energy impelled him to display certain histrionic mannerisms on the podium, which elicited invidious comments on the part of some music critics who objected to his "choreography." But even the skeptics could not deny Bernstein's ardent devotion to music, both classical and modern. His interpretations of Mahler's symphs. seemed to respond to Mahler's innermost creative impulses. Whatever judgment may ultimately be rendered about Bernstein, he remains a phenomenal apparition. History knows of many significant composers who were also excellent conductors, but Bernstein seems to be unique in his protean power to be equally proficient as a symph. conductor, a composer of complex music, and last, not least, of highly original and enormously popular musical stage productions. In his *West Side Story* he created a significant social music drama, abounding in memorable tunes. In his score *The Age of Anxiety* he reflected the turbulence of modern life. A socially conscious individual, Bernstein espoused many libertarian causes, and was once derisively dubbed by a columnist as a devotee of "radical chic." Ever cognizant of his Jewish heritage, Bernstein wrote a devout choral symph., *Kaddish;* as a testimony to his ecumenical religious feelings, he produced a *Mass,* based on the Roman liturgy. On Sept. 9, 1951, he married the Chilean actress Felicia Montealegre (she died in 1978). (A debate rages as to the proper pronunciation of Bernstein's name; intimates used to refer to him as Bern*steen,* and he himself once said he preferred the "democratic Yiddish" Bern*steen* to the "aristocratic Germanic" Bern*styne,* but

on his formal appearances on the radio or television, he reverted to the more universal "Bernstyne.")
WORKS: FOR ORCH.: Symph. No. 1, subtitled *Jeremiah* (Pittsburgh, Jan. 28, 1944, composer conducting; received the N.Y. Music Critics' Circle Award); *The Age of Anxiety* (Symph. No. 2), after a poem by W.H. Auden, traversing many styles and moods, from the religious to the ultramodern, including a spectacular episode in the jazz idiom, scored for Piano and Orch. (Boston Symph. Orch., Koussevitzky conducting; Bernstein, piano soloist, April 8, 1949); *Fugue and Riffs* for Band (1949); *Serenade* for Violin Solo, Strings, and Percussion, after Plato's *Symposium* (Venice Festival, Sept. 12, 1954, Isaac Stern, soloist; Bernstein conducting); *Kaddish* (Symph. No. 3), for Narrator, Chorus, and Orch. (Tel Aviv, Dec. 9, 1963, Bernstein conducting); *Chichester Psalms* for Chorus and Orch. (commissioned by the Dean of Chichester, England; first performed by Bernstein and the N.Y. Phil., July 14, 1965); *Mass*, "a theater piece" for Orch., Chorus, a group of Boy Singers, Dancers, and Dancer-Singers, to a text partly consisting of the Roman liturgy in Latin, partly in vernacular (first produced at the opening of the John F. Kennedy Center for the Performing Arts, Washington, D.C., Sept. 7, 1971); *Songfest*, 12 pieces for 6 Singers and Orch. (Washington, D.C., Oct. 11, 1977); *Divertimento* (Boston, Sept. 25, 1980); *Halil* (Hebrew for "flute"), a Nocturne for Solo Flute, String Orch., and Percussion, dedicated to the memory of an Israeli soldier fallen in the 1973 war (1981; first performed, Tel Aviv, May 1981). FOR THE STAGE: *Fancy Free*, ballet (N.Y., April 18, 1944); *On the Town*, musical comedy, derived from the scenario of the ballet *Fancy Free* (N.Y., Dec. 28, 1944); *Candide*, musical after Voltaire (N.Y., Dec. 1, 1956; new redaction, N.Y., Oct. 13, 1982, as an "opera-house version," produced by the N.Y. City Opera, with a revised orchestration by Bernstein, Hershy Kay, and John Mauceri, and a revised text, largely by Bernstein himself); *Facsimile*, "choreograhic observations in one scene" (N.Y., Oct. 24, 1946); *Trouble in Tahiti*, one-act opera to his own libretto (Brandeis Univ., June 12, 1952); *Wonderful Town*, musical comedy (N.Y., Feb. 25, 1953); *West Side Story*, social music drama, a perennial favorite (Washington, Aug. 19, 1957; N.Y., Sept. 26, 1957; also produced as a motion picture); *Dybbuk*, ballet (N.Y., May 16, 1974); the Bicentennial pageant *1600 Pennsylvania Avenue* (N.Y., May 4, 1976); film score, *On the Waterfront* (1954). CHAMBER MUSIC: Clarinet Sonata (1942); *7 Anniversaries* for Piano (1942–43); *Elegy I* for Horn and Piano (1950); *Elegy II* for Solo Trombone (1950); *Elegy III* for Tuba and Piano (1950). SONGS: *I Hate Music*, subtitled *5 Kid Songs* (1943); *La Bonne Cuisine*, 4 recipes for Voice and Piano (1945); *2 Love Songs* for Voice and Piano, to texts by Rilke (1949). WRITINGS: *The Joy of Music*, a collection of television talks (N.Y., 1959; revised and amplified as *Young People's Concerts*, N.Y., 1970); *The Infinite Variety of Music* (N.Y., 1966); *Six Talks at Harvard* (Cambridge, Mass., 1976); *Findings* (N.Y., 1982).

Bernstein, Martin, American musicologist; b. New York, Dec. 14, 1904. He was educated at N.Y. Univ. (graduated in 1925; B.Mus., 1927); played the double bass in the N.Y. Symph. Orch. (1925), the N.Y. Phil. Orch. (1926–28), and the Chautauqua Symph. Orch. (1929–36). He was for 48 years a member of the faculty of N.Y. Univ. (1924–72); then a prof. of music at Lehman College, City Univ. of N.Y. (1972–73). He publ. *Score Reading* (1932; 2nd ed., 1949); the successful textbook *An Introduction to Music* (N.Y., 1937; 4th ed., 1972); contributed chapters on music to *An Intellectual and Cultural History of the Western World,* Harry Elmer Barnes, ed. (N.Y., 1937). A Festschrift, *A Musical Offering: Essays in Honor of Martin Bernstein,* edited by E.H. Clinkscale and C. Brook, was publ. in 1977. A brother, **Artie Bernstein** (b. Brooklyn, Feb. 3, 1909; d. Los Angeles, Jan. 4, 1964), a classically trained cellist, became a leading jazz bassist in the 1930s and '40s, playing with many big bands, including Jimmy Dorsey's; from 1939–41 he was part of the Benny Goodman Sextet; after World War II he became a studio musician.

Béroff, Michel, French pianist; b. Epinal, Vosges, May 9, 1950. He studied piano with Yvonne Loriod at the Paris Cons., made his debut in Paris at 16; then toured as a concert pianist, often programming works of French avant-garde composers.

Berr, Friedrich, German clarinetist and bassoonist; b. Mannheim, April 17, 1794; d. Paris, Sept. 24, 1838. He studied with Fétis and Reicha in Paris, and settled there in 1823; served as the 2nd clarinetist at the Théâtre-Italien; in 1828 became first clarinetist. In 1931 he was appointed to the faculty of the Paris Cons.; in 1836 he became director of the new School of Military Music. He was the author of a *Traité complet de la clarinette à 14 clefs* (1836); also composed many works for clarinet and bassoon, and some 500 pieces of military music.

Berry, Walter, Austrian bass-baritone; b. Vienna, April 8, 1929. He first studied engineering; later decided to engage in a musical career, and enrolled at the Vienna Academy of Music. In 1950 he sang at the Vienna State Opera. On Oct. 2, 1966, he made his American debut at the Metropolitan Opera in N.Y. as Barak in *Die Frau ohne Schatten* by Richard Strauss. He distinguished himself in Wagnerian operas. He was married to **Christa Ludwig** in 1957, and appeared with her numerous times in corresponding roles (Carmen and Escamillo, Ortrud and Telramund, etc.); they were divorced in 1970, but continued to sing in tandem in the same operas.

Berté, Heinrich, Hungarian composer; b. Galgócz, May 8, 1857; d. Vienna, Aug. 23, 1924. He studied with Hellmesberger, Fuchs, and Bruckner in Vienna. He produced ballets: *Das Märchenbuch* (Prague, 1890); *Amor auf Reisen* (Vienna, 1895); *Der Karneval in Venedig* (Vienna, 1900); and *Automatenzauber* (Vienna, 1901); operettas: *Die Schneeflocke* (Prague, 1896); *Der neue Bürgermeister* (Vienna, 1904); *Die Millionenbraut* (Munich, 1905); *Der*

Kleine Chevalier (Dresden, 1907); *Der schöne Gardist* (Breslau, 1907); *Der Glücksnarr* (Vienna, 1909); *Kreolenblut* (Hamburg, 1911); *Der Märchenprinz* (Hannover, 1914); *Das Dreimäderlhaus* (Vienna, Jan. 15, 1916). This last, based on Schubert melodies, was produced in English under the title *Blossom Time,* arranged by Romberg (N.Y., Sept. 21, 1921; very popular); also as *Lilac Time,* arranged by Clutsam (London, Dec. 22, 1922).

Berteau, Martin, famous French cellist; b. c.1700; d. Angers, Jan. 23, 1771. He studied the bass viol with Kozecz in Germany; then took up the cello, achieving mastery of its technique. He is regarded as the protagonist of the French school of cello playing. He also composed a number of effective pieces for cello.

Bertin, Louise-Angélique, French composer; b. Les Roches, near Paris, Feb. 15, 1805; d. Paris, April 26, 1877. She was a pupil of Fétis; composed the operas *Guy Mannering* (Les Roches, Aug. 25, 1825); *Le Loup-garou* (Paris, March 10, 1827); *Fausto* (Paris, March 7, 1831); *La Esmeralda* (to a libretto adapted by Victor Hugo from his novel *Notre-Dame de Paris;* Paris, Nov. 14, 1836). She also wrote a number of instrumental works, of which *Six Ballades* for Piano was publ.

Bertini, Henri (-Jérôme), known as "Bertini le jeune," pianist and composer; b. London, Oct. 28, 1798; d. Meylau, near Grenoble, Oct. 1, 1876. When 6 months old, he was taken to Paris, where he was taught music by his father and his elder brother, **Benoît-Auguste;** at the age of 12, made a concert tour through the Netherlands and Germany; then studied further in Paris and Great Britain; lived in Paris as a concert pianist from 1821–59, when he retired to his estate at Meylau. He wrote valuable technical studies, some of which have been publ. in editions by G. Buonamici and by Riemann; also arranged Bach's *48 Preludes and Fugues* for Piano, 4-hands; composed much chamber music, many piano pieces.

Bertoldo, Sperindio (Sper'in Dio), Italian organist and composer; b. Modena, c.1530; d. Padua, Aug. 13, 1570. He served as chief organist at the Cathedral of Padua. His surviving compositions include 2 books of madrigals in 5 Voices, publ. in Venice (book 1, 1561; book 2, 1562); the first book includes an *Echo a 6 voci* and a *Dialogo a 8 voci.* Several other madrigals are included in a collection by Cipriano and Annibale (Venice, 1561). Bertoldo's *Toccate, ricercari e canzoni francese...per sonar d'organo* (Venice, 1591) was publ. posthumously. Two ricercari for Organ are included in L. Torchi, *L'Arte musicale in Italia* (vol. III).

Berton, Henri-Montan, French conductor and composer, son of **Pierre-Montan Berton;** b. Paris, Sept. 17, 1767; d. there, April 22, 1844. He was a pupil of Rey and Sacchini; in 1782 he joined the orch. of the Paris Opéra as a violinist; in 1795 he was appointed to the staff of the Paris Cons., and in 1818 succeeded Méhul as prof. of composition. From 1807 to 1809 he conducted at the Opéra-Bouffe; in 1809 became chorusmaster at the Paris Opéra; in 1815 he was elected a member of the French Academy. He wrote 47 operas, of which the most successful were *Montano et Stéphanie* (1799), *Le Délire* (1799), and *Aline, reine de Colconde* (1803); other works included several oratorios, 8 cantatas, and 4 ballets. He also publ. some theoretical works expressing his own views on musical values; they are curious in content but otherwise devoid of significance.

Berton, Pierre-Montan, French composer; b. Maubert-Fontaines, Ardennes, Jan. 7, 1727; d. Paris, May 14, 1780. He studied organ and composition at the choir school of Senlis Cathedral; was a member of the chorus at the Paris Opéra; then became director of the Grand-Théâtre in Bordeaux. In 1755 he was appointed conductor of the Grand Opéra in Paris and was its general director from 1775 to 1778. In that capacity he supplemented the music of the operas of Lully, Rameau, and Gluck. He produced, in Paris, his operas *Erosine* (Aug. 29, 1766), *Théonis, ou Le Toucher* (Oct. 11, 1767), and *Adèle de Ponthieu* (Dec. 1, 1772).

Bertoni, Ferdinando Gioseffo, Italian organist and composer; b. island of Salò, near Venice, Aug. 15, 1725; d. Desenzano, Dec. 1, 1813. He studied with Padre Martini; in 1752 was appointed first organist of San Marco in Venice; made two trips to London, where several of his operas were produced; on Jan. 21, 1785, he succeeded Galuppi as maestro di cappella at San Marco; retired in 1808. From 1757 to 1797 he also served as choirmaster at the Cons. de' Mendicanti. He wrote about 50 operas; of these the following are important: *La Vedova accorta* (Venice, 1745); *Quinto Fabio* (Milan, Jan. 31, 1778); *Demofoonte* (London, Nov. 28, 1778); and *Nitteti* (Venice, Feb. 6, 1789). He also wrote a number of oratorios; harpsichord sonatas; and chamber music.

Bertram, Theodor, German baritone; b. Stuttgart, Feb. 12, 1869; d. (suicide) Bayreuth, Nov. 24, 1907. He studied with his father, the baritone **Heinrich Bertram;** made his debut as the Hermit in *Der Freischütz* in Ulm in 1889; then sang at the Hamburg Opera (1891) and the Berlin Kroll Opera (1892); was a member of the Munich Court Opera (1893–99). He made his Metropolitan Opera debut in N.Y. on Jan. 6, 1900, as the Flying Dutchman, remaining on the roster for a year; he also sang at Covent Garden, London (1900, 1903, 1907), and at Bayreuth (1901–6). He was married to the soprano **Fanny Moran-Olden;** following her death, he became despondent and took his own life.

Berutti, Arturo, Argentine opera composer; b. San Juan, March 27, 1862; d. Buenos Aires, Jan. 3, 1938. He was of Italian extraction, and naturalized the spelling of his last name as **Beruti.** He received his early training in music with his father; then went to Leipzig, where he became a student of Jadassohn. He subsequently lived in Italy, where he produced 3 of his operas: *La Vendetta* (Vercelli, May 21, 1892); *Evangelina* (Milan, Sept. 19, 1893); *Taras Bulba* (Turin, March 9, 1895). Returning to Argentina in 1896, he produced the following operas in various theaters in Buenos Aires: *Pampa* (July 27, 1897); *Yupanki* (July 25, 1899); *Khrise* (June 21, 1902); *Horrida Nox,* the first opera by a native Argentine composer, written to a Spanish libretto, which was produced in Argentina (Buenos Aires, July 7, 1908); *Los Heroes* (Aug. 23, 1919; his only opera produced at the Teatro Colón).

Berwald, Franz Adolf, foremost Swedish composer of the 19th century; son of **Christian Friedrich Berwald;** brother of **Christian August Berwald;** cousin of **Johann Friedrich Berwald;** b. Stockholm, July 23, 1796; d. there, April 3, 1868. He was a member of a musical family of German extraction that settled in Sweden in the 18th century. He studied violin with his father and with his cousin Johann Friedrich Berwald; took lessons in composition with J.B.E. du Puy. He served as a violinist and violist in the orch. of the Royal Chapel in Stockholm (1812–28). In 1819 he played in Finland with his brother; also toured in Russia. In 1829 he went to Berlin and became engaged in business; in 1835 he opened an orthopedic establishment there. In 1841 he went to Vienna; then returned to Sweden, where he served as manager of a glassworks in Angermanland (1850–58); in 1853 was a part owner of a sawmill. In 1864 he was made a member of the Swedish Royal Academy of Music in Stockholm; also gave courses at the Stockholm Cons. In his music Berwald followed the Romantic traditions of the German school of composition; his works reveal influences of Spohr, Weber, and Mendelssohn; there is in his music a certain nostalgia that exudes the sweet odor of slow decay. A renewed interest in Berwald led to a revival of his long–forgotten pieces. A complete edition of his works, *Franz Berwald: Sämtliche Werke,* began publ. in 1966.
WORKS: OPERAS: *Estrella di Soria* (1841; Stockholm, April 9, 1862; modern version by Moses Pergament, Göteborg, March 2, 1931); *Drottningen av Golconda* (1864; first perf. more than a century later, Stockholm, April 3, 1968); the early operas *Gustaf Wasa* (1827), *Leonida* (1829), and *Der Verräter* (1830) remain unperf. FOR ORCH.: *Sinfonie sérieuse,* No. 1 (Stockholm, Dec. 2, 1843); *Sinfonie capricieuse,* No. 2, (1842; perf. in a realization from short score in Stockholm, 72 years later, on Jan. 9, 1914); *Sinfonie singulière,* No. 3 (1845; first perf. 60 years later, Stockholm, Jan. 10, 1905); No. 4 (1845; Stockholm, April 9, 1878); Violin Concerto (Stockholm, March 3, 1821); *Concertstück* for Bassoon and Orch. (1827); Piano Concerto (1855; first perf. in Stockholm in 1904 with Berwald's granddaughter as soloist); 5 symph. poems: *Elfenspiel* and *Erinnerung an die norwegischen Alpen* (Vienna, March 6, 1842); *Ernste und heitere Grillen* (Stockholm, May 19, 1842); *Bayaderen-Fest* (Stockholm, Dec. 6, 1842); 5 piano trios and other chamber music; choral pieces.

Berwald, Johan Fredrik (Johann Friedrich), Swedish violinist and composer; cousin of **Franz Berwald;** b. Stockholm, Dec. 4, 1787; d. there, Aug. 26, 1861. He was a member of a musical family of German nationality which settled in Sweden. A precocious musician, he played the violin in public at the age of 5; took lessons in composition with Abbé Vogler during the latter's stay in Sweden. At the age of 16 he went to St. Petersburg and served as concertmaster in the Russian Imperial Court orch. (1803–12). Returning to Sweden, he was appointed chamber musician to the King of Sweden, a post he held from 1815 until 1849; also conducted (from 1819) the Royal Orch. in Stockholm. He wrote his first symph. when he was 9 years old, but in his mature years he devoted himself mainly to theatrical productions. One of his light operas, *L'Héroïne de l'amour,* to a French libretto, was produced in St. Petersburg in 1811. In Stockholm he was also active as a teacher; among his pupils was his cousin Franz Berwald.

Besard, Jean-Baptiste, French lutenist and composer; b. Besançon, 1567; d. probably in Augsburg, in 1625. He studied philosophy at the Univ. of Dôle; after his marriage in 1602, he went to Rome and studied with the lutenist Lorenzini. Later lived in Germany, publishing at Cologne his *Thesaurus harmonicus* (1603), and at Augsburg his *Novus partus, sive Concertationes musicae duodena trium ...* (1617) and *Isagoge in artem testudinariam* (1617). Some of the compositions in these works have been trans. by O. Chilesotti in *Biblioteca di rarità musicali.*

Besekirsky, Vasili. See **Bezekirsky, Vasili.**

Besozzi, Alessandro, celebrated Italian oboist; b. Parma, July 22, 1702; d. Turin, July 26, 1793. He was a musician at the ducal chapel in Parma (1728–31); made concert tours with his brother, Girolamo (see 3 below); appeared with him in Paris in 1735; then lived in Turin. He publ. numerous trio sonatas for Flute, Violin, and Cello; 6 violin sonatas (with Basso Continuo); etc. Other members of the family who specialized in wind instruments were: (1) **Antonio,** oboist, nephew of Alessandro (b. Parma, 1714; d. Turin, 1781); (2) **Carlo,** oboist, son of Antonio (b. Naples, c.1738; d. Dresden, March 22, 1791); played in the Dresden orch. (1754); wrote several oboe concertos; (3) **Girolamo,** bassoonist, brother of Alessandro (b. Parma, April 17, 1704; d. Turin, 1778); (4) **Gaetano,** oboist, nephew of Alessandro (b. Parma, 1727; d. London, 1794); (5) **Girolamo,** oboist, son of Gaetano (b. Naples, c.1750; d. Paris, 1785); (6) **Henri,** flutist, son of Girolamo; played at the Opéra-Comique; (7) **Louis-Désiré,** son of Henri (b. Versailles, April 3, 1814; d. Paris, Nov. 11, 1879), a student of Lesueur and Barbereau; he won the Prix de Rome in 1837, defeating Gounod.

Bessel, Vasili, Russian music publisher; b. St. Petersburg, April 25, 1842; d. Zürich, March 1, 1907. He was the founder (1869) of the music publishing firm of Bessel & Co. at St. Petersburg, which has publ. works by many distinguished Russian composers (Anton Rubinstein, Rimsky-Korsakov, Tchaikovsky, Mussorgsky); also 2 short-lived periodicals, *Musical Leaflet* (1872–77) and the *Russian Musical Review* (1885–89). Bessel wrote *Reminiscences of Tchaikovsky,* who was his fellow student at the St. Petersburg Cons. In 1920 the firm was transferred to Paris, where it continued under the direction of Bessel's sons, Vasili and Alexander.

Besseler, Heinrich, eminent German musicologist; b. Hörde, Dortmund, April 2, 1900; d. Leipzig, July 25, 1969. He studied mathematics and natural sciences; then turned to musicology; attended the courses of Gurlitt in Freiburg, of Adler in Vienna, and of Ludwig in Göttingen. He received his doctorate in Freiburg in 1923; then taught classes at the univs. at Heidelberg (1928–48), Jena (1948–56), and Leipzig (1956–65). In 1967 he received the honorary degree of Doctor of Humane Letters of the Univ. of Chicago. A Festschrift in his honor was publ. on his 60th birthday. He contributed valuable articles to various music journals, mostly on the musical problems of the Middle Ages and the Renaissance, but also on general subjects of musical esthetics; wrote several basic articles for *Die Musik in Geschichte und Gegenwart.* He was also an editor of the collected works of Dufay, Okeghem, and other musicians of their period.

Best, William Thomas, eminent English organist; b. Carlisle, Aug. 13, 1826; d. Liverpool, May 10, 1897. He studied organ in Liverpool; held various posts as a church organist in Liverpool and London. At his numerous concerts he introduced arrangements of symph. works, thus enabling his audiences to hear classical works in musicianly manner at a time when orch. concerts were scarce. His own works, popular in type, though classical in form, included sonatas, preludes, fugues, concert studies, etc. for organ. He publ. *Handel Album* (20 vols.); *Arrangements from the Scores of the Great Masters* (5 vols.); *Modern School for the Organ* (1853); *The Art of Organ Playing* (1870); etc.

Bethune, Thomas Greene (called **"Blind Tom"**), black American pianist and composer; b. Columbus, Ga., May 25, 1849; d. Hoboken, N.J., June 13, 1908. Born blind in slavery, he was purchased, along with his parents (Charity and Mingo Wiggins), by a Colonel Bethune in 1850. His master's wife was a music teacher who fostered his musical talent. At the age of 9 he was "leased" for 3 years to one Perry Oliver, who arranged concert appearances for him throughout the U.S., including a performance at the White House before President Buchanan. Col. Bethune then took full charge of Tom's career, obtaining legal custody and a major part of his earnings. Bethune played in Europe and in America; his programs usually included Bach, Liszt, Chopin, Gottschalk, and his own compositions, mostly impro-

vised character pieces in salon manner, arranged and supplied with appropriate titles by his managers, e.g. *Rainstorm* (1865); *Wellenlänge* (1882; publ. under the pseudonym **François Sexalise**); *Imitation of the Sewing Machine* (1889); *Battle of Manassas* (1894); etc. He also improvised on themes given by members of the audience.

Beversdorf, Thomas, American trombone player and composer; b. Yoakum, Texas, Aug. 8, 1924; d. Bloomington, Ind., Feb. 15, 1981. He studied trombone and baritone horn with his father, a band director; took courses in composition with Kent Kennan, Eric DeLamarter, and Anthony Donato at the Univ. of Texas (B.M., 1945) and with Bernard Rogers at the Eastman School of Music in Rochester, N.Y. (M.M., 1946); later attended a summer course in composition with Honegger and Copland at Tanglewood (1947); also had some lessons with Anis Fuleihan. He was trombone player with the Rochester Phil. (1945–46), the Houston Symph. (1946–48), and the Pittsburgh Symph. (1948–49); had special engagements as first trombonist with the Metropolitan Opera in N.Y., Ballets Russes de Monte Carlo, and Sadler's Wells Ballet in London. He was an instructor at the Univ. of Houston (1946–48); in 1951 joined the faculty of Indiana Univ. in Bloomington as prof. of composition; in 1977 lectured at the Univ. of Guadalajara in Mexico.

Bevin, Elway, Welsh composer and organist; b. c.1554; d. Bristol, Oct. (buried, Oct. 19) 1638. He was a pupil of Tallis; served as organist of the Bristol Cathedral in 1589 and Gentleman Extraordinary of the Chapel Royal in 1605. He published *A Briefe and Short Instruction in the Art of Musicke* (London, 1631); wrote songs; among them, *Hark, Jolly Shepherds* was popular; also composed an anthem, arranged in a canon of 20 voices.

Beyer, Frank Michael, German organist and composer; b. Berlin, March 8, 1928. He received his earliest musical training from his father, a writer and amateur pianist; spent his childhood in Greece, returning to Berlin in 1938. He studied sacred music and organ; took composition lessons with Ernst Pepping (1952–55). In 1960 he was appointed to the faculty of the Berlin Hochschule für Musik. He founded a concert series, "Musica Nova Sacra." As a composer, he applies the techniques of Bach's counterpoint to modern structures in the manner of Anton von Webern, with thematic materials based on secundal formations and the tritone; the rhythmic patterns of his music are greatly diversified; in dynamic coloration, he explores the finest gradations of sound, particularly in pianissimo.

Beyer, Johanna Magdalena, German-American composer and musicologist; b. Leipzig, July 11, 1888; d. New York, Jan. 9, 1944. She studied piano and music theory in Germany. In 1924 she went to America and studied at the David Mannes School in N.Y.; received a teacher's certificate in 1928. She also took private lessons with Dane Rudhyar, Ruth

Crawford, Charles Seeger, and Henry Cowell. She wrote music and several plays for various projects in N.Y. During Cowell's term in San Quentin prison (1937–41), Johanna Beyer acted as his secretary and took care of his scores. Her own compositional style is dissonant counterpoint. She composed much chamber music; among her more interesting works are *4 Pieces for Oboe and Bassoon,* Clarinet Sonata, 4 string quartets, and *3 Songs for Soprano, Piano and Percussion.*

Bezekirsky, Vasili, Russian violinist; b. Moscow, Jan. 26, 1835; d. there, Nov. 8, 1919. He studied violin in Moscow; in 1858 he went to Brussels, where he took violin lessons with Leonard and lessons in composition with Damcke. Returning to Moscow in 1860, he was concertmaster at the Bolshoi Theater (1861–91); from 1882 to 1902 he was prof. at the Moscow Phil. Inst. As a violin virtuoso, he was greatly regarded in Russia. Tchaikovsky wrote about him: "Although not a Czar of the first magnitude, Bezekirsky is brilliant enough on the dim horizon of present violin playing." Bezekirsky was also a composer; he wrote a violin concerto (Moscow, Feb. 26, 1873); contributed cadenzas to the violin concertos of Beethoven and Brahms. He publ. a vol. of reminiscences, *From the Notebook of an Artist* (St. Petersburg, 1910).

Bhatkhande, Vishnu Narayan, eminent Indian musicologist; b. Bombay, Aug. 10, 1860; d. there, Sept. 19, 1936. He studied jurisprudence; concurrently investigated the systems of Indian ragas; while earning a living as a lawyer, he traveled throughout India to collect authentic ragas. In 1910 he abandoned his legal practice and dedicated himself exclusively to Indian folk music. His compilations of ragas are invaluable resources. He publ. *Hindusthāni sangit paddhati* (4 vols., Marathi, 1910–32), *Srimal-laksya saṅgitam* (Bombay, 1910), and *Kramik pustak mālikā* (6 vols., Marathi, 1919–37).

Bianchi, Francesco, Italian composer; b. Cremona, 1752; d. (suicide) London, Nov. 27, 1810. He studied in Naples with Jommelli and Cafaro. He wrote nearly 80 operas, some quite pleasing, but ephemeral. His first opera was *Giulio Sabino* (Cremona, 1772); it was followed by *Il Grand Cidde* (Florence, 1773). From 1775 to 1778 he was in Paris serving as maestro al cembalo at the Comédie Italienne; there he produced his opera *La Réduction de Paris* (Sept. 30, 1775). In 1778 he went to Florence; in 1783 he became 2nd maestro at the Cathedral of Milan, a post he held until 1793; concurrently he worked in Venice from 1785 to 1791, and again from 1793 to 1797, when he served as 2nd organist at San Marco. He subsequently was in Naples, where he produced his most significant opera, *La Vendetta de Nino* (Nov. 12, 1790). In 1794 he went to London, where he officiated as conductor at the King's Theatre (1795–1801); several of his operas were produced there under his supervision. Apart from his operas, he wrote several pieces of instrumental music, and

also publ. a theoretical treatise, *Dell' attrazione armonica,* which was publ. in excerpts, in Eng., in *The Quarterly Musical Magazine and Review* (1820–21). Bianchi was also a successful teacher; among his English pupils was Henry Bishop.

Bibalo, Antonio, Italian-born Norwegian composer; b. Trieste, Jan. 18, 1922, of Slovak descent (his family name was **Bibalitsch**). He studied piano and composition at the Trieste Cons.; during the disruption caused by World War II, he earned his living as a nightclub pianist and a sanitation worker. He was in Australia briefly before going to England in 1953; studied advanced composition with Elisabeth Lutyens in London. In 1956 he went to Norway and became a naturalized citizen.

WORKS: He attracted the attention of the musical world with the production of his opera *The Smile at the Foot of the Ladder* (1958–62), after a short story by Henry Miller; the original libretto was in Italian as *Sorrisi ai piedi d'una scala,* but the production was in German under the name *Das Lächeln am Fusse der Leiter* at the Hamburg State Opera on April 6, 1965. His other works include a chamber opera, *Frøken Julie (Miss Julie),* after Strindberg (Århus, Denmark, Sept. 8, 1975); a ballet, *Pinocchio* (Hamburg, Jan. 17, 1969); a television ballet, *Nocturne for Apollo* (Norwegian Television, 1971); 2 piano concertos: No. 1 (1953; Oslo, Aug. 1, 1972) and No. 2 (1971; Bergen, Norway, April 27, 1972); Piano Sonatina (1953); 2 chamber concertos: No. 1 for Piano and Strings (1954) and No. 2 for Harpsichord, Violin, and Strings (1974); Fantasy for Violin and Orch. (1954; received 3rd prize at the Wieniawski Composer Competition, Warsaw, 1956); *4 Balkan Dances* for Piano or Orch. (1956); *12 Miniatures* for Piano (1956); *Concerto Allegorico* for Violin and Orch. (1957); *3 Hommages* for Piano (1957); Toccata for Piano (1957); *Pitture Astratte* for Orch. (1958); *Elegia per un'era spaziale (Elegy for a Space Age)* for Soprano, Baritone, Chorus, and Instrumental Ensemble (1963); *Sinfonia Notturna* (1968); *Overture,* after Goldoni's "Servant with Two Masters" (1968); *Autumnale,* suite de concert for Piano, Flute, Vibraphone, and Double Bass (1968); 2 sonatinas for Wind Quintet (1971, 1972); String Quartet No. 1 (1973); 2 piano sonatas (1974, 1975); Suite for Orch. (1974); *Games* for Trombone and Flute (1975).

Biber, Heinrich Ignaz Franz von, famous Bohemian violinist and composer; b. Wartenberg, Bohemia, Aug. 12, 1644; d. Salzburg, May 3, 1704. He was in the service of the Emperor Leopold I, who ennobled him on Dec. 5, 1690; he also served at other courts. In 1670 he was a member of the Kapelle at Salzburg; in 1679 he was appointed Vice-Kapellmeister there, and in 1684 became Kapellmeister. He was one of the founders of the German school of violin playing and was among the first to employ the "scordatura," a system of artificial mistuning to facilitate performance. He publ. a number of violin sonatas, several of which were reprinted in David's *Hohe Schule* and in Denkmäler der Tonkunst in

Österreich; composed 2 operas, *Chi la dura la vince* (Salzburg, 1687) and *L'ossequio de Salisburgo* (Salzburg, 1699); several scores of sacred music, including a requiem and numerous choruses.

Biehle, Herbert, German voice teacher and theorist, son and pupil of **Johannes Biehle;** b. Dresden, Feb. 16, 1901. He studied composition with Georg Schumann, and musicology with Johannes Wolf. He became active mainly as a vocal pedagogue. He publ. several monographs dealing with vocal techniques, among them *Die Stimmkunst* (2 vols., Leipzig, 1931); also several informative essays on the role of the "Sprechstimme" in vocal literature, and a monograph dealing with contributions to the science of organ bells, invented by his father.

Biehle, Johannes, German organist; b. Bautzen, June 18, 1870; d. there, Jan. 4, 1941. He studied at the Dresden Cons.; served as music director and organist in Bautzen (1898–1914). He publ. 2 valuable vols. dealing with the acoustics of church and organ building: *Theorie der pneumatischen Orgeltraktur* (Leipzig, 1911) and *Theorie des Kirchenbaues* (Wittenberg, 1913). He was generally regarded as a founder of the modern organ carillon.

Bielawa, Herbert, American composer; b. Chicago, Feb. 3, 1930, of Polish (paternal) and German (maternal) descent. He studied music at home; from 1954 to 1956 served in the U.S. Army in Germany, stationed in Frankfurt, where he also studied conducting with Bruno Vondenhoff. Returning to the U.S., he took courses in piano with Soulima Stravinsky at the Univ. of Illinois (B.M., 1954); enrolled at the Univ. of Southern Calif. in Los Angeles, and took courses in composition with Ingolf Dahl (1960–61), Halsey Stevens (1961–64), and Ellis Kohs (1961–63); also studied music for cinema with Miklós Rosza and David Raksin. In 1966 he was appointed to the faculty of San Francisco State Univ.; in 1967 established there the Electronic Music Studio. In his own music he makes use of the entire field of practical resources, without prejudice.

Bierdiajew, Walerian, Polish conductor; b. Grodno, March 7, 1885; d. Warsaw, Nov. 28, 1956. He studied composition with Max Reger and conducting with Arthur Nikisch at the Leipzig Cons.; began his conducting career in Dresden in 1906; in 1908 became regular conductor at the Maryinsky Opera Theater in St. Petersburg; then conducted in various Russian opera houses; from 1921–25 he lived in Poland; from 1925–30 was again engaged as a conductor in Russia and in the Ukraine. In 1930 he was appointed prof. of conducting at the Warsaw Cons.; in 1947–49 was conductor of the Cracow Phil.; then taught at the Cons. of Poznan (1949–54) and at the Warsaw Cons. (1954–56).

Biggs, E. Power (Edward George Power), eminent concert organist; b. Westcliff, England, March 29, 1906; d. Boston, March 10, 1977. He studied at Hurstpierpoint College (1917–24); then entered the Royal Academy of Music in London, graduating in 1929. In 1930 he came to the U.S. and became naturalized in 1937. He made his N.Y. debut as an organist at the Wanamaker Auditorium in 1932. He was an organist in Newport, R.I. (1929–31); then moved to Cambridge, Mass., where he served as organist at Christ Church, and later became music director of the Harvard Church in Brookline. In the interim he toured Europe, and made a wide survey of old church organs in England, Iceland, Sweden, Norway, Denmark, Germany, the Netherlands, Austria, Italy, and Spain in search of the type of organ that Bach and Handel played. His repertoire consisted mostly of the Baroque masters, but he also commissioned works from American composers, among them Walter Piston, Roy Harris, Howard Hanson, and Quincy Porter; Benjamin Britten also wrote a work for him. Biggs became well known to American music lovers through his weekly broadcasts of organ recitals over the CBS network, which he gave from 1942–58; he continued to give concerts until arthritis forced him to reduce his concert activities, but he was able to continue recording organ music, and he also edited organ works for publication. Biggs refused to perform on electronic organs, which in his opinion vulgarized and distorted the classical organ sound. His own style of performance had a classical austerity inspired by the Baroque school of organ playing.

Bignami, Carlo, renowned Italian violinist; b. Cremona, Dec. 6, 1808; d. Voghera, Oct. 2, 1848. He studied violin with his father and elder brother. He played in theater orchs. in Cremona and Milan; in 1829 he was appointed director of the Teatro Sociale in Mantua; then was in Milan and Verona. Returning to Cremona in 1837 as director and first violinist of the orch., he made it one of the best in Lombardy. Paganini called him "*il primo violinista d'Italia,*" but he may have meant this phrase to express his low opinion of other Italian violinists in comparison. Bignami wrote a number of violin pieces, including a concerto, a *Capriccio, Studi per violino, Grande Adagio, Polacca,* fantasias, variations, etc.

Bigot, Eugène, French conductor; b. Rennes, Feb. 28, 1888; d. Paris, July 17, 1965. He studied violin and piano at the Rennes Cons., and later at the Paris Cons. In 1913 he was named chorus master at the Théâtre des Champs-Elysées; subsequently toured Europe with the Ballets Suédois; also conducted the Paris Cons. Orch. (1923–25); then served as music director at the Théâtre des Champs-Elysées (1925–27). In 1935 he became president and director of the Concerts Lamoureux, a post he held until 1950; also held the post of principal conductor of the Opéra-Comique (1936–47). In 1947 he became chief conductor of the Radio Orch. in Paris, a post he held until his death.

Bigot, Marie (née **Kiéné**), pianist; b. Colmar, Alsace, March 3, 1786; d. Paris, Sept. 16, 1820. After her marriage in 1804, she lived in Vienna, where she was known and esteemed by Haydn and Beethoven; went to Paris in 1808, where she gave piano lessons from 1812 on; Mendelssohn was briefly her pupil in Paris at the age of 7.

Bihari, János, Hungarian violinist; b. Nagyabony (baptized, Oct. 21), 1764; d. Pest, April 26, 1827. He led a Gypsy band in Pest, and improvised violin pieces in a Hungarian manner, which were later notated by an amanuensis (he himself could not read music); in this manner he became a mediator for Hungarian popular music, and his melodies were used as genuine source material by real composers in Hungary.

Bikel, Theodore, Austrian-American singer and actor; b. Vienna, May 2, 1924. After the Anschluss in 1938, he fled with his family to Palestine; then made his way to London, where he studied at the Royal Academy of Dramatic Arts. He subsequently had a fine career as an actor on stage, screen, and television; concurrently established himself as a folksinger; in 1959 he scored a major Broadway success in the role of Georg von Trapp in the Rogers and Hammerstein musical *The Sound of Music.* He became an American citizen in 1961.

Bildstein, Hieronymus, important Austrian organist and composer; b. Bregenz, c.1580; d. c.1626. After studying music in Bregenz, he went to Konstanz, where he was active as court organist. He wrote 25 motets publ. as *Orpheus chritianus seu Symphoniarum sacrarum prodromus, 5–8 vocum cum basso generali* (Regensburg, 1624); publ. in a modern edition in the Denkmäler der Tonkunst in Österreich, CXXII (1971) and CXXVI (1976).

Billings, William, pioneer American composer of hymns and anthems and popularizer of "fuging tunes"; b. Boston, Oct. 7, 1746; d. there, Sept. 26, 1800. A tanner's apprentice, he acquired the rudiments of music from treatises by Tans'ur; he compensated for his lack of education by a wealth of original ideas and a determination to put them into practice. His first musical collection, *The New England Psalm Singer* (Boston, 1770), contained what he described at a later date as "fuging pieces . . . more than twenty times as powerful as the old slow tunes." The technique of these pieces was canonic, with "each part striving for mastery and victory." His other publ. books were: *The Singing Master's Assistant* (1778); *Music in Miniature* (1779); *The Psalm Singer's Amusement* (1781); *The Suffolk Harmony* (1786); and *The Continental Harmony* (1794). In one instance, he harmonized a tune, *Jargon,* entirely in dissonances; this was prefaced by a "Manifesto" to the Goddess of Discord. There was further a choral work, *Modern Music,* in which the proclaimed aim was expressed in the opening lines: "We are met for a concert of modern invention—To tickle the ear is our present intention." Several of his hymns became popular, particularly *Chester* and *The Rose of Sharon;* an interesting historical work was his *Lamentation over Boston,* written in

Watertown while Boston was occupied by the British. However, he could not earn a living by his music; appeals made to provide him and his large family with funds bore little fruit, and Billings died in abject poverty. The combination of reverence and solemnity with humor makes the songs of Billings unique in the annals of American music, and aroused the curiosity of many modern American musicians; Henry Cowell wrote a series of "fuging tunes" for Orch.

Billington, Elizabeth (née **Weichsel**), famous English soprano; b. London, Dec. 27, 1765; d. near Venice, Aug. 25, 1818. Her mother, a singer, was a pupil of Johann Christian Bach; Elizabeth, too, had some lessons with him. She received her early musical training from her father, a German oboist. She also studied with James Billington, a double-bass player by profession, whom she married on Oct. 13, 1783. Her operatic debut took place in Dublin (1784), as Eurydice in Gluck's opera; she went to London, where she appeared as Rosetta in *Love in a Village* at Covent Garden on Feb. 13, 1786. Her success was immediate; she was reengaged at Covent Garden and also sang at the Concerts of Antient Music in London. Her career was briefly disrupted by the publication, in 1792, of anonymous *Memoirs* attacking her private life. This was immediately followed by an equally anonymous rebuttal, "written by a gentleman," defending her reputation. In 1794 she went to Italy, where she sang for the King of Naples. He made arrangements for her appearances at the San Carlo, where she performed in operas by Bianchi, Paisiello, Paer, and Himmel, all written specially for her. Her husband died in 1794; she remained in Italy for 2 more years; then lived in France, where she married M. Felissent. Returning to London in 1801, she sang alternately at Drury Lane and Covent Garden, with great acclaim, at 4,000 guineas a season. This period was the peak of her success. She retired in 1809, except for occasional performances. After a temporary separation from Felissent, she returned to him in 1817; they settled at their estate at St. Artien, near Venice.

Billroth, Theodor, eminent surgeon and amateur musician; b. Bergen, on the island of Rügen, April 26, 1829; d. Abazzia, Feb. 6, 1894. He received a thorough musical education; was an intimate friend of Hanslick and Brahms; the musical soirees at his home in Vienna were famous. Almost all the chamber music of Brahms was played there (with Billroth as violist) before a public performance. He wrote the treatise *Wer ist musikalisch?* (1896, ed. by Hanslick). Billroth originated 2 crucial intestinal surgical operations, known in medical literature as Billroth I and Billroth II.

Bilson, Malcolm, American pianist; b. Los Angeles, Oct. 24, 1935. He studied at the Vienna Academy of Music and at the Ecole Normale de Musique in Paris; subsequently received a Doctor of Musical Arts degree from the Univ. of Illinois at Urbana. In his concerts he revived the use of the fortepiano, performing on original instruments of the 18th century and modern replicas. In 1968 he became a prof. at Cornell Univ.

Bimboni, Alberto, Italian-American pianist and composer; b. Florence, Aug. 24, 1882; d. New York, June 18, 1960. He studied in Florence; came to the U.S. in 1912 as an opera conductor. In 1930 he was appointed to the faculty of the Curtis Inst. in Philadelphia; taught opera classes at the Juilliard School of Music in N.Y. from 1933; appeared as a pianist in concerts with Ysaÿe, John McCormack, and other celebrated artists. He wrote the operas *Winona* (Portland, Oregon, Nov. 11, 1926); *Karina* (Minneapolis, 1928); *Il Cancelleto d'oro* (N.Y., March 11, 1936); *In the Name of Culture* (Rochester, N.Y., May 9, 1949); numerous songs (many of them publ.).

Binchois (de Binche), Gilles, Burgundian composer; b. Mons in Hainaut, c.1400; d. Soignies, near Mons, Sept. 20, 1460. His father was Jean de Binche, counselor to 2 rulers of Hainaut. Binchois was in the service of William de la Pole, Earl of Suffolk, in Paris (1424). From 1430 he was at the Burgundian court; advanced from 5th to 2nd chaplain; probably visited Italy at some time. Tinctoris considered him the equal of Dunstable and Dufay. He is best known for his secular works; his chansons rank with the finest. Modern reprints of his works are contained in: J. Marix, *Les Musiciens de la cour de Bourgogne au XVe siècle* (1937); L. Feininger, ed., *Documenta polyphoniae liturgicae Sanctae Ecclesiae Romanae,* Ser. I (1947); W. Gurlitt, ed., *Gilles Binchois, 16 weltliche Lieder zu 3 Stimmen,* in *Das Chorwerk,* 22; J. Stainer, ed., *Dufay and His Contemporaries* (1898); Denkmäler der Tonkunst in Österreich (vols. 14/15, 22, 61; formerly 7, 11.i, 31); A.W. Ambros, *Geschichte der Musik,* vol. II (1862–78, 1882); E. Droz and G. Thibault, eds., *Poètes et musiciens du XVe siècle* (1924); A. Schering, ed., *Geschichte der Musik in Beispielen* (Leipzig, 1931; reprinted N.Y., 1950); E. Droz, G. Thibault, and Y. Rokseth, eds., *Trois Chansonniers français du XVe siècle* (1927); H. Besseler, *Die Musik des Mittelalters und der Renaissance,* in Bücken's Handbuch series (1931); C. van den Borren, ed., *Polyphonia Sacra: A Continental Miscellany of the Fifteenth Century* (1932); O. Dischner, ed., *Kammermusik des Mittelalters. Chansons der 1. und 2. niederländischen Schule für drei bis vier Streichinstrumenten herausgegeben* (1927); A. Davison and W. Apel, eds., *Historical Anthology of Music,* vol. I (Cambridge, Mass., 1950); H.E. Wooldridge, *Oxford History of Music,* vol. II (1932); C. Parrish and J.F. Ohl, *Masterpieces of Music before 1750* (N.Y., 1951); G. de Van, "A Recently Discovered Source of Early Fifteenth Century Polyphonic Music, The Aosta Manuscript," *Musica Disciplina,* II (1948); J. Wolf, *Geschichte der Mensural-Notation von 1250–1460,* III (1904); J. Wolf, ed., *Music of Earlier Times* (1946); *Die Chansons von Gilles Binchois,* in *Musikalische Denkmäler,* 2.

Binet, Jean, Swiss composer; b. Geneva, Oct. 17, 1893; d. Trélex, Feb. 24, 1960. He studied academic subjects at the Univ. of Geneva, and simultaneously obtained a diploma from the Institut Jaques-Dalcroze; then took lessons in musicology and composition with Otto Barblan, William Montillet, and Templeton Strong. In 1919 he went to America, where he organized the first school of Dalcroze eurhythmics, and also took lessons with Ernest Bloch. In 1921 he was instrumental in founding, with Bloch, the Cleveland Cons. In 1923 he returned to Europe, and lived in Brussels, where he taught the Dalcroze method. In 1929 he went back to Switzerland, and settled in Trélex. Many of his works are based on Swiss national folk songs. Binet's musical idiom is determined by pragmatic considerations of performance and does not transcend the natural borders of traditional harmonies.

WORKS: Primarily interested in the musical theater, he wrote 6 operettas and radiophonic cantatas; ballets; *L'Ile enchantée* (Zürich, 1947); *Le Printemps* (1950); *La Colline* for 5 Narrators and Orch. (1957); also several scores of incidental music for plays of Sophocles, Shakespeare, and contemporary writers. Other works include a number of sacred and secular choruses; songs with orch. accompaniment; String Quartet (1927); *Divertissement* for Violin and Orch. (1934); Sonatina for Flute and Piano (1942); *6 pièces* for Flute Solo (1947); *Petit concert* for Clarinet and String Orch. (1950); *Variations sur un chant de Noël* for Bassoon and Piano (1957); *3 Dialogues* for 2 Flutes (1957); educational pieces for piano; also harmonizations of popular melodies for chorus.

Bing, Sir Rudolf, international operatic impresario; b. Vienna, Jan. 9, 1902. He studied at the Univ. of Vienna; took singing lessons; then entered the managerial field in opera. After filling various positions with German agencies, he went to England in 1934; became a British subject in 1946. He was one of the most active organizers of the Edinburgh Festivals, and was their music director from 1947 to 1950. In 1950 he was appointed general manager of the Metropolitan Opera in N.Y., inaugurating one of the most eventful and, at times, turbulent periods in the history of the Metropolitan; his controversial dealings with prima donnas were legendary. He resigned in 1972; published an entertaining summary of his managerial experiences in a volume entitled *5,000 Nights at the Opera* (N.Y., 1972) and in his memoir, *A Knight at the Opera* (N.Y., 1981). In 1971 Queen Elizabeth II of England conferred on him the title of Knight Commander of the Order of the British Empire.

Bingham, Seth, American organist and composer; b. Bloomfield, N.J., April 16, 1882; d. New York, June 21, 1972. He studied with Horatio Parker; later in Paris with d'Indy, Widor (composition), and Guilmant (organ). Returning to America, he graduated from Yale Univ. (B.A., 1904); took his M.B. at Yale in 1908, and taught there until 1919; was an instructor and associate prof. at Columbia Univ. until 1954.

WORKS: *Wall Street Fantasy* (1912; perf. as *Symphonic Fantasy* by the N.Y. Phil., Feb. 6, 1916); *La*

Charelzenn, opera (1917); *Tame Animal Tunes* for 18 Instruments (1918); *Memories of France,* orch. suite (1920); *Wilderness Stone* for Narrator, Soli, Chorus, and Orch. (1933); Concerto for Organ and Orch. (Rochester, Oct. 24, 1946); *Connecticut Suite* for Organ and Strings (Hartford, March 26, 1954); Concerto for Brass, Snare Drum, and Organ (Minneapolis, July 12, 1954). Among his compositions for Organ, the following have been frequently performed: *Suite* (1926); *Pioneer America* (1928); *Harmonies of Florence* (1929); *Carillon de Château-Thierry* (1936); *Pastoral Psalms* (1938); *12 Hymn-Preludes* (1942); *Variation Studies* (1950); *36 Hymn and Carol Canons* (1952).

Biordi, Giovanni, Italian composer; b. Rome, 1691; d. there, March 11, 1748. He was maestro di cappella at Tivoli Cathedral (1714–16); in 1717 he became a chapel singer to the Pope. He was named maestro di cappella at the church of S. Giacomo degli Spagnuoli in Rome in 1722, and remained in this post until his death. He also was a voice teacher at the Papal College from 1724; was named secretary (1730) and then chamberlain (1737) of the Sistine Chapel. He composed many sacred works.

Birchard, Clarence C., American music publisher; b. Cambridge Springs, Pa., July 13, 1866; d. Carlisle, Mass., Feb. 27, 1946. He established his firm in Boston in 1901 and specialized in educational books for public schools; of these, a 10-book series, *A Singing School,* introduced lavish profusion of color in design and illustration; the firm has also issued community songbooks, of which the most popular is *Twice 55 Community Songs* (several million copies sold). The catalogue includes orch. scores by many American composers (Berezowsky, Bloch, Converse, Hadley, Ives, Janssen, Josten, Kelley, Loeffler, Mason, Morris, Shepherd, and Sowerby); cantatas by Cadman, Converse, Hanson, Rogers, and Whithorne; and Copland's school opera, *Second Hurricane.* After Birchard's death, Thomas M. Moran succeeded to the presidency of the firm; after Moran's death in 1949, Donald F. Malin became president. The firm publishes a house organ, *The Birchard Broadsheet.*

Bird, Arthur, American composer; b. Belmont, Mass., July 23, 1856; d. Berlin, Dec. 22, 1923. He studied in Berlin with Loeschhorn; spent several months with Liszt at Weimar in 1885; returned to America briefly in 1886, and then lived in Berlin, identifying himself with conservative circles there. He was the Berlin correspondent for American music magazines; in his articles he violently attacked Richard Strauss and other modern composers. Among his own works is a Symph.; *2 Decimettes* for Wind Instruments (won a Paderewski prize in 1901); a comic opera, *Daphne* (N.Y., Dec. 13, 1897); and many piano pieces.

Bird, Henry Richard, eminent English organist; b. Walthamstow, Nov. 14, 1842; d. London, Nov. 21, 1915. He was a pupil of his father; then studied with James Turle; came to London in 1859, where he held various positions as organist, and conducted the Chelsea Choral and Orch. Society; was appointed organist at St. Mary Abbott's in Kensington, and occupied this post until his death; was also a prof. of piano at the Royal College of Music and at Trinity College from 1896. He was famous throughout England as an unexcelled accompanist, and was in constant demand by the foremost artists.

Birkenstock, Johann Adam, German violinist and composer; b. Alsfeld, Feb. 19, 1687; d. Eisenach, Feb. 26, 1733. He studied in Kassel with Ruggiero Fedeli; then in Berlin with Volumier and in Bayreuth with Fiorelli; was employed in the Kassel Court Orch. (1709–30); in 1730 went to Eisenach, where he served as Kapellmeister. His sonatas for violin with basso continuo (Amsterdam, 1722) are included in several anthologies.

Birnie, Tessa, New Zealand pianist and conductor; b. Ashburton, July 19, 1934. She studied piano with Paul Schramm in Wellington; then went to Europe and took lessons with Lefebure in Paris and K.U. Schnabel in Como; subsequently toured as a pianist in Australia and Asia; also played in the U.S. She organized the Sydney Camerata Orch. in 1963, appearing with it as both pianist and conductor.

Birtwistle, Harrison, noted English composer; b. Accrington, Lancashire, July 15, 1934. He studied clarinet; won a scholarship in 1952 to the Royal Manchester College of Music, where he studied composition; also studied clarinet playing with Kell at the Royal Academy of Music in London. In 1966 he was visiting prof. at Princeton Univ.; in 1975 he became music director at the National Theatre, South Bank, London. In his compositions he departed completely from the folkloric trends popular in British modern music and adopted an abstract idiom, often with satirical overtones in his stage works.

WORKS: *Refrains and Choruses* for Wind Quintet (1957); *Monody for Corpus Christi* for Soprano Solo, Flute, Violin, and Horn (1959); *Précis* for Piano Solo (1959); *The World Is Discovered,* Instrumental motet (1960; Festival of the International Society for Contemporary Music, Copenhagen, June 2, 1964); *Chorales* for Orch. (1963); *Narration: The Description of the Passing of a Year* for a cappella Choir (1964); *3 Movements with Fanfares* for Chamber Orch. (1964); *Ring a Dumb Carillon* for Soprano, Clarinet, and Percussion (1965); *Verses* for Clarinet and Piano (1965); *Tragoedia* for Wind Quintet, Harp, and String Quartet (1965); *Carmen paschale* for Chorus and Organ (1965); *The Visions of Francesco Petrarca,* 7 sonnets for Baritone, Chamber Ensemble, and School Orch. (1966); *Punch and Judy,* chamber opera (1966–67; Aldeburgh Festival, June 8, 1968; revised version, London, March 3, 1970); *Monodrama* for Speaker and Instrumental Ensemble (London, May 30, 1967); *Nomos* for 4 Amplified Wind Instruments and Orch. (London, Aug. 23, 1968); *Linoi* for Clarinet and Piano (1968); *Down by the Greenwood Side,* dramatic pastorale (1968; Brighton, May 8, 1969); *Medusa* for Chamber Orch. and Percussion (London, Oct. 22, 1969; revised version, London, March 3, 1970); *4 Interludes* for Clarinet and Pre-recorded Tape (1970); *Verses and Ensembles* for 12 Players (London, Aug. 31, 1970); *Nenia on the Death of Orpheus* for Soprano and Instrumental Ensemble (1970); *The Triumph of Time* for Orch., after a painting of Breughel (1970; London, June 1, 1972); *Meridian* for Mezzo-soprano, Chorus, and an Instrumental Ensemble (1971); *Prologue to Agamemnon* by Aeschylus, for Tenor, Bassoon, Horn, 3 Trumpets, Trombone, Violin, and Double Bass (1971); *Chronometer* for 8-track Electronic Tapes (1971); *The Fields of Sorrow* for 2 Sopranos, Mixed Choir, and Instrumental Ensemble (1971); *An Imaginary Landscape* for Brass, Percussion, and 8 Double Basses (1971); *Epilogue: Full Fathom Five* for Tenor, Brass, and Percussion (1972); *La Plage,* 8 Arias of Remembrance for Soprano, 3 Clarinets, Piano, and Marimba (1972); *Tombeau,* in memory of Stravinsky (1972); *Grimethorpe Aria* for Brass Band (1973); *Orpheus,* opera (1974–77); *Melancholia I* for Clarinet, Harp, and 2 String Orchs. (1976); *Silbury Air* for Woodwind Quartet, Trumpet, Horn, Trombone, String Quintet, Piano, Harp, and Percussion (1977); *Frames, Pulses and Interruptions,* ballet (1977); *Bow Down,* musical theater (London, July 4, 1977); *For O, for O the Hobby Horse Is Forgot* for 6 Percussion Players (1977); *Carmen Arcadiae Mechanicae Perpetuum* for Instrumental Ensemble (1977); *Aventures des Mercures* for Instrumental Ensemble (1980); *On the Sheer Threshold of the Night,* madrigal (1980).

Bischoff, Hermann, German composer; b. Duisburg, Jan. 7, 1868; d. Berlin, Jan. 25, 1936. He was a pupil of Jadassohn at the Leipzig Cons.; lived for a time in Munich, where he was associated with Richard Strauss; then went to Berlin. He composed 2 symphs.; the First Symph. had its world premiere in Essen, May 24, 1906; was given by the Boston Symph. under Karl Muck twice in one season (Jan. 4, 1908, and Feb. 29, 1908); attracted a great deal of attention at the time, but sank into oblivion later on. He also composed the symph. poems *Pan* and *Gewittersegen;* publ. an essay, *Das deutsche Lied* (1905).

Bischoff, Marie. See **Brandt, Marianne.**

Bishop, Anna, English soprano; b. London, Jan. 9, 1810; d. New York, March 18, 1884. She was of French descent (her maiden name was **Rivière**). She studied at the Royal Academy of Music in London; in 1831 she married **Henry Bishop.** She made her London debut on April 20, 1831. In 1839 she appeared in concerts with the French harpist Bochsa, with whom she apparently became intimate. In 1847 she went to America; she obtained a divorce in 1858 and married Martin Schultz. In 1866 she toured China and Australia; the ship she was on became grounded on a coral reef in the Marianas for 21 days, but despite this experience she completed her tour,

eventually returning to N.Y.

Bishop, Sir Henry Rowley, noted English composer; b. London, Nov. 18, 1786; d. there, April 30, 1855. He was a pupil of Francesco Bianchi; attracted attention with his first opera, *The Circassian Bride* (Drury Lane, Feb. 23, 1809); from 1810–24, was conductor at Covent Garden; in 1813 was alternate conductor of the Phil.; in 1819 oratorio conductor at Covent Garden; in 1825 conductor at the Drury Lane Theatre; in 1830 music director at Vauxhall; took the degree of B.Mus. at Oxford (1839); from 1840 was music director at Covent Garden; then prof. of music at Edinburgh (1841–43); was knighted in 1842; conducted the Concerts of Antient Music in 1840–48; was then appointed (succeeding Dr. Crotch) prof. of music at Oxford, where he received the degree of D.Mus. in 1853. He was a remarkably prolific dramatic composer, having produced about 130 operas, farces, ballets, adaptations, etc. His operas are generally in the style of English ballad opera; some of the best are: *Cortez, or The Conquest of Mexico* (1823); *The Fall of Algiers* (1825); *The Knight of Snowdoun* (after Walter Scott, 1811); *Native Land* (1824). His *Clari, or The Maid of Milan* (Covent Garden, May 3, 1823) contains the famous song *Home Sweet Home,* with text by the American John Howard Payne; it appears repeatedly throughout the opera. The tune, previously publ. by Bishop to other words, was thought to have been of Sicilian origin, but after much litigation was accepted as Bishop's original composition (the MS is owned by the Univ. of Rochester in N.Y.). A version of the melody was used by Donizetti in his opera *Anne Boleyn,* giving rise to the erroneous belief that Donizetti was its composer. Bishop also wrote an oratorio, *The Fallen Angel;* a cantata, *The Seventh Day* (1834); many additions to revivals of older operas, etc.; his glees and other lyric vocal compositions are deservedly esteemed. Bishop also publ. vol. I of *Melodies of Various Nations;* and 3 vols. of *National Melodies,* to which Moore wrote the poems.

Bismillah Khan, Indian virtuoso on the shehnai; b. Dumraon, March 21, 1916. He studied instrumental and vocal music; earned great renown in India; appeared as soloist at the Commonwealth Arts Festival in London in 1965.

Bispham, David (Scull), American baritone; b. Philadelphia, Jan. 5, 1857; d. New York, Oct. 2, 1921. He first sang as an amateur in church choruses in Philadelphia; in 1886 went to Milan, where he studied with Vannuccini, and Francesco Lamperti; later studied in London with Shakespeare and Randegger; made his operatic debut as Longueville in Messager's *Basoche* (English Opera House, London, Nov. 3, 1891), in which his comic acting ability, as well as his singing, won praise; made his first appearance in serious opera as Kurwenal in *Tristan und Isolde* (Drury Lane, June 25, 1892). He was particularly effective in the Wagnerian baritone roles; made his American debut with the Metropolitan Opera as Beckmesser (Nov. 18, 1896); was on the

Metropolitan roster 1896–97, 1898–99, and 1900–1903. He was a strong advocate of opera in English; a Society of American Singers was organized under his guidance, presenting light operas in the English language. He publ. an autobiography, *A Quaker Singer's Recollections* (N.Y., 1920). A Bispham Memorial Medal Award was established by the Opera Society of America in 1921 for an opera in English by an American composer; among its winners were Walter Damrosch, Victor Herbert, Henry Hadley, Deems Taylor, Charles Cadman, Louis Gruenberg, Howard Hanson, Otto Luening, Ernst Bacon, George Antheil, and George Gershwin. Bispham left all the biographical and bibliographical material connected with his career to the Music Division of the N.Y. Public Library.

Bittner, Julius, Austrian composer; b. Vienna, April 9, 1874; d. there, Jan. 9, 1939. He first studied law; then music with Bruno Walter and Josef Labor; was a magistrate in Vienna until 1920. At the same time he composed industriously. He devoted most of his energy to opera and also wrote his own librettos; composed 2 symphs., sacred choruses, and numerous songs for his wife, Emilie Bittner, a contralto. During his last years, he suffered from a crippling illness, necessitating the amputation of both legs. WORKS: Operas: *Die rote Gret* (Frankfurt, Oct. 26, 1907); *Der Musikant* (Vienna, April 12, 1910); *Der Bergsee* (Vienna, Nov. 9, 1911; revised 1938); *Der Abenteurer* (Cologne, Oct. 30, 1913); *Das höllisch Gold* (Darmstadt, Oct. 15, 1916); *Das Rosengärtlein* (Mannheim, March 18, 1923); *Mondnacht* (Berlin, Nov. 13, 1928); *Das Veilchen* (Vienna, Dec. 8, 1934); also operettas, ballets, and mimodramas.

Bizet, Georges (baptismal names, **Alexandre-César-Léopold**), great French opera composer; b. Paris, Oct. 25, 1838; d. Bougival, June 3, 1875. His parents were both professional musicians: his father, a singing teacher and composer; his mother, an excellent pianist. Bizet's talent developed early in childhood; at the age of 9 he entered the Paris Cons., his teachers being Marmontel (piano), Benoist (organ), Zimmermann (harmony), and (for composition), Halévy, whose daughter, Geneviève, married Bizet in 1869. In 1852 he won a first prize for piano, in 1855 for organ and for fugue, and in 1857 the Grand Prix de Rome. In the same year he shared (with Lecocq) a prize offered by Offenbach for a setting of a one-act opera, *Le Docteur miracle;* Bizet's setting was produced at the Bouffes-Parisiens on April 9, 1857. Instead of the prescribed Mass, he sent from Rome during his first year a 2-act Italian opera buffa, *Don Procopio* (not produced until March 10, 1906, when it was given in Monte Carlo in an incongruously edited version); later he sent 2 movements of a symph., an overture (*La Chasse d'Ossian*), and a one-act opera (*La Guzla de l'Emir;* accepted by the Paris Opéra-Comique, but withdrawn by Bizet prior to production). Returning to Paris, he produced a grand opera, *Les Pêcheurs de perles* (Théâtre-Lyrique, Sept. 30, 1863); but this work, like *La Jolie Fille de Perth* (Dec. 26, 1867), failed to win popular

approval. A one-act opera, *Djamileh* (Opéra-Comique, May 22, 1872), fared no better. Bizet's incidental music for Daudet's play *L'Arlésienne* (Oct. 1, 1872) was ignored by the audiences and literary critics; it was not fully appreciated until its revival in 1885. But an orch. suite from *L'Arlésienne* brought out by Pasdeloup (Nov. 10, 1872) was acclaimed; a 2nd suite was made by Guiraud after Bizet's death. Bizet's next major work was his masterpiece, *Carmen* (based on a tale by Mérimée, text by Halévy and Meilhac), produced, after many difficulties with the management and the cast, at the Opéra-Comique (March 3, 1875). The reception of the public was not enthusiastic, and several critics attacked the opera for its lurid subject, and the music for its supposed adoption of Wagner's methods. Bizet received a generous sum (25,000 francs) for the score from the publisher Choudens and won other honors (he was named a Chevalier of the Légion d'Honneur on the eve of the premiere of *Carmen*); although the attendance was not high, the opera was maintained in the repertoire. There were 37 performances before the end of the season; the original cast included Galli-Marie as Carmen, Lhérie as Don José, and Bouhy as Escamillo. Bizet was chagrined by the controversial reception of the opera, but it is a melodramatic invention to state (as some biographers have done) that the alleged failure of *Carmen* precipitated the composer's death (he died on the night of the 31st perf. of the opera). Soon *Carmen* became a triumphant success all over the world; it was staged in London (in Italian at Her Majesty's Theatre, June 22, 1878), St. Petersburg, Vienna, Brussels, Naples, Florence, Mainz, N.Y. (Academy of Music, Oct. 23, 1878), etc. The Metropolitan Opera produced *Carmen* first in Italian (Jan. 9, 1884), then in French, with Calvé as Carmen (Dec. 20, 1893). It should be pointed out that the famous *Habanera* is not Bizet's own, but a melody by the Spanish composer Yradier; Bizet inserted it in *Carmen* (with slight alterations), mistaking it for a folk song. Bizet also wrote an operetta, *La Prêtresse* (1854); the operas *Numa* (1871) and *Ivan le Terrible,* in 4 acts (Bordeaux, Oct. 12, 1951; the score was believed to have been destroyed by Bizet, but was discovered among the manuscripts bequeathed to the Paris Cons. by the 2nd husband of Bizet's widow); the cantatas *David* (1856) and *Clovis et Clothilde* (1857); *Vasco da Gama,* symph. ode with Chorus (1859); *Souvenirs de Rome,* symph. suite in 3 movements (Paris, Feb. 28, 1869; publ. in 1880 as a 4-movement suite, *Roma*); orch. overture, *Patrie* (Paris, Feb. 15, 1874); *Jeux d'enfants* (suite for Piano, 4-hands); about 150 piano pieces of all kinds (Bizet was a brilliant pianist); etc. Bizet's First Symph., written at the age of 17, was discovered in the Bizet collection at the Paris Cons. in 1933, and was given its first performance anywhere by Felix Weingartner in Basel on Feb. 26, 1935; it rapidly became popular in the concert repertoire. Bizet also completed Halévy's biblical opera, *Noë* (1869).

Björkander, Nils (Frank Frederik), Swedish composer; b. Stockholm, June 28, 1893; d. Soedertälje,

March 5, 1972. He studied at the Stockholm Cons.; in 1917 he established a music school of his own. Some of his piano pieces achieved considerable popularity, especially *Fyra Skärgårdsskisser* (*4 Sketches from the Skerries;* 1923); he also wrote *Concert-Fantasy* for Piano and Orch.; *Cavatina* for Violin and Orch.; Piano Quintet; Flute Sonata; Violin Sonata; etc.

Björling, Jussi (baptismal names, **Johan Jonatan**), eminent Swedish tenor; b. Stora Tuna, Feb. 5, 1911; d. Siarö, near Stockholm, Sept. 9, 1960. He studied singing with his father, a professional singer; made his first public appearance in 1916 as a member of the vocal Björling Male Quartet, which included his father, David Björling (1873–1926), and 2 other brothers, Johan Olof "Olle" (1909–65) and Karl Gustaf "Gösta" (1912–57), both of whom pursued careers as singers; another brother, Karl David "Kalle" (1917–75), was also a singer. The Björling Male Quartet gave concerts throughout Sweden (1916–19); made an extensive tour of the U.S. (1919–21); then continued to sing in Sweden until 1926. Jussi Björling had an excellent professional training with John Forsell at the Royal Academy of Music in Stockholm. He made his operatic debut as the Lamplighter in *Manon Lescaut* at the Royal Theater in Stockholm on July 21, 1930, and remained there until 1939; also sang as a guest artist with the Vienna State Opera, the Dresden State Opera, and at the Salzburg Festival. He made his professional U.S. debut in a concert broadcast from Carnegie Hall in N.Y. on Nov. 28, 1937, and his first appearance with the Metropolitan Opera as Rodolfo in *La Bohème* on Nov. 24, 1938; continued to sing there until 1941, when his career was interrupted by war. He resumed his appearances at the Metropolitan Opera in 1945 and sang there until 1954, and then again in 1956–57 and 1959. On March 15, 1960, he suffered a heart attack as he was preparing to sing the role of Rodolfo at the Royal Opera House, Covent Garden, London, but in spite of his great discomfort, went through with the performance. He appeared for the last time at a concert in Stockholm on Aug. 20, 1960. Björling was highly regarded for his fine vocal technique and his sense of style. He excelled in the Italian and French roles, and also essayed some Russian operas. He wrote an autobiography, *Med bagaget i strupen* (Stockholm, 1945). The Jussi Björling Memorial Archive was founded in 1968 to perpetuate his memory.

Björling, Sigurd, Swedish baritone; b. Stockholm, Nov. 2, 1907; d. Helsingborg, April 8, 1983. He studied at the Royal Cons. in Stockholm, made his debut in 1930 at the Royal Theater there; also had guest appearances at La Scala in Milan, Covent Garden in London, and in Paris. In 1951 he sang at the Bayreuth Festival; on Nov. 15, 1952, he made his Metropolitan Opera debut in N.Y. as Telramund in *Lohengrin;* then returned to Sweden. He was no relation to his famous namesake Jussi Björling.

Björnsson, Árni, Icelandic composer; b. Loni i Kel-duhverfi, Dec. 23, 1905. He studied theory, composition, piano, and organ at the Reykjavik College of Music; later went to England, where he enrolled at the Royal Manchester College of Music; subsequently returned to Reykjavik, where he was appointed to the faculty of the College of Music. He composed orch. pieces and much choral music in a general Romantic vein.

Blacher, Boris, remarkable German composer; b. Newchwang, China (of half-German, quarter-Russian, and quarter-Jewish ancestry), Jan. 19 (Jan. 6 according to the Russian old-style calendar), 1903; d. Berlin, Jan. 30, 1975. His family moved to Irkutsk, Siberia, in 1914, remaining there until 1920. In 1922 Blacher went to Berlin; studied architecture, and then took a course in composition with F.E. Koch. From 1948 until 1970 he was prof. at the Hochschule für Musik in West Berlin, and from 1953 to 1970 served as its director. An exceptionally prolific composer, Blacher was equally adept in classical forms and in experimental procedures. He initiated a system of "variable meters," with time signatures following the arithmetical progression, alternatively increasing and decreasing, with permutations contributing to metrical variety. For the theater he developed a sui generis "abstract opera," incorporating an element of organized improvisation. In 1960 he was appointed director of the Seminar of Electronic Composition at the Technological Univ. in Berlin, and subsequently made ample use of electronic resources in his own compositions.

WORKS: OPERAS: *Habemeajaja* (1929; not extant); *Fürstin Tarakanowa* (1940; Wuppertal, Feb. 5, 1941); *Romeo und Julia,* after Shakespeare (1943; Berlin Radio, 1947); *Die Flut* (1946; Berlin Radio, Dec. 20, 1946; stage premiere, Dresden, March 4, 1947); *Die Nachtschwalbe (The Night Swallow),* "dramatic nocturne" (Leipzig, Feb. 22, 1948; aroused considerable commotion because of its subject, dealing with prostitutes and pimps); *Preussisches Märchen,* ballet-opera (1949; Berlin, Sept. 23, 1952); *Abstrakte Oper* No. 1 (text by Werner Egk, 1953; Frankfurt Radio, June 28, 1953; stage premiere, Mannheim, Oct. 17, 1953; revised version, Berlin, Sept. 30, 1957); *Rosamunde Floris* (1960; Berlin, Sept. 21, 1960); *Zwischenfälle bie einer Notlandung (Incidents at a Forced Landing),* "reportage in 2 phases and 14 situations" for Singers, Instruments, and Electronic Devices (1965; Hamburg, Feb. 4, 1966); *200,000 Taler,* after Sholom Aleichem (1969; Berlin, Sept. 25, 1969); *Yvonne, Prinzessin von Burgund* (1972; Wuppertal, Sept. 15, 1973); *Das Geheimnis des entwendeten Briefes,* after *The Purloined Letter* by Edgar Allan Poe (1974; Berlin, Feb. 14, 1975).

BALLETS: *Fest im Süden* (1935; Kassel, Feb. 4, 1935); *Harlekinade* (1939; Krefeld, Feb. 14, 1940); *Das Zauberbuch von Erzerum* (1941; Stuttgart, Oct. 17, 1942; revised, 1950, as *Der erste Ball;* Berlin, June 11, 1950); *Chiarina* (1946; Berlin, Jan. 22, 1950); *Hamlet* (1949; Munich, Nov. 19, 1950); *Lysistrata* (1950; Berlin, Jan. 22, 1951); *Der Mohr von Venedig,* after Shakespeare (1955; Vienna, Nov. 29, 1955);

Demeter (1963; Schwetzingen, June 4, 1964); *Tristan* (1965; Berlin, Oct. 10, 1965); incidental music for *Romeo and Juliet* (1951), *Lulu,* after Wedekind (1952), Molière's *Georges Dandin* (1955), *War and Peace,* after Tolstoy (1955), *Robespierre,* after Romain Rolland (1963), *Henry IV,* after Shakespeare (1970).

FOR ORCH.: Concerto for 2 Trumpets and 2 String Orchs. (1931); *Kleine Marchmusik* (1932; Berlin, Nov. 22, 1932); *Capriccio* (1933; Hamburg, May 14, 1935); Piano Concerto (1935; Stuttgart, Nov. 13, 1935); Divertimento for Wind Instruments (1936; Berlin, Feb. 24, 1937); *Geigenmusik* for Violin and Orch. (1936); *Concertante Musik* (1937; Berlin, Dec. 6, 1937); Symphony (1938; Berlin, Feb. 5, 1939); Concerto da camera for 2 Violins, Solo Cello, and String Orch. (1939); *Hamlet,* symph. poem (1940; Berlin, Oct. 28, 1940); Concerto for String Orch. (1940; Hamburg, Oct. 18, 1942); Partita for String Orch. and Percussion (1945); 16 Variations on a Theme of Paganini (1947; Leipzig, Nov. 27, 1947); Concerto for Jazz Orch. (1947); Piano Concerto No. 1 (1947; Göttingen, March 20, 1948); Violin Concerto (1948; Munich, Nov. 17, 1950); Concerto for Clarinet, Bassoon, Horn, Trumpet, Harp, and Strings (1950; Berlin, June 14, 1950); *Dialog* for Flute, Violin, Piano, and Strings (1950); Piano Concerto No. 2 (1952; Berlin, Sept. 15, 1952); *Orchester-Ornament,* based on "variable meters" (1953; Venice Festival, Sept. 15, 1953); *Studie im Pianissimo* (1953; Louisville, Kentucky, Sept. 4, 1954); *Zwei Inventionen* (1954; Edinburgh Festival, Aug. 28, 1954); Viola Concerto (1954; Cologne, March 14, 1955); *Orchester-Fantasie* (1955; London, Oct. 12, 1956); *Hommage à Mozart* (1956; Berlin, Dec. 10, 1956); *Music for Cleveland* (1957; Cleveland, Nov. 21, 1957); *Musica giocosa* (1959; Saarbrücken; April 30, 1959); Variations on a Theme of Muzio Clementi, for Piano and Orch. (1961; Berlin, Oct. 4, 1961); *Konzertstück* for Wind Quintet and Strings (1963; Donaueschingen, Oct. 19, 1963); Cello Concerto (1964; Cologne, March 19, 1965); *Virtuose Musik* for Solo Violin, 10 Wind Instruments, Percussion, and Harp (1966; Dartmouth College, Hanover, N.H., Aug. 19, 1967); arrangement of Bach's *Das musikalische Opfer* (1966); *Collage* (1968; Vienna, Oct. 5, 1969); Concerto for Trumpet and Strings (1970; Nuremberg, Feb. 11, 1971); Concerto for Clarinet and Chamber Orch. (1971; Schwetzingen, May 12, 1972); *Stars and Strings* for Jazz Ensemble and Strings (1972; Nuremberg, Jan. 12, 1973); *Poème* (1974; Vienna, Jan. 31, 1976); *Pentagram* for Strings (1974; Berlin, April 4, 1975).

Blackwood, Easley, American composer; b. Indianapolis, April 21, 1933. He studied piano in his hometown and appeared as a soloist with the Indianapolis Symph. at age 14; studied composition during summers at the Berkshire Music Center (1948–50), notably with Messiaen in 1949; then with Bernhard Heiden at Indiana Univ. and Hindemith at Yale (1949–51); received his M.A. from Yale in 1954; then went to Paris to study with Nadia Boulanger (1954–56). In 1958 he was appointed to the faculty of the Univ. of Chicago. His music is marked by impassioned Romantic éclat and is set in a highly evolved chromatic idiom. Blackwood is an accomplished pianist, particularly notable for his performances of modern works of transcendental difficulty, such as the Concord Sonata of Ives and the 2nd Piano Sonata of Boulez.

WORKS: 4 symphs.: No. 1 (1954–55; Boston, April 18, 1958; won the Koussevitzky Music Foundation prize); No. 2 (1960; Cleveland, Jan. 5, 1961; commissioned for the centenary of the music firm G. Schirmer); No. 3 for Small Orch. (1964; Chicago, March 7, 1965); No. 4 (Chicago, Nov. 22, 1978); Chamber Symph. for 14 Wind Instruments (1955); Clarinet Concerto (Cincinnati, Nov. 20, 1964); *Symphonic Fantasy* (Louisville, Sept. 4, 1965); Concerto for Oboe and String Orch. (1966); Violin Concerto (Bath, England, June 18, 1967); Concerto for Flute and String Orch. (Dartmouth College, Hanover, N.H., July 28, 1968); Piano Concerto (1969–70; Ravinia Festival, Highland Park, Ill., July 26, 1970); Viola Sonata (1953); 2 string quartets (1957, 1959); Concertino for 5 Instruments (1959); 2 violin sonatas (1960, 1975); Fantasy for Cello and Piano (1960); *Pastorale and Variations* for Wind Quintet (1961); Fantasy for Flute, Clarinet, Violin, and Piano (1965); *3 Short Fantasies* for Piano (1965); *Symphonic Movement* for Organ (1966); *Un Voyage à Cythère* for Soprano and 10 Players (1966); Piano Trio (1968).

Blagrove, Henry Gamble, English violinist; b. Nottingham, Oct. 20, 1811; d. London, Dec. 15, 1872. He was extremely precocious in his development; at the age of 12 he was admitted to the Royal Academy of Music in London at its opening in 1823. In 1832–34 he was in Germany and took lessons with Spohr in Kassel. He is credited with having established the first regular series of chamber music concerts in London in 1835.

Blahetka, Marie Léopoldine, Austrian pianist and composer; b. Guntramsdorf, near Vienna, Nov. 15, 1811; d. Boulogne, France, Jan. 12, 1887. She was a piano pupil of Kalkbrenner and Moscheles; also studied composition with Sechter. In 1840 she settled in Boulogne. She wrote a romantic opera, *Die Räuber und die Sänger,* which was produced in Vienna in 1830, and a considerable number of salon pieces for piano.

Blainville, Charles-Henri, French cellist and music theorist; b. probably in or near Rouen, 1710; d. Paris, c.1770. His claim to musicological attention resides in his "discovery" of a 3rd "mode hellénique" (actually the Phrygian mode); in 1751 he wrote a symph. in which he made use of this mode. Rousseau, always eager to welcome a "historical" discovery, expressed his admiration for Blainville. Among Blainville's theoretical writings are *L'Harmonie théorico-pratique* (1746); *Essai sur un troisième mode,* expounding the supposed "mode hellénique"(1751); *L'Esprit de l'art musical* (1754); and *Histoire générale, critique et philologique de la musique* (1767). He composed 5 symphs., publ. a book of sonatas "pour le dessus de viole avec la basse continue," and arranged Tartini's sonatas in the form of concerti grossi.

Blake, David (Leonard), British composer; b. London, Sept. 2, 1936. He studied music at Cambridge; then went to East Berlin, where he took lessons with Hanns Eisler. In 1964 he was appointed lecturer in music at York Univ. His early works were in a tonal idiom influenced by Bartók and Mahler, but later he began writing in the 12-tone system as promulgated by Schoenberg and Eisler. He then experimented in a wide variety of styles, including oriental scales and aleatory improvisation. While serving in the British army in the Far East, he learned Chinese. WORKS: String Quartet No. 1 (1961–62); String Quartet No. 2 (1973); *It's a Small War,* musical for schools (1962); *3 Choruses* to poems by Robert Frost (1964); *Beata l'Alma* for Soprano and Piano (1966); Symph. for Chamber Orch. (1966); *Lumina,* cantata after Ezra Pound, for Soprano, Baritone, Chorus, and Orch. (1968–69); *Metamorphoses* for Orch. (1971); *Scenes* for Solo Cello (1972); Nonet (1971; London, June 21, 1971); *The Bones of Chuang Tzu* for Baritone and Chamber Orch. (1972; Glasgow, March 25, 1975); *In Praise of Krishna* for Soprano and 9 Players (1973; Leeds, March 7, 1973); *Toussaint,* opera in 3 acts (1974–76; London, Sept. 28, 1977); Violin Concerto No. 1 (1976; London, Aug. 19, 1976); *Sonata alla Marcia* for Chamber Orch. (1978; London, May 17, 1978); *From the Mattress Grave* for High Voice and 11 Players (1978; Durham, Feb. 3, 1979); *9 Poems of Heine* for High Voice and Piano (1978); *Cassation* for Wind Octet (1979; Sheffield, May 19, 1979); Clarinet Quintet (1980); *Capriccio* for 7 Players (1980); *The Spear* for Male Speaker, Mezzo-soprano, and 4 Players (1982); *Rise, Dove* for Baritone and Orch. (1982); String Quartet No. 3 (1982); Violin Concerto No. 2 (1983).

Blake, Eubie, black American centenarian jazz piano player, seeded buckdancer, vaudevillian, composer of musicals, rags, etudes, waltzes, and a plethora of miscellaneous popular numbers; b. Baltimore, Feb. 7, 1883; d. Brooklyn, Feb. 12, 1983, 5 days after reaching his 100th birthday. Both his parents were former slaves. He was baptized **James Hubert Blake;** relatives and friends called him Hubie, which was abbreviated to Eubie. He grew up in an atmosphere of syncopated music and sentimental ballads played on music boxes, and had some piano lessons from a friendly church organist in Baltimore. At the age of 15 he got a regular job as a standard pianist in a "hookshop" (a sporting house) run by Aggie Sheldon, a successful madam, which provided him with tips from both the inmates and their customers. He improvised rag music (his long fingers could stretch to 12 keys on the keyboard) and soon began to compose in earnest. In 1899 he wrote his *Charleston Rag,* which became a hit. In 1915 he joined a singer named Noble Sissle, and they appeared on the vaudeville circuit together, advertised as The Dixie Duo. They broke the tradition of blackface white comedians and devised an all-black musical, *Shuffle Along,* which opened in N.Y. on May 23, 1927, billed as "a musical mélange." The score included the song *I'm just wild about Harry,* which became a hit and was actually used as a campaign song for Harry Truman in 1948. Another hit song was *Memories of You,* which Eubie Blake wrote for the musical *Blackbirds of 1930.* Remarkably enough, he was moved by a purely scholarly interest in music and as late as 1949 took courses in the Schillinger System of Composition at N.Y. Univ. In 1969 he recorded the album *The Eighty-Six Years of Eubie Blake* and in 1972 he formed his own record company. As his centennial approached there was a growing appreciation of his natural talent, and a Broadway musical billed simply *Eubie!* was produced with resounding success. In 1981 he received the Medal of Freedom from President Reagan at the White House. He made his last public appearance at the age of 99, at Lincoln Center in N.Y., on June 19, 1982.

Blanc, Giuseppe, Italian song composer; b. Bardonecchia, April 11, 1886; d. Santa Margherita Ligure, Dec. 7, 1969. He studied composition with Bolzoni; produced a number of comic operas, among them *La festa dei fiori* (Rome, Jan. 29, 1913). His only claim to fame is that he was the author of the song *Giovinezza,* which was adopted ex post facto by Mussolini as the national Fascist anthem.

Blanchard, Esprit Joseph Antoine, French composer; b. Pernes, Comtat-Venaissin, Feb. 29, 1696; d. Versailles, April 19, 1770. He studied with Poitevin at the choir school of the St. Sauveur Cathedral in Aix-en-Provence. In 1717 he became maître de musique to the chapter of St. Victor in Marseilles; was then maître de chapelle at the Toulon, Besançon, and Amiens cathedrals. He succeeded Bernier as sous-maître at the Chapelle du Roi in Versailles in 1738; was maître de chapelle there from 1761–65. He wrote mainly sacred choral music for performance at the churches where he was employed.

Blanchet, Emile R., Swiss pianist and composer; b. Lausanne, July 17, 1877; d. Pully, March 27, 1943. He studied with his father, Charles Blanchet (1833–1900); with Seiss, Franke, and Strässer at the Cologne Cons.; and with Busoni in Weimar and Berlin. From 1904–17 he was a teacher of piano at the Lausanne Cons. Among his works are *64 Preludes for Pianoforte in Contrapuntal Style,* a valuable pedagogical work; *Konzertstück* for Piano and Orch.; Violin Sonata; Ballade for 2 Pianos; many études and other piano works; songs; etc.

Blanck, Hubert de, conductor and educator; b. Utrecht, June 11, 1856; d. Havana, Nov. 28, 1932. He studied at the Liège Cons. with Ledent (piano) and Dupuy (composition); subsequently served as a theater conductor in Warsaw (1875); toured Europe as a pianist; visited South America with the violinist E. Dengremont (1880). After teaching at the N.Y. College of Music, he settled in Havana (1883) and founded the first cons. in Cuba, based upon European models (1885). He was exiled in 1896 for participation in the revolution; after the reestablishment of peace, he reopened his school in Havana and set up branches in other towns. He composed piano pieces and songs, but it is as an enlightened educator that he is honored in the annals of Cuban music.

Bland, James A., black American song composer; b. Flushing, N.Y., Oct. 22, 1854; d. Philadelphia, May 5, 1911. He learned to play the banjo and joined a minstrel troupe, improvising songs in the manner of Negro spirituals. His most famous ballad, *Carry Me Back to Old Virginny,* was publ. in 1878; in 1940 it was designated the official song of the state of Virginia. From 1881–1901 Bland lived in England, enjoying excellent success as an entertainer, including a command performance for Queen Victoria, but he dissipated his savings and died in abject poverty.

Blanter, Matvei, Russian composer of popular songs; b. Potchep, Tchernigov district, Feb. 10, 1903. He studied in Moscow with G. Conus; then devoted himself exclusively to the composition of light music. He wrote an operetta, *On the Banks of the Amur* (1939), and some incidental music. Of his songs, the most popular is *Katyusha* (famous during World War II), which combines the melodic inflection of the typical urban ballad with the basic traits of a Russian folk song. Blanter is regarded in Russia as a creator of the new Soviet song style.

Blatný, Josef, Czech organist and composer, father of **Pavel Blatný;** b. Brno, March 19, 1891. He studied composition with Janáček at the Brno Organ School (1909–12); then served as his assistant; subsequently became a prof. of organ at the Brno Cons., where he taught for 28 years (1928–56).
WORKS: *Sinfonia brevis* for String Orch. (1957); *2 Symphonic Dances* (1959); Chamber Symph. (1961); oratorio, *Lotr na pravici (The Thief on the Right;* 1953); 3 violin sonatas (1926, 1957, 1968); 3 string quartets (1929, 1954, 1962); Suite for 2 Flutes, Clarinet, and Bassoon (1947); Piano Trio (1950); Piano Quartet (1968); Piano Sonata (1960); many organ pieces; songs.

Blatný, Pavel, Czech composer and conductor, son of **Josef Blatný;** b. Brno, Sept. 14, 1931. He began his musical studies with his father; then studied piano and music theory at the Brno Cons. (1950–55) and musicology at the Univ. of Brno (1954–58); also took composition lessons with Bořkovec at the Prague Academy of Music (1955–59); attended summer courses of new music at Darmstadt (1965–69); in 1968 traveled to the U.S. and took lessons in jazz piano and composition at the Berklee College of Music. He became an exceedingly active musician in Czechoslovakia; wrote about 600 works, some of them paralleling the development of "third-stream music" initiated in the U.S. by Gunther Schuller, which constitutes a fusion of jazz and classical

forms; played something like 2,000 piano recitals in programs of modern music; conducted a great many concerts and participated in programs of the Czech Radio; in 1971 he was appointed chief of the music division of the television station in Brno.

Blauvelt, Lillian Evans, American soprano; b. Brooklyn, N.Y., March 16, 1874; d. Chicago, Aug. 29, 1947. After studying violin for several years, she took vocal lessons in N.Y. and Paris; gave concerts in France, Belgium, and Russia; made her operatic debut at Brussels (1893); sang before Queen Victoria (1899); sang the coronation ode and received the coronation medal from King Edward (1902); appeared for several seasons at Covent Garden. She married the composer **Alexander Savine** in 1914; created the title role in his opera *Xenia* (Zürich, 1919).

Blaze (called **Castil-Blaze**), **François-Henri-Joseph,** French writer on music; b. Cavaillon, Vaucluse, Dec. 1, 1784; d. Paris, Dec. 11, 1857. He studied with his father, a lawyer and amateur musician; went to Paris in 1799 as a law student; held various administrative posts in provincial towns in France. At the same time he studied music and compiled information on the opera in France. The fruit of this work was the publication in 2 vols. of his book *De l'opéra en France* (Paris, 1820; 1826). He became music critic of the influential Paris *Journal des Débats* in 1822, signing his articles "XXX." He resigned from this post in 1832 but continued to publ. books on music, including valuable compilations of musical lexicography: *Dictionnaire de musique moderne* (1821, 2 vols.; 2nd ed., 1825; 3rd ed., edited by J.H. Mees, with historical preface and a supplement on Netherlandish musicians, 1828, in one vol.); *Chapelle-musique des Rois de France* (1832); *La Danse et les ballets depuis Bacchus jusqu'à Mlle. Taglioni* (1832); *Mémorial du Grand Opéra* (from Cambert, 1669, down to the Restoration); "Le Piano; Histoire de son invention," *Revue de Paris* (1839–40); *Molière musicien* (1852); *Théâtres lyriques de Paris,* 2 vols., on the Grand Opéra (1855) and on the Italian opera (1856); *Sur l'opéra français; Vérités dures mais utiles* (1856); *L'Art des jeux lyriques* (1858); trans. into French many librettos of German and Italian operas. He himself wrote 3 operas; compiled a collection of *Chants de Provence;* some of his popular ballads attained considerable popularity.

Blazhkov, Igor, Ukrainian conductor and music scholar; b. Kiev, Sept. 23, 1936. He studied at the Kiev Cons., graduating in 1959; appeared as guest conductor in Moscow and Leningrad, specializing in modern music, including American works. From 1958–62 he was assistant conductor of the Ukrainian State Orch. in Kiev.

Blech, Harry, English violinist and conductor; b. London, March 2, 1910. He received his musical training at the Trinity College of Music in London and at the Royal Manchester College of Music; later was a violinist in the Hallé Orch. in Manchester

(1929–30) and the BBC Symph. Orch., London (1930–36); organized the Blech String Quartet in 1933 (disbanded in 1950). In 1942 he founded the London Wind Players, in 1946 the London Symph. Players, and in 1949 the London Mozart Players; conducted numerous concerts with these ensembles, mostly in programs of Haydn and Mozart. In 1964 he was made an Officer of the Order of the British Empire.

Blech, Leo, eminent German opera conductor and composer; b. Aachen, April 21, 1871; d. Berlin, Aug. 25, 1958. As a young man he was engaged in a mercantile career; then studied briefly at the Hochschule für Musik in Berlin; returned to Aachen to conduct at the Municipal Theater there (1893–99); also took summer courses in composition with Humperdinck (1893–96). He was subsequently engaged as opera conductor in Prague (1899–1906); then became conductor at the Berlin Court Opera in 1906; was named Generalmusikdirektor in 1913. In 1923 he became conductor of the Deutsches Opernhaus in Berlin; in 1924 was with the Berlin Volksoper, and in 1925 with the Vienna Volksoper. In 1926 he returned to Berlin as a conductor with the Staatsoper, remaining there until 1937; then went to Riga as a conductor of the Riga Opera (1937–41). From 1941 to 1949 he conducted in Stockholm. In 1949 he returned to Berlin and served as Generalmusikdirektor of the Städtische Oper there, remaining at that post until 1953. He was considered a fine interpreter of the standard German and Italian repertoire, particularly in the works of Wagner and Verdi. His own music is in the Wagnerian tradition; his knowledge and understanding of instrumental and vocal resources enabled him to produce competent operas; however, after initial successes, they suffered total oblivion.

Bledsoe, Jules, black American baritone and composer; b. Waco, Texas, Dec. 29, 1898; d. Hollywood, July 14, 1943. He studied at the Chicago Musical College (B.A., 1919); then went to Europe, taking singing lessons in Paris and Rome. Returning to America, he distinguished himself as a fine performer in musical comedies and opera. He sang the central role in the premiere of Jerome Kern's *Show Boat* (1927), appeared in grand opera as Rigoletto and Boris, and sang the title role in Gruenberg's opera *Emperor Jones*. As a composer, he wrote an *African Suite* for Orch. and several songs in the manner of Negro spirituals.

Bleyer, Georg, German composer, poet, and court functionary; b. Tiefurt, near Weimar, (baptized, Oct. 28) 1647; d. c.1694. He studied law and music in Jena (1664–66); was named chamber secretary at the court in Rudolstadt; was awarded the garland of poet laureate in 1672; then was active as a musician in Darmstadt at the court (1677–78). He composed sacred vocal music; also publ. a collection of dances for 4 and 5 instruments as *Lust-Music* (2 vols., Leipzig, 1670).

Blind Tom. See **Bethune, Thomas Greene.**

Bliss, Sir Arthur (Edward Drummond), significant English composer; b. London, Aug. 2, 1891; d. there, March 27, 1975. He studied at Pembroke College, Cambridge; then at the Royal College of Music in London, with Stanford, Vaughan Williams, and Holst. He served in the British Army during World War I; was wounded in 1916, and gassed in 1918. He resumed his musical studies after the Armistice; his earliest works, *Madam Noy,* for Soprano and 6 Instruments (1918), and *Rout,* for Soprano and Orch. (1919; Salzburg Festival, Aug. 7, 1922), were highly successful, and established Bliss as one of the most effective composers in the modern style. From 1923 to 1925 Bliss was in the U.S. as a teacher, living in California. Returning to London, he wrote the musical score for the film *Things to Come,* after H.G. Wells (1935). During World War II he was music director of the BBC (1942–44). He was knighted in 1950; in 1953 was named Master of the Queen's Musick as a successor to Sir Arnold Bax.

WORKS: OPERAS: *The Olympians* (London, Sept. 29, 1949) and *Tobias and the Angel* (London, BBC television, May 19, 1960).

BALLETS: *Checkmate* (Paris, June 15, 1937), *Miracle in the Gorbals* (London, Oct. 26, 1944), *Adam Zero* (London, April 8, 1946), and *The Lady of Shalott* (unofficially known also as *The Towers;* Berkeley, Calif., May 2, 1958).

FOR ORCH.: *Mêlée fantasque* (1921, revised 1965); *A Colour Symphony* (the title refers to 4 heraldic colors, one for each movement: purple, red, blue, and green; premiere, Gloucester, Sept. 7, 1922, under the composer's direction; revised 1932); Concerto for 2 Pianos and Orch. (1924; originally for Piano, Tenor, Strings, and Percussion, 1921); *Introduction and Allegro* (1926, revised 1937); *Hymn to Apollo* (1926, revised 1966); *Things to Come,* concert suite from music to the film (1934–35); *Music for Strings* (1935); *Conquest of the Air,* concert suite from music to the film (1937); Piano Concerto (commissioned by the British Council for the British Week at the N.Y. World's Fair, dedicated "to the people of the United State of America"; N.Y., June 10, 1939); *Theme and Cadenza* for Violin and Orch. (1946); Violin Concerto (London, May 11, 1955); *Meditations on a Theme of John Blow* (Birmingham, England, Dec. 13, 1955); *Edinburgh,* overture (1956); *Discourse* (Louisville, Kentucky, Oct. 23, 1957; recomposed 1965); Cello Concerto (1969–70; Aldenburgh Festival, June 24, 1970; Rostropovich, soloist); *Metamorphic Variations* (London, April 21, 1973; Stokowski conducting; originally titled simply *Variations*); 2 Contrasts for String Orch. (1972; from movements 2 and 3 of Quartet No. 2).

VOCAL MUSIC: *Madame Noy* for Soprano and 6 Instruments (1918); *Rhapsody* for Wordless Mezzo-soprano and Tenor, Flute, English Horn, String Quartet, and Double Bass (1919; London, Oct. 6, 1920); *Rout* for Soprano and Orch. (1920); *The Women of Yueh,* cycle for Voice and Chamber Ensemble (1923–24); *Pastorale* for Mezzo-soprano, Chorus, Strings, Flute, and Drums (1928); *Serenade* for Baritone and Orch. (1929); *Morning Heroes,* symphony for Orator, Chorus, and Orch., dedicated to his brother, killed in action (Norwich, Oct. 22, 1930);

The Enchantress for Contralto and Orch. (1951); *A Song of Welcome,* for the return of Queen Elizabeth II from her Australian journey, for Soprano, Baritone, Chorus, and Orch. (BBC, May 15, 1954; Joan Sutherland, soprano soloist); *Elegiac Sonnet* for Tenor, String Quartet, and Piano (1955); *The Beatitudes,* cantata (Coventry Festival, May 25, 1962); *Mary of Magdala,* cantata (Birmingham, Sept. 1, 1963); *A Knot of Riddles* for Baritone and 11 Instruments (1963); *The Golden Cantata* (1964); *The World Is Charged with the Grandeur of God,* chamber cantata for Chorus, 2 Flutes, 3 Trumpets, and 4 Trombones (1969); *2 Ballads* for Female Chorus, and Orch. or Piano (1971); several song cycles with piano; motets; and anthems.

CHAMBER MUSIC: *Conversations* for Flute, Oboe, and String Trio (1920; a humorous work); Oboe Quintet (1927); Clarinet Quintet (1931); Viola Sonata (1933); 2 string quartets (1940, 1950; 2 earlier quartets are lost); *Flourish: Greeting to a City* for 2 Brass Choirs and Percussion (1961); *Belmont Variations* for Brass (1963).

PIANO MUSIC: Sonata (1952); *Triptych* (1971).

Blitzstein, Marc, significant American composer; b. Philadelphia, March 2, 1905; d. Fort-de-France, Martinique, Jan. 22, 1964, from a brain injury sustained after a political altercation with a group of men in a bar. He studied piano and organ in Pennsylvania; composition with Scalero at the Curtis Inst. in Philadelphia; also took piano lessons with Siloti in N.Y. In 1926 he went to Europe, and took courses with Nadia Boulanger in Paris and Schoenberg in Berlin. Returning to America, he devoted himself chiefly to the cultivation of theatrical works of "social consciousness" of the type created in Germany by Bertolt Brecht and Kurt Weill; accordingly he wrote his stage works for performances in small theaters of the cabaret type. In 1940 he received a Guggenheim fellowship; during World War II he was stationed in England with the U.S. Armed Forces. His theater works include *Triple Sec,* opera-farce (Philadelphia, May 6, 1929); *Parabola and Circula,* one-act opera-ballet (1929); *Cain,* ballet (1930); *The Harpies,* musical satire commissioned by the League of Composers (1931; first production, Manhattan School of Music, N.Y., May 25, 1953); *The Cradle Will Rock,* one-act opera of "social significance" (N.Y., June 16, 1937, with the composer at the piano); *No for an Answer,* short opera (N.Y., Jan. 5, 1941); musical play, *I've Got the Tune* (CBS Radio, Oct. 24, 1937); also musical revues, one of which, *Regina,* to Lillian Hellman's play *The Little Foxes,* was expanded into a full-fledged opera (Boston, Oct. 11, 1949). Shortly before his death the Ford Foundation commissioned Blitzstein to write an opera on the subject of Sacco and Vanzetti, for production by the Metropolitan Opera House, but the work was never finished. Blitzstein further composed *Gods* for Mezzo-soprano and String Orch. (1926); oratorio, *The Condemned* (1930); *Airborne Symphony* (N.Y., March 23, 1946); *Cantatina* for Women's Voices and Percussion; *Jig-Saw,* ballet-suite (1927); *Romantic Piece* for Orch.

(1930); Piano Concerto (1931); *Freedom Morning,* symph. poem (London, Sept. 28, 1943); String Quartet; *Percussion Music* for Piano (1929); many other piano pieces. Blitzstein translated Kurt Weill's *Threepenny Opera* into English (1954), and his version scored great success.

Bloch, Alexander, American violinist and conductor; b. Selma, Ala., July 11, 1881; d. New York, March 16, 1983, at the age of 101. He studied violin with Edouard Herman in N.Y., with Otakar Sevčik in Vienna, with W. Hess and Henri Marteau in Berlin, and with Leopold Auer in St. Petersburg. He took conducting lessons with Chalmers Clifton in N.Y. From 1918 until 1930 he served as a teaching assistant to Auer in N.Y. He then devoted himself mainly to conducting; was conductor of the Central Florida Symph. Orch. at Winter Park (1936–43). In 1950 he took charge of the newly organized Florida West Coast Symph. Orch. in Saratoga; also had guest engagements with the National Symph. Orch. in Washington, D.C. He composed a Christmas opera, *The Lone Tree,* and a children's operetta, *Roeliff's Dream;* also publ. the violin studies *Principles and Practice of Bowing* and *How to Practice.*

Bloch, André, French composer; b. Wissembourg, Alsace, Jan. 18, 1873; d. Paris, Aug. 7, 1960. He studied at the Paris Cons. with Guiraud and Massenet; received the Premier Grand Prix de Rome in 1893. He was conductor of the orch. of the American Cons. at Fontainebleau. His works include operas: *Maida* (1909); *Une Nuit de Noël* (1922); *Broceliande* (1925); *Guignol* (1949); ballet, *Feminaland* (1904); symph. poems: *Kaa* (1933) and *L'Isba nostaligique* (1945); *Les Maisons de l'éternité* for Cello and Orch. (1930); *Suite palestinienne* for Cello and Orch. (Paris, Nov. 14, 1948; his most successful instrumental work).

Bloch, Ernest, remarkable Swiss-born American composer of Jewish ancestry; b. Geneva, July 24, 1880; d. Portland, Oreg., July 15, 1959. He studied solfeggio with Jaques-Dalcroze and violin with Louis Rey in Geneva (1894–97); then went to Brussels, where he took violin lessons with Ysaÿe and composition with Rasse (1897–99); while a student, he wrote a string quartet and a "symphonie orientale," indicative of his natural attraction to non-European cultures and coloristic melos. In 1900 he went to Germany, where he studied music theory with Iwan Knorr at the Hoch Cons. in Frankfurt and took private lessons with Ludwig Thuille in Munich; there he began the composition of his first full-fledged symphony, in C-sharp minor, with its 4 movements originally bearing titles expressive of changing moods. He then spent a year in Paris, where he met Debussy; Bloch's first published work, *Historiettes au crépuscule* (1903), shows Debussy's influence. In 1904 he returned to Geneva, where he began the composition of his only opera, *Macbeth,* after Shakespeare; the project of another opera, *Jézabel,* on a biblical subject, never materialized beyond a few initial sketches. As a tribute to his homeland, he outlined the orchestral work *Helvetia,* based on Swiss motifs, as early as 1900, but the full score was not completed until 1928. During the season 1909–10 Bloch conducted symphonic concerts in Lausanne and Neuchâtel. In 1916 he was offered an engagement as conductor on an American tour accompanying the dancer Maud Allan; he gladly accepted the opportunity to leave war-torn Europe, and expressed an almost childlike delight upon docking in the port of N.Y. at the sight of the Statue of Liberty. Maud Allan's tour was not successful, however, and Bloch returned to Geneva; in 1917 he received an offer to teach at the David Mannes School of Music in N.Y., and once more he sailed for America; he became an American citizen in 1924. This was also the period when Bloch began to express himself in music as an inheritor of Jewish culture; he explicitly articulated his racial consciousness in several verbal statements. His *Israel Symphony, Trois Poèmes juifs,* and *Schelomo,* a "Hebrew rhapsody" for Cello and Orch., mark the height of Bloch's greatness as a Jewish composer; long after his death, *Schelomo* still retains its popularity at symphony concerts. In America, he found sincere admirers and formed a group of greatly talented students, among them Roger Sessions, Ernst Bacon, George Antheil, Douglas Moore, Bernard Rogers, Randall Thompson, Quincy Porter, Halsey Stevens, Herbert Elwell, Isadore Freed, Frederick Jacobi, and Leon Kirchner. From 1920–25 he was director of the Inst. of Music in Cleveland, and from 1925–30, director of the San Francisco Cons. When the magazine *Musical America* announced in 1927 a contest for a symphonic work, Bloch won the first prize for his "epic rhapsody" entitled simply *America;* Bloch fondly hoped that the choral ending extolling America as the ideal of humanity would become a national hymn; the work was performed with a great outpouring of publicity in 5 cities, but as happens often with prizewinning works, it failed to strike the critics and the audiences as truly great, and in the end remained a mere by-product of Bloch's genius. From 1930–39 Bloch lived mostly in Switzerland; then returned to the U.S. and taught classes at the Univ. of Calif., Berkeley (1940–52); finally retired and lived at his newly purchased house at Agate Beach, Oreg. In his harmonic idiom Bloch favored sonorities formed by the bitonal relationship of 2 major triads with the tonics standing at the distance of a tritone, but even the dissonances he employed were euphonious. In his last works of chamber music he experimented for the first time with thematic statements of 12 different notes, but he never adopted the strict Schoenbergian technique of deriving the entire contents of a composition from the basic tone row. In his early Piano Quintet, Bloch made expressive use of quarter-tones in the string parts. In his Jewish works, he emphasized the interval of the augmented second, without a literal imitation of Hebrew chants.

WORKS: OPERA: *Macbeth* (1904–9; Opéra-Comique, Paris, Nov. 30, 1910). FOR ORCH.: *Poèmes d'automne,* songs for Mezzo-soprano and Orch. (1906); Prelude and 2 Psalms (Nos. 114 and 137) for Soprano and Orch. (1912–14); *Vivre-aimer,* symph. poem (1900; Geneva, June 23, 1901); Symph. in C-sharp minor (1901; first complete perf., Geneva, 1910; first American perf., N.Y. Phil., May 8, 1918, composer conducting); *Hiver-printemps,* symph. poem (1904–5; Geneva, Jan. 27, 1906); *Trois Poèmes juifs* (1913; Boston, March 23, 1917, composer conducting); *Israel,* symph. (1912–16; N.Y., May 3, 1917, composer conducting); *Schelomo,* Hebrew rhapsody for Cello and Orch. (1916; N.Y., May 3, 1917, composer conducting); Concerto Grosso No. 1 for Strings and Piano (1924–25; Cleveland, June 1, 1925, composer conducting); *America,* symph. poem (1926; N.Y., Dec. 20, 1928; next day simultaneously in Chicago, Philadelphia, Boston, and San Francisco); *Helvetia,* symph. poem (1928; Chicago, Feb. 18, 1932); *Voice in the Wilderness,* with Cello Obbligato (1936; Los Angeles, Jan. 21, 1937); *Evocations,* symph. suite (1937; San Francisco, Feb. 11, 1938); Violin Concerto (1938; first perf. by Szigeti, Cleveland, Dec. 15, 1938); *Suite symphonique* (Philadelphia, Oct. 26, 1945); *Concerto symphonique* for Piano and Orch. (Edinburgh, Sept. 3, 1949); *Scherzo fantasque* for Piano and Orch. (Chicago, Dec. 2, 1950); *In Memoriam* (1952); *Suite hébraïque* for Viola and Orch. (Chicago, Jan. 1, 1953); *Sinfonia breve* (BBC, London, April 11, 1953); Concerto Grosso No. 2 for String Orch. (BBC, London, April 11, 1953); Symph. for Trombone Solo and Orch. (1953–54; Houston, April 4, 1956); Symph. in E-flat (1954–55; London, Feb. 15, 1956); *Proclamation* for Trumpet and Orch. (1955). CHAMBER MUSIC: *Episodes* for Chamber Orch. (1926); Quintet for Piano and Strings, with use of quarter-tones (1923; N.Y., Nov. 11, 1923); First String Quartet (N.Y., Dec. 29, 1916); 2 Suites for String Quartet (1925); 3 Nocturnes for Piano Trio (1924); Suite for Viola and Piano (won the Coolidge prize, 1919); First Violin Sonata (1920); 2nd Violin Sonata, *Poème mystique* (1924); *Baal Shem* for Violin and Piano (1923); *Méditation hébraïque* and *From Jewish Life,* both for Cello and Piano (1925); Piano Sonata (1935); 2nd String Quartet (London, Oct. 9, 1946; received the N.Y. Music Critics Circle Award for chamber music, 1947); 3rd String Quartet (1951); 4th String Quartet (Lenox, Mass., June 28, 1954); 5th String Quartet (1956); 3 Suites for Cello Unaccompanied (1956); Piano Quintet No. 2 (1956; Dec. 6, 1959); *Suite Modale* for Flute Solo and Strings (1957; Kentfield, Calif., April 11, 1965); 2 Suites for Unaccompanied Violin (1958); Suite for Unaccompanied Viola (1958; the last movement incomplete); *2 Last Poems* for Flute and Chamber Orch.: *Funeral Music* and *Life Again?* (1958; anticipatory of death from terminal cancer). PIANO MUSIC: *Poems of the Sea, In the Night, Nirvana, 5 Sketches in Sepia.* FOR VOICE: A modern Hebrew ritual, *Sacred Service* (1930–33; world premiere, Turin, Italy, Jan. 12, 1934); *Historiettes au crépuscule,* 4 songs for Mezzo-soprano and Piano (1903). Bloch contributed a number of informative annotations for the program books of the Boston Symph., N.Y. Phil., and other orchs.; also contributed articles to music journals, among them "Man and Music" in *Musical Quarterly* (Oct. 1933). An Ernest Bloch Society was formed in London in 1937 with the objective of promoting performances of Bloch's music, with Albert Einstein as honorary president and with vice-presidents including Sir Thomas Beecham, Havelock Ellis, and Romain Rolland.

Bloch, Suzanne, lutenist and harpsichordist, daughter of **Ernest Bloch;** b. Geneva, Aug. 7, 1907. She came to the U.S. with her father; studied there with him and with Roger Sessions; then in Paris with Nadia Boulanger. She became interested in early polyphonic music and began to practice on old instruments to be able to perform music on the instruments for which it was written.

Blockx, Jan, significant Flemish composer; b. Antwerp, Jan. 25, 1851; d. Kapellenbos, near Antwerp, May 26, 1912. He studied organ with Callaerts and composition with Benoit. In 1885 he became a lecturer at the Flemish Music School; also was music director of the Cercle Artistique and other societies in Belgium. With Benoit, he is regarded as the strongest representative of the national Flemish school of composition; while the melodic and rhythmic materials in his music strongly reflect Flemish folk elements, the treatment, contrapuntal and harmonic, is opulent, approaching Wagnerian sonorities.
WORKS: Operas: *Jets vergeten* (Antwerp, Feb. 19, 1877); *Maître Martin* (Brussels, Nov. 30, 1892); *Herbergprinses* (Antwerp, Oct. 10, 1896; produced in French as *Princesse d'Auberge,* N.Y., March 10, 1909); *Thyl Uylenspiegel* (Brussels, Jan. 12, 1900); *De Bruid der Zee* (Antwerp, Nov. 30, 1901); *De Kapel* (Antwerp, Nov. 7, 1903); *Baldie* (Antwerp, Jan. 25, 1908; revised and performed under the title *Liefdelied;* Antwerp, Jan. 6, 1912); a ballet, *Milenka* (1887); *Rubens,* overture for Orch.; *Romance* for Violin and Orch.; several choral works with Orch., among them: *Vredezang; Het droom vant paradies; De klokke Roelandt; Op den stroom; Scheldezang.*

Blom, Eric, preeminent English writer on music; b. Bern, Switzerland, Aug. 20, 1888; d. London, April 11, 1959. He was of Danish and British extraction on his father's side; his mother was Swiss. He was educated in England. He was the London music correspondent for the *Manchester Guardian* (1923–31); then was the music critic of the *Birmingham Post* (1931–46) and of *The Observer* in 1949; edited *Music & Letters* from 1937–50 and from 1954 to the time of his death; he was also the editor of the Master Musicians series. In 1946 he was elected a member of the music committee of the British Council; in 1948, became member of the Royal Musical Assoc. In 1955 he was made a Commander of the Order of the British Empire in recognition of his services to music and received the honorary degree of D.Litt. from Birmingham Univ. In his writings Blom combined an enlightened penetration of musical esthetics with a literary capacity for presenting his subjects and stating his point of view in a brilliant journalistic manner. In his critical opinions he never concealed his disdain for some composers of great

fame and renown, such as Rachmaninoff. In 1946 he was entrusted with the preparation of a newly organized and greatly expanded edition of *Grove's Dictionary of Music and Musicians,* which was brought out under his editorship in 1954, in 9 vols., and to which Blom himself contributed hundreds of articles and translated entries by foreign contributors. In his adamant determination to make this edition a truly comprehensive work, he insisted on the inclusion of complete lists of works of important composers and exact dates of performance of operas and other major works. In 1946 Blom publ. his first lexicographical work, *Everyman's Dictionary of Music,* which was reissued in an amplified edition by Jack Westrup in 1971. His other books include: *Stepchildren of Music* (1923); *The Romance of the Piano* (1927); *A General Index to Modern Musical Literature in the English Language* (1927; indexes periodicals for the years 1915–26); *The Limitations of Music* (1928); *Mozart* (1935); *Beethoven's Pianoforte Sonatas Discussed* (1938); *A Musical Postbag* (1941; collected essays); *Music in England* (1942; revised 1947); *Some Great Composers* (1944); *Classics, Major and Minor, with Some Other Musical Ruminations* (London, 1958).

Blomdahl, Karl-Birger, significant Swedish composer; b. Växjö, Oct. 19, 1916; d. Kungsängen (near Stockholm), June 14, 1968. He studied composition with Hilding Rosenberg and conducting with Thor Mann in Stockholm; in 1946 he traveled in France and Italy on a state stipend; in 1954–55 he attended a seminar at Tanglewood on a grant of the American-Scandinavian Foundation. Returning to Sweden, he taught composition at the Royal College of Music in Stockholm (1960–64); in 1964 he was appointed music director at the Swedish Radio. He was an organizer (with Bäck, Carlid, Johanson, and Lidholm) of a "Monday Group" in Stockholm, dedicated to the propagation of an objective and abstract idiom as distinct from the prevalent type of Scandinavian romanticism. Blomdahl's early works are cast in a neo-Classical idiom, but he then turned to advanced techniques, including the application of electronic music. His 3rd symph., subtitled *Facetter (Facets),* utilizes dodecaphonic techniques. In 1959 he brought out his opera *Aniara,* which made him internationally famous; it pictures a pessimistic future when the remnants of the inhabitants of the planet Earth, devastated by atomic wars and polluted by radiation, are forced to emigrate to saner worlds in the galaxy; the score employs electronic sounds, and its thematic foundation is derived from a series of 12 different notes and 11 different intervals.
WORKS: Trio for Oboe, Clarinet, and Bassoon (1938); String Quartet No. 1 (1939); *Symphonic Dances* (Göteborg, Feb. 29, 1940); *Concert Overture* (Stockholm, Feb. 14, 1942); Suite for Cello and Piano (1944); Viola Concerto (Stockholm, Sept. 7, 1944); Symph. No. 1 (Stockholm, Jan. 26, 1945); Concerto Grosso (Stockholm, Oct. 2, 1945); *Vaknatten (The Wakeful Night),* theater music (1945); *3 Polyphonic Pieces* for Piano (1945); String Trio (1945); Suite

Blomstedt – Blum

for Cello and Piano (1945); *Little Suite* for Bassoon and Piano (1945); Concerto for Violin and String Orch. (Stockholm, Oct. 1, 1947); Symph. No. 2 (1947; Stockholm, Dec. 12, 1952); *Dance Suite No. 1* for Flute, Violin, Viola, Cello, and Percussion (1948); String Quartet No. 2 (1948); *Pastoral Suite* for String Orch. (1948); *Prelude and Allegro* for Strings (1949); Symph. No. 3, *Facetter* (*Facets*; 1950; Frankfurt Festival, June 24, 1951); *Dance Suite No. 2* for Clarinet, Cello, and Percussion (1951); *I speglarnas sal (In the Hall of Mirrors),* oratorio of 9 sonnets from Erik Lindegren's "The Man without a Road," for Soli, Chorus, and Orch. (1951–52; Stockholm, May 29, 1953); Chamber Concerto for Piano, Woodwinds, and Percussion (Stockholm, Oct. 30, 1953); *Sisyfos,* choreographic suite for Orch. (Stockholm, Oct. 20, 1954; produced as a ballet, Stockholm, April 18, 1957); Trio for Clarinet, Cello, and Piano (1955); *Anabase* for Baritone, Narrator, Chorus, and Orch. (Stockholm, Dec. 14, 1956); *Minotaurus,* ballet (Stockholm, April 5, 1958); *Aniara,* futuristic opera with electronic sound, after Harry Martinson's novel about an interplanetary voyage; libretto by Erik Lindegren (1957–59; Stockholm, May 31, 1959; numerous perfs. in Europe); *Fioriture* for Orch. (Cologne, June 17, 1960); *Forma ferritonans* for Orch. (Oxelösund, June 17, 1961); *Spel för åtta (Game for 8),* ballet (Stockholm, June 8, 1962; also a choreographic suite for Orch., 1964); *Herr von Hancken,* comic opera (Stockholm, Sept. 2, 1965); *Altisonans,* electronic piece from natural sound sources (1966); *. . . resan i denna natt (. . . the voyage in this night),* cantata, after Lindegren, for Soprano and Orch. (Stockholm, Oct. 19, 1966). At the time of his death, Blomdahl was working on an opera entitled *The Saga of the Great Computer,* incorporating electronic and concrete sounds, and synthetic speech.

Blomstedt, Herbert, American-born Swedish conductor; b. Springfield, Mass., July 11, 1927. He was educated at the Royal Academy of Music in Stockholm and the Univ. of Uppsala; then studied conducting with Igor Markevitch in Paris, and with Jean Morel and Leonard Bernstein in N.Y. He was music director of the Norrköping Symph. Orch. (1954–61); then conductor of the Oslo Phil. Orch. (1962–68) and of the Danish State Radio Symph. Orch. of Copenhagen (1967–77). Subsequently he was appointed chief conductor of the Swedish Radio Symph. Orch. In 1975 he became principal conductor of the Dresden State Orch.; he toured the U.S. with this ensemble in the fall of 1979.

Bloomfield, Fannie. See **Zeisler, Fannie Bloomfield.**

Bloomfield, Theodore, American conductor; b. Cleveland, June 14, 1923. He studied piano at the Oberlin Cons. (Mus.B., 1944); then took courses in conducting at the Juilliard School in N.Y.; also studied piano with Claudio Arrau and conducting with Pierre Monteux. In 1946–47 he was apprentice conductor to George Szell at the Cleveland Orch.; then conducted the Cleveland Little Symph. and the Civic Opera Workshop (1947–52). He was subsequently music director of the Portland (Oreg.) Symph. (1955–59) and of the Rochester (N.Y.) Phil. (1959–63). He then settled in Germany; was first conductor of the Hamburg State Opera (1964–66) and generalmusikdirektor of Frankfurt (1966–68). In 1975 he became chief conductor of the West Berlin Symph. Orch. He has established a fine reputation for his programs of rarely performed works by old and contemporary composers.

Blow, John, great English composer and organist; b. Newark-on-Trent, Nottinghamshire, Feb. (baptized, Feb. 23) 1648 or 1649; d. Westminster (London), Oct. 1, 1708. In 1660–61 he was a chorister at the Chapel Royal, under Henry Cooke; he later studied organ with Christopher Gibbons. His progress was rapid, and on Dec. 3, 1668, he was appointed organist of Westminster Abbey. In 1679 he left this post and Purcell, who had been Blow's student, succeeded him. After Purcell's untimely death in 1695, Blow was reappointed, and remained at Westminster Abbey until his death; he was buried there, in the north aisle. He married Elizabeth Braddock in 1674; she died in 1683 in childbirth, leaving 5 children. Blow held the rank of Gentleman of the Chapel Royal from March 16, 1673 or 1674; on July 23, 1674, he succeeded Humfrey as Master of the Children of the Chapel Royal; was Master of the Choristers at St. Paul's (1687–1702 or 1703); in 1699 he was appointed Composer of the Chapel Royal. He held the honorary Lambeth degree of D.Mus., conferred on him in 1677 by the Dean of Canterbury. While still a young chorister of the Chapel Royal, Blow began to compose church music; in collaboration with Humfrey and William Turner, he wrote the *Club Anthem* ("I will always give thanks"); at the behest of Charles II, he made a 2-part setting of Herrick's poem "Goe, perjur'd man." He wrote many secular part-songs, among them an ode for New Year's Day 1681/82, "Great sir, the joy of all our hearts," an ode for St. Cecilia; 2 anthems for the coronation of James II; *Epicedium for Queen Mary* (1695); *Ode on the Death of Purcell* (1696). Blow's collection of 50 songs, *Amphion Anglicus,* was publ. in 1700. His best-known work is *Masque for the Entertainment of the King: Venus and Adonis,* written c.1685; this is his only complete score for the stage, but he contributed separate songs for numerous dramatic plays. Purcell regarded Blow as "one of the greatest masters in the world." Fourteen large works by Blow, anthems and harpsichord pieces, have been preserved; 11 anthems are printed in Boyce's *Cathedral Musick* (1760–78). Selected anthems are publ. in *Musica Britannica,* 7. The vocal score of his masque *Venus and Adonis* was publ. by G.E.P. Arkwright in the Old English Edition (No. 25; 1902); the complete score was publ. by the Editions de l'Oiseau Lyre, as ed. by Anthony Lewis (Paris, 1939).

Blum, Robert, important Swiss composer; b. Zürich, Nov. 27, 1900. He studied at the Zürich Cons. with Andreae, Jarnach, and others; in 1924 he took

140

some lessons with Busoni. Upon his return to Switzerland, he devoted himself to choral conducting and teaching. In 1943 he was appointed prof. at the Music Academy in Zürich. In his own compositions he cultivates polyphonic music in the traditional style, enhanced by modern harmonies and occasionally dissonant contrapuntal lines.

WORKS: Opera, *Amarapura* (1926); oratorio, *Kindheit Jesu* (1936); many sacred choral works and Psalms for Voice and Orch.; 6 symphs. (1924, 1926, 1935, 1959, 1961, 1969); *Passionskonzert* for Organ and String Orch. (1943); *Seldwyla-Symphonie* (1968); *4 Partite* for Orch. (1929, 1935, 1953, 1967); Concerto for Orch. (1955); *Overture on Swiss Themes* (1944); *Christ ist erstanden,* orch. variations (1962); *Lamentatio angelorum* for Chamber Orch. (1943); Viola Concerto (1951); Oboe Concerto (1960); Concerto for Wind Quintet (1962); Triple Concerto for Violin, Oboe, Trumpet, and Chamber Orch. (1963); Flute Quartet (1963); Sonata for Flute and Violin (1963); *Concertante Symphonie* for Wind Quintet and Chamber Orch. (1964); *Divertimento* on a 12-tone row for 10 Instruments (1966); *Le Tombe di Ravenna* for 11 Woodwind Instruments (1968); Quartet for Clarinet and String Trio (1970); String Quartet (1970); numerous songs, organ pieces, and arrangements of old vocal compositions.

Blume, Friedrich, preeminent German musicologist and editor; b. Schlüchtern, Jan. 5, 1893; d. there, Nov. 22, 1975. He was the son of a Prussian government functionary; first studied medicine in Eisenach; in 1911 he went to the Univ. of Munich, where he began his musicological studies; then went to the univs. of Leipzig and Berlin. During World War I he was in the German army; was taken prisoner by the British and spent three years in a prison camp in England. In 1919 he resumed his studies at the Univ. of Leipzig, where he took his Ph.D. in 1921 with the dissertation *Studien zur Vorgeschichte der Orchestersuite im 15. und 16. Jahrhundert* (publ. in Leipzig, 1925); in 1923 he became a lecturer in music at the Univ. of Berlin; in 1925 he completed his Habilitation there with *Das monodische Prinzip in der protestantischen Kirchenmusik* (publ. in Leipzig, 1925); was made Privatdozent there that same year; also lectured in music history at the Berlin-Spandau School of Church Music from 1928 to 1934. In 1934 he joined the faculty of the Univ. of Kiel, where he was prof. from 1938 until his retirement in 1958; was then made prof. emeritus. He was an authority on Lutheran church music; his *Die evangelische Kirchenmusik* was published in Bücken's *Handbuch der Musikwissenschaft*, X (1931; 2nd ed., revised, as *Geschichte der evangelischen Kirchenmusik*, 1965; in Eng., as *Protestant Church Music: A History*, 1974). He prepared a collected edition of the works of M. Praetorius (21 vols., Berlin, 1928–41); was general editor of *Das Chorwerk,* a valuable collection of old polyphonic music (1929–38); also editor of *Das Erbe deutscher Musik* (1935–43). In 1943 he was entrusted with the preparation of the monumental encyclopedia *Die Musik in Geschich-*

te und Gegenwart (14 vols., Kassel, 1949–68); following its publication, he undertook the further task of preparing an extensive Supplement, which contained numerous additional articles and corrections of ascertainable errors; its publication was continued after his death by his daughter, Ruth Blume. He also wrote *Wesen und Werden deutscher Musik* (Kassel, 1944); *Johann Sebastian Bach im Wandel der Geschichte* (Kassel, 1947; Eng. trans. as *Two Centuries of Bach,* 1950); *Goethe und die Musik* (Kassel, 1948); *Was ist Musik?* (Kassel, 1959); *Umrisse eines neuen Bach-Bildes* (Kassel, 1962). His life's work was a study in the practical application of his vast erudition and catholic interests in musicological scholarship.

Blumenfeld, Felix, Russian composer and conductor; b. Kovalevka, near Kherson, April 19, 1863; d. Moscow, Jan. 21, 1931. He studied piano in Elizavetgrad; then went to St. Petersburg, where he studied composition with Rimsky-Korsakov; upon graduation in 1885, he joined the staff of the Cons. and taught there until 1905, and again from 1911–18; from 1895–1911 he was the conductor at the Imperial Opera in St. Petersburg; he was also a guest conductor in the Russian repertoire in Paris during the "Russian seasons" in 1908. He was a pianist of virtuoso caliber; was also active as an accompanist for Chaliapin and other famous singers. From 1918–22 he was a prof. of piano at the Cons. of Kiev, and from 1922 to his death he taught at the Moscow Cons. Among his piano students was Vladimir Horowitz. As a composer, Blumenfeld excelled mainly in his piano pieces and songs, many of them publ. by Belaiev. He also wrote a symph., entitled *To the Beloved Dead;* a String Quartet; some other pieces.

Blumental, Felicja, pianist; b. Warsaw, Dec. 28, 1918. She studied piano at the Warsaw Cons.; in 1945, she emigrated to Brazil and became a Brazilian citizen. Villa-Lobos dedicated his 5th Piano Concerto to her; she played this work many times under his direction. Penderecki wrote his *Partita for Harpsichord and Orchestra* for her.

Blumenthal, Jacob, German pianist; b. Hamburg, Oct. 4, 1829; d. London, May 17, 1908. He studied music in Hamburg and Vienna; in 1846 went to Paris, where he became a student of piano with Herz and of composition with Halévy. In 1848 he settled in London, where he became court pianist to Queen Victoria. He composed a number of melodious piano pieces in a fashionable salon style.

Blüthner, Julius (Ferdinand), celebrated German piano maker; b. Falkenhain, near Merseburg, March 11, 1824; d. Leipzig, April 13, 1910. In 1853 he founded his establishment at Leipzig with 3 workmen; by 1897 it had grown to a sizable company, producing some 3,000 pianos yearly. Blüthner's specialty was the "Aliquotflügel," a grand piano with a sympathetic octave-string stretched over and parallel with each unison struck by the hammers. He was awarded many medals for his contributions to the advancement of piano construction. He was co-author, with H. Gretschel, of *Der Pianofortebau* (1872; 3rd ed., revised by R. Hannemann, Leipzig, 1909).

Boccherini, Luigi, famous Italian composer; b. Lucca, Feb. 19, 1743; d. Madrid, May 28, 1805. He grew up in a musical environment and became a cello player. In 1757 he was engaged as a member of the orch. of the Court Theater in Vienna. From 1761 to 1763 he was in Lucca; after a year in Vienna he returned to Lucca and played cello at the theater orch. there. He then undertook a concert tour with the violinist Filippo Manfredi in 1766. Then he went to Paris, where he appeared at the Concert Spirituel in 1768. He became exceedingly popular as a performer, and his own compositions were publ. in Paris; his first publications were 6 string quartets and 2 books of string trios. In 1769 he received a flattering invitation to the Madrid Court, and became chamber composer to the Infante Luis; after the latter's death he served as court composer to Friedrich Wilhelm II of Prussia; was appointed to the German Court on Jan. 21, 1786. After the death of the King in 1797 he returned to Madrid. In 1800 he enjoyed the patronage of Napoleon's brother, Lucien Bonaparte, who served as French ambassador to Madrid. Despite his successes at various European courts, Boccherini lost his appeal to his patrons and to the public. He died in Madrid; in a belated tribute to a native son, the authorities in Lucca had his remains transferred there and reinterred with great solemnity in 1927. Boccherini had profound admiration for Haydn; indeed, so close was Boccherini's style to Haydn's that this affinity gave rise to the saying, "Boccherini is the wife of Haydn." He was an exceptionally fecund composer, specializing almost exclusively in chamber music. The list of his works includes 20 chamber symphs.; 2 octets; 16 sextets; 125 string quintets; 12 piano quintets; 18 quintets for Strings and Flute (or Oboe); 102 string quartets; 60 string trios; 21 violin sonatas; 6 cello sonatas; also 4 cello concertos. He further wrote much guitar music, a Christmas cantata, and some sacred works.

Bochsa, Robert-Nicolas-Charles, celebrated French harpist; b. Montmédy, Meuse, Aug. 9, 1789; d. Sydney, Australia, Jan. 6, 1856. He first studied music with his father; played in public at the age of 7; wrote a symph. when he was 9, and an opera, *Trajan*, at 15. He then studied with Franz Beck in Bordeaux, and later at the Paris Cons. with Méhul and Catel (1806). His harp teachers were Nadermann and Marin. Of an inventive nature, Bochsa developed novel technical devices for harp playing, transforming the harp into a virtuoso instrument. He was the court harpist to Napoleon, and to Louis XVIII. He wrote 8 operas for the Opéra-Comique (1813–16); several ballets, an oratorio, and a great number of works for the harp; also a method for harp. In 1817 he became involved in some forgeries, and fled to London to escape prison. He became very popular as a harp teacher in London society; organized a series of oratorio productions with Sir George Smart (1822). He was also the first prof. of harp at the Academy of Music in London, but in 1827 he lost his position when a story of his dishonest conduct became widely known. However, he obtained a position as conductor of the Italian Opera at the King's Theatre (1826–30). Another scandal marked Bochsa's crooked road to success and notoriety when he eloped with the soprano **Ann Bishop,** the wife of Sir Henry Bishop, in Aug. 1839. He gave concerts with her in Europe, America, and Australia, where he died.

Bockelmann, Rudolf, German bass-baritone; b. Bodenteich, April 2, 1892; d. Dresden, Oct. 9, 1958. He studied singing with Karl Scheidemantel and Oscar Lassner in Leipzig. He then sang at the Neues Theater (1921–26) and at the Stadttheater in Hamburg (1926–32); appeared at the Bayreuth Festival in 1928; in 1929 and in 1934–38 he sang at Covent Garden, London; from 1930 to 1932 he was on the roster of the Chicago Opera Co. In 1932 he returned to Germany and became a member of the Staatsoper in Berlin for the duration of the war. His crypto-Nazi inclinations precluded further engagements outside Germany. He was particularly noted for his congenial interpretations of villainous Wagnerian bass roles. His own notations on operatic techniques were publ. in the *Sammelbände der Robert-Schumann-Gesellschaft,* II/1966 (Leipzig, 1967).

Bodanzky, Artur, famous Austrian conductor; b. Vienna, Dec. 16, 1877; d. New York, Nov. 23, 1939. He studied at the Vienna Cons., and later with Zemlinsky. He began his career as a violinist at the Vienna Opera. In 1900 he received his first appointment as a conductor, leading an operetta season in Budweis; in 1902 he became assistant to Mahler at the Vienna Opera; conducted in Berlin (1905) and in Prague (1906–9). In 1909 he was engaged as music director at Mannheim. In 1912 he arranged a memorial Mahler Festival, conducting a huge ensemble of 1,500 vocalists and instrumentalists. He conducted *Parsifal* at Covent Garden in London in 1914; his success there led to an invitation to conduct the German repertoire at the Metropolitan Opera House; he opened his series with *Götterdämmerung* (Nov. 18, 1915). From 1916–31 he was director of the Society of Friends of Music in N.Y.; in 1919 he also conducted the New Symph. Orch. He made several practical arrangements of celebrated operas (*Oberon, Don Giovanni, Fidelio,* etc.), which he used for his productions with the Metropolitan Opera. His style of conducting was in the Mahler tradition, with emphasis on climactic effects and contrasts of light and shade.

Bode, Rudolf, German acoustician and theorist of rhythmic gymnastics; b. Kiel, Feb. 3, 1881; d. Munich, Oct. 7, 1970. He studied physiology and philosophy at the Univ. of Leipzig, and music theory at the Leipzig Cons. After attending the Dalcroze Inst. of Eurhythmics in Hellerau, he formulated a system of "rhythmic gymnastics." In 1911 he founded a school in Munich with courses embodying his body theories, intended to achieve perfect physical and mental health. He publ. a number of books and essays on the subject: *Der Rhythmus und seine Bedeutung für die Erziehung* (Jena, 1920); *Ausdruckgymnastik* (Munich, 1922; in English as *Expressions-Gymnastic*, N.Y., 1931); *Musik und Bewegung* (Kassel, 1930); *Energie und Rhythmus* (Berlin, 1939). He also wrote a manual of piano study as a rhythmic muscular action, *Rhythmus und Anschlag* (Munich, 1933).

Bodin, Lars-Gunnar, Swedish composer; b. Stockholm, July 15, 1935. He studied composition with Lennart Wenström (1955–59); attended the Darmstadt summer courses (1961); in 1972 became director of the electronic studio at the Stockholm Cons. In collaboration with the Swedish concrete poet and composer Bengt Emil Johnson, he produced a series of pieces described as "text-sound compositions."
WORKS: Brass Quartet (1960); *Arioso* for Piano, Percussion, Cello, Clarinet, and Trombone (1962); *Calendar Music* for Piano (1963); *Semicolon* for Piano and Semaphoring Chorus (1964); *My World Is Your World* for Organ and Tape (1966); *". . . from any point to any other point"* for Electronic Sound (1968; also produced as a ballet, in Stockholm, Sept. 20, 1968); electronic pieces: *Place of Plays; Winter Events* (1967); Toccata (1969); *Traces I* and *II* (1970–71); *From the Beginning to the End* (1973); *Seeings (Earth, Sky, Winds)* (1973); television ballet, *Händelser och handlingar* (*Events and Happenings;* 1971); 3 compositions entitled *Dedicated to You* for Organ and Tape (1971).

Boeck, August de, Belgian composer; b. Merchtem, May 9, 1865; d. there, Oct. 9, 1937. He studied organ at the Brussels Cons.; subsequently was church organist in Brussels; later taught harmony at the Royal Flemish Cons. at Antwerp and at the Brussels Cons. In 1930 he returned to his native town. He wrote operas and incidental music for stage plays; *Rapsodie Dahoméenne* for Orch., on exotic African themes (1893); an orch. fantasy on Flemish folk songs (1923); many songs to French and Flemish texts. Much of his orch. music is infused with impressionistic colors.

Boehe, Ernst, German composer and conductor; b. Munich, Dec. 27, 1880; d. Ludwigshafen, Nov. 16, 1938. He studied with Rudolf Louis and Thuille in Munich; in 1907 was associate conductor, with Courvoisier, of the Munich Volkssymphoniekonzerte; from 1913–20 was court conductor at Oldenburg; then conducted concerts in Ludwigshafen. His works are of a programmatic type, the orchestration emphasizing special sonorities of divided strings, massive wind instruments, and various percussive effects; his tone poems show a decisive Wagnerian influence, having a system of identification motifs. His most ambitious work was an orch. tetralogy on Homer's *Odyssey,* under the general title *Odysseus' Fahrten,* comprising: *Odysseus' Ausfahrt und Schiffbruch* (Munich, Feb. 20, 1903; Philadelphia, Dec. 3, 1904); *Die Insel der Kirke; Die*

Klage der Nausikaa; and *Odysseus' Heimkehr;* also the symph. poem *Taormina* (Essen, 1906; Boston Symph., Nov. 29, 1907).

Boehmer, Konrad, German composer and writer on music; b. Berlin, May 24, 1941. He studied composition, musicology, sociology, and related sciences at Cologne Univ. (Ph.D., 1966); in 1967 he went to the Netherlands, where he lectured on music at the Royal Cons. in The Hague. He adopted a strong political stand of the extreme Marxist persuasion and delivered some sharp criticism against Stockhausen and other proponents of the avant-garde for their isolation from the musical masses, even classifying them as implicit adherents to imperialistic capitalism. In his own music he followed the ideas of Hanns Eisler; he also made use of electronic sound; typical of his belligerent sociomusical projections are *Potential* for Piano (1961); *Information* for Percussion and 2 Pianos (1964–65); and *Song without Words* for Voice and Chamber Orch., to a text by Ho Chi Minh.

Boekelman, Bernardus, Dutch pianist; b. Utrecht, the Netherlands, June 9, 1838; d. New York, Aug. 2, 1930. He studied with his father and at the Leipzig Cons. with Moscheles, Richter, and Hauptmann. In 1864 he emigrated to Mexico; in 1866 settled in N.Y. and then taught in various private schools. He publ. some piano pieces, edited the collection *Century of Music.* His analytical edition of Bach's *Well-Tempered Clavichord* and *2-Part Inventions* using colors to indicate part-writing is unique.

Boëllmann, Léon, French composer; b. Ensisheim, Alsace, Sept. 25, 1862; d. Paris, Oct. 11, 1897. He studied organ with Gigout; later was an organ teacher in Paris. He left 68 publ. works; his *Variations symphoniques* for Cello and Orch. became part of the repertoire of cello players. He wrote a symph., *Fantaisie dialoguée,* for Organ and Orch.; *Suite gothique* for Organ; Piano Quartet; Piano Trio; Cello Sonata; *Rapsodie carnavalesque* for Piano, 4-hands; publ. a collection of 100 pieces for organ under the title *Heures mystiques.*

Boelza, Igor, Russian music scholar and composer; b. Kielce, Poland, Feb. 8, 1904. He studied philology at the Univ. of Kiev; then taught at the Kiev Cons. (1929–41); then was on the staff of the Moscow Cons. (1942–49); was also a member of the board of the State Music Publishing House in Moscow (1941–48) and on the staff of the Inst. for the History of the Arts (1954–61); in 1961 he became a member of the Inst. for Slavonic Studies at the Academy of Sciences of the U.S.S.R. He contributed numerous informative articles dealing with the music of the Slavic countries to various publications; publ. *Handbook of Soviet Musicians* (London, 1943); *Czech Opera Classics* (Moscow, 1951); *History of Polish Musical Culture* (Moscow, 1954); and *History of Czech Musical Culture* (2 vols., Moscow, 1959–73).

Boepple, Paul, choral conductor and pedagogue; b. Basel, Switzerland, July 19, 1896; d. Brattleboro, Vt., Dec. 21, 1970. He took courses at the Dalcroze Inst. in Geneva, and adopted the Dalcroze system in his own method of teaching music; from 1918–26 he was a member of the faculty of the Inst. In 1926 he emigrated to the U.S.; directed the Dalcroze School of Music in N.Y. (1926–32); then taught at the Chicago Musical College (1932–34) and at Westminster Choir School in Princeton (1935–38); subsequently he taught at Bennington College in Vermont. As a choral conductor, he gave numerous performances of modern works.

Boero, Felipe, Argentine opera composer; b. Buenos Aires, May 1, 1884; d. there, Aug. 9, 1958. He studied with Pablo Berutti; received a government prize for further study in Europe and attended the classes of Vidal and Fauré at the Paris Cons. (1912–14). Returning to Buenos Aires, he became active as a teacher. Among his operas, the following were produced at the Teatro Colón: *Tucumán* (June 29, 1918); *Ariana y Dionisios* (Aug. 5, 1920); *Raquela* (June 25, 1923); *Las Bacantes* (Sept. 19, 1925); *El Matrero* (July 12, 1929); *Siripo* (June 8, 1937).

Boetius (or **Boethius**), **Anicius Manlius Torquatus Severinus,** Roman philosopher and mathematician; b. Rome, A.D. c.480; executed in 524 on suspicion of treason, by the Emperor Theodoric, whose counselor he had been for many years. Boetius wrote a treatise in 5 books, *De Institutione Musica,* which was the chief source book for the theorizing monks of the Middle Ages; this treatise was publ. in Venice (1491, 1499), in Basel (1570), in Leipzig (1867), and in a German trans. by Oscar Paul (Leipzig, 1872); a French trans. by Fétis remains in MS. Whether the notation commonly called "Boetian" (using Latin indices to denote traditional Greek notation) is properly attributable to him has been questioned for about 3 centuries (cf. Meibom, *Antiquae musicae auctores septem;* p. 7 of introduction on Alypius). For a defense of its authenticity, see F. Celentano, "La Musica presso i Romani," *Rivista musicale italiana* (1913). In this connection see also H. Potizon, *Boèce, théoricien de la musique grecque* (Paris, 1961). L. Schrade wrote several essays on Boetius: "Das propädeutische Ethos in der Musikanschauung des Boetius," *Zeitschrift für Geschichte der Erziehung und des Unterrichts* (1930); "Die Stellung der Musik in der Philosphie des Boetius," *Archiv für Geschichte der Philosophie* (1932); and "Music in the Philosophy of Boetius," *Musical Quarterly* (April 1947).

Boetticher, Wolfgang, noted German musicologist; b. Bad Ems, Aug. 19, 1914. He studied musicology at the Univ. of Berlin with Schering, Schünemann, Blume, and others; received his Ph.D. there in 1939 with the dissertation *Robert Schumann: Einführung in Persönlichkeit und Werk* (publ. in Berlin, 1941); completed his Habilitation in musicology there in 1943 with his *Studien zur solistischen Lautenpraxis des 16. und 17. Jahrhunderts*

(publ. in Berlin, 1943). In 1948 he joined the faculty of the Univ. of Göttingen; was prof. of musicology (1956–59); from 1958 also taught at the Technical Univ. in Clausthal. He is an acknowledged authority on the music of the Renaissance and the 19th century; his writings on lute music, Orlando di Lasso, and Robert Schumann are valuable.

Boguslawski, Edward, Polish composer; b. Chorzów, Sept. 22, 1940. He studied composition with Szabelski in Katowice and with Haubenstock-Ramati in Vienna. In 1963 he joined the faculty of the State College of Music in Katowice. His music makes use of impressionistic techniques.

WORKS: *Intonazioni I* for 9 Instruments (1962); *Intonazioni II* for Orch. (1967); *Apocalypse* for Narrator, Chorus, and Instruments (1965); *Signals* for Orch. (1965–66); *Metamorphoses* for Oboe, Clarinet, 2 Violins, Viola, and Cello (1967); *Canti* for Soprano and Orch. (1967); Concerto for Oboe, Oboe d'Amore, English Horn, Musette, and Orch. (1967–68); *Versions* for 6 Instruments (1968); *Musica per Ensemble MW–2* for Flute, Cello, and 2 Pianos (1970); Trio for Flute, Oboe, and Guitar (1970); *Per Pianoforte* (1971); *Capriccioso-Notturno* for Orch. (1972); *Impromptu* for Flute, Viola, and Harp (1972); *L'Etre* for Soprano, Flute, Cello, and 2 Pianos (1973); *Pro Varsovia* for Orch. (1973–74); *Musica Notturna* for Musette and Piano (1974); *Evocations* for Baritone and Orch. (1974); *Divertimento* for Chamber Ensemble (1975); Concerto for Oboe, Soprano, and Orch. (1975–76).

Böhm, Georg, German organist; b. Hohenkirchen, Thuringia, Sept. 2, 1661; d. Lüneburg, May 18, 1733. He studied at the Univ. of Jena; was in Hamburg in 1693; in 1698 he became organist at the Johanneskirche in Lüneburg. His organ preludes and harpsichord pieces are exemplars of keyboard works of his time; Bach himself was influenced by Böhm's style of writing. A complete ed. of Böhm's work was begun by Johannes Wolgast in 1927 in 2 vols.; a revised ed. of both vols. was publ. in Wiesbaden in 1952 and 1963, respectively.

Böhm, Joseph, violinist; b. Budapest, March 4, 1795; d. Vienna, March 28, 1876. He was a pupil of his father; at 8 years of age he made a concert tour to Poland and St. Petersburg, where he studied for some years under Pierre Rode. His first concert at Vienna (1815) was very successful; after a trip to Italy, he was appointed (1819) violin prof. at the Vienna Cons.; retired in 1848. He formed many distinguished pupils, including Joachim, Ernst, Auer, Rappoldi, and Hellmesberger (Sr.).

Böhm, Karl, Austrian conductor of great renown; b. Graz, Aug. 28, 1894; d. Salzburg, Aug. 14, 1981. He studied law before enrolling at the Cons. of Graz, where he took lessons in piano playing; subsequently he studied music theory with Mandyczewsky at the Cons. of Vienna. After service in the Austrian army during World War I he was appointed conductor at the Municipal Theater at Graz. He completed his studies of law, receiving a degree of Dr.Jur. in 1919. Although he never took formal lessons in conducting, he soon acquired sufficient technique to be engaged at the State Opera in Munich (1921). He made rapid progress in his career; in 1927 he was appointed Generalmusikdirektor in Darmstadt; having already mastered a number of works by Mozart, Wagner, and Richard Strauss, he included in his repertoire modern operas by Krenek and Hindemith. In 1931 he conducted *Wozzeck* by Alban Berg, a performance which Berg himself warmly praised. From 1931 to 1933 Böhm held the post of Generalmusikdirektor of the Hamburg Opera; from 1934 to 1943 he was music director of the Dresden State Opera, where he gave the first performances of two operas by Richard Strauss: *Die Schweigsame Frau* (June 24, 1935) and *Daphne* (Oct. 15, 1938), which Strauss dedicated to him. During the last two years of the raging war, he was conductor at the Vienna State Opera. The rumors were rife of his at least passive adherence to the Nazis, although he categorically denied that he was ever a member of the party. After the war he was not allowed by the Allied authorities to give performances pending an investigation of his political past; he was cleared and resumed his career in 1947. In 1950 he went to Argentina, where he organized and conducted a German opera repertoire at the Teatro Colón in Buenos Aires; returning to Europe, he again served as principal conductor of the Vienna State Opera (1954–56). On Nov. 5, 1955, he conducted Beethoven's *Fidelio* at the opening in the reconstructed State Opera House. He made his first appearance in the U.S. with the Chicago Symph. Orch. on Feb. 9, 1956; on Oct. 28, 1957, he led the opening of the season at the Metropolitan Opera in N.Y. with Mozart's *Don Giovanni.* He continued to conduct occasional performances at the Metropolitan until 1974. He conducted a program of symphonic music with the N.Y. Phil. Orch. on Dec. 8, 1960; in 1961 he took the Berlin Phil. to the U.S., and in 1963–64 he made a tour in Japan with it. In 1975 he conducted an American tour with the Deutsche Oper of Berlin. In 1979 he brought the Vienna State Opera to America for its first U.S. tour. He also conducted radio and television performances. Böhm received numerous honors and tokens of distinction, among them the Golden Mozart Memorial Medal from the International Mozarteum Foundation in Salzburg, the Brahms Medal from Hamburg, and the Bruckner Ring from the Vienna Symph. On his 70th birthday in 1964 a Böhm Day was celebrated in Vienna; his 80th birthday was observed in 1974 in Salzburg and Vienna. In 1977 Böhm was elected president of the London Symph. Orch. In the annals of the art of conducting, Böhm may well be regarded as a worthy successor of the glorious pleiad of German and Austrian conductors such as Karl Muck, Bruno Walter, and Wilhelm Furtwängler. He was admired for his impeccable rendition of classical opera scores, particularly those of Mozart, in which he scrupulously avoided any suggestion of improper romanticization; he was equally extolled for his productions of the operas of Wagner and Richard Strauss, and he earned additional respect for his audacious espous-

al of modern music. He publ. *Begegnung mit Richard Strauss* (Munich, 1964) and a personal memoir, *Ich erinnere mich ganz genau* (*I Remember It Quite Clearly;* Zürich, 1968).

Böhm, Theobald, German flutist and inventor of the "Böhm flute"; b. Munich, April 9, 1794; d. there, Nov. 25, 1881. He was the son of a goldsmith and learned mechanics in his father's workshop; studied the flute, achieving a degree of virtuosity that made him one of the greatest flute players of his time; he was appointed court musician in 1818; gave concerts in Paris and London. His system of construction marks a new departure in the making of woodwind instruments. To render the flute acoustically perfect, he fixed the position and size of the holes so as to obtain, not convenience in fingering, but purity and fullness of tone; all holes are covered by keys, whereby prompt and accurate "speaking" is assured; and the bore is modified, rendering the tone much fuller and mellower. He publ. *Über den Flötenbau und die neuesten Verbesserungen desselben* (Mainz, 1847; Eng. trans. by W.S. Broadwood, London, 1882); *Die Flöte und das Flötenspiel* (Munich, 1871).

Böhner, Ludwig, German composer; b. Töttelstedt, Gotha, Jan. 8, 1787; d. there, March 28, 1860. He studied with his father and with Johann Christian Kittel, a pupil of Bach. Having achieved considerable fame as a pianist and a composer, he failed to establish himself socially and economically, owing to his personal eccentricities. He wandered through Germany, often on foot, and worked irregularly as a theatrical conductor and a concert pianist. The claim he advanced, that other composers plagiarized him, is supported by the fact that Weber had unintentionally borrowed one of the themes in *Der Freischütz* from Böhner's piano concerto. Böhner's life and character were understood to have inspired the figure of the eccentric genius Kreisler in E.T.A. Hoffmann's *Capellmeister Kreisler* as well as Schumann's *Kreisleriana.*

Boieldieu, François-Adrien, celebrated French opera composer; b. Rouen, Dec. 16, 1775; d. Jarcy, near Grosbois, Oct. 8, 1834. His father was a clerical functionary who at one time served as secretary to Archbishop Larochefoucauld; his mother owned a millinery shop; the parents were divorced in 1794, and Boieldieu received his musical instruction from Charles Broche; he then was apprenticed to Broche as an assistant organist at the church of St. André in Rouen. When he was 17 his first opera, *La Fille coupable* (to his father's libretto), achieved a production in Rouen (Nov. 2, 1793). He composed patriotic pieces which were in demand during the revolutionary period. His *Chant populaire pour la Fête de la Raison* for chorus and orch. was presented at the Temple of Reason (former cathedral) in Rouen on Nov. 30, 1793. His second opera, *Rosalie et Myrza,* was also staged in Rouen (Oct. 28, 1795). He was befriended by the composer Louis Jadin and the piano manufacturer Erard; he met Cherubini and

Méhul; made a tour in Normandy with the tenor Garat. His songs, of a popular nature, were printed in Paris; also publ. were his piano sonatas; a complete edition of these sonatas was reprinted by G. Favre in 2 albums (1944–45). A facile composer, Boieldieu produced one opera after another and had no difficulties in having them staged in Paris. Particularly successful was his opera *Le Calife de Bagdad* (Paris, Sept. 16, 1800), which appealed to the public because of its exotic subject and pseudo-oriental arias.

On March 19, 1802, Boieldieu married the dancer Clotilde Mafleurai, but separated from her the following year. Opportunely, he received an invitation to go to Russia. His contract called for an attractive salary of 4,000 rubles annually, in return for writing operas for the Imperial theaters in St. Petersburg. He attended to his duties conscientiously, and produced operas every year. His salary was raised, but Boieldieu decided to leave Russia in 1811 and return to Paris. His estranged wife died in 1826, and Boieldieu married the singer Jenny Phillis. True to his custom, he resumed composing operas for the Paris theaters. In 1817 he was appointed prof. of composition at the Paris Cons.; he resigned in 1826. In 1821 he was named a Chevalier of the Legion of Honor. After a number of insignificant productions, he achieved his greatest success with his Romantic opera *La Dame blanche*, fashioned after Walter Scott's novels *The Monastery* and *Guy Mannering;* the dramatic subject and the effective musical setting corresponded precisely to the tastes of the public of the time. It was produced at the Opéra-Comique in Paris on Dec. 10, 1825, and became a perennial success in Paris and elsewhere; it was produced in London on Oct. 9, 1826, and in N.Y. on Aug. 24, 1827. In 1833 he received a grant of 6,000 francs from the French government and retired to his country house at Jarcy, where he died. During the last years of his life he became interested in painting; his pictures show a modest talent in landscape. He was also successful as a teacher; among his pupils were Fétis, Adam, and P.J.G. Zimmerman.

Boieldieu composed about 40 operas, of which several were written in collaboration with Méhul, Berton, Hérold, Cherubini, Catel, Isouard, Kreutzer, and Auber; 9 of these operas are lost. Boieldieu's significance in the history of French opera is great, even though the nationalistic hopes of the French music critics and others that he would rival Rossini did not materialize; Boieldieu simply lacked the tremendous power of invention, both in dramatic and comic aspects, that made Rossini a magician of 19th-century opera. Boieldieu's natural son, **Adrien-Louis-Victor Boieldieu** (b. Paris, Nov. 3, 1815; d. Quincy, July 9, 1883), was also a composer; his mother was Thérèse Regnault, a singer. He wrote 2 operas, *Marguerite*, which was sketched by his father but left incomplete, and *L'Aïeule.* WORKS: OPERAS: *La Fille coupable* (Rouen, Nov. 2, 1793); *Rosalie et Myrza* (Rouen, Oct. 28, 1795); *La Famille suisse* (Paris, Feb. 11, 1797); *Zoraine et Zulnare* (Paris, May 10, 1798); *La Dôt de Suzette* (Paris, Sept. 5, 1798); *Beniowski* (Paris, June 8, 1800); *Le Calife de Bagdad* (Paris, Sept. 16, 1800); *Ma tante Aurore* (Paris, Jan. 13, 1803); *Aline, reine de Golconda* (St. Petersburg, March 17, 1804); *Abderkhan* (St. Petersburg, Aug. 7, 1804); *Un Tour de soubrette* (St. Petersburg, April 28, 1806); *Télémaque dans l'isle de Calypso* (St. Petersburg, Dec. 28, 1806); *Les Voitures verseés* (St. Petersburg, April 16, 1808); *Rien de trop ou Les Deux Paravents* (St. Petersburg, Jan. 6, 1811); *Jean de Paris* (Paris, April 4, 1812); *Le Nouveau Seigneur de village* (Paris, June 29, 1813); *La Fête du village voisin* (Paris, March 5, 1816); *Le Petit Chaperon rouge* (Paris, June 30, 1818; highly successful); *La Dame blanche* (Paris, Dec. 10, 1825; his masterpiece; nearly 1,700 performances before 1914 in Paris alone). The following operas were products of collaboration: *La Prisonnière,* with Cherubini (1799); *Le Baiser et la quittance,* with Méhul, Kreutzer, and others (1803); *Bayard à Mézières,* with Cherubini, Catel, and Isouard (1803); *Les Béarnais, ou Henry IV en voyage,* with Kreutzer (1814); *Angéla, on L'Atelier de Jean Cousin,* with Mme. Gail, a pupil of Fétis (1814); *Charles de France, ou Amour et gloire,* with Hérold (1816); *Blanche de Provence, ou La Cour des fées,* with Cherubini, Berton, and others (1821); *Les 3 Genres,* with Auber (1824); *La Marquise de Brinvilliers,* with Berton and others (1831).

Boismortier, Joseph Bodin de, French composer; b. Thionville (Moselle), Dec. 23, 1689; d. Roissy-en-Brie, Oct. 28, 1755. He lived in Metz and Perpignan before settling in Paris in 1724. A prolific composer of instrumental music, he wrote more than 100 opus numbers; of these there are several for block flutes (i.e., recorders) and transverse flutes; 2 suites for clavecin; trio sonatas, among them one with the viola da gamba (1732; modern ed., Mainz, 1967); collections of pieces designed for amateurs (in the positive sense of this abused word), scored with a drone instrument, either the musette (a wind instrument) or the vielle (a string instrument), and publ. under such coaxing titles as "Gentillesses," or "Divertissements de campagne." He also wrote 3 ballet-operas: *Les Voyages de L'Amour* (1736); *Don Quichotte* (1743); *Daphnis et Chloé* (1747), and a number of cantatas.

Boito, Arrigo, important Italian poet and opera composer; b. Padua, Feb. 24, 1842; d. Milan, June 10, 1918. He studied at the Milan Cons. with Alberto Mazzucato and Ronchetti-Monteviti; his 2 cantatas, *Il 4 Giugno* (1860) and *Le Sorelle d'Italia* (1861), written in collaboration with Faccio, were performed at the Cons., and attracted a great deal of favorable attention; as a result, the Italian government granted the composers a gold medal and a stipend for foreign travel for 2 years. Boito spent most of his time in Paris, and also went to Poland to meet the family of his mother (who was Polish); he also visited Germany, Belgium, and England. He was strongly influenced by new French and German music; upon his return to Milan, he undertook the composition of his first and most significant large opera, *Mefistofele,* which contains elements of conventional Italian opera but also dramatic ideas stemming from Beethoven and Wagner. It was performed for the first time at La Scala (March 5, 1868). A controversy followed when a part of the audience objected to the unusual treatment of the subject and the music, and there were actual disorders at the conclusion of the performance. After the 2nd production, the opera was taken off the boards, and Boito undertook a revision to effect a compromise. In this new version, the opera had a successful run in Italian cities; it was also produced in Hamburg (1880), in London (in Italian, July 6, 1880), and in Boston (in Eng., Nov. 16, 1880). It was retained in the repertoire of the leading opera houses, but its success never matched that of Gounod's *Faust.* Boito never completed his 2nd opera, *Nerone,* on which he worked for more than half a century (from 1862–1916). The orch. score was revised by Toscanini and performed by him at La Scala on May 1, 1924. There are sketches for an earlier opera, *Ero e Leandro,* but not enough material to attempt a completion. Boito's gift as a poet is fully equal to that as a composer. He publ. a book of verses (Turin, 1877) under the anagrammatic pen name of **Tobia Gorrio;** he wrote his own librettos for his operas and made admirable translations of Wagner's operas (*Tristan und Isolde; Rienzi*); wrote the librettos of *Otello* and *Falstaff* for Verdi (these librettos are regarded as his masterpieces); also for *Gioconda* by Ponchielli, *Amleto* by Faccio, etc. Boito also publ. novels. He held various honorary titles from the King of Italy; in 1892 he was appointed inspector-general of Italian conservatories; was made honorary D.Mus. by Cambridge Univ. and Oxford Univ.; in 1912 he was made a senator by the King of Italy.

Bok, Mary Louise Curtis, American patroness of music; b. Boston, Aug. 6, 1876; d. Philadelphia, Jan. 4, 1970. She inherited her fortune from Cyrus H.K. Curtis, founder of the Curtis Publishing Co. In 1924 she established in Philadelphia the Curtis Inst. of Music and endowed it initially with a gift of $12.5 million in memory of her mother. The school had a faculty of the most distinguished American and European musicians, and it provided tuition exclusively on a scholarship basis; many talented composers and performers were its students; among them were Leonard Bernstein, Samuel Barber, and Lukas Foss. Josef Hofmann was engaged to head the piano dept.; from 1926 to 1938 he served as director of the Curtis Inst. Mrs. Bok was first married to Edward W. Bok, in 1896; he died in 1930; in 1943 she married **Efrem Zimbalist,** who was director of the Curtis Inst. from 1941 until 1968. She purchased in England the famous Burrell Collection of Wagneriana and brought it to the U.S. In 1932 she received an honorary doctorate from the Univ. of Pennsylvania, and in 1934, an honorary doctorate from Williams College.

Bolcom, William (Elden), American pianist and composer; b. Seattle, May 26, 1938. He studied at the Univ. of Washington in Seattle with John Verrall (B.A., 1958); took a course in composition with Dari-us Milhaud at Mills College in Oakland, Calif. (M.A., 1961); attended classes in advanced composition with Leland Smith at Stanford Univ. (D.M.A., 1964); also studied at the Paris Cons. (2nd prize in composition, 1965). He received Guggenheim fellowships in 1964–65 and 1968–69. He taught at the Univ. of Washington in Seattle (1965–66), Queens College of the City Univ. of N.Y. (1966–68), and the N.Y. Univ. School of the Arts (1969–70). He joined the faculty of the school of music at the Univ. of Michigan in 1973; was made a full prof. in 1983. After absorbing a variety of techniques *sine ira et studio,* he began to experiment widely and wildly in serial thematics, musical collage, sophisticated intentional plagiarism, and microtonal electronics. He was also active as a pianist, recording and giving recitals of ragtime piano and, with his wife, the singer **Joan Morris,** in concerts of popular American songs from olden times. He publ., with Robert Kimbass, a book on the black American songwriting and musical comedy team of Noble Sissle and Eubie Blake, *Reminiscing with Sissle and Blake* (N.Y., 1973); also edited the collected essays of George Rochberg, under the title *The Aesthetics of Survival: A Composer's View of the 20th Century* (Ann Arbor, Mich., 1984).

Bolet, Jorge, brilliant Cuban-American pianist; b. Havana, Nov. 15, 1914. He went to the U.S. in 1926 and studied piano with David Saperton and conducting with Fritz Reiner at the Curtis Inst. in Philadelphia. In 1932 he took lessons with Leopold Godowsky and with Moriz Rosenthal; he also studied briefly with Rudolf Serkin. During World War II he was stationed in Japan; returning to the U.S., he took private lessons with Abram Chasins. Eventually he was appointed head of the piano dept. at the Curtis Inst. A virtuoso of maximal powers, he seems to be a natural heir of his teachers Godowsky and Rosenthal.

Bologna, Jacopo da. See **Jacopo da Bologna.**

Bolzoni, Giovanni, Italian composer and conductor; b. Parma, May 14, 1841; d. Turin, Feb. 21, 1919. He studied at the Parma Cons.; was active as a conductor in Perugia; served as director and prof. of composition at the Liceo Musicale in Turin (1887–1916); also conducted at the Teatro Regio there (1884–89). He composed several operas; among them the most successful were *Il matrimonio civile* (Parma, 1870), *La stella delle Alpi* (Savona, 1876), and *Jella* (Piacenza, 1881). A melodious minuet from one of his string quartets became a perennial favorite in numerous arrangements.

Bomtempo, João Domingos, Portuguese pianist; b. Lisbon, Dec. 28, 1775; d. there, Aug. 18, 1842. He studied in Paris; then went to London, where he stayed until 1811. Returning to Lisbon, he was active on the concert stage; in 1816 he went to London again; finally went to Portugal in 1820. In 1822 he founded a phil. society in Lisbon; in 1833 became director of the Lisbon Cons. He wrote 6 symphonies,

4 piano concertos, 14 piano sextets, a piano quintet, and several piano sonatas; also an opera, *Alessandro in Efesso*. He publ. a piano method (London, 1816).

Bona (or **Buona**), **Valerio**, Italian composer; b. Brescia, c.1560; date of death unknown, but he was still living in 1619. He was a Franciscan monk; maestro di cappella at the cathedrals of Vercelli (1591) and Mondovi, and at the Church of San Francesco in Milan (1596); musician at St. Francesco in Brescia (1611) and prefect at St. Fermo Maggiore in Verona (1614). He was a prolific composer, in polyphonic style, of sacred and secular vocal music (masses, litanies, Lamentations, motets, madrigals, etc.), many of which he wrote for 2 choirs. Also a theorist, he publ.: *Regole del contrapunto, et compositione brevemente raccolte da diuersi auttori* (Casale, 1595); *Esempii delli passagi delle consonanze, et dissonanze* (Milan, 1596); etc.

Bonaventura, Mario di, American conductor, educator, and music publisher; b. Follansbee, W.Va., Feb. 20, 1924. He studied violin; won an award at the N.Y. Phil. in the Young Composers' Composition Competition in 1941; in 1947 went to Paris to study composition with Nadia Boulanger; also took a course in piano accompaniment at the Paris Cons. He subsequently studied conducting with Igor Markevitch at the Mozarteum in Salzburg and later in Paris; received a prize at the 1952 International Conducting Competition at Besançon; in 1953 was awarded the Lili Boulanger Memorial Prize in Composition. In 1954–56 he served as staff pianist with the Pasdeloup Orch. in Paris; made jazz arrangements for the guitarist Django Reinhardt. Returning to the U.S., he conducted the Fort Lauderdale Symph. (1959–62); in 1962 was appointed to the faculty of Dartmouth College; in 1963 inaugurated there an auspicious series of summer festivals under the title "Congregation of the Arts" and commissioned a great number of special works from contemporary composers; all together, 389 modern works were performed during 7 summers, which included 38 world premieres. Among composers-in-residence during this period were Zoltán Kodály, Frank Martin, Boris Blacher, Hans Werner Henze, Ernst Krenek, Witold Lutoslawski, Luigi Dallapiccola, Roberto Gerhard, Walter Piston, Roger Sessions, Carlos Chávez, Easley Blackwood, Elliott Carter, Aaron Copland, Henry Cowell, Ross Lee Finney, Alberto Ginastera, Peter Mennin, and Vincent Persichetti. In 1968 Bonaventura produced and directed the 4th International Anton von Webern Festival; also initiated programs for the furtherance of new music, which awarded 55 commissions to composers in 19 countries. As a conductor, he led orchs. on several European tours. In 1974 he was appointed vice-president and director of publications of G. Schirmer/Associated Music Publishers, N.Y.; in that capacity, too, he promoted publications of modern music; he resigned in 1979 and dedicated himself mainly to univ. teaching.

Bonci, Alessandro, Italian lyric tenor; b. Cesena, Feb. 10, 1870; d. Viserba, Aug. 8, 1940. He studied with Carlo Pedrotti and Felice Coen in Pesaro; later took singing lessons with Della Sedie in Paris. He made his operatic debut in Parma on Jan. 20, 1896, as Fenton in *Falstaff;* then sang at La Scala, Milan, and later undertook a grand tour of Europe; also made appearances in South America and Australia. In 1906 he made his N.Y. debut at the new Manhattan Opera House, and remained on its roster for 3 seasons; on Nov. 22, 1907, he sang the role of the Duke in *Rigoletto* at his debut at the Metropolitan Opera, N.Y., and remained with it for 3 seasons. His voice was of great lyric charm; he was one of the few Italian artists to achieve distinction as a singer of German lieder.

Bond, Carrie Jacobs, American composer of sentimental songs; b. Janesville, Wis., Aug. 11, 1862; d. Glendale, Calif., Dec. 28, 1946. She was naturally gifted in music and painting, and improvised songs to her own words at the piano. She organized a music-selling agency and publ. her own songs under the imprint Carrie Jacobs Bond and Son. Although deficient in musical training, she succeeded in producing sweet melodies in lilting rhythms with simple accompaniment that became extremely popular in America. Her first song was *Is My Dolly Dead?* This was followed by her greatest hit, *A Perfect Day,* and a series of other successful songs: *I Love You Truly, God Remembers When the World Forgets, Life's Garden,* and many others. She publ. an autobiography, *The Roads of Melody* (1927), and an album of her poems with philosophical comments under the title *The End of the Road.*

Bondeville, Emmanuel de, French composer; b. Rouen, Oct. 29, 1898. He studied organ in Rouen and composition with Jean Déré in Paris; subsequently held administrative positions as music director of the Eiffel Tower Radio Station (1935–49), artistic director of the Monte Carlo Opera (1945–49), and director of the Paris Opéra (1952–70). He wrote 2 operas, both produced at the Opéra-Comique in Paris: *L'École des maris* (June 19, 1935) and *Madame Bovary* (June 1, 1951); also composed a symph. triptych after Rimbaud's poem *Illuminations: Le Bal des pendus* (Paris, Dec. 6, 1930), *Ophélie* (Paris, March 29, 1933), and *Marine* (Paris, March 11, 1934). Other works include *Symphonie lyrique* (1957); *Symphonie choréographique* (1966); choral pieces; a piano sonata; songs. In 1959 he was elected successor to Florent Schmitt as a member of the Académie des Beaux-Arts (Institut de France).

Bondon, Jacques, French composer; b. Boulbon (Bouches-du-Rhône), Dec. 6, 1927. He studied violin and painting in Marseilles. In 1945 he went to Paris, where he took courses in composition with Kœchlin, Milhaud, and Jean Rivier. After early experimentation with ultramodern techniques, he tergiversated to prudential modernism. He became associated with Martenot, and wrote a Concerto for Ondes Martenot and Orch. (1955); also composed music for films and for the radio.

Bonelli, Richard, American baritone; b. Port Byron, N.Y., Feb. 6, 1887; d. Los Angeles, June 7, 1980. His real name was **Bunn,** but he changed it to Bonelli when he began his career, since in his time it was difficult to succeed as a singer with an Anglo-Saxon name. He studied with Jean de Reszke in Europe; made his operatic debut as Valentine in *Faust* at the Brooklyn Academy of Music, N.Y., April 21, 1915; then sang at the Monte Carlo Opera, at La Scala in Milan, and in Paris. From 1925 to 1931 he was a member of the Chicago Opera Co.; he made his Metropolitan Opera debut as Germont in *La Traviata* on Dec. 1, 1932. He retired in 1945.

Bonhomme, Pierre, South Netherlandish composer; b. c.1555; d. Liège, June 12, 1617. He was educated in Liège; received the tonsure in 1579; in 1594 was awarded a canonry at the collegiate church of Sainte-Croix in Liège, where he spent the rest of his life. He publ. the *Melodiae sacrae* for 5 to 9 Voices (Frankfurt, 1603) and the *Missae* for 6, 8, 10, and 12 Voices (Antwerp, 1616).

Bonini, Severo, Italian composer, organist, and writer on music; b. Florence, Dec. 23, 1582; d. there, Dec. 5, 1663. He received the habit of the Vallombrosan Benedictines in 1595; professed in 1598; then studied theology and other subjects at the Univ. at Passignano; subsequently resided in an abbey in Florence. In 1611 he became organist at the abbey of Santa Trinità; in 1613 assumed a similar position at S. Mercuriale in Forlì. In 1615 he was made camarlingo at the abbey of S. Michele in Forcole, Pistoia, and in 1619 at S. Mercuriale in Forlì. In 1623 he became curate at S. Martino in Strada, where he remained until 1637. In 1640 he was named organist and maestro di cappella at Santa Trinità, posts he retained until his death. He wrote a valuable treatise on the beginnings of monody and opera, *Discorsi e regole sovra la musica et il contrappunto* (modern ed. and trans. by M. Bonino, Provo, Utah, 1978).

Bonnet, Joseph, eminent French organist; b. Bordeaux, March 17, 1884; d. Ste. Luce-sur-Mer, Quebec, Aug. 2, 1944. He studied with his father, organist at Ste. Eulalie; at the age of 14 he was appointed regular organist at St. Nicholas, and soon after at St. Michel; entered the class of Guilmant at the Paris Cons. and graduated with the first prize. In 1906 he won the post of organist at St. Eustache over many competitors. After extensive tours on the Continent and in England, he became organist of the Concerts du Conservatoire as successor to Guilmant (1911). He made his American debut in N.Y. (Jan. 30, 1917), followed by successful tours of the U.S. He wrote many pieces for his instrument, and edited for publication all the works played in his series of N.Y. concerts as *Historical Organ Recitals* (6 vols.); also publ. an anthology of early French organ music (N.Y., 1942).

Bonno, Giuseppe, noted Austrian composer of Italian descent; b. Vienna, Jan. 29, 1711; d. there, April 15, 1788. His father, Lucrezio Bonno, was the imperial footman. He began his musical studies with Johann Georg Reinhardt, the court organist. Charles VI sent Bonno to Naples in 1726 for further musical education; there he studied composition with Durante and Leo. His first opera, *Nigella e Nise,* was performed in Naples in 1732. In 1736 he returned to Vienna, where he brought out his 2nd opera, *L'amore insuperabile.* In 1737 he was made a court scholar in composition, and in 1739 was named court composer. In 1739 he brought out his oratorio *Eleazaro,* which proved highly successful. He subsequently joined Gluck and Dittersdorf as a Kapellmeister to Field Marshall Joseph Friedrich, Prince of Sachsen-Hildburghausen, in Schlosshof and Mannersdorf. In 1774 he succeeded Gassmann as Imperial Court Kapellmeister. Bonno was greatly esteemed as a teacher; Dittersdorf and Marianne von Martinez were among his pupils. He was a friend of the Mozart family, and recognized the budding genius of Mozart at an early date.

Bononcini, Antonio Maria (not **Marco Antonio,** as he is often listed), Italian opera composer, son of **Giovannia Maria** and brother of **Giovanni;** b. Modena, June 18, 1677; d. there, July 8, 1726. He studied with his father; his first success came with the production of his opera *Il trionfo di Camilla, regina dei Volsci* (Naples, Dec. 26, 1696). This opera was produced in many other theaters in Italy, sometimes under different titles, as *Amore per amore, La fede in cimento,* etc. It was presented in London (March 31, 1706) with great acclaim. In 1702 Bononcini was in Berlin; from 1704–11 he was in Vienna, where he produced the operas *Teraspo* (Nov. 15, 1704); *Arminio* (July 26, 1706); *La conquista delle Spagne di Scipione Africano* (Oct. 1, 1707); *La presa di Tebe* (Oct. 1, 1708); *Tigrane, re d'Armenia* (July 26, 1710). Returning to Italy, he produced the following operas in Milan: *Il tiranno eroe* (Dec. 26, 1715); *Sesostri, re di Egitto* (Feb. 2, 1716); *Griselda* (Dec. 26, 1718). In his native town of Modena, he directed his operas *L'enigma disciolto* (Oct. 15, 1716) and *Lucio Vero* (Nov. 5, 1716). His last opera, *Rosiclea in Dania,* was staged in Naples (Oct. 1, 1721). He wrote 19 operas in all, and 3 oratorios. His most famous opera, *Il trionfo di Camilla,* has often been erroneously attributed to his brother; several songs from it were publ. in London by Walsh.

Bononcini, Giovanni (not **Giovanni Battista,** despite the fact that this name appears on some of his compositions), the best-known composer of the Bononcini family, son of **Giovanni Maria;** b. Modena, July 18, 1670; d. Vienna, July 9, 1747 (buried July 11). His first teacher was his father; he also studied with G.P. Colonna in Bologna, and took cello lessons from Giorgio. In 1687 he was a cellist in the chapel of San Petronio in Bologna; in the same year he became maestro di cappella at San Giovanni in Monte. He publ. his first work, *Trattenimenti da camera* for String Trio, in Bologna at the age of 15. This was followed in quick succession by a set of chamber concertos, "sinfonie" for small ensembles, masses, and instrumental duos (1685–91). In 1691 he went to Rome, where he produced his first opera, *Serse* (Jan. 25, 1694), and shortly afterward, another opera, *Tullo Ostilio* (Feb. 1694). In 1698 he went to Vienna as court composer; there he brought out his operas *La fede pubblica* (Jan. 6, 1699) and *Gli affetti più grandi vinti dal più giusto* (July 26, 1701). He spent 2 years (1702–4) at the court of Queen Sophie Charlotte in Berlin; at her palace in Charlottenburg he produced, in the summer of 1702, the opera *Polifemo;* here he also presented a new opera, *Gli amori di Cefalo e Procri* (Oct. 16, 1704). After the Queen's death (Feb. 1, 1705) the opera company was disbanded; Bononcini returned to Vienna and staged the following operas: *Endimione* (July 10, 1706); *Turno Aricino* (July 26, 1707); *Mario fuggitivo* (1708); *Abdolonimo* (Feb. 3, 1709); *Muzio Scevola* (July 10, 1710). In 1711 Bononcini returned to Italy with his brother (who had also been in Vienna). In 1719 he was in Rome, where he produced the opera *Erminia*. In 1720 he received an invitation to join the Royal Academy of Music in London, of which Handel was director, and the Italian Opera Co. connected with it. A famous rivalry developed between the supporters of Handel, which included the King, and the group of noblemen (Marlborough, Queensberry, Rutland, and Sunderland) who favored Bononcini and other Italian composers. Indicative of the spirit of the time was the production at the King's Theatre of the opera *Muzio Scevola,* with the first act written by Amadei, the 2nd by Bononcini (he may have used material from his earlier setting of the same subject), and the 3rd by Handel (April 15, 1721). By general agreement Handel won the verdict of popular approval; this episode may have inspired the well-known poem publ. at the time ("Some say, compar'd to Bononcini, That Mynheer Handel's but a ninny," etc.). Other operas brought out by Bononcini in London were: *Astarto* (Nov. 19, 1720); *Crispo* (Jan. 10, 1722); *Farnace* (Nov. 27, 1723); *Calpurnia* (April 18, 1724); *Astianatte* (May 6, 1727). He then suffered a series of setbacks, first the death of his chief supporter, Marlborough (1722), and then the revelation that a madrigal he had submitted to the Academy of Music was an arrangement of a work by Lotti, which put Bononcini's professional integrity in doubt. To this was added his strange association with one Count Ughi, a self-styled alchemist who claimed the invention of a philosopher's stone, and who induced Bononcini to invest his earnings in his scheme for making gold. After his London debacle, Bononcini went (in 1732) to Paris, where he was engaged as a cellist at the court of Louis XV. He was referred to in *Le Mercure de France* (Feb. 7, 1735) as the composer of 78 operas. In 1735 he was in Lisbon; in 1737, in Vienna, where he produced the oratorio *Ezechia* (April 4, 1737) and a *Te Deum* (1740). Reduced to poverty, he petitioned the young Empress Maria Theresa for a pension, which was granted in Oct. 1742, giving him a monthly stipend of 50 florins, received regularly until his death on July 9, 1747, at the age of 77. This date and the circumstances of his last years in Vienna were first made known in the valuable paper by Kurt Hueber, *Gli ultimi anni di Giovanni Bononcini, Notizie e documenti inediti,* publ. by the Academy of Sciences, Letters and Arts of Modena (Dec. 1954). Among Bononcini's works, other than operas, are 7 oratorios (including *Ezechia;* all on various biblical subjects), and instrumental works publ. in London by Walsh: several suites for harpsichord; *Cantate e Duetti,* dedicated to George I (1721); Divertimenti for Harpsichord (1722); *Funeral Anthem for John, Duke of Marlborough* (1722); *12 Sonatas or Chamber Airs for 2 Violins and a Bass* (1732); etc. For further details regarding Bononcini's operas, see Loewenberg's *Annals of Opera* (1943; 2nd ed., 1955).

Bononcini, Giovanni Maria, Italian composer; father of **Giovanni** and **Antonio Maria Bononcini;** b. Montecorone, Sept. 23, 1642; d. Modena, Nov. 18, 1678. In 1671 he was awarded a ducal appointment as violinist at the Cathedral of Modena; also served as chamber musician to the Dowager Duchess Laura d'Este. He had 8 children, of whom the only two who survived infancy were Giovanni and Antonio Maria Bononcini. He publ. 11 sets of instrumental works: *I primi frutti del giardino musicale* (Venice, 1666); *Varii fiori* (Bologna, 1669); *Arie, correnti, sarabande, gighe e allemande* (Bologna, 1671); *Sonate* (Venice, 1672); *Ariette, correnti, gighe, allemande e sarabande* (Bologna, 1673); *Trattenimenti musicali* (Bologna, 1675); *Arie e correnti* (Bologna, 1678); also vocal works: *Cantate da camara* for Solo Voice and 2 Violins (Bologna, 1677); *Madrigali* for 5 Voices (Bologna, 1678). He further publ. a didactic manual, *Musico prattico* (Bologna, 1673; a German trans. was publ. in Stuttgart, 1701).

Bononcini, Marco Antonio. See **Bononcini, Antonio Maria.**

Bonporti, Francesco Antonio, Italian composer; b. Trento (baptized, June 11), 1672; d. Padua, Dec. 19, 1748. He studied theology in Innsbruck and Rome; in 1695 returned to Trento; was ordained a priest and served as a cleric at the Cathedral of Trento. He publ. 3 sets of 10 trio sonatas each (Venice, 1696, 1698, and 1703); 10 sonatas for Violin and Bass (Venice, 1707); 10 "concerti a 4" and 5 "concertini" for Violin and Bass; 6 motets for Soprano, Violin, and Bass. He also wrote 2 sets of minuets (50 in each set), which are lost. Four of his "invenzioni" were mistaken for Bach's works and were included in the Bachgesellschaft edition (XLV, part 1, p. 172). Henry Eccles publ. the 4th of these pieces as his own, incorporating it in his Violin Sonata No. 11.

Bontempi (real name, **Angelini**), **Giovanni Andrea,** Italian singer and composer; b. Perugia, c.1624; d. Torgiano, July 1, 1705. He was a castrato, and sang in the choir of San Marco in Venice (1643–50). After studies with Mazzocchi, he was appointed joint Kapellmeister in Dresden, with Schütz and Vincenzo Albrici, in 1656. He assumed the name Bontempi after his patron, Cesare Bontempi. In 1680 he returned to Italy; sang at the Collegiata di S. Maria at

Sapello, near Foligno, in 1682; was maestro di cappella there during the first half of 1686. He was one of the earliest composers of Italian operas and oratorios. His first opera, *Il Paride in musica,* to his own libretto, was produced in Dresden, on Nov. 3, 1662; it was the first Italian opera ever produced there. Two later operas, both produced in Dresden, were *Apollo e Dafne,* written in collaboration with Peranda and produced in Dresden on Sept. 3, 1671, and *Giove e Io* (also with Peranda), produced in Dresden on Jan. 16, 1673. He also composed an oratorio, *Martirio di San Emiliano;* published the treatises *Nova quatuor vocibus componendi methodus* (Dresden, 1660); *Tractus in quo demonstrantur occultae convenientiae sonorum systematis participati* (Bologna, 1690); *Historia musica, nella quale si ha piena cognitione della teorica e della pratica antica della musica harmonica secondo la dottrina de' Greci* (Perugia, 1695).

Bonynge, Richard, Australian conductor; b. Sydney, Sept. 29, 1930. He studied at the New South Wales Cons. of Music; began his career as a pianist. In 1954 he married **Joan Sutherland,** the famed Australian soprano. To assist her, Bonynge turned to conducting, making his debut in 1962. In 1976 he was named music director of the Australian Opera in Sydney. In 1977 he was made a Commander of the Order of the British Empire.

Boone, Charles, American composer of the avant-garde; b. Cleveland, June 21, 1939. He studied with Karl Schiske at the Vienna Academy of Music (1960–61); after returning to the U.S., he took private lessons with Ernst Krenek and Adolph Weiss in Los Angeles (1961–62); attended the Univ. of Southern Calif. (B.M., 1963) and San Francisco State College (M.A., 1968); served as chairman of the San Francisco Composers' Forum and coordinator of the Mills College Performing Group and Tape Music Center. His music creates a sonic environment on purely structural principles, employing serial matrices, coloristic contrasts, and spatial parameters of performing instruments, with resulting styles ranging from lyrical pointillism to static sonorism. Electronic resources make up part of his musical equipment.
WORKS: *Icarus* for Flute Solo (1964); *Song of Suchness* for Soprano, Flute, Piccolo, Viola, Piano, and Celesta (1964); *Parallels* for Violin and Piano (1964); *Oblique Formation* for Flute and Piano (1965); *Starfish* for Flute, E-flat Clarinet, Percussion, 2 Violins, and Piano (1966); *The Yellow Bird* for Orch. (1967); *Constant Comment* for Stereophonic Tape (1967); *Shadow* for Oboe Solo, Tape, and Orch. (1968); *The Edge of the Land* for Orch. (1968); *Not Now* for Clarinet Solo (1969); Quartet for Violin, Clarinet, Cello, and Piano (1970); *Zephyrus* for Oboe and Piano (1970); *Vermilion* for Oboe Solo (1970); *Chinese Texts* for Soprano and Orch. (1971); *Second Landscape* for Chamber Orch. (1973); *Raspberries* for 3 Drummers (1974); *Linea Meridiana* for Chamber Ensemble (1975); *San Zeno/Verona* for Chamber Ensemble (1976); *Fields/Singing* for Soprano and Chamber Ensemble (1976); *Shunt* for 3 Drummers (1978); *String Piece* for String Orch. (1978); *Streaming for Solo Flute* (1979); *Winter's End* for Soprano, Countertenor, Viola da Gamba, Harpsichord (1980); *The Watts Towers* for Solo Drummer (1981); *Trace* for Flute and 10 Players (1981).

Boosey & Hawkes, British music publishers. **Thomas Boosey** was a London bookseller and a continental traveler since 1792. He was often asked to handle music, and in 1816 founded a music publishing house on Holles Street. On the Continent he met eminent musicians of the time; he visited Vienna and negotiated about publication with Beethoven (who mentions Boosey's name in one of his letters to the Royal Phil. Society in London). Boosey's main stock consisted of Italian and French operas; he owned copyrights of Bellini, Donizetti, and Verdi (until 1854); publ. inexpensive Eng. editions of standard European works. In the 1820s he put his son, **Thomas,** in charge of musical publications. In 1846 the firm of Boosey & Sons began publishing band music; in 1855 (in conjunction with the flutist R.S. Pratten) the manufacture of improved flutes was begun; in 1868 the firm acquired Henry Distin's factory for musical instruments, and supplied band instruments for the British and Colonial armies. It was this development that eventually brought about the merger of Boosey and Hawkes. **William Henry Hawkes** was a trumpeter-in-ordinary to Queen Victoria. He established in 1865 a workshop of band instruments and an edition of concert music for orch. and became a strong competitor of Boosey & Sons from 1885 on. Economic pressure forced the amalgamation of the two firms in 1930, combining valuable editions covering a whole century of music. A branch of Boosey & Sons had been established in N.Y. (1892), discontinued in 1900 and reestablished in 1906; after the merger, Boosey & Hawkes opened offices in N.Y., Chicago, and Los Angeles. In Canada, the business was inaugurated in 1913; the Editions Hawkes started a Paris branch in 1922; further affiliates were established in Australia (1933), India (1937), Argentina (1945), South Africa (1946), and Germany (1950). After World War II the factories for the manufacture of band instruments in London were greatly expanded; quantity production of wind instruments, harmonicas, and drums enabled the firm to extend the market to all parts of the world. For a few years after World War II Boosey & Hawkes leased Covent Garden. In 1927 the firm acquired the American rights of Enoch & Sons; in 1943 the catalogue of Adolph Fürstner, containing all the operas of Richard Strauss, was bought for certain territories. In 1947, the Koussevitzky catalogue (Edition Russe de Musique and Edition Gutheil) was purchased, including the major output of Stravinsky, Prokofiev, and Rachmaninoff. Other acquisitions include the copyrights of publications of Winthrop Rogers and Rudall Carte.

Boott, Francis, American composer; b. Boston,

June 24, 1813; d. there, March 2, 1904. He was educated at Harvard (graduated in 1831); lived for a time in Florence, Italy, where he studied music; returned to the U.S. in 1874, settling in Cambridge, Mass. He bequeathed to Harvard Univ. $10,000 (which was increased through capital gains to $15,246 in 1960), the interest to form an annual prize for the best 4-part vocal composition written by a Harvard man. He was a prolific composer of secular and sacred songs, anthems, and chorales, many of which were included in the service book of King's Chapel in Boston. His songs *Here's a Health to King Charles, When Sylvia Sings,* and *Lethe* were once very popular.

Borchard, Adolphe, French pianist and composer; b. Le Havre, June 30, 1882; d. Paris, Dec. 13, 1967. He studied at the Paris Cons. with Diémer and Lenepveu, where he won prizes for piano (1903) and composition (1905, 1907); toured extensively as a pianist, making his American debut in 1910; later settled in Paris as director of various musical activities sponsored by the French government. He composed *Es Kual Herria (The Basque Country)* for Piano and Orch. (Paris, 1922); *En Marge de Shakespeare* for Orch. (1923); *L'Elan* for Orch. (1923); *Sept estampes amoureuses* for Orch. (1927); numerous songs.

Borck, Edmund von, talented German composer; b. Breslau, Feb. 22, 1906; killed in action near Nettuno, Italy, Feb. 16, 1944. He studied composition in Breslau (1920–26), and music history at the Univ. of Berlin; held several positions as opera conductor in Berlin and Frankfurt; then taught theory and composition in Berlin until drafted into the army in 1940. His progress as a composer was rapid; his early works indicated an original creative ability, and his death in combat was a great loss to German music. His style of composition is neo-Classical, with strong contrapuntal structure; the rather austere and reticent mode of expression assumes in Borck's music a colorful aspect through a variety of melodic and rhythmic devices, often in a rhapsodically romantic vein.

Borde, Jean Benjamin de la. See **La Borde, Jean Benjamin de.**

Bordes, Charles, French choral conductor; b. Roche-Corbon, near Vouvray-sur-Loire, May 12, 1863; d. Toulon, Nov. 8, 1909. He studied piano with Marmontel and composition with César Franck. In 1894, in association with Guilmant and Vincent d'Indy, he organized the Schola Cantorum in Paris, and in subsequent years organized chapters of the Schola Cantorum in Avignon and Montpellier. He made numerous tours with his choral group. In 1889 he was commissioned by the French government to make a study of Basque folk songs; he publ. 100 of these in *Archives de la tradition basque.* He also wrote several pieces based on Basque motifs, among them *Suite basque* for Flute and String Quartet (1888) and *Rapsodie basque* for Piano and

Orch. (1890); also edited several anthologies of old French music, publ. by the Schola Cantorum.

Bordoni, Faustina. See **Hasse, Faustina.**

Borel-Clerc (real name, **Clerc**), **Charles,** French composer of popular music; b. Pau, Sept. 22, 1879; d. Cannes, April 9, 1959. He studied music at first in Toulouse; at the age of 17 he went to Paris, where he studied the oboe at the Paris Cons. with Gillet, and composition with Lenepveu; then played oboe in various Paris orchs. He wrote numerous operettas, music revues, and a great number of songs; his greatest success came with *La Matchiche* (1903), a song that became world-famous. His other celebrated songs are *C'est jeune et ça n'sait pas; Madelon de la Victoire* (1918; a sequel to the war song *Madelon* by Camille Robert); many chansonettes for Maurice Chevalier and other artists.

Borg, Kim, noted Finnish bass; b. Helsinki, Aug. 7, 1919. He first studied chemistry; then enrolled in the Sibelius Academy of Music; also took singing lessons in Sweden, Denmark, Austria, Italy, and America. He began his operatic career at Aarhus in 1951; made his Metropolitan Opera debut in N.Y. on Oct. 30, 1959, as Count Almaviva in *Le nozze di Figaro,* remaining on its roster until 1962. He was one of the few non-Russian artists to sing the title role of *Boris Godunov* at the Bolshoi Opera in Moscow. In 1972 he became a member of the faculty of the Royal Cons. of Music in Copenhagen. He furthermore distinguished himself as a composer; wrote 3 trios, a String Quartet, a Trombone Concerto, and a Double-bass Concerto; published a didactic manual, *ABC for the Finnish Singer.*

Borge, Victor (real name, **Borge Rosenbaum**), Danish pianist; b. Copenhagen, Jan. 3, 1909. He studied with his father, Bernhard Rosenbaum (1847–1932); then with V. Schioler. He developed a type of humorous piano concert *sui generis* and appeared in Danish musical revues. In 1940, he settled in the U.S. and became extremely successful in his specialty in radio and television; in autumn 1953 he opened a series of daily recitals on Broadway, billed as "comedy in music," which ran for two and a half seasons, unprecedented in N.Y. theatrical annals for a one-man show. In 1951 he was named "Funniest Man" in music.

Bori, Lucrezia (real name, **Lucrecia Borja y Gonzalez de Riancho**), lyric soprano; b. Valencia, Dec. 24, 1887; d. New York, May 14, 1960. She studied with Melchior Vidal; made her debut in Rome on Oct. 31, 1908, as Micaëla; then sang in Milan, Naples, and, in 1910, in Paris as Manon Lescaut, with the Metropolitan Opera Co., then on a European tour. In 1911 she sang at La Scala; made her debut at the Metropolitan Opera House in N.Y. as Manon Lescaut on Nov. 11, 1912, and sang there until the end of the season 1914–15. After a period of retirement, occasioned by a vocal affliction, she reappeared in

1919 at Monte Carlo as Mimi, returning to the Metropolitan in 1921 in the same role. Thereafter she appeared in N.Y. with increasing success and popularity until the end of the 1935–36 season, when she retired permanently from opera.

Borkh, Inge, famous German soprano; b. Mannheim, May 26, 1917. She first appeared as a stage actress, then decided upon a singing career. She studied at the Cons. in Milan and at the Mozarteum in Salzburg. She made her debut as Czipra in Johann Strauss's *Zigeunerbaron* at the Lucerne Opera in 1940; remained a member there until 1944; then sang at the Bern Opera until 1951. She made her American debut at the San Francisco Opera in 1953; on Jan. 24, 1958, she appeared at the Metropolitan Opera in N.Y. as Salome; she was on its roster also during the seasons of 1960–61 and 1970–71.

Borodin, Alexander, celebrated Russian composer; b. St. Petersburg, Nov. 12, 1833; d. there, Feb. 27, 1887. He was the illegitimate son of a Georgian prince, Ghedeanov; his mother was the wife of an army doctor. In accordance with customary procedure in such cases, the child was registered as the lawful son of one of Ghedeanov's serfs, Porfiry Borodin; hence, the patronymic, Alexander Porfirievich. He was given an excellent education; learned several foreign languages, and was taught to play the flute. He played 4-hand arrangements of Haydn's and Beethoven's symphonies with his musical friend M. Shchiglev. At the age of 14 he tried his hand at composition; wrote a piece for flute and piano and a String Trio on themes from *Robert le Diable.* In 1850 he became a student of the Academy of Medicine in St. Petersburg, and developed a great interest in chemistry; he graduated in 1856 with honors, and joined the staff as assistant prof.; in 1858 received his doctorate in chemistry; contributed several important scientific papers to the bulletin of the Russian Academy of Sciences; traveled in Europe on a scientific mission (1859–62). Although mainly preoccupied with his scientific pursuits, Borodin continued to compose. In 1863 he married Catherine Protopopova, who was an accomplished pianist; she remained his faithful companion and musical partner; together they attended concerts and operas in Russia and abroad; his letters to her from Germany (1877), describing his visit to Liszt in Weimar, are of great interest. Of a decisive influence on Borodin's progress as a composer was his meeting with Balakirev in 1862; later he formed friendships with the critic Stasov, who named Borodin as one of the "mighty five" (actually, Stasov used the expression "mighty heap"), with Mussorgsky and other musicians of the Russian national school. He adopted a style of composition in conformity with their new ideas; he particularly excelled in a type of Russian orientalism which had a great attraction for Russian musicians at the time. He never became a consummate craftsman, like Rimsky-Korsakov; although quite proficient in counterpoint, he avoided purely contrapuntal writing; his feeling for rhythm and orchestral color was extraordinary, and his evocation of exotic scenes in his orch. works and in his opera *Prince Igor* is superb. Composition was a very slow process for Borodin; several of his works remained incomplete, and were edited after his death by Rimsky-Korsakov and Glazunov.

WORKS: OPERAS: *Prince Igor,* opera in 4 acts (begun in 1869, on the subject of the famous Russian medieval chronicle *Tale of Igor's Campaign;* completed posthumously by Rimsky-Korsakov and Glazunov; first perf., St. Petersburg, Nov. 4, 1890; London, June 8, 1914, in Russian; N.Y., Dec. 30, 1915, in Italian); an opera-farce, *Bogatyry (The Valiant Knights,* anonymously produced in Moscow on Oct. 29, 1867; rediscovered in 1932, and produced in Moscow, Nov. 12, 1936, with a new libretto by Demian Biedny, to serve propaganda purposes in an antireligious campaign, but 2 days later banned by the Soviet government for its mockery of Russian nationalism); sketches for the 4th act of an opera, *Mlada* (never produced), each act of which was to have been written by a different composer. FOR ORCH.: Symph. No. 1 in E-flat (1862–67; St. Petersburg, Jan. 16, 1869); Symph. No. 2 in B minor (1869–76; St. Petersburg, March 10, 1877); Symph. No. 3 in A minor (1886; unfinished; 2 movements orchestrated by Glazunov); symph. sketch, *In the Steppes of Central Asia* (1880); *Polovtzian Dances* from *Prince Igor* (perf. as an orch. piece, St. Petersburg, March 11, 1879). CHAMBER MUSIC: String Quartet No. 1 in A (1874–79); String Quartet No. 2 in D (1881); *Serenata alla Spagnola,* 3rd movement of a quartet on the name B-la-f, for their publisher Be-la-ieff, by Borodin, Rimsky-Korsakov, Liadov, and Glazunov (1886); Scherzo for String Quartet in the collective set *Les Vendredis.* A String Trio (dated 1860) and a Piano Quintet were discovered in 1915. FOR PIANO: *Polka, Requiem, Marche funèbre,* and *Mazurka* in the series of paraphrases on the theme of the *Chopsticks Waltz* (includes variations by Borodin, other members of the Russian school, and Liszt; 1880); *Petite suite,* comprising 7 pieces (*Au couvent, Intermezzo, Deux mazurkas, Rêverie, Sérénade, Nocturne;* 1885). FOR VOICE: *Sérénade de 4 galants à une dame* for a cappella Male Quartet (comical; no date); songs: *Sleeping Princess* (1867); *The Princess of the Sea, The Song of the Dark Forest, The False Note, My Songs Are Full of Venom* (1867–68); *The Sea* (1870); *From My Tears* (1873); *For the Shores of Your Distant Country* (1881); *Conceit* (1884); *Arabian Melody* (1885); *The Wondrous Garden* (1885).

Borovsky, Alexander, Russian-American pianist; b. Mitau, March 18, 1889; d. Waban, Mass., April 27, 1968. He first studied with his mother (a pupil of Safonov), then with A. Essipova at the St. Petersburg Cons., winning the Rubinstein Prize in 1912. He taught master classes at the Moscow Cons. from 1915 to 1920; then went to Turkey, Germany, France, and England and gave a number of piano recitals; was a soloist with virtually all major European orchs.; he also made several successful tours in South America. In 1941 he settled in the U.S., and became a prof. at Boston Univ. (1956).

Borowski, Felix, English-American composer and critic; b. Burton, England, March 10, 1872; d. Chicago, Sept. 6, 1956. He studied violin with his father, a Polish émigré; took lessons with various teachers in London, and at the Cologne Cons.; then taught in Aberdeen, Scotland. His early *Russian Sonata* was praised by Grieg; this provided impetus to his progress as a composer. In 1897 he accepted a teaching engagement at the Chicago Musical College; was its president from 1916 to 1925. Subsequently he became active in musical journalism; in 1942 was appointed music editor of the *Chicago Sun;* also served as program annotator for the Chicago Symph. Orch., beginning in 1908. For 5 years he taught musicology at Northwestern Univ. (1937–42). Among his many musical works, the violin piece entitled *Adoration* became widely popular.

Borris, Siegfried, German composer; b. Berlin, Nov. 4, 1906. He studied piano as a child, and began to compose tentatively while still a schoolboy. He entered the Univ. of Berlin as a student of economics; in 1927 became a pupil of Paul Hindemith at the Berlin Hochschule für Musik; in 1933 he obtained a B.Mus. at the Univ. of Berlin as a student of Arnold Schering, but with the advent of the Nazi regime he was compelled to abandon all his activities as a pianist and teacher. In 1945 he joined the staff of the Berlin Hochschule für Musik, and in 1967 became director of the composition class at the Stern Cons. Borris is a prolific composer; he describes his idiom of composition as "vitalism," which connotes a pragmatic type of harmony and counterpoint enlivened by dance-like rhythms; functional tonality is preserved without excluding modernistic dissonant combinations.

Bortkiewicz, Sergei, Russian pianist and composer; b. Kharkov, Feb. 28, 1877; d. Vienna, Oct. 25, 1952. He was a pupil of Liadov at the St. Petersburg Cons. (1896–99); later studied with Jadassohn in Leipzig. He made his debut as a pianist in Munich, in 1902, and subsequently made concert tours of Germany, Australia, Hungary, France, and Russia. From 1904 to 1914, he lived in Berlin, and taught at the Klindworth-Scharwenka Cons.; then went back to Russia; was in Vienna from 1920 to 1929; in Berlin from 1929 to 1934; and again in Vienna after 1934. His compositions include an opera, *Acrobats;* 2 symphs.; *Austrian Suite* and *Yugoslav Suite* for Orch.; 4 piano concertos; Violin Concerto; Cello Concerto; piano pieces; songs. He was the author of the book *Die seltsame Liebe Peter Tschaikowskys und der Nadezhda von Meck* (1938).

Bortniansky, Dimitri, Russian composer; b. Glukhov, Ukraine, 1751; d. St. Petersburg, Oct. 10, 1825. He was a choirboy in the court chapel, where he attracted the attention of Galuppi, who was at the time conductor there; was sent to Italy, where he studied with Galuppi and with other Italian masters in Venice, Bologna, Rome, and Naples (1769–79). In Italy he produced his operas *Creonte* (Venice, Nov. 26, 1776; lost) and *Quinto Fabio* (Modena, Dec. 26, 1778). In 1779 he returned to St. Petersburg and became director of vocal music at the court chapel (1796); as a conductor of the chapel choir he introduced radical reforms for improvement of singing standards; composed for his choir a number of sacred works of high quality, among them a Mass according to the Greek Orthodox ritual; 35 sacred concerti in 4 parts; 10 Psalms in 8 parts; 10 concerti for double choir; etc. He also continued to compose for the stage; produced the comic operas, in French, *Le Faucon* (Gatchina, Oct. 22, 1786) and *Le Fils rival* (Pavlovsk, Oct. 22, 1787). His sacred choral works are published in 10 vols., edited by Tchaikovsky.

Bos, Coenraad Valentyn, Dutch pianist and noted accompanist; b. Leiden, Dec. 7, 1875; d. Chappaqua, N.Y., Aug. 5, 1955. He was a pupil of Julius Röntgen at the Amsterdam Cons. (1892–95); later studied in Berlin. With 2 other countrymen, Jan van Veen (violin) and Jan van Lier (cello), he formed a trio in Berlin which enjoyed an enviable reputation during its active period (1896–1910). His masterly accompaniments on a tour with Ludwig Wüllner attracted more than ordinary attention, and made him one of the most celebrated accompanists both in Europe and the U.S., where he eventually settled. He was the accompanist of Julia Culp, Frieda Hempel, Helen Traubel, Fritz Kreisler, Ernestine Schumann-Heink, Pablo Casals, Elena Gerhard, Jacques Thibaud, Geraldine Farrar, and many others. He taught at the Juilliard School of Music from 1934 to 1952; publ. (in collaboration with Ashley Pettis) a book, *The Well-Tempered Accompanist* (1949).

Boschot, Adolphe, French music critic; b. Fontenay-sous-Bois, near Paris, May 4, 1871; d. Paris, June 1, 1955. He was music critic of *Echo de Paris* from 1910; of *Revue Bleue* from 1919; founded, with Théodore de Wyzewa, the Paris Mozart Society; was elected to the Institut de France in 1926, succeeding Widor as permanent secretary of the Académie des Beaux-Arts. His greatest work is an exhaustive biography of Berlioz in 3 vols.: *La Jeunesse d'un romantique, Hector Berlioz, 1803–31* (Paris, 1906); *Un Romantique sous Louis-Philippe, Hector Berlioz, 1831–42* (Paris, 1908); and *Crépuscule d'un romantique, Hector Berlioz, 1842–69* (Paris, 1913). For this work Boschot received a prize of the Académie. Other books are: *Le Faust de Berlioz* (1910; new ed., 1945); *Carnet d'art* (1911); *Une Vie romantique, Hector Berlioz* (an abridgement of his 3-vol. work, 1919; 27th ed., 1951; also in Eng.; a definitive ed. appeared in Quebec in 1965); *Chez les musiciens* (3 vols., 1922–26); *Entretiens sur la beauté* (1927); *La Lumière de Mozart* (1928); *Le Mystère musical* (1929); *La Musique et la vie* (2 vols., 1931–33); *Théophile Gautier* (1933); *Mozart* (1935); *La Vie et les œuvres d'Alfred Bruneau* (1937); *Musiciens-Poètes* (1937); *Maîtres d'hier et de jadis* (1944); *Portraits de musiciens* (3 vols., 1946–50); *Souvenirs d'un autre siècle* (1947). Boschot trans. into French the librettos of several of Mozart's operas. He was also prominent as a poet; publ. the collections *Poèmes dialogués* (1901) and *Chez nos poètes* (1925).

Bösendorfer, firm of piano makers at Vienna, specializing in concert grands. It was established by **Ignaz Bösendorfer** (b. Vienna, July 27, 1794; d. there, April 14, 1859) in 1828; later managed by his son **Ludwig** (b. Vienna, April 10, 1835; d. there, May 9, 1919). The firm, retaining its original name, was taken over by Carl Hutterstrasser (1863–1942). The Bösendorfer Saal (opened by Hans von Bülow in 1872, and used until 1913) was one of the finest chamber music concert halls in Europe.

Bosio, Angiolina, Italian soprano; b. Turin, Aug. 22, 1830; d. St. Petersburg, April 13, 1859. She studied in Milan with Cattaneo; made her stage debut there in 1846 as Lucrezia in Verdi's opera *I due foscari;* subsequently sang in Paris, N.Y., Philadelphia, Boston, and London; she later visited Russia, where she lived until her untimely death.

Boskovsky, Willi, Austrian violinist and conductor; b. Vienna, June 16, 1909. He studied at the Vienna Academy of Music; in 1933 joined the Vienna Phil. and remained a member until 1970. In 1948 he organized the Wiener Oktet; in 1955 succeeded Clemens Krauss as conductor of the New Year's Day Concerts of the Vienna Phil. In 1969 he became principal conductor of the Johann Strauss Orch. of Vienna, originally founded by Eduard Strauss in 1890; the ensemble was reorganized by the nephew of the older Eduard Strauss, and namesake of the original founder, who died in 1966. Boskovsky assumed the direction of the ensemble as successor to Eduard Strauss, Jr. He resigned as conductor of the New Year's Day Concerts of the Vienna Phil. in 1979. Boskovsky conducted his orch. holding the violin relaxedly in his left hand à la Johann Strauss, and directing his group in an ingratiatingly, authentically Viennese manner in flowing waltz time or rapid polka rhythm, with expressive Luftpausen to emphasize the syncopation.

Bosmans, Henriette, Dutch pianist and composer; b. Amsterdam, Dec. 5, 1895; d. there, July 2, 1952. She studied piano with her mother at the Amsterdam Cons., and embarked on a career as a concert pianist. In 1927 she took lessons in composition with Willem Pijper. In her own music she cultivated an agreeable neo-Classical idiom, with coloristic éclat, suggesting the techniques and devices of French Impressionism; wrote many songs to texts by French poets. In her instrumental works she particularly favored the cello (her father was a well-known cellist, but he died when she was a year old).
WORKS: Cello Sonata (1919); 2 Cello Concertos (1922, 1924); *Poem* for Cello and Orch. (1926); Violin Sonata (1918); Piano Trio (1921); String Quartet (1928); Concertino for Piano and Orch. (1928; Geneva Festival of the International Society for Contemporary Music, April 6, 1929); *Konzertstück* for Flute and Orch. (1929); *Konzertstück* for Violin and Orch. (1934); *Doodenmarsch (March of the Dead)* for Narrator and Chamber Orch. (1946); piano pieces.

Bossi, Costante Adolfo, Italian composer, brother of **Enrico Bossi;** b. Morbegno, Dec. 25, 1876; d. Milan, Jan. 4, 1953. He studied at the Milan Cons.; subsequently was a prof. there (1914–41). He wrote an opera, *La mammola e l'eroe* (Milan, 1916); a Requiem (1920); numerous choruses and songs.

Bossi, (Marco) Enrico, Italian composer; b. Salò, Brescia, April 25, 1861; d. at sea (en route from America to Europe), Feb. 20, 1925. Son and pupil of the organist **Pietro Bossi,** of Morbegno (1834–96), he studied at the Liceo Rossini in Bologna (1871–73), and at Milan (1873–81) under Sangali (piano), Fumagalli (organ), Campanari (violin), Boniforti (counterpoint), and Ponchielli (composition). He subsequently was maestro di cappella and organist at Como Cathedral (1881–89); then, until 1896, prof. of organ and harmony in the Royal Cons. San Pietro at Naples; prof. of advanced composition and organ at the Liceo Benedetto Marcello in Venice (1896–1902); and director of the Liceo Musicale at Bologna (1902–12). After a brief period of retirement from teaching, he was director of the Music School of the Santa Cecilia Academy in Rome (1916–23); toured Europe, England, and the U.S. as a pianist and organist.

Bote & Bock, German music publishing firm established in Berlin in 1838 by **Eduard Bote** (retired 1847) and **Gustav Bock** (b. 1813; d. 1863); the directorship was assumed after Gustav Bock's death by his brother **Eduard Bock** (d. 1871), followed by his son **Hugo Bock** (b. Berlin, July 25, 1848; d. there, March 12, 1932), who handled the affairs of the firm for over 60 years. He acquired for the firm a great number of operas and operettas, and also a number of instrumental works by celebrated 19th-century composers. In 1904 Hugo Bock purchased the catalogue of Lauterbach & Kuhn of Leipzig, including the works of Max Reger (from op. 66 on). His successor was his son **Gustav Bock** (b. Berlin, July 17, 1882; d. July 6, 1953), who headed the firm until 1938, and again from 1947. The headquarters of the firm remained in Berlin; in 1948 a branch was formed in Wiesbaden. Apart from its musical publications, the firm publ. the *Neue Berliner Musikzeitung* (1847–96). A centennial vol. was issued in 1938 as *Musikverlag Bote & Bock, Berlin, 1838–1938.*

Botstiber, Hugo, Austrian music scholar and writer; b. Vienna, April 21, 1875; d. Shrewsbury, England, Jan. 15, 1941. He was a pupil of R. Fuchs, Zemlinsky, H. Rietsch, and Guido Adler; in 1896, assistant librarian of the Vienna Cons.; in 1900, secretary of the Konzertverein there; and in 1905, secretary of the Academy of Music; until 1938 was general secretary of the Vienna Konzerthaus-Gesellschaft; Knight of the Order of Franz Josef. He went to England in 1939. He edited the *Musikbuch aus Österreich* (1904–11); also organ compositions by Pachelbel, piano works of the Vienna masters, and waltzes of Johann Strauss for Denkmäler der Tonkunst in Österreich; was the author of *Joseph Haydn und das Verlagshaus Artaria* (with Franz Artaria; Vienna, 1911); *Geschichte der Ouvertüre* (Leipzig, 1913);

Beethoven im Alltag (Vienna, 1927); completed Pohl's biography of Haydn (vol. III, 1927); publ. a new ed. of Kretzschmar's *Führer durch den Konzertsaal* (1932). Of special interest to American musicians is his article "Musicalia in der New York Public Library" in the bulletin of the Société Internationale de Musique (Oct. 1903), calling international attention for the first time to the important music collection of the N.Y. Public Library.

Bottesini, Giovanni, Italian virtuoso on the double bass, conductor, and composer; b. Crema, Dec. 22, 1821; d. Parma, July 7, 1889. He took lessons in double-bass playing with Rossi at the Milan Cons. (1835–39); played in various orchs.; in 1847 he visited the U.S.; and in 1848 he went to England, where he appeared as a cello soloist; made his independent concert debut in London on June 26, 1849. In 1853 he was once more in America; also was active as a conductor in Paris, in Russia, and in Scandinavian countries. In 1871 he was invited by Verdi to conduct the world premiere of *Aida* in Cairo. He eventually retired to Parma as director of the cons. there. Bottesini was the first great virtuoso on the double bass, regarded as an unwieldy instrument, and thus became a legendary paragon for the few artists who essayed that instrument after him; thus Koussevitzky was often described as the Russian Bottesini during his early career as a double-bass player. Bottesini was the composer of a number of passable operas which had several performances in his lifetime.

Bottrigari, Ercole, Italian music theorist; b. Bologna (baptized, Aug. 24), 1531; d. San Alberto, near Bologna, Sept. 30, 1612. He was an illegitimate son of the nobleman Giovanni Battista Bottrigari; studied mathematics and music in the house of his father; learned to sing and play several instruments; his house teacher was Bartolomeo Spontone. In 1551 he married a rich lady. In his residence he met many celebrated poets of the day, including Tasso. Having acquired profound learning in several scientific and artistic disciplines, he devoted much of his energies to theoretical musical subjects; publ. numerous papers, many of a polemical nature.

Boucher, Alexandre-Jean, famous French violinist; b. Paris, April 11, 1778; d. there, Dec. 29, 1861. A brilliant violin virtuoso, he styled himself "l'Alexandre des violons." Boucher began his career at the age of 6, playing with the Concert Spirituel in Paris; was soloist in the court of Charles IV of Spain (1787–1805); traveled extensively on the Continent and in England. He wrote 2 violin concertos.

Boughton, Rutland, English composer; b. Aylesbury, Jan. 23, 1878; d. London, Jan. 24, 1960. He studied at the Royal College of Music in London with Stanford and Walford Davies; without obtaining his diploma, he engaged in professional activity; was for a time a member of the orch. at Haymarket Theatre in London; taught at Midland Inst. in Birmingham (1905–11); also conducted a choral society

there. He became a firm believer in the universality of arts on Wagnerian lines; formed a partnership with the poet Reginald Buckley; their book of essays, *The Music Drama of the Future,* expounding the neo-Wagnerian idea, was publ. in 1911. To carry out these plans, he organized stage festivals at Glastonbury, helped by his common-law wife, Christina Walshe. Boughton's opera, *The Immortal Hour,* was performed there on Aug. 26, 1914; his choral music drama *The Birth of Arthur* had a performance in 1920; these productions were staged with piano instead of an orch. After an interruption during World War I, Boughton continued the Glastonbury festivals until 1926. In 1927 he settled in the country, in Gloucestershire. He continued to compose, however, and produced a number of stage works, as well as instrumental pieces, few of which have been performed. His ideas of universal art had in the meantime been transformed into concepts of socialist realism, with an emphasis on the paramount importance of folk music as against formal constructions. WORKS: FOR THE STAGE: *The Birth of Arthur* (1909; Glastonbury, Aug. 16, 1920); *The Immortal Hour* (1913; Glastonbury, Aug. 26, 1914); *The Round Table* (Glastonbury, Aug. 14, 1916); *The Moon Maiden,* choral ballet for girls (Glastonbury, April 23, 1919); *Alkestis,* music drama (1922; Glastonbury, Aug. 26, 1922; Covent Garden, London, Jan. 11, 1924); *The Queen of Cornwall,* music drama after Thomas Hardy (Glastonbury, Aug. 21, 1924); *May Day,* ballet (1926); *The Ever Young,* music drama (1928; Bath, Sept. 9, 1935); *The Lily Maid,* opera (1934; Gloucester, Sept. 10, 1934); *Galahad,* music drama (1944); *Avalon,* music drama (1946). FOR ORCH.: *The Skeleton in Armour,* symph. poem with Chorus (1898); *The Invincible Armada,* symph. poem (1901); *A Summer Night* (1902); *Oliver Cromwell,* symph. (1904); *Love and Spring* (1906); *Midnight* (1907); *Song of Liberty* for Chorus and Orch. (1911); *Bethlehem,* choral drama (1915; his most successful work); *Pioneers,* after Walt Whitman, for Tenor, Chorus, and Orch. (1925); *Deirdre,* symph. (1927); Symphony in B minor (1937); Trumpet Concerto (1943). CHAMBER MUSIC: Violin Sonata (1921); Quartet for Oboe and Strings (1930); String Trio (1944); Piano Trio (1948); Cello Sonata (1948); numerous choral works. He publ. several pamphlets and essays: *The Death and Resurrection of the Music Festival* (1913); *The Glastonbury Festival Movement* (1922); *Bach, the Master* (1930); *Parsifal: A Study* (1920); *The Nature of Music* (1930); *The Reality of Music* (1934).

Bouhy, Jacques-Joseph André, Belgian-born French baritone; b. Pepinster, June 18, 1848; d. Paris, Jan. 29, 1929. He studied at the Liège Cons.; then went to Paris and entered the Paris Cons., where he studied piano, organ, and theory of composition, as well as singing. He made his debut as Méphistophélès in Gounod's *Faust* at the Paris Opéra on Aug. 2, 1871; on March 3, 1875, he sang Escamillo in the first performance of *Carmen* at the Opéra-Comique in Paris. He appeared at Covent Garden, London, on

April 22, 1882; then sang at various opera houses in Europe, including that in St. Petersburg. In 1885 he went to N.Y. and served as director of the N.Y. Cons. (until 1889); was again in N.Y. from 1904 to 1907; then returned to Paris and settled there as a singing teacher.

Boulanger, Lili, talented French composer, sister of **Nadia Boulanger;** b. Paris, Aug. 21, 1893; d. Mézy (Seine-et-Oise), March 15, 1918. She studied composition with Paul Vidal at the Paris Cons. (1909–13), and attracted considerable attention when she won the Grand Prix de Rome at graduation with her cantata *Faust et Hélène,* as the first woman to receive this distinction. Her early death at the age of 24 was lamented by French musicians as a great loss. Her talent, delicate and poetic, continued the tradition of French Romanticism on the borderline of Impressionism. Besides her prize-winning cantata she wrote 2 symph. poems, *D'un soir triste* and *D'un matin de printemps;* her opera to Maeterlinck's play *La Princesse Maleine* remained incomplete. She also wrote several choral works with orch.: *Soir sur la plaine; Hymne au soleil; La Tempête; Les Sirènes; Sous bois; La Source; Pour les funerailles d'un soldat; 3 psaumes; Vieille prière bouddhique;* sacred chorus, *Pie Jesu,* for Voice, Strings, Harp, and Organ; cycle of 13 songs to texts of Francis Jammes, *Clairières dans le ciel;* some flute pieces.

Boulanger, Nadia, illustrious French composition teacher, sister of **Lili Boulanger;** b. Paris, Sept. 16, 1887; d. there, Oct. 22, 1979. Both her father and grandfather were teachers at the Paris Cons.; her mother, Countess Myshetskaya, was a Russian and a professional singer; it is from her that Nadia Boulanger received her Russian diminutive (for Nadezhda) name, and it was from her that she had her first music lessons. She entered the Paris Cons., where she studied organ with Guilmant and Vierne, and composition with Gabriel Fauré; she graduated with prizes in organ and theory; in 1908 she received the 2nd Prix de Rome for her cantata *La Sirène;* she completed the composition of the opera by Raoul Pugno, *La Ville Morte,* left unfinished after his death; also composed cello music, piano pieces, and songs; realizing that she could not compare with her sister Lili in talent as a composer, she devoted herself to teaching, and it is in that profession, often regarded as ancillary and uncreative, that she found her finest vocation. She was assistant in a harmony class at the Paris Cons. (1909–24); was engaged as a teacher at the Ecole Normale de Musique in Paris (1920–39); when the American Cons. was founded in 1921 at Fontainebleau, she joined its faculty as a teacher of composition and orchestration; she became its director in 1950. She also had a large class of private pupils from all parts of the world; many of them achieved fame in their own right; among Americans who went to Paris to study with her were Aaron Copland, Roy Harris, Walter Piston, Virgil Thomson, Elliott Carter, David Diamond, Elie Siegmeister, Irving Fine, Easley Blackwood, Arthur Berger, John Vincent, and Harold

Shapero; others were Igor Markevitch, Jean Françaix, Lennox Berkeley, and Dinu Lipatti. Not all of her students were enthusiastic about her methods; some of them complained about the strict, and even restrictive, discipline she imposed on them; but all admired her insistence on perfection of form and accuracy of technique. Her tastes were far from the catholicity expected of teachers; she was a great admirer of Stravinsky, Debussy, and Ravel, but had little appreciation of Schoenberg and the modern Vienna School. She visited the U.S. several times; played the organ part in Aaron Copland's Organ Symph. (which she advised him to compose) with the N.Y. Symph. Orch., under the direction of Walter Damrosch (Jan. 11, 1925), and was the first woman to conduct regular subscription concerts of the Boston Symph. Orch. (1938) and of the N.Y. Phil. (Feb. 11, 1939). During World War II she stayed in America; taught classes at Radcliffe College, Wellesley College, and the Juilliard School of Music; returning to Paris in 1946, she took over a class in piano accompaniment at the Paris Cons.; continued her private teaching as long as her frail health permitted; her 90th birthday was celebrated in September 1977, with sincere tributes from her many students in Europe and America.

Boulez, Pierre, celebrated French composer and conductor; b. Montbrison, March 26, 1925. He studied composition with Olivier Messiaen at the Paris Cons., graduating in 1945; later took lessons with René Leibowitz, who initiated him into the procedures of serial music. In 1948 he became a theater conductor in Paris; made a tour of the U.S. with a French ballet troupe in 1952. In 1954 he organized in Paris a series of concerts called "Domaine Musical," devoted mainly to avant-garde music. In 1963 he delivered a course of lectures on music at Harvard Univ., and on May 1, 1964, made his American debut as conductor in N.Y. In 1958 he went to Germany, where he gave courses at the International Festivals for New Music in Darmstadt. It was in Germany that he gained experience as conductor of opera; he was one of the few Frenchmen to conduct Wagner's *Parsifal* in Germany; in 1976 he was engaged to conduct the *Ring* cycle in Bayreuth. The precision of his leadership and his knowledge of the score produced a profound impression on both the audience and the critics. He was engaged to conduct guest appearances with the Cleveland Orch., and in 1971 he was engaged as music director of the N.Y. Phil., a choice that surprised many and delighted many more. From the outset he asserted complete independence from public and managerial tastes, and proceeded to feature on his programs works by Schoenberg, Berg, Webern, Varèse, and other modernists who were reformers of music, giving a relatively small place to Romantic composers. This policy provoked the expected opposition on the part of many subscribers, but the management decided not to oppose Boulez in his position as music director of the orch. The musicians themselves voiced their full appreciation of his remarkable qualities as a professional of high caliber, but they described him derisively as a "French correction," with reference to his extraordinary sense of rhythm, perfect pitch, and memory, but a signal lack of emotional participation in the music. In America, Boulez showed little interest in social amenities and made no effort to ingratiate himself with men and women of power. His departure of the season 1977–78 and the accession of the worldly Zubin Mehta as his successor were greeted with a sigh of relief, as an antidote to the stern regimen imposed by Boulez. While attending to his duties at the helm of the N.Y. Phil., he accepted outside obligations; from 1971 to 1975 he served as chief conductor of the London BBC Symph. Orch.; as a perfect Wagnerite he gave exemplary performances of Wagner's operas both in Germany and elsewhere. He established his residence in Paris, where he had founded, in 1974, the Institut de Recherche & Coordination Acoustique/Musique, a futuristic establishment generously subsidized by the French government; in this post he could freely carry out his experimental programs of electronic techniques with the aid of digital synthesizers and a complex set of computers capable of acoustical feedback. His own music is an embodiment of such futuristic techniques; it is fiendishly difficult to perform and even more difficult to describe in the familiar terms of dissonant counterpoint, free serialism, or indeterminism. He specifically disassociated himself from any particular modern school of music. He even publ. a pamphlet with the shocking title *Schoenberg est mort*, shortly after Schoenberg's actual physical death; he similarly distanced himself from other current trends.

WORKS: *Le Visage nuptial* for Soprano, Contralto Chorus, and Orch. (1946, revised 1951; Cologne, Dec. 4, 1957, composer conducting); *Le Soleil des eaux*, cantata for Soprano, Men's Chorus, and Orch. (original music for radio play, 1948, revised 1958 and 1965; Darmstadt, Sept. 9, 1958); *Livre pour quatuor* (1948–49; radically revised as *Livre pour cordes*, 1968; Brighton, Dec. 8, 1968, composer conducting); *Symphonie concertante* for Piano and Orch. (1950); *Polyphonie X* for 18 Solo Instruments (Donaueschingen Music Festival, Oct. 6, 1951); *Le Marteau sans maître*, cantata for Contralto, Flute, Viola, Guitar, Vibraphone, and Percussion (1953–55; International Festival of the Society for Contemporary Music, Baden-Baden, June 18, 1955); *Poésie pour pouvoir*, spatial work for 5-track Tape and 2 Orchs. (1958, revised 1982–83; Donaueschingen Festival, Oct. 19, 1958, under the direction of Boulez and Hans Rosbaud); *Pli selon Pli, Portrait de Mallarmé*, for Soprano and Orch. (Donaueschingen, Oct. 20, 1962); *Doubles* for Orch. (1958; Paris, March 16, 1958; expanded as *Figures-Doubles-Prismes* and performed at Strasbourg, Jan. 10, 1964); *Eclat* for Chamber Orch. (1965; Los Angeles, March 26, 1965; revised as *Eclats/Multiples;* London, Oct. 21, 1970); *Domaines,* for Solo Clarinet and 21 Instruments (1968; Brussels, Dec. 20, 1968, composer conducting); *cummings ist der dichter*, for 16 Voices and 24 Instruments (1970: Stuttgart, Sept. 25, 1970); . . . . *explosante-fixe* . . . . for Vibraphone, Harp, Violin, Viola, Cello, Flute, Clarinet, Trumpet, and something called a Halaphone, run by a set of Computers

(N.Y., Jan. 5, 1973; revised 1973–74; La Rochelle, July 6, 1974); *Rituel in memoriam Bruno Maderna* (1974–75; London, April 2, 1975, composer conducting); *Messagesquisse* for 7 Cellos (1977); *Pour le docteur Kalmus* for Clarinet, Flute, Violin, Cello, and Piano (1977); *Répons* for Chamber Orch. and 6 Solo Instruments with Computer (1981; Donaueschingen, Oct. 18, 1981; revised, London, Sept. 6, 1982); *Notations* for Orch. (1980; Paris, June 18, 1982); *Sonatine* for Flute and Piano (1946); Piano Sonata (1946); Sonata for 2 Pianos (Paris, April 29, 1950); *Structures I* for 2 Pianos (1951); *Structures II* for 2 Pianos (1956–61); Piano Sonata No. 2 (1948; Paris, April 29, 1950); Piano Sonata No. 3 (1957); music for the film *Symphonie mécanique* (1955); incidental music for Claudel's version of the *Oresteia* by Aeschylus (1955).

Boulnois, Joseph, French composer; b. Paris, Jan. 28, 1884; killed in battle at Chalaines, Oct. 20, 1918. He studied piano and composition at the Paris Cons.; later became church organist, and from 1909 was choir leader at the Opéra-Comique. He wrote an opera, *L'Anneau d'Isis*, a *Symphonie funèbre*, a Cello Sonata, and various pieces for organ, piano, and voice. His works remain mostly in MS. There has been a revival of interest in his music, which has resulted in some performances of his songs and choruses.

Boult, Sir Adrian (Cedric), eminent British conductor; b. Chester, April 8, 1889; d. Tunbridge Wells, Feb. 22, 1983. His mother, a professional writer on music, gave him piano lessons; at 12 he received some instruction in music from a science teacher, H.E. Piggott, at the Westminster School in London. At 19 he entered Christ Church in Oxford, where he sang in a school chorus under the direction of Sir Hugh Allen; earned a doctorate in music at Oxford Univ.; then went to Leipzig, where he was allowed to attend rehearsals of the Gewandhaus Orch., conducted by Nikisch, who offered him some advice on the technique of conducting; he also took courses in music theory at the Leipzig Cons. with Stephan Krehl and Hans Sitt, and had occasional lessons with Max Reger. He returned to England in 1913; held for a season a subsidiary position on the musical staff of Covent Garden; made his conducting debut with an amateur orch. at West Kirby in 1914. In 1916 he conducted a concert of the Liverpool Phil., and in 1918 led 4 concerts at Queen's Hall, London. During the season 1919–20 he was engaged by Diaghilev to conduct several productions of his Ballets Russes in London. On Jan. 30, 1919, he made his first appearance as guest conductor of the Royal Phil. Society in London; from 1919 to 1924 he led the British Symph., with the personnel of former soldiers of the British Army; concurrently, he taught a class in conducting at the Royal College of Music; in 1924–30 he also led a school orch. there. During the same period he conducted concerts of the Birmingham City Orch. (1924–1930). In 1930 he was appointed music director of the British Broadcasting Co. and organized the BBC Symph., which eventually became one of the finest orch. groups in Europe. Boult led it on a European tour, visiting Brussels in 1935 and Vienna, Zürich, and Budapest in 1936. He remained its music director until 1950. From 1950 until 1957 he served as principal conductor of the London Phil. Orch. During the 1959–60 season he was music director of the Birmingham Symph. Orch. He also filled numerous guest engagements outside England; led a concert of British music at the Salzburg Festival in 1935, and also in 1935 conducted 4 concerts with the Boston Symph. Orch. In 1938 he was guest conductor with the NBC Symph. in N.Y.; on June 9 and 10, 1939, he presented at the N.Y. World's Fair the world premieres of the 7th Symph. of Arnold Bax and the Piano Concerto of Arthur Bliss. Throughout his career he consistently promoted the cause of British music, particularly that of Vaughan Williams; he gave first performances, in London, of his *Pastoral Symphony* (March 8, 1936), 4th Symph. (April 10, 1935), 6th Symph. (April 21, 1948), and 9th Symph. (April 2, 1958). In 1937 he was knighted. In 1953 he conducted at Westminster Abbey the music for the coronation of Queen Elizabeth II. His style of conducting was quite devoid of glamorous self-assertion; his ideal was to serve the music with a minimum display of histrionics; he was greatly respected by the musicians of the orchs. he conducted. He publ. *Thoughts on Conducting* (London, 1963) and an autobiography, *My Own Trumpet: Memoirs of Sir Adrian Boult* (London, 1973).

Bourgeois, Loys (Louis), French composer; b. Paris, c.1510; d. there, c.1561. He was a follower of Calvin, with whom he lived (1545–57) in Geneva; then returned to Paris; was still living in 1561. He is renowned for having composed, or adapted, almost all the melodies the Calvinists sang to Marot's and Bèze's French versions of the Psalms. Clément Marot, poet in the service of Francis I as "valet de chambre," trans. (1533–39) 30 Psalms in metrical form, which found great favor with the Court, who sang them to light melodies. However, the Sorbonne soon condemned them, and in 1542 Marot had to flee to Geneva. The first ed. of Calvin's Genevan Psalter, containing Marot's 30 Psalms, his versifications of the Paternoster and Credo, 5 Psalms of Calvin, and his versions of the Song of Simeon and the Decalogue, was publ. at Geneva in 1542; 17 of the melodies, all but 3 of which were more or less altered, were adapted by Bourgeois from the earlier Strasbourg Psalter of Calvin (1539), and 22 new ones were added. After arriving at Geneva, Marot added 19 other Psalms and the Song of Simeon; these, together with the 30 previously publ., compose the so-called "Cinquante Pseaumes," which, with Marot's Décalogue, Ave, and Graces (all with music), were added in the 1543 edition of the Psalter. By 1549, 17 of the melodies previously used were more or less altered by Bourgeois, and 8 others replaced; in 1551 he modified 4 and substituted 12 new tunes. Thus, several of the melodies are of later date than the Psalms. On Marot's death, in 1544, Théodore de Bèze undertook completing the Psalter. In 1551 he

added 34 Psalms, in 1554 6 more, and in 1562 the remaining 60. Bourgeois composed, or adapted, the tunes to all except the last 40, these being set, supposedly, by Pierre Dubuisson, a singer. In 1557 Bourgeois left Geneva and severed his immediate contact with the work there, although he still continued his activity on the Psalter. Claude Goudimel publ. harmonized editions of the Genevan Psalter after 1562, thereby creating the erroneous belief that he was the author of the melodies themselves. Bourgeois himself harmonized, and publ. in 1547, 2 sets of Psalms in 4–6 parts, intended for private use only. His treatise *Le Droict Chemin de musique,* etc. (Geneva, 1550) proposed a reform in the nomenclature of the tones to fit the solmisation syllables, which was generally adopted in France (see Fétis, *Biographie des musiciens,* vol. II, p. 42).

Bourgeois, Thomas-Louis (-Joseph), French singer and composer; b. Fontaine-L'Evêque, Oct. 24, 1676; d. Paris, 1750. He was maître de musique at the Strasbourg Cathedral (1703–6); sang with the Paris Opéra (1708–11); then was in the service of the Duke of Bourbon (1715–21). As a composer, he produced a number of fine cantatas, of which 19 are extant; he also wrote divertissements and ballets.

Bournonville, Jacques de, French harpsichordist and composer; b. probably in Amiens, c.1675; d. Paris, c.1754. He was either the grandson or the great-grandson of **Jean de Bournonville.** He studied with Bernier; subsequently established himself as a harpsichord player. His motets for one and 2 voices with continuo were publ. in 1711.

Bournonville, Jean de, French composer; b. Noyon, c.1585; d. Paris, May 27, 1632. In 1612 he was appointed director of music at the choir school of the collegiate church of St. Quentin; then was active in Amiens (1618–31). In 1631 he was named director of the choir school of the Sainte-Chapelle. He composed masses, Psalms, motets, and other church music.

Bournonville, Valentin de, French composer, son of **Jean de Bournonville;** b. probably in St. Quentin, c.1610; d. probably in Chartres, Dec. 1663. He studied with his father; became active as a musician in Amiens. In 1646 he became maître de musique at Notre Dame in Paris. In 1653 he was appointed choir director of the school in Chartres. In 1662 he returned to his former post at Notre Dame in Paris.

Bovy, Vina, Belgian soprano; b. Ghent, May 22,1900; d. there, May 16, 1983. at the Ghent Cons. (1915–17); made her operatic debut at the Théâtre Flamand in Ghent in 1918; then sang at the Théâtre de la Monnaie in Brussels (1922–25) and at the Opéra-Comique in Paris. After a series of performances in Italy, she was engaged by Toscanini to join La Scala in Milan. She made her American debut as Violetta in *La Traviata* at the Metropolitan Opera in N.Y. on Dec. 24, 1936, remaining there for a single season; she then returned to Europe. From 1947 to 1955 she served as managing director of the Ghent Opera. She retired from her active career in 1964.

Bovy-Lysberg, Charles-Samuel, Swiss pianist and composer; b. Lysberg, near Geneva, Feb. 1, 1821; d. Geneva, Feb. 15, 1873. He went to Paris and was one of the few young pianists to study with Chopin (1835). Returning to Switzerland, he settled at Dardagny, near Geneva, in 1848; taught piano at the Geneva Cons., and gave recitals in the French cantons. His opera, *La Fille du Carillonneur,* was produced in Geneva in 1854; he also wrote a romantically inspired piano sonata, *L'Absence;* but he became known chiefly by his effective salon pieces for piano (numbering about 130), among them *La Napolitaine, Le Réveil des oiseaux, Le Chant du rouet, Idylle, Les Ondines, Sur l'onde,* etc. His real name was **Bovy,** but he hyphenated it with Lysberg, the name of his birthplace.

Bowen, Edwin York, English composer and pianist; b. London, Feb. 22, 1884; d. Hampstead, Nov. 23, 1961. He studied at the Royal Academy of Music, where he won the Erard and Sterndale Bennett scholarships; his teachers were Matthay (piano) and F. Corder (composition). Upon graduation, he was appointed instructor in piano there. A prolific composer, Bowen wrote 3 symphs.; 3 piano concertos; Violin Concerto; Viola Concerto; Rhapsody for Cello and Orch.; several symph. poems (*The Lament of Tasso, Eventide,* etc.); orch. suites; many practical piano pieces in miniature forms. Bowen was the author of a manual, *Pedalling the Modern Pianoforte* (London, 1936).

Bowles, Paul Frederic, American composer and novelist; b. Jamaica, N.Y., Dec. 30, 1910. He studied at the Dunning School of Music in N.Y.; in 1928 enrolled in the School of Design and Liberal Arts in N.Y.; then went to Paris, where he earned his living as a telephone operator at the offices of the Paris *Herald Tribune.* He returned to N.Y. in 1930, and worked as a bookshop clerk. While thus occupied, he acquired some knowledge of composition, and was accepted as a private student of Aaron Copland in Saratoga, N.Y. In 1931 he studied counterpoint with Nadia Boulanger at the Ecole Normale de Musique in Paris; also took some lessons with Virgil Thomson. He became a habitué of the modernistic and surrealistic gatherings in Paris and wrote works in a post-impressionistic vein modeled after Erik Satie. To this period belong his Piano Sonatina No. 1 (1932), Flute Sonata (1932), Cantata, *Par le détroit* (1933), and *Scènes d'Anabase,* for Voice, Oboe, and Piano (1932). In 1936 he returned to the U.S., where he wrote his first stage work, the ballet *Yankee Clipper,* which was performed by the American Ballet Caravan in Philadelphia on July 19, 1937. He also wrote a number of scores of incidental music for various plays. Other works of the N.Y. period included the opera *Denmark Vesey* (1938), the ballet *Pastorela* (1941), and the opera *The Wind Remains,* to a text by García Lorca; it was produced in

N.Y. in 1943, with Leonard Bernstein conducting. Always attracted by exotic lands and their art, Bowles went to Morocco, settling in Tangier. A total change in his artistic orientation occurred in 1949 when he publ. his first novel, *The Sheltering Sky,* with the action laid in Morocco; it was acclaimed by sophisticated critics; in 1972 he publ. an autobiography entitled *Without Stopping.* From then on, literature became his vocation and music an avocation. In 1980 he opened in Tangier a writing workshop under the aegis of the School of Visual Arts, N.Y. He continued to compose. Among his later works are *A Picnic Cantata* for Women's Voices, 2 Pianos, and Percussion (N.Y., March 23, 1954); and *Yerma* (1959), to a libretto by García Lorca.

Boyce, William, significant English musician, organist, and composer; b. London, Sept. (baptized, Sept. 11) 1711; d. Kensington, Feb. 7, 1779. As a youth he was a chorister in St. Paul's Cathedral under Charles King; then studied organ with Maurice Greene, the cathedral organist. In 1734–36 he was organist at the Earl of Oxford's Chapel; then was at St. Michael's, Cornhill, from 1736 to 1768. Concurrently he was named in 1736 composer to the Chapel Royal. In 1759 he was Master of the King's Musick. An increasing deafness forced him to abandon active musical duties after 1769. His main task consisted in providing sacred works for performance; he also contributed incidental music to theatrical productions. He conducted the Festivals of the Three Choirs (Gloucester, Worcester, Hereford) in 1737, and served as Master of the Royal Band in 1755. His magnum opus was the compilation of the collection *Cathedral Music,* in 3 vols. (1760, 1768, and 1773; 2nd ed., 1788; later eds., 1844 and 1849). This collection comprises morning and evening services, anthems, and other church music by a number of British composers, namely Aldrich, Batten, Bevin, Blow, Bull, Byrd, Child, Clarke, Creyghton, Croft, Farrant, Gibbons, Goldwin, Henry VIII, Humfrey, Lawes, Locke, Morley, Mundy, Purcell, Rogers, Tallis, Turner, Tye, Weldon, and Wise. Of his own music, there are remarkable instrumental works: 12 overtures (London, 1720; reprinted in *Musica Britannica,* vol. XIII); 12 sonatas for 2 Violins and Bass (London, 1747); 8 symphs. (London, 1760; modern ed. by M. Goberman, Vienna, 1964); 10 voluntaries for Organ or Harpsichord (London, 1779). Two overtures erroneously attributed to Boyce, and publ. in Lambert's edition under the titles *The Power of Music* and *Pan and Syrinx,* were works by John Stanley, not by Boyce. His stage works include the following, all produced in London: *The Chaplet* (Dec. 2, 1749); *The Roman Father,* not extant (Feb. 24, 1750); *The Shepherd's Lottery* (Nov. 19, 1751); and *Harlequin's Invasion* (with M. Arne and T. Aylward, Dec. 31, 1759). Several of his vocal works were publ. in *Lyra Britannica* (1745–55); there were also 15 anthems (1780) and a collection of anthems (1750), which were republ. in Novello's edition in 4 vols.; also, various songs were originally publ. in the anthologies *The British Orpheus, The Vocal Musical Mask,* and others.

Brade, William, English-born German violinist and composer; b. 1560; d. Hamburg, Feb. 26, 1630. He settled in Germany about 1590; thereafter was a court musician in various localities, including Brandenburg, Copenhagen, Bückeburg, Hamburg, Güstrow, and Berlin. He composed a number of popular collections of dances.

WORKS: *Newe ausserlesene Paduanen, Galliarden, Canzonen, Allmand und Coranten...auff allen musicalischen Instrumenten lieblich zu gebrauchen* (Hamburg, 1609); *Newe ausserlesene Paduanen und Galliarden...auff allen musicalischen Instrumenten und insonderheit auff Fiolen lieblich zu gebrauchen* (Hamburg, 1614); *Newe ausserlesene liebliche Branden, Intraden, Mascharaden, Balletten, All'manden, Couranten, Volten, Aufzüge und frembde Tänze... insonderheit auff Fiolen zu gebrauchen* (Hamburg and Lübeck, 1617); *Melodieuses paduanes, chansons, galliardes* (Antwerp, 1619); *Newe lustige Volten, Couranten, Balletten, Paduanen, Galliarden, Masqueraden, auch allerley arth newer frantzösischer Täntze* (Berlin, 1621).

Braga, Gaetano, Italian cellist and composer; b. Giulianova, Abruzzi, June 9, 1829; d. Milan, Nov. 21, 1907. He studied at the Naples Cons. with C. Gaetano (1841–52); made tours as a cellist in Europe and America; lived mostly in Paris and London. His *Leggenda valacca,* known in English as *Angel's Serenade,* originally written for voice with cello (or violin) obbligato, attained tremendous popularity and was arranged for various instrumental combinations. Braga wrote several operas: *Alina,* or *La spregiata* (1853); *Estella di San Germano* (Vienna, 1857); *Il ritratto* (Naples, 1858); *Margherita la mendicante* (Paris, 1859); *Mormile* (La Scala, Milan, 1862); *Ruy Blas* (1865); *Reginella* (Lecco, 1871); *Caligola* (Lisbon, 1873); sacred choruses; and a valuable *Metodo di violoncello.*

Braga-Santos, Joly. See **Santos-Braga, Joly.**

Braham (real name, **Abraham**), **John,** renowned English tenor; b. London, March 20, 1774; d. there, Feb. 17, 1856. He studied with Leoni in London, with Rauzzini in Bath, and with Isola in Genoa. He made his debut at Covent Garden (April 21, 1787); then appeared at Drury Lane in 1796, in the opera *Mahmoud* by Storace. He was subsequently engaged to sing at the Italian Opera House in London. In 1798 he undertook an extensive tour in Italy; also appeared in Hamburg. Returning to England in 1801, he was increasingly successful. Endowed with a powerful voice of 3 octaves in compass, he knew no difficulties in operatic roles. He was the original Huon in Weber's *Oberon* (1826). As a ballad writer, he was very popular; he wrote much of the music for the operatic roles which he sang; often he added portions to operas by other composers, as in *The Americans* (1811), with its famous song *The Death of Nelson;* contributed incidental music to 12 productions. In 1831 he entered upon a theatrical business venture; he acquired the Colosseum in Re-

gent's Park; in 1836 he had built the St. James's Theatre, but failed to recoup his investment and lost much of his considerable fortune. He made an American tour in 1840–42 despite the weakening of his voice with age; however, his dramatic appeal remained undiminished and he was able to impress the American public in concert appearances. He then returned to London; made his final appearance in 1852.

Brahms, Johannes, great German composer; b. Hamburg, May 7, 1833; d. Vienna, April 3, 1897. His father, who played the double bass in the orchestra of the Phil. Society in Hamburg, taught Brahms the rudiments of music; later he began to study piano with Otto F.W. Cossel, and made his first public appearance as a pianist with a chamber music group at the age of 10. Impressed with his progress, Cossel sent him to his own former teacher, the noted pedagogue Eduard Marxsen, who accepted him as a scholarship student, without charging a fee. Soon Brahms was on his own, and had to eke out his meager subsistence by playing piano in taverns, restaurants, and other establishments (but not in brothels, as insinuated by some popular biographers). On Sept. 21, 1848, at the age of 15, Brahms played a solo concert in Hamburg under an assumed name. In 1853 he met the Hungarian violinist Eduard Reményi, with whom he embarked on a successful concert tour. While in Hannover, Brahms formed a friendship with the famous violin virtuoso Joseph Joachim, who gave him an introduction to Liszt in Weimar. Of great significance was his meeting with Schumann in Düsseldorf. In his diary of the time, Schumann noted: "Johannes Brahms, a genius." He reiterated his appraisal of Brahms in his famous article "Neue Bahnen" ("New Paths"), which appeared in the *Neue Zeitschrift für Musik* on Oct. 28, 1853; in a characteristic display of metaphor, he described young Brahms as having come into life as Minerva sprang in full armor from the brow of Jupiter. Late in 1853, Breitkopf und Härtel publ. his 2 piano sonatas and a set of 6 songs. Brahms also publ., under the pseudonym of G.W. Marks, a collection of 6 pieces for piano, 4-hands, under the title *Souvenir de la Russie* (Brahms never visited Russia). Schumann's death in 1856, after years of agonizing mental illness, deeply affected Brahms. He remained a devoted friend of Schumann's family; his correspondence with Schumann's widow Clara reveals a deep affection and spiritual intimacy, but the speculation about their friendship growing into a romance exists only in the fevered imaginations of psychologizing biographers. Objectively judged, the private life of Brahms was that of a middle-class bourgeois who worked systematically and diligently on his current tasks while maintaining a fairly active social life. He was always ready and willing to help young composers (his earnest efforts on behalf of Dvořák were notable). Brahms was entirely free of professional jealousy; his differences with Wagner were those of style. Wagner was an opera composer, while Brahms never wrote for the stage. True, some

Brahms

ardent admirers of Wagner (such as Hugo Wolf) found little of value in the music of Brahms, while admirers of Brahms (such as Hanslick) were sharp critics of Wagner, but Brahms held aloof from such partisan wranglings.

From 1857 to 1859 Brahms was employed in Detmold as court pianist, chamber musician, and choir director. In the meantime he began work on his first piano concerto. He played it on Jan. 22, 1859, in Hannover, with Joachim as conductor. Other important works of the period were the two serenades for orchestra and the first string sextet. He expected to be named conductor of the Hamburg Phil. Society, but the directoriat preferred to engage, in 1863, the singer Julius Stockhausen in that capacity. Instead, Brahms accepted the post of conductor of the Singakademie in Vienna, which he led from 1863 to 1864. In 1869 he decided to make Vienna his permanent home. As early as 1857 he began work on his choral masterpiece, *Ein deutsches Requiem;* he completed the score in 1868, and conducted its first performance in the Bremen Cathedral on April 10, 1868. In May 1868 he added another movement to the work (the 5th, "Ihr habt nun Traurigkeit") in memory of his mother, who died in 1865. The title of the German Requiem had no nationalistic connotations; it simply stated that the text was in German rather than Latin. His other important vocal scores include *Rinaldo*, a cantata; the *Liebeslieder* waltzes for vocal quartet and piano 4-hands; the *Alto Rhapsody;* the *Schicksalslied;* and many songs. In 1869 he publ. 2 vols. of *Hungarian Dances* for piano duet; these were extremely successful. Among his chamber music works, the Piano Quintet in F minor, the String Sextet No. 2 in G major, the Trio for French Horn, Violin, and Piano, the two string quartets, op. 51, and the String Quartet op. 67 are exemplary works of their kind. In 1872 Brahms was named artistic director of the concerts of Vienna's famed Gesellschaft der Musikfreunde; he held this post until 1875. During this time, he composed the *Variations on a Theme by Joseph Haydn,* op. 56a. The title was a misnomer; the theme occurs in a Feldpartita for military band by Haydn, but it was not Haydn's own; it was originally known as the St. Anthony Chorale, and in pedantic scholarly editions of Brahms it is called St. Anthony Variations. Otto Dessoff conducted the first performance of the work with the Vienna Phil. on Nov. 2, 1873.

For many years friends and admirers of Brahms urged him to write a symphony. He clearly had a symphonic mind; his piano concertos were symphonic in outline and thematic development. As early as 1855 he began work on a full-fledged symph.; in 1862 he nearly completed the first movement of what was to be his first symph. The famous horn solo in the finale of the first symph. was jotted down by Brahms on a picture postcard to Clara Schumann dated Sept. 12, 1868, from his summer place in the Tyrol; in it Brahms said that he heard the tune played by a shepherd on a Alpine horn; and he set it to a rhymed quatrain of salutation. Yet Brahms was still unsure about his symphonic capacity. (A frivolous suggestion was made by an irresponsible psychomusicologist that it was when Brahms grew his famous luxuriant beard that he finally determined to complete his symphonic essay; such pogonological speculations illustrate the degree to which musical criticism can contribute to its own ridiculosity.) The great C minor Symph., his first, was completed in 1876 and first performed at Karlsruhe on Nov. 4, 1876, conducted by Dessoff. Hans von Bülow, the German master of the telling phrase, called it "The Tenth," thus placing Brahms on a direct line from Beethoven. It was also Hans von Bülow who cracked a bon mot that became a part of music history, in referring to the three B's of music, Bach, Beethoven, and Brahms. The original saying was not merely a vacuous alphabetical generalization; Bülow's phrase was deeper; in answering a question as to what was his favorite key, he said it was E-flat major, the key of Beethoven's *Eroica,* because it had 3 B's in its key signature. (In German, B is specifically B flat, but by extension may signify any flat)—one for Bach, one for Beethoven, and one for Brahms. The witty phrase took wing, but its sophisticated connotation was lost at the hands of professional popularizers.

Brahms composed his 2nd symph. in 1877; it was performed for the first time by the Vienna Phil. on Dec. 30, 1877, under the direction of Hans Richter, receiving a fine acclaim. Brahms led a second performance of the work with the Gewandhaus Orch. in Leipzig on Jan. 10, 1878. In 1878 Brahms wrote his violin concerto; the score was dedicated to Joachim, who gave its premiere with the Gewandhaus Orch. on Jan. 1, 1879. Brahms then composed his 2nd piano concerto, in B-flat major, and was soloist in its first performance in Budapest, on Nov. 9, 1881. There followed the 3rd symph. in F major, first performed by the Vienna Phil., under the direction of Hans Richter, on Dec. 2, 1883. The 4th symph. in E minor followed in quick succession; it had its first performance in Meiningen on Oct. 25, 1885. The symph. cycle was completed in less than a decade; it has been conjectured, without foundation, that the tonalities of the four symphs. of Brahms—C, D, F, and E—correspond to the fugal subject of Mozart's Jupiter Symph., and that some symbolic meaning was attached to it. All speculations aside, there is an inner symmetry uniting these works. The four symphs. contain four movements each, with a slow movement and a scherzo-like Allegretto in the middle of the corpus. There are fewer departures from the formal scheme than in Beethoven, and there are no extraneous episodes interfering with the grand general line. Brahms wrote music pure in design and eloquent in sonorous projection; he was a true classicist, a quality that endeared him to the critics who were repelled by Wagnerian streams of sound, and by the same token alienated those who sought something more than mere geometry of thematic configurations from a musical composition.

The chamber music of Brahms possesses similar symphonic qualities; when Schoenberg undertook to make an orch. arrangement of the piano quartet of Brahms, all he had to do was to expand the sonorities and enhance instrumental tone colors already present in the original. The string quartets of Brahms are edifices of Gothic perfection; his 3 violin sonatas, his 2nd piano trio (the first was a student work and yet it had a fine quality of harmonious construction) all contribute to a permanent treasure of musical classicism. The piano writing of Brahms is severe in its contrapuntal texture, but pianists for a hundred years included his rhapsodies and intermezzos in their repertoire; and Brahms was able to impart sheer delight in his Hungarian rhapsodies and waltzes; they represented the Viennese side of his character, as contrasted with the profound Germanic quality of his symphs. The song cycles of Brahms continued the evolution of the art of the lieder, a natural continuation of the song cycles of Schubert and Schumann.

Brahms was sociable and made friends easily; he traveled to Italy, and liked to spend his summers in the solitude of the Austrian Alps. But he was reluctant to appear as a center of attention; he declined to receive the honorary degree of Mus.D. from the Univ. of Cambridge in 1876, giving as a reason his fear of seasickness in crossing the English Channel. He was pleased to receive the Gold Medal of the Phil. Society of London in 1877. In 1879 the Univ. of Breslau proffered him an honorary degree of Doctor of Philosophy, citing him as "Artis musicae severioris in Germania nunc princeps." As a gesture of appreciation and gratitude he wrote an *Akademische Festouvertüre* for Breslau, and since there was no Channel to cross on the way, he accepted the invitation to conduct its premiere in Breslau on Jan. 4, 1881; its rousing finale using the German student song "Gaudeamus igitur" pleased the academic assembly. In 1887 he was presented with the Prussian Order "Pour le Mérite." In 1889 he received the freedom of his native city of Hamburg; also in 1889, Franz Joseph, the Emperor of Austria, made him a Commander of the Order of Leopold. With success and fame came a sense of self-sufficiency, which found its external expression in the corpulence of his appearance, familiar to all from photographs and drawings of Brahms conducting or playing the piano. Even during his Viennese period Brahms remained a sturdy Prussian; his ideal was to see Germany a dominant force in Europe philosophically and militarily. In his workroom he kept a bronze relief of Bismarck, the "Iron Chancellor," crowned with laurel. He was extremely meticulous in his working habits (his manuscripts were clean and legible), but he avoided wearing formal dress, preferring a loosely fitting flannel shirt and a detachable white collar, but no cravat. He liked to dine in simple restaurants, and he drank a great deal of beer. He was indifferent to hostile criticism; still, it is amazing to read the outpouring of invective against Brahms by George Bernard Shaw and by American critics; the usual accusations were of dullness and turgidity. When Symph. Hall was opened in Boston in 1900 with the lighted signs Exit in Case of Fire, someone cracked that they should more appropriately announce Exit in Case of Brahms. Yet, at the hands of successive German conductors Brahms became a standard symphonist in N.Y., Boston, Philadelphia, and Baltimore. From the perspective of a century, Brahms appears as the greatest master of counterpoint after Bach; one can

learn polyphony from a studious analysis of the chamber music and piano works of Brahms; he excelled in variation forms; his piano variations on a theme of Paganini are exemplars of contrapuntal learning, and they are also among the most difficult piano works of the 19th century. Posterity gave him a full measure of recognition; Hamburg celebrated his sesquicentennial in 1983 with great pomp. Brahms had lived a good life, but died a bad death, stricken with cancer of the liver.

WORKS: FOR ORCH.: 4 symphs.: No. 1 in C minor, op. 68 (1855–76; Karlsruhe, Nov. 4, 1876, Dessoff, conductor); No. 2 in D major, op. 73 (1877; Vienna, Dec. 30, 1877, Richter conductor); No. 3 in F major, op. 90 (1883; Vienna, Dec. 2, 1883, Richter, conductor); No. 4 in E minor, op. 98 (1884–85; Meiningen, Oct. 17, 1885, Brahms, conductor [private perf.]; public perf., Oct. 25, 1885, Bülow, conductor).

OTHER WORKS FOR ORCH.: Piano Concerto No. 1 in D minor, op. 15 (1854–58; Hannover, Jan. 22, 1859, Brahms, soloist; Joachim, conductor); Serenade No. 1 in D major, op. 11 (first version, for small orch., 1857–58; Hamburg, March 28, 1859, Joachim, conductor; 2nd version, for larger orch., 1859; Hannover, March 3, 1860, Joachim, conductor); Serenade No. 2 in A major, op. 16 (1858–59; Hamburg, Feb. 10, 1860, Brahms, conductor; revised, 1875); *Variations on a Theme by Joseph Haydn,* op. 56a (the theme, from the *St. Anthony Chorale,* may not be by Haydn; 1873; Vienna, Nov. 2, 1873, Dessoff, conductor); Violin Concerto in D major, op. 77 (1878; Leipzig, Jan. 1, 1879, Joachim, soloist; Brahms, conductor); Piano Concerto No. 2 in B-flat major, op. 83 (1878–81; Budapest, Nov. 9, 1881, Brahms, soloist; Erkel, conductor); *Akademische Festouvertüre*, op. 80 (1880; Breslau, Jan. 4, 1881, Brahms, conductor); *Tragische Ouvertüre*, op. 81 (1880; Vienna, Dec. 26, 1880, Richter, conductor; rev., 1881); Concerto in A minor for Violin and Cello, op. 102, the *Double* Concerto (1887; Cologne, Oct. 18, 1887, Joachim, violinist; and Hausmann, cellist; and Wüllner, conductor); also 3 Hungarian Dances arranged for Orch. (1873): No. 1 in G minor, No. 3 in F major, and No. 10 in F major.

CHAMBER MUSIC: Piano Trio No. 1 in B major, op. 8 (1853–54; N.Y., Nov. 27, 1855; revised, 1889); Sextet No. 1 in B-flat major for 2 Violins, 2 Violas, and 2 Cellos, op. 18 (1858–60; Hannover, Oct. 20, 1860); Piano Quartet No. 1 in G minor, op. 25 (1861; Hamburg, Nov. 16, 1861); Piano Quartet No. 2 in A major, op. 26 (1861–62; Vienna, Nov. 29, 1862); Piano Quintet in F minor, op. 34 (1861–64; Paris, March 24, 1868); Sextet No. 2 in G major for 2 Violins, 2 Violas, and 2 Cellos, op. 36 (1864–65; Vienna, Feb. 3, 1867); Cello Sonata No. 1 in E minor, op. 38 (1862–65); Trio in E-flat major for Violin, Horn or Viola, and Piano, op. 40 (1865; Karlsruhe, Dec. 7, 1865); String Quartet No. 1 in C minor, op. 51 (1865?–73; Vienna, Dec. 1, 1873); String Quartet No. 2 in A minor, op. 51 (1865?–73?; Vienna, Oct. 18, 1873); Piano Quartet No. 3 in C minor, op. 60 (1855–75; Ziegelhausen, Nov. 18, 1875); String Quartet No. 3 in B-flat major, op. 67 (1876; Berlin, Oct. 1876); Violin Sonata No. 1 in G major, op. 78 (1878–79; Vienna, Nov. 29, 1879); Piano Trio No. 2 in C major, op. 87 (1880–82; Frankfurt, Dec. 28,

1882); Quintet No. 1 in F major for 2 Violins, 2 Violas, and Cello, op. 88 (1882; Frankfurt, Dec. 28, 1882); Cello Sonata No. 2 in F major, op. 99 (1886; Vienna, Nov. 24, 1886); Violin Sonata No. 2 in A major, op. 100 (1886; Vienna, Dec. 2, 1886); Piano Trio No. 3 in C minor, op. 101 (1886; Budapest, Dec. 20, 1886); Violin Sonata No. 3 in D minor, op. 108 (1886–88; Budapest, Dec. 22, 1888); Quintet No. 2 in G major for 2 Violins, 2 Violas, and Cello, op. 111 (1890; Vienna, Nov. 11, 1890); Trio in A minor for Clarinet or Viola, Cello, and Piano, op. 114 (1891; Berlin, Dec. 1, 1891); Quintet in B minor for Clarinet and String Quartet, op. 115 (1891; Berlin, Dec. 1, 1891); Two sonatas: No. 1 in F minor and No. 2 in E-flat major for Clarinet or Viola and Piano, op. 120 (1894; Vienna, Jan. 7, 1895); also a Scherzo in C minor for Violin and Piano, a movement from the Sonata in A minor by Brahms, Schumann, and A. Dietrich. In 1924 a copy from the original score of a Trio in A major, presumably composed by Brahms when he was about 20 years old (see letter to R. Schumann, 1853), was discovered in Bonn; it was publ. in 1938.

FOR SOLO PIANO: Scherzo in E-flat minor, op. 4 (1851; Vienna, March 17, 1867); Sonata No. 1 in C major, op. 1 (1852–53; Leipzig, Dec. 17, 1853); Sonata No. 2 in F-sharp minor, op. 2 (1852; Vienna, Feb. 2, 1882); Sonata No. 3 in F minor, op. 5 (1853; Vienna, Jan. 6, 1863); *Variations on a Theme by Schumann* in F-sharp minor, op. 9 (1854; Berlin, Dec. 1879); 4 Ballades, op. 10: D minor, D major, B minor, and B major (1854); Gavotte in A minor (1854); Gavotte in A major (1855); 2 Gigues: A minor and B minor (1855); 2 Sarabandes: A minor and B minor (1855; Vienna, Jan. 20, 1856); *Variations [13] on a Hungarian Song* in D major, op. 21 (1853; London, March 25, 1874); *Variations [11] on an Original Theme* in D major, op. 21 (1857; Copenhagen, March 1868); *Variations [25] and Fugue on a Theme by Handel* in B-flat major, op. 24 (1861; Hamburg, Dec. 7, 1861); *Variations [28] on a Theme by Paganini* in A minor, op. 35 (1862–63; Zürich, Nov. 25, 1865); 16 Waltzes, op. 39 (1865); 8 Piano Pieces, op. 76 (1871–78; Leipzig, Jan. 4, 1880); 2 Rhapsodies: B minor and G minor, op. 79 (1879; Krefeld, Jan. 20, 1880); *Fantasien* [7], op. 116 (1892); 3 Intermezzos: E-flat major, B-flat minor, and C-sharp minor, op. 117 (1892); Piano Pieces [6], op. 118 (1892; London, Jan. 1894); Piano Pieces [4], op. 119 (1892; London, Jan. 1894); also 5 *Studien* for Piano (I, Study after Frédéric Chopin, in F minor, an arrangement of Chopin's Etude No. 2, op. 25; II, Rondo after Carl Maria von Weber, in C major, an arrangement of the finale of Weber's *Moto perpetuo*, op. 24; III and IV, Presto after J.S. Bach, in G minor [2 arrangements of the finale of BWV 1001]; V, *Chaconne* by J.S. Bach, in D minor, (an arrangement of the finale of BWV 1016); Theme and Variations in D minor (an arrangement of the slow movement of the Sextet No. 1; 1860; Frankfurt, Oct. 31, 1865); Gavotte in A major (an arrangement from Gluck's *Paris ed Elena;* Vienna, Jan. 20, 1856; publ. 1871); 10 Hungarian Dances (an arrangement of nos. 1–10 from the original version for piano, 4-hands; publ. 1872); 51 Exercises (publ. 1893); cadenzas to concertos by Bach (Harpsichord Concerto No. 1 in D minor, BWV 1052), Mozart

(Piano Concertos Nos. 17 in G major, K. 453, 20 in D minor, K. 466, and 24 in C minor, K. 491), and Beethoven (Piano Concerto No. 4 in G major, op. 58).

FOR PIANO, 4-HANDS: *Variations on a Theme by Schumann* in E-flat major, op. 23 (1861; Vienna, Jan. 12, 1864); 16 Waltzes, op. 39 (1865; Vienna, March 17, 1867); *Liebeslieder,* 18 waltzes, op. 52a (1874; an arrangement from the original version for 4 Voices and Piano, 4-hands); *Neue Liebeslieder,* 15 waltzes, op. 65a (1874; an arrangement from the original version for 4 Voices and Piano, 4-hands); Hungarian Dances (21 dances in 4 books; 1852–69).

FOR TWO PIANOS: Sonata in F minor, op. 34b (1864; Vienna, April 17, 1874); Variations on a Theme by Haydn, op. 56b (1873; Vienna, March 17, 1882); also arrangements of Joachim's *Demetrius* Overture and Overture to *Henry IV.*

FOR ORGAN: Fugue in A-flat minor (1856); *O Traurigkeit, O Herzeleid,* chorale prelude and fugue in A minor (1856; Vienna, Dec. 2, 1882); 2 preludes and fugues: A minor and G minor (1856–57); 11 *Choralvorspiele,* op. 122 (1896).

VOCAL MUSIC: Choral Works: *Geistliches Lied* for 4-part Chorus and Organ or Piano, op. 30 (1856); *Ein deutsches Requiem* for Soprano, Baritone, Chorus, and Orch., op. 45 (1857–68; first 3 movements, under Herbeck, Vienna, Dec. 1, 1867; movements 1–4 and 6, under Brahms, Bremen, April 10, 1868; first complete perf., under Reinecke, Leipzig, Feb. 18, 1869); *Ave Maria* for Women's Voices and Orch. or Organ, op. 12 (1858); *Begräbnisgesang* for Choir and Wind Instruments, op. 13 (1858; Hamburg, Dec. 2, 1859); *Marienlieder* for Mixed Chorus, op. 22 (7 songs; 1859); 4 Songs for Women's Voices, 2 Horns, and Harp, op. 17 (1859–60); *Der 13. Psalm* for Women's Voices and Organ or Piano, with Strings ad libitum, op. 27 (1859; Hamburg, Sept. 19, 1864); 2 Motets for 5-part Chorus a cappella, op. 29 (1860; Vienna, April 17, 1864); 3 Sacred Choruses for Women's Voices a cappella, op. 37 (1859–63); 5 *Soldatenlieder* for 4-part Male Chorus a cappella, op. 41 (1861–62); 3 Songs for 6-part Mixed Chorus with Piano ad libitum, op. 42 (1859–61); 12 Songs and Romances for Women's Voices with Piano ad libitum, op. 44 (1859–63); *Rinaldo,* cantata for Tenor, Male Chorus, and Orch., op. 50, after Goethe (1863–68; Vienna, Feb. 28, 1869); *Rhapsodie* for Contralto, Male Chorus, and Orch., op. 53, after Goethe's *Harzreise im Winter* (1869; Jena, March 3, 1870); *Schicksalslied* for Chorus and Orch., op. 54 (1868–71; Karlsruhe, Oct. 18, 1871); Triumphlied for 8-part Chorus, Baritone, and Orch., op. 55 (1870–71; Karlsruhe, June 5, 1872); 7 Songs for 4- and 6-part a cappella Chorus, op. 62 (1874); *Nänie* for Chorus and Orch., op. 82, after Schiller (1880–81; Zürich, Dec. 6, 1881); Two Motets for 4- and 6-part a cappella Chorus, op. 74 (1877; 2nd motet probably composed between 1860 and 1865; Vienna, Dec. 8, 1878); *Gesang der Parzen* for 6-part Chorus and Orch., op. 89, after Goethe's *Iphigenie auf Tauris* (1882; Basel, Dec. 10, 1882); 6 Songs and Romances for 4-part a cappella Chorus, op. 93a (1883–84; Krefeld, Jan. 27, 1885); *Tafellied* for 6-part Chorus and Piano, op. 93b (1884; Krefeld, Jan. 28, 1885); Five Songs for 4- and 6-part a cappella Chorus, op. 104 (1888; Vienna, April 3, 1889); *Fest-*

und Gedenksprüche for a Double a cappella Chorus, op. 109 (1886–88; Hamburg, Sept. 14, 1889); Three Motets for 4- and 8-part a cappella Chorus, op. 110 (1889; Cologne, March 13, 1890); also 13 Canons, for Women's Voices, op. 113 (1860–67); *Deutsche Volkslieder* (26 songs arranged for 4-part Chorus; 1854–73; publ. in 2 books, dated 1926–27). Vocal quartets: For Soprano, Alto, Tenor, Bass, and Piano: 3 Quartets, op. 31 (1859–63); *Liebeslieder,* 18 waltzes, with Piano, 4-hands, op. 52 (1868–69; Vienna, Jan. 5, 1870); 3 Quartets, op. 64 (1862–74); *Neue Liebeslieder,* 15 waltzes, with Piano, 4-hands, op. 65 (1874; Mannheim, May 8, 1875); 4 Quartets, op. 92 (1877–84); *Zigeunerlieder,* op. 103 (1887); 6 Quartets, op. 112 (1888–91); also *Liebeslieder,* Nos. 1, 2, 4–6, 8, 9, and 11 from op. 52 and No. 5 from op. 65, with Orch. (1870); *Kleine Hochzeitskantate* (1874). Vocal duets: With Piano Accompaniment: 3 Duets for Soprano and Alto, op. 20 (1858–60; Vienna, Jan. 29, 1878); 4 Duets for Alto and Baritone, op. 28 (1860–62; Vienna, Dec. 18, 1862); 4 Duets for Soprano and Alto, op. 61 (1874); 5 Duets for Soprano and Alto, op. 66 (1875; Vienna, Jan. 29, 1878); 4 Ballads and Romances, op. 75 (1877–78). Songs: With Piano Accompaniment: 6 Songs, op. 7 (1851-52); 6 Songs, op. 3, for Tenor or Soprano (1852–53); 6 Songs, op. 6, for Soprano or Tenor (1852–53); 8 Songs and Romances, op. 14 (1858); 5 Poems, op. 19 (1858); Romances [15] from L. Tieck's "Magelone" (1861–68); Songs [9], op. 32 (1864); 7 Songs, op. 48 (1855–68); 4 Songs, op. 43 (1857–64); 5 Songs, op. 47 (1860–68); 4 Songs, op. 46 (1864–68); 5 Songs, op. 49 (1868); Songs [8], op. 57 (1871); Songs [8], op. 58 (1871); Songs [8], op. 59 (1871–73); Songs [9], op. 63 (1874); 4 Songs, op. 70 (1875–77); 9 Songs, op. 69 (1877); 5 Songs, op. 72 (1876–77); 5 Songs, op. 71 (1877); 6 Songs, op. 86 (1877–79); 6 Songs, op. 85 (1877–82); Romances and Songs [15] for one or 2 Female Voices, op. 84 (1881); 2 Songs for Alto, Viola, and Piano, op. 91 (first song may have been begun as early as 1864, the 2nd in 1878; publ. 1884); 5 Songs, op. 94 (1884); 7 Songs, op. 95 (1884); 4 Songs, op. 96 (1884); 6 Songs, op. 97 (1884–85); 5 Songs, op. 105 (1886); 5 Songs, op. 106 (1886); 5 Songs, op. 107 (1886); *Vier ernste Gesänge* for Baritone, op. 121 (1896); also *Mondnacht* (1854); *Regenlied* (1872); 5 *Songs of Ophelia* for Soprano, with Piano *ad libitum* (1873); 14 *Volkskinderlieder,* arrangements for Voice and Piano (1858); 28 *Deutsche Volkslieder,* arrangements for Voice and Piano (1858; publ. 1926); arrangement of Schubert's *Memnon* for Voice and Orch. (1862); arrangement of Schubert's *An Schwager Kronos* for Voice and Orch. (1862); arrangement of Schubert's *Geheimes* for Voice, Horn, and Strings; 8 *Gypsy Songs,* an arrangement of op. 103, nos. 1–7 and 11, for Voice and Piano (1887); 49 *Deutsche Volkslieder,* arrangements for Voice and Piano (1894).

Brăiloiu, Constantin, Rumanian ethnomusicographer; b. Bucharest, Aug. 25, 1893; d. Geneva, Dec. 20, 1958. He studied in Austria and Switzerland; in 1928 founded the Archive of Folklore in Bucharest; also was a member of ethnomusicological organizations in Geneva and Paris.

WRITINGS: *Esquisse d'une méthode de folklore musical* (Paris, 1930); *La Musique populaire roumaine* (Paris, 1940); *Le Folklore musical* (Zürich, 1948); *Le Rythme aksak* (Paris, 1952); *La Rythmique enfantine* (Brussels, 1956); "Outline of a Method of Musical Folklore" (trans. by M. Mooney; ed. by A. Briegleb and M. Kahane), *Ethnomusicology* (Sept. 1970).

Brailowsky, Alexander, noted Russian pianist; b. Kiev, Feb. 16, 1896; d. New York, April 25, 1976. After study with his father, a professional pianist, he was taken to Vienna in 1911 and was accepted by Leschetizky as a pupil; made his debut in Paris after World War I; presented a complete cycle of Chopin's works in Paris (1924), and repeated it there several times. He made a highly successful tour all over the world; made his American debut at Aeolian Hall in N.Y., Nov. 19, 1924; made a coast-to-coast tour of the U.S. in 1936; first gave the Chopin cycle in America during the 1937–38 season, in 6 recitals in N.Y.

Brain, Aubrey, English French-horn player; b. London, July 12, 1893; d. there, Sept. 20, 1955. He studied at the Royal College of Music in London; joined the London Symph. Orch.; then played in the BBC Symph. Orch.; retired in 1945. He was appointed prof. at the Royal Academy of Music in 1923, and held this position for 30 years. His father was also a horn player, as was his brother **Alfred** and his son **Dennis.**

Brain, Dennis, English French-horn virtuoso; b. London, May 17, 1921; d. in a automobile accident in Hatfield, Hertfordshire, Sept. 1, 1957. He studied with his father, **Aubrey Brain;** served as first horn player in the Royal Phil., and later with the Philharmonia Orch. He rapidly acquired the reputation of a foremost performer on his instrument. Benjamin Britten's *Serenade* for Tenor, Horn, and Strings was written for Dennis Brain. He was killed when he drove at a high speed, at night, from Birmingham to London, and hit a tree. His death caused a profound shock among English musicians.

Braithwaite, Nicholas, English conductor; son of **Warwick Braithwaite;** b. London, Aug. 26, 1939. He was educated at the Royal Academy of Music in London; later went to Vienna, where he studied with Hans Swarowsky. He served as associate conductor of the Bournemouth Symph. Orch. (1967–70) and as associate principal conductor of the Sadler's Wells Opera (1970–74). From 1976 to 1980 he was music director of the Glyndebourne Touring Opera. In 1980 he was engaged as an assistant to Sir Georg Solti when the London Phil. Orch. made its tour of Japan and South Korea. In 1981 he became chief conductor of the Stora Theater Opera in Göteborg, Sweden.

Braithwaite, Sam Hartley, English composer; b. Egremont, Cumberland, July 20, 1883; d. Arnside,

Westmoreland, Jan. 13, 1947. He studied at the Royal Academy of Music; upon graduation, joined its faculty as an instructor. His compositions include *Military Overture* and *A Night by Dalegarth Bridge,* a tone poem.

Braithwaite, Warwick, British conductor; b. Dunedin, New Zealand, Jan. 9, 1896; d. London, Jan. 18, 1971. He studied at the Royal Academy of Music in London; won the Challen Gold Medal and the Battison Hayes Prize. He began his career as a conductor with the O'Mara Opera Co.; then conducted with the British National Opera Co. He was assistant music director of the BBC; then went to its Cardiff studio in Wales as music director; also conducted the Cardiff Musical Society (1924–31). He was a founder of the Welsh National Orch. From 1932 to 1940 he was a conductor at the Sadler's Wells Opera; then he led the Scottish Orch. in Glasgow (1940–46). Later he was a ballet conductor at the Royal Opera, Covent Garden, in London (1950–53); then conducted the National Orch. of New Zealand and served as artistic director of the National Opera of Australia (1954–55). From 1956 to 1960 he was music director of the Welsh National Opera; then was again a conductor at Sadler's Wells until 1968. He publ. *The Conductor's Art* (London, 1952).

Brancour, René, French music critic; b. Paris, May 17, 1862; d. there, Nov. 16, 1948. Educated at the Paris Cons., he became curator of its collection of musical instruments; in 1906 began a course of lectures on esthetics at the Sorbonne; also wrote newspaper criticism. A brilliant writer, he poured invective on the works of composers of the advanced school; his tastes were conservative, but he accepted French music of the Impressionist period. He wrote biographies of Félicien David (1911) and Méhul (1912) in the series Musiciens Célèbres; of Massenet (1923) and Offenbach (1929) in Les Maîtres de la Musique. Other books are *La Vie et l'œuvre de Georges Bizet* (1913); *Histoire des instruments de musique* (1921); *La Marseillaise et le chant du départ;* etc.

Brand, Max, Austrian composer; b. Lemberg, April 26, 1896; d. Langenzersdorf, near Vienna, April 5, 1980. He studied with Franz Schreker at the Vienna Academy of Music. He made use of the 12-tone method of composition as early as 1927, but did not limit himself to it in his later works. His most spectacular work was the opera *Maschinist Hopkins,* to his own libretto, chosen as the best operatic work of the year by the Congress of German Composers, and first produced at Duisburg on April 13, 1929; it was later staged in 37 opera houses in Europe, including Russia; it marked the climactic point of the "machine era" in modern music between the two wars. Brand was also active in the field of experimental musical films in the triple capacity of author, composer, and director. From 1933–38 he remained in Vienna; then went to Brazil; in 1940 arrived in the U.S., becoming an American citizen in 1945. In 1975 he returned to Austria.
WORKS: *Nachtlied,* from Nietzsche's *Also sprach Zarathustra,* for Soprano and Orch. (1922); 3 songs to poems by Lao-Tse (Salzburg Festival, 1923); *Eine Nachtmusik* for Chamber Orch. (1923); String Trio (1923); *Die Wippe,* ballet (1925); *Tragœdietta,* ballet (1926); *5 Ballads,* a study in 12 tones (1927); *Maschinist Hopkins,* opera in 3 acts (1928); *The Chronicle,* scenic cantata for Narrator, Soli, Chorus, and Orch. (1938); *Piece for Flute and Piano,* in 12 tones (1940); *Kyrie Eleison,* study in 12 tones for Chorus (1940; perf. by Villa-Lobos, Rio de Janeiro, 1940); *The Gate,* scenic oratorio, with Narrator (N.Y., May 23, 1944); *The Wonderful One-Hoss Shay,* symph. rondo for Orch., after Oliver Wendell Holmes (Philadelphia, Jan. 20, 1950); *Night on the Bayous of Louisiana,* tone poem (1953); *Stormy Interlude,* opera in one act, libretto by the composer (1955). About 1958 Brand became absorbed in electronic music; wrote *The Astronauts, An Epic in Electronics* (1962); *Ilian 1 & 2* (1966); numerous pieces of music for modern plays.

Brandt, Jobst vom (or **Jodocus de Brant**), German musician; b. Waltersof, near Marktredwitz, Oct. 28, 1517; d. Brand, near Marktredwitz, Jan. 22, 1570. In 1530 he enrolled at Heidelberg Univ.; in 1548 had become Captain of Waldsassen and Administrator of Liebenstein. He was one of the most important composers of the Senfl school; his music is distinguished by deep feeling and a skillful use of counterpoint.

Brandt, Marianne (real name, **Marie Bischoff**), Austrian contralto; b. Vienna, Sept. 12, 1842; d. there, July 9, 1921. She studied voice in Vienna, and later with Pauline Viardot-Garcia in Baden-Baden (1869–70); she made her debut as Rachel in *La Juive* in Olmütz on Jan. 4, 1867; then sang in Hamburg and at the Berlin Opera (1868–82). In 1872 she appeared in London; made her American debut as Leonore at the Metropolitan Opera in N.Y. on Nov. 19, 1884, and remained on its staff until 1888; she also sang Italian roles in operas by Verdi and Meyerbeer. In 1890 she settled in Vienna as a singing teacher.

Brandts-Buys, Jan, composer; b. Zutphen, the Netherlands, Sept. 12, 1868; d. Salzburg, Dec. 7, 1933. He was a pupil of M. Schwarz and A. Urspruch at the Raff Cons. in Frankfurt; lived for a time in Vienna; later settled in Salzburg. His first opera, *Das Veilchenfest* (Berlin, 1909), met with opposition; a 2nd opera, *Das Glockenspiel* (Dresden, 1913), was received more kindly; while a 3rd, *Die drei Schneider von Schönau* (Dresden, April 1, 1916), was quite successful. Subsequent operas were: *Der Eroberer* (Dresden, 1918); *Micarême* (Vienna, 1919); *Der Mann im Mond* (Dresden, 1922); *Traumland* (Dresden, 1927). He also wrote a ballet, *Machinalität* (Amsterdam, 1928); 2 piano concertos; a *Konzertstück* for Cello and Orch.; chamber music; piano pieces; songs.

Brandukov, Anatol, eminent Russian cellist; b. Moscow, Dec. 22, 1856; d. there, Feb. 16, 1930. He studied cello at the Moscow Cons. with Fitzenhagen

(1868–77), and also attended Tchaikovsky's classes in harmony. In 1878 he undertook a concert tour of Europe; lived mostly in Paris until 1906. His artistry was appreciated by Tchaikovsky, who dedicated his *Pezzo capriccioso* for Cello and Orch. to him; he enjoyed the friendship of Saint-Saëns and Liszt. In 1906 he returned to Moscow, where he was prof. at the Phil. Inst.; from 1921 to 1930 he taught cello at the Moscow Cons. He composed a number of cello pieces and made transcriptions of works by Tchaikovsky, Rachmaninoff, and others.

Branscombe, Gena, Canadian-born American educator, chorus leader, and composer; b. Picton, Ontario, Nov. 4, 1881; d. New York, July 26, 1977. She attended the Chicago Musical College, where she studied piano and composition with Felix Borowski; then went to Berlin, where she took a course with Engelbert Humperdinck. Returning to America, she took conducting lessons with Frank Damrosch and Albert Stoessel; became a U.S. citizen in 1910. In 1935 she organized the Branscombe Chorale, a women's ensemble that she conducted until 1953. She composed mostly choral works, often to her own texts; of these the most notable are *Conventry's Choir, The Phantom Caravan, A Wind from the Sea, Youth of the World,* and *Pilgrims of Destiny,* a choral drama (1928–29). She also composed a symph. suite, *Quebec,* and some 150 songs. Amazingly energetic, she continued to be active until an improbable old age, and at the time of her death she was working on her autobiography.

Brant, Henry Dreyfus, American ultramodern composer and a pioneer of spatial music; b. Montreal, of American parents, Sept. 15, 1913. He learned the rudiments of music from his father, a violinist who taught at the McGill Univ. Conservatorium in Montreal. In 1929 his family moved to N.Y., where Brant studied piano with James Friskin and composition with Leonard Mannes at the Inst. of Musical Art; also took private lessons with Wallingford Riegger (1930–31) and George Antheil (1934–35) and attended classes of Rubin Goldmark at the Juilliard School of Music (1933); in 1938–39 he studied conducting with Fritz Mahler in N.Y. Having absorbed a totality of quaquaversal techniques of composition, he became a teacher; was on the faculty at Columbia Univ. (1945–52), at the Juilliard School of Music (1947–54), and at Bennington College in Vermont (1957–80). In 1982 he settled in Santa Barbara, Calif. He held Guggenheim fellowships in 1946 and 1955. An audacious explorer of sonic potentialities, he draws without prejudice on resources ranging from common objects of everyday American life, such as kitchen utensils and tin cans, to the outermost reaches of euphonious cacophony; he became a pioneer in the field of spatial music, in which the participating instruments are placed at specified points in space, on the stage, on the balcony, and on the aisles. In conducting his spatial music, he developed an appropriate technique, using body language, turnabouts of 90, 135, and 180 degrees to address his instrumentalists, and also resorting to verbal instructions. He is a minor virtuoso on blowing, squeaking, and squealing instruments, excelling on the flageolet, ocarina, and tin whistle. Brant expounded the rationale of spatial music in his article "Space as an Essential Aspect of Musical Composition" in *Contemporary Composers on Contemporary Music,* eds. E. Schwartz and B. Childs (N.Y., 1967). Among his future projects is the construction of a flexible concert hall of plywood parts changing configurations according to acoustical requirements.

Branzell, Karin Maria, noted Swedish contralto; b. Stockholm, Sept. 24, 1891; d. Altadena, Calif., Dec. 14, 1974. She studied with Thekla Hofer in Stockholm, with Bachner in Berlin, and with Rosati in N.Y.; made her operatic debut in 1911. From 1912 to 1918 she was a member of the Stockholm Royal Opera; then sang with the Berlin State Opera (1919–23). She made her American debut as Fricka in *Die Walküre* with the Metropolitan Opera in N.Y. on Feb. 6, 1924, and remained on its roster for 20 seasons, retiring in 1944. Possessing a voice of exceptional range and power, she occasionally sang soprano roles. She was active as a voice teacher in N.Y.; in 1969 she moved to California.

Braslau, Sophie, American contralto; b. New York, Aug. 16, 1892; d. there, Dec. 22, 1935. She studied voice with Buzzi-Peccia; made her debut at the Metropolitan Opera in *Boris Godunov* (Nov. 26, 1914); was a member of the company until 1921; in 1931 toured Scandinavia and the Netherlands. A large collection of her programs, reviews, and biographical materials was given by the family to the Music Division of the N.Y. Public Library (1938).

Brassin, Louis, French pianist; b. Aix-la-Chapelle, June 24, 1840; d. St. Petersburg, May 17, 1884. He was a pupil of Moscheles at the Leipzig Cons.; made concert tours with his brothers **Leopold** and **Gerhard**; taught at the Stern Cons. in Berlin (1866); at the Brussels Cons. (1869–79); then at the St. Petersburg Cons. He publ. the valuable *Ecole moderne du piano;* composed 2 piano concertos, salon pieces for piano, and songs. His effective piano transcription of the Magic Fire music from *Die Walküre* is well known.

Braun, Peter Michael, German composer; b. Wuppertal, Dec. 2, 1936. He studied in Dortmund; later took courses in Cologne with Frank Martin, Bernd Alois Zimmermann, and Herbert Eimert, and also in Detmold with Giselher Klebe. His musical style is governed by structural considerations; in his varied techniques he applies the resources of "organized sound" as formulated by Varèse, the theory of sets and devices of synthetic *musique concrète.* He wrote *Thesis-Medium* for Piano (1960); *Monophonie* for Electric Guitar (1961–67); *Wind Sextet* (1961); *Transfer* for Orch. (1968).

Braun, Wilhelm. See **Brown, William.**

Braunfels, Walter, German composer; b. Frankfurt, Dec. 19, 1882; d. Cologne, March 19, 1954. He studied piano in Vienna with Leschetizky and composition in Munich with L. Thuille. He became active both as an educator and a composer. From 1913 to 1925 he lived near Munich; in 1925 he became a co-director of the Hochschule für Musik in Cologne. With the advent of the Nazi regime, he was compelled to abandon teaching; from 1933 to 1937 he was in Godesberg; from 1937 to 1945 in Überlingen. He excelled mainly as an opera composer; the following operas are notable: *Prinzessin Brambilla* (Stuttgart, March 25, 1909; revised 1931); *Ulenspiegel* (Stuttgart, Nov. 9, 1913); *Die Vögel,* after Aristophanes (Munich, Dec. 4, 1920; his most successful opera; given also in Berlin and Vienna); *Don Gil* (Munich, Nov. 15, 1924); *Der gläserne Berg* (Cologne, Dec. 4, 1928); *Galathea* (Cologne, Jan. 26, 1930); *Der Traum, Ein Leben* (1937); *Die heilige Johanna* (1942); also a mystery play, *Verkündigung,* after Paul Claudel (1936). He further wrote 2 piano concertos; Organ Concerto; *Revelation of St. John* for Tenor, Double Chorus, and Orch.; piano music and songs. He believed in the artistic and practical value of Wagnerian leading motifs; in his harmonies he was close to Richard Strauss, but he also applied impressionistic devices related to Debussy.

Bravničar, Matija, Slovene composer; b. Tolmin Feb. 24, 1897; d. Ljubljana, Nov 25, 1977. After service in the Austrian army (1915–18) he was a violinist at the opera theater in Ljubljana; meanwhile he studied composition at the Cons. there, graduating in 1932; was director of the Ljubljana Academy of Music (1945–49) and later taught composition there (1952–68); was president of the Society of Slovene Composers (1949–52) and of the Union of Yugoslavian Composers (1953–57). In his works, Bravničar cultivates a neo-Classical style, with thematic material strongly influenced by the melorhythmic inflections of Slovenian folk music.

Bream, Julian, noted English guitarist and lutenist; b. London, July 15, 1933. He was educated at the Royal College of Music in London; made his debut at the age of 17. In 1960 he founded the Julian Bream Consort; also directed the Semley Festival of Music and Poetry from 1971. Through his numerous concerts and recordings he has helped to revive interest in Elizabethan lute music. He was named an Officer of the Order of the British Empire in 1964.

Brecher, Gustav, conductor and editor; b. Eichwald, near Teplitz, Bohemia, Feb. 5, 1879; d. Ostend, May 1940. His family moved to Leipzig in 1889, and he studied there with Jadassohn. His first major work, the symph. poem *Rosmersholm,* was introduced by Richard Strauss at a Liszt-Verein concert in Leipzig (1896); Brecher made his debut as a conductor there (1897); was vocal coach and occasional conductor of operas in Leipzig (1898); conducted in Vienna (1901); served as first Kapellmeister in Olmütz (1902), in Hamburg (1903), and Cologne (1911–16); then went to Frankfurt (1916–24) and Leipzig

(1924–33). He committed suicide with his wife aboard a boat off the Belgian coast while attempting to flee from the advancing Nazi troops. His compositions include a symph. fantasia, *Aus unserer Zeit.* He was the author of several essays: *Über die veristische Oper; Analysen zu Werken von Berlioz und Strauss;* and *Über Operntexte und Opernübersetzungen* (1911).

Brecknock, John, English tenor; b. Long Eaton, Nov. 29, 1937. He received his vocal training in Birmingham; then joined the chorus of the Sadler's Wells Opera; in 1967 he appeared in a minor role there, soon rising to prominence as one of its principal members; also sang at Covent Garden, London, the Scottish National Opera, and the Glyndebourne Festival. He made his American debut with the Metropolitan Opera in N.Y. on March 23, 1977, as Tamino in *Die Zauberflöte.* He was especially praised for his performances of the early 19th-century Italian operatic repertoire.

Bredemeyer, Reiner, East German composer; b. Velez, Colombia, of German parents, Feb. 2, 1929. He studied composition with Karl Höller at the Akademie der Tonkunst in Munich (1949–53); then moved to East Germany, where he took courses with Wagner-Régeny at the Akademie der Künste in East Berlin (1955–57). In 1961 he was appointed conductor of the German Theater in East Berlin; in 1978 joined the faculty of the Akademie der Künste in East Berlin. In his own music he is an astute experimenter, but he adheres to the tenets of classical forms and avoids the extremes of modernism.

Brediceanu, Tiberiu, Rumanian composer; b. Lugoj, Transylvania, April 2, 1877; d. Bucharest, Dec. 19, 1968. He studied music mainly in Rumania; was a founding member of the Rumanian Opera and National Theater in Cluj (1919) and the Society of Rumanian Composers in Bucharest (1920); later became director of the Astra Cons. in Brasov (1934–40) and director-general of the Rumanian Opera (1941–44). He publ. valuable collections of Rumanian songs and dances, including 170 Rumanian folk melodies, 810 tunes of the Banat regions, and 1,000 songs of Transylvania.

Breil, Joseph Carl, American composer; b. Pittsburgh, June 29, 1870; d. Los Angeles, Jan. 23, 1926. He studied voice in Milan and Leipzig, and for a time sang in various opera companies. He was the composer of one of the earliest motion picture scores, *Queen Elizabeth* (Chicago, 1912); wrote words and music for the comic operas *Love Laughs at Locksmiths* (Portland, Maine, Oct. 27, 1910); *Prof. Tattle* (1913); and *The Seventh Chord* (1913). His serious opera, *The Legend,* was produced by the Metropolitan Opera on March 12, 1919. His opera *Asra* (after Heine) had a single performance, in Los Angeles (Nov. 24, 1925).

Breitkopf & Härtel, important German firm of

book and music publishers. As an established printing firm in Leipzig, it was bought in 1745 by **Bernhard Christoph Breitkopf** (b. Klausthal Harz, March 2, 1695; d. Leipzig, March 23, 1777). His son, **Johann Gottlob Immanuel** (b. Nov. 23, 1719; d. Jan. 28, 1794), entered the business in 1745; it was his invention which made the basis for the firm's position in the publication of music. In 1756 he devised a font with much smaller division of the musical elements, and this greatly reduced the cost of printing chords (and hence piano music). The firm soon began to issue numerous piano reductions of popular operas for amateur consumption. The earliest music publications, such as the *Berlinische Oden und Lieder* (3 vols., 1756, 1759, 1763), were made by Johann Gottlob Immanuel Breitkopf himself, and bore the imprint "Leipzig, Druckts und Verlegts Johann Gottlob Immanuel Breitkopf"; from 1765–77 the firm name appears as "Bernhard Christoph Breitkopf und Sohn"; from 1777–87 (after Christoph's death) Johann's name again appears alone; his second son, **Christoph Gottlob** (b. Leipzig, Sept. 22, 1750; d. there, April 4, 1800), joined the firm in 1787; from 1787–95 publications were issued as "im Breitkopfischen Verlage" (or Buchhandlung, or Musikhandlung); in 1795 (the year after Immanuel's death) Christoph Gottlob Breitkopf took as his partner his close friend **Gottfried Christoph Härtel** (b. Schneeburg, Jan. 27, 1763; d. near Leipzig, July 25, 1827); since 1795 the firm has been known as Breitkopf und Härtel, although no Breitkopf has been actively associated with the firm since Christoph Gottlob's death in 1800. Härtel's tremendous energy revitalized the firm. He added a piano factory; founded the important periodical *Allgemeine musikalische Zeitung* (1798; editor, J.F. Rochlitz); introduced pewter in place of the harder copper for engraving music; used Senefelder's new lithographic process for either title pages or music where suitable; issued so-called "complete" editions of the works of Mozart, Haydn, Clementi, and Dusek. The firm also began the practice of issuing catalogues with thematic indexes and keeping stocks of scores. From 1827–35 **Florenz Härtel** was head of the firm; **Hermann Härtel** (b. Leipzig, April 27, 1803; d. there, Aug. 4, 1875) and his brother, **Raimund Härtel** (b. Leipzig, June 9, 1810; d. there, Nov. 9, 1888), together dominated the book business of Leipzig (and thus all Germany) for many years; the sons of two sisters of Raimund and Hermann, **Wilhelm Volkmann** (b. Halle, June 12, 1837; d. Leipzig, Dec. 24, 1896) and **Dr. Oskar von Hase** (b. Jena, Sept. 15, 1846; d. Leipzig, Jan. 26, 1921), succeeded them. After Wilhelm Volkmann's death, his son, **Dr. Ludwig Volkmann** (1870–1947), headed the firm jointly with von Hase; von Hase's son, **Hermann** (1880–1945), entered the firm in 1904 and was a co-partner from 1910–14. Hermann von Hase publ. essays tracing the relation of J. Haydn, C.P.E. Bach, and J.A. Hiller to the firm; in 1915 he became a partner in the book business of K.F. Koehler. His brother **Dr. Hellmuth von Hase** (b. Jan. 30, 1891; d. Wiesbaden, Oct. 18, 1979) became director of the firm in 1919. The old house was destroyed during the air bombardment of Dec. 4, 1943; it was rebuilt after the war. In 1950 Dr.von Hase moved to Wiesbaden, where he established an independent business, reclaiming the rights for the firm in West Germany. Important enterprises of the firm throughout its existence are editions of Bach, Beethoven, Berlioz, Brahms, Chopin, Gluck, Grétry, Handel, Haydn, Lassus, Liszt, Mendelssohn, Mozart, Palestrina, Schein, Schubert, Schumann, Schütz, Victoria, and Wagner. The German government supported the publication by Breitkopf & Härtel of the two series of Denkmäler Deutscher Tonkunst (1892–1931 and 1900–1931). Other publications of the firm are: *Der Bär,* yearbook (since 1924); *Katalog des Archivs von Breitkopf und Härtel,* edited by Dr. F.W. Hitzig (2 vols., 1925–26); *Allgemeine musikalische Zeitung* (weekly; 1798–1848 and 1863–65); *Monatshefte für Musikgeschichte* (1869–1905); *Mitteilungen des Hauses Breitkopf und Härtel* (1876–1940; resumed in 1950); *Vierteljahrsschrift für Musikwissenschaft* (1869–1906); *Zeitschrift der Internationlen Musikgesellschaft* (monthly; Oct. 1899–Sept. 1914); *Sammelbände der Internationalen Musikgesellschaft* (quarterly; 1899–1914); *Korrespondenzblatt des Evangelischen Kirchengesangvereins für Deutschland* (monthly; 1886–1922); *Zeitschrift für Musikwissenschaft* (monthly; 1919–35); *Archiv für Musikforschung* (1936–43).

Brel, Jacques, Belgian-born French singer and songwriter; b. Brussels, April 8, 1929; d. Paris, Oct. 9, 1978. He rose to fame in France in the 1950s as a singer and songwriter of popular music, which emphasized such themes as unrequited love, loneliness, death, and war. In 1967 he quit the concert stage and turned to the theater, as a producer, director, and actor. In 1968 the composer Mort Shuman brought Brel's songs to Broadway in his musical *Jacques Brel Is Alive and Well and Living in Paris.* The title proved ironic; stricken with cancer, Brel abandoned his career in 1974 and made his home in the Marquesas Islands; in 1977 he returned to Paris to record his final album, *Brel;* then died.

Brema, Marie (real name, **Minny Fehrman**), English mezzo-soprano of German-American parentage; b. Liverpool, Feb. 28, 1856; d. Manchester, March 22, 1925. She studied singing with Georg Henschel; made her concert debut in London performing Schubert's *Ganymed* on Feb. 21, 1891, under the name of **Bremer** (her father being a native of Bremen). In 1894 she sang at the Bayreuth Festival, the first English singer to be so honored. On Nov. 27, 1895, she appeared as Brangäne in *Tristan und Isolde* at the Metropolitan Opera in N.Y., and remained on its roster through the 1895–96 season. Returning to England, she taught singing at the Royal Manchester College of Music.

Brendel, Alfred, eminent Austrian pianist; b. Wiesenberg, Moravia, Jan. 5, 1931. His principal teacher was Edwin Fischer; he also took some piano lessons with Paul Baumgartner, and later with Eduard Steuermann; he studied composition with Michl. He made his concert debut in Graz in 1948; then began a successful career in Europe. He played for the first time in America in 1963; also toured in South America, Japan, and Australia. He is particularly distinguished as an interpreter of the Vienna classics; but he also included in his active repertoire Schoenberg's difficult Piano Concerto. In May 1983 he presented in N.Y. a cycle of 7 concerts of the complete piano sonatas of Beethoven. He publ. *Musical Thoughts and Afterthoughts* (London, 1976; 2nd ed., 1982).

Brendel, Karl Franz, German writer on music; b. Stolberg, Nov. 26, 1811; d. Leipzig, Nov. 25, 1868. He was educated at the univs. of Leipzig and Berlin: studied piano with Wieck and through him entered the Schumann circle; edited Schumann's periodical *Neue Zeitschrift für Musik* from 1845 until his death in 1868; also was co-editor, with R. Pohl, of the monthly *Anregungen für Kunst.* In 1846 he joined the faculty of the Leipzig Cons.; was also one of the founders, in 1861, of the Allgemeiner Deutscher Musikverein. In his articles he boldly championed the cause of the new German music, as symbolized by the works of Wagner and Liszt. He publ. a successful general music history, *Geschichte der Musik in Italien, Deutschland und Frankreich von den ersten christlichen Zeiten bis auf die Gegenwart* (1852; 7th ed., ed. by Kienzl, 1888; new augmented ed., ed. by R. Hövker, 1902, and reissued in 1906); also publ. a treatise commenting on the "music of the future," *Die Musik der Gegenwart und die Gesamtkunst der Zukunft* (1854), and other similar publications dealing with new developments in German music.

Brenta, Gaston, Belgian composer; b. Brussels, June 10, 1902; d. there, May 30, 1969. He studied music theory with Paul Gilson; in 1925, he and 7 other pupils of Gilson formed the Belgian "Groupe des Synthétistes," advocating a more modern approach to composition. From 1931 he was associated with the Belgian Radio, and from 1953 to 1967 he was music director of the French Services there. His music follows the traditions of cosmopolitan romanticism, with exotic undertones.

Bresgen, Cesar, German composer; b. Florence (of German parents), Oct. 16, 1913. He studied composition with Haas in Munich; in 1939 he went to Salzburg, where he taught at the Mozarteum. After the war he devoted himself mainly to teaching. In his compositions he cultivates the spirit of pragmatic communication; his musical fairy tales and school operas have become widely known; among them the most successful are *Der Igel als Brautigam* (1950); *Brüderlein Hund* (1953); *Der Mann im Mond* (1958); short operas: *Die Freier* (1936); *Dornröschen* (1939); *Das Urteil des Paris* (1943); *Paracelsus* (1943); scenic cantatas: *Der ewige Arzt* (1955); *Salzburger Passion* (1966); Chamber Concerto for 8 Solo Instruments (1934); Concerto for 2 Pianos (1936); Chamber Concerto for Guitar and Small Orch. (1962); Wind Quintet (1964); numerous choral works for school performance. Bresgen has published articles and valuable collections of Austrian folk songs.

Bretan, Nicolae, remarkable Rumanian composer; b. Năsăud, April 6, 1887; d. Cluj, Dec. 1, 1968. He studied at the Cons. of Cluj, composition and singing with Farkas and violin with Gyémánt (1906–8); then at the Vienna Academy of Music (1908–9) and at the Magyar Királyi Zeneakademia in Budapest (1909–12) with Siklos (theory) and Szerémi (violin). His primary career was that of an opera singer, performing baritone parts at the opera houses in Bratislava, Oradea, and Cluj between 1913 and 1944, also acting as a stage director. At the same time he surprisingly asserted himself as a composer of operas and lieder in an effective veristic manner, marked by a high degree of professional expertise and considerable originality.
WORKS: One-act operas: *Luceafărul (The Evening Star;* in Rumanian; trans. by the composer into Hungarian and German; Cluj, Feb. 2, 1921); *Golem* (in Hungarian; trans. by the composer into Rumanian and German; Cluj, Dec. 23, 1924); *Eroii de la Rovine* (in Rumanian; Cluj, Jan. 24, 1935); *Horia* (in Rumanian; also trans. into German by the composer; Cluj, Jan. 24, 1937); *Arald* (in Rumanian; 1939); *Requiem;* mystery play, *An Extraordinary Seder Evening* (in Hungarian; also trans. into Eng.); *Mein Liederland,* about 230 songs to Rumanian, Hungarian, and German words.

Bretón y Hernández, Tomás, Spanish opera composer; b. Salamanca, Dec. 29, 1850; d. Madrid, Dec. 2, 1923. As a youth he played in restaurants and theaters; graduated from the Madrid Cons. (1872); conducted at the Madrid Opera; in 1901 joined the faculty of the Madrid Cons. A fertile composer, he contributed greatly to the revival of the zarzuela. He was at his best in the one-act comic type (*género chico).* Among his operas and zarzuelas (all produced in Madrid) are: *Los amantes de Teruel* (1889); *Juan Garín* (1892); *La Dolores* (1895); *El Domingo de Ramos* (1896); *La Verbena de la Paloma* (1894); *Raquel* (to his own libretto; Jan. 20, 1900); *El caballo del señorito* (1901); *Farinelli* (1903); *Tabaré* (1913). He also wrote an oratorio, *Apocalipsia* (Madrid, 1882), and works for Orch.: *Escenas Andaluzas; Funeral March for Alfonso XII;* Violin Concerto; etc.

Breval, Jean-Baptiste Sébastien, outstanding French cellist and composer; b. Paris, Nov. 6, 1753; d. Colligis, Aisne, March 18, 1823. He studied cello with Jean-Baptiste Cupis; made his debut in 1778 at a Concert Spirituel performing one of his own sonatas; subsequently was a member of its orch. (1781–91); then played in the orch. of the Théâtre Feydeau (1791–1800). He composed a great quantity of instrumental music, including symphs., cello concertos, string quartets, trios, duos, and sonatas. He also wrote an opéra comique, *Ines et Leonore, ou La Sœur jalouse,* performed in Versailles on Nov. 14, 1788.

Bréville, Pierre-Onfroy de, French composer; b. Bar-le-Duc, Feb. 21, 1861; d. Paris, Sept. 24, 1949. He studied at the Paris Cons. with Théodore Dubois (1880–82) and later with César Franck. He was a prof. of counterpoint at the Schola Cantorum from 1898 to 1902; was active also as a music critic. He completed (with Vincent d'Indy and others) Franck's unfinished opera *Ghiselle;* in his own music he followed the traditions of French Romanticism. His opera, *Eros Vainqueur,* was produced in Brussels on March 7, 1910; he also wrote an overture to Maeterlinck's play *La Princesse Maleine,* and to his *Les Sept Princesses;* also composed the orch. suites *Nuit de décembre* and *Stamboul,* as well as numerous choral pieces.

Brian, Havergal, English composer of extraordinary fecundity and longevity; b. Dresden, Staffordshire, Jan. 29, 1876; d. Shoreham-by-the-Sea, Sussex, Nov. 28, 1972. He studied violin, cello, and organ with local teachers; left school at 12 to earn his living and help his father, who was a potter's turner. At the same time he taught himself elementary music theory and also learned French and German without an instructor. From 1904 to 1949 he engaged in musical journalism. He attained a reputation in England as a harmless eccentric possessed by inordinate ambitions to become a composer; he attracted supporters among English musicians, who in turn were derided as gullible admirers of a patent amateur. But Brian continued to write music in large symph. forms; some of his works were performed, mostly by non-professional organizations; amazingly enough, he increased his productivity with age; he wrote 22 symphs. after reaching the age of 80, and 7 more after the age of 90. The total number of symphs. at the time of his death was 32. Finally, English musicians, critics, conductors, and concert organizations became aware of the Brian phenomenon, and performances, mostly posthumous, followed. A Havergal Brian Society was formed in London, and there were a few timorous attempts to further the Brian cause outside of England. The slow acceptance of Brian's music was not due to his overindulgence in dissonance. Quite the contrary is true; Brian was not an innovator; he followed the Germanic traditions of Richard Strauss and Mahler in the spirit of unbridled grandiosity, architectural formidability, and rhapsodically quaquaversal thematicism. Brian's modernism tended to be programmatic, as in the ominous whole-tone progressions in his opera *The Tigers,* illustrating the aerial attacks on London by zeppelins during World War I. Brian's readiness to lend his MSS to anyone showing interest in his music resulted in the loss of several of his works; a few of them were retrieved after years of search.

WORKS: OPERAS: *The Tigers,* to his own libretto (1916–19; orchestrated 1928–29; the score was regarded as lost, but was recovered in 1977, and a perf. was given by the BBC Radio, London, on May 3, 1983); *Deirdre of the Sorrows,* after Synge (1947; incomplete); *Turandot,* to a German libretto after Schiller (1950–51); *The Cenci,* after Shelley (1952); *Faust,* after Goethe (1955–56); *Agamemnon,* after Aeschylus, to an English libretto (1957).

32 SYMPHS: No. 1, *The Gothic,* for Vocal Soloists, Chorus, 4 Mixed Choirs, Children's Choir, 4 Brass Bands, and Very Large Orch. (1919–27; first perf., in London, June 24, 1961, by amateur forces; first professional perf., London, Oct. 30, 1966; broadcast to the U.S. by satellite, BBC-NPR, Washington, D.C., May 25, 1980); No. 2 (1930–31; Brighton, May 19, 1973); No. 3 (1931–32; private broadcast perf., BBC studios, London, Oct. 18, 1974); No. 4, *Das Siegeslied,* a setting of Psalm 68 in the Lutheran version, for Soprano, Double Mixed Chorus, and Orch., with a German text (1932–33; Manchester, July 3, 1967); No. 5, *Wine of Summer,* for Baritone and Orch., in one movement (1937; London, Dec. 11, 1969); No. 6, *Sinfonia tragica,* in one movement (1948; London, Sept. 21, 1966); No. 7 (1948; London, March 13, 1968); No. 8, in one movement (1949; London, Feb. 1, 1954); No. 9 (1951; London, March 22, 1958); No. 10, in one movement (1953–54; London, Nov. 3, 1958); No. 11 (1954; London, Nov. 5, 1959); No. 12, in one movement (1957; London, Nov. 5, 1959); No. 13, in one movement (1959; London, May 14, 1978); No. 14, in one movement (1959–60; London, May 10, 1970); No. 15, in one movement (1960; London, May 14, 1978); No. 16, in one movement (1960; private broadcast perf., BBC studios, London, June 18, 1975); No. 17, in one movement (1960–61; London, May 14, 1978); No. 18 (1961; London, Feb. 26, 1962); No. 19 (1961; Glasgow, Dec. 31, 1976); No. 20 (1962; London, Oct. 5, 1976); No. 21 (1963; London, May 10, 1970); No. 22, *Symphonia brevis* (1964–65; London, Aug. 15, 1971); No. 23 (1965; Univ. of Illinois, Urbana, Oct. 4, 1973); No. 24, in one movement (1965; private broadcast perf., BBC studios, London, June 18, 1975); No. 25 (1965–66; Glasgow, Dec. 31, 1976); No. 26 (1966; Stoke-on-Trent, May 13, 1976); No. 27 (1966; London, March 18, 1979); No. 28 (1967; London, Oct. 5, 1973); No. 29 (1967; Stoke-on-Trent, Nov. 17, 1976); No. 30 (1967; London, Sept. 24, 1976); No. 31, in one movement (1968; London, March 18, 1979); No. 32 (1968; London, Jan. 28, 1971).

Briard, Etienne, type-founder at Avignon, active in the early 16th century. In his engraving he employed round note heads instead of the ordinary angular ones, and separate notes instead of ligatures. Peignot holds that another printer, Granjon, used these methods prior to Briard (see his *Dictionnaire de la bibliologie,* supplement, p. 140). In any case, Briard's characters are much better formed and more easily read; Schmidt's *Ottaviano Petrucci* contains a facsimile of them. The *Liber primum missarum Carpentras* (works of Eleazar Genet, called "Il Carpentrasso"), printed with them at Avignon in 1532, is in the library of the Paris Cons.

Brico, Antonia, American pianist and conductor; b. Rotterdam, June 26, 1902. She moved to California in 1906 and studied at the Univ. of Calif. at Berkeley, graduating in 1923; then went to Berlin, where she took lessons in conducting with Karl Muck at the State Academy of Berlin; also studied piano with Sigismund Stojowski. She gave piano recitals in Europe and America, but her prime interest was in conducting. Overcoming many difficulties, she organized a special concert with the Berlin Phil. on Jan. 10, 1930, which aroused considerable curiosity, women conductors being a rare species at the time. Returning to America, she obtained an engagement with the Los Angeles Phil. at the Hollywood Bowl (Aug. 1, 1930); also arranged a few concerts in N.Y., which she had to finance out of her own resources. After some disheartening experiences (a famous male singer on whom the management counted for public success refused to appear at the last moment), she sought opportunity in Europe; gave concerts in Finland and received a commendation from Sibelius for her conducting of his music. About 1949 she became associated with Albert Schweitzer, visiting his hospital in West Africa; he gave her some suggestions about performances of Bach. Eventually she settled in Denver as a piano teacher; to satisfy her unquenchable thirst for orch. conducting, she managed to lead concerts of the community orch. there. In 1974 she produced an autobiographical film called simply *Antonia,* in which she eloquently pleaded for equality of the sexes on the conducting podium; it was nominated for an Academy Award, and on the strength of it, she was able to obtain several bona fide orch. engagements.

Bridge, Frank, distinguished English composer; b. Brighton, Feb. 26, 1879; d. Eastbourne, Jan. 10, 1941. He took violin lessons from his father; entered the Royal College of Music in 1899 and studied composition with Stanford, graduating in 1904; received an Arthur Sullivan Prize and the Gold Medal of the Rajah of Tagore for "the most generally deserving pupil." He specialized in viola playing; was a member of the Joachim String Quartet in 1906 and later of the English String Quartet. He also appeared as a conductor; was in charge of the New Symph. Orch. during Marie Brema's season (1910–11) at the Savoy Theatre in London; then conducted at Covent Garden during the seasons of Raymond Roze and Beecham; he also appeared as conductor at the Promenade Concerts. With a stipend from Elizabeth Sprague Coolidge, he toured the U.S. in 1923, conducting his own works with the orchs. of Rochester, Boston, Detroit, Cleveland, and N.Y.; he revisited the U.S. in 1934 and 1938. As a composer he received a belated recognition toward the end of his life, and posthumously; although he wrote a great deal of instrumental music, his name appeared but rarely in the programs of modern music festivals. Much of his music is generated by passionate emotionalism, soaring in the harmonic realms of euphonious dissonances, while most of his chamber music maintains a classical spirit of Baroque construction. Although he was greatly impressed by the works of the 2nd Vienna School, he never embraced serial methods of composition. Most remarkable of these advanced works was his 4th String Quartet, written in 1937. Benjamin Britten, who was an ardent student and admirer of Frank Bridge, wrote his *Variations on a Theme of Frank Bridge* based on the materials of this Quartet.

WORKS: FOR THE STAGE: *The Christmas Rose,* children's opera (1919–29; London, Dec. 8, 1932; composer conducting). FOR ORCH.: *Symphonic Poem* (1904); *The Hag* (1904); *Isabella,* symph. poem (London, Oct. 3, 1907); *Dance Rhapsody* (1908); incidental music for *The Two Hunchbacks* (London, Nov. 17, 1910; composer conducting); *The Sea,* orch. suite (London, Sept. 24, 1912); *Dance Poem* (1913; London, March 16, 1914; composer conducting); *Summer,* symph. poem (1914; London, March 13, 1916; composer conducting); *Two Poems* (London, Jan. 1, 1917); *Lament* for String Orch., in memory of the victims of the sinking of the *Lusitania* (London, Sept. 15, 1915); Suite for Strings (1908); incidental music for Frank Stayton's play *Threads* (1921; London, Aug. 23, 1921); *Sir Roger de Coverley* for String Orch. (London, Oct. 21, 1922); *Enter Spring* for Orch. (1926; Norwich, Oct. 27, 1927; composer conducting); *There Is a Willow Grows Aslant a Brook* (1927; London, Aug. 20, 1927); *Oration* for Cello and Orch. (1930; London, Jan. 17, 1936); *Phantasm* for Piano and Orch. (1931; London, Jan. 10, 1934); *Rebus* (1940; London, Feb. 23, 1941). CHAMBER MUSIC: Piano Trio No. 1 (London, Nov. 14, 1900); String Quartet No. 1 (London, March 14, 1901); String Quartet No. 2 (London, Dec. 4, 1901); Piano Quartet (London, Feb. 23, 1903); *Phantasie* for String Quartet (1905); *Three Idylls* for String Quartet (London, March 8, 1907); *Phantasie* for Piano Trio (1908); *Novellettes* for String Quartet (1910); *Phantasie* for Piano Quartet (1910); Viola Duos (1912); String Sextet (1912; London, June 18, 1913); Cello Sonata (1913–17; London, July 13, 1917); String Quartet No. 2 (1915); 2 old English songs, *Sally in Our Alley* and *Cherry Ripe,* for String Quartet (1916); *Sir Roger de Coverley* for String Quartet (1922; also arranged for Orch.); String Quartet No. 3 (1926–27; Vienna, Sept. 17, 1927); *Rhapsody* for String Trio (1928); Piano Trio No. 2 (1928–29; London, Nov. 4, 1929); Violin Sonata (1932); String Quartet No. 4 (1937; Pittsfield, Mass., Sept. 13, 1938); Piano Sonata (1922–25); *Four Characteristic Pieces* for Piano (1914). FOR VOICE: *Romeo and Juliet: A Prayer* for Chorus and Orch. (1916); *Blow Out, You Bugles* for Tenor and Orch. (1918); *Three Tagore Songs* (1922–25); about 100 other songs and choruses.

Bridge, Sir (John) Frederick, English organist, conductor, and composer; b. Oldbury, near Birmingham, Dec. 5, 1844; d. London, March 18, 1924. At the age of 14 he was apprenticed to John Hopkins, organist of Rochester Cathedral; later studied under John Goss; was principal organist at Westminster Abbey (1882–1918); took the degree of D.Mus. at Oxford in 1874 with his oratorio *Mount Moriah;* then taught harmony and organ at various music schools, including the Royal College of Music (from 1883); was conductor of the Highbury Phil. Society (1878–86), the Madrigal Society, and the Royal Choral Society (1896–1922); also served as chairman of Trinity College of Music. He was knighted in 1897.

Bridge, Joseph Cox, English organist and composer, brother of **John Frederick Bridge;** b. Rochester, Aug. 16, 1853; d. St. Albans, March 29, 1929. He studied with his brother and with John Hopkins; from 1877–1925 was organist of Chester Cathedral; in 1879 he revived the Chester Triennial Music Festival and became its conductor until 1900; also founded (1883) and conducted for 20 years the Chester Musical Society; from 1908 was a prof. of music at Durham Univ.

WORKS: Oratorio, *Daniel* (1885); cantatas: *Rudel* (1891) and *Resurgam* (1897); *Evening Service* with Orch. (1879); *Requiem Mass* (1900); operetta, *The Belle of the Area;* Symph. (1894); String Quartet; Cello Sonata; anthems, organ music, piano pieces, songs.

Bridgetower, George Auguste Polgreen, mulatto violinist; b. Biala, Poland, Oct. 11, 1778; d. Peckham, Surrey, Feb. 28, 1860. His father was an Abyssinian; his mother, of Polish extraction. He studied with Giornovichi; as a youth he went to England and entered the service of the Prince of Wales. In 1791, at the age of 13, he played in the violin section of the Haydn-Salomon Concerts in London. On Oct. 4, 1807, he was elected to the membership of the Royal Society of Musicians in London. In 1811 he received his Bachelor of Music degree from Cambridge Univ. From about 1829 to 1843 he resided mostly in Paris and Rome, eventually returning to England, where he married and settled in Surrey. His name is historically important because of his association with Beethoven; it was Bridgetower who gave the first performance, from MS, of the *Kreutzer Sonata,* with Beethoven himself at the piano, in Vienna on May 17, 1803. Beethoven spelled his name in a German orthography as Brischdower.

Brinsmead, John, English piano maker; b. Weare Giffard, Devon, Oct. 13, 1814; d. London, Feb. 17, 1908. He founded his firm in London in 1835. In 1863 his sons, **Thomas** and **Edgar,** were admitted to partnership; in 1900 the firm was incorporated and assumed its permanent title, John Brinsmead & Sons, Ltd. In 1868 they patented an improvement in piano construction, "Perfect Check Repeater Action." In 1908, upon the death of John Brinsmead, the controlling interest was purchased by W. Savile, a director of J.B. Cramer & Co. The Brinsmead and Cramer pianos continued to be manufactured until 1967, when the firm was sold to Kemble & Co. **Edgar Brinsmead** (d. Nov. 28, 1907) wrote a *History of the Piano forte* (1868; revised and republ., 1879).

Bristow, George Frederick, patriotic American composer; b. Brooklyn, N.Y., Dec. 19, 1825; d. New York, Dec. 13, 1898. His father, **William Richard Bristow,** a professional English musician, came to America in 1824; he gave his son primary instruction in violin playing; Bristow's other teachers were Henry Christian Timm and Sir George Alexander Macfarren, who taught him orchestration. He also took violin lessons with Ole Bull. He began his career at the age of 13 by playing in the orch. of the Olympic Theater in N.Y.; in 1843 he joined the violin section of the newly formed N.Y. Phil., and re-

mained with the orch. for 36 years; he also conducted the Harmonic Society from 1851 to 1863 and the Mendelssohn Society from 1867 to 1871. He began to compose with a determination to prove the possibility and the necessity of forming a national American school of composition; he orated at various public occasions defending his cause. He even withdrew from the N.Y. Phil. for several months in 1854 in protest against the neglect of American music in favor of foreigners. Actually, the N.Y. Phil. frequently placed his works on its programs. He was the concertmaster of the circus orch. when P.T. Barnum brought Jenny Lind to America as a special attraction. He also played in the orch. at the N.Y. concerts led by the sensational French conductor Louis Antoine Jullien, and elicited from him a statement praising Bristow's String Quartet as a "truly classical work." Unfortunately, Bristow's own ostensibly American music sounded like a feeble imitation of German models. He merits his place in the annals of American music not for the originality of his own works but for his pioneering efforts to write music on American subjects.

WORKS: Opera, *Rip Van Winkle* (N.Y., Sept. 27, 1855); unfinished opera, *Columbus* (overture perf. by the N.Y. Phil., Nov. 17, 1866); oratorios: *Praise to God* (N.Y. Harmonic Society, March 2, 1861) and *Daniel* (N.Y., Dec. 30, 1867); cantatas: *The Great Republic* (Brooklyn Phil. Society, May 10, 1879) and *Niagara* for Soli, Chorus, and Orch. (Manuscript Society, Carnegie Hall, N.Y., April 11, 1898); Symph. in D minor (Jullien's concert, N.Y. Phil., March 1, 1856); Symph. in F-sharp minor (N.Y. Phil., March 26, 1859); *Arcadian Symphony* (N.Y. Phil., Feb. 14, 1874); overture, *Jibbenainosay* (Harlem Phil., N.Y., March 6, 1889); 2 string quartets; organ pieces; piano pieces; songs.

WRITINGS: *New and Improved Method for Reed or Cabinet Organ* (N.Y., 1888).

Britt, Horace, cellist; b. Antwerp, June 18, 1881; d. Austin, Texas, Feb. 3, 1971. He studied at the Paris Cons. with Jules Delsart (cello) and Albert Lavignac (harmony); was later a private pupil of André Caplet; made his American debut with the Chicago Symph. Orch. (1907); then toured extensively in the U.S. with Georges Barrère and Carlos Salzedo; was co-founder of the Barrère-Britt Concertino, a chamber music group organized in 1937.

Britten, Lord Benjamin, one of the most remarkable composers of England; b. Lowestoft, Suffolk, Nov. 22, 1913; d. Aldeburgh, Dec. 4, 1976. He grew up in moderately prosperous circumstances; his father was an orthodontist, his mother an amateur singer. He played the piano and improvised facile tunes; many years later he used these youthful inspirations in a symph. work which he named *Simple Symphony.* In addition to piano, he began taking viola lessons with Audrey Alston. At the age of 13 he was accepted as a pupil in composition by Frank Bridge, whose influence was decisive on Britten's development as a composer. In 1930 he entered the Royal College of Music in London, where he studied piano with Arthur Benjamin and Harold Samuel, and composition with John Ireland. He progressed rapidly; even his earliest works showed a mature mastery of technique and a fine lyrical talent of expression. His *Fantasy Quartet* for Oboe and Strings was performed at the Festival of the International Society for Contemporary Music in Florence on April 5, 1934. He became associated with the theater and the cinema and began composing background music for films. He was in the U.S. at the outbreak of World War II; returned to England in the spring of 1942; was exempted from military service as a conscientious objector. After the war he organized the English Opera Group (1947), and in 1948 founded the Aldeburgh Festival, in collaboration with Eric Crozier and the singer Peter Pears; this festival, devoted mainly to production of short operas by English composers, became an important cultural institution in England; many of Britten's own works were performed for the first time at the Aldeburgh Festivals, often under his own direction; he also had productions at the Glyndebourne Festival. In his operas he observed the economic necessity of reducing the orch. contingent to 12 performers, with the piano part serving as a modern version of the Baroque *ripieno*. This economy of means made it possible for small opera groups and univ. workshops to perform Britten's works; yet he succeeded in creating a rich spectrum of instrumental colors, in an idiom ranging from simple triadic progressions, often in parallel motions, to ultrachromatic dissonant harmonies; upon occasion he applied dodecaphonic procedures, with thematic materials based on 12 different notes; however, he never employed the formal design of the 12-tone method of composition. A sui generis dodecaphonic device is illustrated by the modulatory scheme in Britten's opera *The Turn of the Screw*, in which each successive scene begins in a different key, with the totality of tonics aggregating to a series of 12 different notes. A characteristic feature in Britten's operas is the inclusion of orchestral interludes, which become independent symph. poems in an impressionistic vein related to the dramatic action of the work. The cries of seagulls in Britten's most popular and musically most striking opera, *Peter Grimes*, create a fantastic quasi-surrealistic imagery. Britten was equally successful in treating tragic subjects, as in *Peter Grimes* and *Billy Budd;* comic subjects, exemplified by his *Albert Herring;* and mystical evocation, as in *The Turn of the Screw*. He was also successful in depicting patriotic subjects, as in *Gloriana*, composed for the coronation of Queen Elizabeth II. He possessed a flair for writing music for children, in which he managed to present a degree of sophistication and artistic simplicity without condescension. Britten was an adaptable composer who could perform a given task according to the specific requirements of the occasion. He composed a "realization" of Gay's *Beggar's Opera*. He also wrote modern "parables" for church performance, and produced a contemporary counterpart of the medieval English miracle play *Noye's Fludde*. Among his other works, perhaps the most remarkable is *War Requiem*, a profound tribute to

the dead of many wars. In 1952 Britten was made a Companion of Honour; in 1965 he received the Order of Merit. In June 1976 he was elevated to the peerage of Great Britain by Queen Elizabeth II and became a Lord, the first composer to be so honored. WORKS: OPERAS: *Paul Bunyan*, to a text by W.H. Auden (Columbia Univ., N.Y., May 5, 1941; revised 1974; BBC, Feb. 1, 1976; Aldeburgh, June 14, 1976); *Peter Grimes*, after a poem by Crabbe, Britten's most popular opera (London, June 7, 1945; originally commissioned by the Koussevitzky Foundation; Tanglewood, Aug. 6, 1946, Leonard Bernstein conducting); *The Rape of Lucretia*, to a text by Ronald Duncan, after Shakespeare (Glyndebourne, July 12, 1946; Chicago, June 1, 1947); *Albert Herring*, after Maupassant (Glyndebourne, June 20, 1947, composer conducting; Tanglewood, Aug. 8, 1949); *The Beggar's Opera*, a new realization of the ballad opera by John Gay (Cambridge, May 24, 1948, composer conducting); *The Little Sweep*, or *Let's Make an Opera*, "an entertainment for young people" to a text by Eric Crozier, with optional audience participation (Aldeburgh, June 14, 1949; St. Louis, March 22, 1950); *Billy Budd*, after Melville (first version in 4 acts; Covent Garden, Dec. 1, 1951, composer conducting; NBC, N.Y., Oct. 19, 1952; revised version in 2 acts, 1960; BBC, Nov. 13, 1960; Covent Garden, Jan. 6, 1964, Solti conducting; Chicago, Nov. 6, 1970); *Gloriana*, on the subject of Elizabeth and Essex (first perf. during Coronation Week, June 8, 1953, at Covent Garden, conducted by Pritchard, in the disgruntled presence of Queen Elizabeth II, who was not amused by a stage presentation of her predecessor's amorous dallyings; Cincinnati, May 8, 1956); *The Turn of the Screw*, chamber opera after Henry James (Venice, Sept. 14, 1954, composer conducting; N.Y. College of Music, March 19, 1958); *Noye's Fludde*, one-act children's opera (Aldeburgh, June 18, 1958; N.Y., March 16, 1959); *A Midsummer Night's Dream*, after Shakespeare (Aldeburgh, June 11, 1960, composer conducting; San Francisco, Oct. 10, 1961); *Curlew River*, church parable (Aldeburgh, June 12, 1964, composer conducting; N.Y. Caramoor Festival, June 26, 1966); *The Burning Fiery Furnace*, church parable (Aldeburgh, June 9, 1966, composer conducting; N.Y. Caramoor Festival, June 25, 1967); *The Prodigal Son*, church parable (Aldeburgh, June 10, 1968, composer conducting; Katonah, June 29, 1969); *Owen Wingrave*, after Henry James (May 16, 1971, composer conducting; simultaneous production by the BBC and the NET Opera Theater in N.Y.; stage premiere, Covent Garden, London, May 10, 1973; Santa Fe, Aug. 9, 1973); *Death in Venice*, after Thomas Mann (Aldeburgh, June 16, 1973; N.Y., Metropolitan Opera, Oct. 18, 1974); 2 realizations of operas by Purcell: *Dido and Aeneas* (London, May 1, 1951, composer conducting) and *The Fairy Queen*, a shortened version for concert performance (Aldeburgh, June 25, 1967); a ballet, *The Prince of the Pagodas* (Covent Garden, Jan. 1, 1957, composer conducting).
VOCAL WORKS: *A Hymn to the Virgin*, anthem for Mixed Voices (1930; Lowestoft, Jan. 5, 1931); *A Boy Was Born*, choral variations (1933; BBC, Feb. 23, 1934; revised 1955); *Friday Afternoons* for Chil-

dren's Voices (1935); *Te Deum in C* (1935; London, Jan. 27, 1936); *Our Hunting Fathers,* symph. cycle for High Voice and Orch. (1936; Norwich, Sept. 25, 1936, composer conducting); *On This Island,* 5 songs, to texts by W.H. Auden (1937; BBC, London, Nov. 19, 1937); *4 Cabaret Songs,* to texts by W.H. Auden (1937–39); *Ballad of Heroes* for High Voice, Chorus, and Orch. (London, April 5, 1939); *Les Illuminations* for High Voice and Strings, to poems by Rimbaud (1939; London, Jan. 30, 1940); *7 Sonnets of Michelangelo* for Tenor and Piano (1940; London, Sept. 23, 1942); Hymn to St. Cecilia for 5-part Chorus (London, Nov. 22, 1942); *A Ceremony of Carols* for Treble Voices and Harp (Norwich, Dec. 5, 1942); *Rejoice in the Lamb* for Chorus, Soloists, and Organ (Northampton, Sept. 21, 1943); *Serenade* for Tenor, Horn, and Strings (London, Oct. 15, 1943); *Festival Te Deum* (1944; Swindon, April 24, 1945); *The Holy Sonnets of John Donne* for High Voice and Piano (London, Nov. 22, 1945); *Canticle I, "My Beloved Is Mine"* for High Voice and Piano (Aldeburgh, Nov. 1, 1947); *A Charm of Lullabies* for Mezzo-soprano and Piano (1947; The Hague, Jan. 3, 1948); *Saint Nicolas,* cantata (Aldeburgh, June 5, 1948); *Spring Symphony* for Soloists, Chorus, and Orch. (Amsterdam, July 9, 1949; Tanglewood, Aug. 13, 1949, Koussevitzky conducting); *5 Flower Songs* for Chorus (Dartington, South Devon, April 3, 1950); *Canticle II, Abraham and Isaac* (Nottingham, Jan. 21, 1952); *Choral Dances* from *Gloriana* (1953); *Winter Words* for High Voice and Piano, to poems by Thomas Hardy (Harewood House, Leeds, Oct. 8, 1953); *Canticle III, Still Falls the Rain,* for Tenor, Horn, and Piano, to a text by Edith Sitwell (London, Jan. 28, 1955); *Songs from the Chinese* for High Voice and Guitar (1957; Aldeburgh, June 17, 1958); *Nocturne* for Tenor, Obbligato Instruments, and Strings, to English poems (Leeds, Oct. 16, 1958); *Six Hölderlin Fragments* for Voice and Piano (Schloss Wolfsgarten, Nov. 20, 1958); *Cantata Accademica* for Soloists, Chorus, and Orch. (1959; Basel, July 1, 1960); *Missa Brevis in D* for Boys' Voices and Organ (London, July 22, 1959); *War Requiem,* to the texts of the Latin Requiem Mass and 9 poems of Wilfred Owen, for Soloists, Chorus, and Orch. (Coventry, May 30, 1962, composer conducting; Tanglewood, July 27, 1963); *Cantata Misericordium* for Soloists, Small Chorus, and Orch., for the centenary of the International Red Cross (Geneva, Sept. 1, 1963); *Songs and Proverbs of William Blake* for Baritone and Piano (Aldeburgh, June 24, 1965); *Voices for Today,* anthem for Chorus, for the 20th anniversary of the United Nations (triple premiere, N.Y., Paris, and London, Oct. 24, 1965); *The Poet's Echo* for High Voice and Piano, to texts by Pushkin (Moscow, Dec. 2, 1965); *The Golden Vanity,* vaudeville for Boys' Voices and Piano (1966; Aldeburgh, June 3, 1967, with the Vienna Boys' Choir); *Children's Crusade,* ballad for Children's Voices and Orch., to a text by Brecht (1968; London, May 19, 1969); *Who Are These Children?,* song cycle for Tenor and Piano (1969; Edinburgh, May 4, 1971); *Canticle IV, Journey of the Magi,* to a text by T.S. Eliot, for Tenor, Countertenor, Baritone, and Piano (Aldeburgh, June 26, 1971); *Canticle V, The Death of St. Narcissus* for

Tenor and Harp, to a text by T.S. Eliot (1974; Schloss Elmau, Bavaria, Jan. 15, 1975); *Sacred and Profane,* 8 medieval lyrics for Chorus (Aldeburgh, Sept. 14, 1975); *A Birthday Hansel* for Voice and Harp, to poems by Robert Burns (1975; Cardiff, March 19, 1976); *Phaedra,* cantata for Mezzo-soprano and Chamber Orch. (1975; Aldeburgh, June 16, 1976); *Welcome Ode* for Children's Chorus and Orch. (1976; Ipswich, July 11, 1977); *8 British Folksongs,* arranged for Voice and Orch.; *6 French Folksongs,* arranged for Voice and Orch.; 6 vols. of British folksong arrangements, with Piano Accompaniment (1943–61); realizations of Purcell's *Orpheus Brittanicus,* with Peter Pears; *4 chansons françaises* for High Voice and Orch. (1928; first perf. in concert form at Aldeburgh, June 10, 1980).

FOR ORCH.: Sinfonietta (1932; London, Jan. 31, 1933); *Simple Symphony* (1934; Norwich, March 6, 1934, composer conducting); *Soirées musicales,* suite from Rossini (1936); *Variations on a Theme of Frank Bridge* for String Orch. (Salzburg, Aug. 27, 1937); *Mont Juic,* suite of Catalan dances, with Lennox Berkeley (1937; BBC, Jan. 8, 1938); Piano Concerto (London, Aug. 18, 1938; revised 1945; with an added 3rd movement, perf. in Cheltenham, July 2, 1946); Violin Concerto (1939; N.Y., March 28, 1940); *Young Apollo* for Piano, String Quartet, and Strings (1939; Toronto, Aug. 27, 1939); *Canadian Carnival* (1939; BBC, June 6, 1940); *Sinfonia da Requiem* (1940; N.Y., March 29, 1941); *An American Overture* (1942); *Diversions* for Piano, Left-hand, and Orch. (1940; revised 1954; Philadelphia, Jan. 16, 1942; Paul Wittgenstein, left-hand pianist, soloist); *Matinées musicales,* suite from Rossini (1941); *Scottish Ballad* for 2 Pianos and Orch. (Cincinnati, Nov. 28, 1941); *Prelude and Fugue* for 18 Strings (London, June 23, 1943); *4 Sea Interludes,* from *Peter Grimes* (Cheltenham, June 13, 1945); *The Young Person's Guide to the Orchestra,* variations and fugue on a theme of Purcell (Liverpool, Oct. 15, 1945); Symph. Suite from *Gloriana* (Birmingham, Sept. 23, 1954); *Pas de Six* from *The Prince of the Pagodas* (Birmingham, Sept. 26, 1957); *Cello Symphony* (1963; Moscow, March 12, 1964; composer conducting; Rostropovich, soloist); *The Building of the House,* overture for the opening of the Maltings concert hall (Aldeburgh, June 2, 1967; composer conducting); *Suite on English Folk Tunes* (1974; Aldeburgh, June 13, 1975); *Lachrymae, Reflections on a Song of John Dowland* for Viola and String Orch. (1976; Recklinghausen, May 3, 1977).

CHAMBER MUSIC: *Quartettino* for String Quartet (1930; London, May 23, 1983); *Phantasy in F minor* for String Quintet (1932; July 22, 1932); *Phantasy* for Oboe and String Trio (1932; Florence, April 5, 1934); Suite for Violin and Piano (1935; London, Jan. 27, 1936); *2 Insect Pieces* for Oboe and Piano (1935; Manchester, March 7, 1979); *3 Divertimenti* for String Quartet (1936; London, Feb. 25, 1936); *Temporal Variations* for Oboe and Piano (1936; London, Dec. 15, 1936); 3 string quartets: No. 1 (1941; London, April 28, 1943); No. 2 (1945; London, Nov. 21, 1945); No. 3 (1975; Aldeburgh, Dec. 19, 1976); *Lachrymae, Reflections on a Song of John Dowland* for Viola and Piano (1950; Aldeburgh; June 20, 1950); *6 Meta-*

morphoses, after Ovid, for Oboe Solo (1951; Thorpress, June 14, 1951); *Alpine Suite* for 3 Recorders (1955); Sonata in C for Cello and Piano (1961; Aldeburgh, July 7, 1961); *Nocturnal,* after John Dowland, for Guitar (1963; Aldeburgh, June 12, 1964); *3 Suites* for Solo Cello: No. 1 (1964; Aldeburgh, June 27, 1965); No. 2 (1967; Aldeburgh, June 17, 1968); No. 3 (1971; Aldeburgh, Dec. 21, 1974); String Quartet in D (1931; revised 1974; Aldeburgh, June 7, 1975); *Gemini Variations* for Flute, Violin, and Piano, 4-hands (1965; Aldeburgh, June 19, 1965); Suite for Harp (1969; Aldeburgh, June 24, 1969).

FOR PIANO: 5 waltzes (1923–25; revised 1969); *Holiday Diary,* suite (1934); *Sonatina romantica* (1940; Aldeburgh, June 16, 1983).

Brixi, Franz (František) Xaver, Bohemian composer of church music; b. Prague, Jan. 2, 1732; d. there, Oct. 14, 1771. He was a pupil of Segert in Prague; held several positions as a church organist; became Kapellmeister at St. Vitus's Cathedral in Prague on Jan. 1, 1759. He wrote a great number of sacred works: 105 masses; 263 offertories and anthems; 6 oratorios; 3 organ concertos; etc.

Broadwood & Sons, oldest keyboard instrument manufacturer in existence; established in London in 1728 by the Swiss harpsichord maker **Burkhard Tschudi,** or **Shudi** (b. Schwanden, Switzerland, March 13, 1702; d. London, Aug. 19, 1773). **John Broadwood** (b. Cockburnspath, Scotland, 1732; d. London, 1812), a Scottish cabinetmaker, was Shudi's son-in-law and successor; in 1773 he began to build square pianos modeled after Zumpe's instruments; in 1780 he marketed his own square pianos, which he patented in 1783; in these, he dispensed with the old clavichord arrangement of the wrest-plank and tuning-pins and transformed the harpsichord pedals into damper and piano pedals; another important invention came in 1788, when he divided the long bridge, which until then had been continuous. Broadwood's improvements were soon adopted by other manufacturers. In 1794 the range of the keyboard was extended to 6 octaves. John Broadwood's sons, **James Shudi Broadwood** (b. London, Dec. 20, 1772; d. there, Aug. 8, 1851) and **Thomas Broadwood,** were admitted to the firm in 1795 and 1807, respectively, and the business was then carried on under the name of John Broadwood & Sons. Beethoven received a Broadwood piano in 1817. **Henry John Tschudi Broadwood** (d. Feb. 8, 1911), great-grandson of the founder, patented the so-called "barless" grand piano; he became a director of John Broadwood & Sons, Ltd., established in 1901, with W.H. Leslie as chairman. In 1925 the firm moved to new quarters in New Bond Street. Members of the Broadwood family are still active in its affairs.

Brod, Max, significant Czech-born writer and composer; b. Prague, May 27, 1884; d. Tel Aviv, Dec. 20, 1968. In Prague he associated himself with Kafka and other writers of the New School, and himself publ. several psychological novels. He studied music at the German Univ. in Prague and became a music critic in various Czech and German publications. In 1939 he emigrated to Tel Aviv, where he continued his literary and musical activities. Among his compositions are *Requiem Hebraicum* (1943); *2 Israeli Peasant Dances* for Piano and Small Orch. (Tel Aviv, April 24, 1947); several piano suites and 14 song cycles. He wrote an autobiography, *Streitbares Leben* (Munich, 1960), and a book on music in Israel (Tel Aviv, 1951).

Brodsky, Adolf, famous Russian violinist; b. Taganrog, April 2, 1851; d. Manchester, England, Jan. 22, 1929. A precocious violinist, he made his public debut at the age of 9 in Odessa; he was then sent to Vienna, where he studied with Joseph Hellmesberger, Sr., and played the 2nd violin in his string quartet. In 1866–68 he was appointed a violinist in the Vienna court orch.; in 1873 he returned to Moscow, where he studied with Ferdinand Laub, whom he succeeded in 1875 as prof. at the Moscow Cons. In 1881 he made a European tour, and on Dec. 4, 1881, in Vienna, gave the world premiere of Tchaikovsky's Violin Concerto, which Tchaikovsky in gratitude dedicated to him, after it had been rejected by Leopold Auer as unplayable. He was praised for his virtuosity, but Tchaikovsky's Violin Concerto was damned as badly written for the violin; the review by Eduard Hanslick, which described the music as emitting a stench, became notorious for its grossness, and caused Tchaikovsky great pain. From 1883 to 1891 Brodsky taught violin at the Leipzig Cons., and also organized a string quartet there (with Hugo Becker, Hans Sitt, and Julius Klengel), which enjoyed an international reputation. In 1891 he went to America and served as concertmaster of the N.Y. Symph. Orch. (until 1894); in 1895 he went to England, where he became concertmaster of the Halle Orch. in Manchester (1895–96); also taught violin at the Royal Manchester College of Music; in 1896 he became its principal. In England he changed the spelling of his first name to **Adolph.** His wife publ. *Recollections of a Russian Home* (London, 1904).

Broekman, David, Dutch-born American conductor; b. Leiden, May 13, 1899; d. New York, April 1, 1958. He studied music with Van Anrooy in The Hague; came to the U.S. in 1924 as music editor for M. Witmark & Sons; then went to Hollywood, where he wrote film scores and conducted pageants and various other shows. He contributed the sound track for several motion pictures, including *All Quiet on the Western Front* and *The Phantom of the Opera;* he further wrote 2 symphs. (1934, 1947), and publ. an autobiography, *The Shoestring Symphony,* exhibiting a mandatory jaundiced view of Hollywood's life-style.

Brogi, Renato, Italian composer; b. Sesto Fiorentino, Feb. 25, 1873; d. San Domenico di Fiesole, Florence, Aug. 25, 1924. He studied music in Florence; then at the Milan Cons.; won the Steiner Prize in Vienna with his opera *La prima notte* (Florence, Nov. 25, 1898). He also composed the operas *L'Oblio*

(Florence, Feb. 4, 1890) and *Isabella Orsini* (Florençe, April 24, 1920); the operettas *Bacco in Toscana* and *Follie Veneziane* (both produced in Florence, 1923); Violin Concerto; String Quartet; Piano Trio; songs.

Broman, Sten, eminent Swedish composer, conductor and music critic; b. Uppsala, March 25, 1902; d. Lund, Oct. 29, 1983. He studied at the German Music Academy in Prague, attending a master class in violin playing with Henri Marteau; subsequently studied musicology with Curt Sachs in Berlin. From 1929–51 he played the viola in various Swedish string quartets; from 1946 to 1966 was conductor of the Phil. Society in Malmö. He was an influential music critic; served as chairman of the Swedish section of the International Society for Contemporary Music from 1933 to 1962. A prolific composer, he wrote 8 symphs. and a number of chamber music pieces. In his idiom he followed a median line of Scandinavian Romanticism, but beginning about 1960 he adopted serial techniques and later experimented with electronic sound.

Bronsart von Schellendorf, Hans, German pianist and composer; b. Berlin, Feb. 11, 1830; d. Munich, Nov. 3, 1913. He studied piano with Kullak in Berlin and took lessons with Liszt in Weimar. In 1897 he undertook a concert tour through Germany, France, and Russia; from 1860–67 he was active as a conductor in Leipzig, Dresden, and Berlin. In his compositions he followed the Romantic trend in Schumann's tradition. His most successful was his youthful Piano Trio, his first opus number (1856); some of his piano pieces retained their popularity for a brief while. He also wrote a dramatic tone poem, *Manfred,* for Chorus and Orch., to his own text (Weimar, Dec. 1, 1901); 2 programmatic symphs. and choruses. In 1861 he married the pianist **Ingeborg Starck** (1840–1913).

Bronsart von Schellendorf, Ingeborg (née **Starck**), pianist and composer; b. (of Swedish parents) St. Petersburg, Aug. 24, 1840; d. Munich, June 17, 1913. She studied piano with Liszt at Weimar; in 1861 she married **Hans Bronsart von Schellendorf.** She composed 4 operas: *König Hjarne* (Berlin, 1891); *Jery und Bätely* (Weimar, 1873); *Die Sühne* (Dessau, 1909); *Die Gottin zu Sais;* also piano concertos, piano sonatas, salon pieces, violin pieces, cello pieces, and songs.

Brook, Barry Shelley, eminent American music scholar; b. New York, Nov. 1, 1918. He studied piano privately with Mabel Asnis; then entered the Manhattan School of Music, where he was a student of Louise Culver Strunsky in piano, of Hugh Ross in conducting, and of Roger Sessions in composition. He subsequently studied at the College of the City of N.Y., obtaining his B.S. in social sciences (1939); then took courses in musicology with Paul Henry Lang at Columbia Univ., receiving his M.A. with the dissertation *Clément Janequin* (1942). From 1942 to 1945 he was a member of the U.S. Air Corps. Select-

ing as his major subject French music history, he went to Paris, where he studied at the Sorbonne; in 1959 he received his doctorate there with his dissertation *La Symphonie française dans la seconde moitié du XVIIIᵉ siècle*. In 1945 he was appointed to the faculty of Queens College; also taught at Brooklyn College. His other engagements were those of visiting prof. at N.Y. Univ. (1964–65), Université de Paris (1967–68), Eastman School of Music in Rochester, N.Y. (1973), Univ. of Adelaide in Australia (1974), and Aspen Music School (1975). From 1966 he served as editor in chief of RILM (Répertoire International de Littérature Musicale); from 1970 was also Chairman of RIdM (Répertoire International d'Iconographie Musicale); from 1977 he was acting president of the International Association of Music Libraries. The main subject of his studies was the music of the Renaissance; he was also an authority on French music of the 18th century. In appreciation of his work he received in 1965 the Dent Medal of the Royal Musical Association of Great Britain. An innovation in his bibliographical studies was the consistent use of modern computers.
WRITINGS: *La Symphonie française dans la seconde moitié du XVIIIe siècle* (3 vols., Paris, 1962); *The Breitkopf Thematic Catalogue, 1878–1962* (N.Y., 1966); *Musicology and the Computer* (N.Y., 1970); *Perspectives in Musicology* (with B. Downes and S. van Solkema; N.Y., 1972); *Thematic Catalogues in Music: An Annotated Bibliography* (N.Y., 1972); numerous valuable articles in *Die Musik in Geschichte und Gegenwart, The New Grove,* and scholarly journals dealing with French symph. literature; also eds. of works of Gossec, Rigel, Bréval, and others (Paris, 1962–63).

Broqua, Alfonso, Uruguayan composer; b. Montevideo, Sept. 11, 1876; d. Paris, Nov. 24, 1946. He studied with Vincent d'Indy at the Schola Cantorum in Paris, where he settled. His works are characterized by a fine feeling for exotic material, which he presents in the brilliant manner of French modern music.
WORKS: Opera, *Cruz del Sur* (1918); *Thelen at Nagouëy,* Inca ballet (1934); *Isabelle,* romantic ballet (1936); *Tabaré,* poetic cycle for Soli, Women's Chorus, and Piano or Orch. (1908); *Poema de las Lomas,* triptych for Piano (1912); Piano Quintet; *3 Cantos del Uruguay* for Voice, Flute, and 2 Guitars (1925); *Cantos de Parana* for Voice and Guitar (1929); *Evocaciones Criollas,* 7 pieces for Guitar (1929); *3 Préludes Pampéens* for Piano (1938; also in orch. version).

Broschi, Carlo. See **Farinelli.**

Brossard, Sébastien de, French composer; b. Dompierre, Orne (baptized, Sept. 12), 1655; d. Meaux, Aug. 10, 1730. He studied theology at Caen (1670–76); was then in Paris (1678–87); in 1687 he went to Strasbourg; in 1689 became "maître de chapelle" at the Strasbourg Cathedral; in 1698 received a similar post at the Cathedral of Meaux; in 1709 he became canon there. His fame rests upon the authorship of what was erroneously regarded as the earliest dictionary of musical terms; it was in fact preceded by many publications: by the medieval compilation *De musica antica et moderna* (c.1100), the last section of which is a vocabulary of musical terms (to be found in Lafage's *Essais de dipthérographie musicale,* vol. I, pp. 404–7); by Joannes Tinctoris's *Terminorum musicae diffinitorium* (c.1475); and by Janowka's *Clavis ad thesaurum magnae artis musicae* (1701); Brossard had access to none of these, however. The title of Brossard's own volume is *Dictionnaire de musique, contenant une explication des termes grecs, latins, italiens et français les plus usités dans la musique,* etc. (Paris, 1703; 2nd ed., 1705; there is an Amsterdam reprint, marked 6th ed., but this designation is erroneous; Eng. trans. by Grassineau, 1740). Brossard also wrote *Lettre à M. Demotz sur sa nouvelle méthode d'écrire le plain-chant et la musique* (1729); a considerable variety of church music, including *Canticum Eucharisticum* on the Peace of Ryswick (1697; new ed. by F.X. Mathias); motets; etc. He brought out several vols. of *Airs sérieux et à boire.* His library of MSS was acquired by Louis XV in 1724, and formed the nucleus of the music collection of the Bibliothèque Nationale.

Brott, Alexander, Canadian conductor, violinist, and composer; b. Montreal, March 14, 1915. He studied piano, violin, and composition at the McGill Cons. in Montreal (1928–35); then composition with Bernard Wagenaar, and conducting at Juilliard in N.Y. (1935–39). In 1939 he returned to Montreal, where he was engaged as concertmaster and assistant conductor of the Montreal Symph. Orch. (1945–58). In his music he follows the Romantic tradition, with impressionistic harmonies imparting an aura of modernity.

Brouillon-Lacombe, Louis. See **Lacombe, Louis.**

Brown, David, English musicologist; b. Gravesend, July 8, 1929. He studied at the Univ. of Sheffield (B.A., 1951; B.Mus., 1952); then was music librarian at the Univ. of London Library, Senate House (1959–62). In 1962 he was appointed a lecturer at the Univ. of Southampton. He was awarded a Ph.D. in 1971 by the Univ. of Southampton for his book *Thomas Weelkes: A Biographical and Critical Study* (London, 1969); also wrote *John Wilbye* (London, 1974); then specialized in Russian music; publ. *Mikhail Glinka* (London, 1974) and an extended 3-vol. biography of Tchaikovsky; its merits are marred by an easy acceptance of the untenable theory that Tchaikovsky committed suicide. He contributed articles on Russian music to the *New Grove Dictionary of Music and Musicians* (1980).

Brown, Earle, American composer of the avant-garde; b. Lunenburg, Mass., Dec. 26, 1926. He played trumpet in school bands; then enrolled in Northeastern Univ. in Boston to study engineering; played trumpet in the U.S. Army Air Force Band; also served as a substitute trumpet player with the San Antonio Symph. in Texas. Returning to Boston, he began to study the Schillinger system of composition; also took private lessons in music theory with Rosalyn Brogue Henning. He soon adopted the most advanced types of techniques in composition, experimenting in serial methods as well as in aleatory improvisation. He was fascinated by the parallelism existing in abstract expressionism in painting, mobile sculptures, and free musical forms; to draw these contiguities together he initiated the idea of open forms, using graphic notation with visual signs in musical terms. The titles of his works give clues to their contents: *Folio* (1952–53) was a group of 6 compositions in which the performer was free to vary the duration, pitch, and rhythm; *25 Pages* (1953) was to be played by any number of pianists up to 25, reading the actual pages in any desired order, and playing the notes upside down or right side up. Further development was represented by *Available Forms I* for 18 instruments, consisting of musical "events" happening in accordance with guiding marginal arrows. Brown made much use of magnetic tape in his works, both in open and closed forms. Apart from his creative endeavors, he had numerous lecturing engagements in Europe and the U.S. He was composer-in-residence with the Rotterdam Phil. in the Netherlands in 1947, and guest prof. at the Basel Cons. in Switzerland in 1975; also served as visiting prof. at the Univ. of Southern Calif. at Los Angeles (1978). He professes no *parti pris* in his approach to techniques and idioms of composition, whether dissonantly contrapuntal or serenely triadic; rather, his music represents a mobile assembly of plastic elements, in open-ended or closed forms. As a result, his usages range from astute asceticism and constrained constructivism to soaring sonorism and lush lyricism, *sine ira et studio.*

Brown, Eddy, American violinist; b. Chicago, July 15, 1895; d. Abano Terme, Italy, June 14, 1974. He was given his first lessons in violin playing by his father; then was taken to Europe, and studied in Budapest with Jenö Hubay. He won a violin competition at the age of 11 playing the Mendelssohn Concerto in Budapest. He then proceeded to London, and eventually to Russia, where he became a pupil of Leopold Auer. Returning to the U.S. in 1915, he made several transcontinental tours; was a soloist with the N.Y. Phil., the Chicago Symph. Orch., the Philadelphia Orch., and the Boston Symph. Orch. In 1922 he founded the Eddy Brown String Quartet; in 1932 he became president of the Chamber Music Society of America, which he organized. He became active in educational programs over the radio; was music director of the Mutual Broadcasting System (1930–37) and of station WQXR in N.Y. (1936–55). From 1956–71 he was artistic coordinator of the Cincinnati College-Cons. of Music.

Brown, Howard Mayer, American musicologist; b. Los Angeles, April 13, 1930. He studied composition with Walter Piston and musicology with Otto

Gombosi at Harvard Univ. (B.A., 1951; M.A., 1954; Ph.D., 1959). He held a Guggenheim fellowship in Florence (1963–64); returning to the U.S., he was a member of the faculty at Wellesley College (1958–60); in 1960 was appointed to the staff of the Univ. of Chicago; in 1967 was named prof. there; in 1970 became chairman of the music dept. In 1972–74 he taught at King's College, Univ. of London; then returned to the Univ. of Chicago. He publ. *Music in the French Secular Theater, 1400–1550* (Cambridge, Mass., 1963); *Instrumental Music Printed before 1600: A Bibliography* (Cambridge, Mass., 1965); *Music in the Renaissance* (Englewood Cliffs, N.J., 1976). In 1970 he was named editor of the compendium *Italian Opera, 1640–1770: Major Unpublished Works in a Central Baroque and Early Classical Tradition* (N.Y., 1977—; planned in 60 vols.).

Brown, Iona, English violinist and conductor; b. Salisbury, Siltshire, Jan. 7, 1941. She studied violin as a child; in 1955 joined the National Youth Orch. of Great Britain, remaining its member for 5 years; she also studied with Hugh Maguire in London, Remy Principe in Rome, and Henryk Szeryng in Paris and Nice. In 1963–66 she played in the Philharmonia Orch. of London; in 1964 she joined the Academy of St. Martin-in-the Fields, and served as its director in 1974. In 1980 she was named music director of the Norwegian Chamber Orch. in Oslo.

Brown, Newel Kay, American composer and pedagogue; b. Salt Lake City, Feb. 29, 1932. He studied composition with Leroy Robertson at the Univ. of Utah (B.F.A., 1953; M.F.A., 1954) and with Howard Hanson, Wayne Barlow, and Barnard Rogers at the Eastman School of Music in Rochester, N.Y. (Ph.D., 1967). From 1961 to 1967 he taught at Centenary College for Women at Hackettstown, N.J.; from 1967 to 1970 he was on the faculty of Henderson State College, Arkadelphia, Ark.; in 1970 became prof. of composition at North Texas State Univ. in Denton. As a member of the Mormon Church, he wrote a number of choral works which entered the permanent repertoire; of these, the Mormon children's choral work *I Hope They Call Me on a Mission* (1968) was translated into 17 languages.

Brown, Rosemary, British musical medium; b. London, July 27, 1917. She led a middle-class life as a housewife, and liked to improvise at the piano. Possessed of a certain type of musical mimicry, she began playing passages in the manner of her favorite compositions by Mozart, Beethoven, Schubert, Chopin, or Liszt; they usually consisted of short melodies invariably accompanied by broken triads and seventh-chords. Under the influence of popular literature dealing with communication with ghosts, she became convinced that the music she played was actually dictated to her by departed composers, and willingly recited stories about their human kindness to her (Chopin warned her to turn off the leaking faucet in the bathtub to prevent flooding). On an errand to a grocery store as a small child, she was approached by a tall, gray-haired gentleman who, observing that she carried a music book, introduced himself as Franz Liszt and volunteered to teach her piano without remuneration. She had similar happy encounters with other famous composers, and soon arranged to take dictation of posthumous works from them. She appeared on British television writing down notes under the dictation of Beethoven, but Beethoven's image failed to materialize on the screen, owing no doubt to some last-moment scruples on the part of the producers. She put out a couple of maudlin, maundering, meandering pamphlets dealing with her transcendental experiences, and a professional journalist publ. the story of her contacts with dead composers. Also transmitted were some postmortem essays by Tovey, well-known for his belief in spooks.

Brown, William, flute player and composer who settled in America in the middle of the 18th century. He gave a concert on the flute in Baltimore on Jan. 30, 1784; then went to Philadelphia, where he participated in numerous benefit concerts; in 1785 he established a series of Subscription Concerts in N.Y. and Philadelphia (with Alexander Reinagle and Henri Capron). He composed *3 Rondos for the Pianoforte or Harpsichord* (dedicated to Francis Hopkinson). He was probably a German; may be identical with Wilhelm Braun of Kassel.

Browning, John, brilliant American pianist; b. Denver, May 22, 1933. His father was a professional violinist, his mother an accomplished pianist. Browning studied with her from childhood; played a Mozart piano concerto at the age of 10, and was accepted as a student by Rosina Lhévinne, who was giving a master course in Denver at the time. The family later moved to Los Angeles, where Browning became a private student of Lee Pattison. He soon moved to N.Y., where he entered the class of Rosina Lhévinne at the Juilliard School of Music; in 1954 he received the $2,000 Steinway Centennial Award. In 1955 he won the Leventritt Award. He made his N.Y. debut in 1956; then went to Belgium to compete for the International Piano Competition sponsored by Queen Elisabeth; he won 2nd prize, after Vladimir Ashkenazy, who received first prize. Returning to the U.S., he developed a nonstop career of uninterrupted successes. On Sept. 24, 1962, he gave the world premiere of Samuel Barber's Piano Concerto with the Boston Symph., conducted by Erich Leinsdorf at Lincoln Center for the Performing Arts in N.Y. The work became his honorific cachet; it was modern, it was difficult to play, but he performed it, according to his own calculations, more than 400 times in the 20 years following its premiere. He has also performed virtually the entire standard repertoire of piano concertos from Beethoven to Prokofiev, 43 concertos in all. In 1965 Browning was soloist with the Cleveland Orch. on a European tour under the auspices of the State Dept.; the itinerary included the Soviet Union; so successful was he there that he was reengaged for appearances in the U.S.S.R. in 1967 and in 1970. In 1971 he played in Japan.

Brubeck, Dave (David), American pianist and jazz improviser, brother of **Howard Brubeck;** b. Concord, Calif., Dec. 6, 1920. He played piano in jazz bands as a boy; then took lessons with Milhaud at Mills College, and with Schoenberg in Los Angeles. During World War II he was assigned to a band in Europe; after demobilization, he organized a highly successful band of his own. In his half-improvised compositions he employs a contrapuntal idiom combining elements of jazz with baroque textures. He wrote the oratorio *Truth Has Fallen* for the opening of the new Midland (Mich.) Center for the Arts, May 1, 1971. In the 1970s he drafted into his band his 3 rock-musician sons: **Darius** (named after Darius Milhaud), b. San Francisco, June 14, 1947 (plays acoustic and electric keyboards); **Chris,** b. Los Angeles, March 19, 1953 (trombone, bass, keyboards); and **Danny,** b. Oakland, Calif., May 5, 1955 (percussion).

Brubeck, Howard, American composer, brother of **Dave Brubeck;** b. Concord, Calif., July 11, 1916. After studying with Darius Milhaud and others, he devoted himself to teaching; was chairman of the music dept. at Palomar Junior College in San Marcos, Calif.
    WORKS: *Elizabethan Suite* for Chamber Orch. and Women's Chorus (1944); *California Suite* for Orch. (1945); *Overture to the Devil's Disciple* (1954); *Four Dialogues* for Jazz Combo and Orch. (San Diego, Aug. 1, 1956); *The Gardens of Versailles,* suite for Orch. (1960); Woodwind Quintet (1950); choruses; piano pieces; arrangements for jazz combo and orch. on Dave Brubeck's themes.

Bruch, Max, celebrated German composer; b. Cologne, Jan. 6, 1838; d. Friedenau, near Berlin, Oct. 2, 1920. His mother, a professional singer, was his first teacher. He afterward studied theory with Breidenstein in Bonn; in 1852 he won a scholarship of the Mozart Foundation in Frankfurt for 4 years, and became a pupil of Ferdinand Hiller, Reinecke, and Breuning. At the age of 14, he brought out a symph. at Cologne, and at 20 produced his first stage work, *Scherz, List und Rache,* adapted from Goethe's Singspiel (Cologne, Jan. 14, 1858). Between 1858 and 1861 he taught music in Cologne; also made prolonged visits to Berlin, Leipzig, Dresden, and Munich; in 1863 he was in Mannheim, where he produced his first full-fledged opera, *Die Loreley* (April 14, 1863), to the libretto by Geibel, originally intended for Mendelssohn. About the same time he wrote an effective choral work, *Frithjof,* which was presented with great success in various German towns, and in Vienna. From 1865–67 Bruch was music director of a concert organization in Koblenz; there he wrote his First Violin Concerto (in G minor), which became a great favorite among violinists; then was court Kapellmeister in Sonderhausen. In 1870 he went to Berlin; his last opera, *Hermione,* based on Shakespeare's *The Winter's Tale,* was produced at the Berlin Opera on March 21, 1872. In 1880 he accepted the post of conductor of the Liverpool Phil., and remained in England for 3 years; in 1883 he

visited the U.S. and conducted his choral work *Arminius* in Boston. From 1883–90 he was music director of an orch. society in Breslau; in 1891 he became a prof. of composition at the Hochschule für Musik in Berlin, retiring in 1910. Bruch was married to the singer **Clara Tuczek** (d. 1919). Cambridge Univ. conferred upon him the honorary degree of D.Mus. (1893); the French Academy elected him corresponding member; in 1918 the Univ. of Berlin gave him the honorary degree of Dr.Phil.
    Bruch's music, although imitative in its essence and even in its melodic and harmonic procedures, has a great eclectic charm; he was a master of harmony, counterpoint, and instrumentation; he was equally adept at handling vocal masses. He contributed a great deal to the development of the secular oratorio, using soloists, chorus, and orch. In this genre he wrote *Odysseus, Arminius, Das Lied von der Glocke,* and *Achilleus;* also *Frithjof* for Baritone, Female Chorus, and Orch.; *Normannenzug* for Baritone, Male Chorus, and Orch.; and several other works for various vocal ensembles. Among his instrumental works, the so-called *Scottish Fantasy* for Violin and Orch. (1880) was extremely successful when Sarasate (to whom the work was dedicated) performed it all over Europe; but the most popular of all works by Bruch is his *Kol Nidrei,* a Hebrew melody for cello and orch., composed for the Jewish community of Liverpool in 1880; its success led to the erroneous assumption that Bruch himself was Jewish (he was, in fact, of a clerical Protestant family). His Concerto for 2 Pianos and Orch. was commissioned by the American duo-piano team Ottilie and Rose Sutro; when they performed it for the first time (Philadelphia Orch., Stokowski conducting, 1916), they drastically revised the original. In 1971 the authentic version was discovered in Berlin, and was given its first performance by Nathan Twining and Mer Berkofsky with the London Symph., Antal Dorati conducting, on May 6, 1974.

Bruchollerie, Monique de la, French pianist; b. Paris, April 20, 1915; d. there, Dec. 15, 1972. She studied with Isidor Philipp; graduated from the Paris Cons. at the age of 13; toured widely as a concert pianist; also was active as a teacher. In 1964 she made a bold proposal to modernize the piano as a performing instrument by constructing a crescent-shaped keyboard to facilitate simultaneous playing in high treble and low bass. She further proposed to install electronic controls enabling the pianist to activate a whole chord by striking a single key.

Bruck (or **Brouck**), **Arnold von** (known also as **Arnold de Bruges** and **Arnoldo Flamengo**), Flemish composer; b. Bruges, c.1500; d. Linz, Feb. 6, 1554. He served as a choirboy in the chapel of Charles V; in 1527 he was named court Kapellmeister to Ferdinand I; retired on Dec. 31, 1545. Many of his motets, hymns, and German part-songs are preserved in MS collections of the 16th century; printed editions are found in Denkmäler der Tonkunst in Österreich, 72 (37.ii) and 99; R. Eitner in *Publikationen älterer Musik* (vol. 2); A. Schering in *Geschichte der Musik in Beispielen* (no. 110); J. Wolf in Denkmäler Deutscher Tonkunst (vol. 34); Otto Kade in A.W. Ambros's *Geschichte der Musik* (vol. 5); C.G. Winterfeld in *Der evangelische Kirchengesang;* A.T. Davison and W. Apel, *Historical Anthology of Music* (no. 111b); see also O. Wessely, ed., *A. von Bruck: Sämtliche lateinschule Motetten,* Denkmäler der Tonkunst in Österreich, XCIX (1961).

Bruckner, (Josef) Anton, inspired Austrian composer; b. Ansfelden, Sept. 4, 1824; d. Vienna, Oct. 11, 1896. He studied music with his father, a village schoolmaster and church organist; also took music lessons at Hörsching with his cousin Johann Baptist Weiss. After his father's death in 1837, Bruckner enrolled as a chorister at St. Florian, where he attended classes in organ, piano, violin, and music theory. In 1840–41 he entered the special school for educational training in Linz, where he received instruction from J.N.A. Dürrnberger; he also studied music theory with Leopold Edler von Zenetti in Enns. While in his early youth, Bruckner held teaching positions in elementary public schools in Windhaag (1841–43) and Kronstorf (1843–45); later he occupied a responsible position as a schoolteacher at St. Florian (1845–55); also served as provisional organist there (1848–51). Despite his professional advance, he felt a lack of basic techniques in musical composition, and at the age of 31 went to Vienna to study harmony and counterpoint with the renowned pedagogue Simon Sechter. He continued his studies with him off and on until 1861. In 1856 he became cathedral organist in Linz, having successfully competed for this position against several applicants. Determined to acquire still more technical knowledge, he sought further instruction and began taking lessons in orchestration with Otto Kitzler, first cellist of the Linz municipal theater (1861–63). In the meantime he undertook an assiduous study of the Italian polyphonic school, and of masters of German polyphony, especially Bach. These tasks preoccupied him so completely that he did not engage in free composition until he was nearly 40 years old. Then he fell under the powerful influence of Wagner's music, an infatuation that diverted him from his study of classical polyphony. In 1865 he attended the premiere of *Tristan und Isolde* in Munich, and met Wagner. He also made the acquaintance of Liszt in Pest, and of Berlioz during his visit in Vienna. His adulation of Wagner was extreme; the dedication of his Third Symph. to Wagner reads: "To the eminent Excellency Richard Wagner the Unattainable, World-Famous, and Exalted Master of Poetry and Music, in Deepest Reverence Dedicated by Anton Bruckner." Strangely enough, in his own music Bruckner never embraced the tenets and practices of Wagner, but followed the sanctified tradition of Germanic polyphony. Whereas Wagner strove toward the ideal union of drama, text, and music in a new type of operatic production, Bruckner kept away from the musical theater, confining himself to symphonic and choral music. Even in his harmonic techniques, Bruckner

seldom followed Wagner's chromatic style of writing, and he never tried to emulate the passionate rise and fall of Wagnerian "endless" melodies depicting the characters of his operatic creations. To Bruckner, music was an apotheosis of symmetry; his symphs. were cathedrals of Gothic grandeur; he never hesitated to repeat a musical phrase several times in succession so as to establish the thematic foundation of a work. The personal differences between Wagner and Bruckner could not be more striking: Wagner was a man of the world who devoted his whole life to the promotion of his artistic and human affairs, while Bruckner was unsure of his abilities and desperately sought recognition. Devoid of social graces, being a person of humble peasant origin, Bruckner was unable to secure the position of respect and honor that he craved. A signal testimony to this lack of self-confidence was Bruckner's willingness to revise his works repeatedly, not always to their betterment, taking advice from conductors and ostensible well-wishers. He suffered from periodic attacks of depression; his entire life seems to have been a study of unhappiness, most particularly in his numerous attempts to find a woman who would become his life companion. In his desperation, he made half-hearted proposals in marriage to women of the people; the older he grew, the younger were the objects of his misguided affections; a notorious episode was his proposal in marriage to a chambermaid at a hotel in Berlin. Bruckner died a virgin.

A commanding trait of Bruckner's personality was his devout religiosity. To him the faith and the sacraments of the Roman Catholic Church were not mere rituals but profound psychological experiences. Following the practice of Haydn, he signed most of his works with the words *Omnia ad majorem Dei gloriam;* indeed, he must have felt that every piece of music he composed redounded to the greater glory of God. His original dedication of his *Te Deum* was actually inscribed *"an dem lieben Gott."* From reports of his friends and contemporaries, it appears that he regarded each happy event of his life as a gift of God, and each disaster as an act of divine wrath. His yearning for secular honors was none the less acute for that. He was tremendously gratified upon receiving an honorary doctorate from the Univ. of Vienna in 1891; he was the first musician to be so honored there. He unsuccessfully solicited similar degrees from the univs. of Cambridge, Philadelphia, and even Cincinnati. He eagerly sought approval in the public press. When Emperor Franz Josef presented him with a snuffbox as a sign of imperial favor, it is said that Bruckner pathetically begged the emperor to order Hanslick to stop attacking him. Indeed, Hanslick was the nemesis of the so-called "New German School" of composition exemplified by Wagner and Liszt, and to a lesser extent, also by Bruckner. Wagner could respond to Hanslick's hostility by caricaturing him in the role of Beckmesser (whom he had originally intended to name Hanslich), and Liszt, immensely successful as a virtuoso pianist, was largely immune to critical attacks. But Bruckner was highly vulnerable. It was not until the end of

Bruckner

his unhappy life that, thanks to a group of devoted friends among conductors, Bruckner finally achieved a full recognition of his greatness.

Bruckner himself was an inadequate conductor, but he was a master organist. In 1869 he appeared in organ recitals in France, and in 1871 he visited England, giving performances in the Royal Albert Hall and the Crystal Palace in London. He was also esteemed as a pedagogue. In 1868 he succeeded his own teacher Sechter as professor of harmony, counterpoint, and organ at the Vienna Cons.; also in 1868 he was named provisional court organist, an appointment formally confirmed in 1878. Concurrently he taught piano, organ, and music theory at St. Anna College in Vienna (1870–74). In 1875 he was appointed lecturer in harmony and counterpoint at the Univ. of Vienna. In failing health, Bruckner retired from the Vienna Cons. in 1891 and a year later relinquished his post as court organist; in 1894 he resigned his lecturer's position at the Univ. of Vienna. The remaining years of his life he devoted to the composition of his Ninth Symph., which, however, remained unfinished at his death.

Bruckner's symphs. constitute a monumental achievement; they are characterized by a striking display of originality and a profound spiritual quality. His sacred works are similarly expressive of his latent genius. Bruckner is usually paired with Mahler, who was a generation younger, but whose music embodied qualities of grandeur akin to those that permeated the symphonic and choral works of Bruckner. Accordingly, Bruckner and Mahler societies sprouted in several countries, with the express purpose of elucidating, analyzing, and promoting their music.

The textual problems concerning Bruckner's works are numerous and complex. He made many revisions of his scores, and dejectedly acquiesced in alterations suggested by conductors who expressed interest in his music. As a result, conflicting versions of his symphs. appeared in circulation. With the founding of the International Bruckner Society, a movement was begun to publ. the original versions of his manuscripts, the majority of which he bequeathed to the Hofbibliothek in Vienna. A complete edition of Bruckner's works, under the supervision of Robert Haas and Alfred Orel, began to appear in 1930; in 1945 Leopold Nowak was named its editor in chief. An excellent explication of the textual problems concerning Bruckner's works is found in Deryck Cook's article "The Bruckner Problem Simplified," in the *Musical Times* (Jan.–Feb., April–May, and Aug. 1969).

WORKS: Bruckner rejected his first symph. as a student work; it is in F minor and is known as his *Schul-Symphonie* or *Studien-Symphonie (Study Symphony)* (1863; movements 1, 2, and 4 first perf. under Moissl, Klosterneuburg, March 18, 1924; movement 3 first perf. under Moissl, Klosterneuburg, Oct. 12, 1924). A second early symph., in D minor, apparently held some interest for him, as he marked it No. 0, "Die Nullte" (1863–64; revised, 1869; movements 3 and 4 first perf. under Moissl, Klosterneuburg, May 17, 1924; first complete perf. under Moissl, Klosterneuburg, Oct. 12, 1924). The follow-

ing list of his nine symphs. is based upon the research of Leopold Nowak: No. 1 in C minor (Version I, "Linz," 1865–66; first perf. with minor additions and alterations, under Bruckner, Linz, May 9, 1868; Version II, "Vienna," 1890–91, a thorough revision; first perf. under Richter, Vienna, Dec. 13, 1891); No. 2 in C minor (Version I, 1871–72; first perf., with minor revisions, under Bruckner, Vienna, Oct. 26, 1873; Version II, 1876–77, with cuts and alterations); No. 3 in D minor, the "Wagner" Symph. (Version I, 1873; first perf. in the Nowak ed. under Schönzeler, Adelaide, March 19, 1978; Version II, 1876–77, a thorough revision; first perf. under Bruckner, Vienna, Dec. 16, 1877; Version III, 1888–89, a thorough revision; first perf. under Richter, Vienna, Dec. 21, 1890; a second Adagio [1876], unrelated to the other versions, was first perf. under C. Abbado, Vienna, May 24, 1980); No. 4 in E-flat major, the "Romantic" Symph. (Version I, 1874; first perf. in the Nowak ed. under K. Wöss, Linz, Sept. 20, 1975; Version II, 1877–78, with Finale of 1880, a thorough revision with a new Scherzo; first perf. under Richter, Vienna, Feb. 20, 1881; Version III, 1887–88, a major revision by Löwe, including a new Finale; first perf. under Richter, Vienna, Jan. 22, 1888); No. 5 in B-flat major (1875–76; minor revisions, 1876–78; first perf. in a recomposed version by F. Schalk, under his direction, Graz, April 8, 1894; first perf. in the Haas ed. under Hausegger, Munich, Oct. 20, 1935); No. 6 in A major (1879–81; Adagio and Scherzo under Jahn, Vienna, Feb. 11, 1883; with major cuts, under Mahler, Vienna, Feb. 26, 1899; first complete perf. under Pohlig, Stuttgart, March 14, 1901); No. 7 in E major (1881–83; first perf. under Nikisch, Leipzig, Dec. 30, 1884); No. 8 in C minor (Version I, 1884–87; first perf. in the Nowak ed. under Schönzeler, BBC, London, Sept. 2, 1973; Version II, 1889–90, a thorough revision; first perf. under Richter, Vienna, Dec. 18, 1892; first perf. in the Haas ed. [a composite version of I and II] under Furtwängler, Hamburg, July 5, 1939); No. 9 in D minor (movements 1–3, 1887–94; Finale [unfinished], 1894–96; first perf. in a recomposed version by Löwe, under his direction, Vienna, Feb. 11, 1903, with Bruckner's *Te Deum* substituted for the Finale; first perf. in the Haas ed. under Hausegger, Munich, April 2, 1932). Other major works are 3 masses: D minor (1864; Linz, Nov. 20, 1864; revised, 1876 and 1881); E minor (1866; Linz, Sept. 29, 1869; revised, 1869, 1876, and 1882); F minor (1867–68; Vienna, June 16, 1872; many revisions); String Quintet in F major (1878–79); *Te Deum* (1881; revised, 1883–84; first perf. with orch. under Richter, Vienna, Jan. 10, 1886); Psalm 150 (1892; Vienna, Nov. 13, 1892). Selected minor works are a Mass in C major (1842?); *Requiem* in D minor (1848–49; St. Florian, March 13, 1849); *Missa Solemnis* in B-flat minor (1854; St. Florian, Sept. 14, 1854); *Apollomarsch,* for Military Band (1862; authenticity not established); March in D minor, for Orch. (1862); 3 orch. pieces in E-flat major, E minor, and F major (1862); String Quartet in C minor (1862); Overture in G minor (1862–63; Klosterneuburg, Sept. 8, 1921); *Germanenzug,* for Male Choir and Brass Instruments (1863); March in E-flat major, for Military Band (1865); *Abendzauber,* for Male Choir and 4 Horns (1878);

Intermezzo, for String Quintet (1879); *Helgoland,* for Male Choir and Orch. (1893); other choral settings; motets; etc.

Brüggen, Frans, distinguished Dutch recorder player, flutist, and conductor; b. Amsterdam, Oct. 30, 1934. He studied the recorder with Kees Otten and flute at the Amsterdam Muzieklyceum; in addition, took courses in musicology at the Univ. of Amsterdam; then launched a major career as a virtuoso performer of music for the recorder; as a flute soloist, he was equally at home in performances of the Baroque masters and contemporary avant-garde composers; also gave informative lectures and illustrative performances of recorder music in Europe, and taught at the Royal Cons. in The Hague.

Brüll, Ignaz, Austrian pianist and composer; b. Prossnitz, Moravia, Nov. 7, 1846; d. Vienna, Sept. 17, 1907. He studied in Vienna with Epstein (piano) and Dessoff (composition); subsequently made extended recital tours; eventually settled in Vienna, where he was a prof. of piano at the Horak Inst. (1872–78). He was an intimate friend of Brahms, who greatly valued his advice.
WORKS: Operas: *Die Bettler von Samarkand* (1864); *Das goldene Kreuz* (Berlin, Dec. 22, 1875; his most successful opera); *Der Landfriede* (Vienna, Oct. 4, 1877); *Bianca* (Dresden, Nov. 25, 1879); *Königin Marietta* (Munich, 1883); *Gloria* (Hamburg, 1886); *Das steinerne Herz* (Vienna, 1888); *Gringoire* (Munich, March 19, 1892); *Schach dem Könige* (Munich, 1893); *Der Husar* (Vienna, 1898; very successful); *Rübezahl* (unfinished); ballet, *Ein Märchen aus der Champagne* (1896); overture, *Im Walde;* 3 serenades and a Dance Suite for Orch.; 2 piano concertos; Violin Concerto; piano pieces; songs.

Brumby, Colin, Australian composer; b. Melbourne, June 18, 1933. He graduated from the Melbourne Univ. Cons. of Music in 1957; studied in London with Alexander Goehr and John Carewe (1963). He lectured at the Brisbane Teacher's Training College (1959–64) and in 1964 became a senior lecturer at the Univ. of Queensland. His music is medium modern, with liberal application of avant-garde techniques.

Brumel, Antoine, celebrated Flemish (or French) musician, contemporary of Josquin des Prez; b. 1460; d. after 1520. He served as a chorister at the Cathedral of Notre Dame in Chartres in 1483; in 1486 became a Master of the Innocents at St. Peter's in Geneva, where he remained until 1492. In 1497 he was Canon at Laon Cathedral. He was a singer at the ducal court in Chambéry in 1501; took up his duties at the court of Alfonso I, Duke of Ferrara, in Aug. 1506; remained in his service there until the chapel was disbanded in 1510. A number of his sacred works were publ. during his lifetime; other pieces are scattered in various anthologies. A complete edition of his works was begun by A. Carapetyan in 1951 in Rome under the aegis of the American Inst. of Musicology. He composed masses, motets, Magnificats, and other sacred works. B. Hudson edited the collection *A. Brumel: Opera omnia,* Corpus Mensurabilis Musicae, V/1–6 (1969–72).

Bruna, Pablo, Spanish organist and composer; b. Daroca, near Saragossa (baptized, June 22), 1611; d. there, June 26 or 27, 1679. He was blinded by smallpox as a child and was later known as "El ciego de Daroca." He overcame his deficiency by successfully learning to play the organ, and was employed as a church organist in his native town. He also improvised a number of organ pieces which were notated by an amanuensis.

Bruneau, (Louis-Charles-Bonaventure-) Alfred, French opera composer; b. Paris, March 3, 1857; d. there, June 15, 1934. In 1873 he entered the Paris Cons., where he was a pupil of Franchomme; won the first cello prize in 1876; later studied harmony with Savard and composition with Massenet; in 1881 he won the Prix de Rome with his cantata *Sainte-Geneviève.* He was a music critic for *Gil Blas* (1892–95); then for *Le Figaro* and *Le Matin;* from 1903–4 was first conductor at the Opéra-Comique; in 1900 he was made a member of the "Conseil Supérieur" at the Paris Cons. and in 1909 succeeded Reyer as inspector of music instruction. He made extensive tours of Russia, England, Spain, and the Netherlands, conducting his own works. He was made a Knight of the Légion d'Honneur in 1895; received the title "Commandeur de St.-Charles" in 1907; became a member of the Académie des Beaux Arts in 1925. His role in the evolution of French opera is of great importance; he introduced realistic drama on the French musical stage, working along lines parallel with Zola in literature. He used Zola's subjects for his most spectacular opera, *L'Ouragan,* and also for the operas *Messidor* and *L'Enfant-Roi.* In accordance with this naturalistic trend, Bruneau made free use of harsh dissonance when it was justified by the dramatic action of the plot.
WORKS: Operas (most of them produced in Paris at the Opéra-Comique): *Kérim* (June 9, 1887); *Le Rêve* (June 18, 1891); *L'Attaque du Moulin* (Nov. 23, 1893); *Messidor* (Feb. 19, 1897); *L'Ouragan* (April 29, 1901); *Lazare* (1902); *L'Enfant-Roi* (March 3, 1905); *Naïs Micoulin* (Monte Carlo, Feb. 2, 1907); *La Faute de l'Abbé Mouret* (March 1, 1907); *Les Quatre Journées* (Dec. 25, 1916); *Le Roi Candaule* (Dec. 1, 1920); *Angelo, tyran de Padoue* (Jan. 16, 1928); *Virginie* (Jan. 7, 1931); ballets: *L'Amoureuse Leçon* (Feb. 6, 1913) and *Les Bacchantes* (after Euripides; Oct. 30, 1912); overtures: *Ode héroïque* and *Léda;* symph. poem, *La Belle au Bois dormant;* symph. poem, with Chorus, *Penthésilée;* a Requiem; *Lieds de France* and *Chansons à danser* (both to poems by C. Mendès); *Les Chants de la vie* (to poems by H. Bataille, F. Gregh, etc.); *Le Navire* for Voice and Orch.; pieces for various combinations of String and Wind Instruments. He publ. *Musiques d'hier et de demain* (1900); *La Musique française* (1901); *Musiques de Russie et musiciens de France* (1903; German trans. by M. Graf in *Die Musik,* Berlin, 1904);

La Vie et les œuvres de Gabriel Fauré (1925); *Massenet* (1934).

Brunelli, Antonio, Italian theorist and composer; b. Pisa, c.1575; d. there, c.1630. He was a pupil of G.M. Nanini; served as an organist at San Miniato in Tuscany from 1604 to 1607; then went to Prato, where he served as maestro di cappella at the Cathedral. On April 12, 1612, he was appointed maestro di cappella of the Grand Duke of Tuscany. Between 1605 and 1621 he publ. motets, canzonette, Psalms, madrigals, Requiems, and others sacred works; some of them were included in Donfried's *Promptuarium musicum* (1623). He publ. the theoretical treatises *Regole utilissime per li scolari che desiderano imparare a cantare* (Florence, 1606; one of the first publ. methods for voice); *Esercizi ad 1 e 2 voci* (Florence, 1607); and *Regole et dichiarazioni de alcuni contrappunti doppii* (Florence, 1610).

Brunetti, Domenico, Italian composer; b. Bologna, c.1580; d. there, April or May 1646. He was organist at the Church of S. Domenico (c.1609); then was maestro di cappella at the Bologna Cathedral (1618); with F. Bertacchi he founded the Accademia dei Filaschici (1633), which later was absorbed into the Accademia Filarmonica. His publications include *Euterpe* (Venice, 1606); *Varii Concentus unica, voce, duabus, tribus, quatuor vel pluribus cum gravi et acuto ad Organum* (Venice, 1609); *Canticum Deiparae Virginis Octies iuxta singulos Rhytmorum Sacrorum* (Venice, 1621). Several of his compositions (motets, madrigals, etc.) were publ. in contemporary collections (1611–26) of A. Schadeo, G. Donfried, A.N. di Treviso, F. Sammaruco, Z. Zanetti, and G.P. Biandrà.

Brunetti, Gaetano, Italian violinist and composer; b. probably in Fano, 1744; d. Culminal de Oreja, near Madrid, Dec. 16, 1798. He studied with Nardini, and in about 1762 went to Madrid; in 1767 was appointed violinist in the Royal Chapel in Madrid; in 1788 became director of the Royal Chamber Orch., remaining in this post until his death. He composed many works for the Spanish Court, and also for the Duke of Alba; Boccherini, who was in Madrid during the same years as Brunetti, was also favored by the Court and the aristocracy, but there was apparently no rivalry between them, as commissions were plentiful. Brunetti's productivity was astounding; he wrote 32 symphs., 6 overtures, numerous dances for orch.; 12 sextets, 72 quintets, 50 quartets, 30 trios; 67 duos for violin and basso continuo; 23 divertimenti for violin, viola, and cello; also an opera, *Jason,* produced in Madrid on Oct. 4, 1768. The Library of Congress in Washington has a large collection of Brunetti's MSS.

Bruni, Antonio Bartolomeo, Italian violinist and composer; b. Cuneo, Jan. 28, 1757; d. there, Aug. 5, 1821. He studied with Pugnani in Turin. In 1780 he went to Paris, and on May 15, 1780, appeared as a violinist at the Concert Spirituel; then served as a member of the orch. of the Comédie-Italienne (1781–89). He was subsequently director of the orch. of the Opéra-Comique (1799–1801); then at the Opéra-Italienne (1801–6). He wrote 22 operas, of which the most successful were *Célestine* (Paris, Oct. 15, 1787), *Claudine* (Paris, March 6, 1794), and *La Rencontre en voyage* (Paris, April 28, 1798). He also wrote music for the violin; publ. a violin method and a viola method (the latter reprinted in 1928).

Brunold, Paul, French pianist, organist, and writer on music; b. Paris, Oct. 14, 1875; d. there, Sept. 14, 1948. He was a pupil of Marmontel (piano) and Lavignac (theory) at the Paris Cons.; later studied with Paderewski. In 1915 he became organist at St. Gervais, in Paris. With H. Expert, he edited the *Anthologie des maîtres français du clavecin des XVIIe et XVIIIe siècles;* with A. Tessier, he bought out a complete edition of Chambonnière's works; he also edited 2 vols. of works by Dieupart for the Lyre-Bird Press of Paris (*6 Suites pour clavecin* and *Airs et Chansons*). He publ. the book *Histoire du grand orgue de l'Eglise St. Gervais à Paris* (1934).

Brusilow, Anshel (real name, **Brusilovsky**), American conductor; b. Philadelphia, Aug. 14, 1928, of Russian-Jewish parents. He studied violin at the Curtis Inst. of Music. Upon graduation, he served as concertmaster of the New Orleans Symph. (1954–55), associate concertmaster of the Cleveland Orch. (1955–59), and concertmaster of the Philadelphia Orch. (1959–66). He was also the founder of the Philadelphia Chamber Orch. (1961–65) and the Chamber Symph. of Philadelphia (1966–68). From 1970 to 1973 he was executive director and conductor of the Dallas Symph. In 1973 he joined the faculty of North Texas State Univ. in Denton.

Bryant, Allan, American composer; b. Detroit, July 12, 1931. He attended Princeton Univ.; then went to Germany, where he worked at the electronic studio in Cologne. Returning to the U.S., he wrote music with multimedia resources designed for theatrical representation. His works include *Quadruple Play* for Amplified Rubber Bands utilizing Contact Microphones and coordinated with an Audio-controlled Lighting System (1966); *Impulses* for a Variety of Percussion, Concussion, and Discussion Sounds (1967); *Bang-Bang* for Loud Instruments, including an Amplified Circular Violin (1967); *X-es Sex,* an intersexual happening, with Boots and Balloons (1967); also political works, e.g. *Liberate Isang Yun* (1967) for a Multimillion-decibel Electronic Sound calculated to reach the ears of the South Korean abductors of the dissident Korean composer Isang Yun from West Berlin (he was liberated in 1969 in response to the tremendous acoustical pressure of the Bryant piece).

Brymer, Jack, distinguished English clarinetist; b. South Shields, Jan. 27, 1915. He studied at the Univ. of London; then served in the Royal Air Force in World War II. In 1947 he joined the Royal Phil. Orch. as principal clarinet; then held this position with the BBC Symph. Orch. (1963–71) and the London

Symph. Orch. (from 1971). He was director of the London Wind Soloists; was prof. at the Royal Academy of Music, London (1950–59); also taught at Kneller Hall (1967–71). In 1960 he was made an Officer of the Order of the British Empire. He wrote an autobiography under the title *From Where I Sit*, publ. in 1979.

Bryn-Julson, Phyllis, American soprano; b. Bowdon, N.D., Feb. 5, 1945 (of Norwegian parentage). She studied piano, organ, violin, and voice at Concordia College, Moorhead, Minn.; then spent several summers at the Berkshire Music Center at Tanglewood and completed her studies at Syracuse Univ. In 1973 she made her first of many regular appearances with the N.Y. Phil.; also sang frequently with the Boston Symph. and other major American orchs. She is particularly renowned as a concert singer, at ease in all periods and styles of music.

Bubalo, Rudolph, American composer; b. Duluth, Minn., Oct. 21, 1927. He played jazz piano as a young man; then studied at the Chicago Musical College and Roosevelt Univ. with John Becker, Vittorio Rieti, Karel Jirak, Rudolph Ganz, and Ernst Krenek. Helped by numerous grants, he made rapid progress in writing works with unusual titles and of unusual content, among them *Valances, Soundposts,* and *Conicality;* most of his works employ electronic sound; perhaps the most striking is *Spacescape* for Orch. and Tape (Cleveland, Feb. 1, 1979), which consists of a series of overlapping variations, with the main theme of 45-second duration.

Bucchi, Valentino, Italian composer; b. Florence, Nov. 29, 1916; d. Rome, May 9, 1976. He studied composition with Frazzi and Dallapiccola, and music history with Torrefranca at the Univ. of Florence, graduating in 1944; subsequently held teaching posts at the Florence Cons. (1945–52 and 1954–57), the Venice Cons. (1952–54), and the Cons. of Perugia (1957–58); was music director of the Accademia Filarmonica Romana (1958–60) and artistic director of the Teatro Communale in Bologna (1963–65). In his works he continued the national Italian tradition of the musical theater, while in his techniques he attempted to modernize the polyphony of the Renaissance along the lines established by Malipiero.

Bucci, Mark, American composer; b. New York, Feb. 26, 1924. He studied with Jacobi and Giannini at the Juilliard School of Music and with Copland at the Berkshire Music Center in Tanglewood; adopted a pragmatic method of composition in a strong rhythmic style, in modern but tonal harmonies, particularly effective in his stage works.
WORKS: One-act operas: *The Boor* (after Chekhov, N.Y., Dec. 29, 1949); *The Dress* (N.Y., Dec. 8, 1953); *Sweet Betsy from Pike* (N.Y., Dec. 8, 1953); *The 13 Clocks* (N.Y., Dec. 29, 1953); *Tale for a Deaf Ear* (Tanglewood, Aug. 5, 1957); *The Hero* (Educational Television, N.Y., Sept. 24, 1965). His *Concerto for a Singing Instrument* was first performed as a *Concerto for Kazoo* by the N.Y. Phil., Leonard Bern-

stein conducting, on March 26, 1960, with Anita Darian as kazoo virtuoso.

Bucharoff (real name, **Buchhalter**), **Simon,** Russian-American pianist and composer; b. Berditchev, April 20, 1881; d. Chicago, Nov. 24, 1955. He settled in America as a youth; studied piano with Paolo Gallico in N.Y., and later with Julius Epstein and Emil Sauer in Vienna. He occupied various teaching posts; lived principally in Chicago and Hollywood.

Bücher, Karl, German economist and writer on music; b. Kirchberg, near Wiesbaden, Feb. 16, 1847; d. Leipzig, Nov. 12, 1930. As a prof. of economics at Leipzig Univ. (1892–1916), he became interested in the correlation between social conditions among primitive peoples and music; he publ. a book, *Arbeit und Rhythmus* (1896), in which the origin of music is traced to natural rhythmic exertions during manual labor, with group singing in unison as a natural expedient for teamwork. The book aroused a great deal of controversy, and went through several printings; the 6th edition was publ. in 1924.

Bucht, Gunnar, Swedish composer; b. Stocksund, Aug. 5, 1927. He studied musicology at Uppsala Univ. (1947–53); concurrently took lessons in theory with Blomdahl (1947–51); received his Ph.D. at Uppsala in 1953; later studied composition in Germany with Orff (1954), in Italy with Petrassi (1954–55), and in Paris with Max Deutsch (1961–62). He taught at Stockholm Univ. (1965–69); was also employed in diplomatic service as cultural attaché at the Swedish Embassy in Bonn (1970–73). In 1975 he was appointed prof. of composition at the Musikhögskolan in Stockholm. His music retains traditional forms while adopting diverse modern techniques.

Büchtiger, Fritz, German composer; b. Munich, Feb. 14, 1903; d. Starnberg, Dec. 26, 1978. He studied organ, flute, voice, conducting, and music theory at the Music Academy of Munich; his instructors in composition were Beer-Walbrunn and Wolfgang von Waltershausen. He followed the contemporary trends of German music, but with the advent of the Nazis, when modernism became strictly *verboten,* he was compelled, as a certified Aryan, to write nationalistic and racially blatant stuff. In 1948 he swerved back to his original interests, formed a studio for new music in Munich, and began writing in a dodecaphonic idiom, adroitly applying it even to his religious compositions. He was also active internationally as chairman of the German section of "Jeunesses musicales."

Buck, Dudley, noted American organist, composer, and pedagogue; b. Hartford, Conn., March 10, 1839; d. West Orange, N.J., Oct. 6, 1909. He studied piano with W.J. Babcock; then traveled to Germany, where he took courses at the Leipzig Cons. with Plaidy and Moscheles (piano), Hauptmann (composition), and J. Rietz (instrumentation); later was in

Paris (1861–62). Returning to the U.S., he served as church organist in Hartford, Chicago, Boston, and Brooklyn. He was one of the first American composers to achieve recognition for his church music.

Buck, Sir Percy Carter, English organist; b. London, March 25, 1871; d. there, Oct. 3, 1947. He studied at the Guildhall School and Royal College of Music; subsequently served as church organist. From 1901–27 he was music director at Harrow School; was prof. of music at Trinity College in Dublin (1910–20); at the Univ. of London (1925–37); also taught at the Royal College of Music in London. He was knighted in 1937. His works include an overture for Orch., *Cœur de Lion;* String Quartet; Piano Quintet; sonatas, piano pieces, etc. He was the author of *Ten Years of University Music in Oxford* (1894; with Mee and Woods); *Unfigured Harmony* (1911); *Organ Playing* (1912); *First Year at the Organ* (1912); *The Organ: A Complete Method for the Study of Technique and Style; Acoustics for Musicians* (1918); *The Scope of Music* (Oxford, 1924); *Psychology for Musicians* (London, 1944); also was editor of the introductory vol. and vols. I and II of the 2nd ed. of the *Oxford History of Music.*

Bücken, Ernst, eminent German musicologist; b. Aachen, May 2, 1884; d. Overath, near Cologne, July 28, 1949. He studied musicology at the Univ. of Munich with Sandberger and Kroyer; also took courses in composition with Courvoisier; received his Ph.D. there in 1912 with the dissertation *Anton Reicha; Sein Leben und seine Kompositionen* (publ. in Munich, 1912); completed his Habilitation at the Univ. of Cologne in 1920 with his *Der heroische Stil in der Oper* (publ. in Leipzig, 1924); was a prof. there from 1925 to 1945; then retired to Overath. His elucidation of musical styles remains an important achievement in his work as a musicologist; as such, he edited the monumental Handbuch der Musikwissenschaft in 10 vols., which began publication in 1927; for this series he contributed *Musik des Rokokos und der Klassik* (1927), *Die Musik des 19. Jahrhunderts bis zur Moderne* (1929–31), and *Geist und Form im musikalischen Kunstwerk* (1929–32); he was also editor of the series Die Grossen Meister der Musik from 1932. His further writings include *Tagebuch der Gattin Mozarts* (Munich, 1915); *München als Musikstadt* (Leipzig, 1923); *Führer und Probleme der neuen Musik* (Cologne, 1924); *Musikalische Charakterköpfe* (Leipzig, 1924); ed. of *Handbuch der Musikerziehung* (Wildpark-Potsdam, 1931); *Ludwig van Beethoven* (Wildpark-Potsdam, 1934); *Richard Wagner* (Wildpark-Potsdam, 1934; 2nd ed., 1943); *Deutsche Musikkunde* (Wildpark-Potsdam, 1935); *Musik aus deutscher Art* (Cologne, 1936); *Musik der Nationen* (Leipzig, 1937; 2nd ed., revised, as *Geschichte der Musik,* ed. by J. Völckers, 1951); ed. of *Richard Wagner: Die Hauptschriften* (Leipzig, 1937); *Das deutsche Lied: Probleme und Gestalten* (Hamburg, 1939); *Robert Schumann* (Cologne, 1940); *Wörterbuch der Musik* (Leipzig, 1940); *Musik der Deutschen: Eine Kulturgeschichte der deutschen Musik* (Cologne, 1941);

Wolfgang Amadeus Mozart: Schöpferische Wandlungen (Hamburg, 1942); *Richard Strauss* (Kevelaar, 1949).

Budd, Harold, American composer of extreme avant-garde tendencies; b. Los Angeles, May 24, 1936. He studied composition and acoustics with Gerald Strang and Aurelio de la Vega at Calif. State Univ. at Northridge (B.A., 1963) and with Ingolf Dahl at the Univ. of Southern Calif. (M.Mus., 1966). From 1969 to 1976 he was on the faculty of the Calif. Inst. of the Arts. An exponent of optically impressive music, he judged the quality of a work by its appearance on paper, in the firm conviction that visual excellence is cosubstantial with audible merit. His compositions are mostly designed for mixed media; some of them are modular, capable of being choreographed one into another; some are mere verbalizations of the intended mode of performance, calculated to stultify, confuse, or exasperate the listening beholder. Perhaps the most arresting and bewildering of such misleading works in his catalogue is something called *Intermission Piece,* to be played at random with a "barely audible amplitude spectrum" during intermission, with the audience "physically or conceptually absent," so that the number of performances runs into thousands, including every time an intermission during a concert occurs any place in the world.

Bühler, Franz, German composer; b. Schneidheim, near Nördlingen, April 12, 1760; d. Augsburg, Feb. 4, 1823. He was a Benedictine monk at Donauwörth; a choral conductor at Botzen (1794) and at Augsburg Cathedral (1801); wrote an opera, *Die falschen Verdachte;* an oratorio, *Jesus, der göttliche Erlöser;* sonatas and preludes for organ; also several theoretical pamphlets.

Buhlig, Richard, American pianist; b. Chicago, Dec. 21, 1880; d. Los Angeles, Jan. 30, 1952. He studied in Chicago, and in Vienna with Leschetizky (1897–1900); made his debut in recital in Berlin (1901); then toured Europe and the U.S. (American debut with the Philadelphia Orch. in N.Y., Nov. 5, 1907). In 1918 he was appointed teacher of piano at the Inst. of Musical Arts in N.Y.; later returned to Europe; eventually settled in Los Angeles as a performer and teacher.

Buketoff, Igor, American conductor; b. Hartford, Conn., May 29, 1915. He studied music at the Juilliard School in N.Y. (1939–42). In 1943 he began his conducting career; appeared as a guest conductor in America and in Europe; led the Young People's Concerts of the N.Y. Phil. (1948–53); then was director of the Fort Wayne (Ind.) Phil. (1948–66); also conducted the Iceland Symph. Orch. (1964–65); served as music director of the St. Paul Opera Assoc. (1968–74); was a visiting prof. at the Univ. of Houston (1977–79).

Bukofzer, Manfred F., eminent German-American musicologist; b. Oldenburg, March 27, 1910; d. Oakland, Calif., Dec. 7, 1955. He studied at the Hoch Cons. in Frankfurt, and at the univs. of Heidelberg, Berlin, and Basel (Dr.Phil., 1936); also took courses with Hindemith in Berlin. He lectured in Basel (1933–39); also at the univs. of Oxford and Cambridge. In 1939 he settled in the U.S.; became a naturalized citizen in 1945. He taught at Case Western Reserve Univ. in Cleveland (1940–41). In 1941 he became a member of the faculty of the Univ. of Calif. at Berkeley; a year before his untimely death he was appointed chairman of the music dept. His numerous publications are distinguished by originality of historical and musical ideas coupled with precision of factual exposition; having mastered the English language, he was able to write brilliantly in British and American publications; he was also greatly esteemed as a teacher.

Bull, John, famous English organist and composer; b. Old Radnor, Radnorshire, c.1562; d. Antwerp, March 12, 1628. He was a pupil of William Blitheman in the Chapel Royal; received his Mus.B. from Oxford in 1586. He was sworn in as a Gentleman of the Chapel Royal in Jan. 1586, becoming an organist in 1591. In 1596, on Queen Elizabeth's recommendation, he was appointed prof. of music at Gresham College, and on March 6, 1597, was elected first public lecturer there. He got into difficulties with Gresham College when he impregnated premaritally a maiden named Elizabeth Walter, and was forced to resign on Dec. 20, 1607; he hastened to take a marriage license 2 days later. In 1610 he entered the service of Prince Henry, but in 1613 was charged with adultery and had to flee England. In Sept. 1615 he became assistant organist at the Antwerp Cathedral in Belgium, and was named its principal organist on Dec. 29, 1617. In the Netherlands he became acquainted with the great Dutch organist and composer Sweelinck; both he and Bull exerted considerable influence on the development of contrapuntal keyboard music of the time. Altogether about 200 compositions are attributed to John Bull; they are listed in Ward's vol. *The Lives of the Professors of Gresham College* (1740). Exercises and variations for the virginal, as well as other works, were printed in the following collections: the *Fitzwilliam Virginal Book* (modern ed. by J.A. Fuller-Maitland and W. Barclay Squire, London, 1899); *Benjamin Cosyn's Virginal Book* (23), *William Forster's Virginal Book* (3), Leighton's *The Tears or Lamentacions of a Sorrowfull Soule;* in *Parthenia* (pieces for virginal by Bull, Byrd, and Gibbons; new ed. by Margaret H. Glyn, London, 1927); and others. The complete keyboard works appear in *Musica Britannica*, XIV, ed. by J. Steele, F. Cameron, and T. Dart (1960; 2nd ed., revised, 1967), and XIX, ed. by T. Dart (1963; 2nd ed., revised, 1970). The conjecture put forward by some writers, notably Leigh Henry in his book *Dr. John Bull* (London, 1937), that Bull was the author of *God Save the King* does not have a scintilla of evidence in its support.

Bull, Ole (Bornemann), eccentric Norwegian violinist; b. Bergen, Feb. 5, 1810; d. Lyso, near Bergen, Aug. 17, 1880. He was extremely precocious, and played the violin experimentally even before acquiring the rudiments of music. At the age of 9 he played solos with the Bergen Harmonic Society. His teachers were then Niels Eriksen and J.H. Poulsen; later he had regular instruction with M. Ludholm. Ignoring academic rules, he whittled the bridge almost to the level of the fingerboard, so as to be able to play full chords on all 4 strings. He was sent by his father to Christiania (Oslo) to study theology, but failed the entrance examinations; instead, he organized a theater orch., which he led with his violin. In 1829 he played in Copenhagen and Kassel. In 1831 he went to Paris, where he heard Paganini and became obsessed with the idea of imitating his mannerisms and equaling his success, a fantasy devoid of all imagined reality because of Bull's amateurish technique. However, he developed a personal type of playing that pleased the public, particularly in localities rarely visited by real artists. During the season 1836–37 he played 274 concerts in England and Ireland; in 1839 he visited the great German violinist and composer Spohr in Kassel, in the hope of receiving useful advice from him. In 1840 he played Beethoven's *Kreutzer Sonata* in London, with Liszt at the piano. On July 23, 1849, he announced the formation of a Norwegian Theater in Bergen, which was opened on Jan. 2, 1850. While he failed to impress serious musicians and critics in Europe, he achieved his dream of artistic success in America; he made 5 concert tours across the U.S., playing popular selections and his own compositions on American themes with such fetching titles as *Niagara, Solitude of the Prairies,* and *To the Memory of Washington,* interspersing them with his arrangements of Norwegian folk songs. He entertained a strong conviction that Norway should generate its own national art, but the practical applications of his musical patriotism were failures because of his lack of formal study and a concentration on tawdry effects; still, it may be argued that he at least prepared the ground for the emergence of true Norwegian music; indeed, it is on his recommendation that Grieg was sent to study at the Leipzig Cons. Characteristically, Ole Bull became attracted by the then-current ideas of communal socialism. In 1852 he purchased 11,144 acres in Pennsylvania for a Norwegian settlement, but his lack of business sense led his undertaking to disaster. The settlement, planned on strict socialist lines, was given the name Oleana, thus establishing a personal connection with the name of its unlucky founder. Oleana soon collapsed, but Ole Bull earned admiration in Norway as a great national figure. Many of his violin pieces, mostly sentimental or strident in nature, with such titles as *La preghiera d'una madre, Variazioni di bravura, Polacca guerriera,* etc., were publ., but they sank into predictable desuetude.

Bullock, Sir Ernest, English organist and educator; b. Wigan, Sept. 15, 1890; d. Aylesbury, May 24, 1979. He studied organ with Bairstow in Leeds; also took courses at the Univ. of Durham (B.Mus., 1908; D.Mus., 1914). After serving as suborganist at Manchester Cathedral (1912–15), he was organist and choirmaster at Exeter Cathedral (1919–27). In 1928 he was named organist and Master of the Choristers at Westminster Abbey, and as such participated in several coronations. He became Gardiner Prof. of Music at the Univ. of Glasgow in 1941. He was then director of the Royal College of Music in London from 1952 until his retirement in 1960. He was knighted by King George VI in 1951.

Bülow, Hans (Guido) von, celebrated German pianist and conductor of high attainment; b. Dresden, Jan. 8, 1830; d. Cairo, Egypt, Feb. 12, 1894. At the age of 9 he began to study piano with Friedrich Wieck and theory with Max Eberwein; then went to Leipzig, where he studied law at the univ. and took a music course with Moritz Hauptmann; he also studied piano with Plaidy. From 1846 to 1848 he lived in Stuttgart, where he made his debut as a pianist. In 1849 he attended the Univ. of Berlin; there he joined radical social groups; shortly afterward he went to Zürich and met Wagner, who was there in exile. After a year in Switzerland where he conducted theater music, Bülow proceeded to Weimar, where he began to study with Liszt. In 1853 he made a tour through Germany and Austria as a pianist. In 1855 he was appointed head of the piano dept. at the Stern Cons. in Berlin, retaining this post until 1864. He married Liszt's natural daughter, Cosima, in 1857. In 1864 he was called by Ludwig II to Munich as court pianist and conductor; the King, who was a great admirer of Wagner, summoned Wagner to Munich from exile. Hans von Bülow himself became Wagner's ardent champion; on June 10, 1865, he conducted at the court opera in Munich the first performance of *Tristan und Isolde,* and on June 21, 1868, he led the premiere of *Die Meistersinger von Nürnberg.* It was about this time that Wagner became intimate with Cosima; after her divorce she married Wagner, in 1870. Despite this betrayal, Bülow continued to conduct Wagner's music; his growing admiration for Brahms cannot be construed as his pique against Wagner. It was Bülow who dubbed Brahms "the third B of music," the first being Bach, and the second Beethoven. In fact, the context of this nomination was more complex than a mere alphabetical adumbration; according to reports, Bülow was asked to name his favorite key; he replied that it was E-flat major, the key signature of the *Eroica,* with the 3 B's (German colloquialism for flats) signifying Bach, Beethoven, and Brahms. Then he was asked why he did not rather nominate Bruckner for the 3rd B, and he is supposed to have replied that Bruckner was too much of a Wagnerian for him. Bülow was indeed renowned for his wit, and his aptitude for alliterative punning; his writings are of elevated literary quality. In 1872 Bülow lived in Florence; then resumed his career as a pianist, winning triumphant successes in England and Russia; during his American tour in 1875–76 he gave 139 concerts; he revisited America in 1889 and 1890. An important

chapter in his career was his conductorship in Meiningen (1880–85). In 1882 he married a Meiningen actress, Marie Schanzer. He was conductor of the Berlin Phil. from 1887 to 1893, when a lung ailment forced him to seek a cure in Egypt. He died shortly after his arrival in Cairo.

As a conductor, Hans von Bülow was an uncompromising disciplinarian; he insisted on perfection of detail, and he was also able to project considerable emotional power on the music. He was one of the first conductors to dispense with the use of the score. His memory was fabulous; it was said that he could memorize a piano concerto by just reading the score, sometimes while riding in a train. The mainstay of his repertoire was Classical and Romantic music, but he was also receptive toward composers of the new school. When Tchaikovsky, unable to secure a performance of his First Piano Concerto in Russia, offered the score to Bülow, he accepted it, and gave its world premiere as soloist with a pickup orch. in Boston, on Oct. 25, 1875; however, the music was too new and too strange to American ears of the time, and the critical reactions were ambiguous. Hans von Bülow encouraged the young Richard Strauss, and gave him his first position as conductor. Bülow was a composer himself, but his works belong to the category of "Kapellmeister Musik," competent, well structured, but devoid of originality. Among his compositions were a symph. "mood picture," *Nirwana;* incidental music to Shakespeare's *Julius Caesar;* piano pieces and numerous songs. He made masterly transcriptions of the prelude to Wagner's *Meistersinger* and the entire opera *Tristan und Isolde;* also arranged for piano the overtures to *Le Corsaire* and *Benvenuto Cellini* by Berlioz. He annotated and edited Beethoven's piano sonatas, which were widely used by piano teachers, even though criticism was voiced against his cavalier treatment of some passages and his occasional alterations of Beethoven's original to enhance the resonance.

Bumbry, Grace (Ann), greatly talented black American mezzo-soprano; b. St. Louis, Jan. 4, 1937. She sang in church choirs as a child; in 1955 went to Northwestern Univ. to study voice with Lotte Lehmann, and continued her lessons with her at the Music Academy of the West in Santa Barbara. She made her professional debut in a concert in London in 1959; then made a spectacular operatic appearance as Amneris at the Paris Opéra in 1960. In a lucky strike, Wieland Wagner engaged her to sing Venus in *Tannhäuser* at the Bayreuth Festival on July 23, 1961; she was the first Afro-American to be featured in the role of a goddess. This event created immediate repercussions in liberal circles, and Grace Bumbry was invited by Jacqueline Kennedy to sing at the White House on Feb. 20, 1962. She then undertook a grand tour of concerts in the U.S.; in 1963 she performed the role of Venus again at the Chicago Lyric Opera, and also sang it at Lyons, France. On Oct. 7, 1965, she made her Metropolitan Opera debut in N.Y. as Princess Eboli in Verdi's opera *Don Carlos.* In 1966 she sang Carmen at the

Salzburg Festival under the direction of Herbert von Karajan; she repeated this role at the Metropolitan with extraordinary success. The sensational element of her race was no longer the exclusive attraction; the public and the press judged her impartially as a great artist. In 1970 she sang Salome in the Strauss opera at Covent Garden in London, and she sang it again, in German, at the Metropolitan Opera on Sept. 19, 1973. She proved her ability to perform mezzo-soprano and high soprano roles with equal brilliance by singing both Aida and Amneris in Verdi's opera, and both Venus and Elisabeth in *Tannhäuser.* In 1963 she married the Polish tenor **Erwin Jaeckel,** who also became her business manager.

Bunger, Richard Joseph, American pianist and composer; b. Allentown, Pa., June 1, 1942. He studied at Oberlin College Cons. (B.Mus., 1964) and the Univ. of Illinois (M.Mus., 1965). In 1973 he was appointed to the faculty of Calif. State College, Dominguez Hills. He became absorbed in the modern techniques of composition, particularly in the new resources of prepared piano; publ. an illustrated vol., *The Well-Prepared Piano* (1973), with a foreword by John Cage; also evolved a comprehensive notational system called "Musiglyph" which incorporates standard musical notation and musical graphics indicating special instrumental techniques. He is the inventor of a "Bungerack," a music holder for the piano, particularly convenient for scores of large size.

Bungert, August, German composer; b. Mülheim, Ruhr, March 14, 1845; d. Leutesdorf, Oct. 26, 1915. He studied piano and composition at Cologne and Paris; lived mostly in Berlin. An ardent admirer of Wagner, Bungert devoted his life to the composition of a parallel work to Wagner's *Ring,* taking Homer's epics as the source of his librettos. The result of this effort was the creation of two operatic cycles: *The Iliad,* comprising *Achilleus* and *Klytemnestra;* and *The Odyssey,* a tetralogy. *The Iliad* was never completed for performance, but all four parts of *The Odyssey* were performed in Dresden: *Kirke* (Jan. 29, 1898); *Nausikaa* (March 20, 1901); *Odysseus' Heimkehr* (Dec. 12, 1896, prior to premieres of parts I and II); *Odysseus' Tod* (Oct. 30, 1903). There were also subsequent productions in other German cities, but everywhere Bungert's operas were received without enthusiasm, and the evident ambition to emulate Wagner without comparable talent proved his undoing. Among other works are the programmatic score *Zeppelins erste grosse Fahrt;* several symph. overtures; *Symphonia Victrix; German Requiem;* many songs. His most successful work was a comic opera, *Die Studenten von Salamanka* (Leipzig, 1884); he also wrote a mystery play, *Warum? woher? wohin?* (1908); incidental music to Goethe's *Faust,* etc.

Bunting, Edward, historiographer of Irish music; b. Armagh, Feb. 1773; d. Dublin, Dec. 21, 1843. He played organ at Belfast; then moved to Dublin. He

publ. 3 collections of old Irish airs in 1796, 1809, and 1840; these were reprinted in 2 vols. in 1969 under the title *The Ancient Music of Ireland;* many of these were publ. for the first time; the first vol. contained songs by O'Conolan and O'Carolan; the 2nd included piano arrangements and a discussion of the Irish, British, and Egyptian harps; the 3rd contained a long dissertation on the history of Irish popular music. Bunting collected his material from old singers and harpers; his publications, therefore, have the value of authenticity.

Buonamente, Giovanni Battista, Italian composer; b. c.1600; d. Assisi, Aug. 29, 1642. He was maestro di cappella at the Austrian court in Vienna from 1626 to 1631; then served in a similar position at the Basilica of S. Francesco in Assisi, beginning in 1633. His importance rests on his sonatas for violin, some of which are the earliest examples of this form; he publ. 7 books of such works in Vienna during his stay there; also wrote trio sonatas for 2 violins and bass.

Buonamici, Giuseppe, Italian pianist; b. Florence, Feb. 12, 1846; d. there, March 17, 1914. He first studied with his uncle, Giuseppe Ceccherini; then at the Munich Cons. with Hans von Bülow and Rheinberger (1868–70); in 1873 returned to Florence, where he was active as a teacher and choral conductor. He publ. a compilation of the technical figures found in Beethoven's piano music, in the form of daily studies; edited the *Biblioteca del Pianista* and the complete Beethoven sonatas; also publ. piano pieces of his own.

Buononcini. See **Bononcini.**

Burbure de Wesembeek, Léon-Philippe-Marie, Belgian music scholar; b. Dendermonde, Aug. 16, 1812; d. Antwerp, Dec. 8, 1889. A scion of an aristocratic family, he studied law at the Univ. of Ghent; he also received an excellent musical education at home with private teachers. In 1846 he settled at Antwerp, and became the keeper of Archives at the Cathedral. He made a profound study of materials on old music accessible to him, and publ. a number of valuable monographs dealing with the Renaissance music guilds of Antwerp, on lute makers, etc. He also composed some 200 works, including an opera, 25 orch. pieces, numerous choral works, etc.
WRITINGS: *Aperçu sur l'ancienne corporation des musiciens instrumentistes d'Anvers, dite de St. Job et de Ste. Marie-Madeleine* (Brussels, 1862); *Recherches sur les facteurs de clavecins et luthiers d'Anvers, depuis le XVIᵉ jusqu'au XIXᵉ siècle* (Brussels, 1869); *Notice sur Charles-Louis Hanssens* (Brussels, 1872); *Charles Luython (1550–1620), compositeur de musique de la Cour impériale* (Brussels, 1880); *Les Œuvres des anciens musiciens belges* (Brussels, 1882).

Burck (real name, **Moller**), **Joachim à,** German church composer; b. Burg, near Magdeburg, 1546; d.

Mühlhausen, Thuringia, May 24, 1610. In 1563 he settled in Mühlhausen; became organist at the Protestant Church of St. Blasius in 1566.

WORKS: *Harmoniae sacrae* (5 books of motets; Nuremberg, 1566); *Die deutsche Passion* (Wittenberg, 1568); *Crepundia sacra* (4 books; Mühlhausen, 1578); several books of motets, odes, and German songs, reprinted in various collections.

Burco, Ferruccio, precocious Italian conductor; b. Milan, April 5, 1939; killed in an automobile accident near Ostuni, April 27, 1965. Phenomenally gifted, he was trained by his mother, a singer, and on May 30, 1943, at the age of 4, conducted an orch. in Milan by memorizing gestures to give cues. With his father acting as his manager, he was exhibited throughout Italy; in 1948 he was brought to the U.S. and conducted a concert at Carnegie Hall in N.Y.; also led sympathetic symph. groups in Philadelphia, Detroit, Boston, Chicago, Los Angeles, and San Francisco. At a special opera performance at the Triborough Stadium at Randalls Island in N.Y., he conducted *Cavalleria rusticana,* with his mother singing the role of Santuzza. During his American tour he weighed only 82 pounds. His subsequent development failed to do justice to his fantastic beginnings, and at the time of his death he was the leader of an itinerant provincial Italian band.

Burgess, Anthony, celebrated British novelist, author of *A Clockwork Orange* and other imaginative novels, who began his career as a professional musician; b. Manchester, England, Feb. 25, 1917. He played piano in jazz combos in England, at the same time studying classical compositions without a tutor. Despite his great success as a novelist, he continued to write music, and developed a style of composition that, were it not for his literary fame, would have earned him a respectable niche among composers. His music is refreshingly rhythmical and entirely tonal, but not without quirky quartal harmonies and crypto-atonal melodic flights. He publ. *This Man and Music* (London, 1982).

WORKS: 3 symphs. (1937; 1956, subtitled *Sinfoni Melayu,* and based on Malaysian themes; 1975); *Sinfonietta* for Jazz Combo (1941); symph. poem, *Gibraltar* (1944); *Song of a Northern City* for Piano and Orch. (1947); *Partita* for String Orch. (1951); *Ludus Multitonalis* for Recorder Consort (1951); Concertino for Piano and Percussion (1951); *Cantata for Malay College* (1954); Concerto for Flute and Strings (1960); Passacaglia for Orch. (1961); Piano Concerto (1976); Cello Sonata (1944); 2 piano sonatas (1946, 1951); incidental music for various plays; songs.

Burgin, Richard, American violinist and conductor; b. Warsaw, Oct. 11, 1892; d. Gulfport, Fla., April 29, 1981. He studied violin with Auer at the St. Petersburg Cons.; played as a soloist with the Warsaw Phil. at the age of 11; in 1907 he made an American tour as a concert violinist. Abandoning a concert career, he served as concertmaster of the Helsingfors Symph. Orch. (1912–15) and of the Oslo Symph. Orch. (1916–19). In 1920 he went to the U.S.; was appointed concertmaster of the Boston Symph., and in 1927 became its assistant conductor; he also conducted orchs. in various cities in New England, and was for many years active as instructor in conducting at the Berkshire Music Center, Tanglewood. In 1967 he went to Tallahassee, Fla., where he continued his activities as a conductor and violin teacher. He was greatly esteemed by orch. members for his pragmatic and reliable technique; however, he never aspired to major orch. posts. He was married to the violinist **Ruth Posselt.**

Burgmüller, Johann August Franz, German organist and conductor; b. Magdeburg, April 28, 1766; d. Düsseldorf, Aug. 21, 1824. He was of a clerical family; having received a good education, he became a teacher and then a traveling theatrical conductor; he founded a musical society in Düsseldorf, and enjoyed a considerable reputation among musicians as a scholar. His two sons, **Johann Friedrich Franz** and **Norbert,** were both musicians.

Burgmüller, Johann Friedrich Franz, German composer of piano music; b. Regensburg, Dec. 4, 1806; d. Beaulieu, near Paris, Feb. 13, 1874. He was the son of **Johann August Franz Burgmüller,** and brother of **Norbert;** having settled in Paris, he adopted a light style to satisfy the demands of Parisian music lovers, and wrote numerous pieces of salon music for piano; he also publ. several albums of piano studies that have become standard works.

Burgmüller, Norbert, German composer, son of **Johann August Franz** and brother of **Johann Friedrich Franz;** b. Düsseldorf, Feb. 8, 1810; d. Aachen, May 7, 1836. He was extremely gifted, and composed music since his early childhood. After study at home, he took lessons with Spohr; wrote many songs and a symph. His 2nd Symph. remained incomplete at the time of his death at the age of 26; Schumann, who thought highly of him, orchestrated the 3rd movement, a scherzo; in this form, the symph. had many performances in Europe and America, and Norbert Burgmüller was mourned by musicians as another Schubert. The point of coincidence was that his unfinished symph. was in the same key as that of Schubert.

Burgon, Geoffrey, significant English composer; b. Hambledon, July 16, 1941. He studied with Peter Wishart and Lennox Berkeley at the Guildhall School of Music in London; earned his living as a jazz trumpeter. As a composer, he became particularly successful in providing background music for television shows; he wrote the score for Evelyn Waugh's *Brideshead Revisited* and for Le Carré's thriller *Tinker, Tailor, Soldier, Spy.* His wide range of musical expression includes the English ecclesiastical tradition as well as medieval French music.

Burgstaller, Alois, German tenor; b. Holzkirchen,

Sept. 21, 1871; d. Gmund, April 19, 1945. He was trained as a watchmaker, and also sang; encouraged by Cosima Wagner, he made a serious study of singing, and performed the role of Siegfried at the Bayreuth Festival in 1896. He made his American debut at the Metropolitan Opera in N.Y. as Siegmund in *Die Walküre* on Feb. 12, 1903; remained on it roster until his final appearance, again as Siegmund, on Jan. 14, 1909. He also sang the title role in the first staged American performance of *Parsifal,* in N.Y., on Dec. 24, 1903. In 1910 he returned to Germany.

Burian, Emil František, Czech composer; b. Pilsen, June 11, 1904; d. Prague, Aug. 9, 1959. He grew up in a musical family; his father, **Emil Burian** (1876–1926), was an operatic baritone; his uncle, **Karl Burian,** was a famous tenor. He studied with Foerster at the Prague Cons. From his first steps in composition, he adopted an extreme modernistic method—an eclectic fusion of jazz, Czech folk art, and French Impressionism; was also active as a film producer, dramatist, poet, jazz singer, actor, piano accompanist, and journalist. In 1927 he organized a "voice band" that sang according to prescribed rhythm but without a definite pitch; his presentation of the voice band at the Siena Festival of the International Society for Contemporary Music (Sept. 12, 1928) aroused considerable interest, and achieved further notoriety through his association with his Dada theater in Prague (1933–41, 1945–49). During World War II Burian was put in a concentration camp by the Nazis, but he survived and returned to active life.

Burian, Karl, Czech tenor; b. Rusinov, near Rakovnik, Jan. 12, 1870; d. Senomaty, Sept. 25, 1924. He studied with F. Piwoda in Prague; made his operatic debut in Brno on March 28, 1891, as Jeník in Smetana's *The Bartered Bride;* then sang in Germany and Russia. In 1898 he was engaged to sing Parsifal at Bayreuth, and was extremely successful in this role. He sang the part of Herod in *Salome* at its world premiere in Dresden on Dec. 9, 1905. He made his American debut as Tannhäuser, on Nov. 30, 1906, at the Metropolitan Opera in N.Y.; remained on the Metropolitan's roster until 1913; then became a member of the Vienna Opera. In America he used the name **Carl Burrian.**

Burk, John N., American writer on music; b. San José, Calif., Aug. 28, 1891; d. Boston, Sept. 6, 1967. He graduated from Harvard Univ. (A.B., 1916). In 1934 he succeeded Philip Hale as program annotator of the Boston Symph. Orch. He edited Philip Hale's Boston Symph. program notes (1935); annotated *Letters of Richard Wagner,* from the Burrell Collection (N.Y., 1950). He is the author of the books *Clara Schumann, A Romantic Biography* (N.Y., 1940); *The Life and Works of Beethoven* (N.Y., 1943); *Mozart and His Music* (N.Y., 1959).

Burkhard, Paul, Swiss conductor and composer; b. Zürich, Dec. 21, 1911; d. Tösstal, Sept. 6, 1977. He studied at the Cons. in Zürich. From 1932 to 1934 he conducted at the Bern Stadttheater; he was then engaged as a conductor at a Zürich theater (1939–45); then became conductor of the Beromünster Radio Orch. in Zürich (1945–57). As a composer he was successful mainly in light music; several of his operettas enjoyed considerable success in Switzerland; among them are *Hopsa* (1935; revised 1957), *Dreimal Georges* (1936), *Der schwarze Hecht* (1939; revived under a new title, *Feuerwerk,* 1950), *Tic-Tac* (1942), *Casanova in der Schweiz* (1944), *Die kleine Niederdorfoper* (1954), and *Die Pariserin* (1957). He also wrote the fairy-tale operas *Die Schneekönigin* (1964) and *Bunbury* (1966); and the Christmas opera *Ein Stern geht auf aus Jaakob* (1970).

Burkhard, Willy, significant Swiss composer; b. Evillard sur Bienne (Leubringen bei Biel), April 17, 1900; d. Zürich, June 18, 1955. He studied with Teichmüller and Karg-Elert in Leipzig (1921), Courvoisier in Munich (1922–23), and Max d'Ollone in Paris (1923–24). Returning to Switzerland, he taught at the Bern Cons. (1928–33) and at the Zürich Cons. (1942–55). His music is neo-Classical in form and strongly polyphonic in structure; his astringent linear idiom is tempered by a strong sense of modal counterpoint.

Burleigh, Cecil, American composer, violinist, and teacher; b. Wyoming, N.Y., April 17, 1885; d. Madison, Wis., July 28, 1980. In 1902 he went to Berlin, where he studied with Anton Witek (violin) and Hugo Leichtentritt (composition); returning to the U.S. in 1905, he studied with Felix Borowski and Emile Sauret at the Chicago Musical College. He subsequently taught at various colleges in Colorado, Iowa, and Montana (1909–19); was a concert violinist in N.Y. (1919–21); appeared in joint recitals with Rosa Ponselle, Louis Graveure, and Rudolf Ganz; in 1921, settled as a violin and composition teacher at the Univ. of Wisconsin. After retiring in 1955, he devoted himself mainly to painting.

Burleigh, Henry Thacker, black American baritone and songwriter; b. Erie, Pa., Dec. 2, 1866; d. Stamford, Conn., Sept. 12, 1949. He studied at the National Cons. in N.Y. In 1894 he became baritone soloist at St. George's Church in N.Y.; retired in 1946 after 52 years of service. He gained wide popularity as a songwriter. On May 16, 1917, the National Association for the Advancement of Colored People awarded him the Spingarn Medal for highest achievement by an American citizen of African descent during the year 1916.

Burmeister, Joachim, German musician; b. Lüneburg, March 5, 1564; d. Rostock, May 5, 1629. He received a master's degree from Rostock Univ.; publ. there the treatises *Hypomnematum Musicae Poeticae* (1599) and *Musicae Practicae sive artis canendi ratio* (1601); wrote several sacred songs, which were publ. in 1601.

Burmeister, Richard, German composer and pianist; b. Hamburg, Dec. 7, 1860; d. Berlin, Feb. 19, 1944. He studied with Liszt at Weimar, Rome, and Budapest, accompanying him on his travels; later taught at the Hamburg Cons., at the Peabody Inst. in Baltimore, Dresden Cons. (1903–6), and Klindworth-Scharwenka Cons. in Berlin (1907–25). Burmeister also made extensive concert tours of Europe and the U.S. His works include the symph. fantasy *Die Jagd nach dem Glück;* Piano Concerto; *The Sisters* (after Tennyson) for Alto with Orch.; Romanza for Violin and Orch.; songs; piano pieces. He also re-scored Chopin's F minor Concerto, Liszt's *Mephisto Waltz* and 5th Rhapsody (with new orch. accompaniment), and Weber's *Konzertstück* for Piano and Orch.

Burney, Charles, celebrated English music historian; b. Shrewsbury, April 7, 1726; d. Chelsea, April 12, 1814. He was a pupil of Edmund Baker (organist of Chester Cathedral), of his eldest half brother, James Burney, and, from 1744–47, of Dr. Arne in London. In 1749 he became organist of St. Dionis-Backchurch, and harpsichord player at the subscription concerts in the King's Arms, Cornhill; resigned these posts in 1751, and until 1760 was organist at King's Lynn, Norfolk, where he planned and began work on his *General History of Music.* He returned to London in 1760; received the degrees of B.Mus. and D.Mus. from Oxford Univ. in 1769. Having exhausted such material as was available in London for his *History of Music,* he visited France, Switzerland, and Italy in 1770 and Germany, the Netherlands, and Austria in 1772, consulting the libraries, attending the best concerts of sacred and secular music, and forming contacts with the leading musicians and scholars of the period (Gluck, Hasse, Metastasio, Voltaire, etc.). The immediate result of these journeys was the publication of *The Present State of Music in France and Italy,* etc. (1771, in diary form) and *The Present State of Music in Germany, the Netherlands,* etc. (1773). His *General History of Music* appeared in 4 vols. (1776–89; new ed. by Frank Mercer in 2 vols. with "Critical and Historical Notes," London and N.Y., 1935), the first vol. concurrently with the complete work of his rival, Sir John Hawkins. From 1806 he received a government pension. Other publications: *La musica che si canta annualmente nelle funzioni della settimana santa nella Cappella Pontificia, composta de Palestrina, Allegri e Bai* (1771; a book of sacred works with Burney's preface); *An Account of the Musical Performances in Westminster Abbey ... in Commemoration of Handel* (1785); *Memoirs of the Life and Writings of the Abate Metastasio* (3 vols., 1796); the articles on music for Rees's *Cyclopedia;* etc. He composed, for Drury Lane, music to the dramas *Alfred* (1745), *Robin Hood* and *Queen Mab* (1750), and *The Cunning Man* (1765; text and music adapted from *Le Devin du village* by Rousseau); also sonatas for piano and for violin; violin and harpsichord concertos, cantatas, flute duets, etc.

Burrowes, John Freckleton, English composer; b.

London, April 23, 1787; d. there, March 31, 1852. He was a pupil of William Horsley; was organist of St. James' Church in Piccadilly for many years. He wrote works for flute and other instruments, and made arrangements for operas. His 2 manuals, *Thorough-Bass Primer* and *The Pianoforte Primer,* were very successful and went through many editions before they became obsolete.

Burrowes, Norma, Welsh soprano; b. Bangor, April 24, 1944. She studied at the Queen's Univ. in Belfast and the Royal Academy, London; made her debut with the Glyndebourne Touring Opera in 1970; also in 1970 she sang at Covent Garden, London; in 1971 she joined the Sadler's Wells Opera; also appeared at the Bayreuth and Aix-en-Provence festivals; made her American debut at the Metropolitan Opera, N.Y., on Oct. 12, 1979.

Burrows, Stuart, Welsh tenor; b. Pontypridd, Feb. 7, 1933. He was educated at Trinity College, Carmarthen, Wales. He made his debut in 1963 at the Welsh National Opera. In 1967 he sang at the San Francisco Opera; in 1970 appeared at the Vienna State Opera. On April 13, 1971, he made his Metropolitan Opera debut in N.Y. as Ottavio in *Don Giovanni.* He is regarded as one of the finest interpreters of Mozart roles.

Burt, Francis, English composer; b. London, April 28, 1926. He studied at the Royal Academy of Music with Howard Ferguson (1948–51) and at the Hochschule für Musik in Berlin with Boris Blacher (1951–54); was awarded the German Mendelssohn Scholarship; went for further study to Rome; in 1956 he received a stipend from the Fondation Européenne de la Culture; from 1957 lived mostly in Vienna.

Busby, Thomas, English writer on music; b. Westminster, Dec. 1755; d. London, May 28, 1838. He was a chorister in London; then studied with Battishill (1769–74); served as church organist at St. Mary's, Newington, Surrey, and St. Mary Woolnoth, Lombard Street. He obtained the degree of B.Mus. from Cambridge Univ. in 1801. In collaboration with Arnold, he publ. *A Complete Dictionary of Music* (1801); he then publ. *A Grammar of Music* (1818) and *A General History of Music* (2 vols., compiled from Burney and Hawkins; London, 1819; reprinted 1968). In 1825 he brought out a set of 3 little vols. entitled *Concert Room and Orchestra Anecdotes of Music and Musicians, Ancient and Modern,* a compilation of some topical value, even though many of the stories are apocryphal. He also publ. *A Musical Manual, or Technical Directory* (1828). His anthology of sacred music, *The Divine Harmonist* (1788), is valuable. His own compositions (oratorios and odes) are imitative of Handel. A melodrama, *Tale of Mystery,* with Busby's music, was produced at Covent Garden (Nov. 13, 1807).

Busch, Adolf, noted violinist, brother of **Hermann** and **Fritz Busch;** b. Siegen, Westphalia, Aug. 8, 1891;

d. Guilford, Vt., June 9, 1952. He studied at Cologne and Bonn; then served as concertmaster of the Vienna Konzertverein (1912–18); subsequently taught at the Hochschule für Musik in Berlin. In 1919 he organized the Busch Quartet and the Busch Trio (with his younger brother Hermann Busch, and his son-in-law **Rudolf Serkin**). The Busch Quartet gained renown with the appointment of Gösta Andreasson and Karl Doktor as its members; Busch's brother Hermann became cellist in the Busch Trio in 1926 and in the Busch Quartet in 1930. Adolf Busch went to Basel in 1927; in 1939 he emigrated to America, and remained there until his death. In 1950 he organized the Marlboro School of Music in Vermont; Rudolf Serkin carried on his work after Busch's death.

Busch, Carl, Danish-American conductor and composer; b. Bjerre, March 29, 1862; d. Kansas City, Dec. 19, 1943. He studied at the Royal Cons. in Copenhagen with Hartmann and Gade; then went to Paris; in 1887 settled in Kansas City, where he was active as a conductor and teacher. From 1912–18 he was conductor of the Kansas City Symph.; also conducted his own works with various orchs. in the U.S., Denmark, and Germany.
WORKS: For Orch.: *The Passing of Arthur* (after Tennyson) and *Minnehaha's Vision; Elegy* for String Orch.; cantatas: *The Four Winds; King Olaf; The League of the Alps; America;* etc.; also many compositions for violin; songs.

Busch, Ernst, German actor and singer; b. Kiel, Jan. 22, 1900; d. East Berlin, June 8, 1980. He first worked for Krupp, but then turned to acting; went to Berlin in 1925, where he became associated with Bertolt Brecht and Kurt Weill in their collaboration. Long a member of the Communist Party, he left Germany in 1933; fought in the International Brigade during the Spanish Civil War; was imprisoned by the Gestapo during World War II but survived his ordeal; after the war, he settled in East Berlin.

Busch, Fritz, eminent German conductor (brother of **Adolf** and **Hermann Busch**); b. Siegen, Westphalia, March 13, 1890; d. London, Sept. 14, 1951. He studied at the Cologne Cons. with Steinbach, Boettcher, Uzielli, and Klauwell; was then conductor of the Deutsches Theater in Riga (1909–10); in 1912 he became music director of the city of Aachen, and then of the Stuttgart Opera in 1918. In 1922 he was named Generalmusikdirektor of the Dresden State Opera; during his tenure, he conducted many notable productions, including the world premieres of Strauss's *Intermezzo* and *Die Aegyptische Helena.* In 1933 he was dismissed from his Dresden post by the Nazi government; leaving Germany, he made many appearances as a conductor with the Danish Radio Symph. Orch. and the Stockholm Phil.; from 1934 to 1939 he served as music director of the Glyndebourne Festivals; from 1940 to 1945 he was active mainly in South America. On Nov. 26, 1945, he made his first appearance with the Metropolitan Opera in N.Y., conducting *Lohengrin;* he continued on its roster until 1949. He was equally distinguished as an operatic and symph. conductor; he was renowned for his performances of Mozart's works. He wrote an autobiography, *Aus dem Leben eines Musikers* (Zürich, 1949; in Eng. as *Pages from a Musician's Life,* London, 1953). Recordings and publications are issued by the Bruder-Busch Gesellschaft.

Busch, Hermann, noted German cellist (brother of **Adolf** and **Fritz Busch**); b. Siegen, Westphalia, June 24, 1897; d. Bryn Mawr, Pa., June 3, 1975. He studied at the Cologne Cons. and the Vienna Academy of Music; played cello in the Vienna Symph. Orch. (1923–27); in 1926 became a member of the Busch Trio; was also a member of the renowned Busch Quartet from 1930 until the death of his brother Adolf in 1952; during his last years of life he taught at the Marlboro School of Music in Vermont.

Busch, William, English pianist and composer; b. London, June 25, 1901; d. Woolacombe, Devon, Jan. 30, 1945. Of German origin, he received his education in America and England; then studied in Germany with Leonid Kruetzer (piano) and Hugo Leichtentritt (theory). He made his debut in London (Oct. 20, 1927). His music shows competent craftsmanship; among his works are: Piano Concerto (1939); Cello Concerto (1941); Piano Quartet (1939); pieces for piano solo.

Bush, Alan Dudley, notable English composer; b. Dulwich, Dec. 22, 1900. He studied piano with Matthay and composition with Corder at the Royal Academy of Music in London; also took private piano lessons with Artur Schnabel and composition with John Ireland. In 1929 he went to Berlin and took courses in musicology and philosophy. Returning to England, he was on the staff of the Royal Academy of Music, from 1925–55. In 1935 he joined the Communist Party; in 1936 he organized in London the Workers' Music Association, remaining its president for 40 years. His early works contain some radical modernist usages, but in accordance with his political views on art, he adopted the precepts of socialist realism, demanding a tonal idiom more easily appreciated by audiences. He made numerous trips to Russia and other countries of the socialist bloc; several of his works had their first performance in East Germany.

Busnois (properly, **De Busne**), **Antoine,** French musician, singer, and composer; b. Béthune, c.1430; d. Bruges, Nov. 6, 1492. In 1467 he entered the ducal chapel in Dijon as a singer; in 1477 he joined the court of Charles the Bold of Burgundy; was in the service of Mary of Burgundy, and remained in that post until her death in 1482. He professed to be a pupil of Okeghem, but there is no confirmation for that claim. Several of his works are found in various anthologies; 7 chansons were publ. by Petrucci (1501–3); a number of his masses, including one on *L'Homme armé,* are extant.

Busoni, Ferruccio (Dante Michelangelo Ben-

venuto), greatly admired pianist and composer of Italian-German parentage; b. Empoli, near Florence, April 1, 1866; d. Berlin, July 27, 1924. His father played the clarinet; his mother, Anna Weiss, was an amateur pianist; Busoni grew up in an artistic atmosphere, and learned to play the piano as a child; at the age of 8 he played in public in Trieste. He gave a piano recital in Vienna when he was 10, and included in his program some of his own compositions. In 1877 the family moved to Graz, where Busoni took piano lessons with W. Mayer. He conducted his own choral work in Graz at the age of 12. At 15 he was accepted as a member of the Accademia Filarmonica in Bologna; he performed there his oratorio *Il sabato del villaggio* in 1883. In 1886 he went to Leipzig; there he undertook a profound study of Bach's music. In 1889 he was appointed a prof. of piano at the Helsingfors Cons., where among his students was Sibelius (who was actually a few months older than his teacher). At that time Busoni married Gerda Sjostrand, whose father was a celebrated Swedish sculptor; they had 2 sons, both of whom became well-known artists. In 1890 Busoni participated in the Rubinstein Competition in St. Petersburg, and won first prize with his *Konzertstück* for Piano and Orch. On the strength of this achievement he was engaged to teach piano at the Moscow Cons. (1890–91). He then accepted the post of prof. at the New England Cons. of Music (1891–94); however, he had enough leisure to make several tours, maintaining his principal residence in Berlin. During the season of 1912–13, he made a triumphant tour of Russia. In 1913 he was appointed director of the Liceo Musicale in Bologna. The outbreak of the war in 1914 forced him to move to neutral Switzerland; he stayed in Zürich until 1920; then returned to Berlin, remaining there until his death in 1924. In various cities, at various times, he taught piano in music schools; among his piano students were Brailovsky, Rudolf Ganz, Egon Petri, Mitropoulos, and Percy Grainger. Busoni also taught composition; Kurt Weill, Jarnach, and Wladimir Vogel were his pupils. He exercised great influence on Edgar Varèse, who was living in Berlin when Busoni was there; Varèse greatly prized Busoni's advanced theories of composition.

Busoni was a philospher of music who tried to formulate a universe of related arts; he issued grandiloquent manifestos urging a return to classical ideals in modern forms; he sought to establish a unifying link between architecture and composition; in his editions of Bach's works he included drawings illustrating the architectonic plan of Bach's fugues. He incorporated his innovations in his grandiose piano work *Fantasia contrappuntistica,* which opens with a prelude based on a Bach chorale, and closes with a set of variations on Bach's acronym, B-A-C-H (i.e., B-flat, A, C, B-natural). In his theoretical writings, Busoni proposed a system of 113 different heptatonic modes, and also suggested the possibility of writing music in exotic scales and subchromatic intervals; he expounded those ideas in his influential essay *Entwurf einer neuen Aesthetic der Tonkunst* (Trieste, 1907; Eng. trans. by T. Baker, N.Y., 1911). Busoni's other publi-

cations of significance were *Von der Einheit der Musik* (1923; in Italian, Florence, 1941; in Eng., London, 1957) and *Über die Möglichkeiten der Oper* (Leipzig, 1926). But despite Busoni's great innovations in his own compositions and his theoretical writing, the Busoni legend is kept alive, not through his music but mainly through his sovereign virtuosity as a pianist. In his performances he introduced a concept of piano sonority as an orchestral medium; indeed, some listeners reported having heard simulations of trumpets and French horns sounded at Busoni's hands. The few extant recordings of his playing transmit a measure of the grandeur of his style, but they also betray a tendency, common to Busoni's era, toward a free treatment of the musical text, surprisingly so, since Busoni preached an absolute fidelity to the written notes. On concert programs Busoni's name appears most often as the author of magisterial and eloquent transcriptions of Bach's works. His gothic transfiguration for piano of Bach's *Chaconne* for Unaccompanied Violin became a perennial favorite of pianists all over the world.

Busoni was honored by many nations. In 1913 he received the order of Chevalier de la Légion d'Honneur from the French government, a title bestowed on only 2 Italians before him: Rossini and Verdi. In 1949 an annual Concorso Busoni was established, with prizes given to contestants in piano playing. Another international award honoring the name of Busoni was announced by the Santa Cecilia Academy of Rome, with prizes given for the best contemporary compositions; at its opening session in 1950 the recipient was Stravinsky.

Busser, Henri-Paul, French composer, organist, and conductor; b. Toulouse, Jan. 16, 1872; d. Paris, Dec. 30, 1973, at the age of 101. After primary musical studies in his native town, he went to Paris, where he studied with Guiraud at the Paris Cons.; also took private lessons with Gounod, Widor, and César Franck. He won 2nd Premier Prix de Rome in 1893 with his cantata *Antigone.* A year before, he was appointed organist at St. Cloud; later served as choirmaster of the Opéra-Comique; in 1902, appointed conductor of the Grand Opéra, a post which he held for 37 years until his resignation in 1939; was reappointed after the war in 1946, and served his term until 1951. He also was for several years president of the Académie des Beaux Arts. He taught composition at the Paris Cons. from 1930 until 1948. During his long career as a conductor, he led several important productions, including the 3rd performance of Debussy's opera *Pelléas et Mélisande.* His centennial was grandly celebrated in January 1972 with performances of his works by the leading Paris orchs. and by an exhibition of his MSS at the Opéra. In 1958 he married the French opera singer **Yvonne Gall** (1885–1972).

Bussler, Ludwig, German music theorist and pedagogue; b. Berlin, Nov. 26, 1838; d. there, Jan. 18, 1900. His father was the painter, author, and privy councillor Robert Bussler; his maternal grandfather was the famous tenor singer **Karl Bader.** He studied with Dehn, Grell, and Wieprecht; then taught theory at the Ganz School of Music in Berlin (1865) and at the Stern Cons. (from 1879); was also active as a conductor at various Berlin theaters. In 1883 he became the music critic for the *National-Zeitung.* His eminently practical writings are: *Musikalische Elementarlehre* (1867; 3rd ed., 1882; Eng. trans., N.Y., 1895; also in Russian); *Der strenge Satz* (1877); *Harmonische Übungen am Klavier* (1877; in Eng., N.Y., 1890); *Kontrapunkt und Fuge im freien Tonsatz* (1878); *Musikalische Formenlehre* (1878; Eng. ed., N.Y., 1883); *Praktische musikalische Kompositionslehre:* Part I, *Lehre vom Tonsatz* (1878), and Part II, *Freie Komposition* (1879); *Instrumentation und Orchestersatz* (1879); *Elementar-Melodik* (1879); *Geschichte der Musik,* 6 lectures (1882); *Modulationslehre* (1882); *Lexikon der musikalischen Harmonien* (1889).

Bussotti, Sylvano, Italian composer of the avant-garde; b. Florence, Oct. 1, 1931. He studied violin; at the age of 9 was enrolled in the Cherubini Cons. in Florence, where he studied theory with Roberto Lupi, and also took piano lessons with Luigi Dallapiccola, while continuing his basic violin studies. In 1957 he went to Paris, where he studied privately with Max Deutsch. He became active as a theatrical director; also exhibited his paintings at European galleries. As a composer he adopted an extreme idiom, in which verbalization and pictorial illustrations are combined with aleatory discursions within the framework of multimedia productions. Many of his scores look like abstract expressionist paintings, with fragments of musical notation interspersed with occasional realistic representations of human or animal forms.

Butler (real name, **Whitwell**), **O'Brien,** Irish composer; b. Cahersiveen, c.1870; d. May 7, 1915 (lost on the *Lusitania*). He began his musical studies in Italy, then became a pupil of C.V. Stanford and W. Parratt at the Royal College of Music in London; later traveled extensively, and spent some time in India, where he wrote an opera, *Muirgheis,* the first opera to be written to a libretto in the Gaelic language; it was produced in Dublin, Dec. 7, 1903. Other compositions include a Sonata for Violin and Piano (on Irish themes) and songs.

Butt, Dame Clara, English contralto; b. Southwick, Sussex, Feb. 1, 1872; d. North Stoke, Oxfordshire, July 13, 1936. She studied with J. H. Blower at the Royal College of Music in London; later took lessons with Bouhy in Paris and Etelka Gerster in Berlin; made her operatic debut as Ursula in Sullivan's *Golden Legend* (London, Dec. 7, 1892); then sang at the music festivals at Hanley and Bristol. She visited the U.S. in 1899 and 1913; in 1913–14 made a world tour with her husband, **R. Kennerley Rumford,** a noted baritone. Several composers wrote special works for her, among them Elgar's *Sea-Pictures* and H. Bedford's *Romeo and Juliet.* In 1920 she was made a Dame of the British Empire.

Butterworth, George Sainton Kaye, talented English composer; b. London, July 12, 1885; killed in the battle of Pozières, Aug. 5, 1916. He inherited his love for music from his mother, a singer, Julia Wigan; learned to play organ at school in Yorkshire; then studied piano at Eton. He later entered Trinity College, Oxford; then engaged in music teaching and writing music criticism; also became an ardent collector of folk songs, and prepared material for Vaughan Williams's *London Symphony.* He made several arrangements of folk songs and wrote an orch. piece, *The Banks of Green Willows,* on folk themes (London, March 20, 1914). He enlisted in the British army at the outbreak of World War I. He wrote *Six Songs from "A Shropshire Lad"* (1911); 11 folk songs from Sussex (1912); *On Christmas Night* for Mixed Chorus (1912); *Cherry Tree,* a prelude for Orch. (1912); *Love Blows as the Wind Blows* for Baritone and String Quartet (1914).

Butting, Max, German composer; b. Berlin, Oct. 6, 1888; d. there, July 13, 1976. He studied organ in Berlin and composition in Munich. Returning to Berlin, he was a successful teacher, but in 1933 was deprived of his various positions for political reasons, being the former editor of a socialist publication. He was able to return to his professional activities after the end of the war. In 1948 he was appointed a lecturer in the music division of the East Berlin Radio; in 1968 he received an honorary doctor's degree from the Univ. of Berlin.

Büttner, Erhard, German composer and writer on music; b. Römhild, Thuringia (baptized, July 19), 1592; d. (suicide) Coburg, Jan. 19, 1625. He studied at the Univ. of Jena; from 1616 until his death he was Kantor at the municipal school in Coburg. He took his own life, being stricken by the sin of having been unfaithful to his wife. He publ. *Rudimenta musica* (Coburg, 1623; 2nd ed., 1625).

Buus, Jacques (**Jachet de** or **van Paus; Jacobus Bohusius**), Flemish contrapuntist; b. c.1500; d. Vienna, late August 1565. His first publications were 2 French songs, printed in Lyons in 1538. In 1541 he went to Italy and was engaged as assistant organist at San Marco in Venice; in 1550 he settled in Vienna. He publ., in Venice, 2 books of instrumental *Canzoni francese* (1543, 1550); 2 books of *Ricercari* (1547, 1549); and one book of *Motetti* (1549); several of his madrigals were publ. in various collections of the period, and also reprinted in a number of anthologies.

Buxtehude, Dietrich, great Danish organist and composer; b. Oldesloe (Holstein), c.1637; d. Lübeck, May 9, 1707. His father, **Johannes Buxtehude** (1602–74), an organist of German extraction, was active in Holstein, which was then under Danish rule. It is to be assumed that Dietrich Buxtehude received a thorough training from his father. He was about 20 years old when he was appointed organist at Helsingborg; in 1660 he became organist in Helsingor. On April 11, 1668, he was elected as successor to the famous organist Franz Tunder at the St. Mary Church in Lübeck; it was a custom in such successions that the newcomer was to marry the incumbent's daughter. Indeed, Dietrich Buxtehude did marry Tunder's daughter, on Aug. 3, 1668. In 1673 he revived the Abendmusik concerts in Lübeck which were originally organized by Tunder, and which were made up of organ music and concerted pieces for chorus and orch.; they were held annually on the 5 Sundays before Christmas, in the afternoon. Both Mattheson and Handel visited Buxtehude on Aug. 17, 1703, with the ostensible purpose of being considered as his successor, but it is a valid surmise that the notorious marriage clause which would have compelled Mattheson or Handel to marry one of Buxtehude's 5 daughters, allegedly lacking in feminine attraction, deterred them from further negotiations. In 1705 Bach, then 20 years old, was supposed to make a trip of some 200 miles from Arnstadt, where he was employed at the time, to Lübeck, to hear Buxtehude; however, the report of Bach's journey is open to serious doubts, for it would have been impossible for him to make such a trip in a short time during his leave of absence; and if he made it he was probably employed as a valet to a stagecoach traveler; any supposition that he walked to Lübeck and back, considering the usual inclement weather and the well-nigh impassable hilly terrain, is untenable. But there can be no doubt that Buxtehude exercised a profound influence on Bach, both as organist and composer. A complete edition of Buxtehude's organ works was publ. in 2 vols. by Spitta in 1875–76, and another edition was issued in 3 vols. by Josef Hedar in 1952. A complete edition of Buxtehude's vocal music under the editorship of W. Gurlitt, in 8 vols., was issued between 1927 and 1958. The complete vocal music began publication in 1925; the thematic catalogue was edited by G. Karstädt and publ. in Wiesbaden in 1974. The instrumental works are in vol. 11 of Denkmäler Deutscher Tonkunst; Abendmusiken and church cantatas are in vol. 14; 19 newly discovered keyboard suites by Buxtehude were brought out by E. Bangert (Copenhagen, 1942).

Byrd (or **Byrde, Bird**), **William,** great English composer; b. Lincoln, 1543; d. Stondon Massey, Essex, July 4, 1623. There are indications that Byrd studied music with Tallis. On March 25, 1563, Byrd was appointed organist of Lincoln Cathedral; in 1568 he married Juliana Birley; early in 1570 he was elected a member of the Chapel Royal, while retaining his post at Lincoln Cathedral until 1572; he then assumed his duties, together with Tallis, as organist of the Chapel Royal. In 1575, both Byrd and Tallis were granted a patent by Queen Elizabeth for the exclusive privilege of printing music and selling music paper for a term of 21 years; however, the license proved unprofitable and they petitioned the Queen in 1577 to give them an annuity in the form of a lease; this petition was granted. In 1585, after the death of Tallis, the license passed wholly into Byrd's hands. The earliest publication of the printing press of Byrd and Tallis was the first set of *Can-*

tiones sacrae for 5 to 8 Voices (1575), printed for them by Vautrollier and dedicated to the Queen; works issued by Byrd alone under his exclusive license were *Psalmes, Sonnets, and Songs of Sadness and Pietie* in 5 Voices (1588; publ. by Thomas East; reprinted as vol. XIV by Fellowes, *English Madrigal School*); *Songs of Sundrie Natures* for 3–6 Voices (1589; reprinted in vol. XV of the *English Madrigal School*); *Liber Primus Sacrarum Cantionum* for 5 Voices (1589); *Liber Secundus Sacrarum Cantionum* for 5–6 Voices (1591); also in 1591 appeared the famous collection of virginal music by Byrd, *My Ladye Nevells Booke* (42 pieces; modern ed. publ. by Hilda Andrews, London, 1926; reprinted, N.Y., 1969). In 1593 Byrd moved to Stondon Massey, Essex, between Chipping Ongar and Ingatestone; owing to various litigations and disputes concerning the ownership of the property, Byrd was limited to the publication of 3 masses, between c.1593 and 1595, separately, and lacking title pages. In 1605 he brought out the first book of *Gradualia;* 2 years later there followed the 2nd book (both books republ. in *Tudor Church Music,* Vol. 7). In 1611 the book of *Psalms, Songs and Sonnets* was publ. (reprinted in vol. XVI of the *English Madrigal School*); in the same year Byrd contributed several pieces to *Parthenia,* a collection of virginal compositions by Byrd, Bull, and Gibbons (newly ed. by Margaret H. Glyn, London, 1927); in 1614 he contributed 4 anthems to Leighton's *Teares or Lamentacions of a Sorrowful Soule;* separate numbers were publ. in various other collections (*Musica Transalpina,* 1588; Watson's *Italian Madrigales,* 1590; Barnard's *Selected Church Music,* 1641; Boyce's *Cathedral Music*); other music for virginal and organ in the *Virginal Book of Queen Elizabeth, Fitzwilliam Virginal Book* (70 pieces), *W. Forster's Virginal Book* (2 pieces). New editions (besides those previously mentioned): *Tudor Church Music* (vol. 2, English church music; vol. 9, masses, cantiones, and motets); Psalms, sonnets, and madrigals, by E.H. Fellowes (1920); *The Collected Works of William Byrd* by E.H. Fellowes (London, 1937–50; revised by T. Dart, P. Brett, and K. Elliott, London, 1962); the *Byrd Organ Book,* a collection of 21 pieces edited for piano from the virginal MSS by Margaret H. Glyn (London, 1923); 14 pieces for keyboard instruments, by J.A. Fuller-Maitland and W. Barclay Squire (London, 1923). A new publication of complete works, edited by P. Brett under the title *The Byrd Edition,* began publication in London in 1970.

C

Caamaño, Roberto, Argentinian pianist and composer; b. Buenos Aires, July 7, 1923. He studied at the Cons. Nacional in Buenos Aires; toured South America as a concert pianist; from 1961 to 1964 was artistic director of the Teatro Colón in Buenos Aires. In 1964 he was appointed a prof. of composition at the Pontífica Universita Católica Argentina. He was the editor of a valuable compendium in 3 vols., *La historia del Teatro Colón (1908–1968),* publ. in Buenos Aires in 1969, illustrated with color plates, drawings, and photographs.

Caba, Eduardo, Bolivian composer; b. Potosí, Oct. 13, 1890; d. La Paz, March 3, 1953. He was educated in Buenos Aires; then went to study with Turina in Spain; in 1942 he settled in La Paz. His ballets and other music are inspired by the pentatonic structure of certain Bolivian folk songs.

Caballé, Montserrat, celebrated Spanish soprano; b. Barcelona, April 12, 1933. She learned to sing at a convent which she attended as a child; at the age of 9 she was accepted at the Conservatorio del Liceo in Barcelona; her teachers there were Eugenie Kemini, Conchita Badia, and Napoleone Annovazzi. She graduated in 1953; then went to Italy, where she sang some minor roles. After a successful appearance as Mimi in *La Bohème* at the Basel Opera, she advanced rapidly, singing Tosca, Aida, Violetta, and other standard opera parts; she also proved her ability to master such modern and difficult parts as Salome, Elektra, and Marie in *Wozzeck.* She filled guest engagements at the Vienna State Opera, then made a grand tour through Germany. In 1964 she sang Manon in Mexico City. She made a triumphant American debut on April 20, 1965, when she was summoned to substitute for another singer in the title role of Donizetti's *Lucrezia Borgia* in a concert performance at Carnegie Hall in N.Y.; the usually restrained N.Y. critics praised her without reservation for the beauty of her voice and expressiveness of her dramatic interpretation. There followed several other American appearances, all of which were highly successful. She made her debut at the Metropolitan Opera in N.Y. as Marguerite in *Faust* on Dec. 22, 1965; she continued her appearances with the Metropolitan Opera; among her most significant roles were Violetta, Mimi, Aida, Norma, Donna Anna, and other roles of the standard operatic repertoire. In 1964 she married **Bernabé Marti,** a Spanish tenor. Subsequently they appeared together in joint recitals.

Cabanilles, Juan Bautista José, Spanish organist

and composer; b. Algemesí, province of Valencia, Sept. 4, 1644; d. Valencia, April 29, 1712. He studied for the priesthood at Valencia and probably received his musical training at the Cathedral there; was appointed organist of the Valencia Cathedral, May 15, 1665 (succeeding J. de la Torre) and retained that post until his death; was ordained a priest on Sept. 22, 1668. He was the greatest of the early Spanish composers for organ, and the most prolific. He composed chiefly "tientos," remarkable for the ingenious use of the variation form (on liturgical or popular themes). A complete edition of his works, in 4 vols., has been edited by H. Anglès (Barcelona, 1927–52). The *Obras vocales* are edited by J. Climent (Valencia, 1971).

Cabezón (Cabeçon), Antonio de, great Spanish organist and composer; b. Castrillo de Matajudíos, near Burgos, 1510 (the exact date is unknown; see S. Kastner's letter to the editor of *Music & Letters,* April 1955); d. Madrid, March 26, 1566. He became blind in infancy; went to Palencia about 1521 to study with the Cathedral organist García de Baeza and with Tomás Gómez. He was appointed organist to the court of the Emperor Charles V and Empress Isabel (1526); after her death, Cabezón entered the service of Prince Philip and accompanied him to Italy, Germany, the Netherlands (1548–51), and England (1554); he returned to Spain (1556) and remained court organist until his death. His keyboard style greatly influenced the development of organ composition on the Continent and the composers for the virginal in England; Pedrell called him "the Spanish Bach." The series Libro de Cifra Nueva (1557), which contains the earliest editions of Cabezón's works, was reprinted by H. Anglès in *La música en la corte de Carlos V* (1944). His son and successor at the court of Philip II, **Hernando** (b. Madrid; baptized, Sept. 7, 1541; d. Valladolid, Oct. 1, 1602), publ. his instrumental works as *Obras de música para tecla, arpa y vihuela* (Madrid, 1578). This vol. contains exercises in 2 and 3 parts, arrangements of hymn tunes, 4-part "tientos," arrangements of motets in up to 6 parts by Josquin and other Franco-Flemish composers, and variations on tunes of the day (*El caballero,* etc.). Copies are in the British Museum, in Sir Percy Wyndham's Collection, at Brussels, Berlin, Madrid, and Washington, D.C. A modern edition appears in *Hispaniae schola musica sacra* (F. Pedrell, 1898; 4 vols.). The Inst. of Medieval Music has issued several vols. of Cabezón's *Collected Works* (C. Jacobs, ed.; N.Y., 1967—). A short MS work for 5 voices is in the Medinaceli Library in Madrid.

Caccini, Francesca (nicknamed **"La Cecchina"**), daughter of **Giulio Caccini;** b. Florence, Sept. 18, 1587; d. c.1640. She was probably the first woman composer of operas. Her opera-ballet *La liberazione di Ruggiero dall'isola d'Alcina* was produced at a palace near Florence on Feb. 2, 1625, and a book of songs from it was publ. in the same year. A modern reprint, edited by Doris Silbert, was publ. in Northampton, Mass. (1945). Francesca Caccini wrote further a *Ballo delle zingare* (Florence, Feb. 24, 1615) in which she acted as one of the gypsies. Her sacred opera *Il martirio di Sant' Agata* was produced in Florence, Feb. 10, 1622.

Caccini, Giulio, Italian composer (called **Romano,** because he lived mostly in Rome); b. Tivoli, c.1550; d. Florence, (buried, Dec. 10) 1618. He was a pupil of Scipione delle Palla in singing and lute playing. His first compositions were madrigals in the traditional polyphonic style, but the new ideas generated in the discussions of the artists and literati of the "Camerata," in the houses of Bardi and Corsi at Florence, inspired him to write vocal soli in recitative form (then termed "musica in stile rappresentativo"), which he sang with consummate skill to his own accompaniment on the theorbo. These first compositions in a dramatic idiom were followed by his settings of separate scenes written by Bardi, and finally by the opera *Il combattimento d'Apolline col serpente* (poem by Bardi); next was *Euridice* (1600; poem by Rinuccini) and *Il rapimento di Cefalo* (in collaboration with others; first perf., Oct. 9, 1600, at the Palazzo Vecchio in Florence). Then followed *Le nuove musiche,* a series of madrigals for solo voice, with bass (Florence, 1602; new eds., Venice, 1607 and 1615; a modern ed. of the 1602 publication, prepared by H. Wiley Hitchcock [Madison, Wis., 1970], includes an annotated Eng. trans. of Caccini's preface, realizations of the solo madrigals, airs, and the final section of *Il rapimento di Cefalo,* an introductory essay on Caccini, the music, the poetry, MSS, other editions, and a bibliography. A trans. of the preface is also available in O. Strunk, *Source Readings in Music History* [N.Y., 1950]). The song *Amarilli mia bella* from the first series became very popular. Caccini also publ. *Fuggilotio musicale* (Venice, 2nd ed., 1613; including madrigals, sonnets, arias, etc.). From 1565 Caccini lived in Florence as a singer at the Tuscan court. He was called, by abbate Angelo Grillo, "the father of a new style of music"; Bardi said of him that he had "attained the goal of perfect music." But his claim to priority in writing vocal music in the "stile rappresentativo" is not supported by known chronology. Caccini's opera *Il rapimento di Cefalo* was performed 3 days after Peri's path-breaking *Euridice;* the closeness in time of operatic productions by both Caccini and Peri is further emphasized by the fact that when Peri produced *Euridice* in Florence (1600), he used some of Caccini's songs in the score. Caccini later made his own setting of *Euridice* (1600), but it was not produced until Dec. 5, 1602. On the other hand, Caccini was undoubtedly the first to publish an operatic work, for his score of *Euridice* was printed early in 1601, before the publication of Peri's work of the same title.

Cadman, Charles Wakefield, American composer; b. Johnstown, Pa., Dec. 24, 1881; d. Los Angeles, Dec. 30, 1946. His great-grandfather was Samuel Wakefield, the inventor of the so-called "Buckwheat Notation." Cadman studied organ with Leo Oehmler in Pittsburgh, and with Emil Paur. He was especially interested in American Indian music; gave lecture recitals with the Indian mezzo-soprano Tsianina Redfeather.

WORKS: For the stage: Opera, *Shanewis (The Robin Woman),* his most successful work (Metropolitan Opera, March 23, 1918); *The Sunset Trail,* operatic cantata (Denver, Dec. 5, 1922); *The Garden of Mystery* (N.Y., March 20, 1925); *A Witch of Salem* (Chicago, Dec. 8, 1926); radio play, *The Willow Tree* (NBC, October 3, 1933). For Orch.: *Thunderbird Suite* (Los Angeles, Jan. 9, 1917); *Oriental Rhapsody* (1917); *Dark Dancers of the Mardi Gras* (1933); *Suite on American Folktunes* (1937); symph. poem, *Pennsylvania* (Los Angeles, March 7, 1940). Cantatas: *Father of Waters* (1928); *House of Joy; Indian Love Charm* for Children's Choir; *The Vision of Sir Launfal* for Male Voices, written for the Pittsburgh Prize Competition (1909). Also, Piano Sonata; violin pieces; about 180 songs, of which *At Dawning* acquired enormous popularity.

Caduff, Sylvia, Swiss conductor; b. Chur, Jan. 7, 1937. She studied at the Lucerne Cons., receiving a piano diploma in 1961; then attended Karajan's conducting classes at the Berlin Cons.; continued conducting studies with Kubelik, Matacic, and Otterloo in Lucerne, Salzburg, and Hilversum (The Netherlands); made her debut with the Tonhalle-Orch. of Zürich. She won first prize in the 1966 Dimitri Mitropoulos conducting competition in N.Y.; as a result, she was an assistant conductor under Bernstein with the N.Y. Phil. (1966–67); taught orch. conducting at the Bern Cons. (1972–77). In 1977 she became the first woman in Europe to be appointed a Generalmusikdirektor, when she took that position with the orch. of the city of Solingen, Germany.

Caffarelli (real name, **Gaetano Majorano**), artificial soprano (*musico*); b. Bitonto, April 12, 1710; d. Naples, Jan. 31, 1783. A poor peasant boy, endowed with a beautiful voice, he was discovered by a musician, Domenico Caffarelli, who taught him, and later sent him to Porpora at Naples. In gratitude to his patron, he assumed the name of Caffarelli. He studied for 5 years with Porpora, who predicted a brilliant career for him. Caffarelli became a master of pathetic song, and excelled in coloratura as well; read the most difficult music at sight, and was an accomplished harpsichord player. His debut at the Teatro Valle (Rome, 1724) in a female role (as was the custom for artificial sopranos) was a triumph. From 1737 to 1745 he sang in London, then in Paris and Vienna. His last public appearance took place on May 30, 1754, in Naples. He was in Lisbon until the earthquake of 1755; he retired from the opera in 1756; upon his return to Naples, he bought the dukedom of Santo-Durato with the fortune he had amassed during his career, and assumed the title of duke.

Cage, John, American composer of ultramodern tendencies; b. Los Angeles, Sept. 5, 1912. His father, John Milton Cage, Sr., was an inventor of devices for detection of submarines; his mother was active as a clubwoman in California. John Cage studied piano with Fannie Dillon and Richard Buhlig in Los Angeles and with Lazare Lévy in Paris; returning to America, he studied composition in California with Adolph Weiss and with Henry Cowell in N.Y.; also attended Schoenberg's classes at the Univ. of Calif., Los Angeles. He developed Cowell's piano technique, making use of tone clusters and playing directly on the piano strings, and initiated a type of procedure which he called "prepared piano." The "preparation" consists of placing on the piano strings a variety of objects, such as screws, copper coins, rubber bands, and the like, which alter the tone color of individual keys. As a performer on the "prepared piano," John Cage attracted considerable attention at his concerts in America and Europe. Eventually the term and the procedure gained acceptance among many avant-garde composers and was listed as a legitimate innovative method in many music dictionaries. On June 7, 1935, Cage married, in Los Angeles, Xenia Kashevaroff; they were divorced in 1945. In 1938–39 he was employed as an accompanist in a dance class at the Cornish School in Seattle, where he also organized a percussion group. He taught for a season at the School of Design in Chicago (1941–42); then moved to N.Y., where he began his fruitful association with the dancer Merce Cunningham, for whom he wrote many special works. An even more important association was his collaboration with the pianist David Tudor, who was able to reify Cage's exotic inspirations, works in which the performer shares the composer's creative role. In 1949 Cage received a Guggenheim fellowship. With the passing years he departed from the musical pragmatism of precise notation and definite ways of performance, electing instead to mark his creative intentions in graphic symbols and pictorial representations. He soon established the principle of indeterminacy in musical composition, borrowing the term from modern physics; in this sense no 2 performances of a composition can be identical. In the meantime he became immersed in the study of mycology, and acquired a formidable expertise in mushroom gathering; he even won a prize in Italy in competition with professional mycologists. He also became interested in chess and played demonstration games with Marcel Duchamps, the famous painter turned chessmaster, on chessboards designed by Lowell Cross to operate on aleatory principles with the aid of a computer and a system of laser rays. In his endeavor to achieve the ultimate in freedom of musical expression, he produced a piece entitled *4'33",* "tacet, any instrument or combination of instruments," in 3 movements, during which no sounds are intentionally produced. It was "performed" in Woodstock, N.Y., on Aug. 29, 1952, by David Tudor, who sat at the piano playing nothing for the length of time stipulated in the title. This was followed by another "silent" piece, *0'00",* an idempotent "to be performed in any way by anyone," presented for the first time in Tokyo, Oct. 24, 1962. Any sounds, noises, coughs, chuckles, groans, and growls produced by the captive listeners to silence are automatically regarded as an integral part of the piece itself, so that the wisecrack about the impossibility of arriving at a fair judgment of a silent piece, since one cannot tell whose music is not being played, is invalidated by the uniqueness of Cage's art. Cage is a consummate showman, and his exhibitions invariably attract music-lovers and music-haters alike, expecting to be exhilarated or outraged, as the case may be. In many such public happenings he departs from musical, unmusical, or even antimusical programs in favor of a free exercise of surrealist imagination, often instructing the audience to participate actively, as for instance going out in the street and bringing in garbage pails needed for percussion effects, with or without garbage. Cage is a brilliant writer, much influenced by the manner, grammar, syntax, and glorified illogic of Gertrude Stein. A detailed annotated catalogue of his works was publ. by Edition Peters (N.Y., 1962). In view of the indeterminacy of so many of Cage's works, such a catalogue can serve only as a list of titles and suggestions of contents. In order to eliminate the subjective element in composition, Cage resorts to a method of selecting the components of his pieces by dice throwing, suggested by the Confucian classic *I Ching,* an ancient Chinese oracle book; the result is a system of total serialism, in which all elements pertaining to acoustical pulses, pitch, noise, duration, relative loudness, tempi, combinatory superpositions, etc., are determined by previously drawn charts. In 1981 Cage was a recipient of the prestigious Mayor's Award of Honor in N.Y. City. On March 9, 1982, his 70th birthday was celebrated anticipatorily by a 13-hour-long exhibit, "Wall-to-Wall John Cage and Friends."

WORKS: Sonata for Solo Clarinet (1933); *Imaginary Landscape* No. 1 for 2 Variable-speed Phonograph Turntables, Muted Piano, and Cymbal (1939); *A Valentine Out of Season* for Prepared Piano (1944); ballet, *The Seasons,* for Chamber Orch. (N.Y., May 13, 1947); *Sonata and Interludes* for Prepared Piano (1948); String Quartet (1950); Concerto for Prepared Piano and Chamber Orch. (1951); *Imaginary Landscape* No. 4 for 12 Radios, 24 Players, and Conductor (1951); *Musical Changes* for Piano, according to the Chinese book of numbers *I Ching* (1951); *Water Music* for Pianist, Radio Receiver, and Drums (1952); *4'33",* tacet piece for Piano (unplayed by David Tudor in Woodstock, N.Y., Aug. 29, 1952); *Music for Piano 4–84* for 4, 5, 6 . . . , 84 Pianists (1953–56); *Winter Music* for 1, 2, 3, 4 . . . , 20 Pianists (1957); Concerto for Piano and Orch. (N.Y., May 15, 1958); *Fontana Mix* for 10 Transparencies permutated quaquaversally in 3 or more dimensions (N.Y., April 26, 1959); *Music for Amplified Toy Pianos* (Middletown, Conn., Feb. 25, 1960); *Cartridge Music* (Cologne, Oct. 6, 1960); *Atlas Eclipticalis* for Orch. (Montreal, Aug. 3, 1961); 0'00", silent piano piece (listened to but unheard, Tokyo, Oct. 24, 1962); *Cheap Imitation* for Piano, a memorized set of Erik Satie's pieces (1969; also for 24, 25, 26 . . . , 95 Pianists); *Reunion* for Electronic Chessboard (Toronto, March 5, 1968); *Renga* with *Apartment House 1776* for 2 Synchronized Orchs. and 4 Vocalists, a bicentennial work (Boston Symph., Sept. 29, 1976); *HPSCHD* ("harpsichord minus the vowels and the r's"), a multimedia event, with Lejaren Hiller, realized for 7 Amplified Harpsichords, Tapes, Slides, and Films programmed by a Computer with 52 Projectors and 52-channeled Tapes (Urbana, Ill., May 16, 1969); *32 études australes* for Piano (1970); *Lecture on the Weather* for 12 Vocalists reading excerpts from the writings of Thoreau, accompanied by electronically realized Wind, Rain, and Thunder (1975); *Roaratorio, An Irish Circus on Finnegans Wake* for 8 Irish Musicians spaced around the audience (1980); *Dance* for 4 Orchs. and 4 Conductors (Cabrillo Festival, Aptos, Calif., Aug. 22, 1982); a work played pizzicato on 8 Cactus Plants, as part of the television program "Good Morning, Mr. Orwell" (1984).

PUBLICATIONS: *Silence* (Middletown, Conn., 1961); *A Year from Monday* (Middletown, 1967); *Notations* (N.Y., 1969); *Writings '67-'72* (Middletown, 1973); *Empty Words: Writings '63-'78* (London, 1980); *For the Birds: John Cage in Conversation with Daniel Charles* (Boston and London, 1981).

Cahier, Mme. Charles (née **Sara Jane Layton-Walker**), distinguished American contralto; b. Nashville, Jan. 8, 1870; d. Manhattan Beach, Calif., April 15, 1951. She studied in Paris with Jean de Reszke and in Vienna with Gustav Walter. She made her operatic debut in Nice (1904); married Charles Cahier on March 30, 1905. She was engaged at the Vienna Hofoper, and toured Europe and America for many years as a concert artist; later she taught at the Curtis Inst. of Music in Philadelphia. Her repertoire included Carmen, and Wagnerian contralto roles.

Cahn, Sammy, American song composer; b. New York, June 18, 1913. He played violin in variety shows and organized a dance band; in 1940 he went to Hollywood and wrote film scores. In 1955 he started a music publishing company. His tune *High Hopes* became J.F. Kennedy's campaign song in 1960. Among his film title songs were *Three Coins in the Fountain, Pocketful of Miracles,* and *Come Blow Your Horn.* He publ. *The Songwriter's Rhyming Dictionary* (N.Y.,1983).

Caix d'Hervelois, Louis de, French viola da gamba player; b. Amiens, c.1680; d. Paris, 1760. He probably studied with Sainte-Colombe and Marin Marais; was active as a musician in the court of the Duc d'Orléans. His works include 5 vols. of *Pièces de viole* (1725–52) and 2 vols. of *Pièces pour la flûte* (1726, 1731). Some of these compositions have been edited by Karl Schroeder; various arrangements of his viola da gamba pieces have been made for contemporary instruments.

Caldara, Antonio, Italian cellist and composer; b. Venice, 1670; d. Vienna, Dec. 26, 1736. He was a pupil of Legrenzi; was maestro di cappella da chiesa e dal teatro to Ferdinando Carlo in Mantua (1699–1707); from 1709 served as maestro di cappella to Prince Ruspoli in Rome; on April 1, 1716, he was appointed assistant choirmaster to J.J. Fux in Vienna. He also lived in Milan, Bologna, and Madrid. Caldara composed 90 operas and sacred dramas, 43 oratorios, about 30 masses, other church music, chamber music, etc. A selection of his church music is reprinted in Denkmäler der Tonkunst in Österreich, 26 (formerly 13.i; ed. by Mandyczewski); other vocal works (cantatas, madrigals, and canons) are in vol. 75 (formerly 39; ed. by Mandyczewski, with introduction and explanatory notes by Geiringer); *Dafne,* ed. by C. Schneider and R. John, is in vol. 91; further vocal works are reprinted in *Musique d'église des XVIIe et XVIIIe siècles* (ed. by Charles Pineau); a madrigal and 18 canons were ed. by Geiringer in *Das Chorwerk* (1933); 28 3-part instrumental canons from Caldara's *Divertimenti musicali* are in *Spielkanons* (Wolfenbüttel, 1928).

Caldwell, Sarah, remarkable American opera conductor; b. Maryville, Mo., March 6, 1924. She learned to play violin at home and appeared at local events as a child; then enrolled as a psychology student at the Univ. of Arkansas. She undertook serious violin study at the New England Cons. in Boston with Richard Burgin, concertmaster of the Boston Symph. Orch.; also studied viola with Georges Fourel. In 1947 she was engaged by Boris Goldovsky, head of the opera dept. at the New England Cons., as his assistant, which proved a valuable apprenticeship for her. In 1952 she was engaged as head of the Boston Univ. opera workshop. In 1957 she formed her own opera company in Boston, called Opera Group; this was the beginning of an extraordinary career, in which she displayed her peculiar acumen in building up an operatic enterprise with scant musical and financial resources. In 1965 she changed the name of her enterprise to Opera Co. of Boston, making use of a former vaudeville theater for her performances. In most of her productions she acts as producer, conductor, administrator, stage director, scenery designer, and publicity manager. Among her productions were *La Traviata* and *Falstaff* by Verdi, *Benvenuto Cellini* by Berlioz, *Don Quichotte* by Massenet, Bellini's *I Capuletti ed i Montecchi,* and several modern operas, among them Prokofiev's *War and Peace,* Schoenberg's *Moses and Aron,* Alban Berg's *Lulu,* Luigi Nono's *Intolleranza,* and *Montezuma* by Roger Sessions. She produced the American premieres in Boston of *The Ice Breaks* by Typpett and *The Soldiers* by Zimmermann. She was able to induce famous singers to lend their participation, among them Beverly Sills, Marilyn Horne, Tito Gobbi, Nicolai Gedda, and Placido Domingo. Because of her imposing corpulence (c.300 lbs.) she conducts performances sitting in a large armchair. Sober-minded critics heap praise on Sarah Caldwell for her musicianship, physical and mental energy, imagination, and a sort of genius for opera productions. On Jan. 13, 1976, she became the first woman to conduct at the Metropolitan Opera (in a perf. of *La Traviata*).

Calegari, Antonio, Italian composer and music theorist; b. Padua, Feb. 17, 1757; d. there, July 22, 1828. He studied with Scalabrin and Betoni in Ven-

ice; was active as a composer there and in Padua. He was a conductor at the Teatro Nuovo in Padua (c.1790–96); spent the last years of his life, from 1801, as organist at the Church of San Antonio in Padua. He brought out 3 operas in Venice: *Le Sorelle rivali* (1784), *L'amor soldato* (1786), and *Il matrimonio scoperto* (1789); the authorship of all 3 is dubious, the last perhaps attributable to Luigi Caligari. Antonio Calegari publ. a curious treatise on composition, *Gioco pittagorico musicale* (Venice, 1801), which was republ. in Paris, during his residence there, as *L'Art de composer la musique sans en connaître les éléments* (1802). A harmonic system, *Sistema armonico* (1829), and a vocal method, *Modi generali del canto* (1836), were publ. posthumously.

Callas, Maria, celebrated American soprano; b. New York, Dec. 3, 1923; d. Paris, Sept. 16, 1977. Her real name was **Maria Anna Sofia Cecilia Kalogeropoulos;** her father was a Greek immigrant. The family went back to Greece when she was 13; she studied voice at the Royal Academy of Music in Athens with the Spanish soprano Elvira de Hidalgo, and made her debut as Santuzza in the school production of *Cavalleria rusticana,* in Nov. 1938. Her first professional appearance was in a minor role in Suppé's *Boccaccio* at the Royal Opera in Athens when she was 16; her first major role, as Tosca, was there in July 1942. She went back to N.Y. in 1945; auditioned for the Metropolitan Opera Co. and was offered a contract, but decided to go to Italy, where she made her operatic debut in the title role of *La Gioconda* (Verona, Aug. 3, 1947). She was encouraged in her career by the famous conductor Tullio Serafin, who engaged her to sing Isolde and Aida at various Italian productions. In 1950 she was accepted as a member of the staff of La Scala in Milan. She was greatly handicapped by her absurdly excessive weight (210 lbs.); by a supreme effort of will she slimmed down to 135 pounds; with her classical Greek profile and penetrating eyes, she made a striking impression on the stage; in the tragic role of Medea in Cherubini's opera she mesmerized the audience by her dramatic representation of pity and terror. Some critics opined that she lacked a true bel canto quality in her voice and that her technique was defective in coloratura, but her power of interpretation was such that she was soon acknowledged to be one of the greatest dramatic singers of the century. Her personal life was as tempestuous as that of any prima donna of the bygone era. In 1949 she married the Italian industrialist Meneghini (d. Jan. 20, 1981), who became her manager, but they separated 10 years later. Her romance with the Greek shipping magnate Aristotle Onassis was a recurrent topic of sensational gossip. Given to outbursts of temper, she made newspaper headlines when she walked off the stage following some altercation, or failed to appear altogether at scheduled performances, but her eventual return to the stage was all the more eagerly welcomed by her legion of admirers. Perhaps the peak of her success was her appearance as Norma at the Metropolitan on Oct.

29, 1956; then again she quit the company as a result of disagreement with the management; but once more an accommodation was reached, and she sang Violetta (N.Y., Feb. 6, 1958); she left the company later in 1958; eventually returned to sing Tosca in 1965, after which she abandoned the stage altogether. In 1971 she gave a seminar on opera at the Juilliard School of Music, and her magic worked even in the novel capacity as instructor; her classes were enthusiastically received by the students. In 1974 she went on a concert tour with the tenor Giuseppe di Stefano; then she returned to Europe. She died suddenly of a heart attack in her Paris apartment. Her body was cremated; her ashes were scattered on the Aegean Sea. A radio commentator's characterization of Callas was that "If an orgasm could sing, it would sound like Maria Callas." Pleonastically speaking, she was an incarnation of carnality.

Callcott, John Wall, English organist and composer; b. London, Nov. 20, 1766; d. Bristol, May 15, 1821. Early in life he developed a particular talent for composing glees and catches; won 3 prize medals at a contest of the Catch Club of London (1785) for his catch *O Beauteous Fair;* a canon, *Blessed Is He;* and a glee, *Dull Repining Sons of Care.* He received his Mus.Bac. and Mus.Doc. from Oxford (1785, 1800); was a co-founder of the Glee Club (1787). During Haydn's visit to London in 1791, Callcott took a few lessons with him and wrote a symph. in imitation of his style. His mind gave way from overwork on a projected biographical dictionary of musicians, and he was institutionalized just before he reached the quirky letter Q. He recovered; but not sufficiently to continue his work, and was released in 1812. In addition to numerous glees, catches, and canons, he wrote *A Musical Grammar* (London, 1806), a standard elementary textbook that went through numerous editions in England and America. A 3-vol. collection of glees, catches, and canons, with a biographical memoir, was publ. posthumously by his son-in-law, William Horsley (London, 1824).

Callinet, François, French organ manufacturer; b. Ladoix, Bourgogne, Oct. 1, 1754; d. Rouffach, Alsace, May 21, 1820. He was apprenticed to K. Riepp in Dijon, and later worked with Joseph Rabiny, with whom he became associated in organ building in 1786. His 2 sons, **Joseph** and **Claude-Ignace,** and the latter's son **Louis-François** carried on the family trade; **Louis Callinet,** a nephew of the founder of the firm, joined Daublaine & Co., and continued organ manufacture.

Callinet, Louis, French organ manufacturer; b. Weiler Ladoix, Bourgogne, April 19, 1786; d. Paris, Aug. 1, 1845. He was a nephew of **François Callinet.** He entered the partnership with Daublaine, who attended to the commercial interests of the firm known as Daublaine & Callinet, but broke with him and destroyed all the instruments that he had built.

Calloway, Cab, black American jazz singer; b. Rochester, N.Y., Dec. 25, 1907. He became a propo-

nent of scat singing, characterized by nonsense syllabization and rapid glossolalia with the melodic line largely submerged under an asymmetric inundation of rhythmic heterophony. He led bands and appeared in the movies; also compiled *Hepster's Dictionary,* listing jazz terms (1938), and publ. an informal autobiography, *Of Minnie the Moocher and Me* (N.Y., 1976).

Calvé, Emma, famous French soprano; b. Décazeville (Aveyron), Aug. 15, 1858; d. Millau, Jan. 6, 1942. She studied voice with Puget in Paris and with Marchesi and Laborde; made her operatic debut as Marguerite in Gounod's *Faust* at the Théâtre de la Monnaie in Brussels, on Sept. 23, 1881; then sang at the Opéra-Comique in Paris 3 years later. She sang at La Scala in 1887. In 1892 she appeared at Covent Garden in London. She made her American debut at the Metropolitan Opera House on Nov. 29, 1893, and remained on its staff until 1904; her greatest role was that of Carmen. Subsequently she made sporadic, but successful, appearances in Europe and America; after 1910 she sang mainly in recitals. Calvé's biography was publ. in 1902 (A. Gallus, *Emma Calvé, Her Artistic Life*), and so great was the aura of her successes that her life was made the subject of a novel by Gustav Kobbé, *Signora, A Child of the Opera House* (N.Y., 1903). She publ. an autobiography, in Eng., *My Life* (N.Y., 1922); toward the end of her life she publ. an additional vol. of memoirs, *Sous tous les ciels j'ai chanté* (Paris, 1940). Forty of her letters, along with an extended biographical sketch, appear in A. Lebois, "Hommages à Emma Calvé (1858–1942)," *Annales, Faculté des Lettres de Toulouse* (Sept. 1967).

Calvisius, Sethus (real name, **Seth Kallwitz**), theorist; son of a poor peasant at Gorsleben, Thuringia; b. Feb. 21, 1556; d. Leipzig, Nov. 24, 1615. He supported himself while studying in the Gymnasia of Frankenhausen and Magdeburg, and the univs. at Helmstadt and Leipzig. In Leipzig he became music director at the Paulinerkirche (1581); from 1582–92 he was cantor at Schulpforta, then cantor of the Thomasschule at Leipzig, and in 1594 became music director at the Thomaskirche and Nicolaikirche there. Calvisius was not only a musician, but a scholar of high attainments. His writings are valuable sources: *Melopoeia seu melodiae condendae ratio* (1582; 2nd ed., 1592); *Compendium musicae practicae pro incipientibus* (1594; 3rd ed. as *Musicae artis praecepta nova et facillima,* 1612); *Harmoniae cantionum ecclesiasticarum a M. Luthero et aliis viris piis Germaniae compositarum 4 voc.* (1596); *Exercitationes musicae duae* (1600); *Auserlesene teutsche Lieder* (1603); *Exercitatio musicae tertia* (1611); *Biciniorum libri duo* (1612).

Calvocoressi, Michel Dimitri, eminent writer on music; b. (of Greek parents) Marseilles, Oct. 2, 1877; d. London, Feb. 1, 1944. He studied music in Paris, but was mostly autodidact; also pursued the social sciences. In 1914 he settled in London. He wrote music criticism and correspondences for French and other journals. He mastered the Russian language and became an ardent propagandist of Russian music; made excellent translations into English and French of Russian and German songs. Among his books are *La Musique russe* (Paris, 1907); *The Principles and Methods of Musical Criticism* (London, 1923; revised 1933); *Musical Taste and How to Form It* (London, 1925); *Musicians' Gallery: Music and Ballet in Paris and London* (London, 1933); also monographs on Liszt (Paris, 1906), Mussorgsky (Paris, 1908), Glinka (Paris, 1911), Schumann (Paris, 1912), Debussy (London, 1941); a new extensive biography of Mussorgsky was posthumously publ. (London, 1946). With Gerald Abraham he publ. the valuable *Masters of Russian Music* (London, 1936).

Calzabigi, Ranieri di, Italian poet and music theorist; b. Livorno, Dec. 23, 1714; d. Naples, July 1795. In 1750 he went to Paris, proceeded to Brussels in 1760; from 1761 until 1772 he remained in Vienna, and was in Pisa by 1775. He engaged in polemics regarding the relative merits of French and Italian operas; lent energetic support to Gluck in his ideas of operatic reform. He wrote for Gluck the libretti of *Orfeo, Alceste,* and *Paride ed Elena.* In 1780 he returned to Italy. He publ. *Dissertazione su le poesie drammatiche del Sig. Abate Pietro Metastasio* (1755), a controversial work concerning Metastasio and Hasse.

Cambert, Robert, the first French opera composer, preceding Lully; b. Paris, c.1628; d. London, 1677. He was a pupil of Chambonnières. His first venture on the lyric stage was *La Pastorale,* written by Perrin and successfully produced at the Château d'Issy in 1659; it was followed by *Ariane, ou Le Mariage de Bacchus* (rehearsed in 1661) and *Adonis* (1662; not perf.; MS lost). In 1669 Perrin received letters patent for establishing the Académie Royale de Musique (the national operatic theater, now the Grand Opéra); he brought out, in collaboration with Cambert, the opera *Pomone* (1671); another opera, *Les Peines et les plaisirs de l'amour,* was written, and produced in Paris in March 1671, before Lully secured the patent. In 1673, Cambert's disappointment drove him to London, where he became a bandmaster.

Cameron, Basil, English conductor; b. Reading, Aug. 18, 1884; d. Leominster, June 26, 1975. He studied music in York with Tertius Noble; then at the Berlin Hochschule für Musik, 1902–6; also took a course in composition with Max Bruch. Returning to England, he sought to obtain a conducting position by Germanizing his name as **Basil Hindenberg,** seeing that German conductors dominated the field in England, but changed it back to his real name when England went to war with Germany in 1914. He served in the British army and was wounded in action in 1918. He conducted the Hastings Municipal Orch. (1923–30); then was guest conductor of the San Francisco Symph. Orch.; from 1932 to 1938 he was conductor of the Seattle Symph. Orch.; during

his tenure he played many new works by modern composers. He belonged to the category of "objective" conductors more interested in the music itself than in his individual communication, an attitude that in the end hampered his American success. He filled in a few engagements in Europe and eventually returned to London, where he was made a Commander of the Order of the British Empire in 1957.

Campagnoli, Bartolommeo, renowned Italian violinist; b. Cento di Ferrara, Sept. 10, 1751; d. Neustrelitz, Germany, Nov. 6, 1827. He studied in Bologna with Dall'Occa and in Florence with Nardini; for several years gave concerts in Italy; became music director to the Duke of Kurland in Dresden (1779–97); then was concertmaster at the Gewandhaus in Leipzig (1797–1818). He made several successful concert tours while in his service; from 1797–1818 was active as a violinist in Leipzig. He composed 41 *Capricci per l'alto viola* (revised by E. Kreuz and A. Consolini as *Caprices pour le viola,* 1922); a Violin Concerto; études for violin; chamber music. He was the author of several pedagogic manuals for the violin: *Nouvelle méthode de la mécanique progressive du jeu de violon* (1791; in Eng., 1856), and *Metodo per violino* (1797; his chief work; publ. and reprinted in all European languages).

Campanari, Giuseppe, Italian dramatic baritone, brother of **Leandro Campanari;** b. Venice, Nov. 17, 1855; d. Milan, May 31, 1927. He began his career as a cellist; played in the orch. of La Scala, and started to study singing; went to the U.S. in 1884, and played cello in the Boston Symph. Orch. until 1893, when he joined Hinrich's Opera Co. in N.Y. as a baritone; made his debut (June 15, 1893) as Tonio in *Pagliacci;* after several years at the Metropolitan Opera he devoted himself to concert work and teaching.

Campanari, Leandro, Italian violinist and conductor, brother of **Giuseppe Campanari;** b. Rovigo, Oct. 20, 1857; d. San Francisco, April 22, 1939. He studied in Padua; attended the Milan Cons., graduating in 1877; after a tour of Europe, he came to the U.S. in 1881 and settled in Boston, where he organized the Campanari String Quartet. He became a proficient conductor and was in charge of the Grand Orch. Concerts at La Scala in Milan from 1897 till 1905. In Feb. 1907 he was engaged to complete the season of the Philadelphia Orch. after the sudden illness of the regular conductor, Fritz Scheel. Campanari failed to impress the orch. or the audience, and was not reengaged.

Campanini, Cleofonte, eminent Italian-American operatic conductor, brother of the famous tenor **Italo Campanini;** b. Parma, Sept. 1, 1860; d. Chicago, Dec. 19, 1919. He studied violin at the Parma Cons. and later at the Cons. of Milan; made his conducting debut with *Carmen* at Parma (1882); conducted the first American performance of *Otello* at the N.Y. Academy of Music (April 16, 1888) while his brother, Italo, was impresario. Between 1888 and 1906, he conducted in Italy, in England, and in South America. A larger field opened to him in 1906, when Hammerstein engaged him for the new Manhattan Opera House in N.Y. Differences with Hammerstein led him to resign in 1909. In the following year he was engaged as principal conductor of the newly formed Chicago Opera Co.; in 1913 he was appointed general director, which post he held until his death. Among opera conductors he occupied a place in the first rank; he seemed to be equally at home in all styles of music. He introduced many new operas in the U.S., among them Massenet's *Hérodiade*, Debussy's *Pelléas et Mélisande*, Charpentier's *Louise*, Wolf-Ferrari's *Il Segreto di Susanna*, etc. On May 15, 1887, he married, in Florence, **Eva Tetrazzini** (sister of **Luisa Tetrazzini**).

Campanini, Italo, famous Italian tenor, brother of **Cleofonte Campanini**; b. Parma, June 30, 1845; d. Corcagno, near Parma, Nov. 22, 1896. In his early years he was an apprentice in his father's blacksmith shop; joined Garibaldi's army and was wounded in the Italian struggle for unification. Subsequently, he studied with Griffini and Lamperti; appeared at Bologna in *Lohengrin* (Nov. 1, 1871), which started him on the road to fame. He made his London debut as Gennaro in *Lucrezia Borgia* (May 4, 1872), and his American debut, also as Gennaro, at the N.Y. Academy of Music (Oct. 1, 1873). He appeared in *Faust* at the opening of the Metropolitan Opera (Oct. 22, 1883); was on its roster until 1894; was briefly active as an impresario; brought over his brother Cleofonte Campanini to conduct the American premiere of Verdi's *Otello* at the N.Y. Academy of Music (April 16, 1888).

Campenhout, François van, Belgian composer, author of the Belgian national anthem; b. Brussels, Feb. 5, 1779; d. there, April 24, 1848. Beginning as violinist in the Théâtre de la Monnaie, he studied singing under Plantade, and became a fine stage tenor, appearing in Belgium, Holland, and France. He wrote 6 operas, 9 cantatas, etc. He is, however, chiefly remembered as the composer of *La Brabançonne*, which was written during the revolution of 1830, and eventually became the national anthem of Belgium.

Campion (Campian), Thomas, English physician, also poet, composer, and dramatist; b. London, Feb. 12, 1567; d. there, March 1, 1620. He studied at Cambridge from 1581–84, residing at Peterhouse; entered Gray's Inn on April 27, 1586. He received his M.D. degree from the Univ. of Caen in France on Feb. 10, 1605. He was first called a "Doctor of Physick" in an English publication in Barnabe Barnes's *Four Books of Offices* in 1606; earlier evidence of his having studied medical science is an oblique reference of Philip Rosseter in 1601, speaking of Campion's poetry and music as "the superfluous blossoms of his deeper studies." Campion was primarily a lyric poet; his music was to enhance the beauty of the poetry by supplying unobtrusive and simple harmonies; in this he differed from such contemporaries as John Dowland, who contrived elaborate lute accompaniments.

WORKS: 3 songs (1596); *A Booke of Ayres, Set Foorth to be sung to the Lute Orpherian, and Base Violl* (1601; consists of 2 separate books, one by Campion and one by Rosseter; Campion wrote both the words and the music for his half of the work); *First and Second Books of Airs* (1613?); *Third and Fourth Books of Airs* (1617?); songs for masques at the marriages of Sir James Hay (1607), Princess Elizabeth (1613), and Robert, Earl of Somerset (1613); songs for a masque at Caversham House (1613); *Songs of Mourning* (for Prince Henry; 1613; words by Campion, music by John Coperario); *A New Way for Making Foure Parts in Counterpoint* (1618; also in Playford's *Introduction to the Skill of Musick*, with additions by Christopher Simpson, 1655 and following years). Campion also publ. *Poemata*, a vol. of Latin epigrams and elegiacs (1595; reprinted 1619), *Observations on the Art of English Poesie* (1602; condemns "the vulgar and unartificial custom of riming"), etc. The 4 books of airs and the songs from Rosseter's *Booke of Ayres* are reprinted in E.H. Fellowes, *English School of Lutenist Song-Writers*.

Campioni, Carlo Antonio, French-born Italian composer; b. Lunéville, Nov. 16, 1720; d. Florence, April 12, 1788. He went to Florence in 1763, and was active there as a composer of church music and maestro di cappella to the ducal court at the Cathedral of S. Maria del Fiore, and in the oratory of S. Giovanni Battista. He also publ. instrumental works among them 6 sonatas for 2 violins, which were fraudulently issued in Amsterdam as the works of Haydn, and were reprinted still under Haydn's name in Mainz in 1953. The very fact that these pieces could pass as Haydn's for 2 centuries obliquely testifies to Campioni as a highly competent composer.

Campra, André, historically important French opera composer; b. Aix (Provence), Dec. 4, 1660; d. Versailles, June 14, 1744. He studied with Guillaume Poitevin; then embraced an ecclesiastical vocation; was made chaplain at Aix on May 27, 1681; served as maître de musique at St. Etienne in Toulouse from 1683–94, and at Notre Dame from 1694–1700; then became conductor at the Paris Opéra. In 1723 he received a court appointment as sous-maître with Bernier and Gervais. His operas had numerous performances in Paris.

WORKS: (all produced in Paris): *L'Europe galante,* opéra-ballet (Oct. 24, 1697); *Le Carnaval de Venise,* ballet (Jan. 20, 1699; Act 3 includes the Italian opera *Orfeo nell' inferni*); *Hésione,* tragédie lyrique (Dec. 20, 1700); *Aréthuse, ou La Vengeance de l'Amour,* tragédie lyrique (July 14, 1701); *Tancrède,* tragédie lyrique (Nov. 7, 1702); *Les Muses,* opéra-ballet (Oct. 28, 1703); *Iphigénie en Tauride,* tragédie lyrique based on the unfinished work of Desmarets (May 6, 1704); *Télémaque,* extracts from operas by Campra et al. (Nov. 11, 1704); *Alcine,* tragédie lyrique (Jan 15, 1705); *Hippodamie,* tragédie lyrique (March 6, 1708); *Les Fêtes vénitiennes,* opéra-ballet (June 17, 1710); *Idoménée,* tragédie lyrique (Jan. 12, 1712); *Les Amours de Vénus et de Mars,* ballet (Sept. 6, 1712); *Téléphe,* tragédie lyrique (Nov. 28, 1713); *Camille, Reine des volsques,* tragédie lyrique (Nov. 9, 1717); *Ballet représenté à Lion devant M. le marquis d'Harlincourt,* ballet (Lyon, May 17, 1718; not extant); *Les Ages,* opéra-ballet (Oct. 9, 1718); *Achille et Deidamie,* tragédie lyrique (Feb. 24, 1735); several divertissements (most of them not extant); 3 books of *Cantates françoises* (1708, 1714, 1728); 5 books of motets (1695–1720); Mass (1700); 2 books of Psalms (1737–38).

Canal, Marguerite, French composer; b. Toulouse, Jan. 29, 1890; d. there, Jan. 27, 1978. She studied at the Paris Cons. with Paul Vidal; in 1920 won the Grand Prix de Rome for her symph. scene *Don Juan.* In 1919 she was appointed to the faculty of the Paris Cons. Her works include a Violin Sonata (1922); *Spleen* for Cello and Chamber Ensemble (1926); several piano pieces; about 100 songs.

Cannabich, Christian, German composer, violinist, and conductor; b. Mannheim, Dec. 28, 1731; d. Frankfurt, Jan. 20, 1798. He studied with Johann Stamitz in Mannheim; became a violinist in the Mannheim Orch. (1746); was sent by the Elector to Rome, where he studied with Jommelli (1750–53); he returned to Mannheim and, after Stamitz's death (1757), became first violinist of the orch.; in 1774 was director of the instrumental music; in 1778 he moved to Munich. Cannabich is usually credited with bringing the Mannheim Orch. to a degree of perfection theretofore never attained, particularly in the carefully graduated crescendo and diminuendo. He was also a prolific composer.

Cantelli, Guido, brilliant Italian conductor; b. Novara, April 27, 1920; d. in an airplane crash at Orly, near Paris, Nov. 24, 1956. He played in his father's military band as a boy; studied piano at the Cons. of Milan. After Italy withdrew from the war in 1943 he, among others, was sent to a German concentration camp in Stettin. After the end of the war he conducted opera at La Scala in Milan. By invitation of Toscanini, he was engaged to conduct the NBC Symph. Orch. in N.Y., making his debut on January 15, 1949, and producing an immediate impression of great excellence. Possessing an extraordinary memory, he conducted both rehearsals and performances of operatic and symph. works without score. He lost his life flying to America to conduct a series of concerts with the N.Y. Phil.

Canteloube (de Malaret), (Marie-) Joseph, French pianist, composer, and writer on music; b. Annonay, near Tournon, Oct. 21, 1879; d. Gridny (Seine-et-Oise), Nov. 4, 1957. His name was simply Canteloube, but he added "de Malaret" after the name of his ancestral estate. He studied piano in Paris with Amélie Doetzer, a pupil of Chopin, and composition with Vincent d'Indy at the Schola Cantorum. He became an ardent collector of French folk songs and arranged and publ. many of them for voice with instrumental accompaniment. His *Chants d'Auvergne* (4 sets for Voice, with Piano or Orch., 1923–30) are frequently heard. Among his other albums, *Anthologie des chants populaires français* (4 sets, 1939–44) is a comprehensive collection of regional folk songs.

WORKS: 2 operas: *Le Mas* (1910–13; Paris Opéra, April 3, 1929) and *Vercingetorix* (1930–32; Paris Opéra, June 26, 1933); symph. poem, *Vers la princesse lointaine* (1910–11); 3 symph. sketches: *Lauriers* (Paris, Feb. 22, 1931); *Pièces françaises* for Piano and Orch. (1935); *Poème* for Violin and Orch. (1937); *Rustiques* for Oboe, Clarinet, and Bassoon (1946). He also publ. a biography of Vincent d'Indy (Paris, 1949).

Capet, Lucien, distinguished French violinist; b. Paris, Jan. 8, 1873; d. there, Dec. 18, 1928. He studied at the Paris Cons.; in 1896–99 was concertmaster of the Lamoureux Orch.; from 1899 to 1903 taught violin at the Cons. of Ste. Cécile in Bordeaux. In 1904 he founded the celebrated Capet Quartet, and played first violin in it until 1921, specializing particularly in the later Beethoven quartets. In 1924 he was appointed director of the Institut de Violon in Paris. He composed *Le Rouet,* symph. poem; *Prélude religieux* for Orch.; *Devant la mer* for Voice and Orch.; *Poème* for Violin and Orch.; 5 string quartets; 2 violin sonatas; 6 violin études. He publ. *La Technique supérieure de l'archet* (Paris, 1916); *Les 17 Quatuors de Beethoven;* also a philosophical work, *Espérances.*

Caplet, André, French composer; b. Le Havre, Nov. 23, 1878; d. Paris, April 22, 1925. He studied violin in Le Havre, and played in theater orchs. there and in Paris; entered the Paris Cons. (1896), where he studied with Leroux and Lenepveu; in 1901 received the Grand Prix de Rome for his cantata *Myrrha.* His *Marche solennelle* for the centennial of the Villa Medicis was performed in Rome (April 18, 1903). He was active in France as a choral and operatic conductor; conducted the first performance of Debussy's *Le Martyre de St. Sebastien* (Paris, May 22, 1911); also conducted opera in the U.S. with the Boston Opera Co. (1910–14) and in London at Covent Garden (1912). He served in the French army during World War I; later continued his musical activities. Caplet's music is unequivocally impressionistic, with a lavish use of wholetone scales and parallel chord formations; he combined this impressionism with neo-archaic usages and mystic programmatic ideas.

WORKS: Oratorio, *Miroir de Jésus* (Paris, May 1, 1924); *Prières* for Voice and Chamber Orch.; *The Masque of the Red Death,* after Poe, for Harp and Orch. (Paris, March 7, 1909; later arranged for Harp and String Quartet and retitled *Conte fantastique;* perf. Paris, Dec. 18, 1923); *Epiphanie* for Cello and Orch. (Paris, Dec. 29, 1923); Double Wind Quintet (Paris, March 9, 1901); *Messe des petits de St. Eustache* (Paris, June 13, 1922); Sonata for Voice, Cello, and Piano; Septet for Strings and 3 Female Voices;

Suite persane for Woodwind Instruments; piano duets; piano pieces; minor choral works and songs. He left unfinished a *Sonata da chiesa* for Violin and Organ (1924) and *Hommage à Ste. Cathérine de Sienna* for Organ and Orch. He was a close friend of Debussy; recent discoveries show that he collaborated with Debussy on several of his orch. works and even completed sections left unfinished by Debussy. His correspondence with Debussy was publ. in Monaco in 1957.

Capocci, Gaetano, Italian organist, composer, and teacher; b. Rome, Oct. 16, 1811; d. there, Jan. 11, 1898. He studied music with Valentino Fioravanti and organ with Sante Pascoli; at the same time he took courses in theology. In 1830 he was appointed organist and music director at the Church of S. Maria in Rome; was then organist at S. Maria Maggiore (from 1839) and at S. Giovanni in Laterano (from 1855). He had numerous students, among them Margherita of Savoy, the future Queen of Italy. His chief merit as a composer was a successful revival of the Classical oratorio. He wrote the oratorios *Il Battista* (Rome, March 31, 1833) and *Assalonne* (Rome, Dec. 8, 1842); numerous sacred choruses and organ pieces.

Carafa de Colobrano, Michele Enrico, prolific composer of operas; b. Naples, Nov. 17, 1787; d. Paris, July 26, 1872. He was a son of Prince Colobrano, Duke of Alvito; began to study music at an early age. Though he became an officer in the army of Naples, and fought in Napoleon's Russian campaign, he devoted his leisure time to music, and after Waterloo adopted it as a profession. In 1827 he settled in Paris; succeeded Lesueur as a member of the Academy (1837); in 1840 was appointed a prof. of composition at the Paris Cons.
  WORKS: Operas: *Gabriella di Vergy* (Naples, July 3, 1816); *Ifigenia in Tauride* (Naples, June 19, 1817); *Berenice in Siria* (Naples, July 29, 1818); *Elisabetta in Derbyshire* (Venice, Dec. 26, 1818); the following operas were produced at the Opéra-Comique in Paris: *Jeanne d'Arc* (March 10, 1821); *Le Solitaire* (Aug. 17, 1822); *Le Valet de chambre* (Sept. 16, 1823); *L'Auberge supposée* (April 26, 1824); *Sangarido* (May 19, 1827); *Masaniello* (Dec. 27, 1827; on the same subject as Auber's *La Muette de Portici*, staged at the Paris Opéra 2 months later; yet Carafa's *Masaniello* held the stage in competition with Auber's famous opera for 136 nights); *La Violette* (Oct. 7, 1828); *Jenny* (Sept. 26, 1829); *Le Livre de l'ermite* (Aug. 11, 1831); *La Prison d'Edimbourg* (July 20, 1833); *Une Journée de la Fronde* (Nov. 7, 1833); *La Grande Duchesse* (Nov. 16, 1835); *Thérèse* (Sept. 26, 1838). He also composed ballets, cantatas, and much church music.

Cardew, Cornelius, English composer of extreme avante garde tendencies; b. Winchcombe, Gloucester, May 7, 1936; d. in a road accident, London, Dec. 13, 1981. He sang in the chorus at Canterbury Cathedral until puberty; then studied composition with Howard Ferguson at the Royal Academy of Music in London (1953–57); in 1957 he went to Cologne and worked at the electronic studio there as an assistant to Karlheinz Stockhausen (1958–60). Returning to England, he organized concerts of experimental music; in 1963–65 he was in Italy, where he had some private lessons with Goffredo Petrassi in Rome. In 1967 he was appointed to the faculty of the Royal Academy of Music in London. In 1969, together with Michael Parsons and Howard Skempton, he organized the Scratch Orchestra, a heterogeneous group for performances of new music, militantly latitudinarian and disestablishmentarian. Under the influence of the teachings of Mao Zedong, Cardew renounced his modernistic past as a bourgeois deviation detrimental to pure Marxism, and subsequently attacked his former associate, Stockhausen, in a book ominously entitled *Stockhausen Serves Imperialism* (London, 1974). He also repudiated his own magnum opus, *The Great Learning,* which was originally performed at the 1968 Cheltenham Festival, scored for a non-singing chorus to the words of Ezra Pound's translation of Confucius, a chorus which was admonished to bang on tapped stones, to whistle and shriek, but never to stoop to vocalizing. In the revised version of the work he appended to the title the slogan "Apply Marxism–Leninism–Mao Zedong Thought in a living way to the problems of the present." This version was first performed by the Scratch Orch. in the Promenade Concert in London on Aug. 24, 1972. His other works include *Volo Solo* for any handy musical instrument (1965); *3 Winter Potatoes* for piano and various assorted concrete sounds, as well as for newspapers, balloons, noise, and people working (Focus Opera Groups, London, March 11, 1968). He also publ. several pamphlets containing some confusing confutations of Confucius. In addition, he compiled a seminal manual, *Scratch Music* (London, 1970).

Cardus, Sir Neville, British writer on music and cricket; b. Manchester, April 2, 1889; d. London, Feb. 28, 1975. He studied singing, then turned to journalism; became an active contributor to the *Manchester Guardian;* wrote essays on numerous subjects, but primarily on cricket and music. He was cricket coach at Shrewsbury School (1912–16); in 1917 joined the staff of the *Manchester Guardian;* became its chief music critic (1927–39); from 1939–47 he was in Australia, writing on cricket and music for the *Syney Morning Herald.* Returning to London, he became music critic for the *Manchester Guardian* in 1951. He received the Wagner Medal of the City of Bayreuth in 1963; was knighted in 1967. His literary style is quasi-Shavian in its colloquial manner and stubborn persuasion.
  WRITINGS: *A Cricketer's Book* (1921); *Autobiography* (1947); *Second Innings: More Autobiography* (1950); *Cricket All the Year* (1952); *A Composer's Eleven* (1958); *Sir Thomas Beecham: A Portrait* (1961); *The Playfair Cardus* (1963); *Gustav Mahler: His Mind and His Music,* Vol. I (1965); *The Delights of Music* (1966); *Full Score* (1970); R. Daniels, ed., *Conversations with Cardus* (London, 1976).

Carey, Henry, English writer for the theater; b. probably in Yorkshire, c.1687; d. (suicide) London, Oct. 5, 1743. He was a natural son of Henry Savile, Lord Eland; studied music with Linnert, Roseingrave, and Geminiani; settled c.1710 in London, where he was active as a poet, librettist, playwright, and composer; wrote 6 ballad-operas, of which *The Contrivances* (Drury Lane, London, June 20, 1729) achieved the greatest success. He wrote the words of the popular song *Sally in Our Alley* and composed a musical setting for it, but his setting was replaced in 1790 by the tune *What though I am a Country Lass,* which has since been traditionally sung to Carey's original poem; also popular was his intermezzo with singing, *Nancy, or The Parting Lovers* (1739). He publ. a collection of 100 ballads, *The Musical Century* (2 vols., 1737 and 1740); also *6 Cantatas* (1732) and *3 Burlesque Cantatas* (1741). Carey's claim to the authorship of *God Save the King* was put forth by his son, George Savile Carey (1743–1807), more than 50 years after his father's death, without any supporting evidence; many anthologies still list Carey's name as the author of the British national anthem. For a complete account of this misattribution of the tune, see P.A. Scholes, *God Save the Queen!* (London, 1954; Appendix I; pp. 284–88). Further discussion of the authorship of the anthem is to be found in W.H. Cummings, *"God Save the King," The Origin and History of the Music and Words* (London, 1902); O.G. Sonneck, *Report on the Star-Spangled Banner* (1909); F.S. Boas and J.E. Borland, *The National Anthem* (London, 1916); J.A. Fuller-Maitland, "Facts and Fictions about *God Save the King," Musical Quarterly* (Oct. 1916); E.A. Maginty, "*America:* The Origin of Its Melody," *Musical Quarterly* (July 1934).

Carissimi, Giacomo, Italian composer of sacred music; b. Marino, near Rome (baptized, April 18, 1605); d. Rome, Jan. 12, 1674. In 1625–27 he was organist at the Cathedral of Tivoli; from 1628 to his death, maestro di cappella in the Church of S. Apollinare in Rome; he also served as maestro di cappella of the Collegio Germanico in Rome. A prolific and original composer, he broke with the Palestrina tradition, devoting himself to perfecting the monodic style, as is evidenced by his highly developed recitative and more pleasing and varied instrumental accompaniments. His MSS were dispersed at the sale of the library of the Collegio Germanico, and many are lost, but a few printed works are still extant. There were publ. the 4 oratorios *Jephte* (his masterpiece), *Judicium Salomonis, Jonas, Balthazar;* 2 collections of motets *a* 2, 3, and 4 (Rome, 1664, 1667); masses *a* 5 and 9 (Cologne, 1663, 1667); *Arie de camera* (1667); and separate pieces in several collections. The finest collection of his works is that made by Dr. Aldrich at Christ-Church College, Oxford. Carissimi also wrote a treatise, publ. only in German: *Ars cantandi, etc.* (Augsburg; 2nd ed., 1692; 3rd ed., 1696; another ed., 1718). F. Chrysander publ. 4 oratorios (*Jephte, Judicium Salomonis, Balthazar, Jonas*) in Denkmäler der Tonkunst 2; *Jonas, Judicium Salomonis* and *Jephte* were also publ. in

I Classici della Musica Italiana, No. 5 (Milan, 1919); vocal duets are reprinted in L. Landshoff's *Alte Meister des Bel canto* (1927); a motet was publ. in *Musique d'Eglise des XVIIᵉ et XVIIIᵉ siècles,* ed. by Ch. Pineau; *6 Solo Cantatas,* ed. with commentary by G. Rose (London, 1969). The complete works are being publ. by the Istituto Italiano per la Storia della Musica (1951—). Claudio Sartori has compiled *Carissimi, Catalogo delle opere attribuite* (1975).

Carlos, Wendy (née **Walter**), transsexual American organist, composer, and electronics virtuoso; b. Pawtucket, R.I., Nov. 14, 1939. He played piano as a child; then studied music and physics at Brown Univ. and at Columbia Univ., where he took courses with Vladimir Ussachevsky. At the same time he began working with the electronic engineer Robert Moog in perfecting the Moog Synthesizer. The result of their experiments with versified tone-colors was a record album under the title "Switched-on-Bach," which became unexpectedly successful, especially among the wide-eyed, susceptible American youth, selling some million copies. This was followed in 1969 by "The Well-Tempered Synthesizer," engineered entirely by Carlos. In 1971 Carlos composed and synthesized the sound track for the film *A Clockwork Orange,* based on the futuristic novel by Anthony Burgess. Then, at the age of 32, he suddenly became aware of his sexual duality, a woman's psyche imprisoned in a man's body. To remedy this sundering nature, he underwent a transsexual operation with his penis being everted to create a fairly respectable and conceivably receptive vagina; on St. Valentine's Day, Feb. 14, 1979, he officially changed his first name Walter to Wendy. She/he described his sexual tergiversation in a candid interview in *Playboy* (May 1979), illustrated with photographs "before and after."

Carlstedt, Jan, Swedish composer; b. Orsa, June 15, 1926. He studied composition with Lars-Erik Larsson at the Royal Academy of Music in Stockholm (1948–52), and later in England (1952–53) and Italy (1954–55). Returning to Stockholm, he became active in furthering the cause of modern music; was a founder of the Society of Contemporary Music in Stockholm (1960).
WORKS: 4 string quartets (1951–52, 1966, 1967, 1972); 2 symphs.: No. 1 (1952–54; revised 1960; Stockholm, Oct. 4, 1961); No. 2, in memory of Martin Luther King (1968; N.Y., Dec. 20, 1970); String Trio (1955–56); Sonata for String Orch. (1956); Sonata for 2 Violins (1956); *12 Miniatures* for Violin, Clarinet, and Cello (1958); 8 Duets for 2 Violins (1958); Sinfonietta for Wind Quintet (1959); Sonata for Solo Violin (1959); *Ballata* for Solo Cello (1960); Divertimento for Oboe and String Trio (1962); Wind Quintet (1962); *Pentastomos* for Wind Quintet (1972–73).

Carmichael, Hoagy, American jazz pianist and composer of popular music; b. Bloomington, Ind., Nov. 22, 1899; d. Rancho Mirage, near Palm Springs, Calif., Dec. 27, 1981. His ambition as a youth was to become a lawyer, and in fact, he graduated from the

Indiana Univ. Law School, and played the piano only for relaxation. In 1929 he went to Hollywood but failed to obtain work as a musician. Working on his own, he organized a swing band and composed songs for it. Although unable to write music professionally, he revealed a natural gift for melody, and soon made a success with such songs as *Riverboat Shuffle* and *Washboard Blues.* He made a hit with his song *Stardust,* which became the foundation of his fame and fortune. Among his other popular tunes were *Ivy, I Get Along without You Very Well, Heart and Soul,* and *In the Cool, Cool, Cool of the Evening,* which won the Academy Award as the best movie song for 1951.

Carneyro, Claudio, Portuguese composer; b. Oporto, Jan. 27, 1895; d. there, Oct. 18, 1963. He studied composition with Lucien Lambert at the Oporto Cons. and later in Paris with Widor (1919–22) and Paul Dukas (1934); taught composition at the Oporto Cons. (1922–58); was its director in 1955–58. In his music, he made ample use of authentic Portuguese motives, adorning them by sonorous impressionistic harmonies.

Carnicer, Ramón, Spanish composer; b. Tárrega, near Lérida, Oct. 24, 1789; d. Madrid, March 17, 1855. He studied in Barcelona with Francisco Queralt and Carlos Baguer; from 1818–20 conducted the Coliseo Theater orch. in Barcelona; in 1828–30 was conductor of the Royal Opera in Madrid; in 1830–54, was a prof. of composition at the Madrid Cons. One of the creators of Spanish national opera (the zarzuela), he composed 10 operas, wrote much church music, many symphs., Spanish songs, etc.; also *Dulce Patria,* the national hymn of Chile.

Carol-Bérard, French composer and theorist; b. Marseilles, April 5, 1881; d. Paris, Dec. 13, 1942. He studied with Albéniz in Barcelona; then settled in Paris. His music, impressionistic with an oriental flavor, remains largely unpubl. He evolved a theory of "chromophonie" (color in movement) and wrote several papers on the subject in *La Revue Musicale* and other publications. He also wrote poetry under the pseudonym **Olivier Realtor.**

Carolan, Turlough, Irish song composer; b. near Nobber, County Meath, 1670; d. near Kilronan, March 25, 1738. He was an itinerant harper, and improvised Irish verses and tunes; these were publ. in various 18th-century collections of Irish music; the number of his original tunes is about 220. He is also known under the name **O'Carolan.**

Caron, Philippe, famous Burgundian contrapuntist of the 15th century, a pupil of Binchois or Dufay. O.J. Gombosi, in his monograph *Jacob Obrecht, Eine stilkritische Studie* (Leipzig, 1925), groups Caron with composers of the Cambrai school interested in continuing Dufay's style; this work also contains a reprint of a 3-part chanson, *Vive Carloys,* MSS of which are in libraries at Rome and Flor-

ence. Other extant works include 4 masses *a* 4 in the Papal Chapel and a MS of 3- and 4-part chansons at Paris. Petrucci publ. a 5-part chanson, *Hélas que pourra deuenir,* in his *Odhecaton* (1501). The Inst. of Medieval Music (Brooklyn, N.Y.) began issuing the complete works in 1971.

Caron, Rose (née **Meuniez**), French dramatic soprano; b. Monerville, Nov. 17, 1857; d. Paris, April 9, 1930. She entered the Paris Cons. in 1880, leaving in 1882 to study with Marie Sasse in Brussels, where her debut was made as Alice in *Robert le Diable* (1884). She sang for 2 years at the Paris Opéra, and again in Brussels, creating Lorance (in *Jocelyn*), Richilde, and Salammbô (1890); in 1890 she returned to the Paris Opéra, where she sang Sieglinde (1893) and Desdemona (1894) in the first performances of *Die Walküre* and *Otello* in France; in 1898 she sang Fidelio at the Opéra-Comique. From 1900 she appeared almost exclusively on the concert stage; in 1902 she was appointed a prof. of singing at the Paris Cons.

Carpenter, John Alden, American composer; b. Park Ridge, Chicago, Feb. 28, 1876; d. Chicago, April 26, 1951. He received his B.A. degree from Harvard Univ. in 1897; also studied music there with John K. Paine; entered his father's shipping supply business, and from 1909–36 was vice-president of the firm. During his earlier years in business he continued his musical studies in Rome (1906) and with Bernard Ziehn in Chicago (1908–12); was made a Knight of the French Legion of Honor (1921); received an honorary M.A. from Harvard Univ. (1922) and an honorary Mus.Doc. from the Univ. of Wisconsin (1933). After his retirement from business in 1936, he devoted himself entirely to composing; in 1947 was awarded the Gold Medal of the National Inst. of Arts and Letters. From his musical contacts abroad he absorbed mildly modernistic and impressionistic techniques and applied them to his music based on American urban subjects, adding the resources of jazz rhythms. His first work in this American idiom was a "jazz pantomime," *Krazy Kat,* after a well-known cartoon series (1921); he then wrote a large-scale musical panorama, *Skyscrapers* (1926), performed as a ballet and an orch. suite in America and abroad, attracting much critical comment as the first symph. work descriptive of modern American civilization; as such, the score has historical significance.
WORKS: Ballets: *Birthday of the Infanta* (Chicago Opera, Dec. 23, 1919); *Krazy Kat* (Chicago, Dec. 23, 1921); *Skyscrapers* (Metropolitan Opera, N.Y., Feb. 19, 1926; Munich, 1928); orch. suite, *Adventures in a Perambulator* (Chicago, March 19, 1915); Concertino for Piano and Orch. (Chicago, March 10, 1916; revised 1947); Symph. No. 1, in C (Litchfield County Choral Union Festival, Norfolk, Conn., 1917; revised for the 50th anniversary of the Chicago Symph. and perf. there, Oct. 24, 1940); *A Pilgrim Vision* for Orch. (Philadelphia, Nov. 23, 1920; for the tercentenary Mayflower Celebration); *Patterns* for Piano and Orch. (Boston, Oct. 21, 1932); *Sea-*

Drift, symph. poem after Whitman (Chicago, Nov. 30, 1933; revised version, 1944); *Danza* for Orch. (Chicago, 1935); Violin Concerto (1936; Chicago, Nov. 18, 1937); Symph. No. 2 (N.Y., Oct. 22, 1942); symph. poem, *The Anxious Bugler* (N.Y., Nov. 17, 1943); *The 7 Ages,* symph. suite (N.Y., Nov. 29, 1945); *Carmel Concerto* for Orch. (1948); *Song of Faith* for Chorus and Orch. (Washington Bicentennial Commission, 1932); *Song of Freedom* for Chorus and Orch. (1941); Violin Sonata (1912); String Quartet (Elizabeth Coolidge Festival, Washington, D.C., 1928); Piano Quintet (1934); *Improving Songs for Anxious Children* (1904); *Gitanjali,* song cycle to poems by Tagore (1913; also arranged for Voice and Orch.); *Water Colors,* 4 Chinese songs with Chamber Orch. (1918); many other songs and piano pieces.

Carpentras (Il Carpentrasso in Italian; real name, **Elzéar Genet),** composer and priest; b. Carpentras (Vaucluse), c.1470; d. Avignon, June 14, 1548. In 1508 he was the leading singer in, and from 1513–21 maestro di cappella of, the Pontifical Chapel in Rome; in 1521 he was sent to Avignon on negotiations connected with the Holy See; in 1524 he made his last visit to Rome; in 1526 he went to France, where he became dean of St. Agricole. Four vols. of his works (masses, 1532; Lamentations, 1532; hymns, 1533; Magnificats, 1537), printed at Avignon by Jean de Channey, are of great interest for being the first works to introduce Briard's new types, with round instead of diamond-shaped and square notes, and without ligatures; a complete copy is in the Vienna Staatsbibliothek, an incomplete one in the Paris Cons. library. His works, though severe and dignified in style, were highly esteemed by his contemporaries. A few motets are printed in Petrucci's *Motetti della Corona* (vol. I, 1514; vol. III, 1519); other works in various contemporary collections, including the edition by A. Seay in Corpus Mensurabilis Musicae, LVIII (1972–73).

Carr, Benjamin, composer and publisher; b. London, Sept. 12, 1768; d. Philadelphia, May 24, 1831. He studied music with Samuel Arnold, Samuel Wesley, and Charles Wesley; established himself as a composer in London. He went to America with his father and brother in 1793; settled in Philadelphia and established Carr's Musical Repository, one of the most important early American music stores and music publishing houses; the following year (1794) they opened branches in N.Y. and Baltimore. He was co-founder in 1820 of the Musical Fund Society in Philadelphia. A versatile musician, he was proficient as a singer, pianist, and organist, and was an influential figure in early American musical life.
    WORKS: *Philander and Silvia,* pastoral piece (London, Oct. 16, 1792); *The Archers, or Mountaineers of Switzerland,* ballad opera (N.Y., April 18, 1796); *Dead March for Washington* (1799); numerous songs and ballads. The N.Y. Public Library owns the only known copy of Carr's *Federal Overture* (Philadelphia, 1794), a medley of popular airs, including the first printing of *Yankee Doodle.*

Carreño, (Maria) Teresa, famous Venezuelan pianist; b. Caracas, Dec. 22, 1853; d. New York, June 12, 1917. As a child she studied with her father, an excellent pianist; driven from home by a revolution, the family in 1862 settled in N.Y., where she studied with Gottschalk. At the age of 8 she gave a public recital in N.Y. (Nov. 25, 1862). She began her career in 1866, after studying with Mathias in Paris and A. Rubinstein. She lived mainly in Paris from 1866 to 1870; then in England. She developed a singing voice and made an unexpected appearance in opera in Edinburgh as the Queen in *Les Huguenots* (May 24, 1872), in a cast that included Tietjens, Brignoli, and Mario; was again in the U.S. early in 1876, when she studied singing in Boston. For the Bolivar centenary celebration in Caracas (Oct. 29, 1885), she appeared as singer, pianist, and composer of the festival hymn, written at the request of the Venezuelan government; hence the frequent but erroneous attribution to Carreño of the national hymn of Venezuela, *Gloria al bravo pueblo* (the music of which was actually composed in 1811 by J. Landaeta, and officially adopted as the Venezuelan national anthem on May 25, 1881). In Caracas she once again demonstrated her versatility, when for the last 3 weeks of the season she conducted the opera company managed by her husband, the baritone **Giovanni Tagliapietra.** After these musical experiments she resumed her career as a pianist; made her German debut in Berlin, Nov. 18, 1889; in 1907 toured Australia. Her last appearance with an orch. was with the N.Y. Phil. Society (Dec. 8, 1916); her last recital was in Havana (March 21, 1917). She impressed her audiences by the impetuous élan of her playing, and was described as "the Valkyrie of the piano." She was married 4 times: to the violinist **Emile Sauret** (June, 1873), to the baritone **Giovanni Tagliapietra** (1876), to **Eugène d'Albert** (1892–95), and to **Arturo Tagliapietra,** a younger brother of Giovanni (June 30, 1902). Early in her career, Teresa Carreño wrote a number of compositions, some of which were publ.: a String Quartet; *Petite danse tsigane* for Orch.; 39 concert pieces for piano; a waltz, *Mi Teresita,* which enjoyed considerable popularity; and other small pieces. She was one of the first pianists to play MacDowell's compositions in public; MacDowell took lessons from her in N.Y. She was greatly venerated in Venezuela; her mortal remains were solemnly transferred from N.Y., where she died, and reburied in Caracas, on Feb. 15, 1938.

Carreras, José, Spanish tenor; b. Barcelona, Dec. 5, 1946. He was educated at the Barcelona Cons.; then sang at the Liceo there. In 1971 he appeared at the opera in Parma and scored a notable success; then sang at the N.Y. City Opera (1972) and Covent Garden, London (1974). He made his Metropolitan Opera debut in N.Y. as Cavaradossi on Nov. 18, 1974; then sang at La Scala, Milan (1975) and at the Salzburg Festival (1976). He possesses a fine lyrical voice and is regarded as one of the outstanding tenors of his generation.

Carrillo, Julián, Mexican composer; b. Ahualulco, San Luis Potosí, Jan. 28, 1875; d. Mexico City, Sept. 9, 1965. He was of Indian extraction; lived mostly in Mexico City, where he studied violin with Pedro Manzano and composition with Melesio Morales. He graduated from the National Cons. in 1899 and received a government stipend for study abroad as a winner of the President Diaz Prize. He took courses at the Leipzig Cons. with Hans Becker (violin), Jadassohn (theory), and Hans Sitt (orchestration); played violin in the Gewandhaus Orch. under Nikisch. In 1902–4 he studied at the Ghent Cons., winning first prize as violinist. He returned to Mexico in 1905 and made numerous appearances as a violinist; also conducted concerts; was appointed general inspector of music, and director of the National Cons. (1913–14 and again 1920–24). He visited the U.S. many times, and conducted his works in N.Y. and elsewhere. During his years in Leipzig he wrote a Symph., which he conducted there in 1902; at the same time he began experimenting with fractional tones; developed a theory which he named *Sonido 13,* symbolically indicating divisions beyond the 12 notes of the chromatic scale. He further devised a special number notation for quarter-tones, eighth-tones, and sixteenth-tones, and constructed special instruments for performance of his music in these intervals, such as a harpzither with 97 strings to the octave; his Concertino for Fractional Tones was performed by Leopold Stokowski with the Philadelphia Orch. on March 4, 1927. Carrillo also publ. several books dealing with music of fractional tones, and edited a monthly magazine, *El Sonido 13,* in 1924–25.

Carse, Adam von Ahn, English composer and writer on music; b. Newcastle upon Tyne, May 19, 1878; d. Great Missenden, Buckinghamshire, Nov. 2, 1958. He studied with F. Corder and Burnett at the Royal Academy of Music in London; from 1909–22 taught music at Winchester College; taught harmony and composition at the Royal Academy of Music (1923–40). He assembled a collection of about 350 wind instruments, which he presented in 1947 to the Horniman Museum in London; publ. a catalogue of this collection in 1951.

Cartan, Jean, talented French composer; b. Nancy, Dec. 1, 1906; d. Bligny, March 26, 1932. His father was the famous mathematician Elie Cartan. Jean Cartan studied music with Marcel Samuel Rousseau; then with Paul Dukas at the Paris Cons. His works, composed within the brief period of 6 years, showed extraordinary promise, and his death at the age of 25 was mourned as a great loss to French music. He left a cantata, *Pater Noster;* 2 string quartets; a Sonatina for Flute and Clarinet (International Festival for Contemporary Music, Oxford, July 25, 1931); piano pieces and several cycles of songs.

Carte, Richard D'Oyly, English impresario; b. London, May 3, 1844; d. there, April 3, 1901. He studied at Univ. College in London; wrote an opera, *Dr. Ambrosias,* and songs; later turned to music man-agement; he represented, among others, Gounod, Adelina Patti, and the tenor Mario. He then became interested in light opera and introduced in England Lecocq's *Giroflé-Girofla,* Offenbach's *La Périchole,* and other popular French operettas. His greatest achievement was the launching of comic operas by Gilbert and Sullivan; he commissioned and produced at the Royalty Theatre their *Trial by Jury* (1875) and then formed a syndicate to stage other productions of works by Gilbert and Sullivan at the London Opéra-Comique Theatre. Dissension within the syndicate induced him to build the Savoy Theatre (1881), which subsequently became celebrated as the home of Gilbert and Sullivan productions, with Carte himself as the leading "Savoyard." He successfully operated the Savoy Theatre until his death; the enterprise was continued by his wife (Helen Lenoir) until her death in 1913; and thereafter by his sons. In 1887 Carte attempted to establish serious English opera through the building of a special theater (now known as Palace Theatre), and the production in 1891 of Sullivan's grand opera *Ivanhoe,* followed by commissions to other English composers (Hamish McGunn, F.H. Cowen, Goring Thomas) to write operas. D'Oyly Carte introduced many improvements in theatrical management, including the replacement of gaslight by electric illumination.

Carter, Bennett Lester ("Benny"), black American jazz alto saxophonist, trumpeter, and composer; b. New York, Aug. 8, 1907. He began to study piano as a child; later mastered the alto saxophone, and played in the bands of Horace Henderson, Duke Ellington, Fletcher Henderson, and Chick Webb; also played trumpet, and began to arrange music for bandleaders. In 1935 he went to Europe, where he played in Paris and Amsterdam. Returning to the U.S. in 1938, he led his own groups; then settled in Los Angeles as a film composer-arranger.

Carter, Betty, black American jazz singer; b. Flint, Mich., May 16, 1930. She studied piano at the Detroit Cons.; began singing in local jazz clubs, on the same bill with such celebrated jazz artists as Charlie Parker, Miles Davis, and Dizzy Gillespie; then joined Lionel Hampton's band (1948–51). She gained widespread acclaim at the Newport Jazz Festivals at Carnegie Hall in 1977 and 1978. She soon rose to the loftiest plateau on the jazz firmament; her voice was remarkable for its operatic qualities and resourceful adaptation to quaquaversal situations.

Carter, Elliott Cook, Jr., outstanding American composer; b. New York, Dec. 11, 1908. After graduating from the Horace Mann High School in 1926, Carter entered Harvard Univ., majoring in literature and languages; at the same time studied piano at the Longy School of Music in Cambridge, Mass. In 1930 he devoted himself exclusively to music, taking up harmony and counterpoint with Walter Piston, and orchestration with Edward Burlingame Hill; also attended in 1932 a course given at Harvard Univ. by Gustav Holst. He obtained his M.A. in 1932, and then went to Paris, where he studied with Nadia Boulanger at the Ecole Normale de Musique, receiving there a *licence de contrepoint;* in the interim he learned mathematics, Latin, and Greek. In 1935 he returned to America; was music director of the Ballet Caravan (1937–39); gave courses in music and also in mathematics, physics, and classical Greek at St. John's College in Annapolis, Md. (1939–41); then taught at the Peabody Cons. in Baltimore (1946–48). He was appointed to the faculty of Columbia Univ. (1948–50) and also taught at Yale Univ. from 1958 to 1962. In 1962 he was the American delegate at the East-West Encounter in Tokyo; in 1963 was composer-in-residence at the American Academy in Rome, and in 1964 held a similar post in West Berlin. In 1967–68 he was a professor-at-large at Cornell Univ. He held Guggenheim fellowships in 1945 and 1950, and the American Prix de Rome in 1953. In 1965 he received the Creative Arts Award from Brandeis Univ. In 1953 he received first prize in the *Concours International de Composition pour Quatuor à Cordes* in Liège for his First String Quartet; in 1960 he received the Pulitzer Prize for his 2nd String Quartet, which also received the N.Y. Music Critics Circle Award and was further elected as the most important work of the year by the International Rostrum of Composers. He again won the Pulitzer, for his 3rd String Quartet, in 1973. His reputation as one of the most important American composers grew with every new work he produced; Stravinsky was quoted as saying that Carter's Double Concerto was the first true American masterpiece. The evolution of Carter's style of composition is marked by his constant preoccupation with taxonomic considerations. His early works are set in a neo-Classical style. He later absorbed the Schoenbergian method of composition with 12 tones; finally he developed a system of serial organization in which all parameters, including intervals, metric divisions, rhythm, counterpoint, harmony, and instrumental timbres, become parts of the total conception of each individual work. In this connection he introduced the term "metric modulation," in which secondary rhythms in a polyrhythmic section assume dominance expressed in constantly changing meters, often in such unusual time signatures as 10/16, 21/8, etc. Furthermore, he assigns to each participating instrument in a polyphonic work a special interval, a distinctive rhythmic figure, and a selective register, so that the individuality of each part is clearly outlined, a distribution which is often reinforced by placing the players at a specified distance from one another. WORKS: *Tom and Lily,* comic opera in one act (1934); Flute Sonata (1934); *Tarantella* for Male Chorus and Orch. (1936); ballet, *The Ball Room Guide* (1937); *The Bridge,* oratorio (1937); *Madrigal Book* for Mixed Voices (1937); Concerto for English Horn (1937); ballet, *Pocahontas* (N.Y., May 24, 1939); *Heart Not So Heavy as Mine* for a cappella Chorus (1939); Suite for Quartet of Alto Saxophones (1939); *The Defense of Corinth,* after Rabelais, for Speaker, Men's Chorus, and Piano, 4-hands (Cambridge, Mass., March 12, 1942); Adagio for Viola and Piano (1943); Symph. No. 1 (Rochester, April 27, 1944); *The*

Harmony of Morning for Female Chorus and Small Orch. (N.Y., Feb. 25, 1945); *Canonic Suite* for 4 Clarinets (1945); *Warble for Lilac Time,* after Walt Whitman, for Soprano and Instruments (Yaddo, Sept. 14, 1946); Piano Sonata (1946); *The Minotaur,* ballet (N.Y., March 26, 1947); *Holiday Overture* for Orch. (Baltimore, Jan. 7, 1948); Woodwind Quintet (N.Y., Feb 27, 1949); 8 pieces for 4 Timpani (1949; Nos. 3 and 6 composed and added in 1966); Cello Sonata (N.Y., Feb. 27, 1950); String Quartet (1951); 8 Etudes and a Fantasy, for Flute, Oboe, Clarinet, and Bassoon (N.Y., Oct. 28, 1952); Sonata for Flute, Oboe, Cello, and Harpsichord (N.Y., Nov. 19, 1953); Variations for Orch. (Louisville, Ky., April 21, 1956); 2nd String Quartet (1959); Double Concerto for Harpsichord and Piano with 2 Chamber Orchs. (N.Y., Sept. 6, 1961); Piano Concerto (Boston, Jan. 6, 1967); Concerto for Orch. (N.Y. Phil., Feb. 5, 1970); String Quartet No. 3 (1971); Brass Quintet (1974); Duo for Violin and Piano (1974); *A Mirror on Which to Dwell* for Soprano and 9 Players, to a cycle of 6 poems by Elizabeth Bishop (N.Y., Feb. 24, 1976); *A Symphony of 3 Orchestras* (N.Y., Feb. 17, 1977); *Syringa,* cantata for Soprano and Small Ensemble (N.Y., Dec. 10, 1978); *Night Fantasies* for Piano (1980); *In Sleep, in Thunder,* song cycle for Tenor and 14 Players, to poems by Robert Lowell (1981); *Triple Duo* for Paired Instruments: Flute/Clarinet; Violin/Cello; Piano/Percussion (1982; London, April 23, 1983); *Changes* for Guitar Solo (1983).

Carulli, Ferdinando, Italian guitar player and composer; b. Naples, Feb. 20, 1770; d. Paris, Feb. 17, 1841. He went to Paris in 1808 and prospered there as a guitar teacher. He is generally regarded as the first guitarist to use his instrument for artistic performances; he publ. a method, *L'Harmonie appliquée à la guitarre* (Paris, 1825). His works number nearly 400 items, including concertos, quartets, trios, duos, fantasias, variations, and solos of all descriptions. In 1830 he composed a piece of program music for guitar entitled *Les Trois Jours,* descriptive of the days of the July 1830 revolution.

Caruso, Enrico, celebrated Italian tenor; b. Naples, Feb. 27, 1873; d. there, Aug. 2, 1921. He was the 18th child of a worker's family, his father being a machinist. All 17 children born before him died in infancy; 2 born after him survived. He sang Neapolitan ballads by ear; as a youth he applied for a part in *Mignon* at the Teatro Fondo in Naples, but was unable to follow the orch. at the rehearsal and had to be replaced by another singer. His first serious study was with Guglielmo Vergine (1891–94); he continued with Vincenzo Lombardi. His operatic debut took place at the Teatro Nuovo in Naples on Nov. 16, 1894, in *L'Amico Francesco,* by an amateur composer, Mario Morelli. In 1895 he appeared at the Teatro Fondo in *La Traviata, La Favorita,* and *Rigoletto;* during the following few seasons he added *Aida, Faust, Carmen, La Bohème,* and *Tosca* to his repertoire. The decisive turn in his career came when he was chosen to appear as leading tenor in the first performance of Giordano's *Fedora* (Teatro

Lirico, Milan, Nov. 17, 1898), in which he made a great impression. Several important engagements followed. In 1899 and 1900 he sang in St. Petersburg and Moscow; between 1899 and 1903 he appeared in 4 summer seasons in Buenos Aires. The culmination of these successes was the coveted opportunity to sing at La Scala; he sang there in *La Bohème* (Dec. 26, 1900), and in the first performance of Mascagni's *Le Maschere* (Jan. 17, 1901). At the Teatro Lirico in Milan he took part in the first performances of Franchetti's *Germania* (March 11, 1902) and Cilea's *Adriana Lecouvreur* (Nov. 6, 1902). In the spring season of 1902 he appeared (with Melba) in Monte Carlo, and was reengaged there for 3 more seasons. He made his London debut as the Duke in *Rigoletto* (Covent Garden, May 14, 1902) and was immediately successful with the British public and press. He gave 25 performances in London until July 28, 1902, appearing with Melba, Nordica, and Calvé. In the season of 1902–3, Caruso sang in Rome and Lisbon; during the summer of 1903 he was in South America. Finally, on Nov. 23, 1903, he made his American debut at the Metropolitan Opera, in *Rigoletto*. After that memorable occasion, Caruso was connected with the Metropolitan to the end of his life. He traveled with various American opera companies from coast to coast; he happened to be performing in San Francisco when the 1906 earthquake nearly destroyed the city. He achieved his most spectacular successes in America, attended by enormous publicity. In 1907 Caruso sang in Germany (Leipzig, Hamburg, Berlin) and in Vienna; he was acclaimed there as enthusiastically as in the Anglo-Saxon and Latin countries. A complete list of his appearances is given in the appendix of his biography by Pierre Key and Bruno Zirato (Boston, 1922). Caruso's fees soared from $2 as a boy in Italy in 1891 to the fabulous sums of $15,000 for a single performance in Mexico City in 1920. He made recordings in the U.S. as early as 1902; his annual income from this source alone netted him $115,000 at the peak of his career. He excelled in realistic Italian operas; his Cavaradossi in *Tosca* and Canio in *Pagliacci* became models which every singer emulated. He sang several French operas; the German repertoire remained completely alien to him; his only appearances in Wagnerian roles were 3 performances of *Lohengrin* in Buenos Aires (1901). His voice possessed such natural warmth and great strength in the middle register that as a youth he was believed to be a baritone. The sustained quality of his bel canto was exceptional and enabled him to give superb interpretations of lyrical parts. For dramatic effect, he often resorted to the "coup de glotte" (which became known as the "Caruso sob"); here the singing gave way to intermittent vocalization without tonal precision. While Caruso was criticized for such usages from the musical standpoint, his characterizations on the stage were overwhelmingly impressive. Although of robust health, he abused it by unceasing activity. He was stricken with a throat hemorrhage during a performance at the Brooklyn Academy of Music (Dec. 11, 1920), but was able to sing in N.Y. one last time, on Dec. 24, 1920. Several surgical operations were performed in an effort to arrest a pleurisy; Caruso was taken to Italy, but succumbed to the illness after several months of remission. He was known as a convivial person and a lover of fine food (a brand of macaroni was named after him). He possessed a gift for caricature; a collection of his drawings was publ. in N.Y. in 1922 (2nd ed., 1951). His private life was turbulent; his liaison (never legalized) with Ada Giachetti, by whom he had 2 sons, was painfully resolved by court proceedings in 1912, creating much disagreeable publicity; there were also suits brought against him by 2 American women. In 1906 the celebrated "monkey-house case" (in which Caruso was accused of improper behavior toward a lady while viewing the animals in Central Park) threatened for a while his continued success in America. On Aug. 20, 1918, he married Dorothy Park Benjamin of N.Y., over the strong opposition of her father, a rich industrialist. Caruso received numerous decorations from European governments, among them the Order of Commendatore of the Crown of Italy; the Légion d'Honneur; and the Order of the Crown Eagle of Prussia. A fictional film biography, *The Great Caruso*, was made of his life in 1950.

Carvalho, Eleazar de, brilliant Brazilian conductor and composer; b. Iguatú (Ceará), July 28, 1912. His father was of Dutch extraction and his mother was part Indian. He studied in Fortaleza at the Apprentice Seaman's School; later joined the National Naval Corps in Rio de Janeiro and played tuba in the band. In 1941 he became assistant conductor of the Brazilian Symph. Orch. in Rio de Janeiro. In 1946 he went to the U.S. to study conducting with Koussevitzky at the Berkshire Music Center, and Koussevitzky invited him to conduct a pair of concerts with the Boston Symph. Orch. Carvalho demonstrated extraordinary ability and musicianship by leading all rehearsals and the concerts without score in a difficult program; his sense of perfect pitch is exceptional. He subsequently conducted a number of guest engagements with orchs. in America and in Europe. In 1963–68 he was conductor of the St. Louis Symph. Orch.; during his tenure he introduced many modern works into his programs, much to the discomfiture of the financial backers of the orch.; still, he lasted a few seasons in St. Louis. From 1969 to 1973 he was conductor of the Hofstra Univ. Orch. in Hempstead, N.Y., which offered him a more liberal esthetic climate; then returned to Brazil.
WORKS: 2 operas on Brazilian subjects: *Descuberta do Brasil* (Rio de Janeiro, June 19, 1939) and *Tiradentes* (Rio de Janeiro, Sept. 7, 1941, dealing with the exploits of a revolutionary dentist during the war of liberation); *Sinfonia branca* (1943); symph. poems: *A Traicao* (1941); *Batalha Naval de Riachuelo* (1943); *Guararapes* (1945); 3 overtures; 2 trios; 2 string quartets; Violin Sonata; songs. He is the husband of the avant-garde composer and pianist **Jocy de Oliveira.**

Carvalho (real name, **Carvaille**), **Léon,** distinguished French baritone and opera manager; b. Port-Louis, near Paris, Jan. 18, 1825; d. Paris, Dec. 29, 1897. He studied at the Paris Cons.; began his career as a singer; in 1853 married the French soprano **Marie Miolan.** From 1856–68 he was director of the Théâtre-Lyrique; from 1869–75 was chief producer at the Paris Opéra; concurrently was manager of the Théâtre du Vaudeville (1872–74); then acted as stage manager at the Opéra; in 1876–87 was director of the Opéra-Comique, succeeding du Locle. After the fire at the Opéra-Comique in 1887, in which 131 persons perished, he was arrested and sentenced to 6 months' imprisonment, but was acquitted on appeal, and reinstated in 1891. He had the reputation of an enlightened administrator, encouraging young artists and young composers.

Carvalho-Miolan, Caroline-Marie-Félix, French dramatic soprano; b. Marseilles, Dec. 31, 1827; d. near Dieppe, July 10, 1895. She entered the Paris Cons. at 12; studied under Duprez; made her operatic debut on Dec. 14, 1849, in *Lucia di Lammermoor* at the Opéra-Comique, where she was engaged from 1849–55; from 1856–67 she sang at the Théâtre Lyrique, where she created the soprano parts in Gounod's *Faust, Roméo et Juliette,* and *Mireille,* and in Clapisson's *La Fanchonette;* from 1868–85 she sang at the Paris Opéra and at the Opéra-Comique; also appeared in London, Berlin, Brussels, St. Petersburg, etc.; retired in 1885. In 1853 she married **Léon Carvalho.**

Carver, Robert, Scottish composer; b. 1487; d. after 1546. He was a Monk of Scone Abbey; developed a melismatic style of composition; wrote masses on the medieval song *L'Homme armé* and many motets, one of them in 19 independent parts. He is regarded as an equal of Dunstable in melodic and rhythmic excellence. Vol. 1 of his collected works was publ. by the American Inst. of Musicology, edited by Denis Stevens, in 1959.

Cary, Annie Louise, celebrated American contralto; b. Wayne, Kennebec County, Maine, Oct. 22, 1841; d. Norwalk, Conn., April 3, 1921. She studied in Boston and Milan; made her operatic debut in Copenhagen as Azucena; studied under Mme. Viardot-García at Baden-Baden; was engaged at Hamburg, Stockholm, Brussels, London, and St. Petersburg. Returning to the U.S., she continued her operatic career in N.Y. theaters; was the first American woman to sing a Wagnerian role in the U.S. (Ortrud in *Lohengrin,* 1877). She married C.M. Raymond in 1882, and retired at the height of her powers. She appeared in concert or oratorio in all leading cities of America.

Casadesus, François Louis, French conductor and composer; b. Paris, Dec. 2, 1870; d. Suresnes, near Paris, June 27, 1954. He studied at the Paris Cons.; conducted the Opéra and the Opéra-Comique on tour in France (1890–92); in 1895 conducted the Opéra on a European tour; was the founder and director (1918–22) of the American Cons. at Fontaine-

bleau; later was active as a radio conductor; wrote music criticism. A collection of valedictory articles was publ. in honor of his 80th birthday (Paris, 1950).
WORKS: Operas: *Cachaprès* (Brussels, 1914); *La Chanson de Paris* (1924); *Bertran de Born* (Monte Carlo, 1925); *Messie d'Amour* (Monte Carlo, 1928); *Symphonie scandinave; Au beau jardin de France* for Orch.; Symph. in E major; smaller compositions for orch.; numerous songs.

Casadesus, Henri, French violinist, brother of the preceding; b. Paris, Sept. 30, 1879; d. there, May 31, 1947. He studied with Lavignac and Laforge in Paris; from 1910–17 was a member of the Capet Quartet; was a founder and director of the Société Nouvelle des Instruments Anciens, in which he played the viola d'amore; subsequently toured in the U.S., playing at the Elizabeth Sprague Coolidge Festivals, Library of Congress, Washington, D.C. Rare and ancient instruments collected by Casadesus are in the museum of the Boston Symph. Orch.

Casadesus, Jean, French pianist, son of **Robert** and **Gaby Casadesus;** b. Paris, July 7, 1927; d. in an automobile accident, near Renfrew, Ontario, Canada, Jan. 20, 1972. He studied piano with his parents; at the outbreak of World War II, he went to the U.S.; studied at Princeton Univ.; won the contest for young soloists held by the Philadelphia Orch. in 1946; appeared as soloist with the N.Y. Phil. and with major European orchs.; made tours of the U.S. and Canada.

Casadesus, Jean-Claude, French conductor, nephew of **Robert** and **Gaby Casadesus;** b. Paris, Dec. 7, 1935. He studied at the Paris Cons.; in 1959 he received first prize as a percussion player there; he was then engaged as timpanist of the Concerts Colonne and of the Domaine Musical; also studied conducting with Dervaux at the Ecole Normale de Musique and with Boulez in Basel. In 1969 he became resident conductor of the Paris Opéra and of the Opéra-Comique. In 1971 he became assistant conductor to Dervaux with the Orch. Phil. des Pays de la Loire in Angers. In 1976 he founded the Lille Phil. Orch.; also appeared as a guest conductor with the BBC Symph., Leningrad Phil., Scottish National Orch., Covent Garden, English National Opera, and other orchs. and opera houses in Europe. In 1983 he was named general secretary of the Major Council of Music in Paris. He was made an officer of the National Order of Merit for his services to French culture.

Casadesus, Marius, French violinist, brother of **François Casadesus;** b. Paris, Oct. 24, 1892; d. Suresnes (Paris), Oct. 13, 1981. He studied at the Paris Cons., graduating in 1914 with first prize in violin; subsequently toured in Europe and America; gave numerous sonata recitals with his nephew, the pianist **Robert Casadesus.** He was a founding member of the Société Nouvelle des Instruments Anciens (1920–40), organized with the purpose of reviving old string instruments, such as the Quinton and Diskantgambe. He wrote a number of pieces for the violin, some choral music, and songs, but his most notorious contribution to violin literature was the so-called Adelaide Concerto, supposedly composed by Mozart when he was 10 years old and dedicated to the oldest daughter of Louis XV, Adelaide (hence the nickname). It was performed in Paris on Dec. 24, 1931, with considerable publicity, but skepticism arose when Casadesus failed to produce either the manuscript or a contemporary copy of it. In 1977, in the course of a litigation for his copyright as the arranger of the "Adelaide Concerto," Casadesus admitted that the piece was entirely his own work. A detailed discussion of the whole hullabaloo is in the entry "Misattributed Compositions" in Percy A. Scholes, *The Oxford Companion to Music.*

Casadesus, Robert, eminent French pianist and composer; b. Paris, April 7, 1899; d. there, Sept. 19, 1972. A scion of a remarkable musical family, he absorbed music at home from his earliest childhood. His uncles were **Henri** and **François Casadesus;** another uncle, **Marcel Louis Lucien** (1882–1917), was a cellist, and his aunt **Rose** was a pianist. He received his formal musical education studying piano with Diémer and composition with Leroux at the Paris Cons. In 1922 he embarked on a wide-ranging tour as a concert pianist; after the outbreak of World War II he went to the U.S.; taught classes at various schools. After the war he taught at the American Cons. at Fountainebleau. He was a prolific composer; wrote 7 symphs., of which the last was performed posthumously in N.Y. on Nov. 8, 1972. He appeared with his wife, **Gaby Casadesus,** in his Concerto for 2 Pianos and Orch. with the N.Y. Phil. on Nov. 25, 1950. He also wrote a Concerto for 3 Pianos and String Orch., which he performed for the first time with his wife and his son **Jean** in N.Y., July 24, 1965. As a pianist, Casadesus was distinguished for his Gallic sense of balance and fine gradation of tonal dynamics.

Casals, Pablo (Pau Carlos Salvador Defilló), great Spanish cellist; b. Vendrell, Catalonia, Dec. 29, 1876; d. San Juan, Puerto Rico, Oct. 22, 1973. He was the second child of a progeny originally numbering 11, 7 of whom died at birth. Legend has it that Pablo Casals barely escaped the same fate when the umbilical cord became entangled around his neck and nearly choked him to death; another legend (supported by Casals himself) is that he was conceived when Brahms began his B-flat Major Quartet, of which Casals owned the original MS, and that he was born when Brahms completed its composition. This legend is rendered moot by the fact that the quartet in question was completed and performed before Casals was born. But even the ascertainable facts of the life of Casals make it a glorious legend. His father, the parish organist and choirmaster in Vendrell, gave Casals instruction in piano, violin, and organ. When Casals was 11 he first heard the cello performed by a group of traveling musicians, and decided to study the instrument. In 1888 his mother took him to Barcelona, where he enrolled in

the Escuela Municipal de Música. There he studied cello with José García, and also took music theory with José Rodoreda, and studied piano with Joaquín Malats and Francisco Costa Llobera. His progress as a cellist was nothing short of prodigious, and he was able to give a solo recital in Barcelona at the age of 14, on Feb. 23, 1891; he graduated with honors in 1893. Albéniz, who heard him play in a café trio, gave him a letter of introduction to Count Morphy, the private secretary to María Cristina, the Queen Regent, in Madrid. Casals was asked to play at informal concerts in the palace, and was granted a royal stipend for study in composition with Tomás Bretón. In 1893 he entered the Cons. de Música y Declamación in Madrid, where he attended chamber music classes of Jesús de Monasterio. He also played in the newly organized Quartet Society there (1894–95). In 1895 he went to Paris and, deprived of his stipend from Spain, earned a living by playing the second cello in the theater orch. of the Folies Marigny. He decided to return to Spain, where he received, in 1896, an appointment to the faculty of the Escuela Municipal de Música in Barcelona; he was also principal cellist in the orch. of the Gran Teatro del Liceo. In 1897 he appeared as soloist with the Madrid Symph. Orch., and was awarded the Order of Carlos III from the Queen. His career as a cello virtuoso was now assured. In 1899 he played at the Crystal Palace in London, and was later given the honor of playing for Queen Victoria at her summer residence at Cowes, Isle of Wight. On Nov. 12, 1899, he appeared as a soloist at a prestigious Lamoureux Concert in Paris, and played with Lamoureux again on Dec. 17, 1899, obtaining exceptional success with both the public and the press. He toured Spain and the Netherlands with the pianist Harold Bauer (1900–1901); then made his first tour of the U.S. (1901–2). In 1903 he made a grand tour of South America. On Jan. 15, 1904, he was invited to play at the White House for President Theodore Roosevelt. In 1906 he became associated with the talented young Portuguese cellist Guilhermina Suggia, who studied with him and began to appear in concerts as Mme. P. Casals-Suggia, although they were not legally married. Their liaison was dissolved in 1912; in 1914 Casals married the American socialite and singer Susan Metcalfe; they became separated in 1928, but were not divorced until 1957. Continuing his brilliant career, Casals organized, in Paris, a concert trio with the pianist Cortot and the violinist Thibaud; they played concerts together until 1937. Casals also became interested in conducting, and in 1919 he organized, in Barcelona, the Orquesta Pau Casals and led its first concert on Oct. 13, 1920. With the outbreak of the Spanish Civil War in 1936, the Orquesta Pau Casals ceased its activities. Casals was an ardent supporter of the Spanish Republican Government, and after its defeat vowed never to return to Spain until democracy was restored there. He settled in the French village of Prades, on the Spanish frontier; between 1939 and 1942 he made sporadic appearances as a cellist in the unoccupied zone of southern France and in Switzerland. So fierce was his opposition to the Franco regime in Spain that he even declined to appear in countries that recognized the totalitarian Spanish government, making an exception when he took part in a concert of chamber music in the White House on Nov. 13, 1961, at the invitation of President Kennedy, whom he admired. In June 1950 he resumed his career as conductor and cellist at the Prades Festival, organized in commemoration of the bicentennial of the death of Bach; he continued leading the Prades Festivals until 1966. He made his permanent residence in 1956, when he settled in San Juan, Puerto Rico (his mother was born there when the island was still under Spanish rule). In 1957 an annual Festival Casals was inaugurated there. During all these years he developed energetic activities as a pedagogue, leading master classes in Switzerland; Italy; Berkeley, California; and Marlboro, Vermont; some of these sessions were televised. Casals was also a composer; perhaps his most effective work is *La sardana*, for an ensemble of cellos, which he composed in 1926. His oratorio *El pessebre* (*The Manger*) was performed for the first time in Acapulco, Mexico, on Dec. 17, 1960; in subsequent years he conducted numerous performances of the score. One of his last compositions was the *Himno a las Naciones Unidas* (*Hymm of the United Nations);* he conducted its first performance in a special concert at the United Nations on Oct. 24, 1971, 2 months before his 95th birthday. On Aug. 3, 1957, at the age of 80, Casals married his young pupil Marta Montañez; following his death, she married the pianist Eugene Istomin, on Feb. 15, 1975. Casals did not live to see the liberation of Spain from the Franco dictatorship, but he was posthumously honored by the Spanish government of King Juan Carlos I, which issued in 1976 a commemorative postage stamp in honor of his 100th birthday.

Case, Anna, American soprano; b. Clinton, N.J., Oct. 29, 1888; d. New York, Jan. 7, 1984. She studied voice in N.Y. with Mme. Ohrstrom-Renard; on Nov. 20, 1909, made her operatic debut at the Metropolitan Opera as a page in *Lohengrin;* remained on its roster until 1919; among the roles in which she excelled were Aida and Carmen. On July 18, 1931, she married Clarence H. Mackay, chairman of the board of the Postal Telegraph Corp., whose daughter, by his first marriage, was Ellin Mackay, who married Irving Berlin.

Casella, Alfredo, outstanding Italian composer; b. Turin, July 25, 1883; d. Rome, March 5, 1947. He began to play the piano at the age of 4 and received his early instruction from his mother; in 1896 he went to Paris, and studied with Diémer and Fauré at the Paris Cons.; won first prize in piano in 1899. He made concert tours as pianist in Europe, including Russia; appeared as guest conductor with European orchs.; in 1912 conducted the Concerts Populaires at the Trocadéro; taught piano classes at the Paris Cons. from 1912–15; returned to Rome and was appointed a prof. of piano at the Santa Cecilia Academy, as successor to Sgambati. In 1917 he founded the Società Nazionale di Musica (later the Società

Italiana di Musica Moderna; since 1923 as the Corporazione delle Musiche Nuove, Italian section of the International Society for Contemporary Music). On Oct. 28, 1921, Casella made his American debut with the Philadelphia Orch. in the triple capacity of composer, conductor, and piano soloist; he also appeared as a guest conductor in Chicago, Detroit, Cincinnati, Cleveland, and Los Angeles; was conductor of the Boston Pops in 1927–29, introducing a number of modern works, but failing to please the public. In 1928 he was awarded the first prize of $3,000 given by the Musical Fund Society in Philadelphia; in 1934 won the Coolidge Prize. In 1938 he returned to Italy, where he remained until his death. Apart from his activities as pianist, conductor, and composer, he was a prolific writer on music, and contributed numerous articles to various publications in Italy, France, Russia, Germany, and America; he possessed an enlightened cosmopolitan mind, which enabled him to penetrate the musical cultures of various nations; at the same time he steadfastly proclaimed his adherence to the ideals of Italian art. In his music he applied modernistic techniques to the old forms; his style may be termed neo-Classical, but in his early years he cultivated extreme modernism.

WORKS: OPERAS: *La donna serpente* (Rome, March 17, 1932); *La favola d'Orfeo* (Venice, Sept. 6, 1932); *Il deserto tentato,* mystery in one act (Florence, May 6, 1937). BALLETS: *Il convento veneziano* (1912; La Scala, Feb. 7, 1925); *La Giara,* "choreographic comedy" after Pirandello (Paris, Nov. 19, 1924); his most successful work); *La camera dei disegni,* for children (Rome, 1940); *La rosa del sogno* (Rome, 1943). ORCH. WORKS: Symph. No. I, in B minor (1905); Symph. No. II, in C minor (1908–9); Symph. No. III, op. 63 (Chicago, March 27, 1941); Suite in C (1909); *Italia,* rhapsody based on folk themes (Paris, April 23, 1910); *Le Couvent sur l'eau,* symph. suite based on the ballet *Il convento veneziano* (Paris, April 23, 1914); *Notte di Maggio* for Voice and Orch. (Paris, March 29, 1914); *Elegia eroica* (Rome, Jan. 21, 1917); *Pagine di guerra* (1916); *Pupazzetti,* 5 pieces for Puppets (1918); *Partita* for Piano and Orch. (N.Y., Oct. 29, 1925); *Scarlattiana,* on themes by Scarlatti, for Piano and Orch. (N.Y., Jan. 22, 1927); *Concerto romano* for Organ and Orch. (N.Y., March 11, 1927); Violin Concerto in A minor (Moscow, Oct. 8, 1928); *Introduzione, Aria e Toccata* (Rome, April 5, 1933); Concerto for Trio and Orch. (Berlin, Nov. 17, 1933); Concerto (Amsterdam, 1937); *Paganiniana,* on themes by Paganini (Vienna, 1942). VOCAL WORKS: *L'Adieu à la vie,* cycle of 4 Hindu lyrics after Tagore's *Gitanjali* (1915; also for Voice and Orch.), 1926); *4 favole romanesche* (1923); *Ninna nanna popolare genovese* (1934); *3 canti sacri* for Baritone and Orch. (1943); *Missa solemnis pro pace* (1944). CHAMBER WORKS: *Barcarola e scherzo* for Flute and Piano (1904); 2 cello sonatas (1907, 1927); *Siciliana e burlesca* for Flute and Piano (1914; 2nd version for Piano Trio, 1917); *5 pezzi* for String Quartet (1920); Concerto for String Quartet (1923–24; also arranged for String Orch.); *Serenata* for Clarinet, Bassoon, Trumpet, Violin, and Cello (1927); *Sinfonia* for Clarinet, Trumpet, Cello, and

Piano (1932); Piano Trio (1933). FOR PIANO: Many pieces, including 2 series of stylistic imitations, *A la manière de* ... : Wagner, Fauré, Brahms, Debussy, Strauss, Franck (1911), and (in collaboration with Ravel) Borodin, d'Indy, Chabrier, Ravel (1913); Sonatina (1916); *A notte alta* (1917; also for Piano and Orch., 1921); *11 pezzi infantili* (1920); *2 ricercari sul nome Bach* (1932); 3 pieces for Pianola (1918). Casella orchestrated Balakirev's *Islamey;* edited Beethoven's sonatas and piano works of Albéniz; arranged Mahler's 7th Symph. for piano, 4-hands.

WRITINGS: *L'evoluzione della musica* (publ. in Italian, French, and Eng. in parallel columns; 1919); *Igor Stravinsky* (1926; new ed., Milan, 1951); *"21 + 26"* (about Rossini, Tolstoy, Busoni, etc.; 1931); *Il pianoforte* (1938); a manual of orchestration, *La tecnica dell'orchestra contemporanea* (completed by V. Mortari; Milan, 1950). In 1941 Casella publ. his memoirs, under the title *I segreti della Giara;* transl. into Eng. as *Music in My Time: The Memoirs of Alfredo Casella* (Oklahoma Univ. Press, 1955).

Casini, Giovanni Maria, Italian organist and composer; b. Florence, Dec. 16, 1652; d. there, Feb. 25, 1719. He studied composition in Florence, and later in Rome with Matteo Simonelli and Bernardo Pasquini (organ). He became a priest and served as organist at the Cathedral of Florence from 1703; retired in 1711 owing to ill health. As a keyboard composer, Casini represents the late Baroque style. As a theorist, he was a follower of Nicolo Vicentino and Giovanni Battista Doni in their studies of the music of Greek antiquity.

Cassadó, Gaspar, distinguished Spanish cellist, son of **Joaquín Cassadó;** b. Barcelona, Sept. 30, 1897; d. Madrid, Dec. 24, 1966. He studied cello with Casals; toured Europe; made his debut in America, in N.Y., on Dec. 10, 1936; made another U.S. tour in 1949. He composed a Cello Sonata, a Cello Concerto, and other pieces for his instrument. His *Catalonian Rhapsody* for Orch. was performed by the N.Y. Phil. on Nov. 8, 1928. Cassadó also made arrangements for cello and orch. of a Mozart horn concerto and Weber's Clarinet Concerto.

Cassadó (Valls), Joaquín, Spanish organist and composer; b. Mataró, near Barcelona, Sept. 30, 1867; d. Barcelona, March 25, 1926. He served as a choir director and organist at several churches in Barcelona; wrote a comic opera, *El monjo negro* (Barcelona, Jan. 24, 1920); *Hispania* for Piano and Orch.; church music.

Cassiodorus, Magnus Aurelius, historian, statesman, and monk; b. Scyllacium (Squillace), Bruttii, c.485; d. Vivarese, Calabria, c.580. He was a contemporary of Boetius; held various civil offices under Theodoric and Athalaric until c.540, when he retired. He founded the monasteries of Castellum and Vivarium; at the latter he wrote his *De artibus ac disciplinis liberalium litterarum;* the section treating of music, *Institutiones musicae,* a valuable source, is printed in Gerbert's *Scriptores,* vol. I; a partial reproduction is to be found in Strunk's *Source Readings in Music History* (N.Y., 1950).

Cassuto, Alvaro, Portuguese conductor and composer; b. Oporto, Nov. 17, 1938. He studied violin and piano as a small child; then took courses in composition with Artur Santos and Lopes Graça. During the season 1960–61 he attended classes in new music in Darmstadt, Germany, with Ligeti, Messiaen, and Stockhausen, and at the same time had instruction in conducting with Herbert von Karajan. He further studied conducting with Pedro de Freitas Branco in Lisbon and Franco Ferrara in Hilversum, the Netherlands. He served as an assistant conductor of the Gulbenkian Orch. in Lisbon (1965–68) and with the Little Orch. in N.Y. (1968–70). In 1970 he was appointed permanent conductor of the National Radio Orch. of Lisbon, and in 1975 was elected its music director. In 1974 he was appointed a lecturer in music and conductor of the Symph. Orch. of the Univ. of Calif. at Irvine, remaining there unitl 1979. He also was guest conductor of numerous orchs. in Europe, South America, and the U.S. In 1969 he received the Koussevitzky Prize in Tanglewood. A progressive-minded and scholarly musician, he amassed a large repertoire of both classical and modern works, displaying a confident expertise. He is also a composer of several orch. works in a modern idiom, as well as of chamber pieces.

Castagna, Bruna, Italian mezzo-soprano; b. Bari, Oct. 15, 1905; d. Pinamar, Argentina, July 10, 1983. She learned to play the piano; then went to Milan to study voice with Tina Scognamiglio; made her debut at Mantua in 1925; then traveled to South America, where she sang for 3 seasons at the Teatro Colón in Buenos Aires and in the provinces (1927–30). Returning to Italy, she sang at La Scala in Milan; then made guest appearances in the U.S. in Chicago, St. Louis, and San Francisco. On March 2, 1936, she successfully performed at the Metropolitan Opera House in N.Y. as Azucena in *Il Trovatore;* there followed a far-flung tour in Australia, Brazil, Egypt, Rumania, and Spain. Eventually she made her home in Argentina. Her most applauded role was Carmen.

Castan, Count Armand de. See **Castelmary.**

Castel, Louis-Bertrand, French acoustician; b. Montpellier, Nov. 11, 1688; d. Paris, Jan. 9, 1757. He became interested in Newton's observation on the correspondence, in proportionate breadth, of the 7 prismatic rays with the string-lengths required for the scale *re, mi, fa, sol, la, si, do;* acting upon this observation, he attempted the construction of a "clavecin oculaire," to produce color-harmonies for the eye as the ordinary harpsichord produces tone-harmonies for the ear. His theory is explained in an essay, *Nouvelles expériences d'optique et d'acoustique* (1735; Eng. trans., London, 1757).

Castelmary (stage name of Count **Armand de Cas-**

tan), French baritone; b. Toulouse, Aug. 16, 1834; d. New York, Feb. 10, 1897, on the stage of the Metropolitan Opera House, just after the first act of *Martha.* He made his operatic debut at the Paris Opéra (1863); remained there till 1870; then sang in London and N.Y.; made his debut at the Metropolitan on Nov. 29, 1893, as Vulcan in *Philemon;* was particularly successful as Méphistophélès in *Faust.*

Castelnuovo-Tedesco, Mario, greatly significant Italian-American composer; b. Florence, April 3, 1895; d. Los Angeles, March 16, 1968. He studied at the Cherubini Inst. with del Valle (piano) and Pizzetti (composition); he began to compose at an early age; his first organized composition, *Cielo di Settembre* for Piano, revealed impressionistic tendencies. He wrote a patriotic song, *Fuori i Barbari,* during World War I. He attained considerable eminence in Italy between the 2 wars, and his music was often heard at European festivals. Political events forced him to leave Italy; in 1939 he settled in the U.S. He became active as a composer for films in Hollywood, but continued to write large amounts of orch. and chamber music. His style is remarkably fluent and adaptable to the various moods evoked in his music, often reaching rhapsodic eloquence.

WORKS: OPERAS: *La mandragola* (libretto by the composer, after Machiavelli; Venice, May 4, 1926; won the National Prize); *The Princess and the Pea,* after Andersen, overture with Narrator (1943); *Bacco in Toscana,* dithyramb for Voices and Orch. (Milan, May 8, 1931); *Aucassin et Nicolette,* puppet show with Voices and Instruments (1938; first perf. in Florence, June 2, 1952); *All's Well That Ends Well,* after Shakespeare (1959); *Saul,* biblical opera (1960); *Il Mercante di Venezia,* after Shakespeare's play *The Merchant of Venice,* to the composer's libretto in Italian (won first prize at the International Competition at La Scala, Milan; first perf. at the Maggio Musicale, Florence, May 25, 1961); *The Importance of Being Earnest,* after Oscar Wilde, chamber opera (1962); *The Song of Songs,* scenic oratorio (Hollywood, Aug. 7, 1963); *Tobias and the Angel,* scenic oratorio (1965). BIBLICAL ORATORIOS: *Ruth* (1949) and *Jonah* (1951). FOR ORCH.: *Cipressi* (Boston Symph., Koussevitzky conducting, Oct. 25, 1940; originally for Piano, 1920); Piano Concerto No. 1 (Rome, Dec. 9, 1928); Piano Concerto No. 2 (N.Y. Phil., Nov. 2, 1939, composer soloist); 3 violin concertos: *Concerto italiano* (Rome, Jan. 31, 1926); *The Prophets* (Jascha Heifetz and the N.Y. Phil., Toscanini conducting, April 12, 1933); 3rd Violin Concerto (1939); Cello Concerto (N.Y. Phil., Jan. 31, 1935, Piatigorsky soloist; Toscanini conducting); *Variazioni sinfoniche* for Violin and Orch. (Rome, 1930); overtures to Shakespeare's plays: *The Taming of the Shrew* (1930); *Twelfth Night* (1933); *The Merchant of Venice* (1933); *Julius Caesar* (1934); *A Midsummer Night's Dream* (1940); *Coriolanus* (1947); etc.; *Poem* for Violin and Orch. (1942); *The Birthday of the Infanta* (1942; New Orleans, Jan. 28, 1947); *Indian Songs and Dances,* suite (Los Angeles, Jan. 7, 1943); *An American Rhapsody* (1943); Serenade for Guitar and Orch. (1943); *Octoroon Ball,* ballet

suite (1947); *Noah's Ark,* movement for Narrator and Orch., from *Genesis,* a suite; other movements by Schoenberg, Stravinsky, Toch, Milhaud, Tansman, and N. Shilkret, who commissioned the work (Portland, Oreg., Dec. 15, 1947). CHAMBER MUSIC: *Signorine: 2 profili* for Violin and Piano (1918); *Ritmi* for Violin and Piano (1920); *Capitan Fracassa* for Violin and Piano (1920); *Notturno adriatico* for Violin and Piano (1922); *I nottambuli* for Cello and Piano (1927); Cello Sonata (1928); First Piano Trio (1928); First String Quartet (1929); *Sonata quasi una fantasia* for Violin and Piano (1929); *The Lark* for Violin and Piano (1930); First Piano Quintet (1932); 2nd Piano Trio (1932); Toccata for Cello and Piano (1935); *Capriccio diabolico* for Guitar (1935; later arranged as a guitar concerto); Concertino for Harp and 7 Instruments (1937); *Ballade* for Violin and Piano (1940); Divertimento for 2 Flutes (1943); Sonata for Violin and Viola (1945); Clarinet Sonata (1945); Sonatina for Bassoon and Piano (1946); 2nd String Quartet (1948); Quintet for Guitar and Strings (1950); Sonata for Viola and Cello (1950); Fantasia for Guitar and Piano (1950); *Concerto da camera* for Oboe and Strings (1950); Sonata for Violin and Cello (1950); 2nd Piano Quintet (1951). FOR PIANO: *English Suite* (1909); *Questo fu il carro della morte* (1913); *Il raggio verde* (1916); *Alghe* (1919); *I naviganti* (1919); *La sirenetta e il pesce turchino* (1920); *Cantico* (1920); *Vitalba e Biancospino* (1921); *Epigrafe* (1922); *Alt-Wien,* Viennese rhapsody (1923); *Piedigrotta* (1924); *Le stagioni* (1924); *Le danze del Re David* (1925); *3 poemi campestri* (1926); *3 corali su melodie ebraiche* (1926); Sonata (1928); *Crinoline* (1929); *Candide,* 6 pieces (1944); *6 canoni* (1950). SONGS: *Le Roy Loys* (1914); *Ninna-Nanna* (1914; very popular); *Fuori i barbari,* a patriotic song (1915); *Stelle cadenti* (1915); *Coplas* (1915); *Briciole* (1916); *3 fioretti di Santo Francesco* (1919; also with Orch.); *Girotondo de golosi* (1920); *Etoile filante* (1920); *L'infinito* (1921); *Sera* (1921); *2 preghiere per i bimbi d'Italia* (1923); *1830,* after Alfred de Musset (1924); *Scherzi,* 2 series (1924–25); music to 33 Shakespeare songs (1921–25); *Indian Serenade* (1925); *Cadix* (1926); *3 Sonnets from the Portuguese,* after E.B. Browning (1926); *Laura di Nostra Donna* (1935); *Un sonetto di Dante* (1939); *Recuerdo* (1940); *Le Rossignol* (1942); *The Daffodils* (1944). FOR CHORUS: 2 madrigals a cappella (1915); *Lecho dodi,* synagogue chant for Tenor, Men's Voices, and Organ (1936); *Sacred Synagogue Service* (1943); *Liberty, Mother of Exiles* (1944). Numerous pieces for guitar, including: *Les Guitares bien temperées,* 24 preludes and fugues for 2 Guitars (1962); 2 guitar concertos (1939, 1953); Concerto for 2 Guitars and Orch. (1962); 3rd String Quartet (1964); Sonatina for Flute and Guitar (1965); Sonata for Cello and Harp (1966).

Castiglioni, Niccolò, Italian pianist and composer of avant-garde tendencies; b. Milan, July 17, 1932. He studied composition with Ghedini, Desderi, and Margola at the Verdi Cons. in Milan, and piano with Gulda at the Mozarteum in Salzburg; also took composition lessons with Blacher. He began his career as a pianist; in 1966 emigrated to the U.S.; was composer-in-residence at the Center of Creative and Performing Arts at the State Univ. of N.Y. in Buffalo (1966–67); then was on the faculty of the Univ. of Michigan (1967) and Univ. of Washington at Seattle (1968–69); in 1970 he was appointed instructor at the Univ. of Calif. in San Diego. In his music he follows a pragmatically modernistic line of composition, making use of any and all mannerisms of the neo-Classical, neo-Romantic, and experimental resources while preserving a necessary minimum of communicable sound production.

WORKS: Opera, *Uomini e no* (1955); radio opera, *Attraverso lo specchio* (*Through the Looking Glass*), after Lewis Carroll (1961; Italian Radio, Oct. 1, 1961); chamber opera, *Jabberwocky*, after Lewis Carroll (1962); one-act opera, *Sweet*, for Baritone, Piano, Bells, and Winds (Rome, 1968); opera-triptych, *3 Mystery Plays* (Rome, Oct. 2, 1968; material made up of *Silence, Chordination*, and *The Rise and Rebellion of Lucifer and Aria*); *Concertino per la notte di Natale* for Strings and Woodwinds (1952); Symph. No. 1 for Soprano and Orch., to a text by Nietzsche (Venice, Sept. 15, 1956); Symph. No. 2 (1956–57; Italian Radio, Nov. 23, 1957); *Canti* for Orch. (1956); *Ouverture in tre tempi* (1957); *Elegia* for 19 Instruments and Soprano (1957); *Impromptus* for Orch. (1957–58); *Inizio di movimento* for Piano (1958); *Movimento continuato* for Piano and 11 Instruments (1958–59); *Sequenze* for Orch. (1959); *Tropi* for 6 Players (1959); *Aprèslude* for Orch. (1959); *Cangianti* for Piano (1959); *Eine kleine Weihnachtsmusik (A Little Christmas Music)* for Chamber Orch. (1959–60); *Disegni* for Chamber Orch. (1960); *Gymel* for Flute and Piano (1960); *Rondels* for Orch. (1960–61); *Décors* for Orch. (1962); *Consonante* for Flute and Chamber Orch. (1962); *Synchromie* for Orch. (1963); Concerto for Orch. (1963); *A Solemn Music I*, after Milton, for Soprano and Chamber Orch. (1963); *Gyro* for Chorus and 9 Instruments (1963); *Caractères* for Orch. (1963); *A Solemn Music II*, a revised version of *I* (1964–65); *Figure*, a mobile for Voice and Orch. (1965); *Alef* for Solo Oboe (1965); *Anthem*, composition in 5 strophes for Chorus and Orch. (1966); *Ode* for 2 Pianos, Wind Instruments, and Percussion (1966); *Canzoni* for Soprano and Orch. (Naples, Oct. 18, 1966); *Carmina* for Chamber Ensemble (1967); *Sinfonia guerriere et amorose* for Organ (1967); *Granulation* for 2 Flutes and 2 Clarinets (1967); *Masques* for 12 Instruments, a bouillabaisse of polytonally arranged fragments of dimly remembered tunes by other composers (1967); *The New Melusine* for String Quartet (1969); *La Chant du signe*, concerto for Flute and Orch. (1969); *Sinfonia in Do*, after Ben Jonson, Dante, Shakespeare, and Keats, for Chorus and Orch. (1968–69; Rome, May 21, 1971).

Castil-Blaze. See **Blaze, François-Henri-Joseph.**

Castro, José María, Argentine composer and conductor, brother of **Juan José Castro;** b. Avellaneda, near Buenos Aires, Dec. 15, 1892; d. Buenos Aires, Aug. 2, 1964. He studied in Buenos Aires; then went to Paris, and like his brother, took a course with Vincent d'Indy. Returning to Argentina in 1930, he became conductor of the Orquesta Filharmónica in Buenos Aires; from 1933 to 1953 also led the Banda Municipal de la Ciudad de Buenos Aires.

WORKS: 3 ballets: *Georgia* (1937; Teatro Colón, Buenos Aires, June 2, 1939; composer conducting), *El sueño de la botella* (1948), and *Falarka* (1951); a monodrama, *La otra voz* for Voice and Orch. (1953); Concerto Grosso for Chamber Orch. (1932; Buenos Aires, June 11, 1933); *Obertura para una ópera cómica* (1934); Piano Concerto (Buenos Aires, Nov. 17, 1941; revised 1956); Concerto for Orch. (1944); Concerto for Cello and 17 Instruments (1945); *3 Pastorales* for Orch. (1945); *Preludio y Toccata* for String Quartet and String Orch. (1949); *Tema coral con variaciones* for Orch. (1952); Concerto for Violin and 18 Instruments (1953); *10 improvisaciones breves* for Chamber Orch. or Piano (1957); *Preludio, Tema con variaciones y Final* for Orch. (1959); *Sinfonía de Buenos Aires* (1963); *El libro de los sonetos* for Voice and Orch. (1947); *5 líricas* for Voice and Orch. (1958); 13 sonnets, *Con la patria adentro*, for Tenor and Orch. (1964); Violin Sonata (1918); Cello Sonata (1933); Sonata for 2 Cellos (1938); 3 string quartets (1944, 1947, 1956); *Sonata poética* for Violin and Piano (1957); 6 piano sonatas (1919; 1924; 1927; 1931; *Sonata de primavera*, 1939; *Sonata dramática*, 1944); piano pieces.

Castro, Juan José, eminent Argentine composer and conductor, brother of **José María Castro;** b. Avellaneda, near Buenos Aires, March 7, 1895; d. Buenos Aires, Sept. 3, 1968. After study in Buenos Aires he went to Paris, where he took a course in composition with Vincent d'Indy. Returning to Argentina in 1929, he organized in Buenos Aires the Orquesta de Nacimiento, which he conducted; in 1930 he conducted the ballet season at the Teatro Colón; conducted opera there from 1933; also became the music director of the Asociación del Profesorado Orquestal and Asociación Sinfónica, with which he gave first local performances of a number of modern works. In 1934 he received a Guggenheim Foundation grant. From 1947 to 1951 he conducted in Cuba and Uruguay; from 1952 to 1953 he was principal conductor of the Victorian Symph. Orch. in Melbourne, Australia; in 1955 he returned to Argentina; from 1956 to 1960 was conductor of the Orquesta Sinfónica Nacional in Buenos Aires; from 1959 to 1964 was director of the Cons. of San Juan, Puerto Rico. He was proficient in all genres of composition, but his works were rarely performed outside of South America, and he himself conducted most of his symph. compositions.

WORKS: His most signal success on the international scene was the prize he received at the contest for the best opera at La Scala in Milan, for *Proserpina e lo straniero* (in the original Spanish, *Proserpina y el extranjero*), of which he conducted the first perf. at La Scala in Milan on March 17, 1952; his other operas were *La Zapatera prodigiosa*, after García Lorca (Montevideo, Dec. 23, 1949); *Bodas de sangre*, also after Lorca (Buenos Aires, Aug. 9, 1956);

Cosecha negra (1961). Other works: Ballets: *Mekhano* (Buenos Aires, July 17, 1937) and *Offenbachiana* (Buenos Aires, May 25, 1940); 5 symphs.: No. 1 (1931); *Sinfonía biblica* for Orch. and Chorus (1932); *Sinfonía Argentina* (Buenos Aires, Nov. 29, 1936); *Sinfonía de los campos* (Buenos Aires, Oct. 29, 1939); No. 5 (1956); *Dans le jardin des morts* (Buenos Aires, Oct. 5, 1924); *A una madre* (Buenos Aires, Oct. 27, 1925); *La Chellah*, symph. poem based on an Arabian theme (Buenos Aires, Sept. 10, 1927); *Allegro, Lento y Vivace* (1931); *Anunciación, Entrada a Jerusalem, Golgotha* (Buenos Aires, Nov. 15, 1932); *Corales criollos* No. 3, symph. poem (1953); won first prize at the Caracas Music Festival, 1954); *Epitafio en ritmos y sonidos* for Chorus and Orch. (1961); *Negro* for Soprano and Orch. (1961); *Suite introspectiva* (1961; Los Angeles, June 8, 1962); Violin Concerto (1962); Violin Sonata (1914); Cello Sonata (1916); String Quartet (1942); Piano Concerto (1941); 2 piano sonatas (1917, 1939); *Corales criollos* No. 1 and No. 2 for Piano (1947); songs.

Castro, Washington, Argentine composer, brother of **José María** and **Juan José Castro;** b. Buenos Aires, July 13, 1909. He studied cello; in 1947 devoted himself mainly to conducting and teaching.

WORKS: *Sinfonía primaveral* (1956); Piano Concerto (1960); *Sinfonía breve* for Strings (1960); Concerto for Orch. (1963); *Rhapsody* for Cello and Orch. (1963); *3 Pieces* for Orch. (1970); 3 string quartets (1945, 1950, 1965); piano pieces; songs.

Castrucci, Pietro, Italian violinist; b. Rome, 1679; d. Dublin, Feb. 29, 1752. He was a pupil of Corelli; came to London (1715) as leader of Handel's opera orch. He was a fine player on the "violetta marina," a stringed instrument invented by himself, and resembling the viola d'amore in tone. In *Orlando,* Handel wrote an air accompanied on 2 "violette marine" "per gli Signori Castrucci" (Pietro, and **Prospero,** his brother). Castrucci publ. violin concertos and 2 books of violin sonatas.

Catalani, Alfredo, greatly talented Italian composer; b. Lucca, June 19, 1854; d. Milan, Aug. 7, 1893. He studied music with his father, a church organist; in 1872 studied with Fortunato Magi and Bazzini at the Istituto Musicale Pacini in Lucca; then went to Paris, where he attended classes of Bazin (composition) and Marmontel (piano). He returned to Italy in 1873; in 1886 became the successor of Ponchielli as prof. of composition at the Milan Cons. It was in Milan that he became acquainted with Boito, who encouraged him in his composition; he also met young Toscanini, who became a champion of his music. Catalani was determined to create a Wagnerian counterpart in the field of Italian opera, and he selected for his libretti fantastic subjects suitable for dramatic action. After several unsuccessful productions he finally achieved his ideal in his last opera, *La Wally;* he died of tuberculosis the year after its production. WORKS: His operas include *La Falce* (Milan, July 19, 1875); *Elda* (Turin, Jan. 31, 1880; revised and pro-

duced under the title *Loreley,* Turin, Feb. 16, 1890); *Dejanice* (Milan, March 17, 1883); *Edmea* (Milan, Feb. 27, 1886); *La Wally* (Milan, Jan. 20, 1892); he further composed *Sinfonia a piena orchestra* (1872); *Il Mattino,* romantic symph. (1874); *Ero e Leandro,* symph. poem (Milan, May 9, 1885); a number of piano pieces and songs.

Catalani, Angelica, Italian soprano; b. Sinigaglia, May 10, 1780; d. Paris, June 12, 1849. She was taught at the convent of Santa Lucia di Gubbio in Rome; made her operatic debut at the Teatro la Fenice in Venice (1795); then sang at La Pergola in Florence (1799), and at La Scala in Milan (1801). In 1801, while engaged at the Italian Opera in Lisbon, she married Paul Valabrègue, an attaché of the French embassy; subsequently gave highly successful concerts in Paris and London. In 1814–17 she undertook, without signal success, the management of the Théâtre des Italiens in Paris while continuing her singing career, appearing in major European cities and at provincial festivals until 1828, when she retired to her country home near Florence. She won great acclaim for her commanding stage presence, wide vocal range, and mastery of the bravura singing style.

Catel, Charles-Simon, French composer and music pedagogue; b. l'Aigle, Orne, June 10, 1773; d. Paris, Nov. 29, 1830. He studied in Paris with Gossec and Gobert at the Ecole Royale du Chant (later merged with the Cons.); served as accompanist and teacher there (1787); in 1790 was accompanist at the Opéra and assistant conductor (to Gossec) of the band of the Garde Nationale. In 1795, on the establishment of the Cons., he was appointed prof. of harmony, and was commissioned to write a *Traité d'harmonie* (publ. 1802; a standard work at the Cons. for 20 years thereafter). In 1910 with Gossec, Méhul, and Cherubini, he was made an inspector of the Cons., resigning in 1816; was named a member of the Académie des Beaux-Arts in 1817. As a composer, Catel was at his best in his operas, written in a conventional but attractive style of French stage music of the time.

WORKS: Operas, performed at the Paris Opéra and the Opéra-Comique: *Sémiramis* (May 4, 1802); *L'Auberge de bagnères* (April 23, 1807); *Les Artistes par occasion* (Jan. 22, 1807); *Les Bayadères* (Paris Opéra, Aug. 8, 1810; his most successful work); *Les Aubergistes de qualité* (June 11, 1812); *Bayard à Mézières* (Feb. 12, 1814); *Le Premier en date* (Nov. 3, 1814); *Wallace, ou Le Ménestrel écossais* (March 24, 1817); *Zirphile et Fleur de Myrte, ou Cent ans en jour* (June 29, 1818); *L'Officier enlevé* (May 4, 1819); also several symphs. and chamber works.

Catoire, Georgi Lvovitch, Russian composer of French descent; b. Moscow, April 27, 1861; d. there, May 21, 1926. While a student of mathematics at the Univ. of Berlin, he took lessons in piano with Klindworth and in composition with Rüfer; later studied with Liadov in St. Petersburg; lived in Moscow and devoted himself to composing; also taught composition at the Moscow Cons.

Caturla, Alejandro García, Cuban composer; b. Remedios, March 7, 1906; assassinated at Remedios, Nov. 12, 1940. He studied with Pedro Sanjuán in Havana; then with Nadia Boulanger in Paris (1928); was founder (1932) and conductor of the Orquesta de Conciertos de Caibarién (chamber orch.) in Cuba; served as district judge in Remedios. His works have been performed in Cuba, Europe, and the U.S. In Caturla's music, primitive Afro-Cuban rhythms and themes are treated with modern techniques and a free utilization of dissonance.

WORKS: Suite of 3 Cuban dances: *Danza del tambor, Motivos de danzas, Danza Lucumí* (Havana, 1928; also perf. in Barcelona, Seville, and Bogotá); *Bembé* for 14 Instruments (Paris, 1929); *Dos poemas Afro-Cubanos* for Voice and Piano (Paris, 1929; also arranged for Voice and Orch.); *Yambo-O,* Afro-Cuban oratorio (Havana, Oct. 25, 1931); *Rumba* for Orch. (1931); *Primera suite cubana* for Piano and 8 Wind Instruments (1930); *Manita en el Suelo,* "mitologia bufa Afro-Cubana" for Narrator, Marionettes, and Chamber Orch., to the text of Alejo Carpentier (1934).

Caurroy, Eustache du. See **Du Caurroy, François-Eustache.**

Cavaccio, Giovanni, Italian composer; b. Bergamo, 1556; d. there, Aug. 11, 1626. He was maestro di cappella at the Cathedral of Bergamo (1581–98) and at Santa Maria Maggiore in Bergamo from 1604 until his death. Among his publ. works are collections of madrigals (1583, 1591, 1599); Psalms (1585); a Requiem (Milan, 1611); and a collection of keyboard pieces, *Sudori musicali* (Venice, 1626). Music by Cavaccio was included in a publication of Psalms dedicated to Palestrina (1592), and pieces by him were printed in Bonometti's *Parnassus Musicus. A Canzon francese per organo* and a toccata are reprinted in L. Torchi, *L'Arte Musicale in Italia* (vol. III.)

Cavaillé-Coll, Aristide, celebrated French organ builder; b. Montpellier, Feb. 4, 1811; d. Paris, Oct. 13, 1899. His father, Dominique Hyacinthe (1771–1862), was also an organ builder. Aristide went to Paris in 1833; built the organ at St.-Denis, and thereafter many famous organs in Paris (St.-Sulpice, Madeleine, etc.), the French provinces, Belgium, the Netherlands, and elsewhere. He invented the system of separate wind chests with different pressures for the low, medium, and high tones; also the "flûtes octaviantes." He publ. *Etudes expérimentales sur les tuyaux d'orgues* (report for the Académie des Sciences, 1849) and *Projet d'orgue monumental pour la Basilique de Saint-Pierre de Rome* (1875).

Cavalieri, Emilio del, Italian composer; b. c.1550; d. Rome, March 11, 1602. He was a nobleman who served as Inspector-General of Art and Artists at the Tuscan court in Florence (1588). He was one of the "inventors" and most ardent champions of the monodic style, or "stile recitativo," which combines melody with accompanying harmonies. His chief work, *La rappresentazione di anima e di corpo* (publ. by A. Guidotti, Rome, 1600, with explanatory preface; reprints: L. Guidiccioni-Nicastro, Livorno, 1911; Munich, 1921), once regarded as the first oratorio, is really a morality play set to music; other dramatic works (*Il satiro,* 1590; *Disperazione di Filene,* 1590; *Giuoco della cieca,* 1595) exemplify in similar manner the beginnings of modern opera form. In all of Cavalieri's music there is a *basso continuato* with thoroughbass figuring; the melodies are also crudely figured. A facsimile ed. of the libretto for *La rappresentazione* was publ. by D. Alaleona (Rome, 1912); a facsimile ed. of the orch. score is to be found in Mantica's *Collezione di prime fioriture del melodramma italiano* (Rome, 1912).

Cavalieri, Katharina, Austrian soprano of Italian descent; b. Währing, near Vienna, Feb. 19, 1760; d. Vienna, June 30, 1801. She studied with Salieri; sang with great success at the Italian Opera and then at the German Opera in Vienna. Although she never sang outside of Vienna, a passage in one of Mozart's letters, describing her as "a singer of whom Germany might well be proud," procured for her deserved recognition. She retired in 1793. Mozart wrote for her the role of Constanze in *Die Entführung,* and the aria "Mi tradi" in *Don Giovanni.*

Cavalieri, Lina, Italian dramatic soprano; b. Viterbo, Dec. 25, 1874; d. Florence, Feb. 8, 1944. As a young woman she was renowned for her beauty, and became the cynosure of the Paris boulevardiers when she appeared at the Folies-Bergère. During her Russian trip in 1900, she married Prince Bariatinsky, who persuaded her to abandon vaudeville and engage in an operatic career. After a few singing lessons with Maddalena Mariani-Masi, she sang in opera in St. Petersburg and Warsaw. In 1906 she was engaged to sing at the Metropolitan Opera in N.Y. (debut Dec. 5, 1906, as Fedora), where she was praised for her dramatic performances as Tosca and Mimi. In 1907, after a Russian divorce from her aristocratic first husband, she contracted a lucrative marriage with the American millionaire Winthrop Chandler, but left him in a week, precipitating a sensational scandal that, given the mores of the time, caused the Metropolitan to break her contract; made her farewell appearance there in a concert on March 8, 1908. In 1909 she returned to N.Y. for guest appearances at the Manhattan Opera House. In 1913 she married the French tenor Lucien Muratore; in 1919 she abandoned him, and opened a beauty salon in Paris. She then married her 4th husband, Paolo D'Arvanni, and went to live at her Villa Cappucina near Florence. Her life ended tragically, when both she and her last husband were killed during an air raid in 1944. She was the subject of an Italian film under the telling title *La donna più bella dello mondo,* with Gina Lollabrigida in the role of Lina Cavalieri.

Cavalli (Caletti), Pier Francesco, historically significant Italian opera composer; b. Crema, Feb. 14, 1602; d. Venice, Jan. 14, 1676. His father, Giovanni Battista Caletti (known also as Bruni), was maestro di cappella at the Cathedral in Crema; he gave him his first instruction in music; as a youth he sang under his father's direction in the choir of the Cathedral. The Venetian nobleman Federico Cavalli, who was also mayor of Crema, took him to Venice for further musical training; and as it was a custom, he adopted his sponsor's surname. In December 1616 he entered the choir of San Marco in Venice, beginning an association there which continued for the rest of his life; he sang there under Monteverdi; also served as an organist at SS. Giovanni e Paolo (1620–30). In 1638, he turned his attention to the new art form of opera, and helped to organize an opera company at the Teatro San Cassiano. His first opera, *Le nozze di Teti e di Peleo,* was performed there on Jan. 24, 1639; 9 more were to follow within the next decade. In 1639 he successfully competed against 3 others for the post of second organist at San Marco. In 1660 Cardinal Mazarin invited him to Paris, where he presented a restructured version of his opera *Serse* for the marriage festivities of Louis XIV and Maria Theresa. He also composed the opera *Ercole Amante* while there, which was given at the Tuileries on Feb. 7, 1662. He returned to Venice in 1662; on Jan. 11, 1665, he was officially appointed first organist at San Marco; on Nov. 20, 1668, he became maestro di cappella there. After Monteverdi, Cavalli stands as one of the most important Venetian composers of opera in the mid-17th century. In recent years several of his operas have been revived; Raymond Leppard edited *L'Ormindo* (London, 1969) and *Calisto* (London, 1975); Jane Glover edited *L'Eritrea* (London, 1977). Cavalli also composed much sacred music; several works are available in modern editions.

WORKS: Operas: *Le nozze di Teti e di Peleo* (Venice, Jan. 24, 1639); *Gli amori d'Apollo e di Dafne* (Venice, 1640); *Didone* (Venice 1641); *Amore innamorato* (Venice, Jan. 1, 1642; music not extant); *La virtù de' strali d'Amore* (Venice, 1642); *Egoisto* (Venice, 1643); *L'Ormindo* (Venice, 1644); *Doriclea* (Venice, 1645); *Titone* (Venice, 1645; music not extant); *Giasone* (Venice, Jan. 5, 1649); *Euripo* (Venice, 1649; music not extant); *Orimonte* (Venice, Feb. 20, 1650); *Oristeo* (Venice, 1651); *Rosinda* (Venice, 1651); *Calisto* (Venice, 1652); *L'Eritrea* (Venice, 1652); *Veremonda l'amazzone di Aragona* (Naples, Dec. 21, 1652); *L'Orione* (Milan, June 1653); *Ciro* (originally composed by Francesco Provenzale; prologue and arias added by Cavalli for Venice, Jan. 30, 1654); *Serse* (Venice, Jan. 12, 1655); *Statira principessa di Persia* (Venice, Jan. 18, 1656); *Erismena* (Venice, 1656); *Artemisia* (Venice, Jan. 10, 1657); *Hipermestra* (Florence, June 12, 1658); *Antioco* (Venice, Jan. 21, 1659; music not extant); *Elena* (Venice, Dec. 26, 1659); *Ercole Amante* (Paris, Feb. 7, 1662); *Scipione africano* (Venice, Feb. 9, 1664); *Mutio Scevola* (Venice, Jan. 26, 1665); *Pompeo ma-*

gno (Venice, Feb. 20, 1666); *Eliogabalo* (composed in 1668; not perf.); *Coriolano* (Piacenza, May 27, 1669; music not extant); *Massenzio* (composed in 1673; not perf.; music not extant). The following operas have been ascribed to Cavalli but are now considered doubtful: *Narciso et Ecco immortalati; Deidamia; Il Romolo e 'l Remo; La prosperità infelice di Giulio Cesare dittatore; Torilda; Bradamante; Armidoro; Helena rapita da Theseo;* also *La pazzia in trono, overo Caligola delirante,* which is a spoken drama with some music. None of the music is extant for any of these works.

Cavazzoni, Girolamo, Italian organist and composer; b. Urbino, c.1520; d. Venice, c.1577. He was a son of **Marco Antonio Cavazzoni** and godson of Cardinal Pietro Bembo. He was organist at San Barbara in Mantua until 1577; supervised the building of the organ there in 1565–66. His *Intavolatura cioè Ricercari, Canzoni, Hinni, Magnificati* (Venice, 1542) contains the first examples of the polyphonic ricercare of the 16th century. His organ ricercari, though related to the motet, differ from it in their extension of the individual sections by means of more numerous entries of the subject and more definite cadences between sections. The 2 canzonas from the same work mark the beginnings of an independent canzona literature for the keyboard. Reprints of Cavazzoni's works are found in L. Torchi, *L'Arte Musicale in Italia* (vol. III); Tagliapietra, *Antologia di Musica* (vol. I); Davison and Apel, *Historical Anthology of Music;* and Schering, *Geschichte der Musik in Beispielen.* O. Mishiati edited his organ works (2 vols., Mainz, 1959 and 1961).

Cavazzoni (also called **da Bologna** and **detta d'Urbino**), **Marco Antonio,** Italian composer and singer, father of **Girolamo Cavazzoni;** b. Bologna, c.1490; d. c.1570 (the date appearing on his will is April 3, 1569). He went to Urbino about 1510 and became acquainted with Cardinal Pietro Bembo; then became a musician in the private chapel of Pope Leo X (1515). In Venice (1517) he was employed by Francesco Cornaro, nephew of the Queen of Cyprus. Back in Rome (1520) he was again in the employ of Pope Leo X. From 1522–24 and from 1528–31 he was in Venice, and in 1536–37 was organist at Chioggia. From 1545–59 he was a singer at San Marco (Venice), where Adriaen Willaert was maestro di cappella. As a youth Cavazzoni wrote a mass, *Domini Marci Antonii,* so named because he derived its theme from the solmization syllables of his Christian names. His most important work is a collection of keyboard pieces, *Recerchari, motetti, canzoni, Libro I* (Venice, 1523). The ricercari are toccata-like rather than contrapuntal, and the motets and canzonas are instrumental transcriptions of vocal pieces. Modern reprints (with biographical notes) are found in Benvenuti's *I classici musicali italiani* (Milan, 1941) and in K. Jeppesen, *Die italienische Orgelmusik am Anfang des Cinquecento* (Copenhagen, 1943).

Cavos, Catterino, Italian-Russian composer; b.

Venice, Oct. 30, 1775; d. St. Petersburg, May 10, 1840. He studied with Francesco Bianchi; his first work was a patriotic hymn for the Republican Guard, performed at the Teatro Fenice (Sept. 13, 1797); he then produced a cantata, *L'eroe* (1798). That same year he received an invitation to go to Russia as conductor at the Imperial Opera in St. Petersburg. He was already on his way to Russia when his ballet *Il sotterraneo* was presented in Venice (Nov. 16, 1799). He remained in St. Petersburg for the rest of his life. His Russian debut as a composer was in a collaborative opera, *Rusalka* (adapted from *Das Donauweibchen* by F. Kauer; Nov. 7, 1803). This was followed by the operas *The Invisible Prince* (May 17, 1805), *The Post of Love* (1806), *Ilya the Bogatyr* (Jan. 12, 1807), *3 Hunchback Brothers* (1808), *The Cossack Poet* (May 27, 1812), and several ballets. His most significant work was *Ivan Susanin*, which he conducted at the Imperial Theater on Oct. 30, 1815. The subject of this opera was used 20 years later by Glinka in his opera *A Life for the Tsar;* the boldness of Cavos in selecting a libretto from Russian history provided the necessary stimulus for Glinka and other Russian composers. (Cavos conducted the premiere of Glinka's opera.) His subsequent operas were also based on Russian themes: *Dobrynia Nikitich* (1818) and *The Firebird* (1822). Cavos was a notable voice teacher; among his pupils were several Russian singers who later became famous.

Cebotari, Maria, Moldavian soprano; b. Kishinev, Bessarabia, Feb. 23, 1910; d. Vienna, June 9, 1949. She sang in a church choir; in 1924–29 studied at the Kishinev Cons.; then went to Berlin, where she took voice lessons with Oskar Daniel at the Hochschule für Musik. In 1929 she sang with a Russian émigré opera troupe in Bucharest and in Paris. In 1931 she made an auspicious debut as Mimi in *La Bohème* at the Dresden Opera; also appeared at the Salzburg Festival. In 1935 she joined the Berlin State Opera; in 1943 became a member of the Vienna State Opera. She also filled guest engagements in other European opera houses. She had a large repertoire which included the standard soprano roles, among them Violetta, Madama Butterfly, Pamina, and Manon; she also gave brilliant performances in modern operas; Richard Strauss greatly prized her abilities, and entrusted to her the role of Aminta in the premiere of his opera *Die schweigsame Frau.* Thanks to her cosmopolitan background, she sang the part of Tatiana in Russian in Tchaikovsky's opera *Eugene Onegin* and the part of Antonida in Glinka's *A Life for the Tsar.* She also appeared in sound films. She was married to the Russian nobleman Count Alexander Virubov; she divorced him in 1938 and married the film actor Gustav Diessl.

Ceccato, Aldo, Italian conductor; b. Milan, Feb. 18, 1934. He studied at the Cons. of Milan, and at the Academy of Music in Berlin. In 1969 he won first prize in the International Competition of Italian Radio for young conductors. He made his American debut with the Chicago Lyric Opera in 1969; then conducted the N.Y. Phil. on Nov. 5, 1970, with excellent success. From 1973 to 1977 he was conductor of the Detroit Symph. Orch. In 1975 he was named Generalmusikdirektor of the Hamburg Phil.

Celibidache, Sergiu, transcendently endowed Rumanian conductor; b. Roman, June 28, 1912. He studied at the Hochschule für Musik in Berlin with Kurt Thomas, Heinz Gmeindl, and Fritz Stein, and also attended the musicology classes of Schering and Schünemann at the Univ. of Berlin; apart from music, he studied advanced mathematics and formalistic philosophy. In 1945 he was suddenly thrust into the position of conductor pro tem of the Berlin Phil. until the regular conductor, Furtwängler, was cleared of any suspicion of Naziphilia. Celibidache served as Furtwängler's assistant from 1947, and continued in this capacity in Berlin until 1952. From 1964 to 1971 he was engaged as music director of the Swedish Radio Symph. Orch.; in 1970 was named Knight of the Swedish Vasa Order; in 1971–77 he was conductor of the Stuttgart Radio Orch.; in 1980 was appointed Generalmusikdirektor of the Munich Phil. Orch. In 1983 he joined the faculty of the Curtis Inst. of Music in Philadelphia, where he also conducted the student orch. On Feb. 27, 1984, he conducted it at Carnegie Hall, N.Y., in his formal American debut as conductor, arousing hosannas and hurrahs from the delighted audience and astonishing critics, in a diversified program of works by Rossini, Wagner, Debussy, and Prokofiev. A cosmopolitan existentialist, he lectured on musical phenomenology at Mainz Univ., and composed music in his leisure time; he wrote 4 symphs., a Piano Concerto, and a variety of minor pieces. As an interpreter, he strives for humanly attainable perfection, and to achieve his goal demands an unconscionable number, sometimes as many as 18, of rehearsals; this precluded most American orch. managements from snaring him into permanent employment. His name is not unpronounceable, however (Cheh-lee-bee-dáh-key, with the stress on the 4th syllable).

Cerha, Friedrich, Austrian composer of the avantgarde; b. Vienna, Feb. 17, 1926. He studied violin with Vasa Prihoda and composition with Alfred Uhl at the Vienna Music Academy (1946–51); also attended courses in musicology and philosophy at the Univ. of Vienna (1946–50). Upon graduation, he became active in the modernistic movement as a violinist, conductor, and composer. In 1958 he organized (with Kurt Schwertsik) the Vienna concert ensemble Die Reihe, devoted to new music. In 1960 he became director of the electronic-music studio and a lecturer at the Vienna Academy, becoming a prof. in 1969. His music pursues the aim of "atomization of thematic materials" as a means toward total integration of infinitesimal compositional quantities, with minimal variations of successive temporal units.

Černohorsky, Bohuslav. See **Czernohorsky, Bohuslav.**

Cerone, Domenico Pietro, Italian tenor and music theorist; b. Bergamo, 1566; d. Naples, 1625. In 1592 he went to Spain and became a singer in the court choir; later was appointed teacher of plainsong to the clergy of the church of the Annunciation at Naples; from 1610 until his death, sang in the Royal Chapel Choir there. He publ. the manual *Regole per il canto fermo* (Naples, 1609) and *El Melopeo y Maestro, tractado de música teórica y práctica* (Naples, 1613). This treatise, written in Spanish, numbers 1,160 pages, containing a compendium of early music theory; it is divided into 22 books and 849 chapters; its pedantic exposition and inordinate length were the main target of Eximeno's satirical novel *Don Lazarillo Vizcardi;* Book XII is publ. in Eng. in O. Strunk's *Source Readings in Music History* (N.Y., 1950); in the U.S., copies of the entire work are to be found in the Library of Congress, the N.Y. Public Library, the Hispanic Society of N.Y., and the Sibley Music Library in Rochester, N.Y.

Certon, Pierre, French contrapuntist; b. c.1510; d. Paris, Feb. 23, 1572. He was a pupil of Josquin des Prez; was choirmaster of the Sainte-Chapelle in Paris (from 1536); composed masses, motets, Psalms, Magnificats, and 4-part chansons, which were printed in the collections of Ballard, Attaignant, Susato, Phalèse, and others, between 1527 and 1560. Reprints of his masses (*Sur le pont d'Avignon; Adjuva me; Regnum mundi*) are to be found in H. Expert's *Monuments de la musique française au temps de la Renaissance,* vol. 2 (1925); 10 chansons in vol. 82 of *Das Chorwerk.*

Cervantes (Kawanag), Ignacio, Cuban pianist and composer; b. Havana, July 31, 1847; d. there, April 29, 1905. He studied with Gottschalk (1859–61) and at the Paris Cons. (1866–68), with Alkan and Marmontel; in 1870 returned to Cuba; in 1898 went to Mexico; also visited the U.S. He was one of the pioneers of native Cuban music; in his *Danzas Cubanas* for Piano he employs Cuban rhythms in an effective salon manner; he also wrote 3 operas, *El submarino Peral, Los Saltimbanquis,* and *Maledetto* (1895; unfinished), and some orch. pieces.

Červený, Wenzel Franz (Václav František), inventor of brass instruments; b. Dubeč, Bohemia, Sept. 27, 1819; d. Königgrätz, Jan. 19, 1896. He was a good performer on most brass instruments when he was only 12 years old; learned his trade with Bauer, a music instrument maker in Prague; worked at various times in Brünn, Bratislava, Vienna, and Budapest; in 1842 established his own shop at Königgrätz. He invented the following instruments: Cornon (1844), Contrabass (1845), Phonikon (1848), Baroxiton (1853), Contrafagotto in metal (1856), Althorn obbligato (1859), Turnerhorn, Jägerhorn, army trombones (1867), and Primhorn (1873). After the success of the Primhorn, he created the complete Waldhorn quartet, which he considered his greatest achievement. Then followed the Subcontrabass and the Subcontrafagotto, and finally an entire family of improved cornets ("Kaiserkornette") and the "Triumph" cornet. His "roller" cylinder-mechanism is an invention of the greatest importance. He also improved the Euphonion, the Russian Signal-horns, the Screw-drum, and the church kettledrum. His instruments took first prizes at exhibitions in Europe and America.

Cesti, Antonio (baptismal name, **Pietro**), renowned dramatic composer; b. Arezzo, Aug. 5, 1623; d. Florence, Oct. 14, 1669. He was a choirboy in Arezzo; then joined the Franciscan order (1637) in Votterra; was probably a pupil of Carissimi at Rome in 1640–45; later was maestro di cappella to Ferdinand II de' Medici, at Florence; in 1660, became a tenor singer in the Papal choir; in 1666–68, was assistant Kapellmeister to Emperor Leopold I at Vienna; then he returned to Florence.

WORKS: His first opera, *Orontea* (Venice, Jan. 20, 1649), was much applauded; other dramatic ventures were also successful; *Cesare amante* (Venice, 1651); *Argia* (Innsbruck, 1655); *Dori* (Innsbruck, 1657; selections printed in vol. XII of *Publikationen der Gesellschaft für Musikforschung*); *Il Principe generoso* (Vienna, 1665; authorship disputed); *Tito* (Venice, Feb. 13, 1666); *Nettuno e Flora festeggianti* (Vienna, July 12, 1666); *Il Pomo d'oro* (Vienna, 1667; publ. in its entirety in Denkmäler der Tonkunst in Österreich, 6, 9 [3.ii, 4.ii]); *Semiramide* (Vienna, June 9, 1667); *Le disgrazie d'Amore* (Vienna, 1667); *Argene* (Venice, 1668); *Genserico* (Venice, Jan. 31, 1669). Cesti wrote numerous cantatas which are preserved in various European libraries; his dramatic flair is reflected in the theatrical forms of his cantatas; he also wrote madrigals, songs, etc. A. Schering's *Geschichte der Musik in Beispielen* contains an aria from *Argia* (No. 203); H. Riemann's *Kantaten-Frühling* (Leipzig, 1912; no. 9), F. Vatielli's *Antiche cantate d'amore* (Bologna, 1920; no. 8), and G. Adler's *Handbuch* (2nd ed., 1930; pp. 439ff.).

Chabrier, (Alexis-) Emmanuel, famous French composer; b. Ambert, Puy de Dôme, Jan. 18, 1841; d. Paris, Sept. 13, 1894. He studied law in Paris (1858–61); also studied composition with Semet and Hignard, piano with Edouard Wolff, and violin with Hammer. He served in the government from 1861; at the same time cultivated his musical tastes; with Duparc, Vincent d'Indy, and others he formed a private group of music lovers, and was an enthusiastic admirer of Wagner. He began to compose in earnest, and produced 2 light operas: *L'Etoile* (Paris, Nov. 28, 1877) and *Une Éducation manquée* (Paris, May 1, 1879). In 1879 he went to Germany with Duparc to hear Wagner's operas; returning to Paris, he publ. some piano pieces; then traveled to Spain; the fruit of this journey was his most famous work, the rhapsody *España* (Paris, Nov. 4, 1883), which produced a sensation when performed by Lamoureux in 1884. Another work of Spanish inspiration was the *Habanera* for piano (1885). In the meantime he served as chorus master for Lamoureux; this experience developed his knowledge of vocal writing; he wrote a brief cantata for mezzo-soprano and women's chorus, *La Sulamite* (March 15, 1885), and his 2 operas *Gwendoline* (Brussels, April 10, 1886) and *Le Roi malgré lui* (Opéra-Comique, Paris, May 18, 1887); another opera, *Briséis,* remained unfinished. In his operas Chabrier attempted a grand style; his idiom oscillated between passionate Wagnerianism and a more conventional type of French stage music; although these operas enjoyed a *succès d'estime,* they never became popular, and Chabrier's place in music history is secured exclusively by his *España,* and piano pieces such as *Bourrée fantasque* (1891; orchestrated by Felix Mottl); his *Joyeuse Marche* for Orch. (originally entitled *Marche française,* 1888) is also popular. Other works are *Ode à la musique* for Voices and Orch. (1890); *10 pièces pittoresques* for Piano (1880; 4 of them orchestrated and perf. as *Suite pastorale*); *3 valses romantiques* for 2 Pianos (1883); songs.

Chadwick, George Whitefield, eminent American composer; b. Lowell, Mass., Nov. 13, 1854; d. Boston, April 4, 1931. He first studied music with Eugene Thayer in Boston; then became head of the music dept. at Olivet College in Michigan (1876); from 1877–78 studied at the Leipzig Cons. with Reinecke and Jadassohn; his graduation piece was an overture to *Rip Van Winkle,* which he conducted with the Leipzig Cons. Orch. on June 20, 1879; then studied organ and composition at Munich under Rheinberger; in 1880 returned to Boston as organist of the South Congregational Church; in 1882 became a teacher of harmony and composition at the New England Cons.; in 1897 succeeded Faelten as director. He received the honorary degree of M.A. from Yale, and an honorary LL.D. from Tufts College in 1905; received the Gold Medal of the Academy of Arts and Letters in 1928; for several seasons was conductor of the Worcester Music Festival; also head of music festivals in Springfield and Worcester, Mass.; was a member of the Boston Academy of Arts and Letters. Chadwick was one of the leading American composers; usually regarded as a pillar of the "Boston Classicists," he was actually an ardent romanticist; his musical style was formed under the influence of the German programmatic school; his harmonies are Wagnerian, his orchestration full and lush.
WORKS: FOR THE STAGE: Comic Operas: *The Quiet Lodging* (privately perf., Boston, 1892) and *Tabasco* (Boston, Jan. 29, 1894); *Judith,* lyric drama (Worcester Festival, Sept. 26, 1901); *The Padrone,* opera (1915); *Love's Sacrifice,* pastoral operetta (1916; Chicago, Feb. 1, 1923); incidental music to *Everywoman* (N.Y. and London, 1911). FOR ORCH.: 3 symphs.: No. 1, in C (1883–85); No. 2, in B-flat (Boston Symph., Dec. 11, 1886); No. 3, in F (Boston Symph., Oct. 20, 1894); overtures: *Rip Van Winkle, Thalia, The Miller's Daughter, Melpomene* (Boston, Dec. 24, 1887; also arranged for Piano, 4-hands), *Adonais* (Boston, Feb. 3, 1900), *Euterpe* (Boston Symph., April 23, 1904, composer conducting), and *Anniversary Overture* (Norfolk Festival, 1922); Serenade in F for String Orch.; *A Pastoral Prelude* (Boston, 1894); Sinfonietta in D (Boston, Nov. 21, 1904); symph. poems: *Cleopatra* (Worcester Festival, 1905)

and *Angel of Death* (N.Y., 1919); *Symphonic Sketches,* suite (*Jubilee, Noël, Hobgoblin,* and *A Vagrom Ballad;* 1895–1904; Boston Symph., Feb. 7, 1908); Theme, Variations, and Fugue for Organ and Orch. (Boston, 1908; arranged by J. Wallace Goodrich for Organ Solo); *Suite symphonique* (Philadelphia, 1911; first prize of the National Federation of Music Clubs); *Aphrodite,* symph. fantasy (Norfolk Festival, 1912); *Tam O'Shanter,* symph. ballad (Norfolk Festival, 1915). CHORAL WORKS: *Dedication Ode* (1886) for Soli, Chorus, and Orch.; *Lovely Rosabelle,* ballad for Solo, Chorus, and Orch. (Boston, 1889); *The Pilgrims* for Chorus and Orch. (Boston, 1891); *Ode for the Opening of the Chicago World's Fair* for Chorus, with Piano or Orch. (1892); *Phoenix Expirans* for Soli, Chorus, and Orch. (Springfield Festival, 1892); *The Lily Nymph,* cantata (1893); *Lochinvar* for Baritone and Orch. (Springfield Festival, 1897); *Noël,* Christmas pastoral for Soli, Chorus, and Orch. (Norfolk Festival, 1908); *Aghadoe,* ballad for Alto and Orch.; numerous sacred works: *Ecce jam noctis* (Yale, 1897); *The Beatitudes; Jubilate;* etc.; many choruses for men's, women's, and mixed voices; also school choruses. CHAMBER MUSIC: 5 string quartets (I, in G minor; II, in C; III, in D; IV, in E minor; V, in D minor); Piano Quintet (1888); violin and cello pieces; etc. He composed about 100 songs with piano, organ, or orch. (*Allah, Ballad of the Trees and Masters, The Danza, Before the Dawn,* etc.). ORGAN WORKS: *10 Canonic Studies for Organ* (1885); *Progressive Pedal Studies for Organ* (1890); miscellaneous pieces (*Requiem, Suite in Variation Form,* etc.); also numerous piano pieces.
WRITINGS: He was the author of *Harmony, A Course of Study* (Boston, 1897; revised ed., 1922) and *Key to the Textbook on Harmony* (Boston, 1902); was co editor of *A Book of Choruses for High Schools and Choral Societies* (N.Y., 1923).

Chaikovsky. See **Tchaikovsky.**

Chailley, Jacques, eminent French musicologist; b. Paris, March 24, 1910. He studied composition with Nadia Boulanger, Delvincourt, and Busser; musicology with Pirro, Rokseth, and Smijers; conducting with Mengelberg and Monteux; also took courses in the history of medieval French literature at the Sorbonne (1932–36; received his Ph.D. there in 1952 with 2 dissertations: *L'Ecole musicale de Saint-Martial de Limoges jusqu'à la fin du XIᵉ siècle* [publ. in Paris, 1960] and *Chansons de Gautier du Coinci* [publ. as *Les Chansons à la Vierge de Gautier de Coinci* in *Monuments de la musique ancienne,* XV, 1959]). He was general secretary (1937–47), vice-principal (1947–51), and prof. of the choral class (1951–53) at the Paris Cons.; in 1952 he became director of the Inst. of Musicology at the Univ. of Paris; also taught at the Lycée La Fontaine (1951–69); in 1962 he became director of the Schola Cantorum. He has written authoritatively on many subjects, including medieval music, the music of ancient Greece, musical history, and the music of Bach, Mozart, Wagner, and others. He also wrote 2 operas, a ballet, orch. works, etc.

Chailly, Luciano, Italian composer; b. Ferrara, Jan. 19, 1920. He studied in Bologna and then with Renzo Bossi in Milan; in 1948 took courses with Hindemith in Salzburg. In 1962 he was appointed head of Rome Television. He was artistic director at La Scala in Milan in 1968–71 and in Turin from 1972; in 1969 joined the faculty at the Milan Cons. He composes in a communicative neo-Classical idiom, with some dodecaphonic incrustations and electronic effects.

WORKS: Operas: *Ferrovia sopraelevata* (Bergamo, Oct. 1, 1955); *Il canto del cigno* (Bologna, Nov. 16, 1957); *Una domanda di matrimonio,* after Chekhov (Milan, May 22, 1957); *La riva delle Sirti* (Monte Carlo, March 1, 1959); *Procedura penale* (Como, Sept. 30, 1959); *Il mantello,* surrealist opera (Florence, May 11, 1960); *Era probita* (Milan, March 5, 1963); *L'Idiota,* after Dostoyevsky (Rome, Feb. 14, 1970); also music for television.

Chailly, Riccardo, Italian conductor; b. Milan, Feb. 20, 1953. He studied music with his father, the renowned **Luciano Chailly.** As a young boy, he conducted a concert in Padua; then moved to Milan, which became his home town. He enrolled at the Giuseppe Verdi Cons. in the class of Bruno Bettinelli, and later went to Siena, where he took courses in conducting with the famous Franco Ferrara; his other teachers in conducting were Piero Guarino and Franco Caracciolo. He was only 19 when he was appointed assistant conductor at La Scala, in 1972. At 21 he was engaged to conduct *Madama Butterfly* with the Chicago Lyric Opera, marking the beginning of his international career. In 1976 he founded, with Hans Werner Henze, the Cantiere Internazionale d'Arte in Montepulciano. He made his debut as conductor of the Metropolitan Opera in N.Y. on March 8, 1982, in a new production of Offenbach's *Les Contes d'Hoffmann.* Apart from his operatic engagements, Chailly was appointed, in 1982, chief conductor of RIAS (West Berlin Radio Symph. Orch.); also in 1982, he became principal guest conductor of the London Phil.

Chaliapin, Feodor, celebrated Russian bass; b. Kazan, Feb. 13, 1873; d. Paris, April 12, 1938. He was of humble origin; at the age of 10 he was apprenticed to a cobbler; at 14 he got a job to sing in a chorus in a traveling opera company; his companion was the famous writer Maxim Gorky, who also sang in a chorus; together they made their way through the Russian provinces, often forced to walk the railroad tracks when they could not afford the fare. Chaliapin's wanderings brought him to Tiflis, in the Caucasus, where he was introduced to the singing teacher Dimitri Usatov (1847–1913), who immediately recognized Chaliapin's extraordinary gifts and taught him free of charge, helping him besides with board and lodgings. In 1894 Chaliapin received employment in a summer opera company in St. Petersburg, and shortly afterward he was accepted at the Imperial Opera during the regular season. In 1896 he sang in Moscow with a private opera com-

pany and produced a great impression by his dramatic interpretation of the bass parts in Russian operas. He also gave numerous solo concerts, which were sold out almost immediately; young music lovers were willing to stand in line all night long to obtain tickets. Chaliapin's first engagement outside Russia was in 1901, at La Scala in Milan, where he sang the role of Mefistofele in Boito's opera of that name; he returned to La Scala in 1904 and again in 1908. On Nov. 20, 1907, he made his American debut at the Metropolitan Opera as Mefistofele; then sang Mephistophélès in Gounod's *Faust* on Jan. 6, 1908; sang Leporello in Mozart's *Don Giovanni* on Jan. 23, 1908. He did not return to America until 1921, when he sang one of his greatest roles, that of the Czar Boris in *Boris Godunov* (Dec. 9, 1921); he continued to appear at the Metropolitan between 1921 and 1929. He sang in Russian opera roles at Covent Garden in London in 1913; returned to Russia in 1914, and remained there during World War I and the Revolution. He was given the rank of People's Artist by the Soviet government, but this title was withdrawn after Chaliapin emigrated in 1922 to Paris, where he remained until his death, except for appearances in England and America. The critical attitude toward Chaliapin in Russia on account of his emigration changed when he was recognized as a great Russian artist who elevated the art of Russian opera to the summit of expressive perfection; numerous articles dealing with Chaliapin's life and career were publ. in the Russian language. He was indeed one of the greatest singing actors of all time; he dominated every scene in which he appeared, and to the last he never failed in his ability to move audiences, even though his vocal powers declined considerably during his last years. He was especially famed for his interpretation of the role of Boris Godunov in Mussorgsky's opera; both dramatically and vocally he created an imperishable image. He was equally great as Mephistophélès in *Faust* and in the buffo roles of Don Basilio in *The Barber of Seville* and Leporello in *Don Giovanni.* He also played the title role in a film version of *Don Quixote.* His last American recital took place in N.Y. on March 3, 1935.

Chamberlain, Houston Stewart, English writer on music; b. Portsmouth, Sept. 9, 1855; d. Bayreuth, Jan. 9, 1927. He received his earliest education at Versailles, and then studied at Cheltenham College in Gloucester. Because of ill health he was obliged to abandon his intention of following a military career (his father was a British admiral), and in 1870 he went to Stettin. His association with Prof. Kuntze there filled him with enthusiasm for Germanic culture and civilization, to the study of which he devoted many years. The results of these studies he publ. in a remarkable work, *Die Grundlagen des 19. Jahrhunderts* (Munich, 1899–1901; 10th ed., 1914; Eng. trans. by Lord Redesdale, London, 1910). The years 1879–81 he spent in Geneva, studying science at the Univ. (taking his degree with the dissertation *Recherches sur la sève ascendante*) and music with A. Ruthardt. During his residence at Dresden (1885–89) he began his activities as a contributor to various German, French, and English journals, writing with equal facility in 3 languages. From 1889–1908 he lived in Vienna. In 1908 he married Wagner's daughter, Eva, then lived in Bayreuth. Chamberlain was one of the most ardent apostles of Wagner's art, and he was also the chief protagonist of Wagner's ideas of German supremacy, which Chamberlain presented in a simplified and vulgar manner, combined with pseudo-scientific speculation and spiced with heavy doses of anti-Semitism. As early as 1923, Chamberlain was attracted to Hitler, but he did not live to see the full flowering of the Nazi millennium. Chamberlain's books on Wagner are of value as a reflection of the time, even though biographical sections are incomplete and out of focus.

Chambonnières, Jacques Champion (called **Champion de Chambonnières**), French clavecinist and composer; b. c.1601–2; d. Paris, April 1672. He was first chamber musician to Louis XIV until 1662, and the teacher of the elder Couperins, d'Anglebert, Le Bègue, Hardelle, and others. Considered the founder of the French clavecin school, he was famed throughout Europe and his style strongly influenced that of contemporary German composers, among them Froberger. Two books of his clavecin pieces were printed (Paris, 1670; reprint of *Les Pièces de clavessin* in the series Monuments of Music . . . in Facsimile, Paris, 1967). Chambonnières's complete works were publ. by Brunold & Tessier (Paris, 1925; reprinted with Eng. trans. and new preface, 1961).

Chaminade, Cécile, French composer and pianist; b. Paris, Aug. 8, 1857; d. Monte Carlo, April 13, 1944. She was a pupil of Lecouppey, Savard, and Marsick; later studied composition with Benjamin Godard. She became successful as a concert pianist; wrote a great number of agreeable piano pieces, in the salon style, which acquired enormous popularity in France, England, and America; her more serious works were much less successful. She made her American debut playing the piano part of her *Concertstück* with the Philadelphia Orch. (Nov. 7, 1908); also wrote a lyric symph., *Les Amazones* (Antwerp, 1888); 2 orch. suites; 2 piano trios; more than 200 piano pieces in a Romantic style, including *Etude symponique, Valse-Caprice, Les Sylvains, La Lisonjera, Arabesque, Impromptu, 6 Airs de ballet,* etc.; numerous songs.

Chamlee, Mario (real name, **Archer Cholmondeley**), American lyric tenor; b. Los Angeles, May 29, 1892; d. there, Nov. 13, 1966. He made his operatic debut as the Duke in *Rigoletto* (San Francisco Opera, 1917); from 1917–19 served with the U.S. Army in France; married the soprano **Ruth Miller** (d. Los Angeles, June 28, 1983, at the age of 90) on Oct. 2, 1919; first appeared with the Metropolitan Opera as Cavaradossi in *Tosca* (Nov. 22, 1920); made extensive concert tours of the U.S. In 1940 he settled in Hollywood as a voice teacher.

Champagne, Claude, Canadian composer; b. Montreal, May 27, 1891; d. there, Dec. 21, 1965. He studied violin, piano, and composition in Montreal; then went to Paris, where he took courses in composition with Gédalge, Koechlin, and Laparra (1921–29). Returning to Canada, he joined the staff of McGill Univ. in Montreal (1932–41). From 1942 to 1962 he served as associate coordinator at the Cons. of Quebec. In his music he follows the modern French tradition.

WORKS: *Hercule et Omphale,* symph. poem (1918; Paris, March 31, 1926); *Prelude et Filigrane* for Piano (1918); *Suite canadienne* for Chorus and Orch. (Paris, Oct. 20, 1928); *Habanera* for Violin and Piano (1929); *Danse villageoise* for Violin and Piano (1929; also orchestrated); *Quadrilha brasileira* for Piano (1942); *Images du Canada français* for Chorus and Orch. (1943; Montreal, March 9, 1947); *Evocation* for Small Orch. (1943); *Symphonie gaspésienne* (1945); Piano Concerto (1948; Montreal, May 30, 1950); String Quartet (1951); *Paysanna* for Small Orch. (1953); *Suite miniature* for Flute, Cello, and Harpsichord (1958); *Altitude* for Chorus and Orch., with Ondes Martenot (Toronto, April 22, 1960); *Concertino grosso* for String Orch. (1963); organ pieces; songs.

Champion, Jacques. See **Chambonnières, Jacques Champion.**

Chanler, Theodore Ward, American composer; b. Newport, R.I., April 29, 1902; d. Boston, July 27, 1961. He studied in Boston with Hans Ebell (piano) and with Arthur Shepherd (composition); then at the Cleveland Inst. of Music with Ernest Bloch; later went to England, where he took courses at Oxford Univ. (1923–25); also studied with Nadia Boulanger in Paris. He returned to America in 1933. His music, mostly in smaller forms, is distinguished by a lyrical quality; his songs are particularly expressive; he employed the modern idiom of polytonal texture without overloading the harmonic possibilities; the melody is free, but usually within tonal bounds.

Chanot, François, French violin maker; b. Mirecourt, March 25, 1788; d. Rochefort (Charente-Maritime), Nov. 12, 1825. He was the son of an instrument maker; became a naval engineer, was retired on half-pay, and during his forced inactivity constructed a violin on the principle that the vibratory power would be increased by preserving the longitudinal wood fibers intact as far as possible. Thus his violin had no bouts, but slight incurvations like a guitar; the sound holes were almost straight, and the belly nearly flat; the strings were attached to the edge of the belly, instead of to a tailpiece. The violin was submitted to the Academy, whose report after testing it rated it equally with those of Stradivari and Guarneri; despite this evaluation, Chanot's violin never became popular. His brother, a *luthier* at Paris, manufactured a number of them, but gave it up when a few years had demonstrated their unpractical character.

Chapí y Lorente, Ruperto, Spanish composer of light opera; b. Villena, near Alicante, March 27, 1851; d. Madrid, March 25, 1909. He studied at the Cons. of Madrid; received a stipend from the Spanish Academy for further study in Rome (1874); wrote some operas (*La hija de Jefte, La hija de Garcilaso,* etc.), but discovered that his talent found more suitable expression in the lighter zarzuela, in which form his first success was won with *La Tempestad* (1882); his work is noted for elegance, grace, and exquisite orchestration; of one of his last zarzuelas (*La revoltosa*), Saint-Saëns remarked that Bizet would have been proud to sign his name to the score. His last zarzuela, *Margarita la Tornera* (Madrid, Feb. 24, 1909), was produced shortly before his death. Chapí y Lorente wrote 155 zarzuelas and 6 operas. In 1893 he founded the Sociedad de Autores, Compositores y Editores de Música.

Chappell & Co., London music publishers, concert agents, and piano manufacturers. Founded in 1810 by Samuel Chappell, J.B. Cramer (the pianist), and F.T. Latour. Cramer retired in 1819, Latour in 1826, and S. Chappell died in 1834, when his son **William** (1809–88) became the head of the firm. In 1840 he established the Musical Antiquarian Society, for which he edited Dowland's songs; he also edited and publ. *A Collection of National English Airs* (2 vols., 1838–39), later enlarged as *Popular Music of the Olden Time* (2 vols., 1855–59; revised by H.E. Wooldridge and publ. in 2 vols., 1893); he left an unfinished *History of Music* (vol. I, London, 1874). His brothers, **Thomas Patey** (1819–1902) and **S. Arthur** (1834–1904), were respectively the founder and manager of the Monday and Saturday Popular Concerts. In 1897 the partnership became a limited company, and Thomas was succeeded by his son, **T. Stanley** (d. 1933), as board chairman; later, William Boosey became managing director. In 1929 the firm was acquired by **Louis Dreyfus.** The American branch, under the direction of **Max Dreyfus,** brother of Louis, has publ. the songs and musical comedies of Richard Rodgers, Jerome Kern, Cole Porter, Harold Arlen, and other popular composers.

Chapple, Stanley, English conductor; b. London, Oct. 29, 1900. He studied at the London Academy of Music; became accompanist with the British National Opera Co. (1918–21); music director of the Vocalion Gramophone Co. (1924–29); and opera conductor at the Guildhall School of Music (1935–39). He had, meanwhile, been making annual summer appearances in the U.S. (1929–39) and was assistant conductor at the Berkshire Music Center (1939–47). In 1948 he became director of the School of Music at the Univ. of Washington in Seattle; resigned from there in 1971 and was then named a prof. emeritus.

Charles, Ernest, American songwriter; b. Minneapolis, Nov. 21, 1895; d. Beverly Hills, Calif., April 16, 1984. He began his career as a singer in Broadway revues and in vaudeville; also wrote songs in an appetizing semi-classical genre, suitable for recitals. His first commercial success came in 1932 when the popular baritone John Charles Thomas sang his song *Clouds* in a N.Y. recital. Encouraged, Charles put out something like 50 solo songs, many of which made the top listing among recitalists: *Let My Song Fill Your Heart; My Lady Walks in Loneliness; When I Have Sung My Songs; If You Only Knew; Sweet Song of Long Ago; Oh, Lovely World.*

Charpentier, Gustave, famous French opera composer; b. Dieuze, Lorraine, June 25, 1860; d. Paris, Feb. 18, 1956. He studied at the Paris Cons. (1881–87), where he was a pupil of Massart (violin), Pessard (harmony), and Massenet (composition). He received the Grand Prix de Rome in 1887 with the cantata *Didon.* Charpentier evinced great interest in social problems of the working classes, and in 1900 formed the society L'Œuvre de Mimi Pinson, devoted to the welfare of the poor, which he reorganized during World War I as an auxiliary Red Cross society. He owes his fame to one amazingly successful opera, *Louise,* a "roman musical" to his own libretto (his mistress at the time was also named Louise, and like the heroine of his opera, was employed in a dressmaking shop), which was produced at the Opéra-Comique in Paris on Feb. 2, 1900. The score is written in the spirit of naturalism and includes such realistic touches as the street cries of Paris vendors. Its success was immediate, and it entered the repertoire of opera houses all over the world; its first American production, at the Metropolitan Opera in N.Y., took place on Jan. 15, 1921. Encouraged by this success, Charpentier wrote a sequel under the title *Julien* (June 4, 1913), but it failed to arouse interest comparable to that of *Louise.* Nor did Charpentier in his very long life (he lived to be 95) succeed in producing any other memorable scores. He wrote an orch. suite, *Impressions d'Italie* (1892); a cycle of songs, *Les Fleurs du mal,* to Baudelaire's words; etc.

Charpentier, Jacques, French composer; b. Paris, Oct. 18, 1933. He studied piano with Maria Cerati-Boutillier; lived in Calcutta (1953–54), where he made a study of Indian music; prepared a valuable thesis, *Introduction à l'étude de la musique de l'Inde.* Upon his return to Paris he studied composition with Tony Aubin and musical analysis with Messiaen at the Paris Cons. In 1954 he was appointed organist at the church of St-Benoit-d'Issy; in 1966 was named chief inspector of music of the French Ministry of Cultural Affairs, and in 1975 was made Inspector General of the Secretariat of State for Culture; he traveled to Brazil and the U.S.S.R.; in 1974 was named official organist of the Church of St. Nicolas du Chardonnet in Paris. Several of his works are based on Hindu melorhythms.

Charpentier, Marc-Antoine, significant French composer; b. Paris, c.1645–50; d. there, Feb. 24, 1704. While he studied painting in Italy, his admiration for Carissimi's music led him to take up serious musical study with him. He then returned to Paris and was appointed maître de chapelle to the Dauphin, but lost the post through Lully's opposition.

This episode so embittered Charpentier against Lully that he totally eschewed Lully's style, often to the detriment of his own compositions. Louis XIV granted him a pension in 1683. He was appointed maître de musique and music teacher to Mlle. de Guise (until 1688); then intendant to the Duke of Orleans; maître de chapelle of the Jesuit collegial church and monastery; and maître de musique of Sainte-Chapelle, a post he held from 1698 until his death. He composed operas and lesser works for the stage; several "tragédies spirituelles" for the Jesuits; masses, motets, pastorales, drinking songs, etc. It has been claimed that Charpentier was Lully's superior in learning, if not in inventive power. Reprints: in *Musique d'Eglise des XVIIe et XVIIIe siècles* (ed. by Pineau); H.W. Hitchcock, ed., *Judicum Salomonis* (New Haven, Conn., 1964); *Médée* (facsimile of Paris ed., 1694; Ridgewood, N.J., 1968); D. Launay, ed., *Te Deum,* in *Le Pupitre* 13 (Paris, 1969); C. de Nys, ed., Mass for Soloists, Double Chorus, and Orch. (London, 1971). H. Wiley Hitchcock edited *The Works of Marc-Antoine Charpentier* (Paris, 1982).

Charpentier, Raymond, French composer and music critic; b. Chartres, Aug. 14, 1880; d. Paris, Dec. 27, 1960. He studied composition with André Gédalge; from 1921 to 1943 he was music director of the Comédie Française; then was active on the French radio (1944–50). Beginning in 1908, he wrote music criticism for various journals. As a composer, he wrote some 20 scores of incidental music for the plays produced at the Comédie Française and a comic opera, *Gérard et Isabelle* (Paris, 1912); also several symph. overtures; 2 string quartets; Wind Quartet; Viola Sonata; piano pieces; songs to texts by Ronsard and Baudelaire.

Chase, Gilbert, eminent American musicologist; b. Havana, Cuba (of American parents), Sept. 4, 1906. He studied at Columbia Univ. and at the Univ. of North Carolina at Chapel Hill; also studied piano. From 1929 to 1935 he lived in Paris and was active as a music correspondent for British and American music periodicals. In 1935 he returned to the U.S.; during 1940–43 he was consultant on Spanish and Latin American music at the Library of Congress in Washington; simultaneously was active in an advisory capacity to musical radio programs. From 1951 to 1953 he was cultural attaché at the American Embassy in Lima, and from 1953 to 1955 served in the same capacity in Buenos Aires. He then became director of the School of Music at the Univ. of Oklahoma (1955–57); from 1958 to 1960 was cultural attaché in Belgium; from 1960 to 1966 he was a prof. of music and director of Latin American studies at Tulane Univ. in New Orleans; in 1965 he became editor of the *Yearbook of Inter-American Musical Research.* In 1963 he organized the First Inter-American Conference on Musicology in Washington. In 1955 the Univ. of Miami bestowed upon him the title of Honorary Doctor of Letters. He also taught at the State Univ. of N.Y. in Buffalo (1973–74) and at the Univ. of Texas in Austin from 1975. WRITINGS: *The Music of Spain* (N.Y., 1941; new ed., 1959; in Spanish, Buenos Aires, 1943); *A Guide to the Music of Latin America* (Washington, 1962); *America's Music: From the Pilgrims to the Present* (N.Y., 1955; new revised ed., 1966; very valuable; also trans. into German, French, Portuguese, and Spanish); *Introducción a la musica americana contemporánea* (Buenos Aires, 1958); *The American Composer Speaks: A Historical Anthology, 1770 to 1965* (Baton Rouge, 1966); *Two Lectures in the Form of a Pair: 1, Music, Culture and History; 2, Structuralism and Music* (Brooklyn, 1973).

Chasins, Abram, multitalented American pianist, composer, writer, educator, and adjudicator; b. New York, Aug. 17, 1903. He went to the Ethical Culture School in N.Y. as a child; then took courses at the Juilliard School of Music, where he studied piano with Ernest Hutcheson and composition with Rubin Goldmark; he was also a protégé of Josef Hofmann, the dean of the Curtis Inst. of Music in Philadelphia, who guided his progress as a concert pianist. At Hofmann's recommendation, Chasins was appointed, at the age of 23, a member of the faculty at the Curtis Inst. and also head of the supplementary piano dept. (1926–36). In the summer of 1931 he took a course in music analysis with Donald Tovey in London. In the meantime he developed a brilliant career as a pianist and composer. On Jan. 18, 1929, he appeared as soloist in his own Piano Concerto with the Philadelphia Orch., Ossip Gabrilowitsch conducting, and was again the soloist in his 2nd Piano Concerto on March 3, 1933, with the Philadelphia Orch. under the direction of Leopold Stokowski. He also wrote a set of 24 preludes for piano (1928), and made virtuoso arrangements for 2 pianos of excerpts from *Carmen* and an equally effective *Fantasy on Themes from Weinberger's Schwanda.* His *Narrative* is an evocative pianistic tone poem. But the most popular piano work of Chasins was his set of *3 Chinese Pieces* ("written with all the expertise of one who had never been near the Orient," as Chasins himself described it). Hofmann, Josef Lhévinne, and other famous pianists invariably included this number as an ultimate applausemaker in their programs. Toscanini became interested, and asked Chasins to orchestrate one of the numbers, *Flirtation in a Chinese Garden,* and also his piano piece *Parade;* Toscanini conducted both pieces at his concert with the N.Y. Phil. on April 8, 1931; this was the first time that Toscanini, so wary of American music, conducted the premiere of a work by a contemporary American composer (Chasins was only 27 years old at the time). In 1932 Chasins was invited by the Moore School of Engineering at the Univ. of Pa. to join Leopold Stokowski in conducting acoustical experiments; several of their findings were incorporated into the writings of the British physicist James Jeans. In 1939–40 Chasins was on the faculty of the Berkshire Center in Tanglewood, where he was engaged by Serge Koussevitzky to give a series of lectures on the niceties of ornamentation in Bach's B-minor Mass; among those who attended these lectures were Leonard Bernstein and Putnam Aldrich. Turning to the new potentialities of the radio, Chasins initiated a Master Class of the Air, broadcasting "Piano Pointers" over the national networks of CBS and NBC. In 1941 he began a series of classical music broadcasts over the radio station WQXR; it was continued under his direction until 1965. He taught and coached a number of brilliant pianists, among them William Kapell, Shura Cherkassky, Jorge Bolet, and **Constance Keene**. He married Constance Keen in 1949, and subsequently gave numerous duo-piano recitals with her. In 1972 he returned to school pedagogy as musician-in-residence at the Univ. of Southern Calif.; at the same time he was engaged as music director of the Univ. radio station, KUSC; he held this position until 1977. In 1976 Chasins received the Award of the National Federation of Music Clubs for "outstanding service to American music during the Bicentennial Year."

During his remarkable career, Chasins formed close relationships with the greatest artists of the century: Stokowski, Hofmann, Godowski. Rachmaninoff himself voiced appreciation of Chasins's piano music. His first publication, *Speaking of Pianists* (N.Y., 1957), records some of these associations. Then came *The Van Cliburn Legend*, telling the extraordinary story of an American winning the International Tchaikovsky Competition in Moscow (N.Y., 1959; also publ. in Russian trans. in Moscow); *The Appreciation of Music* (N.Y., 1966); *Music at the Crossroads* (N.Y., 1972); and *Leopold Stokowski: A Profile* (N.Y., 1979). He contributed articles and reviews to a number of national magazines, among them *Saturday Review* and the "Sunday Magazine" of the *New York Times.* As an adjudicator, Chasins acted on the juries of several important competitions, including the Leventritt Foundation, Metropolitan Opera Auditions, N.Y. Phil. Youth Concerts, the Chopin Prize, the Rachmaninoff Award, and the prestigious Van Cliburn Competition. He also served as consultant on the Columbia Pictures film *The Competition.*

Chausson, (Amédée-) Ernest, distinguished French composer; b. Paris, Jan. 20, 1855; d. Limay, near Mantes, June 10, 1899 (in a bicycle accident). He studied with Massenet at the Paris Cons.; then took private lessons with César Franck, and began to compose. The influence of Wagner as well as that of Franck determined the harmonic and melodic elements in Chausson's music; but despite these derivations, he succeeded in establishing an individual style, tense in its chromaticism and somewhat flamboyant in its melodic expansion. The French character of his music is unmistakable in the elegance and clarity of its structural plan. He was active in musical society in Paris and was secretary of the Société Nationale de Musique. He composed relatively little music; possessing private means, he was not compelled to seek employment as a professional musician.

WORKS: Operas: *Les Caprices de Marianne* (1882–84); *Hélène* (1883–84); *Le Roi Arthus* (perf. posthumously, Brussels, Nov. 30, 1903); incidental music to *La Légende de Sainte Cécile* (Paris, Jan. 25, 1892); *Viviane,* symph. poem (1882; revised 1887); *Solitude dans les bois* (1886); Symph. in B-flat major (Paris, April 18, 1898; still in the repertoire); *Poème* for Violin and Orch. (Concerts Colonne, Paris, April 4, 1897; very popular among violinists); *Poème de l'amour et de la mer* for Voice and Orch. (1882–92; revised 1893); *Chanson perpetuelle* for Voice and Orch. (1898); *Hymne védique* for Chorus, with Orch. (1886); *Chant nuptial* for Women's Voices and Piano (1887); Piano Trio; Piano Quartet; String Quartet (unfinished); songs: *Chansons de Miarka,* to words by Jean Richepin; *Serres chaudes,* to words by Maeterlinck; *2 poèmes,* to words by Verlaine; etc.

Chávez, Carlos, distinguished Mexican composer and conductor; b. Calzada de Tacube, near Mexico City, June 13, 1899; d. Mexico City, Aug. 2, 1978. He studied piano as a child with Pedro Luis Ogazón; studied harmony with Juan B. Fuentes and Manuel Ponce. He began to compose very early in life; wrote a symph. at the age of 16; made effective piano arrangements of popular Mexican songs and also wrote many piano pieces of his own. His first important work was a ballet on an Aztec subject, *El fuego nuevo,* which he wrote in 1921, commissioned by the Secretariat of Public Education of Mexico. Historical and national Mexican subject matter remained the primary source of inspiration in many works of Chávez, but he rarely resorted to literal quotations from authentic folk melodies in his works; rather, he sublimated and distilled the melorhythmic Mexican elements, resulting in a sui generis style of composition. In 1922–23 he traveled in France, Austria, and Germany, and became acquainted with the modern developments in composition. The influence of this period of his evolution as a composer is reflected in the abstract titles of his piano works, such as *Aspectos, Energía, Unidad.* Returning to Mexico, he organized and conducted a series of concerts of new music, giving the first Mexican performances of works by Stravinsky, Schoenberg, Satie, Milhaud, and Varèse. From 1926 to 1928 he lived in N.Y. In the summer of 1928 he organized the Orquesta Sinfónica de Mexico, of which he remained the principal conductor until 1949. Works of modern music occupied an important part in the program of this orch., including 82 first performances of works by Mexican composers, many of them commissioned by Chávez; Silvestre Revueltas was among those encouraged by Chávez to compose. During his tenure as conductor Chávez engaged a number of famous foreign musicians as guest conductors, as well as numerous soloists. In 1949 the orch. was renamed Orquesta Sinfónica Nacional; it remains a permanent institution. Chávez served as director of the Conservatorio Nacional de Música from 1928 to 1935 and was general director of the Instituto Nacional de Bellas Artes from 1946 to 1952. Beginning in 1936 Chávez conducted a great number of concerts with major American orchs., and also conducted concerts in Europe and South America. Culturally, Chávez maintained a close connection with progressive artists and authors of Mexico, particularly the painter Diego Rivera; his

Sinfonía proletaria for Chorus and Orch. reflects his political commitment. In 1958–59 Chávez was Charles Eliot Norton Lecturer at Harvard Univ.; these lectures were publ. in book form under the title *Musical Thought* (Cambridge, 1960); Chávez also publ. a book of essays, *Toward a New Music* (N.Y., 1937). A detailed catalogue of his works in 3 languages, Spanish, Eng., and French, was publ. in Mexico City in 1971.

WORKS: OPERA: *Panfilo and Lauretta,* first produced in Eng. (1953; N.Y., May 9, 1957; then revised and produced in a Spanish version as *El Amor propiciado,* Mexico City, Oct. 28, 1959; still later retitled *The Visitors*).

BALLETS: *El fuego nuevo* (1921; Mexico City, Nov. 4, 1928), *Los cuatro soles* (1925; Mexico City, July 22, 1930), *Caballos de Vapor* (1926; first produced in Eng. under the title *HP,* i.e., *Horsepower,* Philadelphia, March 31, 1932), *Antígona* (Mexico City, Sept. 20, 1940; originally conceived as incidental music for Sophocles' *Antigone,* 1932), *La hija de Cólquide* (*Daughter of Colchis,* 1943; presented by Martha Graham under the title *Dark Meadow,* N.Y., Jan. 23, 1946) and *Pirámide* (1968).

FOR ORCH.: *Sinfonía* (1915); *Cantos de Méjico* for Mexican Orch. (1933); *Sinfonía de Antígona,* Symph. No. 1, derived from his incidental music for *Antigone* (Mexico City, Dec. 15, 1933); *Obertura republicana* (Mexico City, Oct. 18, 1935); *Sinfonía India,* Symph. No. 2 (1935; broadcast, N.Y., Jan. 23, 1936; also Boston Symph. Orch., April 10, 1936; composer conducting; Concerto for 4 Horns (1937; Washington, D.C., April 11, 1937; composer conducting; revised 1964); Piano Concerto (1938–40; N.Y. Phil., Jan. 1, 1942); *Cuatro nocturnos* for Soprano, Contralto, and Orch. (1939); *Toccata* (1947); Violin Concerto (1948; Mexico City, Feb. 29, 1952); Symph. No. 3 (1951; Caracas, Dec. 11, 1954; composer conducting; N.Y. Phil., Jan. 26, 1956); *Sinfonía romántica,* Symph. No. 4 (1952; Louisville, Feb. 11, 1953; composer conducting); Symph. No. 5, for Strings (1953; Los Angeles, Dec. 1, 1953, composer conducting); Symph. No. 6 (1961; N.Y., May 7, 1964); *Soli No. 3* for Bassoon, Trumpet, Viola, Timpani, and Orch. (1965; Baden-Baden, West Germany, Nov. 24, 1965); Symph. No. 7 (1960– ; unfinished); *Resonancias* (Mexico City, Sept. 18, 1964); *Elatio* (Mexico City, July 15, 1967); *Discovery* (Aptos, Calif., Aug. 24, 1969); *Clio,* symph. ode (Houston, Texas, March 23, 1970); *Initium* (1972); *Mañanas Mexicanas* (1974; originally for Piano, 1967); *Sonante* for String Orch. (1974); Trombone Concerto (1975–76; Washington, D.C., May 9, 1978; composer conducting.

CHORAL WORKS: *Tierra mojada* for Chorus, Oboe, and English Horn (Mexico City, Sept. 6, 1932); *El Sol* for Chorus and Orch. (Mexico City, July 17, 1934); *Sinfonía proletaria* (*Llamadas)* for Chorus and Orch. (Mexico City, Sept. 29, 1934); *La paloma azul* for Chorus and Chamber Orch. (1940); *Prometheus Bound,* cantata (1956; Aptos, Calif., Aug. 27, 1972).

CHAMBER MUSIC: Piano and String Sextet (1919); 3 string quartets (1921, 1932, 1944); *3 Pieces* for Guitar (1923); Violin Sonatina (1924); Cello Sonatina (1924); *Energía* for 9 Instruments (1925; Paris, June 11, 1931); Sonata for 4 Horns (1929); 3 of 4 pieces under the generic title *Soli* (No. 1 for Oboe, Clarinet, Trumpet, and Bassoon, 1933; No. 2 for Wind Quintet, 1961; No. 4 for Brass Trio, 1966); *3 Espirales* for Violin and Piano (1934); *Xochipilli Macuilxochitl* for 4 Wind Instruments and 6 Percussionists (N.Y., May 16, 1940; composer conducting; *Toccata* for 6 Percussionists (1942; Mexico City, Oct. 31, 1947); 2 of 3 instrumental pieces, under the generic title *Invention* (No. 2 for String Trio, 1965; No. 3 for Harp, 1967), introducing an inductive method of thematic illation in which each musical phrase is the logical consequent of the one immediately preceding it; *Upingos* for Solo Oboe (1957); *Fuga HAG,C* for Violin, Viola, Cello, and Double Bass (1964); *Tambuco* for 6 Percussionists (1964); Variations for Violin and Piano (1969).

FOR PIANO: 6 sonatas (*Sonata Fantasía,* 1917; 1919; 1928; 1941; 1960; 1961); *Berceuse* (1918); *7 Madrigals* (1921–22); *Polígonos* (1923); *Aspectos I* and *II* (1923); Sonatina (1924); *Blues* (1928); *Fox* (1928); *Paisaje* (1930); *Unidad* (1930); *10 Preludes* (1937); *Fugas* (1942); *4 Etudes* (1949); *Left Hand Inversions of 5 Chopin Etudes* (1950); *Invention* No. 1 (1958); *Estudio a Rubinstein,* in minor seconds (1974); *5 caprichos* (1975–76).

FOR VOICE AND PIANO: *3 exágonos* (1923); *Inutil epigrama* (1923); *Otros 3 exágonos* (1924); *3 poemas* (1938); *La casada infiel* (1941).

Cherepnin. See **Tcherepnin.**

Cherkassky, Shura, Russian pianist; b. Odessa, Oct. 7, 1911. He was a pupil of his mother; then studied with Josef Hofmann at the Curtis Inst. in Philadelphia. He played all over the world; was at his best in the Romantic repertoire; made his home in France.

Cherubini, Luigi (full baptismal name, **Maria Luigi Carlo Zenobio Salvatore**), famous Italian composer; b. Florence, Sept. 14, 1760; d. Paris, March 15, 1842. As a young child he studied music with his father, cembalist at the Pergola Theater; his subsequent teachers were Bartolomeo and Alessandro Felici; then Bizarri and Castrucci; in 1777 he was sent by Duke Leopold II of Tuscany (the future Emperor Leopold III) to Milan to perfect himself in counterpoint under Sarti. At 13 he had already written a Mass, and a stage-intermezzo for a society theater; at 15 he composed another intermezzo, *Il Giuocatore;* during his years of study with Sarti he confined himself to contrapuntal work and church music; in 1780, *Quinto Fabio* (perf. at Alessandria della Paglia) opened the series of his dramatic works; its cool reception spurred him to renewed study, and *Armida* (Florence, 1782), *Adriano in Siria* (Livorno, 1782), *Messenzio* (Florence, 1782), *Quinto Fabio* (revised; Rome, 1783), *Lo sposo di tre e marito di nessuna* (Venice, 1783), *Idalide* (Florence, 1784), and *Alessandro nelle Indie* (Mantua, 1784) received public approbation. Invited to London in the autumn of 1784, he brought out 2 operas: *La finta principessa* (1785), an opera buffa which had fair success; and *Giulio Sabino* (1786), which was less fortunate. Cherubini held the position of Composer to the King for one year, and in July 1786 went to Paris for a one-year visit; in 1788 he brought out *Ifigenia in Aulide* at Turin; then settled permanently in Paris. His first French opera, *Demofoonte* (Grand Opéra, 1788), was a failure owing to his attempt to adapt his style of flowing melody to the ill-turned style of Marmontel, the librettist. The next year Léonard, the Queen's hairdresser, obtained a license to establish Italian opera in a little playhouse called the Théâtre de la Foire de St.-Germain; and here Cherubini conducted, until 1792, the best works of Anfossi, Paisiello, and Cimarosa. During this period he developed, inspired by the text of his opera *Lodoïska* (Théâtre de Monsieur, 1791), a new dramatic style destined to work a revolution on the French stage; the increased breadth and force of the ensemble numbers, the novel and rich orch. combinations, and the generally heightened dramatic effect were imitated or expanded by a host of composers of the French school: Méhul, Berton, Lesueur, Grétry. Cherubini's next operas, *Eliza ou Le Voyage au mont St.-Bernard* (1794) and *Médée* (1797), were hampered by poor libretti. In 1795 Cherubini was appointed one of the Inspectors of the new Cons. Composing steadily, he brought out *L'Hôtellerie portugaise* (1798), *La Punition* (1799), *La Prisonnière* (1799; pasticcio, with Boïeldieu), and in 1800, at the Théâtre Feydeau, *Les Deux Journées* (perf. in London, 1801, as *The Water-carrier;* in Germany as *Der Wasserträger*), his greatest operatic work. Cherubini had fallen into disfavor with Napoleon, whose opinion in musical matters he had slighted; but after the success of *Les Deux Journées,* he was able to produce at the Grand Opéra *Anacréon, ou L'Amour fugitif* (1803) and the ballet *Achille à Scyros* (1804), neither of which, however, had good fortune. At this juncture Cherubini was invited to write an opera for Vienna; *Faniska,* brought out in 1807 at the Kärnthnerthor Theater, was an overwhelming success; so much so that a Vienna critic who ventured the prophecy that Beethoven's *Fidelio* would one day be equally esteemed, was laughed at. Returning to Paris after the French occupation of Vienna, Cherubini wrote *Primmalione* for the Italian opera at the Tuileries (1808), but did not win the Emperor's favor, and retired for a time to the château of the Prince of Chimay, where he occupied his leisure with botanizing. The request to write a mass for the church of Chimay turned the current of his thoughts; he composed the celebrated 3-part Mass in F, the success of which was so marked that Cherubini thenceforward devoted more time to sacred than dramatic composition, though he did bring out *Le Crescendo* (1810), *Les Abencérages* (Opéra, April 6, 1813), *Bayard à Mézières* (1814), *Blanche de Provence* (1821), and *Ali Baba* (Opéra, July 22, 1833). On a visit to London, in 1815, he wrote for the Phil. Society a symph., an overture, and a Hymn to Spring. In this year he lost his place in the Cons. during the troublous times of the Restoration, but was recompensed by his appointment as superintendent of the Royal Chapel, succeeding Martini. In 1816 he was made prof. of composition at the Cons., and its director in 1821; he retired in 1841. Cherubini was one of the great modern masters of counterpoint, and his scores, particularly in his admirable sacred music, bear witness on every page to his skill and erudition. As an opera composer, his main failing was the undue musical prolongation of scenes in which swifter dramatic action would have been preferable.

WORKS: His own catalogue of his works, *Notice des manuscrits autographes de la musique composée par feu M.-L.-C.-Z.-S. Cherubini* (publ. 1843; reprinted, London, 1967), includes 15 Italian and 14 French operas (an uncatalogued, newly discovered opera, *Don Pistacchio,* was perf. at Dresden, Nov. 27, 1926); a ballet; 17 cantatas and "occasional" vocal works with orch.; many detached airs, romances, nocturnes, duets, etc.; 14 choruses; 4 sets of solfeggi (over 160 numbers); 11 Solemn Masses, 2 Requiems, many detached Kyries, Glorias, Credos, etc.; a Credo in 8 parts with Organ; an oratorio (Florence, 1777); motets, hymns, graduals, etc., with orch.; a Magnificat, a Miserere, a Te Deum (each with orch.); 4 litanies, 2 Lamentations, 20 antiphons, etc.; a Symph., an overture, 11 marches, 11 dances, etc.; 6 string quartets, a String Quintet; Sonata for 2 Organs; for piano: 6 sonatas, a grand fantasia, a minuet, a chaconne, etc.

WRITINGS: Cherubini's *Cours de Contrepoint et de Fugue* was prepared for publication by his pupil Halévy. It appeared in a German trans. by Stöpel (1835–36), in Eng. trans. by J. Hamilton (1837) and C. Clarke (1854). Two new German eds. were prepared by G. Jensen (1896) and R. Heuberger (1911).

Chevalier, Maurice, popular French chansonnier; b. Paris, Sept. 12, 1888; d. there, Jan. 1, 1972. He began his career as a singer in Parisian cafés and music halls; then acted in films. In 1929 he went to Hollywood, and soon established himself as one of the foremost musical comedy stars, speaking and singing in English with an ingratiating French accent, affecting a debonair mien, carrying a cane, and wearing a straw hat. His early films included *The Innocents of Paris* (1929), *Love Me Tonight* (1932), and *The Merry Widow* (1934). He remained in France during the German occupation and gave shows for French prisoners of war in Germany. This activity led to accusations of collaboration with the enemy, but Chevalier was able to explain his conduct as a desire to maintain the public spirit among Frenchmen, and he was exonerated. His later films included *Gigi* (1958), *Can-Can* (1960), and *Fanny* (1961). A special Academy Award was presented to him in 1958 in appreciation of his contributions to popular entertainment.

Chevé, Emile-Joseph-Maurice, French music theorist; b. Douarnenez, Finistère, May 31, 1804; d. Fontenay-le-Comte, Aug. 26, 1864. A physician of great merit, he became a zealous advocate of Pierre Galin's method of musical instruction, explained in Galin's *Exposition d'une nouvelle méthode pour l'enseignement de la musique* (1818; 3rd ed., 1831), which attained considerable popularity; married **Nanine Paris** (d. 1868) and collaborated with her in a *Méthode élémentaire de musique vocale* (Paris, 1844; later ed., 1863; German trans. by F.T. Stahl, 1878), in the preface to which he "exposes" and attacks the "defective" methods of the Cons. He and his wife also publ. *Méthode élémentaire d'harmonie* (with Galin; Paris, 1846); and Mme. Chevé wrote *Nouvelle théorie des accords, servant de base à l'harmonie* (Paris, 1844). He publ. a long series of essays and articles by which he vainly sought to draw out the profs. of the Cons. Acrimonious polemics raged for years, and numerous pamphlets were issued in Paris by adherents and foes of the Chevé method.

Chevillard, Camille, French composer and conductor; b. Paris, Oct. 14, 1859; d. Chatou (Seine-et-Oise), May 30, 1923. He studied piano with Georges Mathias; was chiefly self-taught in composition. In 1897 he became assistant conductor of the Lamoureux Concerts; in 1899 succeeded Lamoureux as conductor after having married his daughter; from 1914 was conductor at the Grand Opéra.
WORKS: For Orch. (all perf. in Paris): *Ballade symphonique* (Feb. 23, 1890); *Le Chêne et le roseau* (March 8, 1891); *Fantaisie symphonique* (Oct. 21, 1894); also *Etude chromatique* for Piano; Piano Quintet, Piano Quartet, Piano Trio; String Quartet; Violin Sonata; Cello Sonata; songs with Orch., *L'Attente* and *Chemins d'amour*.

Chiari, Giuseppe, Italian composer of extreme avant-garde tendencies; b. Florence, Sept. 26, 1926. He studied piano; organized the group Musica e Segno in association with Sylvano Bussotti; participated in the Fluxus festival in Wiesbaden (1962), and in avant-garde manifestations in N.Y. (1964) and at the Centre de Musique in Paris (1965). Eventually he returned to Florence, where he owned a clothing store. In his productions he follows the most latitudinarian and disestablishmentarian trends of metadadaistic fragmentationarianism, both in tonal and verbal structures. He publ. *Musica senza contrappunto,* a varitype anthology of disjected observations (Rome, 1969). In it he launched the slogan "Musica gestuale," which deals with audiovisual and tactile events, volitional as well as aleatory. His works include: *Intervalli* for Piano (1956); *Per arco* for Cello (1962); *Teatrino* for Actor-Pianist, Rubber Dolls, Alarm Clocks, and Handsaw (1963); *Don't Trade Here* for Action Theater (1965).

Chickering, Jonas, American piano maker; b. New Ipswich, N.H., April 5, 1798; d. Boston, Dec. 8, 1853. In 1818 he was apprenticed to John Osborn, a Boston piano maker; in 1823, he founded (with James Stewart) the firm of Stewart & Chickering, from 1829 known as Chickering & Mackay (John Mackay, d. 1841), later as Chickering & Sons. Jonas Chickering pioneered in the development of the upright piano, and the full metal plate for square and grand pianos. His son and successor, **Col. Thomas E. Chickering** (b. Boston, Oct. 22, 1824; d. there, Feb. 14, 1871), was named a Chevalier of the Legion of Honor, in addition to taking the first prize for pianofortes at the Paris Exposition of 1867. His 3 sons and their successors carried on the factory, which was famous for quality and high rate of production, until 1908, when it became part of the American Piano Co., and the factory was moved from Boston to East Rochester, N.Y. Later the firm became a subsidiary of the Aeolian American Corp.

Chihara, Paul, American composer of Japanese descent; b. Seattle, July 9, 1938. After the outbreak of the war, his family was relocated, with many other Japanese-Americans, to Minadoka, Idaho. He studied piano as a child; took courses in English literature at the Univ. of Washington (B.A., 1960) and at Cornell Univ. (M.A., 1961); then went to Europe, where he studied composition with Nadia Boulanger in Paris (1962–63) and with Ernst Pepping in West Berlin (1965–66); in the interim he obtained his A.M.D. at Cornell Univ. (1965). From 1966 till 1974 he was on the music faculty of the Univ. of Calif., Los Angeles; traveled to Japan for research in 1967. In his music he utilizes advanced forms of serial techniques, occasionally extending them to aleatory procedures. In his choral compositions he follows the time-honored polyphonic methods of the Renaissance.
WORKS: Viola Concerto (1963); String Quartet (1965); *Tree Music* for 3 Violas and 3 Trombones (1966); *Branches* for 2 Bassoons and Percussion (1966); *Magnificat* for Treble Voices (1966); *The 90th Psalm,* choral cantata (1966); Nocturne for 24 Solo Voices (1966); *Redwood* for Viola and Percussion (1967); *Willow, Willow* for Bass Flute, Tuba, and Percussion (1968); *Rain Music,* tape collage using brewery noises, commissioned by Rainier Breweries in Seattle (1968); *Forest Music* for Orch. (1968; Los Angeles, May 2, 1971); *Driftwood* for Violin, 2 Violas, and Cello (1969); *Logs XVI* for Amplified String Bass and Magnetic Tape (1970); *Ceremony I* for Oboe, 2 Cellos, Double Bass, and Percussion (1971); *Ceremony II* for Flute, 2 Cellos, and Percussion (1972); *Ceremony III* for Small Orch. (1973); *Ceremony IV* for Orch. (1974); *Ceremony V, Symphony in Celebration* (1973–75; Houston, Sept. 8, 1975); *Grass,* concerto for Double Bass and Orch. (1971; Oberlin [Ohio] Cons., April 14, 1972); *Wild Song* for Cello and Orch. (1972). *Missa Carminum* for Chorus a cappella (Los Angeles, Jan. 15, 1976); Saxophone Concerto (Boston, Jan. 30, 1981); Symph. No. 2 (Los Angeles, March 20, 1982); *Sequoia* for String Quartet and Tape (1984).

Child, William, English organist and composer of sacred music; b. Bristol, 1606; d. Windsor, March 23, 1697. He was a boy chorister at Bristol Cathedral under Elway Bevin; studied at Oxford (B.Mus., 1631); in 1632 was in Windsor as organist at St. George's Chapel (succeeding J. Mundy) and then in London at the Chapel Royal; in 1643–60 he apparently lived in retirement, devoting himself to composition; in 1660 he was appointed chanter at the Chapel Royal, and a member of the King's private band. He received his Mus.Bac. in 1631 or 1639; his Mus.Doc. from Oxford in 1663.

WORKS: He publ. Psalms (1639; later eds., 1650 and 1656), services, anthems, compositions in "Court Ayres," canons, catches, etc. (included in collections of Arnold Boyce, Hilton, Playford, and others); also instrumental works. Numerous services, anthems (including *O Lord, grant the King a long life*), a motet (*O bone Jesu*), and chants exist in MS.

Childs, Barney, American composer; b. Spokane, Wash., Feb. 13, 1926. He studied sporadically and intermittently with Leonard Ratner, Carlos Chávez, Aaron Copland, and Elliott Carter; obtained a B.A. degree in English from the Univ. of Nevada (1949), an M.A. from Oxford Univ. as a Rhodes Scholar (1955), and a Ph.D. in literature from Stanford Univ. (1959). He taught English at the Univ. of Arizona (1956–65); then served as dean of Deep Springs College in California (1965–69). From 1969 to 1971 he taught music theory at Wisconsin College-Cons. in Milwaukee; in 1971 joined the faculty at Johnston College of the Univ. of Redlands in California; became a prof. there in 1973. Not overly concerned with public tastes and current fashions of cosmopolitan styles, he cultivates indeterminate structures. He edited, with Elliott Schwarz, *Contemporary Composers on Contemporary Music* (N.Y., 1967).

Chisholm, Erik, Scottish composer; b. Glasgow, Jan. 4, 1904; d. Rondebosch, South Africa, June 7, 1965. He first studied music in Glasgow; then in London and in Edinburgh with Donald Tovey (composition) and Puishnov (piano); received his Mus.Bac. in 1931, and his Mus.Doc. from Edinburgh Univ. in 1934. He was conductor of the Glasgow Grand Opera Society in 1930–39; in 1940 joined the Carl Rosa Opera Co. as conductor; in 1943 toured with the Anglo-Polish Ballet; later went to the Far East; organized the Singapore Symph. Orch., and conducted 50 concerts in Malaya; in 1946 was appointed prof. of music and director of the South African College of Music at Cape Town Univ.; also conducted operas in South Africa. His book, *The Operas of Leoš Janáček*, was publ. posthumously (N.Y., 1971). Chisholm's style of composition is marked by considerable complexity; elements of oriental scale formations are notable.

Chladni, Ernest Florens Friedrich, eminent German acoustician; b. Wittenberg, Nov. 30, 1756; d. Breslau, April 3, 1827. At first a student and prof. of law at Wittenberg and Leipzig, he turned to physics, and made highly important researches in the domain of acoustics. He discovered the "Tonfiguren" (tone-figures; i.e., the regular patterns assumed by dry sand on a glass plate set in vibration by a bow); invented the Euphonium (glass-rod harmonica) and Clavicylinder (steel-rod keyboard harmonica). To introduce his ideas and inventions, he made long journeys and delivered many scientific lectures.

Chlubna, Osvald, Czech composer; b. Brno, June 22, 1893; d. there, Oct. 30, 1971. He studied composition with Janáček in Brno (1914–15) and later at the Brno branch of the Master School of the Prague Cons. (1923–24); taught in Brno at the Cons. (1919–35) and at the Janáček Academy of Music (1953–59). His music is marked by rhapsodic élan; many of his works reflect national events. In 1948 he completed Janáček's unfinished symph. poem, *Dunaj (The Danube;* 1923–28).

Cholmondeley, Archer. See **Chamlee, Mario.**

Chopin, (François-) Frédéric, incomparable genius of the piano who created a unique romantic style of keyboard music; b. Zelazowa Wola, near Warsaw, in all probability on March 1, 1810, the date given by Chopin himself in his letter of acceptance of membership in the Polish Literary Society in Paris in 1833 (but in his certificate of baptism the date of birth is given as Feb. 22, 1810); d. Paris, Oct. 17, 1849. His father, Nicolas Chopin, was a native of Marainville, France, who went to Warsaw as a teacher of French; his mother, Justyna Krzyzanowska, was Polish. He was brought up in his father's private school, among sons of the Polish nobility. Chopin's talent was manifested in early childhood; at the age of 8 he played in public a piano concerto by Gyrowetz, and he had already begun to compose polonaises, mazurkas, and waltzes. He received his primary musical instruction from the Bohemian pianist Adalbert Żywny, who resided in Warsaw at the time. A much more important teacher was Joseph Elsner, director of the Warsaw School of Music, who gave Chopin a thorough instruction in music theory and form. Chopin was 15 years old when his Rondeau for Piano was publ. in Warsaw as op. 1. In the summer of 1829 Chopin set out for Vienna, where he gave a highly successful concert on Aug. 11, 1829, and appeared there again on Aug. 18, 1829. While in Vienna he made arrangements to have his variations on Mozart's aria *Là ci darem la mano,* for Piano and Orch., publ. by Haslinger as op. 2. It was this work that attracted the attention of Schumann, who saluted Chopin in his famous article publ. in the *Allgemeine Musikalische Zeitung* of Dec. 7, 1831, in which Schumann's alter ego, Eusebius, is represented as exclaiming, "Hats off, gentlemen! A genius!" The common impression in many biographies that Schumann "launched" Chopin on his career is deceptive; actually Schumann was some months younger than Chopin, and was referred to editorially merely as a student of Prof. Wieck. Returning to Warsaw, Chopin gave the first public performance of his Piano Concerto in F minor, op. 21, on March 17, 1830. On Oct. 11, 1830, he was soloist in his Piano Concerto in E minor, op. 11. A confusion resulted in the usual listing of the E minor Concerto as first, and the F minor Concerto as his 2nd; chronologically, the composition of the F minor Concerto preceded the E minor. He spent the winter of 1830–31 in Vienna. The Polish rebellion against Russian domination, which ended in defeat, determined Chopin's further course of action, and he proceeded to Paris, visiting Linz, Salzburg, Dresden, and Stuttgart on the way. He arrived in Paris in Sept. 1831, and was introduced to Rossini, Cherubini, and Paër. He also met Bellini, Meyerbeer, Berlioz, Victor Hugo, and Heinrich Heine; he became particularly friendly with Liszt. Paris was then the center of Polish emigration, and Chopin maintained his contacts with the Polish circle there. He presented his first Paris concert on Feb. 26, 1832. He also taught the piano. The Paris critics found an apt Shakespearean epithet for him, calling him "the Ariel of the piano." In 1836 he met the famous novelist Aurore Dupin (Mme. Dudevant), who publ. her works under the affected masculine English name George Sand. They became intimate, even though quite incompatible in character and interests. George Sand was involved in social affairs and held radical views; Chopin was a poet confined within his inner world; it has been said that she was the masculine and he the feminine partner in their companionship. In the winter of 1838–39 Chopin accompanied George Sand to the island of Majorca, where she attended to him with total devotion; yet she portrayed Chopin in her novel *Lucrézia Floriani* as a weakling. Indeed, she was quite overt in her reference to Chopin as a lover; in a personal letter dated 1838 she said that she had difficulty in inducing Chopin to submit to a sensual embrace, and implied that they lived as an immaculate virgin most of the time they were together. They parted in 1847; by that time Chopin was quite ill with tuberculosis; a daguerreotype taken of him represents a prematurely aged man with facial features showing sickness and exhaustion, with locks of black hair partly covering his forehead. Yet he continued his concert career. He undertook a tour as pianist in England and Scotland in 1848; he gave his last concert in Paris on Feb. 16, 1848. *La Revue et Gazette Musicale* of Feb. 20, 1848, gives a precious account of the occasion: "The finest flower of feminine aristocracy in the most elegant attire filled the Salle Pleyel," the paper reported, "to catch this musical sylph on the wing." He died the following year; Mozart's Requiem was performed at Chopin's funeral at the Madeleine, with Habeneck conducting the orch. and chorus of the Paris Cons. and Pauline Viardot and Lablache singing the solo parts. Chopin was buried at Père Lachaise between the graves of Cherubini and Bellini; however, at his own request, his heart was sent to Warsaw for entombment in his homeland.

Chopin represents the full liberation of the piano from traditional orch. and choral influences, the authoritative assumption of its role as a solo instrument. Not seeking "orchestral" sonorities, Chopin may have paled as a virtuoso beside the titanic Liszt, but the poesy of his pianism, its fervor of expression, the pervading melancholy in his nocturnes and ballades, and the bounding exultation of his scherzos and études were never equaled. And, from a purely technical standpoint, Chopin's figurations and bold modulatory transitions seem to presage the elaborate transtonal developments of modern music.

WORKS: FOR SOLO PIANO: *Albumleaf (Moderato)* in E major (1843); *Allegro de concert*, op. 46 (1832–41); *Andante spianato* in G major, op. 22 (1834);

Andantino in G minor (1838); ballades: G minor, op. 23 (1831–35); F major/A minor, op. 38 (1836–39); A-flat major, op. 47 (1840–41); F minor, op. 52 (1842); *Barcarolle* in F-sharp major, op. 60 (1845–46); *Berceuse* in D-flat major, op. 57 (1843–44); *Bolero* in C major/A major, op. 19 (1833); *2 Bourrées,* in G minor and A major (1846); *Canon* in F minor (1839?); *Cantabile* in B-flat major (1834); *Contredanse* in G-flat major (1827?); *3 Ecossaises,* in D major, G major, and D-flat major, op. 72, no. 3 (1826); études: 4, in F major, F minor, A-flat major, and E-flat major, op. 10, nos. 8–11 (1829); 2, in G-flat major and E-flat minor, op. 10, nos. 5–6 (1830); 2, in C major and A minor, op. 10, nos. 1–2 (1830); C minor, op. 10, no. 12 (1830); C major, op. 10, no. 7 (1832); E major, op. 10, no. 3 (1832); C-sharp minor, op. 10, no. 4 (1832); 6, in A minor, E minor, G-sharp minor, D-flat major, G-flat major, and B minor, op. 25, nos. 4–6 and 8–10 (1832–34); A minor, op. 25, no. 11 (1834); F minor, op. 25, no. 2 (1836); C-sharp minor, op. 25, no. 7 (1836); 2, in F major and C minor, op. 25, nos. 3 and 12 (1836); A-flat major, op. 25, no. 1 (1836); *Fantaisie* in F minor/A-flat major, op. 49 (1841); *Fantaisie-impromptu* in C-sharp minor, op. 66 (1835); *Fugue* in A minor (1841–42); *Funeral March* in C minor, op. 72, no. 2 (1827); *Impromptu* in A-flat major, op. 29 (1837); *Impromptu* in F-sharp minor, op. 36 (1839); *Impromptu* in G-flat major, op. 51 (1842); *Introduction and Variations on the German air Der Schweizerbub* in E major (1826); *Introduction* in C major and *Rondo* in E-flat major, op. 16 (1832); *Introduction and Variations on Hérold's "Je vends des scapulaires" from Ludovic* in B-flat major, op. 12 (1833); *Largo* in E-flat major (1837?); mazurkas: D major (1820?); A-flat major (1825; earlier version of op. 7, no. 4); A minor (1825; earlier version of op. 17, no. 4); 2, in G major and B-flat major (1826); A minor, op. 68, no. 2 (1827); F major, op. 68, no. 3 (1829); C major, op. 68, no. 1 (1829); G major (1829); A minor (1829; earlier version of op. 7, no. 2); 4, in F-sharp minor, C-sharp minor, E major, and E-flat major, op. 6 (1830); 5, in B-flat major, A minor, F minor, A-flat major, and C major, op. 7 (1831); B-flat major (1832); 4, in B-flat major, E minor, A-flat major, and A minor, op. 17 (1832–33); C major (1833); A-flat major (1834); 4, in G minor, C major, A-flat major, and B-flat minor, op. 24 (1834–35); 2, in G major and C major, op. 67, nos. 1 and 3 (1835); 4, in C minor, B minor, D-flat major, and C-sharp minor, op. 30 (1836–37); 4, in G-sharp minor, D major, C major, and B minor, op. 33 (1837–38); E minor, op. 41, no. 2 (1838); 3, in E major, B major, and A-flat major, op. 41, nos. 1, 3, and 4 (1839–40); A minor (1840); A minor (1840); 3, in G major, A-flat major, and C-sharp minor, op. 50 (1842); 3, in B major, C major, and C minor, op. 56 (1843); 3, in A minor, A-flat major, and F-sharp minor, op. 59 (1845); 3, in B major, F minor, and C-sharp minor, op. 63 (1846); A minor, op. 67, no. 4 (1846); G minor, op. 67, no. 2 (1849); F minor, op. 68, no. 4 (1849); *Military March* (1817; not extant); nocturnes: E minor, op. 72, no. 1 (1827); C-sharp minor (1830); 3, in B-flat minor, E-flat major, and B major, op. 9 (1830–31); 2, in F major and F-sharp major, op. 15, nos. 1–2 (1830–31); G minor, op. 15, no. 3 (1833); C-sharp minor, op. 27, no. 1 (1835); D-flat major, op.

27, no. 2 (1835); 2, in B major and A-flat major, op. 32 (1836–37); C minor (1837); G minor, op. 37, no. 1 (1838); G major, op. 37, no. 2 (1839); 2, in C minor and F-sharp minor, op. 48 (1841); 2, in F minor and E-flat minor, op. 55 (1843); 2, in B major and E major, op. 62 (1846); polonaises: G minor (1817); B-flat major (1817); A-flat major (1821); G-sharp minor (1822); D minor, op. 71, no. 1 (1825?); B-flat minor, *Adieu* (1826); B-flat major, op. 71, no. 2 (1828); F minor, op. 71, no. 3 (1828); G-flat major (1829); 2, in C-sharp minor and E-flat minor, op. 26 (1834–35); A major, op. 40, no. 1 (1838); C minor, op. 40, no. 2 (1839); F-sharp minor, op. 44 (1840–41); A-flat major, op. 53 (1842); *Polonaise-fantaisie* in A-flat major, op. 61 (1845–46); preludes: A-flat major (1834); 24, op. 28 (1836–39); C-sharp minor, op. 45 (1841); rondos: C minor, op. 1 (1825); F major, op. 5, "à la Mazur" (1826); C major (1828; earlier version of the Rondo in C major for 2 Pianos, op. 73); scherzos: B minor, op. 20 (1831–32); B-flat minor/D-flat major, op. 31 (1837); C-sharp minor, op. 39 (1839); E major, op. 54 (1842); sonatas: C minor, op. 4 (1828); B-flat minor, op. 35, *Funeral March* (1839; 3rd movement is a *Funeral March* in B-flat minor, composed in 1837); B minor, op. 58 (1844); *Tarantelle* in A-flat major, op. 43 (1841); *3 nouvelles études*, for Moscheles's *Methode* (1839); Variation No. 6, in E major, from the *Hexameron (Variations on the March from Bellini's I puritani)* (1837; other variations by Liszt, Thalberg, Pixis, Herz, and Czerny); Variations in A major, *Souvenir de Paganini* (1829); waltzes: A-flat major (1827); B minor, op. 69, no. 2 (1829); D-flat major, op. 70, no. 3 (1829); E major (1829); E-flat major (1829–30); E minor (1830); E-flat major, op. 18 (1831); A minor, op. 34, no. 2 (1831); G-flat major, op. 70, no. 1 (1833); A-flat major, op. 34, no. 1 (1835); A-flat major, op. 69, no. 1, *L'Adieu* (1835); F major, op. 34, no. 3 (1838); A-flat major, op. 42 (1840); E-flat major, *Sostenuto* (1840); F minor, op. 70, no. 2 (1841); A minor (1843?); 3, in D-flat major (*Minute*), C-sharp minor, and A-flat major, op. 64 (1846–47); B major (1848; not extant). — For Piano, 4-hands: *Introduction, Theme, and Variations* in D major (1826). — For 2 Pianos: Rondo in C major, op. 73 (1828; later version of Rondo in C major for Solo Piano).

FOR PIANO AND ORCH.: *Variations on Mozart's "Là ci darem la mano" from Don Giovanni* in B-flat major, op. 2 (1827); *Fantasia on Polish Airs* in A major, op. 13 (1828); *Krakowiak*, rondo in F major, op. 14 (1828); Piano Concerto No. 2, in F minor, op. 21 (1829–30; Warsaw, March 17, 1830, composer soloist; although listed as "No. 2," it was his first concerto in order of composition); Piano Concerto No. 1, in E minor, op. 11 (1830; Warsaw, Oct. 11, 1830, composer soloist; although listed as "No. 1," it was his 2nd concerto in order of composition); *Grand Polonaise* in E-flat major, op. 22 (1830–31).

CHAMBER MUSIC: *Variations on Rossini's "Non più mesta" from "La Cenerentola"* for Flute and Piano, in E major (1824); Piano Trio in G minor, op. 8 (1828–29); *Introduction and Polonaise* for Cello and Piano, in C major, op. 3 (1829–30); *Grand Duo on Themes from Meyerbeer's "Robert le diable"* for Cello and Piano, in E major (1832); Cello Sonata in

G minor, op. 65 (1845–46).

SONGS: 17, op. 74 (to Polish texts; 1829–47).

Chorley, Henry Fothergill, English writer on music; b. Blackley Hurst, Lancashire, Dec. 15, 1808; d. London, Feb. 16, 1872. He was at various times active as a dramatist, translator, art critic, poet, novelist, and journalist; from 1831–68 was music critic of the London *Athenaeum.* During his extensive travels he heard all the best music of the day and met many musical celebrities; a partisan of Mendelssohn and Spohr, he was intolerant toward new musical ideas and attacked Chopin, Schumann, and particularly Wagner, with extraordinary violence.

WRITINGS: *Music and Manners in France and Germany* (3 vols., London, 1841); *Modern German Music* (2 vols., 1854); *Thirty Years' Musical Recollections* (2 vols., 1862; abridged American ed., N.Y., 1926); an interesting *Autobiography, Memoirs and Letters* (2 vols., 1873; ed. by H.G. Hewlett); *National Music of the World* (1880; ed. by Hewlett; 3rd ed., 1911); *Handel Studies* (1859); a novel, *A Prodigy: A Tale of Music* (3 vols., 1866).

Choron, Alexandre Etienne, French music editor and theorist; b. Caen, Oct. 21, 1771; d. Paris, June 28, 1834. A student of languages, and passionately fond of music, he took interest in music theory and through it in mathematics, which he studied till the age of 25; then, by several years' serious application to the Italian and German theorists, he acquired a thorough knowledge of the theory and practice of music. Becoming (in 1805) a partner in a music publishing firm, he devoted his entire fortune to editing and publishing classic and theoretical works and compositions, meanwhile contributing new works of his own. In 1811 he became a corresponding member of the Académie Française; he was entrusted with the reorganization of the maîtrises (training schools for church choirs), and was appointed conductor of religious festivals. In 1816, as director of the Académie Royale de Musique, he reopened the Cons. (closed in 1815) as the Ecole Royale de Chant et de Déclamation. Losing his directorship (1817) because he favored new works by unknown composers, he established, with a very moderate subsidy, the Institution de Musique Classique et Religieuse, for which he labored indefatigably until the July Revolution (1830).

Chotzinoff, Samuel, American pianist and music critic; b. Vitebsk, Russia, July 4, 1889; d. New York, Feb. 9, 1964. He was brought to America as a child; studied piano with Oscar Shack and music theory with Daniel Gregory Mason at Columbia Univ., graduating in 1912. He subsequently became an expert accompanist; toured with Zimbalist and Heifetz. In 1925 he turned to music criticism; served as music critic of the *N.Y. World* (1925–30) and the *N.Y. Post* (1934–41). He then occupied various teaching and administrative positions; was for several years music director of the National Broadcasting Co. He wrote a novel on Beethoven's life, entitled *Eroica;* a book of reminiscences, *A Lost Paradise*

Chou Wen-Chung – Christou

(1955); and a monograph, *Toscanini, An Intimate Portrait* (N.Y., 1956). His autobiographical *Days at the Morn* and *A Little Night Music* were publ. posthumously in 1964.

Chou Wen-Chung, remarkable Chinese-American composer; b. Cheefoo, June 29, 1923 (corresponding to May 16, 1923, according to the lunar calendar in the Chinese Year of the Bear). He studied at the National Univ. of Chungking (1941–45); then went to the U.S.; took private lessons with Varèse in N.Y. and with N. Slonimsky in Boston; then entered Columbia Univ., where he was a student of Otto Luening (M.A., 1954). In 1957 he received a Guggenheim fellowship. In 1964 he joined the faculty of Columbia Univ. as a teacher of composition; became a prof. of music in 1972; was named vice-dean in 1976. His music combines Chinese elements of structure and scale formation with free dissonant counterpoint related to the theory of "organized sound" of Varèse.

WORKS: *Landscapes* for Orch. (San Francisco, Nov. 19, 1953); *7 Poems of the T'ang Dynasty* for Tenor, 7 Wind Instruments, Piano, and Percussion (N.Y., March 16, 1952); *And the Fallen Petals,* triolet for Orch. (Louisville, Ky., Feb. 9, 1955); *In the Mode of Shang* for Chamber Orch. (N.Y., Feb. 2, 1957); *Metaphors* for Wind Instruments (1960–61); *Cursive* for Flute and Piano (1963); *Riding the Wind* for Wind Ensemble (1964); *Pien* for Piano, Wind Instruments, and Percussion (1966); *Yun* for Wind Instruments, 2 Pianos, and Percussion (1969). In 1968 Wen-Chung Chou completed Varèse's unfinished work *Nocturnal* for Voices and Instruments.

Christiansen, Fredrik Melius, Norwegian-American choral conductor, b. Eidsvold, April 1, 1871; d. Northfield, Minn., June 1, 1955. He emigrated to the U.S. in 1888; studied at the Northwestern Cons. of Music; then went to Germany, where he took courses at the Leipzig Cons. (1897–99). Returning to America, he served as director of the School of Music at St. Olaf's College in Northfield, Minn.; he organized the important St. Olaf's Lutheran Choir there. He publ. several useful choral collections: *St. Olaf Choir Series* (6 vols., 1920); *Young Men's Choral Assembly for Schools* (1936); edited *50 Famous Hymns for Women's Voices* (1914); and publ. *Practical Modulation* (1916).

Christiansen, Olaf, American choral conductor of Norwegian descent, son of **Fredrik Melius Christiansen;** b. Minneapolis, Aug. 12, 1901; d. Northfield, Minn., April 12, 1984. He was trained by his father, and upon his death in 1955 succeeded him as director of the St. Olaf Lutheran Choir in Northfield, remaining at this post until his own retirement in 1968. He was also co-founder of the Christiansen Choral School, which had a very large attendance among choral conductors.

Christoff, Boris, eminent Bulgarian bass-baritone; b. Plovdiv, May 18, 1914. He studied law, and at the same time sang in a chorus in Sofia. A private sti-

pend enabled him to go to Rome, where he studied voice with Stracciari. In 1946 he made a successful debut in a solo recital in Rome, and in 1947 sang at La Scala in Milan. He excelled particularly in the role of Boris Godunov, which he sang in Russia; his interpretation recalled that of Chaliapin; he made his American debut in that role at the San Francisco Opera House on Sept. 25, 1956 with great acclaim. His operatic repertoire includes about 40 parts in 6 languages.

Christou, Jani, remarkable Greek composer; b. Heliopolis, Egypt, Jan. 8, 1926, to Greek parents; d. in an automobile accident, with his wife, near Athens, on his 44th birthday, Jan. 8, 1970. He studied at Victoria College in Alexandria; then took courses in philosophy under Wittgenstein at King's College in Cambridge, England (M.A., 1948); concurrently studied composition with Hans Redlich in Letchworth (1945–48); then enrolled in the summer courses of the Accademia Musicale Chigiana in Siena (1949–50); during the same period he attended Karl Jung's lectures on psychology in Zürich. Christou returned to Alexandria in 1951; then lived on his family estate on the island of Chios. He evolved a system of composition embracing the totality of human and metaphysical expression, forming a "philosophical structure" for which he designed a surrealistic graphic notation involving a "psychoid factor," symbolized by the Greek letter psi; aleatory practices are indicated by the drawing of a pair of dice; a sudden stop, by a dagger, etc. His score *Enantiodromia (Opposed Pathways)* for Orch. (1965; revised 1968; first perf. in Oakland, Calif., Feb. 18, 1969), in such a graphic notation, is reproduced in the avant-garde publication *Source* 6 (1969). His notation also includes poetry, choreographic acting, special lighting, film, and projection meant to envelop the listener on all sides. At his death he left sketches for a set of 130 multimedia compositions of a category he called *Anaparastasis* ("proto-performances, meant to revive primeval rituals as adapted to modern culture").

WORKS: *Phoenix Music* for Orch. (1948–49); Symph. No. 1 (1950; London, April 29, 1951); *Latin Mass* for Chorus, Brass, and Percussion (1953; posthumous, Athens, Sept. 26, 1971); *David's Psalms* for Baritone, Chorus, and Orch. (1953); *6 Songs* for Voice and Piano, to poems by T.S. Eliot (1955; orchestrated 1957); Symph. No. 2 for Chorus and Orch. (1954–58; uses an adapted version of the *Latin Mass* as its finale); *Gilgamesh,* oratorio (1958); *Patterns and Permutations* for Orch. (1960; Athens, March 11, 1963); Symph. No. 3 (1959–62); Toccata for Piano and Orch. (1962); *The 12 Keys* for Mezzo-soprano and Chamber Ensemble (1962); *The Breakdown,* opera (1964); *Tongues of Fire,* Pentecost oratorio (1964; English Bach Festival, Oxford, June 27, 1964); *Mysterion,* oratorio for Soli, 3 Choirs, Actors, Orch., and Tape, to ancient Egyptian myths (1965–66); *Praxis for 12* for 11 Strings and Pianist-Percussionist-Conductor (1966; Athens, April 18, 1966; an alternate version exists, titled simply *Praxis,* for 44 Strings and Pianist-Percussionist-Conductor); *Oresteia,*

236

unfinished "super-opera," after Aeschylus (1967–70). Performable works from the cycle *Anaparasta-sis* are: *The Strychnine Lady* for Female Viola Player, 2 groups of Massed Strings, Brass, Percussion, Tapes, Metal Sheet, Sound-producing Objects and Toys, Red Cloth, and 5 Actors (Athens, April 3, 1967); *Anaparastasis I (Astron)* for Baritone and Instrumental Ensemble (Munich, Nov. 12, 1968); *Anaparastasis III (The Pianist)* for Actor, Variable Instrumental Ensemble, and 3 Stereo Tapes (Munich, Nov. 13, 1969); *Epicycle* for Variable Instrumental Ensemble that may take a chiliad or a hebdomad, a nanosecond or a quindecillion of non-zero moments to perform (concise version, Athens, Dec. 15, 1968; extended version, Athens, Dec. 20, 1968); stage music for *The Persians* (1965), *The Frogs* (1966), and *Oedipus Rex* (1969).

Christy, Edwin P., American minstrel show promoter and performer; b. Philadelphia, Nov. 28, 1815; d. New York, May 21, 1862. In 1842 he founded the Christy Minstrels, which played a decisive role in the formation of a typical American variety show, consisting of songs, comic skits, and short plays and parodies. He opened his enterprise in Buffalo; in 1846 he introduced his troupe in N.Y. and played there for 8 years, then went to San Francisco; retired from performing in 1855. It was Christy who had Stephen Foster write his most famous "Ethiopian" songs for him; as was common in his time, Christy appropriated the authorship of these songs, but was decent enough to give Foster credit when the songs became greatly popular. Christy became mentally deranged and ended his life by jumping out of a window.

Chrysander, (Karl Franz) Friedrich, eminent German musicologist and editor; b. Lübtheen, Mecklenburg, July 8, 1826; d. Bergedorf, near Hamburg, Sept. 3, 1901. He began his career as a private tutor; in 1855 he received his Ph.D. from Rostock Univ. His major undertaking was a biography of Handel, but it remained incomplete, bringing the account only to 1740 (3 vols., 1858–67; reprint, 1966). With Gottfried Gervinus, the literary historian, he organized the Deutsche Händelgesellschaft in 1856 for the purpose of publishing a complete edition of Handel's works. After the first vol. was issued in 1858, disagreements among the members caused Chrysander and Gervinus to carry the task alone. King George of Hannover granted them, in 1860, an annual subvention of 1,000 thaler, which they continued to receive until the annexation of Hannover by Prussia in 1866; in 1870, Prussia renewed the subvention from Hannover; after the death of Gervinus in 1871, Chrysander continued the task alone. The resulting publication, *Georg Friedrich Händels Werke: Ausgabe der Drutschen Handelgesellschaft* (100 vols., Leipzig and Bergedorf bei Hamburg, 1858–94; 6 supplementary vols., 1888–1902), was a monumental achievement, but it was superseded by the new critical edition edited by M. Schneider and R. Steglich (Kassel, 1955—). Chrysander also served as editor of the *Allgemeine Musikalische Zeitung*

(1868–71 and 1875–82), to which he contributed many articles. He edited an important collection of essays in the *Jahrbuch für musikalische Wissenschaft* in 1863, and again in 1867. In 1885 he helped to found (with Philipp Spitta and Guido Adler) the *Vierteljahrsschrift für Musikwissenschaft,* and contributed to it until 1894. His other writings include *Über die Molltonart in den Volksgesängen* (Schwerin, 1853), *Über das Oratorium* (Schwerin, 1853), and *Händels biblische Oratorien in geschichtlicher Betrachtung* (Hamburg, 1897; 4th ed., 1922).

Chrysanthos of Madytos, learned Greek cleric and music theorist; b. Madytos, Turkey (hence, known as "of Madytos"); c.1770; d. Bursa, Turkey, 1846. He was bishop of the Greek Orthodox Church in Istanbul, and taught at the music school of the Patriarchate there from 1815 to 1821. He subsequently served as bishop in Durazzo, in Smyrna, and finally in Bursa, where he died. He undertook the reform of the post-Byzantine music notation by reducing the number of neumes and interval indexes; also revived the division of scales into the ancient Greek modes—diatonic, chromatic, and enharmonic. He publ. 2 manuals in the Greek language: *Introduction into the Theory and Practice of Church Music* (Paris, 1821) and *Great Music Instruction* (Trieste, 1832).

Chueca, Federico, Spanish composer of zarzuelas; b. Madrid, May 5, 1846; d. there, June 20, 1908. He was a medical student; organized a band at the Univ. of Madrid; also conducted theater orchs. He began to compose for the stage in collaboration with Valverde, who helped him to harmonize and orchestrate his melodies. Thanks to his prodigious facility, he wrote a great number of zarzuelas, of which *La gran via*, produced in Madrid (July 2, 1886), became his greatest success, obtaining nearly 1,000 performances in Madrid alone; it has also been performed many times in Latin America and the U.S. The march from his zarzuela *Cadiz* served for a time as the Spanish national anthem; dances from his *El año pasado por agua* and *Locuras madrileñas* also enjoyed great popularity. Chueca is regarded as one of the creators of the "género chico" (light genre) of Spanish stage music.

Chung, Kyung-Wha, brilliant Korean violinist; sister of **Myung-Wha Chung** and **Myung-Whun Chung;** b. Seoul, March 26, 1948. She began to study the violin as a small child; made her orch. debut in Seoul at the age of 9, playing the Mendelssohn Concerto; in 1961 she went to the U.S., where she studied with Ivan Galamian at the Juilliard School of Music in N.Y. In 1967 she shared first prize with Pinchas Zukerman in the Leventritt Competition. In 1968 she appeared as soloist with the N.Y. Phil.; made her European debut in 1970 with the London Symph. Orch. She then embarked upon a wide-flung concert tour in Europe and Asia. She gave numerous trio concerts with her sister and brother, and also appeared as a soloist with her brother acting as conductor.

Chung, Myung-Wha, Korean cellist; sister of **Kyung-Wha Chung** and **Myung-Whun Chung;** b. Seoul, March 19, 1944. She studied cello in Seoul; made her orch. debut here in 1957; in 1961 she went to the U.S., where she studied at the Juilliard School of Music in N.Y.; then attended a master class given by Gregor Piatigorsky at the Univ. of Southern Calif. in Los Angeles. She appeared as soloist with orchs. in Europe and America; also played trio concerts with her sister and brother.

Chung, Myung-Whun, Korean pianist and conductor; brother of **Myung-Wha Chung,** and **Kyung-Wha Chung;** b. Seoul, Jan. 22, 1953. He began to play piano as a child in Seoul; then went to the U.S., where he studied at the Mannes College of Music; he received his diplomas in piano and conducting from the Juilliard School of Music in 1974. In 1971 he made his conducting debut in Seoul; in 1974 he won 2nd prize in the International Tchaikovsky Competition in Moscow as a pianist. He subsequently engaged in a double career as pianist and conductor; from 1978–81 he served as assistant conductor of the Los Angeles Phil. Orch.; also gave trio concerts with his sisters.

Ciccolini, Aldo, Italian pianist; b. Naples, Aug. 15, 1925. He studied with Paolo Denza at the Naples Cons.; in 1949 he was the winner of the Long-Thibaud prize in Paris. He toured in France, Spain, and South America; on Nov. 2, 1950, he made his American debut with Tchaikovsky's Concerto No. 1 (N.Y. Phil.). He has since appeared with several major orchs. in the U.S., and has also continued his concerts in Europe. In 1971 he was appointed prof. at the Paris Cons. Ciccolini possesses a virtuoso technique combined with a lyrical sense of phrasing.

Ciconia, Jean (Johannes), Walloon theorist and composer; b. Liège, c.1335; d. Padua, between Dec. 11 and Dec. 24, 1411. Little is known about his life; he was in Italy from 1358 to 1367; was in Liège from 1372 until 1401. In 1402 he went to Padua, where he was a canon. A treatise by him entitled *De proportionibus musicae,* which he completed shortly before his death, is extant. Several of his musical compositions are preserved in Italian libraries; modern reprints are in Denkmäler der Tonkunst in Österreich (vols. VII and XXXI). Ciconia's significance lies in his early use of musical devices that did not become current until much later; he applied the technique of French isorhythmic style as well as canonic imitation.

Cifra, Antonio, Italian composer; b. probably near Terracina, 1584; d. Loreto, Oct. 2, 1629. He was a choirboy in the church of San Luigi dei Francesi in Rome; in 1594–96, was a pupil of G.B. Nanino; also studied with Palestrina; in 1609, was maestro di cappella at the Collegio Germanico in Rome; in 1609–22 and from 1626, was maestro di cappella at

Santa Casa di Loreto; in 1623–26, was maestro di cappella at San Giovanni in Laterano, Rome. A prolific composer, he is considered one of the best of the Roman school; he publ. (between 1600 and 1638) 5 books of motets; 3 of Psalms; 5 of masses; 10 sets of *concerti ecclesiastici* (over 200 numbers); many more motets and Psalms (in 2–12 parts); antiphons; litanies; madrigals; ricercari; *Scherzi ed arie a 1, 2, 3 e 4 voci, per cantar del clavicembalo;* etc.

Cikker, Ján, eminent Slovak composer; b. Banská Bystrica, July 29, 1911. He studied composition at the Prague Cons. with Jaroslav Křička and Vítězslav Novák; also took a course in conducting with Felix Weingartner in Vienna. In 1938–51 he was a prof. of theory at the Bratislava Cons.; then was a prof. of composition at the Bratislava Academy. An exceptionally prolific composer, Cikker is distinguished particularly in his works for the musical theater; his operas enjoyed greatly merited success in their productions in Czechoslovakia and Germany. In his music he has developed an idiom deeply rooted in the melorhythmic patterns of Slovak folk songs, while his harmonic and contrapuntal treatment is marked by effective modernistic devices, making use of unresolved dissonances and atonal melodic patterns.

Cilèa, Francesco, Italian opera composer; b. Palmi, Calabria, July 23, 1866; d. Varazze, Nov. 20, 1950. He studied at the Naples Cons. (1881–89) with Cesi (piano) and Serrao (composition); taught piano there (1894–96); then harmony at the Istituto Musicale in Florence (1896–1904); was head of the Palermo Cons. (1913–16); director of the Majella Cons. in Naples (1916–35). He was a member of the Reale Accademia Musicale in Florence (1898) and a knight of the Order of the Crown of Italy (1893).
WORKS: Operas: *Gina* (Naples, Feb. 9, 1889); *La Tilda* (Florence, April 7, 1892); *L'Arlesiana,* after Daudet (Milan, Nov. 27, 1897; later revised from 4 to 3 acts and produced in Milan, Oct. 22, 1898); *Adriana Lecouvreur,* after Scribe (Milan, Nov. 6, 1902; Covent Garden, Nov. 8, 1904; Metropolitan Opera, Nov. 26, 1906; his most famous opera); *Gloria* (La Scala, Milan, April 15, 1907); *Il matrimonio Selvaggio* (1909); *Poema sinfonico* for Solo, Chorus, and Orch. (Genoa, July 12, 1913); Piano Trio (1886); Cello Sonata (1888); Variations for Violin and Piano (1931); piano pieces; songs.

Cimarosa, Domenico, eminent Italian composer; b. Aversa, near Naples, Dec. 17, 1749; d. Venice, Jan. 11, 1801. The son of a poor mason, and orphaned early, he attended the charity school of the Minorites; his first music teacher was Polcano, organist of the monastery. His talent was so marked that in 1761 he obtained a free scholarship to the Cons. di Santa Maria di Loreto, where he was taught singing by Manna and Sacchini, counterpoint by Fenaroli, and composition by Piccinni. In 1770 his oratorio *Giuditta* was performed in Rome; in 1772 he produced his first opera, *Le stravaganze del Conte,* at Naples, with moderate success. But with *La finta* *parigina,* given the next season at the Teatro Nuovo in Naples, he was fairly launched on a dramatic career singularly free from artistic reverses. His ease and rapidity of composition were phenomenal; in 29 years he wrote nearly 80 operas. His fame grew steadily, eventually rivaling that of Paisiello. In 1778 Cimarosa brought out *L'Italiana in Londra* in Rome, and lived, until 1781, alternately in Rome and Naples; following the custom of the period, he wrote one opera after another specially for the city in which it was to be performed. His speed of composition was such that during the year 1781 he brought out 2 operas in Naples, one in Rome, and 2 in Turin. His works became known far beyond the bounds of Italy; they were performed not only by Italian opera troupes in all European capitals, but also by foreign opera companies, in translation. After Paisiello's return from St. Petersburg, where he had served from 1776 to 1785 as court composer, his post was offered to Cimarosa. He accepted, and set out for St. Petersburg in the autumn of 1787. His journey there was like a triumphant procession; at the courts of Florence, Vienna, and Warsaw, he was overwhelmed with attentions; and he arrived in St. Petersburg on Dec. 2, 1787, wayworn and suffering from the wintry weather, but confident of success. Here he produced 3 operas, and during the 3 years of his stay wrote various other compositions for the court and nobility, including a ballet, *La felicità inaspettata* (Feb. 24, 1788), and a dramatic cantata, *Atene edificata* (June 29, 1788). But as Catherine the Great did not care for his choral works, he was replaced by Sarti, and in 1791 he left Russia; in the autumn of that year he arrived in Vienna, where Emperor Leopold engaged him at a salary of 12,000 florins as Kapellmeister. At Vienna, at the age of 42, he brought out his masterpiece, *Il matrimonio segreto* (Feb. 7, 1792), the success of which eclipsed not only that of his former works but that of the works of all rivals, not excepting Mozart. It is probably the sole survivor, on the present-day stage, of all Cimarosa's dramatic works. Cimarosa remained long enough in Vienna to write 2 more operas; 1793 found him once more at home in Naples, where his *Il matrimonio segreto* aroused unexampled enthusiasm, having 67 consecutive performances, the illustrious composer himself playing the cembalo for the first 7 representations. In 1794 he visited Venice to bring out *Gli Orazi e Curiazi;* in 1796 and 1798 he was in Rome, periodically returning to Naples, and all the time actively engaged in operatic composition. In 1798, he was seriously ill at Naples; the year after, having openly taken part in the Neapolitan revolutionary demonstration on the entrance of the French army into the city, he was imprisoned for a number of days. He then went to Venice, and was at work on a new opera, *Artemisia,* when death suddenly overtook him. It was rumored abroad that he had been poisoned by order of Queen Caroline of Naples, as a dangerous revolutionist; the rumor was so persistent, and popular embitterment so great, that the Pope's personal physician, Piccioli, was sent to make an examination; according to his sworn statement, Cimarosa died of a gangrenous abdominal tumor.

Comedy opera was Cimarosa's forte: in his happiest moments he rivals Mozart; even in "opera seria" many of his efforts are worthy of a place in the repertoire. The fluidity and fecundity of his melodic vein, his supreme command of form, and his masterly control of orch. resources still excite astonishment and admiration. He was the peer of his great Italian contemporary Paisiello.

WORKS: Of the 76 operas known to be his, some of the finest are: *La finta parigina* (Naples, 1773); *Il Fanatico per gli antichi Romani* (Naples, 1777); *L'italiana in Londra* (Rome, Dec. 28, 1778); *L'infedeltà fedele* (Naples, July 20, 1779); *Caio Mario* (Rome, Jan. 1780); *Il convito di pietra* (Venice, Dec. 27, 1781); *Giannina e Bernardone* (Venice, Nov., 1781); *La ballerina amante* (Naples, 1782); *Artaserse* (Turin, Dec. 26, 1784); *Le trame deluse* (Naples, Sept. 1786); *L'Impressario in angustie* (Naples, Oct. 1786); *Le vergine del sole* (St. Petersburg, Nov. 6, 1789); *Il matrimonio segreto* (Vienna, Feb. 7, 1792; given in Eng. with great success at the Metropolitan Opera in 1937); *Le astuzie femminili* (Naples, Aug. 16, 1794); *Orazi e Curiazi* (Venice, Dec. 26, 1796). He also produced at least 3 oratorios; several cantatas; masses in 4 parts, with instrumental accompaniment; Psalms, motets, Requiems, arias, cavatinas, solfeggi, and a great variety of other vocal works; 7 symphs.; cembalo sonatas (of which 32 were ed. and publ. by F. Boghen, Paris, 1926).

Cipra, Milo, Croatian composer; b. Vares, Oct. 13, 1906. He studied composition with Bersa at the Zagreb Music Academy, graduating in 1933; taught there after 1941 and was its dean (1961–71). In his early composition he followed the national school, with thematic elements derived from folk-song patterns of Croatia; he then adopted a severe structural idiom, gradually increasing in modernity.

Cisneros (née **Broadfoot**), **Eleanora de,** American contralto; b. New York, Nov. 1, 1878; d. there, Feb. 3, 1934. She studied singing in N.Y. with Mme. Murio-Celli and later in Paris with Jean de Reszke. In 1901 she married Count Francesco de Cisneros of Havana, Cuba, and appeared professionally under this name. She enjoyed a brilliant career; first appeared with the Metropolitan Opera Co. on tour in Chicago on Nov. 24, 1899, as Rossweisse in *Die Walküre;* then made her N.Y. Metropolitan Opera debut in the same role on Jan. 5, 1900; sang in Italy between 1902 and 1914, and annually in London from 1903 to 1908. Between 1906 and 1911 she was the principal contralto singer at the Manhattan Opera, and later was a member of the Chicago Opera. In 1915 she toured Australia; then lived in Paris until 1929, when she returned to N.Y.

Čiurlionis, Mikolajus, Lithuanian composer; b. Varena, Oct. 4, 1875; d. Pustelnik, near Warsaw, April 10, 1911. He studied composition with Noskowski, and at the Leipzig Cons. with Carl Reinecke and Jadassohn. From 1902 till 1909 he was active in Warsaw as a choral conductor. His music reflects the Germanic Romantic tendencies, but he also developed interesting theories of so-called "tonal ground formations," anticipating the serial methods of Schoenberg and Hauer. Čiurlionis was also a remarkable painter in an abstract expressionist manner; many of his paintings carry musical titles, such as "Prelude and Fugue," "Spring Sonata," etc. His musical works include the symph. poems *In the Forest* (1901) and *The Ocean* (1907); cantata, *De profundis* (1899); String Quartet; numerous piano pieces and songs.

Civil, Alan, noted English horn–player; b. Northampton, June 13, 1929. He studied with Aubrey Brain in London and with Willy von Stemm in Hamburg. He was principal horn of the Royal Phil. Orch. (1952–55), and later co-principal horn, with Dennis Brain, of the Philharmonia Orch. (1955–57); after Brain's tragic death, was principal horn (1957–66); from 1966, principal horn of the BBC Symph. Orch. In 1966 he became a prof. of horn at the Royal College of Music in London.

Claflin, (Alan) Avery, American composer; b. Keene, N.H., June 21, 1898; d. Greenwich, Conn., Jan. 9, 1979. He studied law and banking, and pursued a business career; also took music courses at Harvard Univ. He attracted attention as a composer by his amusing choral work, a fiscal madrigal entitled *Lament for April 15* (1955), to the text of an Internal Revenue tax form. Among his other compositions are the operas *Hester Prynne* (after *The Scarlet Letter* of Hawthorne), of which Scene II of Act II was performed at Hartford on Dec. 15, 1934; *The Fall of Usher* (not performed); *La Grande Bretèche,* after Balzac's story (NBC Radio, Feb. 3, 1957); *Uncle Tom's Cabin* (1961–64); 2 symphs.; *Teen Scenes* for Strings (1955); *Pop Concert Concerto* for Piano and Orch. (1958); Piano Trio; other chamber music.

Clapp, Philip Greeley, American composer and pedagogue; b. Boston, Aug. 4, 1888; d. Iowa City, April 9, 1954. He studied piano with his aunt Mary Greeley James (1895–99); and violin with Jacques Hoffman in Boston (1895–1905); also took lessons in music theory with John Marshall (1905). He then entered Harvard Univ., studying music theory and composition with Spalding, Converse, and Edward Burlingame Hill; received his B.A. (1908), M.A. (1909), and Ph.D. (1911). He also studied composition and conducting in Stuttgart with Max von Schillings (1910). He became a teaching fellow at Harvard (1911–12); was music director at Dartmouth College (1915–18); in 1919 he was appointed director of the music dept. at the Univ. of Iowa, and remained at that post for the rest of his life. Clapp was a prolific composer and a competent teacher; he was also a brilliant pianist, but did not dedicate himself to a concert career; he also appeared as conductor of his own works and was in charge of the univ. orch. at Iowa City. His music is conceived in an expansive Romantic idiom much influenced by the modern German style of composition, and yet introducing some advanced melodic and harmonic patterns, such as building harmonies in

fourths.

Clari, Giovanni Carlo Maria, Italian composer and choral director; b. Pisa, Sept. 27, 1677; d. there, May 16, 1754. He studied with his father and with Francesco Alessi in Pisa; then under Colonna at Bologna, where his opera *Il Savio delirante* was produced in 1695; from 1703 to 1724 he was in Pistoia as maestro di cappella of the Cathedral; then went to Pisa. His best-known work is a collection of madrigals for 2 and 3 voices (1720; reprinted by Carli, Paris, 1825); he also wrote masses, Psalms, a Requiem, and other sacred music.

Claribel. See **Charlotte Barnard.**

Clark, Melville, one of the pioneers of the player-piano industry; b. Oneida County, N.Y., 1850; d. Chicago, Nov. 5, 1918. In 1875 he established himself as an organ builder in Oakland, Calif.; moved to Chicago in 1880; in 1894 he also opened a piano factory, after he had become interested in pneumatic actions; his experiments leading to practical results which convinced him of the possibilities of the player piano, he sold his organ factory, and, in 1900, organized the Melville Clark Piano Co., of which he was president. In 1901 he patented and placed on the market the 88-note roll, utilizing the full compass of the piano, and thus gave the impetus to the phenomenal player-piano industry which later developed. In 1911 he patented a recording mechanism which aimed to reproduce the actual performance of great pianists. He also held many other important patents.

Clark, Melville Antone, harpist and harp manufacturer, nephew of the preceding; b. Syracuse, N.Y., Sept. 12, 1883; d. there, Dec. 11, 1953. He received his first instruction on the harp from his father; was a pupil of Van Veachton Rogers (1896–99) and of John Aptommas in London (1908). While on a tour of Great Britain in 1908 he acquired a small Irish harp, formerly the property of the poet Thomas Moore; by the application of acoustic principles he improved the model and succeeded in producing a small, portable harp (39 inches high) of considerable tone volume; founded the Clark Harp Manufacturing Co. at Syracuse, which turned out the first small Irish harps in 1913; on a tour of the U.S. with John McCormack (1913–14) the inventor demonstrated the possibilities of the new instrument; took out 14 patents on improvements for the portable harp, and developed a new method of pedaling the concert harp; played about 4,000 recitals in the U.S., Canada, and England; was co-founder of the Syracuse Symph. Orch.; treasurer of the National Association of Harpists; president of the Clark Music Co. (1910).
    WRITINGS: *How to Play the Harp, Romance of the Harp, Singing Strings.*

Clarke, Henry Leland, American musicologist and composer; b. Dover, N.H., March 9, 1907. He studied piano and violin; then took courses at Harvard Univ. (M.A., 1929; Ph.D., 1947). In 1929 he went to Paris, where he took composition lessons with Nadia Boulanger at the Ecole Normale de Musique. Upon returning to the U.S., he occupied himself mainly with teaching; was on the faculty of Westminster Choir College (1938–42), the Univ. of Calif., Los Angeles (1947–58), and the Univ. of Washington, Seattle (1958–77). As a composer, Clarke applies a number of interesting innovations, e.g., "Intervalescent Counterpoint" (with interval values constantly changing from one voice to another), "Lipophony" (with certain notes systematically omitted), "Word Tones" (whenever a word recurs, it is assigned to the same pitch), and "Rotating Triskaidecaphony" (a 12-tone series returning to note one for the 13th note, with the next row starting and ending on note 2, etc.).

Clarke, Jeremiah, English composer and organist; b. London, c.1673; d. there (suicide), Dec. 1, 1707. He was a chorister in the Chapel Royal; in 1700 was made Gentleman Extraordinary of the Chapel Royal; in 1704 was appointed joint organist (with Croft) there. A hopeless love affair caused Clarke to take his own life.
WORKS: He composed (with others) the stage works *The World in the Moon* (1697) and *The Island Princess* (1699); wrote incidental music to several plays; was the first composer to set Dryden's *Alexander's Feast* to music (for St. Cecilia's Day, Nov. 22, 1697); also wrote a cantata, an ode, anthems, songs, etc. He was the real author of the famous *Trumpet Voluntary*, erroneously ascribed to Purcell, and popularized by Sir Henry Wood's orch. arrangement.

Clarke, Rebecca, English composer and viola player; b. Harrow, Aug. 27, 1886; d. New York, Oct. 13, 1979. She studied composition at the Royal College of Music in London with Sir Charles Stanford. She was originally a violinist, but specialized later as a viola player. In 1916 she went to the U.S. Among her compositions are Piano Trio (1921), *Chinese Puzzle* for Violin and Piano (1922), Rhapsody for Cello and Piano (1923), and *3 Irish Country Songs* for Violin and Cello. Her music is quite advanced, on the fringe of atonality in melodic outline. She was actively at work in N.Y. until her death at the age of 93. An entry on her chamber music is found in Cobbett's *Cyclopedic Survey of Chamber Music* (London, 1929).

Claudin le Jeune. See **Le Jeune, Claudin.**

Clemencic, René, Austrian recorder player and conductor; b. Vienna, Feb. 27, 1928. He studied the recorder with Hans Staeps and Johannes Collette; also keyboard instruments with Eta Harich-Schneider. In 1958 he founded the Musica Antiqua in Vienna, which became the Ensemble Musica Antiqua in 1959; with this group he gave performances of music covering the period from the Middle Ages to the Baroque, utilizing authentic instruments. In 1969 he founded the Clemencic Consort, and led it in a vast repertoire, extending from the medieval period to the avant-garde.

Clemens (Clement), Jacobus (called **"Clemens non Papa"**), eminent Netherlandish contrapuntist; b. Ypres, c.1510; d. Dixmude, c.1556 (death date is surmised from the fact that vol. 1 of *Novum et insigne opus musicum,* publ. in 1558, contains the motet *Nanie,* composed by Jacob Vaet on Clemens's death). The exact meaning of "non Papa" is not clear; it was once thought to mean "not the Pope," to distinguish the composer from Clement VII; but a more recent interpretation suggests that "non Papa" was intended to differentiate Clemens from a poet also living in the town of Ypres, named Jacobus Papa. His teachers are not known; he was in France for a time; returned in 1540 to the Netherlands and settled in Bruges; in 1545 he went to Antwerp; later lived in Dixmude, where he was buried.
WORKS: 15 masses, numerous motets, chansons, etc., publ. by Phalèse (Louvain, 1555–80); 4 books of *Souterliedekens a 3,* i.e., psalms set to popular Netherlandish tunes, publ. by T. Susato (Antwerp, 1556–57); and many miscellaneous pieces in collections of the period. Reprints are to be found in K. Proske's *Musica divina* (vol. II); R.J. van Maldeghem's *Trésor musical;* and F. Commer's *Collectio operum musicorum Batavorum.* El. Mincoff-Marriage republ. the text of the *Souterliedekens* (The Hague, 1922); a selection of 15 of these pieces, with music, was ed. by W. Blanke (Wolfenbüttel, 1929).

Clément, Edmond, French tenor; b. Paris, March 28, 1867; d. Nice, Feb. 24, 1928. He was a pupil of Warot at the Paris Cons. in 1887; took first prize in 1889; his debut was at the Opéra-Comique, Nov. 29, 1889, as Vincent in Gounod's *Mireille.* His success was instantaneous, and he remained there until 1910 with frequent leave for extended tours; sang in the principal theaters of France, Belgium, Spain, Portugal, England, and Denmark; in 1909–10 sang at the Metropolitan Opera House; in 1911–13, with the Boston Opera Co. His voice was a light tenor of very agreeable quality, with a range of 2 octaves. He created the chief tenor parts in the following operas (all at the Opéra-Comique): Bruneau's *L'Attaque du Moulin* (1893); Saint-Saëns's *Phryné* (1893); Cui's *Le Flibustier* (1894); Godard's *La Vivandière* (1895); Dubois's *Xavière* (1895); Hahn's *L'Ile du rêve* (1898); Erlanger's *Le Juif polonais* (1900); Saint-Saëns's *Hélène* (1904); Dupont's *La Cabrera* (1905); Vidal's *La Reine Fiammette* (1908). He was particularly famous for his portrayal of Des Grieux in Massenet's opera *Manon.*

Clement, Franz, Austrian violinist and composer; b. Vienna, Nov. 17, 1780; d. there, Nov. 3, 1842. He learned to play the violin as a child, and at the age of 10 went to London, where he appeared as a soloist at concerts directed by Salomon and Haydn. Returning to Vienna, he continued his successful career; was conductor at the Theater an der Wien (1802–11); made a tour in Germany and Russia

(1813–18); participated in the concerts of the famous singer Angelica Catalani. He was greatly esteemed as a violinist and musician by his contemporaries; Beethoven wrote his Violin Concerto for him, and Clement gave its first performance in Vienna (Dec. 23, 1806). He wrote 6 concertos and 25 concertinos for violin, as well as numerous technical studies.

Clement, Jacobus. See **Clemens, Jacobus.**

Clementi, Aldo, Italian composer of avant-garde tendencies; b. Catania, May 25, 1925. He took piano lessons as a child in Catania and later was a piano pupil of Pietro Scarpini in Siena; subsequently studied composition with Alfredo Sangiorgi, a pupil of Schoenberg, in Catania (1945–52) and with Petrassi in Rome (1952–54); then attended summer courses in new music at Darmstadt (1955–62). After an initial period of writing music in a neo-Baroque manner, he adopted serial techniques, employing rhythmic indeterminacy and dense, clustered sonics.

Clementi, Muzio, celebrated Italian pianist and composer; b. Rome, Jan. 23, 1752; d. at his country seat at Evesham, England, March 10, 1832. His father, a goldsmith, was a devoted amateur of music, and had his son taught carefully, from early years, by Antonio Buroni, maestro di cappella in a Roman church. From 1759 the organist Condiceli gave him lessons in organ playing and harmony. So rapid was their pupil's progress that when but 9 he obtained a position as an organist, in competition with other, more mature, players. Until 14 years of age he pursued his studies in Italy, G. Carpani (composition) and Sartarelli (voice) being his next instructors. At a piano concert which Clementi gave in 1766, an English gentleman named Beckford was so delighted with his talent that he obtained the father's permission to educate the boy in England. Clementi lived and studied till 1770 in his patron's house in Dorsetshire; then, a thoroughly equipped pianist and musician, he took London by storm. In 1773 his op. 2 (3 piano sonatas dedicated to Haydn, and warmly praised by C.P.E. Bach) was publ.; it may be considered as finally establishing the form of the piano sonata. From 1777–80 he conducted, as cembalist, the Italian Opera. In 1781 he began a pianistic tour, giving concerts at Paris, Strasbourg, Munich and Vienna. Here, on Dec. 24, 1781, he met Mozart in "friendly" rivalry (Mozart's letters make no pretense of concealing his dislike of the "Italian" composer and player); though the palm of final victory was awarded to neither, yet Clementi tacitly admitted, by changing from a mechanically brilliant to a more suave and melodious piano style, the musical superiority of Mozart. In Vienna his opp. 7, 9, and 10 were publ. by Artaria. Excepting a concert season at Paris, in 1785, Clementi now remained in London for 20 years (1782–1802). He not only made his mark, and incidentally amassed quite a fortune, as a teacher, pianist, and composer, but also (after losses through the failure of Longman & Broderip, the instrument makers and music sellers) estab-

lished, with John Longman, a highly successful piano factory and publishing house (now Collard & Collard). With his pupil Field, Clementi set out for St. Petersburg in 1802, passing through Paris and Vienna; their tour was attended by brilliant success, and Field was so well received in St. Petersburg that he accompanied his master no further. Clementi resided for several years alternately in Berlin, Dresden, and St. Petersburg; then, after visiting Vienna, Milan, Rome, and Naples, he again settled in London. The businessman in Clementi now gained the upper hand; he no longer played in public, but devoted himself to composition and the management of his prosperous mercantile ventures. He never again went far from London, except during the winter of 1820–21, which he spent in Leipzig. As a teacher, Clementi trained many distinguished musicians: Field, Cramer, Moscheles, Kalkbrenner, Alexander Klengel, Ludwig Berger, Zeuner, even Meyerbeer, all owed much to his instruction.

WORKS: His compositions include symphs. (which failed in competition with Haydn's) and overtures for orch.; 106 piano sonatas (46 with violin, cello, or flute); 2 duos for 2 pianos; 6 4-hand duets; fugues, preludes, and exercises in canon form; toccatas, waltzes, variations, caprices; *Points d'orgue . . .* (op. 19); *Introduction à l'art de toucher le piano, avec 50 leçons*, etc. (Eng. trans., London, 1801; reprinted, N.Y., 1973); by far the greater part of these are wholly forgotten. But his great book of études, the *Gradus ad Parnassum* (publ. 1817), is a living reminder that he was one of the greatest of piano teachers. Bülow's excellent selection of 50 of these études has been outdone by several later complete eds. (German, Italian, Eng.), including that of Vogrich, arranged progressively (N.Y., 1898). The Library of Congress in Washington, D.C., acquired, largely through the efforts of Carl Engel, numerous MSS by Clementi, including 4 symphs. (almost complete); other fragments are in the British Museum. The first 2 of these symphs. were restored and ed. for publication by Alfredo Casella, who performed them (using Clementi's original instrumentation) for the first time (No. 1, Turin, Dec. 13, 1935; No. 2, Rome, Jan. 5, 1936). The *Collected Works* (5 vols., Leipzig, 1802–5) is now available in reprint (N.Y., 1973). Pietro Spada revised and edited Symphs. Nos. 1–4 and the 2 symphs. of op. 18.

Clemm, John (Johann Gottlob), German-American organ builder; b. Dresden, 1690; d. Bethlehem, Pa., May 5, 1762. Clemm reputedly learned organ making from A. Silbermann, probably while serving the Moravian Church settlement at Herrnhut, Saxony. He came to America with a group of Schwenkfelders in 1735, became a Separatist, and settled in Philadelphia in 1736. His first known organ was installed at Trinity Church in N.Y., in 1741. Subsequently, he assisted the Swedish-American organ builder Hesselius in Philadelphia. He reunited with the Moravians and moved to Bethlehem, Pa. (1756–58). There he continued his work with his assistant, David Tannenberg, until his death. His descendants were important music dealers and publishers in Philadelphia up to 1879. His son, **John Clemm, Jr.,** was the first organist at N.Y.'s Trinity Church.

Cleonides, Greek writer on music; lived in the first half of the 2nd century A.D. His treatise *Eisagoge harmonike (Introductio harmonica)*, based on the theories of Aristoxenus, was for a long time ascribed to the mathematician Euclid, because it had been publ. under Euclid's name by Pena (Paris, 1557) and Meibom (Amsterdam, 1652), although it had been printed with the real author's name by Valla (Venice, 1497). A new critical edition was publ. by K. von Jan in *Musici Scriptores Graeci.* There is a French trans. by Ruelle (1896); for an Eng. trans., see Strunk's *Source Readings in Music History* (N.Y., 1950).

Clérambault, Louis Nicolas, French composer and organist; b. Paris, Dec. 19, 1676; d. there, Oct. 26, 1749. He studied with André Raison; was organist at various Paris churches. He was a successful composer of theatrical pieces for the court: *Le Soleil vainqueur* (Paris, Oct. 21, 1721); *Le Départ du roi* (1745); etc. He also wrote a number of solo cantatas, in which genre he excelled; composed much organ music; some of his organ works are republ. in Guilmant's *Archives des maîtres de l'orgue.* His son, **César François Nicolas Clérambault** (1700–60), was also an organist and composer.

Cleva, Fausto, Italian conductor; b. Trieste, May 17, 1902; d. Athens (collapsed while conducting), Aug. 6, 1971. He studied in Milan; began his conducting career as a youth; in 1920 emigrated to the U.S.; became an American citizen in 1931. He was chorus master and later conductor of the Metropolitan Opera until 1942; then was conductor of the San Francisco Opera Co. (1942–44 and 1949–55); then again with the Metropolitan (1951 until his death). In 1971 he was presented with a gold cigarette case by the directors of the Metropolitan on the occasion of his 50th anniversary as a regular member, since the age of 18, of its conducting staff.

Cliburn, Van (Harvey Lavan, Jr.), brilliant American pianist; b. Shreveport, La., July 12, 1934. He studied piano with his mother; then with Rosina Lhévinne at the Juilliard School of Music in N.Y., graduating in 1954. He made his debut with the Houston Symph. Orch. at the age of 13; appeared with the N.Y. Phil. in 1954; toured as a concert pianist in the U.S. He became suddenly famous when he won the Tchaikovsky Competition in Moscow in 1958, the first American to score such a triumph in Russia, where he became a prime favorite. Upon his return to N.Y. he received a hero's welcome in a street parade. In 1964 he made his debut as an orch. conductor. His playing combines a superlative technique with a genuine Romantic sentiment; this style is particularly effective in the music of Tchaikovsky and Rachmaninoff.

Clicquot, French family of organ builders, of whom the earliest was **Robert Clicquot,** builder of the organ in the Versailles Chapel for Louis XIV (1711), and organs in the cathedrals of Rouen (1689) and Saint-Quentin (1703). His sons **Jean-Baptiste** (b. Rheims, Nov. 3, 1678; d. Paris, March 16, 1746) and **Louis-Alexandre** (b. c.1680; d. Paris, Jan. 25, 1760) were his helpers. The most renowned of the family was **François-Henri Clicquot** (b. 1732; d. Paris, May 24, 1790), who constructed the great organ of Versailles Cathedral (installed Oct. 31, 1761) and the organ of St. Sulpice, with 5 manuals, 66 stops, and a 32-foot pedal (1781).

Clutsam, George H., Australian pianist and composer; b. Sydney, Sept. 26, 1866; d. London, Nov. 17, 1951. As a young pianist, he made tours of Australia, India, China, and Japan; settled in London in 1889 and became a professional accompanist; gave concerts with Melba (1893). From 1908 until 1918 he was a music critic of the *Observer* in London; at the same time wrote music for the stage.
WORKS: Operas: *The Queen's Jester* (1905); *A Summer Night* (London, July 23, 1910); *After a Thousand Years* (1912); *König Harlekin* (Berlin, 1912); several musical comedies: *Gabrielle, Lavender, The Little Duchess* (Glasgow, Dec. 15, 1922). His greatest popular success was the production of *Lilac Time,* an arrangement of Heinrich Berté's operetta *Das Dreimäderlhaus,* based on Schubert's melodies; Clutsam's version in English was first staged in London on Dec. 22, 1922, and had many revivals. Another theatrical medley, arranged from Chopin's melodies, was Clutsam's musical comedy *The Damask Rose* (London, June 17, 1929).

Cluytens, André, noted Belgian conductor; b. Antwerp, March 26, 1905; d. Neuilly, near Paris, June 3, 1967. He studied piano at the Antwerp Cons. His father, conductor at the Théâtre Royal in Antwerp, engaged him as a choral coach; later he conducted opera there (1927–32). He then settled in France, and became a French citizen in 1932. He served as music director at the Toulouse Opera (1932–35); in 1935 was appointed opera conductor in Lyons. In 1944 he conducted at the Paris Opéra; in 1947 he was appointed music director of the Opéra-Comique. In 1949 he was named conductor of the Société du Conservatoire de Paris, and in 1955 he became the first French conductor to appear at the Bayreuth Festival. On Nov. 4, 1956, he made his U.S. debut in Washington, D.C., as guest conductor of the Vienna Phil. during his first American tour. In 1960 he became chief conductor of the Orch. National de Belgique in Brussels, a post he held until his death. Cluytens was highly regarded as a fine interpreter of French music.

Coates, Albert, eminent English conductor, b. St. Petersburg, Russia (of an English father and a mother of Russian descent), April 23, 1882; d. Milnerton, near Cape Town, South Africa, Dec. 11, 1953. He went to England for his general education; enrolled in the science classes of Liverpool Univ., and studied organ with an elder brother who was living there at the time. In 1902 he entered the Leipzig Cons., studying cello with Klengel, piano with Robert Teichmüller, and conducting with Artur Nikisch; served his apprenticeship there and made his debut as conductor in Offenbach's *Les Contes d'Hoffmann* at the Leipzig Opera. In 1906 he was appointed (on Nikisch's recommendation) as chief conductor of the opera house at Elberfeld; in 1910 he was a joint conductor at the Dresden Opera (with Schuch); then at Mannheim (with Bodanzky). In 1911 he received the appointment at the Imperial Opera of St. Petersburg, and conducted many Russian operas. From 1913 he conducted in England, specializing in Wagner and the Russian repertoire; was a proponent of Scriabin's music. In 1920 he made his American debut as guest conductor of the N.Y. Symph. Orch.; during 1923–25 he led conducting classes at the Eastman School of Music in Rochester, N.Y.; also conducted the Rochester Symph. Orch. and appeared as guest conductor with other American orchs. Subsequent engagements included a season at the Berlin State Opera (1931) and concerts with the Vienna Phil. (1935). In 1946 he settled in South Africa, where he conducted the Johannesburg Symph. Orch. and taught at the Univ. of South Africa at Cape Town. Coates was a prolific composer, but his operas and other works had few performances (usually conducted by himself).

WORKS: Symph. poem, *The Eagle* (Leeds, 1925; unsuccessful); operas: *Assurbanipal* (planned for perf. in Moscow in 1915, but abandoned in view of wartime conditions); *Samuel Pepys* (produced in German, Munich, Dec. 21, 1929); *Pickwick* (London, Nov. 20, 1936); *Tafelberg se Kleed* (Eng. title, *Van Hunks and the Devil;* produced at the South African Music Festival in Cape Town, March 7, 1952).

Coates, Edith (Mary), English mezzo-soprano; b. Lincoln, May 31, 1908; d. Worthing, Jan. 7, 1983. She studied at the Trinity College of Music in London; later took lessons with Clive Carey and Dino Borgioli; in 1924 she joined the Old Vic Theatre; sang major roles there from 1931; she appeared at Covent Garden in 1937; was on its roster from 1947 to 1967. She sang the leading roles in the world premieres of Britten's *Peter Grimes* (1945) and *Gloriana* (1953), and in *The Olympians* by Arthur Bliss (1949). In 1977 she was named an Officer of the Order of the British Empire.

Coates, Eric, English composer and viola player; b. Hucknall, Nottinghamshire, Aug. 27, 1886; d. Chichester, Dec. 21, 1957. He took instruction at the Royal Academy of Music with Tertis (viola) and Corder (composition). He was a member of the Hambourg String Quartet, with which he made a tour of South Africa (1908); was first violist in Queen's Hall Orch. (1912–19). In 1946 he visited the U.S., conducting radio performances of his works; in 1948 toured in South America. He gives a detailed account of his career in his autobiography *Suite in Four Movements* (London, 1953). As a composer, Coates specialized in semi-classical works for orch.

His valse serenade *Sleepy Lagoon* (1930) attained enormous popularity all over the world, and was publ. in numerous arrangements. His *London Suite* (1933) was equally successful; its *Knightsbridge* movement became one of the most frequently played marches in England and elsewhere. He further wrote an orch. suite, *4 Centuries* (1941), tracing typical historical forms and styles in 4 sections (*Fugue, Pavane, Valse, and Jazz*); *3 Elizabeths* for Orch.; a great number of songs and instrumental pieces.

Coates, John, English tenor; b. Girlington, Yorkshire, June 29, 1865; d. Northwood, Middlesex, Aug. 16, 1941. He studied with his uncle, J.G. Walton, at Bradford; sang as a small boy at a Bradford church; began serious study in 1893, and took lessons with William Shakespeare in London. He sang baritone parts in Gilbert & Sullivan operettas, making his debut at the Savoy Theatre in *Utopia Limited* (1894); toured in the U.S. with a Gilbert & Sullivan company. He made his debut in grand opera as Faust at Covent Garden (1901); also sang Lohengrin in Cologne and other German cities with considerable success; later sang nearly all the Wagner parts in English with the Moody-Manners Co., with the Carl Rosa Co., and with Beecham (1910); from 1911–13 he toured with Quinlan's opera company in Australia and South Africa. He served in the British army during World War I; in 1919, returned to London, devoting himself chiefly to teaching; also gave recitals of songs by English composers.

Cobbett, Walter Wilson, English patron of music; b. London, July 11, 1847; d. there, Jan. 22, 1937. He was a businessman and amateur violinist. An ardent enthusiast, he traveled widely in Europe and met contemporary composers. He was particularly active in promoting the cause of British chamber music, and arranged a series of Cobbett Competitions; also commissioned special works and established a Cobbett Medal for services to chamber music; the recipients included Thomas Dunhill (1924), Mrs. E.S. Coolidge (1925), and A.J. Clements (1926). Among composers who received the Cobbett commissions and awards were Frank Bridge, York Bowen, John Ireland, Vaughan Williams, James Friskin, Waldo Warner, and Herbert Howells. Cobbett edited the extremely valuable *Cobbett's Cyclopedic Survey of Chamber Music* (2 vols., London; vol. I, 1929; vol. II, 1930; a supplement to vol. I. was publ. in London in 1957; to vol. II, in 1963).

Coccia, Carlo, Italian opera composer; b. Naples, April 14, 1782; d. Novara, April 13, 1873. He studied music theory with Pietro Casella, singing with Saverio Valente, and composition with Paisiello; in 1820 went to Lisbon as maestro concertatore at the San Carlos Opera. In 1824–27 he was conductor at the King's Theatre in London, where he produced his own opera *Maria Stuarda* (1827). He returned to Italy in 1827. Coccia wrote 37 operas; 2 of them, *Clotilda* (Venice, June 8, 1815) and *Caterina di Guise* (Milan, Feb. 14, 1833), were fairly successful.

Cocks & Co., London firm of music publishers, founded 1823 by **Robert Cocks;** his sons, **Arthur Lincoln Cocks** and **Stroud Lincoln Cocks,** became partners in 1868. Upon the death of the original founder in 1887, **Robert Macfarlane Cocks** became the proprietor and carried on the business until 1898, when he retired and transferred the house to Augener and Co. The catalogue of publications comprised 16,000 numbers.

Coclico, Adrianus Petit, Flemish musician and theorist; b. in Flanders, c.1500; d. Copenhagen, 1563 (of the plague). He was a disciple of Josquin; held a teaching post at the Univ. of Wittenberg (1545); then was in Frankfurt an der Oder (1546), in Königsberg (1547), and in Nuremberg (1550). In 1555 he was in Wismar; was compelled to leave Germany when a charge of bigamy was made against him; he settled in Copenhagen in 1556 as organist and singer at the court chapel. He was the author of the important tracts *Compendium musices* (1552; reproduced in facsimile [Kassel, 1955] in the series Documenta Musicologica, ed. by M. Bukofzer; Eng. trans. by A. Seay in Translations Series 5 [Colorado Springs, 1973]) and *Musica reservata* (1552).

Coelho, Ruy, eminent Portuguese composer; b. Alcaçer do Sal, March 3, 1891. He studied piano and composition in Lisbon; in 1910 he went to Germany, where he took lessons in composition with Engelbert Humperdinck, Max Bruch, and Schoenberg (1910–13); subsequently took a course at the Paris Cons. with Paul Vidal; returning to Portugal, he was active as a concert pianist; also wrote music criticism in the *Diario de Noticias.*
WORKS: As a composer, he devoted himself mainly to operas. Most of these were produced at the Lisbon Opera: *Inês de Castro* (Jan. 15, 1927); *Belkiss* (June 9, 1928); *Entre gestas* (1929); *Tá-Mar* (June 16, 1937); *Don João IV* (Dec. 1, 1940); *Rosas de todo o ano* (May 30, 1940); *A rosa de papel* (Dec. 18, 1947); *Auto da barca do Inferno* (Jan. 15, 1950); *Inês Pereira* (1952); *O vestido de novia* (Jan. 4, 1959); *Orfeu em Lisboa* (1963); *A bela dama sem pecado* (*Beautiful Lady without Sin;* 1968); *Auto da barca da Gloria* (1970); also *Serão da Infanta, Vagabundo, Soror Mariana,* and *Cavaleiro das maõs irresistiveis.* Ballets: *A Princesa dos sapatos de ferro* (1912); *A Feira* (1930); *Dom Sebastião* (1943); *Arraial na Ribeira* (1951); *Fatima,* oratorio (1960); *Oratorio da paz* (1967). Orch. works: *5 Sinfonias camoneanas* (1912, 1917, 1943, 1951, 1957); *Nun Alvares,* symph. poem (1922); *Rainha santa,* symph. legend (1926); *Suite Portuguesa No. 1* (1926) and *No. 2* (1928); *Petites symphonies* Nos. 1 and 2 (1928, 1932); *Sinfonia d'alem mar* (1969); Piano Concerto No. 1 (1909); Piano Concerto No. 2 (1948); Violin Sonata No. 1 (1910); Violin Sonata No. 2 (1924); Piano Trio (1916); *Cancões de Saudade e Amor* for Voice and Piano (1917); songs.

Coerne, Louis Adolphe, American composer; b. Newark, N.J., Feb. 27, 1870; d. Boston, Sept. 11, 1922. He studied violin with Kneisel and composition at Harvard Univ. with J.K. Paine (1888–90); then went to Germany, where he took courses with Rheinberger in Munich. Returning to America, he became the first recipient of the degree of Ph.D. in music given by an American univ., with the thesis *The Evolution of Modern Orchestration* (1905; publ. in N.Y., 1908); he then occupied teaching positions at Harvard Univ., Smith College, the Univ. of Wisconsin, etc.
WORKS: Opera, *Zenobia* (1902; produced in Bremen, Germany, Dec. 1, 1905); *Hiawatha,* symph. poem (1893); *Romantic Concerto* for Violin and Orch.; *Beloved America,* patriotic hymn for Male Chorus and Orch.; many part-songs; *Swedish Sonata* for Violin and Piano; 3 piano trios in canon. Most of his MS works are in the Boston Public Library.

Cogan, Philip, Irish composer; b. Cork, 1748; d. Dublin, Feb. 3, 1833. He was a chorister at Cork; in 1772 went to Dublin, where he occupied various posts as a church organist. He acquired great renown as a teacher and performer; Michael Kelly and Thomas Moore were his pupils. Cogan wrote numerous pieces for the harpsichord and the piano, 2 piano concertos, and 2 comic operas: *The Ruling Passion* (Dublin, Feb. 24, 1778) and *The Contract* (Dublin, May 14, 1782; revived under the title *The Double Stratagem,* 1784). In some of his piano works he incorporated Irish rhythms, and is therefore regarded as a pioneer composer of instrumental music in Ireland.

Cohan, George M(ichael), celebrated American composer of popular songs; b. Providence, July 3, 1878 (Cohan, himself, believed that he was born on July 4, but the discovery of his birth certificate proves July 3 to be correct); d. New York, Nov. 5, 1942. He was a vaudeville performer and had a natural talent for writing verses and simple melodies in the ballad style. His greatest song, *Over There* (1917), became sweepingly popular during World War I. A congressional medal was given to him for this song. The film *Yankee Doodle Dandy* (1942) and the Broadway musical *George M!* (1968) were both based on his life.

Cohen, Harriet, distinguished English pianist; b. London, Dec. 2, 1895; d. there, Nov. 13, 1967. She studied piano with her parents; then took an advanced course in piano playing with Matthay; made her first public appearance as a solo pianist at the age of 13. She then engaged in a successful career in England, both as a soloist with major orchs. and in chamber music concerts. She made a specialty of old keyboard music, but also played many contemporary compositions; Vaughan Williams, Arnold Bax, and other English composers wrote special works for her. In 1938 she was made a Dame Commander of the Order of the British Empire in appreciation of her services. She publ. a book on piano playing, *Music's Handmaid* (London, 1936; 2nd ed., 1950). Her memoirs, *A Bundle of Time,* were publ. posthumously (London, 1969).

Cohn, Arthur, American composer, conductor, and publishing executive; b. Philadelphia, Nov. 6, 1910. He studied at the Combs Cons. of Music in Philadelphia (1920–28), and with William F. Happich; also studied violin with Sascha Jacobinoff (1930–31); in 1933–34 he studied composition at the Juilliard School of Music with Rubin Goldmark. Returning to Philadelphia, he was appointed director of the Edwin A. Fleisher Collection at the Free Library of Philadelphia (1934–52); also served as executive director of the Settlement Music School in Philadelphia (1952–56). From 1942 to 1965 he conducted the Symph. Club of Philadelphia; also the Germantown Symph. Orch. (1949–55), the Philadelphia Little Symph. (1952–56), and in 1958 was appointed conductor of the Haddonfield, N.J., Symph. Orch.; made guest appearances at Children's Concerts with the Philadelphia Orch. From 1956 to 1966 he was head of symph. and foreign music at Mills Music Co., and from 1966 to 1972 held a similar position with MCA Music. In 1972 he was appointed Director of Serious Music at Carl Fischer.

Cohn, Heinrich. See **Conried, Heinrich.**

Colasse, Pascal, French opera composer; b. Rheims, Jan. 22, 1649; d. Versailles, July 17, 1709. He was a pupil of Lully, who entrusted him with writing out the parts of his operas from the figured bass and melody. Later Colasse was accused of appropriating scores thrown aside by his master as incomplete. In 1683 he was appointed Master of the Music; in 1696, royal chamber musician. He was a favorite of Louis XIV, and obtained the privilege of producing operas at Lille, but the theater burned down; his opera *Polyxène et Pyrrhus* (1706) failed, and his mind became disordered. Of 10 operas, *Les Noces de Thétys et Pélée* (1689) was his best. He also composed songs, sacred and secular.

Colbran, Isabella (Isabel Angela Colbran), famous Spanish soprano; b. Madrid, Feb. 2, 1785; d. Bologna, Oct. 7, 1845. She studied with Pareja in Madrid, then with Marinelli and Crescentini in Naples; made her debut in a concert in Paris in 1801. After her successful appearances in Bologna (1807) and La Scala in Milan (1808), the impresario Barbaja engaged her for Naples in 1811; she became his mistress, only to desert him for Rossini, whom she married on March 16, 1822 (they were legally separated in 1837). She created the leading soprano roles in several of Rossini's operas, beginning with *Elisabetta, Regina d'Inghilterra* (1815) and concluding with *Semiramide* (1823); with her voice in decline, she retired from the stage in 1824. During the early years of the 19th century she was acclaimed as the leading dramatic coloratura soprano.

Cole, Nat "King" (Nathaniel Adams Coles), black American pianist and singer; b. Montgomery, Ala., March 17, 1917; d. Santa Monica, Calif., Feb. 15, 1965. He worked as a jazz pianist in Los Angeles nightclubs; in 1939 formed the original King Cole Trio (piano, guitar, bass); then turned to singing. He was the first black artist to acquire a sponsor on a radio program; also had a brief series on television. He created a distinct style of velvet vocalization and satin softness in the rendition of intimate, brooding, sentimental songs. His appeal was universal; his tours in South America, Europe, the Middle East, and the Orient attracted great multitudes of admirers who knew him by his recordings. The sole exception was his native state; at his concert in Birmingham, Ala., on April 10, 1956, he was attacked by 6 white men and suffered a minor back injury.

Coleridge-Taylor, Samuel, British composer of African descent (his father was a native of Sierra Leone; his mother English); b. London, Aug. 15, 1875; d. Croydon, Sept. 1, 1912. He studied violin at the Royal Academy of Music (1890); won a composition scholarship (1893); studied under Stanford until 1896. In 1903 he founded at Croydon an amateur string orch. which was very successful; later he added professional woodwind and brass; was appointed a violin teacher at the Royal Academy of Music (1898); became a prof. of composition at Trinity College in London (1903) and at the Guildhall School (1910); was conductor of the London Handel Society (1904–12); lived as a composer and teacher in Croydon. He made 3 concert tours of the U.S., in 1904, 1906, and 1910, conducting his own works. From the very beginning his compositions showed an individuality that rapidly won them recognition, and his short career was watched with interest.

WORKS: 3-act opera, *Thelma;* operettas: *Dream Lovers* and *The Gitanos;* for Soli, Chorus, and Orch.: the successful trilogy *The Song of Hiawatha,* including *Hiawatha's Wedding Feast* (London, 1898), *The Death of Minnehaha* (North Staffordshire, 1899), and *Hiawatha's Departure* (Albert Hall, 1900); the entire trilogy was first performed in Washington, D.C. (Nov. 16, 1904, composer conducting); *The Blind Girl of Castel Cuille* (Leeds, 1901); *Meg Blane* (Sheffield, 1902); *The Atonement* (Hereford, 1903); *Kubla Khan* (Handel Society, London, 1906); *Endymion's Dream,* one-act opera (Brighton, England, Feb. 3, 1910); *A Tale of Old Japan* (London Choral Society, 1911); for orch.: Ballade for Violin and Orch.; Symph. in A minor (London, 1896); *Legend* for Violin and Orch.; Ballade in A minor (Gloucester Festival, 1898); *African Suite;* Romance for Violin and Orch.; *Solemn Prelude* (Worcester, 1899); *Scenes from an Everyday Romance,* suite (London Phil. Society, 1900); *Idyll* (Gloucester Festival, 1901); *Toussaint l'Ouverture,* concert overture (Queen's Hall Symph. Concerts, London, Oct. 26, 1901); *Hemo Dance; Ethiopa Saluting the Colours,* concert march; *4 Novelletten* for String Orch.; *Symphonic Variations on an African Air* (London, June 14, 1906, composer conducting); *Bamboula,* rhapsodic dance (Norfolk [Conn.] Festival, 1910); Violin Concerto in G minor (Norfolk Festival, 1911); *Petite suite de concert;* incidental music to Phillips's *Herod* (1900), *Ulysses* (1902), *Nero* (1906), *Faust* (1908), etc.; chamber music: Piano Quintet; Nonet for Piano, Strings and Woodwind

(1894); *Fantasiestücke* for String Quartet (1895); Clarinet Quintet; String Quartet; Violin Sonata; vocal works: *Zara's Earrings,* rhapsody for Voice and Orch.; *Land of the Sun,* part-song; *In Memoriam,* 3 rhapsodies for Voice and Piano; *The Soul's Expression,* 4 songs for Contralto and Orch.; *Sea Drift,* rhapsody for Chorus; services, anthems, solo songs; for Piano: *Silhouettes; Cameos; Scènes de ballet;* etc. Also other compositions for violin and organ, and arrangements.

Colgrass, Michael (Charles), American composer; b. Chicago, April 22, 1932. He studied at the Univ. of Illinois (Mus.B., 1956); attended classes at the Berkshire Music Center in Tanglewood (1952–54). His principal teachers were Darius Milhaud, Lukas Foss, Wallingford Riegger, and Ben Weber. A percussion player by profession, he was employed in various ensembles in N.Y. In his own music, percussion plays a significant melorhythmic role. He also studied theater arts, including special techniques of the Commedia dell' Arte of the Piccolo Teatro of Milan and physical training for actors at the Polish Theater Laboratory; wrote drama and poetry. He received Guggenheim fellowship awards in 1964 and 1968; won the Pulitzer Prize in 1978. WORKS: *Chamber Music* for 4 Drums and String Quartet (1954); Percussion Quintet (1955); Divertimento for 8 Drums, Piano, and Strings (1960); Rhapsody for Clarinet, Violin, and Piano (1962); *Light Spirit* for Flute, Viola, Guitar, and Percussion (1963); *Sea Shadow* for Orch. (1966); *As Quiet As . . .* for Orch. (1966); *New People,* song cycle for Mezzo-soprano, Viola, and Piano (1969); *The Earth's a Baked Apple* for Chorus and Orch. (1969); *Letter from Mozart,* collage for Piano and Orch. (N.Y., Dec. 3, 1976); *Best Wishes, U.S.A.* for Black Chorus, White Chorus, Jazz Band, Folk Instruments, 4 Vocalists, and Orch. (1976); *Concertmasters,* concerto for 3 Violins and Orch. (1976). *Déjà vu,* concerto for 4 Percussionists and Orch. (1978; received the Pulitzer Prize); Piano Concerto (Miami, Fla., June 25, 1982), Viola Concerto (Toronto, Sept. 26, 1984).

Collard, a family of pianoforte makers in London. M. Clementi, in partnership with John Longman, bought out the music publishers Longman & Broderip in 1798. Longman left to establish his own enterprise, and Clementi entered into a new partnership including himself, Banger, F.A. Hyde, F.W. Collard, and Davis; after several changes, the firm was known as Clementi, Collard & Collard (1823); following Clementi's death in 1832, it has been known as Collard & Collard. While Clementi undoubtedly played an important part in the success of the business, it was Collard's patented inventions which gave the pianofortes their distinctive character, and established the firm's reputation in that field.

Collard, Jean-Philippe, French pianist; b. Mareuil, Jan. 27, 1948. He began piano studies as a child; then studied at the Paris Cons. with Pierre Sancan, graduating at age 16 with a first prize; subsequently won several honors, including the first prize in the Marguerite Long–Jacques Thibaud Competition; appeared as soloist with the leading European orchs. and in recitals. He made his American debut in 1973 with the San Francisco Symph. Orch.; then made a number of coast-to-coast tours of the U.S.; in 1983 appeared as soloist with the Indianapolis Symph. Orch. at Carnegie Hall in N.Y.

Colles, Henry Cope, eminent British music scholar; b. Bridgnorth, Shropshire, April 20, 1879; d. London, March 4, 1943. He studied at the Royal College of Music with Parry (music history), Walter Alcock (organ), and Walford Davies (theory). Subsequently he received a scholarship at Worcester College, Oxford, to study organ; then entered Oxford Univ., obtaining his B.A. (1902), Mus.Bac. (1903), and M.A. (1907); also received an honorary Mus.Doc. (1932). In 1905 he became music critic of the *Academy;* from 1906–19 was music critic of the *Times;* in 1919 was appointed teacher of music history and criticism at the Royal College of Music; was also music director of Cheltenham Ladies' College; in 1923, became member of the board of profs. at the Royal College of Music. He was the editor of the 3rd and 4th eds. of *Grove's Dictionary of Music and Musicians* (1927–29 and 1939–40).

Collet, Henri, French music critic and composer; b. Paris, Nov. 5, 1885; d. there, Nov. 23, 1951. He was a pupil of J. Thibaut and Barès in Paris; then studied Spanish literature with Menéndez Pidal in Madrid, continuing his music studies under Olmeda. He coined the title Les Six Français for a group of young French composers comprising G. Auric, L. Durey, A. Honegger, D. Milhaud, F. Poulenc, and G. Tailleferre.

Colobrano, Michele Enrico Carafa de. See **Carafa de Colobrano, Michele Enrico.**

Colonna, Giovanni Paolo, eminent Italian composer of church music; b. Bologna, June 16, 1637; d. there, Nov. 28, 1695. He studied organ with Filipucci in Bologna; composition in Rome with Carissimi, Benevoli, and Abbatini. In 1659 he became organist at San Petronio in Bologna; was appointed maestro di cappella in 1674. He was several times elected president of the Accademia Filarmonica.

Colonne, Edouard (real name, **Judas**), French conductor and violinist; b. Bordeaux, July 23, 1838; d. Paris, March 28, 1910. He studied at the Paris Cons. under Girard and Sauzay (violin) and with Elwart and Ambroise Thomas (composition). In 1874 he founded the Concerts Nationaux (which later became famous as the Concerts du Châtelet; then Concerts Colonne), at which he brought out the larger works of Berlioz, and many new orch. scores by contemporary German and French composers. In 1878 he conducted the official Exposition concerts; was conductor at the Grand Opéra in 1892; appeared frequently as a visiting conductor in London; also in Russia and Portugal, and with the N.Y. Phil. (1905).

Coltrane, John William, remarkable black American jazz musician, a virtuoso on the tenor saxophone, whose theory and practice stimulated the creation of sophisticated jazz performance which came to be known as "the new black music"; b. Hamlet, N.C., Sept. 23, 1926; d. Huntington, Long Island, N.Y., July 17, 1967. He studied at the Ornstein School of Music in Philadelphia; played in the bands of Dizzy Gillespie, Johnny Hodges, Miles Davis, and Thelonious Monk. He enhanced the resources of his style by studying ancestral African and kindred Asian music, absorbing the fascinating modalities of these ancient cultures.

Combarieu, Jules (-Léon-Jean), eminent French music historian; b. Cahors, Lot, Feb. 4, 1859; d. Paris, July 7, 1916. He studied at the Sorbonne; later in Berlin with Spitta; received the degree of docteur ès lettres; was a prof. of music history at the Collège de France (1904–10).
WRITINGS: *Les Rapports de la poésie et de la musique considérées du point de vue de l'expression* (Diss., 1893); "L'Influence de la musique allemande sur la musique française," *Jahrbuch Peters* (1895); *Etudes de philologie musicale: 1. Théorie du rhythme dans la composition moderne d'après la doctrine antique* (1896; critique and simplification of Westphal); 2. *Essai sur l'archéologie musicale au XIXᵉ siècle et le problème de l'origine des neumes* (1896; these last 2 were awarded prizes by the Académie); 3. *Fragments de l'Enéide en musique d'après un manuscrit inédit* (1898); *Eléments de grammaire musicale historique* (1906); *La Musique: ses lois, son évolution* (1907; numerous eds.; in Eng., 1910); *Histoire de la musique des origines au début du XXᵉ siècle* (3 vols., Paris, 1913–19; an authoritative work; 8th ed. of vol. I, 1948; 6th ed. of vol. II, 1946; new ed. of vol. III, 1947).

Comes, Juan Bautista, Spanish composer; b. Valencia, c.1582; d. there, Jan. 5, 1643. He studied with Juan Perez; was a choirboy at the Valencia Cathedral in 1594–96; in 1605 became choirmaster at the Cathedral of Lérida; then was at the Royal College in Valencia (1605–13); became maestro of the Cathedral there (1613); in 1618 was called by Philip III to Madrid, serving as vice-maestro of the Royal Chapel; from 1628 was again in Valencia; served as maestro of the Cathedral there in 1632–38. He left over 200 works, sacred (masses, Psalms, litanies, etc.) and secular (villancicos, tonadas), most of them in MS, preserved at the Escorial. Two vols. of selected numbers were publ. in Madrid in 1888.

Comettant, Jean-Pierre-Oscar, French music critic and composer; b. Bordeaux, April 18, 1819; d. Montvilliers, near Le Havre, Jan. 24, 1898. He entered the Paris Cons. in 1839 and studied with Elwart and Carafa; developed considerable proficiency as a composer of semipopular songs and marches; also publ. piano transcriptions of famous operas, variations, and fantasias. From 1852–55 he lived in America, where he continued to write salon music. Returning to France, he became the music *feuilletoniste* for *Le Siècle,* and a contributor to various music journals; founded (with his wife, a singer) a musical inst. (1871).

Comissiona, Sergiu, Rumanian conductor; b. Bucharest, June 16, 1928. He studied violin and theory in Bucharest; conducting with Constantin Silvestri. He was one of the principal conductors of the Rumanian State Opera and the Bucharest Phil.; subsequently was music director of the Haifa Symph. Orch. (1959–64); was guest conductor with the London Phil. (1960–63), Stockholm Phil. (1964–66), Berlin Radio Symph. Orch. (1965–67); also was a guest conductor with major symph. orchs. in the U.S. In 1969 he was appointed music director and conductor of the Baltimore Symph. Orch. He was an Israeli citizen (1959–76); on July 4, 1976, he became a U.S. citizen. Symbolically, the ceremony was held at Fort McHenry in Baltimore Harbor, site of the battle which inspired the writing of *The Star-Spangled Banner.* From 1978 to 1982 Comissiona was principal conductor of the American Symph. Orch. in N.Y.; he led the Baltimore Symph. Orch. until 1984; in 1980 he became artistic director, and in 1983–84, music director, of the Houston Symph. Orch.; in 1982 he was also named principal guest conductor of the Radio Phil. Orch. in Hilversum, the Netherlands.

Como, Perry (Pierino), American singer of popular music; b. Canonsburg, Pa., May 18, 1913. After a stint as a barber, he joined the Freddie Carlone Orch. as a singer; then sang with the Ted Weems Orch. (1937–43); subsequently he became one of the most successful popular vocalists through his numerous radio and television appearances. His recordings included such favorites as *I Think of You, It's Impossible,* and *Shadow of Your Smile.*

Compère, Loyset (real name, **Louis**), important composer of the Flemish School; b. Hainaut, c.1445; d. St. Quentin, Aug. 16, 1518. He was a chorister in St. Quentin; then a singer in the chapel of the Duke of Milan (1474–75); in 1486 was singer in the service of Charles VIII of France; was subsequently canon of St. Quentin. He was greatly esteemed by his contemporaries.

Concone, Giuseppe, Italian singing teacher and composer; b. Turin, Sept. 12, 1801; d. there, June 1, 1861. From 1837 until 1848 he lived in Paris, where he became a popular singing teacher. His collection of solfeggi in 5 vols. (*50 Lezioni, 30 Esercizi, 25 Lezioni, 15 Vocalizzi,* and *40 Lezioni per Basso*) became a standard work for singing teachers, showing no signs of obsolescence and continuing much in use all over the world. He also wrote an opera, *Un episodio del San Michele,* which was produced in Turin in 1836.

Confalonieri, Giulio, Italian pianist and writer on

music; b. Milan, May 23, 1896; d. there, June 29, 1972. He studied at the Univ. of Milan and the Cons. of Bologna; lived for some years in London; returned to Milan, where he settled as a teacher and music critic. He wrote an opera, *Rosaspina* (Bergamo, 1939); edited works by Cimarosa and Cherubini; publ. a comprehensive biography of Cherubini under the title *Prigionia di un artista: Il romanzo di Luigi Cherubini* (2 vols., Milan, 1948).

Confrey, Zez (Edward Elezear), American pianist and composer of light music, especially of a style known as "novelty piano"; b. Peru, Ill., April 3, 1895; d. Lakewood, N.J., Nov. 22, 1971. He studied at the Chicago Musical College and privately with Jessie Dunn and Frank Denhart. He appeared as piano soloist, along with George Gershwin, at Paul Whiteman's concert "Experiment in Modern Music" (1924), at which Gershwin's *Rhapsody in Blue* was premiered.
WORKS: *Kitten on the Keys* (1921; his most popular piece); *Stumbling* (1922); *Dizzy Fingers, Valse Mirage,* and *3 Little Oddities* (1923); *Concert Etude* (1922); *Buffoon* (1930); *Grandfather's Clock* (1933); *Oriental Fantasy* (1935); *Ultra Ultra* (1935); *Rhythm Venture* (1936); *Della Robbia* (1938); *Champagne;* etc.

Conley, Eugene, American tenor; b. Lynn, Mass., March 12, 1908; d. Denton, Texas, Dec. 18, 1981. He studied voice with Ettore Verna; began his career as a radio singer in 1939, when the National Broadcasting Co. put him on the air in a program entitled "NBC Presents Eugene Conley." He made his operatic debut at the Brooklyn Academy of Music as the Duke in *Rigoletto;* then sang with the San Carlo Opera Co. in N.Y., the Chicago Opera Co., and the Cincinnati Summer Opera. In 1942 he joined the Army Air Corps. In 1949 he became the first American opera singer to open the season at La Scala, Milan; he later appeared with the Opéra-Comique in Paris, the Covent Garden Opera in London, and the Royal Opera of Stockholm. On Jan. 25, 1950, he made his first appearance at the Metropolitan Opera in N.Y., in the title role of Gounod's *Faust.* He remained on its roster until 1956. In 1960 he was appointed artist-in-residence at North Texas State Univ. in Denton, retiring in 1978. He died of cancer.

Conlon, James, American conductor; b. New York, March 18, 1950. He was graduated from the Juilliard School of Music in N.Y., and conducted the Juilliard Orch. He was the youngest conductor ever invited to lead a subscription concert of the N.Y. Phil. He then appeared with virtually every major orch. in the U.S.; made his Metropolitan Opera debut in N.Y. in 1976. In 1979 he became music director of the Cincinnati May Festival.

Connolly, Justin Riveagh, English composer; b. London, Aug. 11, 1933. He studied composition with Peter Racine Fricker at the Royal College of Music in London; held a Harkness Fellowship at Yale Univ. (1963–65); was then instructor in music theory

there (1965–66). Returning to London, he joined the faculty of his alma mater. As a composer he followed the structural techniques of the avant-garde; in this direction he was influenced by new American trends, such as the theory of combinatoriality of Milton Babbitt and the practice of metrical modulation of Elliott Carter; he also made use of electronic sound. His works are often arranged in sets unified by a generic title and a numerical rubric; in this he also paid tribute to the mathematical concepts of sets and matrixes.

Conradi, August, German opera composer; b. Berlin, June 27, 1821; d. there, May 26, 1873. He was a pupil of Rungenhagen (composition); organist of the "Invalidenhaus" in 1843; went in 1846 to Vienna, and brought out a symph. with marked success; was for years an intimate friend of Liszt at Weimar; then conducted in Stettin, Berlin, Düsseldorf, Cologne, and (from 1856) again in Berlin.
WORKS: Operas (all produced in Berlin): *Rübezahl* (1847); *Musa, der letzte Maurenfürst* (1855); *Die Braut des Flussgottes* (1850); *Die Sixtinische Madonna* (1864); *Knecht Ruprecht* (1865); *So sind die Frauen; Im Weinberge des Herrn* (1867); *Das schönste Mädchen im Städtchen* (1868); also vaudevilles, farces, 5 symphs., overtures, string quartets, etc. He arranged many popular potpourris.

Conried (real name, **Cohn**), **Heinrich,** Austro-American operatic impresario; b. Bielitz, Austria, Sept. 13, 1848; d. Meran, Tyrol, April 27, 1909. He started as an actor in Vienna; in 1877 he managed the Bremen Municipal Theater; came to the U.S. in 1878 and took over the management of the Germania Theater in N.Y.; then was in charge of various theatrical enterprises; from 1892 was director of the Irving Place Theater in N.Y., which he brought to a high degree of efficiency. From 1903 till 1908 he was the manager of the Metropolitan Opera and was instrumental in engaging numerous celebrated artists, including Caruso. During his first season he gave the first American production of *Parsifal,* despite the heated controversy regarding the rights of Wagner's heirs; his decision to produce the opera *Salomé* by Richard Strauss in 1907 also aroused a storm of protests. Conried resigned in 1908 because of dissension within the management of the Metropolitan, and retired in Europe. He was decorated by several European governments; received an honorary M.A. from Harvard Univ.

Constant, Marius, Rumanian-born French composer and conductor; b. Bucharest, Feb. 7, 1925. He graduated from the Bucharest Cons. in 1944; then went to Paris, where he studied conducting with Fournet and composition with Messiaen, Nadia Boulanger, and Honegger (1945–49); he was director of the Ballets de Paris of Roland Petit (1956–66); was founder, president, and music director of Ars Nova (1963–71), a Parisian ensemble for new music; in 1967 he was a guest lecturer at Stanford Univ.; in 1970 gave lectures in Hilversum, the Netherlands. His early compositions are impressionistic; later he adopted serial and aleatory procedures, particularly in multimedia productions.

WORKS: Improvised opera, *La Serrure* (*The Lock;* 1969) other operas: *Le Souper* for Baritone and Vocal Orch. (1969) and *La Tragédie de Carmen* (Paris, Nov. 5, 1981); ballets: *Joueur de flûte* (*The Flute Player;* 1952); *Haut-Voltage* (1956); *Cyrano de Bergerac* (1960); *Eloge de la folie*, with Soprano (1966); *Paradise Lost* (1967); *Candide* (1970; Hamburg, Jan. 24, 1971; material reworked for a concert piece with Solo Harpsichord, 1971); *Le Jeu de Sainte Agnes*, "ecclesiastical action" on a 14th-century MS, for 6 Singers, 5 Actors, Dancer, Hammond Organ, Electric Guitar, Trombone, and Percussion (Besançon, Sept. 6, 1974); *Chants de Maldoror* for Narrator, Dancer-Conductor, 23 Improvising Instrumental Soloists, and 10 Cellos (1962); Piano Concerto (1954); *24 préludes* for Orch. (1957); Concerto for Tuba and String Orch. (1958); *Concert Music* for Saxophone and 11 Instruments (1960); *Turner*, 3 essays for Orch. (1961); *Chaconne et marche militaire* for Orch. (1967); *5 chants et une vocalise* for Dramatic Soprano and Orch. (1968); *Winds* for 13 Winds and Double Bass (1968); *Traits*, based on the 1930s game of surrealist poets, "exquisite corpse," for 6 to 25 Musicians (1969); *Equal* for 5 Percussionists (1969); *14 Stations* for 92 Percussion Instruments (one Player) and 6 Instrumentalists (1969–70); *Candide* for Amplified Harpsichord and Orch. (1971); *Strings* for Strings (1972); *Faciebat Anno 1973* for 24 Violins and Orch. (Paris, July 19, 1973); *Piano Personnage* for Piano and Chamber Ensemble (Paris, Jan. 15, 1974); *For Clarinet* for Solo Clarinet (1974); Symph. for Winds (Montreal, March 17, 1978); *Alleluias* for Trumpet and Organ (1980); *D'une élégie slave* for Solo Guitar (1981); *103 regards dans l'eau* for Violin and Orch. (1981); *Précis de décomposition* for Clarinet, Bassoon, Horn, String Quartet, and Tape (1982).

Constantinescu, Paul, eminent Rumanian composer; b. Ploesti, July 13, 1909; d. Bucharest, Dec. 20, 1963. He studied composition at the Bucharest Cons. with Castaldi, Cuclin, and Jora; then went to Vienna, where he took courses with Schmidt and Joseph Marx. He was first engaged as a violinist in his native town of Ploesti (1927–34); then taught at the academy for religious music in Bucharest (1937–41). In 1941 he was appointed a prof. at the Bucharest Cons., and retained this post until his death.

WORKS: 2 operas: *O noapte furtunoasă* (Bucharest, Oct. 25, 1935; revised 1950; Bucharest, May 19, 1951) and *Pană Lesnea Rusalim* (Bucharest, June 27, 1956; enjoyed excellent success); 5 ballets: *Nunta în Carpați* (1938); *Spune, povesteste, spune* (1947); *Pe malul Dunării* (1947); *Tîrg pe muntele Găina* (1953); *Înfrățire* (1959); 2 Byzantine oratorios: *Patimile și Invierea Domnului* (1946; revised 1948) and *Nașterea Domnului* (1947); Violin Sonatina (1933); *Burlesque* for Piano and Orch. (1937); Sinfonietta (1937); Symph. (1944; revised 1955); Concerto for String Quartet (1947); Piano Concerto (1952); *Rapsodie oltenească* for Orch. (1956); Violin Concerto (1957); Harp Concerto (1960); *Sinfonia Ploieşteană* (1961); Concerto for Violin, Cello, Piano, and Orch. (1963; posthumous, Bucharest, Dec. 28, 1963); piano pieces; songs and choruses. His biography, by V. Tomescu, was publ. in Bucharest in 1967.

Conti, Carlo, Italian composer and pedagogue; b. Arpino, Oct. 14, 1796; d. Naples, July 10, 1868. He studied at the Naples Cons. with Zingarelli and J.S. Mayr; taught there in 1819–21; rejoined its faculty as a teacher of counterpoint in 1846–58; in 1862 became its assistant director. An industrious composer, he wrote 11 operas and much church music. Rossini called him "the best Italian contrapuntist of the day." His distinction lies principally in his excellence as a teacher; among his famous pupils was Bellini.

Conti, Francesco Bartolomeo, Italian composer; b. Florence, Jan. 20, 1681; d. Vienna, July 20, 1732. He was assistant court theorbist (1701–8), principal theorbist (1708–26), and court composer (from 1713); wrote about 30 stage works to Italian and German texts, of which the finest were *Clotilda* (Vienna, 1706) and *Don Chisciotte in Sierra Morena* (after Cervantes; Vienna, 1719); also 10 oratorios, many secular cantatas, and songs.

Conus, Georgi, Russian composer and theorist; b. Moscow, Sept. 30, 1862; d. there, Aug. 29, 1933. He studied at the Moscow Cons. with Taneyev and Arensky; from 1891–99 he taught there; from 1902, was a prof. at the music school of the Phil. Society. He developed an original theory of metric analysis and publ. a brief outline of it; also wrote several symph. works, piano pieces, and songs.

Conus, Julius, Russian violinist and composer, brother of **Georgi Conus;** b. Moscow, Feb. 1, 1869; d. Malenki, Ivanov District, Jan. 3, 1942. He studied at the Moscow Cons.; later taught violin there. He was a friend of Tchaikovsky and was greatly esteemed in Moscow musical circles. His Violin Concerto, first performed by him in Moscow in 1898, has retained its popularity in Russia.

Converse, Frederick Shepherd, distinguished American composer; b. Newton, Mass., Jan. 5, 1871; d. Westwood, Mass., June 8, 1940. He graduated from Harvard Univ. (1893); studied music in Boston with Carl Baermann and Chadwick (1894–96); then in Munich at the Royal Academy of Music with Rheinberger, graduating in 1898. Returning to Boston, he taught harmony at the New England Cons. (1900–2) and 1920–36; was an instructor of composition at Harvard Univ. (1901–7). He was vice-president of the Boston Opera Co. (1911–14); served as a captain in the U.S. Army (1917–19); was dean of the New England Cons. (1931–37); received a Mus.Doc. from Boston Univ. (1933); became a member of the American Academy of Arts and Letters (1937). His early works reflect the influence of academic German training; later he began to apply more advanced harmonies; in his *Flivver Ten Million*, written to glorify the 10-millionth Ford car, he adopted a frankly modern idiom, modeled after Honegger's *Pacific 231*. He sketched some material for a 5th Symph. in 1937, but did not complete it. He had renumbered his symphs. in 1936, calling his previously unnumbered Symph. No. 1 and upping Nos. 1, 2, and 3 by one, giving the title of Symph. 5 to the undeveloped sketches for that work. But his Symphs. Nos. 2, 3, and 4 were premiered, respectively, as Nos. 1, 2, and 3.

WORKS: OPERAS: *The Pipe of Desire* (Boston Opera, Jan. 31, 1906; first American opera to be produced by the Metropolitan Opera Co., March 18, 1910; won the David Bispham medal); *The Sacrifice* (Boston, March 3, 1911); *Sinbad the Sailor* (1913; not perf.); *The Immigrants* (1914; not perf.). ORATORIOS: *Job*, dramatic poem for Soli, Chorus, and Orch. (Worcester Festival, Oct. 2, 1907; also in Hamburg, Nov. 23, 1908; the first American oratorio to be heard in Germany); *Hagar in the Desert*, dramatic narrative for Low Voice and Orch. (written for Mme. Schumann-Heink; sung by her in Hamburg, 1908). CANTATAS: *The Peace Pipe* (1914); *The Answer of the Stars* (1919); *The Flight of the Eagle* (1930). OTHER VOCAL WORKS: *La Belle Dame sans merci*, ballade for Baritone with Orch. (1902); psalm, *I Will Praise Thee, O Lord* (1924).

FOR ORCH.: Symphs.: in D minor, not numbered (Munich, July 14, 1898); No. 1 (Boston, Jan. 30, 1920); No. 2 (Boston, April 21, 1922); No. 3 (1936); No. 6 (posthumously perf. by the Indianapolis Symph. Orch., Nov. 29, 1940); concert overture, *Youth; Festival of Pan* (Boston, Dec. 21, 1900); *Endymion's Narrative* (1901; Boston, April 9, 1903); *Night* and *Day*, 2 poems for Piano and Orch. (Boston, Jan. 21, 1905); overture, *Euphrosyne* (Boston, 1903); orch. fantasy, *The Mystic Trumpeter* (Philadelphia, March 3, 1905; many subsequent perfs.); symph. poem, *Ormazd* (St. Louis, Jan. 26, 1912); symph. poem, *Ave atque Vale* (St. Louis, Jan. 26, 1917); Fantasia for Piano and Orch. (1922); *Song of the Sea* (Boston, April 18, 1924); *Elegiac Poem* (Cleveland, Dec. 2, 1926); fantasy, *Flivver Ten Million* (Boston, April 15, 1927); *California*, festival scenes (Boston, April 6, 1928); symph. suite, *American Sketches* (Boston, Feb. 8, 1935).

Conyngham, Barry, Australian composer; b. Sydney, Aug. 27, 1944. He studied jurisprudence; in 1966 entered the New South Wales Cons.; also took private lessons with Meale, and later with Sculthorpe at the Univ. of Sydney. In 1970 he traveled to Japan and had instruction in advanced techniques with Toru Takemitsu. Returning to Australia, he became a lecturer in Perth at the Univ. of Western Australia; then went to the U.S. to study electronic music at the Univ. of Calif. in San Diego and at Princeton Univ.; eventually received an appointment to teach at Melbourne Univ.

WORKS: Opera, *Ned Mark II* (1975–76); *Jazz Ballet* for Saxophone, Double Bass, Drums, Flute, and Piano (1964); Cello Sonata (1965); Piano Sonata (1966–67); *Dialogue* for String Trio (1967); *Lyric*

Dialogues for 5 Flutes, Oboe, and Cello (1967); *Crises: Thoughts in a City* for 2 String Orchs. and Percussion (1968); *Prisms* for 6 Violins (1968); *Three* for 2 Percussion Groups and String Quartet (1969); *5 Windows* for Orch. (1969); *Ice Carving* for Amplified Violin and 4 String Orchs. (1970); *Water ... Footsteps ... Time* for Solo Piano, Harp, Electric Guitar, Tam-tam, and Orch. (1970–71); *Ends* for Piano (1970); theater piece, *Edward John Eyre*, for Female Voice, Actors, Wind Quintet, and String Orch. (1971); *Five* for Wind Quintet (1970–71); *Six* for 6 Percussionists and Orch. (1971); *Voss* for Female Voice, Chorus, Piano, and Orch. (1972); *Snowflake* for Electric Piano, interchangeable with Harpsichord and Celesta (1973); *Without Gesture* for Percussion and Orch. (1973); *Mirror Images* for 4 Actors, Saxophone, Cello, Double Bass, and Percussion (1975); Percussion Concerto (1977); *Sky* for Strings (1977); *The Apology of Bony Anderson*, musical theater for 4 Voices and Instrumental Ensemble (1978); *Shadows of Noh*, double-bass concerto (1978); *Mirages* for Orch. (1979); String Quartet (1979); *Horizons*, concerto for Orch. (1981); *Southern Cross*, double concerto for Violin, Piano, and Orch. (1981); *Basho* for Soprano and Instruments, after verses by Matsuo Basho (London, Oct. 13, 1981).

Cooke, Benjamin, English organist and composer; b. London, 1734; d. there, Sept. 14, 1793. He studied with Pepusch, whom he succeeded in 1752 as conductor at the Academy of Ancient Music; in 1757 he became choirmaster (after Gates), in 1758 lay vicar, and in 1762 organist, of Westminster Abbey; received a Mus.Doc. from Cambridge (1775) and from Oxford (1782); became organist of St. Martin-in-the-Fields, 1782; in 1789 he resigned the Academy conductorship in favor of Arnold. His best works are in the form of glees, canons, and catches, for which he took several Catch Club prizes (*Collection of 20 Glees, Catches, and Canons for 3-6 Voices in Score*, London, 1775; *9 Glees and 2 Duets*, 1795). He also wrote odes, instrumental concertos, church music, pieces for organ and harpsichord, etc., and added choruses and accompaniments to Pergolesi's *Stabat Mater* (1759) and Galliard's *Morning Hymn* (1772) for the Academy of Ancient Music. His son **Robert** (b. Westminster, 1768; d. Aug. 13, 1814) became organist of St. Martin-in-the-Fields after his father's death in 1793, and on the death of Dr. Arnold, in 1802, was appointed organist and choirmaster of Westminster Abbey; ended his life by drowning himself in the Thames. He publ. a collection of glees in 1805.

Cooke, Deryck, English musicologist; b. Leicester, Sept. 14, 1919; d. London, Oct. 26, 1976. He studied piano privately and composition at Cambridge Univ. with Patrick Hadley and Robin Orr, earning his B.A. in 1940, M.A. in 1943, and Mus.B. in 1947. From 1947 to 1959 he was a member of the music staff of the BBC (rejoined in 1965); after 1959, he devoted most of his time to writing on music and broadcasting. He attracted considerable attention by his scholarly and congenial arrangement of Mahler's unfinished 10th Symph., which he completed using authentic fragments from Mahler's sketch; this version was approved by Alma Mahler, the composer's widow. It was first performed at a BBC Henry Wood Promenade Concert at the Albert Hall in London, on Aug. 13, 1964. Cooke publ. *The Language of Music* (London, 1959) and *Mahler 1860–1911* (BBC centenary booklet, 1960); *I Saw the World End: A Study of Wagner's Ring* (London, 1979); *Gustav Mahler: An Introduction to His Music* (N.Y., 1980); *Variations: Essays on Romantic Music* (posthumous, London, 1982).

Cooke, James Francis, eminent American writer on music and composer; b. Bay City, Mich., Nov. 14, 1875; d. Philadelphia, March 3, 1960. He was educated in Brooklyn and studied music with R.H. Woodman and W.H. Hall; went to Germany in 1900, and continued his studies with Meyer-Obersleben and H. Ritter. As editor of the *Etude* for 40 years (1908–49), he brought it to a high degree of popularity by promoting special features (columns dealing with performance and technique; simple arrangements of classics; etc.). He composed a number of successful piano pieces (*White Orchids, Moon Mist, Ballet Mignon, Sea Gardens, Italian Lake Suite*), and songs.
    WRITINGS: *A Standard History of Music* (Philadelphia, 1910); *Great Pianists on Piano Playing* (4th ed., 1914); *Mastering the Scales and Arpeggios* (1913); *Musical Playlets for Children* (1917); *Great Singers on the Art of Singing* (1921); *Great Men and Famous Musicians* (1925); *Young Folks' Picture-History of Music* (1925); *Light, More Light* (1925); *Johannes Brahms* (1928); *Claude Debussy* (1928); *Musical Travelogues* (1934); *How to Memorize Music* (1947); many non-musical works, including plays and poems.

Coolidge, Elizabeth Sprague (Mrs. Frederick Shurtleff Coolidge), American music patron and accomplished composer; b. Chicago, Oct. 30, 1864; d. Cambridge, Mass., Nov. 4, 1953. In 1918 she established at Pittsfield, Mass., the Berkshire Festivals of Chamber Music, which were held annually under her auspices and later transferred to Washington, D.C. She was the sponsor of the Elizabeth Sprague Coolidge Foundation in the Library of Congress, created in 1925 for the purpose of producing concerts, music festivals, awarding prizes, etc., under the administration of the Music Division of the Library. Numerous modern composers, including Loeffler, Schoenberg, Malipiero, Bartók, Casella, Stravinsky, Prokofiev, Piston, and Hanson, have written works commissioned for it. The auditorium of the Library, of Congress was likewise a gift of Mrs. Coolidge. In 1932 she founded the Elizabeth Sprague Coolidge Medal "for eminent services to chamber music," awarded annually (until 1949) to one or more persons; its recipients included Adolfo Betti, Walter W. Cobbett, Carl Engel, and E.T. Rice. She also initiated performances of modern and classical chamber music throughout the U.S. and Europe. Her sponsorship of the appearances of artists in the U.S. and abroad (the Pro Arte, Coolidge, Roth quartets, etc.) was an important factor in the musical life of the U.S. In recognition of her many cultural contributions she was made honorary M.A. (Yale Univ., Smith College, Mills College), L.D. (Mt. Holyoke College), Mus.Doc. (Pomona College), LL.D. (Univ. of Calif.). She received the Cobbett Medal and various foreign decorations.

Cooper, Emil, Russian conductor; b. Kherson, Dec. 20, 1877; d. New York, Nov. 16, 1960. He studied at the Odessa Cons., then went to Vienna, where he took lessons in violin with Joseph Hellmesberger; later studied in Moscow with Taneyev. At the age of 22 he began to conduct at the Kiev Opera. In 1909 he conducted the Russian Ballet and Opera with the Diaghilev troupe in Paris. He then conducted in Moscow; in 1923 he went abroad; in 1929 he conducted the Chicago Civic Opera; in 1944–50 was on the staff of the Metropolitan Opera Co.; then became music director of the Montreal Opera Guild; subsequently lived in N.Y.

Cooper, Kenneth, highly talented American harpsichordist; b. New York, May 31, 1941. He studied harpsichord playing with Sylvia Marlowe at the Mannes College of Music in N.Y.; also took harpsichord lessons with Fernando Valenti; then entered Columbia Univ. (B.A., 1962; M.A., 1964; Ph.D. in musicology, 1971). He subsequently developed an energetic schedule of teaching; was an instructor of music at Barnard College (1967–71), lecturing on all academic music subjects; an adjunct assistant prof. at Brooklyn College (1971–73); in 1975 was appointed prof. of harpsichord at the Mannes College of Music. A man of latitudinarian and panoramic faculties, Kenneth Cooper encompasses a 360° range of activities, specializing in playing piano and harpsichord, improvisation, authentication of performing usages of the Baroque, translation from musically important languages (Italian, German), and last but not least, revivification of ragtime. He has publ. a number of scholarly articles dealing with the Baroque period; directed stage performances of neglected operas by Handel; and gave concerts of Bach's music at midnight. He has further commissioned works for harpsichord to composers of the avant-garde; played recitals in England, at the Salzburg Festival; traveled as a concert artist in Russia, Rumania, and Greece under the auspices of the U.S. Dept. of State; made frequent appearances with his wife, the soprano **Josephine Mongiardo,** whom he married in 1969.

Coperario (John Cooper, an Englishman who Italianized his patronymic after study in Italy), famous lutenist and viola da gamba player; b. c.1575; d. London, 1626. He went to Italy about 1600, and upon his return to England became an acknowledged authority in the field of instrumental and vocal music, patterned closely on the Italian model. He became music teacher to the children of James I, and of Henry and William Lawes. His improvisations on the organ were greatly admired. He wrote a set of "Fancies" for organ, and a set for viols; music for 2 masques; songs (*Funeral Teares*, 1606; *Songs of Mourning*, 1613, etc.). Two of his anthems are included in Leighton's *Teares of Lamentations;* numerous works for string instruments, with organ, are in the Christ Church library at Oxford; compositions for viols are preserved at the Royal College of Music in London, and other works at the British Museum. His treatise *Rules How to Compose* (c.1610) was publ. in facsimile in Los Angeles in 1951, with an introduction by the editor, Manfred Bukofzer.

Copland, Aaron, a greatly distinguished and exceptionally gifted American composer; b. Brooklyn, Nov. 14, 1900. He was educated at the Boys' High School in Brooklyn; began to study piano with Victor Wittgenstein and Clarence Adler as a young child. In 1917 he took lessons in harmony and counterpoint with Rubin Goldmark in N.Y., and soon began to compose. His first publ. piece, *The Cat and the Mouse* for piano (1920), subtitled *Scherzo humoristique,* shows the influence of Debussy. In 1921 he went to Paris, where he studied composition and orchestration with Nadia Boulanger. Returning to America in 1924, he lived mostly in N.Y.; became active in many musical activities, not only as a composer but also as a lecturer, pianist, and organizer in various musical societies. He attracted the attention of Serge Koussevitzky, who gave the first performance of his early score *Music for the Theater* with the Boston Symph. Orch. in 1925; then engaged Copland as soloist in his Concerto for Piano and Orch. in 1927; the work produced a considerable sensation because of the jazz elements incorporated in the score, and there was some subterranean grumbling among the staid subscribers to the Boston Symph. concerts. Koussevitzky remained Copland's steadfast supporter throughout his tenure as conductor of the Boston Symph. Orch., and later as the founder of the Koussevitzky Music Foundation. In the meantime, Walter Damrosch conducted in N.Y. Copland's Symph. for Organ and Orch., with Nadia Boulanger as soloist. Other orchs. and their conductors also performed his music, which gained increasing recognition. Particularly popular were Copland's works based on folk motifs; of these the most remarkable are *El Salón México* (1933–36) and the American ballets *Billy the Kid* (1938), *Rodeo* (1942), and *Appalachian Spring* (1944). A place apart is occupied by Copland's *Lincoln Portrait* for narrator and orch. (1942), with the texts arranged by the composer from speeches and letters of Abraham Lincoln; this work has had a great many performances, with the role of the narrator performed by such notables as Adlai Stevenson and Eleanor Roosevelt. His patriotic *Fanfare for the Common Man* (1942) achieved tremendous popularity and continued to be played on various occasions for decades; Copland incorporated it *in toto* into the score of his 3rd Symph. He was for many years a member of the board of directors of League of Composers in N.Y.; with Roger Sessions he organized the Copland-Sessions Concerts (1928–31), and was also a founder of the Yaddo Festivals (1932) and of the American Composers' Alliance (1937); was also a participant in such organizations as the Koussevitzky Music Foundation, the Composers Forum, the Cos Cob Press, etc. He was head of the composition dept. at the Berkshire Music Center at Tanglewood from 1940 to 1965, and from 1957 to 1965 was chairman of the faculty. He has lectured extensively and has given courses at The New School for Social Research in N.Y. and at Harvard Univ. (1935 and 1944); was the Charles Eliot Norton Lecturer at Harvard in 1951–52. He is the recipient of many awards: Guggenheim fellowship (1925–27); RCA Victor award of $5,000 for his *Dance Symphony;* Pulitzer Prize and N.Y. Music Critics' Circle Award for *Appalachian Spring* (1945); N.Y. Music Critics' Circle Award for the 3rd Symph. (1947); Oscar award for the film score *The Heiress* from the Academy of Motion Picture Arts and Sciences (1950); Gold Medal for Music from the American Academy of Arts and Letters (1956); Presidential Medal of Freedom (1964); Howland Memorial Prize of Yale Univ. (1970); was also decorated with a Commander's Cross of the Order of Merit in West Germany; was elected to honorary membership of the Santa Cecilia Academy in Rome. He holds numerous honorary doctor's degrees: Princeton Univ. (1956); Brandeis Univ. (1957); Wesleyan Univ. (1958); Temple Univ. (1959); Harvard Univ. (1961); Rutgers Univ. (1967); Ohio State Univ. (1970); N.Y. Univ. (1970); Columbia Univ. (1971); also York Univ. in England (1971). About 1955 Copland developed a successful career as a conductor, and has led major symph. orchs. in Europe, the U.S., South America, and Mexico; he also traveled to Russia under the auspices of the State Dept. As a composer, Copland makes use of a broad variety of idioms and techniques, tempering dissonant textures by a strong sense of tonality. He enlivens his musical textures by ingenious applications of syncopation and polyrhythmic combinations; but in such works as Piano Variations he adopts an austere method of musical constructivism. He uses a modified 12-tone technique in his Piano Quartet (1950) and an integral dodecaphonic idiom in the score of *Connotations* (1962). A chronological list of his works was publ. by Boosey & Hawkes in 1960.

WORKS: FOR THE STAGE: *Grohg,* ballet in one act (1922–25; not perf.; material incorporated into *A Dance Symphony*); *Hear Ye! Hear Ye!,* ballet (1934); *The 2nd Hurricane,* play-opera for high school (1936; N.Y., April 21, 1937); *Billy the Kid,* ballet (Ballet Caravan Co., Chicago, Oct. 16, 1938; N.Y., May 24, 1939); *From Sorcery to Science,* music for a puppet show (1939); *Rodeo,* ballet in one act (Ballets Russes de Monte Carlo, N.Y., Oct 16, 1942); *Appalachian Spring,* ballet (Martha Graham Ballet, Washington, D.C., Oct. 30, 1944); *The Tender Land,* opera (N.Y., April 1, 1954); *Dance Panels,* ballet in 7 movements (1959; revised 1962; Munich, Dec. 3, 1963, composer conducting; arranged for Piano, 1965).

FILM MUSIC: *The City* (1939); *Of Mice and Men* (1939); *Our Town* (1940); *North Star* (1943); *The*

Cummington Story (1945); *The Red Pony* (1948); *The Heiress* (1948; received an Academy Award, 1949); *Something Wild* (1961).

INCIDENTAL MUSIC TO PLAYS: *Miracle at Verdun* (1931); *The 5 Kings* (1939); *Quiet City* (1939).

FOR ORCH.: *Music for the Theater* (N.Y., League of Composers, Nov. 28, 1925, Koussevitzky conducting); Symph. for Organ and Orch. (N.Y., Jan. 11, 1925, Nadia Boulanger, organist; Walter Damrosch conducting; revised version without organ, designated as Symph. No. 1, 1928; also as *Prelude* for Chamber Orch., 1934); Concerto for Piano and Orch. (1926; Boston, Jan. 28, 1927, composer soloist, Koussevitzky conducting); *Symphonic Ode* (1927–29; composed for the 50th anniversary of the Boston Symph. Orch.; Boston Feb. 19, 1932, Koussevitzky conducting; revised 1955 for the 75th anniversary of the Boston Symph. Orch. and rededicated to the memory of Koussevitzky; Boston, Feb. 3, 1956, Munch conducting); *A Dance Symphony* (1930; based on the ballet *Grohg;* received the RCA Victor Competition prize; Philadelphia, April 15, 1931, Stokowski conducting); *Short Symphony* (Symph. No. 2) (1932– 33; Mexico City, Nov. 23, 1934, Chávez conducting); *Statements* (1932–35; first complete perf., N.Y., Jan. 7, 1942); *El Salón Mexico* (1933–36; Mexico City, Aug. 27, 1937, Chávez conducting); *Music for Radio (Prairie Journal),* subtitled *Saga of the Prairie* (CBS, N.Y., July 25, 1937); *An Outdoor Overture* (N.Y., Dec. 16, 1938; arranged for Band, 1941); *John Henry* for Chamber Orch. (CBS, N.Y., March 5, 1940; revised 1952); *Our Town,* suite from the film (CBS, N.Y., June 9, 1940); *Quiet City,* suite from the film, for English Horn, Trumpet, and Strings (1939; N.Y., Jan. 28, 1941); *Billy the Kid,* suite from the ballet (Boston, Jan. 30, 1942); *Lincoln Portrait* for Speaker and Orch. (commissioned by Kostelanetz; Cincinnati, May 14, 1942, Carl Sandburg, speaker; Kostelanetz conducting; highly successful, numerous perfs. by orchs. in America and abroad); *Rodeo,* 4 dance episodes from the ballet (1942); *Music for Movies* for Chamber Orch. (from the films *The City, Of Mice and Men,* and *Our Town;* 1942; N.Y., Feb. 17, 1943); *Fanfare for the Common Man* for Brass and Percussion (1942; Cincinnati, March 12, 1943, Goossens conducting; highly successful on television and radio); *Letter from Home* (N.Y. broadcast, Oct. 17, 1944; revised 1962); *Variation of a Theme by Eugene Goossens* (with 9 other composers; 1944; Cincinnati, March 23, 1945, Goossens conducting); *Appalachian Spring,* suite from the ballet (N.Y., Oct. 4, 1945, Rodzinski conducting; Copland's most popular orch. work; received the Pulitzer Prize for 1945); *Danzón Cubano* (originally for 2 Pianos, 1942; orch. version, 1944; Baltimore, Feb. 17, 1946); Symph. No. 3 (in memory of Mme. Natalie Koussevitzky; 1944–46; Boston, Oct. 18, 1946, Koussevitzky conducting); Concerto for Clarinet, Strings, Harp, and Piano (1947–48; N.Y., Nov. 6, 1950, Benny Goodman, soloist; Reiner conducting); *The Red Pony,* suite from the film (Houston, Nov. 1, 1948); *Preamble for a Solemn Occasion* for Speaker and Orch. (N.Y., 1949, Laurence Olivier, speaker, Bernstein conducting; arranged for Organ, 1953; arranged for Band, 1973); Orch. Variations (orch. version of the Piano Varia-

tions; 1930; 1957); *Connotations* (composed entirely in the 12-tone technique; commissioned for the opening of Phil. Hall, Lincoln Center, N.Y., Sept. 23, 1962, Bernstein conducting); *Music for a Great City* (symph. suite descriptive of life in N.Y. City; London, May 26, 1964, composer conducting); *Emblems* for Band (1964); *Down a Country Lane* for School Orch. (1965); *Inscape* (commissioned by the N.Y. Phil. and first perf. by that orch. at the Univ. of Michigan, Ann Arbor, Sept. 13, 1967, Bernstein conducting); *Inaugural Fanfare* (1969; revised 1975); *3 Latin American Sketches: Estribillo, Paisaje mexicano, Danza de Jalisco* (N.Y., June 7, 1972, Kostelanetz conducting).

VOCAL MUSIC: Choral: 4 Motets (1921); *The House on the Hill* for Women's Voices (1925); *An Immorality* for Soprano, Women's Voices, and Piano (1925); *What Do We Plant?* for Women's Voices and Piano (1935); *Lark* for Bass and Mixed Chorus (1938); *Las agachadas* for Mixed Chorus (1942); *Song of the Guerrillas* for Baritone, Men's Voices, and Piano (1943); *The Younger Generation* for Mixed Chorus and Piano (1943); *In the Beginning* for Mezzo-soprano and Mixed Chorus (commissioned for the Harvard Symposium; Cambridge, Mass., May 2, 1947, Robert Shaw conducting); *Canticle of Freedom* (1955; revised 1965). Songs: *Melancholy* (1917); *Spurned Love* (1917); *After Antwerp* (1917); *Night* (1918); *A Summer Vacation* (1918); *My Heart Is in the East* (1918); *Simone* (1919); *Music I Heard* (1920); *Old Poem* (1920); *Pastorale* (1921); *As It Fell Upon a Day* (1923); *Poet's Song* (1927); *Vocalise* (1928); *12 Poems of Emily Dickinson* (1949–50); *Old American Songs* for Voice and Orch. (arrangements in 2 sets, 1950 and 1959); *Dirge in Woods* (1954).

CHAMBER MUSIC: *Capriccio* for Violin and Piano; *Poem* for Cello and Piano; *Lament* for Cello and Piano; *Preludes* for Violin and Piano; String Quartet (unfinished); Piano Trio (unfinished); *Rondino* for String Quartet (1923); *Nocturne* for Violin and Piano (1926); *Ukelele Serenade* for Violin and Piano (1926); *Lento molto* for String Quartet (1928); *Vitebsk, Study on a Jewish Theme* for Piano Trio (1928; League of Composers, N.Y., Feb. 16, 1929); *Elegies* for Violin and Viola (1932); Sextet for Clarinet, Piano, and String Quartet (arranged from *Short Symphony;* 1932–33; 1937; N.Y., Feb. 26, 1939); Sonata for Violin and Piano (1942–43); Quartet for Piano and Strings (Washington, D.C., Oct. 29, 1950); *Nonet* for 3 Violins, 3 Violas, and 3 Cellos (1960; Washington, March 2, 1961, composer conducting); Duo for Flute and Piano (1971); *Threnody I: Igor Stravinsky, In Memoriam* for Flute and String Trio (1971); *Vocalise* for Flute and Piano (arrangement of *Vocalise;* 1928; 1972); *Threnody II: Beatrice Cunningham, In Memoriam* for G-Flute and String Trio (1973).

FOR PIANO: *Moment musical* (1917); *Danse caractéristique* for Piano Duet or Orch. (1918); *Waltz Caprice* (1918); Sonnets, 1–3 (1918–20); *Moods (3 esquisses): Amertume, pensif, jazzy* and *Petit portrait,* a supplement (1920–21); Piano Sonata in G major (1920–21); *Scherzo humoristique: Le Chat et la souris* (1920); Passacaglia (1921–22); *Sentimental Melody* (1926); Piano Variations (1930; orch. version, 1957); *Sunday Afternoon Music (The Young Pioneers)* (1935); Piano Sonata (1939–41; Buenos Aires, Oct. 21, 1941, composer pianist); 4 Piano Blues (1926–48); Piano Fantasy (1952–57); *Down a Country Lane* (1962); *Rodeo* (arrangement from the ballet; 1962); *Danza de Jalisco* for 2 Pianos (1963; orch. version, 1972); *Dance Panels* (arrangement from the ballet; 1965); *In Evening Air* (excerpt arranged from the film score *The Cummington Story;* 1969); *Night Thoughts (Homage to Ives)* (1972).

WRITINGS: He has publ. the following books: *What to Listen for in Music* (N.Y., 1939; 2nd ed., 1957; trans. into German, Italian, Spanish, Dutch, Arabic and Chinese); *Our New Music* (N.Y., 1941; 2nd ed., revised and enlarged as *The New Music, 1900–1960,* N.Y., 1968); *Music and Imagination,* a collection of lectures delivered at Harvard in 1951–52 (Cambridge, Mass., 1952); *Copland on Music* (N.Y., 1960).

Coppet, Edward J. de, American patron of art and founder of the Flonzaley Quartet; b. New York, May 28, 1855; d. there, April 30, 1916. A man of wealth and refined artistic tastes, he engaged various artists for private quartet performances at his residence. When he realized that constant practice was indispensable for the attainment of a perfect ensemble, he commissioned A. Pochon, in 1902, to find 4 men of the highest artistic standing who were willing to devote all their time to quartet playing. In the summer of the following year Adolfo Betti, Alfred Pochon, Ugo Ara, and Ivan d'Archambeau (first violin, 2nd violin, viola, and cello, respectively) began to practice at Flonzaley, de Coppet's summer residence near Lausanne, Switzerland; in the spring of 1904 they made their first European tour, arousing admiration by the perfection of their ensemble; on Dec. 5, 1905, they gave their first public concert in America (Carnegie Chamber Music Hall, N.Y.), with overwhelming success. They then appeared regularly in America and Europe. After de Coppet's death, his son, **André,** continued the original policy until 1929, when the quartet disbanded.

Coppola, Piero, Italian conductor and composer; b. Milan, Oct. 11, 1888; d. Lausanne, March 13, 1971. He studied at the Milan Cons., graduating in 1909; in 1913 he filled engagements as a conductor at La Scala; in 1914 was in London; in 1921 settled in Paris, where he was active as music director of the recording company "His Master's Voice" (1923–34); eventually settled in Switzerland. He wrote 2 operas, *Sirmione* and *Nikita* (1914); a Symph. (Paris, Nov. 13, 1924, composer conducting); a symph. sketch, *La Ronde sous la cloche* (1924); and various other pieces.

Coppola, Pietro Antonio (Pierantonio), Italian composer; b. Castrogiovanni, Sicily, Dec. 11, 1793; d. Catania, Nov. 13, 1877. For a short time he studied at the Naples Cons.; then began to compose operas, which obtained sufficient success to enable his friends and admirers to present him as a rival to Rossini.

WORKS: From the time he was 19, he produced one opera after another, but without much success until he composed *La Pazza per amore* (Rome, Feb. 14, 1835). This was his 5th opera and it became popular all over Europe (presented in Paris under the title *Eva*). In 1839–43, and again from 1850 till 1871, he was conductor of the Lisbon Royal Opera. His other operas were: *Gli Illinesi* (Turin, Dec. 26, 1835); *Enrichietta di Baienfeld* (Vienna, June 29, 1836); *La bella Celeste degli Spadari* (Milan, June 14, 1837); *Giovanna prima di Napoli* (Lisbon, Oct. 11, 1840); *Il folletto* (Rome, June 18, 1843). He also wrote church music, notably a *Salve Regina* which was highly regarded. His son publ. his biography (1899).

Corder, Frederick, English composer and eminent teacher of composition; b. London, Jan. 26, 1852; d. there, Aug. 21, 1932. He was a pupil at the Royal Academy of Music (1873–75); in 1875 won the Mendelssohn Scholarship; studied with Ferdinand Hiller at Cologne (1875–78); was conductor of the Brighton Aquarium Concerts from 1880 to 1882, and greatly improved their quality; from 1886, was a prof. of composition at the Royal Academy of Music and, from 1889, also curator. In 1905 he founded the Society of British Composers. He was remarkably successful as a teacher, many prominent British composers having been his pupils; a zealous apostle of Wagner, he and his wife made the first English translation of *The Ring of the Nibelung, Die Meistersinger,* and *Parsifal* for the original scores publ. by Schott; was also a contributor to *Grove's Dictionary.*

Cordero, Roque, Panamanian composer; b. Panama, Aug. 16, 1917. He first studied in Panama; then came to the U.S. (1943); studied with Krenek in Minneapolis and with Stanley Chapple (conducting) at the Berkshire Music Center at Tanglewood. He was a prof. at the National Inst. of Music in Panama in 1950–66, and its director in 1953–64; taught at Indiana Univ. in Bloomington (1966–69) and at Illinois State Univ. from 1972; was also active as a conductor.

WORKS: *Capriccio interiorano* for Band (1939); Piano Concerto (1944); Symph. No. 1 (1947); *8 Miniatures* for Orch. (1948); *Rapsodia campesina* for Orch. (1949); Quintet for Flute, Clarinet, Violin, Cello, and Piano (1949); Symph. No. 2 (1956); *5 mensajes breves* for Orch. (1959); 2 string quartets (1969, 1968); Cello Sonata (1962); Violin Concerto (1962); Symph. No. 3 (1965); *Sonata breve* for Piano (1966); *Circunvoluciones y moviles* for 57 Players (1967); *Permutaciones 7* for 7 Instrumentalists (1967); *Paz, Paix, Peace* for 4 Trios and Harp (1969); *Variations and Theme for 5* for Woodwind Quartet and Horn (1975).

Corelli, Arcangelo, famous Italian violinist and composer; b. Fusignano, near Imola, Feb. 17, 1653; d. Rome, Jan. 8, 1713. His violin teacher was G. Benvenuti in Bologna; he learned counterpoint with Matteo Simonelli. Little is known of his early life;

about 1671 he went to Rome, where he was a violinist at the French Church (1675); in the beginning of 1679, he played in the orch. of the Teatro Capranica; Rome remained his chief residence to the end of his life, except for visits to Modena (1689–90) and Naples (1702). There is no substance to the story that in 1672 he went to Paris and was driven out by the intrigues of Lully; biographers mention also his stay at the court of the Elector of Bavaria in Munich about 1680, but there is no documentary evidence of this stay. Equally unfounded is the story that while he was in Naples, a mediocre violinist, Giuseppe Valentini, won the favor of the Roman public so that Corelli returned to Rome a broken man and died shortly afterward. Quite contrary to these fanciful legends, Corelli enjoyed respect, security, and fame. In Rome he had a powerful protector in Cardinal Benedetto Panfili; later he lived in the palace of Cardinal Pietro Ottoboni, conducting weekly concerts which were attended by the elite of Roman society. One of Corelli's admirers was Queen Christina of Sweden, who lived in Rome at the time. Among his pupils were Baptiste Anet, Geminiani, Locatelli, and Giovanni Somis. Corelli was famous as a virtuoso on the violin and may be regarded as the founder of modern violin technique; he systematized the art of proper bowing, and was one of the first to use double stops and chords on the violin. His role in music history is very great despite the fact that he wrote but few works; only 6 opus numbers can be definitely attributed to him. His greatest achievement was the creation of the concerto grosso. Handel, who as a young man met Corelli in Rome, was undoubtedly influenced by Corelli's instrumental writing. Corelli was buried in the Pantheon in Rome.

WORKS: 12 *sonate a 3, 2 violini e violone o arcileuto col basso per l'organo,* op. 1 (Rome, 1681; dedicated to Queen Christina of Sweden); 12 *sonate da camera a 3, 2 violini e violone o cembalo,* op. 2 (Rome, 1685); 12 *sonate a 3, 2 violini e violone o arcileuto, col basso per l'organo,* op. 3 (Rome, 1689); 12 *sonate a 3,* op. 4 (Rome, 1694; in Amsterdam as *Balleti da camera*); 12 *sonate a violino e violone o cembalo,* op. 5 (Rome, 1700; later arranged by Geminiani as *Concerti grossi;* the 12th sonata of op. 5 is *La Follia,* the celebrated set of variations for Violin); *Concerti grossi con 2 violini e violoncello di concertino obbligati, e 2 altri violini, viola, e basso di concerto grosso ad arbitrio che si potranno raddoppiare,* op. 6 (Amsterdam, 1714). All these were variously reprinted at the time; an important ed. is by Pepusch (London, opp. 1–4 and 6); Joachim and Chrysander issued the "complete works" in 1888–91 (London; opp. 1–6); a new critical ed. has been started at the Musikwissenschaftliches Institut der Universität Basel (1976—).

Corelli, Franco, outstanding Italian tenor; b. Ancona, April 8, 1921. He studied naval engineering at the Univ. of Bologna; in 1947 entered the Pesaro Cons. to study voice; dissatisfied with the academic training, he left the Cons. and proceeded to learn the repertoire by listening to recordings of great singers. He made his operatic debut at the Spoleto Festival in 1952 as Don José in *Carmen;* then sang at the Rome Opera in 1953 and at La Scala, Milan, in 1954; he appeared at London's Covent Garden in 1957. On Jan. 27, 1961, he made his Metropolitan Opera debut in N.Y. as Manrico in *Il Trovatore;* from that time he appeared with most of the major opera houses of the world. Among his finest roles are Radames, Ernani, and Don Alvaro.

Corigliano, John, American violinist; b. New York, Aug. 28, 1901; d. Norfolk, Conn., Sept. 1, 1975. He studied with Leopold Auer in N.Y.; gave violin recitals; in 1935 he was appointed assistant concertmaster of the N.Y. Phil., and in 1943 concertmaster; he resigned his position in 1966; subsequently served as concertmaster of the San Antonio Symph.

Corigliano, John, American composer, son of the violinist **John Corigliano;** b. New York, Feb. 16, 1938. He studied at Columbia Univ. with Otto Luening (B.A., 1959), with Vittorio Giannini at the Manhattan School of Music, and privately with Paul Creston. He was subsequently employed as a scriptwriter for radio station WQXR in N.Y. and as assistant director for musical television shows there; later he was in charge of the music section at WBAI. He held a Guggenheim fellowship in 1968–69. In 1971 he joined the faculty of the Manhattan School of Music, and from 1973 taught at Lehman College. His style of composition shows a fine capacity for lyrical expression, and an incisive sense of rhythm, in the generic tradition of Béla Bartók and Prokofiev. Despite the dissonant freedom of his polyphonic writing, his music retains a firm tonal anchorage.

WORKS: *Kaleidoscope* for 2 Pianos (1959); *Pastorale* for Cello and Piano (1958), *Fern Hill* for Chorus and Orch., to words by Dylan Thomas (N.Y., Dec. 19, 1961); Violin Sonata (1963; received first prize in the Spoleto Festival Competition of 1964); *The Cloisters,* cycle of songs (1965); *Elegy* for Orch. (San Francisco, June 1, 1966); *Tournaments Overture* (1967); Piano Concerto (San Antonio, Texas, April 7, 1968, Hilde Somer, soloist); *Poem in October* for Tenor and 8 Instruments (1969); Oboe Concerto (N.Y., Nov. 9, 1975); *Poem on His Birthday* for Baritone, Chorus, and Orch. (Washington, D.C., April 24, 1976); Clarinet Concerto (N.Y., Dec. 6, 1977); *3 Hallucinations for Orchestra,* derived from his score for the film *Altered States* (1981). Also incidental music for Molière's *Le Malade imaginaire,* Sheridan's *The Rivals,* Sophocles' *Oedipus Rex,* Brecht's *Galileo;* special scores for the N.Y. Shakespeare Festival of 1970. He arranged Bizet's *Carmen* for singers, rock and pop groups, Moog synthesizer, and instruments, issued on a record under the title *The Naked Carmen.*

Cornelis, Evert, Dutch conductor and pianist; b. Amsterdam, Dec. 5, 1884; d. Bilthoven, Nov. 23, 1931. He was a pupil of de Pauw at the Amsterdam Cons.; in 1904, won the organ prize; was conductor at the Amsterdam Opera (1908); assistant conductor of the Concertgebouw Orch. (1910–19); from 1922 conductor of the orch. at Utrecht, later choral director at Rotterdam; conductor of the Netherlands Bach Society (1927); toured Europe, the Dutch East Indies, Australia, etc., as a guest conductor. He pioneered extensively for modern music.

Cornelius, Peter, important German composer and writer; b. Mainz, Dec. 24, 1824; d. there, Oct 26, 1874. Danish tenor; b. Labjerggaard, Jan. 4, 1865; d. A nephew of the painter Peter von Cornelius, he at first became an actor, but after an unsuccessful debut changed his mind; he studied theory with Dehn at Berlin (1845–52) and then joined Liszt's following in Weimar as a champion of Wagner, contributing frequent articles to the *Neue 25, 1934. He studied in Copenhagen; made his debut as a Zeitschrift für Musik.* His masterpiece, the opera *Der Barbier von Bagdad,* was produced at Weimar (Dec. 15, 1858) under the direction of Liszt, who resigned his position there because of hostile demonstrations while he was conducting the opera. In 1861 Cornelius went to Wagner 1892; then studied in Berlin with Hermann Spiro and at Vienna, and followed him to Munich (1865), where he was appointed reader to King Ludwig II, and prof. of harmony and rhetoric at the Royal Music School. A 2nd opera, *Der Cid,* was produced at Weimar on May 21, 1865; a 3rd, *Gunlöd* (from the Edda), remained unfinished (completed by Lassen his debut as a tenor in Copenhagen in 1899, where he and produced at Weimar, May 6, 1891). *Der Barbier von Bagdad* was revived at Karlsruhe on Feb. 1, 1884, in a drastically altered version by F. Mottl. Cornelius publ. *Lieder-Cyclus* (op. 3); duets for Soprano and Baritone (op. 6); *Weinachtslieder* (op. 8); *Trauerchöre Danish Theater until 1922; also sang at Bayreuth (1906)* for Male Chorus (op. 9). A vol. of *Lyrische Poesien* was issued in 1861. A complete ed. of Cornelius's works was issued by Breitkopf & Härtel (1905–6). in London (1907–14); made guest appearances in Paris, Stockholm, Oslo, Karlsruhe, and other cities; after his retirement, he taught voice in Copenhagen. He was particularly renowned for his Wagnerian roles. A biography of him by C. Cornelius was publ. in 1925.

Corner, Philip, American composer; b. New York, April 10, 1933. He studied piano; began composing autogenetically at 13, gestated a 3-minute piano piece in 9 months, learned to play the trombone. In 1955 he went to Paris, where he took a course in musical philosophy with Olivier Messiaen; spent a year in Korea studying oriental calligraphy in order to apply it to the needs of graphic music notation. In 1958 he turned to serial music, but mitigated its stern doctrines by aleatory indeterminacy; he often composes works after their first performance to avoid the stigma of premeditation. The titles of his compositions show a surrealistic flavor: *Passionate Expanse of the Law, Certain Distilling Processes, Expressions in Parallel, Air Effect,* and *Music Reserved until Now.* In his *Punishment Piece,* using the naked strings of a grand piano, musical material is determined by tossing spotted transparent pa-

per on the manuscript. In 1965 he composed a timeless piece for indefinitely prolonged chanting on a single note. In 1968 he verbalized a work with the injunction: "One anti-personnel type CBU bomb will be thrown into the audience" (publ. in *Source 6,* 1969, but never perf).

Correa de Arauxo, Francisco, one of the most important Spanish organists of the Renaissance; b. Seville, c.1576; d. Segovia, Oct. 31, 1654. He held the post of organist at the Church of San Salvador in Seville (1599–1636), at the Cathedral of Jaen (1636–40), and at Segovia (from 1640 until his death). His *Facultad orgánica* (originally publ. in Alcaláde Henares, 1626) contains 70 pieces for organ in tablature (most of them his own compositions), reproduced in the series Monumentos de la Música Española, ed. by Santiago Kastner (Madrid, 1950).

Correa de Azevedo, Luis Heitor, Brazilian musicologist; b. Rio de Janeiro, Dec. 13, 1905. He studied at the Instituto Nacional de Música in Rio de Janeiro; in 1932 was appointed librarian there; in 1939 became prof. of national folklore; in 1943 organized the Centro de Pesquisas Folklóricas at the Escuela Nacional de Música. He publ. numerous valuable studies on Brazilian music: *Escala, ritmo e melodia na música dos Indios brasileiros* (Rio de Janeiro, 1938); *Relação das operas de autores brasileiros* (Rio de Janeiro, 1938); *A música brasileira e seus fundamentos* (Washington, D.C., 1948); *Música e músicos do Brasil* (Rio de Janeiro, 1950); *150 años de música no Brasil* (Rio de Janeiro, 1956); *La Musique en Amérique latine* (Paris, 1957); several informative articles in Brazilian, French, and American magazines. From 1947 to 1965 he was in charge of the music division of UNESCO in Paris; in 1967–68 he gave lectures at the Newcomb College of Tulane Univ. in Louisiana.

Corri, Domenico, Italian composer; b. Rome, Oct. 4, 1744; d. London, May 22, 1825. He was a pupil of Porpora in Naples; in 1781 went to Edinburgh as an opera conductor. His attempt to organize his own opera company and a publishing firm there was a failure, and he sought better fortune in London (1790). There he engaged in various enterprises as a publisher, composer, and impresario. His opera, *The Travelers, or Music's Fascination,* was given at Drury Lane on Jan. 22, 1806, with little success. He publ. 4 music manuals in English: *A Complete Musical Grammar* (1787); *A Musical Dictionary* (1798); *The Art of Fingering* (1799); and *The Singer's Preceptor* (1810). His daughter, **Sophia Giustina,** a talented pianist and singer, married Dussek; his sons, **Montague Corri** (1784–1849) and **Haydn Corri** (1785–1860), were also musicians.

Corsi (Corso), Giuseppe (called **Celano** after his birthplace), Italian composer; b. Celano, May 1630; d. May 1690. He studied with Carissimi; served as maestro di cappella at Santa Maria Maggiore in Rome (1659–61); at the Lateran Palace chapel (1661–65); at Santa Casa di Loreto (1668–75); then returned to Rome, but because of his dissemination of books placed on the Church Index, was persecuted and forced to leave (1678); from 1681 to 1688 he was at the court of the Duke of Parma. Among his pupils were Jacopo Perti (at Parma) and Petronio Franceschini. He publ. *Motetti a 2, 3 e 4 voci* (Rome, 1667), *Miserere a 5,* and *Motetti a 9;* various other vocal works, in MS, are preserved in the library of the Liceo Musicale and the Archivio Musicale di S. Petronio at Bologna. Several of his works appeared in collections of the time. He is mentioned in Giuseppe Pitoni's *Guida armonica.*

Corsi, Jacopo, Florentine nobleman and patron of art; b. Florence, July 17, 1560; d. there, Dec. 29, 1602. In his palace, as in that of his friend Bardi, were held the memorable meetings of the "Camerata" in which Peri, Caccini, Emilio del Cavaliere, Galilei, the poet Rinuccini, and others took part, leading to the creation of the earliest operas. Corsi was a good musician, a skillful player on the harpsichord, and a composer; he wrote the concluding 2 numbers of the first opera by Peri, *Dafne,* which was performed at his home in 1598; these settings are preserved in the library of the Brussels Cons.; they were publ. in Solerti's *Albori del Melodramma* (Milan, 1905).

Corso, Giuseppe. See **Corsi, Giuseppe.**

Corte, Andrea della. See **Della Corte, Andrea.**

Corteccia, Francesco Bernardo (baptismal names, **Pier Francesco**), Italian composer and organist; b. Florence, July 27, 1502; d. there, June 27, 1571. He studied music with Bernardo Pisano; was a choirboy at S. Giovanni Battista in Florence; later prepared for the priesthood, and was chaplain at S. Giovanni in 1527–31; in 1531 was organist at S. Lorenzo, then at S. Giovanni (1535–39); was maestro di cappella there and at the Florence Cathedral from 1540 until his death. He wrote musical intermezzi for the opera *Il furto* by Francesco d'Ambra (1544); wedding music (for Duke Cosimo the Great); 9 pieces *a* 4, 6, and 8 (Venice, 1539); 3 books of madrigals (1544, 1547, 1547); *Responsoria et lectiones* (1570); 32 hymns *a* 4; *Canticorum liber primus* (1571); many others. Modern editions of his works include *Francesco Corteccia: Hinnario secondo l'uso della chiesa romana e fiorentina,* ed. by G. Haydon (Cincinnati, 1958 and 1960); A.C. Minor and B. Mitchell, eds., *A Renaissance Entertainment: Festivities for the Marriage of Cosimo I, Duke of Florence, in 1539* (Columbia, Mo., 1968); *Francesco Corteccia: Eleven Works to Latin Texts,* ed. by A. McKinley in *Recent Researches in the Music of the Renaissance,* XXVI (1969).

Cortot, Alfred (Denis), famous French pianist; b. (of a French father and a Swiss mother) Nyon, Switzerland, Sept. 26, 1877; d. Lausanne, June 15, 1962. He was a pupil at the Paris Cons., and studied with Decambes, Rouquou, and Diémer; he won the first prize for piano in 1896; the same year he made his

debut in Paris, playing Beethoven's C minor Concerto at one of the Colonne concerts, and won signal success; he went to Bayreuth (1898) and studied Wagner's works with J. Kniese, and acted as répétiteur at the festivals from 1898–1901. Returning to Paris, he began a most active propaganda for the works of Wagner; on May 17, 1902, he conducted the French premiere of *Götterdämmerung* at the Théâtre du Château d'Eau, and in the same year established the Association des Concerts A. Cortot, which he directed for 2 years, educating the public to an appreciation of Wagner; in 1904 he became conductor of the orch. concerts of the Société Nationale and of the Concerts Populaires at Lille (till 1908). In 1905, together with Jacques Thibaud (violin) and Pablo Casals (cello), he formed a trio, which soon gained a great European reputation. He founded, with A. Mangeot, the Ecole Normale de Musique (1919), and became its director, also giving a summer course in piano interpretation there annually; gave many lecture recitals and appeared as a guest conductor with various orchs. WRITINGS: Articles on the piano works of Debussy, Fauré, Franck, and Chabrier in *Revue Musicale* (1920–26); he publ. a new working ed. of Chopin's Preludes and Etudes; also publ. *Principes rationnels de la technique pianistique* (French and Eng., Paris, 1928; American ed., Boston, 1930); *La Musique française de piano* (vol. I, 1930; Eng. trans., London, 1932; vol. II, 1932); *Cours d'interprétation* (vol. I, Paris, 1934; in Eng., London, 1937); *Aspects de Chopin* (Paris, 1949; in Eng., as *In Search of Chopin,* London, 1951). The publication of a classified catalogue of Cortot's library, entitled *Bibliothèque Alfred Cortot,* ed. by F. Goldbeck and A. Fehr with preface by H. Prunières, was begun in 1936.

Cossutta, Carlo, Italian tenor; b. Trieste, May 8, 1932. He was taken to Argentina while young; received his musical training there. He sang at the Teatro Colón in Buenos Aires in 1958; in 1964 appeared at Covent Garden, London. On Feb. 17, 1973, he made his Metropolitan Opera debut in N.Y. as Pollione in *Norma.* He also sang with the Chicago Lyric Opera, the Paris Opéra, and the Vienna State Opera. He distinguished himself in dramatic roles.

Costa, Mary, American soprano; b. Knoxville, Tenn., April 5, 1932. She received her primary musical training in Los Angeles; sang at the Hollywood Bowl and with the San Francisco Opera. On Jan. 6, 1964, she made her debut at the Metropolitan Opera in N.Y. as Violetta in *La Traviata;* in 1970 she sang opera at the Bolshoi Theater in Moscow. She also made many concert appearances.

Costa, Sir Michael (properly, **Michele**), eminent conductor and opera composer; b. Naples, Feb. 4, 1806; d. Hove, England, April 29, 1884. He studied with his maternal grandfather, **Giacomo Tritto;** with his father, **Pasquale Costa** (a composer of church music); and with Giovanni Furno. He then studied at the Naples Cons. with Crescentini (singing) and Zingarelli (composition). His operas *Il so-*

spetto funesto (Naples, 1826), *Il delitto punito* (1827), *Il carcere d'Ildegonda* (Naples, 1828), and *Malvina* (Naples, 1829) were well received; when Zingarelli was commissioned to write a Psalm (*Super Flumina Babilonis*) for the Music Festival at Birmingham, England, he sent Costa to conduct it. When Costa arrived in Birmingham, the directors of the Festival refused to accept him as a conductor owing to his extreme youth, but offered to pay him a similar fee for performance as tenor in Zingarelli's Psalm and in other works. He was compelled to accept, but his debut as a singer was disastrous. Despite this setback, he decided to remain in England, a decision in which he was encouraged by Clementi, who was impressed by Costa's scoring of a Bellini aria. In 1830 Costa was engaged as maestro al cembalo at the King's Theatre in London; in 1832 he became music director; and in 1833, director and conductor. During this time he produced 3 of his ballets, *Kenilworth* (1831), *Une Heure à Naples* (1832), and *Sir Huon* (1833, for Taglioni). In 1846 he became conductor of the Phil. and of the Royal Italian Opera; in 1848–82, he conducted the Sacred Harmonic Society. From 1849 he was the regular conductor of the Birmingham Festivals; from 1847 to 1880, of the Handel Festivals. He was knighted in 1869; was appointed "director of the music, composer, and conductor" at Her Majesty's Opera, Haymarket, in 1871, serving till 1881. He produced 2 operas in London: *Malek Adel* (May 18, 1837; a revision of *Malvina*) and *Don Carlos* (June 20, 1844).

Costeley, Guillaume, French organist; b. probably at Pont-Audemer (Normandy), 1531; d. Evreux, Jan. 28, 1606. The theory that he was an Irishman named Costello who settled in France, as well as the theory that he was of Scottish extraction, has been discarded. He was court organist to Charles IX of France. In 1571 he became the first annually elected "prince" or "maître" of a society organized in honor of St. Cecilia, which, beginning in 1575, awarded a prize each year for a polyphonic composition. Costeley excelled as a composer of polyphonic chansons; his *Musique,* a book of such works for 4–6 voices, appeared in 1570. Modern editions of some of those for 4 voices are in H. Expert, Maîtres Musiciens de la Renaissance Française (vols. III, XVIII, XIX); an example for 5 voices in Cauchie's *Quinze chansons.*

Cotton, John (or **Johannis Cottonis;** also **Joannes Musica, Johannes filius Dei,** and **Johannes of Afflighem**), early music theorist (11th to 12th century), probable author of the treatise *Epistola ad Fulgentium* (printed by Gerbert in *Scriptores,* vol. II), a valuable work on music describing the modal system of the time and a phase of the development of organum. Six MS copies are preserved: one each in Leipzig, Paris, Antwerp, and the Vatican Library, and 2 in Vienna. Various theories have been advanced concerning its authorship. In the copies at Antwerp and Paris the author is referred to as Cotton or Cottonius, while 2 others give the author's name as Joannes Musica. In an anonymous work,

De script. eccles., quoted by Gerbert, there is a reference to a certain Joannes, an erudite English musician; the dedication of this volume, "Domino et patri sua venerabili Anglorum antistiti Fulgentio," adds further strength to the contention that the author of the *Epistola* was English. However, J. Smits van Waesberghe identifies him with the Flemish theorist Johannes of Afflighem, author of the treatise *De Musica cum tonario* (reprinted Rome, 1950). Other sources suggest that Cotton is also one Johannes filius Dei.

Cottrau, Teodoro, Italian composer of Neapolitan ballads; b. Naples, Nov. 27, 1827; d. there, March 30, 1879. His father, **Guglielmo Louis Cottrau** (b. Paris, Aug. 9, 1797; d. Naples, Oct. 31, 1847), was also a composer of Neapolitan canzonettas (some of them used by Liszt in his piano work *Venezia e Napoli*), as was his brother **Giulio Cottrau** (b. Naples, Oct. 29, 1831; d. Rome, Oct. 25, 1916). Teodoro Cottrau was the composer of the perennial favorite *Santa Lucia* (1850).

Couperin, a renowned family of French musicians. Its musical prominence dates from the 3 sons of **Charles Couperin,** merchant and organist of Chaume, in the dept. of Brie (now part of the dept. of Seine et Marne), and his wife, Marie Andry. The eldest of these, **Louis,** established the family in Paris, where it remained until the extinction of the male line in 1826. He was also the first of his name to hold the post of organist at St.-Gervais in Paris. He was followed in this position by his youngest brother, **Charles; François le Grand,** son of Charles, and the family's most illustrious representative; **Nicolas,** son of **François** (called **Sieur de Crouilly**); **Armand-Louis,** son of Nicolas; and by the 2 sons of Armand-Louis, **Pierre-Louis** and **Gervais-François.** The following articles, arranged alphabetically, give the individual histories of the members of the Couperin family.

Couperin, Armand-Louis (son of **Nicolas**), b. Paris, Feb. 25, 1727; d. there, Feb. 2, 1789. His virtuosity on the organ was extraordinary; in 1748, succeeded his father as organist at St.-Gervais; was also organist to the King (1770–89), and held appointments at St.-Barthélemy, Ste.-Marguerite, Ste.-Chapelle, St.-Jean-en-Grève, etc. He was one of the 4 organists of Notre-Dame. He died a violent death, having been knocked down by a runaway horse. His compositions include sonatas, a trio, motets, and other church music. His wife, **Elisabeth-Antoinette** (née **Blanchet;** b. Paris, Jan. 14, 1729), was also a remarkable organist and clavecinist, still playing in public at the age of 81 (in 1810). She was the daughter of **Blanchet,** the famous clavecin maker, and sister-in-law to **Pascal Joseph Taskin,** the court instrument keeper under Louis XV. D. Fuller edited *A.-L. Couperin: Selected Works for Keyboard* (Madison, Wis., 1975).

Couperin, Charles, b. Chaumes (baptized, April 9), 1638; d. Paris, 1679. He succeeded his brother **Louis**

as organist at St.-Gervais in 1661. He married Marie Guérin (Feb. 20, 1662), and is principally remembered as being the father of the celebrated **François le Grand.**

Couperin, François, b. Chaumes, c.1631; d. Paris, after 1708. He was a pupil of Chambonnières in harmony and clavecin playing; was active as a music teacher and organist. His daughter, **Marguerite Louise** (b. Paris, 1676; d. Versailles, May 30, 1728), was a well-known singer and harpsichordist. She was a fellow member of the Chambre du Roi with her cousin **François le Grand,** who wrote for her the verset *Qui dat nivem* and other pieces.

Couperin, François (surnamed **le Grand** on account of his superiority in organ playing), the most illustrious member of a distinguished family, and one of the greatest of early French composers; b. Paris, Nov. 10, 1668; d. there, Sept. 11, 1733. He was the son of **Charles Couperin,** who was his first teacher; later was a pupil of Jacques-Denis Thomelin, organist of the King's chapel; in 1685 he became organist of St.-Gervais, which post he held until his death; on Dec. 26, 1693, after a successful competition, he succeeded Thomelin as organist of the Chapelle Royale, receiving the title of "organiste du roi"; in 1701 he was appointed "claveciniste de la chambre du roi, et organiste de sa chapelle," and in 1717 he received the title "Ordinaire de la musique de la chambre du roi"; also was made a chevalier of the Order of Latran; he was music master to the Dauphin and other members of the royal family, and ranked high in the favor of Louis XIV, for whom he composed the *Concerts royaux,* which, during 1714–15, were played in Sunday concerts in the royal apartments. He married Marie-Anne Ansault (April 26, 1689), by whom he had 2 daughters: **Marie-Madeleine** (b. Paris, March 9, 1690; d. Montbuisson, April 16, 1742), who became organist of the Abbey of Montbuisson, and **Marguerite-Antoinette** (b. Paris, Sept. 19, 1705; d. there, 1778), who was a talented clavecin player; from 1731–33, she substituted for her father as claveciniste to the King, being the first woman to hold this position (cf. C. Bouvet, "Les Deux d'Anglebert et Marguerite-Antoinette Couperin," *Revue de Musicologie,* 1928); there were also 2 sons, **Nicolas-Louis** (b. July 24, 1707), who died young, and **François-Laurent,** b. c.1708. Famed as an organist, Couperin also acquired a high reputation for his remarkable ability as a performer on the clavecin.

WORKS: His compositions may be conveniently divided into 3 categories: those written for the church, those for the King, and those for the general public. More than half of his creative life was taken up with the religious compositions of the first 2 periods. These include *Pièces d'orgue consistantes en deux Messes* (1690, a total of 42 pieces), formerly attributed to his uncle **François,** and, indeed, publ. under the latter's name in vol. 5 of *Archives des maîtres de l'orgue,* ed. by Guilmant, but now established, through the researches of A. Tessier and P. Brunold, as the early work of **Couperin le Grand;**

motets; *Elévations; Leçons de ténèbres;* etc. Couperin's last and most prolific period was concerned exclusively with instrumental works, and in this field he achieved his greatest and most enduring distinction. In 1713, 1716, 1722, and 1730, he publ. the 4 vols. of his *Pièces de clavecin,* consisting of about 230 pieces or 27 "Ordres" or Suites, each suite being a series of dance forms, programmatic in title and content (*La Majestueuse, La Nanette, Les Petits Moulins à vent, Le Carillon de Cythère, Les Barricades mystérieuses, Les Tic-Toc-Choc ou Les Maillotins,* etc.). In 1716 he publ. an expository work pertaining to the execution of his clavecin pieces, *L'Art de toucher le clavecin,* which attained wide celebrity, and which influenced the keyboard style of Couperin's great contemporary, J.S. Bach. Couperin also introduced the trio sonata to France, his first works in this form being an imitation of Corelli. Later, in 1726, he publ. 4 sonatas, *Les Nations,* described as "Sonades" or "Suites de symphonies en trio," 3 of which are partial reworkings of earlier pieces. They are composed alternately in the strict primitive form, *sonata de chiesa,* and the more flexible composite of dance forms, *sonata de camera.* The 3rd of the series, *L'Impériale,* perhaps represents his most mature and inspired style. Living at a time during which the rivalry between French and Italian music reached its climax, Couperin sought to adapt the new Italian forms to his own personal, and essentially French, style. In his *Les Goûts réunis* (1724), a series of concerted pieces with strings very similar in form and spirit to the *Pièces de clavecin,* one finds titles such as *Sicilienne* and *Ritratto dell' amore.* In the following year he publ. an *Apothéose de Lully,* in which the rivals, Lully and Corelli, are made to unite for the furtherance of art. Couperin's style of composition was based on the basso continuo, the most important voices usually being the uppermost, carrying the melody, and the bass. Nevertheless, his music sometimes attains considerable complexity (on occasion requiring as many as 3 harpsichordists for its proper execution). His melodic invention, particularly in his use of the rondeau, was virtually inexhaustible, his themes swift and expressive. An outstanding feature was his inventive mode of ornamentation, in the "gallant style" of the period. In 1933 the Lyrebird Press in Paris publ. a "complete" ed. of Couperin's works, in 12 vols., under the chief editorship of Maurice Cauchie, assisted by P. Brunold, A. Gastoué, A. Tessier, and A. Schaeffner. The contents are as follows: Vol. I, Didactic works: *Règle pour l'accompagnement* and *L'Art de toucher le clavecin;* Vols. II–V, the 4 books of *Pièces de clavecin;* Vol. VI, *Pièces d'orgue consistantes en deux Messes;* Vols. VII–X, chamber music, including *Concerts royaux, Les Goûts réunis ou Nouveaux concerts à l'usage de toutes les sortes d'instruments de musique, Les Nations, Le Parnasse ou l'Apothéose de Corelli, Apothéose de Lully, Pièces de violes avec la basse chiffrée,* and *Sonades inédites;* Vols. XI and XII, secular vocal music and religious music I and II. More recent eds. are in the LePupitre series, vols. 8 (*Leçons de ténèbres;* 1968), 21–24 (*Pièces de clavecin,* books 1-4; 1969–72), 45 (*9 motets;* 1972), and 51

(*Pièces de violes;* 1974), also separate eds. of *Pièces de clavecin,* ed. by M. Cauchie (1968–72) and by K. Gilbert (1969–72).

Couperin, Gervais-François, 2nd son of **Armand-Louis;** b. Paris, May 22, 1759; d. there, March 11, 1826. He succeeded his brother, **Pierre-Louis,** as organist at St.-Gervais in 1789, also taking over his other appointments. He composed sonatas, variations, etc. He was the last of the Couperins to serve as organist at St.-Gervais, although his daughter, **Céleste** (b. 1793; d. Belleville, Feb. 14, 1860), played there at the time of her father's death. She was a teacher of singing and piano at Beauvais for about 10 years.

Couperin, Louis, b. Chaumes, c.1626; d. Paris, Aug. 29, 1661. He went to Paris with Chambonnières, whose pupil he was; in 1653 became organist of St.-Gervais, a post in which he was succeeded, without interruption, by other members and descendants of the Couperin family until 1826; from 1656, he was a violinist and violist in the orchs. of the court ballets, and musician of the Chambre du Roi. He composed *Pièces de clavecin, Carillons* for Organ, violin pieces, etc. He was one of the earliest of French composers for the harpsichord in the new harmonic style employing the basso continuo, possibly being preceded only by his teacher, Chambonnières. The Lyrebird Press in Paris publ. a "complete" edition of his works, ed. by P. Brunold. His *Pièces de clavecin* is publ. as vol. 18 of Le Pupitre (1970).

Couperin, Nicolas, son of **François de Crouilly;** b. Paris, Dec. 20, 1680; d. there, July 25, 1748. In 1733 he succeeded his cousin **François le Grand** as organist at St.-Gervais.

Couperin, Pierre-Louis (called **"M. Couperin l'aîné"** or **"Couperin fils"**), son of **Armand-Louis;** b. Paris, March 14, 1755; d. there, Oct. 10, 1789. He was organist to the King, later at Notre-Dame, St.-Jean, St.-Merry, and at St.-Gervais (succeeded his father early in 1789; died 8 months later). Some of his compositions were publ. in contemporary collections; others are in MS.

Courtois, Jean, Franco-Flemish contrapuntist of the first half of the 16th century. He was maître de chapelle at Cambrai Cathedral in 1539, when a 4-part motet of his, *Venite populi terrae,* was performed before Charles V of Spain. Many of his motets, Psalms, and songs appeared in publications of the period (printed at Paris, Lyons, Antwerp, Nuremberg, etc.); H. Expert reprinted some of his songs in Les Maîtres Musiciens de la Renaissance Française. Masses, motets, and songs in MS are in the Munich State Library and the library at Cambrai.

Coussemaker, Charles-Edmond-Henri de, French music scholar; b. Bailleul, Nord, April 19, 1805; d. Bourbourg, Jan. 10, 1876. He studied music as a child. His main profession was the law; while studying law at the Univ. of Paris, he took private lessons with Pellegrini in singing and Anton Reicha in harmony. He continued his studies with Lefebvre in Douai, after becoming a practicing lawyer. At this time (1831–35) he found leisure to compose music of the most varied description, all of which, with the exception of a few *romances* and 2 sets of songs, is unpubl., and apparently lost. His interest in history and archaeology led him to the study of the authentic documents of music; he was also influenced by the scholarly articles in *La Gazette et Revue Musicale* (then edited by Fétis). During successive terms as judge in Hazebrouck, Dunkirk, and Lille, he continued to accumulate knowledge of musical documentation; he assembled a vast library; 1,075 items in his library are listed in the *Catalogue de's livres, manuscrits et instruments de musique du feu M. Charles Coussemaker* (Brussels, 1877; issued for an auction).

WRITINGS: A great number of valuable treatises and collections: *Mémoire sur Hucbald* (Paris, 1841); *Notice sur les collections musicales de la bibliothèque de Cambrai . . .* (1843); "Essai sur les instruments de musique au moyen-âge," in Dindron, *Annales archéologiques,* illustrated; *Histoire de l'harmonie au moyen-âge* (1852); *Trois chants historiques* (1854); *Chants populaires des Flamands de France* (1856); *Drames liturgiques du moyen-âge* (1860); *Les Harmonistes des XIIe et XIIIe siècles* (1865); a great work, intended for a supplement to Gerbert, entitled *Scriptorum de musica medii ævi nova series* (4 vols., 1864–76; new ed., Graz, 1908; anastatic reprint, 1931, by *Bolletino Bibliografico Musicale*); *L'Art harmonique aux XIIe et XIIIe siècles* (1865); *Œuvres complètes d'Adam de la Halle* (1872); etc.

Coward, Sir Noel, British playwright and author of musical comedies; b. Teddington, Middlesex, Dec. 16, 1899; d. Port Maria, Jamaica, March 25, 1973. At the age of 11, he appeared on the stage, and was associated with the theater ever since, in the triple capacity of actor, playwright, and producer. Having had no formal education in music, he dictated his songs to a musical amanuensis. Among the musical comedies for which he wrote both words and music are *This Year of Grace* (N.Y., Nov. 7, 1928); *Bitter Sweet* (London, July 18, 1929); *Conversation Piece* (London, Feb. 16, 1934); *Pacific 1860* (London, Dec. 19, 1946); *Ace of Clubs* (London, July 7, 1950); *After the Ball,* to Wilde's *Lady Windermere's Fan* (London, June 10, 1954); 51 songs from his musical plays are publ. in the *Noel Coward Song Book* (N.Y., 1953) with the author's introduction. He also publ. an autobiography, *Present Indicative* (London, 1937); 2nd vol., *Future Indefinite* (London, 1954). He was knighted in 1970.

Coward, Sir Henry, English choral conductor; b. Liverpool, Nov. 26, 1849; d. Sheffield, June 10, 1944. He was apprenticed to be a cutler but attended classes of solfeggio. He organized a choral group at Sheffield and became its conductor. After a period of hard study, he obtained the B.Mus. degree at Oxford (1889), and later D.Mus. (1894). He organized spectacular choral festivals in Sheffield, in which thousands of choristers participated; gave concerts with his chorus in Germany (1906); in 1908 he presented 16 concerts in Canada with members of the Sheffield Choral Union, headed by him. There followed in 1911 a world tour, which included the U.S., Canada, Australia, and South Africa. Coward was the leader of choral groups at Leeds and Glasgow; acted as a judge at competition festivals. He was knighted in 1926. He composed several cantatas and other choral works; ed. a collection of Methodist hymns (1901); publ. *Choral Technique and Interpretation* (1914) and *Reminiscences* (1919).

Cowell, Henry Dixon, remarkable, innovative American composer; b. Menlo Park, Calif., March 11, 1897; d. Shady, N.Y., Dec. 10, 1965. His father, of Irish birth, was a member of a clergyman's family in Kildare; his mother was an American of progressive persuasion. Cowell studied violin with Henry Holmes in San Francisco; after the earthquake of 1906, his mother took him to N.Y., where they were compelled to seek support from the Society for the Improvement of the Condition of the Poor; they returned to Menlo Park, where Cowell was able to save enough money, earned from menial jobs, to buy a piano. He began to experiment with the keyboard by striking the keys with fists and forearms; he named such chords "tone clusters" and at the age of 13 composed a piece called *Adventures in Harmony,* containing such chords. Later he began experimenting in altering the sound of the piano by placing various objects on the strings, and also by playing directly under the lid of the piano *pizzicato* and *glissando.* He first exhibited these startling innovations on March 5, 1914, at the San Francisco Musical Society at the St. Francis Hotel, much to the consternation of its members, no doubt. The tone clusters per se were not new; they were used for special sound effects by composers in the 18th century to imitate thunder or cannon fire. The Russian composer Vladimir Rebikov applied them in his piano piece *Hymn to Inca,* and Charles Ives used them in his *Concord Sonata* to be sounded by covering a set of white or black keys with a wooden board. However, Cowell had a priority by systematizing tone clusters as harmonic amplifications of tonal chords, and he devised logical notation for them. The tone clusters eventually acquired legitimacy in the works of many European and American composers. Cowell also extended the sonorities of tone clusters to instrumental combinations and applied them in several of his symph. works. In the meantime Cowell did not neglect formal studies; he began taking lessons in composition with E.C. Strickland and Wallace Sabin at the Univ. of Calif. in Berkeley, and later with Frank Damrosch at the Inst. of Musical Art in N.Y., and privately, with Charles Seeger (1914–16). After brief service in the U.S. Army in 1918, where he was employed first as a cook and later as arranger for the U.S. Army Band, he became engaged professionally to give a series of lectures on new music, illustrated by his playing his own works on the piano. In 1928 he went to Russia, where he attracted considerable attention as the first American composer to visit there; some of his pieces were publ. in a Russian edition, the first such publications by an American. Upon return to the U.S., he was appointed lecturer on music at The New School in N.Y.

In 1931 he received a Guggenheim fellowship grant, and went to Berlin to study ethnomusicology with Erich von Hornbostel. This was the beginning of his serious study of ethnic musical materials. He had already experimented with some Indian and Chinese devices in some of his works; in his *Ensemble* for Strings (1924) he included Indian thundersticks; the piece naturally aroused considerable curiosity. In 1931 he formed a collaboration with the Russian electric engineer Leon Theremin, then visiting the U.S.; with his aid he constructed an ingenious instrument which he called the Rhythmicon; it made possible the simultaneous production of 16 different rhythms on 16 different pitch levels of the harmonic series. He demonstrated the Rhythmicon at a lecture-concert in San Francisco on May 15, 1932. He also wrote an extensive work entitled *Rhythmicana,* but it did not receive a performance until Dec. 3, 1971, at Stanford Univ., using advanced electronic techniques. In 1927 Cowell founded the *New Music Quarterly* for publication of ultramodern music, mainly by American composers.

Cowell's career was brutally interrupted in 1936, when he was arrested in California on largely contrived and falsified evidence, on charges of homosexuality (then a heinous offense in California) involving the impairment of the morals of a minor. Lulled by the deceptive promises of a wily district attorney of a brief confinement in a sanatorium, Cowell pleaded guilty to a limited offense, but he was vengefully given a maximum sentence of imprisonment, up to 15 years. Incarcerated at San Quentin, he was assigned to work in a jute mill, but indomitably continued to write music in prison. Thanks to interventions in his behalf by a number of eminent musicians, he was paroled in 1940 to Percy Grainger as a guarantor of his good conduct; he was pardoned in the spring of 1941. On Sept. 27, 1941, he married Sidney Robertson, a noted ethnomusicologist. He was now able to resume his full activities as editor and instructor; he held teaching positions at The New School for Social Research in N.Y. (1940–62), the Univ. of Southern Calif., Mills College, and the Peabody Cons. of Music in Baltimore (1951–56); was also appointed adjunct prof. at summer classes at Columbia Univ. (1951–65). In 1951 Cowell was elected a member of the National Academy of Arts and Letters; received an honorary Mus.D. from Wilmington College (1953) and from Monmouth (Ill.) College (1963). In 1956–57 he undertook a world tour with his wife through the Near East, India, and Japan, collecting rich prime materials for his compositions, which by now had acquired a decisive turn toward the use of ethnomusicological melodic and rhythmic materials, without abandoning, however, the experimental devices which were the signposts of most of his works.

In addition to his symph. and chamber music, Cowell publ. in 1930 an important book, *New Musical Resources.* He also edited a symposium, *American Composers on American Music;* in collaboration with his wife he wrote the basic biography of Charles Ives (1955).

WORKS: FOR THE STAGE: Unfinished opera, *O'Higgins of Chile* (1949); a pageant, *The Building of Bamba* (Halcyon, near Pismo Beach, Calif., Aug. 18, 1917).

16 HYMN AND FUGUING TUNES (based on fuguing tunes of William Billings): No. 1 for Band (1943); No. 2 for String Orch. (1944); No. 3 for Orch. (1944); No. 4 for 3 Instruments (1944); No. 5 for String Orch. (1945; version for Orch. incorporated into Symph. No. 10); No. 6 for Piano (1946); No. 7 for Viola and Piano (1946); No. 8 for String Quartet or String Orch. (1947–48); No. 9 for Cello and Piano (1950); No. 10 for Oboe and Strings (1955); No. 11, became *A Thanksgiving Psalm from the Dead Sea Scrolls* for Male Chorus and Orch. (1956); No. 12 for 3 Horns (1957); No. 13 for Trombone and Piano (1960); No. 14 for Organ (1961); No. 15 for 2 Violins or any combination (1961); No. 16 for Orch. (1965; posthumous, N.Y., Oct. 6, 1966).

20 SYMPHS.: No. 1 (1916–17); No. 2, *Anthropos* (*Mankind,* 1938); No. 3, *Gaelic Symphony* (1942); No. 4, *Short Symphony* (1946; Boston, Oct. 24, 1947); No. 5 (1948; Washington, D.C., Jan. 5, 1949); No. 6 (1950–55; Houston, Nov. 14, 1955); No. 7 (1952; Baltimore, Nov. 25, 1952); No. 8, *Choral,* for Chorus and Orch. (1952; Wilmington, Ohio, March 1, 1953); No. 9 (1953; Green Bay, Wis., March 14, 1954); No. 10 for Chamber Orch. (1953; U.S. premiere, N.Y., Feb. 24, 1957); No. 11, *Lines from the Dead Sea Scrolls* (1953; Louisville, May 29, 1954); No. 12 (1955–56; Houston, March 28, 1960); No. 13, *Madras Symphony,* for Small Orch. and 3 Indian Instruments (1957–58; Madras, India, March 3, 1959); No. 14 (1960–61; Washington, D.C., April 27, 1961); No. 15, *Thesis* (1961; Louisville Orch., Murray, Ky., Oct. 7, 1961); No. 16, *Icelandic Symphony* (1962; Reykjavik, March 21, 1963); No. 17, *Lancaster* (1962); No. 18 (1964); No. 19 (1965; Nashville, Oct. 18, 1965); No. 20 (1965).

OTHER WORKS FOR ORCH.: *Vestiges* (1914–20); *Some Music* (1915); *Some More Music* (1915–16); *Communication* (1920); Sinfonietta for Small Orch. (1924–28; Boston, Nov. 23, 1931, Slonimsky conducting); Suite for Solo String and Percussion Piano, and Chamber Orch. (1928; Boston, March 11, 1929, Slonimsky conducting; a scoring of the piano pieces *The Banshee, Leprechaun,* and *Fairy Bells* with Chamber Orch. accompaniment); Piano Concerto (1929; first complete perf., Havana, Cuba, Dec. 28, 1930; first complete U.S. perf., Omaha, Oct. 12, 1978); *Irish Suite* for Chamber Orch. (1929); *Polyphonica* for 12 Instruments (1930); *Synchrony* (1930; Paris, June 6, 1931, Slonimsky conducting); *Reel No. 1* and *No. 2* (1930, 1932); 2 *Appositions* for String Orch. (1931); *Rhythmicana,* Concerto for Rhythmicon and Orch. (1931; Stanford Univ. Orch., Dec. 3, 1971); 3 pieces for Chamber Orch.: *Competitive Sport, Steel and Stone,* and *Heroic Dance* (all 1931); *4 Continuations* for String Orch. (1933); *Old American Country Set* (1937; Indianapolis, Feb. 28, 1940);

American Melting Pot (1939); *Symphonic Set* (1939; orchestration of *Toccanta*); *Celtic Set* (1939; also for band); *Shoonthree* (*Sleep Music,* 1939; also for band); *Pastoral & Fiddler's Delight* (1940; N.Y., July 26, 1949, Stokowski conducting); *Ancient Desert Drone* (1940); *Tales of Our Countryside* for Piano and Orch. (1940; Atlantic City, May 11, 1941, Cowell, soloist; Stokowski conducting; based on piano pieces written 1922–30); *Vox Humana* (1940); *Little Concerto* for Piano, and Orch. or Band (1942; also known as *Concerto Piccolo;* Suite for Piano and String Orch. (1943); *American Pipers* (1943); *United Music* (1944); *Big Sing* (1945); *Festival Overture* for 2 Orchs. (1946); *Saturday Night at the Firehouse* (1948); *Aria* for Violin and String Orch. (1952); *Rondo* (1953); *Ballad* for Strings (1955); *Variations* (1956); *Persian Set* for 12 Instruments (1956–57); *Music 1957* (1957); *Ongaku* (1957; Louisville, March 26, 1958); *Antiphony* for 2 Orchs. (1958); Percussion Concerto (1958; Kansas City, Jan. 7, 1961); *Mela and Fair* (New Delhi, India, Dec. 11, 1959); *Characters* (1959); *Chiaroscuro* (1960); *Variations on Thirds* for 2 Solo Violas and Strings (1960); *Concerto Brevis* for Accordion and Orch. (1960); Harmonica Concerto (1960); *Air and Scherzo* for Saxophone and Small Orch. (1961); *Duo Concertante* for Flute, Harp, and Orch. (1961; Springfield, Ohio, Oct. 21, 1961); 2 koto concertos: No. 1 (1963; Philadelphia, Dec. 18, 1964) and No. 2 (1965); *Concerto Grosso* for 5 Instruments and Orch. (1963; Univ. of Miami, Fla., Jan. 12, 1964); Harp Concerto (1965); *Carol* (1965; new orchestration of slow movement of Koto Concerto No. 1).

OTHER WORKS FOR BAND: *A Curse and a Blessing* (1938); *Shoonthree* (1940; also for Orch.); *Celtic Set* (1943; originally for Orch., 1939); *Animal Magic* (1944); *Grandma's Rumba* (1945); *Fantaisie* (U.S. Military Academy Band, West Point, N.Y., May 30, 1952); *Singing Band* (1953).

OTHER WORKS FOR VOICE: *The Thistle Flower* for Women's Voices a cappella (1928); *Vocalise* for Voice, Flute, and Piano (1937); *Chrysanthemums* for Soprano, 2 Saxophones, and 4 Strings (1937); *Toccanta* for Soprano, Flute, Cello, and Piano (1938); *The Coming of Light* for Chorus a cappella (1939); *Fire and Ice,* after Frost's poem, for 4 Male Soloists, and Orch. or Band (1942); Sonatina for Baritone, Violin, and Piano (1942); *American Muse* for Soprano, Alto, and Piano (1943); *To America* for Chorus a cappella (1947); *The Commission,* cantata for 4 Soloists and Orch. (1954); *. . . if He Please* for Mixed and either Boys' or Women's Choruses, and Orch. (1954); Septet for 5 Voices without words, Clarinet, and Piano (1955–56); *A Thanksgiving Psalm from the Dead Sea Scrolls* for Male Chorus and Orch. (1956; originally *Hymn and Fuguing Tune* No. 11); *Edson Hymns and Fuguing Tunes* for Chorus and Orch. (1960); *The Creator* for Chorus and Orch. (1963); *Ultima Actio* for Chorus a cappella (1965).

OTHER CHAMBER WORKS: *Quartet Romantic* for 2 Flutes, Violin, and Viola (1915–17); 5 string quartets: No. 1, *Pedantic* (1915–16); *Quartet Euphometric* (1916–19); No. 3, *Movement* (1934); No. 4, *Mosaic* (1935); No. 5, *United* Quartet (1936), based on folk melodies of the world; No. 6 (1956; revised 1962);

also unnumbered *Ensemble* for 2 Violins, Viola, 2 Cellos, and 3 Thundersticks (1924; version for String Orch. without Thundersticks, 1959); 7 *Paragraphs* for String Trio (1925); Suite for Violin and Piano (1927); *Exultation* for 10 Strings (1928); Suite for Wind Quintet (1930); 3 works for Percussion: *Pulse, Return,* and *Ostinato Pianissimo* (1930–34); *6 Casual Developments* for Clarinet and Piano (1935); *Sound-form for Dance* for Flute, Clarinet, Bassoon, and Percussion (1936); *Sarabande* for Oboe, Clarinet, and Percussion (1937); *Trickster Coyote* for Flute and Percussion (1941); *Action in Brass* for 5 Brasses (1943); Violin Sonata (1945, revised 1947); Saxophone Quartet (1946); *Tall Tale* for Brass Sextet (1947); *Set for Two* for Violin and Piano (1948); *4 Declamations and Return* for Cello and Piano (1949); *Set of 5* for Violin, Piano, and Percussion (1951); *Set* for Harpsichord, Flute, Oboe, and Cello (1953); *Set of 2* for Harp and Violin (1955); *Homage to Iran* for Violin and Piano (1957); *Iridescent Rondo* for Solo Accordion (1959); *Air and Scherzo* for Saxophone and Piano (1961); Quartet for Flute, Oboe, Cello, and Harp (1962); *Gravely and Vigorously,* in memory of John F. Kennedy, for Solo Cello (1963); *26 Simultaneous Mosaics* for Violin, Cello, Clarinet, Piano, and Percussion (N.Y., Dec. 1, 1964); Piano Trio (1965); *Cleistogamy* (self-pollinating flowerlets), a collection of pieces written between 1941 and 1963.

FOR PIANO: *The Tides of Manaunaun* (1912); *Advertisements* (1914, revised 1959); *Dynamic Motion* (1914); *6 Ings: Floating-Fleeting-Wafting-Seething-Frisking-Scooting* (1916); *It Isn't It* (1922); *The Snows of Fujiyama* (1922); *Aeolian Harp* (1923); *Piece for Piano with Strings* (Paris, 1924); *The Banshee* (1925); *Lilt of the Reel* (1925); *Sinister Resonance* (1925); *Tiger* (1927); *2 Woofs* (1930); *Hilarious Curtain Opener and Ritournelle* (1937); hundreds of other pieces with similar fanciful titles; also some organ pieces.

WRITINGS: *New Musical Resources* (N.Y., 1930); ed., *American Composers on American Music: A Symposium* (Stanford, Calif., 1933; reprinted, N.Y., 1962); *Charles Ives and His Music* (N.Y., 1955; in collaboration with his wife, Sidney Cowell).

Cowen, Sir Frederic Hymen, English composer; b. Kingston, Jamaica, Jan. 29, 1852; d. London, Oct. 6, 1935. His evident talent for music caused his parents to take him to England to study at the age of 4. He was a pupil of Benedict and Goss in London; studied at Leipzig under Hauptmann, Moscheles, Reinecke, Richter, and Plaidy (1865–66); in Berlin under Kiel (1867–68); was conductor of the Phil. Society of London (1888–92), succeeding Sullivan, and again from 1900–7; was music director of the Melbourne Centennial Exhibition (1888–89); conductor of the Liverpool Phil. from 1896–1913; Sir Charles Hallé's successor as conductor of the Manchester Concerts (1896–99); conducted the Handel Triennial Festival (Crystal Palace, 1903–12); the Cardiff Festival (1902–10). He received the degree of Mus.Doc. from Edinburgh Univ. (1910); was knighted in 1911.

WORKS: 4 operas; *Pauline* (London, Nov. 22, 1876); *Thorgrim* (London, April 22, 1890); *Signa* (London, June 30, 1894); *Harold, or The Norman Conquest* (London, June 8, 1895); oratorios: *The Deluge* (1878); *St. Ursula* (1881); *Ruth* (1887); *The Veil* (Cardiff Festival, Sept. 20, 1910; his most successful work); cantatas. For Orch.: 6 symphs.: No.1, in C minor (1869); No.2, in F minor (1872); No. 3, in C minor, *Scandinavian* (1880); No. 4, in B-flat minor, *Welsh* (1884); No. 5, in F (1887); No. 6, in E, *Idyllic* (1897); 3 suites: *The Language of Flowers, In the Olden Time, In Fairyland;* Sinfonietta; Piano Concerto; 4 overtures; *Of Life and Love,* fantasy. Chamber music: 2 piano trios; 2 string quartets; piano pieces; over 250 songs; etc. He publ. his memoirs as *My Art and My Friends* (London, 1913), and an amusing glossary of musical terms, *Music as she is wrote* (London, 1915); also, for the Masterpieces of Music series, books (with biography and music) on Haydn, Mozart, Mendelssohn, and Rossini.

Cowie, Edward, English composer; b. Birmingham, Aug. 17, 1943. He studied at Trinity College, and later took courses at the univs. of Southampton and Leeds with Fricker, Goehr, and Lutoslawski. An artist of wide-ranging attainments, he studied not only music but also painting and ornithology; often his compositions portrayed his pictorial visions of birds, not by literal imitation or suggestion but rather through inner kinship; his intellectual inspirations were Leonardo da Vinci and Goethe in their universal thinking and practice. Eschewing musicological pedantry, he used techniques ranging from static triadic tonality to serialistic atonality, from abstract tonal formations to concrete references to external objects.

Craft, Robert, American conductor and brilliant writer on music; b. Kingston, N.Y., Oct. 20, 1923. He studied at the Juilliard School of Music and the Berkshire Music Center; took courses in conducting with Monteux. During World War II he was in the U.S. Army Medical Corps. In 1947 he conducted the N.Y. Brass and Woodwind Ensemble. A decisive turn in his career was his encounter with Stravinsky, whom he greatly impressed by his precise knowledge of Stravinsky's music; gradually he became Stravinsky's closest associate. He was also instrumental in persuading Stravinsky to adopt the 12-tone method of composition, a momentous turn in Stravinsky's creative path. He collaborated with Stravinsky on 6 vols. of a catechumenical and discursive nature: *Conversations with Igor Stravinsky* (N.Y., 1959); *Memories and Commentaries* (N.Y., 1960); *Expositions and Developments* (N.Y., 1962); *Dialogues and a Diary* (N.Y., 1963); *Themes and Episodes* (N.Y., 1967); *Retrospections and Conclusions* (N.Y., 1969). Resentful of frequent referral to him as a musical Boswell, Craft insists that his collaboration with Stravinsky was more akin to that between the Goncourt brothers, both acting and reacting to an emerging topic of discussion, with Stravinsky evoking his ancient memories in his careful English, or fluent French, spiced with unrestrained discourtesies toward professional colleagues on the American scene, and Craft reifying the material with an analeptic bulimia of quaquaversal literary, psychological, physiological, and culinary references in a flow of finely ordered dialogue. His other publications include *Prejudices in Disguise* (N.Y., 1974); *Stravinsky in Photographs and Documents* (London, 1976; N.Y., 1978); *Current Convictions: Views and Reviews* (N.Y.,1977).

Cramer, Johann Baptist, famous German pianist and pedagogue, eldest son of **Wilhelm Cramer;** b. Mannheim, Feb. 24, 1771; d. London, April 16, 1858. He was brought to London as an infant, and throughout his life regarded it as his home. He received a fine musical education, first from his father, then from Clementi (1783–84) and C.F. Abel (1785). He began to travel as a concert pianist in 1788; visited Vienna, where he met Haydn and Beethoven (1799–1800); in later years (1832–45) spent considerable time as a teacher in Munich and Paris, finally returning to London. His greatest work is his piano method,*Grosse Praktische Pianoforte Schule* (1815) in 5 parts, the last of which, *84 Studies* (op. 50; later revised and publ. as op. 81, including *16 nouvelles études*) is famous in piano pedagogy. Hans von Bülow made a selection of 50 studies from this collection, later revised and annotated in collections of 52 and 60; Henselt issued a different selection, with accompaniment of a 2nd piano; other eds. of Cramer's studies are by Coccius, Riemann, Pauer, Lack, and Lickl; *100 Progressive Etudes* is also well known. Apart from his pedagogic collections, Cramer wrote 9 piano concertos; over 50 piano sonatas; 2 piano quartets; 2 piano quintets; and numerous piano pieces of the salon type; but all these are quite forgotten, while his piano studies, with those of Czerny, maintained their value for more than a century. He first entered the music publishing business in 1805, as head of the firm Cramer & Keys; was in partnership with Samuel Chappell (1810–19). In 1824, together with R. Addison and T.F. Beale, Cramer established a music publishing house (now J.B. Cramer & Co., Ltd.), of which he was director until 1842; in 1844 Addison retired and was succeeded by W. Chappell, the firm then becoming Cramer, Beale & Chappell; after Cramer's death in 1858, and Chappell's retirement in 1861, G. Wood became Beale's partner; about 1862 the firm began to devote much attention to the manufacture of pianos; on Beale's death in 1863, Wood became sole director, continuing it successfully until his death in 1893, although devoting more consideration to piano manufacture than to music publishing. His 2 nephews succeeded him. In 1897 the firm became a limited company.

Cramer, Wilhelm, German violinist, father of **Johann Baptist Cramer;** b. Mannheim, June (baptized, June 2) 1746; d. London, Oct. 5, 1799. He received his musical training from his father, Jacob Cramer (1705–70), who was a violinist in the Mannheim Orch., and also studied with Johann Stamitz and Cannabich; in 1752–69 he was a member of the Mannheim Orch.; then went to Paris. In 1772 he

went to London, where he became a successful violinist and conductor. He was concertmaster of the orch. of the Anacreontic Society during its most prestigious years (1773–91); was chamber musician to the King. He wrote 11 violin concertos, 6 string quartets, 6 violin sonatas, and other string music.

Cras, Jean Emile Paul, French composer; b. Brest, May 22, 1879; d. there, Sept. 14, 1932. He was an officer in the French navy, reaching the rank of vice-admiral; he grew up in a musical atmosphere and when still a child began to compose; took lessons with Henri Duparc. Under the influence of Duparc's style, Cras composed a number of miniatures in an impressionistic vein; he was at his best in lyrical songs and instrumental pieces. WORKS: Opera, *Polyphème* (Paris, Opéra-Comique, Dec. 28, 1922; won the Prize of the City of Paris); *Journal de Bord,* symph. suite (1927); *Légende* for Cello and Orch. (1929); Piano Concerto (1931); for Voice and Orch.: *L'Offrande lyrique* (1920); *Fontaines* (1923); *3 Noëls* (1929); many pieces of chamber music; a number of songs.

Crawford, Ruth Porter, remarkable American composer; b. East Liverpool, Ohio, July 3, 1901; d. Chevy Chase, Md., Nov. 18, 1953. She studied composition with **Charles Seeger,** whom she later married; her principal piano teacher was Heniot Lévy. She dedicated herself to teaching and to collecting American folk songs; when still very young, she taught at the School of Musical Arts in Jacksonville, Fla. (1918–21); then gave courses at the American Cons. in Chicago (1925–29) and at the Elmhurst College of Music in Illinois (1926–29). In 1930 she received a Guggenheim fellowship. She became known mainly as a compiler of American folk songs; publ. *American Folk Songs for Children* (1948), *Animal Folk Songs for Children* (1950), and *American Folk Songs for Christmas* (1953). Her own compositions, astonishingly bold in their experimental aperçus and insights, often anticipated many techniques of the future avant-garde; while rarely performed during her lifetime, they had a remarkable revival in the subsequent decades. WORKS: Violin Sonata (1926); Suite for Piano and Woodwind Quintet (1927; perf. for the first time in Cambridge, Mass., Dec. 14, 1975); *4 Diaphonic Suites* for Various Instruments (1930); *3 Songs* for Contralto, Oboe, Percussion, and Piano, to words by Carl Sandburg (*Rat Riddles; Prayers of Steel; In Tall Grass;* perf. at the Amsterdam Festival of the International Society for Contemporary Music, June 15, 1933); String Quartet (1931; contains a slow movement anticipating the "static" harmonies and "phase shifts"); *Sacco and Vanzetti* for Chorus (Workers' Olympiad, 1933); *Risselty Rosselty* for Small Orch. (1941); Suite for Wind Quintet (1952); several sets of piano pieces; *2 Ricercari* for Voice and Piano (*Sacco, Vanzetti; Chinaman, Laundryman;* 1932).

Crécquillon (Créquillon), Thomas, Franco-Flemish contrapuntist; b. probably in Ghent; d. Béthune,

1557. It is known that he was maître de chapelle at Béthune in 1540; was court musician to Charles V of Spain; later was canon at Namur, Termonde, and Béthune. His works, which rank with the best of that period, consist of 16 masses in 4 and 5 parts, 116 motets, *cantiones,* and 192 French chansons in 4, 5, and 6 parts. Reprints appear in Commer's *Collectio operum musicorum Batavorum saeculi XVI* and Maldeghem's *Trésor musical.* An edition of his works was publ. by N. Bridgman and B. Hudson, *Thomas Crécquillon: Opera omnia,* in Corpus Mensurabilis Musicae, LXIII/1 (1974—). For a complete list of his works (publ. mostly between 1545 and 1636) and a detailed bibliography, see the article on him in *Die Musik in Geschichte und Gegenwart.*

Crescentini, Girolamo, one of the last and finest of the Italian artificial mezzo-sopranos; b. Urbania, near Urbino, Feb. 2, 1762; d. Naples, April 24, 1846. He studied singing with Gibelli at Bologna, and made a highly successful debut at Rome in 1783; subsequent successes in other European capitals earned him the surname of "Orfeo Italiano." He sang at Livorno, Padua, Venice, Turin, London (1786), Milan, and Naples (1788–89). Napoleon, having heard him in 1805, decorated him with the Iron Crown, and engaged him to teach singing to his family in 1806–12; Crescentini then retired from the stage and left Paris, on account of vocal disorders induced by the climate; in 1816 he became a prof. of singing in the Royal Cons. in Naples. Cimarosa wrote his *Orazi e Curiazi* for him. Crescentini publ. several collections of *Ariette* (Vienna, 1797) and a *Treatise on Vocalization in France and Italy,* with vocal exercises (Paris, 1811).

Crespin, Régine, French soprano; b. Marseilles, Feb. 23, 1927. She studied pharmacology; then began taking voice lessons with Suzanne Cesbron-Viseur and Georges Jouatte in Paris. She made her debut in Mulhouse as Elsa in 1950 and then sang at the Paris Opéra. She later acquired a European reputation as one of the best Wagnerian singers; she sang Kundry in *Parsifal* at the Bayreuth Festivals (1958–60); appeared also at La Scala in Milan, at Covent Garden in London, and on Nov. 19, 1962, made her debut with the Metropolitan Opera in N.Y. in the role of the Marschallin in *Der Rosenkavalier;* she remained on the staff of the Metropolitan since 1971; sang the parts of Elsa in *Lohengrin,* Sieglinde in *Die Walküre,* and Amelia in *Un ballo in maschera.*; also appeared as a concert singer. Her sonorous, somewhat somber voice suits dramatic parts excellently.

Creston, Paul (real name, **Giuseppe Guttoveggio**), distinguished American composer; b. New York, Oct. 10, 1906. He studied piano with Randegger and Déthier and organ playing with Yon; he was essentially autodidact in composition. He adopted the name Creston, an anglicized version of his high-school nickname, Crespino, a role he acted in a play. He began to compose tentatively at the age of 8, but he did not compose his full-fledged first opus, 5 *Dances* for piano, until he was 26. In 1938 he obtained a Guggenheim fellowship, and in a few years advanced to the front ranks of American composers, with an impressive catalogue of major works. He filled various jobs as a theater organist for silent movies; then obtained the post of organist at St. Malachy's Church in N.Y. (1934–67); concurrently he taught at the N.Y. College of Music (1963–67). From 1968–75 he was a prof. of music at Central Washington State College. In 1976 he moved to San Diego. He has written more than 100 major compositions, including 6 symphs. and 15 concertos for various instruments, as well as 35 other symph. works, chamber music for various instrumental combinations, choral works, piano pieces, and songs. His music is characterized by engaging spontaneity, with strong melodic lines and full-bodied harmonies; his instrumental writing is highly advantageous for virtuoso performance. He publ. 2 books: *Principles of Rhythm* (N.Y., 1964) and *Creative Harmony* (N.Y., 1970). In his theoretical writings, he militates against the illogic of binary meters and proposes to introduce such time signatures as 6/12 or 3/9; some of these metrical designations he uses in his own works.

WORKS: FOR ORCH.: 6 symphs.: No. 1 (N.Y., Feb. 22, 1941; received N.Y. Music Critics' Circle Award); No. 2 (N.Y., Feb. 15, 1945; highly successful); No. 3 (Worcester Festival, Oct. 27, 1950); No. 4 (Washington, D.C., Jan. 30, 1952); No. 5 (Washington, April 4, 1956); No. 6 for Organ and Orch. (Washington, June 28, 1982); Partita for Flute, Violin, and Strings (1937); *Threnody* for Orch. (1938); 2 *Choric Dances* for Woodwinds, Piano, Percussion, and Strings (1938); Concertino for Marimba and Orch. (1940); *Prelude and Dance* for Piano, Strings, and Orch. (1941); *Pastorale and Tarantella* for Piano, Strings, and Orch. (1941); Saxophone Concerto (1941; N.Y., Jan. 27, 1944); *A Rumor,* symph. sketch (N.Y., Dec. 13, 1941); *Dance Variations* for Soprano and Orch. (1942); *Frontiers* for Orch. (Toronto, Oct. 14, 1943); *Poem* for Harp and Orch. (1945); Fantasy for Trombone and Orch. (Los Angeles, Feb. 12, 1948); Piano Concerto (1949); Concerto for 2 Pianos and Orch. (1951; Montevallo, Ala., Nov. 18, 1968); *Walt Whitman,* symph. poem (1952); *Invocation and Dance* for Orch. (Louisville, Ky., May 15, 1954); *Dance Overture* (1954); *Lydian Ode* (1956); Violin Concerto No. 1 (1956; Detroit, Jan. 14, 1960); Toccata (1957); *Pre-Classic Suite* for Orch. (New Orleans, April 3, 1958); Accordion Concerto (1958); *Janus* for Orch. (Denver, July 17, 1959); Violin Concerto No. 2 (Los Angeles, Nov. 17, 1960); *Corinthians XIII,* symph. poem (Phoenix, March 30, 1964); *Choreografic Suite* for Orch. (1966); *Pavane Variations* for Orch. (La Jolla, Calif., Aug. 21, 1966); *Chthonic Ode,* an "homage to Henry Moore" (Detroit, April 6, 1967); *The Psalmist* for Contralto and Orch. (1967); *Anatolia (Turkish Rhapsody)* for Symph. Band (1967); *Thanatopsis* for Orch. (1971); *Square Dance 76* for Wind Symph. Orch. (1975); *Suite for Strings* (1978); *Sadhana,* op. 117, for Cello and Chamber Orch., inspired by the philosophy of the Indian poet Rabindranath Tagore, cast in the form of a theme and variations (Los Angeles, Oct. 3, 1981).

CHAMBER MUSIC: Suite for Saxophone and Piano (1935); String Quartet (1936); Suite for Viola and Piano (1937); Suite for Violin and Piano (1939); Sonata for Saxophone and Piano (1939); Suite for Flute, Viola, and Piano (1952); Suite for Cello and Piano (1956); Concertino for Piano and Woodwind Quintet (1969); *Ceremonial* for Percussion Ensemble (1972); *Rapsodie* for Saxophone and Organ (1976); Trio for Piano, Violin, and Cello (1979).

CHORAL WORKS: *3 Chorales from Tagore* (1936); *Requiem Mass* for Tenor, Bass, and Organ (1938); *Missa Solemnis* (1949); *Isaiah's Prophecy*, Christmas oratorio (1961); *The Northwest* for Chorus and Orch. (1969); *Hyas Illahee* for Chorus and Orch. (Shreveport, La., March 14, 1976); *Thanksgiving Anthem* for Chorus and Orch. (1982); also liturgical vocal works, with piano or organ accompaniment; piano pieces (*5 Little Dances, 5 Inventions*, etc.).

Crist, Bainbridge, American composer; b. Lawrenceburg, Ind., Feb. 13, 1883; d. Barnstable, Mass., Feb. 7, 1969. He studied piano and flute; later law at the George Washington Univ. (LL.B.); was a lawyer in Boston for 6 years (until 1912), continuing his music as an avocation. He went to Europe to complete his musical training (theory with P. Juon in Berlin and C. Landi in London, and singing with William Shakespeare); he taught singing in Boston (1915–21) and Washington, D.C. (1922–23); returned to Europe (1923) and spent 4 years in Florence, Paris, Lucerne, and Berlin; then came back to the U.S. and settled in Washington.

Cristofori, Bartolommeo, celebrated Italian instrument maker; b. Padua, May 4, 1655; d. Florence, Jan. 27, 1731. He was the inventor of the first practical piano as opposed to the clavichord (which also employs a type of hammer action), although 2-keyed instruments called "Piano e Forte" are known to have existed in Modena in 1598, and a 4-octave keyboard instrument shaped like a dulcimer, with small hammers and no dampers, dating from 1610, is yet in existence. He was a leading maker of clavicembali in Padua; about 1690 went to Florence, where he was instrument maker to Ferdinando de' Medici; on the latter's death in 1713, he was made custodian of the court collection of instruments by Cosimo III. According to an article by Maffei (publ. 1711, *Giornale dei Letterati d'Italia*), Cristofori had up to that year made 3 "gravecembali col piano e forte," these having, instead of the usual jacks plucking the strings with quills, a row of little hammers striking the strings from below. The principle of this hammer action was adopted, in the main, by Gottfried Silbermann, the Streichers, and Broadwood (hence called the "English action"). Following the designation by its inventor, the new instrument was named piano-forte. A piano of Cristofori's make is in the possession of the Metropolitan Museum of Art in N.Y.

Crivelli, Giovanni Battista, Italian composer of the Lombardy school; b. Scandiano, Modena; d. Modena, 1652. He was organist at the Reggio Emilia

Cathedral (1614–19); then served as director at the Accademia dello Spirito Santo in Ferrara (1626); subsequently was organist at the electoral court in Munich. He became maestro di cappella at the Milan Cathedral (1638–42) and at S. Maria Maggiore in Bergamo (1642–48). He publ. *Motetti concertati* (1626; 3rd ed., 1635) and *Madrigali concertati* (1626; 2nd ed., 1633).

Croce, Giovanni, eminent Venetian composer; b. Chioggia (hence surnamed "**il Chiozzotto**"), c.1560; d. Venice, May 15, 1609. He was a pupil of Zarlino; was chorister at San Marco; succeeded Donato as maestro di cappella there in 1603.

WORKS: Sonatas *a* 5 (1580); 2 vols. of motets *a* 8 (1589, 1590; vol. II reprinted 1605 with organ bass; both vols. with organ bass in 1607); 2 vols. of madrigals *a* 5 (1585, 1588); *Triacca musicale* (caprices, or humorous songs in Venetian dialect, *a* 4–7; went through 4 eds. (1596, 1601, 1607, 1609), and was his most popular and famous work; it includes the contest between the cuckoo and the nightingale, judged by the parrot); madrigals *a* 5–6 (1590–1607); *Cantiones sacrae a* 8, with Basso Continuo, for Organ (1622; a 2nd vol. was publ. in 1623); canzonette *a* 4 (1588; new eds., 1595, 1598); masses *a* 8 (1596); Lamentations *a* 4 (1603, 1605) and *a* 6 (1610); Magnificats *a* 6 (1605); vesper psalms *a* 8 (1589); etc. Younge printed some of Croce's madrigals in his *Musica Transalpina* (1588), and a selection of his church music was publ. with Eng. words as *Musica sacra, Penetentials for 6 voyces,* in London in 1608. Modern reprints include 3 masses publ. at Regensburg in 1888, 1891, and 1899, and other works in Proske's *Musica Divina*, Haberl's *Repertorium*, Torchi's *L'Arte musicale in Italia*, Bäuerle's *12 Hymnen und Motetten alter Meister*, and the publications of the Motet Society (London).

Croft (or **Crofts**), **William,** English organist and composer; b. Nether Ettington, Warwickshire (baptized, Dec. 30), 1678; d. Bath, Aug. 14, 1727 (buried in Westminster Abbey). He was a chorister in the Chapel Royal, under Dr. Blow; became a Gentleman of the Chapel Royal in 1700, and (with J. Clarke) joint organist in 1707; he succeeded Blow as organist of Westminster Abbey, Master of the Children, and Composer of the Chapel Royal (1708).

WORKS: *Musica sacra,* numerous anthems *a* 2–8, and a burial service in score (1724; in 2 vols.; the first English work of church music engraved in score on plates); *Musicus apparatus academicus* (2 odes written for his degree of Mus.Doc., received from Oxford, 1713); overtures and act tunes for several plays; violin sonatas; flute sonatas; etc. Modern editions include H. Ferguson and C. Hogwood, eds., *William Croft: Complete Harpsichord Works* (London, 1974); R. Platt, ed., *William Croft: Complete Organ Works* (London, 1976–77).

Crooks, Richard Alexander, American tenor; b. Trenton, N.J., June 26, 1900; d. Portola Valley, Calif., Sept. 29, 1972. He studied voice for 5 years with Sydney H. Bourne and also took lessons with Frank La

Forge; was a boy soprano soloist in N.Y. churches, later tenor soloist; after his war service, made his debut with the N.Y. Symph. Orch. under Damrosch in 1922; gave concerts in London, Vienna, Munich, Berlin, and in the U.S. (1925–27); made his American debut as Cavaradossi with the Philadelphia Grand Opera Co. (Nov. 27, 1930); debut as Des Grieux at the Metropolitan Opera (Feb. 25, 1933); toured Australia (1936–39); gave concerts from coast to coast in the U.S. and Canada; appeared in recitals, as an orch. soloist, and in festivals.

Crosby, Bing (real name, **Harry Lillis**), popular American singer; b. Tacoma, Wash., May 2, 1901; d. while playing golf at La Moraleja golf course outside Madrid, Oct. 14, 1977. He was a drummer in school bands; intermittently attended classes in law at Gonzaga Univ. in Spokane, Wash.; when he became famous, the school gave him an honorary degree of doctor of music. In 1926 he went to Los Angeles, where he filled engagements as a singer. He made his mark on the radio, and his success grew apace; he used his limited vocal resources to advantage by a cunning projection of deep thoracic undertones. He never deviated from his style of singing—unpretentious, sometimes mock-sentimental, and invariably communicative; he became a glorified crooner. Apart from his appearances in concert and with bands, he also made movies; his series with Bob Hope, beginning with *Road to Morocco,* made in 1942, with their invariable girl companion Dorothy Lamour, became classics of the American cinema. He continued his appearances until the last months of his life. The origin of his nickname is in dispute; it was derived either from the popular comic strip "The Bingville Bugle," or from his habit of popping a wooden gun in school, shouting, "Bing! Bing!" In 1953 he publ. his autobiography under the title *Call Me Lucky.* His brother **Bob Crosby** is a bandleader; Bing Crosby's 4 sons from his first marriage are also crooners.

Cross, Joan, English soprano; b. London, Sept. 7, 1900. She was educated at Trinity College, London. In 1931 she joined Sadler's Wells Opera; also appeared at Covent Garden. Subsequently she helped to found the English Opera Group in London, devoted to performances of new works; sang in several first performances of Benjamin Britten's operas. In 1948 she founded the Opera School (now the National School of Opera), serving as one of its teachers for many years. In 1955 she began to produce opera at Sadler's Wells and Covent Garden.

Cross, Lowell Merlin, American composer and electro-musicologist; b. Kingsville, Texas, June 24, 1938. He studied mathematics and music at Texas Technological College, graduating in 1963; then entered the Univ. of Toronto in Canada, obtaining his M.A. in musicology in 1968; attended classes of Marshall McLuhan in environmental technology there; took a course in electronic music with Myron Schaeffer and Gustav Ciamaga. In 1970 he served as resident programmer for Experiments in Art and Technology at Expo '70 in Osaka, Japan, and guest consultant in electronic music at the National Inst. of Design in Ahmedabad, India; in 1971 he was engaged as artist-in-residence at the Univ. of Iowa's Center for New Performing Arts. Eschewing any preliminary serial experimentation, Cross espoused a cybernetic totality of audiovisual, electronic, and theatrical arts.
WORKS: *4 Random Studies* for Tape (1961); *0.8 Century* for Tape (1962); *Eclectic Music* for Flute and Piano (1964); *Antiphonies* for Tape (1964); *After Long Silence* for Soprano and Quadraphonic Tape (1964); *3 Etudes* for Tape (1965); *Video I* and *Video II* for Variable Media, including Tape, Audio System, Oscilloscope, and Television (1965–68); *Musica Instrumentalis* for Acoustical Stereophonic Instruments, Monochrome and Polychrome Television (1965–68); *Video III* for Television and Phase-derived Audio System (1968); *Reunion* for Electronic Chessboard (constructed by Cross and first demonstrated in Toronto, March 5, 1968, the main opponents in the chess game being John Cage and the painter Marcel Duchamp, who won readily); *Electro-Acustica* for Instruments, Laser Deflection System, Television, and Phase-Derived Audio System (1970–71). The notation of Cross's audiovisual compositions consists of color photographs of television images resulting from the programmed manipulation of sound-producing mechanisms in the acoustical space (see his technical paper *Audio/Video/Laser,* publ. in *Source,* Sacramento, Calif., No. 8, 1970). He compiled a valuable manual, *A Bibliography of Electronic Music* (Toronto, 1967). As a pioneer in astromusicology, he created the selenogeodesic score *Lunar Laser Beam* (broadcast as a salutatory message on Nicolas Slonimsky's 77th birthday, April 27, 1971, purportedly via Leningrad, the subject's birthplace; the Sea of Tranquillity on the moon; and the Ciudad de Nuestra Señora Reina de Los Angeles in California). As director of the Video/Laser Laboratory at the Univ. of Iowa, Cross was responsible for the production of Scriabin's *Prometheus* by the Iowa Univ. Orch., conducted by James Dixon, with color projections coordinated with the "color organ" *(luce)* as prescribed in the score (Iowa City, Sept. 24, 1975).

Crosse, Gordon, English composer; b. Bury, Lancashire, Dec. 1, 1937. He studied at Oxford Univ., where he took courses in music history with Egon Wellesz; did postgraduate work in medieval music. In 1962 he went to Rome, where he attended the classes of Goffredo Petrassi at the Santa Cecilia Academy. Returning to England, he taught at Birmingham Univ. (extramurally); in 1969 was appointed to the music dept. of Essex Univ. His absorption in the studies of old music, in combination with an engrossment in modern techniques, determines the character of his own compositions.
WORKS: *Concerto da camera* for Violin and Orch. (Violin Concerto No. 1, 1962; London, Feb. 18, 1968); *Carol* for Flute and Piano (1962); *For the Unfallen* for Tenor, Horn, and Strings (1963; Liverpool, Sept. 17, 1968); *Meet My Folks,* a multi-child presen-

tation for Voices, Instruments, and Adults (1964); Symphs. for Chamber Orch. (Birmingham, Feb. 13, 1965); *Sinfonia Concertante* for Orch. (Cheltenham, July 15, 1965); *Changes,* nocturnal cycle for Soprano, Baritone, Chorus, and Orch. (1965); *Purgatory,* opera after Yeats (Cheltenham, July 7, 1966); *Ceremony* for Cello and Orch. (London, Aug. 4, 1966); *The Grace of Todd,* one-act opera (Aldeburgh, June 7, 1967); *The Demon of Adachigahara* for Speaker, Adolescent Chorus, Mime, and Instruments (1968); Concerto for Chamber Orch. (Budapest, July 3, 1968); Violin Concerto No. 2 (Oxford, Jan. 29, 1970); *The History of the Flood* for Children's Voices and Harp (London, Dec. 6, 1970); *Some Marches on a Ground* for Orch. (1970); *Memories of Morning: Night,* monodrama for Soprano and Orch. (London, Dec. 8, 1971); *Wheel of the World,* "entertainment" based on Chaucer's *Canterbury Tales,* for Actors, Children's Chorus, Mixed Chorus, and Orch. (Aldeburgh Festival, June 5, 1972); *Ariadne* for Solo Oboe and 12 Players (Cheltenham Festival, July 11, 1972); *The Story of Vasco,* opera (London, March 13, 1974); *Celebration* for Chorus (London, Sept. 16, 1974); *Holly from the Bongs,* opera (Manchester, Dec. 9, 1974); *Potter Thompson,* children's opera (London, Jan. 9, 1975); Symph. No. 2 (London, May 27, 1975); *Epiphany Variations: Double Variations for Orchestra* (N.Y., March 18, 1976); *Playground* for Orch. (1977; Manchester, March 2, 1978); *Wildboy* for Clarinet and Ensemble (1977; version for Full Orch., 1980); *Dreamsongs* for Chamber Orch. (1978); Cello Concerto (1979); String Quartet (1980); sacred and secular choruses.

Crossley-Holland, Peter, English ethnomusicologist and composer; b. London, Jan. 28, 1916. He studied physiology at St. John's College, Oxford (B.A., 1936; M.A., 1941); then took courses in composition with Ireland, Seiber, and Julius Harrison at the Royal College of Music in London (B.Mus., 1943); subsequently pursued postgraduate work in Indian music at the London School of Oriental and African Studies. From 1943 to 1945 he was regional director of the British Arts Council; in 1948–63 was engaged in the music division of the BBC; then became assistant director of the Inst. of Comparative Music Studies and Documentation in Berlin. In 1969 he joined the faculty at the Univ. of Calif. in Los Angeles; became a prof. there in 1972; retired in 1984. In 1965 he became editor of the *Journal of the International Folk Music Council.* As an ethnomusicologist, he has concentrated mostly on Celtic, Tibetan, and native American music. He edited *Music in Wales* (London, 1948) and *Artistic Values in Traditional Music* (Berlin, 1966); also publ. *Music: A Report on Musical Life in England* (London, 1949). He composed songs; also pieces for chorus and for recorders.

Crotch, William, eminent English composer; b. Norwich, July 5, 1775; d. Taunton, Dec. 29, 1847. His extraordinary precocity may be measured by the well-authenticated statement (Burney's paper, "Account of an Infant Musician," in the *Philosophical*

Transactions of 1779) that when 2 and a half years old he played on a small organ built by his father, a master carpenter. In 1779, he was brought to London, and played in public. At the age of 11 he became assistant to Dr. Randall, organist of Trinity and King's colleges at Cambridge; at 14, he composed an oratorio, *The Captivity of Judah* (Cambridge, June 4, 1789); he then studied for the ministry (1788–90); returning to music, he was organist of Christ Church, Oxford; graduated from Oxford with a Mus.Bac. in 1794; received a Mus.Doc. in 1799. In 1797 he succeeded Hayes as prof. of music at the Univ. and as organist of St. John's College. Crotch lectured in the Music School (1800–4), and in the Royal Institution in London (1804, 1805, 1807, and again from 1820); was principal of the new Royal Academy of Music from 1822 to 1832.

WORKS: 2 oratorios: *Palestine* (London, April 21, 1812) and *The Captivity of Judah* (Oxford, June 10, 1834; a different work from his juvenile oratorio of the same name); 10 anthems (1798); 3 organ concertos; piano sonatas; an ode, *Mona on Snowdown calls;* a glee, *Nymph, with thee;* a motet, *Methinks I hear the full celestial choir* (these last 3 were very popular); other odes; other glees, fugues; he also wrote *Elements of Musical Composition* (London, 1812; reprint, 1833; 2nd ed., 1856); *Practical Thorough-bass;* etc. A complete list of his compositions appeared in *Musical News* (April 17 and 24, 1897). The Crotch Society of London promotes research and performances.

Crouch, Frederick Nicholls, English conductor and composer; b. London, July 31, 1808; d. Portland, Maine, Aug. 18, 1896. He studied with Bochsa (cello), and entered the Royal Academy of Music in 1822 (teachers: Crotch, Attwood, Howes, Lindley, and Crivelli). At the age of 9 he was a cellist in the Royal Coburg Theater; played in Queen Adelaide's private band till 1832; was a teacher and singer in Plymouth, and cellist in various theaters. He went to N.Y. in 1849; was in Philadelphia in 1856 as conductor of Mrs. Rush's Saturday Concerts; served in the Confederate Army, and settled in Baltimore as a singing teacher. Cora Pearl, the famous Parisian courtesan of the Second Empire, was his daughter. He composed 2 operas; many collections of songs, some original (including the well-known *Kathleen Mavourneen*).

Crüger, Johann, noted German composer of church music; b. Grossbreesen, near Guben, April 9, 1598; d. Berlin, Feb. 23, 1662. A student of divinity at Wittenberg in 1620, he had received thorough musical training at Regensburg under Paulus Homberger. He then traveled in Austria and Hungary; spent some time in Bohemia and Saxony before settling in Berlin, where he was cantor at the Nicolaikirche from 1622 until his death. His fame rests on the composition of many fine chorales (*Jesu, meine Freude; Jesu, meine Zuversicht; Nun danket alle Gott;* etc.), which were originally publ. in the collection *Praxis pietatis melica* (Berlin, 1644; reprinted in 45 eds. before 1736). In addition, he publ. the following collections: *Neues vollkömmliches Gesangbuch Augsburgischer Konfession* ... (1640); *Geistliche Kirchenmelodeyen* ... (1649); *Dr. M. Luthers wie auch andrer gottseliger christlicher Leute Geistliche Lieder und Psalmen* (1657); *Psalmodia sacra* ... (1658); the valuable theoretical works *Synopsis musica* (1630; enlarged 1634), *Praecepta musicae figuralis* (1625), and *Quaestiones musicae practicae* (1650).

Crumb, George (Henry Jr.), distinguished and innovative American composer; b. Charleston, W.Va., Oct. 24, 1929. He was brought up in a musical environment; his father played the clarinet and his mother was a cellist; he studied music at home; began composing while in school, and had some of his pieces performed by the Charleston Symph. Orch. He then took courses in composition at Mason College in Charleston (B.M., 1950); later enrolled at the Univ. of Illinois (M.M., 1952) and continued his studies in composition with Ross Lee Finney at the Univ. of Michigan (D.M.A., 1959); in 1955 he received a Fulbright fellowship for travel to Germany, where he studied with Boris Blacher at the Berlin Hochschule für Musik. He further received grants from the Rockefeller (1964), Koussevitzky (1965), and Coolidge (1970) foundations; in 1967 held a Guggenheim fellowship, and also was given the National Inst. of Arts and Letters Award. In 1968 he was awarded the Pulitzer Prize in music for his *Echoes of Time and the River.* Parallel to working on his compositions, he was active as a music teacher. From 1959 to 1964 he taught piano and occasional classes in composition at the Univ. of Colorado at Boulder; in 1965 he joined the music dept. of the Univ. of Pa.; in 1983 he was named Annenberg Prof. of the Humanities there. In his music, Crumb is a universalist. Nothing in the realm of sound is alien to him; no method of composition is unsuited to his artistic purposes; accordingly, his music can sing as sweetly as the proverbial nightingale, and it can be as rough, rude, and crude as a primitive man of the mountains. The vocal parts especially demand extraordinary skills of lungs, lips, tongue, and larynx to produce such sound effects as percussive tongue clicks, explosive shrieks, hissing, whistling, whispering, and sudden shouting of verbal irrelevancies, interspersed with portentous syllabification, disparate phonemes, and rhetorical logorrhea. In startling contrast, Crumb injects into his sonorous kaleidoscope citations from popular works, such as the middle section of Chopin's *Fantaisie-Impromptu,* Ravel's *Bolero,* or some other "objet trouvé," a procedure first introduced facetiously by Erik Satie. In his instrumentation, Crumb is no less unconventional. Among the unusual effects in his scores is instructing the percussion player to immerse the loudly sounding gong into a tub of water, having an electric guitar played with glass rods over the frets, or telling wind instrumentalists to blow soundlessly through their tubes. Spatial distribution also plays a role: instrumentalists and singers are assigned their reciprocal locations on the podium or in the hall. All this is, of course, but an illustrative décor;

the music is of the essence. Like most composers who began their work around the middle of the 20th century, Crumb adopted the Schoenbergian idiom, seasoned with pointillistic devices. After these preliminaries, he wrote his unmistakably individual *Madrigals,* to words by the martyred poet Federico García Lorca, scored for voice and instrumental groups. There followed the most extraordinary work, *Ancient Voices of Children,* performed for the first time at a chamber music festival in Washington, D.C., on Oct. 31, 1970; the text is again by Lorca; a female singer intones into the space under the lid of an amplified grand piano; a boy's voice responds in anguish; the accompaniment is supplied by an orch. group and an assortment of exotic percussion instruments, such as Tibetan prayer stones, Japanese temple bells, a musical saw, and a toy piano. A remarkable group of 4 pieces, entitled *Makrokosmos,* calls for unusual effects; in one of these, the pianist is ordered to shout at specified points of time. Crumb's most grandiose creation is *Star-Child,* representing, in his imaginative scheme, a progression from tenebrous despair to the exaltation of luminous joy. The score calls for a huge orch., which includes 2 children's choruses and 8 percussion players performing on all kinds of utensils, such as pot lids, and also iron chains and metal sheets, as well as ordinary drums; it had its first performance under the direction of Pierre Boulez with the N.Y. Phil. on May 5, 1977.

WORKS: Sonata for Solo Cello (1955); *Variazioni* for Orch. (1959; Cincinnati, May 8, 1965); *5 Pieces for Piano* (1962); *Night Music I* for Soprano, Piano or Celesta, and Percussion, to verses by Federico García Lorca (1963; Paris, Jan. 30, 1964); *4 Nocturnes (Night Music II)* for Violin and Piano (1963; Buffalo, N.Y., Feb. 3, 1965); *Madrigals, Book I* for Soprano, Contrabass, and Vibraphone, to a text by García Lorca (1965; Philadelphia, Feb. 18, 1966); *Madrigals, Book II* for Soprano, Flute, and Percussion, to a text by García Lorca (1965; Washington, D.C., March 11, 1966); *11 Echoes of Autumn, 1965 (Echoes I)* for Violin, Alto Flute, Clarinet, and Piano (Brunswick, Maine, Aug. 10, 1966); *Echoes of Time and the River (Echoes II: 4 Processionals for Orchestra)* (Chicago, May 26, 1967); *Songs, Drones, and Refrains of Death* for Baritone, Electric Guitar, Electric Contrabass, Amplified Piano (and Amplified Harpsichord), and 2 Percussionists, to a text by García Lorca (1968; Iowa City, Iowa, March 29, 1969); *Madrigals, Book III* for Soprano, Harp and One Percussion Player, to a text by García Lorca (1969; Seattle, March 6, 1970); *Madrigals, Book IV* for Soprano, Flute, Harp, Contrabass, and One Percussion Player, to a text by García Lorca (1969; Seattle, March 6, 1970); *Night of the 4 Moons* for Alto, Alto Flute, Banjo, Electric Cello, and One Percussion Player, to a text by García Lorca (Washington, Pa., Nov. 6, 1969); *Black Angels (13 Images from the Dark Land: Images I)* for Electric String Quartet (Ann Arbor, Mich., Oct. 23, 1970); *Ancient Voices of Children* for Soprano, Boy Soprano, Oboe, Mandolin, Harp, Electric Piano (and Toy Piano), and 3 Percussion Players, to a text by García Lorca (Washington, D.C., Oct. 31, 1970); *Lux aeterna for 5 Masked*

Players for Soprano, Bass Flute (and Soprano Recorder), Sitar, and 2 Percussion Players (1971; Richmond, Va., Jan. 16, 1972); *Vox balaene (Voice of the Whale) for 3 Masked Players* for Electric Flute, Electric Cello, and Amplified Piano (1971; Washington, D.C., March 17, 1972); *Makrokosmos, Volume I (12 Fantasy-Pieces after the Zodiac for Amplified Piano)* (1972; Colorado Springs, Feb. 8, 1973); *Makrokosmos, Volume II (12 Fantasy-Pieces after the Zodiac for Amplified Piano)* (1973; N.Y., Nov. 12, 1974); *Music for a Summer Evening (Makrokosmos III)* for 2 Amplified Pianos and 2 Percussion Players (Swarthmore, Pa., March 30, 1974); *Dream Sequence (Images II)* for Violin, Cello, Piano, One Percussion Player, and 2 Offstage Musicians playing Glass Harmonica (1976); *Star-Child,* a parable for Soprano, Antiphonal Children's Voices, Male Speaking Choir, Bell Ringers, and Large Orch., demanding the coordinating abilities of 4 conductors (N.Y. Phil. May 5, 1977, under the general direction of Pierre Boulez); *Celestial Mechanics (Makrokosmos IV),* cosmic dances for Amplified Piano, 4-hands (N.Y., Nov. 18, 1979); *Apparition,* elegiac songs and vocalises for Soprano and Amplified Piano, to a text by Walt Whitman (1979; N.Y., Jan. 13, 1981); *A Little Suite for Christmas, A.D. 1979* for Piano (Washington, D.C., Dec. 14, 1980); *Gnomic Variations* for Piano (1981); *Pastoral Drone* for Organ (1982); *Processional* for Piano (1983); *A Haunted Landscape* for Orch. (N.Y. Phil., June 7, 1984).

Crusell, Bernhard Henrik, noted Finnish clarinetist and composer; b. Uusikaupunki, near Turku, Oct, 15, 1775; d. Stockholm, July 28, 1838. He took clarinet lessons from a member of the military band at Svaeborg Castle; then moved to Stockholm in 1791; there he had a chance to study with the renowned German music scholar and composer Abbé Vogler, who was a frequent visitor to Sweden. While improving his general knowledge of music, Crusell continued to play the clarinet; in 1798 he went to Berlin to study with Franz Tausch. In 1803 he went to Paris, where he studied composition with Berton and Gossec. In his instrumental music Crusell followed the tradition of Gluck; his vocal works reveal Nordic traits. In Sweden he acted as translator of opera librettos for Stockholm productions; among these were Beethoven's *Fidelio,* Rossini's *The Barber of Seville,* Meyerbeer's *Robert le Diable,* and Auber's *La Muette de Portici.* The Swedish Academy awarded him its gold medal shortly before his death.

Ctesibius, inventor of the hydraulis. He flourished between 246 and 221 B.C., and is known in literature as Ctesibius of Alexandria. The weight of evidence collected by H.G. Farmer tends to demonstrate that the first hydraulis was indeed constructed by Ctesibius.

Cuclin, Dimitri, prolific Rumanian composer; b. Galatz, April 5, 1885; d. Bucharest, Feb. 7, 1978. He studied with Castaldi in Bucharest; in 1907 went to Paris, where he took courses with Vincent d'Indy at the Schola Cantorum. Returning to Rumania, he taught violin at the Bucharest Cons. (1918–22). From 1924 to 1930 he was in America as violin teacher at the Brooklyn College of Music; in 1930 he returned to Rumania, devoting himself mainly to teaching and composition; he continued to write symph. and other music well into his 90s.

WORKS: 20 symphs.: No. 1 (1910); No. 2, subtitled *Triumph of the People's Union* (1938); No. 3 (1942); No. 4 (1944); No. 5, with Soloists and Chorus (1947); No. 6 (1948); No. 7 (1948); No. 8 (1948); No. 9 (1949); No. 10, with Chorus (1949); No. 11 (1950); No. 12, with Soloists and Chorus (1951); No. 13 (1951); No. 14 (1952); No. 15 (1954); No. 16, subtitled *Triumph of Peace* (1959); No. 17 (1965); No. 18 (1967); No. 19 (1971); No. 20 (1972); 5 operas: *Soria* (1911), *Trian si dochia* (1921), *Agamemnon* (1922), *Bellérophon* (1924), and *Meleagridele;* Violin Concerto (1920); Piano Concerto (1939); *Rumanian Dances* for Orch. (1961); Clarinet Concerto (1968); 3 string quartets (1914, 1948, 1949) and numerous other chamber works; piano pieces; sacred choruses; songs. A detailed list of Cuclin's works and his theoretical publications, as well as an extensive bibliography, is contained in Viorel Cosma's *Muzicieni romani* (Bucharest, 1970).

Cui, César, Russian composer, one of "The Five"; b. Vilna, Jan. 18, 1835; d. Petrograd, March 26, 1918. He was the son of a soldier in Napoleon's army who remained in Russia, married a Lithuanian noblewoman, and settled as a teacher of French in Vilna. Cui learned musical notation by copying Chopin's mazurkas and various Italian operas; then tried his hand at composition on his own. In 1849 he took lessons with Moniuszko, who was in Vilna at the time. In 1850 he went to St. Petersburg, where he entered the Engineering School in 1851 and later the Academy of Military Engineering (1855). After graduation in 1857 he became a topographer and later an expert in fortification. He participated in the Russo-Turkish War of 1877; in 1878 he became a prof. at the Engineering School and was tutor in military fortification to Czar Nicholas II. In 1856 Cui met Balakirev, who helped him master the technique of composition. In 1858 he married Malvina Bamberg; for her he wrote a scherzo on the theme *BABEG* (for the letters in her name) and *CC* (his own initials). In 1864 he began writing music criticism in the St. Petersburg *Vedomosti* and later in other newspapers, continuing as music critic until 1900. Cui's musical tastes were conditioned by his early admiration for Schumann; he opposed Wagner, against whom he wrote vitriolic articles; he attacked Strauss and Reger with even greater violence. He was an ardent propagandist of Glinka and the Russian national school, but was somewhat critical toward Tchaikovsky. He publ. the first comprehensive book on Russian music, *Musique en Russie* (Paris, 1880). Cui was grouped with Rimsky-Korsakov, Mussorgsky, Borodin, and Balakirev as one of the "Mighty Five"; the adjective in his case, however, is not very appropriate, for his music lacks grandeur; he was at his best in delicate miniatures, e.g., *Orientale*, from the suite *Kaleidoscope*, op. 50.

WORKS: 6 operas produced in St. Petersburg: *The Mandarin's Son* (1859; Dec. 19, 1878); *The Prisoner of the Caucasus* (1857–58; 1859; rewritten 1881; produced Feb. 16, 1883); *William Ratcliff* (Feb. 26, 1869); *Angelo* (Feb. 13, 1876); *The Saracen* (Nov. 14, 1899); *The Captain's Daughter* (1907–9; Feb. 27, 1911). Other operas: *Le Flibustier* (Opéra-Comique, Paris, Jan. 22, 1894); *Mam'zelle Fifi* (Moscow, Nov. 16, 1903); *Matteo Falcone* (Moscow, Dec. 27, 1907). *A Feast in Time of Plague*, written originally as a dramatic cantata, was produced as a one-act opera (Moscow, Nov. 23, 1901). Children's operas: *The Snow Giant; Little Red Ridinghood; Puss in Boots; Little Ivan the Fool*. Orch. works: *Tarantella* (1859); *Marche solennelle* (1881); *Suite miniature* (1882); *Suite concertante* for Violin, and Orch. or Piano (1884); *2 morceaux* for Cello, and Orch. or Piano (1886); Suite No. 2 (1887); Suite No. 4, *A Argenteau* (1887); Suite No. 3, *In modo populari* (1890); 3 Scherzos (op. 82; 1910). Chamber music: 3 string quartets (c. 1890, 1907, 1913); *5 Little Duets* for Flute and Violin; violin pieces: *2 Miniatures;* Violin Sonata; *Petite Suite; 12 Miniatures* (op. 20); *Kaleidoscope*, 24 numbers; *6 Bagatelles* (op. 51); many songs; piano pieces; choruses. Cui contributed a number to a set of variations on "Chopsticks" (with Borodin, Liadov, and Rimsky-Korsakov). In 1914–16 Cui completed Mussorgsky's opera *The Fair at Sorotchinsk*. A vol. of his *Selected Articles* (1864–1917) was publ. in Leningrad in 1953.

Culp, Julia, Dutch contralto; b. Groningen, Oct. 6, 1880; d. Amsterdam, Oct. 13, 1970. She first studied violin as a child; then became a voice pupil of Cornelia van Zanten at the Amsterdam Cons. (1897), and later of Etelka Gerster in Berlin; made her formal debut in Magdeburg in 1901; her tours of Germany, Austria, the Netherlands, France, Spain and Russia were highly successful from an artistic standpoint, establishing her as one of the finest singers of German lieder. Her American debut took place in N.Y. on Jan. 10, 1913; for many years, she visited the U.S. every season. In private life Mme. Culp was the wife of Erich Merten; after his death in 1919 she married an Austrian industrialist, Willy Ginzkey; lived in Czechoslovakia; after his death (1934) she returned to Amsterdam.

Culshaw, John, English recording producer; b. London, May 28, 1924; d. there, April 27, 1980. He studied music while serving in the British army. From 1954 to 1967 he was manager and chief producer with the Decca Recording Co.; from 1967 to 1975 he held the same post with the BBC. He was awarded the rank of Officer of the Order of the British Empire in 1966. He made a mark in the recording industry by introducing the stereo-reproduction process, which created a three-dimensional effect. His principal achievement was the stereophonic recording of the entire *Ring of the Nibelung*, issued by the Decca Record Co. under the direction of Sir Georg Solti. Culshaw related the

background of this undertaking in his books *Ring Resounding* (London, 1967) and *Reflections on Wagner's Ring* (London, 1976). His other publications are *Sergei Rachmaninoff* (London, 1949) and *A Century of Music* (London, 1952). He also publ. an autobiography, *Odyssey of a Recording Pioneer: Putting the Record Straight* (N.Y., 1981; posthumous).

Cummings, William Hayman, English singer and music antiquarian; b. Sidbury, Devonshire, Aug. 22, 1831; d. London, June 6, 1915. He was a chorister in London at St. Paul's and at the Temple Church; was organist of Waltham Abbey (1847); tenor singer in the Temple, Westminster Abbey, and Chapel Royal; was a prof. of singing at the Royal Academy of Music (1879–96); from 1882–88 was conductor of the Sacred Harmonic Society; was precentor of St. Anne's, Soho (1886–98); principal of the Guildhall School of Music (1896–1910); received an honorary degree of Mus.Doc. from Trinity College in Dublin (1900). He was a cultivated singer and a learned antiquarian; was instrumental in founding the Purcell Society, and edited its first publications; was the author of a biography of Purcell (in the Great Musicians Series; London, 1882; 2nd ed., 1911); also publ. *Primer of the Rudiments of Music* (1877), and *Biographical Dictionary of Musicians* (1892); contributed to *Grove's Dictionary*. His library of 4,500 vols. contained many rare autographs. He composed a cantata, *The Fairy Ring* (1873); sacred music; glees; part- songs; etc.

Curschmann, Karl Friedrich, German composer; b. Berlin, June 21, 1805; d. Langfuhr, near Danzig, Aug. 24, 1841. Originally a law student, he devoted himself to music, studying with Hauptmann and Spohr at Kassel, where his one-act opera *Abdul und Erinnieh* was produced (Oct. 29, 1828). His songs possess a fine poetic quality; a collection of 83 lieder and 9 duets and trios was publ. posthumously in 2 vols. (Berlin, 1871). He was also a noted singer and gave concerts in Germany and Italy.

Curtin, Phyllis, American soprano; b. Clarksburg, W.Va., Dec. 3, 1922. She studied with Olga Avierino in Boston; sang with the New England Opera Co.; was a member of the N.Y. City Opera; made successful appearances at the Teatro Colón in Buenos Aires (1959) and at the Vienna State Opera (1960–61). She made her debut with the Metropolitan Opera Co. on Nov. 4, 1961. Among her most successful roles is Salome; she also sang leading parts in first performances of several American operas. She was married to Phillip Curtin in 1946; divorced and married Eugene Cook in 1956. She taught master classes at the Berkshire Music Center in Tanglewood; then was head of the voice dept. at Yale Univ., and later dean of the School of Fine Arts at Boston Univ.

Curwen, Rev. John, English music theorist; b. Heckmondwike, Yorkshire, Nov. 14, 1816; d. Manchester, May 26, 1880. He was a Congregational minister; studied at Wymondley College and Univ.

College in London; in 1844 was pastor at Plaistow, Essex. Becoming interested in Miss S.A. Glover's "Tonic Sol-Fa" system of teaching, he labored to improve it; established the Tonic Sol-Fa Assoc. and the *Tonic Sol-Fa Reporter* in 1853, and the Tonic Sol-Fa College in 1869, having resigned his pastorate in 1867 to devote himself entirely to propagating the system. His numerous publications relate chiefly to Tonic Sol-Fa (issued by Novello). In 1863 Curwen founded the firm of John Curwen & Sons, publishers of works for school use, choral music. etc., also of the periodicals *Musical News and Herald* (weekly) and *Sackbut* (monthly; discontinued in 1934). In 1923 the business merged with F. & B. Goodwin.

Curwen, John Spencer, English music theorist, son of the **Rev. John Curwen;** b. Plaistow, Sept. 30, 1847; d. London, Aug. 6, 1916. He was a pupil of his father and G. Oakey, and later of G.A. Macfarren, Sullivan, and Prout at the Royal Academy of Music. Like his father, he was an active promoter of the Tonic Sol-Fa system; became president of the Tonic Sol-Fa College in 1880; was a frequent contributor to the *Tonic Sol-Fa Reporter* and its continuation, the *Musical Herald.* He publ. *Studies in Worship Music* (1880) and a 2nd series in 1885; *Memorials of John Curwen* (London, 1882); *Musical Notes in Paris* (1882); etc.

Curzon, Sir Clifford, eminent English pianist; b. London, May 18, 1907; d. there, Sept. 1, 1982. His father was an antique dealer; both he and his wife were music lovers and they encouraged their son's studies, first in violin playing and then as a pianist. In 1919 he enrolled at the Royal Academy of Music, where he studied piano with Charles Reddie and Katharine Goodson; he won two scholarships and the Macfarren Gold Medal. At the age of 16, he made a prestigious appearance as soloist at the Queen's Hall in London. He was only 19 years old when he was given a post as a teacher at the Royal Academy of Music, but he decided to continue his studies and went to Berlin, where he was tutored by Artur Schnabel, and then to Paris, where he took courses with Wanda Landowska in harpsichord and with Nadia Boulanger in general music culture. On Feb. 26, 1939, he made an auspicious American debut in N.Y., and in subsequent years made regular concert tours in the U.S. One of his last American appearances took place on May 2, 1978, when he played the Mozart C-minor Concerto with the Philadelphia Orch. Curzon was a scholarly virtuoso who applied his formidable technique with a careful regard for the music. He was particularly praised for his congenial interpretations of works by Romantic composers, especially Schubert, Schumann, and Brahms. He was a recipient of many official honors in England. In 1958 he was made a Commander of the Order of the British Empire. He received the degree of D.Mus. *honoris causa* from Leeds Univ. in 1970. He was knighted by Queen Elizabeth II in 1977. In 1980 he received the Gold Medal of the Royal Phil. Society in London.

Cuvillier, Charles, French composer of light opera; b. Paris, April 24, 1877; d. there, Feb. 14, 1955. He studied privately with Fauré and Messager, and with Massenet at the Paris Cons.; then became interested in the theater; his first operetta, *Avanthier matin,* was produced at the Théâtre des Capucines in Paris (Oct. 20, 1905); at the same theater, Cuvillier produced *Son petit frère* (April 10, 1907); *Algar* (1909); *Les Muscadines* (1910); and *Sapho* (1912). His most successful operetta, *La Reine s'amuse,* was first staged in Marseilles (Dec. 31, 1912); was revised and produced in Paris as *La Reine joyeuse* (Nov. 8, 1918) and in London as *The Naughty Princess* (1920). His other operettas were *La Fausse Ingénue* (Paris, 1918); *Bob et moi* (1924); *Boufard et ses filles* (Paris, 1929); etc. Cuvillier was also active in musical administration as music director at the Odéon in Paris. The waltz from *La Reine joyeuse* has retained its popularity in numerous arrangements.

Cuzzoni, Francesca, celebrated Italian soprano; b. Parma, c.1700; d. Bologna, 1770. She studied with Lanzi; sang in Parma, Bologna, Genoa, and Venice (1716–18); was engaged at the Italian opera in London, making her debut as Teofane in Handel's opera *Ottone* (Jan. 12, 1723). She made a profound impression on London opera lovers, and was particularly distinguished in lyric roles; but later her notorious rivalry with Faustina Bordoni nearly ruined her career. Following some appearances in Venice, she returned to London (1734); after several seasons she went to the Netherlands, where she became impoverished and was imprisoned for debt. Eventually, she returned to Bologna, where she subsisted by making buttons.

Czernohorsky (Černohorsky), Bohuslav, Bohemian composer; b. Nimburg, Feb. 16, 1684; d. Graz, July 1, 1742. He studied at Prague Univ. A Minorite monk, he was organist at Assisi in 1710–15 (Tartini was one of his pupils) and choirmaster at San Antonio in Padua, in 1715–20. Returning to Bohemia, he was Kapellmeister at the Teinkirche in Prague, and (1735) at St. Jacob's (Gluck was among his pupils); he was again organist in Padua in 1731–41. Many of his MSS were lost at the burning of the Minorite monastery (1754). An offertory *a* 4 and several organ fugues and preludes were publ. by O. Schmid in *Orgelwerke altböhmischer Meister;* 5 organ fugues have been ed. by K. Pietsch; a *Regina Coeli* for Soprano, Organ, and Cello obbligato, and a motet, *Quem lapidaverunt,* are also extant; *Composizioni per organo* constitute vol. 3 of *Musica antiqua Bohemica* (Prague, 1968). The contrapuntal skill of Czernohorsky's fugal writing is remarkable; Kretzschmar described him as "the Bach of Bohemia"; Czech writers refer to him as "the father of Bohemian music" despite the fact that Czernohorsky never made thematic use of native rhythms or melodies.

Czerny, Carl, celebrated Austrian pianist, composer, and pedagogue; b. Vienna, Feb. 20, 1791; d. there,

July 15, 1857. He was of Czech extraction (*czerny* means "black" in Czech), and his first language was Czech. He received his early training from his father, Wenzel Czerny, a stern disciplinarian who never let his son play with other children and insisted on concentrated work. Czerny had the privilege of studying for 3 years with Beethoven, and their association in subsequent years became a close one. Czerny also received advice as a pianist from Hummel and Clementi. He made trips to Leipzig (1836); visited Paris and London (1837) and Italy (1846); with these exceptions, he remained all his life in Vienna. His self-imposed daily schedule for work was a model of diligence; he denied himself any participation in the social life of Vienna and seldom attended opera or concerts. Very early in life he demonstrated great ability as a patient piano teacher; Beethoven entrusted to him the musical education of his favorite nephew. When Czerny himself became a renowned pedagogue, many future piano virtuosos flocked to him for lessons, among them Liszt (whom he taught without a fee), Thalberg, Theodore Kullak, Döhler, Jaëll, and Ninette Belleville-Oury. Despite the heavy teaching schedule, Czerny found time to compose a fantastic amount of piano music, 861 opus numbers in all, each containing many individual items; these included not only piano studies and exercises, for which he became celebrated, but also sonatas, concertos, string quartets, masses, and hymns. In addition, he made numerous piano arrangements of classical symphs., including all of Beethoven's, and wrote fantasies for piano on the themes from famous operas of the time. So dedicated was he to his chosen work that he renounced all thoughts of marriage (but a secret confession of his Platonic adoration of an unnamed female person was found among his MSS); in this wistful deprivation, Czerny's fate paralleled Beethoven's. For a century there has been a fashion among musical sophisticates to deprecate Czerny as a pathetic purveyor of manufactured musical goods; his contemporary John Field, the originator of the genre of piano nocturnes, described Czerny as a "Tintenfass"—an inkpot. A quip was circulated that Czerny hated children, and that he publ. his voluminous books of piano exercises to inflict pain on young pianists. Of late, however, there has been a change of heart toward Czerny as a worthy composer in his own right. Stravinsky expressed his admiration for Czerny, and modern composers have written, with a half-concealed smile, pieces "à la manière de Czerny." Czerny was unexpectedly revealed to be a musician of imaginative fancy and engaging pedantic humor, as for instance in his Brobdingnagian arrangement of Rossini's Overture to *William Tell* for 16 pianists playing 4-hands on 8 pianos; pieces for 3 pianists playing 6-hands on a single keyboard; etc. Obsessed by an idea of compassing all musical knowledge at once, he publ. an *Umriss der ganzen Musikgeschichte* (Mainz, 1851), and also a vol. in English entitled *Letters to a Young Lady on the Art of Playing the Pianoforte from the Earliest Rudiments to the Highest State of Cultivation* (the young lady in the title was never identified). Of his studies the most famous are *Schule der Geläufigkeit*, op. 299, and *Schule der Fingerfertigkeit*, op. 740; others are *Die Schule des Legato und Staccato*, op. 335; *40 Tägliche Studien*, op. 337; *Schule der Verzierungen*, op. 355; *Schule des Virtuosen*, op. 365; *Schule der linken Hand*, op. 399; etc. His Sonata, op. 7, was popular; among his piano transcriptions to be mentioned is *Fantaisie et Variations brilliantes* on an aria from Persiani's opera *Ines de Castro*. Czerny's autobiography, *Erinnerungen aus meinem Leben*, was ed. by W. Kolneder (Baden-Baden, 1968; publ. in part in Eng. in the *Musical Quarterly,* July 1956).

Cziffra, György, noted Hungarian pianist; b. Budapest, Sept. 5, 1921. He studied with Dohnányi at the Budapest Academy of Music; his education was interrupted by World War II, when he served in the Hungarian army; after the war he continued his studies at the Budapest Academy of Music with Ferenczi, but was once more distracted from music when he was arrested in 1950 for his rebellious political views. He was released from jail in 1953, but was again endangered by the abortive Hungarian revolt in 1956. Convinced that he could have no peace under Communist rule, he went to Paris, where he made successful appearances as a concert pianist; eventually he became a French citizen. He was best known for his interpretations of the works of the Romantic repertoire; especially brilliant are his renditions of the music of Liszt.

Czyż, Henryk, Polish conductor and composer; b. Grudziadz, June 16, 1923. He studied law at Torun Univ.; then went to the Poznan Academy of Music, where he studied conducting with Bierdiajew and composition with Szeligowski. In 1952 he was appointed conductor at the Poznan Opera; from 1953–56 he conducted the Polish Radio Symph. Orch. in Warsaw. He was subsequently chief conductor of the Lodz Phil. (1957–60); from 1964–68 he conducted the Cracow Phil.; in 1971–74 served as Generalmusikdirektor of the Düsseldorf Symph.; in 1972–80 again assumed the post of chief conductor of the Lodz Phil. He made his American debut with the Minnesota Orch. in 1973. In 1980 he became a prof. at the Warsaw Academy. His works include *Etude for Orch.* (1949); *Symphonic Variations* (1952); the musical *Bialowlosa* (1960); and the comic opera *Kynolog w rosterce* (1964).

D

Dachs, Joseph, pianist and pedagogue; b. Regensburg, Sept. 30, 1825; d. Vienna, June 6, 1896. He studied in Vienna with Czerny and Sechter; in 1861 was appointed prof. of piano at the Vienna Cons.; he had numerous distinguished pupils, among them Vladimir de Pachmann, Laura Rappoldi, and Isabelle Vengerova. He also gave concerts which were well received in Vienna.

Daffner, Hugo, German composer and musicologist; b. Munich, June 2, 1882; perished in the concentration camp in Dachau, Oct. 9, 1936. He studied composition with Thuille and musicology with Sandberger and Kroyer at the Royal Academy in Munich; received his degree of Dr.Phil. in 1904; subsequently took private lessons with Max Reger. He conducted at the Munich opera house in 1904–6; was active as a music critic in Königsberg and Dresden. After World War I he decided to study medicine, and obtained the degree of M.D. in 1920; in 1924 he went to live in Berlin as a practicing physician. He became a victim of the Nazi program of extermination of Jews.

Dahl, Ingolf, distinguished composer; b. Hamburg, Germany (of Swedish parents), June 9, 1912; d. Frutigen, near Bern, Switzerland, Aug. 6, 1970. He stud-ied composition at the Cons. of Cologne and musicology at the Univ. of Zürich. He came to the U.S. in 1935; settled in California (1938), where he became active as a conductor and composer; was appointed an assistant prof. at the Univ. of Southern Calif. (1945); received 2 Guggenheim fellowships (1952 and 1960). He taught at the Berkshire Music Center, Tanglewood, in the summers of 1952–55. As a composer, he adhered to an advanced polyphonic style in free dissonant counterpoint.
WORKS: *Andante and Arioso* for Flute, Clarinet, Oboe, Horn, and Bassoon (1942); *Music for Brass Instruments* (1944); *Concerto a tre* for Clarinet, Violin, and Cello (1946); Duo for Cello and Piano (1946); Divertimento for Viola and Piano (1948); Concerto for Saxophone and Wind Orch. (1949); *Symphony concertante* for 2 Clarinets and Orch. (1953); *Sonata seria* for Piano (1953); *The Tower of Saint Barbara,* symph. legend (Louisville, Jan. 29, 1955); Piano Quartet (1957); *Sonata Pastorale* for Piano (1960); *Serenade* for 4 Flutes (1960); *Sinfonietta* for Concert Band (1961); Piano Trio (1962); *Aria sinfonica* (Los Angeles, April 15, 1965); *Elegy Concerto* for Violin and Small Orch. (1963; completed by Donal Michalsky, 1971); *Duo concertante* for Flute and Percussion (1966); *Sonata da camera* for Clarinet and Piano (1970); *Intervals* for String Orch. (1970).

Dahlhaus, Carl, eminent German musicologist and editor; b. Hannover, June 10, 1928. He studied musicology at the Univ. of Göttingen with Gerber; also at the Univ. of Freiburg with Gurlitt; received his Ph.D. from the Univ. of Göttingen in 1953 with the dissertation *Studien zu den Messen Josquins des Prés.* He was a dramatic adviser for the Deutsches Theater in Göttingen from 1950 to 1958; from 1960 to 1962 was an editor of the *Stuttgarter Zeitung;* then joined the Inst. für Musikalische Landesforschung of the Univ. of Kiel; completed his Habilitation there in 1966 with his *Untersuchungen über die Entstehung der harmonischen Tonalität* (publ. in Kassel, 1968). In 1966–67 he was a research fellow at the Univ. of Saarbrücken; in 1967 he became prof. of music history at the Technical Univ. of Berlin. He is the editor in chief of the complete edition of Wagner's works, which began publication in 1970; was also an editor of the Supplement to the 12th edition of the *Riemann Musik-Lexikon* (2 vols., Mainz, 1972, 1975) and (with Hans Eggebrecht) of the *Brockhaus-Riemann Musik-Lexikon* (2 vols., Wiesbaden and Mainz, 1978); in addition, was co-editor of the *Neue Zeitschrift für Musik* (from 1972) and of the *Archiv für Musikwissenschaft* (from 1973).

Dahms, Walter, German music critic; b. Berlin, June 9, 1887; d. Lisbon, Oct. 5, 1973. He studied with Adolf Schultze in Berlin (1907–10), then engaged in music criticism; also composed some minor piano pieces and songs. About 1935 he went to Lisbon, Portugal, where he changed his name to **Gualtério Armando,** and continued to publ. books on music in the German language, but for some unfathomable reason he persistently denied his identity. The reasons for his leaving Germany are obscure; he was not a Jew (in fact, he wrote some anti-Semitic articles, directed against Schoenberg and others as early as 1910), and presumably had nothing to fear from the Nazi government, unless he regarded it as unduly liberal. A clue to his true identity was the synonymity of his first names in German (Walter) and in Portuguese (Gualtério).
  WRITINGS: *Schubert* (Berlin, 1912); *Schumann* (1916); *Mendelssohn* (1919); *Die Offenbarung der Music: Eine Apotheose Friedrich Nietzsches* (Munich, 1921); *Music des Südens* (1923), *Paganini* (Berlin, 1960); *Liszt* (Berlin, 1961); and *Wagner* (Berlin, 1962).

Dalayrac, Nicolas (-Marie), French composer; b. Muret (Haute-Garonne), June 8 (baptized, June 13), 1753; d. Paris, Nov. 26, 1809. (He signed his name **d'Alayrac,** but dropped the nobiliary particle after the Revolution.) His early schooling was in Toulouse; returning to Muret in 1767, he studied law and played violin in a local band. He then entered the service of the Count d'Artois in his Guard of Honor, and at the same time took lessons in harmony with François Langlé at Versailles; he also received some help from Grétry. In 1781 he wrote 6 string quartets; his first theater work was a one-act comedy, *L'Eclipse totale* (Paris, March 7, 1782).

From then on, he devoted most of his energies to the theater. He wrote over 56 operas; during the Revolution he composed patriotic songs for special occasions. He also enjoyed Napoleon's favors later on. During his lifetime, and for some 3 decades after his death, many of his operas were popular not only in France but also in Germany, Italy, and Russia; then they gradually disappeared from the active repertoire, but there were several revivals even in the 20th century. Dalayrac's natural facility enabled him to write successfully in all operatic genres. The list of his operas produced in Paris (mostly at the Opéra-Comique) includes the following: *Le Petit Souper, ou L'Abbé qui veut parvenir* (1781); *Le Chevalier à la mode* (1781); *Nina* (May 15, 1786; one of his most successful operas); *Sargines* (May 14, 1788); *Les Deux Petits Savoyards* (Jan. 14, 1789); *Raoul, Sire de Créqui* (Oct. 31, 1789); *La Soirée orageuse* (May 29, 1790); *Camille* (March 19, 1791); *Philippe et Georgette* (Dec. 28, 1791); *Ambroise* (Jan. 12, 1793); *Adèle et Dorsan* (April 27, 1795); *Marianne* (July 7, 1796); *La Maison isolée* (May 11, 1797); *Gulnare* (Dec. 30, 1797); *Alexis* (Jan. 24, 1798); *Adolphe et Clara* (Feb. 10, 1799); *Maison à vendre* (Oct. 23, 1800; many revivals); *Léhéman* (Dec. 12, 1801); *L'Antichambre* (Feb. 26, 1802); *La Jeune Prude* (Jan. 14, 1804); *Une Heure de mariage* (March 20, 1804); *Gulistan* (Sept. 30, 1805); *Deux mots* (June 9, 1806); *Koulouf* (Dec. 18, 1806); *Le Poète et le musicien* (posthumous, Paris, May 30, 1811).

Dalberg, Johann Friedrich Hugo, German pianist, composer, and writer on music; b. Aschaffenburg, May 17, 1760; d. there, July 26, 1812. He studied theology; became a canon in Trier; was also counsellor to the Elector of Trier at Coblenz. He traveled in Italy (1775) and England (1798); gave private concerts as a pianist. Although he was not a professional musician, his compositions and particularly his writings reveal considerable musical culture. He publ. many vocal works; set to music Schiller's *Ode an die Freude* (1799); also wrote songs to Eng. and French texts.

D'Albert, Eugène. See **Albert, Eugène d'.**

Dalcroze, Emile Jaques. See **Jaques-Dalcroze, Emile.**

D'Alembert, Jean le Rond. See **Alembert, Jean le Rond d'.**

D'Alheim, Marie. See **Olénine d'Alheim, Marie.**

D'Alheim, Pierre, French journalist; b. Laroche (Yonne), Dec. 8, 1862; d. Paris, April 11, 1922. In 1893 he married the singer **Marie Olénine,** and organized her concerts in Moscow and in Paris. He became a propagandist of Russian music; publ. a book on Mussorgsky (Paris, 1896), and trans. into French the librettos of *Boris Godunov* and *Khovanshchina* and Mussorgsky's songs.

Dall'Abaco, Evaristo Felice. See **Abaco, Evaristo Felice dall'.**

Dallapiccola, Luigi, distinguished Italian composer; b. Pisino (Pazin), Istria (now a part of Yugoslavia), Feb. 3, 1904; d. Florence, Feb. 19, 1975. He took piano lessons at an early age; went to school at the Pisino Gymnasium (1914–21), except for a period of over a year (1917–18) in which his family was politically exiled in Graz; studied piano and harmony in nearby Trieste (1919–21); in 1922 moved to Florence, where he took courses at the Cherubini Cons., studying piano with Ernesto Consolo (graduated 1924) and composition with Vito Frazzi (graduated 1931); was active in the Italian section of the International Society for Contemporary Music (ISCM) from the early 1930s. In 1934 Dallapiccola was appointed to the faculty of the Cherubini Cons., where he stayed until 1967. As a composer Dallapiccola became interested from the very first in the melodic application of atonal writing; in 1939 he adopted the dodecaphonic method of Schoenberg with considerable innovations of his own (for example, the use of mutually exclusive triads in thematic structure and harmonic progressions). He particularly excelled in his handling of vocal lines in a difficult modern idiom. He visited London in 1946 and traveled on the Continent; taught several courses in American colleges: Berkshire Music Center, Tanglewood, Mass. (1951); Queens College, N.Y. (1956, 1959); the Univ. of Calif., Berkeley (1962); Dartmouth College (summer, 1969); Aspen Music School (1969); and Marlboro (1969).
WORKS: FOR THE STAGE: *Volo di notte (Night Flight),* one-act opera after the St. Exupéry novel *Vol de nuit* (1937–39; Florence, May 18, 1940); *Il Prigioniero (The Prisoner),* one-act opera with a prologue, after Villiers de l'Isle and Charles de Coster (1944–48; revised in 1950 for Reduced Orch.; Turin Radio, Dec. 4, 1949; stage premiere, Florence, May 20, 1950; *Ulisse,* 2-act opera with prologue, after Homer's *Odyssey* (1959–68; premiere, as *Odysseus,* Berlin, Sept. 29, 1968, to a German libretto; Italian, Milan, 1969); *Marsia,* ballet in one act (1942–43; Venice Music Festival, Sept. 9, 1948). INSTRUMENTAL WORKS: *Partita* for Orch., with Soprano in the last movement (1930–32; Florence, Jan. 22, 1933); *Musica* for 3 Pianos (1935); *Piccolo Concerto per Muriel Couvreaux* for Piano and Chamber Orch. (1939–41; Rome, May 1, 1941); *Sonatina canonica,* after Paganini's *Caprices,* for Piano (1942–43); *Ciaccona, Intermezzo e Adagio* for Solo Cello (1945); *Due studi* for Violin and Piano (1946–47); *Due pezzi* for Orch. (1947; arrangement and elaboration of the *Due studi); Tartiniana,* divertimento on themes from Tartini sonatas, for Violin and Chamber Orch. (1951; Bern, March 4, 1952); *Quaderno musicale di Annalibera* for Piano (1952, revised 1953; transcribed for organ by Rudy Shackelford, 1970); *Variazioni per orchestra* (1953–54; Louisville, Ky., Oct. 2, 1954; orch. version of the *Quaderno musicale di Annalibera); Piccola musica notturna* for Orch. (1954; Hannover, June 7, 1954; arranged for 8 Instruments, 1961); *Tartiniana seconda* for Violin and

Piano (1955–56; chamber orch. version made with an added movement, 1956; chamber orch. version, Turin Radio, March 15, 1957); *Dialoghi* for Cello and Orch. (1959–60; Venice, Sept. 17, 1960); *Three Questions with Two Answers* for Orch. (1962; based on material from *Ulisse;* New Haven, Conn., Feb. 5, 1963). VOCAL WORKS: *Due Canzoni di Grado* for Mezzo-soprano, Small Female Chorus, and Small Orch. (1927); *Dalla mia terra,* song cycle for Mezzo-soprano, Chorus, and Orch. (1928); *Due laudi di Fra Jacopone da Todi* for Soprano, Baritone, Chorus, and Orch. (1929); *La Canzone del Quarnaro* for Tenor, Male Chorus, and Orch. (1930); *Due liriche del Kalewala* for Tenor, Baritone, Chamber Chorus, and 4 Percussion Instruments (1930); *3 Studi* for Soprano and Chamber Orch. (1932; also based on the Kalevala epos); *Estate* for Male Chorus a cappella (1932); *Rhapsody* for Voice and Chamber Orch. (1934); *Divertimento in quattro esercizi* for Soprano, Flute, Oboe, Clarinet, Viola, and Cello (1934); *Cori de Michelangelo* in 3 sets: I for Chorus a cappella (1933), II for Female Chorus and 17 Instruments (1935), and III for Chorus and Orch. (1936); *3 Laudi* for Soprano and Chamber Orch. (1936–37); *Canti de prigionia (Songs of Captivity)* for Chorus, 2 Pianos, 2 Harps, and Percussion (1938–41; first complete perf., Rome, Dec. 11, 1941); *Liriche greche* in 3 sets: I, *Cinque frammenti di Saffo* for Voice and 15 Instruments (1942); II, *Due liriche de Anacreonte* for Soprano, 2 Clarinets, Viola, and Piano (1945); III, *Sex carmina Alcaei,* for Soprano and 11 Instruments (1943); *Roncesvals* for Voice and Piano (1946); *Quattro liriche di Antonio Machado* for Soprano and Piano (1948; version with Chamber Orch., 1964); *3 Poemi* for Soprano and Chamber Ensemble (1949); *Job,* biblical drama for 5 Singers, Narrator, Chorus, Speaking Chorus, and Orch. (1949–50; Rome, Oct. 30, 1950); *Goethe-Lieder* for Female Voice and 3 Clarinets (1953); *Canti di liberazione (Songs of Liberation)* for Chorus and Orch. (1951–55; Cologne, Oct. 28, 1955); *An Mathilde,* cantata for Female Voice and Orch. (1955); *Cinque canti* for Baritone and 8 Instruments (1956); *Concerto per la notte di Natale dell'anno 1956 (Christmas Concerto for the Year 1956)* for Soprano and Chamber Orch. (1957; Tokyo, Oct. 11, 1957); *Requiescant* for Mixed Chorus, Children's Chorus, and Orch. (1957–58; Hamburg Radio, Nov. 17, 1959); *Preghiere (Prayers)* for Baritone and Chamber Orch. (1962; Berkeley, Calif., Nov. 10, 1962); *Parole di San Paolo* for Medium Voice and Chamber Ensemble (1969; Washington, D.C., Oct. 10, 1969); *Sicut umbra . . .* for Mezzo-soprano and 4 Instrumental Groups (1969–70; Washington, Oct. 30, 1970); *Tempus destruendi/Tempus aedificandi* for Chorus a cappella (1970–71); *Commaito* for Soprano and Chamber Ensemble (1972; Styrian Autumn Festival, Murau, Austria, Oct. 15, 1972; his last completed work). The *Revue Musical Suisse* dedicated a special issue to Dallapiccola (July/Aug. 1975). A complete catalogue of his works is publ. in the March 1976 issue of *Tempo* (No. 115). A collection of Dallapiccola's own essays was publ. under the title *Appunti incontri meditazioni* (Milan, 1970).

Dallapozza, Adolf, Italian-born Austrian tenor; b. Bolzano, March 14, 1940. His parents settled in Austria when he was 5 months old. He received his musical education at the Vienna Cons.; then joined the Chorus of the Volksoper; in 1962 made his debut as soloist in the role of Ernesto in Donizetti's *Don Pasquale*. In 1967 he became a member of the Vienna State Opera; also sang with the Bavarian State Opera in Munich and made appearances in Milan, Basel, Hamburg, Zürich, and Buenos Aires. In 1976 the President of Austria made him a Kammersänger. He is highly regarded for his versatility, being equally competent in opera, oratorio, and operetta.

Dalla Rizza, Gilda, Italian soprano; b. Verona, Oct. 2, 1892; d. Milan, July 4, 1975. She received her musical training in Bologna; made her debut there in 1912; in 1915 she sang at La Scala; Puccini so admired her singing that he created the role of Magda in *La Rondine* for her (Monte Carlo, March 27, 1917). Toscanini engaged her at La Scala in Milan, and she remained on its roster until 1939. She subsequently taught voice at the Cons. of Venice.

Dal Monte, Toti, Italian coloratura soprano; b. Mogliano, near Treviso, June 27, 1893; d. Pieve di Soligo, Treviso, Jan. 26, 1975. Her original name was **Antonietta Meneghelli.** She studied piano and singing; made her operatic debut at La Scala in Milan in 1916; made her first American appearance at the Metropolitan Opera House in N.Y. in *Lucìa di Lammermoor* on Dec. 5, 1924, remaining at the Metropolitan for the 1924–25 season; also sang in Chicago in 1924–28; at Covent Garden in London in 1926; toured Australia in 1929. After the end of her operatic career, about 1949, she devoted herself to teaching. She publ. her autobiography, *Una voce nel mondo* (Milan, 1962).

Dalmorès, Charles, French dramatic tenor; b. Nancy, Jan. 1, 1871; d. Hollywood, Dec. 6, 1939. After taking first prizes at the local Cons. for solfeggio and French horn at 17, he received from the city of Nancy a stipend for study at the Paris Cons., where he took first prize for horn at 19; played in the Colonne Orch. (2 years) and the Lamoureux Orch. (2 years); at 23, became a prof. of horn playing at the Lyons Cons. His vocal teacher was Dauphin, the bass singer; his debut as a tenor took place on Oct. 6, 1899, at Rouen; later he sang at the Théâtre de la Monnaie in Brussels; 7 seasons at Covent Garden; at the Manhattan Opera House in N.Y. (1906–10; debut as Faust, Dec. 7, 1906); then was with the Chicago Opera Co. (1910–18). His repertoire was large, and included Wagnerian as well as French operas; in Chicago he sang Tristan and the title role in the first performance of *Parsifal* to be presented there.

d'Alvimare, Martin-Pierre. See **Dalvimare, Martin-Pierre.**

Dalvimare (real name, **d'Alvimare**), **Martin-Pierre,** French harpist and composer for harp; b. Dreux (Eure-et-Loire), Sept. 18, 1772; d. Paris, June 13, 1839. In 1800 he was harpist at the Paris Opéra; became harpist to Napoleon in 1806; harp teacher to the Empress Josephine (1807); retired to his estate at Dreux in 1812. He wrote several sonatas for harp and violin; duets for 2 harps, for harp and piano, and for harp and horn; fantasies, variations, etc.

Damase, Jean-Michel, French composer and pianist; b. Bordeaux, Jan. 27, 1928. He studied with Delvincourt at the Paris Cons.; received the Grand Prix de Rome in 1947; made his U.S. debut April 20, 1954, in N.Y. as a pianist-composer.
WORKS: Ballets: *Le Saut du Tremplin* (Paris, 1944); *La Croqueuse de diamants* (Paris, 1950); *Interludes* for Orch. (Nice, 1948); Rhapsody for Oboe and String Orch. (Paris Radio, 1948); Piano Concerto (Cannes, 1950); Violin Concerto (Paris, Dec. 22, 1956); 2nd Piano Concerto (Paris, Feb. 6, 1963); chamber music: Quintet for Violin, Viola, Cello, Flute, and Harp (1947); Trio for Flute, Harp, and Cello (1949); piano pieces and songs; operas: *Colombe* (Bordeaux, May 5, 1961) and *Eurydice* (Bordeaux Festival, May 26, 1972). A list of works and bibliography is publ. in C. Chamfray, "Jean-Michel Damase," *Courrier Musical de France,* 18 (1967).

Damoreau, Laure-Cinthie (née **Montalant;** first known as **"Mlle. Cinti"**), noted French operatic soprano; b. Paris, Feb. 6, 1801; d. Chantilly, Feb. 25, 1863. She studied at the Paris Cons.; made her debut in 1819 at the Théâtre Italien; later was engaged at the Opéra (1826–35). Rossini wrote leading roles for her in *Le Siège de Corinthe* and *Mosè*, as did Auber, during her engagement (1835–43) at the Opéra-Comique (*Domino noir, L'Ambassadrice,* etc.). Retiring from the stage, she made concert tours to England, the Netherlands, and Russia, and (with Artôt, the violinist) to the U.S. and Havana (1843). She was a prof. of singing at the Paris Cons. in 1834–56; then retired to Chantilly. Her husband was an actor at Brussels. She publ. *Album de romances* and *Méthode de chant.*

Da Motta, José Vianna, noted Portuguese pianist; b. on Isle St. Thomas, Portuguese Africa, April 22, 1868; d. Lisbon, May 31, 1948. His family returned to Lisbon when he was a year old; he studied with local teachers; gave his first concert at the age of 13; then studied piano in Berlin with Xaver Scharwenka and composition with Philipp Scharwenka. In 1885 he went to Weimar, where he became a pupil of Liszt; also took lessons with Hans von Bülow in Frankfurt (1887). He then undertook a series of concert tours throughout Europe (1887–88), the U.S. (1892–93; 1899), and South America (1902). He was in Berlin until 1915; then became director of the Geneva Cons. In 1919 he returned to Lisbon and was appointed director of the Lisbon Cons., retiring in 1938. At the height of his career he was greatly esteemed as a fine interpreter of Bach and Beethoven. He was also the author of many articles in German, French, and Portuguese; wrote *Studien bei Bülow* (1896); *Betrachtungen über Franz Liszt* (1898); *Die*

Entwicklung des Klavierkonzerts (as a program book to Busoni's concerts); essays on Alkan; critical articles in the *Kunstwart, Klavierlehrer, Bayreuther Blätter*, etc. He was a prolific composer; among his works are *Die Lusiaden* for Orch. and Chorus; Symph.; String Quartet; many piano pieces, in some of which (e.g., the 5 *Portuguese Rhapsodies* and the Portuguese dance *Vito*) he employs folk themes with striking effect.

Damrosch, Frank, German-American choral conductor, son of **Leopold Damrosch;** b. Breslau, June 22, 1859; d. New York, Oct. 22, 1937. He studied with Bruckner, Jean Vogt, and von Inten, and composition with his father and Moszkowski. In 1882–85 he was conductor of the Denver (Colo.) Chorus Club, and in 1884–85, supervisor of music in public schools, and organist at different churches. In 1885–91, he was chorus master and assistant conductor at the Metropolitan Opera House in N.Y.; till 1887 was conductor of the Newark Harmonic Society; in 1892, organized the People's Choral Union, an enterprise for the popularization of choral singing, for which he publ. in 1894 *Popular Method of Sight Singing*; in 1897–1905, he was supervisor of music in N.Y. City public schools; conducted the Oratorio Society (1898–1912). In 1893 he founded the Musical Art Society, a chorus of 60 trained voices for the performance of a cappella music, which he conducted till 1920. In 1905 he established an exemplary organization, the splendidly equipped Inst. of Musical Art, which, in 1926, became affiliated with the Juilliard School of Music; he retained his position as dean until his retirement in 1933. He received the degree of D.Mus. (*honoris causa*) from Yale Univ. in 1904; publ. vocal numbers (songs, choruses); also wrote *Some Essentials in the Teaching of Music* (N.Y., 1916) and *Institute of Musical Art, 1905–26* (N.Y., 1936).

Damrosch, Leopold, eminent German-American conductor and violinist; b. Posen, Oct. 22, 1832; d. New York, Feb. 15, 1885. He studied with Ries, Dehn, and Böhmer; took the degree of M.D. at Berlin Univ. in 1854, but then, against his parents' wishes, embraced the career of a musician; he appeared at first as a solo violinist in several German cities, later as a conductor at minor theaters, and in 1885 procured, through Liszt, the position of solo violinist in the Grand Ducal Orch. at Weimar. While here he was intimate with Liszt and many of his most distinguished pupils, and won Wagner's lifelong friendship; in Weimar, too, he married the singer **Helene von Heimburg** (b. Oldenburg, 1835; d. New York, Nov. 21, 1904). In 1858–60, Damrosch was conductor of the Breslau Phil. Concerts; gave up the post to make tours with von Bülow and Tausig; organized the Breslau Orch. Society in 1862. Besides this, he founded quartet *soirées,* and a choral society; conducted the Society for Classical Music, and a theater orch. (for 2 years); frequently appeared as a solo violinist. In 1871 he was called to N.Y. to conduct the Arion Society, and made his debut, on May 6, 1871, as conductor, composer, and violinist. In

N.Y. his remarkable capacity as an organizer found free scope; besides bringing the Arion to the highest pitch of efficiency and prosperity, he founded the Symphony Society in 1878, the latter's concerts succeeding those of the Thomas Orch. at Steinway Hall. In 1880 Columbia College conferred on him the degree of D.Mus.; in 1881 he conducted the first major music festival held in N.Y., with an orch. of 250 and a chorus of 1,200; in 1883 he made a highly successful Western tour with his orch.; in 1884–85 he organized the German Opera Co., and, together with Anton Seidl, conducted a season of German opera at the Metropolitan Opera House, presenting Wagner's *Ring des Nibelungen, Tristan und Isolde,* and *Die Meistersinger* for the first time in the U.S. He composed 7 cantatas; Symph. in A; music to Schiller's *Joan of Arc*; marches for orch.; 3 violin concertos; several pieces for violin and orch., and for solo voice and orch.; choruses for mixed voices and male voices; duets; many songs.

Damrosch, Walter Johannes, famous German-American conductor, composer, and educator, son of **Leopold Damrosch;** b. Breslau, Jan. 30, 1862; d. New York, Dec. 22, 1950. He studied harmony with his father, also with Rischbieter and Draeseke in Dresden; piano with von Inten, Boekelmann, and Max Pinner in the U.S.; and conducting with his father and with Hans von Bülow. He was conductor of the N.Y. Oratorio Society (1885–98) and of the N.Y. Symph. Society (1885–1903); assistant conductor of German opera at the Metropolitan Opera House (1885–91); organized the Damrosch Opera Co. (1894), which he directed for 5 seasons, giving German opera (chiefly Wagner) in the principal cities of the U.S.; among the artists whom he first brought to the U.S. were Mmes. Klafsky, Gadski, and Ternina. On March 3, 1886, he presented *Parsifal* in N.Y., in concert form for the first time in America; in 1900–1902 he conducted Wagner's operas at the Metropolitan; then was conductor of the N.Y. Phil. Society (1902–3); in 1903 the N.Y. Symph. Society was reorganized with Damrosch as its regular conductor, a post he held until 1927; he again conducted the Oratorio Society (1917); organized at the request of General Pershing the American Expeditionary Force bands and founded schools for bandmasters in Chaumont, France (1918); conducted a concert by the N.Y. Symph. Society Orch. in the first chain broadcast over the network of the newly organized NBC (Nov. 15, 1926); was appointed musical adviser to NBC (1927, retired 1947); was conductor of the NBC Symph. Orch. in a weekly series of music appreciation hours for the schools and colleges of the U.S. and Canada (1928–42). He conducted many famous works for the first time in the U.S. (Brahms' 3rd and 4th symphs.; Tchaikovsky's 4th and 6th symphs.; etc.); was U.S. delegate at the Paris International Music Congress (1937). He received degrees of D.Mus. (*honoris causa*) from Columbia Univ. (1914), Princeton Univ. (1929), Brown Univ. (1932), Dartmouth College (1933), and N.Y. Univ. (1935); was awarded the David Bispham medal (1929) and the gold medal of the National Inst. of

Arts and Letters (1938).

WORKS: Operas: *The Scarlet Letter* (Damrosch Opera Co., Boston, Feb. 10, 1896); *Cyrano de Bergerac* (Metropolitan Opera House, Feb. 27, 1913; revised 1939); *The Man without a Country* (Metropolitan, May 12, 1937); *The Opera Cloak*, one-act opera (N.Y. Opera Co., Nov. 3, 1942); comic opera, *The Dove of Peace* (Philadelphia, Oct. 15, 1912). Other works: *Manila Te Deum* (N.Y., 1898); *An Abraham Lincoln Song* (N.Y., 1936); incidental music to Euripides' *Iphigenia in Aulis* and *Medea* (Berkeley, Calif., 1915), and to Sophocles' *Electra* (N.Y., 1917); Violin Sonata; *At Fox Meadow* (1899); *Dunkirk*, a setting of R. Nathan's poem, for Baritone, Solo, Male Chorus, and Chamber Orch. (NBC broadcast, May 2, 1943); many songs, including *Death and General Putnam* (1936), *Danny Deever*, etc. He publ. an autobiography, *My Musical Life* (N.Y., 1923; 2nd ed., 1930); was co-editor, with Gartlan and Gehrkens, of the Universal School Music Series.

Dan, Ikuma, Japanese composer; b. Tokyo, April 7, 1924. He studied at the Tokyo Music Academy with K. Shimofusa and S. Moroi; taught at the Tokyo Music School (1947–50); has been active as a film music director and composer, and, since 1967, has presented pop music concerts on television.

WORKS: 5 operas: *Yûzuru* (*The Twilight Crane;* 1950–51; Tokyo, Jan. 30, 1952; revised 1956); *Kikimi-mi-zukin* (*The Listening Cap;* 1954–55; Tokyo, March 18, 1955); *Yang Kwei-fei* (1957–58; Tokyo, Dec. 11, 1958); *Chanchiki* (*Cling-Clang;* 1961–63); *Hikarigoke* (1972; Osaka, April 27, 1972); *Symphonic Poem* (1948); 5 symphs. (1949–50, 1955–56, 1959–60, 1964–65, 1965); *Sinfonia Burlesca* (1953; Tokyo, Jan. 26, 1959); dance suite for Orch., *The Silken Road* (1953–54; Tokyo, June 23, 1955); *Journey through Arabia*, symph. suite (1958); *Olympic Games Overture* (1964); *Festival Overture* (1965); *Japanese Poem* No. 1 for Orch. (1967; Tokyo, Sept. 25, 1967, Arthur Fiedler conducting); *Hymn to the Sai-kai* for Chorus and Orch. (1969); *A Letter from Japan* No. 2 for Orch. (1969); *Rainbow Tower* for Orch. (1970); String Trio (1947); Piano Sonata (1947); String Quartet (1948); Divertimento for 2 Pianos (1949); *Futari Shizuka*, dance drama for Flute, Percussion, and String Ensemble (1961); Concerto Grosso for Harpsichord and String Ensemble (1965); choruses.

Danckerts, Ghiselin, Flemish contrapuntist and theorist; b. Tholen, Zeeland, c.1510; d. c.1565. He entered the Papal Chapel in Rome as a chorister in 1538; was pensioned in 1565. He publ. (1559) 2 books of motets for 4–6 voices; single motets are included in Augsburg collections of 1540 and 1545. His ingenuity in counterpoint is demonstrated in the so-called Chessboard Canon for 4 voices with alternating black and white notes. His autograph MS, pronouncing judgment on the theoretical dispute between Vincentino and Lusitano on the nature of ancient modes, is in the Vatican Library in Rome.

Dancla, (Jean-Baptiste-) Charles, French violinist and composer; b. Bagnères-de-Bigorre, Dec. 19, 1817; d. Tunis, Nov. 9, 1907. He entered the Paris Cons. in 1828, his teachers being Baillot (violin), Halévy, and Berton. In 1834, he was a violinist in the Opéra-Comique orch.; became renowned by his playing in the Société des Concerts, and was appointed prof. of violin at the Paris Cons. in 1857. His quartet *soirées* were famous. Besides 4 symphs., he composed some 130 works for violin; 14 string quartets; 4 piano trios.

Dandrieu, Jean François, French composer; b. Paris, 1682; d. there, Jan. 17, 1738. He was organist at Saint-Merry, Paris, in 1704; in 1721 became organist at the Royal Chapel. He publ. *Livre de sonates en trio* (1705); *Livre de sonates* for Solo Violin (1710); *Principes de l'accompagnement du clavecin* (1718); *Pièces de clavecin* (3 albums, 1724); organ pieces, airs. His importance lies in his works for clavecin, written in a style closely resembling Couperin's.

Daniel, Oliver, American music critic and editor; b. De Pere, Wis., Nov. 24, 1911. He was editor of the American Composers' Alliance (1951–54); in 1954 became director of the Concert Music Administration of Broadcast Music, Inc. He was co-founder, with Leopold Stokowski, of the Contemporary Music Society in 1952; represented the U.S. at the International Music Council of UNESCO. He edited the collections *The Harmony of Maine, Down East Spirituals,* and *The Music of William Billings.*

Daniel, Salvador (real name, **Francisco Daniel;** also known as **Salvador-Daniel**), French composer and political revolutionary; b. Bourges, Feb. 17, 1831; killed during the Paris Commune, May 23, 1871. For a brief time he was director of the Paris Cons. under the Commune. He taught music in an Arab school in Algiers; studied native folk songs of North Africa; wrote a valuable book, *La Musique arabe* (Algiers, 1863, publ. in Eng. as *The Music and Musical Instruments of the Arabs,* London, 1915).

Daniel-Lesur. See **Lesur, Daniel.**

Daniélou, Alain, French musicologist, authority on music of Asia; b. Paris, Oct. 4, 1907. He devoted himself mainly to the study of Asian music; lived mostly in India; lectured at the Univ. of Benares (1949–54); was director of research in Madras (1954–56) and at the Inst. of Indology in Pondicherry (1956–59). In 1959 he was appointed instructor at the Ecole Français d'Extrême Orient in Paris. In 1963 he assumed the post of director of the International Inst. for Comparative Studies.

WRITINGS: *Introduction to the Study of Musical Scales* (London, 1943); *Northern Indian Music* (2 vols., Calcutta, 1949, 1953; 2nd ed., revised, as *The Ragas of Northern Indian Music,* 1968); *La Musique du Cambodge et du Laos* (Pondicherry, 1957); *Traité de musicologie comparée* (Paris,

1959); *Purānas: Texts des Purānas sur la théorie musicale* (Pondicherry, 1959); *Bharata, Muni, Le Gitālamkāra* (Pondicherry, 1960); *Inde* (Paris, 1966); *Sémantique musicale* (Paris, 1967); *La Situation de la musique et des musiciens dans les pays d'orient* (Florence, 1971; Eng. trans., 1971).

Daniels, Mabel Wheeler, American composer; b. Swampscott, Mass., Nov. 27, 1878; d. Boston, March 10, 1971. She studied at Radcliffe College (B.A., magna cum laude, 1900) and with Chadwick in Boston; then with Thuille in Munich; was director of the Radcliffe Glee Club (1911–13); head of music at Simmons College in Boston in 1913–18; received an honorary M.A. from Tufts College in 1933; an honorary D.Mus. from Boston Univ. in 1939. As a composer, she excelled in vocal writing; her instrumental pieces are cautiously modernistic.

WORKS: Operetta, *The Court of Hearts* (Cambridge, Mass., Jan. 2, 1901; she sang the part of Jack of Hearts); operatic sketch, *Alice in Wonderland Continued* (Brookline, Mass., May 20, 1904). Vocal works with Orch.: *The Desolate City* (1913); *Peace with a Sword* (Handel and Haydn Society, Boston, 1917); *Songs of Elfland* (St. Louis Symph. Orch., Feb. 2, 1924); *The Holy Star* (1928); *Exultate Deo* (for the 50th anniversary of Radcliffe College; Boston, May 31, 1929); *Song of Jael,* cantata for Dramatic Soprano, Mixed Voices, and Orch. (Worcester Festival, Oct. 5, 1940); *A Psalm of Praise* (composed for the 75th anniversary of the founding of Radcliffe College; Cambridge, Dec. 3, 1954; Boston Symph. Orch., April 27, 1956); choral cycle for Women's Voices, *In Springtime* (1910); 3-part women's choruses, with Piano and 2 Violins: *Eastern Song* and *The Voice of My Beloved* (prize of the National Federation of Music Clubs, 1911); sacred choruses a cappella (*The Christ Child, Salve festa dies,* etc.); duets; partsongs. For Orch.: *Deep Forest,* prelude for Small Orch. (Barrère Little Symph., N.Y., June 3, 1931; rescored for Full Orch., 1934; Boston Symph., April 16, 1937, Koussevitzky conducting); *Pirates' Island* (Harrisburg Symph., Feb. 19, 1935). Chamber music: *Pastoral Ode* for Flute and Strings (1940); *3 Observations* for Oboe, Clarinet, and Bassoon (1943); *Digressions,* a ballet for Strings (Boston, 1947). She wrote a lively book, *An American Girl in Munich* (Boston, 1905).

Danjou, Jean-Louis-Félix, French music teacher; b. Paris, June 21, 1812; d. Montpellier, March 4, 1866. He studied organ with François Benoist at the Paris Cons.; then played organ at various churches from 1830; was organist at Notre Dame from 1840 till 1847. With his essay *De l'état de l'avenir du chant ecclésiastique* (1844), he became the pioneer in the movement for reforming plainchant; and his journal *Revue de la Musique Religieuse, Populaire et Classique* (1845–49) showed profound erudition gained by assiduous historical research. He was the discoverer (1847) of the celebrated "Antiphony of Montpellier." He labored to promote organ building in France; made a special study of organ manufacture in Germany and the Netherlands; entered into partnership with the organ builders Daublaine & Callinet of Paris, but lost his entire capital, gave up music, and in 1849 became a political journalist in Marseilles and Montpellier.

Dankevich, Konstantin, eminent Ukrainian composer; b. Odessa, Dec. 24, 1905. He studied with Zolotarev at the Odessa Cons., graduating in 1929. In 1942 he was artistic director of the Red Army Ensemble of Songs and Dance in Tiflis. From 1944 to 1953 he was a prof. of composition at the Odessa Cons.; in 1953 he was appointed to the faculty of the Kiev Cons. In his works he successfully presents the motifs of Ukrainian and Russian folk songs. He first attracted attention with his opera *Bogdan Khmelnitzky* (Moscow, June 15, 1951), on a subject from Ukrainian history; the opera was attacked for its libretto and its unsuitable music, and Dankevich revised the score, after which it gained favorable notices in Russia. He also wrote the opera *Nazar Stodolya* (Kharkov, May 28, 1960). His most popular score is *Lileya,* a ballet, produced in 1939 and retained in the repertoire of the Russian theater. Other works include 2 symphs. (1937, 1945), several overtures, and patriotic choruses, including *Poem of the Ukraine* (1960) and the ideological cantata to his own words, *The Dawn of Communism Has Risen over Us* (1961). A monograph on Dankevich was publ. in Ukrainian in Kiev (1959).

Dannreuther, Edward George, pianist and music scholar, brother of **Gustav;** b. Strasbourg, Nov. 4, 1844; d. London, Feb. 12, 1905. He went with his parents in 1849 to Cincinnati, where he was taught by F.L. Ritter; then studied at the Leipzig Cons. with Richter, Moscheles, and Hauptmann (1859–63). On April 11, 1863, he made his debut in London, playing Chopin's Concerto in F minor. He introduced into England the piano concertos of Liszt, Grieg, and Tchaikovsky. In 1872 he founded the London Wagner Society, and conducted its concerts in 1873–74; was an active promoter of the Wagner Festival (1877); was appointed a prof. at the Royal Academy of Music in 1895. An indefatigable champion of the new composers, he was equally active on behalf of the older masters; the chamber music concerts that he gave at his home (1874–93) were famous. Dannreuther visited the U.S. several times.

Dannreuther, Gustav, American violinist, brother of **Edward;** b. Cincinnati, July 21, 1853; d. New York, Dec. 19, 1923. He studied at the Hochschule für Musik, Berlin, under de Ahna and Joachim (violin) and Heitel (theory); then lived in London; in 1877 he joined the Mendelssohn Quintette Club of Boston, traveling through the U.S., Canada, and Newfoundland. In 1882–84 he was director of the Buffalo Phil. Society (a chamber music organization), and during this period gave 60 concerts. In 1884 he founded the Beethoven String Quartet of N.Y. (renamed the Dannreuther Quartet in 1894). From 1907 he taught violin at Vassar College.

Danzi, Franz, German composer and teacher; b.

Schwetzingen, June 15, 1763; d. Karlsruhe, April 13, 1826. He received primary instruction in music from his father, **Innocenz Danzi,** a cellist; later took theory lessons with Abbé Vogler. In 1783 he joined the court orch. in Munich; then (1807–12) served as assistant Kapellmeister at Stuttgart, where he was the teacher of Carl Maria von Weber.

Da Ponte, Lorenzo, famous librettist; b. Ceneda, near Venice, March 10, 1749; d. New York, Aug. 17, 1838. His real name was **Emanuele Conegliano;** he was of a Jewish family; was converted to Christianity at the age of 14, and assumed the name of his patron, Bishop of Ceneda Lorenzo da Ponte. He then studied at the Ceneda Seminary and at the Portogruaro Seminary, where he taught in 1770–73; in 1774 obtained a post as prof. of rhetoric at Treviso, but was dismissed in 1776 for his beliefs concerning natural laws. He then went to Venice, where he led an adventurous life, and was banished in 1779 for adultery; subsequently lived in Austria and in Dresden; in 1782 he settled in Vienna and became official poet to the Imperial Theater; met Mozart and became his friend and librettist of his most famous operas, *Le nozze di Figaro, Don Giovanni,* and *Così fan tutte.* In 1792–98 he was in London; traveled in Europe; then went to N.Y. in 1805. After disastrous business ventures, with intervals of teaching, he became interested in various operatic enterprises. In his last years he was a teacher of Italian at Columbia College. He publ. *Memorie* (4 vols., N.Y., 1823–27; Eng. trans., London, 1929, and Philadelphia, 1929).

Daquin, Louis-Claude, French organist and composer; b. Paris, July 4, 1694; d. there, June 15, 1772. He was a pupil of Marchand; at 6 played on the clavecin before Louis XIV; at 12 became organist at St.-Antoine, where his playing attracted crowds of curious listeners. From 1727 until his death he was organist at St.-Paul, having won the position in competition with Rameau. He publ. a book of *Pièces de clavecin* (1735; contains the celebrated piece *Le Coucou;* selections reprinted in Expert's *Les Maîtres du clavecin;* also revised by Brunold in 1926); a collection of *Noëls pour l'orgue ou le clavecin* (reprinted by Guilmant in *Archives des Maîtres de l'Orgue*), and a cantata, *La Rose.* The first complete modern edition of his *Pièces de clavecin* was edited by Christopher Hogwood (London, 1983).

D'Aranyi, Jelly. See **Aranyi, Jelly.**

Dargomyzhsky, Alexander, outstanding Russian composer; b. in Tula province, Feb. 14, 1813; d. St. Petersburg, Jan. 17, 1869. From 1817 he lived in St. Petersburg; studied piano with Schoberlechner and Danilevsky, and violin with Vorontsov. At 20 he was a brilliant pianist; in 1827–43 he held a government position, but then devoted himself exclusively to music, studying assiduously for 8 years; visited Germany, Brussels, and Paris in 1845; at Moscow (Dec. 17, 1847) produced an opera, *Esmeralda* (after Victor Hugo's *Notre-Dame de Paris*), with great suc-

cess (excerpts publ. in piano score, Moscow, 1948). In 1845–55 he publ. over 100 minor works (vocal romances, ballads, airs, and duos; waltzes, fantasies, etc.); on May 16, 1856, he brought out his best opera, *Rusalka,* at St. Petersburg (vocal score, with indications of instruments, publ. at Moscow, 1937); in 1867, an opera-ballet, *The Triumph of Bacchus* (written in 1845; perf. in Moscow, Jan. 23, 1867); a posthumous opera, *Kamennyi gost (The Stone Guest,* after Pushkin's poem of the same title), was scored by Rimsky-Korsakov and produced at St. Petersburg on Feb. 28, 1872; of *Rogdana,* a fantasy-opera, only a few scenes were sketched. At first a follower of Rossini and Auber, Dargomyzhsky gradually became convinced that dramatic realism with nationalistic connotations was the destiny of Russian music; he applied this realistic method in treating the recitative in his opera *The Stone Guest* and in his songs (several of these to satirical words). His orch. works (*Finnish Fantasia, Cossack Dance, Baba-Yaga,* etc.) enjoyed wide popularity. In 1867 he was elected president of the Russian Music Society.

Dart, (Robert) Thurston, eminent English musicologist; b. London, Sept. 3, 1921; d. there, March 6, 1971. He studied keyboard instruments at the Royal College of Music in London (1938–39); also took courses in mathematics at Univ. College, Exeter (B.Sc., 1942). In 1947 he became an assistant lecturer in music at the Univ. of Cambridge, then a full lecturer in 1952, and finally a prof. of music in 1962. In 1964 he was named King Edward Prof. of Music at King's College of the Univ. of London. As a performing musician, he made numerous appearances on the harpsichord; also appeared as organist and performer on Baroque keyboard instruments. He served as editor of the *Galpin Society Journal* (1947–54) and secretary of the documentary edition *Musica Britannica* (1950–65). His magnum opus was *The Interpretation of Music* (London, 1954; 4th ed., 1967; also in German, under the title *Practica musica,* Bern, 1959, and in Swedish, Stockholm, 1964). He also edited works by Morley, Purcell, John Bull, and others.

Dauprat, Louis-François, celebrated French horn player and composer for horn; b. Paris, May 24, 1781; d. there, July 16, 1868. He studied with Kenn at the Paris Cons.; joined the band of the Garde Nationale, and in 1799 the band of the Garde des Consuls, with which he passed through the Egyptian campaign. In 1801–5 he studied theory at the Cons. under Catel and Gossec, and studied again with Reicha in 1811–14; in 1806–8 was first horn at the Bordeaux Theater; succeeded Kenn in the Opéra orch., and Duvernoy (as *cor solo*), retiring in 1831. He was chamber musician to Napoleon (1811) and Louis XVIII (1816); in 1816 he was appointed prof. of horn in the Cons., resigning in 1842.

Daussoigne-Méhul, Louis-Joseph, French composer; b. Givet, Ardennes, June 10, 1790; d. Liège, March 10, 1875. He was the nephew and foster son of **Etienne-Nicolas Méhul;** studied under him and

Catel at the Cons.; took the Grand Prix de Rome in 1809; after writing 4 operas, which were rejected, he at length produced his one-act *Aspasie* at the Grand Opéra (1820) with moderate success. He did still better with *Valentine de Milan,* a 3-act opera left unfinished by his foster father which he completed. In 1827 he accepted the directorship of the Liège Cons., which he retained, with great benefit to the school, until 1862. Daussoigne-Méhul was an associate of the Royal Academy, Brussels. He brought out a cantata with full orch. in 1828, and a choral symph., *Une Journée de la Révolution,* in 1834.

Dauvergne, Antoine, French composer and conductor; b. Clermont-Ferrand, Oct. 3, 1713; d. Lyons, Feb. 11, 1797. He received his first instruction from his father, went for further study to Paris in 1739, and was appointed a violinist in the Royal Orch. (1741); in 1755 was appointed composer to the Royal Orch.; in 1762, conductor of the Concert Spirituel; after 1769 was active as a conductor and manager of various enterprises until his retirement to Lyons in 1790. He introduced into France the forms of the Italian intermezzo, substituting spoken dialogue for the recitative, and thus was the originator of a style that soon became typical of French dramatic composition. He wrote 15 operas, the first of which, *Les Troqueurs,* was produced at Paris in 1753, and is regarded as the first opéra-comique; wrote 2 books of symphs., 12 sonatas for Violin and Basso Continuo, etc.

David, Félicien (-César), French composer; b. Cadenet, Vaucluse, Apr. 13, 1810; d. St.-Germain-en-Laye, Aug. 29, 1876. Of precocious talent, he was taught in the maîtrise of St.-Sauveur at Aix in 1818–25. He had a fine voice, and composed hymns, motets, and other music. He then studied in the Jesuit college for 3 years; became assistant conductor in the theater at Aix, and in 1829 maître de chapelle at St.-Sauveur; but in 1830 a longing to widen his musical horizons drew him to Paris, where he submitted specimens of his compositions to Cherubini, and was admitted to the Cons., studying harmony with Reber and Millault, counterpoint and fugue with Fétis, and organ with Benoist. In 1831, when the meager allowance given him by a rich and avaricious uncle had been withdrawn, he joined the socialistic movement of the St.-Simonists at Ménilmontant; here he composed a series of 4-part *hymns* for men's voices (later publ. with the words, as the *Ruche harmonieuse*). On the dispersion of the society in 1833, David went to Marseilles with a group of the brotherhood, giving concerts on the way; they proceeded to Constantinople, Smyrna, and Egypt, where they finally dispersed; with an imagination stimulated by his long sojourn in the East, David returned alone to Paris in 1835. He now publ. a collection of *Mélodies orientales;* they met with small success, and he retired to the country, giving himself up to study and composition (2 symphs., 24 small string quintets, 2 nonets for wind instruments, romances, etc.). In 1838 his First Symph. was produced. On Dec. 8, 1844, he at last reaped the fruit of many years' study: his symph. ode *Le Désert* was received at its first performance in the hall of the Cons. with "delirious" applause, and a series of repeat performances were given to crowded houses at the Salle Ventadour for a month. The oratorio *Moïse au Sinaï* followed in 1846, but, like a 2nd symph. ode, *Christophe Colomb* (Paris, March 7, 1847), and *L'Eden* (a "mystery" in 2 parts, Grand Opéra, Aug. 25, 1848), it met with a cool reception. However, his opera *La Perle du Brésil* (Théâtre-Lyrique, Nov. 22, 1851) was quite successful; a 2nd, *Le Dernier Amour,* was rejected by the Grand Opéra and by the Théâtre-Lyrique; but the Grand Opéra accepted it in 1859 as *Herculanum,* and for this opera the great state prize of 20,000 francs was awarded to David in 1867. *Lalla Roukh* (May 12, 1862) and *Le Saphir* (March 8, 1865) were given at the Opéra-Comique (the former with great success, the latter with scarcely a *succès d'estime*). David now abandoned dramatic composition, withdrawing his last opera, *La Captive.* In 1869 he was elected to the Académie, taking Berlioz's chair, and succeeding him also as librarian of the Cons. Besides the above works, he wrote 12 melodies for cello; *Les Brises d'Orient,* piano pieces; *Les Minarets,* 3 piano pieces; *Les Perles d'Orient,* 6 melodies for Voice and Piano; etc.

David, Ferdinand, German violinist and pedagogue; b. Hamburg, Jan. 19, 1810; d. near Klosters, Switzerland, July 18, 1873. In 1823–24 he studied with Spohr and Hauptmann at Kassel; played in the Gewandhaus Orch. in Leipzig, 1825; in 1826–29 was a member of the Königstadt Theater in Berlin. In 1829 he became the first violinist in the private string quartet of the wealthy amateur Baron von Liphardt of Dorpat, Russia, whose daughter he married. He remained in Russia until 1835, giving concerts in Riga, Moscow, and St. Petersburg with great acclaim. In 1836, at Mendelssohn's suggestion, he was appointed first violinist of the Gewandhaus Orch., of which Mendelssohn was the conductor. They became warm friends; Mendelssohn had a great regard for him, and consulted him constantly while writing his Violin Concerto; it was David who gave its first performance (Leipzig, March 13, 1845). When the Leipzig Cons. was established in 1843, David became one of its most important teachers; his class was regarded as the finishing school of the most talented violinists in Europe; among his pupils were Joachim and Wilhelmj. He publ. many valuable editions of violin works by classical composers, notably *Die hohe Schule des Violinspiels,* containing French and Italian masterpieces of the 17th and 18th centuries. His pedagogical activities did not interfere with his concert career; he played in England in 1839 and 1841 with excellent success and was compared with Spohr as a virtuoso; also made occasional appearances on the Continent.

David, Hans Theodor, American musicologist; b. Speyer, Palatinate, July 8, 1902; d. Ann Arbor, Mich., Oct. 30, 1967. He studied at the univs. of Tübingen and Göttingen; received the degree of Dr.Phil. at

Berlin (1928). In 1936 he emigrated to the U.S.; occupied various positions as a researcher and librarian; headed the dept. of musicology at Southern Methodist Univ. in Dallas, Texas (1945–50); in 1950 was appointed to the faculty of the Univ. of Michigan. He publ. *J.S. Bach's Musical Offering, History, Interpretation and Analysis* (N.Y., 1945); edited, with A. Mendel, *The Bach Reader* (N.Y., 1945; 2nd ed., revised, 1966); was co-author, with A.G. Rau, of *A Catalogue of Music of American Moravians, 1742–1842, from the Archives of the Moravian Church at Bethlehem, Pa.* (Bethlehem, Pa., 1938); edited Bach's *Art of the Fugue, Musical Offering,* and *Overture in the French Manner* (first version); *English Instrumental Music of the 16th and 17th Centuries;* etc.

David, Johann Nepomuk, outstanding Austrian composer; b. Eferding, Nov. 30, 1895; d. Stuttgart, Dec. 22, 1977. He studied with Joseph Marx at the Vienna Academy (1920–33); in 1934 was engaged as a prof. of composition at the Leipzig Cons., becoming its director in 1939. He was subsequently director at the Salzburg Mozarteum (1945–47). In 1947 he was appointed a prof. of composition at the Musikhochschule in Stuttgart, serving until 1963. David's music is severely polyphonic in its structure; almost all of his instrumental works are cast in forms of late Baroque; his mastery of counterpoint is revealed in his many choral pieces.
WORKS: FOR ORCH.: Concerto Grosso for Chamber Orch. (1923); Flute Concerto (1934); 2 partitas (1935, 1940); 8 numbered symphs. (1936; 1938; 1940; 1948; 1951, revised 1953; 1954; 1956; 1964–65); *Kume, kum, geselle min,* divertimento on old folk songs (1939; also a sextet for Winds and Piano); *Variations on a Theme of J.S. Bach* for Chamber Orch. (1942); *Symph. Variations on a Theme of H. Schütz* for Chamber Orch. (1942); 3 concertos for String Orch. (1949, 1949, 1975); 2 violin concertos: No. 1 (1952; Stuttgart, April 25, 1954) and No. 2 (1957; Munich, April 22, 1958); *Sinfonia preclassica super nomen H-A-S-E* for 2 Flutes, 2 Horns, and Strings (1953); *Deutsche Tänze* for Strings (1953); *Sinfonia breve* (1955); *Melancholia* for Solo Viola and Chamber Orch. (1958); *Magische Quadrate,* fantasy on serial principles (1959; Recklinghausen, March 23, 1960); *Sinfonia per archi* (1959); *Spiegelkabinett,* waltzes (1960); Organ Concerto (1964–65; Cologne, Nov. 28, 1966); *Variations on a Theme of Josquin des Pres* for Flute, Horn, and Strings (1966); Concerto for Violin, Cello, and Small Orch. (1969); Chaconne (1972).
FOR VOICE: *Requiem chorale* for Soloists, Chorus, and Orch. (1956; Vienna, June 11, 1957); *Ezzolied,* oratorio (1957; West Berlin, May 17, 1960); *Komm, Heiliger Geist,* cantata for 2 Choruses and Orch. (1972; Linz, March 26, 1974); *Stabat Mater,* in 6 parts, for a cappella Chorus (1927); *Deutsche Messe* for a cappella Chorus (1952); *O, wir armen Sünder,* cantata for Alto, Chorus, and Organ (1966); several motets.
CHAMBER MUSIC: Clarinet Quintet (1924); 3 string quartets; String Trio (1931, revised 1935); *Duo con-*

certante for Violin and Cello (1937); Sonata for Flute, Viola, and Guitar (1939); *Introitus, Choral, and Fugue* for Organ and 9 Winds (1939); Trio for Flute, Violin, and Viola (1942); Solo Sonatas for Flute, for Viola, for Cello, and for Lute (1942–44); 2 Solo Sonatas for Violin (1943 and 1963); Sonata for 2 Violins (1945); 4 string trios (1945–48); Partita for Solo Violin (1949); Sonata for 3 Cellos (1962); Trio for Flute, Violin, and Cello (1973); Partita for Violin and Organ (1975). Also numerous organ works (*Ricercare, Chaconne, Fantasia super L'Homme armé, Toccata and Fugue, Partita,* etc.). He wrote a study of Mozart's Jupiter Symph. (2nd ed., 1956).

Davidov, Carl, outstanding Russian violoncellist; b. Goldingen, Latvia, March 15, 1838; d. Moscow, Feb. 26, 1889. He studied cello in Moscow with Heinrich Schmidt and in St. Petersburg with K. Schuberth; in 1859 went to Leipzig, where he studied composition with Hauptmann. In 1860, at the age of 22, he was appointed an instructor at the Leipzig Cons. In 1862 he returned to Russia; from 1862 till 1887 was a prof. at the St. Petersburg Cons., and acting director from 1876 to 1887. He made several European tours, during which he played recitals with Anton Rubinstein, Saint-Saëns, and Liszt. Davidov was also a reputable composer; he wrote 4 cello concertos; a fantasy on Russian songs for Cello and Orch.; a symph. poem, *The Gifts of the Terek River;* String Quartet; String Sextet; Piano Quintet; songs. He also publ. a cello method (Leipzig, 1888; Russian ed., supervised by L. Ginsburg, Moscow, 1947).

Davidovich, Bella, Russian pianist; b. Baku, July 16, 1928. She studied at the Moscow Cons. with Igumnov and Flier, graduating in 1951; in 1962 she joined the faculty of the Moscow Cons. In 1949 she won the first prize at the International Chopin Contest. In 1977 she emigrated to the U.S. She achieved success as soloist with American and European orchs. and in recital, being praised particularly for her peculiarly "Russian" interpretation of 19th-century music, marked by a pervasive Romantic quality.

Davidovsky, Mario, Argentinian composer; b. Buenos Aires, March 4, 1934. He studied there with Ernesto Epstein and others; went to the U.S. in 1958; held 2 consecutive Guggenheim fellowships (1960–62); worked in the electronic music centers of Columbia Univ. and Princeton Univ. In 1971 he was appointed a prof. at the City College of N.Y.; in 1981 he joined the faculty at Columbia Univ. His method of composition tends toward mathematical parameters; his series of *Synchronisms* derives from the numerical coordinates of acoustical elements; electronic sound is integral to most of his work.
WORKS: String Quartet No. 1 (1954); Clarinet Quintet (1956); Nonet (1957); Concerto for Strings and Percussion (1957); String Quartet No. 2 (1958); *Suite sinfónica para el Payaso* (1958); *Serie sinfónica* (1959); *Planos* for Orch. (1961); *2 Studies* for Electronic Sound (1961, 1962); *Contrasts* for Strings

and Electronic Sound (1962); *Inflexions* for 14 Instruments (1965); 7 pieces under the generic title *Synchronisms:* Nos. 1–6 for different Instrumental Groups (1963–70) and No. 7 for Orch. and Tape (1974; N.Y. Phil., Dec. 4, 1975); *Chacona* for Piano Trio (1972); cantata-opera, *Scenes from Shir Hashirim,* for 4 Voices and Chamber Ensemble (1975–76). His *Synchronisms No. 6* for Piano and Electronic Sound was awarded the 1971 Pulitzer Prize.

Davies, Dennis Russell, American conductor; b. Toledo, Ohio, April 16, 1944. He studied at the Juilliard School of Music in N.Y.; became a member of its faculty (1968–71) and co-founder, with Luciano Berio, of the Juilliard Ensemble. He was subsequently music director of the Norwalk (Conn.) Symph. Orch. (1968–73); then was music director of the St. Paul Chamber Orch. (1972–80). In 1980 he became Generalmusikdirektor of the Württemberg State Theater in Stuttgart.

Davies, Fanny, English pianist; b. Guernsey, June 27, 1861; d. London, Sept. 1, 1934. She studied at the Leipzig Cons. with Reinecke and Paul (piano) and Jadassohn (theory) in 1882–83, and at the Hoch Cons. in Frankfurt with Clara Schumann (1883–85); also was a pupil of Scholz in fugue and composition. Her London debut took place at the Crystal Palace, Oct. 17, 1885; then she made successful tours in England, Germany, France, and Italy.

Davies, Peter Maxwell, remarkable British composer of variegated avant-garde pursuits; b. Manchester, Sept. 8, 1934. He went to Leigh Grammar School and then to the Royal Manchester College of Music and Manchester Univ. In 1957 he won a scholarship from the Italian government and proceeded to Rome, where he studied with Goffredo Petrassi; his orch. work *Prolation* (named after the medieval metrical division) received the Olivetti Prize in 1958 and was performed at the Festival of the International Society for Contemporary Music in Rome on June 10, 1959. Returning to England, he served as director of music at Cirencester Grammar School (1959–62); it was there that he introduced for the first time his neo-Socratic method of schooling, encouraging his students to exercise their curiosity. In 1962 he went to the U.S. on a Harkness fellowship and took a fruitful succession of sessions with Sessions at Princeton Univ. In 1965 he joined the UNESCO Conference on Music in Education and traveled around the world on a lecture tour. In 1966–67 he served as composer-in-residence at the Univ. of Adelaide in Australia. In 1967 he organized with Harrison Birtwistle in London an ensemble called the Pierrot Players; in 1970 they decided to rename it The Fires of London, with programs of provocative modernistic works. In 1970 Davies made his home in the Orkney Islands; in 1977 he organized there the annual St. Magnus Festival, which gave its presentations at the Norse Cathedral of St. Magnus; there he also staged many of his own compositions, inspired by medieval chants. Despite the remoteness of the Orkney Islands from musical

centers, the festival attracted attention. In 1979 Maxwell Davies was awarded an honorary doctorate of music at Edinburgh Univ.; he was also appointed successor to Sir William Glock as director of music at Dartington Summer School and was named Composer of the Year by the Composers' Guild of Great Britain. He was commissioned to write a symph. for the Boston Symph. Orch. on the occasion of its centennial in 1981. In his own works Maxwell Davies combines seemingly incongruous elements, which include reverential evocations of medieval hymnody, surrealistic depictions of historical personages, and hedonistic musical theatrics. His most arresting work in this synthetic manner is a set of *8 Songs for a Mad King,* a fantastic suite of heterogeneously arranged pieces representing the etiology of the madness of King George III; at the other end of the spectrum is *Vesalii Icones,* inspired by the anatomical drawings of Christ's Passion and Resurrection by the Renaissance artist Vesalius. Davies is a fervent political activist, a participant in the movement combating the spread of nuclear weapons, and a staunch defender of the planetary environment against industrial pollution.

WORKS: FOR THE STAGE: *Nocturnal Dances,* ballet (London, May 31, 1970); *Blind Man's Buff,* masque for High Voice, Mime, and Chamber Orch. (London, May 29, 1972); *Taverner,* opera to a libretto by Davies, descriptive of the life of the English composer Taverner (1962–70; London, July 12, 1972); *The Martyrdom of Saint Magnus,* chamber opera in 9 scenes (Kirkwall, Orkney, June 18, 1977); *The 2 Fiddlers,* opera for young people (Kirkwall, Orkney, June 16, 1978); *Le Jongleur de Notre Dame,* masque (Kirkwall, Orkney, June 18, 1978); *Salome,* ballet (Copenhagen, Nov. 10, 1978; concert suite drawn from the score, London, March 6, 1979); *The Lighthouse,* chamber opera (1979; Edinburgh, Sept. 2, 1980); *Cinderella,* pantomime for Child Actors (Kirkwall, Orkney, June 21, 1980; first American perf., Washington, D.C., April 16, 1982); *The Rainbow,* theatrical work for children (Kirkwall, Orkney, June 20, 1981).

FOR ORCH.: *Antechrist* for Chamber Ensemble (London, May 30, 1967); *Stedman Caters* for Chamber Ensemble (London, May 30, 1968); *Worldes Blis* (London, Aug. 28, 1968); *Vesalii Icones* for Dancer, Solo Cello, and Instruments, in 14 movements, after 14 anatomical drawings by Andreas Vesalius depicting Christ's Passion and Resurrection (London, Dec. 9, 1969); *Ave Maris Stella* for Chamber Ensemble (Bath, May 27, 1975); Symph. No. 1 (1976; London, Feb. 2, 1978); Symph. No. 2, commissioned by the Boston Symph. Orch. for its centennial (1980; Boston, Feb. 26, 1981); *Image, Reflection, Shadow* (Lucerne Festival, Switzerland, Aug. 22, 1981); *Sinfonia Concertante* for Chamber Orch. (1982; Aug. 12, 1983); *Sinfonietta Accademica* (Edinburgh, Oct. 6, 1983).

CHAMBER MUSIC: Sonata for Trumpet and Piano (1955); *Alma Redemptoris Mater* for Flute, Oboe, 2 Clarinets, Horn, and Bassoon (1957); *St. Michael* for 17 Wind Instruments (London, July 13, 1959); *Hymnos* for Clarinet and Piano (1967); *Canon in Memo-*

riam Igor Stravinsky for Flute, Clarinet, Harp, and String Quartet (London, June 17, 1972); *All Sons of Adam* for Flute, Clarinet, Marimba, Celesta, Guitar, Viola, and Cello (London, Feb. 20, 1974); *Little Quartet* for String Quartet (1980); *A Welcome to Orkney* for Flute, Oboe, Clarinet, Bassoon, Horn, 2 String Quartets, and Double Bass (Kirkwall, Orkney, June 20, 1980); *Brass Quintet* (1981; N.Y., March 19, 1982); *Birthday Music for John* for Viola, Flute, and Cello (London, Jan. 25, 1983).

VOCAL WORKS: *O Magnum Mysterium*, 4 carols for Chorus a cappella (Cirencester, Dec. 8, 1960); *Leopardi Fragments* for Soprano, Contralto, and Instruments (1962); *Veni Sancte Spiritus* for Solo Soprano, Contralto, and Bass, plus Chorus and Chamber Ensemble (Cheltenham Festival, July 10, 1964); *The Shepherds' Calendar* for Chorus and Instruments (Sydney, Australia, May 20, 1965); *Revelation and Fall* for Soprano and 16 Instruments (London, Feb. 26, 1968, composer conducting); *8 Songs for a Mad King* for Male Voice and Instruments, his most important and popular work (London, April 22, 1969, composer conducting); *From Stone to Thorn* for Mezzo-soprano and Instrumental Ensemble (Oxford, June 30, 1971, composer conducting); *Hymn to Saint Magnus* for Mezzo-soprano obbligato and Instrumental Ensemble (London, Oct. 13, 1972, composer conducting); *Notre Dame des Fleurs* for Soprano, Mezzo-soprano, Countertenor, and Instruments, to an obscene French text by the composer (London, March 17, 1973); *Dark Angels* for Mezzo-soprano and Guitar (1974); *Miss Donnithorne's Maggot* for Mezzo-soprano and Instruments (Adelaide Festival, March 9, 1974, composer conducting); *Fiddlers at the Wedding* for Mezzo-soprano and Instruments (Paris, May 3, 1974); *The Blind Fiddler*, song cycle for Soprano and Instrumental Ensemble (Edinburgh, Feb. 16, 1976, composer conducting); *Anakreontika* for Mezzo-soprano and Instrumental Ensemble (London, Sept. 17, 1976) composer conducting); *Westerlings* for Chorus a cappella (London, Oct. 15, 1977); *Solstice of Light* for Tenor Solo, Chorus, and Organ (St. Magnus Festival, Kirkwall, Orkney, June 18, 1979); *Black Pentecost*, cantata for Mezzo-soprano, Baritone, and Orch., decrying industrial air pollution (1979; London, May 11, 1982); *The Yellow Cake Revue* for Singers and Piano, to texts by the composer inveighing against the ominous threat of uranium mining in the Orkney Islands (Kirkwall, Orkney, June 21, 1980, composer conducting); *Into the Labyrinth*, cantata (Kirkwall, Orkney, June 22, 1983).

FOR SOLO INSTRUMENTS: Organ Fantasia from *O Magnum Mysterium* (Cirencester, Dec. 8, 1960); *The Door of the Sun* for Viola (1975); *Farewell to Stromness* (a town in the Orkney Islands), piano interlude from *The Yellow Cake Revue* (St. Magnus Festival, Kirkwall, Orkney, June 21, 1980, composer conducting); Piano Sonata (1981); Organ Sonata (1982); *Sea Eagle* for Solo Horn (1982).

WORKS FOR YOUNG PERFORMERS: *5 Klee Pictures* for School Orch. (1959; revised 1976); *3 Studies for Percussion* for 11 Percussionists (1975); *Kirkwall Shopping Songs* for Children's Voices, Recorders, Percussion, and Piano, to words by the composer (1979);

Songs of Hoy for Children's Voices and Instruments, to a text by the composer (1981); *7 Songs Home* for Unaccompanied Children's Voices, to texts by Davies (1981).

Davies, Sir (Henry) Walford, eminent English organist, educator, and composer; b. Oswestry, Sept. 6, 1869; d. Wrington, Somerset, March 11, 1941. He was a pupil of Sir Walter Parratt at St. George's Chapel in Windsor, where he also served as organist (1885–90); then held positions as organist at Christ Church, Hampstead (1891–98), at the Temple Church (1898–1918), and at St. George's Chapel (1927–32); was a prof. of music at the Univ. of Wales (1919–26). Between 1924 and 1934 he led the novel broadcasting series "Music Lessons in Schools." He was knighted in 1922; was appointed Master of the King's Musick in 1934. He composed mostly sacred choruses.

Davis, Andrew, English conductor; b. Ashbridge, Feb. 2, 1944. He studied at King's College, Cambridge, and at the Royal Academy of Music in London; then went to Rome, where he studied conducting with Franco Ferrara at the Santa Cecilia Academy. Returning to England, he served as assistant conductor of the BBC Scottish Symph. Orch. in Glasgow (1970–73); later was assistant conductor of the New Philharmonia Orch. in London. In 1975 he was named music director of the Toronto Symph. Orch. He also made an American tour as guest conductor.

Davis, Sir Colin (Rex), eminent English conductor; b. Weybridge, Sept. 25, 1927. He studied the clarinet at the Royal College of Music in London, and played in the band of the Household Cavalry while serving in the army. He began his conducting career with the semi-professional Chelsea Opera Group; in 1958 he conducted a performance of *Die Entführung aus dem Serail* at London; from 1961–65 served as music director of Sadler's Wells. He made his U.S. debut as a guest conductor with the Minneapolis Symph. Orch. on Dec. 30, 1960; subsequently had engagements with the N.Y. Phil., the Philadelphia Orch., and the Los Angeles Phil. From 1972–83 he served as principal guest conductor of the Boston Symph. Orch. On Jan. 20, 1967, he made his Metropolitan Opera debut in N.Y., conducting *Peter Grimes*. From 1967–71 he was chief conductor of the BBC Symph. Orch. in London. In 1965 he conducted at the Royal Opera at Covent Garden; he succeeded Solti as its music director in 1971. Among his notable achievements was the production at Covent Garden of the entire cycle of *Der Ring des Nibelungen* in 1974–76; in 1977 he became the first British conductor to appear at the Bayreuth Festival, conducting *Tannhäuser*. He conducted the Royal Opera during its tours in South Korea and Japan in 1979. In 1983 he was appointed chief conductor of the Bavarian Radio Symph. Orch. in Munich, while continuing his regular engagements in London. He was made a Commander of the Order of the British Empire in 1965, and was knighted in 1980.

Davis, Ivan, American pianist; b. Electra, Texas, Feb. 4, 1932. He studied piano with Silvio Scionti at North Texas State Univ. in Denton and later at the Santa Cecilia Academy in Rome with Carlo Zecchi. He also took private lessons with Vladimir Horowitz, beginning in 1961. He obtained first prizes at the Busoni Competition in Bolzano (1958), the Casella Competition at Naples (1958), and the Franz Liszt Competition in N.Y. (1960). He appeared as a soloist with the N.Y. Phil., Boston Symph. Orch., Philadelphia Orch., Chicago Symph., London Symph., Concertgebouw Orch. in Amsterdam, etc. In 1970 he was artist-in-residence at the Univ. of Miami at Coral Gables, Fla.

Davis, Miles (Dewey), Jr., black American jazz trumpeter; b. Alton, Ill., May 25, 1926. He organized a band with Sonny Stitt and Clark Terry; as a youngster: contributed to the flowering of bebop in the company of "bird" Charlie Parker, Coleman Hawkins, Benny Carter, and Billy Eckstine. His bebop syle was modified in 1948 when a band which he led included such an untypical jazz instrument as the French horn (played by Gunther Schuller), and which was exemplified by such numbers as *Boplicity.* He introduced a "cool" manner of playing as contrasted with the frantic "hot" bebop. His arranger was Gil Evans; he had John Coltrane on the saxophone and Philly Joe Jones on the drums. In his own songs he introduced the lyrical and quiet "modal" type of setting, favoring the Lydian scale with its enervating tritone base, and he found suitable harmonies for it. By 1958 he abandoned standard pop practices and plunged into the mystical depths of exotic jazz in such far-out numbers as *Nefertiti* and *Sorcerer.* Then he annexed electronics, forming a "fusion style" with hard rock. To emphasize his departure from his native territory, he affected pseudo-African vestments at his public appearances. Inevitably, or so it seemed, he began to use hallucinogenic drugs, and had some close encounters with unfeeling law enforcers. As he prospered from megamillion sales of record discs, he became the target of extortionists eager to muscle in on the action; some inartistic malefactors peppered his snazzy Ferrari car with machine-gun bullets; he suffered a hip injury which required the implantation of an artificial bone. Davis summarized his creative evolution in his 1981 album egotistically named *We Want Miles.*

Davison, Archibald Thompson, eminent American music educator; b. Boston, Oct. 11, 1883; d. Brant Rock, Cape Cod, Mass., Feb. 6, 1961. He studied at Harvard Univ. (B.A., 1906; M.A., 1907; Ph.D., 1908); took lessons in organ with Widor in Paris. Returning to America, he was organist and choirmaster at Harvard Univ. (1910–40); conducted the Harvard Glee Club (1912–33) and the Radcliffe Choral Society (1913–28); he was a prof. of music at Harvard until his retirement in 1954. He held numerous honorary degrees, including those of D.Mus. at Williams College and Oxford Univ.; Fellow of the Royal College of Music, London; Litt.D. from

Washington Univ. (1953); and L.H.D. from Temple Univ. (1955). He wrote a musical comedy, *The Girl and the Chauffeur,* upon his graduation from Harvard (perf. in Boston, April 16, 1906) and the overtures *Hero and Leander* (1908) and *Tragic Overture* (1918). His greatest achievement was as an educator and popularizer of musical subjects: his lectures on music appreciation were broadcast and enjoyed considerable success among radio listeners. He was associate editor, with Thomas W. Surette, of a multivolume collection of vocal and instrumental pieces, the Concord Series, for which he made numerous arrangements.
    WRITINGS: *Music Education in America* (1926); *Protestant Church Music in America* (1920; enlarged ed., 1933); *Harvard University Hymn Book* (with E.C. Moore, 1926); *Choral Conducting* (1945); *The Technique of Choral Composition* (Cambridge, Mass., 1946); ed., with W. Apel, *Historical Anthology of Music* (Cambridge, 2 vols., 1946; revised ed., 1949); *Bach and Handel: The Consummation of the Baroque in Music* (Cambridge, 1951); *Church Music: Illusion and Reality* (Cambridge, 1952). A dedicatory vol., *Essays on Music in Honor of A.T. Davison by His Associates,* was publ. at Cambridge in 1957.

Dawson, Ted, Canadian composer; b. Victoria, British Columbia, April 28, 1951. He studied violin, viola, and piano at the Victoria Cons. (1964–68); took courses in music theory with Cherney and Komorous at the Univ. of Victoria (1968–72), then in composition with Hambraeus and electronic music with Alcides Lanza at McGill Univ. in Montreal (1973–74); he subsequently engaged in teaching.
    WORKS: *Pentad* for String Quartet (1971); *Concerto Grosso I* for Quadraphonic Tape, or Amplified Viola, Amplified Bassoon, Trombone, Percussion, and Stereo Tape (1973–74); *Concerto Grosso II* for 5 Instrumental Soloists and Orch. (1973); *Chameleon* for Solo Amplified Viola (1974); *Chameleon* for Solo Amplified Flute (1974–75); *The Clouds of Magellan* for 3 Slide Projectors, Computerized Dissolver, Synchronization Tape, and Quadraphonic Audiotape (1976–77); *Binaries in Lyrae* for 4 Dancers, 2 Amplified Percussion Ensembles, Amplified Piano, and Lights (1977–78); *Megatherium* for 2 Amplified Pianos, Synthesizer, and Audiotape (1977–78).

Dawson, William Levi, American composer; b. Anniston, Ala., Sept. 26, 1898. At the age of 13, he ran away from home to enter the Tuskegee Inst.; later played trombone on the Redpath Chautauqua Circuit; graduated from the Tuskegee Inst. in 1921; later studied with Carl Busch in Kansas City and at the American Cons. in Chicago. He received his M.A. in 1927. He played first trombone in the Chicago Civic Orch. (1926–30); then conducted the Tuskegee Choir. Among his works is a Negro folk symph. in 3 movements (Philadelphia Orch., Stokowski conducting, Nov. 16, 1934).

De Angelis, Nazzareno, noted Italian bass; b. Aquila, Nov. 17, 1881; d. Rome, Dec. 14, 1962. As a boy he sang in the Sistine and Justine chapel choirs in Rome; made his operatic debut in Aquila in 1903; then appeared with major Italian opera houses; in America, he was on the roster of the Manhattan Opera House in N.Y. (1909–10); then of the Chicago Opera (1910–11; 1915–20); later made appearances with the Rome Opera (until 1938); also gave song recitals. He was regarded as one of the most cultured bass singers of the Italian school of opera; and he was equally appreciated in Wagnerian roles.

Debain, Alexandre-François, the inventor of the harmonium; b. Paris, 1809; d. there, Dec. 3, 1877. He established a factory of pianos and organs in Paris (1834), and after long experimentation with free reeds patented his harmonium in 1840. He also invented the antiphonel and the harmonichorde, and improved the accordion.

Debussy, Claude (Achille-Claude), great French composer; b. St.-Germain-en-Laye, Aug. 22, 1862; d. Paris, March 25, 1918. Mme. de Fleurville, a pupil of Chopin, prepared him for the Paris Cons., where he was admitted at the age of 10. Here he continued his study of piano with Marmontel, and won 2nd prize in 1877; in the solfeggio class of Lavignac he won the medal 3 years in succession (1874, 1875, 1876). Emile Durand was his teacher in harmony (1876–80); he received no awards there. After his graduation in 1880, Debussy was recommended to Mme. Nadezhda von Meck, Tchaikovsky's patroness, as a household pianist to teach piano to her children and play 4-hands with them. She summoned him to Switzerland, where she was traveling (he was not quite 18 at the time), and took him to Italy and Russia; he stayed with her family in Moscow and at her country estate in the summers of 1881 and 1882. There he had an opportunity to acquaint himself with the music of Borodin and Mussorgsky, which was to influence him greatly in the subsequent period of his creative activity. Although he played Tchaikovsky's scores for Mme. von Meck (including the MS of the 4th Symph., dedicated to her), Debussy did not evince great interest in Tchaikovsky's works. Another influence in his youth was Mme. Vasnier, an excellent singer, whom he met during the years he was preparing for the Grand Prix (1881–84); he spent much of his time at the Vasnier residence at Ville-d'Avray; the first of his *Fêtes galantes,* on poems of Verlaine (as well as some other works), is dedicated to her. In the composition class of Guiraud he won a prize for counterpoint and fugue in 1882; the next year he was the winner of the 2nd Prix de Rome, and finally, in 1884, he won the much coveted Grand Prix, with his cantata *L'Enfant prodigue.* From the Villa Medici in Rome he sent as the fruit of the first year a fragment of a choral work, *Zuleïma* (after Heine's *Almanzor*), which he later destroyed; he also worked on a composition for the stage, *Diane au bois,* which he had begun in Paris, but this was never finished. The 2nd year he wrote *Printemps,* a symph. suite, which found no favor with the jury at the Academy. This did not prevent Debussy from following the path on

which he had commenced, and, returning to Paris, he composed another cantata, *La Damoiselle élue,* even more advanced; at this time (1887) he also visited London. The work of the last year in Rome (1888) was a *Fantaisie* for Piano and Orch. The customary performance of the "envois de Rome" never took place; the committee refused to put *Printemps* on the program, and Debussy insisted that either all or none be produced. At about that time Debussy became an intimate of a group of French poets of the symbolist school, and was particularly fascinated by Mallarmé; he also made a visit to Bayreuth (1888), where he heard *Parsifal;* he repeated this visit in 1889; in that year he also became greatly interested in the oriental music which was presented at the Paris Exposition, and acquired a taste for exotic musical colors. His early enthusiasm for Wagner soon petered out, and he became actually antagonistic to Wagner's ideas. Contacts with the impressionist movement, added to the influence of modern French poetry, contributed to Debussy's mature style, in which formal structure becomes less important, while mood, atmosphere, and color assume special significance. His *Ariettes oubliées* (1888), to Verlaine's words, and *Cinq poèmes* (1890), to Baudelaire's verses, are the first revelations of this new style. He wrote *Petite suite* for Piano, 4-hands (1889; arranged for orch. by H. Busser); in 1890 he began *Suite bergamasque* for Piano, which includes the most celebrated single piece by Debussy, *Clair de lune* (the title is from Verlaine's poem, which also contains the word "bergamasque," adopted by Debussy); it is interesting to observe that in the framework of a classical suite, Debussy applies his novel methods of musical coloring. The year 1892 marked the beginning of the composition of his orchestral *Prélude à l'Après-midi d'un faune* (after Mallarmé; Paris, Dec. 23, 1894) and his only opera, *Pelléas et Mélisande.* Debussy continued his productive work; he wrote a String Quartet (1893; designated as *Premier Quatuor,* although it was the only quartet he wrote); the song vols. *Proses lyriques* (1894) and *Chansons de Bilitis* to poems of Pierre Louÿs (1898), the latter being one of his most poetic invocations; another work, also entitled *Chansons de Bilitis,* for 2 Flutes, 2 Harps, and Celesta was performed semi-privately (Paris, Feb. 7, 1901), in the form of a mimo-melo-drama. Debussy's major composition at the turn of the century was *3 Nocturnes* for Orch. (the first 2, *Nuages* and *Fêtes,* were perf. in Paris, Dec. 9, 1900; the 3rd, *Sirènes,* for Orch. and Wordless Choir of Women's Voices, was perf. with the others on Oct. 27, 1901).

On Oct. 19, 1899, Debussy married Rosalie Texier. (The *Nocturnes* are dedicated to her under the affectionate name "Lily-Lilo.") However, in 1904 he eloped with Mme. Emma Bardac, the wife of a banker; Rosalie shot herself in despair, but recovered; the divorce followed on Aug. 2, 1904, and Debussy finally married Mme. Bardac on Oct. 15, 1905. A daughter born to this marriage ("Chouchou," to whom Debussy dedicated his *Children's Corner*) died at the age of 14 on July 14, 1919.

Pelléas et Mélisande was produced at the Opéra-

Comique on April 30, 1902, after many difficulties, among them the open opposition of Maeterlinck, on whose play the opera was based. Mary Garden sang Mélisande, arousing admiration as well as wonderment as to the reason why an American singer with imperfect French pronunciation should have been selected; Maeterlinck's own choice for the part was his mistress, Georgette Leblanc. The opera was attacked violently by some critics for its decadent character, and for many years was a center of musical controversy. Performances followed, but slowly; it was produced at the Manhattan Opera House in N.Y. on Feb. 19, 1908; at Covent Garden in London on May 21, 1909; at the Metropolitan Opera House in N.Y. on March 21, 1925. At various times it was reported that Debussy had completed other dramatic works; in fact, the Metropolitan even announced its acquisition of the rights to the production of *Le Diable dans le beffroi, La Chute de la maison Usher,* and *La Légende de Tristan;* 2 versions of Debussy's libretto for *La Chute de la maison Usher* are in existence, but nothing is known of any music for these works beyond mention of it in correspondence or conversations. *La Mer,* his next important composition, was completed at Eastbourne, England, in March 1905; it was first performed by Chevillard in Paris, Oct. 15, 1905. Then followed the orch. suite *Images,* of which *Ibéria* (1908), descriptive of a Spanish fiesta, with guitarlike strumming on the violins, was the most successful. On Dec. 18, 1908, Harold Bauer played the first performance, at the Cercle Musical in Paris, of Debussy's *Children's Corner;* an orchestration by Caplet was performed in Paris on March 25, 1911. In 1908 Debussy conducted *La Mer* and *Prélude à l'Après-midi d'un faune* in London; in 1909 he appeared there again to conduct the *Nocturnes;* following this he filled various engagements as a conductor in Paris, Vienna, and Budapest (1910), Turin (1911), Moscow and St. Petersburg (1913), and The Hague, Amsterdam, and Rome (1914). Diaghilev produced his ballet *Jeux* in Paris on May 15, 1913. Debussy contemplated an American tour with the violinist Arthur Hartmann in 1914, but abandoned the idea because of illness; thereafter his health failed rapidly owing to cancer, and, after 2 operations, he finally succumbed. Debussy's last appearance in public was on May 5, 1917, when he played (with Gaston Poulet) the piano part in his Violin Sonata.

Debussy is regarded as the creator and chief protagonist of musical Impressionism, despite the fact that he deprecated the term and denied his role in the movement. This, however, cannot alter the essential truth that, like Monet in painting and Mallarmé in poetry, Debussy created a style peculiarly sensitive to musical mezzotint from a palette of half-lit, delicate colors. To accomplish the desired effect, Debussy introduced many novel technical devices. He made use of the oriental pentatonic scale for exotic evocations, and of the whole-tone scale (which he did not invent, however; samples of its use are found in Glinka and Liszt); he emancipated dissonance, so that unresolved discords freely followed one another; he also revived the archaic practice of consecutive perfect intervals (par-

ticularly fifths and fourths). In Debussy's formal constructions, traditional development is abandoned and the themes themselves are shortened and rhythmically sharpened; in instrumentation, the role of individual instruments is greatly enhanced and the dynamic range subtilized. These applications aroused intense criticism on the part of traditionalists; a book, *Le Cas Debussy* (1910), gave expression to this opposition; see also N. Slonimsky, *Lexicon of Musical Invective* (N.Y., 1953).

WORKS: PUBLISHED: FOR THE STAGE: *Pelléas et Mélisande,* opera (1892–1902); *Le Martyre de Saint Sébastien,* music to the mystery play by d'Annunzio, for Soli, Chorus, and Orch. (1911); ballets: *Jeux* (1912) and *Khamma* (1912).

CHORAL WORKS: *Printemps* for Women's Voices (1882); *Invocation* for Men's Voices (1883); *L'Enfant prodigue,* cantata (1884); *La Damoiselle élue* for Soli, Chorus, and Orch. (1887–88); *3 Chansons de Charles d'Orléans* for Unaccompanied Chorus (1908); *Ode à la France* for Solo, Chorus, and Orch. (1916–17).

FOR ORCH.: *Printemps,* symph. suite (1886–87); *Fantaisie* for Piano and Orch. (1888–89); *Prélude à l'Après-midi d'un faune* (1892–94); *Nocturnes* (1893–99); *La Mer,* 3 symph. sketches: *De l'aube à midi sur la mer, Jeux de vagues, Dialogue du vent et de la mer* (1903–5); incidental music to Shakespeare's *King Lear* (1904); *Danse sacrée* and *Danse profane* for Harp and Strings (1904); *Images: Gigues, Ibéria, Rondes de Printemps* (1906–12).

CHAMBER MUSIC: String Quartet (1893); *Rapsodie* for Saxophone and Piano (1903–5; also with Orch.); *Première rapsodie* for Clarinet and Piano (1909–10); *Petite pièce* for Clarinet and Piano (1910); *Syrinx* for Flute alone (1912); Cello Sonata (1915); Sonata for Flute, Viola, and Harp (1915); Violin Sonata (1916–17).

FOR PIANO SOLO: *Danse bohémienne* (1880); *2 arabesques* (1888); *Rêverie, Ballade, Danse, Valse romantique, Nocturne* (1890); *Suite bergamasque* (1890–1905); *Mazurka* (1891); *Pour le piano* (1896–1901); *Estampes* (1903); *D'un cahier d'esquisses* (1903); *Masques* (1904); *L'Isle joyeuse* (1904); *Images,* first series (1905); *Images,* 2nd series (1907); *Children's Corner* (1906–8); *Hommage à Haydn* (1909); *La Plus que lente* (1910); *12 préludes* (first book, 1910; 2nd book, 1910–13); *La Boîte à joujoux,* children's ballet (1913); *Berceuse héroïque pour rendre hommage à S.M. le Roi Albert Ier de Belgique et à ses soldats* (1914); 2 books of *12 études* (1915).

FOR PIANO DUET: One movement of a *Symphonie en si* (1880; intended for Orch.); *Triomphe de Bacchus* (1881); *Petite suite* (1889); *Marche écossaise sur un thème populaire* (1891; also for Orch.); *6 épigraphes antiques* (1914).

FOR 2 PIANOS: *Lindaraja* (1901); *En blanc et noir* (1915). 60 songs to texts by Verlaine, Bourget, Villon, Baudelaire, Louÿs, Girod, Mallarmé, and others; various arrangements and orchestrations; also *Masques et Bergamasques,* scenario for a ballet written in 1910.

WORKS: UNPUBLISHED: FOR THE STAGE: *Rodrigue et Chimène,* opera (1891–92; unfinished); *F.E.A. (Frères en art),* 3 scenes of a play (1900; with René Peter);

Le Diable dans le beffroi, opera after Poe's *The Devil in the Belfry* (1902–3; unfinished; only notes for the libretto and a sketch for Scene I are extant); 2 versions of a libretto for *La Chute de la maison Usher* (after Poe; 1908–18).

CHORAL WORKS: *Daniel,* cantata (1880–84); *Le Gladiateur* (1883).

FOR ORCH.: *Intermezzo* (after a passage from Heine's *Intermezzo;* 1882; also arranged for Piano Duet).

CHAMBER MUSIC: Trio in G for Piano, Violin, and Cello (1880); *Chansons de Bilitis,* incidental music for Louÿs's poems, for 2 Flutes, 2 Harps, and Celesta (1900).

SONGS: *Caprice* (1880); *Chanson espagnole* for 2 Voices, *Rondel chinois, Romance, Aimons-nous, La Fille aux cheveux de lin, Eclogue* (1880–84); *Berceuse* for the play *La Tragédie de la mort* (1908). An Intermezzo for Cello and Piano was found by Gregor Piatigorsky in Paris in 1938.

WRITINGS: Debussy contributed numerous criticisms and essays to the *Revue Blanche, Gil Blas, Musica, Mercure de France, La Revue S.I.M.,* etc. Collected essays and criticisms publ. in various journals were issued as *Monsieur Croche, Antidilettante* (Paris, 1923; Eng. trans. 1928, 1948; new ed. with commentary by F. Lesure, Paris, 1971).

Decaux, Abel, French organist and composer; b. Auffay, 1869; d. Paris, March 19, 1943. He studied organ with Widor and Guilmant and composition with Massenet at the Paris Cons. He served as organist at the church of Sacré-Cœur in Montmartre; then was prof. of organ playing at the Schola Cantorum; from 1923 to 1937 he taught organ at the Eastman School of Music in Rochester, N.Y. Decaux composed very little; but he attracted posthumous attention by the discovery, and performance, of his group of piano pieces under the title *Clairs de Lune* (the plural being of the essence): *Minuit passe, La Ruelle, Le Cimétière,* and *La Mer,* written between 1900 and 1907 and publ. in 1913; seem to represent early examples of piano writing usually associated with Debussy and Ravel; the similarity of styles is indeed striking, which indicates that Impressionism was "in the air," and in the ears, of impressionable French musicians early in the new century.

Decoust, Michel, French composer; b. Paris, Nov. 19, 1936. He studied at the Paris Cons. with Olivier Messiaen and others; received the Premier 2nd Grand Prix de Rome (1963). His works include *Mouvement* for Strings and Percussion (1964); Etudes for Flutes and Cellos (1966); *Polymorphée* for Orch. (Royan, April 1, 1967); *Instants-Stabiles* for Chamber Ensemble (1967); *Actions* for Voice and Piano, with Audience Participation (Angers, April 18, 1972); *T' Ai* for Double Bass, Electric Guitar, Percussion, Harpsichord, and Voice (Paris, Jan. 25, 1972); *Et, ée* for Chorus and Orch. (Paris, July 23, 1973).

Decsey, Ernst, German-Austrian writer on music; b. Hamburg, April 13, 1870; d. Vienna, March 12, 1941. He studied law in Vienna (receiving a doctorate in law in 1894); then studied composition with Bruckner and Robert Fuchs at the Vienna Cons.; was active as a music critic in Graz and in Vienna. He was the author of the standard biography of Hugo Wolf (in 4 vols., Berlin, 1903–6; several subsequent printings; an abridged one-vol. ed. appeared in 1921). He also wrote the monographs *Anton Bruckner* (Berlin, 1920); *Johann Strauss* (Stuttgart, 1922; 2nd ed., 1947); *Franz Lehár* (Vienna, 1924); *Franz Schubert* (Vienna, 1924); *Maria Jeritza* (Vienna, 1931); *Claude Debussy* (Graz, 1936); and *Debussys Werke* (Graz and Vienna, 1948).

Deering (or **Dering**), **Richard,** English composer; b. Kent, c.1580; d. London (buried, March 22), 1630. He was educated in Italy; returned to England as a well-known musician and practiced in London; in 1610, took the degree of B.Mus. at Oxford; in 1617, became organist at the convent of English nuns at Brussels; in 1625, was appointed organist to Queen Henrietta Maria.

WORKS: *Cantiones sacrae sex vocum cum basso continuo ad organum* (Antwerp, 1597); *Cantiones sacrae quinque vocum* (1617); *Cantica sacra ad melodium madrigalium elaborato senis vocibus* (Antwerp, 1618); *Cantiones sacrae quinque vocum* (1619); 2 books of *Canzonette,* one for 3 Voices and one for 4 (1620; author's name given as Richardo Diringo Inglese); *Cantica sacra ad duos et tres voces, composita cum basso continuo ad organum* (posthumous; London, 1662). Sir Frederick Bridge ed. and publ. an elaborate work of Deering's entitled *The Cryes of London.* Various other compositions (anthems, motets, viol music) are preserved in MS in the libraries of the British Museum, Christ Church, Oxford, the Royal College of Music, Peterhouse, Cambridge, Durham Cathedral, etc.

Defauw, Désiré, Belgian conductor and violinist; b. Ghent, Sept. 5, 1885; d. Gary, Ind., July 25, 1960. He was a pupil of Johan Smit (violin); in 1914–18, led his own quartet (with L. Tertis, C. Woodhouse, and E. Doehard); was a prof. at the Antwerp Cons.; later conductor of the Defauw Concerts in Brussels; was also conductor of the Royal Cons. Orch. there and director of the National Inst. of Radio. In 1938 he was a guest conductor with the NBC Symph. Orch. in N.Y.; in Sept. 1940 he returned to the U.S.; was conductor of the Chicago Symph. Orch. (1943–47) and the Gary Symph. Orch. (1950–58).

Defossez, René, Belgian composer and conductor; b. Spa, Oct. 4, 1905. He studied with his father, then at the Liège Cons. with Rasse; received the Belgian Prix de Rome in 1935 for his opera-cantata *Le Vieux Soudard.* He was then active as a conductor; from 1936 to 1959 was conductor of the Théâtre Royal de la Monnaie in Brussels; in 1946 succeeded Defauw as prof. of conducting at the Brussels Cons.; retired from there in 1971. He was an inspector of state-subsidized music schools (1961–71). In 1969 he was elected a member of the Royal Belgian Academy.

DeGaetani, Jan, remarkable American mezzo-soprano; b. Massillon, Ohio, July 10, 1933. She studied with Sergius Kagen at the Juilliard School of Music in N.Y.; in 1973 was appointed prof. of voice training at the Eastman School of Music in Rochester, N.Y. She achieved distinction as a virtuoso vocalist in her performances of ultramodern works requiring accurate rendition of unusual intervallic skips, and often quarter-tones and other fractional intervals, in addition to special effects such as percussive tongue-clicking and a variety of finely calibrated dynamic nuances. In this field she has become a unique phenomenon; several vocal works have been written specially for her by grateful modern composers. As a lieder singer, DeGaetani excels in an analytical capacity to express the most minute vocal modulations of the melodic line while parsing the words with exquisite intellectual penetration of their meaning, so that even experienced music critics are rendered helpless in search of congenial superlatives to describe her artistry.

Degeyter, Pierre, wood-carver and author of the famous workers' song *Internationale* (1888); b. Oct. 8, 1848; d. St. Denis, near Paris, Sept. 27, 1932. The authorship of the song was contested by Pierre's brother, Adolphe, a blacksmith (b. 1858; d. Lille, Feb. 15, 1917), but after 18 years of litigation, the Paris Appellate Court decided in favor of Pierre.

Degner, Erich Wolf, German composer; b. Hohenstein-Ernstthal, April 8, 1858; d. Berka, near Weimar, Nov. 18, 1908. He studied at the grand-ducal school of music at Weimar, and later at Würzburg; taught at Regensburg and Gotha; in 1885 became director of the music school at Pettau, Styria; in 1888, instructor at the grand-ducal music school at Weimar; in 1891, director of the music school of the Styrian Music Society at Graz; in 1902 was again in Weimar as director of the music school.

Dehn, Siegfried Wilhelm, famous German music theorist; b. Altona, Feb. 24, 1799; d. Berlin, April 12, 1858. He was a law student at Leipzig in 1819–25; also studied harmony and cello playing. He studied theory assiduously with Bernhard Klein in Berlin; at Meyerbeer's insistence he was appointed librarian of the music dept. of the Royal Library in 1842. In 1842–48 he was also editor of the *Caecilia;* then was a prof. at the Royal Academy of Arts (1849–58). Dehn was a profound theorist, and very successful as a teacher of theory, numbering among his pupils Anton Rubinstein and Glinka.
WRITINGS: *Theoretisch-praktische Harmonielehre* (Berlin, 1840; 2nd ed., Leipzig, 1860; his most important work); *Analyse dreier Fugen aus J.S. Bachs Wohltemperiertem Clavier und einer Vokaldoppelfuge G.M. Buononcinis* (Leipzig, 1858); *Eine Sammlung älterer Musik aus dem 16. und 17. Jahrhundert* (Berlin; 12 books of vocal compositions *a* 4–10); trans. Delmotte's work on Orlandus Lassus, *Biogr. Notiz über Roland de Lattre* (Vienna, 1837). A posthumous *Lehre vom Kontrapunkt, dem Kanon und der Fuge* (Berlin, 1859; 2nd ed.,

1883) was ed. by B. Scholz.

De Jong, Conrad, American composer; b. Hull, Iowa, Jan. 13, 1934. He studied trumpet at North Texas State Univ. in Denton, majoring in music education; received his B.M.Ed. in 1954; later studied composition with Bernhard Heiden at Indiana Univ. in Bloomington, obtaining his M.M. in 1959. He was appointed to the music faculty of Wisconsin State Univ. at River Falls in 1959.
WORKS: *Unicycle* for Harpsichord (1960); *3 Studies* for Brass Septet (1960); *Music for 2 Tubas* (1961); *Essay* for Brass Quintet (1963); String Trio (1964); *Fun and Games* for Any Instrument with Piano (1966); *Aanraking (Contact)* for Solo Trombone (1969); *Hist Whist* for Soprano, Flute, Viola, and Percussion (1969); *Grab Gab* for Tuba Ensemble (1970); *Peace on Earth* for Unison Chorus and Organ (1970).

De Koven, (Henry Louis) Reginald, American composer; b. Middletown, Conn., April 3, 1859; d. Chicago, Jan. 16, 1920. He was educated in Europe from 1870, taking his degree at St. John's College, Oxford, in 1879. Before this he studied piano under W. Speidel at Stuttgart, and after graduation studied there another year under Lebert (piano) and Pruckner (harmony). After a 6-month course in Frankfurt under Dr. Hauff (composition), he studied singing with Vannucini at Florence, and operatic composition under Genée in Vienna and Delibes in Paris. In 1902 he organized the Phil. Orch. at Washington, D.C., which he conducted for 3 seasons. He was music critic for the *Chicago Evening Post* (1889–90), *Harper's Weekly* (1895–97), *N.Y. World* (1898–1900 and 1907–12), and later for the *N.Y. Herald.*
WORKS: He wrote several successful operettas: *The Begum* (Philadelphia, Nov. 7, 1887); *Don Quixote* (Boston, Nov. 18, 1889); *Robin Hood* (his best-known work; Chicago, June 9, 1890; London, Jan. 5, 1891; the celebrated song *O Promise Me* was introduced into the score shortly after its first perf.; it was originally publ. as a separate song in 1889); *The Fencing Master* (Boston, 1892); *The Knickerbockers* (Boston, 1893); *The Algerian* (Philadelphia, 1893); *Rob Roy* (Detroit, 1894); *The Tzigane* (N.Y., 1895); *The Mandarin* (Cleveland, 1896); *The Paris Doll* (Hartford, Conn., 1897); *The Highwayman* (New Haven, 1897); and the following, all of which had their premieres in N.Y.: *The Tree Dragoons* (1899); *Red Feather* (1903); *Happyland* (1905); *Student King* (1906); *The Golden Butterfly* (1907); *The Beauty Spot* (1909); *The Wedding Trip* (1911); *Her Little Highness* (1913). A grand opera, *The Canterbury Pilgrims,* was produced at the Metropolitan Opera House on March 8, 1917; another opera, *Rip van Winkle,* was performed by the Chicago Opera Co. (Jan. 2, 1920). In addition, he wrote some 400 songs and a Piano Sonata.

Dela, Maurice, French-Canadian composer and organist; b. Montreal, Sept. 9, 1919; d. Montreal, April 28, 1978. He studied composition with Champagne at the Montreal Cons. and orchestration with Leo Sowerby in Chicago. He subsequently became a church organist in the province of Quebec. His music is pragmatic in style and idiom, tending toward Baroque consistency but energized by an injection of euphonious dissonance.

Delacôte, Jacques, French conductor; b. Remiremont, Vosges, Aug. 16, 1942. He studied conducting with Hans Swarowsky at the Vienna Academy of Music; in 1971 he won the Mitropoulos Competition in N.Y.; in 1972 he appeared as a conductor with the N.Y. Phil.; subsequently conducted at the Hamburg State Opera, the Düsseldorf Opera, the Paris Opéra, and Covent Garden in London. As a symph. conductor, he had engagements with the London Symph., the Cleveland Orch., and the San Francisco Symph. Naturally, he is especially praised for his congenial performances of French operas.

Delage, Maurice, French composer; b. Paris, Nov. 13, 1879; d. there, Sept. 19, 1961. He was engaged as a clerk in a maritime agency in Paris and in a fishery in Boulogne; in 1900 was in the army; then became interested in music and took lessons with Ravel. Subsequently he made voyages to the Orient, and was greatly impressed with Japanese art. His music reveals oriental traits in subject matter as well as in melodic progressions. An ardent follower of Debussy's principles, Delage wrote music in a highly subtilized manner with distinctive instrumental colors. After 1920 he lived mostly in Paris.

Delalande, Michel-Richard, French organist and composer; b. Paris, Dec. 15, 1657; d. Versailles, June 18, 1726. He was the 15th child of a Paris tailor; was apprenticed as a boy chorister at the Saint-Germain Auxerrois; when his voice broke, he began to study organ playing, in which he succeeded so well that Louis XIV entrusted him with giving keyboard lessons to the royal princesses. In 1683 he received the position of "surintendant" of the Royal Chapel. In 1704 he became master of the Royal Chapel; in 1722, he was joined in this directorship by Campra, Bernier, and Gervais. WORKS: Delalande was the composer of excellent ballets, even though they yielded in quality to those of Lully; of these, *Ballet de la jeunesse* (1686), *Le Palais de Flore* (1689), *Adonis* (1698), *Le Ballet des fées* (1699), *L'Hymen champestre* (1700), *Le Ballet de la paix* (1713), and *Les Folies de Gardenio* (1720) were produced at the court in Versailles. With Destouches, he wrote the ballet *Les Elements,* which was produced at the Tuileries Palace in Paris on Dec. 31, 1721. (Vincent d'Indy edited the score and publ. it in 1883.) Delalande also wrote 42 motets, which were publ. in 1729, and a number of "symphonies pour les soupers du roi" (intermezzos to be played at court dinners) and "symphonies de Noël" (instrumental interludes for performances at Christmas time at the court); 22 "Noëls" (arranged in a series of 4 "symphonies") by Delalande were ed. by A. Cellier (Paris, 1937).

De Lamarter, Eric, American organist, music critic, and composer; b. Lansing, Mich., Feb. 18, 1880; d. Orlando, Fla., May 17, 1953. He studied organ with Fairclough in St. Paul, Middleschulte in Chicago, and Guilmant and Widor in Paris (1901–2); then was organist of various churches in Chicago till 1936; assistant conductor of the Chicago Symph. Orch. in 1918–36; also conducted the Chicago Civic Orch. He was music critic of the *Chicago Record-Herald* (1908–9), *Chicago Tribune* (1909–10), and *Inter-Ocean* (from 1910); held teaching positions at the Chicago Musical College and Olivet College. WORKS: Ballet, *The Betrothal* (N.Y., Nov. 19, 1918); ballet suite, *The Black Orchid* (Chicago Symph. Orch., Feb. 27, 1931, composer conducting); 4 symphs. (1914, 1926, 1931, 1932); overture, *The Faun* (1914); *Serenade* for Orch. (1915); overture, *Masquerade* (1916); *Fable of the Hapless Folktune* for Orch. (1917); 2 organ concertos (1920, 1922); *Weaver of Tales* for Organ and Chamber Orch. (1926); ballet suite, *The Dance of Life* (1931); *The Giddy Puritan,* overture on 2 early New England tunes (1921; NBC, June 6, 1938; Chicago Symph., March 9, 1942); organ works; songs.

De Lancie, John Sherwood, American oboe virtuoso; b. Berkeley, Calif., July 26, 1921. His father was an electrical engineer and an amateur clarinet player; his brother played the violin. In 1935 he won an audition for the Philadelphia Orch., and was also accepted to study oboe in the class of Marcel Tabuteau at the Curtis Inst. of Music. He was engaged as principal oboist with the Pittsburgh Symph. under Fritz Reiner, who was also conductor of the Curtis Student Orch. He was then engaged as oboist with the Denver Orch.; in 1942 he was drafted into the U.S. Army as a member of the U.S. Army Band; in 1943 the band was sent to Algiers, to Eisenhower's headquarters; he was subsequently employed by the Office of Strategic Services (now the CIA). After the war De Lancie succeeded Tabuteau as first oboist of the Philadelphia Orch. In 1977 he was appointed Director of the Curtis Inst., succeeding Rudolf Serkin. De Lancie rapidly advanced to the position of one of the greatest virtuosos on his instrument. An interesting episode in his career concerns his meeting with Richard Strauss, during which he asked Strauss why he would not compose a concerto for oboe, in view of the fact that there are so many beautiful oboe solos in many of his works. This suggestion bore fruit, but De Lancie was not the first to play it; the first performance was given by Marcel Saillet on Feb. 26, 1946, in Zürich.

Delannoy, Marcel, French composer; b. La Ferté-Alais, July 9, 1898; d. Nantes, Sept. 14, 1962. He served in the French army in World War I; then took lessons with Gédalge and Honegger. After a few years of instruction, he produced an effective stage work, *Poirier de Misère* (Paris, Feb. 21, 1927), which obtained excellent success. Other works are the ballet-cantata *Le Fou de la dame* (in concert form, Paris, Nov. 9, 1928; stage production, Geneva, April 6, 1929); *Cinderella,* ballet (Chicago, Aug. 30, 1931; revised and perf. as *La Pantoufle de vair* at the Opéra-Comique, Paris, May 14, 1935); a Symph. (Paris, March 15, 1934); *Ginevra,* comic opera in 3 acts (Paris, Opéra-Comique, July 25, 1942); *Arlequin radiophile,* chamber opera (Paris, April 1, 1946); *Puck,* fairy opera after Shakespeare (Strasbourg, Jan. 29, 1949); *Concerto de mai* for Piano and Orch. (Paris, May 4, 1950); *Travesti,* ballet (Enghien-les-Bains, June 4, 1952); ballet, *Les Noces fantastiques* (Paris, Feb. 9, 1955); Symph. for Strings and Celesta (1952–54); *Le Moulin de la galette,* symph. poem (1958).

De Lara (real name, **Cohen**), **Isidore,** English composer of operas; b. London, Aug. 9, 1858; d. Paris, Sept. 2, 1935. He began to study the piano at the age of 10 with H. Aguilar; also studied singing with Lamperti and composition with Mazzucato at the Milan Cons. He then went to Paris to study with Lalo; returning to London, he wrote one opera after another, and easily secured performances.
WORKS: *The Light of Asia* (1892); *Amy Robsart* (London, July 20, 1893); *Moina* (Monte Carlo, March 14, 1897); *Messalina* (Monte Carlo, March 21, 1899; his most successful work); *Sanga* (Nice, Feb. 21, 1906); *Solea* (Cologne, Dec. 12, 1907); *Les Trois Masques* (Marseilles, Feb. 24, 1912); *Naïl* (Paris, April 22, 1912); *Les Trois Mousquetaires* (Cannes, March 3, 1921).

Deldevez, Edouard-Marie-Ernest, French conductor and composer; b. Paris, May 31, 1817; d. there, Nov. 6, 1897. He studied violin with Habeneck and music theory with Halévy and Berton at the Paris Cons. In 1859 he was appointed assistant conductor at the Grand Opéra and of the Conservatoire Concerts; in 1872–75 was principal conductor; concurrently was principal conductor of the Paris Opéra (1873–77); taught orchestral playing at the Paris Cons. (1874–85).

Delgadillo, Luis Abraham, Nicaraguan composer; b. Managua, Aug. 26, 1887; d. there, Dec. 20, 1961. He studied at the Milan Cons.; returning to Nicaragua, he became a band conductor and opened a music school, which later became a cons. His music is permeated with native rhythm and melos; virtually all of his output is descriptive of some aspect of Latin American culture and history.
WORKS: For Orch.: *Sinfonia indigena* (1921); *Sinfonia mexicana* (1924); *Teotihuacan* (1925); *Sinfonia incaica* (1926; Caracas, May 20, 1927, composer conducting); *Sinfonia serrana* (1928); 12 short symphs., all composed in one year (1953) and couched in different styles, from classical to modernistic; overtures in the styles of Debussy and Schoenberg (*Obertura Debussyana* and *Obertura Schoenbergiana,* 1955); 7 string quartets; church music; piano pieces in various forms.

Delibes, (Clément-Philibert-) Léo, famous French composer; b. St.-Germain-du-Val, Sarthe, Feb. 21, 1836; d. Paris, Jan. 16, 1891. He received his early musical training with his mother and an un-cle; then enrolled in the Paris Cons. in 1847 as a student of Tariot; won a premier prix in solfège in 1850; also studied organ with Benoist and composition with Adam. In 1853 he became organist of St. Pierre de Chaillot and accompanist at the Théâtre-Lyrique. In 1856 his first work for the stage, *Deux sous de charbon,* a one-act operetta, humorously subtitled "asphyxie lyrique," was produced at the Folies-Nouvelles. His 2nd work, the opérette bouffe *Deux vielles gardes,* won considerable acclaim at its premiere at the Bouffes-Parisiens on Aug. 8, 1856. Several more operettas were to follow, as well as his first substantial work for the stage, *Le Jardinier et son seigneur,* given at the Théâtre-Lyrique on May 1, 1863. In 1864 he became chorus master of the Paris Opéra. With Louis Minkus he collaborated on the ballet score *La Source,* which was heard for the first time at the Paris Opéra on Nov. 12, 1866. It was with his next ballet, *Coppelia, ou La Fille aux yeux d'émail,* that Delibes achieved lasting fame after its premiere at the Paris Opéra, on May 25, 1870. Another ballet, *Sylvia, ou La Nymphe de Diane* (Paris Opéra, June 14, 1876), was equally successful. He then wrote a grand opera, *Jean de Nivelle* (Opéra-Comique, March 8, 1880), which was moderately successful; it was followed by his triumphant masterpiece, the opera *Lakmé* (Opéra-Comique, April 14, 1883), in which he created a most effective lyric evocation of India; the "Bell Song" from *Lakmé* became a perennial favorite in recitals. In 1881 he was appointed prof. of composition at the Paris Cons.; in 1884 was elected a member of the Institut. His last opera, *Kassya,* was completed but not orchestrated at the time of his death; Massenet orchestrated the score, and it was premiered at the Opéra-Comique on March 24, 1893. Delibes was a master of melodious elegance and harmonious charm; his music possessed an autonomous flow in colorful timbres, and a finality of excellence that seemed effortless while subtly revealing a mastery of the Romantic technique of composition.

Delius, Frederick (baptismal names, **Fritz Theodor Albert**), significant English composer of German parentage; b. Bradford, Jan. 29, 1862; d. Grez-sur-Loing, France, June 10, 1934. His father was a successful merchant, owner of a wool company; he naturally hoped to have his son follow a career in industry, but did not object to his study of art and music. Delius learned to play the piano and violin. At the age of 22 he went to Solano, Florida, to work on an orange plantation owned by his father; a musical souvenir of his sojourn there was his symph. suite, *Florida.* There he met an American organist, Thomas F. Ward, who gave him a thorough instruction in music theory; this study, which lasted 6 months, gave Delius a foundation for his further progress in music. In 1885 he went to Danville, Virginia, as a teacher. In 1886 he enrolled at the Leipzig Cons., where he took courses in harmony and counterpoint with Reinecke, Sitt, and Jadassohn. It was there that he met Grieg, becoming his friend and admirer. Indeed Grieg's music found a deep resonance in his own compositions. An

293

Delius

even more powerful influence was Wagner, whose principles of continuous melodic line and thematic development Delius adopted in his own works. Euphonious serenity reigns on the symph. surface of his music, diversified by occasional resolvable dissonances. In some works he made congenial use of English folk motifs, often in elaborate variation forms. Particularly successful are his evocative symphonic sketches *On Hearing the First Cuckoo in Spring, North Country Sketches, Brigg Fair, A Song of the High Hills,* etc. His orch. nocturne *Paris: The Song of a Great City* is a tribute to a city in which he spent many years of his life. Much more ambitious in scope is his choral work *A Mass of Life,* in which he draws on passages from Nietzsche's *Also sprach Zarathustra.*

Delius settled in Paris in 1888; in 1897 he moved to Grez-sur-Loing, near Paris, where he remained for the rest of his life, except for a few short trips abroad. In 1903 he married the painter Jelka Rosen. His music began to win recognition in England and Germany; he became a favorite composer of Sir Thomas Beecham, who gave numerous performances of his music in London. But these successes came too late for Delius; a syphilitic infection which he had contracted early in life eventually grew into an incurable illness accompanied by paralysis and blindness; as Beecham phrased it, "Delius had suffered a heavy blow in the defection of his favorite goddess Aphrodite Pandemos who had returned his devotions with an affliction which was to break out many years later." Still eager to compose, Delius engaged as his amanuensis the English musician Eric Fenby, who wrote down music at the dictation of Delius, including complete orch. scores. In 1929, Beecham organized a Delius Festival in London (6 concerts; Oct. 12 to Nov. 1, 1929), and the composer was brought from France to hear it. In the same year Delius was made Companion of Honour by King George V and an Hon.Mus.D. by Oxford. A motion picture was made by the British filmmaker Ken Russell on the life and works of Delius. However, Delius remains a solitary figure in modern music. Affectionately appreciated in England, in America, and to some extent in Germany, his works are rarely performed elsewhere.

WORKS: FOR THE STAGE: *Zanoni,* incidental music (1888); *Irmelin,* opera (1890–92; first perf., Oxford, May 4, 1953, Beecham conducting); *The Magic Fountain,* opera (1893–95; first perf., BBC, London, Nov. 20, 1977); *Koanga,* opera (1895–97; Elberfeld, March 30, 1904; first English perf., London, Sept. 23, 1935); *Folkeraadet,* incidental music for G. Heiberg's drama (1897; Christiania, Oct. 1897, Delius conducting); *A Village Romeo and Juliet,* opera (1900–1; Berlin, Feb. 21, 1907; first English perf., London, Feb. 22, 1910); *Margot la Rouge,* opera (1902; first perf., BBC, London, Feb. 21, 1982); *Fennimore and Gerda,* opera after J.P. Jacobsen's novel *Niels Lhyne* (1909–10; Frankfurt, Oct. 21, 1919); *Hassan, or The Golden Journey to Samarkand,* incidental music for J.E. Flecker's drama (1920–23; Darmstadt, June 1, 1923; first English perf., a full version of the score, London, Sept. 23, 1923).

FOR ORCH.: *Florida Suite* (1887; first perf. private-

ly, Leipzig, 1888; first public perf., London, April 1, 1937); *Hiawatha,* tone poem (1888); *Marche Caprice* and *Schlittenfahrt* (1887–88); *Rhapsodic Variations* (unfinished; 1888); *Pastorale* for Violin and Orch. (1888); *Petite Suite* (1889); *Idylle de Printemps* (1889); *Summer Evening* (1890; first perf., London, Jan. 2, 1949); *Legends* for Piano and Orch. (unfinished; 1890); *Paa Vidderne (Sur les Cimes),* concert overture after Ibsen (1890–91; Christiania, Oct. 10, 1891); *Legend* for Violin and Orch. (1893; London, May 30, 1899); *Over the Hills and Far Away,* tone poem (1895; London, May 30, 1899); Piano Concerto in C minor (first version in 3 movements, 1897; 2nd version in one movement, 1906; London, Oct. 22, 1907); *La Ronde se déroule,* tone poem (1899; London, May 30, 1899; revised 1901, as *Life's Dance;* 2nd revision, 1912; Berlin, Nov. 12, 1912); *Paris: The Song of a Great City* (1898; Elberfeld, 1901); *Appalachia,* orch. variations with final chorus (1898–1902; Elberfeld, 1904); *Brigg Fair, An English Rhapsody* (1907; Basel, 1907; first English perf., Liverpool, Jan. 18, 1908); *In a Summer Garden,* rhapsody (1908; London, Dec. 11, 1908, Delius conducting); *Dance Rhapsody* No. 1 (1908; Hereford, Sept. 8, 1909, Delius conducting); *Summer Night on the River* (1911) and *On Hearing the First Cuckoo in Spring* (1912; Leipzig, Oct. 2, 1913; first English perfs. of both pieces, London, Jan. 20, 1914); *North Country Sketches* (1913–14; London, May 10, 1915); *Air and Dance* for Strings (1915; London, Oct. 16, 1929); Double Concerto for Violin, Cello, and Orch. (1915–16; London, Feb. 21, 1920); Violin Concerto (1916; London, Jan. 30, 1919); *Dance Rhapsody* No. 2 (1916); *Eventyr (Once Upon a Time),* ballad for Orch. (1917; London, Jan. 11, 1919); *A Song before Sunrise* for Small Orch. (1918); Cello Concerto (1921; Frankfurt, Jan. 30, 1921); *Caprice and Elegy* for Cello and Chamber Orch. (1930); *A Song of Summer* (dictated by Delius to Eric Fenby in France, 1930; London, Sept. 17, 1932); *Fantastic Dance* (1931; London, Jan. 12, 1934).

VOCAL WORKS: *Paa Vidderne,* after Ibsen, for Reciter with Orch. (1888); *Sakuntala* for Tenor and Orch. (1889); *Maud,* after Tennyson, song cycle for Tenor and Orch. (1891); *Seven Danish Songs* for Voice and Orch. (1897; Paris, 1901, d'Indy conducting); *Mitternachtslied (Zarathustra's Night Song),* after Nietzsche (1898); *Sea Drift,* setting of extract of Walt Whitman's *Out of the Cradle Endlessly Rocking,* for Baritone, Chorus, and Orch. (1903–4; Essen, May, 24, 1906; first English perf., Sheffield, Oct. 7, 1908); *A Mass of Life,* after Nietzsche's *Also sprach Zarathustra,* for Soprano, Alto, Tenor, Baritone, Chorus, and Orch. (1904–5; London, June 7, 1909); *Cynara,* to words by Ernest Dowson, for Baritone and Orch. (1907; London, Oct. 18, 1929); *Songs of Sunset,* after poems of Ernest Dowson, for Mezzo-soprano, Baritone, Chorus, and Orch. (1908; London, June 16, 1911); *On Craig Dhu* (1907) and *Midsummer Song* (1908), both for Unaccompanied Chorus; *Wanderer's Song* for Unaccompanied Men's Chorus (1908); *A Song of the High Hills* for Wordless Chorus and Orch. (1911; London, Feb. 20, 1920); *Arabesk* for Baritone, Chorus, and Orch. (1911; Newport, 1920; first London perf., Oct. 18,

1929); *Requiem,* after Nietzsche, for Soprano, Baritone, Chorus, and Orch., dedicated "to the memory of all young artists fallen in the war" (1914–16; London, March 23, 1922); *Songs of Farewell,* after Walt Whitman, for Double Chorus and Orch. (1930; London, March 21, 1932); *Idyll: Once I Passed through a Populous City,* after Walt Whitman, for Soprano, Baritone, and Orch. (1930–32; London, Oct. 3, 1933; reworking of portions of *Margot la Rouge*) also numerous songs, including several of the above to original piano accompaniments.

Chamber music: 2 string quartets (1888 and 1893; unpubl.); Violin Sonata No. 1 (1905–14); String Quartet (1916; London, Feb. 1, 1919); Cello Sonata (1916; London, Jan. 11, 1919); Violin Sonata No. 2 (1923; London, Oct. 7, 1924); Violin Sonata No. 3 (1930; London, Nov. 6, 1930); also pieces for piano, and a Dance for Harpsichord (1919).

Della Casa, Lisa, noted Swiss Soprano; b. Burgdorf, Feb. 2, 1919. She was educated at the Cons. in Bern, and later at the Zürich Cons. She made her debut in Biel in 1941; from 1943 to 1950 she sang at the Stadttheater in Zürich; also appeared at Salzburg, Glyndebourne, and Munich. From 1952 she was a leading member of the Vienna State Opera. On Nov. 20, 1953, she made her debut at the Metropolitan Opera in N.Y. as the Countess in *The Marriage of Figaro;* continued to make appearances there until 1968; retired in 1974.

Della Ciaia, Azzolino Bernardino, Italian organist and composer; b. Siena, March 21, 1671; d. Pisa, Jan. 15, 1755. He was an organist and also an experienced organ builder; constructed a large organ with 4 manuals and 100 stops for the St. Stephen Church in Pisa. He publ. *Salmi concertati* for 4 Voices, with Instruments (Bologna, 1700); *Cantate de camera* (Lucca, 1701); *Sonate per cembalo* (Rome, 1727). Much of his church music is extant in MS. He is regarded by some as an Italian originator of the sonata form; his instrumental music, however, is more interesting for its florid ornamentation than for strict formal development.

Della Corte, Andrea, eminent Italian musicologist; b. Naples, April 5, 1883; d. Turin, March 12, 1968. He was self-taught in music; devoted himself mainly to musical biography and analysis. He taught music history at the Turin Cons. (1926–53) and at the Univ. of Turin (from 1939). From 1919 till 1967 he was music critic of *La Stampa.*

WRITINGS: A prolific writer, he publ. *Paisiello* (Turin, 1922); *Saggi di critica musicale* (Turin, 1922); *L'opera comica italiana del 1700* (2 vols., Bari, 1923); *Piccola antologia settecentesca, XXIV pezzi inediti o rari* (Milan, 1925); *Disegno storico dell'arte musicale* (Turin, 5th ed., 1950); *Antologia della storia della musica* (2 vols., Turin, 1927–29; 4th ed., 1945); *Niccolò Piccinni* (Bari, 1928); *Scelta di musiche per lo studio della storia* (Milan, 3rd ed., 1949); *La vita musicale di Goethe* (Turin, 1932); *Vincenzo Bellini* (in collaboration with Guido Pannain, Turin, 1936); *Ritratto di Franco Alfano* (Turin, 1936); *Pergolesi* (Turin, 1936); *Un Italiano all'estero: Antonio Salieri* (Turin, 1937); *Tre secoli di opera italiana* (Turin, 1938); *Verdi* (Turin, 1939); *Toscanini* (Vicenza, 1946; in French, Lausanne, 1949); *Satire e grotteschi di musiche e di musicisti d'ogni tempo* (Turin, 1947); *Le sei più belle opere di Verdi: Rigoletto, Il Trovatore, La Traviata, Aida, Otello, Falstaff* (Milan, 1947); *Gluck* (Florence, 1948); *Baldassare Galuppi* (Siena, 1949); *Arrigo Serato* (Siena, 1949); *Storia della musica* (3 vols., in collaboration with Guido Pannain, Turin, 3rd ed., 1952; 2nd ed., trans. into Spanish, 1950); *L'interpretazione musicale e gli interpreti* (Turin, 1951). He ed. song textbooks for the Italian schools. With Guido M. Gatti, he compiled a valuable *Dizionario di musica* (1926; 6th ed., 1959).

Della Maria, Pierre-Antoine-Dominique, French opera composer; b. Marseilles, June 14, 1769; d. Paris, March 9, 1800. Son of an Italian mandolinist, he was remarkably precocious; played the mandolin and cello at an early age, and at 18 produced a grand opera at Marseilles. He then studied composition in Italy (for a time with Paisiello) and produced in Naples a successful opera, *Il maestro di cappella* (1792). He went to Paris in 1796; obtaining a libretto (*Le Prisonnier*) from Duval, he set it to music in 8 days, brought it out at the Opéra-Comique (Jan. 29, 1798), and was at once famous. Before his death he finished 6 more operas, 4 of which were produced during his lifetime; a posthumous opera, *La Fausse Duègne* (completed by Blangini), was produced at Paris in 1802; several church compositions are in MS.

Deller, Alfred, English countertenor; b. Margate, May 31, 1912; d. while visiting Bologna, Italy, July 16, 1979. He studied voice with his father; began singing as a boy soprano, later developing the alto range. He sang in the choirs of the Canterbury Cathedral (1940–47) and at St. Paul's in London. In 1950 he formed his own vocal and instrumental ensemble, the Deller Consort, acting as conductor and soloist in a repertoire of old English music. This unique enterprise led to a modest revival of English madrigals of the Renaissance. In 1963 he founded the Stour Music Festival in Kent. Britten wrote the part of Oberon in his *A Midsummer Night's Dream* for Deller. In 1970 Deller was named a Commander of the Order of the British Empire.

Delle Sedie, Enrico, Italian baritone and singing teacher; b. Livorno, June 17, 1822; d. Garennes-Colombes, near Paris, Nov. 28, 1907. His teachers were Galeffi, Persanola, and Domeniconi. After imprisonment as a revolutionist (1848), he resumed the study of singing and made his debut in San Casciano (1851) in Verdi's *Nabucco.* Until 1861 he sang in the principal Italian cities; appeared in London in 1861; was then engaged at the Théâtre des Italiens, Paris, and appointed prof. of singing in the Cons. (1867–71); was regarded as one of the best singing teachers in Paris. His basic manuals, *Arte e fisiologia del canto* (Milan, 1876; in French as *L'Art* *lyrique*, Paris, 1876) and *L'estetica del canto e dell'arte melodrammatica* (Milan, 1886), were publ.in N.Y. in Eng. as *Vocal Art* (3 parts) and *Esthetics of the Art of Singing, and of the Melodrama* (4 vols.). A condensation (by the author) of both manuals was publ. in one vol. as *A Complete Method of Singing* (N.Y., 1894).

Dello Joio, Norman, able American composer of pleasurable music; b. New York, Jan. 24, 1913, of an Italian-American family whose original surname was Ioio. His father, his grandfather, and his great-grandfather were church organists. Dello Joio acquired skill as an organist and pianist at home; at the age of 12 he occasionally substituted for his father on his job at the Church of Our Lady of Mount Carmel in Manhattan. He took additional organ lessons from his well-known godfather, **Pietro Yon,** and studied piano with Gaston Déthier at the Inst. of Musical Art (1933–38); in the meantime he played jazz piano in various groups in N.Y. From 1939 to 1941 he studied composition with Bernard Wagenaar at the Juilliard School of Music; in 1941 he enrolled in the summer class of composition led by Hindemith at the Berkshire Music Center in Tanglewood; he continued to attend Hindemith's courses at Yale Univ. in 1941–43. During this period he wrote several works of considerable validity, among them a piano trio, a ballet entitled *The Duke of Sacramento*, a Magnificat, a piano sonata, and other pieces. He taught composition at Sarah Lawrence College (1945–50); held two consecutive Guggenheim fellowships (1944, 1945); and composed music with utmost facility and ingratiating felicity. His *Concert Music* was played by the Pittsburgh Symph., conducted by Fritz Reiner, on Jan. 4, 1946, and his *Ricercari* for Piano and Orch. was introduced by the N.Y. Phil. on Dec. 19, 1946, with George Szell conducting, and the piano part played by Dello Joio himself. There followed a number of major works in a distinctive Joioan manner, some of them deeply rooted in medieval ecclesiasticism, profoundly liturgical, and yet overtly modern in their neo-modal moderately dissonant counterpoint. He also exhibited a flair for writing on topical American themes, ranging from impressions of the Cloisters in N.Y. to rhythmic modalities of Little Italy. On May 9, 1950, at Sarah Lawrence College, where he taught, he produced his first opera, *The Triumph of St. Joan;* he later used its thematic material in a symph. in 3 movements, *The Triumph of St. Joan*, originally titled *Seraphic Dialogue*. He then wrote another opera on the subject of St. Joan, to his own libretto, *The Trial of Rouen*, first performed on television by the NBC Opera Theater, April 8, 1956; still another version of the St. Joan theme was an opera in which Dello Joio returned to the original title, *The Triumph of St. Joan*, but composed the music anew; it had its production at the N.Y. City Opera on April 16, 1959. In 1957 Dello Joio received the Pulitzer Prize for his *Meditations on Ecclesiastes*, scored for string orch.; it was first performed in Washington on Dec. 17, 1957, but the material was used previously for a ballet, *There Is*

a Time. In 1961 Dello Joio produced an opera, *Blood Moon*, brought out by the San Francisco Opera, to a scenario dealing with the life and times of an adventurous actress, Adah Menken, who exercised her charms in New Orleans at the time of the Civil War. Returning to liturgical themes, Dello Joio composed three masses, in 1968, 1975, and 1976. He continued his activities as a teacher; from 1956 to 1972 he was on the faculty of the Mannes College of Music in N.Y.; from 1972 to 1979 he taught at Boston Univ. In 1964 he traveled to Rumania, Bulgaria, and the Soviet Union under the auspices of the Cultural Program of the State Dept. He held honorary doctorates in music from Lawrence College in Wisconsin (1959), Colby College in Maine (1963), and the Univ. of Cincinnati (1969). On Feb. 16, 1958, he was the subject of a CBS television documentary titled "Profile of a Composer." He received the N.Y. Music Critics' Award twice, in 1947 and 1959. WORKS: FOR THE STAGE: Operas on the subject of St. Joan: *The Triumph of St. Joan* (Sarah Lawrence College, May 9, 1950); *The Trial at Rouen*, to the composer's libretto (NBC-TV Opera Theater; April 8, 1956); *The Triumph of St. Joan*, a new version of the St. Joan theme, bearing the identical title of the original work (N.Y. City Opera, April 16, 1959; received a N.Y. Music Critics' Circle Award). Other operas: *The Ruby* (Bloomington, Ind., May 13, 1955); *Blood Moon* (San Francisco, Sept. 18, 1961). FOR DANCE: *The Duke of Sacramento* (1942); *Diversion of Angels*, dance by Martha Graham (New London, Conn., Aug. 13, 1948); *Seraphic Dialogue*, choreographed by Martha Graham (Louisville, Ky., Dec. 5, 1951; material taken from *The Triumph of St. Joan Symphony*). FOR ORCH.: Sinfonietta (1940); Concerto for 2 Pianos and Orch. (1941); *Magnificat* (1942); *To a Lone Sentry* for Chamber Orch. (1943); *On Stage* (Cleveland, Nov. 23, 1945); *Concert Music* (Pittsburgh, Jan. 4, 1946); *Ricercari* for Piano and Orch. (N.Y., Dec. 19, 1946, composer soloist with the N.Y. Phil., George Szell conducting); Harp Concerto (N.Y., Oct. 20, 1947); *Variations, Chaconne and Finale* (originally titled *3 Symphonic Dances;* Pittsburgh, Jan. 30, 1948); *Concertato* for Clarinet and Orch. (Chautauqua, May 22, 1949); *Serenade* (Cleveland, Oct. 20, 1949); *New York Profiles* (La Jolla, Calif., Aug. 21, 1949); *The Triumph of St. Joan Symphony* (Louisville, Dec. 5, 1951); *Epigraph* (Denver, Jan. 29, 1952); *Meditations on Ecclesiates* for String Orch. (Washington, D.C., Dec. 17, 1957; received the Pulitzer Prize); *Air Power*, suite (1957); *Anthony and Cleopatra* for Chamber Group (1960); *Fantasy and Variations* for Piano and Orch. (Cincinnati, March 9, 1962); *Variants on a Medieval Tune* for Band (Duke Univ., May 8, 1963); *From Every Horizon* for Band (1964); *Antiphonal Fantasy on a Theme of Vincenzo Albrici*, dedicated to the memory of Hindemith (1966); *5 Images* (1967); *Homage to Haydn* (Little Rock, Ark., June 3, 1969); *Songs of Abélard* for Band (1969; earlier version titled *A Time of Snow*); *Satiric Dances for a Comedy by Aristophanes* for Band (Concord, Mass., July 17, 1975); *Colonial Variants* (Philadelphia, May 27, 1976); *Ballabili* (1981).

Dell'Orefice, Giuseppe, Italian composer; b. Fara, Abruzzio Chietino, Aug. 22, 1848; d. Naples, Jan. 3, 1889. He was a pupil of Fenaroli and Miceli at the Naples Cons.; from 1878, was conductor at the San Carlo Theater in Naples; wrote the ballet *I fantasmi notturni* (Naples, 1872) and the operas *Romilda de' Bardi* (Naples, 1874), *Egmont* (Naples, 1878), *Il segreto della Duchesa* (Naples, 1879), and *L'oasi* (Vicenza, 1886); also songs and piano pieces.

Del Mar, Norman, English conductor; b. London, July 31, 1919. He studied composition with R.O. Morris and Vaughan Williams at the Royal College of Music in London; also played the violin and the French horn in the student orch. He then took lessons in conducting with Constant Lambert. During World War II he played in the Royal Air Force bands and visited the U.S. with the Royal Air Force Symph. in 1944. After the war he organized the Chelsea Symph. Orch. in London; in 1948 he conducted the Sadler's Wells Ballet during its tour in Germany. He was principal conductor of the English Opera Group from 1949–55; was conductor and prof. at the Guildhall School of Music (1953–60); then conducted the BBC Scottish Symph. (1960–65), the Göteborg (Sweden) Symph. (1969–73), and the Chamber Orch. of the Royal Academy of Music (1973–77). In 1972 he was appointed instructor in conducting at the Royal College of Music. In 1975 he was made a Commander of the Order of the British Empire. In 1982 he was named principal guest conductor of the Bournemouth Sinfonietta. He publ. several valuable monographs: *Paul Hindemith* (London, 1957); *Richard Strauss, A Critical Commentary of His Life and Works* (3 vols., London, 1962, 1968); *Modern Music and the Conductor* (London, 1960; paperback ed., 1970); *Anatomy of the Orchestra* (London and Berkeley, 1981).

Delmas, Jean-François, famous French dramatic bass; b. Lyons, April 14, 1861; d. St. Alban de Monthel, France, Sept. 29, 1933. He was a pupil of the Paris Cons., where he won first prize for singing in 1886; made his debut at the Grand Opéra in 1886, as St.-Bris in *Les Huguenots;* then was a regular member of the Opéra, idolized by the public, and unexcelled as an interpreter of Wagner, in whose works he created the principal bass parts at all the French premieres; he created also the chief roles in Massenet's *Le Mage* (1891) and *Thaïs* (1894), Leroux's *Astarté* (1901), Saint-Saëns's *Les Barbares* (1901), Erlanger's *Le Fils de l'étoile* (1904), etc.; besides an enormous French repertoire, he also sang in the operas of Gluck, Mozart, and Weber.

Delmas, Marc-Jean-Baptiste, talented French composer; b. St. Quentin, March 28, 1885; d. Paris, Nov. 30, 1931. He was a pupil of Vidal and Leroux; won the Prix de Rossini (1911), the Grand Prix de Rome (1919), the Chartier Prix for chamber music, the Prix Cressent, and other awards for various compositions. He also wrote the books *G. Bizet* (Paris, 1930) and *G. Charpentier et le lyrisme française* (1931).

WORKS: OPERAS: *Jean de Calais* (1907); *Laïs* (1909); *Stéfano* (1910); *Cyrce* (1920; perf. 1927); *Iriam* (1921); *Anne-Marie* (1922); *Le Giaour* (1925). ORCH. MUSIC: *Les Deux Routes* (1913); *Au pays wallon* (1914); *Le Poète et la fée* (1920); *Le Bateau ivre* (1923); *Penthésilée* (1922); *Rapsodie ariégeoise* for Cello and Orch.; chamber music; piano pieces.

Del Monaco, Mario, powerful Italian tenor; b. Florence, July 27, 1915; d. Mestre, near Venice, Oct. 16, 1982. His father was a government functionary, but his mother loved music and actually sang. Del Monaco haunted provincial opera theaters, determined to be a singer; indeed, he was allowed to sing a minor part in a theater at Mondolfo, near Pesaro, when he was only 13. Rather than take regular voice lessons, he listened to operatic recordings; at 19 he entered the Rossini Cons. in Pesaro, but left it after an unhappy semester of academic vocal training with unimaginative teachers. In 1935 he won a prize in a singing contest in Rome. On Jan. 1, 1941, he made his professional debut in Milan as Pinkerton in *Madama Butterfly,* but had to serve time out in the Italian army during the war. After the war's end he developed a busy career singing opera in a number of Italian theaters, including La Scala of Milan. In 1946 he sang at the Teatro Colón in Buenos Aires, and also in Rio de Janeiro and Mexico City. On Sept. 26, 1950, he sang the role of Radames in *Aida* at the San Francisco Opera; on Nov. 27, 1950, he made his Metropolitan Opera debut in N.Y. as Des Grieux in *Manon Lescaut;* he continued to sing at the Metropolitan until 1959 in virtually every famous tenor part, as Don José in *Carmen,* Manrico in *Il Trovatore,* Cavaradossi in *Tosca,* Canio in *Pagliacci,* etc. On Nov. 16, 1954, he scored considerable success in the role of Andrea Chénier. He sang 102 times at the Metropolitan and appeared in its tours 38 times. Numerically, the maximum of his appearances in the same role was as Otello, which he sang at various opera theaters 427 times. In 1973 he deemed it prudent to retire, and he spent the rest of his life in a villa near Venice, devoting his leisure to his favorite avocations, sculpture and painting. Unlike most Italian tenors who tend to grow corpulent with success, Del Monaco managed to preserve his lean, slender figure, which ensured his mobility on the stage and enabled him to honor the Italian operatic tradition of scurrying to the footlights at the approach of the high C. So energetic was he at climactic scenes that he nearly broke the wrist of Risé Stevens when he threw her down in the last act of *Carmen.* Del Monaco was buried in his Otello costume, while the funeral hymns were intoned in his own voice on a phonograph record.

Delna (real name, **Ledan**), **Marie,** French contralto; b. Meudon, near Paris, April 3, 1875; d. Paris, July 23, 1932. She made her debut at the Opéra-Comique, June 9, 1892, as Dido in Berlioz's *Les Troyens;* sang there for 6 years with great success; in 1898–1901 was at the Opéra; then again at the Opéra-Comique in 1903 she married a Belgian, A.H. de Saone, and retired temporarily from the stage; her reappearance at the Opéra-Comique in 1908 was acclaimed with great applause; after that she was a prime favorite. In 1910 she sang Orfeo (in Gluck's opera) and Marcelline in Bruneau's *L'Attaque du moulin* at the New Theater, making a deep impression; then returned to Paris, where she continued to sing at the Opéra-Comique for many years.

Del Tredici, David (Walter), remarkable American composer; b. Cloverdale, Calif., March 16, 1937. He studied piano, and made his debut as a soloist with the San Francisco Symph. at the age of 16; then enrolled at the Univ. of Calif. in Berkeley, studying composition with Seymour Shifrin, Andrew Imbrie, and Arnold Elston (B.A., 1959). He undertook additional studies at Princeton Univ., where his teachers were Earl Kim and Roger Sessions (M.F.A., 1964). He also continued his pianistic practice, taking private lessons with Robert Helps in N.Y. During the summers of 1964 and 1965 he served as pianist at the Berkshire Music Center in Tanglewood. In 1966 he received a Guggenheim fellowship award; in 1966–67 he was resident composer at the Marlboro Festival in Vermont. From 1966 to 1972 he was assistant prof. of music at Harvard Univ.; in 1973 he joined the music faculty at Boston Univ. While thus retained by pedagogy, he composed avidly. Fascinated by the creation of new literary forms and the novel language of James Joyce, he wrote the work *I Hear an Army,* based on a Joyce poem, scored for soprano and string quartet, which was performed at Tanglewood on Aug. 12, 1964, and immediately caught the fancy of the cloistered but influential cognoscenti, literati, and illuminati; another significant Joyce poem set by Del Tredici was *Night Conjure-Verse* for soprano, mezzo-soprano, woodwind septet, and string quartet, which he conducted in San Francisco on March 4, 1966. Yet another work inspired by the verbal music of James Joyce was *Syzygy* for soprano, horn, bells, drums, and chamber orch., performed in N.Y. on July 6, 1968. For these works Del Tredici plied a modified dodecaphonic course in a polyrhythmic context, gravid with meaningful pauses without fear of triadic encounters. But Del Tredici achieved rare fame with a series of brilliant tone pictures after *Alice in Wonderland* by Lewis Carroll, in which he projected, in utter defiance of all modernistic conventions, overt tonal proclamations, fanfares, and pretty tunes that were almost embarrassingly attractive, becoming melodiouser and harmoniouser with each consequent tone portrait of Alice. And in a couple of the *Alice* pieces he disarmingly attached a personal signature, the vocal countdown of 13, his last name Tredici, in Italian. In 1980 he received the Pulitzer Prize for his score *In Memory of a Summer Day.*

WORKS: : *Soliloquy* for Piano (1958); 4 songs to poems of James Joyce for Voice and Piano (1959); String Trio (1959); *Fantasy Pieces* for Piano (1960); *Scherzo* for Piano, 4-hands (1960); *I Hear an Army* for Soprano and String Quartet, to words of James Joyce (Berkshire Music Center, Tanglewood, Aug. 12, 1964); *Night Conjure-Verse* for Voices and Instruments, to words by James Joyce (1965); *The Last Gospel* for Soprano (amplified), Rock Group, and Orch. (San Francisco, June 15, 1968, composer conducting); *Syzygy* for Soprano, Horn, Bells, and Chamber Orch., to words by James Joyce (N.Y., July 6, 1968); *Pop-Pourri* for Voices, Rock Group, and Orch., to text from Lewis Carroll (La Jolla, Calif., July 28, 1968); *The Lobster Quadrille* for Soprano, Folk Group, Mandolin, Banjo, Accordion, and Orch. (London, Nov. 14, 1969, Aaron Copland conducting; revised 1974; first perf., Aspen Festival, Colo., July 29, 1975); *Vintage Alice* for Soprano, Folk Group, and Chamber Orch. (1971; Saratoga, Calif., Aug. 5, 1972, composer conducting); *Adventures Underground* (1971; Buffalo, April 13, 1975); *An Alice Symphony (Illustrated Alice;* San Francisco, Aug. 8, 1976, composer conducting); *Final Alice* (1975–76; Chicago, Oct. 7, 1976, Solti conducting); *Child Alice,* Part I, *In Memory of a Summer Day* for Soprano (amplified) and Orch. (St. Louis, Feb. 23, 1980; received the Pulitzer Prize); *Child Alice,* Part II, *Happy Voices* for Soprano and Orch. (San Francisco, Sept. 16, 1980); *Child Alice,* Part III, for Soprano (amplified) and Orch. (Philadelphia, May 8, 1981); *All in the Golden Afternoon* for Orch. (Rotterdam, the Netherlands, March 11, 1983).

De Luca, Giuseppe, Italian baritone; b. Rome, Dec. 25, 1876; d. New York, Aug. 26, 1950. He studied music with Vinceslao Persichini at the Santa Cecilia Academy in Rome; made his first professional appearance in Piacenza (Nov. 6, 1897) as Valentine in *Faust;* then sang in various cities of Italy; from 1902, was chiefly in Milan at the Teatro Lirico, and from 1903 at La Scala; he created the principal baritone role in the world premiere of Cilea's *Adriana Lecouvreur* and in *Madama Butterfly.* He made his American debut at the Metropolitan Opera as Figaro in *Il Barbiere di Siviglia* on Nov. 25, 1915, with excellent success, immediately establishing himself as a favorite; on Jan. 28, 1916, he sang the part of Paquiro in the world premiere of *Goyescas* by Granados, at the Metropolitan Opera, of which he became a member until 1935; after a sojourn in Italy, he returned to the U.S. in 1940, and made a few more appearances at the Metropolitan, his vocal powers undiminished by age; he made his farewell appearance in N.Y. in 1947. He sang almost exclusively the Italian repertoire; his interpretations were distinguished by fidelity to the dramatic import of his roles; he was praised by the critics for his finely graduated dynamic range and his mastery of bel canto.

De Lucia, Fernando, famous Italian tenor; b. Naples, Oct. 11, 1860; d. there, Feb. 21, 1925. He made his debut in Naples on March 9, 1885, as Faust; then appeared in London at Drury Lane (1887); on Oct. 31, 1891, he created in Rome the role of Fritz in Mascagni's *L'Amico Fritz;* on Jan. 10, 1894, he made his American debut at the Metropolitan Opera, again as Fritz in Mascagni's opera; then returned to Europe. He retired from the stage in 1917, and taught voice in Naples; sang for the last time in public at Caruso's funeral (1921). De Lucia was one of the finest representatives of the *bel canto* era; he was especially praised for his authentic interpretations of Italian operatic roles.

Delune, Louis, Belgian composer and conductor; b. Charleroi, March 15, 1876; d. Paris, Jan. 5, 1940. He studied with Tinel at the Brussels Cons.; won the Belgian Prix de Rome with his cantata *La Mort du roi Reynaud* (1905); then traveled as accompanist for César Thomson. He lived many years in Paris, and wrote most of his works there; composed *Symphonie chevaleresque;* the opera *Tania;* a ballet, *Le Fruit défendu;* Piano Concerto; violin pieces; etc.

Delvincourt, Claude, outstanding French composer; b. Paris, Jan. 12, 1888; d. in an automobile accident in Orbetello, province of Grosseto, Italy, April 5, 1954. He studied with Boellmann, Busser, Caussade, and Widor at the Paris Cons.; in 1913 received the Prix de Rome for his cantata *Faust et Hélène* (sharing the prize with Lili Boulanger). He was in the French army in World War I, and on Dec. 31, 1915, suffered a crippling wound. He recovered in a few years, and devoted himself energetically to musical education and composition. In 1931 he became director of the Cons. of Versailles; in 1941 he was appointed director of the Paris Cons. His music is distinguished by strong dramatic and lyric quality; he was most successful in his stage works.
WORKS: *Offrande à Siva,* choreographic poem (Frankfurt, July 3, 1927); *La Femme à barbe,* musical farce (Versailles, June 2, 1938); *Lucifer,* mystery play (Paris Opéra, Dec. 8, 1948); 2 orch. suites from the film score *La Croisière jaune: Pamir* (Paris, Dec. 8, 1935) and *Films d'Asie* (Paris, Jan. 16, 1937). He also wrote *Ce monde de rosée* for Voice and Orch. (Paris, March 25, 1935); some chamber music (Trio for Oboe, Clarinet, and Bassoon; Violin Sonata; etc.); piano pieces.

Demantius, (Johannes) Christoph, German composer; b. Reichenberg, Dec. 15, 1567; d. Freiberg, Saxony, April 20, 1643. He became cantor at Zittau in 1597; was at Freiberg in 1604–43; as a prolific composer of sacred and secular music, he ranks with Hassler, M. and H. Prätorius, and Eccard. He wrote *Deutsche Passion nach Johannes* (1631; ed. and publ. by F. Blume, 1934); *Triades precum vespertinarum* (1602); etc. He was the author of an instruction book, *Isagoge artis musicae* (Nuremberg, 1605; 10th ed., 1671).

Demény, Desiderius, Hungarian composer; b. Budapest, Jan. 29, 1871; d. there, Nov. 9, 1937. He was a pupil of V. Herzfeld and S. von Bacho; was ordained as a priest at Gran in 1893; became court chaplain (1897); on 3 different occasions he won the Géza Zichy Prize (with *Ungarische Tanzsuite, Festouvertüre,* and *Rhapsodie*); in 1902 he founded *Zeneközlöny,* an important Hungarian music journal.
WORKS: 8 masses; *Hungarian Suite* for Mixed Chorus; *Scherzo* for Male Chorus; 2 *Bilder aus Al-*

gier; Serenata sinfonica; operetta, *Der sieghafte Tod;* several melodramas; many other choral and vocal works, including about 100 songs (most to German texts).

Demessieux, Jeanne, French organist; b. Montpellier, Feb. 14, 1921; d. Paris, Nov. 11, 1968. At the age of 12 she played organ at the church of Saint-Esprit; she studied at the Paris Cons. with Tagliafero, Jean and Noël Gallon, and Dupré; won premiers prix in harmony (1937), piano (1938), and fugue and counterpoint (1940). She gave her first public recital in Paris in 1946; then toured widely in Europe; made her first highly successful visit to the U.S. in 1953. In 1952 she became a prof. at the Liège Cons.; also served as organist at the Madeleine in 1962. She possessed a phenomenal technique and was regarded as one of the most brilliant improvisers on the organ.

Demus, Jörg, noted Austrian pianist; b. St. Polten, Dec. 2, 1928. At the age of 11 he entered the Vienna Academy; also took lessons in conducting with Swarowsky and Krips and in composition with Joseph Marx; continued his piano studies with Gieseking at the Saarbrücken Cons.; then worked with Kempff, Benedetti Michelangeli, and Edwin Fischer. He made his debut as a concert pianist at the age of 14 in Vienna; made his London debut in 1950; then toured South America (1951). In 1956 he won the Busoni prize of the International Competition for Pianists. Apart from his solo recitals, he distinguished himself as a lieder accompanist to Dietrich Fischer-Dieskau and other prominent singers. Demus assembled a large collection of historic keyboard instruments; publ. a book of essays, *Abenteuer der Interpretation,* and, with Paul Badura-Skoda, an analysis of Beethoven's piano sonatas.

Demuth, Leopold, Austrian baritone; b. Brno, Nov. 2, 1861; d. (during a concert) Czernowitz, March 4, 1910. His real Czech name was **Leopold Pokorný,** but he changed it for professional use. He studied with Joseph Gänsbacher in Vienna; made his debut in 1889 in Halle as Hans Heiling; sang in Leipzig (1891–95) and Hamburg (1895–97); then joined the Vienna Court Opera, remaining on its roster until his death; he also sang at Bayreuth (1899), where he gained recognition as a fine Wagnerian singer.

Demuth, Norman, English composer and writer on music; b. London, July 15, 1898; d. Chichester, April 21, 1968. He studied with Parratt and Dunhill at the Royal College of Music in London. As a youth he joined the British army, in 1915. After the war he played organ in London churches. Later he became a choral conductor; in 1930 became a prof. of composition at the Royal Academy of Music. His works are influenced mainly by French music; in later years he became better known as the author of many books and unorthodox essays on music.
WORKS: 5 symphs. (2 of which are entitled *Symphonic Study*); *Threnody* for Strings (1942); *Overture for a Joyful Occasion* (1946); Violin Concerto

(1937); Saxophone Concerto (1938); Piano Concerto (1943); Piano Concerto for the Left Hand (1947); 3 violin sonatas; Cello Sonata; Flute Sonata; many piano pieces.

WRITINGS: (all publ. in London except the last): *The Gramophone and How to Use It* (1945); *Albert Roussel* (1947); *Ravel*, in the Master Musicians Series (1947); *An Anthology of Musical Criticism* (1948); *César Franck* (1949); *Paul Dukas* (1949); *The Symphony: Its History and Development* (1950); *Gounod* (1950); *Vincent d'Indy* (1951); *A Course in Musical Composition* (1951); *Musical Trends in the 20th Century* (1952); *Musical Forms and Textures* (1953); *French Piano Music: A Survey with Notes on Its Performance* (1959); *French Opera: Its Development to the Revolution* (Sussex, 1963).

Dencke, Jeremiah, American Moravian minister, organist, and composer; b. Langenbilau, Silesia, Oct. 2, 1725; d. Bethlehem, Pa., May 28, 1795. In 1748 he became organist at Herrnhut, the center of the European Moravians; came to America (1761) and served the Moravian settlements in Pennsylvania in various capacities. During the Revolutionary War he was warden of the Bethlehem congregation. Dencke was apparently the first individual to compose vocal concerted church music in the Moravian settlements in Pennsylvania, and possibly the first to write such music in colonial America. He was an able composer. The earliest work he is known to have composed in America is a simple anthem for chorus, strings, and figured bass, written for a *Liebesmahl* ("love feast," a service of spiritual devotion and earthly fraternalism, composed of hymn singing and a light meal of a roll and beverage) on Aug. 29, 1765. His finest works are 3 sets of sacred songs for soprano, strings, and organ, composed in 1767–68. The first, written for the annual festival of the "choir" of small girls, is included in the first vol. of the series Music of the Moravians in America, issued by the N.Y. Public Library in 1938. The other sets of solos were written for Christmas services. Dencke's compositions are listed in A.G. Rau and H.T. David, *A Catalogue of Music by American Moravians, 1742–1842* (Bethlehem, Pa., 1938).

Denisov, Edison, remarkable, innovative Soviet composer; b. Tomsk, April 6, 1929. He was named after Thomas Alva Edison by his father, an electrical engineer; another aspect in so naming him was that the surname Denisov is anagrammatic with Edison, leaving out the last letter. He studied mathematics at the Univ. of Moscow, graduating in 1951, and composition at the Moscow Cons. with Shebalin (1951–56). In 1959 he was appointed to the faculty of the Cons. An astute explorer of tonal possibilities, Denisov writes instrumental works of an empirical genre; typical of these is *Crescendo e diminuendo* for Harpsichord and 12 String Instruments, composed in 1965, with the score written partly in graphic notation. The titles of his pieces reveal a lyric character of subtle nuances, often marked by impressionistic colors: *Aquarelle, Silhouettes, Peinture, Le Vie en rouge, Signes en blanc, Nuages noires.*

WORKS: FOR THE STAGE: Opera, *Soldier Ivan* (1959); *L'Ecume des jours,* lyric drama (1981); *Confession,* ballet after Alfred de Musset (1984). FOR ORCH.: Symph. in C (1955); *Sinfonietta on Tadzhik Themes* (1957); *Peinture* (Graz, Oct. 30, 1970); Cello Concerto (Leipzig, Sept. 25, 1973); Flute Concerto (Dresden, May 22, 1976); Violin Concerto (Milan, July 18, 1978); Piano Concerto (Leipzig, Sept. 5, 1978); *Partita* for Violin and Orch. (Moscow, March 23, 1981); Concerto for Bassoon, Cello, and Orch. (1982); *Tod ist ein langer Schlaf,* variations on a theme by Haydn, for Cello and Orch. (Moscow, May 30, 1982); Chamber Symph. (Paris, March 7, 1983); *Epitaphe* for Chamber Orch. (Reggio Emilia, Italy, Sept. 11, 1983). CHAMBER MUSIC: Sonata for 2 Violins (1958); *Musique* for 11 Wind Instruments and Timpani (Leningrad, Nov. 15, 1965); String Quartet No. 2 (1961); Violin Sonata (1963); *Crescendo e diminuendo* for Harpsichord and 12 String Instruments (Zagreb, May 14, 1967); *Ode in Memory of Ché Guevara* for Clarinet, Piano, and Percussion (Moscow, Jan. 22, 1968); *Musique romantique* for Oboe, Harp, and String Trio (Zagreb, May 16, 1969); *3 Pieces* for Cello and Piano (1969); String Trio (1969); *D-S-C-H,* a monogram for Shostakovich (1969); Wind Quintet (1969); *Silhouettes* for Flute, 2 Pianos, and Percussion (1969); *Chant des oiseaux* for Prepared Piano and Tape (1969); Sonata for Alto Saxophone and Piano (1970); Piano Trio (1971); Cello Sonata (1971); *Solo per flauto* (1971); *Solo per oboe* (1971); *Canon in Memory of Igor Stravinsky* for Flute, Clarinet, and Harp (1971); Sonata for Clarinet Solo (1972); *3 Pieces* for Harpsichord and Percussion (1972); *2 Pieces* for Alto Saxophone and Piano (1974); *Choral varié* for Trombone and Piano (1975); *Aquarelle* for 24 String Instruments (1975); *4 Pieces* for Flute and Piano (1977); *Concerto piccolo* for 4 Saxophones and 6 Percussionists (Bordeaux, April 28, 1979); Sonata for Flute and Guitar (1977); Sonata for Solo Violin (1978); Concerto for Guitar Solo (1981); Trio for Oboe, Cello, and Harpsichord (1981); Sonata for Bassoon Solo (1982); Sonata for Violin and Organ (1982); *Musique de chambre* for Viola, Harpsichord, and Strings (1982); 5 études for Bassoon Solo (1983); Sonata for Flute and Harp (1983); *Es ist genug,* variations for Viola and Piano on a theme of Bach (1984); *Diane dans le vent d'automne* for Viola, Vibraphone, Piano, and Double Bass (1984). FOR VOICES: *Canti di Catulli* for Bass and 3 Trombones (1962); *Soleil des Incas* for Soprano and Instrumental Ensemble, to poems by Gabriela Mistral (Leningrad, Nov. 30, 1964); *Chansons italiennes* for Soprano, Flute, Horn, Violin, and Harpsichord (1966); *Pleurs* for Soprano, Piano, and Percussion, on texts from Russian folk songs (1966); *5 Geschichten vom Herrn Keuner* for Tenor and 7 Instruments, to Brecht's poems (1968); *Automne,* 13 poems to surrealist vocables by Khlebnikov (1969); 2 songs for Soprano and Piano, to poems by Bunin (1970); *Chant d'automne* for Soprano and Orch., to poems by Baudelaire (1971); *La Vie en rouge* for Voice, Flute, Clarinet, Violin, Cello, and Piano (1973); *Requiem* for Soprano, Tenor, Chorus, and Orch. (1980); *Colin et Chloé,* suite from the opera

L'Ecume des jours, for Soloists, Chorus, and Orch. (1981); *Lumière et ombres* for Bass and Piano, to poems by Vladimir Soloviev (1982); *Ton image charmante* for Voice and Orch., to words by Pushkin (1982); *Venue du printemps* for Chorus a cappella (1984). FOR PIANO: *Variations* (1961); *3 Pieces* for Piano, 4-hands (1967); *Signes en blanc* (1974); also *Feuilles mortes* for Harpsichord. ORCHESTRATIONS: Mussorgsky: *Nursery Songs, Sunless,* and *Songs and Dances of Death;* Mossolov: *Advertisements,* arranged for Voice and Orch.; also several Schubert dances.

Dennée, Charles (Frederick), American pianist and pedagogue; b. Oswego, N.Y., Sept. 1, 1863; d. Boston, April 29, 1946. At the New England Cons. in Boston he studied piano with A.D. Turner and composition with S.A. Emery; also studied piano with Hans von Bülow during von Bülow's last visit to the U.S. (1889–90); in 1883 he was appointed a teacher of piano at the New England Cons.; an accident to his right wrist caused his retirement in 1897, after he had played almost 1,100 recitals; subsequent devotion to teaching was fruitful, for many of his pupils held prominent positions on the faculties of various conservatories and music colleges. He was among the first to give illustrated lecture-recitals in the U.S. A selection of his essays was publ. as *Musical Journeys* (Brookline, Mass., 1938). Some of his teaching pieces achieved steady popularity with piano students; he also publ. a manual, *Progressive Technique.*

Dent, Edward Joseph, eminent English musicologist, teacher, and critic; b. Ribston, Yorkshire, July 16, 1876; d. London, Aug. 22, 1957. He studied music with C.H. Lloyd at Eton College; then went to Cambridge to continue his studies with Charles Wood and Stanford (Mus.B., 1899; M.A., 1905); he was elected a Fellow of King's College there in 1902, and subsequently taught music history, harmony, counterpoint, and composition until 1918. He was also active in promoting operatic productions in England by preparing translations of libretti for performances at Cambridge, particularly of the operas of Mozart. From 1918 he wrote music criticism in London; in 1919 he became one of the founders of the British Music Society, which remained active until 1933. The International Society for Contemporary Music came into being in 1922 largely through his efforts, and he served as its president until 1938 and again in 1945; he also was president of the Société Internationale de Musicologie from 1931 until 1949. In 1926 he was appointed prof. of music at Cambridge, a position he held until 1941. He was made an honorary Mus.D. at Oxford (1932), Harvard (1936), and Cambridge (1947) univs. After his death, the Royal Musical Association created, in 1961, the Dent Medal, which is given annually to those selected for their important contributions to musicology. A scholar of the widest interests, he contributed numerous articles to music journals, encyclopedias, dictionaries, and symposia.
WRITINGS: *Alessandro Scarlatti* (London, 1905;

2nd ed., revised by F. Walker, 1960); *Mozart's Operas: A Critical Study* (London, 1913; 3rd ed., revised, 1955); *Terpander, or Music and the Future* (London, 1926); *Foundations of English Opera: A Study of Musical Drama in England during the Seventeenth Century* (Cambridge, 1928); *Ferruccio Busoni* (London, 1933; 2nd ed., 1966); *Handel* (London, 1934); *Opera* (Harmondsworth, 1940; 5th ed., revised, 1949); *Notes on Fugue for Beginners* (Cambridge, 1941); *A Theatre for Everybody: The Story of the Old Vic and Sadler's Wells* (London, 1945; 2nd ed., revised, 1946); *The Rise of Romantic Opera* (ed. by W. Dean; Cambridge, 1976); *Selected Essays* (ed. by H. Taylor; Cambridge, 1979).

Denza, Luigi, Italian song composer; b. Castellammare di Stabia, Feb. 24, 1846; d. London, Jan. 26, 1922. He studied with Serrao and Mercadante at the Naples Cons. Besides the opera *Wallenstein* (Naples, May 13, 1876), which was not especially successful, he wrote about 600 songs (some in Neapolitan dialect), many of which won great popularity. In 1879 he settled in London; was appointed prof. of singing at the Royal Academy of Music (1898); was made a Chevalier of the order of the Crown of Italy. His most famous song is *Funiculi-Funicula,* which was used (under the mistaken impression that it was a folk song) by Richard Strauss in *Aus Italien.*

De Peyer, Gervase, English clarinetist; b. London, April 11, 1926. He studied at the Royal College of Music with Frederick Thurston; also in Paris with Louis Cahuzac. In 1955 he became first clarinetist of the London Symph. Orch.; in 1959 was appointed to the faculty of the Royal Academy of Music. He made appearances also as a soloist, and encouraged composers to write works for the clarinet, of which he gave first performances.

Deppe, Ludwig, famous German piano pedagogue; b. Alverdissen, Lippe, Nov. 7, 1828; d. Bad Pyramont, Sept. 5, 1890. He was a pupil of Marxsen at Hamburg in 1849; later of Lobe at Leipzig. He settled in Hamburg in 1857 as a music teacher, and founded a singing society, which he conducted till 1868. He went to Berlin in 1874, and from 1886 to 1888 was court conductor; also conducted the Silesian Musical Festivals established by Count Hochberg in 1876. He wrote a symph. and 2 overtures, *Zriny* and *Don Carlos.*

De Preist, James, greatly talented black American conductor; b. Philadelphia, Nov. 21, 1936. He was educated in his native city. He conducted the Contemporary Music Guild there (1959–62); then was a music specialist for the U.S. State Dept. in Bangkok, Thailand. In 1964 he won first prize in the Mitropoulos Competition in N.Y.; served for a season as assistant conductor of the N.Y. Phil. (1965–66). He then was associate conductor of the National Symph. Orch. in Washington, D.C. (1972–75). In 1976 he was appointed music director of the Quebec Symph. Orch.; in 1980 became music director of the Oregon Symph. at Portland, but continued at his

Quebec post until 1982. He is a nephew of the renowned singer **Marian Anderson.**

De Reszke, Edouard, famous Polish bass, brother of the tenor **Jean de Reszke** and of the soprano **Josephine de Reszke;** b. Warsaw, Dec. 22, 1853; d. Garnek, May 25, 1917. He studied with an Italian teacher, Ciaffei, in Warsaw; also was trained by his older brother, Jean, and by Steller and Coletti. He then went to Italy, where he continued his study with various teachers. His professional debut was at the Théâtre des Italiens in Paris, when he sang Amonasro in *Aida* under Verdi's direction (April 22, 1876). He continued to make appearances in Paris for 2 seasons, and later sang at La Scala in Milan. In 1880–84 he sang in London with extraordinary success. He made his American debut in Chicago as the King in *Lohengrin* (Nov. 9, 1891); then as Frère Laurent in *Roméo et Juliette* at the Metropolitan Opera House in N.Y. (Dec. 14, 1891); his brother Jean made his N.Y. debut as Roméo at the same performance. Edouard de Reszke's greatest role was that of Méphistophélès in *Faust;* he sang this part at its 500th performance at the Paris Opéra (his brother Jean sang the title role), on Nov. 4, 1887; he made a special final appearance at a Metropolitan gala on April 27, 1903, in the last act of *Faust.* He then retired, and died in extreme poverty as a result of the depredations brought on by World War I.

De Reszke, Jean (Jan Mieczislaw), celebrated Polish tenor, brother of **Edouard** and **Josephine de Reszke;** b. Warsaw, Jan. 14, 1850; d. Nice, April 3, 1925. His mother gave him his first singing lessons; he then studied with Ciaffei and Cotogni. He sang at the Warsaw Cathedral as a boy; then went to Paris, where he studied with Sbriglia. He was first trained as a baritone, and made his debut in Venice (1874) as Alfonso in *La Favorita* under the name of **Giovanni di Reschi.** He continued singing in Italy and France in baritone parts; his first appearance as a tenor took place in Madrid on Nov. 9, 1879, in *Robert le Diable.* He created the title role of Massenet's *Le Cid* at the Paris Opéra (Nov. 30, 1885) and became a favorite tenor there. He appeared at Drury Lane in London as Radames on June 13, 1887 (having previously sung there as a baritone in 1874). He then sang at Covent Garden (until 1900). On Nov. 9, 1891, he made his American debut with the Italian Opera Co.; he made his Metropolitan Opera debut in N.Y. on Dec.14, 1891, as Roméo; he remained with the Metropolitan for 11 seasons. In order to sing Wagnerian roles, he learned German, and made a sensationally successful appearance as Tristan (N.Y., Nov. 27, 1895). His last appearance at the Metropolitan was as Tristan on April 29, 1901, in Act 2 during a postseason gala performance. The secret of his success rested not so much on the power of his voice (some baritone quality remained in his singing to the end) as on his controlled interpretation, musical culture, and fine dynamic balance. When he retired from the stage in 1902, settling in Paris as a voice teacher, he was able to transmit his method to many of his students, several of whom later became

famous on the opera stage.

De Reszke, Josephine, Polish soprano, sister of **Jean** and **Edouard de Reszke;** b. Warsaw, June 4, 1855; d. there, Feb. 22, 1891. She studied at the St. Petersburg Cons.; first appeared in public under the name of **Giuseppina di Reschi** at Venice in 1875; sang Marguerite in Gounod's *Faust* (Aug. 1, 1874), with her brother Jean as Valentin; then was engaged at the Paris Opéra, where she made her debut as Ophelia in *Hamlet* by Ambroise Thomas (Paris, June 21, 1875); later sang in Madrid and Lisbon; appeared as Aida at Covent Garden in London on April 18, 1881. She retired from the stage upon her marriage in 1885 and settled in Poland.

Dering, Richard. See **Deering, Richard.**

Dérivis, Henri Etienne, French bass, father of **Prosper Dérivis;** b. Albi, Aug. 2, 1780; d. Livry, Feb. 1, 1856. He made his debut at the Paris Opéra as Sarastro in the French version of *Die Zauberflöte* under the title of *Les Mystères d'Isis* in 1803; during the next 25 years he was a principal singer there, creating roles in works by Spontini (*La Vestale, Fernand Cortez,* and *Olympie*), Cherubini (*Les Abencérages*), Rossini (*Le Siège de Corinthe*), and others.

Dérivis, Prosper, distinguished French bass, son of **Henri Etienne Dérivis;** b. Paris, Oct. 28, 1808; d. there, Feb. 11, 1880. He studied with Pellegrini and Nourrit in Paris; made his debut at the Paris Opéra in 1831; subsequently created roles there in operas by Berlioz (*Benvenuto Cellini*), Meyerbeer (*Les Huguenots*), Donizetti (*Les Martyrs*), etc.; appeared at La Scala in Milan (1842–43), singing in the premieres of Verdi's *Nabucco* and *I Lombardi;* also sang in the first performance of Donizetti's *Linda di Chamounix* in Vienna in 1842; retired from the stage in 1857; then taught voice in Paris.

De Rogatis, Pascual, Argentine composer; b. Teora, Italy, May 17, 1880; d. Buenos Aires, April 2, 1980, a few weeks before his 100th birthday. He was taken to Buenos Aires as a child; studied piano and composition with Alberto Williams and violin with Pietro Melani and Rafael Albertini. He subsequently established himself in Buenos Aires as a violin teacher and composer. His music followed the Italian tradition, but he often selected local subjects from history and folklore for his operas and choral works. The following operas by him were produced in Buenos Aires: *Anfión y Zeto,* Greek tragedy (Aug. 18, 1915); *Huémac,* to a story of ancient Mexico (July 22, 1916); *La novia del hereje* (*The Heretic's Bride;* June 13, 1935). He further composed a symph. poem, *Atipac* (Buenos Aires, April 7, 1928), and numerous vocal pieces on Argentine themes.

De Sabata, Victor, outstanding Italian conductor and composer; b. Trieste, April 10, 1892; d. Santa Margherita Ligure, Dec. 11, 1967. He studied with Michele Saladino and Giacomo Orefice at the Milan

Cons. (1901–11). An extremely versatile musician, he could play piano with considerable élan, and also took lessons on cello, clarinet, oboe, and bassoon. He was encouraged in his career as conductor by Toscanini; at the same time he began to compose operas; his first production was *Il Macigno,* first performed at the La Scala Opera in Milan on March 30, 1917. His symph. poem *Juventus* (1919) was conducted at La Scala by Toscanini. De Sabata's style of composition involved Romantic Italian formulas, with lyric and dramatic episodes receiving an equal share of his attention. In the meantime he filled engagements as an opera and symph. conductor in Italy. In 1927 he conducted concerts in N.Y. and Cincinnati, in 1936 he conducted opera at the Vienna State Opera, in 1939 he was a guest conductor with the Berlin Phil. Orch., and in 1946 he conducted in Switzerland. On April 21, 1946 he was invited to conduct a symph. concert in London, the first conductor from an "enemy country" to conduct in England after the war. He conducted the Chicago Symph. Orch. in Oct. 1949; in March 1950 he conducted 14 concerts at Carnegie Hall with the N.Y. Phil.; the following August he was guest conductor with the Boston Symph. Orch. In April 1951 he conducted 6 concerts with the N.Y. Phil. in Carnegie Hall. He became popular with American audiences, and in 1952 was engaged to conduct in N.Y., Philadelphia, Washington, Baltimore, St. Louis, and Detroit. In 1953 he conducted in Philadelphia, Los Angeles, San Francisco, and Santa Barbara, Calif. He returned to Italy in 1955; on Feb. 18, 1957, he conducted at the funeral of Toscanini; this was his last appearance on the podium. He died of a heart attack at Santa Margherita Ligure during the night of Dec. 10–11, 1967.

WORKS: Operas; *Il Macigno (The Rock;* La Scala, Milan, March 30, 1917; 2nd version, *Driada,* Turin, Nov. 12, 1935); *Lisistrata* (1920); theater music for Max Reinhardt's production of *The Merchant of Venice (Il Mercanto di Venezia;* Venice, July 18, 1934); ballet, *Le mille e una notte* (La Scala, Milan, Jan. 20, 1931); symph. poems, *Juventus* (1919); *La notte di Platon* (1924); *Gethsemani* (1925).

De Segurola, Andrés, Spanish bass; b. Valencia, March 27, 1874; d. Barcelona, Jan. 22, 1953. He studied with Pietro Farvaro; sang at the Teatro Liceo in Barcelona; made his American debut at the Metropolitan Opera as Alvise in *La Gioconda* (Nov. 15, 1909). For 20 years (1931–51) he lived in Hollywood as a teacher; then returned to Spain.

Des Marais, Paul, American composer; b. Menominee, Mich., June 23, 1920. He was taken to Chicago as an infant; studied there with Leo Sowerby; then with Nadia Boulanger in Cambridge, Mass., and with Walter Piston at Harvard Univ. (B.A., 1949; M.A., 1953). He received the Lili Boulanger prize (1947–48); the Boott prize in composition from Harvard (1949); a John Knowles Paine Traveling Fellowship (1949–51); joined the staff of the Univ. of Calif., Los Angeles, in 1960; received the Inst. of Creative Arts Award there in 1964–65. His early mu-

sic was oriented toward neo-classicism, with pandiatonic excrescences in harmonic structures; in 1959 he evolved a decaphonic idiom using series of no more than 10 notes, while preserving a free, not necessarily nontonal, style of writing.

Desmarets, Henri, important French composer; b. Paris, Feb. 1661; d. Lunéville, Sept. 7, 1741. He was a boy soprano in the Paris Royal Chapel until 1678; was maître de chapelle at Louise-le-Grand, a Jesuit college. He was regarded as one of the most skillful musicians during the reign of Louis XIV. His first stage work produced was the opera *Endymion* (Versailles, March 16, 1682; not extant); there followed (all at Paris) *Didon* (Sept. 11, 1693); *Circé* (Oct. 1, 1694); *Théagène et Cariclée* (Feb. 3, 1695); *Les Amours de Momus,* ballet (May 25, 1695); *Vénus et Adonis,* serious opera (March 17, 1697); *Les Fêtes galantes,* ballet (May 10, 1698); *Iphigénie en Tauride,* opera (May 6, 1704); *Renaud, ou La Suite d'Armide* (March 5, 1722); etc. His personal life was stormy and included an abduction, for which he was sentenced to death in absentia, prompting him to flee France for Brussels (1699). He was then musician to Philip V of Spain, and intendant of music to the Duke of Lorraine at Lunéville (from 1707). He was able to return to France in 1722 after his marriage to the abducted woman was recognized as valid by the French courts.

Desmond, Paul, American jazz alto saxophonist; b. San Francisco, Nov. 25, 1924; d. New York, May 30, 1977. His real name was **Paul Emil Breitenfeld;** he picked up his professional name from a telephone book at random. He gained the rudiments of music from his father, who played the organ for silent movies; Desmond played the clarinet in the school orch.; then switched to the alto saxophone. He made rapid strides toward recognition and modest fame when he joined the Dave Brubeck Quartet, and continued with it until it was disbanded in 1967. He wrote some pieces for the Brubeck Quartet, of which *Take Five,* a jazz composition in 5/4 meter, was adopted as their signature song and became popular.

Desormière, Roger, brilliant French conductor; b. Vichy, Sept. 13, 1898; d. Paris, Oct. 25, 1963. He studied at the Paris Cons.; conducted the Swedish Ballet in Paris (1924–25) and the Ballets Russes (1925–29), and later at La Scala, at Covent Garden, and in Monte Carlo; was at the Opéra-Comique (1937–46); at the Grand Opéra (1945); conducted the BBC in London (1946–47). In 1950 he was stricken with aphasia and other disorders, and was compelled to give up his career.

Des Prez, Josquin, the greatest of the Franco-Flemish contrapuntists; b. c.1440 in Hainault or Henegouwen (Burgundy); d. Condé-sur-Escaut, as provost of the Cathedral Chapter, Aug. 27, 1521. His surname was variously spelled: *Després, Desprez, Deprés, Depret, Deprez, Despretz, Dupré,* and by the Italians *Del Prato* (Latinized as *a Prato, a Pratis,*

Pratensis), etc.; while Josquin (contracted from the Flemish Jossekin, "little Joseph") appears as *Jossé, Jossien, Jusquin, Giosquin, Josquinus, Jacobo, Jodocus, Jodoculus*, etc. His epitaph reads *Jossé de Prés.* However, in the motet *Illibata Dei Virgo* (contained in vol. 9 of the Josquin ed.), of which the text is quite likely of Josquin's authorship, his name appears as an acrostic, thus: *I, O, S, Q, V, I, N, D[es], P, R, E, Z;* this seems to leave little doubt as to its correct spelling. Few details of Josquin's early life are known. He was a boy chorister of the Collegiate Church at St.-Quentin, later becoming canon and choirmaster there; possibly was a pupil of Okeghem, whom he greatly admired (after Okeghem's death, in 1495, he wrote *La Déploration de Johan Okeghem*); from 1459–72 he sang at the Milan Cathedral; by July 1474, was at the Court of Duke Galeazzo Maria Sforza, Milan, as chorister; in 1486–94, was a singer in the Papal choir under the Popes Innocent VIII and Alexander VI; he was also active, for various periods, in Florence, where he met the famous theorist Pietro Aron; in Modena; and in Ferrara (where Isaac was also) as maestro di cappella in 1503–4. Later Josquin returned to Burgundy, settling in Condé-sur-Escaut (1504), where he became provost of Notre Dame. As a composer, he was considered by contemporary musicians and theorists to be the greatest of his period, and he had a strong influence on all those who came into contact with his music or with him personally, as a teacher; Adriaan Petit Coclicus, one of Josquin's distinguished pupils (publ. a method in 1552, entitled *Compendium musices,* based on Josquin's teaching), termed him "princeps musicorum." His works were sung everywhere, and universally admired; in them he achieves a complete union between word and tone, thereby fusing the intricate Netherlandish contrapuntal devices into expressive and beautiful art forms. Two contrasting styles are present in his compositions: some are intricately contrapuntal, displaying the technical ingenuity characteristic of the Netherlands style; others, probably as a result of Italian influence, are homophonic. WORKS: Masses: (In Petrucci's Lib. I, Venice, 1502): *L'Omme armé; La sol fa re mi; Gaudeamus; Fortunata desperata; L'Omme armé, sexti toni.* (Ibid., II, 1505): *Ave Maris stella; Hercules, dux Ferrarae; Malheur me bat; Lami Baudichon; Una musque de Buscaya; Dung aultre amor.* (Ibid., III, 1514): *Mater patris; Faysans regrets; Ad fugam; Di dadi; De Beata Virgine; Sine nomine.* (These 3 books republ. by Junta, Rome, 1526.)—(In Graphäus's *Missae III*): *Pange lingua; Da pacem; Sub tuum praesidium.* Some of these are scattered in other collections, and fragments are found in still others; several more masses are in MS at Rome, Munich, and Cambrai. Motets were publ. by Petrucci (8 in the *Odhecaton,* 1501; others in his books of motets); by Peutinger (*Liber selectarum cantionum,* 1520); and by others of the period. French chansons were publ. by T. Susato (1545), P. Attaignant (1549), and Du Chemin (1553). A complete ed. of Josquin's works was issued (1921–69; 55 vols.) by the Vereeniging voor Nederlandsche Muziekgeschiedenis under the general editorship of A. Smi-jers, M. Amlonowycz, and W. Elders.

Dessau, Paul, German composer of socialist convictions; b. Hamburg, Dec. 19, 1894; d. East Berlin, June 27, 1979. He learned to play the violin at an early age and gave a concert when he was 11 years old. In 1910 he enrolled at the Klindworth-Scharwenka Cons. in Berlin, where he studied violin with Florian Zajic and composition with Eduard Behm and Max Loewengard. In 1913 he worked as répétiteur at the Hamburg City Theater; in 1914 he was drafted into the German army. After the Armistice in 1918 he became engaged as a composer and conductor in various chamber groups in Hamburg; then served as coach and conductor at the Cologne Opera (1919–23) and in Mainz (1924). In 1925 he was appointed conductor at the Städtische Oper in Berlin, holding this position until 1933; with the usurpation of power by the Nazis, he left Germany, lived in various European cities, and also visited Palestine. In 1939 he emigrated to America; lived for some time in N.Y., and in 1944 went to Hollywood, where he worked on the background scores for 14 films as a composer or orchestrator. He returned to Berlin in 1948 and took an active part in German musical life, aligning himself with the political, social, and artistic developments in the German Democratic Republic; he became closely associated with Bertolt Brecht and composed music for several of his plays. Dessau's operas, choral works, songs, and instrumental music are imbued with the progressive ideals of socialist realism; while he believed in the imperative of music for the masses, he made use of modern techniques, including occasional applications of Schoenberg's method of composition with 12 tones. WORKS: FOR THE STAGE: Opera, *Lanzelot und Sanderein* (Hamburg, 1918); 2 children's operas: *Das Eisenbahnspiel* (1931) and *Tadel der Unzuverlässigkeit* (1931); opera, *Die Verurteilung des Lukullus,* after Brecht (Berlin, March 17, 1951; original title, *Das Verhör des Lukullus;* new version, 1968); *Geschäftsbericht,* "minimal" opera of 600 seconds' duration (Leipzig, April 29, 1967); stage music for Brecht's plays: *Furcht und Elend des Dritten Reiches* (1938; originally entitled *99%*); *Mutter Courage und ihre Kinder* (1946); *Der gute Mensch von Sezuam* (1947); *Herr Puntila und sein Knecht Matti* (1949); *Mann ist Mann* (1951); *Der kaukasische Kreidekreis* (1954); also music to Brecht's productions of classical drama: *Faust,* after Goethe (1949); *Don Juan,* after Molière (1953); *Coriolan,* after Shakespeare (1964). FOR ORCH.: Symph. No. 1 (1926); Symph. No. 2 (derived from *Hommage à Bartók;* 1962); *Sozialistische Festouvertüre* (originally, *Symphonischer Marsch;* 1953; revised 1963); *In memoriam Bertolt Brecht* (1957); *Bach-Variationen* (on themes of J.S. Bach and C.P.E. Bach, 1963); *Divertimento* for Chamber Orch. (1964); *Meer der Stürme,* symph. poem (East Berlin, Oct. 14, 1967); *Lenin,* with a choral finale (1970).

Dessoff, (Felix) Otto, eminent German conductor; b. Leipzig, Jan. 14, 1835; d. Frankfurt, Oct. 28, 1892. He studied at the Leipzig Cons. with Moscheles, Hauptmann, and Rietz; then was a theater conductor in various German cities (1854–60). In 1860–75 he was a conductor of the Vienna Opera; also conducted the Vienna Phil. Orch., and taught at the Vienna Cons. In 1875–81 he occupied similar posts at Karlsruhe; in 1881 he became an opera conductor in Frankfurt. He was greatly esteemed by his many celebrated friends for his musicianship; his correspondence with Brahms was publ. by the Brahms Society. He also wrote chamber music (Piano Quintet; Piano Quartet; etc.).

Dessoff, Margarethe, Austrian choral conductor; b. Vienna, June 11, 1874; d. Locarno, Switzerland, Nov. 19, 1944. She was educated at the Frankfurt Cons.; taught there in 1912–17. She organized a madrigal singing group, and traveled with it in Germany (1916–21). In 1922 she settled in America, where she presented interesting programs of choral music (gave the first complete perf. in N.Y. of Vecchi's *L'Amfiparnaso*, 1933). In 1936 she went to Switzerland, where she remained until her death. The leadership of the Dessoff Choir, which she established in N.Y., was taken over in 1936 by Paul Boepple.

Destinn (real name, **Kittl**), **Emmy,** famous dramatic soprano; b. Prague, Feb. 26, 1878; d. Budějovice (Bohemia), Jan. 28, 1930. She first studied the violin; her vocal abilities were revealed later by Mme. Loewe-Destinn, whose second name she adopted as a token of appreciation. She made her debut as Santuzza at the Kroll Opera in Berlin (July 19, 1898) and was engaged at the Berlin Opera as a regular member until 1908. She then specialized in Wagnerian operas, and became a protégée of Cosima Wagner in Bayreuth; because of her ability to cope with difficult singing parts, Richard Strauss selected her for the title role in the Berlin and Paris premieres of his *Salome.* She made her London debut at Covent Garden on May 2, 1904, as Donna Anna; her success in England was spontaneous and unmistakable, and she continued to sing opera in England until the outbreak of World War I. She made her American debut in *Aida* with the Metropolitan Opera Co., Toscanini conducting, on Nov. 16, 1908, and remained with the company until 1914. She returned to America after World War I to sing *Aida* at the Metropolitan (Dec. 8, 1919); retired from the opera stage in 1920 but continued to make concert appearances until shortly before her death. For a few years following World War I she used her Czech name, **Ema Destinnová,** but dropped it later on. Her voice was a pure soprano of great power; she was a versatile singer; her repertoire included some 80 parts. A film biography of her life, *The Divine Emma,* was produced in Czechoslovakia in 1982.

Destouches, André-Cardinal, French operatic composer; b. Paris, April (baptized, April 6) 1672; d. there, Feb. 7, 1749. After attending a Jesuit school in Paris, he went as a boy to Siam with his teacher, the missionary Gui Tachard (1686). He returned to France in 1688; served in the Royal Musketeers (1692–94), and later took lessons from André Campra, contributing 3 airs to Campra's opera-ballet *L'Europe galante* (1697). After this initiation, Destouches produced his first independent work, *Issé,* a "heroic pastorale" in 3 acts (Fontainebleau, Oct. 7, 1697); its popularity was parodied in several productions of a similar pastoral nature (*Les Amours de Vincennes* by P.F. Dominique, 1719; *Les Oracles* by J.A. Romagnesi, 1741). Among his other operas, the following were produced in Paris: *Amadis de Grèce* (March 22, 1699), *Omphale* (Nov. 10, 1701), and *Callirhoé* (Dec. 27, 1712). With Delalande, he wrote the ballet *Les Eléments,* which was produced at the Tuileries Palace in Paris on Dec. 22, 1721. In 1713 Louis XIV appointed him inspector general of the Académie Royale de Musique; in 1728 he became its director, retiring in 1730. A revival of *Omphale* in 1752 evoked Baron Grimm's famous *Lettre sur Omphale,* inaugurating the so-called "Guerre des Bouffons" between the proponents of the French school, as exemplified by Destouches, and Italian opera buffa.

Destouches, Franz (Seraph) von, German composer; b. Munich, Jan. 21, 1772; d. there, Dec. 10, 1844. He was a pupil of Haydn in Vienna in 1787; was appointed music director at Erlangen (1797); then was 2nd concertmaster at the Weimar theater (1799), later becoming first concertmaster and director of music (1804–8); in 1810 was a prof. of theory at Landshut Univ.; then a conductor at Hamburg (1826–42); retired to Munich in 1842.

WORKS: *Die Thomasnacht,* opera (Munich, Aug. 31, 1792); *Das Missverständniss,* operetta (Weimar, April 27, 1805); comic opera, *Der Teufel und der Schneider* (1843; not perf.); incidental music: to Schiller's version of Gozzi's *Turandot* (1802); to Schiller's *Die Braut von Messina* (1803), *Die Jungfrau von Orleans* (1803), and *Wilhelm Tell* (1804); to Kotzebue's *Die Hussiten vor Naumburg* (1804); and to Zacharias Werner's play *Wanda, Königin der Sarmaten* (1808); also a Piano Concerto; piano sonatas; fantasias; variations for piano; Piano Trio; Clarinet Concerto; Mass; oratorio, *Die Anbetung am Grabe Christi.*

Déthier, Edouard, Belgian violinist, brother of **Gaston-Marie Déthier;** b. Liège, April 25, 1886; d. New York, Feb. 19, 1962. He studied at the Liège Cons. (1895–1901); then at the Brussels Cons. (1901–2); subsequently taught there (1902–4). He settled in the U.S. in 1906, appearing in recitals with the principal orchs.; taught at the Inst. of Musical Art and at the Juilliard Graduate School.

Déthier, Gaston-Marie, Belgian organist, brother of **Edouard Déthier;** b. Liège, April 18, 1875; d. New York, May 26, 1958. He studied at the Liège Cons. and later with Guilmant in Paris; came to the U.S. in 1894; was organist at St. Francis Xavier's, N.Y.; taught at the Inst. of Musical Art; in 1915, gave a series of successful sonata recitals as a pianist, with his brother playing violin.

Dett, R(obert) Nathaniel, distinguished black composer, conductor, and anthologist; b. Drummondville, Quebec, Canada, Oct. 11, 1882; d. Battle Creek, Mich., Oct. 2, 1943. He came from a musical family; both his parents were amateur pianists and singers. In 1893 the family moved to Niagara Falls, N.Y.; Dett studied piano with local teachers. He earned his living by playing at various clubs and hotels; then enrolled at the Oberlin (Ohio) Cons., where he studied piano with Howard Handel Carter and theory of composition with Arthur E. Heacox and George Carl Hastings, obtaining his B.Mus. in 1908. He also conducted a school choir; eventually, choral conducting became his principal profession. Upon graduation he occupied various teaching jobs, at Lane College in Jackson, Tenn. (1908–11), the Lincoln Inst. in Jefferson, Mo. (1911–13), the Hampton Inst. in Virginia (1913–32), and Bennett College in Greensboro, N.C. (1937–42). Concerned about his lack of technical knowledge in music, he continued taking courses, mostly during summers, when he was not engaged in teaching and choral conducting; he took lessons with Karl Gehrkens at Oberlin in 1913; attended classes at Columbia Univ., the American Cons. of Music in Chicago, Northwestern Univ., the Univ. of Pa., and, during the academic year 1919–20, Harvard Univ., where he studied composition with Arthur Foote. In the summer of 1929, at the age of 47, he went to France to study with Nadia Boulanger at the American Cons. in Fontainebleau; during the year 1931–32 he attended the Eastman School of Music in Rochester, N.Y., obtaining his M.Mus. in 1932. In the meantime he developed the artistic skills of the Hampton Choir, which toured in Europe in 1930 with excellent success, receiving encomiums in England, France, Belgium, the Netherlands, Germany, and Switzerland. He also periodically led his choir on the radio; in 1943 he became a musical adviser for the USO, and worked with the WAC (Women's Army Corps) on service duty at Battle Creek, where he died. His dominating interest was in cultivating Negro music, arranging Negro spirituals, and publishing collections of Negro folk songs. All of his works were inspired by black melos and rhythms; some of his piano pieces in Negro idiom became quite popular, among them, the suite *Magnolia* (1912); *In the Bottoms* (1913), which contained the rousing *Juba Dance;* and *Enchantment* (1922). He also wrote a number of choral pieces, mostly on biblical themes, such as his oratorios *The Chariot Jubilee* (1921) and *The Ordering of Moses* (Cincinnati, May 7, 1937). His choruses *Listen to the lambs, I'll never turn back no more,* and *Don't be weary, traveler,* became standard pieces of the choral repertoire. He publ. the anthologies *Religious Folk Songs of the Negro* (1926) and *The Dett Collection of Negro Spirituals* (4 vols., 1936). His piano compositions were reprinted in 1973 in Evanston, Ill., with introductory articles by Dominique-René de Lerma and Vivian McBrier.

Deutekom, Cristina, Dutch soprano; b. Amsterdam, Aug. 28, 1932. She was educated in Amsterdam; sang with the Netherlands Opera; also appeared in Munich, Hamburg, Vienna, London, and Milan. She made her American debut at the Metropolitan Opera in N.Y., as the Queen of the Night in *Die Zauberflöte,* on Sept. 28, 1967; also appeared in concerts. She was acknowledged as one of the finest coloratura sopranos of her generation.

Deutsch, Max, Austrian-born French composer, conductor, and pedagogue; b. Vienna, Nov. 17, 1892; d. Paris, Nov. 22, 1982. He studied composition privately with Schoenberg; also took courses at the Univ. of Vienna. He began his career by conducting operetta in Vienna; in 1923 he went to Berlin, where he organized his own orch. group concentrating mainly on modern music, emulating Schoenberg's Society for Private Performances of Vienna. In 1925 he settled in Paris, where he founded a Jewish theatrical ensemble, Der Jiddische Spiegel; also conducted concerts of modern music. From 1933–35 he was in Madrid, where he was in charge of a film enterprise; in 1939 he went to France; served in the Foreign Legion until 1945; then returned to Paris, where he devoted himself to teaching, using Schoenberg's method. In 1960 he founded the Grands Concerts de la Sorbonne. In his own compositions, he pursued novel ideas; he was the first to write a complete film symph., in 5 movements, for the production of the German motion picture *Der Schutz* (1923); he furthermore composed 2 symphs. and a choral symph., *Prière pour nos autres mortels,* after the text of Charles Peguy.

Deutsch, Otto Erich, eminent Austrian musicologist; b. Vienna, Sept. 5, 1883; d. there, Nov. 23, 1967. He studied literature and the history of art at the univs. of Vienna and Graz; was the art critic of Vienna's *Die Zeit* (1908–9); then served as an assistant at the Kunsthistorisches Institut of the Univ. of Vienna (1909–12); later was a bookseller, and then music librarian of the important collection of Anthony van Hoboken in Vienna (1926–35); In 1939 he emigrated to England and settled in Cambridge; in 1947 he became a British subject, but returned to Vienna in 1951. A scholar of impeccable credentials, he was considered one of the foremost authorities on Handel, Mozart, and Schubert; his documentary biographies of these composers constitute primary sources; he was also responsible for initiating the critical edition of Mozart's letters, which he edited with W. Bauer and J. Eibl as *Mozart: Briefe und Aufzeichnungen* (7 vols., Kassel, 1962–75). WRITINGS: *Schubert-Brevier* (Berlin, 1905); *Beethovens Beziehungen zu Graz* (Graz, 1907); *Franz Schubert: Die Dokumente seines Lebens und Schaffens* (in collaboration, first with L. Scheibler, then with W. Kahl and C. Kinsky), which was planned as a comprehensive work in 3 vols. containing all known documents, pictures, and other materials pertaining to Schubert, arranged in chronological order, with a thematic catalogue, but of which only 2 vols. were publ.: vol. III, *Sein Leben in Bildern* (Munich, 1913), and vol. II, part 1, *Die Dokumente Seines Lebens* (Munich, 1914; Eng.

trans. by Eric Blom, titled *Schubert: A Documentary Biography*, London, 1946; American ed., titled *The Schubert Reader: A Life of Franz Schubert in Letters and Documents*, N.Y., 1947; a 2nd German ed., enlarged, publ. in the *Neue Ausgabe sämtlicher Werke* of Schubert, in 1964); *Franz Schuberts Briefe und Schriften* (Munich, 1919; in Eng., London, 1928; 4th German ed., Vienna, 1954); *Die historischen Bildnisse Franz Schuberts in getreuen Nachbildungen* (Vienna, 1922); *Die Originalausgaben von Schuberts Goethe-Liedern* (Vienna, 1926); *Franz Schubert: Tagebuch: Faksimile der Originalhandschrift* (Vienna, 1928); *Mozart und die Wiener Logen* (Vienna, 1932); *Leopold Mozarts Briefe an seine Tochter* (with B. Paumgartner; Salzburg, 1936); *Das Freihaustheater auf der Wieden 1787–1801* (Vienna, 1937); *Wolfgang Amadé Mozart: Verzeichnis aller meiner Werke. Faksimile der Handschrift mit dem Beiheft "Mozarts, Werkverzeichnis 1784–1791"* (Vienna, 1938; in Eng., 1956); *Schubert: Thematic Catalogue of All His Works in Chronological Order* (with D. Wakeling; London, 1951; in German as *Franz Schubert: Thematisches Verzeichnis seiner Werke,* publ. in the *Neue Ausgabe sämtlicher Werke* of Schubert in a revised ed., 1978); *Handel: A Documentary Biography* (N.Y., 1954; London, 1955); *Franz Schubert: Die Erinnerungen seiner Freunde* (Leipzig, 1957; in Eng., 1958); *Mozart: Die Dokumente seines Lebens* (Kassel, 1961; in Eng. as *Mozart: A Documentary Biography,* Palo Alto, Calif., 1965; 2nd ed., 1966; supplement, 1978); *Mozart und seine Welt in zeitgenössischen Bildern* (completed by M. Zenger, Kassel, 1961); also numerous articles on Mozart, Haydn, Beethoven, and others contributed to German, English, and American music publications.

Devienne, François, versatile French musician; b. Joinville, Haute-Marne, Jan. 31, 1759; d. in the insane asylum at Charenton, Sept. 5, 1803. A flutist and bassoonist, member of the band of the Gardes Suisses, bassoonist at the Théâtre de Monsieur (1789–1801), and a prof. at the Paris Cons. (from 1795), he was an extraordinarily prolific composer of peculiar importance from the impulse which he gave to perfecting the technique of wind instruments.

Devrient, Eduard, German writer on musical subjects; b. Berlin, Aug. 11, 1801; d. Karlsruhe, Oct. 4, 1877. He studied singing and thorough-bass with Zelter; gave his first public performance as a baritone in 1819; then joined the Royal Opera, but after the loss of his voice (1834) went over to the spoken drama, without losing his interest in music. He sang the role of Christ in the famous performance of Bach's *St. Matthew Passion* under Mendelssohn on March 11, 1829; was chief producer and actor at the Dresden Court Theater (1844–46) and director at the Karlsruhe Court Theater (1852–70); he was the author of the text to Marschner's *Hans Heiling,* and also created the title role (1833). His chief work is *Geschichte der deutschen Schauspielkunst* (5 vols., 1848–74); his works concerning music are *Briefe aus Paris* (1840, about Cherubini) and *Meine Erinnerungen an Felix Mendelssohn-Bartholdy und seine Briefe an mich* (Leipzig, 1869). Within weeks after publication of the latter, Wagner issued a polemical pamphlet entitled *Herr Eduard Devrient und sein Styl* (Munich, 1869) under the pseudonym Wilhelm Drach, violently attacking Devrient for his literary style. Devrient's book was publ. in Eng. in the same year (London, 1869; 3rd ed., 1891).

Diabelli, Anton, Austrian composer and publisher; b. Mattsee, near Salzburg, Sept. 5, 1781; d. Vienna, April 8, 1858. He was a choirboy in the monastery at Michaelbeurn, and at Salzburg Cathedral; studied for the priesthood at the Munich Latin School, but continued his musical work, submitting his compositions to Michael Haydn, who encouraged him. On the secularization of the Bavarian monasteries, Diabelli, who had already entered that at Raichenhaslach, embraced the career of a musician, went to Vienna (where Joseph Haydn received him kindly), taught piano and guitar for a living, and in 1818 became a partner of Cappi, the music publisher, assuming control of the firm (Diabelli & Co.) in 1824. He publ. much of Schubert's music, but underpaid the composer, and complained that he wrote too much. In 1852 he sold his firm to C.A. Spina. A facile composer, Diabelli produced an opera, *Adam in der Klemme* (Vienna, 1809; one perf.), masses, cantatas, chamber music, etc., which were consigned to oblivion; his sonatinas are still used for beginners. His name was immortalized through Beethoven's set of 33 variations (op. 120) on a waltz theme by Diabelli.

Diaghilev, Sergei, creator and director of the famous Russian Ballet; b. Gruzino, Novgorod district, March 31, 1872; d. Venice, Aug. 19, 1929. He was associated with progressive artistic organizations in St. Petersburg, but his main field of activity was in western Europe. He established the Ballets Russes in Paris; he commissioned Stravinsky to write the ballets *The Firebird, Petrouchka,* and *Le Sacre du Printemps;* also commissioned Prokofiev, Milhaud, Poulenc, Auric, and other composers of the younger generation. Ravel and Manuel de Falla also wrote works for Diaghilev. The great importance of Diaghilev's choreographic ideas lies in the complete abandonment of the classical tradition; in this respect Diaghilev was the true originator of the modern dance.

Diamond, David, outstanding American composer; b. Rochester, N.Y., July 9, 1915. He studied composition with Bernard Rogers at the Eastman School of Music in his hometown (1930–34); then took courses with Roger Sessions in N.Y. In 1936 he went to Paris, where he studied with Nadia Boulanger and became associated with the most important musicians and writers of the time. Returning to N.Y., he devoted his time exclusively to composition; various grants and awards enabled him to continue his work in relative financial prosperity. He received the Juilliard Publication Award for his

Psalm (1937), 3 Guggenheim fellowships (1938, 1941, 1958), an American Academy in Rome award (1942), the Paderewski Prize (1943), and a grant of $1,000 from the National Academy of Arts and Letters (1944). In 1965–67 he taught at the Manhattan School of Music, and in 1973 joined the faculty at the Juilliard School of Music. His early music is marked by a great complexity of harmonic writing, with the sense of tonality clearly present; the element of rhythm, often inspired by natural folklike patterns, is very strong in all of his works. In his later symphs. he adopted a modified dodecaphonic method of composition, while keeping free of doctrinaire serialism. His instrumental and vocal writing is invariably idiomatic, which makes his music welcome to performers and audiences alike.

WORKS: FOR ORCH.: 8 symphs.: No. 1 (N.Y., Dec. 21, 1941); No. 2 (Boston, Oct. 13, 1944); No. 3 (1945; Boston, Nov. 3, 1950); No. 4 (Boston, Jan. 23, 1948); No. 5 (1947–64; N.Y., April 28, 1966); No. 6 (Boston, March 8, 1957); No. 7 (N.Y., Jan. 26, 1962); No. 8 (N.Y., Oct. 26, 1961, prior to Symph. No. 7); *To Music,* choral symph. for Soloists, Chorus, and Orch. (1967); 3 violin concertos: No. 1 (N.Y., March 24, 1937); No. 2 (Vancouver, Feb. 29, 1948); No. 3 (N.Y., April 1, 1976); *Hommage à Satie* (1934); *Threnody* (1935); *Psalm* for Orch. (Rochester, Dec. 10, 1936); first suite from the ballet *Tom* (1936); *Variations on an Original Theme* (1937; Rochester, April 23, 1940); *Elegy in Memory of Maurice Ravel* for Brass, Harp, and Percussion (Rochester, April 28, 1938); *Heroic Piece* (Zürich, July 29, 1938); *Cello Concerto* (1938; Rochester, April 30, 1942); *Concert Piece* (N.Y., May 16, 1940); Concerto for Chamber Orch. (Yaddo, N.Y., Sept. 7, 1940, composer conducting); *Rounds* for String Orch. (Minneapolis, Nov. 24, 1944; his most successful work); *Romeo and Juliet* (N.Y., Oct. 20, 1947); *The Enormous Room,* after e.e. cummings (Cincinnati, Nov. 19, 1949); *Timon of Athens,* symph. portrait after Shakespeare (Louisville, 1949); Piano Concerto (1949; N.Y., April 28, 1966); *Ahavah* for Narrator and Orch. (Washington, D.C., Nov. 17, 1954); *Diaphony* for Brass, 2 Pianos, Timpani, and Organ (N.Y., Feb. 22, 1956); *Sinfonia concertante* (Rochester, March 7, 1957); *World of Paul Klee,* orch. suite (Portland, Oreg., Feb. 15, 1958); *Music* for Chamber Orch. (1969); *A Buoyant Music,* overture No. 2 (1970). CHAMBER MUSIC: Partita for Oboe, Bassoon, and Piano (1935); Concerto for String Quartet (1937); String Trio (1937); Quintet for Flute, String Trio, and Piano (1937); Piano Quartet (1938); Cello Sonata (1938); 10 string quartets (1940, 1943, 1946, 1951, 1960, 1962, 1963, 1964, 1966–68, 1966); Violin Sonata (1945); *Canticle for Perpetual Motion* for Violin and Piano (1947); Chaconne for Violin and Piano (1947); Quintet for Clarinet, 2 Violas, and 2 Cellos (1951); Piano Trio (1951); Nonet for 3 Violins, 3 Violas, and 3 Cellos (1962). VOCAL MUSIC: *This is the Garden,* Chorus a cappella (1935); *3 Madrigals,* after James Joyce, for Chorus a cappella (1937); *Young Joseph,* after Thomas Mann, for Women's Chorus and String Orch. (1944); *L'Ame de Claude Debussy,* extracts from Debussy's letters to Jacques Durand (1949); *The Midnight Meditation,* cycle of 4 songs (1950); *This Sacred Ground* for

Chorus, Male Voice, and Orch. (Buffalo, Nov. 17, 1963); *A Secular Cantata,* to texts from James Agee's *Permit Me Voyage* (N.Y., Feb. 5, 1977). FOR PIANO: Sonatina (1935); Concerto for 2 Pianos (1941); *Album for the Young* (1946); Sonata (1947).

Dianda, Hilda, Argentinian composer; b. Córdoba, April 13, 1925. She studied in Europe with Scherchen and Malipiero; in 1958–62 worked at Radiodiffusion Française in Paris. Upon returning to Argentina, she devoted herself to composition and organization of concerts of ultramodern music.

WORKS: 3 string quartets (1947, 1960, 1962); Concertante for Cello and Chamber Orch. (1952); Trio for Flute, Oboe, and Bassoon (1953); Wind Quintet (1957); *Díptico* for 16 Instruments (1962); *Núcleos* for String Orch., 2 Pianos, and Percussion (1964); works for various ensembles under the generic titles *Resonancias* and *Ludus* (1964–69).

Dibdin, Charles, English composer; b. Dibdin, near Southampton (baptized, March 4), 1745; d. London, July 25, 1814. In 1756–59 he was a chorister at Winchester Cathedral; took lessons there from Kent and Fussell, but was chiefly self-taught in composition; at 15 went to London; was engaged at Covent Garden as a singing actor, and soon began to write for the stage. His first piece, *The Shepherd's Artifice,* was produced at his benefit performance, at Covent Garden, on May 21, 1764. He was engaged at Birmingham in 1763–65, and at Covent Garden again till 1768, when he went over to Drury Lane. Falling out with Garrick, he went to France in 1776 to avoid imprisonment for debt, remaining there until 1778, when he was appointed composer to Covent Garden, having up to that time brought out 8 operas. In 1782–84, he was manager of the newly erected Royal Circus (later the Surrey Theatre). After the failure of certain theatrical enterprises, and a projected journey to India, he commenced a series of monodramatic "table-entertainments," of which song was a principal feature, and which were extremely popular from 1789 to 1805; in these Dibdin appeared as author, composer, narrator, singer, and accompanist. He then built and managed a small theater of his own, which opened in 1796; he retired in 1805 on a pension, which was withdrawn for a time, but subsequently restored. Dibdin also composed numerous sea songs which were very popular at the time. He publ. *The Musical Tour of Mr. Dibdin* (1788), *History of the Stage* (5 vols., 1795), *The Professional Life of Mr. Dibdin* (4 vols., 1803), and various novels. His grandson, **Henry Edward Dibdin** (b. London, Sept. 8, 1813; d. Edinburgh, May 6, 1866), was an organist, harpist, and teacher who compiled the collection *The Standard Psalm Tune Book* (1851).

Di Capua, Eduardo, Italian composer of Neapolitan ballads; b. Naples, 1864; d. there, 1917. He earned his living by playing in small theaters and cafés in and around Naples, and later in the cinemas; also gave piano lessons. His most famous song was *O sole mio* (1898); its popularity was immense, and never abated. Other celebrated songs were *Maria Mari* (1899); *Torna maggio* (1900); *Canzona bella;* etc. Di Capua sold these songs to publishers outright, and so did not benefit by their popularity. He died in extreme poverty.

Dichter, Misha, talented American pianist; b. Shanghai, of Polish-Jewish refugees, Sept. 27, 1945. He was reared in Los Angeles; at the age of 15 he won a contest of the Music Educators National Conference, Western Division. While attending the Univ. of Calif. at Los Angeles, he enrolled in a master class conducted by Rosina Lhévinne; later joined her class at the Juilliard School of Music in N.Y. In 1966 he entered the International Tchaikovsky Competition in Moscow and won 2nd prize, scoring popular acclaim among Russian audiences. Returning to the U.S., he made his Boston Symph. Orch. debut as soloist at the Tanglewood Festival in 1966; numerous appearances with major American and European orchs. followed; he also gave recitals. His wife, **Cipa** (b. Rio de Janeiro, May 20, 1944), is a fine pianist in her own right; they frequently appear together in duo recitals. Dichter's natural predilections lie in the Romantic repertoire; his playing possesses a high emotional appeal; but he also can render full justice to Classical masterpieces, as demonstrated by his appropriate rendition of Mozart's concertos.

Dick, Marcel, Hungarian-American violinist and composer; b. Miskolcz, Hungary, Aug. 28, 1898. He came from a musical family; the famous Hungarian violinist **Eduard Reményi** was his great-uncle. Dick studied violin with Joseph Bloch and composition with Kodály. He was first violist in the Vienna Symph. Orch. (1924–27), and was also a member of the Kolisch Quartet and of the Rosé Quartet. In 1934 he went to the U.S.; was first violist of the Cleveland Orch. (1943–49); in 1948 was appointed head of the dept. of theory of the Cleveland Inst. of Music; he retired in 1973. He wrote a Symph. (Cleveland, Dec. 14, 1950) and a Symph. for 2 String Orchs. (1964); also some chamber music and songs.

Dickinson, Peter, English composer; b. Lytham St. Annes, Lancashire, Nov. 15, 1934. Of a musical family, he studied piano and began to compose early in life. He entered Cambridge Univ.; after obtaining his M.A. degree in music there, he went to the U.S. on a Rotary Foundation fellowship, and studied with Bernard Wagenaar at the Juilliard School of Music in N.Y. (1958–60). Returning to England, he became a lecturer at the College of St. Mark and St. John in London (1962–66); then at the Univ. of Birmingham (1966–70). In 1973 he became a prof. at Keele Univ. In his music he combines the esoteric techniques of serialism with pragmatic considerations for performance.
WORKS: *Postlude on Adeste Fideles* for Organ (1954); *Jesus Christ Is Risen Today* for Chorus a cappella (1955); Sonatina for Flute and Piano (1955); *4 W.H. Auden Songs* for Voice and Piano (1956); Variations for Piano (1957); *5 Blake Songs* for Tenor, Horn, Clarinet, and Bassoon (1957); String Quartet (1958); *Air* for Solo Flute (1958); *Monologue* for String Orch. (1959); *A Dylan Thomas Song Cycle* for Baritone and Piano (1959); *Study in Pianissimo* for Organ (1959); Fantasia for Solo Violin (1959); *Vitalitas,* ballet (1960); Violin Sonata (1961); 4 Duos for Flute and Cello (1962); Trio for Flute, Oboe, and Harpsichord (1962); *5 Forgeries* for Piano Duet (1963); *5 Diversions* for Keyboard Instruments (1963); *Carillon* for Organ (1964); *The Judas Tree,* musical drama for Speakers, Singers, Chorus, and Chamber Orch. (London, May 27, 1965); *Outcry* for Chorus and Orch. (Leamington, May 10, 1969); *Diversions* for Small Orch. (Leamington, Nov. 23, 1969); *Transformations: Homage to Satie* for Orch. (Cheltenham, July 3, 1970); Organ Concerto (Gloucester Cathedral, Aug. 22, 1971); Concerto for Strings, Percussion, and Electronic Organ (Birmingham, Jan. 22, 1971).

Diderot, Denis, illustrious projector and editor of the celebrated "Encyclopédie"; b. Langres, Oct. 5, 1713; d. Paris, July 30, 1784. In his work *Mémoirs sur différents sujets de mathématiques* (The Hague, 1748) are the essays "Des principes d'acoustique" and "Projet d'un nouvel orgue," the latter being an impracticable idea for a new kind of barrel organ.

Didur, Adamo, famous Polish bass; b. Wola Sekowa, near Sanok, Galicia, Dec. 24, 1874; d. Katowice, Jan. 7, 1946. He studied with Wysocki and Emerich; in 1894 made his operatic debut in Rio de Janeiro, thereafter appearing at the La Scala Opera in Milan, at the Warsaw Opera, in Moscow, St. Petersburg, Barcelona, Madrid, London, and Buenos Aires; in 1907–8 he appeared with the Manhattan Opera Co.; in 1908, made his debut as Méphistophélès at the Metropolitan Opera House, of which he was a leading member until 1932. After his retirement from the Metropolitan, he returned to Poland; eventually settled in Katowice, where he taught voice and founded an opera company; also served as director of the Katowice Academy of Music.

Didymus, grammarian of Alexandria; b. 63 B.C. The number of his works was estimated by Seneca at 4,000; he wrote a tract on music, now known only by an epitome of Porphyry's, and some quotations by Ptolemy. In his system the octave of the diatonic genus is formed by 2 precisely similar tetrachords, and in all 3 species of tetrachord (diatonic, chromatic, enharmonic) the ratio for the interval of the major third is 4:5. He also recognized the difference between the major and minor whole tone; this difference $(9/8:10/9 = 81:80)$ is, therefore, rightly termed the "comma of Didymus." Salinas and Doni have written on his musical system.

Diémer, Louis, distinguished French pianist; b. Paris, Feb. 14, 1843; d. there, Dec. 21, 1919. He was a pupil of Marmontel at the Paris Cons., where he took first piano prize in 1856; also of Ambroise Thomas and Bazin for composition, taking first harmony prize, 2d organ prize, and first prize for fugue.

He played with great success at the Alard, Pasdeloup, and Paris Cons. concerts; succeeded Marmontel (1887) as prof. of piano at the Cons. The immense success of his series of historical recitals, in 1889, made him resolve to specialize in early music, and led to his establishing the Société des Anciens Instruments. Widor, Saint-Saëns, Lalo, and others wrote pieces for him which he played at the Colonne and Lamoureux concerts. He edited a number of old French keyboard pieces; his collection *Clavecinistes français* was publ. posthumously in 1928.

Diepenbrock, Alphons, eminent Dutch composer; b. Amsterdam, Sept. 2, 1862; d. there, April 5, 1921. He learned to play violin and piano in his childhood. In 1880 he entered the Univ. of Amsterdam, where he studied classical philology; received his Ph.D. in 1888; taught academic subjects at the grammar school at 's-Hertogenbosch (1888–94); then abandoned his pedagogical activities and devoted himself primarily to music; studied works of the Flemish School of the Renaissance, and later perused the scores of Berlioz, Wagner, and Debussy. Despite this belated study, he succeeded in developing a rather striking individual style of composition, in which Wagnerian elements curiously intertwine with impressionistic modalities. However, he had difficulty in putting the results into definite shape, and he left more than 100 incomplete MSS at his death. His Catholic upbringing led him to concentrate mainly on the composition of sacred choral music; he wrote no symphs., concertos, or instrumental sonatas.
WORKS: *Stabat Mater* for Men's Chorus; *Missa in Die festo* for Tenor, Male Chorus, and Organ (1890–91); *Les Elfes* for Soprano, Baritone, Women's Chorus, and Orch. (1896); *Te Deum* for Soloists, Double Chorus, and Orch. (1897); 2 *Hymnen an die Nacht,* after Novalis, one each for Soprano and Contralto, with Orch. (1899); *Vondel's vaart naar Agrippine (Vondel's Journey to Agrippina)* for Baritone and Orch. (1902–3); *Im grossen Schweigen,* after Nietzsche, for Baritone and Orch. (Amsterdam, May 20, 1906); *Hymne aan Rembrandt* for Soprano, Women's Chorus, and Orch. (1906); incidental music to Verhagen's mythical comedy *Marsyas of De betooverde bron (Marsyas or The Enchanted Well;* 1909–10); *Die Nacht,* after Hölderlin, for Mezzo-Soprano and Orch. (1910–11); *Lydische Nacht* for Baritone and Orch. (1913); incidental music to Aristophanes' *The Birds* (1917; a concert overture from this music is fairly popular); incidental music to Goethe's *Faust* (1918); incidental music to Sophocles' *Electra* (1920); numerous choruses and songs. A collection of Diepenbrock's writings, *Verzamelde geschriften,* ed. by Eduard Reeser, was publ. in Utrecht (1950); a catalogue of his works was issued in Amsterdam in 1962. Eduard Reeser brought out *Brieven en documenten* (letters and documents of Diepenbrock; 2 vols., Amsterdam, 1962–67); he also wrote "Some Melodic Patterns in the Music of Alphons Diepenbrock," *Composers' Voice, 3* (1976/1; pp. 16–25).

Dieren, Bernard van, important composer and writer; b. Rotterdam, Dec. 27, 1884; d. London, April 24, 1936. After studying in Germany and the Netherlands, he settled in 1909 in London as music correspondent of the *Nieuwe Rotterdamsche Courant;* later devoted his time exclusively to composing. His works show radical tendencies.
WORKS: *6 Sketches* for Piano (1911); 4 string quartets (1912; 1917, perf. at the Donaueschingen Music Festival in 1920; 1919; 1923, perf. at the Frankfurt International Music Festival in 1925); Symph. for Soli, Chorus, and Orch., on Chinese texts (1914); *Diaphony* for Baritone and Chamber Orch., on 3 Shakespearean sonnets; *Overture to an Ideal Comedy* (1916); *Les Propous des Beuveurs,* introit for Orch. (after Rabelais; London, 1921); *Sonata Tyroica* for Violin and Piano (1927); many songs (also with string quartet and chamber orch.). He wrote a book on the modern sculptor Jacob Epstein (1920); and a collection of essays, *Down among the Dead Men* (London, 1935).

Diet, Edmond-Marie, French dramatic composer; b. Paris, Sept. 25, 1854; d. there, Oct. 30, 1924. He was a pupil of César Franck and Guiraud; produced the operas *Stratonice* (1887), *Le Cousin Placide* (1887), *Fleur de Vertu* (1894), *La Revanche d'Iris* (1905); also ballets and pantomimes: *Scientia* (1889); *La Grève; Masque rose; M. Ruy-Blas* (1894); *La Belle et la bête* (1895); *L'Araignée d'or* (1896); *Rêve de Noël* (1896); *Watteau* (1900; with Pujet); 3-act operetta, *Gentil Crampon* (Paris, 1897); songs; church music.

Dietrich (or Dieterich), Sixtus, composer; b. Augsburg, c.1492–94; d. St. Gall, Switzerland, Oct. 21, 1548. He was a boy chorister at Constance in 1504–6; in 1508–9, studied in Freiburg; in 1517 was a choirmaster in Constance, becoming a priest in 1522; in 1540 and 1544 he was in Wittenberg. He was one of the most important early Protestant composers of sacred music. A book of Magnificats (1535) and 2 collections of antiphons *a* 4 (1541, 1545) were publ.; motets, songs, etc., are scattered through various German collections printed in 1536–68; 5 pieces are in Glareanus' *Dodecachordon* (1547). Reprints have been publ. in Denkmäler Deutscher Tonkunst, 34, and by H. Zenck (13 hymns).

Dietsch, Pierre-Louis-Philippe, French conductor; b. Dijon, March 17, 1808; d. Paris, Feb. 20, 1865. He was a pupil of Choron at the Paris Cons.; in 1830 became maître de chapelle at St.-Eustache, and later at Ste.-Madeleine; in 1860–63 was conductor at the Paris Opéra; composed 25 masses and other sacred music. He would have been forgotten long ago were his name not connected with that of Wagner. In 1842 he brought out at the Opéra *Le Vaisseau fantôme,* written on Wagner's original sketch of *Der fliegende Holländer,* and in 1861 he conducted (most incompetently) the notorious 3 Paris performances of *Tannhäuser.* See references to Dietsch in Wagner's *Mein Leben* (vols. I and III).

Dietz, Howard, American lyricist; b. New York,

Sept. 9, 1896; d. (of Parkinson's disease) July 30, 1983. He began writing lyrics for popular songs in 1918; wrote texts for Jerome Kern, Gershwin, and Vernon Duke; also collaborated in writing lyrics with Arthur Schwartz. In 1919 he joined the Goldwyn Pictures Corp. as publicity director; when the firm merged into Metro-Goldwyn-Mayer in 1924 he remained with it, becoming its vice-president in 1940. He devised its pseudo-Latin logo, Ars Gratia Artis (the correct word sequence would be Ars Artis Gratia). In 1974 he publ. an autobiography, *Dancing in the Dark*. Of his hobbies, to be noted is the invention of the 2-handed bridge game which was named after him. He also painted and translated librettos. As a publicity man for Metro-Goldwyn-Mayer, he popularized, and possibly made up, Greta Garbo's line "I want to be alone," which became famous.

Dieupart, Charles François, French violinist and harpsichordist; b. c.1670; d. London, c.1740. He went to London in 1700; was maestro al cembalo, for several years, of Handel's operas; and died almost destitute. He publ. *6 Suites de clavecin . . . composées et mises en concert pour un violon et une flûte, avec basse de viole et un archiluth.* Bach copied 2 of Dieupart's clavecin suites, and used various themes in his own *English Suites.* The Lyrebird Press of Paris publ. 2 vols. of Dieupart's works, edited by P. Brunold (vol. I, *6 suites pour clavecin;* vol. II, *Airs et Chansons*).

Diller, Angela, American pianist and pedagogue; b. Brooklyn, Aug. 1, 1877; d. Stamford, Conn., April 30, 1968. She studied music at Columbia Univ. with Edward MacDowell and Percy Goetschius; also with Johannes Schreyer in Dresden; in 1899–1916 was head of the theory dept. of the Music School Settlement in N.Y.; in 1916–21, was an administrator at the David Mannes School; then director of the Diller-Quaile School of Music in N.Y.; was on the faculty of the Univ. of Southern Calif. (1932), Mills College (1935), and the New England Cons. (1936 and 1937); was co-founder, with Margarethe Dessoff, of the Adesdi Chorus and A Cappella Singers of N.Y.; edited, with E. Quaile, K. Stearns Page, and Harold Bauer, many educational music works. In 1953 she received a Guggenheim fellowship award. She publ. *First Theory Book* (1921); *Keyboard Harmony Course* (4 books, 1936, 1937, 1943, 1949), and *The Splendor of Music* (1957).

Dilling, Mildred, noted American harpist; b. Marion, Indiana, Feb. 23, 1894; d. New York, Dec. 30, 1982. She studied with Louise Schellschmidt-Koehne and later, in Paris, with Henriette Renié. After her concert debut in Paris, she played in N.Y. (1913) with the Madrigal Singers of the MacDowell Chorus; appeared in joint recitals in Europe with the de Reszkes and Yvette Guilbert, and in the U.S. with Alma Gluck and Frances Alda; toured the U.S. and Great Britain many times; also made concert tours in South America, in the Middle East, and in the Orient. She had 7 engagements to play at the White House. She had numerous private pupils who became well-known harp players; her most famous student was the comedian Harpo Marx. She cultivated calluses on her fingers to achieve sonority. She was the owner of a large collection of harps which she acquired in different parts of the world. She publ. *Old Tunes for New Harpists* (1934) and *30 Little Classics for the Harp* (1938).

D'Indy, Vincent. See **Indy, Vincent d'.**

Dinicu, Grigoraş, Rumanian composer of light music; b. Bucharest, April 3, 1889; d. there, March 28, 1949. He was of a family of musicians; in 1902 studied violin with Carl Flesch, who taught at the Bucharest Cons. At his graduation in 1906, Dinicu played a violin piece of his own based on popular Rumanian rhythms, *Hora staccato;* Jascha Heifetz made a virtuoso arrangement of it in 1932. Subsequently Dinicu played in hotels, restaurants, nightclubs, and cafés in Bucharest and in Western Europe. Apart from *Hora staccato,* he composed numerous other pieces of light music in the gypsy and Rumanian manner.

Dippel, Andreas, dramatic tenor and impresario; b. Kassel, Germany, Nov. 30, 1866; d. Hollywood, May 12, 1932. In 1882–87 he was employed in a banking house at Kassel, meanwhile beginning vocal study with Frau Zottmayr, a well-known singer at the court theater; he was engaged at the Bremen Stadttheater (1887–92); made his American debut at the Metropolitan Opera in N.Y. (Nov. 26, 1890); then sang at Covent Garden in London, in Munich, and at Bayreuth. His repertoire included nearly 150 roles; he was particularly successful in Wagner's operas. In 1908 he became administrative manager of the Metropolitan; in 1910 he assumed control of the Chicago Opera Co.; was its manager till 1913; then organized his own company, specializing in light opera.

Diruta, Girolamo, celebrated Italian organist; b. Deruta, province of Perugia, c.1554; d. after 1610. He was a pupil, in Venice, of Zarlino, Costanzo Porta, and Claudio Merulo, the last of whom mentions the fact with pride in the preface of Diruta's *Il Transilvano.* In 1574, Diruta was in the Minorite monastery at Correggio; then was church organist in Venice (1582–93); was at the Cathedral of Chioggia (1593–1603); and at Agobbio (Gubbio) Cathedral (1609–12). His *Il Transilvano* is a valuable treatise on organ playing, the first work to treat the organ and its playing technique as distinct and separate from the clavier. It is in 2 parts, in dialogue form: *Dialogo sopra il vero modo di sonar organi e istromenti da penna* (Venice, 1593; further eds., 1597, 1609, 1612, 1625) and *Dialogo diviso in quattro libri . . . il vero modo e la vera regola d'intavolare ciascun canto* (Venice, 1609; 2nd ed., 1622). Dannreuther, in his *Musical Ornamentation,* gives a thorough analysis of Diruta's system of ornamentation. Vol. III of L. Torchi's *L'arte musicale in Italia* contains a Ricercare and 2 toccatas for organ by Diruta.

Di Stefano, Giuseppe, noted Italian tenor; b. Motta Santa Anastasia, near Catania, July 24, 1921. He studied with Luigi Montesanto in Milan; then was conscripted into the Italian army in the infantry, and was taken prisoner; he escaped and went to Switzerland. Returning to Italy after the war, he made his operatic debut in Reggio Emilia in 1946; then sang in Rome and at La Scala in Milan. On Feb. 25, 1948, he made his debut as the Duke of Mantua in *Rigoletto* at the Metropolitan Opera in N.Y.; he was on its roster until 1952, and again in 1955–56 and 1964–65. On Oct. 8, 1950, he sang the role of Rodolfo in *La Bohème* at the San Francisco Opera. He also appeared as a guest artist with the Chicago Lyric Opera during the season 1965–66; his other engagements were at La Scala, the Vienna State Opera, the Berlin State Opera, Covent Garden in London, the Paris Opéra, and Teatro Colón in Buenos Aires. In 1973–74 he made a much-publicized concert tour with Maria Callas. His opera roles were limited almost exclusively to the Italian repertoire, but he also sang Faust in Gounod's opera, Don José in *Carmen,* and Des Grieux in *Manon.*

Distler, Hugo, important German composer; b. Nuremberg, June 24, 1908; d. (suicide) Berlin, Nov. 1, 1942. He studied at the Leipzig Cons. with Grabner and Martienssen. In 1931 he became a church organist at Lübeck; joined the faculty of the Lübeck Cons. (1933–37); also was a teacher at an ecclesiastical school in Spandau (1933–37); taught at the Hochschule für Musik in Wurttemberg (1937–40); from 1940 he was in Berlin. His early training and his connection with church music determined his style as a composer; his music is marked by a strong sense of polyphony. He wrote few works, mostly chamber music and choral pieces: Concerto for Cembalo and String Orch. (1935–36); cantatas: *An die Natur* (1933); *Das Lied von der Glocke* (1933–34); *Lied am Herde* (1940). His oratorio *Die Weltalter* (1942) remained unfinished. Distler's works have been heard in frequent performances since his death. He also publ. *Funktionelle Harmonielehre* (Kassel and Basel, 1941).

Ditson, Oliver, American music publisher, founder of the firm of **Oliver Ditson & Co.;** b. Boston, Oct. 20, 1811; d. there, Dec. 21, 1888. He established himself as a music seller and publisher in Boston in 1835; became a partner of G.H. Parker, his employer, under the firm name of Parker & Ditson; carried on the business in his own name (1842–57); when J.C. Haynes joined the firm, Ditson changed its name to O. Ditson & Co. His eldest son, **Charles,** took charge of the N.Y. branch (**Ch. H. Ditson & Co.**) in 1867, the business being continued until his death. A Philadelphia branch, opened in 1875 by **J. Edward Ditson** as **J. E. D. & Co.,** was in existence until 1910. A branch for the importation and sale of instruments, etc., was established at Boston in 1860 as John C. Haynes & Co. On Oliver Ditson's death, the firm of Oliver Ditson & Co. was reorganized as a corporation, with J.C. Haynes as president (d. May 3, 1907); from 1907 until his death, on May 14, 1929,

Charles H. Ditson managed the business; he was succeeded by H.H. Porter. In 1931 Theo. Presser Co., of Philadelphia, took over the management of the firm; its catalogue embraced about 52,000 titles; it publ. the *Musical Record* (a monthly periodical) from 1878 to 1903, the *Musician* from 1896 to 1918, and several library series. The music house Lyon & Healy was founded by Oliver Ditson in Chicago in 1864 as a western branch.

Dittersdorf, Karl Ditters von (original name, **Karl Ditters**), eminent Austrian composer and violinist; b. Vienna, Nov. 2, 1739; d. Schloss Rothlhotta, Neuhof, Bohemia, Oct. 24, 1799. He played violin as a child; then studied with König and Ziegler; the Prince of Sachsen-Hildurghausen made it possible for him to take private violin lessons with Trani and to study composition with Bono; he played in the Prince's orch. from 1751 to 1761. In 1761 he went to Vienna, where he was engaged as a member of the court theater orch. (until 1764). He was befriended by Gluck, who took him along on his Italian journey, where he had an occasion to appear in public as a violinist. In 1765 he assumed the post of Kapellmeister to the Bishop of Grosswardein in Hungary, where he remained until 1769. His career as a composer began in earnest at this time; he wrote an oratorio, *Isacco, figura del redentore;* several cantatas; and many pieces of orch. and chamber music. In 1770 he became Kapellmeister to the Prince-Bishop of Breslau, Count von Schaffgotsch, at Johannisberg in Silesia. There he wrote mostly for the stage, bringing out 12 works between 1771 and 1776. However, he wrote his most important dramatic works in Vienna and for the ducal theater in Oels. He gained fame with his first singspiel, *Doctor und Apotheker,* produced in Vienna on July 11, 1786; it was followed by other successful stage works, *Betrug durch Aberglauben, Die Liebe im Narrenhause, Das rote Käppchen,* and *Hieronymus Knicker.* He received several honors during his lifetime; in 1770 the Pope bestowed upon him the Order of the Golden Spur; in 1773 he was ennobled by the Emperor as von Dittersdorf. Upon his death of the Prince-Bishop in 1795, he was granted a small pension, and found himself in straitened circumstances until a friend, Baron von Stillfried, took him into his castle, Rothlhotta, where he remained until his death. Dittersdorf was an important figure in the Viennese Classical school of composition, although he lacked the genius of Haydn and Mozart. He was able to fuse the common folksong elements of the period with brilliant ensembles characteristic of opera buffa. His singspiels reveal a jovial humor, melodic charm, and rhythmic vitality. His symphs. and concertos are also of interest as characteristic specimens of the period.

WORKS: FOR THE STAGE: *Il viaggiatore americano in Joannesberg,* farce (Johannisberg, May 1, 1771; not extant); *L'amore disprezzato (Pancratio; Amore in musica),* operetta buffa (Johannisberg, 1771); *Il finto pazzo per amore,* operetta giocosa (Johannisberg, June 3, 1772); *Il tutore e la pupilla,* dramma giocoso (Johannisberg, May 1, 1773); *Lo sposo burlato*, operetta giocosa (Johannisberg, 1773 or 1775; another version as *Der gefoppte Bräutigam*); *Il tribunale di Giove*, serenade with prologue (Johannisberg, 1774); *Il maniscalco*, operetta giocosa (Johannisberg, May 1, 1775); *La contadina fedele*, opera giocoso (Johannisberg, 1776); *La moda ossia Gli scompigli domestici*, dramma giocoso (Johannisberg, June 3, 1776); *L'Arcifanfano, re de' matti*, opera giocosa (Johannisberg, 1776); *Il barone di rocca antica*, operetta giocosa (Johannisberg, 1776); *I visionari* (Johannisberg, 1776; not extant); *Doctor und Apotheker (Der Apotheker und der Doctor)*, singspiel (Vienna, July 11, 1786); *Betrug durch Aberglauben oder Die Schatzgräber (Der glückliche Betrug; Die dienstbaren Geister)*, singspiel (Vienna, Oct. 3, 1786); *Democrito corretto*, opera giocosa (Vienna, Jan. 24, 1787; performed under various titles); *Die Liebe im Narrenhause*, singspiel (Vienna, April 12, 1787); *Das rote Käppchen oder Hilft's nicht so schadt's nicht (Die rote Kappe; Das Rotkäppchen)*, comic operetta (Vienna, 1788); *Im Dunkeln ist nicht gut munkeln oder Irrung über Irrung (25,000 Gulden)*, comic opera (Vienna, Feb. 1789); *Hieronymus Knicker (Lucius Knicker; Chrisostomus Knicker; Hokus Pokus oder Die Lebensessenz)*, singspiel (Vienna, July 7, 1789); *Die Hochzeit des Figaro*, singspiel (Brno, 1789?; music not extant); *Der Schiffspatron oder Der neue Gutsherr*, singspiel (Vienna, 1789); *Hokus-Pokus oder Der Gaukelspiel*, comic opera (Vienna, 1790); *Der Teufel ein Hydraulikus*, comedy (Gratz, 1790); *Der Fürst und sein Volk*, pasticcio (Leipzig, March 5?, 1791; music not extant; in collaboration with F. Piterlin and F. Bertoni); *Das Gespenst mit der Trommel (Geisterbanner)*, singspiel (Oels, Aug. 16, 1794); *Don Quixote der Zweyte (Don Chisciotto)*, singspiel (Oels, Feb. 4, 1795); *Gott Mars und der Hauptmann von Bärenzahn (Gott Mars oder Der eiserne Mann)*, singspiel (Oels, May 30, 1795); *Der Durchmarsch*, an arrangement of J. Paneck's *Die christliche Judenbraut* (Oels, Aug. 29, 1795); *Der Schach von Schiras*, singspiel (Oels, Sept. 15, 1795); *Die befreyten Gwelfen (Die Guelfen)*, prologue (Oels, Oct. 29, 1795); *Ugolino*, serious singspiel (Oels, June 11, 1796); *Die lustigen Weiber von Windsor*, singspiel (Oels, June 25, 1796); *Die schöne Herbsttag*, dialogue (Oels, Oct. 29, 1796); *Der Ternengewinnst oder Der gedemütigte Stolz (Terno secco)*, singspiel (Oels, Feb. 11, 1797); *Der Mädchenmark*, singspiel (Oels, April 18, 1797); *Die Opera buffa*, comic opera (Vienna, 1798); *Don Coribaldi ossia L'usurpata prepotenza*, drama (Dresden, 1798?); *Ein Stück mit kleinen Liedern*, opera based on *Frau Sybilla trinkt keinen Wein* and *Das Reich der Toten*; comic opera version based on *Amore in musica* (Grosswardein, 1767?; not extant); etc.

OTHER VOCAL WORKS: *Isacco, figura del redentore*, oratorio (Grosswardein, 1766); *Il Davide nella Valle di Terebintho (Davidde penitente)*, oratorio (Johannisberg, 1771); *L'Esther ossia La Liberatrice del popolo giudaico nella Persia*, oratorio (Vienna, Dec. 19, 1773); *Giobbe (Hiob)*, oratorio (Vienna, April 8–9, 1786); also several cantatas, both sacred and secular; masses; offertories; graduals; motets; etc.

FOR ORCH: A great number of symphs. have been attributed to Dittersdorf, with over 100 being most likely by him. Most famous are the 12 symphs. on Ovid's *Metamorphoses*; only Nos. 1–6 are extant, although Nos. 7–12 have survived in arrangements for Piano, 4–hands, by Dittersdorf. He also composed many concertos, including 18 for violin, 3 for 2 violins, one for cello, 5 for viola, 4 for oboe, 5 for harpsichord, and one for flute.

CHAMBER MUSIC: 15 divertimentos, including *Il combattimento dell'umane passioni;* 4 string serenades (with 2 horns); numerous string quartets; many sonatas for 4-hands; preludes; etc.

Dittrich, Paul-Heinz, German composer; b. Gornsdorf, Erzgebirge, Dec. 4, 1930. He studied composition with Fidelio Finke and choral conducting with Günther Ramin at the Leipzig Hochschule für Musik (1951–56). Later he took a seminar in advanced composition with Rudolf Wagner-Régeny at the Academy of Arts in East Berlin (1958–60). He was a choral director in Weimar (1956–58) and taught counterpoint and harmony at the Hanns Eisler Hochschule für Musik in East Berlin (1963–76). In 1980 he visited America. In his music, Dittrich reveals himself as an astute creator of modern forms and technical idioms, while carefully observing and preserving the pragmatic elements of instrumental and vocal components. He obtained numerous awards for his compositions, among them a prize of the International Society for Contemporary Music (1975) and a UNESCO prize (1976).

Divitis (de Ryche, le Riche), Antonius (Antoine), celebrated French (or Flemish) contrapuntist of the late 15th and early 16th centuries; b. Louvain, c.1475; d. probably after 1526, in which year he is mentioned as very likely being at St. Peter's in Rome as **Antonius Richardus.** He was a singer and choirmaster at St. Donatien in Bruges (Brugge) in 1501–4; in 1504–5, was choirmaster at St. Rombaut in Malines; then was in the service of Philippe le Beau in Brussels; was a chapel singer to Louis XII from 1506 to 1515.

WORKS: Motets and chansons are scattered in collections, e.g., *Motetti de la corona* (1514), and others printed by Rhaw, Attaingnant, etc. At Cambrai is a mass in MS; at Munich, 2 credos and a Salve Regina *a* 5; at Rome, *Quem dicunt homines* for 4 Voices.

Dixon, Dean, black American conductor; b. New York, Jan. 10, 1915; d. Zug, near Zürich, Nov. 3, 1976. He showed a musical talent as a child and began to take violin lessons. At the age of 17 he organized at his high school in the Bronx a group that he was pleased to call the Dean Dixon Symphony Society. He studied violin at the Juilliard School of Music (1932–36); on a conducting fellowship he took lessons with Albert Stoessel at the Juilliard Graduate School (1936–39); also enrolled in academic classes at Columbia Univ. Teachers College, receiving an M.A. in 1939. Eleanor Roosevelt became interested in his career, and helped him to obtain some conducting engagements, including an appearance with the N.Y. Phil. at the Lewisohn Stadium on Aug. 10, 1941, making him the first of his race to conduct this orch. In 1944 Dixon organized the American Youth Orch., which had a limited success. In 1949 he went to Europe in the hopes of securing wider opportunities. These hopes were fully realized; he was engaged as music director of the Hessian Radio Orch. in Frankfurt (1961–75); concurrently he served as music director of the Sydney (Australia) Symph. (1964–67); also filled special engagements in France, Italy, Spain, and Austria. Returning briefly to the U.S. in 1970, he was guest conductor for a series of N.Y. Phil. summer concerts in Central Park, then went back to Europe and settled in Switzerland in 1974. His career was cut short when he underwent open-heart surgery in 1975; yet he managed to conduct several engagements in Europe before suffering a final collapse.

Dixon, James, American conductor; b. Estherville, Iowa, April 26, 1928. He studied at the Univ. of Iowa (B.M., 1952; M.M., 1956); was conductor of the U.S. 7th Army Symph. Orch. in Germany (1951–54); the Univ. of Iowa Symph. Orch. in Iowa City (1954–59); the New England Cons. Symph. Orch. in Boston (1959–61). In 1962 he returned to the Univ. of Iowa Symph. Orch. as its permanent conductor; from 1965, served as conductor of the Tri-City Symph. Orch. in Davenport, Iowa, and Rock Island, Ill. In addition, he was associate conductor of the Minneapolis Symph. Orch. (1961–62); guest conductor with the following orchs.: National Orch. of Greece in Athens (1955, 1959, 1961), Norddeutscher Rundfunk (1963), Westdeutscher Rundfunk (1964), Tanglewood (1965), Chicago Civic Symph. (1967), and Chicago Symph. Orch. (1972). He was the recipient of the Gustav Mahler Medal in 1963. As an interpreter, he follows the style of Mitropoulos, under whose influence he began his career, combining precision of rhythmic flow with expressive shaping of melodic phrases.

Dizi, François-Joseph, famous French harpist; b. Namur, Jan. 14, 1780; d. Paris, Nov., 1847. He set out for London when only 16; lost his harp on the way but went on without it, and introduced himself to Erard, who gave him a harp and obtained pupils for him. Besides winning fame as a concert player and as a harpist at the principal theaters, he invented the "perpendicular harp" (which was unsuccessful), and composed sonatas, romances, variations, studies, etc., for harp; also publ. *Ecole de Harpe, Being a Complete Treatise on the Harp* (London, 1827). In 1830 he went to Paris, and established a harp factory with Pleyel, which did not do well. There he was appointed harp teacher to the royal princesses.

Dlugoszewski, Lucia, American composer; b. Detroit, June 16, 1931. She studied piano, and concurrently attended classes in physics at Wayne State Univ. (1946–49). Fascinated with the mathematical aspects of music, she began to study with Edgar Varèse, whose works illuminated this scientific relationship for her. Accordingly, in her own works she emphasizes the sonorific element of music; inspired by the example of Varèse's *Ionisation,* she invented or perfected a number of percussion instruments; one of her inventions is the timbre piano, in which she makes use of bows and plectra on the piano strings. In 1960 she joined the Foundation for Modern Dance as a teacher and composer.

WORKS: Her dance scores include *Openings of the Eye* for Flute, Percussion, and Timbre Piano (1958); *8 Clear Places* for Percussion Ensemble (1958–61); *Geography of Noon* for New Percussion Instruments (1964); *Dazzle on a Knife's Edge* for Timbre Piano and Orch. (1966); *Agathlon Algebra* for Timbre Piano and Orch. (1968); and a series of works for various instrumental combinations under the title *Lords of Persia.* Other works are: *50 Transparencies* "for everyday sounds" (1951); *Arithmetic Points* for Orch. (1955); *Instants in Form and Movements* for Timbre Piano and Chamber Orch. (1957); *Delicate Accidents in Space* for Rattle Quintet (1959); *Archaic Aggregates* for Timbre Piano, Ladder Harps, Tangent Rattles, Unsheltered Rattles, and Gongs (1961); *4 Attention Spans* for Orch. (1964); *Strange Tenderness of Naked Leaping* for Orch. (Santa Fe, N.Mex., Nov. 13, 1977); several pieces entitled *Beauty Music,* and *Music for the Left Ear in a Small Room* and other bafflingly and provocatively yclept productions.

Dobbs, Mattiwilda, American soprano; b. Atlanta, July 11, 1925. She studied with Lotte Lehmann; also in Paris with Pierre Bernac. She began her concert career in Europe in 1948; won first prize in the International Competition for Singers in Geneva in 1951; then sang at La Scala, Glyndebourne, and other leading European opera houses. She made her Metropolitan Opera debut in N.Y. on Nov. 9, 1956, as Gilda in Verdi's *Rigoletto.*

Dobiáš, Václav, Czech composer; b. Radčice, near Semily, Sept. 22, 1909; d. Prague, May 18, 1978. He studied violin and composition at the Prague Cons., where he also took courses in microtonal music with Alois Hába, and wrote a *Lento* for 3 Harps (1940) and a Violin Concerto (1941) making use of quarter-tones. After 1945 he became involved in the political problems of musical education; in conformity with the ideology of the Communist Party, he began to write music for the masses in the manner of socialist realism; in 1958 he was elected to the Central Committee of the Communist Party of Czechoslovakia, and was a member of the National Assembly from 1960 to 1969.

Dobrowen, Issay, Russian conductor; b. Nizhny-Novgorod, Feb. 27, 1891; d. Oslo, Dec. 9, 1953. His real name was **Barabeichik;** his orphaned mother was adopted by Israil Dobrovel; Issay Dobrowen changed his legal name, Dobrovel, to Dobrowein, and later to Dobrowen. He studied at the Nizhny-Novgorod Cons. as a small child (1896–1900); then entered the Moscow Cons. and studied with Igumnov (piano) and Taneyev (composition); went to Vienna for additional study with Leopold Godowsky (piano). Returning to Moscow, he became conductor of the Moscow Opera; in 1922 he led the Dresden State Opera in the German premiere of Mussorgsky's opera *Boris Godunov;* in 1924 he conducted opera in Berlin; during the season 1927–28 he conducted opera in Sofia, Bulgaria. In 1931 he made his American debut; conducted the San Francisco Symph. Orch.; was guest conductor with the Minneapolis Symph. Orch., Philadelphia Orch., and the N.Y. Phil. However, he was received indifferently by American audiences, and returned to Europe. He was a regular conductor of the Budapest Opera in 1936–39; at the outbreak of World War II he went to Sweden, where he won his greatest successes, as conductor of both opera and symph., at the Stockholm Opera and the Phil. of Göteborg. In 1948 he conducted at La Scala in Milan. On frequent occasions Dobrowen acted as stage director as well as conductor in German, Italian, and Swedish opera houses. He was a prolific composer; wrote several piano concertos and pieces for piano solo, in a Romantic vein; also an orch. fairy tale, *1,001 Nights* (Moscow, May 27, 1922).

Dobrowolski, Andrzej, Polish composer; b. Lwow, Sept. 9, 1921. He studied organ, singing, clarinet, theory, and composition at the State College of Music in Cracow (1947–51); in 1954 joined the faculty of the Warsaw State College of Music; in 1976 was appointed to the faculty of the Graz Hochschule für Musik. His music is a paradigm of modern structuralism and textural abstraction.
  WORKS: *Symphonic Variations* (1949); *Overture* (1950); Oboe Concerto (1953); *Popular Overture* (1954); Trio for Oboe, Clarinet, and Bassoon (1954); Symph. No. 1 (1955); *8 Studies* for Oboe, Trumpet, Bassoon, and Double Bass (1959); *Music No. 1* for Tape (1962); *Music* for Strings and 4 Groups of Wind Instruments (1964); *Music* for Tape and Solo Oboe (1965); *Music* for Strings, 2 Groups of Wind Instruments, and 2 Loudspeakers (1966); *Music* for Orch. (1968–69); *Krabogapa* for Clarinet, Trombone, Cello, and Piano (1969); *Music No. 2* for Orch. (1970); *Music* for Tape and Solo Piano (1972); *Music* for Solo Tuba (1972); *Music No. 3* for Orch. (1972–73); *Music No. 4* for Orch. (1974); *Music* for Chorus, 2 Groups of Winds, Double Bass, and Percussion (1975).

Dodge, Charles, American composer; b. Ames, Iowa, June 5, 1942. He studied composition with Philip Benzanson at the Univ. of Iowa (B.A., 1964); Darius Milhaud at the Aspen Summer School (1961); Gunther Schuller and Arthur Berger at the Berkshire Music Center in Tanglewood (1964); and Jack Beeson, Chou Wen-Chung, Otto Luening, and Vladimir Ussachevsky at Columbia Univ. (M.A., 1966). He subsequently was on the faculty of Columbia (1967–77) and Princeton (1969–70) univs., teaching electronic music; in 1977 joined the faculty at Brooklyn College; received numerous commissions, grants, and awards, including one from the Koussevitzky Foundation in 1969. He composes in an empirical manner, following serial ideas; in most of his works he makes use of electronic media.
  WORKS: *Folia* for 7 Instruments and Percussion (1963); *Rota* for Orch. (1966); *Changes* for Electronic Tape with the aid of a digital computer storing a succession of numbers made audible by an analog converter (first perf. at the Coolidge Festival, Washington, D.C., Oct. 31, 1970); *Palinode* for Computerized Tape and Orch. (N.Y., Feb. 7, 1977).

Döhler, Theodor, Italian pianist and composer; b. Naples, April 20, 1814; d. Florence, Feb. 21, 1856. He was a pupil of Julius Benedict at Naples and of Czerny (piano) and Sechter (composition) at Vienna. In 1831 he became pianist to the Duke of Lucca; lived for a time in Naples; made brilliant pianistic tours in 1836–46 in Germany, Italy, France, the Netherlands, and England; in 1843 went to Copenhagen, thence to Russia, and in 1846 to Paris; settled in Florence in 1848. In 1846 the Duke, his patron, ennobled him, and he married a Russian countess. He wrote an opera, *Tancreda,* which was performed posthumously in Florence in 1880; many piano pieces; nocturnes; tarantellas; *12 études de concert; 50 études de salon;* variations, fantasias, and transcriptions.

Dohnányi, Christoph von, eminent German-born conductor; grandson of **Ernö (Ernst von) Dohnányi;** b. Berlin, Sept. 8, 1929. He began to study the piano as a child; his musical training was interrupted by World War II. His father, Hans von Dohnányi, a jurist, and his uncle, Dietrich Bonhoeffer, the Protestant theologian and author, were executed by the Nazis for their involvement in the July 20, 1944, attempt on Hitler's life. After the war, he studied jurisprudence at the Univ. of Munich; in 1948 he enrolled at the Hochschule für Musik in Munich, and won the Richard Strauss Prize for composition and conducting. Making his way to the U.S., he continued his studies with his grandfather at Florida State Univ. at Tallahassee; also attended sessions at the Berkshire Music Center at Tanglewood. Returning to Germany, he received a job as a coach and conductor at the Frankfurt Opera (1952–57). Progressing rapidly, he served as Generalmusikdirektor in Lübeck (1957–63) and Kassel (1963–66), chief conductor of the Cologne Radio Symph. Orch. (1964–70) and director of the Frankfurt Opera (1968–77). From 1977 to 1984 he was Staatsopernintendant of the Hamburg State Opera. In 1984 he assumed the position of music director of the Cleveland Orch., having been appointed music director-designate in 1982, succeeding Lorin Maazel. In the meantime he had engagements as guest conductor of the Vienna State Opera, Covent Garden in London, La Scala in Milan, the Metropolitan Opera in N.Y., the Berlin Phil., the Vienna Phil., and the Concertgebouw Orch. in Amsterdam. Both as symph. and opera conductor, Dohnányi proved himself a master technician and a versatile musician capable of congenial interpretation of all types of music, from Baroque to the avant-garde. He is regarded as a leading exponent of the works of the Modern Vienna School, excelling in fine performances of the works of Schoenberg, Berg, and Webern. He is married to the noted German soprano **Anja Silja.**

Dohnányi, Ernö (Ernst von), eminent Hungarian pianist, composer, conductor, and pedagogue; b. Pressburg (Bratislava), July 27, 1877; d. New York, Feb. 9, 1960. He began his musical studies with his father, an amateur cellist; then studied piano and music theory with Károly Forstner. In 1894 he entered the Royal Academy of Music in Budapest, where he took courses in piano with István Thomán and in composition with Hans Koessler. In 1896 he received the Hungarian Millennium Prize, established to commemorate the thousand years of existence of Hungary, for his symph. He graduated from the Academy of Music in 1896, and then went to Berlin for additional piano studies with Eugen d'Albert. He made his debut in a recital in Berlin on Oct. 1, 1897; on Oct. 24, 1898, he played Beethoven's 4th Piano Concerto in London; then followed a series of successful concerts in the U.S. Returning to Europe, he served as prof. of piano at the Hochschule für Musik in Berlin (1908–15). He then returned to Budapest, where he taught piano at the Royal Academy of Music; served briefly as its director in 1919, when he was appointed chief conductor of the Budapest Phil. Orch. In 1928 he became head of the piano composition classes at the Academy of Music; in 1934 he became its director. In 1931 he assumed the post of music director of the Hungarian Radio. As Hungary became embroiled in war and partisan politics which invaded even the arts, Dohnányi resigned his directorship in 1941, and in 1944 he also resigned his post as conductor of the Budapest Phil. Personal tragedy also made it impossible for him to continue his work as a musician and teacher: both of his sons lost their lives; one of them, the German jurist Hans von Dohnányi, was executed for his role in the abortive attempt on Hitler's life; the other son was killed in combat. Late in 1944, Dohnányi moved to Austria. At the war's end rumors were rife that Dohnányi used his influence with the Nazi overlords in Budapest to undermine the position of Bartók and other liberals, and that he acquiesced in anti-Semitic measures. But in 1945 the American occupation authorities exonorated him of all blame; even some prominent Jewish-Hungarian musicians testified in his favor. In 1947–48 he made a tour of England as a pianist; determined to emigrate to America, he accepted the position of piano teacher at Tucumán, Argentina; in Sept. 1949 he reached the U.S., where he became composer-in-residence at Florida State Univ. in Tallahassee.

Dohnányi was a true virtuoso of the keyboard, and was greatly esteemed as a teacher; among his pupils were Georg Solti, Geza Anda, and Bálint Vázsonyi. His own music represented the terminal flowering of European Romanticism, marked by passionate eloquence of expression while keeping within the framework of Classical forms. Brahms praised his early efforts. In retrospect, Dohnányi

appears as a noble epigone of the past era, but pianists, particularly Hungarian pianists, often put his brilliant compositions on their programs. Dohnányi's most popular work with an orch. is *Variations on a Nursery Song;* also frequently played is his Orch. Suite in F-sharp minor. Dohnányi himself presented his philosophy of life in a poignant pamphlet under the title *Message to Posterity* (Jacksonville, Fla., 1960). His grandson **Christoph von Dohnányi** is a talented conductor.

WORKS: FOR THE STAGE: *Der Schleier der Pierrette (Pierrette's Veil),* op. 18, pantomime (1908–9; Dresden, Jan. 22, 1910); *Tante Simona,* op. 20, comic opera (1911–12; Dresden, Jan. 20, 1913); *A vajda tornya (The Tower of the Voivod),* op. 30, opera (1915–22; Budapest, March 19, 1922); *Der Tenor,* op. 34, comic opera (1920–27; Budapest, Feb. 9, 1929).

FOR ORCH.: Symph. in F major (not numbered) and *Zrinyi,* overture (both were awarded the Hungarian Millennium Prize in 1896; first perf., Budapest, June 3, 1897); Piano Concerto No. 1 in E minor, op. 5 (1897–98; Budapest, Jan. 11, 1899; won the Bösendorfer Prize in Vienna, 1899); Symph. No. 1 in D minor, op. 9 (1900–1; Manchester, Jan. 30, 1902); *Konzertstück* for Cello and Orch., op. 12 (1903–4; Budapest, March 7, 1906); Suite in F-sharp minor for Orch., op. 19 (1908–9; Budapest, Feb. 21, 1910); *Variationen über ein Kinderlied (Variations on a Nursery Song),* for Piano and Orch., op. 25 (1913; Berlin, Feb. 17, 1914, Dohnányi, soloist); Violin Concerto No. 1 in D minor, op. 27 (1914–15, Copenhagen, March 5, 1919); *Unnepi nyitány (Festival Overture),* op. 31 (1923); *Ruralia hungarica,* 5 pieces for Orch., op. 32b (1924; Budapest, Nov. 17, 1924, Dohnányi, conductor); *Szimfonikus percek (Symphonic Minutes),* op. 36 (1933); *Suite en valse,* op. 39 (1942–43); Symph. No. 2 in E major, op. 40 (1943–44; London, Nov. 23, 1948; revised 1953–56; Minneapolis, March 15, 1957); Piano Concerto No. 2 in B minor, op. 42 (1946–47; Sheffield, England, Dec. 3, 1947); Violin Concerto No. 2, op. 43 (scored for Orch. without Violins; 1949–50; San Antonio, Jan. 26, 1952); Concertino for Harp and Chamber Orch., op. 45 (1952); *American Rhapsody,* op. 47 (1953; Athens, Ohio, Feb. 21, 1954, Dohnányi, conductor).

VOCAL WORKS: *Magyar hiszekegy (Hungarian Credo)* for Tenor, Choir, and Orch. (1920); *Missa in Dedicatione Ecclesiae (Mass of Szeged)* for Soloist, Chorus, Organ, and Orch., op. 35 (1930; consecration of the Cathedral of Szeged, Oct. 25, 1930); *Cantus vitae,* symph. cantata, op. 38 (1939–41); *Stabat Mater* for 3 Soloists, Children's Chorus, and Orch., op. 46 (1952–53; Wichita Falls, Tex., Jan. 16, 1956); also songs, including 6 Poems, op. 14 (1905–6); *Im Lebenslenz,* op. 16 (1906–7); 3 Songs, with Orch., op. 22 (1912); Hungarian Folk Songs (1922).

CHAMBER MUSIC: Piano Quintet No. 1, op. 1 (1895); String Quartet No. 1, op. 7 (1899); Sonata for Cello and Piano, op. 8 (1899); *Serenade* for String Trio, op. 10 (1902); String Quartet No. 2, op. 15 (1906); Sonata for Violin and Piano, op. 21 (1912); Piano Quintet No. 2, op. 26 (1914); *Ruralia hungarica,* 3 pieces for Violin and Piano, op. 32c (1924); *Ruralia hungarica,* 1 piece for Cello or Violin and Piano, op. 32d (1924); String Quartet No. 3, op. 33 (1926); Sextet for Piano,

Clarinet, Horn, and String Trio, op. 37 (1935); *Aria, for Flute and Piano* (1958); *Passacaglia* for Flute, op. 48 (1959).

FOR PIANO: 4 Pieces, op. 2: *Scherzo* in C-sharp minor, *Intermezzo* in A minor, *Intermezzo* in F minor, *Capriccio* in B minor (1896–97); *Waltz* in F-sharp minor, for 4 hands, op. 3 (1897); Variations and Fugue on a Theme of E(mma) G(ruber), op. 4 (1897); Gavotte and Musette in B-flat major (1898); Passacaglia in E-flat minor, op. 6 (1899); 4 Rhapsodies, in G minor, F-sharp minor, C major, E-flat minor, op. 11 (1902–3); *Winterreigen*, 10 bagatelles: *Widmung, Marsch der lustigen Bruder, An Ada, Freund Viktor's Mazurka, Sphärenmusik, Valse aimable, Um Mitternacht, Tolle Gesellschaft, Morgengrauen, Postludium*, op. 13 (1905); *Humoresken in Form einer Suite:* March, Toccata, Pavane with Variations, Pastorale, Introduction, and Fugue, op. 17 (1907); 3 Pieces: *Aria, Valse impromptu, Capriccio*, op. 23 (1912); Fugue, for left hand or 2 hands (1913); *Suite im alten Stil:* Prelude, Allemande, Courante, Sarabande, Menuet, Gigue, op. 24 (1913); 6 Concert Etudes, op. 28 (1916); Variations on a Hungarian Folk Song, op. 29 (1917); Pastorale, Hungarian Christmas Song (1920); *Ruralia hungarica,* 7 pieces, op. 32a (1923); Essential Finger Exercises (1929); *Suite en valse* for 2 pianos, op. 39a (1945); 6 Pieces: Impromptu, Scherzino, Canzonetta, Cascade, Ländler, Cloches, op. 41 (1945); 12 Short Studies for the Advanced Pianist (1950); 3 Singular Pieces: *Burletta, Nocturne (Cats on the Roof), Perpetuum mobile,* op. 44 (1951); Daily Finger Exercises (3 vols., 1960).

Doležálek, Jan Emanuel, Czech musician; b. Chotěboř, May 22, 1780; d. Vienna, July 6, 1858. He studied music in Vienna with Beethoven's teacher, Albrechtsberger, and through him came to know Beethoven himself. It is owing chiefly to this association that Doležálek's name is known in music history. He arranged a number of Czech songs, and publ. a collection of them.

Dolmetsch, Arnold, English music antiquarian; b. Le Mans, France, Feb. 24, 1858; d. Haslemere, Surrey, Feb. 28, 1940. While apprenticed in his father's piano factory he learned to play both piano and violin, making such marked progress on the latter instrument that his father sent him to Brussels, where he became a pupil of Vieuxtemps (1881–83); then went to the Royal College of Music in London, where he studied violin with Henry Holmes and harmony with Bridge; after completing his studies he went to Dulwich, was appointed instructor of violin at the College, and soon won a reputation as a teacher (1885–89). From his earliest years he had shown a decided predilection for the music of Bach and the old masters; when by chance he became the possessor of a well-preserved viola d'amore, he did not rest until he had mastered the instrument; gradually he acquired the same skill on all the members of the viol family. He then gave up his large class of violin pupils and devoted his entire time to lecturing and giving recitals on the old in-

struments. In his quest for old music he found in the British Museum MSS of almost-forgotten English composers (Simon Ives, Matthew Locke, Thomas Tomkins, John Jenkins, etc.). To become an authoritative interpreter of all this music, he found it necessary to extend his investigations to the virginal, spinet, harpsichord, and clavichord. He began by collecting old books in which those instruments were described by contemporary authorities; the mechanical skill he had acquired in his father's shop he turned to account in repairing the instruments he collected, and before long he was acknowledged as an authority on old music and instruments; he was not only a connoisseur and skilled workman, but also a masterly performer on every instrument in his large collection; with his wife and a pupil, **Kathleen Salmon,** he established the Dolmetsch Trio, devoted exclusively to the performance of old music on the original instruments. A tour of the U.S. attracted so much attention that Chickering & Sons, of Boston, placed their factory and a force of their best workmen at Dolmetsch's disposal. The beginning was made with the restoration of a virginal by Hans Ruckers (1620); then a number of stringed and keyed instruments were built after the best models extant. The interest excited by the revival of these instruments induced several other artists (Wanda Landowska, Fuller-Maitland, the brothers Casadesus, etc.) to give recitals on them. In 1902–9 Dolmetsch lived in Boston, supervising the construction of his instruments and concertizing; he went to Paris to work for Gaveau in 1911–14; after that, he resided in England. In 1925 he founded at Haslemere, Surrey, annual historical chamber music festivals, where the works were played (many by himself) on modern reconstructions of the original historic instruments (clavichord, harpsichord, viols, recorders, etc.). The Dolmetsch Foundation, a society for the purpose of cultivating old music and making his ideas more widely known, was founded by his friends in 1929.

WRITINGS: *Select English Songs and Dialogues of the 16th and 17th Centuries* (2 vols., London, 1898, 1912) and *The Interpretation of the Music of the 17th and 18th Centuries* (London, 1915; new ed., 1944).

Dolmetsch, Carl Frederick, French specialist in recorder music, son of **Arnold Dolmetsch;** b. Fontenay-sous-Bois, near Paris, Aug. 23, 1911. He received thorough training in instrumentation from his father; eventually succeeded him as a leader of the Haslemere Festival. He devoted himself mainly to the publication of music for the recorder; publ. a survey, *Recorder and German Flute during the 17th and 18th Centuries* (London, 1957), and *An Introduction to the Recorder in Modern British Music* (London, 1960). He also publishes the annual bulletin *The Consort.*

Domingo, Placido, Spanish operatic tenor; b. Madrid, Jan. 21, 1941. He went to Mexico at the age of 9 with his parents, who were performers of Spanish zarzuelas; took part in these performances as a child; learned to play the piano and soon developed a pleasing baritone voice, from which he changed to a fine tenorino. He studied operatic parts, accompanying himself at the piano. His first important engagement was in Tel Aviv, where he was engaged as an opera singer for 2 years. He then went to America, where his first engagement was at the N.Y. City Opera as Pinkerton in *Madama Butterfly,* on Oct. 17, 1965; he made his debut with the Metropolitan Opera in N.Y. at the Lewisohn Stadium as Turiddu in a concert performance of *Cavalleria rusticana,* on Aug. 9, 1966. In quick succession he sang Canio in *Pagliacci,* Cavaradossi in *Tosca,* Pinkerton in *Madama Butterfly,* Manrico in *Il Trovatore,* Alfredo in *La Traviata,* Rhadames in *Aida,* and Don José in *Carmen.* He also sang in Hamburg, Milan, and other European cities. Addicted to precise statistics, he calculated the number of his appearances from 1966 to April 1977 at the Metropolitan as 108, and the total of his appearances since his very first engagement up to the same terminal date as 1,209 in 74 roles. His voice possesses a liquidity that is the essence of bel canto; he excels particularly in lyric parts in Italian operas, but he has also essayed Wagnerian roles. He publ. his autobiography, *My First Forty Years* (N.Y., 1983).

Dominiceti, Cesare, Italian composer; b. Desenzano, July 12, 1821; d. Sesto di Monza, June 20, 1888. He studied in Milan, where all his operas were brought out; lived for a long time in Bolivia; made a fortune there. Some years after his return to Italy, he was appointed prof. of composition at the Milan Cons. He wrote the operas *Due mogli in una* (Milan, June 30, 1853), *La maschera* (Milan, March 2, 1854), *Morovico* (Milan, Dec. 4, 1873), *Il lago delle fate* (Milan, May 18, 1878), and *L'Ereditiera* (Milan, Feb. 14, 1881).

Donalda, Pauline (real name, **Lightstone,** translated by her father from **Lichtenstein** when he became a British subject), dramatic soprano; b. Montreal, March 5, 1882; d. there, Oct. 22, 1970. She received her first musical training at Royal Victoria College in Montreal, and then was a private pupil of Duvernoy in Paris; made her debut as Manon (Massenet) at Nice, Dec. 30, 1904; the next year she appeared at La Monnaie in Brussels and at Covent Garden; in 1906–7, at the Manhattan Opera House in N.Y.; then chiefly at the Opéra-Comique. From the time of her retirement, in 1922, to 1937, she had a singing school in Paris; in 1937, returned to Montreal. In 1938 she presented her valuable music library (MSS, autographs, and music) to McGill Univ. In 1940 she founded the Opera Guild in Montreal, serving as its president until it ceased operations in 1969. In 1967 she was made an Officer of the Order of Canada. Her stage name was taken in honor of Sir Donald Smith (later Lord Strathcona), who endowed the Royal Victoria College and was her patron (1975).

Donath, Helen, American soprano; b. Corpus Christi, Texas, July 10, 1940. She was educated at Del Mar College. She then settled in West Germany; made her debut at the Cologne Opera in 1962; sang with fine success in Hannover, Frankfurt, and Munich; also appeared at Bayreuth, being one of the few American singers to gain such distinction. In America, she sang at the San Francisco Opera. She was a favorite singer at Herbert von Karajan's annual Easter Festival in Salzburg.

Donati (Donato), Baldassare, famous Italian composer of motets and madrigals; b. Venice, c.1530; d. there, 1603. He was choirmaster of the so-called "small choir" at San Marco in Venice in 1562–65; this was disbanded by Zarlino when he was appointed maestro di cappella in 1565, and Donati became a simple chorister; he was appointed maestro di canto to the Seminario Gregoriano di San Marco (1580); in 1590, he succeeded Zarlino as maestro di cappella. His compositions are distinguished by their well-defined rhythm and originality. Extant works include *Canzoni Villanesche alla Napoletana* (1550–58); several books of madrigals for 4 parts (1550–68); a vol. of madrigals for 5–6 parts (1553; new eds., 1557, 1560); a vol. of motets for 5–8 parts (1597); etc.

Donati, Ignazio, Italian composer; b. Casalmaggiore, c.1570; d. Milan, Jan. 21, 1638. He was maestro di cappella at the Urbino Cathedral (1612–16); then at Ferrara (1616–18); Casalmaggiore (1618–23); Novara and Lodi (1626–30). In 1631 he became maestro di cappella at the Cathedral of Milan. He publ. 8 books of *concerti ecclesiastici,* 7 books of motets, masses, and Psalms.

Donati, Pino, Italian composer and conductor; b. Verona, May 9, 1907; d. Rome, Feb. 24, 1975. He studied violin; then took composition lessons with G.C. Paribeni. He served as artistic coordinator of the Chicago Lyric Opera from 1958. He wrote 2 operas: *Corradino lo Svevo* (Verona, April 4, 1931) and *Lancillotto del lago* (Bergamo, Oct. 2, 1938); also chamber music.

Donato, Anthony, American violinist and composer; b. Prague, Nebr., March 8, 1909. He studied at the Eastman School of Music in Rochester, N.Y., with Hanson, Rogers, and Royce; obtained the degrees of M.Mus. (1937) and Ph.D. (1947). He was a violin teacher at Drake Univ. (1931–37); Iowa State Teachers College (1937–39); the Univ. of Texas (1939–46); Northwestern Univ. (1947–77).

Donatoni, Franco, Italian composer; b. Verona, June 9, 1927. He studied with Desderi in Milan, Liviabella in Bologna, and Pizzetti at the Santa Cecilia Academy in Rome, graduating in 1953. He was then an instructor at the Cons. of Bologna, the Verdi Cons. in Milan, the Verdi Cons. in Turin, and, since 1970, at the Accademia Musicale Chigiana in Siena. In his music he adopts a system of serial techniques while retaining a fairly strict Baroque structure.

Donington, Robert, distinguished English musicologist; b. Leeds, May 4, 1907. He studied at Queen's College, Oxford (B.A., 1930; B. Litt., 1946); also took a course in composition with Egon Wellesz at Oxford; became associated with Arnold Dolmetsch in his workshop in Haslemere and studied the technique of old instruments; in the capacity of an expert, he contributed to the revival of Elizabethan instruments and music. He was a member of the English Consort of Viols (1935–39); then played with the London Consort (1950–60); in 1956 he founded the Donington Consort, and led it until 1961. He lectured extensively in the U.S.; in 1974 was appointed a prof. at the Univ. of Iowa. He was made a Commander of the Order of the British Empire in 1979.

WRITINGS: *The Work and Ideas of Arnold Dolmetsch* (Haslemere, 1932); *A Practical Method for the Recorder* (with Edgar Hunt; 2 vols., London, 1935); *The Instruments of Music* (London, 1949; 3rd ed., revised, 1970); *Music for Fun* (London, 1960); *Tempo and Rhythm in Bach's Organ Music* (London, 1960); *The Interpretation of Early Music* (N.Y., 1963; 3rd ed., revised, 1974); *Wagner's "Ring" and Its Symbols* (London, 1963; 3rd ed., revised and enlarged, 1974); *A Performer's Guide to Baroque Music* (London, 1973); *String-playing in Baroque Music* (London, 1977); *The Opera* (London, 1978); *The Rise of Opera* (London, 1981).

Donizetti, Gaetano, one of the brilliant triumvirate (Donizetti, Rossini, and Bellini) of Italian opera composers in the first half of the 19th century; b. Bergamo, Nov. 29, 1797; d. there, April 8, 1848. His father, a weaver by trade, later obtained a position in the local pawnshop and desired that his son should become a lawyer. But Donizetti's inclinations were toward art; besides being strongly attracted to music, he studied drawing. His father finally allowed him to enter the Bergamo school of music; his teachers were Salari (voice), Gonzales (piano), and J.S. Mayr (harmony). In 1815 he enrolled in the Bologna Liceo Filarmonico, here completing his contrapuntal studies under Pilotti and Padre Mattei. From his earliest attempts at composition Donizetti was determined to write operas. His first opera was *Il Pigmalione,* which was not produced; but he gained production with his next opera, *Enrico di Borgogna* (Venice, 1818). Two operas —*Una follia* (1818) and *I piccoli, virtuosi ambulanti* (1819)—intervened before the success of *Il Falegname di Livonia* (Venice, 1819; given at first as *Pietro il Grande, Czar delle Russie*). However, *Le nozze in villa* (Mantua, 1820) was a failure. At least a year before his next successful opera, *Zoraide di Granata* (Rome, Jan. 28, 1822), he was exempted from military service thanks to the intercession of an influential noblewoman. In 7 years, between 1822 and 1829, he produced no fewer than 23 operas, none of which left a lasting impression. But with the next production, *Anna Bolena* (Milan, 1830), Donizetti established himself as a master of the musical theater. Written for Pasta and Rubini, after the Italian fashion of adapting roles for singers, its

vogue was more than local; in 1831 it was produced in London, with the bass Lablache as Henry VIII. There followed *L'elisir d'amore* (Milan, 1832), the tragic *Lucrezia Borgia* (La Scala, Milan, 1833), and the immensely popular *Lucia di Lammermoor* (Naples, 1835). Donizetti's life was now spent in traveling from place to place, bringing out opera after opera. He visited Paris in 1835, and produced *Marino Faliero* at the Théâtre des Italiens. In May 1837, he succeeded Zingarelli as director of the Naples Cons. On July 30, 1837, he suffered a grievous loss when his wife died after 9 years of happy marital life. The censor's veto prevented the production of *Poliuto* (written for Nourrit after Corneille's *Polyeucte*) in Naples, and Donizetti decided to go to France. He produced at the Opéra-Comique in Paris the highly successful *La Fille du régiment* (1840), and, at the Grand Opéra, *Les Martyrs,* a revision of the forbidden *Poliuto* (1840). His next opera, *La Favorite* (1840), made a veritable sensation at its production at the Grand Opéra. After this series of Paris successes, Donizetti went back to Italy, where he produced *Adelia* (Rome, 1841) and *Maria Padilla* (Milan, 1841). His next travels took him to Vienna, where his new opera *Linda di Chamounix* evoked such enthusiasm that the Emperor conferred on him the titles of court composer and Master of the Imperial Chapel. In the interim, Donizetti composed a *Miserere* and an *Ave Maria* for the Austrian Court Chapel, in a severe purity of style. After the production of *Don Pasquale* (Paris, 1843), Donizetti had reached the height of his fame and prosperity; but he began to suffer from nervous fatigue and circulatory disturbance. The last opera produced in his lifetime was *Caterina Cornaro* (Naples, 1844); in 1845 he had a paralytic stroke from which he never recovered; he died a madman 3 years later. Posthumous works were *Rita,* produced in 1860; *Gabriella di Vergy* (1869); and *Le Duc d'Albe* (1882). Besides operas, Donizetti wrote many songs, ariettas, duets, and canzonets; 7 masses, one being a Requiem; cantatas; vespers, Psalms, motets; 12 string quartets; piano music.

WORKS: OPERAS: *Il Pigmalione* (1817; not produced in Donizetti's lifetime, but had a modern revival in Bergamo, Oct. 13, 1960); *Enrico di Borgogna* (Venice, Nov. 14, 1818); *Una follia* (Venice, Dec. 15, 1818); *Pietro il Grande, Czar delle Russie,* better known under the title *Il Falegname di Livonia* (Venice, Dec. 26, 1819); *Le nozze in villa* (Mantua, Jan. 23, 1821); *Zoraide di Granata* (Rome, Jan. 28, 1822); *La Zingara* (Naples, May 12, 1822); *La lettera anonima* (Naples, June 29, 1822); *Chiara e Serafina* (Milan, Oct. 26, 1822); *Alfredo il Grande* (Naples, July 2, 1823); *Il fortunato inganno* (Naples, Sept. 3, 1823); *L'Aio nell' imbarazzo* (Rome, Feb. 4, 1824); *Emilia di Liverpool* (Naples, July 28, 1824); *I voti dei sudditi,* cantata (Naples, March 6, 1825); *Alahor di Granata* (Palermo, Jan. 7, 1826); *Elvida* (Naples, July 6, 1826); *Olivo e Pasquale* (Rome, Jan. 7, 1827); *Gli Esiliati in Siberia,* commonly known as *Otto Mesi in due ore* (Naples, May 13, 1827); *Il Borgomastro di Saardam* (Naples, Aug. 19, 1827); *Le convenienze ed inconvenienze teatrali* (Naples, Nov. 21, 1827); *L'Esule di Roma* (Naples, Jan. 1, 1828);

Alina, regina di Golconda (Genoa, May 12, 1828); *Gianni di Calais* (Naples, Aug. 2, 1828); *Il Paria* (Naples, Jan. 12, 1829); *Elisabetta al Castello di Kenilworth* (Naples, July 6, 1829); *I Pazzi per progetto* (Naples, Feb. 7, 1830); *Il diluvio universale* (Naples, Feb. 28, 1830); *Il ritorno desiderato,* cantata, which may be identical with *Il fausto ritorno* (Naples, may have been perf. in Aug. 1830 as a ceremonial piece to celebrate the return of Francesco I and Isabella Maria from Spain); *Imelda de' Lambertazzi* (Naples, Aug. 23, 1830); *Anna Bolena* (Milan, Dec. 26, 1830); *Francesca di Foix* (Naples, May 30, 1831); *La Romanziera e l'uomo nero* (Naples, date cannot be established); *Fausta* (Naples, Jan. 12, 1832); *Ugo, conte di Parigi* (Milan, March 13, 1832); *L'elisir d'amore* (Milan, May 12, 1832); *Sancia di Castiglia* (Naples, Nov. 4, 1832); *Il Furioso all'isola di San Domingo* (Rome, Jan. 2, 1833); *Parisina* (Florence, March 17, 1833); *Torquato Tasso* (Rome, Sept. 9, 1833); *Lucrezia Borgia* (Milan, Dec. 26, 1833); *Rosmonda d'Inghilterra* (Florence, Feb. 26, 1834); *Maria Stuarda* (Naples, Oct. 18, 1834); *Gemma di Vergy* (Milan, Dec. 26, 1834); *Marino Faliero* (Paris, March 12, 1835); *Lucia di Lammermoor* (Naples, Sept. 26, 1835); *Belisario* (Venice, Feb. 4, 1836); *Il campanello di notte* (Naples, June 1, 1836); *Betly* (Naples, Aug. 24, 1836); *L'assedio di Calais* (Naples, Nov. 19, 1836); *Pia de' Tolomei* (Venice, Feb. 18, 1837); *Roberto Devereux,* known also as *Il Conte d'Essex* (Naples, Oct. 29, 1837); *Maria di Rudenz* (Venice, Jan. 30, 1838); *Gianni di Parigi* (Milan, Sept. 10, 1839); *La Fille du régiment* (Paris, Feb. 11, 1840); *Les Martyrs* (Paris, April 10, 1840; French version of his Neapolitan opera *Poliuto*); *La Favorite* (Paris, Dec. 2, 1840; derived from his unfinished opera *L'Ange de Nisida*); *Adelia* (Rome, Feb. 11, 1841); *Maria Padilla* (Milan, Dec. 26, 1841); *Linda di Chamounix* (Vienna, May 19, 1842); *Don Pasquale* (Paris, Jan. 3, 1843); *Maria di Rohan* (Vienna, June 5, 1843); *Dom Sébastien, roi de Portugal* (Paris, Nov. 13, 1843; revised several times by Donizetti and Giacomo Panizza); *Caterina Cornaro* (Naples, Jan. 12, 1844); *Rita, ou Le Mari battu* (1840; Paris, May 7, 1860; posthumously produced); *Il Duca d'Alba* (written for the Paris Opéra in 1839, but the score was incomplete; it was largely supplemented by Matteo Salvi, with new material added, for the Rome premiere on March 22, 1882; Thomas Schippers ed. the original Donizetti score and orchestrated parts of it for his perf., in Italian, in Spoleto in 1959; the libretto was by Scribe, who also wrote the book on the same subject for Verdi's opera, *Les Vêpres siciliennes,* 1855).

Donizetti, Giuseppe, Italian bandmaster and composer, brother of **Gaetano Donizetti;** b. Bergamo, Nov. 9, 1788; d. Constantinople, Feb. 10, 1856. In 1832 he was summoned by the sultan of Turkey to take charge of Turkish military bands. He accepted, and successfully accomplished the task of introducing Western instruments and modernizing the repertoire. The sultan richly rewarded him with honors and money, and Donizetti remained in Constantinople to the end of his life.

Donohoe, Peter, talented English pianist; b. Manchester, June 18, 1953. He studied at Chetham's School of Music in Manchester; made his debut at the age of 12 playing Beethoven's 3rd Piano Concerto at Manchester's Free Trade Hall; then enrolled in the Royal Manchester College of Music; took lessons in Paris with Yvonne Loriod. International recognition followed in 1982, when he became joint first-prize winner in the International Tchaikovsky Competition in Moscow. He subsequently made several world tours, performing in Japan, Canada, the U.S., Australia, and throughout Europe; he was particularly popular in Russia. His repertoire includes the entire range of Classical and Romantic works, but he also cultivates modern piano music, delivering such transcendentally difficult pieces as Liszt's opera transcriptions and Stravinsky's *Petrouchka.*

Donostia, José Antonio de, Basque composer and student of folklore; b. San Sebastián, Jan. 10, 1886; d. Lecároz, Navarra, Aug. 30, 1956. Donostia is his Basque name, corresponding to Dominus Sebastianus, or San Sebastián, his religious name; his full family name was José Antonio Zulacia y Arregui. He attended the Capuchin College in Lecaroz (Navarra); at the age of 16 entered the Franciscan order; was ordained a priest. He studied organ and violin with various teachers; composition with Eugène Cools in Paris. He lived many years in France; also traveled in South America; was compelled to leave Spain during the civil war of 1936–39. He was one of the founders of the Instituto Español de Musicología, and corresponding member of the Academia de Bellas Artes in Madrid. His chief accomplishment is the collection of more than 1,000 Basque folk songs, which he wrote down and transcribed during his methodical journeys through the Basque countryside; 493 of these were publ. in his Basque cancionero, *Euskel Eres-Sorta* (1912); he also publ. *De la música popular vasca; Como canta el vasco;* etc. He wrote several cantatas (*La Vie profonde de Saint François d'Assise; Les Trois Miracles de Sainte Cécile; La Quête héroïque de Graal*); *Préludes basques* for Piano; many motets and other sacred choruses; *Itinerarium mysticum* for Organ (3 vols., based on Gregorian themes); compiled a bibliography of Basque folk music.

Dont, Jakob, Austrian violinist, teacher, and composer; b. Vienna, March 2, 1815; d. there, Nov. 17, 1888. He was the son of the cellist **Joseph Valentin Dont** (b. Georgenthal, Bohemia, April 15, 1776; d. Vienna, Dec. 14, 1833); was a pupil of Böhm and Hellmesberger (Sr.) at the Vienna Cons.; joined the orch. of the Hofburgtheater in 1831, and the court orch. in 1834. He taught in the Akademie der Tonkunst and the Seminary at St. Anna; Leopold Auer was his pupil. From 1873 he was a prof. at the Vienna Cons. His book of violin studies, *Gradus ad Parnassum,* is widely known; he publ. altogether some 50 works.

Dopper, Cornelis, eminent Dutch composer and conductor; b. Stadskanaal, near Groningen, Feb. 7,

1870; d. Amsterdam, Sept. 18, 1939. He studied at the Leipzig Cons.; returning to the Netherlands, he became assistant conductor of the Concertgebouw Orch. in Amsterdam (1908), and was associated with that orch. until 1931. He also traveled as an opera conductor in America (1906–8).

WORKS: 4 operas: *Het blinde meisje von Castel Cuille* (1892); *Het Eerekruis* (Amsterdam, 1894); *Fritjof* (1895); *Willem Ratcliff* (1901); ballet, *Meidevorn,* with Soli and Chorus; 8 symphs.: No. 1, *Diana,* ballet symph. (1896); No. 2 (1903; finished after the 3rd); No. 3, *Rembrandt* (1892; later rewritten); No. 4, *Symphonietta* (1906); No. 5, *Symphonia epica,* with Chorus and Soli (1914); No. 6, *Amsterdam* (1912); No. 7, *Zuiderzee;* No. 8; symph. rhapsody, *Paris;* 5 suites; Divertimento; *Ciaconna gotica,* symph. variations (his best-known work; Concertgebouw, Amsterdam, Oct. 24, 1920, composer conducting); Concertino for Trumpet and 3 Kettledrums; Cello Concerto; 2 overtures; String Quartet; violin sonatas; Cello Sonata; Scherzo for Woodwinds and Piano; many choral works; songs; piano pieces.

Doppler, Albert Franz, Austrian composer and conductor; b. Lwow, Oct. 16, 1821; d. Baden, near Vienna, July 27, 1883. He studied music with his father; played first flute in the Pest Opera Orch.; in 1858 settled in Vienna as ballet conductor at the court opera; taught flute at the Vienna Cons. from 1865. His first opera, *Benjowsky,* was well received in Budapest (Sept. 29, 1847) and had several revivals under the title *Afanasia;* the following operas were also produced in Budapest: *Ilka* (Dec. 29, 1849); *Wanda* (Dec. 16, 1856); *2 Hussars* (March 12, 1853); his last opera, *Judith,* was produced in Vienna (Dec. 30, 1870). He also wrote 15 ballets.

Doppler, Árpád, Hungarian pianist, son of **Karl Doppler;** b. Pest, June 5, 1857; d. Stuttgart, Aug. 13, 1927. He went to Stuttgart as a young man and studied there; was engaged to teach in N.Y. and spent 3 years there (1880–83); later returned to Stuttgart and taught at the Cons. He publ. a number of salon pieces for piano; also wrote a comic opera, *Caligula* (Stuttgart, 1891).

Doppler, Karl, Austrian composer and conductor, brother of **Albert Franz Doppler;** b. Lwow, Sept. 12, 1825; d. Stuttgart, March 10, 1900. Like his father and his brother, he became an excellent flute player; gave concerts in all the major cities of Europe. He was then appointed as court Kapellmeister in Stuttgart, and held this position for 33 years (1865–98). He wrote an opera and pieces for the flute.

Dorati, Antal, distinguished Hungarian-American conductor and composer; b. Budapest, April 9, 1906. He studied harmony with Leo Weiner and composition with Kodály at the Liszt Academy in Budapest (1920–24). He made his debut as an opera conductor in Budapest at the age of 18; was on the staff of the Budapest Opera (1924–28); then conducted at the Dresden Opera (1928–29); was named General-

musikdirektor at the Münster State Opera (1929–32). As the political situation, both racially and artistically, darkened in Central Europe in 1933, Dorati went to France, where he conducted the Ballets Russes de Monte Carlo, which he took over to Australia. He made his American debut with the National Symph. Orch. in Washington (1937); settled in the U.S. in 1940, and became a naturalized American citizen in 1947. In America he held with great distinction the posts of symph. conductor and music director of the Dallas Symph. Orch. (1945–49) and Minneapolis Symph. Orch. (1949–60); then was engaged as chief conductor of the BBC Symph. Orch. in London (1963–66), and of the Stockholm Phil. (1966–70); subsequently was conductor of the National Symph. Orch. in Washington, D.C. (1970–77). In 1977–81 he was conductor and music director of the Detroit Symph. Orch. Simultaneously, he held the position of principal conductor of the Royal Phil. Orch. of London (1975–79); was then named conductor laureate. Through the years he has acquired the reputation of an orch. builder able to handle not only the music but also the musicians; not only the public, but also the business management. He recorded all of the Haydn symphs. Dorati was married to the pianist **Ilse von Alpenheim;** in 1984 was made an Honorary Knight Commander of the Most Excellent Order of the British Empire. He is an active composer; among his works are a String Quartet; String Octet; Oboe Quintet; *Divertimento* for Orch.; ballet, *Graduation Ball,* arranged from the waltzes of Johann Strauss; dramatic cantata, *The Way of the Cross* (Minneapolis, April 19, 1957); Symph. (Minneapolis, March 18, 1960); 7 *Pieces* for Orch. (1961; perf. as a ballet, *Maddalena*); Piano Concerto (1974; Washington, Oct. 28, 1975); Cello Concerto (Louisville, Ky., Oct. 1, 1976).

Doret, Gustave, Swiss composer; b. Aigle, Sept. 20, 1866; d. Lausanne, April 19, 1943. He received his first instruction at Lausanne; studied violin with Joachim in Berlin; then entered the Paris Cons. as a pupil of Marsick (violin) and Dubois and Massenet (composition); was conductor of the Concerts d'Harcourt and of the Société Nationale de Musique in Paris (1893–95); of the concerts at the National Exposition at Geneva (1896); of the Saint-Saëns Festival at Vevey (1913); at the Opéra-Comique (1907–9); also appeared as a visiting conductor in Rome, London, and Amsterdam. Doret was a member of the commission for editing Rameau's collected works. In his music Doret cultivated the spirit of Swiss folk songs; his vocal writing is distinguished by its natural flow of melody.

WORKS: Operas: *Les Armaillis* (Paris, Oct. 23, 1906; enlarged version, Paris, May 5, 1930); *Le Nain du Hasli* (Geneva, Feb. 6, 1908); dramatic legend, *Loÿs* (Vevey, 1912); *La Tisseuse d'Orties* (Paris, 1926); *Voix de la Patrie,* cantata (1891); oratorio, *Les Sept Paroles du Christ* (1895); *La Fête des vignerons* (1905); incidental music to Shakespeare's *Julius Caesar* and to plays by René Morax: *Henriette, Aliénor, La Nuit des quatre-temps, Wilhelm Tell, Davel* (all produced at Mézières); String Quartet;

Piano Quintet; about 150 songs. He publ. *Musique et musiciens* (1915); *Lettres à ma nièce sur la musique en Suisse* (1919); *Pour notre indépendance musicale* (1920); *Temps et contretemps* (1942).

Dorian, Frederick (real name, **Friedrich Deutsch**), eminent Austrian-born American music scholar and commentator; b. Vienna, July 1, 1902. He studied musicology with Guido Adler at the Univ. of Vienna (Dr.Phil., 1925); also took piano lessons with Eduard Steuermann and studied composition privately with Anton von Webern. He was also closely associated with Schoenberg; Dorian's family apartment housed the headquarters of the famous Society for Private Musical Performances, organized by Schoenberg, Alban Berg, and Webern. He also took courses in conducting, achieving a high degree of professionalism. He served as music critic of the *Berliner Morgenpost* (1930–33); with the advent of the Nazi regime to power in Germany, he emigrated to the U.S., becoming an American citizen in 1941. From 1936–54 he was a member of the Carnegie-Mellon Univ. in Pittsburgh (formerly named Carnegie Inst. of Technology); there he organized an opera dept., and conducted its inaugural performance; from 1971–75 he served as Andrew Mellon Lecturer there. From 1975–77 he was visiting lectures on music history at the Curtis Inst. in Philadelphia. In 1978 he gave lectures on musicology at the Hebrew Univ. in Jerusalem. He also served, beginning in 1945, as program annotator for the Pittsburgh Symph. program magazine.

Dorn, Heinrich (Ludwig Egmont), German composer, conductor, and pedagogue; b. Konigsberg, Nov. 14, 1800; d. Berlin, Jan. 10, 1892. He was a law student at Königsberg in 1823, but studied music diligently, continuing in Berlin under L. Berger (piano), Zelter, and B. Klein. After teaching in Frankfurt, he became Kapellmeister of the Königsberg Theater in 1828; in 1829, became music director (and Schumann's teacher) at Leipzig, where he met young Wagner; was music director at the Cathedral of St. Peter's in Riga (1831–42); Kapellmeister and city music director at Cologne (1843), where he founded (1845) the Rheinische Musikschule (which became the Cologne Cons. in 1850); in 1844–47, he conducted the Lower Rhenish Music Festivals. In 1849–69 he was court Kapellmeister at the Royal Opera, Berlin; was pensioned, with the title of Royal Professor, and busied himself with teaching and musical criticism.

Dorsey, Jimmy (James), American clarinet and saxophone player, brother of **Tommy Dorsey;** b. Shenandoah, Pa., Feb. 29, 1904; d. New York, June 12, 1957. He played clarinet in school bands, and at one time led a band of his own; later joined his brother's group, rapidly climbing the ladder of commercial success, epitomized in the film *The Fabulous Dorseys* (1947).

Dorsey, Tommy (Thomas), American trombonist and bandleader, brother of **Jimmy Dorsey;** b. Ma-

honey Plains, Pa., Nov. 19, 1905; d. Greenwich, Conn., Nov. 26, 1956. He played trumpet and other instruments in school bands; then took up the trombone and developed a virtuoso technique using a unique method of convex breathing that enabled him to maintain miraculously long passages legato. His brother regularly played the clarinet and alto saxophone in his band from 1953 on. The film *The Fabulous Dorseys* (1947) bears eloquent testimony to the brothers' fame.

Doubrava, Jaroslav, Czech composer; b. Chrudim, April 25, 1909; d. Prague, Oct. 2, 1960. He studied privately with Otakar Jeremiáš (1931–37); was active mainly in the musical theater. He wrote the operas *A Midsummer Night's Dream*, after Shakespeare (1942–49; completed by Jiří Jaroch, 1966; posthumous premiere, Opava, Dec. 21, 1969), and *Lazy John* (1952); *Balada o lásce* (*Ballad of Love;* 1959–60; completed by Jan Hanuš; posthumous premiere, Prague, June 21, 1962); 3 ballets: *The Tale of the Pea* (1935); *King Lavra* (1951); *Don Quixote* (1954–55); 3 symphs.: No. 1, with Chorus (1938–40); No. 2, *Stalingrad* (1943–44); No. 3 (1956–58); oratorio, *The Message* (1939–40); *Ballad about a Beautiful Death* for Women's Chorus and Orch. (1941); symph. marches: *Partisan March* and *Festive March* (1945); *Autumn Pastorale* (1960; fragment of his unfinished 4th Symph., arranged by Otmar Mácha); Piano Sonatina (1937); 2 violin sonatas (1942, 1958); Sonata for Solo Violin (1942); Piano Sonata (1948–49); piano pieces for children; song cycles.

Dounis, Demetrius Constantine, Greek-American violinist and teacher; b. Athens, Dec. 7, 1886; d. Los Angeles, Aug. 13, 1954. He studied violin with Ondriček in Vienna and simultaneously enrolled as a medical student at the Univ. of Vienna; made several tours as a violinist in Europe, including Russia; after World War I he was appointed prof. at the Salonika Cons. He then lived in England and eventually settled in America; established his N.Y. studio in 1939; went to Los Angeles in 1954. He originated the technique of the "brush stroke," in which the bow is handled naturally and effortlessly.

Dowland, John, great English composer of songs and famous lutenist; b. probably in London, 1563; d. there Feb. (buried, Feb. 20) 1626. In 1580 he went to Paris in the service of Sir Henry Cobham; by 1584 he was back in England, where he eventually married; on July 8, 1588, he was admitted to his Mus.B. from Christ Church, Oxford; in 1592 he played before the Queen. Unsuccessful in his effort to secure a position as one of the Queen's musicians, he set out in 1594 for Germany, where he received the patronage of the Duke of Braunschweig in Wolfenbüttel and the Landgrave of Hesse in Kassel; he then went to Italy and visited Venice, Padua, Genoa, Ferrara, and Florence; in Florence he played before Ferdinando I, the Grand Duke of Tuscany; he then made his way home, returning to England in 1595. In 1598 he was appointed lutenist to King Christian IV of Denmark, remaining in his service until 1606;

he then returned to England, where he became lutenist to Lord Howard de Walden. In 1612 he became one of the lutenists to King Charles I. Dowland was a foremost representative of the English school of lutenist-composers. He was also noted for his songs, in which he made use of novel chromatic developments; he treated the accompanying parts as separate entities, thereby obtaining harmonic effects quite advanced for his time.

WORKS: *The First Booke of Songes or Ayres of fowre partes with Tableture for the Lute* ... (London, 1597); *The Second Booke of Songs or Aires, of 2. 4. and 5. parts; With Tableture for the Lute or Orpherian* ... (London, 1600); *The Third and Last Booke of Songs or Aires* ... (London, 1603); *Lachrimae, or Seven Teares Figvred in Seaven Passionate Pauans,* ... *set forth for the Lute, Viols, or Violons, in fiue parts* (London, 1604); songs in *A Mvsicall Banquet* (London, 1612) and *A Pilgrimes Solace. Wherein is contained Musicall Harmonie of 3. 4. and 5. parts, to be sung and plaid with the Lute and Viols* (London, 1612).

EDITIONS: These include E. Fellowes's eds. of *The First Book of Songs* (London, 1920; revised ed., 1965, by T. Dart), *The Second Book of Songs* (London, 1922; revised ed., 1969, by T. Dart), *The Third and Last Book of Songs* (London, 1923; revised ed., 1970, by T. Dart), *A Pilgrimes Solace* (London, 1924; revised ed., 1969, by T. Dart), and *Seven Hymn Tunes* ... *Lamentatio Henrici Noel* (London, 1934); P. Warlock, *Lachrimae or Seven Tears* ... *Transcribed from the original edition of 1605* (without tablature; London, 1927); T. Dart and N. Fortune, eds., *Ayres for Four Voices*, in *Musica Britannica* (vol. 6, London, 1953; 2nd ed., revised, 1963); D. Poulton and B. Lam, eds., *The Collected Lute Music of John Dowland* (London, 1974).

Dowland, Robert, English composer and lute player, son of **John Dowland;** b. London, 1591; d. there, Nov. 28, 1641. He remained in London after his father went to Denmark; in 1626, succeeded his father as lutenist to Charles I. He publ. *Varietie of Lute Lessons* (1610); edited *A Musicall Banquett*, a collection of English, French, Spanish, and Italian airs (reprinted in *The English Lute Songs*, vol. 20).

Downes, Edward (Thomas), English conductor; b. Aston (Birmingham), June 17, 1924. He studied at the Univ. of Birmingham (1941–44), taking a B.A. in music; and at the Royal College of Music in London (1944–46), studying horn, theory, and composition. In 1948 he was awarded the Carnegie Scholarship, which he used for taking a course in conducting with Hermann Scherchen. His first professional post as conductor was with the Carl Rosa Opera (1950); in 1952 he became a staff conductor at the Covent Garden Opera in London, with which he conducted every work in the repertoire, including the complete *Ring of the Nibelung* cycle; in 1969 he left the Covent Garden staff as a regular member in order to devote himself to symph. conducting, but continued to fill in occasional opera engagements. In 1972–76 he was music director of the Australian

Opera; in 1980 became chief conductor of the Omroeporkest in Hilversum. He conducted the world premiere of Richard Rodney Bennett's opera *Victory* (April 13, 1970). He also conducted the world premieres of Havergal Brian's 14th and 21st symphs. with the London Symph. Orch. on May 10, 1970.

Downes, Edward O(lin) D(avenport), American music critic and lecturer, son of **Olin Downes;** b. Boston, Aug. 12, 1911. He studied at Columbia Univ. (1929–30), the Univ. of Paris (1932 33), the Univ. of Munich (1934–36, 1938), and Harvard Univ. (Ph.D., 1958). Under the tutelage of his father, he entered the career of a music critic; wrote for the *N.Y. Post* (1935–38), the *Boston Transcript* (1939–41), and the *N.Y. Times* (1955–58); was program annotator for the N.Y. Phil. (1960–74); from 1958 acted as quizmaster for the Metropolitan Opera broadcasts. He was a lecturer in music at Wellesley College (1948–49), Harvard Univ. (1949–50), the Univ. of Minnesota (1950–55), and (from 1966) Queens College.

WRITINGS: *Verdi, The Man and His Letters* (trans. of correspondence, N.Y., 1942); *Adventures in Symphonic Music* (N.Y., 1943); *The New York Philharmonic Guide to the Symphony* (N.Y.,1976); co-edited J.C. Bach's opera *Temistocle* (Vienna, 1965); also *Perspectives of Musicology* (N.Y., 1972); contributed a great number of articles on a variety of subjects to music periodicals.

Downes, Olin, eminent American music critic; b. Evanston, Ill., Jan. 27, 1886; d. New York, Aug. 22, 1955. He studied piano with L. Kelterborn and Carl Baermann; harmony with Homer Norris, Clifford Heilman and J.P. Marshall; then devoted himself mainly to musical journalism. From 1906 to 1924 he was music critic of the *Boston Post;* in 1924 was appointed music critic of the *N.Y. Times;* held this post until his death. He was awarded the Order of Commander of the White Rose, Finland (1937); an hon. Mus.Doc., Cincinnati Cons. of Music (1939).

WRITINGS: *The Lure of Music* (1918); *Symphonic Broadcasts* (1931); *Symphonic Masterpieces* (1935). He edited *Select Songs of Russian Composers* (1922); compiled and annotated *Ten Operatic Masterpieces, from Mozart to Prokofiev* (1952). A selection from his writings was publ. in 1957 under the title *Olin Downes on Music*, edited by his widow, Irene Downes.

Draeseke, Felix (August Bernhard), significant German composer; b. Coburg, Oct. 7, 1835; d. Dresden, Feb. 26, 1913. He studied privately with Julius Rietz in Leipzig; became a friend of Liszt and Wagner, and an ardent champion of the New German School. In 1862 he went to Switzerland; taught at the Cons. of Lausanne (1864–74) and later in Geneva. In 1876 he returned to Germany and became a prof. at the Dresden Cons. A Wagnerian in his youth, he was regarded as a radical, but he never accepted the modern tendencies of the 20th century, which he attacked in his pamphlet *Die Konfusion in der Musik* (1906), directed chiefly against Richard Strauss. He was a prolific composer, but his works are virtually unknown outside Germany. A Draeseke Society was formed in Germany in 1931, and issued sporadic bulletins.

WORKS: 6 operas: *König Sigurd* (1853–57; only a fragment perf., in Meiningen, 1867); *Herrat* (1879; Dresden, March 10, 1892); *Gudrun* (Hannover, Jan. 11, 1884); *Bertrand de Born* (1894); *Fischer und Kalif* (Prague, April 15, 1905); *Merlin* (perf. posthumously, Gotha, May 10, 1913); choral trilogy, *Christus* (his major work), consisting of a prelude, *Die Geburt des Herrn;* I. *Christi Weihe,* II. *Christus der Prophet,* III. *Tod und Sieg des Herrn* (produced in its entirety in Dresden and Berlin, 1912); Symph. in G (1872); Symph. in F (1876); *Symphonia tragica* (1886); *Symphonia comica* (1912); sacred and secular choruses; many songs; Piano Concerto; Violin Concerto; 3 string quartets; Quintet for Piano, Violin, Viola, Cello, and Horn; Clarinet Sonata, etc. A complete list of works is found in H. Stephani's article on Draeseke in *Die Musik in Geschichte und Gegenwart.* Draeseke's theoretical publications include: *Anweisung zum kunstgerechten Modulieren* (1875); *Zur Beseitigung des Tritonus* (1876); a versified *Lehre von der Harmonia* (1885); *Der gebundene Stil: Lehrbuch für Kontrapunkt und Fugue* (Hannover, 1902).

Draghi, Antonio, Italian composer of operas and oratorios; b. Rimini, 1635; d. Vienna, Jan. 16, 1700. He was a singer in Venice; in 1658 he settled in Vienna; became Kapellmeister to the Empress Eleanora in 1669; was appointed Hoftheater-Intendant to Leopold I in 1673; named Imperial Court Kapellmeister in 1682. In 1661–99 he produced 67 operas, 116 festival plays ("feste teatrali") and serenades, 32 oratorios, 11 cantatas, 2 masses, etc. Reprints are in Denkmäler der Tonkunst in Österreich, 46 (23.i; 2 masses, a Stabat Mater, and 2 hymns) and in A. Schering's *Geschichte der Musik in Beispielen,* no. 226 (an opera scene).

Drăgoi, Sabin, eminent Rumanian composer and folklorist; b. Seliște, June 18, 1894; d. Bucharest, Dec. 31, 1968. He studied with Novák and Ostrčil in Prague (1920–22); from 1924 to 1942 taught at the Timișoara Cons.; then was a prof. at the Cluj Cons. (1942–46); was director of the Folklore Inst. of Bucharest (1950–64) and a prof. of folklore at the Bucharest Cons. (1950–52).

WORKS: Operas: *Năpasta* (*Disaster;* 1927; Bucharest, May 30, 1928; revised 1958; Bucharest, Dec. 23, 1961); *Kir Ianulea* (1937; Cluj, Dec. 22, 1939); *Horia* (1945); *Păcală* (1956; Brasov, May 6, 1962); oratorio, *Povestea bradului* (1952); 3 cantatas: *Slăvită lumină* (1937); *Mai multă lumină* (1951); *Cununa* (1959); *3 Symphonic Tableaus* (1922); *Divertissement Rustic* for Orch. (1928); *Divertissement sacru* for Chamber Orch. (1933); Piano Concerto (1941); Concertino for Tarogato and Orch. (1953); 7 *Popular Dances* for Orch. (1960); *Suită tătară* for Small Orch. (1961); *Suită lipovană* for Small Orch. (1962); Violin Sonata (1949); String Quartet (1952); *Dixtour* for Winds, Strings, and Piano (1955); *50 Colinde* for Piano (1957); *10 Minia-*

tures for Piano (1960); *12 Miniatures* for Piano (1968); songs; film music.

Dragon, Carmen, American conductor of popular music; b. Antioch, Calif., July 28, 1914; d. Santa Monica, Calif., March 28, 1984. He learned to play piano, double bass, accordion, trumpet, and trombone. He studied music at San Jose State College; then went to San Francisco, where he played the piano in a nightclub. His next move was to Hollywood, where he effloresced as an arranger for movie stars who could not read music. He conducted background music for radio shows. In a higher elevation, he composed a patriotic band piece, *I'm an American.* His concerts supplied pleasurable fare for contented music-lovers. His son **Daryl Dragon** became one-half of the popular music team Captain and Tennille.

Dragonetti, Domenico, noted Italian double-bassist; b. Venice, April 7, 1763; d. London, April 16, 1846. The "Paganini of the contra-basso" was self-taught, excepting a few lessons from Berini, bassist at San Marco, whom he succeeded in 1782; he had already played in the orchs. of the Opera Buffa and Opera Seria for 5 years, and composed concertos with double-bass parts impracticable for anyone but himself. He appeared at London in 1794; with the cellist Lindley, his close friend for 52 years, he played at the Antient Concerts and the Phil. As late as 1845, his virtuosity still unimpaired, he led the double basses, at the unveiling of the Beethoven monument in Bonn, in the C minor Symph. To the British Museum he left a remarkable collection of scores, engravings, and old instruments; to San Marco, his favorite cello (a Gasparo da Salò).

Drdla, Franz, Bohemian composer and violinist; b. Saar, Moravia, Nov. 28, 1868; d. Gastein, Sept. 3, 1944. After 2 years at the Prague Cons. he studied at the Vienna Cons. under Hellmesberger (violin) and Krenn (composition), winning first prize for violin and the medal of the Gesellschaft der Musikfreunde; for several years was a violinist in the orch. of the Hofoper; then made successful tours of Europe; in 1923–25, lived in the U.S.; then in Vienna and Prague. His pieces for violin and piano have won enormous popularity, especially *Souvenir, Vision,* and the first Serenade in A (dedicated to, and played by, Jan Kubelik); he also composed 2 operettas, *Das goldene Netz* (Leipzig, 1916) and *Die Ladenkomtesse* (Prague, 1917).

Drechsler, Joseph, Austrian composer; b. Wällisch-Birken, Bohemia, May 26, 1782; d. Vienna, Feb. 27, 1852. He was a pupil of the organist Grotius at Florenbach; chorus master and Kapellmeister (1812) at the Vienna Court Opera, then conductor in the theaters at Baden (near Vienna) and Pressburg; returning to Vienna, he became organist of the Servite church; in 1816 precentor at St. Ann's; in 1823 Kapellmeister at the University church and the Hofpfarrkirche; in 1822–30 he was also Kapellmeister at the Leopoldstadt Theater, and from 1844, Kapellmeister at St. Stephen's.

WORKS: 6 operas, and about 30 operettas, vaudevilles, and pantomimes; a Requiem, 10 other masses, 3 cantatas, offertories, etc.; string quartets, organ fugues, piano sonatas, other piano music, songs, etc.; a method for organ, and a treatise on harmony. He reedited Pleyel's *Piano School,* and publ. a theoretico-practical guide to preluding.

Dresden, Sem, notable Dutch composer; b. Amsterdam, April 20, 1881; d. The Hague, July 30, 1957. He studied first in Amsterdam with Zweers; then went to Berlin, where he took a course in composition with Hans Pfitzner (1903–5). Returning to the Netherlands, he was active as a choral conductor; from 1919 to 1924 taught composition at the Amsterdam Cons.; then became its director (1924–37); subsequently was director of The Hague Cons. (1937–49, with a break during World War II). From 1914 till 1926 he led the Motet and Madrigal Society in Amsterdam. As a composer, Sem Dresden was influenced primarily by German neo-Romanticism, but his harmonic idiom reveals some impressionistic usages; in many of his works there is a distinctive strain of Dutch melodic rhythms.

Dreyfus, George, German-born Australian composer, bassoonist, and conductor; b. Wuppertal, July 22, 1928. His family left Germany in 1939, settling in Australia. He studied clarinet and then bassoon at the Melbourne Univ. Cons.; played the bassoon in various Australian orchs.; founded the Dreyfus Chamber Orch. in Melbourne. His music is pragmatically constructed and designed for performance by any competent instrumentalists or vocalists.

WORKS: Opera for 8 Characters and Chamber Orch., *Garni Sands* (1965–66; Sydney, July 12, 1972); opera, *The Gilt-Edged Kid* (1970; Melbourne, April 11, 1976); 12-minute opera for Children's Choruses, *Song of the Maypole* (1968); school opera, *The Takeover* (1969); ballet, *The Illusionist* (1965); Trio for Flute, Clarinet, and Bassoon (1956); *Galgenlieder* for Baritone, Flute, Clarinet, Bassoon, and Violin (1957); *Songs Comic and Curious* for Baritone, Flute, Oboe, Clarinet, Horn, and Bassoon (1959); *Wilhelm Busch Lieder* for High Voice and Wind Trio, to words from a famous German children's book (1959); *Music in the Air* for Baritone, Flute, Viola, and Percussion (1961); *From Within Looking Out* for Soprano, Flute, Viola, Vibraphone, and Celesta (1962); *The Seasons* for Flute, Viola, Vibraphone, and Percussion (1963); *Ned Kelly Ballads*, 3 folk songs for Folksinger, 4 Horns, and Rhythm Section (1963); Wind Quintet (1965); *Music for Music Camp* for Orch. (1967); 2 symphs. (1967, 1976); *Jingles*, 5 pieces for Orch. (1968; a potpourri of styles from Mahler, Stravinsky, rock and roll, ballads, and the Tijuana Brass); Wind Quintet (No. 2), after the notebook of J.G. Noverre (1968); *Reflections in a Glass-House*, an image of Captain James Cook, for Narrator, Children's Chorus, and Orch. (1969); Sextet for Didjeridu and Wind Quintet (1971); *MO* for Baritone and String Orch. (1971); *... and more Jin-*

gles, 5 further pieces for Orch. (1972); *The Grand Aurora Australis Now Show* for Orch. (1973); *Old Melbourne* for Bassoon and Guitar (1973); *Hallelujah for Handel* for Orch. (1976); *Kaffeekonzert* for Soprano and Piano Trio (1977); *Terrigal* for Chorus and Orch. (1977); Concerto for Bassoon and Strings (1978); film and television scores.

Dreyschock, Alexander, brilliant Bohemian pianist; b. Zack, Oct. 15, 1818; d. Venice, April 1, 1869. A student of Tomaschck, he acquired a virtuoso technique and was regarded as a worthy rival of Liszt in technical dexterity. At 8 he was able to play in public; toured North Germany (1838); spent 2 years in Russia (1840–42); visited Brussels, Paris, and London, then the Netherlands and Austria. In 1862 he was called to St. Petersburg as a prof. at the newly founded Cons. In 1868, he went to Italy, where he died. His astounding facility in playing octaves, double sixths, and thirds, and performing solos with the left hand alone cast a glamour about his performance; he reached the zenith of his fame about 1850.

Dreyschock, Felix, German pianist, son of **Raimund Dreyschock;** b. Leipzig, Dec. 27, 1860; d. Berlin, Aug. 1, 1906. He studied under Grabau, Ehrlich, Taubert, and Kiel; gave successful concerts, and was a prof. at the Stern Cons. in Berlin. His piano pieces are well-written and effective; he also publ. a Violin Sonata and songs.

Dreyschock, Raimund, Bohemian violinist, brother of **Alexander Dreyschock;** b. Zack, Bohemia, Aug. 20, 1824; d. Leipzig, Feb. 6, 1869. He was a pupil of Pixis in Prague; was concertmaster at the Gewandhaus concerts (1850–69) and a violin teacher in the Cons. at Leipzig. His wife, **Elizabeth** (b. Cologne, 1832; d. there, July, 1911), was a contralto singer who founded and managed a vocal academy in Berlin.

Drieberg, Friedrich von, German music historian and composer; b. Charlottenburg, Dec. 10, 1780; d. there, May 21, 1856. He served in the Prussian army until 1804, when he went to Paris to study composition with Spontini; also traveled to Vienna. He produced 2 operas, *Don Cocagno* (Berlin, 1812) and *Der Sänger und der Schneider* (Berlin, Nov. 23, 1814), but became known mainly through his speculative publications concerning Greek music, promulgating theories and conclusions that were utterly unfounded. However, they were publ. and seriously discussed, if only in refutation. These are *Die mathematische Intervallenlehre der Griechen* (1818); *Aufschlüsse über die Musik der Griechen* (1819); *Die praktische Musik der Griechen* (1821); *Die pneumatischen Erfindungen der Griechen* (1822); *Wörterbuch der griech. Musik* (1835); *Die griechische Musik, auf ihre Grundgesetze zurückgeführt* (1841); *Die Kunst der musikalishen Composition ... nach griechischen Grundsätzen bearbeitet* (1858).

Drigo, Riccardo, Italian composer and conductor; b. Padua, June 30, 1846; d. there, Oct. 1, 1930. He studied music in Venice; conducted opera in Venice and Milan. In 1879 he was engaged to conduct the Italian opera in St. Petersburg; in 1886 became permanent ballet conductor of the Imperial Theater there; conducted first performances of Tchaikovsky's ballets *The Sleeping Beauty* and *The Nutcracker.* After Tchaikovsky's death, Drigo edited the score of the ballet *Swan Lake* and orchestrated a number of Tchaikovsky's piano pieces. Drigo's own ballets, melodious and easy to listen to, also enjoyed excellent success in Russia. Particularly popular was his ballet *Les Millions d'Arlequin (Harlequin's Millions),* which includes the famous *Serenade* for a soulful cello solo and the ingratiating *Valse Bluette.* Drigo conducted the first performance of this ballet in St. Petersburg on Feb. 10, 1900. In 1914–16 he was in Italy; in 1916–20 he was again in St. Petersburg, finally returning to Italy and remaining there until his death.

Dring, Madeleine, English violinist, pianist, singer, and composer; b. Hornsey, Sept. 7, 1923; d. London, March 26, 1977. She studied violin in the Junior Dept. of the Royal College of Music in London, and also acquired professional skill as a pianist, singer, and actress. She took courses in composition at the Royal College of Music with Hubert Howells and Vaughan Williams; developed a knack for writing attractively brief pieces. She also wrote a short opera called *Cupboard Love,* several trios, a suite for Harmonica and Piano, and incidental-music scores for radio and television.

Drouet, Louis François-Philippe, famous French flute player and composer; b. Amsterdam, April 14, 1792; d. Bern, Sept. 30, 1873. He studied composition at the Paris Cons.; at the age of 16, was appointed solo flutist to King Louis of the Netherlands, and at 19 became solo flutist to Napoleon; after Napoleon's defeat, he played the flute with fine impartiality for King Louis XVIII. In 1817 he went to London, and subsequently made concert tours across Europe. In 1840 he was appointed Kapellmeister at Coburg; in 1854 he visited America for a few months; then lived in Gotha and Frankfurt before going to Switzerland, where he died. He composed mainly for the flute; among his works are 10 flute concertos; 2 fantasias for flute and piano; 3 trios for 3 flutes; numerous sonatas and variations for flute and assorted instruments. Drouet is credited with the arrangement of the French popular air *Partant pour la Syrie,* supposedly sung for him by Queen Hortense of the Netherlands.

Druckman, Jacob, outstanding American composer; b. Philadelphia, June 26, 1928. He took private lessons in composition as a youth with Louis Gesensway in Philadelphia; played jazz trumpet as a teenager. Then he entered the Juilliard School of Music in N.Y. and studied with Bernard Wagenaar, Vincent Persichetti, and Peter Mennin (B.S., 1954; M.S., 1956); also in Tanglewood with Aaron Copland

(1949, 1950). In 1954–55 he was at the Ecole Normale de Musique in Paris, where he studied with Tony Aubin. In 1957 he was appointed instructor in the dept. of literature and materials of music at Juilliard; from 1967 he was also an associate at the Columbia-Princeton Electronic Music Center; taught at Brooklyn College from 1972 to 1974; in 1975 was appointed a prof. at Yale Univ. He held Guggenheim grants in 1957 and 1968. In 1972 he received the Pulitzer Prize for music for his orch. work *Windows.* In his music he happily combines the strict elements of polyphonic structure, harking back to Palestrina, with modern techniques of dissonant counterpoint, while refusing to adhere to any doctrinaire system of composition. In his orchestration he makes use of a plethora of percussion instruments, including primitive drums; electronic sonorities also have an increasing importance in his works.
WORKS: Violin Concerto (1956); *4 Madrigals* for Chorus (1959); *Dark upon the Harp* for Mezzo-soprano, Brass Quintet, and Percussion (1962); *Antiphonies* for 2 Choruses (1963); *The Sound of Time* for Soprano and Orch. (1965); *Animus I* for Trombone and Tape (1966); *Incenters* for 13 Players (1968); *Animus II* for Mezzo-soprano, Percussion, and Tape (1969); *Animus III* for Clarinet and Tape (1969); *Windows* for Orch. (Chicago Symph. Orch., May 16, 1972); *Lamia* for Soprano and Orch. (1974); *Valentine* for Double-bass Solo (1975); *Chiaroscuro* for Orch. (1976); Viola Concerto (N.Y., Nov. 2, 1978); *Bo* for Marimba, Harp, and Bass Clarinet (N.Y., Juilliard, March 3, 1979); *Aureole* (N.Y., June 6, 1979); 2 string quartets; other chamber music; songs.

Drury, Stephen, American pianist; b. Spokane, Wash., April 13, 1955. His mother taught him piano; he then went to Harvard Univ., where he worked at the Electronic Music Studio. In 1977 he continued his piano studies in N.Y., with William Masselos; then returned to Harvard and organized an Experimental Music Festival, during which he gave a complete performance of Satie's piano piece *Vexations,* repeated 840 times. He also played the piano sonatas of Ives and piano pieces by John Cage. While preoccupied with avant-garde music, he took occasional lessons in classical piano playing with Claudio Arrau in N.Y. On the musical far-out frontier, he became a member of a conceptual team called Beaux Eaux Duo.

Dubois, (Clément-François) Théodore, eminent French organist and composer; b. Rosnay, Marne, Aug. 24, 1837; d. Paris, June 11, 1924. He entered the Paris Cons. in 1853, working under Marmontel (piano), Benoist (organ), and Bazin and Ambroise Thomas (composition); he graduated in 1861; was the recipient of the Grand Prix de Rome with the cantata *Atala,* after having taken first prizes in all depts. Returning to Paris, he was maître de chapelle at Sainte-Clothilde until 1869 and at the Madeleine until 1877, and then succeeded Saint-Saëns there as organist. In 1871 he was made prof. of harmony at the Paris Cons., succeeding Elwart; in 1891 became prof. of composition; in 1894 was elected to the chair in the Academy left vacant by Gounod's death; in 1896 he succeeded Ambroise Thomas as director of the Paris Cons.; retired in 1905.

WORKS: Comic operas: *La Guzla de l'émir* (Paris, April 30, 1873) and *Le Pain bis, ou La Lilloise* (Opéra-Comique, Feb. 26, 1879); *Aben Hamet* (produced in Italian, Théâtre du Châtelet, Dec. 16, 1884); "idylle dramatique," *Xavière* (Opéra-Comique, Nov. 26, 1895); ballet, *La Farandole* (Paris Opéra, Dec. 14, 1883); 2 oratorios: *Les Sept Paroles du Christ* (1867) and *Le Paradis perdu* (1878; won the City of Paris prize); several cantatas (*L'Enlèvement de Proserpine, Hylas, Bergerette, Les Vivants et les morts, Délivrance*); masses and other church music; many orch. works: *Marche heroïque de Jeanne d'Arc; Fantaisie triomphale* for Organ and Orch.; *Hymne nuptiale; Méditation-Prière* for Strings, Oboe, Harp, and Organ; *Concerto-Capriccio* for Piano; 2nd Piano Concerto; Violin Concerto; 2 symph. poems: *Notre Dame de la Mer* and *Adonis; Symphonie française* (1908); *Fantasietta* (1917); piano pieces (*Chœur et danse des lutins; 6 poèmes sylvestres*); pieces for organ and for harmonium; a cappella choruses; etc. Dubois publ. a practical manual, *Traité de contrepoint et de fugue* (1901), which was a standard work at the Paris Cons.

Dubuc, Alexander, Russian pianist, composer, and teacher; b. Moscow, March 3, 1812; d. there, Jan. 8, 1898. He was a pupil of John Field, about whom he publ. a vol. of memoirs; was a prof. at the Moscow Cons. (1866–72). He wrote piano pieces, songs, and a work on piano technique (1866).

Du Cange, Charles Du Fresne, Sieur, French scholar; b. Amiens, Dec. 18, 1610; d. Paris, Oct. 23, 1688. He belonged to the famed group of 17th-century French writers who established the precepts of modern historical criticism; he is important to musicology because he included definitions of Latin musical terms in his lexicographies. The most valuable of his many works are the *Glossarium ad scriptores mediae et infimae latinitatis* (Paris, 3 vols., 1678; 6 vols., 1733–36; 7 vols., 1840–50; 10 vols., 1883–87) and the *Glossarium ad scriptores mediae et infimae graecitatis* (Lyons, 1688; Breslau, 1889). Almost all his works are preserved in the Bibliothèque Nationale in Paris.

Du Caurroy, François-Eustache, Sieur de St.-Frémin; French composer; b. Beauvais (baptized, Feb. 4), 1549; d. Paris, Aug. 7, 1609. He was a member of the French nobility; his father was "procureur du roi." He entered the Royal Chapel as a singer in 1569; in 1575 received a prize for a chanson, *Beaux yeux;* in 1578 he was "sous-maître"; in 1599 became superintendent of "la musique du roi." Influenced by Le Jeune, he began to compose "musique mesurée"; advanced in the favor of the court, receiving honors and awards; held the ecclesiastical titles of canon at the Ste. Chapelle of Dijon, Ste. Croix of Orleans, and other provincial posts. His greatest work was the collection *Meslanges de la musique,* containing Psalms, "chansons mesurées," noëls, in 4, 5, and 6 voices (posthumously publ., Paris, 1610; some specimens reprinted in Expert's *Maîtres musiciens,* vol. XIII). Other works: *Missa pro defunctis;* 2 vols. of *Preces ecclesiasticae;* instrumental *Fantaisies* for 3, 4, 5, and 6 parts (Paris, 1610; several nos. publ. separately by Expert); 5 vols. of his works in score are in the Bibliothèque Sainte-Geneviève in Paris.

Ducis (Duch), Benedictus, distinguished composer of the 16th century; b. probably near Constance, c.1490; d. Schalckstetten, near Ulm, 1544. He may or may not be identical with **Benedictus de Opitiis,** who was organist at the Antwerp Cathedral (1514–16) and at the Chapel Royal in London (1516–22). It is known for a certainty that Benedictus Ducis was in Vienna c.1515; he probably studied there; in 1532 he applied for a pastorate at Ulm (under the name **Benedict Duch**), but failed to obtain it. In 1533 he succeeded in receiving a pastorate at Stubersheim, near Geislingen; in 1535 he became pastor at Schalckstetten and remained there till his death. Benedictus Ducis has been confused by many writers with Benedictus Appenzeller; the long list of Ducis's works given by Fétis is spurious; Barclay Squire, in *Sammelbände der Internationalen Musik-Gesellschaft* (Jan. 1912), brought conclusive evidence that a considerable number of these works must be attributed to Benedictus Appenzeller. Two works by Ducis were publ. in facsimile by M. Nijhoff (The Hague, 1925); 10 sacred motets are reprinted in Denkmäler Deutscher Tonkunst, vol. XXXIV (ed. by Johannes Wolf).

Dufallo, Richard, American clarinetist and conductor; b. East Chicago, Ind., Jan. 30, 1933. He played clarinet as a youngster; then enrolled at the American Cons. of Music in Chicago. He subsequently studied composition with Lukas Foss at the Univ. of Calif., Los Angeles; in 1957 he joined the Improvisation Chamber Ensemble organized by Foss, and showed an exceptional talent for controlled improvisation in the ultramodern manner. He then joined Lukas Foss as his associate conductor with the Buffalo Phil. (1962–67); also served on the faculty of the State Univ. of N.Y. at Buffalo (1963–67), where he directed its Center of Creative and Performing Arts. He attended a conducting seminar with William Steinberg in N.Y. (1965); Pierre Boulez gave him additional instruction in Basel (1969). In 1967 he went to Japan and other Asian countries as assistant tour conductor with the N.Y. Phil. In 1971 he made his European conducting debut in Paris. He served as conductor of the "Mini-Met," an adjunct to the Metropolitan Opera in N.Y. (1972–74), and was director of the series of new music sponsored by the Juilliard School of Music in N.Y. (1972–79). In 1970 he became artistic director of the Aspen Music Festival's Conference on Contemporary Music. From 1980 he has also served as artistic adviser of Het Gelders Orkest in Arnhem, the Netherlands. He made guest appearances with the Concertgebouw Orch. of Amsterdam, London Symph.,

Chicago Symph., Berlin Phil., Pittsburgh Symph., and Philadelphia Orch.

Dufay, Guillaume, chief representative of the Burgundian school, and famed particularly for his 3-part chansons, masses, and motets; b. probably at Hainault, c.1400; d. Cambrai, Nov. 27, 1474. The last name is pronounced "du-fah-ee," in 3 syllables, as indicated by the way he set his name to music in *Ave regina caelorum,* asking for the Lord's mercy: "Miserere tui labentis *Du-fa-y.*" He was a choirboy at the Cathedral of Cambrai, where he received an excellent training; his teachers were Loqueville and Grenon. He was in Rimini and Pesaro (1419–26); then returned to Cambrai, where he was chapel master (1426–28); then member of the Papal Chapel in Rome (1428–33); in the service of the Duke of Savoy (1433); again in Cambrai (1434); entered again the Papal Chapel (1435–37; not in Rome, however, but in Florence and Bologna); was again in Savoy (1438–44); studied jurisprudence at the Univ. of Turin, obtaining the degree "Baccalarius in decretis" (c.1445). In 1445 he settled at Cambrai, holding the important position of canon at the cathedrals of Cambrai and Mons. Under these fortunate circumstances, which enabled him to live in comfort, he spent the rest of his life, greatly esteemed by both the Church authorities and musicians; he was described by Compère as "the moon of all music, and the light of all singers." Dufay wrote music in almost every form practiced in his time, and was successful in each. A complete list of works, including MS sources and approximate dates of composition, is found in Charles E. Hamm's *A Chronology of the Works of Guillaume Dufay* (1964). The *Opera omnia* (issued by the American Inst. of Musicology, Rome, 1947–50; first ed. by Guillaume de Van, continued by Heinrich Bessler) also contains a valuable commentary.

Dufourcq, Norbert, distinguished French music historian and organist; b. St. Jean-de-Braye (Loiret), Sept. 21, 1904. He was educated at the Sorbonne (1921–23), where he studied history and geography; then at the Ecole Nationale des Chartes (1924–28), graduating as an archivist-palaeographer; also studied piano and music history with Gastoué (1913–20), organ with André Marchal (1920–40), and harmony, counterpoint, and fugue with Marie-Rose Hublé. He took his Ph.D. at the Univ. of Paris in 1935 with the dissertation *Esquisse d'une histoire de l'orgue en France: XIIIe–XVIIIe siècles* (publ. in Paris, 1935). He was a teacher of history at the Collège Stanislas in Paris (1935–46); also prof. of Music History and Musicology at the Paris Cons. (1941–76). In addition to other teaching positions, he also appeared as an organist. He edited performing and scholarly editions of works for the organ and harpsichord of 17th- and 18th-century French composers.

Dugazon, Louise Rosalie, famous opera singer; b. Berlin, June 18, 1755; d. Paris, Sept. 22, 1821. She was brought up in the atmosphere of the theater; her father, F.J. Lefebvre, was a French dancer at the Berlin Opera; she herself began her career as a ballet dancer; then she became a singer, encouraged mainly by Grétry, who thought highly of her talent. She made her debut in Paris in Grétry's opera *Sylvain* (June 19, 1774); in 1775 she married an actor who used the professional name Dugazon; although they were soon separated, she adopted this name for her professional appearances. She sang mostly at the Opéra-Comique; created some 60 new roles; her last public appearance was at the Paris Opéra on Feb. 29, 1804. She was greatly admired by her contemporaries, and her name became a designation of certain types of operatic parts ("jeune Dugazon"; i.e., an ingenue).

Duiffoprugcar (properly, **Tieffenbrucker**), **Gaspar,** Bavarian viol maker; b. Tieffenbrugg, Bavaria, 1514 (date established by Dr. Coutagne of Lyons, in his work *Gaspar Duiffoproucart et les luthiers lyonnais du XVIe siècle,* Paris, 1893); d. Lyons, Dec. 16, 1571. He was long reputed to be the first maker of violins; but Vidal, in his *Les Instruments à archet,* states that all the so-called Duiffoprugcar violins are spurious, having been made by Vuillaume, who in 1827 conceived the idea of making violins after the pattern of a viola da gamba by Duiffoprugcar. Apparently, the latter learned his trade in Italy, the usual spellings of his name showing it to be Italianized rather than gallicized; he settled in Lyons in 1553, and was naturalized in 1559.

Dukas, Paul, famous French composer; b. Paris, Oct. 1, 1865; d. there, May 17, 1935. In 1882–88 he was a student at the Paris Cons., studying under G. Mathias (piano), Théodore Dubois (harmony), and E. Guiraud (composition); won first prize for counterpoint and fugue in 1886, and the 2nd Prix de Rome with a cantata, *Velléda* (1888); began writing music reviews in 1892; was music critic of the *Revue Hebdomadaire* and *Gazette des Beaux-Arts;* also a contributor to the *Chronique des Arts, Revue Musicale,* etc.; in 1906, was made a Chevalier of the Légion d'Honneur; in 1910–13, and again in 1928, was prof. of the orch. class at the Cons.; in 1918, was elected Debussy's successor as a member of the *Conseil de l'enseignement supérieur* there; in 1927, was appointed prof. of composition at the Paris Cons.; also taught at the Ecole Normale de Musique; assisted in the revising and editing of Rameau's complete works for Durand of Paris. Although he was not a prolific composer, he wrote a masterpiece of modern music in his orch. scherzo *L'Apprenti Sorcier;* his opera *Ariane et Barbe-Bleue* is one of the finest French operas in the impressionist style. Shortly before his death he destroyed several MSS of his unfinished compositions.

WORKS: 3 overtures: *King Lear* (1883); *Götz von Berlichingen* (1884); *Polyeucte* (1891); Symph. in C (Paris, Jan. 3, 1897); *L'Apprenti Sorcier* (May 18, 1897; his most famous work); opera, *Ariane et Barbe-Bleue* (Opéra-Comique, May 10, 1907); ballet, *La Péri* (Paris, April 22, 1912); *Villanelle* for Horn and Piano (1906); for Piano: Sonata in E-flat minor;

Variations, Interlude et Finale, on a theme by Rameau; *Prélude élégiaque.* Together with Saint-Saëns, he completed Guiraud's opera *Frédégonde.*

Duke, Vernon. See **Dukelsky, Vladimir.**

Dukelsky, Vladimir (pen name as composer of light music: **Vernon Duke**), versatile composer of both "serious" and popular music; b. Oct. 10, 1903, in the railroad station of the Russian village of Parfianovka (during his mother's trip to Pskov); d. Santa Monica, Calif., Jan. 16, 1969. He was a pupil at the Kiev Cons. of Glière and Dombrovsky; left Russia in 1920 and went to Turkey, coming to the U.S. shortly afterward; later lived in Paris and London; settled in N.Y. in 1929 (naturalized, 1936); was a lieutenant in the Coast Guard (1939–44); went back to France (1947–48), but then returned to the U.S. to live in N.Y. and Hollywood. He began to compose at a very early age; was introduced to Diaghilev, who commissioned him to write a ballet, *Zéphyr et Flore,* the production of which put Dukelsky among the successful group of ballet composers. Another important meeting was with Koussevitzky, who championed Dukelsky's music in Paris and in Boston. In the U.S. Dukelsky began writing popular music; many of his songs, such as *April in Paris,* have enjoyed great popularity. At George Gershwin's suggestion, he adopted the name Vernon Duke for popular music works; in 1955 he dropped his full name altogether, and signed both his serious and light compositions Vernon Duke.

WORKS: FOR THE STAGE: *Zéphyr et Flore* (Paris, Jan. 31, 1925); *Demoiselle Paysanne,* opera in 2 acts (1928); *Le Bal des blanchisseuses,* ballet (Paris, Dec. 19, 1946); *Souvenir de Monte Carlo,* ballet (1949–56). FOR ORCH.: Piano Concerto (1924; not orchestrated); 3 symphs.: No. 1 (Paris, June 14, 1928); No. 2 (Boston, April 25, 1930); No. 3 (Brussels Radio Orch., Oct. 10, 1947); *Ballade* for Piano and Small Orch. (1931); *Dédicaces* for Soprano, Piano, and Orch. (Boston Symph., Dec. 16, 1938); Violin Concerto (Boston, March 19, 1943); Cello Concerto (Boston, Jan. 4, 1946); *Ode to the Milky Way* (N.Y., Nov. 18, 1946). CHORAL MUSIC: *Dushenka,* duet for Women's Voices and Chamber Orch. (1927); *Epitaph* (on the death of Diaghilev) for Soprano Solo, Chorus, and Orch. (Boston Symph., April 15, 1932); *The End of St. Petersburg,* oratorio (Schola Cantorum, N.Y., Jan. 12, 1938); *Moulin-Rouge* for Mixed Chorus (1941). CHAMBER MUSIC: Trio (Variations) for Flute, Bassoon, and Piano (1930); Etude for Bassoon and Piano (1932); *Capriccio mexicano* for Violin and Piano (1933); *3 Pieces* for Woodwind (1939); Violin Sonata (1949); String Quartet (1956). SONGS: *The Musical Zoo,* 20 songs to Ogden Nash's lyrics (1946); *A Shropshire Lad,* song cycle (1949). FOR PIANO: Sonata (1927); *Surrealist Suite* (1944); *Souvenir de Venise* (1948); *Serenade to San Francisco* (1956). He wrote songs for the musical comedies *The Show Is On, Garrick Gaieties, Walk a Little Faster, Three's a Crowd, Americana, Ziegfeld Follies, Cabin in the Sky,* etc.; added 2 ballets and several songs to *Goldwyn Follies,* an unfinished film score by George

Gershwin (1937). He publ. an amusing autobiography, *Passport to Paris* (Boston, 1955), and the polemical book *Listen Here! A Critical Essay on Music Depreciation* (N.Y., 1963). See Igor Stravinsky, "A Cure for V.D.," in the unperiodical magazine *Listen* (Sept. 1964), a curiously undignified polemical incursion.

Dulcken, Ferdinand Quentin, pianist and composer; b. London, June 1, 1837; d. Astoria, N.Y., Dec. 10, 1901. He was the son of **Luise Dulcken** and nephew of **Ferdinand David;** was a pupil of Moscheles and Gade at the Leipzig Cons.; also received encouragement from Mendelssohn. He subsequently taught at the Warsaw Cons., and also at Moscow and St. Petersburg; made many concert tours in Europe as a pianist with Wieniawski, Vieuxtemps, and others. In 1876 he emigrated to America and gave concerts with Reményi; settled in N.Y. as a teacher and composer. He publ. nearly 400 piano pieces of the salon type and also some vocal works.

Dulcken (née **David**), **Luise,** pianist, sister of **Ferdinand David;** b. Hamburg, March 29, 1811; d. London, April 12, 1850. She was taught by C.F.G. Schwencke and Wilhelm Grund; played in public (in Germany) when 11 years of age. She married in 1828, and went to London, where she met with brilliant success as a pianist and teacher. Queen Victoria was one of her many pupils.

Dulichius (Dulich, Deilich, Deulich), Philippus, German composer and music theorist; b. Chemnitz, Dec. 18 (baptized, Dec. 19), 1562; d. Stettin, March 24 (buried, March 25), 1631. He studied at the Univ. of Leipzig; there is no evidence that he went to Italy and studied with Gabrieli, although this assertion appears in his biographies. He was a cantor in Stettin from 1587 until his retirement in 1630; was also in Danzig in 1604–5 to deputize for the cantor of the Marienkirche.

WORKS: (EXCLUSIVELY VOCAL): *Novum opus musicum duarum partium continens dicta insigniora ex evangeliis* (Stettin, 1599); *Centuriae octonum et septenum vocum harmonias sacras laudibus sanctisimae Triados consecratas continentes* (4 parts, Stettin 1607). R. Schwartz publ. 7 choruses from the *Centuriae* (1896); the complete *Centuriae* are publ. in Denkmäler Deutscher Tonkunst (XXXI, XLI).

Du Locle, Camille Théophile Germain du Commun, French librettist; b. Orange, Vacluse, July 16, 1832; d. Capri, Oct. 9, 1903. He was secretary of the Opéra under Perrin's direction; later, director of the Opéra-Comique. He commissioned Bizet to compose *Carmen;* was also instrumental in the preparation of the libretto for Verdi's opera *Aida.*

Dumesnil, Maurice, French-American pianist; b. Angoulême, Charente, April 20, 1886; d. Highland Park, Mich., Aug. 26, 1974. He studied at the Paris Cons. with Isidor Philipp, graduating in 1905. He received personal coaching from Debussy in playing Debussy's piano works, and was subsequently considered as an authority on the subject. He publ. *How to Play and Teach Debussy* (1933) and *Claude Debussy, Master of Dreams* (1940). Apart from his principal occupation as a piano teacher, he was also active as a conductor in Mexico (1916–20); eventually settled in N.Y.

Dumitrescu, Gheorghe, Rumanian composer, brother of **Ion Dumitrescu;** b. Oteșani, Dec. 28, 1914. He studied with Cuclin, Perlea, and Jora at the Bucharest Cons. (1934–41); was active as a violinist; served as director at the National Theater in Bucharest (1935–46); was composer-counselor for the Armatei artistic ensemble (1947–57); in 1951 was appointed a prof. at the Bucharest Cons. His music is marked by a vivacious quality typical of the operetta style.

WORKS: Operetta, *Tarsița și Roșiorul* (1949); 5 operas: *Ion Vodă cel Cumplit (Ion Voda the Terrible;* 1955); *Decebal* (1957); *Răscoala* (1959); *Fata cu garoafe* (1961); *Meșterul Manole* (1969); oratorios: *Tudor Vladimirescu* (1950); *Grivița noastră* (1963); *Zorile de aur* (1964); *Din lumea cu dor în cea fără dor* (1966); *Pămînt dezrobit* (1968); numerous cantatas and other vocal-symphonic works; 4 symphs.: No. 1 (1945); No. 2, *A Republicii,* with Chorus (1962); No. 3 (1965); No. 4 (1970); *Poem rustic* for Orch. (1939); *Poemul amurgului* for Orch. (1941); *Suită pitorească* for Orch. (1942); *4 Symphonic Frescoes* (1943); *Suită primaverii* for Orch. (1944); Cello Concerto (1947); *Suită cîmpenească* for Orch. (1963); 2 piano sonatas (1938, 1939); Viola Sonata (1939); Violin Sonata (1939); Piano Quintet (1940); songs; choruses.

Dumitrescu, Ion, Rumanian composer, brother of **Gheorghe Dumitrescu;** b. Oteșani, June 2, 1913. He studied conducting with Perlea and composition with Cuclin at the Bucharest Cons. (1934–41); was a composer and conductor at the National Theater in Bucharest (1940–47); has taught at the Bucharest Cons. since 1944. He writes in classical forms with undertones of Rumanian folk music.

WORKS: 3 suites for Orch. (1938, 1940, 1944); *2 Pieces* for Orch. (1940); *Poeme* for Cello and Orch. (1940); Symph. No. 1 (1948); *Symphonic Prelude* (1952); Concerto for String Orch. (1956); Suite from the film *Muntele Retezat* (1956); *Sinfonietta* (1955–57); Piano Sonata (1938); *Suite în stil vechi* for Viola and Piano (1939); Piano Sonatina (1940); *2 Pieces* for Piano (1942); String Quartet No. 1 (1949; transcribed for String Orch., 1961); film music; songs.

Dumont (Du Mont), Henri (Henry), significant Belgian-French composer of motets; b. Villers l'Evèque, near Liège, 1610; d. Paris, May 8, 1684. He served as a chorister at Maastricht, and was ordained a priest at Liège; then was organist at St. Paul's Church in Paris (1640–63); maître de chapelle at the French court (1663–83); concurrently was maître de la musique for the Queen of France (1673–81).

Dunhill, Thomas Frederick, English composer; b. London, Feb. 1, 1877; d. Scunthorpe, Lincolnshire, March 13, 1946. He entered the Royal Academy of Music in 1893, and studied with Franklin Taylor (piano) and Stanford (theory); in 1905 was appointed a prof. at the Royal Academy of Music; in 1907 he founded the Concerts of British Chamber-Music, which he conducted until 1916.

WORKS: Operas: *The Enchanted Garden* (London, 1927); *Tantivy Towers* (London, Jan. 16, 1931); *Happy Families* (Guildford, Nov. 1, 1933); ballet, *Gallimaufry* (Hamburg, Dec. 11, 1937); *Phantasy* for String Quartet; Piano Quintet; Quintet for Violin, Cello, Clarinet, Horn, and Piano; Quintet for Horn and String Quartet; Piano Quartet; Viola Sonata; 2 violin sonatas; *The Wind among the Reeds,* song cycle for Tenor and Orch.; violin pieces; compositions for cello. He publ.: *Chamber Music* (a treatise for students, 1912); *Mozart's String Quartets* (2 vols., 1927); *Sullivan's Comic Operas* (1928); *Sir Edward Elgar* (1938).

Duni, Egidio Romoaldo, Italian composer of opera; b. Matera, Feb. 9, 1708; d. Paris, June 11, 1775. He first studied in the Cons. "della Madonna di Loreto," then in the Cons. "della Pietà de' Turchini." His first opera, *Nerone* (Rome, May 21, 1735), was a popular success. He went to London (1737) and the Netherlands (1738); in 1739 he returned to Italy; in 1743 he was maestro di cappella at S. Nicolo di Bari, in Naples; became tutor at the Court of Parma, where, encouraged by the Duke, he began composing French operettas, one of which, *Le caprice amoureux ou Ninette à la cour* (Parma, 1756), was so well received that Duni decided to try his fortune in Paris, where he brought out light and frivolous stage pieces which suited the prevailing taste; he is regarded by some music historians as a founder of French opéra-bouffe. He wrote about 13 Italian operas, and 22 in French.

Dunn, James Philip, American composer; b. New York, Jan. 10, 1884; d. Jersey City, N.J., July 24, 1936. He studied at the College of the City of N.Y. (B.A., 1903); then at Columbia Univ. with MacDowell, and subsequently with Cornelius Rybner. He was then active as a teacher and church organist in N.Y. and elsewhere. As a composer, he attracted attention by his symph. poem descriptive of Lindbergh's transatlantic flight, *We* (N.Y., Aug. 27, 1927). He also wrote an *Overture on Negro Themes* (N.Y., July 22, 1922), some chamber music, and organ pieces.

Dunn, Mignon, American mezzo-soprano; b. Memphis, Tenn., June 17, 1932. At the age of 17 the Metropolitan Opera awarded her a scholarship for vocal studies; she made her operatic debut with the N.Y. City Opera in 1956 as Carmen; on Oct. 29, 1958, she made her first appearance at the Metropolitan Opera, and within a few years became a member of the company; also sang with the Vienna State Opera, the Paris Opéra, at Covent Garden, London, the San Francisco Opera, and the Chicago Lyric Opera. A versatile artist, her repertoire includes roles in

Italian and French operas, as well as those of Wagner.

Dunstable (Dunstaple), John, English composer; b. probably at Dunstable, Bedfordshire, between 1380 and 1390; d. Dec. 24, 1453; buried in St. Stephen's Walbrook, London. He was the most important English composer of the early 15th century, rivalling his contemporaries Binchois and Dufay; was also an astrologer and mathematician. From April 28, 1419, to May 1440 he was canon of Hereford Cathedral and prebendary of Putson Minor; for some time he was in the service of John, Duke of Bedford; the Duke, as Regent of France, represented King Henry V in Paris for a number of years, and probably took his musicians with him. Practically nothing further is known of Dunstable's life. Much of his music is contained in the 6 MSS discovered by F.X. Haberl in the library of the Cathedral of Trent in 1884 ("Trent Codices"). The *Complete Works* are publ. as vol. VIII of *Musica Britannica*, ed. by M.F. Bukofzer (London, 1953; 2d ed., revised, 1970). An examination of these compositions reveals not only the existence of a highly developed art in England early in the 15th century, antedating the full flowering of the Burgundian school (Binchois, Dufay), but also Dunstable's most important contributions to the music of the period in making use of the declamatory motet (in which the rhythm of the spoken word largely governs the musical rhythm) and, apparently, introducing the motet with double structure (which provided the predominant technique of composition of masses in the 15th century).

Duparc, Henri, one of the chief innovators in the domain of French song; b. Paris, Jan. 21, 1848; d. Mont-de-Marsan, Feb. 12, 1933. He studied with César Franck, who regarded him as his most talented pupil. Duparc suffered from a nervous affliction, which forced him to abandon his composition and seek rest in Switzerland. He destroyed the MS of his Cello Sonata, and several symph. suites; of his instrumental works only a few MSS have survived, including the symph. poems *Aux étoiles* (perf. in Paris, April 11, 1874) and *Lénore* (1875) and a suite of 6 piano pieces, *Feuilles volantes.* His songs, to words by Baudelaire and other French poets, are distinguished by exquisitely phrased melodies arranged in fluid modal harmonies; among the best are: *Invitation au voyage, Extase, Soupir, Sérénade, Chanson triste, La Vague et la cloche, Phidilé, Elégie, Testament, Lamento,* and *La Vie antérieure.*

Dupin, Paul, prolific French composer; b. Roubaix, Aug. 14, 1865; d. Paris, March 6, 1949. He worked in a factory; then was a menial clerk, but turned to music against all odds; took some lessons with Emile Durand, and then proceeded to compose with fanatic compulsion; somehow he managed to have more than 200 works actually publ. Of these, the most original were about 500 canons for 3–12 voices, and 40 string quartets titled *Poèmes;* he wrote much other chamber music; some pretty piano pieces

with fanciful titles such as *Esquisse fuguées, Dentelles,* etc.; he even wrote a grand opera, *Marcelle,* which he later hopefully renamed *Lyszelle* for exotic effect. He was much admired in Paris for his determination to succeed, but his works were rarely performed.

Dupont, Gabriel, French composer; b. Caen, March 1, 1878; d. Vésinet, Aug. 2, 1914. He was a pupil of his father, the organist at the Cathedral; later, of Gédalge; then of Massenet and Widor at the Paris Cons.; won the 2nd Prix de Rome in 1901. In a contest conducted in 1903 by Sonzogno, the publishing house in Milan, his opera *La Cabrera* was selected, along with 2 others, to be performed and judged by the public (237 works were submitted); it was produced at Milan on May 17, 1904, with great success, thereby winning for Dupont the prize of 50,000 lire. He wrote other operas: *La Glu,* libretto by Jean Richepin (Nice, Jan. 24, 1910); *La Farce du cuvier* (Brussels, March 21, 1912); *Antar* (1913; the outbreak of war in 1914 prevented its planned production, and the opera was staged posthumously at the Paris Opéra on March 14, 1921); also *Les Heures dolentes* for Orch., 4 pieces from a suite of 14 compositions for Piano (1903–5); *Poèmes d'automne* for Piano; symph. poems: *Hymne à Aphrodite* and *Le Chant de la destinée; Poème* for Piano Quintet; many other piano pieces; etc.

Dupont, Pierre, French songwriter; b. Rochetaillée, near Lyons, April 23, 1821; d. St. Etienne, July 25, 1870. The son of a laborer, and himself uneducated, he attracted attention by his political and rustic ditties. He wrote the words, and then sang the airs to Reyer, who put them into shape. His political songs (*Le Pain, Le Chant des ouvriers,* etc.) created such disturbances that he was banished in 1851, but in 1852 he was pardoned. His song *Les Bœufs* enjoyed some popularity.

Duport, Jean-Louis, famous French cellist; b. Paris, Oct. 4, 1749; d. there, Sept 7, 1819. He made his public debut at the Concerts Spirituels (1768); joined his brother, Jean Pierre, in Berlin at the outbreak of the Revolution; returning in 1806, he became musician to Charles IV, the ex-king of Spain, at Marseilles; in 1812 returned to Paris, where he was soon regarded as the foremost French cellist; taught at the Paris Cons. (1813–15). He wrote 6 cello concertos, sonatas, duos, airs variées, 9 nocturnes (for harp and cello), etc. His *Essai sur le doigté du violoncelle et la conduite de l'archet, avec une suite d'exercises* is still a standard textbook, and practically laid the foundations of modern cello virtuosity.

DuPré, Jacqueline, English cello player; b. Oxford, Jan. 26, 1945. The Gallic name of her family dates back to Norman times. Both her parents were musicians; her mother even wrote a ballet score. Jacqueline DuPré studied cello at the Guildhall School of Music in London and later with Paul Tortelier in Paris, in Switzerland with Casals, and with Rostropovich in Moscow. She owns the famous "Davidov cello" made by Stradivarius in 1712. She made her American debut in N.Y. on May 14, 1965, with electrifying success, playing Elgar's Cello Concerto and eliciting rapturous reviews from the critics. On June 15, 1967, she married the Israeli pianist and conductor **Daniel Barenboim.** In 1972 she was stricken with multiple sclerosis and was obliged to give up her public appearances. In 1976 she was made an Officer of the Order of the British Empire.

Dupré, Marcel, celebrated French organist and composer; b. Rouen, May 3, 1886; d. Meudon, near Paris, May 30, 1971. He was a pupil of his father, **Albert Dupré;** also an organist; studied organ with Guilmant in 1898; he then entered the Paris Cons. (1902–14) and studied with Vierne, Diémer, and Widor, winning first prizes for organ (1907) and for fugue (1909); in 1914 he won the Grand Prix de Rome for the cantata *Psyché.* He was interim organist at Notre-Dame in 1916; in 1920 he gave at the Paris Cons. a cycle of 10 recitals of Bach's complete organ works, playing from memory. On Nov. 18, 1921, he made his N.Y. debut, followed by a transcontinental tour, performing 94 recitals in 85 American cities; a 2nd U.S. tour in 1923 included 110 concerts; he made his 10th tour of the U.S. in 1948. In 1939 he gave 40 concerts in Australia on his world tour. He had, meanwhile, been appointed prof. of organ at the Paris Cons. In 1926; in 1934 he succeeded Widor as organist at St. Sulpice; continued there until his death at the age of 85; became general director of the American Cons. in Fontainebleau in 1947 and was appointed director of the Paris Cons., in succession to Delvincourt, in 1954 (until 1956). Dupré wrote his first work, the oratorio *La Vision de Jacob,* at the age of 14; it was performed on his 15th birthday at his father's house in Rouen, in a domestic production assisted by a local choral society. Most of his organ works are products of original improvisations. Thus *Symphonie-Passion,* first improvised at the Wanamaker organ in Philadelphia (Dec. 8, 1921), was written down much later and performed in its final version at Westminster Cathedral in London (Oct. 9, 1924). Similarly, *Le Chemin de la Croix* was improvised in Brussels (Feb. 13, 1931) and performed in a definitive version in Paris the following year (March 18, 1932). Among precomposed works there are symphs. for Organ: No. 1 (Glasgow, Jan. 3, 1929) and No. 2 (1946); Concerto for Organ and Orch. (Groningen, Netherlands, April 27, 1938, composer soloist); *Psalm XVIII* (1949); 76 chorales and several a cappella choruses; also numerous "verset-préludes." He is the author of *Traité d'improvisation à l'orgue* (1925) and *Méthode d'orgue.*

Duprez, Louis-Gilbert, French tenor; b. Paris, Dec. 6, 1806; d. there, Sept. 23, 1896. His fine boy-voice gained him admission to Choron's Inst.; after diligent vocal and theoretical study, he made his debut as Count Almaviva at the Odéon, in 1825. Dissatisfied with the results, he subjected himself to a long course of training in Italy, and in 1836 succeed-

ed Nourrit at the Opéra. He was appointed prof. of lyrical declamation at the Cons. in 1842, but resigned in 1850 to establish a vocal school of his own, which flourished. He publ. the vocal methods *L'Art du chant* (1845) and *La Mélodie, Etudes complémentaires vocales et dramatiques de l'Art du chant* (1846); also wrote *Souvenirs d'un chanteur* (1880); composed several operas.

Dupuis, Albert, outstanding Belgian composer; b. Verviers, March 1, 1877; d. Brussels, Sept. 19, 1967. He studied piano, violin, and flute at the Music Academy in Verviers; later entered the classes of Vincent d'Indy at the newly created Schola Cantorum in Paris (1897); returned to Belgium in 1899 and later won the Belgian Prix de Rome with his cantata *La Chanson d'Halewyn* (Brussels, Nov. 25, 1903; arranged and perf. as a 3-act opera, Antwerp, Feb. 14, 1914). He became director of the Verviers Cons. in 1907, retiring in 1947.
    WORKS: His other operas, the largest body of lyrical works by a Belgian composer, include *Bilitis* (Verviers, 1899); *Jean Michel* (1901–2; Brussels, March 5, 1903); *Martille* (1904; Brussels, March 3, 1905); *Fidélaine* (Liège, 1910); *Le Château de la Grande Bretèche* (Nice, 1913); *La Passion* (Monte Carlo, April 2, 1916; over 150 perfs. in Europe); *La Captivité de Babylone* (biblical drama); *La Barrière* (Verviers, 1920); *La Délivrance* (Lille, 1921); *Le Sacrifice* (Antwerp, 1921); *La Victoire* (Brussels, 1923); *Ce n'était qu'un rêve* (Antwerp, 1935); *Hassan,* oriental fairy tale (Brussels, 1938); *Un Drame sous Philippe II* (Brussels, Jan. 18, 1938); oratorios: *Les Cloches nuptiales* (1899); *Œdipe à Colone; Psalm 118;* ballets: *Rêve d'enfant,* after Schumann (1951); *Au temps jadis* (1952); *Evocations d'Espagne* (1954); cantatas: *Vers le progrès, Pour la Paix, La Gileppe,* and a *Cantata jubilaire* for Belgian independence; 2 symphs. (1904, 1922–23); *Fantaisie rhapsodique* for Violin and Orch. (1906); *Poème oriental* for Cello and Orch. (1924); *Hermann et Dorothée,* overture (1921); Cello Concerto (1926); *Epitaphe* for Orch. (1929); *Aria* for Viola and Orch. (1933); Piano Concerto (1940); *Caprice rhapsodique* for Orch. (1941); Violin Concerto (1944); *Caprice* for Flute and Orch.; *Solo de concours* for Horn and Orch. and for Trombone and Orch.; *Valse Joyeuse* for Orch.; *La Navarraise* for Orch.; 2 concertinos for Timpani and Orch.; Violin Sonata (1904); String Quartet; 2 piano trios; Piano Quartet; *Scherzo* for Solo Horn; Variations for Solo Horn; *5 pièces paradoxales* for Piano; many other works for piano; choruses; songs; etc. In 1955 he was awarded a prize by the Société des Auteurs Lyriques de Paris for his creative output.

Durand, Marie-Auguste, French organist and publisher; b. Paris, July 18, 1830; d. there, May 31, 1909. He studied organ with Benoist; in 1849, was organist at St. Ambroise; then at Ste.-Geneviève, St.-Roch, and (1862–74) St. Vincent de Paul. He also occupied himself with music criticism and composition (his Chaconne and *Valse* for piano are especially popular). In 1870 he entered into partnership with Schönewerk (acquiring Flaxland's music publishing business), the firm then being known as Durand & Schönewerk; when his son, **Jacques** (b. Paris, Feb. 22, 1865; d. Bel-Ebat, Aug. 22, 1928), replaced Schönewerk in 1891, the title became Durand & Fils. The house is now known as Durand & Cie.; it has made a specialty of publishing works of the outstanding French composers (Joncières, Lalo, Massenet, Debussy, Saint-Saëns, Chausson, Ravel, and many others), and has also brought out French editions of Wagner's *Tannhäuser, The Flying Dutchman,* and *Lohengrin,* as well as several editions of old masters, including a complete critical edition of Rameau, edited by Saint-Saëns. Jacques Durand publ. the following works: *Cours professionel à l'usage des employés du commerce de musique* (2 vols., 1923); *Quelques souvenirs d'un éditeur de musique* (2 vols., 1924–25); *Lettres de Cl. Debussy à son éditeur* (Paris, 1927).

Durante, Francesco, celebrated Italian church composer and noted teacher; b. Frattamaggiore, near Naples, March 31, 1684; d. Naples, Sept. 30, 1755. He studied in Rome and, under the guidance of his uncle, D. Angelo, at the Cons. di Sant' Onofrio, where he taught in 1710–11; then became maestro at the Cons. di Santa Maria di Loreto, and at the Cons. dei Poveri di Gesù Cristo from 1742; again at Sant' Onofrio from 1745 until his death. After Alessandro Scarlatti, and with Leo, Durante ranks as one of the founders and a chief representative of the "Neapolitan school" of composition. He devoted himself almost exclusively to sacred music, in which the breadth, vigor, and resourcefulness of his style are more in evidence than marked originality. He was a very great teacher; his pupils, Duni, Traetta, Vinci, Jommelli, Piccinni, Guglielmi, Pergolesi, Paisiello, and others, took almost complete possession of the European lyric stage during the latter half of the 18th century. The library of the Paris Cons. contains a rich collection of his works.

WORKS: 13 masses, and fragments of masses; 16 Psalms; 19 motets; several antiphons and hymns; 12 madrigals; 6 harpsichord sonatas; etc. His *Lamentations of Jeremiah* and *Pastoral Mass* are in the Vienna Library (in MS). The libraries of the Naples and Bologna Cons. also possess MSS of Durante. Karmrodt of Halle printed a grand Magnificat (with additional accompaniments by Robert Franz); Breitkopf & Härtel publ. 12 *duetti da camera;* H. Schletterer ed. a selection of his keyboard pieces; other reprints of keyboard pieces were publ. by A. Diversi in *Arte antica e moderna* (vol. I; 3 studies), F. Boghen in *Antichi maestri italiani* (4 fugues, 3 toccatas), A. Longo in *Biblioteca d'oro* (vol. II; *Aria danzante*), G. Tagliapietra in *Antologia di musica antica e moderna* (vol. XI), M. Vitali in *Composizioni scelte* (vol. II). A. Diversi publ. a 4-voiced *Christe eleison* in his *Biblioteca mus. sacra.* Concertos for orch. are printed in Le Pupitre, 26.

Durey, Louis, French composer; b. Paris, May 27, 1888; d. St. Tropez, July 3, 1979. He studied music with Léon Saint-Requier (1910–14); became known as a member of Les Six, a group of young French composers dedicated to modern music, the other 5 being Darius Milhaud, Arthur Honegger, Georges Auric, Francis Poulenc, and Germaine Tailleferre. Durey wrote music fashionable during a wave of anti-Romanticism, proclaiming the need of constructive simplicity in modern dress, with abundant use of titillating discords. Although he was the oldest of Les Six, he wrote the least music; most of his works are in miniature forms. Durey's esthetic code was radically altered in 1936 when he joined the French Communist Party. During the German occupation of France he was active in the Resistance, for which he wrote anti-Fascist songs. In 1948 he was elected vice-president of the Association Française des Musiciens Progressives; in 1950 he became the music critic of the Paris Communist newspaper *L'Humanité.* He subscribed to the tenets of the Prague Manifesto of 1948, which called upon progressive musicians to initiate a "democratization of musical forms," to abandon artistic individualism, and to write music derived from national folk songs. In 1961 he received the Grand Prix de la Musique Française.

WORKS: *Le Navire* for Voice and Orch., to words by André Gide (1916); *Le Bestiaire* for Voice and 12 Instruments, after Apollinaire (1919); *Le Printemps au fond de la mer* for Voice and Wind Instruments, to a text by Jean Cocteau (1920); *L'Occasion*, lyric drama after Mérimée (1928); *Fantaisie concertante* for Cello and Orch. (1947); *3 poèmes de Paul Eluard* for Voice and Orch. (1952); *Trio-Serenade* for Violin, Viola, and Cello, in memory of Béla Bartók (1955); overture, *Ile-de-France* (1955); Concertino for Piano, 16 Wind Instruments, Double Bass, and Timpani (1956); *10 chœurs de métiers* for Chorus, 2 Flutes, Clarinet, Violin, Celesta, and Piano (1957); *3 Polyphonies vocales et intrumentales* for Vocal Quartet and 8 Instruments (1963); *Mouvement symphonique* (1964); *Les Soirées de Valfère* for Wind Instruments (1964); *Cantate de la rose et de l'amour* for Soprano and Strings (1965); Sinfonietta (1966); *4 octophonies* for 8 String Instruments (1966); *Dilection* for Strings (1969); *Obsession* for Wind Instruments, Harp, Double Bass, and Percussion (1970); political cantatas, *Paix aux hommes par millions,* to words by Mayakovsky (1949); *La Longue Marche,* after Mao Tse-tung (1949); 3 string quartets; numerous solo songs; piano pieces.

Durkó, Zsolt, Hungarian composer; b. Szeged, April 10, 1934. He studied composition at the Academy of Music at Budapest with Ferenc Farkas (1955–60) and at the Santa Cecilia Academy in Rome with Petrassi (1961–63). Many of his works have scientific connotations, at least in their titles; but some are rooted in Hungarian melorhythmic patterns.

WORKS: *11 Pieces* for String Quartet (1962); *Episodi sul tema B-A-C-H* for Orch. (1962–63); *Organismi* for Violin and Orch. (1963–64); *Psicogramma* for Piano (1964); *Una rapsodia ungherese (A Hungarian Rhapsody)* for 2 Clarinets and Orch. (1964–65); *Improvisations* for Wind Quintet (1965); *Dartmouth Concerto* for Soprano and Chamber

Orch. (1966); 2 string quartets (1966, 1969); *Fioriture* for Orch. (1966); *Altimara* for Chorus and Orch. (1967–68); *Cantilene* for Piano and Orch. (1968); *Symbols* for Horn and Piano (1968–69); *Colloïdes* for Flute, Piccolo, Bassoon, String Quartet, and 5 Alto Voices (1969); *Quartetto d'Ottoni* for 2 Trumpets, Trombone, and Tuba or 2nd Trombone (1970); Concerto for 12 Flutes and Orch. (1970); 2 *Iconographies:* No. 1 for 2 Cellos and Harpsichord (1970) and No. 2 for Horn and Chamber Ensemble (1971); *Fire Music* for Flute, Clarinet, Piano, and String Trio (1970–71); Cantata No. 1 (1971); Cantata No. 2 (1972); *Assonance* for Organ (1972); *Halotti beszéd (Funeral Oration),* oratorio (1972); *Colloïdes* for Flute, Chamber Ensemble, and 3 Contraltos (1975); *Turner Illustrations* for Solo Violin and 14 Instruments (1976); opera, *Moses* (Budapest, May 15, 1977).

Duruflé, Maurice, noted French organist, teacher, and composer; b. Louviers, Eure, Jan. 11, 1902. He studied piano and organ with local teachers; in 1919 went to Paris, where he studied organ with Tournemire, Guilmant, and Louis Vierne. In 1920 he enrolled at the Paris Cons., where he took courses in organ playing with Gigout (first prize, 1922), harmony with Jean Gallon (first prize, 1924), fugue with Caussade (first prize, 1924), and composition with Paul Dukas (1928). In 1930 he was appointed organist of the church of St. Etienne-du-Mont in Paris. In 1943 he became a prof. at the Paris Cons., remaining on its staff until 1969. He composed a number of sacred works and organ pieces. His best known compositions are a Requiem (1947) and a Mass (1967).

Dushkin, Samuel, American violinist; b. Suwalki, Poland, Dec. 13, 1891; d. New York, June 24, 1976. He was brought to America as a child and was adopted by the composer Blair Fairchild, who gave him primary musical education. He studied violin with Leopold Auer in N.Y. and later took several lessons with Fritz Kreisler. He made his European debut as a violinist in 1918, and subsequently toured widely in Europe and America. In 1928 he became associated with Stravinsky and helped him in solving the technical problems in the violin part of his Violin Concerto, and was the soloist in the first performance of this work in Berlin on Oct. 23, 1931, with Stravinsky conducting. He also gave the first performance of Stravinsky's *Duo Concertant* for Violin and Piano, with Stravinsky playing the piano part (Berlin, Oct. 28, 1932). He recounted the details of his collaboration with Stravinsky in his article "Working with Stravinsky," publ. in the Merle Armitage collection *Stravinsky* (N.Y., 1936).

Dussek or **Dušek (Dusík), Franz (František Xaver),** Bohemian pianist and composer; b. Chotěborky, Bohemia, Dec. 8, 1731; d. Prague, Feb. 12, 1799. He studied in Prague with F. Habermann and in Vienna with Wagenseil. He settled in Prague by 1770, as a teacher and performer; was a close friend of Mozart. He wrote several keyboard sonatas and concertos, symphs., quartets, and trios.

Dussek (Dusík), Jan Ladislav, outstanding composer; b. Čáslav (Tschaslau), Bohemia, Feb. 12, 1760; d. St.-Germain-en-Laye, March 20, 1812. At first a boy soprano at the Minorite church in Iglau, he was taught music by Father Spinar while attending the Jesuit college; was organist at the Jesuit church in Kuttenberg for 2 years, and while studying theology at Prague Univ. found time to get a thorough musical training so that after graduation he obtained, through Count Männer, his patron, the post of organist at the church of St.-Rimbaut in Malines (now Mechelen). Thence he went to Bergen-op-Zoom, and in 1782 to Amsterdam; then spent a year at The Hague, and in 1783 studied under C.P.E. Bach at Hamburg; won renown as a pianist and as a performer on Hessel's "harmonica" in Berlin and St. Petersburg, then accepted an appointment from Prince Radziwill, with whom he lived in Lithuania for over a year. He played before Marie Antoinette in 1786, in Paris; soon went to Italy, and returned to Paris in 1788, whence the Revolution drove him to London. Here he married **Sofia Corri,** a singer, in 1792, and undertook a music business with his father-in-law; but his careless habits, and love of luxury and ease, ill fitted him for commercial pursuits; the enterprise failed, and he fled to Hamburg in 1800 to escape his creditors. Here he appears to have stayed about 2 years, giving concerts and teaching. In 1802 he gave a concert at Prague, and paid a visit to his father at Čáslav; he then entered the service of Louis Ferdinand of Prussia (1804–6), whose heroic death in battle (1806) inspired one of Dussek's finest pieces, *Elégie harmonique* for Piano. Afterward, he was briefly attached to the Prince of Isenburg (1806–7); then went to Paris as maître de chapelle to Prince Talleyrand. Dussek's significance in music history is unjustly obscured; he was a master craftsman; some canonic devices in his piano sonatas are remarkable for their skill; his piano writing had both brilliance and science; there are some idiomatic harmonies that presage Schumann and Brahms. He was a virtuoso at the keyboard; with Clementi he shares the honor of having introduced the "singing touch." A composer of amazing industry, Dussek wrote 16 piano concertos (one for 2 pianos), numerous accompanied sonatas, string quartets, a Piano Quartet, Piano Quintet, 53 violin sonatas (some interchangeable with flute), about 40 piano sonatas, 9 sonatas for piano, 4-hands, a number of sets of variations, dances, etc., for piano, as well as topical pieces on world events (*The Sufferings of the Queen of France; The Naval Battle and Total Defeat of the Dutch Fleet by Admiral Duncan;* etc.). He also wrote an opera, *The Captive of Spilberg* (London, Nov. 14, 1798) and incidental music to Sheridan's play *Pizarro* (London, May 24, 1799); publ. a piano method. His *Collected Works* were publ. in Leipzig in 1813–17 (12 vols.; reprinted in 6 vols., N.Y., 1973).

Dutilleux, Henri, talented French composer; b. Angers, Jan. 22, 1916. He studied at the Paris Cons. with H. Busser and with Jean and Noël Gallon; won the first Grand Prix de Rome in 1938; was director of singing at the Paris Opéra in 1942; subsequently was active on the Paris radio (1943–63). In 1961 he was a prof. at the Ecole Normale de Musique and in 1970 at the Paris Cons. He has developed a modernistic style which incorporates many procedures of Impressionism. His instrumental works have had numerous performances in France, England, and America; his most impressive work is his Symph. No. 1 (Paris, June 7, 1951; also perf. in Germany, England, and America). Other works: *Les Hauts de Hurle-Vent,* symph. suite; *Symphonie de danses; Salmacis,* ballet; *Sarabande* for Orch. (1941); Sonatine for Flute and Piano (1943); *La Giole* for Voice and Orch. (1944); *La Princesse d'Elide,* incidental music to Molière's play (1946); Piano Sonata (1946–48); *Monsieur de Pourceaugnac,* incidental music to Molière's play (1948); *Le Loup* (Paris, March 18, 1953); Symph. No. 2 (Boston, Dec. 11, 1959); *5 métaboles* for Orch. (Cleveland, Jan. 14, 1965); *Tout un monde lointain* for Cello and Orch. (Aix-en-Provence, July 25, 1970); *Timbres, espace, mouvement* for Orch. (Washington, D.C., Jan. 10, 1978); chamber music; piano pieces; film music and songs.

Dutoit, Charles, Swiss conductor; b. Lausanne, Oct. 7, 1936. He was of multinational heritage: his father was Swiss French; his mother was part German, part English, and, in her remote ancestry, part Brazilian. He learned to play the violin, viola, piano, and drums; studied conducting by watching Ansermet's rehearsals with the Suisse Romande. He studied music theory at the Lausanne Cons. and at the Academy of Music in Geneva; acquired fluency in the major European languages. He then took courses at the Accademia Musicale in Siena and at the Cons. Benedetto Marcello in Venice; also attended a summer seminar at the Berkshire Center in Tanglewood. Returning to Switzerland, he joined the Lausanne Chamber Orch. as a viola player. He made his conducting debut with the Bern Symph. Orch. in 1963; in 1964 he conducted *Le Sacre du printemps,* and was engaged as music director of the Bern Orch. Later he served in a similar capacity with the Tonhalle Orch. in Zürich. In 1967 he became conductor and artistic director of the Zürich Radio Orch.; then undertook a tour of South America, Australia, Japan, Israel, and Egypt. For several years he was artistic director of the National Orch. in Mexico City. In 1975 he was appointed conductor of the Göteborg Symph. Orch. in Sweden. In 1977 he was engaged as permanent conductor and music director of the Montreal Symph. Orch.; he found the work congenial, since it was centered on French culture; he greatly expanded the orch.'s repertoire; conducted 25 Haydn symphs., much music of Mozart and Beethoven, and especially French music, beginning with Berlioz and including Debussy and Ravel. He also promoted new Canadian music. Articulate in several languages, he speaks volubly of his future plans, which include new opera productions, and guest appearances in the U.S. In 1983 he was appointed principal guest conductor of the Minnesota Orch. in Minneapolis. Dutoit was married 3 times; his 2nd wife was the pianist **Mar-**

tha Argerich.

Dux, Claire, soprano; b. Bydgoszcz, Poland, Aug. 2, 1885; d. Chicago, Oct. 8, 1967. She studied voice with Teresa Arkel in Berlin; made her operatic debut in Cologne in 1906; in 1911–18, was a member of the Berlin State Opera (made her debut in *La Bohème* with Caruso); in 1912–14, sang at Covent Garden in London; in 1918–21, was a member of the Royal Opera in Stockholm; came to the U.S. in 1921 and joined the Chicago Civic Opera Co.; toured the U.S.; then retired. She was married to Charles Swift of Chicago, where she settled.

Dvořák, Antonin, famous Bohemian composer; b. Mühlhausen, Sept. 8, 1841; d. Prague, May 1, 1904. His father, an innkeeper, wished him to enter the butcher's trade; but he, having learned to play the violin from the village schoolmaster, left home at the age of 16 and entered the Prague Organ School, studying under Pitzsch and earning a precarious livelihood as a violinist in a small orch. For about a decade (1861–71), he played the viola in the orch. of the National Theater in Prague. It was not until 1873 that he brought out an important work, *Hymnus* for Mixed Chorus and Orch., which was performed on March 9 of that year and attracted wide notice; in 1875 he was awarded the Austrian State Prize for his Symph. in E-flat (perf. in Prague by Smetana in 1874), and he received that stipend repeatedly thereafter. He then devoted himself to composition with increasing success, becoming the most celebrated of Czech national composers. Liszt, Brahms, and Hans von Bülow, by securing performances and publication of his work, did much to obtain for his compositions the vogue they deservedly enjoy. In 1873 Dvořák gave up playing in orchs. when he was appointed organist at St. Adalbert's Church in Prague. His fame as a composer spread, and numerous pupils flocked to him; finally, a professorship in composition at the Prague Cons. was offered him. In 1884 he was invited to conduct his *Stabat Mater* in London. It was received with such enthusiasm that in the fall of the same year he conducted it at the Worcester Festival, and was commissioned to write a new work for the Birmingham Festival of 1885 (*The Spectre's Bride*). The following year (1886) he visited England again to direct his oratorio *St. Ludmila* at the Leeds Festival; in 1891 he was made an honorary Mus.Doc. by Cambridge Univ. and an honorary Dr.Phil. by the Czech Univ. in Prague. In 1892 he accepted an invitation to head the National Cons. in N.Y. It was in America that he wrote his most celebrated work, the symph. *From the New World* (first perf. by the N.Y. Phil., Dec. 15, 1893); the themes seemed to reflect Negro spirituals, but Dvořák denied any conscious design in this approximation. The work, though, by proposing the use of Negro themes—or Negro-like themes—in symphonic music, had an enormous impact on American musical nationalism. He discussed the idea further in an article, "Music in America," *Harper's New Monthly Magazine* (Feb. 1895), stating that although Americans had accomplished marvels in most fields of endeavor, in music they were decidedly backward and were content to produce poor imitations of European music; the way to salvation, he suggested, was in the development of a national style, a style based on the melodies of Negroes and Indians. This proposal was greeted with enthusiasm by one segment of America's musical world, but by another, fearing a musical miscegenation, it was rejected with disdain. The controversy that ensued raged for more than 2 decades. Upon returning to Prague in 1895, Dvořák resumed his professorship at the Cons.; was appointed its artistic director in 1901. He was the first musician to be made a life member of the Austrian House of Lords. He was a composer of singular versatility and fecundity; the most prominent characteristics of his music are an inexhaustible, spontaneous melodic invention, rhythmic variety, free employment of national folk tunes, and an intensity of harmony which, in his finest works, has an electrifying effect, though sometimes bordering on the crude. His musical style was eclectic; the conflicting influences of Brahms and Wagner occasionally effected an inner incompatibility; however, his very lack of startling originality, combined with an uninhibited emotionalism, contributed to the lasting success of his music.

WORKS: 10 OPERAS (All except the first produced in Prague): *Alfred*, without op. (1870; posthumous, Olomouc, Dec.10, 1938); *Král a uhlíř (The King and the Coal Burner)*, op. 14 (1871; Nov. 24, 1874); *Tvrdé palice (The Blockheads* or *The Pig-Headed Peasants)*, op. 17 (1874; Oct. 2, 1881); *Vanda*, op. 25 (April 17, 1876); *Šelma sedlák (The Peasant a Rogue)*, op. 37 (1877; Jan. 27, 1878); *Dimitrij*, op. 64 (Oct. 8, 1882; revised 1883, 1894); *Jakobin*, op. 84 (*The Jacobin*, 1887–88; Feb. 12, 1889; revised 1897); *Čert a Káča (The Devil and Kate)*, op. 112 (Nov. 23, 1899); *Rusalka*, op. 114 (1900; March 31, 1901; Dvořák's most popular opera); *Armida*, op. 115 (1902–3; March 25, 1904).

FOR ORCH.: 9 symphs., in a chronological renumbering: No. 1, *The Bells of Zlonice*, in C minor, op. 3 (1865; recovered in Prague in 1936 and first perf. there, Oct. 4, 1936); No. 2, in B-flat, op. 4 (1865); No. 3, in E-flat, op. 10 (1873); No. 4, in D minor, op. 13 (1874); No. 5, in F, op. 76 (originally op. 24; 1875); No. 6, in D, op. 60 (1880); No. 7, in D minor, op. 70 (1884–85); No. 8, in G, op. 88 (1888); No. 9, *From the New World*, in E minor, op. 95 (1892–93; N.Y. Phil., Dec. 15, 1893); Piano Concerto in G minor, op. 33 (1875); Violin Concerto in A minor, op. 53 (1879–80); Cello Concerto in B minor, op. 104 (1894–95); *Romance* for Violin and Orch., op. 11 (1873); *Mazurek* for Violin and Orch., op. 49 (1879); *Silent Woods* for Cello and Orch., op. 68 (1893); *Rondo* for Cello and Orch., op. 94 (1892); *Nocturne* in B for Strings, op. 40 (1870); *Serenade* in E for Strings, op. 22 (1875); *Symphonic Variations on an Original Theme*, op. 78 (1877); *Serenade* in D minor, op. 44, for Winds, Cellos, and Double Basses (1878); *Czech Suite* in D, op. 39 (1879); *10 Legends*, op. 59 (1881; originally for Piano, 4-hands); *American Suite* in A, op. 98b (1895; originally for Piano); 5 symph. poems: *The Watersprite*, op. 107 (1896); *The Midday Witch*, op. 108 (1896); *The Golden Spinningwheel*, op. 109 (1896); *The Wood Dove*, op. 110 (1896); *Heroic Song*, op. 111 (1897); overtures: *Dramatic (Tragic) Overture* (1870; from the opera *Alfred*); *My Home*, op. 62 (1881); *Husitská*, op. 67 (1883); *Amid Nature*, op. 91 (1891); *Carnival*, op. 92 (1891); *Othello*, op. 93 (1892); *3 Slavonic Rhapsodies*, op. 45 (1878); *Slavonic Dances*, in 2 sets, opp. 46, 72 (1878, 1886).

VOCAL WORKS: *Hymnus*, from Hálek's "The Heirs of the White Mountain," op. 30, for Chorus and Orch. (1872; revised 1880); *Stabat Mater*, op. 58, oratorio (1876–77); *Psalm 149*, op. 79, for Chorus and Orch. (1879); *The Spectre's Bride*, op. 69, cantata (1884); *St. Ludmila*, op. 71, oratorio (1885–86; amplified and perf. as an opera, *Svatá Ludmila*, Prague, Nov. 30, 1901); Mass in D, op. 86, for Solo Voices and Chorus (1887); *Requiem*, op. 89, for Soloists, Chorus, and Orch. (1890); *Te Deum*, op. 103, for Soprano, Baritone, Chorus, and Orch. (1892); *The American Flag*, op. 102, cantata (1893); choruses.

CHAMBER MUSIC: 3 string quintets (1861, 1875, 1893); 14 string quartets (1862–95); 2 piano quintets (1872, 1887); 2 piano quartets (1875, 1889); 4 piano trios (1875, 1876, 1883, 1891); String Sextet in A, op. 48 (1878); Bagatelles for 2 Violins, Cello, and Harmonium or Piano, op. 47 (1878); Violin Sonata in F, op. 57 (1880); *Terzetto* for String Trio, op. 74 (1887); *4 Romantic Pieces*, op. 75, for Violin and Piano (1887); Violin Sonatina in G, op. 100 (1893); piano pieces. A complete ed. of Dvořák's works, under the general editorship of O. Šourek, was begun in Prague in 1955 and continued after Šourek's death in 1956 by a committee of Czech scholars.

Dwight, John Sullivan, American music critic, and editor of *Dwight's Journal of Music;* b. Boston, May 13, 1813; d. there, Sept. 5, 1893. He graduated from Harvard in 1832, and was one of the founders and most active members of the Harvard Musical Assoc. After studying for the ministry, in 1840 he took charge of the Unitarian Church at Northampton, Mass. His literary and socialistic proclivities, however, gained the mastery; he gave up his pastorate, and entered the ill-starred Brook Farm Community as a teacher of German music and the classics. Returning to Boston in 1848, after the failure of the socialistic experiment, he devoted himself to literature, founded the journal in 1852, and remained its editor in chief until its discontinuance in 1881. A prominent feature in this periodical was the valuable historical essays of A.W. Thayer. The entire journal is available in reprint (N.Y., 1968). Dwight also publ. the excellent *Translations of Select Minor Poems from the German of Goethe and Schiller, with Notes.*

Dyer, Louise (Mrs. Louise B.M. Hanson), patroness of music and publisher; b. Melbourne, Australia, July 16, 1890; d. Monaco, Nov. 9, 1962. She established in Monaco an important publishing enterprise, L'Oiseau-Lyre (The Lyre-Bird Press), financing it entirely out of her own resources. The Lyre-Bird Press has issued a great number of unpubl. or obscure works of medieval and Renaissance French music.

Dylan, Bob (real name, **Robert Zimmerman**), American folksinger and songwriter; b. Duluth, Minn., May 24, 1941. He adopted the name Dylan out of admiration for the poet Dylan Thomas. Possessed by wanderlust, he rode freight trains across the country; played guitar and crooned in the coffeehouses of N.Y. He also improvised songs to his own lyrics. His nasalized country-type semi-Western style, and his self-haunted soft guitar-strumming captured the imagination not only of untutored adolescents but also of certified cognoscenti in search of convincing authenticity. In 1966 he broke his neck in a motorcycle accident, which forced him to interrupt his charismatic career for 2 years. In 1970 he was awarded an honorary doctorate from Princeton Univ., the first such honor given to a popular singer innocent of all academic training. A group of militants in the Students for a Democratic Society adopted the name "Weathermen" after a line from Dylan's song *Subterranean Homesick Blues,* "You don't need a weatherman to know which way the wind blows." The Weathermen claimed credit for several bombings in N.Y. City during 1969 and 1970.

Dyson, Sir George, English composer; b. Halifax (Yorkshire), May 28, 1883; d. Winchester, Sept. 28, 1964. He studied at the Royal College of Music in London; was its music director in 1937–52. He was knighted in 1941. His works include a Symph. (1937); Violin Concerto (1943); an oratorio, *Quo Vadis* (1949); Suite for Small Orch.; *3 Rhapsodies* for String Quartet; piano pieces; numerous pedagogic pieces and songs. His cantata *The Canterbury Pilgrims,* to words modernized from Chaucer's *Canterbury Tales,* is his best-known work; the overture to it was extracted in 1946, and performed separately under the title *At the Tabard Inn.* He further composed numerous sacred choruses; publ. the books *The New Music* (1924), *The Progress of Music* (1932), and a candid autobiography, *Fiddling While Rome Burns: A Musician's Apology* (London, 1954).

Dzerzhinsky, Ivan, Russian composer; b. Tambov, April 9, 1909; d. Moscow, Jan. 18, 1978. He studied with Asafiev at the Leningrad Cons. (1932–34). As a composer he espoused the doctrine of socialist realism. Possessing a facile gift of flowing melodiousness, he made a mark in Soviet music by his first opera, *Quiet Flows the Don,* to a libretto from the novel by the Soviet writer Sholokhov; in it he made use of peasant folk-song elements, emphasizing mass choruses. It was produced in Leningrad on Oct. 22, 1935, and became immediately successful when Stalin attended a performance in Moscow and personally congratulated the composer on his ability to create music in a characteristically Soviet style. He followed it with a sequel, *Virgin Soil Upturned,* which was produced in Moscow on October 23, 1937. His subsequent operas were *The Storm* (after Ostrovsky, 1940); *The Blood of the People* (Leningrad, Jan. 21, 1942); *The Blizzard* (after Pushkin, 1946); *Nadezhda Svetlova* (Orenburg, Sept. 8, 1943); and *A Man's Destiny* (Moscow, Sept. 30, 1961). He further wrote 3 piano concertos (1932, 1934, 1945); numerous piano pieces; songs.

E

Eames, Emma, famous soprano; b. of American parentage in Shanghai, China, Aug. 13, 1865; d. New York, June 13, 1952. Her mother, who was her first teacher, took her to America as a child; she then studied with Clara Munger in Boston and with Mme. Marchesi in Paris. She made her operatic debut at the Grand Opéra, March 13, 1889, as Juliette in Gounod's *Roméo et Juliette.* She subsequently sang at Covent Garden in London, and on Dec. 14, 1891, made her debut at the Metropolitan Opera House in N.Y., again in the role of Juliette. She remained with the Metropolitan until 1909, appearing as Marguerite in *Faust,* Desdemona in *Otello,* Elisabeth in *Tannhäuser,* Aida, Tosca, and Donna Anna in *Don Giovanni.* From 1923 to 1936 she made her home intermittently in Paris and Bath, Maine; in 1936 she settled in N.Y., where she remained until her death. She received the Jubilee Medal from Queen Victoria, and was decorated by the French Academy with the order of Les Palmes Académiques. Her emotional life was turbulent; she married the painter Julian Story in 1891, but they were separated in the midst of a widely publicized scandal; in 1911 she married the baritone **Emilio de Gogorza,** but left him too. She publ. an autobiography, *Some Memories and Reflections* (N.Y., 1927).

East (Easte, Este), Thomas, English music printer and publisher of Elizabethan madrigals; b. London, c.1535; d. there, Jan. 1608. He received his license as a printer in 1565; his first musical publication was Byrd's collection *Psalmes, Sonets and Songs of Sadnes and Pietie* (1588); he was also the assignee of Byrd's patent for printing music paper and musical compositions. In 1592 he brought out *The Whole Booke of Psalmes, with their wonted tunes as they are sung in Churches, composed in four parts,* containing harmonizations by Allison, Blancks, Cavendish, Cobbold, Dowland, Farmer, Farnaby, Hooper, Johnson, and Kirbye (republ. 1594 and 1604; reprinted in score by the Musical Antiquarian Society, 1844). This collection is of historical significance, for it was the first to be printed in score rather than in separate part-books; also for the first time, the tunes were designated by specific names, such as "Kentish" and "Cheshire." Other works printed by East are Yonge's *Musica Transalpina* (1588); Byrd's *Songs of Sundrie Natures* (1589); Watson's *Madrigals* (1590); Byrd's *Cantiones Sacrae* (2 books, 1589, 1591); Morley's *Canzonets* (1593); Mundy's *Songs and Psalmes* (1594); Kirbye's *Madrigals* (1596); Wilbye's *Madrigals* (1598); Dowland's *Ayres* (1600); Bateson's *Madrigals* (1603); Michael East's *Madrigals* (1604); Pilkington's *Songs or Ayres*

(1604); Byrd's *Gradualia* (1605); Youll's *Canzonets* (1607). East's presumed son **Michael East** (c.1580–1648) was a composer; his set of madrigals was publ. by Thomas East in 1604. He served as organist at Lichfield Cathedral; received the degree of B.Mus. at Cambridge (1606); he publ. 6 sets of vocal pieces (madrigals, anthems, etc.) and a set of instrumental works (1638).

Eastman, George, American industrialist; b. Waterville, N.Y., July 12, 1854; d. (suicide, when he learned he had cancer) Rochester, March 14, 1932. Eastman made important and far-reaching contributions to the cause of education; invested immense sums in scientific institutions, particularly the Univ. of Rochester, which includes the Eastman Theater and School of Music (one of the leading music schools of the U.S.). This alone he endowed with $3.5 million.

Easton, Florence, operatic soprano; b. South Bank, Yorkshire, Oct. 25, 1882; d. New York, Aug. 13, 1955. She studied singing with Agnes Larkcom and piano with Charles Reddie at the Royal Academy of Music in London, and singing with Elliott Haslam in Paris. Made her debut at Covent Garden in 1903; in 1906 she married the tenor **Francis Maclennan** (divorced in 1929); her 2nd husband was Stanley Rogers. She toured the U.S. with the Savage Grand Opera; then was engaged at the Berlin Opera (1907–13) and at Hamburg (1912–15). She was with the Chicago Opera from 1915 to 1917; from 1917 to 1929 she was a member of the Metropolitan Opera Co.; after a sojourn in Europe, she reappeared meteorically on leap-year day in 1936 at the Metropolitan as Brünnhilde in *Die Walküre.*

Eaton, John, American composer; b. Bryn Mawr, Pa., March 30, 1935. He received his A.B. and M.F.A. degrees from Princeton Univ., where he studied composition with Milton Babbitt, Edward Cone, and Roger Sessions; subsequently won 3 American Prix de Rome awards and two Guggenheim grants. In 1970 he became prof. of music at the Indiana Univ. School of Music in Bloomington. He lectured at the Salzburg Center in American Studies (1976) and was composer-in-residence at the American Academy in Rome (1976–77). In his works he avails himself of all resources of modern music, including serial techniques, microtones, and electronic media. In several of his scores he makes use of the Syn-Ket (a portable electronic synthesizer built by the Roman sound engineer Ketoff). WORKS: Operas: *Ma Barker* (1957); *Heracles* (1964; Turin, Italy, Oct. 10, 1968); *Myshkin,* after Dostoevsky's novel *The Idiot* (1971; Bloomington, Ind., April 23, 1973); *The Lion and Androcles,* for children (1973; Indianapolis, May 1, 1974); *Danton and Robespierre* (1978; Bloomington, April 21, 1978); *The Cry of Clytaemnestra* (1979; Bloomington, March 1, 1980). Other Works: *Song Cycle on Holy Sonnets of John Donne,* for Voice and Piano (1956); Piano Variations (1957); String Quartet (1958); *Tertullian Overture* (1958); *Adagio and Allegro* for Flute, Oboe, and Strings (1960); *Concert Piece* for Clarinet and Piano (1960); *Concert Music* for Solo Clarinet (1961); *Songs for R.P.B.* for Voice, Piano, and Synthesizer (1964); *Microtonal Fantasy* for 2 Pianos (1965); *Concert Piece* for Syn-Ket (1966); *Thoughts on Rilke* for Soprano, 2 Syn-Kets, and Syn-Mill (1966); *Concert Piece* for Syn-Ket and Symph. Orch. (1966; Berkshire Music Festival, Tanglewood, Mass., Aug. 9, 1967); *Soliloquy* for Electronic Sound Synthesizer (1967); *Vibrations* for 2 Oboes, 2 Clarinets, and Flute (1967); Duet for Syn-Ket and Moog Synthesizer (1968); *Blind Man's Cry* for Soprano and Orch. of Electronic Synthesizers (1968); Mass for Soprano, Clarinet, 3 Syn-Kets, Moog Synthesizer, and Syn-Mill (1970); *Sonority Movement* for Flute and 9 Harps (1971); *In Memoriam Mario Cristini,* piano trio (1971); *Ajax* for Baritone and Orch., after Sophocles (1972); *Guillen Songs* for Voice and Piano (1974); *Duo* for Mixed Chorus (1977); *A Greek Vision* for Soprano, Flute, and Electronics (1981; Chicago, Dec. 7, 1981); Symph. No. 2 (1980–81).

Eberl, Anton Franz Josef, Austrian pianist and composer; b. Vienna, June 13, 1765; d. there, March 11, 1807. On Feb. 27, 1787, he produced the singspiel *La Marchande des modes;* there followed several other stage works, including *Die Zigeuner* (1793). His symphs. and piano music were praised by Mozart and Gluck. He made a concert tour with Mozart's widow in 1795; lived in St. Petersburg from 1796 to 1799; revisited Russia in 1801; gave concerts there on Dec. 8, 15, and 28, 1801, presenting the first performances in Russia of Haydn's *The Creation;* returned to Vienna early in 1802; traveled through Germany in 1806. Besides 4 more stage works, he wrote 2 cantatas, symphs., piano concertos, much chamber music, many piano works (especially sonatas), songs, etc.

Eberlin (Eberle), Johann Ernst, German composer; b. Jettingen, Bavaria, March 27, 1702; d. Salzburg, June 19, 1762. He studied at Benedictine Univ. in Salzburg in 1721–23; was 4th organist at the Salzburg Cathedral (1726), and from 1729, organist and choirmaster there; from 1749, was court Kapellmeister to the Prince-Archbishop in Salzburg.

Eccard, Johannes, eminent German composer; b. Mühlhausen, 1553; d. Berlin, 1611. He was a chorister in the Kapelle at the Weimar court from 1567–71; then in the Bavarian Hofkapelle in Munich, where he was a pupil (1571–74) of Orlandus Lassus; was director of J. Fugger's private orch. at Augsburg (1577); in 1578 he moved to Königsberg, as a member of the Prussian chapel; in 1580 became its assistant conductor, and in 1604, chief conductor. In 1608 he was called to Berlin to serve as court musician to the Elector. He was an important composer of sacred music.

Eccles, John, English violinist and composer; b. London, c.1668; d. Kingston, Surrey, Jan. 12, 1735. He was the son and pupil of the violist **Solomon Eccles**

(1618–83). He became a member of the Queen's Band in 1694, and Master of it in 1700. He was active as a composer for the theater; in 1694 wrote music for *Don Quixote* (with Purcell) and *Don Carlos, Prince of Spain* (after T. Otway); in 1700, for Congreve's *The Judgment of Paris* (March 1701) and *The Way of the World* (March 1700); in 1710, he publ. a collection of his own songs (about 100), which enjoyed wide popularity. He also publ. 3 vols. of "Theatre Music" (c.1700). In all, he wrote music for 12 masques and 62 pieces of incidental music for the stage.

Eckard (Eckardt, Eckart), Johann Gottfried, German composer of keyboard music; b. Augsburg, Jan. 21, 1735; d. Paris, July 24, 1809. He was a copper engraver by profession and learned music in his spare time. In 1758 he was taken to Paris by the piano manufacturer J.A. Stein, and remained there. He acquired a great facility as a pianist, and gave successful concerts in Paris. In the preface to his album of 6 sonatas he states that his task was to compose music suitable for any keyboard instrument, but the indications of dynamics in the MS show that he had mainly the then-novel piano in view. Mozart admired Eckard's works, and there are traits in Mozart's keyboard music of the Paris period that may be traced to Eckard's usages. A complete edition of Eckard's works for piano, ed. by Eduard Reeser and annotated by J. Ligtelijn, has been publ. (Amsterdam, 1956).

Eckhard, Jacob, one of the early German organists in America; b. Eschwege (Hesse), Nov. 24, 1757; d. Charleston, S.C., Nov. 10, 1833. He came to the U.S. in 1776 and settled in Richmond, Va. In 1786 he was organist of St. John's Lutheran Church in Charleston; in 1809 received the post of organist at St. Michael's Episcopal Church. He publ. a hymn book (printed in Boston, 1816); wrote 2 patriotic naval songs, *The Pillar of Glory* and *Rise, Columbia, Brave and Free.*

Ecorcheville, Jules, French writer on music; b. Paris, July 17, 1872; d. Feb. 19, 1915 (fell in battle at Perthesles-Hurlus). He was a pupil of César Franck, 1887–90; a student of literature and art history in Paris and (1904–5) Leipzig; received a doctorat ès lettres (Paris, 1906); was editor of *La Revue Musicale S.I.M.* and a writer on the history and esthetics of music.

Edelmann, Jean-Frédéric, Alsatian musician of considerable accomplishments and a tempestuous and tragic life; b. Strasbourg, May 5, 1749; executed by guillotine in Paris, July 17, 1794. He studied law, matriculating from the Univ. of Strasbourg in 1770. In 1774 he went to Paris, where he became a successful music teacher; among his students was the opera composer Méhul. It was Edelmann who in his teaching and in his compositions made the piano a fashionable instrument in Paris. He joined the Jacobins during the Revolution, and this proved his undoing when the Revolution took a more violent turn.

Edwards, Julian, operetta composer; b. Manchester, England, Dec. 11, 1855; d. Yonkers, N.Y., Sept. 5, 1910. He was a pupil in Edinburgh of Sir H. Oakeley, and in London of Sir George Macfarren; conducted the Royal English Opera Co. (1877) and the English Opera at Covent Garden (1883); came to the U.S. in 1888, settling in Yonkers and devoting himself entirely to composition. Some of his comic operas achieved more than average success, among them *Victoria* (Sheffield, March 6, 1883); *Jupiter* (N.Y., April 14, 1892); *Friend Fritz* (N.Y., Jan. 26, 1893); *King Rene's Daughter,* lyric drama (N.Y., Nov. 22, 1893); *Madeleine* (N.Y., July 31, 1894); *The Goddess of Truth* (N.Y., Feb. 26, 1896); *Brian Boru,* romantic Irish opera (N.Y., Oct. 19, 1896); *The Wedding Day* (N.Y., April 8, 1897); *The Patriot* (1907; N.Y., Nov. 23, 1908; revived, July 24, 1975, at the Newport, R.I., Music Festival; the libretto deals with an attempted assassination of George Washington).

Edwards, Richard, English composer; b. Somersetshire, near Yeovil, c.1522; d. London, Oct. 31, 1566. He studied at Oxford (M.A. in 1547); was (from 1561) master of the children of the Chapel Royal. With these choirboys he presented in 1565 his musical play *Damon and Pithias* (publ. in 1571). Edwards is best known for his madrigal "In going to my naked bed," written about 20 years before the madrigal became popular in England (this piece is reprinted by Fellowes in *The English Madrigal School,* 36).

Eeden, Jean-Baptiste van den, Belgian composer; b. Ghent, Dec. 26, 1842; d. Mons, April 4, 1917. He was a pupil in the conservatories at Ghent and Brussels, winning at the latter the first prize for composition (1869) with the cantata *Faust's laatste nacht.* In 1878, he was appointed director of the Mons Cons., succeeding Huberti.
WORKS: Operas: *Numance* (Antwerp, Feb. 2, 1897) and *Rhena* (Brussels, Feb. 15, 1912); oratorios: *Brutus; Jacqueline de Bavière; Jacob van Artevelde; Le Jugement dernier;* dramatic scene for 3 Voices, *Judith;* 2 cantatas: *Het Woud* and *De Wind;* symph. poem, *La Lutte au XVIᵉ siècle; Marche des esclaves;* etc.; also choruses and songs.

Effinger, Cecil, American composer; b. Colorado Springs, July 22, 1914. He studied violin and oboe; then went to Paris, where he attended classes in composition with Nadia Boulanger. Returning to America, he was first oboist in the Denver Symph. Orch.; then served as bandmaster in the U.S. Army in France (1942–45). Beginning with 1936, he taught music at the Univ. of Colorado, in Boulder, retaining this post until 1981; then continued as composer-in-residence there. In his own music, he maintains a median modern style, making use of polytonal and atonal procedures, without abandoning the basic sense of tonality. Effinger is the inventor of a practical music typewriter patented in 1955 under the name "Musicwriter."
WORKS: Opera, *Cyrano de Bergerac* (Univ. of

Colorado, Boulder, July 21, 1965); children's opera, *Pandora's Box* (1962); 5 symphs. (1946–58); 2 sinfoniettas (1945, 1958); Piano Concerto (1946); Choral Symph. (Denver, Dec. 2, 1952); cantata, *The St. Luke Christmas Story* (1953); *Symphonie concertante* for Harp, Piano, and Orch. (1954); *Tone Poem on the Square Dance* for Orch. (1955); oratorio, *The Invisible Fire* (1957); *Trio concertante* for Trumpet, Horn, Trombone, and Chamber Orch. (1964); 4 string quartets (1943, 1944, 1948, 1963); Viola Sonata (1944); Suite for Cello and Piano (1945); *Pastoral* for Oboe and Strings (1948); *Landscape* for Brass and Strings (1966); Violin Concerto (1974); *The Long Dimension* for Baritone, Chorus, and Orch., (1970); *A Cantata for Easter* (1971); *Quiet Evening* for Flute, Marimba, and Strings (1972); *This We Believe*, oratorio (1975); *Capriccio* for Orch. (1975); music drama, *The Gentleman Desperado and Miss Bird* (1976).

Egenolff, Christian, early German music printer; b. Hadamar, July 26, 1502; d. Frankfurt, Feb. 9, 1555. He publ. 2 collections of 4-part songs, *Gassenhawerlin* and *Reutterliedlin* (1535; facsimile ed. publ. by Moser, Augsburg, 1927), which are of decided value.

Egge, Klaus, prominent Norwegian composer; b. Gransherad, Telemark, July 19, 1906; d. Oslo, March 7, 1979. He studied piano with Nils Larsen and composition with Fartein Valen; after a brief period of further instruction at the Hochschule für Musik in Berlin, he became engaged in organizational work in Norway; was president of the Society of Norwegian composers from 1945. In 1949 he received the State Salary of Art (a government life pension for outstanding artistic achievement). His style of composition is conditioned by Scandinavian modalities, within a framework of euphonious and resonantly modernistic harmonies. He likes to sign his scores with the notes E-g-g-e of his name, a motto which also serves him occasionally as a basic theme.
WORKS: 3 piano concertos: No. 1 (Oslo, Nov. 14, 1938); No. 2 (Oslo, Dec. 9, 1946); No. 3 (Bergen, April 25, 1974); *Sveinung Vreim* for Soli, Chorus, and Orch. (Oslo, Dec. 1, 1941); *Fjell-Norig (Mountainous Norway)* for Voice and Orch. (Oslo, Oct. 1, 1945); *Noreg-songer (The Norway Song)* for Chorus and Orch. (Oslo, May 2, 1952); 5 symphs.: No. 1, *Lagnadstonar (Sounds of Destiny;* Oslo, Oct. 4, 1945); No. 2, *Sinfonia giocosa* (Oslo, Dec. 9, 1949); No. 3, commissioned by the Louisville Orch. (Louisville, Ky., March 4, 1959); No. 4, *Sinfonia seriale sopra B.A.C.H—E.G.G.E* (Detroit, March 28, 1968); No. 5, *Sinfonia dolce quasi passacaglia* (Oslo, Sept. 27, 1969); *Elskhugskvaede (Love Song)* for Voice and Strings (1942); *Draumar i stjernesno (Starsnow Dreams)*, 3 songs for Soprano and Orch. (1943); *Fanitullen (Devil's Dance)*, ballet (Oslo, 1950); *Tärn over Oslo*, overture (1950); Violin Concerto (Oslo, Nov. 5, 1953); Cello Concerto (Oslo, Sept. 9, 1966); Violin Sonata (1932); 2 piano sonatas: No. 1, *Draumkvede (Dream Vision;* 1933), and No. 2, *Patética* (1955); String Quartet (1933; revised 1963); 3 Fantasies for Piano in the rhythms of the Norwegian dances Halling, Springar, and Gangar, (1939);

2 wind quintets (1939, 1976); Piano Trio (1941); *Duo concertante* for Violin and Viola (1950); Sonatina for Harp (1974); choruses and songs.

Eggebrecht, Hans Heinrich, eminent German musicologist and editor; b. Dresden, Jan. 5, 1919. He attended the Gymnasium in Schleusingen, of which his father was superintendent; was drafted into the army during World War II, through which he went unscathed, and then studied music education in Berlin and Weimar; he received his teacher's certificate in 1948. He subsequently studied musicology with H.J. Moser, R. Münnich, and M. Schneider; received his Ph.D. in 1949 from the Univ. of Jena with the dissertation *Melchior Vulpius.* He was assistant lecturer under W. Vetter in music history at the Univ. of Berlin from 1949 to 1951; then did lexicographical work in Freiburg and taught musicology at the univ. there (1953–55); he completed his Habilitation there in 1955 with his *Studien zur musikalischen Terminologie* (publ. in Mainz, 1955; 2nd ed., 1968). He was Privatdozent at Erlangen Univ. (1955–56) and taught musicology at the Univ. of Heidelberg (1956–57). In 1961 he succeeded W. Gurlitt as prof. of musicology at the Univ. of Freiburg. In 1964 he became editor of the *Archiv für Musikwissenschaft.* One of his major musicological contributions was his publ. of the vol. on musical terms and historical subjects (*Sachteil*) for the 12th edition of the *Riemann Musik-Lexikon* (Mainz, 1967), in which he settles many debatable points of musical terminology. Equally important has been his editorship of the *Handwörterbuch der musikalischen Terminologie* since 1972. He also was an editor of the *Brockhaus-Riemann Musik-Lexikon* with Carl Dahlhaus (2 vols., Wiesbaden and Mainz, 1978).

Egk, Werner, significant German composer; b. Auchsesheim, near Donauwörth, May 17, 1901; d. Inning, near Munich, July 10, 1983. His original name was **Mayer,** and rumor had it that he took the name Egk as a self-complimentary acronym for "ein grosser (or even ein genialer) Komponist." Egk himself rejected this frivolous suspicion, offering instead an even more fantastic explanation that Egk was a partial acronym of the name of his wife Elisabeth Karl, with the middle guttural added "for euphony." He studied piano with Anna Hirzel-Langenhan and composition with Carl Orff in Munich, where he made his permanent home. Primarily interested in theater music, he wrote several scores for a Munich puppet theater; was also active on the radio; then wrote ballet music to his own scenarios and a number of successful operas. He was also active as opera conductor and music pedagogue. He conducted at the Berlin State Opera from 1938 to 1941, and was head of the German Union of Composers from 1941 to 1945. He was commissioned to write music for the Berlin Olympiad in 1936, for which he received a Gold Medal. He also received a special commission of 10,000 marks from the Nazi Ministry of Propaganda. The apparent favor that Egk enjoyed during the Nazi reign made it necessary for him to stand trial before the Allied Committee for the de-Nazification proceedings in 1947; it absolved him of political taint. In 1950–53 he was director of the Berlin Hochschule für Musik. As a composer, Egk continued the tradition of Wagner and Richard Strauss, without excluding, however, the use of acidulous harmonies, based on the atonal extension of tonality. The rhythmic investiture of his works is often inventive and bold.

WORKS: Piano Trio (1922); Passacaglia for Strings (1923); String Quartet (1924); String Quintet (1924); radio opera, *Columbus* (Munich, July 13, 1933; first stage perf., Frankfurt, Jan. 13, 1942); *Die Zaubergeige*, opera in 3 acts (Frankfurt, May 19, 1935); *Fürchtlosigkeit und Wohlwollen* (Baden-Baden, April 3, 1936); *Olympische Festmusik* for Orch. (Berlin Olympiad, Aug. 1, 1936); cantatas: *Natur-Liebe-Tod* and *Mein Vaterland* (both perf. at Göttingen, June 26, 1937); *Peer Gynt*, opera (Berlin, Nov. 24, 1938, composer conducting; highly successful despite the inevitable comparisons with Grieg); *Joan von Zarissa*, ballet (Berlin, Jan. 20, 1940); *La Tentation de Saint Antoine* for Contralto and String Quartet (Baden-Baden, May 18, 1947); Piano Sonata (1947); *Abraxas*, ballet (Baden-Baden Radio, Dec. 7, 1947; stage perf., June 6, 1948, in Munich); *Circe*, opera after Calderón (Berlin, Dec. 18, 1948, composer conducting); 2 sonatas for Orch. (1948, 1969); *Französische Suite*, after Rameau, for Orch. (Munich, Jan. 28, 1950); *Ein Sommertag*, ballet (Berlin, June 11, 1950); *Allegria*, suite for Orch. (Baden-Baden radio, April 25, 1952); *Die chinesische Nachtigall*, ballet after Andersen (Munich, May 6, 1953); *Chanson et Romance* for Coloratura Soprano and Chamber Orch. (Aix-en-Provence, July 19, 1953); *Irische Legende*, opera after Yeats (Salzburg, Aug. 17, 1955); *Der Revisor*, opera after Gogol (Schwetzingen, May 9, 1957); *Variations on a Caribbean Theme* for Orch. (Baden-Baden, Jan. 18, 1960); *Die Verlobung in San Domingo*, opera (Munich, Nov. 27, 1963); *17 Days & 4 Minutes*, burlesque opera (Stuttgart, June 2, 1966); *Casanova in London*, ballet (Munich, Nov. 23, 1969); *Moria* for Orch. (Nuremberg, Jan. 12, 1973).

Ehlert, Louis, German composer, conductor, and writer on music; b. Königsberg, Jan. 13, 1825; d. Wiesbaden, Jan. 4, 1884. In 1845 he entered the Leipzig Cons., where he studied with Mendelssohn and Schumann; then took music courses in Vienna and Berlin, where he lived from 1850 to 1863. He visited Italy; conducted the Società Cherubini in 1869; from 1869 to 1871 taught piano at Tausig's school for advanced pianists; then was active in Meiningen and Wiesbaden mainly as a piano teacher. He wrote a great many piano pieces; also *Frühlingssinfonie* and *Requiem für ein Kind*. His collection of essays, *Aus der Tonwelt* (Berlin, 1877), was publ. also in Eng. under the title *From the Tone World* (N.Y., 1885); he also wrote an entertaining vol., *Briefe über Musik an eine Freundin* (Berlin, 1859), which was issued in an Eng. trans. as *Letters on Music, to a Lady* (Boston, 1870).

Ehrling, Sixten, noted Swedish pianist and conductor; b. Malmö, April 3, 1918. He studied piano, organ, composition, and conducting at the Royal Academy of Music's Cons. in Stockholm. After a brief career as a concert pianist he joined the staff of the Royal Opera in Stockholm as a rehearsal pianist, and made his conducting debut there in 1940. He then took conducting lessons with Karl Böhm in Dresden (1941) and, after the end of the war, with Albert Wolff in Paris. In 1942 he was appointed conductor in Göteborg; in 1944 he became a conductor at the Royal Opera in Stockholm, where he served as chief conductor from 1953 to 1960. From 1963 to 1973 he was music director of the Detroit Symph. Orch.; then headed the orch. conducting class at the Juilliard School of Music, N.Y. In 1978 he became music adviser and principal guest conductor of the Denver Symph. Orch., and from 1979, principal guest conductor. He excels in the repertoire of Romantic music, and particularly in his authentic interpretation of works by Scandinavian composers.

Eichberg, Julius, German violinist and composer; b. Düsseldorf, June 13, 1824; d. Boston, Jan. 19, 1893. His first teachers were J. Fröhlich (at Würzburg) and J. Rietz (at Düsseldorf); he then (1843–45) attended the Brussels Cons., studying under Fétis, Meerts, and Bériot; in 1846 was appointed prof. of violin and composition at the Geneva Cons.; in 1856 came to N.Y.; settled in Boston in 1859 as director of the Museum Concerts (till 1866). He also became director of the Boston Cons. and superintendent of music in the public schools; he founded the Eichberg School for Violin.

WORKS: Light operas: *The Doctor of Alcantara* (Boston, April 7, 1862); *The Rose of Tyrol* (1865); *The 2 Cadis* (Boston, March 5, 1868); studies, duets, and characteristic pieces for violin; trios and quartets for strings; songs.

Eichheim, Henry, American composer and violinist; b. Chicago, Jan. 3, 1870; d. Montecito, near Santa Barbara, Calif., Aug. 22, 1942. He received his elementary musical training from his father, **Meinhard Eichheim,** a cellist in the Theodore Thomas Orch.; then studied with C. Becker and L. Lichtenberg at the Chicago Musical College. After a season as a violinist in the Thomas Orch. in Chicago, he was a member of the Boston Symph. Orch. (1890–1912); then devoted himself to concert work and composition. He made 4 trips to the Orient (1915, 1919, 1922, 1928) and collected indigenous instruments, which he subsequently used in his orch. music. All of his works are on oriental subjects.

WORKS: *Oriental Impressions,* or *The Story of the Bell* (Boston Symph., March 24, 1922, composer conducting); *The Rivals,* ballet based on an ancient Chinese legend (Chicago, Jan. 1, 1925; as an orch. piece, under the title *Chinese Legend* Boston Symph., April 3, 1925, composer conducting); *Malay Mosaic* (International Composers' Guild, N.Y., March 1, 1925); *Impressions of Peking* and *Korean Sketch* for Chamber Orch. and a group of Oriental Instruments (Venice Festival of the International

Society for Contemporary Music, Sept. 3, 1925); *Burma,* symph. poem (Neighborhood Playhouse Co., N.Y., March 16, 1926, as incidental music for a play; Chicago Symph. Orch., Feb. 18, 1927, composer conducting); *Java* (Philadelphia Orch., Nov. 8, 1929, composer conducting; contains a "gamelan" section, with 45 instruments); *Bali* (Philadelphia Orch., Stokowski conducting, April 20, 1933, at a Youth Concert); Violin Sonata (1934); other chamber music. The harmonic idiom of these works is derived from Debussy and Scriabin.

Eimert, Herbert, German music theorist; b. Bad Kreuznach, April 8, 1897; d. Cologne, Dec. 15, 1972. He studied at the Cons. and the Univ. of Cologne (musicology and philosophy); became interested in new musical techniques and publ. several essays on the subject, among them *Atonale Musiklehre* (Leipzig, 1924) and *Lehrbuch der Zwölftontechnik* (Wiesbaden, 1950). He composed several pioneering electronic works including *Chimes* (1953–54); *Etude on Sound Mixtures* (1954); and *5 Compositions* (1955–56).

Einem, Gottfried von, outstanding Austrian composer; b. Bern, Switzerland (where his father was attached to the Austrian embassy), Jan. 24, 1918. He went to Germany as a child; studied at Plön, Holstein; then was opera coach at the Berlin Staatsoper. In 1938 he was arrested by the Gestapo, and spent 4 months in prison. After his release he studied composition with Boris Blacher in Berlin (1941–43); was later (1944) in Dresden, where he became resident composer and music adviser at the Dresden State Opera; was then active in Salzburg. In 1953 he visited the U.S.; then settled in Vienna; in 1965 was appointed prof. at the Hochschule für Musik there. Having absorbed the variegated idioms of advanced techniques, Einem produced a number of successful short operas and ballets; in his music he emphasized the dramatic element by dynamic and rhythmic effects; his harmonic idiom is terse and strident; his vocal line often borders on atonality, but remains singable.
WORKS: OPERAS: *Dantons Tod* (Salzburg, Aug. 6, 1947); *Der Prozess (The Trial),* after Kafka (Salzburg Festival, Aug. 17, 1953); *Der Zerrissene* (Hamburg, Sept. 17, 1964); *Der Besuch der alten Dame,* after Dürrenmatt's play (Vienna, May 23, 1971); *Kabale und Liebe,* after Schiller's play (Vienna, Dec. 17, 1976); *Jesu Hochzeit* (Vienna, May 18, 1980; caused a scandal for depicting Christ as having taken a wife). BALLETS: *Prinzessin Turandot* (Dresden, Feb. 5, 1944); *Rondo vom goldenen Kalb* (Hamburg, Feb. 1, 1952); *Pas de cœur* (Munich, July 22, 1952); *Glück, Tod und Traum* (Alpbach, Aug. 23, 1954); *Medusa* (Vienna, Jan. 16, 1957; revised 1971). FOR ORCH.: *Capriccio* (Berlin, March 3, 1943); Concerto for Orch. (1943; Berlin, April 3, 1944, Karajan conducting); *Orchestra Music* (1947; Vienna, June 21, 1948, Böhm conducting); *Serenade* for Double String Orch. (1949; Berlin, Jan. 31, 1950); *Hymnus* for Alto, Chorus, and Orch. (1949; Vienna, March 31, 1951); *Meditations* (Louisville, Nov. 6, 1954); Piano Concerto (1955; Berlin, Oct. 6, 1956); *Symphonic Scenes* (1956; Boston, Oct. 11, 1957); *Ballade* (1957; Cleveland, March 20, 1958, Szell conducting); *Das Stundenlied* for Chorus and Orch., after Brecht (Hamburg, March 1, 1959); *Dance Rondo* (Munich, Nov. 13, 1959); *Nachtstück* (1960; Kassel, Nov. 16, 1962); *Von der Liebe,* lyrical fantasies for High Voice and Orch. (Vienna, June 18, 1961); *Philadelphia Symphony* (Vienna, Nov. 11, 1961, Solti conducting; Philadelphia, Nov. 9, 1962); *Chamber Songs* for Voice and Orch. (1964); Violin Concerto (1966; Vienna, May 31, 1970); *Hexameron* (1969; Los Angeles, Feb. 19, 1970); *Bruckner Dialog* (1971; Linz, March 23, 1974); *Rosa Mystica* for Voice and Orch. (1972; Vienna, June 4, 1973; Fischer-Dieskau, soloist); *An die Nachgeborenen* for Soloists, Chorus, and Orch. (N.Y., Oct. 24, 1975); *Wiener Symphonie* (1976; Minneapolis, Nov. 16, 1977); *Arietten* for Piano and Orch. (1977; Berlin, Feb. 20, 1978); *Ludi Leopoldini,* variations on a theme of Emperor Leopold I (Berlin, Oct. 12, 1980). CHAMBER WORKS: Sonata for Violin and Piano (1949); *Sacred Sonata* for Soprano, Trumpet, and Organ (1971); *Die traumenden Knaben* for Chorus, Bassoon, and Clarinet (1972); 3 string quartets (1975, 1977, 1980); Wind Quintet (1975); Sonata for Solo Violin (1976); Sonata for Solo Viola (1980); *Steinbeis Serenade* for 8 Instruments (1981); 8 sets of lieder (1944–80).

Einstein, Alfred, preeminent German musicologist; b. Munich, Dec. 30, 1880; d. El Cerrito, Calif., Feb. 13, 1952. Although he was friendly with Albert Einstein, the two were not related; a search through the genealogies of both revealed no common ancestor. Alfred Einstein first studied law, then turned to music and took courses with Sandberger and Beer-Walbrunn at the Univ. of Munich, receiving a Dr.Phil. in 1903 with the thesis *Zur deutschen Literatur für Viola da Gamba im 16. und 17. Jahrhundert* (Leipzig, 1905); in 1918–33 he was editor of the *Zeitschrift für Musikwissenschaft;* lived in Munich until 1927 as music critic of the *Münchner Post;* in 1927–33 he was an influential critic of the *Berliner Tageblatt;* in 1933 he left Germany; lived in London and Italy (near Florence); in 1938 settled in the U.S.; taught at Smith College (retired, 1950); was naturalized as an American citizen on March 2, 1945.
WRITINGS: Revised eds. of Riemann's *Musiklexikon* (9th ed., 1919; 10th eds., 1922; 11th enlarged ed., 1929); *Neues Musiklexikon* (German ed. of A. Eaglefield-Hull's *Dictionary of Modern Music and Musicians,* 1926); *Geschichte der Musik,* with *Beispielsammlung zur älteren Musikgeschichte* (1917–18; 6th ed., revised, 1953; new ed. (3rd) of Köchel's *Mozart Verzeichnis* (Leipzig, 1937; very valuable; reprint ed. with numerous corrections, Ann Arbor, 1947); *A Short History of Music* (London, 1936; N.Y., 1937; 4th ed., 1954; trans. of *Geschichte der Musik*); *Gluck* (London, 1936). He contributed a great many valuable papers to the publications of the International Music Society and to other learned editions, to Festschriften, Jahrbücher, etc.; his articles for the *Musical Quarterly* are

especially notable: "The Madrigal" (Oct. 1924); "Dante, on the Way to the Madrigal" (Jan. 1939; also "A Supplement," Oct. 1939); etc. He also prepared a modern ed. of Andrea Antico's publication of 1517, *Canzoni, Sonetti, Strambotti, et Frottole* (Northampton, Mass., 1941); ed. a collection, *The Golden Age of the Madrigal* (N.Y., 1942). His writings in America (publ. in Eng. trans. from his original German) include: *Greatness in Music* (N.Y., 1941; German ed., *Grösse in der Musik*, Zürich, 1951); *Mozart: His Character, His Work* (N.Y., 1945; 4th ed., 1949; German original, 1947); *Music in the Romantic Era* (N.Y., 1947; German ed., *Die Romantik in der Musik*, Vienna, 1950); *The Italian Madrigal* (3 vols., Princeton, 1949; of fundamental importance); *Schubert: A Musical Portrait* (N.Y., 1950; German trans., 1952); *Essays on Music*, ed. by P. Lang (N.Y., 1956; posthumous; 2nd ed., revised, 1958). A profound scholar, Einstein was also a brilliant journalist, with a vivid, richly metaphorical style, capable of conveying to the reader an intimate understanding of music of different eras.

Eisenberg, Maurice, outstanding cellist; b. Königsberg, Feb. 24, 1900; d. (while teaching a cello class at the Juilliard School of Music) New York, Dec. 13, 1972. He was brought to the U.S. as a child; studied violin; then, at the age of 12, took up the cello. He played as a youth in café orchs., and studied at the Peabody Cons. in Baltimore; was a cellist of the Philadelphia Orch. (1917–19); then joined the N.Y. Symph. (under Walter Damrosch). He went to Europe in 1927 and studied in Berlin with Hugo Becker; in Leipzig with Julius Klengel; in Paris with Alexanian; and in Spain with Casals; then taught at the Ecole Normale in Paris (1930–37); returning to the U.S., he gave a concert in N.Y. (Dec. 27, 1937) with excellent success; then appeared with major symph. orchs.; taught at various colleges; publ. a book, *Cello Playing of Today* (1957).

Eisler, Hanns, remarkable German composer; b. Leipzig, July 6, 1898; d. Berlin, Sept. 6, 1962. He studied at the New Vienna Cons.; was a pupil of Arnold Schoenberg in composition; won the Music Prize of the City of Vienna (1924); taught in Berlin from 1925 to 1933; came to the U.S. in 1933; lectured on music at The New School for Social Research in N.Y. (1935–36); was musical assistant to Charlie Chaplin in Hollywood (1942–47); left the U.S. under the terms of "voluntary deportation" in 1948, on account of his radical political past; then lived in Vienna and in Berlin. Under Schoenberg's influence, he adopted the 12-tone method of composition; most of his symph. works are in this advanced style. However, he demonstrated his capacity for writing simple songs for use of choral ensembles; several of his choruses for workers and for the Red Army have become popular in Russia. Eisler was the author of the music of the national anthem of the German Democratic Republic, *Auferstanden aus Ruinen*, adopted in 1949. An edition of his collected works was initiated by the German Academy of the Arts in East Berlin in connection with the Hanns Eisler Archive in 1968, in 3 vols.: I, vocal music; II, instrumental music; III, writings and documents. WORKS: Opera, *Johannes Faustus* (East Berlin, March 11, 1953); over 40 scores of incidental music, to plays by Brecht (*Rote Revue; Die Rundköpfe und die Spitzköpfe; Galileo Galilei; Die Tage der Kommune;* etc.), Ernst Toller (*Feuer aus der Kesseln*), Feuchtwanger (*Kalkutta, 4. Mai*), Shakespeare, Schiller, Aristophanes; about 40 film scores (*Der Rat der Götter; Die Hexen von Salem; Trübe Wasser;* etc.); cantatas (*Tempo des Zeit; Die Massnahme; Kalifornische Ballade;* etc.); several cantatas to texts by Brecht (*Die Weissbrotkantate; Kantate im Exil; Kriegskantate; Kantate auf den Tod eines Genossen;* etc.); *Deutsche Symphonie* for Soli, 2 Speakers, Chorus, and Orch. (Paris, June 25, 1937); 6 orch. suites (Nos. 2–6 from film scores; 1930–34); *Kleine Symphonie* (1931–32); 5 *Orchestral Pieces* (1938); *Kammersinfonie* (1940); *Rhapsody* for Orch. and Soprano (1949); *Ernste Gesänge* for Baritone and String Orch. (1962); chamber music: 2 nonets (1939); 2 septets (1941–47); *Divertimento* for Wind Quintet (1923); *14 Arten, den Regen zu beschreiben* for Flute, Clarinet, Violin, Cello, and Piano (1947); String Quartet (1941); Quintet for Flute, Clarinet, Violin, Cello, and Piano (1941–44); Sonata for Flute, Oboe, and Harp (1935); Duo for Violin and Cello (1925); Violin Sonata (1937); 3 piano sonatas (1922, 1923, 1943); piano albums for children; numerous choruses; mass songs, among them several to Brecht's words (*Das Einheitsfrontlied,* etc.). He publ. a book, *Composing for the Films* (N.Y., 1947).

Eisler, Paul, Austrian pianist and conductor; b. Vienna, Sept. 9, 1875; d. New York, Oct. 16, 1951. He was a pupil of Bruckner at the Vienna Cons.; conducted in Riga, Vienna, and at the Metropolitan Opera in N.Y.; made numerous tours as accompanist for Caruso, Ysaÿe, and other celebrated artists; composed several operettas (*Spring Brides; The Sentinel; The Little Missus; In the Year 1814*).

Eitner, Robert, eminent German musicologist; b. Breslau, Oct. 22, 1832; d. Templin, Feb. 2, 1905. He was a pupil of M. Brosig; settled (1853) in Berlin as a teacher, and gave concerts (1857–59) of his own compositions. He established a piano school in 1863, and publ. *Hilfsbuch beim Klavierunterricht* (1871). He devoted himself chiefly to musical literature, and especially to research on works of the 16th and 17th centuries. One of the founders of the Berlin *Gesellschaft für Musikforschung*, he edited its *Monatshefte für Musikgeschichte* from 1869 till his death; also the *Publikationen älterer praktischer und theoretischer Musikwerke*. WRITINGS: "Verzeichnis neuer Ausgaben alter Musikwerke aus der frühesten Zeit bis zum Jahr 1800," *Monatshefte* (1871); *Bibliographie der Musiksammelwerke des 16. und 17. Jahrhunderts* (with Haberl, Lagerberg, and Pohl); "Verzeichnis der gedruckten Werke von Hans Leo Hassler und Orlandus de Lassus," *Monatshefte* (1873–74); "S.G.

Staden's 'Seelewig,' " *Monatshefte* (1881); *Die Oper von ihren ersten Anfängen bis 1750* (3 vols., 1881–85); *Quellen und Hilfswerke beim Studium der Musikgeschichte* (1891); *Buch- und Musikaliendrucker nebst Notenstecher* (1904; as supplement to *Monatshefte*). His principal work is the great *Biographisch-bibliographisches Quellenlexikon der Musiker und Musikgelehrten der Christlichen Zeitrechnung bis zur Mitte des 19. Jahrhunderts* (10 vols., Leipzig, 1899–1904; additions and corrections publ. from 1913–16 in a quarterly, *Miscellanea Musicae Bio-bibliographica,* ed. by H. Springer, M. Schneider, and W. Wolffheim; reprinted N.Y., 1947). Among Eitner's compositions (several of which were publ.) are a biblical opera, *Judith;* an overture; a piano fantasia on themes from *Tristan und Isolde;* songs.

Eklund, Hans, Swedish composer; b. Sandviken, July 1, 1927. He studied at the Royal Academy of Music in Stockholm with Lars-Erik Larsson (1949–52); then went to Berlin, where he took lessons with Ernst Pepping (1954). His music follows a tradition of neo-Classicism; most of his instrumental works are set in Baroque forms.
    WORKS: Radio opera, *Moder Svea (Mother Svea)* for Soloists, Chorus, Trumpet, and Strings (Swedish Radio, Oct. 7, 1972); Variations for Strings (1952); *Symphonic Dances* (1954); 6 numbers of *Musica da camera:* No. 1, for Cello and Chamber Orch. (1955); No. 2, *Art Tatum in Memoriam,* for Trumpet, Piano, Percussion, and Strings (1956); No. 3, for Violin and Chamber Orch. (1957); No. 4, for Piano and Orch. (1959); No. 5, Fantasia, for Cello and String Orch. (1970); No. 6, for Oboe and Chamber Orch. (1970); 4 symphs.: No. 1, *Sinfonia seria* (1958); No. 2, *Sinfonia breve* (1964); No. 3, *Sinfonia rustica* (1967–68); No. 4, *Hjalmar Branting in memoriam,* for Narrator, Orch., and Tape (1973–74); *Music for Orchestra* (1960); *Bocetos españoles* for Chamber Orch. (1961); *Songs from Stahl,* cantata (1961); *Variazioni brevi* for Orch. (1962); *Introduzione-Versioni e Finale* for Strings (1962–63); *Facce* for Orch. (1964); Toccata for Orch. (1966); *Interludio* for Orch. (1967); *Primavera* for Strings (1967); *Pezzo elegiaco* for Cello, Percussion, and Strings (1969); *Introduction and Allegro* for Harpsichord and String Orch. (1972); Concerto for Trombone, Winds, and Percussion (1972); 4 string quartets (withdrawn, 1954, 1960, 1964); *Little Serenade* for Violin, Clarinet, and Double Bass (1954); Solo Violin Sonata (1956); *Improvisata* for Wind Quintet (1958); *Canzona and Dance* for Solo Violin (1962); Piano Trio (1963); *4 Pieces* for Solo Clarinet (1963); *Invocazione* for Chorus, Piano, and Percussion (1963); *4 Temperamenti* for 4 Clarinets (1963); *Zodinai* for Flute, 2 Clarinets, Bassoon, and Piano (1966); *Per Violoncello* (1967); *Sommarparafras* for Wind Quintet (1968); Toccata and Fugue for Piano (1971); *Notturno,* 3 pieces for Piano (1972); *5 Bagatelles* for Solo Oboe (1973); *4 Pieces* for Solo Bassoon (1973).

El-Dabh, Halim, Egyptian composer; b. Cairo, March 4, 1921. He studied agriculture, and graduated from Cairo Univ. as an agrarian engineer (1945); then became interested in Egyptian musical instruments and composition; in 1950 received a Fulbright fellowship for music study in America; took courses at the New England Cons. in Boston and at the Berkshire Music Center in Tanglewood, Mass. (with Irving Fine and Copland). From 1966 to 1968 he taught at Howard Univ., and from 1969 at Kent State Univ. in Ohio, specializing in African ethnomusicology. Most of his music is derived from authentic Egyptian melodies and rhythms, but the contrapuntal and harmonic accoutrements are of a Western modern type.
    WORKS: 3 symphs. (1952–56); Concerto for an Egyptian Drum with String Orch. (1955); *Tahmela,* symph. poem (Cairo, Jan. 22, 1960); *Ballet of Lights (Cairo, Before the Sphinx,* July 23, 1960); *Opera Flies,* on the story of the Kent State Univ. killings of 1969, the "flies" in the title being an ironically bitter reference to the student victims (Washington, D.C., May 5, 1971); String Quartet (1951); Sextet for Wind Instruments and Percussion (1952); songs; and music for drums (for which he devised his own system of notation).

El-tour, Anna, Russian soprano; b. Odessa, June 4, 1886; d. Amsterdam, May 30, 1954. She studied at the St. Petersburg Cons. (voice with Mme. von Hecke; piano with Essipova). From 1913–20, she taught in Moscow; then left Russia; from 1922–25 was in Berlin; from 1925–48, she taught at the Cons. Internaional de Paris. After 1948, she was a prof. of singing at the Amsterdam Cons. She traveled widely in the Far East; gave recitals in Israel in 1953.

Elgar, Sir Edward (William), eminent English composer; b. Broadheath, near Worcester, June 2, 1857; d. Worcester, Feb. 23, 1934. He received his musical education from his father, who was organist at St. George's Roman Catholic Church in Worcester for 37 years. At an early age he assisted his father at the organ, and took part in the rehearsals and concerts at the Worcester Glee Club; in 1879 he took a few violin lessons in London from Adolf Pollitzer; in the same year, he accepted an appointment as bandmaster at the County Lunatic Asylum in Worcester; he also played in Stockley's orch. in Birmingham; in 1882, was appointed conductor of the Worcester Amateur Instrumental Society; in 1885 succeeded his father as organist at St. George's. After his marriage (1889) to a daughter of Sir Henry Roberts, he tried his fortune in London but found conditions unfavorable, and in 1891 settled in Malvern, where he remained for 13 years. He went to Hereford in 1904, and later to London, until 1920, when he returned to Worcester following the death of his wife. The first composition of Elgar that had a public performance was an orchestral intermezzo (Birmingham, Dec. 13, 1883); his first signal success was with the concert overture *Froissart* (Worcester Festival, Sept. 9, 1890). His cantata *The Black Knight* was produced by the Festival Choral Society in Worcester (April 18, 1893) and was also heard in London, at the Crystal Palace (Oct. 23, 1897); the production of his cantata *Scenes from the Saga of King Olaf* at the North Staffordshire Festival (Oct. 30, 1896) attracted considerable attention; from then on, Elgar's name became familiar to the musical public. There followed the cantata *Caractacus* (Leeds Festival, Oct. 5, 1898), and Elgar's masterpiece, the oratorio *The Dream of Gerontius* (Birmingham Festival, Oct. 3, 1900). In the meantime, Elgar gave more and more attention to orchestral music. On June 19, 1899, Hans Richter presented the first performance in London of Elgar's *Variations on an Original Theme* (generally known as *Enigma Variations*). This work consists of 14 sections, each marked by initials of fancied names of Elgar's friends; in later years, Elgar issued cryptic hints as to the identities of these persons, which were finally revealed. Elgar also stated that the theme itself was a counterpoint to a familiar tune, but the concealed subject was never discovered; various guesses were advanced in the musical press from time to time; a contest for the most plausible answer to the riddle was launched in America by the *Saturday Review* (1953) with dubious results. It is most probable that no such hidden theme existed, and that Elgar, who had a stately sense of humor, indulged in harmless mystification. The success of the *Enigma Variations* was followed (1901–30) by the production of Elgar's *Pomp and Circumstance* marches, the first of which became Elgar's most famous piece through a setting to words by Arthur Christopher Benson, used by Elgar in the *Coronation Ode* (1902), and then publ. separately as *Land of Hope and Glory;* another successful orch. work was the *Cockaigne Overture* (London, June 20, 1901). Elgar's 2 symphs., written in close succession in 1908 and 1910, received respectful attention in England, but never became popular elsewhere. His Violin Concerto, first performed by Fritz Kreisler (London, Nov. 10, 1910), was more successful; there was also a Cello Concerto (London, Oct. 26, 1919). The emergence of Elgar as a major composer about 1900 was all the more remarkable since he had no formal academic training. Yet he developed a masterly technique of instrumental and vocal writing. His style of composition may be described as functional Romanticism; his harmonic procedures remain firmly within the 19th-century tradition; the formal element is always strong, and the thematic development logical and precise. Elgar had a melodic gift, which asserted itself in the earliest works such as the popular *Salut d'amour;* his oratorios, particularly *The Apostles,* were the product of Elgar's fervent religious faith (he was a Roman Catholic); however he avoided archaic usages of Gregorian chant; rather, he presented the sacred subjects in a communicative style of secular drama. Elgar's stature in England is very great. During his lifetime he was a recipient of many honors. He was knighted in 1904. He received honorary degrees of Mus.Doc. from Cambridge (1900), Oxford (1905), Aberdeen (1906); also an LL.D., from Leeds (1904). During his first visit to the U.S. in 1905 he received a D.Mus. degree from Yale Univ.; in 1907 he received the same degree from the Univ. of Western Pa. (now the Univ. of Pittsburgh). He received the

Order of Merit in 1911; was made K.C.V.O. in 1928 and a baronet in 1931; was appointed Master of the King's Musick in 1924, succeeding Sir Walter Parratt. Although he was not a proficient conductor, he appeared on various occasions with orchs. in his own works; during the 3rd of his 4 visits to the U.S. (1905, 1906, 1907, 1911) he conducted his oratorio *The Apostles* (N.Y., 1907); also led the mass chorus at the opening of the British Empire Exhibition in 1924.

WORKS: OPERA: *The Spanish Lady,* in 2 acts, to a libretto based on Ben Jonson, op. 89 (unfinished; sketches date from 1878; 15 excerpts orchestrated by Percy M. Young; BBC, London, Dec 4, 1969). ORATORIOS: *The Light of Life,* op. 29 (Worcester, 1896); *The Dream of Gerontius,* op. 38 (Birmingham, 1900); *The Apostles,* op. 49 (Birmingham, 1903); *The Kingdom,* op. 51 (Birmingham, 1906).

CANTATAS: *The Black Knight,* op. 25 (1893); *Scenes from the Saga of King Olaf,* op. 30 (1896); *The Banner of St. George,* op. 33 (1897); *Caractacus,* op. 35 (1898); *Coronation Ode,* op. 44 (Sheffield, 1902); *The Music Makers* op. 69 (Birmingham, 1912).

CHORAL WORKS WITH ORCH.: *Star of the Summer Night,* op. 23 (1892); *Scenes from the Bavarian Highlands,* op. 27 (1896); *The Spirit of England,* op. 80 (1916).

FOR ORCH.: *The Wand of Youth,* suite in 7 movements, op. 1a (subtitled *Music to a Child's Play,* written at the age of 12 and orchestrated 37 years later; London, Queen's Hall Orch., Dec. 14, 1907); 2nd suite, *The Wand of Youth,* op. 1b (1908); *Sevillana,* op. 7; *3 Pieces* op. 10 (Mazurka, Sérénade mauresque, Contrasts); *Salut d'amour* op. 12 (Crystal Palace, London, Nov. 11, 1889); *2 Pieces,* op. 15 (*Chanson du Matin, Chanson du soir;*) *Froissart,* op. 19, overture (1890); *Serenade* for String Orch. op. 20 (1892); *Imperial March,* op. 32, for Queen Victoria's Diamond Jubilee (1897); *Enigma Variations,* op. 36 (1899); *Pomp and Circumstance,* op. 39, 4 military marches (1901–7; a 5th composed in 1930); *Cockaigne,* op. 40, overture (1901); *Dream Children,* op. 43, 2 pieces for Small Orch. (London Symph. Orch., March 8, 1905, composer conducting); *Introduction and Allegro* for Strings, op. 47 (London, March 8, 1905); *In the South,* op. 50, overture (1904); Symph. No. 1, op. 55 (Manchester, Dec. 3, 1908); *Elegy* for Strings, op. 58 (1909); Violin Concerto, op. 61 (London, Nov. 10, 1910); *Romance,* op. 62, for Bassoon and Orch. (1910); Symph. No. 2, op. 63 (London, May 24, 1911); *Coronation March* op. 65 (1911); *Falstaff,* op. 68, symph. study (Leeds Festival, Oct. 2, 1913, composer conducting); *Sospiri,* op. 70, for String Orch., Harp, and Organ (1914); *Carillon,* op. 75, for Recitation, with Orch. (1914); *Polonia,* op. 76, symph. prelude (1915); *Une voix dans le désert,* op. 77, for Recitation, with Orch. (1915); *Le Drapeau belge,* op. 79, for Recitation with Orch. (1917); Cello Concerto, op. 85 (1919); *Severn Suite,* op. 87, for Brass Band (1930); *Nursery Suite* for Orch. (1931); incidental music for *Grania and Diarmid,* op. 42; *The Crown of India,* op. 66, masque (1912); *The Starlight Express,* op. 78 (1915); music for Laurence Binyon and J.M. Harvey's play *King Arthur* (London, 1923).

CHAMBER MUSIC: Quintet for Wind Instruments, op. 6; String Quartet, op. 8 (MS destroyed); Violin Sonata, op. 9; Violin Sonata in E minor, op. 82 (MS destroyed); String Quartet in C minor, op. 83 (1918); Piano Quintet, op. 84 (1919). Organ works: Voluntaries, op. 14; Sonata in G, op. 28; also choruses and solo songs.

Elias, Salomon (Salomonis), French monk at Sainte-Astère, Périgord. He wrote in 1274 a treatise, *Scientia artis musicae* (printed by Gerbert, *Scriptores,* vol. III), of value as the first practical work giving rules for improvised counterpoint.

Elizalde, Federico, Spanish composer; b. Manila, Philippines (of Spanish parents), Dec. 12, 1908; d. there, Jan. 16, 1979. He entered the Madrid Cons. as a child and received the first prize as pianist at the age of 14. Later he went to California, and studied law at Stanford Univ. At the same time he took composition lessons with Ernest Bloch. He was subsequently active as a conductor of hotel orchs. in England; also visited Germany. Returning to his native islands, he became conductor of the Manila Symph. Orch. (1930). On April 23, 1936, he conducted his *Sinfonia Concertante* at the Festival of the International Society for Contemporary Music in Barcelona. He was in France during World War II; in 1948 he assumed the post of president of the Manila Broadcast Co., but continued his travels in both hemispheres. His music is influenced mainly by Mañuel de Falla; beginning with dancelike works in the Spanish vein, Elizalde has gradually changed his style toward neo-Classicism. He wrote the opera *Paul Gauguin* for the centennial of Gauguin's birth (1948); a Violin Concerto (1943); a Piano Concerto (1947); much chamber music.

Elkan, Henri, American conductor and music publisher; b. Antwerp, Nov. 23, 1897. He studied viola and piano at the conservatories of Antwerp (1914) and Amsterdam (graduated 1917); in 1920 came to the U.S.; played the viola in the Philadelphia Orch. (1920–28); was conductor of the Philadelphia Grand Opera Co. (1928–36) and of the Philadelphia Ballet Co. (1926–39). In 1926 he founded the Henri Elkan Music Publishing Co. in Philadelphia; it became the Elkan-Vogel Music Publishing Co. in 1928, when Adolphe Vogel, a cellist in the Philadelphia Orch., joined Elkan; the partnership was dissolved in 1952; in 1956 Elkan formed a publishing firm under his own name, specializing in works by American and Latin American composers.

Ellberg, Ernst Henrik, Swedish composer and pedagogue; b. Söderhamn, Dec. 11, 1868; d. Stockholm, June 14, 1948. He studied violin and composition at the Stockholm Cons., and was a teacher there from 1904 to 1933; among his pupils were Hilding Rosenberg, Dag Wirén, and Gunnar de Frumerie. He wrote an opera, *Rassa,* which received a prize; several ballets and concert overtures; some chamber music.

Eller, Heino, noted Estonian composer and pedagogue; b. Dorpat (Tartu), March 7, 1887; d. Tallinn, June 16, 1970. He studied law at St. Petersburg Univ. (1908–11), and later took music courses at the Cons. there, graduating in composition in 1920 in the class of Kalafati. From 1920 to 1940 he taught at the music high school in Tartu; in 1940 he joined the faculty of the Cons. in Tallinn. Together with Artur Kapp, Eller established the modern national school of Estonian music, derived from folk materials but framed in modern harmonic structures. He was also renowned as a pedagogue.

WORKS: 3 symphs. (1936, 1947, 1962); several symph. poems, including *Oö hüded* (*Nocturnal Sounds;* 1920; revised 1960); *Symphonic Scherzo* (1921); Violin Concerto (1933; revised 1965); *Fantasy for Violin and Orch.* (1916; revised 1963); 5 string quartets (1925, 1930, 1945, 1954, 1959); 2 violin sonatas (1922, 1946); 4 piano sonatas (1920, 1937, 1944, 1958).

Ellington, Edward Kennedy (known as **Duke Ellington**), black American pianist, bandleader, and composer; one of the most remarkable musicians of jazz; b. Washington, D.C., April 29, 1899; d. New York, May 24, 1974. He played ragtime as a boy; worked with various jazz bands in Washington during the 1910s and early 1920s, and in 1923 went to N.Y., where he organized a "big band" (originally 10 pieces) that he was to lead for the next half-century, a band that revolutionized the concept of jazz: no longer was jazz restricted to small combos of 4–6 "unlettered" improvisers; with the Ellington band complex arrangements were introduced, requiring both improvising skill and the ability to read scores; eventually these scores were to take on the dimensions and scope of classical compositions while retaining an underlying jazz feeling. In the early days his chief collaborator in composition and arrangements was trumpeter James "Bubber" Miley; baritone saxophonist Harry Carney, another arranger, was with the band from its inception until Ellington's death; from 1939 the main collaborator was pianist-composer Billy Strayhorn. Ellington possessed a social elegance and the gift of articulate verbal expression that inspired respect, and he became known as "Duke" Ellington. He was the only jazz musician to receive an honorary degree from Columbia Univ. (1973). He was also the recipient of the Presidential Medal of Freedom on his 70th birthday at the White House in 1969. He made several European trips under the auspices of the State Dept.; toured Russia in 1970 and also went to Latin America, Japan, and Australia. So highly was he esteemed in Africa that the Republic of Togo issued in 1967 a postage stamp bearing his portrait. Since Duke's death, his band has been led by his son **Mercer Ellington** (b. Washington, D.C., March 11, 1919).

WORKS: More than 1,000 compositions, including *East St. Louis Toodle-Oo* (pronounced "toad-lo"; 1926); *Black and Tan Fantasy* and *Creole Love Song* (1927); *Mood Indigo* (1930); *Sophisticated Lady* (uses a whole-tone scale; 1932); *Diminuendo and*

Crescendo in Blue (1937); *Black, Brown and Beige,* (a tonal panorama of black history in America (1943); *Liberian Suite* (1948); *My People,* commissioned for the 100th anniversary of the Emancipation Proclamation (1963); *First Sacred Concert* (first perf., Grace Cathedral, San Francisco, 1965); *Second Sacred Concert* (first perf., Cathedral of St. John the Divine, N.Y., 1968); *The River,* ballet (1970). He publ. a book, *Music Is My Mistress* (Garden City, N.Y., 1973).

Elman, Mischa, remarkable Russian violinist; b. Talnoy, Jan. 20, 1891; d. New York, April 5, 1967. At the age of 6 he was taken by his father to Odessa, where he became a violin student of Fidelmann and a pupil of Brodsky. His progress was extraordinary, and when Leopold Auer heard him play in 1902, he immediately accepted him in his class at the St. Petersburg Cons. In 1904 he made his debut in St. Petersburg with sensational acclaim; his tour of Germany was equally successful; in 1905 he appeared in England, where he played the Glazunov Violin Concerto. On Dec. 10, 1908, he made his American debut in N.Y. and was hailed as one of the greatest virtuosos of the time; he played with every important symph. orch. in the U.S.; with the Boston Symph. alone he was a soloist at 31 concerts. In the following years he played all over the world, and, with Jascha Heifetz, became a synonym for violinistic prowess. His playing was the quintessence of Romantic interpretation; his tone was mellifluous but resonant; he excelled particularly in the concertos of Mendelssohn, Tchaikovsky, and Wieniawski; but he could also give impressive performances of Beethoven and Mozart. He publ. several violin arrangements of Classical and Romantic pieces, and he also composed some playable short compositions for his instrument. His father publ. a sentimental book, *Memoirs of Mischa Elman's Father* (N.Y., 1933).

Eloy, Jean-Claude, French composer; b. Mont-Saint-Aignan (Seine-Maritime), June 15, 1938. He studied in Paris with Darius Milhaud and in Basel with Pierre Boulez. From his earliest works he adopted the advanced techniques of serialism; his main influences are Boulez, Varèse, and Webern; there is an extreme miniaturization in his instrumental music. He composed *Etude III* for Orch. (1962); *Equivalences* (1963); *Polychronies* (1964), *Macles* (1967), and *Faisceaux-Diffractions* (1970), all for Chamber Orch.; also *Kamakala* for Chorus and 3 Orch. Ensembles (1971); *Kshara-Akshara* for Soprano Chorus and 3-sectioned Orch. with 3 Conductors (1974); *Shanti* (Tibetan for "good fortune"), an electronic work lasting 2½ hours without interruption, probably the longest uninterrupted piece ever composed (London, April 6, 1975).

Elsner, Joseph, noted Polish composer, teacher of Chopin; b. Grottkau, June 1, 1769 (of German descent); d. Elsnerowo, near Warsaw, April 18, 1854. He studied violin, voice, and organ at Grottkau, Breslau, and Vienna. In 1791 he became concert-master of the Brünn Opera Theater; then was Kapellmeister at Lemberg (from 1792 to 1799). He was Chopin's teacher at Warsaw, and founded a school there for organists which later became the Warsaw Cons. He also headed the Opera there for 25 years. His autobiography (1840–49), written in German, was publ. posthumously in a Polish trans. (1855; new ed., Cracow, 1957).

WORKS: 32 operas, including *King Wladislaw* (Warsaw, April 3, 1818), duo-dramas, and musical plays, of which 2 were produced in German at Lemberg (*Die seltenen Brüder,* 1794; *Der verkleidete Sultan,* 1796) and the rest in Warsaw; 17 masses; several ballets; sacred and secular choral works; 8 symphs.; 11 string quartets; 2 piano quartets; 3 violin sonatas (a number of these works were publ. by Breitkopf & Härtel and by French and Polish publishers). He also publ. 2 treatises on the vocal treatment of Polish texts (Warsaw, 1818). A medal was struck in his honor in 1849, on the occasion of his 80th birthday.

Elson, Louis Charles, American music historian; b. Boston, April 17, 1848; d. there, Feb. 14, 1920. He studied voice with Kreissmann at Boston and music theory with Karl Gloggner Castelli in Leipzig. Returning to Boston, he was for many years music editor of the *Boston Advertiser;* in 1880 became lecturer on music history at the New England Cons.; was also editor in chief of the *University Encyclopedia of Music* (10 vols., 1912). In his music criticism he attacked the modernists with vicious eloquence, reserving the choicest invective for Debussy; he called *La Mer* "Le Mal de Mer," and said that the faun of *L'Après-midi d'un faune* needed a veterinary surgeon.

WRITINGS: *Curiosities of Music* (1880); *History of German Song* (1888); *The Theory of Music* (1890; revised by F. Converse, 1935); *European Reminiscences* (Chicago, 1891; new ed., Philadelphia, 1914); *The Realm of Music* (1892); *Great Composers and Their Work* (1898); *The National Music of America and Its Sources* (1899; new ed., revised by Arthur Elson, 1924); *Famous Composers and Their Works* (with Philip Hale; new series, Boston, 1900); *Shakespeare in Music* (1901); *History of American Music* (N.Y., 1904; 2nd ed., 1915; revised ed. by A. Elson, 1925); *Music Dictionary* (1905); *Pocket Music Dictionary* (1909; many reprints); *Folk Songs of Many Nations* (1905); *Mistakes and Disputed Points in Music* (1910); *Woman in Music* (1918); *Children in Music* (1918).

Elwell, Herbert, American composer and music critic; b. Minneapolis, May 10, 1898; d. Cleveland, April 17, 1974. He studied at the Univ. of Minnesota; then took courses with Ernest Bloch in N.Y. (1919–21) and Nadia Boulanger in Paris (1921–24); received a Prix de Rome in 1923; from 1924 to 1927 held a fellowship at the American Academy in Rome. Returning to the U.S., he held a post as teacher of composition at the Cleveland Music Inst. (1928–45); from 1932 to 1964 served as music critic for the Cleveland *Plain Dealer.*

WORKS: His most successful work was the ballet *The Happy Hypocrite,* after Max Beerbohm (an orch. suite drawn from the score was perf. in Rome on May 21, 1927, with Elwell himself conducting); *Introduction and Allegro* for Orch. (N.Y., July 12, 1942); *I Was with Him,* cantata for Male Chorus, Tenor Solo, and 2 Pianos (Cleveland, Nov. 30, 1942); *Blue Symphony* for Voice and String Quartet (Cleveland, Feb. 2, 1945); *Lincoln: Requiem Aeternam* for Chorus and Orch. (Oberlin, Feb. 16, 1947); *Pastorale* for Voice and Orch. (Cleveland, March 25, 1948); *Ode* for Orch. (1950); *The Forever Young* for Voice and Orch. (Cleveland, Oct. 29, 1953); *Concert Suite* for Violin and Orch. (Louisville, Feb. 5, 1958); 2 string quartets; Piano Sonata; Violin Sonata; etc.

Emmanuel, Maurice, eminent French music scholar; b. Bar-sur-Aube, May 2, 1862; d. Paris, Dec. 14, 1938. He received his primary education in Dijon; sang in the church choir in Beaune; then studied at the Paris Cons. (1880–87) with Savard, Dubois, Delibes, and Bourgault-Ducoudray; then specialized in the musical history of antiquity under Gevaert in Brussels; also studied ancient languages at the Sorbonne, receiving a licencié ès lettres (1887) and a docteur ès lettres (1895) with the theses *De saltationis disciplina apud Graecos* (publ. in Latin, Paris, 1895) and *La Danse grecque antique d'après les monuments figurés* (Paris, 1896; in Eng. as *The Antique Greek Dance after Sculptured and Painted Figures,* N.Y., 1916). He was a prof. of art history at the Lycée Racine and Lycée Lamartine (1898–1905); maître de chapelle at Ste.-Clotilde (1904–7); in 1909 he succeeded Bourgault-Ducoudray as prof. of music history at the Paris Cons., and held this post until 1936; he edited vols. 17 and 18 of the complete works of Rameau; also Bach's works in Durand's ed. of the classical masters.
WRITINGS: *Histoire de la langue musicale* (2 vols., Paris, 1911; new ed., 1928); *Traité de l'accompagnement modal des psaumes* (Lyons, 1912); *La Polyphonie sacrée* (with R. Moissenet; Dijon, 1923); *Pelléas et Mélisande de Claude Debussy* (Paris, 1926); *César Franck* (Paris, 1930); *Antonin Reicha* (Paris, 1937); also articles in the *Revue Musicale, Musical Quarterly,* etc.
WORKS: Opera, *Salamine* (Paris, June 28, 1929); opéra-bouffe, *Amphitryon* (Paris, Feb. 20, 1937); 2 symphs. (1919, 1931); 2 string quartets and other chamber music; 6 piano sonatinas; vocal music (much of it publ.).

Emmett, Daniel Decatur, American composer of *Dixie* and other popular songs; b. Mt. Vernon, Ohio, Oct. 29, 1815; d. there, June 28, 1904. He began his career as a drummer in military bands; then joined the Virginia Minstrels, singing and playing the banjo; later was a member of Bryant's Minstrels. He wrote the lyrics and the music of *Dixie* in 1859, and it was performed for the first time in N.Y., on April 4, 1859; upon publication, the popularity of the song spread, and it was adopted as a Southern fighting song during the Civil War (even though Emmett was a Northerner). His other songs, *Old Dan Tucker, The Road to Richmond, Walk Along,* etc., enjoyed great favor for some years, but were eclipsed by *Dixie.*

Encina, Juan del, Spanish poet and composer; b. Salamanca, July 12, 1468; d. León, Aug. 29 or 30, 1529. He was the son of a shoemaker of Salamanca named Juan de Fermoselle; became chorister at Salamanca Cathedral; studied music under his elder brother, Diego de Fermoselle, and under Fernando de Torrijos; took his degree in law at Salamanca Univ., where he enjoyed the favor of the chancellor, Don Gutiérrez de Toledo. In 1492 he entered the household of the 2nd Duke of Alba, for whom he wrote a series of pastoral eclogues that form the foundation of the Spanish secular drama. These eclogues included "villancicos," or rustic songs, for which Encina composed the music. He went to Rome in 1500; on May 12, 1500, was appointed canon at the Cathedral of Salamanca; from Feb. 2, 1510, until 1512, he was archdeacon and canon of Málaga; on May 2, 1512, he again went to Rome; his *Farsa de Plácida e Vittoriano* was performed there in the presence of Julius II on Jan. 11, 1513. In 1517, he was "subcollector of revenues to the Apostolic Chamber." In 1519 he was appointed prior of León, and that same year made a pilgrimage to Jerusalem, where he was ordained a priest. He described his sacred pilgrimage in *Tribagia o Via Sacra de Hierusalem* (Rome, 1521). After the death of Leo X in 1521, Encina returned to Spain and spent his last years as prior at León. Besides being the creator of the Spanish drama, Encina was the most important Spanish composer of the reign of Ferdinand and Isabella; he cultivated with notable artistry a type of part-song akin to the Italian "frottola," setting his own poems to music; 68 of these songs are preserved in the valuable *Cancionero musical de los siglos XV y XVI,* ed. by F. A. Barbieri (Madrid, 1890; new ed., in 3 vols., by H. Anglès, 1947, 1951, 1953). Another modern ed. was publ. by C. Terni, *Juan del Encina: L'opera musicale* (Florence, 1974—). No religious music by Encina is known to exist.

Enesco (Enescu), Georges, foremost Rumanian composer and violinist; b. Liveni-Virnaz, Aug. 19, 1881; d. Paris, May 4, 1955. He began to play violin when only 4 years old, taking lessons with a Rumanian gypsy violinist, Nicolas Chioru; then studied with the violinist and composer Caudella; from 1888–93 he was a pupil at the Vienna Cons. under Hellmesberger (violin) and R. Fuchs (theory), winning first prize in violin and harmony (1892); in 1894–99 he studied at the Paris Cons. with Marsick (violin), Fauré and Massenet (composition); won 2nd *accessit* for counterpoint and fugue (1897) and first prize for violin (1899); at the same time he studied cello, organ, and piano, attaining more than ordinary proficiency on all these instruments. His talent for composition manifested itself very early, his first efforts dating from his student days in Vienna; on June 11, 1897, when he was not quite 16, he presented in Paris a concert of his own works (String Quintet, Piano Suite, Violin Sonata, and songs), which attracted the attention of Colonne, who produced the following year the youthful composer's op. 1, *Poème roumain.* On March 8, 1903, he conducted in Bucharest the first performances of his 2 *Rumanian Rhapsodies,* the first of which was to become his most enduring work. He was appointed court violinist to the Queen of Rumania; gave master classes in violin interpretation at the Ecole Normale de Musique; among his pupils was Yehudi Menuhin. In 1912 he offered an annual prize for Rumanian composers (won by Jora, Enacovici, Stan Golestan, Otescu, and others); then toured Europe; first visited the U.S. in 1923, making his debut as conductor, composer, and violinist in a N.Y. concert of the Philadelphia Orch. (Jan. 2, 1923); returned to the U.S. in 1937, and conducted the N.Y. Phil. on Jan. 28, 1937, and several subsequent concerts with remarkable success; reengaged in 1938 and conducted the N.Y. Phil. in 14 concerts; appeared twice as a violinist; also conducted 2 concerts of Rumanian music at the N.Y. World's Fair (May 1939). The outbreak of World War II found Enesco in Rumania, where he lived on his farm in Sinaia, near Bucharest. He remained there through the war years; in 1946 he came again to the U.S. to teach in N.Y. On Jan. 21, 1950, on the 60th anniversary of his first public appearance at the age of 8, he played a farewell concert in N.Y. in the multiple capacity of violinist, pianist, conductor, and composer, in a program comprising Bach's Double Concerto (with Enesco's pupil Yehudi Menuhin), his own Violin Sonata (playing the piano part with Menuhin), and his *First Rumanian Rhapsody* (conducting the orch.). He then returned to Paris; in July 1954 he suffered a stroke, and became an invalid for his remaining days. In homage to his accomplishment in Rumanian music, his native village was renamed Enescu and a street in Bucharest was also named after him. Periodical Enescu Festivals and international performing contests were established in Bucharest in 1958. Enesco had an extraordinary range of musical interests. His compositions include artistic stylizations of Rumanian folk strains; his style was neo-Romantic, but he made occasional use of experimental devices, such as quarter-tones in his opera *Œdipe.* He possessed a fabulous memory and was able to play complete symph. works without the scores.

WORKS: LYRIC TRAGEDY: *Œdipe* (1931; Grand Opéra, Paris, March 10, 1936; Bucharest, posthumous production, Sept. 22, 1958). FOR ORCH.: 3 early symphs., unnumbered (1895, 1896, 1898); 5 numbered symphs.: No. 1 (Paris, Jan. 21, 1906); No. 2 (Bucharest, March 28, 1915); No. 3 (1918; Bucharest, May 25, 1919); No. 4 (1934; unfinished); No. 5, with Tenor and Women's Chorus (1941; unfinished); *Ballad* for Violin and Orch. (1895); *Tragic Overture* (1895); Violin Concerto (1896; Paris, March 26, 1896, at a Paris Cons. concert); Fantasy for Piano and Orch. (1896; Bucharest, March 26, 1900); *Rumanian Poem* (1897; Paris, Feb. 9, 1898); *Pastorale* (1899; Paris, Feb. 19, 1899); *Rumanian Rhapsody No. 1* (1901) and *No. 2* (1902; both perf. for the first time in Bucharest, March 8, 1903, composer conducting); *Symphonie concertante* for Cello and Orch. (1901; Par-

is, March 14, 1909); Suite No. 1 (1903; Paris, Dec. 11, 1904); Suite No. 2 (1915; Bucharest, March 27, 1916, composer conducting); Suite No. 3, *Villageoise* (1938; N.Y. Phil., Feb. 2, 1939, composer conducting); *Concert Overture on Popular Rumanian Themes* (1948; Washington, D.C., Jan. 23, 1949, composer conducting); *Symphonie de chambre* (1954; Paris, Jan. 23, 1955); *Vox maris,* symph. poem (1955; posthumous, Bucharest, Sept. 10, 1964). CHAMBER MUSIC: *Ballad* for Violin and Piano (1895); Piano Quintet (1895); Violin Sonata No. 1 (1897); *Nocturne et Saltarelle* for Cello and Piano (1897); Cello Sonata No. 1 (1898); Violin Sonata No. 2 (1899); *Aubade* for String Trio (1899); Octet for 4 Violins, 2 Violas, and 2 Cellos (1900); *Intermezzo* for Strings (1903); *Allegro de concert* for Harp and Piano (1904); *Dixtuor* for Wind Instruments (1906); *Au soir,* nocturne for 4 Trumpets (1906); *Legenda* for Trumpet and Piano (1906); *Konzertstück* for Viola and Piano (1906); Piano Quartet No. 1 (1909); String Quartet No. 1 (1920); Violin Sonata No. 3, "in popular Rumanian character" (1926); Cello Sonata No. 2 (1935); Piano Quintet No. 2 (1940); *Impressions d'enfance* for Violin and Piano (1940); Piano Quartet No. 2 (1944); String Quartet No. 2 (1951). FOR PIANO: *Variations on an Original Theme* for 2 Pianos (1899); 2 suites for Piano Solo: No. 1, *Dans le style ancien* (1897), and No. 2 (1903); *Pièces impromptues* (1915–16); 3 sonatas (1924, 1927, 1934). VOCAL WORKS: *La Vision de Saul,* cantata (1895); *L'Aurore,* cantata (1898); *Waldgesang* for Chorus (1898); many songs to words by the Queen of Rumania, who wrote poetry in German under the pen name Carmen Sylva, among them *Armes Mägdlein* (1898); *Der Schmetterlingskuss* (1898); *Schlaflos* (1898); *Frauenberuf* (1898); *Sphynx* (1898); *Königshusarenlied* (1899); *Ein Sonnenblick* (1901); *Regen* (1903); *Entsagen* (1907); *Morgengebet* (1908); also several cycles of songs to French texts.

Engel, Carl, German musical historiographer; b. Thiedeweise, near Hannover, July 6, 1818; d. by suicide, London, Nov. 17, 1882. He studied organ with Enckhausen at Hannover and piano with Hummel at Weimar. After residing in Hamburg, Warsaw, and Berlin, he went to Manchester, England, in 1846, and in 1850 to London. There he became an influential writer, and an authority on musical history and musical instruments.

WRITINGS: *The Pianist's Handbook* (1853); *Piano School for Young Beginners* (1855); *Reflections on Church Music* (1856); his lifework began with *The Music of the Most Ancient Nations, Particularly of the Assyrians, Egyptians, and Hebrews* (1864), followed by *An Introduction to the Study of National Music* (1866); *Musical Instruments of All Countries* (1869); *Catalogue of the Special Exhibition of Ancient Musical Instruments* (2nd ed., 1873); *Descriptive Catalogue of the Musical Instruments in the South Kensington Museum* (1874); *Musical Myths and Facts* (1876); *The Literature of National Music* (1879); *Researches into the Early History of the Violin Family* (1883). Among his unpublished MSS is a large history of the musical instruments of the world (4 quarto vols. with over 800 illustrations).

Engel, Carl, distinguished American musicologist and writer on music; b. Paris, July 21, 1883; d. New York, May 6, 1944. He was a great-grandson of **Josef Kroll,** founder of Kroll's Etablissement in Berlin, and grandson of **J.C. Engel,** who made the Kroll Opera famous. Carl Engel was educated at the univs. of Strasbourg and Munich; studied composition in Munich with Thuille. He came to the U.S. in 1905 and established himself as an editor, musicologist, librarian, and publisher. He was editor and musical adviser of the Boston Music Co. (1909–21); chief of the Music Division of the Library of Congress (1922–34); president of G. Schirmer, Inc. (1929–32); in 1929 became editor of the *Musical Quarterly;* remained with it until 1942; from 1934 was again president of G. Schirmer, Inc., and honorary consultant in musicology for the Library of Congress; was U.S. delegate to the Beethoven Centenary, Vienna, 1927; U.S. representative of the International Society of Musicology; first chairman of the Committee on Musicology, American Council of Learned Societies; president of the American Musicological Society (1937–38); was an honorary member of the Harvard Musical Association; also a Fellow of the American Academy of Arts and Letters; received an honorary Mus.Doc. from Oberlin College (1934); was made a Chevalier of the Légion d'Honneur (1937); was a recipient of the Elizabeth Sprague Coolidge medal "for eminent services rendered to chamber music" (1935). A writer with a brilliant style and of wide learning, Carl Engel contributed valuable essays to the *Musical Quarterly* (*Views and Reviews;* articles on Chadwick, Loeffler, etc.); publ. 2 collections of essays: *Alla Breve, from Bach to Debussy* (N.Y., 1921) and *Discords Mingled* (N.Y., 1931). Carl Engel was also a composer; his music was in the French tradition, in an impressionistic vein; his songs, particularly his settings of poems by Amy Lowell, were often sung (the best known among them is *Sea-Shell*); other works include *Triptych* for Violin and Piano; *Perfumes* for Piano (an album of 5 pieces); *Presque valse* for Piano was publ. posthumously.

Engel, Hans, eminent German musicologist; b. Cairo, Egypt, Dec. 20, 1894; d. Marburg, May 15, 1970. He studied at the Akademie der Tonkunst in Munich with Klose and at the Univ. of Munich with Sandberger; received his Ph.D. from the Univ. of Munich in 1925 with the dissertation *Die Entwicklung des deutschen Klavierkonzertes von Mozart bis Liszt* (publ. in Leipzig, 1927); completed his Habilitation at the Univ. of Greifswald in 1926; then taught there (1926–35). He was on the faculty of the Univ. of Königsberg (1935–46) and Marburg Univ. (1946–63).

Engel, Joel, Russian writer on music; b. Berdiansk, April 16, 1868; d. Tel Aviv, Feb. 2, 1927. He studied at Kharkov; later with Taneyev and Ippolitov-Ivanov in Moscow. In 1922 he went to Berlin, where he orga-

nized a publishing house for propaganda of Jewish music; issued a collection of Jewish folk songs in 3 vols. His publications in Russian are: *Pocket Music Dictionary* (Moscow, 1913); *Essays on Music History* (Moscow, 1911); *In the Opera* (1911).

Engel, Lehman, American composer, conductor, and writer on music; b. Jackson, Miss., Sept. 14, 1910; d. New York, Aug. 29, 1982. He began to take piano lessons with local teachers as a child; then went to Cincinnati, where he studied with Sidney Durst at the Cincinnati College of Music (1927–29) and later with Eduardo Trucco in N.Y.; in 1930–34 he took courses in composition with Rubin Goldmark at the Juilliard School of Music and also took private composition lessons with Roger Sessions (1931–37). While still a student, he began to write music for ballet and theatrical plays; in 1934 he wrote incidental music for Sean O'Casey's play *Within the Gates,* which he conducted. From 1935 to 1939 he led the Madrigal Singers for the Works Progress Administration; later worked with the Mercury Theater as composer and conductor. During World War II Engel enlisted in the U.S. Navy and conducted a military orch. at the Great Lakes Naval Training Stations; later was appointed chief composer of the Navy's film division in Washington, D.C. He wrote a great many scores of incidental music for Broadway productions, which he also conducted, among them for T.S. Eliot's *Murder in the Cathedral* and Tennessee Williams's *A Streetcar Named Desire.* As a composer, Engel was happiest in writing for the theater; he had a special knack for vivid musical illustration of the action on the stage. Of importance are his numerous books on the American music theater. He was also active as a teacher of composition and led in N.Y. a seminar on musical lyrics. He conducted the first American performance of Kurt Weill's *The Threepenny Opera;* also conducted the productions of *Showboat, Brigadoon, Annie Get Your Gun, Fanny, Guys and Dolls,* and *Carousel.* Engel received 2 Antoinette Perry (Tony) Awards, in 1950 for conducting Menotti's opera *The Consul,* and in 1953 for conducting the operettas of Gilbert and Sullivan. In 1971 he received the honorary degree of D.M. from the Univ. of Cincinnati.

WORKS: OPERAS: *Pierrot of the Minuet* (Cincinnati, April 3, 1928); *Malady of Love* (N.Y., May 27, 1954); *The Soldier* (N.Y., Nov. 25, 1956, a concert version); *Golden Ladder,* a musical (Cleveland, May 28, 1953). BALLETS: *Phobias* (N.Y., Nov. 18, 1932); *Ceremonials* (N.Y., May 13, 1933); *Transitions* (N.Y., Feb. 19, 1934); *The Shoebird* (Jackson, Miss., April 20, 1968). INCIDENTAL MUSIC TO SHAKESPEARE'S PLAYS: *Hamlet* (1938); *Macbeth* (1941); *Julius Caesar* (1955); *The Tempest* (1960); also music to plays by contemporary authors. FOR ORCH.: 2 symphs. (1939, 1945); Viola Concerto (1945); *The Creation* for Narrator and Orch. (1947); overture, *Jackson* (Jackson, Miss., Feb. 13, 1961). CHAMBER MUSIC: Cello Sonata (1945); Violin Sonata (1953). FOR CHORUS: *Rain* (1929); *Rest* (1936); *Chansons innocentes* (1938); *Let Us Now Praise Famous Men* (1955).

WRITINGS: *The Bright Day,* an autobiography

(N.Y., 1956; revised 1974); an instruction book, *Planning and Producing the Musical Show* (N.Y., 1957; revised 1966); *The American Musical Theater: A Consideration* (N.Y., 1967); ed. the collection *Three Centuries of Choral Music: Renaissance to Baroque* (N.Y., 1939–56); *The Musical Book* (N.Y., 1971); *Words and Music* (N.Y., 1972); *Their Words Are Music* (N.Y., 1975); *Getting the Show On: The Complete Guidebook for Producing a Musical in Your Theater* (N.Y., 1983). A detailed list of Lehman Engel's works for the theater is found in Walter Rigdon, ed., *Who's Who of the American Theater* (N.Y., 1966).

Engelmann, Hans Ulrich, German composer; b. Darmstadt, Sept. 8, 1921. He had piano lessons while in high school; after the end of the disrupting war, he took courses in composition with Wolfgang Fortner in Heidelberg (1945–49); in 1948–50 he attended the classes of René Leibowitz and Ernst Krenek in Darmstadt; enrolled at the Univ. of Frankfurt (1946–52), taking classes in musicology (with Gennrich and Osthoff) and philosophy (with Adorno); in 1952, received his Dr.Phil. with a thesis on Béla Bartók's *Mikrokosmos* (publ. in Würzburg, 1953). Parallel to these pursuits, he took courses in architecture. In 1949 he held a Harvard Univ. stipend at the Salzburg Seminar in American Studies; was active in radio programming and in composition for films and for the theater; spent a season in Iceland (1953–54); then was theater composer in Darmstadt (1954–61). In 1969 he was appointed an instructor at the Frankfurt Hochschule für Musik. His early works are impregnated by chromaticism with an impressionistic tinge. He adopted the 12-tone method of composition, expanding it into a sui generis "field technique" of total serialism, in which rhythms and instrumental timbres are organized systematically. In his theater music he utilizes aleatory devices, *musique concrète,* and electronic sonorities.

Enna, August, eminent Danish composer; b. Nakskov, May 13, 1859; d. Copenhagen, Aug. 3, 1939. He was partly of German and Italian blood; his grandfather, an Italian soldier in Napoleon's army, married a German girl, and settled in Denmark. Enna was brought to Copenhagen as a child, and went to school there. He learned to play piano and violin; had sporadic instruction in theory; later became a member of a traveling orch. and played with it in Finland (1880). Upon his return to Copenhagen, he taught piano and played for dancers; in 1883 he conducted a theater orch. and wrote his first stage work, *A Village Tale,* which he produced the same year. After these practical experiences, he began to study seriously; took lessons with Schjorring (violin), Matthesson (organ), and Rasmussen (composition) and soon publ. a number of piano pieces, which attracted the attention of Niels Gade, who used his influence to obtain a traveling fellowship for Enna; this made it possible for Enna to study in Germany (1888–89) and acquire a complete mastery of instrumental and vocal writing.

WORKS: He followed the German Romantic school, being influenced mainly by Weber's type of opera, and by Grieg and Gade in the use of local color; the first product of this period was his most successful work, in the opera *Heksen (The Witch),* produced in Copenhagen (Jan. 24, 1892), then in Germany. Enna's other operas also enjoyed a modicum of success; these are *Cleopatra* (Copenhagen, Feb. 7, 1894); *Aucassin and Nicolette* (Copenhagen, Feb. 2, 1896); *The Match Girl,* after Andersen (Copenhagen, Nov. 13, 1897); *Lamia* (Antwerp, Oct. 3, 1899); *Ung Elskov* (first produced in Weimar, under the title *Heisse Liebe,* Dec. 6, 1904); *Princess on the Pea,* after Andersen (Aarhus, Sept. 15, 1900); *The Nightingale,* also after Andersen (Aarhus, Sept. 15, 1900); *The Nightingale,* also after Andersen (Copenhagen, Nov. 10, 1912); *Gloria Arsena* (Copenhagen, April 15, 1917); *Comedians,* after Victor Hugo's *L'Homme qui rit* (Copenhagen, April 8, 1920); *Don Juan Mañara* (Copenhagen, April 17, 1925). He further wrote the ballets *The Shepherdess and the Chimney Sweep* (Copenhagen, Oct. 6, 1901); *St. Cecilia's Golden Shoe* (Copenhagen, Dec. 26, 1904); *The Kiss* (Copenhagen, Oct. 19, 1927); also a Violin Concerto, 2 symphs.; an overture, *Hans Christian Andersen;* choral pieces.

Enríquez, Manuel, Mexican composer and violinist; b. Ocotlán, June 17, 1926. He studied violin with Camarena and composition with Bernal Jiménez at the Guadalajara Cons. (1942–50); then went to N.Y. and took lessons in composition with Peter Mennin and violin with Ivan Galamian at the Juilliard School of Music (1955–57); also had private theory lessons with Stefan Wolpe and attended the Columbia-Princeton Electronic Music Center (1971). Returning to Mexico, he was concertmaster of the Guadalajara Symph. Orch.; later supervised music courses at the Inst. of Fine Arts in Mexico City. In 1975 he went to France under a special commission from the Mexican government. As a composer, he follows the median line of cosmopolitan modernism, making use of a severe constructivist idiom, employing graphic optical notation.

WORKS: *Suite* for Violin and Piano (1949); 2 violin concertos (1955, 1966); Symph. No. 1 (1957); 3 string quartets (1959, 1967, 1974); *Preámbulo* for Orch. (1961); Sonatina for Solo Cello (1962); *Divertimento* for Flute, Clarinet, and Bassoon (1962); *4 Pieces* for Viola and Piano (1962); *Obertura lírica* for Orch. (1963); *Pentamúsica* for Wind Quintet (1963); *3 formas concertantes* for Violin, Cello, Clarinet, Bassoon, Horn, Piano, and Percussion (1964); Violin Sonata (1964); *3 invenciones* for Flute and Viola (1964); *Módulos* for 2 Pianos (1965); *Transición* for Orch. (1965); *Poema* for Cello and Small String Orch. (1966); *Ego* for Female Voice, Flute, Cello, Piano, and Percussion (1966); *Trayectorias* for Orch. (1967); *Ambivalencia* for Violin and Cello (1967); *Si Libet* for Orch. (1968); *5 Plus 2* for Flute, Viola, Trombone, Piano, and Percussion, with Actress and Director (1969); *Concierto para 8* (1969); *Ixamatl* for Orch. (1969); *Díptico I* for Flute and Piano (1969); *Díptico II* for Violin and Piano (1971); *Presagios* for Piano (1970); *Móvil I* for Piano (1969); Piano Concerto (1971); *El y Ellos* for Solo Violin and

Orch. Ensemble (1973).

Enriquez de Valderrabano, Enrique, 16th-century Spanish lutenist; native of Peñaranda de Duero. He wrote the tablature book *Libro de música de vihuela, intitulado Silva de Sirenas* (Valladolid, 1547), containing transcriptions for vihuela (large 6-stringed guitar) of sacred and secular vocal works (some arranged for 2 vihuelas), also some original pieces.

Enthoven, Emile, Dutch composer; b. Amsterdam, Oct. 18, 1903; d. New York, Dec. 26, 1950. He studied composition with Johan Wagenaar in Utrecht, and at the age of 15 wrote an adolescent but well-crafted symphony, which Mengelberg performed with the Concertgebouw Orch. in Amsterdam (1918). But this precocious success was not a manifestation of enduring talent; his later works lacked originality. Soon he abandoned composition altogether and took up jurisprudence; for a time he lectured on political science at the Univ. of Leiden; in 1939 emigrated to America and settled in N.Y.

Entremont, Philippe, eminent French pianist and conductor; b. Rheims, June 6, 1934. Both his parents were professional musicians and teachers, and he received his first training from them. He subsequently studied piano with Marguerite Long; then entered the Paris Cons.; won first prize in solfège at 12, in chamber music at 14, and in piano at 15. In 1951 he was the winner of the Belgian State Competition in Brussels. He then toured in Europe; on Jan. 5, 1953, he made his American debut with the National Orch. Association in N.Y.; appeared also as soloist with other American orchs. In 1976 he became music director of the Vienna Chamber Orch.; in 1980 was appointed music adviser and principal conductor of the New Orleans Phil., and in 1981–84 was its music director; in 1982 he took that orch. on a European tour.

Epstein, Julius, Austrian pianist; b. Agram, Croatia, Aug. 7, 1832; d. Vienna, March 1, 1926. He was a pupil at Agram of Ignaz Lichtenegger, and at Vienna of Anton Halm (piano) and Johann Rufinatscha (composition). From 1867 to 1901 he was a prof. of piano at the Vienna Cons.; one of the editors of Breitkopf & Härtel's monumental edition of Schubert's works. Among his pupils were Gustav Mahler and Ignaz Brüll.

Erard, Sébastien, famous maker of pianos and harps; b. Strasbourg, April 5, 1752; d. in his château, La Muette, near Paris, Aug. 5, 1831. His family name was originally **Erhard;** his father was a cabinetmaker by trade, and in his shop Sébastien worked until he was 16, when his father died. He was then engaged by a Paris harpsichord maker, who dismissed him "for wanting to know everything"; under a 2nd employer his ingenuity made a stir in the musical world, and the invention of a "clavecin mécanique" (described by Abbé Roussier, 1776) made him fa-

mous. The Duchess of Villeroy became his patroness, and fitted up in her home a workshop for Erard in which (1777) he finished the first pianoforte made in France. In the meantime, his brother, **Jean-Baptiste,** joined him, and they founded an instrument factory in the Rue Bourbon. Their growing success led to a conflict with the fan-makers' guild (to which the brothers did not belong), which tried to prevent them from working. But the Erards obtained a special "brevet" from Louis XVI for the manufacture of "forté-pianos" and this enabled them to continue their trade unmolested. In the following years, Erard invented the "piano organisé" with 2 keyboards, one for piano and the other for a small organ; he also became interested in the harp, and invented the ingenious double-action mechanism, perfected in 1811. From 1786–96 he was in London; returning to Paris, he made his first grand piano, and employed the English action until his invention, in 1809, of the repetition action, which is regarded as his supreme achievement. An "orgue expressif," built for the Tuileries, was his last important work. His nephew, **Pierre Erard** (1796–1855), succeeded him; he publ. *The Harp in its present improved state compared with the original Pedal Harp* (1821), and *Perfectionnements apportés dans le mécanisme du piano par les Erards depuis l'origine de cet instrument jusqu'à l'exposition de 1834* (1834). Pierre's successor was his wife's nephew, **Pierre Schäffer** (d. 1878); the firm is still the leading French manufacturer of pianos and harps.

Eratosthenes, Greek philosopher; b. Cyprene, c.276 B.C.; d. Alexandria, Egypt, c.194 B.C. He wrote on numerous subjects, chiefly mathematics, and was custodian of the Alexandria library. The *Catasterismi,* attributed to Eratosthenes, contain scattered notes on Greek music and instruments, especially the "lyra" (German trans. by Schaubach, 1795; Bernhardy publ. in 1822 an ed. of the original text). His work on music is lost; Ptolemy quotes his division of the tetrachord.

Erb, Donald, significant American composer; b. Youngstown, Ohio, Jan. 17, 1927. His family moved to Cleveland when he was a child; he studied cornet with a local musician. After a period of service in the U.S. Navy, he enrolled at Kent State Univ. in Ohio, where he continued to study trumpet and also took courses in composition with Harold Miles and Kenneth Gaburo (B.S., 1950), earning his living by playing trumpet in dance bands. In 1950 he entered the Cleveland Inst. of Music, in the class of Marcel Dick (M.M., 1953). On June 10, 1952, he married Lucille Hyman, and went with her to Paris to study with Nadia Boulanger. Returning to Cleveland, he was engaged as a member of the faculty of the Cleveland Inst. (1953). In 1961 he moved to Bloomington, Ind., where he studied composition with Bernard Heiden at Indiana Univ., receiving his doctorate in music in 1964. In 1964–65 he was an assistant prof. of composition at Bowling Green State Univ. In 1965 he received a Guggenheim fellowship grant. In 1965–67 he was a visiting assistant prof. for research in electronic music at Case Inst. of Technology in Cleveland; in 1966–81 was composer-in-residence at the Cleveland Inst. of Music; in 1975–76, visiting prof. of composition at Indiana Univ. in Bloomington. In the summer of 1968 he headed the composition workshop at the centennial Alaska Festival. From 1969–74 he served as staff composer at the Bennington Composers Conference in Vermont. In 1981 he was appointed prof. of composition at the Southern Methodist Univ. in Dallas. As a composer, he is exceptionally liberal in experimenting in all useful types of composition, from simple folklike monody to the strict dodecaphonic structures; as a former trumpeter in jazz bands, he also makes use of the jazz idiom as freely as of neo-Classical pandiatonic techniques. His most popular composition, *The 7th Trumpet* for Orch., is an epitome of his varied styles. He furthermore applied electronic sound in several of his works. In his band compositions he achieves an extraordinary degree of pure sonorism, in which melody, harmony, and counterpoint are subordinated to the purely aural effect. He also cleverly introduces strange-looking and unusual-sounding musical and unmusical and antimusical instruments, such as euphonious goblets, to be rubbed on the rim, and telephone bells. Thanks to the engaging manner of Erb's music, even when ultradissonant, his works safely traverse their premieres and endure through repeated performances.

WORKS: FOR ORCH.: Chamber Concerto for Piano and Chamber Orch. (Chicago, Feb. 12, 1961); *Spacemusic* for Symph. Band (1963); *Symphony of Overtures* (1964; Bloomington, Feb. 11, 1965); Concerto for Solo Percussion and Orch. (Detroit, Dec. 29, 1966); *Christmasmusic* (Cleveland, Dec. 21, 1967); *The 7th Trumpet* (Dallas, April 5, 1969; his most successful work; received the UNESCO Award in 1971); *Treasures of the Snow* for Youth Orch. (1973; Bergen, N.J., June 8, 1974); Cello Concerto (1975; Rochester, N.Y., Nov. 4, 1976); Trombone Concerto (St. Louis, March 11, 1976); Concerto for Keyboards and Orch. (1978; Akron, Ohio, March 23, 1981); Trumpet Concerto (1980; Baltimore, April 29, 1981); *Sonneries* for Orch. (1981; Rochester, N.Y., March 18, 1982); *Prismatic Variations* for Orch. and Children (St. Louis, Jan. 28, 1984).

CHAMBER MUSIC: *Dialog* for Violin and Piano (1958); String Quartet No. 1 (1960); *Music for Brass Choir* (1960); Quartet for Flute, Oboe, Alto Saxophone, and Double Bass (1961); Sonata for Harpsichord and String Quartet (1962); *Four* for Percussion (1962); *Dance Pieces* for Violin, Piano, Trumpet, and Percussion (1963); *Hexagon* for Flute, Alto Saxophone, Trumpet, Trombone, Cello, and Piano (1963); *Concertante* for Harpsichord and Strings (1963); *Antipodes* for String Quartet and Percussion Quartet (1963); *Phantasma* for Flute, Oboe, Double Bass, and Harpsichord (1965); *Diversion for 2 (other than sex)* for Trumpet and Percussion (1966); *Andante* for Piccolo Flute and Alto Flute (1966); String Trio for Violin, Electric Guitar, and Cello (1966); *Reconnaissance* for Violin, Double Bass, Piano, Percussion, and 2 Electronic Setups (1967); *3 Pieces* for Brass Quintet and Piano (1968);

Trio for 2 for Alto Flute, Percussion, and Double Bass (1968); *Fanfare* for Brass and Percussion (1971); *Harold's Trip to the Sky* for Viola, Piano, and Percussion (1972); Quintet for Violin, Cello, Flute, Clarinet, and Piano (1976); Trio for Piano, Electric Piano, and Celesta (1977); Sonata for Clarinet and Percussion (1980); *3 Pieces* for Harp and Percussion (1981); *Déjà Vu*, 6 études for Double-bass Solo (1981); *The St. Valentine's Day* for Brass Quintet (1981); *Aura* for String Quartet (1981); *The Last Quintet* for Woodwinds (1982); *Devil's Quickstep* for Flute, Clarinet, Violin, Cello, Electric Piano, Harp, Percussion, Harmonicas, Tuned Goblets, Telephone Bells, and Audience (1982); *Fantasy for Cellist and Friends* for 8 to 12 Participants (1983).

VOCAL MUSIC: *Cummings Cycle* for Mixed Chorus and Orch. (1963); *Fallout* for Narrator, Chorus, String Quartet, and Piano (1964); *God Love You Now* for Chorus, Hand Percussion, and Harmonicas (1971); *New England's Prospect* for Choruses, Narrator, and Orch., commissioned for the 100th anniversary of the Cincinnati May Festival (Cincinnati, May 17, 1974).

FOR ELECTRONIC SOUND: *Reticulation* for Symph. Band and Electronic Tape (1965); *Reconnaissance* for Moog Synthesizer (1965); *Stargazing* for Dance and Electronic Tape (1966); *Fission* for Electronic Tape, Soprano Saxophone, Piano, Dancers, and Lights (1968); *In No Strange Land* for Tape, Trombone, and Double Bass (1968); *Basspiece* for Double Bass and 4 tracks of prerecorded Double Bass (1969); *Souvenir* for Tape, Instruments, Lights, etc. (1970); *Klangfarbenfunk I* for Orch., Rock Band, and Electronic Sound (Detroit, Oct., 1, 1970); *Z milosci do Warszawy* for Piano, Clarinet, Cello, Trombone, and Electronic Sound (1971); *The Purple-roofed Ethical Suicide Parlor* for Wind Ensemble and Electronic Sound (1972); *Autumnmusic* for Orch. and Electronic Sound (New Haven, Oct. 20, 1973); *The Towers of Silence* for Electronic Sound (1974); *Music for a Festive Occasion* for Orch. and Electronic Sound (1975; Cleveland, Jan. 11, 1976).

Erdmannsdörfer, Max von, German conductor; b. Nuremberg, June 14, 1848; d. Munich, Feb. 14, 1905. He studied at the Leipzig Cons. (1863–67), and in Dresden (1868–69). From 1871 to 1880 he was court conductor at Sondershausen; then was active in Vienna, Leipzig, and Nuremberg. In 1882 he was engaged as conductor of the Imperial Musical Society in Moscow; in 1885 became prof. at the Moscow Cons. His symph. concerts in Moscow were of great importance to Russian music; he introduced many new works by Russian composers, and his influence was considerable in Moscow musical circles, despite the mediocrity of his conducting. Returning to Germany, he became conductor of the Bremen Phil. Concerts (until 1895); in 1897 he settled in Munich.

Erede, Alberto, Italian conductor; b. Genoa, Nov. 8, 1908. He studied at the Milan Cons. (piano, cello, theory); then in Basel with Weingartner (conducting). He conducted opera in England (1934–39);

from 1951 to 1955 was a guest conductor at the Metropolitan Opera in N.Y.; from 1958 to 1962 was Generalmusikdirektor of the German Opera Theater in Düsseldorf; in 1961 became conductor of the Göteborg (Sweden) Orch.; first conducted in Bayreuth in 1968, leading a performance of *Lohengrin*.

Erickson, Robert, American composer; b. Marquette, Mich., March 7, 1917. He studied music with Wesley La Violette at the Chicago Cons.; with Ernst Krenek at Hamline Univ. in St. Paul (B.A., 1943); in 1950, attended a seminar in composition under Roger Sessions at the Univ. of Calif., Berkeley; in 1966 held a Guggenheim fellowship. In 1967 he was appointed prof. of composition at the Univ. of Calif., San Diego. In his music he explores electronic and serial techniques.
WORKS: *Introduction and Allegro* for Orch. (Minneapolis, March 11, 1949); Piano Sonata (1948); String Quartet No. 1 (1950); Piano Trio (1953); Divertimento for Flute, Clarinet, and Strings (1953); Fantasy for Cello and Orch. (1953), String Quartet No. 2 (1956); Variations for Orch. (1957); Duo for Violin and Piano (1959); *Chamber Concerto* (1960); Toccata for Piano (1962); Concerto for Piano and 7 Instruments (1963); *Sirens and Other Flyers* for Orch. (1965); *Piece for Bells and Toy Pianos* (1965); *Ricercar a 5* for Trombone and Tape (1966); *Scapes,* a "contest for 2 groups" (1966); *Birdland* for Electronic Tape (1967); *Ricercar a 3* for Solo Double Bass and Electronic Tape (1967); *Cardenitas,* dramatic aria for Singer, Mime, Conductor, 7 Musicians, and Stereophonic Prerecorded Tape (1968); *Pacific Sirens* for Instruments and Tape (1969); *General Speech* for Trombone (1969); *The Idea of Order at Key West* for Voice and Instruments (1979).

Erk, Ludwig (Christian), German music scholar and educator; b. Wetzlar, Jan. 6, 1807; d. Berlin, Nov. 25, 1883. He received good training in music from his father, **Adam Wilhelm Erk** (1779–1820), who was organist at Wetzlar. His further studies were under André in Offenbach and Spiess in Frankfurt. In 1826 he became a prof. at the seminary in Mörs, where he taught until 1835; from 1836 to 1840 he was an instructor in liturgical singing at Berlin, and conducted a choir. In 1852, he founded the Erk Gesangverein for mixed voices. During his years as a conductor of choral societies, he became interested in folk songs, and accumulated a great collection of authentic materials on the subject; also publ. songbooks for schools, which attained considerable popularity; some of these were written jointly with his brother **Friedrich Erk,** and his brother-in-law, **Greef.** He also publ. *Die deutschen Volkslieder mit ihren Singweisen* (1838–45); *Volkslieder, alte und neue* (1845–46); *Deutscher Liederhort* (folk songs; vol. 1 publ. 1856; MS of the remainder was bought—with the rest of his valuable library—for the Royal Hochschule für Musik in Berlin; continued and ed. by Magnus Böhme, and publ. in 4 vols., 1894); *Mehrstimmige Gesänge* (1833–35); *Volksklänge* (1851–60); *Deutscher Liederschatz* (1859–72); *Vierstim-mige Choralgesänge der vornehmsten Meister des 16. and 17. Jahrhunderts* (1845); *J.S. Bachs mehrstimmige Choralgesänge und geistliche Arien* (1850–65); *Vierstimmiges Choralbuch für evangelische Kirchen* (1863); *Choräle für Männerstimmen* (1866); *Methodischer Leitfaden für den Gesangunterricht in Volksschulen* (1834, Part I).

Erkel, Franz (Ferenc), the creator of Hungarian national opera; b. Gyula, Hungary, Nov. 7, 1810; d. Budapest, June 15, 1893. He was taught by his father; at 24 became director of the Kaschau opera troupe, and went with it to Pest, where he was appointed conductor at the National Theater on its opening in 1837. He was the founder and director of the Budapest Phil. Concerts (1853), and first prof. of piano and instrumentation at the National Musical Academy. His numerous songs, in the national vein, became very popular. He composed the Hungarian National Hymn (1845).
WORKS: Operas (all first presented in Budapest): *Báthory Mária* (Aug. 8, 1840); *Hunyady László* (Jan. 27, 1844; the first truly national Hungarian opera; given almost 300 perfs. in the first 50 years); *Erzsébet* (May 6, 1857); *Kúnok* (1858); *Bánk-Bán* (March 9, 1861; highly successful in Hungary); *Sarolta,* comic opera (June 26, 1862); *Dózsa György* (April 6, 1867); *Brankovics György* (May 20, 1874); *Névtelen hosök* (Nov. 30, 1880); *István király* (March 14, 1885); music for plays; *Festival Overture* for Orch. (1887); many songs and anthems. A symposium of essays on Erkel was publ. in *Zenetudományi Tanulmányok* (Budapest, 1954, II) under the editorship of B. Szabolcsi.

Erkin, Ulvi Cemal, Turkish composer; b. Istanbul, March 14, 1906; d. Ankara, Sept. 15, 1972. He studied piano with Isidor Philipp in Paris and composition with Nadia Boulanger in Fontainebleau. Returning to Turkey, he became a piano instructor at the Ankara Cons.
WORKS: *Bayram,* tone poem (Ankara, May 11, 1934); Symph. No. 1 (Ankara, April 20, 1946); Symph. No. 2 (1948–51); Violin Concerto (Ankara, April 2, 1948); chamber music; piano pieces.

Erlanger, Camille, French composer; b. Paris, May 25, 1863; d. there, April 24, 1919. He was a pupil of the Paris Cons. under Delibes, Durand, and Matthias; in 1888, took the Grand Prix de Rome for his cantata *Velléda.* He earned fame with his opera *Le Juif polonais* (Paris, April 11, 1900), which has remained in active repertoire; other operas are: *Kermaria* (Paris, Feb. 8, 1897); *Le Fils de l'étoile* (Paris, April 20, 1904); *Aphrodite* (Paris, March 27, 1906); *Bacchus triomphant* (Bordeaux, Sept. 11, 1909); *L'Aube rouge* (Rouen, Dec. 29, 1911); *La Sorcière* (Paris, Dec. 18, 1912); *Le Barbier de Deauville* (1917); *Forfaiture* (perf. posthumously at the Opéra-Comique in 1921). He also wrote several symph. poems (*Maître et serviteur,* after Tolstoy, etc.) and a French Requiem.

d'Erlanger, Baron Frédéric, member of the family

of bankers; composer and opera director; b. Paris, May 29, 1868; d. London, April 23, 1943. In 1897 he assumed the pseudonym **Regnal**, formed by reading backward the last 6 letters of his name. He lived in London, where for many years he was one of the directors of the Covent Garden Opera.

WORKS: Operas: *Jehan de Saintre* (Aix-les-Bains, Aug. 1, 1893); *Inez Mendo* (London, July 10, 1897, under the pseudonym Regnal); *Tess,* after Thomas Hardy (Naples, April 10, 1906); *Noël* (Paris, Dec. 28, 1910; Chicago, 1913); Piano Quintet; String Quartet; Violin Concerto (London, March 12, 1903, Kreisler soloist); Violin Sonata; *Andante* for Cello and Orch.

d'Erlanger, Rodolphe, French musicologist, specialist in Arab studies; b. Boulogne-sur-Seine, June 7, 1872; d. Sidi-bou-Sadi, Tunisia, Oct. 29, 1932. He went to Tunis in 1910, and began a thorough study of the theory and history of Arabian music, The result was a series of publications of primary importance, most of them issued posthumously, including a monumental work in 6 volumes under the general title *La Musique arabe* (Paris, 1930–59).

Erlebach, Philipp Heinrich, important German composer; b. Esens, East Frisia, July 25, 1657; d. Rudolstadt, April 17, 1714. He was Hofkapellmeister at Rudolstadt from at least 1681; remained there until 1714. His style was strongly influenced by that of Lully. He wrote orch. suites (6 overtures, publ. 1693); suites for violin, viola da gamba, and continuo (1694), one of which was reprinted by Einstein in *Zur deutschen Literatur für Viola da Gamba* (1905); cantatas; sacred and secular songs, including *Harmonische Freude* (2 parts: 1697, 1710; reprinted by Kinkeldey in vol. 46/47 of Denkmäler deutscher Tonkunst); organ works; etc. Examples from his *Gottgeheilige Singstunde* (1704) are printed in M. Friedlaender's *Das deutsche Lied im 18. Jahrhundert* (1902).

Ernst, Heinrich Wilhelm, violinist and composer; b. Brünn, May 6, 1814; d. Nice, Oct. 8, 1865. He was a pupil of Böhm (violin) and Seyfried (composition) in Vienna, with further study under Mayseder; from 1832–38, lived in Paris. From 1838 to 1850 he was almost continually on concert tours; then settled in London (1855). His works for violin are brilliant and effective; the *Elégie,* the Concerto in F-sharp minor (new ed. by Marteau, 1913), and *Carnaval de Venise* are a few of the most celebrated.

Erös, Peter, Hungarian conductor; b. Budapest, Sept. 22, 1932. He studied piano with Lajos Hernadi, composition with Zoltán Kodály, conducting with László Somogyi, and chamber music with Leo Weiner. After the abortive revolution in Hungary in 1956, he emigrated to the Netherlands. There he served as assistant to Otto Klemperer at the Holland Festival of 1958; from 1958–61 was assistant to Ferenc Fricsay, working with the Deutsche Grammophon Gesellschaft; in 1960 he attended the master classes at Bayreuth. His subsequent professional engage-ments were: assistant conductor of the Concertgebouw Orch. in Amsterdam (1960–65); chief conductor of the Malmö Symph. Orch. (1966–68); permanent guest conductor of the Melbourne Symph. (1969–70). In 1972 he was appointed music director and conductor of the San Diego Symph. Orch.; was active as conductor of the West Australian Symph. Orch. of the Australian Broadcasting Commission. He was also a guest conductor of orchs. all over the world. He resigned from the San Diego Symph. post in 1980, and in 1982 was appointed conductor of the Peabody Symph. Orch. in Baltimore.

Ershov, Ivan, celebrated Russian tenor; b. in the village of Maly Nesvetai, near Novocherkassk, Nov. 20, 1867; d. Tashkent, Nov. 21, 1943. He studied voice in Moscow with Alexandrova-Kochetova and in St. Petersburg with Gabel and Paleček. In 1893 he made his operatic debut at the Maryinsky Theater in St. Petersburg as Faust, which became one of his most popular roles; then went to Italy for a year and took voice lessons with Rossi in Milan; appeared in Turin as Don José in *Carmen.* He returned to Russia in 1894 and joined the Kharkov Opera; in 1895 he became a member of the Maryinsky Opera Theater, and served with it until 1929. He achieved fabulous success as the greatest performer of the tenor roles in the Russian repertoire, and he also was regarded by music critics and audiences as the finest interpreter of the Wagnerian operas; he sang Siegfried, Tannhäuser, Lohengrin, and Tristan with extraordinary lyric and dramatic penetration; as an opera tenor in his time he had no rivals on the Russian stage. In 1929, at the age of 62, he sang Verdi's Otello; he also appeared in oratorio and solo recitals. From 1916 to 1941 he taught voice at the Petrograd (Leningrad) Cons. At the beginning of the siege of Leningrad in 1941, Ershov was evacuated with the entire personnel of the Cons. to Tashkent in Central Asia, where he died shortly afterward.

Erskine, John, American educator and writer on music; b. New York, Oct. 5, 1879; d. there, June 1, 1951. He studied piano with Carl Walter; composition with MacDowell; then took up an academic and literary career, becoming highly successful as a novelist and essayist. He was educated at Columbia Univ. (B.A., 1900; M.A., 1901; Ph.D., 1903; LL.D., 1929); was a prof. of English there (1909–37), then prof. emeritus. In 1923 he resumed piano study under Ernest Hutcheson; played as soloist with the N.Y. Symph. Orch. and the Baltimore Civic Orch.; was president of the Juilliard School of Music in N.Y. (1928–37); president of the Juilliard Music Foundation from 1948 until his death. He was editor of *A Musical Companion* (1935). He received the degree of Mus.Doc. from Rollins College in Florida (1931), Cornell College, Iowa (1935); also the degree of Litt.D. from Amherst College (1923) and the Univ. of Bordeaux, France (1929). Erskine was an Officer of the French Legion of Honor. He publ. books on music, including *Is There a Career in Music?* (N.Y., 1929); *Song without Words: The Story of Felix Mendelssohn* (1941); *The Philharmonic-Sym-*

phony Society of N.Y., Its First Hundred Years (N.Y., 1943); *What Is Music?* (Philadelphia, 1944); *The Memory of Certain Persons* (Philadelphia, 1947); *My Life as a Teacher* (N.Y., 1948); *My Life in Music* (N.Y., 1950).

Eschenbach, Christoph, remarkably talented German pianist and conductor; b. Breslau, Feb. 20, 1940. His real name was Christoph Ringman; his mother died in childbirth, and his father died shortly afterward. He was adopted by his mother's relatives, whose name was Eschenbach; this became his legal name. His foster mother, a professional musician, gave him his first music lessons. He later studied piano with Eliza Hansen in Hamburg and Hans-Otto Schmidt in Cologne. His career proceeded most auspiciously; he won several school prizes; in 1962 he received the important prize of the International Competition in Munich; in 1965 he won the first prize of the Haskil Competition in Lucerne; in the same year he was soloist in a recording of Beethoven's First Piano Concerto with the Berlin Phil. under the direction of Herbert von Karajan. He was selected to represent West Germany at Expo 1967 in Montreal, Canada; on Jan. 16, 1969, he made his first appearance in the U.S., playing Mozart's Piano Concerto in F major with the Cleveland Orch. under the direction of George Szell. Eschenbach became interested in modern music; he gave the premiere of Hans Werner Henze's Second Piano Concerto in 1969. From then on, Eschenbach made several world tours which took him to Russia, South America, South Africa, Israel, and Japan. In 1976 he turned to conducting; on Aug. 10, 1976, he conducted in N.Y. a Mozart program, leading the orch. from the keyboard in two Mozart concertos. He made his home in the Canary Islands, while continuing his tours. He is regarded as one of the finest interpreters of the piano concertos of Mozart and Beethoven; he has also distinguished himself in conducting the Classical repertoire.

Escher, Rudolf, noted Dutch composer; b. Amsterdam, Jan. 8, 1912; d. De Koog (Texel), March 17, 1980. He studied harmony, violin, and piano at the Toonkunst Cons. in Rotterdam (1931–37); was a student in composition of Pijper (1934); worked in the electronic music studios in Delft (1959–60) and in Utrecht (1961). He taught at the Amsterdam Cons. (1960–61) and at the Inst. for Musical Science at the Utrecht Univ. (1964–75). In 1977 he was awarded the Johan Wagenaar Prize for his compositions. Escher's music was very much influenced by the modern French school.
WORKS: FOR ORCH.: *Sinfonia in memoriam Maurice Ravel* (1940); *Musique pour l'esprit en deuil (Music for the Soul in Mourning;* 1941–43; Amsterdam, Jan. 19, 1947); Passacaglia (1945; withdrawn); Concerto for Strings (1947–48; withdrawn); *Hymne de Grand Meaulnes* (1950–51); 2 symphs.: No. 1 (1953–54) and No. 2 (1958; revised 1964 and 1971); *Summer Rites at Noon* for 2 facing Orchs. (1962–68); orchestration of Debussy's *6 épigraphes antiques* for Piano Duet (1976–77; Hilversum Radio,

July 6, 1978).
FOR VOICE: *3 poèmes de Tristan Corbière* for Soprano and Piano (1936); *Horcajo* for Mezzo-soprano and Piano (1941); *Lettre du Mexique* for Baritone and Piano (1942); *Protesilaos en Laodamia,* musical comedy for Mezzo-soprano, Tenor, Baritone, and Orch. (1946–48; withdrawn); *De poort van Ishtar,* incidental music for Chorus and Orch. (1947; withdrawn); *Poèmes de Vion Dalibray* for Tenor and Piano (1947–49); *Chants du désir* for Mezzo-soprano and Piano (1951); *Nostalgies* for Tenor and Orch. (1951; revised 1961); *Strange Meeting,* after Owen, for Baritone and Piano (1952); *Le Vrai Visage de la paix,* after Eluard, for Chorus a cappella (1953; revised 1957); *Song of Love and Eternity,* after Dickinson, for Chorus a cappella (1955); *Ciel, air et vents,* after Ronsard, for Chorus a cappella (1957); *De Perzen (The Persians),* after Aeschylus, incidental music for Narrator, Men's Choir, and Orch. (1963); *Univers de Rimbaud,* 5 songs after Rimbaud for Tenor and Orch. (1970); *3 Poems by W.H. Auden* for Chorus a cappella (1975).
WRITINGS: The monographs *Toscanini en Debussy* (Rotterdam, 1938) and "Maurice Ravel," *Groot Nederland* (July 1939); "Debussy and the Musical Epigram," *Key Notes, 10* (1979/2).

Eschig, Max, French music publisher; b. Opava, now Czechoslovakia, May 27, 1872; d. Paris, Sept. 3, 1927. He settled in Paris and founded a publishing firm under his name in 1907, prospering continually and forming an impressive catalogue of modern works by Ravel, Manuel de Falla, and many other French, Spanish, and English composers.

Eschmann, Johann Karl, Swiss pianist and pedagogue; b. Winterthur, April 12, 1826; d. Zürich, Oct. 27, 1882. He studied in Leipzig with Moscheles, and also had some lessons with Mendelssohn. He then settled in Zürich as a piano teacher; publ. a valuable manual, *Wegweiser durch die Klavierliteratur* (Zürich, 1879; 8th ed., 1914), and *100 Aphorismen aus dem Klavierunterricht* (2nd ed., 1899).

Escobedo, Bartolomé, Spanish composer; b. Zamora, c.1515; d. Nov. 1563 as canon at Segovia. From 1536–41, and again from 1545–54, he was a singer in the Papal Choir at Rome. He was a judge in the famous dispute between Nicola Vicentino and Vincento Lusitano (1551) over the qualities of Greek modes. He composed 2 masses and a number of motets.

Escudier, Léon, French music journalist; b. Castelnaudary, Aude, Sept. 17, 1816; d. Paris, June 22, 1881. He was a brother and partner of **Marie Escudier** (b. Castelnaudary, June 29, 1809; d. Paris, April 18, 1880). In 1838, the brothers began publishing the periodical *La France Musicale* and soon afterward established a music shop. Industrious writers, they issued jointly the following works: *Etudes biographiques sur les chanteurs contemporains* (1840); *Dictionnaire de musique d'après les théoriciens, historiens et critiques les plus célèbres* (2 vols.,

1844; reprinted in 1854 as *Dictionnaire de musique, théorique et historique*); *Rossini, sa vie et ses œuvres* (1854); *Vie et aventures des cantatrices célèbres, précédées des musiciens de l'Empire, et suivies de la vie anecdotique de Paganini* (1856). Léon broke up partnership with his brother in 1862, retaining the music business; he established a new paper, *L'Art Musical,* which continued to appear until Sept. 27, 1894. Marie retained the publishing and editorial rights to *La France Musicale,* which ceased publication in 1870.

Eshpai, Andrei, Soviet composer, son of **Yakov Eshpai;** b. Kozmodemiansk, May 15, 1925. He studied with Aram Khatchaturian in Moscow; during the war he acted as a translator from German. In his music he makes use of folk motifs of the Mari nation from which he descended.
   WORKS: 4 symphs. (1959, 1962, 1964, 1982); *Symphonic Dances* (1951); *Hungarian Melodies* for Violin and Orch. (1952); 2 piano concertos (1954, 1972); 2 violin sonatas (1966, 1970); Concerto for Orch., with Solo Trumpet, Vibraphone, Piano, and Double Bass (1967); *Festival Overture* for Chorus, 12 Violins, 8 Cellos, 6 Harps, 4 Pianos, and Orch. (1970); ballet, *The Circle* (Kuibishev, Feb. 23, 1981); Oboe Concerto (1982).

Eshpai, Yakov, Russian composer of Mari extraction; b. near Zvenigorodsk, Oct. 30, 1890; d. Moscow, Feb. 20, 1963. He studied violin and singing in Kazan, and later at the Moscow Cons. He publ. important collections of national songs of the Ural region, particularly of the Mari ethnic group; also wrote vocal and instrumental music on native themes.

Eslava y Elizondo, Miguel Hilarión, Spanish composer and scholar; b. Burlada, Navarra, Oct. 21, 1807; d. Madrid, July 23, 1878. He was a choirboy at the Cathedral of Pamplona; studied organ and violin; in 1827 he went to Calahorra, where he studied with Francisco Secanilla; at the age of 21 he was appointed music director at the Cathedral of Burgo de Osma, where he was ordained a priest. In 1832 he became music director at Seville; in 1847 he obtained the appointment as chapel master to Queen Isabella in Madrid; in 1854 he became a prof. at the Madrid Cons. He also edited a periodical, *Gaceta Musical de Madrid* (1855–56). He wrote 3 operas with Italian texts: *Il Solitario del Monte Selvaggio* (Cádiz, 1841), *La tregua di Ptolemaide* (1842), and *Pietro il crudele* (1843); his fame rests, however, not on his musical compositions, but on his great collection in 10 vols., *Lira sacro-hispana* (Madrid, 1869), an anthology of Spanish sacred music from the 16th to the 19th century, including some of Eslava's own works (Requiem, Te Deum, etc.). He also publ. *Método de solfeo* (1846) and *Escuela de Armonía y Composición* (1861).

Esplá, Oscar, Spanish composer; b. Alicante, Aug. 5, 1886; d. Madrid, Jan. 6, 1976. He at first studied engineering and philosophy; then turned to music, traveling and studying for some years in Germany.

He was the first president of the Junta Nacional de Música under the Spanish Republic (1934) and in 1936 was director of the Madrid Cons.; then lived in Brussels and Paris; eventually returned to Spain.
   WORKS: *La bella durmiente,* opera (Vienna, 1909); *La Balteira,* opera (1939); ballets: *Ciclopes de Ifach* and *El contrabandista* (1930); orch. works: *Suite levantina; El sueño de Eros; Don Quixote; Ambito de la danza; Las cumbres;* scenic cantata, *Nochebuena del diablo* (1924); *Sonata del sur* for Piano and Orch. (1936–43); *Sinfonía Aitana* (Madrid, Oct. 31, 1964); String Quartet (1947); *De profundis* for 4 Soloists, Chorus, and Orch. (1967); piano pieces; songs. He publ. the books *El arte y la musicalidad* and *Las actividades del espíritu y su fundamento estético.*

Essipoff (Essipova), Anna, famous Russian pianist and pedagogue; b. St. Petersburg, Feb. 13, 1851; d. there, Aug. 18, 1914. She was a pupil of **Leschetizky,** and married him in 1880 (divorced 1892). She made her debut in St. Petersburg; subsequently made long concert tours throughout Europe and in America; her distinguishing artistic quality was a singing piano tone and "pearly" passage work. From 1870 to 1885 she gave 669 concerts. In 1893 she was engaged as a prof. of piano at the St. Petersburg Cons., and continued to teach there until the last years of her life. Many famous pianists and composers, Prokofiev among them, were her students.

Estes, Simon, black American bass-baritone; b. Centerville, Iowa, March 2, 1938. He studied voice at the Juilliard School of Music in N.Y.; then began his career as a singer of oratorio and lieder. On June 10, 1976, he made his Metropolitan Opera debut in N.Y. as Oroveso in *Norma;* he also appeared at La Scala in Milan, the Bolshoi Theater in Moscow, and the Hamburg State Opera. In 1978 he sang at the Bayreuth Festival in the title role of *Der Fliegende Holländer.* His major operatic roles include Wotan, Boris Godunov, and King Philip in Verdi's *Don Carlos.*

Estrada, Carlos, Uruguayan composer and conductor; b. Montevideo, Sept. 15, 1909; d. there, May 7, 1970. He studied in Paris with Roger-Ducasse and Henri Busser (composition) and with Philippe Gaubert (conducting). Returning to Montevideo, he was associated with the State Radio (1940–54) and later became director of the National Cons. in Montevideo (1954–68). He wrote 2 symphs. (1951, 1967); chamber music; effective piano pieces. A complete list of his works is found in vol. 16 of *Composers of the Americas* (Washington, D.C., 1970).

Euclid, famous Greek geometer; lived at Alexandria about 300 B.C. He is the reputed author of a treatise on music, *Katatomè kanonos (Sectio canonis),* following the theories of Pythagoras (new critical ed. by K. von Jan in *Musici scriptores graeci*). For another treatise long ascribed to Euclid, see the entry on Cleonides.

Eulenburg, Ernst, German music publisher, b. Berlin, Nov. 30, 1847; d. Leipzig, Sept. 11, 1926. He studied at the Leipzig Cons.; in 1874 established in Leipzig the publ. house bearing his name; after his acquisition of Payne's *Kleine Partitur-Ausgabe* (1892) he enormously increased the scope of that publication so that large orch. scores could be included. Upon his death the firm was taken over by his son **Kurt Eulenburg.**

Eulenburg, Kurt, German music publisher, son of **Ernst Eulenburg;** b. Berlin, Feb. 22, 1879; d. London, April 10, 1982 (at the age of 103!). Apprenticed by his father, he joined the Eulenburg firm in 1911, and upon his father's death in 1926 became its sole owner. He extended the dept. of miniature scores and also publ. the original text ("Urtext") of many of Mozart's works, edited by Alfred Einstein, Blume, Kroyer, and others. During the war, he lived in Switzerland. He settled in London in 1945 and took over the management of the London branch of his publishing business. He retired in 1968.

Euler, Leonhard, great mathematician; b. Basel, April 15, 1707; d. St. Petersburg, Sept. 18, 1783. He was a prof. of mathematics at St. Petersburg (1730) and Berlin (1741); publ. several important works on music theory and acoustics, chief among them being the *Tentamen novae theoriae musicae* (1739). Euler was the first to employ logarithms to explain differences in pitch.

Evangelisti, Franco, Italian composer; b. Rome, Jan. 21, 1926; d. there, Jan. 29, 1980. He first studied engineering at the Univ. of Rome; then went to Germany, where he took courses in composition at the Univ. of Freiburg; also attended summer courses with Ernst Krenek and René Leibowitz at Darmstadt. In his own music he explored the musical resources of electronics; the titles of his works betray his preoccupation with mathematical terminology, as exemplified by *4!* (factorization of the numbers from 1 to 4) for Violin and Piano (1955); *Ordini* for Orch. (1955); *Random or Not Random* for Orch. (1956–62); *Proporzioni* for Flute (1958); *Campi integrati* (1959); *Aleatorio* for String Quartet (1959); *Condensazioni* for Orch. (1962). He also lectured on electronic music.

Evans, Bill (William John Evans), American jazz pianist and composer; b. Plainfield, N.J., Aug. 16, 1929; d. New York, Sept. 15, 1980. After taking up the piano, he joined the band of Miles Davis and soon became a leading jazz pianist; after making the classic jazz recording of *Kind of Blue* with the Davis group, he formed his own jazz trio. He received Grammy awards for his recordings *Conversations with Myself* (1963), *Alone* (1970), and *The Bill Evans Album* (1971).

Evans, Edwin, Sr., English organist and writer; b. London, 1844; d. there, Dec. 21, 1923. An assiduous and thorough scholar, he publ. basic analytic vols. on Beethoven and Brahms: *Beethoven's 9 Sympho-*

nies, fully described and analyzed (London, 1923–24) and the remarkable 4-vol. edition (1,581 pages; over 1,000 musical examples) *Historical, Descriptive and Analytical Account of the Entire Works of Johannes Brahms:* vol. I, vocal works (1912); vol. II, chamber and orch. music up to op. 67 (1933; reprinted 1950); vol. III, chamber and orch. music from op. 68 to the end (1935; reprinted 1949); vol. IV, piano works (1936; reprinted 1950). Vols. II, III, and IV were publ. posthumously. He also wrote *Accompaniment of Plainchant* (1911); *Wagner's Teachings by Analogy* (1915); *How to Compose; How to Accompany at the Piano* (London, 1917); *Method of Instrumentation* (vol. I, *How to Write for Strings*); *Technics of the Organ* (London, 1938); trans. Wagner's *Oper und Drama;* made organ arrangements of operatic overtures.

Evans, Sir Geraint, Welsh baritone; b. Pontypridd, South Wales, Feb. 16, 1922. He studied in Hamburg and Geneva; was associated with the Glyndebourne Festivals from 1949 to 1961; appeared in San Francisco in 1959, and also sang at La Scala in Milan in 1960 and at the Vienna Opera in 1961. He made his Metropolitan Opera debut in N.Y. on March 25, 1964, as Falstaff. He distinguished himself particularly in the roles of Figaro, Leporello, and Papageno. He was knighted in 1969 after having been made a Commander of the Order of the British Empire in 1959. He publ. *A Knight at the Opera* (London, 1984).

Ewald, Victor, Russian composer; b. St. Petersburg, Nov. 27, 1860; d. Leningrad, April 26, 1935. He studied engineering; from 1895 to 1915 was a prof. at the Inst. of Civil Engineering. Music was his avocation; he played the cello and the French horn; took part in Belaieff's quartet evenings and wrote a number of chamber music works; of these, his brass quintet is still popular. After the Revolution he continued to work in his primary profession as a civil engineer and instructor; also was active as an ethnomusicologist and participated in the expeditions in the north of European Russia collecting folk songs. His daughter **Zinaida** (1894–1942) continued his work in folklore and publ. several collections of Russian songs, in collaboration with her husband, **Evgeny Gippius** (b. 1903).

Ewen, David, prolific American writer on music; b. Lwow, Poland, Nov. 26, 1907. He came to the U.S. in 1912. He attended the College of the City of N.Y.; studied music theory with Max Persin; was enrolled as a student at the Music School Settlement and at Columbia Univ. He was music editor of *Reflex Magazine* (1928–29) and *The American Hebrew* (1935); was active briefly as a publisher (1946–49); in 1965 joined the music faculty of the Univ. of Miami, which awarded him in 1974 the honorary degree of D.Mus.. In all probability, Ewen has publ. more books on music and edited more reference publications than anyone else in the 20th century (82 at the last count in 1984). Some of his publications have been trans. into 17 languages.

WRITINGS: (not including revisions publ. with the amplificatory modifier "New"): *The Unfinished Symphony* (1931); *Hebrew Music* (1931); *Wine, Women, and Waltz* (1933); *Composers of Today* (1934); *The Man with the Baton* (1936); *Composers of Yesterday* (1937); *Men and Women Who Make Music* (1939); *Musical Vienna* (with Frederic Ewen, 1939); *Living Musicians* (1940); *Pioneers in Music* (1941); *Music Comes to America* (1942; revised 1947); *Dictators of the Baton* (1943; revised 1948); *Men of Popular Music* (1944; revised 1952); *Music for the Millions* (1944; revised 1946, 1949; publ. under title *Encyclopedia of Musical Masterpieces*, 1950); *American Composers Today* (revised ed., 1949); *The Story of Irving Berlin* (1950); *The Story of Arturo Toscanini* (1951; in Italian, Milan, 1952); *Fun with Musical Games and Quizzes* (with N. Slonimsky, 1952); *The Complete Book of 20th Century Music* (1952); *European Composers Today* (1953); *The Story of Jerome Kern* (1953); *The Milton Cross Encyclopedia of Great Composers and Their Music* (with Milton Cross, 1953); *Encyclopedia of the Opera* (1955); *A Journey to Greatness, George Gershwin* (1956; rewritten in 1970 under the title *George Gershwin: His Journey to Greatness*); *Panorama of American Popular Music* (1957); *Complete Book of the American Musical Theater* (N.Y., 1958; extremely valuable; brought up to date as *The New Complete Book of the American Musical Theater*, 1970); *Encyclopedia of Concert Music* (N.Y., 1959); *The World of Jerome Kern* (N.Y., 1960); *Leonard Bernstein* (N.Y., 1960; revised 1967); *History of Popular Music* (N.Y., 1961); *The Story of America's Musical Theater* (N.Y., 1961; revised 1969); *Ewen's Lighter Classics in Music* (N.Y., 1961); *David Ewen Introduces Modern Music* (N.Y., 1962; revised 1969); *The Book of European Light Opera* (N.Y., 1962); *Popular American Composers* (N.Y., 1962); *The Complete Book of Classical Music* (N.Y., 1963); *The Life and Death of Tin Pan Alley* (N.Y., 1964); *American Popular Songs: From the Revolutionary War to the Present* (N.Y., 1966); *Great Composers: 1300–1900* (N.Y., 1966); *The World of 20th-Century Music* (N.Y., 1968); *Composers since 1900* (N.Y., 1969); *Great Men of American Popular Songs* (N.Y., 1970); *Composers of Tomorrow's Music* (N.Y., 1971); *New Encyclopedia of the Opera*, a radical revision of *Encyclopedia of the Opera* (1971); *Popular American Composers: First Supplement* (N.Y., 1972); *Mainstreams of Music* (in 4 vols., N.Y., 1972, 1973, 1974, 1975); *All the Years of American Popular Music* (Englewood Cliffs, N.J., 1977); *Musicians since 1900* (N.Y., 1978); *American Composers: A Biographical Dictionary* (N.Y., 1982). He also publ. a number of books for young people (on Gershwin, Bernstein, Haydn, Irving Berlin, Toscanini, Johann Strauss, Jerome Kern, Richard Rodgers, and Cole Porter). He rewrote, revised, and expanded the *Milton Cross Encyclopedia of Great Composers* (N.Y., 1960). Revised eds. of *The Book of Modern Composers*, originally publ. in 1943, appeared as *The New Book of Modern Composers* in 1960 and 1967. He further edited *From Bach to Stravinsky* (1933) and *The World of Great Composers* (Englewood Cliffs, N.J., 1962).

Ewing, Maria (Louise), American soprano; b. Detroit, March 27, 1950. She studied at the Cleveland Inst. of Music with Eleanor Steber and Jennie Tourèl; made her professional debut in 1973 at the Ravinia Festival with the Chicago Symph. Orch.; subsequently appeared with opera companies in Chicago, Washington, D.C., Santa Fe, and Houston. She made her Metropolitan Opera debut in N.Y. in 1976 as Cherubino in *Le nozze di Figaro;* in 1976 she sang at La Scala in Milan. She returned to the Metropolitan Opera to sing the part of Dorabella in a new production of *Così fan tutte.* She was a periodic soloist at the Glyndebourne Festival, where her husband, **Sir Peter Hall,** was artistic director.

Eximeno (y Pujades), Antonio, one of the most important Spanish writers on music; b. Valencia, Sept. 26, 1729; d. Rome, June 9, 1808. He entered the Company of Jesus at the age of 16; became a prof. of rhetoric at the Univ. of Valencia; in 1764 was appointed prof. of mathematics at the military academy in Segovia. When the Jesuits were expelled from Spain in 1767, he went to Rome, and in 1768 began to study music. In 1774 he publ. *Dell' origine e delle regole della musica colla storia del suo progresso, decadenza e rinnovazione* (Rome; Spanish trans. by Gutierrez, 1776, 3 vols.), in which he protested against pedantic rules and argued that music should be based on the natural rules of prosody. His theories were strongly controverted, especially by Padre Martini; in answer to the latter, Eximeno publ. *Dubbio di Antonio Eximeno sopra il Saggio fondamentale, pratico di contrappunto del Maestro Giambattista Martini* (Rome, 1775). His dictum that the national song should serve as a basis for the art-music of each country was taken up by Pedrell and led to the nationalist movement in modern Spanish music. Eximeno also wrote a satirical musical novel, *Don Lazarillo Vizcardi,* directed against the theories of Pietro Cerone (publ. by Barbieri, 1872–73, 2 vols.).

Expert, Henry, eminent French music editor; b. Bordeaux, May 12, 1863; d. Tourettes-sur-Loup (Alpes-Maritimes), Aug. 18, 1952. He attended a Jesuit school in Bordeaux; went to Paris in 1881 and studied with César Franck and Eugène Gigout; taught at the Ecole Nationale de Musique Classique, and lectured at the Ecole des Hautes Etudes Sociales; from 1909, he was deputy-librarian of the Paris Cons.; became chief of the library in 1921; was the founder (in 1903, with Maury) of the Société d'Etudes Musicales et Concerts Historiques, also of the choral society Chanterie de la Renaissance (1924). In 1933 he retired. His life work was the editing and publication of Franco-Flemish music of the 15th and 16th centuries, in 6 parts: I. *Les Maîtres-Musiciens de la Renaissance française* (works by Orlando di Lasso, Goudimel, Costeley, Janequin, Brumel, La Rue, Mouton, Fevin, Mauduit, Claude Le Jeune, Regnart, Du Caurroy, Gervaise, and Attaingnant's collection of chansons, all in modern notation, with facsimiles, etc.; 23 vols., publ. 1894–1908); II. *Bibliographie thématique* (2 vols., catalogue of publications of Attaingnant); III. *Les Théoriciens de la musique au temps de la Renaissance* (works of Michel de Menhou); IV. 2 vols. of music by Antoine de Bertrand; V. *Commentaires;* VI. *Extraits des Maîtres Musiciens* (selected single compositions, arranged for modern use; a large number have been publ., including works by some composers not found in Part I, viz.: Bertrand, Bonnet, Certon, De La Grotte, Gardanne, Josquin des Prez, Le Heurteur, Le Pelletier, Passereau, Thoinot-Arbeau). In 1924 Expert began the publication of a new series of French music of the 16th century entitled *Monuments de la musique française au temps de la Renaissance* (with scores in modern notation), of which 10 vols. were publ.; these contain works by Le Jeune, in 2 vols. *(Octonaires de la vanité et inconstance du monde);* Certon (3 masses); Le Blanc *(Airs de plusieurs musiciens);* Bertrand, in 4 vols. *(Amours de P. de Ronsard);* Goudimel *(Messes à 4 voix);* L'Estocart *(Octonaires de la vanité du monde).* Expert also edited *Chansons mondaines des XVIIᵉ et XVIIIᵉ siècles français* (80 songs); *Airs français des XVIᵉ et XVIIᵉ siècles* (Boesset, Guedron, Tessier, Lambert) *Florilège du concert vocal de la Renaissance* (1928–29), in 8 parts (Janequin, Lassus, Costeley, Bonnet, Le Jeune, Mauduit); *Les Maîtres du clavecin des XVIIᵉ et XVIIIᵉ siècles* (Dandrieu, Daquin, Corrette); *Amusements des maîtres français du XVIIIᵉ siècle* (Chédeville, J. Aubert, Baton); *Répertoire de musique religieuse et spirituelle* (Campra, Charpentier, Dumont, Lully, Bernier, Couperin le Grand, Clérambault, Lalande, Rameau, etc.); *La Fleur des musiciens de P. de Ronsard* (1923); instrumental *Fantaisies* by Le Jeune and Du Caurroy; and *Le Pseautier huguenot du XVIᵉ siècle* (the Huguenot Psalter; 1902). He contributed the chapter on the music of France during the 16th century to Lavignac's *Encyclopédie de la Musique.*

Eybler, Joseph, Austrian composer; b. Schwechat, near Vienna, Feb. 8, 1765; d. Schönbrunn, July 24, 1846. He studied with Albrechtsberger in Vienna; was a friend of Haydn and Mozart; in 1792, became choirmaster at the Carmelite Church; was tutor to the princes in 1810, and first court Kapellmeister in 1824, on Salieri's retirement. He composed symphs., concertos, quartets, sonatas, etc.; also 2 oratorios, 32 masses, a Requiem, 7 Te Deums, and 30 offertories.

Eysler, Edmund S., Austrian operetta composer; b. Vienna, March 12, 1874; d. there, Oct. 4, 1949. He produced a great number of stage works; in 1915 he wrote no fewer than 4 operettas (*Leutnant Gustl, Der grosse Gabriel, Ein Tag im Paradies, Die oder Keine*). His most successful operetta was *Bruder Straubinger* (Vienna, Feb. 20, 1903; over 100 perfs. in that year). Other successful operettas: *Pufferl* (Vienna, April 13, 1905); *Künstlerblut* (1906); *Das Glückschweinchen* (1908); *Der unsterbliche Lump* (1910); *Das Zirkuskind* (1911); *Die goldene Meisterin* (Vienna, Sept. 13, 1927).

F

Faber, Heinrich (known as **Magister Henricus Faber**), German theorist; b. Lichtenfels, c.1500; d. Ölsnitz, Saxony, Feb. 26, 1552. He entered the Univ. of Wittenberg in 1542; received the degree of Master of Liberal Arts in 1545; was then rector of the school of St. George's Monastery near Naumburg; in 1551 was appointed lecturer at Wittenberg Univ.; then was rector at Ölsnitz. He publ. *Compendiolum musicae pro incipientibus* (1548; reprinted many times and also issued in German trans. as *Musica, Kurtzer Inhalt der Singkunst*, 1572; ed. by Adam Gumpelzhaimer and publ. as *Compendium musicae pro illius artis tironibus*, 1591). Faber further publ. *Ad Musicam practicam introductio* (1550); a *Musica poetica* remains in MS.

Fabini, Eduardo, Uruguayan composer; b. Solís del Mataojo, May 18, 1882; d. Montevideo, May 17, 1950. He studied violin in Montevideo, and later in Europe with César Thomson at the Brussels Cons., winning first prize; then gave concerts as a violinist in South America and in the U.S. (1926); eventually returned to Montevideo, and was active there as a composer and educator. His music is inspired entirely by South American folklore; the idiom is mildly modernistic, with lavish use of whole-tone scales and other external devices of Impressionism.

WORKS (all first perf. in Montevideo): Ballets: *Mburucuyá* (April 15, 1933) and *Mañana de Reyes* (July 31, 1937); symph. poem, *Campo* (April 29, 1922); overture, *La isla de los Ceibos* (Sept. 14, 1926); *Melga sinfónica* (Oct. 11, 1931); Fantasia for Violin and Orch. (Aug. 22, 1929); choral works; piano pieces; songs.

Fabricius, Johann Albert, eminent bibliographer, son of **Werner Fabricius;** b. Leipzig, Nov. 11, 1668; d. Hamburg, April 30, 1736. A learned man, he was a prof. of elocution; publ. important books of reference, valuable to musicology for the information they contain on musical topics: *Thesaurus antiquitatum hebraicarum* (7 vols., 1713); *Bibliotheca latina mediae et infimae aetatis* (6 vols., 1712–22; 2nd ed., 1734); *Bibliotheca graeca sive notitia scriptorum veterum graecorum* (14 vols., 1705–28).

Fabricius, Werner, German composer; b. Itzehoe, April 10, 1633; d. Leipzig, Jan. 9, 1679. He studied with Thomas Selle and Heinrich Scheidemann in Hamburg; then took courses in law in Leipzig, where he also served as organist of the Nicolaikirche and Paulinerkirche.

WORKS: He publ. a collection of pavanes, allemandes, etc., for viols and other instruments, under the title *Deliciae harmonicae* (Leipzig, 1656); also *Geistliche Lieder* (Jena, 1659); *Geistliche Arien, Dialogen, Concerten, etc.* (Leipzig, 1662); motets; etc.

Faccio, Franco, Italian composer and conductor; b. Verona, March 8, 1840; d. near Monza, July 21, 1891. His first teacher was G. Bernasconi; in 1855–64 he studied at the Milan Cons.; Arrigo Boito was his fellow pupil and friend; they wrote together a patriotic music drama, *Le Sorelle d'Italia,* which was produced by the students; the 2 served together under Garibaldi in 1866. His first opera was *I profughi fiamminghi* (La Scala, Nov. 11, 1863); this was followed by the Shakespearian opera *Amleto,* for which Boito wrote the libretto (Genoa, May 30, 1865). In 1866–68 Faccio made a tour in Scandinavia as a symph. conductor; in 1868 he became a prof. at the Milan Cons., and in 1871 succeeded Terziani as conductor at La Scala; on April 25, 1886, he conducted for the 1,000th time there. His performances of Verdi's operas were regarded as most authentic; he gave the world premiere of *Otello* at La Scala (1887).

Fachiri, Adila, Hungarian violinist, grandniece of **Joachim,** sister of **Jelly d'Aranyi;** b. Budapest, Feb. 26, 1886; d. Florence, Dec. 15, 1962. She studied with Joachim, and received from him a Stradivarius violin. In 1909 she settled in London, where she married Alexander Fachiri, a lawyer. She appeared many times with her sister in duets; on April 3, 1930, the sisters gave in London the first performance of Holst's Concerto for 2 Violins, written especially for them.

Faelten, Carl, pianist and teacher, brother of **Reinhold Faelten;** b. Ilmenau, Thuringia, Dec. 21, 1846; d. Readfield, Maine, July 20, 1925. He studied in Frankfurt, and profited by advice from Raff. In 1878–82 he taught at the Hoch Cons. in Frankfurt; then was engaged at the Peabody Inst. in Baltimore (1882–85) and at the New England Cons. in Boston (1885–97); was director of the Cons. from 1890 until 1897, when with his brother he founded the Faelten Pianoforte School in Boston.

Faelten, Reinhold, pianist and teacher, brother of **Carl Faelten;** b. Ilmenau, Thuringia, Jan. 17, 1856; d. Worcester, Mass., July 17, 1949. He was a pupil of Klughardt and Gottschalk at Weimar; taught in Frankfurt, Baltimore, and Boston; in 1897 he founded, with his brother, the Faelten Pianoforte School in Boston. Jointly with his brother, he wrote several books on the Faelten method: *100 Ear-training Exercises; Keyboard Harmony;* also a *Transposition System.*

Fagan, Gideon, South African conductor and composer; b. Somerset West, Cape Province, Nov. 3, 1904; d. Cape Town, March 21, 1980. He studied at the South African College of Music in Cape Town with W.H. Bell (1916–22) and later in London at the Royal College of Music (1922–26), where his teachers were Boult and Sargent (conducting) and Vaughan Williams (composition). With the exception of a brief return to South Africa (1926–27), Fagan established residence in London, where he led theatrical companies, arranged light music for broadcasts and films, and acted as guest conductor with the BBC and other orchs. In 1949 he went back to South Africa, where he became active as arranger and conductor at the Johannesburg Radio (SABC); later was appointed its head of music (1963–66). He also taught composition and conducting at the Univ. of Cape Town (1967–73). In 1979 he received the Medal of Honor of the South African Academy for Science and Art.

Fago, Nicola, Italian composer, called "Il Tarantino" after his place of birth; b. Taranto, Feb. 26, 1677; d. Naples, Feb. 18, 1745. He was a pupil of Provenzale at the Cons. della Pietà in Naples (from 1693); he became his assistant in 1697 and his successor in 1705. From 1704 to 1708 he was maestro di cappella at the Cons. di Sant' Onofrio; from 1709 to 1731, maestro di cappella at the Tesoro di San Gennaro; retired on a modest pension in 1740. He was the teacher of Leonardo Leo, Francesco Feo, Jommelli, and Sala. His son **Lorenzo Fago** (b. Naples, Aug. 13, 1704; d. there, April 30, 1793), an organist and composer, was his successor at the Tesoro di San Gennaro (1731–66 and 1771–80), and taught at the Cons. della Pietà dei Turchini for 56 years (1737–93) until his death.
   WORKS: 4 operas: *Radamisto* (1707); *Astarto* (1709); *La Cassandra indovina* (1711); *Lo Masillo* (1712); 3 oratorios, including *Faraone sommerso* and *Il monte fiorito;* a Te Deum and other sacred music, much of it still preserved in the archives of Naples, Paris, and London.

Fahrbach, Philipp, Austrian conductor and composer; b. Vienna, Oct. 26, 1815; d. there, March 31, 1885. He was a pupil of Lanner; conducted his own orch. for years, and then a military band. His dances and marches (over 400 works) were very popular. His 3 brothers, his son, and his nephews were all active as band musicians.

Fairchild, Blair, American composer; b. Belmont, Mass., June 23, 1877; d. Paris, April 23, 1933. He studied composition with J.K. Paine and Walter Spalding at Harvard Univ. (B.A., 1899); then took courses with Giuseppe Buonamici in Florence. From 1901 till 1903 he was an attaché in the American embassies in Turkey and Persia. From 1905 he lived mostly in Paris, where he continued his musical studies with Charles Widor. Influenced by his travels in the Orient, and fascinated by the resources of exotic melos and rhythm, he wrote a number of pieces for orch. and for piano, and many songs in a pseudo-oriental manner; despite the imitative qualities of his music, Fairchild must be regarded as one of the few Americans who tried to transplant exotic folkways, both in subject matter and in melodic turns.

Faith, Percy, American conductor and arranger of popular music; b. Toronto, April 7, 1908; d. Los Angeles, Feb. 9, 1976. He studied with Louis Waizman and Frank Wellman at the Toronto Cons.; played piano in movie theaters and in dance bands. In 1931 he joined the Canadian Broadcasting Corp. and conducted the radio orch. in popular programs of Canadian music; in 1940 moved to the U.S. to fill a conducting post for the NBC Carnation Contented Hour; in 1950 he became music director of Columbia Records and made more than 45 albums of his own. He composed numerous film scores for Hollywood movies and in 1955 won an Academy Award nomination for *Love Me or Leave Me.* An amiably disposed composer of music "for listening pleasure," he described his goal as "satisfying the millions of devotees of that pleasant American institution known as the quiet evening at home, whose idea of perfect relaxation is the easy chair, slippers and good music."

Falchi, Stanislao, Italian composer; b. Terni, Jan. 29, 1851; d. Rome, Nov. 14, 1922. He studied in Rome with C. Maggi and S. Meluzzi; in 1877 he became a teacher at the Santa Cecilia Academy; from 1902 till 1915 was its director. Among his pupils were A. Bonaventura, A. Bustini, V. Gui, B. Molinari, L. Refice, and F. Santoliquido. He wrote the operas *Lorhelia* (Rome, Dec. 4, 1877), *Giuditta* (Rome, March 12, 1887), and *Il Trillo del diavolo* (Rome, Jan. 29, 1899); also a Requiem for the funeral of Victor Emmanuel II (Jan. 17, 1883).

Falcon, Marie-Cornélie, French soprano; b. Paris, Jan. 28, 1814; d. there, Feb. 25, 1897. She studied with Bordogni and A. Nourrit; made her debut at the Paris Opéra on July 20, 1832, as Alice in *Robert le Diable.* She sang at the Paris Opéra with excellent success; appeared as Valentine in *Les Huguenots* on Jan. 15, 1838, when, though still a very young woman, she unaccountably lost her voice. She made an unsuccessful attempt to return to the stage in a special benefit performance at the Paris Opéra on March 14, 1840; in desperation she resorted to consuming all sorts of quack medicines provided by bogus doctors, but in the end had to give up her career. She retired to her villa near Paris; she lived another 60 years. Still, her singing in the roles of Valentine in *Les Huguenots* and Rachel in *La Juive* became a legendary memory, so that the description "Falcon type" was applied to singers who excelled in her roles.

Falconieri, Andrea, Italian composer and lutenist; b. Naples, 1586; d. there, July 29, 1656. He was in the service of the house of Farnese at Parma; studied with Santino Garsi there until 1614; in 1615 was in Florence; in 1616, in Rome; in 1619, again in Florence; in 1620–21, at the court of Modena; then traveled in Spain and France; in 1629–35, was again at Parma; from 1639, was maestro di cappella at the royal court in Naples; in 1642, was in Genoa; in 1650, was in Naples. His *Libro Primo di Villanelle a 1, 2 e 3 voci* (with alphabetical tablature for Spanish guitar) was publ. in Rome, 1616 (reprinted by Gardano at Venice); various other books followed, the *Libro V delle musiche* appearing in 1619; probably one of his last works was the valuable instrumental collection *Primo Libro di Canzone, Sinfonie, Fantasie, Capricci per Violini e Viole, overo altri Strumenti a 1, 2 e 3 voci con il basso continuo* (Naples, 1650). Reprints: arias (2 books) in the *Raccolta nazionale delle musiche italiane;* in A. Parisotti's *Arie antiche* and *Piccolo album di musica antica;* in L. Torchi's *Eleganti canzoni ed arie italiane del secolo XVII* and *L'arte musicale in Italia* (vol. VII); *17 Arie a una voce,* publ. by G. Benvenuti; *2 Villanelle a 3,* ed. by C. Sabatini; 4 songs in *La Flora,* ed. by Knud Jeppesen (Copenhagen, 1949).

Falik, Yuri, greatly talented Soviet cellist and composer; b. Odessa, July 30, 1936. He studied cello with A. Strimer at the Leningrad Cons.; in 1962 won first cello prize at the International Competition in Helsinki. He composed music from adolescence; in 1955 enrolled in the composition class of Boris Arapov at the Leningrad Cons., graduating in 1964. He subsequently joined the staff of the Leningrad Cons., teaching both cello and composition. In his own music Falik reveals a quasi-Romantic quality, making use of tantalizingly ambiguous melodic passages approaching the last ramparts of euphonious dissonance. His angular rhythms, with their frequently startling pauses, suggest a theatrical concept.
WORKS: For the stage: *Till Eulenspiegel,* "mystery ballet" (1967); *Oresteia,* choreographic tragedy (1968). For Orch.: Concertino for Oboe and Chamber Orch. (1961); Symph. for String Orch. and Percussion (1963); Concerto for Orch. on the themes of *Till Eulenspiegel* (1967); *Music for Strings* (1968); *Easy Symphony* (1971); Violin Concerto (1971); *Elegiac Music in Memoriam Igor Stravinsky* for Chamber Orch. (1975); Concerto for Orch. No. 2, *Symphonic Etudes* (1977). Chamber music: 5 string quartets (1955, 1965, 1974, 1976, 1978); Trio for Oboe, Clarinet, and Piano (1959); Wind Quintet (1964); *The Tumblers* for 4 Woodwinds, 2 Brasses, and 19 Percussion Instruments (1966); *Inventions* for Vibraphone, Marimba, and 5 Tam-tams (1972); *English Divertimento* for Flute, Clarinet, and Bassoon (1978). Vocal music: *Solemn Song,* cantata (1968); *Winter Songs* for Chorus a cappella (1975); solo songs.

Fall, Fritz (Frederick), opera conductor, nephew of Leo Fall; b. Vienna, July 25, 1899; d. Washington, D.C., Nov. 24, 1974. He studied at the Vienna Academy; was an opera conductor in Austria, Germany, and Czechoslovakia (1925–37); in 1937 he went to America; in 1938–42, conducted and taught in Tyler, Texas; during World War II was with the Office of Strategic Services of the U.S., in 1945–48, was with the Allied Military Government in Europe; from 1948, taught and conducted the Dept. of Agriculture Symph. Orch. in Washington, D.C. He changed his first name from Fritz to Frederick after becoming an American citizen.

Fall, Leo(pold), Austrian composer of light opera;

b. Olmütz, Feb. 2, 1873; d. Vienna, Sept. 16, 1925. His father was a military bandmaster, and it was from him that Leo Fall received his training in practical music making; then he took up academic courses at the Vienna Cons. with Johann Fuchs and others. For some years he was a theater conductor in Berlin, Hamburg, and Cologne, but lived for most of his life in Vienna. His operettas are typical Viennese products, light-hearted, romantic, and melodious. Although they never reached the height of international success obtained by such masters of the genre as Lehár, at least one of them, *Die Dollarprinzessin* (Vienna, Nov. 2, 1907), was famous for many years. The list of his operettas includes also *Der fidele Bauer* (Mannheim, July 27, 1907), *Eternal Waltz* (London, Dec. 22, 1911), *Die Rose von Constantinople* (Vienna, Dec. 2, 1916), and *Mme. Pompadour* (Vienna, March 2, 1923). His operetta *Der Rebell*, a failure at its first production (Vienna, Nov. 29, 1905), was revised and staged under the new title *Der liebe Augustin* (Berlin, Feb. 3, 1912), scoring excellent success.

Falla (y Matheu), Manuel de, one of the greatest Spanish composers; b. Cádiz, Nov. 23, 1876; d. Alta Gracia, in the province of Córdoba, Argentina, Nov. 14, 1946. He studied with J. Tragó (piano) and F. Pedrell (composition) in Madrid; composed some zarzuelas, which he later discarded. His opera, *La vida breve*, won the prize awarded by the Academia de Bellas Artes, Madrid, in 1905; in that year he also won the Ortiz y Cussó Prize for pianists. In 1907 he went to Paris, where he became friendly with Debussy, Dukas, and Ravel, who aided and encouraged him. Under their influence he adopted the principles of Impressionism without, however, giving up his personal and national style; in 1914 he returned to Spain and in 1921 made his home in Granada, frequently touring Europe as conductor of his own works. In May 1938 he was made president of the Instituto de España. In 1939, at the end of the Spanish Civil War, he went to Argentina; after conducting a few concerts of his music in Buenos Aires, he withdrew to the small locality of Alta Gracia, where he lived the last years of his life in seclusion. His art is rooted both in the folk music of Spain and in the purest historical traditions of Spanish music. Up to 1919 his works were cast chiefly in the Andalusian idiom, and his instrumental technique was often conditioned by effects peculiar to Spain's national instrument, the guitar. In *El retablo de Maese Pedro* he turns to the classical tradition of Spanish (especially Castilian) music; the keyboard style of his Harpsichord Concerto shows, in the classical lucidity of its writing, a certain kinship with Domenico Scarlatti (who lived in Spain for many years). Falla taught composition privately, his most gifted pupils being Ernesto Halffter and Joaquín Nin-Culmell.

WORKS: Opera, *La vida breve* (Nice, 1905; revised 1913; April 1, 1913; Metropolitan Opera, N.Y., March 7, 1926); *El retablo de Maese Pedro* for Marionettes and Singers (1919–22; perf. in Madrid, in concert form, March 23, 1923; a private stage perf.

was given in the salon of the Princesse de Polignac, in Paris, on June 25, 1923; first public stage perf., Paris, Nov. 13, 1923, under the composer's direction); ballets: *El amor brujo* (Madrid, April 15, 1915; a tremendously effective work; numerous perfs. as an orch. suite) and *El sombrero de tres picos* (London, July 22, 1919; very successful); *Noches en los jardines de España* for Piano and Orch. (1909–15; Madrid, April 9, 1916); Concerto for Harpsichord (or Piano), Flute, Oboe, Clarinet, Violin, and Cello, written at the suggestion of Wanda Landowska (Barcelona, Nov. 5, 1926, composer conducting; Wanda Landowska, soloist); *Homenajes*, in 4 parts: 1. *Pour le tombeau de Debussy* (originally for Guitar, 1920); 2. *Fanfare pour Arbós* (1933); 3. *Pour le tombeau de Paul Dukas* (originally for Piano, 1935); 4. *Pedrelliana* (1938; first perf. of the entire suite, Buenos Aires, Nov. 18, 1939, composer conducting); for Piano: *4 pièces espagnoles: Aragonesa, Cubana, Montañesa, Andaluza; Fantasia Bética;* songs: *3 mélodies* (1909); *7 canciones populares españolas* (1914; very popular); *Psyché* for Voice, Flute, Harp, Violin, Viola, and Cello (1924); *Soneto a Córdoba* for Voice and Harp (1927). A posthumous opera, *La Atlántida*, begun in 1928 and based on M.J. Verdaguer's Catalan poem, was completed by Ernesto Halffter and produced at La Scala in Milan on June 18, 1962. Falla's writings on music were collected and ed. by F. Sopeña and publ. as *Escritos sobre música y músicos* (Buenos Aires, 1950); another collection, in German trans. and ed. by J. Grünfeld, is *Spanien und die neue Musik. Ein Lebensbild in Schriften, Bildern Erinnerungen* (Zürich, 1968); in Eng., trans. by D. Urman and J. Thomson, as *On Music and Musicians* (London, 1979).

Fanciulli, Francesco, Italian conductor and composer; b. Porto San Stefano, July 17, 1850; d. New York, July 17, 1915. He studied in Florence; after some years as an opera conductor in Italy, he came to America (1876) and earned his living as an organist and theatrical conductor; in 1893 he succeeded Sousa as conductor of the Marine Band in Washington, D.C.; was then bandmaster of the 71st Regiment in N.Y. (1898–1904); after that, conducted his own band. He wrote an opera, *Priscilla*, which was produced in Norfolk, Va., on Nov. 1, 1901.

Fanelli, Ernest, French composer; b. Paris, June 29, 1860; d. there, Nov. 24, 1917. He played drums in orchs. as a small boy; entered the Paris Cons. in 1876, in the class of Delibes. He worked as a copyist and music engraver for many years; in 1912 he applied to Gabriel Pierné for work, submitting the score of his own symph. poem *Thèbes* as a specimen of his handwriting. This score, composed by Fanelli as early as 1883, seemed to anticipate the instrumental and harmonic usages of Debussy and other composers of impressionist music, and Pierné decided to perform it as a curiosity; he conducted it at the Colonne concert in Paris (March 17, 1912), and the novelty created a mild sensation in French musical circles; other works by Fanelli (*Impressions pastorales; L'Effroi du Soleil; Suite rabelai-*

sienne; etc.), all written before 1893, were also found interesting. However, the sensation proved of brief duration, and the extravagant claims for Fanelli's talent collapsed.

Farberman, Harold, American conductor and composer; b. New York, Nov. 2, 1929. He studied at the Juilliard School of Music in N.Y. and the New England Cons. in Boston; served as percussion player with the Boston Symph. Orch. (1952–63); then engaged on an independent career as a symph. conductor; from 1971 to 1979 he conducted the Oakland (Calif.) Symph. Orch. In his own music he often cultivates the idiom of jazz and rock.

WORKS: Rock Opera, *Medea* (Boston, March 26, 1961); *The Losers,* opera (N.Y., March 26, 1971); *Evolution* for Soprano, Horn, and Percussion (1954); Timpani Concerto (1962); Trio for Violin, Piano, and Percussion (1963); Concerto for Bassoon and String Orch.; *5 Images* for Brass Quintet (1964); *Elegy, Fanfare and March* for Orch. (1964–65); Concerto for Saxophone and String Orch. (1965); Symph. No. 1 for Strings and Percussion; *Greek Scene* for Soprano and Orch.; *Progressions* for Flute, Percussion, and Orch.; *Variations* for Piano, Percussion, and Orch.; *Paramount Concerto* for Piano and Orch.; *If Music Be* for Rock Group, Jazz Organ, and Orch. (1969); *Pilgrim's Progress* for Jazz Organ and Orch. (1969); *There's Us, There's Them ... Together?* for Voice, Jazz Combo, and Orch.; *Initiation Ballet* for Jazz Quartet and Orch. (from the opera *The Losers*); Violin Concerto (1972); *Impressions* for Oboe, Strings, and Percussion; *War Cry on a Prayer Feather* for Soprano, Baritone, and Orch. (Colorado Springs, Nov. 11, 1976).

Farinelli (real name, **Carlo Broschi**), celebrated Italian artificial soprano; b. Andria, Jan. 24, 1705; d. Bologna, Sept. 16, 1782. His father was a merchant of flour (*farina* in Italian), and called him Farinelli ("little flour"); at puberty, he had him castrated to promote his singing career. Porpora took the boy as a pupil, and he became famous in Naples as "il ragazzo" (the boy) singing in the streets. At the age of 16 he sang in Rome in Porpora's opera *Eomene;* his fame spread in Italy and abroad. In 1727 he met the famous castrato singer Bernacchi in Bologna; in a singing contest with him, Farinelli acknowledged defeat, and persuaded Bernacchi to give him lessons to achieve virtuosity in coloratura. He visited Vienna in 1724, 1728, and 1731. In 1734 he was sent by Porpora to London to join the Italian opera there. He made his London debut on Oct. 27, 1734, in *Artaserse* by Hasse, appearing with Senesino and Cuzzoni; he remained in London for 2 years, amassing a fortune; he then went to Paris, and in 1737 to Madrid, where he attained unparalleled success as court singer to King Philip V; his duty was to sing several arias every night to cure the king's melancholy. His influence on the ailing monarch, and on the Queen, was such that he was able to command considerable funds to engage famous performers at the Madrid court. He also persuaded Philip V to cut his beard. When Farinelli's voice began to fail, he undertook to serve as impresario, decorator, and stage director. He continued to enjoy the court's favor under Philip's successor, Ferdinand VI, but at the accession to the Spanish throne of Carlos III in 1759, Farinelli was dismissed. He went back to Italy in possession of great wealth; he assembled his family in a palatial villa which he built near Bologna, and spent his last 20 years of life in contentment.

Farley, Carole Ann, American soprano; b. LeMars, Iowa, Nov. 29, 1946. She studied at Indiana Univ.; then with Marianne Schech at the Hochschule für Musik in Munich, and with Cornelius Reid in N.Y. She made her debut in Linz, Austria, in 1969; married José Serebrier. Her singing of the title role in Alban Berg's *Lulu* at the Metropolitan Opera in N.Y. in 1977 placed her at the foremost rank of musicianly artists and singing intellectuals. She also appeared as Lulu in Cologne. Other roles are: Manon, Donna Anna, Mimi, Violetta.

Farmer, Henry George, eminent musicologist; authority on oriental music; b. Birr, Ireland, Jan. 17, 1882; d. Law, Lanarkshire, Dec. 30, 1965. He studied piano and violin, and as a boy joined the Royal Artillery Orch. in London, playing the French horn at its concerts. He then studied philosophy and languages at Glasgow Univ. An extremely prolific writer, he publ. a number of original works, dealing with such varied subjects as military music and Arabic musical theories. He was the founder and conductor of the Glasgow Symph. Orch. (1919–43); wrote several overtures and some chamber music.

Farmer, John, Elizabethan madrigal composer, active from 1591 to 1601. In 1595 he was organist at the Christ Church Cathedral in Dublin; in 1599 he left Dublin and went to London. Among his madrigals the best known are *Fair Phyllis I saw sitting all alone, You pretty flowers,* and *A little pretty bonny lass,* included in his *First Set of English Madrigals to Fowre Voices* (London, 1599; reprinted in vol. 8 of E.H. Fellowes's *English Madrigal School*). He contributed a 6-part madrigal, *Fair Nymphs, I heard one telling,* to *The Triumphes of Oriana,* and several canticles and hymns to Thomas East's *Whole Booke of Psalmes* (1592). Extant MSS are in the Christ Church Library and Music School at Oxford, and in the British Museum. Farmer was also the author of *Divers and sundry waies of two parts in one* (London, 1591).

Farnaby, Giles, English composer; b. probably in Cornwall, c.1565; d. London, Nov. (buried, Nov. 25) 1640. He graduated from Oxford in 1592, receiving the degree of B.Mus.; later moved to London, where he remained until his death.

WORKS: *Canzonets to Fowre Voyces* (1598; includes an added madrigal for 8 Voices, one of the few such works in the English school; reprint by E.H. Fellowes, in vol. 20 of the *English Madrigal School*); vocal religious works in various collections, and motets, psalms, etc.; more than 50 virginal pieces in the *Fitzwilliam Virginal Book* (ed. by J.A. Fuller-Maitland and W. Barclay Squire, London, 1899); a madrigal, *Come, Charon,* is in MS at the Royal College of Music; part of another is in the British Library. Farnaby's son, **Richard Farnaby,** was also a gifted composer.

Farnadi, Edith, Hungarian-born Austrian pianist; b. Budapest, Sept. 25, 1921. She entered the Budapest Academy of Music at the age of 9; studied with Bartók and Weiner; made her debut at 12; was granted her diploma at 16. She made appearances with the violinists Hubay and Hubermann; taught at the Budapest Academy; then moved to Austria and became a teacher in Graz. She is noted for her performances of Hungarian music.

Farquhar, David, New Zealand composer; b. Cambridge, England, April, 5, 1928. He studied first at Victoria Univ. in Wellington; went to England and studied at Cambridge Univ. and took composition from Benjamin Frankel at the Guildhall School of Music in London. His music is contrapuntal in structure and neo-Romantic in mood.
WORKS: *Ring around the Moon,* dance suite for Orch. (1954); *Harlequin Overture* (1958); Symph. (1959; Wellington, Aug. 13, 1960; the first symph. by a New Zealand composer to be given a premiere at a public concert); Concertino for Piano and Strings (1960); 2 *Anniversary Suites* for Orch. (1961, 1965); Elegy for Strings (1961); an opera, *A Unicorn for Christmas* (1962); *3 Pieces* for Violin and Piano (1967).

Farrant, John, English organist and composer, active in the 16th century. He served as lay clerk at Salisbury, and subsequently organist at the Salisbury Cathedral (1587–92); he was briefly organist at Hereford (1593). Contemporary records testify to his intractable temper, which resulted in physical clashes with the dean of the Salisbury Cathedral, and led to his expulsion from there. As a composer, Farrant is chiefly distinguished for his Service in D minor (misattributed in a 19th-century ed. to Richard Farrant). His son, also named **John Farrant** (baptized in Salisbury, Sept. 28, 1575; d. there, 1618), was a chorister at the Salisbury Cathedral in 1585, and organist there from 1598 till 1616. Another John Farrant, possibly related to the preceding, was organist at Christ Church, Newgate, London; he was the author of a Magnificat; this work, sometimes referred to as "Farrant in G minor," is often confused with Richard Farrant's Cathedral Service in A minor.

Farrant, Richard, English composer; b. c.1530; d. Windsor, probably Nov. 30, 1580. He was a Gentleman of the Chapel Royal during the reign of Edward VI; then became master of the choristers (1564) at St. George's Chapel, Windsor; also served as a lay clerk and organist there. Beginning with 1567 Farrant presented a play annually before the Queen. In 1569 he returned to the Chapel Royal. Farrant wrote mainly church music; his Cathedral

Service in A minor and 2 anthems, *Hide Not Thou Thy Face* and *Call to Remembrance,* are regarded as the most beautiful examples of English sacred music of the 16th century. A Service in D minor was publ. as by Richard Farrant, but this was a misattribution, the real author being John Farrant of Salisbury. Several of Richard Farrant's works are in the British Library and at Durham Cathedral.

Farrar, Ernest Bristow, English organist and composer; b. London, July 7, 1885; d. in the battle of the Somme, France, Sept. 18, 1918. He studied at the Royal College of Music with Stanford and Parratt; served as organist of the English Church in Dresden (1909); then at various churches in England (1910–14). His orch. suite *English Pastoral Impression* won the Carnegie Award; he further wrote the orch. pieces *The Open Road, Lavengro, The Forsaken Merman,* and *Heroic Elegy;* also *3 Spiritual Studies* for Strings; variations on an old English sea song, for Piano and Orch.; the cantatas *The Blessed Damozel* and *Out of Doors;* chamber music (*Celtic Suite* for Violin and Piano, etc.); songs; preludes for organ; etc.

Farrar, Geraldine, celebrated American soprano; b. Melrose, Mass., Feb. 28, 1882; d. Ridgefield, Conn., March 11, 1967. She studied music with Mrs. J.H. Long of Boston; at 17, she went to Europe; took lessons with Emma Thursby in N.Y., Trabadello in Paris, and Graziani in Berlin; made a successful debut at the Berlin Opera on Oct. 15, 1901, as Marguerite, under the direction of Karl Muck; then studied with Lilli Lehmann. She sang at the Monte Carlo Opera for 3 seasons (1903–6). Her career in Europe was well established before her American debut as Juliette at the Metropolitan Opera (Nov. 26, 1906); she remained on the staff for 16 years; made her farewell appearance in *Zaza* on April 22, 1922, but continued to sing in concert; gave her last public performance at Carnegie Hall in 1931; then retired to Ridgefield, Conn. Her greatest success was *Madama Butterfly,* which she sang with Caruso in its American premiere at the Metropolitan on Feb. 11, 1907; subsequently sang this part in America more than 100 times. Her interpretation of Carmen was no less remarkable. She also appeared in silent motion pictures between 1915 and 1919; her film version of Carmen aroused considerable interest. On Feb. 8, 1916, she married the actor Lou Tellegen, from whom she was subsequently divorced. She made adaptations of pieces by Kreisler, Rachmaninoff, and others, for which she publ. the lyrics. She wrote an autobiography, *Such Sweet Compulsion* (N.Y., 1938; reprinted in 1970), which had been preceded in 1916 by *Geraldine Farrar: The Story of an American Singer.* Her scrapbooks, many letters, the fan she used in *Madama Butterfly,* etc., are in the Music Division of the Library of Congress in Washington, D.C.

Farrell, Eileen, brilliant American soprano; b. Willimantic, Conn., Feb. 13, 1920. Her parents were vaudeville singers; she received her early vocal training with Merle Alcock in N.Y., and later studied with Eleanor McLellan. In 1940 she sang on the radio; in 1947–48 made a U.S. tour as a concert singer; toured South America in 1949. Her song recital in N.Y. on Oct. 24, 1950, was enthusiastically acclaimed and secured for her immediate recognition. She was soloist in Beethoven's 9th Symph. with Toscanini and the NBC Symph. Orch.; also appeared many times with the N.Y. Phil. She made her operatic debut as Santuzza with the San Carlo Opera in Tampa, Fla., in 1956. In 1958 she joined the San Francisco Opera Co. and in 1957 became a member of the Lyric Opera of Chicago. On Dec. 6, 1960, she made a successful debut with the Metropolitan Opera Co. in N.Y., in Gluck's *Alcestis;* she remained on its roster until 1964; then returned in 1965–66; was a Distinguished Professor of Music at the Indiana Univ. School of Music in Bloomington from 1971 to 1980.

Farrenc, Aristide, French flutist and music editor; b. Marseilles, April 9, 1794; d. Paris, Jan. 31, 1865. He studied flute; went to Paris in 1815, and studied at the Cons.; at the same time was engaged as 2nd flutist at the Théâtre Italien. In 1821 he established a music shop and printing press; publ. French editions of Beethoven; also composed music for the flute. He married **Louise Dumont,** a talented musician in her own right. He diligently collected material for the rectification of existing biographies, but generously turned it over to Fétis for use in the 2nd edition of his great work, of which Farrenc also read proofs. Jointly with Fétis's son, Edouard, he began the publication of *Le Trésor des pianistes* (23 vols., 1861–72; reprinted N.Y., 1977, foreword by Bea Friedland), a collection of piano music from the 16th century to Mendelssohn, with historical notes; it was continued after his death by his wife. From 1854 he contributed papers to *La France Musicale* and other journals.

Farrenc (neé **Dumont**), **Louise,** French pianist and composer; b. Paris, May 31, 1804; d. there, Sept. 15, 1875. She studied music with Reicha; in 1821 married **Aristide Farrenc,** but was not entirely eclipsed by his acknowledged eminence. While most female composers of her time hardly ever rose above the level of barely tolerable salon music, she actually labored and produced works of such competence that they might well have been written by Onslow or some other male contemporary. Her 3 symphs. had respectable performances: No. 1 in Brussels, Feb. 23, 1843; No. 2 in Paris, May 3, 1846; No. 3 in Paris, April 22, 1849; the latter received an accolade in the prestigious, and definitely male-oriented, *Gazette Musicale,* which conceded that "she revealed, alone among her sex in musical Europe, genuine learning, united with grace and taste." She also wrote a Piano Concerto; 30 études in all major and minor keys for Piano; 4 piano trios; Cello Sonata; 2 violin sonatas; 2 piano quintets; a Sextet and a Nonet for Winds and Strings; one of her overtures (1840) was reviewed by Berlioz, who remarked that it was orchestrated "with a talent rare among wom-

en." Louise Farrenc was a brilliant pianist; she taught piano at the Paris Cons. from 1842 till 1872, the only woman ever to hold a permanent position as an instrumentalist there in the 19th century. Her daughter **Victorine** (1827–59) was also a talented pianist whose promising career was cut short by an early death. After the death of her husband in 1865, Louise Farrenc assumed the editorship of the monumental collection *Le Trésor des pianistes* begun by him.

Farwell, Arthur, American composer and music educator; b. St. Paul, Minn., April 23, 1872; d. New York, Jan. 20, 1952. He studied at the Mass. Inst. of Technology, graduating in 1893; then studied music with Homer Norris in Boston, Humperdinck in Berlin, and Guilmant in Paris. He was a lecturer on music at Cornell Univ. (1899–1901); in 1909–14 was on the editorial staff of *Musical America;* then directed municipal concerts in N.Y. City (1910–13); was director of the Settlement Music School in N.Y. (1915–18); in 1918 he went to California; lectured on music there; was acting head of the music dept. at the Univ. of Calif., Berkeley (1918–19); in 1919 he founded the Santa Barbara Community Chorus, which he conducted until 1921; was the first holder of the composers' fellowship of the Music and Art Association of Pasadena (1921–25); taught music theory at Michigan State College in East Lansing (1927–39); eventually settled in N.Y. Farwell was a pioneer in new American music, and tirelessly promoted national ideas in art. He contributed to various ethnological publications. In 1901–11 he operated the Wa-Wan Press (Newton, Mass.), a periodical (quarterly, 1901–7; monthly, 1907–11) that printed piano and vocal music of "progressive" American composers of the period, the emphasis being on works that utilized indigenous (black, Indian, and cowboy) musical materials (reprinted N.Y., 1970, under the direction of Vera Lawrence Brodsky). Disillusioned about commercial opportunities for American music, including his own, he established at East Lansing, in April 1936, his own lithographic handpress, with which he printed his music, handling the entire process of reproduction, including the cover designs, by himself.

WORKS: For Orch.: *Symbolistic Study No. 3,* after Walt Whitman (1905; revised 1922; Philadelphia Orch., March 30, 1928); *Pageant Scene* (1913); *The Gods of the Mountain* (Minneapolis Symph. Orch., Dec. 13, 1929); music for pageants, including Percy MacKaye's *Caliban by the Yellow Sands* (N.Y., May 1916; written for the Shakespeare tercentenary); *Pilgrimage Play* (Hollywood, 1921); *Symphonic Song on "Old Black Joe"* (Hollywood, 1923); *Symphonic Hymn on "March! March!";* also *The Hako* for String Quartet (1922); *Violin Sonata* (1928); Concerto for 2 Pianos and String Orch., a version of *Symbolistic Study No. 6* (1931; won first prize of the National Federation of Music Clubs Competition; broadcast by CBS, May 28, 1939); numerous school choruses, and vocal compositions; piano pieces (many of them arranged for various instrumental ensembles); several collections of American Indian melodies and folk songs of the South and West; arrangements of Indian melodies (*Dawn,* a fantasy on Indian themes, in various versions, dated between 1901 and 1926, is characteristic of these works).

Fasch, Johann Friedrich, German composer; b. Buttelstadt, near Weimar, April 15, 1688; d. Zerbst, Dec. 5, 1758. He studied with Kuhnau at Leipzig, and later (1713) with Graupner and Grunewald at Darmstadt; in 1721 he went to Lukaveč, Bohemia, as Kapellmeister to Count Morzin; after 1722, was Kapellmeister at Zerbst. A catalogue of his works, compiled in 1743, enumerates 12 complete series of church cantatas, 16 masses and Mass sections, 4 operas, over 90 overtures, 61 concertos (for violin, flute, oboe, etc.), some of which have been printed in modern editions; most of his vocal works are not extant. Many scores are preserved in MS in the libraries of Darmstadt, Dresden, Leipzig, and Brussels; in the archives of the Thomasschule at Leipzig are the parts of 5 orch. suites of Fasch in the handwriting of J.S. Bach, who entertained a very high opinion of the works of his contemporary. Hugo Riemann publ. 5 trio sonatas and a String Quartet in *Collegium Musicum* and 2 orch. suites in Breitkopf & Härtel's *Orchesterbibliothek;* a Violin Concerto in D was ed. by A. Hoffmann (Wolfenbüttel, 1961). Fasch's autobiography appeared in vol. III of F.W. Marpurg's *Historisch-kritische Beyträge zur Aufnahme der Musik* (Berlin, 1754–78).

Fasch, Karl Friedrich Christian, German composer, son of **Johann Friedrich Fasch;** b. Zerbst, Nov. 18, 1736; d. Berlin, Aug. 3, 1800. He learned to play the violin and harpsichord as a child; studied all musical subjects with Hertel at Strelitz. At the age of 15, he joined the violinist Franz Benda as his accompanist, and at the age of 20 he was recommended by Benda as harpsichordist to Frederick the Great, jointly with C.P.E. Bach. He also taught music and composed contrapuntal pieces of considerable ingenuity and complexity. He was conductor at the Berlin Opera (1774–76). In 1790 he organized a choral society, which led to the foundation of the famous Singakademie. Fasch was greatly admired by musicians for his contrapuntal skill; the renown of his name was still strong in the first part of the 19th century; in 1839, 6 vols. of his sacred works were publ. by the Singakademie.

Fassbänder, Brigitte, German mezzo-soprano; b. Berlin, July 3, 1939. She studied with her father, the noted baritone **Willi Domgraf-Fassbänder.** She made her debut at the Bavarian State Opera, Munich, in 1961; soon established herself as one of its leading singers. She also made appearances at La Scala, Milan, the Vienna State Opera, Covent Garden, London, etc. Her repertoire ranges from Gluck to Richard Strauss in opera; she is also adept in lieder.

Fassbender, Zdenka, soprano; b. Děčín, Bohemia, Dec. 12, 1879; d. Munich, March 14, 1954. She studied voice in Prague; made her operatic debut in Karlsruhe in 1899; from 1906 to 1919 she was one of the principal singers at the Munich Opera; she also sang at Covent Garden in London (1910, 1913). The famous conductor **Felix Mottl** married her on his deathbed to sanction a lifelong alliance.

Fauchet, Paul Robert, French composer; b. Paris, June 27, 1881; d. there, Nov. 12, 1937. He studied at the Paris Cons., and later taught harmony there; also was maître de chapelle of Saint-Pierre de Chaillot in Paris. He wrote a number of sacred works, but is remembered mainly for his *Symphonie* for Band, the earliest example of a classical symph. written for the medium (1936); its *Scherzo* is profusely enmeshed with whole-tone scales.

Fauré, Gabriel-Urbain, great French composer; b. Pamiers (Ariège), May 12, 1845; d. Paris, Nov. 4, 1924. His father was a provincial inspector of primary schools; noticing the musical instinct of his son, he took him to Paris to study with Louis Niedermeyer; after Niedermeyer's death in 1861, Fauré studied with Saint-Saëns, from whom he received a thorough training in composition. In 1866 he went to Rennes as organist at the church of Saint-Sauveur; returned to Paris on the eve of the Franco-Prussian War in 1870, and volunteered in the light infantry. He was organist at Notre-Dame de Clignancourt, Saint-Honoré d'Eylau, and Saint-Sulpice (1871–74); subsequently became 2nd organist, and in 1877 choirmaster, at the Madeleine; in 1896 he was appointed chief organist there, and prof. of composition at the Paris Cons. He was an illustrious teacher; among his students were Ravel, Enesco, Koechlin, Roger-Ducasse, Laparra, Florent Schmitt, Louis Aubert, and Nadia Boulanger. In 1905 he succeeded Théodore Dubois as director; resigned in 1920, when growing deafness and ill health made it impossible for him to continue to direct the Cons. From 1903 till 1921 he wrote occasional music reviews in *Le Figaro* (publ. as *Opinions Musicales;* posthumous, Paris, 1930); he was elected a member of the Académie des Beaux Arts in 1909; became a Commander of the Légion d'Honneur in 1910. Fauré's stature as composer is undiminished by the passage of time. He developed a musical idiom all his own; by subtle application of old modes he evoked the aura of eternally fresh art; by using unresolved mild discords and special coloristic effects in his instrumental music, he anticipated the procedures of Impressionism; in his piano works he shunned virtuosity in favor of the classical lucidity of the French masters of the clavecin; the precisely articulated melodic line of his songs is in the finest tradition of French vocal music. Several of his works (significantly, those of his early period) have entered the general repertoire: the great Requiem, First Violin Sonata, *Elégie* for Cello and Piano; also songs (*Ici-bas, Les Roses d'Ispahan, Clair de lune, Au cimetière,* etc.). WORKS: FOR THE STAGE: *Caligula,* incidental music to a play by A. Dumas, Jr. (Paris, Nov. 8, 1888); *Shylock,* after Shakespeare (Paris, Dec. 11, 1889); *Pelléas et Mélisande,* after Maeterlinck (London, June 21, 1898; often perf. as an orch. suite); *Promé-*

thée, lyric tragedy (Béziers, Aug. 27, 1900); *Le Voile du bonheur*, incidental music for Clémenceau's play (Paris, Nov. 4, 1901); *Pénélope* (Monte Carlo, March 4, 1913); *Masques et bergamasques*, stage music (Monte Carlo, April 10, 1919). FOR ORCH.: Symph. in D minor (Paris, March 15, 1885); Suite (1875; only one movement, *Allegro symphonique*, was publ.); *Pavane* (1887); *Ballade* for Piano and Orch. (Paris, April 23, 1881); Romance for Violin and Orch. (1882); *Fantaisie* for Piano and Orch. (1919). CHORAL WORKS: *Cantique de Jean Racine* for Mixed Chorus, Harmonium, and String Quartet (1873); *Les Djinns* for Chorus and Orch. (1875); *La Naissance de Vénus* for Soli, Chorus, and Orch. (1882; Paris, April 3, 1886); *Messe de Requiem* for Soli, Chorus, Organ, and Orch. (1887); *Ave Verum* and *Tantum Ergo* for Female Voices and Organ (1894); offertories and other church music. CHAMBER MUSIC: 2 violin sonatas (1876, 1916); 2 piano quartets (1879, 1886); 2 piano quintets (1906, 1921); 2 cello sonatas (1918, 1922); Piano Trio (1923); String Quartet (1924); *Berceuse* for Piano and Violin (1879); *Elégie* for Piano and Cello (1894); Andante for Violin and Piano (1894); *Papillon* for Cello and Piano (1897); *Sicilienne* for Cello and Piano (1893); *Sérénade* for Cello and Piano (1908); *Fantaisie* for Flute and Piano (1898). PIANO WORKS: 13 nocturnes; 13 barcarolles; 5 impromptus; 4 waltzes; *Dolly*, 6 pieces for 4-hands (1889; orchestrated by Rabaud); 96 songs: 4 to words by Victor Hugo, 4 after Théophile Gautier, 3 after Baudelaire, 16 after Paul Verlaine (including the cycle *La Bonne Chanson*), etc.

Faure, Jean-Baptiste, famous French baritone; b. Moulins, Allier, Jan. 15, 1830; d. Paris, Nov. 9, 1914. He was a choirboy at the Madeleine and other Paris churches; entered the Paris Cons. at the age of 21; after a short period of study he made his debut at the Opéra-Comique, in Massé's opera *Galathée* (Oct. 20, 1852); from 1861–76 he was on the staff of the Paris Opéra; his farewell appearance was in the title role of *Hamlet* by Ambroise Thomas (May 13, 1876), the role that he created in 1868. Subsequently he sang in concerts, appearing with enormous success in Vienna and in London. He was particularly impressive in dramatic roles in Meyerbeer's operas and also in Gounod's *Faust*, as Méphistophélès. He wrote a number of songs, of which several became fairly successful (*Crucifix, Les Rameaux*, etc.).

Favart, Charles-Simon, French librettist; b. Paris, Nov. 13, 1710; d. Belleville, near Paris, March 12, 1792. He publ. satirical plays as a youth; after a successful performance of one of his vaudevilles at the Opéra-Comique, he was appointed stage manager there; in 1758 he became its director. He wrote about 150 plays used for operas by Duni, Philidor, and Gluck; he was also the author of *Les Amours de Bastien et Bastienne* (1753), used by Mozart in a German version for his early opera (1768).

Favart, Marie, French soprano; b. Avignon, June 15, 1727; d. Paris, April 21, 1772. Her maiden name was **Marie-Justine-Benoît Buronceray;** she married

the impresario **Charles-Simon Favart** in 1745; went with him to Paris, where she sang soubrette roles at the Théâtre-Italien with notable success, often appearing in works for which her husband had prepared the librettos. She became involved in various theatrical intrigues in Paris; an account of these was publ. by Pougin in his book *Madame Favart* (1912).

Fay, Amy, American pianist; b. Bayou Goula, La., May 21, 1844; d. Watertown, Mass., Feb. 28, 1928. She studied in Berlin with Tausig and Kullak; then became a pupil of Liszt in Weimar. She publ. a vivid book of impressions, *Music-Study in Germany* (Chicago, 1881), which went through more than 20 printings and was trans. into French and German. See H.L. Kaufman in *Notable American Women* (Cambridge, Mass., 1971), vol. 1.

Fayrfax, Robert, English composer; b. Deeping Gate, Lincolnshire (baptized, April 23), 1464; d. St. Alban, Hertfordshire, Oct. 24, 1521. He was a Gentleman of the Chapel Royal in 1496, and organist at St. Alban's Abbey and at King's Chapel (1497–98); received a B.Mus. (1501) and a D.Mus. (1504) from Cambridge Univ. and a D.Mus. from Oxford Univ. (1511; with his mass *O quam glorifica*). In 1520 he led the Royal Singers accompanying King Henry VIII to the Field of the Cloth of Gold in France. Of his works, 29 are extant: 6 masses (4 are in the Oxford Museum School Collection), 2 Magnificats, 10 motets, 8 part-songs, 3 instrumental pieces. His sacred and secular vocal works are in the *Fayrfax Book* (British Library MS Add. 5465); lute arrangements of several sacred compositions and an instrumental piece for 3 parts are in the British Library. Reprints of some of his compositions are in J. Stafford Smith's *Musica Antiqua* (1812). E. Warren edited *Robert Fayrfax: Collected Works,* in Corpus Mensurabilis Musicae, XVII/1–3 (1959–66).

Feather, Leonard, British-American writer on music, expert on jazz; b. London, Sept. 13, 1914. He studied at St. Paul School in London; in 1935 he came to the U.S.; was naturalized in 1948. He held various jobs as an arranger, lyricist, adviser for jazz festivals, radio commentator, and lecturer; specialized in the field of jazz and folk music; publ. *Inside Bebop* (N.Y., 1949); a compendious *Encyclopedia of Jazz* (N.Y., 1955), which he supplemented by the *New Encyclopedia of Jazz* (1960) and the *Encyclopedia of Jazz in the 60's* (1966). He makes his home in Hollywood.

Feinberg, Samuel, eminent Russian pianist and composer; b. Odessa, May 26, 1890; d. Moscow, Oct. 22, 1962. He moved to Moscow in 1894; studied piano with Goldenweisser at the Moscow Cons.; also took theory lessons with Zhilayev; graduated in 1911. In 1922 he was appointed prof. of piano at the Cons., holding this post until his death; also gave regular piano recitals in Russia in programs emphasizing new Russian music; he performed all of Beethoven's sonatas and the complete set of Bach's *Wohl-*

temperiertes Clavier, as well as Chopin and Schumann. As a composer he limited himself almost exclusively to piano music, which was influenced mainly by Chopin and Scriabin in its fluidity and enhanced tonality. His 6th Piano Sonata was played at the Venice Festival in 1925.

Felciano, Richard, American composer; b. Santa Rosa, Calif., Dec. 7, 1930. He studied with Darius Milhaud at Mills College; subsequently took courses at the Paris Cons. In 1958–59 he took private lessons with Luigi Dallapiccola in Florence. He holds a Ph.D. from the Univ. of Iowa (1959). He was the recipient of the Guggenheim fellowship in 1969 and 2 fellowships from the Ford Foundation (1964, 1971–73). He is also the holder of the American Academy of Arts and Letters Award (1974). In 1967 he was appointed resident composer at the National Center for Experiments in Television in San Francisco. At the same time he was also on the music faculty of the Univ. of Calif. at Berkeley.

Feld, Jindřich, Czech composer; b. Prague, Feb. 19, 1925. He studied violin with his father; took composition with Hlobil at the Prague Cons. (1945–48) and with Řídký at the Prague Academy of Music (1948–52); also studied musicology at Charles Univ. (1945–52). During the academic year 1968–69 he was a visiting prof. at the Univ. of Adelaide in Australia; returning to Prague, he was appointed to the staff of the Prague Cons. His early music is in a neo-Baroque manner, but he soon adopted a variety of modern techniques.

Feldman, Morton, American composer of the avant-garde; b. New York, Jan. 12, 1926. He studied piano with Vera Maurina-Press and had composition lessons with Wallingford Riegger in 1941 and with Stefan Wolpe in 1944. Profoundly impressed by the abstract expressionism of modern painting in the late 1940s and by his first meeting with John Cage in 1950, Feldman evolved a congenial set of musical concepts and introduced an element of predetermined indeterminacy into the performance of his music, as exemplified in his *Projections I–IV* for different instrumental combinations (1950–51). In such works he indicates only an approximation of the notes to be played in a musical "action," specifying the instrumental range (high, medium, low) and the number of notes per time unit in any voluntary or involuntary rhythmic distribution. He uses graphic optical notation optionally, transcribing it into traditional scores for practical performance; he abandoned graphic notation altogether during two periods (1953–58 and in the early 1960s), employing precise notation.
WORKS: *Projections I–IV* (1950–51); *Intersections I* for Orch. (1951), *II* and *III* for Piano (1952, 1953), and *IV* for Cello (1953); *Marginal Intersection* for Orch. (1951); *4 Songs to E.E. Cummings* for Soprano, Cello, and Piano (1951); *Extensions I* for Violin and Piano (1951), *III* for Piano (1952), *IV* for 3 Pianos (1952–53), and *V* for 2 Cellos; *Intermissions I–VI* (1951–53); *Intersection* for Tape (1951); *Struc-*

tures for String Quartet (1951); *2 Pieces* for 2 Pianos (1954); *3 Pieces* for String Quartet (1954–56); *Piece* for 4 Pianos (1957); *2 Pianos* for 2 Pianos (1957); *2 Instruments* for Cello and Horn (1958); *Atlantis* for Orch. (1958); *Last Pieces* for Piano (1959); Trio for 3 Pianos (1959); Trio for 2 Pianos and Cello (1959); a ballet, *Ixion (Summerspace)* for 10 Instruments or 2 Pianos (1960; as a classical ballet, N.Y., April 14, 1966; choreographed by Merce Cunningham); a cantata, *The Swallows of Salangan,* for Chorus and 23 Instruments (1960); *Out of "Last Pieces"* for Orch. (1960–61); *Journey to the End of the Night* for Soprano and 4 Wind Instruments (1960); *Structures* for Orch. (1960–62); *Intervals* for Baritone and Instruments (1961); *2 Pieces* for Clarinet and String Quartet (1961); *Philip Guston* for Small Orch. (1962); *For Franz Kline* for Soprano, Violin, Cello, Horn, Chimes, and Piano (1962); *The Straits of Magellan* for 7 Instruments (1963); *De Kooning* for Piano, Violin, Cello, Horn, and Percussion (1963); *4 Instruments* for Violin, Cello, Glockenspiel, and Piano (1963); *Chorus and Instruments I–II* (1963, 1967); *Vertical Thoughts I–V* for different instrumental combinations (1963); *Numbers* for 9 Instruments (1964); *Rabbi Akiba* for Soprano and 10 Instruments (1964); *The King of Denmark* for Percussion (1965); *Christian Wolff at Cambridge* for Chorus a cappella (1965); *2 Pieces* for 3 Pianos (1966); *First Principles* for Large Instrumental Ensemble (1966–67); *In Search of an Orchestration* for Orch. (1967); *False Relationships and the Extended Ending* for Violin, Cello, Trombone, 3 Pianos, and Chimes (1968); *On Time and the Instrumental Factor* for Orch. (1969); *Between Categories* for 2 Pianos, 2 Chimes, 2 Violins, and 2 Cellos (1969); *Madame Press Died Last Week at Ninety* for Chamber Ensemble (St. Paul de Vence, July 20, 1970; Foss conducting); *The Viola in My Life I* for Solo Viola and 6 Instrumentalists, *II* for Solo Viola and 7 Instrumentalists, *III* for Viola and Piano, and *IV* for Viola and Orch. (1970–71); *3 Clarinets, Cello and Piano* (1971); *Chorus and Orchestra I–II* (1971–72); *I Met Heine on the Rue Fürstenberg* for Voice and 6 Instrumentalists (1971); *The Rothko Chapel* for Solo Viola, Chorus, and Percussion (1971; Houston, April 9, 1972); *Cello and Orchestra* (1971–72); *Voice and Instruments I* for Soprano and Chamber Orch. (1972), and *II* for Voice, Clarinet, Cello, and Double Bass (1974); *Voices and Instruments I* for Chorus and 9 Instrumentalists, and *II* for 3 Voices, Flute, 2 Cellos, and Double Bass (both 1972); *Pianos and Voices I* for 5 Pianists that hum, and *II* for 5 Pianos and 5 Voices (both 1972); *For Frank O'Hara* for 7 Instrumentalists (1973); *String Quartet and Orchestra* (1973); *Voices and Cello* for 2 Voices and Cello (1973); *Instruments I* for 5 Instruments, and *II* for 9 Instrumentalists (1974–75); *Piano and Orchestra* (1975); *4 Instruments* for piano quartet (1975); *Oboe and Orchestra* (1976); *Orchestra* (1976); *Voice, Violin and Piano* (1976); *Routine Investigations* for Oboe, Trumpet, Piano, Viola, Cello, and Double Bass (1976); *Elemental Procedures* for Chorus and Orch. (1976); *The Spring of Chosroes* for Violin and Piano (1977); *Neither,* monodrama after an original text by Beckett, for Soprano and Orch. (1977; Rome,

May 13, 1977; N.Y., Nov. 21, 1978).

Fellerer, Karl Gustav, eminent German musicologist and editor; b. Freising, July 7, 1902; d. Munich, Jan. 7, 1984. He studied at the Regensburg School of Church Music and took courses in composition with Heinrich Schmid and Joseph Haas in Munich; then studied musicology at the Univ. of Munich with Sandberger and at the Univ. of Berlin with Hornbostel, Abert, Wolf, and Sachs; received his Ph.D. in 1925 from the Univ. of Munich with the dissertation *Beiträge zur Musikgeschichte Freisings von den ältesten christlichen Zeiten bis zur Auflösung des Hofes 1803* (Freising, 1926); completed his Habilitation in 1927 at the Univ. of Münster with his *Der Palestrina stil und seine Bedeutung in der vokalen Kirchenmusik des 18. Jahrhunderts* (Augsburg, 1929). In 1927 he became a lecturer at the Univ. of Münster; in 1931 prof. in Freiburg, Switzerland; in 1934 he became head of the dept. of musicology at the Univ. of Münster; in 1939 he succeeded Theodor Kroyer as prof. of music history at the Univ. of Cologne; he retired in 1970. Fellerer distinguished himself as an outstanding authority on the history of music of the Roman Catholic church; he contributed valuable studies on the music of the Middle Ages, the Renaissance, and the 19th century; he also served as editor of several important music journals and other publications. His 60th birthday was honored by the publication of three *Festschriften.*

Fellowes, Rev. Edmund Horace, eminent English musicologist and editor; b. London, Nov. 11, 1870; d. Windsor, Dec. 20, 1951. He attended Winchester and Oriel Colleges, Oxford; studied music with P.C. Buck, Fletcher, and L. Straus; received a Mus.Bac. degree from Oxford (1896); honorary Mus.Doc. degrees from Dublin Univ. (1917), Oxford (1938), and Cambridge (1950). In 1897–1900, he was precentor at Bristol Cathedral; in 1900, canon; in 1923–27, conductor at St. George's Chapel, Windsor Castle; in 1918, librarian at St. Michael's College, Tenbury; in 1927–29, he toured the U.S. and Canada with the Choir of St. George's Chapel and Choristers of Westminster Abbey; also lectured on old English music at various univs.; in 1932–33, was a lecturer on music at Liverpool Univ. He ed. the valuable collections *The English Madrigal School,* including the works of Thomas Morley, Orlando Gibbons, John Wilbye, John Farmer, Thomas Weelkes, William Byrd, Henry Lichfild, John Ward, Thomas Tomkins, Giles Farnaby, Thomas Bateson, John Bennet, George Kirbye, etc. (36 vols., 1913–36), and *The English School of Lutenist Songwriters,* containing the collected works of John Dowland, Thomas Campion, Thomas Ford, Francis Pilkington, Robert Jones, etc. (32 vols., 1920–32); was co-editor of the Carnegie edition *Tudor Church Music,* including works of White, Tallis, Taverner, Byrd, and Gibbons (10 vols., 1919–47); was also ed. of collected works of William Byrd (20 vols., 1937–50); 11 fantasies for Strings by Orlando Gibbons (1925); songs of Fletcher and Beaumont; etc. Fellowes was also a composer of church music; in his early years he wrote many anthems, *Morning and Evening Service,* songs, and a String Quartet.

Felsenstein, Walter, influential Austrian opera producer; b. Vienna, May 30, 1901; d. East Berlin, Oct. 8, 1975. He studied at a Graz technical college; then went to Vienna, where he enrolled in drama courses at the Burgtheater. In 1923 he appeared as an actor in Lübeck; in 1924 went to Mannheim. In 1925 he became dramatic adviser and producer in Beuthen, Silesia; in 1927 he was called to Basel to become chief opera and drama producer at the Stadttheater; in 1929 he went to Freiburg im Breisgau as both actor and dramatic adviser and producer. He served as chief producer at the Cologne Opera in 1932 and at the Frankfurt Opera in 1934. Despite his differences with the policies of the Nazi authorities, he as able to continue producing operas and dramas. From 1938–40 he produced plays in Zürich; he then served as producer in Berlin (1940–44); he was drafted by the military despite his age, and served for a year. After the war he was director of the Komische Oper in East Berlin, a position he held until his death. During his tenure, the Komische Oper established itself as one of the best opera houses of Europe; his productions of *Die Fledermaus, Carmen, Le nozze di Figaro, Otello, Les Contes d'Hoffmann,* and *Die Zauberflöte* were artistically of the first rank. He also made operatic films and gave courses on theater arts. Among his students were the opera producers Götz Friedrich and Joachim Herz. With S. Melchinger, he compiled *Musiktheater* (Bremen, 1961); with G. Friedrich and J. Herz, he publ. *Musiktheater: Beiträge zur Methodik und zu Inszenierungs-Konzeptionen* (ed., S. Stomper; Leipzig, 1970).

Felsztyn (Felstin, Felstinensis, Felsztynski), Sebastian von, notable Polish theorist and composer; b. Felsztyn, Galicia, c.1490; d. c.1543. He studied (1507–9) at the Univ. of Cracow (bachelor's degree); was chaplain at Felsztyn, later at Przemysl; then was provost in Sanok. He wrote a compendium on Gregorian chant and mensural music, publ. in several eds. (1515, 1519, 1522, 1534, 1539) as *Opusculum utriusque musicae tam choralis quam etiam mensuralis.* He further publ. a practical manual for church singing, *Directiones musicae ad cathedralis ecclesiae Premisliensis usum* (Cracow, 1543); edited St. Augustin's *Dialogus de musica* (with comments); and composed a vol. of hymns, *Aliquot hymni ecclesiastici vario melodiarum genere editi* (Cracow, 1522; partly lost). His significance as a composer lies in the fact that he was the first Polish musician to employ consistent 4-part writing; one selection for 4 voices is reprinted in Surzynski's *Monumenta musices sacrae in Polonia* (vol. II).

Felumb, Svend Christian, Danish composer; b. Copenhagen, Dec. 25, 1898; d. there, Dec. 16, 1972. He studied in Copenhagen with L. Nielsen and Bruce, and in Paris with Blenzel and Vidal; from 1924 till 1947 he was an oboist in the Danish Royal Orch.; in

1947–1962 he conducted the Tivoli Orch. He was the founder of the Ny Musik society in Copenhagen and a leader of the movement for modern national Danish music.

Fenaroli, Fedele, Italian music theorist; b. Lanciano, April 25, 1730; d. Naples, Jan. 1, 1818. He studied with his father, who was a church organist; then went to Naples, where he became a pupil of Francesco Durante and Leonardo Leo at the Cons. of Santa Maria di Loreto; in 1762 became 2nd master there, and in 1777 the first; also taught at the Cons. della Pietà. He trained many famous musicians (Cimarosa, Conti, Mercadante, Zingarelli, etc.); his theoretical manuals were highly regarded, not only in Italy, but in France; he publ. *Partimento ossia Basso numerato* (Rome, 1800); *Studio del contrappunto* (Rome, 1800); *Regale musicali per i principianti di cembalo* (Naples, 1775). He was a prolific composer of church music, which, however, did not sustain its initial renown; composed 2 oratorios, *Abigaille* (1760) and *L'arca nel Giordano.*

Fenby, Eric, English composer; b. Scarborough, April 22, 1906. He studied piano and organ; after a few years as an organist in London, he went (1928) to Grez-sur-Loing, France, as amanuensis for Frederick Delius, taking down his dictation note by note, until Delius's death in 1934. Two years later he publ. his experiences in a book entitled *Delius as I Knew Him* (London; 4th ed., N.Y., 1981). He was director of music of the North Training School (1948–62); from 1964 was a prof. of composition at the Royal Academy of Music. Because of the beneficent work he undertook, he neglected his own compositions; however he also wrote some pleasant music for strings.

Fendler, Edvard, German-American conductor; b. Leipzig, Jan. 22, 1902. He studied conducting with G. Brecher and composition with Leichtentritt; conducted in Germany, France, and the Netherlands (1927–41); was conductor of the National Symph. Orch., Ciudad Trujillo, the Dominican Republic (1942–44); then was in the U.S. (1945–47); was conductor of the National Symph. Orch. in San José, Costa Rica (1948–49); returned to the U.S. in 1949; from 1952 till 1970 he was conductor of the Mobile (Ala.) Symph. Orch.

Fennell, Frederick, American band conductor; b. Cleveland, July 2, 1914. He began conducting during the summers of 1931–33 at the National Music Camp at Interlochen, Mich.; went on to study at the Eastman School of Music in Rochester, N.Y. (B.M., 1937; M.M., 1939); then served on its faculty as conductor of the Little Symph. and Symph. Band (1939–65). In 1952 he founded the Eastman Wind Ensemble, with which he made numerous record albums; he was also a guest conductor at the Boston Pops. In 1965 he was appointed conductor-in-residence of the Univ. of Miami School of Music at Coral Gables, Fla.; he also made European tours with the School Orch. of America (1965, 1966) and produced a series of specially recorded concerts at the Library of Congress, using 19th-century band instruments and music (1972, 1973, 1977). He is the recipient of an honorary Mus.D. degree from the Univ. of Oklahoma City; in 1958 was made an Honorary Chief by the Kiowa Indian tribe. He publ. *Time and the Winds* (Kenosha, Wis., 1954) and *The Drummer's Heritage* (Rochester, 1957).

Fennelly, Brian, American composer; b. Kingston, N.Y., Aug. 14, 1937. He attended Union College in Schenectady (1954–58), earning a bachelor's degree in mechanical engineering; served in the Air Force (1958–61); upon discharge, returned to Union College, obtaining the degree of B.A. in 1963. He then took postgraduate courses at Yale Univ. School of Music, where he studied with Mel Powell, Gunther Schuller, and Allen Forte (M.M., 1965; Ph.D., 1968); also took cello lessons. As a doctoral student, he wrote the dissertation *A Descriptive Notation for Electronic Music.* In 1968 he was appointed to the faculty of the School of Arts and Sciences at N.Y. Univ. In 1980 he received the Guggenheim fellowship grant. He traveled widely as a pianist, conductor, and lecturer; was delegate to World Music Days, under the auspices of the International Society for Contemporary Music, in Iceland, the Netherlands, France, Austria, Czechoslovakia, Finland, Greece, and Israel. He is extremely liberal in his choice of idiom for his own music, free of fashionable elitism, willing and eager to use all effective means of composition, ranging from stark homophony to dodecaphonic structuralism, traversing on the way through the unblushing expression of soulful Romanticism. For purely practical purposes he produced 9 pieces, each for a solo instrument, under the general title *Tesserae* (that is, regularly shaped pieces of stone or glass used for mosaic material; the word itself, meaning "four" in Greek, refers to a 4-cornered plate). He also made use of electronic sound.

Feo, Francesco, celebrated Italian composer; b. Naples, 1691; d. there, Jan. 18, 1761. He was a pupil of Andrea Basso and Nicola Fago at the Cons. della Pietà from 1704; his first opera was *Amor tirannico* (Naples, Jan. 18, 1713); then followed *La forza della virtù* (Naples, Jan. 22, 1719), *Teuzzone* (Naples, Jan. 20, 1720), *Siface, re di Numidia* (Naples, Nov. 4, 1720), *Andromaca* (Rome, Feb. 5, 1730), *Arsace* (Turin, Dec. 26, 1740), etc. He also wrote pieces for special occasions, including a serenade for the marriage of Charles of Bourbon, King of the 2 Sicilys, to Princess Maria Amalia of Poland (1737) and a piece for the Spanish King's birthday (1738). Feo spent most of his life in Naples; he was first maestro di cappella at the Cons. of Sant' Onofrio (1723–39); then at the Cons. dei Poveri di Gesù Cristo (1739–43). Most of his works (over 150 in all) are extant in MS at Naples.

Fere, Vladimir, Russian composer and ethnomusicologist; b. Kamyshin, in the Saratov district, May 20, 1902; d. Moscow, Sept. 2, 1971. He studied piano with Goldenweiser and composition with Glière and Miaskovsky at the Moscow Cons. (1921–29). In 1936 he went to Frunze, Kirghizia; composed (in collaboration with Vlasov) a number of operas based on native folk motifs; all these operas were first produced in Frunze: *Golden Girl* (May 1, 1937); *Not Death but Life* (March 26, 1938); *Moon Beauty* (April 15, 1939); *For People's Happiness* (May 1, 1941); *Patriots* (Nov. 6, 1941); *Son of the People* (Nov. 8, 1947); *On the Shores of Issyk-Kul* (Feb. 1, 1951); *Toktogul* (July 6, 1958); *The Witch* (1965); *One Hour before Dawn* (1969). He wrote several symph. pieces on Kirghiz themes; numerous choruses; also chamber music.

Ferencsik, János, eminent Hungarian conductor; b. Budapest, Jan. 18, 1907; d. there, June 12, 1984. He studied organ and music theory at the Budapest Cons.; then served as choral conductor at the Hungarian State Opera. In 1930–31 he was an assistant at the Bayreuth Festival. In 1948–50 he conducted the Vienna State Opera. From 1957 to 1974 he was chief conductor of the Hungarian State Opera, and concurrently led concerts of the Hungarian National Phil. Orch. In 1951 and again in 1961 he was awarded and prestigious Kossuth Prize. In 1958 he undertook a series of tours as a guest conductor in Europe and America. On his 70th birthday, in 1977, the Hungarian government bestowed upon him the Order of the Banner.

Ferguson, Howard, British composer and music editor; b. Belfast, Oct. 21, 1908. He studied composition with R.O. Morris at the Royal College of Music in London; piano with Harold Samuel; conducting with Sargent. From 1948 to 1963 he was a prof. at the Royal Academy of Music in London. His music is neo-Classical in its idiom; in some of his compositions he makes use of English, Scottish, and Irish folk songs. WORKS: 5 *Irish Folktunes* for Cello or Viola, and Piano (1927); 2 *Ballads* for Baritone, Chorus, and Orch. (1928–32); Violin Sonata No. 1 (1931); 3 *Medieval Carols* for Voice and Piano (1932–33); Octet for Clarinet, Bassoon, Horn, String Quartet, and Double Bass (1933); 5 *Pipe Pieces* for 3 Bamboo Pipes (1934–35); *Partita* for Orch. (1935–36; also for 2 Pianos); 4 *Short Pieces* for Clarinet or Viola and Piano (1932–36); 4 *Diversions on Ulster Airs* for Orch. (1939–42); Flute Sonata (1938–40); 5 *Bagatelles* for Piano (1944); Violin Sonata No. 2 (1946); *Chauntecleer*, ballet (1948); Concerto for Piano and Strings (1950–51; London, May 29, 1952, Myra Hess, soloist); *Discovery* for Voice and Piano (1951); *3 Sketches* for Flute and Piano (1932–52); 2 *Fanfares* for 4 Trumpets and 3 Trombones (1952), *Overture for an Occasion* for Orch. (1952–53); 5 *Irish Folksongs* for Voice and Piano (1954); *Amore langueo* for Tenor, Chorus, and Orch. (1955–56); *The Dream of the Rood* for Soprano or Tenor, Chorus, and Orch. (1958–59); piano pieces. He edited many old keyboard works, among them those by Purcell (1964) and Blow (1965); also the anthologies *Style and Interpretation* (4 vols., 1963–64), *Early French Keyboard Music* (2 vols., 1966); *Early Italian Keyboard Music* (2 vols., 1968); *Early German Keyboard Music* (2 vols., 1970); *Early English Keyboard Music* (1971); also edited *W. Tisdall: Complete Keyboard Works* (London, 1958); with C. Hogwood, *W. Croft: Complete Harpsichord Works* (2 vols., London, 1974); *Anne Cromwell's Virginal Book, 1638* (London, 1974); *F. Schubert, Piano Sonatas* (London, 1979); *Keyboard Works of C.P.E. Bach* (4 vols., London, 1983).

Fernandez, Oscar Lorenzo, Brazilian composer; b. Rio de Janeiro, Nov. 4, 1897; d. there, Aug. 26, 1948. He studied music at the Instituto Nacionale de Musica, and appeared as composer, conductor, and pianist in his own works in Brazil and other Latin American countries. He won several prizes. In 1925 he became a prof. at the Instituto Nacionale, and organized a choral society there. In his music he adopted a strongly national style, derived from Brazilian folk songs but without actual quotation. WORKS: Opera, *Malazarte* (Rio de Janeiro, Sept. 30, 1941, composer conducting); ballet on Inca themes, *Amayá* (Rio de Janeiro, July 9, 1939); suite for Orch., *Imbapará* (Rio de Janeiro, Sept. 2, 1929); suite for Orch., *Reisado do pastoreio* (Rio de Janeiro, Aug. 22, 1930; the last movement of this suite, *Batuque*, a Brazilian dance, became popular); Violin Concerto (1942); Symph. (perf. posthumously by the Boston Symph. Orch., Eleazar de Carvalho conducting, Feb. 25, 1949); also a number of chamber music compositions: *Trio Brasileiro* (1924); Suite for Flute, Oboe, Clarinet, Bassoon, and Horn (Rio de Janeiro, Sept. 20, 1927); several piano works; songs. A complete bibliography of magazine articles on Fernandez is found in Vasco Mariz, *Dicionario Bio-Bibliografico Musical* (Rio de Janeiro, 1948).

Fernández Arbós, Enrique. See **Arbós, Enrique Fernández.**

Fernández Caballero, Manuel, Spanish composer; b. Murcia, March 14, 1835; d. Madrid, Feb. 20, 1906. He was a precocious musician; learned to play the violin, piano, and piccolo as a child, and at the age of 7, played in a school band. He then studied violin with Soriano Fuertes in Murcia; in 1850 he entered the Madrid Cons., where his teachers were Eslava and Pedro Albéniz; in 1856 he received first prize in composition; then conducted various orchs. and became interested in theatrical composition. During his career as a conductor and composer, he wrote more than 200 zarzuelas, several of which attained great popularity: *Los dineros del Sacristan* and *Los Africanistas* (Barcelona, 1894); *El cabo primero* (Barcelona, 1895); *La rueda de la fortuna* (Madrid, 1896); *Los estudiantes* (Madrid, 1900). He also wrote sacred music.

Ferneyhough, Brian, English composer; b. Coventry, Jan. 16, 1943. He studied at the Birmingham School of Music (1961–63); then took courses with Lennox Berkeley and Maurice Miles at the Royal Academy of Music in London (1966–67); furthermore, received instruction in advanced composition with Ton de Leeuw in Amsterdam and Klaus Huber in Basel (1969–73). In 1971 he was appointed to the faculty at the Hochschule für Musik in Freiburg, Germany; in 1976, 1978, and 1980, lectured at the Darmstadt summer courses.

WORKS: *4 Miniatures* for Flute and Piano (1965); *Coloratura* for Oboe and Piano (1966); Sonata for 2 Pianos (1966); *Prometheus* for Wind Sextet (1967); *Sonatas* for String Quartet (1967); *Epicycle* for 20 Strings (Hilversum, Sept. 7, 1969); *Missa Brevis* for 12 Solo Voices (1971); *Firecycle Beta* for Orch., with 5 Conductors (1969–71); *7 Sterne* for Organ (1971); *Time and Motion Study I* for Solo Bass Clarinet (1971–77), *II* for Cello and Electronics (1973–75), and *III* for 16 Solo Voices and Percussion (1974); *Transit* for 6 Amplified Voices and Chamber Orch. (1972–75; London Sinfonietta in Royan, France, March 25, 1975; first British perf., London, Nov. 16, 1977); *Perspectivae Corporum Irregularum* for Oboe, Viola, and Piano (1975); *Unity Capsule* for Solo Flute (1975–76); *Funérailles,* version I, for String Sextet, Double Bass, and Harp (1969–77); *La Terre est un homme* for Orch. (1976–79); *Funérailles,* version II, for 7 Strings and Harp (1980); String Quartet No. 2 (1980); *Lemmacon-Epigram* for Piano (1981); *Superscriptio* for Solo Piccolo (1981); *Carceri d'Invenzione* for Chamber Ensemble (London, Nov. 16, 1982).

Fernström, John (Axel), Swedish conductor and composer; b. I-Chang, Hupei, China (the son of a Swedish missionary), Dec. 6, 1897; d. Hälsingborg, Oct. 19, 1961. He studied first at the Cons. in Malmö, then took violin lessons in Copenhagen, where he also studied with P. Gram (1923–30). He took courses in conducting at Sonderhausen, Germany, and later settled in Hälsingborg.

WORKS: An exceptionally prolific composer, he wrote 3 operas: *Achnaton* (1931); *Isissystrarnas bröllop* (1942); *Livet en dröm* (1946); 12 symphs.: No. 1 (1920); No. 2 (1924); No. 3, *Exotica* (1928); No. 4 (1930); No. 5 (1932); No. 6 (1938); No. 7, *Sinfonietta in forma di sonata de chiesa* (1941); No. 8, *Amore studiorum* (1942); No. 9, *Sinfonia breve* (1943); No. 10, *Sinfonia discrète* (1944); No. 11, *Utan mask* (1945); No. 12 (1951); *Symphonic Variations* (1930); 2 violin concertos (No. 2, 1952); Chaconne for Cello and Orch. (1936); Clarinet Concerto (1936); Viola Concerto (1937); Concertino for Flute, Female Chorus, and Small Orch. (1941); Bassoon Concerto (1946); Cello Concertino (1949); *Ostinato* for Strings (1952); Mass for Soli, Chorus, and Orch. (1931); *Stabat Mater* for Soli, Chorus, and Strings (1936); *Songs of the Sea,* suite for Soprano and Strings (1943); *Den mödosamma vä gen,* profane oratorio (1947); 8 string quartets (1920, 1925, 1931, 1942, 1945, 1947, 1950, 1952); many other chamber works; songs and choral works. He publ. an autobiographical book, *Confessions* (1946).

Ferrabosco, Alfonso, Italian composer, son of **Domenico Ferrabosco;** b. Bologna, Jan. (baptized, Jan. 18) 1543; d. there, Aug. 12, 1588. He went to England as a youth; in 1562 he was in the service of

Queen Elizabeth; went back to Italy in 1564; was again in England from 1564 to 1569. He lived in France for some time, and married a woman from Antwerp; after another sojourn in England (1572–78) he was in Turin in the service of the Duke of Savoy, whom he accompanied to Spain (1585); eventually he returned to Bologna. The historical position of Alfonso Ferrabosco is important for the influence of Italian music that he brought to the court of Queen Elizabeth. Some of his madrigals are found in Young's *Musica transalpina* (London, 1588, 1597), Morley's *Madrigals to Five Voyces* (London, 1598), Pevernage's *Harmonia celesta* (1593), and other collections up to 1664; further compositions appear in collections of P. Phalèse (1583, 1591, 1593), A. Morsolina (1588), G.B. Besardo (1603), etc. MSS are in the Bodleian Library and Music School at Oxford, British Library, St. Michael's College, Tenbury, and Royal College of Music Library.

Ferrabosco, Alfonso, Italian-English composer, natural son of the preceding; b. Greenwich, England, c.1575; d. there, March (buried, March 11) 1628. He was educated in England, and remained there after his father returned to Italy in 1578. He was supported from the funds of the English court; was one of the King's Musicians for the Violins from about 1602 until his death; was named teacher to the Prince of Wales in 1604. In 1626 he was made Composer of the King's Music; also Composer of Music in Ordinary to the King. He was highly regarded as composer of the music for masques of Ben Jonson, of whom he was a close friend: *The Masque of Blackness* (1604–5); *The Masque of Hymen* (1605–6); *The Masque of Beauty* (1607–8); *The Masque for Lord Haddington's Marriage* (1607–8); and *The Masque of Queens* (1608–9). In 1609 he publ. a vol. of *Ayres* (dedicated to Prince Henry) and a book of *Lessons for 1, 2 and 3 Viols;* also contributed 3 compositions to Leighton's *Teares or Lamentacions* (1614). MSS are in libraries of the British Museum, the Music School and Church, Oxford, and the Royal College of Music. His works for viol demonstrate extraordinary ability in contrapuntal writing, while preserving the rhythmic quality of the dance forms (pavans, etc.) and the free ornamental style of the fantasies.

Ferrabosco, Domenico Maria, Italian composer; b. Bologna, Feb. 14, 1513; d. there, Feb. 1574. He was maestro di cappella at San Petronio in Bologna; in 1546 he was at the Vatican, returning to Bologna in 1548; was again at the Vatican from 1550 until 1555; eventually returned to Bologna. He is chiefly known as a composer of madrigals; his book of 45 madrigals, *Il primo libro de' madrigali a 4 voci,* was publ. by Gardano in 1542; Gardano also publ. motets (1554) and other madrigals (1557) by Ferrabosco; some madrigals and a 4-voiced canzona, the latter in lute tablature, appeared in 1584 (publ. by Scotto).

Ferrari, Benedetto, Italian opera librettist and composer, called "Della Tiorba" from his proficiency on the theorbo; b. Reggio, c.1603; d. Modena, Oct.

22, 1681. He studied music in Rome; served as a choirboy at the Collegio Germanico in Rome (1617–18); subsequently was a musician at the Farnese court in Parma (1619–23). In 1637 he proceeded to Venice; there he wrote the libretto for Manelli's opera *L'Andromeda,* produced at the Teatro di San Cassiano in 1637; it was the first opera performed in a theater open to the public. He then wrote libretti for *La Maga fulminata* by Manelli (1638); *L'inganno d'Amore* by Bertoli (Regensburg, 1653); *La Licasta* by Manelli (Parma, 1664); and 4 of his own operas, all produced in Venice: *Armida* (Feb. 1639), *Il Pastor regio* (Jan. 23, 1640), *La Ninfa avara* (1641), and *Il Principe giardiniero* (Dec. 30, 1643). In 1651–53 he was in Vienna. From 1653–62 he served as court choirmaster in Modena; after a hiatus of employment, he was reinstated in 1674, remaining in this post until his death. In Modena he produced the opera *Erosilda* (1658) and 2 cantatas, *Premo il giogo delle Alpi* and *Voglio pur di vita uscir* (reprinted in Riemann's *Kantaten Frühling,* vol. 1, Leipzig, 1909). Six of Ferrari's libretti were publ. in Milan in 1644 under the title *Poesie drammatiche.*

Ferrari, Gabrielle, French pianist and composer; b. Paris, Sept. 14, 1851; d. there, July 4, 1921. She studied at the Milan Cons. and later in Paris, where she had lessons with Gounod. She wrote a number of effective piano pieces (*Rapsodie espagnole, Le Ruisseau, Hirondelle,* etc.) and songs (*Larmes en songe, Chant d'exil, Chant d'amour,* etc.); finally ventured to compose operas, producing *Le Dernier Amour* (Paris, June 11, 1895), *Sous le masque* (Vichy, 1898), *Le Tartare* (Paris, 1906), and *Le Cobzar,* which proved to be her most successful opera (Monte Carlo, Feb. 16, 1909; several subsequent revivals).

Ferrari, Giacomo Gotifredo, Italian composer; b. Rovereto, Tyrol (baptized, April 2), 1763; d. London, Dec. 1842. He studied piano at Verona with Marcola and theory with Marianus Stecher at the Monastery of Mariaberg in Switzerland. He then went to Naples, where he studied with Latilla. There he met Chevalier Campan, household master for Marie Antoinette; he was then appointed as court musician at the Tuileries. He arrived in Paris in 1787; after the Revolution he went to London, where he settled as a singing teacher. He produced in London the operas *I due Svizzeri* (May 14, 1799), *Il Rinaldo d'Asti* (March 16, 1802), *L'eroina di Raab* (April 8, 1813), and *Lo sbaglio fortunato* (May 8, 1817); he also wrote 2 ballets and several instrumental works (4 septets, 2 piano concertos, etc.).

Ferrari, Gustave, Swiss pianist and composer; b. Geneva, Sept. 28, 1872; d. there, July 29, 1948. He studied at the Geneva Cons., and later in Paris. In 1900 he went to London, where he remained for many years. From 1917 till 1925 he conducted operetta in America; then returned to Europe and toured with Yvette Guilbert, as her accompanist in a repertoire of French folk songs; later on he gave song recitals himself, singing with his own accompaniment folk songs of France and French Canada; also lectured on the subject, and edited collections of French folk music. As a composer, he wrote mostly incidental music for the stage; composed a cantata for the Rousseau Festival (Geneva, 1912); *The Wilderness,* a Greek dance ballad (London, 1915); other choral works; a song cycle, *Le Livre pour toi.*

Ferrari-Trecate, Luigi, Italian composer; b. Alessandria, Piedmont, Aug. 25, 1884; d. Rome, April 17, 1964. He studied with Antonio Cicognani at the Cons. of Pesaro, and also with Mascagni. Subsequently he was engaged as a church organist; was prof. of organ at the Liceo Musicale in Bologna (1928–31); in 1929–55 was director of the Parma Cons. He wrote several operas which had considerable success: *Pierozzo* (Alessandria, Sept. 15, 1922); *La Bella e il mostro* (Milan, March 20, 1926); *Le astuzie di Bertoldo* (Genoa, Jan. 10, 1934); *Ghirlino* (Milan, Feb. 4, 1940); *Buricchio* (Bologna, Nov. 5, 1948); *L'Orso Re* (Milan, Feb. 8, 1950); *La capanna dello Zio Tom* (*Uncle Tom's Cabin;* Parma, Jan. 17, 1953); *La fantasia tragica; Lo spaventapasseri* (1963); he also wrote music for a marionette play, *Ciottolino* (Rome, Feb. 8, 1922); a sacred cantata, *In hora calvarii* (1956); and *Contemplazioni* for Orch. (1950).

Ferrer, Mateo, Catalan composer; b. Barcelona, Feb. 25, 1788; d. there, Jan. 4, 1864. A highly gifted musician, he was famous for his improvisations on the organ. He was organist at the Barcelona Cathedral for 52 years, from 1812 until his death. His Sonata (1814), printed by Joaquín Nín in his collection *16 sonates anciennes d'auteurs espagnols* (Paris, 1925), shows a certain affinity with early Beethoven.

Ferrero, Willy, precocious Italian conductor; b. Portland, Maine, May 21, 1906; d. Rome, March 24, 1954. He was taken to Italy in his infancy; as a child of 6 he conducted a performance at the Teatro Costanzi in Rome; at age 8 he conducted symph. concerts in European capitals with sensational success, and was the object of extravagant praise as a phenomenal musician. World War I interrupted his career; he continued to conduct operas and concerts in Italy, but failed to fulfill the extraordinary promise of his early youth. He received an excellent academic education; studied at the Vienna Academy (graduated in 1924); composed a symph. poem, *Il mistero dell' aurora,* and some chamber music.

Ferretti, Dom Paolo, eminent Italian musicologist; b. Subiaco, Dec. 3, 1866; d. Bologna, May 23, 1938. He studied theology at the Benedictine College of San Anselmo in Rome; then taught in Malta, Genoa, and Parma; was abbot of the Benedictine Monastery of San Giovanni in Parma; in 1922 was appointed by Pope Pius XI director of the Scuola Pontificia (until 1931, when it became the Pontifical Inst. of Sacred Music). During the summers of 1925, 1927, and 1928 he taught courses in Gregorian chant at the Pius X School of Liturgical Music in N.Y. The importance of his investigations lies in a scholarly analysis of the rhythmic treatment and especially the forms of Gregorian chant. He publ. *Principii teorici e practici del Canto Gregoriano* (Rome, 1905); *Il Cursus Metrico e il ritmo delle melodie del Canto Gregoriano* (Rome, 1913); *Estetica gregoriana* (Rome, 1934; also in French, Tournai, 1938).

Ferri, Baldassare, celebrated Italian artificial soprano; b. Perugia, Dec. 9, 1610; d. there, Nov. 18, 1680. At the age of 11 he was choirboy in Orvieto to Cardinal Crescenzio, in whose service he remained until 1625, when he entered the service of Prince Ladislaus of Poland in Warsaw, remaining with him until 1655, with some interruptions for trips to Italy. From 1655 he was in Vienna at the court of Ferdinand III; appeared briefly in London (about 1671); then returned to Italy. His success at the various courts, and with the public in several countries, must have been great, for he accumulated a fortune. According to contemporary accounts (e.g., A. Bontempi, *Historia Musica,* 1695), he possessed a phenomenal voice.

Ferrier, Kathleen, remarkable English contralto; b. Higher Walton, Lancashire, April 22, 1912; d. London, Oct. 8, 1953. She grew up in Blackburn, where she studied piano; also began voice lessons there with Thomas Duerden; for a time she was employed as a telephone operator. In 1937 she won first prizes for piano and singing at the Carlisle Competition; she then decided on a career as a singer, and subsequently studied voice with J.E. Hutchinson in Newcastle upon Tyne and with Roy Henderson in London. After an engagement as a soloist in the *Messiah* at Westminster Abbey in 1943, she began her professional career in full earnest. Britten chose her to create the title role in his *Rape of Lucretia* (Glyndebourne, July 12, 1946); she also sang Orfeo in Gluck's *Orfeo ed Euridice* there in 1947 and at Covent Garden in 1953. She made her American debut with the N.Y. Phil. on Jan. 15, 1948, singing *Das Lied von der Erde,* with Bruno Walter conducting. She made her American recital debut in N.Y. on March 29, 1949. Toward the end of her brief career, she acquired in England an almost legendary reputation for vocal excellence and impeccable taste, so that her untimely death (from cancer) was greatly mourned. In 1953 she was made a Commander of the Order of the British Empire; she also received the Gold Medal of the Royal Phil. Society.

Ferroud, Pierre-Octave, French composer; b. Chasselay, near Lyons, Jan. 6, 1900; d. near Debrecen, Hungary (killed in an automobile accident), Aug. 17, 1936. He attended the Univ. of Lyons, and studied there and in Strasbourg with Erb, Ropartz, Witkowski, and Florent Schmitt; in 1923 settled in Paris, where he developed varied activities as a composer, music critic, and adviser for radio broadcasting. He first attracted attention with the performance of his ballet *Le Porcher* (Ballets Suédois, Paris, Nov. 15, 1924); there followed the symph. poem *Foules* (Paris, March 21, 1926); an operatic sketch, *Chirurgie,* after Chekhov (Monte Carlo, March 20, 1928); and Symph. in A (Paris, March 8, 1931, Monteux conducting; also at the Prague Festival of the International Society for Contemporary Music, Sept. 6, 1935); other works are the ballets *Jeunesse* (Paris, April 29, 1933) and *Vénus ou L'Equipée planétaire* (1935); Cello Sonata (1933); *Andante cordial* for Violin, Cello, and Piano; Trio for Oboe, Clarinet, and Bassoon (1934); also several song cycles and piano pieces. Ferroud's music is distinguished by an adroit application of contrapuntal methods to compositions of an essentially popular style; his chief influence was Florent Schmitt, about whom he wrote a book, *Autour de Florent Schmitt* (Paris, 1927).

Fesca, Alexander Ernst, German pianist and composer, son of **Friedrich Ernst Fesca;** b. Karlsruhe, May 22, 1820; d. Braunschweig, Feb. 22, 1849. He studied with his father, and later with Taubert. He was extremely successful as a concert pianist in 1839; in 1841 he became chamber musician to Prince Fürstenberg; settled in Braunschweig in 1842, where he brought out his operas *Der Troubadour* (July 25, 1847) and *Ulrich von Hutten* (1849); he also wrote a piano sextet, 2 piano trios, a violin sonata, and many songs, some of which became popular. His early death at the age of 28 was regretted by many admirers who believed that he was a composer of uncommon talent.

Fesca, Friedrich Ernst, German composer; b. Magdeburg, Feb. 15, 1789; d. Karlsruhe, May 24, 1826. He studied violin; made a debut in his own Violin Concerto; in 1806 he joined the orch. of the Duke of Oldenburg; in 1808 he obtained a similar position at the Westphalian court at Kassel; in 1813 he was in Vienna; in 1814 became a member of the Karlsruhe Orch. He was a prolific composer of chamber music (20 quartets and 5 quintets); also wrote 2 operas, *Cantemire* (Karlsruhe, April 27, 1820) and *Omar und Leila* (Karlsruhe, Feb. 26, 1824); 3 symphs.; 4 overtures; etc.

Festa, Costanzo, Italian composer; b. Rome, c.1480; d. there, April 10, 1545. He was a singer in the Pontifical Chapel from about 1517. He was a composer of much importance, being regarded as a forerunner of Palestrina, whose works were strongly influenced by those of Festa; was the first important Italian musician who successfully fused the Flemish and Italian styles, melodically and harmonically. He may well be considered one of the first, if not the first, of the native Italian madrigalists. The earliest known publ. work of his appeared in 1519. Of his numerous compositions, many sacred works were publ. in various collections from 1513 till 1549; a *Te Deum a 4* (publ. in Rome, 1596) is still sung in the Vatican on solemn festivals. A complete list of Festa's works, together with reprints, is found in A. Cametti's "Per un precursore del Palestrina: Il compositore piemontese Costanzo Festa," *Bollettino Bibliografico Musicale* (April 1931); also, A. Main edited *Costanzo Festa, Opera omnia,* in Corpus

Mensurabilis Musicae, XXV (1962–68).

Fétis, Edouard-Louis François, Belgian music editor, son of **François-Joseph Fétis;** b. Bouvignes, near Dinant, May 16, 1812; d. Brussels, Jan. 31, 1909. He edited his father's *La Revue Musicale* (1833–35); was for years librarian of the Brussels Library. He publ. *Les Musiciens belges* (1848) and *Les Artistes belges à l'étranger* (1857–65), and compiled a catalogue of his father's library. His brother, **Adolphe-Louis-Eugène Fétis** (b. Paris, Aug. 20, 1820; d. there, March 20, 1873), was a pupil of his father, and of Herz (piano); lived in Brussels and Antwerp, and from 1856 in Paris as a music teacher. He composed music for piano and harmonium.

Fétis, François-Joseph, erudite Belgian musical theorist, historian, and critic; b. Mons, March 25, 1784; d. Brussels, March 26, 1871. He received primary instruction from his father, an organist at the Mons Cathedral; learned to play the violin, piano, and organ when very young, and in his 9th year wrote a Concerto for Violin, with Orch.; as a youth, was organist to the Noble Chapter of Sainte-Waudru. In 1800 he entered the Paris Cons., where he studied harmony with Rey and piano with Boieldieu and Pradher; in 1803 he visited Vienna, there studying counterpoint, fugue, and masterworks of German music. Several of his compositions (a symph., an overture, sonatas and caprices for piano) were publ. at that time. In 1806 Fétis began the revision of the plainsong and entire ritual of the Roman Church, a vast undertaking, completed, with many interruptions, after 30 years of patient research. A wealthy marriage in the same year, 1806, enabled him to pursue his studies at ease for a time; but the fortune was lost in 1811, and he retired to the Ardennes, where he occupied himself with composition and philosophical researches into the theory of harmony; in 1813 he was appointed organist for the collegiate church of St.-Pierre at Douai. In 1818 he settled in Paris; in 1821 became a prof. of composition at the Paris Cons.; in 1824 his *Traité du contrepoint et de la fugue* was publ. and accepted as a regular manual at the Cons. In 1827 he became librarian of the Cons., and in the same year founded his unique journal *La Revue Musicale,* which he edited alone until 1832; his son edited it from 1833 until 1835, when its publication ceased. Fétis also wrote articles on music for *Le National* and *Le Temps.* In 1828 he competed for the prize of the Netherlands Royal Inst. with the treatise *Quels ont été les mérites des Néerlandais dans la musique, principalement aux XIVe–XVIe siècles . . . ;* Kiesewetter's essay on the same subject won, but Fétis's paper was also printed by the Inst. In 1832 he inaugurated his famous series of historical lectures and concerts. In 1833 he was called to Brussels as maître de chapelle to King Leopold I, and director of the Cons.; during his long tenure in the latter position, nearly 40 years, the Cons. flourished as never before. He also conducted the concerts of the Academy, which elected him a member in 1845. Fétis was a confirmed believer in the possibility of explaining music history and music theory scientifically; in his scholarly writings he attempted a thorough systematization of all fields of the art; he was opinionated and dogmatic, but it cannot be denied that he was a pioneer in musicology. He publ. the first book on music appreciation, *La Musique mise à la portée de tout le monde* (Paris, 1830; numerous reprints and translations into Eng., German, Italian, Spanish, Russian); further pedagogical writings are: *Solfèges progressifs* (Paris, 1837); *Traité complet de la théorie et de la pratique de l'harmonie* (Brussels, 1844). As early as 1806 Fétis began collecting materials for his great *Biographie universelle des musiciens et bibliographie générale de la musique* in 8 vols. (Paris, 1833–44; 2nd ed., 1860–65; supplement of 2 vols., 1878–80; edited by A. Pougin). This work of musical biography was unprecedented in its scope; entries on composers and performers whom Fétis knew personally still remain prime sources of information. On the negative side are the many fanciful accounts of composers' lives taken from unreliable sources; in this respect Fétis exercised a harmful influence on subsequent lexicographers for a whole century. His *Histoire générale de la musique,* in 5 vols., goes only as far as the 15th century (Paris, 1869–76); this work exhibits Fétis as a profound scholar, but also as a dogmatic philosopher of music propounding opinions without convincing evidence to support them. Of interest are his *Esquisse de l'histoire de l'harmonie considerée comme art et comme science systématique* (Paris, 1840); *Notice biographique de Nicolo Paganini* (Paris, 1851; with a short history of the violin); *Antoine Stradivari* (Paris, 1856; with a commentary on bowed instruments); reports on musical instruments at the Paris Expositions of 1855 and 1867; etc. Fétis was also a composer; between 1820 and 1832 he wrote 7 operas, serious and light, for the Opéra-Comique; composed church music, 3 string quartets, 3 string quintets, 2 symphs., and a Flute Concerto. His valuable library of 7,325 vols. was acquired after his death by the Bibliothèque Royale of Brussels; a catalogue was publ. in 1877.

Fetler, Paul, American composer; b. Philadelphia, Feb. 17, 1920. His family moved to Europe when Fetler was a child, and he had early musical studies in Latvia, Holland, Sweden, and Switzerland. He returned to the U.S. in 1939 and studied composition with Van Vactor at Northwestern Univ., graduating in 1943. He studied briefly with Celibidache in Berlin (1945–46) and, returning to the U.S., with Quincy Porter and Hindemith and Yale Univ. (1946–48). In 1948 he was appointed a teacher at the Univ. of Minnesota and in 1960 became a prof. there. His numerous awards include two Guggenheim grants (1953, 1960) and National Endowment grants (1975, 1977).

Feuermann, Emanuel, greatly gifted Austrian-born American cellist; b. Kolomea, Galicia, Nov. 22, 1902; d. New York, May 25, 1942. As a child he was taken to Vienna where he first studied cello with his father; subsequently studied cello with Friedrich

Buxbaum and Anton Walter; made his debut in Vienna in 1913 in a recital. He went to Leipzig in 1917 to continue his studies with Julius Klengel; his progress was so great that he was appointed to the faculty of the Gürzenich Cons. in Cologne by Abendroth at the age of 16; he also was first cellist in the Gürzenich Orch. and was a member of the Bram Eldering Quartet. In 1929 he was appointed prof. at the Hochschule für Musik in Berlin; as a Jew he was forced to leave Germany after the advent of the Nazis to power; he then embarked on a world tour (1934–35). He made his American debut on Dec. 6, 1934, with the Chicago Symph. Orch.; then appeared as soloist with many of the leading American orchs.; also played chamber music with Schnabel and Huberman, and later with Rubinstein and Heifetz.

Fevin, Antoine de, French composer; b. probably in Arras, 1474; d. Blois, Jan. 1512. He was a younger contemporary of Josquin des Prez, whose style he emulated. He composed 12 masses, 6 of which were printed in collections by Petrucci (1515) and Antico (1516); also 29 motets, 3 Magnificats, and Lamentations (publ. by Montanus in 1549); 3 works by Fevin are in the archives of Toledo Cathedral (cf. F. Rubio Piqueras, *Música y músicos toledanos,* 1923); 6 motets were printed in Petrucci's *Motetti della corona* (1514), and some French chansons in various collections. Fevin's mass *Mente tota* is reprinted in Expert's *Maîtres musiciens* (vol. 5); a 6-voice motet and parts of masses are in Eslava's *Lira sacro-hispana;* a 4-voice *Kyrie* in Burney's *General History of Music* (vol. 2); the mass *Ave Maria* and *Benedictus et Hosanna* is in Delporte's *Collection de polyphonie classique;* several motets were reprinted by B. Kahmann (Amsterdam, 1951).

Février, Henri, French opera composer; b. Paris, Oct. 2, 1875; d. there, July 6, 1957. He studied at the Paris Cons. with Fauré, Leroux, Messager, Pugno, and Massenet; composed the operas *Le Roi aveugle* (Paris, May 8, 1906); *Monna Vanna* (Paris, Jan. 13, 1909); *Gismonda* (Chicago, Jan. 14, 1919; Paris, Oct. 15, 1919); *La Damnation de Blanche-Fleur* (Monte Carlo, March 13, 1920); *La Femme nue* (Monte Carlo, March 23, 1929); operettas: *Agnès, dame galante* (1912); *Carmosine* (1913); *Ile désenchantée* (Paris, Nov. 21, 1925); etc. Février wrote the monograph *André Messager; Mon maître, mon ami* (Paris, 1948).

Ffrangcon-Davies, David Thomas (real name, **David Thomas Davis;** the surname Ffrangcon was taken from the Nant-Ffrangcon mountain range near his birthplace), prominent British baritone; b. Bethesda, Caernarvon, Wales, Dec. 11, 1855; d. London, April 13, 1918. He was ordained a priest in 1884, but later left the church to take up a musical career; studied singing with Richard Latter, Shakespeare, and Randegger in London; made his concert debut in Manchester (Jan. 6, 1890), his stage debut at Drury Lane Theatre (April 26, 1890). In 1896–98, he sang in festivals throughout the U.S. and Canada;

then lived in Berlin (1898–1901); from 1903, he was a prof. of singing at the Royal College of Music in London. After a nervous breakdown in 1907 he gave up public singing. His book, *The Singing of the Future* (London, 1905; preface by Elgar), was republ. by his daughter, Marjorie Ffrangcon-Davies, as Part II of *David Ffrangcon-Davies, His Life and Book* (London, 1938; introduction by Ernest Newman).

Fibich, Zdenko (Zdeněk), significant Czech composer; b. Seboriče, Dec. 21, 1850; d. Prague, Oct. 15, 1900. He studied first in Prague, then at the Leipzig Cons. with Moscheles (piano) and Richter (theory). Upon his return to Prague, he occupied the posts of deputy conductor and choirmaster at the Provisional Theater (1875–78) and director of the Russian Church choir (1878–81). From then on, he continued to live in Prague, devoting himself mainly to composition. In his music, he was greatly influenced by Wagner, and applied quasi-Wagnerian methods even when treating national Bohemian subjects. His main distinction was a gift for facile melody, and he was at his best in his short pieces, such as *Poème,* op. 41, no. 6, for piano, which has become extremely popular through many arrangements for various instrumental combinations.

WORKS: Operas (produced at Prague): *Bukovín* (April 16, 1874); *Blaník* (Nov. 25, 1881); *Nevésta Messinská* (*The Bride of Messina;* March 28, 1884; very popular); *Bouře* (*The Tempest;* March 1, 1895); *Hédy,* after Byron's *Don Juan* (Feb. 12, 1896); *Šárka* (Dec. 28, 1897); *Pad Arkuna* (*The Fall of Arkun;* produced posthumously, Nov. 9, 1900; his most important work); music to the dramatic trilogy *Hippodamia* by Vrchlický, a sequence of 3 scenic melodramas with actors reciting to orch. accompaniment: *Námluvy, Pelopovy* (*The Wooing of Pelops;* Feb. 21, 1890); *Smír Tantalúv* (*The Atonement of Tantalus;* June 2, 1891); *Smrt Hippodamie* (*Hippodamia's Death;* Nov. 8, 1891). For Orch.: 3 symphs.: No. 1 (1883); No. 2 (1893); No. 3, in E minor (1898); symph. poems: *Othello* (1873); *Zaboj, Slavoj a Luděk* (1873); *Toman a lesni panna* (*Toman and the Wood Nymph;* 1875); *Bouře* (*The Tempest;* 1880); *Vesna* (*Spring;* 1881); *Vigiliae* for Small Orch. (1883); *V podvečer* (*At Twilight;* 1893); choral ballad, *Die Windsbraut;* melodramas: *Stědry den* (*Christmas Day;* 1875); *Vodník* (*The Water Sprite;* 1883); *Hákon* (1888); *Věčnost* (*Eternity;* 1878); *Spring Romanza* for Chorus and Orch. (1880); 2 string quartets; Piano Quartet; *Romance* for Violin and Piano; piano pieces; songs; choruses. He also publ. a method for piano.

Ficher, Jacobo, Russian-Argentine composer; b. Odessa, Jan. 14, 1896; d. Buenos Aires, Sept. 9, 1978. He studied violin with Stolarsky and Korguev in Odessa and composition with Kalafati and Steinberg at the St. Petersburg Cons., graduating in 1917. In 1923 he left Russia and emigrated to Argentina. In 1956 he was appointed prof. of composition at the National Cons. of Music in Buenos Aires. His music is characterized by a rhapsodic fluency of development and a rich harmonic consistency. A prolific composer, he wrote for the stage, for orch., and for voice; he particularly excelled in chamber music.

Fickenscher, Arthur, American composer and pianist; b. Aurora, Ill., March 9, 1871; d. San Francisco, April 15, 1954. He studied at the Munich Cons.; toured the U.S. as accompanist to famous singers, among them Bispham and Schumann-Heink. From 1920 till 1941 he was head of the music dept. of the Univ. of Virginia, Charlottesville. In 1947 he settled in San Francisco. A musician of an inquisitive mind, he elaborated a system of pure intonation; contrived the "Polytone," an instrument designed to play music in which the octave is subdivided into 60 tones; publ. an article, "The Polytone and the Potentialities of a Purer Intonation," *Musical Quarterly* (July 1941).

WORKS: His major work was the *Evolutionary Quintet,* evolved from a violin sonata and an orch. scherzo written in the 1890s; the MSS were burned in the San Francisco earthquake and fire of 1906; the musical material was then used from memory for a quintet for piano and strings, in 2 movements; the 2nd movement, entitled *The 7th Realm,* became a separate work. He also wrote *Willowwave and Welloway* for Orch. (1925); *The Day of Judgment* for Orch. (1927; Grand Rapids, Feb. 10, 1934); *Out of the Gay Nineties* for Orch. (Richmond, Va., Dec. 4, 1934, composer conducting); *Variations on a Theme in Medieval Style* for String Orch. (1937); *Dies Irae* for Chamber Orch. (1927); *The Chamber Blue,* mimodrama for Orch., Soli, Women's Chorus, and Dancers (Univ. of Virginia, April 5, 1938); large choral work, with Orch., *The Land East of the Sun and West of the Moon* (after William Morris).

Ficker, Rudolf von, distinguished German musicologist; b. Munich, June 11, 1886; d. Igls, near Innsbruck, Aug. 2, 1954. In 1905–12 he studied at the Univ. of Vienna with Adler (musicology), and in Munich with Thuille and Courvoisier (composition); received his Ph.D. from the Univ. of Vienna with the dissertation *Die Chromatik im italienischen Madrigal des 16. Jahrhunderts.* He taught at the Univ. of Innsbruck from 1920; became a prof. there in 1923; at the Univ. of Vienna in 1927; and in 1931 at the Univ. of Munich. He was a specialist in early Gothic music.

Fiedler, Arthur, highly popular American conductor; b. Boston, Dec. 17, 1894; d. Brookline, Mass., July 10, 1979. Of a musical family, he studied violin with his father, **Emanuel Fiedler,** a member of the Boston Symph. Orch.; his uncle, **Benny Fiedler,** also played violin in the Boston Symph. In 1909 Fiedler was taken by his father to Berlin, where he studied violin with Willy Hess, and attended a class of chamber music with Ernst von Dohnányi; he also had some instruction in conducting with Arno Kleffel and Rudolf Krasselt. In 1913 he formed in Berlin the Fiedler Trio with 2 other Fiedlers. In 1915, with the war raging in Europe, Fiedler returned to America, and joined the 2nd-violin section of the Boston Symph.

Orch. under Karl Muck; later he moved to the viola section; he also doubled on the celesta, when required. In 1924 he organized the Arthur Fiedler Sinfonietta, a professional ensemble of members of the Boston Symph. In 1929 he started a series of free open-air summer concerts at the Esplanade on the banks of the Charles River in Boston, presenting programs of popular American music intermingled with classical numbers. The series became a feature in Boston's musical life, attracting audiences of many thousands each summer. In 1930 Fiedler was engaged as conductor of the Boston Pops, which he led for nearly half a century. Adroitly combining pieces of popular appeal with classical works and occasional modern selections, Fiedler built an eager following, eventually elevating the Boston Pops to the status of a national institution. He was seemingly undisturbed by the clinking of beer steins, the pushing of chairs, the shuffling of feet, and other incidental sound effects not provided for in the score but which were an integral part of audience participation at Pops concerts. For Fiedler was a social man, gregarious, fond of extracurricular activities; one of his favorite pastimes was riding on fire engines; this addiction was rewarded by a number of nominations as honorary chief of the fire depts. of several American cities. He became commercially successful and willingly accepted offers to advertise for whisky or for orange juice ("that is not only for breakfast anymore"); this popularity, however, cost him a degradation to a lower rank of music-makers, so that his cherished ambition to conduct guest engagements in the regular subscription series of the Boston Symph. Orch. never materialized. On Jan. 4, 1977, President Gerald Ford bestowed upon him the Medal of Freedom. As a mark of appreciation from the city of Boston, a footbridge near the Esplanade was named after him, with the first 2 notes of the Prelude to *Tristan and Isolde,* A and F, marking the initials of Arthur Fiedler's name, engraved on the plaque. His death was mourned by Boston music-lovers in a genuine outpouring of public grief.

Fiedler, Max, German conductor; b. Zittau, Dec. 31, 1859; d. Stockholm, Dec. 1, 1939. He was a piano pupil of his father, and studied the organ and theory with G. Albrecht; attended the Leipzig Cons. (1877–80). In 1882 he was appointed a teacher at the Hamburg Cons.; in 1903, became its director. In 1904 he succeeded Barth as conductor of the Hamburg Phil. Society; remained there until 1908. Although he had won an enviable reputation as a concert pianist, he soon abandoned that career and rapidly won distinction as a conductor. He was guest conductor of the N.Y. Phil. Orch. during the season of 1905–6; in 1907, conducted the London Symph. Orch. The climax of his career was the prestigious appointment as conductor of the Boston Symph. Orch., the position he held from 1908 to 1912. In 1916 he was named music director in Essen, Germany; after 1933 appeared as conductor with the Berlin Phil. and the Berlin Radio. In 1934 he conducted in Sweden. He composed a Symph., a Piano Quintet, a String Quartet, a *Lustspiel* overture, piano pieces, and songs.

Field, John, remarkable Irish pianist and composer; b. Dublin, July 26, 1782; d. Moscow, Jan. 23, 1837. His father was a violinist; his grandfather, an organist; it was from his grandfather that he received his first instruction in music. He then had lessons with Clementi, and was also employed in the salesrooms of Clementi's music establishment in London. In 1802 he accompanied Clementi to Paris, and in 1803 to St. Petersburg, where Field settled as a teacher and performer. After many concert tours in Russia, he returned to England temporarily, and performed his Concerto in E-flat with the Phil. Society of London (Feb. 27, 1832); he continued a European tour in 1833, playing in Paris, in Switzerland, and in Italy. He was stricken with an ailment at Naples, and remained in a hospital for 9 months; at the end of his resources, he was persuaded by a friendly Russian family to return to Moscow. On the way, he was able to give a concert in Vienna, with extraordinary success; but the combination of alcoholism and general ill health led to his death 2 years after arriving in Moscow. Field's historical position is of importance, even though his music in itself does not reveal a great original talent. He was undoubtedly a precursor of Chopin in his treatment of piano technique; he was also the originator of keyboard nocturnes. He greatly developed the free fantasias and piano recitative, while following the basic precepts of Classical music. Like Chopin after him, Field wrote mainly for the piano; he composed 7 piano concertos, 4 sonatas, 18 nocturnes, polonaises, and other pieces; also Quintet for Piano and Strings and 2 divertimenti for Piano, Strings, and Flute.

Fielitz, Alexander von, German conductor and composer; b. Leipzig, Dec. 28, 1860; d. Bad Salzungen, July 29, 1930. He was of partly Slavic origin; his mother was Russian. He studied piano with Julius Schulhoff and composition with Kretschmer in Dresden; in conducting he profited by the advice of Nikisch. He conducted opera in various German towns; a nervous disorder caused him to take a prolonged rest in Italy (1887–97); then he settled in Berlin as a teacher. In 1905–8 he was in Chicago, where he organized an orch. and conducted it for a season; in 1908 he returned to Berlin as a teacher at, and later (1916) director of, the Stern Cons. He wrote a number of songs and piano pieces; his song cycle *Eliland* and his songs based on Tuscan folk music were quite popular; he also wrote 2 operas, *Vendetta* (Lübeck, 1891) and *Das stille Dorf* (Hamburg, March 13, 1900).

Fiévet, Paul, French composer; b. Valenciennes, Dec. 11, 1892; d. Paris, March 15, 1980. His father, **Claude Fiévet** (1865–1938), was a composer in his own right. Paul Fiévet studied piano and music theory at the Paris Cons., where he was a student of Xavier Leroux, Caussade, and Widor, obtaining first prize in harmony in 1913, and first prize in composition in 1917, 1918, and 1919. He received the Grand

Prix International in Ostende in 1931 and the Grand Prix of Paris in 1932. Among his works are an operetta, *Le Joli Jeu* (Lyons, 1933), and several symph. suites of the type of "landscape music," e.g., *Les Horizons dorés* (Paris, 1932), *Puerta del Sol* (Paris, 1933), *Images de France* (Paris, 1964), *Orient* (Paris, 1929), *En hiver*, etc. He also wrote several string quartets (one of which he whimsically entitled *Sputnik*), a Brass Sextet, and numerous choruses and piano pieces.

Figner, Medea, famous Italian-Russian soprano; b. Florence, April 3, 1858; d. Paris, July 8, 1952. Her complete name was **Zoraide Amedea Mei.** She studied voice with Bianchi, Carlotta Carozzi-Zucchi, and Panofka in Florence; made her debut as Azucena in Sinalunga, near Florence, in 1875; then sang in the opera theaters of Florence. From 1877 to 1887 she toured in Italy, Spain, and South America; she met the celebrated Russian tenor **Nicolai Figner** during her travels, and followed him to Russia; they were married in 1889, divorced in 1903. She became extremely successful on the Russian operatic stage; was a member of the Maryinsky Imperial Opera Theater in St. Petersburg until 1912. She then devoted herself mainly to voice teaching. In 1930 she emigrated to Paris. Her voice was described by contemporary critics as engagingly soft, rich, "velvety," and "succulent." She could sing mezzo-soprano roles as impressively as those in the soprano range. She was fortunate in having been coached by Tchaikovsky in the role of Liza in his opera *The Queen of Spades*, which she sang in its first production; her husband sang the role of her lover in the same opera. Her other successful roles were Tosca, Mimi, Donna Anna, Elsa, Brünnhilde, Marguerite, Desdemona, Aida, Amneris, and Carmen. In 1912 she publ., in St. Petersburg, her memoirs.

Figner, Nicolai, celebrated Russian tenor; b. Nikiforovka, in the Kazan government, Feb. 21, 1857; d. Kiev, Dec. 13, 1918. He was a lieutenant in the Russian navy before his voice was discovered; made his debut in Naples in 1882; then he studied diligently in Milan; in 1887 he returned to Russia and was engaged as a tenor at the Imperial Theater in St. Petersburg. He was the favorite tenor of Tchaikovsky and was selected to sing the leading role in the premiere of *The Queen of Spades;* his interpretation of Lensky in *Eugene Onegin* was also famous. In 1889 he married the Italian soprano **Medea Mei,** who wrote a book of memoirs (St. Petersburg, 1912) in which she described their careers.

Figulus (real name, **Töpfer**), **Wolfgang,** German writer on music; b. Naumburg, c.1525; d. Meissen, Sept. 1589. He studied in Leipzig; in 1549–51 was cantor at the Thomaskirche in Leipzig; in 1551–88, at the Fürstenschule in Meissen. He wrote *Elementa musicae* (1555; many other eds.); revised Martin Agricola's *Deutsche Musica* (1560); publ. a book of motets, *Precationes* (Leipzig, 1553); *Cantiones sacrae* (1575); and *Hymni sacri et scholastici* (revised by his son-in-law, Friedrich Birck, 1604); a collection of Christmas songs, containing works of his own, of Martin Agricola, and others, was publ. post-humously in 2 books (1594 and 1605).

Filippi, Filippo, Italian composer and critic; b. Vicenza, Jan. 13, 1830; d. Milan, June 24, 1887. He studied law at Padua, taking his degree in 1853. In 1852 he began his career as a music critic with a warm defense of Verdi's *Rigoletto;* from 1858 till 1862 was editor of the *Gazzetta Musicale,* and in 1859 music critic of the newly founded *Perseveranza.* He publ. a collection of essays on great musicians, *Musica e musicisti* (Milan, 1876); as a zealous Wagnerite he wrote a pamphlet, *Riccardo Wagner* (in German, as *Richard Wagner: Eine musikalische Reise in das Reich der Zukunft,* 1876); also publ. a monograph, *Della vita e delle opere di Adolfo Fumagalli* (Milan, 1857); composed a String Quintet; 9 string quartets; Piano Trio; piano pieces; songs.

Filke, Max, German composer; b. Steubendorf-Leobschütz, Silesia, Oct. 5, 1855; d. Breslau, Oct. 8, 1911. He studied with Brosig in Breslau and with Haberl at the Kirchenmusikschule in Regensburg (1877); then with Piutti at the Leipzig Cons. (1880); was engaged as choirmaster at Straubing (1881) and conductor of the Sängerkreis at Cologne (1890); then became director at the Cathedral in Breslau and prof. at the inst. for church music there. His numerous compositions for the church assign him a distinguished position among composers of sacred music.

Fillmore, Henry (full name, **James Henry Fillmore, Jr.**), American bandleader and composer; b. Cincinnati, Feb. 3, 1881; d. Miami, Fla., Dec. 7, 1956. His paternal grandfather was August Damerin Fillmore (2nd cousin of President Millard Fillmore); his father, James Henry Fillmore, and his uncles Fred A. and Charles M. Fillmore were the founders of the Cincinnati music publishing firm of Fillmore Bros. Co. Henry Fillmore was educated at the Miami (Ohio) Military Inst., and later at the Cincinnati College of Music. As a bandmaster, he led the Syrian Shrine Band of Cincinnati to national prominence in the period 1920–26, making several transcontinental tours; in 1915 he founded the Fillmore Band, which was one of the earliest bands to make regular radio broadcasts (1927–34). In 1938 he moved to Miami, Fla., where he conducted bands at the Orange Bowl. He is best known, however, as the composer of numerous popular marches (*Americans We, Men of Ohio, His Honor* et al.), 2nd only to Sousa's in their tuneful liveliness. He was also the leading proponent of the "trombone smear," a humorous effect of the trombone glissando. He used numerous pseudonyms in his publ. pieces (**Al Hayes, Harry Hartley, Ray Hall, Gus Beans, Henrietta Moore,** and **Harold Bennett,** under which name he publ. the popular *Military Escort March*). He was also a compiler of sacred songs and tune books. In 1956 he received an honorary D.Mus. degree from the Univ. of Miami, Fla.

Fillmore, John Comfort, American music educator; b. New London, Conn., Feb. 4, 1843; d. there, Aug. 15, 1898. He was a pupil of G.W. Steele at Oberlin College in Ohio; then at the Leipzig Cons. (1865–67). He was director of the music dept. at Oberlin College (1867); at Ripon College in Wisconsin (1868–78); at Milwaukee College for Women (1878–84). He founded (1884) the Milwaukee School of Music, of which he was director until 1895, when he took charge of the School of Music of Pomona College in Claremont, Calif.

WRITINGS: *Pianoforte Music: Its History, with Biographical Sketches and Critical Estimates of Its Greatest Masters* (Chicago, 1883); *New Lessons in Harmony* (1887); *Lessons in Music History* (1888); *A Study of Omaha Indian Music* (with Alice C. Fletcher and F. La Flesche, 1893).

Filtz, Anton, talented German composer; b. Eichstätt, Sept. (baptized, Sept. 22) 1733; d. Mannheim, March (buried, March 14) 1760. He was a pupil of J. Stamitz; from 1754, first cellist in the Mannheim Orch. He belongs to the school of Mannheim Symphonists, early practitioners of classic instrumental style. That his works must have enjoyed great popularity seems to be proved by the numerous reprints issued at London and Amsterdam, pirated from the original Paris editions. He was exceptionally prolific; in the span of his brief life he completed 41 symphs., many trio sonatas, string trios, sonatas for violin, cello, flute, etc., and concertos for various instruments. Riemann publ. 4 symphs. by Filtz in Denkmäler der Tonkunst in Bayern (4 and 13; formerly 3.i and 7.ii); 2 trios (ibid., 27; formerly 15); and one in *Collegium Musicum.*

Finck, Heinrich, German composer; b. Bamberg, 1445; d. in the Schottenkloster, Vienna, June 9, 1527. He was in the service of 3 Polish kings: Johann Albert (1492), Alexander (1498), and Sigismund (1506); was in Cracow from at least 1491; in 1492 visited Budapest, Vienna, and Torgau, but returned to Poland; in 1510–13 was Kapellmeister to Duke Ulrich at Stuttgart; then at the court of Maximilian I, in Augsburg; in 1520 was appointed composer of the Cathedral chapter at Salzburg; in 1525–26, Hofkapellmeister to Ferdinand I at Vienna, where he was succeeded by his pupil Arnold von Bruck.

WORKS: *Schöne auserlesene Lieder des hochberühmten Heinrich Finckens* (Nuremberg, 1536; reprinted in R. Eitner's *Publikationen,* vol. VIII); other songs publ. by Salblinger (1545) and by Rhaw (1542). Reprints are to be found in Blume's *Das Chorwerk* (hymns ed. by R. Gerber; the *Missa in summis*); in A.W. Ambros's *Geschichte der Musik* (vol. 5); in the Denkmäler der Tonkunst in Österreich (72; formerly 37.ii); in H.J. Moser's *Kantorei der Spätgotik* and in L. Hoffmann-Erbrecht's *Heinrich Finck: Ausgewählte Werke,* I, in *Das Erbe deutscher Musik* (1962).

Finck, Henry Theophilus, American music critic and editor; b. Bethel, Mo., Sept. 22, 1854; d. Rumford Falls, Maine, Oct. 1, 1926. He was brought up in

Oregon; then entered Harvard Univ., where he studied with J.K. Paine. After graduation in 1876 he went to Germany; studied comparative psychology in Berlin and Vienna, and publ. a book, *Romantic Love and Personal Beauty* (1887), propounding a theory that romantic love was unknown to the ancient nations. He was music editor of the *N.Y. Evening Post* from 1881 to 1924, and occasionally wrote for other journals. Finck was a brilliant journalist; in his books on music he stressed the personal and psychological elements.

Finck, Hermann, German composer, great-nephew of **Heinrich Finck;** b. Pirna, Saxony, March 21, 1527; d. Wittenberg, Dec. 28, 1558. He was educated at the court chapel of King Ferdinand of Bohemia; studied at Wittenberg Univ. (1545); then taught music there (1554); was appointed organist in 1557. His major work is the treatise *Practica musica,* publ. by Rhaw (1556), and subdivided into 5 parts. Some of Hermann Finck's works are reprinted by Eitner in his *Publikationen* (vol. VIII, 1879).

Findeisen, Nicolai, Russian music historian and editor; b. St. Petersburg, July 23, 1868; d. Leningrad, Sept. 20, 1928. He studied with Nicolai Sokolov; in 1893 he founded the *Russian Musical Gazette* and remained its editor until it ceased publication in 1917. His writings include monographs on Verstovsky (1890), Serov (1900), Dargomyzhsky (1902), Anton Rubinstein (1905), and Rimsky-Korsakov (1908); he publ. a series of brochures and books on Glinka; the first vol. of a projected large biography, *Glinka in Spain,* appeared in 1896; a catalogue of Glinka's MSS, letters, and portraits was publ. in 1898; he also edited Glinka's correspondence (1908). Findeisen's major achievement was the extensive history of Russian music up to the year 1800, publ. in 2 vols. (partly posthumously) in Leningrad (1928–29) under the title *Sketches of Music in Russia from the Most Ancient Times until the End of the 18th Century.*

Fine, Irving, remarkable American composer; b. Boston, Dec. 3, 1914; d. there, Aug. 23, 1962. He studied with Walter Piston at Harvard Univ. (B.A., 1937; M.A., 1938) and with Nadia Boulanger in Cambridge, Mass. (1938), and in France (1939); also took a course in choral conducting with A.T. Davison. He was an assistant prof. of music at Harvard (1947–50); in 1950 was appointed prof. at Brandeis Univ.; also was a member of the faculty at the Berkshire Music Center in Tanglewood, Mass. (1946–57). He was at first influenced by Stravinsky and Hindemith, and adopted a cosmopolitan style of composition in which contrapuntal elaboration and energetic rhythm were his main concerns; later on, however, he developed a distinctive style of his own, with a lyrical flow of cohesive melody supported by lucid polyphony.
WORKS: Violin Sonata (1946); *Toccata concertante* for Orch. (Boston, Oct. 22, 1948); Partita for Wind Quintet (1948); *Alice in Wonderland,* suite for Chorus and Orch. (1949); Nocturne for Strings and Harp (1951); String Quartet (1952); *Serious Song,* lament for String Orch. (1955); Fantasy for String Trio (1956–57); *Diversions* for Orch. (1958–68); several ingenious piano pieces for children; and his capital work, *Symphony 1962* (Boston Symph. Orch., March 23, 1962).

Fine, Vivian, American composer; b. Chicago, Sept. 28, 1913. She was accepted as a piano student at the Chicago Musical College at an incredible one-digit age; as she grew she took piano lessons with Djane Lavoie-Herz, who claimed to be a pupil of Scriabin, and who instilled the love of Scriabin's polychromatic, anxious melorhythms in Vivian Fine herself. She then had harmony lessons with Ruth Crawford; later received instruction in modern composition from Henry Cowell; also had some help from Adolph Weidig. Progressing precociously, she wrote a piece for oboe solo, which rated a performance in N.Y.; in 1931 her *4 Pieces* for 2 flutes was performed at the Bauhaus in Dessau, Germany. She settled in N.Y. in 1931 and for fully 10 years had sessions with Sessions; she also took piano lessons with Abby Whiteside (1937–45) and had a brief series of lessons in orchestration with George Szell. In 1935 she married the sculptor Benjamin Karp, but continued her career under her maiden name. Although her musical environment in N.Y. was suffused with atonality and dodecaphony, she wrote basically tonal music; she was particularly adept in intimate theatrical productions for a chamber ensemble with voices, and for ballet. In 1974 she received a grant from the National Endowment for the Arts to write an opera; the result was a rather pleasing opus, to her own libretto, *The Women in the Garden,* produced in San Francisco on Feb. 12, 1978. The women in the plot were Emily Dickinson, Isadora Duncan, Gertrude Stein, and Virginia Woolf, disporting themselves in their characteristically erratic fashion. Vivian Fine held several teaching jobs: at N.Y. Univ. (1945–48); at the Juilliard School of Music in N.Y., for a brief semester in 1948; at the College School of Dance in Connecticut (1963–64), and at Bennington College in Vermont (from 1964). She further gave lectures at various small artistic schools in places like Oshkosh (1968). In 1980 she received a Guggenheim fellowship and also became a member of the National Academy and Inst. of Arts and Letters.
WORKS: FOR THE STAGE: *A Guide to the Life Expectancy of a Rose* for Soprano, Tenor, and Chamber Ensemble (N.Y., May 16, 1956); *The Women in the Garden,* chamber opera for 5 Singers and 9 Instruments (1977; San Francisco, Feb. 12, 1978); the ballets *The Race of Life* (1937; N.Y., Jan. 23, 1938), *Opus 51* (Bennington Dance Festival, Aug. 6, 1938), *Tragic Exodus* (N.Y., Feb. 19, 1939), *They Too Are Exiles* (N.Y., Jan. 7, 1940), *Alcestis* (N.Y., April 29, 1960), and *My Son, My Enemy* (Connecticut College, Aug. 14, 1965). FOR ORCH.: Concertante for Piano and Orch. (1944); *Drama* for Orch. (San Francisco, Jan. 5, 1983). CHAMBER MUSIC: *Solo* for Oboe (1929); *4 Pieces* for 2 Flutes (1930); Sonatina for Oboe and Piano (1939); *Capriccio* for Oboe and String Trio

(1946); *Divertimento* for Cello and Percussion (1951); Violin Sonata (1952); String Quartet (1957); *Duo* for Flute and Viola (1961); *Fantasy* for Cello and Piano (1962); *Melos* for Solo Double Bass (1964); *The Song of Persephone* for Solo Viola (1964); Concertino for Piano and Percussion Ensemble (1965); Chamber Concerto for Cello and 6 Instruments (1966); Quintet for Violin, Viola, Cello, Trumpet, and Harp (1967); Concerto for Piano Strings and Percussion for One Performer (1972); *The Flicker* for Solo Flute (1973); *3 Buddhist Evocations* for Violin and Piano (1977); Brass Quartet (1978); *Nightingales,* motet for 6 Instruments (1979); *Music* for Flute, Oboe, and Cello (1980); Piano Trio (1980). VO-CAL MUSIC: *The Passionate Shepherd to His Love and Her Reply* for 3-part Women's Chorus (1938; Madison, Wis., April 23, 1975); *4 Elizabethan Songs* (1938–41); *The Great Wall of China* for Voice, Flute, Cello, and Piano, to the text of Kafka (1947); *Valedictions* for Mixed Chorus, Soprano, Tenor, and 10 Instruments (1959); *Morning* for Mixed Chorus, Narrator, and Organ (1962); *Paean* for Women's Chorus, Brass Ensemble, and Narrator (1969); *Sounds of the Nightingale* for Soprano, Chorus, and Chamber Orch. (1971); *Missa brevis* for 4 Cellos and Taped Voice (1972); *Teisho* for 8 Singers and String Quartet (1975); *Meeting for Equal Rights: 1866,* cantata (N.Y., April 23, 1976); *Oda a las Ranas* for Women's Chorus, Flute, Oboe, Cello, and Percussion (1980); piano pieces; songs.

Finke, Fidelio Fritz, significant German composer and pedagogue; b. Josefsthal, Northern Bohemia, Oct. 22, 1891; d. Dresden, June 12, 1968. He studied with Vítězslav Novák at the Prague Cons.; from 1915–20 was on its faculty. In 1920 he was named supervisor of German music schools in Czechoslovakia; in 1926 was appointed prof. at the Prague Cons. From 1927–58 he was a prof. of composition at the Hochschule für Musik in Leipzig, and in 1959 held a similar post at the Hochschule für Musik in Dresden. As a composer, he followed the evolutionary path of German music, from the classicism of Brahms through the deeply contrapuntal constructions of Max Reger, finally adopting the liberating precepts of the New Vienna School, with its integration of thematic elements and concomitant emancipation of dissonance. As a pedagogue, he was highly regarded in the academic community.
WORKS: Operas: *Die versunkene Glocke* (1915–18); *Die Jakobsfahrt* (Prague, 1936); *Der schlagfertige Liebhaber* (1950–54); *Der Zauberfisch* (Dresden, June 3, 1960). For Orch.: *Pan,* a symph. (1919); Piano Concerto (1930); Concerto for Orch. (1931); *Das Lied der Zeit,* choreographic tone poem (1946); 2 *Symphonische Märsche* (1960); *Festliche Musik* (1964); 8 suites for various Instrumental Groupings (1947–61). Chamber music: 5 string quartets (1914–64); Sonata for Harp Solo (1945); Horn Sonata (1946); Clarinet Sonata (1949); Viola Sonata (1954); Wind Quintet (1955); *Primula veris* for Violin and Piano (1957); *Divertimento* for Chamber Orch. (1964); numerous choruses; Toccata for Piano, Left-hand; organ works; songs.

Finney, Ross Lee, distinguished American composer and teacher; b. Wells, Minn., Dec. 23, 1906. He studied at the Univ. of Minn. with Donald Ferguson; received a B.A. in 1927 from Carleton College. In 1928 he went to Paris, where he took lessons with Nadia Boulanger; returning to America, he enrolled at Harvard Univ., where he studied with Edward Burlingame Hill; in 1935 had instructive sessions with Sessions. From 1929–49 he was on the faculty of Smith College; concurrently taught at Mt. Holyoke College (1938–40). In 1931–32 he was in Vienna, where he took private lessons with Alban Berg; in 1937 he studied with Gian Francesco Malipiero in Asolo. He then taught composition at the Hartt School of Music in Hartford, Conn. (1941–42), and at Amherst College (1946–47). In the interim he served with the Office of Strategic Services in Paris; was slightly injured when he stepped on a land mine while working in the war zone; this earned him the Purple Heart and Certificate of Merit. His professional career was facilitated by 2 Guggenheim fellowships (1937, 1947) and a Pulitzer traveling fellowship (1937). In 1948–49 he was a visiting lecturer at the Univ. of Michigan in Ann Arbor; from 1949–73 he was a prof. there, and also served as chairman of the dept. of composition; furthermore, he established there an electronic laboratory. Because of the wide diversification of his stylistic propensities, Finney's works represent a veritable encyclopedic inventory of styles and idioms, from innocently pure modalities to highly sophisticated serialistic formations. About 1950 Finney devised a sui generis dodecaphonic method of composition which he called "complementarity." In it a 12-tone row is formed by 2 mutually exclusive hexachords, often mirror images of each other; tonal oases make their welcome appearances; a curious air of euphony theoretically dissonant combinations is created by the contrapuntal superposition of such heterophonic ingredients, and Finney's harmonies begin to sound seductively acceptable despite their modernity.
WORKS: FOR ORCH.: 4 symphs.: No. 1, subtitled *Communiqué* (1942); No. 2 (1958; Philadelphia, Nov. 13, 1959); No. 3 (1960; Philadelphia, March 6, 1964); No. 4 (1972; Baltimore, March 31, 1973); Violin Concerto No. 1 (1935; revised 1952); *Barbershop Ballad* (CBS Radio, Feb. 6, 1940); *Overture for a Drama* (Rochester, N.Y., Oct. 28, 1941); *Slow Piece* for String Orch. (1940); *Variations, Fuguing, and Holiday* for Orch., based on a hymn tune of William Billings (1943; Los Angeles, May 17, 1947); Piano Concerto No. 1 (1948); *Variations* for Orch. (1957; Minneapolis, Dec. 30, 1965); *Three Pieces* for Chamber Orch. and Tape Recorder (1962); Concerto for Percussion and Orch. (1965); Symph. Concertante (1967); Piano Concerto No. 2 (1968); *Landscapes Remembered* (1971); *Summer in Valley City* for Concert Band (Ann Arbor, April 1, 1971); *Spaces* (Fargo, N. Dak., March 26, 1972); Violin Concerto No. 2 (1973; Dallas, March 31, 1976; revised 1977); Concerto for Alto Saxophone, with Wind Orch. (1974); *Variations on a Memory* for 10 Players (1975); *Narrative* for Cello and 14 Instruments (1976); Concerto for Strings (1977; N.Y., Dec. 5, 1977);

Chamber Concerto for 7 Players (1981). CHAMBER MUSIC: 8 string quartets (1935–60); 2 piano trios (1938, 1954); Piano Quartet (1948); 2 piano quintets (1953, 1961); *Chromatic Fantasy* for Solo Cello (1957); String Quintet (1958); *Fantasy in 2 Movements* for Solo Violin (1958; commissioned by Yehudi Menuhin and first perf. by him at the World's Fair in Brussels, June 1, 1958); *Divertissement* for Piano, Clarinet, Violin, and Cello (1964); *Three Studies in Four* for Solo Percussionists (1965); *Two Acts for Three Players* for Clarinet, Percussion, and Piano (1970); *Two Ballades* for Flutes and Piano (1973); *Tubes I* for one to 5 Trombones (1974); *Quartet* for Oboe, Cello, Percussion, and Piano (1979); *Two Studies* for Saxophones and Piano (1981); also 2 viola sonatas; 2 cello sonatas; 3 violin sonatas. FOR SOLO PIANO: 5 piano sonatas (1933–61); *Fantasy* (1939); *Nostalgic Waltzes* (1947); *Variations on a Theme by Alban Berg* (1952); *Sonata quasi una fantasia* (1961). CHORAL WORKS: *Pilgrim Psalms* (1945); *Spherical Madrigals* (1947); *Edge of Shadow* for Chorus and Orch. (1959); *Still Are New Worlds* for Narrator, Tape, Choir, and Orch. (1962; Ann Arbor, May 10, 1963); *Nun's Priest's Tale,* after Chaucer, for Folksinger, Electric Guitar, and Small Orch. (Hanover, N.H., Aug. 21, 1965); *The Martyr's Elegy* for High Voice, Chorus, and Orch. (Ann Arbor, April 23, 1967); *The Remorseless Rush of Time* for Choir and Orch. (1969); *Earthrise* for Soloist, Choir, and Orch. (1978; Ann Arbor, Dec. 11, 1979).
PUBLICATIONS: Editions of Geminiani's 12 sonatas for Violin and Piano (Northampton, Mass., 1935); a book, *The Game of Harmony* (N.Y., 1947).

Finnila, Birgit, Swedish contralto; b. Falkenberg, Jan. 20, 1931. She studied in Göteborg; later took courses at the Royal Academy of Music in London with Roy Henderson; made her concert debut in Göteborg in 1963; then made numerous appearances with the major orchestras of Europe; later sang in America, Australia, and Israel.

Finnissy, Michael, English composer; b. London, March 17, 1946. He studied composition with Searle and Bernard Stevens at the Royal College of Music (1964–66); taught in the music dept. of the London School of Contemporary Dance (1969–74).
WORKS: FOR THE STAGE: *Mysteries,* musical theater in 8 parts to Latin texts from the Bible, for varying vocal and instrumental combinations (1972–79; the separately performable parts are titled *The Parting of Darkness, The Earthly Paradise, Noah and the Great Flood, The Prophesy of Daniel, The Parliament of Heaven, The Annunciation, The Betrayal and Crucifixion of Jesus of Nazareth,* and *The Deliverance of Souls*); *Circle, Chorus and Formal Act* for Soloists, Choruses, Percussionists, Instrumentalists, Dancers, and Mimes (1973); *Orfeo* for Soloists and Instrumentalists (1974–75); *Medea* for Soloists, Actors, and Instrumentalists (1973–76); *Tom Fool's Wooing* for 14 a cappella Voices (1975–78); *Mr. Punch* for Voice and Instrumentalists (1976–77). FOR ORCH.: 5 concertos for Piano and Ensemble: No. 1 (1975); No. 2 (1975–76);

No. 3 (1978); No. 4 for Piano Alone (1978–80); No. 5, with Mezzo-soprano (1980); *Offshore* (1975–76); *Long Distance* for Concertante Piano and Chamber Orch. (1977–78); *Alongside* for Chamber Orch. (1979); *Sea and Sky* (1979–80). CHAMBER MUSIC: *Song 2, 4, 6,* and *10* for Chamber Ensemble (1967–68); *Transformation of the Vampire* for Clarinet, 3 Percussionists, Violin, and Viola (1968–71); *Alice III* for Cello and Percussionist (1970–75); *Kagami-Jashi* for Flute and Harp (1979). FOR PIANO: *Song 5, 7, 8,* and *9* (1963–68); *Jazz* (1976); *All Fall Down* (1977); Piano Concerto No. 4 (1978–80); *Grainger* (1979); *Boogie-Woogie* (1980); *Nancarrow* (1980). VOCAL WORKS: *World* for 6 Voices and 27 Instruments (1968–74); *Jeanne d'Arc* for Soprano, Tenor, Solo Cello, and Chamber Orch. (1967–71); *Babylon* for Mezzo-soprano and Ensemble (1971); *Goro* for Tenor and Ensemble (1978); *Sir Tristan* for Mezzo-soprano and Instruments (1978); *Talawva* for Mezzo-soprano and Instruments (1979).

Fino, Giocondo, Italian composer; b. Turin, May 2, 1867; d. there, April 19, 1950. He studied oriental languages and theology; concurrently took music lessons with Giovanni Bolzoni; he remained in Turin practically all his life. He wrote the operas *La festa del grano* (Turin, 1910) and *Campana a gloria* (Turin, 1916); several stage works in the Piedmont dialect; biblical cantata, *Noemi e Ruth* (Bergamo, 1908); ballets, pantomimes, choral works; chamber music and piano pieces.

Finzi, Gerald, English composer; b. London, July 14, 1901; d. Oxford, Sept. 27, 1956. He began his study of music with Ernest Farrar (1914–16) and Edward Bairstow (1917–22); studied counterpoint with R.O. Morris in 1925. He was a teacher of composition at the Royal Academy of Music in London (1930–33); in 1939 he organized the Newbury String Players, which did much to develop interest in 18th-century English music. He edited overtures by Boyce for the Musica Britannica. As a composer, Finzi's music reflects the influence of Elgar and Vaughan Williams, while the basic materials are rooted in English folk songs.
WORKS: *A Severn Rhapsody* (1923; Bournemouth, June 4, 1924); *By Footpath and Stile,* song cycle for Baritone and String Quartet to poems by Thomas Hardy (1921–22; London, Oct. 23, 1923); *Introit,* for Violin and Small Orch. (1925; London, May 4, 1927; revised, 1935 and 1942); *Interludium* for Oboe and String Quartet (1936); *Dies Natalis,* cantata for Soprano or Tenor Solo and Strings (1938–39; London, Jan. 26. 1940); *Prelude and Fugue* for String Trio (1942); *Farewell to Arms* for Tenor and Chamber Orch. (1944; Manchester, April 1, 1945); *Let Us Garlands Bring,* 5 Shakespeare songs for Baritone and Strings (1929–42; BBC, London, Oct. 18, 1942); 5 cycles for Voice and Piano of settings of poems by Thomas Hardy: *Before and after Summer* (1932), *Earth and Air and Rain* (1928–32), *I said to Love* (1928), *Till Earth Outwears* (1927), and *A Young Man's Exhortation* (1926–29); *Intimations of Immortality,* ode after Wordsworth for Tenor, Chorus,

and Orch. (1949–50; Gloucester, Sept. 5, 1950); *Nocturne: New Year Music* for Orch. (1949); *For St. Cecilia,* ceremonial ode for Tenor, Chorus, and Orch. (1947; London, Nov. 22, 1947); Concerto for Clarinet and Strings (1948–49; Hereford, Sept. 9, 1949); *Grand Fantasia and Toccata* for Piano and Orch. (1953); Cello Concerto (1951–55; Cheltenham, July 19, 1955); *In Terra Pax,* Christmas scene for Soprano, Baritone, Chorus, Strings, and Antique Cymbals (1954; revised 1956).

Fiocco, Jean-Joseph, Belgian composer, 2nd son of **Pietro Antonio Fiocco** (of the first marriage); b. Brussels, Dec. (baptized, Dec. 15) 1686; d. there, March 30, 1746. He succeeded his father as music master at the ducal chapel, and held this post for 30 years (1714–44); wrote 5 oratorios, 8 Psalms, 9 Requiems, motets, etc. Two copies of his *Sacri concentus* for 4 Voices and 3 Instruments are known to exist; most of his other works are lost.

Fiocco, Joseph-Hector, Belgian composer, 8th child of **Pietro Antonio Fiocco** (of his 2nd marriage); b. Brussels, Jan. 20, 1703; d. there, June 22, 1741. He was sous-maître at the royal chapel c.1729–31; from 1731 to 1737 was maître de chapelle at the Antwerp Cathedral; was master of the collegiate church of SS. Michel and Gudule in Brussels until his death. He wrote numerous sacred works, publ. in *Monumenta Musicae Belgicae* (vol. III); also wrote *Pièces de clavecin* (2 suites of 12 pieces each).

Fiocco, Pietro Antonio, Italian composer; b. Venice, c.1650; d. Brussels, Sept. 3, 1714. He traveled to Germany, then settled in Brussels, marrying a Belgian lady in 1682; she died in 1691, and Fiocco remarried in 1692. He was music master of the ducal chapel in Brussels; in 1694 he established an opera enterprise; until 1698 was director, with Giovanni Paolo Bombarda, of the Opéra du Quai du Forn; wrote special prologues for the operas of Lully; also wrote music for the court; his pastoral play *Le Retour du printemps* was produced in 1699. A collection of his sacred concertos was publ. in Antwerp (1691). Among his instrumental works only a few, including *Sonate à 4,* are extant. Two of his sons, **Jean-Joseph** and **Joseph-Hector,** became professional musicians.

Fiorillo, Federigo, violinist and composer; b. Braunschweig, Germany (baptized, June 1), 1755; d. after 1823. He was taught by his father, **Ignazio Fiorillo;** he traveled as a violinist and conductor; appeared as a violinist in St. Petersburg in 1777, then in Poland (1780–81); conducted in Riga (1782–84); in 1785 he went to Paris, where he participated in the Concert Spirituel; in 1788 he was in London, where he played the viola in Salomon's quartet. He probably remained in London until c.1815; then he was in Amsterdam and again in Paris. He was a prolific composer for violin and various combinations of string instruments; but he is known chiefly through his useful collection *Etudes de violon,* comprising 36 caprices, which was frequently reprinted.

Fiorillo, Ignazio, Italian composer, father of **Federigo Fiorillo;** b. Naples, May 11, 1715; d. Fritzlar, near Kassel, Germany, June 1787. He studied with Durante and Leo in Naples; composed his first opera, *Mandane,* at the age of 20 (Venice, 1736). Other operas were *Artimene* (Milan, 1738), *Partenope nell' Adria* (Venice, 1738), and *Il Vincitor di se stesso* (Venice, 1741). He traveled as a theater conductor; was appointed court conductor at Braunschweig (1754); in 1762 he received a similar post at Kassel, retiring in 1780. He wrote a number of German operas in Braunschweig and 3 Italian operas in Kassel. An oratorio, *Isacco;* a Requiem; and other church works are also noteworthy.

Firkušný, Rudolf, eminent Czech pianist; b. Napajedla, Feb. 11, 1912. Janáček, impressed by his musical talent, accepted him as a private pupil in composition in 1919; he also studied piano with Růzena Kurzová at the Brno Cons. He made his concert debut in Prague on June 14, 1920, at the age of 8, as soloist in a Mozart piano concerto. He also studied music theory with Vilém Kurz and Rudolf Karel at the Prague Cons. He began his professional career in Czechoslovakia. On Jan. 13, 1938, he made his American debut in N.Y.; also took private piano lessons with Artur Schnabel, who lived in N.Y. at the time. In 1943 he toured South America; in 1944 he made a tour of Mexico, Cuba, and Central America. In 1946 he participated in the Prague Festival; but this was his last professional appearance in Czechoslovakia. Eventually, he became an American citizen; he was soloist with the Boston Symph. Orch. on Nov. 2, 1945, in the world premiere of Menotti's Piano Concerto, and again on Dec. 31, 1948, in the premiere of Howard Hanson's Piano Concerto. Bohuslav Martinu wrote for Firkušný his 3rd Piano Concerto, which he performed for the first time with the Dallas Symph. on Nov. 20, 1949; he also gave the first performance of Martinu's 4th Piano Concerto with the Symph. of the Air in N.Y., under Leopold Stokowski, on Oct. 4, 1956. In 1958–59 he toured Australia and the politically available countries in Asia. By 1973, the count of his tours aggregated to 25 in Europe, 10 in South America, 12 in Mexico, 3 in Israel, and 2 in Australia; to these must be added a greater number of American concerts. In all of his programs he included works by Czech composers, particularly those by his teacher Janáček. In 1982, on his 70th birthday, he celebrated his 60th anniversary as a concert pianist. In his career he shunned the appurtenances and perquisites of a typical virtuoso; even his physical appearance did not suit the consecrated image of a flamboyant matinée idol; he was too deeply concentrated on the proper interpretation of the music he played to flaunt the externals; he earned the admiration of critics for his musical integrity. His technical equipment was always of the highest caliber; his lyrical talent enhanced the physical aspects of his virtuosity. Firkušný was also a composer; he wrote a Piano Concerto and a number of attractive piano études and miniatures. In 1979 he began the publication, with the violinist Rafael Druian, of a complete edition of the Mozart violin sonatas. An excellent teacher, he gave master classes in piano at the Juilliard School of Music in N.Y. and at the Aspen Music School in Colorado.

Fischer, Annie, distinguished Hungarian pianist; b. Budapest, July 5, 1914. She studied at the Academy of Music in Budapest with Ernst von Dohnányi; in 1933 she won first prize in the International Liszt Competition in Budapest. Her career was interrupted by World War II, but she eventually resumed her concert activities. She became well known for her authentic performances of the piano music of Mozart and Beethoven.

Fischer, Carl, music publisher; b. Buttstädt, Thuringia, Dec. 7, 1849; d. New York, Feb. 14, 1923. He studied music in Gotha; entered a partnership in an instrument manufacturing business with his brother **August Emil Fischer** in Bremen. In 1872 he went to N.Y. and opened a music store at 79 East 4th Street; in 1923 the store was moved to 62 Cooper Square. He secured the rights for republishing orch. scores and parts by German composers, eventually becoming one of the most important of American music publishing firms. From 1907 to 1931 the firm publ. a monthly periodical, the *Musical Observer,* edited by Gustav Sänger; in 1923 the business was incorporated and Carl Fischer's son **Walter S. Fischer** (b. New York, April 18, 1882; d. there, April 26, 1946) became president; after his death, Frank H. Connor (1903–77) was elected president; upon his death he was succeeded by his son. In 1909 the firm established a branch in Boston, which was expanded in 1960 through the purchase of the Charles Homeyer Music Co. of Boston; in 1935 a branch was also opened in Los Angeles, and in 1969 one in San Francisco. In 1947 the firm occupied a new building in N.Y. at 165 West 57th Street, which also housed a concert hall. The catalogue of the firm is representative of all genres of musical composition; early acquisitions were works by composers living in America, including Rachmaninoff and Ernest Bloch; in the last quarter of the century, the firm publ. a number of instrumental and vocal works by composers of the avant-garde, including some in graphic notation.

Fischer, Edwin, eminent Swiss pianist; b. Basel, Oct. 6, 1886; d. Zürich, Jan. 24, 1960. He studied with Hans Huber in Basel and Martin Krause in Berlin; then taught at the Stern Cons. in Berlin (1905–14); taught at the Berlin Hochschule für Musik from 1931; between 1926 and 1932 he was also engaged as a conductor in Lübeck, Munich, and Berlin. In 1942 he returned to Switzerland. He was renowned as one of the most intellectual pianists of his time and a distinguished pedagogue. He founded the Edwin-Fischer-Stiftung to assist needy and young musicians. He also publ. several valuable books on music: *J.S. Bach* (Potsdam, 1945); *Musikalische Betrachtungen* (Wiesbaden, 1949; in Eng. as *Reflections on Music,* London, 1951); *Beethovens Klaviersonaten* (Wiesbaden, 1956; Eng. trans., 1959); and *Von den Aufgaben des Musikers* (Wiesbaden, 1960).

Fischer, Emil, German operatic bass; b. Braunschweig, June 13, 1838; d. Hamburg, Aug. 11, 1914. He received his vocal training entirely from his parents, who were opera singers; made his debut in Graz in 1857; then was with the Danzig Opera (1863–70); in Rotterdam (1875–80); and with the Dresden Opera (1880–85); then went to America; made his debut with the Metropolitan Opera Co. on Nov. 23, 1885, and remained on the staff for 5 years; lived mostly in N.Y. as a vocal teacher; returned to Germany shortly before his death. On March 15, 1907, a testimonial performance was held in his honor at the Metropolitan Opera, at which he sang one of his greatest roles: that of Hans Sachs in *Die Meistersinger* (Act 3, Scene 1). He was particularly famous for his Wagnerian roles.

Fischer, Ivan, Hungarian conductor; b. Budapest, Jan. 20, 1951. He studied cello and composition at the Bartók Cons. in Budapest (1965–70); then took lessons in conducting with Hans Swarowsky at the Vienna Academy of Music; during the 1975–76 season he conducted concerts in Milan, Florence, Vienna, and Budapest; beginning in 1976, he filled engagements with the BBC Symph. Orch. in London and the BBC regional orchs. From 1979–82 he was music director of the Northern Sinfonia Orch. at Newcastle upon Tyne. In 1983 he took the London Symph. Orch. on a tour of the Far East. Also in 1983 he made his first appearance in the U.S., as a guest conductor with the Los Angeles Phil., and was appointed music director of the Kent Opera.

Fischer, Jan, Czech composer; b. Louny, Sept. 15, 1921. He studied at the Prague Cons. (1940–45) and took lessons in composition from Řídký at the master class there (1945–48). His music occupies the safe ground of Central European Romanticism, not without some audacious exploits in euphonious dissonance.

WORKS: 5 operas: *Ženichové (Bridegrooms;* 1956; Brno, Oct. 13, 1957); *Romeo, Julie a tma (Romeo, Juliet and Darkness;* 1959–61; Brno, Sept. 14, 1962); *Oh, Mr. Fogg,* comic chamber opera after Jules Verne's *Around the World in 80 Days* (1967–70; Saarbrücken, June 27, 1971); *Miracle Theater,* radio opera (1970); *Decamerone,* chamber opera (1975–76); ballet, *Eufrosyne* (1951; Pilsen, 1956); *Pastoral Sinfonietta* (1944); Violin Concerto (1946); *Essay* for Jazz Orch. and Solo Piano (1947); *Popular Suite* for Wind Orch. and Piano (1950); *Dance Suite* for Orch. (1957); *Fantasia* for Piano and Orch. (1953); Symph. No. 1, *Monothematic* (1959); Clarinet Concerto (1965); *Obrazy (Pictures) I* and *II* for Orch. (1970, 1973); Harp Concerto (1972); Flute Sonata (1944); Suite for Wind Sextet (1944); Suite for English Horn and Piano (1945); *Ballada* for String Quartet and Clarinet (1949); Piano Quintet (1949); *Ut stellae* for Soprano, 2 Pianos, Flute, Bass Clarinet, Percussion, and Tape (1966); *Amoroso* for Clarinet and Piano (1970); Wind Quintet (1971); *4 Studies* for Solo Harp (1971).

Fischer, Johann Caspar Ferdinand, German composer of keyboard music; b. c.1665; d. Rastatt, Aug. 27, 1746. He served as house musician to the Margrave of Baden (1696–1716); continued to serve the court after it moved to Rastatt in 1716.

WORKS: During his lifetime he publ. the following: *Le Journal du printemps,* op. 1 (airs and ballet numbers in the style of Lully; 1696; reprinted in the Denkmäler Deutscher Tonkunst, X/1); *Les Pièces de clavecin,* op. 2 (1696; reprinted 1698, under the title *Musikalisches Blumen-Büschlein*); *Vesper Psalms,* op. 3 (1701); *Ariadne musica neo-organoedum,* op. 4 (Schlackenworth, 1702; contains 20 preludes and fugues for Organ in 20 different keys, thus foreshadowing Bach's *Well-Tempered Clavier*); *Litaniae Lauretanae,* op. 5 (1711); also *Musikalischer Parnassus* (9 keyboard suites named after the 9 Muses; Augsburg, 1738) and *Blumenstrauss* (Augsburg, 1732; a series of 8 preludes and fugues in 8 church modes). His *Sämtliche Werke für Klavier und Orgel,* ed. by E.V. Werra, was publ. in Leipzig, 1901.

Fischer, Joseph, music publisher; b. Silberhausen, Germany, April 9, 1841; d. Springfield, Ohio, Nov. 24, 1901. He emigrated to the U.S. as a youth, and in 1864 established the firm of J. Fischer & Bro. in Dayton, Ohio, with his brother **Ignaz Fischer;** in 1875 the firm moved to N.Y. Joseph Fischer was succeeded, at his death, by his sons **George** and **Carl;** the sons of George Fischer, **Joseph** and **Eugene,** became proprietors of the firm in 1920. During its early years, J. Fischer & Bro. specialized in music for the Roman Catholic Church, but later expanded its activities to include instrumental music by contemporary composers, organ works, and also light opera.

Fischer, Kurt von, distinguished Swiss musicologist; b. Bern, April 25, 1913. He studied piano at the Bern Cons. with F.J. Hirt and with Czeslaw Marek; later took the courses in musicology with Kurth and Gurlitt at the Univ. of Bern, where he received his Ph.D. in 1938 with the dissertation *Griegs Harmonik und die nordländische Folklore* (publ. in Bern, 1938); subsequently completed his Habilitation in 1948 there with his *Die Beziehungen von Form und Motiv in Beethovens Instrumentalwerken* (publ. in Strasbourg, 1948; 2nd ed., 1972). He taught piano at the Bern Cons. from 1939–57, and concurrently was lecturer in musicology at the Univ. of Bern (1948–57). In 1957 he became prof. of musicology and chairman of the dept. at the Univ. of Zürich. In 1965 he assumed the post of co-editor of the *Archiv für Musikwissenschaft.* In 1967–72 he served as president of the International Musicological Society.

Fischer, Ludwig, German bass; b. Mainz, Aug. 18, 1745; d. Berlin, July 10, 1825. He first studied violin and cello; then took vocal lessons with Anton Raaff in Mannheim; in 1772 he was named virtuoso da camera at the Mannheim court; followed the court when it moved to Munich in 1778; proceeded to Vienna, where he sang opera in 1780–83; then obtained excellent success in Paris (1783) and Italy; also sang in Prague and Dresden (1785) and in Regensburg (1785–88). In 1788 he was granted a lifetime appointment in Berlin; retired in 1815. Mozart wrote the part of Osmin in *Die Entführung aus dem Serail* for Fischer.

Fischer, Res, German contralto; b. Berlin, Nov. 8, 1896; d. Stuttgart, Oct. 4, 1974. She studied in Stuttgart and Prague; then took lessons in Berlin with Lilli Lehmann; made her debut in 1927 in Basel, where she sang until 1935; then appeared with the Frankfurt Opera (1935–41); in 1941 she joined the Stuttgart Opera, remaining on its roster until 1961; was made its honorary member in 1965. She also sang at the festivals of Salzburg and Bayreuth, and with the state operas in Vienna, Hamburg, and Munich. She created the title role in Orff's *Antigonae* (Salzburg, 1949) and sang in the first performance of Wagner-Régeny's *Bergwerk von Falun* (Salzburg, 1961).

Fischer, Wilhelm, eminent Austrian musicologist; b. Vienna, April 19, 1886; d. Innsbruck, Feb. 26, 1962. He studied with Guido Adler at the Univ. of Vienna, where he received his Ph.D. with the dissertation *Matthias Georg Monn als Instrumentalkomponist* in 1912; he obtained his Habilitation there with his *Zur Entwicklungsgeschichte des Wiener klassischen Stils* in 1915; then joined the faculty of the Univ. of Vienna in 1919; subsequently was lecturer in musicology at the Univ. of Innsbruck from 1928 until the Anschluss of 1938, when he was removed from this position and was conscripted as a forced laborer; after World War II, he was restored to the faculty of the Univ. of Innsbruck as a prof., serving there from 1948 until his retirement in 1961. In 1951 he was elected president of the Central Inst. of Mozart Research at the Mozarteum in Salzburg; he publ. numerous essays on Mozart and other Classical composers; among his most important writings, apart from his *Habilitationsschrift,* are *Zur Geschichte des Fugenthemas* (Leipzig, 1925) and *Beethoven als Mensch* (Regensburg, 1928). In 1956 he was presented with a Festschrift on the occasion of his 70th birthday.

Fischer-Dieskau, Dietrich, celebrated German baritone; b. Zehlendorf, a suburb of Berlin, May 28, 1925. His original family name was Fischer, but his grandfather made it Fischer-Dieskau, after the name of a small castle near Leipzig that the family owned in years past. Both his parents were musical, and he studied piano and took voice lessons with Georg Walter; in 1942 he entered the Berlin Hochschule für Musik as a student of Hermann Weissenborn, but was soon conscripted into the German army, to tend horses. In 1945 he was taken prisoner of war in Italy, during which time he was allowed to make appearances as a singer; finally released in 1947, he returned to Berlin and resumed his vocal studies with Weissenborn. He made his operatic debut as Posa in *Don Carlos* at the Berlin Städtische Oper in 1948; he then sang opera in Munich, Vienna,

Milan, and Bayreuth; he also made numerous appearances in song recitals and concerts. In a few years he established himself as a master of the art of German song; and he sang with equal penetration the Italian and French repertoire. His specialty became complete cycles of Schubert's great lieder; he elicited great encomiums for such performances from the British critics after his London recitals in 1950 and 1951. He made his American debut as soloist with the Cincinnati Symph. on April 5, 1955, singing the baritone part in the *German Requiem* of Brahms. On May 2, 1955, he gave a recital in N.Y., in a program of Schubert's lieder, with excellent acclaim. Remarkably, he achieved equal successes in opera and in concert; critics and commentators freely referred to him as one of the greatest singers of the century; remarkable also was his ability to embrace the largest repertoire in opera and concerts; as a matter of course, he sang the major baritone parts in standard operas, among them Don Giovanni, Count Almaviva in *Le nozze di Figaro,* Hans Sachs, Wolfram, Valentin, Rigoletto, Renato, and Falstaff; he demonstrated his extraordinary musicianship by singing the title role in Alban Berg's opera *Wozzeck;* the baritone solo part in Stravinsky's sacred ballad *Abraham and Isaac;* the title role in Busoni's opera *Doktor Faust;* Mandryka in Richard Strauss's *Arabella;* roles in operas of Hindemith; and Mittenhofer in the world premiere of Hans Werner Henze's *Elegy for Young Lovers* (Schwetzingen, May 20, 1961). In his recital programs he audaciously tackled the songs of Charles Ives. He proved his ability in oratorio, both traditional and modern, no less than in opera and concert. Bravely, he ventured into the circumscribed field of conducting; he made his American debut with the Los Angeles Phil. on March 24, 1974. Then, in an apparent effort to round off the entire domain of music, he publ. books of surprising excellence: *Auf den Spuren der Schubert-Lieder* (Wiesbaden, 1971; Eng. trans. as *Schubert: A Biographical Study of His Songs,* London, 1976), *Wagner und Nietzsche* (Stuttgart, 1974; Eng. trans., N.Y., 1976), and *The Fischer-Dieskau Book of Lieder* (N.Y., 1976). He married often. His 4th wife, **Julia Varadi,** is a soprano.

Fišer, Luboš, outstanding Czech composer; b. Prague, Sept. 30, 1935. He studied composition with Hlobil at the Prague Cons. (1952–56) and with Bořkovec at the Prague Academy of Music, graduating in 1960. In 1971 he emigrated to the U.S.; was a composer-in-residence with the American Wind Symph. Orch. in Pittsburgh. His music is often associated with paintings, archeology, and human history; his style of composition employs effective technical devices without adhering to any particular doctrine.

WORKS: FOR THE STAGE: Chamber opera, *Lancelot* (1959–60; Prague, May 19, 1961); musical, *Dobrý voják Švejk (The Good Soldier Schweik;* Prague, 1962); ballet, *Changing Game* (1971). FOR ORCH.: *Suite* (1954); 2 symphs. (1956, 1958–60); *Symphonic Fresco* (1962–63); *Chamber Concerto* for Piano and Orch. (1964; revised 1970); *15 Prints after Dürer's*

Apocalypse (1964–65; Prague, May 15, 1966; his most successful work; winner of a UNESCO prize in Paris, 1967); *Pietà* for Chamber Ensemble (1967); *Riff* (1968); *Double* (1969); *Report* for Wind Instruments (1971; commissioned by the American Wind Symph. Orch.); *Kreutzer Etude* for Chamber Orch. (1974); *Labyrinth* (1977); *Serenade for Salzburg* for Chamber Orch. (1978); *Albert Einstein,* portrait for Organ and Orch. (1979); Piano Concerto (1980); *Meridian* (1980); *Romance* for Violin and Orch. (1980); *Centaures* (1983). CHAMBER MUSIC: *4 Compositions* for Violin and Piano (1955); String Quartet (1955); Sextet for Wind Quintet and Piano (1956); *Ruce (Hands),* sonata for Violin and Piano (1961); *Crux* for Violin, Kettledrums, and Bells (1970); Cello Sonata (1975); *Variations on an Unknown Theme* for String Quartet (1976); Piano Trio (1978); Sonata for 2 Cellos and Piano (1979); *Testis* for String Quartet (1980); Sonata for Solo Violin (1981). FOR VOICE: *Caprichos* for Vocalists and Chorus, after a text drawn from Goya's paintings (1966); Requiem for Soprano, Baritone, 2 Choruses, and Orch. (Prague, Nov. 19, 1968); *Lament over the Destruction of the City of Ur,* after Ur-Sumerian tablets, for Soprano, Baritone, 3 Narrators, Chorus, Children's and Adult's Speaking Choruses, 7 Timpani, and 7 Bells (1969; as a ballet, 1978); *Ave Imperator* for Solo Cello, Male Chorus, 4 Trombones, and Percussion (1977); *The Rose* for Chorus a cappella (1977); *Per Vittoria Colona* for Solo Cello and Female Chorus (1979); *Istanu,* melodrama for Narrator, Alto Flute, and 4 Percussionists (1980); *Znameni (The Sign)* for Soloists, Chorus, and Orch. (1981); *Address to Music,* melodrama for Narrator and String Quartet (1982). FOR PIANO: 6 sonatas: No. 1 (1955); No. 2 (1957); No. 3, *Fantasia* (1960); No. 4 (1962–64); No. 5 (1974); No. 6, *Fras* (1978).

Fisher, Avery, American pioneer in audio equipment and munificent patron of music; b. New York, March 4, 1906. He was educated at N.Y. Univ. (B.S., 1929); then worked for the publishing house of Dodd, Mead as a graphics designer (1933–43). In 1937 he founded the Phil. Radio firm, later known as Fisher Radio; it became one of the foremost manufacturers of audio equipment in the world, producing high-fidelity and stereophonic components. Having amassed a substantial fortune, he sold the firm in 1969. In 1973 he gave the N.Y. Phil. $10 million to renovate the interior of Phil. Hall; in 1976 it was inaugurated at a gala concert in which it was officially renamed Avery Fisher Hall in his honor. He also created the Avery Fisher Prize, which is awarded to outstanding musicians of the day.

Fisher, Sylvia, Australian soprano; b. Melbourne, April 18, 1910. She studied at the Melbourne Cons.; then sang in local productions. In 1948 she became a member of the Covent Garden Opera in London, remaining on its roster until 1958. In 1959 she sang in Chicago; then was a member of the English Opera Group (1963–71). She created the role of Miss Wingrave in Britten's *Owen Wingrave* (London, BBC, May 16, 1971); also sang in other contemporary operas.

Fitelberg, Gregor, eminent Polish conductor and composer; b. Dvinsk, Latvia, Oct. 18, 1879; d. Katowice, June 10, 1953. He studied at the Warsaw Cons. with Barcewicz and Noskowski; then played the violin in the Warsaw Phil.; became its concertmaster, and eventually (1908) conductor. After the outbreak of World War I he went to Russia as a conductor of symph. concerts; in 1921 he went to Paris; conducted performances of Diaghilev's Ballets Russes; in 1923 he returned to Poland and conducted the Warsaw Phil. (1923–34); then founded and led the Polish Radio Symph. Orch. in Warsaw from 1934 to 1939; in 1940 he was in Buenos Aires, after fleeing Warsaw via Vienna, Italy, and Paris; from 1942–45 he was in the U.S.; in 1947 he went back to Poland, and became conductor at the Polish Radio Symph. Orch. in Katowice. At his symph. concerts he gave many performances of works by Polish composers; was one of the best interpreters of Szymanowski. In 1951 the Polish government awarded him a state prize. Fitelberg was also a composer; he wrote 2 symphs. (1903, 1906); 2 Polish rhapsodies for Orch. (1913, 1914); symph. poem, *In der Meerestiefe* (1913); Violin Concerto (1901); and some chamber music; his Violin Sonata received the Paderewski prize in 1896.

Fitelberg, Jerzy, talented Polish composer, son of **Gregor Fitelberg;** b. Warsaw, May 20, 1903; d. New York, April 25, 1951. He received his musical education mainly from his father; then took courses in the Hochschule für Musik in Berlin. In 1933 he went to Paris; in May 1940 he came to the U.S., where he remained until his death. In 1936 he received an Elizabeth Sprague Coolidge award for his String Quartet No. 4, which was performed at the Coolidge Festival of Chamber Music in Washington, D.C. (1937); his orch. and chamber music was often performed in Europe; much of it was publ. His works are couched in the neo-Classical style, and are cosmopolitan in thematic substance; they are distinguished by energetic rhythm and strong contrapuntal texture; only a few of his compositions reflect Polish melos.
  WORKS: 3 suites for Orch. (1926–30); Concerto for String Orch. (1928; arrangement of the 2nd String Quartet); Violin Concerto No. 1 (Vienna Festival of the International Society for Contemporary Music, June 20, 1932); Violin Concerto No. 2 (Paris Festival, June 22, 1937); *The Golden Horn* for String Orch. (1942); Nocturne for Orch. (N.Y. Phil., March 28, 1946, Rodzinski conducting); Octet for Wind Instruments; 5 string quartets; Sonata for 2 Violins and 2 Pianos; Sonatina for 2 Violins; *3 Polish Folksongs* for Women's Voices (1942).

Fitzgerald, Ella, black American jazz singer; b. Newport News, Va., April 25, 1918. She began singing in small clubs in Harlem in the early 1930s; discovered by Chick Webb (one of Harlem's most popular musicians) in 1935, she joined his band; upon his death in 1939, she became its leader; in 1942 she became a free-lance singer and has since worked with most major jazz musicians and groups. She is particularly adept at scat singing and improvising, frequently creating new melodies over given harmonies much in the manner of a jazz instrumentalist. Stylistically, she is equally at ease in swing and bebop; developing, over the years, a superlative blend of musicianship, vocal ability, and interpretive insight, she has achieved a popularity and respect rarely acquired by jazz singers.

Fitzwilliam, Viscount Richard, wealthy British collector of paintings, engravings, books, and musical MSS; b. Richmond, Surrey, Aug. 1745; d. London, Feb. 4, 1816. He bequeathed his library to Cambridge Univ. The musical MSS include especially valuable works: the immensely important *Fitzwilliam Virginal Book* (often wrongly termed *Virginal Booke of Queen Elizabeth*), anthems in Purcell's hand, sketches by Handel, and many early Italian compositions. Vincent Novello edited and publ. 5 vols. of the Italian sacred music as *The Fitzwilliam Music* (London, 1825); J.A. Fuller-Maitland and A.H. Mann made a complete catalogue of it (1893). The entire contents of the *Fitzwilliam Virginal Book* were edited and publ. by J.A. Fuller-Maitland and William Barclay Squire (2 vols., Leipzig and London, 1894–99; facsimile reprint, N.Y., 1954).

Fizdale, Robert, American pianist; b. Chicago, April 12, 1920. He studied with Ernest Hutcheson at the Juilliard School of Music; formed a piano duo with Arthur Gold; they made a professional debut at N.Y.'s New School for Social Research in 1944, in a program devoted entirely to John Cage's music for prepared pianos. They toured widely in the U.S., Europe, and South America; works were written specially for them by Samuel Barber, Milhaud, Poulenc, Auric, Virgil Thomson, Norman Dello Joio, and Ned Rorem. With Arthur Gold he publ. a successful book, *Misia* (N.Y., 1979), on the life of Maria Godebsky, a literary and musical figure in Paris early in the century.

Flagello, Nicolas (Oreste), prolific and brilliant American composer and conductor; b. New York, March 15, 1928. He was of Italian antecedents; his father, a professional dress designer, loved music and played the oboe; his mother assisted him tastefully in his successful shop, and also sang. His maternal grandfather, Domenico Casiello, was a musician in Naples. With such genetic endowment, it was inevitable that Flagello should become a musician. He began his piano lessons at the incredible age of 3, or so they say, and played in public at 5, according to undocumented reports. At 6 he began taking violin lessons with Francesco di Giacomo. He also learned to play the oboe, and was a member of the school band, performing on these instruments according to demand. In 1945–46 he played the violin in Stokowski's All-American Youth Orch. in N.Y. In 1946 he entered the Manhattan School of Music (B.M., 1949; M.M., 1950), studying with a variety of teachers in multifarious subjects (Harold

Bauer, Hugo Kortschak, Hugh Ross, Vittorio Giannini). He also took conducting lessons with Mitropoulos. It was with Giannini that he had his most important training in composition, for 15 years, from 1935 to 1950, and it was Giannini who influenced him most in his style of composition—melodious, harmonious, euphonious, singingly Italianate, but also dramatically modern. After obtaining his master's degree, Flagello went to Italy, where he took lessons with Ildebrando Pizzetti at the Santa Cecilia Academy in Rome (Mus.D., 1956). Returning to the U.S., he taught composition and conducting at the Manhattan School of Music until 1977; appeared as a guest conductor with the Chicago Lyric Opera and the N.Y. City Opera; also toured as accompanist to Tito Schipa, Richard Tucker, and other singers.

WORKS: *Lyra* for 6 Brass Instruments (1945); *Beowulf,* symph. poem (1949); Piano Concerto No. 1 (1950); *Mirra,* opera in 3 acts (1953); *The Wig,* one-act opera (1953); Piano Concerto No. 2 (1955); Violin Concerto (1956); *Rip Van Winkle,* children's operetta (1957); *Missa sinfonica* for Orch. without Voices (1957); *The Sisters,* one-act opera (1958; N.Y., Feb. 23, 1961); Concerto for String Orch. (1959); *The Judgment of St. Francis,* one-act opera (1959; N.Y., March 18, 1966); Divertimento for Piano and Percussion (1960); *Capriccio* for Cello and Orch. (1961); *Burlesca* for Flute and Guitar (1961); Piano Concerto No. 3 (1962); Concertino for Piano, Brass, and Timpani (1963); Concerto for Harp (1963); Violin Sonata (1963); *Lautrec,* ballet suite (1965); Symph. No. 1 (1967; N.Y., April 23, 1971); *Passion of Martin Luther King* for Soloists, Orch., and Chorus (1968); *Te Deum for All Mankind* for Chorus and Orch. (1968); *The Piper of Hamelin,* children's opera to Flagello's own libretto (1970); Symph. No. 2, *Symphony of the Winds,* for Wind Instruments and Percussion (1970); *Philos* for Brass Quintet (1970); *Ricercare* for Brass and Percussion (1971); *Remembrance* for Soprano, Flute, and String Quartet (1971); *Credendum* for Violin and Orch. (1973); *Benedictus* for a cappella Chorus (1974); *Prisma* for Horn Septet (1974); Piano Concerto No. 4 (1975); *Canto* for Soprano and Orch. (1978); *Furanna* for Flute (1978); *Diptych* for Brass Trio (1979); *Odyssey* for Symphonic Band (1981); *Quattro amori,* song cycle for Mezzo-soprano and Piano (1983); *Beyond the Horizon,* 3-act opera (1983).

Flagstad, Kirsten, famous Norwegian soprano; b. Hamar, July 12, 1895; d. Oslo, Dec. 7, 1962. She studied with her mother (coach at the Oslo Opera) and with Ellen Schytte-Jacobsen in Oslo; in 1912 she made her debut there at the National Theater as Nuri in d'Albert's opera *Tiefland;* then sang in oratorio, operettas, and musical comedies in Oslo; in 1928–30 was engaged at the Storm Theater at Göteborg; in 1931–32, again at the National Theater; in 1933 and 1934, appeared at the Bayreuth Festival. On Feb. 2, 1935, she made a very successful debut at the Metropolitan Opera in N.Y. as Sieglinde in *Die Walküre,* and sang Isolde (her most celebrated role), Brünnhilde, Elisabeth, Elsa, and Kundry in

her first season there; appeared at Covent Garden in London, as Isolde, on May 18, 1936. She also sang with the San Francisco Opera (1935–38) and the Chicago City Opera (1937), and made numerous guest appearances through the U.S. and Australia. In 1941 she returned to Norway; in 1951 she reappeared at the Metropolitan Opera, singing Isolde and Leonore; made her farewell appearance there on March 19, 1952. She was director of the Norwegian Opera from 1958 to 1960.

Flament, Edouard, French composer, conductor, and bassoon virtuoso; b. Douai, Aug. 27, 1880; d. Bois-Colombes (Seine), Dec. 27, 1958. He studied at the Paris Cons. with Bourdeau (bassoon), Lavignac, Caussade, and Lenepveu (composition). After graduation (1898), he played the bassoon in the Lamoureux Orch. (1898–1907) and in the Société des Instruments à Vent (1898–1923); conducted opera and concerts in Paris (1907–12), Algiers (1912–14), and Marseilles (1919–20); summer concerts at Fontainebleau (1920–22); then with the Diaghilev ballet in Monte Carlo, Berlin, London, and Spain (1923–29). In 1930 he became conductor at the Paris Radio.

WORKS: An exceptionally prolific composer, he wrote between 1894 and 1957 some 175 opus numbers, including the operas *La Fontaine de Castalie, Le Cœur de la rose,* and *Lydéric et Rosèle;* 8 symphs.; *Oceano Nox,* symph. poem; *Variations radio-phoniques;* 5 piano concertos; *Concertstück* for Bassoon and Orch.; Divertimento for 6 Bassoons; Quintet for 5 Bassoons; Quartet for 4 Bassoons; 3 string quartets; Violin Sonata, Viola Sonata, 2 cello sonatas, etc.; about 180 film scores. Few of his works are publ.; most of the larger ones remain unperformed.

Flanagan, William, American composer; b. Detroit, Aug. 14, 1923; d. New York, Aug. 31, 1969 (found dead in his apartment, a victim of an overdose of barbiturates). He studied composition at the Eastman School of Music in Rochester, N.Y., with Burrill Phillips and Bernard Rogers; then at the Berkshire Music Center in Tanglewood with Arthur Honegger, Arthur Berger, and Aaron Copland; also, in N.Y., with David Diamond. Concurrently, he became engaged in musical journalism; was a reviewer for the *N.Y. Herald Tribune* (1957–60). His style of composition is characterized by an intense pursuit of an expressive melodic line, projected on polycentric but firmly tonal harmonies.

WORKS: One-act opera, *Bartleby,* after Melville's short story (1952–57; N.Y., Jan. 24, 1961); *A Concert Ode* for Orch. (1951; Detroit, Jan. 14, 1960); *A Concert Overture* (1948; N.Y., Dec. 4, 1959); *Divertimento for Classical Orchestra* (1948; Toledo, Ohio, Jan. 9, 1960); *Notations* for Large Orch. (1960); *Chapter from Ecclesiastes* for Mixed Chorus and String Quintet (N.Y., March 21, 1963); *Narrative* for Orch. (Detroit, March 25, 1965); Divertimento for String Quartet (1947); Chaconne for Violin and Piano (1948); Passacaglia for Piano (1947); Piano Sonata (1950); song cycles. He wrote background music for Edward Albee's plays *The Sandbox* (1961) and *The Ballad of the Sad Café* (1963).

Flecha, Mateo, Spanish composer; b. Prades, Tarragona, 1530; d. Solsona, Lérida, Feb. 20, 1604. He received his musical education from his uncle, also named **Mateo Flecha** (1481–1553); was boy chorister in the court chapel at Arevalo. In 1564 he entered the imperial chapel in Vienna; by 1579 was in Prague with the Emperor; Philip III made it possible for him to return to Spain as abbot of Portella in 1599. He publ. a book of madrigals in Venice (1568), and the collection *Las ensaladas* (Prague, 1581), containing "ensaladas" (quodlibets, comic songs) by his uncle, and some by himself. This collection was brought out in a modern edition by Higinio Anglés, with an introductory essay on the Flechas (Barcelona, 1954).

Fleisher, Edwin A., American patron of music; b. Philadelphia, July 11, 1877; d. there, Jan. 9, 1959. He studied at Harvard Univ. (B.A., 1899). He founded a Symph. Club in Philadelphia (1909) and engaged conductors to rehearse an amateur orch. there; at the same time he began collecting orch. scores and complete sets of parts, which became the nucleus of the great Edwin A. Fleisher Collection, presented by him to the Free Library of Philadelphia. A cumulative catalogue covering the period from 1929 to 1977 was publ. in Boston in 1979.

Fleisher, Leon, distinguished American pianist; b. San Francisco, July 23, 1928, of Jewish-Russian immigrant parents. His father was a tailor; his mother a singing teacher. He received the rudiments of music from his mother; then studied piano with Lev Shorr. He played in public at the age of 6; then was sent to Europe for studies with Artur Schnabel at Lake Como, Italy; continued his studies with him in N.Y. At the age of 14 he appeared as soloist with the San Francisco Symph. Orch.; at 16 he was soloist with the N.Y. Phil. (Nov. 4, 1944); in 1952 he became the first American to win first prize at the Queen Elisabeth of Belgium International Competition in Brussels; this catapulted him into a brilliant career. He made several European tours; in 1958 played at the Bayreuth and Salzburg festivals; also gave highly successful recitals in South America. In 1961–62 he was a soloist with the San Francisco Symph. Orch. to observe its 75th anniversary. At the peak of his career, a pianistic tragedy befell him; he was stricken with a mysterious and mystifying neurological ailment that made the fingers of his right hand curl up on itself, completely incapacitating him as a pianist; this thing was diagnosed as carpal-tunnel syndrome. A possible treatment was surgical, by cutting the ligament and removing the tenosynovium around the tendons to relieve the pressure on the nerve. Disabled as he was, Fleisher turned to piano works written for left hand alone commissioned by Paul Wittgenstein, the Austrian pianist who lost his right arm during World War I, to Ravel, Prokofiev, and others. Fleisher learned these concertos and performed them successfully. He also began to conduct. He studied conducting with Pierre Monteux in San Francisco and at the conducting school established by Monteux in Hancock, Maine; he also profited from advice from George Szell. In 1968 he became artistic director of the Theater Chamber Players in Washington, D.C.; in 1970 he became music director of the Annapolis Symph. Orch. as well. From 1973 to 1977 he was associate conductor of the Baltimore Symph. Orch.; then was its resident conductor in 1977–78. He appeared as a guest conductor at the Mostly Mozart Festival in N.Y., and also with the Boston Symph., San Francisco Symph., Cincinnati Symph., and the Los Angeles Chamber Orch. A treatment with cortisone injections and even acupuncture and the fashionable biofeedback to control the electrophysiological motor system did not help. In 1981 he decided to undergo surgery; it was miraculously successful, and on Sept. 16, 1982, he made a spectacular comeback as a bimanual pianist, playing the *Symphonic Variations* by César Franck with Sergiu Comissiona and the Baltimore Symph. He then resumed his active career.

Fleisher devoted much time to teaching; he joined the faculty of the Peabody Cons. of Music in Baltimore in 1959, and subsequently was named to the Andrew W. Mellon Chair in Piano; was also a visiting prof. at the Rubin Academy of Music in Jerusalem. Among his brilliant pupils were André Watts and Lorin Hollander.

Flesch, Carl, celebrated violinist and pedagogue; b. Moson, Hungary, Oct. 9, 1873; d. Lucerne, Switzerland, Nov. 14, 1944. He was a violin pupil of Grün at the Vienna Cons. (1886–89), then of Sauzay and Marsick at the Paris Cons. (1890–94). From 1897 to 1902 he was a prof. at the Cons. in Bucharest; in 1903–8, a prof. at the Cons. in Amsterdam. From 1924 till 1928 Flesch was head of the violin dept. of the Curtis Inst. in Philadelphia; then divided his time between the U.S. and Germany; in 1933 he went to England; eventually went to Hungary and then to Switzerland, where he taught at the Lucerne Cons. He issued the standard pedagogic work for violin, *Die Kunst des Violinspiels* in 2 vols. (Berlin, 1923, 1928; new ed., 1954), which was translated into English (Boston, 1924–30), Italian (Milan, 1953), Polish (Cracow, 1964), and Russian (vol. 1, Moscow, 1964); also wrote *Das Klangproblem im Geigenspiel* (Berlin, 1931; in Eng., N.Y., 1934). His MS work *Die Hohe Schule des Violin-Fingersatzes* was publ. first in Italian (Milan, 1960), then in Eng., as *Violin Fingering, Its Theory and Practice* (N.Y., 1966). His *Erinnerungen eines Geigers* was publ. posthumously (Freiburg im Breisgau, 1960), and appeared previously in English translation, edited by Hans Keller and C.F. Flesch, under the title *The Memoirs of Carl Flesch* (London, 1957; 3rd ed., 1974). Carl Flesch publ. new editions of Kreutzer's études, Mozart's violin sonatas (with Schnabel), 20 études of Paganini, and the violin concertos of Beethoven, Mendelssohn, and Brahms.

Fleury, Louis, eminent French flutist; b. Lyons, May 24, 1878; d. Paris, June 11, 1926. He studied at the Paris Cons.; from 1905 until his death was head of the famous Société Moderne d'Instruments à

Vent, also (from 1906) of the Société des Concerts d'Autrefois, with which he gave concerts in England; made appearances with Melba and Calvé. Debussy composed *Syrinx* for Unaccompanied Flute for him. He edited much old flute music, including sonatas and other pieces by Blavet, Naudet, Purcell, J. Stanley, etc., and contributed to French and English periodicals ("Souvenirs d'un flûtiste," *Le Monde Musical;* etc.).

Flodin, Karl, Finnish composer, b. Wasa (Vaasa), July 10, 1858; d. Helsinki, Nov. 30, 1925. He studied music with Faltin in Helsinki (1877–83), and with Jadassohn at the Leipzig Cons. (1890–92). In 1908 he went to Buenos Aires as music critic for a German paper there; returned to Finland in 1921. He publ. numerous essays on Finnish music (in Finnish and German); wrote a biography of Martin Wegelius (1922); composed a *Cortège* for Horn and Orch., as well as incidental music to various plays; publ. some 80 piano pieces. He was married to the singer **Adée Leander** (1873–1935).

Floquet, Etienne Joseph, French composer; b. Aix-en-Provence, Nov. 23, 1748; d. Paris, May 10, 1785. After studying in his native town, he went to Paris; there he wrote the opera-ballet *L'Union de l'amour et des arts,* produced with great success at the Académie Royale de Musique (Sept. 7, 1773); his 2nd opera, *Azolan, ou Le Serment indiscret* (Nov. 22, 1774, also at the Académie), was a fiasco. Floquet then went to Italy, where he perfected his knowledge by studying with Sala in Naples and with Martini in Bologna. Returning to Paris, he had 2 operas performed at the Académie: *Hellé* (Jan. 5, 1779) and *Le Seigneur bien-faisant* (Dec. 14, 1780). He also wrote a comic opera, *La Nouvelle Omphale* (Comédie-Italienne, Nov. 22, 1782). In an attempt to challenge Gluck's superiority, Floquet wrote the opera *Alceste* on the same subject as Gluck's famous work, but it was never produced.

Floridia, Pietro, Italian composer; b. Modica, Sicily, May 5, 1860; d. New York, Aug. 16, 1932. He studied in Naples with Cesi (piano) and Lauro Rossi (composition); while at the Naples Cons. he publ. several piano pieces which became quite popular. On May 7, 1882, he brought out in Naples a comic opera, *Carlotta Clepier.* From 1888 to 1892 he taught at the Cons. of Palermo; then lived in Milan. In 1904 he emigrated to the U.S.; taught at the Cincinnati College of Music (1906–8); in 1908 settled in N.Y.; in 1913 organized and conducted an Italian Symph. Orch. there. His music (mostly for the stage) is written in a competent manner, in the style of the Italian *verismo.*

Flothuis, Marius, eminent Dutch composer; b. Amsterdam, Oct. 30, 1914. He received his rudimentary musical education at home from his uncle, who taught him piano; then had piano lessons with Arend Koole and studied music theory with Brandts-Buys. He took academic courses at the Univ. of Amsterdam, and musicology at the Univ. of Utrecht (1932–37); served as assistant manager of the Concertgebouw Orch. After the occupation of the Netherlands by the Germans in 1940 he was dismissed from his job (his wife was half Jewish). On Sept. 18, 1943, he was arrested by the Nazis on the charge of hiding Jews, and transported to the concentration camp in Vught, the Netherlands, and a year later to a German labor camp. His liberation came on May 4, 1945, in a forest near Schwerin; he returned to Amsterdam and was reinstated at his managerial job at the Concertgebouw. From 1955 till 1974 he was artistic director of the Concertgebouw. In 1974 he was appointed prof. of musicology at the Univ. of Utrecht. He publ. several books, including a monograph on W.A. Mozart (The Hague, 1940) and the essay *Mozarts Bearbeitungen eigener und fremder Werke* (Kassel, 1969). In his compositions he adopts the motivic method of melodic writing and its concomitant form of variations in freely dissonant counterpoint and largely neo-Classical format. Dissatisfied with his youthful works, he destroyed his MSS dating before 1934, including some perfectly acceptable symph. pieces.

Flotow, Friedrich (Adolf Ferdinand) von, famous German opera composer; b. Teutendorf, April 27, 1813; d. Darmstadt, Jan. 24, 1883. He was a scion of an old family of nobility; he received his first music lessons from his mother; then was a chorister in Güstrow. At the age of 16 he went to Paris, where he entered the Cons. to study piano with J.P. Pixis and composition with Reicha. After the revolution of 1830, he returned home, where he completed his first opera, *Pierre et Cathérine,* set to a French libretto; it was premiered in a German translation in Ludwigslust in 1835. Returning to Paris, he collaborated with the Belgian composer Albert Grisar on the operas *Lady Melvil* (1838) and *L'Eau merveilleuse* (1839). With the composer Auguste Pilati, he composed the opera *Le Naufrage de la Méduse* (Paris, May 31, 1839; performed in a German trans. as *Die Matrosen,* Hamburg, Dec. 23, 1845). He scored a decisive acclaim with his romantic opera, *Alessandro Stradella,* based on the legendary accounts of the life of the Italian composer; it was first performed in Hamburg on Dec. 30, 1844, and had numerous subsequent productions in Germany. He achieved an even greater success with his romantic opera *Martha, oder Der Markt zu Richmond* (Vienna, Nov. 25, 1847); in it he demonstrated his ability to combine the German sentimental spirit with Italian lyricism and Parisian elegance. The libretto was based on a ballet, *Lady Henriette, ou La Servante de Greenwich* (1844), for which Flotow had composed the music for Act I; the ballet in turn was based on a vaudeville, *La Comtesse d'Egmont;* the authentic Irish melody *The Last Rose of Summer* was incorporated into the opera by Flotow, lending a certain nostalgic charm to the whole work. Flotow's aristocratic predilections made it difficult for him to remain in Paris after the revolution of 1848; he accepted the post of Intendant at the grand ducal court theater in Schwerin (1855–63); then moved to Austria; he returned to Germany in 1873, settling in

Darmstadt in 1880.

WORKS: OPERAS: *Pierre et Cathérine* (first perf. in a German version, Ludwigslust, 1835); *Die Bergknappen; Alfred der Grosse; Rob-Roy* (Royaumont, Sept. 1836); *Sérafine* (Royaumont, Oct. 30, 1836); *Alice* (Paris, April 8, 1837); *La Lettre du préfet* (Paris, 1837; revised 1868); *Le comte de Saint-Mégrin* (Royaumont, June 10, 1838; revised as *Le Duc de Guise*, Paris, April 3, 1840; in German, Schwerin, Feb. 24, 1841); *Lady Melvil* (with Albert Grisar; Paris, Nov. 15, 1838); *L'eau merveilleuse* (with Grisar; Paris, Jan. 30, 1839); *Le Naufrage de la Méduse* (with Auguste Pilati; Paris, May 31, 1839; in German as *Die Matrosen*, Hamburg, Dec. 23, 1845); *L'Esclave de Camoëns* (Paris, Dec. 1, 1843; subsequent revisions under different titles); *Alessandro Stradella* (Hamburg, Dec. 30, 1844); *L'Âme en peine (Der Förster;* Paris, June 29, 1846); *Martha, oder Der Markt zu Richmond* (Vienna, Nov. 25, 1847); *Sophie Katharina, oder Die Grossfürstin* (Berlin, Nov. 19, 1850); *Rübezahl* (Retzien, Aug. 13, 1852, private perf.; Frankfurt, Nov. 26, 1853, public perf.); *Albin, oder Der Pflegesohn* (Vienna, Feb. 12, 1856; revised as *Der Müller von Meran*, Königsberg, 1859); *Herzog Johann Albrecht von Mecklenburg, oder Andreas Mylius* (Schwerin, May 27, 1857); *Pianella* (Schwerin, Dec. 27, 1857); *La Veuve Grapin* (Paris, Sept. 21, 1859; in German, Vienna, June 1, 1861); *La châtelaine (Der Märchensucher,* 1865); *Naida* (St. Petersburg, Dec. 11, 1865); *Zilda, ou La Nuit des dupes* (Paris, May 28, 1866); *Am Runenstein* (Prague, April 13, 1868); *L'Ombre* (Paris, July 7, 1870; in German as *Sein Schatten,* Vienna, Nov. 10, 1871); *Die Musikanten,* or *La Jeunesse de Mozart* (Mannheim, June 19, 1887).

BALLETS: *Lady Henriette, ou La Servante de Greenwich* (Act II by R. Burgmüller and Act III by E. Deldevez; Paris, Feb. 21, 1844); *Die Libelle,* or *La Demoiselle, ou Le Papillon ou Dolores* (Schwerin, Aug. 8, 1856); *Die Gruppe der Thetis* (Schwerin, Aug. 18, 1858); *Der Tannkönig* (Schwerin, Dec. 22, 1861); *Der Königsschuss* (Schwerin, May 22, 1864).

INSTRUMENTAL MUSIC: Symph. (1833; not extant); 2 piano concertos (1830 and 1831); *Jubel-Ouverture* (1857); also *Trio de salon* for Violin, Piano, and Cello (1845); Violin Sonata (1861); songs.

Floyd, Carlisle, American opera composer; b. Latta, S.C., June 11, 1926. He studied at Syracuse Univ. with Ernst Bacon (A.B., 1946; M.A., 1949); also took private lessons with Rudolf Firkušný. and Sidney Foster. In 1947 he joined the staff of the School of Music of Florida State Univ., Tallahassee; in 1976 became a prof. of music at the Univ. of Houston. His musical drama in 2 acts and 10 scenes, *Susannah,* was produced there (Feb. 24, 1955); it was later staged at the City Center in N.Y. (Sept. 27, 1956); received the N.Y. Music Critics Circle Award as the best opera of the year. Floyd's other works include *Slow Dusk,* a musical play in one act (1949); *Fugitives,* a musical drama in 3 acts (1951); operas: *Wuthering Heights* (Santa Fe, July 16, 1958); *The Passion of Jonathan Wade* (N.Y., Oct. 11, 1962); *The Sojourner and Mollie Sinclair* (Raleigh, N.C., Dec.

2, 1963); *Markheim* (New Orleans, March 31, 1966); *Of Mice and Men,* after John Steinbeck's novel (Seattle, Jan. 22, 1970); *Bilby's Doll,* for the Bicentennial (Houston, Feb. 29, 1976); *Willie Stark* (Houston, April 24, 1981); *All the King's Men* (1981). He further wrote the ballet *Lost Eden* for 2 Pianos (1952); *Pilgrimage,* a cycle of 5 songs (1955); *The Mystery (5 Songs of Motherhood)* for Soprano and Orch. (1962); *In Celebration: An Overture* (1970); other vocal and instrumental pieces.

Foch (real name, **Fock**), **Dirk,** composer and conductor; b. Batavia, Java (where his father was governor general of the Dutch East Indies), June 18, 1886; d. Locarno, Switzerland, May 24, 1973. He studied in the Netherlands and Germany; began his career in Sweden; conducted the Göteborg Symph. Orch. (1913–15); was guest conductor of the Concertgebouw Orch. in Amsterdam and of the orch. at The Hague (1917–19). He made his American debut as conductor with a specially assembled orch. at Carnegie Hall in N.Y., April 12, 1920; also conducted orch. groups elsewhere in the U.S., and in Vienna. WORKS: *Ein hohes Lied,* 5 fragments from the Bible for Recitation and Orch. (Amsterdam, 1931); a musical pageant in the style of the medieval mystery plays, *From Aeon to Aeon;* 3 ballades for Piano (1913); a cycle of songs from the Chinese (1921); *Java Sketches* for Piano (1948).

Fodor-Mainvielle, Joséphine, famous French soprano; b. Paris, Oct. 13, 1789; d. Saint-Génis, near Lyons, Aug. 14, 1870. She made her debut in 1808 in St. Petersburg in Fioravanti's *Le Cantatrici villane;* gained renown for her performances in the operas of Mozart and Rossini at the King's Theatre in London (1816–18); was likewise successful in her many engagements in Paris, Naples, and Vienna. During a performance of the title role of *Sémiramide* in Paris on Dec. 9, 1825, she suddenly lost her voice and was eventually compelled to quit the stage. She went to Naples in the hopes of recovery under the warm sun, but her attempts to renew her career in 1828 and 1831 failed, and she spent the rest of her long life in retirement.

Foerster, Adolph Martin, American composer; b. Pittsburgh, Feb. 2, 1854; d. there, Aug. 10, 1927. He owed his first musical training to his mother; studied at the Leipzig Cons. with Richter; then returned to Pittsburgh, where he was active as a teacher of singing and piano. He composed *Dedication March* for the opening of the Carnegie Music Hall in Pittsburgh (Nov. 7, 1895); symph. poem, *Thusnelda;* Violin Concerto; 2 piano trios; 2 piano quartets; 2 string quartets; numerous piano works; songs.

Foerster, Joseph Bohuslav, significant Czech composer; b. Prague, Dec. 30, 1859; d. Nový Vestec, near Stará Boleslav, May 29, 1951. He was the son of the Czech organist **Joseph Förster** (1833–1907). He studied at the Prague Organ School; in 1882–88 was organist at St. Vojtěch; subsequently was choirmaster of Panna Marie Sněžná (1889–94); also wrote music criticism. He married the opera singer **Berta Lauterer** in 1888; when she was engaged to sing at the Municipal Theater of Hamburg in 1893, Foerster followed her, and became a prof. at the Hamburg Cons. in 1901 and also music critic of the *Hamburger Nachrichten,* the *Neue Hamburger Zeitung,* and the *Hamburger Freie Presse.* Subsequently his wife was engaged by Mahler for the Vienna Court Opera (1903), and Foerster obtained a position at the New Cons. in Vienna. In 1918 he returned to Prague, where he held teaching positions: taught composition at the Prague Cons. (1919–22); then taught at its master school (1922–31) and at the Univ. of Prague (1920–36). He was president of the Czech Academy (1931–39); in 1945 received the honorary title of National Artist of the Republic of Czechoslovakia. He continued to teach privately and to compose almost to the end of his very long life; many Czech composers of the 20th century were his students. Foerster wrote in every genre; his music is suffused with lyric melos, and reveals characteristic national traits in his treatment of melodic and rhythmic material. His harmonic idiom represents the general style of Central European Romanticism, stemming from Dvořák, and ultimately from Wagner and Brahms.

WORKS: Operas (all first perf. in Prague): *Deborah* (Jan. 27, 1893); *Eva* (Jan. 1, 1899); *Jessika* (April 16, 1905); *Nepřemožení (The Conquerers;* Dec. 19, 1918); *Srdce (The Heart;* Nov. 15, 1923); *Bloud (The Simpleton;* Feb. 28, 1936); incidental music for Shakespeare's plays *Love's Labour's Lost, Twelfth Night,* and *Julius Caesar,* and for Strindberg's *Journey of Fortunate Peter;* 4 masses; oratorio, *St. Venceslas* (1928); cantata, *May* (1936); cantata on the subject of the Thirty Years' War (1940); *1945,* cantata written to celebrate the liberation of Czechoslovakia; 5 symphs. (1888, 1893, 1895, 1905, 1929); symph. poems: *My Youth* (1900) and *Enigma* (1909); symph. suite, *Cyrano de Bergerac* (1903); *Solemn Overture* (1907); 2 violin concertos (1911, 1926); Cello Concerto (1931); *Capriccio* for Flute and Small Orch. (1940); 4 string quartets (1882, 1893, 1907, 1944); 3 piano trios (1883, 1894, 1921); String Quintet (1886); Wind Quintet (1909); Nonet for String and Wind Instruments (1931); 2 violin sonatas (1889, 1892); *Sonata quasi una fantasia* for Violin and Piano (1943); Suite for Viola and Piano (1940). He publ. a book of memoirs, *Poutník v Cizině* (Prague, 1947; in German as *Der Pilger,* 1955).

Foerstrová-Lautererová, Berta, Czech soprano; b. Prague, Jan. 11, 1869; d. there, April 9, 1936. She studied in Prague; made debut as Agathe in *Der Freischütz* at the Prague National Theater in 1887; during her tenure there, she created roles in Dvořák's operas *Jakobín* and *Dimitrij;* was a member of the Hamburg Opera (1893–1901); then sang with the Vienna Court Opera (1901–13), appearing under the name of **Foerster-Lauterer;** she retired in 1914. He husband was the composer **Josef Bohuslav Foerster.**

Foldes, Andor, Hungarian pianist; b. Budapest, Dec. 21, 1913. He was given piano lessons by his mother as a child, and at the age of 8 already played a Mozart concerto with the Budapest Phil. From 1922 to 1932 he studied composition with Leo Weiner, conducting with Ernst Unger, and piano with Dohnányi at the Liszt Academy of Music in Budapest; in 1933 he received the Liszt Prize, and in 1934 began his first European tour as a concert pianist. In 1939 he went to N.Y., and became a naturalized American citizen in 1948; then he returned to Europe; lived in Germany and in Switzerland. In 1969 he toured India and Japan; also gave concerts in Argentina and South Africa. Apart from the regular piano repertoire, Foldes played almost all piano works by Bartók. With his wife, **Lili Foldes,** he publ. an entertaining booklet, *Two on a Continent* (N.Y., 1947); he further publ. a lively piano manual, *Keys to the Keyboard* (N.Y., 1948), which was translated into German, Hungarian, Italian, Spanish, Norwegian, Polish, Dutch, Japanese, and Korean, and *Gibt es einen Zeitgenössischen Beethoven-Stil und andere Aufsätze* (Wiesbaden, 1963).

Fontanelli, Alfonso, Italian madrigal composer; b. Reggio Emilia, Feb. 15, 1557; d. Rome, Feb. 11, 1622. He was in the service of Duke Alfonso II of Este in Ferrara (1588–97) and of his successor, Cesare II, until 1601, when Fontanelli left the court to save himself from prosecution for suspected complicity in the assassination of his 2nd wife's lover. However, he was again in the service of the Estes in 1605, when he was in Rome as emissary of the Duke of Modena; in 1608 he was in Modena; in 1612–13, at the Spanish court. He took Holy Orders in 1621. He was a friend of Gesualdo, Prince of Venosa, and may have been influenced by him in his madrigals. He publ. anonymously 2 books of madrigals in 5 voices: *Primo libro* (Ferrara, 1595; reprint, Venice, 1603); *Secondo libro* (Venice, 1604; reprints 1609 and 1619). He was greatly esteemed by his contemporaries; Orazio Vecchi contributed an introduction to the 1603 edition of his *Primo libro,* praising him for the inventiveness and dignity of his music.

Foote, Arthur (William), eminent American composer; b. Salem, Mass., March 5, 1853; d. Boston, April 8, 1937. He studied piano with a local teacher in Salem; in 1870 he entered Harvard Univ., studying composition with J.K. Paine; he received the A.M. degree in 1875 (the first such degree in music given in America). He also studied organ with B.J. Lang. In 1876 he attended the Wagner Festival in Bayreuth. In 1878 he became organist in the Boston First Unitarian Church, a post that he held until 1910. In 1881 he organized in Boston a series of chamber music concerts which continued until the end of the century; he was frequently pianist with the Kneisel Quartet (1890–1910), performing several of his own works. For 50 years, from 1883, he was a successful teacher in Boston. He was a member of the Music Teachers National Assoc.; a founding member of the American Guild of Organists, and its president from 1909–12; was also a member of the National Inst. of Arts and Letters and a Fellow of the American Academy of Arts and Sciences. His music is distinguished by a fine lyrical feeling, in a Romantic tradition.

WORKS: Many of his orch. works were presented for the first time by the Boston Symph. Orch.: overture, *In the Mountains* (Feb. 5, 1887; also perf. at the Paris Exposition, July 12, 1889); Suite for Strings in D, op. 21 (Nov. 23, 1889); symph. prologue, *Francesca da Rimini* (Jan. 24, 1891); Suite in D minor, op. 36 (March 7, 1896); Suite for Strings in E, op. 63 (April 16, 1909; particularly popular). Other works include: Serenade in E for Strings, op. 25; *4 Character Pieces*, after Omar Khayyám, op. 48, for Orch.; Cello Concerto; *A Night Piece* for Flute and Strings; cantatas (for Chorus, and Piano or Orch.): *The Farewell of Hiawatha* for Men's Voices, op. 11; *The Wreck of the Hesperus*, op. 17; *The Skeleton in Armor*, op. 28. Chamber music: 3 string quartets; 2 piano trios; Violin Sonata; Piano Quartet; Piano Quintet; Cello Sonata; various pieces for instruments with piano accompaniment; more than 100 songs, of which the following are the best known: *The Night Has a Thousand Eyes; I Know a Little Garden Path; Constancy; In Picardie; Ashes of Roses;* also vocal quartets; church music.

WRITINGS: He was the author of several manuals: *Modern Harmony in Its Theory and Practice* (jointly with W.R. Spalding, 1905; reprinted 1936; revised 1959; republ. as *Harmony,* 1969); *Some Practical Things in Piano-Playing* (1909); *Modulation and Related Harmonic Questions* (1919); also trans. Richter's *Treatise on Fugue;* ed. vol. 9 of *The American History and Encyclopedia of Music* (1908–10). His autobiography was privately printed by his daughter, Katharine Foote Raffy (Norwood, Mass., 1946). See also his article "A Bostonian Remembers," *Musical Quarterly* (Jan. 1937).

Forbes, Sebastian, Scottish composer, organist, and choral conductor; b. Amersham, Buckingham, May 22, 1941. He is the son of the Scottish violist **Watson Forbes** (b. St. Andrews, Nov. 16, 1909), a performer in several English chamber groups, prof. of viola at the Royal Academy of Music in London, and head of the music dept. of the BBC for Scotland. Sebastian Forbes studied with Howard Ferguson at the Royal Academy (1958–60) and with Philip Radcliffe and Thurston Dart at King's College of Cambridge Univ. (1960–64). He subsequently held positions as conductor of the Aeolian Singers (1965–69) and Seiriol Singers (1969–72), and was a univ. lecturer at Bangor (1968–72) and Surrey (since 1972).

WORKS: *Pageant of St. Paul,* suite for orch. (1964); Piano Trio (1964); *Antiphony* for Violin and Piano (1965); Partita for Clarinet, Cello, and Piano (1966); Chaconne for Orch. (1967); *Sequence of Carols* for Chorus a cappella (1967); *Second Sequence of Carols* for Male Chorus, String Orch., and Organ (London, May 1, 1968); String Quartet (1969); *Essay* for Clarinet and Orch. (London, July 28, 1970); *Third Sequence of Carols* for Chorus a cappella (1971); Symph. in 2 movements (Edinburgh Festival, Sept. 2, 1972); *Fantasy* for Solo Cello (1974).

Ford, Ernest, English conductor and composer; b. London, Feb. 17, 1858; d. there, June 2, 1919. He was a pupil of Arthur Sullivan at the Royal Academy of Music and of Lalo in Paris; for some years was conductor at the Royal English Opera House (where he conducted the premiere of Sullivan's *Ivanhoe* in 1891), then at the Empire Theatre, and in 1897–1908 at the Royal Amateur Orch. Society; from 1916, was a prof. of singing at the Guildhall School of Music; was a Fellow of the Royal Academy of Music from 1899. He wrote operas and operettas; a motet, *Domine Deus* (for the 250th anniversary of Harvard Univ.); songs, duets, etc.; publ. *Short History of Music in England* (1912).

Ford, Thomas, English composer and lutenist; b. c.1580; d. Nov. (buried, London, Nov. 17) 1648. He was appointed musician to Prince Henry in 1611, and to Charles I in 1626. He was especially successful in the "ayre," a type of composition developed by Dowland, in which melodic prominence is given to the upper voice. These "ayres" appear in alternative settings, either as solo songs with lute accompaniment or as 4-part a cappella songs. He wrote *Musicke of Sundrie Kindes* (1607; the first part contains 11 ayres); 2 anthems in Leighton's *Teares;* canons in Hilton's *Catch that catch can;* and the famous madrigal *Since first I saw your face.* MSS are at Christ Church, Oxford, and at the British Library.

Fordell, Erik, Finnish composer; b. Kokkola, July 2, 1917; d. Kaarlela, Dec. 21, 1981. He studied at the Sibelius Academy and the Helsinki Inst. of Church Music. He was unquestionably the most prolific symph. composer in Finland. He wrote 45 symphs. in 32 years: No. 1 (1949); No. 2 (1949); No. 3 (1952); Nos. 4–9 (1956); No. 10 (1956); Nos. 11–13 (1957); No. 14 (1958); No. 15 (1961); No. 16 (1955; revised 1966); No. 17 (1966); No. 18 (1955; revised 1966); No. 19 (1967); Nos. 20–21 (1968); Nos. 22–25 (1969); No. 26, *Kaustby* (1970); No. 27 (1973–74); No. 28, *Chou-Enlai* (1974); No. 29 (1974); No. 30, *China's Folk* (1974); Nos. 31–34 (1976); No. 35 (1977); Nos. 36–39 (1978); No. 40 (1978–79); Nos. 41–42 (1979); No. 43 (1980); and 2 unnumbered symphs.: *Nature Symphony* (1970–71) and Symph. in One Movement (1981). He also wrote 2 violin concertos (1955, 1959); 4 piano concertos (1961, 1962, 1962, 1962); Horn Concerto (1956); *Oratorium profanum* (1968); *Trilogy* for Orch. (1969); *Symphonic Trilogy* (1970); 8 suites for Strings; 5 cantatas; 4 wind quintets; 7 string quartets; Violin Sonata; Flute Sonata; songs; choral music; piano pieces.

Forkel, Johann Nikolaus, erudite German music historian; b. Meeder, near Coburg, Feb. 22, 1749; d. Göttingen, March 20, 1818. He was a chorister at Lüneburg (1762–66) and at Schwerin (1766). In 1769 he began the study of law in Göttingen, supporting himself by teaching music. He served as a church organist; in 1778 was appointed music director at the Univ. of Göttingen.
WRITINGS: *Über die Theorie der Musik, sofern sie Liebhabern und Kennern derselben nothwen-*

dig und nützlich ist (1774); *Musikalischkriti-sche Bibliothek* (3 vols., Gotha, 1778–79); *Über die beste Einrichtung öffentlicher Concerte* (1779); *Genauere Bestimmung einiger musikalischer Begriffe* (1780); *Musikalischer Almanach für Deutschland* (1782, 1783, 1784, and 1789); *Allgemeine Geschichte der Musik* (Leipzig, 1788 and 1801, 2 vols., covering the period up to 1550; his materials for later times went to the publisher Schwickert); *Allgemeine Literatur der Musik, oder Anleitung zur Kenntniss musikalischer Bücher* (1792; important as the pioneer work of its class); *Über Johann Sebastian Bachs Leben, Kunst und Kunstwerke* (Leipzig, 1802; the first full biography of Bach, based on information supplied by Bach's sons; in Eng., London, 1820; new trans., London, 1920, by Terry). Forkel's unique transcriptions, in modern notation, of Graphäus's *Missae XIII* (1539) and of the *Liber XV. missarum* of Petrejus (1538; masses by Ockeghem, Obrecht, Josquin, and others) were engraved, and a proof pulled, but the invading French army melted down the plates for cannonballs. The proof sheets, corrected by Forkel, are in the Berlin Library. His publ. compositions include piano sonatas and songs; in MS are the oratorio *Hiskias;* 2 cantatas: *Die Macht des Gesangs* and *Die Hirten an der Krippe zu Bethlehem;* symphs., trios, choruses, etc.

Fornerod, Aloys, Swiss violinist and composer; b. Montet-Cudrefin (Vaud), Nov. 16, 1890; d. Fribourg, Jan. 8, 1965. He studied violin and theory at the Cons. of Lausanne and at the Schola Cantorum in Paris. Returning to Switzerland, he was a member of the Lausanne Symph. Orch.; in 1954 he was appointed director of the Fribourg Cons. As a composer, he followed the French modern style, in the spirit of fin-de-siècle Impressionism. He publ. *Les Tendances de la musique moderne* (Lausanne, 1924); was for 40 years a critic for *La Tribune de Lausanne.*

Forrest, Hamilton, American composer; b. Chicago, Jan. 8, 1901. He sang as a chorister in Chicago churches; studied with Adolf Weidig; has written mainly for the stage, including the operas *Yzdra* (1925; received the Bispham Memorial Medal of the American Opera Society of Chicago) and *Camille* (Chicago, Dec. 10, 1930, with Mary Garden in the title role); ballet music; and *Watercolors* for 14 Wind Instruments and Harp.

Forrester, Maureen, outstanding Canadian contralto; b. Montreal, July 25, 1930. She studied piano as a child; had vocal training in Montreal with Sally Martin, and later with Frank Rowe and Bernard Diamant. She made her professional debut in a recital in Montreal on March 29, 1953; then traveled to Paris, and gave a recital there on Feb. 14, 1955. She made her American debut at N.Y.'s Town Hall on Nov. 12, 1956; on Feb. 17, 1957, she was soloist in Mahler's *Resurrection Symphony* with the N.Y. Phil. under Bruno Walter, scoring a remarkable success. From 1965–74 she was a member of the Bach

Aria Group. She made her first appearance with the Metropolitan Opera in N.Y. on Feb. 10, 1975, as Erda in *Das Rheingold.* She also taught voice; served as head of the voice dept. of the Philadelphia Academy of Music (1966–71).

Forsell, (Carl) Johan (John), famous Swedish baritone; b. Stockholm, Nov. 6, 1868; d. there, May 30, 1941. He was in the Swedish army before embarking on his vocal studies. He made his debut in 1896 at the Stockholm Opera; sang there from 1896 to 1901, and again in 1903–9. He was on the roster of the Metropolitan Opera during the season of 1909–10. In 1924 he was appointed director of the Stockholm Opera, a post he held until 1939; also taught singing at the Stockholm Cons. from 1924 until 1931. A jubilee collection of essays, *Boken om J. Forsell,* was publ. on his 70th birthday (Stockholm, 1938).

Förster, August, German piano manufacturer; b. Löbau, July 30, 1829; d. there, Feb. 18, 1897. He founded a piano factory in Bohemia; also owned the Förster Saal in Berlin. His firm constructed the first quarter-tone piano with 2 manuals (1924).

Förster, Emanuel Aloys, German composer and theorist; b. Niederstein, Silesia, Jan. 26, 1748; d. Vienna, Nov. 12, 1823. After service in the Prussian army, during which he played the oboe in a band, he went to Vienna for a thorough course in music, eventually becoming a teacher himself, although without a school position. He became friendly with Beethoven, who expressed esteem for him. Förster was a prolific composer; he wrote 48 string quartets, 5 oboe concertos, 10 violin sonatas, 21 piano sonatas, etc. His variations on arias from operas by Mozart, Sarti, and others enjoyed great popularity. He also publ. a manual, *Anleitung zum Generalbass* (1805; several later eds.).

Forster, Georg, German composer and compiler of music; b. Amberg, c.1510; d. Nuremberg, Nov. 12, 1568. He sang at the Heidelberg chapel in 1521, matriculating in classical studies in 1528. In 1531 he undertook medical studies at Ingolstadt; in 1534–39, studied humanities in Wittenberg with Melanchthon. In 1544 he received his degree of doctor of medicine at Tübingen Univ.; then was a medical practitioner in Amberg, Würzburg, Heidelberg, and Nuremberg (1544–47). He edited the valuable collection *Ein Auszug guter alter und neuer teutscher Liedlein* (in 5 parts; Nuremberg, 1539–56). Reprints are found in Jöde's *Das Chorbuch* and Schering's *Geschichte der Musik in Beispielen* (no. 88). Part II of the collection is publ. in R. Eitner's *Publikationen,* vol. 29. The first 3 parts were publ. in *Das Erbe deutscher Musik:* XX (1942), LX (1969), and LXI (1976); the other 2 parts are in preparation.

Förster, Joseph, Czech organist and composer; b. Osojnitz, Bohemia, Feb. 22, 1833; d. Prague, Jan. 3, 1907. He was organist in several churches in

Prague, and a prof. of theory at the Prague Cons. He wrote organ pieces, church music, and a treatise on harmony. He was the father of the celebrated Czech composer **Joseph Bohuslav Foerster.**

Forsyth, Cecil, English composer and writer on music; b. Greenwich, Nov. 30, 1870; d. New York, Dec. 7, 1941. He received his general education at Edinburgh Univ.; then studied at the Royal College of Music with Stanford and Parry. He joined the viola section in the Queen's Hall Orch.; also was connected with the Savoy Theatre, where he produced 2 of his comic operas, *Westward Ho!* and *Cinderella.* After the outbreak of World War I he went to N.Y., where he remained for the rest of his life. He composed a Viola Concerto and *Chant celtique* for Viola and Orch.; also songs, sacred music, and instrumental pieces. He was the author of a comprehensive manual, *Orchestration* (N.Y., 1914; 2nd ed., 1935; reprinted 1948); *Choral Orchestration* (London, 1920); also a treatise on English opera, *Music and Nationalism* (London, 1911). He publ. (in collaboration with Stanford) *A History of Music* (London, 1916) and a collection of essays, *Clashpans* (N.Y., 1933).

Forti, Anton, famous Austrian tenor and baritone; b. Vienna, June 8, 1790; d. there, June 16, 1859. He first sang in Esterháza (1807–11); then went to Vienna, where he appeared at the Theater an der Wien (1811–13); in 1813 he joined the Court Theater, singing both tenor and baritone roles; also sang in Prague, Hamburg, and Berlin; continued to sing until late in his life. He was particularly esteemed for his performances in the roles of Figaro and Don Giovanni.

Fortner, Wolfgang, important German composer; b. Leipzig, Oct. 12, 1907. He studied composition with Hermann Grabner at the Leipzig Cons., and musicology with Theodore Kroyer at the Univ. there (1927–31). Upon graduation he was engaged for 22 years as instructor in music theory at the Inst. of Sacred Music in Heidelberg; then was a prof. of composition at the Music Academy in Detmold (1954–57) and held a similar position at the Hochschule für Musik in Freiburg im Breisgau (1957–73). Concurrently he led the concerts of Music Viva in Heidelberg, Freiburg, and Munich; and after 1954 was also a lecturer at the Academy of the Arts in West Berlin. In 1961 he was engaged to conduct a seminar at the Berkshire Music Center at Tanglewood; he visited the U.S. again in 1968. His music is marked by exceptional contrapuntal skills, with the basic tonality clearly present even when harmonic density reaches its utmost; in some of his works since 1947, Fortner gives a dodecaphonic treatment to melodic procedures; in his textures he often employs a "rhythmic cell" device. He is equally adept in his works for the musical theater and purely instrumental compositions; the German tradition is maintained throughout, both in the mechanics of strong polyphony and in rational innovations. WORKS: FOR THE STAGE: 5 operas: *Bluthochzeit*

(after García Lorca's *Bodas de Sangre,* 1956; Cologne, June 8, 1957; revised 1963), which is a reworking of a dramatic scene, *Der Wald,* for Voices, Speaker, and Orch. (Frankfurt, June 25, 1953); *Corinna,* opera buffa (1958; Berlin, Oct. 3, 1958); *In seinem Garten liebt Don Perlimlín Belisa* (also after García Lorca's *Bodas de Sangre,* 1961–62; Schwetzingen, May 10, 1962); *Elisabeth Tudor* (1968–71; Berlin, Oct. 23, 1972); *That Time (Damals),* after Beckett, for Mime, Narrator, Mezzo-soprano, Baritone, Harpsichord, Guitar, Piano, and Live Electronics (1977; Baden-Baden, April 24, 1977). 3 ballets: *Die weisse Rose* (after Wilde's *The Birthday of the Infants,* 1949; concert perf., Baden-Baden, March 5, 1950; stage premiere, Berlin, April 28, 1951); a pantomime, *Die Witwe von Ephesus* (1952; Berlin, Sept. 17, 1952); *Carmen,* a Bizet-collage (1970; Stuttgart, Feb. 29, 1971).

FOR ORCH.: *Suite,* on music of Sweelinck (1930); Concerto for Organ and String Orch. (1932; reused as a Harpsichord Concerto, 1935); Concerto for String Orch. (1933); Concertino for Viola and Small Orch. (1934); *Capriccio und Finale* (1939); *Ernste Musik* (1940); Piano Concerto (1942); *Streichermusik II* for String Orch. (1944); Violin Concerto (1946; Baden-Baden, Feb. 16, 1947); Symph. (1947; Baden-Baden, May 2, 1948; his first use of dodecaphony); *Phantasie über die Tonfolge B-A-C-H* for 2 Pianos, 9 Solo Instruments, and Orch. (1950); Cello Concerto (1951; Cologne, Dec. 17, 1951); *Mouvements* for Piano and Orch. (1953; Baden-Baden, Feb. 6, 1954; as a ballet, Essen, Feb. 26, 1960); *La Cecchina,* Italian overture after Piccini (1954); *Impromptus* (1957; Donaueschingen, Oct. 20, 1957); *Ballet blanc* for 2 Solo Violins and String Orch. (1958; as a ballet, Wuppertal, Dec. 30, 1959); *Aulodie* for Oboe and Orch. (1960, revised 1966); *Triplum* for Orch. and 3 Obbligato Pianos (1965–66; Basel, Dec. 15, 1966; as a ballet, Munich, 1969); *Immagini* for Small or Large String Orch. (1966–67; also version for Large String Orch. and Soprano); *Marginalien* (1969; Kiel, Jan. 12, 1970); *Zyklus* for Cello, Winds, Harp, and Percussion (1969; originally for Cello and Piano, 1964); *Prolegomena* (concert suite from the opera *Elisabeth Tudor,* 1973; Nuremberg, April 19, 1974); *Prismen* for Flute, Oboe, Clarinet, Harp, Percussion, and Orch. (1974; Basel, Feb. 13, 1975); *Triptychon* (1976–77; consists of 3 parts: *Hymnus I* for 6 Brasses; *Improvisation* for Large Orch., and *Hymnus II* for 18-Voice String Orch.; first complete performance, Düsseldorf, April 6, 1978).

FOR VOICE: *Fragment Maria,* chamber cantata (1969); *Grenzen der Menschheit,* cantata (1930); *Nuptiae Catulli* for Tenor, Chamber Chorus, and Chamber Orch. (1937; Basel, April 5, 1939); *An die Nachgeborenen,* cantata (1947; Baden-Baden, April 4, 1948); *2 Exerzitien* for 3 Female Voices and 15 Instruments (1948); *Mitte des Lebens,* cantata for Soprano and 5 Instruments (1951); *Isaaks Opferung,* oratorio-scene for 3 Soloists and 40 Instruments (1952; Donaueschingen, Oct. 12, 1952); *The Creation,* after James Weldon Johnson's poem, for Voice and Orch. (1954; Basel, Feb. 18, 1955; Fischer-Dieskau, soloist); *Chant de naissance,* cantata for Soprano, Chorus, Solo Violin, Strings, Winds, Percussion, and Harp (1958; Hamburg, April 12, 1959); *Berceuse royale* for Soprano, Solo Violin, and String Orch. (a section from *Chant de naissance,* 1958; revised in 1975 for Soprano and 7 Instruments); *Prélude und Elegie,* parergon to the Orch.; *Impromptus* for Soprano and Orch., after Hölderlin (1959); *Die Pfingstgeschichte nach Lukas,* for Tenor, Chorus, 11 Instruments or Chamber Orch., and Organ (1962–63; Düsseldorf, May 7, 1964); *Der 100. Psalm* for Chorus, 3 Horns, 2 Trumpets, and 2 Trombones (1962); *"Versuch eines Agon um . . . ?"* for 7 Singers and Orch. (1973; Hannover, Nov. 8, 1973); *Gladbacher Te Deum* for Baritone, Chorus, Tape, and Orch. (1973; Mönchengladbach, June 6, 1974); *Machaut-Balladen* for Voice and Orch. (1973; Saarbrücken, Jan. 19, 1975); choruses; songs.

Fortune, Nigel (Cameron), English musicologist; b. Birmingham, Dec. 5, 1924. He studied at the Univ. of Birmingham (B.A., 1950); received his Ph.D. in 1954 from Gonville and Caius College, Cambridge with the dissertation *Italian Secular Song from 1600 to 1635: The Origins and Development of Accompanied Monody.* He was music librarian at the Univ. of London (1956–59); in 1959 he became a lecturer at the Univ. of Birmingham; in 1969 was appointed a reader in music there. He was a senior consulting editor of the *New Grove Dictionary of Music and Musicians* (London, 1980). With D. Arnold, he edited *The Monteverdi Companion* (London, 1968) and *The Beethoven Companion* (London, 1971). He also edited works by Dowland and Purcell.

Foss, Hubert James, English writer on music; b. Croydon, May 2, 1899; d. London, May 27, 1953. He attended Bradfield College; in 1921 became a member of the educational dept. of the Oxford Univ. Press, and in 1924 founded the music dept., which he headed till 1941. He composed *7 Poems by Thomas Hardy* for Baritone, Male Chorus, and Piano; instrumental pieces; songs. He was the author of *Music in My Time* (1933); *The Concertgoer's Handbook* (London, 1946); *Ralph Vaughan Williams* (London, 1950); collected and edited *The Heritage of Music, Essays . . .* (2 vols., London, 1927–34). His book *London Symphony: Portrait of an Orchestra* remained unfinished at his death, and was completed by Noël Goodwin (London, 1954).

Foss, Lukas (real surname, **Fuchs**), brilliant American pianist, conductor, and composer; b. Berlin, Aug. 15, 1922. He was a scion of a cultural family; his father was a prof. of philosophy; his mother, a talented modern painter. He studied piano and music theory with Julius Goldstein-Herford. When the dark shadow of the Nazi dominion descended upon Germany, the family prudently moved to Paris; there Foss studied piano with Lazare Lévy, composition with Noël Gallon, and orchestration with Felix Wolfes. He also took flute lessons with Marcel Moÿse. In 1937 he went to the U.S. and enrolled at the Curtis Inst. in Philadelphia, where he studied piano with Isabelle Vengerova, composition with Rosario Scalero, and conducting with Fritz Reiner;

spent several summers at Tanglewood, Mass., where he studied conducting with Koussevitzky at the Berkshire Music Center; in 1940–41 he took a course in advanced composition with Hindemith at Yale Univ. He became a naturalized American citizen in 1942. Foss began to compose at a very early age; was the youngest composer to be awarded a Guggenheim fellowship (1945); in 1960 he received his 2nd Guggenheim fellowship. His first public career was that of a concert pianist, and he elicited high praise for his appearances as a piano soloist with the N.Y. Phil. and other orchs. He made his conducting debut with the Pittsburgh Symph. Orch. in 1939. From 1944 to 1950 he was pianist of the Boston Symph. Orch.; then traveled to Rome on a Fulbright fellowship (1950–52). From 1953 to 1962 he taught composition at the Univ. of Calif. in Los Angeles, where he also established the Improvisation Chamber Ensemble to perform music of "controlled improvisation." In 1960 he traveled to Russia under the auspices of the U.S. State Dept. In 1963 he was appointed music director and conductor of the Buffalo Phil. Orch.; during his tenure there he introduced ultramodern works, much to the annoyance of some regular subscribers; he resigned his position there in 1970. In 1964–65 he led in N.Y. a series of "Evenings for New Music." In 1965 he served as music director of the American-French Festival at Lincoln Center, N.Y. In 1971 he became principal conductor of the Brooklyn Philharmonia; also established the series "Meet the Moderns" there. From 1972–75 he conducted the Jerusalem Symph. Orch. In 1980 he was appointed music director of the Milwaukee Symph. Orch.; also conducted several guest engagements with the N.Y. Phil. Throughout the years he evolved an astounding activity as conductor, composer, and lately college instructor, offering novel ideas in education and performance. As a composer he traversed a protean succession of changing styles, idioms, and techniques. His early compositions were marked by the spirit of Romantic lyricism, adumbrating the musical language of Mahler; some other works reflected the neo-Classical formulas of Hindemith; still others suggested the hedonistic vivacity and sophisticated stylization typical of Stravinsky's productions. But the intrinsic impetus of his music was its "pulse," which evolves the essential thematic content into the substance of original projection. His earliest piano pieces were publ. when he was 15 years old; there followed an uninterrupted flow of compositions in various genres. Foss was fortunate in being a particular protégé of Koussevitzky, who conducted many of his works with the Boston Symph.; and he had no difficulty in finding other performers. As a virtuoso pianist he often played the piano part in his chamber music, and he conducted a number of his symph. and choral works.

WORKS: Incidental music to Shakespeare's play *The Tempest* (N.Y., March 31, 1940); *The Prairie,* cantata after Carl Sandburg's poem (N.Y., May 15, 1944; an orch. suite from it was performed earlier by the Boston Symph. Orch., Oct. 15, 1943); Piano Concerto No. 1 (1944); *Symphony in G* (Pittsburgh, Feb. 4, 1945, composer conducting); *Ode* for Orch.

(N.Y., March 15, 1945); *Gift of the Magi*, ballet after O. Henry (Boston, Oct. 5, 1945); *Song of Anguish*, biblical solo cantata (1945); Boston, March 10, 1950); *Song of Songs*, biblical solo cantata (Boston, March 7, 1947); String Quartet (1947); *Recordare* for Orch. (Boston, Dec. 31, 1948); Oboe Concerto (N.Y., radio premiere, Feb. 6, 1950); opera, *The Jumping Frog of Calaveras County*, after Mark Twain (Bloomington, Ind., May 18, 1950); Piano Concerto No. 2 (Venice, Oct. 7, 1951, composer soloist; revised 1953; N.Y. Music Critics' Award, 1954); *A Parable of Death*, cantata after Rilke (Louisville, Ky., March 11, 1953); opera, *Griffelkin* (NBC Television, Nov. 6, 1955); *Psalms* for Voices and Orch. (N.Y., May 9, 1957); *Symphony of Chorales*, based on Bach's chorales (Pittsburgh, Oct. 24, 1958); *Introductions and Goodbyes*, miniature opera (N.Y., May 6, 1960); *Time Cycle*, suite for Soprano and Orch. in 4 movements to texts by Auden, Housman, Kafka, and Nietzsche with intercalative improvisations by a combo of Clarinet, Cello, Percussion, and Piano (N.Y., Oct. 21, 1960; won the N.Y. Music Critics' Award); *Echoi* for Piano, Percussion, Clarinet, and Cello (N.Y., Nov. 11, 1963); *Elytres* for 21 Instruments (Los Angeles, Dec. 8, 1964); *Fragments of Archilochos* for Contratenor, Narrator, 4 Small Choruses, Large Chorus ad lib., Mandolin, Guitar, and Percussion (1965); *For 24 Winds* (1966); *Phorion* for Electric Guitar, Electric Piano, and Electric Organ, with thematic material derived from Bach's E-major Partita for Solo Violin (hence the title, *Phorion*, meaning "borrowed" in Greek; first perf., N.Y., April 27, 1967; later incorporated into *Baroque Variations*, consisting of the *Largo* from Handel's Suite in E, Scarlatti's Sonata in E, and *Phorion*); *Concert* for Cello and Orch. (N.Y., March 5, 1967; Rostropovich, soloist); *Geod* (abbreviation of Geodesics), musical action for Orch. (Hamburg, Dec. 6, 1969; composer conducting); *MAP* (acronym for "Men at Play"), musical play for 5 Instrumentalists (1970); *Paradigm* for Percussionist, Electric Guitar, and 3 Instruments (Buffalo, N.Y., 1969); *The Cave of the Winds*, wind quintet (1972); *Orpheus* for Cello or Viola or Guitar, with Orch. (1972); *Divertissement* for String Quartet (1972; Ojai, Calif., 1973); *Ni bruit ni vitesse* for 2 Pianists playing on the Keyboard and 2 Percussionists playing on Piano Strings (1973); *Fanfare* for Chamber Orch. with 3 Folk Instruments (Istanbul, June 28, 1973); *The Percussion Concerto* for Chamber Orch. with a "percussionist/magician" perambulating about the stage telling the players what to do, and a "mechanical metronomic conductor" (1975); *Folksong* for Orch. (Baltimore, Jan. 21, 1976); *Quartet Plus* for Narrator and Double String Quartet (N.Y., April 29, 1977); *American Cantata* for Tenor, Soprano, 2 Speakers, Chorus, and Orch. (N.Y., Dec. 1, 1977); *Quintets for Orchestra* (Cleveland, May 2, 1979); *Round a Common Center* for Piano Quartet or Piano Quintet, with or without Voice, with or without Narration (Lake Placid, N.Y., Jan. 30, 1980); *Curriculum vitae* with a "Time-Bomb" for a Miscellaneous Ensemble, ending with a Cap-gun Explosion; *Exeunt*, dissertation for Orch. (1982); *Solo Observed* for Chamber Orch. (1983).

Foster, Lawrence, American conductor; b. Los Angeles, Oct. 23, 1941. He made his first conducting appearance with the Young Musicians Foundation Debut Orch. in 1960. At the age of 24 he was appointed assistant conductor of the Los Angeles Phil. Orch.; in 1966 received the Koussevitzky Memorial Conducting Prize at the Berkshire Music Festival in Tanglewood, Mass. In 1969–74 he was chief guest conductor of the Royal Phil. Orch. of London. In 1971–78 he was conductor-in-chief of the Houston Symph. Orch. He became Generalmusikdirektor in the city of Duisburg, West Germany, in 1981. He is particularly notable for his dynamic interpretations of modern works, but has also been acclaimed for his precise and intelligent presentations of the Classical and Romantic repertoire.

Foster, Sidney, American pianist; b. Florence, S.C., May 23, 1917; d. Boston, Feb. 7, 1977. He began playing piano when he was 4 years old, and at the age of 10 was admitted to the Curtis Inst. in Philadelphia, where he studied with Isabelle Vengerova and David Saperton. In 1940 he won the first Leventritt Foundation Award, which entitled him to an appearance as soloist with the N.Y. Phil. This was the beginning of a brilliant international career. In 1964 he played 16 concerts in Russia. He taught piano at Florida State Univ. (1949–51); in 1952 he joined the piano faculty of Indiana Univ. at Bloomington.

Foster, Stephen Collins, American composer of famous songs; b. Lawrenceville, Pa., July 4, 1826; d. New York, Jan. 13, 1864. He learned to play the flute as a child; publ. a song, *Open Thy Lattice, Love*, at the age of 18. His father was a government worker and businessman, active in politics; his brothers were engaged in commerce. About 1846 he went to Cincinnati as accountant for his brother Dunning. Foster wrote a total of 189 songs, for most of which he wrote both words and music. Of these, *Old Folks at Home*, sometimes referred to as *Swanee Ribber* (from its initial line, "Way down upon de Swanee ribber"), was publ. on Oct. 21, 1851, with the subtitle "Ethiopian Melody as sung by Christy's Minstrels." E.P. Christy (1815–62) was the organizer of one of the first traveling minstrel companies; his name was given as author, in consideration of a small sum of money received by Foster, whose name was not attached to the song until 1879, upon the expiration of the original copyright. About 40,000 copies of this song were sold during the year after publication. Foster was greatly encouraged and, as he wrote to Christy, hoped to establish himself as "the best Ethiopian song writer." Of other songs, the most notable are *Oh! Susanna* (1848; became popular in the gold rush of 1849), *My Old Kentucky Home, Massa's in de Cold Ground, Jeanie with the Light Brown Hair, Old Black Joe, Nelly Was a Lady, Laura Lee*, etc. The title page of *Beautiful Dreamer* (publ. 1864) bears the legend "the last song ever written by Stephen C. Foster. Composed but a few days previous to his death," but this maudlin claim (an appeal for sales) is false, as the work was prepared for publication in 1862. It is not known which song was Foster's last. On July 22, 1850, Foster married Jane McDowell in Pittsburgh; they had a daughter, but the marriage was not happy. In 1853 Foster went to N.Y. and stayed there alone for a year; in 1854 he was living in Hoboken, N.J.; went to N.Y. again in 1860, while his wife remained with relatives. Foster died penniless at Bellevue Hospital, yet his earnings were not small; in 1849–60 he received about $15,000 in royalties. Apart from the songs, Foster wrote 12 instrumental pieces in salon music style, and made numerous arrangements for flute, guitar, violin, etc., for the collection *Foster's Social Orchestra* (N.Y., 1854). He had some knowledge of instrumental writing; his harmonies, though simple, are adequate. The extant MSS are mostly in the Foster Hall Collection at the Univ. of Pittsburgh (dedicated on June 2, 1937); bibliographical bulletins are issued periodically by this organization. A one-cent stamp bearing Foster's picture was brought out by the U.S. post office in 1940. In 1915 W.R. Whittlesey and O.G. Sonneck publ. a *Catalogue of First Editions of S. Foster*. There are hundreds of reprints of Foster's songs, but almost all are in "improved" arrangements. A facsimile reprint of the original sheet music of 40 songs was publ., with valuable commentary by Richard Jackson, in N.Y. in 1974.

Fou Ts'ong, Chinese pianist; b. Shanghai, March 10, 1934. He studied piano in his native city; then won third prizes in the Bucharest Piano Competition (1953) and the Warsaw International Chopin Competition (1955); continued his studies at the Warsaw Cons. In 1958 he decided to make his home in London; appeared with many of the major orchs. of Europe and the U.S.; also gave many recitals. He was particularly noted for his expressive playing of works by Chopin and Debussy.

Foulds, John Herbert, significant English composer and musical theorist; b. Manchester, Nov. 2, 1880; d. Calcutta, April 24, 1939. He was precocious and began to compose at a single-digit age; learned to play cello; earned a living by playing in theater orchs. In 1900 he joined the prestigious Hallé Orch. in Manchester, until 1910; then moved to London, where he served as music director for the London Central YMCA (1918–23); also conducted at the Univ. of London Music Society (1921–26). In 1935 he left England and went to India; there he undertook a thorough study of Indian folk music; served as director of European music for the All-India Radio at Delhi Station and at Calcutta Station (1937–39); he also formed an experimental "Indo-European" orch., which included both European and Asian instruments. He was the first English composer to experiment with quarter-tones, and as early as 1898 wrote a string quartet with fractional intervals; he also composed semi-classical pieces using traditional Indian instruments. Unfortunately, most of his MSS are lost, but enough remain to confute the Kipling dictum that East and West shall never meet.

WORKS: FOR THE STAGE: Concert opera, *The Vision of Dante* (1905–8); miniature opera, *Cleopatra* (1909; lost); *The Tell-Tale Heart*, melodrama after Edgar Allan Poe, for Actor and Chamber Orch. (1910); 3-act opera, *Avatara* (1919–30; lost); music for the ritual play *Veils* (1926; unfinished). FOR ORCH.: *Undine Suite* (c.1899); *Epithalamium* (London, Oct. 9, 1906); *Lento e scherzetto* for Cello and Orch. (c.1906); 2 Cello Concertos (1908–9; Manchester, March 16, 1911); *Apotheosis* for Violin and Orch. (1908–9); *Mirage*, symph. poem (1910); *Suite française* (1910); *Keltic Suite* (1911); *Music Pictures (Group III)*, suite (London, Sept. 4, 1912); *Hellas* for Double String Orch., Harp, and Percussion (1915–32); *Miniature Suite* (1915); *Peace and War*, meditation (1919); *3 Mantras* (1919–30); *Le Cabaret*, overture to a French comedy (1921); *Suite fantastique* (1922); *Music Pictures (Group IV)* for Strings (c.1922); *Saint Joan Suite* (1924–25); *Henry VIII Suite* (1925–26); *April-England*, tone poem (1926–32); *Dynamic Triptych* for Piano and Orch. (1929; Edinburgh, Oct. 15, 1931); *Keltic Overture* (1930); *Indian Suite* (1932–35); *Pasquinades symphoniques*, symph. in 3 movements (1935; finale left unfinished); *Deva-Music* (1935–36; only fragments remain); *Chinese Suite* (1935); *3 Pasquinades* (c.1936); *Symphony of East and West* for European and Indian Instruments (1937–38; lost); *Symphonic Studies* (1938; lost). FOR VOICE: *The Song of Honor* for Speaker, Chamber Orch., and ad lib. Female Chorus (1918); *A World Requiem* for 4 Soloists, Small Boys' Chorus, Mixed Chorus, and Orch. (1919–21; London, Nov. 11, 1923; perf. each Armistice Night in London from 1923 to 1926); choruses; songs. CHAMBER MUSIC: 10 string quartets: Nos. 1–3 (before 1899; lost), No. 4 (1899), No. 5 (lost), No. 6, *Quartetto romantico* (1903), No. 7 (lost), No. 8 (1907–10), No. 9, *Quartetto intimo* (1931–32), and No. 10, *Quartetto geniale* (1935; only the 3rd movement, *Lento quieto*, is extant); Cello Sonata (1905; revised 1927); *Impromptu on a Theme of Beethoven* for 4 Cellos (1905); *Music Pictures (Group I)* for Piano Trio (1910; lost); *Ritornello con variazioni* for String Trio (1911); *Aquarelles (Music Pictures—Group II)* for String Quartet (c.1914); *Sonia* for Violin and Piano (1925). FOR PIANO: *Dichterliebe*, suite (1897–98); *Essays in the Modes*, 6 studies (1920–27); *Egotistic*, modal essay (1927); *2 Landscapes* (c.1928); *Scherzo chromatico* (1927; lost).
WRITINGS: *Music To-Day: Its Heritage from the Past, and Legacy to the Future* (London, 1934).

Fourdrain, Félix, French composer; b. Nice, Feb. 3, 1880; d. Paris, Oct. 22, 1923. He studied with Widor; wrote operas: *Echo* (Paris, 1906); *La Légende du point d'Argentan* (Paris, April 17, 1907); *La Glaneuse* (Lyons, 1909); *Vercingétorix* (Nice, 1912); *Madame Roland* (Rouen, 1913); *Les Contes de Perrault* (Paris, 1913); *Les Maris de Ginette; La Mare au diable; La Griffe;* operettas: *Dolly* (Paris, 1922); *L'Amour en cage; Le Million de Colette; La Hussarde* (Paris, 1925); incidental music to Cain's *Le Secret de Polichinelle* (Cannes, 1922); *Anniversaire* for Orch.; many songs (*Le Papillon, Sérénades,*

Revanche d'amour, Pays des cours, etc.).

Fourestier, Louis, French composer and conductor; b. Montpellier, May 31, 1892; d. Boulogne-Billancourt, Sept. 30, 1976. He studied at the Paris Cons. under Gédalge and Leroux; won the Rossini Prize in 1924 (for his cantata *Patria*), the Grand Prix de Rome in 1925 (for the cantata *La Mort d'Adonis*), and the Heugel Prize in 1927 (for the symph. poem *Polynice*); served as a conductor in Marseilles and Bordeaux; in 1938 was appointed conductor at the Paris Opéra; in 1945–63 was a prof. at the Paris Cons.; on Nov. 11, 1946, he made his conducting debut at the Metropolitan Opera in N.Y.; conducted also in 1947–48; then returned to Paris.

Fournet, Jean, distinguished French conductor; b. Rouen, April 14, 1913. He studied at the Paris Cons., graduating with the highest honors. He then became conductor of the French Radio Orch.; also conducted at the Paris Opéra and the Opéra-Comique. Concurrently he taught conducting at the Ecole Normale de Musique. In 1961 he was appointed a permanent conductor of the Radio Phil. Orch. at Hilversum, the Netherlands. He also was chief conductor of the Rotterdam Phil. Orch. (1968–73). He is especially renowned for his interpretations of new French music, tempering its orchestral brilliance with Classical restraint.

Fournier, Pierre, famous French cellist; b. Paris, June 24, 1906. He studied cello with Paul Bazelaire and G. Hekking at the Paris Cons. He taught at the Ecole Normale de Musique (1937–39) and at the Paris Cons. (1941–49); then he decided to devote himself entirely to his concert career, which took him all over the world, including South America, Japan, Australia, New Zealand, and South Africa; he also made regular appearances in the U.S.; was praised for his natural *bel canto* quality on his instrument, as well as for his impeccable musical taste. Several composers wrote special works for him; he gave first performances of the cello concertos of Albert Roussel, Frank Martin, Bohuslav Martinů, and Jean Martinon. He also possessed the entire repertoire of cello works of Bach, Beethoven, and Brahms. In 1970 he settled in Switzerland, where he holds summer courses in interpretation in Zürich. In 1953 he was made a Chevalier of the Legion of Honor.

Fournier, Pierre-Simon, French cutter and founder of music type; b. Paris, Sept. 15, 1712; d. there, Oct. 8, 1768. Instead of the lozenge-shaped types in the style of Hautin's (1525), Fournier introduced round-headed notes, described in his *Essai d'un nouveau caractère de fonte* ... (1756); he also publ. a *Traité historique sur l'origine et le progrès des caractères de fonte pour l'impression de la musique* (Paris, 1765).

Fowler, Jennifer, Australian composer; b. Bunbury, Western Australia, April 14, 1939. She attended the Univ. of Western Australia, graduating in the arts (1961) and later in music (1968); studied electronic music at the Univ. of Utrecht (1968–69); then went to live in England.
  WORKS: *Variations* for Voice, Violin, Clarinet, and Percussion (1966); String Quartet (1967); *Fanfare* for Brass and Strings (1968); *Sculpture in 4 Dimensions* for Orch. (1969); *Chimes, Fractured* for Antiphonally Placed Chamber Ensemble (1970); *Hours of the Day* for 4 Mezzo-sopranos, 2 Oboes, and 2 Clarinets (1970); *Revelation* for String Quintet (1970–71); *Look on This Oedipus* for Orch. (1973); *Piece for an Opera House* for 2 Pianos, or for Piano and Tape (1973); *Chant with Garlands* for Orch. (1974).

Fox, Charles Warren, American musicologist; b. Gloversville, N.Y., July 24, 1904; d. there oct. 15, 1983. He took courses in psychology at Cornell Univ. (B.A., 1926; Ph.D., 1933); also studied musicology there with Otto Kinkeldey. In 1932 he became a part-time instructor in psychology at the Eastman School of Music in Rochester, N.Y.; in 1933 began giving courses in music history and musicology; he retired in 1970. From 1952–59 he was editor of the *Journal of the American Musicological Society.* From 1954–56 he served as president of the Music Library Association.

Fox Strangways, A(rthur) H(enry), noted English writer on music and ed.; b. Norwich, Sept. 14, 1859; d. Dinton, near Salisbury, May 2, 1948. He studied at Wellington College, London; received his M.A. in 1882 from Balliol College, Oxford; then was a schoolmaster at Dulwich College (1884–86) and Wellington College (1887–1910). From 1911–25 he wrote music criticism for the *Times* of London; in 1925 he became music critic of the *Observer.* In 1920 he founded the quarterly journal *Music & Letters,* which he edited until 1937 (he was succeeded by Eric Blom). He was a specialist in Indian music and wrote several books on the subject, including *The Music of Hindostan* (Oxford, 1914); also publ. a collection of essays, *Music Observed* (London, 1936), and a biography of Cecil Sharp (with M. Karpeles; London, 1933; 2nd ed., 1955). He contributed the article "Folk-Song" to the introductory vol. of *The Oxford History of Music* (London, 1929).

Fox, Virgil, American concert organist; b. Princeton, Ill., May 3, 1912; d. Palm Beach, Fla., Oct. 25, 1980. He studied piano as a child, but soon turned to the organ as his favorite instrument. He played the organ at the First Presbyterian Church in his hometown at the age of 10, and gave his first public recital in Cincinnati at 14. He then enrolled in the Peabody Cons. in Baltimore, graduating in 1932. To perfect his playing he went to Paris, where he took lessons with Marcel Dupré at St. Sulpice and Louis Vierne at Notre Dame. He returned to the U.S. in 1938 and became head of the organ dept. at the Peabody Cons. In 1946 he was appointed organist at the Riverside Church in N.Y., where he played on a 5-manual 10,561-pipe organ specially designed for him. He then launched a remarkable career as an organ soloist. He was the first American to play at the Thomaskirche in Leipzig, where Bach had served as organist, and also played at Westminster Abbey in London. As a solo artist, he evolved an idiosyncratic type of performance in which he embellished the stodgy Baroque music with romantic extravaganza; he also took to apostrophizing his audiences in a whimsical mixture of lofty sentiment and disarming self-deprecation. This type of personalized art endeared him to the impatient emancipated musical youth of America, and he became one of the few organists who could fill a concert hall. He also displayed a robust taste for modern music; he often played the ear-stopping discordant arrangement of *America* by Charles Ives. Wracked by cancer, he gave his last concert in Dallas on Sept. 26, 1980.

Frackenpohl, Arthur (Roland), American composer; b. Irvington, N.J., April 23, 1924. He studied at the Eastman School of Music in Rochester, N.Y., with Bernard Rogers; also with Milhaud at the Berkshire Music Center in Tanglewood, Mass., and with Nadia Boulanger at Fontainebleau. In 1949 he was appointed a member of the faculty at the State Univ. Teachers' College in Potsdam, N.Y.
WORKS: Sonatina for Clarinet and Piano (1948); Brass Quartet (1949); Trio for Oboe, Horn, and Bassoon (1949); cantata, *A Child This Day Is Born* (1951); Suite for Strings (1953); *An Elegy on the Death of a Mad Dog* (1955); *Allegro Giocoso* (1955); *A Jubilant Overture* for Orch. (1956); cantata, *The Natural Superiority of Men* (1959); Symph. No. 2 for Strings (1960); chamber opera, *Domestic Relations ("To Beat or Not to Beat"),* after O. Henry (1964); Suite for Trumpet and Strings (1964); String Quartet (1971); *French Suite* for Woodwind Quintet (1972); *American Folk Song Suite* for Band (1973); Variations for Tuba and Winds (1974); Duo for Clarinet and Percussion (1974).

Fradkin, Fredric, American violinist; b. Troy, N.Y., April 2, 1892; d. New York, Oct. 3, 1963. At the age of 5 he became a pupil of Schradieck; later studied with Max Bendix and Sam Franko in N.Y.; then went to Paris; studied at the Cons. there with Lefort, graduating in 1909 with first prize. He was concertmaster of the Bordeaux Opera Co.; then took instruction with Ysaÿe in Brussels. Returning to America, he made his debut as a concert violinist in N.Y. on Jan. 10, 1911; then gave concerts in Europe; in 1918–19 he was concertmaster of the Boston Symph. Orch.; later settled in N.Y. as a private teacher.

Fraenkel, Wolfgang, German composer; b. Berlin, Oct. 10, 1897; d. Los Angeles, March 8, 1983. He studied violin, piano, and music theory at the Klindworth-Scharwenka Cons. in Berlin; at the same time took courses in jurisprudence and was a judge in Berlin until the advent of the Nazi regime in 1933; he was interned in the Sachsenhausen concentration camp, but as a 50 percent Jew (his mother was an Aryan, as was his wife), he was released in 1939, and went to China, where he enjoyed the protection of Chiang Kai-shek, who asked him to organize music education in Nanking and Shanghai. In 1947, when China exploded into a civil war, he emigrated to the U.S. and settled in Los Angeles. He earned a living by composing background music for documentary films in Hollywood, supplementing his income by copying music (he had a calligraphic handwriting). Fraenkel's own music has evolved from the standard German traditions, but at a later period he began to experiment with serial methods of composition.
WORKS: Opera, *Der brennende Dornbusch* (1924 –27); 3 string quartets (1924, 1949, 1960; the 3rd Quartet received the Queen Elisabeth Prize and was performed at the Liège Festival of the International Society for Contemporary Music in 1962); Flute Concerto (1930); *Der Wegweiser,* cantata (1931); Cello Sonata (1934); Violin Sonata (1935); *Filippo* for Speaker and Orch. (1948); Sonata for Solo Violin (1954); *Variations and a Fantasy on a Theme by Schoenberg* for Piano (1954); *Frescobaldi,* transcription for Orch. of 5 organ pieces by Frescobaldi (1957); Viola Sonata (1963); *Klavierstück* for Tape and Piano (1964); *Symphonische Aphorismen* for Orch. (1965; awarded first prize at the International Competition of the City of Milan); *Joseph* for Baritone and Orch., to a text by Thomas Mann (1968); *Missa aphoristica* for Chorus and Orch. (1973); String Quintet (1976). All his works, both publ. and in MS, are deposited in the Moldenhauer Archive in Spokane, Wash.

Frager, Malcolm, American pianist; b. St. Louis, Jan. 15, 1935. He studied languages at Columbia Univ.; majored in Russian, graduating in 1957. He studied piano with Carl Friedberg in N.Y. (1949–55); received various prizes in the U.S. In 1960 he won the Queen Elisabeth of Belgium International Competition, which marked the beginning of his worldwide career; he was particularly successful in Russia.

Framery, Nicolas Etienne, French composer, writer on music, and poet; b. Rouen, March 25, 1745; d. Paris, Nov. 26, 1810. He composed the text and music for the comic opera *La Sorcière par hasard* (1768); its performance at Villeroy earned him the position of superintendent of music with the Count of Artois. The opera was played at the Comédie-Italienne (Paris, Sept. 3, 1783), but suffered a fiasco because of the antagonism against Italian opera generated by the adherents of Gluck. He also wrote librettos for Sacchini, Salieri, Paisiello, Anfossi, and other Italian composers; edited the *Journal de Musique* in Paris from 1770 till 1778, and *Calendrier Musical Universal* (1788–89); compiled, together with Ginguène and Feytou, the musical part of vol. I of *Encyclopédie méthodique* (1791; vol. II by Momigny, 1818); besides smaller studies, he wrote *De la nécessité du rythme et de la césure dans les hymnes ou odes destinées à la musique* (1796); translated into French Azopardi's *Musico prattico* (*Le Musicien pratique;* 2 vols., 1786).

Françaix, Jean, talented French composer; b. Le Mans, May 23, 1912. He first studied at the Le Mans Cons., of which his father was director; then at the Paris Cons. with Isidor Philipp (piano) and Nadia Boulanger (composition). In his music, Françaix associates himself with the new French school of composers, pursuing the twofold aim of practical application and national tradition; his instrumental works represent a stylization of Classical French music; in this respect, he comes close to Ravel.

WORKS: FOR THE STAGE: Comic chamber opera, *Le Diable boiteux* (1937; Paris, June 30, 1938, Nadia Boulanger conducting); opera, *La Main de gloire* (1945; Bordeaux, May 7, 1950); comic operas: *Paris à nous deux* (Fontainebleau, Aug. 7, 1954) and *La Princesse de Clèves* (1961–65); ballets: *Scuola di Ballo* (1933); *Les Malheurs de Sophie* (1935); *Le Roi nu,* after Andersen's tale (Paris, June 15, 1936); *Le Jeu sentimental* (1936); *La Luthérie enchantée* (1936); *Verreries de Venise* (1938); *Le Jugement du fou* (1938); *Les Demoiselles de la nuit* (1948); *La Dame dans la lune* (Paris, Feb. 11, 1958); *L'Apostrophe,* musical comedy, after Balzac (1940; Amsterdam, July 1, 1951); oratorio, *L'Apocalypse selon St. Jean* (Paris, June 11, 1942); *Cantate de Méphisto* for Bass Solo and Strings (Paris, Oct. 8, 1955). FOR ORCH.: Symph. (Paris, Nov. 6, 1932); Concertino for Piano and Orch. (1932); Suite for Violin and Orch. (1934); *Sérénade* for Chamber Orch. (1934); *Fantaisie* for Cello and Orch. (1934; revised 1955); *Quadruple Concerto* for Flute, Oboe, Clarinet, Bassoon, and Orch. (1935); *Au Musée Grévin,* suite for Orch. (1936); Piano Concerto (Berlin, Nov. 8, 1936); *Musique de cour,* suite for Flute, Violin, and Orch. (1937); *Invocation à la volupté* for Baritone and Orch. (1946); *Les Bosquets de Cythère,* 7 waltzes for Orch. (1946); *La Douce France,* suite for Orch. (1946); *Rhapsodie* for Viola and Small Orch. (1946); Symph. for Strings (1948); *Les Ziques de Mars,* "petit ballet militaire" for Orch. (1950); Symph. (1953; La Jolla, Calif., Aug. 9, 1953); *Si Versailles m'était conté,* suite for Orch. from the film (1954); *Sérénade B E A,* "game" for String Orch. on 3 notes (1955); *Divertimento* for Horn and Small Orch. (1958); Concerto for Harpsichord and Instrumental Ensemble (1959); *Le Dialogue des Carmelites,* suite for Orch. (1960); *L'Horloge de Flore,* suite for Oboe and Orch. (Philadelphia, March 31, 1961); *6 préludes* for Chamber String Orch. (1963); 2-Piano Concerto (1965); Flute Concerto (Schwetzingen, May 13, 1967); *Jeu poétique en 6 mouvements* for Harp and Orch. (1969); *Les Inestimables Chroniques du grand Gargantua* for Narrator and String Orch. (1970); Violin Concerto (1970); *Theme and Variations* for Orch. (Bochum, Germany, Dec. 12, 1973); *Fantaisie Burlesque* for Orch. (Nuremberg, March 15, 1974); Concerto for Double Bass and Orch. (Frankfurt, Nov. 1, 1974); *Cassazione per 3 orchestre* (1975). CHAMBER MUSIC: *Divertissement* for Violin, Viola, Cello, Winds, Percussion, Harp, and Double Bass (1933); *Divertissement* for Bassoon and String Quartet (1944); *Cantate satirique,* after Juvenal, for 4 String Instruments and Piano, 4-hands (1947); *L'Heure de Berger* for Strings and Piano (1947); Wind Quintet (1948); *Variations sans thème* for Cello and Piano (1951); *Sonatine* for Trumpet and Piano (1952); *Ode à la gastronomie* for Chorus (1953); Piano Sonata (1960); Quartet for English Horn, Viola, and Cello (1971).

Francescatti, Zino, brilliant violinist; b. Marseilles, Aug. 9, 1902. His father, a Frenchman of Italian extraction, was a violin pupil of Paganini; prodded by him, Zino Francescatti appeared in public as a violinist at the age of 5, and played the Beethoven Violin Concerto with an orch. at 10. In 1927 he went to Paris, where he began teaching at the Ecole Normale de Musique; also conducted occasional performances of the Paris symph. organization Concerts Poulet. Between 1931 and 1939 he made several world tours; in 1939 made his home in the U.S., appearing in concert recitals and as a soloist with orchs. He made his U.S. debut on Nov. 1, 1939, with the N.Y. Phil.

Franchetti, Alberto, Italian composer; b. Turin, Sept. 18, 1860; d. Viareggio, Aug. 4, 1942. He studied in Turin with Niccolò Coccon and Fortunato Magi; then with Rheinberger in Munich and with Draeseke in Dresden. He devoted his entire life to composition, with the exception of a brief tenure as director of the Cherubini Cons. in Florence (1926–28).

WORKS: Operas: *Asrael* (Reggio Emilia, Feb. 11, 1888); *Cristoforo Colombo* (Genoa, Oct. 6, 1892); *Fior d'Alpe* (Milan, March 15, 1894); *Il Signor di Pourceaugnac* (Milan, April 10, 1897); *Germania* (his most successful opera; produced at La Scala, March 11, 1902; also had repeated perfs. in N.Y., London, Buenos Aires, etc.); *La figlia di Jorio* (Milan, March 29, 1906); *Notte di leggenda* (Milan, Jan. 14, 1915); *Giove a Pompei* (with Umberto Giordano; Rome, June 5, 1921); *Glauco* (Naples, April 8, 1922); Symph. (1886); symph. poems: *Loreley* and *Nella selva nera; Inno* for Soli, Chorus, and Orch. (for the 800th anniversary of the Univ. of Bologna); several pieces of chamber music and songs.

Franchomme, Auguste-Joseph, famous French cellist; b. Lille, April 10, 1808; d. Paris, Jan. 21, 1884. He studied at the Lille Cons.; then with Levasseur and Norblin at the Paris Cons.; then played cello in various opera houses; in 1828 became solo cellist of the Royal Chapel and was founding member of the Société des Concerts du Conservatoire. In 1846 he was appointed prof. at the Paris Cons. He was an intimate friend of Chopin; established evenings of chamber music in Paris with Hallé and Alard. He wrote cello pieces, mostly in variation form, and operatic potpourris.

Franck, César (-Auguste-Jean-Guillaume-Hubert), great Belgian composer and organist; b. Liège, Dec. 10, 1822; d. Paris, Nov. 8, 1890. He studied first at the Royal Cons. of Liège with Daussoigne and others; at the age of 9 he won first prize for singing, and at 12 first prize for piano. As a child prodigy, he gave concerts in Belgium. In 1835 his family moved to Paris, where he studied privately with Anton Reicha; in 1837 he entered the Paris Cons., studying with Zimmermann (piano), Benoist (organ), and Leborne (theory). A few months after his entrance examinations he received a special award of "grand prix d'honneur" for playing a fugue a third lower at sight; in 1838 he received the first prize for piano; in 1839, a 2nd prize for counterpoint; in 1840, first prize for fugue; and in 1841, 2nd prize for organ. In 1842 he was back in Belgium; in 1843 he returned to Paris, and settled there for the rest of his life. On March 17, 1843, he presented there a concert of his chamber music; on Jan. 4, 1846, his first major work, the oratorio *Ruth*, was given at the Paris Cons. On Feb. 22, 1848, in the midst of the Paris revolution, he married; in 1851 he became organist of the church of St.-Jean-St.-François; in 1853, maître de chapelle and, in 1858, organist at Ste.-Clotilde, which position he held until his death. In 1872 he succeeded his former teacher Benoist as prof. of organ at the Paris Cons. Franck's organ classes became the training school for a whole generation of French composers; among his pupils were d'Indy, Chausson, Bréville, Bordes, Duparc, Ropartz, Pierné, Vidal, Chapuis, Vierne, and a host of others, who eventually formed a school of modern French instrumental music. Until the appearance of Franck in Paris, operatic art dominated the entire musical life of the nation, and the course of instruction at the Paris Cons. was influenced by this tendency. By his emphasis on organ music, based on the contrapuntal art of Bach, Franck swayed the new generation of French musicians toward the ideal of absolute music. The foundation of the famous Schola Cantorum by d'Indy, Bordes, and others in 1894 realized Franck's teachings. After the death of d'Indy in 1931, several members withdrew from the Schola Cantorum and organized the Ecole César Franck (1938).

César Franck was not a prolific composer; but his creative powers rose rather than diminished with advancing age; his only symph. was completed when he was 66; his remarkable Violin Sonata was written at the age of 63; his String Quartet was composed in the last year of his life. Lucidity of contrapuntal design and fullness of harmony are the distinguishing traits of Franck's music; in melodic writing he balanced the diatonic and chromatic elements in fine equilibrium. Although he did not pursue innovation for its own sake, he was not averse to using unorthodox procedures. The novelty of introducing an English horn into the score of his symph. aroused some criticism among academic musicians of the time. Franck was quite alien to the Wagner-Liszt school of composition, which attracted many of his own pupils; the chromatic procedures in Franck's music derive from Bach rather than from Wagner.

WORKS: OPERAS: *Le Valet de Ferme* (1851–53); *Hulda* (1882–85; Monte Carlo, March 8, 1894); *Ghisèle* (unfinished; orchestration completed by d'Indy, Chausson, Bréville, Rousseau, and Coquard; first perf., Monte Carlo, March 30, 1896). ORATORIOS: *Ruth* (1843–46; Paris, Jan. 4, 1846; revised 1871); *La Tour de Babel* (1865); *Les Béatitudes* (1869–79; Dijon, June 15, 1891); *Rédemption* (first version, Paris, April 10, 1873; final version, Paris, March 15, 1875); *Rébecca* (Paris, March 15, 1881; produced as a one-act sacred opera at the Paris Opéra, May 25, 1918). SYMPH. POEMS: *Les Eolides* (Paris, May 13, 1877); *Le Chasseur maudit* (Paris, March 31, 1883); *Les Djinns* (Paris, March 15, 1885); *Psyché* (Paris, March 10, 1888). OTHER WORKS FOR ORCH.: *Variations symphoniques* for Piano and Orch. (Paris, May 1, 1886); Symph. in D minor (Paris, Feb. 17, 1889). CHAMBER MUSIC: 4 piano trios (early works; 1841–42); *Andante quietoso* for Piano and Violin (1843); *Duo pour piano et violon concertants,* on themes from Dalayrac's *Gulistan* (1844); Quintet in F minor for Piano and Strings (1879); Violin Sonata (1886); String Quartet (1889). ORGAN WORKS: *6 pièces* (Fantaisie; Grande pièce symphonique; Prélude, Fugue, et Variations; Pastorale; Prière; Finale); *3 pièces* (Fantaisie; Cantabile; Pièce heroïque); *Andantino; 3 chorales;* an album of 44 *Petites pièces;* an album of 55 pieces, entitled *L'Organiste;* etc. SACRED MUSIC: *Messe solennelle* (1858); *Messe à 3 voix* (1860); *Panis angelicus* for Tenor, Organ, Harp, Cello, and Double Bass; offertories, motets, etc.; 16 songs, among them *La Procession* (also arranged for Voice and Orch.). PIANO PIECES: *4 fantaisies; Prélude, Choral et Fugue; Prélude, Aria et Final; 3 petits riens; Danse lente;* etc.

Franck, Johann Wolfgang, German composer; b. Unterschwaningen, June (baptized, June 17) 1644; d. c.1710. He was brought up in Ansbach, and served there as court musician from 1665 till 1679; produced 3 operas at the Ansbach court: *Die unvergleichliche Andromeda* (1675); *Der verliebte Föbus* (1678); and *Die drei Töchter Cecrops* (1679). On Jan. 17, 1679, in a fit of jealousy, he allegedly killed the court musician Ulbrecht, and was forced to flee. He found refuge in Hamburg with his wife, Anna Susanna Wilbel (whom he had married in 1666), and gained a prominent position at the Hamburg Opera; between 1679 and 1686 he wrote and produced 17 operas, the most important of which was *Diokletian* (1682). His private life continued to be stormy; he deserted his wife and their 10 children, and went to London, where he remained from 1690 to about 1702. The exact place and date of his death are unknown. In London he organized (with Robert King) a series of Concerts of Vocal and Instrumental Music; publ. 41 English songs. Other publications are: *Geistliche Lieder* (Hamburg, 1681, 1685, 1687, 1700; republ. in 1856 by D.H. Engel, with new words by Osterwald; newly ed. by W. Krabbe and J. Kromolicki in vol. 45 of Denkmäler Deutscher Tonkunst; 12 arrangements for 4 voices by A. von Dommer, publ. 1859; separate reprints by Riemann, Friedlaender, and others); *Remedium melancholiae* (25 secular solo songs with Basso Continuo; London, 1690); arias; etc.

Franck, Joseph, Belgian composer and organist, brother of **César Franck;** b. Liège, Oct. 31, 1825; d. Issy, near Paris, Nov. 20, 1891. He studied organ with Benoist at the Paris Cons., obtaining the first prize

(1852); then was organist at the church of St. Thomas d'Aquin in Paris. He composed sacred music and piano works, and publ. several manuals on harmony, piano technique, and other pedagogical subjects.

Franck, Melchior, German composer; b. Zittau, c.1579; d. Coburg, June 1, 1639. He went to Nuremberg in 1601, and in 1602 obtained the post of Kapellmeister at Coburg, where he remained to the end of his life. He was an excellent contrapuntist; composed sacred and secular vocal music, and exerted considerable influence on his contemporaries. Selections from his instrumental works, edited by F. Bölsche, constitute vol. XVI of Denkmäler Deutscher Tonkunst; vol. XVII of the *Monatshefte für Musikgeschichte* contains a careful description of his printed works, also of MSS preserved in public libraries. Reprints of his sacred vocal works have been publ. by F. Commer, E. Mauersberger, and F. Jöde; secular works in the *Staatliches Liederbuch, Kaiser-Liederbuch,* and other collections.

Franckenstein, Clemens von, German composer; b. Wiesentheid, July 14, 1875; d. Hechendorf, Aug. 19, 1942. He spent his youth in Vienna; then went to Munich, where he studied with Thuille; later took courses with Knorr at the Hoch Cons. in Frankfurt. He traveled with an opera company in the U.S. in 1901; then was engaged as a theater conductor in London (1902–7). In 1912–18 and in 1924–34 was Intendant at the Munich Opera. He wrote several operas, the most successful of which was *Des Kaisers Dichter* (on the life of the Chinese poet Li-Tai Po), performed in Hamburg (Nov. 2, 1920) and elsewhere in Germany. Other operas are *Griselda* (Troppau, 1898), *Fortunatus* (Budapest, 1909), and *Rahab* (Hamburg, 1911). He also wrote several orch. works.

Franco of Cologne, medieval theorist and practical musician. His identity is conjectural; there was a learned man known as Magister Franco of Cologne who flourished as early as the 11th century; several reputable scholars regard him as identical with the musical theorist Franco; against this identification is the improbability of the emergence of theories and usages found in Franco's writings at such an early date. The generally accepted period for his activities is the middle of the 13th century (from 1250 to about 1280). The work on which the reputation of Franco of Cologne rests is the famous treatise *Ars cantus mensurabilis.* Its principal significance is not so much the establishment of a new method of mensural notation as the systematization of rules that had been inadequately or vaguely explained by Franco's predecessors. The treatise is valuable also for the explanation of usages governing the employment of concords and discords. It was reprinted, from different MSS, in Gerbert's *Scriptores* (vol. III) and in Coussemaker's *Scriptores* (vol. I). Gerbert attributes it to a Franco of Paris, a shadowy figure who may have been the author of a treatise and 3 summaries, all beginning

with the words "Gaudent brevitate moderni." The *Ars cantus mensurabilis* is reproduced in English in O. Strunk's *Source Readings in Music History* (N.Y., 1950).

Franco, Johan, American composer; b. Zaandam, the Netherlands, July 12, 1908. He studied at the Cons. of Amsterdam (1929–34); in 1936 he emigrated to America; became a U.S. citizen in 1942; served in the U.S. Army during World War II. He wrote 5 symphs. (1933, 1939, 1940, 1950, 1958); symph. poem, *Péripétie* (1935); 5 "concertos liricos": No. 1 for Violin and Chamber Orch. (1937); No. 2 for Cello and Orch. (1962); No. 3 for Piano and Chamber Orch. (1967); No. 4 for Percussion and Chamber Orch. (1970); No. 5 for Guitar and Chamber Orch. (1973); Violin Concerto (Brussels, Dec. 6, 1939); *Serenata concertante* for Piano and Chamber Orch. (N.Y., March 11, 1940); symph. poem, *Baconiana* (1941); Divertimento for Flute and String Quartet (1945); 6 string quartets (1931–60); 6 partitas for Piano (1940–52); 8 toccatas for Carillon (1953–58); *American Suite* for Carillon (1952); *Supplication* for Orch. (1964); Sonata for Violin and Cello (1965); Sonata for Solo Saxophone (1965); *Triumphe* for Orch. (1967); *Ode* for Male Chorus and Wind Orch. (1968); *Saga of the Sea* for Carillon (1970); numerous vocal works with Orch. and Chorus a cappella; many songs. In all his works Franco follows the ideal of cyclic construction, with Classical symmetry governing not only the larger forms but separate sections of each individual work. His instrumental writing is invariably functional.

Francœur, François, French violinist; b. Paris, Sept. 8, 1698; d. there, Aug. 5, 1787. He was a member of the orch. of the Paris Opéra, a chamber musician to the King, and one of the "24 violons du roi" (1730). Conjointly with his inseparable friend François Rebel, he was director of the Opéra (1751) and Superintendent of the King's Music (1760). He wrote 2 books of violin sonatas; produced 10 operas (in collaboration with Rebel).

Francœur, Louis-Joseph, French violinist, nephew of **François Francœur;** b. Paris, Oct. 8, 1738; d. there, March 10, 1804. He entered the orch. of the Paris Opéra at the age of 14; became its conductor at 27. During the Revolution he was imprisoned as a suspect, but was released after the Thermidor coup d'état (1794) and was appointed director of the Paris Opéra. He wrote an act for the opera *Lindor et Ismène* (Paris, Aug. 29, 1766); publ. a treatise, *Diapason général de tous les instruments à vent* (1772). The MS of his *Essai historique sur l'établissement de l'opéra en France* is preserved in the library of the Paris Cons.

Frandsen, John, respected Danish conductor; b. Copenhagen, July 10, 1918. He was educated at the Royal Danish Cons. in Copenhagen; then was organist at the Domkirke there (1938–53); also made appearances as a conductor. After serving as conductor with the Danish Radio Symph. (1945–46), he became a conductor at the Royal Danish Theater; also made appearances with the Royal Danish Orch. In 1958 he toured the U.S. with the Danish Radio Symph. He was also active as a teacher, both at the Royal Danish Cons. and the Opera School of the Royal Danish Theater. In 1980 he was named orch. counselor of the Danish Radio. He is particularly noted for his outstanding performances of contemporary Danish music.

Frank, Ernst, German conductor and composer; b. Munich, Feb. 7, 1847; d. Oberdöbling, near Vienna, Aug. 17, 1889. He studied with M. de Fontaine (piano) and F. Lachner (composition); in 1868, was conductor at Würzburg; in 1869, chorus master at the Vienna Opera; in 1872–77, conductor at Mannheim; in 1877–79, at Frankfurt; in 1879–87, at the Hannover court opera. He wrote the operas *Adam de la Halle* (Karlsruhe, April 9, 1880), *Hero* (Berlin, Nov. 26, 1884), and *Der Sturm* (after Shakespeare; Hannover, Oct. 14, 1887); completed H. Götz's opera *Francesca da Rimini* and produced it at Mannheim (1877). Frank was a friend of Brahms. Mental illness led to his being committed to an asylum in April 1887.

Frankel, Benjamin, noted English composer; b. London, Jan. 31, 1906; d. there, Feb. 12, 1973. He worked as an apprentice watchmaker in his youth; then went to Germany to study music; returning to London, he earned his living by playing piano or violin in restaurants. It was only then that he began studying composition seriously. In the interim he made arrangements, played in jazz bands, and wrote music for films; some of his film scores, such as that for *The Man in the White Suit,* are notable for their finesse in musical characterization. In 1946 he was appointed to the faculty of the Guildhall School of Music and Drama in London. Frankel also took great interest in social affairs; was for many years a member of the British Communist Party and followed the tenets of socialist realism in some of his compositions.
WORKS: 8 symphs.: No. 1 (1952); No. 2 (Cheltenham, July 13, 1962); No. 3 (1965); No. 4 (London, Dec. 18, 1966); No. 5 (1967); No. 6 (London, March 23, 1969); No. 7 (London, June 4, 1970); No. 8 (1972); *The Aftermath* for Tenor, Trumpet, Harp, and Strings (1947); Violin Concerto (dedicated "to the memory of the 6 million"; Stockholm Festival, June 10, 1956); Bagatelles for 11 Instruments (1959); *Serenata concertante* for Piano Trio and Orch. (1961); Viola Concerto (1966); *A Catalogue of Incidents* for Chamber Orch. (1966); *Overture for a Ceremony* (1970); *Pezzi melodici* for Orch. (Stroud Festival, Oct. 19, 1972); Quintet for Clarinet and String Quartet (1953); 5 string quartets; Piano Quartet; *Pezzi pianissimi* for Clarinet, Cello, and Piano; 2 string trios; 2 sonatas for Solo Violin; *Sonata ebraica* for Cello and Harp; *Elégie juive* for Cello and Piano; Trio for Clarinet, Cello, and Piano; songs.

Frankenstein, Alfred, American writer on music and art; b. Chicago, Oct. 5, 1906; d. San Francisco,

June 22, 1981. He played clarinet in the Civic Orch. of Chicago before turning to writing; from 1935 to 1975 he was music critic of the *San Francisco Chronicle;* concurrently served as its principal art critic; from 1937 to 1963 he was program annotator of the San Francisco Symph. He publ., besides innumerable special articles, a book of essays, *Syncopating Saxophones* (Chicago, 1925); *Modern Guide to Symphonic Music* (N.Y., 1966), and several publications dealing with modern American art. He was the first to publ. the sketches of Victor Hartmann that inspired Mussorgsky's *Pictures at an Exhibition* (*Musical Quarterly,* July 1939).

Frankl, Peter, brilliant Hungarian pianist; b. Budapest, Oct. 2, 1935. He studied at the Franz Liszt Academy of Music in Budapest; his teachers included Zoltán Kodály, Leo Weiner, and Lajos Hernadi. In 1957 he won first prize in the Marguerite Long Competition; also won prizes at competitions in Munich and Rio de Janeiro, which catapulted him into an international career. He made his debut in America in a Dallas recital in 1965. Eventually he moved to London and became a British subject in 1967. In England he formed the Frankl-Pauk-Kirshbaum Trio. His repertoire is extensive, ranging from classical music to contemporary works.

Franklin, Benjamin, great American statesman; b. Boston, Jan. 17, 1706; d. Philadelphia, April 17, 1790. An amateur musician, he invented (1762) the "armonica," an instrument consisting of a row of glass discs of different sizes, set in vibration by light pressure. A string quartet mistakenly attributed to him came to light in Paris in 1945, and was publ. there (1946); the parts are arranged in an ingenious "scordatura"; only open strings are used, so that the quartet can be played by rank amateurs. Franklin also wrote entertainingly on musical subjects; his letters on Scottish music are found in vol. VI of his collected works.

Franko, Nahan, American violinist and conductor, brother of **Sam Franko;** b. New Orleans, July 23, 1861; d. Amityville, N.Y., June 7, 1930. As a child prodigy, he toured with Adelina Patti; then studied in Berlin with Joachim and Wilhelmj. Returning to America, he joined the orch. of the Metropolitan Opera; was its concertmaster from 1883 to 1905; made his debut there as a conductor on April 1, 1900; was the first native-born American to be engaged as conductor there (1904–7).

Franko, Sam, American violinist; b. New Orleans, Jan. 20, 1857; d. New York, May 6, 1937 (from a skull fracture resulting from a fall). He was educated in Germany; studied in Berlin with Joachim, Heinrich de Ahna, and Eduard Rappoldi. Returning to the U.S. in 1880, he joined the Theodore Thomas Orch. in N.Y., and was its concertmaster in 1884–91; in 1883 he toured the U.S. and Canada as a soloist with the Mendelssohn Quintette Club of Boston. In order to prove that prejudice against native orch. players was unfounded, he organized in 1894 the American

Symph. Orch., using 65 American-born performers; this orch. he later used for his Concerts of Old Music (1900–9). In 1910 he went to Berlin and taught at the Stern Cons.; he returned to N.Y. in 1915 and remained there for the rest of his life. At the celebration of his 79th birthday (1936), he gave his valuable collection of music MSS to the Music Division of the N.Y. Public Library. He publ. for piano: *Album Leaf* (1889); *Viennese Silhouettes* (a set of 6 waltzes, 1928); etc.; several violin pieces; practical arrangements for violin and piano of works by Bach, Chopin, Mendelssohn, Rimsky-Korsakov, etc.; also edited classical music albums. His memoirs were publ. posthumously under the title *Chords and Discords* (N.Y., 1938).

Franz, Robert, famous German song composer; b. Halle, June 28, 1815; d. there, Oct. 24, 1892. His family name was **Knauth;** his father, Christoph Franz Knauth, legally adopted the name Franz in 1847. The parents did not favor music as a profession, but Franz learned to play the organ and participated as an accompanist in performances in his native city. In 1835 he went to Dessau, where he studied with Friedrich Schneider; in 1837 he returned to Halle. He publ. his first set of songs in 1843; they attracted immediate attention and were warmly praised by Schumann. Shortly afterward he received an appointment as organist at the Ulrichskirche in Halle, and also as conductor of the Singakademie there; later he received the post of music director at Halle Univ. (1851–67), which conferred on him the title of Mus.Doc. in 1861. The successful development of his career as a musician was interrupted by a variety of nervous disorders and a growing deafness, which forced him to abandon his musical activities in 1868. Liszt, Joachim, and others organized a concert for his benefit, collecting a large sum of money (about $25,000); admirers in America (Otto Dresel, S.B. Schlesinger, B.J. Lang) also contributed funds for his support.

WORKS: Franz was undoubtedly one of the finest masters of the German lied. He publ. about 350 songs; among the best known are *Schlummerlied, Die Lotosblume, Die Widmung,* and *Wonne der Wehmuth.* He also wrote: *117th Psalm* for Double Chorus a cappella; *Kyrie* for Chorus a cappella and Solo Voices; *Liturgy;* arranged works by Bach (*St. Matthew Passion; Christmas Oratorio;* 10 cantatas; etc.) and Handel (*Messiah; L'Allegro, Il Penseroso, ed Il Moderato;* etc.). He publ. *Mitteilungen über J.S. Bachs Magnificat* (Leipzig, 1863); *Offener Brief an Ed. Hanslick über Bearbeitungen älterer Tonwerke, namentlich Bachscher und Händelscher Vokalwerke* (Leipzig, 1871); both were reprinted by R. Bethge as *Gesammelte Schriften über die Wiederbelebung Bachscher und Händelscher Werke* (Leipzig, 1910).

Fränzl, Ferdinand, German violinist and composer, son of **Ignaz Fränzl;** b. Schwetzingen, May 20, 1770; d. Mannheim, Oct. 27, 1833. He studied with his father; later was a pupil in composition of F.X. Richter and Pleyel at Strasbourg, and of Mattei at Bologna. He entered the Mannheim court orch. at the age of 22; in 1785 began to travel on concert tours with his father. He was appointed conductor of the Munich Opera in 1806, but continued his tours; retired in 1826; finally settled in Mannheim. As a master violinist, he enjoyed great renown. A prolific composer, he wrote 8 violin concertos; Double Concerto for 2 Violins; 6 operas; 9 string quartets; 6 string trios; symphs.; overtures; songs.

Fränzl, Ignaz, German violinist and composer, father of **Ferdinand Fränzl;** b. Mannheim, June 3, 1736; d. there, Sept. 3, 1811. He entered the Mannheim court orch. as a boy of 11; became co-concertmaster in 1774, and was conductor from 1790 to 1803. He made several concert tours with his son; composed symphs. and music for the violin, and also wrote for the stage. His singspiel *Die Luftbälle* was produced in Mannheim with excellent success (April 15, 1787); he also wrote music for Shakespeare's plays.

Fraschini, Gaetano, noted Italian tenor; b. Pavia, Feb. 16, 1816; d. Naples, May 23, 1887. He studied with F. Moretti; made his debut in Pavia in 1837; subsequently sang in Milan, Venice, Trieste, Rome, and other Italian cities; also appeared in London at Her Majesty's Theatre (1847) and Drury Lane (1868). He created the role of Genaro in Donizetti's *Caterina Cornaro;* much esteemed by Verdi, he sang in the premieres of *Attila, Il Corsaro, La battaglia di Legnano, Alzira, Stiffelio,* and *Un ballo in maschera.* The opera house in his native city of Pavia is named for him.

Frederick II (Frederick the Great) of Prussia; b. Berlin, Jan. 24, 1712; d. Potsdam, Aug. 17, 1786. He was an enlightened patron of music, a flute player of considerable skill, and an amateur composer. He studied flute with Quantz; in 1740, when he ascended to the throne, he established a court orch. and an opera house; Bach's son Carl Philipp Emanuel was his harpsichordist until 1767. In 1747 J.S. Bach himself was invited to Potsdam; the fruit of this visit was Bach's *Musical Offering,* written on a theme by Frederick II. A collection of 25 flute sonatas and 4 concertos by Frederick was publ. by Spitta (3 vols., Leipzig, 1889; reprinted, N.Y., 1967); other works were publ. in vol. XX of *Die Musik am preussischen Hofe.* Selections from different compositions were edited by Barge, G. Lenzewski, E. Schwarz-Reiflingen, H. Osthoff, G. Müller, G. Thouret, and others. Besides instrumental works, Frederick contributed arias to several operas: *Demofoonte* by Graun (1746); *Il Re pastore* (1747; with Quantz and others); *Galatea ed Acide* (1748; with Hasse, Graun, Quantz, and Nichelmann); and *Il trionfo della fedeltà* (1753; with Hasse and others).

Freed, Isadore, American composer; b. Brest-Litovsk, Russia, March 26, 1900; d. Rockville Center, Long Island, N.Y., Nov. 10, 1960. He came to the U.S. at an early age; graduated from the Univ. of Pa. in 1918 (Mus.Bac.); then studied with Ernest Bloch and with Vincent d'Indy in Paris; returned to the U.S. in

1934; held various teaching positions; in 1944 was appointed head of the music dept. at Hartt College of Music in Hartford, Conn.

WORKS: FOR THE STAGE: *Vibrations*, ballet (Philadelphia, 1928); operas: *Homo Sum* (1930) and *The Princess and the Vagabond* (Hartford, May 13, 1948). FOR ORCH.: *Jeux de timbres* (Paris, 1933); Symph. No. 1 (1941); *Appalachian Symphonic Sketches* (Chautauqua, N.Y., July 31, 1946); *Festival Overture* (San Francisco, Nov. 14, 1946); Rhapsody for Trombone and Orch. (radio premiere, N.Y., Jan. 7, 1951); Symph. No. 2 for Brass (San Francisco, Feb. 8, 1951, composer conducting); Violin Concerto (N.Y., Nov. 13, 1951); Cello Concerto (1952); Concertino for English Horn and Orch. (1953). CHAMBER MUSIC: 3 string quartets (1931, 1932, 1937); Trio for Flute, Viola, and Harp (1940); *Triptych* for Violin, Viola, Cello, and Piano (1943); Passacaglia for Cello and Piano (1947); Quintet for Woodwinds and Horn (Hartford, Dec. 2, 1949); Sonatina for Oboe and Piano (Boston, March 31, 1954); also choral works; piano and organ pieces; songs. He was co-editor of *Masters of Our Day*, contemporary educational material for piano (N.Y., 1936–37).

Freed, Richard (Donald), distinguished American music critic; b. Chicago, Dec. 27, 1928. He studied at the Univ. of Chicago; then held various newspaper jobs and subsequently wrote for the *Saturday Review* and the *New York Times* (1965). From 1966 to 1970 he was assistant to the director of the Eastman School of Music in Rochester, N.Y.; in 1973 he joined the staff of *Stereo Review;* other positions were as a record critic for the *Washington Star* (1972–75) and the *Washington Post* (since 1976); program annotator for the St. Louis Symph. Orch. (since 1973), the Philadelphia Orch. (since 1974), the Houston Symph. Orch. (1977–80), and the National Symph. Orch. of Washington, D.C. (since 1977). In 1974 he was appointed executive director of the Music Critics Association. He also contributed reviews and articles to numerous periodicals and served as a consultant to performing and funding organizations.

Freeman, Harry Lawrence, black American composer; b. Cleveland, Oct. 9, 1869; d. New York, March 24, 1954. He studied theory with J.H. Beck and piano with E. Schonert and Carlos Sobrino; taught at Wilberforce Univ. (1902–4) and the Salem School of Music (1910–13); organized and directed the Freeman School of Music (1911–22) and the Freeman School of Grand Opera (from 1923); conducted various theater orchs. and opera companies. In 1920 he organized the Negro Opera Co.; in 1930 received the Harmon Gold Award; conducted a pageant, *O Sing a New Song*, at the Chicago World's Fair in 1934. He was the first black composer to conduct a symph. orch. in his own work (Minneapolis, 1907), and the first of his race to write large operatic compositions. All his music is written in folk-song style; his settings are in simple harmonies; his operas are constructed of songs and choruses in simple concatenation of separate numbers.

WORKS: Grand operas (all on Negro, oriental,

and Indian themes): *The Martyr* (Denver, 1893); *Valdo* (Cleveland, May 1906); *Zuluki* (1898); *African Kraal* (Wilberforce Univ., Chicago, June 30, 1903, with an all-black cast, composer conducting; revised 1934); *The Octoroon* (1904); *The Tryst* (N.Y., May 1911); *The Prophecy* (N.Y., 1912); *The Plantation* (1914); *Athalia* (1916); *Vendetta* (N.Y., Nov. 12, 1923); *American Romance*, jazz opera (1927); *Voodoo* (N.Y., Sept. 10, 1928); *Leah Kleschna* (1930); *Uzziah* (1931); *Zululand*, a tetralogy of music dramas: *Nada, The Lily* (1941–44; vocal score contains 2,150 pp.), *Allah* (1947), and *The Zulu King* (1934); *The Slave*, ballet for Choral Ensemble and Orch. (Harlem, N.Y., Sept. 22, 1932); songs (*Whither, If thou did'st love*, etc.).

Freer, Eleanor (née **Everest**), American composer; b. Philadelphia, May 14, 1864; d. Chicago, Dec. 13, 1942. She studied singing in Paris (1883–86) with Mathilde Marchesi; then took a course in composition with Benjamin Godard. Upon her return to the U.S., she taught singing at the National Cons. of Music in N.Y. (1889–91). On April 25, 1891, she married Archibald Freer of Chicago; they lived in Leipzig in 1892–99; then settled in Chicago, where she studied theory with Bernard Ziehn (1902–7). She publ. some light pieces under the name Everest while still a young girl, but most of her larger works were written after 1919.

WORKS: 9 operas, of which the following were performed: *The Legend of the Piper* (South Bend, Ind., Feb. 28, 1924); *The Court Jester* (Lincoln, Nebr., 1926); *A Christmas Tale* (Houston, Dec. 27, 1929); *Frithiof* (Chicago, Feb. 1, 1931; in concert form); *A Legend of Spain* (Milwaukee, June 19, 1931; in concert form); a song cycle (settings of Elizabeth Barrett Browning's entire *Sonnets from the Portuguese*); about 150 songs; piano pieces. She also wrote an autobiography, *Recollections and Reflections of an American Composer* (Chicago, 1929).

Freitas Branco, Luíz de, significant Portuguese composer; b. Lisbon, Oct. 12, 1890; d. there, Nov. 27, 1955. He studied in Lisbon with Tomás Borba; became influenced by the theories of the Belgian modernist Désiré Pâque, who lived in Lisbon at the time. In 1910 Freitas Branco went to Berlin to study with Humperdinck, and then to Paris for studies with Gabriel Grovlez; returning to Portugal in 1916, he engaged primarily in teaching. His music is cast in an impressionistic vein.

WORKS: *Manfredo*, after Byron's poem, for Soloists, Chorus, Organ, and Orch. (1905); symph. poems: *Depois de uma Leitura de Antero de Quental* (1907–8) and *Paraísos artificiais* (1913); 2 symph. pieces, each entitled *Suite Alentejana* (1910, 1927); *Vathek*, symph. variations on an oriental theme (1914); Violin Concerto (1916); *Balada* for Piano and Orch. (1917); *Cena lírica* for Cello and Orch. (1917); 4 symphs. (1924, 1926, 1943, 1952); 2 violin sonatas (1907, 1928); String Quartet (1911); Cello Sonata (1913); *10 Preludes* for Piano (1918); Piano Sonatina (1930); choruses; songs.

Fremaux, Louis, eminent French conductor; b. Aire-sur-la-Lys, Aug. 13, 1921. He attended the Cons. in Valenciennes, but his education was interrupted by World War II. He served in the Résistance during the Nazi occupation. After the war he studied conducting at the Paris Cons. with Louis Fourestier, graduating in 1952 with the first prize. From 1956 to 1966 he was chief conductor of the Monte Carlo National Opera and Orch. In 1968 he founded the Orch. de Lyon; was its music director until 1971. From 1969 to 1978 he was music director of the City of Birmingham Symph. Orch. In 1979 he became chief conductor of the Sydney (Australia) Symph. Orch.

Fremstad, Olive, famous Swedish-born American dramatic soprano; b. Stockholm, March 14, 1871 (entered into the parish register as the daughter of an unmarried woman, Anna Peterson); d. Irvington-on-Hudson, N.Y., April 21, 1951. She was adopted by an American couple of Scandinavian origin, who took her to Minnesota; she studied piano in Minneapolis; came to N.Y. in 1890 and took singing lessons with E.F. Bristol; then held several church positions; in 1892 she sang for the first time with an orch. (under C. Zerrahn) in Boston. In 1893 she went to Berlin to study with Lilli Lehmann; made her operatic debut in Cologne as Azucena in *Il Trovatore* (1895); sang contralto parts in Wagner's operas at Bayreuth during the summer of 1896; in 1897 made her London debut; also sang in Cologne, Vienna, Amsterdam, and Antwerp. From 1900 to 1903 she was at the Munich Opera. She made her American debut as Sieglinde at the Metropolitan Opera on Nov. 25, 1903. Subsequently she sang soprano parts in Wagnerian operas; at first she was criticized in the press for her lack of true soprano tones; however, she soon triumphed over these difficulties, and became known as a soprano singer to the exclusion of contralto parts. She sang Carmen with great success at the Metropolitan (March 5, 1906), with Caruso; her performance of Isolde under Mahler (Jan. 1, 1908) produced a deep impression; until 1914 she was one of the brightest stars of the Metropolitan Opera, specializing in Wagnerian roles, but she was also successful in *Tosca* and other Italian operas. She sang Salomé at the first American performance of the Strauss opera (N.Y., Jan. 22, 1907) and in Paris (May 8, 1907). After her retirement from the Metropolitan, she appeared with the Manhattan Opera, the Boston Opera, and the Chicago Opera, and in concerts; presented her last song recital in N.Y. on Jan. 19, 1920. In 1906 she married Edson Sutphen of N.Y. (divorced in 1911); in 1916 she married her accompanist, **Harry Lewis Brainard** (divorced in 1925). In Willa Cather's novel *The Song of the Lark,* the principal character was modeled after Olive Fremstad.

French, Jacob, American composer of psalm tunes; b. Stoughton, Mass., July 15, 1754; d. Simsbury, Conn., May 1817. He was co-founder, with William Billings, of the Stoughton Music Society in 1774; fought at the battle of Bunker Hill in the Revolutionary War; was one of the few survivors of the Cherry Valley Massacre. After the war he became a singing teacher, retiring in 1814. He publ. *New American Melody* (1789), *Psalmodist's Companion* (1793), and *Harmony of Harmony* (1802).

Freni, Mirella (real last name, **Fregni**), noted Italian soprano; b. Modena, Feb. 27, 1935. Curiously enough, her mother and the mother of the future celebrated tenor Luciano Pavarotti worked for a living in the same cigarette factory; curiouser still, the future opera stars shared the same wet nurse. Mirella Freni studied voice with her uncle, Dante Arcelli; made her first public appearance at the age of 11; her accompanist was a child pianist named Leone Magiera, whom she married in 1955. She later studied voice with Ettore Campogalliani; made her operatic debut in Modena on Feb. 3, 1955, as Micaela in *Carmen;* then sang in provincial Italian opera houses. In 1959 she sang with the Amsterdam Opera Co. at the Holland Festival; then at the Glyndebourne Festival (1960), Covent Garden in London (1961), and La Scala in Milan (1962). She gained acclaim as Mimi in the film version of *La Bohème,* produced at La Scala on Jan. 31, 1963, with Herbert von Karajan conducting; when La Scala toured Russia in 1964, Freni joined the company and sang Mimi at the Bolshoi Theater in Moscow. She also chose the role of Mimi for her American debut with the Metropolitan Opera in N.Y. on Sept. 29, 1965. She subsequently sang with the Vienna State Opera, the Munich Opera, the San Carlo Co. in Naples, and the Rome Opera. In 1976 she traveled with the Paris Opéra during its first American tour. In addition to Mimi, she sang the roles of Susanna in *Le nozze di Figaro,* Zerlina in *Don Giovanni,* Violetta in *La Traviata,* Amelia in *Simon Boccanegra,* and Manon.

Freschi, (Giovanni) Domenico, Italian composer; b. Bassano, Vicenza, c.1625; d. Vicenza, July 2, 1710. He was maestro di cappella at the Cathedral of Vicenza from 1656 until his death; publ. 2 masses and a number of Psalms (1660, 1673). In 1677 he went to Venice, remaining there for 8 years; wrote 15 operas, which were successfully produced there, and a series of short pieces for an opera house in Piazzola, near Padua. He also wrote at least 3 oratorios, including *Giuditta* and *Il Miracolo del mago.*

Frescobaldi, Girolamo, one of the greatest Italian organists and composers of the Renaissance; b. Ferrara (baptized, Sept. 9), 1583; d. Rome, March 1, 1643. He studied with Luzzasco Luzzaschi in Ferrara; by the age of 14 was organist at the Accademia della Morte in Ferrara; in early 1607 became organist of S. Maria in Trastevere; then, in June 1607, traveled to Brussels in the retinue of the Papal Nuncio; publ. his first work, a collection of 5-part madrigals, in Antwerp in 1608, printed by Phalèse. Returning to Rome in the same year, he was appointed organist at St. Peter's as successor to Ercole Pasquini. He retained this all-important post until his death, with the exception of the years 1628 to 1634, when he was court organist in Florence. A significant indication of Frescobaldi's importance among musicians of his time was that Froberger, who was court organist in Vienna, came to Rome especially to study with Frescobaldi (1637–41). Frescobaldi's place in music history is very great; particularly as a keyboard composer, he exercised a decisive influence on the style of the early Baroque; he enlarged the expressive resources of keyboard music so as to include daring chromatic progressions and acrid passing dissonances, "durezze" (literally, "harshnesses"); in Frescobaldi's terminology "toccata di durezza" signified a work using dissonances; he used similar procedures in organ variations on chorale themes, "fiori musicali" ("musical flowers"). His ingenious employment of variations greatly influenced the entire development of Baroque music.

WORKS: *Fantasie a 2, 3 e 4* (Milan, 1608, Book I); *Ricercari e canzoni francese* (Rome, 1615); *Toccate e partite d'intavolatura di cembalo* (Rome, 1615); *Il 2° libro di toccate, canzoni, versi d'inni, magnificat, gagliarde, correnti ed altre partite d'intavolatura di cembalo ed organo* (Rome, 1616); *Capricci sopra diversi soggetti* (Rome, 1624); *Arie musicale a più voci* (Florence, 1630); *Fiori musicali di diverse compositioni Toccate, Kirie, Canzoni, Capricci e Recercari in partitura* (Venice, 1935); *Canzoni alla francese* was publ. posthumously in Rome, 1945. A complete ed. of organ and other keyboard works by Frescobaldi was issued in 5 vols., ed. by P. Pidoux in Kassel (1950–54); *Keyboard Compositions Preserved in Manuscripts*, No. 30 of Corpus of Early Keyboard Music (3 vols., 1968); selected organ works, in 2 vols., were publ. in Leipzig in 1943–48; *Fiori musicale & Toccate e Partite* in 2 vols. was publ. in Rome in 1936–37; *Fiori musicale* was also brought out by J. Bonnet and A. Guilmant (Paris, 1922); *25 Canzoni, 7 Toccate & Correnti* was ed. by F. Boghen (Milan, 1918); *Toccate, Ricercari, Canzoni*, etc. was issued by Casella in *I classici della musica italiana* (Milan, 1919); numerous other eds. of selected pieces are also available. A "complete works" ed. is now in progress, under the auspices of the Comune di Ferrara and the Società Italiana di Musicologica; the first vol., issued in 1975, is *Due messe a otto voci.*

Freund, John Christian, English-American music journalist; b. London, Nov. 22, 1848; d. Mt. Vernon, N.Y., June 3, 1924. He studied music in London and Oxford; in 1871 arrived in N.Y., where he became the editor of the *Musical and Dramatic Times;* in 1890 began publishing a commercial magazine, *Music Trades.* In 1898 he founded the weekly magazine *Musical America* and was its editor until his death. In his editorials he fulminated against the rival magazine *Musical Courier,* and also wrote sharp polemical articles denouncing composers and music critics who disagreed with his viewpoint; in this respect he was a typical representative of the personal type of musical journalism of the time.

Freund, Marya, remarkable German soprano; b. Breslau, Dec. 12, 1876; d. Paris, May 21, 1966. She first studied violin, taking lessons with Sarasate; then began to study singing; made successful appearances in Europe and America with symph. orchs. and in recital. Her career as a singer was mainly significant, however, not for the excellence of her performances in the standard repertoire, but for her devotion to modern music. She sang the principal vocal works by Schoenberg, Stravinsky, Ravel, Bloch, Milhaud, and many others; eventually settled in Paris as a singing teacher.

Frey, Emil, eminent Swiss pianist and composer; b. Baden, in the canton of Aargau, April 8, 1889; d. Zürich, May 20, 1946. He studied musical subjects with Otto Barblan at the Geneva Cons.; at the age of 15 was accepted as a student of Louis Diémer in piano and Widor in composition; in 1907 went to Berlin, and later to Bucharest, where he became a court pianist. In 1910 he won the Anton Rubinstein prize for his Piano Trio in St. Petersburg; on the strength of this success he was engaged to teach at the Moscow Cons. (1912–17). Returning to Switzerland after the Russian Revolution, he joined the faculty of the Zürich Cons.; he continued his concert career throughout Europe and also in South America. He wrote 2 symphs. (the first with a choral finale), Piano Concerto, Violin Concerto, Cello Concerto, Swiss Festival Overture, Piano Quintet, String Quartet, Piano Trio, Violin Sonata, Cello Sonata, several piano sonatas, piano suites, and sets of piano variations; publ. a piano instruction manual, *Bewusst gewordenes Klavierspiel und seine technischen Grundlagen* (Zürich, 1933).

Frey, Walter, Swiss pianist, brother of **Emil Frey;** b. Basel, Jan. 26, 1898. He studied piano with F. Niggli and theory with Andreae. From 1925 to 1958 he was, jointly with his brother, an instructor in piano at the Zürich Cons.; concurrently evolved an active concert career in Germany and Scandinavia; specialized in modern piano music and gave first performances of several piano concertos by contemporary composers. He publ. (with Willi Schuh) a collection, *Schweizerische Klaviermusik aus der Zeit der Klassik und Romantik* (Zürich, 1937).

Fricker, Peter Racine, significant English composer; b. London, Sept. 5, 1920. He studied at the Royal College of Music and later with Mátyás Seiber. In 1952 he was appointed music director at Morley College in London; taught composition at the Royal College of Music in 1955–64. In 1964 he went to Santa Barbara, Calif., as a visiting prof. at the Univ. of Calif.; in 1970 he became chairman of the music dept. there.

WORKS: *Rondo scherzoso* for Orch. (1948); Symph. No. 1 (1949; Cheltenham Festival, July 5, 1950; awarded the Koussevitzky prize); Symph. No. 2 (Liverpool, July 26, 1951); *Canterbury Prologue,* ballet (London, 1951); Concerto for Viola and Orch. (Edinburgh, Sept. 3, 1953); Piano Concerto (London, March 21, 1954); *Rapsodia concertante* for Violin and Orch. (Cheltenham Festival, July 15, 1954); *Litany* for Double String Orch. (1955); *Concertante* for 3 Pianos, Strings, and Timpani (London, Aug. 10,

1956); *The Death of Vivien*, radio opera (1956); *A Vision of Judgment*, oratorio (Leeds, Oct. 13, 1958); *Comedy Overture* (1958); Toccata for Piano and Orch. (1959); Symph. No. 3 (London, Nov. 8, 1960); *O longs désirs*, song cycle for Soprano and Orch. (1964); Symph. No. 4, "in memoriam Mátyás Seiber" (Cheltenham, Feb. 14, 1967); *3 Scenes* for Orch. (Santa Barbara, Feb. 26, 1967); *7 Counterpoints* for Orch. (Pasadena, Oct. 21, 1967); *Magnificat* for Soloists, Chorus, and Orch. (Santa Barbara, May 27, 1968); *The Roofs* for Coloratura Soprano and Percussion (1970); *Nocturne* for Chamber Orch. (1971); *Introitus* for Orch. (Canterbury, June 24, 1972); Symph. No. 5 (1975). Chamber music: Wind Quintet (1947); *3 Sonnets of Cecco Angiolieri* for Tenor, Wind Quintet, Cello, and Double Bass (1947); String Quartet in One Movement (1948; Brussels Festival, 1950); *Prelude, Elegy and Finale* for Strings (1949); Concerto for Violin and Chamber Orch. (1950); Violin Sonata (1950); *Concertante* for English Horn and Strings (1950); String Quartet No. 2 (1953); Horn Sonata (1955; premiered by Dennis Brain); Suite for Recorders (1956); Cello Sonata (1957); Octet for Wind and String Instruments (1958); *Serenade No. 1* for 6 Instruments (1959); *Serenade No. 2* for Flute, Oboe, and Piano (1959); *4 Dialogues* for Oboe and Piano (1965); *5 Canons* for 2 Flutes and 2 Oboes (1966); Fantasy for Viola and Piano (1966); *Concertante No. 4* for Flute, Oboe, Violin, and Strings (Santa Cruz, Calif., Feb. 25, 1969); *Some Superior Nonsense* for Tenor, Flute, Oboe, and Harpsichord (Santa Barbara, Feb. 26, 1969); *Serenade No. 3* for Saxophone Quartet (1969); *3 Arguments* for Bassoon and Cello (1969); Suite for Harpsichord (1957); *14 Aubades* for Piano (1958); 12 studies for Piano (1961); *Commissary Report* for Men's Voices (1965); *Refrains* for Solo Oboe (1968); *Paseo* for Guitar (1969); *Concertante No. 5* for Piano and String Quartet (Santa Barbara, Jan. 29, 1972); *Come Sleep* for Contralto, Alto, and Bass Clarinet (1972); *The Groves of Dodona* for 6 Flutes (1973); *Spirit Puck* for Clarinet and Percussion (1974); *Trio-Sonata* for Organ (1974); String Quartet No. 3 (1975).

Fricsay, Ferenc, Hungarian conductor; b. Budapest, Aug. 9, 1914; d. Basel, Feb. 20, 1963. He received his early musical training from his father, a military-band leader; he was barely 6 years old when he was accepted as a pupil in the music class for beginners at the Budapest high school; as he grew up he took piano lessons with Bartók and composition with Kodály. He also learned to play almost all orch. instruments. At the age of 15 he conducted a radio performance of his father's military band; in 1934 he became orch. conductor at Szeged, and in 1936 conducted the opera there. In 1944 he returned to Budapest; in 1945 made his debut as conductor at the Budapest Opera. In 1947 he conducted at the Salzburg Festival; subsequently made a European tour as guest conductor; also toured South America. In 1948–52 he was Generalmusikdirektor of the Berlin City Opera; from 1949 to 1954 was artistic director of the radio orch. RIAS in the American sector of divided Berlin, and was regular conductor there

until 1961. On Nov. 13, 1953, he made a highly successful American debut with the Boston Symph. Orch.; in 1954 was engaged as conductor of the Houston Symph. Orch., but soon resigned, owing to disagreement on musical policy with the management. He was Generalmusikdirektor of the Bavarian State Opera in Munich from 1956–58. He then settled in Switzerland, continuing to conduct occasional guest engagements, until his illness (leukemia) forced him to abandon all activities.

Fried, Oskar, German conductor and composer; b. Berlin, Aug. 10, 1871; d. Moscow, July 5, 1941. He studied with Humperdinck in Frankfurt and P. Scharwenka in Berlin; played the horn in various orchs. until the performance of his choral work with orch. *Das trunkene Lied*, given by Karl Muck in Berlin (April 15, 1904), attracted much favorable attention; he continued to compose prolifically; wrote *Verklärte Nacht* for Solo Voices and Orch.; *Andante und Scherzo* for Wind Instruments, 2 Harps, and Kettledrums; *Präludium und Doppelfuge* for String Orch.; etc. At the same time he began his career as a conductor, achieving considerable renown in Europe; he was conductor of the Stern Choral Society in Berlin (from 1904), of the Gesellschaft der Musikfreunde in Berlin (1907–10), and of the Berlin Symph. Orch. (1925–26); left Berlin in 1934 and went to Russia; became a Soviet citizen in 1940. For several years before his death he was conductor of the Tiflis Opera, in the Caucasus; later was chief conductor of the All-Union Radio Orch. in Moscow.

Friedberg, Carl, German pianist; b. Bingen, Sept. 18, 1872; d. Merano, Italy, Sept. 8, 1955. He studied piano at the Frankfurt Cons. with Kwast, Knorr, and Clara Schumann; also took a course in composition with Humperdinck; subsequently taught piano at the Frankfurt Cons. (1893–1904) and at the Cologne Cons. (1904–14). In 1914 he made his first American tour, with excellent success; taught piano at the Inst. of Musical Art in N.Y.; was a member of the faculty of the Juilliard School of Music in N.Y. Among his pupils were Percy Grainger, Ethel Leginska, Elly Ney, and other celebrated pianists.

Friedheim, Arthur, pianist; b. St. Petersburg (of German parents), Oct. 26, 1859; d. New York, Oct. 19, 1932. He was a pupil of Anton Rubinstein and Liszt, and became particularly known as an interpreter of Liszt's works. He made his first American tour in 1891; taught at the Chicago Musical College in 1897; then traveled; lived in London, Munich, and (after 1915) N.Y. as a teacher and pianist; composed a Piano Concerto and many pieces for solo piano, as well as an opera, *Die Tänzerin* (Karlsruhe, 1897). His memoirs, *Life and Liszt: The Recollections of a Concert Pianist*, were publ. posthumously (N.Y., 1961).

Friedhofer, Hugo, American composer of film music; b. San Francisco, May 3, 1901; d. Los Angeles, May 17, 1981. He played cello in theater orchs.; studied composition with Domenico Brescia. In 1929 he went to Hollywood, where he worked as an arranger and composer for early sound films. In 1935 he was engaged as an orchestrator for Warner Brothers, and received valuable instruction from Erich Wolfgang Korngold and Max Steiner. In Los Angeles he attended Schoenberg's seminars and took additional lessons in composition with Ernst Toch and Kanitz; he also had some instruction with Nadia Boulanger during her sojourn in California. He wrote his first complete film score for *The Adventures of Marco Polo* in 1938, and in thc following ycars composed music for about 70 films. His film music for *The Best Years of Our Lives* won the Academy Award in 1946. His other film scores included *Vera Cruz, Violent Saturday, The Sun Also Rises,* and *The Young Lions.* Friedhofer was highly esteemed by the Hollywood theatrical community and by his colleagues in the film studios for his ability to create a congenial musical background, alternatively lyrical and dramatic, for the action on the screen, never sacrificing the purely musical quality for the sake of external effect. He was the only California native of all the famous film composers in Hollywood, the majority of whom were Germans and Austrians. When a Hollywood mogul told Friedhofer to use numerous French horns since the film in question was taking place in France, he acquiesced and, by extension of the dictum, used an English-horn solo to illustrate the approach to the cliffs of Dover of the film characters fleeing the French Revolution.

Friedlaender, Max, eminent German musicologist; b. Brieg, Silesia, Oct. 12, 1852; d. Berlin, May 2, 1934. He was first a bass; studied voice with Manuel García in London and Julius Stockhausen in Frankfurt; appeared at the London Monday Popular Concerts in 1880. He returned to Germany in 1881 and took a course at Berlin Univ. with Spitta; obtained the degree of Dr.Phil. at Rostock with the thesis *Beiträge zur Biographie Franz Schuberts* (1887); then was Privatdozent at Berlin Univ. in 1894, and a prof. and director of music there from 1903. He was exchange prof. at Harvard Univ. in 1911; lectured at many American univs. and received the degree of LL.D. from the Univ. of Wisconsin; retired in 1932. He discovered the MSS of more than 100 lost songs by Schubert and publ. them in his complete edition (7 vols.) of Schubert's songs. Together with Johann Bolte and Johann Meier, he searched for years in every corner of the German Empire in quest of folk songs still to be found among the people; some of these he publ. in a vol. under the title *100 deutsche Volkslieder* in *Goethe Jahrbuch* (1885); was editor of *Volksliederbuch für gemischten Chor* (1912); edited songs of Mozart, Schumann, and Mendelssohn, Beethoven's "Scotch Songs," the first version of Brahms's *Deutsche Volkslieder* (1926), *Volksliederbuch für die deutsche Jugend* (1928), etc.

Friedman, Erick, distinguished American violinist; b. Newark, N.J., Aug. 16, 1939. He first studied violin with his father, an amateur violinist; at the age of 10 he enrolled at the Juilliard School of Music in N.Y., in the class of Ivan Galamian; at 17 he commenced studies with Jascha Heifetz; he also received guidance from Nathan Milstein. His progress was rapid, and he soon garnered prizes in several violin competitions; he then appeared as soloist with the Boston Symph., Chicago Symph., Pittsburgh Symph., N.Y. Phil., Philadelphia Orch., Berlin Phil., Orch. de Paris, and other orchs.; made many extensive concert tours, playing in Europe, the Far East, and South America. Friedman's performances are characterized by a careful regard for the composer's intentions and a technical skill that rank him among the finest violinists of his generation.

Friedman, Ignaz, famous Polish pianist; b. Podgorze, near Cracow, Feb. 14, 1882; d. Sydney, Australia, Jan. 26, 1948. He studied music theory with Hugo Riemann in Leipzig and piano with Leschetizky in Vienna. In 1904 he launched an extensive career as a concert pianist; gave about 2,800 concerts in Europe, America, Australia, Japan, China, and South Africa. In 1941 he settled in Sydney. He was renowned as an interpreter of Chopin; prepared an annotated edition of Chopin's works in 12 vols., publ. by Breitkopf & Härtel; also edited piano compositions of Schumann and Liszt for Universal Edition in Vienna. Friedman was himself a composer; he wrote a hundred or so pieces for piano in an effective salon manner, among them a group of *Fantasiestücke.*

Friedman, Ken, American avant-garde composer; b. New London, Conn., Sept. 19, 1939. He became associated with Richard Maxfield, who initiated him into the arcana of modern music. Friedman developed feverish activities in intellectual and musical fields; edited ephemeral magazines; directed an underground radio program, "Garnisht Kigele," in Mt. Carroll, Ill.; was a founder of the avant-garde group Fluxus. As an avant-garde artist and designer, he exhibited his products in Brno, Nice, Cologne, Copenhagen, Trieste, and San Diego; staged happenings and audiovisual events in California, announcing himself as "The Truly Incredible Friedman." Most of his works are verbal exhortations to existentialist actions, e.g., *Scrub Piece* (scrubbing a statue in a public square), *Riverboat Brawl* (starting a brawl in a riverboat at Disneyland), *Goff Street* (a "theft event," transplanting a street sign), *Come Ze Revolution* (chanting pseudo-Greek songs), *Watermelon* (splitting a watermelon with a karate blow), etc. He also composed a *Quiet Sonata* (1969) for 75 Truncated Guitar Fingerboards with no strings attached; realized for Nam June Paik his alleged *Young Penis Symphony* for 10 ditto, and had it performed at a hidden retreat in San Francisco.

Friedman, Richard, American composer; b. New York, Jan. 6, 1944. He received his formal education in exact sciences, specializing in electronics. He worked at the Intermedia Electronic Music Studio at N.Y. Univ. (1966–68) in collaboration with Morton Subotnick; prepared electronic tape pieces, mostly of scientific inspiration: *Lumia Mix* (1967); *Crescent* (1967); and *To the Star Messenger* (1968), a melodrama depicting the discovery of the moons of Jupiter by Galileo. Another piece of the period was *Alchemical Manuscript* (1968), inspired by the arcane lore of the searchers for the philosopher's stone. In 1968 Friedman moved to California; worked with the music dept. of the radio station KPFA in Berkeley; arranged numerous broadcasts of electronic materials, notably *Serenade* for Viola on Tape and *4-Pole Neuro-Magnet with Double Cross*, composed in 1970. Taking advantage of the techniques of amplification, Friedman was able to create the sound of an orch. of violas with a single viola player. In most of his works he applies the avant-garde philosophy of tonal frugality, limiting his resources to a few notes. Apart from his radio work, he conducted information/media performances at the San Francisco Museum of Art under the general title "Outside/Inside," utilizing closed-circuit television, inflatable structures, and sculptures activated by light beams.

Friedrich II (der Grosse). See **Frederick II.**

Fries, Wulf (Christian Julius), German-American cellist and teacher; b. Garbeck, Jan. 10, 1825; d. Roxbury, Mass., April 29, 1902. As a cellist, he played in Norway, in the Bergen theater orch. (from 1842), and at Ole Bull's concerts. In 1847 he went to Boston, where he became a founding member of the Mendelssohn Quintette Club, with A. Fries (first violin), Gerloff (2nd violin), Edward Lehmann (first viola), Oscar Greiner (2nd viola), and himself as cellist. He belonged to it for 23 years; also figured in the Musical Fund Society and the Harvard Musical Assoc.; played in trios with Anton Rubinstein, and until 1901 took part in concerts in New England.

Frijsh, Povla (real name, **Paula Frisch**), concert soprano; b. Aarhus, Denmark, Aug. 3, 1881; d. Blue Hill, Maine, July 10, 1960. She first studied piano and theory in Copenhagen with O. Christensen, later voice in Paris with Jean Périer; made her debut in Paris at the age of 19; appeared in concert and recital in Paris and briefly in opera in Copenhagen; made her American debut in 1915; gave many first performances of modern vocal music (Bloch's *Poèmes d'automne*, Loeffler's *Canticle of the Sun*, songs by Griffes, etc.), and made a specialty of modern international song literature. She introduced Negro spirituals to Paris and Copenhagen.

Friml, Rudolf, famous Bohemian-American operetta composer; b. Prague, Dec. 2, 1879; d. Hollywood, Nov. 12, 1972. His original family name was **Frimel.** He was a pupil at the Prague Cons. of Juranek (piano) and Foerster (theory and composition); toured Austria, England, Germany, and Russia as accompanist to Kubelik, the violinist, coming with him to the U.S. in 1900 and again in 1906; remained in the U.S. after the 2nd tour; gave numerous recitals, appeared as soloist with several of the large symph. orchs. (played his Piano Concerto with the N.Y. Symph. Orch.), and composed assiduously; lived in N.Y. and Hollywood, composing for motion pictures.
WORKS: Operettas: *The Firefly* (Syracuse, Oct. 14, 1912); *High Jinks* (Syracuse, Nov. 3, 1913); *Katinka* (Morristown, N.Y., Dec. 2, 1915); *You're in Love,* musical comedy (Stamford, Conn., 1916); *Glorianna* (1918); *Tumble In* (1919); *Sometime* (1919); *Rose Marie* (N.Y., Sept. 2, 1924; very popular); *Vagabond King* (N.Y., Sept. 21, 1925; highly successful); also wrote a great number of piano pieces in a light vein. In 1937 Metro-Goldwyn-Mayer made a film of *The Firefly,* the popular *Donkey Serenade* being added to the original score.

Frisch, Paula. See **Frijsh, Povla.**

Frischenschlager, Friedrich, Austrian composer and musicographer; b. Gross Sankt Florian, Styria, Sept. 7, 1885; d. Salzburg, July 15, 1970. He studied music in Graz; in 1909 went to Berlin, where he studied musicology with Johann Wolf and Kretzschmar, and also attended Humperdinck's master classes in composition. In 1918 he was engaged as a music teacher at the Mozarteum in Salzburg; remained there until 1945; also edited the bulletin of the Mozarteum. An industrious composer, he wrote the fairy-tale operas *Der Schweinehirt,* after Hans Christian Andersen (Berlin, May 31, 1913); *Die Prinzessin und der Zwerg* (Salzburg, May 12, 1927); and *Der Kaiser und die Nachtigall,* after Andersen (Salzburg, March 27, 1937); also several choral works; *Symphonische Aphorismen* for Orch.; and teaching materials for voice.

Friskin, James, American pianist and composer; b. Glasgow, March 3, 1886; d. New York, March 16, 1967. He studied with E. Dannreuther (piano) and Stanford (composition) at the Royal College of Music in London; then taught at the Royal Normal College for the Blind (1909–14). In 1914 he came to the U.S. In 1934 he gave 2 recitals in N.Y. consisting of the complete *Wohltemperierte Clavier* of Bach. In 1944 he married Rebecca Clarke. Among his works are *Phantasie* for String Quartet; *Phantasie* for Piano Trio; *Phantasy* for Piano, 2 Violins, Viola, and Cello (1912); Quintet for Piano and Strings; Violin Sonata. He publ. *The Principles of Pianoforte Practice* (London, 1921; new ed., N.Y., 1937); also (with Irwin Freundlich) *Music for the Piano* (N.Y., 1954).

Froberger, Johann Jakob, famous German organist and composer; b. Stuttgart, May 18, 1616; d. Héricourt, Haute-Saône, France, May 7, 1667. About 1634 he went to Vienna, where he entered the Inst. of Singer oder Canthoreyknaben; there it was the custom to allow the choirboys, when their voices had changed and when they had attained a certain degree of musical scholarship, to serve as apprentices to famous masters of the time on stipends given by Emperor Ferdinand II. Froberger, however,

did not apply for the subvention until late 1636, when it was refused him; thereupon, he held the position of 3rd organist at the court from Jan. 1 to Oct. 30, 1637. He then again applied, with success, and was granted a stipend of 200 gulden; in October of that year he left to study under Frescobaldi in Rome, remaining there for 3½ years. In March 1641 he returned to Vienna, where he again was organist in 1641–45 and 1653–58; after this he made long concert tours (to Paris and London). Stories of his adventures in London, and of his appointment first as organ blower at Westminster Abbey and then as court organist to Charles II (first publ. by Mattheson, but not corroborated by any English sources), must be dismissed as apocryphal. He spent his last years in the service of Princess Sybille of Württemberg at her château near Héricourt. Although 2 collections of toccatas, canzoni, and partitas were publ. long after his death (1693 and 1696), there is internal evidence that the majority of these works were written before 1650.
WORKS: Organ toccatas, fantasias, canzoni, fugues, etc., of which 3 MS vols. are in the Vienna Library; in Berlin are 2 printed vols., *Diverse ingegnosissime, rarissime, et non maj più viste curiose partite di toccate, canzoni, ricercari, capricci,* etc. (1693; reprinted at Mainz, 1695) and *Diverse curiose e rare partite musicali,* etc. (1696); also a vol. of suites for clavecin. Froberger's works, ed. by G. Adler, are in Denkmäler der Tonkunst in Österreich (vols. 8, 13, 21; formerly vols. 4.i, 6.ii, 10.ii).

Froidebise, Pierre, important Belgian composer, organist, and teacher; b. Ohey, May 15, 1914; d. Liège, Oct. 28, 1962. He began studies in harmony and organ playing with Camille Jacquemin (1932–35); then entered the classes at the Namur Cons. with René Barbier, and at the Brussels Cons. with Moulaert and Léon Jongen. His chosen specialty was the history of organ music; he publ. in 1958 a monumental *Anthologie de la musique d'orgue des primitifs à la Renaissance.* But he also was deeply interested in the techniques of new music, particularly Schoenberg's method of composition with 12 tones; in 1949 he formed in Liège a progressive society under the name Variation. As a teacher of composition in Liège, he attracted many students of the avant-garde, among them Henri Pousseur.
WORKS: 2 radio operas: *La Bergère et le ramoneur* and *La Lune amère* (both 1957); *De l'aube à la nuit* for Orch. (1934–37); *Antigona* for Soli, Chorus, and Orch. (1936); Violin Sonata (1938); *La Légende de Saint-Julien l'Hospitalier,* symph. poem after Flaubert (1941); *3 poèmes japonais* for Voice and Piano (1942–43); *5 comptines* for Voice and 11 Instruments (1947; International Society for Contemporary Music Festival, Brussels, June 27, 1950); *Amerœur,* cantata for Voice, Wind Quintet, and Piano (1948); *Stèle pour sei Shonagon* for Soprano and 19 Instruments (1958; contains aleatory passages); *Justorum animae* and *Puer natus est* for Chorus and Orch.

Frölich, Theodor, Swiss composer; b. Brugg (Aar-

gan), Feb. 20, 1803; d. (suicide) Aarau, Oct. 16, 1836. He studied composition with Zelter in Berlin; returning to Switzerland, was active mainly as an educator. He is remembered chiefly through his colorful songs, *Persische Lieder,* to Rückert's words, and his choruses, *Lieder im Volkston;* one of these choruses, *Wem Gott will rechte Gunst erweisen,* became popular.

Froschauer, Johann, an Augsburg printer (end of 15th century), once thought to have been the first to print music with movable type, in Michael Keinspeck's *Lilium musicae planae* (1498); however, it is now known that wood blocks were employed for the music illustrations in that work; it also appears fairly certain that music printing with movable type preceded Froschauer's work.

Früh, Armin Leberecht, German musical inventor; b. Mühlhausen, Thuringia, Sept. 15, 1820; d. Nordhausen, Jan. 8, 1894. He invented, in 1857, the "Semeiomelodicon" (an apparatus for facilitating musical instruction, consisting of a series of note heads which, when pressed by the finger, produced tones of corresponding pitch); he traveled to introduce his invention to prominent musicians, and established a factory in Dresden in 1858, but it soon failed.

Früh, Huldreich Georg, Swiss pianist and composer; b. Zürich, June 16, 1903; d. there, April 25, 1945. He studied piano with Walter Frey and music theory with Andreae at the Zürich Cons.; then became an instructor at the Volksklavierschule, and later joined the group of avant-garde musicians at the cabaret Cornichon. He wrote mainly theatrical pieces and songs on politically oriented radical subjects.

Frühbeck de Burgos, Rafael, Spanish conductor of German parentage; b. Burgos, Sept. 15, 1933. He studied violin and piano at the Bilbao Cons. and later at the Cons. of Madrid and at the Hochschule für Musik in Munich. In 1959 he was appointed music director of the Bilbao Symph. Orch., becoming the youngest musician ever to lead an orch. in Spain. In 1962 he was appointed conductor of the Orquesta Nacional in Madrid; remained at this post until 1977. In the meantime, he toured as a guest conductor in the European music centers. In 1968–70 he was a guest conductor with major orchs. in the U.S.; from 1975 to 1976 he was conductor of the Montreal Symph. Orch.; in 1980 was named principal guest conductor of the National Symph. Orch. in Washington, D.C.

Frumerie, (Per) Gunnar (Fredrik) de, eminent Swedish composer; b. Nacka, near Stockholm, July 20, 1908. He enrolled at the Stockholm Cons., where he studied piano with Lundberg and composition with Ernst Ellberg; was a stipendiary of the Jenny Lind Foundation (1929–32) in Vienna, where he took courses in piano with Emil von Sauer and in composition with Erwin Stein; then went to Paris, where he took piano lessons with Alfred Cortot and composition with Leonid Sabaneyev. After returning to Sweden, he was active as a concert pianist; in 1945 was appointed to the piano faculty at the Stockholm Musikhögskolan; was a prof. there from 1962. As a composer, he adheres to the Scandinavian Romantic tradition.

WORKS: Opera, *Singoalla* (Stockholm, March 16, 1940); ballet, *Johannesnatten (The Night of St. John;* 1947); 2 piano concertos (1929, 1932); *Suite in an Ancient Style* for Chamber Orch. (1930); *En moder,* melodrama to a text by Andersen (1932); Variations and Fugue for Piano and Orch. (1932); Violin Concerto (1936); Partita for String Orch. (1937); *Pastoral Suite* for Flute and Piano (1933; revised for Flute, String Orch., and Harp, 1941); *Symphonic Variations* (1941); *Symphonic Ballad* for Piano and Orch. (1943–44); cantata, *Fader vår (Our Father;* 1945); Divertimento for Orch. (1951); 2-piano Concerto (1953); *8 Psalms* for Chorus and Orch. (1953–55); Concerto for Clarinet, String Orch., Harp, and Percussion (1958); Trumpet Concerto (1959); Concertino for Oboe, String Orch., Harp, and Percussion (1960); Flute Concerto (1969); Horn Concerto (1971–72); *Ballad* for Orch. (1975); 2 piano trios (1932, 1952); 2 violin sonatas (1934, 1944); 2 piano quartets (1941, 1963); *Elegiac Suite* for Cello and Piano (1946); 2 piano sonatinas (1950); *Ballad* for Piano (1965); *Circulus quintus,* 24 miniatures for Piano (1965); 2 piano sonatas (1968); Suite for Wind Quintet (1973); String Quintet (1974); a cappella choral works; solo songs.

Fry, William Henry, American composer and journalist; b. Philadelphia, Aug. 10, 1813; d. Santa Cruz, West Indies, Sept. 21, 1864. He was one of the most vociferous champions of American music, and particularly of opera on American subjects in the English language. Ironically, his own opera *Leonora* (perf. in Philadelphia, June 4, 1845), for which he claimed the distinction of being the first grand opera by a native American composer, was a feeble imitation of Italian vocal formulas in the manner of Bellini, with a libretto fashioned from a novel by Bulwer-Lytton, *The Lady of Lyons. Leonora* ran for 16 performances before closing; a revival of some numbers in concert form was attempted in N.Y. on Feb. 27, 1929, as a period piece, but was met with puzzled derision. Fry continued his campaign in favor of American opera in English, and composed 3 more operas, one of which, *Notre Dame de Paris,* after Victor Hugo, was produced in Philadelphia on May 3, 1864; 2 other operas, *The Bridal of Dunure* and *Aurelia the Vestal,* were not performed. He also wrote several symphs., including *The Breaking Heart* (1852; not extant); *Santa Cluus (Christmas Symphony)* (N.Y., Dec. 24, 1853); *A Day in the Country* (1853?; not extant); *Childe Harold* (N.Y., May 31, 1854; not extant); as well as a symph. poem, *Niagara* (N.Y., May 4, 1854). Fry's various proclamations, manifestos, and prefaces to publ. editions of his works are interesting as illustrations of the patriotic bombast and humbug that agitated American musicians in the mid-19th century.

Frye, Walter, English composer of the 15th century. Nothing is known regarding his life, but from indirect indications, it appears that he was attached to the court of Burgundy. Of his 3 masses (in MS at the Royal Library in Brussels), 2 are without a Kyrie, a lack characteristic of the English school; his *Ave Regina* is an early example of the "song motet." His works have been edited by S. Kenney in *Walter Frye: Collected Works,* in Corpus Mensurabilis Musicae, XIX (1960).

Fryer, George Herbert, English pianist and pedagogue; b. London, May 21, 1877; d. there, Feb. 7, 1957. He studied at the Royal College of Music; then with Matthay in London and Busoni in Weimar. He made his debut as a pianist in London (Nov. 17, 1898); then traveled in Europe; in 1914 he made a tour in the U.S.; in 1915 gave recitals for the British army in France; in 1917 returned to London; taught at the Royal College of Music (1917–47). He wrote miscellaneous pieces for piano; also publ. a book, *Hints on Pianoforte Practice* (N.Y., 1914).

Fuchs, Carl Dorius Johannes, distinguished German music scholar; b. Potsdam, Oct. 22, 1838; d. Danzig, Aug. 27, 1922. He studied piano with Hans von Bülow, thoroughbass with Weitzmann, and composition with Kiel; took the degree of Dr.Phil. at Greifswald, with the dissertation *Präliminarien zu einer Kritik der Tonkunst* (1871). In 1868 he became a teacher at the Kullak Academy in Berlin; then gave piano concerts in Germany. In 1874 he went to Hirschberg; in 1879, to Danzig, where he was organist at the Petrikirche and music critic of the *Danziger Zeitung* (1887–1920); was also organist for many years at the Synagogue in Danzig, and wrote *Andachts-lieder für Tempel und Haus.* Fuchs was a friend of Nietzsche, with whom he corresponded.

Fuchs, Johann Nepomuk, Austrian composer and conductor, brother of **Robert Fuchs;** b. Frauenthal, Styria, May 5, 1842; d. Vöslau, near Vienna, Oct. 5, 1899. He studied with Sechter at Vienna; conducted the Pressburg Opera in 1864; held similar positions at Brno, Kassel, Cologne, Hamburg, Leipzig, and (from 1880) at the Vienna Opera. In 1894 he succeeded Hellmesberger as director of the Vienna Cons. He produced the opera *Zingara* (Brünn, 1892) and several others.

Fuchs, Peter Paul, Austrian conductor; b. Vienna, Oct. 30, 1916. He studied piano with Leonie Gombrich, composition with Eugene Zador and Karl Weigl, and conducting with Felix Weingartner and Josef Krips. He subsequently had conducting engagements at the Vienna Volksoper and in the German Theater in Brno. In the wake of the Nazi-fomented Anschluss of Austria to the German thousand-year Reich, Fuchs went to the U.S. in 1938; served in the U.S. Army; was accompanist periodically at the San Francisco Opera and at the Metropolitan Opera in N.Y.; organized a small opera company, Opera for Everyone, presenting performances of operas in English at colleges and music schools. From 1950 to 1976 he was on the faculty of Louisiana State Univ. in Baton Rouge as head of the opera workshop there; from 1960 to 1976 also served as conductor of the Baton Rouge Symph. He further made a European tour conducting opera in Rumania, the Netherlands, Greece, West Germany, and Austria. He eventually became music director and conductor of the Greensboro (N.C.) Symph. Orch. He publ. a manual, *The Psychology of Conducting* (N.Y., 1969) and edited *The Music Theater of Walter Felsenstein* (N.Y., 1975); composed a comic opera, *Serenade at Noon* (Baton Rouge, La., March 22, 1965); *Partita ricercata* for Flute, Oboe, Harpsichord, and Double Bass (1973); *Polyphony* for Orch. (1976); 3 string quartets; choruses.

Fuchs, Robert, renowned Austrian composer and pedagogue, brother of **Johann Nepomuk Fuchs;** b. Frauenthal, Feb. 15, 1847; d. Vienna, Feb. 19, 1927. He studied at the Vienna Cons.; from 1875 till 1912 was a prof. of harmony there, and established himself as a teacher of historical importance; among his students were Gustav Mahler, Hugo Wolf, and Schreker. His own compositions are, however, of no consequence, and there is no evidence that he influenced his famous pupils stylistically or even technically; the only pieces that were at all successful were his 5 serenades for String Orch. He wrote also 5 symphs., Piano Concerto, 2 piano trios, 3 string quartets, 2 piano quartets, Piano Quintet, and numerous pieces for piano solo and for piano, 4-hands.

Fučik, Julius, Czech composer of band music; b. Prague, July 18, 1872; d. Leitmeritz, Sept. 25, 1916. He was a bassoon player at the German Opera in Prague (1893) and later in Zagreb and Budapest; studied composition with Dvořák; was bandmaster of the 86th and 92nd Austrian regiments. He wrote a great number of dances and marches for band, including the immensely popular march *Entrance of the Gladiators.*

Fuenllana, Miguel de, blind Spanish vihuela virtuoso and composer; b. Navalcarnero, Madrid, early in the 16th century; date of death unknown. He was chamber musician to the Marquesa de Tarifa, and later at the court of Philip II, to whom he dedicated (1554) his *Libro de música para vihuela, intitulado Orphenica Lyra.* From 1562 to 1568 he was chamber musician to Queen Isabel de Valois, 3rd wife of Philip II. The *Libro* gives evidence of a high state of musical art in Spain during the 16th century; besides fantasias and other compositions for vihuela by Fuenllana and old Spanish ballads (such as the famous *Ay de mi, Alhama*), it contains arrangements for vihuela of works by Vásquez, Morales, P. and F. Guerrero, Flecha, Bernal, and several Flemish masters.

Fuerstner, Carl, German-American pianist, conductor, and composer; b. Strasbourg, June 16, 1912. He attended the Hochschule für Musik in Cologne (1930–34), studying composition and conducting; his teachers there were Hermann Abendroth, Walter Braunfels, Philipp Jarnach, and Ernst Klussmann. While still a student, he composed incidental music for theatrical plays. In 1939 he went to the U.S. as assistant conductor of the San Francisco Opera Co.; served as head coach of the opera dept. at the Eastman School of Music in Rochester, N.Y., and conducted the Rochester Civic Community Orch.; then was engaged as a piano teacher at Brigham Young Univ. in Provo, Utah; toured as piano accompanist to many famous artists, among them the violinists Menuhin, Ricci, and Spivakovsky, the cellist Nelsova, and the singers Martinelli, Kipnis, Traubel, Peerce, Siepi, and Leontyne Price; conducted an impressive repertoire of classical and modern operas with various operatic groups in America and in Europe. In 1963 he was appointed head coach of the opera dept. at Indiana Univ. in Bloomington. In 1973 Fuerstner was elected to the faculty of the International Summer Courses at the Mozarteum in Salzburg.

Führer, Robert (Johann Nepomuk), composer and organist; b. Prague, June 2, 1807; d. Vienna, Nov. 28, 1861. He studied with Johann Vitásek; was an organist in provincial towns before succeeding his teacher as Kapellmeister at the Prague Cathedral in 1839. He became involved in fraudulent transactions and was dismissed from his post in 1845. He then held various positions as an organist and choral conductor in Vienna, Salzburg, Munich, Augsburg, and Gmunden. A series of embezzlements and other criminal offenses perpetrated by him resulted in his dismissal from several of his positions, but he continued to compose and perform; in 1856 he was Bruckner's competitor for the post of organist in Linz, arousing great admiration for his skill, even though Bruckner was selected. He served a prison term in 1859, but was given full freedom to write music. He publ. numerous sacred works (32 masses, 14 Requiems, 4 litanies, etc.) and many organ pieces; also handbooks on harmony and organ playing. Despite his notoriously dishonest acts and professional untrustworthiness (he publ. one of Schubert's masses under his own name), he enjoyed a fine reputation for his musicianship.

Fuleihan, Anis, American pianist, conductor, and composer; b. Kyrenia, Cyprus, April 2, 1900; d. Palo Alto, Calif., Oct. 11, 1970. He studied at the English School in Kyrenia; came to the U.S. in 1915 and continued his study of the piano in N.Y. with Alberto Jonás; toured the U.S., also the Near East, from 1919 to 1925; then lived in Cairo, returning to the U.S. in 1928; was on the staff of G. Schirmer, Inc. (1932–39); in 1947 became a prof. at Indiana Univ.; in 1953, director of the Beirut Cons. in Lebanon. In 1962 he went to Tunis under the auspices of the State Dept.; in 1963 organized the Orch. Classique de Tunis; remained there until 1965.

WORKS: Opera, *Vasco* (1960); for Orch.: *Mediterranean Suite* (1930; Cincinnati, March 15, 1935); *Preface to a Child's Story Book* (1932); Symph. No. 1 (N.Y. Phil., Dec. 31, 1936); Concerto No. 1 for Piano and String Orch. (Saratoga Springs, N.Y., Sept. 11, 1937, composer soloist); Concerto No. 2 for Piano and Orch. (N.Y., 1938); Fantasy for Viola and Orch. (1938); Violin Concerto (1930); *Fiesta* (Indianapolis Symph. Orch., Dec. 1, 1939); *Symphonie concertante* for String Quartet and Orch. (N.Y. Phil., April 25, 1940); Concerto for 2 Pianos and Orch. (Hempstead, N.Y., Jan. 10, 1941); *Epithalamium* for Piano and Strings (Philadelphia, Feb. 7, 1941); Concerto for Theremin and Orch. (N.Y., Feb. 26, 1945); *Invocation to Isis* (Indianapolis Symph. Orch., Feb. 28, 1941); Concerto for Violin, Piano, and Orch. (1943); Ondes Martinot Concerto (1944); *3 Cyprus Serenades* for Orch. (Philadelphia Orch., Dec. 13, 1946, Ormandy conducting); Rhapsody for Cello and String Orch. (Saratoga Springs, Sept. 12, 1946); *Overture for 5 Winds* (N.Y., May 17, 1947); *The Pyramids of Giza,* symph. poem (1952); Toccata for Piano and Orch. (1960); *Islands,* symph. suite (1961); Flute Concerto (1962); Piano Concerto No. 3 (1963); Cello Concerto (1963); Viola Concerto (1963); Violin Concerto No. 2 (1965); Symph. No. 2 (N.Y., Feb. 16, 1967); Violin Concerto No. 3 (1967); *Le Cors anglais s'amuse,* diversions for English Horn and Strings (1969); Piano Quintet (1967); Piano Trio (1969); 5 string quartets (1940–67); 14 piano sonatas (1940–68); Horn Quintet (1959); Clarinet Quintet; Violin Sonata; Viola Sonata; Cello Sonata; choral pieces, songs.

Fulkerson, James, American composer and trombonist; b. Streator, Ill., July 2, 1945. He studied at Wesleyan Univ. (B.M., 1966) and the Univ. of Illinois (M.M., 1968); took lessons in trombone playing with Carmine Caruso and John Silber; studied composition with Gaburo, Hiller, Johnston, and Martinano. He was a creative associate of the Center for the Creative and Performing Arts in Buffalo, N.Y. (1969–72); composer-in-residence at the Deutscher Akademischer Austauschdienst in Berlin (1973) and at the Victorian College of the Arts in Melbourne (since 1978). He is a virtuoso on the trombone, and he makes a specialty of playing the most fantastically difficult modern pieces. His own compositions are no less advanced.

Fuller, Albert, American harpsichordist; b. Washington, D.C., July 21, 1926. He studied organ with Paul Callaway at the National Cathedral in Washington, D.C.; then attended classes at the Peabody Cons. and at Georgetown and Johns Hopkins univs. He studied harpsichord with Ralph Kirkpatrick at Yale Univ. and also theory there with Hindemith, graduating with a M.Mus. in 1954. He then went to Paris on a Ditson fellowship; upon his return to the U.S., he made his N.Y. recital debut in 1957; his European debut followed in 1959. In 1964 he became a prof. of harpsichord at the Juilliard School of Music in N.Y.

Fuller Maitland, John Alexander, eminent English music scholar; b. London, April 7, 1856; d. Carnforth, Lancashire, March 30, 1936. He studied at Westminster School and Trinity College in Cambridge (M.A., 1882); then took piano lessons with Dannreuther and W.S. Rockstro. He was music critic of the *Pall Mall Gazette* (1882–84) and of the *Manchester Guardian* (1884–89); lectured extensively on the history of English music; appeared as a pianist with the Bach Choir and as a performer on the harpsichord in historical concerts. He contributed to the first edition of *Grove's Dictionary* and edited the Appendix; was editor in chief of the 2nd edition (1904–10); was also editor of *English Carols of the 15th Century* (1887); *English Country Songs* (1893; with L.E. Broadwood); *Fitzwilliam Virginal Book* (1899; with W. Barclay Squire, his brother-in-law); 12 trio sonatas and the *St. Cecilia Ode* of Purcell in the monumental edition of the Purcell Society, the piano works of Purcell's contemporaries (1921). Together with Clara Bell he translated Spitta's *Bach* (3 vols., 1884; 2nd ed., 1899); compiled the catalogue of the music division of the Fitzwilliam Museum (1893). He is the author of the following books: *Schumann* (1884); *Masters of German Music* (1894); *The Musician's Pilgrimage* (1899); *English Music in the 19th Century* (1902); *The Age of Bach and Handel* (vol. IV of *The Oxford History of Music,* 1902; new ed., 1931); *Joseph Joachim* (1905); Brahms (1911; in German, 1912); *The Concert of Music* (1915); *The "48"—Bach's Wohltemperiertes Clavier* (2 vols., 1925); *The Keyboard Suites of J.S. Bach* (1925); *The Spell of Music* (1926); *A Door-Keeper of Music* (1929); *Bach's Brandenburg Concertos* (1929); *Schumann's Concerted Chamber Music* (1929); *The Music of Parry and Stanford* (Cambridge, 1934).

Fumet, Dynam-Victor, French organist and composer; b. Toulouse, May 4, 1867; d. Paris, Jan. 2, 1949. He studied with César Franck and with Guiraud at the Paris Cons. At an early age he became involved in the political activities of French anarchists and was forced to leave school. For a time he earned his living as a piano player in Paris nightclubs; in 1910 became organist of St. Anne's Church in Paris. His music follows the precepts of French Wagnerism; the influence of Franck is also noticeable. Fumet wrote several orch. works on mystic themes, among them *Magnetisme céleste* for Cello and Orch. (1903); *Trois âmes* (1915); *Transsubstantiation* (1930); *Notre mirage, notre douleur* (1930). During the German occupation he wrote *La Prison glorifiée* (1943).

Furno, Giovanni, Italian composer and pedagogue; b. Capua, Jan. 1, 1748; d. Naples, June 20, 1837. He studied at the Cons. di Saint Onofrio in Naples, and in 1775 became a teacher of theory of composition there; retired in 1835. Among his pupils were Bellini and Mercadante. He wrote 2 operas, sacred choral music, and some instrumental pieces.

Fürstner, Adolph, German publisher; b. Berlin,

April 3, 1833; d. Bad Nauheim, June 6, 1908. He was a member of a family of merchants; although lacking in musical education, he showed a keen understanding of the commercial value of good music. He founded a music publishing firm under his own name in Berlin in 1868; in 1872 he acquired the catalogue of the Dresden firm of C.F. Meser, which owned several operas by Wagner and some works of Liszt; he subsequently purchased the rights of operas by Massenet, and later demonstrated his business acumen by securing *Pagliacci.* His firm distinguished itself as the earliest publisher of Richard Strauss. Fürstner was succeeded after his death by his son **Otto** (b. Berlin, Oct. 17, 1886; d. London, June 18, 1958); in 1933 Otto Fürstner was compelled to leave Germany; he went to England, where he resumed his business and gradually won back the German rights to the original editions of the firm. After the death of Otto Fürstner his widow, **Ursula Fürstner,** took over the ownership of the firm; in 1970, it was incorporated as Fürstner, London.

Furtwängler, Wilhelm, celebrated German conductor; b. Berlin, Jan. 25, 1886; d. Ebersteinburg, Nov. 30, 1954. His father, Adolf Furtwängler, was a noted archaeologist. He grew up in Munich, where he received a private education; his musical studies were with Schillings, Rheinberger, and Beer-Walbrunn; he also studied piano with Conrad Ansorge. He later served as répétiteur with Mottl in Munich (1908–9). In 1910 he became 3rd conductor at the Strasbourg Opera; then conducted the symph. concerts in Lübeck (1911–15); in 1915 he was engaged as conductor in Mannheim. From 1919 to 1924 he conducted the Vienna Tonkünstler Orch.; concurrently (from 1921) he served as director of the Gesellschaft der Musikfreunde in Vienna. In the interim he led the Berlin Staatskapelle (1920–22); also served as conductor of the Frankfurt Museum concerts. A decisive turn in his career was his appointment in 1922 as chief conductor of the Berlin Phil. as successor to Nikisch; he also assumed the vacant post of Kapellmeister of the Leipzig Gewandhaus Orch., which he held until 1928. On Jan. 3, 1925, he made his American debut with the N.Y. Phil., which was greeted with general acclaim; he conducted this orch. again in 1926 and 1927. In 1927 he was elected conductor of the Vienna Phil. in succession to Weingartner, holding the post of artistic director until 1930, and continuing as guest conductor later on. In 1927 the Univ. of Heidelberg conferred upon him the title of Dr.Phil.; in 1928 the city of Berlin named him Generalmusikdirektor. In 1931 he conducted at the Bayreuth Festival for the first time; on April 17, 1932, he was awarded the prestigious Goethe Gold Medal. In 1933 he was appointed director of the Berlin State Opera and vice-president of the Reichsmusikkammer. He maneuvered adroitly to secure his independence from the increasing encroachment of the Nazi authorities on both his programs and the personnel of the Berlin Phil., and succeeded in retaining several Jewish players. On March 12, 1934, he conducted Hindemith's symph. *Mathis der Maler* and was sharply berated by Goeb-

bels, who called Hindemith a "cultural Bolshevist" and "spiritual non-Aryan" (this with reference to Hindemith's half-Jewish wife). In the face of continued Nazi interference, Furtwängler decided to resign all of his posts on Dec. 4, 1934; however, a few months later, he made an uneasy peace with the Nazi authorities and agreed to return as a conductor with the Berlin Phil., giving his first concert on April 25, 1935. In 1936 he was offered a contract as permanent conductor of the N.Y. Phil. in succession to Toscanini, but had to decline the prestigious offer to quiet the rising accusations, on the part of American musicians, of his being a Nazi collaborator. In 1937 he went to London to participate in the musical celebrations in honor of the coronation of King George VI; in 1939 he was made a Commander of the Legion of Honor by the French government. After the outbreak of World War II, he confined his activities to Germany and Austria. Continuing to be loyal to Germany but with ambivalent feelings toward the Nazi government, Furtwängler went to Switzerland, where he remained during the last months of the war. He returned to Germany in 1946; faced the Allied Denazification Court, and was absolved from the charges of pro-Nazi activities (Dec. 17, 1946). On May 25, 1947, he conducted the Berlin Phil. for the first time since the end of the war, leading an all-Beethoven concert to great acclaim; he also renewed his close association with the Vienna Phil. and the Salzburg Festival. He was tentatively engaged to conduct the Chicago Symph. in 1949, but the project was canceled when public opinion proved hostile. In Western Europe, however, he took both the Vienna and Berlin phil. orchs. on a number of major tours and was received most enthusiastically; he also became a regular conductor with the Phil. Orch. of London. In 1951 he reinaugurated the Bayreuth Festival by conducting Beethoven's 9th Symph.; in 1952 he resumed his post as chief conductor of the Berlin Phil. His last years of life were clouded by increasing deafness, so that his podium had to be wired for sound. He was to conduct the Berlin Phil. on its first American tour in the spring of 1955, but death intervened, and Herbert von Karajan was elected his successor.

Furtwängler was a perfect embodiment of the great tradition of the German Romantic school of conducting; his interpretations of the music of Beethoven, Schubert, Schumann, Brahms, Bruckner, and Wagner were models of formal purity. He never strove to achieve personal magic with the audience, and never ranked with such charismatic conductors as Stokowski or Koussevitzky in this respect. But to professional musicians he remained a legendary master of the orch. sound and symmetry of formal development of symph. music. Like most German conductors, Furtwängler was himself a composer; quite naturally, the style of his works followed the Romantic tradition, with potential exuberance controlled by a severe sense of propriety. He left behind 3 symphs. (1903, 1947, 1954), a Te Deum (1910), Piano Quintet (1935), Symph. Concert for Piano and Orch. (1937), 2 violin sonatas (1937, 1940), and some minor pieces. He publ. a critical essay, *Johannes Brahms und Anton Bruckner*

(Leipzig, 1941; 2nd ed., 1952); *Gespräche über Musik* (Zürich, 1948; in Eng. as *Concerning Music*, London, 1953); *Ton und Wort* (Wiesbaden, 1954); *Der Musiker und sein Publikum* (Zürich, 1954); *Vermächtnis* (Wiesbaden, 1956).

Furuhjelm, Erik Gustaf, Finnish composer; b. Helsinki, July 6, 1883; d. there, June 13, 1964. He studied violin; then took lessons in composition with Sibelius and Wegelius; continued his studies in Vienna with Robert Fuchs. From 1909 to 1935 he lectured on music theory at the Helsinki School of Music, and from 1920 to 1935 served as assistant director there. He founded the magazine *Finsk Musikrevy;* in 1916 he wrote the first book-length biography of Sibelius.
WORKS: Piano Quintet (1906); 2 symphs. (1906–11, 1925–26); *Romantic Overture* (1910); *Konzertstück* for Piano and Orch. (1911); *Intermezzo and Pastorale* for Orch. (1920–24); *Fem bilder (5 Pictures)* for Orch. (1924–25); *Phantasy* for Violin and Orch. (1925–26); *Folklig svit (Rustic Suite)* for Orch. (1939); *Solitude* for Orch. (1940); String Quartet.

Futterer, Carl, Swiss composer; b. Basel, Feb. 21, 1873; d. Ludwigshafen, Nov. 5, 1927. He studied to be a lawyer; then began taking lessons in composition with Hans Huber; wrote operas and other works but kept them hidden until late in life. His comic opera *Don Gil mit den grünen Hosen* (1915) was produced in Freiburg im Breisgau in 1922; another opera, *Der Geiger von Gmünd* (1917), was produced in Basel in 1921. He further wrote a Sinfonietta (1917); Octet (1921); Quartet for Oboe, Clarinet, Horn, and Bassoon (1921); Trio for Clarinet, Cello, and Piano (1924); Piano Trio (1927); Violin Sonata (1927); Piano Concerto (1927).

Fux, Johann Joseph, Austrian composer and learned theorist; b. Hirtenfeld, Styria, 1660; d. Vienna, Feb. 13, 1741. He enrolled at the Jesuit Univ. in Graz as a "grammatista" in 1680; in 1681 entered the Ferdinandum, a Jesuit inst. for gifted music students; also studied at the Jesuit Univ. of Ingolstadt; was organist at St. Moritz there until 1688. In 1696–1702 he was organist at the Schottenkirche in Vienna; in 1698 he was made court composer; in 1705, vice-Kapellmeister at St. Stephen's, and principal Kapellmeister there in 1712–15; was named assistant Kapellmeister to the court in 1713, succeeding Ziani as first Kapellmeister (the highest position attainable for a musician) in 1715. This office he held until his death, under 3 successive emperors, and received many tokens of imperial favor. Over 200 works have been added to the original 405 catalogued works; the greatest and the most enduring is his treatise on counterpoint, *Gradus ad Parnassum,* publ. originally in Latin (Vienna, 1725), since then in German, Italian, French, and Eng. (1791; part of the *Gradus ad Parnassum* was publ. in Eng. as *Steps to Parnassus,* N.Y., 1943; 2nd ed., revised, 1965, as *The Study of Counterpoint*); Mozart and Haydn studied it; Cherubini and Albrechtsberger adopted its method, which was sanctioned by Piccinni and Padre Martini. Vogler, however, con-

demned it (see introduction to Vogler's *Choral-System,* p. 1; Fröhlich's biography of Vogler, p. 18). Fux was well aware of the weakness of contemporary music practice and, in trying to arrive at a satisfactory remedy, disregarded the modern idiom already established when he was writing and chose, as the basis of his theory, the style of Palestrina. Although his presentation of that style is not very strong or even authentic (for, among other things, he could not have been very well acquainted with the main body of Palestrina's works because they were not commonly available at the time), the method is still valuable for its organization and the discipline it affords (cf. K. Jeppesen's *Counterpoint,* 1931; in Eng., N.Y., 1939).
WORKS: 20 operas; 12 oratorios; about 80 partitas and overtures (among them the *Concentus musico-instrumentalis*); much sacred music: about 80 masses (the *Missa canonica* is a contrapuntal masterpiece); 3 Requiems; 2 *Dies irae;* 57 vespers and Psalms; etc.; 38 "sacred sonatas." The Johann Joseph Fux Gesellschaft began issuing the Collected Works in 1959, a series that is still in progress; to date, 11 vols. have been publ.; in addition, a selection from his works is publ. in Denkmäler der Tonkunst in Österreich, vols. 1 (1.i; 4 masses), 3 (2.i; 27 motets), 19 (9.ii; 2 sacred sonatas, 2 overtures), 34/35 (17; the opera *Costanza e fortezza;* later ed. by G.P. Smith, Northampton, Mass., 1936), 47 (23.ii; the *Concentus musico-instrumentalist*), 85 (keyboard works).

G

Gabrieli, Andrea (also known as **Andrea di Cannaregio**), eminent Italian organist and composer; b. Venice, c.1510; d. there, 1586. He was a pupil of Adrian Willaert at San Marco and chorister there (1536); was organist at S. Geremia in Cannaregio in 1557–58; was in Bavaria in 1562 and went to Frankfurt, to the coronation of Maximilian II, as court organist of Duke Albrecht V of Bavaria. In 1566 he returned to Venice and was appointed 2nd organist at San Marco; became first organist on Jan. 1, 1585, succeeding Merulo. He enjoyed a great reputation as an organist (his concerts with Merulo, on 2 organs, were featured attractions). Among his pupils were his famous nephew, **Giovanni Gabrieli,** and Hans Leo Hassler. A prolific composer, he wrote a large number of works of varied description, many of which were publ. posthumously, edited by his nephew. His versatility is attested by the fact that he was equally adept in sacred music of the loftiest spirit, and in instrumental music, as well as in madrigals, often of a comic nature.

WORKS: *Sacrae cantiones* (37 motets; 1565); *Libro I di madrigali a 5 voci* (30 madrigals; 1566); *Libro II di madrigali a 5 voci* (28 madrigals; 1570); *Greghesche e justiniane* (15 numbers; 1571); *Primus Liber Missarum 6 vocum* (4 masses; 1572); *Libro I di madrigali a 6 voci* (30 madrigals; 1574); *Libro di madrigali a 3 voci* (30 madrigals; 1575); *Ecclesiasticae cantiones a 4 voci* (58 motets; 1576); *Libro II de madrigali a 6 voci* (22 madrigals; 1580); *Psalmi Davidici a 6 voci* (7 Psalms; 1583); *Sonate a 5 strumenti* (lost; 1586); *Concerti di Andrea et di Giovanni Gabrieli* (39 motets; 26 madrigals, 1587); *Edippo Tiranno* (choruses for Sophocles' *Oedipus,* perf. in Vicenza in 1585, 1588); *Libro III di madrigali a 5 voci* (22 madrigals; 1589); *Madrigali et ricercari* (24 madrigals, 7 ricercari; 1589); *Intonazioni d'organo* (12 *intonazioni;* 1593); *Ricercari di Andrea Gabrieli* (13 ricercari; 1595); *Libro III de ricercari* (6 ricercari, one fantasia, one motet, one canzone, 2 madrigals, one capriccio on the *passamezzo antico;* 1596); *Mascherate di Andrea Gabrieli et altri* (3 *mascherate,* 3 madrigals; 1601); *Canzoni alla francese et ricercari* (4 canzoni, 7 ricercari; 1605); *Canzoni alla francese* (9 canzoni, one Ricercare; 1605); and a large number of detached works in contemporary and later collections.—Modern eds.: G. Benvenuti, *Istituzioni e monumenti dell' arte musicale italiana* (vols. I and II; vocal and instrumental pieces); L. Torchi, *L'arte musicale in Italia* (vols. II and III; 16 motets and pieces for organ); K. von Winterfeld, in *Joh. Gabrieli und sein Zeitalter* (1834; 2 vols. and a musical supplement); J. von Wasielewski, in *Geschichte der Instrumental-Musik im 16.*

Gabrieli – Gabrieli Giovanni

Jahrhundert (1878) and in the music supplement of *Die Violine im 17. Jahrhundert* (2nd ed., 1905); A.G. Ritter, *Geschichte des Orgelspiels im 14.–18. Jahrhundert* (1884; revised by Frotscher, 1933); G. d'Alessi, *Classici della musica italiana* (vol. VI); de la Moskowa, *Recueil des morceaux de musique ancienne* (1843); H. Riemann, *Alte Kammermusik* (8-voiced ricercare); O. Kinkeldey in *Orgel und Klavier in der Musik des 16. Jahrhunderts* (organ arrangements by Andrea Gabrieli of Orlando di Lasso's chanson *Susanne un jour*); J. Wolf, in *Sing- und Spielmusik* (a *canzone francese*); H. Bäuerle (*Missa brevis,* 1932); W. Schöllgen (Easter motet, 1932); A. Einstein, in Denkmäler der Tonkunst in Österreich, vol. 77 (41; 3 madrigals in 6, 7, 8 voices, 1934); idem, in the musical supplement (no. 21) of *A Short History of Music* (N.Y., 1938); idem, in *The Golden Age of Music* (N.Y., 1942); idem, in *The Italian Madrigal* (vol. III; Princeton, 1949); A. Schering, *Geschichte der Musik in Beispielen* (no. 130); Davison and Apel, *Historical Anthology of Music* (vol. I, nos. 135, 136); Parish and Ohl, *Masterpieces of Music before 1750* (no. 21); *Das Chorwerk*, 96 (3 motets). The *Opera Omnia*, ed. by Denis Arnold, is being issued by the American Inst. of Musicology; as of 1977, 6 vols. had appeared.

Gabrieli, Domenico (Gabrielli) (called the "Menghino dal violoncello," Menghino being the diminutive of Domenico), Italian composer; b. Bologna, April 15,1651; d. there, July 10, 1690. He studied composition with Legrenzi in Venice and cello with Petronio Franceschini in Bologna. An excellent cellist, he played in the orch. of San Petronio, Bologna (1680–87); was a member of the Bologna Phil. Academy (1676); then became its president (1683). He was one of the earliest composers for cello solo. WORKS: He produced 12 operas in Bologna, Venice, Modena, and Turin; his last opera, *Tiberio in Bisanzio,* was perf. posthumously in Lucca (Jan. 20, 1694). Other works: *Ricercari per violoncello solo* (1689; MS at the Liceo in Bologna); *Balletti, gighe, correnti e sarabande* for 2 Violins, Cello, and Basso Continuo (1684; 2nd ed., 1704); *Vexillum pacis* (motets for Contralto, with Instrumental Accompaniment; posthumous, 1695). L. Landshoff ed. 3 *Arie* with Instrumental Obbligato (in *Alte Meister des Bel Canto,* 1912) and 2 cello sonatas (1930); A. Einstein printed a chamber cantata in the music supplement (no. 28) of his *A Short History of Music* (N.Y., 1938).

Gabrieli, Giovanni, celebrated Venetian composer, nephew and pupil of **Andrea Gabrieli;** b. Venice, between 1554 and 1557; d. there, Aug. 12, 1612. He lived in Munich from 1575 to 1579. On Nov. 1, 1584, he was engaged to substitute for Merulo as first organist at San Marco in Venice; on Jan. 1, 1585, was permanently appointed as 2nd organist (his uncle meanwhile took charge of the first organ); retained this post until his death. As a composer, he stands at the head of the Venetian school; he was probably the first to write vocal works with parts for instrumental groups in various combinations, partly spe-cified, partly left to the conductor, used as accompaniment as well as interspersed instrumental *sinfonie (Sacrae Symphoniae).* His role as a composer and teacher is epoch-making; through his innovations and his development of procedures and devices invented by others (free handling of several choirs in the many-voiced vocal works, "concerted" solo parts and duets in the few-voiced vocal works, trio-sonata texture, novel dissonance treatment, speech rhythm, root progressions in fifths, use of tonal and range levels for structural purposes, coloristic effects) and through his numerous German pupils (particularly Schütz) and other transalpine followers, he gave a new direction to the development of music. His instrumental music helped to spark the composition of German instrumental ensemble music, which reached its apex in the symph. and chamber music works of the classical masters. Of interest also is the fact that one of his ricercari, a 4-part work in the 10th tone (1595), is an early example of the "fugue with episodes" (reprinted in Riemann's *Musikgeschichte in Beispielen,* no. 52, Leipzig, 1913).

WORKS: Publications (very few) contain both sacred and secular vocal, as well as instrumental, works: *Concerti di Andrea et di Giovanni Gabrieli* (5 motets, 5 madrigals; 1587); *Intonazioni d'organo di Andrea Gabrieli et di Giovanni suo nepote* (11 *intonazioni;* 1593); *Sacrae Symphoniae Joannis Gabrielii* (42 motets, Mass, 12 instrumental canzoni, 3 sonatas; 1597); *Sacrarum Symphoniarum Continuatio* (9 motets, of which 5 are reprints; 1600); *Canzoni per sonare* (6 canzoni; 1608); *Sacrae Symphoniae Diversorum Autorum* (26 motets; 1613); *Sacrae Symphoniae, Liber II* (26 motets, Mass, 3 Magnificats; 1615); *Canzoni et Sonate* (15 canzoni, 5 sonatas; 1615); *Reliquiae Sacrorum Concentum* (one Magnificat, 19 motets, of which 10 are reprints; 1615). Detached pieces in collections up to 1625: 25 more madrigals, one canticle, Magnificats, motets, ricercari, toccatas, fantasias. Modern publications: G. Benvenuti publ. 3 secular vocal pieces in vol. I (1931), and G. Cesari 13 canzoni and 2 sonatas, (from *Sacrae Symphoniae,* 1597) in vol. II (1932), of the *Istituzioni e monumenti dell'arte musicale italiana (Andrea e Giovanni Gabrieli e la musica strumentale in S. Marco);* K. von Winterfeld, *Johannes Gabrieli und sein Zeitalter* (1834; 2 vols. and a vol. of music supplements); Proske, Griesbacher, Commer, etc. (motets); J. von Wasielewski, *Geschichte der Instrumental-Musik im 16. Jahrhundert* (1878), and in the music supplement of *Die Violine im 17. Jahrhundert* (2nd ed., 1905); Riemann, *Alte Kammermusik* (*Sonata a 3 violini* and *Canzona a 8*); L. Torchi, *L'arte musicale in Italia* (vols. II, III); H. Besseler, *Das Chorwerk* (vols. 10 and 67; 3 motets in each); A. Schering, *Geschichte der Musik in Beispielen* (nos. 130, 148); G. Tagliapietra *Antologia di musica antica e moderna per piano* (vol. II, 1931); A. Einstein (*Canzoni a 4,* 1933, Schott Antiqua; motet in the music supplement of his *Short History of Music,* no. 19, 1938; madrigal in *The Golden Age of the Madrigal,* 1942, no. 6); W. Danckert (*Sonata a 3 violini,* 1934); Davison and Apel, *Historical Anthology of Music* (vol. I, nos. 157,

173); F. Stein (*Sonata pian e forte,* 1931); J.F. Williamson (motet, 1932); G.W. Woodworth (3 motets; 1950–52); Bongiovanni (5 motets; 1954). Hans David has adapted several of Gabrieli's canzoni for modern use. An *Opera Omnia,* in 10 vols., ed. by Denis Arnold, is being issued by the American Inst. of Musicology in its Corpus Mensurabilis Musicae series.

Gabrielli, Caterina, famous soprano; b. Rome, Nov. 12, 1730; d. there, Feb. 16, 1796. She was known under the nickname "La Coghetta" (that is, "Little Cook," for her father was a cook in a Roman nobleman's palace). She made her debut at Venice in 1754; then went to Vienna, where she was hailed as a "new star on the musical firmament" and was coached by Gluck and Metastasio; she sang many parts in the Vienna productions of Gluck's operas, up to 1761; made triumphant appearances in Milan, Turin, and Naples; then went to Russia (with Traetta) and sang in St. Petersburg with unfailing acclaim (1772–74). In 1775 she made her first appearance in London, arousing admiration among the cognoscenti; but she was also the object of common gossip related to her notoriously loose morals. She returned to Italy after only one season in London, and eventually settled in Rome.

Gabrielli, Domenico. See **Gabrieli, Domenico.**

Gabrilowitsch, Ossip, notable pianist and conductor; b. St. Petersburg, Feb. 7, 1878; d. Detroit, Sept. 14, 1936. In 1888–94 he was a pupil at the St. Petersburg Cons., studying piano with A. Rubinstein and composition with Navrátil, Liadov, and Glazunov; graduated as winner of the Rubinstein Prize, and then spent 2 years (1894–96) in Vienna studying with Leschetizky; then toured Germany, Austria, Russia, France, and England. His first American tour (debut Carnegie Hall, N.Y., Nov. 12, 1900) was eminently successful, as were his subsequent visits (1901, 1906, 1909, 1914, 1915, 1916). During the season 1912–13 he gave in Europe a series of 6 historical concerts illustrating the development of the piano concerto from Bach to the present day; on his American tour in 1914–15 he repeated the entire series in several of the larger cities, meeting with an enthusiastic reception. On Oct. 6, 1909, he married the contralto **Clara Clemens** (daughter of Mark Twain), with whom he frequently appeared in joint recitals. He conducted his first N.Y. concert on Dec. 13, 1916; was appointed conductor of the Detroit Symph. Orch. in 1918. In 1928 and the following years he also conducted the Philadelphia Orch., sharing the baton with Leopold Stokowski, but still retaining his Detroit position.

Gaburo, Kenneth, American composer; b. Somerville, N.J., July 5, 1926. He studied composition with Bernard Rogers at the Eastman School of Music, Rochester, N.Y. (M.M., 1949), and at the Univ. of Illinois, Urbana (D.M.A., 1962); then went to Rome, where he studied with Goffredo Petrassi. Returning to America, he occupied teaching posts at Kent

State Univ., Ohio (1949–50); at McNeese State Univ. in Lake Charles, La. (1950–54); and at the Univ. of Illinois, Urbana (1955–68); in 1968 was appointed to the faculty of the Univ. of Calif. at San Diego; remained there until 1975. In 1967 he held a Guggenheim fellowship. He founded and directed the New Music Chorale Ensemble in concerts in the U.S. and Europe. His music is quaquaversal.
WORKS: Operas: *The Snow Queen* (Lake Charles, May 5, 1952) and *The Widow* (Urbana, Feb. 26, 1961); *Bodies,* abstract theater piece (1957); *The Dog-King,* play with music (1959); *On a Quiet Theme* for Orch. (1952); *4 Inventions* for Clarinet and Piano (1953); *Music for 5 Instruments* (1954); set of 3 *Ideas and Transformations* for Strings (1955); String Quartet (1956); *Line Studies* for 4 Instruments (1957); electronic score for the play *The Hydrogen Jukebox; Lingua I–IV,* massive theater play exploring the structural properties of language in a musical context (1965–70); Viola Concerto (1959); *Antiphony I* for 3 String Groups and Electronic Sound; *Antiphony II* for Piano and Electronic Sound; *Antiphony III* for Singers and Electronic Sound; *Antiphony IV* for Piccolo, Double Bass, Trombone, and Electronic Sound; *Antiphony V* for Piano and Electronic Sound; *Shapes and Sounds* for Orch. (1960); *2* for Mezzo-soprano, Alto Flute, and Double Bass (1963); *Circumcision* for 3 Groups of Male Voices (1964); *The Flow of E,* based on a synthesized vowel *e* and its electronic transformations (1965); *Inside,* quartet for a Single Doublebass Player (1969); *Mouthpiece,* sextet for Solo Trumpet and 5 Projection Slides (1970).

Gade, Jacob, Danish composer; b. Vejle, Nov. 29, 1879; d. Copenhagen, Feb. 21, 1963. He studied violin; was a member of the N.Y. Symph. Orch. (1919–21); then returned to Copenhagen and was active there as a conductor. Among his light compositions, *Jalousie* (1925) attained great popularity. He also wrote several symph. poems (*Den sidste Viking, Leda and the Swan,* etc.).

Gade, Niels (Wilhelm), Danish composer and founder of the modern Scandinavian school of composition; b. Copenhagen, Feb. 22, 1817; d. there, Dec. 21, 1890. He was the only child of an instrument maker; studied violin with a member of the Danish court band, and gave a concert in Copenhagen at the age of 16. He then took composition lessons with A.P. Berggreen; soon he began writing songs to German texts. At the age of 23, he wrote his overture *Nachklänge von Ossian,* for which he was awarded a prize by the Copenhagen Musical Society. The work was performed in Copenhagen on Nov. 19, 1841, and was soon publ.; this early overture remained the most popular work of Gade, and endured in the orch. repertoire for many years. His next important work was Symph. in C minor. Gade sent this to Mendelssohn in Leipzig, and Mendelssohn performed it at a Gewandhaus concert on March 2, 1843. Subsequently, Gade received a government stipend for travel in Germany; he went to Leipzig, where Mendelssohn accepted him as a friend, and let him conduct some of the Gewand-haus concerts. Gade's talent flourished in the congenial atmosphere; an ardent admirer of Mendelssohn and Schumann, he adopted a Romantic style in the prevalent Germanic spirit. After Mendelssohn's death in 1847, Gade assumed the conductorship of the Gewandhaus concerts, but on the outbreak of the Schleswig-Holstein war in the spring of 1848, he returned to Copenhagen. In 1850, he became chief conductor of the Copenhagen Musical Society; also was a co-founder of the Copenhagen Cons. in 1866. He visited Birmingham in 1876 to conduct his cantata *Zion* at the festival there. In the same year, the Danish government granted him a life pension. In Denmark, his position as a prime musician was by then fully established; but he was accepted in Germany, too, as a master composer. Despite his adherence to the Germanic school, he infused elements of national Danish melodies into his works, and so led the way to further development of Scandinavian music.

WORKS: 8 symphs. (1841–71); overtures: *Nachklänge von Ossian* (1840); *Im Hochlande* (1844); *Hamlet* (1861); *Michelangelo* (1861); Violin Concerto (1880); cantatas: *Comala* (1846); *Elverskud* (1853); *The Holy Night* (1861); *At Sunset* (1865); *Kalanus* (1871); *Zion* (1873); *The Crusaders* (1873); *The Mountain Thrall* (1873); *Gefion* (1875); *Psyche* (1882); *Der Strom*, after Goethe's *Mahomet* (1889); chamber music: 2 string quintets, String Octet, Piano Trio, String Quartet, 3 violin sonatas, *Folk Dance* for Violin and Piano, *Pictures of the Orient* for Violin and Piano; for Piano Solo: *Spring Flowers*, *Aquarelles* (3 books), *Idylls*, 4 *Fantastic Pieces*, *Folk Dance*, Sonata in E minor; also 21 vocal works for various combinations, in the style of folk songs; incidental music for a play, *Mariotta;* ballet music; etc.

Gadski, Johanna (Emilia Agnes), celebrated German soprano; b. Anclam, June 15, 1872; d. Berlin, Feb. 22, 1932, as a result of an automobile accident. She studied voice with Frau Schroeder-Chaloupka at Stettin; made her opera debut at the age of 17 in Berlin with the Kroll Opera; she then sang in Mainz, Bremen, and Stettin. On March 1, 1895, she made her American debut with the Damrosch Opera Co. in N.Y. as Elsa in *Lohengrin*, and subsequently sang other Wagnerian roles, including Elisabeth, Eva, and Sieglinde. On Dec. 28, 1899, she made her debut with the Metropolitan Opera on tour, and established herself as a prime interpreter of dramatic parts, excelling in particular as Brünnhilde and Isolde; remained with the Metropolitan until 1904; made her debut at Covent Garden in London on May 15, 1899; in 1904–6 she made 2 transcontinental tours of the U.S., as a concert singer. In 1907 she returned to the Metropolitan Opera, where she continued to appear until her final appearance on April 13, 1917. She left the U.S. for Germany when America entered the war in 1917; returned to the U.S. in 1929, remaining until 1931. On Nov. 11, 1892, she was married to Lieutenant Hans Tauscher.

Gadzhibekov, Uzeir, Azerbaijani composer; b. Agdzhabedy, near Shusha, Sept. 17, 1885; d. Baku, Nov. 23, 1948. He studied in Shusha; then lived in Baku, where he produced his first opera on a native subject, *Leyly and Medzhnun* (Jan. 25, 1908). His comic opera *Arshin Mal Alan* (Baku, Nov. 27, 1913) had numerous performances; another opera, *Kyor-Oglu (A Blind Man's Son),* was produced at the Azerbaijan Festival in Moscow (April 30, 1937).

Gaffurio, Franchino. See **Gaforio, Franchino.**

Gaforio (or **Gafori, Gafuri, Gaffurio**), **Franchino** (Latinized as **Franchinus Gafurius;** often simply **Franchinus**), celebrated Italian theorist; b. Lodi, Jan. 14, 1451; d. Milan, June 24, 1522. He studied theology and music; lived in Mantua, Verona, and Genoa (1477); he formed an intimacy with the Doge Prospero Adorno (then in exile) and fled with him to Naples (1478). There he met various distinguished musicians, and held public disputation with Johannes Tinctoris, Guarnier, and Hycart. The plague and the Turkish invasion compelled him to return to Lodi (1480); was a teacher and choirmaster at Monticello for 3 years, made a short visit to Bergamo in 1483, and in 1484 until his death was maestro di cappella at the Milan Cathedral, and first singer in the choir of Duke Lodovico Sforza. In 1485 he also founded a music school at Milan, which prospered.

WRITINGS: *Theoricum opus harmonicae disciplinae* (Naples, 1480; 2nd ed., Milan, 1492, as *Theorica musicae;* facsimile reprint, Rome, 1934); *Practica musicae Franchino Gaforio Laudensis... in IV libris* (Milan 1496; his magnum opus, with examples of mensural notation in block-print; other eds., 1497, 1502, 1508, 1512, 1522); *Angelicum ac divinum opus musicae materna lingua scriptum* (Milan, 1496); *De harmonia musicorum instrumentorum* (Milan, 1518; with biography of Gaforio by P. Meleguli); *Apologia Franchini Gafurii musici adversus Ioannem Spatarium et complices musicos Bononienses* (Turin, 1520; concerning the controversy between the Milanese and Bolognese schools). A complete ed. of his compositions, edited by Lutz Finscher, was begun in 1955.

Gagliano, the name of a family of famous violin makers at Naples. **Alessandro,** who worked from 1695 to 1725, was a pupil of Stradivari, and he, as well as his sons **Nicola** (1695–1758) and **Gennaro** (1700–88), followed largely the Stradivari model. The instruments of **Ferdinando Gagliano** (c.1724–81), a son of Nicola, exhibit less skillful workmanship than those of the older members of the family.

Gagliano, Marco da, Italian opera composer; b. Florence, May 1, 1582; d. there, Feb. 25, 1643. He was a pupil of L. Bati; in 1608, became maestro at S. Lorenzo in Florence, and shortly after at the Medici court as well; was made canon in 1610, and in 1615, Apostolic Protonotary. In 1607 he founded the Accademia degli Elevati. Gagliano was among the first composers to write in the "stile rappresentativo," which he developed further by ornamentation.

WORKS: *Dafne*, "opera in musica" (his most important work; first played at Mantua, 1608; publ. in Florence, 1608, and reprinted in shortened form by R. Eitner in vol. 10 of the *Publikationen älterer Musikwerke*); *La Flora*, opera (with Peri; Florence, 1628); *Due Messe, a 4, 5* (Florence, 1594); 6 vols. of madrigals *a 5* (1602–17); *Sacrae cantiones* (*I a 6*, with a Mass, 1614; *II a 1–6*, with Basso Continuo, 1622); *Musiche a 1, 2, e 3 voci* (Venice, 1615, with Continuo).

Gagnebin, Henri, Swiss composer and pedagogue; b. Liège (of Swiss parents), March 13, 1886; d. Geneva, June 2, 1977. He studied organ with Vierne and composition with Vincent d'Indy at the Schola Cantorum in Paris; served as a church organist in Paris (1910–16) and in Lausanne (1916–25); was director of the Geneva Cons. from 1925 to 1957. He publ. the books *Entretiens sur la Musique* (Geneva, 1943), *Musique, mon beau souci* (Paris, 1968), and *Orgue, musette et bourbon* (Neuchâtel, 1975).

WORKS: 4 symphs. (1911, 1918–21, 1955, 1970); 3 *Tableaux symphoniques d'après F. Hodler* (1942); *Suite d'orchestre sur des Psaumes huguenots* for Orch. (1950); Piano Concerto (1951); Clarinet Concerto (1971); Concerto for Oboe, Bassoon, and String Orch. (1972); String Trio (1968); Wind Octet (1970); Brass Quintet (1970); Wind Sextet (1971); other chamber music, including several string quartets; many organ pieces.

Gailhard, Pierre, French operatic singer; b. Toulouse, August 1, 1848; d. Paris, Oct. 12, 1918. He began his vocal studies in his native city, and entered the Paris Cons. in 1866. After one year of study under Révial he graduated in 1867, winning 3 first prizes. He made his debut at the Opéra-Comique (Dec. 4, 1867) as Falstaff in Thomas's *Songe d'une nuit d'été;* on Nov. 3, 1871, he made his debut at the Opéra as Méphistophélès in Gounod's *Faust.* At the height of his powers and success he gave up the stage when, in 1884, he accepted, jointly with M. Ritt, the management of the famous institution; on the appointment of M. Bertrand as successor to Ritt, in 1892, he retired, but joined Bertrand the following year as co-director; after the latter's death, in 1899, he remained sole director till 1907. His administration was remarkably successful, considering both the novelties produced and the engagement of new singers (Melba, Eames, Bréval, Caron, Ackté, Alvarez, Saléza, Renaud, the 2 de Reszkes, etc.). Against violent opposition he introduced, and maintained in the repertoire *Lohengrin* (1895), *Die Walküre* (1893), *Tannhäuser* (1895; the first perf. after the notorious fiasco of 1861), *Meistersinger* (1897), *Siegfried* (1902). His son, **André Gailhard** (b. Paris, June 29, 1885; d. Ermont, Val d'Oise, July 3, 1966), composed the operas *Amaryllis* (Toulouse, 1906), *Le Sortilège* (Paris, 1913), and *La Bataille* (Paris, 1931), and the cantata *La Sirène.*

Gaillard, Marius-François, French composer and conductor; b. Paris, Oct. 13, 1900; d. Evecquemont (Yvelines), July 23, 1973. He studied with Diémer and Leroux at the Paris Cons. He began his career as a pianist; then started a series of symph. concerts in Paris, which he conducted from 1928 till 1949. He traveled all over the world, collecting materials of primitive music. His compositions follow a neo-impressionist trend.

Gaito, Constantino, Argentine composer; b. Buenos Aires, Aug. 3, 1878; d. there, Dec. 14, 1945. He studied in Naples with Platania; lived in Buenos Aires as a teacher; wrote the operas (all produced at Buenos Aires) *Shafras* (1907), *I Doria* (1915), *I paggi di Sua Maestà* (1918), *Caio Petronio* (Sept. 2, 1919), *Flor de nieve* (Aug. 3, 1922), *Ollantay* (July 23, 1926), *Lázaro* (1929), and *La sangre de las guitarras* (Aug. 17, 1932); the ballet *La flor del Irupé* (Buenos Aires, July 17, 1929); oratorio, *San Francisco Solano* (1940); symph. poem, *El ombú* (1924); songs; piano pieces.

Gál, Hans, Austrian composer and music scholar; b. Brunn, near Vienna, Aug. 5, 1890. He studied at the Univ. of Vienna with Mandyczewski and Guido Adler; in 1919–29 he lectured at the Vienna Univ.; then went to Germany; was director of the Mainz Cons. in 1929–33; returned to Vienna in 1933; after the advent of the Nazi government, was compelled to leave Vienna in 1938, and settled in Edinburgh, where he became a lecturer on music at the univ. (1945-65) while continuing to compose.

WRITINGS: *The Golden Age of Vienna* (London, 1948); *Johannes Brahms* (Frankfurt, 1961; Eng. trans., 1964); *Richard Wagner* (Frankfurt, 1963); *The Musician's World: Great Composers in Their Letters* (London, 1965; German trans., 1966); *Franz Schubert, oder Die Melodie* (Frankfurt, 1970; Eng. trans., 1974).

WORKS: Operas: *Der Arzt der Sobeide* (Breslau, 1919); *Die heilige Ente* (Düsseldorf, April 29, 1923); *Das Lied der Nacht* (Breslau, April 24, 1926); *Der Zauberspiegel* (Breslau, 1930; also as an orch. suite); *Die beiden Klaas* (1933); 3 symphs. (1928, 1949, 1952); *A Pickwickian Overture* (1939); Violin Concerto (1931); Cello Concerto (1944); Piano Concerto (1947); *Idyllikon* for Small Orch. (1969); Triptych for Orch. (1970); 2 string quartets (1916, 1929); String Trio (1931); Piano Quartet (1915); Piano Trio (1948); Violin Sonata (1921); numerous choral works, sacred and secular. He publ. a manual, *Anleitung zum Partiturlesen* (Vienna, 1923; in Eng. under the title *Directions for Score-Reading,* 1924).

Galamian, Ivan, eminent American violinist and pedagogue; b. Tabriz, Persia, of Armenian parents, Feb. 5, 1903; d. New York, April 14, 1981. He studied violin in Moscow and later in Paris, where he took private lessons with Lucien Capet. In 1930 he settled in the U.S.; was on the staff of the Curtis School of Music in Philadelphia (1944–46); then joined the faculty of the Juilliard School of Music in N.Y. In later years he taught privately in his own apartment, and during the summer at the Meadowmount School in Westport, N.Y. Among his violin pupils were Pinchas Zukerman, Jaime Laredo, Michael Rabin, Paul Zukofsky, and Itzhak Perlman. He publ. *Principles of Violin Playing and Teaching* (Englewood Cliffs, N.J., 1962); *Contemporary Violin Technique* (N.Y., 1966).

Galilei, Vincenzo, celebrated writer on music, father of Galileo Galilei, the astronomer; b. S. Maria a Monte, near Florence, c.1520; d. Florence, June (buried, July 2) 1591. A skillful lutenist and violinist, and student of ancient Greek theory, he was a prominent member of the artistic circle meeting at Count Bardi's house; his compositions for solo voice with lute accompaniment may be regarded as the starting point of the monody successfully cultivated by Peri, Caccini, etc., the founders of the "opera in musica." A zealous advocate of Grecian simplicity, in contrast with contrapuntal complexity, he publ. a *Dialogo ... della musica antica et della moderna* (Florence, 1581; to the 2nd ed. [1602] is appended a polemical *Discorso ... intorno all' opere di messer Gioseffo Zarlino da Chioggia,* which had appeared separately in 1589) and *Fronimo. Dialogo ...* (in 2 parts: Venice, 1568 and 1569; new ed., 1584), all of considerable historical interest. Vol. IV of *Istituzioni e monumenti dell' arte musicale italiana* (Milan, 1934), edited by F. Fano, is devoted entirely to Galilei; it contains a large selection of music reprints from his *Fronimo. Dialogo* (lute transcriptions by Galilei and original compositions), *Libro d'intavolatura di liuto* (1584), *Il secondo libro de madrigali a 4 et a 5 voci* (1587), and a 4-part *Cantilena,* together with biographical details, list of works, notes about extant MSS, reprints, transcriptions, etc. His *Contrapunti a due voci* (1584) was edited by Louise Read (Northampton, Mass., Smith College Music Archives, vol. VIII, 1947).

Galindo (Dimas), Blas, Mexican composer; b. San Gabriel, Jalisco, Feb. 3, 1910. He studied harmony, counterpoint, and fugue with Rolón, musical analysis with Huízar, composition with Chávez, and piano with Rodriguez Vizcarra at the National Cons. in Mexico City (1931–42); had special composition lessons with Aaron Copland at the Berkshire Music Center in Tanglewood, Mass. (1941–42); in 1934 he formed, together with Ayala, Contreras, and Moncayo, the Grupo de los Cuatro for the presentation of modern music (disbanded after a few years). He was a prof. of music and director of the National Cons. in Mexico City from 1942 till 1961; in 1955 became director of the orch. of the Mexican Inst. of Social Security; was pensioned by the government in 1965 and devoted himself mainly to composition thereafter. In his music he stresses native elements, while adhering to classical forms; in his later works he made use of electronic sound.
WORKS: 7 BALLETS: *Entre sombras anda el fuego* (*Among Shadows Walks Fire;* Mexico City, March 23, 1940); *Danza de las fuerzas nuevas* (*Dance of the New Forces;* 1940); *El Zanate* (Mexico City, Dec. 6, 1947); *La Manda* (Mexico City, March 31, 1951); *El sueño y la presencia* (Mexico City, Nov. 24, 1951); *La*

hija del Yori (Mexico City, 1952); *El maleficio* (Mexico City, Oct. 28, 1954). FOR ORCH.: *Sones de mariachi* (1940); 2 piano concertos: No. 1 (Mexico City, July 24, 1942) and No. 2 (Mexico City, Aug. 17, 1962); *Nocturno* (1945); *Don Quijote* (1947); *Homenaje a Cervantes,* suite (1947); *Astucia* (1948); *Poema de Neruda* for String Orch. (1948); *Pequeñas variaciones* (1951); *Los signos del zodíaco* for Small Orch. (1951); 3 symphs.: No. 1, *Sinfonía breve,* for Strings (Mexico City, Aug. 22, 1952); No. 2 (Caracas, March 19, 1957; shared first prize at the Caracas Festival); No. 3 (Washington, D.C., April 30, 1961); *Obertura mexicana* (1953); Flute Concerto (1960; New Orleans, April 3, 1965); *4 Pieces* (1961; Mexico City, Nov. 15, 1963); *Edipo Rey* (1961; incidental music for Sophocles' *Oedipus Rex*); Violin Concerto (1962; Mexico City, Sept. 13, 1970); *3 Pieces* for Clarinet and Orch. (1962); *Obertura* for Organ and Strings (1963); *3 Pieces* for Horn and Orch. (1963); Concertino for Electric Guitar and Orch. (1973; Mexico City, June 12, 1977); *En busca de un muro* (1973). FOR VOICE: *Jicarita* for Voice and Orch. (1939); *Primavera,* youth cantata for Wind Orch. and Children's Chorus (1944); *Arrullo* for Voice, and Small Orch. or Piano (1945); *La Montana* for Chorus a cappella (1945); *A la Patria,* cantata (1946); *3 canciones de la Revolución* for Orch. and Chorus (1953); *Homenaje a Juárez,* cantata with Narrator (1957); *A la Independencia,* cantata (Mexico City, Nov. 24, 1960); *Quetzalcoatl* for Orch. and Narrator (1963); *Tríptico Teotihuacán* for Wind Orch., Indigenous Mexican Percussion Instruments, Chorus, and Soloists (Teotihuacán, Sept. 14, 1964); *Letanía erótica para la paz* for Orch., Organ, Chorus, Soloists, Narrator, and Tape (1963–65; Mexico City, May 2, 1969); *La ciudad de los dioses* (*Luz y Sonido*) for Orch., Chorus, and Narrators (1965); *Homenaje a Rubén Dario* for Narrator and String Orch. (1966); choruses; songs. CHAMBER MUSIC: Suite for Violin and Cello (1933); Quartet for 4 Cellos (1936); *Bosquejos* for Wind Instruments (1937); *2 Preludes* for Oboe, English Horn, and Piano (1938); *Obra para orquesta mexicana* for Indigenous Instruments (1938); Sextet for Flute, Clarinet, Bassoon, Horn, Trumpet, and Trombone (1941); Violin Sonata (1945); Cello Sonata (1949); Suite for Violin and Piano (1957); Quintet for Piano and String Quartet (1960); *3 sonsonetes* for Wind Quintet and Electronic Sound (1967); String Quartet (1970); *Titoco-tico* for Indigenous Percussion Instruments (1971); *Tríptico* for Strings (1974). FOR PIANO: *Llano Alegre* (1938); *5 preludios* (1945); *7 piezas* (1952); Sonata (1976); numerous small pieces. FOR ORGAN: *Estudio* (1971). A list of his works up to 1965 is found in *Composers of the Americas,* vol. 11 (Washington, 1965).

Galkin, Elliott, American conductor, music critic, and educator; b. Brooklyn, Feb. 22, 1921. He studied at Brooklyn College (B.A., 1943); then served with the U.S. Air Force (1943–46); was stationed in France, and received conducting diplomas from the Paris Cons. and the Ecole Normale de Musique. Returning to the U.S., he studied at Cornell Univ. (M.A., 1950; Ph.D., 1960, with the dissertation *The*

Theory and Practice of Orchestral Conducting from 1752). During 1955–56 he was an apprentice conductor with the Vienna State Opera; in 1956 he joined the faculty of Goucher College in Towson, Md.; named prof. there in 1964. In 1957 he joined the faculty of the Peabody Cons. of Music in Baltimore as a conductor; also wrote music criticism for the *Baltimore Sun.* From 1977–82 he served as director of the Peabody Cons. of Music.

Gall, Yvonne, French soprano; b. Paris, March 6, 1885; d. there, Aug. 21, 1972. The spelling of her original name was **Galle.** She studied at the Paris Cons.; made her debut at the Paris Opéra in 1908, and remained on its roster until 1935; also sang at the Opéra-Comique (1921–34). In 1918–21 she was a member of the opera in Chicago, then sang in San Francisco (1931). After her retirement, she taught voice at the Paris Cons. She was highly successful in the French and Italian operatic repertoire. In 1958 she married the French composer and conductor **Henri Paul Busser,** who although much older, outlived her and reached the age of 101.

Gallenberg, Wenzel Robert, Austrian composer; b. Vienna, Dec. 28, 1783; d. Rome, March 13, 1839. He studied under Albrechtsberger; in 1803 he married Countess Giulietta Guicciardi (to whom Beethoven dedicated his Sonata No. 2, op. 27). In Naples, shortly thereafter, he made the acquaintance of the impresario Barbaja; wrote numerous successful ballets for him, and in 1821–23 was his partner when Barbaja was director of opera in Vienna. He attempted the management of the Kärnthnertor-Theater in 1829 but failed, and was obliged to return to Italy, rejoining Barbaja. He wrote about 50 ballets; a sonata, marches, fantasies, etc., for piano. On one of his themes Beethoven wrote a set of variations.

Galli, Filippo, celebrated Italian bass; b. Rome, 1783; d. Paris, June 3, 1853. He made his debut as a tenor in Naples in 1801; after an interruption caused by an illness, he returned to the stage as a bass in Venice in 1812, singing in the premiere of Rossini's *L'inganno felice;* his success was so great that Rossini wrote several other roles for him, including Fernando in *La gazza ladra* and the title role in *Maometto II;* Donizetti wrote the role of Henry VIII for him in *Anna Bolena.* He sang in London at the King's Theatre (1827 and subsequent years). His voice began to decline about 1840, and he abandoned the stage; was then active as a chorus master in Lisbon and Madrid; taught voice at the Paris Cons. (1842–48).

Galli-Curci, Amelita, brilliant Italian soprano; b. Milan, Nov. 18, 1882; d. La Jolla, Calif., Nov. 26, 1963. She studied in Milan and intended to be a pianist; graduated in 1903 from the Milan Cons., winning the first prize. She never took regular voice lessons, but acquired an excellent vocal technique by devising a unique method of self-instruction, listening to recordings of her own voice. She received advice from Mascagni and William Thorner. She made her debut in Trani as Gilda (Dec. 26, 1906), then sang in various opera houses in Italy and in South America (1910). She continued her successful career as an opera singer in Europe until 1915; after the entry of Italy into the war, she went to America; made a sensationally successful debut with the Chicago Opera Co. as Gilda (Nov. 18, 1916); she made her first appearance with the Metropolitan Opera as Violetta (Nov. 14, 1921); remained as a member of the Metropolitan until 1930; then gave concert recitals; eventually retired to California. She was married twice: to the painter Luigi Curci (1910; divorced 1920) and to **Homer Samuels,** her accompanist.

Galli-Marié, Célestine (née **Marié de l'Isle**), French dramatic mezzo-soprano; b. Paris, Nov. 1840; d. Vence, near Nice, Sept. 22, 1905. Her father, an opera singer, was her only teacher. She made her debut at Strasbourg (1859); sang in Toulouse (1860) and in Lisbon (1861). She sang *La Bohème* at Rouen (1862) with such success that she was immediately engaged for the Paris Opéra-Comique; made her debut there (1862) as Serpina in *La Serva padrona.* She created the roles of Mignon (1866) and Carmen (1875).

Galliard, Johann Ernst, German oboist and composer; b. Celle, c.1680; d. London, 1749. He was a pupil of A. Steffani at Hannover. A skillful oboist, he went to London (1706) as chamber musician to Prince George of Denmark; succeeded Draghi as organist at Somerset House; in 1713, played in the Queen's Theatre orch.; in 1717–36, engaged in writing music for the stage productions at Covent Garden and Lincoln's Inn Fields. He last appeared as an oboist probably in 1722.

Gallico, Paolo, composer and pianist; b. Trieste, May 13, 1868; d. New York, July 6, 1955. At the age of 15, he gave a recital at Trieste; then studied at the Vienna Cons. under Julius Epstein, graduating at 18 with highest honors. After successful concerts in Italy, Austria, Russia, Germany, etc., he settled in N.Y. in 1892 as a concert pianist and teacher; toured the U.S. frequently as pianist in recitals and as a soloist with the principal orchs. He won the prize of the National Federation of Music Clubs in 1921 with his dramatic oratorio *The Apocalypse* (perf. by the N.Y. Oratorio Society, Nov. 22, 1922). His symph. episode, *Euphorion,* was performed in Los Angeles (April 6, 1923), N.Y., and Detroit; his Sextet was performed by the Society of the Friends of Music in N.Y. He also wrote an opera, *Harlekin;* piano pieces; and songs. His son, Paul Gallico, is a well-known writer.

Gallignani, Giuseppe, Italian composer and writer on music; b. Faenza, Jan. 9, 1851; d. (suicide) Milan, Dec. 14, 1923. He studied at the Milan Cons.; was then choir leader at the Milan Cathedral; edited the periodical *Musica Sacra* (1886–94); was director of the Parma Cons. (1891–97); from 1897, director of the Milan Cons. He produced the operas *Il Grillo del* *focolare* (Genoa, Jan. 27, 1873), *Atala* (Milan, March 30, 1876), and *Nestorio* (Milan, March 31, 1888), which were unsuccessful; but his church music was greatly appreciated (particularly his Requiem for King Umberto I).

Gallo, Fortune, impresario; b. Torremaggiore, Italy, May 9, 1878; d. New York, March 28, 1963. He studied the piano in Italy; migrated to the U.S. in 1895; first directed the tours of a number of famous bands (1901–9), then founded the San Carlo Opera Co. (1909); in 1920, brought Anna Pavlova and her Russian Ballet to America; in 1923, organized an opera season in Havana, Cuba; in 1925, was director of the tour of Eleanora Duse; in 1926, built and operated the Gallo Theater; in 1928, made a film version of *Pagliacci;* presented performances of operetta in N.Y. and elsewhere.

Gallon, Jean, French composer and pedagogue; b. Paris, June 25, 1878; d. there, June 23, 1959. He studied piano with Diémer and theory with Lavignac and Lenepveu at the Paris Cons.; was chorus director of the Société des Concerts du Cons. (1906–14) and at the Paris Opéra (1909–14). From 1919 till 1949 he taught harmony at the Paris Cons. Among his pupils were Robert Casadesus, Marcel Delannoy, Henri Dutilleux, Olivier Messiaen, and Jean Rivier. He publ. harmony exercises for use at the Cons.; with his brother **Noël Gallon,** he composed several pieces of theater music, among them a ballet, *Hansli le Bossu* (1914); also composed some chamber music and songs.

Gallon, Noël, French composer, brother of **Jean Gallon;** b. Paris, Sept. 11, 1891; d. there, Dec. 26, 1966. He studied piano with I. Philipp and Risler; theory with Caussade and Lenepveu at the Paris Cons., and also with Rabaud. In 1910 he received the First Prix de Rome. From 1920 he was on the faculty of the Paris Cons. as an instructor in solfège, counterpoint, and fugue. As a composer, he was influenced by his brother, who was his first tutor in music; with him he wrote a ballet, *Hansli le Bossu* (1914); his own works comprise a few symph. pieces; Suite for Flute and Piano (1921); Quintet for Horn and Strings (1953); teaching pieces.

Gallus (also **Gallus Carniolus**), **Jacobus,** important Slovenian composer; b. Carniola (probably in Ribniča), between April 15 and July 31, 1550; d. Prague, July 24, 1591. His Slovenian name was **Petelin** (which means "cockerel"); its Germanic equivalent was **Handl,** or **Hähnel** (diminutive of Hahn, "rooster"); he publ. most of his works under the corresponding Latin name Gallus ("rooster"). As a master of polychoral counterpoint, Gallus was highly regarded in his time; he held several important positions as an organist and music director; was Kapellmeister to the Bishop of Olomouc and later was employed at the church St. Johannes in Vado in Prague. A number of his works were publ. during his lifetime. Of these there are several masses: *Selectiores quaedam Missae* (Prague, 1580), con-

taining 4 books of 16 masses, from 4 to 8 voices; a modern edition by Paul A. Pisk was publ. in Denkmäler der Tonkunst in Österreich (Vienna, 1935; reprinted in 1959, 1967, and 1969); 4 books of motets were publ. in Prague in 1586–91 under the title *Opus musicum:* first part (1586) from 4 to 8 voices (exact title, *Tomus primus musici operis harmonium quatuor, quinque, sex, octo et pluribus vocum*); 2nd and 3rd were publ. in 1587, and 4th in 1591; 5 additional motets were printed individually from 1579 to 1614. *Opus musicum* was reprinted in a modern edition by Emil Bezecny and Josef Mantuani in Denkmäler der Tonkunst in Österreich (Vienna, 1899, 1905, 1908, 1913, 1917, 1919; all reprinted again in 1959); *Moralia 5, 6 et 8 vocibus concinnata,* originally publ. in 1596, was reprinted in a modern edition by Dragotin Cvetko (Ljubljana, 1968) and Allen B. Skei (Madison, Wis., 1970). His secular works include *Harmoniae morales* (Prague, 1589–90; modern ed. by Dragotin Cvetko, Ljubljana, 1966) and *Moralia* (Prague, 1596). A motet by Gallus, *Ecce quomodo moritur justus,* was borrowed by Handel for his *Funeral Anthem.*

Gallus, Johannes (Jean le Cocq, Maître Jean, Mestre Jhan), Flemish contrapuntist; d. c.1543. He was maestro di cappella to Duke Ercole of Ferrara in 1534 and 1541. Many of his pieces were publ. in collections and in a vol. of motets printed by Scotto (1543). He was long confused with Jhan Gero.

Galpin, Rev. Francis William, English writer on music; b. Dorchester, Dorset, Dec. 25, 1858; d. Richmond, Surrey, Dec. 30, 1945. He graduated with classical honors from Trinity College, Cambridge (B.A., 1882; M.A., 1885); received his music education from Dr. Garrett and Sterndale Bennett; held various posts as vicar and canon (1891–1921); Hon. Freeman, Worshipful Company of Musicians (1905); wrote many articles on the viola pomposa and other old instruments in *Music & Letters* and *Monthly Musical Record* (1930–33). A Galpin Society was formed in London in 1946 with the object of bringing together all those interested in the history of European instruments and to commemorate the pioneer work of Galpin; it publishes, once a year, the *Galpin Society Journal* (1948–).
WRITINGS: *Descriptive Catalogue of the European Instruments in the Metropolitan Museum of Art, N.Y.* (1902); *The Musical Instruments of the American Indians of the North West Coast* (1903); *Notes on the Roman Hydraulus* (1904); *The Evolution of the Sackbut* (1907); *Old English Instruments of Music* (1910; new ed., London, 1932); *A Textbook of European Musical Instruments* (London, 1937); *The Music of the Sumerians, Babylonians and Assyrians* (1937); *The Music of Electricity* (1938). Galpin was the editor of the revised and augmented ed. of Stainer's *Music of the Bible* (1913).

Galston, Gottfried, Austrian-American pianist; b. Vienna, Aug. 31, 1879; d. St. Louis, April 2, 1950. He was a pupil of Leschetizky in Vienna, and of Jadassohn and Reinecke at the Leipzig Cons.; in 1903–7, he taught at the Stern Cons. in Berlin. On his extended concert tours he proved himself a player of keen analytical powers and intellectual grasp; in 1902, he toured Australia; then Germany, France, and Russia; in 1912–13, he toured in America; toured Russia 11 times (last, in 1926); in 1921–27, lived in Berlin; returned to the U.S. in 1927 and settled in St. Louis. He publ. a *Studienbuch* (1909; 3rd ed., Munich, 1920); analytical notes to a series of 5 historical recitals.

Galuppi, Baldassare, Italian composer, called **Il Buranello** after the island of Burano, near Venice, on which he was born; b. Oct. 18, 1706; d. Venice, Jan. 3, 1785. He studied with his father, a barber and violin player; in 1722 he brought out at Vicenza an opera, *La fede nell'incostanza,* which attracted attention to his talent; he then studied under Lotti in Venice, and in 1729 produced his opera *Dorinda,* with G.B. Pescetti. He cultivated comic opera with such success as to earn the title of "padre dell'opera buffa." He was also a distinguished player on the harpsichord. In 1740 he was appointed maestro del coro at the Ospizio dei Mendicanti; in 1741–43, visited London; in 1748, returned to Venice, where he was 2nd maestro at San Marco; in 1762–64, was principal maestro there. From 1765 to 1768 he acted as maestro to the Russian court; taught many Russian singers and composers; Bortniansky, who later followed him to Venice, was one of his pupils; then he resumed his duties in Venice as maestro del coro. Galuppi wrote a prodigious amount of music: some 112 operas and 20 oratorios; also sacred music and 12 harpsichord sonatas.

Galvani, Giacomo, noted Italian tenor; b. Bologna, Nov. 1, 1825; d. Venice, May 7, 1889. He studied in Bologna with Gamberini and Zamboni; made his debut in *I Masnadieri* in Spoleto in 1849; subsequently sang in Bologna, Milan, London, Barcelona, and other cities with great success; after his retirement, he taught voice in Venice. He was acclaimed for his performances in the operas of Rossini and Donizetti.

Galway, James, Irish flute virtuoso; b. Belfast, Dec. 8, 1939. His first instrument was the violin, but he soon began to study the flute. At the age of 14 he went to work in a piano shop in Belfast; a scholarship enabled him to go to London, where he continued to study flute, and also took academic courses in music at the Royal College of Music and the Guildhall School of Music and Drama. He then received a grant to go to Paris to study with the celebrated flutist Jean-Pierre Rampal at the Paris Cons. His first professional job as a flutist was with the wind band at the Royal Shakespeare Theatre in Stratford-upon-Avon. He subsequently played with the Sadler's Wells Opera Co., the Royal Opera House Orch., and the BBC Symph. Orch.; then was appointed principal flutist of the London Symph. Orch., and later with the Royal Phil. As his reputation grew, he was engaged in 1969 by Herbert von Karajan as first flutist in the Berlin Phil., a post he held until 1975. Abandoning his role as an orch. flutist, he devoted himself to a career as a concert artist; in a single season, 1975–76, he appeared as a soloist with all 5 major London orchs.; also toured in the U.S., Australia, and the Orient, as well as in Europe. He became successful on television, playing his 18-karat-gold flute. He publ. *James Galway: An Autobiography* (N.Y., 1979) and *Flute* (London, 1982).

Gamba, Piero, Italian conductor; b. Rome, Sept. 16, 1936. From a musical family (his father was a professional violinist), he was trained in music at home; his precocity was so remarkable that he was reportedly able to read an orch. score at the age of 8, and at 9 was actually allowed to conduct a regular symph. concert in Rome. He also composed. Unlike the talent of so many child musicians, his gift did not evaporate with puberty; he became a professional artist. According to ecstatic press reports, he conducted in 40 countries and 300 cities, so that his name became familiar to uncounted multitudes (including a billion people in China). From 1970 to 1981 he served as conductor and music director of the Winnipeg Symph. Orch., Canada; in 1982 he was appointed principal conductor of the Symph. Orch. of Adelaide, Australia.

Ganche, Edouard, French writer on music; b. Baulon (Ille-et-Vilaine), Oct. 13, 1880; d. Lyons, May 31, 1945. He studied with Imbert, Henry Expert, and others in Paris. He devoted his life to the study of Chopin and publ. *La Vie de Chopin dans son œuvre* (1909); *Frédéric Chopin, sa vie et ses œuvres* (1913). He was also the editor of the Oxford edition of Chopin's works (1932).

Gange, Fraser, distinguished baritone; b. Dundee, Scotland, June 17, 1886; d. Baltimore, July 1, 1962. He studied in Dundee with his father; later was a pupil of Amy Sherwin in London; made his debut as a basso at the age of 16; toured England, Scotland, Australia, and New Zealand twice; taught singing at the Royal Academy of Music in London; in 1923, came to the U.S.; made his American debut in N.Y. (Jan. 18, 1924); from 1932 to 1946 was a prof. of voice at the Juilliard Summer School in N.Y.; from 1931 to 1957 taught at the Peabody Cons. in Baltimore. His repertoire included 40 oratorios and more than 2,000 songs; he presented in Baltimore a concert of songs on his 70th birthday, in 1956.

Ganne, Louis Gaston, French composer; b. Buxières-les-Mines, Allier, April 5, 1862; d. Paris, July 13, 1923. He was a pupil of T. Dubois, Massenet, and César Franck at the Paris Cons. He was conductor of the balls at the Opéra, and at the municipal Casino at Monte Carlo; wrote successful comic operas, ballets, and divertissements.

WORKS: Operas: *Rabelais* (Paris, Oct. 25, 1892); *Les Colles des femmes* (Paris, 1893); *Les Saltimbanques* (Paris, Dec. 30, 1899); *Miss Bouton d'or* (Paris, Oct. 14, 1902); *Hans le joueur de flûte* (his most successful operetta; Monte Carlo, April 14,

1906); *Les Ailes* (Paris, Sept. 1, 1910); ballets: *Au Japon* (1903; very successful) and *Kermesse flamande* (1917); many orch. dances, of which *La Czarine* and *La Tsigane* became favorites; the patriotic tunes *La Marche Lorraine* and *Le Père de la Victoire,* immensely popular in France; about 150 piano pieces.

Gänsbacher, Johann, Austrian composer; b. Sterzing, Tyrol, May 8, 1778; d. Vienna, July 13, 1844. He studied with Abbé Vogler (1803–4) and Albrechtsberger in Vienna (1806); visited Prague, Dresden, and Leipzig; then resumed study under Vogler, at Darmstadt (Weber and Meyerbeer were his fellow pupils). With Weber, he went to Mannheim and Heidelberg, and rejoined him later in Prague. In Vienna Gänsbacher also met Beethoven. He served in the war of 1813, led a roving life for several years, and finally (1823) settled in Vienna as Kapellmeister of the Cathedral. Of his 216 compositions (masses, Requiems, orch. works, piano pieces, songs, etc.), only a small part has been publ.

Ganz, Rudolph, distinguished pianist and conductor; b. Zürich, Feb. 24, 1877; d. Chicago, Aug. 2, 1972. He studied music assiduously, first as a cellist (with Friedrich Hegar), then as a pianist (with Robert Freund) in Zürich; he continued his piano study with his great-uncle **C. Eschmann-Dumur,** and also took composition lessons with Charles Blanchet at the Cons. of Lausanne; in 1897–98, he studied piano with F. Blumer in Strasbourg; and in 1899 took a course in advanced piano playing with Ferruccio Busoni in Berlin. He made his first public appearance at the age of 12 as a cellist, and at 16 as a pianist. In 1899, he was the soloist in Beethoven's *Emperor Concerto* and Chopin's E-minor Concerto with the Berlin Phil.; and in May 1900 the Berlin Phil. performed his First Symph. In 1901 he went to the U.S. and was engaged as a prof. of piano at the Chicago Musical College; between 1905 and 1908 he made several tours of the U.S. and Canada, and in 1908–11 toured Europe, playing 16 different piano concertos. After 1912 he divided his time touring in Europe and America; in 1921 he added one more profession to his career, that of a symph. conductor; in 1921–27 he was music director and conductor of the St. Louis Symph.; in 1938–49 he conducted a highly successful series of Young People's Concerts with the N.Y. Phil.; concurrently, in 1929–54 he served as director of the Chicago Musical College. He played first performances of many important works by modern composers, including Ravel, Bartók, and Busoni. In July 1900 he married **Mary Forrest,** an American concert singer. He was a highly successful pedagogue, and continued to teach almost to the time of his death, at the age of 95. Besides the early symph., he wrote a lively suite of 20 pieces for Orch., *Animal Pictures* (Detroit, Jan. 19, 1933, composer conducting); Piano Concerto (Chicago Symph. Orch., Feb. 20, 1941, composer soloist); *Laughter—Yet Love, Overture to an Unwritten Comedy* (1950); solo piano pieces; and a couple of hundred songs to words in German, French, Eng., and Swiss and Alsatian dialects. He publ. *Rudolph*

Ganz Evaluates Modern Piano Music (N.Y., 1968).

Ganz, Wilhelm, German pianist; b. Mainz, Nov. 6, 1833; d. London, Sept. 12, 1914. He studied music with his father, **Adolf Ganz** (b. Mainz, Oct. 14, 1796; d. London, Jan. 11, 1870), and with Anschütz. He followed his father to London, where he appeared as a pianist; in 1856 he became accompanist to Jenny Lind. In 1879 he organized the Ganz Orch. Concerts in London, and gave first London performances of works by Liszt and Berlioz; many celebrated artists (Saint-Saëns, Pachmann, etc.) made their English debuts at his concerts. After the discontinuance of his enterprise, in 1883, he devoted himself mainly to teaching. He publ. *Memories of a Musician* (London, 1913).

Garant, Serge, Canadian composer; b. Quebec City, Sept. 22, 1929. He studied piano and clarinet in Sherbrooke and composition in Montreal with Claude Champagne. In 1951 he went to Paris to take a course in musical analysis with Messiaen. Returning to Canada in 1953, he worked as a pianist and music arranger; with the composers Morel and Joachim and the pianist Jeanne Landry he organized in Montreal a modern group, Musique de Notre Temps, dedicated to the presentation of new European and American music; in 1967 he was appointed to the music faculty of the Univ. of Montreal. His music is constructed with formal precision from given thematic, metric, and rhythmic elements, and developed along classical lines.

Garat, Pierre-Jean, famous French concert singer and teacher; b. Ustaritz (Bas-Pyrénées), April 25, 1762; d. Paris, March 1, 1823. His talent was discovered early, and he studied theory and singing with Franz Beck in Bordeaux; his father wished him to become a lawyer, and sent him to the Univ. of Paris in 1782. However, Garat neglected his legal studies, and, aided by the Count d'Artois, he was introduced to Marie Antoinette, whose special favor he enjoyed up to the Revolution. He earned his livelihood as a concert singer; accompanied Rode, in 1792, to Rouen, where he gave numerous concerts before being arrested as a suspect during the Terror; subsequently he went to Hamburg. He returned to Paris in 1794, and sang (1795) at the Feydeau Concerts, where his triumphs speedily procured him a professorship of singing in the newly established Cons.. For 20 years longer, his fine tenor-baritone voice, trained to perfection, made him the foremost singer on the French concert stage. Nourrit, Levasseur, and Ponchard were his pupils.

Garaudé, Alexis de, French singer and composer; b. Nancy, March 21, 1779; d. Paris, March 23, 1852. He studied theory under Cambini and Reicha, and singing under Crescentini and Garat; was a singer in the royal choir in 1808–30 and prof. of singing in the Cons. in 1816–41. He publ. 3 string quintets; many ensemble pieces for violin, flute, clarinet, and cello; sonatas and variations for piano; a solemn Mass; vocalises, arias, duets, and songs; also a *Mé-*

thode de chant (1809, op. 25; 2nd revised ed. as *Méthode complète de chant,* op. 40); *Solfège, ou Méthode de musique; Méthode complète de piano;* and *L'Harmonie rendue facile, ou Théorie pratique de cette science* (1835). He also arranged the vocal scores of Meyerbeer's *Le Prophète* and other operas.

Garay Narciso, Panamanian violinist, composer, and diplomat; b. Panama, June 12, 1876; d. there, March 27, 1953. He studied at the Brussels Cons., graduating with a Premier Prix; later he attended courses at the Schola Cantorum in Paris. He publ. a Violin Sonata and a valuable treatise on Panamanian folk music, *Tradiciones y cantares de Panama* (1930). He also occupied diplomatic posts and at one time was Minister of Foreign Affairs.

Garbin, Edoardo, Italian tenor; b. Padua, March 12, 1865; d. Brescia, April 12, 1943. He studied with Alberto Selva and Vittorio Orefice in Milan; made his debut in 1891 in Vicenza as Alvaro in *La forza del destino;* also sang in Milan (Teatro dal Verme), Naples, and Genoa; in 1893 he created the role of Fenton in Verdi's *Falstaff* at La Scala in Milan; made guest appearances in Rome, Vienna, Berlin, London, Russia, and South America. He married the soprano **Adelina Stehle.** He was particularly distinguished in *verismo* roles.

Garbousova, Raya, brilliant Russian cellist; b. Tiflis, Oct. 10, 1905. She studied at the Cons. there, graduating in 1923; later studied with Hugo Becker, Felix Salmond, and Pablo Casals. After many concerts in Europe, she settled in the U.S. (1927); appeared as a soloist with major American orchs. She played the first performance of the Cello Concerto by Samuel Barber (Boston, April 5, 1946) and the Cello Concerto by Rieti (1960).

García, Francisco Javier (**Padre García,** called in Rome "lo Spagnoletto"), Spanish composer of church music; b. Nalda, 1731; d. Saragossa, Feb. 26, 1809. He lived for some years in Rome as a student and singing teacher; in 1756 he was appointed maestro at Saragossa Cathedral. His works show a marked contrast to the fugal style prevailing before, being more natural and simple. He wrote an oratorio, *Tobia* (1773); the operas *La finta schiava* (Rome, 1754), *Pompeo Magno in Armenia* (Rome, 1755), *La Pupilla* (Rome, 1755), *Lo Scultore deluso* (Rome, 1756); masses; motets, chiefly in 8 parts. His most noted pupil was Caterina Gabrielli.

García, Manuel (**del Popolo Vicente Rodriguez**), famous Spanish tenor, singing teacher, and dramatic composer; b. Seville, Jan. 21, 1775; d. Paris, June 9, 1832. A chorister in the Seville Cathedral at 6, he was taught by Ripa and Almarcha, and at 17 was already well known as a singer, composer, and conductor. After singing in Cadiz, Madrid, and Málaga, he proceeded (1807) to Paris, and sang to enthusiastic audiences at the Théâtre-Italien; in 1809, at his benefit, he sang his own monodrama *El*

poeta calculista with extraordinary success. From 1811 to 1816 he was in Italy. On his return to Paris, his disgust at the machinations of Catalani, the manageress of the Théâtre-Italien, caused him to break his engagement and go to London (1817), where his triumphs were repeated. In 1819–24 he was again the idol of the Parisians at the Théâtre-Italien; sang as first tenor at the Royal Opera in London (1824) and in 1825 embarked for N.Y. with his wife, his son Manuel, and his daughter Maria (Malibran), and the distinguished artists Crivelli *fils,* Angrisani, Barbieri, and de Rosich; from Nov. 29, 1825, to Sept. 30, 1826, they gave 79 performances at the Park and Bowery theaters in N.Y.; the troupe then spent 18 months in Mexico. García returned to Paris, and devoted himself to teaching and composition. His operas, all forgotten, comprise 17 in Spanish, 18 in Italian, and 8 in French, besides a number never performed, and numerous ballets. He was a preeminently successful teacher; his 2 daughters, Mme. Malibran and Pauline Viardot-García, as well as Nourrit, Rimbault, and Favelli, were a few of his best pupils.

García, Manuel Patricio Rodriguez, distinguished Spanish vocal teacher, son of preceding; b. Madrid, March 17, 1805; d. London, July 1, 1906 (aged 101). He was intended to be a stage singer; in 1825 went to N.Y. with his father, but in 1829 adopted the vocation of a singing teacher (in Paris), with conspicuous success. An exponent of his father's method, he also carefully investigated the functions of the vocal organs; invented the laryngoscope, for which the Königsberg Univ. made him a Dr.Phil. In 1840 he sent to the Academy a *Mémoire sur la voix humaine,* a statement of the conclusions arrived at by various investigators, with his own comments. He was appointed prof. at the Paris Cons. in 1847, but resigned in 1848 to accept a similar position at the London Royal Academy of Music, where he taught uninterruptedly from Nov. 10, 1848, until 1895. Among García's pupils were his wife, Eugénie, Jenny Lind, Henriette Nissen, and Stockhausen. His *Traité complet de l'art du chant* was publ. in 1847 (Eng. ed., 1870; revised ed. by García's grandson, **Albert García** as *García's Treatise on the Art of Singing,* London, 1924). He also publ. (in Eng.) a manual, *Hints on Singing* (London, 1894).

García, Pauline Viardot-. See **Viardot-García, Pauline.**

Gardano, Antonio, one of the earliest and most celebrated Italian music-printers; b. 1509; d. Venice, Oct. 28, 1569. From 1537 he reprinted many current publications as well as important novelties, and compositions of his own, e.g., *Motetti del frutto* (1538) and *Canzoni franzese* (1539). His works also appeared in various collections of the time. After 1569 his sons **Alessandro** and **Angelo** carried on the business till 1575, when they separated; the former later set up for himself in Rome (1582–91), while the latter remained in Venice till his death (1610); his heirs continued publishing under his name till 1677.

Gardelli, Lamberto, distinguished Italian conductor; b. Venice, Nov. 8, 1915. He studied at the Liceo Musicale Rossini in Pesaro; after a brief career as a concert pianist he went to Stockholm as a guest conductor of symph. concerts there (1946–55). He then conducted concerts of the Danish State Radio Symph. Orch. in Copenhagen (1955–61); in 1973 was appointed a regular conductor of the Royal Opera in Copenhagen.

Garden, Mary, celebrated operatic soprano; b. Aberdeen, Scotland, Feb. 20, 1874; d. Inverurie, Scotland, Jan. 3, 1967. She came to the U.S. as a child; lived in Hartford, Conn., and then in Chicago. She studied violin and piano; in 1893 she began the study of singing with Mrs. Robinson Duff in Chicago; in 1895 she went to Paris, where she studied with many teachers (Sbriglia, Bouhy, Trabadello, Mathilde Marchesi, and Lucien Fugère). Her funds, provided by a wealthy patron, were soon depleted, and Sybil Sanderson, an American soprano living in Paris, came to her aid and introduced her to Albert Carré, director of the Opéra-Comique. Her operatic debut was made under dramatic circumstances on April 10, 1900, when the singer who performed the title role of Charpentier's *Louise* at the Opéra-Comique was taken ill during the performance, and Mary Garden took her place. She revealed herself not only as a singer of exceptional ability, but also as a skillful actress. She subsequently sang in several operas of the general repertoire; also created the role of Diane in Pierné's opera *La Fille de Tabarin* (Opéra-Comique, Feb. 20, 1901). A historic turning point in her career was reached when she was selected to sing Mélisande in the world premiere of Debussy's opera (Opéra-Comique, April 30, 1902); she also became the center of a raging controversy, when Maurice Maeterlinck, the author of the drama, voiced his violent objection to her assignment (his choice for the role was Georgette Leblanc, his common-law wife), and pointedly refused to have anything to do with the production. Mary Garden won warm praise from the critics for her musicianship, despite the handicap of her American-accented French. She remained a member of the Opéra-Comique; also sang at the Grand Opéra, and at Monte Carlo. She made her American debut as Thaïs at the Manhattan Opera House, N.Y. (Nov. 25, 1907), and presented there the first American performance of *Pelléas et Mélisande* (Feb. 19, 1908). She also undertook the performance of *Salome* at its 2nd production in N.Y. (Jan. 27, 1909). In 1910 she joined the Chicago Opera Co.; she became its impresario in the season 1921–22, during which the losses mounted to about $1,000,000. She sang in the first American performances of Honegger's *Judith* (Chicago, Jan. 27, 1927), Alfano's *Resurrection* (1930), and Hamilton Forrest's *Camille* (1930), an opera she commissioned specially. After 1930 she made sporadic appearances in opera and concerts; in 1935, she gave master classes in opera at the Chicago Musical College; acted as technical adviser for opera sequences in motion pictures in Hollywood; in 1939 she returned to Scotland; made a lecture tour in the U.S. in 1947. With Louis Biancolli she wrote a book of memoirs, *Mary Garden's Story* (N.Y., 1951).

Gardiner, Henry Balfour, English composer; b. London, Nov. 7, 1877; d. Salisbury, England, June 28, 1950. He was a pupil of Iwan Knorr in Frankfurt; taught singing for a short time in Winchester, but then devoted his whole time to composition. He was also an ardent collector of English folk songs; his own compositions reflect the authentic modalities of the English countryside. He wrote a *Phantasy* for Orch.; *English Dance;* Symph. in D; String Quintet; *News from Wydah* for Soli, Chorus, and Orch.; piano pieces; songs. His most successful piece was *Shepherd Fennel's Dance* for Orch.

Gardiner, John Eliot, English conductor; b. Springhead, Dorset, April 20, 1943. He was educated at King's College, Cambridge; while still a student there, he founded the Monteverdi Choir (1964); then went to France to study with Nadia Boulanger; upon his return to England, took postgraduate courses with Thurston Dart at King's College, London. He made his first major conducting appearance at the Promenade Concerts in London in 1968; also conducted at the Sadler's Wells Opera and at Covent Garden. He continued giving concerts with his Monteverdi Choir; also founded the English Baroque Soloists, a group which played works of the Baroque on original instruments. In 1980 he was appointed principal conductor of the Canadian Broadcasting Corp. Radio Orch. in Vancouver; in 1981 he served as artistic director of the Göttingen Handel Festival. He is credited with the discovery of the manuscript of Rameau's opera *Les Boréades* in Paris in 1971.

Gardiner, William, British writer on music; b. Leicester, March 15, 1770; d. there, Nov. 16, 1853. His father, a hosiery manufacturer, was an amateur musician from whom he acquired the rudiments of music. During his travels on the Continent on his father's business he gathered materials for a collection, *Sacred Melodies* (1812–15), adapted to English words from works by Mozart, Haydn, and Beethoven. His book *The Music of Nature* (London, 1832) enjoyed a certain vogue; he also publ. memoirs, *Music and Friends, or Pleasant Recollections of a Dilettante* (3 vols.; I–II, London, 1838; III, 1853); *Sights in Italy, with some Account of the Present State of Music and the Sister Arts in that Country* (London, 1847).

Gardner, John Linton, English composer; b. Manchester, March 2, 1917. He studied organ at Exeter College, Oxford, with Sir Hugh Allen, Ernest Walker, R.O. Morris, and Thomas Armstrong (Mus.B., 1939). In 1946–52 he was opera coach at Covent Garden; in 1953 was appointed instructor at Morley College; served as its director of music (1965–69); concurrently he was director of music at St. Paul's Girls' School in 1962, and taught at the Royal Academy of Music in London (from 1956); retired in 1975.

His style is characteristically fluent and devoid of attempts at experimentation; modernistic devices are used sparingly. He was made a Commander of the Order of the British Empire in 1976.

WORKS: Operas: *The Moon and Sixpence,* after Somerset Maugham (London, May 24, 1957); *The Visitors* (Aldeburgh Festival, June 10, 1972); *Bel and the Dragon* (1973); *The Entertainment of the Senses* (London, Feb. 2, 1974); *Tobermoray* (1976); for Orch.: Symph. (Cheltenham, July 5, 1951); *A Scots Overture* (London, Aug. 16, 1954); Piano Concerto No. 1 (1957); *Sinfonia piccola* for Strings (1974); *An English Ballad* (1969); *3 Ridings* (1970); Sonatina for Strings (1974); chamber music: *Rhapsody* for Oboe and String Quartet (1935); Oboe Sonata (1953); *Concerto da camera* for 4 Instruments (1968); *Chamber Concerto* for Organ and 11 Instruments (1969); sacred and secular choruses; piano pieces; songs.

Gardner, Samuel, American violinist and composer; b. Elizavetgrad, Russia, Aug. 25, 1891; d. New York, Jan. 23, 1984. He came early to the U.S. and studied violin with Felix Winternitz and Franz Kneisel; composition with Goetschius, and later with Loeffler in Boston. He was a member of the Kneisel String Quartet (1914); also played violin in American orchs. From 1924 to 1941 he taught violin at the Inst. of Musical Art in N.Y. He wrote a number of pleasant pieces: *Country Moods* for String Orch. (Staten Island Civic Symph., Dec. 10, 1946); a tone poem, *Broadway* (Boston Symph., April 18, 1930, composer conducting); his *From the Canebrake,* op. 5, no. 1, enjoyed popularity; he also publ. *Essays for Advanced Solo Violin* (1960).

Garlandia, Johannes de (sometimes called **Johannes de Garlandia the Elder** to distinguish him from a hypothetical Joh. Garlandia the Younger, proposed by H. Riemann on rather suppositional grounds), 13th-century writer on mathematics, theology, and alchemy; b. England, c.1195. He studied at Oxford; in 1217 went to Paris; joined the Crusade against the Albigenses; was probably still living in 1272. He is the author of several tracts on music, among them the *De musica mensurabili positio,* a valuable treatise on mensural music, 2 versions of which were printed by Coussemaker in his *Scriptores,* vol. I.; a modern edition was prepared by F. Reimer (Wiesbaden, 1972). There are altogether 4 works printed under his name in Gerbert and Coussemaker.

Garreta, Julio, Catalan composer; b. San Feliu, March 12, 1875; d. there, Dec. 2, 1925. Entirely self-taught, he learned piano and composition. He wrote a great number of "sardanas" (the Catalan national dance); a friendship with Casals stimulated several larger works; his *Impressions symphoniques* for String Orch. was performed in Barcelona on Oct. 29, 1907. His *Suite Empordanesa* for Orch. received first prize at the Catalan Festival in 1920. He also wrote a Cello Sonata, a Piano Sonata, and a Piano Quartet.

Garrison, Mabel, American coloratura soprano; b. Baltimore, April 24, 1886; d. New York, Aug. 20, 1963. She was a pupil of W.E. Heimendahl and P. Minetti at the Peabody Cons. (1909–11); then of O. Saenger in N.Y. (1912–14), and of H. Witherspoon (1916). She made her debut as Filina (*Mignon*) in Boston, April 18, 1912; was a member of the Metropolitan Opera from 1914 to 1921; made a world tour; in 1933 she taught singing at Smith College; then retired.

Gasparini, Francesco, Italian composer; b. Camaiore, near Lucca, March 5, 1668; d. Rome, March 22, 1727. He was a pupil of Corelli and Pasquini in Rome, where he taught for a time; in 1701–13 was maestro di coro at the Ospedale della Pietà, Venice; became maestro di cappella at S. Lucina in Rome in 1717. In 1725 he was appointed maestro di cappella at the Lateran, Rome. Between 1702 and 1723 he produced about 50 operas at Venice, Rome, and Vienna, with great success; he also wrote masses, motets, cantatas, Psalms, oratorios, etc. His chief work was a method of thorough-bass playing, *L'armonico pratico al cimbalo* (Venice, 1708; 7th ed., 1802), used in Italy for nearly a hundred years. His most famous pupil was Benedetto Marcello.

Gasparo da Salò (family name, **Bertolotti**), Italian instrument maker; b. Polpenazzi (baptized in Salò, May 20), 1540; d. Brescia (buried, April 14), 1609. He came to Brescia in 1562, and settled there as a maker of viols, viole da gamba, and contrabass viols, which gained much celebrity; his violins were less valued. His pupils were his eldest son, **Francesco;** Giovanni Paolo Maggini; and Giacomo Lafranchini. Dragonetti's favorite double bass was an altered "viola contrabassa" of Gasparo's.

Gassmann, Florian Leopold, important Austrian composer; b. Brüx, Bohemia, May 3, 1729; d. Vienna, Jan. 20, 1774. He learned to play the violin and harp from a local chorus master; at the age of 13 ran away from home, and reached Italy; there is no corroboration for the claim that he became a student of Padre Martini in Bologna. After living in Venice in the service of Count Leonardo Veneri, he was asked by the Austrian Emperor Francis I in 1764 to be theater conductor in Vienna. In 1772 he succeeded Reutter as court Kapellmeister, and founded the Tonkünstler-Societät for the relief of the widows and orphans of musicians. He was greatly esteemed as a teacher; among his students was Salieri. Gassmann's 2 daughters, **Maria Anna** (b. Vienna, 1771; d. there, Aug. 27, 1852) and **Therese Maria** (b. Vienna, April 1, 1774; d. there, Sept. 8, 1837), were opera singers. Gassmann was a remarkably prolific opera composer; he wrote about 25 operas, several of which were produced during his travels in Italy: *Achille in Sciro* (Venice, 1766), *Ezio* (Rome, 1770); his "dramma giocoso," *La Contessina,* was one of the earliest comic operas treating the social world of aristocrats and merchants. He further composed many cantatas, some 50 sacred works, numerous trio sonatas and quartets, and about 50 "symphonien" in the concertante manner, some derived from the instrumental portions of his operas. Mozart greatly appreciated some of Gassmann's chamber music. One of the symphs., in B minor, was edited by Karl Geiringer for Universal Edition (1933). *La Contessina* and a selection of Gassmann's sacred music are publ. in Denkmäler der Tonkunst in Österreich, vols. 42–44 and 83 (former nos. 21.i and 45).

Gassner, Ferdinand Simon, Austrian violinist; b. Vienna, Jan. 6, 1798; d. Karlsruhe, Feb. 25, 1851. In 1816, he was violinist at the National Theater in Mainz; in 1818, he became music director at Giessen Univ., which in 1819 made him Dr. Phil. and lecturer on music. In 1826 he joined the court orch. at Karlsruhe, and afterward became teacher of singing and chorus master at the theater. In 1822–35 he publ. the *Musikalischer Hausfreund* at Mainz; he edited (1841–45) the *Zeitschrift für Deutschlands Musikvereine und Dilettanten.* He wrote *Partiturkenntniss, Ein Leitfaden zum Selbstunterricht* (1838; French ed., 1851, as *Traité de la partition*) and *Dirigent und Ripienist* (1846); contributed to the Supplement of Schilling's *Universallexikon der Tonkunst* (1842) and edited an abridgment of the entire work (1849). He composed 2 operas, several ballets, a cantata, songs, etc.

Gastinel, Léon-Gustave-Cyprien, French composer; b. Villers, near Auxonne, Aug. 13, 1823; d. Fresnes-les-Rurgis, Oct. 20, 1906. He was a pupil of Halévy at the Paris Cons., taking first Grand Prix de Rome for his cantata *Vélasquez* in 1846. A successful composer of operas, he produced *Le Miroir* (1853), *L'Opéra aux fenêtres* (1857), *Titus et Bérénice* (1860), *Le Buisson vert* (1861), *Le Barde* (Nice, 1896), and the ballet *Le Rêve* (Paris Opéra, 1890), besides other stage works: *La Kermesse, Eutatès, Ourania,* and *La Tulipe bleue;* also 4 oratorios and 3 solemn masses, orch. compositions, chamber music, choruses, etc.

Gastoldi, Giovanni Giacomo, Italian composer; b. Caravaggio; d. 1622. In 1581 he was a singer at the court of Mantua; contributed part of the score of *L'Idropica,* produced in Mantua on June 2, 1608. In 1609 he was maestro di cappella in Milan. A number of his works were publ.: 4 books of madrigals (1588, 1589, 1592, 1602); 4 books of canzonette (1592, 1595, 1596, 1597); many individual pieces are reproduced in contemporary collections. His "balletti" (dance songs) are remarkable for their rhythmic vigor in folk-song style.

Gatti, Guido, eminent Italian music critic and writer; b. Chieti, May 30, 1892; d. Grottaferrata, near Rome, May 10, 1973. He was editor of *La Riforma Musicale* (Turin, 1913–15) and *Il Pianoforte* (Turin 1920–27), which changed its name in 1927 to *La Rassegna Musicale.*
WRITINGS: *Guida musicale della Giovanna d'Arco di Enrico Bossi; Biografia critica di Bizet* (1914); "Figure di musicisti francesi," *Biblioteca della Riforma Musicale* (Turin, 1915); *Musicisti moderni d'Italia e di fuori* (Bologna, 1920; 2nd ed.,

1925); *Le Barbier de Séville de Rossini* (Paris, 1925); *Debora e Jaele di I. Pizzetti* (1922); *Dizionario musicale* (in collaboration with A. della Corte; 1925; 2nd ed., 1930; revised ed., 1952); *Ildebrando Pizzetti* (Turin, 1934; in Eng., London, 1951); *Alfredo Casella* (with F. D'Amico; Milan, 1958); *Victor de Sabata* (Milan, 1958); contributed to *Grove's Dictionary;* wrote numerous articles for music magazines in Europe and America.

Gatti-Casazza, Giulio, Italian impresario; b. Udine, Feb. 3, 1868; d. Ferrara, Sept. 2, 1940. He was educated at the univs. of Ferrara and Bologna, and graduated from the Naval Engineering School at Genoa; when his father, who had been chairman of the board of directors of the Municipal Theater at Ferrara, accepted a position in Rome in 1893, Gatti-Casazza abandoned his career as engineer and became director of the theater. His ability attracted the attention of the Viscount di Modrone and A. Boito, who, in 1898, offered him the directorship of La Scala at Milan. During the 10 years of his administration the institution came to occupy first place among the opera houses of Italy. In 1908–35 he was general director of the Metropolitan Opera, and the period of his administration was, both artistically and financially, the most flourishing in the history of the house; he vastly improved the orch., chorus, and all the mechanical depts.; one of his first suggestions to the board of directors was to offer a $10,000 prize for the encouragement of native operatic composers (won by Horatio Parker with *Mona,* 1912); the doors were opened to American composers (starting with Converse, Damrosch, and Herbert), and eminent foreign composers gladly accepted invitations to have the world premiere of new works take place at the Metropolitan (Humperdinck's *Königskinder,* Puccini's *Girl of the Golden West,* Granados's *Goyescas,* Giordano's *Madame Sans-Gêne,* etc.); the list of novelties produced is a long one, numbering 110 works; besides, there were noteworthy revivals of older works, e.g., Gluck's *Iphigénie en Tauride* (revised by Richard Strauss), etc. During this period, Giulio Setti was chorus master and set a high standard for the opera chorus. Gatti-Casazza procured the services of the best conductors available, bringing with him from La Scala the master Arturo Toscanini, and such able conductors as Polacco and Panizza. He resigned in 1935, Giulio Setti leaving with him, and went to Italy, where he lived in retirement. On April 3, 1910, Gatti-Casazza married the soprano **Frances Alda;** they were divorced in 1929; in 1930 he married Rosina Galli (d. April 30, 1940), premiere danseuse and ballet mistress.

Gatty, Nicholas Comyn, English composer; b. Bradfield, Sept. 13, 1874; d. London, Nov. 10, 1946. He was educated at Downing College, Cambridge (B.A., 1896; Mus.B., 1898); then studied with Stanford at the Royal College of Music; was organist to the Duke of York's Royal Military School at Chelsea; music critic of *Pall Mall Gazette,* 1907–14; also acted as assistant conductor at Covent Garden.

WORKS: One-act operas (all produced in London): *Greysteel* (1906); *Duke or Devil* (1909); *The Tempest* (April 17, 1920); *Prince Ferelon* (1921; received the Carnegie Award for this opera); *Macbeth,* 4-act opera (MS); *King Alfred and the Cakes; Ode on Time* for Soli, Chorus, and Orch., after Milton; *3 Short Odes;* Variations for Orch. on *Old King Cole;* Piano Concerto; Piano Trio; String Quartet; waltzes for piano; songs.

Gaubert, Philippe, renowned French conductor and composer; b. Cahors, July 3, 1879; d. Paris, July 8, 1941. He studied flute with Taffanel at the Paris Cons.; in 1905, won the 2nd Prix de Rome; in 1919–38, was conductor of the Paris Cons. concerts; in 1920 was first conductor at the Opéra in Paris.

Gaudimel, Claude. See **Goudimel, Claude.**

Gauk, Alexander, Russian conductor; b. Odessa, Aug. 15, 1893; d. Moscow, March 30, 1963. He studied composition with Kalafati and Vitols, and conducting with N. Tcherepnin, at the Petrograd Cons., where he graduated in 1917; then conducted at the State Opera and Ballet Theater there (1920–31). He was chief conductor of the Leningrad Phil. Orch. (1930–34), the U.S.S.R. State Symph. Orch. of Moscow (1936–41), and the All-Union Radio Symph. Orch. of Moscow (1953–63). He also taught conducting at the conservatories of Leningrad (1927–33), Tiflis (1941–43), and Moscow (1939–63). His pupils included such distinguished conductors as Mravinsky, Melik-Pashayev, Simeonov, and Svetlanov. He championed the music of Russian composers; restored Rachmaninoff's First Symphony to the active Russian repertoire from orch. parts found in the archives of the Moscow Cons. He was also a composer; wrote a symph., a harp concerto, a piano concerto, and songs.

Gaultier, Denis, famous French lute player and composer; b. Marseilles, c.1600; d. Paris, late Jan. 1672. He was active as a composer from about 1625 or 1630; was a lutenist in Paris in 1626. Much of his work is in the form of dance suites, each selection in the various groups bearing a descriptive title. As a composer, Gaultier developed a type of ornamentation which influenced the keyboard style of Froberger and Chambonnières. Among his pupils were Mouton, DuFaux, and Gallot.

Gauthier, Eva, soprano; b. Ottawa, Canada, Sept. 20, 1885; d. New York, Dec. 26, 1958. She studied voice in Ottawa and at the Paris Cons. with Frank Buels and Jacques Bouhy, later with Schoen-René in Berlin; in 1909, she made her operatic debut as Micaela in Pavia, Italy; in 1910, appeared at Covent Garden, London (Yniold in *Pelléas et Mélisande*); later devoted herself to a concert career; performed many works of contemporary composers; during her world tours she also made a study of Javanese and Malayan folk songs.

Gavazzeni, Gianandrea, Italian composer and conductor; b. Bergamo, July 25, 1909. He studied at the Santa Cecilia Academy in Rome (1921–24); then at the Milan Cons. (1925–31), where his principal teacher was Pizzetti. He then became engaged in musical journalism and in conducting; it was as a conductor that he became mostly known in Italy and abroad; he conducted concerts in England, Moscow, and Canada (1965–67). He was music director of La Scala, Milan, from 1965 to 1972; led the La Scala Opera in Moscow (1965) and in Montreal (1967); on Oct. 11, 1976, made his American debut at the Metropolitan Opera in N.Y.

Gaviniès, Pierre, French violinist and composer; b. Bordeaux, May 11, 1728; d. Paris, Sept. 8, 1800. He learned to play the violin as a child in the workshop of his father, who was a lute maker. In 1734, the family moved to Paris. Gaviniès made his first public appearance in a Concert Spirituel at the age of 13; he reappeared at these concerts as a youth of 20; his success with the public was such that Viotti described him as "the French Tartini." From 1773 to 1777 he was director (with Gossec) of the Concert Spirituel. When the Paris Cons. was organized in 1795, he was appointed prof. of violin. His book of technical exercises, *Les 24 Matinées* (violin studies in all the 24 keys), demonstrates by its transcendental difficulty that Gaviniès must have been a virtuoso; he attracted numerous pupils, and is regarded as the founder of the French school of violin pedagogy. His original works are of less importance; he wrote 3 sonatas for violin accompanied by cello (publ. posthumously; the one in F minor is known as *Le Tombeau de Gaviniès*); his most celebrated piece is an air, *Romance de Gaviniès,* which has been publ. in numerous arrangements; he wrote further 6 sonatas for 2 Violins and 6 violin concertos, and produced a comic opera, *Le Prétendu* (Paris, Nov. 6, 1760).

Gavoty, Bernard, French writer on music; b. Paris, April 2, 1908; d. there, Oct. 24, 1981. He took courses in philosophy and literature at the Sorbonne; also studied organ at the Paris Cons. In 1942 he was appointed organist at Saint-Louis des Invalides in Paris; in 1945 he became music critic for *Le Figaro,* under the nom de plume Clarendon, a position he continued to hold until his death. He publ. *Louis Vierne, Le musicien de Notre-Dame* (Paris, 1943); *Jehan Alain, Musicien Français* (Paris, 1945); *Souvenirs de Georges Enesco* (Paris, 1955); *Pour ou contre la musique moderne?* (with Daniel-Lesur, Paris, 1957); *Chopin amoureux* (with Emile Vuillermoz; Paris, 1960); *Vingt grands interprètes* (Lausanne, 1966; also in German); a number of lavishly illustrated monographs about contemporary artists, under the general title *Les Grands Interprètes* (Geneva, 1953, et seq.), containing biographies of Gieseking, Furtwängler, Menuhin, etc.; also made documentary films on famous musicians.

Gay, John, English librettist of *The Beggar's Opera;* b. Barnstaple, Devon (baptized, Sept. 16), 1685;

d. London, Dec. 4, 1732. The opera was brought out in London on Jan. 29, 1728, and was immensely popular for a century, chiefly because of its sharp satire and the English and Scots folk melodies it used. It has had a number of successful revivals. The government disliked *The Beggar's Opera,* and forbade the performance of its sequel, *Polly,* the score of which was printed in 1729. When *Polly* was finally performed in 1777 it was a fiasco, because the conditions satirized no longer prevailed.

Gayarre, Julián, famous Spanish tenor; b. Valle de Roncal, Jan. 9, 1844; d. Madrid, Jan. 2, 1890. His original name was Gayarre Sebástian. He studied in Madrid; attracted attention at his appearance at Covent Garden, in London, in 1877; continued to sing there until 1881, and again in 1886–87. He was generally regarded as one of the finest lyrico-dramatic tenors of his time, and was described by enthusiasts as having "the voice of an angel."

Gaztambide, Joaquín, Spanish composer; b. Tudela, Navarre, Feb. 7, 1822; d. Madrid, March 18, 1870. He studied at Pamplona and at the Madrid Cons. with Pedro Albéniz (piano) and Ramón Carnicer (composition). After a stay in Paris, he returned to Madrid as manager of several theaters and as conductor of the Cons. concerts; he became director of the Concert Society in 1868. He was best known, however, for his zarzuelas, the satiric musical productions which are identified with the Madrid stage. Gaztambide wrote 44 zarzuelas, many of which became popular; one, *El juramento,* first produced in 1858, was revived in Madrid in 1933. He took a zarzuela company to Mexico and Havana in 1868–69.

Gazzaniga, Giuseppe, Italian opera composer; b. Verona, Oct. 5, 1743; d. Crema, Feb. 1, 1818. He was a pupil of Porpora in Naples; after the production of his early opera *Il Barone di Trocchia* there (1768), he traveled to Venice and to Vienna; his opera *Don Giovanni Tenorio* (Venice, Feb. 5, 1787) anticipated Mozart's *Don Giovanni;* in all he wrote 50 operas, several of which became quite popular at the time (*La locanda, L'isola di Alcina, La vendemmia, La Moglie capricciosa,* etc.). Mozart's librettist, Lorenzo da Ponte, wrote the libretto of Gazzaniga's opera *Il finto cieco* (Vienna, Feb. 20, 1786).

Gebel, Georg (Jr.), German composer; b. Brieg, Silesia, Oct. 25, 1709; d. Rudolstadt, Sept. 24, 1753. He studied with his father; was organist at St. Maria Magdalene (1729) in Breslau, and Kapellmeister to the Duke of Oels. In 1735 he joined Count Brühl's orch. at Dresden, where he met Hebenstreit, the inventor of the "Pantaleon," and learned to play that instrument. In 1747 he was appointed Kapellmeister to the Prince of Schwarzburg-Rudolstadt. He was a precocious composer, and wrote a number of light operas (to German rather than Italian librettos, thus upholding the national tradition), and more than 100 symphs., partitas, and concertos.

Gédalge, André, eminent French theorist, composer, and pedagogue; b. Paris, Dec. 27, 1856; d. Chessy, Feb. 5, 1926. He began to study music rather late in life, and entered the Paris Cons. at the age of 28. However, he made rapid progress, and obtained the 2nd Prix de Rome after a year of study (under Guiraud). He then elaborated a system of counterpoint, later publ. as *Traité de la fugue* (Paris, 1901; Eng. trans., 1964), which became a standard work. In 1905, Gédalge was engaged as a prof. of counterpoint and fugue at the Paris Cons.; among his students were Ravel, Enesco, Koechlin, Roger-Ducasse, Milhaud, and Honegger. He also publ. *Les Gloires musicales du monde* (1898) and other pedagogic works. As a composer, Gédalge was less significant. Among his works are a pantomime, *Le Petit Savoyard* (Paris, 1891); an opera, *Pris au piège* (Paris, 1895); and 3 operas that were not performed: *Sita, La Farce du Cadi,* and *Hélène;* he also wrote 3 symphs., several concertos, some chamber music, and songs.

Gedda, Nicolai (real last name, **Ustinov**), noted Swedish tenor; b. Stockholm, July 11, 1925, of Russian-Swedish extraction. Gedda was his mother's name, which he assumed in his professional life. His father was a Russian, Michael Ustinov, who fought in the White Army and emigrated after the civil war; he then earned his living by singing in the Don Cossack Choir; later he served as chorus master of a Russian Orthodox church in Stockholm; Nicolai Gedda joined him in a children's chorus. In 1950 Gedda entered the opera school at the Stockholm Cons.; on April 8, 1952, he made a successful debut as the leading tenor in Adam's comic opera *Le Postillon de Longjumeau.* In 1953 he made his debut at La Scala in Milan; in 1954 he sang Faust at the Paris Opéra; then had an engagement at Covent Garden in London; in 1957 he sang Don José in *Carmen* at the Vienna State Opera. He made his U.S. debut as Faust with the Pittsburgh Opera on April 4, 1957; his Metropolitan Opera debut followed in N.Y. on Nov. 1, 1957; he created the role of Anatol in Barber's *Vanessa* at the Metropolitan on Jan. 15, 1958. Because of his natural fluency in Russian and his acquired knowledge of German, French, Italian, and English, he was able to sing with total freedom the entire operatic repertoire. In 1980 and in 1981 he made highly successful appearances in Russia, both in opera and on the concert stage, in programs of Russian songs.

Gehot, Jean (also **Joseph**), Belgian violinist and composer; b. Brussels, April 8, 1756; d. in the U.S. c.1820. He went to London after 1780; there he publ. *A Treatise on the Theory and Practice of Music* (1784), *The Art of Bowing the Violin* (1790), and *Complete Instructions for Every Musical Instrument* (1790). In 1792, he went to America; gave concerts in N.Y., where he presented his work *Overture in 12 movements, expressive of a voyage from England to America.* He then played violin at the City Concerts in Philadelphia, under the management of Reinagle and Capron. However, he failed to prosper in America; most of his works were publ. in London, among them 17 string quartets, 12 string trios, and 24 "military pieces" for 2 Clarinets, 2 Horns, and Bassoon.

Geiringer, Karl, eminent Austrian-American musicologist; b. Vienna, April 26, 1899. He studied composition with Hans Gál and Richard Stöhr, and musicology with Guido Adler and Wilhelm Fischer in Vienna; continued his musicological studies with Curt Sachs and Johannes Wolf in Berlin; received his Ph.D. from the Univ. of Vienna with the dissertation *Die Flankenwirbelinstrumente in der bildenden Kunst (1300–1550)* in 1923 (publ. in Tutzing, 1979). In 1930 he became librarian and museum curator of the Gesellschaft der Musikfreunde in Vienna. He left Austria after 1938 and went to London, where he worked for the BBC; also taught at the Royal College of Music (1939–40); he then emigrated to the U.S.; was a visiting prof. at Hamilton College, Clinton, N.Y. (1940–41); in 1941 he became a prof. at Boston Univ. and head of graduate studies in music; in 1962 he was made a prof. at the Univ. of Calif., Santa Barbara; he retired in 1972. In 1955–56 he was president of the American Musicological Society. In 1959 he was elected a Fellow of the American Academy of Arts and Sciences; also was an honorary member of the Österreichische Gesellschaft für Musikwissenschaft and of the American chapter of the Neue Bach-Gesellschaft; in addition, was a member of the Joseph Haydn Inst. of Cologne. A music scholar and writer of great erudition, he contributed valuable publications on the Bach family, Haydn, and Brahms. As a member of the editorial board of the Denkmäler der Tonkunst in Österreich, he edited the collected works of Paul Peuerl and the instrumental works of Isaac Posch (vol. 70); also, with E. Mandyczewski, selected works by Antonio Caldara (vol. XXXIX). He edited Gluck's opera *Telemaco, Sämtliche Werke,* I/2; Haydn's opera *Orlando Paladino, Werke,* XXV/11, and 100 arrangements of Scottish folk songs by Haydn, *Werke,* XXXII/1. He was general editor of the Harbrace History of Musical Forms and of the Univ. of Calif., Santa Barbara, Series of Early Music; edited Isaac Posch's *Harmonia concertans 1623.* WRITINGS: *Führer durch die Joseph Haydn Kollektion im Museum der Gesellschaft der Musikfreunde in Wien* (with H. Kraus; Vienna, 1930); "Joseph Haydn," in Bücken's *Grosse Meister* (Potsdam, 1932); *Wiener Meister um Mozart und Beethoven* (a collection of piano works; Vienna, 1935); *Johannes Brahms: Leben und Schaffen eines deutschen Meisters* (a major study; Vienna, 1935; Eng. trans., London and N.Y., 1936; 3rd ed., revised and enlarged, N.Y., 1981); *Musical Instruments: Their History in Western Culture from the Stone Age to the Present Day* (London, 1943; 3rd ed., revised and enlarged, published as *Instruments in the History of Western Music,* N.Y., 1978); *Haydn: A Creative Life in Music* (N.Y., 1946; 2nd ed., 1963); *A Thematic Catalogue of Haydn's Settings of Folksongs from the British Isles* (Superior, Wis., 1953); *The Bach Family: Seven Generations of Creative Genius* (an important study; N.Y., 1954); *Music of the Bach Family: An Anthology* (a valuable collection; Cambridge, Mass., 1955); *Johann Sebastian Bach: The Culmination of an Era* (an excellent study; N.Y., 1966).

Geissler, Fritz, East German composer; b. Wurzen, near Leipzig, Sept. 16, 1921; d. Bad Saarow, Jan. 11, 1984. He studied at the Hochschule für Musik in Leipzig with Max Dehnert and Wilhelm Weismann (1948–50); later taught there (1962–70); then joined the faculty of the Dresden Cons.; was named a prof. there in 1974. Geissler's music is dialectical and almost Hegelian in its syllogistic development and climactic synthesis; the ground themes are carefully adumbrated before their integration in a final catharsis; formal dissonances are emancipated by a freely modified application of the Schoenbergian method of composition with 12 tones related only to one another. The human quality of the tightly elaborate polyphonic structure of Geissler's works is expressed with considerable élan by means of variegated rhythmic designs and quasi-aleatory instrumental soliloquies. The formal element remains strictly observed; Geissler favors classical paradigms of symph. and concerto.

Gelinek (properly, **Jelinek**), **Joseph,** composer; b. Seltsch, near Beroun, Bohemia, Dec. 3, 1758; d. Vienna, April 13, 1825. He studied philosophy in Prague and at the same time took lessons in music with Segert; became a good pianist (Mozart praised him); was ordained a priest in 1786, but did not abandon music; went to Vienna and settled there as a piano teacher; c.1810 became music master to Prince Esterhazy. He was a prolific composer; 92 opus numbers are listed in a catalogue issued by André; his fantasias, variations, and dances for piano were quite successful.

Geminiani, Francesco, Italian violinist and writer; b. Lucca (baptized, Dec. 5), 1687; d. Dublin, Sept. 17, 1762. He studied with Carlo Ambrogio Lonati in Milan, and with Corelli in Rome and Alessandro Scarlatti in Naples; in 1706 returned to Lucca and played violin in the town orch. until 1710; in 1711 was concertmaster in the Naples Opera orch. In 1714 he went to London, where he won a reputation as a teacher and performer; in 1731 he presented a series of subscription concerts in London; in 1733 he went to Dublin, where he established a concert hall and gave concerts; in 1734 he returned to London; in 1740 he was briefly in Paris; he was again in Paris for a longer period between 1749 and 1755, when he went back once more to London; in 1759 he settled in Dublin, where he was music master to Charles Coote, later the Earl of Bellamont. Both in London and Dublin he was financially successful; besides music, he was interested in art, and bought and sold pictures. As a virtuoso, Geminiani continued the tradition established by his teacher Corelli, and made further advances in violin technique by the use of frequent shifts of position, and by a free application of double-stops. In his compositions, he adopted the facile method of the Italian school; he excelled particularly in brisk allegro movements. During his years in England and Ireland he made a determined effort to please English tastes; his works are often extremely effective, but his inherent talents fell far short of Corelli's, and in music history he remains but a secondary figure. The claim that Geminiani was the author of the first publ. violin method, *The Art of Playing on the Violin,* which appeared anonymously in vol. V of Prelleur's *The Modern Musick Master* (London, 1730), is erroneous; upon examination it proves to be an edited republication of an earlier anonymous violin method titled *Volens Nolens,* originally publ. in London in 1695; perpetuating the misattribution, this text was later publ. under Geminiani's own name as *The Compleat Tutor for the Violin;* in 1751 a 3rd edition appeared under the original title, *The Art of Playing on the Violin;* it was subsequently trans. into French (Paris, 1752) and German (Vienna, 1785); a facsimile edition of the original, prepared by D.D. Boyden, was issued in 1952. Boyden established the relevant facts in the matter in his paper "Geminiani and the First Violin Tutor" (*Acta Musicologica,* Feb. 1960). Apart from the question of authorship, *The Art of Playing on the Violin* is of historic importance because it sets forth the principles of violin playing as formulated by Corelli, with many of the rules still in common use. Other papers and manuals publ. under Geminiani's name, and assumed to be authentic, are: *Rules for Playing in a true Taste on the Violin, German Flute, Violoncello and Harpsichord* (London, 1745); *A Treatise on good Taste, being the second Part of the Rules* (London, 1749); *Guida Armonica o Dizionario Armonico, being a Sure Guide to Harmony and Modulation* (London, 1742; in French, 1756; in Dutch, 1756); *A Supplement to the Guida Harmonica* (London, 1745); *The Art of Accompaniament* [sic] *or a new and well digested method to learn to perform the Thorough Bass on the Harpsichord* (London, 1775); *The Art of Playing the Guitar or Cittra, Containing Several Compositions with a Bass for the Violoncello or Harpsichord* (London, 1760); he also compiled *The Harmonical Miscellany* (London, 1758).

WORKS (all instrumental): Op. 1, 12 sonatas for Violin and Figured Bass (1716); op. 2, 6 concerti grossi (1732); op. 3, 6 concerti grossi (1733); op. 4, 12 sonatas for Violin and Figured Bass (1739); op. 5, 6 sonatas for Cello and Figured Bass (1739); op. 6, 6 concerti grossi (1741); op. 7, 6 concerti grossi (1746); also 12 string trios and arrangements of Corelli's works for various instrumental combinations. The concerti grossi have been publ. in modern editions by P. Mies (op. 2, no. 2), in *Musik im Haus* (1928); M. Esposito (op. 2, no. 2, arranged for String Orch., London, 1927); H.J. Moser (op. 2, nos. 4, 5, 6, arranged for strings and piano), in *Das Musik-Kränzlein* (Leipzig, 1937); R. Hernried (op. 3, nos. 1–6, Leipzig, 1935). Violin sonatas have been publ. by R.L. Finney (op. 1, nos. 1–12, Northampton, Mass., 1935) and A. Moffat (op. 4, no. 8, Mainz, 1910; op. 4, no. 11, Berlin, 1899).

Gemünder, August Martin Ludwig, violin maker; b. Ingelfingen, Württemberg, Germany, March 22, 1814; d. New York, Sept. 7, 1895. He established a shop at Springfield, Mass., in 1846; then moved to Boston, where he was joined by his brother **Georg** (b. April 13, 1816; d. Jan. 15, 1899), also a violin maker, a pupil of J.B. Vuillaume in Paris. In 1852, the brothers settled in N.Y., where they established themselves as the foremost manufacturers of musical instruments; between 1860 and 1890 they received numerous medals for excellence at expositions in Europe and America. After the death of August Gemünder, the business was continued by 3 of his sons, as August Gemünder & Sons. Georg Gemünder wrote an autobiographical sketch with an account of his work, *Georg Gemünder's Progress in Violin Making* (1880, in German; 1881, in Eng.).

Generali (real name, **Mercandetti**), **Pietro,** Italian opera composer; b. Masserano, Oct. 23, 1773; d. Novara, Nov. 3, 1832. He studied in Rome; began to compose sacred music at an early age, but soon turned to opera. He traveled all over Italy as producer of his operas and also went to Vienna and Barcelona. Returning to Italy, he became maestro di cappella at the Cathedral of Novara. He anticipated Rossini in the effective use of dynamics in the instrumental parts of his operas, and was generally praised for his technical knowledge. He wrote about 50 stage works, in both the serious and comic genres, but none survived in the repertoire after his death. The following were successful at their initial performances: *Pamela nubile* (Venice, April 12, 1804); *Le lagrime di una vedova* (Venice, Dec. 26, 1808); *Adelina* (Venice, Sept. 16, 1810); *L'Impostore* (Milan, May 21, 1815); *I Baccanali di Roma* (Venice, Jan. 14, 1816; reputed to be his best work); *Il servo padrone* (Parma, Aug. 12, 1818); *Il divorzio persiano* (Trieste, Jan. 31, 1828).

Gentele, Goeran, brilliant Swedish opera manager; b. Stockholm, Sept. 20, 1917; killed in an automobile crash near Olbia, Sardinia, July 18, 1972. He studied political science in Stockholm, and art at the Sorbonne in Paris. He was first engaged as an actor, and then was stage director at the Royal Drama Theater in Stockholm (1941–52) and at the Royal Opera (1952–63), where he was appointed director in 1963. In 1970 he became engaged as general manager of the Metropolitan Opera House in N.Y., effective June 1972; great expectations for his innovative directorship in America were thwarted by his untimely death during a vacation in Italy.

Georges, Alexandre, French opera composer; b. Arras, Feb. 25, 1850; d. Paris, Jan. 18, 1938. He studied at the Niedermeyer School in Paris, and later became a teacher of harmony there. He occupied various posts as organist in Paris churches, and was a successful organ teacher. As a composer, he was mainly interested in opera; the following operas were produced in Paris: *Le Printemps* (1888); *Poèmes d'amour* (1892); *Charlotte Corday* (March 6, 1901); *Miarka* (Nov. 7, 1905; his most successful work; revived and shortened, 1925); *Myrrha* (1909); *Sangre y sol* (Nice, Feb. 23, 1912). He also wrote the oratorios *Notre Dame de Lourdes, Balthazar,* and *Chemin de Croix;* the symph. poems *Léila, La Naissance de Vénus,* and *Le Paradis perdu.* He wrote some chamber music for unusual combinations: *A la Kasbah* for Flute and Clarinet; *Kosaks* for Violin and Clarinet; etc. He is best known, however, for his melodious *Chansons de Miarka* for Voice and Piano (also with Orch.). His arrangement of *Chansons champenoises à la manière ancienne,* by G. Dévignes, is also well known.

Georgiades, Thrasybulos, Greek musicologist; b. Athens, Jan. 4, 1907; d. Munich, March 15, 1977. He studied piano in Athens; then studied musicology with Rudolf von Ficker at the Univ. of Munich, where he received his Ph.D. in 1935 with the dissertation *Englische Diskanttraktate aus der ersten Hälfte des 15. Jahrhunderts* (published in Würzburg, 1937); he also studied composition with Carl Orff. In 1938 he became a prof. at the Athens Odeon; was its director from 1939 to 1941. He completed his Habilitation at the Univ. of Munich in 1947 with his *Der griechische Rhythmus: Musik, Reigen, Vers und Sprache* (publ. in Hamburg, 1949). In 1948 he joined the faculty of the Univ. of Heidelberg; in 1956 he became a prof. at the Univ. of Munich, retiring in 1972. He contributed valuable papers to German music journals on ancient Greek, Byzantine, and medieval music. His other writings include *Volkslied als Bekenntnis* (Regensburg, 1947); *Musik und Sprache* (Berlin, 1954); *Musik und Rhythmus bei den Griechen; Zum Ursprung der abendländischen Musik* (Hamburg, 1958); *Das musikalische Theater* (Munich, 1965); *Schubert, Musik und Lyrik* (Göttingen, 1967). His book on Greek music was publ. in Eng. under the title *Greek Music, Verse, Dance* (N.Y., 1956).

Gerber, Ernst Ludwig, celebrated German lexicographer, son and pupil of the organist and composer **Heinrich Nikolaus Gerber;** b. Sondershausen, Sept. 29, 1746; d. there, June 30, 1819. He studied organ and theory with his father; then studied law and music in Leipzig, becoming a skillful cellist and organist, in which latter capacity he became (1769) his father's assistant, and succeeded him in 1775. He was also a chamber musician. He was able to visit Weimar, Kassel, Leipzig, and other cities, and gradually gathered together a large collection of musicians' portraits; to these he appended brief biographical notices, and finally conceived the plan of writing a biographical dictionary of musicians. Though his resources (in a small town without a public library, and having to rely in great measure on material sent him by his publisher, Breitkopf) were hardly adequate to the task he undertook, his *Historisch-biographisches Lexikon der Tonkünstler* (Leipzig, 2 vols., 1790–92; reprinted 1976) was so well received, and brought in such a mass of corrections and fresh material from all quarters, that he prepared a supplementary edition, *Neues historisch-biographisches Lexikon der Tonkünstler* (4

vols., 1812–14; reprinted 1966). Though the former was intended only as a supplement to Walther's dictionary, and both are, of course, out of date, they contain much material still of value, and have been extensively drawn upon by more recent writers. He composed sonatas for piano, chorale preludes for organ, and music for wind band. The Viennese Gesellschaft der Musikfreunde purchased his large library.

Gerhard, Roberto, eminent Catalonian composer; b. Valls, near Tarragona (Spain), Sept. 25, 1896; d. Cambridge, England, Jan. 5, 1970. Although of Swiss parentage and nationality, he was prominently associated with the Catalonian musical movement. He studied piano in Barcelona with Granados (1915–16) and was the last composition student of Felipe Pedrell (1916–22). The currents of Central European music were already becoming apparent in his music even before he joined Schoenberg's master classes in Vienna and Berlin (1923–28). Gerhard held a brief professorship in Barcelona and served as head of the music dept. of the Catalan Library there until the defeat of the Republic in the Spanish Civil War; lived in Paris until June 1939, then settled in England and became a British subject. He was a guest prof. of composition at the Univ. of Michigan in the spring of 1960 and at the Berkshire Music Center, Tanglewood, during the summer of 1962. In 1967 he was made a Commander of the Order of the British Empire. In his music written in England, Gerhard makes use of serialistic procedures, extending the dodecaphonic principle into the domain of rhythms (12 different time units in a theme, corresponding to the intervallic distances of the notes in the tone row from the central note).

Gerhardt, Elena, celebrated German lieder singer (mezzo-soprano); b. Leipzig, Nov. 11, 1883; d. London, Jan. 11, 1961. She studied at the Leipzig Cons. (1899–1903) with Marie Hedmont; made her public debut on her 20th birthday in a recital, accompanied by Nikisch; toured Europe as a lieder singer with great success; made her English debut in London in 1906, and her American debut in N.Y., Jan. 9, 1912. In 1933 she settled in London, making appearances as a singer, and teaching. She compiled *My Favorite German Songs* (1915), edited a selection of Hugo Wolf's songs (1932), and wrote her autobiography, *Recital* (London, 1953; preface by Dame Myra Hess).

Gericke, Wilhelm, noted Austrian conductor; b. Schwanberg, April 18, 1845; d. Vienna, Oct. 27, 1925. He studied with Dessoff at the Vienna Cons. (1862–65); after a number of engagements as guest conductor in provincial theaters, he became conductor of the municipal theater in Linz. In 1874 he joined the staff of the Vienna Court Opera as an assistant conductor; in 1880 he took charge of the Gesellschaft der Musikfreunde concerts, and also led the Singverein. From 1884 to 1889 he was conductor of the Boston Symph. Orch.; returning to Vienna, he once again served as conductor of the Gesellschaft der Musikfreunde concerts from 1890–95. He was called again to America in 1898 to lead the Boston Symph. Orch., conducting its concerts until 1906; then returned to Vienna. Gericke was the only conductor in the history of the Boston Symph. Orch. to serve two separate terms; as such, he did much to make it a fine ensemble, for he was a remarkably able conductor and a highly efficient drillmaster.

Gerl, Franz Xaver, German bass and composer; b. Andorf, Nov. 30, 1764; d. Mannheim, March 9, 1827. He sang in the choir at Salzburg; in 1789 became principal bass at the Theater auf der Wieden in Vienna, remaining on its roster until 1793; he created the role of Sarastro in Mozart's *Die Zauberflöte* in 1791; his wife, **Barbara Reisinger** (1770–1806), created the role of Papagena in that production. He composed several works for the stage, collaborating with Bendikt Schack.

Gerlach, Theodor, German conductor and composer; b. Dresden, June 25, 1861; d. Kiel, Dec. 11, 1940. A student of Fr. Wüllner, Gerlach first attracted attention with an effective cantata, *Luthers Lob der Musica.* In. 1886, he became conductor of the German Opera in Posen. After several other posts as conductor, he settled in Karlsruhe as director of the Musikbildungsanstalt. He wrote an opera, *Matteo Falcone,* to his own libretto, which was produced with considerable success in Hannover (1898); of greater interest are his experiments with "spoken opera," employing inflected speech; of these, *Liebeswogen* was produced in Bremen on Nov. 7, 1903; later revised and produced under the title *Das Seegespenst* in Altenburg, April 24, 1914; he applied the same principle, using the spoken word over an instrumental accompaniment, in his *Gesprochene Lieder.* Also of interest is his early *Epic Symphony* (1891).

Gerle, Hans, German lutenist; b. Nuremberg, c.1500; d. there, 1570. He was well known in his time both as a performer on the lute and as a manufacturer of viols and lutes. His works in tablature are of considerable historic value: *Musica Teusch auf die Instrument der grossen unnd kleinen Geygen, auch Lautten* (Nuremberg, 1532; 2nd ed., 1537; 3rd ed., under the title *Musica und Tabulatur,* 1546); *Tabulatur auff die Laudten* (Nuremberg, 1533); *Ein newes sehr künstlichs Lautenbuch* (Nuremberg, 1552; with pieces by Francesco da Milano, Ant. Rotta, Joan da Crema, Rosseto, and Gintzler). Reprints of his works have been edited by W. Tappert in *Sang und Klang aus alter Zeit* (1906) and by H.D. Bruger in *Schule des Lautenspiels,* I/2, and *Alte Lautenkunst I.*

German, Sir Edward (real name, **Edward German Jones**), English composer; b. Whitchurch, Feb. 17, 1862; d. London, Nov. 11, 1936. He began serious music study in Jan. 1880, under W.C. Hay at Shrewsbury; in Sept. he entered the Royal Academy of Music, studying organ (Steggall), violin (Weist-Hill and Burnett), theory (Banister), and composition and or-

chestration (Prout), graduating with a symph.; he was elected a Fellow of the Royal Academy of Music in 1895. In 1888–89 he conducted the orch. at the Globe Theatre; here his incidental music to Richard Mansfield's production of *King Richard III* was so successful that Sir Henry Irving commissioned him to write the music to *Henry VIII* (1892). German was then enabled to give up teaching and to devote himself entirely to composition. He was knighted in 1928; awarded the gold medal of the Royal Phil. Society in 1934.

Germani, Fernando, Italian organist; b. Rome, April 5, 1906. He studied at the Santa Cecilia Academy; precociously gifted, he was appointed organist in the Augusteo Orch. at the age of 15; in 1927 made an American tour; also taught organ at the Curtis Inst. in Philadelphia. Returning to Italy, he joined the faculty of the Music Academy in Siena in 1932; in 1935 became a prof. at the Rome Cons. and in 1948 was named first organist at St. Peter's Cathedral in the Vatican. In Rome he presented a series of concerts of all the organ works of Bach; he gave a similar series at Westminster Abbey which was broadcast by BBC. In 1961 he gave organ recitals in San Francisco and in 1962 played in N.Y., in varied programs that included, besides Bach's music, works by César Franck and Max Reger. He took part in music festivals in Berlin, Edinburgh, and other cities. He prepared a new complete edition of works by Frescobaldi as *Opere per organo e cembalo* (3 vols., Rome, 1964).

Gernsheim, Friedrich, German composer and conductor; b. Worms, July 17, 1839; d. Berlin, Sept. 11, 1916. He studied at the Leipzig Cons. with Moscheles (piano) and Hauptmann (theory); then was in Paris (1855–61) for further studies. Returning to Germany, he became a prof. at the Cologne Cons. (1865–74); then conducted choral concerts in Rotterdam (1874–80); subsequently taught at the Stern Cons. in Berlin (1890–97). His works are marked by a characteristic Romantic flair, as an epigone of Schumann; he was also influenced by Brahms, who was his friend. He wrote 4 symphs., several overtures, a Piano Concerto, a Violin Concerto, 4 string quartets, 3 piano quartets, 2 piano trios, a String Quintet, 3 violin sonatas, 2 cello sonatas, and numerous choral works, songs, and piano pieces, totaling 92 opus numbers.

Gero, Jhan (Jehan), Flemish composer who flourished in the 16th century. He was a fine madrigal writer; publ. 2 books of madrigals for 4 voices (1549), 2 books of madrigals for 3 voices (1553), and a book of madrigals for 2 voices (1541); he also wrote motets. He was at one time confused with **Johannes Gallus.**

Gershkovitch, Jacques, Russian conductor; b. Irkutsk, Siberia, Jan. 3, 1884; d. Sandy, Oreg., Aug. 12, 1953. He studied at the St. Petersburg Cons. with Rimsky-Korsakov, Glazunov, and Nicolas Tcherepnin. He graduated with honors, and received a scholarship to study in Germany under Artur Nikisch. Upon his return to Russia, he became director of the Irkutsk Cons.; after the Revolution, he joined the orch. of Pavlova's ballet troupe as a flutist, and traveled with it to the Orient. He settled in Tokyo, where he organized special concerts for young people; after the earthquake of 1923, he went to the U.S.; conducted guest engagements with the San Francisco Symph.; then was in Portland, Oreg., where he founded the Portland Junior Symph.; he conducted it for 30 years, until his death.

Gershwin, George, immensely gifted American composer; b. Brooklyn, N.Y., Sept. 26, 1898; d. Beverly Hills, Calif., July 11, 1937. His real name was **Jacob Gershvin,** according to the birth registry; his father was an immigrant from Russia whose original name was Gershovitz. Gershwin's extraordinary career began when he was 16, playing the piano in music stores to demonstrate new popular songs. His studies were desultory; he took piano lessons with Ernest Hutcheson and Charles Hambitzer in N.Y.; studied harmony with Edward Kilenyi and with Rubin Goldmark; later on, when he was already a famous composer of popular music, he continued to take private lessons; he studied counterpoint with Henry Cowell and with Wallingford Riegger; during the last years of his life, he applied himself with great earnestness to studying with Joseph Schillinger in an attempt to organize his technique in a scientific manner; some of Schillinger's methods he applied in *Porgy and Bess.* But it was his melodic talent and a genius for rhythmic invention, rather than any studies, that made him a genuinely important American composer. As far as worldly success was concerned, there was no period of struggle in Gershwin's life; one of his earliest songs, *Swanee,* written at the age of 19, became enormously popular (more than a million copies sold; 2,250,000 phonograph records). He also took time to write a lyrical *Lullaby* for String Quartet (1920). Possessing phenomenal energy, he produced musical comedies in close succession, using fashionable jazz formulas in original and ingenious ways. A milestone of his career was *Rhapsody in Blue,* for Piano and Jazz Orch., in which he applied the jazz idiom to an essentially classical form. He played the solo part at a special concert conducted by Paul Whiteman at Aeolian Hall in N.Y. on Feb. 12, 1924. The orchestration was by Ferde Grofé, a circumstance that generated rumors of Gershwin's inability to score for instruments; these rumors, however, were quickly refuted by his production of several orch. works, scored by himself in a brilliant fashion. He played the solo part of his Piano Concerto in F, with Walter Damrosch and the N.Y. Symph. Orch. (Dec. 3, 1925); this work had a certain vogue, but its popularity never equaled that of the *Rhapsody in Blue.* Reverting again to a more popular idiom, Gershwin wrote a symph. work, *An American in Paris* (N.Y. Phil., Dec. 13, 1928, Damrosch conducting). His *Rhapsody No. 2* was performed by Koussevitzky and the Boston Symph. on Jan. 29, 1932, but was unsuccessful; there followed a *Cuban Overture*

(N.Y., Aug. 16, 1932) and Variations for Piano and Orch. on his song *I Got Rhythm* (Boston, Jan. 14, 1934, Gershwin soloist). In the meantime, Gershwin became engaged in his most ambitious undertaking: the composition of *Porgy and Bess,* an American opera in a folk manner, for black singers, after the book by Dubose Heyward. It was first staged in Boston on Sept. 30, 1935, and shortly afterward in N.Y. Its reception by the press was not uniformly favorable, but its songs rapidly attained great popularity (*Summertime; I Got Plenty o' Nuthin'; It Ain't Neccessarily So; Bess, You Is My Woman Now*); the opera has been successfully revived in N.Y. and elsewhere; it received international recognition when an American company of black singers toured South America and Europe in 1955, reaching a climax of success with several performances in Russia (Leningrad, Dec. 26, 1955, and also Moscow); it was the first American opera company to visit Russia. Gershwin's death (of a gliomatous cyst in the right temporal lobe of the brain) at the age of 38 was mourned as a great loss to American music; memorial concerts have been held at Lewisohn Stadium in N.Y. on each anniversary of his death, with large attendance. His musical comedies include: numbers for *George White's Scandals* of 1920–24; *Our Nell* (1922); *Sweet Little Devil* (1923); *Lady Be Good* (1924); *Primrose* (1924); *Tip Toes* (1925); *Song of the Flame* (1925); *135th Street* (one act, 1923; produced in concert form Dec. 29, 1925, Paul Whiteman conducting); *Oh Kay!* (1926); *Strike Up the Band* (1927); *Funny Face* (1927); *Rosalie* (1928); *Treasure Girl* (1928); *Show Girl* (1929); *Girl Crazy* (1930); *Of Thee I Sing* (1931; a political satire which was the first musical to win a Pulitzer Prize); *Pardon My English* (1932); *Let 'Em Eat Cake* (1933); for motion pictures: *Shall We Dance, Damsel in Distress, Goldwyn Follies* (left unfinished at his death; completed by Vernon Duke). A collection of his songs and piano transcriptions, *George Gershwin's Song Book,* was publ. in 1932; reprinted as *Gershwin Years in Song* (N.Y., 1973).

Gershwin, Ira, one of the most talented American librettists and lyricists, brother of **George Gershwin;** b. New York, Dec. 6, 1896; d. Beverly Hills, Calif., Aug. 17, 1983. He attended night classes at the College of the City of N.Y., wrote verses and humorous pieces for the school paper, and served as cashier in a Turkish bath of which his father was part owner. He began writing lyrics for shows in 1918, using the pseudonym **Arthur Francis.** His first full-fledged show as a lyricist was the musical comedy *Be Yourself,* for which he used his own name for the first time. He achieved fame when he wrote the lyrics for his brother's musical comedy *Lady Be Good* (1924). He remained his brother's collaborator until George Gershwin's death in 1937, and his lyrics became an inalienable part of the whole, so that the brothers George and Ira Gershwin became artistic twins, like Gilbert and Sullivan, indissolubly united in some of the greatest productions of the musical theater in America: *Strike Up the Band* (1930), *Of Thee I Sing* (1931), etc., and the culminating product of the brotherly genius, the folk opera *Porgy and Bess* (1935). Ira Gershwin also wrote lyrics for other composers, among them Vernon Duke (*The Ziegfeld Follies of 1936*), Kurt Weill (*Lady in the Dark,* and several motion pictures), and Jerome Kern (the enormously successful song *Long Ago and Far Away* from the film *Cover Girl*).

Gerster, Etelka, Hungarian dramatic soprano; b. Kaschau, June 25, 1855; d. Pontecchio, near Bologna, Aug. 20, 1920. She studied with Mathilde Marchesi in Vienna, then made her debut in Venice as Gilda in *Rigoletto,* Jan. 8, 1876. Her great success resulted in engagements in Berlin and Budapest in Italian opera under the direction of Carlo Gardini. She married Gardini on April 16, 1877, and continued her successful career, making her London debut on June 23, 1877, as Amina in *Sonnambula,* and her U.S. debut in the same role on Nov. 11, 1878, at the N.Y. Academy of Music. She returned to London for 3 more seasons (1878–80), then sang again in N.Y. in 1880–83 and in 1887. After retiring, she taught singing in Berlin, and in N.Y. at the Inst. of Musical Art (1907). She wrote the book *Stimmführer* (1906; 2nd. ed., 1908).

Gerster, Ottmar, eminent German violinist, composer, and pedagogue; b. Braunfels, June 29, 1897; d. Leipzig, Aug. 31, 1969. He studied music theory with Bernhard Sekles at the Frankfurt Cons. (1913–16); then was mobilized during the last years of World War I; after the war, studied violin with Adolf Rebner (1919–21); played the viola in string quartets (1923–27), and concurrently was concertmaster of the Frankfurt Symph. Orch. From 1927 to 1939 he taught violin and theory at the Folkwang-Schule in Essen; in 1940 was again in the army. After that war he was on the faculty of the Hochschule für Musik in Weimar (1947–52) and then in Leipzig (1952–62). His music is marked by melodious polyphony in a neo-Classical vein; in his operas he used folklike thematic material.

Gervaise, Claude, French composer of the 16th century. He was a viol player, and chamber musician to François I and Henri II. He composed many dances and *chansons;* 6 vols. of his *Danceries à 4 et 5 parties* were publ. by Attaignant from about 1545 to 1556, but only 3 vols. remain; a selection of his dances is included in vol. 23 (Danceries) of *Les Maîtres musiciens* edited by H. Expert (1908). Several *chansons* by Gervaise appear in 16th-century collections.

Gesualdo, Don Carlo, Prince of Venosa, lutenist and composer; b. Naples, c.1560; d. there, Sept. 8, 1613. He probably studied with Pomponio Nenna; in 1590, his unfaithful wife and first cousin, Maria d'Avalos, and her lover were murdered at Gesualdo's orders; in 1594, he was at the court of the Estensi in Ferrara, where he married his 2nd wife, Leonora d'Este, in that year; sometime after the death of the Duke of Ferrara, in 1597, Don Carlo returned to Naples, where he remained till death. Living at the epoch when the "new music" (the homophonic style) made its appearance, he was one of the most original musicians of the time. Like Rore, Banchieri, and Vincentino, he was a so-called chromaticist; his later madrigals reveal a distinctly individual style of expression and are characterized by strong contrasts, new (for their time) harmonic progressions, and a skilful use of dissonance; he was a master in producing tone color through the use of different voice registers and in expressing the poetic contents of his texts. He publ. 6 vols. of madrigals *a* 5 (Genoa, 1585, each part separately; an ed. in score was publ. by G. Pavoni, Venice, 1613). A complete edition of his works was begun by the Istituto Italiano per la Storia della Musica (Rome), but only one vol. (2 books of madrigals) appeared (1942); a new edition of the 6 books of madrigals, edited by F. Vatelli and A. Bizzelli, was publ. in 1956–58. A new edition of his works, in 10 vols. (6 books of madrigals, 3 vols. of sacred works, and one vol. of instrumental works, canzonette, and Psalms), edited by W. Weisman and G.E. Watkins, was publ. in 1957–67.

Geszty, Sylvia, Hungarian soprano; b. Budapest, Feb. 28, 1934. She studied at the Budapest Cons.; made her debut at the National Theater in Budapest in 1959. In 1966 she sang the Queen of the Night in Peter Hall's production of *The Magic Flute* at Covent Garden in London; she repeated the role at the Salzburg Festival in 1967 and also sang Zerbinetta at the Munich Opera Festival; her agile voice and attractive stage presence made her a favorite in this soubrette role, and she chose it for her 1971 debut with the Glyndebourne Festival. She joined the Hamburg Opera in 1970; in the same year she sang at the Teatro Colón in Buenos Aires; then made her North American debut in the same role with the N.Y. City Opera. Her other roles include Olympia in *The Tales of Hoffmann,* and Alcina in Handel's opera.

Gevaert, François Auguste, eminent Belgian composer and musicologist; b. Huysse, near Audenarde, July 31, 1828; d. Brussels, Dec. 24, 1908. He was a pupil of De Somère (piano) and Mengal (composition) at the Ghent Cons. (1841–47), taking the Grand Prix de Rome for composition; from 1843 he was also organist at the Jesuit church. He produced 2 operas in 1848, with some success; lived in Paris for a year (1849–50), and was commissioned to write an opera for the Théâtre-Lyrique; then spent a year in Spain, his *Fantasía sobre motivos españoles* winning him the Order of Isabella la Católica; he also wrote a *Rapport sur la situation de la musique en Espagne* (Brussels, 1851). After a short visit to Italy and Germany, he returned to Ghent in 1852, and up to 1861 brought out 9 operas in quick succession. In 1857 his festival cantata *De nationale verjaerdag* won him the Order of Léopold. In 1867 he was appointed music director at the Opéra, Paris; in 1870, the German invasion caused him to return home, and from 1871 he was director of the Brussels Cons., succeeding Fétis. In this position he gave evidence of remarkable talent for organization. As conductor of the "Concerts du Conservatoire," he exerted a far-reaching influence through his historical concerts, producing works of all nations and periods. In 1873 he was elected a member of the Academy, succeeding Mercadante; in 1907 he was made a baron.

WORKS: 12 operas; 3 cantatas; a *Missa pro defunctis* and *Super flumina Babylonis* (both for Male Chorus and Orch.); overture, *Flandre au lion; ballads (Philipp van Artevelde,* etc.); songs (many in the collection *Nederlandsche Zangstukken*).

WRITINGS: Even more important than Gevaert's compositions are his scholarly books: *Leerboek van den Gregoriaenschen Zang* (1856); *Traité d'instrumentation* (1863; revised and enlarged as *Nouveau traité de l'instrumentation,* 1885; German trans. by Riemann, 1887; Spanish trans. by Neuparth, 1896; Russian trans. by Rebikov, 1899); *Histoire et théorie de la musique de l'antiquité* (2 vols., 1875, 1881); *Les Origines du chant liturgique de l'église latine* (1890; German trans. by Riemann; threw new light on the Gregorian tradition); *Cours méthodique d'orchestration* (2 vols., 1890; complement of *Nouveau traité); La Mélopée antique dans l'église latine* (1895; a monumental work); *Les Problèmes musicaux d'Aristote* (3 vols., 1899–1902; adopts the theories of Westphal, certain of which were later proved untenable); *Traité d'harmonie théorique et pratique* (2 vols., 1905, 1907). He ed. *Les Gloires de l'Italie* (a collection of vocal numbers from operas, oratorios, cantatas, etc., of the 17th and 18th centuries); *Recueil de chansons du XVe siècle* (transcribed in modern notation); *Vademecum de l'organiste* (classic transcriptions).

Geyer, Stefi, Swiss violinist of Hungarian descent; b. Budapest, Jan. 28, 1888; d. Zürich, Dec. 11, 1956. She studied violin with Hubay at the Budapest Academy; toured in Europe and the U.S. at an early age. In 1919 she settled in Zürich and married the composer **Walter Schulthess.** She taught at the Zürich Cons. for 30 years (1923–53). She was an object of passion on the part of Béla Bartók, who wrote a violin concerto for her (1907), but she never performed it; it was finally discovered and performed in Basel in 1958. Another composer who was enamored of her was Othmar Schoeck, who also wrote a concerto for her.

Ghezzo, Dinu, Rumanian composer; b. Tusla, July 2, 1941. He studied music at the Bucharest Cons., graduating in 1966; then went to the U.S., where he enrolled at the Univ. of Calif., Los Angeles (Ph.D., 1973). In 1974 he was appointed to the faculty of Queens College. In 1976 he organized in N.Y. the New Repertory Ensemble, for the purpose of presenting programs of new music. His works are of a distinctly modern character, making use of electronic instruments. His compositions include Clarinet Sonata (1967); String Quartet (1967); *Segmenti* for Clarinet, Cello, and Piano (1968); *Music* for Flutes and Tapes (1971); *Kanones* for Flutes, Cello, Harpsichord, and Tapes (1972); *Images* for Bass Flute, Divider, and Echoplex (1972); *Thalla* for

Piano, Electric Piano, and 16 Instruments (1974); Concertino for Clarinet and Winds (1975); *Ritualen* for Prepared Piano (1969); *Ritualen II* for Prepared Piano and Tape (1970); *Cantos nuevos,* ballet (1977).

Ghiaurov, Nicolai, Bulgarian bass; b. Lydjene, near Velingrad, Sept. 13, 1929. He studied violin and piano in Bulgaria; then went to Moscow, where he received his vocal training. He made his debut in Sofia as Don Basilio in *The Barber of Seville* in 1955; then appeared in Moscow (1958) and at La Scala in Milan (1959). He soon established himself as a fine singer; his quality of voice is that of basso cantante. He sang Méphistophélès in *Faust* at his debut with the Metropolitan Opera in N.Y. (Nov. 8, 1965).

Ghignone, Giovanni Pietro. See **Guignon, Jean-Pierre.**

Ghis, Henri, French pianist and composer; b. Toulon, May 17, 1839; d. Paris, April 24, 1908. He studied at the Paris Cons. with Marmontel (piano); received first prize in 1854; also studied organ with Benoist (graduated in 1855). He became a fashionable piano teacher in Paris; many aristocratic ladies (to whom he dedicated his pieces) were his pupils. He was the first teacher of Ravel. He publ. salon music for piano: waltzes, mazurkas, polonaises, polkas, gavottes, caprices, etc., often with superinduced titles, as *Séduction, Menuet de la petite princesse, La Marquisette,* etc.; but his name is mostly known through his extremely popular arrangement of an old aria, which he publ. for piano as *Air Louis XIII* (1868); the actual melody was definitely not by Louis XIII; its authorship is unknown; in all probability it is an old French folk song.

Gialdini, Gialdino, Italian conductor and composer; b. Pescia, Nov. 10, 1843; d. there, March 6, 1919. He was a pupil of T. Mabellini at Florence. His first opera, *Rosamunda* (prize opera in a competition instituted by the Pergola Theater, Florence), given in 1868, was unsuccessful; after producing 2 "opere buffe," *La Secchia rapita* (Florence, 1872) and *L'Idolo cinese* (1874), in collaboration with other musicians, he gave up opera writing, and devoted himself with success to conducting. Later he again turned to dramatic composition, producing the operas *I due soci* (Bologna, Feb. 24, 1892), *La Pupilla* (Trieste, Oct. 23, 1896), and *La Bufera* (Pola, Nov. 26, 1910); these operas were successful. He also publ. *Eco della Lombardia,* a collection of 50 folk songs.

Gianettini (or **Zanettini**), **Antonio,** Italian composer; b. Fano, 1648; d. Munich, July 12, 1721. He was organist at San Marco, Venice (1676–86); produced 3 operas in Venice, winning a reputation that led to his appointment as maestro di cappella at the court of Modena; was organist at Modena from 1686 till 1721, except during 1695, when he brought out 3 operas in Hamburg. He moved to Munich with his family in May 1721. He composed 6 operas; 6 oratorios; several cantatas; a Kyrie *a* 5; and Psalms *a* 4, with Instruments (Venice, 1717).

Gianneo, Luis, Argentine composer; b. Buenos Aires, Jan. 9, 1897; d. there, Aug. 15, 1968. He studied composition with Gaito and Drangosch. From 1923 to 1943 he taught at the Inst. Musical in Tucumán; then was a prof. of music at various schools in Buenos Aires. He was especially interested in the problems of musical education of the very young; in 1945 he organized and conducted the Orquesta Sinfónica Juvenil Argentina; from 1955 to 1960 he was director of the Cons. of Buenos Aires.

WORKS: Ballet, *Blanca nieves* (1939); 3 symphs. (1938, 1945, 1963); *Turay-Turay,* symph. poem (Buenos Aires, Sept. 21, 1929); *Obertura para una comedia infantil* (1939); Piano Concerto (1941); Sinfonietta (Buenos Aires, Sept. 20, 1943); Violin Concerto (Buenos Aires, April 13, 1944); *Cantica Dianae* for Chorus and Orch. (1949); *Variaciones sobre tema de tango* for Orch. (1953); *Angor Dei* for Soprano and Orch. (1962); *Poema de la Saeta* for Soprano and Orch. (1966); 4 string quartets (1936, 1944, 1952, 1958); 2 piano trios; String Trio; Violin Sonata; Cello Sonata; teaching pieces for piano; 3 Piano Sonatas (1917, 1943, 1957); songs.

Giannetti, Giovanni, Italian composer; b. Naples, March 25, 1869; d. Rio de Janeiro, Dec. 10, 1934. He studied in Naples, Trieste, and Vienna; in 1912–13, was director of the Liceo Musicale, Siena; in 1915, was in Rome, where (from 1920) he was music director of the Teatro dei Piccoli, with which he toured Europe and South America.

WORKS: Operas: *L'Erebo* (Naples, April 9, 1891); *Padron Maurizio* (Naples, Sept. 26, 1896); *Milena* (Naples, Nov. 15, 1897); *Il Violinaro di Cremona* (Milan, Nov. 23, 1898); *Don Marzio* (Venice, March 2, 1903); *Il Cristo alla festa di Purim* (Rio de Janeiro, Dec. 16, 1904); *Il Nazareno* (Buenos Aires, Jan. 20, 1911); *La Serenata di Pierrot,* pantomime (Rome, April 18, 1917); *Cuore e bautte* (Rome, June 5, 1918); *Il Principe Re,* operetta (Rome, July 7, 1920).

Giannini, Dusolina, American soprano, sister of **Vittorio Giannini;** b. Philadelphia, Dec. 19, 1900. She received her earliest musical education at home; her mother was a violinist; her father, **Ferruccio Giannini** (1869–1948), was an Italian tenor who made one of the earliest phonograph recordings, in 1896. She studied voice with Marcella Sembrich; made her concert debut in N.Y., on March 14, 1920. On Sept. 12, 1925, she made her operatic debut in Hamburg, and subsequently sang in opera in London, Berlin, and Vienna. On Feb. 12, 1936, she appeared with the Metropolitan Opera in the role of Aida, and remained on its staff until 1941. She sang the part of Hester in the first performance of the opera *The Scarlet Letter,* by her brother, Vittorio Giannini (Hamburg, June 2, 1938).

Giannini, Vittorio, American composer, brother of **Dusolina Giannini;** b. Philadelphia, Oct. 19, 1903; d. New York, Nov. 28, 1966. Brought up in a musical family, he showed a precocious talent. He was sent to Italy at the age of 10, and studied at the Cons. of Milan (1913–17). After returning to the U.S., he took private lessons with Martini and Trucco in N.Y.; in 1925 he entered the Juilliard graduate school, where he was a pupil of Rubin Goldmark in composition and Hans Letz in violin; in 1932 he won the American Prix de Rome; was in Rome for a period of 4 years. Upon his return to N.Y., he was appointed to the faculty of the Juilliard School of Music in 1939 as a teacher of composition and orchestration; in 1941 he also became an instructor in music theory; furthermore, he was appointed prof. of composition at the Curtis Inst. of Music in Philadelphia in 1956. As a composer, Giannini was at his best in opera, writing music of fine emotional éclat, excelling in the art of bel canto and avoiding extreme modernistic usages; in his symph. works he also continued the rich Italian tradition; these qualities endeared him with opera singers, but at the same time left his music out of the mainstream of the modern century.

WORKS: Operas: *Lucedia* (Munich, Oct. 20, 1934); *Flora* (1937); *The Scarlet Letter* (Hamburg, June 2, 1938); *Beauty and the Beast* (1938; concert version, CBS Radio, Nov. 24, 1938; stage premiere, Hartford, Conn., Feb. 14, 1946); *Blennerhasset,* radio opera (CBS Radio, Nov. 22, 1939); *The Taming of the Shrew* (his most appreciated opera; in concert form, Cincinnati Symph. Orch., Jan. 31, 1953; in color telecast, NBC opera theater, March 13, 1954); *The Harvest* (Chicago, Nov. 25, 1961); *Rehearsal Call,* opera buffa (N.Y., Feb. 15, 1962); *The Servant of 2 Masters* (posthumous, N.Y., March 9, 1967); for Orch.: Symph., subtitled "In Memoriam Theodore Roosevelt" (1935; N.Y., NBC Orch., Jan. 19, 1936, composer conducting); I.B.M. Symph., commissioned for the N.Y. World's Fair (1939); 4 numbered symphs.: No. 1, *Sinfonia* (Cincinnati, April 6, 1951); No. 2 (St. Louis, April 16, 1956); No. 3 for Band (1958); No. 4 (N.Y., May 26, 1960); 3 divertimentos (1953, 1961, 1964); *Psalm 130,* concerto for Double Bass and Orch. (Brevard, N.C., Aug. 9, 1963); *The Medead,* monodrama for Soprano and Orch. (Atlanta, Ga., Oct. 20, 1960); Piano Concerto (1937); Organ Concerto (1937); Concerto for 2 Pianos (1940); several sacred works for chorus; *Canticle of the Martyrs* (commissioned for the 500th anniversary of the Moravian Church, 1957, at Winston-Salem, N.C.); Concerto Grosso for Strings (1931); Piano Quintet (1931); Woodwind Quintet (1933); Piano Trio (1933); 2 violin sonatas (1926, 1945); Piano Sonata; many songs.

Giardini, Felice de', Italian violinist and composer; b. Turin, April 12, 1716, d. Moscow, June 8, 1796. He was a chorister at the Cathedral of Milan; studied singing and harpsichord with Paladini and violin with Somis in Turin. As a young man he played in various theater orchs. in Rome and Naples; often improvised cadenzas at the end of operatic numbers. He acquired popularity in Italy and made a tour in Germany (1748); then went to London (1750), where he made a series of successful appearances as a concert violinist. In 1752 he joined the Italian opera in London as concertmaster and conductor; he became its impresario in 1756, and was connected with the management, with interruptions, for several more seasons, returning to the career of virtuoso and teacher in 1766. He conducted the Three Choirs festival (1770–76) and was concertmaster at the Pantheon Concerts (1774–80); also conducted other theater orchs. In 1784–89 he was in Italy; returned to London in 1789 and led 3 seasons of Italian opera, without financial success. In 1796 he was engaged as a violinist in Russia and gave his initial concert in Moscow, on March 24, 1796, but soon became ill, and died shortly afterward. As a violinist, he was eclipsed in London by Salomon and Cramer, but he left his mark on musical society there.

Gibbons, Christopher, English organist and composer; b. London (baptized, Aug. 22), 1615; d. there, Oct. 20, 1676. He was the son of **Orlando Gibbons;** was a pupil at the Chapel Royal; in 1638, he became organist at Winchester Cathedral; in 1660, he was appointed organist of the Chapel Royal, private organist to Charles II, and organist at Westminster Abbey. He received the degree of Mus.D. from Oxford in 1663, at the special request of the King. He wrote anthems and many string fantasies, now in MS in the British Library, Christ Church, Oxford; the Royal College of Music; Marsh's Library, Dublin; and Durham and Ely cathedrals; some of his motets are in Playford's "Cantica sacra" (1674). He also collaborated with Matthew Locke in the music for Shirley's masque *Cupid and Death*. C. Rayner prepared the modern edition, *Christopher Gibbons: Keyboard Compositions*, in *Corpus of Early Keyboard Music*, XVIII (1967).

Gibbons, Edward, English musician; b. Cambridge, 1568; d. probably Exeter, c.1650. The eldest living son of **William Gibbons,** who founded this musical family, he was the brother of **Ellis** and **Orlando.** He received a B.Mus. degree from both Oxford and Cambridge; after serving as a lay clerk at King's College, Cambridge, he became master of choristers in 1593, and kept the post until 1598; then he went to the Exeter Cathedral, where he served for many years, with the titles of "priest-vicar" and succentor, though he remained a layman. Little of his music is in existence; a few of his compositions, all for the church, are in the British Library, at Christ Church, Oxford, and in the Bodleian Library.

Gibbons, Ellis, English composer and organist, brother of **Edward** and **Orlando Gibbons;** b. Cambridge, 1573; d. May 1603. The only compositions of his which are known to exist are 2 madrigals included by Morley in his collection *The Triumphes of Oriana* (*Long live fair Oriana* and *Round about her charret*).

Gibbons, Orlando, celebrated English composer and organist, brother of **Edward** and **Ellis Gibbons;** b. Oxford (baptized, Dec. 25), 1583; d. Canterbury, June 5, 1625. He was taken to Cambridge as a small child; in 1596, he became chorister at King's College there; matriculated in 1598; composed music for various occasions for King's College (1602–3). On March 21, 1605, he was appointed organist of the Chapel Royal, retaining this position until his death. He received the degree of B.Mus. from Cambridge Univ. in 1606, and that of D.Mus. from Oxford in 1622. In 1619 he became chamber musician to the King; in 1623, organist at Westminster Abbey. He conducted the music for the funeral of James I (1625); died of apoplexy 2 months later. His fame as a composer rests chiefly on his church music; he employed the novel technique of the "verse anthem" (a work for chorus and solo voices, the solo passages having independent instrumental accompaniment, for either organ or strings); other works followed the traditional polyphonic style, of which Gibbons became a master. He was also one of the greatest English organists of the time.

WORKS: *Fantasies of 3 Parts ... composed for viols* (1610; described on the title page as "Cut in copper, the like not heretofore extant in England"; ed. by E.F. Rimbault in *Musical Antiquarian Society*, vol. 9; new ed. by E.H. Fellowes, 1924); pieces for the virginal, in *Parthenia* (21 pieces of Gibbons, Byrd, and John Bull; 1611; reprinted in *Musical Antiquarian Society*, vol. 18; new ed. by Margaret H. Glyn, 1927); *The First Set of Madrigals and Mottets of 5 Parts* (London, 1612; reprinted in *Musical Antiquarian Society*, vol. 3; new ed. by E.H. Fellowes in *The English Madrigal School*, vol. 5, 1921); 9 Fancies, appended to *20 konincklijke Fantasien op 3 Fiolen* by T. Lupo, Coperario, and W. Daman (Amsterdam, 1648); 2 anthems in Leighton's *Teares or Lamentacions of a Sorrowfull Soule* (the only sacred works by Gibbons publ. during his lifetime). A "complete" ed. of all extant sacred compositions is in *Tudor Church Music*, 4; Gibbons's entire keyboard works were ed. by Margaret H. Glyn in 5 vols. (London, 1925); also in *Musica Britannica*, 20 (1962). Further new eds. follow: The madrigal *God give you good morrow* (from *The Cryes of London*, an early 17th-century MS [in the Brit. Museum] containing 2 other sets of street cries likewise polyphonically treated by T. Weelkes and R. Deering), ed. by Sir Fred. Bridge (London, 1920); 2 Fantazias for String Quartet or Small String Orch., and a Pavan and Galliard for String Sextet or Small String Orch., ed. by E.H. Fellowes (London, 1925); 10 pieces from the virginal book of B. Cosyn, arranged for modern organ by J.A. Fuller-Maitland (London, 1925); Verse Anthems, in *Early English Church Music*, III (1964).

Gibbs, Cecil Armstrong, English composer; b. Great Baddow, near Chelmsford, Aug. 10, 1889; d. Chelmsford, May 12, 1960. He studied at Trinity College, Cambridge, and at the Royal College of Music in London; later became an instructor there (1921–39); in 1934 he received the Cobbett Gold Medal for his services to British chamber music.

WORKS: Operas: *The Blue Peter* (1924); *Twelfth Night* (1947); *The Great Bell of Burley* (children's opera, 1949); 3 symphs.; *Spring Garland* for Strings;

Gibson – Gieseking

Oboe Concerto; *Peacock Pie,* suite for Piano and Strings; Rhapsody for Violin and Orch.; *Essex Suite* for Strings; several string quartets; Lyric Sonata for Violin and Piano; Piano Trio; cantatas: *La Belle Dame sans merci, The Lady of Shalott, Deborah and Barak, Before Daybreak, Odyssey;* also a Pastoral Suite for Baritone, Chorus, and Orch. (1951). Gibbs wrote more than 100 songs, many of them to poems of Walter de la Mare. His musical style adheres to the Romantic school; the influence of folk melodies and rhythms is also noticeable.

Gibson, Sir Alexander, distinguished Scottish conductor; b. Motherwell, Feb. 11, 1926. he was educated at Glasgow Univ. and the Royal College of Music in London; also took courses at the Salzburg Mozarteum and in Siena. He made his debut as conductor at the Sadler's Wells Opera in London in 1951; was subsequently conductor of the BBC Scottish Symph. Orch. in Glasgow (1952–54). In 1959 he was appointed principal conductor of the Scottish National Orch. in Glasgow. In 1962 he founded the Scottish Opera, becoming its first music director. In 1977 Queen Elizabeth II knighted him for his services in behalf of the musical life of his native Scotland and Great Britain. In 1981 he became principal guest conductor of the Houston Symph. Orch. He is mainly renowned for his congenial performances of the works of modern Romantic composers, particularly those of the English school.

Gideon, Miriam, American composer; b. Greeley, Colo., Oct. 23, 1906. She studied piano with Hans Barth in N.Y. and with Felix Fox in Boston; then enrolled at Boston Univ. (B.A., 1926) and took courses in musicology at Columbia Univ. (M.A., 1946); studied composition privately with Lazare Saminsky and Roger Sessions. She served on the music faculty of Brooklyn College (1944–54); in 1955 became a prof. of music at the Jewish Theological Center; in 1967 joined the faculty at the Manhattan School of Music; then was a prof. of music at the City Univ. of N.Y. (1971–76); was elected to the American Academy and Inst. of Arts and Letters in 1975. She wrote music in all genres, in a style distinguished by its attractive modernism.
WORKS: Opera, *Fortunato* (1958); *The Adorable Mouse,* French folk tale for Narrator and Chamber Orch. (1960); *Lyric Piece* for String Orch. (1941); *Symphonia brevis* (1953); *Songs of Youth and Madness* for Voice and Orch. on poems of Friedrich Hölderlin (1977); String Quartet (1946); Viola Sonata (1948); *Fantasy on a Javanese Motive* for Cello and Piano (1948); Divertimento for Woodwind Quartet (1948); *Biblical Masks* for Violin and Piano (1960); Cello Sonata (1961); Suite for Clarinet and Piano (1972); *Fantasy on an Irish Folk Motive* for Oboe, Viola, Bassoon, and Vibraphone (1975); *The Hound of Heaven,* to the poem by Francis Thompson, for Voice, Violin, Viola, Cello, and Oboe (1945); *Sonnets from Shakespeare* for Voice, Trumpet, and String Quartet (1950); *Sonnets from "Fatal Interview,"* after Edna St. Vincent Millay, for Voice, Violin, Viola, and Cello (1952); *The Condemned Play-ground* for Soprano and Instruments (1963); *Questions on Nature* for Voice, Oboe, Piano, Tam-tam, and Glockenspiel (1965); *Rhymes from the Hill,* after the *Galgenlieder* of Christian Morgenstern, for Voice, Clarinet, Cello, and Marimba (1968); *The Seasons of Time,* after Japanese poetry, for Voice, Flute, Cello, and Piano (1969); Clarinet Sonata (1973); *Nocturnes* for Voice, Flute, Oboe, Violin, Cello, and Vibraphone (1976); *Canzona* for Piano (1945); *6 Cuckoos in Quest of a Composer* for Piano (1953); Piano Sonata (1977); choruses and songs.

Gielen, Michael, German conductor; b. Dresden, July 20, 1927. He was a son of Josef Gielen, an opera director who emigrated to Buenos Aires in 1939, and a nephew of the pianist **Eduard Steuermann.** He studied piano and composition in Buenos Aires with Erwin Leuchter; in 1951 went to Vienna; from 1954–60 he served as conductor of the Vienna State Opera. He then was principal conductor of the Royal Swedish Opera in Stockholm (1960–65); also was a conductor with the Cologne Radio Symph. Orch. (1965–69). From 1969–72 he was chief conductor of the Orch. National de Belgique in Brussels; in 1972 was appointed chief conductor of the Netherlands Opera in Amsterdam. In 1977 he became director of the Frankfurt Opera and chief conductor of the Museumgesellschaft Concerts; in 1980 he was appointed music director of the Cincinnati Symph. Orch. He won a solid reputation as a congenial interpreter of contemporary music. He is also a composer in his own right; his works include a Violin Sonata (1946); Trio for Clarinet, Viola, and Bassoon (1948); *Variations* for String Quartet (1949); *Music* for Baritone, Strings, Piano, Trombone, and Percussion (1954); *4 Songs of Stefan George* for Chorus and Instruments (1955); Variations for 40 Instruments (1959); *Pentaphonie* for Piano, 5 Soloists, and 5 Quintets (1960–63).

Gieseking, Walter, distinguished pianist; b. Lyons, France, of German parents, Nov. 5, 1895; d. London, Oct. 26, 1956. He studied with Karl Leimer at the Hannover Cons., graduating in 1916; then served in the German army during World War I; began his concert career with extensive tours of Europe; made his American debut at Aeolian Hall, N.Y., Feb. 22, 1926, and after that appeared regularly in the U.S. and Europe with orchs. and in solo recitals. He became one of the most brilliant and musicianly pianists of his generation, capable of profound and intimate interpretations of both classical and modern piano music. His dual German-French background enabled him to project with the utmost authenticity the piano masterpieces of both cultures. His playing of Debussy was remarkable; he was also an excellent performer of works by Prokofiev and other modernists. He composed some chamber music and made piano transcriptions of songs by Richard Strauss. He became the center of a political controversy when he arrived in the U.S. early in 1949 for a concert tour; he was accused of cultural collaboration with the Nazi regime, and public protests forced the cancellation of his scheduled performances at Carnegie Hall. However, he was later cleared by an Allied court in Germany and was able to resume his career in America. He appeared again at a Carnegie Hall recital on April 22, 1953, and until his death continued to give numerous performances in both hemispheres. His autobiography, *So Wurde ich Pianist,* was publ. posthumously in Wiesbaden (1963).

Gigli, Beniamino, famous Italian tenor; b. Recanati, March 20, 1890; d. Rome, Nov. 30, 1957. He studied with Rosati in Rome; made his operatic debut in Rovigo, near Venice, in 1914, as Enzo in *La Gioconda;* then sang in many Italian cities. His first American appearance was as Faust in Boito's *Mefistofele* with the Metropolitan Opera (Nov. 26, 1920); he remained on its staff until 1932, and returned there for one season, 1938–39. He then went back to Italy, where he remained during World War II. He revisited the U.S. in 1955 and gave a series of concerts with considerable success, despite his age. At the height of his career, he ranked among the best tenors in opera; he was particularly impressive in the lyric roles of Verdi's and Puccini's operas; he also sang in the German and French repertoire; his interpretation of Lohengrin was acclaimed. His voice possessed great strength and a variety of expressive powers.

Gigout, Eugène, French organ virtuoso and composer; b. Nancy, March 23, 1844; d. Paris, Dec. 9, 1925. He began music studies in the *maîtrise* of Nancy Cathedral; at 13 he entered the Niedermeyer School at Paris, in which he subsequently taught (1863–85 and 1900–1905); for a time, was a pupil of Saint-Saëns. From 1863, Gigout was organist at the church of St.-Augustin; he won fame as a concert organist in France, England, Germany, Switzerland, Spain, and Italy; he was especially famous for his masterly improvisations. In 1885 he founded at Paris an organ school subsidized by the government, from which many excellent pupils graduated (Boëllmann, Fauré, Messager, A. Georges, A. Roussel, C. Terrasse, etc.); from 1911, he was a prof. of organ and improvisation at the National Cons., Paris. He was also an esteemed writer on music and a critic; he was a Commander of the Order of Isabella la Católica; Officer of Public Instruction (from 1885); and Chevalier of the Legion of Honor (from 1895). As a composer, he followed the severe style.

Gil-Marchex, Henri, French pianist; b. St. Georges d'Espérance (Isère), Dec. 16, 1894; d. Paris, Nov. 22, 1970. He studied at the Paris Cons., then with L. Capet and A. Cortot; toured Europe, Russia, and Japan, and performed modern works at various festivals in Europe. In 1956, he was director of the Cons. at Poitiers.

Gilardi, Gilardo, Argentine composer; b. San Fernando, May 25, 1889; d. Buenos Aires, Jan. 16, 1963. He studied with Pablo Berutti, then devoted himself to teaching and composing. Two of his operas were produced at the Teatro Colón in Buenos Aires: *Ilse*

(July 13, 1923) and *La leyenda de Urutaú* (Oct. 25, 1934). He also wrote *Sinfonia cíclico* (1961), 3 piano trios, 2 string quartets, *Sonata Popular Argentina* for Violin and Piano (1939), and many dances and songs based on native melodies.

Gilbert, Anthony, English composer; b. London, July 26, 1934. He studied piano at the Trinity College of Music and later at Morley College, where he took composition classes with Milner and Goehr (1959–60); also studied privately with Seiber (1960); then again with Goehr (1960–63). His professional career evolved mainly in teaching; he was on the faculty at Lancaster Univ. (1971–73), at Morley College (from 1971), and at the Royal Northern College of Music in Manchester (from 1973). A modernist by nature, he nevertheless wrote music in classical forms, and was not averse to representational music; on the purely structural side, he adopted various attenuated forms of serial music, and in thematic development used disparate aggregative blocks.

WORKS: Opera, *The Scene-Machine* (1970; Kassel, Germany, April 4, 1971); *Sinfonia* for Chamber Orch. (London, March 30, 1965); *Regions* for 2 Chamber Orchs. (1966); *Peal II* for Jazz or School Orch. (1968); Symph. (Cheltenham Festival, July 12, 1973); *Ghost and Dream Dancing* for Orch. (Birmingham, Sept. 19, 1974); Duo for Violin and Viola (1963); Serenade for 6 Instruments (1963); *Brighton Piece* for 2 Percussionists and Instrumental Ensemble (1967); *9 or 10 Osannas* for Clarinet, Horn, Violin, Cello, and Piano (1967); *The Incredible Flute Music* for Flute and Piano (1968); *Spell Respell* for Electric Bassett Clarinet and Piano (1968); *Mother* for Solo Cello, Clarinet, Flute, Violin or Viola, Keyboard, and Percussion (1969); *A Treatment of Silence* for Violin and Tape (1970); *Love Poems* for Soprano, Clarinet, Cello, and Accordion (1970); *O'Grady Music* for Clarinet, Cello, and Toy Instruments (Los Angeles, Jan. 10, 1972); *String Quartet with Piano Pieces* (1972); *Cantata: A Man Who Tried to Hijack an Airplane* for 3 Voices and Renaissance Instruments (1972); *Canticle* for Wind Ensemble (1973); *Inscapes* for Soprano, Reader, and Instrumental Ensemble (1975); 2 piano sonatas (1962, 1966); *Charm against the Gout* for Chorus (1965); several melodramas for wireless.

Gilbert, Henry Franklin Belknap, remarkable American composer; b. Somerville, Mass., Sept. 26, 1868; d. Cambridge, Mass., May 19, 1928. He studied at the New England Cons. and with E. Mollenhauer; in 1889–92, was a pupil of MacDowell (composition) in Boston. Rather than do routine music work to earn his livelihood (he had previously been a violinist in theaters, etc.), he took jobs of many descriptions, becoming, in turn, a real estate agent, a factory foreman, a collector of butterflies in Florida, etc., and composed when opportunity afforded. In 1893, at the Chicago World's Fair, he met a Russian prince who knew Rimsky-Korsakov and gave him many details of contemporary Russian composers whose work, as well as that of Bohemian and Scandinavian composers which was based on folk song, influenced Gilbert greatly in his later composition. In 1894 he made his first trip abroad and stayed in Paris, subsequently returning to the U.S.; when he heard of the premiere of Charpentier's *Louise,* he became intensely interested in the work because of its popular character, and, in order to hear it, earned his passage to Paris, in 1901, by working on a cattle boat; the opera impressed him so much that he decided to devote his entire time thereafter to composition. In 1902 he became associated with Arthur Farwell, whose Wa-Wan Press publ. Gilbert's early compositions. During this time (from 1903) he employed Negro tunes and rhythms extensively in his works. The compositions of his mature period (from 1915) reveal an original style, not founded on any particular native American material but infused with elements from many sources, and are an attempt at "un-European" music, expressing the spirit of America and its national characteristics. WORKS: OPERA: *The Fantasy in Delft* (1915). FOR ORCH.: *2 Episodes* (Boston, Jan. 13, 1896); *Humoresque on Negro-Minstrel Tunes* (originally entitled *Americanesque,* 1903; Boston Pops, May 24, 1911); *Comedy Overture on Negro Themes* (1905; perf. at a N.Y. municipal concert, Aug. 17, 1910; Boston Symph., April 13, 1911; also perf. by Glière, in Feodosia, Crimea, July 22, 1914, and in Odessa, Aug. 1, 1914); symph. poem, *The Dance in Place Congo* (1906; perf. as a ballet at the Metropolitan Opera, N.Y., March 23, 1918); *Strife* (1910); *Negro Rhapsody* (Norfolk, [Conn.] Festival, June 5, 1913, composer conducting); symph. prologue for Synge's *Riders to the Sea* (1904; MacDowell Festival, Peterboro, N.H., Aug. 20, 1914; revised version, N.Y. Phil., Nov. 11, 1917); *American Dances* (1915); *Indian Sketches* (Boston Symph., March 4, 1921); Suite from *Music to Pilgrim Tercentenary Pageant* (Boston Symph., March 31, 1922); *Symphonic Piece* (Boston Symph., Feb. 26, 1926); Nocturne, a "symph. mood" after Walt Whitman (Philadelphia, March 16, 1928); Suite for Chamber Orch. (commissioned by the E.S. Coolidge Foundation; first perf., Chamber Orch. of Boston, Slonimsky conducting, April 28, 1928); *To Thee, America,* hymn for Chorus and Orch. (MacDowell Festival, Peterboro, N.H., Jan. 25, 1915); *Salammbô's Invocation to Tänith,* aria for Soprano and Orch. (N.Y., Elise Stevens, with the Russian Symph. Orch., March 10, 1906); an early String Quartet. FOR PIANO: *Negro Episode, Mazurka, Scherzo,* 2 *Verlaine Moods, The Island of the Fay* (also for Orch.), *Indian Scenes, A Rag Bag, Negro Dances.* SONGS: *Pirate Song,* after Stevenson; *Celtic Studies,* cycle of 4 songs to poems by Irish poets; *The Lament of Deirdre; Faery Song;* 2 *South American Gypsy Songs; Fish Wharf Rhapsody; Give Me the Splendid Sun; The Owl; Orlamonde; Zephyrus; Homesick; Tell Me Where Is Fancy Bred?; Croon of the Dew;* 8 *Simple Songs; Perdita; The Curl; School Songs;* also ed. *100 Folksongs* (Boston, 1910); contributed articles to the *Musical Quarterly* ("The American Composer," April 1915; "The Survival of Music," July 1916; "Originality," Jan. 1919), and to other magazines.

Gilbert, Jean (pen name of **Max Winterfeld**), German operetta composer; b. Hamburg, Feb. 11, 1879; d. Buenos Aires, Dec. 20, 1942. He studied with Scharwenka; was active as a theater conductor in Hamburg and Berlin. In 1933 he left Germany, eventually settling in Buenos Aires. WORKS: Operettas: *Die keusche Susanne* (1910); *Polnische Wirtschaft* (1910); *Die Kino-Königin* (1911); *Puppchen* (1912); *Die Frau im Hermelin* (1918); *Die Braut des Lucullus* (1920); *Katja, die Tänzerin* (1922); *Das Weib im Purpur* (1923); *In der Johannisnacht* (1926); *Hotel Stadt Lemberg* (1929); *Das Mädel am Steuer* (1930). The song *Puppchen, du bist mein Augenstern,* from the operetta *Puppchen,* achieved immense popularity in Europe.

Gilbert, Kenneth, Canadian harpsichordist, organist, and musicologist; b. Montreal, Dec. 16, 1931. He studied organ in Montreal with Conrad Letendre, piano with Yvonne Hubert, and theory with Gabriel Cusson at the Montreal Cons.; he won the Prix d'Europe for organ in 1953, and subsequently studied in Europe with Nadia Boulanger (theory), Gaston Litaize (organ), and Gustav Leonhardt and Ruggero Gerlin (harpsichord). From 1952–67 he was organist and music director of the Queen Mary Road United Church in Montreal; gave concerts as organist and harpsichordist. He taught at the Montreal Cons. (1957–74), McGill Univ. (1964–72), and Laval Univ. (1969–76). He edited the complete harpsichord works of François Couperin (4 vols., 1969–72); also the complete works of Domenico Scarlatti (11 vols., 1971—).

Gilbert, Sir William Schwenck, British playwright, creator, with Sir Arthur Sullivan, of the famous series of comic operas; b. London, Nov. 18, 1836; d. Harrow Weald, Middlesex, May 29, 1911 (of cardiac arrest following a successful attempt to rescue a young woman swimmer from drowning). He was given an excellent education (at Boulogne and at King's College, London) by his father, who was a novelist. After a routine career as a clerk, Gilbert drifted into journalism, contributing drama criticism and humorous verse to London periodicals. His satirical wit was first revealed in a theater piece, *Dulcamara* (1886), in which he ridiculed grand opera. He met Sullivan in 1871, and together they initiated the productions of comic operas which suited them so perfectly. Some plots borrow ludicrous situations from actual Italian and French operas; Gilbert's librettos, in rhymed verse, were nonetheless unmistakably English. This insularity of wit may explain the enormous popularity of the Gilbert & Sullivan operas in English-speaking countries, while they are practically unknown on the Continent. Despite the fact that the targets of Gilbert's ridicule were usually the upper classes of Great Britain, the operas were often performed at court. He was knighted in 1907. After 20 years of fruitful cooperation with Sullivan, a conflict developed, and the 2 severed their relationship for a time. A reconciliation was effected, but the subsequent productions fell short of their greatest successes. The most popular of the Gilbert & Sullivan operettas are

H.M.S. Pinafore (1878); *The Pirates of Penzance* (1880); *Iolanthe* (1884); *The Mikado* (1885); and *The Gondoliers* (1889). A special theater, the Savoy, was built for the Gilbert & Sullivan productions in London in 1881 by the impresario Richard D'Oyly Carte.

Gilels, Emil, outstanding Russian pianist; b. Odessa, Oct. 19, 1916. He studied at the Odessa Cons. with Yakov Tkatch and Berthe Ringold; then with Reingbald, graduating in 1935; then went to Moscow for advanced piano studies with Heinrich Neuhaus at the Moscow Cons. (1935–38). He made his first public appearance at the age of 13 in Odessa; in 1933 he received first prize at the Moscow competition; in 1936 he carried 2nd prize at the international piano competition in Vienna, and in 1938 won the first prize at the prestigious international competition in Brussels, which marked the highest point of his career; also in 1938 he was appointed a prof. at the Moscow Cons. He made numerous appearances in concert recitals and as soloist with major orchs. of Europe, America, and the Far East; made his first American tour in 1955, and returned at regular intervals; in 1977 he toured the U.S. for the 12th time. His playing is distinguished by a quality of Romantic intellectuality, with a fine understanding of the special pianistic sonorities. On several of his tours he played all 5 Beethoven piano concertos in succession.

Giles, Nathaniel, English organist and composer of church music; b. Worcester, c.1558; d. Windsor, Jan. 24, 1633. A son of **William Giles,** organist of St. Paul's Cathedral, London, he studied at Oxford; was organist at Worcester Cathedral from 1581 to 1585, when he became clerk, organist, and choirmaster at St. George's Chapel, Windsor; in 1597, became Gentleman and Master of the Children there. He wrote 4 services for the church; a great number of anthems; several motets and a 5-part madrigal (incomplete or in MS). Some of his compositions are included in Leighton's *Teares or Lamentacions of a Sorrowfull Soule* (1614); a service and an anthem are in Barnard's *Church Music* (1641); Hawkins's *History of Music* contains Giles's *Lesson of Descant of thirty-eighte Proportions of sundrie Kindes.*

Gilibert, Charles, dramatic baritone; b. Paris, Nov. 29, 1866; d. New York, Oct. 11, 1910. He sang one season at the Opéra-Comique, and then went to the Théâtre de la Monnaie, Brussels, where he became a great favorite; from 1900 to 1903 he was a member of the Metropolitan Opera; at his debut on Dec. 18, 1900, and throughout the entire season, he failed to make a decided impression, but on his appearance in the 2nd season he took the public by storm; in 1906–10, he was at the Manhattan Opera House in N.Y.; he was then reengaged for the Metropolitan, and was to have created Jack Rance in *The Girl of the Golden West,* but died just before the opening of the season. He was also a distinguished concert singer and interpreter of old French songs.

Gillespie, John Birks ("Dizzy"), black American jazz trumpeter and bandleader; b. Cheraw, S.C., Oct. 21, 1917. He picked up the rudiments of music from his father; at the age of 18 he went to Philadelphia, where he joined a local jazz band; in 1939 he became a member of the Cab Calloway orch., and in 1944 he was with the Billy Eckstine band. Soon he emerged as a true innovator in jazz playing, and was one of the founders of the style variously known as bebop, bop, and rebop. He received the nickname "Dizzy" because of his wild manner of playing, making grimaces and gesticulating during his performances. Gillespie is doubtless one of the greatest trumpeters in jazz history and practice, a true virtuoso on his instrument, extending its upper ranges and improvising long passages at breakneck speed.

Gillet, Ernest, French composer; b. Paris, Sept. 13, 1856; d. there, May 6, 1940. He studied cello at the Paris Cons., and was for many years a cellist in the orch. of the Paris Opéra. He publ. a number of melodious pieces, of which *Loin du bal* for Piano became a perennial drawing-room favorite, available also in numerous arrangements.

Gilman, Lawrence, renowned American music critic; b. Flushing, N.Y., July 5, 1878; d. Franconia, N.H., Sept. 8, 1939. He was self-taught in music; in 1901–13, he was music critic of *Harper's Weekly;* in 1915–23, music, dramatic, and literary critic of the *North American Review;* from 1921, author of the program notes of the N.Y. Phil. and Philadelphia Orch. concerts; from 1923, was music critic of the *N.Y. Herald Tribune;* was a member of the National Inst. of Arts and Letters.

WRITINGS: *Phases of Modern Music* (1904); *Edward MacDowell* (1905, in the Living Masters of Music series; revised and enlarged as *Edward MacDowell: A Study,* 1909); *The Music of To-Morrow* (1906); *Stories of Symphonic Music* (1907); *Aspects of Modern Opera* (1909); *Nature in Music* (1914); *A Christmas Meditation* (1916); "Taste in Music," *Musical Quarterly* (Jan. 1917); *Music and the Cultivated Man* (1929); *Wagner's Operas* (1937); *Toscanini and Great Music* (1938). He set to music 3 poems of W.B. Yeats (*The Heart of the Woman, A Dream of Death,* and *The Curlew*).

Gilmore, Patrick Sarsfield, American bandmaster; b. County Galway, Ireland, Dec. 25, 1829; d. St. Louis, Sept. 24, 1892. He went to Canada with an English band, but soon settled in Salem, Mass., where he conducted a military band. In 1859 in Boston he organized the famous Gilmore's Band. As bandmaster in the Federal army at New Orleans (1864), he gave a grand music festival with several combined bands, introducing the novel reinforcement of strong accents by cannon shots. He won wide renown through the National Peace Jubilee (1869) and the World's Peace Jubilee (1872), 2 monster music festivals held in Boston; in the former, Gilmore led an orch. of 1,000 and a chorus of 10,000; in the latter, an orch. of 2,000 and a chorus of 20,000; the orch. was reinforced by a powerful organ, cannon fired by electricity, anvils, and chimes of bells.

After the 2nd jubilee, Gilmore went to N.Y., and, as a popular bandmaster, traveled with his men throughout the U.S. and Canada, and also (1878) to Europe. He also led bands or orchs. in various resorts in and near N.Y.

WORKS: Military music; dance music; many arrangements for band. Some of his songs were popular. He claimed to be the composer of *When Johnny Comes Marching Home* (1863), a song that remained a favorite long after the Civil War. The song bears the name of Louis Lambert as composer; this may have been one of Gilmore's many aliases—at any rate, he introduced the song and started it on its way to popularity.

Gilson, Paul, Belgian composer, critic, and educator; b. Brussels, June 15, 1865; d. there, April 3, 1942. He studied with Auguste Cantillon and Charles Duyck; took lessons from Gevaert; in 1889, he won the Belgian Prix de Rome with his cantata, *Sinai,* performed at Brussels in 1890. His subsequent works, both choral and orch., won him a foremost place among modern Flemish composers. In addition to his composing, he wrote numerous books and articles on music, and taught, beginning in 1899, as a prof. of harmony at the Brussels Cons.; in 1904, he was also on the faculty of the Antwerp Cons.; in 1909, he left both posts to become music inspector in the Belgian schools. He was also an important music critic: for *Soir* from 1906 to 1914, for *Le Diapason* from 1910 to 1914, and later for *Midi.* He was the founder of the *Revue Musicale Belge* (1924). In 1942, he publ. his memoirs, *Notes de musique et souvenirs.* He also publ. *Les Intervalles, Le Tutti orchestral, Quintes et octaves, Traité d'harmonie, Traité d'orchestre militaire.*

Gimpel, Bronislaw, Austrian-born American violinist, brother of **Jakob Gimpel;** b. Lemberg (Lwow), Jan. 29, 1911; d. Los Angeles, May 1, 1979. He studied with R. Pollack in Vienna (1922–26) and Carl Flesch in Berlin (1928–29). From 1929–31 he was concertmaster at the Radio Orch. in Königsberg; from 1931–36 was in Göteborg, Sweden. In 1937 he emigrated to the U.S.; from 1937–42 he was concertmaster of the Los Angeles Phil.; from 1967–73 was on the faculty of the Univ. of Conn. In 1962 he organized the Warsaw String Quartet and toured with it in the U.S., Europe, and Japan. In 1968 he also became the concertmaster of the New England Quartet. He was to play a joint recital with his brother, Jakob Gimpel, in Los Angeles on May 9, 1979, but died 8 days before the scheduled concert; instead, his brother played a piano recital in his memory.

Gimpel, Jakob, Austrian-born American virtuoso pianist, brother of the violinst **Bronislaw Gimpel;** b. Lemberg (Lwow), April 16, 1906. He received his earliest musical training at home; his father was an excellent musician. After a preliminary study at the Lemberg Cons., he went to Vienna, where he took piano lessons with Eduard Steuermann; also had private instruction in music theory with Alban Berg. He made his concert debut in Vienna in 1923; then engaged in a brilliant concert career; he was especially successful in Germany; in one particular season he gave 80 concerts there, including 5 recitals in Hamburg. He also was a frequent soloist with orchs. His specialty was Romantic music; he infused the works of Beethoven, Schumann, and Chopin with a peculiarly lyrico-dramatic poetry which seemed to recreate the zeitgeist to perfection. When Germany was usurped by the Nazis, he went to Palestine, where he became closely associated with the violinist Bronislaw Huberman, the founder of the Israel Phil. In 1938 he emigrated to America, settling in Los Angeles, where he became active as an artist and a teacher; he also supplied background music to motion pictures, and had several appearances with the Los Angeles Phil. He continued to concertize in Europe; he received the Ben-Gurion Award of the State of Israel and the Order of Merit, First Class, of the Federal Republic of Germany for his "great services as an interpreter of German music," an exquisitely ironic but all the more precious gesture of the country that during its period of darkness closed its doors to Gimpel as a Jew. In 1971 Gimpel joined the music faculty of the Calif. State Univ., Northridge, as Distinguished Professor-in-Residence. He continued to give recitals in programs of Schumann and Chopin. On May 9, 1979, Jakob Gimpel was to give a joint recital in Los Angeles with his brother, the violinist Bronislaw Gimpel, who died suddenly 8 days before the scheduled concert. Instead, Jakob Gimpel played a solo recital in memory of his brother.

Ginastera, Alberto, greatly talented Argentinian composer; b. Buenos Aires, April 11, 1916; d. Geneva, June 25, 1983. His father was of Catalan descent, and Ginastera often preferred to pronounce his name with a soft "g," as in the Catalan language; the standard pronunciation, however, is with a hard "g". His mother was of Italian origin. Ginastera took private lessons in music as a child; then entered the National Cons. of Music in Buenos Aires, where he studied composition with José Gil, Athos Palma, and José André; also took piano lessons with Argenziani. He began to compose in his early youth; in 1934 won first prize of the musical society El Unísono for his *Piezas infantiles* for Piano. His next piece of importance was *Impresiones de la Puna* for Flute and String Quartet, in which he made use of native Argentinian melodies and rhythms; he discarded it, however, as immature; he withdrew a number of his other works, some of them of certain value, for instance, his *Concierto argentino,* which he wrote in 1935, at the age of 19, and *Sinfonía Porteña,* his first symph. (which may be identical in its musical material with *Estancia*). Also withdrawn was his 2nd Symph., the *Sinfonía elegíaca,* written in 1944, even though it was successfully performed. In 1946–47 Ginastera traveled to the U.S. on a Guggenheim fellowship grant. Returning to Argentina, he was appointed to the faculty of his alma mater, the National Cons. in Buenos Aires, where he taught intermittently from 1948 to 1958; he also served as dean of the faculty of musical arts and sciences at the Argentine Catholic Univ. In 1969 he left Argentina and lived mostly in Geneva, Switzerland. From his earliest steps in composition, Ginastera had an almost amorous attachment for the melodic and rhythmic resources of Argentinian folk music, and he evolved a fine harmonic and contrapuntal setting congenial with native patterns. His first significant work in the Argentinian national idiom was *Panambí*, a ballet, composed in 1935 and performed at the Teatro Colón in Buenos Aires on July 12, 1940, conducted by Juan José Castro. There followed a group of *Danzas argentinas* for Piano, written in 1937; in 1938 he wrote 3 songs; the first one, *Canción al árbol del olvido*, is a fine evocation of youthful love; it became quite popular. In 1941 he was commissioned to write a ballet for the American Ballet Caravan, to be called *Estancia;* the music was inspired by the rustic scenes of the pampas; a suite from the score was performed at the Teatro Colón in Buenos Aires on May 12, 1943, and the complete work was brought out there on Aug. 19, 1952. A series of works inspired by native scenes and written for various instrumental combinations followed, all infused with Ginastera's poetic imagination and brought to realization with excellent technical skill. Soon, however, Ginastera began to search for new methods of musical expression, marked by modern and sometimes strikingly dissonant combinations of sound, fermented by asymmetrical rhythms. Of these works, one of the most remarkable is *Cantata para América Mágica*, scored for dramatic soprano and percussion instruments, to apocryphal pre-Columbian texts, freely arranged by Ginastera himself; it was first performed in Washington, D.C., on April 30, 1961, with excellent success. An entirely new development in Ginastera's evolution as composer came with his first opera, *Don Rodrigo* (1964), produced on July 24, 1964, at the Teatro Colón. In it Ginastera followed the general formula of Alban Berg's *Wozzeck,* in its use of classical instrumental forms, such as rondo, suite, scherzo, and canonic progressions; he also introduced a *Sprechstimme.* In 1964 Ginastera wrote the *Cantata Bomarzo* on a commission from the Elizabeth Sprague Coolidge Foundation in Washington, D.C. He used the same libretto by Manuel Mujica Láinez in his opera *Bomarzo,* which created a sensation at its production in Washington on May 19, 1967, by its unrestrained spectacle of sexual violence. It was announced for performance at the Teatro Colón on Aug. 9, 1967, but was taken off at the order of the Argentinian government because of its alleged immoral nature. The score of *Bomarzo* reveals extraordinary innovations in serial techniques, with thematical employment not only of different chromatic sounds, but also of serial progressions of different intervals. Ginastera's last opera, *Beatrix Cenci,* commissioned by the Opera Society of Washington, D.C., and produced there on Sept. 10, 1971, concluded his operatic trilogy. Among instrumental works of Ginastera's last period, the most remarkable was his 2nd Piano Concerto (1972), based on a tone-row derived from the famous dissonant opening of the finale of Beethoven's 9th Symph.; the 2nd movement of the con-

certo is written for the left hand alone. Ginastera was married to the pianist **Mercedes de Toro** in 1941; they had a son and a daughter. He divorced her in 1965 and married the Argentinian cellist **Aurora Natola,** for whom he wrote the Cello Sonata, which she played in N.Y. on Dec. 13, 1979, and his 2nd Cello Concerto, which she performed for the first time in Buenos Aires on July 6, 1981. WORKS: Operas: *Don Rodrigo,* in 3 acts and 9 tableaux (Buenos Aires, July 24, 1964); *Bomarzo,* in 2 acts and 15 tableaux, to a libretto from a novel by Manuel Mujica Láinez (Washington, D.C., May 19, 1967); *Beatrix Cenci,* in 2 acts and 14 tableaux (Washington, D.C., Sept. 10, 1971).

BALLETS: *Panambí* (1935; Teatro Colón, July 12, 1940, conducted by Juan José Castro); *Estancia* (Buenos Aires, Aug. 19, 1952).

FOR ORCH.: Suite from the ballet *Panambí* (Buenos Aires, Nov. 27, 1937); *Primer concierto argentino* (Montevideo, July 18, 1941; withdrawn); *Primera sinonía (Porteña)* (1942; withdrawn); *Dances* from the ballet *Estancia* (Buenos Aires, May 12, 1943); *Obertura para el Fausto Criollo* (Santiago, Chile, May 12, 1944); *Sinfonía elegíaca* (2nd Symph.; Buenos Aires, May 31, 1946; withdrawn); *Ollantay,* 3 symph. movements after an Inca poem (Buenos Aires, Oct. 29, 1949); *Variaciones concertantes* for Chamber Orch. (Buenos Aires, June 2, 1953); *Pampeana No. 3,* symph. pastoral (Louisville, Ky., Oct. 20, 1954); Harp Concerto (1956; Philadelphia, Feb. 18, 1965); Piano Concerto No. 1 (Washington, D.C., April 22, 1961); Violin Concerto (N.Y. Phil., Oct. 3, 1963; Ruggiero Ricci, soloist; Leonard Bernstein conducting); Concerto for Strings (Caracas, May 14, 1966); Suite from *Bomarzo* (1967); *Estudios sinfónicos* (Vancouver, March 31, 1968); Cello Concerto No. 1 (1968; Dartmouth College, July 7, 1968; revised 1971–72); Piano Concerto No. 2 (Indianapolis, March 22, 1973; Hilde Somer, soloist); *Popul Vuh* for Orch. (1975–83; unfinished); *Glosses sobre temas de Pau Casals* for String Orch. and String Quintet "in lontano" (San Juan, Puerto Rico, June 14, 1976); Cello Concerto No. 2 (Buenos Aires, July 6, 1981; Aurora Natola, soloist); *Iubilum* (1979–80; Buenos Aires, April 12, 1980).

CHAMBER MUSIC: *Impresiones de la Puna* for Flute and String Quartet (1942; withdrawn); *Dúo* for Flute and Oboe (1945); *Pampeana No. 1* for Violin and Piano (1947); 4 string quartets: No. 1 (1948); No. 2 (1958); No. 3, with Soprano (1973); No. 4, with Baritone, to the text of Beethoven's Heiligenstadt Testament (1974; unfinished); *Pampeana No. 2* for Cello and Piano (1950); Piano Quintet (1963); *Puneña No. 2* for Cello Solo (1976); Guitar Sonata (1976); Cello Sonata (N.Y., Dec. 13, 1979; Aurora Natola, cellist); *Fanfare* for 4 Trumpets in C (1980): *Serenade* for Cello Solo, Flute, Oboe, Clarinet, Bassoon, Horn, Double Bass, Harp, and Percussion (1980).

FOR VOICE: 2 *Canciones:* No. 1, *Canción al árbol del ovido;* No. 2, *Canción a la luna lunanca* (1938); *Cantos del Tucumán* for Voice, Flute, Violin, Harp, and 2 Indian Drums (1938); *Psalm 150* for Mixed Choir, Boys' Choir, and Orch. (1938; Buenos Aires, April 7, 1945); 5 *Canciones populares argentinas* for Voice and Piano (1943); *Las horas de una estancia* for Voice and Piano (1943); *Hieremiae prophetae lamentatiónes* for Mixed Choir a cappella (1946); *Cantata para América Mágica* for Dramatic Soprano and Percussion, to an apocryphal pre-Columbian text (1960; Washington, D.C., April 30, 1961); *Sinfonía Don Rodrigo* for Soprano and Orch. (Madrid, Oct. 31, 1964); *Cantata Bomarzo* for Speaker, Baritone, and Chamber Orch. (Washington, D.C., Nov. 1, 1964); *Milena*, cantata for Soprano and Orch., to texts from Kafka's letters (Denver, April 16, 1973); *Serenata* for Cello, Baritone, and Chamber Ensemble, to texts of Pablo Neruda (1973); *Turbae ad Passionem Gregorianam* for Tenor, Baritone, and Bass, Boys' Chorus, Mixed Chorus, and Orch. (Philadelphia, March 20, 1975).

FOR PIANO: *Piezas infantiles* (1934); *Danzas argentinas* (1937); *3 Piezas* (1940); *Malambo* (1940); *12 Preludios americanos* (1944); *Suite de Danzas criollas* (1946); *Rondó sobre temas infantiles argentinos* (1947); Sonata No. 1 (1952); *Pequeña danza* from *Estancia* (1955); *Toccata*, arranged from *Toccata per organo* by Domenico Zipoli (1972); Sonata No. 2 (1981); Sonata No. 3 (1982); also *Toccata, Villancico y Fuga* for Organ (1947); *Variazioni e Toccata* for Organ (1980); film music.

Gingold, Josef, distinguished Russian-born American violinist and pedagogue; b. Brest-Litovsk, Oct. 28, 1909. He came to the U.S. in 1920. He studied violin in N.Y. with Vladimir Graffman, and later in Brussels with Eugène Ysaÿe. He then served as first violinist in the NBC Symph. Orch. under Toscanini (1937–43); was concertmaster of the Detroit Symph. Orch. (1943–46) and the Cleveland Orch. (1947–60). He taught at Case Western Reserve Univ. (1950–60) and was prof. of chamber music at the Meadowmount School of Music (1955–81). In 1960 he was appointed to the faculty of the Indiana Univ. School of Music in Bloomington; was made a distinguished prof. of music there in 1965. He also gave master classes at the Paris Cons. (1970–81), in Tokyo (1970), in Copenhagen (1979), and in Montreal (1980); held the Mischa Elman Chair at the Manhattan School of Music in N.Y. (1980–81). He was a guiding force in establishing the International Violin Competition of Indianapolis; was its first honorary chairman and president of the jury in 1982.

Giordani, Giuseppe (called **Giordanello**), Italian composer; b. Naples, Dec. 9, 1743; d. Fermo, Jan. 4, 1798. He studied with Fenaroli at the San Loreto Cons., Naples; Cimarosa and Zingarelli were fellow students. His first opera, *Epponina*, was given in Florence in 1779. He continued to write operas for various Italian towns, but they were not outstanding, and few of the 30-odd he wrote have survived. He also wrote several oratorios and church music. From 1791 until his death he was maestro di cappella at the Fermo Cathedral. He is sometimes credited with *Il bacio* and other operas and works produced in London by Tommaso Giordani; Giuseppe was not related to Tommaso, and never left Italy. The famous song *Caro mio ben*, popularized in London by Pacchierotti, was probably written by Giuseppe.

Giordani, Tommaso, Italian composer; b. Naples, c.1730; d. Dublin, late Feb. 1806. His family, which included his father, **Giuseppe;** his mother, **Antonia;** his brother, **Francesco;** and his sisters, **Marina** and **Nicolina** (known later as **Spiletta** from one of her opera roles), together formed a strolling opera company, with the father as impresario and singer and the rest of the family, except Tommaso, as singers. Tommaso was probably a member of the orch. and the arranger of music. They left Naples about 1745 and moved northward, appearing in Italian towns, then in Graz (1748), Frankfurt (1750), and Amsterdam (1752). They made their London debut at Covent Garden on Dec. 17, 1753, and returned in 1756, at which time Tommaso first appeared as a composer, with his comic opera *La Comediante fatta cantatrice* (Covent Garden, Jan. 12, 1756). The Giordani company next went to Dublin, appearing there in 1764; Tommaso continued to be active both in Dublin and in London; he was conductor and composer at the King's Theatre, London, in 1769 and many following seasons, and in Dublin, where he lived after 1783, was conductor and composer at the Smock Alley and Crow Street theaters; he also taught piano between operas. In 1794, he was elected president of the Irish music fund. He played an important part in Irish music circles, and wrote altogether more than 50 English and Italian operas, including pasticcios and adaptations.

WORKS: *L'Eroe cinese* (Dublin, 1766); *Il Padre el il figlio rivali* (London, 1770); *Artaserse* (London, 1772); *Il Re pastore* (London, 1778); *Il bacio* (London, 1782). He also wrote several cantatas, including *Aci e Galatea* (London, 1777); an oratorio, *Isaac* (Dublin, 1767); songs for the original production of Sheridan's *The Critic* (Drury Lane, London, Oct. 29, 1779); many Italian and English songs that were popular for a long time; concertos; string quartets; trios; many piano pieces.

Giordano, Umberto, Italian opera composer; b. Foggia, Aug. 28, 1867; d. Milan, Nov. 12, 1948. He studied with Gaetano Briganti at Foggia, and then with Paolo Serrao at the Naples Cons. (1881–90). His first composition performed in public was a symph. poem, *Delizia* (1886); he then wrote some instrumental music. In 1888 he submitted a short opera, *Marina*, for the competition established by the publisher Sonzogno; Mascagni's *Cavalleria rusticana* received first prize, but *Marina* was cited for distinction. Giordano then wrote an opera in 3 acts, *Mala vita*, which was performed in Rome, Feb. 21, 1892; it was only partly successful; was revised and presented under the title *Il voto* in Milan (1897). There followed a 2-act opera, *Regina Diaz* (Rome, Feb. 21, 1894), which obtained a moderate success. Then Giordano set to work on a grand opera, *Andrea Chénier*, to a libretto by Illica. The production of this opera at La Scala (March 28, 1896) was a spectacular success, which established Giordano as one of the best composers of modern Italian opera. The dramatic subject gave Giordano a fine opportunity to display his theatrical talent; but the opera also revealed his gift for lyric expression. *Andrea Chénier* was produced at the N.Y. Academy of Music shortly after its Milan premiere; a performance at the Metropolitan Opera House came considerably later (March 7, 1920). Almost as successful was his next opera, *Fedora* (Teatro Lirico, Milan, Nov. 17, 1898; Metropolitan Opera, Dec. 5, 1906), but it failed to hold a place in the world repertoire after the initial acclaim; there followed *Siberia*, in 3 acts (La Scala, Dec. 19, 1903; revised 1921, and perf. at La Scala, Dec. 5, 1927). Two short operas, *Marcella* (Milan, Nov. 9, 1907) and *Mese Mariano* (Palermo, March 17, 1910), were hardly noticed and seemed to mark a decline in Giordano's dramatic gift; however, he recaptured the attention of the public with *Madame Sans-Gêne*, produced at a gala premiere at the Metropolitan on Jan. 25, 1915, conducted by Toscanini, with Geraldine Farrar singing the title role. With Franchetti, he wrote *Giove a Pompei* (Rome, July 5, 1921); then he produced *La cena delle beffe* in 4 acts, which was his last signal accomplishment; it was staged at La Scala, Dec. 20, 1924, and at the Metropolitan, Jan. 2, 1926. He wrote one more opera, *Il Re*, in one act (La Scala, Jan. 10, 1929). During his lifetime he received many honors, and was elected a member of the Accademia Luigi Cherubini in Florence and of several other institutions. Although not measuring up to Puccini in musical qualities or to Mascagni in dramatic skill, Giordano was a distinguished figure in the Italian opera field.

Giornovichi, Giovanni Mane, Italian violinist, probably of Croatian extraction (his real name was **Jarnowick**); b. Raguso or Palermo, c.1735; d. St. Petersburg, Russia, Nov. 23, 1804. He was a pupil of Antonio Lolli in Palermo; gave successful concerts in Europe; on the strength of his reputation, he was engaged as court musician to Catherine II, succeeding his teacher Lolli in that post. He was in Russia in 1789–91; then appeared in London (1791–94), Paris, Hamburg, and Berlin. He returned to Russia in 1803, and died there the following year; was a member of the court orch. in St. Petersburg until his death. In his old age he devoted himself to playing billiards for money. Among his works are 22 violin concertos (17 extant); 3 string quartets; *Fantasia e Rondo* for Piano. He was probably the first to introduce the "romance" into the violin concerto as a slow movement, and he helped to set the rondo as the finale.

Giovannelli, Ruggiero, Italian composer; b. Velletri, 1560; d. Rome, Jan. 7, 1625. On Aug. 8, 1583, he was nominated director of the cappella of San Luigi de' Francesi at Rome; later (1591–94) was maestro in the Collegium Germanicum; in 1594 he succeeded Palestrina as maestro at St. Peter's, and in 1599 joined the Pontifical Chapel. He was one of the most famous masters of the Roman School; of his works there have been printed 3 books of madrigals *a* 5 (1586, 1587, 1589; completely reprinted 1600); 2 of *Madrigali sdruccioli a* 4 (1585 [7th ed., 1613], 1589 [5th ed., 1603]); 2 books of motets *a* 5–8 (1589, 1604);

Canzonette and *Villanelle a* 3 (1592, 1593); also scattered works in collections publ. from 1583 to 1620 (Scotto, Phalèse, Schadaeus, etc.). K. Proske's *Musica divina* contains a Psalm (vol. III, 1859); L. Torchi's *L'arte musicale in Italia* includes a motet and Psalm *a* 8 and a madrigal *a* 5 (vol. II). In the Vatican Library are many sacred works in MS. To Giovannelli was entrusted, by Pope Paul V, the preparation of a new edition of the Gradual (2 vols., 1614, 1615).

Giovanni da Cascia (Johannes de Florentia), Italian 14th-century composer. According to his younger contemporary Filippo Villani, in *Liber de civitatis Florentiae famosis civibus*, he was the initiator of the stylistic reform which spread from Florence shortly after 1300. He was organist and probably chorus master at Santa Maria del Fiore at Florence; lived at the court of Mastino II della Scala, Verona, c.1329–51. His compositions included 16 madrigals, 3 *cacce, ballate*, etc.; MSS may be found in libraries at Florence and Paris, and in the British Museum. In all, 28 works by Giovanni, in 2–3 parts, are known. The madrigal *Agnel son bianco* was edited and publ. by Johannes Wolf in *Sammelbände der Internationalen Musik-Gesellschaft* (1902; ex. 4); 2 other compositions were also edited and publ. by Wolf in his *Geschichte der Mensural-Notation* (pp. 61–64; Leipzig, 1904). For further modern editions of his works, see N. Pirrotta, editor, *The Music of 14th Century Italy*, in Corpus Mensurabilis Musicae, VIII/1 (1954), and W. Marrocco, editor, *Italian Secular Music*, in *Polyphonic Music of the Fourteenth Century*, VI (1967).

Giraldoni, Eugenio, famous Italian baritone; b. Marseilles, May 20, 1871; d. Helsinki, June 23, 1924. Both his parents were professional singers; his father, **Leone Giraldoni,** was a renowned baritone, and his mother, **Carolina Ferni-Giraldoni,** a famous soprano. He made his debut in Barcelona as Don José in 1891; then sang in Buenos Aires and in Italy (at La Scala and other theaters); made his debut at the Metropolitan Opera in N.Y. as Barnaba in *La Gioconda* on Nov. 28, 1904; remained there only one season (1904–5); eventually settled in Russia.

Giraldoni, Leone, Italian baritone; father of **Eugenio Giraldoni;** b. Paris, 1824; d. Moscow, Oct. 1, 1897. He studied in Florence with Ronzi; made his debut in 1847 in Lodi; created the title roles of *Il Duca d'Alba* by Donizetti, *Simone Boccanegra* by Verdi, and Renato in Verdi's *Un ballo in maschera*. He retired from the stage in 1885; then taught voice in Italy. From 1891 to 1897 he was on the staff of the Moscow Cons. Among his students were Nicolai and Medea Figner. He published *Guida teorico-practico ad uso dell'artista cantante* (Bologna, 1864).

Girdlestone, Cuthbert (Morton), English music scholar; b. Bovery-Tracey, Sept. 17, 1895; d. St. Cloud, France, Dec. 10, 1975. He was educated at the Sorbonne (licence ès lettres, 1915) and the Schola Cantorum in Paris; then entered Trinity College, Cambridge; became a lecturer at Cambridge in 1922; in

1926 he was appointed prof. of French at the Univ. of Durham, Newcastle division (later the Univ. of Newcastle upon Tyne); retired in 1960 and settled in St. Cloud. He publ. a valuable analysis of Mozart's piano concertos under the title *Mozart et ses concertos pour piano* (Paris, 1939; Eng. trans., 1948; 2nd ed., 1964); also the important monograph *Jean-Philippe Rameau: His Life and Work* (London, 1957; 2nd ed., revised, 1969). He further wrote *La Tragédie en musique (1673–1750) considérée comme genre littéraire* (Paris, 1972).

Giuliani, Mauro, Italian guitar virtuoso; b. Bisceglie, near Bari, July 27, 1781; d. Naples, May 8, 1829. He was entirely self-taught; at the age of 19 undertook a highly successful tour in Europe; settled in Vienna in 1806. where he became associated with Hummel, Moscheles, and Diabelli; Beethoven became interested in him, and wrote some guitar music expressly for his performances. In 1823 he visited London, where he won extraordinary acclaim; a special publication, named after him *The Giulianiad* and devoted to reports about his activities, was initiated there, but only a few issues appeared. Giuliani publ. over 200 works for guitar; he also perfected a new guitar with a shorter fingerboard ("la ghitarra di terza").

Giulini, Carlo Maria, eminent Italian conductor; b. Barletta, May 9, 1914. He began to study the violin as a boy; at 16 he entered the Conservatorio di Musica di Santa Cecilia in Rome, where he studied violin and viola with Remy Principe, composition with Alessandro Bustini, and conducting with Bernardino Molinari; also received instruction in conducting from Casella at the Chigi Academy in Siena; then joined the Augusteo Orch. in Rome in the viola section, under such great conductors as Richard Strauss, Bruno Walter, Mengelberg, and Furtwängler. He was drafted into the Italian army, but went into hiding as a convinced anti-Fascist; after the liberation of Rome by the Allied troops in 1944, he was engaged to conduct the Augusteo Orch. in a special concert celebrating the occasion. He was then engaged as assistant conductor of the RAI Orch. in Rome, and was made its chief conductor in 1946. In 1950 he helped to organize the RAI Orch. in Milan; in 1952 he conducted at La Scala as an assistant to Victor de Sabata; in 1954 he became principal conductor there; his performance of *La Traviata,* with Maria Callas in the title role, was particularly notable. In 1955 he conducted Verdi's *Falstaff* at the Edinburgh Festival, earning great praise. On Nov. 3, 1955, he was a guest conductor with the Chicago Symph., and returned to it for 5 more appearances in subsequent years. During its European tour of 1971 he was joint conductor with Sir Georg Solti. Giulini now became an undisputed master of the art of conducting, in both the operatic and the symph. repertoire; his renown was worldwide. In 1973 he was named principal conductor of the Vienna Symph. Orch., and in 1975 he took it on a world tour, which included the U.S., Canada, and Japan. On Oct. 24, 1975, he led it at a televised concert from the United Nations. In 1978 he succeeded Zubin Mehta as chief conductor and music director of the Los Angeles Phil., and succeeded in maintaining it at a zenith of orchestral brilliance. In 1983 he took the orchestra to Japan. His conducting style embodies the best traditions of the Italian school as exemplified by Toscanini, but is free from explosive displays of temper. He is above all a Romantic conductor who can identify his musical Weltanschauung with the musical essence of Beethoven, Verdi, Mahler, and Tchaikovsky; he leads the classics with an almost abstract contemplation. In the music of the 20th century, he gives congenial interpretations of works by Debussy, Ravel, and Stravinsky; the expressionist school of composers lies outside of his deeply felt musicality, but he does not actively promote the experimental school of modern music. His behavior on the podium is free from self-assertive theatrics, and he treats the orchestra as comrades-in-arms, associates in the cause of music, rather than subordinate performers of the task assigned to them. Yet his personal feeling for music is not disguised; often he closes his eyes in fervent self-absorption when conducting without score the great Classical and Romantic works.

Glanville-Hicks, Peggy, Australian composer and critic; b. Melbourne, Dec. 29, 1912. She studied composition with Fritz Hart at the Melbourne Cons.; in 1931 went to London, where she took courses in piano with Arthur Benjamin, theory with R.O. Morris and C. Kitson at the Royal College of Music, composition with Ralph Vaughan Williams, orchestration with Gordon Jacob, and conducting with Constant Lambert and Sir Malcolm Sargent. She obtained a traveling scholarship which enabled her to go to Paris for lessons with Nadia Boulanger, and to Vienna, where she took a course in musicology and advanced composition with Egon Wellesz. In 1939 she came to the U.S.; became an American citizen; in 1938–48 was married to the English composer **Stanley Bates;** from 1948 to 1958 she wrote music criticism for the *N.Y. Herald Tribune.* In 1957 she received a Guggenheim fellowship; in 1959 she went to Greece, and made her residence in Athens. There she produced her opera *Nausicaa,* to the text of Robert Graves (Athens, Aug. 19, 1961), which had a modicum of success. Her other operas are *Caedmon* (1934); *The Transposed Heads* (Louisville, March 27, 1954); *The Glittering Gate* (N.Y., May 14, 1959); *Sappho* (1963). She wrote the ballets *Hylas and the Nymphs* (1937); *Postman's Knock* (1940); *The Masque of the Wild Man* (1958); *Saul and the Witch of Endor* (1959); *Triad* (1959); *Tragic Celebration* (1966); *A Season in Hell* (1967); *Dance Cantata* for Soloists, Speaking Chorus, Narrator, and Orch. (1947); *Letters from Morocco* for Voice and Orch. to texts from actual letters she received from the composer Paul Bowles (N.Y., Feb. 22, 1953); *Sinfonia da Pacifica* (1953); *Tapestry* for Orch. (1956); Piano Concerto (1936); Flute Concerto (1937); *Concertino da camera* for Flute, Clarinet, Bassoon, and Piano (Amsterdam Festival, June 10, 1948); *3 Gymnopedies* for Harp and Other Instruments (1953);

Etruscan Concerto for Piano and Chamber Orch. (N.Y., Jan. 25, 1956); *Concerto romantico* for Viola and Orch. (1957); *Drama* for Orch. (1966), *Concertino antico* for Harps and String Quartet; several other works inspired by ancient Greek modalities; choral pieces; songs. As a pragmatic composer of functional music with human connotations, Peggy Glanville-Hicks shuns the monopolistic fashion of mandatory dissonance, but explores attentively the resources of folk music, making use of Greek melos in her opera *Nausicaa,* of Hindu rhythmic modes in the opera *The Transposed Heads,* and of allusions to non-Western modalities in *Letters from Morocco.* She ceased to compose after going blind in 1969.

Glareanus, Henricus (also **Heinrich Glarean;** real name, **Heinrich Loris;** Latinized: **Henricus Loritus**), Swiss musical theorist and writer; b. Mollis, in the canton of Glarus, June 1488; d. Freiburg, Baden, March 28, 1563. He studied with Rubellus at Bern, and later with Cochläus at Cologne, where he was crowned poet laureate by Emperor Maximilian I in 1512, as the result of a poem he composed and sang to the emperor. He first taught mathematics at Basel (1515); in 1517 went to Paris, where he taught philosophy; in 1522 returned to Basel, where he stayed till 1529, when he settled in Freiburg. There he was a prof. of poetry, then of theology. His first important work, *Isagoge in musicen,* publ. at Basel in 1516 (Eng. trans. in the *Journal of Music Theory,* III, 1959; pp. 97–139), dealt with solmization, intervals, modes, and tones. A still more important vol., the *Dodecachordon,* was publ. in 1547; in it, Glareanus advanced the theory that there are 12 church modes, corresponding to the ancient Greek modes, instead of the commonly accepted 8 modes. The 3rd part of the *Dodecachordon* contains many works by 15th- and 16th-century musicians. A copy of the *Dodecachordon,* with corrections in Glareanus's own handwriting, is in the Library of Congress, Washington, D.C. A German trans., with the musical examples in modern notation, was publ. by P. Bohn in vol. 16 of *Publikationen der Gesellschaft für Musikforschung* (Leipzig, 1888); Eng. trans. and commentary by C.A. Miller in *Musicological Studies and Documents,* 6 (1965); facsimile edition in *Monuments of Music and Music Literature in Facsimile,* 2/65 (N.Y., 1967). A complete index of Glareanus's works is contained in P. Lichtenthal's *Dizionario e bibliografia della musica,* IV, pp. 274–76 (Milan, 1826). J.L. Wonegger publ. *Musicae epitome ex Glareani Dodekachordo* (1557; 2nd ed., 1559; in German as *Uss Glareani Musik ein Usszug,* 1557).

Glasenapp, Carl Friedrich, music scholar, biographer of Wagner; b. Riga, Oct. 3, 1847; d. there, April 14, 1915. He studied philology at Dorpat; from 1875, was headmaster at Riga. An ardent admirer of Wagner's art, he devoted his entire life to the study of the master's works, and was one of the principal contributors to the *Bayreuther Blätter* from their foundation. His great work is the monumental biography of Wagner *Richard Wagners Leben und Wirken,* of which the first 2 vols. were publ. at Kas-

sel and Leipzig (1876, 1877); after the 2nd enlarged edition (1882) these were rewritten, and the entire work was issued at Leipzig as *Das Leben Richard Wagners* (I, 1813–43 [1894]; II, 1843–53 [1896]; III, 1853–62 [1899]; IV, 1862–72 [1904]; V, 1872–77 [1907]; VI, 1877–83 [1911]). Vols. I, II, and III appeared in Eng. trans. (with amplifications) by W.A. Ellis (London, 1900, 1901, 1903), but after that Ellis continued the biography as an independent work. Though Glasenapp's work was considered the definitive biography in its time, its value is diminished by the fact that he publ. only materials approved by Wagner's family; as a result, it was superseded by later biographies. His other works on Wagner include *Wagner-Lexikon* with H. von Stein (1883); *Wagner-Encyklopädie* (2 vols., 1891); *Siegfried Wagner* (1906); *Siegfried Wagner und seine Kunst* (1911), with sequels, *Schwarzschwanenreich* (1913) and *Sonnenflammen* (1919); he also edited *Bayreuther Briefe, 1871–73* (1907) and *Familienbriefe an Richard Wagner, 1832–74* (1907).

Glass, Philip, remarkable American composer; b. Baltimore, Jan. 31, 1937. He was the grandchild of Orthodox Jewish immigrants from Russia. His father owned a record store, and Glass worked there from the age of 12; he studied flute at the Peabody Cons. in Baltimore; at the age of 15 he entered the Univ. of Chicago, where he took courses in piano and in wrestling in the featherweight category (1952–56); then moved to N.Y. to study at the Juilliard School of Music, where he was a student of Persichetti in composition, earning his M.S. in 1962. In 1964 he received a Fulbright grant and went to Paris, where, inevitably, he was steered to the "boulangerie," the classroom of Nadia Boulanger, the formidable *nourrice* of 3 generations of American composers; from her he learned a rather abecedarian counterpoint, which gave him a needed discipline. Much more important to his future development was his meeting with the great Indian sitar virtuoso Ravi Shankar, who introduced him to the mysterious world of Hindu ragas. He traveled to Morocco, where he absorbed the arcane modalities of North African melorhythms, which taught him the heterodox art of melodic repetition. He wrote music for a group of traveling American actors and actresses; he married one of them, JoAnne Akalaitis, and traveled with her to the foothills of the Himalayas. Eventually he divorced her and in 1980 married a 29-year-old medical doctor, Luba Burtyk. In 1967 he returned to N.Y. in a state of musical transfiguration; his style of composition became an alternately concave and convex mirror image of Eastern modes, undergoing melodic phases of stationary harmonies in lieu of modulations. In the physical world, he had to take a variety of manual jobs, as a furniture mover, carpenter, and cabdriver. He formed associations with modern painters and sculptors who strove to obtain maximum effects with a minimum of means. Glass began to practice a similar method in music, which soon acquired the factitious sobriquet of Minimalism. Other Americans and some Europeans followed this practice, which was basically Eastern in its catatonic homophony; Steve Reich was a close companion in minimalistic pursuits of maximalistic effects. Glass formed his own phonograph company, Chatham Square, which recorded most of his works. He also organized an ensemble of electrically amplified wind instruments, which became the chief medium of his own compositions. On April 13, 1968, he presented the first concert of the Glass Ensemble at Queens College in N.Y. Between 1969 and 1975 he made altogether 8 European tours. In 1970 and 1973 Glass was again in India.

His productions, both in America and in Europe, became extremely successful among young audiences, who were mesmerized by this mixture of rock realism with alluring mysticism; undeterred by the indeterminability and interminability of his productions, some lasting several hours of merciless, relentless, unremitting homophony, they accepted Glass as a true representative of earthly and unearthly art. The mind-boggling titles of these works added to the tantalizing incomprehensibility of the subjects that Glass selected for his inspiration. The high point of his productions was the "opera" *Einstein on the Beach*, to a text by Robert Wilson, which involved deliberate befuddlement in a surrealistic comminution of thematic ingredients and hypnotic repetition of harmonic subjects. It was first produced at the Festival of Avignon in France, on July 25, 1976, and was subsequently performed in Venice, Belgrade, Brussels, Paris, Hamburg, Rotterdam, and Amsterdam, finally reaching, on Nov. 21, 1976, the stage of the Metropolitan Opera at Lincoln Center in N.Y., where it proved something of a sensation of the season; however, it was not produced as part of the regular subscription series. On Sept. 5, 1980, Glass staged in Rotterdam his opera *Satyagraha*, based on an episode of Gandhi's years in South Africa between 1893 and 1913. "Satyagraha" was Gandhi's slogan, composed of 2 Hindu words: *saty* ("truth") and *agraha* ("firmness"). Another significant production was a film, *Koyaanisquatsi*, a Hopi Indian word meaning "life out of balance." The music represented the ultimate condensation of the basic elements of composition as practiced by Philip Glass; here the pitiless ritualistic repetition of chords arranged in symmetrical sequences becomes hypnotic, particularly since the screen action is devoid of narrative; the effect is enhanced by the deep bass notes of an Indian chant. Other works by Glass consist of the following: *Piece in the Shape of a Square* (N.Y., May 19, 1968); *Music in Fifths* (N.Y., Jan. 16, 1970); *Music with Changing Parts* (N.Y., Nov. 10, 1972); *Music in 12 Parts* (first full perf., N.Y., June 1, 1974); *North Star* for 2 Voices and Instruments (1975). On Oct. 6, 1983, the Brooklyn Academy of Music presented the first American performance of a mixed-media piece by Glass called *The Photographer: Far from the Truth*, based on the life of the 19th-century photographer Eadweard Muybridge; it includes a scene in which he murders his wife's lover. This was followed by the exotic opera *Akhnaton*, set in ancient Egypt, with the singing parts in the ancient Accadian language, in Egyptian, and in He-

brew, with an explanatory narration in English; it was produced in Stuttgart on March 24, 1984.

Glaz, Herta, Austrian contralto; b. Vienna, Sept. 16, 1908. She made her debut at the Breslau Opera in 1931, presaging a successful career, but in 1933 was forced to leave Germany. She toured Austria and Scandinavia as a concert singer; sang at the German Theater in Prague during the season 1935–36; in 1936 she took part in the American tour of the Salzburg Opera Guild; subsequently sang at the Chicago Opera (1940–42); on Dec. 25, 1942, she made her debut with the Metropolitan Opera in N.Y., and remained on its staff until 1956; then taught voice at the Manhattan School of Music, retiring in 1977; settled in Los Angeles.

Glazunov, Alexander, notable Russian composer; b. St. Petersburg, Aug. 10, 1865; d. Neuilly-sur-Seine, March 21, 1936. Of a well-to-do family (his father was a book publisher), he studied at a technical high school in St. Petersburg, and also took lessons in music with a private tutor. As a boy of 15, he was introduced to Rimsky-Korsakov, who gave him weekly lessons in harmony, counterpoint, and orchestration. Glazunov made rapid progress, and at the age of 16 completed his first symph., which was performed by Balakirev on March 29, 1882, in St. Petersburg. So mature was this score that Glazunov was hailed by Stasov, Cui, and others as a rightful heir to the masters of the Russian national school. The music publisher Belaiev arranged for publication of Glazunov's works, and took him to Weimar, where he met Liszt. From that time Glazunov composed assiduously in all genres except opera. He was invited to conduct his symphs. in Paris (1889) and London (1896–97). Returning to St. Petersburg, he conducted concerts of Russian music. In 1899 he was engaged as an instructor in composition and orchestration at the St. Petersburg Cons. He resigned temporarily during the revolutionary turmoil of 1905 in protest against the dismissal of Rimsky-Korsakov by the government authorities, but returned to the staff after full autonomy was granted to the Cons. by the administration. On Dec. 14, 1905, Glazunov was elected director and retained this post until 1928, when he went to Paris. In 1929 he made several appearances as conductor in the U.S.; led his 6th Symph. with the Detroit Symph. Orch. (Nov. 21, 1929) and also conducted the Boston Symph. He was the recipient of honorary degrees of Mus.D. from Cambridge and Oxford univs. (1907). Although he wrote no textbook on composition, his pedagogical methods left a lasting impression on Russian musicians through his many students who preserved his traditions. His music is often regarded as academic, yet there is a flow of rhapsodic eloquence that places Glazunov in the Romantic school. He was for a time greatly swayed by Wagnerian harmonies, but resisted this influence successfully; Lisztian characteristics are more pronounced in his works. Glazunov was one of the greatest masters of counterpoint among Russian composers, but he avoided extreme polyphonic complexity. The national spirit of his music is unmistakable; in many of his descriptive works, the programmatic design is explicitly Russian (*Stenka Razin, The Kremlin,* etc.). His most popular score is the ballet *Raymonda.* The major portion of his music was written before 1906, when he completed his 8th Symph.; after that he wrote mostly for special occasions.

WORKS: Incidental music to Grand Duke Konstantin Romanov's mystery play *The King of the Jews* (1914); ballets: *Raymonda* (1896; St. Petersburg, Jan. 19, 1898); *Ruses d'amour* (1898); *The Seasons* (1899).

FOR ORCH.: Symph. No. 1 (1881; St. Petersburg, March 29, 1882); 2 *Overtures on Greek Themes* (1881–85); 2 serenades (1883); *Stenka Razin,* symph. poem (1884); *A la mémoire d'un héros* (1885); *Suite caractéristique* (1885); *Idyll* and *Rêverie orientale* (1886); Symph. No. 2 (1886; Paris, June 29, 1889, composer conducting); *Une Pensée à Franz Liszt* for String Orch. (1886); *Mazurka* (1887); *The Forest,* symph. poem (1888); *Mélodie* and *Sérénade espagnole* for Cello and Orch. (1888); *Marche des Noces* for Large Orch. (1889); *Une Fête slave,* symph. sketch (1890; from *Quatuor slave*); *The Sea,* symph. fantasy (1890); *Oriental Rhapsody* (1890); *The Kremlin,* symph. picture (1890); Symph. No. 3 (1891); *Printemps,* musical picture (1892); *Triumphal March* on the occasion of the famous Columbian Exposition in Chicago (1893); overture *Carnaval* (1894); *Chopiniana,* suite on Chopin's themes (1894); 2 *Valses de concert* (1894); Symph. No. 4 (St. Petersburg, Feb. 3, 1894, composer conducting); *Cortège solennel* (1894); *Scènes de ballet* (1894); *Fantaisie* (1895); Symph. No. 5 (1895); suite from the ballet *Raymonda* (1897); Symph. No. 6 (1896; St. Petersburg, Feb. 21, 1897); *Pas de caractère,* on Slavic and Hungarian themes (1900); *Intermezzo romantico* (1901); *Chant du ménestrel* for Cello and Orch. (1901; also for Cello and Piano); *Ouverture solennelle* (1901); *Marche sur un thème russe* (1901); Symph. No. 7 (St. Petersburg, Jan. 3, 1903); *Ballade* (1903); *From the Middle Ages,* suite (1903); Violin Concerto (1904; St. Petersburg, March 4, 1905, Leopold Auer, soloist; first perf. outside Russia, London, Oct. 17, 1905, Mischa Elman, soloist); *Scène dansante* (1905); Symph. No. 8 (Dec. 22, 1906); *Le Chant du destin,* dramatic overture (1907); 2 preludes: No. 1, *In Memory of V. Stasov* (1906), and No. 2, *In Memory of Rimsky-Korsakov* (1908); *In Memory of Gogol* (1909); *Finnish Fantasy* (Helsingfors, Nov. 7, 1910, composer conducting); Piano Concerto No. 1 (1911); *Finnish Sketches* (1912); *Dance of Salomé,* after Oscar Wilde (1912); *Karelian Legend* (1914); Piano Concerto No. 2 (Petrograd, Nov. 11, 1917); *Concerto-Ballata* for Cello and Orch. (Paris, Oct. 14, 1933, composer conducting; Maurice Eisenberg, soloist); Saxophone Concerto (in collaboration with Sigurd Rascher; first perf. by him in Nykoping, Sweden, Nov. 25, 1934).

VOCAL WORKS: *Coronation Cantata* (1894); *Hymn to Pushkin* for Female Chorus (1899); cantata for Women's Chorus with 2 Pianos, 8-hands (1900); *Memorial Cantata* (1901); 21 songs.

CHAMBER MUSIC: 7 string quartets: No. 1, in D (1882); No. 2, in F (1884); No. 3, in G (*Quatuor slave;* 1889); No. 4, in A (1899); No. 5, in D (1900); No. 6, in B-flat (1930); No. 7, in C (1931); *5 Novelettes* for String Quartet (1888); Suite for String Quartet (1894); String Quintet (1895); Suite for String Quartet (1929); *Pensée à Liszt* for Cello and Piano; *Rêverie* for French Horn and Piano; *In modo religioso* for 4 Brass Instruments; *Elegy* for Viola and Piano; *Oberek* for Violin and Piano.

PIANO MUSIC: 2 sonatas (1898, 1899); *Barcarolle; Novelette;* Prelude and 2 mazurkas; 3 études; *Petite valse; Nocturne; Grande valse de concert: 3 Miniatures; Valse de salon; 3 morceaux; 2 Impromptus;* Prelude and Fugue; Theme and Variations; Suite for 2 Pianos (1920); 4 preludes and fugues (1922). Glazunov also completed and orchestrated the overture to Borodin's *Prince Igor* (from memory, having heard Borodin play it on the piano).

Glebov, Igor. Pen name of **Boris Asafiev.**

Glière, Reinhold, eminent Russian composer; b. Kiev, Jan. 11, 1875; d. Moscow, June 23, 1956. He studied violin with Hrimaly at the Moscow Cons., where he also took courses with Arensky, Taneyev, and Ippolitov-Ivanov (1894–1900), graduating with a gold medal. In 1905 he went to Berlin, where he remained for 2 years; returning to Russia, he became active as a teacher; was appointed prof. of composition at the Kiev Cons., and was its director in 1914–20; then was appointed to the faculty of the Moscow Cons., a post he retained until 1941. He traveled extensively in European and Asiatic Russia, collecting folk melodies; conducted many concerts of his own works; he made his last tour a month before his death, conducting in Odessa, Kishinev, and other cities. He was an extremely prolific composer, and was particularly distinguished in symph. works, in which he revealed himself as a successor of the Russian national school. He never transgressed the natural borderline of traditional harmony, but he was able to achieve effective results. His most impressive work is his 3rd Symph., surnamed *Ilya Muromets,* an epic description of the exploits of a legendary Russian hero. In his numerous songs Glière showed a fine lyrical talent. He wrote relatively few works of chamber music, most of them early in his career. In his opera *Shah-Senem,* he made use of native Caucasian songs. Glière was the teacher of 2 generations of Russian composers; among his students were Prokofiev and Miaskovsky. He received 2 Stalin prizes, for the String Quartet No. 4 (1948) and for the ballet *The Bronze Knight* (1950).

WORKS: OPERAS: *Shah-Senem* (Baku, May 4, 1934); *Leily and Medzhnun* (Tashkent, July 18, 1940); *Rachel,* one-act opera after Maupassant's *Mademoiselle Fifi* (Moscow, April 19, 1947); *Ghulsara* (Tashkent, Dec. 25, 1949). BALLETS: *Chrysis* (Moscow, Nov. 30, 1912); *Cleopatra* (Moscow, Jan. 11, 1926); *Red Poppy* (Moscow, June 14, 1927); *Comedians* (Moscow, April 5, 1931); *The Bronze Knight* (Leningrad, March 14, 1949). INCIDENTAL MUSIC: *King Oedipus* of Sophocles (1921); *Lysistrata* of

Aristophanes (1923); *Marriage of Figaro* of Beaumarchais (1927). FOR ORCH.: Symph. No. 1 (Moscow, Jan. 3, 1903); Symph. No. 2 (Berlin, Jan. 23, 1908, Koussevitzky conducting); *The Sirens*, symph. poem (Moscow, Jan. 30, 1909); Symph. No. 3, *Ilya Muromets* (Moscow, March 23, 1912); *2 Poems* for Soprano and Orch. (1924); *Cossacks of Zaporozh*, symph. poem (1921; Odessa, Dec. 23, 1925); *Trizna*, symph. poem (1915); *For the Festival of the Comintern*, fantasy for Wind Orch. (1924); *March of the Red Army* for Wind Orch. (1924); *Imitation of Jezekiel*, symph. poem for Narrator and Orch. (1919); Concerto for Harp and Orch. (Moscow, Nov. 23, 1938); *Friendship of Nations*, overture (1941); Concerto for Coloratura Soprano and Orch. (Moscow, May 12, 1943); *For the Happiness of the Fatherland*, overture (1942); *25 Years of the Red Army*, overture (1943); *Victory*, overture (Moscow, Oct. 30, 1945); Cello Concerto (Moscow, Feb. 18, 1947); Horn Concerto (Moscow, Jan. 26, 1952, composer conducting); an unfinished Violin Concerto. CHAMBER MUSIC: 5 string quartets (No. 4 won the Stalin Prize, 1948; No. 5 left unfinished at his death); 3 string sextets; String Octet. OTHER MUSIC: 20 pieces for Violin and Piano; 12 duos for 2 Violins; Ballad for Cello and Piano; 4 pieces for Double Bass and Piano; 8 pieces for Violin and Cello; 12 pieces for Cello and Piano; 10 duos for 2 Cellos; miscellaneous pieces for different instruments. He also wrote about 200 songs and 200 piano pieces.

Glinka, Mikhail, great Russian composer, often called "the father of Russina music" for his pioneering cultivation of Russian folk modalities; b. Novospasskoye, Smolensk district, June 1, 1804; d. Berlin, Feb. 15, 1857. A scion of a fairly rich family of landowners, he was educated at an exclusive school in St. Petersburg (1818–22); he also took private lessons in music; his piano teacher was a resident German musician, Carl Meyer; he also studied violin; when the famous pianist John Field was in St. Petersburg, Glinka had an opportunity to study with him, but he had only 3 lessons before Field departed. He began to compose even before acquiring adequate training in theory. As a boy he traveled in the Caucasus; then stayed for a while at his father's estate; at 20 entered the Ministry of Communications in St. Petersburg; he remained in government employ until 1828; at the same time, he constantly improved his general education by reading; he had friends among the best Russian writers of the time, including the poets Zhukovsky and Pushkin. He also took singing lessons with an Italian teacher, Belloli. In 1830 he went to Italy, where he continued irregular studies in Milan (where he spent most of his Italian years); he also visited Naples, Rome, and Bologna. He met Donizetti and Bellini. He became enamored of Italian music, and his early vocal and instrumental compositions are thoroughly Italian in melodic and harmonic structure. In 1833 he went to Berlin, where he took a course in counterpoint and general composition with the famous German theorist Dehn; thus he was nearly 30 when he completed his theoretical

education. In 1834 his father died, and Glinka went back to Russia to take care of the family affairs. In 1835 he was married; but the marriage was unhappy, and he soon became separated from his wife, finally divorcing her in 1846. The return to his native land led him to consider the composition of a truly national opera on a subject (suggested to him by Zhukovsky) depicting a historical episode in Russian history, the saving of the first tsar of the Romanov dynasty by a simple peasant, Ivan Susanin. (The Italian composer Cavos wrote an opera on the same subject 20 years previously, and conducted it in St. Petersburg.) Glinka's opera was produced in St. Petersburg on Dec. 9, 1836, under the title *A Life for the Tsar*. The event was hailed by the literary and artistic circles of Russia as a milestone of Russian culture, and indeed the entire development of Russian national music received its decisive creative impulse from Glinka's patriotic opera. It remained in the repertoire of Russian theaters until the Russian Revolution made it unacceptable, but it was revived, under the original title, *Ivan Susanin*, on Feb. 27, 1939, in Moscow, without alterations in the music, but with the references to the tsar eliminated from the libretto, the idea of saving the country being substituted for that of saving the tsar. Glinka's next opera, *Ruslan and Ludmila*, after Pushkin's fairy tale, was produced on Dec. 9, 1842; this opera, too, became extremely popular in Russia. Glinka introduced into the score many elements of oriental music; one episode contains the earliest use of the whole-tone scale in an opera. Both operas retain the traditional Italian form, with arias, choruses, and orch. episodes clearly separated. In 1844 Glinka was in Paris, where he met Berlioz; he also traveled in Spain, where he collected folk songs; the fruits of his Spanish tour were 2 orch. works, *Jota Aragonesa* and *Night in Madrid*. On his way back to Russia, he stayed in Warsaw for 3 years; the remaining years of his life he spent in St. Petersburg, Paris, and Berlin, where he died.

WORKS: FOR THE STAGE: Operas: *A Life for the Tsar; Ruslan and Ludmila;* sketches for 3 unfinished operas; *Chao-Kang*, ballet (1828–31); incidental music for Kukolnik's tragedy *Prince Kholmsky;* incidental music for the play *The Moldavian Gypsy*. FOR ORCH.: *Andante Cantabile and Rondo; Larghetto;* 2 overtures; Symph. in B-flat; *Trumpet March* (1828); *Overture-Symphony on Russian Themes* (1834; completed in 1938 by V.I. Shebalin); *Valse* (1839); *Polonaise* (1839); *Valse-Fantaisie* (1839); *Capriccio brillante* on the *Jota Aragonesa* (1845; afterward renamed *Spanish Overture No. 1*); *Summer Night in Madrid: Spanish Overture No. 2* (1848); *Kamarinskaya* (1848); symph. poem on Gogol's *Taras Bulba* (unfinished, part of first movement only; 1852); *Festival Polonaise* on a bolero melody (1855). CHAMBER MUSIC: Septet in E-flat (1824); 2 string quartets (1824, 1830); *Trio pathétique* (1827); 2 serenades (1832); Sonata for Piano and Viola (1825–28); about 40 piano numbers (5 valses, 7 mazurkas, nocturnes, etc.); much vocal music, including choral works, quartets, duets, arias, and about 85 songs with piano accompaniment, many set to poems by Pushkin and Zhukovsky.

Globokar, Vinko, French composer of Slovenian descent; b. Anderny, July 7, 1934. He studied trombone in Ljubljana (1949–54) and at the Paris Cons. (1955–59); took composition lessons in Paris with René Leibowitz (1959–63) and with Luciano Berio (1965). He was a trombonist and composer at the Center for Creative Arts at the State Univ. of N.Y. at Buffalo in 1965–66. In 1966 he was appointed trombone instructor at the Cologne Hochschule für Musik. As a composer, he follows the most modern ideas of serial music in aleatory distribution. His works include *Plan* for a Persian Drum and 4 Instruments (1965); *Fluide* for 9 Brasses and 3 Percussion Instruments (1967); *Traumdeutung,* a "psychodrama" (Amsterdam, Sept. 7, 1968); *Etude pour folklore I* for 19 Soloists (1968); *Etude pour folklore II* for Orch. (1968); Concerto Grosso (Cologne, Nov. 6, 1970); *Airs de voyages vers l'interieur* for Ensemble (Stuttgart, Nov. 3, 1972).

Glock, Sir William, English music critic and broadcasting administrator; b. London, May 3, 1908. He studied at Gonville and Caius College, Cambridge; then took piano lessons with Artur Schnabel in Berlin. He made some appearances as a concert pianist, but devoted most of his time and effort to music criticism. In 1934 he joined the staff of the *Observer;* served as its chief music critic from 1939 to 1945. In 1949 he founded *The Score* magazine, and edited it until 1961. In 1948 he established the Summer School of Music at Bryanston, Dorset, which relocated to Dartington Hall, Devon, in 1953; he continued as its music director until 1979. In 1959 he assumed the important post of controller of music of the BBC, retaining it until 1973. In 1964 he was made a Commander of the Order of the British Empire; was knighted in 1970.

Glover, William Howard, English conductor and composer; b. London, June 6, 1819; d. New York, Oct. 28, 1875. He played the violin in the Lyceum Theater orch. in London; conducted opera in Manchester, Liverpool, and London. In 1868 he came to N.Y., where he was conductor at Niblo's Garden until his death.
WORKS: Opera, *Ruy Blas* (London, Oct. 21, 1861); operettas: *Aminta* (London, Jan. 26, 1852); *Once Too Often* (London, Jan. 20, 1862); *Palomita, or The Veiled Songstress* (publ. in N.Y., 1875); cantata, *Tam o' Shanter* (London, July 4, 1855, Berlioz conducting); overtures; piano music; songs.

Gluck, Alma (real name, **Reba Fiersohn**), American soprano; b. Bucharest, Rumania, May 11, 1884; d. New York, Oct. 27, 1938. She was brought to America as a small child and was educated at public schools in N.Y. Her early marriage to Bernard Gluck in 1902 ended in divorce, but they had a talented daughter, Abigail, born in 1903, who became a successful author; in her novel *Of Lena Geyer* (1936) and in her autobiography, *Too Strong for Fantasy* (1967), publ. under her assumed name, Marcia Davenport, she gives many revealing glimpses of her mother's career. From 1906–9 Alma Gluck studied voice with Arturo Buzzi-Peccia, who arranged for her to appear in the role of Sophie in Massenet's opera *Werther* on the stage of the New Theater in N.Y. on Nov. 16, 1909. Shortly afterward, on Nov. 28, 1909, she sang at a Sunday concert at the Metropolitan Opera in N.Y. On Dec. 23, 1909, she appeared in a revival of *Orfeo ed Euridice* at the Metropolitan, with Toscanini conducting. Her success led to further engagements in such diversified roles as Marguerite in *Faust,* Venus in *Tannhäuser,* Gilda in *Rigoletto,* and Mimi in *La Bohème.* On Oct. 10, 1910, she gave a recital in N.Y. Her divorce became final in 1912, and she went to Europe to complete her vocal studies; she coached with Jean de Reszke in Paris and with Marcella Sembrich in Switzerland. Returning to the U.S., she resumed her career, appearing at Sunday concerts under the auspices of the Metropolitan Opera. She rapidly became a favorite with both opera and concert audiences; she also satisfied public demand by recording popular songs such as *Carry Me Back to Old Virginny,* a disc which reportedly sold 2 million copies. On June 15, 1914, she married in London the Russian violinist **Efrem Zimbalist;** their combined artistic genes produced a son, Efrem Zimbalist, Jr., who became a famous actor and whose daughter Stefanie, Alma Gluck's granddaughter, also swam into thespian popularity. Alma Gluck died at the age of 54 of cirrhosis of the liver.

Gluck, Christoph Willibald (Ritter von), renowned composer; b. Erasbach, near Weidenwang in the Upper Palatinate, July 2, 1714; d. Vienna, Nov. 15, 1787. His father was a forester at Erasbach until his appointment as forester to Prince Lobkowitz of Eisenberg about 1729. Gluck received his elementary instruction in the village schools at Kamnitz and Albersdorf near Komotau, where he also was taught singing and instrumental playing. Some biographers refer to his study at the Jesuit college at Komotau, but there is no documentary evidence to support this contention. In 1732 Gluck went to Prague to complete his education, but it is doubtful that he took any courses at Prague Univ. He earned his living in Prague by playing violin and cello at rural dances in the area; also sang at various churches; there he had an opportunity to meet Bohuslav Černohorsky, who was chapelmaster at St. James' Church from 1735; it is probable that Gluck learned the methods of church music from him. He went to Vienna in 1736, and was chamber musician to young Prince Lobkowitz, son of the patron of Gluck's father. In 1737 he was taken to Milan by Prince Melzi; this Italian sojourn was of the greatest importance to Gluck's musical development. There he became a student of G.B. Sammartini and acquired a solid technique of composition in the Italian style. After 4 years of study, Gluck brought out his first opera, *Artaserse,* to the text of the celebrated Metastasio; it was produced in Milan (Dec. 26, 1741) with such success that Gluck was immediately commissioned to write more operas. There followed *Demetrio* or *Cleonice* (Venice, May 2, 1742); *Demofoonte* (Milan, Jan. 6, 1743); *Il Tigrane* (Crema, Sept. 9, 1743); *La Sofonisba* or *Siface* (Milan, Jan. 13, 1744); *Ipermestra* (Venice, Nov. 21, 1744); *Poro* (Turin, Dec. 26, 1744); *Ippolito* or *Fedra* (Milan, Jan. 31, 1745). He also contributed separate numbers to several other operas produced in Italy. In 1745 Gluck received an invitation to go to London; on his way, he visited Paris and met Rameau. He was commissioned by the Italian Opera of London to write 2 operas for the Haymarket Theatre, as a competitive endeavor to Handel's enterprise. The first of these works was *La Caduta dei giganti*, a tribute to the Duke of Cumberland on the defeat of the Pretender; it was produced on Jan. 28, 1746; the 2nd was a pasticcio, *Artamene*, in which Gluck used material from his previous operas; it was produced March 15, 1746. Ten days later, Gluck appeared with Handel at a public concert, despite the current report in London society that Handel had declared that Gluck knew no more counterpoint than his cook (it should be added that a professional musician, Gustavus Waltz, was Handel's cook and valet at the time). On April 23, 1746, Gluck gave a demonstration in London, playing on the "glass harmonica." He left London late in 1746 when he received an engagement as conductor with Pietro Mingotti's traveling Italian opera company. He conducted in Hamburg, Leipzig, and Dresden; on June 29, 1747, he produced a "serenata," *Le nozze d'Ercole e d'Ebe,* to celebrate a royal wedding; it was performed at the Saxon court, in Pillnitz. Gluck then went to Vienna, where he staged his opera *Semiramide riconosciuta,* after a poem of Metastasio (May 14, 1748). He then traveled to Copenhagen, where he produced a festive opera, *La Contesa dei Numi* (March 9, 1749), on the occasion of the birth of Prince Christian; his next productions (all to Metastasio's words) were *Ezio* (Prague, 1750); *Issipile* (Prague, 1752); *La clemenza di Tito* (Naples, Nov. 4, 1752); *Le Cinesi* (Vienna, Sept. 24, 1754); *La danza* (Vienna, May 5, 1755); *L'innocenza giustificata* (Vienna, Dec. 8, 1755); *Antigono* (Rome, Feb. 9, 1756); *Il Re pastore* (Vienna, Dec. 8, 1756).

In 1750 Gluck married Marianna Pergin, daughter of a Viennese merchant; for several years afterward he conducted operatic performances in Vienna. As French influence increased there, Gluck wrote several entertainments to French texts, containing spoken dialogue, in the style of opéra comique; of these, the most successful were *Le Cadi dupé* (Dec. 1761) and *La Rencontre imprévue* (Jan. 7, 1764; perf. also under the title *Les Pèlerins de la Mecque,* his most popular production in this genre). His greatest work of the Vienna period was *Orfeo ed Euridice,* to a libretto by Calzabigi (in a version for male contralto; Oct. 5, 1762, with the part of Orfeo sung by the famous castrato Gaetano Guadagni). Gluck revised it for a Paris performance, produced in French on Aug. 2, 1774, with Orfeo sung by a tenor. There followed another masterpiece, *Alceste* (Vienna, Dec. 16, 1767), also to Calzabigi's text. In the preface to *Alceste,* Gluck formulated his esthetic credo, which elevated the dramatic meaning of

musical stage plays above a mere striving for vocal effects: "I sought to reduce music to its true function, that of seconding poetry in order to strengthen the emotional expression and the impact of the dramatic situations without interrupting the action and without weakening it by superfluous ornaments." Among other productions of the Viennese period were *Il trionfo di Clelia* (Vienna, May 14, 1763); *Il Parnaso confuso* (Schönbrunn Palace, Jan. 24, 1765); *Il Telemacco* (Vienna, Jan. 30, 1765); and *Paride ed Elena* (Vienna, Nov. 30, 1770).

The success of his French operas in Vienna led Gluck to the decision to try his fortunes in Paris, yielding to the persuasion of François du Roullet, an attaché at the French embassy in Vienna, who also supplied Gluck with his first libretto for a serious French opera, an adaptation of Racine's *Iphigénie en Aulide* (Paris, April 19, 1774). Gluck set out for Paris early in 1773, preceded by declarations in the Paris press by du Roullet and Gluck himself, explaining in detail Gluck's ideas of dramatic music. These statements set off an intellectual battle in the Paris press and among musicians in general between the adherents of traditional Italian opera and Gluck's novel French opera. It reached an unprecedented degree of acrimony when the Italian composer Nicola Piccinni was engaged by the French court to write operas to French texts, in open competition with Gluck; intrigues multiplied, even though Marie Antoinette never wavered in her admiration for Gluck, who taught her singing and harpsichord playing. However, Gluck and Piccinni themselves never participated in the bitter polemics unleashed by their literary and musical partisans. The sensational successes of the French version of Gluck's *Orfeo* and of *Alceste* were followed by the production of *Armide* (Sept. 23, 1777), which aroused great admiration. Then followed Gluck's masterpiece, *Iphigénie en Tauride* (May 17, 1779), which established Gluck's superiority to Piccinni, who was commissioned to write an opera on the same subject but failed to complete it in time. Gluck's last opera, *Echo et Narcisse* (Paris, Sept. 24, 1779), did not measure up to the excellence of his previous operas. By that time, Gluck's health had failed; he had several attacks of apoplexy, which resulted in a partial paralysis. In the autumn of 1779 he returned to Vienna, where he lived as an invalid for several more years. His last work was a *De profundis* for Chorus and Orch., written 5 years before his death.

Besides his operas, he wrote several ballets, of which *Don Juan* (Vienna, Oct. 17, 1761) was the most successful; he further wrote a cycle of 7 songs to words by Klopstock, 7 trio sonatas, several overtures, etc. Breitkopf & Härtel publ. excellent editions of Gluck's most important operas; other operas are included in Denkmäler der Tonkunst in Bayern, vol. 26 (14.ii), and Denkmäler der Tonkunst in Österreich, vols. 44a, 60, and 82 (21.ii, 30.ii, and 44); H. Gál edited a Sinfonia in G, identical with the overture to *Ipermestra;* the trio sonatas are found in Riemann's *Collegium musicum;* songs in Delsarte's *Archives du chant.* Wagner, while in Dresden (1842–49), made a complete revision of the score of

Iphigénie en Aulide; this arrangement was so extensively used that a Wagnerized version of Gluck's music became the chief text for performances during the 19th century. A complete edition of Gluck's works was begun by the Bärenreiter Verlag in 1951.

Gnecchi, Vittorio, Italian opera composer; b. Milan, July 17, 1876; d. there, Feb. 1, 1954. He studied at the Milan Cons. His opera *Cassandra* was performed at Bologna on Dec. 5, 1905; some years later, after the premiere of Richard Strauss's *Elektra,* there was considerable discussion when the Italian critic Giovanni Tebaldini pointed out the identity of some 50 themes in both *Cassandra* and *Elektra* ("Telepatia Musicale," *Rivista Musicale Italiana,* Feb.–March 1909). Gnecchi also wrote the operas *Virtù d'amore* (1896) and *La rosiera,* after a comedy by Alfred de Musset (given at Gera, Germany, Feb. 12, 1927; in Italian, at Trieste, Jan. 24, 1931).

Gnessin, Mikhail, Russian composer; b. Rostov-on-the-Don, Feb. 2, 1883; d. Moscow, May 5, 1957. He studied at the St. Petersburg Cons. with Rimsky-Korsakov and Liadov in 1901–8; went to Germany in 1911; in 1914 returned to Rostov, where he composed, taught music, and interested himself in various socialist activities. He made a trip to Palestine in 1921 to study Jewish music; some of his subsequent work reflected this visit. After 1923, he composed and taught alternately in Moscow and Leningrad. In addition to his Jewish music, he composed a number of works in the Romantic vein.
WORKS: DRAMATIC MUSIC: *Balagan,* by Blok (1909); *The Rose and the Cross,* by Blok (1914); *Antigone,* by Sophocles (1909–15); *The Phoenician Women,* by Euripides (1912–16); *Oedipus Rex,* by Sophocles (1914–15); *The Story of the Red-Haired Motele,* by Utkin (1926–29); *The Inspector-General,* by Gogol (1926). OPERAS: *Abraham's Youth* (1921–23) and *The Maccabees.* FOR VOICE AND ORCH.: *Ruth* (1909); *Vrubel* (1912); *The Conqueror Worm* (1913); symph. movement for Solo Voices, Chorus, and Orch.: *1905–1917* (1925). FOR ORCH.: Symph. fragment, *After Shelley* (1906–8); *Songs of Adonis* (1919); symph. fantasy, *Songs of the Old Country* (1919); suite, *Jewish Orchestra at the Town Bailiff's Ball* (1926). CHAMBER MUSIC: Requiem, in memory of Rimsky-Korsakov, for String Quartet and Piano (1913–14); *Variations on a Jewish Theme* for String Quartet (1916); *Azerbaijan Folksongs* for String Quartet (1930); *Adygeya* for Violin, Viola, Cello, Clarinet, Horn, and Piano (1933); *Sonata-Fantasia* for Piano, Violin, Viola, and Cello (1945), *Theme with Variations* for Cello and Piano (1955); several song cycles; piano pieces; arrangements of Jewish folk songs. He publ. *Reflections and Reminiscences of Rimsky-Korsakov* (Moscow, 1956).

Gobbi, Tito, famous Italian baritone; b. Bassano del Grappa, near Venice, Oct. 24, 1913; d. Rome, March 5, 1984. Although he suffered from asthma as a child, he engaged in sports and developed into a fine athlete, an alpinist, and a cyclist. He studied law at the Univ. of Padua; then took singing lessons with Giugio Crimi in Rome. He made his operatic debut as Rodolfo in *La Sonnambula* in Gubbio, near Perugia, in 1935. In 1936 he won first prize in a singing contest in Vienna; in 1937 he sang at the Teatro Adriano in Rome; in 1939 he appeared at the Teatro Costanzi in Rome in the role of Germont *père* in *La Traviata.* In 1942 he sang for the first time at La Scala in Milan as Belcore in *L'elisir d'amore.* In 1948 he made his American debut at the San Francisco Opera; in 1954 he joined the Chicago Opera. On Jan. 13, 1956, he appeared at the Metropolitan Opera in N.Y. in the role that made him famous, the infamous Scarpia in *Tosca.* In subsequent years he toured the whole operatic world, including Covent Garden in London, the Paris Opéra, the Vienna State Opera, the Munich State Opera, Barcelona, Lisbon, the Teatro Colón in Buenos Aires, and Rio de Janeiro; he was also a frequent guest artist at the Maggio Musicale Festival in Florence and at the Salzburg Festival. He gave solo recitals in Scandinavia, Egypt, and Israel. His opera repertoire included about 100 roles; the most notable were Rigoletto, Iago, Falstaff, and Macbeth in Verdi's operas, and the title role in Mozart's *Don Giovanni.* In non-Italian presentations, he gave a congenial rendition of the musically challenging part of Wozzeck in Alban Berg's opera. He retired from the stage in 1979, and devoted himself to his favorite avocation, oil painting. He publ. an entertaining memoir, *Tito Gobbi: My Life* (London, 1979).

Godard, Benjamin (Louis Paul), French composer; b. Paris, Aug. 18, 1849; d. Cannes, Jan. 10, 1895. He studied violin with Richard Hammer and later with Vieuxtemps; composition with Reber of the Paris Cons. He publ. his first work, a Violin Sonata, at the age of 16 and wrote several other chamber music pieces, obtaining the Prix Chartier. In 1878 he received a municipal prize for an orch. work; in the same year he produced his first opera, *Les Bijoux de Jeannette.* His 2nd opera was *Pedro de Zalamea* (Antwerp, Jan. 31, 1884), but it left little impact; then came his masterpiece, *Jocelyn,* after Lamartine's poem (Brussels, Feb. 25, 1888). The famous *Berceuse* from this opera became a perennial favorite, exhibiting Godard's lyric talent at its best. There followed the opera *Dante et Béatrice,* produced at the Opéra-Comique in Paris on May 13, 1890. His opera *La Vivandière* was left unfinished at his death, and the orchestration was completed by Paul Vidal; it was staged posthumously in Paris on April 1, 1895; another posthumous opera, *Les Guelphes,* was produced in Rouen (Jan. 17, 1902). Godard wrote 3 programmatic symphs: *Symphonie gothique* (1883), *Symphonie orientale* (1884), and *Symphonie légendaire* (1886); and a *Concerto Romantique* for Violin and Orch. (1876); he also wrote 3 string quartets, 4 violin sonatas, a Cello Sonata, and 2 piano trios; piano pieces; and more than 100 songs. A 2-vol. collection of Godard's piano works was publ. by G. Schirmer (N.Y., 1895); another collection of piano pieces was edited by Paolo Gallico (N.Y., 1909).

Godfrey, George. See **Müller, Georg Gottfried.**

Godimel, Claude. See **Goudimel, Claude.**

Godowsky, Leopold, famous pianist; b. Soshly, near Vilna, Feb. 13, 1870; d. New York, Nov. 21, 1938. He played in public as a child in Russia; at 14, was sent to Berlin to study at the Hochschule für Musik, but after a few months there, proceeded to N.Y.; gave his first American concert in Boston on Dec. 7, 1884; in 1885, played engagements at the N.Y. Casino; in 1886, toured Canada with the Belgian violinist Ovide Musin. He then went back to Europe; played in society salons in London and Paris, and became a protégé of Saint-Saëns. In 1890 he joined the faculty of the N.Y. College of Music; on May 1, 1891, married Frieda Saxe, and became an American citizen. He taught at the Broad St. Cons. in Philadelphia (1894–95); was head of the piano dept. of the Chicago Cons. (1895–1900); then embarked on a European tour; gave a highly successful concert in Berlin (Dec. 6, 1900), and remained there as a teacher; in 1909–14, conducted a master class at the Vienna Academy of Music; made tours in the U.S. in 1912–14, and settled permanently in the U.S. at the outbreak of World War I. After the war, he traveled in Europe, South America, and Asia as a concert pianist; his career ended in 1930, when he suffered a stroke. Godowsky was one of the outstanding masters of the piano; possessing a scientifically inclined mind, he developed a method of "weight and relaxation"; applying it to his own playing, he became an outstanding technician of his instrument, extending the potentialities of piano technique to the utmost, with particular attention to the left hand. He wrote numerous piano compositions of transcendental difficulty, yet entirely pianistic in style; also arranged works by Weber, Brahms, and Johann Strauss. Particularly remarkable are his 53 studies on Chopin's études, combining Chopin's themes in ingenious counterpoint; among his original works, the most interesting are *Triakontameron* (30 pieces; 1920; no. 11 is the well-known *Alt Wien*) and *Java Suite* (12 pieces). He also wrote simple pedagogical pieces, e.g., a set of 46 *Miniatures* for Piano, 4-hands, in which the pupil is given a part within the compass of 5 notes only (1918); edited piano studies by Czerny, Heller, Köhler, etc.; composed music for the left hand alone (*6 Waltz Poems, Prelude and Fugue,* etc.), and publ. an essay, "Piano Music for the Left Hand," *Musical Quarterly* (July 1935). Maurice Aronson publ. a musical examination paper, providing an analysis of Godowsky's *Miniatures* (N.Y., 1935).

Goehr, Alexander, English composer, son of **Walter Goehr;** b. Berlin, Aug. 10, 1932. He studied at the Royal Manchester College of Music (1952–53); then took courses with Messiaen at the Paris Cons. (1955–57). From 1960–67 he was in charge of the production of orch. concerts for the BBC. In 1968–69 he was composer-in-residence at the New England Cons. in Boston; in 1969–70 taught at Yale Univ. Returning to England, he joined the faculty of Leeds Univ. (1971–76); from 1975 served as artistic director of the Leeds Festivals. In 1976 he was appointed prof. of music at the Univ. of Cambridge. His compositions are marked with a severe, at times austere, polyphony, tending toward integral serialism. WORKS: Piano Sonata (1952); *Fantasias* for Clarinet and Piano (1955); *Fantasia* for Orch. (1955); *Narration,* to words of Blake, for Voice and Piano (1955); String Quartet (1958); *The Deluge,* cantata (1958); *Four Seasons from the Japanese* for Soprano and Orch. (1959); *Sutter's Gold,* cantata (1960); *Hecuba's Lament* for Orch. (1960); Suite for Flute, Clarinet, Horn, Violin, Viola, Cello, and Harp (1961); Violin Concerto (1962); *Little Symphony* (1963); *Pastorals* for Orch. (1965); Piano Trio (1966); *Arden muss sterben,* opera (Hamburg, March 5, 1967); String Quartet No. 2 (1967); *Romanza* for Cello and Orch. (1968); *Konzertstück* for Piano and Orch. (1969); *Nonomiya* for Piano (1969); *Symph.* (London, May 9, 1970); *Triptych,* theater piece for Actors, Singers, and Instruments, consisting of *Naboth's Vineyard* (1968), *Shadowplay,* after Plato's *Republic* (1970), and *Sonata about Jerusalem* (1970); Concerto for 11 Instruments (Brussels, Jan. 25, 1971); Piano Concerto (Brighton Festival, May 14, 1972; Daniel Barenboim, soloist); *Chaconne* for Wind Instruments (Leeds, Nov. 3, 1974); *Lyric Pieces* for Chamber Ensemble (London, Nov. 15, 1974); *Metamorphosis/Dance* for Orch. (London, Nov. 17, 1974); String Quartet No. 3 (London, June 28, 1976); *Psalm 4* for Female Soloists, Chorus, Viola, and Organ (London, July 8, 1976, composer conducting); *Fugue on the Fourth Psalm* for Strings (1976); *Babylon the Great Is Fallen* for Chorus and Orch. (1979); *Das Gesetz der Quadrille* for Baritone and Piano, to texts by Kafka (1979); *Sinfonia* for Orch. (1980); *2 études* for Orch. (1981); *Behold the Sun,* concert aria for Soprano, Vibraphone, and Chamber Ensemble (1981; London, Feb. 9, 1982).

Goehr, Walter, German conductor; b. Berlin, May 28, 1903; d. Sheffield, England, Dec. 4, 1960. He studied theory with Schoenberg in Berlin; then became conductor of Berlin Radio (1925–31). In 1933 he went to England; from 1945 to 1948, was conductor of the BBC Theatre Orch.; was conductor of the Morley College concerts from 1943 until his death.

Goethe, Johann Wolfgang von, illustrious German poet and dramatist; b. Frankfurt am Main, Aug. 28, 1749; d. Weimar, March 22, 1832. Although he could not comprehend Beethoven, and even snubbed him, he had ideas of his own on music (see *Briefwechsel zwischen Goethe und Zelter,* Berlin, 1833; Ferdinand Hiller also shows this in his *Goethes musicalisches Leben* (Cologne, 1883). In recent years Goethe's attitude toward music has been made the subject of investigation by several scholars.

Goetschius, Percy, renowned American music teacher and pedagogue; b. Paterson, N.J., Aug. 30, 1853; d. Manchester, N.H., Oct. 29, 1943. He studied at the Stuttgart Cons., and taught various classes there; also wrote music criticism. He returned to the U.S. in 1890; was on the faculty of Syracuse Univ. (1890–92) and at the New England Cons. of Music in Boston (1892–96). In 1905 he was appointed head of the dept. of music at the N.Y. Inst. of Musical Art; retired in 1925. Goetschius was a product of the fossilized Germanic tradition; convinced that the laws of harmony as set by old German pedagogues were unalterable and inviolate, he stood in horror before any vestige of unresolved dissonances.

Goetz, Hermann, German composer; b. Königsberg, Prussia, Dec. 7, 1840; d. Hottingen, near Zürich, Dec. 3, 1876. He studied at the Stern Cons. in Berlin in 1860–63, with von Bülow in piano and with H. Ulrich in composition. In 1863, he took the post of organist at Winterthur, Switzerland; then lived in Zürich; gave private lessons; conducted a singing society. His most famous work is the opera *The Taming of the Shrew (Der Widerspenstigen Zähmung),* based on Shakespeare's play, which was given in Mannheim, Oct. 11, 1874; it was then given in Vienna, Berlin, Leipzig, and other German cities, and produced in an Eng. version in London (Drury Lane Theatre, Oct. 12, 1878). His other works include the opera *Francesca da Rimini* (Mannheim, Sept. 30, 1877; unfinished; 3rd act completed by Ernst Frank); incidental music for Widmann's play *Die heiligen drei Könige* (Winterthur, Jan. 6, 1866); Symph. in F; Piano Concerto (Basel, Dec. 1, 1867); String Quartet (1865); chamber music; several pieces for piano; 24 songs.

Goeyvaerts, Karel, significant Belgian composer; b. Antwerp, June 8, 1923. He studied at the Antwerp Cons. (1943–47), and with Milhaud, Messiaen, and Maurice Martenot in Paris (1947–50); received the Lili Boulanger Award in 1949. He taught music history at the Antwerp Cons. (1950–57); in 1970 he organized the Ghent Inst. of Psycho-Acoustics and Electronic Music (IPEM). Goeyvaerts is one of the pioneers of serialism, spatial music, and electronic techniques. His works bear pointedly abstract titles with structural connotations; he also applies aleatory devices in audio-visual collages.
WORKS: *3 lieder per sonare a venti-sei* for 6 Solo Instruments (1948–49); Sonata for 2 Pianos, op. 1 (1950–51); *Opus 2* for 13 Instruments (1951); *Opus 3 aux sons frappés et frottés (with Striking and Rubbing Sounds)* for 7 Instruments (1952); *Opus 4 aux sons morts (with Dead Sounds)* for Tape (1952); *Opus 5 aux sons purs (with Pure Sounds)* for Tape (1953); *Opus 6* for 180 Sound Objects (1954); *Opus 7 aux niveaux convergents et divergents (with Converging and Diverging Levels)* for Tape (1955); *Diaphonie,* suite for Orch. (1957); *Improperia,* cantata for Good Friday, for Alto, Double Chorus, and 6 Instruments (1958); *Piece for 3* for Flute, Violin, and Piano (1960); *Jeux d'été* for 3 Orch. Groups (1961); *La Passion* for Orch. (1962); *Cataclysme,* ballet for Orch. and ad libitum Narration (1963); *Piece* for Piano, with Tape (1964); *Goathermala* for Mezzo-soprano and Flute (1966); *Parcours* for 2 to 6 Violins (1967); *Mass in Memory of John XXIII* for Chorus and 10 Winds (1968); *Actief-Reactief* for 2 Oboes, 2 Trumpets, and Piano (1968); *Catch à quatre,* verbal composition for 4 Wandering Musicians (1969); *Al naar gelang* for 5 Instrumental Groups (1971); *Hé,* audio-visual production (1971; in collaboration with Herman Sabbe and Lucien Goethals); Piano Quartet, mobile composition for Violin, Viola, Cello, and Tape (1972); *Belise dans un jardin (Belise in the Garden)* for Chorus and 6 Instruments (1972); *Nachklänge aus dem Theater* for Tape (1972); *Op acht paarden wedden (To Bet on 8 Horses),* electronic mobile composition for 8 Sound Tracks (1973); *Landschap,* mobile composition for Harpsichord (1973); *You'll Never Be Alone Anymore* for Bass Clarinet and Electronics (1974); *Mon doux pilote s'endort aussi* for Choral Ensemble (1976).

Gogorza, Emilio Edoardo de, American baritone; b. Brooklyn, May 29, 1874; d. New York, May 10, 1949. After singing as a boy soprano in England, he returned to the U.S. and studied with C. Moderati and E. Agramonte in N.Y.; made his debut in 1897 with Marcella Sembrich in a concert; sang throughout the country in concerts and with leading orchs. Beginning in 1925, was for several years an instructor of voice at the Curtis Inst. of Music in Philadelphia. He married the American soprano **Emma Eames** in 1911.

Gold, Arthur, Canadian pianist; b. Toronto, Feb. 6, 1917. He studied with Josef and Rosina Lhévinne at the Juilliard School of Music; upon graduation, formed a piano duo with Robert Fizdale; together they gave numerous concerts in Europe and America, in programs of modern music, including works specially written for them by such celebrated composers as Samuel Barber, Darius Milhaud, Francis Poulenc, Georges Auric, and Virgil Thomson. Gold and Fizdale also pioneered performances of works by John Cage for prepared piano. With Fizdale he publ. a successful book, *Misia* (N.Y., 1979), on the life of Maria Godebska, a literary and musical figure in Paris early in the century.

Gold, Ernest, Austrian-American composer; b. Vienna, July 13, 1921. He studied piano and violin at home (his father was an amateur musician); in 1938 emigrated to the U.S.; studied harmony in N.Y. with Otto Cesana. He began writing songs in a popular vein; of these, *Practice Makes Perfect* became a hit. At the same time he composed in classical forms; to this category belong his *Pan American Symphony,* Piano Concerto, String Quartet, and Piano Sonata. In 1945 he went to Hollywood as an arranger; took lessons with George Antheil (1946–48); then was commissioned to write film scores; among them the following were very successful: *The Defiant Ones; On the Beach; Exodus* (Academy Award, 1960); *Judgment at Nuremberg* (1961); *It's a Mad, Mad, Mad, Mad World* (1963); *The Secret of Santa Vittoria* (1969). In 1950 he married the singer **Marni Nixon;** they were divorced in 1968; in 1975 he married the writer Jeannette Keller Light. In 1975 a star with his name was placed in the pavement of Hollywood's Walk of Fame; he was the first screen composer so honored.

Goldberg, Albert, American music critic; b. Shenandoah, Iowa, June 2, 1898. He studied at the Chicago Musical College (1920–22); taught there (1924–26); appeared as pianist and conductor; was music critic of the *Chicago Herald Examiner* (1925–36) and of the *Chicago Tribune* (1943–46). In 1947 he was appointed to the staff of the *Los Angeles Times,* and was still writing for it in 1978.

Goldberg, Johann Gottlieb, remarkable German organist and harpsichord player; b. Danzig (baptized, March 14), 1727; d. Dresden, April 13, 1756. As a child, he was brought to Dresden by his patron, Count Hermann Karl von Keyserlingk; he is reported to have studied with Wilhelm Friedemann Bach, and later with J.S. Bach (1742–43); in 1751 became musician to Count Heinrich Brühl, a post he held till his death. His name is immortalized through the set of 30 variations written for him by Bach, and generally known as the *Goldberg Variations*. Goldberg's own compositions include 2 concertos; 24 polonaises; a Sonata with Minuet and 12 variations for Clavier; 6 trios for Flute, Violin, and Bass; a Motet; a Cantata; and a Psalm.

Goldberg, Szymon, eminent Polish-born American violinist and conductor; b. Wloclawek, June 1, 1909. He played violin as a child in Warsaw; in 1917 he went to Berlin and took regular violin lessons with Carl Flesch. After a recital in Warsaw in 1921, he was engaged as concertmaster of the Dresden Phil. Orch. (1925–29); in 1929 he was appointed concertmaster of the Berlin Phil. Orch. but was forced to leave in 1934 despite Furtwängler's vigorous attempts to safeguard the Jewish members of the orch.; he then toured Europe. He made his American debut in N.Y. in 1938; while on a tour of Asia, he was interned in Java by the Japanese from 1942–45; eventually he came to the U.S.; became an American citizen in 1953. From 1951–65 he taught at the Aspen Music School; concurrently was active as a conductor. In 1955 he founded the Netherlands Chamber Orch. in Amsterdam, which he led with notable distinction for 22 years; he also took the ensemble on tours.

Goldenweiser, Alexander, Russian piano pedagogue; b. Kishinev, March 10, 1875; d. Moscow, Nov. 26, 1961. He studied piano with Pabst and composition with Arensky at the Moscow Cons.; in 1906 became a prof. of piano there, holding this post for 55 years, until his death. Two generations of Russian pianists were his pupils, among them Kabalevsky and Lazar Berman. As a pedagogue, he continued the traditions of the Russian school of piano playing, seeking the inner meaning of the music while achieving technical brilliance. He was a frequent visitor at Tolstoy's house near Moscow, and wrote reminiscences of Tolstoy (Moscow, 1922); publ. several essays on piano teaching; also com-

posed chamber music and piano pieces.

Goldman, Edwin Franko, eminent American bandmaster; b. Louisville, Ky., Jan. 1, 1878; d. New York, Feb. 21, 1956. He was the nephew of **Sam Franko** and **Nahan Franko,** well-known conductors; was brought to N.Y., where he studied composition with Dvořák, and cornet with J. Levy and C. Sohst. He became solo cornetist of the Metropolitan Opera orch. when he was 17, remaining there for 10 years. For the next 13 years he taught cornet and trumpet; he formed his first band in 1911. In 1918, the Goldman Band outdoor concerts were inaugurated. His band was noted not only for its skill and musicianship but for its unusual repertoire, including modern works especially commissioned for the band. Goldman was a founder and first president of the American Bandmasters' Assoc.; he received honorary D.Mus. degrees from Phillips Univ. and Boston Univ., and medals and other honors from governments and associations throughout the world. He wrote more than 100 brilliant marches, of which the best known is *On the Mall;* also other band music; solos for various wind instruments; studies and methods for cornet and other brass instruments; several songs. He was the author of *Foundation to Cornet or Trumpet Playing* (1914); *Band Betterment* (1934); *The Goldman Band System* (1936).

Goldman, Richard Franko (son of **Edwin Franko Goldman**), American bandmaster and composer; b. New York, Dec. 7, 1910; d. Baltimore, Jan. 19, 1980. He graduated from Columbia Univ. in 1931; later studied composition with Nadia Boulanger in Paris. He became an assistant of his father in conducting the Goldman Band in 1937; on his father's death in 1956, he succeeded him as conductor; continued to conduct the band into the summer of 1979, when ill health forced him to retire and allow the band to dissolve. He taught at the Juilliard School of Music (1947–60), was a visiting prof. at Princeton (1952–56), and in 1968 was appointed director of the Peabody Cons. of Music in Baltimore and served as its president (1969–77). He wrote many works for various ensembles: *A Sentimental Journey* for Band (1941); 3 duets for Clarinets (1944); Sonatina for 2 Clarinets (1945); Duo for Tubas (1948); Violin Sonata (1952), etc; many arrangements for band. A progressive musician, Goldman experimented with modern techniques, and his music combines highly advanced harmony with simple procedures accessible to amateurs.

Goldmark, Karl, eminent Austro-Hungarian composer; b. Keszthely, Hungary, May 18, 1830; d. Vienna, Jan. 2, 1915. The son of a poor cantor, he studied at the school of the Musical Society of Sopron (1842–44); the talent he showed there as a violinist resulted in his being sent to Vienna, where he studied with L. Jansa (1844–45); later studied at the Vienna Cons., as a pupil of Preyer (harmony) and Böhm (violin). He spent most of his life in Vienna, where the first concert of his compositions was given on March 20, 1857. Landmarks in his career were the first performance of his *Sakuntala* overture by the Vienna Phil. on Dec. 26, 1865, and the premiere of his first opera, *Die Königin von Saba,* at the Vienna Opera on March 10, 1875; both were very successful. WORKS: Operas (in addition to *Die Königin von Saba*): *Merlin* (Vienna, Nov. 19, 1886); *Das Heimchen am Herd,* based on Dickens's *The Cricket on the Hearth* (Vienna, March 21, 1896); *Die Kriegsgefangene* (Vienna, Jan. 17, 1899); *Götz von Berlichingen,* based on Goethe's play (Budapest, Dec. 16, 1902); *Ein Wintermärchen,* based on Shakespeare's *A Winter's Tale* (Vienna, Jan. 2, 1908). For Orch.: 7 overtures: *Sakuntala, Penthesilea, Im Frühling, Der gefesselte Prometheus, Sappho, In Italien, Aus Jugendtagen;* a symph. poem, *Ländliche Hochzeit (Rustic Wedding;* Vienna, March 5, 1876); 2 symphs.; symph. poem, *Zrinyi* (1903); Violin Concerto No. 1 (Nuremberg, Oct. 28, 1878); other instrumental concertos. Chamber music: 2 piano trios; Piano Quintet; Cello Sonata; Violin Sonata; piano pieces; songs; choral works. He publ. an autobiography, *Erinnerungen aus meinem Leben* (Vienna, 1922; in Eng. as *Notes from the Life of a Viennese Composer,* N.Y., 1927).

Goldmark, Rubin, American composer and teacher, nephew of **Karl Goldmark;** b. New York, Aug. 15, 1872; d. there, March 6, 1936. He studied at the Vienna Cons. with A. Door (piano) and J.N. Fuchs (composition); in 1891–93 he was a student at the National Cons. in N.Y. with Joseffy (piano) and Dvořák (composition). He went to Colorado Springs for his health in 1894; taught at the College Cons. there (1895–1901). Returning to N.Y. in 1902, for the next 20 years he gave private lessons in piano and theory. In 1924, he was appointed head of the composition dept. of the Juilliard School in N.Y., and remained there until his death; among his pupils were Aaron Copland, Abram Chasins, Frederick Jacobi, and other American composers. He was active in promoting such musical clubs as The Bohemians (of N.Y.), of which he was a founder and president (1907–10), the Beethoven Assoc., and the Society for the Publication of American Music. WORKS: Overture, *Hiawatha* (Boston, Jan. 13, 1900); tone poem, *Samson* (Boston, March 14, 1914); Requiem, suggested by Lincoln's Gettysburg Address (N.Y., Jan. 30, 1919); *A Negro Rhapsody* (his most popular work; N.Y., Jan. 18, 1923); Piano Quartet (Paderewski Prize, 1909; N.Y., Dec. 13, 1910); Piano Trio; *The Call of the Plains* for Violin and Piano (1915); songs.

Goldovsky, Boris, Russian-American pianist and conductor, son of the violinist **Lea Luboshutz;** b. Moscow, June 7, 1908. He studied piano with his uncle **Pierre Luboshutz;** later in Berlin with Schnabel and Kreutzer, and in Budapest with Dohnányi. He appeared as soloist with the Berlin Phil. at the age of 13 in 1921; came to America in 1930; was director of the Opera Workshop at the Berkshire Music Center, Tanglewood (1942–64); founded the New England Opera Co. in 1946. A versatile musician, he trans. opera librettos into singable English;

presented popular radio talks on music; acted as moderator for Metropolitan Opera broadcasts. A collection of his comments was publ. as *Accents on Opera* (N.Y., 1953); he also wrote *Bringing Opera to Life* (N.Y., 1968).

Goldschmidt, Berthold, German-born English composer and conductor; b. Hamburg, Jan. 18, 1903. He studied at the Univ. of Hamburg and at the Friedrich Wilhelm Univ. in Berlin; also at the Berlin State Academy of Music with Schreker. He was an assistant conductor at the Berlin State Opera (1926–27) and conductor at the Darmstadt Opera (1927–29); then was a conductor with the Berlin Radio and the Städtische Oper. In 1935 he went to England; became a British citizen in 1947. He made numerous guest appearances in England with various orchs.; also conducted opera. He composed 2 operas: *Der gewaltige Hahnrei* (Mannheim, Feb. 14, 1932) and *Beatrice Cenci* (1949–50); a ballet, *Chronica* (1938); Symphony (1944); Concertino for Violin (1933), Concertino for Cello (1933), Concertino for Harp (1949), and Concertino for Clarinet (1955), as well as miscellaneous works for piano.

Goldschmidt, Otto, German pianist; b. Hamburg, Aug. 21, 1829; d. London, Feb. 24, 1907. He was at first a pupil of Jakob Schmitt and F.W. Grund, then of Mendelssohn at the Leipzig Cons., and of Chopin at Paris (1848). In 1849 he played in London at a concert given by **Jenny Lind;** accompanied her on her American tour (1851) and married her at Boston, Feb. 5, 1852; from 1852 to 1855 they lived in Dresden; from 1858 until her death (1887), in London. He founded the Bach Choir in 1875, and conducted it till 1885. He composed an oratorio, *Ruth* (Hereford, 1867); a choral song, *Music,* for Soprano and Women's Chorus (Leeds, 1898); piano music, including a Concerto, piano studies, 2 duets for 2 Pianos; was co-editor of *The Chorale Book for England,* a collection of hymns (1863).

Goldsmith, Jerry, American composer for films; b. Los Angeles, Feb. 10, 1929. He studied music at the Univ. of Southern Calif.; became a staff composer with the 20th Century-Fox Film Corp.; wrote the scores for *The Sand Pebbles; Freud; Planet of the Apes; 7 Days in May* (1964); *A Patch of Blue* (1966); *Seconds* (1966); *Patton* (1970); *Papillon* (1973); *The Cassandra Crossing* (1976); *Islands in the Stream* (1977); *MacArthur* (1978); etc. He also wrote chamber music and vocal works.

Golestan, Stan, Rumanian composer; b. Vaslui, June 7, 1875; d. Paris, April 21, 1956. He studied composition and orchestration with Vincent d'Indy, Albert Roussel, and Paul Dukas at the Schola Cantorum in Paris (1897–1903). Subsequently he wrote music criticism in *Le Figaro.* WORKS: For Orch.: *La Dembovitza* (1902); *Lăutarul şi Cobzarul,* Rumanian dances (1902); Symph. (1910); *Rapsodie roumaine* (1912); *Rapsodie concertante* for Violin and Orch. (1920); *Concerto roumain* for Violin and Orch. (1933); *Concerto moldave* for Cello and Orch. (1936); Piano Concerto, subtitled *Sur les cîmes des Carpathes,* for Piano and Orch. (1935–38). Chamber music: Violin Sonata (1908); 2 string quartets, *Arioso* and *Concert Allegro* for Viola and Piano (1932); Flute Sonatina (1932). For Piano: *Poèmes et paysages* (1922) and *Thème, variations et dances;* vocal pieces.

Golitzin, Nicolai, Russian nobleman, a music amateur; b. St. Petersburg, Dec. 19, 1794; d. Tambov District, Nov. 3, 1866. He was a talented cello player, but his name is remembered mainly because of his connection with Beethoven, who dedicated to Golitzin the overture op. 124 and the string quartets opp. 127, 130, 132. Golitzin was also responsible for the first Russian performance of Beethoven's *Missa solemnis* (1825).

Göllerich, August, Austrian writer on music; b. Linz, July 2, 1859; d. there, March 16, 1923. He was a pupil of Liszt; studied composition with Bruckner; acquired Ramann's music school in Nuremberg in 1890, and established branches in Erlangen, Fürth, and Ansbach; from 1896, he was conductor of the Musikverein and director of the Cons. in Linz; his wife, **Gisela Pászthory-Voigt** (also a pupil of Liszt), supervised the other schools. He publ. *A. Reissmann als Schriftsteller und Komponist* (1884); *Beethoven* (1904); *Franz Liszt* (1908); guides to Liszt's *Graner Festmesse* and Wagner's *Ring des Nibelungen* (1897). His chief work, a biography of Bruckner (who himself selected Göllerich for this task), in 4 vols., was completed by Max Auer (first vol., Regensburg, 1924; 2nd, 1928; remaining vols., 1932 and 1937).

Golschmann, Vladimir, renowned French conductor; b. Paris, Dec. 16, 1893; d. New York, March 1, 1972. He studied violin and piano at the Schola Cantorum; as early as 1919 he organized the Concerts Golschmann in Paris, in programs featuring many first performances of modern works. In 1923 he conducted ballet in the U.S.; then was conductor of the Scottish Orch. in Glasgow (1928–30). In 1931 he was engaged as conductor of the St. Louis Symph. Orch., and held this post for more than a quarter of a century (1931–58); from 1964 to 1970 was conductor of the Denver Symph. Orch.; also appeared as guest conductor with other American orchs.

Golyscheff, Jefim (Jef), Russian composer and theorist; b. Kherson, Sept. 20, 1897; d. Paris, Sept. 25, 1970. He studied violin in Odessa and played in public as a child. In 1909, in the wake of anti-Jewish pogroms in Russia, he went to Berlin, where he studied chemistry as well as music theory; at the same time he began to paint in the manner of Abstract Expressionism. Golyscheff played a historic role in the development of the serial methods of composition; his String Trio, written about 1914 and publ. in 1925, contains passages described by him as "Zwölftondauer-Komplexen," in which 12 different tones are given 12 different durations in the main theme. As both a painter and a musician, he was close to the Dada circles in Berlin, and participated in futuristic experiments. On April 30, 1919, he presented at a Dada exhibition in Berlin his *Anti-Symphonie,* subtitled *Musikalische Kreisguillotine (Musical Circular Guillotine),* with characteristic titles of its movements: 1, *Provocational Injections;* 2, *Chaotic Oral Cavity, or Submarine Aircraft;* 3, *Clapping in Hyper F-sharp Major.* On May 24, 1919, he appeared at a Berlin Dada soirée with a piece of his composition entitled *Keuchmaneuver (Cough Maneuver).* All this activity ceased with the advent of the Nazis in 1933. As a Jew, Golyscheff had to flee Germany; he went to Paris, but after the fall of France in 1940 was interned by the Vichy authorities. His life was probably spared because of his expertise as a chemist; he was conscripted as a cement laborer. In 1956 he went to Brazil, where he devoted himself exclusively to painting, and had several successful exhibitions in São Paulo. In 1966 he returned to Paris, where he remained until his death.

Gombert, Nicolas, Flemish composer; b. southern Flanders, possibly between Lille and St. Omer, c.1490; d. c.1556. He was one of the most eminent pupils of Josquin des Prez, on whose death he composed a funeral dirge. The details of his early life are obscure and uncertain. The physician Jerome Cardan reported that Gombert violated a boy and was sentenced to the galleys on the high seas. He is first positively accounted for in 1526, when his name appears on the list of singers at the court chapel of Charles V that was issued at Granada in that year; the restless Emperor traveled continually throughout his extensive domain—Spain, Germany, and the Netherlands—and his retinue was obliged to follow him in his round of his courts at Vienna, Madrid, and Brussels; Gombert probably was taken into the service of the Emperor on one of the latter's visits to Brussels. He is first mentioned as "maistre des enffans de la chapelle de nostre sr empereur" ("master of the boys of the royal chapel") in a court document dated Jan. 1, 1529; he remained in the Emperor's employ until 1538–40, during which time he took an active part in the various functions of the court, composing assiduously. After his retirement from his post in the royal chapel, he seems to have returned to his native Netherlands (Tournai), and there continued to compose until his death. He held a canonship at Notre Dame, Courtrai, from June 23, 1537, without having to take up residence there, and was also a canon at the Cathedral of Tournai from June 19, 1534. Despite his many trips abroad and the natural influence of the music of other countries, Gombert remained, stylistically, a Netherlander. The chief feature of his sacred works is his use of imitation, a principle which he developed to a high state of perfection. The parts are always in motion, and pauses appear infrequently; when they do occur, they are very short. In his handling of dissonance he may be regarded as a forerunner of Palestrina. His secular works, of which the earliest known printed examples (9 4-part chansons) are included in Attai gnant's collection of 1529–49, are characterized by a refreshing simplicity and directness. Gombert's greatest contributions to the development of 16th-century music lay in his recognizing the peculiarities of Netherlandish polyphony and his developing and spreading it abroad. He wrote 11 masses, over 160 motets, and 70 chansons, many of which appeared in contemporary (mostly Spanish) lute and guitar arrangements, a fact which shows the great vogue they had. Reprints have been publ. by F. Commer in Collectio Operum Musicorum Batavorum (1839—), VIII (one motet), and XII (2 chansons); A. Reissmann in *Allgemeine Geschichte der Musik* (1863; one chanson); R.J. v. Maldeghem in Trésor Musical (1865—), II (one motet), XI (3 chansons), XII (one motet), XIV (5 chansons), XVI (one motet of doubtful authorship), XVII (one chanson), XX (2 motets); R. Eitner in Publikationen Älterer Praktischer ... Musikwerke, III (1875; 2 chansons); A.W. Ambros in *Geschichte der Musik,* V (3rd ed., 1911; one motet, revised by O. Kade); E.H. Wooldridge in *The Oxford History of Music,* II (1905; one motet); Th. Kroyer in *Der vollkommene Partiturspieler* (1930; 10 Magnificat selections); A. Schering in *Geschichte der Musik in Beispielen* (1931; no. 102, portion of the Mass *Media vita*); a motet is in Attaignant's *Treize livres de motets* (Book I, pp. 167–75), reprinted by the Lyrebird Press (Paris, 1934). Gombert's *Opera omnia,* edited by J. Schmidt-Görg, was publ. in Corpus Mensurabilis Musicae, VI/1–11 (1951–75).

Gomes, Antonio Carlos, Brazilian composer; b. (of Portuguese parents) Campinas, Brazil, July 11, 1836; d. Pará (Belém), Sept. 16, 1896. He was a pupil of his father, then of the Cons. in Rio de Janeiro, where he produced 2 operas, *Noite do Castello* (1861) and *Joanna de Flandres* (1863). The success of these works induced Emperor Don Pedro II to grant him a stipend for further study in Milan; there he soon made his mark with a humorous little piece entitled *Se sa minga* (a song from this work, *Del fucile ad ago,* became popular), produced in 1867. After another piece in the same vein (*Nella Luna,* 1868), he made a more serious bid for fame with the opera *Il Guarany,* produced at La Scala on March 19, 1870, with brilliant success; this work, in which Amazon-Indian themes are used, quickly went the round of Italy, and was given in London (Covent Garden) on July 13, 1872. Returning to Rio de Janeiro, Gomes brought out a very popular operetta, *Telegrapho elettrico.* His other operas are *Fosca* (La Scala, Milan, Feb. 16, 1873), *Salvator Rosa* (Genoa, March 21, 1874), *Maria Tudor* (La Scala, Milan, March 27, 1879), *Lo Schiavo* (Rio de Janeiro, Sept. 27, 1889), and *Condor* (La Scala, Milan, Feb. 21, 1891). He wrote the hymn *Il saluto del Brasile* for the centenary of American independence (1876); also the cantata *Colombo,* for the Columbus Festival in 1892. In 1895 he was appointed director of the newly founded Cons. at Pará, but he died soon after arriving there. Besides his operas, he composed songs (3 books), choruses, and piano pieces.

Gomólka, Mikolaj (Nicolas), Polish composer; b.

Sandomierz, c.1535; date of death unknown. He was a chorister at Cracow (1545), and then played trumpet and flute in the court orch. In 1566 he returned to his native town, where he married and served as a judge. His chief work was *Melodiae na psalterz polski* (Cracow, 1580), containing 150 melodies to words from the Psalms trans. by the poet Jan Kochanowski; a new edition was publ. by J.W. Reiss in 1923; several pieces are included in the anthology by Jachimecki and Lissa, *Music of the Polish Renaissance* (Warsaw, 1954).

Goodall, Reginald, English conductor; b. Lincoln, July 13, 1901. He studied piano with Arthur Benjamin and violin with W.H. Reed at the Royal College of Music in London; from 1936 to 1939 was assistant conductor at Covent Garden; then went to Germany, and was engaged as an assistant to Furtwängler at the Berlin Phil.; also led many operatic performances. He is regarded as a foremost interpreter of Wagner's music dramas; in 1973 he conducted the entire cycle of the *Ring of the Nibelung* at Sadler's Wells Opera in London. In 1975 he was made a Commander of the Order of the British Empire.

Goode, Richard, American pianist; b. New York, June 1, 1943. He studied at the Mannes College of Music with Nadia Reisenberg and at the Curtis Inst. of Music with Rudolf Serkin; then made his debut in N.Y. in 1961; subsequently appeared extensively as a chamber music artist. In 1973 he won the Clara Haskil International Competition.

Goodman, Benny (Benjamin David), American clarinetist and jazz-band leader; b. Chicago, May 30, 1909. He acquired a taste for syncopated music as a child by listening to phonographic recordings of ragtime; was playing professionally by the age of 12 (1921); and in 1926 was working with Ben Pollack, one of the leading Chicago jazz musicians of the period. In 1928 he went to N.Y. as a clarinetist in various bands. In 1934 he formed his own band, which became known nationwide from its weekly appearances on the "Let's Dance" radio program. Both as the leader of a large dance band and for his virtuoso performances in various jazz combos, Goodman was the best-known and most successful musician of the swing era; was called the King of Swing. He also played clarinet parts in classical works in concert and for records, appearing as soloist in Mozart's Clarinet Concerto with the N.Y. Phil. (Dec. 12, 1940), and recording works by Copland, Bartók, Stravinsky, Morton Gould, and Leonard Bernstein. His autobiography, *The Kingdom of Swing,* was publ. in 1939; a biographical movie, *The Benny Goodman Story,* was made in 1955.

Goodrich, (John) Wallace, American organist, conductor, and writer on music; b. Newton, Mass., May 27, 1871; d. Boston, June 6, 1952. He studied at the New England Cons. in Boston (organ with Dunham, composition with Chadwick); then in Munich with Rheinberger (1894–95) and with Widor in Paris. In 1896–97, he was coach at the Leipzig Municipal

Theater. In 1897 he returned to Boston and became an instructor at the New England Cons.; he was appointed dean in 1907, and in 1931 director, a post he held until 1942. He was organist of Trinity Church in 1902–9, and for the Boston Symph. Orch. from 1897 to 1909. He founded the Choral Art Society in 1902 and was its conductor until 1907; he was also, at various periods, conductor of the Cecilia Society, the Boston Opera Co., and the Worcester County Choral Assoc. He composed an *Ave Maria* for Chorus and Orch. (Munich, 1895) and other choral music; wrote *The Organ in France* (Boston, 1917); trans. A. Pirro's *J.S. Bach and His Works for the Organ* (1902) and d'Ortigue's *Méthode d'accompagnement du plain-chant* (1905).

Goodson, Katharine, English pianist; b. Watford, Hertfordshire, June 18, 1872; d. London, April 14, 1958. In 1886–92 she was a pupil of O. Beringer at the Royal Academy of Music, and in 1892–96 of Leschetizky in Vienna; made her debut in London at a Saturday Popular Concert, Jan. 16, 1897, with signal success; then made tours of England, France, Austria, and Germany, which established her reputation; her American debut, with the Boston Symph., took place on Jan. 18, 1907; she subsequently made many tours of the U.S., and of the Netherlands, Belgium, and Italy. In 1903 she married the English composer **Arthur Hinton.**

Goossens, Sir Eugene, outstanding English conductor and composer; b. London, May 26, 1893; d. there, June 13, 1962. A scion of a family of musicians of Belgian extraction, he was educated at the Bruges Cons. (1903); returning to England in 1904, he subsequently studied at the Liverpool College of Music (1906); then won a Liverpool scholarship to the Royal College of Music in London (1907); studied violin with Rivarde, piano with Dykes, and composition with Charles Wood and Stanford; won the silver medal of the Worshipful Company of Musicians; in 1912–15 played the violin in the Queen's Hall Orch. He was associated with Sir Thomas Beecham's operatic enterprises (1915–20); conducted a season of concerts with his own orch. in London (1921). In 1923 he was engaged as conductor of the Rochester (N.Y.) Phil. Orch.; in 1931 he was appointed conductor of the Cincinnati Symph. Orch., remaining at that post until 1946. From 1947 to 1956 he was director of the New South Wales Cons. of Music at Sydney and conductor of the Sydney Symph. Orch.; he was knighted in 1955. Goossens belonged to a group of English composers who cultivated exotic themes with modernistic harmonies stemming from Debussy. He conducted his first orch. piece, *Variations on a Chinese Theme*, at the age of 19 at the Royal College of Music in London (June 20, 1912); continued to write prolifically in all genres (opera, ballet, symph., chamber music); his mature style became a blend of impressionistic harmonies and neo-Classical polyphony; while retaining a clear tonal outline, Goossens often resorted to expressive chromatic melos bordering on atonality. WORKS: *Variations on a Chinese Theme* for

Orch. (1911); *Miniature Fantasy* for String Orch. (1911); Suite for Flute, Violin, and Harp (1914); *5 Impressions of a Holiday* for Flute, Cello, and Piano (1914); symph. poem, *Perseus* (1914); symph. prelude, *Ossian* (1915); *Phantasy Quartet* for Strings (1915); String Quartet No. 1 (1916); 2 sketches for String Quartet: *By the Tarn* and *Jack o' Lantern* (1916); *Kaleidoscope*, suite of piano pieces in a humorous vein (1917–18); Violin Sonata No. 1 (1918); Prelude to Verhaeren's *Philip II* (1918); *The Eternal Rhythm* for Orch. (London, Oct. 19, 1920); *4 Conceits* for Piano (1918); Piano Quintet (1919); *Lyric Poem* for Violin and Piano (1921; also arranged for Violin and Orch.); ballet, *L'Ecole en crinoline* (1921); *Silence* for Chorus and Piano (1922); incidental music to W. Somerset Maugham's *East of Suez* (1922); *Sinfonietta* (London, Feb. 19, 1923); String Sextet (1923); *Pastoral and Harlequinade* for Flute, Oboe, and Piano (1924); Fantasy for Wind Instruments (1924); opera, *Judith* (1925; Covent Garden, June 25, 1929); *Rhythmic Dance* for Orch. (Rochester, March 12, 1927); Concertino for Double String Orch. (1928); Oboe Concerto (London, Oct. 2, 1930; Leon Goossens, soloist); Violin Sonata No. 2 (1930); opera, *Don Juan de Mañara* (1934; Covent Garden, June 24, 1937); Symph. No. 1 (Cincinnati, April 12, 1940); 2nd String Quartet (1942); *Phantasy-Concerto* for Piano and Orch. (Cincinnati, Feb. 25, 1944, composer conducting; Iturbi, soloist); 2nd Symph. (BBC, Nov. 10, 1946); oratorio, *Apocalypse* (1951; Sydney, Nov. 22, 1954, composer conducting). Goossens is the author of *Overture and Beginners; A Musical Autobiography* (London, 1951).

Goossens, Leon, distinguished English oboist, brother of **Sir Eugene Goossens;** b. Liverpool, June 12, 1897. He studied at the Royal College of Music in London (1911–14); then joined the Queen's Hall Orch. (1914–24); subsequently played in the Covent Garden orch., in the Royal Phil. Society's orch., and in the London Phil. (1932–39). From 1924 to 1939 he taught oboe at the Royal College of Music. He commissioned works for oboe to several English composers, among them Elgar and Vaughan Williams. In 1950 he was made a Commander of the Order of the British Empire.

Goovaerts, Alphonse Jean Marie André, Belgian musicologist; b. Antwerp, May 25, 1847; d. Brussels, Dec. 25, 1922. He was a member of a literary family; as a youth he became greatly interested in Flemish literature and in church music. He arranged and publ. a collection of Flemish songs (1868–74); composed several pieces of church music, and performed them with a chorus he established in Antwerp; also made transcriptions for chorus of works by Palestrina and Flemish contrapuntists. He publ. several papers propounding a reform in church music, which aroused opposition from conservative circles (*La Musique de l'église*, 1876; in Flemish as *De kerkmuziek*); also publ. a valuable book, *Histoire et bibliographie de la typographie musicale dans le Pays-Bas* (1880; awarded the gold medal of the Belgian Academy); a monograph on the Belgian music printer Pierre Phalèse; and other studies relating to Flemish music.

Gordon, James Carel Gerhard, flute maker; b. Cape Town, May 22, 1791; d. (insane) Lausanne, c.1845. He was born of a Dutch captain and a Swiss mother in South Africa. He joined the Swiss Guards of Charles X in Paris in 1814; concurrently, studied flute with Tulou; worked on improvements of its mechanism more or less at the same time as Böhm, so that the priority of the invention became a matter of insoluble controversy. He escaped with his life during the attack on the Swiss Guards in the Revolution of 1830; was pensioned and retired to Switzerland when his mind became deranged.

Goss, Sir John, English organist and composer; b. Fareham, Hampshire, Dec. 27, 1800; d. London, May 10, 1880. A son of **Joseph Goss,** the Fareham organist, he became a child chorister of the Chapel Royal; then studied under Attwood. He was successively organist of Stockwell Chapel (1821), St. Luke's, Chelsea (1824), and St. Paul's Cathedral (1838–72). In 1856 he was appointed a composer to the Chapel Royal; he was knighted in 1872, and received the degree of Mus.Doc. from Cambridge Univ. in 1876. His music includes church services, anthems, chants, Psalms, etc.; some orch. pieces; songs and glees. He edited a collection of hymns, *Parochial Psalmody* (1827); *Chants, Ancient and Modern* (1841); *Church Psalter and Hymnbook* (1856; with Rev. W. Mercer). He publ. *The Organist's Companion,* 4 vols. of voluntaries and interludes, and *An Introduction to Harmony and Thorough-bass* (1833; many eds.).

Gossec, François-Joseph, significant Belgian composer; b. Vergnies, Jan. 17, 1734; d. Paris, Feb. 16, 1829. He showed musical inclinations at an early age; as a child, studied at the collegiate church in Walcourt and sang in the chapel of St. Aldegonde in Mauberige; then joined the chapel of St. Pierre there, where he studied violin, harpsichord, harmony, and composition with Jean Vanderbelen; in 1742 was engaged as a chorister at the Cathedral of Notre Dame in Antwerp; received some instruction with André-Joseph Blavier in violin and organ playing there. In 1751 he went to Paris, and in 1754 joined a private musical ensemble of the rich amateur La Pouplinière. There he wrote chamber music and little symphs., in which he seems to have anticipated Haydn; several works for string quartet followed in 1759. After the death of La Pouplinière in 1762, Gossec became a member of the retinue of the Prince de Condé at Chantilly, and continued to compose for private performances. In 1760 he wrote a Requiem; then turned his attention to stage music; produced a 3-act opéra-comique, *Le Faux Lord* (Paris, June 27, 1765); obtained a decisive success with another short opéra-comique, *Les Pêcheurs* (April 23, 1766); there followed the operas (perf. at the Comédie-Italienne and at the Paris Opéra) *Toinon et Toinette* (June 20, 1767); *Le Double*

Déguisement (Sept. 28, 1767); *Sabinus* (Feb. 22, 1774); *Alexis et Daphné* (Sept. 26, 1775); *La Fête du village* (May 26, 1778); *Thésée* (March 1, 1782); *Rosine* (July 14, 1786); several other operas (*Nictocris, La Fédération,* etc.) were not performed. In 1770 he organized a performing society, Concerts des Amateurs; became a director of the Concert Spirituel (1773–77); was also an associate director of the Paris Opéra (1780–85) and manager of the Ecole Royale de Chant (1784–89); when this school became the Cons. in 1795, Gossec became one of the inspectors, and also taught composition there; he publ. a manual, *Exposition des principes de la musique,* for use at the Cons. In 1795 he became a member of the newly founded Académie des Beaux-Arts of the Institut de France. Gossec welcomed the French Revolution with great enthusiasm, and wrote many festive works to celebrate Revolutionary events, among them *L'Offrande à la Liberté* (1792); *Le Triomphe de la République* (1793); *Le Cri de vengeance* (1799); and numerous marches and hymns. During his long life he saw many changes of regime, but retained his position in the musical world and in society throughout the political upheavals. He retired to Passy, then a suburb of Paris, at the age of 80. Gossec's historic role consists in his creation of a French type of symph. composition, in which he expanded the resources of instrumentation so as to provide for dynamic contrasts; he experimented with new sonorities in instrumental and choral writing; his string quartets attained a coherence of style and symmetry of form that laid the foundation of French chamber music. In his choral works, Gossec was a bold innovator, presaging in some respects the usages of Berlioz; his *Te Deum,* written for a Revolutionary festival, is scored for 1,200 singers and 300 wind instruments; in his oratorio, *La Nativité,* he introduced an invisible chorus of angels placed behind the stage; in other works, he separated choral groups in order to produce special antiphonal effects. Among reprints of Gossec's works are a Trio, in Riemann's *Collegium musicum* (Leipzig, 1909); String Quartet, op. 15, no. 2, in *Veröffentlichungen der Musiksammlung W. Höckner* (facsimile reprint; Leipzig, 1932); 2 symphs., edited by S. Beck (N.Y., 1937); a Symph. in Sondheimer's collection *Werke aus dem 18. Jahrhundert* (Berlin, 1922–39); a Symph. for 10 Instruments, in G. Cucuël, *Etudes sur un orchestre de XVIIIᵉ siècle* (Paris, 1913); 3 works edited by Barry Brook (Paris, 1962–63): Symph. in D, op. III/6; Symph. in E-flat, op. VIII/1; Symph. Concertante (from the *Ballet de Mirza*).

Gotovac, Jakov, noted Yugoslav composer; b. Split, Oct. 11, 1895; d. Zagreb, Oct. 16, 1982. He studied law at Zagreb Univ., and music with Antun Dobronic in Zagreb and with Joseph Marx in Vienna. In 1923 he was appointed conductor of the Croatian National Opera in Zagreb, retaining this post until 1958. He composed mostly for the theater; his instrumental music is imbued with the folkways of Croatia, enhancing the simple native materials by carefully proportioned modernistic mutations while preserving the impulsive asymmetrical patterns of the original songs. His music was often performed in Yugoslavia and at occasional Central European festivals, but rarely beyond.

Gottschalk, Louis Moreau, celebrated American pianist and composer; b. New Orleans, May 8, 1829; d. Rio de Janeiro, Dec. 18, 1869. He studied music as a child in New Orleans with François Letellier, organist at the St. Louis Cathedral; then studied in Paris from 1842 to 1846 (piano under Hallé and Stamaty; harmony under Maleden) and became the rage of the salons, winning praise from both Chopin and Berlioz; made his formal debut in the Salle Pleyel on April 17, 1849. He made a successful tour through France, Switzerland, and Spain in 1850–51; returned to the U.S. in 1853 for a grand tour throughout the country, playing his own piano works and conducting his orch. works at huge festivals; his popularity was phenomenal. The impresario Max Strakosch engaged him for an even more extended tour throughout the U.S. Gottschalk died of yellow fever in Rio de Janeiro during his travels. His compositions are mostly for piano, or piano with other instruments, and are cast in both conventional Romantic idioms and in the more exotic Creole, Afro-Hispanic, and "Americanistic" patterns; about 300 works are currently known, but the existence of additional MSS is suspected.
WORKS: 4 operas: *Charles IX* (1859–60; not extant); *Isaura de Salerno* (1859; never perf.); *Amalia Warden* (1860; Act I libretto extant); *Escenas campestras* for Soprano, Tenor, Baritone, and Orch. (Havana, Feb. 17, 1860); 2 symph. poems, *La Nuit des tropiques* and *Montevideo: Grand Marcha solemne* for Orch. (dedicated to the Emperor of Brazil); *Variations on Dixie's Land; The Dying Poet; Morte!!; The Last Hope* (these last 3 being his most popular works). *The Piano Works of Louis Moreau Gottschalk* (5 vols., N.Y., 1969), ed. by V.L. Brodsky, is a collection of facsimiles of early eds.; it contains a valuable essay by Robert Offergeld. Seven additional, previously unpubl. piano pieces appear in *The Little Book of Louis Moreau Gottschalk,* ed. by Richard Jackson and Neil Ratliff (N.Y., 1976). A list of works compiled by Offergeld is publ. as *The Centennial Catalogue of the Published and Unpublished Compositions of Louis Moreau Gottschalk* (N.Y., 1970). Gottschalk's journals were trans. from French and publ. in Eng. under the title *Notes of a Pianist* (Philadelphia, 1881; reprinted, N.Y., 1964).

Goudimel, Claude (his name was variously spelled in contemporary and later editions as **Gaudimel, Gaudiomel, Godimel, Gondimel, Goudmel, Gudmel,** etc.), celebrated French composer and theorist; b. Besançon, c.1510; killed in the St. Bartholomew massacre at Lyons, Aug. 27, 1572. In 1549 Goudimel studied at the Univ. of Paris; he publ. a book of chansons as a joint publisher with Du Chemin. He lived in Metz between 1557 and 1568; there he became a Huguenot; in 1568 he returned to Besançon, and then lived in Lyons, where he perished. It was long supposed that he lived in Rome, where he founded a school of music, but this assertion is totally lacking in foundation. It seems certain that Goudimel never visited Italy, and it is significant that none of his numerous works appeared in Roman publications. Most of his music was publ. by Du Chemin in Paris; other contemporary publishers were Adrien Le Roy and Robert Ballard, who publ. his complete Huguenot psalter in 1564 under the title *Les CL pseaumes de David, nouvellement mis en musique à quatre parties;* it was publ. in Geneva in 1565 as *Les Pseaumes mis en rime françoise par Clément Marot et Th. de Bèze, mis en musique à 4 parties;* it was reprinted in a facsimile edition in Kassel, 1935; a 1580 edition, also issued in Geneva, was republ. by H. Expert in vols. 2–4 of *Les Maîtres Musiciens de la Renaissance* (1895–97). A German trans. of the Psalms, with Goudimel's musical settings, first appeared in 1573; many reprints followed. Goudimel also composed 5 masses, publ. by Du Chemin (one, 1554) and Le Roy and Ballard (4, 1558), together with other sacred music. Two 4-part motets were included in T. Susato's *Ecclesiasticarum cantionum* (Antwerp, 1553–55). Further reprints have been edited by R.J. v. Maldeghem in Trésor Musical, III (1867; 12-part *Salve Regina* and 2 4-part motets) and XI (1875; 3 3-part chansons); C. Bordes in *Anthologie des maîtres religieux primitifs,* II (the mass *Le bien que j'ay*) and III (4-part motet); K. von Winterfeld, A. Ebrard, H. Bellermann, etc. (Psalms). Three masses are in H. Expert's *Monuments de la musique française au temps de la Renaissance,* IX (1928); 9 Psalms in P. Pidoux's *Collection de musique protestante* (1935). Publication of the Complete Works, under the direction of L. Dittmer and P. Pidoux (Inst. of Medieval Music), began in 1967.

Gould, Glenn Herbert, remarkably individualistic Canadian pianist; b. Toronto, Sept. 25, 1932; d. there, Oct. 4, 1982, as a result of a massive stroke. His parents were musically gifted and gladly fostered his precocious development; he began to play piano, and even compose, in his single-digit years. At the age of 10, he entered the Royal Cons. of Toronto, where he studied piano with Alberto Guerrero, organ with Frederick C. Silvester, and music theory with Leo Smith; he received his diploma as a graduate at 14, in 1946. As he began practicing with total concentration on the mechanism of the keyboard, he developed mannerisms that were to become his artistic signature. He reduced the use of the pedal to a minimum in order to avoid a harmonic haze; he cultivated "horizontality" in his piano posture, bringing his head down almost to the level of the keys. He regarded music as a linear art; this naturally led him to an intense examination of the Baroque stuctures; Bach was the subject of his close study rather than Chopin; he also cultivated performances of early polyphonists, Sweelinck, Gibbons, and others. He played Mozart with emphasis on the early pianoforte techniques; he peremptorily omitted the Romantic composers Chopin, Schumann, and Liszt from his repertoire. He found the late sonatas of Beethoven more congenial to his temperament, and, remarkably enough, he played the piano works of the modern Vienna school—Schoenberg, Berg, and Webern—perhaps because of their classical avoidance of purely decorative tonal formations. He attracted great attention and evoked unequivocal praise at his American and European concerts, but in 1964 he abruptly terminated his stage career and devoted himself exclusively to recording, which he regarded as a superior art to concertizing. This enabled him to select the best portions of the music he played in the studio, forming a mosaic unblemished by accidental mishaps. A great part of the interest he aroused with the public at large was due to mannerisms that marked his behavior on the stage. He used a 14-inch-high chair that placed his eyes almost at the level of the keyboard; he affected informal dress; he had a rug put under the piano and a glass of distilled water within reach. He was in constant fear of bodily injury; he avoided shaking hands with the conductor after playing a concerto; and he sued the Steinway piano company for a large sum of money when an enthusiastic representative shook his hand too vigorously. But what even his most ardent admirers could not palliate was his unshakable habit of singing along with his performance; he even allowed his voice to be audible on his carefully wrought, lapidary phonograph recordings. Socially, Gould was a recluse; he found a release from his self-imposed isolation in editing a series of radio documentaries for the Canadian Broadcasting Corp. He called three of them a "solitude tragedy." Symbolically, they were devoted to the natural isolation of the Canadian Arctic, the insular life of Newfoundland, and the religious hermetism of the Mennonite sect. He also produced a radio documentary on Arnold Schoenberg, treating him as a musical hermit. Other activities included conducting a chamber orch. without an audience. Needless to add, Gould never married.

Gould, Morton, extraordinarily talented and versatile American composer and conductor; b. Richmond Hill, N.Y., Dec. 10, 1913. His father was an Austrian; his mother came from Russia; both fostered his early addiction to music. If the affectionate family memories are to be accepted as facts (and why not?), Gould composed a piano waltz at the age of 6 (indeed, it was ultimately publ. under the title *Just Six*). Being a prodigy did not harm Gould. He was bent on learning what music really is. He had piano lessons with Joseph Kardos and Abby Whiteside; later he enrolled in the composition class of Vincent Jones at N.Y. Univ.; there, at the age of 16, he presented a concert of his works. To keep body and soul together he played the piano in silent movies and in loud jazz bands, accompanied dancers, and gave demonstrations of musical skill on college circuits. In 1931–32 he served as staff pianist at Radio City Music Hall; in 1934–42 was in charge of the series "Music for Today" on the Mutual Radio network, and in 1943 became music director of the lucrative "Chrysler Hour" on CBS Radio. These contacts gave great impetus to his

bursting talent for composing singable, playable, and enjoyable light pieces; he was pregnant with the fertile sperm of musical Americana; his *American Symphonette No. 1* (1933) became a popular success; equally accessible to the musical youth of the day was the *Chorale and Fugue in Jazz* for 2 Pianos and Orch. (1934); no less a musical magus than Stokowski put it on the program of the Philadelphia Orch. (Jan. 2, 1936). Gould then produced 3 more symphonettes (1935, 1938, 1941). No. 3 disgorged the luscious *Pavane;* the misspelling *Pavanne* (sic) was a concession to public illiteracy; the piece cloned several arrangements. There followed the *Latin-American Symphonette* (1940), an engaging tetrad of Latin dances (Rhumba, Tango, Guaracha, Conga). His *Spirituals* for Strings and Orch. (1941) is Gould's interpretation of the religious aspect of the American people. His other works touch on American history, as exemplified by *A Lincoln Legend* (1941), which Toscanini placed on his program with the NBC Symph. on Nov. 1, 1942; there followed the rambunctious orchestral *Cowboy Rhapsody* (1943). In 1945 Gould conducted a whole program of his works with the Boston Symph. Orch. He then turned to ballet in his *Fall River Legend,* based on the story of the notorious New England old maid who may or may not have given her mother 40 whacks and "when she saw what she had done she gave her father 41." Gould's *Symphony of Spirituals,* written for the American bicentennial (1976), was a reverential offering; his other bicentennial work, *American Ballads* (1976), is a symph. florilegium of American songs. Gould wrote the music for the Broadway show *Million Dollar Baby* (1945), several scores for Hollywood films, and also background music for the historical television productions *Verdun* (1963), *World War I* (1964–65), and *Holocaust* (1978). But Gould was not so much seduced by public success as not to test his powers in a field known as absolute music. He studied ways and means of Baroque techniques, and wrote several concertos: one for piano (1937), one for violin (1938), one for viola (1944), *Variations* for 2 Pianos and Orch. (1952), and *Inventions* for 4 Pianos and Orch. (1953); on top of these "classical" works he produced a unique shtick, *Concerto for Tap Dancer,* with Orch. (1953). Gould was a conductor of excellent skills; he toured Australia in 1977, Japan in 1979, Mexico in 1980, and Israel in 1981. In 1983 he received the National Arts Award.
   WORKS: Broadway musicals, *Million Dollar Baby* (1945) and *Arms and the Girl* (1950); ballets, *Interplay* (N.Y., Oct. 17, 1945, composer conducting), *Fall River Legend* (N.Y., April 22, 1947), and *Fiesta* (Cannes, France, March 17, 1957); 3 *American Symphonettes* (1933, 1935, 1937); *Chorale and Fugue in Jazz* for 2 Pianos and Orch. (Youth Orch., N.Y., Jan. 2, 1936, Stokowski conducting); Piano Concerto (1937; broadcast June 16, 1938, composer soloist); Violin Concerto (1938); *Stephen Foster Gallery* for Orch. (Pittsburgh, Jan. 12, 1940); *Spirituals* for Orch. (N.Y., Feb. 9, 1941, composer conducting); *Latin-American Symphonette* (Brooklyn, Feb. 22, 1941); *Cowboy Rhapsody* (1942); Symph. No. 1 (Pittsburgh, March 5, 1943); *Interplay* for Piano and

Orch. (broadcast Aug. 25, 1943); Viola Concerto (1943); *Symphony on Marching Tunes,* No. 2 (N.Y., June 2, 1944); Concerto for Orch. (Cleveland, Feb. 1, 1945); *Harvest* for Harp, Vibraphone, and Strings (St. Louis, Oct. 27, 1945); *Minstrel Show* for Orch. (Indianapolis, Dec. 21, 1946); Symph. No. 3 (Dallas, Feb. 16, 1947, composer conducting); *Symphony* for Band (West Point, April 13, 1952, composer conducting); *Inventions* for 4 Pianos, Brass, and Percussion (N.Y., Oct. 19, 1953); *Dance Variations* for 2 Pianos and Orch. (N.Y., Oct. 24, 1953); *Showpiece* for Orch. (Philadelphia, May 7, 1954); *Derivations* for Clarinet and Band, written for Benny Goodman (Washington, D.C., July 14, 1956, composer conducting); *Declaration* for 2 Speakers, Male Chorus, and Orch.; setting of the Declaration of Independence (Washington, D.C., Jan. 20, 1957); *Jekyll and Hyde Variations* for Orch. (N.Y., Feb. 2, 1957); *Dialogues* for Piano and String Orch. (N.Y., Nov. 3, 1958, composer soloist); *Festive Music* for Orch. (N.Y., Jan. 16, 1965, composer conducting); *Venice* for Double Orch. and Brass Bands (Seattle, May 2, 1967); *Vivaldi Gallery* for Orch. (Seattle, March 25, 1968); *Troubadour Music* for 4 Guitars and Orch. (San Diego, March 1969); *Symphony of Spirituals* (Detroit, April 1, 1976); *American Ballads* for Orch. (Queens, N.Y., April 24, 1976, composer conducting); *Something To Do,* cantata-musical (Washington, D.C., Labor Day, 1976); Music for *Holocaust,* the TV mini-series (broadcast April 1978); *Cheers* for Orch. (Boston, May 1, 1979); *Burchfield Gallery* for Orch. (Cleveland, April 9, 1981); *Celebration '81* (for television; broadcast April 27, 1981); Cello Suite (1982); *Housewarming* for Orch. (Baltimore, Sept. 16, 1982); *American Sing,* commissioned for the opening concert of the Los Angeles Olympic Games (Hollywood Bowl, July 29, 1984).

Gounod, Charles François, famous French composer; b. St. Cloud, June 17, 1818; d. Paris, Oct. 18, 1893. His father, Jean François Gounod, was a painter, winner of the 2nd Grand Prix de Rome, who died when Gounod was a small child. His mother, a most accomplished woman, supervised his literary, artistic, and musical education, and taught him piano. He completed his academic studies at the Lycée St. Louis; in 1836, he entered the Paris Cons., studying with Halévy, Lesueur, and Paër. In 1837 he won the 2nd Prix de Rome with his cantata *Marie Stuart et Rizzio;* in 1839 he obtained the Grand Prix with his cantata *Fernand.* In Rome, he studied church music, particularly the works of Palestrina; composed there a Mass for 3 Voices and Orch., which was performed at the church of San Luigi dei Francesi. In 1842, during a visit to Vienna, he conducted a Requiem of his own; upon his return to Paris, he became precentor and organist of the Missions Etrangères; studied theology for 2 years, but decided against taking Holy Orders; yet he was often referred to as l'Abbé Gounod; some religious choruses were publ. in 1846 as composed by Abbé Charles Gounod. Soon Gounod tried his hand at stage music. On April 16, 1851, his first opera, *Sapho,* was produced at the Grand Opéra, with only

moderate success; he revised it much later, extending it to 4 acts from the original 3, and it was performed again on April 2, 1884; but even in this revised form it was unsuccessful. Gounod's 2nd opera, *La Nonne sanglante,* in 5 acts, was staged at the Paris Opéra on Oct. 18, 1854; there followed a comic opera, *Le Médecin malgré lui,* after Molière (Jan. 15, 1858), which also failed to realize Gounod's expectations. In the meantime, he was active in other musical ways in Paris; he conducted the choral society Orphéon (1852–60) and composed for it several choruses. Gounod's great success came with the production of *Faust,* after Goethe (Théâtre-Lyrique, March 19, 1859; perf. with additional recitatives and ballet at the Opéra, March 3, 1869); *Faust* remained Gounod's greatest masterpiece, and indeed the most successful French opera of the 19th century, triumphant all over the world without any sign of diminishing effect through a century of changes in musical tastes. However, it was widely criticized for the melodramatic treatment of Goethe's poem by the librettists, Barbier and Carré, and for the somewhat sentimental style of Gounod's music; in Germany, it is usually produced under the title *Margarete* or *Gretchen* to dissociate it from Goethe's work. The succeeding 4 operas, *Philémon et Baucis* (Paris, Feb. 18, 1860), *La Colombe* (Baden-Baden, Aug. 3, 1860), *La Reine de Saba* (Paris, Feb. 29, 1862), and *Mireille* (Paris, March 19, 1864), were only partially successful, but with *Roméo et Juliette* (Paris, April 27, 1867), Gounod recaptured universal acclaim. In 1870, during the Franco-Prussian War, Gounod went to London, where he organized Gounod's Choir, and presented concerts at the Phil. and the Crystal Palace; when Paris fell, he wrote an elegiac cantata, *Gallia,* to words from the Lamentations of Jeremiah, which he conducted in London on May 1, 1871; it was later performed in Paris. He wrote some incidental music for productions in Paris: *Les Deux Reines,* to a drama by Legouvé (Nov. 27, 1872), and *Jeanne d'Arc,* to Barbier's poem (Nov. 8, 1873). In 1874, he returned to Paris; there he produced his operas *Cinq-Mars* (April 5, 1877), *Polyeucte* (Oct. 7, 1878), and *Le Tribut de Zamora* (April 1, 1881), without signal success. The last years of his life were devoted mainly to sacred works, of which the most important was *La Rédemption,* a trilogy, first performed at the Birmingham Festival in 1882; another sacred trilogy, *Mors et vita,* also written for the Birmingham Festival, followed in 1885. Gounod continued to write religious works in close succession, and produced (among many others) the following: *Te Deum* (1886); *La Communion des saints* (1889); *Messe dite le Clovis* (1890); *La Contemplation de Saint François au pied de la croix* (1890); *Tantum ergo* (1892). A Requiem (1893) was left unfinished, and was arranged by Henri Büsser after Gounod's death. One of Gounod's most popular settings to religious words is *Ave Maria,* adapted to the first prelude of Bach's *Well-tempered Clavier,* but its original version was *Méditation sur le premier Prélude de Piano de J.S. Bach* for Violin and Piano (1853); the words were added later (1859). Other works are: 2 symphs. (1855); *Marche funèbre d'une marionnette* for Orch. (1873); *Petite symphonie* for Wind Instruments (1888); 3 string quartets; a number of piano pieces; songs. Among his literary works were *Ascanio de Saint-Saëns* (1889); *Le Don Juan de Mozart* (1890; in Eng., 1895); and an autobiography, *Mémoires d'un artiste* (publ. posthumously, Paris, 1896; in Eng. trans. by W.H. Hutchenson, *Autobiographical Reminiscences with Family Letters and Notes on Music*, N.Y., 1896).

Grabovsky, Leonid, Ukrainian composer; b. Kiev, Jan. 28, 1935. He studied at the Kiev Cons. with Revutsky and Liatoshinsky, graduating in 1959. His music is marked by modern tendencies, making use of dissonant counterpoint and asymmetric polyrhythmic combinations.
WORKS: *Intermezzo* for Orch. (1958); String Quartet (1958); *4 Ukrainian Songs* for Chorus and Orch. (1959); Sonata for Unaccompanied Violin (1959); *Symphonic Frescoes* (1961); 2 comic operas, after Chekhov, *The Bear* (1963) and *Marriage Proposal* (1964); Trio for Violin, Double Bass, and Piano (1964); *Microstructures* for Oboe Solo (1964); *Constants* for 4 Pianos, 6 Percussion Groups, and Solo Violin (1964); *From Japanese Haiku* for Tenor, Piccolo, Bassoon, and Xylophone (1964); *La Mer* for Narrator, 2 Choruses, Organ, and Orch. (1964–70; Rotterdam, Sept. 10, 1971); *Pastels* for Female Voice, Violin, Viola, Cello, and Double Bass (1964); *Little Chamber Music* No. 1 for 15 String Instruments (1966); *Homeomorphia I, II, and III* for One or 2 Pianos (1968); *Ornaments* for Oboe, Viola, and Harp (1969); *Homeomorphia IV* for Orch. (1970); *Little Chamber Music* No. 2 for Oboe, Harp, and 12 Solo String Instruments (1971); *2 Pieces* for String Orch. (1972); *Concorsuono* for Solo Horn (1974); *St. John's Eve,* symph. legend for Orch., after Gogol (1976).

Gradenwitz, Peter, German-Israeli musicologist; b. Berlin, Jan. 24, 1910. He studied literature and philosophy at Berlin Univ.; composition with Julius Weismann and Josef Rufer. In 1934 he went to Paris; in 1935, to London; in 1936, settled in Tel Aviv, where he became active as a writer, lecturer, and organizer of concerts; established Israeli Music Publications; he was also active on the radio.
WRITINGS: *Johann Stamitz* (Vienna, 1936); *The Music of Israel* (N.Y., 1949); *Wege zur Musik der Gegenwart* (Stuttgart, 1963); books in Hebrew: *Music History* (Jerusalem, 1939); *The World of the Symphony* (Jerusalem, 1945; 7th ed., 1953); *Music and Musicians in Israel* (Tel Aviv, 1959). He wrote a String Quartet; *Palestinian Landscapes* for Oboe and Piano; songs.

Graener, Paul, significant German composer; b. Berlin, Jan. 11, 1872; d. Salzburg, Nov. 13, 1944. He was a chorister at the Berlin Cathedral; studied composition with Albert Becker at the Veit Cons. in Berlin. He traveled in Germany as a theater conductor; in 1896, went to London, where he taught at the Royal Academy of Music (1897–1902). He was then in Vienna as a teacher at the Neues Konservatorium; subsequently directed the Mozarteum in Salzburg (1910–13); then lived in Munich; in 1920, he succeeded Max Reger as a prof. of composition at the Leipzig Cons. (until 1925); was director of the Stern Cons. in Berlin (1930–33). He wrote music in all genres, and was fairly successful as an opera composer; in his style, he followed the Romantic movement, but also emphasized the folk element.
WORKS: OPERAS: *Don Juans letztes Abenteuer* (Leipzig, June 11, 1914); *Theophano* (Munich, June 5, 1918); *Schirin und Gertraude* (Dresden, April 28, 1920); *Hanneles Himmelfahrt* (Dresden, Feb. 17, 1927); *Friedemann Bach* (Schwerin, Nov. 13, 1931); *Der Prinz von Homburg* (Berlin, March 14, 1935); *Schwanhild* (Cologne, Jan. 4, 1941). FOR ORCH.: Symph.; *Romantische Phantasie; Waldmusik; Gothische Suite;* Piano Concerto; Cello Concerto. CHAMBER MUSIC: 6 string quartets; Piano Quintet; 3 violin sonatas. In several of his chamber music works, Graener attempted to carry out a definite programmatic design while maintaining traditional form, as in his *Kammermusik-Dichtung* for Piano Trio.

Graeser, Wolfgang, talented Swiss composer; b. Zürich, Sept. 7, 1906; d. (suicide) Nikolassee, June 13, 1928. He went to Berlin in 1921; studied violin with Karl Klingler, and quickly acquired erudition in general music theory; also made a serious study of various unrelated arts and sciences (mathematics, oriental languages, painting). His signal achievement was an orchestration of Bach's *Kunst der Fuge* (perf. at the Leipzig Thomaskirche by Karl Straube, June 26, 1927). He publ. a book, *Körpersinn* (Munich, 1927).

Graffman, Gary, outstanding American pianist; b. New York, Oct. 14, 1928. He won a scholarship to the Curtis Inst. of Music when he was 8, and studied there with Isabelle Vengerova. He was only 10 years old when he gave a piano recital at Town Hall in N.Y. After graduating from Curtis in 1946, he was a scholarship student at Columbia Univ. (1946–47). In 1946 he won the first regional Rachmaninoff competition, which secured for him his debut with the Philadelphia Orch. in 1947. In 1949 he was honored with the Leventritt Award. Subsequently he received a Fulbright grant to go to Europe (1950–51). Returning to the U.S., he had lessons with Horowitz in N.Y. and Rudolf Serkin in Marlboro, Vt. He was on his way to establishing himself as a pianist of the first rank when disaster struck; about 1979 he began to lose the use of his right hand, a rare ailment, designated by some doctors as a carpal-tunnel syndrome, that attacks instrumentalists. (Leon Fleisher suffered from it but recovered after myotherapy. Schumann had to discontinue his career as a pianist owing to a similar impedimentum, but he applied primitive treatments, such as exercising his weak fingers with a sling and a pulley, which in the end strained the tendons, further weakening the hand.) Happily, the prognosis for Graffman's full recovery remains positive, but he had to cancel his concert appearances pending the process of cure. He brought out an autobiography under the title *I Real-*

ly Should Be Practicing (Garden City, N.Y., 1981).

Grahn, Ulf, Swedish composer; b. Solna, Jan. 17, 1942. He studied piano with Herbert Westrell, violin with Rudolf Forsberg, and composition with Gunnar Johanson and Hans Eklund at the Royal College of Music in Stockholm; also took voice lessons and sang bass in various choruses. In 1972 he and his wife, the pianist **Barbro Dahlman,** went to America; he enrolled at the Catholic Univ. (M.M., 1973); with his wife he founded the Contemporary Music Forum, presenting programs of modern music by American and European composers. In his own music he maintains the golden mean of contemporary idioms, without doctrinaire deviations, scrupulously serving the tastes of the general audience. WORKS: *Musica da camera* for Chamber Orch. (1964); *Serenade* for 2 Oboes (1965); *Fancy* for Orch. (1965); *Elegy* for Oboe, Horn, and Cello (1967); Trio for Flute, Oboe, and Clarinet (1967); Suite for 2 Violins and Viola (1967); *Lamento* for Strings (1967); Symph. No. 1 (1967); *Hommage à Charles Ives* for String Orch. (1968; Trondheim, Norway, Feb. 13, 1969); Chamber Concerto for Double Bass (1968; Santa Barbara, Calif., Feb. 7, 1973); *Dialogue* for Flute and Clarinet (1969); *Joy* for Symphonic Band (1969; Stockholm, Feb. 2, 1970); *Ancient Music* for Piano and Chamber Orch. (1970; Copenhagen, March 20, 1972); *A Dream of a Lost Century* for Chamber Orch. (1971; Stockholm, June 1, 1972); *Lux,* ballet (1972; Stockholm, April 6, 1972); *Alone* for Flute (1972); *This Reminds Me of . . .* for Flute, Clarinet, Horn, Trombone, and Percussion (1972; Washington, D.C., Dec. 15, 1975); Concerto for Orch. (1973; Philadelphia, April 10, 1981); *Soundscapes I* for Flute, Bass Clarinet, English Horn, and Percussion (1973; Washington, D.C., Oct. 28, 1973); *Soundscapes II* for Instruments (1974); *Soundscapes III* for Flute, Clarinet, Percussion, and Tape (1975); *Soundscapes IV* for Soprano, Flute, Bass Clarinet, Percussion, and Piano (1975); Chamber Concerto for Viola d'Amore and 10 Instruments (1975; Washington, D.C., Jan. 17, 1977); *Order-Fragments-Mirror* for Flute, Bass Clarinet, Percussion, and Piano (1975); Flute Sonata (1976); *Magnolias in Snow* for Flute and Piano (1976); Concertino for Piano and Strings (1979; Northern Virginia Symph., Feb. 28, 1981; Barbro Dahlman, soloist); String Quartet No. 2 (1979); *Floating Landscape* for 8 Flutes (1979); Piano Sonata (1980); *Rondeau* for Chamber Orch. (1980); Piano Quartet (1980); *Summer Deviation* for Flute, Violin, Viola, Cello, and Piano (1981); *Images* for Bass Clarinet and Marimba (1981); *Eldorado* for Flute, Violin, Clarinet, Piano, and Baryton (1982); Violin Sonata (1983); Symph. No. 2 (1983).

Grainger, Percy Aldridge, celebrated pianist and composer; b. Melbourne, Australia, July 8, 1882; d. White Plains, N.Y., Feb. 20, 1961. He received his early musical training from his mother; at the age of 10, appeared as pianist at several public concerts; then had lessons with Louis Pabst; in 1894, went to Germany, where he studied with Kwast in Frankfurt; also took a few lessons with Busoni. In 1901 he began his concert career in England; then toured South Africa and Australia. In 1906 he met Grieg, who became enthusiastic about Grainger's talent; Grainger's performances of Grieg's Piano Concerto were famous. In 1914, Grainger settled in the U.S.; made a sensational debut in N.Y., on Feb. 11, 1915; gave summer sessions at the Chicago Musical College from 1919 to 1931; was for one academic year (1932–33) chairman of the music dept. of N.Y. Univ. In 1935 he founded a museum in Melbourne, in which he housed all his MSS and his rich collection of musical souvenirs. After 1940 he lived mostly in White Plains, N.Y. He married Ella Viola Ström in 1928 in a spectacular ceremony staged at the Hollywood Bowl, at which he conducted his work *To a Nordic Princess,* written for his bride. Grainger's philosophy of life and art calls for the widest communion of peoples and opinions; his profound study of folk music underlies the melodic and rhythmic structure of his own music; he made a determined effort to re-create in art music the free flow of instinctive songs of the people; he experimented with "gliding" intervals within the traditional scales and polyrhythmic combinations with independent strong beats in the component parts. In a modest way he was a pioneer of electronic music; as early as 1937 he wrote a quartet for electronic instruments, notating the pitch by zigzags and curves. He introduced individual forms of notation and orch. scoring, rejecting the common Italian designations of tempi and dynamics in favor of colloquial Eng. expressions. An eccentric to the last, he directed that his skeleton, after the removal and destruction of the flesh, be placed for preservation and possible display in the Grainger Museum at the Univ. of Melbourne, but his request was declined and he was buried in an ordinary manner. WORKS: FOR ORCH.: *Mock Morris* (1911); *Irish Tunes from County Derry* (1909); *Molly on the Shore; Shepherd's Hey; Colonial Song* (1913); *The Warriors* (music to an imaginary ballet; 1916); *English Dance* for Orch. and Organ (1925); *Ye Banks and Braes o' Bonnie Doon* (1932); *Harvest Hymn* (1933); *Danish Folk-song Suite* (1937). FOR CHAMBER ORCH.: *The Nightingale and the 2 Sisters* (1931). FOR CHORUS AND ORCH.: *Marching Song of Democracy* (1916); *The Merry Wedding* (1916); *Father and Daughter; Sir Eglamore; The Camp; The March of the Men of Harlech; The Hunter in His Career; The Bride's Tragedy; Love Verses from "The Song of Solomon"; Tribute to Foster* (1931). FOR CHORUS AND BRASS BAND: *I'm 17 Come Sunday; We Have Fed Our Seas for a Thousand Years* (1912); *Marching Tune.* FOR A CAPPELLA CHORUS: *Brigg Fair; The Innuit; Morning Song in the Jungle; A Song of Vermland; At Twilight; Tiger-Tiger!; The Immovable Do;* etc. All these are also issued in various arrangements. CHAMBER MUSIC: *Handel in the Strand* (1913); octet, *My Robin Is to the Greenwood Gone; Walking Tune* for Woodwind Quintet; *Green Bushes* (1921); *Hill-Song No. 1* (1923); *Shallow Brown* (1924); *Hill-Song No. 2* (1929); *Spoon River* (1930); *Free Music for Strings* (1935). FOR MILITARY BAND: *Children's March* (1918); march, *The Lads of Wamphrey; Lincolnshire Posy,* 6 folk songs from Lincolnshire, England; settings, in various combinations, of 20 of Kipling's poems (1911–38); 32 settings of British folk songs (1911–38); piano pieces; etc.

Gram, Hans, Danish-born American composer; b. Copenhagen, May 20, 1754; d. Boston, April 28, 1804. He studied philosophy at the Univ. of Copenhagen, and also had some training in music. About 1785 he went to America, and settled in Boston, where he became organist of the Brattle St. Church. He contributed various musical pieces to the *Massachusetts Magazine,* including a curious composition entitled *The Death Song of an Indian Chief* for Voice, 2 Clarinets, 2 Horns, and Strings, which was publ. in the March 1791 issue; it was apparently the first orch. score publ. in the U.S.; he also wrote *Sacred Lines for Thanksgiving Day* (1793) and some other vocal works for the same magazine. He was a co-editor of *The Massachusetts Compiler,* a rather progressive collection on Psalmody, which also contained a music dictionary.

Gram, Peder, Danish conductor and composer; b. Copenhagen, Nov. 25, 1881; d. there, Feb. 4, 1956. After graduation from the Univ. of Copenhagen, he studied music theory at the Leipzig Cons. with Sitt and Krehl and conducting with Nikisch (1904–7). Returning to Copenhagen, he was chief conductor of the Danish Concert Society (1918–32) and the Danish Radio Orch. (1937–51). He publ. in Danish the books *Musikens formlaere i grundtraek* (1916), *Moderne musik* (1934) and *Analytisk harmonilaere* (1947).
WORKS: 3 symphs. (1913, 1925, 1954); *Symphonic Fantasy* (1908); *Poème lyrique* (1911); *Romance* for Violin and Orch. (1911); *Festouverture* (1913); *Avalon* for Soprano and Orch. (1916); Violin Concerto (1920); *Prologue to a Shakespearean Drama* (1928); *Ballet Suite* (1944); *Intrada seria* (1946); 3 string quartets (1906, 1927, 1941); Piano Trio (1910); Cello Sonata (1914); Oboe Sonatina (1935); Wind Quintet (1942); piano pieces; songs.

Gramm, Donald, American bass-baritone; b. Milwaukee, Feb. 26, 1927; d. New York, June 2, 1983. He was of German ancestry, and his family name was **Grambach;** he abbreviated it to Gramm when he began his career as a singer. He studied piano and organ at the Wisconsin College-Conservatory of Music (1935–44); also studied voice with George Graham. He made his professional debut in Chicago at the age of 17 when he sang the role of Raimondo in Donizetti's opera *Lucia di Lammermoor;* he continued his vocal studies at the Chicago Musical College and at the Music Academy of the West in Santa Barbara, where he was a student of Martial Singher. On Sept. 26, 1952, he made his N.Y. debut at the N.Y. City Opera, as Colline in *La Bohème,* and continued to appear with the company for the rest of his life. He was extremely versatile in his roles; he sang Méphistophélès in *Faust,* Leporello in *Don Giovanni,* Figaro in *Le nozze di Figaro,* Falstaff in Verdi's opera, Baron Ochs in *Der Rosenkavalier,* and Scarpia in *Tosca;* on Jan. 10, 1964, he made his

debut at the Metropolitan Opera in N.Y., in the minor role of Truffaldino in *Ariadne auf Naxos;* he also distinguished himself as an interpreter of such difficult parts as Dr. Schön in Berg's *Lulu* and Moses in Schoenberg's *Moses und Aron.*

Granados, Eduardo, Spanish composer, son of **Enrique Granados;** b. Barcelona, July 28, 1894; d. Madrid, Oct. 2, 1928. He studied in Barcelona with his father; then at the Madrid Cons. with Conrado del Campo; taught at the Granados Academy in Barcelona; was also active as a conductor; presented many works by his father. He wrote several zarzuelas, of which the first, *Bufon y Hostelero,* was performed with some success in Barcelona (Dec. 7, 1917); other stage works are: *Los Fanfarrones,* comic opera; *La ciudad eterna,* mystery play; *Los Cigarrales,* operatic sketch; also musical comedies (*Cocktails del Nuevo,* etc.).

Granados, Enrique, outstanding Spanish composer; b. Lérida, July 27, 1867; d. at sea, March 24, 1916 (victim of the sinking by a German submarine of the S.S. *Sussex* in the English Channel). He studied piano at the Barcelona Cons. with Jurnet and Pujol, winning first prize (1883); then studied composition there with Pedrell (1884–87); in 1887 went to Paris to study with Charles de Beriot; made his recital debut in Barcelona in 1890. He first supported himself by playing piano in restaurants and giving private concerts. He attracted attention as a composer with an opera, *Maria del Carmen* (Madrid, Nov. 12, 1898); in 1900 he conducted a series of concerts in Barcelona; also established a music school, the Academia Granados. He then wrote 4 operas, which were produced in Barcelona with little success: *Picarol* (Feb. 23, 1901); *Follet* (April 4, 1903); *Gaziel* (Oct. 27, 1906); and *Liliana* (1911). He undertook the composition of a work that was to be his masterpiece, a series of piano pieces entitled *Goyescas,* inspired by the paintings and etchings of Goya; his fame rests securely on these imaginative and effective pieces, together with his brilliant *Danzas españolas.* Later, Fernando Periquet wrote a libretto based on the scenes from Goya's paintings, and Granados used the music of his piano suite for an opera, *Goyescas.* Its premiere took place, in the presence of the composer, at the Metropolitan Opera in N.Y., on Jan. 28, 1916, with excellent success; the score included an orch. *Intermezzo,* one of his most popular compositions. It was during his return voyage to Europe that he lost his life. Other works by Granados include an intermezzo to *Miel de la Alcarría* (1893); symph. poems, *La nit del mort* and *Dante; Suite arabe; Suite gallega; Marcha de los vencidos; Serenata;* orch. suites, *Elisenda* and *Navidad;* Piano Trio; String Quartet; *Serenata* for 2 Violins and Piano; *Oriental* for Oboe and Strings; *Trova* for Cello and Piano; *Cant de les Estrelles* for Chorus, Organ, and Piano. Piano works: *Danzas españolas* (4 vols.); *Goyescas:* (Part I) *Los Requiebros, Coloquio en la Reja, El fandango del Candil, Quejas o la Maja y el Ruiseñor;* (Part II) *El Amor y la Muerte (Ballade), Epílogo (Serenade of the*

Specter), El Pelele (Escena goyesca); Escenas romanticas; 6 pieces on Spanish popular songs; *Valses poéticos; Cuentos para la juventud; Marche militaire* and *A la Cubana* (also arranged for Orch.); *2 danses caractéristiques: Danza gitana* and *Danza aragonesa.* Songs: *Colección de Tonadillas, escritas en estilo antiguo; Colección de canciones amatorias.* Granados's music is essentially Romantic, with an admixture of specific Spanish rhythms and rather elaborate ornamentation.

Grancino, a family of violin makers, active in the 17th and early 18th centuries. **Andrea Grancino** established a workshop in Milan in 1646; his son, **Paolo,** worked in Milan between 1665 and 1692; he belonged to the Amati school, and several violins attributed to Amati are apparently the work of Paolo Grancino. Paolo's son, **Giovanni,** began making violins in 1677; he is reputed to have been the best of the family. His 2 sons, **Giovanni Battista** and **Francesco,** were active between 1715 and 1746; their labels are marked **Fratelli Grancini.**

Grancino (Grancini), Michel Angelo, Italian composer; b. Milan, 1605; d. there, April 17, 1669. He was organist at the Paradiso Church in Milan as a youth of 17; then was appointed organist at San Sepolcro (1624) and later at San Ambrogio (1628). In 1630 he became a maestro di cappella of the Milan Cathedral, and retained this post until his death. During his lifetime he publ. some 20 vols. of his works, which included madrigals, motets, and *concerti sacri,* only a few of which are extant.

Grandi, Alessandro, Italian composer; b. 1577, place of birth uncertain; d. Bergamo, 1630. He was maestro di cappella in Ferrara, first at the Accademia della Morte (1597–1604), then at the Accademia dello Spirito Santo (1604–16); in 1617 was a singer at San Marco, Venice; in 1620, 2nd maestro di cappella at San Marco; in 1627, he went to Bergamo as maestro di cappella at Santa Maria Maggiore; he and his family died there in 1630 of the plague. He was one of the leading masters of the "stile nuovo" in Italy. His works include 3 books of *Cantade et arie* (Venice, 1620–29); 2 books of *Madrigali concertati* (Venice, 1615–22); several books of motets (Venice, 1610–29); other music in MS is at the Fitzwilliam Museum, Cambridge; Christ Church, Oxford; in Berlin and Vienna.

Grandjany, Marcel, French harpist; b. Paris, Sept. 3, 1891; d. New York, Feb. 24, 1975. He studied at the Paris Cons., winning first prize for harp (1905); made his Paris debut on Jan. 24, 1909; his American debut, N.Y., Feb. 7, 1924; taught at the Fontainebleau Cons. (1921–35); in 1936 settled in N.Y.; became an American citizen in 1945. In 1938 he joined the staff of the Juilliard School of Music; remained there until shortly before his death; also taught at the Montreal Cons. from 1943 to 1963. He composed a *Poème symphonique* for Harp, French Horn, and Orch., and several other works for harp; also songs to French texts. He publ. *First Grade*

Harp Pieces (N.Y., 1964).

Grappelli (Grappelly), Stéphane, French jazz violinist; b. Paris, Jan. 26, 1908. Trained as a classical musician, he turned to jazz, and in 1934 organized the Quintette du Hot Club de France with the Belgian guitarist Django Reinhardt. He became the foremost jazz violinist in the European style of "Le Jazz hot."

Grassi, Eugène, composer; b. Bangkok, Siam, July 5, 1881; d. Paris, June 8, 1941. He was born of French parents in Siam; went to France as a youth and studied with Vincent d'Indy; he revisited Siam in 1910–13 to collect materials on indigenous music; his works reflect this study as well as, in harmonic idiom, the influence of Debussy. Among his compositions, all with oriental flavor, are *Le Revéil de Bouddha,* symph. poem (Paris, Feb. 20, 1920); *Poème de l'univers* for Orch. (Paris, April 9, 1922); *Les Sanctuaires* (Paris, March 25, 1926); also songs in the impressionist manner.

Grassini, Josephina (Giuseppina), Italian contralto; b. Varese, April 8, 1773; d. Milan, Jan. 3, 1850. She studied in Varese with Domenico Zucchinetti and in Milan with Antonio Secchi. She made her debut as an opera singer in Parma in 1789 in Guglielmi's *La pastorella nobile;* sang at La Scala in 1790, and soon attained popularity on all the leading Italian stages; in 1800 she sang in Milan before Napoleon, and became his mistress; he took her with him to Paris, where she sang at national celebrations. She was in London in 1804–6; then returned to Paris and sang at the French court; she was noted for her beauty and her acting, as well as her voice.

Graun, Carl Heinrich, German composer; b. Wahrenbrück, near Dresden, May 7, 1704; d. Berlin, Aug. 8, 1759. He received his primary education at the Kreuzschule in Dresden (1713–20), where he studied with Grundig (voice) and Petzold (organ). He sang soprano in the town council choir; then began to study composition with Johann Christoph Schmidt. In 1725 he was engaged as operatic tenor at the Braunschweig court; soon he began to compose operas for production at the court theater: *Sancio und Sinilde* (Feb. 3, 1727), *Iphigenia in Aulis* (Aug. 16, 1728), *Polidorus* (1731), and *Scipio Africanus* (1732), all to German librettos. On June 14, 1733, he staged his first Italian opera, *Lo specchio della fedeltà* (also known under the title *Timareta;* June 13, 1733). In 1735 Graun was invited by Frederick the Great (then Crown Prince of Prussia) to Rheinsberg, as music director; Graun gladly accepted, and followed Frederick to Berlin when he became King (1740). In Rheinsberg, Graun wrote a great number of cantatas, in the Italian style; in Berlin, his chief duty was to establish an Italian opera troupe, for which purpose he traveled to Italy in search of good singers. Upon his return to Berlin, Graun produced his first opera for his company, *Rodelinda* (Dec. 13, 1741); there followed *Cesare e Cleopatra* (Dec. 7, 1742), staged for the inauguration of the new opera house. He continued to compose operas with unfailing regularity for each season, 28 in all, among them *Artaserse* (Dec. 2, 1743), *Catone in Utica* (Jan. 24, 1744), *Alessandro nell' Indie* (1744), *Adriano in Siria* (Jan. 7, 1746), *Il Mitridate* (Dec. 18, 1750), and *Semiramide* (March 27, 1754). Frederick the Great himself wrote the librettos (in French) for Graun's operas *Montezuma* (Berlin, Jan. 6, 1755; printed in Denkmäler Deutscher Tonkunst, 15) and *La Merope* (March 27, 1756). In those years Graun enjoyed very high renown and royal favor; only Hasse approached him in public esteem. In his operas, Graun adhered to the Italian tradition, and was preoccupied chiefly with the requirements of the singing voice. During the last years of his life he wrote some excellent church music; his *Te Deum* commemorating Frederick's victory at the battle of Prague (1756) is regarded as one of the finest sacred works in Germany; even more renowned is Graun's Passion oratorio, *Der Tod Jesu* (Berlin, March 26, 1755), which was performed annually for a century. Graun's instrumental music displays a high degree of contrapuntal craftsmanship, as well as a facile melodic gift, but despite these qualities, it failed to sustain interest as well as his sacred works did. He wrote a Concerto Grosso for Flute, Violin, Viola da Gamba, Cello, and Strings; about 30 concertos for Harpsichord; 6 flute concertos; 3 quintets for Harpsichord and Strings; about 35 trio sonatas; duets for various instruments; etc.

Graun, Johann Gottlieb, German composer, brother of **Carl Heinrich Graun;** b. Wahrenbrück, near Dresden, 1703; d. Berlin, Oct. 27, 1771. He studied violin with Pisendel in Dresden and with Tartini in Padua. In 1726 he was appointed Konzertmeister in Merseburg, where he was the teacher of Wilhelm Friedemann Bach. In 1732 he became Konzertmeister for Crown Prince Frederick (later Frederick the Great) at Rheinsberg, and from 1741 held a similar position in the newly founded Royal Opera in Berlin, where his brother, Carl Heinrich, was Kapellmeister. His works include 100 symphs., 60 violin concertos, about 8 string quartets, and a number of sacred works. Only a few are publ.: 6 harpsichord concertos; 8 sonatas for 2 Flutes and Violin. Riemann reprinted 3 trio sonatas in *Collegium musicum* (1906).

Graupner, (Johann) Christoph, German composer; b. Kirchberg, Saxony, Jan. 13, 1683; d. Darmstadt, May 10, 1760. He studied music in Kirchberg with the cantor Michael Mylius and the organist Nikolaus Kuster, and later at the Thomasschule in Leipzig with Johann Kuhnau and Johann Schelle; he then went to Hamburg, where he became harpsichordist at the Oper-am-Gänsemarkt (1707–9); during this time he composed 5 operas. In 1709 he was called to Darmstadt as Vice-Kapellmeister to the Landgraf Ernst Ludwig; in 1712 he was appointed Kapellmeister, a post he held until his death. Graupner was a highly industrious composer; he wrote 8 operas, some 1,400 church cantatas, 24 secular cantatas, about 100 symphs., 50 concertos, 80 overtures, and many instrumental sonatas and keyboard works. Several of his compositions were publ. during his lifetime, including *8 Partien auf das Clavier ... erster Theil* (Darmstadt, 1718), the *Monatliche Clavier Früchte ... meistenteils für Anfänger* (Darmstadt, 1722), and *Vier Partien auf das Clavier, unter der Benennung der Vier Jahreszeiten* (Darmstadt, 1733); he also brought out a *Neu vermehrtes Darmstädtisches Choralbuch* (Darmstadt, 1728). He was proficient as an engraver, and printed several keyboard pieces in his own workshop. His operas include *Dido, Königin von Carthago* (Hamburg, 1707); *Il fido amico, oder Der getreue Freund Hercules und Theseus* (Hamburg, 1708; not extant); *L'amore ammalato: Die Krankende Liebe, oder Antiochus und Stratonica* (Hamburg, 1708); *Bellerophon, oder Das in die preussisch Krone verwandelte Wagenstirn* (Hamburg, Nov. 28, 1708; not extant); *Der Fall des grossen Richters in Israel, Simson, oder Die abgekühlte Liebesrache der Deborah* (Hamburg, 1709; not extant); *Berenice und Lucilla, oder Das tugendhafte Lieben* (Darmstadt, March 4, 1710; not extant); *Telemach* (Darmstadt, Feb. 16, 1711; not extant); *La constanza vince l'inganno* (Darmstadt, 1715). The Denkmäler Deutscher Tonkunst, vols. 51–52 (1926), contains 17 of his cantatas; an incomplete edition of his works was edited by F. Noack (4 vols., Kassel, 1955–57).

Graupner, Johann Christian Gottlieb, composer; b. Verden, near Hannover, Germany, Oct. 6, 1767; d. Boston, April 16, 1836. He was the son of the oboist **Johann Georg Graupner,** and became himself an oboist in military bands. In 1788 he was in London, and played in Haydn's orch. in 1791. About 1795, he emigrated to America, settling in Charleston, S.C.; played his Oboe Concerto there on March 21, 1795; early in 1797, he went to Boston; in 1800, he opened a music store; also taught piano, and all orch. instruments, on which he was fairly proficient; publ. works by himself and other composers; he became an American citizen in 1808. In 1810 he organized the Boston Phil. Society, which was the first semiprofessional orch. in Boston; it gave performances of Haydn's symphs., presented the *Messiah* in 1818 and Haydn's *Creation* in 1819; the orch. continued its activity until Nov. 1824. In 1815, Graupner was a co-founder of a musical organization which became the Handel and Haydn Society of Boston, and which greatly influenced the development of choral music in New England. In view of these accomplishments, Graupner is referred to by some writers as the "father of American orchestral music." In 1806, he publ. *Rudiments of the art of playing the piano forte, containing the elements of music* (reprinted 1819, 1825, and 1827). He was married to **Catherine Hillier,** a professional singer (1770–1821); in Boston on Dec. 30, 1799, she sang a Negro ballad; this fact led to erroneous reports that Graupner himself appeared as a blackface minstrel.

Gray, Cecil, British writer on music; b. Edinburgh, May 19, 1895; d. Worthing, Sept. 9, 1951. He studied music with Healey Willan; in 1920, with Philip Heseltine (Peter Warlock), he edited a new magazine of music criticism, the *Sackbut;* later was music critic for the *Daily Telegraph* and the *Manchester Guardian;* wrote 3 operas (to his own texts) and other music.

WRITINGS: *A Survey of Contemporary Music* (1924); *Carlo Gesualdo, Prince of Venosa; Musician and Murderer* (in collaboration with Philip Heseltine; 1926); *The History of Music* (1928); *Sibelius* (1931); *Peter Warlock* (1934); *Sibelius: The Symphonies* (1935); *Predicaments, or Music and the Future* (1936); *The 48 Preludes and Fugues of Bach* (1938); *Contingencies* (N.Y., 1947); memoirs, *Musical Chairs or Between Two Stools* (London, 1948).

Gray, Linda Esther, Scottish soprano; b. Greenock, May 29, 1948. She studied at the Scottish Academy of Music and in London with Eva Turner; won the Kathleen Ferrier and John Christie awards in 1973. She made her debut with the Glyndebourne Touring Opera in 1972 as Mimi; sang with the Glyndebourne Festival in 1974 and with the Scottish Opera in 1975 in the roles of Donna Elvira, Ariadne, Eva, and Amelia. Her first role with the English National Opera was Micaela in 1978; she later sang Aida, Tosca, and Isolde there. She also sang Isolde with the Welsh National Opera in 1979 and Sieglinde at Covent Garden. She made her U.S. debut in Dallas as Sieglinde in 1981; then appeared as Beethoven's Leonore with the same company in Mexico.

Greatorex, Thomas, English organist, singer, and conductor; b. North Wingfield, Derby, Oct. 5, 1758; d. Hampton, near London, July 18, 1831. He was the son of an amateur organist; the family moved to Leicester in 1767. He studied with Dr. B. Cooke (1772); was befriended by Lord Sandwich and became music director of his household for a time. He sang at the Concerts of Antient Music in London (from 1776) and was organist at Carlisle Cathedral (1781–84). He then traveled in the Netherlands, Italy, and France, and took lessons in Strasbourg with Pleyel. Settling in London, he became a highly popular singing teacher (in one week he gave 84 lessons at a guinea each). In 1793 he was appointed conductor of the Concerts of Antient Music, a post which he held until his death, never missing a single concert. He assisted in the revival of the Vocal Concerts in 1801; from 1819 he was organist at Westminster Abbey; he conducted festivals throughout England, and was one of the founders of the Royal Academy of Music in London (1822). He publ. *A Selection of Tunes* (London, 1829); the collection *Parochial Psalmody* (1825); *12 Glees* (1832); anthems; Psalms; and chants; but it was as an organist that Greatorex was best known.

Greenawald, Sheri, American soprano; b. Iowa City, Nov. 12, 1947. After completing her vocal studies, she quickly rose to prominence through her appearances with the Santa Fe Opera, Cincinnati Opera, San Francisco Opera, Houston Grand Opera, Washington Opera, and others; in addition to her roles in the standard Italian and French operatic repertoires, she sang in the world premieres of Pasatieri's *Signor Deluso* (1974) and *Washington Square* (1976) and Bernstein's *A Quiet Place* (1983). She was also a soloist with the Boston Symph., Philadelphia Orch., San Francisco Symph., Cleveland Orch., and St. Louis Symph.

Greenberg, Noah, American conductor; b. New York, April 9, 1919; d. there, Jan. 9, 1966. He studied music privately; served in the U.S. Merchant Marine (1944–49); organized choruses in N.Y. In 1952 he founded the N.Y. Pro Musica Antiqua, an organization specializing in Renaissance and medieval music, performed in authentic styles and on copies of early instruments; revived the medieval liturgical music dramas *The Play of Daniel* (1958) and *The Play of Herod* (1963); traveled with his ensemble in Europe in 1960 and 1963. It was primarily through the efforts of the N.Y. Pro Musica Antiqua (later known as the N.Y. Pro Musica) that early music, formerly known only to musicologists, became a viable idiom available to modern audiences. Greenberg held a Guggenheim fellowship in 1955 and Ford fellowships in 1960 and 1962.

Greene, Harry Plunket, Irish singer; b. near Dublin, June 24, 1865; d. London, Aug. 19, 1936. He studied in Florence with Vannuccini, and in London under J.B. Welsh and A. Blume; made his debut in the *Messiah* at Stepney (Jan. 21, 1888) and soon became a popular concert artist. He made the first of several tours of the U.S. in 1893; also appeared in Canada. He was noted for his interpretations of Schumann and Brahms; publ. a valuable instruction book for singers, *Interpretation in Song* (London, 1912); a biography of Stanford (London, 1935); and a vol. of musical reminiscences, *From Blue Danube to Shannon.*

Greene, Maurice, English organist and composer; b. London, Aug. 12, 1696; d. there, Dec. 1, 1755. He served as a choirboy in St. Paul's Cathedral; became proficient as an organist; was appointed organist of St. Paul's in 1718. In 1727, he succeeded Croft as composer to the Chapel Royal; in 1730, he was Tudway's successor as prof. of music at the Univ. of Cambridge, receiving the title of Mus.Doc. In 1735, he became Master of the King's Musick. Beginning in 1750, he accumulated and collated a great number of English sacred works; he willed this material to Boyce, who made use of it in his monumental collection, *Cathedral Music.*

WORKS: 3 oratorios: *The Song of Deborah and Barak* (1732); *Jephtha* (1737); *The Force of Truth* (1744); 3 dramatic pastorals: *Florimel, or Love's Revenge* (1734); *The Judgment of Hercules* (1740); *Phoebe* (1747); a collection of 12 English songs, *The Chaplet;* an album of 25 sonnets for Voice, with Harpsichord and Violin, *Spenser's Amoretti;* he collected *40 Select Anthems in Score* (2 vols., 1743); composed numerous catches and canons, organ voluntaries, harpsichord pieces, etc.

Greenhouse, Bernard, American cellist; b. Newark, N.J., Jan. 3, 1916. He studied cello with Felix Salmond at the Juilliard School of Music in N.Y.; subsequently took lessons with Feuermann and Casals. He made his debut in N.Y. in a recital in 1946; in 1955 he became a founding member of the Beaux Arts Trio, which gradually acquired a fine reputation in its genre. He was also active as a teacher; taught at the Juilliard School of Music (1950–62), the Manhattan School of Music (1950–72), the Indiana Univ. School of Music (1956–64), the Univ. of Hartford (1962–71), and N.Y. State Univ. (1965–72).

Gregor, Christian Friedrich, composer and hymnologist; b. Dirsdorf, Silesia, Jan. 1, 1723; d. Zeist, the Netherlands, Nov. 6, 1801. As an organist, music director, composer, and hymnologist, Gregor was the most important musician of the international Moravian Church (Unitas Fratrum) of the 18th century. Joining the Moravian Brethren in 1742, he soon assumed leading positions in its management: was financial agent of Zinzendorf, member of the Unity Elders Conference (1764–1801), and bishop (1789–1801). He made numerous business trips to Germany, the Netherlands, England, Russia, and North America (Pennsylvania, 1770–72); while in Pennsylvania, he gave instruction in composition to Johann Friedrich Peter. During his stay at Herrnhut, Saxony, as organist, Gregor compiled the first hymnal publ. by the Moravians (*Choral-Buch, enthaltend alle zu dem Gesangbuche der Evangelischen Brüder-Gemeinen vom Jahre 1778 gehörige Melodien*; Leipzig, 1784) and arranged the musical liturgies.

Gregory I, "the Great"; b. Rome, 540; d. there, March 12, 604. He was Pope from 590 to 604; was celebrated in music history as the reputed reformer of the musical ritual of the Roman Catholic Church. It is traditionally believed that by his order, and under his supervision, a collection was made in 599 of the music employed in the different churches; that various offertories, antiphons, responses, etc., were revised and regularly and suitably distributed over the entire year in an arrangement which came to be known as Gregorian chant. While for centuries the sole credit for the codification, which certainly took place, had been ascribed to Gregory, investigations by such scholars as Gevaert, Riemann, P. Wagner, Frere, Houdard, Gastoué, Mocquereau, and others have demonstrated that some of Gregory's predecessors had begun this reform and even fixed the order of certain portions of the liturgy, and that the work of reform was definitely completed under some of his immediate successors. Evidence in favor of Gregory's leading part in the reform is marshaled in E.G.P. Wyatt's *Saint Gregory and the Gregorian Music* (1904); evidence against his participation is given in Paul Henry Lang's *Music in Western Civilization* (N.Y., 1941). See also G. Morin, *Les Véritables Origines du Chant grégorien* (Maredsous, 1890); W. Brambach, *Gregorianisch* (Leipzig, 1895); F.H. Duddin, *Gregory the Great* (2 vols., London, 1905); F. Tarducci, *Storia*

di S. Gregorius e del suo tempo (Rome, 1909); P.C. Vivell, *Der gregorianische Gesang: Eine Studie über die Echtheit der Tradition* (Graz, 1904).

Gretchaninov, Alexander, Russian composer; b. Moscow, Oct. 25, 1864; d. New York, Jan. 3, 1956. He studied at the Moscow Cons. (1881–91) with Safonov (piano) and Arensky (composition); then entered the St. Petersburg Cons. as a pupil of Rimsky-Korsakov (1891–1903); was a prof. of composition at the Moscow Inst. until 1922; then lived in Paris; visited the U.S., where he appeared with considerable success as guest conductor of his own works (1929–31); came to the U.S. again in 1939, settling in N.Y. He became an American citizen on July 25, 1946. He continued to compose until the end of his long life. A concert of his works was presented on his 90th birthday at Town Hall in N.Y. (Oct. 25, 1954) in the presence of the composer. A complete catalogue of his works is appended to his autobiography, *My Life.* His music is rooted in the Russian national tradition; influences of both Tchaikovsky and Rimsky-Korsakov are in evidence in his early works; toward 1910 he attempted to inject some impressionistic elements into his vocal compositions, but without signal success. His masterly sacred works are of historical importance, for he introduced a reform into Russian church singing by using nationally colored melodic patterns; in several of his masses he employed instrumental accompaniment contrary to the prescriptions of the Russian Orthodox faith, a circumstance that precluded the use of these works in Russian churches. His *Missa oecumenica* represents a further expansion toward ecclesiastical universality; in this work he makes use of elements pertaining to other religious music, including non-Christian. His instrumental works are competently written, but show less originality than his vocal music. His early *Lullaby* (1887) and the song *Over the Steppes* still retain their popularity, and have been publ. in numerous arrangements.
WORKS: OPERAS: *Dobrinya Nikititch* (Moscow, Oct. 27, 1903); *Sister Beatrice* (Moscow, Oct. 25, 1912; suppressed after 3 perfs. as being irreverent); *The Dream of a Little Christmas Tree,* children's opera (1911); *The Castle Mouse,* children's opera (1921); *The Cat, the Fox, and the Rooster,* children's opera (1919); *Marriage,* comic opera after Gogol (1945–46; Berkshire Music Festival, Aug. 1, 1948); *Idylle forestière,* ballet divertissement for Orch. (N.Y., 1925); incidental music to Ostrovsky's *Snegurotchka* (Moscow, Nov. 6, 1900), A. Tolstoy's *Tsar Feodor* (Moscow, Oct. 26, 1898), and *Death of Ivan the Terrible* (1899). FOR ORCH.: Concert Overture in D minor (1892; St. Petersburg, March 1893); *Elegy in Memory of Tchaikovsky* (1893; St. Petersburg, Dec. 31, 1898, Rimsky-Korsakov conducting); 5 symphs: No. 1 (1893; St. Petersburg, Jan. 26, 1895); No. 2 (1909; Moscow, March 14, 1909); No. 3 (1920–23; Kiev, May 29, 1924); No. 4 (1923–24; N.Y., April 9, 1942); No. 5 (1936; Philadelphia, April 5, 1939); *Poème élégiaque* (Boston, March 29, 1946); *Festival Overture* (Indianapolis, Nov. 15, 1946); *Poème lyrique* (1948). Vo-

CAL WORKS: *Liturgy of St. John Chrysostom* (Moscow, Oct. 19, 1898); *Laudate Deum* (Moscow, Nov. 24, 1915); *Liturgia domestica* (Moscow, March 30, 1918); *Missa oecumenica* for Soli, Chorus, and Orch. (Boston, Feb. 25, 1944); 84 choruses; 14 vocal quartets; 8 duets; 258 songs (some with orch.). CHAMBER MUSIC: 4 string quartets, 2 trios, Violin Sonata, Cello Sonata, 2 clarinet sonatas, 2 *Miniatures* for Saxophone and Piano. FOR PIANO: 2 sonatas (2nd in 1944); *Petits tableaux musicaux* (1947); etc. After the Revolution, Gretchaninov wrote a new Russian national anthem, *Hymn of Free Russia* (sung in N.Y. at a concert for the benefit of Siberian exiles, May 22, 1917), but it was never adopted by any political Russian faction. He wrote 201 opus numbers in all; op. 201 is a chorus a cappella, *Have Mercy O God.*

Grétry, André Ernest Modeste, greatly significant French opera composer; b. Liège, Feb. 8, 1741; d. Montmorency, near Paris, Sept. 24, 1813. His father was a violinist at the church of St. Martin in Liège; at the age of 9, Grétry was entered as a chorister at the St. Denis Church, but was dismissed 2 years later. At 12, he began to study violin and singing; he learned music under Leclerc and the organist Nicolas Rennekin; studied composition with Moreau. About 1754 an Italian opera company gave a season in Liège, and young Grétry thus received his first impulse toward dramatic music. His early works were instrumental; in 1758, he wrote 6 small symphs.; his next work was a Mass, which interested the ecclesiastical authorities; as a result, he was enabled (through the Canon du Harlez) to go to Rome, where he entered the College de Liège (1761–65), a school founded for the education of natives of Liège. There he studied diligently, and composed several church works, 6 string quartets, a Flute Concerto, and 2 intermezzos, including *Le Vendemmiatrici,* which was produced in Rome in 1765. In 1766, he was in Geneva as a music teacher. He met Voltaire, who advised him to go to Paris; before his departure, he produced in Geneva a stage work, *Isabelle et Gertrude,* to a libretto by Favart, after Voltaire. He arrived in Paris in the autumn of 1767; he sought the patronage of aristocrats and diplomats; the Swedish ambassador, Count de Creutz, gave him the first encouragement by obtaining for him Marmontel's comedy *Le Huron;* it was performed with Grétry's music at the Comédie-Italienne (Aug. 20, 1768). From then on, Grétry produced operas one after another, without interruption, even during the years of the French Revolution.

The merit of Grétry's operas lies in their melodies and dramatic expression. He was not deeply versed in the science of music; yet despite this lack of craftsmanship in harmony and counterpoint, he achieved fine effects of vocal and instrumental writing. His operas suffered temporary eclipse when Méhul and Cherubini entered the field, but public interest was revived by the magnificent tenor Elleviou, in 1801. The changes in operatic music during the next 30 years caused the neglect of Grétry's works. Nevertheless, Grétry—"the Molière of music," as he was called—founded the school of

French opéra-comique, of which Boieldieu, Auber, and Adam have been such distinguished alumni. During his lifetime, he was greatly honored: he was elected a member of many artistic and learned institutions in France and abroad; the Prince-Bishop of Liège made him a privy councillor in 1784; a street in Paris was named for him in 1785; he was admitted to the Institut de France in 1795, as one of the first 3 chosen to represent the dept. of musical composition; in 1795 he was also appointed Inspector of the Paris Cons., but resigned in a few months; a bust of him was placed in the Grand Opéra foyer, and a marble statue in the entrance hall of the Opéra-Comique; Napoleon made him a Chevalier of the Legion of Honor in 1802, and granted him a pension of 4,000 francs in compensation for losses during the Revolution. Grétry bought "L'Ermitage," Rousseau's former residence at Montmorency, and lived there in retirement. He was married, and had several children, but survived them all. His daughter, **Lucille** (real name, **Angélique-Dorothée-Lucie;** b. Paris, July 15, 1772; d. there, Aug. 25, 1790), was a gifted musician who died young; at the age of 13, with some assistance from her father, she composed an opera, *Le Mariage d'Antonio,* which was produced at the Opéra-Comique, July 29, 1786; her 2nd opera, *Toinette et Louis,* was produced on March 23, 1787. Grétry's *Mémoires ou Essais sur la musique* was publ. in 1789 (reprinted in 1797 with 2 additional vols. ed. by his friend, Legrand; in German, in 1800 at Leipzig, with critical and historical annotations by K. Spazier; in 3 vols. by Mass in 1829 and an enlarged ed. by P. Magnette, Liège, 1914). In these essays, Grétry set forth his views on the paramount importance of the just declamation of every syllable set to music. He also wrote a *Méthode simple pour apprendre à préluder en peu de temps avec toutes les resources de l'harmonie* (1802) and *De la Vérité,* an ardent avowal of Republican tenets, with remarks on the feelings and the best means of exciting and expressing them by music (1803); his *Réflexions sur l'art,* in 6 vols., was never publ. During the last years of his life he wrote *Réflexions d'un solitaire;* his friends did not think its publication was advisable; the MS was considered lost until C. Malherbe discovered it in 1908; it was publ. in 4 vols., edited by L. Solvay and E. Closson (Brussels and Paris, 1919–22). Besides his dramatic works, Grétry composed a *De Profundis, Confiteor,* a Requiem, an antiphon, motets, and a good deal of instrumental music. Under the auspices of the Belgian government, a complete edition of his works was publ. in 1883–97, under the editorship of Gevaert and others.

WORKS: The list of his operas is long; they include *Lucile* (Paris, Jan. 5, 1769); *Le Tableau parlant* (Paris, Sept. 20, 1769; very popular); *Les Deux Avares* (Fontainebleau, Oct. 27, 1770); *Sylvain* (Paris, Feb. 19, 1770); *L'Amitié à l'épreuve* (Fontainebleau, Nov. 13, 1770); *L'Ami de la maison* (Fontainebleau, Oct. 26, 1771); *Zémire et Azor* (Fontainebleau, Nov. 9, 1771); *Le Magnifique* (Paris, March 4, 1773); *La Rosière de Salency* (Fontainebleau, Oct. 23, 1773); *Céphale et Procris, ou L'Amour conjugal* (Versailles, Dec. 30, 1773); *La Fausse Magie* (Paris,

Feb. 1, 1775); *Les Mariages samnites* (3 acts, from the one-act opera of 1768; Paris, June 12, 1776); *Amour pour amour* (Versailles, March 10, 1777); *Matroco* (Chantilly, Nov. 12, 1777); *Le Jugement de Midas* (Paris, March 28, 1778); *Les Fausses Apparences, ou L'Amant jaloux* (Versailles, Nov. 20, 1778); *Les Événements imprévus* (Versailles, Nov. 11, 1779); *Aucassin et Nicolette, ou Les Mœurs du bon vieux temps* (Versailles, Dec. 30, 1779); *Andromaque* (Paris, June 6, 1780); *Emilie* (Paris, Feb. 22, 1781); *La Double Epreuve, ou Colinette à la Cour* (Paris, Jan. 1, 1782); *Le Sage dans sa retraite* (The Hague, Sept. 19, 1782); *L'Embarras de richesses* (Nov. 26, 1782); *La Caravane du Caire* (Fontainebleau, Oct. 30, 1783); *Théodore et Paulin* (Versailles, March 5, 1784); *Richard Cœur de Lion* (his greatest masterpiece; Paris, Oct. 21, 1784); *Panurge dans l'isle des lanternes* (Paris, Jan. 25, 1785); *Amphitrion* (Versailles, March 15, 1786); *Les Méprises par ressemblance* (Fontainebleau, Nov. 7, 1786); *Le Comte d'Albert* (Fontainebleau, Nov. 13, 1786); *Le Prisonnier anglois* (Paris, Dec. 26, 1787; with alterations in 1793 as *Clarice et Belton*); *Le Rival confident* (Paris, June 26, 1788); *Raoul Barbe-Bleue* (Paris, March 2, 1789); *Aspasie* (Paris, March 17, 1789); *Pierre le grand* (Paris, Jan. 13, 1790); *Guillaume Tell* (Paris, April 9, 1791); *Cécile et Ermancé, ou Les Deux Couvents* (Paris, Jan. 16, 1792); *A Trompeur, trompeur et demi* (Paris, Sept. 24, 1792); *Joseph Barra* (Paris, June 5, 1794); *Denys le tyran, maître d'école à Corinthe* (Paris, Aug. 23, 1794); *La Rosière républicaine, ou La Fête de la vertu* (Paris, Sept. 3, 1794); *Callias, ou Nature et patrie* (Paris, Sept. 18, 1794); *Lisbeth* (Paris, Jan. 10, 1797); *Anacréon chez Polycrate* (Paris, Jan. 17, 1797); *Le Barbier de village, ou Le Revenant* (Paris, May 6, 1797); *Elisca, ou L'Amour maternel* (Paris, Jan. 1, 1799); *Le Casque et les colombes* (Paris, Nov. 7, 1801); *Delphis et Mopsa* (Paris, Feb. 15, 1803).

Grieg, Edvard Hagerup, celebrated Norwegian composer; b. Bergen, June 15, 1843; d. there, Sept. 4, 1907. The original form of the name was **Greig.** His great-grandfather, Alexander Greig, of Scotland, emigrated to Norway about 1765, and changed his name to Grieg (see J. Russell Greig, "Grieg and His Scottish Ancestry," in Hinrichsen's *Music Year Book,* 1952). Grieg received his first instruction in music from his mother, an amateur pianist. At the suggestion of the Norwegian violinist Ole Bull, young Grieg was sent to the Leipzig Cons. (1858), where he studied piano with Plaidy and Wenzel, and later with Moscheles; and theory with E.F. Richter, Robert Papperitz, Moritz Hauptmann, and Reinecke. He became immersed in the atmosphere of German Romanticism, with the esthetic legacy of Mendelssohn and Schumann; Grieg's early works are permeated with lyric moods related to these influences. In 1863 he went to Copenhagen, where he took a brief course of study with Niels Gade. In Copenhagen, he also met the young Norwegian composer Rikard Nordraak, with whom he organized the Euterpe Society for the promotion of national Scandinavian music, in opposition to the German influences dominating Scandinavian music. The premature death of Nordraak at the age of 23 (1866) left Grieg alone to carry on the project. After traveling in Italy, he returned to Norway, where he opened a Norwegian Academy of Music (1867), and gave concerts of Norwegian music; he was also engaged as conductor of the Harmonic Society in Christiania (Oslo). In 1867 he married his cousin, the singer **Nina Hagerup.** At that time he had already composed his 2 violin sonatas and the first set of his *Lyric Pieces* for Piano, which used Norwegian motifs. On April 3, 1869, Grieg played the solo part in the world premiere of his Piano Concerto, which took place in Copenhagen. Thus, at the age of 25, he established himself as a major composer of his time. In 1874–75 he wrote incidental music to Ibsen's *Peer Gynt;* the 2 orch. suites arranged from this music became extremely popular. The Norwegian government granted him an annuity of 1,600 crowns, which enabled him to devote most of his time to composition. Performances of his works were given in Germany with increasing frequency; soon his fame spread all over Europe. On May 3, 1888, he gave a concert of his works in London; he also prepared recitals of his songs with his wife. He revisited England frequently; received the honorary degree of Mus.Doc. from Cambridge (1894) and Oxford (1906). Other honors were membership in the Swedish Academy (1872), the French Academy (1890), etc. Despite his successes, Grieg was of a retiring disposition, and spent most of his later years in his house at Troldhaugen, near Bergen, avoiding visitors and shunning public acclaim. However, he continued to compose at a steady rate. His death, of heart disease, was mourned by all Norway; he was given a state funeral and his remains were cremated, at his own request, and sealed in the side of a cliff projecting over the fjord at Troldhaugen.

Grieg's importance as a composer lies in the strongly pronounced nationalism of his music; without resorting to literal quotation from Norwegian folk songs, he succeeded in re-creating their melodic and rhythmic flavor. In his harmony, he remained well within the bounds of tradition; the lyric expressiveness of his best works and the contagious rhythm of his dancelike pieces imparted a charm and individuality which contributed to the lasting success of his art. His unassuming personality made friends for him among his colleagues; he was admired by Brahms and Tchaikovsky. The combination of lyricism and nationalism in Grieg's music led some critics to describe him as "the Chopin of the North." He excelled in miniatures, in which the perfection of form and the clarity of the musical line are remarkable; the unifying purpose of Grieg's entire creative life is exemplified by his lyric pieces for piano. He composed 10 sets of these pieces in 34 years, between 1867 and 1901. His songs, which he wrote for his wife, are distinguished by the same blend of Romantic and characteristically national inflections. In orch. composition, Grieg limited himself to symph. suites, and arrangements of his piano pieces; in chamber music, his 3 violin sonatas, a Cello Sonata, and a String Quartet are examples of fine instrumental writing. Publication of a complete list of his works began in Frankfurt in 1977.

WORKS: For ORCH.: Symph. in C (1864; Grieg withdrew it after several early perfs.; it was revived at the Bergen Festival on May 30, 1981); *In Autumn,* concert overture (op. 11, 1865); *2 Elegiac Melodies* for String Orch. (op. 34, based on songs from op. 33: *The Wounded One* and *The Last Spring*); Concerto in A minor for Piano and Orch. (op. 16, 1868); *Norwegian Dances* (op. 35, 1881); *Holberg Suite* for String Orch. (op. 40, 1884–85); *Peer Gynt Suite* No. 1 (op. 46, 1876; includes *Morning, Aase's Death, Anitra's Dance, In the Hall of the Mountain King*); *2 Melodies* for String Orch. (op. 53, 1891; based on songs from op. 21 and op. 23: *Norwegian* and *First Meeting*); *Peer Gynt Suite* No. 2 (op. 55, 1876; includes *The Abduction and Ingrid's Lament, Arab Dance, Peer Gynt's Homecoming, Solveig's Song*); *Sigurd Jorsalfar Suite* (op. 56, 1872); *2 Norwegian Melodies* for String Orch. (op. 63, 1894–95; based on melodies from op. 17: *In the Style of a Folk Song* and *Cowkeeper's Tune and Peasant Dance*); *Symphonic Dances* (1898); *Evening in the Mountains* for Oboe, Horn, and Strings (arranged from op. 68, no. 4; 1898); *At the Cradle* for String Orch. (arranged from op. 68, no. 5; 1898); *Funeral March in Memory of Rikard Nordraak* for Military Band (arranged from the Piano Solo written in 1866); *Lyric Suite* (arranged from piano solos, op. 54, 1891; includes *Shepherd Boy, Norwegian March, Nocturne, March of the Dwarfs*). CHAMBER MUSIC: Sonata in F for Violin and Piano (op. 8, 1865); Sonata in G minor for Violin and Piano (op. 13, 1867); String Quartet in G minor (op. 27, 1877–78); Sonata in A minor for Cello and Piano (op. 36, 1883); Sonata in C minor for Violin and Piano (op. 45, 1886–87); String Quartet in F (2 movements only; 1892). CHORAL WORKS: *At a Southern Convent's Gate* (op. 20, 1871); 2 songs from *Sigurd Jorsalfar* (op. 22, 1870); *Album for Male Voices* (op. 30, 1877); *Landsighting* (op. 31, 1872); *Scenes from "Olav Trygvason"* (op. 50, 1873); *Ave Maris Stella* (no opus number); *4 Psalms* (op. 74, 1906); he also wrote *The Bewitched One* for Baritone, with Strings and 2 Horns (op. 32, 1878), and the ballad *Bergliot* for Declamation and Orch. (op. 42, 1870–71). He wrote the incidental music for Björnson's *Sigurd Jorsalfar* (Christiania, April 10, 1872) and Ibsen's *Peer Gynt* (Christiania, Feb. 24, 1876), from which the suites so named were taken. FOR PIANO: Piano solos: 4 pieces (op. 1, 1862); *Poetic Tone-Pictures* (op. 3, 1863); *Humoresker* (op. 6, 1865); Sonata in E minor (op. 7, 1865); *Funeral March in Memory of Rikard Nordraak* (1866); 10 sets of *Lyric Pieces* (Book 1, op. 12, 1867; Book 2, op. 38, 1883; Book 3, op. 43, 1884; Book 4, op. 47, 1888; Book 5, op. 54, 1891; Book 6, op. 57, 1893; Book 7, op. 62, 1895; Book 8, op. 65, 1896; Book 9, op. 68, 1898; Book 10, op. 71, 1901; among the most famous individual numbers of the *Lyric Pieces* are: *Butterfly, Erotik,* and *To Spring* in Book 3; *March of the Dwarfs* in Book 5); *Norwegian Dances and Songs* (op. 17, 1870); *Scenes from Peasant Life* (op. 19, 1872); *Ballad in the Form of Variations on a Norwegian Folk Song* (op. 24, 1875); *Album Leaves* (op. 28, 1864, 1874, 1876, 1878); *Improvisations on Norwegian Folk Songs*

(op. 29, 1878); *Holberg Suite* (op. 40, 1884); *Norwegian Folk Melodies* (op. 66, 1896); *Norwegian Peasant Dances* (op. 72, 1902); *Moods* (op. 73, 1906); *6 Norwegian Mountain Tunes* (no opus number); 3 piano pieces (no opus number; nos. 2 and 3 written in 1898 and 1891); arrangements for piano solo of a number of his songs and orch. works; original piano duets: *Norwegian Dances for 4 Hands* (op. 35, 1881); *Valses-Caprices* (op. 37, 1883); 2nd piano parts to 4 piano sonatas by Mozart (1877). SONGS: 25 sets of songs to German and Norwegian words; of these, *I Love Thee* attained enormous popularity; song cycle, *Haugtussa* (*A Child of the Mountains* op. 67, 1895). An ed. of his works, in 20 vols., is projected by the Edvard Grieg Committee, in Oslo.

Grieg, Nina (née **Hagerup**), Norwegian singer, wife of **Edvard Grieg;** b. near Bergen, Nov. 24, 1845; d. Copenhagen, Dec. 9, 1935. Her father, Herman Hagerup, was a brother of Grieg's mother. She studied singing with Helsted; she met Grieg in Copenhagen, and married him on June 11, 1867. Her interpretations of Grieg's songs elicited much praise from the critics.

Griffes, Charles Tomlinson, outstanding American composer; b. Elmira, N.Y., Sept. 17, 1884; d. New York, April 8, 1920. He studied piano with a local teacher, Mary S. Broughton; also took organ lessons. In 1903, he went to Berlin, where he was a pupil of Gottfried Galston (piano) and of Rüfer and Humperdinck (composition). To eke out his living, he gave private lessons; also played his own compositions in public recitals. In 1907, he returned to the U.S., and took a music teacher's job at the Hackley School for Boys at Tarrytown, N.Y.; at the same time he continued to study music by himself; he was fascinated by the exotic art of the French Impressionists, and investigated the potentialities of oriental scales. He also was strongly influenced by the Russian school, particularly Mussorgsky and Scriabin. A combination of natural talent and determination to acquire a high degree of craftsmanship elevated Griffes to the position of a foremost American composer in the impressionist genre; despite changes of taste, his works retain an enduring place in American music.

WORKS: His best are *The White Peacock* for Piano (1917; also for Orch., Philadelphia, Stokowski conducting, Dec. 19, 1919) and the tone poem *The Pleasure Dome of Kubla Khan,* after Coleridge (Boston Symph. Orch., Nov. 28, 1919); others are *The Kairn of Koridwen,* dance drama for 5 Woodwinds, Celesta, Harp, and Piano (N.Y., Feb. 10, 1917); *Shojo,* Japanese pantomimic drama for 4 Woodwinds, 4 Muted Strings, Harp, and Percussion (1917); *Poem* for Flute and Orch. (N.Y., Nov. 16, 1919); *2 Sketches on Indian Themes* for String Quartet (1922); for Piano: *3 Tone Pictures* (*The Lake at Evening, The Vale of Dreams,* and *The Night Winds;* 1915); *Fantasy Pieces* (*Barcarolle, Notturno,* and *Scherzo;* 1915); *Roman Sketches* (*White Peacock, Nightfall, The Fountain of Acqua Paola,* and *Clouds;* 1917); Sonata in F (Feb. 26, 1918); vocal works: *These*

Things Shall Be for Unison Chorus (1917); songs to German texts (*Auf geheimen Waldespfade, Auf dem Teich*, etc.); songs to Eng. words: *The First Snowfall, The Half-ring Moon, Evening Song; Tone Images* (*La Fuite de la lune, Symphony in Yellow*, and *We'll to the Woods, and Gather May;* 1915); 2 *Rondels* (*Come, love, across the sunlit land* and *This book of hours;* 1915); 3 *Poems* (*In a Myrtle Shade, Waikiki*, and *Phantoms;* 1916); 5 *Poems of Ancient China and Japan* (*So-Fei gathering flowers, Landscape, The Old Temple, Tears*, and *A Feast of Lanterns;* 1917); 3 *Poems* (*The Lament of Ian the Proud, Thy Dark Eyes to Mine*, and *The Rose of the Night;* 1918); *An Old Song Re-sung* (1920).

Grimm, Friedrich Melchior (Baron von), German writer; b. Regensburg, Sept. 25, 1723; d. Gotha, Dec. 19, 1807. He went to Paris in 1750 and remained there till the Revolution, frequenting literary and musical circles and taking an active part in all controversies; his "Lettre sur Omphale" in the *Mercure de France* (1752) took the side of Italian opera in the "guerre des bouffons," but some years later he upheld Gluck against the Italian faction supporting Piccinni. He edited the *Correspondance littéraire, philosophique et critique*, which offers important data on French opera (standard ed. in 16 vols., Paris, 1877–82). He befriended the Mozarts on their first visit to Paris (see the many references to him in E. Anderson, *Letters of Mozart and His Family*, London, 1938; 2nd ed., revised, 1966, by A. Hyatt King and M. Carolan). He also wrote a satire on J. Stamitz, *Le Petit Prophète de Boehmisch-Broda;* reproduced in Eng. in O. Strunk's *Source Readings in Music History* (N.Y., 1950).

Grimm, Heinrich, German composer; b. Holzminden, c.1593; d. Braunschweig, July 10, 1637. He studied with Michael Praetorius; then studied theology at the Univ. of Helmstedt; in 1619, became rector of the Magdeburg town school; in 1631, when the town was destroyed, he fled with his family to Braunschweig, where he became a cantor at the church of St. Catherine; subsequently was a cantor at St. Andreas's church (1632–37). He was an exponent of the concerted style, with thorough-bass, at that time still a novel technique in Germany. His extant works include masses, Psalms, Passions, and several pedagogical works; he publ. *Unterricht, wie ein Knabe nach der alten Guidonischen Art zu solmisieren leicht angeführt werden kann* (Magdeburg, 1624) and *Instrumentum Instrumentorum* (1629); prepared a combined edition of *Melopoeia seu melodiae condendae ratio* by Calvisius and *Pleiades Musicae* by Baryphonus (Magdeburg, 1630).

Grisar, Albert, Belgian dramatic composer; b. Antwerp (of German-Belgian parentage), Dec. 26, 1808; d. Asnières, near Paris, June 15, 1869. He studied for a short time (1830) with Reicha in Paris. Returning to Antwerp, he brought out his opera *Le Mariage impossible* (Brussels, March 4, 1833), and obtained a government subsidy for further study in Paris. On April 26, 1836, he produced *Sarah* at the Opéra-Comique; then *L'An mille* (June 23, 1837), *La Suisse à Trianon* (March 8, 1838), *Lady Melvil* (Nov. 15, 1838, with Flotow), *L'Eau merveilleuse* (Jan. 31, 1839, with Flotow), *Le Naufrage de la Méduse* (May 31, 1839, with Flotow and Pilati), *Les Travestissements* (Nov. 16, 1839), and *L'Opéra à la cour* (July 16, 1840, with Boieldieu, Jr.). In 1840 he went to Naples for further serious study under Mercadante; returning to Paris in 1848, he brought out *Gilles ravisseur* (Feb. 21, 1848), *Les Porcherons* (Jan. 12, 1850), *Bonsoir, M. Pantalon* (Feb. 19, 1851), *Le Carillonneur de Bruges* (Feb. 20, 1852), *Les Amours du diable* (March 11, 1853), *Le Chien du jardinier* (Jan. 16, 1855), *Voyage autour de ma chambre* (Aug. 12, 1859), *Le Joaillier de St. James* (revision of *Lady Melvil;* Feb. 17, 1862), *La Chatte merveilleuse* (March 18, 1862), *Bégaiements d'amour* (Dec. 8, 1864), and *Douze innocentes* (Oct. 19, 1865). He left, besides, 12 finished and unfinished operas; also dramatic scenes, over 50 romances, etc. His statue (by Brackeleer) was placed in the vestibule of the Antwerp Theater in 1870.

Grisi, Giuditta, Italian mezzo-soprano; b. Milan, July 28, 1805; d. Robecco d'Oglio, near Cremona, May 1, 1840. She was a niece of the famous contralto **Josephina Grassini;** a cousin of the dancer Carlotta Grisi; and the elder sister of the celebrated soprano **Giulia Grisi.** She studied at the Milan Cons.; made her first appearance in Vienna in 1826; afterward sang with success in Italy and in Paris at the Théâtre-Italien under Rossini's management; retired in 1838, after her marriage to Count Barni. Bellini wrote for her the part of Romeo in *I Capuleti ed i Montecchi* (Venice, March 11, 1830); her sister sang Juliet.

Grisi, Giulia, celebrated Italian soprano; b. Milan, July 28, 1811; d. Berlin, Nov. 29, 1869. She studied with her sister, **Giuditta Grisi,** and with Filippo Celli and Pietro Guglielmi, son of the composer; also with Marliani in Milan and with Giacomelli in Bologna; made her first appearance at 17 as Emma in Rossini's *Zelmira;* won the admiration of Bellini, who wrote for her the part of Juliet in *I Capuleti ed i Montecchi* (Venice, March 11, 1830); she sang in Milan until 1832; dissatisfied with her contract and unable to break it legally, she fled to Paris, where she joined her sister at the Théâtre-Italien; she made her Paris debut in the title role of Rossini's *Semiramide* (Oct. 16, 1832); her success was phenomenal, and for the next 16 years she sang during the winter seasons at the Théâtre-Italien. She made her London debut in Rossini's *La gazza ladra* (April 8, 1834), and continued to visit London annually for 27 years. With Rubini, Tamburini, and Lablache, she appeared in Bellini's *I Puritani* and other operas; when the tenor **Giovanni Mario** replaced Rubini, Grisi sang with him and Tamburini; she married Mario (her 2nd husband) in 1844; toured the U.S. with him in 1854; retired in 1861, and lived mostly in London, making occasional visits to the Continent; on one visit to Berlin, she died of pneumonia.

Grist, Reri, black American soprano; b. New York, 1932. She studied at the High School of Music and Art and at Queens College; began her professional career on Broadway, appearing in *West Side Story* (1957); made her operatic debut with the Santa Fe Opera as Blonde in *Die Entführung aus dem Serail* in 1959; in 1960 sang at the Cologne Opera as the Queen of the Night. She made her Metropolitan Opera debut in N.Y. on Feb. 25, 1966, as Rosina in *Il Barbiere di Siviglia.* She held several teaching posts; was for several years on the faculty of the Indiana Univ. School of Music in Bloomington.

Griswold, Putnam, American bass; b. Minneapolis, Dec. 23, 1875; d. New York, Feb. 26, 1914. He studied with A. Randegger in London, Bouhy in Paris, Stockhausen in Frankfurt, and Emerich in Berlin; sang at the Berlin Opera in 1904; in 1904–5 toured the U.S. with Savage's company, appearing in the Eng. version of *Parsifal;* from 1906 to 1911 was a popular singer at the Berlin Opera; made his Metropolitan Opera debut on Nov. 23, 1911, in the role of Hagen in *Götterdämmerung.* He was identified with the bass parts in Wagner's works until his death; German critics pronounced him the greatest foreign interpreter of these roles, and he was twice decorated by the Kaiser.

Grofé, Ferde (Ferdinand Rudolph von), American composer, pianist, and arranger; b. New York, March 27, 1892; d. Santa Monica, Calif., April 3, 1972. He attended N.Y. and California public schools; studied music with Pietro Floridia; then was engaged as viola player in the Los Angeles Symph. Orch., at the same time working as popular pianist and conductor in theaters and cafés; joined Paul Whiteman's band in 1920 as pianist and arranger; it was his scoring of Gershwin's *Rhapsody in Blue* (1924) that won him fame. In his own works, Grofé successfully applied jazz rhythms, interwoven with simple ballad-like tunes; his *Grand Canyon Suite* (Chicago, Nov. 22, 1931, Paul Whiteman conducting) has become very popular. Other light pieces in a modern vein include a Piano Concerto (1932–59); *Broadway at Night; Mississippi Suite; 3 Shades of Blue; Tabloid Suite* (N.Y., Jan. 25, 1933); *Symphony in Steel* (N.Y., Jan. 19, 1937); *Hollywood Suite; Wheels Suite; New England Suite; Metropolis; Aviation Suite; San Francisco Suite* for Orch. (San Francisco, April 23, 1960); *Niagara Falls Suite* for Orch. (Buffalo, Feb., 1961); *World's Fair Suite* for Orch. (N.Y., April 22, 1964); *Virginia City: Requiem for a Ghost Town,* symph. poem (Virginia City, Nev., Aug. 10, 1968).

Grosz, Wilhelm (Will), Austrian composer; b. Vienna, Aug. 11, 1894; d. New York, Dec. 10, 1939. He studied composition with Franz Schreker in Vienna; then lived in Berlin (1928–33). In 1933 he went to London; in 1938 went to N.Y. He wrote an opera, *Sganarell,* after Molière (Dessau, Nov. 21, 1925); *Der arme Reinhold,* a "danced fable" (Berlin, Dec. 22, 1928); a modern musical comedy, *Achtung, Aufnahme!* (Frankfurt, March 23, 1930); *Jazzband* for Violin and Piano (1924); Violin Sonata (1925); a song cycle, *Liebeslieder.* As Will Grosz, he wrote light songs.

Grout, Donald Jay, eminent American musicologist; b. Rock Rapids, Iowa, Sept. 28, 1902. He studied philosophy at Syracuse Univ. (A.B., 1923) and musicology at Harvard Univ. (A.M., 1932; Ph.D., 1939). He studied piano in Boston, and gave a solo recital there in 1932. In the interim he went to Europe, where he took a course in French music of the Baroque period in Strasbourg and in the history of opera in Vienna. In 1935–36 he was a visiting lecturer in music history at Mills College in Calif.; from 1936 to 1942 he was on the staff of the music dept. at Harvard Univ.; from 1942 to 1945 was at the Univ. of Texas in Austin; from 1945 to 1970 was a prof. of musicology at Cornell Univ. He held a Guggenheim Foundation grant in 1951. He served as president of the American Musicological Society (1961–63); in 1966 became curator of the Accademia Monteverdiana in N.Y. He is the author of the valuable publications *A Short History of Opera* (2 vols., N.Y., 1948; revised ed., 1965); *A History of Western Music* (N.Y., 1960; 3rd ed., 1980); *Mozart in the History of Opera* (Washington, D.C., 1972); and *Alessandro Scarlatti: An Introduction to His Operas* (Berkeley, 1979). He is a member of the Editorial Board of *The New Grove Dictionary of Music and Musicians* (London, 1980). In his honor a Festschrift was issued, W.W. Austin, edition, *New Looks at Italian Opera: Essays in Honor of Donald J. Grout* (Ithaca, N.Y., 1968).

Grove, Sir George, eminent English musicographer; b. Clapham, in South London, Aug. 13, 1820; d. Sydenham, May 28, 1900. He studied civil engineering; graduated in 1839 from the Institution of Civil Engineers, and worked in various shops in Glasgow, and then in Jamaica and Bermuda. He returned to England in 1846, and became interested in music; without abandoning his engineering profession, he entered the Society of Arts, of which he was appointed secretary in 1850; this position placed him in contact with the organizers of the 1851 Exhibition; in 1852 he became secretary of the Crystal Palace. He then turned to literary work; was an editor, with William Smith, of the *Dictionary of the Bible;* traveled to Palestine in 1858 and 1861 in connection with his research; in 1865 he became director of the Palestine Exploration Fund. In the meantime, he accumulated a private music library; began writing analytical programs for Crystal Palace concerts; these analyses, contributed by Grove during the period 1856–96, established a new standard of excellence in musical exegesis. Grove's enthusiasm for music led to many important associations; with Arthur Sullivan he went to Vienna in 1867 in search of unknown music by Schubert, and discovered the score of Schubert's *Rosamunde.* In 1868 he became editor of *Macmillan's Magazine;* remained on its staff for 15 years; in 1878 he visited America; he received many honors for his literary and musical achievements, among them the D.C.L., Univ. of

Durham (1875), and LL.D., Univ. of Glasgow (1885). In 1883 he was knighted by Queen Victoria. When the Royal College of Music was formed in London (1882), Grove was appointed director, and retained this post until 1894. His chief work, which gave him enduring fame, was the monumental *Dictionary of Music and Musicians,* which Macmillan began to publ. in 1879. It was first planned in 2 vols., but as the material grew, it was expanded to 4 vols., with an appendix, its publication being completed in 1889. Grove himself contributed voluminous articles on his favorite composers, Beethoven, Schubert, and Mendelssohn; he gathered a distinguished group of specialists to write the assorted entries. The 2nd edition of Grove's *Dictionary* (1904–10), in 5 vols., was edited by Fuller-Maitland; the 3rd edition (1927–28), by H.C. Colles; an American supplement, first publ. in 1920, edited by W.S. Pratt and C.H.N. Boyd, was expanded and republ. in 1928; the 4th edition, also edited by H.C. Colles, was publ. in 5 vols., with a supplementary vol. in 1940. Eric Blom was entrusted with the preparation of an entirely revised and greatly enlarged 5th edition, which was publ. in 9 vols. in 1954; it became the largest music reference book in the Eng. language; Grove's original articles on Beethoven, Schubert, and Mendelssohn were publ. separately in 1951, since their bulk was out of proportion even in this edition; revised articles on these composers were included instead. A new, 6th edition, under the editorship of Stanley Sadie, in 20 vols., numbering some 15,000 pages, containing about 22,500 articles and over 3,000 illustrations, reflecting the contributions of some 2,400 scholars from all over the world, was publ. in London in 1980, under the title *The New Grove Dictionary of Music and Musicians.* Grove further publ. *Beethoven and His 9 Symphonies* (London, 1896; 3rd ed., 1898; reprint, 1962); contributed prefaces to Otto Jahn's *Life of Mozart* and Novello's *Short History of Cheap Music;* also numerous articles to the musical press.

Grové, Stefans, South African composer; b. Bethlehem, Orange Free State, July 23, 1922. He studied piano with his mother and his uncle; later took courses with Cameron Taylor at the South African College of Music, with W.H. Bell in Cape Town, and with Walter Piston at Harvard Univ. (1953–55), where he received his M.A. In 1956 he was appointed instructor at the Peabody Cons., Baltimore, where he founded the Pro Musica Rara group for performance of Baroque music; in 1972 he was appointed senior lecturer in composition at the Univ. of Cape Town and in 1972 took a similar post at the Univ. of Pretoria. He edited the orch. score of the newly discovered (1971) Concerto for 2 Pianos and Orch. of Max Bruch. Grové's music is distinguished by clarity of formal presentation and a free flow of melodic line; the contrapuntal structure is often complex, but it is invariably cast within clearly outlined harmonies. WORKS: Clarinet Sonata (1947); String Trio (1948); *Elegy* for String Orch. (Cape Town, July 9, 1948); Duo for Violin and Cello (1950); *Die Dieper*

Reg, ballet (1950); Piano Trio (1952); Trio for Oboe, Clarinet, and Bassoon (1952); Quintet for Flute, Oboe, Viola, Bass Clarinet, and Harp (1952); *Tower Music* for Brass Ensemble (1954); Flute Sonata (1955); Sinfonia Concertante (Johannesburg, Oct. 23, 1956); Quartet for Flute, Oboe, Clarinet, and Bassoon (1956); Violin Concerto (1959); *Alice in Wonderland* for Viola, Piccolo, Alto Flute, Wind Ensemble, and Percussion (1959); *Symphony 1962;* Partita for Orch. (1964); *Ritual,* fantasy for Organ (1969); *An Experience in Style,* 14 imitative pieces for Harpsichord and Piano (1971); *Kaapse Druuie* for Chorus, Piano, Guitar, Marimba, Flute, Clarinet, and Saxophone (1974); Concerto Grosso for Violin, Cello, Piano, and Youth Orch. (1974); *Maya,* concerto for Violin, Piano, and Youth String Orch. (1976); *Warata,* ballet for Young Dancers (1976); *For a Winter Day,* fantasy for Bassoon and Piano (1977); *Chain Rows* for Orch. with Instrumental Soloists (1978); *Rendezvous* for Piccolo and Tuba (1978).

Groven, Eivind, Norwegian composer and musicologist; b. Lårdal, Telemark, Oct. 8, 1901. He studied at the Oslo Cons. (1923–25); d. Oslo, Feb. 8, 1977. In 1932 he was appointed a consultant on folk music for Norwegian Radio; remained there until 1946; in 1940 he received a state composer's pension. He collected about 1,800 Norwegian folk tunes, several of which he used as thematic foundation for his own compositions. In 1965 he patented an electronic organ, with special attachments for the production of non-tempered intervals. WORKS: Symph. poems: *Renaissance* (1935), *Historiske syner* (*Historical Visions,* 1936), *Fjelltonar* (*Tunes from the Hills;* 1938), *Skjebner* (*The Fates;* 1938), and *Bryllup i skogen* (*Wedding in the Wood;* 1939); 2 symphs.: No. 1, *Innover viddene* (*Toward the Mountains;* 1937; revised 1951), and No. 2, *Midnattstimen* (*The Midnight Hour;* 1946); *Hjalarljod,* overture (1950); Piano Concerto (1950); *Symfoniske slåtter* (*Norwegian Folk Dances*), 2 sets: No. 1 (1956) and No. 2, *Faldafeykir* (1967). Vocal music: *Brudgommen* (*The Bridegroom*) for Soprano, 2 Altos, Tenor, Chorus, and Orch. (1928–31); *Naturens tempel* (*The Temple of Nature*) for Chorus and Orch. (1945); *Ivar Aasen,* suite for Soprano, Bass, Chorus, and Orch. (1946); *Soga om ein by* (*The Story of a Town*) for Soprano, Tenor, Bass, Chorus, and Orch. (1956); *Margjit Hjukse* for Chorus and Hardanger Fiddle (1963); *Draumkaede* for Soprano, Tenor, Baritone, Chorus, and Orch. (1965); *Ved foss og fjord* (*By Falls and Fjord*) for Male Chorus and Orch. (1966); among his many songs for solo voice, most scored with piano and later rescored with orch., are: *Moen* (*The Heath;* 1926; orchestrated 1934); *Neslandskyrkja* (*The Nesland Church;* 1929; orchestrated 1942); *Moderens korstegn* (*The Mother's Sign of the Cross;* 1930; orchestrated 1942); *På hospitalet om natten* (*In the Hospital at Night;* 1930; orchestrated 1946); *Høstsanger* (*The Autumn Song;* orchestrated 1946). Chamber music: *Solstemning* (*Sun Mood*) for Solo Flute, or Flute and Piano (1946); *Balladetone* for 2 Hardanger Fiddles (1962); *Regnbogen* (*The Rainbow*) for 2 Hardanger Fiddles

(1962). His many theoretical studies include *Natur-skalaen (The Natural Scale;* Skein, 1927); *Temper-ering og renstemning (Temperament and Non-tempered Tuning,* dealing with a new system of piano tuning according to natural intervals; Oslo, 1948; Eng. trans., 1970); *Eskimomelodier fra Alaska (Eskimo Melodies from Alaska;* Oslo, 1955).

Groves, Sir Charles, distinguished English conductor; b. London, March 10, 1915. He was educated at the Royal College of Music in London. In 1941 he joined the BBC as a choral conductor. He then was music director of the Bournemouth Symph. Orch. (1951–61) and the Welsh National Opera (1961–63). From 1967 to 1977 he was music director of the Royal Liverpool Phil. Orch. In 1978 he became music director of the English National Opera in London, resigning in 1979. He was knighted by Queen Elizabeth II in 1973. He was especially fond of the music of Elgar and Delius, which he performed with great élan, and was also noted for his sensitive readings of the symphs. of Sibelius. He was instrumental in launching the careers of several English conductors of the younger generation, especially in his sponsorship of the Liverpool International Conductors' Competition.

Grovlez, Gabriel (Marie), French conductor, writer, and composer; b. Lille, April 4, 1879; d. Paris, Oct. 20, 1944. He studied at the Paris Cons. under Diémer, Lavignac, Gédalge, and Fauré; won first prize in piano there (1899); was then taught piano at the Schola Cantorum (from 1908); was appointed conductor at the Paris Opéra in 1914; also conducted the Chicago Opera Co. (1921–22 and 1925–26).

Gruber, Franz Xaver, Austrian composer and organist; b. Unterweizburg, Nov. 25, 1787; d. Hallein, near Salzburg, June 7, 1863. He acquired fame as the composer of the Christmas carol *Stille Nacht, Heilige Nacht.* Of a poor family, Gruber had to do manual work as a youth, but managed to study organ; by dint of perseverance he obtained, at the age of 28, his first position, as church organist and schoolmaster at Oberndorf. It was there, on Christmas Eve of 1818, that a young curate, Joseph Mohr, brought him a Christmas poem to be set to music, and Gruber wrote the celebrated song.

Gruber, H(einz) K(arl), Austrian composer; b. Vienna, Jan. 3, 1943. He was a member of the famous Vienna Boys' Choir (1953–57); studied composition with Uhl and Jelinek; also played double bass and French horn; took courses in film music at the Hochschule für Musik in Vienna (1957–63); in 1963–64 attended master classes there held by Einem. He played principal double bass in the Tonkünstler Orch. in Vienna (1963–69); was a co-founder, with Schwertsik and Zukan, of an avant-garde group, MOB art & tone ART (1968). In 1961 he joined the Vienna ensemble *die reihe* as a double-bass player; in 1969 was engaged as double-bass player in the ORF (Austrian Symph. Orch.), where he also performed as an actor. In his own music Gruber maintains a wide amplitude of styles, idioms, and techniques, applying the dodecaphonic method of composition in works of a jazz and pop nature. His "pandemonium," *Frankenstein!!,* which is a megamultimedia affair, with children's verses recited in a bizarre and mock-scary manner, became quite popular.

WORKS: FOR THE STAGE: Melodrama in 5 scenes, *Die Vertreibung aus dem Paradies (The Expulsion from Paradise)* for Speakers and 6 Solo Instruments (1966); musical spectacle, *Gomorrah* (1970–72); "pandemonium," *Frankenstein!!,* after H.C. Artmann, for Baritone Chansonnier and Orch. (1976–77; London, Nov. 25, 1978; U.S. premiere, Berkshire Music Center, Tanglewood, Aug. 13, 1980; version for Vocalist and 12-player Ensemble, Berlin Festival, Sept. 30, 1979).

FOR ORCH.: Concerto for Orch. (1960–64); *Manhattan Broadcasts* for Light Orch. (1962–64); *fürbass,* concerto for Double Bass and Orch. (1965); *Revue* for Chamber Orch. (1968); *Vergrösserung (Magnification,* 1970); *Arien* for Violin and Orch. (1974–75); *Phantom-Bilder (Photo-Fit Pictures)* for Chamber Ensemble (1977); *. . . aus Schatten duft gewebt (. . . of shadow fragrance woven)* for Violin and Orch. (1977–78; Berlin Festival, Sept. 29, 1979); *Entmilitärisierte Zonen (Demilitarized Zones),* march-paraphrases (1979); *Charivari,* subtitled *An Austrian Journal* (1981); *Rough Music,* concerto for Percussion and Orch. (1982–83).

Gruberová, Edita, Czech coloratura sorpano; b. Bratislava, Dec. 23, 1946. She received her musical education in Prague and Vienna; made her debut with the Slovak National Theater in Bratislava in 1968; in 1972 she made a successful appearance at the Vienna State Opera; she also sang at the Bayreuth Festivals, the Hamburg State Opera, the Frankfurt Opera, the Bavarian State Opera in Munich, and other major opera houses, establishing herself as one of the finest coloratura sopranos of her generation.

Gruenberg, Louis, eminent American composer; b. near Brest Litovsk, Poland, Aug. 3, 1884; d. Los Angeles, June 9, 1964. He was brought to the U.S. as an infant; studied piano with Adele Margulies in N.Y.; then went to Berlin, where he studied with Busoni (piano and composition); in 1912 made his debut as a pianist with the Berlin Phil.; intermittently took courses at the Vienna Cons., where he also was a tutor. In 1919 he returned to the U.S. and devoted himself to composing. He was one of the organizers and active members of the League of Composers (1923); became a champion of modern music, and one of the earliest American composers to incorporate jazz rhythms in works of symph. dimensions (*Daniel Jazz, Jazzettes,* etc.); from 1933 to 1936 he taught composition at the Chicago Music College; then settled in Santa Monica, Calif.

WORKS: His opera *The Emperor Jones,* to O'Neill's play (Metropolitan Opera, N.Y., Jan. 7, 1933), attracted a great deal of attention by its dramatic effects and novel devices, particularly in the use of percussion; it received the David Bispham Medal. OTHER STAGE WORKS: *The Witch of Brocken* (1912); *The Bride of the Gods* (1913); *Dumb Wife* (1921); *Jack and the Beanstalk* (libretto by John Erskine; N.Y., Nov. 19, 1931); *Queen Helena* (1936); *Green Mansions,* radio opera (CBS, Oct. 17, 1937); *Volpone,* opera (1945); *The Miracle of Flanders,* mystery play (1950); *Anthony and Cleopatra,* opera (1940–60). FOR ORCH.: 5 symphs.: No. 1 (1919; revised in 1929; won the $5,000 RCA Victor prize in 1930; perf. by Koussevitzky and the Boston Symph., Feb. 10, 1934); Nos. 2–5 (1942–48); *Vagabondia* (1920); *The Hill of Dreams,* symph. poem (won the Flagler prize; N.Y., Oct. 23, 1921); *Jazz Suite* (Cincinnati, March 22, 1929); *The Enchanted Isle,* symph. poem (Worcester Festival, Oct. 3, 1929); *9 Moods* (1929); *Music for an Imaginary Ballet,* 2 sets (1929, 1944); *Serenade to a Beauteous Lady* (Chicago, April 4, 1935); 2 piano concertos (1914; 1938, revised 1961); Violin Concerto (Philadelphia Orch., Dec. 1, 1944, Heifetz, soloist); *Americana,* suite for Orch. (1945). VOCAL WORKS: *Daniel Jazz* for Tenor and 8 Instruments (N.Y., Feb. 22, 1925); *Creation* for Baritone and 8 Instruments (N.Y., Nov. 27, 1926); *Animals and Insects* for Voice and Piano; *4 Contrasting Songs; A Song of Faith,* spiritual rhapsody for Speaker, Voices, Chorus, Orch., and a Dance Group, dedicated to the memory of Mahatma Gandhi (1952–62; brought out in a posthumous perf. for the first time in Los Angeles on Nov. 1, 1981); also publ. 4 vols. of Negro spirituals. CHAMBER MUSIC: Suite for Violin and Piano (1914); 3 violin sonatas (1912, 1919, 1950); *Indiscretions* for String Quartet (1922); *Diversions* for String Quartet (1930); 2 string quartets (1937, 1938); *Jazzettes* for Violin and Piano (1926); 2 piano quintets (1929, 1937); *Poem in Form of a Sonatina* for Cello and Piano (1925); *4 Whimsicalities* for String Quartet (1923). PIANO WORKS: *Jazzberries, Polychromatics, Jazz Masks, 6 Jazz Epigrams, 3 Jazz Dances,* etc.

Grumiaux, Arthur, eminent Belgian violinist; b. Villers-Perwin, March 21, 1921. He studied violin and piano with Fernand Quinet at the Charleroi Cons. and violin with Alfred Dubois at the Royal Cons. in Brussels; also took private lessons in composition with Enesco in Paris. In 1939 he received the Vieuxtemps Prize; in 1940 was awarded the Prix de Virtuosité from the Belgian government. In 1949 he was appointed prof. of violin at the Royal Cons. In 1973 he was knighted by King Baudouin for his services to music; he thus shared the title of baron with Paganini. His performances are characterized by a studied fidelity to the composer's intentions, assured technical command, and a discerning delineation of the inner structure of the music.

Grümmer, Elisabeth, famous German soprano; b. Niederjeutz, March 31, 1911. She first pursued a career as an actress. In 1941 Herbert von Karajan invited her to sing at the Aachen Opera, which marked the beginning of a successful career. In 1951 she appeared at Covent Garden; in 1957 at Bayreuth. In 1959 she became a prof. at the Hochschule

für Musik in West Berlin. In 1961 she toured South America; in 1964 she gave concerts in Korea and Japan. It was not until April 20, 1967, at the age of 56, that she sang for the first time at the Metropolitan Opera in N.Y., as Elsa in *Lohengrin.* Her acting ability greatly redounded to her success in opera.

Grümmer, Paul, German cellist; b. Gera, Feb. 26, 1879; d. Zug, Switzerland, Oct. 30, 1965. He studied in Leipzig and Berlin; in 1899 went to London as cellist at Covent Garden and member of the Jan Kubelik String Quartet; in 1913, he joined the Adolf Busch Quartet; in 1926–33 he taught at the Hochschule für Musik in Cologne; in 1933–40, was a prof. at the Hochschule für Musik in Berlin; in 1940–45, at the Vienna Academy of Music; retired to Zürich in 1945. He wrote pedagogic works for the cello and edited Bach's unaccompanied cello suites. His autobiography, *Begegnungen,* was publ. in Munich in 1963.

Grünbaum, Therese, famous Austrian soprano; b. Vienna, Aug. 24, 1791; d. Berlin, Jan. 30, 1876. She studied with her father, **Wenzel Müller,** the composer and conductor; appeared on stage while still a child; in 1807 she went to Prague; in 1816 she joined the Kärnthnertortheater in Vienna, remaining as a principal member there until 1826; while in Vienna, she gained fame for her Rossini roles; also created the role of Eglantine in Weber's *Euryanthe;* after appearances in Berlin (1828–30), she taught voice. She married the tenor **Johann Christoff** (b. Haslau, Oct. 28, 1785; d. Berlin, Oct. 10, 1870); a daughter, **Caroline** (b. Prague, March 18, 1814; d. Braunschweig, May 26, 1868), was also a soprano.

Grund, Friedrich Wilhelm, German conductor and composer; b. Hamburg, Oct. 7, 1791; d. there, Nov. 24, 1874. He was brought up in a musical family, his father having been a theater conductor. He studied cello, but after a brief concert career devoted himself mainly to conducting. In 1819, he founded in Hamburg the Gesellschaft der Freunde des Religiösen Gesanges, which later became the Hamburg Singakademie. In 1828, was engaged to lead the newly established Phil. Concerts, a post he held until 1862. In 1867 he organized (with Karl Grädener) the Hamburg Tonkünstlerverein. He wrote several operas, which were not performed; a cantata, *Die Auferstehung und Himmelfahrt Christi;* some chamber music (Octet for Wind Instruments and Piano; Quintet for Oboe, Clarinet, Horn, Bassoon, and Piano; *Trio de Salon* for Piano, 4-hands, and Cello); many piano pieces, which enjoyed considerable success and were praised by Schumann.

Grunenwald, Jean-Jacques, French organist and composer of Swiss parentage; b. Cran-Gevrier, near Annecy, Feb. 2, 1911; d. Paris, Dec. 19, 1982. He studied organ with Dupré at the Paris Cons.; received first prize in 1935; studied composition with Henri Busser, obtaining another first prize in 1937. From 1936 to 1945 he was the assistant of Dupré at St.-Sulpice in Paris; in 1955–70 was organist at St.-Pierre-de-Montrouge. He was a prof. at the Schola

Cantorum in Paris from 1958 to 1961, and from 1961 to 1966 was on the faculty of the Cons. of Geneva. Through the years he played more than 1,500 concerts, presenting the complete organ works of Bach and César Franck. He also became famous for the excellence of his masterly improvisations, which rivaled those of his teacher Marcel Dupré. His compositions include *Fêtes de la lumière* for Orch. (1937); Piano Concerto (1940); *Concert d'été* for Piano and String Orch. (1944); lyric drama, *Sardanapale*, after Byron (1945–50); *Ouverture pour un Drame sacre* for Orch. (1954); *Cantate pour le Vendredi Saint* (1955); *Psalm 129 (De profundis)* for Chorus and Orch. (1959); *Fantaisie en dialogue* for Organ and Orch. (1964); Sonata for Organ (1964); piano pieces; etc.

Grünfeld, Alfred, Austrian pianist and composer; b. Prague, July 4, 1852; d. Vienna, Jan. 4, 1924. He studied in Prague, and later at Kullak's Academy in Berlin; settled in Vienna in 1873, and established himself there as a popular concert pianist and teacher; he also made tours in other European countries, including Russia. He composed an operetta, *Der Lebemann* (Vienna, Jan. 16, 1903) and the comic opera, *Die Schönen von Fogaras* (Dresden, 1907); made brilliant arrangements for piano of waltzes by Johann Strauss; also publ. piano studies and various other pieces (*Spanish Serenade, Hungarian Fantasy, Barcarolle, Impromptu,* etc.).

Grünfeld, Heinrich, renowned cellist, brother of **Alfred Grünfeld;** b. Prague, April 21, 1855; d. Berlin, Aug. 26, 1931. He studied at the Prague Cons.; went to Berlin in 1876, and taught cello at Kullak's Academy; also played chamber music with X. Scharwenka and G. Hollander. He publ. a book of memoirs, *In Dur und Moll* (Berlin, 1924).

Grützmacher, Friedrich (Wilhelm Ludwig), renowned German cellist; b. Dessau, March 1, 1832; d. Dresden, Feb. 23, 1903. He received his musical training from his father, a chamber musician at Dessau; at the age of 16 he went to Leipzig, and produced such a fine impression that Ferdinand David secured for him the post of first cellist of the Gewandhaus Orch. (1849). In 1860 he went to Dresden, where he remained for more than 40 years, until his death, as a teacher and chamber music player. Among his pupils were Hugo Becker and several other well-known cellists. He wrote a Cello Concerto; *Hohe Schule des Violoncellspiels* (Leipzig, 1891); several books of cello studies, and numerous arrangements for cello of works by classical composers; also edited cello works by Beethoven, Mendelssohn, Chopin, and Schumann. His brother, **Leopold Grützmacher** (b. Dessau, Sept. 4, 1835; d. Weimar, Feb. 26, 1900), was also a cellist; he studied in Dessau, and later joined the Gewandhaus Orch. in Leipzig; after occupying various posts in theater orchs., he settled in Weimar as a teacher at the court chapel. He wrote 2 cello concertos and a number of salon pieces for his instrument. Leopold's son, **Friedrich** (b. Meiningen, July 20, 1866; d. Cologne, July 25, 1919), carried on the family tradition of cello playing; was a pupil of his father as well as of his uncle; was a member of various theater orchs. in Budapest and elsewhere; finally settled in Cologne as a teacher at the Cons. there. He publ. a number of valuable cello collections and transcriptions.

Guadagni, Gaetano, famous male contralto; b. Lodi, c.1725; d. Padua, Nov., 1792. He began his career in Parma (1746); in 1748, went to London, where he attracted the attention of Handel, who gave him contralto parts in *Messiah* and *Samson;* after many successful appearances in London, he sang in Dublin (1751–52); then went to Paris (1754) and to Lisbon (1755), where he studied with Gizziello. He then returned to Italy; in 1762, Gluck secured an engagement for him in Vienna to sing Orfeo in Gluck's opera. In 1769, Guadagni was again in London. In 1770 he sang in Munich; in 1772, he appeared in Venice; in 1776, he was summoned by Frederick the Great to Potsdam, receiving great acclaim; in 1777, he settled in Padua, where he continued to sing at churches. He was not only a fine singer but an excellent actor; also wrote various arias, one of which, *Pensa a serbarmi,* is preserved in the Bologna library.

Guadagnini, family of famous violin makers of Piacenza, Italy. **Lorenzo** (1695–1748) used the label "Laurentius Guadagnini, alumnus Antonius Stradivarius," and he may have studied with Stradivarius in Cremona shortly before the latter's death in 1737; certainly he followed Stradivarius's models in his violin making. Lorenzo's son, **Giovanni Battista** (b. Cremona, 1711; d. Turin, Sept. 18, 1786), received his training presumably from his father, and may have been with him at the shop of Stradivarius; he followed his father from Cremona to Piacenza in 1737; worked in Milan (1749–58); was in Parma (1759–71); then settled in Turin. His violins are regarded as the finest of the Guadagninis. His two sons, **Giuseppe** (1736–1805) and **Gaetano** (1745–1817), continued the family tradition and manufactured some good instruments, but failed to approach the excellence of their father's creations. Violin-making remained the family's occupation through 4 more generations in Turin; the last representative, **Paolo Guadagnini,** perished in the torpedoing of an Italian ship, on Dec. 28, 1942.

Gualdo, Giovanni (John), Italian musician and wine merchant. He arrived in Philadelphia from London in 1767 and opened a store there; among other things, he sold instruments, taught violin, flute, guitar, and other instruments; also arranged music; presented concerts; the first of these, given in Philadelphia on Nov. 16, 1769, was devoted largely to Gualdo's own compositions, and may well be regarded as the earliest "composer's concert" in America. He died insane at the Pennsylvania Hospital, Philadelphia, Dec. 20, 1771. His *6 easy evening entertainments for 2 mandolins or 2 violins with a thorough bass for the harpsichord or violincello* are in MS in the Library of Congress, Washington, D.C.; the printed op. 2, *6 Sonates for 2 German flutes with a thorough bass* (his name appears here as **Giovanni Gualdo da Vandero**) is in the British Museum. Copies of both sets are owned by the N.Y. Public Library.

Guarneri, famous family of violin makers in Cremona. The Italian form of the name was **Guarnieri;** Guarneri was derived from the Latin spelling, **Guarnerius;** the labels invariably used the Latin form. **Andrea,** head of the family (b. Cremona, c.1625; d. there, Dec. 7, 1698), was a pupil of Nicolo Amati; he lived in Amati's house from 1641 to 1646, and again from 1650 to 1654, when, with his wife, he moved to his own house in Cremona and began making his own violins, labeling them as "alumnus" of Amati and, after 1655, "ex alumnis," often with the additional words of "sub titolo Sanctae Theresiae." Andrea's son **Pietro Giovanni,** known as **Peter of Mantua** (b. Cremona, Feb. 18, 1655; d. Mantua, March 26, 1720), worked first at Cremona; then went to Mantua, where he settled; he also used the device "sub titolo Sanctae Theresiae." Another son of Andrea, **Giuseppe** (b. Cremona, Nov. 25, 1666; d. there, c.1740), worked in his father's shop, which he eventually inherited; in his own manufactures, he departed from his father's model and followed the models of Stradivarius. Giuseppe's son, **Pietro** (b. Cremona, April 14, 1695; d. Venice, April 7, 1762), became known as **Peter of Venice;** he settled in Venice in 1725, and adopted some features of the Venetian masters, Montagnana and Serafin. **(Bartolomeo) Giuseppe Antonio,** known as **Giuseppe del Gesù,** from the initials IHS often appearing on his labels (b. Cremona, Aug. 21, 1698; d. there, Oct. 17, 1744), was a son of Giuseppe. He became the most celebrated member of the family; some of his instruments bear the label "Joseph Guarnerius Andreae Nepos Cremonae," which establishes his lineage as a grandson of Andrea. His violins are greatly prized; only Stradivarius excelled him in the perfection of instrumental craftsmanship; he experimented with a variety of wood materials, and also made changes in the shapes of his instruments during different periods of his work. Paganini used one of his instruments.

Guarnieri, (Mozart) Camargo, outstanding Brazilian composer; b. Tiété, state of São Paulo, Feb. 1, 1907. He studied piano and composition in São Paulo before going, in 1938, to Paris, where he took a course in composition with Charles Koechlin and one in conducting with Rühlmann. In 1942 and 1946 he visited the U.S. as a conductor of his own works. He later returned to Brazil, where he taught at various institutions. His music is permeated with "Brasilidad," a syndrome that is Brazilian in its melody and rhythm; his *Dansa brasileira* is typical in its national quality.
     WORKS: *Pedro Malazarte*, one-act comic opera (1931); opera, *Um homem só* (1960); 4 symphs. (1944, 1946, 1952, 1963); 5 piano concertos (1936, 1946, 1964, 1967, 1970); 2 violin concertos (1940, 1953); *Overture*

concertante (1943); *Dansa brasileira* for Orch. (São Paulo, March 7, 1941; originally for Piano, 1931); *Dansa negra* for Orch. (1947); *Chôro* for Violin and Orch. (1951); *Variations on a Northeast Brazilian Theme* for Piano and Orch. (1953); *Suite IV Centenário* for Orch. (1954; Louisville Orch., Jan. 15, 1955); *Chôro* for Clarinet and Orch. (1956); *Chôro* for Piano and Orch. (1957); *Sêca*, cantata (1957); *Suite Vila Rica* for Orch. (1958); *Chôro* for Cello and Orch. (1961); Piano Concertino (1961); *Seresta* for Piano and Chamber Orch. (1965); *Guaná bará*, cantata (1965); *Homage to Villa-Lobos* for Wind Orch. (1966); *Següencia, Coral e Ricercare* for Chamber Orch. (1966); 3 string quartets (1932, 1944, 1962); 5 violin sonatas (1930, 1933, 1950, 1959, 1962); many songs and piano pieces.

Gubaidulina, Sofia, Soviet composer of the extreme avant-garde; b. Chistopol, Oct. 24, 1931. She studied at the Cons. of Kazan; graduated in 1954; then enrolled at the Moscow Cons. to study composition with Peiko and Shebalin. Her music follows vectorially divergent paths, without adhering to a prearranged doctrine of modern composition. Perhaps her most astounding work is the Concerto for Bassoon and Low String Instruments, in 5 movements (1975), in which the bassoon is embedded in a net of 4 cellos and 3 double basses, creating a claustrophobic syndrome of ingrown low sonorities, while the solo instrument is forced to perform acrobatic feats to escape constriction, such as labial glissandos and rapid repetitions of a single note.
     WORKS: Symph. (1958); Piano Concerto (1959); String Quintet (1957); *Intermezzo* for 16 Harps, 8 Trumpets, and Drums (1961); *Allegro rustico* for Flute and Piano (1963); 5 Etudes for Harp, Double Bass, and Piano (1966); Sonata for Percussion (1966); *Pantomimes* for Double Bass and Piano (1966); *Detto No. 1* for Organ (1969); *Detto No. 2* for Chamber Ensemble; electronic work, *Vivant-non-Vivant* (1970); String Quartet (1971); *Concordanza* for Chamber Group (1971); *Rumore e Silenzio* for Harpsichord, Celesta, and Percussion (1974); Concerto for Bassoon and Low String Instruments (1975); Concerto for Piano and String Orch. (1978); *In croce* for Cello and Organ (1979); *Percussio di Pekarsky* (1979; Pekarsky is a top percussionist in the U.S.S.R.); *Garden of Joy and Sorrow* for Flute, Viola, and Harp (1980); Violin Concerto (Moscow, April 15, 1982); piano pieces; songs.

Gudmel, Claude. See **Goudimel, Claude.**

Gudmundsen-Holmgreen, Pelle, Danish composer; b. Copenhagen, Nov. 21, 1932. He studied theory and composition with Finn Höffding and Svend Westergaard at the Royal Danish Cons. in Copenhagen (1953–58); served as stage manager of the Royal Theater there (1959–64); taught composition at the Jutland Academy of Music in Aarhus (1967–73). He followed serial techniques; then experimented with a "new simplicity" achieved through persistent repetition of notes and patterns; employed optical notation, in which the distance between notes in a score equals the "time span" between the playing of those notes.

Gueden, Hilde, Austrian soprano; b. Vienna, Sept. 15, 1917. Both her parents were musicians. She made her debut in operetta at the age of 16; in 1939 the family moved to Switzerland; in 1941 she sang Zerlina in Munich; in 1942, made her debut in Rome. In 1947 Gueden became a member of the Vienna State Opera; also appeared at La Scala, Milan. She made her American debut at the Metropolitan Opera in N.Y., on Nov. 15, 1951, as Gilda, and sang there until 1961; then continued her career in Europe, mainly appearing with the Vienna State Opera.

Guédron, Pierre, French composer; b. Châteaudun, 1565; d. Paris, 1621. He was a choirboy in the chapel of Cardinal de Guise and later sang in the royal chapel (1588). In 1601 he was appointed Composer of the King's Music. He wrote ballets for the court, which included solo songs. Some of his airs are included in *Airs de Cour* (1615–18), and other contemporary collections. He is regarded as a precursor of Lully in the creation of French ballet music.

Guénin, (Marie) Alexandre, French violinist and composer; b. Maubeuge, Feb. 20, 1744; d. Etampes, Jan. 22, 1835. He showed a precocious talent, and was sent to Paris for study with Gaviniès (violin) and Gossec (composition). In 1771 he joined the orch. of the Paris Opéra; later was active as a conductor in the Paris society called Concert Spirituel; taught at the Ecole Royale de Chant. Several of his works were publ. in his lifetime: 6 symphs.; 6 violin duos; 6 string trios.

Guerrero, Francisco, Spanish composer; b. Seville, 1528 (probably on St. Francis Day, Oct. 4); d. there, Nov. 8, 1599. He was a pupil of his brother, **Pedro,** and for a short time of Morales. In 1546, he became maestro di cappella of Jaén Cathedral; in 1549, he went to Seville as cantor at the Cathedral there. In both 1551 and 1554, he was offered a similar post at the Cathedral of Malaga, but declined it. In 1556, he was in Lisbon; in 1567, in Cordova; in 1570, in Santander; in 1581–82 he went to Rome; in 1588, he was in Venice, whence he undertook a pilgrimage to Palestine. His account of his journey, *El viaje de Jerusalem que hizo Francisco Guerrero,* was publ. in 1611, and went through numerous editions. As a composer he was greatly appreciated by his contemporaries, but the comparisons with Morales or Victoria overestimate his importance.

Guglielmi, Pietro Alessandro, Italian composer; b. Massa di Carrara, Dec. 9, 1728; d. Rome, Nov. 18, 1804. He studied with his father, **Jacob Guglielmi,** and with Durante at the Cons. Santa Maria di Loreto at Naples. His first comic opera, *Lo solachianello 'mbroglione,* was performed at Naples in 1757; during the next 10 years he wrote 24 operas, including *Il ratto della sposa* (Venice, 1765) and *La sposa fedele* (Venice, 1767), which were played all over Europe and became highly popular. He went to London in 1767; during his 5 years there, conducted and wrote several operas, among them *Ezio* (Jan. 13, 1770), in which his wife, **Lelia Achiapati,** sang. He returned to Italy in 1772; in 1793 was appointed maestro di cappella of San Pietro in Vaticano by Pope Pius VI and turned to church music; composed several oratorios, of which *Debora e Sisara* (Naples, Feb. 13, 1789) was regarded as his masterpiece. A detailed list of Guglielmi's operas is found in F. Piovano's articles on him and his son in the *Rivista Musicale Italiana* (1905, 1910).

Guglielmi, Pietro Carlo, Italian composer, son of **Pietro Alessandro Guglielmi;** b. Naples, c.1763; d. there, Feb. 28, 1817. After study at the Cons. di Santa Maria di Loreto at Naples, he went to Spain; his first operas were performed at Madrid in 1793 and 1794; then lived in Italy, producing operas in Naples, Florence, and Rome. He went to London in 1809; presented several operas at the King's Theatre; returned to Italy in 1810, and was appointed maestro di cappella to the Duchess Beatrice at Massa di Carrara. A list of his works, including some 40 operas, oratorios, and cantatas, was publ. by Francesco Piovano in the *Rivista Musicale Italiana* (1909–10).

Gui, Vittorio, Italian composer and conductor; b. Rome, Sept. 14, 1885; d. Florence, Oct. 16, 1975. He studied at the Liceo Musicale di Santa Cecilia in Rome; began his career as an opera conductor; then conducted in Parma, Naples, and at La Scala in Milan (1923); eventually settled in Florence; was founder of the Maggio Musicale Fiorentino in 1933. From 1947 to 1965 he conducted opera in England; was counsellor of Glyndebourne Festival Opera (1960–65).

Guido d'Arezzo (known also as **Guido Aretinus**), famous reformer of musical notation and vocal instruction; b. c.997; d. Pomposa; date of death uncertain; May 17, 1050, often cited, is unfortunately without foundation. He received his education at the Benedictine abbey at Pomposa, near Ferrara. He left the monastery in 1025, as a result of disagreements with his fellow monks, who were envious of his superiority in vocal teaching; he was then summoned by Bishop Theobald of Arezzo to the cathedral school there; it was because of this association that he became known as Guido d'Arezzo. The assertions that he traveled in France and spent several years at the monastery of Saint-Maur des Fossés, near Paris (see, for example, Dom G. Morin in *Revue de l'art chrétien,* 1888) are not borne out by documentary evidence. Still more uncertain are the claims of his travels in Germany, and even in England. However this may be, his fame spread and reached the ears of Pope John XIX, who called him to Rome to demonstrate his system of teaching (1028). In his last years, he was a prior of the Camaldolite fraternity at Avellano. Guido's fame rests on his system of solmization, by which he established the nomenclature of the major hexachord Ut, Re, Mi, Fa, So, La, from syllables in the initial lines of the Hymn of St. John:

Ut queant laxis *Re*sonare fibris
*Mi*ra gestorum *Fa*muli tuorum,
*Sol*ve polluti *La*bii reatum,
Sancte Joannes.

No less epoch-making was Guido's introduction of the music staff of 4 lines, retaining the red *f*-line and the yellow *c*-line of his predecessors, and drawing between them a black *a*-line, above them a black *e*-line, and writing the plainsong notes (which he did *not* invent) in regular order on these lines and in the spaces:

New black line e———————
Old yellow line c———————
New black line a———————
Old red line f———————

He also added new lines above or below these, as occasion required; thus, Guido's system did away with all uncertainty of pitch. Another invention credited to Guido is the so-called Guidonian hand, relating the degrees of the overlapping hexachords to various places on the palm of the left hand, a device helpful in directing a chorus by indicating manually the corresponding positions of the notes. Opinions differ widely as to the attribution to Guido of all these innovations; some scholars maintain that he merely popularized the already-established ideas and that solmization, in particular, was introduced by a German abbot, Poncius Teutonicus, at the abbey of Saint-Maur des Fossés. Guido's treatises are *Micrologus de disciplina artis musicae* (publ. by A. Amelli, Rome, 1904; ed. by J. Smits van Waesberghe, 1955); *Regulae de ignoto cantu; Epistola de ignoto cantu* (publ. in Eng. in Strunk's *Source Readings in Music History*, N.Y., 1950).

Guignon, Jean-Pierre (Giovanni Pietro Ghignone), violinist and composer; b. Turin, Feb. 10, 1702; d. Versailles, Jan. 30, 1774. He went to Paris from Italy in his youth; was engaged as music tutor to the Dauphin, and persuaded the King to revive and bestow on him the title of Roi des Violons et Ménétriers, which had last been used in 1695; every professional musician in France was required to join a guild and to pay a fee to Guignon as holder of the title; so much opposition was aroused by this requirement that Parliament considered the case and deprived Guignon of this prerogative. He wrote several books of concertos, sonatas, and duos for violin.

Guilbert, Yvette, famous French *diseuse* and folksong singer; b. Paris, Jan. 20, 1865; d. Aix-en-Provence, Feb. 2, 1944. She made her debut in Paris as an actress in 1885; in 1890 she began her career as a café singer; at first she sang popular songs in Paris; later, as she toured Europe and the U.S., where she first appeared in 1896, she became noted for her interpretations of French folk songs; she regarded herself as primarily an actress, rather than a singer. She wrote her memoirs, *La Chanson de ma vie* (Paris, 1927) and *Autres temps, autres chants* (Par-

is, 1946).

Guillemain, (Louis-) Gabriel, French violinist and composer; b. Paris, Nov. 7, 1705; d. there (suicide), Oct. 1, 1770. He was a member of the King's orch. and gave concerts as a virtuoso. He was one of the first French composers to write violin sonatas with a developed clavichord accompaniment. He also wrote several ballets, and instrumental music for various combinations.

Guilmant, (Félix) Alexandre, eminent French organist and composer; b. Boulogne, March 12, 1837; d. Meudon, near Paris, March 29, 1911. He studied organ with his father, Jean-Baptiste Guilmant (1793–1890); took harmony lessons with Gustave Carulli in Boulogne. In 1860, he took an advanced course in organ playing with Lemmens in Brussels. When still a child, he substituted for his father at the Church of St.-Nicolas in Boulogne; at 20, he taught at the Boulogne Cons. and conducted choral concerts. He then played organ in various churches in Paris, including St.-Sulpice (1863) and Notre Dame (1868); in 1871, he was appointed organist of Ste. Trinité, remaining at this post for 30 years. He was one of the founders of the Schola Cantorum (1894); in 1896, he was appointed prof. of organ at the Paris Cons.; also appeared as organ soloist with Paris orchs. and subsequently all over Europe and in the U.S. (1893–97). He was not only a virtuoso of the first rank, but a master in the art of improvisation; he formed a great school of students, among whom were René Vierné, Joseph Bonnet, Nadia Boulanger, Marcel Dupré, and the American organist William Carl. He was a prolific composer of works for organ, which include 8 sonatas, 2 symphs. for Organ and Orch., 25 books of organ pieces, 10 books of *L'Organiste liturgiste;* there are also 3 masses, Psalms, vespers, motets, etc. Of greater importance than these are Guilmant's monumental editions of old masters: *Archives des maîtres de l'orgue* (Paris, 1898–1914; 10 vols.) and *Ecole classique de l'orgue* (1898–1903); he also edited selected works of French composers performed at his historical concerts (1902–06); made numerous arrangements for organ of various classical works.

Guion, David (Wendell Fentress), American composer; b. Ballinger, Texas, Dec. 15, 1892; d. Dallas, Oct. 17, 1981. He studied piano with Leopold Godowsky in Vienna; returning to the U.S. in 1915, he occupied various teaching posts in Texas; then lived in N.Y., while continuing to gravitate toward Texas; was commissioned to write a musical panorama, *Cavalcade of America,* for the 1936 Texas centennial; his *Texas Suite* for band followed in 1952. Guion devoted many years to collecting and arranging American folk songs for various folk ensembles. Of these arrangements, the most famous were *Turkey in the Straw, Arkansas Traveler,* and *Home on the Range.* He also wrote an African ballet suite, *Shingandi;* several orch. suites, among them *Southern Nights Suite; Sheep and Goat Walking to the Pasture; Alley Tunes;* and *Mother*

Guiraud – Gundry

Goose Suite.

Guiraud, Ernest, French composer; b. New Orleans, June 23, 1837; d. Paris, May 6, 1892. He studied with his father, Jean Baptiste Guiraud; produced his first opera *Le Roi David,* in New Orleans at the age of 15. He then went to Paris, which was his home for the rest of his life; studied at the Paris Cons., with Marmontel (piano) and Halévy (composition); won the Grand Prix de Rome in 1859 with his cantata *Bajazet et le joueur de flûte.* He stayed in Rome for 4 years; then returned to Paris, where his one-act opera, *Sylvie,* was produced at the Opéra-Comique (May 11, 1864). He was appointed a prof. at the Cons. in 1876; among his students were Debussy, Gédalge, and Loeffler. He wrote the recitatives to Bizet's *Carmen* and completed the orchestration of Offenbach's *Contes d'Hoffmann.* His operas (all first perf. in Paris) include *En prison* (March 5, 1869); *Le Kobold* (July 2, 1870); *Madame Turlupin* (1872); *Piccolino* (April 11, 1876, his most popular stage work); *Galante aventure* (March 23, 1882); *Frédégonde* (completed by Saint-Saëns; Dec. 18, 1895). He also wrote a ballet, *Gretna Green* (1873); 2 suites for Orch.; *Arteveld,* an overture; *Caprice* for Violin and Orch.; and a treatise on instrumentation.

Gulda, Friedrich, Austrian pianist; b. Vienna, May 16, 1930. He studied piano in early childhood (1937–42) with Felix Pazofsky; then enrolled at the Vienna Music Academy as a piano student of Bruno Seidlhofer. At the age of 16 he won first prize at the International Pianists' Contest in Geneva, and immediately embarked on a concert career, giving recitals in Europe (1947–48), South America (1949), and the U.S., making a brilliant American debut in Carnegie Hall, N.Y., on Oct. 11, 1950. He was praised by critics for his intellectual penetration of the music of Bach, Beethoven, and Mozart; about 1955 he became intensely fascinated by jazz, particularly in its improvisatory aspect, which he construed as corresponding to the freedom of melodic ornamentation in Baroque music. He often included jazz numbers (with drums and slap bass) at the end of his recitals; he learned to play the saxophone, began to compose for jazz, and organized the Eurojazz Orch. As a further symptom of his estrangement from musical puritanism he returned the Beethoven Bicentennial ring given to him by the Vienna Music Academy (his old alma mater) in appreciation of his excellence in playing Beethoven's music, and gave a speech explaining the reasons for his action. He composed and performed jazz pieces, among them *Music* Nos. 1 and 2 for Piano and Big Band (1962, 1963); *Music* for 3 Jazz Soloists and Band (1962); Symph. in F for Jazz Band and Orch.; *The Veiled Old Land* for Jazz Band (1964); *The Excursion* for Jazz Orch. (1965, celebrating the flight of the American spaceship Gemini 4); *Concertino for Players and Singers* (1972). He further made a bold arrangement of Vienna waltzes in the manner of the blues; also composed a jazz musical, *Drop-out oder Gustav der Letzte* (1970), freely after Shake-speare's *Measure for Measure;* publ. a book of essays, *Worte zur Musik* (Munich, 1971). He eventually made his home in Munich.

Gumbert, Ferdinand, German composer; b. Berlin, April 22, 1818; d. there, April 6, 1896. He was first trained by his father for book selling, but he pursued his musical studies, developing a particular interest in opera. After a short study of singing, he appeared at the Cologne Opera (1840–42); in 1842 he settled in Berlin as a voice teacher and also began to compose. His songs, written in a facile, eclectic style, enjoyed a considerable vogue; the song *An des Rheines grünen Ufern* is used as an insert in Lortzing's opera *Undine.* He produced several operettas in Berlin: *Der kleine Ziegenhirt* (Jan. 21, 1854), *Bis der Rechte kommt* (Nov. 20, 1856), etc.; publ. *Musik, Gelesenes und Gesammeltes* (Berlin, 1860).

Gumpelzhaimer, Adam, German composer; b. Trostberg, c.1559; d. Augsburg, Nov. 3, 1625. He studied music with Father Jodocus Entzenmüller at the monastery of St. Ulric in Augsburg; from 1581 to his death he was cantor at St. Anna, Augsburg.
WORKS: *Erster (zweiter) Teil des Lustgärtleins teutsch und lateinischer Lieder mit drei Stimmen* (1591 and 1611); *Erster (zweiter) Teil des Wirtzgärtleins 4 stimmiger geistlicher Lieder* (1594 and 1619); *Psalmus LI octo vocum* (1604); *Sacri concentus octonis vocibus modulandi cum duplici basso in organorum usum* (1601 and 1614; 2 parts); *10 geistliche Lieder mit 4 Stimmen* (1617); *2 geistliche Lieder mit 4 Stimmen; 5 geistliche Lieder mit 4 Stimmen von der Himmelfahrt Jesu Christi; Newe teutsche geistliche Lieder mit 3 und 4 Stimmen* (1591 and 1594); *Das Inventar der Kantorei St. Anna in Augsburg* (compiled 1620–22; publ. in the ed. of R. Schaal; Kassel, 1965). A number of Gumpelzhaimer's motets have been reprinted in Bodenschatz's *Florilegium Portense,* Schadaeus's *Promptuarium,* and Vintzius's *Missae.* O. Mayr ed. a selection of his works in Denkmäler der Tonkunst in Bayern, 19 (10.ii).

Gundry, Inglis, English composer; b. London, May 8, 1905. He studied law at Oxford Univ.; 1935 entered the Royal College of Music in London, where he took a music course with Vaughan Williams. In 1942 he was appointed Royal Marines Schoolmaster; then taught music history at London Univ. In 1960 he became music director of the Sacred Music Drama Society. He wrote the operas (all to his own librettos) *Naaman, The Leprosy of War* (1938); *The Return of Odysseus* (1941; revised 1957); *The Partisans* (London, May 28, 1946); *Avon* (London, April 11, 1949); *The Logan Rock* (Portchurno, Aug. 15, 1956); *The Prince of the Coxcombs* (London, Feb. 3, 1965); *The Three Wise Men* (London, Jan. 11, 1968); *The Prisoner Paul* (1969); a ballet, *Sleep* (1943); *Symphonic Fantasy* for Orch. (1948); the song cycles *The Black Mountains* (1956) and *The Year of the Firebird* (1957); he also arranged several old English music dramas.

Gungl, Joseph, famous Hungarian bandmaster and popular composer; b. Zsámbék, Dec. 1, 1810; d. Weimar, Jan. 31, 1889. He played the oboe in an artillery regiment in the Austrian army, and later became that band's conductor; he wrote a number of marches and dances, which became extremely popular; traveled with his band all over Germany. In 1843, he established his own band in Berlin; made an American tour in 1849; then returned to Europe and lived mostly in Munich and Frankfurt.

Gunsbourg, Raoul, Rumanian-French impresario; b. Bucharest, Dec. 25, 1859; d. Monte Carlo, May 31, 1955. After directing opera companies in Russia, he became the director of the Grand Theatre in Lille (1888–89); of the Nice Opera (1889–91); then of the Monte Carlo Opera (1893–1950); his first important production there was the stage version of *The Damnation of Faust* by Berlioz (Feb. 18, 1893). He produced at Monte Carlo several of his own operas (he wrote the piano scores, and the orchestration was done by L. Jehin); of these, *Le Vieil Aigle,* after Maxim Gorky's fable (Monte Carlo, Feb. 13, 1909), had a modicum of success.

Gura, Eugen, operatic baritone; b. Pressern, near Saatz, Bohemia, Nov. 8, 1842; d. Aufkirchen, Bavaria, Aug. 26, 1906. He studied in Vienna and in Munich; sang in Munich (1865–67), Breslau (1867–70), and Leipzig (1870–76), obtaining extraordinary success; then was in Hamburg (1876–83) and Munich (1883–96). He was particularly impressive in Wagnerian roles; his performance of Hans Sachs was greatly praised. He publ. *Erinnerungen aus meinem Leben* (Leipzig, 1905). His son, **Hermann Gura** (b. Breslau, April 5, 1870; d. Bad Wiessee, Bavaria, Sept. 13, 1944), was also a baritone; like his father, he specialized in Wagnerian roles; after a successful career as an opera singer in Germany, he settled in Berlin as voice teacher.

Guridi, Jesús, Spanish composer; b. Vitoria, Basque province of Álava, Sept. 25, 1886; d. Madrid, April 7, 1961. He studied in Madrid, at the Schola Cantorum in Paris, in Brussels (with Jongen), and in Cologne. He returned to Spain in 1909; became an organist at Bilbao, where he remained until 1939; then moved to Madrid; was appointed prof. of organ at the Madrid Cons. in 1944. During his 30 years in Bilbao, he promoted the cause of Basque folk music; publ. an album of 22 Basque songs. His zarzuelas make frequent use of Basque folk music; of these, *El caserio* (Madrid, 1926) attained enormous success in Spain; other stage works are *Amaya,* lyric drama in 3 acts (Bilbao, 1920), *La meiga* (Madrid, 1928), and *Mirentxu,* idyll in 2 acts; he further wrote a symph. poem, *An Adventure of Don Quixote; Sinfonia pirenáica; Basque Sketches* for Chorus and Orch.; an orch. suite, *10 Basque Melodies* (very popular in Spain); a number of choral works a cappella on Basque themes; 4 string quartets; pieces for piano; various songs.

Gurlitt, Cornelius, German composer; b. Altona, Feb. 10, 1820; d. there, June 17, 1901. He was a member of an artistic family; his brother, Louis Gurlitt, was a well-known landscape painter. He studied piano with Johann Peter Reinecke in Altona, and with Weyse in Copenhagen, where he went in 1840. In 1845, he made a journey through Europe; he met Schumann, Lortzing, Franz, and other eminent composers. In 1864 he was appointed organist of the Altona Cathedral, retaining this post until 1898; also taught at the Hamburg Cons. (1879–87). He wrote an opera, *Die römische Mauer* (Altona, 1860); another opera, *Scheik Hassan,* was not performed. He further composed 3 violin sonatas, 3 cello sonatas, several cycles of songs, etc. He is chiefly remembered, however, by his numerous piano miniatures, in Schumann's style; a collection of these was publ. by W. Rehberg, under the title *Der neue Gurlitt* (2 vols.; Mainz, 1931).

Gurlitt, Manfred, German conductor and composer; b. Berlin, Sept. 6, 1890; d. Tokyo, April 29, 1972. He was of an artistic family; his grandfather was the well-known landscape painter Louis Gurlitt, whose brother was the composer **Cornelius Gurlitt.** He studied in Berlin with Humperdinck (composition) and Karl Muck (conducting); rapidly progressed as a professional conductor; was a coach at the Berlin Opera (1908) and at the Bayreuth Festival (1911); was theater conductor in Essen and Augsburg; conductor and music director at the Bremen Opera (1914–27); then at the Berlin Opera and on the German radio. After 1933, he was deprived of his position by the Nazi regime; in 1939 he settled in Japan as a teacher and conductor; organized the Gurlitt Opera Co. in Tokyo.

WORKS: Operas: *Die Heilige* (Bremen, Jan. 27, 1920); *Wozzeck* (Bremen, April 22, 1926; written almost at the same time as Alban Berg's *Wozzeck*); *Soldaten* (1929); *Nana* (1933); *Seguidilla Bolero* (1937); *Nordische Ballade;* and *Wir schreiten aus; 3 politische Reden* for Baritone, Men's Chorus, and Orch.; *Goya Symphony* (1950); *Shakespeare Symphony* (1954) for 5 Solo Voices and Orch.; songs with Orch.; concertos for Piano, for Violin, for Cello; Piano Quartet; songs.

Gurlitt, Wilibald, eminent German musicologist and editor; b. Dresden, March 1, 1889; d. Freiburg im Breisgau, Dec. 15, 1963. He was a grandnephew of the composer **Cornelius Gurlitt,** and a cousin of **Manfred Gurlitt.** He studied musicology at the Univ. of Heidelberg with Philipp Wolfrum; also at the Univ. of Leipzig with Hugo Riemann and Arnold Schering, where he received his Ph.D. in 1914 with the dissertation *Michael Praetorius (Creuzbergensis): Sein Leben und seine Werke* (publ. in Leipzig, 1915); subsequently was an assistant to Riemann. He served in World War I, and was taken prisoner in France. After the Armistice, he became a lecturer at the Univ. of Freiburg; directed its dept. of musicology from 1920; was made a full prof. in 1929, but was removed from his position by the Nazi regime in 1937; resumed his professorship in 1945; retired in 1958. Gurlitt's investigations of the organ music of Praetorius led him to construct (in collaboration with Oscar Walcker) a "Praetorius organ," which was to reproduce the tuning of the period. This gave impetus in Germany to performance of historic works on authentic or reconstructed instruments. Gurlitt's other interests included the problem of musical terminology, resulting in the publ. of his *Handwörterbuch der musikalischen Terminologie.* In 1952 he revived the moribund *Archiv für Musikwissenschaft.* He ed. the first two vols. of the 12th ed. of Riemann's *Musik-Lexikon* (Mainz, 1959 and 1961). He also publ. *Johann Sebastian Bach: Der Meister und sein Werk* (Berlin, 1936; 4th ed., 1959; in Eng., St. Louis, 1957). For a complete list of his writings and scholarly eds., see his autobiographical article in *Die Musik in Geschichte und Gegenwart;* also A. Schmitz, "Wilibald Gurlitt," in *Jahrbuch der Akademie der Wissenschaften und der Literatur* (Mainz, 1964).

Gurney, Ivor, English song composer; b. Gloucester, Aug. 28, 1890; d. Dartford, Kent, Dec. 26, 1937. He was a chorister at Gloucester Cathedral; studied at the Royal College of Music in London with Stanford and Vaughan Williams; served in World War I, was wounded and gassed, and never recovered his physical and mental health; the 2 vols. of his war poems illustrate the turmoil of his inner life. After the Armistice, Gurney began to compose songs; 27 were publ. before his death, and several more were included in a 2-vol. edition of his melodies publ. posthumously. Gurney's gift was not for larger forms; he was at his best in his songs; he also wrote 5 *Western Watercolors,* 5 preludes for piano, and some violin pieces. A memorial Gurney issue of *Music & Letters,* with articles by Vaughan Williams, Walter de la Mare, and others, was publ. in 1938.

Gusikoff, Michel, American violinist and composer; b. New York, May 15, 1893; d. there, July 10, 1978. He was of a musical family; his father was a violin maker and his great-grandfather, **Michal Jozef Guzikov,** was a famous performer on the xylophone. He studied violin with Franz Kneisel and composition with Percy Goetschius; served as concertmaster with the Russian Symph. Orch. in N.Y., the N.Y. Symph. Orch., the Philadelphia Orch., and the NBC Symph. Orch. He subsequently became concertmaster and associate conductor of the Pittsburgh Symph. He made violin arrangements of songs by Gershwin; also wrote an *American Concerto* for Violin and Orch.

Gutchë, Gene (real name, **Romeo E. Gutsche**), American composer; b. Berlin, July 3, 1907. He studied in Germany, then went to the U.S., where he undertook additional academic work at the Univ. of Minnesota with Donald Ferguson and at the Univ. of Iowa with Philip Greeley Clapp (Ph.D., 1953); held two Guggenheim fellowships (1961, 1964). His music is marked by a fairly advanced idiom and a neo-Romantic treatment of programmatic subject matter. In some of his orch. works he applies fractional tones by dividing the strings into two groups tuned at slightly differing pitches.

WORKS: Symph. No. 1 (Minneapolis, April 11, 1950); Symph. No. 2 (1950–54); Symph. No. 3 (1952); *Rondo Capriccioso* (1953; N.Y., Feb. 19, 1960; with the application of fractional tones); Piano Concerto (Minneapolis, June 19, 1956); Cello Concerto (1957); Symph. No. 4 (1960; Albuquerque, March 8, 1962); Symph. No. 5 for Strings (Chautauqua, July 29, 1962); *Bongo Divertimento* for Solo Percussionist and Orch. (1962); *Timpani Concertante* (Oakland, Calif., Feb. 14, 1962); Violin Concerto (1962); *Genghis Khan,* symph. poem (Minneapolis, Dec. 6, 1963); *Rites in Tenochtitlán* for Small Orch. (St. Paul, Jan. 26, 1965); *Gemini* for Orch., with microtones (Minneapolis, July 26, 1966); *Classic Concerto* for Orch. (St. Paul, Nov. 11, 1967); Symph. No. 6 (1968); *Epimetheus USA* for Orch. (Detroit, Nov. 13, 1969); *Icarus,* suite for Orch. (1975); *Bi-Centurion* for Orch. (1975; Rochester, N.Y., Jan. 8, 1976); *Perseus and Andromeda XX* for Orch. (1976; Cincinnati, Feb. 25, 1977); *Akhenaten* for Chorus and Orch. (St. Louis, Sept. 23, 1983). 4 string quartets; 3 piano sonatas; choruses.

Gutheil-Schoder, Marie, German mezzo-soprano; b. Weimar, Feb. 10, 1874; d. Ilmenau, Oct. 4, 1935. She studied in Weimar, made her debut there in 1891; sang with the court opera until 1900, when she went to the Vienna Opera, becoming an outstanding singer-actress in such roles as Carmen, Elektra, Salome; in 1926 she was appointed stage director of the opera. She married the composer and conductor **Gustav Gutheil.**

Guthrie, Woody (full name, **Woodrow Wilson Guthrie**), American folk singer; b. Okemah, Okla., July 14, 1912; d. New York, Oct. 3, 1967. His father was a prizefighter and a professional guitar player. The family suffered adversity during the Depression; Woody Guthrie took to the road; performed in saloons and at labor meetings, improvising songs of social significance. Later he joined Pete Seeger and others in a group known as Almanac Singers; publ. the books *Bound for Glory* and *American Folksong.* Although not a trained singer, Guthrie acquired fame as an impassioned balladeer of disadvantaged Americans. Ignoring for the moment his freely professed radical convictions, the U.S. government bestowed upon him in 1966 an award of merit as "a poet of the American landscape." His career was cut short in 1957 when he contracted Huntington's chorea, which incapacitated him. His son **Arlo Guthrie** (b. New York, July 10, 1947) carried on Woody Guthrie's tradition as a folk singer; became famous for his ballad *Alice's Restaurant,* which is also the title of a motion picture in which he starred as himself, getting busted.

Gutiérrez, Horacio, brilliant Cuban pianist; b. Havana, Aug. 28, 1948. He studied in Havana; made his concert debut there as a young child; continued his studies in Los Angeles and at the Juilliard School in N.Y. He gained fame in 1970, after winning 2nd prize in the world's most prestigious musical arena, the International Tchaikovsky Competi-tion in Moscow. Since then, he has appeared with major American and European orchs.

Gutsche, Romeo E. See **Gutchë, Gene.**

Guy-Ropartz. See **Ropartz, Guy.**

Guyot, Jean, Flemish musician, also known under the names of **Jean de Chatelet** and **Johannes Ca-stileti;** b. Chatelet (Hainaut) in 1512; d. Liège, March 11, 1588. He studied at the Univ. of Louvain, and received the degree of licencié-ès-arts on March 22, 1537; in 1546 he was chaplain at St. Paul's in Liège; publ. his first motets in Antwerp that year; about 1557 assumed the duties of maître de chapelle at the Cathedral of St. Lambert in Liège; on Nov. 1, 1563, was appointed music master at the Imperial Court in Vienna; he returned to Liège in Aug., 1564, and remained maître de chapelle at the Cathedral of St. Lambert to his death.

Guzikov, Michal Jozef, famous performer on the xylophone; b. Szklow, Poland, Sept. 14, 1806; d. Aa-chen, Oct. 21, 1837. Of a Jewish musical family, he showed precocious talent; with four relatives he traveled all over Europe; his virtuosity on the xylo-phone was extraordinary, and elicited praise from the public as well as from celebrated musicians, among them Mendelssohn. Guzikov's programs consisted of arrangements of well-known works and also his own pieces; his most successful number was a transcription of Paganini's *La Campanella.*

Gyrowetz, Adalbert, notable Austrian composer; b. Budweis, Bohemia, Feb. 19, 1763; d. Vienna, March 19, 1850. He studied piano, violin, and composition with his father, a local choirmaster; then went to Prague, where he studied law; at the same time, began to compose band pieces and waltzes; he was befriended by Count Franz von Fünfkirchen, who was a music lover, and whose secretary he became. For the private orch. of Count von Fünfkirchen, Gy-rowetz wrote 6 symphs. in Haydn's style; later, when he was in Vienna, he showed these works to Mozart, who encouraged him and arranged for a performance of one of Gyrowetz's symphs. From Vienna, he traveled through Italy; in Naples, he studied with Sala and Paisiello. In 1789, he went to Milan, Genoa, and finally to Paris, where several of his works were accepted by publishers. He then moved to London, where one of his pieces was per-formed at a Haydn concert (March 23, 1792). He was commissioned to write an opera, *Semiramide,* for the Pantheon Theatre, but before the announced performance the opera building burned down, and with it perished the MS of *Semiramide.* After 3 years in London, he returned to the Continent, even-tually settling in Vienna (1793), where he became Kapellmeister at the Vienna Opera (1804–31). In Vienna, he enjoyed a great reputation as composer, and his name was often coupled with Beethoven's in public prints.

WORKS: He composed a number of operas, which were performed, one after another, at the Vienna Opera: *Selico* (Oct. 15, 1804); *Agnes Sorel* (Dec. 4, 1806); *Die Junggesellen-Wirtschaft* (June 18, 1807); *Die Pagen des Hertzogs von Vendome* (Aug. 5, 1808); *Der betrogene Betrüger* (Feb. 17, 1810); *Der Augenartz* (his most successful opera; Oct. 1, 1811); *Das Winterquartier in Amerika* (Oct. 30, 1812); *Robert* (July 15, 1813); *Helene* (Feb. 16, 1816); *Aladin* (Feb. 7, 1819); *Der blinde Harfner* (Dec. 19, 1827); *Der Geburtstag* (Feb. 11, 1828); *Felix und Adele* (Aug. 10, 1831); also several operettas and singspiels. In 1834, he produced in Dresden an op-era, *Hans Sachs,* using essentially the same literary material as Wagner's *Meistersinger.* He further wrote a number of ballets; much church music; some 60 symphs.; about 60 string quartets; 30 trios; about 40 violin sonatas, as well as piano pieces and songs. The historical reasons for the rapid decline of Gyrowetz's repute as a composer after his death are not easy to explain; attempted revivals of his music proved futile.

Gysi, Fritz, Swiss musicologist; b. Zofingen, Feb. 18, 1888; d. Zürich, March 5, 1967. He studied at the Basel Cons., at Zürich Univ., and at Berlin Univ.; in 1921 became lecturer in music at the Univ. of Zü-rich. He publ. *Mozart in seinen Briefen* (1921); *Max Bruch* (1922); *Claude Debussy* (1926); *Richard Wag-ner und die Schweiz* (1929); *Richard Strauss* (1934); *Hans Georg Nägeli* (1936).

H

Haas, Joseph, eminent German composer and pedagogue; b. Maihingen, March 19, 1879; d. Munich, March 30, 1960. He studied with Max Reger in Munich and with Karl Straube in Leipzig (organ). In 1911 he was appointed composition teacher at the Stuttgart Cons.; in 1921 became a prof. in the Catholic church music dept. at the Akademie der Tonkunst in Munich. From 1945 to 1950 he was president of the Hochschule für Musik in Munich. Through the long years of his pedagogical activities, Haas established himself as one of the most reputable teachers in Germany. As a composer, Haas is equally estimable, but his music has failed to gain popularity outside his circle. He wrote more than 100 opus numbers. At the time of his retirement in 1950, a Joseph Haas Society was organized in Munich, with the aim of issuing bulletins regarding his works.
WORKS: Operas: *Tobias Wunderlich* (Kassel, Nov. 24, 1937) and *Die Hochzeit des Jobs* (Dresden, July 2, 1944); oratorios: *Die heilige Elisabeth* (1931); *Christnacht* (1932); *Das Lebensbuch Gottes* (1934); *Das Lied von der Mutter* (1939); *Das Jahr in Lied* (1952); *Die Seligen* (Kassel, April 12, 1957); *Deutsche Kindermesse* (1958); *Marienkantate* (1959); *Variations on a Rococo Theme* for Orch.; *Ouvertüre zu einem frohen Spiel* (1943); 2 string quartets (1908, 1919); Trio for 2 Violins and Piano (1912); many song cycles. He publ. a biography of Max Reger (Bonn, 1949); contributed articles to various publications.

Haas, Karl, German conductor and musicologist; b. Karlsruhe, Dec. 27, 1900; d. London, July 7, 1970. He studied at the univs. of Munich and Heidelberg; then worked for the Karlsruhe and Stuttgart radios; was active as a collector of valuable old instruments; made microfilms of old music. In 1939 he emigrated to England; in 1943 he organized the London Baroque Ensemble; led it until 1966 in performances of little-known Baroque music. He also edited works by Haydn, Boccherini, and Cherubini.

Haas, Monique, French pianist; b. Paris, Oct. 20, 1906. She studied at the Paris Cons. with Lazare Lévy; became greatly interested in modern music, and gave numerous concerts all over Europe in programs of 20th-century composers; also appeared with orchs. in modern concertos. She is married to the composer **Marcel Mihalovici.**

Haas, Pavel, Czech composer; b. Brno, June 21, 1899; put to death in the concentration camp at Auschwitz (Oswiecim), Poland, Oct. 17, 1944. He studied piano and composition in Brno; was a soldier in the Austrian army in World War I; after the Armistice, continued his study with Petřzelka at the Brno Cons. (1919–21) and at the master class there with Janáček (1921–22). He tried to leave Czechoslovakia after its occupation by the Nazi hordes, but the outbreak of World War II made this impossible; in 1941 he was placed in a concentration camp in Terezín, where he continued to compose until, in Oct. 1944, he was sent to Auschwitz and put to death there.

WORKS: Opera, *Šarlatán (The Charlatan),* to his own libretto (1936; Brno, April 2, 1938); *Zesmutnělé Scherzo (Mournful Scherzo)* for Orch. (1921); *Předehra pro rozhlas (Overture for Radio)* for Orch., Male Chorus, and Narrator (1930); Symph. (1941; unfinished); *Studie* for String Orch. (1943); Variations for Piano and Orch. (1944); cantata, *Introduction and Psalm XXIX* (1931); 3 string quartets (1920, 1925, 1938); *Fata morgana,* piano quintet, with Tenor Solo (1923); Wind Quintet (1929); Suite for Oboe and Piano (1939); Suite for Piano (1935); songs. His extant MSS are preserved in the Moravian Museum in Brno.

Haas, Robert (Maria), distinguished Austrian musicologist; b. Prague, Aug. 15, 1886, d. Vienna, Oct. 4, 1960. He received his primary education in Prague; then studied music history at the univs. of Prague, Berlin, and Vienna; obtained his Ph.D. in 1908 from the Univ. of Prague with his dissertation *Das Wiener Singspiel.* He then was an assistant to Guido Adler at the Inst. for Music History in Vienna (1908–09). During World War I he was in the Austrian army; then joined the staff of the Nationalbibliothek in Vienna, becoming chief of the music division in 1920. He completed his Habilitation at the Univ. of Vienna in 1923 with his *Eberlins Schuldramen und Oratorien;* then became a lecturer there; also devoted much of his time to the music of the Baroque and Classical eras. After the founding of the International Bruckner Society, he became editor of the critical edition of Bruckner's works; he also edited works for Denkmäler der Tonkunst in Österreich. He retired in 1945.

WRITINGS: *Gluck und Durazzo im Burgtheater* (Vienna, 1925); *Die estensischen Musikalien: Thematisches Verzeichnis mit Einleitung* (Regensburg, 1925); *Die Wiener Oper* (Vienna, 1926); *Wiener Musiker vor und um Beethoven* (Vienna, 1927); *Die Musik des Barocks* (Potsdam, 1928); *Aufführungspraxis der Musik* (Potsdam, 1931); *W.A. Mozart* (Potsdam, 1933; 2nd ed., 1950); *Anton Bruckner* (Potsdam, 1934); *Bach und Mozart in Wien* (Vienna, 1951); *Ein unbekanntes Mozart-Bildnis* (Vienna, 1955).

Haas, Werner, talented German pianist; b. Stuttgart, March 3, 1931; d. Nancy, Oct. 13, 1976. He studied at the Hochschule für Musik in Stuttgart and at the Saarbrücken Cons. Following the example of Walter Gieseking, whose master courses he had attended, Haas developed a particular interest in French music, and became a fine interpreter of works of Debussy and Ravel.

Hába, Alois, notable Czech composer of microtonal music; b. Vizovice, Moravia, June 21, 1893; d. Prague, Nov. 18, 1973. He studied with Novák at the Prague Cons. (1914–15); then privately with Schreker in Berlin (1918–22); returned to Prague in 1923; taught there from 1924 to 1951. He became interested in the folk music of the Orient, which led him to consider writing in smaller intervals than the semitone. His first work in the quarter-tone system was the 2nd String Quartet (op. 7, 1920); in his 5th String Quartet (op. 15, 1923) he first applied the sixth-tones; in his 16th String Quartet (op. 98, 1967) he introduced the fifth-tones. He notated these fractional intervals by signs in modified or inverted sharps and flats. The piano manufacturing firm A. Förster constructed for him a quarter-tone piano (1925) and a sixth-tone harmonium (1927); other firms manufactured at his request a quarter-tone clarinet (1924) and trumpet (1931). From 1923–53 Hába led a class of composition in fractional tones at the State Cons. in Prague, attracting a large number of students, among them his brother, **Karel,** the conductors Ančerl and Susskind, and the composers Dobiáš, Ježek, Kowalski, Kubín, Lucký, Ponc, Karel Reiner (who, along with E. Schulhoff, specialized in quarter-tone piano playing and premiered 10 of Hába's works), Seidel, Srnka, Constantin Iliev of Bulgaria, Slavko Osterc of Yugoslavia, and Necil Kâzim Akses of Turkey. Hába publ. an important manual of modern harmony, *Neue Harmonielehre des diatonischen, chromatischen, Viertel-, Drittel-, Sechstel-, und Zwölfteltonsystems (New Principles of Harmony of the Diatonic, Chromatic, Fourth-, Third-, Sixth-, and Twelfth-Tone Systems;* Leipzig, 1927), detailing new usages introduced by him in his classes; he further publ. *Harmonicke základy čtvrttónové soustavy (Harmonic Foundation of the Quarter-Tone System;* Prague, 1922) and *Von der Psychologie der musikalischen Gestaltung, Gesetzmässigkeit der Tonbewegung und Grundlagen eines neuen Musikstils (On the Psychology of Musical Composition; Rules of Tonal Structure and Foundation of New Musical Style;* Vienna, 1925); also *Mein Weg zur Viertel- und Sechstetonmusik* (Düsseldorf, 1971). As a composer, he cultivated a "non-thematic" method of writing, without repetition of patterns and devoid of development.

WORKS: OPERAS: *Matka (Mother;* 1927–29), in quarter-tones, to his own text; it was first perf. in Munich in a German version as *Die Mutter* on May 17, 1931, and subsequently produced in Czech (Prague, May 27, 1947); *Nová Země (The New Land;* 1934–36), written in the traditional tempered scale; never perf., except for the overture, played in Prague on April 8, 1936; *Přijd království Tvé (Thy Kingdom Come),* in fractional tones, to Hába's own text (1937–40; unperf.); cantata, *Za mír (For Peace;* Prague, Nov. 1, 1950). FOR ORCH.: Overture (Berlin, Dec. 9, 1920); *Symphonic Fantasy* for Piano and Orch. (1921); *Cesta života (The Path of Life;* Winterthur, Switzerland, March 15, 1934); *Valašská suita*

(Prague, Oct. 29, 1953); Violin Concerto (1955; Prague, Feb. 17, 1963); Viola Concerto (1955–57). CHAMBER MUSIC: The following are in the tempered scale: 4 nonets for Wind and String Instruments (1931, based on a 12-tone row; 1932, based on a 7-tone row; 1953; 1963); string quartets Nos. 1, 7, 8, 9, 13, and 15 (1919; 1951; 1951; 1952; *Astronautic,* 1961; 1964); Violin Sonata (1915); Fantasy for Flute or Violin, and Piano, op. 34, (1928; op. 34a, version for Bass Clarinet and Piano, 1967); Sonata for Guitar Solo (1943); Sonata for Chromatic Harp, op. 59 (1944); Sonata for Diatonic Harp, op. 60 (1944); *Intermezzo and Preludium* for Diatonic Harp (1945); Suite for Solo Bassoon (1950; op. 69a, version for Bass Clarinet, 1968); Suite, quartet for Bassoons (1951); *Fantasy* and *Fantasy and Fugue* for Organ (both 1951); Solo Clarinet Sonata (1952); Suite for Solo Violin, op. 81a (1955); Suite for Solo Cello, op. 81b (1955); Suite for Solo Cymbalom (1960); Suite for Solo Bass Clarinet, op. 96 (1964); Suite for Solo Saxophone (1968); Suite for Bass Clarinet and Piano (1969); *Observations from a Journal* for Narrator and String Quartet (1970); Suite for Violin and Piano, op. 103 (1972; his last work); *Fugue Suite* for Piano (1918); *Variations on a Canon by Schumann* for Piano (1918); *2 morceaux* for Piano (1917–18; arranged for String Orch. by R. Kubín, 1930); Piano Sonata, op. 3 (1918); *6 Pieces* for Piano (1920); *4 Modern Dances* for Piano (1927); *Toccata quasi una Fantasia* for Piano (1931); *6 Moods* for Piano (1971). Works in quarter-tones: string quartets Nos. 2, 3, 4, 6, 12, and 14 (1920, 1922, 1922, 1950, 1960, 1963); Fantasy for Solo Violin (1921); *Music* for Solo Violin (1922); Fantasy for Solo Cello (1924); Fantasy for Violin and Piano, op. 21 (1925); Suite No. 1 for Clarinet and Piano (1925); Fantasy for Viola and Piano (1926); Fantasy for Cello and Piano (1927); 2 suites for Solo Guitar (1943, 1947); Suite No. 2 for Solo Clarinet (1943–44); Suite for Trumpet and Trombone (1944); Suite for 4 Trombones (1950); Suite for Solo Violin, op. 93 (1961–62); 6 suites for Piano (1922, revised 1932; 1922, revised 1932; 1923; 1924; 1925; 1959); 11 fantasies for Piano (Nos. 1–10, 1923–26; No. 11, 1959); Piano Sonata, op. 62 (1947). Works in fifth-tones: String Quartet No. 16 (1967). Works in sixth-tones: string quartets Nos. 5, 10, and 11 (1923, 1952, 1958); Duo for 2 Violins (1937); Suite for Solo Violin, op. 85a (1955); Suite for Solo Cello, op. 85b (1955); *6 Pieces* for Harmonium (1928). He also wrote songs and choral pieces, many of them in the quarter-tone system.

Hába, Karel, Czech composer, brother of **Alois Hába;** b. Vizovice, Moravia, May 21, 1898; d. Prague, Nov. 21, 1972. He studied violin with Karel Hoffmann and Jan Mařák and music theory with V. Novák, J. Křička, and J.B. Foerster at the Prague Cons.; also attended his brother's class in quarter-tone music (1925–27). He wrote only 3 pieces in quarter-tones, but he faithfully followed the athematic method of composing that was the cornerstone of Alois Hába's esthetics. Karel Hába was employed as a violinist in the orch. of Prague Radio (1929–36); was later a music critic and lecturer in music education at Charles Univ. (1951–63). He

wrote *Violin Manual in the Quarter-tone System* (MS, 1927) and *Modern Violin Technique,* in 2 vols. (Prague, 1928).

Habeneck, François-Antoine, eminent French conductor; b. Mézières, Jan. 22, 1781; d. Paris, Feb. 8, 1849. His father, a native of Mannheim and a member of a regimental band, taught him the violin. In 1800 Habeneck entered the Paris Cons., studying violin with Baillot. In 1804 he became a violinist in the orch. of the Opéra-Comique; shortly thereafter he joined the orch. of the Paris Opéra, becoming principal violin in 1817. From 1806–15 he conducted the student orch. at the Paris Cons., and also taught violin there (1808–16; 1825–48). From 1824–31 he was *premier chef* (with Valentino) of the Paris Opéra, holding that post alone from 1831–46; during his tenure there he conducted the premieres of *Guillaume Tell, La Juive, Les Huguenots,* and *Benvenuto Cellini.* In 1828 he founded the Société des Concerts du Conservatoire de Paris, which initially consisted of an orch. of 86 musicians and a chorus of 79 singers (the average complement of orch. members was 60). At his first concert on March 9, 1828, he conducted Beethoven's *Eroica* Symph.; he subsequently championed Beethoven's symphs. in his concerts, giving the first Paris perf. of the 9th Symph. on March 27, 1831. Under his guidance the orch. became the finest in its day, gaining the praise of such musicians as Mendelssohn and Wagner. He led it for 20 years, conducting his last concert on April 16, 1848. A pioneering figure among conductors, Habeneck retained many of the characteristics of the earlier violin-leader type of conductor (for instance, he used the violin part, with other instruments cued in, instead of a full score; directed with a violin bow; and, at the beginning of his career, played along with his musicians); nevertheless, he assumed a foremost place among the conductors of his era. He was also a composer, but his works are not significant. With Isouard and Benincori he wrote an opera, *Aladin ou La Lampe merveilleuse* (Paris Opéra, Feb. 6, 1822); he composed 2 violin concertos and other violin music; also publ. a *Méthode théorique et pratique de violon* (Paris, 1835).

Haberbier, Ernst, German pianist; b. Königsberg, Oct. 5, 1813; d. Bergen, Norway, March 12, 1869. He studied with his father, an organist; left home in 1832; went to Russia and became a court pianist in St. Petersburg in 1847; gave concerts in London in 1850; in 1852 appeared in Paris, where he scored a sensational success; in 1866 he settled in Bergen. He perfected what he considered a novel system of piano technique, dividing difficult passages between the 2 hands (however, this had been done by Scarlatti and Bach long before). He wrote a number of effective piano pieces, of which *Etudes-Poésies* (op. 53) are the best known.

Haberl, Franz Xaver, eminent German theorist, music editor, and historiographer; b. Oberellenbach, Lower Bavaria, April 12, 1840; d. Regensburg,

Sept. 5, 1910. He studied in the Boys' Seminary at Passau, and took Holy Orders in 1862; in 1862–67 was Cathedral Kapellmeister and music director at the Seminary; in 1867–70 was organist at S. Maria dell' Anima in Rome; in 1871–82 was Cathedral Kapellmeister at Regensburg, where he founded, in 1875, a world-renowned school for church music. He was an authority on Catholic church music, past and present. In 1872 he assumed the editorship of the collection *Musica divina,* and edited the periodical *Musica Sacra* in 1888. In 1876 he began to publ. the *Cäcilienkalender,* the scope of which was greatly widened until, after 1885, it was issued under the more appropriate name of *Kirchenmusikalisches Jahrbuch;* as such it has become one of the most important publications for historical studies concerning the church music of the 15th, 16th, and 17th centuries; Haberl continued as editor until 1907, when he resigned and was succeeded by Karl Weinmann. He founded the Palestrina Society in 1879, and (beginning with vol. X) was editor in chief of Breitkopf & Härtel's complete edition of Palestrina's works (33 vols., completed on the tercentenary of Palestrina's death, 1894), which he aided not only by his experience and learning, but also by rare MSS from his private collection. In 1899 he was elected president of the Allgemeiner Cäcilienverein, and became editor of its official organ, *Fliegende Blätter für Katholische Kirchenmusik.* In 1889 he was made Dr.Theol. (*honoris causa*) by the Univ. of Würzburg; in 1908, "Monsignore." Under his general supervision, a new edition of the *Editio Medicea* (1614) of the plainchant melodies was issued, with papal sanction, at Regensburg (1871–81). When modern scholarship had proved that the original edition had not been publ. with papal sanction and had not been revised by Palestrina; that, in fact, it contained the old melodies in badly distorted and mutilated form, the papal sanction was withdrawn, and the edition suppressed and replaced by a new *Editio Vaticana* in 1904. The result of this was that Haberl's books dealing with plainchant (which had been held in the highest esteem, and had passed through many editions) fell into desuetude. The books thus affected are: *Praktische Anweisung zum harmonischen Kirchengesang* (1864), *Magister Choralis* (1865; 12th ed., 1899; trans. into Eng., French, Italian, Spanish, Polish, and Hungarian), *Officium hebdomadae sanctae* (1887, in German), and *Psalterium vespertinum* (1888). His other writings, the value of which remains unimpaired, are *Bertalotti's Solfeggien* (1880), *Wilhelm Dufay* (1885), *Die römische "Schola Cantorum" und die päpstlichen Kapellsänger bis zur Mitte des 16. Jahrhunderts* (1887), and *Bibliographischer und thematischer Musikkatalog des päpstlichen Kapellarchivs im Vatikan zu Rom* (1888).

Hadley, Henry (Kimball), eminent American composer and conductor; b. Somerville, Mass., Dec. 20, 1871; d. New York, Sept. 6, 1937. He studied piano and violin with his father and then with S. Emery and G.W. Chadwick at the New England Cons. in Boston; in 1894, studied theory with Mandyczewski in Vienna. Returning to America, he became director of music at St. Paul's School in Garden City, N.Y. (1895–1902); toured various cities in Germany, conducting his own works (1905–9); conducted at the Stadttheater in Mainz (1908–9) and brought out there his one-act opera *Safié.* In 1909 he was engaged as conductor of the Seattle Symph. Orch.; from 1911–15 he was conductor of the San Francisco Symph. Orch., and from 1920–27, associate conductor of the N.Y. Phil. Orch. In 1924 he again toured Europe; conducted symph. concerts in Buenos Aires in 1927; was conductor of the Manhattan Symph. Orch. (1929–32), producing many American works. He was conductor at the opening concert of the Berkshire Festival at Stockbridge, Mass., in 1933. He traveled extensively; conducted his own works in Japan and Argentina; spent his last years mostly in N.Y. He received a Mus.D. from Tufts College (1925); was a member of the National Inst. of Arts and Letters and the American Academy of Arts and Letters; received the Order of Merit from the French government. Hadley occupied a position of prominence among American composers. In his style, he frankly adhered to programmatic writing. Although he shunned the unresolved dissonances of the ultramodern school, he was not averse to using fairly advanced harmonies in an impressionist vein; he often applied exotic colors when the subject matter justified it. He was an excellent craftsman, both as composer and conductor, and contributed much to the growth of American music culture.

WORKS: Comic opera, *Nancy Brown;* grand operas: *Safié* (Mainz, April 4, 1909); *Azora, the Daughter of Montezuma* (Chicago, Dec. 26, 1917); *Bianca* (N.Y., Oct. 15, 1918, composer conducting); *The Fire-Prince,* operetta (1917); *Cleopatra's Night* (N.Y., Jan. 31, 1920); *A Night in Old Paris* (N.Y., Feb. 22, 1933); festival play, *The Atonement of Pan* (San Francisco, Aug. 10, 1912); 5 symphs.: No. 1, *Youth and Life* (N.Y. Phil., Dec. 2, 1897); No. 2, *The 4 Seasons* (N.Y. Phil., Dec. 20, 1901; won the Paderewski prize and one offered by the New England Cons.); No. 3 (Berlin Phil., Dec. 27, 1907, composer conducting); No. 4, *North, East, South, West* (Norfolk [Conn.] Festival, Jan. 6, 1911, composer conducting); No. 5, *Connecticut* (Norfolk [Conn.] Festival, 1935); overtures: *Hector and Andromache; In Bohemia* (Boston Symph., Dec. 16, 1901); *Herod; Othello* (Philadelphia Orch., Dec. 26, 1919); *Youth Triumphant; Aurora Borealis* (1931); *Academic Overture; Alma Mater* (1932); *The Enchanted Castle* (1933); tone poems: *Salome* (composed in 1905, before the production of *Salome* by Richard Strauss; publ. in 1906; perf. by Muck and the Boston Symph., April 12, 1907); *Lucifer* (Norfolk [Conn.] Festival, June 2, 1914, composer conducting); *The Ocean* (N.Y. Phil., Nov. 17, 1921, composer conducting); orch. rhapsody, *The Culprit Fay* (Chicago Symph. at Grand Rapids, Mich., May 28, 1909, composer conducting; won a $1,000 prize of the National Federation of Music Clubs); orch. suites: *Oriental* (1903); *Ballet of the Flowers* (1925); *Suite ancienne* (1926); *Silhouettes, San Francisco* in 3 movements (Robin Hood Dell, July 17, 1932, composer conducting); *Streets of Pe-*

kin (Tokyo, Sept. 24, 1930, composer conducting); *Scherzo diabolique* for Orch., "to recall a harrowing personal experience during a terrifying automobile ride at night, exceeding all speed limits" (Century of Progress Exposition, Chicago, Aug. 1934, composer conducting); incidental music to *The Daughter of Hamilcar* and *Audrey; Konzertstück* for Cello and Orch. (1937); Piano Quintet (1920); 2 string quartets; 2 piano trios; Violin Sonata; Elegy for Cello and Piano; choral works with Orch.: *In Music's Praise* (1899; won the Oliver Ditson Prize); *Merlin and Vivien; The Fate of Princess Kiyo; The Nightingale and the Rose; The Golden Prince; The Fairy Thorn; Ode to Music* (1917); *The New Earth* (1919); *Resurgam* (Cincinnati Music Festival, May 1923); *Mirtil in Arcadia* (Harrisburg [Pa.] Festival, May 17, 1928); *Belshazzar* (1932); 6 ballads (*The Fairies; In Arcady; Jabberwocky; Lelawala, a Legend of Niagara; The Princess of Ys; A Legend of Granada*); many anthems; piano pieces; over 150 songs to German and Eng. words. A Henry Hadley Foundation for the Advancement of American Music was organized in 1938.

Hadley, Patrick Arthur Sheldon, British composer; b. Cambridge, March 5, 1899; d. King's Lynn, Norfolk, Dec. 17, 1973. He studied at the Royal College of Music in London with Vaughan Williams and others (1922–25); then taught there in 1925–38; in 1938–46 held a fellowship at Gonville and Caius College in Cambridge; held a chair of music at Cambridge from 1946 to 1962. He composed mostly vocal music; among his works are the cantatas *The Trees So High* (1931); *La Belle Dame sans merci* (1935); *Travelers* (1940); *The Hills* (1946); *Fen and Flood* (1956); *Connemara* (1958); *Cantata for Lent* (1960).

Hadow, Sir William Henry, English music educator; b. Ebrington, Gloucestershire, Dec. 27, 1859; d. London, April 8, 1937. He studied at Malvern College (1871–78) and Worcester College, Oxford (1878–82); received the degrees of M.A. (1888) and Mus.B. (1890). He held various positions in English univs. from 1885–1919; was knighted in 1918. He wrote a cantata, *The Soul's Pilgrimage;* a String Quartet; 2 violin sonatas; a Viola Sonata; and a number of anthems. These, however, are of little significance; Hadow's importance lies in his books, written in a lively journalistic style. His book on Haydn, *A Croatian Composer* (London, 1897), claiming that Haydn was of Slavonic origin, aroused considerable controversy; modern research proves the claim fanciful and devoid of foundation. Of more solid substance are his other writings: *Studies in Modern Music* (2 vols., 1892–95; 10th ed., 1921); *Sonata Form* (1896); *The Viennese Period* (vol. 5 of the *Oxford History of Music,* 1904); *Beethoven* (1917); *William Byrd* (1923); *Music* (in the Home Univ. Library, 1924; 3rd revised ed., by Sir George Dyson, 1949); *Church Music* (1926); *A Comparison of Poetry and Music* (1926); *Collected Essays* (1928); *English Music* (1931); *The Place of Music among the Arts* (1933); *Richard Wagner* (1934). He edited songs of the British Isles (1903); was editor in chief of the *Oxford History of Music* (1901–5 and 1929); contributed articles to various British magazines and to the *Musical Quarterly* (Jan. 1915).

Haeffner, Johann Christian Friedrich, German composer; b. Oberschönau, near Suhl, March 2, 1759; d. Uppsala, Sweden, May 28, 1833. He was a pupil of Vierling at Schmalkalden; studied at the Univ. of Leipzig, and served as proofreader for Breitkopf; then became conductor of a traveling opera troupe; in 1781 he arrived in Stockholm, where he became an organist at a German church. He produced at Stockholm several operas in the style of Gluck which had a favorable reception: *Electra* (July 22, 1787), *Alcides inträde i Världen* (Nov. 11, 1793), and *Renaud* (Jan. 29, 1801). In 1792 he was appointed court conductor; in 1808 he went to Uppsala, where he remained for the rest of his life, acting as organist of the Cathedral and music director of the univ. He took great interest in Swedish national music; publ. Swedish folk songs with accompaniment, and revised the melodies of the Geijer-Afzelius collection; edited a *Svenska Choralbok* (2 parts, 1819–21), in which he restored the choral melodies of the 17th century, and added preludes (1822); also arranged a collection of old Swedish songs in 4 parts (1832–33; he finished only 2 books).

Haendel, Ida, violinist; b. Chelm, Poland, Dec. 15, 1924. She studied at the Warsaw Cons., receiving its gold medal; made a facile London debut when she was only 10 years old by appearing with Sir Henry Wood at a Proms concert in the Brahms Violin Concerto. She then continued her studies with Carl Flesch and Georges Enesco. She settled in England and became a British subject. She was a soloist with the London Phil. on its tour of China in 1973. A facile writer, she publ. an interesting account of her life and career in *Woman with Violin* (London, 1970).

Hafez, Abdel Halim (Abdel Halim Shabana), Egyptian singer; b. Halawat, 1930; d. London, March 30, 1977. He rose to prominence in Egypt, and the Arab world in general, as the foremost interpreter of romantic and nationalistic songs; won renown for his renditions of *Safini Marru* and *Ala Kad el Shouk.* He used Western instruments in his performances, and even utilized the Moog synthesizer. So widespread was his fame at the time of his death, that 100,000 Egyptians lined the streets of the funeral procession in Cairo.

Hagegård, Håkan, Swedish baritone; b. Karlstad, Nov. 25, 1945. He studied at the Royal Academy of Music in Stockholm; also took lessons with Tito Gobbi in Rome, Gerald Moore in London, and Erik Werba in Vienna. He made his operatic debut as Papageno in Mozart's *Die Zauberflöte* at the Royal Opera in Stockholm in 1968; subsequently appeared throughout Europe, following his successful portrayal of Papageno in the film by Ingmar Bergman. He is particularly distinguished as an interpreter of baritone parts in the operas of Mozart, Rossini, Verdi, and Donizetti.

Hageman, Maurits Leonard, Dutch violinist and composer; b. Zutfen, Sept. 25, 1829; d. Nijmegen, April 16, 1906. He studied with Bériot and Fétis at the Brussels Cons., graduating in 1852. After playing violin in the Italian Opera orch. at Brussels, he became a conductor at Groningen; then was director of the Cons. of Batavia, Java (1865–75), and conductor of the orch. there. Returning to the Netherlands, he founded a music school in Leeuwarden. He wrote an oratorio, *Daniel;* several other choral works; piano pieces; songs.

Hageman, Richard, distinguished American pianist, conductor, and composer; b. Leeuwarden, the Netherlands, July 9, 1882; d. Beverly Hills, March 6, 1966. He studied music with his father, **Maurits Hageman;** then took courses at the Brussels Cons. with Gevaert and Arthur de Greef. He held an auxiliary position as conductor at the Royal Opera in Amsterdam (1899–1903). After playing accompaniments for Mathilde Marchesi in Paris (1904–5), he came to the U.S. as accompanist for Yvette Guilbert in 1906; from 1913–21 and again in 1936 was on the conducting staff of the Metropolitan Opera; also conducted the summer opera at Ravinia Park in Chicago and taught voice at the Chicago Musical College. In 1938 he settled in Hollywood, where he was engaged as a composer of film music. He wrote 2 operas: *Caponsacchi* (1931; produced in Freiburg, Germany, as *Tragödie in Arezzo,* Feb. 18, 1932; at the Metropolitan Opera House, N.Y., Feb. 4, 1937; received the David Bispham Memorial Medal) and *The Crucible* (Los Angeles, Feb. 4, 1943). He achieved a lasting reputation mainly through his solo songs, of which *Do Not Go My Love* (to words by Rabindranath Tagore) and *At the Well* became extremely popular.

Hagen, Francis Florentine, American Moravian minister and composer; b. Salem, N.C., Oct. 30, 1815; d. Lititz, Pa., July 7, 1907. He served as a teacher and minister in various Moravian congregations; edited and compiled the *Church and Home Organist's Companion* (several vols.). He wrote a number of anthems, in which a definite sense for distinguished popular melody is noticeable; also a cantata and an overture. His *Morning Star,* a Christmas carol, which in Moravian communities stood in continuous favor for almost a century, was reprinted in 1939. Another anthem is included in the series Music of the Moravians in America, publ. by the N.Y. Public Library.

Hagerup Bull, Edvard, Norwegian composer; b. Bergen, June 10, 1922. He studied composition in Norway with Bjarne Brustad and Ludvig Irgens Jensen; in 1947 went to Paris, where he took courses with Koechlin, Rivier, Messiaen, and Milhaud; continued his studies in Berlin with Boris Blacher. His music bears a pleasing neo-Classical stamp.
WORKS: *Le Soldat de plomb,* ballet suite (1948–49); Serenade for Orch. (1950); *Morceaux rap-*sodiques, divertimento for Orch. (1950); 2 trumpet concertos (1950, 1960); *Sinfonia di teatro,* symph. prelude (1950–51); *Petite suite symphonique* for Small Orch. (1951); *Escapades,* suite for Orch. (1952); Divertimento for Piano and Orch. (1954); 5 symphs.: No. 1, *3 mouvements symphoniques* (1955); No. 2, *In modo d'una sinfonia* (1958–59); No. 3, *Sinfonia espressiva* (1964); No. 4, *Sinfonia humana* (1968); No. 5, *Sinfonia in memoriam* (1971–72); *3 morceaux brefs* for Saxophone and Orch. (1955); *Cassation* for Chamber Orch. (1959); *Münchhausen,* ballet (1961); *Epilogue* for Strings (1961); *Undecim Sumus* for Chamber Orch. of Soloists (1962); *Dialogue* for Flute, Strings, and Piano (1965); *6 épigrammes* for Chamber Ensemble (1969); Concerto for Flute and Chamber Orch. (1969); *Air solennel,* symph. movement (1972); Clarinet Sonata (1951); *3 bucoliques* for Oboe, Clarinet, and Bassoon (1953); Duo for Violin and Piano (1956); *Ad usum amicorum* for Flute, Violin, Cello, and Piano (1957); *Marionnettes sérieuses* for Wind Quintet (1960); *Quadrige* for 4 Clarinets (1963); Sextet for Saxophone and Wind Quintet (1965); *Sonata cantabile* for Flute, Violin, Cello, and Piano (1966); *Concert* for Trumpet, Horn, and Trombone (1966); *Accents* for Piano (1968); *Sonata con spirito* for Piano Quartet (1970).

Hägg, Gustaf Wilhelm, eminent Swedish organist and composer; b. Visby, Nov. 28, 1867; d. Stockholm, Feb. 7, 1925. Hägg was his mother's name, which he legally adopted; his father's name was Peterson. Hägg was a remote relative of **Jacob Adolf Hägg.** He studied organ at the Stockholm Cons.; in 1893 he was appointed organist at the Klara Church in Stockholm, retaining this position for the rest of his life. In the interim he traveled for further study purposes in Germany and France (1897–1900). In 1904 he joined the staff of the Stockholm Cons., as a teacher of harmony and organ playing. He enjoyed a distinguished reputation in Sweden as an organist, and gave numerous recitals in which he played the works of César Franck and other organ composers. He also composed 5 organ concertos and other organ pieces; several cantatas; songs. He arranged and publ. collections of Swedish songs (Stockholm, 1908), and an album, *Songs of Sweden* (N.Y., 1909).

Hägg, Jacob Adolf, Swedish composer; b. Oestergarn, June 27, 1850; d. Hudiksvall, March 1, 1928. He was a remote relative of **Gustaf Wilhelm Hägg.** He studied at the Stockholm Cons.; then received a stipend to take courses in Denmark with Gade, who exercised a decisive influence on his style of composition; he further studied piano with Anton Door in Vienna and music theory with Kiel in Berlin. Ambition to learn and relentless diligence in his studies upset his mental equilibrium so that he had to spend 15 years in a sanatorium (1880–95). He recovered but retired to the country, reducing his activity to a minimum. Despite this misadventure he was able to leave a considerable legacy of works, among them 5 symphs., of which *Nordische Symphonie* (1870; revised 1890) was the best known; 3 overtures;

Hahn – Haieff

Cello Sonata, Piano Trio, String Quartet, and other chamber music; piano pieces; songs.

Hahn, Georg, remarkable Austrian bass; b. Vienna, Jan. 30, 1897; d. Munich, Dec. 9, 1950. He enlisted in the Austrian army in World War I; after demobilization began to study singing with Theodor Lierhammer at the Vienna Academy of Music. In 1927 he joined the Bavarian State Opera in Munich; made guest appearances in Brussels, Berlin, Paris, and London; also sang at La Scala, Milan. He was equally successful in such dramatic roles as Pizarro in *Fidelio,* Sarastro in *Die Zauberflöte,* and Rigoletto, as well as in buffo parts such as Falstaff and Leporello. He performed all his roles in German, even in the Italian repertoire, and continued to sing and record to the very last months of the war, in 1943 and 1944.

Hahn, Reynaldo, Venezuelan-born French composer; b. Caracas, Aug. 9, 1874; d. Paris, Jan. 28, 1947. His father, a merchant from Hamburg, settled in Venezuela c.1850; the family moved to Paris when Reynaldo Hahn was 5 years old. He studied singing and apparently had an excellent voice; a professional recording he made in 1910 testifies to that. He studied music theory at the Paris Cons. with Dubois and Lavignac and composition with Massenet, who exercised the most important influence on Hahn's own music. He also studied conducting, achieving a high professional standard as an opera conductor. In 1906 he was invited to conduct at the Mozart Sesquicentennial Festival in Salzburg (other conductors were Mahler and Richard Strauss). In 1934 he became music critic of *Le Figaro.* He remained in France during the Nazi occupation at a considerable risk to his life, since he was Jewish on his father's side. In 1945 he was named a member of the Inst. de France and music director of the Paris Opéra. Hahn's music is distinguished by a facile, melodious flow and a fine Romantic flair. Socially, he was known in Paris for his brilliant wit. He maintained a passionate youthful friendship with Marcel Proust, who portrayed him as a poetic genius in his novel *Jean Santeuil;* their intimate correspondence was publ. in 1946.
WORKS: OPERAS: *L'ile du rêve,* "Polynesian idyll," after Pierre Loti (Opéra-Comique, Paris, March 23, 1898); *La Carmélite* (Opéra-Comique, Paris, Dec. 16, 1902); *Nausicaa* (Monte Carlo, April 10, 1919); *Fête triomphale* (Paris Opéra, July 14, 1919); *La Colombe de Bouddah* (Cannes, March 21, 1921); *Ciboulette,* light opera (Théâtre des Variétés, Paris, April 7, 1923); *Le Marchand de Venise,* after Shakespeare (Paris Opéra, March 25, 1935). OPERETTAS: *Miousic* (Paris, March 22, 1914); *Mozart,* after a play by Sascha Guitry (Paris, Dec. 2, 1925); *Brummel* (Paris, Jan. 20, 1931); *O mon bel inconnu* (Paris, Oct. 5, 1933); *Malvina* (Gaîté Lyrique, Paris, March 25, 1935). INCIDENTAL MUSIC: To Daudet's *L'Obstacle* (1890); Croisset's *Deux courtisanes* (1902); Racine's *Esther* (1905); Hugo's *Angelo* (1905) and *Lucrèce Borgia* (1911); Wolff and Duvernois's *Le Temps d'aimer* (1926). BALLETS: *Fin d'amour* (1892);

Le Bal de Béatrice d'Este (Paris, April 11, 1907); *La Fête chez Thérèse* (Paris, Feb. 16, 1910); *Medusa* (Monte Carlo, Dec. 24, 1911); *Le Dieu bleu* (Diaghilev's Ballets Russes, Paris, May 14, 1912); *Le Bois sacré* (1912); 2 symph. poems: *Nuit d'amour bergamasque* (1897) and *Promethée triomphant* (1911); Christmas mystery, *La Pastorale de Noël* (1908). A lyric comedy, *Le Oui des jeunes filles,* left unfinished at Hahn's death, was completed and orchestrated by Henri Busser and perf. posthumously at the Opéra-Comique in Paris on June 21, 1949. Hahn further wrote a Violin Concerto (Paris, Feb. 26, 1928); Piano Concerto (Paris, Feb. 4, 1931); Cello Concerto; Piano Quintet; String Quartet; and a number of piano pieces, among them a suite, *Portraits des peintres,* inspired by poems of Marcel Proust. But his most signal accomplishment lies in his songs, such as *Les Chansons grises* (1891–92, written when he was still a cons. student), *L'Heure exquise,* and *Si mes vers avaient des ailes.* Hahn was a brilliant journalist. His articles were collected in the following publications: *Du Chant* (Paris, 1920); *Notes. Journal d'un musicien* (Paris, 1933); *L'Oreille au guet* (Paris, 1937); and *Thèmes variés* (Paris, 1946).

Hahn, Ulrich. See **Han, Ulrich.**

Haibel, (Johann Petrus) Jakob, Austrian composer; b. Graz, July 20, 1762; d. Djakovar, March 24, 1826. He was engaged in Vienna as a tenor; in 1806 settled in Djakovar; there he married Sophie Weber, sister of Mozart's widow. He produced several stage works in Vienna, among them the ballet *Le nozze disturbate* (May 18, 1795) and a singspiel, *Der Tyroler Wastl* (May 14, 1796), which became very popular. Other productions were *Der Papagei und die Gans* (May 25, 1799); *Tsching, Tsching, Tsching* (Feb. 6, 1802); *Der kleine Cesar* (July 25, 1804); etc.

Haieff, Alexei, Russian-American composer; b. Blagoveshchensk, Siberia, Aug. 25, 1914. He received his primary education at Harbin, Manchuria; in 1931 came to the U.S.; studied with Rubin Goldmark and Frederick Jacobi at the Juilliard School of Music in N.Y.; during 1938–39 he studied with Nadia Boulanger in Cambridge, Mass. He held a Guggenheim fellowship in 1946 and again in 1949; was a Fellow at the American Academy in Rome (1947–48), a prof. at the Univ. of Buffalo (1962–68), and composer-in-residence at the Univ. of Utah (1968–70). In his music Haieff follows Stravinsky's type of neo-Classical writing, observing an austere economy of means, but achieving modernistic effects by a display of rhythmic agitation, often with jazzy undertones.
WORKS: Ballets: *The Princess Zondilda and Her Entourage* (1946) and *Beauty and the Beast* (1947); 3 symphs.: No. 1 (1942); No. 2 (Boston, April 11, 1958; received the American International Music Fund Award); No. 3 (New Haven, Conn., April 11, 1961); Divertimento for Orch. (N.Y., April 5, 1946); Violin Concerto (1948); Piano Concerto (N.Y., April 27, 1952; received the Award of the N.Y. Music Critics

Circle); Sonatina for String Quartet (1937); 3 *Bagatelles* for Oboe and Bassoon (1939); Serenade for Oboe, Clarinet, Bassoon, and Piano (1942); *Eclogue* for Cello and Piano (1947); *La Nouvelle Héloïse* for Harp and String Quartet (1963); Cello Sonata (1963); *Eloge* for Chamber Orch. (1967); *Caligula* for Baritone and Orch., after Robert Lowell (N.Y., Nov. 5, 1971); Sonata for 2 Pianos (1945); Piano Sonata (1955); songs.

Haitink, Bernard, eminent Dutch conductor; b. Amsterdam, March 4, 1929. He studied violin at the Amsterdam Cons.; then played in the Radio Phil. Orch. in Hilversum. In 1954–55 he attended the conducting course of Ferdinand Leitner, sponsored by the Netherlands Radio; in 1955 he was appointed to the post of second conductor of the Radio Phil. Orch. in Hilversum, becoming its principal conductor in 1957. In 1956 he made his first appearance as a guest conductor with the Concertgebouw Orch. of Amsterdam. He made his U.S. debut with the Los Angeles Phil. Orch. on Jan. 2, 1958. In 1959 he conducted the Concertgebouw Orch. in England. In 1961 he became co-principal conductor of the Concertgebouw Orch., sharing his duties with Eugen Jochum; that same year he led it on a tour of the U.S., followed by one to Japan in 1962. In 1964 he became chief conductor of the Concertgebouw Orch. In 1967 he also assumed the post of principal conductor and artistic adviser of the London Phil. Orch., becoming its artistic director in 1969; he resigned from this post in 1978. He made his first appearance at the Glyndebourne Festival in 1972, and in 1978 was named its music director. He also acted as a guest conductor with the Berlin Phil., Vienna Phil., N.Y. Phil., Chicago Symph., Boston Symph., and Cleveland Orch. In 1982 he led the Concertgebouw Orch. on a transcontinental tour of the U.S. In his interpretations Haitink avoids personal rhetoric, allowing the music to speak for itself. Yet he achieves eloquent and colorful effect; especially fine are his performances of the symphs. of Bruckner and Mahler; equally congenial are his projections of the Classical repertoire. He has received numerous international honors, including the Netherlands' Royal Order of Orange-Nassau (1969), the Medal of Honor of the Bruckner Society of America (1970), and the Gustav Mahler Society Gold Medal (1971); he was named a Chevalier de l'Ordre des Arts et des Lettres of France (1972). He received the rare distinction of being made an Honorary Knight Commander of the Order of the British Empire by Queen Elizabeth II in 1977.

Hale, Adam de la. See **Adam de la Halle.**

Hale, Philip, eminent American music critic; b. Norwich, Vt., March 5, 1854; d. Boston, Nov. 30, 1934. He took music lessons in his early youth, and as a boy played the organ in the Unitarian Church at Northampton, Mass.; went to Yale Univ. to study law, and was admitted to the bar in 1880. He then took organ lessons with Dudley Buck; subsequently went to Europe (1882–87), where he studied organ

with Haupt in Berlin, and composition with Rheinberger in Munich and with Guilmant in Paris. Returning to America, he served as a church organist in Albany and Troy, N.Y., and in Boston, but soon abandoned this employment for his true vocation, that of drama and music criticism. He was a forceful and brilliant writer; his articles were often tinged with caustic wit directed against incompetent performers and, regrettably, against many modern composers; he also disliked Brahms, and was credited with the celebrated but possibly apocryphal quip that the exits in the newly opened Symph. Hall in Boston should have been marked not "Exit in Case of Fire," but "Exit in Case of Brahms." Another verbal dart attributed to Philip Hale was his dismissal of a singer with the concluding sentence "Valuable time was consumed." Hale was the music critic for the *Boston Home Journal* (1889–91), the *Boston Post* (1890–91), the *Boston Journal* (1891–1903), and the *Boston Herald*, of which he was also drama editor (1904–33). He was also editor of the *Boston Musical Record* (1897–1901). From 1901–33 he compiled the program books of the Boston Symph. Orch., setting a standard of erudition and informative annotation. He edited *Modern French Songs* for The Musician's Library (1904); was joint author, with Louis C. Elson, of *Famous Composers and Their Works* (1900). Hale was succeeded as the program annotator of the Boston Symph. by John N. Burk, who publ. a selection of Hale's articles under the title *Philip Hale's Boston Symphony Programme Notes* (N.Y., 1935; revised ed., 1939). Hale's voluminous archives and collections of newspaper articles are preserved in the Music Division of the Boston Public Library.

Halévy, Jacques-François-Fromental-Elie, celebrated French opera composer; b. Paris, May 27, 1799; d. Nice, March 17, 1862. He was a child prodigy. At 10 he entered the Paris Cons. as an elementary pupil of Cazot. In 1810 he studied piano with Lambert; in 1811, harmony with Berton; and counterpoint for 5 years with Cherubini. At 17 he competed for the Prix de Rome, winning the 2nd prize with his cantata *Les Derniers Moments du Tasse;* in 1817 he again won the 2nd prize, with *La Mort d'Adonis;* in 1819 he gained the Grand Prix de Rome with his *Herminie.* He had previously composed an opera, *Les Bohémiennes* (never perf.), publ. a Piano Sonata for 4-hands, and set to music the 130th Psalm in Hebrew, the De Profundis. During his stay in Italy he wrote another opera. In 1822, on his return to Paris, he made vain attempts to produce his grand opera *Pygmalion* and *Les Deux Pavillons,* a comedy-opera. It was not until 1827 that he brought out a one-act comedy-opera, *L'Artisan,* at the Théâtre Feydeau, though with little success. The same year he succeeded Daussoigne as prof. of harmony and accompaniment at the Cons., following Fétis as prof. of counterpoint and fugue in 1833, and taking a class of advanced composition in 1840. In 1827 he was engaged as the harpsichordist at the Italian Opera. In 1828, with Rifaut, he composed *Le Roi et le bâtelier* in honor of Charles X. On Dec. 9 of the same year, *Clari* (with Malibran as prima donna) was a success at the Théâtre Italien; *Le Dilettante d'Avignon* was produced on Nov. 7, 1829; and on May 3, 1830, the grand ballet *Manon Lescaut.* Halévy was now appointed "chef du chant" at the Opéra, a post he retained for 16 years. In 1831 *La Langue musicale* was produced at the Opéra-Comique; then *La Tentation* (Paris, June 20, 1832; ballet-opera, with Gide), at the Opéra; *Les Souvenirs de Lafleur,* at the Opéra-Comique (March 4, 1833); and on May 16 of 1933, a completion of Hérold's unfinished *Ludovic,* which proved very successful. On Feb. 23, 1835, the Paris Opéra produced Halévy's masterpiece, *La Juive,* which soon became one of the most spectacular successes in opera theaters throughout Europe and America. A few months later appeared *L'Eclair* (Dec. 16, 1835), a sparkling comedy-opera. To add to his growing reputation, Halévy was created a Chevalier of the Legion of Honor. On the death of Reicha (1836), Halévy succeeded him as one of the 3 musical members of the Académie; and in 1854 he was appointed Secretary for life. With *La Juive* Halévy attained not only the zenith of his powers, but also of his triumphs. *La Juive* was followed by *Guido et Ginevra* (March 5, 1838); *Les Treize* (April 15, 1839); *Le Shérif* (Sept. 2, 1839); *Le Drapier* (Jan. 6, 1840); *Le Guitarrero* (Jan. 21, 1841); *La Reine de Chypre* (Dec. 22, 1841); *Charles VI* (Feb. 3, 1843); *Le Lazzarone* (March 23, 1844); and *Les Mousquetaires de la reine* (March 15, 1846). He collaborated with Adam, Auber, and Carafa in *Les Premiers Pas* for the inauguration of the National Opera (1847). His next productions were: *Le Val d'Andorre* (Nov. 11, 1848); *La Fée aux roses* (Oct. 1, 1849); *La Dame de pique* (Dec. 28, 1850). On June 8, 1850, Halévy conducted in London an Italian opera, *La Tempesta.* He then produced in Paris *Le Juif errant* (April 23, 1852); *Le Nabab* (Sept. 1, 1853); *Jaguarita* (May 14, 1855); *L'Inconsolable* (under the nom de plume **Albert;** 1855); *Valentine d'Aubigny* (1856); *La Magicienne* (March 17, 1858). Besides his operas, Halévy wrote a Piano Sonata for 4-hands; romances; nocturnes; part-songs for men's voices; scenes from *Prometheus Unbound* (Paris, March 18, 1849); and the cantatas *Italie* (1849) and *Les Plagues due Nil* (1959); he also left the almost-finished scores of 2 operas, *Vanina d'Ornano* and *Le Déluge* (originally *Noé,* completed by Bizet; perf. April 5, 1885). In the Paris schools his *Leçons de lecture musicale* (Paris, 1857) was adopted as the textbook for singing. *Souvenirs et portraits* (1861) and *Derniers souvenirs et portraits* (1863) were collections of the funeral orations that, as secretary of the Académie, he had delivered at the obsequies of deceased members. At the Paris Cons. he had many distinguished pupils, among them Gounod and Bizet (who married Halévy's daughter).

Halffter, Cristóbal, significant Spanish composer and conductor, nephew of **Ernesto** and **Rodolfo Halffter;** b. Madrid, March 24, 1930. He studied composition with Conrado del Campo at the Cons. in Madrid (1947–51); then had private lessons with

Alexandre Tansman in Paris. He taught at the Madrid Cons. (1960–67) and was associated with the Radio Nacional de España; traveled as a conductor and lecturer in Europe; visited the U.S. in 1966. In his music he adopted a radical modern idiom; evolved a modified technique of dodecaphonic writing, and explored electronic sound.

WORKS: FOR THE STAGE: Opera, *Don Quichotte* (Düsseldorf, 1970); ballet, *Saeta* (Madrid, Oct. 28, 1955). FOR ORCH.: *Scherzo* for Orch. (1951); Piano Concerto (Madrid, March 13, 1954); *2 Movements for Timpani and Strings* (Madrid, June 26, 1957); Concertino for String Orch. (1956; expanded version of his First String Quartet); *5 Microformas* for Orch. (1960); *Rhapsodia española de Albeniz* for Piano and Orch. (1960); Sinfonia for 3 Instrumental Groups (1963); *Sequencias* for Orch. (1964; Madrid, June 16, 1964); *Lineas y puntos* for 20 Winds and Tape (1967; Donaueschingen, Oct. 22, 1967); *Anillos* for Orch. (1967–68; perf. as a ballet, Lyons, April 13, 1971); *Fibonaciana,* concerto for Flute and String Orch. (Lisbon, May 30, 1970); *Planto por las victimas de la violencia (Plaint for the Victims of Violence)* for Chamber Ensemble and Tape (Donaueschingen, Oct. 17, 1971); *Requiem por la libertad imaginada* for Orch. (1971); *Pinturas negras* for Orch. and Concertante Organ (1972); *Procesional* for 2 Pianos, Winds, and Percussion (Strasbourg, June 8, 1974); *Tiempo para espacios* for Harpsichord and 12 Strings (1974); Cello Concerto (1974; Granada, June 24, 1975); *Elegias a la muerte de tres poetas españoles* for Orch. (1974–75); *Pourquoi* for 12 Strings (1974–75); *Officium defunctorum* (Paris, 1979); Violin Concerto. FOR VOICE: *Antifona Pascual a la Virgen (Regina coeli)* for Soprano, Contralto, and Orch. (1951); *Misa ducal* for Chorus and Orch. (Madrid, May 14, 1956); *In exspectatione resurrectionis Domini,* cantata (1962); *Brecht-Lieder* for Voice and Orch. (1967); *In memoriam Anaick* for Child Narrator, Children's Chorus, and ad lib. Instruments (1967); *Symposion* for Baritone, Chorus, and Orch. (1968); *Yes Speak Out Yes,* cantata, after a text by Norman Corwin, in honor of the 20th anniversary of the UN's declaration of human rights (N.Y., Dec. 12, 1968); *Noche pasiva del sentido* for Soprano, 2 Percussionists, and Tapes (1971); *Gaudium et Spes* for 32 Voices and Tapes (1972); *Oración a Platero* for Narrator, Chorus, Children's Chorus, and 5 Percussionists (1975). CHAMBER MUSIC: 2 string quartets: No. 1, *3 Pieces* (1955), and No. 2, *Memories, 1970* (1970); *3 Pieces* for Solo Flute (1959); Solo Violin Sonata (1959); *Codex* for Guitar (1963); *Espejos (Mirrors)* for 4 Percussionists and Tape (1963); *Antiphonismoi* for 7 Players (1967); *Oda* for 8 Players (1969); *Noche activa del espiritu* for 2 Pianos and Electronics (1973); *Mijar* for 2 Flutes and Electronic Ensemble (Basel, June 1, 1980). FOR PIANO: Sonata (1951), and *Formantes* for 2 Pianos (1961).

Halffter, Ernesto, important Spanish composer, brother of **Rodolfo Halffter;** b. Madrid, Jan. 16, 1905. He studied composition with Manuel de Falla and Adolfo Salazar; as a young man he organized a chamber ensemble in Seville, with which he presented works by contemporary Spanish composers. He first attracted the attention of the music world with his *Sinfonietta,* which was included in the program of the Oxford Festival of the International Society for Contemporary Music (July 23, 1931). At the outbreak of the Spanish Civil War in 1936, he went to Lisbon; returned to Madrid in 1960. In his music he continued the tradition of Spanish modern nationalism, following the stylistic and melorhythmic formations of his teacher Manuel de Falla; he also completed and orchestrated Falla's unfinished scenic cantata, *Atlántida,* which was first performed at La Scala in Milan on June 18, 1962. His other significant works are *Fantaisie portugaise* for Orch. (Paris, March 23, 1941); *Automne malade* for Voice and Orch.; *Suite ancienne* for Wind Instruments; chamber opera, *Entr'acte* (1964); ballets: *Sonatina* (1928); *Dulcinea* (1940); *Cojo enamorado* (1954); *Fantasía galaica* (1955; Milan, 1967); *Rapsodia portuguesa* for Piano and Orch. (1962); *Canticum in memoriam P.P. Johannem XXIII* for Soprano, Baritone, Chorus, and Orch. (1964); *Psalmen* for Soloist, Chorus, and Orch. (1967); Guitar Concerto (1968).

Halffter, Rodolfo, eminent Spanish-Mexican composer, brother of **Ernesto** and uncle of **Cristóbal;** b. Madrid, Oct. 30, 1900. He acquired a considerable technique of composition, mainly by the study of classical works; received some instruction and advice from Manuel de Falla in Granada (1929). As a young man he was a member of a group of Spanish composers promoting national Spanish music in a modern idiom. From 1934–36 he was a music critic of *La Voz.* During the Spanish Civil War, he occupied important positions in the cultural sections of the Loyalist government; was chief of the Music Section of the Ministry of Propaganda (1936) and then became a member of the Central Music Council of the Spanish Republic (1937); after the Loyalist defeat, he fled to France and then to Mexico, where he settled in 1939 and became a naturalized citizen. In 1940 he founded the first Mexican company for contemporary ballet, La Paloma Azul; founded the publishing house Ediciones Mexicanas de Música in 1946 and remains its manager; edited the journal *Nuestra Música* (1946–52); was director of the music dept. of the National Inst. of Fine Arts (1959–64).

WORKS: His early music is influenced by Manuel de Falla and is imbued with Spanish melorhythms; he experimented with dodecaphonic structures; his *3 hojas de álbum* (1953) were the earliest pieces of 12-tone music publ. in Mexico. The scores of his opera buffa *Clavileño* (1934–36) and an *Impromptu* for Orch. (1931–32) were lost when a bomb hit the house where he stayed on the Spanish border during the Civil War. His other works include 3 ballets: *Don Lindo de Almería* (1935; Mexico City, Jan. 9, 1940); *La madrugada del Panadero* (*The Baker's Morning;* Mexico City, Sept. 20, 1940); *Elena la Traicionera* (Mexico City, Nov. 23, 1945); Suite for Orch. (1924–28; Madrid, Nov. 5, 1930); *Obertura concertante* for Piano and Orch. (1932; Valencia, May 23, 1937); Divertimento for 9 Instruments (1935; Mexico City, Nov. 18, 1943); Violin Concerto (1939–40; Mexico City, June 26, 1942); an orch. scoring of *3 sonatas* of Antonio Soler (1951); *Obertura festiva* (Mexico City, May 25, 1953); *3 piezas* for String Orch. (Mexico City, Aug. 10, 1955); *Tripartita* for Orch. (Mexico City, July 15, 1960); *Diferencias* for Orch. (Mexico City, Sept. 13, 1970); *Alborada* for Orch. (Mexico City, May 9, 1976); *Giga* for Solo Guitar (1930); *Pastorale* for Violin and Piano (1940); *3 piezas breves* for Solo Harp (1944); String Quartet (1957–58); Cello Sonata (1960); *3 movimientos* for String Quartet (1962); *8 tientos (Fantasias)* for String Quartet (1973). FOR PIANO: *2 sonatas de El Escorial* (1928); *Preludio y fuga* (1932); *Danza de Ávila* (1936); *Pequeñas variaciones elegiacas* (1937); *Homenaje a Antonio Machado* (1944); 3 sonatas (1947, 1951, 1967); *11 bagatelles* (1949); *3 hojas de álbum* (1953); *Música* for 2 Pianos (1965); *Laberinto: Cuatro intentos de acertar con la salida* (Labyrinth: 4 Attempts to Locate the Exit; 1971–72); *Homenaje a Arturo Rubinstein* (1973); *Facetas* (1976). FOR VOICE: *La nuez* for Children's Chorus (1944); *3 epitafios* for Chorus a cappella (1947–53); *Pregón para una Pascua pobre* for Chorus, 3 Trumpets, 2 Tenor Trombones, Bass Trombone, and Percussion (Mexico City, April, 6, 1969); 3 song cycles: *Marinero en tierra* (1925); *2 sonetos* (1940–46); *Desterro* (1967).

Hall, David, American writer on music; b. New Rochelle, N.Y., Dec. 16, 1916. He was educated at Yale Univ. (B.A., 1939) and Columbia Univ. (graduate study in psychology, 1939–40); then worked for Columbia Records and NBC; from 1948 to 1956 he was music director of the classics division of the Mercury Record Corp., where he pioneered in the development of high-fidelity recordings; then was music editor of *Stereo Review* (1957–62); later was named president of Composers Recordings, Inc. (1963–66). From 1967 to 1980 he was head of the Rodgers and Hammerstein Archives of Recorded Sound at the N.Y. Public Library, and from 1980 its curator. He publ. several annotated guides to recordings; also contributed countless articles and record reviews to leading publications.

Hall, Marie (Mary Paulina), English violinist; b. Newcastle upon Tyne, April 8, 1884; d. Cheltenham, Nov. 11, 1956. As a small child she gave performances in the homes of music-lovers in Newcastle, Malvern, and Bristol with her father, an amateur harp player; her uncle (violin); her brother (violin); and her sister (harp). Elgar heard her, and was impressed by her talent; he sent her to Wilhelmj in London for regular study; she also studied with Johann Kruse. At the age of 15 she won the first Wessely Exhibition at the Royal Academy of Music. She was recommended by Jan Kubelik to Ševčík in Prague (1901), from whom she received a rigorous training; she made her professional debut in Prague (1902); then played in Vienna. After a highly successful London concert (Feb. 16, 1903), she made her American debut as soloist with the N.Y. Symph., Walter Damrosch conducting (Nov. 8, 1905); toured Australia (1907) and India (1913). On Jan. 27, 1911, she married her manager, Edward Baring, and settled in Cheltenham; she continued to appear in concerts in England until 1955, with her daughter, **Pauline Baring,** as her accompanist.

Hall, Pauline, Norwegian composer; b. Hamar, Aug. 2, 1890; d. Oslo, Jan. 24, 1969. She studied composition with Catharinus Elling in Oslo (1910–12) and later in Paris (1912–14) and Dresden. From 1934 to 1964 she served as music critic of *Dagbladet.* In her music, Pauline Hall follows the modern French ideal of classical clarity, seasoned with euphonious dissonance.

WORKS: *Verlaine Suite* for Orch. (1929); *Circus Sketches,* orch. suite (1933); Suite for Wind Quintet (1945); *Little Dance Suite* for Oboe, Clarinet, and Bassoon (1958); *4 tosserier* for Soprano, Clarinet, Bassoon, Horn, and Trumpet (1961); *Variations on a Classical Theme* for Solo Flute (1961); *Markisen (The Marquise),* ballet (1964).

Hall, Sir Peter, noted English theater and opera producer; b. Bury St. Edmunds, Nov. 22, 1930. He was educated at St. Catharine's College, Cambridge. In 1955–56 he was director of the Arts Theatre, London. He was managing director of the Royal Shakespeare Theatre from 1960 to 1968; from 1973 he was director of the National Theatre; worked also at the Royal Opera House, Covent Garden. In 1970 he began a long and fruitful association as an opera producer at Glyndebourne. He was knighted in 1977. He is known for his versatility, having produced operas by Cavalli, Mozart, Wagner, Tchaikovsky, Schoenberg, and Tippett. In 1983 he produced the new *Ring* cycle at Bayreuth for the 100th anniversary of Wagner's death, with Solti conducting.

Halle, Adam de la. See **Adam de la Halle.**

Hallé, Sir Charles (real name, **Carl Hallé**), renowned pianist and conductor; b. Hagen, Westphalia, April 11, 1819; d. Manchester, Oct. 25, 1895. The son of a local church organist, he revealed a musical talent as a child, and performed in public at the age of 4; at 16 he was sent to study music seriously with Rinck at Darmstadt; in 1836 he went to Paris, where he entered the friendly circle of Chopin, Liszt, and others. In 1846 he gave concerts of his own as a pianist in chamber music. After the Revolution of 1848, he went to England, settling in Manchester, where he conducted an orch., choruses, and opera. In 1857 he established subscription concerts with an orch. ensemble of his own, which became famous as Charles Hallé's Orch. (debut, Jan. 30, 1858); he conducted it until his death; it endured for 125 years as one of the finest orchs. of Europe, eventually becoming known as the Hallé Orch. Although his chief activities were connected with Manchester, he also conducted the London Popular Concerts; gave piano recitals; in 1861 he presented all of Beethoven's sonatas in 8 concerts, repeating this cycle in 2 successive seasons. From 1873 till 1893 he conducted the Bristol Festivals; in 1883 he became conductor of the Liverpool Phil. So-ciety, as successor to Max Bruch; in 1893 was appointed the first principal of the Royal Manchester College of Music. He was a champion of Berlioz in England, and gave several complete performances of Berlioz's *Damnation de Faust.* His first wife was Désirée Smith de Rilieu; with his 2nd wife, the violinist **Wilma Neruda,** he made 2 Australian tours (1890 and 1891). He was knighted in 1888. He established a very high standard of excellence in orch. performance, which greatly influenced musical life in England. He publ. a *Pianoforte School* (1873) and edited a *Musical Library* (1876). M. Kennedy edited *The Autobiography of Charles Hallé* (London, 1972).

Hallén, (Johannes) Andreas, notable Swedish composer; b. Göteborg, Dec. 22, 1846; d. Stockholm, March 11, 1925. He studied with Reinecke in Leipzig, Rheinberger in Munich, and Rietz in Dresden; upon his return to Sweden, conducted in Göteborg (1872–78 and 1883–84); then was conductor of the Phil. Concerts in Stockholm (1884–92) and of the Royal Opera (1892–97). From 1908–19 he was a prof. of composition at the Stockholm Cons.

WORKS: Operas: *Harald der Viking* (Leipzig, Oct. 16, 1881); *Hexfällan* (Stockholm, March 16, 1896); *The Treasure of Waldemar* (Stockholm, April 8, 1899); *Walpurgis Night* (revised version of *Hexfällan,* Stockholm, March 15, 1902); choral works, with Orch.: *The Page and the King's Daughter; Dream-King and His Love; Goblin's Fate; Christmas Eve; Peace; Missa solemnis* (Stockholm, 1923); symph. poems: *En Sommarsaga; Die Toteninsel; Sphärenklänge;* overtures.

Hallnäs, Hilding, Swedish composer and organist; b. Halmstad, May 24, 1903. He studied at the Royal Academy of Music in Stockholm (1924–29); subsequently served as church organist in Göteborg, where he was also active as a teacher. His works reflect the prevalent Romantic style of Scandinavian music; in later compositions he applies modified serial techniques.

WORKS: He wrote 9 symphs., but withdrew the first 2 and renumbered the others: No. 1, *Sinfonia pastorale* (1944; Göteborg, March 22, 1945); No. 2, *Sinfonia notturna* (Göteborg, March 4, 1948); No. 3, *Little Symphony,* for Strings and Percussion (Göteborg, Oct. 3, 1948); No. 4, *Metamorfose sinfonische* (Göteborg, April 17, 1952; revised 1960); No. 5, *Sinfonia aforistica* (Göteborg, Jan. 24, 1963); No. 6, *Musica intima,* for Strings and Percussion (Malmö, Nov. 7, 1967); No. 7, *A Quite Small Symphony,* for Chamber Orch. (Minneapolis, June 12, 1974). He further wrote 2 ballets, *Kärlekens ringdans (Love's Dance in the Round;* 1955–56) and *Ifigenia* (1961–63; also a suite); *Divertimento* for Orch. (1937); 2 violin concertos (1945, 1965); *Symphonic Ballet Suite* (1955–56); Piano Concerto (1956); *Cantica lyrica* for Tenor, Chorus, and Orch. (1957); 2 concertos for Flute, Strings, and Percussion (1957, 1962); Concerto for String Orch. and Percussion (1959); *Epitaph* for Strings (1963); *Rapsodie* for Chamber Orch. and Soprano (1963); *En grekisk saga (A Greek*

Saga) for Orch. (1967–68; dedicated to Melina Mercouri, Mikis Theodorakis, and the Greek people); *Momenti bucolichi* for Oboe and Orch. (1969); *Horisont och linjespel* for String Orch. (1969); *Triple Concerto* for Violin, Clarinet, Piano, and Orch. (1972–73); 2 string quartets (1949, 1967); Quintet for Flute, Oboe, Viola, Cello, and Piano (1954); *Cantata* for Soprano, Flute, Clarinet, Cello, and Piano (1955); 2 violin sonatas (1957, 1975); piano trio, *Stanze sensitive* (1959); 3 piano sonatas (1963–75); organ sonata, *De Profundis* (1965); *24 Preludes* for Guitar (1967); *Passionsmusik*, 15 pieces for Organ (1968); *3 momenti musicali* for Violin, Horn, and Piano (1971); *Invocatio* for Chorus and String Quartet (1971); *Confessio*, trio for Clarinet, Cello, and Piano (1973); *Triptykon* for Violin, Clarinet, and Piano (1973).

Hallström, Ivar, significant Swedish composer; b. Stockholm, June 5, 1826; d. there, April 11, 1901. He studied jurisprudence at the Univ. of Uppsala; there he became a friend of Prince Gustaf, who was himself a musical amateur; on April 9, 1847, jointly with Gustaf, he produced in Stockholm an opera, *The White Lady of Drottningholm;* in 1853 he became librarian to Prince Oscar; in 1861–72 he was director of Lindblad's music school in Stockholm. His 2nd opera, *Hertig Magnus,* was produced at the Royal Opera in Stockholm on Jan. 28, 1867, but had only 6 performances in all, purportedly because it contained more arias in minor keys (10, to be exact) than those in major (only 8). He then produced another opera, *The Enchanted Cat* (Stockholm, April 20, 1869), which was more successful. With his next opera, *Den Bergtagna (The Bewitched One),* produced in Stockholm on May 24, 1874, he achieved his greatest success; it had repeated performances not only in Sweden, but also in Germany and Denmark. In this work Hallström made use of Swedish folk motifs, a pioneer attempt in Scandinavian operatic art. His next opera, *Vikingarna* (Stockholm, June 6, 1877), was but moderately successful; there followed *Neaga* (Stockholm, Feb. 24, 1885), to a libretto by Carmen Sylva (Queen Elisabeth of Rumania). He also wrote several ballets, cantatas, and arrangements of Swedish folk songs for piano.

Halm, August, German composer and writer; b. Gross-Altdorf, Württemberg, Oct. 26, 1869; d. Saalfeld, Feb. 1, 1929. A member of a family of scholars, he received an excellent general education; then studied theology at Tübingen. In 1892 he went to Munich, where he took courses with Rheinberger. Subsequently he devoted himself mainly to musical pedagogy; taught in various schools in Thuringia; conducted choral societies and also wrote music criticism. An August Halm Society was organized after his death. He was a prolific composer, but his music failed to take hold. He wrote 2 symphs., which were performed in Ulm and Stuttgart; a Piano Concerto; 8 string quartets; 2 suites for String Trio; and a number of piano studies. He publ. *Harmonielehre* (Berlin, 1905); *Von zwei Kulturen der Musik* (Munich, 1913; 3rd ed., 1947); *Die Symphoni-*

en A. Bruckners (Munich, 1914; 2nd ed., 1923); *Von Grenzen und Ländern der Musik* (Munich, 1916); *Einführung in die Musik* (Berlin, 1926); *Beethoven* (Berlin, 1927).

Halvorsen, Johan, Norwegian violinist and composer; b. Drammen, March 15, 1864; d. Oslo, Dec. 4, 1935. He studied violin with Lindberg at the Stockholm Cons.; was concertmaster of the Bergen Orch.; then went to Leipzig to study with Brodsky; subsequently studied with César Thomson in Belgium; returning to Norway in 1892, he became conductor of a theater orch. in Bergen; in 1899 was appointed conductor at the National Theater in Oslo. He was married to a niece of Grieg; this association was symbolic of his devotion to Grieg's art; his music reflects Grieg's influence very strongly. He wrote incidental music to Björnson's *Vasantasena* and *The King,* Drachmann's *Gurre,* Eldegard's *Fossegrimen* and *Dronning Tamara,* and to other works. He further wrote 3 symphs., a Violin Concerto, 2 Norwegian rhapsodies, and several orch. suites on Norwegian themes. His most popular works are the march *Triumphant Entry of the Boyars* and an arrangement of Handel's Passacaglia for Violin, and Viola or Cello.

Hamal, Henri-Guillaume, Belgian organist and composer; b. Liège, Dec. 3, 1685; d. there, Dec. 3, 1752. As a youth he excelled in the various capacities of harpsichord player, singer, and cellist; was also a versatile composer of songs to texts in many languages. However, none of his works is preserved, and his reputation was transmitted mainly by members of his family. His son, **Jean-Noël Hamal** (b. Liège, Dec. 23, 1709; d. there, Nov. 26, 1778), studied with his father and later served as chorus master at the Liège Cathedral; he also traveled in Italy, where he acquired additional knowledge of composition. He wrote a great number of church works: 56 masses, 32 cantatas, 5 oratorios, 179 motets; also operas, overtures, and numerous pieces for the harpsichord. **Henri Hamal** (b. Liège, July 20, 1744; d. there, Sept. 17, 1820), a nephew of Jean-Noël Hamal, studied with him, and later in Italy. He was a chorus master at the Liège Cathedral for some time. He wrote much church music, of which 3 vols. are preserved in the Royal Library at Brussels.

Hambourg a family of musicians of Russian extraction. **Michael Hambourg,** pianist and teacher; b. Yaroslavl, July 12, 1855; d. Toronto, Canada, June 18, 1916. He went to England in 1890; in 1911 moved to Toronto, where he established, with his son Boris, the Hambourg Cons. of Music. **Boris Hambourg,** cellist, son of Michael Hambourg; b. Voronezh, Jan. 8, 1885; d. Toronto, Nov. 24, 1954. He studied cello with Hugo Becker in Frankfurt (1898–1903); in 1910 made an American tour, and in the following year went to Toronto, where he established, with his father, the Hambourg Cons. **Jan Hambourg,** violinist; b. Voronezh, Aug. 27, 1882; d. Tours, France, Sept. 29, 1947. He studied violin with Sauret and Wilhelmj in London, with Sevčik in Prague, and with Eugène

Ysaÿe in Brussels. With his brothers Boris and Mark he established the Hambourg Trio; he died during a concert tour in France. **Mark Hambourg**, pianist; b. Bogutchar, June 12, 1879; d. Cambridge, England, Aug. 26, 1960. He studied piano with his father, Michael Hambourg, and made his debut in Moscow at the age of 9; then went to Vienna to study with Leschetizky. He was highly successful as a concert pianist; traveled all over the world; played his 1,000th concert on June 16, 1906. He toured with his brothers Boris and Jan in the U.S. in 1935; then returned to England. He publ. 2 piano manuals, *How to Play the Piano* (Philadelphia, 1922) and *From Piano to Forte; A Thousand and One Notes* (London, 1931); and a book of memoirs, *The Eighth Octave* (London, 1951).

Hamboys, John. See **Hanboys, John.**

Hambraeus, Bengt, prominent Swedish composer, organist, and musicologist; b. Stockholm, Jan. 29, 1928. He took organ lessons with Alf Linder (1944–48); then entered Uppsala Univ. (M.A., 1956); also attended the summer courses in modern music at Darmstadt (1951–55). In 1957 he joined the music staff of the Swedish Broadcasting Corp.; in 1972 was appointed to the faculty of McGill Univ. in Montreal. His style of composition oscillates between modernistic constructivism based on strong dissonant polyphony and sonoristic experimentalism; he is regarded as a leader of the Swedish musical avant-garde.

Hamel, Marie-Pierre, French organ builder; b. Auneuil, Oise, Feb. 24, 1786; d. Beauvais, July 25, 1879. He was from a family of jurists, and himself pursued a legal career; in 1817 he became a judge at Beauvais. Apart from his professional activities, he was from his childhood interested in music; he manufactured a small organ of 3 octaves at the age of 13, and successfully repaired an old organ in a neighboring village to the satisfaction of the church wardens. He later rebuilt the grand organ of the Cathedral of Beauvais (1826). He publ. several manuals and descriptions of organs in various French cities. His principal writings were *Rapport sur les travaux du grand orgue de l'Eglise de la Madeleine à Paris* (Paris, 1846); *Nouveau manuel complet du facteur d'orgues* (3 vols., Paris, 1849; new ed. by Guédon, 1903; contains a history of organ building).

Hamerik (real name, **Hammerich**), **Asger,** Danish composer; b. Copenhagen, April 8, 1843; d. Frederiksborg, July 13, 1923. He was a son of a prof. of divinity, who discouraged his musical interests; despite this opposition, he studied with Gade in Copenhagen and with Hans von Bülow in Berlin. He met Berlioz in Paris in 1864, and accompanied him to Vienna in 1866, studying orchestration. Hamerik was probably the only pupil that Berlioz had. He received a gold medal for his work *Hymne de la paix,* at the contest for the Paris Exposition. His opera *Tovelille* was performed in Paris in concert form (May 6, 1865); another opera, *Hjalmar and Ingeborg,* was not performed in its entirety. In 1870 he visited Italy and produced his Italian-language opera, *La vendetta* (Milan, Dec. 23, 1870). He then received an invitation to become director of the newly organized Peabody Cons. in Baltimore. He accepted, and remained in Baltimore for 26 years, until 1898, when he returned to Copenhagen. In Baltimore he wrote a number of symph. works, which he conducted with the cons. orch.

WORKS: *5 Nordic Suites* (1872–78); *Symphonie poétique* (1879); *Symphonie tragique* (1881); *Symphonie lyrique* (1885); *Symphonie majestueuse* (1888); *Symphonie sérieuse* (1892); *Symphonie spirituelle* for String Orch. (1895); Choral Symph. (No. 7).

Hamerik, Ebbe, Danish composer, son of **Asger Hamerik;** b. Copenhagen, Sept. 5, 1898; d. there, Aug. 11, 1951 (drowned in the Kattegat). He studied music with his father; was active mainly as a conductor. He composed the operas *Stepan* (Mainz, Nov. 30, 1924); *Leonardo da Vinci* (Antwerp, 1939); *Marie Grubbe* (Copenhagen, May 17, 1940); *Rejsekammeraten,* after Andersen (Copenhagen, Jan. 5, 1946); also 5 symphs., subtitled *Ur cantus firmus I–V* (1937, 1947, 1947–48, 1949, 1950); Wind Quintet (1942); 2 string quartets; piano pieces; songs.

Hamilton, Iain, remarkable Scottish composer; b. Glasgow, June 6, 1922. He was taken to London at the age of 7, and attended Mill Hill School; after graduation he became an apprentice engineer, but studied music in his leisure time. He was 25 years old when he decidedly turned to music as his career; entered the Royal Academy of Music, where he was a piano student of Harold Craxton and a composition student of William Alwyn; concurrently he attended the Univ. of London, obtaining his B.Mus. in 1950. He made astonishing progress as a composer, and upon graduation from the Royal Academy received the prestigious Dove Prize; other awards followed, among them the Royal Phil. Society Prize for his Clarinet Concerto, the Koussevitzky Foundation Award for his 2nd Symph., the Edwin Evans Prize, the Butterworth Award, and the Arnold Bax Gold Medal. From 1952 to 1960 he taught composition at Morley College in London, and during the same period conducted classes in musical analysis at the Univ. of London. In 1962 he received an appointment to the faculty at Duke Univ. in North Carolina; became a prof. there in 1966–67; was resident composer and teacher at Tanglewood in the summer of 1962, and also taught at the Summer School of Music at Dartington Hall in England. In 1970 he received the honorary degree of D.Mus. from Glasgow Univ.; in 1971 he received a professorship at Lehman College, City Univ. of N.Y., but resigned precipitously after a single day because of unacceptable teaching conditions. Apart from his regular pedagogic activities, he has served as a music consultant on various committees, including the Music Advisory Panel of the BBC and the National Music Council. During the first 2 decades of his work as a composer he wrote mainly instrumental music, but beginning in 1966 he devoted himself primarily to the composition of operas, completing 5 opera scores within 10 years; of these, *The Catiline Conspiracy* is acknowledged as his masterpiece. Hamilton's style of composition is marked by terse melodic lines animated by a vibrant rhythmic pulse, creating the impression of kinetic lyricism; his harmonies are built on a set of peculiarly euphonious dissonances, which repose on emphatic tonal centers. For a period of several years he pursued a sui generis serial method, but soon abandoned it in favor of a free modern manner; in his operas he makes use of thematic chords depicting specific dramatic situations.

WORKS: OPERAS: *The Royal Hunt of the Sun,* to his own libretto from a play by Peter Shaffer (1966–68; orchestration completed 1975; produced by the English National Opera in London, Feb. 2, 1977); *Agamemnon,* after Aeschylus (1967–69); *Pharsalia,* dramatic commentary with a libretto by the composer from Lucan (1968); *The Catiline Conspiracy,* to a text by the composer, based on Ben Jonson's play (Stirling, Scotland, March 16, 1974); radio opera, *Tamburlaine* (BBC, London, Feb. 14, 1977); *Anna Karenina* (1977–78; London, May 7, 1981). FOR ORCH.: *Variations on an Original Theme* for String Orch. (1948); Symph. No. 1 (1948); Clarinet Concerto (1950); Symph. No. 2 (1951); Violin Concerto (1952); *Bartholomew Fair,* overture (1952); *Symphonic Variations* (1953); *Scottish Dances* (1956); *Sonata* for Chamber Orch. (1957); *Overture: 1912* (1957); Concerto for Jazz Trumpet and Orch. (1957); *Sinfonia for 2 Orchestras* (1958); *Ecossaise* (1959); Piano Concerto (1960); *Arias* for Small Orch. (1962); *The Chaining of Prometheus* for Wind Instruments and Percussion (1963); *Cantos* (1964); Concerto for Organ and Small Orch. (1964); *Circus* for 2 Trumpets and Orch. (1969); *Alastor* (1970); *Voyage* for Horn and Chamber Orch. (1970); *Amphion* (2nd Violin Concerto) for Violin and Orch. (1971); *Commedia,* concerto for Orch. (London, May 4, 1973); *Aurora* (N.Y., Nov. 21, 1975). CHAMBER MUSIC: Quintet No. 1 for Clarinet and String Quartet (1948); String Quartet (1950); Quartet for Flute and String Trio (1951); *Variations* for Unaccompanied Violin (1951); *3 Nocturnes* for Clarinet and Piano (1951); Viola Sonata (1951); *Capriccio* for Trumpet and Piano (1951); Clarinet Sonata (1954); Octet for Strings (1954); *Songs of Summer* for Soprano, Clarinet, Cello, and Piano (1954); *Serenata* for Violin and Clarinet (1955); Piano Trio (1955); Cello Sonata No. 1 (1959); Sextet for Flute, 2 Clarinets, Violin, Cello, and Piano (1962); *Sonatas and Variants* for 10 Wind Instruments (1963); Brass Quintet (1964); *Sonata notturna* for Horn and Piano (1965); String Quartet No. 2 (1965); *Sonata for 5* for Wind Quintet (1966); Flute Sonata (1966); *Sea Music* (Quintet No. 2) for Clarinet and String Quartet (1971); *5 Scenes* for Trumpet and Piano (1971); Violin Sonata (1974); Cello Sonata No. 2 (1974); *The Alexandrian Sequence* for 12 Instruments (1976). VOCAL WORKS: *The Bermudas* for Baritone, Chorus, and Orch. (1956); Cantata for Tenor and Piano (1957); *5 Love Songs* for Voice and Orch. (1957); *Nocturnal* for 11 Solo

Voices (1959); *A Testament of War* for Baritone and Small Ensemble (1961); *Dialogues* for Coloratura Soprano and Small Ensemble (1965); *Epitaph for This World and Time* for 3 Choruses and 2 Organs (1970); *Te Deum* for Mixed Chorus, Wind Instruments, and Percussion (1972); *To Columbus,* a setting of Walt Whitman's poem, for Mixed Chorus, 3 Trumpets, 3 Trombones, and Percussion, written for the U.S. Bicentennial (1976). FOR KEYBOARD: Organ pieces; 2 piano sonatas (1951, 1970); *Nocturnes with Cadenzas* for Piano (1963); *Palinodes* for Piano (1972); *A Vision of Canopus* for Organ (1975).

Hamlisch, Marvin, American composer of popular music; b. New York, June 2, 1944. His father, an accordionist, trained him in music; he studied piano at the Juilliard School of Music and at Queens College; began writing songs at the age of 15. His first signal success came in 1974, when he won 3 Academy Awards for the music scores for the movies *The Way We Were* and *The Sting.* (For the latter, his award was won for a score written mostly by others: the piano music was by Scott Joplin, composed 60–70 years earlier, and the orchestrations were by Gunther Schuller, adapted from 60-year-old stock arrangements.) In 1975 he wrote the score for the musical *A Chorus Line,* which received the Pulitzer Prize for the play and a Tony award for the best musical score; Universal Pictures bought the cinema rights for $5.5 million. The Broadway production opened on July 25, 1975, to a chorus line of hosannas from otherwise sober-sided critics; a 2nd Broadway production followed in 1976; an international touring company was started in Toronto in May 1976, and a national company began its cross-country tour a few days later.

Hamm, Charles (Edward), American musicologist; b. Charlottesville, Va., April 2, 1925. He studied at the Univ. of Virginia (B.A., 1947) and Princeton Univ. (M.F.A., 1950; Ph.D., 1960, with the dissertation *A Chronology of the Works of Guillaume Dufay,* publ. in Princeton, 1964). He taught at Princeton Univ. (1948–50 and 1958), at the Cincinnati Cons. of Music (1950–57), and at Tulane Univ. (1959–63). In 1963 he was appointed prof. of musicology at the Univ. of Illinois; in 1976 joined the faculty of Dartmouth College. He served as president of the American Musicological Society from 1972–74. A versatile scholar, he publ. books on a variety of subjects; these include *Opera* (Boston, 1966); *Yesterdays: Popular Song in America* (N.Y., 1979); *Music in the New World* (N.Y., 1983).

Hammer, Heinrich Albert Eduard, German-American violinist, conductor, and composer; b. Erfurt, Germany, Oct. 27, 1862; d. Phoenix, Ariz., Oct. 28, 1954. He studied violin with A. Pott and theory with H. Ritter; also took singing lessons with Mme. Viardot-Garcia in Paris. He then lived in the Netherlands (1893–96) and Bochum, Germany (1897–1901); conducted the Lausanne Symph. Orch. (1901–5); in 1905 he organized a symph. orch. in Göteborg, Sweden. In 1908 he settled in America; conducted his own orch. in Washington, D.C., until 1921, when he went to California; lived mostly in Pasadena. He continued to compose until the end of his long life; at the age of 90, married his pupil Arlene Hammer, who helped him to edit his autobiography. Among his works are a Symph.; 3 American Indian rhapsodies for Orch.; a symph. poem, *Sunset at Sea;* an orch. ode, *Columbia Triumphant in Peace* (1915); and much church music.

Hammerich, Angul, Danish writer on music, brother of **Asger Hamerik** (whose real name was Hammerich); b. Copenhagen, Nov. 25, 1848; d. there, April 26, 1931. He studied cello; at the same time, occupied a post in the Dept. of Finance; wrote music criticism; taught musicology at the Univ. of Copenhagen. In 1898 he founded the Collection of Ancient Musical Instruments; was a founder of the Danish Musicological Society (1921).

WRITINGS: *Studies in Old Icelandic Music* (1900; in Danish and German); *The Conservatory of Music at Copenhagen* (1892; in Danish); *Essay on the Music at the Court of Christian IV* (1892; in German, 1893); *On the Old Norse Lurs* (1893; in German, 1894); *Descriptive Illustrated Catalogue of the Historical Musical Museum of Copenhagen* (1909; in Danish; German trans. by E. Bobé, 1911); *Medieval Musical Relics of Denmark* (1912; in Danish; Eng. trans. by Margaret Williams-Hamerik, 1912); *J.P.E. Hartmann, Biographical Essays* (1916); a history of Danish music to c.1700 (1921).

Hammerschmidt, Andreas, important composer of sacred music; b. Brüx, Bohemia, 1612; d. Zittau, Nov. 8, 1675. In 1626 his father took him to Freiberg, Saxony, and it was there that he received his education; he was appointed organist at Freiberg in 1634, and in 1639 at Zittau, retaining this post until his death. A statue was erected to his memory there. His works for the Lutheran services are of great significance. He was one of the earliest composers to adopt the new Italian style of writing elaborate instrumental accompaniments to polyphonic vocal works.

Hammerstein, Oscar, celebrated impresario; b. Stettin, Germany, May 8, 1846; d. New York, Aug. 1, 1919. At the age of 16 he ran away from home; spent some time in England; then went to America, where he worked in a N.Y. cigar factory. Possessing an inventive mind, he patented a machine for shaping tobacco leaves by suction; later edited a tobacco trade journal. At the same time, he practiced the violin; learned to write music, and dabbled in playwriting; in 1868 he produced in N.Y. a comedy in German; also wrote the libretto and music of an operetta, *The Kohinoor* (N.Y., Oct. 24, 1893). His main activity, however, was in management. He built the Harlem Opera House (1888), the Olympia Music Hall (1895), and the Republic Theater (1900), and presented brief seasons of plays and operas there. In 1906 he announced plans for the Manhattan Opera House in N.Y., his crowning achievement. The enterprise was originally planned as a

theater for opera in English, but it opened with an Italian company in Bellini's *Puritani* (Dec. 3, 1906). Hammerstein entered into bold competition with the Metropolitan Opera, and engaged celebrated singers, among them Melba, Nordica, Tetrazzini, and Mary Garden; among the spectacular events presented by him were the first American performances of 5 operas by Massenet, Charpentier's *Louise,* and Debussy's *Pelléas et Mélisande.* The new venture held its own for 4 seasons, but in the end Hammerstein was compelled to yield; in April 1910, he sold the Manhattan Opera House to the management of the Metropolitan for $1.2 million, and agreed not to produce grand opera in N.Y. for 10 years. He also sold to the Metropolitan (for $100,000) his interests in the Philadelphia Opera House, built by him in 1908. (The texts of these agreements were publ. in full in the *Musical Courier* of March 29, 1911.) Defeated in his main ambition in America, Hammerstein transferred his activities to England. There he built the London Opera House, which opened with a lavish production of *Quo Vadis* by Nougès (Nov. 17, 1911). However, he failed to establish himself in London, and after a season there, returned to N.Y. In contravention of his agreement with the Metropolitan, he announced a season at the newly organized American Opera House in N.Y., but the Metropolitan secured an injunction against him, and he was forced to give up his operatic venture.

Hammerstein, Oscar, II, American lyricist, grandson of the preceding; b. New York, July 12, 1895; d. Highland Farms, Doylestown, Pa., Aug. 23, 1960. He studied law at Columbia Univ., graduating in 1917; then became interested in the theater. He collaborated on the librettos for Friml's *Rose Marie* (1924) and Romberg's *The Desert Song* (1926); his greatest success as a lyricist came with the production of Jerome Kern's *Show Boat* (1926), including the celebrated song *Ol' Man River.* In 1943 he joined hands with the composer Richard Rodgers, and together they produced several brilliant musical comedies, with spectacular success: *Oklahoma!* (1943; Pulitzer Prize); *Carousel* (1945); *Allegro* (1947); *South Pacific* (1949; Pulitzer Prize, 1950); *The King and I* (1951); *Me and Juliet* (1953); *Pipe Dream* (1955); etc. His lyrics are characterized by a combination of appealing sentiment and sophisticated nostalgia, making them particularly well suited to the modern theater.

Hammond, Dame Joan, New Zealand soprano; b. Christchurch, May 24, 1912. She studied at the Sydney Cons.; made her operatic debut in Sydney in 1929; then went to London, where she continued vocal studies with Dino Borgioli; also studied in Vienna. She made her London debut in 1938; then sang with the Vienna State Opera; was a member of the Carl Rosa Opera Co. (1942–45). She made her Covent Garden debut in 1948; also sang with the Sadler's Wells Opera; appeared in the U.S. with the N.Y. City Center Opera in 1949; she retired in 1965. In 1974 she was made a Dame of the British Empire.

She wrote an autobiography, *A Voice, a Life* (London, 1970).

Hammond, Laurens, American manufacturer of keyboard instruments; b. Evanston, Ill., Jan. 11, 1895; d. Cornwall, Conn., July 1, 1973. He studied engineering at Cornell Univ.; then went to Detroit to work on the synchronization of electrical motor impulses, a principle which he later applied to the Hammond Organ, an electronic keyboard instrument, resembling a spinet piano, which suggests the sound of the pipe organ. Still later, he developed a newfangled electrical device which he called the Novachord and which was designed to simulate the sound of any known or hypothetical musical instrument; he gave the first demonstration of the Novachord in the Commerce Dept. auditorium in Washington, D.C., on Feb. 2, 1939. In 1940 he introduced the Solovox, an attachment to the piano keyboard which enables an amateur player to project the melody in organlike tones. A further invention that proved attractive to dilettantes was the "chord organ," which he introduced in 1950, and which is capable of supplying basic harmonies when a special button is pressed by the performer.

Hammond-Stroud, Derek, English baritone; b. London, Jan. 10, 1929. He studied with Elena Gerhardt in London and Gerhard Hüsch in Vienna and Munich. He made his debut in London in 1955; in 1962 he joined the Sadler's Wells Opera; was a leading member of the Royal Opera, Covent Garden, from 1971. He made his American debut with the Houston Grand Opera in 1975, and on Dec. 5, 1977, his Metropolitan Opera debut as Faninal in *Der Rosenkavalier*. He was known for his vivid portrayals of the Wagnerian roles of Alberich and Beckmesser; was also a distinguished concert singer.

Hampton, Lionel, American jazz vibraphonist, drummer, pianist, and bandleader; b. Louisville, Ky., April 12, 1909. He played drums in Chicago nightclubs; then moved to Los Angeles, where he formed a band of his own. He was a pioneer in introducing to jazz the vibraphone, on which he is a virtuoso performer; he gained nationwide prominence as a member of the Benny Goodman Quartet from 1936–40. From then on he usually led his own bands, most often playing vibes, but occasionally performing on other instruments; he is the originator of the "trigger-finger" method of piano playing (2 forefingers drumming upon a single note *prestissimo*). Beginning in 1956, he made several successful European tours. In 1965 he gave up his big band and founded a sextet called the Jazz Inner Circle.

Han (Hahn), Ulrich (Udalricus Gallus), German music printer; b. Ingolstadt, c.1425; d. Rome, after 1478. He is believed to be the first to print music with movable type, in his *Missale secundum consuetudinem curie romane* (Rome, 1476). In this work the double-process method was employed, i.e., 2 impressions were made; first, the lines of the staff were printed, following which the note forms (mostly square black heads with a stem at the right side) were superimposed over them.

Hanboys (or **Hamboys**), **John,** English music theorist of the 15th century. He was one of the first Englishmen on whom the degree of Mus.D. was conferred. He also held an ecclesiastic rank. His Latin treatise *Summa super musicam continuam et discretam,* which describes the musical notation of his time, was printed by Coussemaker in his *Scriptores* (vol. 1, p. 416).

Handel, George Frideric (the Anglicized form of the name, adopted by Handel in England; the original German spelling was **Georg Friedrich Händel;** other forms used in various branches of the family were Hendel, Hendeler, Händler, and Hendtler; the early spelling in England was Hendel; in France it is spelled Haendler; the Russian transliteration of the name from the Cyrillic alphabet, which lacks the aspirate, is Ghendel), great German-born English composer; b. Halle, Feb. 23, 1685; d. London, April 14, 1759. His father was a barber-surgeon and valet to the Prince of Saxe-Magdeburg; at the age of 61 he took a second wife, Dorothea Taust, daughter of the pastor of Giebichenstein, near Halle; Handel was the 2nd son of this marriage. As a child, he was taken by his father on a visit to Saxe-Weissenfels, where he had a chance to try out the organ of the court chapel. The Duke, Johann Adolf, noticing his interest in music, advised that he be sent to Halle for organ lessons with Friedrich Wilhelm Zachau, the organist of the Liebfrauenkirche there. Zachau gave him instruction in harpsichord and organ playing and also introduced him to the rudiments of composition. Handel proved to be an apt student, and was able to substitute for Zachau as organist whenever necessary; he also composed trio sonatas and motets for church services on Sundays. After the death of Handel's father in 1697, he entered the Univ. of Halle in 1702, and was named probationary organist at the Domkirche there. In 1703 he went to Hamburg, where he was engaged as "violino di ripieno" by Reinhard Keiser, the famous composer and director of the Hamburg Opera. There he met Johann Mattheson; in 1703 the two undertook a journey to Lübeck together, with the intention of applying for the post of organist in succession to Buxtehude, who was chief organist there. It was the custom for an incoming organist to marry a daughter of the incumbent as a condition of appointment; apparently neither Mattheson nor Handel availed themselves of this opportunity. (Bach made the same journey in 1704, and also returned without obtaining the succession.) There was apparently a quarrel between Mattheson and Handel at a performance of Mattheson's opera *Cleopatra,* in which he sang the leading male role of Antonio, while Handel conducted from the keyboard as maestro al cembalo. When Mattheson completed his stage role he asked Handel to yield his place at the keyboard to him; Handel declined, and an altercation ensued, resulting in a duel with swords, which was called off when Mattheson broke his sword on a metal button of Handel's coat. There is no independent confirmation of this episode, however, and the two apparently reconciled.

Handel's first opera, *Almira,* was produced at the Hamburg Opera on Jan. 8, 1705; his next opera, *Nero,* was staged there on Feb. 25, 1705. He was then commissioned to write 2 other operas, *Florindo* and *Daphne,* originally planned as a single opera combining both subjects. In 1706 Handel undertook a long voyage to Italy, where he visited Florence, Rome, Naples, and Venice. The first opera he wrote in Italy was *Rodrigo,* presented in Florence in 1707. Then followed *Agrippina,* produced in Venice on Dec. 26, 1709; it obtained an excellent success, being given 27 performances. In Rome, Handel composed the serenata *Il trionfo del tempo e del disinganno,* which was performed there in the spring of 1707. Handel's oratorio *La Resurrezione* was given in Rome on April 8, 1708. On July 19, 1708, he brought out in Naples his serenata *Aci, Galatea, e Polifemo;* its score was remarkable for a bass solo that required a compass of 2 octaves and a fifth. During his Italian sojourn Handel met Alessandro and Domenico Scarlatti. In 1710 he returned to Germany and was named Kapellmeister to the Elector of Hannover, as successor to the Italian musician Agostino Steffani. Later that year he visited England, where he produced his opera *Rinaldo* at the Queen's Theatre in London on Feb. 24, 1711; it received 15 performances in all. After a brief return to Hannover in June 1711, he made another visit to London, where he produced his operas *Il pastor fido* (Nov. 22, 1712) and *Teseo* (Jan. 10, 1713). He also wrote an ode for Queen Anne's birthday, which was presented at Windsor Palace on Feb. 6, 1713; it was followed by 2 sacred works, *Te Deum* and *Jubilate,* performed on July 7, 1713, to celebrate the Peace of Utrecht; these performances won him royal favor and an annuity of 200 pounds sterling.

An extraordinary concurrence of events persuaded Handel to remain in London, when Queen Anne died in 1714 and Handel's protector, the Elector of Hannover, became King George I of England. The King bestowed many favors upon Handel and augmented his annuity to 400 pounds sterling. He became a British subject in 1727, and Anglicized his name to George Frideric Handel, dropping the original German umlaut. He continued to produce operas, invariably to Italian librettos, for the London stage. His opera *Silla* was produced in London on June 2, 1713; it was followed by *Amadigi di Gaula* on May 25, 1715. In 1716 Handel wrote *Der für die Sünden der Welt gemarterte und sterbende Jesus,* to the text of the poet Heinrich Brockes. In 1717 Handel produced one of his most famous works, written expressly for King George I, his *Water Music.* On July 17, 1717, an aquatic fête on the Thames River was held by royal order; the King's boat was followed by a barge on which an orch. of 50 musicians played Handel's score, or at least a major portion of it. The final version of *Water Music* combines 2 instrumental suites composed at different times; one was written for the barge party, the other is of an earlier provenance. In 1717 Handel became resident composer to the Duke of

Chandos, for whom he wrote the 11 so-called *Chandos Anthems* (1717–18), the secular oratorio *Acis and Galatea* (1718), and the oratorio *Esther* (1718). He also served as music master to the daughters of the Prince of Wales; for Princess Anne he composed his first collection of *Suites de pièces pour le clavecin* (1720), also known as *The Lessons,* which includes the famous air with variations nicknamed *The Harmonious Blacksmith;* the appellation is gratuitous, and the story that Handel was inspired to compose it after he visited a blacksmith shop, where he was impressed by the steady beat of the artisan's hammer, was a persistent figment of anonymous imagination. In 1719 Handel was made Master of Musick of a new business venture under the name of the Royal Academy of Music, established for the purpose of presenting opera at the King's Theatre. The first opera he composed for it was *Radamisto* (April 27, 1720). In the fall of 1720 the Italian composer Giovanni Bononcini joined the company. A rivalry soon developed between him and Handel which was made famous by a piece of doggerel by the poet John Byrom ("Some say, compar'd to Bononcini, that Mynheer Handel's but a ninny. Others aver that he to Handel is scarcely fit to hold a candle. Strange all this difference should be twixt tweedledum and tweedledee."). Handel won a Pyrrhic victory when Bononcini had the unfortunate idea of submitting to the London Academy of Music a madrigal which he had appropriated *in extenso* from a choral piece by the Italian composer Antonio Lotti; Lotti discovered it, and an embarrassing controversy ensued, resulting in Bononcini's disgrace and expulsion from London (he died in obscurity in Vienna, where he sought refuge). The irony of the whole episode is that Handel was no less guilty of plagiarism. An article on Handel in the 1880 edition of the *Encyclopædia Britannica* spares no words condemning Handel's conduct: "The system of wholesale plagiarism carried on by Handel is perhaps unprecedented in the history of music. He pilfered not only single melodies but frequently entire movements from the works of other masters, with few or no alterations, and without a word of acknowledgment." Between 1721 and 1728 Handel produced the following operas at the King's Theatre: *Florindante, Ottone, Flavio, Giulio Cesare, Tamerlano, Rodelinda Scipione, Alessandro, Admeto, Riccardo Primo, Siroe,* and *Tolomeo;* of these, *Giulio Cesare* and *Rodelinda* became firmly established in the operatic repertoire and had numerous revivals. In 1727 he composed 4 grand anthems for the coronation of King George II and Queen Caroline. In the spring of 1728 the Royal Academy of Music ceased operations, and Handel became associated with the management of the King's Theatre. The following year, he went to Italy to recruit singers for a new Royal Academy of Music. Returning to London, he brought out the operas *Lotario, Partenope, Poro, Ezio, Sosarme,* and *Orlando;* only *Orlando* proved to be a lasting success. On May 2, 1732, Handel gave a special production of a revised version of his oratorio *Esther* at the King's Theatre; it was followed by the revised version of *Acis and Galatea* (June 10, 1732) and the oratorio

Deborah (March 17, 1733). On July 10, 1733, he produced his oratorio *Athalia* at Oxford, where he also appeared as an organist; he was offered the degree of Mus.Doc. (*honoris causa*), but declined the honor. Discouraged by the poor reception of his operas at the King's Theatre, Handel decided to open a new season under a different management. But he quarreled with the principal singer, the famous castrato Senesino, who was popular with audiences, and thus lost the support of a substantial number of his subscribers, who then formed a rival opera company, called The Opera of the Nobility. It engaged the famous Italian composer Porpora as director, and opened its first season at Lincoln's Inns Fields on Dec. 29, 1733. Handel's opera *Arianna in Creta* had its premiere at the King's Theatre on Jan. 26, 1734, but in July of that year both Handel's company and the rival enterprise were forced to suspend operations. Handel set up his own opera company at Covent Garden, inaugurating his new season with a revised version of *Il pastor fido* (Nov. 9, 1734); this was followed by *Ariodante, Alcina, Atalanta, Arminio, Giustino,* and *Berenice,* all staged between 1735 and 1737; only *Alcina* sustained a success; Handel's other operas met with an indifferent reception. On Feb. 19, 1736, Handel presented his ode *Alexander's Feast* at Covent Garden, and on March 23, 1737, he brought out a revised version of his oratorio *Il trionfo del tempo e della verità.* His fortunes improved when he was confirmed by the Queen as music master to Princesses Amelia and Caroline. He continued to maintain connections with Germany; he traveled to Aachen in 1737. Upon his return to London he suffered from attacks of gout, an endemic illness of British society at the time, but he managed to resume his work. On Jan. 3, 1738, he produced his opera *Faramondo,* and on April 15, 1738, presented his opera *Serse* (a famous aria from this opera, *Ombra mai fu,* became even more famous in an instrumental arrangement made by parties unknown, under the title "Handel's Celebrated Largo"). There followed a pasticcio, *Giove in Argo* (May 1, 1739), and *Imenea* (Nov. 22, 1740). On Jan. 10, 1741, he produced his last opera, *Deidamia,* which marked the end of his operatic enterprise. In historical perspective, Handel's failure as an operatic entrepreneur was a happy turn of events, for he then directed his energy toward the composition of oratorios, in which he achieved greatness. For inspiration he turned to biblical themes, using English texts. On Jan. 16, 1739, he presented the oratorio *Saul;* on April 4, 1739, there followed *Israel in Egypt.* He also wrote an *Ode for St. Cecilia's Day,* after Dryden (Nov. 22, 1739), and his great set of 12 *Concerti grossi,* op. 6. Milton's *L'Allegro* and *Il Penseroso* inspired him to write *L'Allegro, il Penseroso, ed il Moderato* (Feb. 27, 1740). In 1741 Handel was invited to visit Ireland, and there he produced his greatest masterpiece, *Messiah;* working with tremendous concentration of willpower, and imagination, he completed Part I in 6 days, Part II in 9 days, and Part III in 6 days. The work on orchestration took him only a few more days; he signed the score on Sept. 14, 1741. The first performance of *Messiah* was given in Dublin on

April 13, 1742, and its London premiere was presented on March 23, 1743. If contemporary reports can be trusted, King George II rose to his feet at the closing chords of "Hallelujah," and the entire audience followed his example. This established a tradition, at least in England; since then every performance of *Messiah* moved the listeners to rise during this celebratory chorus. Handel's oratorio *Samson,* produced in London on Feb. 18, 1743, was also successful, but his next oratorio, *Semele* (Feb. 10, 1744), failed to arouse public admiration. Continuing to work, and alternating between mythological subjects and religious themes, he produced *Joseph and His Brethren* (March 2, 1744), *Hercules* (Jan. 5, 1745), and *Belshazzar* (March 27, 1745). His subsequent works, composed between 1746 and 1752, were a pasticcio under the titles *Occasional Oratorio, Judas Maccabaeus, Joshua, Alexander Balus, Susanna, Solomon, Theodora, The Choice of Hercules,* and *Jephtha.* Of these, *Judas Maccabaeus, Solomon,* and *Jephtha* became favorites with the public. Besides oratorios, mundane events also occupied Handel's attention. To celebrate the Peace of Aachen, he composed the remarkable *Music for the Royal Fireworks,* which was heard for the first time in Green Park in London on April 27, 1749. In 1750 he revisited Germany. But soon he had to limit his activities on account of failing eyesight, which required the removal of cataracts; the operation proved unsuccessful, but he still continued to appear in performances of his music, with the assistance of his pupil John Christopher Smith. Handel's last appearance in public was at the London performance of *Messiah* on April 6, 1759; 8 days later, on April 14, the Saturday between Good Friday and Easter, he died. He was buried at Westminster Abbey; a monument by Roubiliac marks his grave. (It should be noted that the year of birth on Handel's gravestone is marked as 1684 rather than 1685; this discrepancy is explained by the fact that the calendar year in England and other European countries began in March, and not in January.)

A parallel between 2 great German contemporaries, Bach and Handel, is often drawn. Born a few months apart, Bach in Eisenach, Handel in Halle, at a distance of about 130 kilometers, they never met. Bach visited Halle at least twice, but Handel was then away, in London. The difference between their life's destinies was profound. Bach was a master of the Baroque organ who produced religious works for church use, a schoolmaster who regarded his instrumental music as a textbook for study; he never composed for the stage, and traveled but little. By contrast, Handel was a man of the world who dedicated himself mainly to public spectacles, and who became a British subject. Bach's life was that of a German burgher; his genius was inconspicuous; Handel shone in the light of public admiration. Bach was married twice; survivors among his 20 children became important musicians in their own right. Handel remained celibate, but he was not a recluse. Physically, he tended toward healthy corpulence; he enjoyed the company of friends, but had a choleric temperament, and could not brook adverse argument. Like Bach, he was deeply religious, and there was no ostentation in his service to his God. Handel's music possessed grandeur of design, majestic eloquence, and lusciousness of harmony. Music lovers did not have to study Handel's style to discover its beauty, while the sublime art of Bach could be fully understood only after knowledgeable penetration into the contrapuntal and fugal complexities of its structure.

Handel bequeathed the bulk of his MSS to his amanuensis, John Christopher Smith, whose son presented them in turn to King George III. They eventually became a part of the King's Music Library; they comprise 32 vols. of operas, 21 vols. of oratorios, 7 vols. of odes and serenatas, 12 vols. of sacred music, 11 vols. of cantatas, and 5 vols. of instrumental music. Seven vols. containing sketches for various works are in the Fitzwilliam Collection at Cambridge. An edition of Handel's works in 36 vols., edited by Arnold, was publ. by command of George III between 1787 and 1797. A monumental edition in 100 vols. was issued by the German Handel Society under the editorship of F.R. Chrysander between 1856 and 1894. J.M. Coopersmith collected and edited 10 vols. of publ. material to complete Chrysander's edition, and brought out an authentic version of *Messiah* in vocal score. In 1955 a new edition, the Hallische Handel Ausgabe, was begun by Max Schneider and Rudolf Steglich for the Handel Gesellschaft in Halle. A thematic catalog was compiled by A.C. Bell in 1969.

Handl, Jacob. See **Gallus, Jacob Handl.**

Handschin, Jacques, eminent Swiss musicologist; b. Moscow, April 5, 1886; d. Basel, Nov. 25, 1955. He studied organ in Moscow; in 1905 he studied mathematics and history at the Univ. of Basel; then went to Munich to pursue his academic studies; also studied organ and theory with Max Reger; he later attended some of the lectures in musicology given in Leipzig by Riemann and in Berlin by Hornbostel; took additional courses in organ playing with Karl Straube in Leipzig and with Widor in Paris. Returning to Russia, he taught organ at the St. Petersburg Cons. (1909–20); gave numerous organ recitals in Russia, and promoted contemporary organ works by Russian composers, among them Glazunov and Taneyev; included these works in his anthology *Les Maîtres contemporains de l'orgue* (Paris, 1913–14). In 1920 he returned to Switzerland; in 1921 he received his Ph.D. from the Univ. of Basel with the dissertation *Choralbearbeitungen und Kompositionen mit rhythmischem Text in der mehrstimmigen Musik des 13. Jahrhunderts;* he completed his Habilitation there in 1924 with his tract *Über die mehrstimmige Musik der St. Martial Epoche sowie die Zusammenhänge zwischen Notre Dame und St. Martial und die Zusammenhänge zwischen einem dritten Stil und Notre Dame und St. Martial.* In 1924 he became Privatdozent at the Univ. of Basel; was a prof. of musicology there from 1935–55. He also served as a church organist in Zürich and Basel. He was greatly esteemed for his ample erudition and the soundness of his analytical theories; he

evolved philosophical principles of musical esthetics seeking the rational foundations of the art. His most important work is *Der Toncharakter: Eine Einführung in die Tonpsychologie* (Zürich, 1948), which sets down his principles of musical esthetics; other works include *La Musique de l'antiquité* (Paris, 1946) and *Musikgeschichte im Überblick* (Lucerne, 1948).

Handy, W(illiam) C(hristopher), black American composer, "father of the blues"; b. Florence, Ala., Nov. 16, 1873; d. New York, March 28, 1958. His father and grandfather were ministers. In 1892 he was graduated from the Teachers' Agricultural and Mechanical College in Huntsville, Ala.; became a schoolteacher and also worked in iron mills; learned to play the cornet and was a soloist at the Chicago World's Fair (1893); became bandmaster of Mahara's Minstrels. From 1900–2 he taught at the Agricultural and Mechanical College; then from 1903–21, conducted his own orch. and toured the South. He received the award of the National Assoc. for Negro Music, St. Louis (1937). On Jan. 1, 1954, he married his secretary, Irma Louise Logan. His famous song *Memphis Blues* (publ. 1912; the 2nd piece to be publ. as a "blues," and the first blues to achieve popularity) was originally written as a campaign song for the mayor of Memphis, E.H. Crump (1909); this song, along with his more celebrated *St. Louis Blues* (1914), opened an era in popular music, turning the theretofore prevalent spirit of ragtime gaiety to ballad-like nostalgia, with the lowered third, fifth, and seventh degrees ("blue notes") as distinctive melodic traits. He followed these with more blues: *Yellow Dog; Beale Street; Joe Turner;* the march *Hail to the Spirit of Freedom* (1915); *Ole Miss* for Piano (1916); the songs *Aunt Hagar's Children* (1920); *Loveless Love* (1921); *Aframerican Hymn;* etc. He publ. the anthologies *Blues: An Anthology* (also publ. as *A Treasury of the Blues;* N.Y., 1926; 2nd ed., 1949; 3rd ed., revised by J. Silverman, 1972); *Book of Negro Spirituals* (N.Y., 1938); *Negro Music and Musicians* (N.Y., 1944); also *Negro Authors and Composers of the U.S.* (N.Y., 1936); wrote an autobiography, *Father of the Blues* (N.Y., 1941). A commemorative stamp showing Handy playing the trumpet was issued on May 17, 1969, in Memphis, Tenn., the birthplace of his "blues."

Hannay, Roger, talented American composer; b. Plattsburg, N.Y., Sept. 22, 1930. He studied composition with F. Morris and Dika Newlin at Syracuse Univ. (1948–52), H. Norden at Boston Univ. (1952–53), Bernard Rogers and Howard Hanson at the Eastman School of Music in Rochester, N.Y. (1954–56; Ph.D., 1956), and Lukas Foss and Aaron Copland at the Berkshire Music Center (1959); had sessions with Sessions and attended lectures by Elliott Carter at the Princeton Seminar for Advanced Studies (1960). He taught at various colleges; in 1966 joined the music faculty of the Univ. of North Carolina at Chapel Hill; was founder and director of the New Music Ensemble (1967–82), and also served as chairman of the Division of Fine Arts there in 1979–82.

An unprejudiced and liberal music-maker, he makes use of varied functional resources, from neo-Classical pandiatonism to dodecaphony; resorts also to the device of "objets trouvés," borrowing thematic materials from other composers.

WORKS: 2 chamber operas: *2 Tickets to Omaha, The Swindlers* (1960) and *The Fortune of St. Macabre* (1964); *Requiem*, after Whitman's "When Lilacs Last in the Dooryard Bloom'd" (1961); Cantata (1952); *The Inter-Planetary Aleatoric Serial Factory* for Soprano Solo, String Quartet, Rock Band, Actors, Dancers, Tapes, Film, and Slides (1969); 4 symphs.: No. 1 (1953; revised 1973); No. 2 (1956); No. 3, "The Great American Novel," with Chorus and Tape-recorded Sound (1976–77); No. 4, "American Classic" (1977); *Dramatic Overture,* an homage to Schoenberg (1955); *Lament* for Oboe and Strings (1957); Symph. for Band (1963); *Sonorous Image* for Orch. (1968); *Sayings for Our Time,* to a text from the "current news media," for Chorus and Orch. (Winston-Salem, N.C., Aug. 2, 1968); *Fragmentation* for Orch. or Chamber Orch. (1969); *Listen* for Orch. (1971; Guilford College, N.C., July 7, 1973); *Celebration* for Tape and Orch. (N.Y., May 19, 1975); *Suite-Billings* for Youth Orch. (1975); *Rhapsody* for Flute and Piano (1952); Sonata for Brass Ensemble (1957); Divertimento for Wind Quintet (1958); *Concerto da camera* for Recorder, Violin, Viola, Cello, Harpsichord, and Soprano (1958; revised 1975); 4 string quartets: No. 1 (1962); No. 2, *Lyric* (1962); No. 3, *Designs* (1963); No. 4, *Quartet of Solos* (1974; comprising the simultaneous perfs. of the 4 solo pieces *Grande Concerte, Second Fiddle, O Solo Viola,* and *Concert Music*); *The Fruit of Love,* after St. Vincent Millay, for Soprano, and Piano or Chamber Orch. (1964, 1969); *Spectrum* for Brass Quintet (1964); *Structure* for Percussion Ensemble (1965; revised 1974); *Marshall's Medium Message* for Mod-Girl Announcer and Percussion Quartet (1967); *America Sing!* for Tape and Visuals (1967); *Fantome* for Viola, Clarinet, and Piano (1967); *Live and in Color!* for Mod Girl Announcer, Percussion Quartet, 2 Action Painters, Tape, Films, and Slides (1967); *Confrontation* for Tape and Percussion (1969); *Squeeze Me* for Chamber Ensemble and Film (1970); *Tuonelan Joutsen,* vocalise for Soprano, English Horn, and Film (1972, after Sibelius's *Swan of Tuonela*); *Prophecy of Despair* for Male Chorus and Percussion (1972); *Grande Concerte* for Solo Violin (1972); *Concert Music* for Solo Cello (1973); *Sphinx* for Tape and Trumpet (1973); *4 for 5* for Brass Quintet (1973); *O Solo Viola* for Solo Viola (1974); *2nd Fiddle* for Solo Violin (1974); *Phantom of the Opera* for Organ and Soprano (1975); *Pied Piper* for Tape and Clarinet (1975); *Oh Friends!* for Chamber Wind Ensemble and Pitch Percussion (1976); Suite for Piano (1954); *Abstractions* for Piano (1962); Piano Sonata (1964); *Sonorities* for Piano (1966); *The Episodic Refraction* for Tape and Piano (1971); choruses; songs.

Hannikainen, Ilmari, Finnish pianist and composer; b. Jyväskylä, Oct. 19, 1892; d. Kuhmoinen, July 25, 1955. A scion of a musical family (his father, **Pekka Hannikainen,** was a conductor and composer), he studied in Helsinki; then took lessons with Alexander Siloti in St. Petersburg and with Alfred Cortot in Paris. Returning to Finland, he was active as a piano teacher; with his brothers **Tauno** and **Arvo Hannikainen,** he organized a concert trio. He composed a folk play, *Talkoottanssit* (1930); a Piano Concerto; a Piano Quartet; and many solo piano pieces.

Hannikainen, Pekka, Finnish conductor; b. Nurmes, Dec. 9, 1854; d. Helsinki, Sept. 13, 1924. He was the founding member of a musically important family in Finland; his sons **Ilmari, Tauno, Arvo,** and **Väinö** were respectively a pianist, a cellist, a violinist, and a harpist.

Hannikainen, Tauno, Finnish cellist and conductor; b. Jyväskylä, Feb. 26, 1896; d. Helsinki, Oct. 12, 1968. A member of a prominent musical family in Finland (his father, **Pekka Hannikainen,** was a conductor and composer; his brother **Ilmari Hannikainen** was a pianist and composer), he studied in Helsinki, and took some cello lessons with Pablo Casals in Paris. Returning to Finland, he organized a trio with his brothers **Arvo,** a violinist, and Ilmari. He conducted the Symph. Orch. of Turku (1927–40); then went to America, where he was the principal conductor of the Symph. Orch. of Duluth, Minn. (1942–46), and conductor of the Chicago Civic Symph. Orch. (1947–50); at the same time he was assistant conductor of the Chicago Symph. Orch. (1947–49), then its associate conductor (1949–50); he then returned to Finland, where he was conductor of the City Orch. in Helsinki; he retired in 1963, but continued as a guest conductor. He was active in promoting works by contemporary Finnish composers. He was married to the Finnish soprano **Anne Niskanen.**

Hannikainen, Väinö, Finnish harpist and composer, son of **Pekka Hannikainen;** b. Jyväskylä, Jan. 12, 1900; d. Kuhmoinen, Aug. 7, 1960. He studied in Helsinki and Berlin; from 1923–57 was first harpist of the Helsinki Orch. He wrote several symph. poems, a Harp Concerto, a Harp Sonata, some theater music, and songs.

Hanon, Charles-Louis, French pianist and pedagogue; b. Renescure, near Dunkerque, July 2, 1819; d. Boulogne-sur-Mer, March 19, 1900. Next to Czerny, Hanon was the most illustrious composer of piano exercises, embodied in his chef d'œuvre, *Le Pianiste-virtuose,* which for over a century was the vademecum for many millions of diligent piano students all over the face of the musical globe; its validity as a book of exercises remains solid well into the 21st century. He further wrote a collection of 50 instructive piano pieces under the title *Méthode élémentaire de piano;* a useful compilation, *Extraits des chefs-d'œuvres des grands maîtres;* as well as a selection of 50 ecclesiastical chants, *50 cantiques choisis parmi les plus populaires.* He also attempted to instruct uneducated musicians in the art of accompanying plainchant in a curious didactic publication, *Système nouveau pour apprendre à accompagner tout plainchant sans savoir la musique.*

Hansen, Wilhelm, Danish music publishing firm founded in Copenhagen by Jens Wilhelm Hansen (1821–1904). His sons, **Jonas W. Hansen** (1850–1919) and **Alfred W. Hansen** (1854–1922), also played an active part in the business, which was eventually entrusted to the sons of Alfred, **Asger** (b. 1889) and **Svend** (b. 1890). A large proportion of publ. Scandinavian (Danish, Swedish, Norwegian) music is brought out by this firm; it has also bought other smaller firms, and publ. some of the works of Arnold Schoenberg. Branches have been established in Oslo, Stockholm, Frankfurt, and London.

Hanslick, Eduard, greatly renowned music critic; b. Prague, Sept. 11, 1825; d. Baden, near Vienna, Aug. 6, 1904. He studied law at Prague and Vienna; took the degree of Dr.Jur. in 1849, qualifying himself for an official position. But he had already studied music under Tomaschek at Prague; in 1848–49 was music critic for the *Wiener Zeitung,* and soon adopted a literary career. His first work, *Vom Musikalisch-Schönen: Ein Beitrag zur Revision der Aesthetik der Tonkunst* (Leipzig, 1854; in French, 1877; Spanish, 1879; Italian, 1884; Eng., 1891; Russian, 1895), brought him worldwide fame. Its leading idea is that the beauty of a musical composition lies wholly and specifically in the music itself; i.e., it is immanent in the relations of the tones, without any reference whatever to extraneous (non-musical) ideas, and can express no others. Such being his point of view through life, it follows logically that he could not entertain sympathy for Wagner's art; his violent opposition to the music-drama was a matter of profound conviction, not personal spite; he in fact wrote a moving tribute after Wagner's death. On the other hand, he was one of the very first and most influential champions of Brahms. From 1855–64 Hanslick was music editor of the *Presse;* thereafter of the *Neue Freie Presse;* he became a lecturer on music history and esthetics at Vienna Univ., prof. extraordinary in 1861, and full prof. in 1870, retiring in 1895 (succeeded by Guido Adler). At the Paris Expositions of 1867 and 1878, and the Vienna Exposition of 1873, Hanslick was a juror in the dept. of music. What gives his writings permanent value is the sound musicianship underlying their brilliant, masterly style. Yet in music history he is chiefly known as a captious and intemperate reviler of genius; Wagner caricatured him in the part of Beckmesser (in an early version of *Die Meistersinger* the name was to be Hans Lick). WRITINGS: *Geschichte des Concertwesens in Wien* (1869); *Aus dem Concertsaal* (1870); a series begun with *Die moderne Oper* (1875) and followed by 8 more vols., giving a fairly comprehensive view of the development of opera from Gluck to 1900: II, *Musikalische Stationen* (1880); III, *Aus dem Opernleben der Gegenwart* (1884); IV, *Musikalisches Skizzenbuch* (1888); V, *Musikalisches und Litterarisches* (1889); VI, *Aus dem Tagebuch eines Musikers*

(1892); VII, *Fünf Jahre Musik* (1896); VIII, *Am Ende des Jahrhunderts* (1899); IX, *Aus neuer und neuester Zeit* (1900); *Suite, Aufsätze über Musik und Musiker* (1885); *Konzerte, Komponisten und Virtuosen der letzten fünfzehn Jahre* (1886); *Aus meinem Leben* (2 vols., 1894). All these books passed through several eds. He also ed. T. Billroth's posthumous essay *Wer ist musikalisch?* (1895; 4th ed., 1912), and wrote the commentary for the illustrated *Galerie deutscher Tondichter* (1873) and *Galerie französischer und italienischer Tondichter* (1874). A collection of Hanslick's articles in the *Neue Freie Presse* was publ. in Eng. trans. under the title *Vienna's Golden Years of Music, 1850–1900* (N.Y., 1950).

Hanson, Howard, important American composer and educator; b. Wahoo, Nebr., Oct. 28, 1896; d. Rochester, N.Y., Feb. 16, 1981. His parents emigrated from Sweden to America and made their home in Nebraska, which had a large population of Scandinavian settlers; Hanson's northern ancestry played an important part in his spiritual outlook and his own music. His mother taught him piano; he began to compose very early in life; he also learned to play the cello. He attended the Luther College in Wahoo and played piano and organ in local churches; in 1912 he enrolled in the Univ. of Nebraska; in 1913 he went to N.Y. where he took piano lessons with James Friskin and studied composition with Percy Goetschius at the Inst. of Musical Art. In 1915 he enrolled at Northwestern Univ. in Evanston, Ill., where his teachers in composition were Arne Oldberg and P.C. Lutkin; he graduated in 1916 with a B.A. degree. He progressed rapidly as a composer; his *Symphonic Prelude* was performed by the Chicago Symph.; he also wrote a Piano Quintet and some other works. In 1916, at the age of 20, he received an appointment to teach music at the College of the Pacific in San Jose, Calif.; was named its dean in 1919. In 1921 he became the first American to win the prestigious Prix de Rome, which enabled him to spend 3 years at the American Academy there. He composed copiously; the major part of his works reflected his profound sentiment for his ancestral land; his *Scandinavian Suite* for Piano (1919) exemplified this devotion. He believed in music as a function of the natural environment. During his stay in the west, he wrote the score for a *California Forest Play* (1920). The work that gained him admission to Rome was a symph. poem, *Before the Dawn;* in 1923 he completed a piece for chorus and orch. entitled *North and West.* All these works clearly indicated his future path as a composer; they were permeated with the spirit of the northern country, inspired by both Scandinavia and the American West. There followed his first important work, Symph. No. 1, subtitled *Nordic;* he conducted its first performance in Rome on May 30, 1923. In it he expressed, as he himself said, "the solemnity, austerity, and grandeur of the North, of its restless surging and strife, and of its somberness and melancholy." Hanson was often described as an American Sibelius; indeed, he professed profound admiration for the great Finn, with whom he shared an affinity for slowly progressing lyrical modalities and somber harmonies anchored in deep organ points. In 1923 he conducted the American premiere of his *Nordic Symphony* in Rochester, and met George Eastman, the inventor of Kodak film. Eastman, who knew next to nothing about music, had nonetheless a keen appreciation of ability among artists and composers; in 1924 he offered Hanson the position of director of the Eastman School of Music; Hanson was not quite 28 years old at that time. Eastman's insight was justified; Hanson elevated the Eastman School of Music from a provincial conservatory to one of the most important musical institutions in America. He retained his post as director for 40 years; apart from his teaching, he inaugurated annual festivals of American music in Rochester; as director and conductor of these festivals, he showed an extraordinary measure of liberal choice, programming not only musical compositions that were naturally congenial to him, but also modern works in dissonant harmonies; and he maintained a friendly attitude toward his students even when they veered away into the field of cosmopolitan abstractions. All told, during his tenure in Rochester Hanson presented works by 700 composers and something like 1,500 different compositions. In 1925 he completed one of the most significant works, *The Lament of Beowulf,* for chorus and orch., based on an Old English saga. In 1930 he wrote his 2nd symph., entitled *Romantic,* on commission from Koussevitzky and the Boston Symph. on its 50th anniversary; Koussevitzky conducted its first performance on Nov. 28, 1930. Hanson's 3rd symph. (1936–37) glorified the pioneer spirit of Swedish immigrants; it was presented over the NBC Radio network on March 26, 1938, with Hanson himself conducting. In his Symph. No. 4, subtitled *The Requiem,* written in 1943, Hanson paid a tribute to the memory of his father; he conducted its first performance with the Boston Symph. on Dec. 3, 1943; in 1944 the work received the Pulitzer Prize in music. There followed the 5th symph. *Sinfonia Sacra,* in a single movement (1954); in it Hanson invoked his deep-rooted Christian faith; it was first performed by the Philadelphia Orch. on Feb. 18, 1955. Hanson wrote his 6th symph. to commemorate the 125th anniversary of the N.Y. Phil.; Leonard Bernstein conducted it on leap-year day of 1968. Hanson's 7th symph., *A Sea Symphony,* with chorus, derived from Walt Whitman's poem, was first performed on Aug. 7, 1977, at the National Music Camp at Interlochen. Whitman's poetry was close to Hanson's creative imagination; he wrote several other works based on Walt Whitman's poems, among them *3 Songs from "Drum Taps"* (1935); *Song of Democracy,* which Hanson conducted in Philadelphia on April 9, 1957; and *The Mystic Trumpeter,* performed in Kansas City on April 26, 1970. Hanson remained faithful to his musical and philosophical convictions throughout his long career. Like Sibelius, he wrote music of profound personal feeling, set in an idiom which reflected the triumphs and laments of his life and of his double inheritance. In 1933 he composed his opera, *The Maypole of Merry Mount,* based on *The Maypole Lovers of Merry Mount* by Nathaniel Hawthorne. Hanson dedicated the work to the memory of George Eastman, who had committed suicide 2 years before. Hanson conducted its first performance in concert form in Ann Arbor on May 20, 1933; on Feb. 10, 1934, it was produced by the Metropolitan Opera in N.Y., conducted by Tullio Serafin. It was one of the few operas by an American composer staged at the Metropolitan, and the production was very successful; according to reports, there was a total of 50 curtain calls for Hanson and the singers after its 4 acts. Despite this popular reception and favorable critical reviews, the opera had only 4 performances, and was not retained in the repertoire, a fate not unlike that of other American operas produced at the Metropolitan. A symph. suite drawn from the score enjoyed frequent performances at summer symph. concerts and on the radio.

In the meantime, Hanson continued an active career as conductor. In 1932 he led several concerts of American music in major cities of Europe. During the season 1961–62 he took the Eastman School Phil. Orch. on a grand European tour, under the auspices of the State Dept.; the itinerary included Portugal, Spain, Switzerland, France, Luxembourg, Belgium, Sweden, Greece, Cyprus, Syria, Egypt, Lebanon, Turkey, Germany, Poland, and Russia; in each of these countries Hanson received a most gratifying success; he was praised as both composer and able conductor; his school orch. also received its share of appreciation. As an educator, Hanson enjoyed a great prestige; many talented American composers studied under him. He received numerous honorary degrees. In 1935 he was elected a member of the National Inst. of Arts and Letters; in 1938 he became a fellow of the Royal Academy of Music in Sweden. He held, at various times, a presidency of the National Association of Schools of Music; served also as president of the Music Teachers National Association and of the National Music Council. He was awarded 19 honorary doctorates in music, among them from Syracuse Univ., Univ. of Nebraska, Northwestern Univ., New England Cons. of Music, and Univ. of Michigan. In 1945 he received the Ditson Award and in 1946 was given the George Foster Peabody Award. But with the radical changes in contemporary composition, Hanson's own music seemed to recede into an old-fashioned irrelevance; the number of performances of his music dwindled; only occasionally were his symphs. broadcast from old recordings. Hanson never tried to conceal his bitterness at this loss of appreciation in his country for whose artistic progress he labored so mightily. Yet Hanson's music cannot in all fairness be judged as unredeemingly obsolete. His array of sonorous harmonies, often in modulations at a tritone's distance of their respective tonics, reaches the borderline of pungent bitonality; his bold asymmetrical rhythms retain their vitality; his orchestration is masterly in its instrumental treatment. True, Hanson never accepted the modern techniques of serialism or a total emancipation of dissonance; yet he maintained a liberal attitude toward these new developments. Many of his conservative conservatory admirers were surprised by the publ. of his book, *Harmonic Materials of Modern Music,* in which he presented an exhaustive inventory of advanced harmonic formulas, tabulating them according to their combinatory potentialities.

WORKS: FOR THE STAGE: *California Forest Play of 1920,* ballet, with Solo Voices, Chorus, and Orch. (1919; Calif. State Redwood Park, 1920); *Merry Mount,* opera in 3 acts (1933, commissioned by the Metropolitan Opera; concert perf., Ann Arbor, May 20, 1933; first stage perf., Metropolitan Opera, Feb. 10, 1934); *Nymph and Satyr,* ballet (1978; Chautauqua, N.Y., Aug. 9, 1979).

FOR ORCH: *Symph. Prelude* (1916); *Symph. Legend* (San Francisco, 1917); *Symph. Rhapsody* (1920; Los Angeles, May 26, 1921); *Before the Dawn,* symph. poem (Los Angeles, 1920); *Exultation,* symph. poem with Piano obbligato (San Francisco, 1920); Concerto for Organ, Strings, and Harp (1921); 7 symphs.: No. 1, *Nordic Symphony* (1922; Rome, May 30, 1923; composer conducting; first American perf., Rochester, March 19, 1924); No. 2, *Romantic Symphony* (1928–30; commissioned for the 50th anniversary of the Boston Symph. Orch., Koussevitzky conducting, Nov. 28, 1930); No. 3 (1937–38; first complete perf., NBC studio with NBC Symph., March 26, 1938, composer conducting; first public perf., Boston Symph., Nov. 3, 1939, composer conducting); No. 4, *Requiem* (1943; Boston Symph., Dec. 3, 1943, composer conducting; won Pulitzer Prize of 1944); No. 5, *Sinfonia Sacra* (1954; Philadelphia Orch., Feb. 18, 1955); No. 6 (1967; N.Y. Phil. Orch., Feb. 29, 1968); No. 7, *A Sea Symphony,* after Whitman, for Chorus and Orch. (1977; Interlochen, Mich., Aug. 7, 1977; for the 50th anniversary of the National Music Camp there); *North and West,* symph. poem with Choral Obbligato (1923; N.Y., 1924); *Lux Aeterna,* symph. poem with Viola Obbligato (1923); *Pan and the Priest,* symph. poem with Piano Obbligato (1925–26; London, Oct. 26); Concerto for Organ and Orch. (1926; Rochester, Jan. 6, 1927; uses themes from *North and West*); *Merry Mount Suite* (1937; from the opera); *Fantasy* for String Orch. (1939; based on the String Quartet of 1923); *Serenade* for Flute, Harp, and Strings (1945; also arranged for Flute and Piano); Piano Concerto (Boston Symph., Dec. 31, 1948, composer conducting); *Pastorale* for Oboe, Harp, and Strings (1949; also arranged for Oboe and Piano); *Fantasy-Variations on a Theme of Youth* for Piano and Strings (for the Northwestern Univ. Centennial, Feb. 18, 1951); *Elegy in Memory of My Friend, Serge Koussevitzky* (Boston Symph., Jan. 20, 1956, Munch conducting); *Mosaics* (1957; Cleveland Orch., Jan. 23, 1958); *Summer Seascape I* for Orch. (New Orleans, March 10, 1959); *Summer Seascape II* for Strings (1965); *Bold Island Suite* (1959–61; Cleveland Orch., Jan. 25, 1962); *For the First Time* (Rochester Univ., 1963); *Dies natalis I* (1967); *Young Composer's Guide to the 6-tone Scale,* suite for Piano, Winds, and Percussion (1971–72).

FOR BAND: *March Carillon* (1920; arranged for Band by Erik Leidzen); *Chorale and Alleluia* (1953); *Centennial March* (1968); *Dies Natalis II* (1972); *Laude* (1974).

FOR VOICE: *The Lament for Beowulf,* for Chorus and Orch. (1923–25; Ann Arbor Festival, 1926); *Heroic Elegy* for Orch. and Chorus without words (for the Beethoven centenary, 1927); *3 Songs from "Drum Taps,"* after Whitman, for Baritone, Chorus, and Orch. (1935); *Hymn to the Pioneers* for Men's Voices a cappella (1938); *The Cherubic Hymn* for Chorus and Orch. (1948–49); *Centennial Ode* for Narrator, Baritone, Chorus, and Orch. (1950); *How Excellent Thy Name* for Chorus and Piano (1952); *The Song of Democracy* for Chorus and Orch. (1956; Philadelphia, April 9, 1957); *The Song of Human Rights,* cantata for Speaking Chorus and Orch., to the Universal Declaration of Human Rights (Washington, D.C., Dec. 10, 1963); *4 Psalms* for Baritone, Solo Cello, and String Sextet (Washington, D.C., Oct. 31, 1964); *2 Psalms: Psalm 150 (A Jubilant Song)* for Chorus and Orch. (1965) and *Psalm 121* for Chorus and Orch. (1968); *Streams in the Desert* for Chorus and Orch. (1969); *The Mystic Trumpeter* for Narrator, Chorus, and Orch. (1969; Kansas City, Mo., April 26, 1970); *New Land, New Covenant* for Soloist, Children's Chorus, Mixed Chorus, and Orch.; to words by Isaac Watts, T. S. Eliot, and John Newton, and from the Bible and the Declaration of Independence (1976; Byrn Mawr, Pa., May 2, 1976); *Prayer for the Middle Ages* for Chorus a cappella (1976); songs.

CHAMBER MUSIC: Piano Quintet (1916); *Concerto da Camera* for Piano and String Quartet (1916–17; version for Strings Alone, Rome, March 20, 1922); String Quartet (1923).

FOR PIANO: *Prelude and Double Concert Fugue* for 2 Pianos (1915); *4 Poems* (1917–18); Sonata (1918); *3 Miniatures* (1918–19); *Scandinavian Suite* (1919); *3 Etudes* (1920); *2 Yule-Tide Pieces* (1920).

PUBLICATIONS: *Harmonic Materials of Modern Music: Resources of the Tempered Scale* (N.Y., 1960).

Hanuš, Jan, Czech composer; b. Prague, May 2, 1915. He studied composition privately with Jeremiáš, and conducting with Pavel Dědeček at the Prague Cons. He then devoted himself to editorial work in music publishing houses; was an assistant in preparing the complete critical edition of Dvořák's collected works; also completed the instrumentations of the unfinished operas *Tkalci* by Nejedlý and *Balada o lásce* by Doubrava. His own music is marked by lyrical Romanticism, not without stringent dissonant textures.

Harasiewicz, Adam, Polish pianist; b. Chodziez, western Poland, July 1, 1932. He studied with Kazimierz Mirski until 1950; then at the State School of Music in Cracow. He entered the Chopin Contest in 1949, but failed to win a prize. In March 1955 he competed again, at the 5th International Chopin Contest in Warsaw, in which pianists of 27 countries took part, and won the first prize of 30,000 zlotys.

Harbison, John (Harris), American composer; b. Orange, N.J., Dec. 20, 1938. He grew up in an intellectual environment; his father was a prof. of history at Princeton Univ.; his mother was a magazine writer; both were musical. Exceptionally versatile, he studied violin, viola, piano, voice, and tuba at Princeton High School; also took theory lessons and won an award at a BMI contest at the age of 16. In 1956 he entered Harvard Univ. as a composition student (B.A., 1960); got a bundle of prestigious prizes, not only for music but even for poetry. He also received a Paine Traveling Fellowship from Harvard for a season of study in Berlin; there he took composition lessons with Boris Blacher, and also sang in a choir. Returning to the U.S., he studied composition with Roger Sessions and Earl Kim at Princeton Univ. (M.F.A., 1963). From 1963 to 1968 he was a member of the Society of Fellows at Harvard; from 1969 to 1982 he taught at the Mass. Inst. of Technology; then was composer-in-residence of the Pittsburgh Symph. Orch. (1982–84). He also made appearances as a conductor; led the Cantata Singers from 1969 to 1973 and again from 1980 to 1982. In 1977 he held a Guggenheim fellowship. In his music Harbison has freely adopted quaquaversal methods of composition, *sine ira et studio,* without doctrinaire pedestrianism; he makes use of dodecaphonic techniques when they suit his structural design; in his Shakespearean opera, *The Winter's Tale,* he introduces innovative "dumbshows" acted by pantomime, and also uses recordings; in his opera *Full Moon in March* he includes "prepared piano."

WORKS: For the Stage: Operas: *The Winter's Tale,* after Shakespeare (1974; San Francisco, Aug. 20, 1979), and *Full Moon in March,* after Yeats (1977; Cambridge, Mass., April 30, 1979); 2 ballets after Homer: *Ulysses' Raft* (1983) and *Ulysses' Bow* (1983; Pittsburgh, May 11, 1984). For Orch.: *Sinfonia* for Violin and Double Orch. (1963); *Confinement* for Chamber Ensemble (1965); *Elegiac Songs* for Mezzo-soprano and Chamber Orch., to poems by Emily Dickinson (N.Y., Jan. 12, 1974); *Descant-Nocturne* (1976); *Diotima* (1976; Boston, March 10, 1977); Piano Concerto (1978; N.Y., May 12, 1980); *Snow Country* for Oboe and String Orch. (1979); Violin Concerto (1980); Symph. No. 1 (1981; Boston, March 22, 1984). Chamber music: *Serenade* for 6 Players (1968); *Bermuda Triangle* for Tenor Saxophone, Cello, and Electric Organ (1970); *Book of Hours and Seasons* for Mezzo-soprano, Flute, Cello, and Piano (1975); Wind Quintet (1978); Piano Quintet (1981); *Variations* for Violin, Cello, and Piano (1982); also *The Flower-Fed Buffaloes* for Baritone and Chorus (1976) and other choral music; songs.

d'Harcourt, Eugène, French conductor and composer; b. Paris, May 2, 1859; d. Locarno, Switzerland, March 4, 1918. He studied at the Paris Cons. with Massenet, Durand, and Savard (1882–86); then took courses in Berlin with Bargiel. In 1892 he built the "Salle d'Harcourt" in Paris, where he presented 3 seasons of Concerts Eclectiques Populaires. He wrote an unsuccessful opera, *Le Tasse* (Monte Carlo, 1903), in addition to 3 unnecessary symphs. and some passable chamber music.

d'Harcourt, Marguerite, French folk-song collector and composer; b. Paris, Feb. 24, 1884; d. there, Aug. 2, 1964. She studied composition with Vincent d'Indy and Maurice Emmanuel; composed 2 symphs.; *Rapsodie péruvienne* for Oboe, Clarinet, and Bassoon; and many songs. With her husband, **Raoul d'Harcourt,** she publ. a valuable treatise, *Musique des Incas et ses survivances* (2 vols., Paris, 1925), based on materials gathered during their journeys in Peru; another valuable publication which she compiled was a collection of 240 songs, *Chansons folkloriques françaises au Canada* (Quebec, 1956).

Harewood, 7th Earl of, George Hubert Lascelles, British music editor and organizer; b. London, Feb. 7, 1923. He was educated at Eton and King's College, Cambridge; served as captain in the Grenadier Guards in World War II; was wounded and taken prisoner in 1944. He was founder and editor of the magazine *Opera* (1950–53); was a member of the board of directors of the Royal Opera at Covent Garden (1951–53; 1969–72); from 1956–66 served as chairman of the Music Advisory Committee of the British Council; from 1961–65 was artistic director of the Edinburgh International Festival; from 1962–67 was chancellor of the Univ. of York. In 1972 he was appointed managing director of the Sadler's Wells Opera (known after 1974 as the English National Opera). He edited Kobbé's *Complete Opera Book* in 1954, 1963, and 1972; it was finally publ. as *The New Kobbé's Complete Opera Book* in 1976.

Harline, Leigh, American composer; b. Salt Lake City, March 26, 1907; d. Long Beach, Calif., Dec. 10, 1969. He studied music at the Univ. of Utah; went to Los Angeles in 1928, when he became arranger for Walt Disney (1931–42); then worked as a film-music composer in Hollywood; his song *When You Wish upon a Star* received an Academy Award in 1940.

Harnoncourt, Nikolaus, noted cellist, conductor, and musicologist; b. Berlin, Dec. 6, 1929. He was educated at the Vienna Academy of Music; then played in the Vienna Symph. In 1952 he founded the Vienna Concentus Musicus, an ensemble devoted to original performances in the Baroque style. He made many tours with this group.

Harper, Heather, distinguished English soprano; b. Belfast, May 8, 1930. She studied piano and voice at the Trinity College of Music; also took voice lessons with Helene Isepp and Frederic Husler; made her operatic debut in 1954 with the Oxford Univ. Opera; then appeared at the Glyndebourne Festival and with the English Opera Group. She made her Covent Garden debut in 1962; also sang at the Bayreuth Festivals, the Teatro Colón in Buenos Aires, the San Francisco Opera, and the Metropolitan Opera in N.Y. In 1965 she was made a Commander of the Order of the British Empire.

Harrell, Lynn, outstanding American cellist; b.

New York, Jan. 30, 1944. His father was the baritone **Mack Harrell;** his mother was a violinist. He studied at the Juilliard School of Music in N.Y. with Leonard Rose and at the Curtis Inst. of Music in Philadelphia with Orlando Cole; also attended master classes with Piatigorsky in Dallas (1962) and Casals in Marlboro, Vt. (1963). He made his debut at a young people's concert of the N.Y. Phil. in 1961; then was first cellist of the Cleveland Orch. (1965–71). In 1975 he was named co-recipient (with the pianist Murray Perahia) of the first Avery Fisher Prize. He taught at the Univ. of Cincinnati College-Cons. of Music from 1971 to 1976; then joined the faculty of the Juilliard School of Music, while continuing his concert career. His playing is marked by ingratiating tonal mellowness and a facile, unforced technical display.

Harrell, Mack, American baritone; b. Celeste, Texas, Oct. 8, 1909; d. Dallas, Jan. 29, 1960. He studied violin and voice at the Juilliard School of Music in N.Y.; after some concerts as a soloist he joined the staff of the Metropolitan Opera (1939–45) and continued to make appearances there between 1947 and 1954; also taught voice at the Juilliard School (1945–56). He publ. a book, *The Sacred Hour of Song* (N.Y., 1938).

Harris, Sir Augustus, celebrated English impresario; b. Paris, 1852; d. Folkestone, England, June 22, 1896. An actor by profession, he became a stage manager and producer (with his brother Charles) with the Mapleson Co. in Manchester in 1873. In 1879 he leased the Drury Lane Theatre in London; in 1887 took up the promotion of Italian opera and secured control of Her Majesty's Theatre, Covent Garden, the Olympia, and various provincial stages. He introduced to the English public many of the most famous singers of his time, among them Melba, Maurel, and the de Reszkes. He was knighted in 1891.

Harris, Charles K(assell), American song composer; b. Poughkeepsie, N.Y., May 1, 1865; d. New York, Dec. 22, 1930. He played banjo and piano as a child, and soon began to write songs; went into business for himself at 18 and put out the shingle "Banjoist and song writer/Songs written to order." He established his own publishing firms in Milwaukee and N.Y. His most spectacular success was the song *After the Ball* (1892); characteristically, he entitled his autobiography *After the Ball: 40 Years of Melody* (N.Y., 1926).

Harris, Roy, significant American composer; b. Chandler, Lincoln County, Okla., Feb. 12, 1898; d. Santa Monica, Calif., Oct. 1, 1979. His parents, of Irish and Scottish descent, settled in Oklahoma; in 1903 the family moved to California, where Roy Harris had private music lessons with Henry Schoenfeld and Arthur Farwell. In 1926 he went to Paris, where he studied composition with Nadia Boulanger; was able to continue his stay in Paris thanks to 2 consecutive Guggenheim fellowship awards (1927, 1928). Upon return to the U.S. he lived in California and in N.Y.; several of his works were performed and attracted favorable attention; his former teacher Arthur Farwell publ. an article in the *Musical Quarterly* (Jan. 1932) in which he enthusiastically welcomed Harris as an American genius. In his compositions, Harris showed a talent of great originality, with a strong melodic and rhythmic speech that is indigenously American. He developed a type of modal symbolism akin to Greek ethos, with each particular mode related to a certain emotional state. Instrumental music is the genre in which Harris particularly excelled. He never wrote an opera or an oratorio, but made astute use of choral masses in some of his works. He held the following teaching positions: Westminster Choir School, Princeton (1934–35); Cornell Univ. (1941–43); Colorado College (1943–48); Utah State Agricultural College in Logan (1948–49); Peabody College for Teachers at Nashville (1949–51); Sewanee, Tenn. (1951); Pa. College for Women (1951–56); Univ. of Southern Illinois (1956–57); Indiana Univ. (1957–60); Inter-American Univ., San Germán, Puerto Rico (1960–61); Univ. of Calif., Los Angeles (1961–73). In 1973 he was appointed composer-in-residence at Calif. State Univ., Los Angeles, a post he held until his death. He received honorary D.Mus. degrees from Rutgers Univ. and the Univ. of Rochester in N.Y.; in 1942 he was awarded the Elizabeth Sprague Coolidge Medal "for eminent services to chamber music." In 1936 he married the pianist **Johana Harris** (née **Beula Duffey;** b. Ottawa, Canada, Jan. 1, 1913); she assumed her professional name Johana in honor of J.S. Bach; the single *n* is used owing to some esoteric numerologic considerations to which Roy Harris was partial. After Roy Harris's death, she married, on Dec. 17, 1982, her 21-year-old piano student John Hegge.

WORKS: FOR ORCH.: 13 symphs.: No. 1 (Boston, Jan. 26, 1934); No. 2 (Boston, Feb. 28, 1936); No. 3 (Boston, Feb. 24, 1939; his best-known and most frequently performed work; it was the first American symph. to be played in China, during the 1973 tour of the Philadelphia Orch. under the direction of Eugene Ormandy); No. 4, *Folksong Symphony,* with Chorus (Cleveland, Dec. 26, 1940); No. 5 (Boston, Feb. 26, 1943); No. 6, *Gettysburg Address* (Boston, April 14, 1944); No. 7 (Chicago, Nov. 20, 1952); No. 8 (San Francisco, Jan. 17, 1962); No. 9 (Philadelphia, Jan. 18, 1963); No. 10, *Abraham Lincoln Symphony* for Chorus, Brass, 2 Amplified Pianos, and Percussion (Long Beach, Calif., April 14, 1965); No. 11 (N.Y., Feb. 8, 1968); No. 12 (partial perf., Milwaukee, Feb. 24, 1968); No. 13 for Chorus and Orch. (1969; Washington, D.C., Feb. 10, 1976); Symph. for Band (West Point, N.Y., May 30, 1952); *When Johnny Comes Marching Home,* symph. overture (Minneapolis, Jan. 13, 1935); *Farewell to Pioneers,* symph. elegy (Philadelphia, March 27, 1936); Concerto for 2 Pianos and Orch. (Denver, Jan. 21, 1947); *Kentucky Spring* (Louisville, Ky., April 5, 1949); Piano Concerto (Louisville, Dec. 9, 1953); *Fantasy* for Piano and Orch. (Hartford, Conn., Nov. 17, 1954); *Epilogue to Profiles in Courage: J.F.K.* (Los Angeles, May 10, 1964); *These Times* for Orch., with Piano (1962);

Concerto for Amplified Piano, Wind Instruments, and Percussion (1968). VOCAL WORKS: *Whitman Triptych* for Women's Voice and Piano (1927); *A Song for Occupations,* after Whitman, for Chorus a cappella (1934); *Symphony for Voices,* after Walt Whitman, for Chorus a cappella (Princeton, May 20, 1936); *American Creed* for Chorus and Orch. (Chicago, Oct. 30, 1940); Mass for Men's Voices and Organ (N.Y., May 13, 1948); *Canticle to the Sun* for Coloratura Soprano and Chamber Orch., after St. Francis (Washington, Sept. 12, 1961); *Jubilation* for Chorus, Brasses, and Piano (San Francisco, May 16, 1964). CHAMBER MUSIC: Concerto for Clarinet, Piano, and String Quartet (Paris, May 8, 1927); 3 string quartets (1930, 1933, 1939); String Sextet (1932); Fantasy for Piano, Flute, Oboe, Clarinet, Bassoon, and Horn (Pasadena, Calif., April 10, 1932); Piano Trio (1934); Quintet for Piano and Strings (1936); *Soliloquy and Dance* for Viola and Piano (1939); String Quintet (1940). FOR PIANO: Sonata (1929); *Variations on an Irish Theme* (1938); *Little Suite* (1938); *American Ballads* (1942).

Harrison, George, English rock singer, member of the celebrated group The Beatles; b. Liverpool, Feb. 25, 1943. Like his co-Beatles, he had no formal musical education, and learned to play the guitar by osmosis and acclimatization. Not as extraverted as John Lennon, not as exhibitionistic as Paul McCartney, and not as histrionic as Ringo Starr, he was not as conspicuously projected into public consciousness as his comrades-in-rock. Yet he exercised a distinct influence on the character of the songs that The Beatles sang. He became infatuated with the mystical lore of India; sat at the feet of a hirsute guru; introduced the sitar into his rock arrangements. He is the author of *Something,* one of the greatest successes of The Beatles. When the group broke up in 1970, Harrison proved sufficiently talented to impress his individual image in his own music; he also collaborated on songs of social consciousness with Bob Dylan.

Harrison, Guy Fraser, American conductor; b. Guildford, Surrey, England, Nov. 6, 1894. He studied at the Royal College of Music, where he won an organ scholarship; served as an organist of the Episcopal Cathedral in Manila (1914–20); then emigrated to America; was organist of St. Paul's Cathedral in Rochester, N.Y. (1920–24); then was conductor of the Eastman Theater Orch. in Rochester (1924–49). In 1951 he was appointed conductor of the Oklahoma City Orch.; retired in 1973.

Harrison, Julius Allan Greenway, English conductor and composer; b. Stourport, Worcestershire, March 26, 1885; d. Harpenden, Hertfordshire, April 5, 1963. He studied music with Granville Bantock; subsequently was active mainly as a conductor; filled in engagements with the Beecham Opera Co., the Scottish Symph. Orch., the Handel Society, the Hastings Orch. (1930–40), etc. In his music he makes competent use of English folk songs. He wrote an opera, *The Canterbury Pilgrims;* an orch. suite,

Worcestershire Pieces; cantatas; some chamber music; many songs.

Harrison, Lou, American composer of the avantgarde; b. Portland, Oreg., May 14, 1917. After a period of study with Henry Cowell at San Francisco State College, he plunged headlong into the crosscurrents of modern music. In 1941 he attended the classes of Schoenberg at the Univ. of Calif. at Los Angeles; in 1943 moved to N.Y., where he worked as a music critic for the *N.Y. Herald-Tribune* (1945–48); for a while taught at the progressive Black Mt. College in North Carolina. He held 2 Guggenheim Foundation awards (1952 and 1954); eked out his finances by accompanying modern dancers, and also performing himself as a dancer; at one time he was employed as a florist. He tried his luck as an instrument maker; invented 2 new principles of clavichord construction; built a Phrygian aulos; developed a process for direct composing on a phonograph disc; in 1938 proposed a theory in interval control, and in 1942 supplemented it by a device for rhythm control; also wrote plays and versified poematically. He was one of the earliest adherents of an initially small group of American musicians who promoted the music of Charles Ives, Carl Ruggles, Varèse, and Cowell; he prepared for publication the 3rd Symph. of Charles Ives, which he conducted in its first performance, in 1947. He visited the Orient in 1961, and fortified his immanent belief in the multiform nature of music by studying Japanese and Korean modalities and rhythmic structures. Returning to California, he taught at San Jose State College. Seeking new sources of sound production, he organized a percussion ensemble of multitudinous drums and such homely sound makers as coffee cans and flowerpots. He wrote texts in Esperanto for his vocal works.

WORKS: Opera, *Rapunzel* (N.Y., May 14, 1959); *Young Caesar,* puppet opera (Aptos, Calif., Aug. 21, 1971); ballet scores: *Marriage at the Eiffel Tower* (1948); *Perilous Chapel* (1949); *Solstice* (1950); other works for dance: *Changing World, Johnny Appleseed, Almanac of the Seasons, Changing Moment, Omnipotent Chair, Praises for Hummingbirds and Hawks, Something to Please Everybody,* etc.; *Jephthah's Daughter,* "a theater kit" (Cabrillo College, March 9, 1963); for Orch.: *Elegiac Symphony* (1942–75); *Symphony on G* (1947–53; Oakland, Calif., Feb. 8, 1966); Suite for Solo Violin, Solo Piano, and Orch. (N.Y., Jan. 11, 1952, composer conducting); *Simfony from Simfonies* in free style for Orch. (1956); *Koncerto por la Violono kun perkuta orkestro* (title in Esperanto; N.Y., Nov. 19, 1959); *Suite for Simfoniaj Kordoj* (Esperanto for "Suite for String Orch."; 1960); *Concerto in Slendro* for Violin, Celesta, and Percussion (1961); *Nova Odo* for Chorus and Oriental Instruments (Seoul, Korea, 1963); 14 or more sinfonias for Percussion Orch.; *Recording Piece* for Concert Boobams, Talking Drums, and Percussion (1955); Mass, and other sacred works for chorus.

Harsányi, Tibor, Hungarian composer; b. Magyarkanizsa, Hungary, June 27, 1898; d. Paris, Sept. 19, 1954. He studied at the Budapest Academy of Music with Kodály; in 1923 he settled in Paris, where he devoted himself to composition. The melodic material of his music stems from Hungarian folk melos; his harmonic idiom is largely polytonal; the rhythms are sharp, often with jazz-like syncopation; the form remains classical.

WORKS: FOR THE STAGE: Chamber opera, *Les Invités* (Gera, Germany, 1930); radio opera, *Illusion* (Paris, June 28, 1949); 4 ballets: *Le Dernier Songe* (Budapest, Jan. 27, 1920); *Pantins* (Paris, 1938); *Chota Roustaveli* (in collaboration with Honegger and A. Tcherepnin; Monte Carlo, 1945); *L'Amour et la vie* (1951); puppet show, *L'Histoire du petit tailleur* for 7 Instruments and Percussion (1939). FOR ORCH.: *La Joie de vivre* (Paris, March 11, 1934, composer conducting); 2 divertissements (1940–41, 1943); Violin Concerto (Paris Radio, Jan. 16, 1947); *Figures et rythmes* (Geneva, Nov. 19, 1947, composer conducting); *Danses variées* (Basel, Feb. 14, 1950, composer conducting); Symph. (Salzburg Festival, June 26, 1952). CHAMBER MUSIC: Sonatina for Violin and Piano (1918); *3 Pieces* for Flute and Piano (1924); 2 string quartets (1918, 1935); Cello Sonata (1928); Nonet for String and Wind Instruments (Vienna Festival, June 21, 1932); Rhapsody for Cello and Piano (1939); *Picnic* for 2 Violins, Cello, Double Bass, and Percussion (1951); many piano pieces, among them *5 études rythmiques* (1934), *3 pièces lyriques,* and albums for children. He also wrote several choral works, including *Cantate de Noël* for Voices, Flute, and Strings (Paris, Dec. 24, 1945).

Harshaw, Margaret, outstanding American opera singer; b. Narberth, Pa., May 12, 1909. She began her career as a contralto; later expanded her voice to mezzo-soprano and soprano, while retaining her capacity as a contralto. She was a scholarship student at the Juilliard Graduate School of Music in N.Y., where she studied voice with Anna Schoen-René, graduating in 1942. Shortly after graduation, she won the Metropolitan Opera Auditions of the Air and made her debut with the company in N.Y. as a mezzo-soprano in the role of the Second Norn in *Götterdämmerung* on Nov. 25, 1942; subsequently she sang contralto and mezzo-soprano roles in German, Italian, and French operas; she also acquitted herself brilliantly as a dramatic soprano in her appearance as Senta in *Der fliegende Holländer* at the Metropolitan Opera on Nov. 22, 1950; was particularly successful in Wagnerian roles; she sang Isolde, Sieglinde, Kundry, Elisabeth, and all 3 parts of Brünnhilde. She also excelled as Donna Anna in *Don Giovanni* and Leonore in Beethoven's *Fidelio.* She was a guest soloist with the opera companies of Philadelphia, Cincinnati, San Francisco, and Covent Garden in London, and at the Glyndebourne Festivals. In 1962 she joined the faculty of the Indiana Univ. School of Music in Bloomington; she retired from the Metropolitan Opera in 1963.

Hart, Fritz, English conductor and composer; b. Brockley, Kent, Feb. 11, 1874; d. Honolulu, July 9, 1949. He studied at the Royal College of Music in London in 1893–96; in 1908 he went to Australia and settled there; in 1915 he became director of the Melbourne Cons.; in 1928 was appointed joint artistic director of the Melboune Symph. Orch.; conducted both the Manila Symph. and the Honolulu Orch. (1932 until his death); settled in Honolulu in 1936 when appointed prof. of music at the Univ. of Hawaii; retired in 1942. He wrote operas, operettas, orch. works, chamber music, choruses, and songs.

Hart, Lorenz, American lyricist; b. New York, May 2, 1895; d. there, Nov. 22, 1943. He began as a student of journalism at Columbia Univ. (1914–17); then turned to highly successful theatrical writing. During his 18-year collaboration with Richard Rodgers, he wrote the lyrics for *Connecticut Yankee* (1927); *On Your Toes* (1936); *Babes in Arms* (1937); *The Boys from Syracuse* (1938); *I Married an Angel* (1938); *Too Many Girls* (1939); *Pal Joey* (1940); *By Jupiter* (1942). Some of their best songs (*Manhattan, Here in My Arms, My Heart Stood Still, Small Hotel, Blue Moon, Where or When, I Married an Angel*) are publ. in the album *Rodgers & Hart Songs* (N.Y., 1951).

Hart & Sons, a firm of London violin makers, founded in 1825 by **John Hart.** His son, **John Thomas Hart** (b. Dec. 17, 1805; d. London, Jan. 1, 1874), a pupil of Gilkes, made a complete study of Cremonese and other violins of Italian make, establishing a reputation as an expert in his field. John Thomas's son, **George Hart** (b. London, March 23, 1839; d. near Newhaven, April 25, 1891), succeeded him. He was a good violinist himself; publ. valuable books, *The Violin: Its Famous Makers and Their Imitators* (London, 1875; French ed., Paris, 1886) and *The Violin and Its Music* (London, 1881). His sons, **George** and **Herbert Hart,** inherited the business.

Harth, Sidney, American violinist, conductor, and pedagogue; b. Cleveland, Oct. 5, 1929. He studied at the Cleveland Inst. of Music (Mus.B., 1947); then took lessons with Joseph Fuchs and Georges Enesco; was a recipient of the Naumburg prize in 1948; made his debut at Carnegie Hall in N.Y. in 1949. He later served as concertmaster and assistant conductor of the Louisville Orch. (1953–58), and taught at the Univ. of Louisville. For 3 seasons he was concertmaster of the Chicago Symph. Orch. (1959–62) and concurrently taught at De Paul Univ.; was also concertmaster of the Casals Festival Orch. in San Juan (1959–65; 1972). From 1963–73 he was a prof. of music and chairman of the music dept. at Carnegie-Mellon Univ. in Pittsburgh. He then went to California and served as concertmaster and associate conductor of the Los Angeles Phil. (1973–79); was interim concertmaster of the N.Y. Phil. in 1980; also served as music director of the Puerto Rico Symph. Orch. (1977–79). In 1981 he became orch. director at the Mannes College of Music and a prof. of violin at the State Univ. of N.Y. at Stony Brook. With his wife, **Teresa Testa Harth,** he gave duo violin concerts.

Hartmann, Arthur, Hungarian-American violinist; b. Maté Szalka, Hungary, July 23, 1881; d. New York, March 30, 1956. He was brought to Philadelphia as a child and first studied with his father; then was a pupil of Loeffler (violin) and Homer Norris (composition). He made his debut in Philadelphia (1887) as a child prodigy; by the time he was 12, he had played practically the entire modern violin repertoire. He toured the U.S., Canada, and Scandinavia; played in Paris in recitals with Debussy, and became his intimate friend. In 1939 he settled in N.Y.; retired in 1954. He made numerous transcriptions and arrangements; discovered and edited 6 sonatas of Felice de' Giardini; wrote an essay on Bach's Chaconne which has been translated into 14 languages.

Hartmann, August Wilhelm, Danish organist and composer, son of **Johann Ernst Hartmann;** b. Copenhagen, Nov. 6, 1775; d. there, Nov. 15, 1850. He studied with his father; was first violinist in the Royal Chapel (1796–1817); then was appointed organist at the Garrison Church in Copenhagen. His organ works and other compositions are found in the Royal Library.

Hartmann, Emil, Danish composer, son of **Johan Peter Emilius Hartmann;** b. Copenhagen, Feb. 21, 1836; d. there, July 18, 1898. He received his early education from his father and from **Niels Gade** (who was his brother-in-law); from 1861 till his death was organist in various churches in Denmark. After Gade's death, Hartmann conducted a season of the Musical Society at Copenhagen (1891–92).
WORKS: Operas: *Elverpigen* (Copenhagen, Nov. 5, 1867); *Korsikaneren* (Copenhagen, April 7, 1873); *Ragnhild* (1896); *Det store Lod* (1897); ballet, *Fjeldstuen* (Copenhagen, May 13, 1859); 7 symphs.; other instrumental works.

Hartmann, Johan Peter Emilius, celebrated Danish composer; b. Copenhagen, May 14, 1805; d. there, March 10, 1900. He was the most famous of the Hartmann family in Denmark; was grandson of **Johann Ernst Hartmann** and son of **August Wilhelm Hartmann.** He studied law at the Univ. of Copenhagen, and for many years occupied a public position as a jurist (1828–70), but he was also profoundly interested in music; studied with his father and became his assistant as organist at the Copenhagen Cathedral (1843), remaining in that capacity until his death. He also taught at the Cons. of Copenhagen (from 1827). In 1836 he was one of the organizers of the Danish Music Society; in 1868 was appointed its director. He was also co-director (with **Niels Gade,** his son-in-law) of the new Copenhagen Cons., established in 1867. He spent almost his entire life in Denmark; the only extensive traveling he undertook was in 1836, when he visited Germany and France. He was greatly esteemed in Denmark. A Hartmann Scholarship was founded on the occasion of his 50th jubilee, and he received the Daneborg order.
WORKS: Operas: *The Raven* (Copenhagen, Oct. 29, 1832); *The Corsairs* (Copenhagen, April 23, 1835); *Little Christina* (Copenhagen, May 12, 1846); ballets: *Valkyrien* (Copenhagen, Sept. 13, 1861) and *Thrymskviden* (Copenhagen, Feb. 21, 1868); melodrama, *The Golden Horns* (1834); 2 symphs.: in G minor (1835) and in E major (1848); overtures; Violin Concerto; Flute Sonata; Violin Sonata; pieces for piano; songs.

Hartmann, Johann Ernst, German-Danish composer and violinist, founder of the "Hartmann dynasty" of musicians active in Denmark; b. Glogau, Silesia, Dec. 24, 1726; d. Copenhagen, Oct. 21, 1793. He studied violin in Silesia, and held various posts as a band violinist. In 1766 he settled in Copenhagen; became conductor of the Royal Orch. in 1768. Most of his MSS were lost in a fire (1794), but his violin method and a few instrumental works are extant. His chief claim to fame is the fact that the melody of the present national anthem of Denmark, *Kong Christian stod ved hojen Mast,* was used in the score he wrote for the melodrama *Fiskerne* (Copenhagen, Jan. 31, 1780), and was for a long time regarded as his own composition, although it may have been borrowed from some unknown source of folk origin. A study of this melody is included in Angul Hammerich's book *J.P.E. Hartmann, Biographical Essays* (Copenhagen, 1916).

Hartmann, Karl Amadeus, outstanding German composer; b. Munich, Aug. 2, 1905; d. there, Dec. 5, 1963. He studied with Joseph Haas at the Music Academy in Munich (1923–27) and later with Scherchen. He began to compose rather late in life; his first major work was a Trumpet Concerto, which was performed in Strasbourg in 1933. During the war he studied advanced musical composition and analysis with Anton von Webern in Vienna (1941–42). After the war he organized in Munich the society Musica Viva. He received a prize from the city of Munich in 1948; in 1952 was elected a member of the German Academy of Fine Arts, and soon after became president of the German section of the International Society for Contemporary Music. Despite his acceptance of a highly chromatic, atonal idiom and his experimentation in the domain of rhythm (patterned after Boris Blacher's "variable meters"), Hartmann retained the orthodox form and structural cohesion of basic Classicism. He was excessively critical of his early works, and discarded many of them, but some have been retrieved and performed after his death.
WORKS: Chamber opera, *Des Simplicius Simplicissimus Jugend* (1934–35; Cologne, Oct. 20, 1949; a revised, reduced scoring of the work was made in 1955 and retitled *Simplicius Simplicissimus*); 8 symphs.: No. 1, *Versuch eines Requiems (Attempt at a Requiem),* to words by Walt Whitman, for Soprano and Orch. (1936–40; Vienna, June 22, 1957); No. 2, *Adagio* (1941–46; Donaueschingen, Sept. 10, 1950); No. 3 (1948–49; Munich, Feb. 10, 1950); No. 4 for String Orch. (1946–47; Munich, April 2, 1948); No. 5, *Symphonie concertante,* for Wind Instruments, Cellos, and Double Basses (1950; Stuttgart, April 21,

1951; based on "variable meters"); No. 6 (1951–53; Munich, April 24, 1953); No. 7 (1958; Hamburg, March 15, 1959); No. 8 (1960–62; Cologne, Jan. 25, 1963); *Miserae* (Prague, Sept. 1, 1935); *Concerto funebre* for Violin and String Orch. (1939; revised 1959; Braunschweig, Nov. 12, 1959); *Symphonischen Hymnen* (1942; Munich, Oct. 9, 1975); symph. overture, *China kämpft* (*China at War;* 1942; Darmstadt, July 1947); Concerto for Piano, Winds, and Percussion (Donaueschingen, Oct. 10, 1953); Concerto for Viola, Piano, Winds, and Percussion (Frankfurt, May 25, 1956); *Gesangsszene,* on German texts of Jean Giraudoux's "Sodome et Gomorrhe," for Baritone and Orch. (1962–63; unfinished; Frankfurt, Nov. 12, 1964); *Kammerkonzert* for Clarinet, String Quartet, and String Orch. (Zürich, June 17, 1969); *Jazz-Toccata und -Fugue* for Piano (1928); *Tanzsuite* for Wind Quintet (1931; Frankfurt, April 20, 1975); Piano Sonatina (1931); 2 string quartets (*Carillon,* 1933; 1945–46); *Burleske Musik* for 6 Winds, Percussion, and Piano (c.1933; Rotterdam, June 30, 1967); *Friede Anno 48,* after Gryphius, for Soprano, Chorus, and Piano (1937; Cologne, Oct. 22, 1968; the sections for soprano and piano also exist as a separate piece called *Lamento,* a cantata for Soprano and Piano); *Kleines Konzert* for String Quartet and Percussion (version for String Orch. and Percussion, Braunschweig, Nov. 29, 1974).

Hartmann, Thomas de, Russian composer; b. Khoruzhevka, Ukraine, Sept. 21, 1885; d. Princeton, N.J., March 26, 1956. He studied piano with Anna Essipova at the St. Petersburg Cons.; composition with Taneyev and Arensky. His first important work, the ballet *The Little Crimson Flower,* was produced at the Imperial Theater in St. Petersburg in 1907 with Pavlova, Karsavina, Nijinsky, and Fokine. After the Revolution he went to the Caucasus; taught at the Tiflis Cons. (1919); then went to Paris, where he remained until 1951, when he settled in N.Y. His early music is in the Russian national style, influenced particularly by Mussorgsky; from about 1925, he made a radical change in his style of composition, adopting many devices of outspoken modernism (polytonality, etc.).
WORKS: *The Little Crimson Flower,* ballet (St. Petersburg, Dec. 16, 1907); *Babette,* ballet (Nice, March 10, 1935); opera, *Esther* (not perf.); 4 symphs. (1915; 1944; 1953; 1955, unfinished); Cello Concerto (1935; Boston, April 14, 1938); Piano Concerto (1940; Paris, Nov. 8, 1942); Double-bass Concerto (1943; Paris, Jan. 26, 1945); Harp Concerto (1944); Violin Concerto (Paris, March 16, 1947); Flute Concerto (Paris, Sept. 27, 1950); *12 Russian Fairy Tales* for Orch. (Houston, April 4, 1955, Stokowski conducting); Violin Sonata (1937); Cello Sonata (1942); Trio for Flute, Violin, and Piano (1946); 3 song cycles to words by Verlaine, Proust, and James Joyce; other songs; piano pieces. His music to Kandinsky's spectacle *The Yellow Sound,* arranged by Gunther Schuller from Hartmann's sketches, was played in N.Y. in a series of performances beginning Feb. 9, 1982.

Harty, Sir Hamilton, eminent conductor and composer; b. Hillsborough, County Down, Ireland, Dec. 4, 1879; d. Brighton, England, Feb. 19, 1941. He received his entire education from his father, an organist; so well grounded was he as a performer that on Feb. 12, 1894, at the age of 14, he was formally appointed as organist at Magheragall Church, in County Antrim; later he also filled positions as church organist in Belfast and in Bray, outside Dublin. In 1901 he went to London, where he began to compose; his Piano Quintet, String Quartet, and *Irish Symphony* won prizes; in London he also began to conduct. On July 15, 1904, he married the singer **Agnes Nicholls.** In 1920 he was appointed conductor of the renowned Hallé Orch. in Manchester, remaining at that post for 13 seasons. In 1932 he became conductor of the London Symph. Orch. In 1931 he made his first American tour, during which he conducted in Boston, Chicago, and Cleveland, and at the Hollywood Bowl. In 1934 he conducted in Australia. He was knighted in 1925. Harty's arrangements of Handel's *Water Music* and *Royal Fireworks Music* for large orch. became standard repertoire pieces; of his original works, only his *Irish Symphony,* first performed under his direction in Manchester on Nov. 13, 1924, received praise; he also wrote *Comedy Overture* (1906); *Ode to a Nightingale,* after Keats, for Soprano and Orch. (1907); Violin Concerto (1908–9); *With the Wild Geese,* symph. poem (1910); *The Mystic Trumpeter* for Baritone, Chorus, and Orch. (1913); *The Children of Lir,* symph. poem (London, March 1, 1939). He arranged *A John Field Suite* for Orch., based on piano pieces by Field.

Harvey, Jonathan, significant British composer; b. Sutton, Goldfield, May 3, 1939. He served as a chorister at St. Michael's College, Tenbury (1948–52); won a scholarship to St. John's College, Cambridge; studied music there with Erwin Stein and Hans Keller; gained his Ph.D. from Glasgow Univ. in 1964; then joined the music faculty of Southampton Univ. In 1969–70 he lectured at Princeton Univ.; in 1980 became prof. of music at Sussex Univ. As a composer, Harvey absorbed and astutely synthesized a number of quaquaversal idioms and techniques ranging from medieval modalities to ultra-modern procedures; he also made use of electronic resources.
WORKS: FOR ORCH.: Symph. (1966); Chaconne on *Iam dulcis amica* (1967); *Benedictus* (1970); *Persephone's Dream* (London, Jan. 18, 1973); *Inner Light* (London, March 3, 1976); *Smiling Immortal* for Chamber Orch. (London, July 11, 1977); *Whom ye adore* (Glasgow, Sept. 19, 1981). CHAMBER MUSIC: Variations for Violin and Piano (1965); *Studies* for 2 Clarinets (1970); Trio for Violin, Cello, and Piano (1971); *Inner Light I* for 7 Players (London, Nov. 26, 1973); *Quantumplation* for Instrumental Ensemble (1973); *Meditation* for Cello and Quadrophonic Tape (1976); String Quartet (1977); *Album,* 7 miniatures for Wind Quintet (1978); *Be(com)ing* for Clarinet and Piano (1979); *Concelebration* for Instrumental Ensemble (London, Jan. 6, 1980); *Mortuos*

plango, vivos, voco for Computerized Concrete Sounds (1980; Lille, Nov. 30, 1980); *Modernsky Music* for 2 Oboes, Bassoon, and Harpsichord (Sounthorpe, Sept. 19, 1981). VOCAL MUSIC: 4 songs of Yeats for Bass and Piano (1965); Cantata I for Soloists, Chorus, Organ, and Strings (1965); Cantata II, *Three Lovescapes* for Soprano and Piano (1967); Cantata III for Soprano and 6 Players (1968); Cantata IV, *Ludus Amoris,* for Soloists, Speaker, Chorus, and Orch. (1969); Cantata V for Soloists and Wind Quintet (1970); Cantata VI, *On Faith,* for Chorus and Strings (1970); Cantata VII, *On Vision* (1971); Cantata VIII (1971); Cantata IX (1973); Cantata X, *Spirit Music,* for Soprano, 3 Clarinets, and Piano (Sheffield, Feb. 20, 1976); *Inner Light II* for Soloists, Instruments, and Tape (Cheltenham, July 8, 1977); *Hymn* for Chorus and Orch. (1979, for the 900th anniversary of Winchester Cathedral, July 12, 1979); *Passion and Resurrection,* church opera (Winchester Cathedral, March 21, 1981); *Resurrection* for Double Chorus and Organ (Worcester, Aug. 28, 1981).

Harwood, Basil, English organist and composer; b. Woodhouse, Gloucestershire, April 11, 1859; d. London, April 3, 1949. He studied piano with J.L. Roeckel and organ with George Risely; also studied with Reinecke and Jadassohn at the Leipzig Cons. Returning to England, he occupied various posts as an organist: at St. Barnabas Church, Pimlico (1883–87); Ely Cathedral (1887–92); and Christ Church Cathedral, Oxford (1892–1909). He edited the *Oxford Hymn Book* (1908); wrote a number of sacred works for chorus; organ pieces (2 sonatas, Organ Concerto, Christmastide, *Dithyramb,* etc.); a cantata, *Ode on May Morning,* after Milton (Leeds Festival, 1913).

Harwood, Elizabeth, English soprano; b. Kettering, May 27, 1938. She studied at the Royal Manchester College of Music; won the Kathleen Ferrier Memorial Prize in 1960. In 1961 she joined the Sadler's Wells Opera; was a winner of the Verdi Sesquicentennial Competition in Busetto in 1963; subsequently sang with the Scottish Opera, Covent Garden, and the English Opera Group; also made guest appearances at La Scala in Milan and at the Salzburg Festival. She made her Metropolitan Opera debut in N.Y. on Oct. 15, 1975, as Fiordiligi in *Così fan tutte.*

Häser, August Ferdinand, German composer; b. Leipzig, Oct. 15, 1779; d. Weimar, Nov. 1, 1844. He was a member of a musical family; his 3 brothers and a sister were musicians. He was educated at the Thomasschule in Leipzig, and studied theology at Leipzig Univ. In 1797 he went to Lemgo, Westphalia, where he taught mathematics in high school. He traveled in Italy from 1806–13; then returned to Lemgo. In 1817 he was engaged in Weimar as music teacher to Princess Augusta (the future German empress); also conducted the chorus at the Court Opera there; was a church organist and a teacher of Italian.

Häser, Charlotte, German soprano; b. Leipzig, June 24, 1784; d. Rome, May 1, 1871. She studied with her father, **Johann Georg Häser,** a composer; then sang in Dresden; she went to Italy in 1806, where she enjoyed tremendous success; she was also one of the first women to sing male roles. After she left the stage, she settled in Rome. Her brother, **August Ferdinand Häser,** was a composer.

Haskil, Clara, brilliant Rumanian pianist; b. Bucharest, Jan. 7, 1895; d. Brussels, Dec. 7, 1960. A precocious musician, she played in public at the age of 7; then entered the Paris Cons., where she studied piano with Cortot and won a first prize at the age of 14. Busoni heard her in Basel and invited her to study with him in Berlin. She played programs of Beethoven sonatas with Enesco, Ysaÿe, and Casals; subsequently gave piano recitals and appeared as a soloist with major symph. orchs. in Europe and America. A muscular deficiency severely impeded her concert career; however, she continued playing concerts during periods of remission of her ailment. Music critics praised her fine musicianship and her penetrating interpretation of classical piano music.

Haslinger, Tobias, Austrian music publisher; b. Zell, March 1, 1787; d. Vienna, June 18, 1842. He went to Vienna in 1810 after studying music in Linz; was bookkeeper in Steiner's music establishment; later became a partner and, after Steiner's retirement in 1826, sole proprietor. A gregarious and affable person, he made friends with many musicians, and was on excellent terms with Beethoven, who seemed to enjoy Haslinger's company; many letters to him from Beethoven are extant, among them the humorous canon *O Tobias Dominus Haslinger.* He was succeeded by his son **Carl Haslinger** (b. Vienna, June 11, 1816; d. there, Dec. 26, 1868). The latter studied with Czerny and became a brilliant pianist as well as an industrious composer; he publ. more than 100 works of various kinds. Continuing the tradition of his father, he publ. several symphs., piano concertos, overtures, and other works by Beethoven, and later Liszt's Piano Concerto in E-flat; he was also the publisher of many Strauss waltzes. In 1875 the firm was bought from his widow by Schlesinger of Berlin (subsequently, R. & W. Lienau).

Hasse (née **Bordoni**), **Faustina,** famous Italian mezzo-soprano, wife of **Johann Adolf Hasse;** b. Venice, c.1700; d. there, Nov. 4, 1781. She studied with Gasparini and Benedetto Marcello. She made her debut in 1716 in Pollarolo's opera *Ariodante,* and obtained such success that soon she was called the "New Siren." When she sang in Florence a few years later (1722), a special medal was issued in her honor; she was equally successful in Naples. She became a member of the court theater in Vienna in 1724, at a high salary. Handel heard her there, and engaged her for his opera enterprise in London, where she made her debut on May 5, 1726, winning high praise. She remained in London for 2 seasons; her quarrel with Francesca Cuzzoni in a competition for public attention resulted in her departure from England.

She went back to Venice; in 1730 she married Hasse, and devoted her life thenceforth to his success, without abondoning her own career. From 1731 till 1763 they lived in Dresden; then in Vienna (until 1773), finally settling in Venice. According to Burney, she could sustain a note longer than any other singer; her trills were strong and rapid; her intonation, perfect. Burney also praised her physical qualities.

Hasse, Johann Adolf, important German composer; b. Bergedorf, near Hamburg, March 25, 1699; d. Venice, Dec. 16, 1783. He received his first instruction in music from his father, a schoolmaster and organist. In 1714–17 he studied in Hamburg; then, in 1718, at the recommendation of J. Ulrich von König, the poet, he was engaged by Keiser, director of the Hamburg Opera, as a tenor; he sang there 4 seasons, and from 1719 was tenor at the Braunschweig theater; it was there that Hasse first appeared as a composer, with his opera *Antioco* (Aug. 11, 1721). He then went to Naples to study the craft of composition more thoroughly; there he was a pupil of Porpora and later of Alessandro Scarlatti. In 1725 he wrote a serenade for 2 voices which was performed by Farinelli and Vittoria Tesi, and this further promoted Hasse's career in Italy; there followed a successful production of his new opera, *Sesostrate* (Naples, May 13, 1726). In 1727 he was appointed to the staff of the Scuola degl'Incurabili in Venice; there he wrote his *Miserere*, which enjoyed excellent success throughout Italy for many years afterward. His ability to ingratiate himself with society, his affable manners, and his handsome appearance contributed to his artistic success; he was often referred to as "il caro Sassone" (even though he was not a Saxon). In 1729 he met the famous singer **Faustina Bordoni,** and married her in Venice the following year. She sang the leading roles in many of his operas, and together they attained the highest positions in the operatic world. He wrote 2 operas for her, *Artaserse* and *Dalisa,* produced in Venice shortly after their marriage; he also brought out his 11th opera, *Tigrane* (Nov. 4, 1729). In 1731 Hasse received an appointment as music director of the Dresden Opera, with Faustina Hasse as prima donna; his first operatic production in Dresden was *Cleofide,* on Sept. 13, 1731, in which his wife scored a brilliant success. During frequent leaves of absence they traveled in Italy, where Hasse produced the following operas: *Catone in Utica* (Turin, Dec. 26, 1731); *Caio Fabrizio* (Rome, Jan. 12, 1732); *Siroe, re di Persia* (Bologna, May 2, 1733); and *Tito Vespasiano* (Pesaro, Sept. 24, 1735). In Dresden he produced *Senocrita* (Feb. 27, 1737); *Atalanta* (July 26, 1737); *Asteria* (Aug. 3, 1737); *Alfonso* (May 11, 1738); *Numa Pompilio* (Oct. 7, 1741); *Arminio* (Oct. 7, 1745); *La Spartana generosa* (June 14, 1747); *Demofoonte* (Feb. 9, 1748); *Attilio Regolo* (Jan. 12, 1750); *Ciro riconosciuto* (Jan. 20, 1751); *Adriano in Siria* (Jan. 17, 1752); *Solimano* (Feb. 5, 1753); *Artemisia* (Feb. 6, 1754); *L'Olimpiade* (Feb. 16, 1756); etc. Among other capital cities he visited during this period was Warsaw, where he produced *Il sogno di Scipione* (Oct.

7, 1738; not extant). His productions in Vienna were *Ipermestra* (Jan. 8, 1744); *Alcide al Bivio* (Oct. 8, 1760); *Zenobia* (Oct. 7, 1761); *Il trionfo di Clelia* (April 27, 1762); *Egeria* (April 24, 1764); *Partenope* (Sept. 9, 1767); and *Piramo e Tisbe* (Nov. 1768). His last opera was *Ruggerio,* produced in Milan on Oct. 16, 1771.

Although Hasse was fortunate in his artistic life and never lacked the support of the public, he had to face strong rivalry on the part of the Italian composer Porpora, who was engaged by the Dresden court in 1747. Furthermore, Porpora's pupil, a young singer named Regina Mingotti, became a formidable competitor to Faustina Hasse, no longer in her prime. Hasse succeeded in maintaining his firm position in Dresden, and Porpora departed for Vienna in 1752. In 1760, during the siege of Dresden in the course of the Seven Years' War, Hasse's house was set afire by gunfire, and nearly all of his MSS perished. Hasse's vitality and determination overcame these challenges, and he never ceased to produce new works with astounding facility. His music did not break new paths in operatic art, but he was a master of singing melody in the Italian style, and a fine craftsman in harmony and instrumentation. *Pallido è il sole* and *Per questo dolce amplesso,* from his opera *Artaserse,* were the 2 airs that Farinelli sang every evening for 10 years to soothe the melancholy of the ailing Spanish King Philip. In addition to his operas, Hasse wrote 11 oratorios, many masses, 3 Requiems, 23 Psalms, 5 litanies, 22 motets, a Te Deum, and a *Salve regina* (publ. in London in 1740, under the title *The Famous Salve Regina Composed by Signor Hasse*); he also wrote instrumental concertos, string trios, sonatas, etc. An important collection of Hasse's MSS is in the Dresden Library. A selection of his works was publ. by A. Schering in Denkmäler Deutscher Tonkunst (vols. 20, 29/30) and by Otto Schmid in *Musik am sächsischen Hofe* (vols. 1, 2, 6, 7, 8); G. Göhler edited *10 ausgewählte Orchesterstücke* (1904). Other reprints are by Christian I. Latrobe in his *Selection of Sacred Music* (6 vols., 1806–26), by B. Engländer (keyboard sonatas; Leipzig, 1930), etc.; cantatas for solo female and orch. are in Le Pupitre, 11. S.H. Hansell's *Works for Solo Voice of Johann Adolph Hasse* (Detroit, 1968) is a thematic index of 132 solo vocal works with orch. or continuo accompaniment: cantatas, motets, and antiphons.

Hasselmans, Louis, French cellist and conductor; b. Paris, July 25, 1878; d. San Juan, Puerto Rico, Dec. 27, 1957. He was the son of a harpist and grandson of a conductor. He studied the cello with Jules Delsart at the Paris Cons., winning first prize at the age of 15, and theory with Lavignac and B. Godard. From 1893 to 1909 he was cellist in the Capet Quartet; made his debut as a conductor in Paris in 1905; then conducted at the Opéra-Comique (1909–11) and in Montreal (1911–13); was conductor of the Chicago Opera (1918–20) and was engaged as conductor of French operas at the Metropolitan Opera in N.Y. (1921–36); then taught at Louisiana State Univ. in Baton Rouge (1936–48).

Hassler, Caspar, German composer, brother of **Hans Leo Hassler;** b. Nuremberg (baptized, July 17), 1562; d. there, Aug. 19, 1618. In 1586 he was appointed organist at the Lorenz-Kirche; also supervised the building of the organ in the Würzburg Cathedral. He wrote a number of organ pieces; edited several collections of sacred works by various authors.

Hassler, Hans Leo, celebrated German composer; b. Nuremberg, Oct. 25, 1564; d. Frankfurt, June 8, 1612. He studied with his father, Isaak Hassler (1530–91), and from his earliest years became extremely proficient on the organ. In 1584 he went to Venice to study with Andrea Gabrieli. Hassler was the first notable German composer to go to Italy for musical study; however, he did not remain long in Venice; after 18 months there, he was recalled to Germany, where he obtained the post of chamber musician to Count Octavianus Fugger in Augsburg (1586); following the latter's death in 1600, Hassler became director of town music in Nuremberg and also organist at the Frauenkirche there. On Jan. 1, 1602, he received the post of chamber organist to the Court of Rudolf II at Prague; this was an honorary position rather than an actual occupation, and Hassler appeared but infrequently, if at all, at the imperial court in Prague. At the time he was busily engaged in the manufacture and installation of musical clocks; his commercial pursuits led to numerous litigations with business rivals. In 1604 he took a leave of absence from Nuremberg and went to Ulm; in 1608 he became organist to the Elector of Saxony in Dresden, and in 1612 accompanied him to Frankfurt; but Hassler was weakened by tuberculosis and died shortly after his arrival there. The style of Hassler's music is greatly influenced by his teacher Andrea Gabrieli, and by the latter's nephew, Giovanni Gabrieli, with whom Hassler became friendly in Venice. Having absorbed the Italian techniques, Hassler applied his knowledge to the composition of strongly national German songs, and became one of the founders of national musical art in Germany. WORKS: *Canzonette a 4* (Nuremberg, 1590); *Cantiones sacrae a 4–12* (Augsburg, 1591); *Neue teutsche Gesäng nach Art der welschen Madrigalien und Canzonetten a 4–8* (Augsburg, 1596); *Madrigali a 5–8* (Augsburg, 1596); 8 masses *a 4–8* (Nuremberg, 1599); *Sacri concentus a 4–12* (Augsburg, 1601; 2nd ed., 1612); *Lustgarten neuer teutscher Gesäng, Balletti, Gailliarden und Intraden a 4–8* (Nuremberg, 1601; later eds., 1605, 1610; reprints in Eitner's *Publikationen älterer praktischer und theoretischer Musikwerke,* vol. 15); *Psalmen und christliche Gesäng mit vier Stimmen auf die Melodien fugweis componirt* (Nuremberg, 1607); *Kirchengesänge, Psalmen und geistliche Lieder, auf die gemeinen Melodien mit vier Stimmen simpliciter gesetzt* (Nuremberg, 1608; 2nd enlarged ed., 1637); *Venusgarten oder Neue lustige liebliche Tänz a 4–6* (with V. Haussmann; Nuremberg, 1615); numerous motets, litanies, and organ works in various contemporary collections. Reprints are in Denkmäler Deutscher Tonkunst, vols. 2, 7, 24/25; Denkmäler der Tonkunst in Bayern, vols. 7, 9, 20 (4.ii, 5.ii, 11.i); Riemann's *Illustrationen zur Musikgeschichte* and *Musikgeschichte in Beispielen;* Schering's *Geschichte der Musik in Beispielen;* Leichtentritt's *Meisterwerke deutscher Tonkunst;* etc. R. von Saalfeld ed. the Psalms and sacred songs (1925); H. Bäuerle ed. 2 masses. A chronological list of Hassler's printed works was publ. by Eitner in the *Monatshefte für Musik-Geschichte* (1874). Publication of the *Collected Works,* ed. by C. Russell Crosby, was begun in 1961 (Wiesbaden).

Hassler, Jakob, German organist and composer, brother of **Hans Leo Hassler;** b. Nuremberg, (baptized, Dec. 18) 1569; d. Eger, between April and Sept. 1622. Like his famous brother, he enjoyed the patronage of the Fugger family; was enabled to go to Italy in 1590 to improve his musical education; upon his return to Germany, on his brother's recommendation, he received the honorary post of organist to Emperor Rudolf II in Prague. In 1611 he settled in Eger. He publ. a collection of Italian madrigals (Nuremberg, 1600) and a book of sacred works (Nuremberg, 1601). E. von Werra publ. several keyboard pieces by Jakob Hassler in Denkmäler der Tonkunst in Bayern, 7 (4.ii).

Hässler, Johann Wilhelm, German composer and pianist; b. Erfurt, March 29, 1747; d. Moscow, March 29, 1822. His father was a maker of men's headwear; he followed his father's trade while studying organ with his uncle, Johann Christian Kittel. At the age of 14, he was able to earn his living as organist at an Erfurt church. After his father's death, in 1769, he maintained for some years a manufactory of fur muffs. A meeting in Hamburg with Carl Philipp Emanuel Bach gave him a fresh impetus toward continuing his musical activities. He gave concerts as a pianist, and publ. several piano sonatas. On Feb. 8, 1779, he married his pupil Sophie Kiel. In 1780 he opened public winter concerts in Erfurt; his wife appeared there as a singer and choral director. In 1789 he played in Berlin and Potsdam; in Dresden he took part in a contest with Mozart, as organist and pianist, without producing much impression either on Mozart himself or on the listeners. In 1790 he went to London, where he performed piano concertos under the direction of Haydn. In 1792 he went to Russia, where he remained for 30 years, until his death. In Moscow he became greatly renowned as a pianist, as a composer, and particularly as a teacher. Most of his works were publ. in Russia; these included sonatas, preludes, variations, fantasies, etc., and also pieces for piano, 4-hands. His style represents a transition between Bach and Beethoven, without attaining a degree of the imagination or craftsmanship of either. However, his piano pieces in the lighter vein have undeniable charm. His Gigue in D minor was well known. His autobiography is included in Willi Kahl, *Selbstbiographien deutscher Musiker* (Cologne, 1948). See also W. Georgii, *Klavier-Musik* (Zürich, 1950); R.-A. Mooser, *Annales de la musique et des musiciens en Russie au XVIIIᵉ siècle* (Geneva, 1951; vol. II, pp. 659–61).

Hastings, Thomas, American composer of hymn tunes; b. Washington, Litchfield County, Conn., Oct. 15, 1784; d. New York, May 15, 1872. The family moved to Clinton, N.Y., when Hastings was 12; he became interested in practical music and was a leader of a village chorus. He collected hymns, which were later publ. in a collection, *Musica Sacra* (Utica, N.Y., 1815; 2nd ed., 1816); it was later combined with S. Warriner's *Springfield Collection* (Boston, 1813) as *Musica Sacra: or, Springfield and Utica Collection* (Utica, 1818; 9 subsequent eds. to 1830). He moved to Utica in 1823 and was a member of a Handel and Haydn society there; he also edited a religious weekly publication, *The Western Recorder.* In 1832 he settled in N.Y., where he was connected with the Normal Inst., in association with Lowell Mason. He received the honorary degree of D.Mus. from N.Y. Univ. (1858). WRITINGS: Among his many publications were *Musical Reader* (1817); *Dissertation on Musical Taste* (in which he discourses on the superiority of German music; Albany, 1822; 2nd enlarged ed., 1853); *The Union Minstrel* (1830); *Spiritual Songs for Social Worship* (with Lowell Mason; 1831); *Devotional Hymns and Religious Poems* (1850); *History of Forty Choirs* (1854); and *Sacred Praise* (1856). His own hymn tunes have been estimated to number more than 1,000, and, next to those of Lowell Mason, are regarded as the finest of his time in America. These include the tune to which the celebrated hymn *Rock of Ages* is sung; the words are by Augustus Toplady, and Hastings entitled his tune simply *Toplady* to honor the author of the words. Other well-known hymn tunes are *Retreat, Zion,* and *Ortonville.* He publ. many of his melodies under foreign-sounding names, and it is not always possible to ascertain their authorship.

Hatton, John Liptrot, British composer of light music; b. Liverpool, Oct. 12, 1809; d. Margate, Sept. 20, 1886. He acquired facility as a pianist and singer, and appeared on the vaudeville stage as a musical comedian. He publ. a great number of songs, among which *Anthea* and *Good-bye, sweetheart, good-bye* became extremely popular. In 1832 he went to London; produced his operetta, *The Queen of the Thames,* there (Feb. 25, 1843). He then went to Vienna, where he staged his opera *Pascal Bruno* (March 2, 1844). For some of his numbers he used the punning pseudonym **Czapek** (genitive plural of the Hungarian word for "hat"). In 1848–50 he made an extensive American tour. Returning to England, he was music director at the Princess's Theatre (1853–59); wrote music for several Shakespeare plays there; wrote a cantata, *Robin Hood* (Bradford Festival, Aug. 26, 1856); a grand opera, *Rose, or Love's Ransom* (London, Nov. 26, 1864); and a sacred drama, *Hezekiah* (Dec. 15, 1877); edited collections of old English songs.

Haubenstock-Ramati, Roman, Polish composer of experimental music; b. Cracow, Nov. 27, 1919. He studied philosophy at the Univ. of Cracow; also took music lessons with Arthur Malawski and Josef Koffler. From 1947 to 1950 he was music director of Radio Cracow; then went to Israel, where he was director of the State Music Library in Tel Aviv (1950–56). In 1957 he settled in Vienna, where he was for a time employed by Universal Edition as reader and adviser for publications of new music. In 1959 he organized in Donaueschingen the first exhibition of musical scores in graphic notation; he himself evolved an imaginative type of modern particella in which the right-hand page gives the outline of musical action for the conductor while the left-hand page is devoted to instrumental and vocal details. This type of notation combined the most advanced type of visual guidance with an aide-mémoire of traditional theater arrangements. In 1967 he inaugurated a weekly seminar for avant-garde music in Bilthoven, the Netherlands. In 1968 he gave lectures in Buenos Aires, and in 1969 he conducted a seminar in Stockholm. Several of his works bear the subtitle "Mobile" to indicate the flexibility of their architectonics. WORKS: *Ricercari* for String Trio (1950); *Blessings* for Voice and 9 Players (1952); *Recitativo ed Aria* for Harpsichord and Orch. (1954); *Papageno's Pocket-Size Concerto* for Glockenspiel and Orch. (1955); *Les Symphonies des timbres* for Orch. (1957); *Chants et Prismes* for Orch. (1957, revised 1967); *Séquences* for Violin and Orch. in 4 groups (1957–58); *Interpolation,* a "mobile" for Solo Flute (1958); *Liaisons,* a "mobile" for Vibraphone and Marimbaphone (1958); *Petite musique de nuit,* a "mobile" for Orch. (1958); *Mobile for Shakespeare* for Voice and 6 Players (1960); *Credentials or "Think, Think Lucky,"* after Beckett, for Speech-voice and 8 Players (1960); *Decisions,* 10 pieces of musical graphics for Variable Instrumentation (1960–68); *Jeux 6,* "mobile" for 6 Percussionists (1960); opera, *Amerika,* after Kafka's novel (1962–64; Berlin, Oct. 8, 1966); *Vermutungen über ein dunkles Haus,* 3 pieces for 3 Orchs., 2 of which are on tape (1963; material from the opera); *Klavierstücke I* for Piano (1963–65); *Jeux 2* and *4,* "mobiles" for 2 and 4 Percussionists (1965, 1966); *Hotel Occidental* for Speech-chorus, after Kafka (in 3 versions, 1967); an anti-opera, *La Comédie,* after Beckett, for One Male and 2 Female Speech-singers, and 3 Percussionists (St. Paul-de-Vence, Alpes-Maritimes, France, July 21, 1969; German version as *Spiel,* Munich, 1970; Eng. version as *Play*); *Tableau I, II,* and *III* for Orch. (1967, 1968, 1970); *Symphonie "K"* (1967; material from the opera *Amerika*); *Psalm* for Orch. (1967); *Divertimento,* text collage for Actors, Dancer, and/or Mime, and 2 Percussionists (1968; after *Jeux 2*); *Catch I* for Harpsichord (1969), *II* for One or 2 Pianos (1970), and *III* for Organ (1971); *Multiple I–VI* for various instrumental combinations (1969); *Alone* for Trombone and Mime (1969); *Describe* for Voice and Piano (1969); *Hexachord I* and *II* for 2 Guitars (1972); *Concerto a tre* for Piano, Trombone, and Percussion (1973); 2 string quartets (1973, 1978); *Shapes (in Memory of Stravinsky) I* for Organ and Tape, and *II* for Organ, Piano, Harpsichord, and Celesta (both 1973); *Endless,* endless "mobile" for 7 Players and Conductor (1974); Solo Cello Sonata (1975); *Musik* for 12 Instruments (1976); *Ulysses,* ballet (1977); *Concerto per archi* (1977; Graz, Oct. 11, 1977); *Symphonien* (1977; Baden-Baden, May 10, 1978); *Self* for Bass Clarinet and 3 Tapes (1978).

Haubiel, Charles Trowbridge (original name, **Charles Trowbridge Pratt**), American composer; b. Delta, Ohio, Jan. 30, 1892; d. Los Angeles, Aug. 26, 1978. His father's last name was Pratt, but he adopted his mother's maiden name, Haubiel, as his own. He had piano lessons with his sister **Florence Pratt,** an accomplished pianist. In 1911 he went to Europe, where he studied piano with Rudolf Ganz in Berlin; also took composition lessons with Alexander von Fielitz in Leipzig. Returning to the U.S. in 1913, he taught music at various schools in Oklahoma. When the U.S. entered the war in 1917, he enlisted in the field artillery and served in France. After the Armistice he resumed a serious study of composition with Rosario Scalero at the David Mannes Music School in N.Y. (1919–24), while continuing taking piano lessons with Rosina and Josef Lhévinne. Intermittently he taught musical subjects at the Inst. of Musical Art in N.Y. (1921–31) and at N.Y. Univ. (1923–47). In 1935 he organized Composers Press, Inc., with the purpose of promoting the publication of American music, and served as its president until 1966. He was a recipient of numerous awards of merit for outstanding contributions to music. His own compositions reveal an excellent theoretical and practical grasp of harmony, counterpoint, instrumentation, and formal design. In his idiom he followed the models of the Romantic school of composition, but he embroidered the basic patterns of traditional music with winsome coloristic touches, approaching the usage of French Impressionism. He was extremely prolific; many of his works underwent multiple transformations from a modest original, usually for solo piano or a chamber group, to a piece for full orch.; in all these forms his compositions remain eminently playable.
WORKS: Mexican folk opera, *Sunday Costs 5 Pesos* (Charlotte, N.C., Nov. 6, 1950). FOR ORCH.: *Gothic Variations* (originally for Violin and Piano, 1919; revised 1942; adapted for Full Orch., and perf. in Los Angeles, June 9, 1970); *Vox Cathedralis* (originally for Organ, 1925; arranged for 2 Pianos, 1928; finally transcribed for Orch., 1934, and perf. in N.Y. May 6, 1938); *Rittrati (Portraits;* originally for Piano, 1919; orch. transcription first perf., Chicago Symph., Dec. 12, 1935); *Karma,* symph. variations (1928; received first prize at the Schubert Centennial in a contest by Columbia Records; revised in 1968 and retitled *Of Human Destiny*); *Suite Passacaglia* (Los Angeles, Jan. 31, 1936; originally for 2 Pianos); *Symphony in Variation Form* (1937); *Miniatures* for String Orch. (N.Y., April 23, 1939); *American Rhapsody* (1948); *Pioneers,* symphonic saga of Ohio (1946; revised 1956; perf. in Los Angeles, Feb. 19, 1960); *Metamorphosis* (1926; set of 29 variations on Stephen Foster's *Swanee River;* filmed as a short subject and produced under the title *Swanee River Goes Hi-Hat*); *1865 A.D.* (1943; revised 1958, under the title *Mississippi Story;* first perf. Los Angeles, April 24, 1959). CHAMBER MUSIC: *Ecchi classici* for

String Quartet (1924); *Duo Forms* for Cello and Piano (1929–31); *Cryptics* for Bassoon and Piano (1932); *Lodando la danza* for Oboe, Violin, Cello, and Piano (1932); *Nuances,* suite for Flute and Piano (1938); Cello Sonata (1941); *In the French Manner* for Flute, Cello, and Piano (1942); String Trio (1943); Violin Sonata (1945); *Shadows* for Violin and Piano (1947); *Pastoral Trio* for Flute, Cello, and Piano (1949); *Epochs* for Violin and Piano (1954–55); *Threnody for Love* for 6 Instruments (1965); *Ohioana,* cycle for Violin and Piano (1966); Trio for Clarinet, Cello, and Piano (1969). Also numerous choral works: *Vision of Saint Joan* (1941); *Jungle Tale* (1943); *Father Abraham* (1944), etc.; piano suite, *Solari* (1932–34); other pieces for piano solo.

Haudebert, Lucien, French composer; b. Fougères, April 10, 1877; d. Paris, Feb. 24, 1963. He studied organ; then went to Paris, where he took lessons in composition with Fauré. He followed in his music the traditions of César Franck, preferring large sonorities and clear tonal harmonies. He stood aloof from modern developments in France and had little recognition even among traditional musicians, despite praise from Romain Rolland. His most effective work is the oratorio *Dieu Vainqueur* (1916–22); other significant works are the oratorio *Moïse* (1928); *Symphonie bretonne* (1936); *Symphonie française* (1941); *Voyage en Bretagne* for Orch. (1953); *Chants de la mer* for Voices and Orch. (1950); also chamber music, including a Quartet for Saxophones.

Hauer, Josef Matthias, significant Austrian composer and original theorist; b. Wiener-Neustadt, near Vienna, March 19, 1883; d. Vienna, Sept. 22, 1959. After attending a college for teachers, he became a public-school instructor; at the same time he studied music. An experimenter by nature, with a penchant for mathematical constructions, he developed a system of composition based on "tropes," or patterns, which aggregated to thematic formations of 12 different notes. As early as 1912 he publ. a piano piece, entitled *Nomos (Law),* which contained the germinal principles of 12-tone music; in his theoretical publications he elaborated his system in greater detail. These were *Vom Wesen des Musikalischen* (Berlin, 1922); *Deutung des Melos* (Vienna, 1923); *Vom Melos zur Pauke* (Vienna, 1925), and finally *Zwölftontechnik* (Vienna, 1926), in which the method of composing in the 12-tone technique was illustrated with practical examples. Hauer vehemently asserted his priority in 12-tone composition; he even used a rubber stamp on his personal stationery proclaiming himself the true founder of the 12-tone method. This claim was countered, with equal vehemence but with more justification, by Schoenberg; indeed, the functional basis of 12-tone composition in which the contrapuntal and harmonic structures are derived from the unifying tone row did not appear until Schoenberg formulated it and put it into practice in 1924. Hauer lived his entire life in Vienna, working as a composer, conductor, and teacher. Despite its forbidding character, his music attracted much attention.

WORKS: 2 operas: *Salammbô*, after Flaubert (1930; unperf.) and *Die schwarze Spinne* (1932; posthumous, Vienna, May 23, 1966); an oratorio, *Wandlungen*, for 6 Soloists, Chorus, and Chamber Orch. (1927; Baden-Baden, April 16, 1928); 2 cantatas: *Emilie vor ihrem Brauttag* for Alto and Orch. (1928) and *Der Menschen Weg*, in 7 sections, to poems by Hölderlin, for 4 Soloists, Chorus, and Orch. (1934; reduced in 1952 to 5 sections; Vienna, June 1953); *Lateinische Messe* for Chorus, Chamber Orch., and Organ (1926, unfinished; posthumous, Vienna, June 18, 1972); *Vom Leben*, after Hölderlin, for Narrator, Small Chorus, and Small Orch. (1928). OTHER WORKS: *Nomos* (Symph. No. 1), in 7 parts, for 1 or 2 Pianos, or Orch. (1912–13; version for 2 Pianos, Sankt Pölten, June 7, 1913); *Nomos* (Symph. No. 2), in 5 parts, for Piano and Small Orch. (1913); *Nomos*, 7 little piano pieces (1913); *Apokalyptische Phantasie* (Symph. No. 3) for 2 Pianos or Orch. (1913; version for 2 Pianos, Wiener-Neustadt, May 9, 1914; version for Orch., posthumous, Styrian Autumn Festival, Graz, Austria, Oct. 21, 1969); *Oriental Tale* for Piano (1916); *Nomos* for Piano and String Ensemble (1919); Quintet for Clarinet, Violin, Viola, Cello, and Piano (1924); 6 string quartets (1924–26); 8 suites for Orch. (1924; 1924; 1925, with Baritone Solo; 1926; 1926; 1926, also for String Quartet; 1926; 1927); *Romantische Fantasie* for Small Orch. (1925); 7 *Variations* for Flute, Clarinet, Violin, Viola, Cello, and Double Bass (1925); *Symphonische Stücke (Kammerstücke)* for String Orch., Piano, and Harmonium (1926); Sinfonietta (1927; Berlin, Dec. 13, 1928); Violin Concerto (1928; Berlin, Nov. 12, 1929); Piano Concerto (1928); *Divertimento* for Small Orch. (1930); *Konzertstücke* for Orch. (1932; from *Die schwarze Spinne*); *Tanzphantasien* Nos. 1 and 2 for 4 Soloists and Orch. (1933) and Nos. 3–7 for Chamber Orch. (1934); 2 *Tanzsuiten* for 9 Solo Instruments (1936); *Labyrinthischer Tanz* for Piano, 4-Hands (1952); *Langsamer Walzer* for Orch. (1953); *Chinesisches Streichquartett* (1953); *Hausmusik* for Piano, 4-Hands (1958). After 1940, Hauer was primarily concerned with composing a series of pieces, each ostentatiously bearing the subtitle *Zwölftonspiel*, for orch. and chamber combinations of all descriptions—their total number exceeding 100—with each one designated by the month and year composed, as, for example, his *Zwölftonspiel* for Orch. (August 1940), *Zwölftonspiel* for Violin and Harpsichord (July 1948), *Zwölftonspiel* for Orch. (September 1957), and *Zwölftonspiel* for String Sextet (May 1958).

Haug, Hans, Swiss composer; b. Basel, July 27, 1900; d. Lausanne, Sept. 15, 1967. He studied piano with Egon Petri and Ernst Levy in Basel, and later with Busoni at the Munich Academy of Music. Returning to Switzerland, he became choral conductor at the Municipal Theater in Basel (1928–34); from 1935–38 he conducted the orch. of the Radio Suisse Romande and also taught at the Cons. of Lausanne, where he finally settled. As a composer, he was most successful in writing for the theater.

WORKS: Operas: *Don Juan in der Fremde* (Basel, Jan. 15, 1930); *Madrisa* (Basel, Jan. 15, 1934); *Tartuffe* (Basel, May 24, 1937); *Le Malade imaginaire*, after Molière (Zürich, Feb. 8, 1947); *Der Spiegel der Agrippina* (1954); *Justice du roi* (1963); radio operas: *Gardien vigilant* (1967) and *Le Souper de Venise* (1967); oratorio, *Michelangelo* (Solothurn, Feb. 28, 1943); operettas: *Barbara* (1938); *Gilberte de Courgenay* (1939); several radio operettas; ballets: *L'Indifférent* and *Pan und Apollo;* incidental music for theatrical plays; numerous cantatas, including a humorous *Cantate gastronomique* for Soli, Chorus, and Orch.; Symph. (1948); *Capriccio* for Wind Instruments and Piano (1957); Concertino for Flute and Small Orch. (1943); Concertino for Oboe, Viola, and Small Orch.; Concertino for Piano and Orch.; Guitar Concerto (1952); 2 piano concertos (1938, 1962); Double Concerto for Oboe and Viola (1953); 3 string quartets; Wind Quartet; Wind Quintet; *Kurze Musik* for Cello and Orch.; etc.; also a curious symph. poem entitled *Charlie Chaplin* (1930).

Hauk, Minnie (real name, **Amalia Mignon Hauck**), celebrated American soprano; b. New York, Nov. 16, 1851; d. Triebschen, near Lucerne, Switzerland, Feb. 6, 1929. Her father was a German carpenter who became involved in the political events of 1848, emigrated to America, and married an American woman; he named his daughter Mignon after the character in Goethe's *Wilhelm Meister*. The family moved to Atchison, Kans., when Minnie was very young; her mother maintained a boarding house at a steamboat landing on the Missouri. In 1860 they moved to New Orleans; there Minnie Hauk began to sing popular ballads for entertainment. She made her operatic debut at the age of 14 in Brooklyn, in *La Sonnambula* (Oct. 13, 1866); then took lessons with Achille Errani in N.Y. On Nov. 15, 1867, she sang Juliette at the American premiere of Gounod's opera in N.Y. She attracted the attention of the rich industrialist Leonard Jerome and the music publisher Gustave Schirmer, who financed her trip to Europe. She sang in opera in Paris during the summer of 1868; made her London debut at Covent Garden on Oct. 26, 1868; in 1870 she sang in Vienna. She sang the title roles in the first American performances of *Carmen* (N.Y. Academy of Music, Oct. 23, 1878) and Massenet's *Manon* (Dec. 23, 1885); made her debut at the Metropolitan Opera in N.Y. as Selika in *L'Africaine* on Feb. 10, 1891; continued to appear there for that season, but following a disagreement with the management, decided to organize her own opera group; with it, she gave the first Chicago performance of *Cavalleria rusticana* (Sept. 28, 1891). She then settled in Switzerland with her husband, Baron Ernst von Hesse-Wartegg, whom she had married in 1881; after his death she lived mostly in Berlin; lost her fortune in the depreciation of her holdings in Germany. In 1919, Geraldine Farrar launched an appeal to raise funds for her in America. Hauk's autobiography, collated by E.B. Hitchcock, was publ. as *Memories of a Singer* (London, 1925).

Hauptmann, Moritz, eminent German theorist and composer; b. Dresden, Oct. 13, 1792; d. Leipzig, Jan. 3, 1868. His father was an architect and hoped to bring up his son in that profession; however, there was no parental opposition to music studies; Hauptmann took lessons with Scholz (violin), Grose (piano and harmony), and Morlacchi (composition) in Dresden; later studied with Weinlig; in 1811 he went to Gotha to study violin and composition with Spohr and became his lifelong friend; went to Vienna in 1813 as a violinist in Spohr's orch. at the Theater an der Wien. In 1812 he joined the Dresden Court Orch. as violinist; in 1815 he became music teacher in the family of the Russian military governor of Dresden, Prince Repnin, and went with them to Russia, where he remained for 5 years. In 1820 he returned to Dresden; in 1822, Spohr engaged him as violinist in the court orch. at Kassel. In 1842, at Mendelssohn's recommendation, he was appointed cantor at the Thomasschule and prof. of composition at the Leipzig Cons., retaining these posts until his death. He became greatly renowned as a teacher of violin and composition. Among his pupils were Ferdinand David, Joachim, Hans von Bülow, Jadassohn, and Arthur Sullivan. A master of classical form, he was a polished composer, in the tradition of Spohr and Mendelssohn; the architectonic symmetry of his instrumental works and the purity of part-writing in his vocal music aroused admiration among his contemporaries; yet his music failed to endure, and rapidly went into decline after his death. He publ. about 60 works, among them 3 violin sonatas, 4 violin sonatinas, 2 string quartets, piano pieces, sacred works, and a number of lieder, a genre in which he excelled. His theoretical work *Die Natur der Harmonik und Metrik* (Leipzig, 1853; 2nd ed., 1873; Eng. trans., London, 1888) is an attempt to apply Hegel's dialectical philosophy to the realm of music. It exercised considerable influence on the later development of German theory of harmony; among other German scholars, Riemann was influenced by it. Hauptmann's other writings are: *Erläuterungen zu J.S. Bachs Kunst der Fuge* (Leipzig, 1841; 2nd ed., 1861); *Die Lehre von der Harmonik* (ed. by Oscar Paul; Leipzig, 1868); *Opuscula* (miscellaneous writings, ed. by E. Hauptmann; Leipzig, 1874). His letters to Spohr and others were edited by F. Hiller (Leipzig, 1876). A.D. Coleridge publ. a selection, in Eng., of Hauptmann's correspondence as *Letters of a Leipzig Cantor* (1892).

Hausegger, Siegmund von, Austrian conductor and composer; b. Graz, Aug. 16, 1872; d. Munich, Oct. 10, 1948. He was trained musically by his father, Friedrich von Hausegger. At the age of 16 he composed a grand Mass, which he himself conducted; at 18 he brought out in Graz an opera, *Helfrid.* Richard Strauss thought well enough of Hausegger as a composer to accept for performance his comic opera *Zinnober,* which he conducted in Munich on June 19, 1898. Hausegger began his own conducting career in Graz as a theater conductor in 1895; in 1897 he was guest conductor in Bayreuth; was conductor of the Volk-Symphonie-Konzerte in Munich (1899–

1902) and of the Museum Concerts in Frankfurt (1903–6). In 1910 he was appointed conductor of the Phil. Concerts in Hamburg. From 1918 to 1934 he was director of the Academy of Musical Art in Munich; in 1920 was named Generalmusikdirektor of the Munich Konzertverein, which became the Munich Phil. in 1928; remained there until his retirement in 1938.

Haussermann, John, American composer; b. Manila, Philippines, Aug. 21, 1909. He was taken to New Richmond, Ohio, as a child and studied piano with local teachers; returned to Manila in 1922 and studied music theory with Dr. Ebeneezer Cook there. In 1924 he enrolled in the Cincinnati Cons. of Music, studying organ with Parvin Titus and music theory with George Leighton. In 1930 he went to Paris, where he studied organ with Marcel Dupré and composition with Paul Le Flem. In 1934 he was again in Manila, where he was active as an organist; then lived in Cincinnati; dedicated himself mainly to composing. His music is marked by a pragmatic sense of formal cohesion, which does not exclude a flair for innovation, as exemplified by his Concerto for Voice and Orch.

WORKS: FOR ORCH.: Symphs.: No. 1 (1938; partial perf., N.Y., May 28, 1939); No. 2 (1941; Cincinnati, March 31, 1944, Eugene Goossens conducting); No. 3 (1947; Cincinnati, April 1, 1949, Thor Johnson conducting); *Rhapsodic Overture* for Piano and Chamber Orch. (1938); *The After Christmas Suite* for Orch. (Cincinnati, March 22, 1938); Concerto for Voice and Orch. (Cincinnati, April 24, 1942); *Ronde carnavalesque* for Orch. (N.Y., Feb. 6, 1949); *Stanza* for Violin and Orch. (Mallorca, Spain, Feb. 22, 1956); *Sacred Cantata* for Baritone and Orch. (Cincinnati, Jan. 31, 1965). CHAMBER MUSIC: Quintet for Flute, Oboe, Clarinet, Bassoon, and Harpsichord (1935); Piano Quintet (1935); String Quartet (1937); *Suite rustique* for Flute, Cello, and Piano (1937); *Divertissements* for String Quartet (1940); *Serenade* for Theremin and Strings (1945); *Poème et Clair de lune* for Violin and Piano (1940); Violin Sonata (1941). FOR PIANO: *24 préludes symphoniques* (1932–33); *Sonatine fantastique* (1932); *Pastoral fantasie* for 2 Pianos, 4-hands (1933); *Sonatine romantique* (1933); *Ballade, Burlesque, et Légende* (1936); 7 *Bagatelles* (1948); 9 *Impromptus* (1958); 5 *Harmonic Etudes* (1968); a great number of organ pieces; songs.

Haussmann, Valentin. Five German musicians in direct lineal descent bore this name: **Valentin Haussmann I,** the eldest, b. Nuremberg, 1484, composed chorales, and was a friend of Luther. His son, **Valentin Haussmann II,** was organist at Gerbstädt, and an industrious composer of motets, canzonets, and dances. A selection of his instrumental works was publ. by F. Bölsche in Denkmäler Deutscher Tonkunst (vol. 16). **Valentin Haussmann III,** son of the preceding, was organist at Löbejün, and an expert in organ construction. His son, **Valentin Haussmann IV,** b. Löbejün, c.1647, occupied the post of chapel musician to the Köthen court. **Valentin Bar-**

tholomäus Haussmann V, son of the preceding, b. Löbejün, 1678, became cathedral organist at Merseburg and Halle, and burgomaster at Lauchstadt.

Hawes, William, English composer and conductor; b. London, June 21, 1785; d. there, Feb. 18, 1846. As a boy he was a chorister at the Chapel Royal (1793–1801); then violinist at Covent Garden (1802); became Gentleman of the Chapel Royal in 1805; vicar-choral and master of choristers at St. Paul's Cathedral (1812); master of the children of the Chapel Royal (1817); and lay-vicar of Westminster Abbey (1817–20). He was director of English opera at the Lyceum; it was at his suggestion that Weber's *Der Freischütz* was given for the first time in England (July 22, 1824); he contributed some airs of his own composition to this production. Subsequently, he adapted and produced many Italian, French, and German operas for the English stage; he wrote and staged several light operas, among them *Broken Promises* (1825), *The Quartette, or Interrupted Harmony* (1828), *The Sister of Charity* (1829), etc. Some of his glees were popular. He edited the publication (in score) of the *Triumphes of Oriana* (1818), various collections of glees, etc.

Hawkins, Coleman (nicknamed **Bean** and **Hawk**), black American jazz tenor saxophonist; b. St. Joseph, Mo., Nov. 21, 1904; d. New York, May 19, 1969. He joined the Kansas City group Jazz Hounds in 1921; from 1923–34 was a member of Fletcher Henderson's band in N.Y.; his full tone and heavy vibrato became the standard for tenor saxophone, and he was considered the foremost performer on the instrument. In 1934–39 he worked in Europe; upon his return to the U.S. in 1939 he made his most influential recording, *Body and Soul;* departing from the usual paraphrase approach of swing improvisation, his extemporized solo became an inspiration to the new generation of jazz musicians and paved the way for the bebop of the 1940s.

Hawkins, Sir John, eminent English music historian; b. London, March 29, 1719; d. there, May 21, 1789. He studied law while serving as a clerk, and soon was able to act as an attorney. An ardent devotee of music, he entered the musical society of the time and was on friendly terms with Handel; he also participated in literary clubs, and knew Samuel Johnson, Goldsmith, and others. A wealthy marriage (1753) enabled him to devote his leisure to literature and music. In the meantime, he progressed on the ladder of success in the legal profession. In 1761 he became a magistrate; in 1763, chairman of the Quarter Sessions; he was knighted in 1772. His first publication dealing with music was brought out anonymously: *An Account of the Institution and Progress of the Academy of Ancient Music* (1770). The culmination of 16 years of labor was his monumental *General History of the Science and Practice of Music,* publ. in 1776 in 5 vols. (quarto), containing 58 portraits of musicians; it was reprinted in 1853 (2 vols.) and 1875 (3 vols.) by Novello (octavo); the 1875 edition was reprinted again, with posthumous notes by Hawkins, in 2 vols., edited by O. Wessely, in Graz, 1969. The first vol. of Burney's *General History of Music* appeared at the same time as the 5 vols. of Hawkins; thus, Hawkins undoubtedly held priority for the first general history of music publ. in England; however, its reception was rather hostile; Burney himself derided Hawkins in an unpubl. poem. Yet the Hawkins work contained reliable information, particularly dealing with musical life in London in the 18th century. Hawkins died of a paralytic stroke and was buried in Westminster Abbey.

Haydn, (Franz) Joseph, illustrious Austrian composer; b. Rohrau, Lower Austria, probably March 31, 1732 (baptized, April 1, 1732); d. Vienna, May 31, 1809. He was the 2nd of 12 children born to Mathias Haydn, a wheelwright, who served as village sexton, and Anna Maria Koller, daughter of the market inspector and a former cook in the household of Count Harrach, lord of the village. Their 2nd son, **Michael,** also became a musician. On Sundays and holidays music was performed at home, the father accompanying the voices on the harp, which he had learned to play by ear. When Haydn was a small child his paternal cousin Johann Mathias Franck, a choral director, took him to Hainburg, where he gave him instruction in reading, writing, arithmetic, and instrumental playing. When Haydn was 8 years old, Karl Georg Reutter, Kapellmeister at St. Stephen's Cathedral in Vienna, engaged him as a soprano singer in the chorus. After Haydn's voice began to break, he moved to the household of Johann Michael Spangler, a music teacher. He obtained a loan of 150 florins from Anton Buchholz, a friend of his father, and was able to rent an attic room where he could use a harpsichord. In the same house lived the famous Italian poet and opera librettist Pietro Metastasio, who recommended Haydn to a resident Spanish family as a music tutor. He was also engaged as accompanist to students of Nicolò Porpora, for whom he performed various menial tasks in exchange for composition lessons. He made a diligent study of *Gradus ad Parnassum* by Fux and *Der volkommene Kapellmeister* by Mattheson. Soon he began to compose keyboard music. In 1751 he wrote the singspiel *Der krumme Teufel.* A noblewoman, Countess Thun, engaged Haydn as harpsichordist and singing teacher; he met Karl Joseph von Fürnburg, for whom he wrote his first string quartets. In 1759 Haydn was engaged by Count Ferdinand Maximilian von Morzin as Kapellmeister at his estate in Lukaveč. On Nov. 26, 1760, Haydn married Maria Anna Keller, the eldest daughter of his early benefactor, a Viennese wigmaker.

A decided turn in Haydn's life was his meeting with Prince Paul Anton Esterházy. Esterházy had heard one of Haydn's symphs. during a visit to Lukaveč, and engaged him to enter his service as 2nd Kapellmeister at his estate in Eisenstadt; Haydn signed his contract with Esterházy on May 1, 1761. Prince Paul Anton died in 1762, and his brother, Prince Nikolaus Esterházy, known as the "Magnificent," succeeded him. He took Haydn to his new palace at Esterház, where Haydn was to provide 2 weekly operatic performances and 2 formal concerts. Haydn's service at Esterház was long-lasting, secure, and fruitful; there he composed music of all descriptions, including most of his known 83 string quartets, about 80 of his 104 symphs., a number of keyboard works, and nearly all his operas; in 1766 he was elevated to the rank of first Kapellmeister. Prince Nikolaus Esterházy was a cultural patron of the arts, but he was also a stern taskmaster in his relationship to his employees. His contract with Haydn stipulated that each commissioned work had to be performed without delay, and that such a work should not be copied for use by others. Haydn was to present himself in the "antichambre" of the palace each morning and afternoon to receive the Prince's orders, and he was obliged to wear formal clothes, with white hose and a powdered wig with a pigtail or a hairbag; he was to have his meals with the other musicians and house servants. In particular, Haydn was obligated to write pieces that could be performed on the viola da gamba, an instrument which the Prince could play; in consequence, Haydn wrote 175 separate numbers for the viola da gamba. He also wrote 3 sets of 6 string quartets each (opp. 9, 17, and 20), which were brought out in 1771–72. His noteworthy symphs. included No. 49 in F minor, *La passione;* No. 44 in E minor, known as the *Trauersinfonie;* No. 45 in F-sharp minor; and the famous *Abschiedsinfonie* (the *Farewell* Symph.), performed by Haydn at Esterház in 1772. The last movement of the *Farewell* Symph. ends in a long slow section during which one musician after another ceases to play and leaves the stage, until only the conductor and a single violinist remain to complete the work. The traditional explanation is that Haydn used the charade to suggest to the Prince that his musicians deserved a vacation after their arduous labors, but another and much more plausible version, found in *Anedotti piacevoli ed interessanti,* publ. in 1830 by G.G. Ferrari, who personally knew Haydn, is that the Prince had decided to disband the orch. and that Haydn wished to impress on him the sadness of such a decision; the known result was that the orch. was retained. In 1780 Haydn was elected a member of the Modena Phil. Society; in 1784 Prince Henry of Prussia sent him a gold medal; in 1785 he was commissioned to write a "passione istrumentale," *The Seven Last Words,* for the Cathedral of Cádiz; in 1787 King Friedrich Wilhelm II gave him a diamond ring; many other distinctions were conferred upon him. During his visits to Vienna he formed a close friendship with Mozart, who was nearly a quarter of a century younger, and for whose genius Haydn had great admiration. If the words of Mozart's father can be taken literally, Haydn told him that Mozart was "the greatest composer known to me either in person or by name." Mozart reciprocated Haydn's regard for him by dedicating to him a set of 6 string quartets. Prince Nikolaus Esterházy died in 1790, and his son Paul Anton (named after his uncle) inherited the estate. Haydn was granted an annuity of 1,000 florins; nominally he remained in the service of the new Prince as Kapellmeister, but he took up permanent residence in Vienna.

In 1790 Johann Peter Salomon, the enterprising London impresario, visited Haydn and persuaded him to travel to London for a series of concerts. Haydn accepted the offer, arriving in London on Jan. 1, 1791. On March 11 of that year he appeared in his first London concert in the Hanover Square Rooms, presiding at the keyboard. Haydn was greatly feted in London by the nobility; the King himself expressed his admiration for Haydn's art. In July 1791 he went to Oxford to receive the honorary degree of Mus.D. For this occasion, he submitted his Symph. No. 92 in G major, which became known as the *Oxford* Symph.; he composed in a 3-part canon, *Thy Voice, O Harmony, Is Divine,* as his exercise piece. It was also in England that he wrote his Symph. No. 94 in G major, the *Surprise* Symph. The surprise of the title was provided by the loud drum strokes at the end of the main theme in the slow movement; the story went that Haydn introduced the drum strokes with the sly intention of awakening the London dowagers, who were apt to doze off at a concert. On his journey back to Vienna in the summer of 1792 Haydn stopped in Bonn, where young Beethoven showed him some of his works, and Haydn agreed to accept him later as his student in Vienna. In 1794 Haydn went to London once more. His first concert, on Feb. 10, 1794, met with great success. His *London* symphs., also known as the *Salomon* symphs., because Haydn wrote them at Salomon's request, were 12 in number, and they included No. 99 in E-flat major; No. 100 in G major, known as the *Military* Symph.; No. 101 in D major, nicknamed *The Clock* because of its pendulum-like rhythmic accompanying figure; No. 102 in B-flat major; No. 103 in E-flat major, known as the *Drum Roll* Symph.; and No. 104 in D major.

Returning to Vienna, Haydn resumed his contact with the Esterházy family. In 1794 Prince Paul Anton had died and was succeeded by his son Nikolaus; the new Prince has plans to revive the Haydn orch. at Eisenstadt, with Haydn again as Kapellmeister. Conforming to the new requirements of Prince Nikolaus, Haydn turned to works for the church, including 6 masses. His Mass in C major was entitled *Missa in tempore belli* (1796), for it was composed during Napoleon's drive toward Vienna. The 2nd Mass, in B-flat major, the *Heiligmesse,* also dates from 1796. In 1798 Haydn composed the 3rd Mass, in D minor, which is often called the *Nelson-messe,* with reference to Lord Nelson's defeat of Napoleon's army at the Battle of the Nile. The 4th Mass, in B-flat major (1799), is called the *Theresien-messe,* in honor of the Austrian Empress Maria Theresa. The 5th Mass, in B-flat major, written in 1801, is known as the *Schöpfungsmesse,* for it contains a theme from the oratorio *Die Schöpfung (The Creation).* The 6th Mass, in B-flat major (1802), is referred to as the *Harmoniemesse,* for its extensive use of wind instruments; the word "harmonie" is here used in the French meaning, as the wind instrument section. Between 1796 and 1798 Haydn composed his great oratorio *Die Schöpfung,* which was first performed at a private concert for the nobility at the Schwarzenburg Palace in Vienna on April 29, 1798. In 1796 he wrote the Concerto in E-flat major for trumpet, which became a standard piece for trumpet players. In 1797 Haydn was instructed by the Court to compose a hymn-tune of a solemn nature that could be used as the national Austrian anthem. Haydn succeeded triumphantly in this task; he made use of this tune as a theme of a set of variations in his String Quartet in C major, op. 76, no. 3, which itself became known as the *Emperor* Quartet. The original text for the hymn, written by Lorenz Leopold Haschka, began "Gott erhalte Franz den Kaiser." This hymn had a curious history: a new set of words was written by August Heinrich Hoffmann during a period of revolutionary disturbances in Germany preceding the general European revolution of 1848; its first line, "Deutschland, Deutschland über alles," later assumed the significance of German imperialism; in its original it meant merely, "Germany above all (in our hearts)." Between 1799 and 1801 Haydn completed the oratorio *Die Jahreszeiten;* its text was trans. into German from James Thomson's poem *The Seasons.* It was first performed at the Schwarzenburg Palace in Vienna on April 24, 1801. In 1802, beset by illness, Haydn resigned as Kapellmeister to Prince Nikolaus. Despite his gradually increasing debility, Haydn preserved the saving grace of his natural humor; in response to the many salutations of his friends, he sent around a quotation from his old song, *Der Alte,* confessing his bodily weakness. Another amusing musical jest was Haydn's reply to a society lady who identified herself at a Vienna party as a person to whom Haydn had dedicated a lively tune ascending on the major scale; she sang it for him, and he replied wistfully that the tune was now more appropriate in an inversion. Haydn made his last public appearance at a concert given in his honor in the Great Hall of the Univ. of Vienna on March 27, 1808, with Salieri conducting *Die Schöpfung.* When Vienna capitulated to Napoleon, he ordered a guard of honor to be placed at Haydn's residence. Haydn died on May 31, 1809, and was buried at the Hundsturm Cemetery. In consequence of some fantastic events, his skull became separated from his body before his reinterment at Eisenstadt in 1820; it was actually exhibited under glass in the hall of the Gesellschaft der Musikfreunde in Vienna for a number of years, before being reunited with his body in the Bergkirche in Eisenstadt on June 5, 1954, in a solemn official ceremony.

Haydn was often called "Papa Haydn" by his intimates in appreciation of his invariable good humor and amiable disposition. Ironically, he never became a papa in the actual sense of the word. His marriage was unsuccessful; his wife was a veritable termagant; indeed, Haydn was separated from her for most his life. Still, he corresponded with her and sent her money, even though, according to a contemporary report, he never opened her letters.

In schoolbooks Haydn is usually described as "father of the symphony," the creator of the classical form of the symph. and string quartet. Historically, this absolute formulation cannot be sustained; the symphonic form was established by Stamitz and his associates at the Mannheim School; the string quartet, an outgrowth of the string trio-sonata, was of an even earlier provenance. But Haydn's music was not limited to formal novelty; its greatness was revealed in the variety of moods, the excellence of variations, and the contrast among the constituent movements of a symph.; string quartets, as conceived by Haydn, were diminutions of the symph.; both were set in sonata form, consisting in 3 contrasting movements, *Allegro, Andante, Allegro,* with a *Minuet* interpolated between the last 2 movements. It is the quality of invention that places Haydn above his contemporaries and makes his music a model of classical composition. A theory has been put forward that Haydn's themes were derived from the folk melodies of Croatian origin that he had heard in the rural environment of his childhood, but no such adumbrations or similarities can be convincingly proved. Genius is a gift bestowed on a musician or poet without external urgencies.

The intimate *Volkstümlichkeit,* a popular impressiveness of Haydn's music, naturally lent itself to imaginative nicknames of individual compositions. There are among his symphs. such appellations as *Der Philosoph* and *Der Schulmeister;* some were titled after animals: *L'Ours* and *La Poule;* others derived their names from the character of the main theme, as in *Die Uhr (The Clock),* the *Paukenschlag (Surprise),* and the *Paukenwirbel (Drum Roll).* Among Haydn's string quartets there are *La Chasse,* so named because of the hunting horn fanfares; the *Vogelquartett,* in which one hears an imitation of bird calls; the *Froschquartett,* which seems to invoke a similarity with frog calls in the finale; the *Lerchenquartett,* containing a suggestion of a lark call; and the *Farmyard* string quartet. The famous *Toy* Symph., scored for an ensemble which includes the rattle, the triangle, and instruments imitating the quail, cuckoo, and nightingale, was long attributed to Haydn but is actually a movement of a work by Leopold Mozart.

Haydn played a historic roll in the evolution of functional harmony by adopting 4-part writing as a fundamental principle of composition, particularly in his string quartets. This practice has also exercised a profound influence on the teaching of music theory.

WORKS: The precise extent of Haydn's vast output will probably never be known. Many works are lost; others, listed in various catalogues, may never have existed or were duplications of extant works; some are of doubtful authenticity, and some are definitely spurious. The following list of his works attempts to be comprehensive in scope, but it is not an exhaustive compilation.

SYMPHS.: The generally accepted list of Haydn's authentic symphs. numbers 104. For detailed information, consult the monumental study by H.C. Robbins Landon, *The Symphonies of Joseph Haydn* (London, 1955; supplement, 1961); see also his exhaustive biography *Haydn: Chronicle and Works* (5 vols., Bloomington, Ind., and London, 1976–80). The numbering follows the thematic catalogue prepared by Anthony van Hoboken. Also included are the descriptive titles, whether authorized by Hadyn or not. No. 1, in D major (1759); No. 2, in C major (1761); No. 3, in G major (1762); No. 4, in D major (1760); No. 5, in A major (1760); No. 6, in D major, *Le Matin* (1761); No. 7, in C major, *Le Midi* (1761); No. 8, in G major, *Le Soir* (1761); No. 9, in C major (1762); No. 10, in D major (1761); No. 11, in E-flat major (1760); No. 12, in E major (1763); No. 13, in D major (1763); No. 14, in A major (1764); No. 15, in D major (1761); No. 16, in B-flat major (1763); No. 17, in F major (1762); No. 18, in G major (1764); No. 19, in D major (1760); No. 20, in C major (1763); No. 21, in A major (1764); No. 22, in E-flat major, *The Philosopher* (1764); No. 23, in G major (1764); No. 24, in D major (1764); No. 25, in C major (1761); No. 26, in D minor, *Lamentatione* (1770); No. 27, in G major (1761); No. 28, in A major (1765); No. 29, in E major (1765); No. 30, in C major, *Alleluja* (1765); No. 31, in D major, *Hornsignal* (1765); No. 32, in C major (1760); No. 33, in C major (1760); No. 34, in D minor/D major (1767); No. 35, in B-flat major (1767); No. 36, in E-flat major (1765); No. 37, in C major (1758); No. 38, in C major (1769); No. 39, in G minor (1765); No. 40, in F major (1763); No. 41, in C major (1770); No. 42, in D major (1771); No. 43, in E-flat major, *Mercury* (1772); No. 44, in E minor, *Trauersinfonie* (1772); No. 45, in F-sharp minor, *Abschiedsinfonie* (1772); No. 46, in B major (1772); No. 47, in A major (1772); No. 48, in C major, *Maria Theresia* (1769); No. 49, in F minor, *La Passione* (1768); No. 50, in C major (1773); No. 51, in B-flat major (1774); No. 52, in C minor (1774); No. 53, in D major, *Imperial* or *Festino* (1778); No. 54, in G major (1774); No. 55, in E-flat major, *The Schoolmaster* (1774); No. 56, in C major (1774); No. 57, in D major (1774); No. 58, in F major (1768); No. 59, in A major, *Fire* (1769); No. 60, in C major, *Il Distratto* (1774); No. 61, in D major (1776); No. 62, in D major (1780); No. 63, in C major, *La Roxelane* or *Roxolana* (1779); No. 64, in A major, *Tempora mutantur* (1773); No. 65, in A major (1773); No. 66, in B-flat major (1776); No. 67, in F major (1776); No. 68, in B-flat major (1774); No. 69, in C major, *Laudon* or *Loudon* (1776); No. 70, in D major (1779); No. 71, in B-flat major (1779); No. 72, in D major (1765); No. 73, in D major, *La Chasse* (1782); No. 74, in E-flat major (1781); No. 75, in D major (1781); No. 76, in E-flat major (1782); No. 77, in B-flat major (1782); No. 78, in C minor (1782); No. 79, in F major (1784); No. 80, in D minor (1784); No. 81, in G major (1784); *Paris* symphs.: No. 82, in C major, *L'Ours* or *The Bear* (1786), No. 83, in G minor, *La Poule* or *The Hen* (1785), No. 84, in E-flat major (1786), No. 85, in B-flat major, *La Reine* or *The Queen* (1785); No. 86, in D major (1786), and No. 87, in A major (1785); No. 88, in G major (1787); No. 89, in F major (1787); No. 90, in C major (1788); No. 91, in E-flat major (1788); No. 92, in G major, *Oxford* (1789); *London* or *Salomon* symphs.: No. 93, in D major (1791; London, Feb. 17, 1792), No. 94, in G major, *Mit dem Paukenschlag* or *The Surprise* (1791; London, March 23, 1792), No. 95, in C minor (1791; London, 1791), No. 96, in D major, *The Miracle* (1791; London, 1791), No. 97, in C major (1792; London, May 3 or 4, 1792), No. 98, in B-flat major (1792; London, March 2, 1792), No. 99, in E-flat major (1793; London, Feb. 10, 1794), No. 100, in G major, *Militär* or *Military* (1793–94; London, March 31, 1794), No. 101 in D major, *Die Uhr* or *The Clock* (1793–94; London, March 3, 1794), No. 102, in B-flat major (1794; London, Feb. 2, 1795), No. 103, in E-flat major, *Paukenwirbel* or *Drum Roll* (1795; London, March 2, 1795), and No. 104, in D major, *London* or *Salomon* (1795; London, May 4, 1795); also the Concertante (now called Sinfonia Concertante) in B-flat major, listed in the Hoboken catalogue as No. 105 (1792; London, March 9, 1792). Hoboken also lists No. 106, in D major (1769; only first movement extant; may have been composed as the overture to *Le Pescatrici*); No. 107, in B-flat major (1761; may be by Wagenseil); and No. 108, in B-flat major (1761).

CONCERTOS: 4 for Violin: No. 1, in C major (1765); No. 2, in D major (1765; not extant); No. 3, in A major (1770); No. 4, in G major (1769); 2 for Cello: No. 1, in C major (1765), and No. 2, in D major (1783); another cello concerto may be lost or has been confused with No. 1; 2 for Organ or Harpsichord: C major (1756) and D major (1767); also most likely by Haydn are 3 others for Organ or Harpsichord, all in C major (1763, 1766, 1771); one for Violin, and Harpsichord or Organ, in F major (1766); 3 for Harpsichord: F major (1771); G major (1770; also for Piano); D major (1784; also for Piano); one for Trumpet, in E-flat major (1796); 5 for 2 Lire Organizzate: C major (1787); F major (1786); G major (1787); F major (1787); G major (1787); also divertimenti, notturni, etc. Several other concertos for oboe, flute, horn, and bassoon are either lost or spurious.

Haydn also composed several miscellaneous orch. works, including overtures to his dramatic pieces: G minor (to *L'isola disabitata*); D major (to *L'incontro improvviso*); G major (to *Lo speziale*); B-flat major (to *La vera costanza*); C major (to *L'infedeltà delusa*); C minor/C major (to *Il ritorno di Tobia*); also the *Musica instrumentale sopra le 7 ultime parole del nostro Redentore in croce ossiano 7 sonate con un'introduzione ed al fine un terremoto* (1786; for Cadiz).

DRAMATIC WORKS: *Der krumme Teufel*, singspiel (1751?; first confirmed perf., Vienna, May 29, 1753; not extant); *Der neue krumme Teufel (Asmodeus, der krumme Teufel)*, singspiel (1758?; music not extant); *Acide*, festa teatrale (1762; Eisenstadt, Jan. 11, 1763; only fragment and libretto extant; revised version, 1773; only fragment extant; *Marchese (La Marchesa Nespola)*, comedia (1762?; only fragment extant; dialogues not extant); *Il Dottore*, comedia (1765?; not extant); *La Vedova*, comedia (1765?; not extant); *Il scanarello*, comedia (1765?; not extant); *La Canterina*, intermezzo in musica (1766; Bratislava, Sept. 11?, 1766); *Lo speziale (Der Apotheker)*, dramma giocoso (1768; Esterháza, Autumn 1768); *Le Pescatrici (Die Fischerinnen)*, dramma giocoso (1769; Esterháza, Sept. 16?, 1770); *L'infedeltà delusa (Liebe macht erfinderisch; Untreue lohnt sich nicht; Deceit Outwitted)*, burletta per musica (1773; Esterháza, July 26, 1773); *Philemon und Baucis oder Jupiters Reise auf die Erde*, singspiel/marionette opera (1773; Esterháza, Sept. 2, 1773); *Hexenschabbas*, marionette opera (1773?; not extant);

Haydn

L'incontro improvviso (Die unverhoffte Zusammenkunft; Unverhofftes Begegnen), dramma giocoso (1775; Esterháza, Aug. 29, 1775); Dido, singspiel/marionette opera (1776?; Esterháza, March ?, 1776; music not extant); Opéra comique vom abgebrannten Haus (not extant; may be identical with the following work); Die Feuerbrunst, singspiel/marionette opera (1775?–78?; may be by Haydn; dialogues not extant); Il mondo della luna (Die Welt auf dem Monde), dramma giocoso (1777; Esterháza, Aug. 3, 1777); Die bestrafte Rachbegierde, singspiel/marionette opera (1779?; Esterháza, 1779; music not extant); La vera costanza, dramma giocoso (1778?; Esterháza, April 25, 1779; only music extant appears in the revised version of 1785, known as Der flatterhafte Liebhaber; Der Sieg der Beständigkeit; Die wahre Beständigkeit; List und Liebe; etc.); L'isola disabitata (Die wüste Insel), azione teatrale (1779; Esterháza, Dec. 6, 1779; revised 1802); La fedeltà premiata (Die belohnte Treue), dramma pastorale giocoso (1780; Esterháza, Feb. 25, 1781); Orlando paladino (Der Ritter Roland), dramma eroicomico (1782; Esterháza, Dec. 6, 1782); Armida, dramma eroico (1783; Esterháza, Feb. 26, 1784); L'anima del filosofo ossia Orfeo ed Euridice, dramma per musica (1791; composed for London but not perf.; first confirmed perf., Florence, June 10, 1951, with Callas and Christoff in the principal roles); Alfred, König der Angelsachsen, oder Der patriotische König (1796; perf. as the incidental music to Haldane, König der Dänen, Eisenstadt, Sept. 1796).

MASSES: Missa Rorate coeli desuper in G major (date unknown; not extant, or identical with the following); Mass in G major (date unknown; composed by G. Reutter, Jr., Arbesser, and Haydn; publ. in London, 1957); Missa brevis in F major (1749?); Missa Cellensis in honorem Beata Maria Virgine in C major, Cäcilienmesse (1766); Missa Sunt bona mixta malis in D minor (1769?; not extant); Missa in honorem Beata Maria Virgine in E-flat major, Missa Sancti Josephi; Grosse Orgelmesse (1769?); Missa Sancti Nicolai in G major, Nicolaimesse; 6/4-Takt-Messe (1772); Missa brevis Sancti Joannis de Deo in B-flat major, Kleine Orgelmesse (1775?); Missa Cellensis in C major, Mariazeller Messe (1782); Missa Sancti Bernardi von Offida in B-flat major, Heiligmesse (1796); Missa in tempore belli in C major, Kriegsmesse; Paukenmesse (1796; Vienna, Dec. 26, 1796?); Missa in D minor, Nelsonmesse; Imperial Mass; Coronation Mass (1798; Eisenstadt, Sept. 23, 1798?); Missa in B-flat major, Theresienmesse (1799); Missa in B-flat major, Schöpfungsmesse (1801; Eisenstadt, Sept. 13, 1801); Missa in B-flat major, Harmoniemesse (1802; Eisenstadt, Sept. 8, 1802).

ORATORIOS: Stabat Mater (1767); Applausus (Jubilaeum virtutis Palatium), allegorical oratorio/cantata (1768; Zwettl, April 17, 1768); Il ritorno di Tobia (1774–75; Vienna, April 2 and 4, 1775, in 2 parts; revised 1784); Die sieben letzten Worte unseres Erlösers am Kreuze (1795–96; Vienna, 1796); Die Schöpfung (The Creation; 1796–98; first private perf., Schwarzenburg Palace, Vienna, April 29, 1798; first public perf., Kärnthnertortheater, Vienna, March 19, 1799); Die Jahreszeiten (The Seasons; 1799–1801; Schwarzenburg Palace, Vienna, April 24, 1801).

Haydn's other vocal works include 2 Te Deums (both in C major); offertories; secular cantatas; secular vocal works for orch.; more than 50 songs with keyboard accompaniment; vocal duets, trios, and quartets with keyboard accompaniment; more than 50 canons; arrangements of Scottish and other songs; and Gott erhalte Franz den Kaiser (God Save the Emperor Franz; 1797; was the Austrian national anthem until 1918).

STRING QUARTETS: Op. 1 (c.1757–59): No. 1, in B-flat major, La Chasse; No. 2, in E-flat major; No. 3, in D major; No. 4, in G major; No. 5, in E-flat major; No. 6, in C major; op. 2 (c.1760–62): No. 1, in A major; No. 2, in E major; No. 4, in F major; No. 6, in B-flat major; op. 9 (1771): No. 1, in C major; No. 2, in E-flat major; No. 3, in G major; No. 4, in D minor; No. 5, in B-flat major; No. 6, in A major; op. 17 (1771): No. 1, in E major; No. 2, in F major; No. 3, in E-flat major; No. 4, in C minor; No. 5, in G major, Recitative; No. 6, in D major; Sun Quartets, op. 20 (1772): No. 1, in E-flat major; No. 2, in C major; No. 3, in G minor; No. 4, in D major; No. 5, in F minor; No. 6, in A major; Russian Quartets; Jungfernquartette, op. 33 (1781): No. 1, in B minor; No. 2, in E-flat major, The Joke; No. 3, in C major, The Bird; No. 4, in B-flat major; No. 5, in G major, How do you do?; No. 6, in D major; op. 42, in D minor (1785); Prussian Quartets, op. 50 (1787): No. 1, in B-flat major; No. 2, in C major; No. 3, in E-flat major; No. 4, in F-sharp minor; No. 5, in F major, Ein Traum; No. 6, in D major, The Frog; Tost Quartets, op. 54 (1788): No. 1, in G major; No. 2, in C major; No. 3, in E major; Tost Quartets, op. 55 (1788): No. 1, in A major; No. 2, in F minor, The Razor; No. 3, in B-flat major; Tost Quartets, op. 64 (1790): No. 1, in C major; No. 2, in B minor; No. 3, in B-flat major; No. 4, in G major; No. 5, in D major, The Lark; No. 6, in E-flat major; Apponyi Quartets, op. 71 (1793): No. 1, in B-flat major; No. 2, in D major; No. 3, in E-flat major; Apponyi Quartets, op. 74 (1793): No. 1, in C major; No. 2, in F major; No. 3, in G minor, The Rider; Erdödy Quartets, op. 76 (1797): No. 1, in G major; No. 2, in D minor, Fifths; No. 3, in C major, Emperor; No. 4, in B-flat major, Sunrise; No. 5, in D major; No. 6, in E-flat major; Lobkowitz Quartets, op. 77 (1799): No. 1, in G major; No. 2, in F major; op. 103, in D minor (1803?; unfinished; only movements 2 and 3 finished).—Haydn also arranged the orch. version of the Musica instrumentale sopra le 7 ultime parole del nostro Redentore in croce . . . for String Quartet (1787), as well as pieces from the operas La vera costanza and Armida.

Other works by Haydn include 21 string trios (3 not extant); a great number of works for baryton, written for Prince Esterházy, who was an avid baryton player: about 125 baryton trios (divertimentos), various works for one or 2 barytons, etc.; 29 keyboard sonatas (3 listed as trios), most of them for harpsichord or piano, with violin and cello; 47 solo keyboard sonatas (7 not extant, one not complete), almost all of them for harpsichord; etc.

Haydn, (Johann) Michael, Austrian composer,

brother of **Franz Joseph Haydn;** b. Rohrau, (baptized, Sept. 14, 1737) d. Salzburg, Aug. 10, 1806. He served as a boy soprano at St. Stephen's Cathedral in Vienna (1745–55); his voice was remarkable for its wide range, reaching 3 octaves. He replaced his brother in solo parts when a younger voice was required. He studied composition mainly by reading books on counterpoint, particularly *Gradus ad Parnassum* by Fux. In 1757 he became chapel master at Grosswardein; in 1762, music director to Archbishop Sigismund at Salzburg. In 1768 he married the daughter of the organist Lipp, Maria Magdalena, an excellent soprano singer who was praised by Mozart. The French occupation of Salzburg in 1800 deprived him of his property, but he was aided by his brother. His fortunes were mended somewhat by the handsomely rewarded commission of a mass which he received from the Empress Teresa, wife of the Emperor Franz I, and which was performed at the Luxemburg Palace on Oct. 4, 1801. He opened a school of composition, and educated many distinguished pupils, including Carl Maria von Weber. In 1833, Martin Bischofsreiter, a Benedictine monk, publ. *Partitur-Fundamente,* a collection of thoroughbass exercises written by Michael Haydn for his scholars. He composed a mass and vespers for Prince Esterházy, who twice offered to make him assistant chapel master; but Haydn declined, hoping that the Salzburg chapel would be reorganized. A prolific composer, his best works were his sacred compositions, which his brother held in high esteem. Although he had advantageous offers for publ. from Breitkopf & Härtel, he was reluctant to accept, so that most of his music remained in MS at the time of his death. WORKS: DRAMATIC: Singspiels, *Rebekka als Braut* (Salzburg, April 10, 1766); *Die Hochzeit auf der Alm* (Salzburg, May 6, 1768); *Die Warheit der Natur* (Salzburg, July 7, 1869); *Der englische Patriot* (1779); *Die Ahrenleserin* (Salzburg, July 2, 1788); the oratorios *Die Schuldigkeit des ersten Gebots,* parts 2 (1767; collaborated with Mozart); *Der Kampf der Busse und Bekehrung* (Salzburg, Feb. 21, 1768); *Der remutige Petrus* (Salzburg, March 11, 1770); *Der büssender Sünder* (Salzburg, Feb. 15, 1771); *Oratorium de Passione Domini nostri Jesu Christi* (1775); several operas, including the opera seria *Andromeda e Perseo* (Salzburg, March 14, 1787); incidental music to Voltaire's *Zaïre* (Salzburg, Sept. 29, 1777). SACRED MUSIC: Over 400 works, including 38 masses, 2 of which are *Missa Hispanica* (Salzburg, Aug. 4, 1786) and *Pro defunctor Archiepscopo Sigismundo* (Salzburg, Dec. 31, 1771; known as Requiem in C minor, which influenced Mozart's Requiem); cantatas, Requiems, settings of the Te Deum, *Litaniae laurentanae,* vespers, responsories, graduals and offertories; also 2 collections of 4-part songs. INSTRUMENTAL MUSIC: About 40 symphs.; 30 divertimenti (1760–95); serenades (1760–85); marches; minuets; partitas; cassations; nocturnes; concertos for flute, violin, and harpsichord; Double Concerto for Viola, Organ, and Strings; string quartets and quintets; a Sextet. A selection of his masses and other church works was edited by A.M. Klafsky in Denkmäler der Tonkunst in Österreich, vols. 45 and 62 (formerly 22 and 32.i); a selection of his instrumental works, edited and partly reorchestrated by L.H. Perger, in vol. 29 (formerly 14.ii), including a Symph. in E-flat (1783), a Symph. in C major (1788), a Turkish March, etc.; additional recent publications are in *Accademia Musicale* (Mainz), vols. 7, 8, 9; *Musica Rinata* (Budapest), vols. 3, 4, 7; and by the Haydn-Mozart Press in Salzburg.

Hayes, Philip, English organist and composer, son of **William Hayes;** b. Oxford, (baptized, April 17) 1738; d. London, March 19, 1797. He studied mainly with his father; received a Mus.B. from Oxford (May 18, 1763); became a Gentleman of the Chapel Royal in 1767; organist of New College, Oxford (1776); succeeded his father as organist of Magdalen College and prof. of music at the univ. (1777); also received his Mus.D. the same year; became organist of St. John's College (1790). WORKS: Oratorio, *Prophecy* (Oxford, 1781); masque, *Telemachus;* odes; anthems; services; Psalms; glees; 6 concertos for Organ, Harpsichord, or Piano (1769); also some numbers in Dibdin's *The 2 Misers* and Dr. Arnold's *2 to One.* He ed. *Harmonia Wiccamica* (London, 1780).

Hayes, Roland, distinguished black tenor; b. Curryville, Ga., June 3, 1887; d. Boston, Jan. 1, 1977. His parents were former slaves. He studied singing with A. Calhoun in Chattanooga, Tenn., and later at Fisk Univ. in Nashville; subsequently continued vocal studies in Boston and in Europe. He made his concert debut in Boston on Nov. 15, 1917, in a program of German lieder and arias by Mozart; then made a successful tour in the U.S. In 1920 he went to London, where he studied the German repertoire with Sir George Henschel. A grand European tour followed, with appearances in Paris, Vienna, Leipzig, Munich, Amsterdam, Madrid, and Copenhagen. In 1924 he gave more than 80 concerts in the U.S., obtaining a veritable triumph for his interpretation of lyrical German and French songs, and most particularly for his poignant rendition of Negro spirituals. In 1925 he was awarded the Spingarn Medal for "most outstanding achievement among colored people," and in 1939 he received the honorary degree of Mus.D. from Wesleyan Univ. in Delaware, Ohio. He publ. expert arrangements of 30 Negro spirituals, *My Songs* (N.Y., 1948).

Hayes, William, English organist and composer; b. Gloucester, Dec. 1707 (baptized, Jan. 26, 1708); d. Oxford, July 27, 1777. He was a chorister at Gloucester Cathedral; was organist of St. Mary's, Shrewsbury (1729–31); then of Worcester Cathedral (1731–34). In 1734 he became organist of Magdalen College, Oxford; received a Mus.Bac. (Oxford, 1735); was univ. prof. of music (1742); in 1749 received a Mus.D. He conducted the Gloucester music festival in 1757, 1760, and 1763. WORKS: His canons *Allelujah* and *Miserere nobis* and his glee *Melting airs soft joys inspire* won prizes offered by the Catch Club in 1763; also a masque, *Circe;* Psalms; odes; glees; canons; ballads;

cantatas. He also wrote *Remarks on Mr. Avison's Essay on Musical Expression* (1762); *Anecdotes of the Five Music-Meetings* (1768); and was co-editor of Boyce's *Cathedral Music.*

Haym (Haim), Nicola Francesco, Italian cellist, composer, and librettist of German descent; b. Rome, July 6, 1678; d. London, Aug. 11, 1729. He was a violone player in the private orch. of Cardinal Ottoboni in Rome under Corelli (1694–1700); then went to London, where he was composer and cellist to the 2nd Duke of Bedford (1701–11); later was a bass player in the employ of the Duke of Chandos. He was a major figure in organizing performances of Italian opera in London. In 1722 he became the official librettist and Italian secretary of the Royal Academy of Music, the business venture responsible for presenting Italian opera in London. His works include 2 oratorios, *David sponsae restitutus* (1699) and *Santa Costanza* (1700); a serenata, *Il reciproco amore di Tirsi e Clori* (1699); a secular cantata, *Lontan del idol mio* (1704); and instrumental pieces, including *12 Sonate e tre* (1703) and a second set of *12 Sonate a tre* (1704).

Hayman, Richard, American composer of the extreme avant-garde; b. Sandia, N.Mex., July 29, 1951. He studied humanities and philosophy at Columbia Univ.; attended classes of Vladimir Ussachevsky in electronic music; also studied flute with Eleanor Laurence at the Manhattan School of Music and had sessions on Indian vocal music with Ravi Shankar; consulted with Philip Corner and John Cage on the problems of ultramodern music; attended Pierre Boulez's conducting seminars at the Juilliard School of Music. He eked out a meager living by intermittent employment as a construction worker, gardener, operating-room assistant in a hospital, and church pipe organ renovator; earned an occasional few dollars as a subject in sleep-laboratory experiments; as a last resort, boldly peddled earplugs in the N.Y. subway. He arranged exhibitions of his graffiti at the Univ. of Buffalo; organized assemblages of objects and sounds at the Avant-Garde Festival at Shea Stadium in N.Y.; wrote provocatively titled articles. In 1975 he was appointed an editor of *Ear* magazine. Perhaps his most mind-boggling musical work is *Dali,* composed at the command of Salvador Dali, scored for large orch., and notated on a toothpick, with instructions to "ascend chromatically in slow pulse." It was "performed" on March 23, 1974. Another work is *it is not here,* a light-and-sound piece, realized in Morse code at the Museum of Modern Art in N.Y. on June 14, 1974. Other pieces are *heartwhistle,* with the audience beating their collective pulses and whistling continuous tones (Aug. 3, 1975); *sleep whistle,* with the composer whistling while asleep in a store window during a paid sleep exhibition (Dec. 7, 1975); *roll,* with the composer rolling, lying down, in the street, covered with bells as a token of Hindu devotion (April 9, 1975); *dreamsound,* a sleep event in which the composer makes various sounds for the benefit of slumbering participants (Berkeley, Calif., Feb.

20, 1976); *home* for a Telephone; *Boo Boo* for Piano; *Buff Her Blind* for Musical Toys and Electronic Instruments; *spirits* for Transduced Piano.

Hays, Doris, American pianist and composer of the avant-garde; b. Memphis, Tenn., Aug. 6, 1941. She attended the Cadek Cons. of Chattanooga, and studied with Richard Hervig at the Univ. of Iowa and later with Paul Badura-Skoda at the Univ. of Wisconsin; then traveled to Europe, where she took courses at the Hochschule für Musik in Munich. In 1971 she won first prize at the International Competition for Interpreters of New Music in Rotterdam. Returning to the U.S., she took lessons in advanced piano playing with Hilde Somer in N.Y.; gave numerous piano recitals in programs of ultramodern music; taught music at Queens College in N.Y. and at the Univ. of Wisconsin; made records of piano works by contemporary American and European composers. In her own compositions she endeavors to unite auditory, visual, and tactile elements; several of her works employ rhythmic patterns of lights and motorized sculptures designed by herself and programmed through computers. Typical of these multimedia works is *SensEvents* (1971–77), scored for a group of instruments instructed to play simultaneously but non-synchronously, of an indeterminate duration, with beams of colored light directed at individual musicians to indicate clues. Other works are: *Scheveningen Beach* (1973) for Piccolo, Several Ordinary Flutes, and Alto Flute; *Duet for Pianist and Audience* (1971); *Chartres Red* (1972) for Piano; *Pieces from Last Year* (1974) for 16 Instruments Playing Non-synchronously; *Breathless* (1975) for Bass Flute; *Sunday Nights* (1976) and *Sunday Mornings* (1980) for Piano; *Southern Voices* for Orch. (Chattanooga, April 6, 1982); numerous pieces for modernistic children.

Hebenstreit, Pantaleon, German musician; b. Eisleben, 1667; d. Dresden, Nov. 15, 1750. In his early years, he was engaged variously as a violinist and a dancing master in Leipzig, but fled from his creditors to Merseburg. There the idea of improving the dulcimer was suggested to him, and he invented the instrument with which he made long and brilliant concert tours, and which Louis XIV named the Pantaleon, after its originator's Christian name. As a precursor of the piano, it has disappeared in the process of evolution. In 1706, Hebenstreit was appointed Kapellmeister and dancing master to the court at Eisenach; in 1714, "pantaleon chamber musician" at the Dresden court.

Heckel, Emil, German music publisher and piano manufacturer; b. Mannheim, May 22, 1831; d. there, March 28, 1908. He was trained by his father, **Karl Ferdinand Heckel** (1800–70), in piano manufacturing. He was a great admirer of Wagner, was one of the most important supporters of the Bayreuth Festivals, and maintained a voluminous correspondence with Wagner himself, which was publ. by his son Karl Heckel under the title *Briefe Richard Wagners an Emil Heckel* (Berlin, 1899; Eng. trans.

by W.A. Ellis, London, 1899). Emil Heckel had an enormous bust of Wagner, sculpted by J. Hoffart, installed in his palatial residence at Mannheim, but the bust was busted during the anti-Wagnerian air bombardment in World War II.

Heckel, Johann Adam, German manufacturer of musical instruments; b. Adorf, July 14, 1812; d. Biebrich, April 13, 1877. From 1824–35 he worked with the bassoonist Carl Almenräder on experiments for improving the clarinet and the bassoon. His son and successor, **Wilhelm** (b. Biebrich, Jan. 25, 1856; d. there, Jan. 13, 1909), continued his experiments with success and constructed the "Heckelphone" (a baritone oboe; used by Strauss in the score of *Salome*) in 1904; also made various changes in the construction of other woodwind instruments. He wrote *Der Fagott. Kurzgefasste Abhandlung über seine historische Entwicklung, seinen Bau und seine Spielweise* (1899; new ed., 1931).

Heckscher, Céleste de Longpré (née **Massey**), American composer; b. Philadelphia, Feb. 23, 1860; d. there, Feb. 18, 1928. Of an artistic family (her grandfather was the artist Louis de Longpré), she studied piano and participated in the musical affairs of her native city; was for many years president of the Philadelphia Operatic Society. She began to compose about 1890; wrote the operas *The Flight of Time* and *Rose of Destiny* (Philadelphia, May 2, 1918); *Dances of the Pyrenees*, an orch. suite (Philadelphia, Feb. 17, 1911); a fantasy, *To the Forest*, for Violin and Piano (1902); songs; and piano pieces. Her style, melodious and without pretensions, is akin to Chaminade's.

Hedley, Arthur, English musicologist; b. Dudley, Northumberland, Nov. 12, 1905; d. Birmingham, Nov. 8, 1969. He studied French literature at the Federal Univ. of Durham (1923–27), and music with W.G. Whittaker at Newcastle. An ardent Chopinist, he learned the Polish language to be able to study Chopin documentation in the original; publ. a biography, *Chopin* (London, 1947; 3rd ed., revised 1974, by M.J.E. Brown); edited and trans. *Selected Correspondence of Fryderyk Chopin* (London, 1962); helped to dispel cumulative misconceptions and deceptions relating to Chopin's life; was instrumental in exposing the falsity of the notorious Potocka-Chopin correspondence produced by Mme. Czernicka (who killed herself in 1949 on the 100th anniversary of Chopin's death, after the fraudulence of her claims was irrefutably demonstrated by Hedley at the Chopin Inst. in Warsaw). Hedley's Chopinolatry was carried to the point of fetishism; he acquired Chopin's cuff links and a lead pencil; proved the authenticity of Chopin's silk waistcoat, which came to light in Paris.

Heger, Robert, Alsatian-born German conductor and composer; b. Strasbourg, Aug. 19, 1886; d. Munich, Jan. 14, 1978. He studied composition with Max Schillings in Munich; then engaged in opera conducting. He conducted at Nuremberg from 1913 to 1921; was subsequently engaged at the State Opera in Vienna (1925–33); was at the Berlin State Opera (1933–45), and after the war at the Berlin City Opera (1945–50); he subsequently led the Bavarian State Opera in Munich.

WORKS: Several operas, among them *Ein Fest auf Haderslev* (Nuremberg, Nov. 12, 1919); *Der Bettler Namenlos* (Munich, April 8, 1932); *Der verlorene Sohn* (Dresden, March 11, 1936); *Lady Hamilton* (Nuremberg, Feb. 11, 1951); 3 symphs.; symph. poem, *Hero und Leander;* Violin Concerto; Cello Concerto; Piano Trio; String Quartet; other pieces of chamber music; also choral works and songs.

Heiden, Bernhard, German-born American composer; b. Frankfurt am Main, Aug. 24, 1910. He studied piano, clarinet, and violin; also theory and harmony; then (1929–33) studied at the Hochschule für Musik in Berlin, where his principal teacher was Paul Hindemith. In 1935 he emigrated to the U.S.; taught at the Art Center Music School in Detroit; was also conductor of the Detroit Chamber Orch., as well as pianist, harpsichordist, and chamber music artist. He served in the U.S. Army (1943–45); then studied musicology with Donald Grout at Cornell Univ. (A.M., 1946). In 1946 he joined the faculty of the Indiana Univ. School of Music in Bloomington; retired in 1981. His music is neo-Classical in its formal structure, and strongly polyphonic in texture; it is distinguished also by its impeccable sonorous balance and effective instrumentation.

Heifetz, Jascha, celebrated violinist; b. Vilna, Feb. 2, 1901. His father, Ruben Heifetz, an able musician, taught him the rudiments of violin playing at a very early age; he then studied with Elias Malkin at the Vilna Music School, and played in public before he was 5 years old; at the age of 6, he played Mendelssohn's Concerto in Kovno. In 1910 he was taken by his father to St. Petersburg, and entered the Cons. there in the class of Nalbandian; after a few months, he was accepted as a pupil by Leopold Auer. He gave his first public concert in St. Petersburg on April 30, 1911. The following year, with a letter of recommendation from Auer, he went to Berlin; his first concert there (May 24, 1912), in the large hall of the Hochschule für Musik, attracted great attention: Artur Nikisch engaged him to play the Tchaikovsky Concerto with the Berlin Phil. (Oct. 28, 1912), and Heifetz obtained sensational success as a child prodigy of extraordinary gifts. He then played in Austria and Scandinavia. After the Russian Revolution of 1917, he went to America, by way of Siberia and the Orient. His debut at Carnegie Hall in N.Y. (Oct. 27, 1917) won for him the highest expression of enthusiasm from the public and in the press; veritable triumphs followed during his tour of the U.S., and soon his fame spread all over the world. He made his first London appearance on May 5, 1920; toured Australia (1921), the Orient (1923), Palestine (1926), and South America. He revisited Russia in 1934, and was welcomed enthusiastically. He became a naturalized American citizen in 1925, and made his home in Beverly Hills, Calif.; in subsequent years he continued to travel as a concert violinist, visiting virtually every country in the world, but about 1970 ceased to appear in public as a soloist; he participated in a trio (with Piatigorsky and Pennario) and also taught classes of exceptionally talented pupils at the Univ. of Southern Calif., Los Angeles.

The quality of his playing is unique in luminous transparency of texture, tonal perfection, and formal equilibrium of phrasing; he never allowed his artistic temperament to superimpose extraneous elements on the music; this inspired tranquillity led some critics to characterize his interpretations as impersonal and detached. Heifetz made numerous arrangements for violin of works by Bach, Vivaldi, and contemporary composers; his most famous transcription is *Hora Staccato* by the Rumanian composer Grigoraş Dinicu (1889–1949), made into a virtuoso piece by adroit ornamentation and rhythmic elaboration. In his desire to promote modern music, Heifetz commissioned a number of composers (Walton, Gruenberg, Castelnuovo-Tedesco, and others) to write violin concertos for him, and performed several of them. Herbert R. Axelrod edited and publ. an "unauthorized pictorial biography" of Heifetz (1977); Heifetz filed a lawsuit for $7.5 million against the publisher and compiler, claiming invasion of privacy.

Heiller, Anton, significant Austrian organist and composer; b. Vienna, Sept. 15, 1923; d. there, March 25, 1979. He studied piano and organ at the Vienna Cons.; in 1952 won first prize at the International Organ Contest in Haarlem, the Netherlands; in 1969 he received the Austrian Grand Prize for Music; in 1971 he was appointed prof. at the Hochschule für Musik in Vienna. His own music is rooted deeply in the tradition of the Renaissance, while his contrapuntal technique adopts modern procedures. He particularly excelled in sacred works, to Latin texts; in these he occasionally made use of the 12-tone method of composition.

WORKS: Chamber oratorio, *Tentatio Jesu* (1952); *Psalmenkantate* (1955); Concerto for Organ and Orch. (1963); cantata, *In principio erat verbum* (1965); *Stabat mater* for Chorus and Orch. (1968); several masses, including *Kleine Messe über Zwolftonmodelle,* a cappella (1962); *English Mass* (1965); *Adventsmusik* for Chorus and Organ (1971).

Heinefetter, 6 sisters, all well known as opera singers. **Sabina** (b. Mainz, Aug. 19, 1809; d. Illemau, Nov. 18, 1872) was an itinerant harpist as a child; at the age of 16, she went to Kassel to study with Spohr; then sang with brilliant success in Vienna, Berlin, and Milan. One of her outstanding roles was Donna Anna in *Don Giovanni.* She died insane. **Maria** (**Mme. Stöckel;** b. Mainz, Feb. 16, 1816; d. Vienna, Feb. 23, 1857) achieved during her short career several notable successes; she also died insane. **Katinka** (1820–58), **Fatima, Eva,** and **Nanette** were the other sisters who appeared professionally on the opera stage.

Heinichen, Johann David, notable German composer and theorist; b. Krössuln, near Weissenfels, April 17, 1683; d. Dresden, July 16, 1729. He was educated at the Thomasschule in Leipzig, studying with Schell and Kuhnau; at the same time, he studied law, and practiced as a lawyer in Weissenfels. His first opera, *Der Karneval von Venedig, oder Der angenehme Betrug,* was performed in Leipzig in 1709; he then held a position as conductor at Zeitz. Councillor Buchta of Zeitz supplied the funds for Heinichen to accompany him to Italy (1710–16), where he produced several operas. In Venice, he joined the Elector of Saxony, Frederick Augustus, and followed him to Dresden as Kapellmeister of the Italian opera company there (1717). However, as a result of confusion brought about by a violent quarrel between Heinichen and the celebrated singer Senesino the Dresden opera was dissolved. Heinichen remained in Dresden as director of church and chamber music. He was a prolific composer; a thematic catalogue of his works is found in G.A. Seibel, *Das Leben des J.D. Heinichen* (Leipzig, 1913), listing, besides his operas, 2 oratorios, 16 masses, 63 cantatas, more than 100 other sacred works, 4 symphs., 2 overtures, 30 concertos, 17 sonatas, 7 pieces for Flute, many separate airs, etc. Most of them were preserved in the Dresden library, but unfortunately many perished in the fire-bombing of Dresden in 1945. Few of his works have been publ. Heinichen's importance lies not so much in his compositions as in his basic theoretical work, *Neu erfundene und gründliche Answeisung zu vollkommener Erlernung des General-Basses* (Hamburg, 1711; new revised ed. as *Der General-Bass in der Composition,* Dresden, 1728).

Heinrich, Anthony Philip (Anton Philipp), American violinist and composer of Bohemian birth; b. Schönbüchel, March 11, 1781; d. in extreme poverty in New York, May 3, 1861. As a boy he acquired proficiency on the piano and violin, but began adult life as a wholesale merchant and banker; in 1810 he emigrated to America, settling in Philadelphia as a merchant and as unpaid music director of the Southwark Theatre. After business reverses in 1817 he moved to the wilds of Kentucky, first to Bardstown and then to nearby Lexington, where he managed to find enough musicians to conduct in a performance of a Beethoven symph. Without any knowledge of harmony, he began to compose in 1818; these first songs and choral and instrumental pieces he publ. later as op. 1, *The Dawning of Music in Kentucky, or The Pleasures of Harmony in the Solitudes of Nature,* and op. 2, *The Western Minstrel* (both 1820; reprinted N.Y., 1972). He became music director at the Southwark Theatre in Philadelphia; later, in Louisville, Ky. The year 1827 found him in London, playing violin in a small orch.; there he also studied theory, and about 1830 began to write for orch.; returned to the U.S. in 1832. In 1834 he again visited England, as well as Germany and Austria (1835), and had some of his works produced at Dresden, Prague, Budapest, and Graz (his symph. *The Combat of the Condor* was perf. at Graz in 1836;

also in France); in Vienna he entered a competition with a symph., but the prize was awarded to Franz Lachner; disappointed, he returned to America and settled in N.Y., where he soon gained immense popularity, and was generally known as "Father Heinrich." He was a commanding figure in the musical affairs of the U.S., publishing many of his piano pieces and songs; grand festivals of his works being arranged in N.Y., Philadelphia, and Boston; and the critics speaking of him as the "Beethoven of America." But a tour of Germany in 1857–58 was a dismal failure. The quality of his works is dubious at best; he wrote for an enormous orch., *à la* Berlioz, and his musical ideas, out of all proportion to the means employed, recall the style of Haydn's imitators; nevertheless, he is historically important, being the first to employ American Indian themes in works of large dimensions and to show decided nationalist aspirations. In 1917 the Library of Congress acquired Heinrich's "Memoranda" (letters, programs, newspaper clippings, etc.), many publ. works, and almost all the orch. scores, enumerated in a list made by Heinrich himself in 1857. A perusal of the titles is amusing and instructive: *Grand American Chivalrous Symphony; The Columbiad, or Migration of American Wild Passenger Pigeons; The Ornithological Combat of Kings, or The Condor of the Andes and the Eagle of the Cordilleras; Pocahontas, the Royal Indian Maid and the Heroine of Virginia, the Pride of the Wilderness; The Wild-wood Spirit's Chant or Scintillations of "Yankee Doodle,"* forming a Grand National Heroic Fantasia scored for a Powerful Orch. in 44 Parts; *Manitou Mysteries, or The Voice of the Great Spirit; Gran Sinfonia Misteriosa-Indiana* (U.S. perf., N.Y., Dec. 2, 1975). Reprints (in addition to opp. 1 and 2): *Songs without Words,* vol. I of Piano Music in Nineteenth Century America (Chapel Hill, N.C., 1975); *Yankeedoodle* (for Piano) in W.T. Marrocco and H. Gleason, *Music in America* (N.Y., 1964); *The Maiden's Dirge,* in E. Gold, *The Bicentennial Collection of American Music* (Dayton, Ohio, 1975).

Heinsheimer, Hans (Walter), American publishing executive and writer on music; b. Karlsruhe, Sept. 25, 1900. He studied law in Heidelberg, Munich, and Freiburg im Breisgau (Juris Dr., 1923); then joined Universal Edition in Vienna, where he was in charge of its opera dept. (1924–38), and supervised the publication of such important stage works as Alban Berg's *Wozzeck,* Krenek's *Jonny spielt auf,* Weinberger's *Schwanda,* Kurt Weill's *Aufstieg und Fall der Stadt Mahagonny,* and George Antheil's *Transatlantic.* He came to the U.S. in 1938 and was associated with the N.Y. branch of Boosey & Hawkes. In 1947 he was appointed director of the symph. and operatic repertoire of G. Schirmer, Inc.; in 1957 became director of publications and in 1972 vice-president of the firm; in these capacities he promoted the works of Samuel Barber, Gian Carlo Menotti, Leonard Bernstein, and Elliott Carter. He retired in 1974 and has devoted himself mainly to writing. A brilliant stylist in both

German and English, he has contributed numerous informative articles to *Melos, Musical Quarterly, Holiday, Reader's Digest,* etc. He publ. the entertaining books *Menagerie in F-sharp* (N.Y., 1947) and *Fanfare for Two Pigeons* (1952); the 2 works were publ. in German in a single vol. entitled *Menagerie in Fis-dur* (Zürich, 1953); he also wrote *Best Regards to Aida* (publ. in German as *Schönste Grüsse an Aida;* Munich, 1968).

Heintze, Gustaf Hjalmar, Swedish pianist and composer; b. Jönköping, July 22, 1879; d. Saltsjöbaden, March 4, 1946. He was of a musical family; his father, **Georg Wilhelm Heintze** (1849–95), was a well-known organist, as was his grandfather, **Gustaf Wilhelm Heintze** (1825–1909). He studied at the Stockholm Cons.; in 1910 was appointed organist at a Stockholm church, a post he held until his death. He wrote cantatas, 2 violin concertos, chamber music, and organ pieces.

Heinze, Sir Bernard Thomas, eminent Australian conductor; b. Shepparton, near Melbourne, July 1, 1894; d. Sydney, June 9, 1982. He studied at the Univ. of Melbourne and the Royal College of Music in London, and attended classes of Vincent d'Indy at the Schola Cantorum in Paris. He also took violin lessons in Berlin with Willy Hess. Returning to Australia after service in the Royal Artillery during World War I, he became a teacher at the Melbourne Conservatorium in 1924; was named a prof. in 1925 and remained on its faculty until 1956. He also served as director of the New South Wales Cons. (1956–66). In 1938 he made a European tour as conductor; from 1933 until 1949 he was also conductor of the Melbourne Symph. Orch. He was knighted in 1949.

Helder, Bartholomäus, German composer; b. Gotha, 1585; d. Remstedt, near Gotha, Oct. 28, 1635. He studied theology in Leipzig; was a schoolteacher at a village near Gotha (1607–16); then was for 20 years a pastor at Remstedt. He died of the plague. He publ. a collection of Christmas and New Year's songs, *Cymbalum genethliacum* (1614), and a book of psalm tunes, *Cymbalum Davidicum;* many of his secular songs are included in contemporary anthologies. His New Year's song *Das alte Jahr vergangen ist* became very popular.

Helfert, Vladimír, Czech musicologist; b. Plánice, Bohemia, March 24, 1886; d. Prague, May 18, 1945. He studied with Hostinsky in Prague and with Kretzschmar and Wolf at Berlin Univ., receiving the degree of Mus.D. in 1908 with the dissertation *G. Benda und J.J. Rousseau;* in 1921 was an instructor, and in 1926 prof. of musicology, at the Univ. of Brno; was director of the Czech Orch. Society there; from 1924, was editor of the paper *Hudebni Rozhledy.* In 1940 he was arrested by the Nazis and held in Breslau; was released in 1943, then rearrested in 1945 and taken to the Terezin concentration camp. He died a few days after his liberation.

Heller, Stephen, celebrated Hungarian pianist and composer; b. Pest, May 15, 1813; d. Paris, Jan. 14, 1888. He was of a Jewish family, but was converted to Christianity as a youth. He studied piano with F. Brauer and showed such extraordinary ability that he was sent to Vienna to continue his studies; there he studied briefly with Czerny before he took lessons with Anton Halm. In 1828 he began a tour through Austria and Germany. However, the exertion of travel proved too much for him; in Augsburg he became ill, and decided to remain there for a time; financial means were provided by a wealthy family. In 1838 he went to Paris, where he became friendly with Berlioz, Chopin, and Liszt. Soon he became very successful as a pianist; some critics even judged him as superior to Chopin. In Paris, Heller began to compose piano pieces somewhat akin to Schumann's: brilliant salon dances, studies, and character pieces that became exceedingly popular. In 1849 he visited London, where his concerts charmed a large circle of music-lovers. A nervous ailment forced him to curtail his appearances; in 1862 he revisited England and played with Hallé at the Crystal Palace. He then returned to Paris, where he remained for the rest of his life.

WORKS: He wrote in all several hundred piano pieces, arranged in groups in 158 opus numbers; of these, the most effective are *Traumbilder; Promenades d'un solitaire; Nuits blanches; Dans les bois; Voyage autour de ma chambre; Tablettes d'un solitaire; Tarentelles;* admirable études; ballades (notably *La Chasse*); 4 sonatas; 3 sonatinas; waltzes; mazurkas; caprices; nocturnes; variations; etc.

Hellmesberger, Georg, Sr., renowned Austrian violinist and conductor; b. Vienna, April 24, 1800; d. Neuwaldegg, near Vienna, Aug. 16, 1873. His father, a country schoolmaster, gave him his first musical instruction; he succeeded Schubert as soprano chorister in the Imperial Chapel; in 1820 became a pupil of the Vienna Cons. under Böhm (violin) and E. Förster (composition); in 1821 became an assistant instructor there; in 1833, a prof. In 1830 he succeeded Schuppanzigh as conductor of the Imperial Opera; also in 1830, became a member of the court chapel; was pensioned in 1867; conducted the Vienna Phil. from 1847 to 1848. He had many distinguished pupils, including Ernst, Hauser, Auer, Joachim, and his own sons, **Georg** and **Joseph.**

Hellmesberger, Georg, Jr., Austrian violinist, son of the preceding; b. Vienna, Jan. 27, 1830; d. Hannover, Nov. 12, 1852. He studied violin with his father and composition with Rotter; made a successful concert tour through Germany and England. At the age of 20, he was appointed concertmaster of the Hannover Royal Orch., and produced there 2 operas, *Die Bürgschaft* and *Die beiden Königinnen* (1851), when his career, so brilliantly begun, was cut short by tuberculosis, to which he succumbed at the age of 22.

Hellmesberger, Joseph, Jr., Austrian violinist, conductor, and dramatic composer, son of the preceding; b. Vienna, April 9, 1855; d. there, April 26, 1907. He studied with his father; from 1870–84 was concertmaster of the Vienna Phil.; in 1884 became ballet conductor at the Vienna court opera, and was engaged as opera conductor there in 1890. In 1887 he succeeded his father as leader of the Hellmesberger Quartet. He also conducted the Vienna Phil. (1901–3) and the Stuttgart Opera (1904–5).

WORKS: 10 operettas, produced in Vienna, Munich, and Hamburg between 1880 and 1906: *Kapitän Ahlström; Der Graf von Gleichen; Der schöne Kurfürst; Rikiki, oder Nelly, das Blumenmädchen; Das Orakel; Der bleiche Gast; Das Veilchenmädel; Die drei Engel; Mutzi;* and *Der Triumph des Weibes.* Also, ballets: *Fata Morgana; Die verwandelte Katze; Das Licht; Die fünf Sinne;* etc.

Hellmesberger, Joseph, Sr., Austrian conductor and violinist; b. Vienna, Nov. 3, 1828; d. there, Oct. 24, 1893. He studied violin with his father, **Georg Hellmesberger, Sr.,** at the Vienna Cons. In 1851 he was appointed conductor of the Gesellschaftskonzerte; also served as director of the Gesellschaft der Musikfreunde in Vienna (1851–59). Concurrently he taught violin at the Vienna Cons. (1851–77) and was concertmaster of the Vienna Phil. (1855–77). He further occupied the post of the concertmaster at the Imperial Austrian Opera (1860), and in 1877 became conductor of the court orch. From 1849 to 1887 he played the first violin in the famous string quartet bearing his name.

Helmholtz, Hermann (Ludwig Ferdinand) von, celebrated German scientist and acoustician; b. Potsdam, Aug. 31, 1821; d. Berlin, Sept. 8, 1894. His father was a schoolteacher in Potsdam, and Helmholtz received his education there. His mother, Caroline Penn, was of English extraction. He studied medicine at the Military Inst. of Berlin; received his M.D. and became a member of the staff of the Charité Hospital there (1842); in 1843 he was appointed a military surgeon at Potsdam; was then recalled to Berlin as a teacher of anatomy (for artists) at the Academy of Fine Arts (1848). In 1849 he obtained a position as prof. of physiology at the Univ. of Königsberg; in 1855 was a prof. at Bonn; in 1858, at Heidelberg. In 1871, abandoning the teaching of physiology and anatomy, he accepted the position of prof. of physics at the Univ. of Berlin; publ. various scientific studies. The work of most interest to musicians, and indispensable for students of acoustics, is his *Lehre von den Tonempfindungen als physiologische Grundlage für die Theorie der Musik* (Braunschweig, 1863); it was trans. by Alexander John Ellis and publ. in London under the title *On the Sensations of Tone as a Physiological Basis for the Theory of Music* (London, 1875; new ed., N.Y., 1948). By a long series of experiments, Helmholtz established a sure physical foundation for the phenomena manifested by musical tones, either single or combined. He supplemented and amplified the theories of Rameau, Tartini, Wheatstone, Corti, and others, furnishing impregnable formulae for all classes of consonant and dissonant tone effects, and proving with scientific precision what Hauptmann and his school sought to establish by laborious dialectic processes. Helmholtz's labors resulted primarily in instituting the laws governing the differences in quality of tone (tone color) in different instruments and voices, covering the whole field of harmonic, differential, and summational tones; and those governing the nature and limits of musical perception by the human ear.

Helps, Robert, American pianist and composer; b. Passaic, N.J., Sept. 23, 1928. He studied at the Juilliard School of Music in N.Y. with Abby Whiteside (piano) and Roger Sessions (composition). He occupied teaching posts at Princeton Univ., the San Francisco Cons. of Music (1968–70), Stanford Univ., and the Univ. of Calif. at Berkeley. In 1970–72 he was on the staff of the New England Cons. of Music; then taught at the Manhattan School of Music (1973–76) and, from 1978, at the Univ. of Southern Florida. His natural pianism helps Helps to write idiomatically for his instrument.

WORKS: Fantasy for Piano (1952); Symph. No. 1 (1955); Piano Trio (1957); *Image* for Piano (1958); *Recollections* for Piano (1959); *Portrait* for Piano (1960); *Cortège* for Orch. (1963); Serenade in 3 parts: (1) Fantasy for Violin and Piano; (2) Nocturne for String Quartet; (3) *Postlude* for Piano, Violin, and Horn (1964); Piano Concerto (1966); *Saccade* for Piano, 4-hands (1967); *Quartet* for Piano Solo, divided into 4 equal parts, each numbering 22 keys (1971).

Hemke, Frederick, American saxophone player; b. Milwaukee, July 11, 1935. He studied at the Univ. of Wisconsin (1953–58) and at the Eastman School of Music in Rochester, N.Y. (1960–62); also took lessons (1955–56) with Marcel Mule in Paris, where he became the first American to win the Premier Prix in saxophone (1956). In 1964 he joined the Chicago Symph. Orch.; from 1962 was on the faculty of Northwestern Univ. In 1966 he made a tour of 11 countries in the Orient under the auspices of the State Dept. On Feb. 24, 1983, in Stockholm, he gave the first performance of the last work of Allan Pettersson, Symph. No. 16 for Alto Saxophone and Orch., commissioned by Hemke in 1979.

Hempel, Frieda, brilliant German coloratura soprano; b. Leipzig, June 26, 1885; d. Berlin, Oct. 7, 1955. In 1900 she entered the Leipzig Cons. as a piano pupil; in 1902–5 she studied singing with Frau Nicklass-Kempner in Berlin; made her debut in Breslau; made her Berlin Opera debut in Nicolai's *Merry Wives of Windsor* (Aug. 22, 1905); in 1905–7 was at the Court Opera in Schwerin; in 1907–12 was a member of the Royal Opera in Berlin; in 1912–19 was one of the foremost members of the Metropolitan Opera, where she made her debut as the Queen in *Les Huguenots* on Dec. 27, 1912. In 1920 she impersonated Jenny Lind in the Lind centenary celebrations in N.Y. and throughout the U.S. (70 concerts). She was married to William B. Kahn in 1918 (divorced in 1926). From 1940 till 1955 she lived in N.Y. A few months before her death, knowing that she was incurably ill, she returned to Berlin. Her memoirs, *Mein Leben dem Gesang,* were publ. posthumously (Berlin, 1955).

Henderson, Alva, American opera composer; b. San Luis Obispo, Calif., April 8, 1940. He studied voice and music theory at the San Francisco State College; devoted himself mainly to vocal works. His first opera, *Medea,* based on the play by Robinson Jeffers, was produced with a modicum of critical favor in San Diego, on Nov. 29, 1972; his 2nd opera was adapted from Shakespeare's play *The Tempest.* He obtained his most decisive success with his 3rd opera, *The Last of the Mohicans,* after the novel of James Fenimore Cooper, produced by the Wilmington Opera Society on June 12, 1976, in Wilmington, Del.

Henderson, "Skitch" (Lyle Russell Cedric Henderson), English-born American conductor; b. Birmingham, England, Jan. 27, 1918. He came to the U.S. in his youth; took up the organ and piano, and then played on a radio station in North Dakota; moving to Hollywood, he was accompanist to Judy Garland and worked at MGM. During World War II he served as a fighter pilot in the Royal Air Force and the U.S. Air Force; after the war, he returned to Hollywood as a conductor for radio and films; also studied with Ernst Toch. In 1949 he joined the music staff of NBC; later was music director for several television shows; also had guest engagements with provincial orchs. In 1983 he organized his own N.Y. Pops Orch., which made its first appearance at Carnegie Hall.

Henderson, William James, American music critic; b. Newark, N.J., Dec. 4, 1855; d. (suicide) New York, June 5, 1937. He was a graduate (1876) of Princeton (M.A., 1886); studied piano with Carl Langlotz (1868–73) and voice with Torriani (1876–77); was chiefly self-taught in theory. He wrote many librettos of light operas, and also *Cyrano de Bergerac* for Walter Damrosch (1913). He was first a reporter (1883), then music critic of the *N.Y. Times* (1887–1902) and, for 35 years, until his death, for the *N.Y. Sun* (1902–37); lectured on music history at the N.Y. College of Music (1899–1902); from 1904, lectured on the development of vocal art at the Inst. of Musical Art in N.Y. A brilliant writer, Henderson was an irreconcilable and often venomous critic of modern music; he loved Wagner, but savagely attacked Debussy and Richard Strauss. Henderson, in turn, was the butt of some of Charles Ives's caustic wit.

Hendl, Walter, American conductor; b. West New York, N.J., Jan. 12, 1917. He studied conducting with Fritz Reiner at the Curtis Inst. of Music in Philadelphia. He was associate conductor of the N.Y. Phil. from 1945–49 and music director of the Dallas Symph. from 1949–58. From 1964–72 he was director of the Eastman School of Music in Rochester, N.Y.; in 1976 he was appointed music director of the Erie (Pa.) Phil. He composed some incidental music for theatrical plays.

Hendricks, Barbara, black American soprano; b. Stephen, Ariz., Nov. 20, 1948. She studied voice with Jennie Tourel; made her debut at the San Francisco Opera in 1974; in Europe, she appeared at the Glyndebourne Festival and at the Netherlands Opera in Amsterdam. In America, she had several engagements with leading orchs.; also gave recitals.

Henkemans, Hans, Dutch composer and pianist; b. The Hague, Dec. 23, 1913. He took lessons in piano and composition with Bernhard van den Sigtenhorst-Meyer and Willem Pijper (1930–36); made his debut as a pianist in his own Piano Concerto at 19. Concurrently he studied medicine at the Univ. of Utrecht, and was active as a practicing psychiatrist. As a composer, he follows the stylistic manner of the modern French school, cultivating sonorous harmonies supporting melodic lines of a modal character.

Henneberg, Johann Baptist, Austrian conductor and composer; b. Vienna, Dec. 6, 1768; d. there, Nov. 26, 1822. He conducted at Vienna theaters (1790–1803); then became a member of the orch. of Count Esterházy; in 1818, returned to Vienna. He wrote a great number of singspiels, of which the most successful were *Die Waldmänner* (Vienna, Oct. 14, 1793) and *Liebe macht kurzen Prozess* (Leipzig, 1799).

Henneberg, Richard, German conductor and composer; b. Berlin, Aug. 5, 1853; d. Malmö, Oct. 19, 1925. He studied piano with Liszt; then traveled as accompanist with various artists, including Wieniawski; held posts as operatic coach at the Italian Opera in London, and at various theaters in Berlin and Stockholm; from 1885–1907 conducted at the Stockholm Opera; from 1914–20 was conductor of the Malmö Orch. Henneberg gave the first performance of *Tannhäuser* in Stockholm (1876) and the first complete production of the *Ring of the Nibelung* in Sweden (1907), and was an ardent propagandist of Wagner's music. He wrote a comic opera, *Drottningens Vallfart* (Stockholm, 1882); incidental music to Ibsen's *Brand;* various Shakespearean pieces; a ballet, *Undine;* some choral works and songs (all in a Wagnerian vein).

Hennessy, Swan, American composer; b. Rockford, Ill., Nov. 24, 1866; d. Paris, Oct. 26, 1929. He was the son of an Irish-American settler; studied general subjects in Oxford, and music in Germany; then traveled in Italy, France, and Ireland, eventually settling in Paris.
WORKS: About 70 compositions, several of which are derived from Irish folk melos; his technical equipment was thorough; his idiom, impressionistic. Among his Irish-inspired works are *Petit trio celtique* for Violin, Viola, and Cello; *Rapsodie celtique* for Violin and Piano; *Rapsodie gaëlique* for Cello and Piano; *Sonata in Irish Style* for Violin

and Piano; several piano albums "*à la manière de ...*"; characteristic piano pieces in a humorous vein, such as *Epigrammes d'un solitaire, Impressions humoristiques,* etc.; 4 string quartets.

Henriques, Fini Valdemar, Danish composer; b. Copenhagen, Dec. 20, 1867; d. there, Oct. 27, 1940. He studied violin with Valdemar Tofte in Copenhagen, and with Joachim at the Hochschule für Musik in Berlin; studied composition with Svendsen; returning to Copenhagen, he was a violinist in the court orch. (1892–96); also appeared as a soloist. He organized his own string quartet, and traveled with it in Europe; also conducted orchs.
WORKS: As a composer, he followed the Romantic school; he possessed a facile gift of melody; his *Danish Lullaby* became a celebrated song in Denmark. He also wrote an opera, *Staerstikkeren* (Copenhagen, May 20, 1922); several ballets (*The Little Mermaid,* after Hans Andersen; *Tata,* etc.); *Hans Andersen Overture;* 2 symphs.; String Quartet; Quartet for Flute, Violin, Cello, and Piano; Violin Sonata; a number of piano pieces (several cycles, *Lyrik, Erotik,* etc.).

Henry, Leigh Vaughan, English writer and conductor; b. Liverpool, Sept. 23, 1889; d. London, March 8, 1958. He received his earliest training from his father, John Henry, a singer and composer; then studied with Granville Bantock in London, Ricardo Viñes in France, and Buonamici in Italy; taught music at Gordon Craig's Theatrical School in Florence (1912); then was in Germany, where he was interned during World War I. Returning to England, he edited a modern-music journal, *Fanfare* (1921–22); also was active in various organizations promoting modern music; in 1930 he went to the U.S.; lectured at various colleges. He was music director of the Shakespeare Festival Week in London in 1938, 1945, and 1946; organized and conducted orch. concerts of British music, and the National Welsh Festival Concerts; also at the BBC.
WRITINGS: *Music: What It Means and How to Understand It* (London, 1920); *The Growth of Music in Form and Significance* (1921); *The Story of Music* (1935); *Dr. John Bull* (largely fictional; London, 1937); *My Surging World,* autobiography (with R. Hale; 1937). Among his compositions are *The Moon Robber,* opera; *Llyn-y-Fan,* symph. poem; various pieces on Welsh themes.

Henry, Michel, a member of the 24 "violons du roi" under Henry IV and Louis XIII; b. Paris, Feb. 1555; date of death unknown. He wrote ballets for the court. His younger brother, known as Le Jeune, also in the "violons du roi," composed some very interesting instrumental music: a *Fantaisie* for 5 Violins; another *Fantaisie,* for 5 *cornetti; Pavane* for 6 Oboes; some of this is reproduced by P. Mersenne in his *Harmonie universelle* (vol. 3, pp. 186–277). Dolmetsch made a modern arrangement of the *Fantaisie* for 5 Violins.

Henry, Pierre, French composer and acoustical inventor; b. Paris, Dec. 9, 1927. He studied with Messiaen at the Paris Cons.; also took courses with Nadia Boulanger; in 1950 was a founder of the Groupe de Recherche de Musique Concrète with Pierre Schaeffer, but in 1958 separated from the group to experiment on his own projects in the field of electro-acoustical music and electronic synthesis of musical sounds. In virtually all of his independent works he applied electronic effects, often with the insertion of pre-recorded patches of concrete music and sometimes "objets trouvés" borrowed partially or in their entirety from pre-existent compositions.

WORKS: In collaboration with Pierre Schaeffer he wrote *Symphonie pour un homme seul* (1950) and the experimental opera *Orphée 53* (1953); independently he wrote *Microphone bien tempéré* (1952); *Musique sans titre* (1951); *Concerto des ambiguités* (1951); *Astrologie* (1953); *Spatiodynamisme* (1955); 4 ballets: *Haut voltage* (1956); *Coexistence* (1959); *Investigations* (1959); *Le Voyage* (1962); also *Messe de Liverpool* (1967); *Ceremony* (1970); *Futuristie 1,* "electro-acoustical musical spectacle," with the reconstruction of the "bruiteurs" introduced by the Italian futurist Luigi Russolo in 1909 (Paris, Oct. 16, 1975).

Henry V, English king; b. Monmouth, Sept. 1387; d. Bois de Vincennes, Aug. 31, 1422. During his reign (1413–22), he established a flourishing musical service at the Chapel Royal; was a musician himself; probably was the author of a Gloria and a Sanctus for 3 Voices in the Old Hall MS (transcribed into modern notation, and publ. by the Plainsong and Medieval Music Society, 1933–38, vols. I and III; in that edition, these works are ascribed to Henry VI).

Henry VI, English king; b. Windsor, Dec. 6, 1421; d. London, May 21, 1471. He reigned from 1422 till 1471. For a long time, he was regarded as the "Roy Henry" who was the author of a Gloria and a Sanctus in the Old Hall MS; however, research by M. Bukofzer tends to indicate that the works may actually be by Henry V.

Henry VIII, English king; b. Greenwich, June 28, 1491; d. Windsor, Jan. 28, 1547. He reigned from 1509 to 1547. He received regular instruction in music; his compositions include 2 masses (lost); a Latin motet for 3 Voices (publ. in the *Baldwin Collection,* 1591); the anthem *O Lord, the Maker of All Things;* a secular ballad, *Passe tyme with good cumpanye,* for 3 Voices (publ. in Chappell's *Popular Music of the Olden Time*); 5 4-part songs and 12 3-part songs; also several pieces for 3 and 4 viols; 35 pieces are printed in *Music at the Court of Henry VIII,* vol. 18 of *Musica Britannica.*

Henschel, Sir George (full name, **Isador Georg Henschel**), German conductor, composer, and singer; b. Breslau, Feb. 18, 1850; d. Aviemore, Scotland, Sept. 10, 1934. Both his parents were of Polish-Jewish descent, but he was converted to Christianity when young. He studied with Julius Shäffer at Bres-

lau, and with Moscheles (piano), Götze (singing), and Reinecke (theory) at the Leipzig Cons. (1867–70); then with Friedrich Kiel (composition) and Adolf Schulze (singing) in Berlin. He was a boy soprano; when his voice broke he gave concerts as a tenor; made his debut in Leipzig (1868) as Hans Sachs (baritone) in a concert performance of *Die Meistersinger;* he then toured throughout Europe; later gave recitals as a bass, and in 1914 appeared in London singing as a basso profondo. At the age of 78 he sang a group of Schubert lieder in London (at the Schubert centennial, 1928). An important turning point in his career came when he was selected as the first conductor of the Boston Symph., which he led for 3 seasons (1881–84); he also gave concerts in Boston and N.Y. as a singer. Settling in England, he founded the London Symph. Concerts (inaugural concert, Nov. 17, 1886), and conducted them until the series was concluded in 1897. He was a vocal teacher at the Royal College of Music (1886–88) and conductor of the Scottish Symph. Orch. (1893–95). In 1905–8 he was a prof. of singing at the Inst. of Musical Art in N.Y. In 1931, at the age of 81, he was engaged to conduct a commemorative concert on the 50th anniversary of the Boston Symph. Orch., identical (except for one number) with his inaugural Boston concert of 1881. In 1881 Henschel married the American singer **Lillian Bailey,** with whom he gave concerts; she died in 1901. In 1907 he was married, for a 2nd time, to Amy Louis. He was knighted in 1914.

WORKS: His musical compositions (mostly vocal) are in the German Romantic tradition. They include the opera *Nubia* (Dresden, Dec. 9, 1899); *Stabat Mater* (Birmingham, Oct. 4, 1894); *Requiem,* in memory of his first wife (Boston, Dec. 2, 1902); Mass for 8 Voices (London, June 1, 1916); String Quartet; about 200 songs (almost all publ.). He was the author of *Personal Recollections of Johannes Brahms* (Boston, 1907) and the autobiographical *Musings and Memories of a Musician* (1918).

Henschel, Lillian June (née **Bailey**), American soprano; b. Columbus, Ohio, Jan. 17, 1860; d. London, Nov. 4, 1901. She made her professional debut in Boston at 16; then went to Paris to study with Mme. Viardot-García. On April 30, 1879, she appeared in London, at a Phil. concert, when she sang, besides her solo number, a duet with **George Henschel.** She then studied with him and on March 9, 1881, married him. When Henschel was appointed first conductor of the Boston Symph. Orch., she appeared as a soloist with him accompanying her at the piano, also in duets at Boston Symph. concerts. Until her untimely death, the Henschels were constantly associated in American artistic life. Her well-trained voice and fine musical feeling won her many admirers.

Hensel, Fanny Cäcilia, pianist and composer; sister of **Felix Mendelssohn;** b. Hamburg, Nov. 14, 1805; d. Berlin, May 14, 1847. Brought up in the cultured atmosphere of the Mendelssohn family, she received an excellent musical education at home. She married the painter W. Hensel on Oct. 3, 1829, but remained very close to her brother, who constantly asked her advice in musical matters; her death, which occurred suddenly, was a great shock to Mendelssohn, who died a few months afterward. She had a talent for composing; publ. 4 books of songs; a collection of part-songs, *Gartenlieder* (reprinted, London, 1878); also *Lieder ohne Worte* for Piano.

Hensel, Heinrich, German dramatic tenor; b. Neustadt, Oct. 29, 1874; d. Hamburg, Feb. 23, 1935. He studied in Vienna and Milan; was a member of the Frankfurt Opera (1900–6), then at Wiesbaden (1906–11), where Siegfried Wagner heard him and engaged him to create the chief tenor part in his opera *Banadietrich* (Karlsruhe, 1910) and also to sing Parsifal at the Bayreuth Festival. He obtained excellent success; subsequently sang at Covent Garden, London (1911). He made his American debut at the Metropolitan Opera House in N.Y. as Lohengrin (Dec. 22, 1911) and was hailed by the press as one of the finest Wagnerian tenors; he also appeared with the Chicago Opera; returned to Germany and sang at the Hamburg Opera (1912–29).

Henselt, Adolph von, distinguished German pianist and composer; b. Schwabach, May 9, 1814; d. Warmbrunn, Silesia, Oct. 10, 1889. The family moved to Munich when he was still an infant, and he studied piano there with Mme. von Fladt. In 1831, an allowance from King Ludwig I enabled him to continue piano study with Hummel at Weimar; he then took a course of theory under Sechter in Vienna. After a highly successful tour in Germany (1837), he went to St. Petersburg (1838), where he established himself as a piano teacher; was appointed chamber pianist to the Empress, and inspector of music at Imperial Institutes for girls in principal Russian cities. He remained in Russia for 40 years; a generation of Russian pianists studied under him. He was a virtuoso of the first rank; like Liszt (whose intimate friend he became), he developed an individual manner of playing, designed to express a personal feeling for the music. His technical specialty was the artful execution, in legato, of widely extended chords and arpeggios, for the achievement of which he composed extremely difficult extension studies. As a composer of piano pieces, he was praised by Schumann and Liszt. His principal works are a Piano Concerto, 2 sets of études, and a number of effective piano pieces (*Frühlingslied, La gondola,* etc.); altogether, he publ. 54 works. He publ. a long-winded but historically and didactically interesting paper entitled *Instructions for Teaching of Playing the Fortepiano, Based on Experience of Many Years, a Manual for the Teachers and Pupils of the Educational Institutions Entrusted to Him by the Government* (in Russian; St. Petersburg, 1868).

Henze, Hans Werner, outstanding German composer of the modern school; b. Gütersloh, Westphalia, July 1, 1926. His early studies at the Braunschweig School of Music were interrupted by military service, and for a year he was in the German army on the Russian front. After the war he took music courses at the Kirchenmusikalisches Inst. in Heidelberg; at the same time he studied privately with Wolfgang Fortner. Early in his career as a composer he became fascinated with the disciplinary aspects of Schoenberg's method of composition with 12 tones, and attended the seminars on the subject given by René Leibowitz at Darmstadt. A musician of restless temperament, he joined a radical political group and proclaimed the necessity of writing music without stylistic restrictions in order to serve the masses. In search of natural musical resources, he moved to Italy; lived in Ischia from 1953 to 1956; then stayed in Naples and finally settled in Marino. He successfully attempted to integrate musical idioms and mannerisms of seemingly incompatible techniques; in his vocal works he freely adopted such humanoid effects as screaming, bellowing, and snorting; he even specified that long sustained tones were to be sung by inhaling as well as exhaling. Nonetheless, Henze manages to compose music that is feasible for human performance. But political considerations continued to play a decisive role in his career. In 1967 he, in company with the German radical composer Paul Dessau, withdrew from the membership of the Academy of the Arts of West Berlin, in a gesture of protest against its artistic policies. He defiantly placed the red flag on the stage at the first performance of his oratorio *Das Floss der Medusa* in Hamburg on Dec. 9, 1968; when the chorus refused to sing under such circumstances, Henze canceled the performance, and declared that revolutionary action was more important than any world première. During his stay in Italy he became a member of the Italian Communist Party.

WORKS: FOR THE STAGE: *Das Wundertheater,* opera for Actors, after Cervantes (1948; Heidelberg, May 7, 1949; revised for Singers, 1964; Frankfurt, Nov. 30, 1965); *Ballet Variations* (concert premiere, Düsseldorf, Oct. 3, 1949; stage premiere, Wuppertal, Dec. 21, 1958); *Jack Pudding,* ballet (1949; Wiesbaden, Jan. 1, 1951); *Rosa Silber* (1950; concert premiere, Berlin, May 8, 1951; stage premiere, Cologne, Oct. 15, 1958); *Labyrinth,* choreographic fantasy (1951; concert perf., Darmstadt, May 29, 1952); *Die schlafende Prinzessin,* ballet after Tchaikovsky (1951; Essen, June 5, 1954); *Ein Landarzt,* radio opera after the story by Kafka (Hamburg, Nov. 19, 1951; broadcast, Nov. 29, 1951; revised as a monodrama for Baritone and Orch., 1964; first perf., Berlin, Oct. 12, 1965; Dietrich Fischer-Dieskau, soloist; radio opera revised for the stage, 1964; first perf., Frankfurt, Nov. 30, 1965); *Boulevard Solitude,* opera (1951; Hannover, Feb. 17, 1952); *Der Idiot,* ballet pantomime after Dostoyevsky (Berlin, Sept. 1, 1952); *Pas d'action,* ballet (Munich, 1952; withdrawn by the composer and revised as *Tancredi,* 1964; Vienna, May 14, 1966); *Das Ende einer Welt,* radio opera (Hamburg, Dec. 4, 1953; revised for the stage, 1964; Frankfurt, Nov. 30, 1965); *König Hirsch,* opera (1952–55; Berlin, Sept. 23, 1956; revised as *Il Re cervo,* 1962; Kassel, March 10, 1963); *Maratona,* ballet (1956; Berlin, Sept. 24, 1957); *Ondine,* ballet (1956–

57; London, Oct. 27, 1958); *Der Prinz von Homburg,* opera (1958; Hamburg, May 22, 1960); *L'Usignolo dell'Imperatore,* pantomime after Andersen (Venice, Sept. 16, 1959); *Elegy for Young Lovers,* chamber opera (1959–61; in German, Schwetzingen, May 20, 1961; first perf. to Auden's original Eng. libretto, Glyndebourne, July 13, 1961); *Der junge Lord,* comic opera (1964; Berlin, April 7, 1965); *The Bassarids,* opera seria (1965; in German, Salzburg, Aug. 6, 1966; first perf. to the original Eng. libretto by Auden and Kallman, Santa Fe, July 7, 1968); *Moralities,* scenic cantatas after Aesop, to texts by Auden (1967; Cincinnati, May 18, 1968); *Der langwierige Weg in die Wohnung der Natascha Ungeheuer,* show (RAI, Rome, May 17, 1971); *La cubana, oder Ein Leben für die Kunst,* vaudeville (1973; NET Opera Theater, N.Y., March 4, 1974; stage premiere, Munich, May 28, 1975); *We Come to the River,* actions for music (1974–76; London, July 12, 1976); *Don Chisciotte,* opera, arrangement of Paisiello (Montepulciano, Aug. 1, 1976); *Orpheus,* ballet in 2 acts by Edward Bond (Stuttgart, March 17, 1979); *Pollicino,* fairy-tale opera (Montepulciano, Aug. 2, 1980); *The English Cat,* chamber opera (Schwetzingen, June 2, 1983).

FOR ORCH: Chamber Concerto for Piano, Flute, and Strings (Darmstadt, Sept. 27, 1946); Concertino for Piano and Winds, with Percussion (Baden-Baden, Oct. 5, 1947, Werner Egk conducting); Symph. No. 1 (Bad Pyrmont, Aug. 25, 1948, Wolfgang Fortner conducting; revised version, Berlin, April 9, 1964, composer conducting); Violin Concerto No. 1 (Baden-Baden, Dec. 12, 1948); Symph. No. 2 (Stuttgart, Dec. 1, 1949); Symph. Variations (1950); Piano Concerto No. 1 (1950; Düsseldorf, Sept. 14, 1952, composer conducting); Symph. No. 3 (Donaueschingen, Oct. 7, 1951); *Ode to the West Wind* for Cello and Orch., to the poem by Shelley (Bielefeld, April 30, 1954); *4 poemi* (Frankfurt, May 31, 1955, Stokowski conducting); Symph. No. 4, in one movement (1955; Berlin, Oct. 9, 1963, composer conducting); Sonata for Strings (Zürich, March 21, 1958, Paul Sacher conducting); *3 Symphonic Studies* (1955–64; first version perf. as *Symphonic Studies,* Hamburg, Feb. 14, 1956); *3 Dithyrambs* for Chamber Orch. (Cologne, Nov. 27, 1958); *Jeux des Tritons,* divertimento from the ballet *Ondine,* for Piano and Orch. (Zürich, March 28, 1960); *Antifone* (1960; Berlin, Jan. 20, 1962, Karajan conducting); Symph. No. 5 (1962; N.Y., May 16, 1963, Bernstein conducting); *Los Caprichos,* fantasia for Orch. (1963; Duisburg, April 6, 1967); *Doppio Concerto* for Oboe, Harp, and Strings (Zürich, Dec. 2, 1966, Paul Sacher conducting); *Telemanniana* (Berlin, April 4, 1967); Fantasia for Strings, from the film *Junge Torless* (Berlin, April 1, 1967); Concerto for Double Bass and Orch. (Chicago, Nov. 2, 1967); Piano Concerto No. 2, in one movement (1967; Bielefeld, Sept. 29, 1968); Symph. No. 6 (Havana, Nov. 24, 1969); *Compases para Preguntas Ensimismadas* (Basel, Feb. 11, 1971, Paul Sacher conducting); *Heliogabalus Imperator,* "allegoria per musica" (Chicago, Nov. 16, 1972, Solti conducting); *Tristan* for Piano, Tape, and Mixed Orch. (1973; London, Oct. 20, 1974, Colin Davis conducting); *Ragtimes and Habaneras* for Brass Instruments (London, Sept. 13, 1975); Concert Suite from

the film *Katharina Blum* (Brighton, May 6, 1976, composer conducting); *Aria de la folia española* for Chamber Orch. (St. Paul, Sept. 17, 1977); *Il Vitalino raddoppiato* for Violin Concertante and Chamber Orch. (Salzburg, Aug. 2, 1978); *Barcorola* (1979; Zürich, April 22, 1980); *Apollo triofante,* suite from *Orpheus* (Gelsenkirchen, Sept. 1, 1980); dramatic scenes from *Orpheus* (1979; Zürich, Jan. 6, 1981, composer conducting); *I sentimenti di Carl Philip Emmanuel Bach,* transcriptions for Flute, Harp, and Strings (Rome, April 14, 1982); *Le Miracle de la rose* for Clarinet and 13 Players (London, May 26, 1982); Symph. No. 7 (Berlin, Dec. 1, 1984).

CHAMBER MUSIC: Violin Sonata (1946); Sonatina for Flute and Piano (1947); String Quartet No. 1 (1947); Serenade for Solo Cello (1949); Variations for Piano (1949); Chamber Sonata for Piano, Violin, and Cello (1948; Cologne, March 16, 1950; revised 1963); *Apollo et Hyazinthus* for Harpsichord, Alto, and 8 Instruments (Frankfurt, June 26, 1949); String Quartet No. 2 (Baden-Baden, Dec. 16, 1952); Wind Quintet (1952; Bremen, Feb. 15, 1953); *Concerto per il Marigny* for Piano and 7 Instruments (Paris, March 9, 1956); Sonata for Piano (1959); *Chamber Music 1958* for Tenor, Guitar, and 8 Instruments (Hamburg, Nov. 26, 1958); *Lucy Escott Variations* for Piano (1963; Berlin, March 21, 1965); Divertimento for 2 Pianos (N.Y., Nov. 30, 1964); *Royal Winter Music,* 2 sonatas on Shakespearean characters, for Guitar (1975–79); String Quartet No. 3 (Berlin, Sept. 12, 1976); *Amicizia* for Clarinet, Cello, and Percussion Instruments (Montepulciano, Aug. 6, 1976); String Quartets Nos. 4 and 5 (Schwetzingen, May 25, 1977); Sonata for Violin Solo (Montepulciano, Aug. 10, 1977); *L'autunno* for Wind Instruments (London, Feb. 28, 1979); Sonata for Viola and Piano (Witten, April 20, 1980).

VOCAL MUSIC: 5 madrigals, to poems by François Villon, for Mixed Chorus and 2 Solo Instruments (1947; Frankfurt, April 25, 1950); *Chorus of the Captured Trojans,* from *Faust,* Part 2, for Mixed Chorus and Large Orch. (1948; Bielefeld, Feb. 6, 1949; revised 1964); *Whispers from Heavenly Death,* cantata from the poem by Walt Whitman, for High Voice and 8 Solo Instruments (1948); *Der Vorwurf (The Reproach),* concert aria to words by Franz Werfel, for Baritone, Trumpet, and Strings (Darmstadt, July 29, 1948); 5 Neapolitan songs for Baritone and Orch. (Frankfurt, May 26, 1956, Dietrich Fischer-Dieskau, soloist); *Nocturnes and Arias* for Soprano and Orch. (Donaueschingen, Oct. 20, 1957); *Novae de Infinito Laudes,* cantata to text by Giordano Bruno (1962; Venice, April 24, 1963); *Ariosi,* to poems by Tasso, for Soprano, Violin, and Orch. (1963; Edinburgh Festival, Aug. 23, 1964); *Being Beauteous,* cantata from the poem by Arthur Rimbaud, for Soprano, Harp, and 4 Cellos (1963; Berlin, April 12, 1964); *Cantata della Fiaba Estrema* for Soprano, Small Chorus, and 13 Instruments (1963; Zürich, Feb. 26, 1965); Choral Fantasy for Small Chorus, 5 Instruments, and Percussion (1964; Berlin, Jan. 23, 1967); *Muses of Sicily* for Chorus, 2 Pianos, Winds, and Timpani (Berlin, Sept. 20, 1966); *Versuch über Schweine (Essay on Pigs)* for Baritone and Chamber Orch. (London, Feb. 14, 1969; the title is an ironic reference to certain revolting students, active during the 1960s); *Das Floss der Medusa (The Raft of the Medusa),* popular and military oratorio to the memory of Ché Guevara (1968; the projected premiere in Hamburg on Dec. 9, 1968, had to be canceled as a result of left-wing political action; concert premiere, Vienna, Jan. 29, 1971; stage premiere, Nuremberg, April 15, 1972); *El Cimarrón* for Baritone, Flute, Guitar, and Percussion, to texts from *The Autobiography of a Runaway Slave* by Esteban Montejo (Aldeburgh Festival, June 22, 1970); *Voices* for Mezzo-soprano, Tenor, and Instrumental Group, to 22 revolutionary texts (London, Jan. 4, 1974, composer conducting); *Jephtha,* oratorio by Carissimi, realized by Henze (London, July 14, 1976, composer conducting); *The King of Harlem* for Mezzo-soprano and Instrumental Ensemble, to a text by Federico García Lorca (Witten, April 20, 1980); *3 Auden Pieces* for Voice and Piano (Aldeburgh, June 15, 1983).

WRITINGS: *Musik und Politik: Schriften und Gespräche, 1955–1975* (Munich, 1976; also in Eng., as *Music and Politics: Collected Writings, 1953–81,* London and Ithaca, N.Y., 1982).

Herbeck, Johann (Franz) von, Austrian conductor and composer; b. Vienna, Dec. 25, 1831; d. there, Oct. 28, 1877. He was a boy chorister at the Heiligenkreuz monastery, where he had instruction in piano; then studied composition with Ludwig Rotter in Vienna; he also studied philosophy and law at the Univ. of Vienna; from 1859 to 1870, and from 1875 to his death, he was conductor of the Gesellschaft der Musikfreunde; in 1866 he was named first Hofkapellmeister and in 1869 first Kapellmeister of the court opera; in 1870 was named its director as well, remaining there until 1875. He was particularly successful as conductor and organizer of several choral societies in Vienna. Herbeck publ. numerous choral works of considerable worth, if not of any originality. His son, Ludwig Herbeck, publ. a biography, *Johann Herbeck, ein Lebensbild* (Vienna, 1885), which contains a complete catalogue of his works. See also the sketch on Herbeck in Hanslick's *Suite* (Vienna, 1885).

Herbert, Victor, famous composer of light music; b. Dublin, Feb. 1, 1859; d. New York, May 26, 1924. He was a grandson of Samuel Lover, the Irish novelist; his father died when he was an infant; soon his mother married a German physician and settled in Stuttgart (1867), taking the boy with her. He entered the Stuttgart high school, but did not graduate; his musical ability was definitely pronounced by then, and he selected the cello as his instrument, taking lessons from the celebrated cellist Bernhard Cossmann in Baden-Baden. He soon acquired a degree of technical proficiency that enabled him to take a position as cellist in various orchs. in Germany, France, Italy, and Switzerland; in 1880 he became a cellist of the Eduard Strauss waltz band in Vienna; in 1881, returned to Stuttgart, where he joined the court orch., and studied composition with Max Seifritz at the Cons. His earliest works were for the cello with orch.; he performed his Suite with the Stuttgart orch. on Oct. 23, 1883, and his First Cello Concerto on Dec. 8, 1885. On Aug. 14, 1886, he married the Viennese opera singer **Therese Förster** (1861–1927); in the same year she received an offer to join the Metropolitan Opera in N.Y., and Herbert was engaged as an orch. cellist there, appearing in N.Y. also as soloist (played his own Cello Concerto with the N.Y. Phil., Dec. 10, 1887). In his early years in N.Y., Herbert was overshadowed by the celebrity of his wife, but soon he developed energetic activities on his own, forming an entertainment orch. which he conducted in a repertoire of light music; he also participated in chamber music concerts; was soloist with the Theodore Thomas and Seidl orchs. He was the conductor of the Boston Festival Orch. in 1891; Tchaikovsky conducted this orch. in Philadelphia in a miscellaneous program, and Herbert played a solo. He was associate conductor of the Worcester Festival (1889–91), for which he wrote a dramatic cantata, *The Captive* (Sept. 24, 1891). In 1893 he became bandmaster of the famous 22nd Regiment Band, succeeding P.S. Gilmore. On March 10, 1894, he was soloist with the N.Y. Phil. in his 2nd Cello Concerto. In the same year, at the suggestion of William MacDonald, the manager of the Boston Ideal Opera Co., Herbert wrote a light opera, *Prince Ananias,* which was produced with encouraging success in N.Y. (Nov. 20, 1894). From 1898 to 1904, Herbert was conductor of the Pittsburgh Symph. Orch., presenting some of his own compositions: *Episodes amoureuses* (Feb. 2, 1900); *Hero and Leander* (Jan. 18, 1901); *Woodland Fancies* (Dec. 6, 1901); *Columbus* (Jan. 2, 1903). In 1900 he directed at Madison Square Garden, N.Y., an orch. of 420 performers for the benefit of the sufferers in the Galveston flood. On April 29, 1906, he led a similar monster concert at the Hippodrome for the victims of the San Francisco earthquake. In 1904 he organized the Victor Herbert N.Y. Orch., and gave concerts in N.Y. and neighboring communities.

But it is as a composer of light operas that Herbert became chiefly known. In the best of these he unites spontaneous melody, sparkling rhythm, and simple but tasteful harmony; his experience as a symph. composer and conductor imparted a solidity of texture to his writing that placed him far above the many gifted amateurs in this field. Furthermore, he possessed a natural communicative power in his music, which made his operettas spectacularly successful with the public. In the domain of grand opera, he was not so fortunate. When the production of his first grand opera, *Natoma,* took place at Philadelphia on Feb. 25, 1911, it aroused great expectations; but the opera failed to sustain lasting interest. Still less effective was his 2nd opera, *Madeleine,* staged by the Metropolitan Opera Co. in N.Y. on Jan. 24, 1914. Herbert was one of the founders of the American Society of Composers, Authors and Publishers (ASCAP) in 1914, and was vice-president from that date until his death. In 1916 he wrote a special score for the motion picture, *The Fall of a Nation,* in synchronization with the screen play.

WORKS: Operettas: *Prince Ananias* (N.Y., Nov.

20, 1894); *The Wizard of the Nile* (Chicago, Sept. 26, 1895); *The Gold Bug* (N.Y., Sept. 21, 1896); *The Serenade* (Cleveland, Feb. 17, 1897); *The Idol's Eye* (Troy, N.Y., Sept. 20, 1897); *The Fortune Teller* (Toronto, Sept. 14, 1898); *Cyrano de Bergerac* (Montreal, Sept. 11, 1899); *The Singing Girl* (Montreal, Oct. 2, 1899); *The Ameer* (Scranton, Pa., Oct. 9, 1899); *The Viceroy* (San Francisco, Feb. 12, 1900); *Babes in Toyland* (Chicago, June 17, 1903); *Babette* (Washington, D.C., Nov. 9, 1903); *It Happened in Nordland* (Harrisburg, Pa., Nov. 21, 1904); *Miss Dolly Dollars* (Rochester, N.Y., Aug. 31, 1905); *Wonderland* (Buffalo, Sept. 14, 1905); *Mlle. Modiste* (Trenton, Oct. 7, 1905; Herbert's most popular work); *The Red Mill* (Buffalo, Sept. 3, 1906); *Dream City* (N.Y., Dec. 25, 1906); *The Tattooed Man* (Baltimore, Feb. 11, 1907); *The Rose of Algeria* (Wilkes-Barre, Sept. 11, 1909); *Little Nemo* (Philadelphia, Sept. 28, 1908); *The Prima Donna* (Chicago, Oct. 5, 1908); *Old Dutch* (Wilkes-Barre, Nov. 6, 1909); *Naughty Marietta* (Syracuse, Oct. 24, 1910; highly successful); *When Sweet Sixteen* (Springfield, Mass., Dec. 5, 1910); *Mlle. Rosita* (later called *The Duchess,* Boston, March 27, 1911); *The Enchantress* (Washington, Oct. 9, 1911); *The Lady of the Slipper* (Philadelphia, Oct. 8, 1912); *The Madcap Duchess* (Rochester, N.Y., Oct. 13, 1913); *Sweethearts* (Baltimore, March 24, 1913); *The Débutante* (Atlantic City, Sept. 21, 1914); *The Only Girl* (Atlantic City, Oct. 1, 1914); *Princess Pat* (Atlantic City, Aug. 23, 1915); *Eileen* (Cleveland, Jan. 1, 1917, as *Hearts of Erin*); *Her Regiment* (Springfield, Mass., Oct. 22, 1917); *The Velvet Lady* (Philadelphia, Dec. 23, 1918); *My Golden Girl* (Stamford, Conn., Dec. 19, 1919); *The Girl in the Spotlight* (Stamford, Conn., July 7, 1920); *Oui, Madame* (Philadelphia, March 22, 1920); *Orange Blossoms* (Philadelphia, Sept. 4, 1922); *The Dream Girl* (New Haven, April 22, 1924). Other stage productions: *Cinderella Man* (1915), *The Century Girl* (1916), *Ziegfeld Follies* (1917, 1920–23), *The Willow Plate* (marionette play by Tony Sarg, 1924). Nonstage works: Serenade, op. 12; First Cello Concerto (Dec. 8, 1885); 2nd Concerto for Cello, op. 30 (N.Y. March 10, 1894); *Pan-Americana; Suite of Serenades* (composed for Paul Whiteman's orch.; perf. 1924); *Golden Days; Dramatic Overture;* orch. arrangements; men's choruses; songs; many pieces for piano, violin and piano, and cello and piano.

Herbig, Günther, German conductor; b. Usti-nad-Labem, Czechoslovakia, Nov. 30, 1931. He studied conducting with H. Abendroth at the Franz Liszt Hochschule in Weimar; then worked with Scherchen, Yansons, and Karajan. In 1956 he conducted at the City Theater in Erfurt; from 1957–62 was conductor at the German National Theater in Weimar; then held the position of music director of the Hans Otto Theater in Potsdam (1962–66). From 1966–72 he was conductor of the East Berlin Symph. Orch.; in 1970 became also Generalmusikdirektor of the Dresden Phil., and in 1972 its chief conductor. In 1977 he was appointed chief conductor of the East Berlin Symph.; later made worldwide tours in the Orient and South America. From 1979–81 he served as principal guest conductor of the Dallas Symph. Orch. In 1983 he was appointed music director-designate of the Detroit Symph. Orch., and in Sept. 1984 was named its music director.

Herbst, Johannes, American Moravian minister and composer; b. Kempten, Swabia, July 23, 1735; d. Salem, N.C., Jan. 15, 1812. Herbst came to the U.S. in 1786 to serve as minister at Lancaster, Pa., and later at Lititz. In 1811 Herbst was elevated to the episcopate and transferred to the Southern Province of the Moravian Church at Salem, where he died the following year. When he emigrated to the U.S. he brought with him a large number of musical MSS, this being the practice of those traveling to the American Moravian settlements. During the following years, in which he was a performing musician, composer, and teacher, he added to his collection, copying MSS brought from Europe by other Moravians, and music composed by American Moravians; altogether there are almost 12,000 pages in his hand, constituting the most extensive individual collection of 18th- and 19th-century Moravian (and non-Moravian) music in the U.S. The Herbst Collection is in the Archives of the Moravian Music Foundation in Winston-Salem, N.C., and is available complete on either microfiche or roll microfilm: A. 493 MS scores of about 1,000 vocal-instrumental pieces (Congregation Music); B. 45 MS scores or parts of larger vocal works by C.P.E. Bach, Mozart, Haydn, and others, including Herbst and other Moravians; C. 6 miscellaneous vols. of keyboard works, texts, etc.; the entire collection totals 11,676 pages. An itemized *Catalog of the Johannes Herbst Collection,* prepared by Marilyn Gombosi, was publ. in Chapel Hill, N.C., in 1970 and includes a biographical sketch of Herbst and a short history of the collection. Herbst was the most prolific of all the American Moravian composers, having to his credit some 127 choral anthems and songs (all included in the above collection; a few pieces were publ. by H.W. Gray, Peters, and Boosey & Hawkes). Many of his works show him to have been a highly skilled musical craftsman. His music collection is particularly important as the principal source of music by American and European Moravian composers.

Herford, Julius, American musician and pedagogue; b. Berlin, Feb. 21, 1901; d. Bloomington, Ind., Sept. 17, 1981. He studied at Stern's Cons. in Berlin; then pursued a rather successful career as a choral conductor and concert pianist. He emigrated to the U.S. in 1939 and devoted himself mainly to teaching; was at various times on the faculty of Columbia Univ., the Juilliard School of Music, and Westminster Choir College. In 1964 he was appointed prof. of music at Indiana Univ. Among his students were Lukas Foss, Robert Shaw, Robert Wagner, and John Nelson.

Héritte-Viardot, Louise-Pauline-Marie, vocal teacher; daughter of **Pauline Viardot-García;** b. Paris, Dec. 14, 1841; d. Heidelberg, Jan. 17, 1918. She was for many years a singing teacher at the St. Petersburg Cons.; then taught in Frankfurt, Berlin, and Heidelberg. She was married to a French consular official, Héritte. She was also a composer; her opera *Lindoro* was performed in Weimar (1879); she further wrote the cantatas *Das Bacchusfest* (Stockholm, 1880) and *Le Feu de ciel;* some chamber music; and vocal exercises. Her memoirs (trans. from the original German) were publ. in Eng. as *Memories and Adventures* (London, 1913), in French as *Mémoires de Louise Héritte-Viardot* (Paris, 1923).

Herman, Jerry, American composer of popular music; b. New York, July 10, 1933. He played piano by ear but never learned to read music. He studied drama at the Univ. of Miami; then became a scriptwriter for television in N.Y. Later he devoted himself entirely to musical comedies, for which he wrote both lyrics and music. His shows *Parade* (1960) and *Milk and Honey* (1961) were fairly successful; but he made his greatest hit with the production of *Hello, Dolly!* (N.Y., Jan. 16, 1964), which had the longest run in the history of Broadway shows, closing on Dec. 26, 1970. A comparable success was achieved by his next musical, *Mame,* which opened in N.Y. on May 24, 1966.

Herman, Reinhold (Ludwig), conductor and composer; b. Prenzlau, Germany, Sept. 21, 1849; d. probably in New York, c.1920. He studied at the Stern Cons. in Berlin; came to the U.S. in 1871 as a singing teacher; from 1884, conducted the choral society Liederkranz; from 1898–1900, conducted the Handel and Haydn Society in Boston; then lived in Italy; returned to N.Y. in 1917. He publ. *An Open Door for Singers* (N.Y., 1912); wrote 3 operas, of which *Wulfrin* was performed in Kassel (Oct. 11, 1898); also several choral works.

Herman, Woody (real given names, **Woodrow Charles**), American clarinetist and bandleader; b. Milwaukee, May 16, 1913. He studied there and at Marquette Univ. In 1931 he joined a jazz band as a clarinet player, and in 1937 formed his first band; has had several since then, most being called "Herds"; i.e., the First Herd, Second Herd, etc. In the mid-1940s Herman's was the first prominent big band to make the transition from swing to a more advanced, bebop-influenced idiom characterized by "progressive" harmonies; it became known as "progressive jazz." On March 25, 1946, he presented in Carnegie Hall the first performance of Stravinsky's *Ebony Concerto,* written specially for him. He is also the composer of numerous popular songs.

Hermann, Hans, German composer; b. Leipzig, Aug. 17, 1870; d. Berlin, May 18, 1931. He studied with W. Rust in Leipzig, E. Kretschmer in Dresden, and H. von Herzogenberg in Berlin; from the age of 18, played the double bass in various European orchs.; then taught at the Klindworth-Scharwenka Cons. in Berlin (1901–7). From 1907–27, he lived in Dresden; then returned to Berlin. He publ. some 100 songs, of which several became fairly well known

(*Drei Wanderer, Alte Landsknechte,* etc.); he had a flair for imitating the simple style of the folk ballad; he further wrote a Symph., subtitled *Lebensepisoden;* a stage work, *Der rote Pimpernell;* pieces for clarinet with piano, etc.

Hermannus (surnamed **Contractus** on account of his paralyzed limbs), Swabian theoretician and composer; b. Saulgau, July 18, 1013; d. Altshausen, near Biberach, Sept. 24, 1054. He was the son of Hermann, Count of Vehringen. He was a student in the Reichenau monastery; under the guidance of his tutor, Abbot Berno, he acquired wide learning. In 1043 he entered the Benedictine order. His best-known work (containing valuable historical notices on music) is a chronology from the time of Christ to 1054. It has been republ. several times, and is to be found in Peres's (Pertz's) *Monumenta* (vol. V). Hermannus was the author of *Opuscula musica,* in which he gives a thorough discussion of the church modes and criticizes the Daseian notation used in the 10th-century tract *Musica enchiriadis.* He proposed his own notation by Greek and Latin letters. In the indication of a change in pitch, it had an advantage over neume notation. Hermannus's notation is written above the neume notation in some MSS of the 11th and 12th centuries in the Munich Library. He was the composer of the Gregorian Marian antiphons *Salve Regina* and *Alma Redemptoris Mater.* A transcription (into modern notation) of his *Versus ad discernendum cantum* is to be found in A. Schering's *Geschichte der Musik in Beispielen* (no. 7).

Hermstedt, (Johann) Simon, famous German clarinetist; b. Langensalza, Dec. 29, 1778; d. Sondershausen, Aug. 10, 1846. He was educated at the Annaberg school for soldiers' children; studied with Knoblauch and Baer; became a clarinetist in the Langensalza regiment; then conducted a military band in Langensalza. He made improvements in his instrument; composed concertos, variations, and other pieces for clarinet. Spohr wrote a Clarinet Concerto for him.

Hernándo (y Palomar), Rafael (José María), Spanish composer; b. Madrid, May 31, 1822; d. there, July 10, 1888. He studied with Carnicer and Saldoni at the Madrid Cons. (1837–43); then went to Paris, where he took lessons with Auber. His *Stabat Mater* was performed there, and a grand opera, *Romilda,* was accepted for performance at the Théâtre des Italiens, but the revolutionary upheaval of 1848 prevented its production. Hernándo returned to Madrid, where he produced a number of zarzuelas, of which the most successful was *El duende* (June 6, 1849); others were *Palo de ciego* (Feb. 15, 1849); *Colegialas y soldados* (March 21, 1849); *Bertoldo y Comparsa* (May 23, 1850); *Cosas de Juan* (Sept. 9, 1854); *El tambor* (April 28, 1860); *Aurora;* etc.; he also collaborated with Barbieri, Oudrid, and Gaztambide in *Escenas de Chamberi* (Nov. 19, 1850) and *Don Simplicio Bobadilla* (May 7, 1853). In 1852 he became secretary of the Madrid Cons.; later taught harmony there.

Herold, (Louis-Joseph) Ferdinand, celebrated French composer; b. Paris, Jan. 28, 1791; d. Thernes, near Paris, Jan. 19, 1833. His father, **François-Joseph Hérold** (pupil of C.P.E. Bach), a piano teacher and composer, did not desire his son to become a musician, and sent him to the Hix school, where his aptitude for music was noticed by Fétis, then assistant teacher there. After his father's death (1802), Herold began to study music seriously; in 1806 he entered the Paris Cons., taking piano lessons with Louis Adam, and winning first prize for piano playing in 1810. He studied harmony under Catel, and (from 1811) composition under Méhul; in 1812 his cantata *Mlle. de la Vallière* won the Prix de Rome (the MS score is in the Cons. library, with works composed during his 3 years' study in Rome). From Rome he went to Naples, where he became pianist to Queen Caroline; here he produced his first opera, *La gioventù di Enrico Quinto* (Jan. 5, 1815), which was well received. From Naples he went to Vienna, and after a few months' stay returned to Paris, where he finished the score of Boieldieu's *Charles de France,* an "opéra d'occasion" (Opéra-Comique, June 18, 1816), and where all the rest of his operas were produced. The flattering reception of *Charles de France* led to the successful production of *Les Rosières* (Jan. 27, 1817), *La Clochette* (Oct. 18, 1817), *Le Premier Venu* (Sept. 28, 1818), *Les Troqueurs* (Feb. 18, 1819), and *L'Auteur mort et vivant* (Dec. 18, 1820); the failure of the last-named opera caused him to distrust his natural talent, and to imitate, in several succeeding stage works, the style then in vogue—that of Rossini. With the comic opera *Marie* (Aug. 12, 1826) Herold returned, however, to his true element, and won instant and brilliant success. Meantime he had obtained the post of chorus master at the Italian Opera (1824); during this period he brought out *Le Muletier* (May 12, 1823), *Lasthénie* (Sept. 8, 1823), *Vendôme en Espagne* (Dec. 5, 1823), *Le Roi René* (Aug. 24, 1824), and *Le Lapin blanc* (May 21, 1825). In 1826 he was appointed to the staff of the Grand Opéra, for which he wrote several melodious and elegant ballets: *Astolphe et Jaconde* (Jan. 29, 1827); *La Somnambule* (Sept. 19, 1827); *Lydie* (July 2, 1828); *La Fille mal gardée* (Nov. 17, 1828); *La Belle au bois dormant* (April 27, 1829); *La Noce de village* (Feb. 11, 1830). *La Somnambule* furnished Bellini with the subject of his popular opera. On July 18, 1829, Herold produced *L'Illusion,* a one-act opera full of charming numbers. *Emmeline,* a grand opera (Nov. 28, 1829), was a failure, but his next opera, *Zampa* (May 3, 1831), was sensationally successful and placed Herold in the first rank of French composers. He then wrote *L'Auberge d'Aurey* (May 11, 1830) jointly with Carafa; *La Marquise de Brinvilliers* (Oct. 31, 1831) in collaboration with Auber, Batton, Berton, Blangini, Boieldieu, Carafa, Cherubini, and Paër; also produced *La Médecine sans médecin* (Oct. 15, 1832). His last work publ. in his lifetime, *Le Pré aux clercs* (Dec. 15, 1832), had a remarkable vogue. He died of consumption shortly before his 42nd birthday. His unfinished opera *Ludovic* was completed by Halévy and produced posthumously at the Opéra-Comique on May 16, 1833. Herold's piano music (55 opus numbers) consists of sonatas, caprices, rondos, divertissements, fantasies, variations, and potpourris.

Herrera Luis, de la Fuente Mexican conductor and composer; b. Mexico City, April 26, 1916. He studied piano and violin; took composition lessons with Rodolfo Halffter. From 1954 to 1972 he served as principal conductor of the National Symph. Orch. in Mexico City; in the interim he led the National Symph. Orch. of Peru (1965–71); was guest conductor of orchs. in the U.S., Canada, Europe, and New Zealand; in 1978 was appointed music director of the Oklahoma Symph. Orch. in Oklahoma City.
   WORKS: Opera, *Cuauhtemoc;* ballets, *La Estrella y la Sirena* and *Fronteras;* he also composed chamber music.

Herrmann, Bernard, American conductor and outstanding composer for films; b. New York, June 29, 1911; d. Los Angeles, Dec. 24, 1975. He won a composition prize at the age of 13; then enrolled at N.Y. Univ., where he studied with Philip James and Percy Grainger; later took courses with Wagenaar in composition and Albert Stoessel in conducting at the Juilliard Graduate School of Music. In 1934 he was appointed to the staff of the Columbia Broadcasting System as a composer of background music for radio programs and conductor of the CBS Symph. Orch. summer radio series; from 1940 till 1955 he was chief conductor of the CBS Symph. Orch. in boldly progressive programs of modern works, including those by Charles Ives. He became associated with Orson Welles and wrote several film scores for the radio broadcasts of the Mercury Theater. His music for *Citizen Kane* (1940), the first of his 61 film scores, is still regarded as a classic of the genre. His use of an electric violin and electric bass in the score for *The Day the Earth Stood Still* (1951) is an example of early application of electronic music in films. He subsequently wrote film scores for the thrillers of Alfred Hitchcock, succeeding in capturing the eerie spirit of Hitchcock's peculiar art by the use of atonal devices; of these, the score for *Psycho* (1960), for strings only, was particularly apt. Among Herrmann's other film scores were *The Devil and Daniel Webster* (1941; also known as *All that Money Can Buy;* received an Academy Award); *Jane Eyre* (1942); *Anna and the King of Siam* (1946); *The Ghost and Mrs. Muir* (1948); *Snows of Kilimanjaro* (1952); *Garden of Evil* (1954); *The Trouble with Harry* (1955); *The Man Who Knew Too Much* (1956); *The Wrong Man* (1957); *Vertigo* (1958); *North by Northwest* (1959); *The Man in the Gray Flannel Suit* (1956); *The 7th Voyage of Sinbad* (1958); *Journey to the Center of the Earth* (1959); *The Birds* (1963); *Fahrenheit 451* (1966); *La Mariée était en noir* (*The Bride Wore Black,* 1967); *Sisters* (1973); and *Obsession* (1975). Herrmann spent the last 10 years of his life in England, but was in Los Angeles in Dec. 1975 to conduct the score for his last film, *Taxi Driver;* he died in his sleep shortly after completing the final recording session. His concert works include the 4-act opera *Wuthering Heights* (1948–50; recorded in England in 1966; first complete stage perf., Portland, Oreg., Nov. 6, 1982); 2 Christmas operas for television: *A Christmas Carol* (CBS Television, N.Y., Dec. 23, 1954) and *A Child Is Born;* 2 cantatas: *Moby Dick* (N.Y., April 11, 1940) and *Johnny Appleseed* (1940). For Orch.: *The City of Brass,* symph. poem (1934); *Sinfonietta* for Strings (1935); *Currier and Ives,* suite (1935); *Nocturne and Scherzo* (1936); *Fiddle Concerto* (1940); Symph. No. 1 (1940; N.Y. Phil., Nov. 12, 1942); *For the Fallen* (N.Y. Phil., Dec. 16, 1943, composer conducting); *The Fantasticks* for Vocal Quartet and Orch. (1944). He also wrote a String Quartet (1932); *Aubade* for 14 Instruments (1933); *Echoes* for String Quartet (1966); clarinet quintet, *Souvenirs de Voyage* (1967).

Herrmann, Hugo, German composer; b. Ravensburg, April 19, 1896; d. Stuttgart, Sept. 7, 1967. He acquired primary knowledge of music without systematic study; was drafted into the German army during World War I and severely wounded in 1918. After the Armistice he took courses in composition with Schreker in Berlin. In 1923 he went to the U.S. and was employed as a church organist; in 1925 he returned to Germany; from 1935 to 1962 he was director of a music school in Trossingen. A believer in practical art, he promoted community music; took especial interest in the accordion and wrote several works for this instrument; he also composed pieces for the mouth organ. He also wrote several operas: *Gazellenhorn; Picknick; Vasantasena; Das Wunder; Paracelsus; Der Rekord; Der Überfall; Die Heinzelmännchen;* 5 symphs.; 5 string quartets, etc. He publ. a manual, *Einführung in die Satztechnik für Mundharmonika-Instrumente* (Trossingen, 1958), containing instructions for performance on the mouth organ.

Hertz, Alfred, eminent German-American conductor; b. Frankfurt, July 15, 1872; d. San Francisco, April 17, 1942. After completing his academic studies he entered the Raff Cons., where he studied with Anton Urspruch; then held positions as an opera conductor in Altenburg (1892–95), Barmen-Elberfeld (1895–99), and Breslau (1899–1902). In 1902 he was engaged as conductor of the German repertoire at the Metropolitan Opera; he conducted the first American performance of *Parsifal* (Dec. 24, 1903), which took place against the wishes of the Wagner family; consequently, Hertz could no longer obtain permission to conduct Wagner in Germany. He made his Covent Garden debut in 1910. In 1915 he was engaged to lead the San Francisco Symph. Orch.; he retained that post until 1930. He also organized the summer series of concerts at the Hollywood Bowl (1922), and conducted more than 100 concerts there; he was affectionately known as the "Father of the Hollywood Bowl."

Hertzka, Emil, Austrian music publisher; b. Budapest, Aug. 3, 1869; d. Vienna, May 9, 1932. He stud-

ied chemistry at the Univ. of Vienna; also took courses in music. He was engaged on the staff of the music publisher Weinberger in Vienna (1893); then joined Universal Edition, organized in 1901. In 1907 he became its director, and remained in that capacity until his death. He purchased the catalogues of other music publishing firms: the Wiener Philharmonischer Verlag and the Albert J. Gutmann Co. (which publ. Bruckner and Mahler), and acquired the rights of publication to works by many celebrated modern composers (Bartók, Schoenberg, Alban Berg, Kurt Weill, Krenek); also represented Soviet composers. An impassioned believer in the eventual worth of experimental music, he encouraged young composers, took active part in the organization of concerts of modern music, etc. An Emil Hertzka Foundation was established by his family after his death, for the purpose of helping unknown composers secure performances and publication of their works.

Hervé (properly, **Florimond Ronger**), French dramatic composer, the creator of French operetta; b. Houdain, near Arras, June 30, 1825; d. Paris, Nov. 3, 1892. He was a chorister and scholar of St.-Roch; became organist at various churches in Paris. With his friend Kelm, in 1848, he sang in *Don Quichotte et Sancho Pansa,* an interlude of his own composition, at the Opéra National. In 1851 he conducted the orch. at the Palais Royal; in 1855 he opened the Folies-Concertantes, a small theater for the production of pantomimes, *saynètes* (musical comediettas for 2 persons), etc., and, with phenomenal activity, developed the light French operetta from these diminutive and frivolous pieces, writing both librettos and music, conducting the orch., and often appearing as an actor on the stage. From 1856 to 1869 he led this feverish life in Paris, producing his works at various theaters, and responding to failures by doubling his efforts. In 1870–71, when the Franco-Prussian War and the Commune stopped theatrical activities in Paris, he went to London, where he produced several of his light operas; he revisited London many times afterward. In all, he wrote about 50 operettas, of which only one became a universal success, *Mam'zelle Nitouche* (Paris, Jan. 26, 1883, followed by numerous productions in European cities); other fairly successful works were *L'Œil crevé* (Paris, Oct. 12, 1867) and *Le Petit Faust* (Paris, April 28, 1869). He also wrote a grand opera, *Les Chevaliers de la table ronde* (Paris, Nov. 17, 1866); the ballets *Sport, La Rose d'Amour, Les Bagatelles,* etc.

Herz, Henri, brilliant Austrian pianist; b. Vienna, Jan. 6, 1803; d. Paris, Jan. 5, 1888. He was taught by his father, and by Hünten at Coblenz; later (1816) by Pradher, Reicha, and Dourlen at the Paris Cons.; he won first piano prize; improved himself in Moscheles's style after that virtuoso's visit in 1821; was in high repute as a fashionable teacher and composer, his compositions realizing 3 and 4 times the price of those of his superior contemporaries. In 1831 he made a tour of Germany with the violinist

Lafont; visited London in 1834, where at his first concert Moscheles and Cramer played duets with him. In 1842, he was appointed a piano prof. at the Paris Cons. He suffered financial losses through partnership with a piano manufacturer, Klepfer, and thereupon undertook a concert tour through the U.S., Mexico, and the West Indies (1845–51). Returning, he established a successful piano factory, his instruments receiving first prize at the Paris Exhibition of 1855. He resigned his professorship at the Cons. in 1874. Herz acknowledged that he courted the popular taste; his numerous works (over 200) include piano concertos, variations, sonatas, rondos, violin sonatas, nocturnes, dances, marches, fantasias, etc. He publ. an interesting and vivid book, *Mes voyages en Amérique* (1866), a reprint of his letters to the *Moniteur Universel.*

Herzogenberg, Heinrich von, Austrian pianist and composer; b. Graz, June 10, 1843; d. Wiesbaden, Oct. 9, 1900. He studied with Dessoff at the Vienna Cons.; then lived in Graz; went to Leipzig in 1872; with Spitta, Holstein, and Volkland, he founded the Bach-Verein there (1874); was its conductor from 1875–85; then was a prof. of composition at the Hochschule für Musik in Berlin (1885–88); was director of the Meisterschule (1889–92 and 1897–1900). He was a very prolific composer; his chief influences were Brahms and Bruch.
WORKS: Oratorios: *Die Geburt Christi; Die Passion; Erntefeier;* choral works with Orch.: *Der Stern des Liedes; Die Weihe der Nacht; Nannas Klage; Totenfeier;* and several Psalms and motets; cantata, *Columbus;* symph. poem, *Odysseus;* 2 symphs.; Piano Quintet; String Quintet; 5 string quartets; Quartet for Piano, Horn, Clarinet, and Bassoon; 2 piano quartets; 2 piano trios; 2 string trios; Trio for Piano, Oboe, and Horn; 3 violin sonatas; 3 cello sonatas; several works for piano, 4-hands; fantasies for organ. Herzogenberg's wife, **Elisabet,** née **von Stockhausen** (b. Paris, April 13, 1847; d. San Remo, Jan. 7, 1892), was an excellent pianist. They were great friends of Brahms, with whom they maintained a long correspondence (see M. Kalbeck, *Johannes Brahms im Briefwechsel mit Heinrich und Elisabet von Herzogenberg,* 1907).

Heseltine, Philip (pen name, **Peter Warlock**), brilliant English composer and writer; b. London, Oct. 30, 1894; d. there, Dec. 17, 1930. He studied at Eton with Colin Taylor (1908–10); a meeting with Delius in France in 1910 influenced him profoundly in the direction of composition; he adopted a style that was intimately connected with English traditions of the Elizabethan period and yet revealed impressionistic undertones in harmonic writing. Another influence was that of Bernard van Dieren, from whom he absorbed an austerely contrapuntal technique. He publ. all his musical works under the name Peter Warlock. He was a conscientious objector during World War I; in 1917 was in Ireland; after the Armistice returned to London; in 1920 he founded the progressive journal of musical opinion *The Sackbut;* wrote criticism; made transcriptions of old English music; participated in organizing the Delius Festival in 1929. Suffering from depression, he committed suicide by gas in his London flat.
WRITINGS: (under the name Philip Heseltine): *Frederick Delius* (London, 1923; revised ed. by Hubert Foss, London, 1952); *Carlo Gesualdo, Prince of Venosa, Musician and Murderer* (in collaboration with Cecil Gray; London, 1926); a pamphlet of 8 pages, *Thomas Whythorne: An Unknown Elizabethan Composer* (Oxford, 1927); as Peter Warlock, publ. a monograph, *The English Ayre* (London, 1926); ed. (with P. Wilson) 300 old songs (*English Ayres, Elizabethan and Jacobean; French Ayres*); was co-editor of *Oxford Choral Songs* and the *Oxford Orchestral Series,* a collection of old English and Italian dances; transcribed for piano some lute music of John Dowland, *Forlorne Hope;* many other transcriptions. Musical compositions: song cycle *The Curlew* (with Flute, English Horn, and String Quartet); *Saudades* (3 songs); *Lilligay* (5 songs); *Peterisms* (2 sets of 3 songs each); *Candlelight* (12 nursery songs), and many separate songs; *Capriol Suite* (on tunes from Arbeau's *Orchésographie,* in 2 versions: for String Orch. and Full Orch.); *Corpus Christi* (2 versions, for Chorus a cappella and for Soprano and Tenor Soli, with String Quartet); numerous other vocal works.

Hess, Ludwig, German tenor; b. Marburg, March 23, 1877; d. Berlin, Feb. 5, 1944. He studied singing with Vidal in Milan; gave concerts of German lieder throughout Europe, specializing in the modern repertoire; made a successful tour of the U.S. and Canada in 1911; conducted a choral society in Königsberg (1917–20); then settled in Berlin. He was also a composer; wrote the operas *Abu und Nu* (Danzig, 1919) and *Vor Edens Pforte* (after Byron); *Kranion* (Erfurt, 1933); a Symph.; symph. poem, *Himmelskönig mit musizierenden Engeln* (after Hans Memling); *Ariadne,* a cantata; many choral works, and numerous songs. He publ. *Die Behandlung der Stimme vor, während und nach der Mutation* (Marburg, 1927).

Hess, Dame Myra, distinguished English pianist; b. London, Feb. 25, 1890; d. there, Nov. 25, 1965. She studied at the Royal Academy of Music with Tobias Matthay; made her concert debut in London on Nov. 14, 1907, at the age of 17, playing Beethoven's G-major Concerto with Thomas Beecham, and producing a highly favorable impression. She then embarked on a successful and steady career; made several tours in Germany and France; played recitals in America in 1922, repeating her American tours at regular intervals. She organized the National Gallery Concerts in 1939, continuing them through the war and the blitz. It was mainly for her work during this period that she was created a Dame of the British Empire by King George VI in 1941. Her playing was marked by classical precision and poetic imagination; although she was never attracted by the modern repertoire of her time, she occasionally performed piano music by contemporary British composers.

Hess, Willy, noted Swiss musicologist; b. Winterthur, Oct. 12, 1906. He studied piano and music theory at the Zürich Cons. and musicology at the Univ. of Zürich. He was also a professional bassoon player; from 1942–71 he played bassoon in the Winterthur Stadtorchester. As a musicologist, he devoted most of his effort to the compilation of a Beethoven catalogue. He edited a valuable *Verzeichnis der nicht der Gesamtausgabe veröffentlichen Werke Ludwig van Beethovens* (Wiesbaden, 1957); also edited the extensive supplement *Ludwig van Beethoven: Sämtliche Werke: Supplement zur Gesamtausgabe* (14 vols., Wiesbaden, 1959–71). His other important writings include *Ludwig van Beethoven* (Geneva, 1946); *Beethovens Oper Fidelio und ihre drei Fassungen* (Zürich, 1953); *Beethoven* (Zürich, 1956; 2nd ed., revised, 1976); *Die Harmonie der Künste* (Vienna, 1960); *Die Dynamik der musikalischen Formbildung* (2 vols., Vienna, 1960; 1964); *Vom Doppelantlitz des Bösen in der Kunst, dargestellt am Beispiel der Musik* (Munich, 1963); *Vom Metaphysischen im Künstlerischen* (Winterthur, 1963); *Parteilose Kunst, parteilose Wissenschaft* (Tutzing, 1967); *Beethoven-Studien* (Munich, 1972); also an autobiography, *Aus meinem Leben: Erlebnisse, Bekenntnisse, Betrachtungen* (Zürich, 1976). He was also a prolific composer; he wrote several fairy-tale operas, a Symph., a Sonata for Bassoon and Small Orch., a Horn Concerto, and numerous pieces of chamber music, including a curious work for double bassoon and string quartet.

Hess, Willy, German violinist; b. Mannheim, July 14, 1859; d. Berlin, Feb. 17, 1939. His first teacher was his father, who was a pupil of Spohr. As a child, he was taken to the U.S.; at the age of 9, he played with the Thomas Orch. He then studied with Joachim in Berlin; later occupied posts as concertmaster in Frankfurt (1878–86), Rotterdam, where he taught at the Cons. (1886–88), and in Manchester, England, with the Hallé Orch. (1888–95). From 1895 to 1903, he was a prof. of violin at the Cons. of Cologne; then taught at the Royal Academy of Music in London (1903–4); in 1904, he was engaged as concertmaster of the Boston Symph. Orch., and remained in that position until 1910; also organized the Hess Quartet in Boston. From 1910–28 he taught at the Hochschule für Musik in Berlin; he remained there until his death.

Hesse, Max, German music publisher; b. Sondershausen, Feb. 18, 1858; d. Leipzig, Nov. 24, 1907. In 1880 he founded under his name a publishing house, with headquarters in Leipzig; in 1915 the firm moved to Berlin. Among its most important publications were the 3rd through 11th editions of Riemann's *Musik Lexikon* (1887–1929) and H.J. Moser's *Musik-Lexikon.* Great devastation was wreaked on the physical materials of the firm by air bombardment during World War II. After the war the firm was re-established in Berlin.

Hessen, Alexander Friedrich, Landgraf von, German musician; b. Copenhagen, Jan. 25, 1863; d. Fronhausen, March 26, 1945. In 1888 he became landgrave of the House of Hessen. Although blind from childhood, he studied music with admirable diligence; took violin lessons in Berlin with Joachim and Bruch; studied composition with Draeseke in Dresden and with Fauré in Paris. By an extraordinary effort he managed to compose a number of works, mostly chamber music and lieder.

Heuberger, Richard (Franz Joseph), Austrian conductor and composer; b. Graz, June 28, 1850; d. Vienna, Oct. 27, 1914. By profession a civil engineer, in 1876 he turned his full attention to music; became choral master of the Vienna Gesangverein and conductor of the Singakademie (1878); in 1902–9, was conductor of the Männergesangverein; was appointed a prof. at the Vienna Cons. (1902). In 1881 he became music critic of the *Wiener Tageblatt,* then of *Neue Freie Presse* (1896–1901); after 1904, of *Neue Musikalische Presse,* and editor of *Musikbuch aus Österreich* (1904–6).

Heugel, Jacques-Léopold, French music publisher; son of **Henry Heugel;** b. La Rochelle, March 1, 1811; d. Paris, Nov. 12, 1883. In 1839 he joined a music publishing establishment founded in Paris by J.A. Meissonnier (1812), and became its director; the name was changed to "Heugel et Cie." After his death his nephew, **Paul Chevalier Heugel** (1861–1931), became its owner. The firm is now managed by **Philippe** and **François Heugel,** successors to their father, **Jacques-Paul Heugel,** who was the grandson of Jacques-Léopold Heugel. The list of publications includes the famous Paris Cons. methods, in all branches of music, and the works of celebrated composers (Bizet, Bruneau, Charpentier, Delibes, Fauré, Franck, Honegger, Ibert, d'Indy, Lalo, Massenet, Milhaud, Offenbach, Poulenc, Ravel, Roussel, Florent Schmitt, Widor, etc.). The firm also publ. the important weekly *Le Ménestrel* (founded in 1833; suspended publication during the Franco-Prussian War, 1870–71, and during World War I; ceased publishing in 1940).

Heward, Leslie, English conductor; b. Littletown, Liversedge, Yorkshire, Dec. 8, 1897; d. Birmingham, May 3, 1943. He was a pupil of his father, an organist; then studied with Stanford and Vaughan Williams at the Royal College of Music in London. He began his conducting career with the British National Opera Co. From 1924–27 he was music director of the South African Broadcasting Corp. and conductor of the Cape Town Symph. Orch. In 1930 he was appointed conductor of the City of Birmingham Orch., a position he held until his death. He was also a composer; he wrote several orch. suites, choruses, and songs, as well as chamber music. A memorial volume was publ. in his honor under the editorship of Eric Blom (London, 1944), and a discography was compiled by William Holmes in *Le Grand Baton* (Dec. 1980, pp. 17–21).

Hewitt, James, American composer, publisher, organist, and violinist; b. Dartmoor, England, June 4,

1770; d. Boston, Aug. 1, 1827. He played in the court orch. in London as a youth. In 1792 he went to America and settled in N.Y., where he was described as one of the "professors of music from the Opera House, Hanover Square, and Professional Concerts under the direction of Haydn, Pleyel, etc., London." On Sept. 21, 1792, he gave a benefit concert with the violinists J. Gehot and B. Bergmann, the flutist W. Young, and a cellist named Phillips, which included Hewitt's *Overture in 9 Movements, expressive of a battle.* Subsequently, Young and Gehot went to Philadelphia, and in 1793 Hewitt, Bergmann, and Phillips gave a series of 6 subscription concerts; at their 5th concert (March 25, 1793) they presented for the first time in America, Haydn's *Passion of Our Saviour* (i.e., *The Seven Last Words*); in 1794 Henri Capron joined Hewitt in promoting his "City Concerts"; meanwhile, Hewitt became the leader of the Old American Co. Orch., and in 1795 gave up his activities in connection with the subscription concerts. In 1798 he bought out the N.Y. branch of Carr's "Musical Repository" and established a publishing business of his own. In 1811 he went to Boston, where he played organ at Trinity Church and was in charge of the music presented at the Federal Street Theatre. In 1816 he returned to N.Y.; also traveled in the South. In N.Y. he was director of the Park Theatre.

WORKS: Ballad operas: *Tammany* (produced in N.Y., 1794, under the auspices of the Tammany Society; only one song, "The Death Song of the Cherokee Indians," survives; reprinted in W.T. Marrocco and H. Gleason, *Music in America*); *The Patriot or Liberty Asserted* (1794); *The Mysterious Marriage* (1799); *Columbus* (1799); *Pizarro, or The Spaniards in Peru* (1800); *Robin Hood* (1800); *The Spanish Castle* (N.Y., Dec. 5, 1800); *The Wild Goose Chase* (1800); overture, *Demophon*; set of 3 piano sonatas; *Battle of Trenton* for Piano (reprinted in the collection *Music from the Days of George Washington*, ed. by Carl Engel and Oliver Strunk); *The 4th of July—A Grand Military Sonata for the Pianoforte*; some other music, much of it extant in the Library of Congress, Washington, D.C.; the N.Y. Public Library; and the Boston Public Library. In 1816 Hewitt publ. a new setting of the *Star-Spangled Banner* to Key's poem, but it never took root. His *Nahant Waltz* is reprinted in J.T. Howard's *A Program of Early American Piano Music* (N.Y., 1931). **John Hill Hewitt** (b. New York, July 12, 1801; d. Baltimore, Oct. 7, 1890), eldest son of James Hewitt, studied at West Point Academy; was a theatrical manager, a newspaper man, and drillmaster of Confederate recruits in the Civil War; wrote poems and plays; about 300 songs (*The Minstrel's Return from the War, All Quiet along the Potomac, Our Native Land, The Mountain Bugle,* etc.); cantatas (*Flora's Festival, The Fairy Bridal, The Revelers,* and *The Musical Enthusiast*); ballad operas (*Rip Van Winkle, The Vivandiere, The Prisoner of Monterey, The Artist's Wife*). His admirers dubbed him the "father of the American ballad," but the ballad form existed in America long before him. He wrote a book of memoirs, *Shadows on the Wall* (1877; reprinted 1971). **James Lang Hewitt** (1807–53), another son of James,

was associated with the publishing firm of J.A. Dickson in Boston (1825); after his father's death he returned to N.Y. and continued his father's publishing business.

Heyer, Wilhelm, German patron of music; b. Cologne, March 30, 1849; d. there, March 20, 1913. A wealthy co-owner of the wholesale paper manufacturing firm Poensgen & Heyer, he was an enthusiastic amateur and was active in the musical affairs of Cologne in advisory capacities. In 1906 he established a historical musical museum in Cologne, in which he assembled more than 2,600 instruments with accessories, about 20,000 autographs of musicians, 3,500 portraits, and a library of books about music, containing many rare editions. Georg Kinsky, curator of the museum from 1909, publ. an illustrated catalogue of the Heyer collections. The museum was dissolved in 1927, and the instruments were acquired by the Musicological Inst. of Leipzig Univ.; the books were dispersed by auction sales.

Hickox, Richard, English conductor; b. Stokenchurch, Buckinghamshire, March 5, 1948. He studied at the Royal Academy of Music in London; was also an organ scholar at Queen's College, Cambridge. He then founded the Richard Hickox Singers and Orch., with which he presented programs ranging from the 14th to 20th centuries. He also served as music director of the City of London Sinfonia and artistic director of the Northern Sinfonia of Newcastle upon Tyne. In 1983 he became associate conductor of the San Diego Symph. Orch. while continuing his various activities in England.

Hidalgo, Juan, one of the earliest and most notable Spanish opera composers; b. c.1600; d. Madrid, March 30, 1685. In 1631 he became a member of the Royal Chapel in Madrid as harpist and also as player of the "clavi-harpa," an instrument he is said to have invented. A document of 1677 attests that he was "of superior skill, and had merited the highest honors from Their Majesties at all times." So great was his reputation that the Duke of Infantado called him "unique in the faculty of music." He composed the opera *Celos aun del aire matan,* to a text by Calderón de la Barca (perf. Madrid, Dec. 5, 1660); the music of Act I (voices and basso continuo) was discovered by J. Subirá and publ. by him in 1933 (this is the longest extant specimen of Spanish operatic music from the 17th century). Hidalgo also wrote music for Calderón's comedies *Ni amor se libra de amor* (1662) and *Hado y divisa de Leónido y de Marfisa* (1680), and for *Los celos hacen estrellas* by Juan Vélez (c.1662). It is very probable that he also composed the opera *La púrpura de la rosa* (1660), text by Calderón. He was likewise known as a composer of sacred and secular songs (some preserved in the National Library, Madrid). Music by Hidalgo is reprinted in Pedrell's *Cancionero* (IV) and *Teatro lírico* (vols. III, IV, and V).

Higgins, Richard C. (Dick), American avantgarde composer; b. Cambridge, England, March 15,

1938. He was taken to America as a child; studied piano in Worcester, Mass.; composition and mycology with John Cage in N.Y. Eventually he moved to California; became active in the mushrooming avant-garde groups; participated in staging "happenings" across the country; joined the ultramodern group Fluxus in 1961; organized the Something Else Press (1964) with the aim of publishing something else. Not averse to academic activities, he joined the faculty of the Calif. Inst. of the Arts in Los Angeles. In his productions he pursues the objective of total involvement, in which music is verbalized in conceptual designs without reification, or expressed in physical action; the ultimate in this direction is achieved by his work *The Thousand Symphonies* (1968), in which the composer shoots machine-gun bullets through MS paper; his Symph. No. 585, shot by a sergeant of the army at the composer's behest, was distributed in holographs in No. 6 of the avant-garde magazine *Source* (1969) under the subtitle "The Creative Use of Police Resources." Other major compositions include: *Graphis,* 146 works for Varying Groups (1958); *A Loud Symphony* (1958); Symph. No. 3½ (duration, 50 seconds; 1959); *In the Context of Shoes,* a happening for Tape, Vacuum Cleaners, Drills, Gardener's Shears, Piano, and Anti-Dancers (1960); *In Memoriam,* 164-part canon (1960); *Musical Processes,* cycle of 5 pieces for Indeterminate Ensembles (1960); *Constellations and Contributions* for Multimedia (1959–60); *Symphoniae sacrae,* conceptual works without a definite realization (1961); *The Peaceable Kingdom,* spoken opera with Bells (1961); *Danger Musics,* a cycle of 43 conceptual pieces (1961–63); *Litany* for 5 Pianos and Tape Recorder (1962–68); *Requiem for Wagner the Criminal Mayor* for Tape Recorder (1962); *Lavender Blue,* opera (1963); *Egg* for Magnetic Tape (1967); *Sophocles I and II,* fatal pieces for Piano (1970). He publ. *foew&ombwhnw,* "a grammar of the mind and a phenomenology of love and a science of the arts as seen by a stalker of the wild mushroom" (N.Y., 1969). His zodiac parameter is Aries, with the sun in Pisces.

Higginson, Henry Lee, founder of the Boston Symph. Orch.; b. New York, Nov. 18, 1834; d. Boston, Nov. 15, 1919. He studied at Boston's Latin School, and attended Harvard in 1851; in 1852–53 was in Europe; in 1856–60 studied voice, piano, composition, and theory in Vienna; in 1868 he became a partner in his father's brokerage firm in Boston (Lee, Higginson & Co.). In 1881, in order to found the Boston Symph. Orch., he assumed the responsibility of providing for about $50,000 yearly of the annual budget of some $115,000, thus clearing the estimated deficit and assuring the organization's successful continuance; the orch., consisting of 67 performers, gave its first concert at the old Music Hall on Oct. 22, 1881; in the summer of 1885, the series of concerts of lighter music, famous as the 'Pops,' were instituted; on Oct. 15, 1900, the Boston Symph. Orch. inaugurated its own permanent home, Symph. Hall; in 1903 the Pension Fund was established, for the benefit of which a special concert is given annually. A firm believer in the superiority of German musicians, Higginson engaged George Henschel as the first conductor of the orch. (1881–84); there followed a line of German conductors: Wilhelm Gericke (1884–89), Artur Nikisch (1889–93), Emil Paur (1893–98), Gericke again (1898–1906), Karl Muck (1906–8), Max Fiedler (1908–12), and again Karl Muck, from 1912 till 1918, when he submitted to arrest to avoid prosecution under the Mann Act as an enemy alien when the U.S. entered World War I. Higginson, distraught over Muck's arrest, resigned his position shortly after and selected a board of directors to control the orch.. He died the following year.

Hignard, (Jean-Louis) Aristide, French composer; b. Nantes, May 20, 1822; d. Vernon, March 20, 1898. He studied with Halévy at the Paris Cons., taking the 2nd Grand Prix de Rome. He was an earnest composer of lofty aims, but brought out operas and other works of secondary importance; his best opera, *Hamlet,* composed in 1868, was to be performed in Paris; unluckily for him, *Hamlet* by Ambroise Thomas was produced that same year, with such spectacular success that Hignard could not compete with it; accordingly, he had to be content with a provincial production in his native city (Nantes, April 21, 1888). His other operas that reached the stage include *Le Visionnaire* (Nantes, 1851); *Le Colin-Maillard* (Paris, 1853); *Les Compagnons de la Marjolaine* (Paris, 1855); *M. de Chimpanzé* (Paris, 1858); *Le Nouveau Pourceaugnac* (Paris, 1860); *L'Auberge des Ardennes* (Paris, 1860); *Les Musiciens de l'orchestre* (Paris, 1861)

Hill, Alfred, Australian composer; b. Melbourne, Nov. 16, 1870; d. Sydney, Oct. 30, 1960. He went to study music in Germany; took violin lessons at the Leipzig Cons., and played violin for 2 years in the Gewandhaus Orch., which was conducted by Brahms, Grieg, and Tchaikovsky, among others. He then went to New Zealand, where he became interested in the study of the aboriginal music of the Maori. From 1916 to 1934 he was a prof. at the Sydney Cons.

WORKS: Operas: *The Weird Flute; Tapu; The Rajah of Shivapore; Giovanni the Sculptor; The Ship of Heaven; Lady Dolly; The Whipping Boy;* cantatas: *Hinemoa* and *Tawhaki;* 12 symphs.; 17 string quartets; other pieces of chamber music; many songs. Several of his works are based on Maori themes. He publ. a manual, *Harmony and Melody* (Sydney, 1927).

Hill, Edward Burlingame, eminent American composer; b. Cambridge, Mass., Sept. 9, 1872; d. Francestown, N.H., July 9, 1960. A member of a distinguished family of educators (his father was a prof. of chemistry at Harvard, and his grandfather, president of Harvard), he pursued regular courses at Harvard Univ.; studied music with J.K. Paine; graduated in 1894 summa cum laude; took lessons in piano with B.J. Lang and A. Whiting, in composition with Chadwick and Bullard; also (for one summer) studied with Widor in Paris. He became greatly interested in the new tonal resources of the impressionist school of composers; wrote articles in the *Boston Evening Transcript,* and other publications dealing with French music; publ. a book, *Modern French Music* (Boston, 1924). In 1908 he joined the faculty of Harvard Univ. as an instructor in music; became associate prof. in 1918; prof. in 1928–37; then James E. Ditson Prof. (1937–40); retired in 1940, and lived mostly in New Hampshire; was a member of the National Inst. of Arts and Letters, American Academy of Arts and Sciences; was a Chevalier of the Légion d'Honneur; lectured at the univs. of Strasbourg and Lyons (1921). In his music, Hill reveals himself as a follower of the French school; clarity of design and elegance of expression are his chief characteristics. His best works are for orch.; but he also composed some fine chamber and choral music.

WORKS: FOR ORCH.: symph. poem, *The Parting of Lancelot and Guinevere* (St. Louis, Dec. 31, 1915); *Stevensoniana Suite No. 1* (N.Y., Jan. 27, 1918); symph. poem, *The Fall of the House of Usher,* after Poe (Boston, Oct. 29, 1920); *Stevensoniana Suite No. 2* (N.Y., March 25, 1923). The following were perf. for the first time by the Boston Symph. Orch: *Waltzes* (Feb. 24, 1922); *Scherzo* for 2 Pianos and Orch. (Dec. 19, 1924); symph. poem, *Lilacs* (his best work in the impressionist manner; Cambridge, March 31, 1927; many subsequent perfs.); Symph. No. 1 (March 30, 1928); *An Ode* (for the 50th anniversary of the Boston Symph. Orch.; Oct. 17, 1930); Symph. No. 2 (Feb. 27, 1931); Concertino for Piano and Orch. (Boston, April 25, 1932); Sinfonietta for String Orch. (Brooklyn, April 3, 1936; also in Boston); Symph. No. 3 (Dec. 3, 1937); Violin Concerto (Nov. 11, 1938); Concertino for String Orch. (April 19, 1940); *Music for English Horn and Orch.* (March 2, 1945); *Prelude* for Orch. (N.Y., March 29, 1953). *Diversion* for Small Ensemble was performed at the Saratoga Festival (Sept. 6, 1947). CHAMBER MUSIC: Flute Sonata (1926); Clarinet Sonata (1927); Sextet for Flute, Oboe, Clarinet, Bassoon, Horn, and Piano (1934); String Quartet (1935); Piano Quartet (1937); Sonata for 2 Clarinets (1938); Quintet for Clarinet and String Quartet (1945); Sonata for Bassoon and Piano (1948); Sonatina for Cello and Piano (1949); Sonatina for Violin and Piano (1951). VOCAL WORKS: *Nuns of the Perpetual Adoration,* cantata for Women's Voices, with Orch. or Piano (1908); *Autumn Twilight* for Soprano and Orch.; *The Wilderness Shall Rejoice,* anthem for Mixed Chorus (1915); 2 pantomimes (with orch. accompaniment): *Jack Frost in Midsummer* (1908) and *Pan and the Star* (1914). FOR PIANO: *Poetical Sketches* (1902); *Country Idyls,* a set of 6 pieces; *Jazz Study* for 2 Pianos (1924).

Hill, Ureli Corelli, American violinist and conductor; b. New York, c.1802; d. Paterson, N.J., Sept. 2, 1875. His father, Uri K. Hill, was a teacher of music in Boston and N.Y., and author of a manual, *Solfeggio Americano, A System of Singing* (N.Y., 1820). An admirer of Corelli, he named his son after him;

the first name (Ureli) is a combination of the father's name, Uri, and a friend's name, Eli. Ureli Corelli Hill played violin in various theaters in N.Y. as a boy; was a violinist in the orch. of Garcia's opera company in 1825; then joined the N.Y. Sacred Musical Society, and conducted it in the first American performance, with orch. accompaniment, of Handel's *Messiah* (1831). In 1835–37 he was in Germany, where he studied a year with Spohr. Returning to N.Y., he became a founder and first president of the N.Y. Phil. (1842–48); then went West in quest of fortune, which, however, failed to materialize. In N.Y. he exhibited a pianoforte of his own invention, in which he used small bell tuning forks in place of strings, so as to secure perfect intonation; the attempt to promote this instrument met with failure. He played the violin in the N.Y. Phil. from 1850 until 1873, when he retired because of age; continued to play engagements in various theater orchs. throughout his life; then moved to Paterson, N.J., where he engaged (unsuccessfully) in real-estate schemes. Depressed on account of constant setbacks in his ventures of promotion in music and in business, he committed suicide by swallowing morphine.

Hill, W.E. & Sons, a firm of violin makers and music dealers in London. It is claimed that "Mr. Hill, the instrument maker," mentioned in Pepys's Diary (1660), was an ancestor of the present owners. The founder of the firm was **Joseph Hill** (1715–84); he was an apprentice to Peter Wamsley; established his business in 1750. He had 5 sons, who were good violinists. **William Ebsworth Hill,** a great-grandson of the founder (b. London, Oct. 20, 1817; d. Hanley, April 2, 1895), adopted the present name of the firm; his instruments took first prize at the expositions in London (1851) and Paris (1867). His sons, **William Henry Hill** (b. London, June 3, 1857; d. there, Jan. 20, 1927), **Arthur Frederick Hill** (b. London, Jan. 24, 1860; d. there, Feb. 5, 1939), and **Alfred Ebsworth Hill** (b. London, Feb. 11, 1862; d. there, April 21, 1940), collaborated in the writing of *Antonio Stradivari, His Life and Work* (London, 1902), a standard work. From material also gathered by them, Lady M.L. Huggins previously wrote *Giovanni Paolo Maggini: His Life and Work* (London, 1892). William Henry, Arthur F., and Alfred Ebsworth Hill are the joint authors of *The Violin-Makers of the Guarneri Family* (with introductory note by E.J. Dent; London, 1931). The Ashmolean Museum at Oxford contains a valuable collection of stringed instruments, including a 1716 Stradivari violin with a bow dated 1694, presented by Arthur F. Hill. The firm continues to exist in the second half of the 20th century, under the direction of the descendants of the founder, **Andrew Hill** (b. London, July 3, 1942) and **David Hill** (b. London, Feb. 28, 1952).

Hillemacher, two brothers, French composers; **Paul** (b. Paris, Nov. 29, 1852; d. Versailles, Aug. 13, 1933) and **Lucien** (b. Paris, June 10, 1860; d. there, June 2, 1909). They both studied at the Paris Cons.; Paul Hillemacher won the 2nd Prix de Rome in 1875, and the first in 1876, with the cantata *Judith;* Lucien Hillemacher obtained the 2nd Prix de Rome in 1879, and the first in 1880. After graduation, they decided to write music in collaboration, and adopted a common signature—P.L. Hillemacher.

WORKS: Together they produced the following stage works: *Saint-Mégrin,* opera (Brussels, March 2, 1886); *Une Aventure d'Arlequin,* opéra-comique (Brussels, March 22, 1888); *Le Régiment qui passe* (Royan, Sept. 11, 1894); *Le Drac,* lyric drama (perf. at Karlsruhe in German as *Der Flutgeist,* Nov. 14, 1896); *Orsola,* lyric drama (Paris, May 21, 1902); *Circé,* lyric drama (Paris, April 17, 1907). Paul Hillemacher, who survived his brother by 24 years, wrote a short "tableau musical," *Fra Angelico,* which was produced at the Paris Opéra-Comique on June 10, 1924. In addition to their operas, the brothers wrote a symph. legend, *Loreley,* which won the prize of the City of Paris (1882); 2 orch. suites, *La Cinquantaine* and *Les Solitudes;* an oratorio, *La Légende de Sainte Geneviève* (1886); songs. They also brought out a biography of Gounod (Paris, 1905).

Hiller, Ferdinand, distinguished German conductor and composer; b. Frankfurt, Oct. 24, 1811; d. Cologne, May 10, 1885. He was a member of a wealthy Jewish family; received a fine education; studied piano with Aloys Schmitt, and appeared in public at the age of 10. In 1825 he went to Weimar to study with Hummel, whom he accompanied to Vienna in 1827, and visited Beethoven. He lived in Paris from 1828–35 and became a friend of Chopin, Liszt, Berlioz, and many other celebrated musicians. When his father died in 1836, he went back to Frankfurt, where he conducted the concerts of the Cäcilien-Verein. He went then to Italy, where he produced an opera, *Romilda* (Milan, 1839). It was unsuccessful, but an oratorio, *Die Zerstörung Jerusalems,* which he wrote in the following year, aroused the interest of Mendelssohn, who invited Hiller to Leipzig, where it was performed by the Gewandhaus Orch. (April 2, 1840). In 1841 he went to Italy, where he studied church music. His subsequent activities consisted mainly of conducting in Germany; he led the Gewandhaus concerts in Leipzig during the 1843–46 season; then conducted in Dresden, where he staged his operas *Der Traum in der Christnacht* (1845) and *Konradin* (Oct. 13, 1847); he was municipal conductor at Düsseldorf (1847–50), then at Cologne. He established the Cologne Cons., and was its first director until his death; also conducted the Lower Rhine Festival, which further enhanced his reputation. His other engagements were at the Italian Opera in Paris (1851–52) and in St. Petersburg, Russia, where he led a group of symph. concerts (1870); he also visited London several times between 1852 and 1872. He never ceased to compose works in large forms, despite their indifferent success; wrote 3 more operas: *Der Advokat* (Cologne, 1854); *Die Katakomben* (Wiesbaden, Feb. 15, 1862); and *Der Deserteur* (Cologne, Feb. 17, 1865); an oratorio, *Saul;* cantatas: *Lorelei; Nal und Damajanti; Israels Siegesgesang;*

Prometheus; Rebecca; Prinz Papagei; a ballad, *Richard Löwenherz,* for Soli, Chorus, and Orch.; 3 symphs.; 3 overtures; 3 piano concertos; 5 string quartets; 5 piano quartets; 5 piano trios; many choral works; more than 100 songs; piano music. In his musical leanings, he was a conservative, and violently attacked Wagner. His classical training and friendly association with Spohr, and especially Mendelssohn, naturally influenced his style. Gifted in many fields of artistic endeavor, he was also a brilliant critic; his writings were publ. in collected form as *Die Musik und das Publikum* (1864); *Beethoven* (1871); *Aus dem Tonleben unserer Zeit* (2 vols.; 1868, 1871); *Musikalisches und Persönliches* (1876); *Briefe von M. Hauptmann an Spohr und andere Komponisten* (1876); *Felix Mendelssohn-Bartholdy, Briefe und Erinnerungen* (1874); *Briefe an eine Ungenannte* (1877); *Künstlerleben* (1880); *Wie hören wir Musik?* (1881); *Goethes musikalisches Leben* (1883); and *Erinnerungsblätter* (1884).

Hiller (Hüller), Johann Adam, significant German composer; b. Wendisch-Ossig, near Görlitz, Dec. 25, 1728; d. Leipzig, June 16, 1804. After completing his primary education in his native town, he went to Dresden, where he studied music with Homilius. In 1751 he entered the Univ. of Leipzig, where he studied law; at the same time he was forced to earn his living by performing at popular concerts as a singer and flute player. In 1754 he became tutor to a nephew of Count Brühl at Dresden, whom he accompanied in 1758 to Leipzig; there he finally settled, and devoted himself to a revival of the Subscription Concerts, known as the Liebhaberkonzerte, in 1763, a concert series originally organized by Johann Doles in 1743; these developed into the famous Gewandhaus concerts, of which he was appointed conductor and led until 1785. In 1771 he founded a singing school, and from 1789 to 1801 was cantor and music director of the Thomasschule as successor of Doles. Hiller was one of the originators of the singspiel; in order to stress the disparity of characters in his operas, he assigned arias in a grand manner to the gentry, while persons of low degree were given simple songs.

WORKS: Singspiels: *Lisuart und Dariolette, oder Die Frage und die Antwort* (Leipzig, Nov. 25, 1766); *Lottchen am Hofe* (Leipzig, April 24, 1767); *Die Liebe auf dem Lande* (Leipzig, May 18, 1768); *Die Jagd* (Weimar, Jan. 29, 1770; his best-known work); *Der Krieg* (Berlin, Aug. 17, 1772); *Die Jubelhochzeit* (Berlin, April 5, 1773); *Das Grab des Mufti, oder Die zwey Geizigen* (Leipzig, Jan. 17, 1779). Several remained unperf. (*Das Orakel, Poltis, Die Friedensfeyer,* etc.). He further wrote many instrumental works, church music, and lieder, in which he excelled; particularly fine are his *Lieder für Kinder,* to words by C.F. Weisse (1769; new ed., 1865); also *Lieder mit Melodien an meinen Canarienvogel* (1759); *Letztes Opfer, in einigen Lieder-Melodien* (1790); setting of Horace's *Carmen ad Aelium Lamian;* 3 string quartets (1796); a Symph.; keyboard compositions. He edited many classical works, and also brought out numerous collections of contemporary pieces by German and Italian composers; publ. *Allgemeines Choral-Melodienbuch für Kirchen und Schulen* (1793). He brought out a weekly publication on music, *Wöchentliche Nachrichten und Anmerkungen, die Musik betreffend* (1766–70; reprinted in 4 vols., Hildesheim, 1970), the first music periodical in Germany to report news regularly. His writings include *Lebensbeschreibungen berühmter Musikgelehrten und Tonkünstler* (1784); *Über Metastasio und seine Werke* (1786); *Anweisung zum musikalisch-richtigen Gesang* (1774); *Anweisung zum musikalisch-zierlichen Gesang* (1780); *Anweisung zum Violinspiel* (1792). His autobiography, *Lebensläufe deutscher Musiker,* was reprinted in an edition by A. Einstein (Leipzig, 1914).

Hillis, Margaret, American conductor; b. Kokomo, Ind., Oct. 1, 1921. She studied piano as a child; also played the tuba and double bass in school bands. An energetic person, she became a junior golf champion and, fantastically, was a civilian flying instructor for the U.S. Navy during World War II. She then enrolled as a music student at Indiana Univ. (B.A., 1947), and studied choral conducting at the Juilliard School of Music in N.Y. (1947–49). Her teacher, Robert Shaw, engaged her as his assistant. She became conductor of the chorus of the American Opera Society in N.Y. in 1952, remaining in this post until 1968. In 1957, at Fritz Reiner's behest, she organized the Chicago Symph. Orch. Chorus, which soon developed into an outstanding choral aggregation. Her various, often synchronous, employments included the following: instructor in choral conducting at the Juilliard School of Music (1951–53); music director of the Kenosha (Wis.) Orch. (1961–68); director of the Cleveland Orch. Chorus (1969–71); resident conductor of the Chicago Civic Orch. (from 1967); director of choral activities at Northwestern Univ. in Chicago (1970–77); music director of the Elgin (Ill.) Symph. Orch. (from 1971). In 1978 she became a visiting professor of conducting at the Indiana Univ. School of Music in Bloomington. In 1981 she was named music director of the Concert Society, Libertyville, Ill.; in 1982 she was appointed director of choral activities for the San Francisco Symph. She had numerous engagements as a guest conductor. On Oct. 31, 1977, in a sort of coup de théâtre, she substituted on short notice for the temporarily incapacitated Sir Georg Solti to conduct a performance of Mahler's monumental Symph. No. 8 at Carnegie Hall in N.Y. She received many awards of merit from various organizations; she is also the recipient of honorary degrees of Mus.D. from Temple Univ. (1967) and Indiana Univ. (1972).

Hilton, John (the Elder), English organist and composer; d. Cambridge, March, 1608. He was appointed organist at Trinity College, Cambridge, on Jan. 26, 1594. He was probably the composer of the anthem *Lord, for Thy tender mercies' sake;* another anthem, *Call to Remembrance* (modern reprint by the Oxford Univ. Press), is also most likely by him. To distinguish him from a younger John Hilton, who may have been his son, he is referred to as John Hilton the Elder.

Hilton, John (the Younger), English composer; b. Oxford, 1599; d. London, March (buried, March 21) 1657. He may have been the son of **John Hilton the Elder**; obtained his degree of Mus.B. from Trinity College at Cambridge (1626); in 1628 he was appointed organist at St. Margaret's, Westminster.
WORKS: *Ayres, or Fa-las for 3 voyces* (London, 1627; reprinted by the Musical Antiquarian Society, XIII, London, 1844); the following works are attributed to him: *Catch that catch can, or, a Choice collection of catches, rounds, and canons for 3 or 4 voyces* (1625); 2 services; *Elegy;* anthems. The British Museum has further MSS. Other compositions are to be found in F. Keel's collection *Elizabethan Love-Songs* (N.Y., 1913), C.K. Scott's *Euterpe* (vol. 12, London, 1910), and E.H. Meyer's *Spielmusik des Barock* (vol. 1, Kassel, 1934). Six pieces for string trio have been arranged by Peter Warlock (London, 1930).

Himmel, Friedrich Heinrich, German opera composer; b. Treuenbrietzen, Brandenburg, Nov. 20, 1765; d. Berlin, June 8, 1814. He studied theology at the Univ. of Halle; at the same time, he cultivated music. He received a stipend from Friedrich Wilhelm II to study with Naumann in Dresden; subsequently he went to Italy, where he acquired skill in stage music. His cantata *Il primo navigatore* was performed in Venice (March 1, 1794), and his opera *La morte di Semiramide,* in Naples (Jan. 12, 1795). He then returned to Berlin and was appointed court conductor. In 1798 he went to St. Petersburg, where he produced his opera *Alessandro* (Jan. 1799). In 1800 he returned from Russia by way of Sweden and Denmark; in Berlin he produced his Italian opera *Vasco di Gama* (Jan. 12, 1801). His subsequent operas, staged in Berlin, were in the nature of singspiels, to German words: *Frohsinn und Schwärmerei* (March 9, 1801); *Fanchon das Leiermädchen* (May 15, 1804; his most successful work; many revivals); *Die Sylphen* (April 14, 1806); etc. His last opera, Der Kobold, was produced in Vienna (May 22, 1813). Many of his songs had great vogue (*An Alexis, Es kann ja nicht immer so bleiben,* etc.). He also composed an oratorio, *Isacco figura del Redentore* (Berlin, 1792); several works of sacred music; a Piano Concerto; Piano Sextet; Piano Quartet; pieces for piano solo.

Hindemith, Paul, eminent German composer, one of the leading masters of 20th-century music; b. Hanau, near Frankfurt, Nov. 16, 1895; d. Frankfurt, Dec. 28, 1963. He began studying violin music at the age of 9; at 14 he entered the Hoch Cons. in Frankfurt, where he studied violin with A. Rebner, and composition with Arnold Mendelssohn and Sekles. His father was killed in World War I, and Hindemith was compelled to rely on his own resources to make a living. He became concertmaster of the orch. of the Frankfurt Opera House (1915–23), and later played the viola in the string quartet of his teacher Rebner; from 1922–29 he was the viola player in the Amar String Quartet; also appeared as soloist on the viola and viola d'amore; later also was engaged as a conductor, mainly in his own works. As a composer, he joined the modern movement and was an active participant in the contemporary music concerts at Donaueschingen, and later in Baden-Baden. In 1927 he was appointed instructor in composition at the Berlin Hochschule für Musik. With the advent of the Hitler regime in 1933, Hindemith began to experience increasing difficulties, both artistically and politically. Although his own ethnic purity was never questioned, he was married to Gertrud Rottenberg, daughter of the Jewish conductor Ludwig Rottenberg, and he stubbornly refused to cease ensemble playing with undeniable Jews. Hitler's propaganda minister, Dr. Goebbels, accused Hindemith of cultural Bolshevism, and his music fell into an official desuetude. Unwilling to compromise with the barbarous regime, Hindemith accepted engagements abroad. Beginning in 1934, he made 3 visits to Ankara at the invitation of the Turkish government, and helped to organize the music curriculum at the Ankara Cons. He made his first American appearance at the Coolidge Festival at the Library of Congress, Washington, D.C., in a performance of his Unaccompanied Viola Sonata (April 10, 1937); after a brief sojourn in Switzerland, he emigrated to the U.S.; was instructor at the Berkshire Music Center in Tanglewood in the summer of 1940; in 1940–53 he was a prof. at Yale Univ.; he was elected a member of the National Inst. of Arts and Letters; and during the academic year 1950–51 he was Charles Eliot Norton Lecturer at Harvard Univ. He became an American citizen in 1946. He conducted concerts in the Netherlands, Italy, and England during the summer of 1947; in 1949, revisited Germany for the first time since the war, and conducted the Berlin Phil. in a program of his own works (Feb. 14, 1949). In 1953 he went to Switzerland; gave courses at the Univ. of Zürich; also conducted orchs. in Germany and Austria. In 1954 he received the prestigious Sibelius Award of $35,000, offered annually to distinguished composers and scientists by a Finnish shipowner. In 1959–61, he conducted guest appearances in the U.S.; in 1963 he visited America for the last time; then went to Italy, Vienna, and finally to Frankfurt, where he died. Hindemith's early music reflects rebellious opposition to all tradition; this is noted in such works as the opera Mörder, Hoffnung der Frauen (op. 12, 1921) and Suite 1922 for Piano (op. 26); at the same time, he cultivated the techniques of constructivism, evident in such a work as his theatrical sketch Hin und Zurück (op. 45a, 1927), in which Krebsgang (retrograde movement) is applied to the action on the stage, so that events are reversed; in a work of a much later period, Ludus Tonalis (1943), the postlude is the upside-down version of the prelude. Along constructive lines is Hindemith's cultivation of so-called Gebrauchsmusik, that is, music for use; he was also an ardent champion of Hausmusik, to be played or sung by amateurs at home; the score of his Frau Musica (as revised in 1944) has an obbligato part for the audience to sing. A neo-Classi-

cal trend is shown in a series of works, entitled Kammermusik, for various instrumental combinations, polyphonically conceived, and Baroque in style. Although Hindemith made free use of atonal melodies, he was never tempted to adopt an integral 12-tone method, which he opposed on esthetic grounds. Having made a thorough study of old music, he artfully assimilated its polyphony in his works; his masterpiece of this genre was the opera Mathis der Maler. An exceptionally prolific composer, Hindemith wrote music of all types for all instrumental combinations, including a series of sonatas for each orch. instrument with piano. Hindemith's style may be described as a synthesis of modern, Romantic, Classical, Baroque, and other styles, a combination saved from the stigma of eclecticism only by Hindemith's superlative mastery of technical means. As a theorist and pedagogue, Hindemith developed a self-consistent method of presentation derived from the acoustical nature of harmonies.

WORKS: OPERAS: Mörder, Hoffnung der Frauen (Murderer, Hope of Women), op. 12, in one act (1919; Stuttgart, June 4, 1921); Das Nusch-Nuschi, op. 20, marionette opera (1920; Stuttgart, June 4, 1921; revised version, Königsberg, Jan. 22, 1931); Sancta Susanna, op. 21, in one act (1921; Frankfurt, March 26, 1922); Cardillac, op. 39, 3 acts (Dresden, Nov. 9, 1926; revised version, Zürich, June 20, 1952); Hin und Zurück, op. 45a, one-act sketch (Baden-Baden, July 15, 1927); Neues vom Tage (News of the Day), in 3 parts (1928–29, revised 1953; Berlin, June 8, 1929; revised version in 2 acts, Naples, April 7, 1954, composer conducting); Mathis der Maler (Matthias the Painter), in 7 scenes (1934–35; Zürich, May 28, 1938; U.S. premiere, Boston, Feb. 17, 1956; Hindemith's best stage work); Orfeo, realization of Monteverdi's opera (1943); Die Harmonie der Welt (The Harmony of the Universe), 5 acts (1950–57; Munich, Aug. 11, 1957, composer conducting); Das lange Weihnachtsmahl (The Long Christmas Dinner; 1960; Mannheim, Dec. 17, 1961; U.S. premiere, N.Y., March 13, 1963); Tuttifäntchen, incidental music for a Christmas fairy tale (1922; Darmstadt, Dec. 13, 1922).

BALLETS: Der Dämon (The Demon), op. 28, a pantomime (1922; Darmstadt, Dec. 1, 1923); Nobilissima Visione, dance legend in 6 scenes (perf. under the title St. Francis by the Ballets Russes de Monte Carlo, in London, July 21, 1938, composer conducting); Theme and Variations: The 4 Temperaments for String Orch. and Piano (1940; N.Y. City Ballet, Nov. 20, 1946; most often perf. as a concert piece); Hérodiade, with recitation, after Mallarmé (produced as Mirror before Me, by the Martha Graham Dance Group, Washington, D.C., Oct. 30, 1944; also as a concert piece, with optional narration).

FOR ORCH.: Cello Concerto, op. 3 (1916); Lustige Sinfonietta, op. 4 (1916); Piano Concerto, op. 29 (1924); Concerto for Orch., with Oboe, Bassoon, and Violin Soli, op. 38 (Duisburg, July 25, 1925); Konzertmusik for Wind Orch., op. 41 (Donaueschingen, July 1926); Konzertmusik for Viola and Orch., op. 48 (Hamburg, March 28, 1930, composer soloist); Konzertmusik for Piano, Brass, and 2 Harps, op. 49

(Chicago, Oct. 12, 1930); *Konzertmusik* for Strings and Brass, op. 50 (for 50th anniversary of the Boston Symph. Orch.; perf. there, April 3, 1931); *Konzertstück* for Trautonium and Strings (1931); *Philharmonisches Konzert,* variations (Berlin, April 14, 1932); *Mathis der Maler,* symph. from the opera (Berlin, March 12, 1934, Furtwängler conducting); *Der Schwanendreher,* concerto for Viola and Small Orch. (Amsterdam, Nov. 14, 1935, composer soloist); *Trauermusik* for Solo Viola or Violin or Cello, and String Orch. (written for a memorial broadcast for King George V, who died on Jan. 20, 1936; London, Jan. 22, 1936, composer soloist); *Symphonic Dances* (London, Dec. 5, 1937); *Nobilissima Visione,* suite from the ballet (Venice, Sept. 13, 1938); Violin Concerto (1939; Amsterdam, March 14, 1940); *Theme and Variations: The 4 Temperaments* for String Orch. and Piano (Boston, Sept. 3, 1940, Foss, soloist; premiered in 1946 as a ballet); Cello Concerto (1940; Boston, Feb. 7, 1941, Piatigorsky, soloist); Symph. in E-flat (1940; Minneapolis, Nov. 21, 1941), Mitropoulos conducting); *Cupid and Psyche,* overture for a ballet (1943; Philadelphia, Oct. 29, 1943); *Symphonic Metamorphosis on Themes of Carl Maria von Weber* (1943; N.Y., Jan. 20, 1944); Piano Concerto (1945; Cleveland, Feb. 27, 1947, Sanromá, soloist); *Symphonia Serena* (1946; Dallas, Feb. 2, 1947, Dorati conducting); Clarinet Concerto (1947; Philadelphia, Dec. 11, 1950, Benny Goodman, soloist); Concerto for 4 Winds, Harp, and Small Orch. (N.Y., May 15, 1949); Concerto for Trumpet, Bassoon, and String Orch., in 2 movements (New Haven, Conn., Nov. 4, 1949; 3rd movement added in 1952); Sinfonietta (1949; Louisville, March 1, 1950, composer conducting); Horn Concerto (1949; Baden-Baden, June 8, 1950, Dennis Brain, soloist); Symph. in B-flat for Concert Band (Washington, April 5, 1951, composer conducting); *Die Harmonie der Welt,* symph. from the opera (1951; Basel, Jan. 24, 1952); *Pittsburgh Symphony* (1958; Pittsburgh, Jan. 30, 1959, composer conducting); Organ Concerto (1962–63; N.Y., April 25, 1963, composer conducting; Heiller, soloist).

CHAMBER MUSIC: *Andante and Scherzo,* op. 1, trio for Clarinet, Horn, and Piano (1914); unnumbered String Quartet in C, op. 2 (1915); Piano Quintet, op. 7 (1917); *3 Stücke* for Cello and Piano, op. 8 (1917); First String Quartet, in F minor, op. 10 (Frankfurt, June 2, 1919); a set of 6 sonatas, opp. 11/1–6, of which 2 are for Violin and Piano (1918); one for Cello and Piano (1919); one for Viola and Piano (1919); one for Solo Viola (1919); one for Solo Violin (1919); 2nd String Quartet, in C, op. 16 (Donaueschingen, Aug. 1, 1921); 3rd String Quartet, op. 22 (Donaueschingen, Nov. 4, 1922); *Kleine Kammermusik,* op. 24/2, for Wind Quintet (1922); a set of 4 sonatas, opp. 25/1–4: for Solo Viola (1922); for Viola d'Amore and Piano (1923); for Solo Cello (1923); for Viola and Piano (1924; publ. 1977); *"Minimax"—Reportorium für Militärmusik,* parody for String Quartet (1923; publ. 1978); Quintet for Clarinet and String Quartet, op. 30 (Salzburg Festival, Aug. 7, 1923); 4th String Quartet, op. 32 (Vienna, Nov. 5, 1923); a set of 4 sonatas, opp. 31/1–4, of which 2 are for Solo Violin (1924); one, a *Canonic Sonatina,* for 2 Flutes (1924);

one for Solo Viola (1924); First Trio for Violin, Viola, and Cello, op. 34 (Salzburg, Aug. 6, 1924); *Rondo* for 3 Guitars (1925); *3 Stücke* for 5 Instruments (1925); 7 numbered pieces titled *Kammermusik: No. 1,* op. 24/1 (Donaueschingen Festival, July 31, 1922); *No. 2,* op. 36/1, for Piano and 12 Instruments (Frankfurt, Oct. 31, 1924); *No. 3,* op. 36/2, for Cello and 10 Instruments (Bochum, April 30, 1925, composer's brother, Rudolf, soloist); *No. 4,* op. 36/3, for Violin and Large Chamber Orch. (Dessau, Sept. 25, 1925); *No. 5,* op. 36/4, for Viola and Large Chamber Orch. (Berlin, Nov. 3, 1927) *No. 6,* op. 46/1, for Viola d'Amore and Chamber Orch. (1927; Cologne, March 29, 1928); *No. 7,* op. 46/2, for Organ and Chamber Ensemble (1927; Frankfurt, Jan. 8, 1928); *8 Pieces* for Solo Flute (1927); Trio for Viola, Heckelphone or Saxophone, and Piano, op. 47 (1928); *2 Canonic Duets* for 2 Violins (1929); *14 Easy Duets* for 2 Violins (1931); 2nd Trio for Violin, Viola, and Cello (Antwerp, March 17, 1933); *Konzertstück* for 2 Saxophones (1933); *Duet* for Viola and Cello (1934); Violin Sonata in E (1935); Flute Sonata (1936); Sonata for Solo Viola (1937); *Meditation* for Violin or Viola or Cello, and Piano (1938); Quartet for Clarinet, Violin, Cello, and Piano (1938); Oboe Sonata (1938); Bassoon Sonata (1938; transcribed for Bass Clarinet in 1959 for Josef Horák); Clarinet Sonata (1939); Horn Sonata (1939); Trumpet Sonata (1939); Solo Harp Sonata (1939); Violin Sonata in C (1939); Viola Sonata in C (1939); English Horn Sonata (1941); Trombone Sonata (1941); *A Frog He Went a-Courting,* variations for Cello and Piano (1941); *Echo* for Flute and Piano (1942); 5th String Quartet, in E-flat (Washington, Nov. 7, 1943); Sonata for Saxophone (or Alto Horn or French Horn) and Piano (1943); 6th String Quartet (Washington, March 21, 1946); Cello Sonata (1948); Septet for Winds (1948); Double-bass Sonata (1949); Sonata for 4 Horns (1952); Tuba Sonata (1955); Octet for Clarinet, Bassoon, Horn, and String Quintet (Berlin, Sept. 23, 1958).

VOCAL WORKS: *3 Songs* for Soprano and Orch., op. 9 (1917); *Melancholie* for Contralto and String Quartet, op. 13 (1918); *Des Todes Tod,* op. 23/1, 3 songs for Female Voice, 2 Violas, and 2 Cellos (1922); *Die junge Magd,* op. 23/2, 6 poems for Contralto, Flute, Clarinet, and String Quartet (1922); *Lieder nach alten Texten* for Mixed Chorus a cappella, op. 33 (1923); *Die Serenaden,* op. 35, little cantata on romantic poems, for Soprano, Oboe, Viola, and Cello (1925); *Der Lindenbergflug* for Soloists and Orch. (1929); *Das Unaufhörliche,* oratorio (Berlin, Nov. 21, 1931); *5 Songs on Old Texts* for Mixed Chorus a cappella (c.1938; includes revisions of some songs of op. 33); *6 Chansons,* after Rilke, for Mixed Chorus a cappella (1939); *3 Choruses* for Male Chorus a cappella (1939); *The Demon of the Gibbet* for Male Chorus a cappella (1939); *When Lilacs Last in the Dooryard Bloom'd,* an American requiem after Walt Whitman, for Mezzo-soprano, Baritone, Chorus, and Orch. (N.Y., May 14, 1946); *Apparebit Repentina Dies* for Chorus and Brass (Harvard Symposium, Cambridge, Mass., May 2, 1947); *Das Marienleben,* after Rilke, for Soprano and Orch. (1938–48; revised, shortened, and orchestrated version of songs originally for Voice and

Piano, 1923); *Ite, angeli veloces,* cantata trilogy: *Chant de triomphe du roi David, Custos quid de nocte,* and *Cantique de l'espérance* (1953–55; first complete perf., Wuppertal, June 4, 1955); *12 Madrigals* for 5-part Mixed Chorus a cappella (1958); *Der Mainzer Umzug* for Soprano, Tenor, Baritone, Mixed Chorus, and Orch.; (Mainz, June 23, 1962); Mass for Mixed Chorus a cappella (Vienna, Nov. 12, 1963; his last work).

For voice and piano: *3 Hymnen,* op. 14, after Whitman (1919); *8 Songs* for Soprano, op. 18 (1920); *Das Marienleben,* op. 27, a cycle of songs after Rilke (Donaueschingen, June 17, 1923; revised radically and perf. in Hannover, Nov. 3, 1948); *6 Lieder* for Tenor and Piano (1933–35); *9 English Songs* (1942–44); *13 Motets* (1941–60).

For piano: *7 Waltzes,* op. 6, for 4-hands (1916); *In einer Nacht,* op. 15, a set of 15 pieces (1920); Sonata, op. 17 (1917); *Tanzstücke,* op. 19 (1922); *Suite "1922,"* op. 26 (1922); *Klaviermusik,* op. 37, incorporating *Übung in drei Stücken,* op. 37/1 (1925) and *Reihe kleiner Stücke,* op. 37/2 (1927); 3 numbered sonatas (1936); Sonata for 4-hands (1938); Sonata for 2 Pianos (1942); *Ludus Tonalis,* studies (Chicago, Feb. 15, 1943).

Gebrauchsmusik: Music for Mechanical Instruments, op. 40: Toccata for Player Piano, and Music for Mechanical Organ (both 1926–27); Music for the film *Felix the Cat* for Mechanical Organ, op. 42 (1927); *Spielmusik (Music to Play)* for Strings, Flutes, and Oboes, op. 43/1 (1927); *Lieder für Singkreise (Songs for Singing Groups)* for a cappella Voices, op. 43/2 (1927); *Schulwerk für Instrumental-Zusammenspiel (Educational Music for Instrumental Ensembles),* op. 44, including the often-performed *5 Pieces* for String Orch., op. 44/4 (1927); *Sing- und Spielmusiken für Liebhaber und Musikfreunde (Music to Sing and Play for Amateurs and Music Lovers),* including: *Frau Musica* for Soli, Chorus, and String Orch., op. 45/1 (1928; revised as *In Praise of Music,* 1943), *8 Canons* for 2 Voices and Instruments, op. 45/2 (1928), *Ein Jäger aus Kurpfalz (The Hunter of Kurpfalz),* for Strings and Winds, op. 45/3 (1928), *Kleine Klaviermusik,* op. 45/4 (1929), and *Martinslied* for Unison Chorus and 3 Instruments, op. 45/5 (1929); *Lehrstück (Lesson Piece),* after Brecht, for Male Soli, Narrator, Chorus, Orch., Dance Group, Clowns, and Community Singing (Baden-Baden, July 28, 1929); *Wir bauen eine Stadt (Let's Build a Town),* play for Children's Soli and Chorus, and Instruments (Berlin, June 21, 1930); *Plöner Musiktag (Music for a Daylong Festival in Plön),* in 4 sections: *Morgenmusik (Morning Music)* for Brass Quintet, *Tafelmusik (Table Music)* for Strings and Brass, *Kantate* for Soli, Children's Chorus, Narrator, Strings, Winds, and Percussion, and *Abendkonzert (Evening Concert),* 6 individual pieces for Chamber and Orch. Grouping (all 1932; Plön, June 1932); *Wer sich die Musik erkiest (The One Who Chooses Music)* for Voices and Instruments (1952). The Auftrag der Hindemith-Stiftung is issuing a Collected Works edition (begun in 1975). Thematic indexes have been compiled by Kurt Stone (for the Associated Music Publishers, N.Y., 1954; verified by the composer) and H. Rösner, *Paul Hindemith—Katalog seiner Werke, Diskographie, Bibliographie, Einführung in das Schaffen* (Frankfurt am Main, 1970).

WRITINGS: *Unterweisung im Tonsatz* (2 vols., 1937, 1939; in Eng. as *The Craft of Musical Composition,* N.Y., 1941; revised, 1945); *A Concentrated Course in Traditional Harmony* (2 vols., N.Y., 1943, 1953); *Elementary Training for Musicians* (N.Y., 1946); *J.S. Bach: Heritage and Obligation* (New Haven, Conn., 1952; German ed., *J.S. Bach: Ein verpflichtendes Erbe,* Wiesbaden, 1953); *A Composer's World: Horizons and Limitations* (Cambridge, Mass., 1952).

Hines, Earl (Kenneth) "Fatha," black American jazz pianist; b. Duquesne, Pa., Dec. 28, 1905; d. Oakland, Calif., April 22, 1983. His father was a professional trumpet player and his mother played piano and organ. He took piano lessons as a child, but became interested mainly in jazz piano. He played with big bands as a young man, and in 1927 joined a quintet led by Louis Armstrong in Chicago. He began recording with Armstrong and under his influence evolved a special type of "trumpet piano style" characterized by sharp accents, octave tremolos in the treble, and insistently repeated melodic notes. In 1928 he organized his own big band in Chicago, and toured with it in the U.S., including the Southern states; his was one of the first black big bands to play in the South; its theme song, *Deep Forest,* became popular. A radio announcer used to introduce him as "Fatha Hines coming through deep forest with his children," and the nickname "Fatha" stuck. After a hiatus of several years, Hines reappeared on the jazz horizon as a solo pianist and made a hit wherever he appeared. In 1957 he toured Europe; played in Berlin in 1965 and in Russia in 1966; he also played in Japan. During his last years he made his residence in San Francisco, where he played his last engagement just a week before his death. He was described by jazz critics as "the last of the great masters."

Hines, Jerome, American singer; b. Hollywood, Calif., Nov. 8, 1921. His real name was **Heinz,** but he changed it to its Anglo-Saxon homonym when he began to sing professionally. He studied mathematics and chemistry at the Univ. of Calif. in Los Angeles, graduating in 1943; at the same time took vocal lessons with Gennaro Curci in Los Angeles, and later with Samuel Margolis in N.Y. After a few performances in light opera, he sang the part of Biterolf in *Tannhäuser* with the San Francisco Opera, on Oct. 24, 1941. In 1944 he sang Méphistophélès in *Faust* with the New Orleans Opera Co. He was not drafted into the U.S. Army during the war because of his excessive height (6 feet 6 inches), but instead was employed as a chemist in war-related work. On Nov. 21, 1946, he made his debut at the Metropolitan Opera in N.Y. in a minor role, as the Sergeant in *Boris Godunov,* and on Feb. 18, 1954, sang its title role. He made numerous guest appearances with European opera houses, the Edinburgh Festival in

1953, at La Scala in Milan in 1958, and at the Bayreuth Festival in 1958. On Sept. 23, 1962, he made history when he sang the role of Boris Godunov, in Russian, at the Bolshoi Theater in Moscow, with the Soviet Premier, Khrushchev, in attendance. He repeated his feat a month later at the Bolshoi Theater, and also performed in Leningrad, Kiev, and Tiflis. On his return to the U.S., he sang the part of Boris Godunov in the original Mussorgsky version with the Metropolitan Opera in N.Y. on Oct. 14, 1975. His other roles included Don Giovanni, Don Basilio, Sarastro, Des Grieux, Wotan, and Rodolfo. His 30th anniversary with the Metropolitan was observed in a special ceremony on Jan. 8, 1976. Altogether, he had sung 454 times with the company. He publ. an autobiography, *This Is My Story, This My Song* (Westwood, N.J., 1968), and a book, *Great Singers on Great Singing* (London, 1983). He also composed an opera, *I Am the Way*, based on the life of Christ.

Hinrichs, Gustav, German-American conductor; b. Ludwigslust, Germany, Dec. 10, 1850; d. Mountain Lake, N.J., March 26, 1942. He studied violin and piano with his father; composition with E. Marxsen in Hamburg. In 1870 he settled in America; was in San Francisco until 1885; then went to Philadelphia, where he organized his own opera company; gave the American premieres of *Cavalleria rusticana* (Philadelphia, Sept. 9, 1891) and *Pagliacci* (N.Y., June 15, 1893). In 1903–4, he conducted at the Metropolitan Opera House; then retired. He was the composer of an opera, *Onti-Ora* (Indian name of the Catskill Mountains; Philadelphia, July 28, 1890).

Hinrichsen, Max, German music publisher; b. Leipzig, July 6, 1901; d. London, Dec. 17, 1965. He worked with his father, **Heinrich Hinrichsen** (1868–1942), at Peters Edition, Leipzig, until 1937, when he went to London, becoming a British subject in 1947. There he established Hinrichsen Edition, Ltd.; in 1944 he began publishing *Hinrichsen's Musical Year Book,* which appeared irregularly until 1961.

Hinrichsen, Walter, music publisher; brother of **Max Hinrichsen;** b. Leipzig, Sept. 23, 1907; d. New York, July 21, 1969. He studied at the Univ. of Leipzig; then was connected with Peters Edition there, headed by his father, **Heinrich Hinrichsen** (1868–1942; see **Peters, Carl Friedrich**). In 1936 Walter Hinrichsen came to America; was in the U.S. Army (1942–45); after the war became a government employee in the U.S. Zone in Germany (1945–47). He then returned to America and in 1948 opened the new offices of the C.F. Peters Corp. in N.Y. After his death the firm has continued with his widow, Evelyn Hinrichsen, as president.

Hinshaw, William Wade, American baritone; b. Union, Iowa, Nov. 3, 1867; d. Washington, D.C., Nov. 27, 1947. He studied voice with L.G. Gottschalk in Chicago; was choir director at various churches; made his operatic debut as Méphistophélès in Gounod's *Faust* with the H.W. Savage Co. (St. Louis, Nov. 6, 1899); in 1903, opened the Hinshaw School of Opera in Chicago, which was later incorporated into the Chicago Cons.; Hinshaw became president of the combined institutions (1903–7). In 1909 he organized the International Grand Opera Co. of Chicago. He made his debut at the Metropolitan Opera House, N.Y., on Nov. 16, 1910, remaining on its roster until 1913; in 1912 he sang in the Wagner festival at Graz, and in 1914, in the special *Ring* festival at Berlin; then returned to America. In 1916 he offered a prize of $1,000 for the best one-act opera by an American composer (awarded to Hadley for his opera *Bianca*). From 1920 to 1926 he produced Mozart's operas in Eng. with his own company in the U.S., Canada, and Cuba (about 800 perfs. in all). He then settled in Washington, D.C.

Hinton, Arthur, English composer; b. Beckenham, Nov. 20, 1869; d. Rottingdean, Aug. 11, 1941. He studied at the Royal Academy of Music in London; then taught violin there; subsequently went to Munich for further study with Rheinberger. There he composed a Symph., which he conducted at one of the concerts of the Munich Cons.; traveled in Italy; returned to London in 1896. He continued to compose; his 2nd Symph. was performed in London in 1903. He married the pianist **Katharine Goodson,** who gave many performances of his piano works, including a concerto. He wrote the children's operettas *The Disagreeable Princess* and *St. Elizabeth's Rose;* also a number of songs.

Hirsch, Paul Adolf, German bibliographer and collector; b. Frankfurt, Feb. 24, 1881; d. Cambridge, England, Nov. 23, 1951. He began collecting rare musical editions as a young man, and publ. successive catalogues of his rapidly growing library. In 1936 he left Germany and was able to transport his entire collection to England; it was purchased by the British Museum in 1946; the total number of items was about 20,000. In 1922 he began the publication of new editions (several in facsimile, and with commentaries) of rare works; these are Francesco Caza, *Tractato vulgare de canto figurato* (Milan, 1492; ed. J. Wolf, 1922); Giovanni Luca Conforto, *Breve et facile maniera d'essercitarsi a far passaggi* (Rome, 1593; ed. J. Wolf, 1922); *Neujahrsgrüsse Seelen; Eine Sammlung von Liedern mit Melodien und Bilderschmuck aus den Jahren 1770–1800* (ed. M. Friedlaender, 1922); Georg Philipp Telemann, *Fantaisies pour le clavessin: 3 douzaines* (ed. Max Seiffert, 1923); Hercole Bottrigari, *Il desiderio, overo de' concerti di varii strumenti musicali* (Venice, 1594; ed. Kathi Meyer, 1924); Karl Friedrich Zelter, *Fünfzehn ausgewählte Lieder* (ed. Moritz Bauer, 1924); Giovanni Spataro, *Dilucide et probatissime demonstratione* (Bologna, 1521; ed. J. Wolf, 1925); Nicolaus Listenius, *Musica, ab authore denuo recognita* (Nuremberg, 1549; ed. Georg Schünemann, 1927); Carl Philipp Emanuel Bach, *Zwölf zwei- und dreistimmige kleine Stücke für die Flöte oder Violine und das Klavier* (1770; ed. Richard Hohenemser, 1928); Christoph Schultze, *Lukas-Passion* (Leipzig, 1653; ed. Peter Epstein, 1930); Martin Luther, *Deutsche Messe* (1526; ed. J. Wolf, 1934);

Wolfgang Amadeus Mozart, *The Ten Celebrated String Quartets*, first authentic ed. in score (ed. Alfred Einstein, 1945).

Hitchcock, H(ugh) Wiley, eminent American musicologist and editor; b. Detroit, Sept. 28, 1923. He was educated at Dartmouth College (A.B., 1943) and the Univ. of Michigan (M.Mus., 1948; Ph.D., 1954, with the dissertation *The Latin Oratorios of Marc-Antoine Charpentier*); taught music at the Univ. of Michigan (1947–61); then was prof. of music at Hunter College (1961–71); in 1971 became prof. of music at Brooklyn College (named Distinguished Prof. of Music in 1980), where he also served as director of the Inst. for Studies in American Music. A recipient of numerous grants, including Fulbright senior research fellowships in 1954–55 (Italy) and 1968–69 (France), and a Guggenheim fellowship in 1968–69, he also served on the boards of the Music Library Association (1965–72) and the American Musicological Society (1966–78, in various capacities), and as president of the Charles Ives Society (since 1973); was also editor of The Prentice-Hall History of Music Series (Englewood Cliffs, N.J., 1965—), *Earlier American Music* (reprints of music; N.Y., 1972), and Recent Researches in American Music (Madison, Wis., 1976—). He was a member of the executive committee and area editor for the Americas of *The New Grove Dictionary of Music and Musicians* (1969–79; publ. in London, 1980); was co-editor, with Stanley Sadie, of *The New Grove Dictionary of Music in the United States* (scheduled for publ. in 1984). His research interests are wide and meritorious, covering French Baroque and American music; his editorial contributions include the works of Caccini, Leonardo Leo, Charpentier, and Lully.
WRITINGS: *Music in the United States: A Historical Introduction* (Englewood Cliffs, N.J., 1969; 2nd ed., revised and enlarged, 1974); *Charles Ives Centennial Festival-Conference 1974* (program book; N.Y., 1974); *Ives* (London, 1977); co-editor, with V. Perlis, of *An Ives Celebration: Papers and Panels of the Charles Ives Centennial Festival-Conference* (Urbana, Ill., 1977); *The Phonograph and Our Musical Life* (Brooklyn, 1980); co-author, with L. Inserra, of *The Music of Ainsworth's Psalter (1612)* (Brooklyn, 1981); *The Works of Marc-Antoine Charpentier: A Catalogue Raisonné* (Paris, 1982).

Hoboken, Anthony van, eminent Dutch music bibliographer; b. Rotterdam, March 23, 1887; d. Zürich, Nov. 1, 1983. He studied with Iwan Knorr at the Hoch Cons. in Frankfurt and with Schenker in Vienna. In 1927 he founded the Archive for Photographs of Musical Manuscripts in the National Library at Vienna; he then began to collect first editions of classical works; his Haydn collection is particularly rich. He publ. the complete thematic catalogue of Haydn's work in 2 vols. (1957, 1971). He also contributed a number of articles on Haydn to music journals. A Festschrift in his honor was publ. on his 75th birthday, edited by J. Schmidt-Görg (Mainz, 1962). His archive of early music publications was purchased by the Austrian government in 1974, and officially opened at the Austrian National Library in Vienna on Hoboken's 90th birthday, March 23, 1977, as a tribute to his signal accomplishments in musical bibliography; although frail, Hoboken was present on this occasion.

Hoddinott, Alun, Welsh composer; b. Bargoed, Aug. 11, 1929. He studied music at the Univ. College of South Wales in Cardiff; also took private instruction with Arthur Benjamin. In 1951 he was appointed lecturer in music at Cardiff College of Music and Drama; in 1959 joined the music faculty of the Univ. College of South Wales. He also serves as organizer of the annual Cardiff Music Festival. His music follows the judicious line of humanitarian modernism, without blundering into musical chaos.
WORKS: 5 OPERAS: *The Beach of Falesá* (Cardiff, March 26, 1974); *Murder, the Magician* (Welsh Television, Feb. 11, 1976); *What the Old Man Does Is Always Right* (1975); *The Rajah's Diamond* (1979); *The Trumpet Major* (Manchester, England, April 1, 1981). FOR ORCH.: Symph. No. 1 (National Eisteddfod of Wales; Pwllheli, Aug. 5, 1955, composer conducting); Symph. No. 2 (Cheltenham Festival, July 11, 1962); Symph. No. 3 (Manchester, Dec. 5, 1968); Symph. No. 4 (Manchester, Dec. 4, 1969); Symph. No. 5 (London, March 6, 1973); Concerto No. 1 for Piano, Wind Instruments, and Percussion (London, Feb. 22, 1960); Concerto No. 2 for Piano and Orch. (National Eisteddfod of Wales, Cardiff, Aug. 5, 1969, composer conducting); Concertino for Viola and Chamber Orch. (Llandaff Festival, June 25, 1958); Harp Concerto (Cheltenham Festival, July 16, 1958); Concerto for Clarinet and String Orch. (Cheltenham Festival, July 16, 1954); Concerto for Organ and Orch. (Llandaff Festival, June 19, 1967); Horn Concerto (Llandaff Festival, June 3, 1969); Concertino for Viola and Small Orch. (Llandaff Festival, June 25, 1958); Violin Concerto (Birmingham, March 30, 1961); Concertino for Trumpet, Horn, and Orch. (Llangefni, April 8, 1971); Concerto Grosso No. 1 (Caerphilly Festival, June 11, 1965); Concerto Grosso No. 2 (1966); *Variants* for Orch. (London, Nov. 2, 1966); *Fioriture* (London, Nov. 24, 1968); Divertimento for Orch. (Llandaff, Nov. 14, 1969); *4 Welsh Dances* (London, June 28, 1958); *Investiture Dances* (commissioned to celebrate the investiture of the Prince of Wales; London, June 22, 1969); *Night Music* (Aberystwyth, Jan. 30, 1967); *Sinfonia* for String Orch. (Bromsgrove Festival, April 19, 1964); *Sinfonietta No. 1* (Cardiff Festival, 1968); *Sinfonietta No. 2* (Cheltenham Festival, July 4, 1969); *Sinfonietta No. 3* (Swansea, March 10, 1970); *Sinfonietta No. 4* (Wales, July 30, 1971); *The Sun, the Great Luminary of the Universe* (Swansea, Oct. 8, 1970); *Sinfonia Fidei* for Soprano, Tenor, Chorus, and Orch. (1977); *The Heaventree of Stars* for Violin and Orch. (1980). CHAMBER MUSIC: 4 violin sonatas (1969, 1970, 1971, 1976); Cello Sonata (1970); Clarinet Sonata (1967); Sonata for Harp (1964); Horn Sonata (1971); Divertimenti for 8 Instruments (1968); Divertimento for Oboe, Clarinet, Horn, and Bassoon (1963); Piano Quintet (1972); Septet for

Wind Instruments, Strings, and Piano (1956); Sextet for Flute, Clarinet, Bassoon, Violin, Viola, and Cello (1960); String Quartet (1966); Variations for Flute, Clarinet, Harp, and String Quartet (1962); 6 piano sonatas (1959–72); *Ritornelli* for Trombone, Wind Instruments, and Percussion (1974); *A Contemplation Upon Flowers* for Soprano and Orch. (1976); organ music; choruses; songs.

Hodges, Edward, English organist and composer; b. Bristol, July 20, 1796; d. Clifton, England, Sept. 1, 1867. He was an organist at Bristol; received his Mus.Doc. at Cambridge (1825); in 1838, went to America, where he became an organist in Toronto and then in N.Y. (1839). He returned to England in 1863. He publ. *An Essay on the Cultivation of Church Music* (N.Y., 1841). The Library of Congress acquired the bulk of his music library (743 vols.), including his own works in MS, in 1919. His daughter, **Faustina Hasse Hodges** (b. Malmesbury, Aug. 7, 1823; d. Philadelphia, Feb. 4, 1895), was also an organist in the U.S. She composed songs and instrumental pieces and publ. a biography of her father (N.Y., 1896). His son, **Rev. John Sebastian Bach Hodges** (b. Bristol, 1830: d. Baltimore, May 1, 1915), an accomplished organist, composed many anthems and services.

Höeberg, Georg, Danish composer, conductor, and violinist; b. Copenhagen, Dec. 27, 1872; d. Vedboek, Aug. 3, 1950. He studied at the Cons. of Copenhagen, and later in Berlin; taught at the Copenhagen Cons. in 1900–14; in 1914–30, was conductor at the Royal Opera; in 1915–49 he appeared as a guest conductor in Scandinavia and Germany. He wrote the opera *Bryllup i Katakomberne* (*The Wedding in the Catacombs*; Copenhagen, March 6, 1909); the ballet *The Paris Cathedral* (Copenhagen, Oct. 25, 1912); several pieces for violin and orch.; a Symph.; choral works; and songs.

Høffding, Finn, Danish composer; b. Copenhagen, March 10, 1899. He studied violin with K. Sandby (1911–21), organ with R.S. Rung-Keller (1919–21), composition and harmony with Knud Jeppesen (1918–21), and music history with Thomas Laub (1920–23); then went to Vienna, where he took lessons with Joseph Marx (1921–22). He subsequently was for 38 years on the faculty of the Royal Academy of Music in Copenhagen (1931–69), during the last 15 of which he acted as director there. His style of composition is influenced by linear counterpoint as practiced by Carl Nielsen.

Hoffman, Grace, American mezzo-soprano; b. Cleveland, Jan. 14, 1925. She was educated at Western Reserve Univ. in Cleveland; then studied voice with Friedrich Schorr in N.Y. and Mario Basiola in Milan; after appearances in the U.S., she went to Europe, where she sang in Florence and Zürich; in 1955 became a member of the Württemberg State Theater in Stuttgart. On March 27, 1958, she made her Metropolitan Opera debut in N.Y. as Brangäne in *Tristan und Isolde.* She made many appearances

at La Scala in Milan, Covent Garden in London, Bayreuth, and the Vienna State Opera. In 1978 she became a prof. of voice at the Hochschule für Musik in Stuttgart. She was noted for her performances of the music of Wagner and Verdi, particularly for her roles of Brangäne, Kundry, and Eboli; also sang widely in concerts.

Hoffman, Richard, pianist and composer; b. Manchester, England, May 24, 1831; d. Mt. Kisco, N.Y., Aug. 17, 1909. He received his first instruction from his father and then studied with Leopold de Meyer, Pleyel, Moscheles, Rubinstein, Döhler, and Liszt. He spent most of his life in the U.S. and was a major figure in American musical life, but chose to retain his British citizenship. (Perhaps this was due to his having the same birthdate as Queen Victoria; on their joint birthday he would place a British flag on the mantel and play *God Save the Queen* on the piano.) He came to N.Y. in 1847; traveled with Jenny Lind on her American tour (1850–52) as joint artist; appeared often with Louis Moreau Gottschalk for duo–piano recitals. He was a prolific composer, mainly of salon music for piano; wrote about 100 opus numbers; also songs, anthems, etc. He publ. *Some Musical Recollections of Fifty Years* (with biographical sketch by his wife; posthumous, 1910).

Hoffmann, Ernst Theodor Amadeus (his third Christian name was Wilhelm, but he replaced it by Amadeus, from love of Mozart), famous German writer, who was also a composer; b. Königsberg, Jan. 24, 1776; d. Berlin, June 25, 1822. He was a student of law, and served as assessor at Poznan; also studied music with the organist Podbielski. He acquired considerable proficiency in music; served as music director at the theater in Bamberg; then conducted opera performances in Leipzig and Dresden (1813–14). In 1814 he settled in Berlin, where he remained. He used the pen name of **Kapellmeister Johannes Kreisler** (subsequently made famous in Schumann's *Kreisleriana*); his series of articles in the *Allgemeine Musikalische Zeitung* under that name were reprinted as *Phantasiestücke in Callot's Manier* (1814). As a writer of fantastic tales, he made a profound impression on his period, and influenced the entire Romantic school of literature; indirectly, he was also a formative factor in the evolution of the German school of composition. His own compositions are passable from the technical viewpoint, but strangely enough, for a man of his imaginative power, they lack the inventiveness that characterizes his literary productions. If his music is occasionally performed, it is only as a curiosity.

Hoffmeister, Franz Anton, German composer and publisher; b. Rothenburg, May 12, 1754; d. Vienna, Feb. 9, 1812. He went to Vienna as a law student, but became greatly interested in music, and in 1783 established his publishing firm, of historic significance owing to its publications of Mozart and Beethoven. In 1800 he went to Leipzig, where he organized (with Kühnel) a "Bureau de Musique," which eventually became incorporated into the celebrated firm of C.F. Peters. In 1805 he returned to Vienna, where he devoted himself mostly to composition. Amazingly prolific, he composed 9 operas, 66 symphs. and overtures, 42 string quartets, 5 piano quartets, 11 piano trios, 18 string trios, and 12 piano sonatas; in addition to these he wrote a very great number of compositions for flute with various instruments. Hoffmeister's craftsmanship was of sufficient excellence to lead to confusion of his music with Haydn's. Regarding this, see E.F. Schmid, "F.A. Hoffmeister und die *Göttweiger Sonaten*," *Zeitschrift für Musik* (1937), and A. Weinmann, *Die Wiener Verlagswerke von Franz Anton Hoffmeister* (Vienna, 1969).

Hofhaimer (Hofheimer), Paul, celebrated organist and composer; b. Radstadt, Jan. 25, 1459; d. Salzburg, 1537. Cuspinianus and Luscinius both wrote of him as an unrivaled organist and lutenist. He was greatly appreciated at the various courts where he served. He was court organist to the Archduke Sigismund of Tyrol from 1480, residing at Innsbruck, and from 1490, at the court of the Emperor Maximilian I there. He was ennobled by the Emperor in 1515, when he played in St. Stephen's Cathedral in Vienna; he was also made Knight of the Golden Spur by King Ladislas of Hungary. Little of his organ music survives; some is preserved in the Berlin State Library. Extant works are *Harmoniae poeticae* (odes of Horace set for 4 Voices; 35 by Hofhaimer and 9 by Senfl; Nuremberg, 1539; republ. by Achtleitner, 1868); 4-part German songs in contemporary collections (5 in Oeglin's *Liederbuch*, 1512; others in Forster's *Liederbuch*, 1539); etc.

Hofmann, Casimir, Polish pianist; father of **Josef Hofmann**; b. Cracow, 1842; d. Berlin, July 6, 1911. He studied at the Vienna Cons.; then conducted opera in Cracow. In 1878 he moved to Warsaw, where he taught and conducted. After the spectacular success of his young son, he followed him on his extended tours throughout Europe and America. From 1886, he lived mainly in Berlin. He wrote numerous works in various genres.

Hofmann, Heinrich (Karl Johann), German pianist and composer; b. Berlin, Jan. 13, 1842; d. Gross-Tabarz, Thuringia, July 16, 1902. He studied in Berlin with Grell, Dehn, and Wüerst. He became a concert pianist, then turned to composition. Exceptionally productive, he wrote a great deal of operatic, symph., and chamber music; choral works; and solo piano pieces; all of which were publ. and frequently performed. His popularity declined precipitously toward the end of his life; his music vanished from concert programs after his death. His style reflected Wagnerian procedures, particularly in heroic moods; he possessed complete mastery of technique, but his music lacked originality or distinction.
   WORKS: Stage works: comic opera, *Cartouche* (Berlin, 1869); heroic drama, *Armin* (Dresden, Oct. 14, 1877); pastoral opera, *Aennchen von Tharau*

(Hamburg, Nov. 6, 1878); historic opera, *Wilhelm von Oranien* (1882); comic opera, *Donna Diana* (Berlin, Nov. 15, 1886). His *Frithjof Symphony* (1874) was enormously popular, having had 43 perfs. during the 1874–75 season in German cities alone; it was also perf. in England and America. Similarly successful was his orchestral *Hungarian Suite* (1873). He also wrote a great number of choral works and songs; characteristic piano pieces; chamber music.

Hofmann, Josef, celebrated pianist; b. Podgorze, near Cracow, Jan. 20, 1876; d. Los Angeles, Feb. 16, 1957. He was the son of the pianist **Casimir Hofmann;** his mother was a professional opera singer. At the age of 4 he began to play the piano, tutored by an older sister and an aunt; at 5, his father began giving him regular lessons. He was barely 6 when he first appeared in public in Ciechocinek; at the age of 10 he played Beethoven's Concerto No. 1 with the Berlin Phil., under Hans von Bülow. He also made a tour of Scandinavia; played in France and England; his concerts as a child prodigy became a European sensation; soon an American offer of a concert tour came from the impresarios Abbey, Schoeffel & Grau. On Nov. 29, 1887, Hofmann appeared at the Metropolitan Opera House, as a soloist in Beethoven's Concerto No. 1, with an orch. conducted by Adolf Neuendorff, and played works by Chopin and some of his own little pieces. He electrified the audience, and hardheaded critics hailed his performance as a marvel. He appeared throughout the U.S., giving 42 concerts in all; then agitation was started by the Society for the Prevention of Cruelty to Children against the exploitation of his talent. Alfred Corning Clark of N.Y. offered $50,000 to the family for his continued education. The offer was accepted, and young Hofmann began serious study with Moszkowski (piano) and Urban (composition) in Berlin. Then Anton Rubinstein accepted him as a pupil in Dresden, where Hofmann traveled twice a week for piano lessons. At the age of 18 he resumed his career, giving recitals in Dresden and elsewhere in Germany with enormous success; made his first tour of Russia in 1896, attaining huge popularity there; he reappeared in Russia frequently. In 1898 he again played in the U.S.; from then on, he appeared in American cities almost every year. At the peak of his career, he came to be regarded as one of the greatest pianists of the century. He possessed the secret of the singing tone, which enabled him to interpret Chopin with extraordinary delicacy and intimacy. He was also capable of summoning tremendous power playing Liszt and other works of the virtuoso school. His technique knew no difficulties; but in his interpretations, he subordinated technical effects to the larger design of the work. When the Curtis Inst. of Music was founded in Philadelphia (1924), Hofmann was engaged to head the piano dept.; in 1926–38 he was director of the Curtis Inst. On Nov. 28, 1937, his golden jubilee in the U.S. was celebrated with a concert at the Metropolitan Opera House, where he had first played as a child 50 years before. He performed the D-minor Concerto of Anton Rubinstein, and his own *Chromaticon* for Piano and Orch. From 1938 to his death he lived mostly in California. He became an American citizen in 1926. Hofmann was also a composer, under the pen name **Michel Dvorsky** (a transliteration of the literal translation into Polish of his German name, meaning "courtyard man"). Among his works are several piano concertos; some symph. works; *Chromaticon* for Piano and Orch. (first played by him with the Cincinnati Symph. Orch., Nov. 24, 1916); numerous piano pieces. He publ. a practical manual, *Piano-Playing with Piano-Questions Answered* (1915).

Hofmann, Peter, outstanding German tenor; b. Marienbad, Aug. 12, 1944. He studied at the Hochschule für Musik in Karlsruhe; made his operatic debut in 1972 in Lübeck as Tamino; in 1973 joined the Württemberg State Theater in Stuttgart. He came to prominence in his performance of the role of Siegmund in the centennial Bayreuth productions of *Der Ring des Nibelungen;* later he appeared as Parsifal at Covent Garden in London. He made his U.S. debut as Siegmund with the San Francisco Opera in 1977; sang Lohengrin with the Metropolitan Opera in N.Y. in 1980. His other roles included Max, Florestan, Alfred in *Die Fledermaus,* Loge, and Bacchus.

Hofmeister, Friedrich, German music publisher; b. Strehlen, Jan. 24, 1782; d. Reudnitz, near Leipzig, Sept. 30, 1864. In 1807 he established in Leipzig the music firm that bears his name; beginning in 1829, he publ. a valuable monthly catalogue, the *Musikalisch-litterarischer Monatsbericht.* His son and successor, **Adolf Hofmeister** (b. c.1802; d. Leipzig, May 26, 1870), publ. a 3rd and enlarged edition of Whistling's *Handbuch der musikalischen Litteratur* (1845), with supplementary vols. filled from issues of Hofmeister's *Monatsbericht.* After 1852, the 12 *Monatsberichte* for each complete year were arranged in alphabetical order and issued as a *Jahresbericht.* All these valuable editions were continued by the firm under the proprietorship of Albert Röthing (b. Leipzig, Jan. 4, 1845; d. there, Aug. 11, 1907). In 1905, Karl Günther became the head of the firm; he was succeeded by Karl Ganzenmüller. In 1935 the firm acquired the catalogue of Merseburger (Leipzig); after World War II the firm had offices both in Frankfurt and Leipzig.

Hofstetter, Romanus, German cleric and composer; b. Laudenbach (Württemberg), April 24, 1742; d. Miltenberg, May 21, 1815. He publ. 12 string quartets under his own name and, more importantly, is the true author of 6 string quartets commonly attributed to Haydn as his op. 3.

Hogwood, Christopher, English harpsichordist, musicologist, and conductor; b. Nottingham, Sept. 10, 1941. He studied at Cambridge Univ. and at the Charles Univ. in Prague. In 1967 he and David Munrow organized the Early Music Consort, an ensemble devoted to the performance of medieval music.

In 1973 he founded the Academy of Ancient Music with the aim of giving authentic renditions of music of the Baroque period; he made an intensive study of the works of Mozart, recording all of the symphs. on instruments of Mozart's time. He made a tour of the U.S. in 1974. In 1979 he became a professor-in-residence at Sydney (Australia) Univ. He edited works by J.C. Bach, Purcell, and Croft; was also a contributor to the 6th edition of *The New Grove Dictionary of Music and Musicians* (1980).

Hoiby, Lee, American composer; b. Madison, Wis., Feb. 17, 1926. After a preliminary music study in his hometown he took piano lessons with Egon Petri at Mills College, where he received his M.A. in 1952; intermittently he studied with Menotti at the Curtis Inst. in Philadelphia, and then attended various courses in Rome and Salzburg. In 1957 he received an award of $1,000 from the National Inst. of Arts and Letters. He is at his best in composing operas on contemporary subjects in a manner reminiscent of Menotti—concise, dramatic, and aurally pleasing, and sometimes stimulating.
WORKS: Operas: *The Scarf,* after Chekhov's story *The Witch* (Spoleto, June 20, 1958); *Beatrice,* after Maeterlinck (Louisville, Ky., Oct. 23, 1959); *Natalia Petrovna,* after Turgenev (N.Y., Oct. 8, 1964); *Summer and Smoke,* after a play by Tennessee Williams (St. Paul, Minn., June 19, 1971); also incidental music to the play *The Duchess of Malfi* (N.Y., March 19, 1957). Other works are *Noctambulation* for Orch. (N.Y., Oct. 4, 1952); *Hearts, Meadows & Flags* for Orch. (Rochester, N.Y., Nov. 6, 1952); *Pastoral Dances* for Flute and Orch. (New Orleans, Nov. 6, 1956); Violin Sonata; 5 Preludes for Piano; *Design for Strings; Diversions* for Woodwind Quintet; *Songs of the Fool* for Mixed Chorus; etc.

Holbrooke, Josef, English composer; b. Croydon, July 5, 1878; d. London, Aug. 5, 1958. He received his primary education from his father; then studied at the Royal Academy of Music in London with F. Corder. After graduation, he conducted ballet and various summer orchs. Although he composed prolifically, and had many ardent admirers of his music, he never succeeded in establishing himself as a representative British composer. Perhaps this was owing to the fact that he stood aloof from modernistic developments of European music, and preferred to write for a hypothetical mass audience, which, however, failed to materialize at the infrequent performances of his music.
WORKS: OPERAS: *Pierrot and Pierrette* (London, Nov. 11, 1909); a trilogy (his main dramatic work), *The Cauldron of Anwyn:* I. *The Children of Don* (London, June 15, 1912), II. *Dylan, Son of the Wave* (London, July 4, 1913), III. *Bronwen, Daughter of Llyr* (Huddersfield, Feb. 1, 1929); *The Enchanter* (Chicago, 1915); *The Snob,* one-act comic opera. BALLETS: *The Red Masque; The Moth; The Enchanted Garden.* ORCH. WORKS: Symph. poems, *The Raven* (London, 1900); *The Viking; Ulalume* (1904); *Byron,* with Chorus; *Queen Mab,* with Chorus (Leeds Festival, 1904); *Homage to E.A. Poe,* with Chorus; *The*

Bells, with Chorus (Birmingham, 1906); *The Skeleton in Armor; The Masque the Red Death;* 5 symphs.; variations on *3 Blind Mice, The Girl I Left behind Me,* and *Auld Lang Syne; Dreamland Suite; Les Hommages,* suite; *The Haunted Palace,* fantasy; *The New Renaissance,* overture. CHAMBER MUSIC: 5 string quartets; 4 string sextets; 3 violin sonatas; 2 piano quartets; 2 clarinet quintets; Piano Quintet; Trio for Violin, Horn, and Piano. He wrote many piano pieces, songs, and clarinet pieces; also a book, *Contemporary British Composers* (1925).

Holden, Oliver, American musician, carpenter, and minister; b. Shirley, Mass., Sept. 18, 1765; d. Charlestown, Mass., Sept. 4, 1844. After serving as a marine in the navy, he settled in Charlestown in 1787 and was active there as a justice of the peace and carpenter; then abandoned carpentry and established a music store (about 1790); also offered music lessons; officiated as preacher of the Puritan Church; served as Charlestown representative in the State House of Representatives (1818–33). He composed psalm tunes and odes; at least 21 hymns are known to be of his authorship, his best being *Coronation* (set to the words of *All Hail the Power of Jesus' Name*), first publ. in vol. I of his *Union Harmony* (1793); it has retained its popularity until modern times. His *From Vernon's mount behold the hero rise,* one of the many works written in commemoration of George Washington's death, was sung at the Old South Meeting House, Boston, in Jan. 1800. Other publications are *The American Harmony* (1792); *The Massachusetts Compiler* (1795; with H. Gram and S. Holyoke); *The Worcester Collection* (1797; ed. and revised by Holden); *Sacred Dirges, Hymns and Anthems* (1800); *Modern Collection of Sacred Music* (1800); *Plain Psalmody* (1800); *Charlestown Collection of Sacred Songs* (1803); *Vocal Companion* (1807); and *Occasional Pieces.*

Holguín, Guillermo. See **Uribe-Holguín, Guillermo.**

Holiday, Billie (called **Lady Day**), black American jazz singer; b. Baltimore, April 7, 1915; d. New York, July 17, 1959. She began singing professionally in Harlem nightclubs at age 15; was discovered by impresario John Hammond and bandleader Benny Goodman in 1933 and appeared with his band; also with Count Basie, Artie Shaw, and others; toured Europe (1954, 1958). Her otherwise brilliant career was marred by personal tragedies and, above all, addiction to narcotics and alcohol. Despite the oft-quoted phrase "Lady Day sings the blues," Billie Holiday rarely sang classic blues; with her unique vocal endowments she managed to make everything she performed—mostly popular tunes of the day—sound "bluesy." She publ. (with some professional journalistic help) an autobiography, *Lady Sings the Blues* (N.Y., 1956).

Hollander, Lorin, American pianist; b. New York, July 19, 1944. He received his early musical training from his father, the violinist **Max Hollander,** and studied violin before tackling the piano. He earned the reputation of an aggressive pianist to whom technical difficulties, whether in Bach or Prokofiev, did not exist. His principal piano teacher was Steuermann at the Juilliard School of Music in N.Y.

Holliger, Heinz, Swiss oboe player and composer; b. Langenthal, May 21, 1939. He studied oboe with Cassagnaud and composition with Veress at the Cons. of Bern; then oboe with Pierlot and piano with Lefebure in Paris and with Boulez in Basel. In 1959 he obtained the first prize for oboe playing in the international competition held in Geneva, and won first prize again in Munich in 1961. He embarked on a career as a concert oboist with his wife, the harpist **Ursula Hänggi,** touring in Europe and in the U.S. Several modern composers wrote special works for him, among them Penderecki, Henze, Stockhausen, Krenek, Berio, and Jolivet. He composes mostly chamber music works, several of them scored, understandably, for oboe and harp.
WORKS: Sonata for Unaccompanied Oboe (1956); 3 *Liebeslieder* for Voice and Orch. (1960); *Erde und Himmel* for Tenor and 5 Instruments (1961); *Studie* for Soprano, Oboe, Cello, and Harpsichord (1962); *Improvisationen* for Oboe, Harp, and 12 Instruments (1963); Trio for Oboe, Viola, and Harp (1968); *Der magische Tänzer,* chamber opera for 2 Men and 2 Marionettes (Basel, April 26, 1970); *Pneuma* for Winds, Percussion, and Organ (Donaueschingen, Oct. 18, 1970); *Cardiophonic* for a Wind Instrument and 3 Magnetophones (1971); String Quartet (1973); *Atenbogen* for Orch. (1975); *Komposition* for Organ and Tape (Baden-Baden, Oct. 18, 1980).

Hollingsworth, Stanley, American composer; b. Berkeley, Calif., Aug. 27, 1924. He studied at San Jose State College; then with Darius Milhaud at Mills College and with Gian Carlo Menotti at the Curtis Inst. of Music in Philadelphia; subsequently was at the American Academy in Rome (1955–56). He received a Guggenheim fellowship in 1958; also was awarded several grants from the National Endowment for the Arts. From 1961 to 1963 he taught at San Jose State College; in 1963 joined the faculty of Oakland Univ. in Rochester, Mich. His music follows the principles of practical modernism; in this respect he emulates Menotti. He used the pseudonym **Stanley Hollier** in some of his works.
WORKS: 4 operas: *The Mother,* after Andersen (1949; Philadelphia, March 29, 1954); *La Grande Bretèche,* after Balzac (1954; NBC TV, Feb. 10, 1957); *The Selfish Giant* (1981); *Harrison Loved His Umbrella* (1981); *Dumbarton Oaks Mass* for Chorus and String Orch.; *Stabat Mater* for Chorus and Orch. (San Jose, May 1, 1957); *Psalm of David* for Tenor, Chorus, and Orch. (1962); Piano Concerto (1980); Divertimento for Orch. (1982); *3 Ladies beside the Sea* for Narrator and Orch. (1983); chamber music: Sonata for Oboe and Piano; 3 impromptus for Flute and Piano (1975); *Ricordanza* for Oboe and String Trio (in memory of Samuel Barber; 1981); *Reflections and Diversions* for Clarinet and Piano (1984).

Holloway, Robin, English composer; b. Leamington Spa, Oct. 19, 1943. He took lessons in composition with Alexander Goehr. In 1974 he was appointed music lecturer at Cambridge Univ. His music is deeply rooted in Englishry; he resists the procrustean deformation of fashionable dodecaphony, preferring the relatively liberal discipline of neo-medieval counterpoint, clinging resolutely to basic tonality and modality. Yet on occasion he audaciously piles tonal Pelion on modal Ossa in his effort to achieve mountainous polyharmony; he also makes use of occasional *objets trouvés* from the music of Brahms, Debussy, and Schoenberg, treating such objects as legitimate flotsam and jetsam. His dramatizations, intensifications, and amplifications of Schumann's lieder are notable.

WORKS: *Garden Music* for 6 Players (1962); 3 Concertinos for Chamber Orch. (1964–69, 1967, 1975); Concerto for Organ and Wind Instruments (1966); Concerto No. 1 for Orch. (1966–72); *Divertimento* No. 1 for Piano and Orch. (1968); *Souvenirs de Schumann* for Orch. (1970); *The Wind Shifts* for High Voice and Strings, to 8 poems of Wallace Stevens (1970); *Fantasy-Pieces* on Schumann's *Liederkreis* (1971); *Clarissa*, opera after the novel by Richardson (1971–77); *Divertimento* No. 2 for Wind Nonet (1972); *Evening with Angels* for 16 Players (1972); *The Death of God*, melodramatic cantata (1973); *Domination of Black* (1974); *Sea Surface Full of Clouds*, cantata to poems by Wallace Stevens (1974–75); *Romanza* for Violin and Chamber Orch. (1976); *The Rivers of Hell* for Chamber Ensemble (1977); Concerto No. 2 for Orch. (1979); *Serenade* for Octet (1979); *Ode* for Chamber Orch. (1980); *The Dark Air* for Chamber Orch. (1980); *Clarissa Symphony* (Birmingham, Dec. 9, 1982); *Sound Idyll* for Chamber Orch. (London, Oct. 10, 1983).

Holmboe, Vagn, eminent Danish composer; b. Horsens, Jutland, Dec. 20, 1909. He studied composition with Knud Jeppesen and Høffding at the Royal Cons. in Copenhagen (1927–29); then took intermittent courses in Berlin (1930–33); traveled in Transylvania (1933–34), where he gained first-hand knowledge of Balkan folk music. Upon return to Copenhagen, he taught at the Royal Danish Inst. for the Blind (1940–49), wrote music criticism for the newspaper *Politiken* (1947–55), and taught at the Copenhagen Cons. (1950–65). A recipient of a government lifetime grant, and remarkably productive, he wrote 22 symphs. (of which he withdrew 3 early ones); 13 chamber concertos for different solo instruments; and 14 extant string quartets (after he withdrew 10 previous ones). His music evolved from the legacy of Sibelius and Carl Nielsen; he then developed a method of composition with "germ themes," that grow metamorphically; his symph. works give an impression of grandeur, with long, dynamic crescendos in expanded tonality.

WORKS: 3-act opera, *Lave og Jon* (*Lave and Jon*, 1946–48); one-act chamber opera, *Kniven* (*The Knife*, 1959–60); symph. fairy play, *Fanden og borgemesteren* (*The Devil and the Mayor*, 1940); radio play, *Fløjten* (1946); ballet, *Den galsindede tyrk* (1942–44). FOR ORCH.: 11 numbered symphs.: No. 1, for Chamber Orch. (1935; Aarhus, Feb. 21, 1938); No. 2 (Copenhagen, Dec. 5, 1939); No. 3, *Sinfonia rustica* (1941; Copenhagen, June 12, 1948); No. 4, *Sinfonia sacra*, with Chorus (1941, revised 1945; Copenhagen, Sept. 2, 1945); No. 5 (1944; Copenhagen, June 16, 1945); No.6 (1947; Copenhagen, Jan. 8, 1948); No. 7 (1950; Copenhagen, Oct. 18, 1951); No. 8, *Sinfonia boreale* (1951–52; Copenhagen, March 5, 1953); No. 9 (Copenhagen, Dec. 19, 1968); No. 10 (1970–71; Detroit, Jan. 27, 1972); No. 11 (Copenhagen, Feb. 17, 1983); *Sinfonia in memoriam* (1954–55); 4 sinfonias for String Orch., known collectively as *Kairos* (1957, 1957, 1958–59, 1962); 3 chamber symphs.: No. 1, *Collegium musicum concerto No. 1* (1951); No. 2 (1968); No. 3, *Frise* (1969–70); 3 works representing symph. metamorphoses: *Epitaph* (1956); *Monolith* (1960); *Epilogue* (1961–62); *Tempo variabile* (1971–72); Concerto for Orch. (1929); Concerto for Chamber Orch. (1931); Concerto for String Orch. (1933); *Rapsodi* for Flute and Chamber Orch. (1935); Violin Concerto (1938); Cello Concerto (1974); Concerto for Recorder, Celeste, Vibraphone, and Strings (1974); Flute Concerto (1976); Tuba Concerto (1976); 13 chamber concertos: No. 1 for Piano, Strings, and Percussion (1939); No. 2 for Flute, Violin, Celesta, Percussion, and String Orch. (1940); No. 3 for Clarinet, 2 Trumpets, 2 Horns, and Strings (1940); No. 4, *Triple Concerto*, for Violin, Cello, Piano, and Chamber Orch. (1942); No. 5 for Viola and Chamber Orch. (1943); No. 6 for Violin and Chamber Orch. (1943); No. 7 for Oboe and Chamber Orch. (1944–45); No. 8, *Sinfonia concertante*, for Chamber Orch. (1945); No. 9 for Violin, Viola, and Chamber Orch. (1945–46); No. 10, *Træ-messing-tarm*, for Chamber Orch. (1945–46); No. 11 for Trumpet, 2 Horns, and String Orch. (1948); No. 12 for Trombone and Chamber Orch. (1950); and No. 13, *Collegium musicum concerto No. 2*, for Oboe, Viola, and Chamber Orch. (1955–56); Concertino No. 1 for Violin, Viola, and String Orch. (1940) and No. 2 for Violin and String Orch. (1940); *Symphonic Overture* for Percussion, Piano, and Strings (1941). CHAMBER MUSIC: 14 string quartets: No. 1 (1948–49); No. 2 (1949); No. 3 (1949–50); No. 4 (1953–54, revised 1956); No. 5 (1955); No. 6 (1961); No. 7 (1964–65); No. 8 (1965); No. 9 (1965–66, revised 1969); No. 10 (1969); No. 11, *Quartetto rustico* (1972); No. 12 (1973); No. 13 (1975); No. 14 (1975); *Musik for fugle og frøer* for 2 Flutes and 16 Bassoons (1971); Sextet for Flute, Clarinet, Bassoon, Violin, Viola, and Cello (1972–73); Wind Quintet (1933); Quintet for Flute, Oboe, Clarinet, Violin, and Viola (1936); *Notturno* for Wind Quintet (1940); *Aspekter* for Wind Quintet (1957); *Tropos* for String Quintet (1960); Brass Quintet (1961–62); *Musik til Morten* for Oboe and String Quartet (1970); Serenade for Flute, Piano, Violin, and Cello (1940); *Primavera* for Flute, Piano, Violin, and Cello (1951); *Quartetto medico* for Flute, Oboe, Clarinet, and Piano (1956); Quartet for Flute, Violin, Viola, and Cello (1966); *Fanden løs i Voldmosen* for Clarinet, 2 Violins, and Double Bass (1971); *Ondata* for Percussion (1972); *Firefir*, quartet for 4 Flutes (1977); *Rhapsody Intermezzo* for Violin, Clarinet, and Piano (1938); *Isomeric* for 2 Violins and Piano (1950); Piano Trio

(1954); Trio for Flute, Piano, and Cello (1968); *Nuigen*, piano trio (1976); an unnumbered Violin Sonata (1929); 3 numbered violin sonatas (1935, 1939, 1965); *Sonatina capricciosa* for Flute and Piano (1942); sonata for Violin and Viola (1963); Oboe Sonatina (1966); *Triade* for Trumpet and Organ (1975). FOR SOLO INSTRUMENTS: Violin Sonata (1953); Flute Sonata (1957); Double-bass Sonata (1962); Cello Sonata (1968–69). For Piano: *Choral Fantasy* (1929); 2 sonatas (1929, 1930); *Allegro affettuoso* (1931); 4 suites (1930–33); *Julen 1931* (1931); *6 Sketches* (1934); *Rumaensk Suite* (1937–38); *6 Pieces* (1939); *Sonatina briosa* (1941); *Suono da bardo* (1949–50); *Moto austero* (1965); *I venti* (1972). For Organ: *Fabula I* (1972); *Fabula II* (1973); *Contrasti* (1972). FOR VOICE: *Requiem for Nietzsche* for Tenor, Baritone, Mixed Chorus, and Orch. (1963–64); *Skoven (The Forest)* for Mixed Chorus, Children's Chorus, and Instruments (1960); *3 Inuit sange (3 Eskimo Songs)* for Baritone, Male Chorus, and Percussion (1956); *Beatus parvo* for Chorus and Chamber Orch. (1962); *Edward* for Baritone and Orch. (1971); *The wee-wee man* for Tenor and Orch. (1971); *Zeit* for Alto and String Quartet (1966–67); a cappella choruses, including *Solhymne* (1960) and the Latin motets *Liber Canticuli I* (1951–52), *II* (1952–53), *III* (1953), *IV* (1953), and *V, Beatus vir* (1967); numerous cantatas for ceremonial events; songs. He wrote a book on contemporary music, *Mellemspil (Interlude;* Copenhagen, 1966).

Holmès, Augusta (Mary Anne), French composer; b. Paris (of Irish parents), Dec. 16, 1847; d. there, Jan. 28, 1903. She progressed very rapidly as a child pianist, and gave public concerts; also composed songs, under the pen name **Hermann Zenta.** She studied harmony with H. Lambert, an organist; later became a pupil of César Franck. She then began to compose works in large forms, arousing considerable attention, mixed with curiosity, for she was undoubtedly one of the very few professional women composers of the time. Her music, impartially considered, lacks individuality or strength; at best, it represents a conventional by-product of French Romanticism, with an admixture of fashionable exotic elements.

WORKS: Operas: *La Montagne noire* (Paris Opéra, Feb. 8, 1895); *Héro et Léandre; Astarte; Lancelot du lac;* for Orch.: *Andante pastoral* (Paris, Jan. 14, 1877); *Lutèce* (Angers, Nov. 30, 1884); *Les Argonautes* (Paris, April 24, 1881); *Irlande* (Paris, March 2, 1882); *Ode triomphale* (Paris, March 4, 1888); *Pologne; Andromède; Hymne à Apollon;* etc.; cantatas: *La Vision de la Reine; La Chanson de la caravane; La Fleur de Neflier;* some piano pieces; 117 songs, some of which have remained in the active repertoire of French singers.

Holmes, Edward, English pianist and author; b. London, 1797; d. there, Aug. 28, 1859. He received a fine education; was a friend of Keats at Enfield. He studied music with Vincent Novello. In 1826 he became a contributor to a literary journal, *Atlas.* He publ. *A Ramble among the Musicians of Germany* (1828; reprint, with a new introduction and indexes by Charles Cudworth, N.Y., 1969); *The Life of Mozart* (his most important work; 1845; 2nd ed., 1878); *Life of Purcell; Analytical and Thematic Index of Mozart's Piano Works;* also articles in the *Musical Times* and other journals.

Holst, Gustav (full baptismal name, **Gustavus Theodore von Holst),** significant British composer; b. Cheltenham, Sept. 21, 1874; d. London, May 25, 1934. He was of Swedish stock; his paternal great-grandfather settled in England in 1807. Holst's father was an organist; his mother, a piano teacher; Holst received his primary musical education from his parents. He played the organ in Wyck Rissington, Gloucestershire; in 1893 enrolled at the Royal College of Music in London, where he took piano lessons with Herbert Sharpe, and also learned to play the trombone; in composition he studied with Charles Villiers Stanford and Rockstro. For some years he earned his living as trombonist in various orchs. in London. In 1905 he was appointed music master at St. Paul's Girls' School, and in 1907 was engaged as music director at Morley College in London, retaining both positions throughout his whole life. Plagued by suspicions of his German sympathies at the outbreak of World War I in 1914, Holst removed the Germanic-looking (but actually Swedish) nobiliary particle "von" from his last name (his early works were publ. under the name **Gustav von Holst**). Upon the advice of Percy A. Scholes, Holst traveled during the later period of the war to Salonika and Constantinople to organize musical activities among British troops, which further enhanced his reputation as a patriot. In 1919 he was appointed teacher of composition at the Royal College of London; from 1919–23 he also was on the faculty of Reading College. Early in his life he became deeply interested in Hindu philosophy, religion, and music; his music of the period reveals his fascination with Sanskrit epics. His most famous work, the symph. suite *The Planets,* is inspired by the astrological significance of the planets. There are 7 movements, each bearing a mythological subtitle: *Mars, the Bringer of War; Venus, the Bringer of Peace; Mercury, the Winged Messenger; Jupiter, the Bringer of Jollity; Saturn, the Bringer of Old Age; Uranus, the Magician;* and *Neptune, the Mystic,* with an epilogue of female voices singing wordless syllables. The suite had a private performance in London on Sept. 29, 1918; 5 movements were played in public on Feb. 15, 1920; the entire work was first given in its entirety on Nov. 15, 1920. Its success was immediate and lasting in England and America; it was featured by some American orchs. at special concerts in celebration of space travel, and was even given in connection with the production of the science-fiction film *2001: A Space Odyssey.* The melodic and harmonic style of *The Planets* epitomizes Holst's musical convictions, in which lyrical, dramatic, and triumphant motifs are alternately presented in coruscatingly effective orch. dress. Holst also contributed greatly to the national style based on English folk songs. He was a master of choral writing, and several of his vocal compositions retain their validity. Some of his orientally inspired pieces also enjoy occasional performances. He was a highly successful teacher and an able conductor. In 1923 and again in 1932 he visited the U.S. as a lecturer and conductor; chronic ill health limited his activities. His daughter Imogen Holst described his mind in the last year of his life as "closed in gray isolation."

WORKS: FOR THE STAGE: *Lansdown Castle*, operetta (Cheltenham, Feb. 7, 1893); *The Revoke* (one act; 1895); *The Youth's Choice* (1902); *Sita* (1899–1906); *Sāvitai*, chamber opera after the Hindu epic *Mahabharata* (1908; London, Dec. 5, 1916); *The Perfect Fool* (Covent Garden, London, May 14, 1923); *At the Boar's Head* (Manchester, April 3, 1925); *The Wandering Scholar* (1929; Liverpool, Jan. 31, 1934); choral ballet, *The Golden Goose* (BBC, London, Sept. 21, 1926, composer conducting); choral ballet, *The Morning of the Year* (London, March 17, 1927, composer conducting); *The Coming of Christ*, mystery play for Chorus, Piano, Strings, and Trumpet (1927; Canterbury, May 28, 1928, composer conducting).

FOR ORCH.: *A Winter Idyll* (1897); overture, *Walt Whitman* (1899); *Suite de Ballet* (1899; London, May 20, 1904); Symph. in F, *The Cotswolds* (1900; Bournemouth, April 24, 1902); symph. poem, *Indra* (1903); *Song of the Night* for Violin and Orch. (1905); *Marching Song* and *Country Song* for Chamber Orch. (1906); *Songs of the West* (1906); 2 *Songs without Words* for Chamber Orch. (1906); *Somerset Rhapsody* (London, April 6, 1910); incidental music to the masque *The Vision of Dame Christian* (London, July 22, 1909); music for the Stepney Pageant (1909); Suite No. 1 for Military Band (1909); oriental suite, *Beni Mora* (1910; London, May 1, 1912); *Invocation* for Cello and Orch. (1911); Suite No. 2 for Military Band (1911); *Phantastic Suite* (1911); *St. Paul's Suite* for String Orch. (1913); *The Planets*, suite for Large Orch. and Voices (1914–16; London, Nov. 15, 1920; Holst's most famous work); *Japanese Suite* (1915; London, Oct. 19, 1919); *Fugal Concerto* for Flute, Oboe, and Strings (London, Oct. 11, 1923); *First Choral Symphony* for Soprano and Mixed Voices (Leeds Festival, Oct. 7, 1925); symph. poem, *Egdon Heath*, after Thomas Hardy (N.Y., Feb. 12, 1928); *Moorside Suite* for Brass Band (London, Sept. 29, 1928); *Double Concerto* for 2 Violins (London, April 3, 1930); *Hammersmith*, prelude and scherzo (London, Nov. 25, 1931); *Capriccio* for Jazz Band (edited by Imogen Holst; 1932; London, Jan. 16, 1968); *Brook Green Suite* for Strings and Woodwinds (1933); *Lyric Movement* for Viola and Chamber Orch. (1933; London, March 18, 1934).

CHAMBER MUSIC: *Fantasy Pieces*, 3 pieces for Oboe and String Quartet (1896; revised 1910); Piano Quintet for Piano and Wind Instruments (1896); Woodwind Quintet (1903; London, Sept. 15, 1982).

VOCAL WORKS: *Clear and Cool* for Chorus and Orch. (1897); *Ornulf's Drapa*, scena for Baritone and Orch. (1898); 5 *Partsongs* and *Ave Maria* for 8-part Women's Chorus (1900); 5 *Partsongs* (1903); 6 *Songs* for Baritone and Piano; 6 *Songs* for Soprano and Piano; *King Estmere*, ballade for Chorus and Orch. (1903; London, April 4, 1908); *The Mystic Trumpeter*, after Walt Whitman (1904; London, June 29, 1905); 5 *Songs* for Female Chorus, after *The Princess* by Tennyson (1905); *Hymns* from the *Rig Veda* for Voice and Piano (1908); 10 *Choral Hymns* from the *Rig Veda* (1908–10); *The Cloud Messenger*, ode for Chorus and Orch. (1910); *Christmas Day* (1910); 4 part-songs for Children, Women's Chorus, and Harp (1911); *Hecuba's Lament* for Contralto, Female Chorus, and Orch. (1911); 2 Psalms for Chorus, Strings, and Organ (1912); *Hymn to Dionysus* (1913); *Dirge for 2 Veterans* for Men's Chorus and Brass Band (1914); part-songs for Mixed Chorus (1916); 3 hymns for Chorus and Orch. (1916); 6 folk songs for Chorus (1916); *Hymn of Jesus* for 2 Choruses, Orch., Piano, and Organ (1917; London, March 25, 1920); *Ode to Death*, with Orch., after Walt Whitman (1919; Leeds Festival, Oct. 6, 1922); choruses to *Alcestis* for Women's Chorus, Harp, and Flutes (1920); motet, *The Evening Watch* (1924); *Choral Fantasia* for Soprano, Chorus, Organ, and Orch. (1930; Gloucester, Sept. 8, 1931); 12 Welsh folk songs for Mixed Chorus (1930–31); 6 *Choruses* for Male Voice and Strings (1932); 6 *Canons* for Chorus a cappella (1932); songs.

FOR PIANO: *Toccata* on the Northumbrian pipe tune *Newburn Lads* (1924); *Chrissemas Day in the Morning* (1926); *Nocturne* (1930); *Jig* (1932).

Holst, Imogen Clare, English musician, daughter of **Gustav Holst;** b. Richmond, Surrey, April 12, 1907; d. Aldeburgh, March 9, 1984. She was a faithful keeper of her father's musical materials and writings. From 1952 to 1964 she was musical assistant to Benjamin Britten; she also conducted the ensemble of the Purcell Singers (1953–67) and served as artistic director of the Aldeburgh Festival (1956–77). She was one of the first women in Britain to conduct brass and military bands. In 1975 she was named by Queen Elizabeth II a Commander of the Order of the British Empire.

WORKS: *Gustav Holst* (London, 1938); *The Music of Gustav Holst* (London, 1951); *A Thematic Catalogue of Gustav Holst's Music* (London, 1974).

Holstein, Franz (Friedrich) von, German composer; b. Braunschweig, Feb. 16, 1826; d. Leipzig, May 22, 1878. His father was an army officer; at his behest, Holstein entered the Cadet School; there he had an opportunity to study musical theory. While a lieutenant, he privately produced his operetta, *Zwei Nächte in Venedig* (1845). He fought in the Schleswig-Holstein campaign; returning to Braunschweig, he wrote a grand opera, *Waverley*, after Walter Scott. He sent the score to Hauptmann at the Leipzig Cons.; the latter expressed his willingness to accept Holstein as a student. Accordingly, he resigned from the army (1853) and studied with Hauptmann until 1856. He then undertook some travels in Italy, finally returning to Leipzig, where he settled. He was also a poet, and wrote his own librettos. The musical style of his operas was close to the French type, popularized by Auber. He was a man of means, and left a valuable legacy for the benefit of indigent music students.

WORKS: Operas: *Der Haideschacht* (Dresden, Oct. 22, 1868); *Der Erbe von Morley* (Leipzig, Jan. 23, 1872); *Die Hochländer* (Mannheim, Jan. 16, 1876); another opera, *Marino Faliero,* remained unfinished; overture, *Frau Aventiure* (left in sketches only; orchestrated by Albert Dietrich; perf. posthumously, Leipzig, Nov. 13, 1879); *Beatrice,* scene for Soprano Solo with Orch.; Piano Trio; other chamber music; part-songs for Mixed and Men's Voices; etc.

Holt, Henry, Austrian-born American conductor and operatic administrator; b. Vienna, April 11, 1934. He studied with Hugo Strelitzer at Los Angeles City College and with Ingolf Dahl at the Univ. of Southern Calif.; made his conducting debut in *Rigoletto* with the American Opera Co. in Los Angeles in 1961; then was general director of the Portland (Oreg.) Opera (1964–66). In 1966 he was appointed general director of the Seattle Opera; conducted its highly acclaimed Wagner Festivals. In 1983 he became music director of the Univ. of Southern Calif. Opera; also continued to lead the Wagner Festivals in Seattle.

Holter, Iver (Paul Fredrik), Norwegian composer; b. Gausdal, Dec. 13, 1850; d. Oslo, Jan. 25, 1941. He entered the Univ. of Christiania (Oslo) as a student of medicine, but devoted much more time to music, which he studied under Svendsen; then was a pupil of Jadassohn, Richter, and Reinecke at the Leipzig Cons. (1876–78); lived in Berlin (1879–81); became Grieg's successor as conductor of the Harmonie in Bergen (1882); from 1886 to 1911 he was conductor of Musikföreningen in Oslo, and from 1890–1905, also of Handvaerkersångföreningen; in 1907, founded (and conducted until 1921) Holters Korförening, a society devoted to the production of large choral works (sacred and secular); was conductor of several of the great Scandinavian festivals; in 1900 he conducted with Svendsen the Northern Concerts in Paris. In 1919 the Norwegian government granted him an artist's stipend. He was editor of the *Nordisk Musik Revue* (1900–6). His compositions include a Symph. (1885); a Violin Concerto; and several cantatas: for the 300-year jubilee of Christiania (1924); for the 900-year Olavs-jubilee (1930); also choruses; chamber music; songs.

Holyoke, Samuel, American composer; b. Boxford, Mass., Oct. 15, 1762; d. East Concord, N.H., Feb. 7, 1820. His father was a clergyman, and Holyoke was naturally drawn to composing hymns. Although he received no formal training in music, he began to compose early, following his innate musical instinct. He wrote his most popular hymn tune, *Arnheim,* when he was only 16. He attended Harvard College, graduating in 1789; in 1793 he organized a school of higher education, known as the Groton Academy (later Lawrence Academy). In 1800 he went to Salem, where he was active as a teacher; was also a member of the Essex Musical Assoc. in Salem. Holyoke was among those who did not favor the application of "fuging" tunes in sacred music, as advocated by Billings, and generally omitted that style of composition from his collections; in the preface to his *Harmonia Americana* he states his reason for this as being because of "the trifling effect produced by that sort of music; for the parts . . . confound the sense and render the performance a mere jargon of words." His first collection was the *Harmonia Americana* (Boston, 1791); then followed *The Massachusetts Compiler* (co-ed. with Hans Gram and Oliver Holden; Boston, 1795); *The Columbian Repository of Sacred Harmony* (publ. Exeter, N.H., and dedicated to the Essex Musical Association; copyright entry dated April 7, 1802; contains 734 tunes, many of his own composition); *The Christian Harmonist* (Salem, 1804); and *The Instrumental Assistant* (Exeter; 2 vols., 1800–7; includes instructions for violin, German flute, clarinet, bass viol, and hautboy). He also publ. the song *Washington* (1790), and *Hark from the Tombs* (music for the funeral of Washington; 1800), etc.

Holzbauer, Ignaz (Jakob), noted Austrian composer; b. Vienna, Sept. 17, 1711; d. Mannheim, April 7, 1783. He studied law and at the same time received instruction in music from members of the choir at St. Stephen's in Vienna; he also perused *Gradus ad Parnassum* by Fux, whom he met later and who advised him to go to Italy for further studies. He then proceeded to Venice, but soon returned home. For a brief period he served as Kapellmeister to Count Rottal of Holešov in Moravia; in 1737 he married Rosalie Andreides, a singer; shortly thereafter they moved to Vienna, where he became a conductor and she a singer at the court theater; they also spent several years in Italy. In 1751 he was named Oberkapellmeister in Stuttgart. In 1753 he became Kapellmeister at the court of the elector Karl Theodor in Mannheim, a post he held until the court moved to Munich in 1778. He visited Rome in 1756, Turin in 1758, and Milan in 1759; during these visits he produced several of his operas. Holzbauer was greatly respected as a composer, especially for his church music; Mozart heard one of his masses in Mannheim in 1777 and found it excellent. Holzbauer was an important figure among symph. composers of the Mannheim school; he wrote some 65 works for orch. Of his operas, *Günther von Schwarzburg* (Mannheim, Jan. 5, 1777) is historically significant for its departure from Italian convention; it is thoroughly German in subject and treatment, and is noteworthy for the inclusion of accompanied recitative in place of the dialogue of the singspiel. It was publ. in Mannheim in 1776; reprinted in *Denkmäler deutscher Tonkunst,* VIII–IX (1902). His other operas include *Il figlio delle selve* (Schwetzingen, 1753); *L'isola disabitata* (Schwetzingen, 1754); *L'issipile* (Mannheim, Nov. 1, 1754); *Don Chisciotte* (Schwetzingen, 1755); *I cinesi* (Mannheim, 1756); *Le nozze d'Arianna* (Mannheim, 1756); *Il filosofo di campagna* (Mannheim, 1756); *La clemenza di Tito* (Mannheim, Nov. 4, 1757); *Nitteti* (Turin, 1758); *Alessandro nell'Indie* (Milan, 1759); *Ippolito ed Aricia* (Mannheim, Nov. 4, 1759); *Adriano in Siria* (Mannheim, Nov. 4, 1768); *Tancredi* (Munich, Jan. 1783). He also wrote ballet music for operas by J.A. Hasse: *L'Ipermestra* (Vienna, Jan. 8, 1744) and *Arminio* (Vienna, May 13, 1747). In addition, he composed 4 oratorios, 21 masses (also a *Deutsche Messe*), 37 motets, a Miserere, and other church music. His instrumental works, in addition to the symphs., include concertos, divertimentos, string quartets, string quintets, etc.

Homer, Louise (née **Louise Dilworth Beatty**), American contralto; b. Shadyside, near Pittsburgh, April 28, 1871; d. Winter Park, Fla., May 6, 1947. She studied in Philadelphia, and later in Boston, where her teacher in harmony was **Sidney Homer,** whom she married in 1895. With him she went to Paris, and there continued her study of voice with Fidèle Koenig; she also took lessons with Paul Lhérie in dramatic action. She made her debut in opera as Leonora in *La Favorita* (Vichy, 1898). In 1899 she was engaged at the Théâtre de la Monnaie in Brussels, singing various parts of the French and Italian repertoires. She subsequently sang Wagnerian contralto roles in German at Covent Garden, London. She made her American debut in opera as Amneris with the Metropolitan Opera Co. (then on tour) at San Francisco (Nov. 14, 1900); sang the same part in N.Y. (Dec. 22, 1900); continued on the staff of the Metropolitan from 1900 to 1919, the 1914–15 season excepted; was then with the Chicago Opera Co. (1920–25); with the San Francisco and Los Angeles Opera companies (1926), and again with the Metropolitan, reappearing there on Dec. 14, 1927. Her classic interpretation of Orfeo at the Paris revival of Gluck's opera (1909) and subsequently in N.Y. (Dec. 23, 1909, under Toscanini) produced a great impression. One of her greatest operatic triumphs was her performance of Dalila, with Caruso singing Samson. She gave her last appearance on Nov. 28, 1929. After retiring from the opera stage, she gave recitals with her daughter, **Louise Homer Stires,** a soprano. Her husband wrote a book of memoirs, *My Wife and I* (N.Y., 1939).

Homer, Sidney, American composer; b. Boston, Dec. 9, 1864; d. Winter Park, Fla., July 10, 1953. He studied in Boston, with Chadwick; then in Leipzig and Munich. In 1895 he married **Louise Dilworth Beatty,** his pupil, and went with her to Paris. He retired in 1940 and settled in Winter Park. He publ. about 100 songs, many of which won great favor, particularly *A Banjo Song;* also *Dearest, Requiem, Prospice, Bandanna* ballads, *It was the time of roses, General William Booth enters into Heaven, The song of the shirt, Sheep and Lambs, Sing me a song of a lad that is gone, The pauper's drive;* also 17 lyrics from Christina Rossetti's *Sing-song.* Other works include Sonata for Organ (1922); Quintet for Piano and Strings (1932); Violin Sonata (1936); String Quartet (1937); Piano Trio (1937). He publ. a book of memoirs, *My Wife and I* (N.Y., 1939).

Homilius, Gottfried August, eminent German organist and composer; b. Rosenthal, Feb. 2, 1714; d. Dresden, June 5, 1785. He studied composition and keyboard playing with J.S. Bach; completed his edu-

cation at the Univ. of Leipzig in 1735; in 1742 became organist of the Frauenkirche in Dresden; then was appointed music director of 3 main churches there (1755). His publ. works are: a Passion (1775); a Christmas oratorio, *Die Freude der Hirten über die Geburt Jesu* (1777); *6 deutsche Arien* (1786); in MS in the Berlin State Library and in the Dresden Kreuzchor archives: Passion according to St. Mark; church music for each Sunday and Feast day in the year; motets, cantatas, fugued chorales, a thorough-bass method, 2 chorus books, etc.

Honegger, Arthur (Oscar), remarkable French composer; b. Le Havre (of Swiss parents), March 10, 1892; d. Paris, Nov. 27, 1955. He studied violin in Paris with Lucien Capet; then went to Switzerland, where he took courses with L. Kempter and F. Hegar at the Zürich Cons. (1909–11). Returning to France in 1912, he entered the Paris Cons., in the classes of Gedalge and Widor; also took lessons with Vincent d'Indy. His name first attracted attention when he took part in a concert of Les Nouveaux Jeunes in Paris on Jan. 15, 1918. In 1920 the Paris critic Henri Collet publ. an article in *Comoedia* in which he drew a fortuitous parallel between the Russian Five and a group of young French composers whom he designated as Les Six. These Six were Honegger, Milhaud, Poulenc, Auric, Durey, and Tailleferre. The label persisted, even though the 6 composers went their separate ways and rarely gave concerts together. Indeed, only Honegger, Milhaud, and Poulenc became generally known; Auric limited his activities mainly to the theater and the cinema, while Germaine Tailleferre produced some musical plays and concert pieces; as to Durey, he was known more as a dedicated member of the French Communist Party than as a composer.

In the early years of his career, Honegger embraced the fashionable type of urban music, with an emphasis on machinelike rhythms and curt, pert melodies. In 1921 he wrote a sport ballet, *Skating Rink,* and a mock-militaristic ballet, *Sousmarine.* In 1923 he composed the most famous of such machine pieces, *Mouvement symphonique No. 1,* subtitled *Pacific 231.* The score was intended to be a realistic tonal portrayal of a powerful American locomotive, bearing the serial number 231. The music progressed in accelerating rhythmic pulses toward a powerful climax, then gradually slackening its pace until the final abrupt stop; there was a simulacrum of a lyrical song in the middle section of the piece. *Pacific 231* enjoyed great popularity and became in the minds of modern-minded listeners a perfect symbol of the machine age. Honegger's 2nd *Mouvement symphonique,* composed in 1928, was a musical rendering of the popular British sport rugby. His *Mouvement symphonique No. 3,* however, bore no identifying subtitle. This abandonment of allusion to urban life coincided chronologically with a general trend away from literal representation and toward absolute music in classical forms, often of historical or religious character. Among his most important works in that genre were *Le Roi David,* to a biblical subject, and *Jeanne d'Arc au bûcher,* glorifying the French patriot saint on the semimillennium of her martyrdom. Honegger's symphs. were equally free from contemporary allusions; the first 2 lacked descriptive titles; his 3rd symph. was entitled *Liturgique,* with a clear reference to an ecclesiastical ritual; the 4th symph. was named *Deliciae Basilienses,* because it was written to honor the city of Basel; the somewhat mysterious title of the 5th symph., *Di tre re,* signified nothing more arcane than the fact that each of its movements ended on the thrice-repeated note D. Honegger spent almost all of his life in France, but he retained his dual Swiss citizenship, a fact that caused some biographers to refer to him as a Swiss composer. In 1926 he married the pianist-composer **Andrée Vaurabourg** (1894–1980), who often played piano parts in his works. In 1929 he paid a visit to the U.S.; he returned to America in 1947 to teach summer classes at the Berkshire Music Center at Tanglewood, but soon after his arrival was stricken with a heart ailment and was unable to complete his term; he returned to Paris and remained there until his death.

WORKS: FOR THE THEATER: *Le Roi David,* dramatic psalm in 3 parts for Narrator, Soloists, Chorus, and 15 Instruments (1921; Mézières, Switzerland, June 11, 1921; revised as an oratorio with Full Orch. in 1923 and produced in Winterthur, Switzerland, Dec. 2, 1923); *Antigone,* opera in 3 acts (1924–27; Brussels, Dec. 28, 1927); *Judith,* biblical drama in 13 scenes (1925; Mézières, June 11, 1925; expanded to a 3-act opera and presented at Monte Carlo Opera, Feb. 13, 1926); *Amphion,* melodrama (1929; Paris, June 23, 1931); *Les Aventures du Roi Pausole,* operetta (1929–30; Paris, Dec. 12, 1930); *Cris du Monde,* stage oratorio for Soprano, Contralto, Baritone, Chorus, and Orch. (1930; Solothurn, Switzerland, May 3, 1931); *La Belle de Moudon,* operetta in 5 acts (1931; Mézières, May 30, 1931); *Jeanne d'Arc au bûcher,* dramatic oratorio in a Prologue and 11 scenes (1934–35; concert version, without Prologue, Basel, May 12, 1938; stage premiere, in German, Zürich, June 13, 1942); *L'Aiglon,* opera in collaboration with Jacques Ibert (1935; Monte Carlo Opera, March 11, 1937); *Les Mille et Une Nuits,* spectacle for Soprano, Tenor, Chorus, and Orch. (1937; Paris Exhibition, 1937); *Les Petites Cardinal,* operetta in collaboration with Jacques Ibert (1937; Paris, Feb. 20, 1938); *Nicolas de Flue,* dramatic legend for Narrator, Mixed Choir, Children's Choir, and Orch. (1939; concert premiere, Solothurn, Oct. 26, 1940; stage production, Neuchâtel, Switzerland, May 31, 1941).

BALLETS: *Vérité-Mensonge,* marionette ballet (1920; Paris, Nov. 1920); *Skating Rink* (1921; Paris, Jan. 20, 1922); *Sousmarine* (1924; Paris, June 27, 1925); *Roses de métal* (Paris, 1928); *Sémiramis,* ballet-melodrama (1931; Paris, May 11, 1934); *Un Oiseau blanc s'est envolé* (1937; Paris, June 1937); *Le Cantique des cantiques* (1937; Paris, Feb. 2, 1938); *La Naissance des couleurs* (1940; Paris, 1949); *Le Mangeur de rêves* (1941; Paris, 1941); *L'Appel de la montagne* (1943; Paris, July 9, 1945); scenes one and 4 of *Chota Roustaveli,* in 4 scenes (also known as *L'Homme à la peau de léopard;* 1945; Monte Carlo Opera, May 5, 1946; scenes 2 and 3 composed by

Harsányi and Alexandre Tcherepnin); *De la musique* (1950).

INCIDENTAL MUSIC: *Les Dit des jeux du monde,* in the form of 10 dances, 2 interludes, and epilogue, for Flute, Trumpet, Percussion, and Strings (1918; as a ballet, Paris, Dec. 2, 1918); *La Mort de Sainte Alméenne* (1918); *La Danse macabre* (1919); *Saül* (Paris, June 16, 1922); *Fantasio* (1922); *Antigone* (1922); *La Tempête* (1923); *Liluli* (1923); *Le Miracle de Notre-Dame* (1925); *L'Impératrice aux rochers* (1925; Paris, Feb. 17, 1927); *Phaedre* (1926); *800 mètres* (1941); *Le Soulier de satin* for Soprano, Baritone, and Orch. (Paris, Nov. 17, 1943); *Charles le Téméraire* for Choir, 2 Trumpets, 2 Trombones, and Percussion (1943–44; Mézières, May 27, 1944); *Hamlet* for Narrator, Chorus, and Orch. (Paris, Oct. 17, 1946); *Prométhée* (1946); *L'Etat de siège* (Paris, Oct. 27, 1948); *Tête d'or* (1948); *Œdipe-Roi* (1948).

FOR ORCH.: *Prélude pour "Aglavaine et Sélysette"* by Maeterlinck (1916–17; Paris Cons. orch. class, April 3, 1917, composer conducting); *Le Chant de Nigamon* (1917; Paris, Jan. 3, 1920); *Entrée, Nocturne et Berceuse* for Piano and Chamber Orch. (1919; Paris, 1919); *Pastorale d'eté* (1920; Paris, Feb. 12, 1921); *Horace Victorieux,* "mimed symph." (1920–21; concert premiere, Lausanne, Oct. 30, 1921; mimed premiere, Essen, Germany, Dec. 28, 1927); *Marche funèbre* (one section of *Les Mariés de la Tour Eiffel,* with other individual sections by Les Six members Auric, Milhaud, Poulenc, and Tailleferre; 1921; Paris, June 18, 1921); *Chant de joie* (1923; Paris, April 7, 1923); *Prélude pour "La Tempête,"* after Shakespeare (1923; Paris, May 1, 1923); *Pacific 231* (designated as *Mouvement symphonique No. 1;* 1923; Serge Koussevitzky's concert, Paris, May 8, 1924); Concertino for Piano and Orch. (1924; Paris, May 23, 1925; Andrée Vaurabourg, soloist); Suite from incidental music to *L'Impératrice aux rochers* (1925); Suite from incidental music to *Phèdre* (1926); *Rugby (Mouvement symphonique No. 2;* 1928; Paris, Oct. 19, 1928; inaugural concert of L'Orchestre Symphonique of Paris, Ernest Ansermet conducting); *Prélude, Fugue et Postlude,* from the melodrama *Amphion* (1929; Geneva, Nov. 3, 1948); Cello Concerto (1929; Boston, Feb. 17, 1930); 5 symphs.: No. 1 (1929–30; Boston, Feb. 13, 1931); No. 2 for String Orch. and optional Trumpet (1941; Zürich, May 18, 1942); No. 3, *Liturgique* (1945–46; Zürich, Aug. 17, 1946); No. 4, *Deliciae Basilienses* (1946; Basel, Jan. 21, 1947); No. 5, *Di tre re* (1950; Boston, March, 9, 1951); *Mouvement symphonique No. 3* (1932–33; Berlin, March 26, 1933); Suite from the film *Les Misérables* (1934; Paris, Jan. 19, 1935); *Prélude, Arioso et Fughetta sur le nom de BACH* for String Orch. (arranged by A. Hoérée, 1936; Paris, Dec. 5, 1936; originally for Piano); *Nocturne* (1936; Brussels, April 30, 1936); *La Marche sur la Bastille* for Band, from incidental music for Romain Rolland's pageant *Le Quatorze Juillet* (1936; Paris, July 14, 1936); *La Grande Barrage,* an "image musicale" (1942); *Jour de fête suisse,* suite from music to the ballet *L'Appel de la montagne* (1943; Winterthur, Nov. 14, 1945); 2 extracts from the film *Mermoz* (1943); *Sérénade à Angélique* for Small Orch. (1945; Zürich Radio, Nov. 19, 1945); *Concerto da camera* for Flute, English Horn, and Strings (1949; Zürich, May 6, 1949); *Toccata* (one section of *La Guirlande de Campra,* with other individual sections by Lesur, Manuel, Tailleferre, Poulenc, Sauguet, and Auric, 1950; complete work, Aix-en-Provence Festival, July 31, 1952); *Suite archaïque* (1950–51; Louisville, Ky., Feb. 28, 1951); *Monopartita* (1951; Zürich, June 12, 1951).

VOCAL MUSIC: *Cantique de Pâques* for 3 Women's Voices, Women's Chorus, and Orch. (1918; Toulouse, March 27, 1923); *Pâques à New York* for Voice and String Quartet (1920); *Chanson de Ronsard* for Voice, Flute, and String Quartet (1924); *3 chansons de la petite sirène* for Voice, Flute, and Strings or String Quartet (1926); *La Danse des morts,* oratorio for Narrator, Soloists, Chorus, Organ, and Orch. (1938; Basel, March 1, 1940); *Chant de libération* for Baritone, Unison Chorus, and Orch. (1942; Paris, Oct. 22, 1944); *Une Cantate de Noël* for Baritone, Mixed Chorus, Children's Chorus, Organ, and Orch. (sketched 1941, completed 1953; Basel, Dec. 18, 1953).

CHAMBER MUSIC: 2 violin sonatas (1916–18, 1919); 3 string quartets (1916–17, 1934–36, 1936–37); *Rapsodie* for 2 Flutes, Clarinet (or 2 Violins, Viola), and Piano (1917); *Danse de la chèvre* for Solo Flute (1919); Sonatina for 2 Violins (1920); Viola Sonata (1920); Cello Sonata (1920); *Hymn* for 10 String Instruments (1920); Sonatina for Clarinet or Cello, and Piano (1921–22); *3 contrepoints* for Flute, English Horn, Violin, and Cello (1923); *Prélude et Blues* for Quartet of Chromatic Harps (1925); Sonatina for Violin and Cello (1932); *Petite suite* for any 2 Treble Instruments and Piano (1934); Solo Violin Sonata (1940); *Sortilèges* for Ondes Martenot (1946); *Intrada* for Trumpet and Piano (1947); *Romance* for Flute and Piano (1953).

RADIO MUSIC: *Les Douze Coups de minuit,* a "radio-mystère" for Chorus and Chamber Orch. (1933; Paris Radio, Dec. 27, 1933); *Radio panoramique* for Tenor, Soprano, Organ, String Quintet, Wind Instruments, and Percussion (1935; Geneva Radio, March 4, 1935; concert premiere, Paris, Oct. 19, 1935); *Christophe Colomb,* radio oratorio for 2 Tenors, Chorus, and Orch. (1940; Lausanne Radio, April 17, 1940); *Les Battements du monde* for Woman's Voice, Child's Voice, Chorus, and Orch. (Lausanne Radio, May 18, 1944); *Saint François d'Assise* for Narrator, Baritone, Chorus, and Orch. (Lausanne Radio, Dec. 3, 1949).

FILM MUSIC: *Les Misérables* (1934); *Mayerling* (1935); *Regain* (1937); *Mlle. Doctor* (1937); *Pygmalion,* after G.B. Shaw's play (1938); *Mermoz* (1943); *Bourdelle* (1950); 36 others.

PIANO MUSIC: *3 pièces (Scherzo, Humoresque,* and *Adagio espressivo;* 1910); *3 pièces: Hommage à Ravel* (1915); *Prélude et Danse* (1919); *Toccata et Variations* (1916); *7 pièces brèves* (1919–20); *Sarabande* (1920); *Le Cahier Romand,* 5 pieces (1921–23); *Hommage à Albert Roussel* (1928); Suite for 2 Pianos (1928); *Prélude, Arioso et Fughetta sur le nom de BACH* (1932; arranged for Strings by A. Hoérée in 1936); *Scenic-Railway* (1937); *Partita* for 2 Pianos (1940; arranged from *3 contrepoints);* 2 *esquisses,* in Nicolas Obouhov's simplified notation

(1943–44); *Souvenir de Chopin* (1947).

SONGS: *4 poèmes* (1914–16); *6 poèmes de Apollinaire* (1915–17; Nos. 1 and 3–6 orchestrated as *5 poèmes de Apollinaire,* 1916–17); *3 poèmes de Paul Fort* (1916); *6 poésies de Jean Cocteau* (1920–23); *2 chants d'Ariel* (1923; also arranged for Orch.); *3 poèmes de Claudel* (1939–40); *3 psalms* (1940–41); *5 mélodies-minute* (1941); *4 Songs* for Low Voice and Piano (1944–45). Honegger publ. a book, *Je suis compositeur* (Paris, 1951; in Eng. as *I Am a Composer,* London, 1966).

Hood, Mantle, American ethnomusicologist; b. Springfield, Ill., June 24, 1918. He studied composition privately with Ernst Toch (1945–50); was enrolled at the Univ. of Calif., Los Angeles (B.A., 1951; M.A. in composition, 1951); continued his studies at the Univ. of Amsterdam, receiving his Ph.D. in 1954 with the dissertation *The Nuclear Theme as a Determinant of Patet in Javanese Music* (publ. in Groningen, 1954). In 1954 he joined the faculty at the Univ. of Calif., Los Angeles, becoming a full prof. there in 1962; in 1961 he was appointed director of the Inst. of Ethnomusicology. In 1956–57 he traveled to Indonesia on a Ford Foundation fellowship, and in 1976 received a Fulbright fellowship for study in India. In 1976 he became an adjunct prof. at the Univ. of Maryland; in 1977 was a visiting prof. at Yale Univ. and at Wesleyan Univ. He publ. *The Ethnomusicologist* (N.Y., 1971); contributed numerous valuable articles on oriental music to various learned journals and musical encyclopedias; also made arrangements of Indonesian melodies. His compositions include a symph. poem, *Vernal Equinox* (1955); Woodwind Trio (1950); 6 duets for Soprano and Alto Recorder (1954); piano pieces.

Hoogstraten, Willem van, Dutch conductor; b. Utrecht, March 18, 1884; d. Tutzing, Germany, Sept. 11, 1965. He studied violin with Alexander Schmuller; then with Bram Eldering at the Cons. of Cologne and with Ševčik in Prague; played concerts with the pianist **Elly Ney,** whom he married in 1911 (divorced in 1927). In 1914–18 he conducted the municipal orch. in Krefeld; in 1922 he was engaged as conductor of the summer concerts of the N.Y. Phil. (until 1938); was its associate conductor (1923–25). He was regular conductor of the Portland (Oreg.) Symph. Orch. in 1925–37. During World War II he was in charge of the Mozarteum Orch. in Salzburg (1939–45). In 1949 he settled in Stuttgart; conducted the Stuttgart Phil.

Hook, James, English organist and composer; b. Norwich, June 3, 1746; d. Boulogne, 1827. He exhibited a precocious talent as a boy; took lessons with Garland, organist of the Norwich Cathedral. In 1764 he went to London, where he played organ at various entertainment places. In 1765 he won a prize for his *Parting Catch.* He was subsequently organist and music director at Marylebone Gardens, London (1769–73) and at Vauxhall Gardens (1774–1820); his last position was at St. John's, Horsleydown.

WORKS: He was a highly industrious composer of songs; he may have written as many as 2,000 numbers; of these, only a few escaped oblivion (*Within a mile of Edinboro' Town; Sweet Lass of Richmond Hill,* etc.); many oratorios and odes; concertos for harpsichord; 117 sonatas, sonatinas, and divertimentos for piano; about 30 theater scores, all produced in London: *Cupid's Revenge* (June 12, 1772); *The Lady of the Manor* (Nov. 23, 1778); *The Fair Peruvian* (March 8, 1786); *Jack of Newbury* (May 6, 1795); *Wilmore Castle* (Oct. 21, 1800); *The Soldier's Return* (April 23, 1805); *The Invisible Girl* (April 28, 1806); *The Fortress* (July 16, 1807); *Safe and Sound* (August 28, 1809); etc. He publ. a manual, *Guida di musica,* in 2 parts (1785; 1794); some of the musical examples from it were reprinted by H. Wall in *Leaves from an Old Harpsichord Book.*

Hopkins, Charles Jerome (first name is sometimes erroneously given as **Edward**), American composer and musical journalist; b. Burlington, Vt., April 4, 1836; d. Athenia, N.J., Nov. 4, 1898. Self-taught in music (he took only 6 lessons in harmony), he learned to play piano sufficiently well to attain professional status. He studied chemistry at the N.Y. Medical College; played organ in N.Y. churches, and was active in various educational enterprises; in 1856 he founded the American Music Assoc., which promoted concerts of music by Gottschalk, Bristow, and other American composers. In 1868 he founded the *N.Y. Philharmonic Journal,* and was its editor until 1885. In 1886 he organized several "Free Singing and Opera Schools," for which he claimed nearly 1,000 pupils. In 1889 he went to England on a lecture tour, announcing himself as "the first American Operatic Oratorio composer and Pianist who has ever ventured to invade England with New World Musical theories and practices." Throughout his versatile career, he was a strong advocate of American music; his sensational methods and eccentric professional conduct brought him repeatedly into public controversy; in England he was sued for libel. Hopkins claimed a priority in writing the first "musicianly and scientific Kinder-Oper" (*Taffy and Old Munch,* a children's fairy tale, 1880). He further wrote an operatic oratorio, *Samuel,* and a great number of choruses and songs, few of which were publ. He compiled 2 collections of church music and an *Orpheon Class-Book.*

Hopkins, Edward John, English organist and composer; b. London, June 30, 1818; d. there, Feb. 4, 1901. He was a chorister at the Chapel Royal (1826–33); then studied theory with T.F. Walmisley. In 1834 he became organist at Mitcham Church; from 1838, was at St. Peter's Islington; from 1841, at St. Luke's; and from 1843, at the Temple Church, London. There he remained for 55 years, retiring in 1898; Walford Davies was his successor. Several of his many anthems have become established in the church repertoire (*Out of the Deep, God is Gone Up, Thou Shalt Cause the Trumpet of the Jubilee to Sound,* etc.). His book, *The Organ: Its History and Construction* (in collaboration with Rimbault, London, 1855; 5th ed., 1887), is a standard work. He contributed articles to *Grove's Dictionary of Music and Musicians* and to various musical publications.

Hopkins, John Henry, American clergyman and writer of hymn tunes; b. Pittsburgh, Oct. 28, 1820; d. Hudson, N.Y., Aug. 13, 1891. He studied at schools of divinity and served as a deacon in several churches. His Christmas carol *We Three Kings of Orient Are* is a perennial favorite. He publ. a collection, *Carols, Hymns and Songs* (1862).

Hopkinson, Francis, American statesman, writer, and composer; signer of the Declaration of Independence; b. Philadelphia, Sept. 21, 1737; d. there, May 9, 1791. By profession a lawyer, he was deeply interested in music; learned to play the harpsichord; studied music theory with James Bremner; was a member of an amateur group in Philadelphia who met regularly in their homes to play music, and also gave public concerts by subscription. He was the composer of the first piece of music written by a native American, *Ode to Music,* which he wrote in 1754, and of the first original American song, *My days have been so wondrous free* (1759). At least, this is the claim he makes in the preface to his 7 *Songs* (actually 8, the last having been added after the title page was engraved) *for the harpsichord or forte piano,* dated Philadelphia, Nov. 20, 1788, and dedicated to George Washington: "I cannot, I believe, be refused the Credit of being the first Native of the United States who has produced a Musical Composition." Other works: *Ode in Memory of James Bremner* (1780); a dramatic cantata, *The Temple of Minerva* (1781); there are also some songs. Hopkinson's music was couched in the conventional English style, modeled after pieces by T.A. Arne, but he undoubtedly possessed a genuine melodic gift. He also provided Benjamin Franklin's glass harmonica with a keyboard, introduced improvements in the quilling of the harpsichord, and invented the Bellarmonic, an instrument consisting of a set of steel bells. He was probably, but not certainly, the compiler of *A Collection of Psalm Tunes with a Few Anthems,* etc. A MS book of songs in Hopkinson's handwriting is in the possession of the Library of Congress. Hopkinson's son, **Joseph Hopkinson,** wrote the words to *Hail Columbia.*

Horák, Josef, Czech bass clarinetist; b. Znojmo, March 24, 1931. He attended the State High School for Musical and Dramatic Arts in Prague; was a clarinetist in the Brno State Phil. and Czech Radio Orch. On Oct. 20, 1955, he made his debut as a performer on the bass clarinet, and began a unique career as a virtuoso on that instrument; along with the Dutch bass clarinetist Harry Sparnaay, Horák is responsible for the revival of interest in the bass clarinet. Hindemith transcribed for Horák his Bassoon Sonata. In 1963 Horák and the pianist Emma Kovárnová formed the chamber duo Due Boemi di Praga, and performed nearly 300 specially commissioned works by Alois Hába, André Jolivet, Frank

Martin, Messiaen, Stockhausen, and many, many others. In 1972 Horák was appointed to the faculty of the Prague Cons.

Horenstein, Jascha, renowned Russian conductor; b. Kiev, May 6, 1898; d. London, April 2, 1973. His family moved to Germany when he was a child; he studied with Max Brode in Königsberg and Adolf Busch in Vienna; also took courses in composition with Franz Schreker in Berlin, where he became an assistant to Wilhelm Furtwängler. He made his conducting debut with the Vienna Symph. Orch. in 1923; then was a guest conductor with the Berlin Phil. Orch.; from 1925 to 1928 was conductor of the Berlin Symph. Orch.; in 1929 he became chief conductor of the Düsseldorf Opera, a post he held until forced to leave in 1933. In 1940 he came to the U.S.; after the war he returned to Europe. He was especially noted for his authoritative interpretations of the symphs. of Bruckner and Mahler.

Horn, Charles Edward, composer and conductor, son of **Karl Friedrich Horn;** b. London, June 21, 1786; d. Boston, Oct. 21, 1849. He studied with his father, and practiced voice under the guidance of Rauzzini. He made his debut as a singer in a light opera (June 26, 1809); sang Kaspar in the Eng. production of *Der Freischütz.* In 1827 he went to N.Y., where he staged several of his operas; returned to London in 1830; in 1832 he emigrated to America; there he wrote several oratorios, including *The Remission of Sin* (later named *Satan*). In 1847 he became conductor of the Handel and Haydn Society in Boston. In the U.S., he was notable primarily as a singer and composer of ballads.

Horn, Karl Friedrich, German composer; b. Nordhausen, April 13, 1762; d. Windsor, England, Aug. 5, 1830. He settled in England at the age of 20, and with the patronage of Count Brühl, Saxon ambassador in London, became a fashionable teacher. In 1823 he became organist of St. George's Chapel at Windsor. With Wesley he prepared an Eng. edition of Bach's *Wohltemperierte Clavier;* also wrote a treatise on thoroughbass; composed 12 sets of piano variations, with flute obbligato; 6 piano sonatas; *Military Divertimentos.*

Hornbostel, Erich Moritz von, eminent musicologist; b. Vienna, Feb. 25, 1877; d. Cambridge, England, Nov. 28, 1935. He studied philosophy in Vienna and Heidelberg; received a Ph.D. in chemistry from the Univ. of Vienna (1900); in 1905–6 was the assistant of Stumpf in Berlin; in 1906, came to the U.S. to record and study Indian music (Pawnee); in 1906–33, was director of the Phonogramm-Archiv in Berlin, and concurrently a prof. at the Univ. of Berlin (1917–33); then went to the U.S. In 1934 he went to England. He was a specialist in Asian, African, and other non-European music; also investigated the problems of tone psychology; contributed hundreds of articles to scholarly publications on these subjects. He edited a collection of records, *Musik des Orients* (Lindström, 1932); from 1922 until his death was co-editor, with C. Stumpf, of the *Sammelbände für vergleichende Musikwissenschaft.* Hornbostel's writings are being prepared for reissue, edited by K.P. Wachsmann et al. (The Hague, 1975—).

Horne, Marilyn, outstanding American mezzo-soprano; b. Bradford, Pa., Jan. 16, 1934. In 1945 the family moved to Long Beach, Calif.; she enrolled as a vocal student of William Vennard at the Univ. of Southern Calif., in Los Angeles; also attended master classes given by Lotte Lehmann. In 1952 she joined the Roger Wagner Chorale and traveled to Europe with it. Returning to California, she gave a recital at the Hollywood Bowl in 1954. She went to Europe again in 1956; spent a year in Vienna, and joined the staff of the Municipal Opera at Gelsenkirchen, where she sang a variety of roles, including Mimi in *La Bohème,* Tatiana in *Eugene Onegin,* Minnie in *The Girl of the Golden West,* and the demanding role of Marie in *Wozzeck.* In 1960 she returned to California, where she married the conductor **Henry Lewis,** who became the first black conductor of a standard American symph. orch. when he was appointed to the post of music director of the New Jersey Symph. Orch. in 1968. Their interracial marriage prospered; a daughter was born to them, but their psychological incompatibility led to a separation in 1976. Marilyn Horne's career progressed with excellent allure; she impressed her audience with her performance of Marie in *Wozzeck* at the San Francisco Opera on Oct. 4, 1960. On March 3, 1970, she made her debut at the Metropolitan Opera in N.Y. in the role of Adalgisa in *Norma;* she subsequently sang there the roles of Rosina in *The Barber of Seville* (Jan. 23, 1971), Carmen (Sept. 19, 1972), Isabella in *L'Italiana in Algeri* (Nov. 10, 1973), and Fides in *Le Prophète* (Jan. 18, 1977). On Oct. 16, 1975, she appeared in the title role of Handel's *Rinaldo* at the Houston Opera; on Oct. 13, 1977, she sang with the Houston Grand Opera the title role of Rossini's *Tancredi.* She wrote (with assistance) an autobiography, *My Life* (N.Y., 1983).

Horovitz, Joseph, Austrian-born British composer; b. Vienna, May 26, 1926. He was taken to England after the Anschluss in 1938, and studied music at Oxford, gaining his degree of B.Mus. there; then went to Paris to take a course with Nadia Boulanger. He developed a series of mannerisms that, when synthesized, became a recognizable style, modernistic without solemnity, appealing without crudity, and often cachinnogenic.
WORKS: Operas: *Gentleman's Island* (Cheltenham, July 9, 1959); *The Dumb Wife* (Antwerp, Jan. 10, 1972). Ballets: *Les Femmes d'Alger* (London, 1952); *Alice in Wonderland* (London, 1953); *Let's Make a Ballet* (London, 1965). For Orch.: *Fantasia on a Theme of Couperin* for Strings (1962); Trumpet Concerto (1965); *Horizon Overture* (1972); *Toy Symphony* (1977); 5 string quartets; Cello Sonata (1951); Oboe Quartet (1956); *Horrortorio* (a horror oratorio; 1959); *Jazz Harpsichord Concerto;* other synthetic pieces.

Horowitz, Vladimir, fabulous Russian-born American pianist; b. Berdichev, Oct. 1, 1904. He began to study piano with his mother, who was herself an excellent pianist, a pupil of Vladimir Puchalsky, who later became Horowitz's own teacher at the Kiev Cons. His other teachers were Sergei Tarnowsky and Felix Blumenfeld. He made his public debut in a recital in Kiev on May 30, 1920, which was the beginning of a remarkable career. He made his first appearance outside Russia in a recital in Berlin on Jan. 2, 1926; then gave concerts throughout Europe. In Paris in 1928 he took a few lessons with Alfred Cortot, confined mostly to suggestions about style and interpretation. On Jan. 12, 1928, he made his American debut, performing Tchaikovsky's First Piano Concerto, with the N.Y. Phil. conducted by Sir Thomas Beecham, who was also making his American debut; he then appeared as a soloist with other American orchs., earning the reputation of a piano virtuoso of the highest caliber, so that his very name became synonymous with pianistic greatness. In 1931 he played at the White House for President Hoover, his family, and guests. In 1933 he married Wanda Toscanini, daughter of Arturo Toscanini. He became an American citizen in 1942. He celebrated the 25th anniversary of his American debut with a recital at Carnegie Hall in N.Y. on Feb. 25, 1953. Horowitz seemed to possess every gift of public success; he was universally admired; his concerts sold out without fail whenever and wherever he chose to play. His idol, Rachmaninoff, became his friend. But amidst all these artistic blessings he developed a nervous ailment that made it impossible for him to play in public; there were anxious moments before his scheduled appearances when his managers and his family were not sure whether he would be able or willing to play. For a period of 12 years, between 1953 and 1965, he withdrew from the stage; public confrontation seemed to lead to physiological impediments. However, he enjoyed making recordings when he was free to change his successive versions in the sanctuary of a studio. He also accepted a few private pupils. On May 9, 1965, he finally returned to the stage in a recital at Carnegie Hall, but another hiatus in his concert activity occurred from 1969–74; once again he had to overcome his reluctance to face an audience; he would announce a concert, only to cancel it at the crucial moment. On Jan. 8, 1978, he performed Rachmaninoff's 3rd Piano Concerto with Eugene Ormandy and the N.Y. Phil.; on Feb. 26, 1978, he played at the White House at the invitation of President Carter; this coincided with the 50th anniversary of his American debut. On May 22, 1982, at the behest of the Prince of Wales, he gave a recital in the Royal Festival Hall in London, marking his first appearance in Europe in 31 years. Through his recordings he formed a large following in Japan; in June 1983 he decided to give a series of concerts in Tokyo and other Japanese cities, which became an event of the season. Horowitz's tastes lie with Romantic music; his performances of works by Chopin, Liszt, Tchaikovsky, and Rachmaninoff are incomparable. He also excels in congenial renditions of Scriabin's music. Among contemporary composers Horowitz prefers those of a lyrical nature. He gave the world premiere of Samuel Barber's Piano Sonata in Havana on Dec. 9, 1949. He himself composed a sparkling piano paraphrase of themes from *Carmen* and made a vertiginous transcription for piano of Sousa's march *Stars and Stripes Forever,* a veritable tour de force of pianistic pyrotechnics, which he performed for years as an encore, to the delight of his audiences.

Horszowski, Mieczyslaw, Polish pianist; b. Lemberg (Lwow), June 23, 1892. He was a certified child prodigy; made his first public appearance at the age of 10, playing Beethoven's First Piano Concerto with the Warsaw Phil. He studied piano with Henryk Melcer in Lemberg; was then sent to Vienna, where Leschetizky accepted him as a private pupil. On Feb. 16, 1906, he played a solo recital at La Scala in Milan. He also played for Pope Pius X in Rome; then gave a command performance for Queen Alexandra at Buckingham Palace in England. He played for Granados in Barcelona; then undertook an extensive concert tour in Europe; also played joint recitals with Casals. In 1954 he gave a series of piano recitals in N.Y. in programs including the piano works of Beethoven. On Nov 13, 1961, he played for President John F. Kennedy at the White House with Alexander Schneider and Casals. In 1942 he joined the faculty of the Curtis Inst. in Philadelphia. In 1981, at the age of 89, he married his longtime companion, the Italian pianist **Bice Costa** of Genoa, whom he had met 26 years before. At the age of 90 he played a Mozart concerto at the Metropolitan Museum of Art in N.Y. His name is pronounced Mee-eh-chee-sláv Hor-shóv-skee.

Horton, Austin Asadata Dafora, Nigerian composer; b. Freetown, Sierra Leone, West Africa, Aug. 4, 1890; d. New York, March 4, 1965. As a youth, he became deeply interested in African folk dance festivals and studied the culture of many African tribes. He then went to Europe and organized a dance group in Germany. He settled in the U.S. in 1921, devoting himself to the propagation of African art, coaching singers, dancers, and drummers for performance of African dances. He utilized authentic African melorhythms in several of his stage spectacles, for which he also arranged the musical scores. Of these, *Kykunkor, the Witch,* produced at the Unity Theater Studio in N.Y. on May 7, 1934, attracted considerable attention. He also produced a dance drama, *Tunguru.*

Horvat, Stanko, Croatian composer; b. Zagreb, March 12, 1930. He studied composition with Šulek at the Zagreb Academy of Music, graduating in 1956; then took a course with Tony Aubin at the Paris Cons. and private composition lessons with René Leibowitz (1958–59); returning to Yugoslavia, he was appointed to the music faculty of the Zagreb Academy in 1961. In his style of composition he traversed successively a period of neo-Classical mannerisms, serialism in its dodecaphonic aspect, aleatory expressionism, and sonorism; eventually he returned to a median technique of pragmatic modernism.

Horwitz, Karl, Austrian composer; b. Vienna, Jan. 1, 1884; d. Salzburg, Aug. 18, 1925. He studied with Arnold Schoenberg, and adopted an atonal idiom. He was active in organizing the Donaueschingen Festivals (from 1921) and in other societies devoted to modern music; among his works are a symph. poem, *Vom Tode;* 2 string quartets; several song cycles. In 1924 he suffered a loss of hearing, as a result of disease, and died shortly afterward.

Hothby, John, English music theorist; b. c.1415; d. probably in England, Nov. 6, 1487. He was a student at Oxford; was a member of the Carmelite order; lived in Florence, Italy, about 1440, and was known there under the Italianized name **Ottobi;** was then in Lucca (1468–86), where he taught in canonic schools. In 1486 he was recalled to England by Henry VII. A. Seay edited *The Musical Works of John Hothby* in Corpus Mensurabilis Musicae, XXXIII (1964). An edition of his theoretical works is in progress.

Hotter, Hans, greatly esteemed German bass-baritone; b. Offenbach, Jan. 19, 1909. He studied voice in Munich in 1929 made his debut at Troppau; sang there from 1930; subsequently was a member at the German Theater in Prague (1932–34). He then sang at the Hamburg State Opera (1934–45), the Bavarian State Opera in Munich (1937–72), the Berlin State Opera (1939–72), and the Vienna State Opera (1939–42). He also made appearances with La Scala in Milan, Covent Garden in London, the Teatro Colón in Buenos Aires, the Paris Opéra, and the Chicago Opera. He made his Metropolitan Opera debut on Nov. 9, 1950, as the Dutchman in *Der fliegende Holländer,* and remained on its roster until 1954. From 1977 he taught at the Vienna Hochschule für Musik. He was particularly acclaimed for his Wagnerian roles; he was ranked as the foremost Wotan at the Bayreuth Festivals.

Hotteterre, a family of French musicians: **Nicolas Hotteterre** (b. 1637; d. Paris, May 10, 1694), a hurdy-gurdy player; his brother **Martin** (d. 1712), also a hurdy-gurdy player and a performer at the court ballets; **Louis Hotteterre** (d. 1719), son of Nicolas, who played the flute at the French court for 50 years (1664–1714); his brother **Nicolas Hotteterre** (d. Paris, Dec. 4, 1727), who (like his brother) played flute and oboe in Lully's orch. at the court of Louis XIV; **Jacques Hotteterre** (b. Sept. 29, 1674; d. Paris, July 16, 1762), surnamed "le Romain," evidently owing to his long sojourns in Rome, popularized the transverse (German) flute at the French court and publ. several manuals on that instrument and others: *Principes de la flûte traversière ou flûte d'Allemagne, de la flûte à bec ou flûte douce et du hautbois* (Paris, 1707; sometimes attributed to his cousin Louis; the 1728 ed. was reprinted in facsimile, Kassel, 1941); *Méthode pour la musette* (1738); *L'Art de préluder sur la flûte traversière, sur la flûte à bec,* *etc.* (Paris, 1712; 2nd ed. under the title *Méthode pour apprendre . . .* , c.1765); he also wrote sonatas, duos, trios, suites, *rondes (chansons à danser),* and minuets for flute.

Hovhaness, Alan (Vaness) Scott, prolific and proficient American composer of Armenian-Scottish descent; b. Somerville, Mass., March 8, 1911. His family name was **Chakmakjian.** He took piano lessons with Adelaide Proctor and with Heinrich Gebhard in Boston; his academic studies were at Tufts Univ.; in 1932 he enrolled in the New England Cons. as a student of Frederick S. Converse. From his earliest attempts at composition, he took great interest in the musical roots of his paternal ancestry, studying the folk songs assembled by the Armenian musician Komitas, and gradually came to believe that music must reflect the natural monody embodied in national songs and ancient church hymns. In his own music he adopted modal melodies and triadic harmonies. This *parti pris* had the dual effect of alienating him from the milieu of modern composers while exercising great attraction for the music consumer at large. By dint of ceaseless repetition of melodic patterns and relentless dynamic tension, he succeeded in creating a sui generis type of impressionistic monody, flowing on the shimmering surfaces of euphony, free from the upsetting intrusion of heterogeneous dissonance; an air of mysticism pervades his music, aided by the programmatic titles which he often assigns to his compositions. After completion of his studies, he served on the faculty of the New England Cons. of Music (1948–51); then moved to N.Y. He was awarded two Guggenheim fellowships (1954 and 1958). In 1959 he received a Fulbright fellowship and traveled to India and Japan, where he collected native folk songs for future use and presented his own works, as pianist and conductor, receiving tremendous acclaim. In 1962 he was engaged as composer-in-residence at the Univ. of Hawaii; he then traveled to Korea. He eventually settled in Seattle. A composer of relentless fecundity, he produced 51 symphs., several operas, quasi-operas, and pseudo-operas, as well as an enormous amount of choral music. The totality of his output is in excess of 370 opus numbers. In a laudable spirit of self-criticism, he destroyed 7 of his early symphs. and began numbering them anew so that his first numbered symph. (subtitled *Exile*) was chronologically his 8th. He performed a similar auto-da-fé on other dispensable pieces. Among his more original compositions is a symph. score *And God Created Great Whales,* in which the voices of humpback whales recorded on tape were used a solo with the orch.; the work was performed to great effect in the campaign to save the whale from destruction by human (and inhuman) predators.
WORKS: OPERAS (each one to the composer's own libretto): *Etchmiadzin* (1946); *The Blue Flame* (San Antonio, Texas, Dec. 13, 1959); *Spirit of the Avalanche* (Tokyo, Feb. 15, 1963); *Wind Drum* and *The Burning House* (both at Gatlinburg, Tenn., Aug. 23, 1964); *Pilate* (Los Angeles, June 26, 1966); *The Travelers* (Foothill College, Los Altos Hills, Calif., April

22, 1967); *Pericles,* grand opera (1975); *Tale of the Sun Goddess Going into the Stone House* (1979). Operetta, *Afton Water,* on the play of William Saroyan (1951).

SYMPHS. (the numbering does not always coincide with the chronological order of composition): No. 1, *Exile* (BBC, London, May 26, 1939); No. 2, *Mysterious Mountain* (Houston, Oct. 31, 1955, Stokowski conducting); No. 3 (N.Y., Oct. 14, 1956); No. 4 for Concert Band (Pittsburgh, June 28, 1959); No. 5, *Short Symphony* (1959); No. 6, *Celestial Gate* (1959); No. 7, *Nanga Parvat,* for Band (1959); No. 8, *Arjuna* (1947; Madras, India, Feb. 1, 1960); No. 9, *St. Vartan* (N.Y., March 11, 1951); No. 10 (1959); No. 11, *All Men Are Brothers* (1960, New Orleans, March 21, 1961; revised, New Orleans, March 31, 1970); No. 12, with Chorus (1960); No. 13 (1953); No. 14, *Ararat* (1960); No. 15, *Silver Pilgrimage* (N.Y., March 28, 1963); No. 16, *Korean Kayageum,* for Strings and Korean Percussion Instruments (Seoul, Jan. 26, 1963); No. 17 for Metal Orch., commissioned by the Amercian Metallurgical Congress (Cleveland, Oct. 23, 1963); No. 18, *Circe* (1964); No. 19, *Vishnu* (N.Y., June 2, 1967); No. 20, *3 Journeys to a Holy Mountain,* for Concert Band (1968); No. 21, *Etchmiadzin* (1968); No. 22, *City of Light* (1970); No. 23, *Ani,* for Band (1972); No. 24, *Majnun,* with Chorus (1973; Lubbock, Texas, Jan. 25, 1974); No. 25, *Odysseus,* for Chamber Orch. (1973; London, April 10, 1974); No. 26, *Consolation* (San Jose, Calif., Oct. 24, 1975); No. 27 (1975); No. 28 (1976); No. 29 for Horn and Orch. (Minneapolis, May 4, 1977); No. 30 (1976); No. 31 for Strings (Seattle, Dec. 7, 1977); No. 32 for Chamber Orch. (1977); No. 33 for Chamber Orch. (1978); No. 34 (1977); No. 35 for Korean Instruments and Orch. (Seoul, June 9, 1978); No. 36 for Flute and Orch., op. 312 (Washington, D.C., Jan. 16, 1979; Rampal, soloist; Rostropovich conducting); No. 37 (1978); No. 38 for Soprano and Orch. (1978); No. 39 for Guitar and Orch. (1978); No. 40 for Brass, Timpani, and Orch. (1979; Interlochen, April 9, 1982); No. 41, *Mountain Sunset* (1979); No. 42 (1979); No. 43 (1979; Aptos, Calif., Aug. 20, 1981); No. 44 (1980); No. 45 (1979); No. 46, *To the Green Mountains* (Burlington, Vt., May 2, 1981); No. 47, *Walla Walla, Land of Many Waters,* for Soprano and Orch. (Walla Walla, Wash., Nov. 24, 1981); No. 48, *Vision of Andromeda* (Miami, Fla., June 21, 1982, by the visiting Minneapolis Symph. Orch.); No. 49, *Christmas,* for Strings (1981); No. 50, *Mount St. Helens* (1982); No. 51 (1982).

23 CONCERTOS: Concerto for Cello and Orch. (1936); *Lousadzak (Coming of Light)* for Piano and Strings (1944; Boston, Feb. 4, 1945); *Return and Rebuild the Desolate Places,* concerto for Trumpet and Strings (N.Y., June 17, 1945); *Asori,* concerto for Flute, Cornet, Bassoon, Trumpet, Timpani, and Strings (1946); *Sosi,* concerto for Violin, Piano, Percussion, and Strings (1948; N.Y., March 6, 1949); *Artik,* concerto for Horn and Orch. (1948; Rochester, N.Y., May 7, 1954); *Zertik Parkim,* concerto for Piano and Chamber Orch. (1948); *Elibris (God of Dawn),* concerto for Flute and Strings (1949; San Francisco, Jan. 26, 1950); *Khaldis,* concerto for 4 Trumpets, Piano, and Percussion (1951); *Talin,* concerto for Viola and String Orch. (1952); Accordion Concerto (1959); Concerto for Harp and Strings (1973); Concerto for Euphonium and Orch. (1977); Concerto for Guitar and Orch. (1979); Concerto for Soprano Saxophone and Orch. (1980); 8 numbered concertos: No. 1, *Arevakal (Season of the Sun),* for Orch. (1951; N.Y., Feb. 18, 1952); No. 2 for Violin and Strings (1951–57); No. 3, *Diran,* for Baritone Horn or Trombone, and Strings (1948); No. 4 for Orch. (1952; Louisville, Ky., Feb. 20, 1954); No. 5 for Piano and Strings (1952); No. 6 for Harmonica and Strings (1953); No. 7 for Orch (1953); No. 8 for Orch. (1953).

OTHER WORKS FOR ORCH.: *Storm on Mt. Wildcat* (1931); *Celestial Fantasy* (1944); *3 Armenian Rhapsodies* (1944); *Khiriam Hairis* for Trumpet and Strings (1944); *Tzaikerk (Evening Song)* for Orch. (1945); *Kohar* for Orch. (1946); *Forest of Prophetic Sounds* for Orch. (1948); *Overture* for Trombone and Strings (1948); *Janabar,* 5 hymns for Violin, Trumpet, Piano, and Strings (1949; N.Y., March 11, 1951); *Prelude and Quadruple Fugue* for Orch. (1955); *Meditation on Orpheus* for Orch. (1957–58); *Copernicus,* tone poem (1960); *Mountain of Prophecy* for Orch. (1960); *Meditation on Zeami,* symph. poem (1963; N.Y., Oct. 5, 1964); *Ukiyo, Floating World,* tone poem (1964; Salt Lake City, Jan. 30, 1965); *Fantasy on Japanese Wood Prints* for Xylophone and Orch. (Chicago, July 4, 1964); *The Holy City* for Orch. (Portland, Oreg., April 11, 1967); *Fra Angelico,* symph. poem (Detroit, March 21, 1968); *Mountain and Rivers without End* for 10 Instruments (1968); *And God Created Great Whales* for Orch., with Voices of Humpback Whales recorded on Tape (1969; N.Y., June 11, 1970); *A Rose for Emily,* ballet for Orch. (1970); *Dawn on Mt. Tahoma* for Orch. (1973); *Fanfare to the New Atlantis* for Orch. (1975); *Ode to Freedom* for Violin and Orch. (Wolf Trap Farm Park, near Washington, D.C., July 3, 1976; Yehudi Menuhin, soloist); *Rubáiyát* for Narrator, Accordion, and Orch. (1975; N.Y., May 20, 1977).

CHAMBER MUSIC: Piano Quintet No. 1 (1926; revised 1962); Piano Trio (1935); String Quartet No. 1 (1936); Violin Sonata (1937); Suite for English Horn and Bassoon (1938); *Varak* for Violin and Piano (1944); *Anahid* for Flute, English Horn, Trumpet, Timpani, Percussion, and Strings (1944); *Saris* for Violin and Piano (1946); *Haroutiun (Resurrection),* aria and fugue for Trumpet and Strings (1948); *Sosi (Forest of Prophetic Sounds)* for Violin, Piano, Horn, Timpani, Giant Tam-tam, and Strings (1948), String Quartet No. 2 (1950); *Khirgiz Suite* for Violin and Piano (1951); *Orbit No. 1* for Flute, Harp, Celesta, and Tam-tam (1952); *Orbit No. 2* for Alto Recorder and Piano (1952); *Koke No Kiwa (Moss Garden)* for English Horn, Clarinet, Harp, and Percussion (1954); Wind Quintet (1960); *Nagooran* for an Ensemble of South Indian Instruments (1962); String Trio (1962); Piano Quintet No. 2 (1964); Sextet for Violin and 5 Percussionists (1966); *6 Dances* for Brass Quintet (1967); *Spirit of Ink,* 9 pieces for 3 Flutes (1968); String Quartet No. 3 (1968); *Vibration Painting* for 13 String Instruments (1969); String Quartet No. 4 (1970); *The Garden of Adonis* for Flute and Harp (1971); Sonata for 2 Bassoons (1973); Clarinet Quartet (1973); *Night of a White Cat* for

Clarinet and Piano (1973); *Fantasy* for Double Bass and Piano (1974); String Quartet No. 5 (1976); Suite for 4 Trumpets and Trombone (1976); Suite for Alto Saxophone and Guitar (1976); Septet for Flute, Clarinet, Bass Clarinet, Trumpet, Trombone, Double Bass, and Percussion (1976); Sonata for 2 Clarinets (1977); *Sunset on Mt. Tahoma* for 2 Trumpets, Trombone, and Organ (1978); Sonata for Clarinet and Harpsichord (1978); Saxophone Trio (1979); 2 Sonatas for 3 Trumpets and 2 Trombones (1979).

PIANO MUSIC: *Mountain Lullaby* (1931); *3 Preludes and Fugues* (1935); *Sonata Ricercare* (1935); *Macedonian Mountain Dance* (1937); *Do you remember the last silence?* (1957); *Poseidon Sonata* (1957); *Child of the Garden*, for Piano, 4-hands (1958); *Madras Sonata* (1947; final revision, 1959); *Bardo Sonata* (1959); *Love Song Vanishing into Sounds of Crickets* (1979); *Sonata Catamount* (1980); *Sonata, Journey to Arcturus* (1981); *Hiroshige's Cat* (1982); *Sonata on the Long Total Eclipse of the Moon, July 6, 1982* (1982); *Tsugouharu Fujita's Cat* (1982); *Lake Sammamish* (1983).

VOCAL WORKS: *Ad Lyram* for Solo Voices, Double Chorus, and Chamber Orch. (Houston, Texas, March 12, 1957); *To the God Who Is in the Fire*, cantata (Urbana, Ill., April 13, 1957); *Magnificat* for Solo Voices, Chorus, and Chamber Orch. (1957); *Fuji*, cantata for Female Voices, Flute, Harp, and String Orch. (1960); *In the Beginning Was the Word* for Vocal Soloists, Chorus, and Orch. (1963); *Lady of Light* for Solo Voices, Chorus, and Chamber Orch. (1969); *Saturn*, 12 pieces for Soprano, Clarinet, and Piano (1971); *The Way of Jesus*, folk oratorio (St. Patrick's Cathedral, N.Y., Feb. 23, 1975); *Revelations of St. Paul*, cantata (1980; N.Y., Jan. 28, 1981); innumerable hymns, anthems, sacred and secular choruses; songs.

Hovland, Egil, Norwegian composer; b. Mysen, Oct. 18, 1924. He studied organ and composition at the Oslo Cons. (1946–49), later studying privately with Bjarne Brustad (1951–52, in Oslo), Vagn Holmboe (1954, in Copenhagen), Aaron Copland (1957, at Tanglewood), and Dallapiccola (1959, in Florence). In Norway he was active as a music critic and as an organist at a church in Fredrikstad. He cultivates a peculiarly Scandinavian type of neo-Classical polyphony, but is apt to use serial techniques.

Howard, John Tasker, eminent American writer on music; b. Brooklyn, Nov. 30, 1890; d. West Orange, N.Y., Nov. 20, 1964. He attended Williams College in Williamstown, Mass.; then studied composition with Howard Brockway and Mortimer Wilson. He then devoted himself primarily to musical journalism; was managing editor of the *Musician* (1919–22); served as educational director of the Ampico Corp. (1922–28); then edited the music section of *McCall's Magazine* (1928–30) and *Cue* (1936–38); taught at Columbia Univ. in 1950–54. From 1940 to 1956 he was the curator of the Americana Music Collection at the N.Y. Public Library, which he enriched to a great extent. His major achievement was the publication of several books and monographs on American music and musicians.

WRITINGS: *Our American Music* (N.Y., 1931; 4 eds., the last one posthumous, 1965); *Stephen Foster, America's Troubadour* (N.Y., 1934; revised 1953); *Ethelbert Nevin* (N.Y., 1935); *Our Contemporary Composers, American Music in the 20th Century* (1941); *This Modern Music* (N.Y., 1942; new ed. by James Lyons, 1957, under the title *Modern Music*); *The World's Great Operas* (N.Y., 1948); *A Short History of Music in America* (N.Y., 1957; with G.K. Bellows). He was also a composer of modest, but respectable, attainments. He wrote a piece for Piano and Orch., entitled *Fantasy on a Choral Theme* (New Jersey Orch., Orange, N.J., Feb. 20, 1929); also *Foster Sonatina* for Violin and Piano; piano pieces; and some songs.

Howard, Kathleen, contralto; b. Niagara Falls, Canada, July 17, 1884; d. Hollywood, Aug. 15, 1956. She studied in N.Y. with Bouhy and in Paris with Jean de Reszke; sang at the Metz Opera (1907–9); at Darmstadt (1909–12); at Covent Garden in London (1913); with the Century Opera in N.Y. (1914–15). She made her first appearance with the Metropolitan Opera in N.Y. in *The Magic Flute* (Nov. 20, 1916); remained on the staff until 1928. After her retirement from the stage, she was engaged in magazine work; was fashion editor of *Harper's Bazaar* (1928–33); publ. an autobiography, *Confessions of an Opera Singer* (N.Y., 1918). She married Edward Kelley Baird on June 27, 1916.

Howe, Mary, American composer; b. Richmond, Va., April 4, 1882; d. Washington, D.C., Sept. 14, 1964. She studied at the Peabody Cons. in Baltimore; was a pupil of Gustav Strube (composition) and Ernest Hutcheson (piano); in 1915, settled in Washington, where she played a prominent part in musical organizations. She was a vice-president of the Friends of Music of the Library of Congress; was a member of the board of directors of the National Orch.

WORKS: Violin Sonata (1922); Suite for String Quartet and Piano (1923); *Sand* for Orch. (1928); *Dirge* for Orch. (1931); *Castellana* for 2 Pianos and Orch. (1935); *Spring Pastoral* for Solo Violin and 13 Instruments (1936); *Stars and Whimsy* for 15 Instruments (1937); *Potomac*, orch. suite (1940); *Agreeable Overture* (1949); *Rock*, symph. poem (Vienna, Feb. 15, 1955); choral works: *Chain Gang Song* (1925) and *Prophecy, 1792* (1943).

Howell, Dorothy, English pianist and composer; b. Handsworth, Feb. 25, 1898; d. London, Jan. 12, 1982. She studied composition with McEwen and piano with Tobias Matthay at the Royal Academy of Music in London; from 1924 to 1970 she taught music theory there. Among her works are a ballet, *Koong Shee;* a symph. poem, *Lamia* (after Keats); an overture, *The Rock;* a Piano Concerto; and some chamber music.

Howells, Herbert, distinguished English composer; b. Lydney, Gloucestershire, Oct. 17, 1892; d. Oxford, Feb. 24, 1983. In 1912 he entered the Royal College of Music in London, where he studied composition with Stanford and counterpoint with Charles Wood; in 1920 he was appointed an instructor in composition there, a position he held for more than 40 years. In 1936 he succeeded Holst as music director at St. Paul's Girls' School, remaining there until 1962; he also was a prof. of music at the Univ. of London (1954–64). In 1953 he was made a Commander of the Order of the British Empire and in 1972 a Companion of Honour. The music Howells wrote during his long life was nobly British, in its national references, its melodic outspokenness, and its harmonic opulence; in this it was a worthy continuation of the fine tradition of Elgar and Vaughan Williams.

WORKS: FOR ORCH.: Piano Concerto No. 1 in C major (1913; London, July 10, 1914); 3 dances for Violin and Orch. (1915); "The B's," suite (1915); *Puck's Minuet* and *Merry-eye* (1917–20); *Procession* (1922); *Pastoral Rhapsody* (1923); Piano Concerto No. 2 in C minor (1924); *Paradise Rondel* (1925); *Pageantry* for Brass Band (1934); *Fantasia* for Cello and Orch. (1937); Concerto for Strings (1939); Suite for Strings (1944); *Music for a Prince,* suite (1949); *Triptych* for Brass Band (1960).

CHORAL MUSIC: *Sine nomine* for 2 Soloists, Chorus, and Orch. (1922); *A Kent Yeoman's Wooing Song* for Soloists, Chorus, and Orch. (1933); *Requiem* for Unaccompanied Chorus (1936); *Hymnus Paradisi* for Soprano, Tenor, Chorus, and Orch. (1938); *A Maid Peerless* for Women's Voices and Strings, or Piano (1949); *Missa Sabrinensis* for Soloists, Chorus, and Orch. (1954; Worcester Festival, Sept. 7, 1954); *An English Mass* (1956); *Stabat Mater* for Tenor, Chorus, and Orch. (1963); *Take him, earth, for cherishing* (Motet on the Death of President Kennedy) (1964); *The Coventry Mass* for Choir and Organ (1968).

CHAMBER MUSIC: Piano Quartet (1916); *Rhapsodic Quintet* for Clarinet and Strings (1917); *Phantasy String Quartet* (1918); *In Gloucestershire,* string quartet (1923); 3 Sonatas for Violin and Piano (1918, 1918, 1923); Sonata for Oboe and Piano (1943); Sonata for Clarinet and Piano (1949).

FOR KEYBOARD: Organ Sonata No. 1 (1911); Organ Sonata No. 2 (1933); *Prelude—De profundis* for Organ (1958); Partita for Organ (1971); 2 sets of pieces for Clavichord: *Lambert's Clavichord* (1926–27) and *Howells' Clavichord* (1951–56); *Sonatina* for Piano (1971).

Howland, William Legrand, American composer; b. Asbury Park, N.J., 1873; d. at his cottage, Douglas Manor, Long Island, N.Y., July 26, 1915. He studied with Philip Scharwenka in Berlin, and lived most of his life in Europe. His one-act opera, *Sarrona,* to his own libretto, was produced in Italian in Bruges, Belgium (Aug. 3, 1903), and subsequently had a number of performances in Italy; it was staged in N.Y. (in Eng.) on Feb. 8, 1910; in Philadelphia (in German) on March 23, 1911. He wrote another opera, *Nita;* 2 oratorios: *The Resurrection* and *Ecce Homo;* and some choral works.

Hřimalý, Adalbert (Vojtech), Czech violinist and composer; b. Pilsen, July 30, 1842; d. Vienna, June 15, 1908. A member of an exceptionally musical family (his father was an organist; his 3 brothers were violinists), he received an early training at home; then studied with Mildner at the Prague Cons. (1855–61); was subsequently active as a conductor, composer, and teacher in various towns in the Netherlands, Sweden, and Rumania. He wrote a great number of works, including an opera, *Zaklety princ (The Enchanted Prince;* Prague, May 13, 1872).

Hřimalý, Johann (Jan), celebrated violinist and teacher; b. Pilsen, April 13, 1844; d. Moscow, Jan. 24, 1915. Like his older brother **Adalbert,** he studied at the Prague Cons. At the age of 24 he went to Moscow, where he became a prof. of violin at the Cons. (1874). He remained in Moscow for 40 years until his death, and was regarded there as a great teacher; 2 generations of Russian violinists studied under him. He also organized a string quartet in Moscow; publ. *Tonleiterstudien und Übungen in Doppelgriffen für die Violine* (Prague, 1895).

Hřimalý, Otakar, Czech violinist, son of **Adalbert Hřimalý;** b. Cernauti, Rumania, Dec. 20, 1883; d. Prague, July 10, 1945. He studied at the Vienna Cons. In 1909 he went to Moscow upon the recommendation of his uncle, **Johann Hřimalý;** became a prof. at the Moscow Cons., and remained there until 1922; then lived in Rumania; in 1939, went to Prague. He was known not only as a violin teacher but also as a composer; wrote an opera; 2 symphs.; the symph. poems *Ganymed* and *Der goldene Topf;* also chamber music and violin pieces.

Hubay, Jenö, celebrated Hungarian violinist; b. Budapest, Sept. 15, 1858; d. Vienna, March 12, 1937. He received his initial training from his father, Karl Hubay, prof. of violin at the Budapest Cons.; gave his first public concert at the age of 11; then studied with Joachim in Berlin (1873–76). His appearance in Paris, at a Pasdeloup concert, attracted the attention of Vieuxtemps, of whom he became a favorite pupil; in 1882 he succeeded Vieuxtemps as prof. at the Brussels Cons. In 1886 he became a prof. at the Budapest Cons. (succeeding his father); from 1919 to 1934 he was its director. In Budapest he formed the celebrated Hubay String Quartet. In 1894 he married the Countess Rosa Cebrain. Among his pupils were Vecsey, Szigeti, Telmányi, Eddy Brown, and other renowned violinists. Hubay was also a prolific composer.

WORKS: Operas (all produced in Budapest): *Alienor* (Dec. 5, 1891); *Le Luthier de Crémone* (Nov. 10, 1894); *A Falu Rossza (The Village Vagabond;* March 20, 1896); *Moosröschen* (Feb. 21, 1903); *Anna Karenina* (Nov. 10, 1923); *Az álarc (The Mask;* Feb. 26, 1931); 4 symphs.: No. 1 (1885); No. 2, *1914–15* (1915); No. 3, *Vita nuova,* for Soli, Chorus, and Organ; No. 4, *Petöfi-Sinfonie,* for Soli, Chorus, and Orch.; also *Biedermeyer Suite* for Orch. (1913); 4 violin concertos; 14 pieces for Violin and Orch., in the Hungarian manner, *Scènes de la Csárda; Sonate romantique* for Violin and Piano; he also ed. the violin études of Kreutzer (1908), Rode, Mayseder, and Saint Lubin (1910).

Huber, Hans, Swiss composer; b. Eppenberg, near Olten, June 28, 1852; d. Locarno, Dec. 25, 1921. He studied at the Leipzig Cons. with Richter, Reinecke, and Wenzel (1870–74); then taught music at Wesserling, at Thann (Alsace), and at Basel; received an honorary degree of Dr.Phil. from Basel Univ. (1892). In 1896 he became director of the Basel Cons., a post that he held until his death. Huber composed prolifically in all genres; his style combined the rhapsodic form typical of Lisztian technique with simple ballad-like writing. He often used Swiss songs for thematic material. In Switzerland his reputation is very great and his works are frequently performed, but they are virtually unknown elsewhere.

WORKS: Operas: *Weltfrühling* (Basel, March 28, 1894); *Kudrun* (Basel, Jan. 29, 1896); *Der Simplicius* (Basel, Feb. 22, 1912); *Die schöne Bellinda* (Bern, April 2, 1916); *Frutta di mare* (Basel, Nov. 24, 1918); 8 symphs. (all except No. 2 perf. first in Basel): No. 1, *William Tell* (April 26, 1881); No. 2, *Böcklinsinfonie* (Zürich, July 2, 1900); No. 3, *Heroische* (Nov. 9, 1917); No. 4, *Akademische* (May 23, 1909); No. 5, *Romantische* (Feb. 11, 1906); No. 6 (Nov. 19, 1911); No. 7, *Swiss* (June 9, 1917); No. 8 (Oct. 29, 1921); 4 piano concertos (Basel, 1878, 1891, 1899, 1910); Violin Concerto (1878); Sextet for Piano and Wind Instruments (1900); Quintet for Piano and Wind Instruments (1914); 2 string quintets (1890, 1907); String Quartet; 2 piano quartets; 5 piano trios; 10 violin sonatas; 5 cello sonatas; a number of piano works, among them 48 preludes and fugues for piano, 4-hands.

Huber, Kurt, eminent Swiss musicologist; b. Chur, Oct. 24, 1893; executed by the Gestapo in Munich, July 13, 1943, for participation in student protests against the Nazi government. He studied with Sandberger and Kroyer in Munich (Dr.Phil., 1917, with the dissertation *Ivo de Vento: Ein Beitrag zur Musikgeschichte des 16. Jahrhunderts*, 1, publ. in Lindenberg, 1918); from 1920, he taught at the Univ. of Munich; publ. *Die Doppelmeister des 16. Jahrhunderts* (Munich, 1920); *Der Ausdruck musikalischer Elementarmotive: Eine experimental psychologische Untersuchung* (Leipzig, 1923). From 1925 he devoted himself to collecting and recording old Bavarian folk songs, and publ. them (with Paul Klem).

Huberman, Bronislaw, famous Polish violinist; b. Częstochowa, Dec. 19, 1882; d. Corsier-sur-Vevey, Switzerland, June 15, 1947. At a very early age he began to study the violin with Michalowicz, a teacher at the Warsaw Cons.; he then studied with Isidor Lotto; in 1892 he was taken to Berlin, where he studied with Joachim. He made public appearances at the age of 11 in Amsterdam, Brussels, and Paris. Adelina Patti heard him in London and engaged him to appear with her at her farewell concert in Vienna (Jan. 12, 1895); on Jan. 29, 1896, he played

Brahms's Violin Concerto in Vienna; Brahms, who was present, commended him warmly. Huberman toured the U.S. in 1896–97; many world tours followed; he gave a series of 14 concerts in Paris (1920), 10 in Vienna (1924), 8 in Berlin (1926); toured America again in 1937. At a concert arranged on May 16, 1909, by the city of Genoa for the victims of the Messina earthquake, Huberman was honored by an invitation to play upon Paganini's Guarneri violin (preserved in the Museum of Genoa). He taught a master class at the Vienna State Academy (1934–36); in 1936 organized a new Palestine Symph. Orch., consisting chiefly of Jewish musicians who had lost their positions in Europe. He came to the U.S. in 1940; returned to Europe after the war. He publ. *Aus der Werkstatt des Virtuosen* (Vienna, 1912); *Mein Weg zu Paneuropa* (1925).

Hucbald (Hugbaldus, Ubaldus, Uchubaldus), Flemish monk and musical theorist; b. at or near Tournai, c.840; d. Saint-Amand, near Tournai, June 20, 930. He was a pupil of his uncle Milo, director of the singing school at Saint-Amand; then was himself director of a similar school at Nevers (860); subsequently returned to Saint-Amand and succeeded his uncle. The following works are printed under his name in Gerbert's *Scriptores* (vol. I): *De Harmonica institutione; Musica enchiriadis* (gives the earliest detailed account of the beginnings of polyphonic music and of the Daseian notation, in which the Greek aspirate sign is used in various combinations and positions to produce 18 symbols indicating that many pitches); *Scholia enchiriadis;* fragments entitled *Alia musica;* and *Commemoratio brevis de tonis et psalmis modulandis.* However, it has been established (by W. Mühlmann, in *Die "Alia Musica";* Leipzig, 1914) that Hucbald was not the author of *Musica enchiriadis.*

Hüe, Georges-Adolphe, French composer; b. Versailles, May 6, 1858; d. Paris, June 7, 1948. He was a pupil at the Paris Cons. of Reber and Paladilhe; took first Grand Prix de Rome in 1879, and the Prix Crescent in 1881; lived in Paris as a teacher and composer; was a member (succeeding Saint-Saëns) of the Académie des Beaux-Arts (1922).

WORKS: Operas: *Les Pantins* (Opéra-Comique, Dec. 28, 1881); *Le Roi de Paris* (Paris Opéra, April 26, 1901); *Titania,* after Shakespeare (Opéra-Comique, Jan. 20, 1903); *Le Miracle* (Paris Opéra, Dec. 30, 1910); *Dans l'ombre de la cathédrale,* after Blasco Ibañez (Opéra-Comique, Dec. 7, 1921); *Riquet à la houppe,* after Perrault (Opéra-Comique, Dec. 21, 1928); ballet, *Cœur brisé* (Paris, 1890); pantomime, *Siang Sin* (Paris Opéra, March 19, 1924); *Rübezahl,* symph. legend in 3 parts (Concerts Colonne, 1886); "féerie dramatique," *La Belle au bois dormant* (Paris, 1894); *Résurrection,* "épisode sacré" (1892); *Le Berger,* ballade and fantaisie for Violin and Orch. (1893); Symph.; *Rêverie* and *Sérénade* for Small Orch.; *Romance* for Violin and Orch.; choral works; songs of more than average merit (6 songs from Heine's *Lyrisches Intermezzo; Croquis d'Ori-*

ent; *Chansons printanières; Berceuse pour les gueux; 2 chansons;* etc.).

Hughes, Dom Anselm, eminent English musicologist; b. London, April 15, 1889; d. Nashdom Abbey, Burnham, Buckinghamshire, Oct. 8, 1974. He studied at Oxford (B.A., 1911; M.A., 1915); lectured on medieval church music in univs. and colleges in the U.S. and Canada (1932, 1934, 1939, and 1940); contributed articles to *Grove's Dictionary of Music and Musicians;* edited (with others) the *Old Hall Manuscript* (1933–38).
  WRITINGS: *Early English Harmony* (vol. II; London, 1912); *Latin Hymnody* (London, 1923); *Worcester Mediaeval Harmony* (Burnham, 1928); *The House of My Pilgrimage* (London, 1929); *Anglo-French Sequelae* (London, 1934); *Index to the Facsimile Edition of MS Wolfenbüttel 677* (Oxford, 1939); *Liturgical Terms for Music Students* (Boston, 1940); *Medieval Polyphony in the Bodleian Library* (Oxford, 1951); *Catalogue of the Musical Manuscripts at Peterhouse, Cambridge* (Cambridge, 1953). He also composed *Missa Sancti Benedicti* (London, 1918) and various small pieces of church music.

Hughes, Herbert, Irish critic and composer; b. Belfast, March 16, 1882; d. Brighton, England, May 1, 1937. He studied at the Royal College of Music in London. He was one of the founders of the Irish Folksong Society and co-editor of its early journals; was music critic of the *Daily Telegraph.* He collected and edited many folk songs, including the collections Boosey's *Modern Festival Series; Irish Country Songs* (in 4 vols.); *Old Irish Melodies* (3 vols.); *Historical Songs and Ballads of Ireland; Songs from Connacht; Songs of Uladh.* He composed incidental music to the comedy *And So to Bed;* the film *Irish Hearts; Nursery Rhymes,* studies in imitation (2 vols.); *Parodies* for Voice and Orch. (2 vols.); *Brian Boru's March* for Piano; *3 Satirical Songs* for Violin, Flute, Clarinet, and Bassoon; *Shockheaded Peter,* cycle for Soprano, Baritone, and Piano; etc.

Hughes, Rupert, American writer on music; b. Lancaster, Mo., Jan. 31, 1872; d. Los Angeles, Sept. 9, 1956. He studied with W.G. Smith in Cleveland (1890–92), E.S. Kelley in N.Y. (1899), and C. Pearce in London (1900–1). His publications include: *American Composers* (Boston, 1900; revised 1914); *The Musical Guide* (2 vols., N.Y., 1903; republ. as *Music Lovers' Encyclopedia,* in one vol., 1912; revised and newly ed. by Deems Taylor and Russell Kerr as *Music Lover's Encyclopedia,* 1939; revised 1954); edited *Thirty Songs by American Composers* (1904). He composed a dramatic monologue for Baritone and Piano, *Cain* (1919); piano pieces; songs. He was principally known, however, as a successful novelist.

Hugo, John Adam, American pianist and composer; b. Bridgeport, Conn., Jan. 5, 1873; d. there, Dec. 29, 1945. In 1888–97 he studied at the Stuttgart Cons. with Speidel, Faiszt, Doppler, and Zumpe; appeared as a concert pianist in Germany, England, and Italy;

returned to the U.S. in 1899. His one-act opera, *The Temple Dancer,* was one of the few operas by American composers presented by the Metropolitan Opera in N.Y. (March 12, 1919); it was also produced in Honolulu (Feb. 19, 1925). His other works are the operas *The Hero of Byzanz* (written while studying at the Stuttgart Cons.) and *The Sun God;* Symph.; 2 piano concertos; Piano Trio; pieces for violin; pieces for cello; piano pieces; and songs.

Hull, Arthur Eaglefield, English writer on music; b. Market Harborough, March 10, 1876; d. London, Nov. 4, 1928. He studied privately with Matthay and Charles Pearce in London; served as organist at Huddersfield Parish Church; was (from 1912) editor of the *Monthly Musical Record.* In 1918 he founded the British Music Society; was its honorary director until 1921; received his Mus.Doc. from Queen's College, Oxford. In 1906 he married **Constance Barratt,** an accomplished violinist. A man of broad culture, he was an enthusiast for new music; was an early champion of Scriabin in England. In 1924 he brought out a *Dictionary of Modern Music and Musicians.* This was a pioneer vol. and, despite an overabundance of egregious errors and misconceptions, is of service as a guide; a German trans. was made by Alfred Einstein, with numerous errors corrected (1926); another vol. which still retains its value is *Modern Harmony: Its Explanation and Application* (London, 1914; 3rd ed., 1923; reprinted 1934). In 1927 he publ. a book, *Music: Classical, Romantic and Modern,* which proved to be a pasticcio of borrowings from various English and American writers; this was pointed out by many reviewers, and the book was withdrawn by the publishers in 1928; this episode led directly to Hull's suicide; he threw himself under a moving train at the Huddersfield Railway Station, suffered grave injuries and loss of memory, and died a few weeks later. The list of his publications also includes *Organ Playing, Its Technique and Expression* (1911); *The Sonata in Music* (1916); *Scriabin* (1916); *Modern Musical Styles* (1916); *Design or Construction in Music* (1917); *Cyril Scott* (1918); he made Eng. translations of Romain Rolland's *Handel* (1916) and *Vie de Beethoven;* edited the complete organ works of Bach and Mendelssohn (with annotations for students); was also editor of the series Music Lovers' Library and Library of Music and Musicians (in which his book on Scriabin appeared); other books by him in the same series were *Bach* and *Three English Composers.*

Hullah, John Pyke, English composer and organist; b. Worcester, June 27, 1812; d. London, Feb. 21, 1884. He was a pupil of William Horsley; in 1833 he studied singing with Crivelli at the Royal Academy of Music; as a composer he was entirely self-taught. At the age of 24 he produced an opera to a story by Charles Dickens, *The Village Coquette* (London, Dec. 6, 1836); 2 other operas followed: *The Barber of Bassora* (London, Nov. 11, 1837) and *The Outpost* (May 17, 1838). In the meantime, he obtained the post of church organist at Croydon. He made several trips to Paris, where he became interested in the new system of vocal teaching established by Wilhem; he modified it to suit English requirements, and, with the sanction of the National Education Committee, he opened his Singing School for Schoolmasters at Exeter Hall (1841). The school became the target of bitter criticism; nonetheless, it prospered; thousands of students enrolled; his wealthy supporters helped him build St. Martin's Hall for performances of vocal music by his students; the hall was inaugurated in 1850; it was destroyed by fire in 1860. From 1844 to 1874 Hullah taught singing at King's College, and later at Queen's College and Bedford College in London. He conducted the student concerts of the Royal Academy of Music (1870–73); in 1872 he became an inspector of training schools. He held the honorary degree of LL.D. from Edinburgh Univ. (1876); was also a member of the Cecilia Society in Rome and of the Academy of Music in Florence. He edited Wilhem's *Method of Teaching Singing Adapted to English Use* (1841); publ. *A Grammar of Vocal Music* (1843); *A Grammar of Harmony* (1852); *A Grammar of Counterpoint* (1864); *The History of Modern Music* (1862); *The Third or Transition Period of Musical History* (1865); *The Cultivation of the Speaking Voice* (1870); *Music in the House* (1877); also brought out useful collections of vocal music: *The Psalter; The Book of Praise Hymnal;* the *Whole Book of Psalms with Chants.* He was the composer of the celebrated song *O that we two were Maying;* other popular songs are *The Storm* and *3 Fishers.* A *Life of John Hullah* was publ. by his wife (London, 1886).

Hüller, Johann Adam. See **Hiller, Johann Adam.**

Hüllmandel, Nicolas-Joseph, Alsatian musician; b. Strasbourg, May 23, 1756; d. London, Dec. 19, 1823. He was an illegitimate son of **Michel Hüllmandel,** organist at the Strasbourg Cathedral and nephew of the French-horn player Jean-Joseph Rodolphe. He studied with Carl Philip Emmanuel Bach in Hamburg; in 1776 he went to Paris, where he taught piano and the glass harmonica; among his pupils in composition were Onslow and Aubert. After the French Revolution he went to London, where he remained until his death. There he publ. a manual, *Principles of Music, Chiefly Calculated for the Pianoforte* (1795).

WORKS: 17 sonatas for Piano; 34 sonatas for Piano with Violin obbligato; 54 Airs for Piano; 12 Suites for Piano; 2 books of divertissements for Piano. He composed in a typical manner of his time; Mozart, in one of his letters to his father, expressed appreciation of Hüllmandel's sonatas.

Hume, Paul, American music critic; b. Chicago, Dec. 13, 1915. He studied at the Univ. of Chicago; took private lessons in piano, organ, and voice; was organist, choirmaster, and baritone soloist at various churches in Chicago and Washington, D.C.; gave song recitals in Boston and in the Midwest; taught voice at Catholic Univ. in Washington; in

1946, became music editor and critic of the *Washington Post* (until 1982); was an instructor in music history at Georgetown Univ. (1950–77); was also a visiting prof. at Yale Univ.; has contributed to the *Saturday Review* (N.Y.); was active as a lecturer and radio commentator on music; publ. *Catholic Church Music* (N.Y., 1956) and *Our Music, Our Schools, and Our Culture* (National Catholic Education Assoc., 1957). Paul Hume leaped to national fame in 1950, when President Truman, outraged by Hume's unenthusiastic review of Margaret Truman's song recital, wrote him a personal letter threatening him with bodily injury. Hume sold the letter to a Connecticut industrialist for an undisclosed sum of money.

Humfrey, Pelham, English composer; b. 1647; d. Windsor, July 14, 1674. He was among the first children appointed to the restored Chapel Royal in 1660, and (together with fellow-choristers John Blow and William Turner) he wrote the famous *Club Anthem.* In 1664 King Charles II sent him to study in France and Italy under the Secret Service Funds; that he worked under Lully remains unverified, nor can it be proved that he got to Italy. He returned to England in 1667 and was appointed Gentleman of the Chapel Royal on Oct. 26, 1667. An entry in Pepys's diary for Nov. 15, 1667, described him as being "full of form, and confidence, and vanity" and disparaging "everything, and everybody's skill but his own." Humfrey's justification of his self-confidence lay in his undoubted mastery of the Italian declamatory style, greater than anyone had yet achieved in England. On July 15, 1672, he was appointed Master of the Children of the Chapel Royal. Two years later he died, at the early age of 27. One of his wards was the young Henry Purcell, whose style clearly shows Humfrey's influence.

Hummel, Ferdinand, German composer and harpist; b. Berlin, Sept. 6, 1855; d. there, April 24, 1928. He gave concerts as a child harpist (1864–67); then studied music at Kullak's Academy in Berlin and later at the Hochschule für Musik there. He established himself as a teacher in Berlin, and also became a prolific composer. Much impressed by the realistic school of Italian opera (Mascagni), he wrote several short operas in the same genre: *Mara* (Berlin, 1893); *Angla* (Berlin, 1894); *Assarpai* (Gotha, 1898); *Sophie von Brabant* (Darmstadt, 1899); *Die Beichte* (Berlin, 1900); *Ein treuer Schelm; Die Gefilde der Seligen* (Altenburg, 1917). He also wrote a Symph., a Piano Concerto, chamber music, and choral works, aggregating to about 120 opus numbers.

Hummel, Johann Nepomuk, celebrated German pianist and composer; b. Pressburg, Nov. 14, 1778; d. Weimar, Oct. 17, 1837. He studied with his father, **Johannes Hummel,** who was music master of the Imperial School for Military Music. In 1786 the father was appointed conductor at Schikaneder's Theater in Vienna; there Mozart interested himself in young Hummel, took him into his house, and for 2 years instructed him. Hummel made his debut in

1787 at a concert given by Mozart in Vienna; in 1788–93 he accompanied his father on professional concert tours as a pianist, visiting Bohemia, Germany, Denmark, Scotland, England, and the Netherlands. In London he studied briefly with Clementi; in Oxford he presented his String Quartet. In 1793 he returned to Vienna and began a course of studies with Albrechtsberger, and also profited by the counsel of Haydn and Salieri in composition; became a friend of Beethoven and of Goethe. In 1804–11 he acted as deputy Kapellmeister for Haydn, in Prince Esterházy's service. In the meantime, he had his opera *Mathilde von Guise* produced in Vienna (March 26, 1810). He settled in Vienna in 1811 as a teacher; in 1816–18 was court Kapellmeister at Stuttgart, and in 1819, at Weimar, a post he held until his death. His duties were not too rigorous, and he was allowed to make frequent professional tours. He traveled to St. Petersburg in 1822; in 1825 he was in Paris, where he was made a Chevalier of the Legion of Honor; in 1826, visited Belgium and the Netherlands; in 1827, was in Vienna; in 1828, in Warsaw; and in 1829, again in France. He conducted a season of German opera at the King's Theatre in London in 1833. The last years of his life were marred by ill health and much suffering. At the peak of his career as a pianist, he was regarded as one of the greatest virtuosos of his time; both as pianist and composer, he was often declared to be the equal of Beethoven. His compositions were marked by excellent craftsmanship; his writing for instruments, particularly for piano, was impeccable; his melodic invention was rich, and his harmonic and contrapuntal skill was of the highest caliber. Yet, with his death, his music went into an immediate eclipse; performances of his works became increasingly rare, until the name of Hummel all but vanished from active musical programs. However, some of his compositions were revived by various musical societies in Europe and America, and, as a result, at least his chamber music was saved from oblivion. He wrote 124 opus numbers; these include 9 operas; several ballets; cantatas; 3 masses for 4 Voices and Organ; *Missa solemnis* (1826); a Graduale and Offertorium, still in use in Austrian churches; 7 concertos and concertinos for Piano and Orch.; many works for piano solo; 6 piano trios; Piano Quintet; Quintet for Violin, Viola, Cello, Double Bass, and Piano; Septet in D minor (his most outstanding work) for Flute, Oboe, Viola, Horn, Cello, Double Bass, and Piano; cadenzas to the Mozart concertos. He also publ. *Anweisung zum Pianofortespiel* (1828), an elaborate instruction book and one of the first to give a sensible method of fingering. His wife, **Elisabeth Hummel-Röckl** (1793–1883), was an opera singer; they had 2 sons, a pianist and a painter. Hummel's great-great-grandson Mike Hummel, an industrialist in Los Angeles, son of Wilhelm Hummel, who came to the U.S. in 1922, sought to restore interest in Hummel and collected his memorabilia, which were kept in Mike's grandfather's place in Florence, and in 1975 shipped everything to Los Angeles. In 1978 Hummel's bicentennial was celebrated in Weimar.

Humperdinck, Engelbert, celebrated German composer; b. Siegburg, near Bonn, Sept. 1, 1854; d. Neustrelitz, Sept. 27, 1921. He first studied architecture in Cologne; there he met Ferdinand Hiller, who discovered his musical talent and took him as a student at the Cologne Cons.; his other teachers there were Gernsheim and Jensen (composition), Seiss and Mertke (piano), Rensberg and Ehlert (cello). In 1876 he won a Mozart scholarship at Frankfurt; studied in Munich with Franz Lachner and Rheinberger; there he publ. his first works, *Humoreske* for Orch. (1880) and *Die Wallfahrt nach Kevelaar* for Chorus, which won the Mendelssohn Prize (1879); he also won the Meyerbeer prize of 7,600 marks (1881), which enabled him to visit Italy and France. In Italy he met Wagner, who invited him to be his guest at Bayreuth. Here Humperdinck assisted in preparing the score of *Parsifal* for publication; from then on the relations between Humperdinck and the Wagner family were most cordial; Siegfried Wagner became Humperdinck's pupil and received his entire musical education from him. In 1885–87 Humperdinck was a prof. at the Cons. in Barcelona; after his return to Germany he taught for a short time in Cologne, and then went to Mainz in the employ of the Schott publishing firm; in 1890 he became a prof. at the Hoch Cons. in Frankfurt, and music critic for the *Frankfurter Zeitung.* On Dec. 23, 1893, in Weimar, he produced the fairy-opera *Hänsel und Gretel* (text by his sister, Adelheid Wette). The work, aside from its intrinsic merit, appeared at the right psychological moment. The German public, weary of the bombast of the Wagner-imitators, were almost willing to accept the blunt realism of the Italian *verismo* as a relief from the labored dullness of pseudo-Wagnerian music dramas. And now a new composer, drawing inspiration from folk music, found musical expression for a thoroughly German subject, and the public was delighted. Before a year had passed, the work was in the repertoire of every German opera house; abroad as well its success was extraordinary and lasting (London, Dec. 26, 1894; N.Y., Oct. 8, 1895). A host of imitators ransacked German fairy-lore, but with ill success. Since Humperdinck's health had never been robust, he determined after this success to give up teaching, and after production of his next work, *Die sieben Geislein* (Berlin, Dec. 19, 1895), a fairy play for children written for voice and piano, he retired (in 1896) to Boppard on the Rhine to devote himself entirely to composition. In 1898 he wrote incidental music to Rosmer's *Königskinder* (Munich, Jan. 23, 1897); in this music Humperdinck made a bold attempt to prescribe definite rhythmic and pitch inflections ("sprechnoten") to the actors in the drama; he later recast the score into an opera, which was produced at the Metropolitan Opera House in N.Y. (Dec. 28, 1910). In 1900 he became director (with practically nominal duties) of the Akademische Meisterschule in Berlin. His other operas are *Dornröschen* (Frankfurt, Nov. 12, 1902); *Die Heirat wider Willen* (Berlin, April 14, 1905); *Die Marketenderin* (Cologne, May 10, 1914); and *Gaudeamus* (Darmstadt, March 18, 1919); he wrote incidental music for Berlin productions of 5 plays of

Shakespeare: *The Merchant of Venice* (Nov. 9, 1905); *The Winter's Tale* (Sept. 15, 1906); *Romeo and Juliet* (Jan. 29, 1907); *Twelfth Night* (Oct. 17, 1907); *The Tempest* (Oct. 8, 1915); also to *Lysistrata,* by Aristophanes (Berlin, Feb. 27, 1908), and to *The Blue Bird,* by Maeterlinck (Berlin, Dec. 23, 1912). He contributed music to Max Reinhardt's production of *The Miracle* (London, Dec. 23, 1911). He further wrote a choral ballade, *Das Glück von Edenhall* (1884); *Maurische Rhapsodie* for Orch. (1898); and a Symph. Among his songs, the cycle *Kinderlieder* is particularly fine. Humperdinck's lasting fame still rests, however, upon one opera, *Hänsel und Gretel,* which succeeded thanks to Humperdinck's ability to write melodies of ingenuous felicity, despite the almost incompatible Wagnerian instrumental and dramatic design.

Huneker, James Gibbons, brilliant American journalist and writer on music; b. Philadelphia, Jan. 31, 1857; d. Brooklyn, Feb. 9, 1921. He studied piano with Michael Cross in Philadelphia, and in 1878 in Paris with Théodore Ritter; later with Joseffy at the National Cons. in N.Y.; then taught piano there (1888–98). He was music and drama critic of the *N.Y. Recorder* (1891–95) and the *Morning Advertiser* (1895–97); music, drama, and art critic for the *N.Y. Sun* (1900–12). In 1917 he was music critic of the *Philadelphia Press;* after one season (1918–19) with the *N.Y. Times* he became music critic for the *N.Y. World,* a position he held until his death; also wrote for various journals in N.Y., London, Paris, Berlin, and Vienna. He publ. a novel dealing with artistic life in N.Y., *Painted Veils* (1921), but devoted most of his uncommon gifts to musical journalism. He was capable of rising to true poetic style when writing about Chopin and other composers whom he loved; but he also possessed a talent for caustic invective; his attacks on Debussy were particularly sharp. He had a fine sense of humor, and candidly described himself as an "old fogy." In addition to his literary publications, he furnished introductory essays for Joseffy's edition of Chopin's works. WRITINGS: *Mezzotints in Modern Music* (1899); *Chopin: The Man and His Music* (1900; in German, 1914); *Melomaniacs* (1902); *Overtones, A Book of Temperaments* (1904); *Iconoclasts: A Book for Dramatists* (1905); *Visionaries: Fantasies and Fiction* (1905); *Egoists: A Book of Supermen* (1909); *Promenades of an Impressionist: Studies in Art* (1910); *Franz Liszt: A Study* (1911; in German, 1922); *The Pathos of Distance* (1913); *Old Fogy, His Musical Opinions and Grotesques* (1913); *New Cosmopolis* (1915); *Ivory Apes and Peacocks* (1915); *Unicorns* (1917); *The Philharmonic Society of New York and Its 75th Anniversary* (1917); *Bedouins* (1920); *Steeplejack* (his memoirs; 1920); *Variations* (1921). A selection of his letters was publ. posthumously by Josephine Huneker (1922); a collection of essays, with an introduction by Mencken, in 1929.

Hungerford, Bruce, Australian pianist; b. Korumburra, Victoria, Nov. 24, 1922; d. in an automobile accident in the Bronx, N.Y., Jan. 26, 1977. He received his education in Melbourne; studied piano with Ignaz Friedman in Sydney (1944), and later with Ernest Hutcheson at the Juilliard School of Music in N.Y. (1945–47); took private lessons with Myra Hess in N.Y. between 1948 and 1958, and also with Carl Friedberg in 1948–55. He gave his first piano recital in N.Y. in 1951; from then until 1965 he appeared under the name **Leonard Hungerford.** Apart from his virtuoso technique, he possessed an extraordinary mastery of dynamic gradations and self-consistent musical phraseology. He also gained recognition as a color photographer and archeologist, specializing in Egyptology; he recorded a 17-part audiovisual lecture entitled "The Heritage of Ancient Egypt" (1971).

Hunt, Jerry, American composer; b. Waco, Texas, Nov. 30, 1943. He studied piano at North Texas State Univ.; developed a successful career as a performer of modern music; was on the faculty of Southern Methodist Univ. in Texas (1967–73) and concurrently was artist-in-residence at the Video Research Center in Dallas. WORKS: The titles of his works indicate a preoccupation with mathematical and abstract concepts, as exemplified by his 8 pieces for varying instrumental groups bearing the generic title *Helix* (1961–71); other works are *Sur Dr. John Dee,* scored for "zero to 11 performers" (1963); *Tabulatura Soyga,* for zero to 11 Instruments (1965); *Preparallel* for Orch. Groups (1965); *Unit,* a "solo situation" (1967); *Infrasolo* for 10 Cymbals "or something else" (1970); *Autotransform glissando* (1970); *Symphony for Electronics* (1971); *Haramand Playing: Recursive/Regenerative* for Electronic Audio and Video Generating Systems (1972); *Quaquaversal Transmission,* a theater work (1973); *21 Segments* for varying numbers of Instruments (1973–77).

Hünten, Franz, German pianist and composer; b. Coblenz, Dec. 26, 1793; d. there, Feb. 22, 1878. He studied with his father, an organist; at the age of 26 he went to Paris and took courses at the Cons. with Pradher (piano) and Cherubini (composition); composed salon music for piano (fantasies, variations on opera themes, waltzes, etc.), some 250 opus numbers in all, most of which he succeeded in publishing; also brought out a *Méthode nouvelle pour le piano,* and other didactic compilations which became popular among teachers and students; Hünten was very much in demand as a piano teacher in Paris. Having accumulated considerable capital from his enterprises, he returned to Coblenz in 1848, and remained there until his death.

Hunter, Rita, English soprano; b. Wallasey, Aug. 15, 1933. She studied voice in Liverpool; later took lessons with Dame Eva Turner; then joined the Sadler's Wells Chorus; also sang with the Carl Rosa Opera Co. In 1959 she joined the Sadler's Wells Opera; obtained success with her interpretation of Brünnhilde (in English) in performances of Wagner's operas. On Dec. 19, 1972, she made her American debut with the Metropolitan Opera in N.Y. as Brünnhilde; in 1975 sang with the San Francisco Opera. In 1980 she was named a Commander of the Order of the British Empire.

Hupfeld, Herman, American composer of popular music, singer, pianist, and lyricist; b. Montclair, N.J., Feb. 1, 1894; d. there, June 8, 1951. He served in the U.S. Navy in World War I. While in the service he wrote and performed his songs to his own words. Possessing a natural flair for sentimental melodies and nostalgic lyrics, he contributed successfully to Broadway shows; occasionally employed jazz rhythms, as in his song *When Yuba Plays the Rhumba on the Tuba.* He achieved fame with the theme song for the movie *Casablanca* (with Ingrid Bergman and Humphrey Bogart), *As Times Goes By,* a tune that indelibly impinged on the hearts of millions.

Hurford, Peter, noted English organist; b. Minehead, Somerset, Nov. 22, 1930. He studied law and music at Jesus College, Cambridge; later took organ lessons with André Marchal in Paris. In 1958 he was named Master of the Music at St. Albans Abbey; in 1963 he founded the International Organ Festival there. He left St. Albans in 1979 to pursue his international career as a leading interpreter of the music of the Baroque period. In 1984 he was made an officer of the Order of the British Empire.

Hurlstone, William Yeates, English composer and pianist; b. London, Jan. 7, 1876; d. there, May 30, 1906. A precocious musician, he composed waltzes as a young child; studied at the Royal College of Music with Stanford (composition) and Edward Dannreuther (piano); performed his own Piano Concerto in 1896. In 1905 he was appointed a prof. at the Royal College of Music but died in the following year; his early death was much regretted.

Hurok, Sol, Russian-American impresario; b. Pogar, April 9, 1888; d. New York, March 5, 1974. Fleeing the political iniquities of the Czarist regime in regard to Jews, he emigrated to the U.S. in 1905, and became a naturalized citizen in 1914. In 1913 he inaugurated a series of weekly concerts announced as "Music for the Masses" at the Hippodrome in N.Y.; then became an exclusive manager for famous Russian artists, among them Anna Pavlova, Feodor Chaliapin, Artur Rubinstein, Mischa Elman, and Gregor Piatigorsky, as well as numerous other celebrities in the field of the ballet and opera. He negotiated the difficult arrangements with the Soviet government for American appearances of the Bolshoi Ballet, the Ukrainian dance company, and the Leningrad Kirov Ballet; made frequent trips to Russia, helped by his fluency in the language. Ironically, his N.Y. office became the target of a bomb attack by a militant Jewish organization which objected to Hurok's importation of Soviet artists, even though many of the artists were themselves Jewish.

Hurst, George, English conductor; b. Edinburgh, May 20, 1926, of Rumanian-Russian parentage. He first studied piano with Isserlis; then took courses in conducting and composition at the Royal Cons. of Music in Toronto; also studied conducting with Monteux. He was a teacher and conductor at the Peabody Cons. of Music in Baltimore (1947–55); then was assistant conductor of the London Phil. Orch. (1955–57) and of the BBC Northern Symph. Orch. at Manchester (1958–68); subsequently served as artistic director of the Bournemouth Sinfonietta; after 1978 he made guest appearances with various orchs. in Europe.

Hurwitz, Emanuel, English violinist; b. London, May 7, 1919. He received a scholarship from Bronislaw Huberman which allowed him to study at the Royal Academy of Music. In 1948 he became concertmaster of the Goldsborough (later English) Chamber Orch., a position he held until 1968; was then concertmaster of the New Philharmonia Orch. (1969–71). He was also active as a chamber music artist; was first violinist of the Hurwitz String Quartet (1946–51), the Melos Ensemble (1956–72), and the Aeolian Quartet (from 1970). In 1968 he founded the Hurwitz Chamber Orch. (from 1972 known as the Serenata of London), a conductorless ensemble. He was made a Commander of the Order of the British Empire in 1978.

Hus-Desforges, Pierre Louis, French cellist and composer; b. Toulon, March 14, 1773; d. Pont-le-Voy, near Blois, Jan. 20, 1838. He studied at the Paris Cons.; played the cello in various orchs.; held numerous posts as a theatrical conductor and teacher. He was conductor at the Théâtre-Français in St. Petersburg early in the 19th century; returning to France, was cellist at the Théâtre Saint-Martin in Paris; from 1819 –22 taught at Metz; in 1823 was in Bordeaux; from 1824, again in Paris. His name as composer appears for the first time as **Citoyen Desforges,** on a song entitled *L'Autel de sa patrie* (Paris, 1798); he was the author of *Méthode de violoncelle à l'usage des commençants* (Paris, 1828); a String Quartet; and a "Sinfonia concertante" with Violin and Cello obbligato; he also publ. a historical novel, *Sapho à Leucade* (Paris, 1818).

Husa, Karel, distinguished Czech-born American composer, conductor, and pedagogue; b. Prague, Aug. 7, 1921. He studied violin and piano in his youth; concurrently took courses in engineering; in 1941 he entered the Prague Cons., studying composition with Jaroslav Řídký; in 1945–46 he attended the Academy of Music; in 1946 was awarded a French government grant to continue his studies in Paris at the Ecole Normale de Musique and the Paris Cons.; his teachers included Arthur Honegger and Nadia Boulanger; he also studied conducting with Jean Fournet and André Cluytens. In 1954 he emigrated to the U.S., and joined the music dept. of Cornell Univ. as teacher of composition and conductor of the student orch. He became an American citizen in 1959. He appeared widely as a guest conductor, frequently including his own music in his programs. In his early works he followed the modern Czech school of composition, making thematic use of folk tunes; later he enlarged his musical resources to include atonal, polytonal, microtonal, and even occasional aleatory procedures, without following doctrinaire prescriptions to the letter. His music is oxygenated by humanistic Romanticism; as a result, it gains numerous performances. In 1969 Husa received the Pulitzer Prize for his 3rd String Quartet.

WORKS: FOR ORCH.: Overture for Large Orch. (first public perf., Prague, June 18, 1946); Sinfonietta for Orch. (Prague, April 25, 1947); *3 Fresques* for Orch. (Prague, April 27, 1949; revised as *Fresque* for Orch., Syracuse, N.Y., May 5, 1963); Divertimento for String Orch. (Paris, Oct. 30, 1949); Concertino for Piano and Orch. (Brussels, June 6, 1952); *Musique d'Amateurs,* 4 Easy Pieces for Oboe, Trumpet, Percussion, and Strings (1953); *Portrait* for String Orch. (Donaueschingen, Oct. 10, 1953); Symph. No. 1 (Brussels, March 4, 1954); 4 Little Pieces for Strings (Fürsteneck, Germany, March 17, 1957); *Fantasies for Orch.* (Ithaca, N.Y., April 28, 1957); Divertimento for Brass and Percussion (Ithaca, N. Y., Feb. 17, 1960); Poem for Viola and Chamber Orch. (Cologne, June 12, 1960); *Mosaïques for Orchestra.* (Hamburg, Nov. 7, 1961); *Elegie et Rondeau* for Alto Saxophone and Orch. (Ithaca, N.Y., May 6, 1962); Serenade for Woodwind Quintet Solo with String Orch., Xylophone, and Harp (Baltimore, Jan. 7, 1964); *Festive Ode* for Chorus and Orch. (1965); Concerto for Brass Quintet and String Orch. (Buffalo, Feb. 15, 1970); Concerto for Alto Saxophone and Concert Band (Ithaca, N.Y., March 17, 1968); *Music for Prague 1968* (2 versions; for Band: Washington, D.C., Jan. 31, 1969; for Orch.: Munich, Jan. 31, 1970); Concerto for Percussion and Wind Instruments (Waco, Texas, Feb. 7, 1972); *Apotheosis of This Earth* for Wind Instruments (Ann Arbor, Mich., April 1, 1971; 2nd version for Chorus and Orch.: Ithaca, N.Y., April 12, 1973); *2 Sonnets from Michelangelo* for Orch. (Evanston, Ill., April 28, 1972); Trumpet Concerto (Storrs, Conn., Aug. 9, 1974); *The Steadfast Tin Soldier* for Narrator and Orch. (Boulder, Colo., May 10, 1975); *Monodrama,* ballet for Orch. (Indianapolis, March 26, 1976); *An American Te Deum* for Baritone, Chorus, and Wind Ensemble (Cedar Rapids, Iowa, Dec. 4, 1976; 2nd version for Baritone, Chorus, and Orch.: Washington, D.C., May 10, 1978); Fanfare for Brass Ensemble (1980); Pastoral for Strings (Miami Beach, April 12, 1980); *The Trojan Women,* ballet for Orch. (Louisville, March 28, 1981); Concerto for Wind Ensemble (Lansing, Mich., Dec. 3, 1982); Cantata for Men's Chorus and Brass Quintet (Crawfordsville, Ind., April 20, 1983). CHAMBER MUSIC: Sonatina for Piano (1943); String Quartet (1942–43); Suite for Viola and Piano (1945); Sonatina for Violin and Piano (1945); String Quartet No. 1 (Prague, May 23, 1948); Piano Sonata No. 1 (1950); *Evocations of Slovakia* for Clarinet, Viola, and Cello (Paris, May 4, 1952); String Quartet No. 2 (Paris, Oct. 23, 1954); *2 Preludes* for Flute, Clarinet, and Bassoon (Ithaca, N.Y., April 21, 1966); Divertimento for Brass Quintet (Ithaca, N.Y., Nov. 20, 1968); String Quartet No. 3 (Chicago, Oct. 14, 1968);

Studies for Percussion (1968); Sonata for Violin and Piano (N.Y., March 31, 1974); Piano Sonata No. 2 (1975); *Landscapes* for Brass Quintet (Kalamazoo, Mich., Oct. 17, 1977); *3 Dance Sketches* for Percussion (Miami Beach, April 12, 1980); *Intradas and Interludes* for 7 Trumpets and Timpani (Columbus, Ohio, June 20, 1980); *3 Moravian Songs* for Chorus a cappella (1981); *Every Day* for Chorus a cappella (1981); *Sonata a tre* for Violin, Clarinet, and Piano (Hong Kong, March 23, 1982); *Recollections* for Woodwind Quintet and Piano (Washington, D.C., Oct. 28, 1982); *12 Moravian Songs* for Voice and Piano (1956); other vocal pieces.

Huss, Henry Holden, American composer and pianist; b. Newark, N.J., June 21, 1862; d. New York, Sept. 17, 1953. He was a descendant of Leonhard Huss, brother of the Bohemian martyr John Huss. His mother, Sophia Ruckle Holden Huss, was a granddaughter of Levi Holden, a member of Washington's staff. Huss studied piano and theory with his father and with Otis B. Boise. In 1882 he went to Germany, and studied organ and composition with Rheinberger at the Munich Cons.; graduated with a *Rhapsody* for Piano and Orch. (1885), which he subsequently performed with several American orchs.; he also played his Piano Concerto in B with the N.Y. Phil., the Boston Symph., etc. In 1904 he married **Hildegard Hoffmann,** a concert singer; they appeared frequently in joint recitals. He continued to compose almost to the very end of his long life.

WORKS: Symph. poems: *Life's Conflicts* (1921) and *La Nuit* (originally for Piano Solo, 1902; orchestrated 1939; first perf., Washington, D.C., March 12, 1942); 4 string quartets; Violin Sonata; Cello Sonata; Viola Sonata; choral works: *The 23rd Psalm; Mankind's Own Song; Winged Messengers of Peace; The Flag; The Fool's Prayer; Captain, Oh My Captain; Lord, Make My Heart a Place Where Angels Sing;* etc.

Hutcheson, Ernest, Australian pianist and teacher; b. Melbourne, July 20, 1871; d. New York, Feb. 9, 1951. He studied piano in Australia with Max Vogrich; played concerts as a very young child; then was sent to the Leipzig Cons. to study with Reinecke, graduating in 1890. In 1898 he performed his own Piano Concerto with the Berlin Phil. In 1900 he arrived in the U.S.; was head of the piano dept. at the Peabody Cons. in Baltimore (1900–12). In 1915 he created a sensation in N.Y. by playing 3 concertos (Tchaikovsky, Liszt, and MacDowell) in a single evening; in 1919 he repeated his feat, playing 3 Beethoven concertos in one evening; during 1924–45 he was dean of the Juilliard School. Among his compositions are several symph. works and numerous piano pieces. He publ. *Elements of Piano Technique* (N.Y., 1907); *Elektra by Richard Strauss: A Guide to the Opera* (N.Y., 1910); *A Musical Guide to the Richard Wagner Ring of the Nibelung* (N.Y., 1940); *The Literature of the Piano* (N.Y., 1948; 2nd ed., revised, 1964).

Hutchings, Arthur, English musicologist; b. Sun-bury-on-Thames, July 14, 1906. He studied violin and piano; then was engaged in teaching music and composing; became prof. of music at Durham Univ. in 1947; was prof. of music at Exeter Univ. from 1968–71. His books include *Schubert* (London, 1945; 4th ed., 1973); *Delius* (London, 1948); *A Companion to Mozart's Piano Concertos* (London, 1948; 3rd ed., 1980); *The Invention and Composition of Music* (London, 1958); *The Baroque Concerto* (London, 1961; 3rd ed., revised, 1973); *Church Music in the Nineteenth Century* (London, 1967); *Mozart: The Man, the Musician* (London, 1976); *Purcell* (London, 1982).

Hüttenbrenner, Anselm, Austrian composer; b. Graz, Oct. 13, 1794; d. Ober-Andritz, near Graz, June 5, 1868. At the age of 7 he studied with the organist Gell; studied law at the Univ. of Graz; in 1815 he went to Vienna to study with Salieri. Schubert was his fellow student, and they became close friends. Hüttenbrenner also knew Beethoven intimately, and was present at his death. He was an excellent pianist and a prolific composer; Schubert praised his works. He wrote 6 operas; an operetta; 8 symphs.; many overtures; 10 masses; 4 Requiems; 3 funeral marches; 2 string quartets; a String Quintet; piano sonatas; 24 fugues; other piano pieces; some 300 male quartets; 200 songs. One of his songs, *Erlkönig,* was included in the collection *12 Lieder der deutschen Romantik,* ed. by H.H. Rosenwald (1929). His reminiscences of Schubert were publ. by Otto Deutsch in 1906. It was Hüttenbrenner who came into the possession of many Schubert MSS after Schubert's death, among them that of the "Unfinished Symph.," which he held until 1865. It has been suggested that Hüttenbrenner had lost the 3rd and 4th movements of Schubert's work, and for that reason was reluctant to part with the incomplete MS, but the extant sketches for the Scherzo make that unlikely.

Huybrechts, Albert, Belgian composer; b. Dinant, Feb. 12, 1899; d. Woluwe-St.-Pierre, near Brussels, Feb. 21, 1938. He studied at the Brussels Cons. with Martin Lunssens, Paulin Marchand, Léon Dubois, and Joseph Jongen. In 1926 he gained international recognition by winning 2 U.S. prizes, the Elizabeth Sprague Coolidge Prize of the Library of Congress for his Violin Sonata, and the Ojai Valley Prize in California for his String Quartet. In 1937 he was appointed a prof. at the Brussels Cons., but a severe attack of uremia led to his premature death. He wrote in a judiciously modern idiom, seasoned with prudential dissonance.

Hyllested, August, Swedish pianist and composer; b. Stockholm, June 17, 1856; d. Blairmore, Scotland, April 5, 1946. He played in public as a child; then studied at the Copenhagen Cons. with Niels Gade, and subsequently with Theodor Kullak (piano) and Friedrich Kiel (composition) in Berlin; then had some lessons from Liszt. He gave concerts as pianist in England (1883) and in America (1885). In 1886–91 he was a prof. and assistant director of the Chicago Musical College; in 1891–94, taught piano at the Gottschalk Lyric School in Chicago. After a concert tour in Europe, he returned to Chicago in 1897; he was in Glasgow in 1903–14; then again in the U.S. (1916–19); in Denmark and Sweden (1919–21); in 1923, retired to Blairmore, where he died shortly before his 90th birthday. He publ. numerous piano pieces in a Romantic style (*Album Leaf, Valse sentimentale, Suite romantique,* etc.); a suite of Scandinavian dances; a fantasia on Scotch tunes; choral pieces; a symph. poem, *Elizabeth,* with Double Chorus (London, 1897, composer conducting).

Hynninen, Jorma, distinguished Finnish baritone and operatic administrator; b. Leppävirta, April 3, 1941. He studied at the Sibelius Academy in Helsinki (1966–70); also took courses in Rome with Luigi Ricci and in Salzburg with Kurt Overhoff. He won first prize at the singing competition in Lappeenranta in 1969, and in the Finnish division of the Scandinavian singing competition in Helsinki in 1971. In 1970 he made his concert debut in Helsinki, as well as his operatic debut as Silvio in *Pagliacci* with the Finnish National Opera there, and subsequently sang leading roles with the company. He also made guest appearances at La Scala in Milan (1977), at the Vienna State Opera (1977, 1982, 1983), at the Hamburg State Opera (1977, 1978), at the Bavarian State Opera (1979, 1980, 1981), and at the Paris Opéra (1980); gave recitals throughout Europe and the U.S. He made his N.Y. debut in a recital in 1980; his operatic debut followed in 1983, when he sang with the Finnish National Opera during its visit to America; made his Metropolitan Opera debut as Posa in 1984. He was appointed artistic director of the Finnish National Opera in 1984. In addition to such traditional operatic roles as Pelléas, Wolfram, Orpheus, and Valentin in *Faust,* he has sung parts in contemporary Finnish operas; he created the role of the King in *The King Goes Forth to France* by Aulis Sallinen, first performed at the Savonlinna Opera Festival on July 7, 1984.

I

Ibach, Johannes Adolf, German piano maker; b. Barmen, Oct. 17, 1766; d. there, Sept. 14, 1848. In 1794, he founded a piano factory at Barmen; also manufactured organs from 1834, with his son **C. Rudolf Ibach;** then traded under the name of Adolf Ibach & Sohn; from 1839, as Rudolf & Söhne, when his son **Richard** joined the firm. From 1862 the firm was known as C. Rudolf & Richard Ibach, to distinguish it from another business founded by a third son, **Gustav J.** The same year C. Rudolf died, and in 1869 his son **Rudolf** (d. Herrenalb, Black Forest, July 31, 1892) continued the piano factory alone as Rudolf Ibach Sohn; he established a branch at Cologne, gained medals for the excellence of his pianos, and became purveyor to the Prussian court. **Richard Ibach** continued the organ factory.

Ibert, Jacques, French composer; b. Paris, Aug. 15, 1890; d. there, Feb. 5, 1962. He studied at the Paris Cons. with Gédalge and Fauré (1911–14); during World War I served in the French navy; returned to the Paris Cons. after the Armistice and studied with Paul Vidal; received the Prix de Rome in 1919 for his cantata *Le Poète et la fée;* while in Rome, he wrote his most successful work, the symph. suite *Escales (Ports of Call),* inspired by a Mediterranean cruise while serving in the navy. In 1937 he was appointed director of the Academy of Rome, and held this post until 1955, when he became director of the united management of the Paris Opéra and Opéra-Comique (until 1957). In his music, Ibert combines the most felicitous moods and techniques of Impressionism and neo-Classicism; his harmonies are opulent; his instrumentation is coloristic; there is an element of humor in lighter works, such as his popular orch. *Divertissement* and an even more popular piece, *Le Petit Ane blanc,* from the piano suite *Histoires.* His craftsmanship is excellent; an experimenter in tested values, he never fails to produce the intended effect.

WORKS: OPERAS: *Angélique* (Paris, Jan. 28, 1927); *Persée et Andromède* (Paris, May 15, 1929); *Le Roi d'Yvetot* (Paris, Jan. 15, 1930); *Gonzague* (Monte Carlo, 1935); *L'Aiglon,* after Edmond Rostand, in collaboration with Honegger (Monte Carlo, March 11, 1937); *Les Petites Cardinal,* with Honegger (Paris, 1938); *Barbebleue,* radio opera (Lausanne Radio, Oct. 10, 1943). BALLETS (all first perf. in Paris): *Les Rencontres* (Nov. 21, 1925); *Diane de Poitiers* (April 30, 1934, produced by Ida Rubinstein); *Les Amours de Jupiter* (March 9, 1946); *Le Chevalier errant* (May 5, 1950); *Tropismes pour des Amours Imaginaires* (1957). FOR ORCH.: Symph. poem, *Noël en Picardie* (1914); *Ballade de la geôle de Reading,* after

Oscar Wilde (Paris, Oct. 22, 1922); *Escales*, 3 symph. pictures (Paris, Jan. 6, 1924); *Féerique*, symph. scherzo (Paris, Dec. 12, 1925); Concerto for Cello and Wind Instruments (Paris, Feb. 28, 1926); *Divertissement*, suite (Paris, Nov. 30, 1930; from incidental music to *Le Chapeau de paille d'Italie); Paris,* suite for Chamber Orch. (Venice, Sept. 15, 1932; from incidental music to *Donogoo,* play by Jules Romains); Flute Concerto (Paris, Feb. 25, 1934); *Concertino da Camera* for Saxophone and Chamber Orch. (Paris, May 2, 1935); *Capriccio* (1938); *Ouverture de fête* (Paris, Jan. 18, 1942); *Suite élisabéthaine* (1944); *Symphonie concertante* for Oboe and String Orch. (Basel, Feb. 11, 1949); *Louisville Concerto* (Louisville, Feb. 17, 1954); *Hommage à Mozart* for Orch. (1957); *Bacchanale* for Orch. (1958); *Bostoniana* for Orch. (1956–61). VOCAL WORKS: *Le Poète et la fée,* cantata (1919); *Chant de folie* for Solo Voices, Chorus, and Orch. (Boston, April 23, 1926); *3 chansons* for Voice, and Orch. or Piano; *La Verdure dorée* for Voice and Piano; *Chanson du rien* for Voice and Piano; *Quintette de la peur* for Chorus and Piano (1946). CHAMBER MUSIC: *2 mouvements* for 2 Flutes, Clarinet, and Bassoon (1923); *Jeux,* sonatina for Flute and Piano (1924); *3 pièces brèves* for Flute, Oboe, Clarinet, Horn, and Bassoon (1930); *Pastoral* for 4 Fifes (in *Pipeaux,* by various composers, 1934); *Entr'acte* for Flute and Guitar (1935); String Quartet (1944); Trio for Violin, Cello, and Harp (1944); *2 Interludes* for Violin and Harpsichord (1949); also 6 pieces for Harp (1917); a piece for Unaccompanied Flute (1936). FOR PIANO: *Histoires* (10 pieces); *Les Rencontres,* arranged from the ballet (5 pieces); *Petite suite en 15 images* (1943).

Idelsohn, Abraham Zevi, eminent Jewish musicologist; b. Pfilsburg, near Libau (Latvia), July 13, 1882; d. Johannesburg, South Africa, Aug. 14, 1938. He studied in Königsberg, in Berlin, and with Jadassohn and Kretzschmar at the Leipzig Cons. He possessed a powerful baritone voice and for a time was cantor of the synagogue at Regensburg (1903); then went to Johannesburg and later (1906–21) was in Jerusalem, where he founded an Inst. for Jewish Music (1910) and a Jewish music School (1919). In 1921, he returned to Germany; then went to the U.S.; lectured at the Hebrew Union College in Cincinnati (1924–34). In 1934 he suffered a paralytic stroke; was taken to Miami, and in 1937 to Johannesburg, where he finally succumbed. Idelsohn was one of the greatest authorities on Jewish music and contributed much towards its establishment on a scientific basis.

WRITINGS: He publ. a quantity of studies in English, German, and Hebrew on oriental and Hebrew music, of which the most important are: *History of Jewish Music* (in Hebrew, 1924; 2nd ed., 1928, also publ. in English); *The Ceremonies of Judaism* (1923 –30); *Diwan of Hebrew and Arabic Poetry of the Yemenite Jews* (in Hebrew; 1930); *Jewish Liturgy and Its Development* (1932; reprint issued by the Hebrew Union College, N.Y., 1956); "Musical Characteristics of East European Jewish Folk-Songs," in the *Musical Quarterly* (Oct. 1932). His most impor-

tant contribution to the study of Jewish music is the monumental *Thesaurus of Hebrew-Oriental Melodies* (10 vols.; 1914–32), in which are collected, with the aid of phonograph recordings, Jewish melodies of North Africa, Asia Minor, Palestine, and other parts of the world. He also composed and publ. 6 synagogue services; Hebrew songs (1929); a music drama, *Jephtah* (1922); and a *Jewish Song Book for Synagogue, Home and School* (1929).

Illica, Luigi, Italian librettist; b. Castell' Arquato, Piacenza, May 9, 1857; d. Colombarone, Piacenza, Dec. 16, 1919. He was engaged as a journalist in Milan; after 1892 devoted himself to writing librettos. He was the author (in collaboration with Giacosa) of librettos for Puccini's operas *La Bohème, Tosca,* and *Madama Butterfly,* and the sole writer of the text for Giordano's *Andrea Chenier* and Mascagni's *Le Maschere.*

Imbrie, Andrew (Welsh), notable American composer; b. New York, April 6, 1921. He studied piano with Leo Ornstein (1930–42); then served in the Signal Corps of the U.S. Army during World War II; spent a summer studying composition with Nadia Boulanger at Fontainebleau; intermittently had fruitful sessions with Sessions, first privately, then at Princeton Univ. and at the Univ. of Calif. at Berkeley (M.A., 1947). In 1947 he was awarded the American Prix de Rome; after a sojourn in Italy, was appointed a prof. of music at Berkeley, in 1960. He held 2 Guggenheim grants (1953–54, 1960–61). His style of composition is marked by a sharp and expressive melodic line, while the polyphony is vigorously motile; harmonic confluence is dissonant but euphoniously tonal. Imbrie's natural propensity is toward instrumental writing; even his choral pieces possess the texture of chamber music.

WORKS: FOR ORCH.: *Ballad in D* (1947; Florence, June 20, 1949); Violin Concerto (1954; San Francisco, April 22, 1958); *Little Concerto* for Piano, 4-hands, and Orch. (1956); *Legend,* symph. poem (San Francisco, Dec. 9, 1959); Symph. No. 1 (San Francisco, May 11, 1966); Symph. No. 2 (1969); Symph. No. 3 (1970); Cello Concerto (1972); Piano Concerto No. 1 (1973); Piano Concerto No. 2 (1974); Flute Concerto (N.Y., Oct. 13, 1977). CHAMBER MUSIC: 4 string quartets (1942, 1953, 1957, 1969); Piano Trio (1946); *Divertimento* for 6 Instruments (1948); *Serenade* for Flute, Viola, and Piano (1952); *Impromptu* for Violin and Piano (1960); Cello Sonata (1966); Chamber Symph. (1968); Piano Sonata (1947). VOCAL WORKS: *On the Beach at Night,* to words by Walt Whitman (1948); *Drum Taps,* cantata to words by Walt Whitman (1961); 2 operas: *Christmas in Peeples Town* (Berkeley, Dec. 3, 1964) and *Angle of Repose,* after the novel of Wallace Stegner (San Francisco, Nov. 6, 1976).

d'India, Sigismondo, Italian madrigal composer; b. c.1580, probably in Palermo; d. 1629, possibly in Modena. He traveled throughout Italy between 1601 and 1610, visiting various courts. From 1611–23 he was director of chamber music at the court of Carlo

Emanuele I, Duke of Savoy, in Turin; then was in the service of Cardinal Maurizio of Savoy, in Rome, and with the Este court in Modena. He publ. 8 books of madrigals in 5 parts; 5 books of arias and cantatas in the monodic style, which was then coming into fashion, entitled simply *Musiche* (possibly by association with Caccini's *Le nuove musiche*); and, in the polyphonic style, 2 books of *Sacri Concentus* (1610) and a book of motets (1627). D'India is reputed for the comparative boldness of his harmonic progressions in the otherwise static monody affected by his Florentine contemporaries. His opera (in recitative), *Zalizura*, is extant. There is an edition of his works edited by J. Joyce and G. Watkins in *Musiche rinascimentali siciliane* (1980—).

d'Indy, (Paul-Marie-Théodore-) Vincent, eminent French composer; b. Paris, March 27, 1851; d. there, Dec. 2, 1931. Owing to the death of his mother at his birth, his education was directed entirely by his grandmother, a woman of culture and refinement who had known Grétry and Monsigny, and who had shown a remarkable appreciation of the works of Beethoven when that master was still living. From 1862–65 he studied piano with Diémer, and later harmony and theory with Marmontel and Lavignac. In 1869 he made the acquaintance of Henri Duparc, and with him spent much time studying the masterpieces of Bach, Beethoven, Berlioz, and Wagner; at that time, he wrote his opp. 1 and 2, and contemplated an opera on Victor Hugo's *Les Burgraves* (1869–72; unfinished). During the Franco-Prussian War he served in the Garde Mobile, and wrote of his experiences in *Histoire du 105ᵉ bataillon de la Garde nationale de Paris en l'année 1870–71* (1872). He then began to study composition with César Franck (1872–80); when the latter was appointed prof. of organ at the Cons. (1873), he joined the class, winning a 2nd *accessit* in 1874 and the first, the following year. On his first visit to Germany in 1873 he met Liszt and Wagner, and was introduced to Brahms; in 1876, he heard the first performances of the *Ring* dramas at Bayreuth, and for several years thereafter made regular trips to Munich to hear all the works of Wagner; he also attended the première of *Parsifal* in 1882. In 1872–76, he was organist at St.-Leu; in 1873–78, chorus master and timpanist with the Colonne Orch.; for the Paris première of *Lohengrin* in 1887 he drilled the chorus and was Lamoureux's assistant. In 1871 he joined the Société Nationale de Musique as a junior member, and was its secretary from 1876 till 1890, when, after Franck's death, he became president. In 1894 he founded, with Bordes and Guilmant, the famous Schola Cantorum (opened 1896), primarily as a school for plainchant and the Palestrina style. Gradually the scope of instruction was enlarged to include all musical disciplines, and the inst. became one of the world's foremost music schools. D'Indy's fame as a composer began with the performance of *Le Chant de la cloche* at a Lamoureux concert in 1886; the work itself had won the City of Paris Prize in the competition of the preceding year. As early as 1874, Pasdeloup had played the overture *Les Piccolomini* (later embodied as the second part in the *Wallenstein* trilogy), and in 1882 the one-act opera *Attendez-moi sous l'orme* had been produced at the Opéra-Comique; but the prize work attracted general attention, and d'Indy was recognized as one of the most important of modern French masters. Although he never held an official position as a conductor, he frequently, and with marked success, appeared in that capacity (chiefly upon invitation to direct his own works); thus, he visited Spain in 1897, Russia in 1903 and 1907, and the U.S. in 1905, when he conducted the regular subscription concerts of Dec. 1 and 2 of the Boston Symph. Orch. In 1892 he was a member of the commission appointed to revise the curriculum of the Cons., and refused a proffered professorship of composition; but in 1912 accepted an appointment as prof. of the ensemble class. Besides his other duties, he was, from 1899, inspector of musical instruction in Paris; made his last U.S. visit in 1921. He was made a Chevalier of the Legion of Honor in 1892, an Officer in 1912; was also a member of many academies and artistic associations (in Belgium, the Netherlands, Spain, Italy, Sweden, etc.). Both as teacher and creative artist, d'Indy continued the traditions of César Franck. Although he cultivated almost every form of composition, his special talent seemed to be in the field of the larger instrumental forms. Some French critics assign to him a position in French music analogous to that of Brahms in German music. His style rests on Bach and Beethoven; however, his deep study of Gregorian chant and the early contrapuntal style added an element of severity, and not rarely of complexity, that renders his approach somewhat difficult, and has prompted the charge that his music is lacking in emotional force.

WRITINGS: In addition to composition, d'Indy did some important editing and wrote several books. For the edition of Rameau's complete works (ed. by Saint-Saëns and Malherbe) he revised *Dardanus, Hippolyte et Aricie,* and *Zaïs;* also ed. Monteverdi's *Orfeo* and *Incoronazione di Poppea;* he also made piano arrangements of orch. works by Chausson, Duparc, and other composers. His numerous articles in various journals are remarkable for their critical acumen and literary finish. He publ. an important manual, *Cours de Composition musicale* (Book I, 1903; Book II: Part 1, 1909, Part 2, 1933); *César Franck* (1906; in Eng., 1910, reprinted, N.Y., 1965); *Beethoven: Biographie critique* (1911; Eng. trans. by T. Baker, Boston, 1913; reprint, N.Y., 1970); *La Schola Cantorum en 1925* (1927); *Wagner et son influence sur l'art musical français* (1930); *Introduction à l'étude de Parsifal* (1937; posthumous).

WORKS: FOR THE STAGE: *Attendez-moi sous l'orme,* op. 14, one-act comic opera (Opéra-Comique, Feb. 11, 1882); *Le Chant de la cloche,* op. 18, dramatic legend (Brussels, Théâtre de la Monnaie, Nov. 21, 1912); *Fervaal,* op. 40, lyric drama (Brussels, March 12, 1897); *L'Etranger,* op. 53, lyric drama (Brussels, Jan. 7, 1903); *La Légende de Saint-Christophe,* op. 67, lyric drama (Paris Opéra, June 9, 1920); *Le Rêve de Cynias,* op. 80, lyric comedy

(Paris, June 10, 1927).

FOR ORCH.: *Jean Hunyade*, op. 5, symph. (Paris, May 15, 1875); *Antoine et Cléopâtre*, op. 6, overture (Paris, Feb. 4, 1877); *La Forêt enchantée*, op. 8, symph. legend (Paris, March 24, 1878); *Wallenstein*, op. 12, symph. trilogy: a) *Le Camp de Wallenstein* (April 12, 1880), b) *Max et Thécla* (Jan. 25, 1874; originally *Les Piccolomini*), c) *La Mort de Wallenstein* (April 11, 1884); *Lied*, op. 19, for Cello and Orch. (Paris, April 18, 1885); *Saugefleurie*, op. 21, legend (Paris, Jan. 25, 1885); *Symphonie Cévenole (sur un chant montagnard français)*, op. 25, for Orch. and Piano (Paris, March 20, 1887); *Sérénade et Valse*, op. 28 (from op. 16 and 17), for Small Orch. (1887); *Fantaisie*, op. 31, for Oboe and Orch. (Paris, Dec. 23, 1888); incidental music to Alexandre's *Karadec*, op. 34 (Paris, May 2, 1891); *Tableaux de Voyage*, op. 36 (Le Havre, Jan. 17, 1892); *Istar*, op. 42, symph. variations (Brussels, Jan. 10, 1897); incidental music to Mendès's *Medée*, op. 47 (1898); *Choral varié*, op. 55, for Saxophone and Orch. (Paris, May 17, 1904); *2nd Symph.*, op. 57, in B-flat (Paris, Feb. 28, 1904); *Jour d'été à la montagne*, op. 61 (Paris, Feb. 18, 1906); *Souvenirs*, op. 62, tone poem (Paris, April 20, 1907); *La Queste de Dieu*, op. 67, descriptive symph. (from *La Légende de Saint-Christophe*; 1917); *3rd Symph.*, op. 70: *Sinfonia brevis de bello Gallico* (1916–18; Paris, Dec. 14, 1919); *Le Poème des rivages*, op. 77 (N.Y., Dec. 1, 1921); *Diptyque méditerranéen*, op. 87 (Paris, Dec. 5, 1926); Concerto for Piano, Flute, Cello, and String Orch., op. 89 (Paris, April 2, 1927).

CHAMBER MUSIC: Piano Quartet in A minor, op. 7 (1878); Suite in D, op. 24, for Trumpet, 2 Flutes, and String Orch. (Paris, March 5, 1887); Trio for Piano, Clarinet, and Cello, op. 29 (1888); String Quartet No. 1, op. 35 (1891); String Quartet No. 2, op. 45 (1898); *Chansons et Danses*, op. 50, *divertissement* for 7 Wind Instruments (Paris, March 7, 1899); Violin Sonata, op. 59 (1905); Piano Quintet in G minor, op. 81 (1925); Cello Sonata, op. 84 (1926); *Suite en 4 parties*, op. 91, for Flute, Strings, and Harp (Paris, May 17, 1930); String Sextet, op. 92 (1928); String Quartet No. 3, op. 96 (1929); Trio No. 2, op. 98, for Piano, Violin, and Cello (1929).

VOCAL WORKS: *Chanson des aventuriers de la mer*, op. 2, for Baritone Solo and Men's Chorus (1870); *La Chevauchée du Cid*, op. 11, for Baritone, Chorus, and Orch. (1879); *Cantate Domino*, op. 22 (1885); *Ste. Marie-Magdeleine*, op. 23, cantata (1885); *Sur la mer*, op. 32, for Women's Voices and Piano (1888); *Pour l'inauguration d'une statue*, op. 37, cantata (1893); *L'Art et le peuple*, op. 39, for Men's Chorus (1894); *Deus Israël*, op. 41, motet (1896); *Ode à Valence*, op. 44, for Soprano and Chorus (1897); *Les Noces d'or du sacerdoce*, op. 46 (1898); *Sancta Maria*, op. 49, motet (1898); *6 Chants populaires français*, opp. 90 and 100, for a cappella Chorus (1928, 1931); *Le Bouquet de printemps*, op. 93, for Women's Chorus (1929); songs (opp. 3, 4, 10, 13, 20, 43, 48, 52, 56, 58, 64).

FOR PIANO: *3 romances sans paroles*, op. 1 (1870); *Petite sonate*, op. 9 (1880); *Poème des montagnes*, op. 15: *Le Chant des bruyères, Danses rythmiques, Plein-air* (1881); *4 pièces*, op. 16 (1882); *Helvetia*, op. 17, 3 waltzes (1882); *Saugefleurie*, op. 21 (1884; also arranged for Orch.); Nocturne, op. 26 (1886); *Promenade*, op. 27 (1887); *Schumanniana*, op. 30, 3 pieces (1887); *Tableaux de voyage*, op. 33, 13 pieces (1889); *Petite chanson grégorienne*, op. 60, for Piano, 4-hands (1904); Sonata, op. 63 (1907); *Menuet sur le nom de Haydn*, op. 65 (1909); *13 Short Pieces*, op. 68; *12 petites pièces faciles*, op. 69, in old style; *7 chants de terroir*, op. 73, for Piano, 4-hands; *Pour les enfants de tous les âges*, op. 74, 24 pieces; *Thème varié, fugue et chanson*, op. 85; *Conte de fées*, op. 86, suite (1926); 6 paraphrases on French children's songs, op. 95; *Fantaisie sur un vieil air de ronde française*, op. 99 (1931).

FOR ORGAN: *Prélude et Petit Canon*, op. 38 (1893); *Vêpres du Commun d'un Martyr*, op. 51 (1889); *Prélude*, op. 66 (1913).

WITHOUT OPUS NUMBER: O *gai Soleil*, canon *a* 2 (1909); incidental music to *Veronica* (1920); *3 chansons anciennes du Vivarais* (1926); *La Vengeance du mari*, for 3 Soli, Chorus, and Orch. (1931).

Infantas, Fernando de las, Spanish musician and theologian; b. Córdoba, 1534; d. after 1609. He belonged to a noble family and enjoyed the protection of the Emperor Charles V and later of Philip II, who employed him on diplomatic missions in Italy. He went to Venice, and then to Rome, where he lived for 25 years (1572–97). He exerted a decisive influence upon the course of Catholic church music by opposing the plan for the reform of the Roman Gradual undertaken by Palestrina in 1578 at the request of Pope Gregory XIII. Backed by the authority of Philip II of Spain, he succeeded in having the project abandoned. He publ. *Sacrarum varii styli cantionum tituli Spiritus Sancti*, a collection of motets in 3 books: I for 4 voices, II for 5 voices (both publ. in Venice, 1578), III for 6–8 voices (Venice, 1579), and *Plura modulationum genera quae vulgo contrapuncta appellantur super excelso gregoriano cantu* (Venice, 1579; contains 100 contrapuntal exercises for 2–8 voices based on one plainsong theme; it pointed the way to a new freedom and elasticity in polyphonic writing); separate compositions were also publ. in various collections of the time. A Sequence for 6 voices, *Victimae paschali*, was publ. by W. Dehn in *Sammlung älterer Musik aus dem 16. und 17. Jahrhundert*, vol. V, pp. 6–11 (Berlin, 1837–40).

Infante, Manuel, Spanish composer; b. Osuna, near Seville, July 29, 1883; d. Paris, April 21, 1958. He studied piano and composition with Enrique Morera; in 1909 he settled in Paris; gave concerts of Spanish music; wrote numerous pieces for piano, mostly on Spanish themes: *Gitancrias; Pochades andalouses; Sevillana*, fantasy (1922); *El Vito* (variations on a popular theme); also an opera, *Almanza.*

Ingegneri, Marco Antonio, Italian composer; b. Verona, c.1545; d. Cremona, July 1, 1592. He was a pupil of Vincenzo Ruffo, organist of the Verona Cathedral. He went to Cremona about 1568 and became maestro di cappella at the Cathedral there (1579). Monteverdi was his pupil.

Ingenhoven, Jan, Dutch composer; b. Breda, May 29, 1876; d. Hoenderlo, May 20, 1951. He studied with L. Brandts-Buys in Rotterdam and Mottl in Munich; lived in Germany and Switzerland; conducted a madrigal choir in Munich (1909–12); then devoted himself mainly to composition. His works are influenced by Debussy, but he preserves an element of peculiarly native melos. Among his works are a symph. fantasy, *Brabant and Holland;* 3 symph. poems (*Lyric; Dramatic; Romantic);* 4 string quartets; Woodwind Quintet; Trio for Violin, Cello, and Harp; Trio for Flute, Clarinet, and Harp; Trio for Piano, Violin, and Cello; several choral works in the classical tradition; songs.

Inghelbrecht, Désiré Emile, French conductor and composer; b. Paris, Sept. 17, 1880; d. there, Feb. 14, 1965. He studied at the Paris Cons.; after graduation, conducted at various theaters in Paris; toured as conductor of the Ballets Suédois (1919–22); was director of the Opéra-Comique (1924–25 and 1932–33), of the Pasdeloup Orch. (1928–32), and of the Algiers Opera (1929–30). In 1945–50 he was conductor of the Paris Opéra; also conducted abroad. He was the founder of the Orch. National de la Radiodiffusion in Paris in 1934. He publ. several books and pamphlets on conducting: *Comment on ne doit pas interpréter Carmen, Faust et Pelléas* (1932); *Diabolus in musica* (1933); *Mouvement contraire: Souvenirs d'un musicien* (1947); and *Le Chef d'orchestre et son équipe* (1948; Eng. trans. as *The Conductor's World,* 1953).

Insanguine, Giacomo (Antonio Francesco Paolo Michele), called **Monopoli,** Italian composer; b. Monopoli, March 22, 1728; d. Naples, Feb. 1, 1795. He studied with Cotumacci at the Cons. of San Onofrio in Naples; then became his master's assistant (1767) and 2nd teacher (1774); after Cotumacci's death (1785), first teacher. He concurrently was 2nd organist at the Cappella del Tesoro di San Gennaro (1774), first organist (1776), and maestro di cappella there (1781).

Ioannidis, Yannis, Greek composer; b. Athens, June 8, 1930. He studied piano in Athens (1946–55), then music theory at the Cons. there; and organ, composition, and conducting at the Vienna Musical Academy (1955–63); taught at Pierce College in Athens (1963–68); in 1968 went to live in Caracas (his family was from Venezuela), where he served as artistic director of the chamber orch. of the National Inst. of Culture and Fine Arts; he was a prof. there from 1969, and at the Caracas Cons. and Univ. from 1971. As a composer, he follows the precepts of the 2nd Vienna School, with a firm foundation of classical forms. WORKS: 2 string quartets (1961, 1971); *Triptych* for Orch. (1962); Duo for Violin and Piano (1962); *Peristrophe* for String Octet (1964); *Versi* for Solo Clarinet (1967); *Arioso* for String Nonet (1960);

Tropic for Orch. (1968); *Schemata (Figures)* for String Ensemble (1968); *Projections* for Strings, Winds, and Piano (1968); *Fragments I* for Cello and Piano (1969) and *Fragments II* for Solo Flute (1970); *Metaplassis A* and *B* for Orch. (1969, 1970); *Actinia* for Wind Quintet (1969); *Transiciones* for Orch. (1971); *Estudio I, II,* and *III* for Piano (1971–73); *Fancy for 6* for 4 Winds, Cello, and Percussion (1972); *Nocturno* for Piano Quartet (1972); transcriptions of Greek folk songs for chorus.

Iparraguirre y Balerdí, José María de, Spanish-Basque composer and poet; b. Villarreal de Urrechu, Aug. 12, 1820; d. Zozobastro de Isacho, April 6, 1881. He led a wandering life; improvised songs, accompanying himself on the guitar; one of his songs, *Guernikako arbola,* a hymn to the sacred tree of Guernica, became the national anthem of the Basques. As a result of the unrest in the Basque country, and his own participation in it, he was compelled to leave Spain; spent many years in South America; was enabled to return to Spain in 1877, and even obtained an official pension.

Ippolitov-Ivanov, Mikhail (real name **Ivanov,** but he assumed his mother's name to distinguish himself from Michael Ivanov, the music critic; the name is pronounced Ippolítov-Ivánov); important Russian composer and pedagogue; b. Gatchina, Nov. 19, 1859; d. Moscow, Jan. 28, 1935. He entered the St. Petersburg Cons. in 1875; studied composition with Rimsky-Korsakov, graduating in 1882. He then received the post of teacher and director of the Music School in Tiflis, in the Caucasus, where he remained until 1893; he became deeply interested in Caucasian folk music; many of his works were colored by the semi-oriental melodic and rhythmic inflections of that region. Upon Tchaikovsky's recommendation, he was appointed in 1893 prof. of composition at the Moscow Cons.; in 1906 became its director, retiring in 1922. Among his pupils were the composers Glière and Vasilenko. From 1899 on, he was conductor of the Mamontov Opera in Moscow; in 1925, he became conductor of the Bolshoi Theater in Moscow. Outside Russia, he is known mainly for his effective symph. suite *Caucasian Sketches* (1895). WORKS: OPERAS: *Ruth* (Tiflis, Feb. 8, 1887); *Azra* (Tiflis, Nov. 28, 1890); *Asya* (Moscow, Sept. 28, 1900); *Treason* (1909); *Ole from Nordland* (Moscow, Nov. 21, 1916); *The Last Barricade* (1934); also completed Mussorgsky's unfinished opera *Marriage* (1931). FOR ORCH.: *Symphonic Scherzo* (St. Petersburg, May 20, 1882); *Yar-Khmel,* spring overture (St. Petersburg, Jan. 23, 1883, composer conducting); *Caucasian Sketches* (Moscow, Feb. 5, 1895, composer conducting); *Iveria* (2nd series of *Caucasian Sketches;* Moscow, 1906); Symph. No. 1 (Moscow, 1908); *Armenian Rhapsody* (Moscow, 1909); *On the Volga* (Moscow, 1910); *Mtzyri,* symph. poem (Moscow, 1922); *Turkish March* (Baku, 1929); *From the Songs of Ossian,* 3 musical pictures (Moscow, 1927); *Episodes of the Life of Schubert* (1929); *In the Steppes of Turkmenistan; Voroshilov March; Musical*

Scenes of Uzbekistan; symph. poem, *Year 1917; Catalan Suite* (1934); suite on Finnish themes, *Karelia* (1935, last work; only the Finale was orchestrated). CHAMBER MUSIC: Violin Sonata; 2 string quartets; *An Evening in Georgia* for Harp, Flute, Oboe, Clarinet, and Bassoon. VOCAL WORKS: *Alsatian Ballad* for a cappella Mixed Chorus; *5 Characteristic Pieces* for Chorus, and Orch. or Piano; *The Legend of a White Swan* for a cappella Mixed Chorus; *Cantata in Memory of Pushkin* for Children's Chorus and Piano; *Cantata in Memory of Zhukovsky* for Mixed Chorus and Piano; *Pythagorean Hymn to the Rising Sun* for Mixed Chorus, 10 Flutes, 2 Harps, and Tuba; *Cantata in Memory of Gogol* for Children's Chorus and Piano; *Hymn to Labor* for Mixed Chorus and Orch.; 116 songs. He publ. *The Science of the Formation and Resolution of Chords* (1897, in Russian) and *50 Years of Russian Music in My Memories* (Moscow, 1934; in Eng. in *Musical Mercury,* N.Y., 1937).

Ireland, John, eminent English composer; b. Inglewood, Bowdon, Cheshire, Aug. 13, 1879; d. Rock Mill, Washington, Sussex, June 12, 1962. A member of a literary family (both his parents were writers), he received a fine general education. As his musical inclinations became evident, he entered the Royal College of Music in 1893, studying piano with Frederick Cliffe and composition with Stanford. His parents died while he was still a student; he obtained positions as organist in various churches; the longest of these was at St. Luke's, Chelsea (1904–26). In 1905 he received the degree of Bac.Mus. at the Univ. of Durham; was awarded an honorary Mus.Doc. there in 1932. He taught at the Royal College of Music for a number of years; Benjamin Britten, Alan Bush, E.J. Moeran, and other British composers were his pupils. He began to compose early in life; during his student years, he wrote a number of works for orch., chamber groups, and voices, but destroyed most of them. His creative catalogue, therefore, begins in 1903 (with the song cycle *Songs of a Wayfarer*). His early compositions were influenced by the German Romantic school; soon he felt the impact of modern musical ideas; he adopted many devices of the French impressionist school; his rhythmic concepts were enlivened by the new Russian music presented by the Diaghilev Ballet. At the same time, he never wavered in his dedication to the English spirit of simple melody; his music re-creates the plainsong and the usages of Tudor music in terms of plagal modalities and freely modulating triadic harmonies. WORKS: FOR ORCH.: *The Forgotten Rite,* symph. prelude (1913); *Mai-Dun,* symph. rhapsody (1921); *A London Overture* (1936); *Concertino pastorale* for Strings (1939); *Epic March* (1942); *Satyricon* (1946); Piano Concerto (London, Oct. 2, 1930). CHORAL WORKS: *Morning Service* for Voices with Organ (1907–20); motet, *Greater love hath no man* (1912); *Communion Service* (1913); *Evening Service* (1915); *These things shall be* for Baritone Solo, Chorus, and Orch. (1937); a number of 4-part songs a cappella; 2-part songs with piano accompaniment; unison choral songs with piano accompaniment. CHAMBER MUSIC: *Fantasy Trio* for Piano, Violin, and Cello (1906); Trio for Violin, Clarinet, and Piano (1913; rewritten for Violin, Cello, and Piano, 1915, and revised again in 1938); Trio No. 2 for Violin, Cello, and Piano (1917); Violin Sonata No. 1 (1909; revised twice, 1917, 1944); Violin Sonata No. 2 (1917); Cello Sonata (1923); *Fantasy Sonata* for Clarinet and Piano (1943). FOR PIANO: *The Daydream* and *Meridian* (1895; revised 1941); *Decorations* (1913); *The Almond Trees* (1913); Rhapsody (1915); *London Pieces* (1917–20); *Leaves from a Child's Sketchbook* (1918); *Summer Evening* (1919); Sonata (1920); *On a Birthday Morning* (1922); *Soliloquy* (1922); Sonatina (1927); Ballade (1929); *Indian Summer* (1932); *Green Ways* (1937); *Sarnia,* "An Island Sequence" (1941); *3 Pastels* (1941); organ works; about 100 songs, to words by D.G. Rossetti, Christina Rossetti, Thomas Hardy, A.E. Housman, Ernest Dowson, etc.

Irino, Yoshirō, Japanese composer; b. Vladivostok, Siberia, Nov. 13, 1921; d. Tokyo, June 28, 1980. Although of pure Japanese ancestry, he was baptized in the Greek Orthodox faith, which he retained throughout his life. He was sent to Tokyo as a child, and studied economics at Tokyo Univ.; at the same time he took composition lessons with Saburo Moroi. In 1954 he was appointed to the faculty of the Tokyo Music School. A prolific composer, he wrote music of all categories, adopting a style decidedly modern in character, marked by fine instrumental coloration, with a complete mastery of contemporary techniques. Most of his vocal and stage music is imbued with a pronounced Japanese sensibility, with touches that are almost calligraphic in their rhythmic precision. WORKS: An operetta, *The Man in Fear of God* (Tokyo, May 25, 1954); a television opera, *Drum of Silk* (1962); a ballet, *Woman-Mask* (1959); *Adagietto and Allegro vivace* for Orch. (1949); Sinfonietta for Chamber Orch. (1953); Ricercari for Chamber Orch. (1954); Double Concerto for Violin, Piano, and Orch. (1955); *Concerto Grosso* (1957); Sinfonia (1959); Concerto for String Orch. (1960); Suite for Jazz Ensemble (1960); *Music* for Harpsichord, Percussion, and 19 String Instruments (1963); Symph. No. 2 (1964); 2 *Fantasies* for 17 and 20 kotos (1969); *Sai-un (Colorful Clouds)* for 15 String Instruments (1972); *Wandlungen* for 2 Shakuhachi and Orch. (1973); 2 string quartets (1945, 1957); Flute Sonatina (1946); Piano Trio (1948); String Sextet (1950); *Chamber Concerto* for 7 Instruments (1951); *Music* for Violin and Piano (1957); Quintet for Clarinet, Saxophone, Trumpet, Cello, and Piano (1958); Divertimento for 7 Winds (1958); *Music* for Violin and Cello (1959); *Music* for Vibraphone and Piano (1961); Partita for Wind Quintet (1962); String Trio (1965); 3 *Movements* for 2 Kotos and Jushichi-gen (1966); 7 *Inventions* for Guitar and 6 Players (1967); Violin Sonata (1967) *3 Movements* for Solo Cello (1969); Sonata for Piano, Violin, Clarinet, and Percussion (1970); Trio for Flute, Violin, and Piano (1970); *A Demon's Bride* for Chorus, Oboe, Horn, Piano, and Percussion (1970); *Globus I* for Horn and Percussion (1970); *Globus II* for Marimba, Double Bass, and Percussion (1971); *Globus III* for Violin, Cello, Piano, Harp, Shō, and 2 ·Dancers (1975); Suite for Solo Viola (1971); *Cloudscape* for String Ensemble (1972); *3 Improvisations* for Solo Flute (1972); *5 Days* for Violin and Viola (1972); *3 Scenes* for 3 Kotos (1972); *Strömung* for Flute, Harp, and Percussion (1973); Shō-yō for Japanese Instruments (1973); *Gafu* for Flute, Shō, and Double Bass (1976); *Klänge* for Piano and Percussion (1976); *Movements* for Solo Marimba (1977); *Cosmos* for Shakuhachi, Violin, Piano, 2 Kotos, and Percussion (1978); *Shi-dai* for Shakuhachi, 20-gen, 17-gen, and Shamisen (1979); Duo Concertante for Alto Saxophone and Koto (1979).

Isaac, Heinrich (or **Isaak, Izak, Yzac, Ysack;** in Italy, **Arrigo Tedesco** [Henry the German]; Low Latin, **Arrighus**), Netherlandish polyphonist (the Italian term "Tedesco" was used at the time for Netherlanders as well as Germans); b. Brabant, c.1450; d. Florence, March 26, 1517. From 1485 to 1492 he was in the service of Lorenzo de' Medici, in the capacities of organist, maestro di cappella, and teacher to Lorenzo's children. He afterward spent several years in Rome, and finally was called to the court of Maximilian I, at Vienna, as "Symphonista regis"; from 1514 until his death he lived in Florence. He was greatly influenced by the music of the countries in which he lived, writing with equal facility in the Netherlandish, Italian, and German styles as they flourished in his day.
WORKS: 23 masses *a* 4–6 (of which 10 were publ. between 1506–39; those in MS are in libraries in Vienna (8), Munich (4), and Brussels (1). Motets and psalms by Isaac were printed in some 40 collections from 1501–64 (see Eitner, *Bibliographie der Musiksammelwerke;* Berlin, 1877). One of the most beautiful of German chorales, *Nun ruhen alle Wälder,* is sung to Isaac's melody *Inspruk, ich muss dich lassen.* A voluminous collection of motets, *Choralis Constantinus,* was ed. by his pupil Ludwig Senfl, in 1550 (3 parts). Parts I and II were republ. in Denkmäler der Tonkunst in Österreich, 10 and 32 (5.i and 16.i); part III, by the Univ. of Michigan Press (1950; ed. by Louise Cuyler). Isaac's secular works were ed. by Joh. Wolf and also republ. in Denkmäler der Tonkunst in Österreich, 28 and 32 (14.i and 16.i). The *Missa carminum* and other works are publ. in F. Blume's *Das Chorwerk,* 7, 81, and 100. Other reprints are in Eitner's *Publikation älterer Musikwerke* I (5 4-voiced vocal works), and A. Schering's *Geschichte der Musik in Beispielen* (a Kyrie and a canzona). Five polyphonic masses from Isaac's *Choralis Constantinus* were transcribed and ed. by Louise Cuyler (Univ. of Michigan, 1956).

Isepp, Martin, Austrian pianist and harpsichordist; b. Vienna, Sept. 30, 1930. He went to England; studied at Lincoln College, Oxford, and at the Royal Academy of Music in London; in 1957 he joined the music staff of the Glyndebourne Festival. From 1973–76 he was on the faculty of the Juilliard School of Music in N.Y. He became best known as an accompanist to many of the foremost singers of the day, including Dame Janet Baker, Hans Hotter, Elisabeth Schwarzkopf, and John Shirley-Quirk.

Ishii, Kan, Japanese composer, brother of **Maki Ishii;** b. Tokyo, March 30, 1921. He is one of two sons of Baku Ishii, a renowned scholar of modern dance. He studied in Tokyo at the Musashino Music School with Goh, Ikenouchi, and Odaka (1939–43); in 1952 went to Germany and took lessons in composition with Carl Orff at the Hochschule für Musik in Munich. Returning to Japan, he taught at the Toho Music Univ. and at the Aichi-Prefectural Arts Univ.; in 1970 was elected president of the All-Japan Chorus League.
WORKS: 4 operas: *Mermaid and Red Candle* (1961); *Kaguyahime* (*Prince Kaguya,* 1963); *En-no-Gyojia* (Tokyo, 1964); *Lady Kesa and Morito* (Tokyo, Nov. 24, 1968); 9 ballets: *God and the Bayadere* (Tokyo, Nov. 6, 1950); *Birth of a Human* (Tokyo, Nov. 27, 1954); *Frökln Julie* (1955); *Shakuntara* (1961); *Marimo* (Tokyo, 1963); *Biruma no tategoto* (*Harp of Burma,* 1963); *Haniwa* (1963); *Hakai* (1965); *Ichiyo Higuchi* (1966); symph. poem, *Yama* (*Mountain,* Tokyo, Oct. 7, 1954); *Kappa's Penny* for Youth Orch. (1956); *Sinfonia Ainu* for Soprano, Chorus, and Orch. (1958–59); *The Reef,* cantata for Baritone, Chorus, 4 Pianos, and Percussion (1967); *Akita the Great* for Chorus and Brass (1968); *Music for Percussion* for 8 Players (1970); Viola Sonata (1960); Music for Solo Flute (1972); *Footsteps to Tomorrow,* cantata for Solo Soprano (1972); folk songs; choruses, etc. He compiled a valuable collection of Japanese folk songs, publ. in 6 vols.

Ishii, Maki, Japanese composer, brother of **Kan Ishii;** b. Tokyo, May 28, 1936. He received an early training in music from his father, a renowned promoter of modern dance; studied composition with Akira Ifukube and Tomojiro Ikenouchi, and conducting with Akeo Watanabe, in Tokyo (1952–58); then went to Germany, where he took courses at the Berlin Hochschule für Musik with Boris Blacher and Josef Rufer (1958–61); after a brief return to Japan he went back to Germany, where he decided to remain. In his works he attempts to combine the coloristic effects of Japanese instruments with European techniques of serial music and electronic sounds.
WORKS: Prelude and Variations for 9 Players (1959–60); 7 *Stücke* for Small Orch. (1960–61); 4 *Bagatelles* for Violin and Piano (1961); *Transition* for Small Orch. (1962); *Aphorismen I* for String Trio, Percussion, and Piano (1963); *Galgenlieder* for Baritone, Male Chorus, and 13 Players (1964); *Characters* for Flute, Oboe, Piano, Guitar, and Percussion (1965); *Hamon* for Violin, Chamber Ensemble, and Tape (1965); *Expressions* for String Orch. (Tokyo, Jan. 11, 1968); *5 Elements* for Guitar and 6 Players (1967); *Piano Piece* for Pianist and Percussionist (1968); *Kyō-ō* for Piano, Orch., and Tape (Tokyo, Feb. 22, 1969); *Kyō-sō* for Percussion and Orch. (Tokyo, Feb. 7, 1969); *La-sen I* for 7 Players and Tape (1969); *La-sen II* for Solo Cello (1970); *Sō-gū I* for Shakuhachi and Piano (1970); *Music for*

Gagaku (1970); *Dipol* for Orch. (1971); *Sō-gū II* for Gagaku and Symph. Orch. (Tokyo, June 23, 1971; work resulting from simultaneous perf. of *Music for Gagaku* and *Dipol*); *Sen-ten* for Percussion Player and Tape (1971); *Aphorismen II* for a Pianist (1972); *Chō-etsu* for Chamber Group and Tape (1973); *Polaritäten* for Soloists and Orch. (1973; work exists in 3 versions, each having different soloists: *I* for Biwa and Harp; *II* for Biwa, Shakuhachi, and Flute; *III* for Shakuhachi and Flute); *Synkretismen* for Marimba, 7 Soloists, Strings, and 3 Percussionists (1973); *Anime Amare* for Harp and Tape (1974); *Jo* for Orch. (1975); *Translucent Vision* for Orch. (1981–82).

Isidore of Seville, Spanish cleric; b. Cartagena, c.560; d. Seville, April 4, 636. He was brought to Seville as a child; in 599 became archbishop there. Between 622 and 633, compiled a treatise on the arts, *Etymologiarum sive originum libri XX;* he expressed the conviction that music can only be preserved through memory, for musical sounds could never be notated (*scribi non possunt*). The text was publ. in Oxford (1911); an Eng. trans. of the pertinent parts is included in Strunk's *Source Readings in Music History* (N.Y., 1950).

Isler, Ernst, Swiss organist and music critic; b. Zürich, Sept. 30, 1879; d. there, Sept. 26, 1944. He studied in Zürich and Berlin; served as an organist in Zürich, and taught organ there. He became music critic of the influential daily paper *Neue Zürcher Zeitung* in 1902, and held this position until his death; from 1910 to 1927 he was editor of the *Schweizerische Musikzeitung.* He publ. monographs on Hans Huber, Max Reger, etc.; also a valuable compendium, *Das Züricherische Konzertleben 1895–1914* (Zürich, 1935), and its sequel, covering the years 1914–31 (Zürich, 1936).

Ísólfsson, Páll, Icelandic organist and composer; b. Stokkseyri, Oct. 12, 1893; d. Reykjavik, Nov. 23, 1974. He studied organ at the Leipzig Cons. with Straube, and later in Paris with Bonnet. Returning to Iceland, he served as organist at the Reykjavik Cathedral (1939–68) and director of the Reykjavik Cons. and of Icelandic Radio. He wrote a number of attractive piano pieces in the manner of Grieg (humoresques, intermezzi, capriccios, etc.), choruses, and a cantata on the millennial anniversary of the Icelandic Parliament (1930); also compiled (with S. Einarsson) a collection of choral pieces by various composers. In 1963–64 he publ. his autobiography in 2 vols. (in Icelandic).

Isouard, Nicolo, important French opera composer; b. Malta, Dec. 6, 1775; d. Paris, March 23, 1818. A son of a prosperous merchant, he was sent to Paris to study engineering; afterward, he served as a clerk in Malta, in Palermo, and in Naples, where he took lessons with Sala and Guglielmi. In the spring of 1794 he produced his first opera, *L'avviso ai maritati,* in Florence; from that time on he abandoned business pursuits, dedicating himself to operatic composition. In order not to embarrass his family, and particularly his father, who was against his career as a musician, he adopted the name **Nicolo de Malte,** or simply **Nicolo.** He served as organist of St. John of Jerusalem at Malta (1795–98); in 1799, went to Paris, where he became increasingly successful as an opera composer; he was also popular as a pianist. In Paris he had to undergo strong competition with Boieldieu; but the lengthy list of productions of his operas up to 1816 shows that he had never relaxed his industry. The music of his operas demonstrates a facile melodic gift in the French manner, as well as sound craftsmanship. Besides operas, he wrote church music. The best known of his operas are *Cendrillon, Joconde,* and *Jeannot et Colin.* A list of his operas, produced in Paris, includes: *Le Petit Page* (with R. Kreutzer; Feb. 14, 1800); *La Statue* (April 26, 1802); *L'Intrigue au sérail* (April 25, 1809); *Cendrillon* (Feb. 22, 1810); *La Victime des arts* (Feb. 27, 1811); *La Fête du village* (March 31, 1811); *Le Billet de loterie* (Sept. 14, 1811); *Le Magicien sans magie* (Nov. 4, 1811); *Lully et Quinault* (Feb. 27, 1812); *Le Prince de Catane* (March 4, 1813); *Les Français à Venise* (June 14, 1813); *Joconde* (Feb. 28, 1814); *Michel-Ange* (Dec. 11, 1802); *Les Confidences* (March 31, 1803); *Le Baiser et la quittance* (June 18, 1803); *Le Médecin turc* (Nov. 19, 1803); *L'Intrigue aux fenêtres* (Feb. 26, 1805); *Le Déjeuner de garçons* (April 24, 1805); *La Ruse inutile* (May 30, 1805); *Léonce* (Nov. 18, 1805); *La Prise de Passaw* (Feb. 8, 1806); *Idala* (July 30, 1806); *Les Rendezvous bourgeois* (May 9, 1807); *Les Créanciers* (Dec. 10, 1807); *Un Jour à Paris* (May 24, 1808); *Cimarosa* (June 28, 1808); *Jeannot et Colin* (Oct. 17, 1814); *Les deux Maris* (March 18, 1816); *L'Une pour l'autre* (May 11, 1816); *Aladin* (Feb. 6, 1822; posthumous work, completed by Benincori and Habeneck).

Istomin, Eugene, American pianist; b. New York, Nov. 26, 1925, of Russian parents. He studied with Rudolf Serkin at the Curtis Inst. in Philadelphia; in 1943 he won the Leventritt Award for an appearance as soloist with the N.Y. Phil. Orch. (Nov. 21, 1943), playing the 2nd Piano Concerto of Brahms. After that he developed a highly successful concert career; appeared with a number of American orchs., and also gave recitals in America and in Europe. On Feb. 15, 1975, he married Martita Casals, widow of Pablo Casals.

Ištvan, Miloslav, Czech composer; b. Olomouc, Sept. 2, 1928. He studied music at the Janáček Academy in Brno with Jaroslav Kvapil (1948–52); subsequently was active mainly as a music teacher. Like many of his compatriots he cultivated a national style of composition, thematically derived from folk-music, but later adopted the *modus operandi* of the cosmopolitan avant-garde. In 1963 he joined the Creative Group A of Brno, dedicated to free musical experimentation "uninhibited by puritanically limited didactical regulations." He also worked in the electronic music studio of Brno Radio.

Iturbi, José, celebrated Spanish pianist; b. Valencia, Nov. 28, 1895; d. Hollywood, June 28, 1980. He took piano lessons with Malats in Barcelona; while still a very young boy he earned a living by playing in street cafés. A local group of music lovers collected a sum of money to send him to Paris for further study; he was accepted as a student at the Paris Cons., and graduated in 1912. After a while he developed a brilliant concert career; his performances of Spanish music were acclaimed for their authentic rhythmic spirit. He made a tour of South America; in 1928 he appeared as soloist in the U.S.; during his second American tour in 1930 he gave 67 concerts. In 1936 he turned to conducting; led the Rochester Phil. until 1944. He wrote a number of pleasing piano pieces in a typical Spanish vein; of these, *Pequeña danza española* exercised considerable attraction. His sister, **Amparo Iturbi** (b. Valencia, March 12, 1898; d. Beverly Hills, Calif., April 21, 1969), was also a talented pianist; she played piano duos with José Iturbi on numerous occasions in Europe and America.

Ivanovici, Ion, Rumanian bandleader and composer of light music; b. Banat, 1845; d. Bucharest, Sept. 29, 1902. He played the flute and clarinet in a military band in Galatz, and in 1880 conducted his own band there. In the same year he wrote the waltz *Valurile Dunării (The Waves of the Danube),* which became a perennial favorite all over the world. He took part in the Paris Exposition of 1889, and conducted there a band of 116 musicians. In 1900 he was appointed Inspector of Military Music in Rumania. He publ. about 150 pieces for piano and dances for band.

Ivanovs, Janis, prolific Latvian composer; b. Preili, Oct. 9, 1906. He studied composition with Wihtol, piano with Dauge, and conducting with Schneevoigt at the Latvian Cons. in Riga, graduating in 1931; then worked at Latvian Radio; in 1949 was appointed to the composition faculty at the Latvian Cons. An exceptionally fecund composer, he wrote 20 symphs., several of a programmatic nature descriptive of the Latvian countryside: No. 1, *Symphonie-Poème* (1933); No. 2, *Atlantida* (1941); No. 6, *Latgales* (*Latvian,* 1949); No. 12, *Sinfonia energica* (1967); No. 13, *Symphonia humana* (1969). His symph. peoms also reflect nature scenes; e.g., *Varaviksne* (*Rainbow,* 1938) and *Padebešu Kalns* (*Mountain under the Sky,* 1939). He further wrote 3 string quartets (1933, 1946, 1961); a Cello Concerto (1938); Violin Concerto (1951); Piano Concerto (1959); choruses; songs; piano pieces; film music.

Ives, Burl, American folksinger; b. Hunt Township, Jasper County, Ill., June 14, 1909. He studied briefly at N.Y. Univ.; traveled through the U.S. and Canada as an itinerant handyman, supplementing his earnings by singing and playing the banjo. He then became a dramatic actor and appeared on the stage and in films, and gave concerts of folk ballads, accompanying himself on the guitar. He publ. an autobiography, *Wayfaring Stranger* (N.Y., 1948), and the anthologies *The Burl Ives Songbook* (1953) and *The Burl Ives Book of Irish Songs* (1958).

Ives, Charles Edward, one of the most remarkable American composers, whose individual genius created music so original, so universal, and yet so deeply national in its sources of inspiration, that it profoundly changed the direction of American music; b. Danbury, Conn., Oct. 20, 1874; d. New York, May 19, 1954. His father, **George Ives,** was a bandleader of the First Connecticut Heavy Artillery during the Civil War, and the early development of Charles Ives was, according to his own testimony, deeply influenced by his father. At the age of 12, he played the drums in the band and also received from his father rudimentary musical training in piano and cornet playing. At the age of 13 he played organ at the Danbury Church; soon he began to improvise freely at the piano, without any dependence on school rules; as a result of his experimentation in melody and harmony, encouraged by his father, Charles Ives began to combine several keys, partly as a spoof, but eventually as a legitimate alternative to traditional music; at 17 he composed his *Variations on America* for organ in a polytonal setting; still earlier he wrote a band piece, *Holiday Quick Step,* which was performed by the Danbury Band in 1888. He attended the Danbury High School; in 1894 he entered Yale Univ., where he took regular academic courses and studied organ with Dudley Buck and composition with Horatio Parker; from Horatio Parker he received a fine classical training; while still in college he composed 2 full-fledged symphs., written in an entirely traditional manner demonstrating great skill in formal structure, fluent melodic development, and smooth harmonic modulations. After his graduation from Yale Univ., in 1898, Ives joined an insurance company; also played organ at the Central Presbyterian Church in N.Y. (1899–1902). In 1907 he formed an insurance partnership with Julian Myrick of N.Y.; he proved himself to be an exceptionally able businessman; the firm of Ives & Myrick prospered, and Ives continued to compose music as an avocation. In 1908 he married Harmony Twichell. In 1918 he suffered a massive heart attack, complicated by a diabetic condition, and was compelled to curtail his work both in business and in music to a minimum because his illness made it difficult to handle a pen. He retired from business in 1930, and by that time had virtually stopped composing. In 1919 Ives publ. at his own expense his great masterpiece, *Concord Sonata,* for piano, inspired by the writings of Emerson, Hawthorne, the Alcotts, and Thoreau. Although written early in the century, its idiom is so extraordinary, and its technical difficulties so formidable, that the work did not receive a performance in its entirety until John Kirkpatrick played it in N.Y. in 1939. In 1922 Ives brought out, also at his expense, a volume of *114 Songs,* written between 1888 and 1921 and marked by great diversity of style, ranging from lyrical Romanticism to powerful and dissonant modern invocations. Both the *Concord Sonata* and the *114 Songs* were distributed gratis by Ives himself to anyone wishing to receive copies. His orch. masterpiece, *Three Places in New England,* also had to wait nearly 2 decades before its first performance; of the monumental 4th Symph., only the 2nd movement was performed in 1927, and its complete performance was given posthumously in 1965. In 1947 Ives received the Pulitzer Prize for his 3rd Symph., written in 1911. The slow realization of the greatness of Ives and the belated triumphant recognition of his music were phenomena without precedent in music history. Because of his chronic ailment, and also on account of his personal disposition, Ives lived as a recluse, away from the mainstream of American musical life; he never went to concerts and did not own a record player or a radio; while he was well versed in the musical classics, and studied the scores of Beethoven, Schumann, and Brahms, he took little interest in sanctioned works of modern composers; yet he anticipated many technical innovations, such as polytonality, atonality, and even 12-tone formations, as well as polymetric and polyrhythmic configurations, which were prophetic for his time. In the 2nd movement of the *Concord Sonata* he specified the application of a strip of wood on the white and the black keys of the piano to produce an echo-like sonority; in his unfinished *Universe Symphony* he planned an antiphonal representation of the heavens in chordal counterpoint and the earth in contrasting orch. groups. He also composed pieces of quarter-tone piano music. A unique quality of his music was the combination of simple motifs, often derived from American church hymns and popular ballads, with an extremely complex dissonant counterpoint which formed the supporting network for the melodic lines. A curious idiosyncrasy is the frequent quotation of the "fate motive" of Beethoven's 5th Symph. in many of his works. Materials of his instrumental and vocal works often overlap, and the titles are often changed during the process of composition. In his orchestrations he often indicated interchangeable and optional parts, as in the last movement of the *Concord Sonata,* which has a part for flute obbligato; thus he reworked the original score for large orch. of his *3 Places in New England* for a smaller ensemble to fit the requirements of Slonimsky's Chamber Orch. of Boston, which gave its first performance, and it was in this version that the work was first publ. and widely performed until the restoration of the large score was made in 1974. Ives possessed an uncommon gift for literary expression; his annotations to his works are both trenchant and humorous; he publ. in 1920 *Essays before a Sonata* as a literary companion vol. to the *Concord Sonata;* his *Memos* in the form of a diary, publ. after his death, reveal an extraordinary power of aphoristic utterance. He was acutely conscious of his civic duties as an American, and once circulated a proposal to have federal laws enacted by popular referendum. His centennial in 1974 was celebrated by a series of conferences at his alma mater at Yale Univ., in N.Y., in Miami and many other American cities, and in Europe, including Russia. While during his lifetime he and a small group of devoted friends and admirers had great difficulties in having his works performed, recorded, or publ., a veritable Ives cult emerged after his death; eminent conductors gave repeated performances of his orch. works, and modern pianists were willing to cope with the forbidding difficulties of his works. In the number of orch. performances, in 1976 Ives stood highest among modern composers on American programs, and the influence of his music on the new generation of composers reached a high mark, so that the adjective "Ivesian" became common in music criticism to describe certain acoustical and coloristic effects characteristic of his music. America's youth expressed especial enthusiasm for Ives, which received its most unusual tribute in the commercial marketing of a T-shirt with Ives's portrait. All of the Ives MSS and his correspondence were deposited by Mrs. Ives at Yale Univ., forming a basic Ives archive.

WORKS: FOR ORCH.: 4 symphs.: No. 1 (1896–98); No. 2 (1897–1902; N.Y., Feb. 22, 1951); No. 3 (1901–4; N.Y., April 5, 1946); No. 4 (1910–16; 2nd movement only perf., N.Y., Jan. 29, 1927; first perf. in its entirety was given in N.Y. on April 26, 1965, Leopold Stokowski conducting the American Symph. Orch.); also incomplete fragments of a *Universe Symphony* (1911–16); *3 Places in New England* (Orchestral Set No. 1: The "St. Gaudens" in Boston Common; Putnam's Camp, Redding, Connecticut; The Housatonic at Stockbridge; 1903–14; N.Y., Jan. 10, 1931, Chamber Orch. of Boston, Nicolas Slonimsky conducting); *Calcium Light Night* for Chamber Orch. (1898–1907); *Central Park in the Dark* (1898–1907; Columbia Univ., N.Y., May 11, 1946); *The Unanswered Question* (1908); *Theater Orchestra Set: In the Cage, In the Inn, In the Night* (1904–11); *The Pond* (1906); *Browning Overture* (1911); *The Gong on the Hook and Ladder, or Firemen's Parade on Main Street* for Chamber Orch. (1911); *Lincoln, the Great Commoner* for Chorus and Orch. (1912); *A Symphony: Holidays,* in 4 parts, also perf. separately: *Washington's Birthday* (1913), *Decoration Day* (1912), *4th of July* (1913), *Thanksgiving and/or Forefathers' Day* (1904); *Over the Pavements* for Chamber Orch. (1913); *Orchestral Set No. 2* (1915); *Tone Roads* for Chamber Orch. (1911–15); *Orchestral Set No. 3* (1919–27). CHAMBER MUSIC: String Quartet No. 1, subtitled *A Revival Service* (1896); *Prelude,* from "Pre-First Sonata," for Violin and Piano (1900); Trio for Violin, Clarinet, and Piano (1902); "Pre-Second String Quartet" (1905); *Space and Duration* for String Quartet and a very mechanical Piano (1907); *All the Way Around and Back* for Piano, Violin, Flute, Bugle, and Bells (1907); *The Innate* for String Quartet and Piano (1908); *Adagio Sostenuto* for English Horn, Flute, Strings, and Piano (1910); Violin Sonata No. 1 (1908); Violin Sonata No. 2 (1910); Trio for Violin, Cello, and Piano (1911); String Quartet No. 2 (1913); Violin Sonata No. 3 (1914); *Set* for String Quartet and Piano (1914); Violin Sonata No. 4, subtitled *Children's Day at the Camp Meeting* (1915). VOCAL WORKS: *Psalm 67* (1898); *The Celestial Country,* cantata (1899); *3 Harvest Home Chorales* for Mixed Chorus, Brass, Double Bass, and Organ (1898–1912); *General William Booth Enters into Heaven* for

Chorus with Brass Band (1914); *114 Songs* (1884–1921). PIANO PIECES: *3-page Sonata* (1905); *Some Southpaw Pitching* (1908); *The Anti-Abolitionist Riots* (1908); Sonata No. 1 (1909); *22* (1912); *3 Protests for Piano* (1914); Sonata No. 2 for Piano, subtitled *Concord, Mass., 1840–1860,* in 4 movements: *Emerson, Hawthorne, The Alcotts, Thoreau* (1909–15; publ. 1919; first perf. in its entirety by John Kirkpatrick, N.Y., Jan. 20, 1939; the 2nd movement requires the application of a strip of wood on the keys to produce tone-clusters); *3 Quartertone Piano Pieces* (1903–24).

WRITINGS: As a companion piece to his "Concord Sonata" (Piano Sonata No. 2), Ives wrote *Essays before a Sonata* (publ. N.Y., 1920), commentaries on the Concord writers who inspired his work, and on various musical and philosophical matters; this has been reprinted as *Essays before a Sonata and Other Writings,* ed. by Howard Boatwright (N.Y., 1961). Most of his other expository writings are publ. as *Memos,* ed. by John Kirkpatrick (N.Y., 1972), composed of autobiography, explanation, and criticism.

Ives (Ive), Simon, English composer; b. Ware (baptized, July 20), 1600; d. London, July 1, 1662. He was organist in Newgate and a choral master at St. Paul's Cathedral in London; wrote music for masques at the court; in 1633 contributed material to Shirley's masque *The Triumph of Peace.* His songs, catches, and rounds were publ. in several 17th-century collections: Playford's *Select Ayres and Dialogues* (1669) and *Musical Companion* (1672), Hilton's *Catch that Catch can* (1652), etc. He also wrote instrumental music, some of which was included in *Musick's Recreation* (1652 and 1661).

Ivogün, Maria, Hungarian soprano; b. Budapest, Nov. 18, 1891. Her real name was **Ilse von Günther,** which she histrionically compressed into I(lse)vo(n)gün(ther) = Ivogün. Her father was an officer, her mother an operetta singer. She went to Vienna to study with Irene Schlemmer-Ambros; then moved to Munich, where she took lessons with Hanny Schöner. She made a successful operatic debut at the Bavarian State Opera in Munich in 1913, as Mimi in *La Bohème;* in 1925 she joined the Städtische Oper in Berlin, remaining on its roster until 1934. In 1922 she went on a concert tour in the U.S. She also appeared at Covent Garden in London, at La Scala in Milan, and at the Salzburg Festivals. She retired from the stage in 1932, and became active as a voice teacher; from 1948–50 she taught at the Vienna Academy of Music, and from 1950–58 was on the faculty of the Berlin Hochschule für Musik. She was married twice: to the tenor **Karl Erb** from 1921–32 and to her accompanist **Michael Raucheisen** in 1933.

Iwaki, Hiroyuki, distinguished Japanese conductor; b. Tokyo, Sept. 6, 1932. He was educated in Tokyo; then conducted many of the major Japanese orchs. In 1969 he assumed the post of chief conductor of the NHK (Japan Broadcasting Corp.) Symph. Orch.; in 1974 he also became chief conductor of the Melbourne (Australia) Symph.; in addition, was principal guest conductor of the Atlanta Symph. In Europe, he received encomiums for his appearances with the Berlin and Vienna Phil. orchs.

J

Jachet di Mantua (Jaquet Collebaud de Vitré), French-born Italian composer; b. Vitré, 1483; d. Mantua, Oct. 2, 1559. He went to Mantua about 1526, and became its citizen in 1534. He was titular maestro di cappella at the Cathedral of Peter and Paul from 1534–59. His publ. works include 4-part motets (Venice, 1539); 5-part motets (Venice, 1540); a Mass in 4 parts (Paris, 1554); masses in 5 parts (Venice, 1555); *Messe dei Fiore* in 5 parts (Venice, 1555); Passions in 5 parts (Venice, 1567); and other sacred pieces. A complete edition of his works began publication in 1970 under the editorship of P. Jackson and G. Nugent in Corpus Mensurabilis Musicae.

Jachimecki, Zdzislaw, eminent Polish musicologist; b. Lwow, July 7, 1882; d. Cracow, Oct. 27, 1953. He studied in Lwow with S. Niewiadomski and H. Jarecki, and in Vienna with Adler (musicology) and Schoenberg (composition); received a Dr.Phil. with the dissertation *150 Psalms by Mikolaj Gomolka* (1906). He then became a member of the faculty at the Univ. of Cracow. Jachimecki was one of the most renowned Polish musicologists; he was also a composer of choral works; was a conductor of symph. concerts in Cracow from 1908–24. Most of his writings were publ. in Polish, in Cracow. They include *The Influence of Italian Music on Polish Music* (1911); *Organ Tablature of the Holy Ghost Cloister in Cracow, 1548* (1913); *Music of the Royal Court of King Wladyslaw Jagiello* (1915); *Outlines of Polish History of Music* (Warsaw, 1919); *Moniuszko* (Warsaw, 1921); *Chopin* (1926; in French as *F. Chopin et son œuvre,* Paris, 1930); monographs on Mozart, Haydn, Wagner, Szymanowski, etc.; he also contributed an article on Moniuszko to the *Musical Quarterly* (Jan. 1928); publ. *Muzyka Polska* (2 vols., 1948, 1951).

Jachino, Carlo, Italian composer; b. San Remo, Feb. 3, 1887; d. Rome, Dec. 23, 1971. He studied with Luporini in Lucca and with Riemann in Leipzig; then taught at the Parma Cons. (until 1936), at Naples (1936–38), and at the Santa Cecilia Academy in Rome (1938–50). He then went to South America; was director of the National Cons. in Bogotá, Colombia (1953–57); returning to Italy, he served as artistic director of the Teatro San Carlo in Naples (1961–69). His opera *Giocondo e il suo rè* was produced in Milan (June 24, 1924). He also wrote several works of chamber music; a treatise on the 12-tone method of composition, *Tecnica dodecafonica* (Milan, 1948); and *Gli strumenti d'orchestra* (Milan, 1950). In his early compositions he followed the Romantic Italian style; later he adopted a modified

12-tone method.

Jackson, George K., English-American organist and theorist; b. Oxford (baptized, April 15), 1757; d. Boston, Mass., Nov. 18, 1822. He was a pupil of Dr. James Narer; became a surplice boy at the Chapel Royal, London; was among the tenor singers at the Handel Commemoration in 1784; in 1791, received a Mus.Doc. from St. Andrew's College. In 1796 he came to Norfolk, Va., then to Elizabeth, N.J., and N.Y. (in 1804, became music director at St. George's Chapel). By 1812 he was in Boston, where he remained as an organist at various churches; also gave a series of oratorios with Graupner and Mallet. A collection of his music is in the library of the Harvard Music Association, Boston. He publ. *First Principles, or a Treatise on Practical Thorough Bass* (London, 1795); *David's Psalms* (1804); *A Choice Collection of Chants* (1816); *The Choral Companion* (1817); *Watt's Divine Hymns set to music.*

Jacob, Gordon, English composer and pedagogue; b. London, July 5, 1895; d. Saffron Walden, England, June 8, 1984. He studied music theory with Stanford at the Royal College of Music, and from 1926 to 1966 was on its faculty; also served as examiner of other music schools. In 1968 he was named a Commander of the Order of the British Empire.

Jacob, Maxime, French composer; b. Bordeaux, Jan. 13, 1906; d. at the Benedictine Abbey at En-Calcat (Tarn), Feb. 26, 1977. He studied music in Paris with Gédalge, Koechlin, and Darius Milhaud. Pursuing a whimsical mode, he became associated with the so-called Ecole d'Arcueil, named after a modest Paris suburb where Erik Satie presided over his group of disciples; then made a 180° turn toward established religion, and in 1930 entered the Benedictine Order, where he served mainly as an organist. He continued to compose prolifically; between 1929 and 1949 he wrote 15 piano sonatas, 3 violin sonatas, 2 cello sonatas, etc.; then produced 8 string quartets (1961–69); a curious *Messe syncopée* (1968); 500 or more songs.

Jacobi, Erwin, Swiss musicologist; b. Strasbourg, Sept. 21, 1909; d. Zürich, Feb. 27, 1979. He studied economics in Berlin, obtaining a diploma of engineering in 1933; from 1934 to 1952 he lived in Israel; there he studied harpsichord with Pelleg and composition with Ben-Haim; in 1952 he went to America, where he took lessons in harpsichord playing with Wanda Landowska, composition with Hindemith, and music history with Curt Sachs. In 1953 he went to Switzerland to work at the Univ. of Zürich as a graduate student, in 1961 he became an assistant lecturer there. In 1970 he was a visiting prof. at the Univ. of Iowa, and in 1971 was active in the same capacity at Indiana Univ. He contributed a great number of valuable papers on Baroque composers to various musicological journals; of these the most important was a dissertation on the evolution of music theory in England (publ. in Stras-bourg, 1957–60; new ed., Baden-Baden, 1971).

Jacobi, Frederick, American composer; b. San Francisco, May 4, 1891; d. New York, Oct. 24, 1952. He studied piano with Paolo Gallico and Rafael Joseffy, and composition with Rubin Goldmark; then took private lessons with Ernest Bloch. Subsequently he was on the faculty of the Juilliard School of Music in N.Y. (1936–50), and served as a member of the executive board of the League of Composers. In his own music he often made use of authentic American Indian themes; also drew from jazz, black music, folk songs, and even some Hebraisms. WORKS: Opera, *The Prodigal Son* (1944); for Orch.: *The Pied Piper,* symph. poem (1915); *A California Suite* (San Francisco, Dec. 6, 1917); 2 symphs.: No. 1, *Assyrian* (San Francisco, Nov. 14, 1924); No. 2 (San Francisco, April 1, 1948); *Ode for Orchestra* (San Francisco, Feb. 12, 1943); Concertino for Piano and String Orch. (Saratoga Springs, Sept. 3, 1946); *2 Assyrian Prayers* for Voice and Orch. (1923); *The Poet in the Desert* for Baritone Solo, Chorus, and Orch. (1925); *Sabbath Evening Service* for Baritone Solo and Mixed Chorus (1931); 3 string quartets (1924, 1933, 1945); *Impressions from the Odyssey* for Violin and Piano (1947); *Meditation* for Trombone and Piano (1947); miscellaneous piano pieces and songs.

Jacobs, Arthur, English music critic, lexicographer, opera librettist and translator; b. Manchester, June 14, 1922. He studied at Oxford Univ. From 1947 to 1952 he was music critic for the *Daily Express* and has since then written articles for a number of publications. From 1960 to 1971 he was an associate editor of the London monthly *Opera.* In 1952 he publ. a book on Gilbert and Sullivan. He then became deeply involved in musical lexicography; compiled an uncommonly intelligent, compact reference work, *A New Dictionary of Music* (London, 1958; 2nd ed., 1967; reprints with revisions, 1968, 1970; completely revised in 1977). In 1964 Jacobs was appointed a lecturer in music history at the Royal Academy of Music, London; was visiting prof. at the Univ. of Illinois (1967), at the Univ. of Calif., Santa Barbara (1969), and at Temple Univ. in Philadelphia (1970, 1971); he also toured Australia and Russia. In 1979 he became head of music at Huddersfield Polytechnic. An accomplished linguist, he mastered Russian, German, French, and Italian; trans., with admirable fidelity to the syllabic and musical values of the originals, some 20 operas, among them Tchaikovsky's *The Queen of Spades,* Schoenberg's *Erwartung,* and Alban Berg's *Lulu;* wrote the libretto of Nicholas Maw's opera *One Man Show* (London, 1964). Several of these translations have been adopted by the Royal Opera, Covent Garden, and Sadler's Wells Opera (from 1974 the English National Opera) in London. In 1971 he was appointed editor of the *Music Yearbook,* publ. in London.

Jacobs, Paul, American pianist; b. New York, June 22, 1930; d. there, a victim of AIDS (Acquired Immune Deficiency Syndrome), Sept. 25, 1983. He was a prototypical child prodigy, but overcame his musical precocity by an extraordinary intellectual endeavor, specializing in the twin aspects of structural composition, Baroque and avant-garde; he played the former on the harpsichord; by disposition and natural selection he eschewed Romantic music. He studied piano with Ernest Hutcheson; from 1951–60 he was in Europe; gave an unprecedented recital in Paris of a complete cycle of piano music of Schoenberg; became associated with the European centers of avant-garde music, at the Domaine Musical in Paris, at the contemporary music festivals in Darmstadt, and in various other localities. Returning to the U.S., he was appointed official pianist of the N.Y. Phil. in 1962; also taught at the Manhattan School of Music and at Brooklyn College, remaining on its faculty until his death. He recorded the piano works of Debussy, Schoenberg, Stravinsky, Elliot Carter, and others.

Jacobs-Bond, Carrie. See **Bond, Carrie Jacobs.**

Jacopo da Bologna (Jacobus de Bononia), 14th-century composer, one of the earliest representatives of the Florentine "Ars nova". He wrote madrigals, *ballate,* etc.; his MSS are in the libraries of Florence and Paris and at the British Museum in London. His complete works are publ. in W.T. Marrocco, *The Music of Jacopo da Bologna* (Berkeley and Los Angeles, 1954). Johannes Wolf publ. 3 madrigals in his *Geschichte der Mensuralnotation* (nos. 40–42); one madrigal is in G. Reese's *Music in the Middle Ages* (N.Y., 1940; p. 363), and another in A.T. Davison and W. Apel, *Historical Anthology of Music* (Cambridge, Mass., 1947).

Jacotin (real name, **Jacques Godebrie**), Flemish composer; b. Antwerp, c.1445; d. there, March 23, 1529. He was for nearly half a century "chapelain" in the choir of Notre Dame in Antwerp (1479–1528). His vocal works were publ. in collections by Attaignant (1529, 1530–35) and Rhaw (1545), in Le Roy's & Ballard's *Chansons nouvellement composées* (1556), etc. He excelled especially in French chansons; of these *Trop dure m'est ta longue demeure* is reproduced in H. Expert's reprint of Attaignant's collection of 1529; and *Mon triste cœur* in Eitner's *Selection of 60 Chansons* (1899). Several motets attributed to Jacotin and publ. by Petrucci are of doubtful authenticity. His *Sancta Divinitas unus Deus* for 8 voices appeared in Uhlhardt's collection of 1546.

Jacques de Liège (Jacobus Leoniensis), Belgian music theorist; b. Liège, c.1260; d. there, after 1330. He studied in Paris; then was a cleric in Liège. About 1330, already at an advanced age, he wrote the important compendium *Speculum musicae* in 7 parts and 293 folios (586 pages; approximating some 2,000 pages in modern typography); it was formerly attributed to Johannes de Muris, but the authorship of Jacques de Liège is proved by the specific indication in the MS (Paris, Bibliothèque Nationale) that the initial letters of the 7 chapters form the name of the author; these letters are I-A-C-O-B-U-S. W. Grossmann, in *Die einleitenden Kapitel des Speculum Musicae von J. Muris* (Leipzig, 1924), overlooks this indication.

Jadassohn, Salomon, noted German pedagogue; b. Breslau, Aug. 13, 1831; d. Leipzig, Feb. 1, 1902. He studied piano and violin in Breslau; in 1848 took courses at the Leipzig Cons.; in 1849 he was in Weimar, where Liszt accepted him as a student; then he returned to Leipzig, and studied privately with Hauptmann. He remained in Leipzig during his entire life; organized a choral society, Psalterion (1866); conducted the concerts of the Euterpe Society. In 1871 he was appointed instructor at the Leipzig Cons.; in 1887 was made Dr.Phil. (honoris causa); in 1893 he became Royal Professor. A scholar of the highest integrity and of great industry, he codified the traditional views of harmony, counterpoint, and form in his celebrated manuals, which have been trans. into many languages. He was a firm believer in the immutability of harmonic laws, and became the Rock of Gibraltar of conservatism in musical teaching; through his many students, who in turn became influential teachers in Germany and other European countries, the cause of orthodox music theory was propagated far and wide. He was also a composer; wrote 4 symphs.; a Piano Concerto; 3 piano quintets; a Piano Quartet; 4 piano trios; 2 string quartets; a Serenade for Flute and String Orch.; a Cavatina for Cello with Orch.; choral works; many piano pieces and songs. He was a master of contrapuntal forms, and wrote a number of vocal duets in canon; other contrapuntal devices are illustrated in many of his works. His music is totally forgotten; but his importance as a theorist cannot be doubted.

Jadin, Louis Emmanuel, French composer and conductor; b. Versailles, Sept. 21, 1768; d. Paris, April 11, 1853. He was at first a page in the household of Louis XVI; after the Revolution, he was on the staff of the Théâtre de Monsieur; there he produced his comic opera, *Joconde* (Sept. 14, 1790). He then wrote all kinds of festive compositions to be performed on special occasions during the revolutionary years. In 1802 he became prof. of piano at the newly established Paris Cons., succeeding his brother, **Hyacinthe Jadin** (1769–1802). During the Napoleonic wars he continued to write patriotic pieces; his orch. overture, *La Bataille d'Austerlitz,* enjoyed great popularity for a while. He also wrote pieces for piano, and piano duets.

Jaëll, Alfred, noted French pianist; b. Trieste, March 5, 1832; d. Paris, Feb. 27, 1882. He studied with his father, Eduard Jaëll; appeared as a child prodigy in Venice in 1843; continual concert tours earned him the nickname of "le pianiste voyageur." He traveled in America in 1852–54; after this, lived in Paris, Brussels, and Leipzig. In 1866 he married **Marie Trautmann;** made piano transcriptions from works of Wagner, Schumann, and Mendelssohn.

Jaëll-Trautmann, Marie, French pianist, wife of **Alfred Jaëll;** b. Steinseltz, Alsace, Aug. 17, 1846; d. Paris, Feb. 4, 1925. She studied with Henri Herz at the Paris Cons., where she won first prize. After her marriage, she accompanied her husband on his travels. She wrote many characteristic pieces for piano, and publ. pedagogical works: *La Musique et la psycho-physiologie* (1895); *Le Mécanisme du toucher* (1896); *Le Toucher* (1899); *L'Intelligence et le rythme dans les mouvements artistiques* (1905); *Le Rythme du regard et la dissociation des doigts* (1906); *La Coloration des sensations tactiles* (1910); *La Résonance du toucher et la topographie des pulpes* (1912); *La Main et la pensée musicale* (posthumous, 1925).

Jaffee, Michael, American instrumentalist; b. Brooklyn, N.Y., April 21, 1938. He studied music at N.Y. Univ. (B.A., 1959; M.A., 1963); while still a student, he married **Kay Jaffee** (née Cross; b. Lansing, Mich., Dec. 31, 1937) in 1961; with her he founded the Waverly Consort, an early-music group dedicated to authentic performances using period instruments and costumes; it obtained considerable success on the concert circuit. His wife played recorder in the Waverly Consort.

Jagel, Frederick, American tenor; b. Brooklyn, N.Y., June 10, 1897; d. San Francisco, July 5, 1982. His parents were both pianists. He studied singing with William Brady in N.Y.; then went to Milan for further study; made his operatic debut in Livorno in 1924; returning to the U.S., he appeared with the Metropolitan Opera in N.Y. as Radames (Nov. 8, 1927). He subsequently sang at the San Francisco Opera Co. and at the Teatro Colón in Buenos Aires. In 1948 he sang the title role in the first American performance of Britten's opera *Peter Grimes.* On June 12, 1928, he married **Nancy Weir,** an opera singer. From 1949 to 1970 he taught voice at the New England Cons. in Boston.

Jahn, Otto, learned German philologist and musicographer; b. Kiel, June 16, 1813; d. Göttingen, Sept. 9, 1869. He studied languages and antiquities at Kiel, Leipzig, and Berlin; then traveled in France and Italy; in 1839 he settled in Kiel as a lecturer on philology; in 1842 became prof. of archeology at Greifswald; was director of the Archeological Museum in Leipzig (1847); he lost this position in the wake of the political upheaval of 1848. In 1855 he was appointed prof. of archeology at Bonn Univ. He went to Göttingen shortly before his death. In the field of music, his magnum opus was the biography of Mozart (Leipzig, 1856–59, in 4 vols.; 2nd ed., 1867, in 2 vols.; 3rd ed., 1889–91, revised by H. Deiters; 4th ed., also revised by Deiters, 1905–7; exhaustively rewritten and revised by Hermann Abert as *Wolfgang Amadeus Mozart: Neu bearbeitete und erweiterte Ausgabe von Otto Jahns "Mozart,"* 2 vols., Leipzig, 1919–21, rendering it the standard biography; further revision by A.A. Abert, 2 vols., Leipzig, 1955–56). The Eng. trans. (by P. Townsend) appeared in 3 vols. in London (1882). Jahn's biography was the first musical life written according to the comparative critical method; it reviews the state of music during the period immediately preceding Mozart; this comprehensive exposition has become a model for subsequent musical biographies. Jahn intended to write a biography of Beethoven according to a similar plan, but could not complete the task; Thayer utilized the data accumulated by Jahn in his own work on Beethoven; Pohl used Jahn's notes in his biography of Haydn. Numerous essays by Jahn were publ. in his *Gesammelte Aufsätze über Musik* (1866). He composed songs, of which 32 were publ. in 4 books; he also brought out a vol. of songs for mixed voices; edited the vocal score of Beethoven's *Fidelio.*

James, Harry (Haag), greatly popular American jazz trumpeter and bandleader; b. Albany, Ga., March 15, 1916; d. of lymphatic cancer, Las Vegas, July 5, 1983. His father was the director and trumpeter in the Mighty Haag Circus, and his mother was a trapeze artist there; Harry James got his middle name from the circus. He was trained to be a contortionist, but exhibited greater talent in blowing the trumpet. He played in his father's band and in dance bands around Texas, where the family moved. In 1937 he joined Benny Goodman's band; in 1939 organized a group of his own. His trumpet playing had a virtuoso quality; he could blow it *dolce* and even *dolcissimo* but when needed he blew it with deafening *fortissimo.* He also could perform ultra-chromatic glissando. Apart from his brilliance as a trumpeter he also possessed an intuitive entrepreneurial sense; after hearing Frank Sinatra sing on the radio, he hired him as a soloist with his band. The popularity of Harry James reached its peak during the era of big bands; his recording albums, some of them bearing such self-proclamatory titles as *"Wild about Harry,"* sold into the millions, even in wartime, when shellac, from which disks were manufactured, was rationed. In 1943 he married Betty Grable, the pin-up girl of the G.I.s in World War II, famous for the lissome beauty of her nether limbs. She was his second wife, out of the total of four. They were divorced in 1965; she died in 1973. Faithful to the slogan that the show must go on, Harry James, wracked with cancerous pain, continued to perform; he played in Denver on June 10 and 11, 1983; he played his last gig in Los Angeles, on June 26, nine days before his death. He observed, as he was dying, "Let it just be said that I went up to do a one-nighter with Archangel Gabriel."

James, Philip (Frederick Wright), notable American composer and conductor; b. Jersey City, N.J., May 17, 1890; d. Southampton, Long Island, N.Y., Nov. 1, 1975. His older sister gave him the rudiments of music; he served also as a choirboy in New Jersey Episcopalian churches. He later studied composition with Rubin Goldmark and Rosario Scalero, and organ with J. Warren Andrews. He was in the army during World War I; after the Armistice, was appointed bandmaster of the American Expeditionary Force General Headquarters Band;

he also took organ lessons with Joseph Bonnet and Alexandre Guilmant in Paris. Returning to the U.S., he held various posts as organist and choirmaster in several churches in N.Y., and also conducted numerous theatrical and symph. organizations, among them the Victor Herbert Opera Co. (1919–22), New Jersey Symph. Orch. (1922–29), Brooklyn Orch. Society (1927–30), Bamberger Little Symph. (Station WOR; 1929–36). In 1933 he was elected a member of the National Inst. of Arts and Letters; won numerous prizes, among them one for his orch. suite *Station WGZBX*, awarded by the National Broadcasting Co. In 1923 he joined the faculty of N.Y. Univ.; became chairman of the music dept. in 1933; retired in 1955.

WORKS: For the stage: *Judith,* dramatic reading with Ballet and Chamber Orch. (1927; N.Y., Feb. 18, 1933). For orch.: *Overture in Olden Style on French Noëls* (1926; revised 1929; N.Y., Feb. 23, 1930); *Sea Symphony* for Bass-baritone and Orch. (1928; Frankfurt, July 14, 1960); *Song of the Night,* symph. poem (1931; N.Y., March 15, 1938); *Station WGZBX,* satirical suite (NBC Symph. Orch., May 1, 1932); Suite for Strings (N.Y. Univ., April 28, 1934); *Gwalia, a Welsh Rhapsody* (N.Y., Nov. 14, 1935); *Bret Harte Overture No. 3* (N.Y., Dec. 20, 1936); *Brennan on the Moor* for Chamber Orch. (N.Y., Nov. 28, 1939); Sinfonietta (N.Y., Nov. 10, 1941; revised 1943); Symph. No. 1 (1943; revised 1961); 2nd Suite for Strings (1943; Saratoga Springs, Sept. 5, 1946); Symph. No. 2 (1946; Rochester, N.Y., May 7, 1966); *Miniver Cheevy* and *Richard Cory* for Narrator and Orch. (Saratoga, N.Y., Sept. 9, 1947); *Chaumont,* symph. poem for Chamber Orch. (1948; N.Y., May 2, 1951). Chamber music: String Quartet (1924; revised 1939); Suite for Woodwind Quintet (1936); Piano Quartet (1937; revised 1948). Choral works: *The Nightingale of Bethlehem,* cantata (1920; revised 1923); *Shirat Ha-Yam,* cantata (1920; revised 1933–58); *Song of the Future* for Mixed Chorus a cappella (1922); *Missa Imaginum* for Mixed Chorus and Orch. (1929); *General William Booth Enters into Heaven* for Tenor, Male Voices, and Chamber Orch. (1932); *World of Tomorrow* for Mixed Chorus and Orch. (1938); *Psalm 150* for Mixed Chorus and Orch. (1940; revised 1956); *Chorus of Shepherds and Angels,* cantata (1956); *To Cecilia,* cantata for Chorus and Chamber Orch. (1966); choruses; hymns; songs. For band: *Perstare et Perstare,* festal march (N.Y., June 10, 1942; arranged for Orch. 1946); *E.F.G. Overture* (1944; N.Y., June 13, 1945); *Fanfare and Ceremonial* (1955; N.Y., June 20, 1956; revised 1962). For organ: *Méditation à Sainte Clotilde* (1915); *Dithyramb* (1921); *Fête* (1921); Sonata No. 1 (1929); *Pantomime* (1941); *Galarnad* (1946); *Novelette* (1946); *Solemn Prelude* (1948); *Alleluia-Toccata* (1949); *Pastorale* (1949); *Requiescat in pace* (1949; revised 1955); *Passacaglia on an Old Cambrian Bass* (1951; arranged for Orch., 1956; for Band, 1957); *Sortie* (1973); piano pieces.

Janáček, Leoš, greatly renowned Czech composer; b. Hukvaldy, Moravia, July 3, 1854; d. Ostrava, Aug. 12, 1928. At the age of 10 he was placed at the Augus-

tine monastery in Brno as a chorister; then studied at the Brno Teachers' Training College (1872–74) and at the Organ School (College of Music) in Prague, where he studied organ with Skuherský (1874–75); later took lessons in composition with L. Grill at the Leipzig Cons. and with Franz Krenn at the Vienna Cons. (1879–80). Returning to Brno, he was active as a teacher; from 1881 to 1888 he conducted the Czech Phil. there; from 1919 to 1925 he taught at the Cons. of Brno; many Czech composers of the younger generation were his students. Although he began to compose early in life, it was not until 1916, with the production of his opera *Její pastorkyňa* (commonly known under its German title, *Jenufa*), that his importance as a national composer was realized in the music world; the work was widely performed in Austria, Germany, and Russia, and was eventually produced in America. In the field of religious music, he created a unique score, *Glagolitic Mass* (also known as *Slavonic Mass* or *Festival Mass*), to a text in old Slavonic, with an instrumental accompaniment. Janáček took great interest in Russian literature and music; he visited Russia 3 times; his operas *Kát'a Kabanová* and *From the House of the Dead* and several other works are based on Russian literary works. There is an affinity between Janáček's method of dramatic prosody and Mussorgsky's ideas of realistic musical speech, but Janáček never consciously imitated the Russian models. He was a firm believer in the artistic importance of folk songs, and collected a number of them in his native Moravia; contributed a paper on the musical structure of national songs to the Prague Academy (1901). During the last 2 decades of his life, Janáček was strongly influenced by the French school; the idiom of his instrumental works of that period clearly reflects impressionist usages.

WORKS: For the stage: 9 operas: *Šárka* (1887, revised in 1918; instrumentation of the 3rd act and final revision of the first and 2nd acts accomplished by Janáček's student Oswald Chlubna in 1918–19 and 1924; Brno, Nov. 11, 1925); *Počátek románu* (*Beginning of a Romance,* 1891; Brno, Feb. 10, 1894); *Její pastorkyňa* (*Her Foster Daughter;* German title, *Jenufa;* 1894–1903; Brno, Jan. 21, 1904; revised 1906, 1911, and 1916; final version first perf., Prague, May 26, 1916); *Osud* (*Fate,* 1903–4; Brno Radio, Sept. 18, 1934; first stage perf., Brno, Oct. 25, 1958); the satiric opera *Výlety páně Broučkovy* (*The Excursions of Mr. Broucek*), made up of 2 separately performable scenes, *Výlet pana Broučka do Měsíce* (*Mr. Broucek's Flight to the Moon,* 1908–17) and *Výlet pana Broučka do XV století* (*Mr. Broucek's Trip to the 15th Century,* 1917; both in Prague, April 23, 1920); *Kát'a Kabanová* (after Ostrovsky's play *The Storm,* 1919–21; Brno, Nov. 23, 1921); *Příhody lišky Bystroušky* (*The Cunning Little Vixen,* 1921–23; Brno, Nov. 6, 1924); *Věc Makropulos,* after Čapek (*The Makropulos Affair,* 1923–25; Brno, Dec. 18, 1926); *Z mrtvého domu,* after Dostoyevsky (*From the House of the Dead,* 1927–28; produced posthumously, Brno, April 12, 1930); and a ballet, *Rákocz Rákoczy* (1891; Prague, July 24, 1891). Choral works: 6 cantatas: *Hospodine pomiluj ny*

(*Lord, Have Mercy Upon Us*) for Solo Quartet and Double Chorus, with Organ, Harp, 3 Trumpets, 3 Trombones, and 2 Tubas (1896); *Amarus* for Solo Trio, Chorus, Harp, and Orch. (1897; revised 1901 and 1906); *Otčenáš (The Lord's Prayer)* for Tenor, Chorus, Harp, and Organ (1901; revised 1906); *Elegie* for Tenor, Mixed Chorus, and Piano (1903–4; Brno, Dec. 20, 1930; written on the death of Janáček's daughter); *Mass in E-flat major*, unfinished, for Mixed Choir and Organ (1908; Brno, March 7, 1943); *Na Soláni Čarták (At the Inn of Solan)* for Male Chorus and Orch. (1911); *Věčné evangelium (The Eternal Gospel)*, cantata-legend for Soprano, Tenor, Chorus, and Orch. (1914) and *Glagolská mše (Glagolitic Mass* or *Slavonic Mass* or *Festival Mass)* for Soli, Chorus, and Orch. (1926; Brno, Dec. 5, 1927); a cappella choruses. CHAMBER VOCAL WORKS: *Zápisník zmizelého (The Diary of One Who Vanished)* for Tenor, Alto, 3 Female Voices, and Piano (1917–19, revised 1924) and *Říkadla (Nursery Rhyme)* for 9 Singers and Chamber Ensemble (1925–27); numerous folk-song arrangements. FOR ORCH.: Suite for String Orch. (Brno, Dec. 2, 1877); *Idyll* for String Orch. (Brno, Dec. 15, 1878); *Moravian Dances* (1888–91); *6 Lašske tance (6 Lachian Dances*, 1889–90; as a ballet, Brno, Feb. 19, 1925); *Suite* (1891); *Žárlivost (Jealousy)*, symph. poem (1894); *Šumařovo dítě (The Fiddler's Child)*, ballad (1912; Prague, Nov. 14, 1917), *Taras Bulba*, rhapsody after Gogol (1915–18; Brno, Oct. 9, 1921); *Balada blanická (The Ballad of Blanik)*, symph. poem (1920; Brno, March 21, 1920); Sinfonietta (1926; Prague, June 29, 1926; his most popular instrumental work); *Dunaj (The Danube)*, symph. poem (1923–28; completed by Chlubna, 1948); Violin Concerto (1927–28; only a fragment was completed). CHAMBER MUSIC: 2 string quartets: No. 1 (inspired by Tolstoy's *Kreutzer Sonata*, 1923) and No. 2, *Intimate Letters* (1928); *Dumka* for Violin and Piano (1880); *Pohádka (Fairytale)* for Cello and Piano (1910); Violin Sonata (1913); *Mládí (Youth)* for Wind Sextet (1924); Concertino for Piano and Ensemble of Clarinet, Bassoon, Horn, 2 Violins, and Viola (1925; Brno, Feb. 16, 1926); *Capriccio* for Piano, left-hand, and Flute, Piccolo, 2 Trumpets, 3 Trombones, and Tuba (1926; Prague, March 2, 1928). FOR PIANO: *Tema con variazioni* (known as the *Zdeňka Variations*, 1880); *3 Moravian Dances* (1892, 1904); *Po zarostlém chodníčku (On an Overgrown Path)*, cycle in 2 series (1901–8); sonata, *1. X. 1905* (also known as *From the Street*, 1905); *V mlhách (In the Mist)*, 4 pieces (1912); *Memory* (1928). A complete list of works with exact dates of composition and performance is found in Gr. Černušák and Vlad. Helfert, *Pazdírkuv Hudebni Slovník Naučny*, vol. 2 (Prague, 1937), and in Kenneth Thompson, *Dictionary of Twentieth-Century Composers 1911–1971* (N.Y., 1973). A complete critical edition of his works began publication in 1979 in Prague and Kassel.

Janeček, Karel, Czech composer and theorist; b. Czestochowa, Poland, Feb. 20, 1903; d. Prague, Jan. 4, 1974. He spent his boyhood in Kiev. After completing his secondary education at an industrial school, he went to Prague, where he took courses in composition with Křička and Novák (1924–27). From 1929 to 1941 he taught at the Pilsen Music School; then was prof. of composition at the Prague Cons. (1941–46) and later at the Prague Academy. In his early works Janeček adopted a traditional national style; later he occasionally employed a personalized dodecaphonic scheme.

WORKS: *Overture* (1926–27); 2 symphs. (1935–40, 1954–55); *Lenin,* symph. triptych (1953); *Legend of Prague,* overture for String Orch. (1956); Fantasy for Orch. (1962–63); Sinfonietta (1967); *Large Symposium* for 15 Soloists (1967); 3 string quartets (1924, 1927, 1934); Divertimento for 8 Instruments (1925–26); String Trio (1930); Trio for Flute, Clarinet, and Bassoon (1931); Duo for Violin and Viola (1938); Violin Sonata (1939); Divertimento for Oboe, Clarinet, and Bassoon (1949); Cello Sonata (1958); *Little Symposium,* chamber suite for Flute, Clarinet, Bassoon, and Piano (1959); Duo for Violin and Cello (1960); *Chamber Overture* for Nonet (1960); Quartet for Flute, Oboe, Clarinet, and Bassoon (1966); *Trifles and Abbreviations* for Piano (1926); *Tema con variazioni* for Piano, inspired by the tragedy of the village of Lidice, destroyed by the Nazis (1942); several choral works, including *To the Fallen* (1950–51), *To the Living* (1951), and *My Dream* (1972); songs.

Janequin, Clément, creator and chief representative of the new 16th-century French polyphonic chanson; b. Châtellerault, c. 1485; d. Paris, 1558. He was a pupil of Josquin. In his youth he may have been in the service of Louis Ronsard, father of the poet Pierre Ronsard, and may have accompanied his master during the Italian campaigns, from 1507 to the battle of Marignano, 1515. About 1520 he was in Paris, and later perhaps in Spain. There is evidence that in 1529 he was in Bordeaux, was subsequently in the service of the Cardinal of Lorraine (d. 1550), then was chaplain of the Duke de Guise, whose victories he celebrated by extended chansons. From 1545 to 1558 he was curate at Unverre. In a 1559 dedication in verse, he bemoans his old age and poverty.

WORKS: Besides many detached pieces in collections of the time (Attaignant's, Gardane's, etc.), and chansons in special editions, there were publ. 2 masses (1532, 1554), *Sacræ cantiones seu motectæ 4 voc.* (1533), *Proverbs de Salomon mis en cantiques et ryme françoise* (1554); *Octante deux psaumes de David* (1559); etc. Among the most interesting "Inventions" (chansons) in 4–5 parts are *La Bataille* (portraying the battle of Marignano; Verdelot added a 5th part to the original 4), *La Prise de Boulogne, Le Chant des oiseaux,* etc. Some of Janequin's works are ambitious examples of program music. Reprints have been made by Henri Expert in his *Maîtres Musiciens de la Renaissance Française* (chansons; vol. 7) and by Maurice Cauchie in *Les Concerts de la Renaissance,* Part 2 (a collection of 30 3- and 4-voiced chansons by Janequin; 1928). Cauchie also edited 2 5-voiced chansons (*Le Caquet des femmes* and *La Jalouzie*). His complete chansons are publ. in 6 vols. as *Chansons polyphoniques,* ed. by T. Merritt and F. Lesure (Monaco, 1965–71).

Janis (real name, **Yanks,** abbreviated from **Yankelevitch**), **Byron,** noted American pianist; b. McKeesport, Pa., March 24, 1928. He began to study piano with a local teacher; at the age of 8 he was taken to N.Y., where he became a pupil of Adele Marcus. Progressing rapidly, he made his important debut in 1943, playing Rachmaninoff's 2nd Piano Concerto with the NBC Symph. Orch.; he played it again with the Pittsburgh Symph. Orch. on Feb. 20, 1944, with the 13-year-old Lorin Maazel on the podium; Vladimir Horowitz happened to be present at the concert and told Janis that he would be willing to take him as a private pupil; these private lessons with Horowitz continued for several years, leaving an indelible mark on Janis's pianism. In 1948 he toured South America, obtaining a particularly resounding success in Buenos Aires. On Oct. 29, 1948, he played in Carnegie Hall, N.Y., with exceptionally favorable reviews in the press. In 1952 he made a tour of Europe. In 1960 he made his first tour of Russia, under the auspices of the U.S. State Dept.; he played in Moscow, Leningrad, Odessa, Minsk, and Kiev; the Soviet critics praised him for his poetic performances of Romantic music; he played again in Russia in 1962. In 1961, on the occasion of the sesquicentennial of the birth of Liszt, he played both of Liszt's piano concertos with the Boston Symph. Orch. During a visit to France in 1967, Janis discovered the autograph MSS of 2 waltzes by Chopin, the G-flat major, op. 70, no. 1, and the E-flat major, op. 18; in 1973 he located 2 variants of these waltzes in the library of Yale Univ. In 1975 he made the film *Frédéric Chopin: A Voyage with Byron Janis,* which was produced by the Public Broadcasting Service. In 1953 he was married, in London, to June Dickinson Wright; they were divorced in 1965, and in 1966 he married Maria Veronica Cooper, the daughter of the movie star Gary Cooper. At the climax of his highly successful career, Byron Janis was stricken with the dreaded amyotrophic lateral sclerosis, which affects the motor neuron cells, gradually depriving the victim of command of his bodily movements.

Janitsch, Johann Gottlieb, Silesian composer and bass viol player; b. Schweidnitz, June 19, 1708; d. Berlin, c.1763. He studied music in Breslau and law at the Univ. of Frankfurt an der Oder (1729–33). In 1733 he became secretary to Franz Wilhelm von Happe, a minister of state. In 1736 Crown Prince Friedrich (later Frederick the Great) made him a member of his personal orch. in Ruppin; he followed Friedrich to Rheinsberg, where he organized a series of famous concerts known as the "Friday Academies." In 1740 he was named "contraviolinist" in Frederick the Great's orch. in Berlin, and continued his "Friday Academies" there. His *Sonata da camera* for Flute, Oboe, Violin, Viola, Cello, and Harpsichord, entitled *Echo,* composed in 1757, is reprinted in *Collegium musicum,* LXVIII (Leipzig, 1938); another work in this genre was publ. in

1970. A collection of his compositions has been assembled from the available MSS by Josef Marx of the McGinnis & Marx firm of music publishers in N.Y.

Janowka, Thomas Balthasar (Janovka, Tomáš Baltazar), Bohemian organist; b. Kuttenberg (baptized, Jan. 6), 1669; d. (buried, June 13) 1741. He received a Jesuit education at the St. Wenceslas seminary in Prague; earned his M.Phil. from Charles Univ. there in 1689. In 1691 he was appointed organist at Tyne Church in Prague, remaining at his post for half a century until his death. He compiled the *Clavis ad thesaurum magnae artis musicae* (Prague, 1701), which was the 2nd (after Tinctoris) music dictionary ever publ. Only a few copies of the original edition are extant, but the book was reprinted in 1973.

Janson, Arvid. See **Yansons, Arvid.**

Jansons, Mariss, conductor; b. Riga, Latvia, Jan. 14, 1943. He was a son of the noted conductor **Arvid Yansons.** He studied at the Leningrad Cons., where he took courses in violin, viola, piano, and conducting. He profited from initial conducting studies with his father; then studied with Swarowsky in Vienna, Karajan in Salzburg, and Mravinsky in Leningrad. In 1971 he won 2nd prize in the Karajan Competition in West Berlin; then made appearances with major orchs. and opera houses in the Soviet Union and Eastern Europe; also conducted in Western Europe and America. In 1979 he was named chief conductor of the Oslo Phil. Orch.

Janssen, Werner, American composer and conductor; b. New York, June 1, 1899. He studied music theory with Frederick Converse in Boston and conducting with Felix Weingartner in Basel and Hermann Scherchen in Strasbourg (1921–25); won the Prix de Rome of the American Academy (1930) and made his debut as a conductor in Rome; he gave a concert of music by Sibelius in Helsinki in 1934 and was praised by Sibelius himself; received the Finnish Order of the White Rose. He made his American debut with the N.Y. Phil. on Nov. 8, 1934; served as regular conductor of the Baltimore Symph. (1937–39); then went to Hollywood, where he organized the Janssen Symph. (1940–52) and commissioned American composers to write special works. He was subsequently conductor of the Utah Symph. Orch., Salt Lake City (1946–47), of the Portland (Oreg.) Orch. (1947–49), and of the San Diego Symph. (1952–54). In 1937 he married the famous motion picture actress Ann Harding; they were divorced in 1963. As a composer, Janssen cultivates the art of literal pictorialism; his most successful work of this nature was *New Year's Eve in New York* (Rochester, May 9, 1929), a symph. poem for Large Orch. and Jazz Instruments; the orch. players were instructed to shout at the end "Happy New Year!" Other works are: *Obsequies of a Saxophone* for 6 Wind Instruments and a Snare Drum (Washington, D.C., Oct. 17, 1929); *Louisiana Suite* for Orch. (1930); *Dixie Fugue* (extracted from the *Louisiana Suite;* Rome, Nov. 27, 1932); *Foster Suite* for Orch., on Stephen Foster's tunes (1937); 2 string quartets.

Janssens, Jean-François-Joseph, Belgian composer; b. Antwerp, Jan. 29, 1801; d. there, Feb. 3, 1835. He studied with his father and later with Lesueur in Paris. Returning to Antwerp, he became a lawyer; was a notary public until the siege of Antwerp (1832); composed in his leisure hours. Going to Cologne, he lost his MSS and other possessions in a fire on the night of his arrival; this misfortune so affected him that he became insane. He wrote 4 operas, 2 cantatas, 2 symphs., 5 masses; a number of motets, anthems, and hymns; also songs.

Jaques-Dalcroze, Emile, composer and creator of "Eurhythmics"; b. (of French parents) Vienna, July 6, 1865; d. Geneva, July 1, 1950. In 1873 his parents moved to Geneva; having completed his course at the Univ. and also at the Cons. there, he went to Vienna for further study under R. Fuchs and A. Bruckner, and then to Paris, where he studied orchestration at the Cons. with Delibes; in 1892 he returned to Geneva as instructor of theory at the Cons. Since he laid special stress on rhythm, he insisted that all his pupils beat time with their hands, and this led him, step by step, to devise a series of movements affecting the entire body. Together with the French psychologist Edouard Claparide, he worked out a special terminology and reduced his practice to a regular system, which he called "Eurhythmics." When his application to have his method introduced as a regular course at the Cons. was refused, he resigned, and in 1910 established his own school at Hellerau, near Dresden. Even before that time the new system had attracted wide attention, and the school flourished from the beginning; within 3 years branches were opened in France, Russia, Germany, England, and the U.S. (Bryn Mawr College, N.Y., and Chicago). Conditions resulting from the war brought about the closing of the school at Hellerau in 1915. After that he founded another school at Geneva, the headquarters of which was later moved to Paris. In 1925 the Hellerau School was established in Laxenburg, near Vienna. Jaques-Dalcroze himself also taught in London; in his later years he lived in Geneva. Without question, the results obtained by Jaques-Dalcroze have contributed toward the recent development of the ballet. Aside from his rhythmical innovations, he also commanded respect as a composer of marked originality and fecundity of invention; many of his works show how thoroughly he was imbued with the spirit of Swiss folk music.

WORKS: Operas: *Le Violon maudit* (Geneva, 1893); *Janie* (Geneva, March 13, 1894); *Sancho Panza* (Geneva, 1897); *Onkel Dazumal* (Cologne, 1905; as *Le Bonhomme Jadis,* Paris, 1906); *Les Jumeaux de Bergame* (Brussels, 1908); *Fête de la jeunesse et de la joie* (Geneva, 1932); operetta, *Respect pour nous* (Geneva, 1898); pantomime, *Echo et Narcisse* (Hellerau, 1912); *Festival vaudois* for Soli, Chorus, and Orch.; *La Veillée* for Soli, Chorus, and Orch.;

Dance Suite in A for Orch.; *Suite de ballet;* 2 violin concertos; String Quartet; Suite for Cello and Piano; *Fantasia appassionata* for Violin and Piano; *Images* (1928); *Dialogues* (1931); *Ariettes* (1931); *Rondeaux* for Piano (1933); several collections of songs (*Chansons romandes et enfantines, Chansons populaires et enfantines, Idylles et chansons, Volkskinderlieder, Tanzlieder für Kinder, Chansons religieuses, Chansons de la gosse,* etc.). He publ. *Le Cœur chante; Impressions d'un musicien* (Geneva, 1900); *L'Education par le rhythme,* a series of lectures (1907); a comprehensive *Méthode Jaques-Dalcroze* (5 parts, 1907–14); *Rhythm, Music and Education* (Basel, 1922; in German, French, and Eng.); *Souvenirs* (Neuchâtel and Paris, 1942); *La Musique et nous* (Geneva, 1945); also "The Child and the Pianoforte," *Musical Quarterly* (April 1928); "Eurhythmics and Its Implications," in the *Musical Quarterly* (July 1930); "L'Improvisation au piano," *Rhythm* (1932).

Jarnach, Philipp, composer; b. Noisy, France, July 26, 1892; d. Bornsen, near Bergedorf, Dec. 17, 1982. He was a son of the Catalonian sculptor E. Jarnach and a German mother. He studied at the Paris Cons. with Risler (piano) and Lavignac (theory). At the outbreak of World War I he went to Zürich, where he met Busoni; this meeting was a decisive influence on his musical development; he became an ardent disciple of Busoni; after Busoni's death, he completed Busoni's last opera, *Doktor Faust,* which was produced in Jarnach's version in Dresden on May 21, 1925. During the years 1922–27 Jarnach wrote music criticism in Berlin. In 1927 he was appointed prof. of composition at the Cologne Cons., and remained at that post until 1949; from 1949 to 1970 he taught at the Hamburg Cons. Jarnach's own music is determined by his devotion to Busoni's ideals; it is distinguished by impeccable craftsmanship, but it lacks individuality. He participated in the modern movement in Germany between the two world wars, and many of his works were performed at music festivals during that period. Among his works are a *Sinfonie brevis* (1923); String Quintet (1920); String Quartet (1924); *Musik zum Gedächtnis des Einsamen* for String Quartet (1952); Sonatina for Flute and Piano; Cello Sonatina; etc.

Järnefelt, Armas, Finnish conductor and composer; b. Vyborg, Aug. 14, 1869; d. Stockholm, June 23, 1958. He studied with Wegelius at the Helsinki Cons. and also with Busoni, who taught there at the time; he then went to Berlin (1890) and to Paris (1892), where he studied with Massenet. He began his career as an opera coach in Magdeburg (1896); then was at Düsseldorf (1897). Returning to Finland in 1898, he was a conductor in his native town; in 1903 he received a government stipend for travel; was for 25 years conductor of the Stockholm Opera (1907–32); was conductor of the Helsinki Opera (1932–36), and of the Helsinki Municipal Orch. (1942–43). He was married to the Finnish singer **Maikki Pakarinen** (1893; divorced in 1908), then to another singer, **Liva Edström.** He wrote several works for orch., in a national Finnish style: *Korsholm, Suomen synty, Laulu Vuokselle, Åbo slott,* etc.; his *Berceuse* and *Praeludium* for Small Orch. became extremely popular.

Järnefelt, Maikki (née **Pakarinen**), Finnish soprano, wife of **Armas Järnefelt;** b. Joensuu, Aug. 26, 1871; d. Turku, July 4, 1929. She studied with Mme. Marchesi in Paris; became a well-known opera singer in Europe; also lived in America for several years. She was married to Järnefelt in 1893 and divorced in 1908; then was married to **Selim Palmgren** (1910).

Jarnowick, Giovanni. See **Giornovichi, Giovanni Mare.**

Jarnowick, Pierre Louis Hus-Desforges. See **Hus-Desforges, Pierre Louis.**

Jarre, Maurice, French composer for films; b. Lyons, Sept. 13, 1924. He studied electrical engineering at Lyons; in 1944 went to Paris and began to study music. He became a successful film composer; won the Academy Award for his emotional score to *Dr. Zhivago* (1966).
WORKS: *Mouvements en relief* for Orch.; *Polyphonies concertantes* for Piano, Trumpet, Percussion, and Orch.; *Passacaille,* in memory of Honegger (Strasbourg Festival, June 15, 1956); *Mobiles* for Violin and Orch. (Strasbourg Festival, June 20, 1961).

Jarrett, Keith, American jazz pianist; b. Allentown, Pa., May 8, 1945. He studied in Boston; then began his career in 1965 with Art Blakey; from 1966 he played with Charles Lloyd's group, and subsequently toured with it. At the height of his career as a jazz virtuoso he bagan giving piano recitals of classical modern music, specializing in performances of Béla Bartók. He also composed several works in a somewhat improvisatory manner.

Järvi, Neeme, conductor; b. Tallinn, Estonia, June 7, 1937. He studied at the Tallinn Music School, graduating with degrees in percussion and choral conducting; then studied conducting at the Leningrad Cons. with Mravinsky. In 1963 he became conductor of the Estonian Radio and Television Orch. and chief conductor of the Estonian Opera Theater. In 1971 he won first prize at the international conducting competition sponsored by the Santa Cecilia Academy in Rome, which resulted in his appointment as chief conductor of the Estonian State Symph. Orch. He made guest appearances throughout the Soviet Union, Europe, and Japan. In 1980 he emigrated to the U.S.; subsequently was a guest conductor with the N.Y. Phil., Boston Symph., Philadelphia Orch., San Francisco Symph., National Symph., and Indianapolis Symph. In 1984 he became music director and principal conductor of the Scottish National Orch. in Glasgow.

Jaubert, Maurice, French composer; b. Nice, Jan. 3, 1900; killed in action in France, June 19, 1940. He studied law and took lessons in piano and composition at the Cons. of Nice. He abandoned the legal profession in 1923, when he went to Paris. He obtained considerable success with the score for the French film *Carnet de bal* (1938). His works include: *Suite française* for Orch. (St. Louis, Nov. 10, 1933); *Sonata a due* for Violin, Cello, and String Orch. (Boston, Dec. 27, 1946); *Jeanne d'Arc,* symph. poem (1937); etc.

Jeffries (Jeffreys), George, English composer; b. c.1610; d. Weldon, July 1, 1685. He served as organist to King Charles I at the Chapel Royal; from 1646 was steward to Sir Christopher (later Lord) Hatton at Kirkby, Northamptonshire. Among his works (preserved in the British Library) are some 190 motets and anthems and several church services (in Latin); also madrigals, masques, and stage pieces.

Jehin, François, celebrated Belgian violinist; b. Spa, Belgium, April 18, 1839; d. Montreal, Canada, May 29, 1899. As a child he studied with Servais and with his uncle, **François Prume,** whose name he added to his own, often performing as **Jehin-Prume;** then took lessons with Bériot at the Brussels Cons.; studied harmony with Fétis; won first prize in violin and in theory; at the age of 16, after completing advanced studies with Vieuxtemps and Wieniawski, he undertook a European tour; appeared with Anton and Nicholas Rubinstein, Jenny Lind, and other celebrities; formed a famous trio with Kontski and Monsigny. In 1863 he traveled through Mexico, Cuba, and N.Y. to Montreal; met and married the singer **Rosita del Vecchio.** Thenceforth, his time was divided between Europe and America; he eventually settled in Montreal. Among his pupils was Eugène Ysaÿe. He wrote 2 violin concertos and many brilliant solo pieces for his instrument. He publ. in Montreal a book of memoirs, *Une Vie d'artiste* (contains a list of his works from op. 1 to op. 88).

Jelich, Vincenz, Austrian composer; b. Fiume, 1596; d. Zabern, Alsace, c.1636. His original name was **Jeličić,** indicating Croatian extraction. From 1606–9 he served as a choirboy in Graz; there he studied music with Matthia Ferrabosco; then was at the Jesuit Univ. (1610–15). In 1618 he went to Zabern in Alsace as a court musician. He publ. *Parnassia militia* (1622), 2 books of sacred songs under the title *Arion* (1628), and a number of motets.

Jelinek, Hanns, Austrian composer; b. Vienna, Dec. 5, 1901; d. there, Jan. 27, 1969. He considered himself self-taught in composition, though he studied briefly with F. Schmidt and Berg in Vienna (1918–19) and had studies with Schoenberg and adopted the 12-tone method. In 1958 Jelinek was appointed a lecturer at the Academy of Music in Vienna, becoming a full prof. in 1965.
WORKS: Operetta, *Bubi Caligula* (1947; from this, the orch. pieces *Ballettmusik* and *Suite*). FOR

ORCH.: 6 symphs.: No. 1 in D (1926–30; Breslau, June 13, 1932; revised in 1940 and in 1945–46); No. 2, *Sinfonia ritmica,* for Jazz Band and Orch. (1929; Vienna, March 14, 1931; revised in 1949); No. 3, *Heitere Symphonie,* for Brass and Percussion (1930–31; Vienna Festival of the International Society for Contemporary Music, June 20, 1932); No. 4, *Sinfonia concertante,* for String Quartet and Orch. (1931; revised 1953; Vienna, May 2, 1958); No. 5, *Symphonie brevis* (1948–50; Vienna, Dec. 19, 1950); No. 6, *Sinfonia concertante* (1953; Venice, Sept. 15, 1953; revised 1957); *Praeludium, Passacaglia und Fuge* for Flute, Clarinet, Bassoon, Horn, and Strings (1922; Wuppertal, March 12, 1954); *Sonata ritmica* for Jazz Band and Orch. (1928; revised 1960; Vienna, Nov. 26, 1960); *Rather Fast,* rondo for Jazz Band and Orch. (1929); Suite for String Orch. (1931); Concertino for String Quartet and String Orch. (1951); *Phantasie* for Clarinet, Piano, and Orch. (1951; Salzburg Festival of the ISCM, June 21, 1952); *Preludio solenne* for Orch. (1956); *Perergon* for Small Orch. (1957); *Rai buba,* étude for Piano and Orch. (1956–61). FOR VOICE: *Prometheus,* after Goethe, for Baritone and Orch. (1936); *Die Heimkehr,* radio cantata for Soloists, Chorus, Orch., and Tape (1954); *Unterwegs,* chamber cantata for Soprano, Vibraphone, and Double Bass (1957); *Begegnung,* dance scene for Chorus and Orch. (1965); songs. CHAMBER MUSIC: *6 Aphorismen* for 2 Clarinets and Bassoon (1923–30); Suite for Solo Cello (1930); 2 string quartets (1931, 1935); *Das Zwölftonwerk,* a collection of 9 individually titled chamber pieces in 2 series: Series one of 6 works for Piano (1947–49) and Series 2 of 3 works for Various Instruments (1950–52); *3 Blue Sketches* for 9 Jazz Soloists (1956); Sonata for Solo Violin (1956); *Ollapotrida,* suite for Flute and Guitar (1957); *2 Blue O's* for 7 Jazz Performers (1959); *10 Zahme Xenien* for Violin and Piano (1960). FOR PIANO: Sonatina (1923–30); *4 Structuren* (1952); *Zwölftonfibel* (1953–54).
WRITINGS: The manual *Anleitung zur Zwölftonkomposition* (2 vols., Vienna, 1952; 2nd ed., 1967).

Jemnitz, Sándor (Alexander), Hungarian composer; b. Budapest, Aug. 9, 1890; d. Balatonföldvár, Aug. 8, 1963. He studied with Koessler at the Budapest Academy (1912–16); then briefly with Max Reger in Leipzig. From 1917 to 1921 he occupied various posts as assistant conductor at German opera theaters; from 1921 to 1924, attended Schoenberg's classes at the Prussian Academy of Music in Berlin. In 1924 he returned to Budapest; was engaged as a music critic. As a composer, he followed the median line of Middle European modernism of the period between the 2 world wars, representing a curious compromise between the intricate contrapuntal idiom of Max Reger and the radical language of atonality modeled after Schoenberg's early works. He wrote mostly instrumental music.
WORKS: Concerto for Chamber Orch. (1931); *Prelude and Fugue* for Orch. (1933); *7 Miniatures* for Orch. (1948); *Overture for a Peace Festival* (1951); Concerto for String Orch. (1954); Fantasy for Orch.

(1956); 3 violin sonatas (1921, 1923, 1925); Cello Sonata (1922); 3 solo violin sonatas (1922, 1932, 1938); Flute Trio (1924); 2 wind trios (1925); Trumpet Quartet (1925); 2 string trios (1925, 1929); Flute Sonata (1931); Partita for 2 Violins (1932); Guitar Trio (1932); Solo Cello Sonata (1933); Solo Harp Sonata (1933); *Duet Sonata* for Saxophone and Banjo (1934); Solo Double-bass Sonata (1935); Solo Trumpet Sonata (1938); Solo Flute Sonata (1941); Solo Viola Sonata (1941); String Quartet (1950); 2 suites for Violin and Piano (1952, 1953); Trio for Flute, Oboe, and Clarinet (1958); *3 Pieces* for Piano (1915); 2 piano sonatinas (1919); *17 Bagatelles* for Piano (1919); 5 piano sonatas (1914, 1927, 1929, 1933, 1954); *Recueil* for Piano (1938–45); Sonata for Pedal Organ (1941); *8 Pieces for Piano* (1951); 2 organ sonatas (1959); songs. His ballet, *Divertimento,* written in 1921, was not produced until 26 years later (Budapest, April 23, 1947). He also publ. brief monographs on Mozart, Beethoven, Mendelssohn, Schumann, and Chopin.

Jenkins, John, English composer; b. Maidstone, 1592; d. Kimberley, Norfolk, Oct. 26, 1678. His father was a carpenter by trade but was apparently musical, for upon his death, in 1617, an inventory of his possessions included "Seven Vialls and Violyns, One Bandora and a Cytherne." In John's early years he was a domestic tutor and lute player to various aristocrats; also played at the courts of Charles I and Charles II. He wrote many *Fancies* for viols or organ, and light pieces which he called *Rants;* of these, *Mitter Rant* was included in Playford's *Musick's Handmaid* (1678); *The Fleece Tavern Rant* and *The Peterborough Rant,* both in Playford's *Apollo's Banquet* (1690); his popular air *The Lady Katherine Audley's Bells* or *The Five Bell Consort* appeared in Playford's *Courtly Masquing Ayres* (1662). He wrote some music for violin; an edition entitled *12 Sonatas for 2 Violins and a Base, with a Thorough Base for the Organ or Theorbo* attributed to Jenkins, and supposedly publ. in London in 1660, is not extant; the claim made by some historians that Jenkins was the first English composer of violin sonatas cannot be sustained inasmuch as William Young had anticipated him by publishing 11 violin sonatas in 1653. Reprints: *John Jenkins, Fancies and Ayres,* ed. by Helen Joy Sleeper (Wellesley, 1950); *J. J. 3 Part Fancy and Ayre Divisions* (Wellesley Ed. 10, 1966); *J. J. Consort Music of 4 Parts,* ed. by Andrew Ashbee (*Musica Britannica,* 26, 1969).

Jensen, Adolf, German composer; b. Königsberg, Jan. 12, 1837; d. Baden-Baden, Jan. 23, 1879. He stemmed from a family of musicians in Königsberg; studied with Ehlert and Köhler; began to compose as a boy; at 19, went to Russia as a music tutor; then was theater conductor in Posen (1857); was in Copenhagen (1858–60), where he studied with Gade; then returned to Königsberg. He subsequently taught at Tausig's school in Berlin (1866–68); then lived in Dresden, Graz, and finally at Baden-Baden, where he died of consumption. A great admirer of

Schumann, he closely imitated him in his songs, of which about 160 were publ. He also wrote an opera, *Die Erbin von Montfort* (1864–65); it was revised by Kienzl, to a new libretto by Jensen's daughter, under the title *Turandot.* Other works are the cantatas *Jephthas Tochter, Der Gang der Jünger nach Emmäus, Adonisfeier,* etc., and many characteristic piano pieces.

Jensen, Gustav, German violinist and composer, brother of **Adolf Jensen;** b. Königsberg, Dec. 25, 1843; d. Cologne, Nov. 26, 1895. He studied with his brother; then with Dehn in Berlin (theory) and with Joachim (violin). In 1872 he became prof. of composition at the Cologne Cons., and held that position until his death. He wrote a Symph.; String Quartet; Violin Sonata; Cello Sonata; *Ländliche Serenade* for String Orch.; various violin pieces; publ. the series Klassische Violinmusik; trans. into German Cherubini's *Manual of Counterpoint.*

Jeppesen, Knud, eminent Danish musicologist and composer; b. Copenhagen, Aug. 15, 1892; d. Aarhus, Denmark, June 14, 1974. He studied at the Univ. of Copenhagen with Laub and Nielsen, and at the Univ. of Vienna with G. Adler and R. Lach (Dr.Phil., 1922, with the dissertation *Die Dissonanzbehandlung in den Werken Palestrinas;* Eng. trans. by Margaret W. Hamerik, as *The Style of Palestrina and the Dissonance,* with introduction by E.J. Dent, Copenhagen, 1927; 2nd ed., 1946; very valuable). From 1920 to 1946, he taught at the Cons. in Copenhagen; in 1946–57 was a prof. of musicology at the Univ. of Aarhus; from 1931 to 1954, editor of *Acta Musicologica.* He edited *Der Kopenhagener Chansonnier* (1927). Other writings: *Kontrapunkt* (1930; Eng. trans., with introduction by Glen Haydon, N.Y., 1939; 2nd German ed., Leipzig, 1956); *Die mehrstimmige italienische Laude um 1500* (1935); *Die italienische Orgelmusik am Anfang des Cinquecento* (Copenhagen, 1943); etc. In his compositions Jeppesen lives up to his reputation as a profound student of polyphonic masterpieces of the Renaissance; his music is the product of his erudition: precise in its counterpoint, unfailingly lucid in its harmonic structure, and set in impeccable classical forms.
WORKS: Opera, *Rosaura* (1946; Copenhagen, Sept. 20, 1950); Symph. (1939); Horn Concerto (1941); *Little Summer Trio* for Flute, Cello, and Piano (1941); *Te Deum Danicum* (1942; Copenhagen, 1945; London, Oct. 27, 1948); *Tvesang (Twin Song)* for Tenor, Bass, Double Chorus, Orch., Piano, and Organ (1965; Danish Radio, Copenhagen, Jan. 12, 1967).

Jeremiáš, Jaroslav, Czech composer, son of the organist and composer **Bohuslav Jeremiáš** (1859–1918); b. Písek, Aug. 14, 1889; d. Budějovice, Jan. 16, 1919. He studied at the Prague Cons.; also took lessons with Novák. He was engaged as an opera conductor at Ljubljana, then returned to Prague. Although he died at the age of 29, he left several significant works: the opera *Starý král (The Old King;* produced posthumously, Prague, April 13, 1919); the oratorio *Jan Hus* (also posthumous;

Prague, June 13, 1919); a Viola Sonata; songs.

Jeremiáš, Otakar, Czech conductor and composer, brother of **Jaroslav Jeremiáš;** b. Písek, Oct. 17, 1892; d. Prague, March 5, 1962. He studied composition, as did his brother, with Vítězslav Novák at the Prague Cons.; also took lessons in cello playing; was a cellist in the Czech Phil. He subsequently directed a music school at Budějovice (1918–28); conducted the orch. of the Prague Radio (1929–45); was director of the Prague Opera (1945–51) and the first chairman of the Czech Composers Guild. His music continues the traditions of the Czech national school, with a pronounced affinity to the style of Smetana, Foerster, and Ostrčil.
WORKS: 2 operas: *Bratři Karamazovi (The Brothers Karamazov,* after Dostoyevsky, 1922–27; Prague, Oct. 8, 1928) and *Enšpígl (Til Eulenspiegel,* 1940–44; Prague, May 13, 1949); 2 cantatas: *Mohamedův zpěv* (1932) and *Písně o rodné zemi (Song of the Native Land,* 1940–41); *Písně jara (Spring Song)* for Orch. (1907–8); *Podzimní suita (Autumn Suite)* for Orch. (1907–8); 2 symphs. (1910–11, 1914–15); *Jarní předehra (Spring Overture,* 1912); *Fantasie* for Orch. and 2 Mixed Choruses (1915; Prague Radio, Oct. 27, 1942); *Romance o Karlu IV,* melodrama with Orch. (1917); *Láska,* 5 songs with Orch. (1921); Piano Trio (1909–10); String Quartet (1910); Piano Quartet (1911); String Quintet (1911); *Fantasie na staročeské chorály (Fantasy on Old Czech Chorales)* for Nonet (1938); 2 piano sonatas (1909, 1913); songs; film music.

Jeritza (real name, **Jedlitzka**), **Maria,** dramatic soprano; b. Brünn, Oct. 6, 1887; d. Orange, N.J., July 10, 1982. She studied voice privately as a young girl, then joined the chorus at the Brünn Opera. She made her professional debut in Olmütz, as Elsa in *Lohengrin* in 1910; later sang at the Vienna Volksoper, where she made her debut in 1911, as Elisabeth in *Tannhäuser.* Emperor Franz Josef heard her sing the part of Rosalinda in *Die Fledermaus* at the summer spa in Bad Ischl, and was so impressed by her physical appearance, as well as her voice, that he decreed that she should be engaged at the Vienna Opera. This was the beginning of a glorious career. On Oct. 25, 1912, she created the title role in the opera *Ariadne auf Naxos* by Richard Strauss at the Stuttgart Opera Theater. She also created the role of the Empress in the first performance of *Die Frau ohne Schatten* by Richard Strauss, in Vienna on Oct. 10, 1919. One of her most impressive subsequent appearances was that of Marietta in Korngold's opera *Die tote Stadt,* which she sang in Hamburg on Dec. 4, 1920. She also sang this role in the American premiere of Korngold's opera, on Nov. 19, 1921, in her American debut at the Metropolitan Opera in N.Y. Her appearance in the title role of *Tosca* at the Metropolitan Opera on Dec. 1, 1921, established her as a prima donna beyond the reach of any female rival; N.Y. critics praised not only her exquisite voice and dramatic power, but also her blonde beauty and other undeniable feminine attractions. She was equally impressive in such diverse roles as Sieglinde, Thaïs, Minnie in *The Girl of the Golden West*, and the title role of *Turandot.* Faithful to the developing talent of Erich Korngold, she sang the title role in the American premiere of his *Violanta* at the Metropolitan Opera, on Nov. 5, 1927. By turning the musical clock around, she sang operettas by Suppé with extraordinary effect; she also toured the U.S. in Rudolf Friml's operetta *Music Hath Charms* in 1934. She was married 3 times: to Baron Leopold Popper de Podhurgen in 1919 (divorced in 1935); to the motion picture executive Winfield Sheehan; and, after Sheehan's death in 1945, to Irving P. Seery, a New Jersey businessman, who died in 1966. A convivial person, she maintained many friends; her 90th birthday was celebrated at her estate in October 1977; she was 94 when she died. She publ. *Sunlight and Song,* an autobiography (N.Y., 1924); a monograph on her life and career by Ernst Decsey was publ. in Vienna in 1931.

Jessel, Léon, German operetta composer; b. Stettin, Jan. 22, 1871; d. Berlin, Jan. 4, 1942. He began his career as a theater conductor in Germany; then produced numerous operettas, some of which enjoyed considerable popular success, among them *Die beiden Husaren* (Berlin, 1913), *Schwarzwaldmädel* (1917), *Verliebte Frauen* (1920), *Die Postmeisterin* (1921), *Schwalbenhochzeit* (1921), *Des Königs Nachbarin* (1924), *Die Luxuskabine* (1929), *Junger Wein* (1933), and *Die goldene Mühle* (1940). His piano piece *Die Parade der Zinnsoldaten (The Parade of Tin Soldiers),* composed in 1905, achieved perennial popularity.

Ježek, Jaroslav, Czech composer; b. Prague, Sept. 25, 1906; d. New York, Jan. 1, 1942. He studied composition with Jirák and Josef Suk; also experimented with quarter-tone techniques under the direction of Alois Hába. In 1928 he became resident composer for the "Liberated Theater," a Prague satirical revue; produced the scenic music for 20 of its plays. In 1939, shortly before the occupation of Czechoslovakia by the Nazis, he emigrated to America.

Jiménez-Mabarak, Carlos, Mexican composer; b. Tacuba, Jan. 31, 1916. He studied piano with Jesús Castillo in Guatemala; attended classes in humanities in Santiago, Chile (1930–33); then studied musicology with Charles Van den Borren in Brussels (1933–36); returned to Mexico in 1937 and studied conducting with Revueltas. After more travel in Europe, he taught music theory at the National Cons. in Mexico (1942–65) and at the School of Arts in Villahermosa (1965–68). He draws his thematic materials from the folk songs of Mexico; his predilection is for the theater; he was one of the first to use electronic music and "musique concrète" in Mexico.
WORKS: Opera, *Misa de seis* (Mexico City, June 21, 1962); incidental music to *Calígula,* after Camus (1947); ballets: *Perifonema* (Mexico City, March 9, 1940); *El amor del agua* (Mexico City, 1950); *El Ratón Pérez* (1955); *El Paraíso de los Ahogados,* "música magnetofónica" (1960); *Pitágoras dijo ...* for Small Ensemble (1966); several cantatas; Piano Concerto (1944); 2 symphs. (1945, 1962); *Sinfonia Concertante* for Piano and Orch. (1966; Mexico City, March 11, 1977); *Concierto del abuelo* for Piano and String Quartet (1938); Concerto for Timpani, Bells, Xylophone, and Percussion (1961); *La ronda junto a la fuente* for Flute, Oboe, Violin, Viola, and Cello (1965); piano pieces; songs.

Jirák, Karel Boleslav, eminent Czech composer and conductor; b. Prague, Jan. 28, 1891; d. Chicago, Jan. 30, 1972. He studied privately with Vítězslav Novák and with J.B. Foerster. In 1915 he was appointed conductor of the Hamburg City Opera; in 1918 went to Brno, where he was conductor at the National Theater for a season (1918–19). He then was choral conductor and prof. of composition at the Prague Cons. (1920–30); from 1930 to 1945, was music director of the Czechoslovak Radio. In 1947 he went to the U.S.; in 1948 became chairman of the theory dept. at Roosevelt College (later Univ.) in Chicago; held the same position also at Chicago Cons. College, from 1967 to 1971. His music represents the finest traditions of Middle-European 20th-century Romanticism.
WORKS: Opera, *A Woman and God* (1911–14; Brno, March 10, 1928); 6 symphs.: No. 1 (1915–16); No. 2 (1924); No. 3 (1929–38; Prague, March 8, 1939); No. 4, *Episode from an Artist's Life* (1945; Prague, April 16, 1947); No. 5 (1949; Edinburgh Festival, Aug. 26, 1951; winner of the Edinburgh International Festival prize); No. 6 (1957–70; Prague, Feb. 17, 1972); *Overture to a Shakespearean Comedy* (1917–21; Prague, Feb. 24, 1927); Serenade for Strings (1939); *Symphonic Variations* (Prague, March 26, 1941); *Overture "The Youth"* (1940–41); Rhapsody for Violin and Orch. (1942); *Symphonietta* for Small Orch. (1943–44); Piano Concerto (1946; Prague, Dec. 12, 1968); *Symphonic Scherzo* for Band or Orch. (1950; orch. version, Chicago, April 25, 1953); Serenade for Small Orch. (1952; first complete perf., Santa Barbara, Calif., March 24, 1965); *Legend* for Small Orch. (1954; Chicago, March 20, 1962); Concertino for Violin and Chamber Orch. (1957; Chicago, May 18, 1963). CHAMBER MUSIC: 7 string quartets (1915, 1927, 1937–40, 1949, 1951, 1957–58, 1960); String Sextet, with Alto Voice (1916–17); Cello Sonata (1918); *Night Music* for Violin and Piano (1918; orchestrated, 1928); Violin Sonata (1919); Viola Sonata (1925); Divertimento for String Trio (1925); Flute Sonata (1927); Wind Quintet (1928); *3 Pieces* for Violin and Piano (1929); *Variations, Scherzo and Finale,* nonet (1943); Serenade for Winds (1944); Piano Quintet (1945); Violin Sonatina (1946); *Mourning Music* for Viola and Organ (1946; also orchestrated); Clarinet Sonata (1947); *Introduction and Rondo* for Horn and Piano (1951); *3 Pieces* for Cello and Piano (1952); Horn Sonata (1952); Oboe Sonata (1953); Trio for Oboe, Clarinet, and Bassoon (1956); *4 Essays* for Violin and Piano (1959–62); Suite for Solo Violin (1964); Piano Trio (1966–67); Bass Clarinet Sonatina (1968–69). VOCAL WORKS: *Psalm 23* for Chorus and Orch. (1919); *Requiem* for Solo Quartet, Chorus, Organ,

and Orch. (1952; Prague, Nov. 17, 1971); several a cappella works for male chorus; song cycles (many also with orch.): *Lyric Intermezzo* (1913); *Tragicomedy,* 5 songs (1913); *Fugitive Happiness,* 7 songs (1915–16); *13 Simple Songs* (1917); *3 Songs of the Homeland* (1919); *Evening and Soul* (1921); *Awakening* (1925); *The Rainbow* (1925–26); *The Year* (1941); *7 Songs of Loneliness* (1945–46); *Pilgrim's Songs* (1962–63); *The Spring* (1965). FOR PIANO: *Summer Nights,* 4 pieces (1914); *Suite in Olden Style* (1920); *The Turning Point* (1923); 2 sonatas (1926, 1950); *Epigrams and Epitaphs* (1928–29); *4 Caprices in Polka Form* (1945); *5 Miniatures* (1954); *4 Pieces for the Right Hand* (1968–69). FOR ORGAN: *5 Little Preludes and Fugues* (1957); Suite (1958–64); Passacaglia and Fugue (1971); also incidental music for plays. He is the author of a textbook on musical form (in Czech, 5 eds., 1924–45).

Joachim, Amalie (née **Weiss**), German concert singer, wife of **Joseph Joachim;** b. Marburg, May 10, 1839; d. Berlin, Feb. 3, 1899. Her real maiden name was **Schneeweiss,** but she abridged it to Weiss in 1854 when she appeared as a singer in Vienna. She began her career as a soprano; after her marriage to Joachim (1863) she abandoned the stage but continued to give recitals as a lieder singer; her interpretations of Schumann's songs were particularly fine.

Joachim, Joseph, one of the greatest masters of the violin; b. Kittsee, near Pressburg, June 28, 1831; d. Berlin, Aug. 15, 1907. He began to study the violin at the age of 5; his first teacher was Szervaczinski, with whom he appeared in public at the age of 7, playing a violin duet. At the age of 10 he was sent to the Vienna Cons., where he studied with Böhm; in 1843 he played in Leipzig at a concert presented by Pauline Viardot; Mendelssohn did him the honor of accompanying him on the piano. He appeared with the Gewandhaus Orch. (Nov. 16, 1843); then made his first tour in England (1844), arousing admiration for his mature musicianship and remarkable technique. Returning to Leipzig, he studied with Ferdinand David; also played as concertmaster of the Gewandhaus Orch. in David's absence. From 1849 till 1854 Joachim served as concertmaster of the court orch. in Weimar. Liszt, who reigned supreme in Weimar, did not favor young Joachim, and in 1854 Joachim went to Hannover as solo violinist at the court; in 1863 he married the singer **Amalie Weiss.** In 1868 he was appointed director of the Hochschule für Ausübende Tonkunst in Berlin. His fame as a teacher spread far and wide, and aspiring violinists from all over Europe flocked there to study with him. He did not, however, abandon his career as a virtuoso; he was particularly popular in England, which he visited annually after 1862; he received an honorary degree of D.Mus. from Cambridge Univ. (1877), and also from Oxford and Glasgow. His style of playing, nurtured on the best Classical models, was remarkable for masterful repose, dignity, and flawless technique. It was his unswerving determination to interpret the mu-

sic in accordance with the intentions of the composer; this noble objectivity made him an authentic exponent of the best of violin literature. As a player of chamber music he was unexcelled in his day. The famous Joachim Quartet, organized in 1869, attained great and merited celebrity in Europe; the Joachim tradition of excellence and faithful interpretation of classical works influenced the subsequent generations of German violinists. From 1882 to 1887 Joachim also served as one of the principal conductors of the Berlin Phil.

WORKS: His compositions for the violin are virtuoso pieces that have never ceased to attract performers; of these, the most famous is the Concerto in D minor, op. 11, known as the *Hungarian Concerto* (marked "in ungarischer Weise"), which he wrote in Hannover in the summer of 1857, and first performed there on March 24, 1860; another Concerto, in G major (Hannover, Nov. 5, 1864, composer soloist), was revised in 1889. Other works are: Variations for Violin and Orch. (Berlin, Feb. 15, 1881, composer soloist); *Andantino* and *Allegro scherzoso* for Violin and Orch.; *3 Stücke (Romanze, Fantasiestück, Frühlingsfantasie)* for Violin and Piano; *3 Stücke (Lindenrauschen, Abendglocken, Ballade)* for Violin and Piano; *Hebrew Melodies* for Viola and Piano; *Variations on an Original Theme* for Viola and Piano; *Notturno* for Violin and Orch.; several overtures; cadenzas for violin concertos by Beethoven and Brahms; songs.

João IV, King of Portugal; b. Villa-Vicosa, March 19, 1604; d. Lisbon, Nov. 6, 1656. As a prince he received a fine musical training at the court chapel. He began collecting church music, gradually accumulating a magnificent library, which was totally destroyed in the earthquake of 1755. However, its contents are known, for a catalogue of it was issued in Lisbon in 1649, and reprinted by Vasconcellos in 1873. João IV was a true music scholar, well acquainted with the flow of conflicting opinions regarding musical theory. He publ. (anonymously) the pamphlets *Defensa de la musica moderna contra la errada opinion del obispo Cyrillo Franco* (in Spanish; 1649); *Respuesta a las dudas que se pusieron a la missa "Panis quem ego dabo" de Palestrina* (1654); Italian translations were made of both. He composed a considerable quantity of church music; his motets *Crux fidelis* and *Adjuva nos* are reprinted in S. Lück's *Sammlung ausgezeichneter Kompositionen für die Kirche* (1884–85).

Jochum, Eugen, German conductor, brother of **Georg Ludwig** and **Otto Jochum;** b. Babenhausen, Bavaria, Nov. 1, 1902. He studied organ and piano at the Augsburg Cons. (1914–22), composition with Waltershausen at the Munich Academy of Music (1922–24), and conducting with Sigmund von Hausegger. He subsequently occupied various posts as opera coach and assistant conductor in Munich, Kiel, Mannheim, and Duisburg. From 1934 to 1949 he was Generalmusikdirektor of the Hamburg Phil.; simultaneously (1934–45) he served as music director of the Hamburg State Opera; then conducted the Radio Orch. in Munich (1949–60); in 1961 he became conductor of the Concertgebouw Orch. in Amsterdam; later was conductor and artistic director of the Bamberg Symph. (1969–73); then held the title of laureate conductor of the London Symph. Orch. from 1977 to 1979. He is reputed as one of the best conductors of the symph. works of Bruckner and Mahler.

Jochum, Georg Ludwig, German conductor, brother of **Eugen** and **Otto Jochum;** b. Babenhausen, Dec. 10, 1909; d. Mülheim an der Ruhr, Nov. 1, 1970. He studied in Munich with Hausegger and Pembaur; occupied numerous posts as conductor: at the Frankfurt Opera (1937–40); in Linz (1940–45); etc. From 1946 to 1958 he was director of the Duisburg Cons.; also filled in numerous appearances as guest conductor in Europe, Japan, and South America.

Jochum, Otto, prolific German composer, brother of **Eugen** and **Georg Ludwig Jochum;** b. Babenhausen, March 18, 1898; d. Bad Reichenhall, Nov. 24, 1969. He studied at the Augsburg Cons. and at the Munich Academy of Music with Heinrich Kasper Schmid, Gustav Geierhaas, and Joseph Haas (1922–31). In 1933 he was appointed director of the Municipal Singing School in Augsburg; in 1949, became director of the Augsburg Cons.; retired in 1952. He composed about 150 opus numbers, among them 2 oratorios (*Der jüngste Tag* and *Ein Weihnachtssingen*); 12 masses; a great number of works for chorus, both accompanied and a cappella; arrangements of folk songs; a *Goethe-Sinfonie* (1941); *Florianer-Sinfonie* (1946); songs.

Johannes Chrysorrhoas (John of Damascus), Christian saint; b. Damascus, c.700; d. at the monastery of St. Sabas, near Jerusalem, 754. He was canonized by both the Greek and Roman Church; was the earliest dogmatist of the Greek Church; wrote many examples of the *kanon,* a special type of Byzantine hymn that usually used a pre-existent melody. John is credited, by what may be a legend, with having arranged the Byzantine Oktoechos and having improved Byzantine notation.

Johannesen, Grant, eminent American pianist and pedagogue; b. Salt Lake City, July 30, 1921. He studied piano with Robert Casadesus at Princeton Univ. (1941–46) and with Egon Petri at Cornell Univ.; also took courses in composition with Roger Sessions and Nadia Boulanger. He made his concert debut in N.Y. in 1944. In 1949 he won first prize at the Ostend Concours International, which was the beginning of his international career. He toured Europe with Mitropoulos and the N.Y. Phil. in 1956 and 1957; made a European tour, including Russia, with Szell and the Cleveland Orch. in 1968; also played at leading music festivals in France, the Netherlands, and Norway. From 1960 to 1966 he taught at the Aspen Music School; in 1973 he became music consultant and adviser of the Cleveland Inst. of Music; was named its music director in 1974, and finally president in 1977. Johannesen ac-

quired a reputation as a pianist of fine musicianly stature, subordinating his virtuoso technique to the higher considerations of intellectual fidelity to the composer's intentions; he was particularly esteemed for his performances of French and American music. He also composed some piano works. He was married to the Canadian cellist **Zara Nelsova** from 1963 to 1973.

Johanos, Donald, American conductor; b. Cedar Rapids, Iowa, Feb. 10, 1928. He studied violin with André de Ribaupierre and Cecil Burleigh at the Eastman School of Music, Rochester, N.Y.; conducting with Eugene Ormandy, George Szell, Eduard van Beinum, and Otto Klemperer (1955–57). From 1963 to 1970 he was principal conductor and music director of the Dallas Symph. Orch., achieving estimable results. Subsequently he was guest conductor with numerous American and European orchs. In 1970 he was appointed associate conductor of the Pittsburgh Symph.; concurrently, he was also conductor of the Honolulu Symph. Orch. and artistic director of the Hawaii Opera Theatre.

Johansen, David Monrad, Norwegian composer; b. Vefsn, Nov. 8, 1888; d. Sandvika, Feb. 20, 1974. He studied piano with Karl Nissen and music theory with Iver Holter; in 1915 he went to Berlin, where he took lessons with Humperdinck; by this time in middle age, he continued his studies in composition in Paris (1927) and in Leipzig (1933–35), where he took a special course in counterpoint with Grabner. In the meantime he pursued an active career as a concert pianist and composer; gave a recital of his own works in Oslo in 1915. He also wrote music criticism in *Aftenposten* (1925–45). His music continued the national Norwegian tradition, in the lyric manner of Grieg; as time went by, Johansen experienced a mild influence of Russian and French music, gradually forming an innocuous modern style with sporadic audacious incursions into the domain of sharp dissonance.

Johansen, Gunnar, Danish-American pianist; b. Copenhagen, Jan. 21, 1906. He studied piano with Victor Schiøler; later in Berlin with Frederic Lamond, Edwin Fischer, and Egon Petri. From 1924 to 1929 he toured Europe as a concert pianist; then lived in California. In 1939 he joined the faculty of the Univ. of Wisconsin in Madison as artist-in-residence, a title that was specially created for him. An early admirer of Busoni, he devoted himself to propagandizing his music. In March 1966 he presented a Busoni Centennial Commemorative program at the Univ. of Wisconsin, including Busoni's formidable *Fantasia Contrappuntistica.* He recorded for Artist Direct Records the complete piano works of Busoni and his Bach transcriptions, the complete piano works of Liszt, and the complete clavier works of Bach. Johansen produced a sensation of seismic proportions on Jan. 14, 1969, when he played with the Philadelphia Orch. in N.Y. the piano version of Beethoven's Violin Concerto at 30½ hours' notice. Johansen is also a composer of truly fantastic fecundity. He wrote 2 piano concertos (1930, 1970); *East-West,* cantata for Wordless Women's Voices, Piano, 3 Woodwinds, and Percussion (1944); 31 piano sonatas (1941–51); and 246 piano sonatas improvised directly on the keyboard and recorded on tape (1952–70). A scholar as well as a musician, Johansen trans. from Danish into Eng. George Brandes's biography of Kierkegaard.

Johansson, Bengt, Finnish composer; b. Helsinki, Oct. 2, 1914. He studied composition with Sulho Ranta and Selim Palmgren; also cello at the Sibelius Academy in Helsinki, graduating in 1947; made study trips to Europe, Italy, and America; upon his return to Finland, he became director of music broadcasting for Finnish Radio (1952); was a teacher at the Helsinki Academy from 1960; in 1965 he became a lecturer in music history at the Sibelius Academy. His music makes use of a wide variety of resources, including electronic sound.

Johnsen, Hallvard, Norwegian composer; b. Hamburg, Germany, June 27, 1916, to Norwegian parents. He went to Norway as a youth; studied music theory with Bjarne Brustad (1937–41) and Karl Andersen (1943–45) in Oslo and with Vagn Holmboe in Denmark. He also learned to play the flute and was employed as a flutist in Norwegian military bands.
WORKS: Opera, *The Legend of Svein and Maria* (1971; Oslo, Sept. 9, 1973); 13 symphs.: No. 1 (1949); No. 2, *Pastorale* (1954); No. 3 (1957); No. 4 (1959); No. 5 (1960); No. 6 (1961); No. 7 (1962); No. 8 (1964); No. 9 (1968); No. 10 (1973); No. 11 (1975); No. 12 (1976); No. 13 (1983); cantata, *Norwegian Nature* (1952); 2 *Overtures* (1954, 1968); 2 flute concertos with String Orch. (1939, 1955); 2 violin concertos with Chamber Orch. (1955, 1967); Trumpet Concerto (1966); *Canzona* for Wind Orch. (1968); Cello Concerto (1977); Trio for Flute, Violin, and Viola (1938); Quartet for Flute and String Trio (1945); *Tema con variazioni* for Piano (1957); 3 string quartets (1962, 1966, 1972); Serenade for Wind Quintet (1962); Suite for Flute and Horn (1964); Quintet for Winds, with Vibraphone (1965); Sextet (1974); *Trio Serenade* for Flute, Viola, and Cello (1974); Quartet for 4 Saxophones (1974); *Divertimento* for 2 Cornets, Horn, Baritone Horn, and Tuba (1974); Duet for 2 Flutes (1975); Quintet for 2 Trumpets, Horn, Trombone, and Bass Trombone (1978); Trio for Trumpet, Trombone, and Vibraphone (1980); *Pastoral* for Flute, Violin, and Vibraphone (1981); choral pieces.

Johnson, Bengt-Emil, Swedish composer and poet; b. Ludvika, Dec. 12, 1936. He studied composition with Knut Wiggen; at the same time pursued his abiding interest in modernistic poetry, publ. 4 collections of poems (1963–66) in a "concrete" idiom polyphonically elaborated in the technique of recited "text-sound compositions," a process electronically combining semantic and abstract sounds. Most of his works are of this nature; in emulation of computer-type identification (also used by Xenakis), he includes the year of composition in the title: *Semikolon; Äventyr på vägen (Semicolon; Adven-*

ture on the Way; 1965); *1/1966: Släpkoppel (Dragleash . . .); 1/1967: Nya släpkoppel med vida världen (New drag-leashes with the wide world); 2/1967: (Meden) (While); "from any point to any other point,"* a ballet in collaboration with Lars-Gunnar Bodin and Margaretha Åsberg (1968); *1/1969: Genom törstspegeln (första passeringen) (Through the mirror of thirst—first passage); 2/1969: För Abraham Jakobsson, på vägen (For Abraham Jakobsson, on the way),* after C.J.L. Almquist; *3/1969: Through the mirror of thirst (second passage); 1/1970: (bland) (among); 2/1970: (among) II; 3/1970: (among) III; 4/1970: Jakter (Hunts),* after C.F. Hills; *6/1970: Hyllning till Mr. Miller (Homage to Mr. Miller),* based on Henry Miller; *1/1971: under publikens jubel (Under the cheers of the people); 1/1972: (among) IV; 2/1972: (While) II; 3/1972: Släpkoppel (uppsläpp); 4/1972: Släpkoppel (Weltanschauung) (Drag-leash—World Outlook)* for a cappella Chorus; *5/1972: Mimicry (Erik Rosenberg in memoriam)* for Voice, Cello, Trombone, Piano, and Percussion; *1/1973: Pierrot på rygg* for Soprano, Cello, Piano, and Percussion; *2/1973: Subsong II; 3/1973: Ej blir det natt* for Chorus; *Disappearances* for Piano and Tape (1974).

Johnson, Edward, Canadian tenor and operatic impresario; b. Guelph, Ontario, Aug. 22, 1878; d. there, April 20, 1959. He studied at the Univ. of Toronto; in 1900, went to N.Y., where he sang in light opera; then went to Italy for further study; appeared there in opera under the name of **Eduardo di Giovanni.** In 1919 he returned to the U.S.; was a member of the Chicago Opera Co.; then joined the Metropolitan Opera Co. (debut, Nov. 16, 1922); in 1935 he was appointed general manager of the Metropolitan, succeeding Herbert Witherspoon. He resigned in 1950. He eventually moved to Toronto, where he taught voice at the Univ. of Toronto.

Johnson, James Weldon, black American lyricist, librettist, anthologist, and writer on music (also a poet, novelist, newspaper editor, lawyer, and international diplomat); b. Jacksonville, Fla., June 17, 1871; d. in an automobile accident at Wiscasset, Maine, June 26, 1938. He studied literature at Atlanta University; then returned to Jacksonville, becoming a teacher and school principal; after self-study, became a lawyer (1898; the first black to pass the Florida bar examinations). A poem written for school use in 1900 to commemorate Abraham Lincoln's birthday, *Lift Every Voice and Sing,* was set to music by his brother, the composer **J. Rosamond Johnson,** and performed in Jacksonville the same year; though its beginnings were inauspicious, the song gradually acquired popularity, and in 15 years became known as "the Negro National Anthem." In the summer of 1899 the brothers visited N.Y. in an attempt to find a producer for their collaborative Gilbert and Sullivan–styled operetta, *Tolosa, or The Royal Document;* while their effort failed, they became acquainted with Oscar Hammerstein and many figures in the black musical life of N.Y. They returned to N.Y. in subsequent summers, selling some 30 songs to various musical reviews, and moved there permanently in 1902, forming, with Bob Cole, an enormously successful songwriting team of Cole and Johnson Bros.; among their hit songs, mostly in black dialect, were *Under the Bamboo Tree* (1902), which was parodied by T.S. Eliot in "Fragment of the Agon," *Congo Love Song* (1903), and, under the pseudonym **Will Handy,** *Oh, Didn't He Ramble* (1902), which was to become a jazz standard; the team's success was such that they became known as "Those Ebony Offenbachs." In 1906 James Weldon Johnson was consul to Venezuela, and later, to Nicaragua. During this period he wrote his only novel, *The Autobiography of an Ex-Colored Man* (publ. anonymously, as if it were a true confession; Boston, 1912), in which he gives vivid descriptions of the "ragtime" musical life in N.Y. during the first decade of the century; soon afterward, his trans. of Granados's *Goyescas* was used for the Metropolitan Opera's first performance of this work. In 1926 he compiled (with a lengthy and valuable introduction) *The Book of American Negro Spirituals* (N.Y.), with arrangements by his brother, and, in 1927, *The 2nd Book of American Negro Spirituals;* his book *Black Manhattan* (N.Y., 1930), a historical study of blacks in N.Y., also draws together considerable information on black musical life. He also wrote an autobiography, *Along This Way* (1931). His papers are on deposit at Yale Univ.

Johnson, J(ohn) Rosamond, black American composer and bass, brother of **James Weldon Johnson;** b. Jacksonville, Fla., Aug. 11, 1873; d. New York, Nov. 11, 1954. He studied at Atlanta Univ. and at the New England Cons. of Music; took voice lessons with David Bispham. He set his brother's poem *Lift Every Voice and Sing* (1900) to music, this later becoming known as "the Negro National Anthem"; the brothers collaborated on many other songs at this time, selling them to various musical reviews in N.Y.; in 1902 they formed, with Bob Cole, the songwriting team of Cole and Johnson Bros., meeting with tremendous success; in addition to popular black-dialect songs, Johnson wrote some songs that were accepted on the concert stage, such as *Li'l Gal* and *Since You Went Away.* In 1912–13 he was music director of Hammerstein's Opera House in London; he also sang in opera; subsequently toured America and Europe in programs of Negro spirituals; with his brother he compiled two vols. of Negro spirituals (1926, 1927), adding piano accompaniments; wrote a ballet, *African Drum Dance,* and many vocal works; also *Rolling Along in Song* (a history of black music with 85 song arrangements). He sang the role of Lawyer Frazier in the early performances of Gershwin's *Porgy and Bess.*

Johnson, Robert Sherlaw, English composer; b. Sunderland, May 21, 1932. He was educated at King's College at the Univ. of Durham; after graduation he enrolled in the Royal Academy of Music in London; in 1957 he went to Paris, where he studied piano with Jacques Février and composi-

tion with Nadia Boulanger; also attended classes of Olivier Messiaen at the Paris Cons.; returning to England, he gave piano recitals in programs of 20th-century music. In 1961 he became a member of the faculty of Leeds Univ., and later was lecturer in music at the Univ. of York (1965–70). In 1970 he was appointed to the staff of Oxford Univ. In his music he re-creates Renaissance forms and mannerisms in a modern modal idiom. He composes mainly for chamber ensembles and vocal groups.

WORKS: Opera, *The Lampton Worm* (1976); 2 string quartets (1966, 1969); *Triptych* for Flute, Clarinet, Violin, Cello, Piano, and Percussion (1973); Quintet for Clarinet, Violin, Viola, Cello, and Piano (1974); Sonata for Alto Flute and Cello (1976); *The Praises of Heaven and Earth* for Soprano, Electronic Tape, and Piano (1969); *Incarnatio* for Chorus a cappella (1970); *Green Whispers of Gold* for Voice, Electronic Tape, and Piano (1971); *Carmina vernalia* for Soprano and Instruments (1972); *Christus resurgens* for Chorus a cappella (1972); *Festival Mass of the Resurrection* for Choir and Chamber Orch. (1974); *Anglorum feriae* for Soprano, Tenor, Chorus, and Orch. (1976); *Veritas veritatus* for 6 Voices (1980); 3 piano sonatas (1963, 1967, 1976); *Asterogenesis* for 8-octave Piano (manufactured by Bösendorfer of Vienna), extending the range to the C below the lowest C on an ordinary piano (1973); *Nymphaea ("Projections")* for Piano (1976).

Johnson, Thor, American conductor; b. Wisconsin Rapids, Wis., June 10, 1913 (of Norwegian parentage); d. Nashville, Tenn., Jan. 16, 1975. He studied at the Univ. of North Carolina and later at the Univ. of Michigan (M.A., 1935); organized the Univ. of Michigan Little Symph., with which he toured in the U.S. in 1935–36 and in 1937–41. In 1936 he won the Huntington Beebe Fellowship. This enabled him to study conducting in Europe during 1936–37. His principal teachers were Malko, Abendroth, Weingartner, and Bruno Walter. Returning to America, he attended Koussevitzky's conducting courses at the Berkshire Music Center; conducted the Grand Rapids (Mich.) Symph. Orch. (1940–42), and was guest conductor of the Philadelphia Orch. at Ann Arbor. He enlisted in the U.S. Army in 1942; from 1947 to 1958 he was principal conductor of the Cincinnati Symph. Orch., one of the few Americans to hold the conductorship of a major American orch. for such a length of time. From 1958 to 1964 he was director of conducting activities at Northwestern Univ., Chicago, and from 1967 till his death, directed the Nashville (Tenn.) Orch. Assoc.; also filled in guest engagements in Europe; in 1971 he conducted in Italy and Rumania. He also traveled as a guest conductor in the Orient.

Johnson, Tom, American composer and music critic; b. Greeley, Colo., Nov. 18, 1939. He studied at Yale Univ. (B.A., 1961; M.Mus., 1967). Subsequently he was employed as instructor of the 52nd Army Band Training Unit at Fort Ord, Calif. (1963–65), and in 1967 was a dance accompanist at N.Y. Univ. In 1971 he became music critic of the radical Greenwich

Village paper *The Village Voice,* and pugnaciously proceeded to preach the gospel of asymptotic modernity. In his own compositions he aims to displease, but much to his chagrin, often fails in his design to shock. The most beguiling of his productions is *The 4-Note Opera* for Soloists, Chorus, Piano, and Tape, to his own libretto, produced at The Cubiculo in N.Y. on May 11, 1972; the score actually makes use of only 4 notes, A, B, D, and E, but employs them with quaquaversal expertise. Among his other works are *Pendulum* for Orch. (1965); *Fission* for Orch. (1966); *4 Violins* for 4 Violins and Percussion (1966); Trio for Flute, Cello, and Piano (1967); *5 Americans* for Orch. (1969); *411 Lines,* theater piece (1970); and several pieces of "Action Music" for dancers and piano. Apart from his activities as a composer and writer, Tom Johnson has also appeared as a singer, even though he grievously lacks the *bel canto* quality in his throaty voice; on June 11, 1976, in the summer gardens of the Museum of Modern Art in N.Y., he gave a rendition of a group of 18 "Secret Songs" of his composition, set to nonsense syllables; after singing each of the songs he burned the MS in a specially provided white bowl in which an eternal flame burns—sustained by alcohol.

Johnston, Benjamin, American avant-garde composer; b. Macon, Ga., March 15, 1926. He was educated at the College of William and Mary (A.B., 1949), at the Cincinnati Cons. of Music (M.Mus., 1950), and at Mills College (M.A., 1952). In 1951 he joined the faculty of the Univ. of Illinois at Urbana. In 1959 he received a Guggenheim fellowship. His works include *Celebration* for Solo Piano; Duo for Flute and String Bass; *9 Variations for String Quartet; Knocking Piece* for Percussion; *Night,* cantata (1955); *Gambit* for Dancers and Orch. (1959); *Sonata for Microtonal Piano* (1965); *Quintet for Groups* (1966) and a "tombstone" piece, *Ci gît Satie,* for the Swingle Singers (1966); also an opera, *Carmilla* (1970).

Jolas, Betsy, French composer of American parentage; b. Paris, Aug. 5, 1926. She went to America in 1939; studied at Bennington College (B.A., 1946); returned to Paris in 1946 and took courses with Olivier Messiaen at the Paris Cons. In her music she applies constructive methods in neo-Baroque forms and quasi-serial techniques.
WORKS: *Figures* for 9 Instruments (1956); *Mots* for 5 Voices and 8 Instruments (1963); *Quatuor* for Coloratura Soprano, Violin, Viola, and Cello (1964); *J.D.E.* for 14 Instruments (1966); *D'un opéra de voyage* for 22 Instruments (1967); *Quatre plages* for String Orch. (1968); *Etats* for Violin and Percussion (1969); *Winter Music* for Organ and Chamber Orch. (1970); *Le Pavillon au bord de la rivière,* musical spectacle after a medieval Chinese play (Avignon, July 25, 1975); *O Wall,* a "mini-opera" as an instrumental counterpart to a line from Shakespeare's *A Midsummer Night's Dream,* for Woodwind Quintet (N.Y., Nov. 5, 1976).

Jolivet, André, prominent French composer; b. Paris, Aug. 8, 1905; d. there, Dec. 20, 1974. A son of artistically inclined parents, he took an interest in the fine arts, wrote poetry, and improvised at the piano; studied cello with Louis Feuillard and music theory with Aimé Théodas at Notre Dame de Clignancourt. At the age of 15 he wrote a ballet and designed a set for it; in 1928 he undertook a prolonged study of musical techniques with Paul Le Flem. Of decisive importance to the maturation of his creative consciousness was his meeting in 1930 with Varèse, then living in Paris, who gave him a sense of direction in composition. In 1935 Jolivet organized in Paris the progressive group La Spirale. In 1936, in association with Yves Baudrier, Olivier Messiaen, and Daniel Lesur, he founded La Jeune France, dedicated to the promotion of new music in a national French style. Jolivet was also active as conductor of his own works, and traveled all around the world, including America, Russia, Egypt, and Japan, in this capacity. He served as conductor and music director of the Comédie Française (1943–59); was technical adviser of the Direction Générale des Artes et des Lettres (1959–62), and president of the Concerts Lamoureux (1963–68); he also was prof. of composition at the Paris Cons. (1965–70). Jolivet injected an empiric spirit into his music, making free use of modernistic technical resources, including the electronic sounds of the Ondes Martenot. Despite these esoteric preoccupations, and even a peripheral deployment of serialism, Jolivet's music is designed mainly to provide aural stimulation and esthetic satisfaction.
WORKS: Opera buffa, *Dolorès,* subtitled *Le Miracle de la femme laide* (1942; Paris Radio, May 4, 1947); 3 ballets: *Guignol et Pandore* for Piano or Orch. (1943; Paris, April 29, 1944); *L'Inconnue* (1950; Paris Opéra, April 19, 1950); *Ariadne* (1964; Paris, March 12, 1965); oratorio, *La Vérité de Jeanne* (1956; Domrémy Festival, May 20, 1956; 3 orch. interludes drawn from it are often played separately); 2 cantatas: *La Tentation dernière* (1941; Paris, May 16, 1941) and *Le Cœur de la matière* (1965; Paris, April 9, 1965); scenic music for radio legends and other productions such as *La Queste de Lancelot* (1943; Paris, Jan. 21, 1944); *Le Livre de Christophe Colomb* (1946; Paris, Feb. 21, 1947); *Hélène et Faust,* after Goethe (1949); 2 productions of *Antigone* (1951; 1960); *Empereur Jones* (1953); *L'Amour médecin* (1955); and *L'Eunuque* (1959). He also wrote *Andante* for String Orch. (1935); *Danse incantatoire* for Orch. with 2 Ondes Martenot (1936); *3 chants des hommes* for Baritone and Orch. (1937); *Poèmes pour l'enfant* for Voice and 11 Instruments (1937; Paris, May 12, 1938); *Cosmogonie,* prelude for Orch. (1938; Paris, Nov. 17, 1947; also for Piano); *5 danses rituelles* (1939; Paris, June 15, 1942); *3 complaintes du soldat* for Voice, and Orch. or Piano (1940); *Symphonie de danses* (1940; Paris, Nov. 24, 1943); *Suite delphique* for Wind Instruments, Harp, Ondes Martenot, and Percussion (1943; Vienna, Oct. 22, 1948); *Psyché* for Orch. (1946; Paris, March 5, 1947); *Fanfares pour Britannicus* for Brass and Percussion (1946); Concerto for Ondes Martenot and Orch. (1947; Vienna, April 23, 1948); 2 trumpet concertos:

Concertino (Concerto No. 1) for Trumpet, String Orch., and Piano (1948) and No. 2 (1954); 2 flute concertos: No. 1, with String Orch. (1949) and No. 2, *Suite en concert,* for Flute and Percussionists (1965); Piano Concerto (1949–50; Strasbourg Music Festival, June 19, 1951); Concerto for Harp and Chamber Orch. (1952); 3 numbered symphs.: No. 1 (1953; International Society for Contemporary Music Festival, Haifa, May 30, 1954), No. 2 (1959; Berlin Festival Oct. 3, 1959), and No. 3 (1964; Mexico City, Aug. 7, 1964, composer conducting); Concerto for Bassoon, String Orch., Harp, and Piano (1954; Paris Radio, Nov. 30, 1954); *Suite transocéane* (1955; Louisville, Ky., Sept. 24, 1955); *Suite française* for Orch. (1957); Percussion Concerto (1958; Paris, Feb. 17, 1959); *Adagio* for Strings (1960); *Les Amants magnifiques* for Orch. (1961; Lyons, April 24, 1961); Symph. for Strings (1961; Paris, Jan. 9, 1962); 2 cello concertos: No. 1 (1962; Paris, Nov. 20, 1962) and No. 2, with String Orch. (1966; Moscow, Jan. 6, 1967); *12 Inventions* for 12 Instruments (1966; Paris, Jan. 23, 1967); *Songe à nouveau rêvé* for Soprano and Orch. (1970); Violin Concerto (1972; Paris, Feb. 28, 1973); *La Flèche du temps* for 12 Solo Strings (1973); *Yin-Yang* for 11 Solo Strings (1974). His chamber and solo instrumental works include *3 Temps* for Piano (1930); Suite for String Trio (1930); String Quartet (1934); *Mana* for Piano (1935); *3 poèmes* for Ondes Martenot and Piano (1935); *5 incantations* for Solo Flute (1936); *Messe pour le jour de la paix* for Voice, Organ, and Tambourine (1940); *Ballet des étoiles* for 9 Instruments (1941); *Suite liturgique* for Voice, Oboe, Cello, and Harp (1942); Nocturne for Cello and Piano (1943); *Pastorales de Noël* for Flute or Violin, Bassoon or Viola, and Harp (1943); *Chant des Linos* for Flute and Piano, or Flute, Violin, Viola, Cello, and Harp (1944); *Sérénade* for Oboe and Piano, or Wind Quintet (1945); 2 piano sonatas (1945, 1957); *Hopi Snake Dance* for 2 Pianos (1948); *Epithalame* for 12-part Vocal "Orch." (1953; Venice, Sept. 16, 1956); *Sérénade* for 2 Guitars (1956); *Rhapsodie à 7* for Clarinet, Bassoon, Trumpet, Trombone, Percussion, Violin, and Double Bass (1957); Flute Sonata (1958); Sonatina for Flute and Clarinet (1961); *Hymne à l'univers* for Organ (1961); *Messe "Uxor tua"* for 5 Voices, and 5 Instruments or Organ (1962); Sonatina for Oboe and Bassoon (1963); *Madrigal* for 4 Voices and 4 Instruments (1963); *Alla rustica* for Flute and Harp (1963); *Suite rhapsodique* for Solo Violin (1965); *Suite en concert* for Solo Cello (1965); *5 églogues* for Solo Viola (1967); *Ascèses,* 5 pieces for Solo Flute or Clarinet (1967); *Cérémonial en hommage à Varèse* for 6 Percussionists (1968); *Controversia* for Oboe and Harp (1968); *Mandala* for Organ (1969); *Arioso barocco* for Trumpet and Organ (1969); *Patchinko* for 2 Pianos (1970); *Heptade* for Trumpet and Percussion (1971–72).

Jommelli, Niccolò, greatly significant Italian composer; b. Aversa, near Naples, Sept. 10, 1714; d. Naples, Aug. 25, 1774. He began his musical studies with Canon Muzzillo, the director of the Cathedral choir in Aversa; in 1725 he entered the Cons. S. Onofrio in Naples, where he studied with Prota and Feo; in 1728 he enrolled in the Cons. Pietà dei Turchini in Naples, where he continued his studies with Fago, Sarcuni, and Basso. In 1737 he composed a comic opera, *L'errore amoroso,* for Naples; this was followed by a 2nd comic opera, *Odoardo* (Naples, 1738). On Jan. 16, 1740, his first serious opera, *Ricimero rè de' Goti,* was produced in Rome. After composing *Astianatte* (Rome, Feb. 4, 1741), he went to Bologna for the premiere of his *Ezio* (April 29, 1741); there he studied with Padre Martini; was also elected to membership in the Accademia Filarmonica. He then proceeded to Venice, where his opera *Merope* was given on Dec. 26, 1741; in 1743 he became music director of the Ospedale degli Incurabili there; during this time he composed several notable sacred works, including the oratorios *Isacco figura del Redentore* and *La Betulia liberata.* In 1747 he left Venice for Rome; in 1749 he went to Vienna, where his opera *Achille in Sciro* was successfully staged on Aug. 30, 1749. Several of his operas had been performed in Stuttgart, resulting in a commission for a new opera from Karl Eugen, the Duke of Württemberg. *Fetonte* was premiered in Stuttgart on the duke's birthday on Feb. 11, 1753. On Jan. 1, 1754, Jommelli became Ober-Kapellmeister in Stuttgart. Among the operas he composed for Stuttgart were *Pelope* (Feb. 11, 1755), *Nitteti* (Feb. 11, 1759), and *L'Olimpiade* (Feb. 11, 1761); he also composed sacred music, including a *Miserere* and a *Te Deum,* both of which were widely performed. In 1768 Jommelli accepted an offer from King José of Portugal to compose operas and sacred music for the court of Lisbon. He left Stuttgart in 1769 and returned to Italy; for Naples he composed the operas *Armida abbandonata* (May 30, 1770) and *Ifigenia in Tauride* (May 30, 1771); also the serenata *Cerere placata* (Sept. 14, 1772). His opera *Il trionfo di Clelia* was produced in Lisbon with great success on June 6, 1774. His last work for Naples was a *Miserere* on Psalm 50, which was heard during Holy Week 1774.

The historical significance of Jommelli lies in his being a mediator between the German and Italian styles of composition, especially in opera. He introduced into Italian opera the German solidity of harmonic texture and also the expressive dynamics associated with the "Mannheim" school of composition; he also abandoned the formal Neapolitan convention of the da capo aria, thus contributing to a more progressive and realistic operatic form; this earned him the sobriquet "the Italian Gluck." On the other hand, he influenced the development, during his long stay in Stuttgart, of German opera in the direction of simple melodiousness and natural rhythmic flow without dependence on contrapuntal techniques. Thus his influence was beneficial both for his native art and for the most austere German operatic traditions.

WORKS: OPERAS: *L'errore amoroso,* comic opera (Naples, 1737; not extant); *Odoardo,* comic opera (Naples, 1738; not extant); *Ricimero rè de' Goti* (Rome, Jan. 16, 1740); *Astianatte* (Rome, Feb. 4, 1741; also known as *Andromaca*); *Ezio* (Bologna, April 29, 1741; 2nd version, Naples, Nov. 4, 1748; 3rd version, Stuttgart, Feb. 11, 1758, not extant; 4th version, 1771; revised by da Silva, Lisbon, April 20, 1772); *Merope* (Venice, Dec. 26, 1741); *Semiramide riconosiuta* (Turin, Dec. 26, 1741; 2nd version, Piacenza, 1753; 3rd version, Stuttgart, Feb. 11, 1762); *Don Chichibio*, intermezzi (Rome, 1742); *Eumene* (Bologna, May 5, 1742; 2nd version, as *Artemisia*, Naples, May 30, 1747); *Semiramide* (Venice, Dec. 26, 1742); *Tito Manlio* (Turin, 1743; 2nd version, Venice, 1746, not extant; 3rd version, Stuttgart, Jan. 6, 1758, not extant); *Demofoonte* (Padua, June 13, 1743; 2nd version, Milan, 1753; 3rd version, Stuttgart, Feb. 11, 1764; revised, Ludwigsburg, Feb. 11, 1765; revised by da Silva, Lisbon, June 6, 1775; 4th version, Naples, Nov. 4, 1770); *Alessandro nell'Indie* (Ferrara, 1744, not extant; 2nd version, Stuttgart, Feb. 11, 1760, not extant; revised by da Silva, Lisbon, June 6, 1776); *Ciro riconosciuto* (Bologna, May 4, 1744; 2nd version, 1747?; 3rd version, Venice, 1749; completely new version, 1751 or 1758); *Sofonisba* (Venice, 1746; not extant); *Cajo Mario* (Rome, Feb. 6, 1746; 2nd version, Bologna, 1751); *Antigono* (Lucca, Aug. 24, 1746); *Didone abbandonata* (Rome, Jan. 28, 1747; 2nd version, Vienna, Dec. 8, 1749; 3rd version, Stuttgart, Feb. 11, 1763); *L'amore in maschera*, comic opera (Naples, 1748; not extant); *La cantata e disfida di Don Trastullo*, intermezzi (Rome, 1749; 2nd version, Lucca, 1762); *Artaserse* (Rome, Feb. 4, 1749; 2nd version, Stuttgart, Aug. 30, 1756); *Demetrio* (Parma, 1749); *Achille in Sciro* (Vienna, Aug. 30, 1749; 2nd version, Rome, Jan. 26, 1771); *Cesare in Egitto* (Rome, 1751; not extant); *La Villana nobile*, comic opera (Palermo, 1751; not extant); *Ifigenia in Aulide* (Rome, Feb. 9, 1751; revised with arias by Traetta, Naples, Dec. 18, 1753); *L'Uccellatrice*, intermezzi (Venice, May 6, 1751; 2nd version as *Il paratajo [ovvero] La Pipée*, Paris, Sept. 25, 1753); *Ipermestra* (Spoleto, Oct. 1751); *Talestri* (Rome, Dec. 28, 1751); *I Rivali delusi*, intermezzi (Rome, 1752); *Attilio Regolo* (Rome, Jan. 8, 1753); *Fetonte* (Stuttgart, Feb. 11, 1753, not extant; 2nd version, Ludwigsburg, Feb. 11, 1768); *La clemenza di Tito* (Stuttgart, Aug. 30, 1753, not extant; 2nd version, Ludwigsburg, Jan. 6, 1765, not extant; revised by da Silva, Lisbon, June 6, 1771); *Bajazette* (Turin, Dec. 26, 1753); *Don Falcone*, intermezzi (Bologna, Jan. 22, 1754); *Lucio Vero* (Milan, 1754); *Catone in Utica* (Stuttgart, Aug. 30, 1754; not extant); *Pelope* (Stuttgart, Feb. 11, 1755; revised by da Silva, Salvaterra, 1768); *Enea nel Lazio* (Stuttgart, Aug. 30, 1755, not extant; revised by da Silva, Salvaterra, 1767); *Creso* (Rome, Feb. 5, 1757); *Temistocle* (Naples, Dec. 18, 1757; 2nd version, Ludwigsburg, Nov. 4, 1765); *Nitteti* (Stuttgart, Feb. 11, 1759, not extant; revised by da Silva, Lisbon, June 6, 1770); *Endimione ovvero Il trionfo d'amore*, pastorale (Stuttgart, 1759, not extant; 2nd version, Queluz, June 29, 1780); *Cajo Fabrizio* (Mannheim, Nov. 4, 1760; includes arias by G. Cola); *L'Olimpiade* (Stuttgart, Feb. 11, 1761; revised by da Silva, Lisbon, March 31, 1774); *L'isola disabitata*, pastorale (Ludwigsburg, Nov. 4, 1761, not extant; 2nd version, Queluz, March 31, 1780); *Il trionfo d'amore*, pastorale (Ludwigsburg, Feb. 16, 1763; not extant); *La pastorella illustre*, pastorale (Stuttgart, Nov. 4, 1763, not extant; revised by da Silva, Salvaterra,

1773); *Il Re pastore* (Ludwigsburg, Nov. 4, 1764, not extant; revised by da Silva, Salvaterra, 1770); *Imeneo in Atene*, pastorale (Ludwigsburg, Nov. 4, 1765; revised by da Silva, Lisbon, March 19, 1773); *La Critica*, comic opera (Ludwigsburg, 1766; revised as *Il giuoco di picchetto*, Koblenz, 1772; revised as *La conversazione [e] L'accademia di musica*, Salvaterra, 1775); *Vologeso* (Ludwigsburg, Feb. 11, 1766; revised by da Silva, Salvaterra, 1769); *Il matrimonio per concorso*, comic opera (Ludwigsburg, Nov. 4, 1766, not extant; revised by da Silva, Salvaterra, 1770); *Il Cacciatore deluso [ovvero] La Semiramide in bernesco*, serious-comic opera (Tübingen, Nov. 4, 1767; revised by da Silva, Salvaterra, 1771); *La Schiava liberata*, serious-comic opera (Ludwigsburg, Dec. 18, 1768; revised by da Silva, Lisbon, March 31, 1770); *Armida abbandonata* (Naples, May 30, 1770; revised by da Silva, Lisbon, March 31, 1773); *L'amante cacciatore*, intermezzi (Rome, 1771; not extant); *Le avventure di Cleomede*, serious-comic opera (Naples, 1771?; revised by da Silva, Lisbon, June 6, 1772); *Ifigenia in Tauride* (Naples, May 30, 1771; revised by da Silva, Salvaterra, 1776); *Il trionfo di Clelia* (Naples, 1774?); etc. His opera *Fetonte* was publ. in Denkmäler Deutscher Tonkunst, vols. 22–23 (1907).

OTHER STAGE WORKS: *Componimento drammatico* (Rome, Feb. 9, 1747; not extant); *Componimento drammatico* (Ronciglione, Feb. 28, 1751; not extant); *La reggia de' Fati* (with G.B. Sammartini; Milan, March 13, 1753); *La pastorale offerta* (with G.B. Sammartini; Milan, March 19, 1753); *Il giardino incanto* (Stuttgart, 1755; not extant); *L'asilo d'amore* (Stuttgart, Feb. 11, 1758; not extant); *Le Cinesi* (Ludwigsburg, 1765; not extant); *L'unione coronata* (Solitude, Sept. 22, 1768; not extant); *Cerere placata* (Naples, Sept. 14, 1772); etc.; also, serenatas, several secular cantatas and other vocal pieces; he also contributed to a number of pasticcios.

ORATORIOS, PASSIONS, AND SACRED CANTATAS: *Che impetuoso è questo torrente* for 2 Sopranos, Tenor, and Orch. (Naples, 1740); *Isacco figura del Redentore* for 2 Sopranos, Alto, Tenor, Bass, 4-part Chorus, and Orch. (Venice, 1742); *La Betulia liberata* for Soprano, Alto, Tenor, Bass, 4-part Chorus, and Orch. (Venice, 1743); *Gioas* for 3 Sopranos, 3 Altos, 4-part Chorus, and Strings (Venice, 1745); *Juda proditor* for 3 Sopranos, 3 Altos, and Chorus (Venice, 1746?; not extant); *Ove son? Chi mi guida?* for Soprano, Alto, Tenor, and Orch. (Naples, 1747); *La passione di Gesù Cristo* for Soprano, Alto, Tenor, Bass, 4-part Chorus, and Orch. (Rome, 1749); *Giuseppe glorificato in Egitto* for 2 Sopranos, Tenor, and Orch. (Rome, 1749); *Le Spose di Elcana* for 4-part Chorus (Palermo, 1750; not extant); *In questa incolte riva* for 2 Sopranos and Orch. (Rome, May 20, 1751); *Non più: L'atteso istante* for Soprano, Alto, Tenor, and Orch. (Rome, 1752); *Il sacrifizio di Gefte* for 4-part Chorus and Strings (Palermo, 1753; not extant); *La reconciliazione della Virtù e della Gloria* for 2-part Chorus (Pistoia, 1754; not extant); *Gerusalemme convertita* (Palermo, 1755; not extant); *Il sogno di Nabucco* (Palermo, 1755; not extant); etc. Additional sacred works include many masses, as well as graduals, offertories, antiphones, Psalms, motets, hymns, etc. His instrumental works include harpsichord concertos, quartets, divertimenti, and sonatas.

Jonás, Alberto, Spanish-American pianist; b. Madrid, June 8, 1868; d. Philadelphia, Nov. 9, 1943. He received primary music training in Madrid; then studied piano and theory of composition at the Brussels Cons. In 1890 he went to St. Petersburg, Russia, where he had some lessons with Anton Rubinstein. After a brief concert career in Europe, he went to the U.S., where he taught piano at the Univ. of Michigan (1894–98) and the Cons. of Detroit (1898–1904). From 1904 to 1914 he lived in Berlin; after the outbreak of World War I he came back to America, settling in N.Y., where he established a fine reputation as a piano pedagogue. In collaboration with 16 pianists, he publ. *Master School of Modern Piano Playing and Virtuosity* (N.Y., 1922), which went through 5 editions, and also brought out several books of piano exercises for beginners. He wrote a number of attractive piano pieces in a salon manner, among them *Northern Dances, Humoresque, Nocturne,* and *Evening Song.*

Joncières, Victorin de (real name, **Felix Ludger Rossignol**), French composer; b. Paris, April 12, 1839; d. there, Oct. 26, 1903. He was first a student of painting; music was his avocation. At the age of 20 he produced a light opera for a student performance; encouraged by its success with the critics, he began to study music seriously, first with Elwart, then with Leborne at the Paris Cons. He was a great admirer of Wagner, and when Leborne expressed his opposition to Wagner, Joncières impulsively left his class.
WORKS: Operas (all produced in Paris): *Sardanapale* (Feb. 8, 1867); *Le Dernier Jour de Pompei* (Sept. 21, 1869); *Dimitri* (May 5, 1876; his most successful work); *La Reine Berthe* (Dec. 27, 1878); *Le Chevalier Jean* (March 11, 1885; successful in Germany under the title *Johann von Lothringen*); *Lancelot du lac* (Feb. 7, 1900); he further wrote music to *Hamlet* (Nantes, Sept. 21, 1867); *Symphonie romantique* (Paris, March 9, 1873); Violin Concerto (Paris, Dec. 12, 1869); a symph. ode, *La Mer;* etc.

Jones, Daniel, remarkable Welsh composer; b. Pembroke, Dec. 7, 1912. Both his parents were musicians, and he absorbed the natural rudiments of music instinctively at home. He attended the Swansea Univ. College; then entered the Royal Academy of Music in London, where he studied a variety of theoretical and practical aspects of music: composition with Farjeon, conducting with Sir Henry Wood, viola with Lockyear, and French horn with Aubrey Brain; in 1935 he was awarded the Mendelssohn Scholarship; received his M.A. for a thesis on Elizabethan lyric poetry and its relations with music; obtained his D.Mus. at the Univ. of Wales in 1951; received an honorary D.Litt. in 1970. During World War II he served in the British Intelligence Corps; continued his interests in literature and was editor

of the collected poems of Dylan Thomas (1971). An exceptionally prolific composer, he wrote 9 symphs. within 30 years, between 1945 and 1974; several oratorios; 2 operas; much chamber music. In 1936 he promulgated a system of "complex metres," in which the numerator in the time signature indicates the succession of changing meters in a clear numerical progression, e.g. 32-322-3222-322-32, followed by 332-3332, 332, etc.; his other innovation is a category of "continuous modes," with the final note of the mode (non-octaval) serving as the initial note of a transposed mode.
WORKS: Symphs.: No. 1 (1944); No. 2 (1950); No. 3 (1951); No. 4 (1954); No. 5 (1958); No. 6 (1964); No. 7 (1971); No. 8 (1972); No. 9 (1974); operas: *The Knife* (London, Dec. 2, 1963) and *Orestes* (1967); oratorios and cantatas: *The Country beyond the Stars* (1958), *St. Peter* (1962), *The 3 Hermits* (1969), *The Ballad of the Standard-Bearer* (1969), *The Witnesses* (1971); *Capriccio* for Flute, Harp, and Strings (1965); Violin Concerto (1966); Sinfonietta (1972); several concert overtures and symph. suites; a "miscellany" for Small Orch. (1947), etc.; 8 string quartets; 5 string trios; String Quintet; Sonata for Unaccompanied Cello (1946); Sonata for Cello and Piano (1972); Kettledrum Sonata (1947); 8 Pieces for Violin and Viola (1948); Wind Septet (1949); Wind Nonet (1950); Sonata for 4 Trombones (1955); 24 bagatelles for Piano Solo (1943–55); 6 piano sonatas; 3 piano sonatinas. He is the author of numerous articles expounding his philosophy of music, some of them incorporated in a book, *Music and Esthetic* (1954).

Jones, Edward, Welsh musician and writer ("Barrd y Brenin"); b. Llanderfel, Merionethshire, March 29, 1752; d. London, April 18, 1824. He was taught by his father, and the family organized a Welsh ensemble, consisting of harps and string instruments. In 1775 he went to London; in 1783, was appointed Welsh bard to the Prince of Wales. He publ. several anthologies of Welsh music, including *Musical and Poetical Relicks of the Welsh Bards* (1784; 2nd ed., 1794; an additional vol. appeared under the title *The Bardic Museum,* 1802; 3rd vol., 1824; a supplementary vol. was publ. posthumously; the entire work contains 225 Welsh melodies); in addition to these, he publ. collections of melodies by other nations; also *Musical Trifles Calculated for Beginners on the Harp.*

Jones, Geraint, Welsh organist, harpsichordist, and conductor; b. Porth, May 16, 1917. He studied at the Royal Academy of Music in London; made his debut as harpsichordist at the National Gallery in 1940; subsequently gave numerous recitals as an organist, often on historical instruments of Europe; in 1951 he founded the Geraint Jones Singers and Orch., which he led in many performances of Baroque music.

Jones, Gwyneth, Welsh soprano; b. Pontnewyndd, Nov. 7, 1936. She was educated at the Royal College of Music in London; also studied in Siena and Geneva. She started her career in Zürich in 1962. In 1963 she joined the Royal Opera at Covent Garden; subsequently sang in Vienna, Bayreuth, Munich, and at La Scala, Milan. On Nov. 24, 1972, she made her American debut at the Metropolitan Opera in N.Y. as Sieglinde in *Die Walküre.*

Jones, Parry, Welsh operatic tenor; b. Blaina, Monmouthshire, Feb. 14, 1891; d. London, Dec. 26, 1963. He studied in London, in Italy, and in Germany; made his debut in London in 1914. He sang in America; survived the German submarine attack on the S.S. *Lusitania* on his return trip to England. In London he sang with the Beecham and D'Oyly Carte opera companies, with the Carl Rosa Opera Co. (1919–22), and with the British National Opera Co. (1922–28). He first sang at Covent Garden in 1920–21; then again in 1925–26, 1930–32, 1935, and 1937. In 1949 he became a principal tenor at Covent Garden and remained on its roster until 1955. Subsequently, he taught voice at the Guildhall School of Music.

Jones, Philip, outstanding English trumpet player; b. Bath, March 12, 1928. He studied at the Royal College of Music in London with Ernest Hall; then served as principal trumpet player in the Royal Phil. (1956–60), Philharmonia Orch. (1960–64), London Phil. (1964–65), New Philharmonia (1965–67), and BBC Symph. (1968–71). In 1957 he founded the Philip Jones Brass Ensemble; he commissioned many composers to write works for his ensemble. He was made an Officer of the Order of the British Empire in 1977.

Jones, Sidney, English composer of light music; b. London, June 17, 1861; d. there, Jan. 29, 1946. At an early age he became conductor of a military band; then toured the English provinces and Australia as conductor of various light opera companies; in 1905 he was appointed conductor at the London Empire Theatre. He owes his fame mainly to his enormously successful operetta *Geisha* (London, April 25, 1896), which was for decades performed all over the world. His other operettas are: *The Gayety Girl* (London, 1893); *An Artist's Model* (London, 1895); *A Greek's Slave* (Vienna, 1899); *San Toy* (Vienna, 1899); *My Lady Molly* (London, 1903); *The Medal and the Maid* (London, 1903); *See See* (London, 1906); *The King of Cadonia* (London, 1908); *The Persian Princess* (London, 1909); *Spring Maid* (London, 1911); *The Girl from Utah* (London, 1913); *The Happy Day* (London, 1916).

Jones, Sissieretta (real name, **Matilda S. Joyner**), black American soprano, known as "the Black Patti" (with reference to Adelina Patti); b. Portsmouth, Va., Jan. 5, 1868; d. Providence, R.I., June 24, 1933. She studied voice at the New England Conservatory of Music; began singing professionally in 1888. Her first success was in 1892 at a Cakewalk Jubilee held in Madison Square Garden in N.Y.; afterward she gave recitals at the Academy of Music; the Metropolitan Opera considered her for African roles in *Aida* and *L'Africaine,* but racial attitudes and conservative management policies would not permit

such parts to be taken by Afro-Americans. She subsequently toured the U.S., including a command performance before President Harrison at the White House. From 1893 to 1910 she led the Black Patti's Troubadours, with which she toured and sang operatic arias.

Jones, "Spike" (Lindley Armstrong), American bandleader; b. Long Beach, Calif., Dec. 14, 1911; d. Los Angeles, May 1, 1965. He played drums as a boy; then led a school band. On July 30, 1942, he made a recording of a satirical song, *Der Führer's Face,* featuring a Bronx-cheer razzer; toured the U.S. with his band, The City Slickers, which included a washboard, a Smith and Wesson pistol, anti-bug Flit guns in E-flat, doorbells, anvils, hammers to break glass, and a live goat trained to bleat rhythmically. Climactically, he introduced the Latrinophone (a toilet seat strung with catgut). With this ensemble, he launched a Musical Depreciation Revue. He retired in 1963, when the wave of extravaganza that had carried him to the crest of commercial success subsided.

Jones, Thad(deus Joseph), black American jazz trumpeter, cornetist, and bandleader; b. Pontiac, Mich., March 28, 1923. While still in school, he formed a jazz combo with his brothers; then served in the U.S. Army (1943–46); resuming his career, he was a featured member of Count Basie's orch. from 1954 to 1963. In 1965 he formed a band with Mel Lewis, which subsequently gained fame through its many tours of the U.S. and Europe, including a visit to the Soviet Union in 1972.

Jongen, (Marie-Alphonse-Nicolas-) Joseph, eminent Belgian composer; brother of **Léon Jongen;** b. Liège, Dec. 14, 1873; d. Sart-lez-Spa, July 12, 1953. He studied at the Liège Cons.; received a premier prix for each of the academic subjects and also for piano and organ. In 1891 he joined the staff of the Liège Cons. as a teacher of harmony and counterpoint. In 1894 he gained attention as a composer when he won 2 national prizes; in 1897 he won the Belgian Prix de Rome. He then went abroad; received advice from Richard Strauss in Berlin and Vincent d'Indy in Paris. After returning to Brussels, he taught at a music academy; from 1898, also held the position of *professeur adjoint* at the Liège Cons., where he became a prof. in 1911. After the outbreak of the war in 1914, he went to London; made appearances as a pianist and organist there, and with Defauw, Tertis, and Doehaerd, organized a piano quartet which became known as the Belgian Quartet. In 1919 he returned to Belgium; in 1920 he became a prof. of counterpoint and fugue at the Brussels Cons.; from 1925–39 he was its director; was succeeded by his brother, Léon. During World War II, he lived in France; then returned to his country estate at Sart-lez-Spa, where he remained until his death. He was a prolific composer and continued to write music to the end of his life; the total of his works aggregates to 137 opus numbers. While not pursuing extreme modern effects, Jongen suc-

ceeded in imparting an original touch to his harmonic style.
WORKS: FOR ORCH.: Symph. (1899); Violin Concerto (1899); Cello Concerto (1900); *Fantasie sur deux Noëls populaires wallons* (1902); *Lalla-Roukh,* symph. poem after Thomas Moore (1904); *Prélude et Danse* (1907); *2 Rondes wallones* (1912; also for Piano); Trumpet Concertino (1913); *Impressions d'Ardennes* (1913); Suite for Violin and Orch. (1915); *Epithalame et Scherzo* for 3 Violins, and Orch. or Piano (1917); *Tableaux pittoresques* (1917); *Poème héroïque* for Violin and Orch. (1919); *Prélude élégiaque et Scherzo* (1920); *Fantasie rhapsodique* for Cello and Orch. (1924); *Hymne* for Organ and Strings (1924); *Symphonie concertante* for Organ and Orch. (1926), his finest work, popularized by the organist Virgil Fox in his appearances with American orchs.; *Pièce symphonique* for Piano and Orch. (1928); *Passacaille et Gigue* (1929); *Suite No. 3, dans le style ancien* (1930); *10 Pièces* (1932); *Triptyque* (1935); *Ouverture Fanfare* (1939); *Alleluia* for Organ and Orch. (1940); *Ouverture de fête* (1941); Piano Concerto (1943); *Bourrée* (1944); Harp Concerto (1944); Mass for Organ, Chorus, and Orch. (1946); *In memoriam* (1947); *Ballade, Hommage à Chopin* (1949); *3 Mouvements symphoniques* (1951). CHAMBER MUSIC: 3 string quartets (1893, 1916, 1921); Piano Trio (1897); Piano Quartet (1901); 2 violin sonatas (1902, 1909); Trio for Piano, Violin, and Viola (1907); Cello Sonata (1912); *2 Serenades* for String Quartet (1918); *2 Pièces* for Flute, Cello, and Harp (1924); *2 Pièces* for 4 Cellos (1929); *Sonata eroica* for Organ (1930); Wind Quintet (1933); Quintet for Harp, Flute, Violin, Viola, and Cello (1940); Concerto for Wind Quintet (1942); Quartet for 4 Saxophones (1942); String Trio (1948); a number of piano pieces, including 24 preludes in all keys (1941); solo pieces for various instruments with piano; many songs with instrumental accompaniment; choral works.

Jongen, Léon, important Belgian composer, brother of **Joseph Jongen;** b. Liège, March 2, 1884; d. Brussels, Nov. 18, 1969. He studied organ and served as a church organist in Liège; received the Belgian Grand Prix de Rome for his cantata *Les Fiancés de Noël* (1913); was in the Belgian army during World War I; after the war traveled to the Far East and became the first conductor of the Opéra Français in Hanoi. Returning to Belgium in 1934, he became an instructor at the Brussels Cons.; from 1939 to 1949 was successor to his brother as its director.
WORKS: Operas: *L'Ardennaise* (1909) and *Thomas l'Agnelet* (1922-23; Brussels, Feb. 14, 1924); musical fairy tale, *Le Rêve d'une nuit de Noël* (1917; Paris, March 18, 1918); ballet, *Le Masque de la Mort rouge,* after Poe (1956). Also 2 lyric scenes for Chorus and Orch.: *Geneviève de Brabant* (1907) and *La Légende de St. Hubert* (1909; first public perf., St. Hubert, July 21, 1968); *Campéador* for Orch. (1932); *Malaisie,* suite for Orch. (1935); *In Memoriam Regis* for Orch. (1935); *Prélude, Divertissement et Final* for Piano and Orch. (1937); *Trilogie de Psaumes* for Chorus and Orch. (1937–39); *Rhapsodia belgica* for Violin and Orch. (1948); *Musique for a Ballet*

(1954); *Divertissement en forme de variations sur un thème de Haydn* for Orch. (1956); Violin Concerto (1962; compulsory work for the 12 finalists of the 1963 Queen Elisabeth violin contest held in Brussels). He further wrote a String Quartet (1919); Fantasia for Piano (1930); *Divertissement* for 4 Saxophones (1937); Trio for Oboe, Clarinet, and Bassoon (1937); Trio for Flute, Violin, and Viola (1937); Piano Quartet (1955); Quintet for Piano, Flute, Clarinet, Horn, and Bassoon (1958); songs.

Joplin, Scott, black American pianist and composer; b. Texarkana, Nov. 24, 1868; d. New York, April 1, 1917. He learned to play the piano at home, and later studied music seriously with a local German musician. He left home at 17 and went to St. Louis, earning his living by playing piano in local emporia. In 1893 he moved to Chicago (drawn by the prospect of music-making and other gaiety of the World's Fair), and in the following year went to Sedalia, Mo., where he took music courses at George Smith College, a segregated school for blacks. His first music publications were in 1895, of genteel, maudlin songs and marches, typical of the period. His success as a ragtime composer came with the *Maple Leaf Rag* (1899; the most famous of all piano rags), which he named after a local dance hall, the Maple Leaf Club. The sheet-music edition sold so well that Joplin was able to settle in St. Louis and devote himself exclusively to composition; he even tried to write a ragtime ballet (*The Ragtime Dance,* 1902) and a ragtime opera, *A Guest of Honor* (copyright 1903, but the music is lost; newspaper notices indicate it was probably perf. by the Scott Joplin Opera Co. in 1903). In 1907 he went to N.Y., where he continued his career as a composer and teacher. Still intent on ambitious plans, he wrote an opera, *Treemonisha,* to his own libretto (the title deals with a black baby girl found under a tree by a woman named Monisha); he completed the score in 1911 and produced it in concert form in 1915 without any success. Interest in the opera was revived almost 60 years later; T.J. Anderson orchestrated it from the piano score, and it received its first complete performance at the Atlanta Symph. Hall on Jan. 28, 1972. Despite Joplin's ambitious attempts to make ragtime "respectable" by applying its principles to European forms, it was with the small, indigenous dance form of the piano rag that he achieved his greatest artistic success. As one noted historian phrased it, these pieces are "the precise American equivalent, in terms of a native dance music, of minuets by Mozart, mazurkas by Chopin, or waltzes by Brahms." Altogether, he wrote about 50 piano rags, in addition to the 2 operas, and a few songs, waltzes, and marches. The titles of some of these rags reflect his desire to transcend the trivial and create music on a more serious plane: *Sycamore,* "A Concert Rag" (1904); *Chrysanthemum,* "An Afro-American Intermezzo" (1904); *Sugar Cane,* "A Ragtime Classic 2 Step" (1908); *Fig Leaf Rag,* "A High Class Rag" (1908); *Reflection Rag,* "Syncopated Musings" (1917). In his last years he lamented at having failed to achieve the recognition he felt his music merited. Suffering from syphilis, he became insane and died shortly afterward in a state hospital. More than 50 years later, in the early 1970s, an extraordinary sequence of events—new recordings of his music and its use in an award-winning film, *The Sting* (1974)—brought Joplin unprecedented popularity and acclaim: among pop recordings, *The Entertainer* (1902) was one of the best-selling discs for 1974; among classical recordings, Joplin albums represented 74 percent of the best sellers of the year. In 1976 he was awarded exceptional posthumous recognition by the Pulitzer Prize Committee. Among the numerous collections of his music, the best is the 2-vol. set, facsimiles of the original eds., issued by the N.Y. Public Library, *The Collected Works of Scott Joplin*, ed. by Vera Brodsky Lawrence (N.Y., 1971; lacks 3 rags, for which reprint permission was denied, and 2 song collaborations, discovered subsequent to publication).

Jora, Mihail, Rumanian composer; b. Roman, Aug. 14, 1891; d. Bucharest, May 10, 1971. He studied piano privately in Iaşi (1901–12) and theory at the Cons. there (1909–11); then went to Germany, where he became a student of Max Reger at the Leipzig Cons. (1912–14); after World War I he went to Paris, where he studied with Florent Schmitt (1919–20). Returning to Rumania, he held the professorship in composition at the Bucharest Cons. (1929–62). He was a founding member of the Society of Rumanian Composers in 1920, and was consultant to the Bucharest Opera (1931–45). He was also a music critic.

Jordá, Enrique, Spanish conductor; b. San Sebastian, March 24, 1911. He was a chorister in the parochial school and played organ at his parish church in Madrid; in 1929 he went to Paris as a medical student, but then turned decidedly to music, studying organ with Marcel Dupré, composition with Paul Le Flem, and conducting with Frans Rühlmann. He made his debut as an orch. conductor in Paris in 1938; then became the regular conductor of the Madrid Symph. Orch.; subsequently was principal conductor of the Cape Town Symph. Orch. in South Africa (1947–51). From 1954 to 1963 he was conductor of the San Francisco Symph. Orch.; in 1970 he became conductor of the Phil. Orch. at Antwerp, Belgium, remaining there until 1976. He publ. a popular book, *El director de orquesta ante la partitura* (Madrid, 1969).

Jordan, Jules, American singer and composer; b. Willimantic, Conn., Nov. 10, 1850; d. Providence, R.I., March 5, 1927. He moved to Providence in 1870 and established himself as a singer, choral conductor, and teacher; for 40 years (1880–1920), conducted the Arion Club (250 voices). He was a successful composer of school operettas (*The Alphabet, Cloud and Sunshine*, etc.); wrote 6 light operas: *Star of the Sea; An Eventful Holiday; The Buccaneers; Princess of the Blood; Her Crown of Glory; A Leap Year Furlough;* the vaudeville sketches *Cobbler or King* and *Managerial Tactics;* etc. His romantic comedy opera, *Rip Van Winkle*, was produced at the Providence Opera House (May 25, 1897); another opera, *Nisiea*, remained unperformed. He wrote his own librettos for his stage works as well as for his cantatas *The Night Service, Barbara Fritchie*, etc.

Jordan, Sverre, Norwegian composer; b. Bergen, May 25, 1889; d. there, Jan. 10, 1972. He studied piano; then traveled to Germany, where he took courses in piano and composition in Berlin with Ansorge and Klatte (1907–14). In 1914 he returned to Bergen; was active as music director of the National Theater (1932–57). In his works he made liberal use of national folk songs, which met the tastes of the general public. Typical of these nationally oriented works are *Suite in Old Style* for Small Orch. (1911); *Norvegiani* for Orch. (1921); *Smeden (The Smith)* for Baritone, Chorus, and Orch. (1924); *Norge i vare hjerter*, cantata for the opening of the Bergen Exhibition (1928); *Suite on Norwegian Folk Tunes and Dances* for Orch. (1936); *Holberg-silhuetter* for Orch. (1938); *Norwegian Rhapsody* for Orch. (1950); *Suite in Old Style on Holberg Themes* for Orch. (1954); *Concerto romantico* for Horn and Orch. (1956); and *Kongen (The King)*, orch. melodrama with narration and choral finale (1957). Other works are a Piano Concerto (1945); Cello Concerto (1947); *Concerto piccolo* for Piano and Orch. (1963); Violin Concerto (1966); 2 violin sonatas (1917, 1943); Flute Sonatina (1955); 2 piano trios (1958, 1963); Piano Sonata (1963); incidental music for many plays; over 200 songs, often with orch. accompaniment.

Jørgensen, Erik, Danish composer; b. Copenhagen, May 10, 1912. He studied theory of music with Knud Jeppesen in Copenhagen (1928–31); then took private lessons with Finn Høffding; in 1936 he took conducting courses with Scherchen in Geneva. He evolved an individual idiom of composition, marked by an abundance of asymmetrical rhythmic configurations in the neo-Baroque manner; he later experimented with dodecaphony; eventually adopted a technique of "controlled coincidences."

Joseffy, Rafael, eminent Hungarian-American pianist and teacher; b. Hunfalu, July 3, 1852; d. New York, June 25, 1915. At the age of 8 he began to study piano with a local teacher at Miskolcz, and later at Budapest. In 1866 he entered the Leipzig Cons., where his principal teacher was E.F. Wenzel, though he also had some lessons with Moscheles. From 1868 to 1870 he studied with Karl Tausig in Berlin, and the summers of 1870 and 1871 he spent with Liszt in Weimar. He made his debut at Berlin in 1870; his excellent technique and tonal variety elicited much praise; his career was then securely launched. He made his American debut in 1879, playing at a symph. concert of Leopold Damrosch in N.Y., where he settled permanently; he taught at the National Cons. from 1888 till 1906. In America he gained appreciation both as a virtuoso and as a musician of fine interpretative qualities; his programs featured many works of Brahms at a time when Brahms was not yet recognized in America as a great master. As a pedagogue, Joseffy was eminently successful; many American concert pianists were his pupils. He brought out an authoritative edition of Chopin's works in 15 vols. (with critico-historical annotations by Huneker); also ed. studies by Czerny, Henselt, Moscheles, Schumann, and others. His *School of Advanced Piano Playing* (1902; in German as *Meisterschule des Klavierspiels*) is a valuable practical method. Joseffy was also a composer; he publ. a number of characteristic piano pieces (*Die Mühle, Romance sans paroles, Souvenir d'Amérique, Mazurka-Fantasie, Spinnlied,* etc.) and arrangements of works by Schumann, Bach, Boccherini, Gluck, and Delibes.

Josephs, Wilfred, English composer; b. Newcastle upon Tyne, July 24, 1927. He studied harmony and dentistry; gained a degree in dental surgery in 1951, and was a military orthodontist in the British army. In 1954 he entered the Guildhall School of Music in London, where he studied with Alfred Nieman; then went to Paris, where he took private lessons with Max Deutsch (1958–59). About that time he turned passionately toward the ideals of his ancestral Judaism; in memory of Jews who perished during World War II, he wrote a Requiem, to the text of the Hebrew prayer, Kaddish, containing 9 slow sections and a single faster movement; it won first prize at the International Competition of La Scala in Milan in 1963. In his instrumental music he adopted the dodecaphonic method of composition without doctrinaire adherence to the idiom; he described his music as "atonal with tonal implications." A highly prolific composer, he wrote music of all genres.
WORKS: FOR THE STAGE: Opera-entertainment, *Pathelin* (1963); television opera, *The Appointment* (1968); children's opera, *Through the Looking Glass and What Alice Found There* (1977–78); 3-act opera, *Rebecca* (1982–83); 3 ballets: *The Magic Being* (1961); *La Répétition de Phèdre* (1964–65); *Equus* (1978; produced in Baltimore, March 21, 1979); children's musical, *The King of the Coast* (1967); *A Child of the Universe* for Narrator, Soloists, Actors, Dancers, Mimes, Ballet, Choruses, Band, and Orch. (1971).
FOR ORCH.: *The Ants,* comedy overture (1955); 9 symphs.: No. 1 (1955; revised 1957–58 and 1974–75); No. 2 (1963–64); No. 3, *Philadelphia,* for Chamber Orch. (1967); No. 4 (1967–70); No. 5, *Pastoral* (1970–71); No. 6, with Solo Singer and Chorus (1972–74); No. 7, *Winter,* for Chamber Orch. (1976); No. 8, *The 4 Elements,* for Symph. Band (1975–77); No. 9, *Sinfonia Concertante,* for Chamber Orch. (1979–80); *Elegy* for Strings (1957); *Concerto da Camera*·for Solo Piano, Solo Violin, and Chamber Orch. (1959); *A Tyneside Overture* (1960); *Meditatio de Boernmundo* for Viola and Orch. (1960–61); *Cantus Natalis,* cello concerto (1961–62); *Aelian Dances,* 5 dances based on Newcastle tunes (1961); *Monkchester Dances,* 6 dances based on Newcastle tunes (1965); Piano Concerto No. 1 (1965); *Canzonas on a Theme of Rameau* for Strings (1965); Concerto for Light Orch. (1966); *Polemic* for Strings (1967); *Rail,*

symph. picture (1967); Oboe Concerto (1967–68); *Serenade* for Chamber Orch. (1968); *Variations on a Theme of Beethoven* (1969); Double Violin Concerto (1969); Piano Concerto No. 2 (1971); *Saratoga Concerto,* triple concerto for Guitar, Harp, Harpsichord, and Chamber Orch. (1972); *The 4 Horsemen of the Apocalypse,* overture (1973–74); Concerto for Brass Band (1974); Clarinet Concerto (1975); *Eve (d'après Rodin),* symph. poem (1977–78); *Divertimento* for 2 Oboes, 2 Horns, and Strings (1979); *Concerto d'Amore* for 2 Violins and Orch. (1979); Double-bass Concerto (1980); *The Brontës,* overture (1981); *High Spirits,* overture (1981–82); Percussion Concerto (1982); Concerto for Viola and Chamber Orch. (1983).

Josten, Werner, American composer; b. Elberfeld, Germany, June 12, 1885; d. New York, Feb. 6, 1963. He studied music theory in Munich; then took courses with Jaques-Dalcroze in Geneva; he lived in Paris from 1912 to 1914; at the outbreak of World War I, he returned to Germany; in 1918 was appointed assistant conductor at the Munich Opera. In 1920 he went to the U.S. and appeared as composer-accompanist with several singers; in 1933 he became an American citizen. He taught at Smith College in Northampton, Mass., from 1923 to 1949; also conducted the Smith College Orch., with which he presented performances of works by Monteverdi and Handel. His own compositions are couched in the lyrical manner of German Romantic music, with a strong undercurrent of euphonious counterpoint within the network of luscious harmonies. During his American period, he became interested in exotic art, and introduced impressionistic devices in his works.

Joubert, John, significant South African composer; b. Cape Town, March 20, 1927. After preliminary studies in South Africa, he traveled to Great Britain with a Performing Right Scholarship in 1946 and took music courses with Howard Ferguson at the Royal Academy of Music in London (1946–50). He was a lecturer in music at the Univ. of Hull (1950–62); then at the Univ. of Birmingham. In his music he cultivates the pragmatic goal of pleasurability, wherein harmony and counterpoint serve the functional role of support for a flowing melody; in several works he makes use of primitive elements derived from Hottentot rites, transmuting the primitive vocalizations into modern polytonal and polyrhythmic formations. His carols *Torches* and *There Is No Rose* enjoy wide popularity.
WORKS: FOR THE STAGE: *Antigone,* radio opera (BBC, London, July 21, 1954); *In the Drought,* chamber opera (Johannesburg, Oct. 20, 1956); *Silas Marner,* after the novel by George Eliot (Cape Town, May 20, 1961); *The Quarry,* opera for young people (Wembley, March 26, 1965); *Under Western Eyes,* after the novel by Joseph Conrad (Camden, England, May 29, 1969); *The Prisoner,* opera for schools (Barnet, March 14, 1973); *Legend of Princess Vlei,* ballet (Cape Town, Feb. 21, 1952). CANTATAS: *The Burghers of Calais* (1954); *Leaves of Life* (1963);

Urbs beata (first perf. at St. George's Cathedral, Cape Town, Nov. 26, 1963); *The Choir Invisible* (Halifax, May 18, 1968); *The Martyrdom of St. Alban* (London, June 7, 1969); *The Raising of Lazarus* (Birmingham, Sept. 30, 1971). VARIOUS CHORAL WORKS: *Pro Pace,* cycle of 3 motets for Unaccompanied Chorus (1960); *The Holy Mountain,* canticle for Chorus and 2 Pianos (1963); numerous sacred works, anthems, and carols, including *Torches, There Is No Rose, Great Lord of Lords, Welcome Yule, Christ Is Risen, The Beatitudes, Te Deum;* secular part-songs, among them *The God Pan* and *Sweet Content;* also *African Sketchbook (Hottentot Animal Songs)* for Vocal Quartet and Wind Instruments (1970); *3 Hymns to St. Oswald* for Vocal Quartet and Organ (1972); *Crabbed Age and Youth* for Countertenor and Ensemble (London, Nov. 9, 1974); *The Magus* for Soloists, Chorus, and Orch. (Sheffield, Oct. 29, 1977); *Herefordshire Canticles* for Soprano, Baritone, Chorus, and Orch. (Hereford, Aug. 23, 1979); *The Turning Wheel* for Soprano and Piano (Ounedin, New Zealand, Oct. 1, 1980). FOR ORCH.: Overture (Cheltenham Festival, June 12, 1953); *Symphonic Prelude* (Durban Centenary Festival, May 15, 1954); Violin Concerto (York, June 17, 1954); Symph. No. 1 (Hull, April 12, 1956); *North Country Overture* (1958); Piano Concerto (Manchester, Jan. 11, 1959); Sinfonietta for Chamber Orch. (1962); *In Memoriam, 1820* (1962); Symph. No. 2 (London, March 24, 1971, composer conducting); Concerto for Bassoon and Chamber Orch. (1974); *Deploration* for Chamber Orch. (Birmingham, Dec. 28, 1978). CHAMBER MUSIC: String Quartet No. 1 (1950); *Miniature String Quartet* (1953); Viola Sonata (1952); String Trio (1958); Octet for Clarinet, Bassoon, Horn, String Quartet, and Double Bass (1960); *Sonata a cinque* for Recorder, 2 Violins, Cello, and Harpsichord (1963); 2 piano sonatas (1956, 1971); Duo for Violin and Cello (1971); *Kontakion* for Cello and Piano (1974); *Threnos* for Harpsichord and Strings (1974); String Quartet No. 2 (1977); organ pieces; songs.

Juch, Emma (Antonia Joanna), American operatic soprano; b. Vienna, July 4, 1863 (of American parents); d. New York, March 6, 1939. She was brought to the U.S. at the age of 4, and studied in N.Y. with Murio Celli; made her debut in the old Chickering Hall in 1881; made her stage debut in London (June, 1881); sang 3 seasons under Mapleson's management in England and in the U.S.; in 1886–87 she was principal soprano of the American Opera Co., and with the National Opera Co. (1887–88); in 1889 she organized the Emma Juch Grand Opera Co., which presented opera in the U.S. and Mexico (until 1891); after that, she confined herself chiefly to concert appearances. On June 26, 1894, she married District Attorney Francis L. Wellman, but they were divorced in 1911.

Judge, Jack, English composer of popular songs; b. 1878; d. West Bromwich, July 28, 1938. His song *It's a long, long way to Tipperary,* written in 1912, attained enormous popularity in England and else-

where as a wartime song during World War I.

Judson, Arthur, American concert manager; b. Dayton, Ohio, Feb. 17, 1881; d. Rye, N.Y., Jan. 28, 1975. He took violin lessons with Max Bendix; played in orchs., and himself conducted summer resort orchs. In 1900 he was appointed dean of the Cons. of Music of Denison Univ., Granville, Ohio. In 1907 he was in N.Y.; was connected with the editorial and advertising depts. of *Musical America.* From 1915 to 1935 he was manager of the Philadelphia Orch.; in 1922 he was appointed manager of the N.Y. Phil. Orch., and held this position for 34 years, resigning in 1956. In 1928 his concert management took over the Wolfsohn Musical Bureau; in 1930, these organizations merged into the Columbia Concerts Corp., with Judson as president.

Juilliard, Augustus D., American music patron; b. at sea, during his parents' voyage on a sailing vessel from Burgundy to America, April 19, 1836; d. New York, April 25, 1919. He was a prominent industrialist; left the residue of his estate for the creation of the Juilliard Musical Foundation (established in 1920). The objects of his foundation are to aid worthy students of music in securing a complete musical education, and to arrange and give concerts for the education of the general public in the musical arts. The Juilliard School of Music was founded and has been maintained by the foundation.

Jullien, Louis Antoine, French conductor; b. Sisteron, April 23, 1812; d. Paris, March 14, 1860. The son of a bandmaster, he went to Paris in 1833 and studied composition with Le Carpentier and Halévy, but could not maintain the discipline of learning music, and began to compose light dances instead; of these, the waltz *Rosita* attained enormous, though transitory, popularity in Paris. He left the Cons. in 1836 without taking a degree, and became engaged as conductor of dance music at the Jardin Turc. He also attempted to launch a musical journal, but an accumulation of carelessly contracted debts compelled him to leave France (1838). He went to London, where he conducted summer concerts at the Drury Lane Theatre (1840) and winter concerts with an enlarged ensemble of instrumentalists and singers (1841). He then opened a series of "society concerts," at which he presented large choral works, such as Rossini's *Stabat Mater,* as well as movements from Beethoven's symphs. In 1847 he engaged Berlioz to conduct at the Drury Lane Theatre, which he had leased. He became insolvent in 1848, but attempted to recoup his fortune by organizing a "concert monstre" with 400 players, 3 choruses, and 3 military bands. He succeeded in giving 3 such concerts in London in 1849. He then essayed the composition of an opera, *Pietro il Grande,* which he produced at his own expense at Covent Garden, on Aug. 17, 1852. He used the pseudonym **Roch Albert** for his spectacular pieces, such as *Destruction of Pompeii;* publ. some dance music (*Royal Irish Quadrille,* etc.) under his own name. In 1853 he was engaged by P.T. Barnum for a series of concerts in the U.S. For his exhibition at the Crystal Palace in N.Y. (June 15, 1854), attended by a great crowd, he staged a simulated conflagration for his *Fireman's Quadrille.* Despite his eccentricities, however, Jullien possessed a true interest in musical progress. At his American concerts he made a point of including several works by American composers: *Santa Claus Symphony* by William Henry Fry and some chamber music by George Frederick Bristow. In 1854 he returned to London; his managerial ventures resulted in another failure. In 1859 he went to Paris, but was promptly arrested for debt, and spent several weeks in prison. He died a few months later in an insane asylum to which he had been confined.

Jurgenson, Pyotr, Russian music publisher; b. Reval, July 17, 1836; d. Moscow, Jan. 2, 1904. The youngest son of indigent parents, he learned the music trade with M. Bernard, owner of a music store in St. Petersburg; Jurgenson served in 3 other music-selling houses there, before opening a business of his own in 1861, in Moscow. With a small investment, he gradually expanded his firm until it became one of the largest in Russia. Through Nicolai Rubinstein he met the leading musicians of Russia, and had enough shrewdness of judgment to undertake the publication of works of Tchaikovsky, beginning with his op. 1. He became Tchaikovsky's close friend, and, while making a handsome profit out of Tchaikovsky's music, he demonstrated a generous regard for Tchaikovsky's welfare; he publ. full scores of Tchaikovsky's symphs. and operas, as well as his songs and piano works. His voluminous correspondence with Tchaikovsky, from 1877 to Tchaikovsky's death, was publ. in 2 vols. in Moscow (1938 and 1952). Jurgenson also publ. many works by other Russian composers; issued vocal scores of Glin-

ka's operas; also publ. the first Russian eds. of the collected works of Chopin, Schumann, and Mendelssohn, and the scores of Wagner's operas. His catalogue contained some 20,000 numbers. After his death, his son **Boris Jurgenson** succeeded to the business; it was nationalized after the Russian Revolution.

Jurinac, Sena, famous Yugoslav soprano; b. Travnik, Oct. 24, 1921. Her father was a Croatian physician; her mother was Viennese. She studied in Zagreb; made her formal debut there as Mimi in *La Bohème;* for her professional appearances she changed her original Slavic first name, **Srebrenka** (literally, the Silver One), to a more mellifluous Sena. She made her debut with the Vienna State Opera on May 1, 1945; subsequently sang in Salzburg, Edinburgh, Glyndebourne, Florence, London, at La Scala in Milan, and at the Teatro Colón in Buenos Aires. She made her American debut with the San Francisco Opera in 1959. In 1953 she married the singer **Sesto Bruscantini.**

Jyrkiäinen, Reijo, Finnish composer; b. Suistamo, April 6, 1934. He studied composition with Nils-Eric Fougstedt and Joonas Kokkonen at the Sibelius Academy in Helsinki (1956–63), and theory at the Univ. of Helsinki (1958–63); later attended modern-music courses at Darmstadt (1962–63) and the electronic sessions at the Bilthoven Radio Studio in the Netherlands (1963). From 1957 to 1966 he was librarian of music recordings at the Finnish Broadcasting Co.; then taught at the Sibelius Academy (1966–67). In 1972 he became managing director of the Helsinki Phil. Orch. In his own works, he has pursued advanced experimentation, ranging from classical Schoenbergian dodecaphony to electronics.

K

Kabalevsky, Dmitri, noted Russian composer; b. St. Petersburg, Dec. 30, 1904. When he was 14 years old, his family moved to Moscow; there he received his primary musical education at the Scriabin Music School (1919–25); also studied music theory privately with Gregory Catoire; in 1925 he entered the Moscow Cons. as a student of Miaskovsky in composition and Goldenweiser in piano; in 1932 he was appointed instructor in composition there; in 1939 became a full prof. As a pedagogue, he developed effective methods of musical education; in 1962 he was elected head of the Commission of Musical Esthetic Education of Children; in 1969 became president of the Scientific Council of Educational Esthetics in the Academy of Pedagogical Sciences of the U.S.S.R.; in 1972 he received the honorary degree of president of the International Society of Musical Education. As a pianist, composer, and conductor, he made guest appearances in Europe and America. Kabalevsky's music represents a paradigm of the Russian school of composition in its Soviet period; his melodic writing is marked by broad diatonic lines invigorated by an energetic rhythmic pulse; while adhering to basic tonality, his harmony is apt to be rich in euphonious dissonances. A prolific composer, he writes in all musical genres; in his operas he successfully reflects both the lyrical and the dramatic aspects of the librettos, several of which are based on Soviet subjects faithful to the tenets of socialist realism. His instrumental writing is functional, taking into consideration the idiomatic capacities of the instruments.

WORKS: OPERAS: *Colas Breugnon,* after Romain Rolland (Leningrad, Feb. 22, 1938); *At Moscow* (Moscow, Nov. 28, 1943; revised and produced under the title *In the Fire* in Moscow, Nov. 7, 1947); *The Family of Taras* (Leningrad, Nov. 7, 1950); *Nikita Vershinin* (Moscow, Nov. 26, 1955); *The Sisters* (1969). FOR ORCH.: 4 symphs.: No. 1 (Moscow, Nov. 9, 1932); No. 2 (Moscow, Dec. 25, 1934); No. 3, subtitled *Requiem for Lenin,* with a choral ending (Moscow, Jan. 21, 1934); No. 4 (Moscow, Oct. 17, 1956); *The Comedians,* orch. suite, from incidental music to a play (1940); *Spring,* symph. poem (1960); *Pathetic Overture* (1960); 3 piano concertos: No. 1 (Moscow, Dec. 11, 1931, composer soloist); No. 2 (Moscow, May 12, 1936); No. 3 (Moscow, Feb. 1, 1953, composer conducting; Vladimir Ashkenazy, soloist); Violin Concerto (Leningrad, Oct. 29, 1948); 2 cello concertos: No. 1 (Moscow, March 15, 1949) and No. 2 (1964). CHAMBER MUSIC: 2 string quartets (1928, 1945); *20 Simple Pieces* for Violin and Piano (1965). FOR PIANO: 3 piano sonatas (1928, 1945, 1946); 24 preludes

(1943); many other piano pieces, including 30 children's pieces (1938); 24 *Simple Pieces* for children (1944). VOCAL WORKS: 7 *Merry Songs* for Voice and Piano (1945); numerous school songs and choruses; *Requiem* for Voices and Orch. (Moscow, Feb. 9, 1963); oratorio, *A Letter to the 30th Century* (1970); also incidental music for plays; film scores.

Kabasta, Oswald, Austrian conductor; b. Mistelbach, Dec. 29, 1896; d. (suicide) Kufstein, Austria, Feb. 6, 1946. He studied at the Vienna Academy of Music and in Klosterneuburg; was a choir director in Florisdorf, and a teacher of singing in Viennese high schools. In 1924 he was appointed music director to the Municipal Theater of Baden near Vienna; in 1926, conductor of opera and concert in Graz and guest conductor of the Gesellschaft der Musikfreunde in Vienna; in 1931–37 was music director of the Austrian Radio. In 1935 he was appointed director of the Gesellschaft der Musikfreunde. As conductor of the Vienna Radio Orch., he toured with it in London (1936), Berlin, Warsaw, Budapest, Amsterdam, etc. He was conductor of the Bruckner Festivals in Linz in 1936 and 1937; in 1938 he succeeded Von Hausegger as conductor of the Munich Phil. Having compromised himself by a close association with the Austrian Nazis, he committed suicide a few months after the conclusion of World War II.

Kabeláč, Miloslav, Czech composer; b. Prague, Aug. 1, 1908; d. there, Sept. 17, 1979. He studied composition with K.B. Jirák and conducting with Pavel Dědeček at the Prague Cons. (1928–31); also took piano lessons with Vilém Kurz there (1931–34). He then served as conductor and music director at the Czech Radio in Prague (1932–39, 1945–54); taught composition at the Prague Cons. from 1958 to 1962. From 1968 to 1970 he lectured on electronic music at the Czech Radio in Plzeň. In his music he followed a fairly advanced modern idiom, occasionally applying dodecaphonic devices, but hewing close to the fundamentals of tonality.

Kadosa, Pál, talented Hungarian composer and pianist; b. Léva (now Levice, Czechoslovakia), Sept. 6, 1903; d. Budapest, March 30, 1983. He studied piano with Arnold Székely and composition with Kodály at the Budapest Academy of Music (1921–27); had a brief career as a concert pianist; then taught piano at the Fodor Music School in Budapest (1927–43). In 1945 he was appointed to the piano faculty at the Budapest Academy of Music. He won the Kossuth Prize for composition in 1950 and the Erkel Prize twice, in 1955 and 1962. In his music he combined the elements of the cosmopolitan modern idiom with strong Hungarian rhythms and folklike melodies; in his treatment of these materials, and particularly in the energetic asymmetrical passages, he was closer to the idiom of Béla Bartók than to that of his teacher Kodály. The lyrical element in modal interludes adds to the Hungarian charm of his music.

WORKS: Opera, *A huszti kaland* (*The Adventure of Huszt;* 1949–50; Budapest, Dec. 22, 1951); 5 cantatas: *De amore fatale* (1939–40); *Terjed a fény* (*Light Is Spreading;* 1949); *Sztálin esküje* (*Stalin's Oath;* 1949); *A béke katonai* (*The Soldiers of Peace;* 1950); *Március fia* (*Son of March;* 1950); Chamber Symph. (1926); 2 divertimentos for Orch. (1933; 1933–34, revised 1960); 8 symphs.: No. 1 (1941–42; Budapest, 1965); No. 2, *Capriccio* (Budapest, 1948); No. 3 (1953–55; Budapest, 1957); No. 4 for String Orch. (1958–59; Budapest, 1961); No. 5 (1960–61; Hungarian Radio, 1962); No. 6 (1966; Hungarian Radio, Aug. 19, 1966); No. 7 (1967; Budapest, 1968); No. 8 (1968; Hungarian Radio, 1969); *Partita* for Orch. (1943–44); *Morning Ode* for Orch. (1945); March, overture (1945); *Honor and Glory,* suite (1951); Suite for Orch. (1954); *Pian e forte,* sonata for Orch. (1962); Suite for Small Orch. (1962); Sinfonietta (1974); 4 piano concertos: No. 1 (1931; Amsterdam International Society for Contemporary Music Festival, June 9, 1933, composer soloist); No. 2, concertino (1938); No. 3 (1953); No. 4 (1966); 2 violin concertos (1932, revised 1969–70; 1940–41, revised 1956); Concerto for String Quartet and Chamber Orch. (1936); Viola Concertino (1937); 3 string quartets (1934–35, 1936, 1957); Serenade for 10 Instruments (1967); solo sonatinas for Violin (1923) and Cello (1924); Sonatina for Violin and Cello (1923); 2 violin sonatas (1925, revised 1969–70; 1963); Suite for Violin and Piano (1926; revised 1970); 2 string trios (1929–30, 1955); *Partita* for Violin and Piano (1931); Suite for Solo Violin (1931); Wind Quintet (1954); Piano Trio (1956); *Improvisation* for Cello and Piano (1957); Flute Sonatina (1961); Violin Sonatina (1962); 3 suites for Piano (1921; 1921–23; 1923, revised 1970); several piano cycles: 7 *Bagatelles* (1923), 8 *Epigrams* (1923–24), 5 *Sketches* (1931), 6 *Hungarian Folksongs* (1934–35), 6 *Little Preludes* (1944), 10 *Bagatelles* (1956–57), 4 *Caprichos* (1961), *Kaleidoscope* (8 pieces, 1966), *Snapshots* (1971); 4 piano sonatas (1926, revised 1970; 1926–27; 1930; 1959–60); Piano Sonatina (1927); 2-piano Sonata (1947); Suite for Piano Duet (1955); 3 *Radnóti Songs* (1961); 7 *Attila József Songs* (1964); folk-song arrangements; piano albums for children.

Kaempfert, Bert, German composer and bandleader; b. Hamburg, Oct. 16, 1923; d. on the island of Majorca, Jan. 20, 1980. He studied clarinet, saxophone, and accordion; was drafted into the German army as a member of a music corps; taken prisoner of war in 1945, he conducted a band in the camp. He returned to Hamburg in 1947; in 1949 he became director of North German Radio, for which he composed numerous songs which attained great popularity, among them *Spanish Eyes, Swinging Safari, Blue Midnight,* and *Strangers in the Night,* which was catapulted to the top of the song hits by Frank Sinatra.

Kagel, Mauricio, leading composer of the cosmopolitan avant-garde; b. Buenos Aires, Dec. 24, 1931. He studied in Buenos Aires with Juan Carlos Paz and Alfredo Schiuma; also attended courses in philosophy and literature at the Univ. of Buenos

Aires. In 1949 he became associated with the Agrupación Nueva Música. From 1949 to 1956 he was choral director at the Teatro Colón. In 1957 he obtained a stipend of the Academic Cultural Exchange with West Germany and went to Cologne, which he made his permanent home. From 1960 to 1966 he was a guest lecturer at the International Festival Courses for New Music in Darmstadt; in 1961 and 1963 he gave lectures and demonstrations of modern music in the U.S., and in 1965 was a prof. of composition at the State Univ. of N.Y. in Buffalo; in 1967 he was a guest lecturer at the Academy for Film and Television in Berlin; in 1968 he presented a course in new music in Göteborg, Sweden; in 1969, returned to Cologne as director of the Inst. for New Music at the Musikschule in Cologne; was named prof. there in 1974. As a composer, Kagel evolved an extremely complex system in which a fantastically intricate and yet wholly rational serial organization of notes, intervals, and durations is supplemented by aleatory techniques; some of these techniques are derived from linguistic permutations, random patterns of lights and shadows on exposed photographic film, and other seemingly arcane processes. In his hyper-serial constructions, Kagel endeavors to unite all elements of human expression, ultimately aiming at the creation of a universe of theatrical arts in their visual, aural, and societal aspects.

WORKS: *Palimpsestos* for Chorus a cappella (1950); String Sextet (1953); *Traummusik* for Instruments and Musique Concrète (1954); *Anagrama* for Speaking Chorus, 4 Vocalists, and Chamber Ensemble (1958); *Transición I* for Electronic Sounds (1958); *Transición II* for Piano, Percussion, and 2 Magnetic Tapes (1959); *Pandora's Box* for Magnetic Tape (1961); *Sonant* for Electric Guitar, Harp, Double Bass, and 20 Instruments (1961); *Sur scène* for 6 Participants in mixed media, with Musicians instructed to interfere with Actors and Singers (concert perf., Radio Bremen, May 6, 1962); *Heterophonie* for Optional Ensemble, in 5 sections, optionally played or unplayed, with the conductor given an option to regard all instructions in the score as binding or not binding (Cologne, May 22, 1962, optionally conducted by the composer with the oboe giving A-sharp for tuning); *Phonophonie*, 4 melodramas for 2 Voices and Sound Sources (1963); *Composition & Decomposition*, a reading piece (1963); *Diaphonie* for Chorus, Orch., and Slide Projections (1964); *Music for Renaissance Instruments* for 23 Performers (1966); String Quartet (1967); *Montage* for different Sound Sources (1967); *Ornithologica multiplicata* for Exotic Birds (1968); *Ludwig van*, a surrealistic film score bestrewed with thematic fragments from Beethoven's works (1970; a bicentennial homage to Beethoven); *Staatstheater,* a "scenic composition" involving a ballet for "non-dancers" and orchestrated for a number of household objects, including a chamber pot and medical appurtenances such as a large clyster filled with water held in readiness to administer a rectal enema (Hamburg Staatsoper, April 25, 1971); *Variations ohne Fuge* for Orch. (1972); *Con voce* for 3 Mute Actors (1972); *Mare nostrum,* scenic play

(1975); *Kantrimiusik* (phonetic rendition into German of "country music"; 1975); *Variété,* "concert-spectacle for Artists and Musicians" (Metz Festival, Fall 1977); opera, *Die Erschöpfung der Welt* (Stuttgart, Feb. 8, 1980).

Kahn, Robert, German pianist and composer; b. Mannheim, July 21, 1865; d. Biddenden, Kent, May 29, 1951. He studied music with Lachner in Mannheim and with Rheinberger in Munich. In 1885 he went to Berlin, and in 1890 moved to Leipzig, where he organized a Ladies' Choral Union, which he conducted; in 1893 he was appointed instructor of piano at the Berlin Hochschule für Musik, retiring in 1931. After the advent of the Nazi government in Germany, he went to England, where he remained until his death. He composed a considerable amount of respectable chamber music and many singable choruses. He was a brother of the banker **Otto Kahn.**

Kaim, Franz, German impresario; b. Kirchheim unter Tech, near Stuttgart, May 13, 1856; d. Munich, Nov. 17, 1935. Having built a concert hall and organized an orch. in Munich, he established there (1893) the celebrated series of concerts bearing his name, the "Kaimkonzerte," which presented classical works and also new compositions by German composers; the successive conductors were Hans Winderstein (1893), Zumpe (1895), Löwe (1897), Hausegger (making guest appearances in 1898), Weingartner (1898–1905), and Schneevoigt (from 1905 until the dissolution of the orch. in 1908). Besides the regular symph. concerts, a series of Volkssinfoniekonzerte was given. Immediately after the orch. broke up, its members formed the Konzertverein under the direction of Löwe (later under Pfitzner and Hausegger). In 1928 the Kaim orch. became the Munich Phil.

Kaiser, Alfred, Belgian-born British composer; b. Brussels, Feb. 29, 1872; d. Bournemouth, Oct. 1, 1917. He studied composition with Bruckner in Vienna and with Foerster in Prague; went to London to live. During World War I he changed his name to **De Keyser** to escape the odium attached to the Kaiser of Germany. Among his works are the operas *Le Billet de Joséphine* (Paris, 1902), *Die schwarze Nina* (Elberfeld, 1905), and *Stella Maris* (Düsseldorf, 1910). He also wrote a Symph., a Piano Concerto, and chamber music.

Kajanus, Robert, outstanding Finnish conductor; b. Helsingfors, Dec. 2, 1856; d. there, July 6, 1933. He studied at the Helsingfors Cons., and later at the Leipzig Cons., with Reinecke, Richter, and Jadassohn (1877–79); then went to Paris, where he studied with Svendsen (1879–80); he then lived for some time in Dresden. In 1882 he returned to Helsingfors, and founded an orch. society which sponsored concerts by the newly organized Helsingfors Phil., an ensemble he led until his death; from 1897–1926 he was music director at the Univ. of Helsingfors. Kajanus was the earliest champion of the music of Sibelius; he made the first recordings of the first and 2nd symphs. of Sibelius with the London Symph. Orch. In 1900 he was engaged by the French government to present a concert of Finnish music with the Helsingfors Phil. at the World Exposition in Paris; he was also awarded the French Legion of Honor. He composed some orch. and choral pieces on Finnish themes, among them the symph. poems *Kullerro* and *Aino;* an orch. suite, *Sommarminnen;* 2 Finnish rhapsodies; piano pieces; songs.

Kalafati, Vasili, Russian composer and pedagogue of Greek extraction; b. Eupatoria, Crimea, Feb. 10, 1869; d. Leningrad, during the siege, Jan. 30, 1942. He studied at the St. Petersburg Cons. with Rimsky-Korsakov, graduating in 1899; subsequently was appointed to the teaching staff. A musician of thorough knowledge of every aspect of music theory, he was held in great esteem by his colleagues and students; Rimsky-Korsakov sent Stravinsky to Kalafati for additional training in harmony. As a composer, Kalafati faithfully continued the traditions of the Russian national school; many of his works were publ. by Belaieff; he wrote a Symph., a Piano Quintet, 2 piano sonatas, and a number of songs, all set in impeccably euphonious harmonies.

Kalinnikov, Vasili, Russian composer; b. Voin, near Mtzensk, Jan. 13, 1866; d. Yalta, Crimea, Jan. 11, 1901. He studied in Orel; in 1884 he enrolled at the Moscow Cons., but had to leave it a year later because of inability to pay; he then studied the bassoon at the Music School of the Moscow Phil. Society, which provided free tuition. He earned his living by playing bassoon in theater orchs.; also studied composition with A. Ilyinsky and Blaramberg. While still a student, he composed his first work, the symph. poem *The Nymphs* (Moscow, Dec. 28, 1889); later wrote another symph. poem, *The Cedar and the Palm;* the overture and entr'actes for *Tsar Boris;* and a prelude to the opera *In the Year 1812.* In 1895 he completed his most successful work, Symph. in G minor (Kiev, Feb. 20, 1897); a 2nd symph., in A (Kiev, March 12, 1898), was not as successful; he also wrote a cantata, *John of Damascus; Ballade* for Women's Chorus and Orch.; songs and piano pieces. Owing to his irregular habits and undernourishment, he contracted tuberculosis, and was sent to Yalta for treatment; there he died a few months later. Kalinnikov possessed a fine lyric talent; there is a definite trend in Russia toward greater recognition of his music. Several of his works in MS (Serenade for Strings; the overture *Bylina;* etc.) were publ. on the 50th anniversary of his death (1951).

Kalisch, Paul, German tenor; b. Berlin, Nov. 6, 1855; d. St. Lorenz am Mondsee, Salzkammergut, Austria, Jan. 27, 1946. He studied architecture; then went to Milan, where he took voice lessons with Leoni and Lamperti; he sang with considerable success in Italy (Milan, Rome, Florence), then at the Munich Opera and in Berlin; in 1889 he sang the Wagner roles at the Metropolitan Opera House with **Lilli Lehmann,** whom he married in N.Y. the following year. At the first Paris performance of *Tristan und Isolde* (1904) he and his wife sang the title roles; they were later separated (though not legally divorced); after Lilli Lehmann's death in 1929, he lived on her estate in Salzkammergut, remaining there until his death at the age of 90.

Kalish, Gilbert, American pianist; b. Brooklyn, July 2, 1935. He studied at Columbia College (1952–56; B.A., 1956); also attended the Graduate School of Arts and Sciences at Columbia Univ. (1956–58). In addition, he took piano lessons with Isabelle Vengerova, Leonard Shure, and Julius Hereford. He was a pianist with both the Contemporary Chamber Ensemble and the Boston Symph. Chamber Players; as a soloist, he toured widely in the U.S., Europe, and Australia, in programs including works by Stravinsky, Charles Ives, and others. He also was a regular accompanist with the American mezzo-soprano Jan DeGaetani. He served as artist-in-residence at the State Univ. of N.Y. at Stony Brook and head of keyboard activities at the Berkshire Music Center at Tanglewood.

Kalkbrenner, Christian, German composer and writer, father of **Friedrich W.M. Kalkbrenner;** b. Minden, Hannover, Sept. 22, 1755; d. Paris, Aug. 10, 1806. He studied piano with Becker and violin with Rodewald in Kassel; was choirmaster at the court of the Queen in Berlin (1788), then in the court of Prince Heinrich at Rheinsberg (1790–96); in 1797, went to Naples; in 1798 he became choirmaster at the Paris Opéra. There he produced his opera *Olimpie* (Dec. 18, 1798); also some pasticcios from music by Mozart and Haydn; he further wrote 2 symphs., a Piano Concerto, and several piano sonatas; publ. *Theorie der Tonkunst* (1789) and *Kurzer Abriss der Geschichte der Tonkunst* (1792).

Kalkbrenner, Friedrich Wilhelm Michael, celebrated German pianist; b. near Kassel, between Nov. 2 and Nov. 8, 1785; d. Deuil, Seine-et-Oise, June 10, 1849. He was taught by his father, **Christian Kalkbrenner.** In 1799–1801 he was enrolled at the Paris Cons., where he studied with Adam and Nicodami (piano) and Catel (harmony), taking first prizes in 1801. From 1803 he studied counterpoint with Albrechtsberger in Vienna; appeared as a concert pianist in Berlin, Munich (1805), and Stuttgart; also in Paris, with great success, in 1806. As a teacher, too, he was in great vogue. The years 1814–23 he spent in London; in 1818 he took up Logier's newly invented Chiroplast, simplified it, and applied it practically. After a German tour in 1823 with the harpist Dizi, Kalkbrenner settled (1824) in Paris as a partner in the Pleyel piano factory (the future Mme. Camilla Pleyel was one of his pupils). He revisited Germany in 1833 and Belgium in 1836. Kalkbrenner was inordinately vain of the success of his method of teaching, which aimed at the independent development of the fingers and wrist; his practical method of octave playing became a standard of modern piano teaching. He also developed left-hand technique, and a proper management of the pedals. As for his playing, his technique was smooth and well-rounded, his fingers supple and of equal strength, and his tone full and rich; his style, while fluent and graceful, lacked emotional power. His numerous études (among them several for left hand alone) are interesting and valuable. Chopin took some advice from him in Paris, but did not become his pupil despite Kalkbrenner's urging.

WORKS: 4 piano concertos (the last, op. 125, for 2 Pianos); Piano Septet, with Strings and 2 Horns; Quintet for Piano, Clarinet, Horn, Bassoon, and Double Bass; 2 piano sextets; piano quintets; 3 piano quartets; 7 piano trios; 15 sonatas; also rondos, fantasies, variations, caprices, etc., of a light character.

WRITINGS: *Méthode pour apprendre le pianoforte à l'aide du guide-mains* (1830); *Traité d'harmonie du pianiste* (1849).

Kallenberg, Siegfried Garibaldi, German composer; b. Schachen, near Lindau, Nov. 3, 1867; d. Munich, Feb. 9, 1944. He studied at the Cons. of Stuttgart with Faisst; from 1892, taught at Stettin, Königsberg, and Hannover. In 1910 he settled in Munich; a Kallenberg Society was established there in 1921 to promote his creative output. As a composer, Kallenberg was inspired by neo-Romanticism; in some of his works there are touches of Impressionism; his absorption in symbolic subjects brought him into a kinship with the Expressionist school in Germany. Apart from works on exotic subjects, he wrote music in a traditional style; he was particularly strong in choral polyphony.

Kalliwoda, Johann Wenzel, famous Bohemian violinist and composer; b. Prague, Feb. 21, 1801; d. Karlsruhe, Dec. 3, 1866. He studied at the Prague Cons. (1811–16) with Pixis (violin) and D. Weber (composition); played in the Prague Orch. (1817–21). In 1822 he became conductor of Prince Fürstenberg's orch. in Donaueschingen; there he spent 30 years, eventually retiring to Karlsruhe. He enjoyed an enviable reputation; some of his music was highly praised by Schumann.

WORKS: 2 operas: *Blanda* (Prague, Nov. 29, 1827) and *Prinzessin Christine* (1827); 10 masses; 7 symphs.; 14 overtures and 13 fantasias for Orch.; Violin Concerto; Concerto for 2 Violins; 7 concertinos; 3 string quartets; 3 string trios; a variety of solos for violin; also choruses, duets, and songs.

Kalliwoda, Wilhelm, German pianist and composer, son of **Johann Wenzel Kalliwoda;** b. Donaueschingen, July 19, 1827; d. Karlsruhe, Sept. 8, 1893. He studied with Hauptmann in Leipzig; also took some lessons from Mendelssohn; wrote piano pieces and songs; was also a reputable conductor.

Kallstenius, Edvin, Swedish composer; b. Filipstad, Aug. 29, 1881; d. Stockholm, Nov. 22, 1967. He first studied science at Lund Univ. (1898–1903); then took courses in music at the Leipzig Cons. (1903–7); returning to Stockholm, he became music critic of the *Svenska Dagbladet;* was a music librarian at Radio Sweden (1928–46) and a board member of the Society of Swedish Composers (1932–61). In his early works he followed the Romantic traditions of Scandinavian music; but later turned to advanced modern techniques, including explicit application of dodecaphonic configurations.

WORKS: FOR ORCH.: *Scherzo fugato* for Small Orch. (1907; revised 1923); *Sista Striden,* dramatic overture (1908); *En serenad i sommarnatten (A Serenade in the Summer Night;* 1918); *Sinfonia concertata* for Piano and Orch. (1922); 4 sinfoniettas (1923; 1946; *Dodicitonica,* 1956; *Semi-seriale,* 1958); 5 symphs. (1926, revised 1941; 1935; 1948; 1954; *Sinfonia su temi 12-tonici,* 1960); *Dalarapsodi* (1931); *Dalslandsrapsodi* (1936); *Romantico,* overture (1938); *Högtid och fest,* trilogy (1940); *Musica gioconda* for Strings (1942); *Cavatina* for Viola and Orch. (1943); *Passacaglia enarmonica* (1943); *Kraus-variationer* (1947); *Sonata concertate* for Cello and Orch. (1951); *Musica sinfonica* for Strings (1953; full orch. version, 1959); *Nytt vin i gamla läglar (New Wine in Old Bottles)* for Small Orch. (1954); *Choreographic Suite* (1957); *Prologo seriale* (1966). VOCAL WORKS: *När vi dö (When Mankind Perishes),* Requiem for Chorus and Orch. (1919); *Sångoffer (Song Offering),* cantata for Baritone and Orch. (1944); *Stjärntändningen* for Chorus and Orch. (1949); *Hymen, o, Hymenaios* for Soli, Chorus, and Orch. (1955). CHAMBER MUSIC: 8 string quartets (1904; 1905; 1913; *Divertimento alla serenata,* 1925; 1945; 1953; *Dodecatonica,* 1957; 1961); Cello Sonata (1908); Violin Sonata (1909); Clarinet Quintet (1930); Suite for Winds and Percussion (1938); Wind Quintet (1943); *Trio divertente* for Flute, Violin, and Viola (1950); *Piccolo trio seriale* for Flute, English Horn, and Clarinet (1956); *Trio svagante* for Clarinet, Horn, and Cello (1959); solo sonatas for Cello (1961), Flute (1962), and Violin (1965); *Lyric Suite* for Flute, Saxophone, and Cello (1962); String Trio (1965).

Kálmán, Emmerich (Imre), Hungarian composer of light opera; b. Siófok, Oct. 24, 1882; d. Paris, Oct. 30, 1953. He studied with Kössler in Budapest; won the Imperial Composition Prize (1907). Settling in Vienna, he produced a great number of tuneful and successful operettas; in 1938 he left Vienna; was in Paris until 1940; then came to America; lived in N.Y. and Hollywood; in 1949 went again to Europe.

WORKS: He made his debut as a composer with the symph. scherzo *Saturnalia,* perf. by the Budapest Phil. Orch. (Feb. 29, 1904); later dedicated himself exclusively to the composition of operettas in the Viennese style. His first success was with *Ein Herbstmanöver* (first perf. in Hungarian, Budapest, Feb. 22, 1908; perf. in N.Y. in the same year as *The Gay Hussars*). His other popular operettas were *Gold gab ich für Eisen* (Vienna, Oct. 16, 1914; N.Y., Dec. 6, 1916, as *Her Soldier Boy);* *Fräulein Susi* (Budapest, Feb. 23, 1915; Eng. and American productions as *Miss Springtime); Die Csardasfürstin* (Vienna, Nov. 17, 1915; in England as *Gypsy Princess;* in America as *The Riviera Girl); Gräfin Mariza* (Vienna, Feb. 28, 1924); *Die Zirkusprinzessin (The Circus Princess;* Vienna, March 26, 1926). The following were moderately successful: *Der gute Kamerad* (first version of *Gold gab ich für Eisen;* Vienna, Oct. 10, 1911); *Der kleine König* (Vienna, Nov. 27, 1912); *Die Faschingsfee* (Vienna, Jan. 31, 1917); *Die Bajadere* (Vienna, Dec. 23, 1921); *Golden Dawn* (N.Y., Nov. 30, 1927); *Die Herzogin von Chicago* (Vienna, April 6, 1928); *Ronny* (Berlin, Dec. 22, 1931); *Kaiserin Josephine* (Zürich, Jan. 18, 1936); *Marinka* (N.Y., July 18, 1945). His last work, *Arizona Lady*, was perf. posthumously in Bern in 1954.

Kalninš, Alfreds, Latvian composer; b. Zehsis, Aug. 23, 1879; d. Riga, Dec. 23, 1951. He studied at the St. Petersburg Cons. with Homilius (organ) and Liadov (composition); was organist at various Lutheran churches in Dorpat, Libau, and Riga; also played organ recitals in Russia. While in Riga, he was active as a teacher and composer. From 1927 till 1933 he lived in N.Y.; then returned to Latvia and settled in Riga.
WORKS: Operas: *Banuta* (first national Latvian opera; Riga, May 29, 1920); *Salinieki (The Islanders;* Riga, 1925); *Dzimtenes atmoda (The Nation's Awakening;* Riga, Sept. 9, 1933); symph. poem, *Latvia;* piano pieces; some 100 choruses; about 200 songs; arrangements of Latvian folk songs (publ. in Riga).

Kalninš, Janis, Latvian composer and conductor, son of **Alfreds Kalninš;** b. Pernav (Pärnu), Nov. 2, 1904. He studied in Riga with Vitols and in Leipzig with H. Abendroth; was conductor at the Latvian National Theater in Riga (1924–33), then at the Riga Opera House (1933–44). In 1948 he settled in Canada. From 1962 to 1968 he conducted the New Brunswick Symph.
WORKS: *Hamlet,* opera (Riga, Feb. 17, 1936); 3 symphs.: No. 1 (1939–44); No. 2, *Symphony of the Beatitudes,* with Chorus (1953); No. 3 (1972–73); Violin Concerto (1945–46); *Theme and Variations* for Clarinet, Horn, and Orch. (1963); String Quartet (1948); choruses; songs.

Kalomiris, Manolis, distinguished Greek composer; b. Smyrna, Turkey, Dec. 26, 1883; d. Athens, April 3, 1962. He studied piano with A. Sturm and composition with Herman Grädener at the Vienna Cons. (1901–6); then went to Russia, where he taught piano at a private school in Kharkov. In 1910 he settled in Greece; was instructor of the Athens School of Music (1911–19) and founder of the Hellenic Cons. of Athens (1919–26). In 1926 he founded the Cons. of Athens; was its director until 1948. As a music educator, he was greatly esteemed in Greece; 2 generations of Greek composers were his pupils. Kalomiris was the protagonist of Greek nationalism in music; almost all his works are based on Greek folk-song patterns, and many are inspired by Hellenic subjects. In his harmonies and instrumentation he followed the Russian school of composition, with a considerable influx of lush Wagnerian sonorities. His catalogue of works, publ. in Athens in 1964, lists 222 opus numbers; he also brought out several textbooks on harmony, counterpoint, and orchestration.
WORKS: OPERAS: *O Protomastoras (The Master-Builder),* to a libretto by Nikos Kazantzakis, the first opera by a Greek composer on a native subject (Athens, March 24, 1916); *Mother's Ring,* music drama (1917); *Anatoli (The Orient),* musical fairy tale, to a libretto by Kalomiris, after Cambyssis (1945–48); *The Shadowy Waters,* opera to a libretto after Yeats (1950–52); *Constantin Palaeologus,* music legend after a story by Kazantzakis (Athens, Aug. 12, 1962). FOR ORCH.: *Greek Suite* (1907); *The Olive Tree* for Women's Chorus and Orch. (1909); *Iambs and Anapests,* suite (1914); *Valor Symphony* for Chorus and Orch. (1920); *Greek Rhapsody* for Piano and Orch. (orchestrated by Gabriel Pierné and conducted by him for the first time in Paris, April 3, 1926); *Island Pictures* for Violin and Orch. (1928); *Symphony of the Kind People* for Mezzo-soprano, Chorus, and Orch. (1931); *3 Greek Dances* (1934); Piano Concerto (1935); *At the Ossios Loukas Monastery* for Narrator and Orch. (1937); *Triptych* (1940); *Minas the Rebel,* tone poem (1940); *The Death of the Courageous Woman,* tone poem (1945); Concertino for Violin and Orch. (1955); *Palamas Symphony* for Chorus and Orch., to texts by the Greek poet Palamas (Athens, Jan. 22, 1956). CHAMBER MUSIC: Piano Quintet, with Soprano (1912); String Trio (1921); *Quartet quasi fantasia* for Harp, Flute, English Horn, and Viola (1921); Violin Sonata (1948). FOR PIANO: *Sunrise* (1902); *3 Ballads* (1906); *For Greek Children* (1910); *2 Rhapsodies* (1921); 5 preludes (1939); choruses; songs.

Kaminski, Heinrich, eminent German composer; b. Tiengen, Baden, July 4, 1886; d. Ried, Bavaria, June 21, 1946. He studied at Heidelberg Univ. with Wolfrum and in Berlin with Kaun, Klatte, and Juon; taught a master class at the Berlin Academy of Music (1930–32). In 1933 he settled in Ried, where he remained to the end of his life. His writing is strictly polyphonic and almost rigid in form; the religious and mystic character of his sacred music stems from his family origins (he was the son of a clergyman of Polish extraction); the chief influences in his work were Bach and Bruckner. Interest in his music was enhanced after his death by posthumous editions of his unpubl. works.
WORKS: FOR THE STAGE: Opera, *Jürg Jenatsch* (Dresden, April 27, 1929); music drama for Narrator and Orch., *Das Spiel vom König Aphelius* (his last work, completed in 1946; produced posthumously, Göttingen, Jan. 29, 1950); a Passion, after an old French mystery play (1920). CHORAL WORKS: *69th Psalm* (1914); *Introitus und Hymnus* (1919); *Magnificat* (1925); *Der Mensch,* motet (1926); *Die Erde,* motet (1928); etc. FOR ORCH.: Concerto Grosso for Double Orch. (1922); *Dorische Musik* (1933); Piano Concerto (Berlin, 1937); *In Memoriam Gabrielae* for Orch., Contralto, and Solo Violin (1940); *Tanzdrama* (1942). CHAMBER MUSIC: Quartet for Clarinet, Viola, Cello, and Piano (1912); 2 string quartets (1913, 1916); Quintet for Clarinet, Horn, Violin, Viola, and Cello (1924); *Music for 2 Violins and Harpsichord* (1931); *Hauskonzert* (1941); *Ballade* for

Horn and Piano (1943). FOR ORGAN: Toccata (1923); *Chorale-Sonata* (1926); 3 chorale preludes (1928); Toccata and Fugue (1939). FOR PIANO: *Klavierbuch* (1934); *10 kleine Übungen für das polyphone Klavierspiel* (1935). SONGS: *Brautlied* for Soprano and Organ (1911); *Cantiques bretons* (1923); *3 geistliche Lieder* for Soprano, Violin, and Clarinet (1924); *Triptychon* for Alto and Organ (1930); *Lied eines Gefangenen* (1936); *Weihnachtsspruch* (1938); *Hochzeitsspruch* for 2 Altos and Organ (1940); *Dem Gedächtnis eines verwundeten Soldaten* for 2 Sopranos and Piano (1941); folk-song arrangements.

Kamu, Okko, Finnish violinist and conductor; b. Helsinki, March 7, 1946. He studied violin at the Sibelius Academy in Helsinki under Onni Suhonen; at the age of 23 he won the international competition for conductors arranged by the Herbert von Karajan Foundation; in 1971 was appointed conductor with the Finnish Radio Symph. Orch.; from 1976 to 1979 was chief conductor of the Oslo Phil. Orch.; in 1979 was appointed chief conductor of the Helsinki Phil.

Kancheli, Giya, Soviet Georgian composer; b. Tiflis, Aug. 10, 1935. He studied composition at the Tiflis Cons. (1959–63); in 1970 was appointed to its faculty. His sources of inspiration are nourished by Caucasian melos, with its quasi-oriental fiorituras and deflected chromatics which impart a peculiar aura of lyric introspection to the music; but his treatment of these materials is covertly modernistic and overtly optimistic, especially in sonoristic effects. He wrote 6 symphs. (1967, 1970, 1973, 1975, 1977, 1981); his 4th Symph., commemorating the semimillennium of the death of Michelangelo, was given its American premiere by the Philadelphia Orch. on Jan. 13, 1978. He also wrote a musical comedy, *The Pranks of Hanum* (1973); *Largo and Allegro* for Strings, Piano, and Timpani (1963); and several film scores.

Kapell, William, brilliant American pianist; b. New York, Sept. 20, 1922, of Russian and Polish parents; d. in an airplane crash at King's Mountain, near San Francisco, Oct. 29, 1953. He studied with Olga Samaroff at the Philadelphia Cons. of Music; made his N.Y. debut on Oct. 28, 1941; subsequently appeared as a soloist with all major American orchs. and also in Europe, specializing in modern music. He met his death returning from an Australian concert tour.

Kaper, Bronislaw, Polish-born American songwriter; b. Warsaw, Feb. 5, 1902; d. (of cancer) Beverly Hills, Calif., April 26, 1983. He received his academic education in music at the Warsaw Cons.; left Poland in the 1920s, and proceeded to Hollywood via Berlin and Paris. An adept and intelligent musician who understood the requirements of the popular idiom, he composed background music for numerous films, among them *San Francisco, Gaslight,* 2 versions of *Mutiny on the Bounty* (with Clark Gable in 1935 and Marlon Brando in 1962), and *Lili* (for

which he received an Academy Award in 1953).

Kaplan, Mark, outstanding American violinist; b. Cambridge, Mass., Dec. 30, 1953. He was brought up in Syracuse, N.Y.; began violin lessons as a small child; at the age of 8 he won a local violin competition, and enrolled as a student of Dorothy DeLay at the Juilliard School of Music in N.Y.; received its Fritz Kreisler Memorial Award. In 1973 he was awarded the prestigious Award of Special Distinction at the Leventritt Competition in N.Y.; subsequently was a soloist with the N.Y. Phil., Philadelphia Orch., Cleveland Orch., Los Angeles Phil., and Minnesota Orch.; also played in Europe with the Berlin Phil., Stockholm Phil., North German Radio Symph. Orch. of Hamburg, and the Scottish National Orch. of Glasgow, meriting praise for his fine musicianship and virtuoso technique.

Kapp, Arthur, Estonian composer; b. Suure-Iani, Feb. 28, 1875; d. Tallinn (Reval), Jan. 14, 1952. He studied at the St. Petersburg Cons. with Rimsky-Korsakov. From 1904 to 1920 he was director of the Cons. of Astrakhan, on the Volga; from 1920 to 1943, director of the Reval (Tallinn) Cons. in Estonia. In his capacity as a prof. of composition there he was the teacher of a generation of Estonian musicians.
WORKS: 4 symphs., concertos (for piano, violin, cello, clarinet, and french horn), and a String Sextet. His Symph. No. 4, subtitled *Youth Symphony* (1949), was awarded the State Prize in 1949, and the First Stalin Prize in 1950; he also wrote a cantata, *For Peace* (1951).

Kapp, Eugen, notable Estonian composer, son of **Arthur Kapp;** b. Astrakhan, May 26, 1908. He studied with his father, who was director of the Astrakhan Cons.; followed him to Estonia in 1920, and graduated from the Tallinn Cons. there in 1931; succeeded his father as prof. of composition at the Tallinn Cons. and served as its director until 1965.
WORKS: His operas, *Flames of Vengeance* (Tallinn, July 21, 1945) and *Freedom's Singer* (Tallinn, July 20, 1950), were awarded Stalin prizes. Other works: ballet, *Kalevipoeg* (1949); *Patriotic Symphony;* cantata, *Power of the People;* 2 violin sonatas; piano pieces; choral works.

Kapp, Julius, German writer on music; b. Seelbach in Baden, Oct. 1, 1883; d. Sonthofen, March 18, 1962. He studied in Marburg, Berlin, and Munich; received his Dr.Phil. in 1906. From 1904 to 1907 he was editor of *Literarischer Anzeiger,* which he founded in 1904; in 1923–45 was stage director of the Berlin State Opera and edited its bulletin, *Blätter der Staatsoper;* in 1948–54 held a similar post at the Berlin Municipal Opera.
WRITINGS: *Wagner und Liszt* (1908); *Franz Liszt* (1909; went through 20 printings before 1924); *Register zu Liszts Gesammelten Schriften* (1909); *Liszt-Brevier* (1910); *Liszt und die Frauen* (1911); *Wagner und die Frauen* (1912; 16th printing, 1929; completely rewritten and publ. in Eng. trans. as *The Loves of Richard Wagner,* London, 1951); *Paganini*

(1913; many eds.; 15th ed., 1969); *Berlioz* (1914); *Das Dreigestirn: Berlioz—Liszt—Wagner* (1920); *Meyerbeer* (1920; 8th printing, 1932); *Franz Schreker* (1921); *Das Opernbuch* (1922; 16th printing, 1928); *Die Oper der Gegenwart* (1922); *Weber* (1922; 5th revised ed., 1931); *Die Staatsoper 1919 bis 1925* (1925); *Wagner und seine erste Elisabeth* (with H. Jachmann, 1926); *185 Jahre Staatsoper* (1928); *Wagner und die Berliner Staatsoper* (1933); *Wagner in Bildern* (1933); *Geschichte der Staatsoper Berlin* (1937); *200 Jahre Staatsoper in Bild* (1942). He ed. Liszt's *Gesammelte Schriften* (4 vols., 1910) and Wagner's *Gesammelte Schriften und Briefe* (24 vols., 1914).

Kapp, Villem, Estonian composer, nephew of **Arthur Kapp,** first cousin of **Eugen Kapp;** b. Suure-Jöani, Sept. 7, 1913; d. Tallinn, March 24, 1964. He studied music at the Tallinn Cons.; from 1944 was a prof. of composition there. He wrote in an expansive Romantic style rooted in folk song; his opera, *Lembitu* (Tallinn, Aug. 23, 1961), glorifies Estes Lembitu, the leader of the Estonian struggle against the invading Teutonic crusaders in 1217. He also wrote 2 symphs., chamber music, and choral pieces.

Kappel, Gertrude, German soprano; b. Halle, Sept. 1, 1884; d. Pullach, April 3, 1971. She studied with Nikisch and Noe at the Leipzig Cons.; made her debut in 1903 at the Hannover Opera, after which she was engaged in Munich, Berlin, and Vienna for the leading Wagnerian roles; appeared also in Amsterdam, Brussels, Madrid, London, and Paris; made her first American appearance as Isolde with the Metropolitan Opera on Jan. 16, 1928, and remained a member until 1936; in 1932, sang the title part in *Elektra* at its first Metropolitan performance; in 1933 she joined the roster of the San Francisco Opera Co.; retired in 1937 and returned to Germany.

Kaprál, Václav, Czech composer, father of **Vítězslava Kaprálová;** b. Určice, near Prostějova, Moravia, March 26, 1889; d. Brno, April 6, 1947. He studied composition with Janáček in Brno (1907–10) and with Novák in Prague (1919–20); then took piano lessons with Alfred Cortot in Paris (1923–24). He established his own music school in Brno in 1911; lectured at the Univ. of Brno (1927–36); then taught at the Brno Cons. from 1936 until his 3-year internment in a concentration camp in Svatobořice during World War II; in 1946, became a prof. at the Music Academy in Brno. In his works he shows a fine eclectic talent.

Kaprálová, Vítězslava, Czech composer, daughter of **Václav Kaprál** (family names in Slavic languages assume adjectival gender endings); b. Brno, Jan. 24, 1915; d. Montpellier, France, June 16, 1940. She received her early education from her father; then (1930–35) studied at the Brno Cons. under Vilém Petrželka (conducting and composition); later at the Prague Cons. with Novák (composition) and Talich (conducting). In 1937 she received a scholarship to Paris, where she took lessons in conducting with Munch and composition with Martinu. Her early death, from tuberculosis, cut short a remarkable career.

WORKS: *Suite en miniature* for Orch. (1932–35); Piano Concerto (Brno, June 17, 1935); *Military Sinfonietta* (Prague, Nov. 26, 1937); *Suita rustica* (Brno, April 16, 1939); *Partita* for String Orch. and Piano (perf. posthumously, Brno, Nov. 12, 1941); *Christmas Prelude* for Chamber Orch. (1939); Concertino for Violin, Clarinet, and Orch. (1940; unfinished); *Legenda a Burleska* for Violin and Piano (1932); *Sonata appassionata* for Piano (1933); String Quartet (1936); *6 Variations on the Bells of the Church of Saint Etienne in Paris* for Piano (1938); *2 Ritournelles* for Cello and Piano (1940).

Karajan, Herbert von, great conductor in the grand Germanic tradition; b. Salzburg, April 5, 1908. He was a scion of a cultured musical family; his great-grandfather **Theodore von Karajan** was a learned music scholar. His parentage was partly Serbian and partly Greek; his father, Ernst von Karajan, was a medical officer; his mother's maiden name was Martha Cosmâc. His father played the clarinet; his brother was a child pianist; and he too began taking piano lessons at a very early age. He attended the Mozarteum in Salzburg, where he studied piano and also took conducting lessons with the director of the Mozarteum, Bernard Paumgartner; later he went to Vienna, where he studied conducting with Franz Schalk at the Vienna Academy of Music. He made his debut as a conductor there on Dec. 17, 1928, with a student orch. In 1929 he received his first appointment as a conductor, at the Ulm Staattheater. From Ulm he went to Aachen, where he was engaged to conduct opera and symph. concerts (1934). In 1936 he conducted *Tristan und Isolde* at the Vienna State Opera; in 1937 he conducted a concert of the Berlin Phil., and in 1938 was engaged to conduct *Fidelio* at the Berlin Städtische Oper (Sept. 30, 1938). His reputation as an impeccable technician and disciplinarian was firmly established during his tenure at the Berlin Opera, so that the *Berliner Tageblatt* once referred to him as "das Wunder Karajan." His capacity of absorbing the music at hand and transmitting its essence to the public became his most signal characteristic; he conducted all his scores from memory, including Wagner's *Ring*. He also began to accept engagements abroad; in 1938 he conducted at La Scala in Milan and also made guest appearances in Belgium, the Netherlands, and Scandinavia. He continued to conduct in Berlin throughout the devastation of the war. There was a dark side to Karajan's character, revealing his lack of human sensitivity and even a failure to act in his own interests. He became fascinated with the organizing solidity of the National Socialist Party in Germany; on April 9, 1933, he registered in the Salzburg office of the Austrian National Socialist Party; his party number was 607525. A month later he joined the German Nazi organization in Ulm under No. 3430914. He lived to regret these actions after the Nazi *Götterdämmerung*, but he was denazified by the Allies' army of occupation in 1946. On June 15, 1932, Karajan married **Elmy Holgerloef,** an operetta soprano; he divorced her in 1942 and married Anita Gutermann; he divorced her, too, after he found out that her ancestry was partly Jewish. He retired to Salzburg to await his political clearance, and on Jan. 12, 1946, he was permitted to lead the Vienna Phil. He was also allowed to make recordings with the Vienna Phil. for the British division of Columbia Gramophone Co. In 1948 he was appointed artistic director of the Gesellschaft der Musikfreunde in Vienna, and was also named music director of the Vienna Symph. In 1950 he was engaged as music director at La Scala in Milan; later he led the Bach Festival in Vienna. In 1951 he conducted the complete cycle of *Der Ring des Nibelungen,* and in 1952 conducted in Bayreuth a new production of *Tristan und Isolde.* He was also engaged as music director of the London Phil. Orch., with which he gave concerts in Germany, Austria, France, and Switzerland. In 1954 he became principal conductor of the Berlin Phil. When Furtwängler died in Nov. 1954, on the eve of an announced tour of the Berlin Phil. in the U.S., Karajan took the orch. over and gave a series of memorable performances with it in American cities. Ironically, there were no organized protests of Karajan's employment, even though Furtwängler's engagement with the N.Y. Phil. some years before were canceled because of his alleged toleration of Nazi philosophy; yet Furtwängler never joined the Nazi party, while Karajan joined it twice. On his 47th birthday, April 5, 1955, the members of the Berlin Phil. elected him artistic director and conductor. He became to all intents and purposes an absolute dictator of the affairs of the Berlin Phil., brooking no insubordination whatsoever; a minor scandal erupted in 1982 when Karajan insisted on engaging a young lady clarinetist as the principal of the clarinet section of the orch., threatening to discontinue the highly lucrative recording activities should his request be refused; a compromise was reached in which she was allowed to play with the orch. on probation; apart from her apparent lack of orch. experience, her engagement would have broken the established tradition of the Berlin Phil. in excluding women from membership. His association with the Berlin Phil. made it impossible for him to continue his formal contract as chief conductor of the Vienna Symph., and he resigned his Vienna position in 1960. His American connections grew stronger when he brought the Berlin Phil. to the U.S. in 1976, and again in 1982, when he conducted a triumphant series of concerts in N.Y. and Los Angeles. About that time he was named permanent conductor and music director of the Berlin Phil. for life. He made an operatic debut in America conducting *Die Walküre* at the Metropolitan Opera in N.Y. on Nov. 21, 1967. He was popular in France, and served as artistic adviser of the Orch. de Paris from 1969–71. In 1968 he established the Karajan Foundation for the purpose of promoting biennial international competitions for young conductors. As his fame spread, he conducted all over the world; in 1962 he took the Vienna Phil. Orch. to Russia; he took the La Scala

Orch. to Russia in 1964, and the Berlin Phil. in 1969. He was the recipient of numerous honorary titles; he received the Mozart Ring in Vienna in 1957 and the Prix France-Allemagne in 1970. Finland awarded him the Order of the White Rose. In 1973 he was elevated to the rank of Honorary Citizen of West Berlin. The great reputation that Karajan earned despite political disadvantages is explained by his extraordinary capacity for systematic work, his emotional strength, and his justified self-assurance; both in opera and in symph. he is capable of achieving superlative performances. His cycles of Beethoven symphs. are recognized as exemplary in fidelity to style and excellence of execution.

Karajan, Theodor Georg von, Austrian writer on music, great-grandfather of **Herbert von Karajan;** b. Vienna, Jan. 22, 1810; d. there, April 28, 1873. He studied history, philology, and law; after holding various minor posts, he became president of the Austrian Academy of Science (1866–69). His important monograph *J. Haydn in London, 1791 und 1792* (Vienna, 1861) contains Haydn's correspondence with Maria Anna von Genzinger; he also publ. *Aus Metastasios Hofleben* (Vienna, 1861).

Karayev, Kara, Soviet composer; b. Baku, Feb. 5, 1918; d. Moscow, May 13, 1982. He studied piano and theory in Baku; then took courses in composition with Shostakovich at the Moscow Cons., graduating in 1946. From 1949 to 1953 he was director of the Azerbaijani Cons. in Baku. His music is derived mainly from his semi-oriental environment, comprising not only the native Tartar motifs, but also other Asian resources; particularly effective are his theatrical spectacles featuring native dances and choral ensembles.

WORKS: Opera, *Fatherland* (1945); ballets: *Seven Beauties* (1952) and *On the Track of Thunder* (1958); cantatas: *The Song of the Heart* (1938) and *The Song of Happiness* (1947); oratorio, *Hymn of Friendship* (1972); for Orch.: 3 symphs. (1944, 1946, 1965); *Leyly and Medzhnun,* symph. poem (1947); *Albanian Rhapsody* (1952); *Don Quixote,* symph. sketches (1960); *Poem of Joy* for Piano and Orch. (1937); Violin Concerto (1967); numerous pieces for folk instruments; 2 string quartets; a series of piano pieces, including 24 preludes; choruses; film music.

Karel, Rudolf, Czech composer; b. Pilsen, Nov. 9, 1880; d. at the Terezín concentration camp, March 6, 1945. He was the last student of Dvořák, with whom he studied in Prague for one year during Karel's term at the Prague Cons. (1901–4). In 1914 he went to Russia as a teacher, and remained there during World War I. After the Revolution he made his way to Irkutsk, Siberia; during the Russian civil war he became a member of the Czechoslovak Legion and conducted an orch. organized by the legionnaires. He returned to Prague in 1920; from 1923 to 1941 taught at the Prague Cons. As a member of the Czech resistance in World War II, he was arrested by the Nazis in March 1943; was transferred to Terezín in Feb. 1945, and died there of dysentery shortly before liberation. His music reflects the Romantic concepts; he had a predilection for programmatic writing; the national element is manifested by his treatment of old modal progressions; his instrumental writing is rich in sonority; the polyphonic structure is equally strong.

WORKS: Lyric comedy, *Ilseino srdce (Ilsea's Heart;* 1906–9; Prague, Oct. 11, 1924); 2 musical fairy tales: *Smrt Kmotřička (Godmother Death;* 1928–33; Brno, Feb. 3, 1933) and *Tři vlasy děda Vševěda (3 Hairs of the Wise Old Man;* 1944–45; his last work, written in camp, left as a draft only, arranged by his student Zbyněk Vostřák, and perf. posthumously in Prague, Oct. 28, 1948); Suite for Orch. (1903–4); *Comedy Overture* (1904–5); Fantasy for Orch. (1905); *Ideály (The Ideals),* symph. epic from an artist's life (1906–9); 2 symphs.: *Renaissance* (1910–11) and *Spring* (1935–38); 2 other symphs., of 1904 and 1917, are lost; *Vzkříšení (Resurrection),* symph. for Soli, Chorus, and Orch. (1923–27; Prague, April 9, 1928); *Capriccio* for Violin and Orch. (1924); *4 Slavonic Dance Moods* for Orch. (1912); *The Demon,* symph. poem (1918–20); *Revolutionary Overture* (1938–41); *Sladká balada dětská (Sweet Ballad for a Child)* for Soprano, Chorus, and Orch. (1928–30); *Černoch (A Negro),* exotic ballad for Baritone, and Orch. or Piano (1934); 3 string quartets (1902–3, 1907–13, 1935–36); Piano Trio (1903–4); Violin Sonata (1912); Nonet for Wind Quintet and String Quartet (1945; left in draft form and completed by F. Hertl); Piano Sonata (1910); other piano pieces: *5 Pieces* (1902); *Notturno* (1906–7); *Thema con variazioni* (1910); *3 Waltzes* (1913); *Burlesques* (1913–14); also, choruses; songs; incidental music.

Karg-Elert, Sigfrid, distinguished German organist and composer; b. Oberndorf, Württemberg, Nov. 21, 1877; d. Leipzig, April 9, 1933. He studied with Reinecke and Jadassohn at the Leipzig Cons.; in 1919 was appointed to its staff. Concurrently with his teaching activities, he began to give organ recitals, and soon became known as one of the greatest virtuosos on the instrument; he also played on the Kunstharmonium, for which he wrote many original compositions. His real name, **Karg,** sounded unattractive to his audiences (it means "avaricious"), and he changed it to Karg-Elert. As a composer, he developed a brilliant style, inspired by the music of the Baroque, but he embellished this austere and ornamental idiom with impressionistic devices; the result was an ingratiating type of music with an aura of originality. In 1932 he undertook a concert tour in the U.S.

Karkoff, Maurice Ingvar, prominent Swedish composer; b. Stockholm, March 17, 1927. He studied piano and conducting at the Royal Academy of Music in Stockholm (1948–53); composition with Blomdahl, Lars-Erik Larsson, Erland von Koch in Stockholm, with Holmboe in Copenhagen, and later with Nadia Boulanger and André Jolivet in Paris (1957), Wladimir Vogel in Switzerland (1959–61), and Alexander Boscovich in Tel Aviv (1963). Returning to Sweden in 1965, he devoted himself principally to teaching. In his music he absorbed many cultures; these are reflected in his style of composition, which may be described as romantic modernism; thematically he is sensitive to exotic resources and coloristic instrumental timbres.

WORKS: FOR ORCH.: *Serenade* for Strings (1953); *Short Variations* for String Quartet (1953; revised 1956); Sinfonietta (1954); Saxophone Concertino (1955); 8 symphs.: No. 1 (1955–56; Bergen, Norway, Oct. 22, 1956); No. 2 (1957; Swedish Radio, Jan. 5, 1959); No. 3, *Sinfonia breve* (1958–59; Gävle, Jan. 10, 1960); No. 4 (1963; Stockholm, April 4, 1964); No. 5, *Sinfonia da camera* (1964–65; Gävle, Nov. 11, 1965); No. 6 (1972–73; Stockholm, Oct. 12, 1974); No. 7, *Sinfonia da camera* (1975); No. 8 (1979–80); *Short Symphony* for Symph. Band (Stockholm, Sept. 27, 1982); Violin Concerto (1956); Piano Concerto (1957); Cello Concerto (1957–58); *Lyric Suites I* and *II* for Chamber Orch. (1958); Trombone Concerto (1958); Horn Concerto (1959); *9 Aphoristic Variations* (1959); Clarinet Concerto (1959); Variations (1961); *Serenata* for Chamber Orch. (1961); *7 pezzi* (1963); *Oriental Pictures* (1965–66; also for Piano); Suite for Harpsichord and Strings (1962); *Concerto da camera* for Balalaika and Orch. (1962–63); Concerto for Orch. (1963); *Transfigurate mutate* (1966); *Tripartita* (1966–67); *Textum* for Strings (1967); *Metamorphoses* (1967); *Sinfonietta grave* (1968–69); *Epitaphium* for Small Chamber Orch. (1968; also for Nonet); *5 Summer Scenes* (1969); *Triptyk* (1970); *Partes caracteris* (1971); *Symphonic Reflexions* (1971); *Passacaglia* for Strings (1971); Trumpet Concerto (1977); *Texture* (1978). VOCAL MUSIC: *6 Allvarliga Songs* for High Voice and Orch. (1955); *Det Svenska Landet,* festival cantata (1956); *Livet,* songs and recitation for Low Voice and Orch. (1959); *Gesang des Abgeschiedenen,* 5 songs for Baritone, and Orch. or Piano (1959–60); *10 Japanese Songs* for High Voice, and Orch. or Piano (1959); *Himmel och Jord,* cantata (1960); *Sieben Rosen später,* cantata (1964); *Das ist sein Erlauten,* cantata (1965); *Landscape of Screams,* after Nelly Sachs, for Soprano, Narrator, and Instruments (1967); *6 Chinese Impressions* for High Voice and Instrumental Ensemble (1973); songs. CHAMBER MUSIC: Flute Sonata (1953); Cello Sonata (1954–55); Violin Sonata (1956); Wind Quintet (1956–57); String Quartet (1957); Quartet for 2 Trumpets, Horn, and Trombone (1958); String Trio (1960); *Chamber Concerto* for 14 Winds, Timpani, Percussion, and String Basses (1961); *Metamorphoses* for 4 Horns (1966); *Terzetto* for Flute, Cello, and Piano (1967); *3 Episodes* for Clarinet, Cello, and Piano (1968); *4 parte* for 13 Brasses and Percussion (1968); *4 momenti* for Violin and Piano (1970); *Epitaphium* for Accordion, Electric Guitar, and Percussion (1970); *6 pezzi breve* for Oboe Solo (1972); minor chamber pieces. PIANO MUSIC: Piano Sonata (1956); *Partita piccola* (1958); *Capriccio on Football* (1961; musical report on a football game); *Monopartita* (1969); *3 Expressions* for 2 Pianos (1971); other pieces for piano. Under the impression of his travels to Israel, he wrote a chamber opera, *The Boundary Kibbutz* (1972–73).

Karkoschka, Erhard, German composer; b. Ostrava, Bohemia, March 6, 1923. He studied music in Stuttgart and in Tübingen; in 1958 was appointed to the staff of the Hochschule für Musik in Stuttgart. He adopted the serial method of composition, following the example of Anton Webern; often incorporated electronics in his works; also resorted to graphic notation in order to achieve greater freedom of resulting sonorities. He wrote *Symphonische Evolutionen* (1953); *Kleines Konzert* for Violin and Chamber Orch. (1955); *Undarum continuum* for Orch. (1960); *Antinomie* for Wind Quintet (1968); *Quattrologe* for String Quartet (1966); *Tempora mutantur* for String Quartet (1971); electronic works; much choral music and stage melodramas. He publ. *Zur rhythmischen Struktur in der Musik von heute* (Kassel, 1962); *Das Schriftbild der neuen Musik* (Celle, 1966; in Eng. as *Notation in New Music*, London, 1972); and many magazine articles dealing with problems of new music.

Karlowicz, Jan, Polish music scholar, father of **Mieczyslaw Karlowicz;** b. Subortowicze, near Troki, May 28, 1836; d. Warsaw, June 14, 1903. He studied music in Wilno, Moscow, Paris, Brussels, and Berlin. Settling in Warsaw, he publ. translations of several German textbooks on harmony; also publ. (in Eng., German, and French) a pamphlet, *Project of a New Way of Writing Musical Notes* (Warsaw, 1876); composed some songs.

Karlowicz, Mieczyslaw, Polish composer, son of the theorist **Jan Karlowicz;** b. Wiszniewo, Dec. 11, 1876; d. Zakopane, Galicia, Feb. 8, 1909. He was sent to Germany to study violin as a child. In 1887 he began composition studies in Warsaw with Noskowski, Roguski, and Maszynski; violin with Barcewicz; later he continued his studies in Berlin with H. Urban (1895–1900). Returning to Warsaw, he devoted himself to composition and teaching; was director of the Warsaw Music Society (1904–6); after a sojourn in Germany (where he studied conducting with Nikisch in Leipzig), he settled in Zakopane; also traveled to France, Austria, and Germany. An enthusiastic mountain climber, he was killed in an accident, under an avalanche. Essentially a Romantic composer, he succeeded in blending the national elements of Polish folk music with the general European genre of mild modernism; there is an influence of Richard Strauss in his expansive tone painting. The appreciation of his music in Poland rose rather than declined after his death; some of his piano pieces and songs have been established in the concert repertoire.
WORKS: Serenade for String Orch. (1898); Symph. in E minor, subtitled *Renaissance* (1900); symph. poem, *Returning Waves* (1904); symph. trilogy, *Eternal Songs* (1907); *Lithuanian Rhapsody* for Orch. (1908); *Stanislaw and Anna of Oswiecim,* symph. poem (1908); *Sad Story,* symph. poem (1908); *Episode at the Masquerade,* symph. poem (1908–9; unfinished; completed by G. Fitelberg). He publ. some previously unknown letters of Chopin (Warsaw, 1904; in French as *Souvenirs inédits de F. Chopin,* Paris, 1904).

Karpath, Ludwig, Austrian singer and music critic; b. Budapest, April 27, 1866; d. Vienna, Sept. 8, 1936. He was a pupil at the Cons. in Budapest; studied singing in Vienna; was a member of the National Opera Co. in the U.S. (singing minor bass roles) for 3 seasons (1886–88); returning to Vienna, he became an influential music critic; for many years (1894–1921) wrote for the *Neues Wiener Tageblatt.* He publ. *Siegfried Wagner als Mensch und Künstler* (1902), *Zu den Briefen Wagners an eine Putzmacherin* (1906), *R. Wagner, der Schuldenmacher* (1914), and *Wagners Briefe an Hans Richter* (1924).

Karpeles Maud, English ethnomusicologist; b. London, Nov. 12, 1885; d. there Oct. 1, 1976. She became an associate with Cecil Sharp in collecting and organizing English folk songs; in 1915 she went to the U.S., where she assembled American songs of English origin, publ. in 2 vols., *English Folk Songs from the Southern Appalachians* (London, 1917; 1932); she further publ. *Songs from Newfoundland* (London, 1934; 2nd ed., 1970). From 1949 to 1963 she edited the annual *Journal of the International Folk Music Council.* In 1961 she was made a Dame Commander of the Order of the British Empire. Among her many publications were *Cecil Sharp* (London, 1933; reprinted 1955, in collaboration with A.H. Fox Strangways); *Folk Songs of Europe* (London, 1956; N.Y., 1964); *An Introduction to English Folk Song* (London, 1973).

Karr, Gary, American virtuoso double-bass player; b. Los Angeles, Nov. 20, 1941. He was a scion of a family of musicians which numbered 7 bass players (his father, grandfather, 2 uncles, and 3 cousins). He absorbed the technique of manipulating this mastodon of string instruments by natural selection: studied with a cellist, a pianist, and a singer (Jennie Tourel) before taking lessons with Herman Reinshagen, former first double-bass player of the N.Y. Phil. He then took an additional course with the cellist Gabor Rejto at the Univ. of Southern Calif.; subsequently studied at the Aspen Music School and finally at the Juilliard School of Music in N.Y. He launched his spectacular career as a soloist with major American orchs., and then played with the London Phil. and the Oslo Phil. His solo recitals attracted a great deal of curiosity and elicited astounded praise from even the most skeptical of music critics. To expand the meager repertoire for the instrument, he commissioned Hans Werner Henze, Gunther Schuller, Alec Wilder, Malcolm Arnold, and other modern composers to write special works for him. He also introduced some works in the jazz manner. As an instructor, he gave courses at several music schools in the U.S. and Canada.

Kasemets, Udo, Estonian-born Canadian composer; b. Tallinn, Nov. 16, 1919. He studied at the Tallinn Cons. and the Stuttgart State Academy of Music, and attended a Darmstadt summer course in new music under Krenek (1950). He emigrated to Canada in 1951 and became an organist, accompanist, and teacher; later became music critic for the

Toronto *Daily Star;* was also lecturer on mixed-media music at the Ontario College of Arts in Toronto. In 1966 he became editor of *Canavangard,* an annotated catalogue of avant-garde Canadian composers. His early music is set in peaceful Romantic modalities with Estonian undertones, but soon he espoused serialism and the pantheatricalism of the most uninhibited avant-garde.

WORKS: *Estonian Suite* for Chamber Orch. (1950); *Sonata da camera* for Solo Cello (1955); Violin Concerto (1956); String Quartet (1957); *Logos* for Flute and Piano (1960); *Haiku* for Voice, Flute, Cello, and Piano (1961); *Squares* for Piano, 4-hands (1962); *5* for 2 Performers on 2 Pianos and Percussion (1962–63); *Trigon* for One, 3, 9, or 27 Performers, a multidimensional score in which thematic information is provided by a deoxyribonucleic matrix (1963; 11 subsequent versions, 1964–66); *Communications, a noncomposition to words by e.e. cummings,* a cybernetic manifestation for singular or plural singers, speakers, instrumentalists, or dancers, of an indeterminate duration (1963); *Cumulus* for any Solo Instrument or Ensemble, and 2 Tape Recorders, the score consisting of 9 segments to be played in any order (1963–64; 2 later versions, 1966, 1968); *Calceolaria,* time/space variations on a floral theme, for any number of Performers (1966; version for 4-channel Tape, 1967); *Contactics,* a choreography for Musicians and Audience (1966); *Variations on Variations on Variations* for Singers, Instrumentalists, and 4 Loudspeakers (1966); *Quartets of Quartets,* 4 separate works for varying ensembles of Readers, Tape, Calibrators, Wind-bells, Wind Generators, Opaque Projectors, and any other sound-producing media: *Music for Nothing, Music for Anything (Wordmusic), Music for Something (Windmusic),* and *Music for Everything* (all 1971–72); *Music(s) for John Cage,* incorporating *Guitarmusic for John Cage* for any number of Guitars, Projections, and Dimmers, *Voicemusic for John Cage* for any number of Voices, *Saladmusic for John Cage* for any number of Salad Makers, and *Walking/Talking* for any number of Walkers/Talkers (all 1972); *Time-Space Interface* for any number of participants and any media, in both indoor and outdoor versions (1971–73); *Quadraphony (Music of the Quarter of the Moon of the Lunar Year),* an acoustical/architectural time/space exploration project (1972–73); *La Crasse du Tympan* for Record/Tape Mix (1973); *WATEARTHUNDAIR: Music of the 10th Moon of the Year of the Dragon,* a nature-sound-mix with verbal and visual commentary (1976); *KANADANAK,* a "celebration of our land and its people . . ." for Readers, Drummers, and Audience participation (1976–77). *Counterbomb Renga,* a spectacle by about 100 poets and musicians, protesting against the proliferation of nuclear weapons, was conceived and coordinated by Kasemets (Canadian Broadcasting Corp., April 3, 1983).

Kassern, Tadeusz Zygfrid, Polish composer; b. Lwow, March 19, 1904; d. New York, May 2, 1957. He studied with M. Soltys at the Lwow Cons. and with Opieński in Poznan. He also took a course in law; in 1931, went to Paris. In 1945 he was appointed cultural attaché at the Polish Consulate in N.Y. However, he broke with the Communist government in Poland, and remained in N.Y.; became an American citizen in 1956. Among Polish composers, he pursued a cosmopolitan trend; although many of his works are inspired by Polish folk music, the idiom and the method are of a general European modern character.

Kässmayer, Moritz, Austrian violinist and composer; b. Vienna, March 20, 1831; d. there, Nov. 9, 1884. He studied with Sechter at the Vienna Cons.; then played violin in the orch. of the Vienna Opera; later became ballet conductor there. He wrote a comic opera, *Das Landhaus zu Meudon* (1869); symphs.; masses and other church music; 5 string quartets; songs. His *Mesalliansen* for String Quartet, with Piano, 4-hands, and *Volksweisen und Lieder* for String Quartet "humoristisch und kontrapunktisch bearbeitet" are amusing specimens of old-fashioned humor.

Kastalsky, Alexander, Russian choral conductor and composer; b. Moscow, Nov. 28, 1856; d. there, Dec. 17, 1926. He was a pupil of Tchaikovsky, Taneyev, and Hubert at the Moscow Cons. (1875–82). In 1887 he became instructor of piano at the Synodal School in Moscow; in 1891, assistant conductor of the Synodal Chorus; in 1910, was appointed director of the school and principal conductor of the choir. In 1911 he took the choir on an extended European tour. In 1918 the Synodal School became a choral academy; in 1923 it merged with the Moscow Cons. Kastalsky was also a teacher of conducting at the Moscow Phil. Inst. (1912–22); in 1923, was appointed prof. of choral singing at the Moscow Cons. He was a notable composer of Russian sacred music, into which he introduced modern elements, combining them with the ancient church modes.

Kastner, Jean Georges (Johann Georg), Alsatian composer and theorist; b. Strasbourg, March 9, 1810; d. Paris, Dec. 19, 1867. He studied organ as a child; later entered the Strasbourg Lutheran Seminary. He then gave up his theological studies and went to Paris. There he resumed his musical education, taking lessons with Berton and Reicha. An industrious scholar, Kastner acquired enormous erudition in various arts and sciences. He pursued the study of acoustics and formulated a theory of the cosmic unity of the arts. At the same time he took great interest in practical applications of music; he was active in organizing the contest of bands of 9 nations held at the Paris Exposition of 1867. He was a founder and vice-president of the Assoc. des Artistes-Musiciens. He was elected a member of the Institut and an Officer of the Legion of Honor. Among the grandiose projects that he carried out were several vols. of "Livres-Partitions," that is, symph.-cantatas illustrating musico-historical subjects, preceded by essays upon them. Of these the following were publ.: *Les Danses des morts; disser-*

tations et recherches historiques, philosophiques, littéraires et musicales sur les divers monuments de ce genre qui existent tant en France qu'à l'étranger and *Danse macabre, grande ronde vocale et instrumentale* (Paris, 1852; 310 pp.); *La Harpe d'Eole, et la musique cosmique* and *Stéphen, ou La Harpe d'Eole, grand monologue avec chœurs* (1856); *Les Sirènes* and *Le Rêve d'Oswald ou Les Sirènes, grande symphonie dramatique vocale et instrumentale* (1858); *Parémiologie musicale de la langue française* and *La Saint-Julien de ménétriers, symphonie-cantate à grand orchestre, avec solos et chœurs* (1862; 659 pages); *Les Voix de Paris* and *Les Cris de Paris, grande symphonie humoristique vocale et instrumentale,* making use of vendors' cries with orch. accompaniment (1875). Kastner wrote several operas, 4 of which were produced in Strasbourg: *Gustav Wasa* (1832); *Oskars Tod* (1833); comic opera, *Der Sarazene* (1834); *Die Königin der Sarmaten* (1835). In Paris he produced 2 operas: *La Maschera* (June 17, 1841) and *Le Dernier Roi de Juda* (1844). He also wrote 5 overtures, Sextet for Saxophones, and 2 collections of men's choruses (*Les Chants de la vie,* 1854; *Chants de l'armée française,* 1855); publ. a useful and highly practical *Manuel général de musique militaire à l'usage des armées françaises* (Paris, 1848). His great project, *Encyclopédie de la musique,* was left uncompleted at his death.

Katchen, Julius, American pianist; b. Long Branch, N.J., Aug. 15, 1926; d. Paris, April 29, 1969. He studied in N.Y. with David Saperton; made his debut with the Philadelphia Orch. on Oct. 21, 1937. He studied academic subjects at Haverford College, graduating in 1945. In 1948 he toured Palestine; then settled in Paris; gave a series of successful concerts in Europe.

Katims, Milton, American conductor and violist; b. New York, June 24, 1909. He attended Columbia Univ.; studied viola and conducting with L. Barzin. In 1935–43 he was a viola player and assistant conductor at station WOR in N.Y.; in 1943, joined the NBC Symph. Orch. as first violist, and subsequently became assistant conductor under Toscanini. From 1954 to 1974 he was conductor and music director of the Seattle Symph. Orch. In 1976 he was appointed artistic director of the School of Music at the Univ. of Houston; he resigned in 1983.

Kauer, Ferdinand, Austrian composer; baptized at Klein-Tajax (Znaim), Moravia, Jan. 18, 1751; d. Vienna, April 13, 1831. As a boy he played organ in a Jesuit church at Znaim; in 1784 he played violin in a Vienna theater, and also supplied music for a number of plays performed there. He wrote some 100 operettas and other stage works; of these, *Das Donauweibchen* (Vienna, Jan. 11, 1798) was sensationally successful and was performed all over Europe for many years; other works (an oratorio, *Die Sündflut;* a quantity of church music; symphs.; concertos; etc.) also enjoyed favor. Most of his MSS were lost in the flood of 1830; a list of extant works

is given by Eitner in his *Quellen-Lexikon.* Kauer publ. *Singschule nach dem neuesten System der Tonkunst* (1790) and *Kurzgefasste Generalbass-Schule für Anfänger* (1800).

Kauffmann, Leo Justinus, Alsatian composer; b. Dammerkirch, Sept. 20, 1901; killed in an air raid, Strasbourg, Sept. 25, 1944. He studied with Marie Joseph Erb in Strasbourg and with Jarnach and Abendroth in Cologne; in 1932–40 was active in radio work in Cologne; then taught at the Strasbourg Cons.; served as its director until he was killed. He wrote the opera *Die Geschichte vom schönen Annerl* (Strasbourg, June 20, 1942); a Mass; a Symph.; Concertino for Double Bass, with Chamber Orch.

Kaufman, Louis, distinguished American violinist; b. Portland, Oreg., May 10, 1905. He studied with Kneisel; won the Loeb Prize in 1927 and the Naumburg Award in 1928. In 1950 he regularly gave concerts in Europe. On Oct. 21, 1950, he presented in Paris, as violinist and conductor, the 12 concertos by Vivaldi, op. 8; in 1954 he played 12 concertos by Torelli, op. 8, in London; also performed Vivaldi's concertos in Rio de Janeiro and Buenos Aires (1952). He gave numerous first performances of works by contemporary composers, among them a violin concerto by Dag Wiren (Stockholm, Oct. 25, 1953), and first American performances of violin works by Darius Milhaud, Lev Knipper, Bohuslav Martinů, and others; also played American works in Europe; gave the first performance in England of Walter Piston's Violin Concerto (London, April 6, 1956). He edited 6 sonatas for violin by G.P. Telemann and *Sonata concertante* by L. Spohr; publ. *Warming Up Scales and Arpeggios* for violinists (1957).

Kaufmann, Walter, German-born American conductor, composer, and musicologist; b. Karlsbad, April 1, 1907; d. Bloomington, Ind., Setp. 9, 1984. He studied composition with Schreker in Berlin; also studied musicology in Prague. In 1935 he traveled to India, where he remained for 10 years; devoted much time to the study of the Hindu systems of composition; also appeared as conductor, serving as music director of the Bombay Radio. In 1947 he moved to Nova Scotia and taught piano at the Halifax Cons. there; from 1949–57 he was music director of the Winnipeg Symph. Orch. In 1957 he settled in the U.S., where he joined the faculty of the Indiana Univ. School of Music in Bloomington. He became an American citizen in 1964. He was awarded a D.Mus. *honoris causa* by the Spokane (Wash.) Cons. in 1946. He wrote *Musical Notations of the Orient* (Bloomington, 1967); *The Ragas of North India* (Bloomington, 1968); *Tibetan Buddhist Chant* (with translations by T. Norbu; Bloomington, 1975); *Involvement with Music: The Music of India* (N.Y., 1976); *Musical References in the Chinese Classics* (Detroit, 1976); *The Ragas of South India* (Bloomington, 1976); *Altinden* (Leipzig, 1981); also valuable articles on Eastern music for American music journals.

WORKS: OPERAS: *Der grosse Dorin* (1932); *Der*

Hammel bringt es an den Tag (1932); *Esther* (1931–32); *Die weisse Göttin* (1933); *Anasuya,* radio opera (Bombay, Oct. 1, 1938); *The Cloak,* after Gogol (1933–50); *A Parfait for Irene* (Bloomington, Feb. 21, 1952); *The Research* (1951); *The Golden Touch,* short opera for children (1953); *Christmas Slippers,* television opera (1955); *Sganarelle* (1955); *George from Paradise* (1958); *Paracelsus* (1958); *The Scarlet Letter,* after Hawthorne (Bloomington, May 6, 1961); *A Hoosier Tale* (Bloomington, July 30, 1966); *Rip van Winkle,* short opera for children (1966). BALLETS: *Visages* (1950); *The Rose and the Ring* (1950); *Wang* (1956). FOR ORCH.: Symph. No. 1 for Strings (1931); *Prag,* suite (1932); Concerto No. 1 for Piano and Orch. (1934); Symph. No. 2 (1935); Symph. No. 3 (1936); Symph. No. 4 (1938); *2 Bohemian Dances* (1942); Concerto No. 1 for Violin and Orch. (1943); *6 Indian Miniatures* (1943); Concerto No. 2 for Violin and Orch. (1944); *Navaratnam,* suite for Piano and Chamber Orch. (1945); *Phantasmagoria* (1946); Variations for Strings (1947); Concertino for Piano and Strings (1947); *Dirge* (1947); *Madras Express* (Boston Pops, June 23, 1948); *Fleet Street Overture* (1948); *Strange Town at Night* (1948); *Faces in the Dark* (1948); *Andhera* for Piano and Orch. (1942–49); Sinfonietta No. 1 (Symph. No. 5; 1949); Divertimento for Strings (1949); Concerto No. 2 for Piano and Orch. (1949); Concerto for Violoncello and Orch. (1950); *Chivaree Overture* (1950); *Main Street* for Strings (1950); *Kalif Storch,* fairy tale for Speaker and Orch. (1951); *Arabesques* for 2 Pianos and Orch. (1952); *Vaudeville Overture* (1952); *Sewanee River Variations* (1952); *Short Suite* for Small Orch. (1953); *Nocturne* (1953); *Pembina Highway* (1953); *4 Skies* (1953); *3 Dances to an Indian Play* (1956); Symph. No. 6 (1956); *4 Essays* for Small Orch. (1956); Sinfonietta No. 2 (1959); Concerto for Timpani and Orch. (1963); *Festival Overture* (1968); Concertino for Violin and Orch. (1977). CHAMBER MUSIC: 10 string quartets (1935–46); 3 piano trios (1942–46); 6 Pieces for Piano Trio (1957); String Quartet (1961); Partita for Woodwind Quintet (1963); *Arabesques* for Flute, Oboe, Harpsichord, and Bass (1963); 8 Pieces for 12 Instruments (1967); *Passacaglia and Capriccio* for Brass Sextet (1967); Sonatina for Piccolo or Flute Solo (1968). FOR PIANO: Concertino (1932); Sonatina No. 1 (1948); Sonata (1948–51); *Arabesques* for 2 Pianos (1952); Sonatina No. 2 (1956); Suite (1957). He further wrote the cantatas *Galizische Bäume* for Chorus and Orch. (1932), *Coronation Cantata* for Soloists, Chorus, and Orch. (1953), and *Rubayyat* for Soloist and Orch. (1954); also songs.

Kaun, Hugo, German composer; b. Berlin, March 21, 1863; d. there, April 2, 1932. He studied piano with Oskar Raif and composition with Friedrich Kiel in Berlin; composed industriously as a very young man. In 1887 he went to live in America, settling in Milwaukee, where he remained for 14 years (1887–1901); was a successful teacher, and continued to compose. In 1902 he returned to Berlin to teach privately; in 1922, became a prof. at the Klindworth-Scharwenka Cons.; publ. an autobiography, *Aus meinem Leben* (Berlin, 1932); also a manual for students, *Harmonielehre und Aufgabenbuch.* A cultured composer, thoroughly versed in the craft, he wrote a great number of works, and enjoyed recognition among large groups of friends; his musical style contained elements of both Brahmsian and Wagnerian idioms.

Kay, Hershy, American composer, arranger, and orchestrator; b. Philadelphia, Nov. 17, 1919; d. Danbury, Conn., Dec. 2, 1981. He studied cello with Felix Salmond and orchestration with Randall Thompson at the Curtis Inst. of Music in Philadelphia (1936–40); then went to N.Y., and began a fruitful career as an arranger of Broadway musicals and ballets. He orchestrated a number of Leonard Bernstein's theater works: *On the Town* (1944), *Peter Pan* (1951), *Candide* (1956; revival, 1973), *Mass* (1971), and the Bicentennial pageant *1600 Pennsylvania Avenue* (1976). His last arrangement for Bernstein was *Olympic Hymn,* performed at the opening of the Olympic Congress in Baden-Baden (Sept. 23, 1981). His other orchestrations for Broadway include Kurt Weill's *A Flag Is Born* (1947), Latouche's *The Golden Apple* (1954), Mary Rogers's *Once upon a Mattress* (1958), Blitzstein's *Juno* (1958), *Sand Hog* (1958), *Livin' the Life* (1958), *Milk and Honey* (1961), *The Happiest Girl in the World* (1961), *110 in the Shade* (1963), *Coco* (1969), *A Chorus Line* (1975), *American Musical Jubilee* (1976), *Music Is* (1976), *On the Twentieth Century* (1977), *Evita* (1979), *Carmelina* (1979), and *Barnum* (1980). He further made numerous arrangements for the N.Y. City Ballet, among them *Cakewalk* (1951, after Gottschalk), *Western Symphony* (1954, after cowboy songs and fiddle tunes; produced by Balanchine on Sept. 7, 1954, and included in his company's Russian tour in 1962), *The Concert* (1956, after Chopin), *Stars and Stripes* (1958, after Sousa's marches), *Who Cares?* (1970, after Gershwin), and *Union Jack* (1976, after popular British music). His ballet arrangements for other companies include *The Thief Who Loved a Ghost* (1950, after Weber), *L'Inconnue* (1965), *The Clowns* (1968; a rare 12-tone arrangement), *Meadowlark and Cortège Burlesque* (1969), *Grand Tour* (1971, after Noel Coward), and *Winter's Court* (1972). He also orchestrated a Gottschalk piano piece, *Grand Tarantella,* for Piano and Orch. (1957) and completed orchestration of Robert Kurka's opera *The Good Soldier Schweik* (N.Y. City Center, April 23, 1958).

Kay, Ulysses Simpson, eminent black American composer; b. Tucson, Ariz., Jan. 7, 1917. He received his early music training at home; on the advice of his mother's uncle **"King" Oliver,** a leading jazz cornetist, he studied piano. In 1934 he enrolled at the Univ. of Arizona at Tucson (Mus.B., 1938); he then went to study at the Eastman School in Rochester, N.Y., where he was a student of Bernard Rogers and Howard Hanson (M.M., 1940); later attended the classes of Paul Hindemith at the Berkshire Music Center in Tanglewood (1941–42). He served in the U.S. Navy (1942–45); went to Rome as winner of the

American Rome Prize, and was attached there to the American Academy (1949–52). From 1953 to 1968 he was employed as a consultant by Broadcast Music Inc. in N.Y.; was on the faculty of Boston Univ. (1965) and of the Univ. of Calif., Los Angeles (1966–67); in 1968 was appointed prof. of music at the Herbert H. Lehman College in N.Y.; was made Distinguished Prof. there in 1972. In 1964 he held a Guggenheim fellowship; in 1969 he was awarded an honorary doctorate in music by the Univ. of Arizona. Kay's music follows a distinctly American idiom, particularly in its rhythmic intensity, while avoiding ostentatious ethnic elements; in harmony and counterpoint, he pursues a moderately advanced idiom, marked by prudentially euphonious dissonances; his instrumentation is masterly.

WORKS: Operas: *The Boor,* after Chekhov (1955; Louisville, April 3, 1968); *The Juggler of Our Lady* (1956; New Orleans, April 23, 1954); *The Capitoline Venus* (Quincy, Ill., March 12, 1971); *Jubilee* (Jackson, Miss., April 12, 1976); Oboe Concerto (Rochester, N.Y., April 16, 1940); *5 Mosaics* for Chamber Orch. (Cleveland, Dec. 28, 1940); ballet, *Dance Calinda* (Rochester, N.Y., April 23, 1941); *Of New Horizons,* overture (N.Y., July 29, 1944); *A Short Overture* (N.Y., March 31, 1947); Suite for Strings (Baltimore, April 8, 1949); *Sinfonia in E* (Rochester, N.Y., May 2, 1951); *6 Dances* for Strings (1954); Concerto for Orch. (N.Y., 1954); *Song of Jeremiah,* cantata (Nashville, April 23, 1954); Serenade for Orch. (Louisville, Sept. 18, 1954); *3 Pieces after Blake* for Soprano and Orch. (1952; N.Y., March 27, 1955); *Fantasy Variations* for Orch. (1963); *Umbrian Scene* for Orch. (New Orleans, March 31, 1964); *Markings,* symph. essay, dedicated to the memory of Dag Hammarskjöld (Rochester, Mich., Aug. 8, 1966; television perf., with scenes from Hammarskjöld's life, on "The Black Composer," shown on educational TV in N.Y. on June 19, 1972); *Theater Set* for Orch. (1968); *Scherzi musicali* for Chamber Orch. (1971); *Aulos* for Flute and Chamber Orch. (Bloomington, Ind., Feb. 21, 1971); *Quintet Concerto* for 5 Brass Soli and Orch. (N.Y., March 14, 1975); *Southern Harmony* for Orch. (North Carolina Symph., Feb. 10, 1976); 2 string quartets (1953, 1956); Quintet for Flute and Strings (1947); Piano Quintet (1949); Piano Sonata (1940); film score for *The Quiet One* (1948); many choral pieces and songs.

Kayser, Philipp Christoph, German composer and pianist; b. Frankfurt, March 10, 1755; d. Zürich, Dec. 23, 1823. In 1775 he settled in Zürich as a teacher. From Goethe's correspondence with him it appears that he wrote music to several of Goethe's singspiels, but only one, *Scherz, Liszt und Rache,* is preserved, in MS. He publ. *Weihnachtskantate: 2 Sonates en symphonie* for Piano and 2 Horns; and songs.

Keats, Donald, significant American composer; b. New York, May 27, 1929. He studied piano at the Manhattan School of Music; then enrolled in Yale Univ., where he attended classes with Quincy Porter and Paul Hindemith in composition (Mus.B.,

1949) and musicology with Alfred Einstein and Leo Schrade; then attended classes in composition at Columbia Univ. with Otto Luening, Douglas Moore, and Henry Cowell (M.A., 1953), and took a course in musicology with Paul Henry Lang. Subsequently he joined the Graduate School of Music at the Univ. of Minnesota, where he studied composition with Paul Felter and Dominick Argento and musicology with Johannes Riedel (Ph.D., 1962). In 1954 he received a Fulbright traveling grant and went to Germany, where he became a student of Philipp Jarnach at the Hochschule für Musik in Hamburg. In 1964–65 he received his first Guggenheim fellowship grant to continue his studies in Paris, Florence, and Vienna; in 1972–73 he obtained a second Guggenheim grant and traveled to France and England. Other awards and prizes were from the National Endowment for the Arts, from Yale Univ., from the Rockefeller Foundation, and from the Ford Foundation. In 1948–49 he served as a teaching fellow at Yale Univ. School of Music; was then called to the army and was an instructor at the U.S. Naval School of Music at Washington, D.C., (1953–54); later was a member of the faculty of Antioch College in Yellow Springs, Ohio (1957–76); in 1969–70 he was visiting prof. of music at the School of Music, Univ. of Washington, in Seattle. In 1976 he was appointed prof. of music and composer-in-residence at the Univ. of Denver School of Music. In the meantime he gave guest performances in various parts of the world as a pianist in his own works; he gave concerts of his own music in Tel Aviv and Jerusalem in 1973; performed at a concert of his music in N.Y. in 1975, under the auspices of the U.S. Dept. of the Interior; and accompanied singers in programs of American songs, including his own. In his own compositions Keats appears as a classical lyricist; his music is sparse in texture but opulent in sonorous substance, frugal in diction but expansive in elaborate developments; its expressive power is a musical equivalent of "Ockham's razor," a medieval law of parsimony which proclaims the principle of *multa paucis,* multitude by paucity, abundance in concision. The titles of his works often indicate this economic precision of design: *Musica Instrumentalis; Polarities; Diptych; Branchings.* In his *Elegiac Symphony* he gives full expression to the lyric nature of his talent; it is an outgrowth of an orchestral *Elegy* inspired by the sadness upon the death of his infant son.

WORKS: For Orch.: Symph. No. 1 (1954); Symph. No. 2, *Elegiac Symph.* (Dayton, Ohio, Jan. 20, 1960; numerous subsequent hearings); *The New Work,* ballet (1967); *Concert Piece* (Columbus, Ohio, Feb. 3, 1968); *Branchings* for Orch. (1976). Chamber music: Sonata for Clarinet and Piano (1948); Piano Trio (1948); *Divertimento* for Wind and String Instruments (1949); 2 string quartets (1951, 1965); String Trio (1951); *Polarities* for Violin and Piano (1968); *Dialogue* for Piano and Wind Instruments (1973); *Diptych* for Cello and Piano (1973); *Epithalamium* for Violin, Cello, and Piano (1977); *Musica Instrumentalis* for 9 Instruments (1980). For Piano: *Theme and Variations* (1954); Sonata (1966). For Voices: *The Hollow Men* for Chorus, Clarinet, 3

Trombones, and Piano, to words by T.S. Eliot (Hamburg, July 12, 1955); *The Naming of Cats* for Vocal Quarter and Piano, to words by T.S. Eliot (1962); *A Love Triptych,* song cycle to poems by Yeats (1970); *Tierras del alma* for Soprano, Flute, and Guitar (Denver, May 23, 1979).

Keene, Christopher, American conductor; b. Berkeley, Calif., Dec. 21, 1946. He studied piano and cello; took courses at the Univ. of Calif., Berkeley, majoring in history in 1963. While still a student he organized an opera company, with which he staged several modern works, including the West Coast premiere of Henze's *Elegy for Young Lovers;* was a guest conductor of the Spoleto Festivals in the summers of 1968, 1969, and 1971. Concurrently, he was music director of the American Ballet Co., for which he wrote a ballet of his own, *The Consort* (1970). In 1970 he joined the conducting staff of the N.Y. City Opera as the winner of the Julius Rudel Award; made a brilliant debut in Ginastera's opera *Don Rodrigo;* on March 12, 1971, conducted the world premiere of Menotti's opera *The Most Important Man;* on Aug. 12, 1971, he conducted the posthumous world premiere of the opera *Yerma* by Villa-Lobos, with the Santa Fe Opera Co. At his N.Y. appearances he was enthusiastically acclaimed by the critics as one of the brightest precocious talents in the profession. In April 1971 he distinguished himself with the N.Y. City Opera by a highly competent performance of *La Traviata,* and later conducted also at the Metropolitan Opera. These accomplishments are all the more remarkable since he never took a regular course in conducting, but learned to lead orchs. by instinctual instrumental navigation. In 1975 he was appointed music director of the Syracuse (N.Y.) Symph. Orch. While retaining this position he also assumed the posts of music director of the Spoleto Festival in Charleston, S.C. (1977), and of the Long Island Phil. (1979). In 1982 he was appointed artistic supervisor of the N.Y. City Opera.

Kegel, Herbert, distinguished German conductor; b. Dresden, July 29, 1920. He studied at the Dresden Cons. In 1946 he became conductor of the Rostock Opera; in 1949 was engaged as a regular conductor of the Leipzig Radio Orch.; in 1960 he was named its chief conductor. From 1975 to 1978 he was a prof. at the Hochschule für Musik in Leipzig, and in 1978 became a prof. at the Dresden Hochschule für Musik. In 1977 was appointed to the prestigious post of chief conductor of the Dresden Phil. He was regarded as one of the most competent conductors of East Germany, combining a thorough knowledge of his repertoire with a fine sense of effective presentation of the music.

Keilberth, Joseph, German conductor; b. Karlsruhe, April 19, 1908; d. Munich, July 20, 1968. He served as a conductor at the Karlsruhe State Opera (1935–40), of the Berlin Phil. Orch. (1940–45), and at the Dresden Opera (1945–51). He assumed the post of chief conductor of the Bamberg Symph. in 1949, retaining this position until his death in 1968; con-

currently he served as Generalmusikdirektor of the Hamburg Phil. (1950–59); from 1959 until his death he also held the post of Generalmusikdirektor of the Bavarian State Opera in Munich. In 1951 he toured with the Bamberg Symph. in Switzerland, the Netherlands, France, Spain, and Portugal. In 1953 he conducted the Wagner Festival in Bayreuth; in 1954 toured with the Bamberg Symph. in Cuba and Mexico. He made his U.S. conducting debut at Carnegie Hall in N.Y. on April 4, 1954.

Keiser, Reinhard, important German opera composer; b. Teuchern, near Weissenfels, Jan. 9, 1674; d. Hamburg, Sept. 12, 1739. He received his early musical training from his father, **Gottfried Keiser,** an organist; was then sent to Leipzig, where he studied at the renowned Thomasschule directed by Johann Schelle. In 1693 he was in Braunschweig, where he began his career as a composer for the stage. His first opera-pastorale, *Der königliche Schäfer oder Basilius in Arcadien,* was performed shortly after his arrival in Braunschweig; in 1894 he produced a singspiel, *Procris und Cephalus;* there followed another pastorale, *Die wiedergefundenen Verliebten,* in 1695; it was revived in Hamburg in 1699 under the title *Die beständige und getreue Ismene.* In 1694 he was named Cammer-Componist in Braunschweig. In 1695 he went to Hamburg, which became his permanent residence. In 1696 he was engaged as Kapellmeister with the Hamburg Opera; in 1702 he became its co-director, retaining this position until 1707. Hamburg was then the main center of opera productions in Germany, and Keiser worked industriously producing not only his own operas there, but also the stage works of Handel and Mattheson. The number of Keiser's stage works was never calculated with credible precision; the best estimate is that he wrote in Hamburg at least 77 operas and 39 singspiels and theatrical intermezzi. The subjects of his operas are still predominantly taken from Greek and Roman mythology, as was customary in the Baroque era, but he introduced a decisive innovation by using the German language in his dramatic works; he further made use of popular local themes; he made a concession, however, in resorting to the Italian language in arias. Thus his last opera, *Circe,* produced in Hamburg on March 1, 1734, contains 21 German arias and 23 Italian arias. Keiser also continued the common tradition of having other composers contribute to the music. In his ballets he followed the French *style galant* and effectively used Rococo devices. In so doing he formed a German Baroque idiom national in essence and cosmopolitan in treatment; this aspect of his work influenced his younger contemporaries Bach and Handel. In 1718 Keiser became a guest Kapellmeister to the Duke of Württemberg in Stuttgart. In 1721 he went to Copenhagen to supervise the productions of his operas *Die unvergleichliche Psyche, Ulysses,* and *Der Armenier.* In 1723 he returned to Hamburg, and in 1725 composed 2 operas on subjects connected with Hamburg history and society: *Der Hamburger Jahrmarkt* and *Die Hamburger Schlachtzeit.* In 1728 he became Canonicus minor and Cantor of the Katharinenkirche in Hamburg. Apart from operas, he wrote many sacred works (oratorios, cantatas, Psalms, Passions), of which several were publ. in the collections *R. Keisers Gemüths-Ergötzung bestehend in einigen Sing-Gedichten mit einer Stimme und unterschiedlichen Instrumenten* (1698); *Divertimenti serenissimi* (airs with harpsichord accompaniment, 1714); *Kaiserliche Friedenpost* (songs and duets with harpsichord, 1715); etc. Several excerpts from his operas were publ. in Denkmäler Deutscher Tonkunst and other collections.

WORKS: FOR THE STAGE: *Der königliche Schäfer oder Basilius in Arcadien* (Braunschweig, 1693); *Procris und Cephalus,* singspiel (Braunschweig, 1694); *Die wiedergefundenen Verliebten,* Schäferspiel (Braunschweig, 1695; revised as *Die beständige und getreue Ismene,* Hamburg, 1699); *Mahumet II,* Trauerspiel (Hamburg, 1696); *Der geliebte Adonis* (Hamburg, 1697); *Die durch Wilhelm den Grossen in Britannien wieder eingeführte Treue* (Hamburg, 1698); *Allerunterthäbigster Gehorsam,* Tantzspiel and singspiel (Hamburg, Nov. 15, 1698); *Der aus Hyperboreen nach Cymbrien überbrachte güldene Apfel zu Ehren Friedrichs und Hedwig Sophiens zu Holstein* (Hamburg, 1698); *Der bey dem allgemeinen Welt-Friede und dem Grossen Augustus geschlossene Tempel des Janus* (Hamburg, 1699); *Die wunderbahr-errettete Iphigenia* (Hamburg, 1699); *Die Verbindung des grossen Hercules mit der schönen Hebe,* singspiel (Hamburg, 1699); *Die Wiederkehr der güldnen Zeit* (Hamburg, 1699); *La forza della virtù, oder Die Macht der Tugend* (Hamburg, 1700); *Das höchstpreissliche Crönungsfest Ihrer Kgl. Majestät zu Preussen,* ballet opera (Hamburg, 1701); *Störtebecker und Jödge Michaels* (2 versions; Hamburg, 1701); *Die wunderschöne Psyche,* singspiel (Hamburg, Oct. 20, 1701); *Circe oder Des Ulisses erster Theil* (Hamburg, 1702); *Penelope oder Des Ulysses ander Theil* (Hamburg, 1702); *Sieg der fruchtbaren Pomona* (Hamburg, Oct. 18, 1702); *Die sterbende Eurydice oder Orpheus erster Theil* (Hamburg, 1702); *Orpheus ander Theil* (Hamburg, 1702); *Neues preussisches Ballet* (Hamburg, 1702); *Die verdammte Staat-Sucht, oder Der verführte Claudius* (Hamburg, 1703); *Die Geburt der Minerva* (Hamburg, 1703); *Die über die Liebe triumphierende Weissheit oder Salomon* (Hamburg, 1703); *Der gestürzte und wieder erhöhte Nebucadnezar, König zu Babylon* (Hamburg, 1704); *Die römische Unruhe oder Die edelmüthige Octavia* (Hamburg, Aug. 5, 1705); *Die kleinmüthige Selbstmörderinn Lucretia oder Die Staats-Thorheit des Brutus,* Trauerspiel (Hamburg, Nov. 29, 1705); *La fedeltà coronata oder Die gekrönte Treue* (Hamburg, 1706); *Masagniello furioso, oder Die Neapolitanische Fischer-Empörung* (Hamburg, June 1706); *La costanza sforzata, Die gezwungene Beständigkeit oder Die listige Rache des Sueno* (Hamburg, Oct. 11, 1706); *Il genio d'Holsatia* (Hamburg, 1706; used as prologue to succeeding work); *Der durchlauchtige Secretarius, oder Almira, Königin von Castilien* (Hamburg, 1706); *Der angenehme Betrug oder Der Carneval von Venedig* (Hamburg, 1707; includes arias by C. Graupner); *La forza dell'amore oder Die von Paris entführte Helena* (Hamburg, 1709); *Die blutdürstige Rache oder Heliates und Olympia* (Hamburg, 1709; with C. Graupner); *Desiderius, König der Langobarden* (Hamburg, July 26, 1709); *Die bis und nach dem Todt unerhörte Treue des Orpheus* (Hamburg, 1709; based on *Die sterbende Eurydice oder Orpheus erster Theil* and *Orpheus ander Theil*); *La grandezza d'animo oder Arsinoe* (Hamburg, 1710); *Le Bon Vivant oder Die Leipziger Messe* (Hamburg, 1710); *Der Morgen des europäischen Glückes oder Aurora,* Schäferspiel (Hamburg, July 26?, 1710); *Der durch den Fall des grossen Pompejus erhöhte Julius Caesar* (Hamburg, Nov. 1710); *Der hochmüthige, gestürtzte und wieder erhabene Croesus,* dramma musicale (Hamburg, 1710); *Die oesterreichische Grossmuth oder Carolus V* (Hamburg, June 1712); *Die entdeckte Verstellung oder Die geheime Liebe der Diana,* Schäferspiel (Hamburg, April 1712; revised 1724); *Die wiederhergestellte Ruh oder Die gecrönte Tapferkeit des Heraclius* (Hamburg, June 1712); *L'inganno fedele oder Der getreue Betrug* (Hamburg, Oct. 1714); *Die gecrönte Tugend* (Hamburg, Nov. 15, 1714); *Triumph des Friedens,* serenata (Hamburg, March 1, 1715); *Fredegunda* (Hamburg, March 1715); *L'amore verso la patria oder Der sterbende Cato* (Hamburg, 1715); *Artemisia* (Hamburg, 1715); *Das römische Aprilfest,* Lust- and Tantz-spiel (Hamburg, June 1716); *Das verewigte und triumphirende Ertz-Haus Oesterreich,* serenata (Hamburg, 1716); *Das zerstörte Troja oder Der durch den Tod Helenen versöhnte Achilles* (Hamburg, Nov. 1716); *Die durch Verstellung und Grossmuth über die Grausamkeit siegende Liebe oder Julia* (Hamburg, Feb. 1717); *Die grossmüthige Tomyris* (Hamburg, Feb. 1717); *Der die Festung Siebenbürgisch-Weissenburg erobernde und über Dacier triumphirende Kayser Trajanus* (Hamburg, Nov. 1717); *Das bey seiner Ruh und Gebuhrt eines Printzen frolockende Lycien unter der Regierung des Königs Jacobates und Bellerophon* (Hamburg, Dec. 28, 1717); *Die unvergleichliche Psyche* (Copenhagen, April 16, 1722); *Ulysses* (Copenhagen, Oct. 1722); *Der Armenier* (Copenhagen, Nov. 1722); *Die betrogene und nochmahls vergötterte Ariadne* (Hamburg, Nov. 25, 1722; based on the opera by Conradi of 1691); *Sancio oder Die siegende Grossmuth* (1723?); *Das wegen Verbannung der Laudplagen am Geburthstage Herrn Friedrich IV zu Dennemark jauchzende Cimbrien,* serenata (Copenhagen, 1724); *Das frohlockende Gross Britannien,* serenata (Hamburg, June 8, 1724); *Der sich rächende Cupido,* Schäferspiel (Hamburg, 1724; based on *Die entdeckte Verstellung oder Die geheime Liebe der Diana*); *Bretislaus oder Die siegende Beständigkeit* (Hamburg, Jan. 27, 1725); *Der Hamburger Jahrmarkt oder Der glückliche Betrug* (Hamburg, June 27, 1725); *Die Hamburger Schlachtzeit oder Der misslungene Betrug* (Hamburg, Oct. 22, 1725); *Prologus beim Geburths Feste Friderici Ludovici von Hannover,* serenata (Hamburg, Jan. 31, 1726); *Mistevojus König der Obotriten oder Wenden* (Hamburg, 1726); *Der lächerliche Printz Jodelet* (Hamburg, 1726); *Buchhofer der stumme Printz Atis,* intermezzo (Hamburg, 1726);

Barbacola, intermezzo (Hamburg, 1726; includes music by Lully); *Lucius Verus oder Die siegende Treue* (Hamburg, Oct. 18, 1728; based on *Berenice* by Bronner of 1702); *Der hochmüthige, gestürtzte und wieder erhabene Croesus,* singspiel (Hamburg, 1730; based on the dramma musicale of 1710); *Jauchzen der Kunste* (1733); *Circe* (Hamburg, March 1, 1734; with arias by other composers). Of these, *Die römische Unruhe oder Die edelmüthige Octavia* was ed. by M. Schneider in the supplement to the Handel *Gesamtausgabe* (Leipzig, 1902); *Der lächerliche Printz Jodelet* was ed. by F. Zelle in the *Publikationen der Gesellschaft für Musikforschung* (1892); the 1730 version of *Der hochmüthige, gesturtzte und wieder erhabene Croesus* was ed. by M. Schneider in the Denkmäler Deutscher Tonkunst, vol. 37 (1912).

Keiser also composed several secular cantatas and other pieces, including *Gemüths-Ergötzung,* cantata (Hamburg, 1698); *Componimenti musicali, oder Teutsche und italiänische Arien, nebst unterschiedlichen Recitativen aus Almira und Octavia* (Hamburg, 1706); *Divertimenti serenissima delle cantate, duette ed arie diverse senza stromenti oder Durchlauchtige Ergötzung* (Hamburg, 1713); *Musikalische Land-Lust, bestehend in verschiedenen moralischen Cantaten* (Hamburg, 1714); *Kayserliche Friedenspost, nebst verschiedenen moralischen Singgedichten und Arien* (Hamburg, 1715). Sacred works by Keiser include *Der blutige und sterbende Jesus* (Hamburg, Holy Week, 1704); *Der für die Sünde der Welt gemartete und sterbende Heiland Jesus* (Hamburg, 1712); *Der zum Tode verurtheilte und gecreutzigte Jesus* (Hamburg, 1715); *Passions Oratorium* (Hamburg, 1717?); *Die über den Triumph ihres Heylandes Jesu jubilirende gläubige Seele* (Hamburg, Nov. 2, 1717; not extant); *Die durch Grossmuth und Glauben triumphirende Unschuld oder Der siegende David* (Hamburg, Aug. 9, 1721); etc. The *Passions Oratorium* has been publ. in a modern ed. in the *Geistliche Chormusik,* vol. X (Stuttgart, 1963).

Kelberine, Alexander, pianist; b. Kiev, Feb. 22, 1903; d. (suicide) New York, Jan. 30, 1940. He studied at the Kiev Cons., then at the Univ. of Vienna; took lessons from Busoni in Berlin; in 1923, came to America and studied at the Juilliard Graduate School in N.Y. with Siloti (piano) and Rubin Goldmark (composition); later also studied with Ernst Toch. A victim of acute depression, he programmed his last recital for pieces in minor keys and of funereal connotations, concluding with Liszt's *Todtentanz;* he then went home and took an overdose of sleeping pills. His body was discovered on Jan. 30, 1940. He was married to the pianist **Jeanne Behrend,** but was estranged from her.

Kelemen, Milko, significant Croatian composer; b. Podrawska Slatina, March 30, 1924. He was taught to play piano by his grandmother; in 1945 entered the Zagreb Academy of Music, where he studied theory with Šulek; then went to Paris, where he took courses with Messiaen and Aubin at the Paris Cons. (1954–55); supplemented his studies at Freiburg with Fortner (1958–60); then worked on electronic music at the Siemens studio in Munich (1966–68); in the interim he taught composition at the Zagreb Cons. (1955–58, 1960–65). He was co-founder of the Zagreb Biennial Festival of New Music, and became its president in 1961. In 1969 he was appointed to the faculty of the Schumann Cons. in Düsseldorf; in 1973 he became a prof. of composition at the Hochschule für Musik in Stuttgart. As a composer, Kelemen began his career following the trend of European modernism well within academically acceptable lines, but changed his style radically about 1956 in the direction of the cosmopolitan avant-garde, adopting successively or concurrently the techniques of serialism, abstract expressionism, constructivism, and sonorism, making use of electronic sound; he further writes alternatively valid versions for a single piece.

WORKS: FOR THE STAGE: A "theater-of-the-absurd" musical scene, *Novi stanar (The New Tenant),* after Ionesco (1964; Münster, Sept. 20, 1964); 2 operas: *König Ubu* (1965; Hamburg, 1965) and *Der Belagerungszustand (State of Siege),* after Camus's novel *The Plague* (1968–69; Hamburg, Jan. 10, 1970); a "scenic action," *Opera bestial* (1973–74); 2 ballets: *Le Héros et son miroir (The Hero and His Mirror;* 1959; Paris, May 10, 1961) and *Napuštene (Abandoned;* 1956; Lübeck, Nov. 4, 1964). FOR ORCH.: *Prelude, Aria and Finale* for String Orch. (1948); Sinfonietta (1950); Symph. (1951; Zagreb, Feb. 18, 1952); Piano Concerto (1952; Zagreb, Dec. 22, 1953); Violin Concerto (1953; Zagreb, April 19, 1957); *Koncertantne improvizacije* for Strings (1955); *Adagio and Allegro* for Strings (1955); *Concerto giocosa* for Chamber Orch. (1956; Zagreb, Jan. 4, 1957); Concerto for Bassoon and Orch. (1956; Zagreb, April 11, 1957); *Simfonijska muzika 1957* (Zagreb, June 4, 1958); *3 Dances* for Viola and Strings (1957); *Konstelacije* for Chamber Orch. (1958; Zagreb, April 27, 1960); Concertino for Double Bass and Strings (1958); *Skolion* (1958); *5 Essays* for Strings (1959); *Ekvilibri* for 2 Orchs. (1961); *Transfiguracije* for Piano and Orch. (1961; Hamburg, April 6, 1962); *Sub Rosa* (1964; Zagreb, May 23, 1965); *Surprise* for Chamber String Orch. (1967; Zagreb, May 13, 1967); *Composé* for 2 Pianos and Orch. Groups (1967; Donaueschingen, Oct. 22, 1967); *Changeant* for Cello and Orch. (1967–68); *Floreal,* in 3 versions (1969–70; Coolidge Festival, Washington, D.C., Oct. 30, 1970); *Oliphant* for 5 Winds and Chamber Ensemble (1971); *Sonabile* for Piano, with Ring Modulator and Orch. (1972); *Abecedarium* for Chamber String Orch. (1973; Graz, Oct. 13, 1974); *Mirabilia II* for Piano, with Ring Modulator and 2 Orch. Groups (Graz, Oct. 12, 1977). FOR VOICE: *Igre (Games),* song cycle for Baritone and Strings (1955; Zagreb, Sept. 29, 1956); *Epitaph* for Mezzo-soprano and Chamber Orch. (1961); *O Primavera,* cantata for Tenor and Strings (1964); *Hommage à Heinrich Schütz* for Chorus a cappella (1964); *Le Mot* for Mezzo-soprano and 2 Orchs. (1964–65); *Musik für Heinssenbüttel* for Voice and Chamber Ensemble (1967); *Passionato* for Flute and Choral Group (1971); *Yebell* for Narrator, Pantomime, and Chamber Ensemble

(1972; Munich, Sept. 1, 1972); *For You* for Voice and Ring Modulator (1972); *Gassho* for 4 Choruses (1974). CHAMBER MUSIC: *Musika* for Solo Violin (1957); *Etudes contrapunctiques* for Wind Quintet (1959); Oboe Sonata (1960); *Studija* for Solo Flute (1961); *Radiant* for Flute, Viola, Piano or Celesta, Harpsichord, and Percussion (1961); *Entrances* for Wind Quintet (1966); *Motion* for String Quartet (1968); *Varia melodia* for String Quartet (1972); *Fabliau* for Solo Flute (1972); *Tantana*, 5 movements of instrumental "happening," with Voices in one movement (1972). FOR PIANO: *Theme and Variations* (1949); Sonata (1954); *5 Studies* (1958); *Dessins commentées* (1963).

Kell, Reginald, English clarinet virtuoso; b. York, June 8, 1906; d. Frankfort, Ky., Aug. 5, 1981. He studied violin at an early age, but later took up the clarinet, and earned a living by playing in silent-movie houses; in 1927 he enrolled at the Royal Academy of Music in London with Haydn Draper; upon Draper's death in 1934 he succeeded him as clarinet teacher at the Royal Academy of Music, a post he held until 1939. He subsequently occupied positions as principal clarinet player at the Royal Phil. (1931–32), London Phil. (1932–36), Covent Garden Opera (1932–36), London Symph. Orch. (1936–39), Liverpool Phil. (1942–45), and the Philharmonia (1945–48). In 1948 he went to the U.S., where he became active as a performer in chamber music ensembles and as a teacher; he was back in London in 1958; retired in 1966, and took up watercolor painting; in 1978 he exhibited his paintings at the Aspen Music Festival.

Keller, Hans, Austrian-British musicologist; b. Vienna, March 11, 1919. He emigrated to England in 1938; studied violin and viola, and played in orchs. and string quartets; mastered the English language to an extraordinary degree, and soon began pointing out solecisms and other infractions on the purity of the tongue to native journalists; wrote articles on film music, and boldly invaded the sports columns in British newspapers, flaunting his mastery of the lingo. In 1947 he founded (with Donald Mitchell) the periodical *Music Survey;* joined the music division of the BBC in 1959. He launched a system of "functional analysis," applying symbolic logic and pseudo-Babbagean taxonomy to render esthetic judgment on the value of a given musical work. He publ. several articles expounding the virtues of his ratiocination, among them the fundamental essay "Functional Analysis: Its Pure Application," *Music Review* (1957).

Keller, Karl, German composer and flutist; b. Dessau, Oct. 16, 1784; d. Schaffhausen, July 19, 1855. His father was a court organist and chamber musician. Keller was a flute virtuoso; he was court musician at Berlin (until 1806), Kassel (until 1814), Stuttgart (until 1816), and Donaueschingen (1817), where he later became chorus master. He married the opera singer **Wilhelmine Meierhofer.** In 1849 he received a pension and retired to Switzerland. He wrote 3 flute concertos; 4 polonaises, with Orch.; 2 divertisse-

ments, with Orch.; 6 part-songs for Male Chorus; duos and solos for flute; songs.

Keller, Matthias, German violinist and composer; b. Ulm, March 20, 1813; d. Boston, Oct. 12, 1875. He studied music in Stuttgart and Vienna; at 16 became first violinist of the Royal Chapel in Vienna (for 5 years); then was bandmaster in the army (for 7 years); in 1846, went to America and played in theater orchs. in Philadelphia; became interested in violin making and founded Keller's Patent Steam Violin Manufactory (1857). He then went to N.Y. and won a \$500 prize for his *American Hymn (Speed our Republic, O Father on high),* for which he wrote both words and music; composed over 100 songs, including some patriotic songs for the Civil War; also *Ravel Polka* (1846). He also publ. *A Collection of Poems* (1874).

Kelley, Edgar Stillman, important American composer and writer; b. Sparta, Wis., April 14, 1857; d. New York, Nov. 12, 1944. He studied first with F.W. Merriam (1870–74), then with Clarence Eddy and N. Ledochowsky in Chicago (1874–76). In 1876 he went to Germany, where he took courses at the Stuttgart Cons. (until 1880) with Seifritz (composition), Krüger and Speidel (piano), and Friedrich Finck (organ). Returning to the U.S., he served as an organist in Oakland and San Francisco; conducted performances of light opera companies in N.Y.; taught piano and theory at various schools and at the N.Y. College of Music (1891–92); was music critic for the *San Francisco Examiner* (1893–95); lecturer on music for the Univ. Extension of N.Y. Univ. (1896–97); then acting prof. at Yale Univ. (1901–2). In 1902 he went to Berlin, where he taught piano and theory (until 1910). In 1910 he was appointed dean of the dept. of composition at the Cincinnati Cons., retaining this post until 1934, at the same time holding a fellowship in composition at Western College in Oxford, Ohio. He received an honorary Litt.D. from Miami Univ. (1916) and an honorary LL.D. from the Univ. of Cincinnati (1917). He contributed articles to various music journals; also publ. correspondence from Germany during his stay there. With his wife, **Jessie Stillman Kelley,** he organized the Kelley Stillman Publishing Co., which publ. several of his scores. Although his stage works and his symph. pieces were quite successful when first performed (some critics described him as a natural successor to MacDowell in American creative work), little of his music survived the test of time.

WORKS: Theme and Variations for String Quartet (c.1880); *Wedding Ode* for Tenor Solo, Men's Chorus, and Orch. (c.1882); incidental music to *Macbeth,* for Orch. and Chorus (San Francisco, Feb. 12, 1885); comic opera, *Puritania* (Boston, June 9, 1892; 100 consecutive perfs.; publ. in vocal score); *Aladdin,* Chinese suite for Orch. (San Francisco, April 1894); incidental music to *Ben Hur,* for Soli, Chorus, and Orch. (N.Y., Oct. 1, 1900; highly successful, used for perfs. of that popular play some 6,000 times up to 1918); music to Fernald's play *The Cat and the Cherub* (N.Y., June 15, 1901); *Alice in Won-*

derland, suite for Orch. (Norfolk [Conn.] Festival, June 5, 1919, composer conducting); First Symph., *Gulliver* (Cincinnati, April 9, 1937); 2nd Symph., *New England* (Norfolk Festival, June 3, 1913, composer conducting); *The Pilgrim's Progress,* musical miracle play for Soli, Chorus, Children's Chorus, Organ, and Orch. (Cincinnati May Festival, May 10, 1918); *A California Idyll* for Orch. (N.Y., Nov. 14, 1918); *The Pit and the Pendulum,* symph. suite, after Poe (1925); *Israfel* and *Eldorado,* for Voice and Orch.; Piano Quintet; 2 piano quartets; many choral works, of which the best known are *My Captain,* after Whitman, and *The Sleeper,* after Poe; 3 pieces for Piano: *The Flower Seekers; Confluentia* (also arranged for String Orch., 1913); *The Headless Horseman;* a song, *The Lady Picking Mulberries* (1888); song cycle, *Phases of Love* (1890). He also publ. *Chopin the Composer* (N.Y., 1913); *Musical Instruments* (Boston, 1925).

Kellogg, Clara Louise, famous American soprano; b. Sumterville, S.C., July 9, 1842; d. New Hartford, Conn., May 13, 1916. She received her vocal training in N.Y., from Manzocchi, Errani, and Muzio; made her professional debut at the Academy of Music in N.Y. (Feb. 27, 1861); then sang in Boston. She sang Marguerite in the N.Y. premiere of *Faust* (Nov. 25, 1863); made her London debut as Marguerite on Nov. 2, 1867. In 1872 she organized an opera company with Pauline Lucca, but the rivalry between them precluded its success. In 1873 she launched an opera enterprise of her own, known as the English Opera Co.; she extended her supervision to the translations of the librettos, the stage settings, and the training of the soloists and chorus. She herself sang 125 performances in the winter of 1874–75. After that, she divided her time between Europe and America. In 1887 she married her manager, Karl Strakosch, nephew of Maurice and Max Strakosch, and retired from the stage. She wrote *Memoirs of an American Prima Donna* (N.Y., 1913).

Kelly, Michael, Irish singer and composer; b. Dublin, Dec. 25, 1762; d. Margate, Oct. 9, 1826. He studied singing under Rauzzini, and in Naples (1779) under Fenaroli and Aprile. He then sang in Palermo, Livorno, Florence, Bologna, and Venice. Visiting Vienna, he was engaged at the court opera for 4 years, becoming the friend of Mozart, and taking the role of Basilio in the production of *Figaro.* In 1787 he appeared for the first time at Drury Lane in London, and sang leading tenor roles there until his retirement. In 1789 his debut as a composer was made with *False Appearances* and *Fashionable Friends;* up to 1820 he wrote the music for 62 stage pieces, also many songs. He had a music shop from 1802 to 1811; when it failed, he went into the wine trade; it was Sheridan who said, considering the quality of his music and wines, that he was "a composer of wines and an importer of music." His *Reminiscences,* publ. in the year of his death (1826), were written by Theodore Hook from material supplied by Kelly (reprinted with a new introduction by A.H. King, N.Y., 1968); the vol. is replete with amusing musical anecdotes.

Kelterborn, Rudolf, Swiss composer; b. Basel, Sept. 3, 1931. He studied piano and rudimentary music theory in high school; then entered the Univ. of Basel and studied musicology with Jacques Handschin; later took a course in composition with Willy Burkhard in Zürich and Boris Blacher in Salzburg; for one semester he studied in Detmold with Wolfgang Fortner (1955). In 1960 he was engaged as a teacher of composition at the Music Academy in Detmold; in 1968 he became a prof. at the Hochschule für Musik in Zürich. In 1975 he was appointed music director of the Basel Radio. He was also active as a conductor, mostly of his own music. In his music, Kelterborn applies a precisely coordinated serial organization wherein quantitative values of duration form a recurrent series; the changes of tempo are also subjected to serialization. Both melody and harmony are derived from a tone row in which the dissonant intervals of major seventh and minor second are the mainstays.

WORKS: OPERAS: *Die Errettung Thebens* (Zürich, June 23, 1963) and *Kaiser Jovian* (Karlsruhe, March 4, 1967). FOR ORCH.: Suite for Woodwinds, Percussion, and Strings (1954); Concertino for Violin and Chamber Orch. (1954); Sonata for 16 Solo Strings (1955); *Canto appassionato* (1959); Concertino for Piano, Percussion, and Strings (1959); *Metamorphosen* (1960); Cello Concerto (1962); *Phantasmen* (1966); Symph. No. 1 (Vienna, April 26, 1968); Symph. No. 2 (1969); *Musik* for Piano and 8 Wind Instruments (1970); *Traummusik* for Small Orch. (1971); *Kommunikationen* for 6 Instrumental Groups (1972); *Changements* (1973); *Tableaux encadrés* (1974). CHAMBER MUSIC: 4 string quartets (1954, 1956, 1962, 1970); *5 Fantasien* for Wind Quintet (1958); *Esquisses* for Harpsichord and Percussion (1962); *Meditationen* for 6 Wind Instruments (1962); *Kammersonate* for Flute, Oboe, String Trio, and Harpsichord (1963); *Fantasia a tre* for Piano, Violin, and Cello (1967); *4 Stücke* for Clarinet and Piano (1970); *9 Momente* for Viola and Piano (1973); *Reaktionen* for Violin and Piano (1974). VOCAL WORKS: *Cantata profana* (1960); *Ewige Wiederkehr,* chamber cantata (1960); *Musica spei* for Soprano, Chorus, and Orch. (1968); *Dies unus* for Voices and Orch. (1971); *3 Fragmente* for Chorus and Orch. (1968); *Dies unus* for Voices and Orch. (1971); *3 Fragmente* for Chorus a cappella (1973).

Kemp, Barbara, German dramatic soprano; b. Cochem, Dec. 12, 1881; d. Berlin, April 17, 1959. She sang in opera in Rostock and Breslau before being engaged as a member of the Berlin State Opera in 1914. She married the composer **Max von Schillings** in 1923; in the same year (on March 1) she sang the title role in his opera *Mona Lisa* at the Metropolitan Opera in N.Y. She returned to Germany in 1924; sang Wagnerian roles at Bayreuth; continued on the roster of the Berlin State Opera until 1932, when she retired, but continued to produce opera in Berlin for several years.

Kempe, Rudolf, eminent German conductor; b. Niederpoyritz, near Dresden, June 14, 1910; d. Zurich, May 11, 1976. He studied oboe at the Orchestral School of the Dresden Staatskapelle; in 1929 became first oboist of the Gewandhaus Orch. in Leipzig. He made his conducting debut at the Leipzig Opera in 1936. He served in the German army during World War II; then conducted in Chemnitz; was director of the Opera there (1945–48) and at the Weimar National Theater (1948–49). From 1949 to 1953 he was Generalmusikdirektor of the Dresden Staatskapelle; then served in an identical capacity with the Bavarian State Opera in Munich (1952–54); also made appearances in opera in Vienna, in London (Covent Garden), and at the Metropolitan Opera in N.Y. In 1960 Sir Thomas Beecham named him associate conductor of the Royal Phil. Orch. of London; upon Beecham's death in 1961, he became its principal conductor; from 1963 till 1975 was artistic director as well. He was chief conductor of the Tonhalle Orch. in Zürich (1965–72) and of the Munich Phil. (from 1967); from 1975 he conducted the BBC Symph. He was a distinguished interpreter of Beethoven, Brahms, Wagner, Bruckner, and Richard Strauss; also conducted light opera.

Kempff, Wilhelm, distinguished German pianist; b. Juterbog, Nov. 25, 1895. He studied piano with his father, also named **Wilhelm Kempff;** at the age of 9 he entered the Berlin Hochschule für Musik, where he studied composition with Robert Kahn and piano with Heinrich Barth; also attended the Univ. of Berlin. He began his concert career in 1916; in 1918 he made the first of many appearances with the Berlin Phil.; from that time he toured throughout Europe, South America, and Japan, featuring improvisation as part of his programs. From 1924 to 1929 he was director of the Stuttgart Hochschule für Musik; from 1957 he gave annual courses in Positano, Italy. He made his London debut in 1951 and his American debut in N.Y. in 1964. He continued to appear in concerts well past his octogenarian milestone; in 1979 he was a soloist with the Berlin Phil., after having had an association with it for more than 50 years. Kempff epitomized the old tradition of German pianism; he eschewed flamboyance in his performances of Mozart, Beethoven, Schubert, and other classics. He publ. a book of memoirs, *Unter dem Zimbelstern* (Stuttgart, 1951). He was also a composer.

Keneman, Feodor, Russian pianist and composer of German descent; b. Moscow, April 20, 1873; d. there, March 29, 1937. He was a piano student of Safonov at the Moscow Cons. (graduated in 1895) and a student of composition of Ippolitov-Ivanov there (graduated in 1897); also attended counterpoint classes of Taneyev. From 1899 to 1932 he taught music theory at the Moscow Cons. He gave piano recitals and was the favorite accompanist of Chaliapin, for whom he composed the popular Russian ballad "As the King Went to War" and arranged the folk song "Ei ukhnem!" which became one of the greatest successes at Chaliapin's concerts. Keneman made an American tour with Chaliapin in 1923–24. He also composed a number of military marches and band pieces.

Kenessey, Jenö, Hungarian composer; b. Budapest, Sept. 23, 1906; d. there, Aug. 19, 1976. He studied with Lajtha and Siklós in Budapest and attended Franz Shalk's conducting course in Salzburg; in 1932 he was appointed a member of the conducting staff at the Budapest Opera House; conducted his opera *Gold and the Woman* (1942) there on May 8, 1943, and his ballet *May Festival* (1948) on Nov. 29, 1948. His other works include 5 more ballets: *Montmartre* (1930); *Johnny in Boots* (1935); *Mine Is the Bridegroom* (1938); *The Kerchief* (1951); *Bihari's Song* (1954); also, *Dance Impressions* for Orch. (1933); Divertimento for Orch. (1945); *Dances from Sárköz* for Orch. (1953); *Beams of Light,* cantata (1960); *Canzonetta* for Flute and Chamber Orch. (1970); *Dawn at Balaton,* symph. poem, with Narrator and Female Voices (1972); Piano Quartet (1928–29); Sonata for Harp and Flute (1940); Sonata for Harp, Flute, and Viola (1940); Divertimento for Viola and Harp (1963); Trio for Violin, Viola, and Harp (1972); *Elegy and Scherzo* for Piano (1973); songs and choruses.

Kennedy, Michael, English writer on music; b. Manchester, Feb. 19, 1926. He received his education in Manchester; then joined the staff of the *Daily Telegraph* there in 1941, becoming its northern editor in 1960.
WRITINGS: *The Hallé Tradition: A Century of Music* (Manchester, 1960); *The Works of Ralph Vaughan Williams* (London, 1964; revised ed., 1980); *Portrait of Elgar* (London, 1968; revised ed., 1982); *Elgar: Orchestral Music* (London, 1969); *Portrait of Manchester* (Manchester, 1970); *A History of the Royal Manchester College of Music* (Manchester, 1971); *Barbirolli: Conductor Laureate* (London, 1971); *Mahler* (London, 1974); *Richard Strauss* (London, 1976). He also ed. *The Autobiography of Charles Hallé, with Correspondence and Diaries* (London, 1976) and *The Concise Oxford Dictionary of Music* (London, 3rd revised ed., 1980).

Kennedy-Fraser, Marjory, Scottish singer, pianist, and folk-song collector; b. Perth, Oct. 1, 1857; d. Edinburgh, Nov. 22, 1930. She was the daughter of the famous Scottish singer **David Kennedy** (1825–86) and traveled with him as his accompanist from the age of 12. She then studied with Mathilde Marchesi in Paris; also took courses in piano with Matthay and in music history with Niecks. Inspired by the example of her father, she became a dedicated collector of folk songs. In 1905 she went to the Outer Hebridean Isles, after which she made a specialty of research in Celtic music, including the adaptation and arranging of Gaelic folk material into art forms; publ. the famous collection *Songs of the Hebrides,* with texts in Gaelic and Eng., in 3 vols. (1909, 1917, 1921); also wrote a *Hebridean Suite* for Cello and Piano (1922), several collections of folk music for schools, piano pieces based on Hebridean folk songs, etc. She publ. the important handbook *Hebridean Song and the Laws of Interpretation* (Glasgow, 1922); a similar vol. for Lowland Scots songs; *From the Hebrides* (London, 1925); an autobiography, *A Life of Song* (London, 1928); wrote the libretto for Bantock's opera *The Seal Woman*, and sang the title role in it. She was married to A.J. Fraser, a schoolteacher in Glasgow.

Kenton, Stan (Stanley Newcomb), American jazz bandleader; b. Wichita, Kans., Feb. 19, 1912; d. Hollywood, Aug. 25, 1979. He spent his youth in California; earned a living playing piano in local saloons and speakeasies and at the same time began experimenting with new sounds in jazz. A volatile but talented musician, he constantly invented slogans to describe his arrangements and his manner of conducting, such as "progressive jazz," "artistry in rhythm," and "innovations in modern music," but above all he believed that music must be loud to overwhelm and subjugate the public. He kept discovering modernistic devices, such as already obsolescent progressions of whole-tone scales and consecutive major ninth-chords. He was ecstatic when he stumbled upon the Schillinger System of Composition, which professed to impart the power of creativity to untutored musicians. Although commercially successful, Kenton suffered mandatory nervous breakdowns, and at one time decided to abandon music and become a psychiatrist; he gave up the idea when he realized that he would have to learn Greek-derived words and unpronounceable German terms. He married frequently; one of his sons was indicted for conspiracy to commit murder (he put a snake in the mailbox of a bothersome attorney).

Kepler, Johannes, illustrious German astronomer; b. Weil, Württemberg, Dec. 27, 1571; d. Regensburg, Nov. 15, 1630. He explored Pythagorean concepts of harmony and relationships among music, mathematics, and physics in books 3 and 5 of his *Harmonices mundi.*

Kerle, Jacobus de, Flemish organist and composer; b. Ypres, 1531 or 1532; d. Prague, Jan. 7, 1591. He served as church organist at the Cathedral of Orvieto (1555–61); then was ordained a priest and in 1561 went to Venice, where he supervised the publ. of his *Liber Psalmorum.* He then proceeded to Rome, where he met Cardinal Otto Truchsess, Lord High Steward and Bishop of Augsburg, who commissioned Kerle to write his *Preces speciales pro salubri generalis concilii successu* for the Council of Trent. In 1563–64 he traveled throughout northern Italy to Barcelona, and later was in Dillingen, Bavaria (1564). He returned to Ypres in 1565; traveled to Rome once more; in 1568 went to Augsburg, where he became vicar-choral and organist at the Cathedral; later held a prebend in Cambrai (1575–87). Early in 1582 he became Kapellmeister to Elector Gebhard Truchsess of Waldburg in Cologne; in Sept. 1582 became chaplain at the imperial court in

Augsburg under Rudolph II; in Oct. 1582 he joined the court chapel in Vienna; in 1583 settled in Prague. He exerted a considerable influence on the musical culture of his time.

Kerll (or **Kerl, Kherl, Cherl**), **Johann Kaspar,** German organist and composer; b. Adorf, Saxony, April 9, 1627; d. Munich, Feb. 13, 1693. He served a musical apprenticeship with his father, an organist and organ manufacturer, **Kaspar Kerll;** in his youth, was court organist in Vienna, where he studied with the imperial court Kapellmeister, Giovanni Valentini; then went to Rome; he converted to Catholicism and received instruction from Carissimi; it is possible that he also met Frescobaldi. He was subsequently court organist in Brussels. On Sept. 22, 1656, he was appointed Kapellmeister in Munich; he resigned this post in 1673. From 1674–77 he served as organist at St. Stephen's Cathedral in Vienna; on March 16, 1677, he was named imperial court organist in Vienna. He was ennobled in 1664.

Kerman, Joseph, American musicologist; b. London (of American parents), April 3, 1924. He studied at the Univ. College School in London; then went to the U.S.; enrolled at N.Y. Univ. (A.B., 1943); subsequently studied musicology at Princeton Univ. with Strunk, receiving his Ph.D. there in 1950 with the dissertation *The Elizabethan Madrigal: A Comparative Study* (publ. in the series American Musicological Society Studies and Documents, N.Y., 1962). He taught at Westminster Choir College (1949–51); in 1951 he joined the faculty of the Univ. of Calif. at Berkeley; was named associate prof. there in 1955, and prof. in 1960; from 1960 to 1963 served as chairman of its music dept. From 1971 to 1974 he was Heather Prof. of Music at Oxford Univ.; then resumed his professorship at Berkeley. His books include *Opera as Drama* (N.Y., 1956); *The Beethoven Quartets* (N.Y., 1967); with H. Janson, *A History of Art and Music* (N.Y., 1968); with V. Kerman, *Listen* (N.Y., 1972).

Kern, Jerome (David), famous American composer; b. New York, Jan. 27, 1885; d. there, Nov. 11, 1945. He was educated in N.Y. public schools; studied music with his mother; then with Paolo Gallico and Alexander Lambert (piano) and Austin Pearce and Albert von Doenhoff (theory); went to Germany, where he continued to study composition; returned to N.Y. in 1904; became a pianist and a salesman for a publishing firm; publ. his first song, *How'd You Like to Spoon with Me,* in 1905, and it became famous; in 1906 he was in London, where he was connected with a theatrical production. In 1911 he obtained his first success as a composer for the stage with his musical comedy *The Red Petticoat* (Nov. 13, 1912). After that he continued to produce musical comedies in rapid succession; in 1917 alone he produced 7 shows on Broadway; altogether, he composed more than 60 works for the stage, including several motion picture scores. His most important productions include *Very Good, Eddie* (N.Y., Dec. 23, 1915); *Have a Heart* (N.Y., Jan. 11, 1917);

Kertész – Ketting

Head over Heels (N.Y., April 29, 1918); *Sally* (N.Y., Dec. 21, 1920; extremely successful); *Stepping Stones* (N.Y., Nov. 6, 1923); *Sunny* (N.Y., Sept. 22, 1925); *Show Boat* (Washington, D.C., Nov. 15, 1927; N.Y., Dec. 27, 1927; his most remarkable score, one of the finest American works of its genre; includes the famous bass aria *Ol' Man River*); *The Cat and the Fiddle* (N.Y., Oct. 15, 1931); *Music in the Air* (N.Y., Nov. 8, 1932); *Roberta* (N.Y., Nov. 18, 1933); *The 3 Sisters* (London, April 9, 1934); *Gentlemen Unafraid* (St. Louis, June 3, 1938); *Very Warm for May* (N.Y., Nov. 17, 1939). He also composed an orch. work, *Portrait of Mark Twain* (Cincinnati, May 14, 1942). A motion picture on his life, *As the Clouds Roll By,* was produced posthumously (1946). A selection of his songs are in *The Jerome Kern Song Book,* with an introduction by Oscar Hammerstein II (N.Y., 1955).

Kertész, István, Hungarian conductor; b. Budapest, Aug. 28, 1929; d. Kfar Saba, Israel, April 16, 1973 (drowned while swimming in the Mediterranean). He studied at the Academy of Music in Budapest and at the Santa Cecilia Academy in Rome (1958); was conductor at Györ (1953–55) and at the Budapest Opera (1953–57); from 1958–64 served as music director in Augsburg; then went to the Cologne Opera. From 1965–68 he was principal conductor of the London Symph. Orch. He made his U.S. debut in 1961 with the Detroit Symph.; his accidental death was deplored.

Ketèlbey, Albert William, English composer of light music; b. Aston, Aug. 9, 1875; d. Cowes, Isle of Wight, Nov. 26, 1959. He was of remote Danish origin. Precociously gifted in music, he wrote a piano sonata at the age of 11, and played it at the Worcester Town Hall; Elgar heard it and praised it. At the age of 13, he competed for a Trinity College scholarship, and was installed as Queen Victoria Scholar; at 16 he obtained the post of organist at St. John's Church at Wimbledon; at 20 began tours as the conductor of a musical comedy troupe. For some years he was music director of Columbia Gramophone Co. and music editor at Chappell's Music Publishing Co. Among his works are: Quintet for Woodwinds and Piano; String Quartet; *Caprice* for Piano and Orch.; comic opera, *The Wonder Worker;* etc. He achieved fame with a series of remarkably popular instrumental pieces on exotic subjects (*In a Persian Market, In a Monastery Garden, Sanctuary of the Heart, In a Chinese Temple Garden,* etc.). He also publ. many small pieces under various pseudonyms.

Ketting, Otto, Dutch composer, son of **Piet Ketting;** b. Amsterdam, Sept. 3, 1935. He studied composition at The Hague Cons. (1952–58); played trumpet in various orchs. (1955–61); taught composition at the Rotterdam Cons. (1967–71) and at the Royal Cons. in The Hague (1971–74). In 1983 he was appointed artistic adviser to the Utrecht Symph. Orch. His music represents a valiant effort to adapt Classical modalities to the esthetics of the 20th century.

WORKS: 2 operas: *Dummies* (The Hague, Nov. 14, 1974) and *O, Thou Rhinoceros* (Holland Festival, June 2, 1977); 6 ballets: *Het laatste bericht (The Last Message;* 1962); *Intérieur* (1963); *Barrière* (1963); *The Golden Key* (1964); *Choreostruction* (1963); *Theater Piece* (1973); *Kerstliederen (Christmas Songs)* for Chorus and Small Orch. (1953); Sinfonietta (1954); *2 canzoni* for Orch. (1957); Passacaglia for Orch. (1957); Concertino for 2 Solo Trumpets, String Orch., 3 Horns, and Piano (1958); Symph. (1957–59); Concertino for Jazz Quintet and Orch. (1960); Variations for Wind Orch., Harp, and Percussion (1960); *Pas de deux,* choreographic commentary for Orch. (1961); a series of "collages," among which the most uninhibited is *Collage No. 9* for 22 Musicians (Conductor, 16 Brass, and 5 Percussionists; 1963; Amsterdam, Jan. 26, 1966; audience reaction, hopefully that of outrage, is part of the perf.: the conductor is instructed to treat his environment with disdain and contempt, to arrive late, leave early, and refuse to acknowledge social amenities); *In Memoriam Igor Stravinsky* for Orch. (1971); *Time Machine* for Winds and Percussion (Rotterdam, May 5, 1972); *For Moonlight Nights* for Flutist (alternating on Piccolo and Alto Flute) and 26 Players (1973; Hilversum, April 17, 1975); *Adagio* for Chamber Orch. (1977); *Symphony* for Saxophones and Orch. (1978); Concerto for Solo Organ (1953); Sonata for Brass Quartet (1955); Piano Sonatina (1956); Serenade for Cello and Piano (1957); *A Set of Pieces* for Flute and Piano (1967); *A Set of Pieces* for Wind Quintet (1968); *Minimal Music* for 28 Toy Instruments (1970).

Ketting, Piet, Dutch composer, conductor, and pianist, father of **Otto Ketting;** b. Haarlem, Nov. 29, 1904. He studied singing and choral conducting at the Utrecht Cons.; then took lessons in composition with Willem Pijper. As a pianist, he formed a duo with the flutist Johan Feltkamp (1927), and a unique trio with Feltkamp and oboist Jaap Stotijn (1935) that toured the Dutch East Indies in 1939; from 1949 to 1960 he conducted the Rotterdam Chamber Orch.; was also founder and conductor of the Rotterdam Chamber Choir (1937–60). From 1960 till 1974 he immersed himself in the numerical symbolism of J.S. Bach's works, with some startling, though unpubl., results. In his own music he pursues a modern Baroque system of composition, with a discreet application of euphonious dissonance. He allowed himself a 20-year hiatus in composition between 1942 and 1962, partly on account of the war, but then resumed production with renewed vigor.

WORKS: 2 symphs. (1929, 1975); Sinfonia for Cello and Orch. (1963; radio perf., Dec. 1, 1965); *De minnedeuntjes (The Love Songs)* for Chorus and Orch. (1966–67; Dutch Radio, May 9, 1968); Bassoon Concertino (1968); Clarinet Concertino (1973); String Trio (1925); 3 string quartets (1927–28); Cello Sonata (1928); Trio for Flute, Clarinet, and Bassoon (1929); Flute Sonata (1930); Sonata for Flute, Oboe, and Piano (1936); *Partita* for 2 Flutes (1936); *Fantasia No. 1* for Harpsichord, Descant, and Treble Recorders and Flute (1969); *Fantasia No. 2* for Harpsichord

(1972); *Preludium e Fughetta* for Alto Flute and Piano (1969); 4 piano sonatinas (1926, 1926, 1927, 1929); *Prelude, Interlude and Postlude* for 2 Pianos (1971); *Jazon and Medea,* dramatic scene for Chorus, Piano, Flute, and Clarinet (1975).

Keussler, Gerhard von, German composer and conductor; b. Schwanenburg, Latvia, July 5, 1874; d. Niederwartha, near Dresden, Aug. 21, 1949. He studied biology in St. Petersburg; then went to Leipzig, where he took courses in music theory with Riemann and Kretzschmar at Leipzig Univ. and with Reinecke and Jadassohn at the Cons. From 1906 to 1910 he conducted a German chorus in Prague; then went to Hamburg, where he conducted the Phil. Orch. until 1920 and led the Singakademie. In 1931 he toured in Australia as a conductor; returning to Germany in 1934, he taught at the Prussian Academy of Arts in Berlin; in 1941 he settled in Niederwartha, near Dresden, where he remained until his death. He wrote operas in a Wagnerian vein, of which several were performed: *Wandlungen* (1904); *Gefängnisse* (Prague, April 22, 1914); and *Die Gesselfahrt* (Hamburg, 1923); he further composed 2 symphs. and a symph. poem, *Australia* (1936).

Key, Francis Scott, a Baltimore lawyer, author of the words of the American national anthem; b. Carroll County, Md., Aug. 1, 1779; d. Baltimore, Jan. 11, 1843. He wrote the text of the anthem aboard a British ship (where he was taken as a civilian emissary to intercede for release of a Maryland physician) on the morning of Sept. 14, 1814, setting it to the tune of the British drinking song *To Anacreon in Heaven,* popular at the time, written by John Stafford Smith. The text and the tune did not become an official national anthem until March 3, 1931, when the bill establishing it as such was passed by Congress and signed by President Herbert Hoover.

Khachaturian, Aram, brilliant Russian composer of Armenian extraction; b. Kodzhori, suburb of Tiflis, June 6, 1903; d. Moscow, May 1, 1978 (buried in Erevan). His father was a bookbinder. The family stayed in Tiflis until 1920; Khachaturian played the tuba in the school band, and also studied biology. He then went to Moscow and entered the Gnessin School to study cello; later studied composition with Gnessin himself. In 1929 he became a student at the Moscow Cons., graduating in 1934 in the class of Miaskovsky. Although he started to compose rather late in life, he developed rapidly, and soon progressed to the first rank of Soviet composers. His music is in the tradition of Russian Orientalism; he applies the characteristic scale progressions of Caucasian melos, without quoting actual folk songs. His *Sabre Dance* from his ballet *Gayane* became popular all over the world. In 1948 Khachaturian was severely criticized by the Central Committee of the Communist Party, along with Prokofiev, Shostakovich, and others, for modernistic tendencies; although he admitted his deviations in this respect, he continued to compose essentially in his typical manner, not shunning highly dissonant harmonic

combinations. As a conductor of his own works, he gave a concert in Reykjavik, Iceland, in 1951; conducted in Bulgaria in 1952, in Finland in 1955, in London in 1955 and again in 1977, in Japan in 1963, and in Greece in 1965. He made his American debut in Washington, D.C., on Jan. 23, 1968, conducting the National Symph. Orch. in a program of his works; on Jan. 28, 1968, he conducted in N.Y. to a rousing audience reception. In 1933 he married the composer **Nina Makarova** (1908–76). Khachaturian's name is to be properly pronounced Hachaturyán, with a stress on the palatalized last syllable, and with the initial consonant "H" ("Kh") pronounced as the German "ch."

WORKS: FOR THE STAGE: 3 ballets: *Happiness* (1939; Erevan, 1939; Moscow, Oct. 24, 1939); *Gayane* (1940–42; Perm, Dec. 9, 1942; revised 1952 and 1957; extracted 3 symph. suites, 1943; includes the immensely popular *Sabre Dance*); *Spartak* (*Spartacus;* 1950–56; Leningrad, Dec. 26, 1956; revised 1957–58; 4 symph. suites extracted: Nos. 1–3, 1955, and No. 4, 1966).

FOR ORCH.: *Dance Suite* (1932–33); 3 symphs.: No. 1 (1932–33; Moscow, April 23, 1935); No. 2 (1943; Moscow, Dec. 30, 1943; revised, Moscow, March 6, 1944); No. 3 for 15 Solo Trumpets, Orch., and Organ (1947; Leningrad, Dec. 13, 1947); Piano Concerto (1936; Leningrad, July 5, 1937); *The Widow of Valencia,* incidental music (1939–40; orch. suite, 1953); *Masquerade,* incidental music to Lermontov's play (1940; orch. suite, 1944); Violin Concerto (1940; Moscow, Nov. 16, 1940; transcribed for Flute in 1968 by Jean-Pierre Rampal); *2 Armenian Dances* for Cavalry Band (1943); *Solemn Overture* (1945); *Russian Fantasy* (1946); Cello Concerto (1945–46; Moscow, Oct. 30, 1946); *Ode in Memory of Lenin* (1948; Moscow, Dec. 26, 1948); *Battle of Stalingrad,* music for film (screened in Moscow, Dec. 9, 1949); *Concerto-Rhapsody* for Piano and Orch. (1955–68); overture, *Salutation* (1958–59); *Concerto-Rhapsody* for Violin and Orch. (1961–62; Yaroslavl, Oct. 7, 1962; Moscow, Nov. 3. 1962); *Concerto-Rhapsody* for Cello and Orch. (1963; Gorky, Jan. 4, 1964).

CHAMBER MUSIC: *Song-Poem* for Violin and Piano (1929); Violin Sonata (1932); String Quartet (1932); Trio for Clarinet, Violin, and Piano (1932); *Jazz Composition* for Solo Clarinet (1966; written for Benny Goodman); *Sonata-Monologue* for Solo Cello (1974); *Sonata-Fantasia* for Solo Violin (1975).

FOR VOICE: *Poem about Stalin* for Orch., with choral ending (1938; Moscow, Nov. 29, 1938); *3 Concert Arias* for Soprano and Orch. (1946); *Ode to Joy* for Mezzo-soprano, Chorus, 10 Harps, Unison Violins, Band, and Orch. (1955); *Ballade about the Fatherland* for Bass and Orch. (1961); *In Memory of the Heroes,* cantata for Soprano, Male Chorus, and Orch. (1976; a reworking of *Battle of Stalingrad*); songs.

FOR PIANO: 2 albums of children's pieces (1926–47, 1965); *Poem* (1927); *Suite* (1932); *Toccata* (1932); *Suite,* 3 pieces for 2 Pianos (1945); Sonatina (1952); Sonata (1961); *7 Fugues with Recitatives* (1928–66); music for films; numerous marches for band.

Khachaturian, Karen, Soviet composer; nephew of

Aram Khachaturian; b. Moscow, Sept. 19, 1920. He studied at the Moscow Cons. with Litinsky; during World War II he served in the entertainment division of the Red Army. He resumed studies in 1945 at the Moscow Cons. with Shebalin, Shostakovich, and Miaskovsky, graduating in 1949; in 1952 he was appointed to the faculty of the Moscow Cons. His music follows the general line of socialist realism, nationalist or ethnic in thematic resources and realistic in harmonic and contrapuntal treatment. He wrote a number of effective scores for films. His name, like the name of his uncle, is stressed on the last syllable.

WORKS: For the stage: Operetta, *An Ordinary Girl* (1959); ballet, *Cipollino,* after Rodari's fairy tale (1973). For Orch.: Sinfonietta (1949); Overture (1949); *New-Year Tree,* suite (1951); *Youth Overture* (1951); *In Mongolia,* suite (1951); *Oriental Suite* (1952); *Sports Suite* (1954); 2 symphs.: No. 1 (Moscow, March 12, 1955) and No. 2 (1968); *Friendship Overture* (1959); *At the Circus,* suite (1968). For Voice: *At the Lone Willow,* cantata (1950); *A Moment of History,* oratorio, to documented texts of the Soviet Revolution of 1917 (1971); choruses, songs. Chamber music: Violin Sonata (1947); Cello Sonata (1966); String Quartet (1969).

Khandoshkin, Ivan, Russian violinist and composer; b. 1747; d. St. Petersburg, March 28, 1804. He was the first Russian violin virtuoso, and the first to write instrumental music on Russian folk themes. He studied in St. Petersburg with an Italian musician, Tito Porta; then was sent to Italy, where he was a student at the Tartini school in Padua; it is probable that he took lessons from Tartini himself. Returning to Russia in 1765, he became a violinist in the Imperial Chapel; was concertmaster of the Court Orch. in 1773; also taught violin at the Academy of Arts in St. Petersburg, and later in Moscow and in Ekaterinoslav. These appointments were highly unusual honors to one of Khandoshkin's origin (he was a liberated serf). The following pieces were publ. during his lifetime: *6 sonates pour deux violons* (Amsterdam, 1781); *Chansons russes variées pour violon et basse* (Amsterdam, 1781); *Nouvelles variations sur des chansons russes* for Violin (St. Petersburg, 1784). A set of Russian songs for unaccompanied violin was publ. in 1820; a number of works by Khandoshkin came to light in Russian archives in recent times; his Concerto for Viola and String Orch. was publ. in 1947; *Sentimental Aria* for Unaccompanied Violin was publ. in 1949.

Khokhlov, Pavel, noted Russian baritone; b. Spassky, Aug. 2, 1854; d. Moscow, Sept. 20, 1919. He studied in Moscow; made his debut with the Bolshoi Theater there in the role of Valentin in *Faust* in 1879; was on its roster until he retired in 1900; also appeared at the Maryinsky Theater in St. Petersburg (1881, 1887–88). He sang the title role in *Eugene Onegin* at the first professional performance of the opera in Moscow in 1881, was also noted for other roles in the Russian repertoire.

Khrennikov, Tikhon, important Soviet composer socially active in music administration; b. Elets, June 10, 1913. He was the 10th child in the family of a provincial clerk, but his parents, his brothers, and sisters were musical, played the Russian guitar and the mandolin, and sang peasant songs. He took piano lessons with a local musician; in 1927 he went to Moscow, where he was introduced to Gniessin, who accepted him as a student in his newly founded musical Technicum; there he studied counterpoint with Litinsky and piano with Ephraim Hellman. After graduation from Gniessin's school, he entered the Moscow Cons., where he studied composition with Shebalin and piano with Neuhaus. At the age of 19 he composed his first important work, a Piano Concerto, which he performed as soloist in Moscow in 1933. He also wrote a piece for a children's theater directed by Natalie Satz, about the time that Prokofiev presented *Peter and the Wolf* at the same theater. In addition, he wrote a number of lyrical ballads and patriotic mass songs. Khrennikov graduated from the Moscow Cons. in 1936; later continued his postgraduate work with Shebalin. In 1961 he joined the faculty of the Moscow Cons., and was named a prof. in 1966. In the meantime he became engaged in the political life of the country. He was attached to the music corps of the Red Army and accompanied it during the last months of the war, entering Berlin in May 1945. In 1947 he joined the Communist party; was also a deputy of the Supreme Soviet; in 1948 he was appointed secretary-general of the Union of Soviet Composers, and in 1949 became president of the music section of the All-Union Society for Cultural Exchange with Europe and America. He further served as head of the organizing committee for the International Festivals and the Tchaikovsky Competitions in Moscow. He held numerous honors, including the Lenin Prize in 1974. Amid all this work he never slackened the tempo of his main preoccupation, that of composition. He wrote operas, ballets, symphs., and concertos, and appeared as a piano soloist. He was a member of the Soviet delegation to the U.S. in 1959. Khrennikov was named a Hero of Socialist Labor in 1973. During his entire career he was a stout spokesman for the Soviet musical policy along the lines of socialist realism, and his own works express forcefully the desirable qualities of Soviet music, a flowing melody suggesting the broad modalities of Russian folk songs, a vibrant and expressive lyricism, and effective instrumental formation.

WORKS: FOR THE STAGE: Operas: *Brothers* (later renamed *In the Storm;* Moscow, May 31, 1939); *Frol Skobeyev* (Moscow, Feb. 24, 1950; 2nd version renamed *Unrelated Son-in-Law*); *Mother,* after the novel by Maxim Gorky (Moscow, Oct. 26, 1957); fairy-tale opera for children, *Boy Giant* (1969); comic opera, *Much Ado about ... Hearts,* a parody on Shakespeare's play *Much Ado about Nothing* (1976); operettas: *100 Devils and a Single Girl* (Moscow, May 16, 1963); *White Nights* (Moscow, Nov. 3, 1967); ballet, *Happy Childhood* (1970). FOR ORCH.: 3 symphs.: No. 1 (Moscow, Oct. 10, 1955); No. 2, expressing "the irresistible will to defeat the Fascist foe" (Moscow, Jan. 10, 1943); No. 3 (1973); 3 piano concertos (1933, 1970, 1982); 2 violin concertos (1959, 1975); Cello Concerto (Moscow, May 13, 1964). INCIDENTAL MUSIC: *A Soldier Returns from the Front* (1938); *Don Quixote* (1941). FILM MUSIC: *Shepherdess and Shepherd* (1941); *At Six o'Clock after the War* (1944); *The Balladeer Goes West* (1947); *Hussar's Ballad* (1962); *We Need Not a Password* (1964). Also chamber music; piano pieces; many songs and choruses.

Kienzl, Wilhelm, Austrian composer; b. Waizenkirchen, Jan. 17, 1857; d. Vienna, Oct. 3, 1941. He studied music at the Graz Gymnasium with Ignaz Uhl, and with W.A. Remy (composition); later with Josef Krejči at Prague, Rheinberger in Munich, and Liszt at Weimar, at length receiving his Ph.D. in Vienna in 1879 for the dissertation *Die musikalische Deklamation* (Leipzig, 1880). A 2nd work, *Miscellen* (Leipzig, 1885), concerning impressions received in Bayreuth (1879), created a stir by its bold criticism. During 1880 he lectured on music in Munich; in 1881–82, made a pianistic tour in Hungary, Rumania, and Germany; in 1883, was appointed conductor of the German opera in Amsterdam. Shortly thereafter, he went to Krefeld to take up a similar position; in 1886 he married the concert singer **Lili Hoke.** In 1886–90 he was artistic director of the Styrian Musikverein at Graz and directed the symph. concerts and the programs of the provincial vocal and instrumental schools. In 1890–92 he held the position of first conductor at the Hamburg Opera; in 1892–94 was court conductor at Munich, before returning to Graz. In 1917, he received the honorary degree of Doc.Mus. from the Univ. of Graz; later, in Vienna, was music critic for various papers. His early operas include *Urvasi* (Dresden, Feb. 20, 1886; rewritten 1909); *Heilmar, der Narr* (Munich, March 8, 1892; very successful); *Der Evangelimann* (Berlin, May 4, 1895; his most famous work). Then followed *Don Quichote,* a "musical tragi-comedy" (Berlin, Nov. 18, 1898); *In Knecht Rupprechts Werkstatt,* a "Märchenspiel" (Graz, 1906); *Der Kuhreigen (Ranz des Vaches)* (Vienna, Nov. 23, 1911); *Das Testament* (Vienna, Dec. 6, 1916); *Hassan der Schwarmer* (Chemnitz, 1925); *Sanctissimum* (Vienna, 1925); *Hans Kipfel,* singspiel (Vienna, 1928). Kienzl finished Adolf Jensen's opera *Turandot,* and edited Mozart's *Titus.* His own publ. compositions include about 120 songs; much light piano music; incidental music to *Die Brautfahrt; Septuaginta* (1937); 3 *Phantasiestücke* for Piano and Violin; Piano Trio; 2 string quartets; choral music. He also composed the new Austrian national anthem, with a text by the future president of Austria, Karl Renner, to replace that written by Haydn in 1797; its adoption was announced by the Republican government on June 6, 1920, but on Dec. 13, 1929, the Haydn melody was once more adopted as a national anthem (with a different set of words). Kienzl edited Brendel's *Grundzüge der Geschichte der Musik* (Leipzig, 1886) and *Geschichte der Musik in Italien, Deutschland und Frankreich* (7th ed., Leipzig, 1889). In addition, he wrote *Richard Wagner* (1904; 2nd ed., 1908); *Aus Kunst und Leben* (1904); *Im Konzert* (1908); *Betrachtungen und Erinnerungen* (1909); *Meine Lebenswanderung,* an autobiography (1926); *Hans Richter* (1930).

Kilpinen, Yrjö, Finnish song composer; b. Helsingfors, Feb. 4, 1892; d. Helsinki, March 2, 1959. He had very little academic education in music; took a few courses at the Helsingfors Cons., in Berlin, and in Vienna. His chosen form was that of lyric song; possessing an exceptional talent for expressing poetic lines in finely balanced melodies, he attained great renown in Finland, and has been called the Finnish Hugo Wolf. He composed about 800 lieder to words in German, Finnish, and Swedish, by classical and modern poets. In 1948 he was appointed a member of the Academy of Finland. About 300 of his songs are publ.; other works are *Pastoral Suite* for Orch. (1944); *Totentanz* for Orch. (1945); 6 piano sonatas; Cello Sonata; Suite for Viola da Gamba, with Piano; etc.

Kim, Earl, American composer; b. Dinuba, Calif., Jan. 6, 1920. He studied at the Univ. of Calif., Berkeley (M.A. 1952); was an associate prof. at Princeton Univ. (1952–67) and subsequently on the staff of Harvard Univ. His works include *Dialogues* for Piano and Orch. (1959); *They Are Far Out* for Soprano, Violin, Cello, and Percussion (1966); *Gooseberries, She Said* for Soprano, 5 Instruments, and Percussion (1968); *Letter Found near a Suicide,* song cycle; *Exercises en route,* multimedia composition. He received in 1971 the Brandeis Univ. Creative Arts Award.

Kim, Young-Uck, South Korean violinist; b. Seoul, Sept. 1, 1947. A typical child prodigy, he began to fiddle with astounding precocity on a minuscule violin. He was sent to the U.S. when he was 11 and accepted as a student of Ivan Galamian at the Curtis Inst. of Music in Philadelphia. On May 10, 1963, he made an auspicious appearance with Ormandy and the Philadelphia Orch. in a nationally televised concert; then toured with them in South America. This was the beginning of a brilliant career; he made a European tour as a soloist with the Berlin Phil., the Concertgebouw Orch. of Amsterdam, the Vienna Phil., and the London Symph. He also organized the Ax-Ma-Kim Trio, with the Polish-born American pianist Emanuel Ax and the Chinese cello virtuoso Yo-Yo Ma.

Kimball, Jacob, Jr., American composer; b. Topsfield, Mass., Feb. 22, 1761; d. in the almshouse there, Feb. 6, 1826. In 1775 he was a drummer in the Massachusetts militia; then entered Harvard Univ. (graduated 1780); subsequently studied law and was admitted to the bar, but soon gave up that profession for music, teaching in various New England towns. He wrote hymns, psalm tunes, and "fuguing pieces," in the style of Billings; compiled *The Rural Harmony* (71 original compositions for 3 and 4 voices; Boston, 1793). Another collection, *The Essex Harmony* (44 tunes and 2 anthems), is also attributed to him; it was publ. in Exeter, N.H., in 1800, and dedicated to the Essex (Mass.) Music Assoc.; the Boston Public Library possesses an imperfect copy.

Kincaid, William, outstanding American flutist and pedagogue; b. Minneapolis, April 26, 1895; d. Philadelphia, March 27, 1967. He studied flute with Georges Barrère at the Inst. of Musical Art in N.Y.; then played in the N.Y. Symph. Orch. (1914–21). In 1921 Stokowski engaged him as first flutist of the Philadelphia Orch., a position he held with great distinction until his retirement in 1960; he also was a distinguished teacher at the Curtis Inst. of Music, where he taught a number of noted flute players. He maintained a valuable collection of historic flutes; his own instrument was a specially made platinum flute.

Kindler, Hans, Dutch-American cellist and conductor; b. Rotterdam, Jan. 8, 1892; d. Watch Hill, R.I., Aug. 30, 1949. He studied at the Rotterdam Cons., receiving first prize for piano and cello in 1906. In 1911 he was appointed prof. at the Scharwenka Cons. in Berlin, and first cellist at the Berlin Opera. In 1912–13 he made a successful tour of Europe; in 1914, came to the U.S. to become first cellist of the Philadelphia Orch., a post he held until 1920. In 1927 he made his debut as a conductor in Philadelphia; in 1928 he conducted the world premiere of Stravinsky's ballet *Apollon Musagète* at the Library of Congress Festival in Washington, D.C.; in 1929 he appeared as a cellist in 110 concerts throughout the U.S. and Europe, also touring as far as Java and India. In 1931 he organized the National Symph. Orch. in Washington, of which he was permanent conductor until his resignation on Nov. 30, 1948.

King, Alec (Alexander) Hyatt, English bibliographer and musicologist; b. Beckenham, Kent, July 18, 1911. He was educated at Culwich College and King's College, Cambridge (B.A., 1933); in 1934 he joined the Dept. of Printed Books of the British Museum; became head of the music division in 1944; retired in 1976. He publ. a number of valuable textual and bibliographical studies.

King, Karl L(awrence), American Midwestern bandmaster and composer of band music; b. Painterville, Ohio, Feb. 21, 1891; d. Fort Dodge, Iowa, March 31, 1971. After 8 grades of public schools in Cleveland and Canton, Ohio, during which he began to play brass instruments (primarily the baritone horn) under the tutelage of local musicians, he quit school to learn the printing trade, but soon began to play in and compose for local bands. In 1910 he initiated his short career as a circus bandsman, bandmaster, and composer, ending it in 1917–18 as bandmaster of the Barnum & Bailey Circus Band (for which he had already written what was to remain his most famous march, *Barnum & Bailey's Favorite*). On Sept. 13, 1920, he conducted his first concert with the Fort Dodge Military Band, with which he was to be associated for half a century. It was a time when the small-town band in the U.S. was passing its heyday; but King took a group of only 18 bandsmen, added to them, and in a very few years had created a notable institution, not only in Iowa but in the whole Midwestern rural culture (and this over a period when most town bands were disappearing under the competition of radio, recordings, the school-band movement, and faster transportation and communications). In 1922 the band began to receive municipal tax support under the Iowa Band Law (for which one of King's marches is named), and its name was changed to the Fort Dodge Municipal Band, although it was known commonly as Karl L. King's Band. For 40 years it toured widely over its region, especially to play at county fairs, and King himself traveled even more widely to conduct or judge at band contests, conventions, massed band celebrations, and all manner of band events. He was one of the founders, in 1930, of the American Bandmasters Assoc.; he served as president of that group in 1939, and in 1967 was named Honorary Life President. Among his 260-odd works for band (most publ. the firm of C.L. Barnhouse in Oskaloosa, Iowa) are concert works, novelties, waltzes, and all manner of dance forms; but marches predominate, from the circus marches of his early days to sophisticated marches for univ. bands (such as *Pride of the Illini* for Illinois and *Purple Pageant* for Northwestern) and especially to easy but tuneful and well-written marches for the less-accomplished school bands. The musical *The Music Man* (1957) was inspired in part by King's music, according to its composer and fellow Iowan, **Meredith Willson.**

Kinkeldey, Otto, eminent American musicologist; b. New York, Nov. 27, 1878; d. Orange, N.J., Sept. 19, 1966. He graduated from the College of the City of N.Y. in 1898 (B.A.) and from N.Y. Univ. in 1900 (M.A.); then took lessons with MacDowell at Columbia Univ. (until 1902). After that he went to Germany, where he undertook a course of study with Radecke, Egidi, and Thiel at the Akademisches Inst. für Kirchenmusik in Berlin; studied musicology at the Univ. of Berlin with Fleischer, Friedlaender, Kretzschmar, and J. Wolf (1902–6); received his Ph.D. from the Univ. of Berlin in 1909. He was organist and choirmaster at the Chapel of the Incarnation in N.Y. (1898–1902); organist and music director of the American Church in Berlin (1903–5); instructor in organ and theory, lecturer on musicology, and music director at the Univ. of Breslau (1909–14); was named Royal Prussian Prof. in 1910. Returning to the U.S. at the outbreak of World War I, he became organist and choirmaster at All-Souls Church in N.Y. (1915–17); was an infantry captain in the U.S. Army (1917–19); in 1915–23, and again in 1927–30, was chief of the Music Division of the N.Y. Public Library; in 1923–27 he was a prof. of music at Cornell Univ.; in 1930–46, a prof. of musicology and librarian there; prof. emeritus, 1946. He was a guest prof. at Harvard Univ. (1946–48), the Univ. of Texas (1948–50), Princeton Univ. (1950–51), North Texas State College (1952–53), the Univ. of Illinois (1953–54), the Univ. of Calif., Berkeley (1954–55), Boston Univ. (1957), and the Univ. of

Washington, Seattle (1958). He was elected president of the American Musicological Society for 1934–36, and reelected for 1940–42; was also nominated an honorary member of the Musical Assoc. in London. In 1947 he received a Litt.D. *honoris causa* from Princeton Univ. He publ. the valuable book *Orgel und Klavier in der Musik des 16. Jahrhunderts* (Ph.D. dissertation, 1909; publ. in Leipzig, 1910); many articles in the *Musical Quarterly,* the *Proceedings* of the Music Teachers' National Assoc., etc.; edited Erlebach's *Harmonische Freude musikalischer Freunde* for vols. 46 and 47 of Denkmäler Deutscher Tonkunst (1914). Later publications include *A Jewish Dancing Master of the Renaissance, Guglielmo Ebreo* (reprinted in 1929 from A.S. Freidus Memorial Volume) and *Music and Music Printing in Incunabula* (reprinted in 1932 from the *Papers of the Bibliographical Society of America,* vol. 26).

Kipnis, Alexander, eminent Russian-born American bass; b. Zhitomir, Feb. 13, 1891; d. Westport, Conn., May 14, 1978. He learned to play trombone and double bass; enrolled in the Warsaw Cons. and graduated in 1912 in conducting; subsequently served in the Russian army as a military bandmaster. Later he decided to study singing and went to Berlin, where he took voice lessons with Ernst Grenzebach at the Klindworth-Scharwenka Cons. In 1913 he sang at Monti's Operetten Theater and in 1914 at the Filmzauber operetta theater. At the outbreak of the war in 1914 he was interned as an enemy alien, but was soon released and made his operatic debut in Hamburg in 1915; then was a member of the Wiesbaden Opera (1917–22). He made his American debut as Pogner in *Die Meistersinger von Nürnberg* with the visiting German Opera Co. in Baltimore on Jan. 31, 1923; he then was a member of the Chicago Civic Opera (1923–32). He also sang regularly at the Deutsches Opernhaus in Berlin (from 1919), at the Berlin State Opera (1932–35), and at the Vienna State Opera (until 1938). He became an American citizen in 1931. During these years he made guest appearances at the Bayreuth, Salzburg, and Glyndebourne festivals, as well as at Covent Garden in London and the Teatro Colón in Buenos Aires. On Jan. 5, 1940, he made his Metropolitan Opera debut in N.Y. as Gernemanz in *Parsifal,* and continued to sing there until 1946; he then devoted himself mainly to teaching. Through the years he appeared as a soloist with Richard Strauss, Siegfried Wagner, and Toscanini. His son, **Igor Kipnis,** is a well-known harpsichordist.

Kipnis, Igor, distinguished American harpsichordist, son of the famous singer **Alexander Kipnis;** b. Berlin, Sept. 27, 1930. In 1938 the family moved to the U.S., where he took piano lessons with his maternal grandfather, the noted musician **Heniot Levy.** Kipnis first studied at the Westport (Conn.) School of Music; for several years served as an accompanist for his father's pupils. He then entered Harvard Univ., where his instructors were Randall Thompson and the visiting British musicologist Thurston Dart. He also took harpsichord lessons with Fernando Valenti. After graduation from Harvard (B.A., 1952), Kipnis served abroad in the Signal Corps of the U.S. Army. Returning to the U.S., he eked out his living as a bookstore salesman in N.Y.; later was employed as an editorial adviser to Westminster Records Co. He made his concert debut as a harpsichordist in N.Y. in 1961. During the summers of 1964, 1965, 1966, and 1967 he was instructor in Baroque performances at the Berkshire Music Center in Tanglewood. In 1967 he made his first European tour; in 1968 he gave concerts in South America; then traveled to Israel in 1969, and in Australia in 1971. He served as an associate prof. of fine arts at Fairfield Univ., Conn. (1971–75), and artist-in-residence there (1975–77); also taught and played at the Festival Music Society in Indianapolis and at its Early-Music Inst. In 1982 he became visiting tutor in Harpsichord and Baroque Music Studies at the Royal Northern College of Music in Manchester, England. He did much to revive the fortepiano, a keyboard instrument that succeeded the harpsichord as the favorite medium of composers in the early 19th century. He also promoted interest in modern music. Several contemporary composers, among them Ned Rorem, George Rochberg, Richard Rodney Bennet, Barbara Kolb, and John McCabe, wrote special works for him.

Kircher, Athanasius, highly significant Jesuit scholar; b. Geisa, near Fulda, Germany, May 2, 1601; d. Rome, Nov. 27, 1680. He attended the Jesuit Seminary in Fulda (1612–18), and was ordained in Paderborn in 1618. He subsequently studied philosophy and theology in Cologne (1622), Koblenz (1623), and Mainz (1624–28); from 1629 to 1631 he taught theology and philosophy at the Univ. of Würzburg; in 1631 he went to Lyons, then to Avignon, and in 1633 to Rome, where he taught at the Collegio Romano; he remained in Rome until the end of his life. His *Oedipus aegiptiacus* contains a curious chapter on hieroglyphic music; in his treatise *De arte magnetica* he gives examples of musical airs which were popularly regarded as a cure for tarantism (a nervous condition supposedly induced by the bite of a tarantula). Indeed, his writings present a curious mixture of scientific speculation and puerile credulity. His principal work is the Latin compendium *Musurgia universalis sive ars magna consoni et dissoni* (Rome, 1650; in German, 1662; a facsimile ed. was issued in 1969).

Kirchner, Leon, significant American composer; b. Brooklyn, Jan. 24, 1919, of Russian-Jewish parents. In 1928 the family moved to Los Angeles; there he studied piano with Richard Buhlig; in 1938 he entered the Univ. of Calif., Berkeley, where he took courses in music theory with Albert Elkus and Edward Strickland (B.A., 1940); he also took lessons with Ernest Bloch in San Francisco. In 1942 he went to N.Y., where he had some fruitful private sessions with Sessions; in 1943 he entered military service in the U.S. Army; after demobilization in 1946 he was appointed to the faculty of the San Francisco Cons., concurrently teaching at the Univ. of Calif., Berkeley; in 1948 he received a Guggenheim fellowship; in 1950 he became associate prof. at the Univ. of Southern Calif., Los Angeles; from 1954 to 1961 he taught at Mills College in Oakland, Calif., and in 1961 was named prof. of music at Harvard Univ.; during the academic year 1970–71 he was a guest prof. at the Univ. of Calif., Los Angeles. He received the N.Y. Music Critics Award in 1950 and 1960, and in 1967 was awarded the Pulitzer Prize. In his music Kirchner takes the prudential median course, cultivating a distinct modern idiom without espousing any particular modernistic technique, but making ample and effective use of euphonious dissonance; the contrapuntal fabric in his works is tense but invariably coherent. Through his natural inclinations toward Classical order, he prefers formal types of composition, often following the established Baroque style.

WORKS: Opera, *Lily,* after Saul Bellow's novel *Henderson, The Rain King* (N.Y., April 14, 1977); Sinfonia (N.Y., Jan. 31, 1952); *Toccata* for Strings, Wind Instruments, and Percussion (San Francisco, Feb. 16, 1956); Piano Concerto No. 1 (N.Y., Feb. 23, 1956, composer soloist); Piano Concerto No. 2 (Seattle, Oct. 28, 1963); *Music for Orchestra* (1969); chamber music: Duo for Violin and Piano (1947); String Quartet No. 1 (1949); *Sonata concertante* for Violin and Piano (1952); Piano Trio (1954); String Quartet No. 2 (1958); Concerto for Violin, Cello, 10 Instruments, and Percussion (1960); String Quartet No. 3, with Electronic Sound (1966; awarded the Pulitzer Prize for 1967); *Lily* for Violin, Viola, Cello, Woodwind Quintet, Piano, Percussion, and Voice (1973; material from this work was used in his opera, *Lily*); vocal works: *Letter* (1943); *The Times Are Nightfall* for Soprano and Piano (1943); *Dawn* for Chorus and Organ (1946); *Of Obedience and the Runner,* after Walt Whitman, for Soprano and Piano (1950); *Words from Wordsworth* for Chorus (1966); Piano Sonata (1948); *Little Suite* for Piano (1949).

Kirchner, Theodor, distinguished German composer; b. Neukirchen, near Chemnitz, Dec. 10, 1823; d. Hamburg, Sept. 18, 1903. On Mendelssohn's advice, he studied in Leipzig with K.F. Becker (theory) and J. Knorr (piano), and, in the summer of 1842, with Johann Schneider in Dresden. He was engaged as organist at Winterthur (1843–62) and then taught at the Zürich Music School (1862–72); later held the post of director of the Würzburg Cons. (1873–75). He then returned to Leipzig; finally went to Hamburg in 1890. As a youth he enjoyed the friendship of Mendelssohn and Schumann, who encouraged and aided him with their advice. He wrote about 90 piano works, in the style of Schumann; some of his miniatures are of very high quality; he also made numerous transcriptions for piano solo and piano duet (*Alte Bekannte in neuem Gewande*); *Kinder-Trios* for Piano, Violin, and Cello; Piano Quartet; String Quartet; 8 pieces for Piano and Cello; etc.

Kirkby, Emma, English soprano; b. Camberley,

Feb. 26, 1949. She made her debut in London in 1974; specialized in early music; was a member of the Academy of Ancient Music, the London Baroque, and the Consort of Musicke. In 1978 she toured the U.S.; then gave concerts in the Middle East with the lutenist Anthony Rooley. Her repertoire ranges from the Italian quattrocento to arias by Handel, Mozart, and Haydn. The careful attention she paid to the purity of intonation free from intrusive vibrato was praised.

Kirkby-Lunn, Louise, English dramatic contralto; b. Manchester, Nov. 8, 1873; d. London, Feb. 17, 1930. She studied voice in Manchester and at the Royal College of Music in London; appeared as an opera singer at various London theaters, making her debut at Drury Lane in 1893; then toured with Sir Augustus Harris's company, and with the Carl Rosa Opera Co. from 1897 until 1899, when she married W.J. Pearson, and retired from the stage for 2 years. In 1901 she reappeared as a member of the Royal Opera at Covent Garden, where she soon became one of the popular favorites. On Dec. 26, 1902, she sang for the first time at the Metropolitan Opera in N.Y., where her interpretations of Wagnerian roles (Ortrud and Brangäne) made a deep impression; in 1904 she sang Kundry in Savage's production of *Parsifal* in English. In 1906–8 she was again with the Metropolitan Opera; sang with the British National Opera Co. in 1919–22; toured in Australia.

Kirkman (real name, **Kirchmann**), **Jakob,** founder of the firm of Kirkman and Sons, the London harpsichord makers; b. Bischweiler, near Strasbourg, March 4, 1710; d. Greenwich, June (buried, June 9) 1792. He settled in London about 1730; there he was associated with a Flemish harpsichord maker, Hermann Tabel. After Tabel's death, Kirkman married his widow and acquired Tabel's tools. In 1755 he was naturalized as a British subject. In 1773 Kirkman, who was childless, formed a partnership with his nephew, **Abraham Kirkman** (1737–94). The descendants of Abraham Kirkman continued the business until 1896, when the firm was merged with Collard; it was eventually absorbed by Chappell. For details and a list of surviving instruments, see the exhaustive article on Kirkman in Donald Boalch, *Makers of the Harpsichord and Clavichord* (London, 1956).

Kirkpatrick, John, eminent American pianist and pedagogue; b. New York, March 18, 1905. He studied at Princeton Univ.; then took courses in Paris with I. Philipp, C. Decreus, and Nadia Boulanger; returning to America in 1931, he became an energetic promoter of the cause of American music. His signal achievement was the first performance of the *Concord Sonata* by Charles Ives, which he gave in N.Y. on Jan. 20, 1939, playing it from memory, an extraordinary feat for the time; this performance, which earned enthusiastic reviews for both Ives and Kirkpatrick, played an important role in the public recognition of Ives. As a pedagogue, Kirkpatrick taught at Mount Holyoke College (1943–46) and at Cornell Univ. (1946–68); later joined the faculty of Yale Univ. (1968–75), where he was also curator of the Charles Ives Collection. His compendia *A Temporary Mimeographed Catalogue of the Music Manuscripts and Related Materials of Charles Edward Ives* (New Haven, 1960; reprinted 1973) and *Charles E. Ives: Memos* (N.Y., 1972) are primary sources of the Ives studies.

Kirkpatrick, Ralph, eminent American harpsichordist and music editor; b. Leominster, Mass., June 10, 1911; d. Guilford, Conn., April 13, 1984. He studied at Harvard Univ. (A.B., 1931); then went to Paris to study theory with Nadia Boulanger, and also took lessons in harpsichord playing with Wanda Landowska. He subsequently worked with Arnold Dolmetsch at Haslemere, England, in order to acquaint himself with the technical problems of performing on old keyboard instruments and on their modern replicas. He also studied with Günther Ramin and Heinz Tiessen in Berlin. In 1937 he was awarded a Guggenheim fellowship for research in Baroque performing practices; he undertook an extensive tour of Europe, studying private collections of MSS. His research was particularly fruitful in Spain; he consulted the Madrid telephone book for descendants of Domenico Scarlatti (who spent his last years of life in Spain) and was fortunate enough to discover that several Scarlattis listed in the directory were indeed related to the family; the MSS he was able to find there became the foundation of his standard biography, *Domenico Scarlatti* (Princeton and London, 1953; 3rd ed., revised, 1968). In 1940 he was appointed to the staff of Yale Univ., remaining on its staff until his retirement in 1978. Kirkpatrick was highly selective in his evaluation of Baroque music; while emphasizing the importance of William Byrd, François Couperin, and Domenico Scarlatti, he regarded Vivaldi and Telemann as minor composers serving the temporary tastes of the general public. He edited 60 sonatas by Scarlatti (1953) and recorded them; he also edited Bach's *Goldberg Variations* and prepared a vol. on Bach's *Well-tempered Clavier* (1984). His interpretations as a harpsichordist were of the highest degree of fidelity to the Baroque style; but he also gave brilliant performances of modern piano works, including those of Stravinsky, Darius Milhaud, Henry Cowell, Walter Piston, and Elliott Carter.

Kirnberger, Johann Philipp, noted German theorist; b. Saalfeld, April 24, 1721; d. Berlin, July 27, 1783. He first studied violin and harpsichord at home; then took organ lessons with P. Kellner at Gräfenroda, and with H.N. Gerber at Sondershausen; also studied violin with Meil there. By 1741 he was a pupil of Bach in Leipzig, and spent 2 years with him. He then traveled in Poland (1741–50) as a tutor in various noble Polish families; in 1751 he became violinist to Frederick the Great, and in 1758, Kapellmeister to Princess Amalie. He was greatly renowned as a teacher; among his pupils were Schulz, Fasch, and Zelter. As a theoretical writer, he was regarded as one of the greatest authorities of his time. In his own compositions he displayed an amazing contrapuntal technique, and seriously strove to establish a scientific method of writing music according to basic rules of combination and permutation; his *Der allezeit fertige Polonaisen- und Menuetten-componist* (1757) expounded the automatic method of composition. Other works are: *Die Konstruction der gleichschwebenden Temperatur* (1760); *Die Kunst des reinen Satzes in der Musik aus sicheren Grundsätzen hergeleitet und mit deutlichen Beispielen versehen* (2 vols., 1771, 1779; his magnum opus); *Grundsätze des Generalbasses, als erste Linien zur Komposition* (1781; often republ.); *Gedanken über die verschiedenen Lehrarten in der Komposition, als Vorbereitung zur Fugenkenntniss* (1782). *Die wahren Grundsätze zum Gebrauch der Harmonie* (1773) was claimed by a pupil of Kirnberger's, J.A.P. Schulz, as his work.

Kirsten, Dorothy, American soprano; b. Montclair, N.J., July 6, 1915. She studied singing at the Juilliard School of Music in N.Y.; Grace Moore took an interest in her and enabled her to go to Italy for further voice training. She studied in Rome with Astolfo Pescia; the outbreak of war in 1939 forced her to return to the U.S. She became a member of the Chicago Opera Co. (debut, Nov. 9, 1940); made her first appearance in N.Y. as Mimi with the San Carlo Opera Co. (May 10, 1942); appeared with the Metropolitan Opera in the same role on Dec. 1, 1945; she sang there in 1945–52, 1954–57, and 1960–75. In 1947 she went to Paris, where she sang Louise in Charpentier's opera, coached by Charpentier himself. On New Year's Eve of 1975 she made her farewell appearance at the Metropolitan Opera, in the role of Tosca, in celebration of the 30th anniversary of her debut with the company. She publ. an autobiography, *A Time to Sing* (Garden City, N.Y., 1982).

Kjerulf, Halfdan, Norwegian song composer; b. Christiania, Sept. 15, 1815; d. Grefsen, near Christiania, Aug. 11, 1868. He was a member of a family of artists and scholars; studied piano as a child; then took up law, subsequently working as a journalist. In 1848–49 he took lessons with a resident German musician, Carl Arnold; then studied with Gade in Copenhagen (1849–50); in 1850–51 he enrolled in the Leipzig Cons.; in 1851 he returned to Norway, where he taught piano. He limited himself to composition in small forms; although he followed the German model, he injected melodic and rhythmic elements of a national Norwegian character into his songs. Grieg was deeply influenced by his example and frequently expressed admiration for his music; many celebrated singers (Jenny Lind, Christine Nilsson, and Henriette Sontag among them) included his songs in their programs, and thus made them known. He wrote about 130 songs in all, among which the most popular are *Last Night, Tell Me, The Nightingale,* and *Synnöve's Song;* he also composed some 30 works for men's chorus and 10 albums of piano pieces marked by a strong Scandinavian cast (*Elfin Dance, Shepherd's Song,*

Cradle Song, Spring Song, Album-leaf, Capriccio, Scherzo, Scherzino, etc.); also publ. the album *25 Selected Norwegian Folk Dances* for Piano (1861) and *Norwegian Folk Songs* for Piano (1867); these are arrangements of Norwegian melodies from collections by Lindeman and others. In 1874 a monument was erected to him in Christiania.

Klafsky, Katharina, Hungarian soprano; b. St. Johann, Sept. 19, 1855; d. Hamburg, Sept. 22, 1896. She studied with Mme. Marchesi in Vienna; began her career as a chorus singer in various opera houses; in 1881 she attracted attention as a Wagnerian singer; appeared in Hamburg (1885), in London (1892, 1894), and in the U.S. (1895–96). She was one of the most spectacular prima donnas of her day, and her early death was mourned by opera-lovers as a great loss.

Klebe, Giselher, German composer; b. Mannheim, June 28, 1925. He studied at the Berlin Cons. with Kurt von Wolfurt (1942–43), with Josef Rufer, and with Boris Blacher (1946–51). He worked in the program division of the Berlin Radio (1946–49); in 1957 was appointed to the faculty of the Nordwestdeutsche Musik Akademie in Detmold; was elected member of the Academy of Arts in Berlin. An experimenter by nature, he writes music in widely ranging forms, from classically conceived instrumental pieces to highly modernistic inventions; his technique is basically dodecaphonic; coloristic and sonoristic schemes also play an important role. WORKS: OPERAS: *Die Räuber,* after Schiller (1951–56; Düsseldorf, June 3, 1957; revised 1962); *Die tödlichen Wünsche,* after Balzac (1957–59; Düsseldorf, June 14, 1959); *Die Ermordung Cäsars,* after Shakespeare (1958–59; Essen, Sept. 20, 1959); *Alkmene,* after Kleist (1961; Berlin, Sept. 25, 1961); *Figaro lässt sich scheiden,* opera buffa after von Horváth (1962–63; Hamburg, June 28, 1963); *Jakobowsky und der Oberst,* comic opera after Werfel (1965; Hamburg, Nov. 2, 1965); *Das Märchen von der schönen Lilie,* fairy-tale opera after Goethe (1967–68; Schwetzingen, May 15, 1969); *Ein wahrer Held,* after Synge's *Playboy of the Western World,* adapted by Boll (1972–73; Zürich Festival, Jan. 18, 1975); *Das Mädchen aus Domremy,* after Schiller (1975–76; Stuttgart, June 19, 1976); *Das Rendez-vous* (Hannover, Oct. 7, 1977). BALLETS: *Pas de trois* (1951; Wiesbaden, 1951); *Signale* (1955; Berlin, 1955); *Fleurenville* (1956; Berlin, 1956); *Menagerie* (1958); *Das Testament* (Symph. No. 4; 1970). FOR ORCH.: *Con moto* (1948; Bremen, Feb. 23, 1953); *Divertissement joyeux* for Chamber Orch. (1949; Darmstadt, July 8, 1949); *Die Zwitschermaschine (The Twittering Machine),* metamorphosis on Klee's famous painting (1950; Donaueschingen, Sept. 10, 1950); *2 Nocturnes* (1951; Darmstadt, July 20, 1952); 4 symphs.: No. 1 for 42 Strings (1951; Hamburg, Jan. 7, 1953); No. 2 (1953); No. 3 (1967); No. 4, *Das Testament,* ballet-symph. for Orch. and 2 Pianos tuned a quarter-tone apart (1970–71; Wiesbaden, April 30, 1971); *Rhapsody* (1953); *Double Concerto* for Violin, Cello, and Orch. (1954; Frankfurt, June 19, 1954); *Moments musicaux* (1955); Cello Concerto (1957); *Omaggio* (1960);

Adagio and Fugue, on a motif from Wagner's *Die Walküre* (1962); *Herzschläge,* 3 symph. scenes for Beat Band and Orch. (1969); Concerto for Electronically Altered Harpsichord and Small Orch. (1971–72); *Orpheus,* dramatic scenes (1976). VOCAL MUSIC: *Geschichte vom lustigen Musikanten* for Tenor, Chorus, and 5 Instruments (1946–47); *5 Römische Elegien,* after Goethe, for Narrator, Piano, Harpsichord, and Double Bass (1952; Donaueschingen, Oct. 10, 1953); *Raskolnikows Traum,* dramatic scene after Dostoyevsky, for Soprano, Clarinet, and Orch. (1956); *5 Lieder* for Alto and Orch. (1962); *Stabat Mater* for Soprano, Mezzo-soprano, Alto, Chorus, and Orch. (1964); *Gebet einer armen Seele (The Prayer of a Poor Soul),* dodecaphonic Mass for Chorus and Organ (1966); choruses; songs. CHAMBER MUSIC: Wind Quintet (1948); 2 string quartets (1949, 1963); Viola Sonata (1949); 2 solo violin sonatas (1952, 1955); 2 violin sonatas (1953, 1972); *Elegia appasionata,* piano trio (1955); *Dithyrambe* for String Quartet (1957); *7 Bagatelles* for Basset Horn, Trombone, Harp, and Tubular Bells (1961); *9 Duettini* for Flute and Piano (1962); *Missa "Miserere nobis"* for 18 Wind Instruments (1965); *Concerto a 5* for Piano, Harpsichord, Harp, Percussion, and Double Bass (1965); *Quasi una fantasia,* piano quintet (1967); *Scene and Aria* for 3 Trumpets, 3 Trombones, 2 Pianos, and 8 Cellos (1967–68); *Variations on a Theme of Berlioz* for Organ and 3 Drummers (1970); Double-bass Sonata (1971); *Nenia* for Solo Violin (1975). FOR PIANO: *Nocturnes* (1949); 2-piano Sonata (1949); *4 Inventions* (1956).

Klecki, Paul. See **Kletzki, Paul.**

Klee, Bernhard, German conductor: b. Schleiz, April 19, 1936. He studied piano and conducting at the Leipzig Cons.; then conducted opera in Cologne and Bern; in 1966 became Generalmusikdirektor in Lübeck; from 1976 to 1979 was chief conductor of the Hannover Radio Orch. In 1977 he became Generalmusikdirektor of the Düsseldorf Symph. In 1974 he made a successful American debut as a guest conductor with the N.Y. Phil.

Kleiber, Carlos, outstanding German conductor, son of **Erich Kleiber;** b. Berlin, July 3, 1930. He accompanied his parents to South America in 1935, and received his musical education in Buenos Aires. He studied chemistry in Zürich before deciding upon a conducting career. He conducted at the Theater am Gärtnerplatz in Munich in 1953, and subsequently in Potsdam (1954); then at the Deutsche Oper am Rhein in Düsseldorf (1956–64) and at the Zürich Opera (1964–66); after 1966 he was on the staff of the Württemberg State Theater in Stuttgart; later conducted at the Bavarian State Opera in Munich (from 1968), and at the Vienna State Opera (from 1973); in 1974 was engaged at the Bayreuth Festival and also at Covent Garden in London. He had guest appearances as an orch. conductor with the Berlin Phil. and the Vienna Phil. On Sept. 8, 1977, he made his American debut conducting Verdi's *Otello* with the San Francisco Opera; in 1979 conducted a guest engagement with the Chicago Symph. Orch. Following in his father's tradition of astutely eloquent interpretation of both operatic and symph. repertoire, Carlos Kleiber advanced securely into the foremost ranks of modern conductors.

Kleiber, Erich, eminent Austrian conductor; b. Vienna, Aug. 5, 1890; d. Zürich, Jan. 27, 1956. He studied at the Prague Cons. and the Univ. of Prague; in 1911, was conductor at the Prague National Theater; then conducted opera in Darmstadt (1912–19), Barmen-Elberfeld (1919–21), Düsseldorf (1921–22), and Mannheim (1922–23). In 1923 he was appointed Generalmusikdirektor of the Berlin State Opera; conducted the world premiere of Berg's opera *Wozzeck* (Dec. 14, 1925). In 1935, in protest against the German National Socialist government, he emigrated to South America, where he toured as a guest conductor; also appeared in Mexico, Cuba, and the U.S.; in 1936–49, conducted German opera at the Teatro Colón in Buenos Aires. He conducted the Havana Phil. Orch. (1944–47); appeared as guest conductor of the NBC Symph. Orch. (1945–46); was engaged as chief conductor of the Berlin State Opera in 1954, but resigned in March 1955, before the opening of the season, because of difficulties with the officials of the German Democratic Republic. He wrote: Violin Concerto; Piano Concerto; orch. variations; *Capriccio* for Orch.; Overture; numerous chamber music works, piano pieces, and songs.

Klein, Fritz Heinrich, Austrian composer and theorist of an original bent; b. Budapest, Feb. 2, 1892; d. Linz, July 11, 1977. He took piano lessons with his father; then went to Vienna, where he studied composition with Schoenberg and Alban Berg, and became their devoted disciple. From 1932 to 1957 he taught music theory at the Bruckner Cons. in Linz. His most ingenious composition is *Die Maschine* (1921; first perf. N.Y., Nov. 24, 1924), subtitled "Eine extonale Selbstsatire" and publ. under the pseudonym "Heautontimorumenos" (i.e., self-tormentor); this work features instances of all kinds of tonal combinations, including a "Mutterakkord," which consists of all 12 different chromatic tones and all 11 different intervals, the first time such an arrangement was proposed. He also publ. an important essay bearing on serial techniques then still in the process of formulation, "Die Grenze der Halbtonwelt," in *Die Musik* (Jan. 1925). He made the vocal score of Alban Berg's opera *Wozzeck*. Among his own works are *Partita* for 6 Instruments (1953); Divertimento for String Orch. (1954); *Ein musikalisches Fliessband* for Orch. (1960); *Musikalisches Tagebuch* for Orch. (1970); he further wrote several stage works, among them a mystery opera, *Nostradamus*.

Klein, Lothar, German-born Canadian composer; b. Hannover, Jan. 27, 1932. He moved to England in 1939 and to the U.S. in 1941; studied composition with Paul Fetler at the Univ. of Minnesota, graduating in 1954, and orchestration with Dorati (1956–58); took courses in composition with Josef Rufer at the Free Univ. of Berlin and with Blacher at the Hochschule für Musik there (1958–60). Returning to the U.S., he taught at the Univ. of Minnesota (1962–64) and the Univ. of Texas at Austin (1964–68); in 1968 was appointed to the faculty of the Univ. of Toronto, where he became chairman of the graduate music dept. (1971–76). His early music is essentially tonal, esthetically derived from neo-Romantic procedures; he then experimented with various branches of serialism; also wrote collage pieces embodying elements of all historical periods through linkage of stylistic similarities.

Kleinheinz, Franz Xaver, German composer and conductor; b. Mindelheim, June (baptized, June 26) 1765; d. Budapest, Jan. 26, 1832. He played in the Munich Orch.; in 1803 he went to Vienna to study with Albrechtsberger; then was active in Brünn; subsequently in Budapest (1814–23). He made transcriptions for string quartet of Beethoven's early piano sonatas; wrote the operas *Harald* (Budapest, March 22, 1814) and *Der Käfig* (Budapest, 1816); much chamber music; sacred choral works; Piano Concerto; etc.

Kleinsinger, George, American composer; b. San Bernardino, Calif., Feb. 13, 1914; d. New York, July 28, 1982. He was apprenticed to study dentistry; then turned to music; studied with Philip James at N.Y. Univ. and later at the Juilliard Graduate School with Jacobi and Wagenaar. From his earliest attempts at composition he adopted a hedonistic regard toward music as a medium of education and entertainment. In this vein he wrote in 1942 a Broadway musical for children entitled *Tubby the Tuba*, which was highly successful; other works in a similarly whimsical manner were *Pee-Wee the Piccolo* (1946); *Street Corner Concerto* for Harmonica and Orch. (1946); and *Brooklyn Baseball Cantata* (1948). His crowning work was the chamber opera *Archy and Mehitabel*, based on the popular comic strip featuring a garrulous cockroach and an emotional cat; it was first performed in N.Y. on Dec. 6, 1954, and later metamorphosed into a Broadway musical under the title *Shinbone Alley*. Kleinsinger's private life reflected the eccentricity of his musical talents; he inhabited the famous bohemian Hotel Chelsea in N.Y., where he maintained a running waterfall, a turtle, a skunk, an iguana, 40 fish, a dog, a python, and a cat. He used to play the piano with a boa constrictor wrapped around him. How he maintained his menagerie in peace was his guarded secret.

Klemm, Johann Gottlob. See **Clemm, Johann Gottlob.**

Klemperer, Otto, celebrated German conductor; b. Breslau, May 14, 1885; d. Zürich, July 6, 1973. He received early musical training from his mother; in 1901 he entered the Hoch Cons. in Frankfurt, where he studied piano with Kwast and music theory with Knorr; later went to Berlin to study composition and conducting with Pfitzner. At the age of 21 he was engaged to conduct Max Reinhardt's production of *Orpheus in the Underworld* in Berlin. He was later appointed chorus master, and subsequently conductor, at the German Theater in Prague. In 1910 he assisted Mahler in his preparations for the Munich premiere of the *Symphony of a Thousand;* also conducted at the Hamburg Opera (1910–12). He subsequently had engagements in the provinces; in 1917 he received the prestigious appointment of music director of the Cologne Opera, where he conducted the first German performance of Janáček's *Kát'a Kabanová.* In 1924 he became music director of the Wiesbaden Opera. On Jan. 24, 1926, he made his U.S. debut as a guest conductor with the N.Y. Symph. Orch. In 1927 he became music director of the Kroll Opera in Berlin; there he presented the first German performances of Stravinsky's *Oedipus Rex* and Schoenberg's *Erwartung.* In 1933 he was forced to leave Germany and he emigrated to the U.S. In 1933 he became music director of the Los Angeles Phil. Orch., and also appeared as a guest conductor in N.Y., Philadelphia, and Pittsburgh. A disaster nearly put an end to his career in 1939 when he had to undergo an operation for a brain tumor. Still, during a period of remission, he accepted the post of conductor with the Budapest Opera, which he led from 1947–50. In 1951 he made a guest appearance with the Philharmonia Orch. However, he could never regain complete control of his body and mind, and on several occasions lost the memory of his own identity, and was found wandering in the streets. In his active years he distinguished himself by a series of Beethoven's symphs. which he presented at the Royal Festival Hall in London. His interpretations of Mahler's symphs. were notable for their Classical restraint without loss of their fervor. In 1970 he conducted in Jerusalem and accepted Israeli citizenship. He retired in 1972, and then lived in Switzerland until his death. Klemperer was also a composer; in his works he was mainly influenced by the Romantic style of his early teacher Hans Pfitzner. He wrote an opera, *Das Ziel* (1915; revised 1970); *Missa sacra* (1916); 6 symphs. (from 1960); 9 string quartets (1948–70); 17 pieces for Voice and Orch. (1967–70); and about 100 lieder. He publ. *Meine Errinerungen an Gustav Mahler* (Zürich, 1960; in Eng. as *Minor Recollections*, London, 1964).

Klenau, Paul (August) von, Danish conductor and composer; b. Copenhagen, Feb. 11, 1883; d. there, Aug. 31, 1946. He studied violin with Hillmer and composition with Malling in Copenhagen; then took lessons in violin with Halir and in composition with Max Bruch at the Berlin Hochschule für Musik (1902). In 1904 he went to Munich, where he studied composition privately with Thuille; in 1908 moved to Stuttgart, where he became a student of Max von Schilling. He began his conducting career at the Freiburg Opera during the season of 1907–8; in 1909 was conductor at the Court Opera Theater there; in 1912 was conductor of the Bach Society in Frankfurt; then returned to the Freiburg Opera (1913). After World War I he studied with Schoenberg. From 1920 to 1926 he was conductor of the Danish

Phil. Society; concurrently conducted the Vienna Konzerthausgesellschaft (1922–30). He returned to Copenhagen in 1940.
   WORKS: 6 operas: *Sulamith,* after Song of Songs (Munich, Nov. 16, 1913); *Kjartan und Gudrun* (Mannheim, April 4, 1918; revised version as *Gudrun auf Island,* Hagen, Nov. 27, 1924); *Die Lästerschule (The School for Scandal,* after Sheridan; Frankfurt, Dec. 25, 1926); *Michael Kolhaas* (after Kleist; Stuttgart, Nov. 4, 1933; new version, Berlin, March 7, 1934); *Rembrandt van Rijn,* libretto by Klenau (simultaneous premiere, Berlin and Stuttgart, Jan. 23, 1937); *Elisabeth von England* (Kassel, March 29, 1939; title changed to *Die Königen* after the outbreak of World War II to avoid mentioning England; produced in Berlin, April 1940); 7 symphs.; *Inferno,* 3 fantasies for Orch. (after Dante); chamber music; piano pieces; songs. His most successful work was a ballet after Han Christian Andersen, *Kleine Idas Blumen* (Stuttgart, 1916).

Klengel, August Alexander, German pianist and composer; b. Dresden, Jan. 27, 1783; d. there, Nov. 22, 1852. He studied with Milchmayer, and from 1803, with Clementi, with whom he traveled through Germany and, in 1805, to St. Petersburg, where he remained as a private tutor to aristocratic families until 1811. He then lived in Paris; visited London in 1815; returned to Dresden in 1816, and was appointed organist at the Roman Catholic Court Church. He was a fine organist and pianist, particularly distinguished by his *legato* piano style; as a composer, he was a master of contrapuntal forms; his canons were so ingenious that he was known under the sobriquet "Kanon-Klengel."

Klengel, Julius, German cellist, brother of **Paul Klengel;** b. Leipzig, Sept. 24, 1859; d. there, Oct. 27, 1933. Brought up in a musical atmosphere (virtually all members of his family were professional or amateur musicians), he developed rapidly; studied cello with Emil Hegar and theory with Jadassohn. He joined the Gewandhaus Orch. in Leipzig when he was 15; in 1881 he became first cellist, and remained in that post until his resignation in 1924. He also taught at the Leipzig Cons. He traveled widely in Europe as a soloist; composed a number of works for his instrument, among them 4 concertos; *Konzertstück* for Cello with Piano; *Hymnus* for 12 Cellos; Double Concerto for Violin and Cello; 2 string quartets; Piano Trio; also edited a number of cello works and publ. cello exercises.

Klengel, Paul, German conductor and composer, brother of **Julius Klengel;** b. Leipzig, May 13, 1854; d. there, April 24, 1935. He studied at the Leipzig Cons. and at Leipzig Univ.; took the degree of Dr.Phil. with the dissertation *Zur Ästhetik der Tonkunst.* In 1881–86 he conducted the Leipzig Euterpe Concerts; in 1888–93, was 2nd court conductor at Stuttgart; then was again in Leipzig. From 1898 to 1902 he conducted German choral societies in N.Y.; then went back to Germany. He was a versatile musician and was proficient as a violinist as well as a pianist, although he did not engage in a concert career. He wrote numerous works for violin, and also publ. many skillful arrangements for various combinations.

Kletzki (originally spelled **Klecki**), **Paul,** Polish conductor; b. Lodz, March 21, 1900; d. Liverpool, March 5, 1973. He studied violin with Emil Mlynarski; during World War I was a member of the Lodz Phil.; then lived in Berlin (1921–33) and in Italy. After World War II he occupied various conducting posts; appeared as a guest conductor with the Liverpool Phil. (1954–55). From 1958 to 1962 he conducted the Dallas Symph.; then went to Switzerland, where he conducted the Bern Orch. (1964–66) and the Orch. de la Suisse Romande (1967–70); also was a guest conductor in South America and Australia. He wrote about 50 compositions for various combinations, including 2 symphs.

Klindworth, Karl, eminent German pianist, pedagogue, and editor; b. Hannover, Sept. 25, 1830; d. Stolpe, near Potsdam, July 27, 1916. He learned to play violin and piano as a child; obtained work as conductor of a traveling opera company when he was only 17; also traveled in Germany as a concert pianist; then went to Weimar to study with Liszt. In 1854 he went to London, where he remained until 1868, establishing himself as a popular piano teacher. When Wagner was in London in 1855, they became friends; as a result of his admiration for Wagner, Klindworth undertook the most important work of his life, the arrangement in vocal scores of Wagner's tetralogy *Der Ring des Nibelungen.* In 1868, he was engaged as a prof. at the newly founded Moscow Cons. at the invitation of its director, Nicolai Rubinstein; after Rubinstein's death in 1881 Klindworth returned to Germany; in 1882–87 was one of the principal conductors of the Berlin Phil. In 1884 he established in Berlin his own Klavierschule; in 1893 it was merged with the Scharwenka Cons. of Music in Berlin, as Konservatorium der Musik Klindworth-Scharwenka, which became one of the most famous music schools in Germany. Klindworth was an exceptionally competent arranger and music editor; apart from his masterly transcriptions of Wagner's operas, he made an arrangement for 2 pianos of Schubert's C major Symph. He also wrote a number of virtuoso pieces for piano, of which the brilliant *Polonaise-Fantaisie* and 24 grand études in all keys enjoyed some vogue among pianists.

Klose, Friedrich, Swiss composer; b. Karlsruhe (of Swiss parents), Nov. 29, 1862; d. Ruvigliana, Lugano, Dec. 24, 1942. He studied in Karlsruhe and Geneva; in 1886 he went to Vienna, where he took a course with Bruckner. He traveled in Germany, Austria, and Switzerland, occupying teaching posts for a year or two in various places, until 1907, when he was appointed prof. of composition at the Akademie der Tonkunst in Munich. In 1920 he went to Switzerland. He wrote several large works that reveal the influence of Bruckner and Wagner; of

these, the most important is *Ilsebill,* described as a "dramatic symphony" (Munich, Oct. 29, 1905); another important work is an oratorio, *Der Sonne-Geist* (Basel, 1918); he further wrote a symph. poem, *Das Leben ein Traum;* organ works; String Quartet; songs. He publ. the books *Meine Lehrjahre bei Bruckner* (Regensburg, 1927) and *Bayreuth* (1929).

Klose, Margarete, German contralto; b. Berlin, Aug. 6, 1902; d. there, Dec. 14, 1968. She studied music at the Klindworth-Scharwenka Cons. in Berlin; made her debut in Ulm in 1927; then sang in Mannheim (1928–31) and at the Berlin State Opera, where she obtained a decisive popular and musical success; she remained there until 1949; then sang at the Berlin City Opera until 1958, returning to the Berlin State Opera until her retirement in 1961; also sang in Italy, England, and the U.S. She was particularly praised for her Wagnerian contralto roles.

Klotz, a family of Bavarian violin makers at Mittenwald. Their instruments were brought into repute by **Matthias Klotz** (b. Mittenwald, June 11, 1653; d. there, Aug. 16, 1743), the son of Ägidius Klotz; he is believed to have learned the art of violin making from Nicola Amati, during his travels in Italy; he manufactured his best instruments between 1670 and 1696. His son **Sebastian Klotz** (b. Mittenwald, Jan. 18, 1696; d. there, Jan. 20, 1775) is regarded as even superior to him in making violins after Italian models. There followed, in the 18th century, several other violin makers named Klotz, but their relationship to the family cannot be established.

Knabe, William (Valentine Wilhelm Ludwig), founder of the celebrated piano manufacturing firm of Baltimore; b. Kreuzberg, near Oppeln, Prussia, June 3, 1803; d. Baltimore, May 21, 1864. He opened his business in 1839 with Henry Gaehle; in 1854 the partnership was dissolved. His successors were his sons **William Knabe** (1841–89) and **Ernest Knabe** (1827–94), joined later by Charles Keidel, and Knabe's grandsons **Ernest J. Knabe** and **William Knabe** (1872–1939). The firm was later amalgamated with the American Piano Corp.

Knappertsbusch, Hans, eminent German conductor; b. Elberfeld, March 12, 1888; d. Munich, Oct. 25, 1965. He studied with Steinbach and Lohse at the Cologne Cons. (1908–12); served as an assistant to Siegfried Wagner and Richter at Bayreuth. He conducted opera in Elberfeld (1913–18), Leipzig (1918–19), and Dessau (1919–22). From 1922 to 1936 he was Generalmusikdirektor of the Bavarian State Opera in Munich, a post he held with great distinction. He then conducted at the Vienna State Opera (1936–45); was also a conductor with the Vienna Phil. (1937–44). After World War II, he returned to Germany, making his home in Munich. He conducted at the Salzburg Festivals (1947–50, 1954–55); from 1951 he conducted at the Bayreuth Festivals; from 1947 to 1964 he was a regular guest conductor with the Vienna Phil. Knappertsbusch was one of the best exponents of the German school of conducting, in which fidelity to the music was the paramount virtue, over and above the pursuits of personal success.

Knecht, Justin Heinrich, German composer and organist; b. Biberach, Sept. 30, 1752; d. there, Dec. 1, 1817. He was an organist and music director in Biberach from 1771 to the end of his life, traveling only briefly to Stuttgart, where he was court conductor from 1807 till 1809. Despite his provincial field of activity he attained considerable repute in Germany through his compositions and theoretical writings. He was a follower of the Vogler system of harmony; taught chord building by thirds up to chords of the eleventh on all degrees of the scale. His publications include: *Erklärung einiger missverstandenen Grundsätze aus der Vogler' schen Theorie* (Ulm, 1785); *Gemeinnütziges Elementarwerk der Harmonie und des Generalbasses* (4 parts, 1792–98); *Kleines alphabetisches Wörterbuch der vornehmsten und interessantesten Artikel aus der musikalischen Theorie* (1795); *Vollständige Orgelschule für Anfänger und Geübtere* (3 parts, 1795–98); *Theoretisch-praktische Generalbass-Schule; Kleine Klavierschule für die ersten Anfänger* (republ. as *Bewährtes Methodenbuch beim ersten Klavierunterricht*); *Allgemeiner musikalischer Katechismus* (Biberach, 1803); *Luthers Verdienst um Musik und Poesie* (1817). He wrote about 15 operas, several sacred works, and a piece for 15 instruments, *Tongemälde der Natur,* to which he supplied a programmatic description, seemingly anticipating Beethoven's "Pastoral" Symph. However, the resemblance is superficial, and there is no reason to believe that Beethoven was influenced by Knecht in this "tone painting" of nature.

Kneisel, Franz, violin virtuoso; b. Bucharest (of German parentage), Jan. 26, 1865; d. New York, March 26, 1926. He studied at the Cons. of Bucharest, graduating at the age of 14; in 1879 went to Vienna, where he became a pupil of Grün and Hellmesberger at the Vienna Cons.; made his debut on Dec. 31, 1882, in Vienna; in 1884 he went to Berlin, where he was concertmaster of the Bilse Orch. (1884–85). In 1885 he was engaged as concertmaster of the Boston Symph. Orch.; made his debut as a soloist in Boston on Oct. 31, 1885, playing the Beethoven Concerto. In 1886 he organized the celebrated Kneisel Quartet (with Emmanuel Fiedler as 2nd violin; Louis Svecenski, viola; Fritz Giese, cello), which gave performances of high quality in Boston, N.Y., and other American cities, and also in Europe, obtaining world fame before dissolving in 1917. Kneisel was admirable in ensemble playing; his service to the cause of chamber music in America was very great. He was made honorary Mus.Doc. by Yale Univ. (1911) and by Princeton Univ. (1915). In 1903 he resigned his post as concertmaster of the Boston Symph.; from 1905 he taught violin at the Inst. of Musical Art in N.Y. He composed *Grand Concert Etude* for Violin; publ. *Advanced Exercises* for the violin (1900); edited a collection of violin pieces (3 vols., 1900).

Knipper, Lev, important Russian composer; b. Tiflis, Dec. 3, 1898; d. Moscow, July 30, 1974. He studied piano, and took lessons in composition with Glière in Moscow; traveled to Germany and took private lessons with Jarnach in Berlin and Julius Weissmann in Freiburg. Under the influence of western European trends he wrote music in a fairly advanced style of composition, but soon abandoned these experiments and devoted himself to the study of folk music of different nationalities of the Soviet Union; notated folk songs of Turkestan, Kirghiziya, etc.

WORKS: An extraordinarily prolific composer, he wrote 20 symphs.; the choral finale of his 4th symph. was arranged as a song, which became extremely popular, not only in Russia, but in the U.S. (as *Meadowland*); several ballets and orch. suites on ethnic motives; overtures; 3 violin concertos (1944, 1965, 1967); 2 cello concertos (1962, 1972); Clarinet Concerto (1966); Oboe Concerto (1967); Bassoon Concerto (1969); 3 string quartets and other chamber music; piano pieces; songs; operas: *The North Wind* (Moscow, March 30, 1930) and *On the Baikal Lake* (1948), making use of Mongol themes.

Knorr, Iwan, eminent German music pedagogue and composer; b. Mewe, Jan. 3, 1853; d. Frankfurt, Jan. 22, 1916. His family went to Russia when he was 3 years old, returning to Germany in 1868; he then entered the Leipzig Cons., where he studied piano with Moscheles and theory with Richter and Reinecke. In 1874 he went back to Russia, where he taught at the Kharkov Cons., and also at the Imperial Inst. for Noble Ladies in St. Petersburg. He finally settled in Frankfurt in 1883 as a teacher at the Hoch Cons.; in 1908, became its director. He had many distinguished pupils, among them Cyril Scott, Pfitzner, Braunfels, and Ernst Toch. He wrote music in a Romantic vein; several of his works are inspired by Ukrainian folk songs, which he had heard in Russia.

Knorr, Julius, eminent German pianist and pedagogue; b. Leipzig, Sept. 22, 1807; d. there, June 17, 1861. He made his debut as a pianist at the Gewandhaus, in Leipzig, in 1831; was an intimate friend of Schumann and an editor of the *Neue Zeitschrift für Musik* during its first year. Knorr introduced the preparatory technical exercises that have become the groundwork of technical study on the piano.

Knussen, Oliver, English composer; b. Glasgow, June 12, 1952. Remarkably precocious, he began playing piano as a very small boy and showed unusual diligence also in his studies of music theory, mostly with John Lambert. On April 7, 1968, he made musical headlines when, at the age of 15, he conducted the London Symph. Orch. in the first performance of his own First Symph., written in an eclectic, but astoundingly effective, modern style. He was awarded fellowships for 3 years (1970, 1971, 1973) at Tanglewood, where he studied advanced composition with Gunther Schuller.

WORKS: 3 symphs.: No. 1 (1966–67; London, April 7, 1968); No. 2 for Soprano and Orch. (1970–71; Tanglewood, Aug. 18, 1971); No. 3 (1973–76; revised 1979; first complete perf., London, Sept. 6, 1979); *Pantomime* for Chamber Ensemble (1968; revised 1971); Concerto for Orch. (1968–69; London, Feb. 1, 1970; revised 1974); *Masks* for Solo Flute (1969); *Fire-Capriccio* for Flute and String Trio (1969); *Tributum,* overture (1969); *Vocalise with Songs of Winnie-the-Pooh* for Soprano and 6 Instruments (1970; revised without text, 1974–75); *Choral* for Wind Orch. (1970–72; Boston, Nov. 8, 1973); *Rosary Songs* for Soprano, Clarinet, Viola, and Piano (1972); *Océan de terre* for Soprano and Chamber Ensemble (1972–73; revised 1975); *Puzzle Music,* 4 pieces after puzzle canons by John Lloyd, for Flute, Clarinet, 2 Percussionists, Harp, Guitar or Mandolin, and Celesta (1972–73); *Chiara* for Soprano, Female Chorus, and Small Orch. (1971–75); *Ophelia Dances,* Book I, for Ensemble (1975); *Coursing* for Chamber Ensemble (1979); *Max and the Maximonsters,* a children's opera (Brussels, Nov. 28, 1980).

Kobbé, Gustav, American writer on music; b. New York, March 4, 1857; killed in his sailboat by a Navy seaplane maneuvering in the bay near Babylon, Long Island, July 27, 1918. He studied piano and composition with Adolf Hagen in Wiesbaden (1867–72), and with Joseph Mosenthal in N.Y. He attended Columbia College (School of Arts, 1877; School of Law, 1879). He was a frequent contributor, on musical and other subjects, to the daily press and to magazines.

WRITINGS: *Wagner's Life and Works* (N.Y., 1890; 2 vols., containing analyses, with the *Leitmotive* of the music dramas); *The Ring of the Nibelung* (1899; part of the preceding, printed separately); *Opera Singers* (1901); a novel, *Signora, A Child of the Opera House* (1902); *Loves of the Great Composers* (1905); *How to Appreciate Music* (1906); *Wagner and His Isolde* (1906); *Famous American Songs* (1906). Shortly before his accidental death, he finished his *Complete Opera Book,* which was publ. posthumously (N.Y., 1919) and proved so successful that 20 printings were issued before 1950; a revised and enlarged ed., *Kobbé's Complete Opera Book,* compiled by the Earl of Harewood (1,246 pages; includes stories of many operas by modern composers), was publ. in 1963 and 1972; in 1976 an ed. appeared as *The New Kobbé's Complete Opera Book.*

Kochanski, Paul, Polish violinist; b. Odessa, Sept. 14, 1887; d. New York, Jan. 12, 1934. He studied with Mlynarski in Warsaw; in 1901 became concertmaster of the Warsaw Phil.; in 1903 went to Brussels to study with César Thomson; in 1907 was appointed prof. at the Warsaw Cons. From 1916 to 1918 he taught violin at the Petrograd Cons.; then joined the staff of the Cons. of Kiev (1919–20); in 1920 he left Russia, reaching America in 1921; made his American debut with the N.Y. Symph. Orch., Feb. 14, 1921. From 1924 he taught at the Juilliard School. He excelled in the performance of modern works; did a

great service in promoting the violin music of Szymanowski; publ. several transcriptions for violin and piano, among them a *Spanish Popular Suite* (after *7 Spanish Popular Songs* of Manuel de Falla).

Köchel, Ludwig von, Austrian musicographer, compiler of the famous Mozart catalogue; b. Stein, near Krems, Jan. 14, 1800; d. Vienna, June 3, 1877. He studied natural sciences and law at the Univ. of Vienna, and attained distinction in botany and mineralogy; music was his hobby; his love for Mozart's art moved him to compile a Mozart catalogue as methodically as he would a descriptive index of minerals; the result of this task of devotion was the monumental *Chronologisch-thematisches Verzeichnis sämmtlicher Tonwerke Wolfgang Amade Mozarts* (Leipzig, 1862; 2nd ed., prepared by Waldersee, 1905; 3rd ed., extensively revised by A. Einstein, who supplemented the "K numbers" used to identify Mozart's works by secondary numbers, 1937; reprinted, with further alterations and corrections and supplement, Ann Arbor, 1947; 6th ed., a major revision, by F. Giegling, A. Weinmann, and G. Sievers, Wiesbaden, 1964; further supplementary material in the *Mozart-Jahrbuch 1971–72,* pp. 342–401, as prepared by P. van Reijen). Köchel himself publ. some supplementary matter in the *Allgemeine Musikalische Zeitung* (1864). His writings on music include further *Über den Umfang der musikalischen Produktivität W.A. Mozarts* (1862), which preceded the publication of the catalogue; *Die kaiserliche Hofmusikkapelle in Wien von 1543 bis 1867* (1869); and *Johann Josef Fux* (1872); he also edited *83 neuaufgefundene Originalbriefe L. van Beethovens an den Erzherzog Rudolph* (1865).

Kocsis, Zoltán, brilliant Hungarian pianist; b. Budapest, May 30, 1952. He studied at the Franz Liszt Academy of Music with Pál Kadosa, Ferenc Rados, and György Kurtág, receiving his diploma there in 1973. In 1970 he won the Hungarian Radio Beethoven Competition, which launched him on an international career; in 1971 he made his first tour of the U.S.; played again in the U.S. in 1982. A pianist of extraordinary versatility, he can deliver authentic performances of works ranging from Bach through Beethoven and Rachmaninoff to the avant-garde music of the present day.

Koczalski, Raoul (Armand Georg), Polish pianist; b. Warsaw, Jan. 3, 1884; d. Poznan, Nov. 24, 1948. He was trained by his mother; at the age of 4 he played at a charity concert in Warsaw and was at once proclaimed an "infant phenomenon"; his progress was watched by psychologists, and a detailed biography of him was publ. by B. Vogel when he was only 12. He gave concerts in Vienna (1892), Russia, Paris, and London (1893); made nearly 1,000 public appearances before 1896. His sensational success diminished as he grew out of the prodigy age, but he was appreciated as a mature pianist for his sensitive playing of Chopin. He lived mostly in France,

Kodály

Germany, and Sweden; after World War II he returned to Poland and taught in Posnan; shortly before his death he was appointed to a state teaching post in Warsaw. He was precocious not only as a pianist but also as a composer; wrote some 50 opus numbers before he was 10. His opera *Rymond*, written at the age of 17, was produced at Elberfeld, Oct. 14, 1902; he wrote another opera, *Die Sühne* (Mühlhausen, 1909); many piano pieces.

Kodály, Zoltán, illustrious Hungarian composer; b. Kecskemét, Dec. 16, 1882; d. Budapest, March 6, 1967. He was brought up in a musical family; received general education at the Archiex Episcopal Grammar School in Nagyszombat; at the same time, he took lessons in piano, violin, viola, and cello; soon began to compose; wrote a Mass at the age of 16. He then enrolled at the Univ. of Budapest, and also studied composition with Hans Koessler at the Budapest Academy of Music. His early works were mostly sacred choral compositions and chamber music; his doctoral thesis, *Strophic Structure in the Hungarian Folk Song* (1906), indicates his growing interest in folk music. He became associated with Béla Bartók in collecting, organizing, and editing the vast wealth of national folk songs; he also made use of these melodies in his own works. He publ. his findings in the bulletins of the Hungarian Ethnographic Society. In Dec. 1906 he went to Berlin, and in April 1907 proceeded to Paris, where he took some lessons with Widor; in 1907 he was appointed instructor at the Budapest Academy of Music; wrote music criticism for several newspapers in Budapest; also contributed correspondence to the *Revue Musicale*, the *Musical Courier*, and other journals. In 1913 he issued, with Bartók, a detailed paper dealing with the subject of collecting national songs. During World War I he continued to teach and compose, but his activity in collecting and publishing Hungarian folk songs was inevitably curtailed. In 1919 Kodály was appointed assistant director of the Academy of Music in Budapest; for political reasons he was relieved of this post; however, he resumed his teaching in 1922. In 1923 he was commissioned to write a commemorative work in celebration of the half-century of the union of Buda and Pest; for this occasion he wrote *Psalmus Hungaricus*, which proved to be one of his most significant works. The initial performance in Budapest was followed by numerous productions all over Europe, and also in America. Another signal success was the presentation of Kodály's national opera, in a comic style, *Háry János* (1926); an orch. suite from this work is widely played. Two suites of folk dances, arranged in a modern manner, *Dances of Marosszék* and *Dances of Galánta*, won for Kodály a worldwide popularity. His reputation as one of the most significant national composers was firmly established with the repeated performances of these works. During the turbulent events of 1939–45, Kodály remained in Budapest, working on his compilations of folk songs. In 1946–47 he visited the U.S. and conducted concerts of his works. His first wife, Emma, whom he married in 1910, died in 1958;

on Dec. 18, 1959, he married Sarolta Péczely, a student (b. 1940). In 1965 he visited the U.S. as a lecturer. Kodály's musical style is not as radical as that of Bartók; he never departs from basic tonality, and his experiments in rhythm do not reach the primitivistic power of Bartók's percussive idiom. Kodály prefers a Romantic treatment of his melodic and harmonic materials; there is also a decided tinge of Impressionism in his orchestration. But there is no mistaking his ability to present nationally colored melorhythms in a pleasing and stimulating manner.

WORKS: FOR THE STAGE: Incidental music, *Notre Dame de Paris* (Budapest, Feb. 1902); *Le Cid* (Budapest, Feb. 1903); *A nagybacsi (The Uncle;* Budapest, Feb. 1904); *Pacsirtaszo (Lark Song;* Budapest, Sept. 14, 1917); singspiel, *Háry János* (Budapest, Oct. 16, 1926; U.S. premiere, N.Y., March 18, 1960; Kodály's most popular work); *Székelyfonó (The Transylvanian Spinning Room),* lyric scenes based on Hungarian folk songs and dances (Budapest, April 24, 1932); singspiel, *Czinka Panna* (Budapest, March 15, 1948); ballet, *Kuruc mese (Kuruc Tale;* 1935; from the music to *Dances of Marosszék* and *Dances of Galánta*).

FOR ORCH.: *Nyári este (Summer Evening),* tone poem (Budapest, Oct. 22, 1906; reorchestrated 1929–30; N.Y. Phil., April 3, 1930, Toscanini conducting); *Hungarian Rondo, on Old Hungarian Soldiers' Songs* for Cello and Orch. (1917; Vienna, Jan. 12, 1918); *Ballet Music* (1925; Budapest, Oct. 16, 1926; originally intended for *Háry János*); orch. suite from *Háry János* (N.Y., Dec. 15, 1927; version for Brass Band, not arranged by Kodály, Barcelona, March 24, 1927); *Theater Overture* (1927; Budapest, Jan. 10, 1928; from *Háry János*); *Dances of Marosszék* (1930; Dresden, Nov. 28, 1930); *Dances of Galánta* (Budapest, Oct. 23, 1933, for the 80th anniversary of the Budapest Phil. Society; Philadelphia, Dec. 11, 1936); *Variations on a Hungarian Folk Song,* known as *Peacock Variations* (1938–39; Amsterdam, Nov. 23, 1939); Concerto for Orch. (1939–40; Chicago Symph., Feb. 6, 1941); *Minuetto serio* (1953; from *Czinka Panna*); Symph. in C (1957–61; Lucerne, Aug. 16, 1961).

CHAMBER MUSIC: Trio for 2 Violins and Viola (1899); *Intermezzo* for String Trio (1905); *Adagio* for Violin or Cello, and Piano (1905); 2 string quartets (1908–9, 1916–18); Cello Sonata (1909); *Duo* for Violin and Cello (1914); Solo Cello Sonata (1915; very popular); *Capriccio* for Solo Cello (1915); *Hungarian Rondo* for Cello and Piano (1917); *Serenade* for 2 Violins and Viola (1919–20); Cello Sonatina (1921–22); *Invitation to the Campfire* for Solo Clarinet (1930); *Epigrams* for Instrument or Voice, and Piano (1954); several transcriptions for Cello or Violin, and Piano, of pieces by J.S. Bach.

FOR VOICE: *Stabat Mater* for Male Chorus a cappella (pre-1900); *Assumpta est* for Chorus and Orch. (1902); *20 Hungarian Folk Songs* for Voice and Piano (with Bartók; 1906); *2 Songs* for Bass and Orch. (1913–16); *Psalmus hungaricus,* based on the 55th Psalm, for Tenor, Chorus, and Orch. (Budapest, Nov. 19, 1923; U.S. premiere, N.Y. Phil., Dec. 19, 1927; his most important work); *Magyar nepzene (Hun-*

garian Folk Music), 57 arrangements of folk songs for Voice and Piano (publ. in Eng., N.Y., 1960); *Pange lingua* for Chorus and Organ (1929); *Te Deum Budavár* for 4 Soloists, Chorus, and Orch. (for the 250th anniversary of the delivery of Buda from the Turks; perf. in the Budapest Cathedral, Sept. 11, 1936); *Molnár Anna* for Chorus and Chamber Orch. (1942; revised 1959); *Kádár Kata* (Transylvanian folk ballad) for Contralto and Chamber Orch. (1943); *Missa brevis* for Chorus, and Organ or Orch. (1942–44; Budapest, Feb. 11, 1945); *Vértanúk sírjánál (At the Graves of the Martyrs)* for Chorus and Orch. (1945); *Kállai kettös (Double Dances of Kálló)* for Chorus, 3 Clarinets, 2 Cimbaloms, and Strings (1950; Budapest, April 4, 1951); *An Ode: The Music Makers*, after O'Shaughnessy, for Chorus, 2 Trumpets, 3 Trombones, and Strings (1964); *Laudes organi* for Chorus and Organ (1966); numerous songs and choruses for children and music students: *Bicinia hungarica* (1937–42); *333 Reading Exercises* (1943); *441 Melodies*, collected in 4 books, subtitled *Pentatonic Music* (1945–48); etc.; also song collections for general use.

FOR PIANO: *Meditation* (1907); *9 Pieces* (1910); *Marosszék Dances* (1930); *24 Little Canons on the Black Keys* (1945); *Children's Dances* (1946).

He publ. numerous articles in ethnographic and musical publications. He ed. the periodical *Studia Musicologica Academiae Scientiarum Hungaricae;* wrote the book *Die ungarische Volkmusik* (Budapest, 1962). His collected writings were publ. as *Kodály Zoltán: Visszatekintés*, ed. by F. Bónis (Budapest, 1964).

Koechlin, Charles, notable French composer; b. Paris, Nov. 27, 1867; d. Canadel, Var, Dec. 31, 1950. He studied at the Paris Cons. with Gedalge, Massenet, and Fauré, graduating in 1897. He lived mostly in Paris, where he was active as a composer, teacher, and lecturer; made 3 visits to the U.S. (1918, 1928, 1937), lecturing on French music (in Eng.); contributed to various journals (*Gazette des Beaux Arts, Chronique des Arts,* etc.) and to Lavignac's *Encyclopédie* (valuable and comprehensive essays on modern music). He also participated in modern-music societies, and worked in various social organizations for the promotion of worldwide music culture. In his own compositions he created a style that is unmistakably French in its clarity and subtlety of nuance and dynamics; although highly sympathetic to all innovation, he stopped short of crossing the borders of perceptible tonality and coherent rhythmic patterns; he was a master of orchestration. As a pedagogue, he possessed a clear insight into the problems of musical technique; publ. several manuals of fundamental value: *Traité d'harmonie* (3 vols., 1927–30); *Etude sur les notes de passage* (1922); *Etude sur l'écriture de la fugue d'école* (1933); *Précis des règles du contrepoint* (1927; also in Eng. as *A Summary of the Rules of Counterpoint*); *Traité d'orchestration* (4 vols.); *Théorie de la musique* (1935); also an advanced paper, *Essai sur la musique polytonale et atonale*. A *Traité de polyphonie modale* is in MS. He also publ. mono-

graphs on Gabriel Fauré (1927) and Debussy (1927).

WORKS: *Jacob chez Laban,* biblical pastoral (1896–1908; Paris, May 19, 1925); ballets: *La Forêt païenne* (Paris, June 17, 1925) and *L'Ame heureuse* (1947); *La Forêt,* symph. poem (1896–1907); *En mer, la nuit,* symph. poem (1899–1904); *L'Automne,* symph. suite (1896–1909); *Nuit de Walpurgis classique,* symph. poem (1901–7); *Etudes antiques,* symph. suite (1908–14); symph. poems: *Le Printemps, L'Hiver, Nuit de juin, Midi en août* (1910–12); *Suite légendaire* (1915–20); *Rapsodie sur des chansons françaises* (1916); *La Course de printemps,* symph. poem after Kipling's *Jungle Book* (1925–27); *The 7 Stars Symphony,* symph. suite (1933); *Symphonie d'hymnes* (1936); *La Loi de la jungle,* after Kipling (1939); Partita for Chamber Orch. (1945); also 2 symphs. arranged mostly from earlier works; *Ballade* for Piano and Orch. (1919); *20 chansons bretonnes* for Cello and Chamber Orch. (1934); *Offrande musicale sur le nom de B.A.C.H.,* 15 pieces for Organ and Orch. (1942); *Silhouettes comiques,* 12 pieces for Bassoon and Orch. (1943); 3 string quartets; several fugues for String Quartet; *Suite en quatuor* for Flute, Violin, Viola, and Piano; Sonata for 2 Flutes; Piano Quintet; *Divertissement* for 2 Flutes and Bass Flute; Trio for Flute, Clarinet, and Bassoon; Modal Sonatina for Flute and Clarinet; *Primavera* for Flute, Violin, Viola, Cello, and Harp; Septet for Flute, Oboe, English Horn, Clarinet, Bassoon, Horn, and Saxophone; Flute Sonata; Viola Sonata; Oboe Sonata; Violin Sonata; Cello Sonata; Horn Sonata; Bassoon Sonata; 2 clarinet sonatas; several suites of pieces for Unaccompanied Flute; several sets of piano pieces (*Paysages et marines, Les Heures persanes, 12 pastorales, L'Ancienne Maison de campagne, 12 petites pièces très facile,* etc.); organ music; vocal duets, trios, and quartets; several cycles of songs.

Koellreutter, Hans Joachim, German composer; b. Freiburg im Breisgau, Sept. 2, 1915. He studied flute, piano, and composition in Berlin and in Geneva. In 1937 he went to Brazil and unfolded an energetic program of performances of modern music. In 1939 he formed in São Paulo the group Música Viva Brasil and also publ. a magazine of the same name. He was a prof. at the Inst. Musical in São Paulo (1942–44) and directed an international course on new music in Teresópolis. In 1952 he founded an orch. in Bahia, which he conducted until 1962; then was in charge of the music programs of the Goethe Inst. in Munich (1963–65); the years 1965–69 he spent in New Delhi, India, where he founded a music school. From 1969 to 1975 he was music instructor and director of performances at the Goethe Inst. in Tokyo; then returned to Brazil. His music follows Classical forms, while the thematic materials are modeled after the 12-tone method of composition; in several of his works he makes use of exotic motives of South America, India, and Japan.

Koenen, Tilly (Mathilde Caroline), Dutch mezzo-soprano; b. Salatiga, Java, Dec. 25, 1873; d. The Hague, Jan. 4, 1941. She studied piano, on which she became a proficient performer; then took up voice with Cornelia van Zanten. She toured Germany and Austria from 1900 with excellent success; visited America in 1909–10 and in 1915–16. She was particularly impressive in her interpretations of German Romantic songs; also performed some songs by her compatriots.

Koessler, Hans, German organist and composer; b. Waldeck, Jan. 1, 1853; d. Ansbach, May 23, 1926. He studied with Rheinberger in Munich; then taught at the Dresden Cons.; in 1882, went to Budapest to teach organ and, later, composition at the Academy of Music, remaining on the staff until 1908. In 1918 he retired to Ansbach. In his music he follows the tradition of Brahms; although his technical achievements inspire respect, his works lack any durable quality that would distinguish them from the mass of other competent compositions by German composers of his generation.

Koffler, Jósef, Polish composer; b. Stryj, Nov. 28, 1896; killed, with his wife and child, in Wieliczka, near Cracow, during a street roundup of Jews in 1943. He was a pupil of Schoenberg and Guido Adler; graduated from the Univ. of Vienna in 1923; then went to Lwow, where he taught at the Cons., edited the Polish monthly review *Orchestra,* and contributed to other music magazines. He was the first Polish composer to use the method of composition with 12 tones according to Schoenberg's principles; his *15 Variations* for String Orch. (Amsterdam Festival, June 9, 1933) are derived from a 12-tone row. He composed 3 symphs.; his 3rd Symph. was performed at the London Festival on June 17, 1938; other works are String Trio (Oxford Festival, July 23, 1931); Divertimento for Oboe, Clarinet, and Bassoon; String Quartet; *40 Polish Folk Songs* for Piano; *Quasi una sonata;* a cycle of piano pieces; *Love Cantata; 4 Poems* for Voice and Piano.

Kogan, Leonid, Soviet virtuoso of the violin; b. Dnepropetrovsk, Nov. 14, 1924; d. on the train, at the Mytishcha railroad station on his way to a concert engagement, Dec. 17, 1982. His father was a photographer who played the violin; when Kogan was 10 years old the family moved to Moscow, and he became a pupil of Abram Yampolsky at the Moscow Cons., graduating in 1948. He was obviously a *wunderkind,* but was prudently spared harmful exploitation. In 1947 he won a prize in Prague at the Youth Festival. In 1951 he went to Brussels to take part in the competition sponsored by the Belgian Queen, and received first prize. His career was instantly assured; he played recitals in Europe to unanimous acclaim. He made an auspicious American debut in 1958, playing the Brahms Violin Concerto with the Boston Symph. In 1965 he received the Lenin Prize. In 1952 he joined the faculty of the Moscow Cons.; was named prof. in 1963 and head of the violin dept. in 1969. his playing exemplified the finest qualities of the Russian School: an emotionally romantic élan and melodious filigree of technical detail. In addition to the standard repertoire, in which he ex-

celled, he also played modern violin works, particularly those by Soviet composers. He was married to Elizabeth Gilels, sister of the Soviet pianist Emil Gilels, who was herself an accomplished violinist. Following the violinistic genetic code, their 2 children were also musical: a girl played the piano, and a boy, **Pavel Kogan** (b. Moscow, June 6, 1952), was so good on the violin that in 1970 he won the Sibelius contest in Finland. On Oct. 16, 1975, Pavel Kogan was soloist with the Philadelphia Orch. The family shunned politics, and Leonid Kogan resolutely declined to participate in any protests, domestic or foreign, against the presumed anti-Semitism in Russian politics, even though he himself was patently Jewish.

Köhler, Louis, German composer of celebrated piano studies; b. Braunschweig, Sept. 5, 1820; d. Königsberg, Feb. 16, 1886. He studied piano in Braunschweig with Sonnemann; then took courses in composition in Vienna (1839–43) with Sechter and Seyfried; also studied piano there with Bocklet. After a season of theater conducting, he settled in Königsberg (1847) and established there a successful school for piano playing. He wrote 3 operas, a ballet, a Symph., overtures, cantatas, and other works, but he is remembered exclusively for his albums of piano studies, which have been adopted in music schools all over the world; next to Czerny, he is the most popular purveyor of didactic piano literature; it must be observed that while his studies are of great instructive value, they are also worthwhile from a purely musical standpoint. His chief work, in which he laid the foundation of methodical piano pedagogy, is *Systematische Lehrmethode für Klavierspiel und Musik,* in 2 vols.: I. *Die Mechanik als Grundlage der Technik* (1856; 3rd ed., revised by Riemann, 1888) and II. *Tonschriftwesen, Harmonik, Metrik* (1858); other publications are *Führer durch den Klavierunterricht* (6th ed., 1879); *Der Klavierfingersatz* (1862); *Der Klavierunterricht, oder Studien, Erfahrungen und Ratschläge* (4th ed., 1877); *Die neue Richtung in der Musik* (1864); *Leichtfassliche Harmonie- und Generalbasslehre* (a valuable manual of harmony; 3rd ed., 1880); *Brahms und seine Stellung in der neueren Klavierliteratur* (1880); *Der Klavierpedalung* (1882); *Allgemeine Musiklehre* (1883).

Kohn, Karl, American pianist and composer; b. Vienna, Aug. 1, 1926. After the Nazi absorption of Austria in 1938, his family emigrated to the U.S.; he studied piano with Carl V. Werschinger and conducting with Prüwer at N.Y. College of Music (1940–44); then took courses in music theory and composition at Harvard Univ. with Walter Piston, Irving Fine, and Randall Thompson (B.A., 1950; M.A., 1955). In 1956 he traveled to Finland on a Fulbright grant; upon return to the U.S. he taught piano and music theory at Pomona College in Claremont, Calif., and at the Claremont Graduate School of Music. He also taught several summers at the Berkshire Music Center at Tanglewood, Mass.; held a Guggenheim fellowship in 1961–62; in 1975 was awarded a grant by the National Endowment for the Arts. As a pianist, he specializes in modern music, deploying a virtuoso technique in tackling the most formidable piano works; also gave duo-piano concerts with his wife, **Margaret Kohn.** In his compositions he tends toward prudential serialism but also explores diatonic modalities, applying the power of pervicacious iteration of pandiatonic chordal complexes; he successfully adapts medieval polyphonic devices to contemporary usages, such as the integration of the precomposed thematic fragments, a technique anciently known as "centone" (literally, "patchwork quilt"). He makes use of topological rearrangements of classical pieces, as in *Son of Prophet Bird,* dislocated and paraphrased from Schumann's *Bird as a Prophet.*

Kohs, Ellis Bonoff, notable American composer; b. Chicago, May 12, 1916. His mother was a good violinist, and when Kohs learned to play the piano he often accompanied her at home. In 1928 the family moved from San Francisco (following his early musical studies there at the Cons.) to Brooklyn, and Kohs studied with Adelaide Belser at the Inst. of Musical Art in N.Y. In 1933 he returned to Chicago and enrolled at the Univ. of Chicago as a student in composition with Carl Bricken (M.A., 1938). Upon graduation he proceeded to N.Y., where he entered the Juilliard School of Music, studying composition with Bernard Wagenaar and musical pedagogy with Olga Samaroff Stokowski. He continued his musical studies at Harvard Univ., with Walter Piston in composition and with Hugo Leichtentritt and Willi Apel in musicology (1939–41); he also attended a seminar given by Stravinsky at Harvard in 1940–41. During the summer of 1940 he was a lecturer in music at the Univ. of Wisconsin in Madison. From 1941 to 1946 he served in the U.S. Army as a chaplain's assistant and organist, and in the U.S. Air Force as a bandleader. After his discharge from service, he engaged in pedagogical work and in active composition; his teaching posts included Wesleyan Univ. (1946–48), the Kansas City Cons. of Music (summers of 1946 and 1947), the College of the Pacific at Stockton, Calif. (1948–50), Stanford Univ. (summer of 1950), and, from 1950, the Univ. of Southern Calif., Los Angeles. In his music he pursues the aim of classical clarity; he is particularly adept in variation structures; the rhythmic patterns in his works are often asymmetrical, and the contrapuntal fabric highly dissonant; in some of his works he makes use of a unifying 12-tone row, subjecting it to ingenious metamorphoses, as revealed in his opera *Amerika,* after the novel by Franz Kafka. A humorous streak is shown in his choral piece *The Automatic Pistol,* to words from the U.S. Army weapons manual, which he composed during his military service. As a pedagogue, he wrote there useful manuals: *Music Theory, a Syllabus for Teacher and Student* (2 vols., N.Y. 1961); *Musical Form: Studies in Analysis and Synthesis* (Boston, 1976); and *Musical Composition: Projects in Ways and Means* (Metuchen, N.J., 1980).

WORKS: FOR THE STAGE: Opera, *Amerika,* after Kafka (1969; abridged concert version produced in Los Angeles, May 19, 1970); incidental music to Shakespeare's *Macbeth* (1947). FOR ORCH.: Concerto for Orch. (Berkeley, Calif., Aug. 9, 1942); *Passacaglia* for Organ and String Orch. (1946); *Legend* for Oboe and String Orch. (Columbus, Ohio, Feb. 27, 1947); Cello Concerto (1947); Chamber Concerto for Viola and String Nonet (1949); Symph. No. 1 (1950); Symph. No. 2, with Chorus (Univ. of Illinois, Urbana, April 13, 1957); Violin Concerto (1980; Los Angeles, April 24, 1981). CHAMBER MUSIC: String Quartet (1942); *Night Watch* for Flute, Horn, and Timpani (1943); Sonatina for Bassoon and Piano (1944); *Short Concert* for String Quartet (1948); Clarinet Sonata (1951); *Variations* for Recorder (1956); Brass Trio (1957); *Studies in Variation* in 4 parts: for Woodwind Quintet, for Piano Quartet, for Piano Solo, for Violin Solo (1962); Sonata for Snare Drum and Piano (1966); *Duo* for Violin and Cello, after Kafka's *Amerika* (1971); Concerto for Percussion Quartet (1978). FOR VOICE: *The Automatic Pistol* for Male Voices a cappella (Washington, D.C., Army Music Chorus, Sept. 5, 1943); *25th Psalm* (1947); *Fatal Interview,* song cycle (text by Edna St. Vincent Millay; 1951); *Lord of the Ascendant* (based on the Gilgamesh legend) for Chorus, Soloists, Dancers, and Orch. (1956); *3 Songs* from the Navajo, for Mixed Chorus (1957); *3 Greek Choruses* for Women's Chorus (1957); *23rd Psalm* for Soloists and Chorus a cappella (1957); *Men* for Narrator and 3 Percussionists, text by Gertrude Stein (1982; Los Angeles, March 15, 1984); *Subject Cases* for Narrator and Percussionist, text by Gertrude Stein (Los Angeles, Feb. 14, 1983). FOR PIANO: *Etude in Memory of Bartók* (1946); *Variations* (1946); *Variations on L'Homme armé* (1947); *Toccata* for Harpsichord or Piano (1948); *Fantasy on La, Sol, Fa, Re, Mi* (1949); *10 Inventions* (1950). FOR ORGAN: *Capriccio* (1948); 3 Chorale-Variations on Hebrew Hymns (1952).

Kojian, Varujan, violinist and conductor; b. Beirut, Lebanon, of Armenian parentage, March 12, 1945. He was taken to France as a child and studied violin at the Paris Cons.; then went to the U.S. and took violin lessons with Ivan Galamian and Jascha Heifetz. He subsequently became assistant concertmaster of the Los Angeles Phil., and also served for a while as assistant conductor. Then he went to Vienna for additional conducting studies with Hans Swarowsky. In 1972 he won first prize in the conducting competition in Sorrento, Italy; from 1973 to 1976 he acted as principal guest conductor with the Seattle Symph. From 1980 to 1983 he served as music director of the Utah Symph. Orch. in Salt Lake City.

Kokkonen, Joonas, prominent Finnish composer; b. Iisalmi, Nov. 13, 1921. He studied composition with Selim Palmgren at the Sibelius Academy in Helsinki, and later taught there. In 1963 he was elected to membership of the Finnish Academy; in 1965 he became chairman of the Union of Finnish Composers. In 1973 he was awarded the Sibelius Prize. Like all composers of his generation in Finland, he experienced the inevitable influence of Sibelius, but he soon abandoned the characteristic diatonic modalities of Finnish folk music and formed an individual style of composition marked by a curiously anfractuous chromaticism and involuted counterpoint, freely dissonant but hewing to clearly identifiable tonal centers. For a period he dabbled in dodecaphonic writing, but found its doctrinaire discipline uncongenial. He derives his techniques from the contrapuntal procedures of Bach and, among the moderns, from Bartók. Thematically, he adopts an objective method of formal structure, in which a free succession of formative motives determines the content.

WORKS: Opera, *Viimeiset Kiusaukset (The Last Temptations)*, on the subject of the life of a 19th-century Finnish evangelist (Helsinki, Sept. 2, 1975); 5 symphs.: No. 1 (1960); No. 2 (1961); No. 3 (Helsinki, Sept. 12, 1967); No. 4 (1970; Helsinki, Nov. 7, 1971); No. 5 (1982; Helsinki, Jan. 12, 1983); *Lintujen Tuonela (The Hades of the Birds)* for Mezzo-soprano and Orch. (1959); *Sinfonia da camera* for String Orch. (1962); *Opus sonorum* for Orch. (1964); Cello Concerto (1969); *Inauguratio,* suite for Orch. (1971); *... durch einen Spiegel* for 12 Strings and Harpsichord (1977); *Requiem* (1981); Piano Trio (1948); Piano Quintet (1953); Duo for Violin and Piano (1955); 3 string quartets (1959, 1966, 1976); Wind Quintet (1973); *Improvvisazione* for Violin and Piano (1982); several sacred choruses; also piano pieces and songs.

Kolar, Victor, American conductor; b. (of Bohemian parentage) Budapest, Feb. 12, 1888; d. Detroit, June 16, 1957. He studied violin with Ševčik and composition with Dvořák at the Prague Cons. In 1900 he emigrated to America; played violin in the Pittsburgh Orch. (1905–8) and in the N.Y. Symph. Orch. (1908–20). In 1920 he became associate conductor at the Detroit Symph. Orch., and later was appointed principal conductor there, until 1941. As assistant conductor of the N.Y. Symph. Orch. he brought out several of his own works, among them his Symph. (Jan. 28, 1916); his other works were *Hiawatha,* a symph. poem (Pittsburgh, Jan. 31, 1908); *3 Humoresques* for Violin and Piano; numerous songs; 7 marches.

Kolb, Barbara, talented American composer; b. Hartford, Conn., Feb. 10, 1939. She was of a musical family; her father was a song composer. She studied the visual arts; also took up clarinet. She enrolled at the Hartt College of Music in Hartford, where she studied composition with Arnold Franchetti (B.A., 1961; M.M., 1964). During the summers of 1960, 1964, and 1968 she attended the classes of Lukas Foss and Gunther Schuller at the Berkshire Music Center in Tanglewood. In 1969 she became the first American woman to win the U.S. Prix de Rome in composition, and spent the years 1969–71 at the American Academy in Rome. In 1971 she received a Guggenheim fellowship; in 1976 she was awarded a 2nd Guggenheim fellowship; she was also the recipient of the award by the National Inst. of Arts and Let-

ters; in 1975 and 1977 she was given the Creative Artists Public Service awards. From 1973 to 1975 she was on the music faculty at Brooklyn College; she further received grants from the National Endowment for the Arts in 1972, 1974, 1977, and 1979. In her music she builds a sui generis melodic, harmonic, and rhythmic environment, making use of variegated techniques; a factor in several of her works is a persistent iteration and emphatic reiteration of thematic materials, creating an aura of quaquaversal melorhythmic rotation invariably reverting to the thematic exordium, while constantly changing the timbres. The most remarkable of her compositions in this manner of flowing recurrence is *Soundings,* of which she made 3 different versions.

WORKS: *Rebuttal* for 2 Clarinets (1964); *Chansons bas* for Voice, Harp, and Percussion (1965); *Fragments* for Flute and Piano (1966); *Three Place Settings* for Narrator, Clarinet, Violin, Double Bass, and Percussion (1968); *Trobar clus* for 13 Instruments, representing wordlessly the ancient Provençal verse form of the rondeau type (Tanglewood, Aug. 29, 1970); *Soundings* for 11 Instruments and Electronic Tape; her most successful work (Lincoln Center, N.Y., Oct. 27, 1972; revised for Full Orch. and perf. by the N.Y. Phil., Pierre Boulez conducting, Dec. 11, 1975; a 2nd revision made in 1977 was first perf. by the Boston Symph. Orch., Seiji Ozawa conducting, Feb. 16, 1978; also conducted by him during the tour of the Boston Symph. in Japan in March 1978, with the tape replaced by a supernumerary orch. group); *Frailties* for Tenor, 4-channel Electronic Tape, and Orch. (1972); *Spring, River, Flowers, Moon, Night* for 2 Pianos and Electronic Tape (1974); *Looking for Claudio* for Guitar and Electronic Tape (1975); *Appello* for Piano Solo (1976); *Musique pour un vernissage* for Flute, Violin, Viola, and Guitar, originally intended as "furniture music" or "music to walk by" à la Satie, to be played at the opening of a Paris art exhibition (1977; first perf. as such in Paris, composer conducting, then arranged as a concert piece and presented at the Kennedy Center for the Performing Arts in Washington, D.C., Feb. 3, 1979, Leon Fleisher conducting); *Songs before an Adieu* for Flute, Guitar, and Voice (1977–79); *Chromatic Fantasy* for Narrator and Chamber Ensemble (1979); *3 Lullabies* for Solo Guitar (1980); *Related Characters* for Viola and Piano (1980); *The Point that Divides the Wind* for Organ and 4 Percussionists (1981).

Kolinski, Mieczyslaw, Polish-born Canadian composer, ethnomusicologist, and music theorist; b. Warsaw, Sept. 5, 1901. He studied piano and composition at the Hochschule für Musik in Berlin; then took courses in musicology, psychology, and anthropology at Berlin Univ. (Ph.D., 1930); concurrently assisted Hornbostel at the Staatliches Phonogramm-Archiv in Berlin (1926–33); then moved to Prague; in 1938 went to Belgium to avoid the Nazis; then settled in N.Y. in 1951. In 1955 he was co-founder, and in 1958–59, president, of the Society for Ethnomusicology; in 1966–76 taught at Toronto Univ.;

became a Canadian citizen in 1974. As an ethnomusicologist, he transcribed over 200 works from ·Samoa, New Guinea, Surinam, West Africa, and Haiti; also edited numerous folk-song editions. As a music theorist, he publ. *Konsonanz als Grundlage einer neuen Akkordlehre* (Prague, 1936).

Kolisch, Rudolf, Austrian violinist; b. Klamm, July 20, 1896; d. Watertown, Mass., Aug. 1, 1978. He studied violin with Ševčik at the Univ. of Vienna; also took private lessons in composition with Schoenberg. In 1922 he organized the Kolisch Quartet, which systematically presented works by modern composers. His was the first string quartet to perform its programs from memory. In 1935 he went to the U.S.; in 1942 he became the leader of the Pro Arte Quartet; taught at the Univ. of Wisconsin until 1967, and then was artist-in-residence at the New England Cons. of Music in Boston. He was one of the few professional left-handed violinists.

Kolodin, Irving, American music critic; b. New York, Feb. 22, 1908. He studied at the Inst. of Musical Art in N.Y.; was music critic on the *N.Y. Sun* (1932–50); in 1947 he became editor of the music section of the *Saturday Review*. He publ. a number of valuable reference works and monographs: *The Metropolitan Opera 1883–1935* (N.Y., 1936; new revised ed., as *The Story of the Metropolitan Opera, 1883–1950*, N.Y., 1953; 4th ed., N.Y., 1966); *The Kingdom of Swing* (with Benny Goodman; N.Y., 1939); *A Guide to Recorded Music* (N.Y., 1941; new ed., as *New Guide to Recorded Music*, Garden City, N.Y., 1946; 3rd revised ed., 1950); *Mozart on Records* (N.Y., 1942); *Orchestral Music*, in the series The Guide to Long-Playing Records (N.Y., 1955); editor, *The Saturday Review Home Book of Recorded Music and Sound Reproduction* (N.Y., 1956); *Musical Life* (N.Y., 1958); *The Continuity of Music: A History of Influence* (N.Y., 1969); *The Interior Beethoven: A Biography of the Music* (N.Y., 1975); *The Opera Omnibus: Four Centuries of Critical Give and Take* (N.Y., 1976); *In Quest of Music* (N.Y., 1980).

Komitas, Sogomon, Armenian composer, pioneer of national folk music; b. Kutina, Turkey, Oct. 8, 1869; d. Paris, Oct. 22, 1935. His family name was **Sogomian;** orphaned at the age of 11, he was sent to study singing at a seminary in Etchmiatsin; upon graduation in 1893, he was given the name Komitas, after a 7th-century Armenian hymn writer. In 1895 he went to Tiflis, where he studied music theory; then lived in Berlin (1896–99), where he took courses in composition and choral conducting. During all these years he studiously collected materials pertaining to Armenian folk music, and publ. numerous papers in German dealing with the subject; also composed original music based on Armenian motifs. In 1910 he moved to Constantinople; the massacre of Armenian populations in Turkey in 1915 so affected him that he became incurably psychotic. He lived afterwards in Paris. Komitas is regarded as the founder of scientific Armenian musicology; his works were publ. in a collected edition on the centennial of his birth; his body was reverently transferred from Paris for reburial in Erevan, capital of Soviet Armenia. There is a considerable body of biographical and bibliographical publications, mostly in the Russian language; the basic biographies are A. Shaverdian, *Komitas and Armenian Music* (Erevan, 1956), and G. Geodakian, *Komitas* (Erevan, 1969).

Kondorossy, Leslie, Hungarian-American composer; b. Pressburg, June 25, 1915. He studied at the Academy of Music in Budapest; after World War II he emigrated to America and settled in Cleveland; there he evolved fruitful activity as a teacher, conductor, and composer. He is especially proficient in producing short operas; among them are *Night in the Puszta* (Cleveland, June 28, 1953); *The Voice* (Cleveland, May 15, 1954); *The Pumpkin* (Cleveland, May 15, 1954); *Unexpected Visitor* and *The 2 Imposters* (Cleveland, Oct. 21, 1956); *The Fox* (Cleveland, Jan. 28, 1961); *The Baksis* (1964); *Nathan the Wise* (1964); radio operas: *The Midnight Duel* (Cleveland Radio, March 20, 1955) and *The String Quartet* (Cleveland Radio, May 8, 1955); children's operas: *The Poorest Suitor* (Cleveland, May 24, 1967); *Shizuka's Dance* (Cleveland, April 22, 1969; also perf. on Tokyo Television, Japan, July 31, 1974); *Kalamona and the 4 Winds* (Cleveland Radio, Sept. 12, 1971); church opera, *Ruth and Naomi* (Cleveland, April 28, 1974); *Kossuth Cantata* (Cleveland, March 16, 1952); *David, a Son of Jesse,* oratorio (Cleveland, June 4, 1967); Trombone Concerto (1958); Trumpet Concerto (1959); Harp Concerto (1961); *Jazz Mass* for Voices and Jazz Band (1968); Harpsichord Concerto (1972); numerous organ pieces.

Kondrashin, Kirill, noted Russian conductor; b. Moscow, March 6, 1914; d. Amsterdam, March 7, 1981. He studied piano and music theory at the Musical Technicum in Moscow; then took a course in conducting with Khaikin at the Moscow Cons. While still a student he began conducting light opera (1934–37); then conducted at the Malyi Opera Theater in Leningrad (1937–41). In 1943 he received the prestigious appointment to the staff of the Bolshoi Theater in Moscow, where he conducted a wide repertoire emphasizing Russian operas. He received Stalin prizes in 1948 and 1949. In 1969 he was named People's Artist of the U.S.S.R. Kondrashin was the first Soviet conductor to appear in the U.S. (1958), and held numerous subsequent engagements in America, the last being a concert he conducted at the Hollywood Bowl in February 1981. In 1960 he was appointed chief conductor of the Moscow Phil., with which he performed numerous new Soviet works, including Shostakovich's controversial 13th Symph. In 1950–53 and 1972–75 he also taught at the Moscow Cons. After 1975 he increased his guest engagements outside Russia, and in 1978 decided to emigrate; in 1979 he assumed the post of permanent conductor of the Concertgebouw Orch. in Amsterdam; in 1981 he died suddenly of a heart attack after a concert. His conducting style was marked by an effective blend of lyrical melodiousness and dramatic romanticism, without deviating from the prevalent Russian traditions. He publ. a book, *On the Art of Conducting* (Leningrad, 1970).

Konetzni, Anny, Austrian soprano, sister of **Hilde Konetzni;** b. Vienna, Feb. 12, 1902; d. there, Sept. 6, 1968. She studied at the Vienna Cons. and later in Berlin with Jacques Stuckgold; made her debut as a contralto at the Vienna Volksoper in 1925; then sang in Augsburg, Elberfeld, and Chemnitz; joined the Berlin State Opera in 1931, and also appeared with the Vienna State Opera, La Scala in Milan, the Paris Opéra, and London's Covent Garden. She made her Metropolitan Opera debut in N.Y. as Brünnhilde in *Die Walküre* on Dec. 26, 1934; remained on the roster until the close of the season. After World War II, she taught voice in Vienna. She was particularly successful as an interpreter of heroic roles in Wagner's operas.

Konetzni, Hilde, famous Austrian soprano, sister of **Anny Konetzni;** b. Vienna, March 21, 1905; d. there, April 20, 1980. She studied at the Vienna Cons., and later in Prague with Prochaska-Neumann; made her debut as Sieglinde in *Die Walküre* in Chemnitz in 1929; then sang at the German Theater in Prague (1932–36). In 1936 she became a member of the Vienna State Opera; also appeared at Salzburg, La Scala in Milan, Covent Garden in London, South America, and the U.S. In 1954 she joined the faculty of the Vienna Academy of Music. She was an outstanding interpreter of the soprano parts in the operas of Wagner and Richard Strauss.

Konius, Georgi. See **Conus, Georgi.**

Konjović, Petar, eminent Serbian composer; b. Sombor, May 6, 1882; d. Belgrade, Oct. 1, 1970. He studied at the Prague Cons. with Novák; was choral director and teacher in Zemun and Belgrade (1906–14). In 1920 he toured Europe as a pianist; in 1921–26 was music director of the Zagreb Opera. In 1927–33 he was director of national theaters in Osijek, Split, and Novi Sad; in 1933–39, intendant of the national theater in Zagreb. In 1939 he settled in Belgrade as rector and prof. of the Açademy of Music.

WORKS: Operas: *Vilin Veo* or *Ženidba Miloševa* (*The Wedding of Milos;* Zagreb, April 25, 1917); *Koštana* (Zagreb, April 16, 1931); *Knez od Zete* (*The Duke of Zeta;* Belgrade, May 25, 1929); *Sel jaci* (*The Peasants;* Belgrade, March 3, 1952); Symph. in C (1908); *Capriccio adriatico* for Violin and Orch. (1920); *Makar Chudra,* symph. poem after Maxim Gorky (1944); 2 string quartets; solo pieces for violin, cello, and piano; 24 songs; *Moja zemlja,* 100 Yugoslav folk songs, of which 25 are arranged for voice and small orch. He publ. a book of essays, *Ličnosti* (*Personalities;* Zagreb, 1920), and a monograph on Miloje Milojević (Belgrade, 1954).

Kono, Kristo, Albanian composer; b. Tirana, July 17, 1907. He studied at the Milan Cons.; wrote the first national Albanian operetta, *The Dawn* (1954); also an opera, *Flowers of Memories* (1959), and many choruses.

Konoye, Hidemarō, Japanese composer and conductor; b. Tokyo, Nov. 18, 1898; d. there, June 2, 1973. A member of an aristocratic Japanese family, he received his education in Japan and in Europe; attended classes in composition of Vincent d'Indy at the Schola Cantorum in Paris; then took courses with Franz Schreker and Georg Schumann at the Berlin Cons. He made his European debut as a conductor with the Berlin Phil., on Jan. 18, 1924. Returning to Japan, he was principal conductor of the New Symph. Orch. in Tokyo (1926–34), specializing in new works of Japanese, European, and American composers. He conducted in the U.S. in 1937 and 1957. He is the composer of several orch. pieces based on Japanese subjects; also orchestrated old Japanese court music for the modern Western orch.; arranged the music of *Madama Butterfly* for the films (inserting many Japanese folk melodies).

Kontarsky, Alfons, German pianist, brother of **Aloys** and **Bernhard Kontarsky;** b. Iserlohn, Westphalia, Oct. 9, 1932. He studied piano with Else Schmitz-Gohr at the Hochschule für Musik in Cologne (1953–55) and with Erdmann in Hamburg (1955–57); in 1955 received, along with his older brother, Aloys, the first prize for duo-piano playing at the International Competition of the Bavarian Radio in Munich; with Aloys, made a concert tour of duo recitals through the U.S., South America, South Africa, and Japan; in 1967 was appointed prof. of piano at the Hochschule für Musik in Cologne.

Kontarsky, Aloys, German pianist, brother of **Alfons** and **Bernhard Kontarsky;** b. Iserlohn, Westphalia, May 14, 1931. He studied piano with Else Schmitz-Gohr at the Hochschule für Musik in Cologne and with Erdmann in Hamburg; in 1955 he received, along with his younger brother Alfons, the first prize for duo-piano playing at the International Competition of the Bavarian Radio in Munich; then embarked with him on a worldwide tour of duo-piano recitals in the U.S., South America, South Africa, and Japan. He specialized in ultramodern music; gave premiere performances of works by Stockhausen, Berio, Earle Brown, Pousseur, Bussotti, and B.A. Zimmermann. In 1960 he joined the faculty of the International Festival Series of New Music in Darmstadt.

Kontarsky, Bernhard, German pianist and conductor, brother of **Alfons** and **Aloys Kontarsky;** b. Iserlohn, Westphalia, April 26, 1937. He studied at the Hochschule für Musik in Cologne and at the Univ. of Cologne. In 1964 he received the Mendelssohn Prize in Chamber Music. He was conductor of the Stuttgart State Opera; was also active as a concert pianist, both as a soloist and in ensemble with his brothers.

Kontski, Antoine de, Polish pianist, brother of **Apollinaire** and **Charles de Kontski;** b. Cracow, Oct. 27, 1817; d. Ivanichi, near Okulova, Novgorod district, Russia, Dec. 7, 1889. He was the most famous member of the Kontski family of precocious musicians. He studied with John Field in Moscow (1830); went to Paris in 1851; then was in Berlin (1853); in 1854–67 he was in St. Petersburg; then he lived in London as a piano teacher. He toured the U.S. in 1883 and again in 1885; lived for a time in Buffalo, N.Y. At the age of nearly 80, he undertook a world tour (1896–98), giving concerts in Australia, Japan, and Siberia. He died at the estate of friends near St. Petersburg.

Kontski, Apollinaire de, Polish violinist, brother of **Antoine** and **Charles de Kontski;** b. Cracow, Oct. 23, 1825; d. Warsaw, June 29, 1879. He studied with his elder brother Charles; he appeared with his brothers as a small child in Russia and later in Germany, frankly exploited by his family for sensational publicity and gain. In 1837 he played for Paganini in Paris; in 1861 he became director of the Warsaw Cons., of which he was a founder, and remained in that post until his death. He publ. some violin music.

Kontski, Charles de, Polish pianist, brother of **Antoine** and **Apollinaire de Kontski;** b. Cracow, Sept. 6, 1815; d. Paris, Aug. 27, 1867. Like his brothers, he was a child prodigy, and made appearances with them at various public exhibitions and concerts. He studied in Warsaw and in Paris, eventually settling in Paris as a private piano teacher, enjoying considerable success in society.

Konwitschny, Franz, German conductor; b. Fulnek, Czechoslovakia, Aug. 14, 1901; d. Belgrade, July 28, 1962. He studied violin at the German Musikverein School in Brünn (Brno) before enrolling at the Leipzig Cons. (1923–25); while still a student he played violin at the Gewandhaus Orch. in Leipzig. In 1927 he became a conductor at the opera in Stuttgart. In 1933 he went to Freiburg as Generalmusikdirektor; then held the same post with the operas in Frankfurt (1938) and Hannover (1945). In 1949 he became chief conductor of the Gewandhaus Orch. in Leipzig, and succeeded in restoring its prestige and competence of performance to its former standard, before World War II. He also served as Generalmusikdirektor of the Dresden State Opera (1953–55); then went to East Berlin as chief conductor of the State Opera. He died in Belgrade during a tour.

Kornauth, Egon, Austrian composer; b. Olmütz (Olomouc), May 14, 1891; d. Vienna, Oct. 28, 1959. He studied in Vienna with Fuchs, Schreker, and Schmidt; took a course in musicology with Guido Adler at the Univ. (Ph.D., 1915). In 1926 he was engaged to organize an orch. in Medan, Sumatra; despite the difficulties of such an undertaking, he maintained this orch. for 2 seasons; later he toured through Java, Celebes, and Ceylon with the Vienna Trio, which he founded. Kornauth's music is marked by considerable contrapuntal skill; his instrumental pieces and songs are mostly in a Romantic vein.

Korngold, Erich Wolfgang, Austrian composer of remarkable and precocious gifts; b. Brno, May 29, 1897; d. Hollywood, Nov. 29, 1957. He received his earliest musical education from his father, **Julius Korngold;** he then studied with Fuchs, Zemlinsky, and Grädener in Vienna. His progress was astounding; at the age of 12 he composed a Piano Trio, which was soon publ., revealing a competent technique and an ability to write in a modern style (strongly influenced by Richard Strauss). About the same time he wrote (in piano score) a pantomime, *Der Schneemann;* it was orchestrated by his teacher Zemlinsky, and performed at the Vienna Court Opera (Oct. 4, 1910), creating a sensation. In 1911 Nikisch played Korngold's *Schauspiel-Ouvertüre* in a concert of the Gewandhaus Orch. at Leipzig; in the same year the youthful composer gave a concert of his works in Berlin, appearing also as a pianist; his Sinfonietta was given by Felix Weingartner and the Vienna Phil. in 1913. Korngold was not quite 19 when his 2 short operas, *Der Ring des Polykrates* and *Violanta,* were produced in Munich. His first lasting success came with the opera *Die tote Stadt,* produced first in Hamburg (1920) and then on many opera stages all over the world. In 1929 he entered a fruitful collaboration with the famous director Max Reinhardt; in 1934 he went to Hollywood to arrange Mendelssohn's music for the Reinhardt film production of *A Midsummer Night's Dream.* He was intermittently in Europe; taught at the Vienna Academy of Music (1930–34) before settling in Hollywood; composed a number of film scores; conducted light opera with the N.Y. Opera Co. in 1942 and 1944. He became an American citizen in 1943; after 1945 he divided his time between the U.S. and Europe; lived for some time in Vienna.

Korngold's music represents the last breath of the Romantic spirit of Vienna; it is marvelously consistent with the melodic, rhythmic, and harmonic style of the judicious modernity of the nascent 20th century. When Mahler heard him play some of his music as a young boy, he kept repeating: "Ein Genie! Ein Genie!" Korngold never altered his established idiom of composition, and was never tempted to borrow modernistic devices, except for some transitory passages in major seconds or an occasional whole-tone scale. After the early outbursts of incautious enthusiasms on the part of some otherwise circumspect critics nominating Korngold as a new Mozart, his star, his erupting nova, began to sink rapidly, until it became a melancholy consensus to dismiss his operas at their tardy revivals as derivative products of an era that had itself little to exhibit that was worthwhile. Ironically, his film scores, in the form of orchestrated suites, experienced long after his death a spontaneous renascence, particularly on records, and especially among the unprejudiced and unopinionated American musical youth, who found in Korngold's music the stuff of their own new dreams.

WORKS: OPERAS: *Der Ring des Polykrates* and *Violanta* (Munich, March 28, 1916); *Die tote Stadt* (Hamburg, Dec. 4, 1920; Metropolitan Opera, N.Y., Nov. 19, 1921); *Das Wunder der Heliane* (Hamburg, Oct. 7, 1927); *Kathrin* (Stockholm, Oct. 7, 1939); *Die stumme Serenade* (Dortmund, Dec. 5, 1954); pantomime, *Der Schneemann* (Vienna, Oct. 4, 1910). FOR ORCH.: *Schauspiel-Ouvertüre* (Leipzig, 1911); Sinfonietta (Vienna, Nov. 28, 1913); Suite from the music to Shakespeare's *Much Ado about Nothing*, for Chamber Orch. (Vienna, 1919); *Sursum Corda*, symph. overture (1919); Piano Concerto for Left Hand Alone (1923; written for Paul Wittgenstein); Cello Concerto (1946); Violin Concerto (Jascha Heifetz with the St. Louis Symph. Orch., Feb. 15, 1947); *Symphonic Serenade* for String Orch. (1949); Symph. in F-sharp (1950; first public perf., Munich, Nov. 27, 1972); *Theme and Variations* for Orch. (1953). CHAMBER MUSIC: Piano Trio (1910); Violin Sonata; String Sextet; Piano Quintet; 3 string quartets (1922, 1935, 1945); 3 piano sonatas (1908, 1910, 1932).

Korngold, Julius, noted Austrian music critic; b. Brno, Dec. 24, 1860; d. Hollywood, Sept. 25, 1945. He was a law student; at the same time he studied music with Franz Krenn at the Vienna Cons. In 1902 he became music critic of the influential *Neue Freie Presse.* He was much in the limelight when his son **Erich** began his spectacular career at the age of 13 as a child composer, and an unfounded suspicion was voiced that Korngold was using his position to further his son's career. He publ. a book on a contemporary German opera, *Deutsches Opernschaffen der Gegenwart* (1922). In 1938 he joined his son in the U.S., settling in Hollywood, where he remained until his death.

Kósa, György, Hungarian composer and pianist; b. Budapest, April 24, 1897; d. Budapest, Aug. 16, 1984. He exhibited a precocious talent for music, and when he was 7 years old Béla Bartók accepted him as a piano student. At 13 he entered the Budapest Academy of Music, where he studied with Kodály, Siklós, and Victor Herzfeld; he continued his piano studies in the class of Dohnányi and received his diploma in 1917. He then traveled as an accompanist with violinists and other artists in Germany, Austria, and Italy; returned to Budapest in 1921 and in 1927 became prof. of piano at the Budapest Academy of Music. He remained in Budapest during World War II and was compelled to serve as a manual laborer in a war camp; after 1945 he resumed his teaching at the Academy, where he stayed until retirement in 1962. The primary influence in his music is that of Bartók, but he also experienced the attraction of impressionist techniques.

Koshetz, Nina, Russian soprano; b. Kiev, Dec. 30, 1894; d. Santa Ana, Calif., May 14, 1965. She studied piano as a child; then began to study singing. She toured Russia with Rachmaninoff, of whose songs she was a congenial interpreter. After the Revolution she went to the U.S.; appeared as a soloist with major American orchs. and also sang recitals of Russian songs. In 1941 she went to California and devoted herself to teaching.

Kössler, Hans. See **Koessler, Hans.**

Kostelanetz, André, Russian-American conductor; b. St. Petersburg, Dec. 22, 1901; d. Port-au-Prince, Haiti, Jan. 13, 1980. He studied at the St. Petersburg Cons. In 1922 he left Russia and went to America. He was employed as a rehearsal accompanist at the Metropolitan Opera in N.Y.; in 1930 was engaged to conduct the CBS Symph. Orch. On June 2, 1938, he married the famous soprano **Lily Pons;** they were divorced some years later. During World War II he organized concerts for the U.S. Armed Forces; subsequently conducted numerous popular concerts in America and in Europe, particularly summer concerts. He also made successful arrangements of light music; his technique of massive concentration of instrumental sonorities and of harmonic saturation by means of filling in harmonies with inner thirds and sixths influenced film music. An intelligent musician, he commissioned special works from American composers, of which the most successful was Copland's *Lincoln Portrait.*

Kotoński, Wlodzimierz, Polish composer of the avant-garde; b. Warsaw, Aug. 23, 1925. He studied theory with Piotr Rytel at the Warsaw Cons. (1945–51) and also took private lessons with Tadeusz Szeligowski in Poznan. He became a research worker in Polish folk music at the State Inst. of Art, and simultaneously began experimenting with alteration of sound by electronic means; produced an *Etude concrète* in which a single stroke of cymbals was electronically metamorphosed and expanded into a work of considerable length (1949). In 1959–60 he attended the summer sessions of new music at Darmstadt; then went to Paris, where he researched the problems of musique concrète with Pierre Schaeffer; in 1966–67 he worked at the Electronic Music Studio of the West German Radio in Cologne; in 1978 lectured at the State Univ. of N.Y. at Buffalo; in 1981 he again visited the U.S. to attend the world premiere of his *Sirocco.*

WORKS: *Etude concrète* for a single stroke of Cymbals electronically metamorphosed (1949; Darmstadt, July 9, 1960); *Poème* for Orch. (1949); *Quartettino* for 4 Horns (1950); *Danses montagnardes* for Orch. (1950); *Prelude and Passacaglia* for Orch. (1953); *6 Miniatures* for Clarinet and Piano (1957); *Chamber Music* for 21 Instruments and Percussion (1958; Warsaw Festival, Oct. 2, 1958); *Musique en relief,* cycle of 5 miniatures for 6 Orch. Groups (1959; Darmstadt, Sept. 5, 1959); Trio for Flute, Guitar, and Percussion (1960); *Concerto per quattro* for Harp, Harpsichord, Guitar, Piano, and Chamber Orch. (1960); *Canto* for 18 Instruments (1961); *Selection I* for 4 Jazz Players (1962); *Pezzo* for Flute and Piano (1962); *Musica per fiati e timpani* (1964); 2 wind quintets (1964, 1967); *Monochromie* for Solo Oboe (1964); *A battere* for Guitar, Viola, Cello, Harpsichord, and Percussion (1966); *Pour quatre* for Clarinet, Trombone, Cello, and Piano (1968); *Action* for Electronic Sound (Cracow, June 5, 1969); *Music* for 16 Cymbals and Strings (1969; Warsaw, Sept. 20, 1969); *Multiplay,* instrumental theater for Brass Quintet (1971); *Musical Games,* instrumental theater for 5 Players (1972); Oboe Concerto (1972); *Aeolian Harp* for Soprano and 4 Instruments (1972–73); *Promenade* for Clarinet, Trombone, and Cello, all electronically amplified, and 2 Synthesizers (1973); *Wind Rose* for Orch. (1976); *Spring Music* for Flute, Oboe, Violin, and Synthesizer (1978); *Bora* for Orch. (1979); *Sirocco* for Orch. (1981). He publ. a book, *Instrumenty perkusyjne we współczesnej orkiestrze (Percussion Instruments in the Modern Orchestra;* Cracow, 1963).

Kotter, Hans, Alsatian organist and composer; b. Strasbourg, c.1480; d. Bern, 1541. He studied organ with Paul Hofhaimer; was organist at the electoral court in Torgau; then served as organist of the collegiate church of St. Nikolaus in Fribourg, Switzerland (1514–30) until he was banished for espousing the doctrines of the reformer Zwingli. In 1534 Kotter was able to return to Switzerland, and he took up residence in Bern as a schoolmaster. He compiled a collection of keyboard pieces in tablature (1513), including preambles, fantasies, dances, transcriptions of vocal music, and settings of plainchant. There is also in existence a setting of a *Nobis post hoc* by Kotter interpolated in a *Salve Regina* by Hofhaimer.

Kottlitz, Adolf, German violinist; b. Trier, Sept. 27, 1820; killed while hunting in Uralsk, Russia, Oct. 26, 1860. He began his career as a child prodigy; gave public concerts at the age of 10; spent 3 years in Paris, where he was a protégé of Liszt; then played violin in the orch. of the Königsberg Opera (1848–56). In 1856 he undertook a long tour in Russia, and finally settled in Uralsk as a violin teacher. He publ. 2 string quartets. His wife, **Clothilde** (née **Ellendt;** 1822–67), was a singing teacher in Königsberg.

Kotzeluch, Leopold Anton. See **Koželuch, Leopold Anton.**

Kotzwara (*recte* **Kočvara**), **Franz,** Bohemian composer; b. Prague, 1730; d. (by hanging himself) London, Sept. 2, 1791. He traveled in Europe; then settled in London toward the end of the 18th century. In 1790 he went to Dublin as a viola player in the orch. at the King's Theatre; returning to London the same year, he played in the orch. at the Handel Commemoration in May. He is remembered solely for his piano piece *The Battle of Prague,* which attained tremendous popularity in the 19th century.

Koussevitzky, Serge, celebrated Russian conductor; b. Vishny-Volochok, July 26, 1874; d. Boston, June 4, 1951. His father and his 3 brothers were all amateur musicians. Koussevitzky learned to play the trumpet and took part, with his brothers, in a small wind ensemble, numbering 8 members in all; they earned their living by playing at balls and weddings and occasionally at village fairs. At the age of 14 he went to Moscow; since Jews were not allowed to live there, he became baptized. He then received a fellowship with free tuition at the Musico-Dramatic Inst. of the Moscow Phil., in the class of the double bass; his teacher was the famous double-bass player Ramboušek; he also studied music theory with Blaramberg and Kruglikov. In 1894 he joined the orch. of the Bolshoi Opera Theater, where Ramboušek held the first chair in the double-bass section. Upon Ramboušek's death in 1901, Koussevitzky succeeded him at his post. Koussevitzky before long became known as a soloist of the first magnitude on the double bass who was able to achieve high artistic performance on this supposedly unwieldy instrument. On March 25, 1901, he gave his first public concert in Moscow in a program which included an adaptation of Handel's Cello Concerto; on subsequent occasions he performed his own arrangement for double bass of Mozart's Bassoon Concerto and of Bruch's *Kol Nidrei.* On March 27, 1903, he gave a double-bass recital in Berlin, attracting great attention. To supplement the meager repertoire, he wrote several pieces for the double bass and performed them at his concerts; with some aid from Glière, he composed a Double-bass Concerto, which he performed for the first time in Moscow on Feb. 25, 1905. On Sept. 8, 1905, he married Natalie Ushkov, of a wealthy tea-merchant family. He soon resigned from the orch. of the Bolshoi Opera Theater; in an open letter to the Russian publication *Musical Gazette,* explained the reason for his resignation as the economic and artistic difficulties in the orch. He then went to Germany, where he continued to give double-bass recitals; played the First Cello Concerto by Saint-Saëns on the double bass. In 1907 he conducted a student orch. at the Berlin Hochschule für Musik; his first public appearance as a conductor took place on Jan. 23, 1908, with the Berlin Phil. In 1909 he established a publishing house, Editions Russes de Musique; in 1915 he purchased the catalogue of the Gutheil Co.; among composers with whom he signed contracts were Scriabin, Stravinsky, Prokofiev, Medtner, and Rachmaninoff; the association with Scriabin was particularly fruitful, and in subsequent years Koussevitzky became the greatest champion of Scriabin's music. In 1909 he organized his own symph. orch. in Moscow, featuring works by Russian composers, but also including classical masterpieces; played many Russian works for the first time, among them Scriabin's *Prometheus.* In the summer of 1910 he took his orch. to the towns along the Volga River in a specially chartered steamboat. He repeated the Volga tour in 1912 and 1914. The outbreak of World War I made it necessary to curtail his activities; however, he continued to give his concerts in Moscow; in 1915 he presented a memorial Scriabin program. After the Revolution of 1917, Koussevitzky was offered the directorship of the

State Symph. Orch. (former Court Orch.) in Petrograd; he conducted it until 1920; also presented concerts in Moscow despite the hardships of the revolutionary times. In 1920 he left Russia; went first to Berlin, then to Rome, and finally to Paris, where he settled for several years. There he organized the Concerts Koussevitzky with a specially assembled orch.; presented many new scores by French and Russian composers, among them Ravel's orchestration of Mussorgsky's *Pictures at an Exhibition*, Honegger's *Pacific 231*, and several works by Prokofiev and Stravinsky. In 1924 Koussevitzky was engaged as permanent conductor of the Boston Symph. Orch., a post that he was to hold for 25 years, the longest tenure of any conductor of that organization; until 1928 he continued his Paris series (during the summer months). Just as in Russia he championed Russian composers, in France the French, so in the U.S. he encouraged American composers to write works for the Boston Symph. Orch. Symphonic compositions by Aaron Copland, Roy Harris, Walter Piston, Samuel Barber, Howard Hanson, Edward Burlingame Hill, William Schuman, and others were performed by Koussevitzky for the first time. For the 50th anniversary of the Boston Symph. Orch. (1931) Koussevitzky commissioned works from Stravinsky (*Symphony of Psalms*), Hindemith, Honegger, Prokofiev, Albert Roussel, Ravel (piano concerto), Copland, Gershwin, etc. In 1950 he conducted in Rio de Janeiro, Israel, and in Europe; also was guest conductor at several concerts of the Boston Symph. after his successor, Charles Munch, became principal conductor. A highly important development in Koussevitzky's American career was the establishment of the Berkshire Music Center at Tanglewood, Mass. This was an outgrowth of the Berkshire Symph. Festival, organized in 1934 by Henry Hadley; Koussevitzky and the Boston Symph. Orch. presented summer concerts at the Berkshire Festival in 1935 for the first time; since then, the concerts have become an annual institution. The Berkshire Music Center was opened on July 8, 1940, with Koussevitzky as director and Copland as assistant director; among the distinguished guest instructors were Hindemith, Honegger, and Messiaen; Koussevitzky himself taught conducting; he was succeeded after his death by his former student Leonard Bernstein. Koussevitzky held many honorary degrees: Mus.Doc. from Brown Univ. (1926), Rutgers Univ. (1937), Yale Univ. (1938), Rochester Univ. (1940), Williams College (1943), and Boston Univ. (1945); LL.D. from Harvard Univ. (1929) and from Princeton Univ. (1947). He was a member of the French Legion of Honor; held the Cross of Commander of the Finnish Order of the White Rose (1936). Besides his Double-bass Concerto, he wrote *Humoresque*, *Valse miniature*, *Chanson triste*, and other small pieces for his instrument; and an orch. work, *Passacaglia on a Russian Theme* (Boston Symph., Oct. 12, 1934). Koussevitzky became an American citizen on April 16, 1941. In 1942 his wife died; he established the Koussevitzky Foundation as a memorial to her, the funds to be used for commissioning works by composers of all nationalities. He married Olga Naoumoff (1901–78), a niece of Natalie Koussevitzky, on Aug. 15, 1947.

As a conductor, Koussevitzky possessed an extraordinary emotional power; in Russian music, and particularly in Tchaikovsky's symphs., he was unexcelled; he was capable of achieving the subtlest nuances in the works of the French school; his interpretations of Debussy were notable. As a champion of modern music, he introduced a great number of compositions for the first time anywhere; his ardor in projecting unfamiliar music before new audiences in different countries served to carry conviction among the listeners and the professional music critics. He was often criticized for the liberties he allowed himself in the treatment of classical masterpieces; undoubtedly his performances of Bach, Beethoven, Brahms, and Schubert were untraditional; but they were nonetheless musicianly in the sincere artistry that animated his interpretations.

Koutzen, Boris, Russian-American violinist and composer; b. Uman, near Kiev, April 1, 1901; d. Mount Kisco, N.Y., Dec. 10, 1966. He studied violin with Leo Zetlin and composition with Glière at the Moscow Cons. (1918–22). In 1922 he went to the U.S. and joined the violin section of the Philadelphia Orch.; also taught violin at the Philadelphia Cons. His music possesses an attractive Romantic flavor in an old Russian manner. He composed a number of orch. pieces, among them *Solitude* (Philadelphia, April 1, 1927, composer conducting); *Valley Forge*, symph. poem (N.Y., Feb. 19, 1940); Concerto for 5 Solo Instruments (Boston, Feb. 23, 1940); Violin Concerto (Philadelphia, Feb. 22, 1952, **Nadia Koutzen,** composer's daughter, soloist); Piano Concertino (1959); opera, *You Never Know* (1962); *Concertante* for 2 Flutes and Orch. (1965).

Kovařovic, Karel, noted Czech conductor and composer; b. Prague, Dec. 9, 1862; d. there, Dec. 6, 1920. He studied clarinet, harp, and piano at the Prague Cons., and composition with Fibich. In 1900 he was appointed opera conductor of the National Theater in Prague, and held this post until his death; he also led symph. concerts in Prague. As a conductor, he demonstrated great craftsmanship and established a high standard of excellence in his operatic productions; his interpretations of Dvořák and Smetana were particularly notable; an ardent believer in the cause of Czech music, he promoted national compositions. In his own music, he also made use of national materials, but his treatment was mostly imitative of the French models; the influences of Gounod and Massenet are particularly noticeable. He publ. some of his lighter works under a series of humorously misspelled names of French opera composers (C. Biset, J. Héral, etc.).
WORKS: Operas (all produced in Prague): *Ženichové* (*The Bridegrooms;* May 13, 1884); *Cesta oknem* (*Through the Window;* Feb. 11, 1886); *Noc Šimona a Judy* (*The Night of Simon and Jude;* original title, *Frasquita;* Nov. 5, 1892); *Psohlavci* (*The Dog-Heads;* April 24, 1898; his most famous

opera); *Na starém bélidle* (*At the Old Bleaching-House;* Nov. 22, 1901); ballets: *Hashish* (June 19, 1884); *Pohádka o nalezeném štěstí* (*A Tale of Found Happiness;* Dec. 21, 1886); *Na zaletech* (*Flirtation;* Oct. 24, 1909); symph. works; Piano Concerto; 2 string quartets; etc.

Koven, Reginald de. See **De Koven, Reginald.**

Kowalski, Max, German composer and pedagogue; b. Kowal, Poland, Aug. 10, 1882; d. London, June 4, 1956. He was taken to Frankfurt as an infant, and received his primary education there; studied law, obtaining his Dr.Juris. at Marburg Univ.; returning to Frankfurt, he studied music with Bernhard Sekles; in 1912 wrote a cycle of songs to Guiraud's *Pierrot Lunaire* (independently from Schoenberg's work of the same year) and during the following 20 years composed a number of lieder, which were widely performed in Germany. After 1933 he was put in the Buchenwald concentration camp, but was released in 1939, and went to England; settled in London as a teacher and a synagogal cantor; eked out his existence by also tuning pianos.

Koželuh (Kozeluch; Koscheluch), Johann Antonín (Jan Evangelista Antonín Tomáš), Bohemian composer, cousin of **Leopold Koželuh;** b. Welwarn, Dec. 14, 1738; d. Prague, Feb. 3, 1814. He began music studies at school in Welwarn; was then a chorister at the Jesuit College in Breznice; subsequently, studied with J.F.N. Seger in Prague; then went to Vienna, where he had instruction from Gluck, Gassmann, and Hasse. Upon his return to Prague, he established himself as a music teacher; in 1784 he became Kapellmeister at St. Vitus' Metropolitan Cathedral, where he remained until his death. His cousin was one of his pupils. He composed 2 operas: *Alessandro nell'Indie* (Prague, 1769) and *Il Demofoonte* (Prague, 1771); much sacred music, including 2 oratorios, about 45 masses, 5 requiems, etc.; 4 symphs.; an oboe concerto; 2 bassoon concertos; and many other instrumental works.

Koželuh (Kozeluch; Kotzeluch), Leopold (Jan Antonín), Bohemian composer, pianist, and teacher, cousin of **Johann Antonín Koželuh;** b. Welwarn, June 26, 1747; d. Vienna, May 7, 1818. He began his musical studies in Welwarn; then had instruction with his cousin and with F.X. Dušek in Prague. He also studied law but turned to a career in music after the success he attained with his ballets and pantomimes. In 1778 he went to Vienna, where he established himself as a pianist, teacher, and composer; also was active as a music publisher. In 1792 he was appointed Kammer Kapellmeister and Hofmusik Compositor, succeeding Mozart; he held this position until his death. Although Beethoven referred to him contemptuously in a letter of 1812 as "miserabilis," Koželuh was an excellent pianist; he composed about 50 solo sonatas, 22 piano concertos, 28 symphs., about 80 piano trios, and other pieces of chamber music. His stage works included operas,

ballets, and pantomimes, but little of this music is extant; his only extant opera is *Gustav Wasa* (c.1792).

Kozina, Marjan, Slovenian composer; b. Novo Mesto, June 4, 1907; d. there, June 19, 1966. He studied at the Cons. of Ljubljana; later took courses with Joseph Marx at the Vienna Academy of Music and with Josef Suk at the Prague Cons. During the occupation of Yugoslavia by the Nazi armies, Kozina took part in the armed resistance movement; after the liberation he taught at the Musical Academy of Ljubljana. He wrote music in a fine, unaffected manner, making circumspect use of modern harmonies, while deriving his melorhythmic essence from native Slovenian folk-song patterns. His most important work is the music drama *Equinox* (Ljubljana, May 2, 1946), which had numerous revivals in Yugoslavia and was also performed in Prague and Moscow. Other works are the ballet *Diptihon* (1952) and a cantata, *Lepa Vida* (*Beautiful Vida;* 1939).

Kraft, Anton, Austrian cello virtuoso, father of **Nicolaus Kraft;** b. Rokitzán, near Pilsen, Dec. 30, 1749; d. Vienna, Aug. 28, 1820. He began to study at an early age with his father, an amateur cellist; then went to Prague, and later to Vienna; there he enjoyed the friendship of Haydn, who recommended him for a post as cellist in the chapel of Prince Esterházy (1778); he was subsequently in the employ of Prince Grassalkowicz; in 1795 entered the service of Prince Lobkowitz in Vienna. Among Kraft's works are 3 sonatas; 3 grand duos for Violin and Cello; several grand duos for 2 Cellos; Divertissement for Cello and Double Bass; etc. For a time it was thought that Haydn's famous Cello Concerto in D was actually written by Kraft, but it is now generally agreed by specialists that it is an authentic work by Haydn. Since it was written for Kraft, he may have made technical suggestions that were adopted by Haydn.

Kraft, Nicolaus, Hungarian cellist and composer, son of **Anton Kraft;** b. Esterház, Dec. 14, 1778; d. Eger, May 18, 1853. He studied cello with his father, and went with him on concert tours while quite young; he and his father played chamber music with Mozart at the Dresden court (1789); when the Krafts went to Vienna in 1790, Nicolaus became a member of the famous Schuppanzigh Quartet. He was subsequently chamber musician to Prince Lobkowitz, who sent him to Berlin in 1791 to study for a year with Duport. After concerts in Germany, he returned to Vienna, and joined the court orch. (1809); then entered the court orch. at Stuttgart in 1814. He retired after an accident to his hand, in 1834. He wrote 5 cello concertos; 6 cello duos; 3 divertissements for 2 Cellos; Cello Fantasia, with String Quartet; *Polonaise* and *Bolero* for Cello, with Orch.; other cello music. His son, **Friedrich Kraft** (b. Vienna, Feb. 13, 1807; d. Stuttgart, Dec. 4, 1874), was also a cellist, and played in the Stuttgart Court Orch. for many years.

Kraft, William, American virtuoso percussionist, composer and conductor; b. Chicago, Sept. 6, 1923. His parental name was **Kashereffsky,** which his parents Americanized to Kraft. The family moved to California and Kraft began to study piano. He took music courses at San Diego State College and at the Univ. of Calif. in Los Angeles, where he also had professional percussion instruction with Murray Spivack. In 1943 he was called to arms, and served in the U.S. forces as pianist, arranger, and drummer in military bands; while in Europe with the army he took time out to attend music courses at Cambridge Univ. Returning to the U.S. after discharge from military duty, he earned a living as percussionist in jazz bands. In the summer of 1948 he enrolled in the Berkshire Music Center in Tanglewood, where he studied composition with Irving Fine and conducting with Leonard Bernstein. In 1949 he entered Columbia Univ., where his instructors in composition were Jack Beeson, Otto Luening, Seth Bingham, Vladimir Ussachevsky, and Henry Cowell; he also attended classes in musicology with Erich Hertzmann and Paul Henry Lang (B.S., 1951; M.A., 1954). He continued to perfect his technique as a percussion player; and took lessons with Morris Goldenberg and Saul Goodman; he attained a high degree of virtuosity as a percussion player, both in the classical tradition and in jazz. In 1955 he was named chief of the percussion section of the Los Angeles Phil. Orch., retaining this position until 1981. In the meantime he developed his natural gift for conducting; from 1969 to 1972 he served as assistant conductor of the Los Angeles Phil.; in a parallel development, he composed assiduously and successfully. In 1981 he was appointed composer-in-residence of the Los Angeles Phil.; then founded the Los Angeles Phil. New Music Group, presenting programs of modern works for chamber orch. combinations. He held 2 Guggenheim fellowship grants (1967, 1972). As a composer, he explores without prejudice a variety of quaquaversal techniques, including serial procedures; naturally, his music coruscates with a rainbow spectrum of asymmetrical rhythms. There is a tendency in the very titles of his works toward textured constructivism, e.g. *Momentum, Configurations, Collage, Encounters, Translucences, Triangles, Mobiles,* but there are also concrete representations of contemporary events, as in *Riots—Decade '60.*

WORKS: Nonet for Brass and Percussion (Los Angeles, Oct. 13, 1958); *3 Miniatures* for Percussion and Orch. (Los Angeles, Feb. 14, 1959); *Variations on a Folksong* for Orch. (Los Angeles, March 26, 1960); *Symphony* for Strings and Percussion (N.Y., Aug. 21, 1961); *Concerto Grosso* (San Diego, March 22, 1963); *Silent Boughs,* song cycle (1963); *6 Pieces* for String Trio (1963); Concerto for 4 Percussion Soloists and Orch. (Los Angeles, March 10, 1966); Double Trio for Piano, Prepared Piano, Amplified Guitar, Tuba, and Percussion (Los Angeles, Oct. 31, 1966); *Configurations* for 4 Percussion Soloists and Jazz Orch. (Los Angeles, Nov. 13, 1966); *Contextures: Riots—Decade '60* (Los Angeles, April 4, 1969); *Games: Collage No. 1* for Brass and Percussion (Pasadena, Calif., Nov. 21, 1969); *Triangles,* concerto for Percussion and 10 Instruments (Los Angeles, Dec. 8, 1969); *Mobiles* for 10 Instruments (Berkeley, Calif., Oct. 18, 1970); *Cadenze* for 7 Instruments (1972); *In Memoriam Igor Stravinsky* for Violin and Piano (1972–74); Piano Concerto (Los Angeles, Nov. 21, 1973); *Des Imagistes* for 2 Readers and Percussion (1974); *Requiescat* for Electric Piano (1975); *Translucences* for Piano (1975); *Encounters I (Soliliquy)* for Percussion (1975); *Encounters II* for Unaccompanied Tuba (1975); *Encounters IV,* a Duel for Trombone and Percussion (1975); *Encounters V (In the Morning of the Winter Sea)* (1975); *The Innocents: The Witch Trial at Salem* for Voices, Percussion, and Celesta (Los Angeles, Oct. 18, 1976); *Andirivieni (Coming and Going)* for Tuba and Orch. (Los Angeles, Jan. 26, 1978); *The Sublime and the Beautiful* for Orch. (1979); *Luminescences* for Piano (1979); *Dialogues and Entertainments* for Wind Ensemble (1980); *Solo Piece* for Horn (1981); *Triple Play* for Orch. (1982); Double Concerto No. 2 for Violin, Piano, and Chamber Orch. (1982); music for the film *Fire and Ice* (1983); Timpani Concerto (Indianapolis, March 9, 1984); *Study for Contextures II: The Final Beast* (Los Angeles, April 2, 1984, composer conducting).

Kramer, A. Walter, American music critic and composer; b. New York, Sept. 23, 1890; d. there, April 8, 1969. He studied music with his father, Maximilian Kramer, and took violin lessons with Carl Hauser and Richard Arnold. After graduating from the College of the City of N.Y. in 1910, he joined the staff of *Musical America* (1910–22) and served as its editor in chief from 1929 till 1936. His music criticism was journalistically voluble and knowledgeable. He wrote many pleasant and entirely singable songs and also essayed an ambitious *Symphonic Rhapsody* for Violin and Orch. (1912).

Kranich & Bach, well-known firm of piano makers founded in N.Y. in 1864 by **Helmuth Kranich, Sr.** (b. Grossbreitenbach, Germany, Aug. 22, 1833; d. New York, Jan. 29, 1902), and **Jacques Bach** (b. Lorentzen, Alsace, June 22, 1833; d. New York, Oct. 29, 1894). The business, incorporated in 1890, has been continued by the founders' descendants: **Frederick Kranich** served as president from 1902 to 1920, and was succeeded by **Louis P. Bach** from 1920 to 1930. In 1930 **Jacques Bach Schlosser** (grandson of Jacques Bach) was elected president. **Helmuth Kranich,** son of Helmuth Sr., was appointed a member of the board of directors in 1894, secretary of the firm in 1902, and president in 1946; retired in 1950; died in N.Y. on Oct. 24, 1956. Other members of the board of directors included **Philip Schlosser** (grandson of Jacques Bach), **Victor Kranich** (son of Helmuth Kranich, Sr.), **Lucy Bach** (daughter of Jacques Bach), and **John J. Kuhn** (grandnephew of Jacques Bach). Frederick Kranich invented the "Isotonic" pedal, doing away with the shifting keyboard in grand pianos, and the "Violyn" plate for upright pianos, and perfected various improvements in piano construction.

Krantz, Eugen, German pianist; b. Dresden, Sept. 13, 1844; d. Gohrisch, near Königstein, May 26, 1898. He studied at the Dresden Cons.; was chorus master at the court opera there (1869–84); taught at the Dresden Cons., becoming director in 1890, when he bought the institution. He publ. some songs and a *Lehrgang im Klavierunterricht* (1882); was also critic for the Dresden *Presse* and the *Nachrichten.*

Krása, Hans, Czech composer; b. Prague, Nov. 30, 1899; d. Auschwitz, Oct. 16, 1944. He was of Czech-German (Jewish) extraction; studied in a German high school in Prague; took lessons in music with Zemlinsky and Keussler in Prague. He made rapid progress, and had his first orch. piece, *Grotesques,* performed in Prague on May 20, 1921; also successful were his beginnings as a conductor; he was engaged as chorus master at the German Theater in Prague; then went to Berlin, where he conducted at the Kroll Opera. He returned to Prague in 1928, and in 1942 was interned at the Theresienstadt concentration camp; nevertheless he continued to compose, and produced an opera, *Brundibár,* which had several performances arranged by an opera group of the Jewish inmates. On Oct. 16, 1944, he was transported to Auschwitz and put to death. He was a composer of some interesting works in a "hedonistic" manner, aiming at sophisticated entertainment; his idiom was mildly atonal. So promising was his career as a composer that his *Pastorale* and *March* (originally first and 2nd movements from a symph.) were performed in Paris (April 24, 1923) and also by the Boston Symph. Orch. (Nov. 19, 1926). His String Trio was performed posthumously at the Aspen (Colo.) Festival (Oct. 22, 1951). He also wrote incidental music to *Lysistrata,* and the cantata *Die Erde ist des Herrn.* Other works were *Theme with Variations* for String Quartet (1942); a group of songs to words by Rimbaud; some piano pieces.

Krasner, Louis, American violinist; b. Cherkassy, Russia, June 21, 1903. He was taken to the U.S. as a small child; studied at the New England Cons. in Boston, graduating in 1923; then went abroad, where he studied violin with Carl Flesch, Lucien Capet, and Ševčik. From 1944 to 1949 he was concertmaster of the Minneapolis Symph. Orch.; then became prof. of violin and chamber music at Syracuse Univ. In 1974 he joined the staff of the New England Cons. He commissioned Alban Berg in 1934 to write a violin concerto for him; gave its world premiere at the Barcelona Festival of the International Society for Contemporary Music (April 19, 1936); also gave the world premiere of Schoenberg's Violin Concerto (Philadelphia, Dec. 6, 1940, Stokowski conducting).

Kraus, Alfredo, noted tenor; b. Las Palmas, Canary Islands, Sept. 24, 1927. He studied in Barcelona, Valencia, and Milan; made his operatic debut in Cairo in 1956; then sang in Rome, London, Milan, Chicago, and San Francisco. He made his debut at the Metropolitan Opera in N.Y. on Feb. 16, 1966, as the Duke in *Rigoletto;* in subsequent years he became its regular member. He is considered to be the finest *tenore di grazia* since Schipa.

Kraus, Joseph Martin, important German-born Swedish composer; b. Miltenberg-am-Main, June 20, 1756; d. Stockholm, Dec. 15, 1792. He attended the Jesuit School in Mannheim; subsequently studied law at the univs. of Mainz (1773–74), Erfurt (1775–76), and Göttingen (1777–78). In 1778 he went to Sweden, making his home in Stockholm; in 1780 was elected a member of the Swedish Academy of Music; in 1781 was appointed deputy conductor of the court orch. His great interest in Swedish culture prompted King Gustavus III to send him to Germany, Austria, Italy, France, and England for study purposes between the years 1782 and 1787. During his travels he met Gluck and Haydn, both of whom warmly praised his music. In 1788 he was appointed Hovkapellmästare in Stockholm, holding this position until his untimely death from tuberculosis. During his short life (he was almost an exact contemporary of Mozart), he composed several distinguished works for the stage; his operas (to Swedish texts) are estimable achievements, especially *Aeneas i Carthago (Dido och Aeneas),* which was premiered posthumously in Stockholm on Nov. 18, 1799. He also composed a *Symphonie funèbre* and *Begravingskantata* for the assassinated Gustavus III. After Kraus's death, his MSS and letters were deposited in the library of the Univ. of Uppsala. In recent years, a number of his works have been publ. His own writings include *Versuch von Schäfergedichten* (Mainz, 1773) and *Etwas von und über Musik fürs Jahr 1777* (Frankfurt, 1778).

Kraus, Lili, Hungarian pianist; b. Budapest, April 3, 1905. Her father was a stonecutter of Czech descent, but her mother sang. Lili Kraus studied piano, and was accepted as a student of Bartók and Kodály at the Academy of Music in Budapest, graduating at the age of 17. She then went to Vienna, where she studied piano with Eduard Steuermann at the Vienna Cons.; in 1926 she received her diploma; from 1930 to 1934 she attended master classes in piano study with Artur Schnabel in Berlin. She became known in Europe as a congenial Chopin player, but after a series of concerts and duo recitals with the violinist Szymon Goldberg in Beethoven programs she was hailed as a true Beethovenian; then she played Mozart and was extolled as an authentic Mozartian. But she also gave performances of piano works by Béla Bartók. Thus equipped, she toured Europe, Japan, Australia, and South Africa. She married the German philosopher Otto Mandl and settled in London. Recklessly, she engaged in a world tour through the Orient in 1942 and was caught in Java when the Japanese captured the island; fortunately she was helped by a Japanese conductor with whom she played in Tokyo, and he made her life tolerable. After the war she acquired New Zealand citizenship, which exorcised her former Austrian affiliation. In 1948 she went to South Africa and taught piano at the Univ. of Cape Town. In 1949 she arrived in the U.S., where she gave a series of highly lauded concerts; she played in London in 1960. In 1967 she was engaged as artist-in-residence at Texas Christian Univ. in Austin; she retired in 1983. A widow since 1956, she eventually settled on her farm in North Carolina, where she engaged in her artistic hobbies, such as dressmaking, painting, and yoga. She continued in her religion as a Roman Catholic. On March 4, 1978, she was awarded by her native Austria the Cross of Honor for Science and Art.

Krause, Anton, German pianist and conductor; b. Geithain, Nov. 9, 1834; d. Dresden, Jan. 31, 1907. He began to study piano at an early age; then studied at Dresden; from 1850 to 1853 studied at the Leipzig Cons. with Wenzel, Moscheles, Hauptmann, Richter, Rietz, and David; taught music and also conducted in Leipzig. In 1859 he succeeded Reinecke at Barmen as director of the Singverein and the Konzertgesellschaft, retiring in 1897. He wrote *Prinzessin Ilse* for Soli, Female Chorus, Piano, and Declamation; choral works; songs; also instructive piano pieces. He publ. a collection of classical sonatinas and *Library for Two Pianofortes* (18 vols.).

Krause, Emil, German piano pedagogue and music critic; b. Hamburg, July 30, 1840; d. there, Sept. 5, 1916. He was a pupil of Hauptmann, Richter, Rietz, Moscheles, and Plaidy at the Leipzig Cons. In 1860 he went to Hamburg, where he taught piano and wrote music criticism for the *Fremdenblatt* from 1864 until 1907. He publ. *Beiträge zur Technik des Klavierspiels,* with supplementary matter in *Ergänzungen; Aufgabenbuch für die Harmonielehre* (1869; 8th ed., 1908); *Praktische Klavierschule* (1892); *Neuer "Gradus ad Parnassum"* (100 études); and *Anleitung zum Studium der Musikgeschichte* (1906); *Johannes Brahms in seinen Werken* (Hamburg, 1892; contains a catalogue of works); *Kurzgefasste Darstellung der Passion, des Oratoriums und modernen Konzertwerkes für Chor, Soli und Orchester* (Langensalza, 1902). His compositions include an oratorio, *Den Heimgegangenen; Trio non difficile* for Piano, Violin, and Cello (1863); songs; piano pieces.

Krause, Martin, German pianist and pedagogue; b. Lobstadt, near Leipzig, June 17, 1853; d. Plattling, Bavaria, Aug. 2, 1918. He was a pupil of his father, a cantor, and of Wenzel and Reinecke at the Leipzig Cons. After successful tours in the Netherlands and Germany (1878–80), he was prostrated by nervous exhaustion for 2 years. He played before Liszt in 1883, and for 3 years, until Liszt's death, was in constant communication with the master and his pupils. In 1885 Krause, Siloti, Frau Moran-Olden, and others gave 2 grand concerts in Leipzig, which marked the establishment of the Lisztverein, of which Krause was the chief promoter, chairman, and manager till 1900, when it was discontinued. After 1900 he taught in Leipzig, Dresden, and at the Stern Cons. in Berlin.

Krause, Tom, Finnish baritone; b. Helsinki, July 5, 1934. He studied in Helsinki, Vienna, and Hamburg; made his concert debut in Helsinki in 1957, his operatic debut at the Berlin Städtische Oper in 1958. In 1962 he joined the Hamburg State Opera; also sang at Bayreuth, Covent Garden in London, Glyndebourne, and the Vienna State Opera. On Oct. 11, 1967, he made his American debut at the Metropolitan Opera in N.Y. as Count Almaviva in *Le nozze di Figaro.*

Krauss, Clemens, eminent Austrian conductor; b. Vienna, March 31, 1893; d. Mexico City, May 16, 1954. He served as a chorister at the Imperial Chapel in Vienna; then studied at the Vienna Cons. with Reinhold (piano), Grädener (composition), and Heuberger (theory), graduating in 1912. He was then choral director at the State Theater in Brünn; subsequently conducted opera in Riga (1913–14), Nuremberg (1915–16), Stettin (1916–21), and Graz (1921–22). In 1922 he became an assistant to Franz Schalk at the Vienna State Opera; also taught conducting at the Vienna Academy of Music and was conductor of the Vienna Tonkünstlerkonzerte (1923–27). In 1924–29 he was director of the Frankfurt Opera and conductor of the Museum Concerts; from 1929 to 1934 he was director of the Vienna State Opera; was also conductor of the Vienna Phil. (1930–33). In 1929 he undertook an American tour, and had a signal success as guest conductor with the N.Y. Phil. and the Philadelphia Orch. Returning to Germany in 1934, he served as director of the Berlin State Opera; in 1937 he assumed the post of Generalmusikdirektor of the Bavarian State Opera in Munich, a position he held until 1944; was also a conductor at the Salzburg Festivals and at the Mozarteum; during the last months of the devastating war (1944–45) he conducted concerts of the Vienna Phil. He was compromised by his mute acquiescence in the Nazi barbarism, but as an artist, he tried to protect Jewish musicians who worked under his direction. Unlike his more tainted colleagues, he was not called to account for his dubious political attitudes, however, and after the war he continued to serve as conductor of the Vienna State Opera; led concerts of the Vienna Phil. from 1947, including its famous New Year's Day Concerts. He was married to the singer **Viorica Ursuleac,** whom he often accompanied at the piano in her recitals. Krauss was a close friend and collaborator of Richard Strauss; he conducted the premieres of his operas *Arabella, Friedenstag, Capriccio* (for which he wrote the libretto), and *Die Liebe der Danae.* He was regarded as one of the foremost operatic and symph. conductors in Austria and Germany; he was particularly praised for his interpretations of the operas of Wagner and Strauss. He died suddenly on a tour of Mexico.

Krauze, Zygmunt, Polish composer and pianist; b. Warsaw, Sept. 19, 1938. He studied composition with Sikorski and piano with Maria Wilkomirska at the Warsaw Cons., graduating in 1962 (M.A., 1964); completed studies with Nadia Boulanger in Paris (1966–67). He is an inventive composer, cultivating with equal devotion primitive rustic instruments and electronic sounds. As a pianist, he specializes in new music; he taught piano at Cleveland State Univ. (1970–71).

WORKS: *3 Malay Pantuns,* to Indonesian texts, for 3 Flutes and Contralto (1961); *5 Unitary Piano Pieces* (1963); *Triptych* for Piano (1964); *Voices* for 5–15 Optional Instruments (1968); *Polychrony* for Clarinet, Trombone, Cello, and Piano (1968); 2 string quartets (1960, 1969); *Piece for Orchestra No. 1* (1969); *Piece for Orchestra No. 2* (1970); *Folk Music* for Orch. (1971–72); *Aus aller Welt stammende* for 10 Strings (1973); *Vibrations* for Piano, 8-hands (1973); *Song for Flute, Clarinet, Bassoon, Violin, Cello, Double Bass, and 3 Automatophones* (1974); *Automatophone* for 15 Musical Boxes and 15 Plucked Instruments (1974); *Fête galante et pastorale,* space music for a castle, for 13 Tapes and 6 Instrumental Groups (1974; Graz, Austria, Oct. 12, 1974); *Idyll* for Tape, 4 Hurdy-gurdies, 4 Bagpipes, 4 Zlobcoki, 8 Fifes, 16 Bells, and 4 Whistles (1974).

Krebs (real name, **Miedcke**), **Carl August,** German composer; b. Nuremberg, Jan. 16, 1804; d. Dresden, May 16, 1880. He studied music with the opera singer **Johann Baptist Krebs,** who legally adopted him. A precocious child, he is said to have composed the opera *Feodore* at the age of 7. He became a conductor at the Vienna Opera in 1826; in 1850 he was appointed principal conductor of the Dresden Opera, succeeding Wagner, who had been involved in revolutionary activities in Saxony; Krebs continued at his Dresden post until 1872. He produced 2 operas: *Silva* (Hamburg, 1830) and *Agnes* (Hamburg, Oct. 8, 1833; revised under the title *Agnes Bernauer* and produced in Dresden in 1858); but he was successful mainly as a song composer; his religious hymn *Vater unser* was popular for many years; he also wrote several masses and some brilliant piano pieces. He was married to the opera singer **Aloysia Michalesi** (1826–1904). Their daughter **Mary Krebs** (1851–1900) was a talented pianist.

Krebs, Johann Ludwig, German organist and composer; b. Buttelstädt, Oct. 10, 1713; d. Altenburg, Jan. 2, 1780. He received methodical training in musical subjects from his father, an organist, and was sent to study at the Thomasschule in Leipzig, where he became a pupil of Bach for 9 years (1726–35); was Bach's assistant at the harpsichord in Bach's Collegium Musicum there. Later he was organist at Zeitz, Zwickau, and Altenburg. He publ.: *Klavierübungen* in 4 parts (Nuremberg, 1743–49); sonatas for clavier and flute; suites and preludes for clavier; string trios; organ pieces (including an organ fugue on the name B-A-C-H); these were reprinted in the series Masterpieces of Organ Music (N.Y., 1944–45); Partita No. 2 is found in Pauer's *Alte Meister;* a Trio with Continuo, in Riemann's *Collegium Musicum;* his organ works were edited by K. Tittel in *Johann Ludwig Krebs: Ausgewählte Orgelwerke,* in *Die Orgel* (Lippstadt, 1963–75).

Krehbiel, Henry Edward, noted American music critic; b. Ann Arbor, Mich., March 10, 1854; d. New York, March 20, 1923. He was music critic of the *Cincinnati Gazette* (1874–80); then editor of the *N.Y. Musical Review* and critic for the *N.Y. Tribune;* the latter post he held for some 40 years, until his death; in 1909, he received the honorary degree of M.A. from Yale Univ. He publ. *Notes on the Cultivation of Choral Music, and the Oratorio Society of New York* (1884); *Review of the N.Y. Musical Seasons 1885–90* (5 vols.); *Studies in the Wagnerian Drama* (1891); *The Philharmonic Society of New York: A Memorial* (1892); *How to Listen to Music* (1896); *Annotated Biography of Fine Art* (with R. Sturgis; 1897); *Music and Manners in the Classical Period* (1898); *Chapters of Opera* (1908; 2nd ed., 1911); *A Book of Operas* (1909); *The Pianoforte, and Its Music* (1911); *Afro-American Folksongs* (1914); *A Second Book of Operas* (1917); *More Chapters of Opera* (1919); translations of Courvoisier's *Technic of Violin Playing* (N.Y., 1880; 2nd ed., 1896), Kerst's *Beethoven* (1905), and Kerst's *Mozart* (1905); also publ. and edited the Eng. version of Thayer's *Beethoven* (3 vols., 1921); he was consulting editor of *The Music of the Modern World* (1895–97) and American editor of the 2nd edition of *Grove's Dictionary of Music and Musicians* (1904–10); was also author, for many years, of the program notes of the N.Y. Phil. Society. He was a brilliant writer of music criticism, and was able to project his opinions (and his prejudices) in vivid prose in his newspaper reviews. He was an ardent champion of Wagner, and he also wrote with warm admiration for the late Romantic composers; but he deprecated the modern school of composition, hurling invectives on Stravinsky, Prokofiev, and Schoenberg (whose music he described as excrement).

Krein, Alexander, Russian composer; b. Nizhny-Novgorod, Oct. 20, 1883; d. Staraya Ruza, near Moscow, April 21, 1951. At the age of 13 he entered the Moscow Cons. and studied cello; also studied composition privately with Nikolayev and Yavorsky. Later he became an instructor at the People's Cons. of Moscow (1912–17); after the Revolution he worked in the music division of the Commissariat of Education and in the Ethnographic Dept. From 1923 he was associated with the productions of the Jewish Drama Theater in Moscow, and wrote music for many Jewish plays. Together with Gnessin, he was a leader of the National Jewish movement in Russia. In general, his style was influenced by Scriabin and Debussy, but he made considerable use of authentic Hebrew material.

Krein, Grigori, Russian composer, brother of **Alexander Krein;** b. Nizhny-Novgorod, March 18, 1879; d. Komarovo, near Leningrad, Jan. 6, 1955. He studied with Juon and Glière. His music underwent the influence of Jewish culture, and he wrote many works on Jewish themes; however, he also cultivated strict classical forms, adapting them to his needs. He wrote a descriptive symph. cycle on Lenin's life (1937); other works are a Violin Concerto; String Quartet; *Hebrew Rhapsody* for Clarinet and Orch.; piano pieces.

Krein, Julian, Russian composer, son of **Grigori Krein;** b. Moscow, March 5, 1913. He studied with his father; wrote his first compositions at the age of 13. In 1927 he went to Paris; took some lessons with Paul Dukas. In 1933 he went back to Moscow and remained there. Besides composing, he also wrote music criticism. His music is marked by a lyric quality; in his harmonic procedures he adopts advanced methods bordering on polytonality. Among his works are *5 Preludes* for Orch. (1927); symph. prelude, *Destruction* (1929); Cello Concerto (Barcelona, Oct. 18, 1931, Eisenberg, soloist); *Spring Symphony* (1938); piano pieces; songs.

Kreisler, Fritz, celebrated violinist; b. Vienna, Feb. 2, 1875; d. New York, Jan. 29, 1962. His talent manifested itself at an early age and was carefully fostered by his father, under whose instruction the boy made such progress that at the age of 6 he was sent to study with Jacob Dont; then was admitted to the Vienna Cons., where he studied with Jacques Auber and Hellmesberger (1882–85); in 1885, he carried off the gold medal. He then entered the Paris Cons., where he was a pupil of Massart (violin) and Delibes (composition); graduated in 1887 as winner of the Grand Prix (gold medal) over 40 competitors. He made his American debut at Steinway Hall in N.Y. on Nov. 10, 1888. In the following year, he made a very successful tour of the U.S. with Moriz Rosenthal. On his return to Europe, he abandoned music for some years; studied medicine in Vienna, and art in Rome and Paris; then entered the Austrian army, serving as an officer in an Uhlan regiment. At his reappearance in Berlin (March 1899) his playing created a sensation. Not only had he regained his outstanding virtuosity, but he had also developed into a great interpreter. On his 2nd visit to the U.S., in 1900–1, when he appeared as a soloist and in ensemble with Hofmann and Gerardy, he carried his audiences by storm; on his tour of England in the spring of 1901, he scored similar triumphs. In 1904 the London Phil. Society honored him by awarding him the Beethoven gold medal. At the outbreak of World War I in 1914, he joined his former regiment; was wounded at Lemberg (Sept. 6, 1914) and excused from further service. Fortunately his wound was slight (his hip and shoulder were injured in a Russian cavalry attack), so that at the end of 1914 he resumed his artistic career in the U.S. He remained in the U.S. throughout the rest of World War I despite the embarrassment of his status as an enemy alien; after the Armistice, went back to Europe, but continued to make frequent visits to America. He was made Commander of the Legion of Honor by the French government, and received many other honors from foreign governments. In 1938 he became a French citizen; in 1940 he returned to N.Y.; in 1943, became an American citizen.

Kreisler's repertoire contained almost everything of value written for the violin since the 17th century. He was the owner of a Guarneri violin and of instruments by other masters; gathered a rich collection of invaluable MSS; in 1949 donated to the Library of Congress the original scores of Brahms's Violin Concerto and Chausson's *Poème* for Violin and Orch. He wrote some of the most popular violin pieces in the world, among them *Caprice viennois, Tambourin chinois, Schön Rosmarin, Liebesfreud,* etc. He also publ. a number of pieces in the classical vein, which he ascribed to various old composers (Vivaldi, Pugnani, Couperin, Padre Martini, Dittersdorf, Francœur, Stamitz, and others). In 1935 he reluctantly admitted that these pieces were his own, with the exception of the first 8 bars from the "Couperin" *Chanson Louis XIII,* taken from a traditional melody; he explained his motive in doing so by the necessity of building up well-rounded programs for his concerts that would contain virtuoso pieces by old composers, rather than a series of compositions under his own, as yet unknown, name. He also wrote the operettas *Apple Blossoms* (N.Y., Oct. 7, 1919) and *Sissy* (Vienna, Dec. 23, 1932); publ. numerous arrangements of early and modern music (Corelli's *La Folia,* Tartini's *The Devil's Trill,* Dvořák's *Slavonic Dances, Spanish Dance* by Granados, *Tango* by Albéniz, etc.). He publ. a book of reminiscences of World War I, *Four Weeks in the Trenches: The War Story of a Violinist* (Boston, 1915).

Krejčí, Iša, important Czech composer and conductor; b. Prague, July 10, 1904; d. there, March 6, 1968. He studied composition with Jirák and Novák and conducting with Talich at the Prague Cons., graduating in 1929; was active as a conductor in Bratislava (1928–32), then at the Prague National Theater (1933–34) and at the Prague Radio (1934–45). From 1945 till 1958 he headed the opera in Olomouc; from 1958 to his death, he was music director of the National Theater in Prague. His music, in a neo-Classical idiom, is distinguished by vivacious rhythms and freely flowing melody; the national Czech element is not ostentatious, but its presence is well marked.

Kremer, Gidon, violinist; b. Riga, Latvia, Feb. 27, 1947. He won the first prize of the Latvian Republic at the age of 16; then went to the Moscow Cons. to study with David Oistrakh. In 1970 he won first prize in the prestigious International Tchaikovsky Competition in Moscow, which catapulted him to a worldwide career. His vast repertoire includes several works by composers of the avant-garde.

Kremer, Isa, Jewish folksinger; b. Beltzi, Bessarabia, 1885; d. Cordoba, Argentina, July 7, 1956. She acquired early fame as a singer of Russian, Yiddish, Polish, and German ballads; made many tours in Russia and Eastern Europe before coming to the U.S. in 1923; in N.Y. she appeared in vaudeville; gave her final concert in America at Carnegie Hall on Dec. 3, 1950. She married Dr. Gregorio Bermann, an Argentine psychiatrist, in 1940.

Krenek, Ernst, noted modern composer; b. Vienna, Aug. 23, 1900. (Being of Czech origin, he used to spell his name Křenek [pronounced Krshenek] with a diacritical sign on the *r,* but dropped it after coming to

America.) He studied in Vienna, and in Berlin with Franz Schreker; lived in Zürich (1923–25); then was an opera coach in Kassel, under Paul Bekker (1925–27); in 1928 he returned to Vienna and became a correspondent of the *Frankfurter Zeitung;* also traveled widely in Europe as a lecturer and an accompanist in programs of his own songs. In 1937 he came to the U.S.; was a prof. of music at Vassar College (1939–42); then head of the music dept. at Hamline Univ. in St. Paul, Minn. (1942–47); lived in Hollywood in 1947–50. In the summer of 1950 and in following years he made successful tours of Germany as a lecturer and a conductor of his own works. He became an American citizen on Jan. 24, 1945. He was married to Anna Mahler (daughter of Gustav Mahler) in 1923; they were divorced in 1925, and he married Berta Hermann, an actress. His evolution as a composer mirrors the development of modern music in general. The tradition of Mahler, strengthened by the domestic ties of Krenek's first marriage, was the dominant influence of his early life in music; he then became associated with the modern groups in Vienna, particularly Schoenberg, Berg, and Anton von Webern. In Germany he was associated with Hindemith as a creator of modern opera in a satiric manner. He achieved a masterly technique of composition in his earliest works, and developed his melodic and harmonic idiom in the direction of atonality and polytonality. His first international success came to him at the age of 26, with the production of his opera *Jonny spielt auf,* generally described as a "jazz opera" (although no such title appears in the score). It deals with a jazz fiddler whose fame sweeps the world; in the apotheosis, Jonny sits atop a gigantic globe. The opera was first performed in Leipzig (Feb. 10, 1927), producing a sensation; it was subsequently translated into 18 languages and performed all over the world; a brand of Austrian cigarettes was named after it; it was staged at the Metropolitan Opera House in N.Y. (Jan. 19, 1929) with the hero as a black-faced musician rather than a Negro as in the original. However, the opera fell into desuetude a few years later. Krenek produced several short operas, to which he wrote his own librettos, with transitory success. He also composed symphonic, choral, and chamber music; wrote books and articles on music history and modern methods of composition. In 1933 he adopted the 12-tone method of composition; his opera *Karl V* was written in this idiom; subsequent works use various ingenious applications of Schoenberg's basic method. In 1950 he completed a voluminous autobiography, the MS of which he deposited at the Library of Congress, not to be opened until 15 years after his death. Excerpts were publ. under the title *Self-Analysis.* He made his home in Palm Springs, Calif., but traveled widely as a conductor and pianist in his own works in Europe. In 1963 he was awarded the Grand State Prize of Austria.

WORKS: OPERAS AND DRAMAS WITH MUSIC: *Zwingburg* (Berlin, Oct. 16, 1924); *Der Sprung über den Schatten* (Frankfurt, June 9, 1924); *Orpheus und Eurydike* (Kassel, Nov. 27, 1926); *Jonny spielt auf* (Leipzig, Feb. 10, 1927); *Leben des Orest* (Leipzig,

Jan. 19, 1930); *Cefalo e Procri* (Venice, Sept. 15, 1934); *Karl V* (Prague, June 15, 1938); *Tarquin* (Vassar College, May 13, 1941; first professional perf., Cologne, July 16, 1950); *What Price Confidence?* (1946); *Dark Waters* (1951); *Pallas Athene weint* (Hamburg, Oct. 17, 1955); *The Bell Tower* (Urbana, Ill., March 17, 1957); 3 short operas: *Der Diktator; Das geheime Königreich; Schwergewicht oder Die Ehre der Nation* (Wiesbaden, May 6, 1928); *Ausgerechnet und verspielt,* comic opera (Vienna, June 27, 1962); *Der goldene Bock,* fantastic chamber opera (Hamburg, June 16, 1964, composer conducting); *Das kommt davon, oder Wenn Sardakai auf Reisen geht (That's What Happened or, If Sardakai Goes Traveling),* to his own libretto (Hamburg State Opera, June 27, 1970).

BALLETS: *Der vertauschte Cupido,* after Rameau (Kassel, Oct. 25, 1925); *Mammon* (Munich, Oct. 1, 1927); *8-column Line* (Hartford, Conn., 1939).

FOR ORCH.: 5 symphs.: No. 1 (1921); No. 2 (1922); No. 3 (1922); No. 4 (N.Y., Nov. 27, 1947); No. 5 (Albuquerque, March 16, 1950); *2 concerti grossi* (1921); *Symphonische Musik* for 9 Solo Instruments (Donaueschingen, July 30, 1922); Piano Concerto No. 1 (1923); Concertino for Flute, Violin, Harpsichord, and String Orch. (1924); Violin Concerto (Dessau, Jan. 5, 1925); *Symphonie* for Brass and Percussion (1924–25); *3 Military Marches* (Donaueschingen, 1926); *Potpourri* (Cologne, Nov. 15, 1927); *Kleine Symphonie* (Berlin, Nov. 1, 1928); *Theme and Variations* (1931); *Music for Wind Orchestra* (1931); Piano Concerto No. 2 (Amsterdam, March 17, 1938); *Symphonic Piece* for String Orch. (Ann Arbor, Mich., Aug. 1, 1939); *Little Concerto* for Piano and Organ, with Chamber Orch. (1940); *I Wonder as I Wander,* variations on a North Carolina folk song (1942); *Tricks and Trifles,* orch. version of the *Hurricane Variations* (1945); *Symphonic Elegy* for Strings, on the death of Anton von Webern (1946); Piano Concerto No. 3 (Minneapolis, Nov. 22, 1946, Mitropoulos, pianist-conductor; the 12-tone system consistently used by Krenek after 1936 is not applied in this concerto); Piano Concerto No. 4 (1950); Double Concerto for Violin, Piano, and Chamber Orch. (Donaueschingen Festival, Oct. 6, 1951); Concerto for Harp and Chamber Orch. (Philadelphia, Dec. 12, 1952); Concerto for 2 Pianos and Orch. (N.Y., Oct. 24, 1953); *Medea* for Contralto and Orch. (Philadelphia, March 13, 1953); *11 Transparencies* (Louisville, Feb. 12, 1955); *Spass mit Karten,* ballet (1957); *Kette, Kreis und Spiegel,* symph. poem (1957); *Spiritus Intelligentiae, Sanctus* for Voices and Electronic Sounds (1957); *Hexaeder,* 6 pieces for Chamber Ensemble (1958); *Missa duodecim tonorum* for Mixed Chorus and Organ (1958); *Sestina* for Soprano and Small Ensemble (1958); *Quaestio temporis* for Chamber Orch. (Hamburg, Sept. 30, 1960); *La Corona,* cantata (1959); *From 3 Make 7* for Chamber Orch. (1961); *5 + 1 (Alpbach Quintet;* 1962).

CHAMBER MUSIC: Violin Sonata (1919); Serenade for Quartet (1919); 8 string quartets: No. 1 (1921); No. 2 (1921); No. 3 (1923); No. 4 (1923–24); No. 5 (1930); No. 6 (1937); No. 7 (1943); No. 8 (1952); Suite for Clarinet and Piano (1924); Solo Violin Sonata

(1924–25); Suite for Cello Solo (1939); Sonatina for Flute and Viola (1942); Sonata for Violin Solo (1942); Sonata for Viola and Piano (1948); String Trio (1948); *Parvula Corona Musicalis ad honorem J.S. Bach* for String Trio (1950); *Fibonacci-Mobile* for String Quartet, 2 Pianos, and Coordinator (Hanover, N.H., July 7, 1965).

For piano: *Double Fugue* for Piano, 2-hands (1918); *Dance Studies,* in *Grotesken-Album* (ed. by K. Seeling, 1922); 6 sonatas: No. 1 (1919); No. 2 (1928); No. 3 (1943); No. 4 (1948); No. 5 (1950); No. 6 (1951); 5 sonatinas (1920); *Toccata and Chaconne* on the chorale *Ja, ich glaub' an Jesum Christum* (1922; also a suite of pieces on the chorale); 2 suites (1924); 5 pieces (1925); *12 Short Piano Pieces* (1938); *Hurricane Variations* (1944); *8 Piano Pieces* (1946); *George Washington Variations* (1950).

For chorus: *Concert Aria,* to text from Goethe's *Stella* (1928); *Von der Vergänglichkeit des Irdischen,* cantata (1932); *Reisebuch aus den Österreichischen Alpen* (1935); 2 a cappella choruses for Women's Voices, on Elizabethan poems (1939); *Proprium Missae in Festo SS. Innocentium* for Women's Voices (1940); *Lamentatio Jeremiae Prophetae, Secundum Brevarium Sacrosanctae Ecclesiae Romanae* (1941); *Cantata for Wartime* (1943); *5 Prayers* for Women's Voices, from the *Litanie* by John Donne (1944); *The Santa Fe Time Table* for Chorus a cappella, to the text of names of railroad stops between Albuquerque and Los Angeles (1945); *In Paradisum,* motet for Women's Voices a cappella (1946). Krenek also composed an Organ Sonata (1941) and revised and orchestrated Monteverdi's *L'incoronazione di Poppea* (1937); he is the author of the books *Über neue Musik* (collected lectures; Vienna, 1937; in Eng. as *Music Here and Now,* N.Y., 1939); *Studies in Counterpoint* (N.Y., 1940; in German as *Zwölfton-Kontrapunkt Studien,* Mainz, 1952); *Selbstdarstellung,* autobiography (Zürich, 1948; in Eng. as *Self-Analysis,* Albuquerque, 1953); *Musik im goldenen Westen: Das Tonschaffen des U.S.A.* (Vienna, 1949); *Johannes Ockeghem* (N.Y., 1953); *De rebus prius factis* (Frankfurt, 1956); *Gedanken Unterwegs* (Munich, 1959).

Kretschmer, Edmund, German composer; b. Ostritz, Aug. 31, 1830; d. Dresden, Sept. 13, 1908. He studied with Julius Otto (composition) and Johann Schneider (organ) in Dresden. In 1863 he became organist of the court, retiring in 1901. He was a successful composer; his choral work *Geisterschlacht* won a prize at the Dresden singing festival (1865); his 3-part Mass for Men's Chorus won the Brussels Academy's prize in 1868. He wrote several operas to his own librettos in a Wagnerian manner; at least 2 of them were successful: *Die Folkunger* (Dresden, March 21, 1874) and *Heinrich der Löwe* (Leipzig, Dec. 8, 1877); he also produced 2 light operas: *Der Flüchtling* (Ulm, 1881) and *Schön Rotraut* (Dresden, 1887); several choral works for festive occasions; church music; etc.

Kretzschmar, August Ferdinand Hermann, emi-nent German music scholar; b. Olbernhau, Jan. 19, 1848; d. Nikolassee, near Berlin, May 10, 1924. He was a chorister and a pupil of Julius Otto in Dresden; then studied with Richter, Reinecke, Oskar Paul, and Papperitz at the Leipzig Cons., where he took his degree of Dr.Phil. with a thesis on ancient notation prior to Guido d'Arezzo, *De signis musicis* (1871). He then became a teacher of organ and harmony at the Leipzig Cons.; also conducted choral societies there. In 1876 he was a theater conductor at Metz; in 1877, music director at Rostock Univ.; in 1880, municipal music director there. In 1887 he joined the faculty of Leipzig Univ.; in 1888–97, was Riedel's successor as conductor of the Riedelverein; conducted the Akademische Orchesterkonzerte initiated by himself (1890–95). In 1904 he went to Berlin as a prof. at the Univ. there; in 1909–20, was also the director of the Berlin Hochschule für Musik. He was a thoroughly educated musician, a good organist as well as choral conductor, and composer of some secular and sacred vocal music. But his importance in musicology lies in his establishment of certain musical and estetic concepts that elucidate the historical process. He introduced a convenient term (taken from theology), "Hermeneutik," applying it to the explanation of musical melodies and intervallic progressions as expressive of human emotions.

Kreutz, Arthur, American composer; b. La Crosse, Wis., July 25, 1906. He studied music at the Univ. of Wisconsin and at Columbia Univ. in N.Y.; then was lecturer at the latter (1946–52); in 1952 he was appointed to the staff of the music dept. of the Univ. of Mississippi, where he remained until 1964. His works include a "ballad opera," *Acres of Sky* (Fayetteville, Ark., Nov. 16, 1951); symph. poem, *Winter of the Blue Snow* (1942); 2 symphs. (1945, 1946); opera, *The University Greys* (Clinton, Miss., March 15, 1954); folk opera, *Sourwood Mountain* (Clinton, Jan. 8, 1959); also *Dance Concerto* for Clarinet and Orch. (1958); Violin Concerto (1965); 2 "jazz sonatas" for Violin and Piano, and other pieces in a jazz vein; also *New England Folksing* for Chorus and Orch. (Brooklyn, Feb. 17, 1948) and *Mosquito Serenade* for Orch. (N.Y. Phil., Feb. 21, 1948).

Kreutzer, Auguste, French violinist, brother of **Rodolphe Kreutzer;** b. Versailles, Sept. 3, 1778; d. Paris, Aug. 31, 1832. He studied with his brother at the Paris Cons.; played in the orch. of the Paris Opéra-Comique and Opéra; also in the court orchs.; taught at the Paris Cons. He wrote 2 violin concertos, 3 sonatas, etc.

Kreutzer, Konradin (later known as **Conrad**), important German composer; b. Messkirch, Baden, Nov. 22, 1780; d. Riga, Dec. 14, 1849. He was a pupil of J.B. Rieger at Zwiefalten Abbey and of Ernst Weihrauch (1792–96). He then studied law at Freiburg for one year (1799–1800) before devoting himself to music. In 1800 he brought out his first operetta, *Die lächerliche Werbung,* in Freiburg. He lived for 5 years in Constance, and then in Vienna until

1811, studying counterpoint under Albrechtsberger. He produced, with considerable success, *Jerry und Bätely,* after Goethe (May 19, 1810); not being able to bring out 2 operas, *Konradin von Schwaben* and *Der Taucher,* in Vienna, he went, after a pianistic tour of a year, to Stuttgart, where, after the production of *Konradin von Schwaben* (March 30, 1812), he was appointed court conductor. In Stuttgart he produced 8 dramatic works, and then went to Donaueschingen in 1818 as conductor to Prince von Fürstenberg. There he produced, in 1819, *Adele von Budoy,* which was later successful in a revision entitled *Cordelia.* Returning to Vienna, he brought out *Libussa* (Dec. 4, 1822); was conductor at the Kärnthnertor Theater (1822–27, 1829–32, and 1835–40) and at the Josephstadt Theater (1833–35); his most successful work, *Das Nachtlager von Granada* (Jan. 14, 1834), appeared, and was followed a month later by *Der Verschwender* (Feb. 20, 1834), incidental music for Ferdinand Raimund's play of that name. Together with *Jerry und Bätely,* these 2 works held the stage until the end of the century. In 1840–42 he was conductor at the Municipal Theater in Cologne; after 2 years in Vienna (1847–49), he accompanied his daughter Cäcilie, a singer, to Riga, where he died. Besides his many operas, he wrote an oratorio, *Die Sendung Mosis,* and a cantata, *Die Friedensfeier;* also church music, chamber music, and piano pieces; songs, and some noteworthy men's choruses (*Die Capelle, Sonntagsmorgen, Der Tag des Herrn,* etc.).

Kreutzer, Léon, French composer and music critic, son of **Auguste Kreutzer;** b. Paris, Sept. 23, 1817; d. Vichy, Oct. 6, 1868. He studied piano with Fleche and composition with Benoist. He wrote for the *Revue et Gazette Musicale, Revue Contemporaine, La Quotidienne, L'Union,* etc.; publ. *Essai sur l'art lyrique au théâtre* (1845) and a treatise on modulation; also wrote an orch. prelude to Shakespeare's *The Tempest;* string quartets, piano sonatas, etc.

Kreutzer, Leonid, Russian pianist and pedagogue; b. St. Petersburg, March 13, 1884; d. Tokyo, Oct. 30, 1953. He studied piano with Anna Essipova and composition with Glazunov at the St. Petersburg Cons. In 1906 he went to Germany; from 1921 to 1932 taught at the Hochschule für Musik in Berlin. After the advent of the Nazi regime in 1933 he went to the U.S., and in 1938 traveled to Japan, where he became a prof. of piano at the Cons. of Tokyo; earned a fine reputation as a teacher there; many Japanese concert pianists were his pupils. He publ. *Das Wesen der Klaviertechnik* (Berlin, 1923).

Kreutzer, Rodolphe, famous violinist; b. Versailles, Nov. 16, 1766; d. Geneva, Jan. 6, 1831. His father, a German violinist and teacher in Versailles, and Anton Stamitz were his teachers. At the age of 13 he played a violin concerto by Stamitz at a Concert Spirituel; performed his own First Concerto there in May 1784; in 1785 he was appointed first violin in the Chapelle du Roi, and in 1790 solo violin in the Théâtre-Italien, bringing out his first

opera, *Jeanne d'Arc à Orleans* (May 10, 1790). It was followed by over 40 others, given at the Opéra, the Opéra-Comique, or the Théâtre-Italien; *Lodoiska* (Aug. 1, 1791) was perhaps his best. A year after his appointment as a teacher of violin at the Cons., he made a triumphant concert tour through Italy, Germany, and The Netherlands (1796); was in Vienna in 1798. In 1801 he succeeded Rode as solo violin at the Opéra, of which he became 2nd conductor in 1816 and was first conductor in 1817–24. From 1802 he was also chamber musician to Napoleon; from 1815, to Louis XVIII; retired in 1826, and so far lost influence that his last opera, *Mathilde,* was contemptuously rejected by the direction of the Opéra. Although his own music could not withstand the test of time, his name became immortal because it was to him that Beethoven dedicated the celebrated *Kreutzer Sonata.*

Křička, Jaroslav, eminent Czech composer and pedagogue; b. Kelč, Moravia, Aug. 27, 1882; d. Prague, Jan. 23, 1969. He first studied law in Prague (1900–2); then studied music at the Cons. there (1902–5) and in Berlin (1905–6); in 1906, taught music in Ekaterinoslav, Russia; in 1909, returned to Prague and conducted (1911–20) the famous choral society Hlahol; in 1919, became a prof. at the Cons., remaining on its staff until 1945; then devoted his time to composition.

WORKS: Operas: *Hypolita* (1910–16; Prague, Oct. 10, 1917); *Bílý pán (The White Gentleman),* after Oscar Wilde's *The Canterville Ghost* (1927–29; Brno, 1929; revised in 1930 as *Today Ghosts Have a Difficult Time;* Breslau, Nov. 14, 1931); *Kral Lavra (King Lawrence;* 1936–37; revised 1938–39; Prague, June 7, 1940); *České jesličky (The Czech Christmas Manger;* 1936–37; revised 1948; Prague, Jan. 15, 1949); *Jáchym a Juliána (Joachim and Julia;* 1945–48; Opava, 1951); *Serenáda,* opera buffa (Pilsen, 1950); *Kolébka (The Cradle),* musical comedy (1950; Opava, 1951); *Zahořanský hon (The Zahořany Hunt;* Opava, 1955); children's operas: *Ogaři (Country Lads;* 1918; Nové Město in Moravia, Sept. 7, 1919); *Dobře to dopadlo* or *Tlustý pradědeček (It Turned Out Well* or *The Fat Great-Grandfather;* 1932) and *Lupici a detekotyvove (Robbers and Detectives;* 1932; both operas, Prague, Dec. 29, 1932); several small operas for children's theater; television opera, *Kalhoty (A Pair of Trousers;* Czech television, 1962). For Orch.: symph., *Jarní (Spring;* 1905–6; revised 1942; *Nostalgie* for String Orch. and Harp (1905); *Faith,* symph. poem (1907); *A Children's Suite* (1907); *Scherzo Idyllic* (1908; Prague, Nov. 13, 1910; 3rd movement of an uncompleted Symph. No. 2); *Modrý pták (A Blue Bird),* overture after a Maeterlinck fairy tale (1911; Prague, March 3, 1912, composer conducting); *Adventus,* symph. poem (1920–21; Prague, Nov. 6, 1921); *Matěj Kopecký,* overture (1928); *Horácká suita (Suite montagnarde;* 1935; Prague, Sept. 8, 1935); Sinfonietta for String Orch. and Timpani (1940–41); *Majales,* overture (1942); Violin Concerto (1944); Concertino for Horn, and String Quartet or String Orch. (1951); *Variations on a Theme of Boccherini* for Bassoon, and String

Quartet or String Orch. (1952); *Sinfonietta semplice* (1962). Cantatas. *Pokušcni na poušti (Temptation in the Desert;* 1921–22); *Jenny, the Thief* (1927–28); *Tyrolese Elegies* (1930–31); *A Eulogy to a Woman* (1933); *Recollections of Student Years* (1934); *Moravian Cantata* (1935–36); *The Golden Spinning Wheel* (1943); *To Prague* (1960); *Small Suite in Old Style* for 2 Violins and Piano (1907); 3 string quartets (1907; 1938–39; *Wallachian,* 1949); *Doma (At Home),* piano trio (1924–25); Violin Sonata (1925); Sonatina for 2 Violins (1926–27; revised for Violin and Viola); Concertino (septet) for Violin, Wind Quintet, and Piano (1940); *Partita* for Solo Violin (1941); Divertimento for Wind Quintet (1950); Flute Sonatina (1951); Variations for Solo Violin (1956); Violin Sonatina (1962); several albums of piano pieces; a number of songs; also, arrangements of folk songs.

Krieger, Adam, German composer; b. Driesen, Neumark, Jan. 7, 1634; d. Dresden, June 30, 1666. He studied organ with Samuel Scheidt in Halle; in 1655–57 he was organist at the Nikolaikirche in Leipzig; then went to Dresden in 1657 as keyboard teacher to the Elector's daughter; in 1658 was made chamber and court organist there. He was one of the most important of the early composers of German lieder; he called his "Arien," and for most of them wrote the words as well as the music; they contain instrumental ritornels, for 2 violins and continuo in the early songs, for 5 strings and continuo in the later ones. Many of these "Arien" have been preserved, although most of his original collection (1657) is lost; it was reconstructed by H. Osthoff (1929); the 2nd collection (1667) is reproduced in vol. 19 of Denkmäler Deutscher Tonkunst.

Krieger (or **Krüger**), **Johann,** famous German contrapuntist and organist, brother of **Johann Philipp Krieger;** b. Nuremberg, Dec. 28, 1651; d. Zittau, July 18, 1735. He studied with his brother, and became his successor as chamber organist at Bayreuth in 1672. He was subsequently a court musician at Greiz (1678–81); then went to Zittau, where he was active as municipal organist; he remained there for 53 years, appearing for the last time on the day before he died. His music was appreciated by Handel; some of his organ compositions are regarded as presaging the grand style of Bach.

Krieger, Johann Philipp, German composer, brother of **Johann Krieger;** b. Nuremberg, Feb. 25, 1649; d. Weissenfels, Feb. 7, 1725. He was a pupil of Johann Drechsel and Gabriel Schütz in Nuremberg; went to Copenhagen, where he became a pupil and later assistant of court organist Johann Schröder (1663–69). In 1670 he was appointed court organist and chamber composer at Bayreuth, with an interval of study in Italy (1673). He was subsequently court musician at Kassel, and at Halle (from 1677); on Dec. 23, 1680, he was appointed court conductor at Weissenfels and Halle, remaining in this capacity until his death. He received the rank of nobility from Emperor Leopold I during a visit to Vienna

(1677). He produced some 20 stage works in Halle, Weissenfels, Hamburg, and other German towns; publ. 12 trio sonatas for 2 Violins, with Continuo (op. 1, 1688); 12 sonatas for Violin, with Viola da Gamba (op. 2, 1693); *Musikalischer Seelenfriede,* 20 sacred arias for Violin, with Bass (1697); *Lustige Feldmusik,* 6 overtures for Wind or other Instruments (1704); etc. Modern reprints, edited by Seiffert, are in vols. 53/54 of Denkmäler Deutscher Tonkunst (contains a selection of 21 sacred compositions by Krieger with critical commentary, as well as a complete list of his sacred works performed at Weissenfels, notes of extant MSS, biographical details, etc.), vol. 6 (2 sacred choral works, one with a practical transcription), and the appendix to vol. 18 (3 keyboard pieces). Other reprints are: instrumental suite from *Lustige Feldmusik,* in *Perlen alter Kammermusik* (ed. by Schering, for Strings; 1912); in *Organum,* edited by Seiffert (vol. 3, containing no. 3 of the *Feldmusik,* for Chamber Orch.); selected organ pieces are in vol. 4 of *Organum,* etc.; 24 arias, in *Haus- und Kammermusik aus dem XVI.–XVIII. Jahrhundert,* edited by H.J. Moser (1930); 2 arias in Schering's *Geschichte der Musik in Beispielen;* Eitner edited 2 partitas, 2 sonatas, and various vocal works in *Monatshefte für Musikgeschichte* (supplement to vol. 30).

Kriens, Christian, Dutch-American pianist, violinist, and composer; b. Brussels, April 29, 1881; d. Hartford, Conn., Dec. 17, 1934. He was taken to the Netherlands as a child; studied with his father, a clarinetist, and later at The Hague Cons. At 14 he made his debut at Amsterdam, playing the *Emperor Concerto* and conducting his own 2nd Symph. From 1896 to 1899 he toured Europe as a violinist; then taught at The Hague Cons. He came to America as conductor of the French Opera Co. (1906); settled in N.Y. in 1907; was a violinist in the N.Y. Symph. and N.Y. Phil., and at the Metropolitan Opera. He then became director of the Traveller's Broadcasting Co., Station WTIC, Hartford, Conn. Despondent over his inability to find further work, he committed suicide.

Krips, Josef, noted Austrian conductor; b. Vienna, April 8, 1902; d. Geneva, Oct. 13, 1974. He studied with Mandyczewski and Weingartner in Vienna; was violinist at the Volksoper there (1918–21); then became operatic coach and choirmaster of the Volksoper (1921); made his operatic conducting debut there in 1921. In 1924 he conducted opera in Aussig; in 1925, at the Municipal Theater in Dortmund; in 1926–33 was Generalmusikdirektor at Karlsruhe. In 1933 he was appointed conductor at the Vienna State Opera; in 1935, became a prof. at the Vienna Academy of Music. In 1938 he lost these positions, after the annexation of Austria to Germany; conducted a season of opera in Belgrade (1938–39). In 1945 he rejoined the staff of the Vienna State Opera; conducted in England, France, and Russia in 1947, producing an excellent impression; also conducted the Vienna Phil. and at the Salzburg Festival. In 1950 he was appointed conductor of the London Symph. Orch.; from 1954 to 1963 he was conductor of the Buffalo Phil. Orch., then conductor of the San Francisco Symph. Orch. (1963–70); also was a guest conductor of the N.Y. Phil. and other American and European orchs.

Krohn, Ilmari (Henrik Reinhold), eminent Finnish music scholar; b. Helsinki, Nov. 8, 1867; d. there, April 25, 1960. After studying with Richard Faltin in Helsinki, he went to Germany, where he took courses at the Leipzig Cons. with Papperitz and Reinecke (1886–90); obtained his Dr.Phil. in 1900 with the thesis *Über die Art und Enstehung der geistlichen Volksmelodien in Finnland* (Helsinki, 1899). Returning to Finland, he joined the staff of the Univ. of Helsinki (1900); also taught at the Cons. there; lectured at musical congresses in London, Paris, Basel, Vienna, and Rome (1891–1914). In 1906 he founded the musical journal *Säveletär;* was a member of the Songbook Commission (1918–23); proposed the construction of an "Acoustic Harmonium" of his own invention, and publ. a paper on it, *System Krohn* (Vienna, 1906). In 1918 he was promoted to prof. of musicology at the Univ. of Helsinki, the first person to hold that post there; he retired in 1935.

Kroll, Franz, German pianist and music editor; b. Bromberg, June 22, 1820; d. Berlin, May 28, 1877. He was first a student of medicine; then took lessons from Liszt; settled in Berlin as a music teacher. He was the editor of Bach's *Well-Tempered Clavier* for the Bach Gesellschaft, to which he contributed an introduction, summarizing bibliographical data; also edited Mozart's piano works.

Kroll, William, American violinist; b. New York, Jan. 30, 1901; d. Boston, March 10, 1980. He studied in Berlin and at the Inst. of Musical Art in N.Y. (graduated in 1922); then became first violinist of the Coolidge String Quartet, and appeared with it at numerous chamber music festivals in the U.S. and in Europe; subsequently organized a string quartet of his own, the Kroll Quartet.

Kroyer, Theodor, eminent German musicologist; b. Munich, Sept. 9, 1873; d. Wiesbaden, Jan. 12, 1945. He studied piano with Lang, counterpoint with Rheinberger, and musicology with Sandberger; took the degree of Dr.Phil. in 1897 from the Univ. of Munich with the dissertation *Die Anfang der Chromatik im italienischen Madrigal des XVI. Jahrhunderts* (publ. Leipzig, 1902); completed his Habilitation there in 1902 with his *Ludwig Senfl und sein Motettenstil* (Munich, 1902); then became music critic of the *Münchener Allgemeine Zeitung;* was on the staff of the univs. of Munich (1902–20), Heidelberg (1920–23), and Leipzig (1923–33). In 1925 he purchased for the Univ. of Leipzig the rich collection of instruments, MSS, and portraits from the famous Heyer Museum in Cologne; also in 1925 he began issuing the valuable series Publikationen Älterer Musik (Deutsche Gesellschaft für Musikwissenschaft). In 1932 be became a prof. at the

Univ. of Cologne; retired in 1938. He edited a vol. (motets and Magnificat) of the complete works of Senfl in Denkmäler der Tonkunst in Bayern, 5 (1903); also edited a selection from the works of G. Aichinger for the same series (vol. 8, 1909).

Krstić, Petar, Serbian composer; b. Belgrade, March 2, 1877; d. there, Jan. 21, 1957. He studied at the Vienna Cons. with R. Fuchs. Returning to Belgrade, he conducted opera at the National Theater; in 1930, became inspector of several music schools. His works, based on Serbian national tunes, included the opera *Zulumćar* (Belgrade, Nov. 23, 1927); cantata, *Jutro Slobode* (1919); several orch. suites of national dances; choruses and songs. He edited a Serbian music dictionary.

Krueger, Karl (Adalbert), American conductor; b. Atchison, Kans., Jan. 19, 1894; d. Elgin, Ill., July 21, 1979. He learned to play the cello and organ in his early youth; then began his formal study at Midland College in his hometown (B.A. 1913) and at the Univ. of Kansas (M.A., 1916); also took an intermediate course in Boston at the New England Cons. of Music (1914–15), where his instructors were Chadwick in composition and Wallace Goodrich in organ playing. Subsequently Krueger played organ at St. Ann's Epsicopal Church in N.Y. (1916–20). In 1920 he made a concert tour of Brazil as an organist; then went to Vienna, where he studied music theory with Robert Fuchs and conducting with Franz Schalk. He also attended classes in economics at the Univ. of Vienna and the Univ. of Heidelberg. Returning to the U.S. in 1922, he married the heiress Emma McCormick Jewett, of Chicago. He held the posts of conductor of the Seattle Symph. Orch. (1926–32), the Kansas City Phil. (1933–43), and the Detroit Symph. Orch. (1943–49); he was thus the first American-born musician to serve as permanent conductor of a major American symph. orch. In 1958 he founded the Society for the Preservation of the American Musical Heritage and made numerous recordings of American works. He wrote *The Way of the Conductor: His Origins, Purpose and Procedures* (N.Y., 1958).

Krumpholtz, Johann Baptist, Bohemian harpist and composer; b. Budenice, near Zlonice, May 8, 1742; d. Paris, Feb. 19, 1790. He received his first instruction from his father, a bandmaster in a Paris regiment; gave concerts in Vienna in 1772; studied composition with Haydn; in 1773–76, was a member of Prince Esterházy's orch. Following a long concert tour in Germany, he returned to France, and in Metz he married **Fräulein Meyer,** a 16-year-old harpist, with whom he subsequently gave concerts in Paris and London. Krumpholtz added to his fame as a harpist by inventing a harp with 2 pedals, loud and soft; he also stimulated Erard to make experiments that led to the invention of the modern pedal mechanism. His life ended tragically; he drowned himself in the Seine when his young wife eloped to England with another man. He wrote 6 concertos for Harp and Orch.; Duo for 2 Harps; 52 sonatas and other works entitled *Sonates pathétiques;* Symph. for Harp, with Small Orch.; many short pieces.

Krumpholtz, Wenzel, Austrian violinist, brother of **Johann Baptist Krumpholtz;** b. Budenice, near Zlonice, 1750; d. Vienna, May 2, 1817. He was a member of the orch. at the Vienna Opera in 1796, and was friendly with Beethoven; when Krumpholtz died, Beethoven was moved to write a *Gesang der Mönche,* dedicated to his memory. Wenzel Krumpholtz wrote several pieces for unaccompanied violin, among them *Abendunterhaltung* and *Eine Viertelstunde für eine Violine.*

Krupa, Gene, American jazz drummer; b. Chicago, Jan. 15, 1909; d. Yonkers, N.Y., Oct. 16, 1973. He joined a jazz band when still in his adolescence; made his first recording at 18. In 1935 he became Benny Goodman's drummer and scaled the heights of the swing world; having a phenomenal technique and being a natural showman, he "popularized" the drums with extended, virtuosic solos. He left Goodman in 1938, forming his own band; he toured Europe and the Orient and became internationally famous. A largely fictional film, *The Gene Krupa Story,* was produced in 1959.

Kruse, Georg Richard, German conductor and writer on music; b. Greiffenberg, Jan. 17, 1856; d. Berlin, Feb. 23, 1944. He studied at the Univ. of Bern and in Leipzig; then was an opera director and conductor in Germany. In 1894–96 he toured the U.S. as conductor of a troupe presenting Humperdinck's *Hansel und Gretel;* returned to Europe and was municipal theater director in Bern, St. Gall, and Ulm (1896–1900); from 1900 to 1909 he edited the *Deutsche Bühnengenossenschaft.* In 1906 he founded and was director of the Lessing Museum in Berlin; in 1908, founded the Lessing Society and the *Musik-Volksbibliothek des Tonkünstlerverein;* also was editor of dramatic and musical works for *Reclams Universalbibliothek* and contributed articles to various journals. He publ. a comprehensive biography of A. Lortzing (1899); *Lortzings Briefe* (1901; enlarged 2nd ed., Regensburg, 1913); biographies of Otto Nicolai and Hermann Götz; essays; etc.

Kruseman, Jacob Philip, Dutch music publisher; b. Amsterdam, Nov. 17, 1887; d. The Hague, Jan. 31, 1955. He studied singing, and appeared in recitals and light opera in the Netherlands until 1909, when he founded a publishing firm in The Hague, specializing in books on music and art; issued about 25 vols. of biographies of famous composers, and himself wrote a booklet, *Beethoven's Eigen Woorden* (The Hague, 1947). His most important publication is *Geïllustreerd muzieklexicon,* edited by himself with G. Keller (The Hague, 1932; supplemented, ed. by Kruseman and Zagwijn, 1949); it is modeled after Riemann's *Musiklexikon,* but contains a great deal of information on Dutch musicians not available in other reference books. After his death, the management of his publishing firm was assumed by his widow.

Kruyf, Ton de, Dutch composer; b. Leerdam, Oct. 3, 1937. He studied violin; attended seminars in new music in Darmstadt led by Maderna, Boulez, Stockhausen, and Ligeti; then took a course in composition with Wolfgang Fortner in Heidelberg. In his music he pursues the goal of maximum effect with a minimum of means; he makes use of serialism when it is structurally justified.

WORKS: Opera, *Spinoza* (Amsterdam, June 15, 1971); short radio opera, *Quauhquauhtinchan in den vreemde (Quauhquauhtinchan in Foreign Parts;* Hilversum, June 3, 1972); ballet, *Chronologie II* (The Hague, 1968); *Mouvements symphoniques* for Orch. (1955; revised 1966); *Sinfonietta,* 3 dances for Strings (1956; revised 1965); *5 Impromptus* for Small Orch. (1958); *Einst dem Grau der Nacht enttäuscht,* after poems by the modern painter Paul Klee, for Mezzo-soprano and Chamber Ensemble (Hilversum, Sept. 15, 1964); *Pour faire le portrait d'un oiseau,* after Jacques Prévert, for Mezzo-soprano and Chamber Ensemble (Hilversum, Sept. 17, 1965); *De blinde zwemmers,* 3 fragments for Youth Chorus and 2 Instrumental Groups (1966); *Töne aus der Ferne,* after a poem by Paul Klee, for Alto and Chamber Orch. (Amsterdam, Sept. 11, 1968); *Sinfonia II* (Hilversum, May 14, 1969; developed from an orch. interlude in the opera *Spinoza*); *4 pas de deux* for Flute and Orch. (1972); *Echoi* for Oboe and String Orch. (1973); *Twee uur (2 Hours)* for Speaker and Orch. (1973); Quartet for Flute, Violin, Trumpet, and Bassoon (1959); Flute Sonatina (1960); *Music* for String Quartet (1962); *Partita* for String Quartet (1962); Solo Cello Sonata (1964); *Aubade* for Horn, 2 Trumpets, Trombone, and Tuba (1965); *Fragments IV from Shakespeare Sonnets* for Mezzo-soprano, Flute, and Cello (1965); *Pas de deux* for Flute and Piano (1968); *Serenata per complesso da camera* for Flute, Clarinet, Harp, and String Quintet (1968); *Mosaico* for Oboe and String Trio (1969); *Séance* for Percussion, Piano, and Harp (1969); *Echoi* for Solo Oboe (1973); *Sgrafitti* for Piano (1960); *Arioso* for Piano, 4-hands (1975).

Kubelík, Jan, famous Czech violinist; b. Michle, near Prague, July 5, 1880; d. Prague, Dec. 5, 1940. He was taught by his father, who was a gardener; since he showed extraordinary talent, he was accepted by Ševčik as a student at the Prague Cons.; later he studied in Vienna, where he made his professional debut on Nov. 26, 1898. In 1900 he began a series of triumphant concerts in Europe and America. He was regarded as a counterpart to Paderewski in virtuosity, dramatic appeal, and ability to communicate his art to audiences everywhere. In 1903 he married a Hungarian countess and became a naturalized Hungarian citizen. His career as a great virtuoso was stopped short with World War I; he appeared less frequently than before; lived mostly in Prague. He gave a series of farewell concerts in 1939–40; his last concert was in Prague on May 8, 1940, after his beloved homeland had been dismembered by the Nazis. He composed 6 violin concertos in a brilliant style; also a Symph.; and some chamber music.

Kubelík, Rafael, eminent Czech conductor, son of **Jan Kubelík;** b. Býchory, near Kolín, June 29, 1914. He studied at the Prague Cons.; made his conducting debut with the Czech Phil. in Prague on Jan. 24, 1934; he was subsequently conductor at the National Theater in Brno (1939–41); from 1942 to 1948 he was music director of the Czech Phil.; between 1948 and 1950 he conducted in England and elsewhere in Europe. In 1950 he was appointed principal conductor of the Chicago Symph. Orch.; he made it a rule to feature modern works (about 60 pieces in all) in his programs; this and his insistence on painstaking work on details in rehearsals antagonized some critics in the Chicago press, so that he was compelled to resign (1953). From 1955 to 1958 he was director of the Covent Garden Opera in London; during his tenure there he presented the complete performance of *Boris Godunov* in Mussorgsky's original version. In 1961 he became chief conductor of the orch. of the Bavarian Radio, and toured with it in Japan (1965) and the U.S. (1968); retired from the post in 1979; for a brief time he was music director of the Metropolitan Opera in N.Y. (1973–74), where he also became the epicenter of controversy; these contretemps, however, did not undermine his artistic integrity. In 1978 he was engaged to conduct 6 weeks of guest appearances with the N.Y. Phil. In 1967 he became a Swiss citizen. Kubelík is also a composer; he wrote 2 operas: *Veronika* (Brno, April 19, 1947) and *Cornelia Faroli* (1966); 3 symphs.; Violin Concerto; Cello Concerto; Requiem; other choral works; *4 Forms* for String Orch. (1965); *Orphikon: Music in 3 Movements* for Orch. (N.Y., April 2, 1981, composer conducting).

Kubik, Gail (Thompson), American composer; b. South Coffeyville, Okla., Sept. 5, 1914; d. Covina, Calif., July 20, 1984, of the side effects of kala-azar, a visceral protozoan infection he had contracted on a trip to Africa. His father was of Bohemian extraction; his mother, of Irish origin, was trained as a concert singer. Kubik studied the rudiments of music with her; then enrolled at the Eastman School of Music, where he studied violin with Samuel Belov, and composition with Bernard Rogers, Edward Royce, and Irving McHose; in 1934 he received his B.M. degree. In the same year he wrote a Piano Trio, and a Violin Concerto in which he was soloist in its premiere with the Chicago Symph. (Jan. 2, 1938). He continued his study in composition with Leo Sowerby at the American Cons. of Music in Chicago (M.M., 1936). In the meantime, he organized a family ensemble with his mother and his 2 brothers, and played concerts with them. In 1936–37 he taught violin at the Dakota Wesleyan Univ. in Mitchell, S.Dak.; in 1937–38 he took a composition course with Walter Piston at Harvard Univ. In 1938–40 Kubik was on the faculty of Teachers College at Columbia Univ. Concurrently he was employed as staff composer for NBC, and wrote incidental music for several radio productions. During World War II he

served in the U.S. Air Force with the rank of sergeant. In 1943 he received a Guggenheim fellowship. After the war he traveled in Europe as a conductor and lecturer. He was awarded the American Prix de Rome in 1950 and 1951 and spent 3 years at the American Academy in Rome. In 1952 he was a guest lecturer at the Santa Cecilia Academy there. One of the most important works of this period was his *Symphonie concertante* for piano, viola, trumpet, and orch., for which he received the Pulitzer Prize in Music. In 1970 he was appointed composer-in-residence at Scripps College in Claremont, Calif.; when he was asked to retire at the age of 65 in 1980, he brought an unsuccessful suit against the school, claiming that productivity and not age should determine the time of retirement for a creative person. Besides his symph. works, Kubik developed great skill in writing for documentary films. His gift of musical humor was expressed at its best in the music he wrote for the animated film cartoon *Gerald McBoing-Boing* (1950), which received both a Motion Picture Academy Award and the British Film Inst. Award, and which incidentally launched a vogue of twangy rhinogenic tunes in popular music. In his symphonic and other scores he cultivated a manner that was expressively modern, without abandoning the basic tenets of tonality; the rhythmic patterns of his music were apt to be stimulatingly asymmetric.

WORKS: FOR THE STAGE: *A Mirror for the Sky,* folk opera on the life of Audubon (Eugene, Oreg., May 23, 1939); *Boston Baked Beans,* "opera piccola" (N.Y., March 9, 1952); *Frankie and Johnnie,* ballet for Dance Band and Folk Singer (1946). FOR ORCH.: *American Caprice* for Piano and Orch. (1936); *Scherzo* (1940); 2 violin concertos: No. 1 (1934; revised 1936; Chicago, Jan. 12, 1938); No. 2 (1940; revised 1941; won first prize in the Jascha Heifetz competition); *Spring Valley Overture* (1947); 3 symphs.: No. 1 (1949); No. 2 (Louisville, Ky., April 7, 1956); No. 3 (N.Y., Feb. 28, 1957); *Symphonie concertante* for Piano, Viola, Trumpet, and Orch. (N.Y., Jan. 27, 1952; received the Pulitzer Prize in 1952); *Thunderbolt Overture* (1953); *Scenario* (1957). CHAMBER MUSIC: *Trivialities* for Flute, Horn, and String Quartet (1934); Piano Trio (1934); Wind Quintet (1937); *Suite* for 3 Recorders (1941); Sonatina for Violin and Piano (1944); *Toccata* for Organ and Strings (1946); *Little Suite* for Flute and 2 Clarinets (1947); *Soliloquy and Dance* for Violin and Piano (1948); Divertimento No. 1 for 13 Players (1959); Divertimento No. 2 for 8 Players (1959); *Prayer and Toccata* for Organ and Chamber Orch. (1968); Divertimento No. 3 for Piano Trio (1970–71); *5 Birthday Pieces* for 2 Recorders (1974). FOR VOICE: *In Praise of Johnny Appleseed* for Bass-baritone, Chorus, and Orch. (1938; revised 1961); *Choral Profiles, Folk Song Sketches* for Chorus (1938); *Puck: A Legend of Bethlehem,* radio music (NBC Network, Dec. 29, 1940); *Litany and Prayer* for Men's Chorus, Brass, and Percussion (1943–45); *Fables and Song* for Voice and Piano (1950–59); *A Christmas Set* for Chorus and Chamber Orch. (1968); *A Record of Our Time,* "protest piece" for Chorus, Narrator, Soloist, and Orch. (Manhattan, Kans., Nov. 11, 1970);

Scholastics for a cappella Chorus (1972); *Magic, Magic, Magic* for Chorus and Chamber Orch. (San Antonio, Texas, April 25, 1976). FILM SCORES: *The World at War* (1942); *Memphis Belle* (1943); *Gerald McBoing-Boing* (1950); *The Miner's Daughter* (1950); *Two Gals and a Guy* (1951); *Translantic* (1952); *The Desperate Hours* (1955); *Down to Earth* (1959); also piano pieces.

Kufferath, Hubert Ferdinand, German pianist and organist, brother of **Johann Hermann** and **Louis Kufferath;** b. Mülheim an der Ruhr, June 11, 1818; d. Brussels, June 23, 1896. He studied first with his brothers; then with Hartmann (violin) in Cologne; with Ferdinand David and Mendelssohn in Leipzig. In 1841–44 he was conductor of the Männergesangverein of Cologne; then settled in Brussels, where he taught members of the royal family; in 1872, became a prof. at the Brussels Cons. He wrote symphs., piano concertos, piano pieces (*Capriccio, Etudes de concert, Charakterstücke,* etc.); also wrote *Praktische Chorschule für 4 Vocal- oder Instrumentalstimmen zum Studium der Harmonie, des Kontrapunktes und der Orgel* (1896).

Kufferath, Johann Hermann, German violinist and composer, brother of **Hubert Ferdinand** and **Louis Kufferath;** b. Mülheim an der Ruhr, May 12, 1797; d. Wiesbaden, July 28, 1864. He studied violin with Spohr and composition with Hauptmann; in 1823, became music director at Bielefeld; in 1830, at Utrecht, where he also taught singing at the School of Music and conducted various societies; retired to Wiesbaden in 1862. He wrote cantatas (*Jubelkantate,* etc.), overtures, and motets; also a *Manuel de chant.*

Kufferath, Louis, pianist and teacher, brother of **Hubert Ferdinand** and **Johann Hermann Kufferath;** b. Mülheim an der Ruhr, Nov. 10, 1811; d. near Brussels, March 2, 1882. He studied with his brother Johann Hermann, and with Schneider at Dessau. In 1836–50 he was director of the Cons. at Leeuwarden in the Netherlands; then in Ghent and Brussels. He publ. a Mass; 250 canons; a cantata, *Artevelde;* songs; etc.

Kufferath, Maurice, Belgian cellist and writer on music, son of **Hubert Ferdinand Kufferath;** b. Brussels, Jan. 8, 1852; d. there, Dec. 8, 1919. He studied cello with the Servais (*père* and *fils*), then at Brussels Univ.; from 1873 to 1900, wrote for *L'Indépendence Belge,* was editor of the *Guide Musical,* then proprietor; in 1900, became director of the Théâtre de la Monnaie, together with Guillaume Guidé; was co-founder of the Ysaÿe concerts, with Ysaÿe and Guidé. He publ. essays on Wagner's operas, and a comprehensive work, *Le Théâtre de Wagner de Tannhäuser à Parsifal* (Brussels, 1891–98; 6 vols.; of these, *Parsifal* was publ. in Eng. trans., N.Y., 1904); also a brochure, *L'Art de diriger l'orchestre* (Brussels, 1891; an account of Hans Richter's conducting in Brussels); a sketch of Henri Vieuxtemps (Brussels, 1883). He wrote the report on the musical instruments at the Brussels Exposition of 1880. Under the pen name **Maurice Reymont** he trans. Wagner's librettos and texts of songs by Brahms into French. He was an ardent propagandist for Wagner's ideas in Belgium.

Kuhlau, Friedrich, prolific German composer; b. Ülzen, Sept. 11, 1786; d. Copenhagen, March 12, 1832. He lost an eye in a childhood accident; during his recovery studied piano; became a private tutor in Hamburg and studied composition there with E.F.G. Schwenke. He went to Copenhagen in 1810 in order to avoid conscription into Napoleon's army; there he prospered, and in 1813 was appointed court musician.

WORKS: He produced several stage works in Copenhagen: *Røverborgen* (*The Robber's Castle;* May 26, 1814); *Trylleharpen* (*The Magic Harp;* Jan. 30, 1817); *Elisa* (April 17, 1820); *Lulu* (Oct. 29, 1824); *William Shakespeare* (March 28, 1826); *Elverhøj* (*The Fairies' Mound;* Nov. 6, 1828; his most celebrated dramatic work); wrote 3 flute quartets; trios concertants, duets, etc., for flute; 8 violin sonatas; 2 piano concertos; instructive piano sonatas and perennially popular sonatinas, much used for teaching purposes; also various pieces for 4 hands; songs and male quartets, once in great vogue.

Kuhlmann, Kathleen, American mezzo-soprano; b. San Francisco, Dec. 7, 1950. She studied in San Francisco and at the Chicago Lyric Opera School, making her debut with that company in 1979; subsequently appeared there in *Andrea Chenier* and *The Love of 3 Oranges.* She made her European debut in 1980 with the Cologne Opera, and in 1982 sang Charlotte in *Werther* and Rosina in *Il Barbiere di Siviglia.* On her 30th birthday (Dec. 7, 1980) she made her debut at Milan's La Scala as Meg Page in *Falstaff.* She made her London debut in 1982 at the Royal Opera, Covent Garden, as Ino and Juno in a new production of Handel's *Semele.* In 1983 she sang the leading role in *La Cenerentola* with the Glyndebourne Opera. Her other appearances included performances in the Promenade Concerts in London and with the Vienna State Opera.

Kuhnau, Johann (real family surname, **Kuhn**), erudite German musician, organist, and theorist; b. Geising, April 6, 1660; d. Leipzig, June 5, 1722. He studied at the Kreuzschule in Dresden with Salomon Krügner and Christoph Kittel; took lessons with Heringk and Albrici, then with Edelmann at Zittau, where he was acting cantor in 1681–82. He attended the Univ. of Leipzig in 1682–88, studying law; meanwhile, in 1684 succeeded Kühnel as organist at the Thomaskirche; in 1688 he organized a Collegium Musicum and also began to practice law. He became music director of the Univ. of Leipzig in 1701, when he was also appointed cantor at the Thomaskirche; was Bach's predecessor in the post. He publ. *Jura circa musicos ecclesiasticos* (Leipzig, 1688); *Der musickalische Quacksalber ... in einer kurtzweiligen und angenehmen Historie ... beschrieben* (Dresden, 1700; a satire on Italian music);

3 treatises are in MS. Kuhnau was the first to publish a harpsichord sonata imitated from the instrumental sonata (properly a suite) in several movements. It is found in Part II of his *Neue Clavier-Übung* (1692) and contains 3 movements, Allegro, Adagio, and Allegro (Rondo); there followed 7 sonatas in his *Frische Clavier-Früchte* (1696), which show a marked advance in treatment and melodic invention; 6 more harpsichord sonatas appeared under the title *Biblische Historien nebst Auslegung in sechs Sonaten,* in the highly original form of illustrations to biblical stories, thus presaging the development of program music; they set forth the fight between David and Goliath, David's cure of Saul, Jacob's Wedding, etc. (1700; new ed. of the first 2 by J.S. Shedlock, 1895; new ed. of the first by H. Bauer, 1927). Kuhnau's complete clavier works were publ. by Päsler in vol. 2 of Denkmäler Deutscher Tonkunst; Schering publ. 4 church cantatas and a list of Kuhnau's sacred works in vols. 58/59.

Kulenkampff, Georg, German virtuoso violinist; b. Bremen, Jan. 23, 1898; d. Schaffhausen, Oct. 4, 1948. He studied violin with Willy Hess in Berlin; in 1916 became concertmaster of the Bremen Phil. From 1923–26 he taught violin at the Hochschule für Musik in Berlin; in 1943 went to Switzerland and taught at the Lucerne Cons. He is regarded as one of the most brilliant German violinists of his generation; his book *Geigerische Betrachtungen,* partly didactic, partly autobiographical in content, was publ. posthumously, ed. by G. Meyer-Stichtung (Regensburg, 1952).

Kullak, Adolf, German music theorist and critic, brother of **Theodor Kullak;** b. Meseritz, Feb. 23, 1823; d. Berlin, Dec. 25, 1862. He studied general subjects at the Univ. of Berlin, and music with Bernhard Marx; then taught at his brother's Academy; contributed music criticism to various periodicals; publ. some piano pieces and songs. He wrote *Das Musikalisch-Schöne* (Leipzig, 1858) and *Ästhetik des Klavierspiels* (Berlin, 1861; 4th ed. by W. Niemann, 1906; 5th ed., 1916; in Eng., N.Y., 1892), a valuable and instructive summary of piano methods.

Kullak, Franz, German pianist and composer, son of **Theodor Kullak;** b. Berlin, April 12, 1844; d. there, Dec. 9, 1913. He studied with his father; also with Liszt for a brief while. In 1867 he became a piano teacher at his father's Academy; assumed its directorship at his father's death in 1882, dissolving the institution in 1890. He wrote an opera, *Ines de Castro* (Berlin, 1877); piano pieces; songs; also an essay, *Der Vortrag in der Musik am Ende des 19. Jahrhunderts* (Leipzig, 1898).

Kullak, Theodor, famous German pianist and pedagogue; b. Krotoschin, Sept. 12, 1818; d. Berlin, March 1, 1882. He studied piano with local teachers; in 1837 he went to Berlin at his father's behest to study medicine; also studied music there with Dehn (theory); then in 1842 went to Vienna, where he took

lessons with Czerny. Returning to Berlin in 1846, he became court pianist to the King of Prussia. In 1850 he founded a cons. in Berlin in partnership with Julius Stern and Bernhard Marx; however, dissension soon arose among them, and in 1855 Kullak established his own school, the Neue Akademie der Tonkunst, which greatly prospered and became famous as Kullak's Academy. He publ. valuable pedagogic works: *Materialien für den Elementar-Unterricht* (3 vols.); *Schule des Oktavenspiel;* various characteristic pieces for piano in a salon manner (*Ondine, Les Etincellese, Les Danaides, La Gazelle,* etc.); also *Kinderleben* (2 albums of piano pieces).

Kullman, Charles, American operatic tenor; b. New Haven, Conn., Jan. 13, 1903; d. there, Feb. 8, 1983. He was of German parentage; his family name was originally spelled with two *n*'s. He entered Yale Univ., and sang at the Yale Glee Club at college; graduated in 1924; then took courses at the Juilliard School of Music in N.Y., graduating in 1927. His first experience in opera was as a member of the American Opera Co., established in Rochester, N.Y., by Vladimir Rosing. Seeking wider opportunities, he went to Berlin, where he made his debut on Feb. 24, 1931, as Pinkerton in *Madama Butterfly,* at the Kroll Opera, a subsidiary of the Berlin State Opera, conducted by Otto Klemperer. He sang at the Berlin State Opera in 1932–35; then appeared at the Vienna State Opera, at Salzburg summer festivals, and at Covent Garden in London (1934–36). On Dec. 19, 1935, he made his debut at the Metropolitan Opera in N.Y. as Faust in Gounod's opera, vociferously greeted by loyal supporters who came specially from New Haven to join in the deserved applause. He remained on the roster of the Metropolitan until 1960; sang for the last time there on Dec. 3, 1960. His repertoire comprised 33 roles, including tenor parts in most standard German and Italian operas. He scored a signal success in the role of Eisenstein in *Die Fledermaus,* which he sang 30 times. After relinquishing his active stage career, he accepted a teaching position at Indiana Univ., where he was prof. of music until his retirement in 1971.

Kunc, Božidar, Croatian-American pianist and composer; b. Zagreb, July 18, 1903; d. Detroit, April 1, 1964. He received his academic training at the Music Academy in Zagreb, graduating in 1927; taught there from 1929 to 1950, when he emigrated to the U.S. He was a brother of the singer **Zinka Milanov.** His music is impressionistic in its harmonic palette.

Kunkel, Charles, German-American pianist and publisher; b. Sipperfeld, Rheinpfalz, July 22, 1840; d. St. Louis, Dec. 3, 1923. He was taken to America in 1848 by his father, who gave him elementary musical training. In 1868 he and his brother, **Jacob,** also a musician, went to St. Louis, where he established a music publishing business and started a music periodical, *Kunkel's Musical Review,* which included sheet music and articles; with his brother he also opened a music store selling pianos and other instruments; in 1872 he founded the St. Louis Cons. of Music, which continued in business for several years; furthermore, he presented an annual series of concerts in St. Louis known as Kunkel's Popular Concerts (1884–1900). He taught piano to the last years of his life; also publ. a method of piano playing, which was commended favorably by Liszt; Anton Rubinstein praised him as a pianist during his visit to St. Louis in 1873. Kunkel was reputed to be quite formidable as a sight reader. Altogether, he was certainly a shining light in the German musical colony in middle America in the 2nd half of the 19th century. With his brother he gave, to tumultuous applause, a series of concerts playing piano duets. His publishing business put out a cornucopia of his own piano solos with such titles as *Nonpareil, Galop Brilliant, Philomel Polka, Snowdrops Waltz,* and *Southern Jollification,* most of these highly perishable; however, one piece, *Alpine Storm,* deserves retrieval, if for no other reason than its dedication: "To my son, Ludwig van Beethoven Kunkel." (This piece also contains "tone clusters" played with the palm of the hand in the bass to imitate thunder.)

Kunkel, Franz Joseph, German theorist and composer; b. Dieburg, Aug. 20, 1808; d. Frankfurt, Dec. 31, 1880. From 1828 to 1954 he was rector and music teacher in the Bensheim Teachers' Seminary. He wrote *Kleine Musiklehre; Die Verurteilung der Konservatorien zu Pflanzschulen des musikalischen Proletariats* (1855); *Kritische Beleuchtung des C.F. Weitzmannischen Harmonie-Systems; Die neue Harmonielehre im Streit mit der alten* (1863); etc.; also a cantata, Psalms, motets, etc.

Kunkel, Jacob, German-American pianist; b. Kleiniedesheim, Oct. 22, 1846; d. St. Louis, Oct. 16, 1882. He studied with his elder brother, **Charles Kunkel,** and was also a nominal pupil of Tausig, who, according to the Kunkel family report, refused to teach him because he thought that the younger man was equal to the master. He was taken to America with his brother, and participated in most of the latter's enterprises, in the music publishing business and in a general music store. The brothers also gave a series of concerts playing piano duets. Jacob Kunkel composed piano pieces in a salon manner.

Künneke, Eduard, German operetta composer; b. Emmerich, Jan. 27, 1885; d. Berlin, Oct. 27, 1953. He studied with Max Bruch in Berlin; was subsequently engaged as a choirmaster in various theaters in Germany; produced 2 operas, *Robins Ende* (Mannheim, 1909) and *Coeur As* (Dresden, 1913), with little success; he then turned to light opera, and his first work in this genre, a singspiel, *Das Dorf ohne Glocke* (Berlin, April 5, 1919), was received with great acclaim. His next light opera, *Der Vetter aus Dingsda* (Berlin, April 15, 1921), was no less successful; there followed *Lady Hamilton* (1926); *Glückliche Reise* (Berlin, Nov. 23, 1932); *Lockende Flamme* (1933); *Herz über Bord* (1935); *Der grosse*

Name (1938); etc. His last operetta was *Hochzeit mit Erika* (1949). Besides his stage works, he wrote many film scores, an Overture, a Piano Concerto, and other instrumental compositions.

Kunst, Jaap (Jakob), Dutch ethnomusicologist; b. Groningen, Aug. 12, 1891; d. Amsterdam, Dec. 7, 1960. He started playing the violin at an early age; soon became interested in the folk songs of the Netherlands. He received a degree in law at the Univ. of Groningen (1917); then toured with a string trio in the Dutch East Indies, and decided to remain in Java, where he worked in a government post. He became interested in indigenous Javanese music, and founded an archive for folk instruments and recordings in Jakarta. He returned to the Netherlands in 1934; in 1936 became curator of the Royal Tropical Inst. in Amsterdam; in 1953 became a lecturer at the Univ. of Amsterdam. Kunst is credited with having coined the word "ethnomusicology" as a more accurate term than "comparative musicology."

WRITINGS: *A Study of Papuan Music* (Weltevreden, 1931); *Musicologisch onderzoek 1930* (Batavia, 1931); *De Toonkunst van Java* (The Hague, 1934; Eng. trans., 1949; enlarged as *Music in Java,* 1973); *Music in Flores: A Study of the Vocal and Instrumental Music among the Tribes Living in Flores* (Leiden, 1942); *The Cultural Background of Indonesian Music* (Amsterdam, 1949); *Metre, Rhythm and Multipart* (Leiden, 1950); *Musicologica: A Study of the Nature of Ethnomusicology, Its Problems, Methods and Representative Personalities* (Amsterdam, 1950; enlarged as *Ethnomusicology,* 1955); *Sociologische bindingen in der muziek* (The Hague, 1953); ed. collections of folk songs of the Netherlands and Northern New Guinea.

Kunwald, Ernst, Austrian conductor; b. Vienna, April 14, 1868; d. there, Dec. 12, 1939. He studied law at Vienna Univ. (Dr.Juris., 1891); at the same time studied piano with Leschetizky and J. Epstein, and composition with H. Grädener; then studied at the Leipzig Cons. with Jadassohn. His first engagement as an opera conductor was in Rostock (1895–97); then he conducted opera in Sondershausen (1897–98), Essen (1898–1900), Halle (1900–1), Madrid (1901–2), and Frankfurt (1902–5), and at Kroll's Theater in Berlin (1905–6); served as 2nd conductor of the Berlin Phil. Orch. (1907–12). In 1906 he was guest conductor of the N.Y. Phil. Society; in 1912, became regular conductor of the Cincinnati Symph. Orch., and from 1914, also of the May Festival. He was arrested as an enemy alien on Dec. 8, 1917, but was released on bail and allowed to continue to conduct until his internment. In 1919 he went to Germany and conducted symph. concerts in Königsberg (1920–27); in 1928–31, conducted the Berlin Symph. Orch.; then returned to Vienna, where he remained until his death.

Kupferberg, Herbert, American journalist and music critic; b. New York, Jan. 20, 1918. He was educated at Cornell Univ. (B.A., 1939) and at Columbia

Univ. (M.A., 1940; M.S., 1941). From 1942–66 he was on the staff of the *N.Y. Herald Tribune;* was also music critic of the *Atlantic Monthly* from 1962–69 and of the *National Observer* from 1967–77. He served as rapporteur for the Twentieth Century Fund's N.Y. task force on cultural exchange with the Soviet Union, which led to the publication of the report *The Raised Curtain* in 1977.
WRITINGS: *Those Fabulous Philadelphians: The Life and Times of a Great Orchestra* (N.Y., 1969); *The Mendelssohns: Three Generations of Genius* (N.Y., 1972); *Opera* (N.Y., 1975); *Tanglewood* (N.Y., 1976); also 2 books for young readers, *Felix Mendelssohn: His Life, His Family, His Music* (N.Y., 1972) and *A Rainbow of Sound: The Instruments of the Orchestra and Their Music* (N.Y., 1973).

Kupferman, Meyer, American composer; b. New York, July 13, 1926. He came from a Jewish family; his father, an immigrant from Rumania, taught him to sing Rumanian folk songs; his mother, who was Russian-Jewish, taught him old Yiddish songs. He studied clarinet with Louis Levy and piano with Joel Newman. He acquired his knack for composition from imitating modern French music, and his early works bear a distinct impressionistic flavor; following the trends of the times, he adopted the 12-tone method, but soon abandoned its strictures in favor of a more general style of composition. Among his most original works is a series of some 50 pieces for various instruments, titled *Infinities.* In 1975 he received a Guggenheim fellowship. In 1981 he was given an award of $5,000 by the American Academy and Inst. of Arts and Letters. About 1970 he turned to the "gestalt" form, which effectuates a creative synthesis of incompatible elements. He was also engaged in teaching; in 1951 he joined the music faculty of Sarah Lawrence College.
WORKS: Operas: *In a Garden* (N.Y., Dec. 29, 1949); *The Curious Fern* and *Voices for a Mirror* (both produced in N.Y. on June 5, 1957); *Draagenfut Girl* (Bronx, N.Y., May 8, 1958); *Dr. Faustus Lights the Lights* (1952); *The Judgement* (*Infinities* No. 18; 1966–67); *Prometheus* (1975–77); 11 symphs. (1950–83); Piano Concerto No. 1 (1948); Concerto for Cello and Jazz Band (1962); Concerto for Cello, Tape, and Orch. (1974); Concerto for 6 Instruments and Orch. (1976); Violin Concerto (1976); Piano Concerto No. 2 (1977); Tuba Concerto (1982); Clarinet Concerto (1984); 7 string quartets; some 35 pieces for various ensembles, entitled *Cycle of Infinities*; Concertino for 11 Brass Instruments; *Sonata on Jazz Elements* for Piano; *Tunnel of Love* for Jazz Combo (N.Y., May 22, 1971); *Abracadabra Quartet* for Piano and String Trio (N.Y., Dec. 5, 1976); *The Red King's Throw* for Clarinet, Piano, Cello, and Percussion (1978); *Richter 7,* "musical earthquake" (1979); a number of works titled *Sound Objects* representing dream images.

Kurka, Robert, American composer of Czech descent; b. Cicero, Ill., Dec. 22, 1921; d. New York, Dec. 12, 1957. He studied violin with Kathleen Parlow

and Hans Letz; composition with Otto Luening and Darius Milhaud; received a Guggenheim fellowship in 1951 and 1952. His opera *The Good Soldier Schweik,* completed shortly before his untimely death from leukemia, was produced with extraordinary success at the N.Y. City Center on April 23, 1958, and has since been widely performed in America and in Europe. His other works include 2 symphs.; Serenade for Chamber Orch.; Violin Concerto; Concerto for 2 Pianos, String Orch., and Trumpet; Concerto for Marimba and Orch.; *Ballad for French Horn and Strings;* 5 string quartets; Piano Trio; 4 violin sonatas; piano pieces; choruses.

Kurt, Melanie, Austrian soprano; b. Vienna, Jan. 8, 1880; d. New York, March 11, 1941. She studied piano at the Vienna Cons. (1887–94), winning the gold medal and Liszt prize; then took singing lessons from Fannie Mütter in Vienna, and made a successful operatic debut as Elisabeth in *Tannhäuser* (Lübeck, 1902). From 1905 to 1908 she sang in Braunschweig; then (1908–12) at the Berlin Opera. She became an outstanding Wagner interpreter and appeared in London, Brussels, Milan, Budapest, etc. When the Deutsches Opernhaus in Charlottenburg was opened in 1912, she was engaged as chief soprano for heroic roles. On Feb. 1, 1915, she made her debut at the Metropolitan Opera House as Isolde. In 1917 she returned to Europe, living in Berlin and Vienna as a singing teacher. In 1939 she settled in N.Y., where she remained until her death.

Kurtág, György, Hungarian composer; b. Lugoj, Feb. 19, 1926. He learned to play piano as a child; then studied composition with Kadosa, Leo Weiner, Veress, and Farkas at the Budapest Academy of Music (1946–53); went to Paris and took lessons with Milhaud and Messiaen (1957–58); upon returning to Budapest, he taught at the Academy of Music. In his music he sometimes applies serial principles to classical melodic configurations and forms.
WORKS: *Suite* for Piano Duet (1950); Piano Suite (1951); *Cantata* (1953); Viola Concerto (1954); String Quartet (1959); Wind Quintet (1959); *8 Piano Pieces* (1960); *8 Duets* for Violin and Cimbalom (1960–61); *Jelek (Signs)* for Solo Viola (1961); *5 Merrycate* for Guitar (1962); *Bornemissza Péter mondásai (The Sayings of Péter Bornemissza),* concerto for Soprano and Piano (1963–68); *In Memory of a Winter Sunset,* 4 fragments for Soprano, Violin, and Cimbalom (1969); *4 Capriccios* for Soprano and Chamber Ensemble (1971–72); *Game* for Piano (1974–75); *4 Songs* (1975); *Szálkák (Splinters)* for Solo Cimbalom (1975); *Messages of the Late Miss R. V. Troussova* for Soprano and Chamber Ensemble (Paris, Jan. 14, 1981); *Omaggio a Luigi Nono* (London, Feb. 3, 1981).

Kurth, Ernst, eminent Austrian musicologist; b. Vienna, June 1, 1886; d. Bern, Aug. 2, 1946. He studied at the Vienna Cons. with Guido Adler; received his Dr.Phil. with the thesis *Der Stil der Opera seria von Chr. W. Gluck bis zum Orfeo* (1908), which was publ. in Adler's *Studien zur Musikwissenschaft* (vol. 1); held various posts as a teacher and a conductor in Germany; then went to Bern in 1912, where he founded a Collegium Musicum; became a prof. in 1927. His principal work, *Grundlagen des linearen Kontrapunkts: Bachs melodische Polyphonie* (Bern, 1917), exercised a profound influence on musicology, and on practical composition as well; the term "linear counterpoint," which he introduced in it, became part of scientific nomenclature in music; a companion vol., *Romantische Harmonik und ihre Krise in Wagners Tristan* (Bern, 1920), is a psychological analysis of Romantic music. His vol. *Musikpsychologie* (Berlin, 1931) represents a synthesis of his theoretical ideas on musical perception. He also publ. a comprehensive biography of Bruckner (2 vols., Berlin, 1925) and several valuable studies: "Zur Ars cantus mensurabilis des Franko von Köln," in *Kirchenmusikalisches Jahrbuch* (1908); *Die Voraussetzungen der theoretischen Harmonik und der tonalen Darstellungssysteme* (Bern, 1913); "Zur Motivbildung Bachs," *Bach Jahrbuch* (1917).

Kurtz, Edward Frampton, American violinist and composer; b. New Castle, Pa., July 31, 1881; d. Cedar Falls, Iowa, June 8, 1965. He studied at the Univ. of Iowa, the Detroit Cons., and the Cincinnati Cons.; took violin lessons with Eugène Ysaÿe while Ysaÿe was conductor of the Cincinnati Symph. Orch.; studied composition with Clapp, Goetschius, and E.S. Kelley. After teaching at various Midwestern colleges, he became head of the music dept. of Iowa State Teachers College, in 1940, and lived mostly in Iowa. He wrote 5 symphs. (1932, 1939, 1940, 1943, 1944); several symph. poems; a Suite for String Quartet, subtitled *From the West;* violin pieces.

Kurtz, Efrem, Russian-American conductor; b. St. Petersburg, Nov. 7, 1900. He studied academic subjects in Riga; then went to Germany and took music courses at the Stern Cons. in Berlin, graduating in 1922. Subsequently he devoted himself to ballet conducting. He came to the U.S. in 1943; was conductor of the Kansas City Phil. (1943–48) and of the Houston Symph. Orch. (1948–54). In 1966 he conducted some concerts in Moscow and Leningrad; then was active as a guest conductor in Europe and America; in 1977 he conducted in Tokyo; also filled in engagements with the Kansas City Phil. and with the Zürich Tonhalle Orch.; in 1979 conducted guest appearances in Houston, Texas. He makes his permanent home in Switzerland. He married the flutist **Elaine Shaffer.**

Kurz, Selma, coloratura soprano; b. Bielitz, Silesia, Nov. 15, 1874; d. Vienna, May 10, 1933. She studied with Ress; made her first appearances in Hamburg in 1895. In 1899 she was engaged by Mahler at the Vienna Court Opera, and remained on the roster until 1926. She made her London debut at Covent Garden as Gilda (June 7, 1904), creating a profound impression; subsequently appeared in America as a concert singer, also with success. She was married to the famous Viennese gynecologist Josef Halban; they were the parents of the soprano **Desi Halban.**

Kusser (or **Cousser**), **Johann Sigismund,** composer; b. Pressburg, Feb. 13, 1660; d. Dublin, Nov. 1727. He received his early musical training from his father, Johann Kusser (1626–75), a minister and organist. He lived in Stuttgart as a boy; then spent 8 years in Paris (1674–82), where he became a pupil of Lully. He subsequently was in Ansbach (1682–83); then in Braunschweig (1690). In 1694 he became co-director of the Hamburg Opera, but left 2 years later, and was active in Nuremberg and Augsburg as an opera composer. He was again in Stuttgart from 1700 to 1704. In 1705 he appeared in London, and after a year proceeded to Dublin, where he was a chapelmaster and teacher. He revisited Stuttgart briefly, but returned to Dublin, and remained there until his death. He was greatly esteemed as an operatic conductor; Mattheson, in his *Volkommener Capellmeister,* holds him up as a model of efficiency. Kusser is historically significant for being the mediator between the French and the German styles of composition, and the first to use Lully's methods and forms in German instrumental music. Lully's influence is shown in Kusser's set of 6 suites for strings, *Composition de musique suivant la méthode française* (Stuttgart, 1682).

WORKS: Operas: produced in Braunschweig: *Julia* (1690); *Kleopatra* (1691); *Ariadne* (Feb. 15, 1692); *Andromeda* (Feb. 20, 1692); *Jason* (Sept. 1, 1692); *Narcissus* (Oct. 14, 1692); *Porus* (1693); in Hamburg: *Erindo* (1694) and *Der grossmüthige Scipio Africanus* (1694); in Stuttgart: *Der verliebte Wald* (1698) and *Erminia* (Oct. 11, 1698); 18 suites from the lost operas *Le Festin des Muses, La Cicala delle cetra d'Eunomio,* and *Apollen enjoué,* 6 operatic overtures, and several arias are extant; an aria from *Erindo* is publ. in Schering's *Geschichte der Musik in Beispielen* (No. 250); an overture was ed. by H. Osthoff (1933).

Kussevitsky, Serge. See **Koussevitzky, Serge.**

Kuula, Toivo, Finnish composer; b. Vasa, July 7, 1883; d. Viipuri (Vyborg), May 18, 1918. He studied at the Helsinki Cons. with Wegelius, Järnefelt, and Sibelius (1900–8); then went to Italy, where he took courses with Bossi in Bologna; also studied in Paris with Marcel Labey; in 1910 he was appointed conductor of the orch. at Oulu; from 1911 to 1916 was assistant conductor of the Helsinki Phil.; then conductor of the orch. in Viipuri. He was shot to death during a street fight in the aftermath of the Finnish Civil War. His music, rooted in Finnish folk song, is occasionally touched with Impressionism. To commemorate his achievement, 2 societies were formed in Helsinki and Stockholm, in 1948 and 1949.

WORKS: At his death he left unfinished a *Jupiter Symphony;* his *Stabat Mater* for Chorus, Organ, and Orch. (1914–18) was completed by Madetoja and first perf. in 1919 in Helsinki. Completed works: 2 *South Ostrobothnian Suites* for Orch. (1906, 1912); *Prelude and Fugue* for Orch. (1909); *Prelude and Intermezzo* for Strings and Organ (1909); *Orjanpoika (The Son of a Slave),* symph. legend (1910); *Kuolemattomuuden toivo (Hope of Immortality)* for Baritone, Chorus, and Orch. (1910); *Merenkyl-pijäneidot (Maids on the Seashore)* for Soprano and Orch. (1910); *Impi ja pajarinpoika (The Maid and the Boyar's Son)* for Soprano and Orch. (1911); *Bothnic Poem* for Orch. (Petrograd, Oct. 26, 1918, composer conducting); Violin Sonata; music for plays; piano pieces; songs.

Kuyper, Elisabeth, Dutch conductor and composer; b. Amsterdam, Sept. 13, 1877; d. Lugano, Feb. 26, 1953. She studied with Max Bruch in Berlin. In 1908–20 she taught theory at the Hochschule für Musik there; was founder (1908) and conductor of the Berlin Tonkünstlerinnen Orch.; in 1922 she led a few concerts of the London Women's Symph. Orch., and in 1923 conducted the N.Y. Women's Symph. Orch.; later returned to Europe and lived at Lago Maggiore in Brissago. She composed a Symph.; Violin Concerto; several violin sonatas; Ballade for Cello and Piano; Piano Trio; songs.

Küzdö, Victor, Hungarian violinist and teacher; b. Budapest, Sept. 18, 1859; d. Glendale, Calif., Feb. 24, 1966, at the age of 106. He studied at the Budapest Cons. with Karl Huber; made his debut there in 1882; toured in Europe, and visited the U.S. in 1884 and 1887. In 1894 he settled in N.Y.; in 1918–31, taught at the summer school of the Chicago Musical College; in 1932, settled in Glendale. He became totally blind in 1950. He publ. several violin pieces, among them a Serenade and *Witches' Dance.*

Kvapil, Jaroslav, significant Czech composer; b. Fryšták, April 21, 1892; d. Brno, Feb. 18, 1958. He studied with Janáček in Brno (1906–9) and at the Leipzig Cons. (1911–13) with Leichmüller (piano) and Max Reger (composition). He was in the Austrian army during World War I; then was music director of the Phil. Society in Brno (1919–47); taught at the Janáček Academy of Music in Brno (1947–57). His works show the double influence of Janáček's national and rhapsodic style and Max Reger's strong polyphonic idiom.
WORKS: Opera, *Pohádka máje (A Romance in May;* 1940–43; Prague, May 12, 1950; revised 1955; Brno, 1955); oratorio, *Lví srdce (The Lion's Heart;* 1928–31; Brno, Dec. 7, 1931); 2 cantatas: *A Song on Time That Is Passing* (1924) and *Small Italian Cantata* (1950); 4 symphs.: No. 1 (1913–14); No. 2 (1921); No. 3 (1936–37); No. 4, *Vítězná (Victory;* 1943); *Thema con variazioni e fuga* for Orch. (1912); 2 violin concertos (1927–28, 1952); *Z těžkých dob (From Anxious Times),* symph. variations (1939); *Slavonic (Jubilee) Overture* (1944); *Burlesque* for Flute and Orch. (1945); *Svítání (Daybreak),* symph. poem (1948–49); Oboe Concerto (1951); Piano Concerto (1954); 3 violin sonatas, with Piano (1910, 1914, 1931); Sonata for Violin and Organ (1931); Piano Trio (1912); Cello Sonata (1913); 6 string quartets (1914, 1926, 1931, 1935, 1949, 1951); Piano Quintet (1914–15); Brass Quintet (1925); Variations for Trumpet and Piano (1929); Suite for Trombone and Piano (1930); *Intimate Pictures* for Violin and Piano (1934); Wind Quintet (1935); Violin Sonatina

(1941); *Fantasy* for Cello and Piano (1942); Nonet (1944); Quartet for Flute, Violin, Viola, and Cello (1948); Duo for Violin and Viola (1949); Suite for Viola and Piano (1955). He also wrote 3 piano sonatas (1912, 1925, 1946); Variations for Piano (1914); *Fantasy in the Form of Variations* for Piano (1952); Piano Sonatina (1956); *10 Pieces* for Piano (1957); Fantasy for Organ (1935); several song cycles; many transcriptions of folk songs; a piano album of 100 folk songs from Moravian Slovakia (1914).

Kwalwasser, Helen, American violinist, daughter of **Jacob Kwalwasser;** b. Syracuse, N.Y., Oct. 11, 1927. She showed a gift for violin playing at an early age; studied with Louis Persinger (1936–39), with Zimbalist at the Curtis Inst. of Music in Philadelphia (1939–41), then with Galamian (1941–48); made her debut in N.Y. on March 25, 1947; then toured Europe (1949); returning to N.Y., was active as a violinist and teacher.

Kwalwasser, Jacob, music psychologist and educator, father of **Helen Kwalwasser;** b. New York, Feb. 27, 1894; d. Pittsburgh, Aug. 7, 1977. He received his education at the Univ. of Pittsburgh and the Univ. of Iowa, obtaining his Ph.D. in 1926; taught in the public schools in Pittsburgh (1918–23); was head of public school music at the Univ. of Iowa (1923–26); in 1926, was appointed prof. and head of the dept. of music education at Syracuse Univ. He is the co-author of the Kwalwasser-Dykema Music Tests; publ. a manual on the subject in 1913; also collaborated in establishing the Kwalwasser-Ruch Musical Accomplishment Test, and various other melodic, harmonic, and instrumental tests; publ. numerous magazine articles on music education.

Kwast, James, famous German pianist and teacher; b. Nijkerk, the Netherlands, Nov. 23, 1852; d. Berlin, Oct. 31, 1927. He studied with his father and Ferdinand Böhme; later with Reinecke and Richter at the Leipzig Cons.; also with Theodor Kullak and Wüerst at Berlin, and with Brassin and Gevaert at Brussels. In 1874 he became an instructor at the Cons. of Cologne; from 1883 till 1903 he taught at the Hoch Cons. in Frankfurt; from 1903 to 1906, was a prof. of piano at the Klindworth-Scharwenka Cons. in Berlin; then at the Stern Cons. there. He was greatly esteemed by his colleagues and students as a piano pedagogue; many well-known pianists were his pupils at Frankfurt and Berlin. His first wife, Antonia (d. Stuttgart, Feb. 10, 1931), was a daughter of Ferdinand Hiller; his 2nd wife, **Frieda Hodapp-Kwast** (b. Bargen, Aug. 13, 1880; d. Bad Wiessee, Sept. 14, 1949), was a concert pianist. He wrote a Piano Concerto and other piano music; edited works of Handel and Clementi for the *Tonmeister* edition.

L

La Barbara, Joan, American composer and experimental vocalist; b. Philadelphia, June 8, 1947. Her grandfather taught her to play nursery songs on the piano; later she sang in church and school choirs; joined a folk music group in Philadelphia; then went to N.Y., where she sang in radio commercials and at the same time made contacts with the most uninhibited representatives of the American avant-garde. In her compositions she usually makes use of graphic notation. Among her works are *Ides of March* for Strings and Voices (1974); *An Exaltation of Larks* for Voice and Electronics (1975); *Cyclone,* a sound sculpture for White Noise and Voices (1975; first perf. in Bonn, Germany, May 14, 1977); *Thunder* for Voice Electronics and Timpani (1976); *Circular Song* for Voice employing circular breathing (1975). She introduced many other vocal improvements, including vocalizing while breathing in and out.

Labarre, Théodore, eminent French harpist; b. Paris, March 5, 1805; d. there, March 9, 1870. He studied privately with Cousineau, Boscha, and Naderman; then at the Paris Cons. with Dourlen, Eler, Fétis, and Boieldieu. In 1824–47 he lived alternately in London and Paris; became conductor of the Opéra-Comique; in 1851, was appointed conductor of Louis Napoleon's private orch.; in 1867, became prof. of harp at the Paris Cons. He wrote 4 operas, 5 ballets, numerous pieces for harp, songs, etc.; also a *Méthode complète* for the harp.

L'Abbé, Joseph Barnabé Saint-Sevin (real name, **Saint-Sevin**), French violinist and composer; b. Agen, June 11, 1727; d. Paris, July 20, 1803. A precocious musician, he began his study with his father and became a member of the orch. of the Comédie-Française at the age of 12; then studied with Leclair; was a violinist at the Opéra (1742–62); also played at the Concert Spirituel (1741–55); devoted his later years to teaching and composition. He had an excellent violin technique, and was an innovator in that he wrote out cadenzas in full.

WORKS: 2 books of violin sonatas, with Continuo (1748–64); symphs. for 3 Violins and Continuo (c.1754); 5 collections of airs arranged for one and 2 violins; a manual, *Les Principes du violon* (1761).

Labey, Marcel, French conductor and composer; b. Le Vésinet, Seine-et-Oise, Aug. 6, 1875; d. Nancy, Nov. 25, 1968. He studied law in Paris, receiving his degree in 1898; then turned his attention to music, studying piano with Delaborde, harmony with Lenormand, and composition with Vincent d'Indy at the Schola Cantorum; taught piano there, and at d'Indy's death in 1931, became vice-principal of the school.

WORKS: Opera, *Bérengère* (1912; Le Havre, April 12, 1929); 3 symphs. (1903, 1908, 1934); *Suite champêtre* for Orch. (1923); *Ouverture pour un drame* (Paris, Jan. 22, 1921); Piano Sonata; Viola Sonata; 2 violin sonatas; String Quartet; Piano Trio; Piano Quartet; Piano Quintet; songs; etc. He publ. piano arrangements of several orch. works of d'Indy (Symph. in B-flat, *Jour d'été à la montagne,* etc.).

Labia, Fausta, Italian opera singer, sister of **Maria Labia;** b. Verona, April 3, 1870; d. Rome, Oct. 6, 1935. She became a great favorite in Sweden, but retired in 1908 after her marriage. She then lived many years in Rome and taught at the Santa Cecilia Academy. Her method, *L'arte del respiro nello recitazione e nel canto,* was publ. posthumously in 1936.

Labia, Maria, Italian soprano, sister of **Fausta Labia;** b. Verona, Feb. 14, 1880; d. Malcesine del Garda, Feb. 10, 1953. She received her musical education from her mother, an excellent amateur singer; made her operatic debut in Stockholm on May 19, 1905, as Mimi. From 1906 to 1908 she was on the roster of the Komische Oper in Berlin. She was then engaged by the Manhattan Opera, where she first appeared on Nov. 9, 1908, as Tosca. After the demise of that company she joined the Vienna Opera; then taught voice at the Music Academy of Siena. She was an actress of great emotional power, and was particularly successful in such dramatic roles as Carmen, Santuzza, Nedda, and Violetta.

Labitzky, August, German violinist and conductor, son of **Joseph Labitzky;** b. Bečov (Petschau), Oct. 22, 1832; d. Reichenhall, Aug. 28, 1903. He studied at the Prague Cons., and with Ferdinand David and Hauptmann in Leipzig. He became conductor of the Karlsbad resort orch. in 1853; composed piano pieces, etc.

Labitzky, Joseph, German dance composer and violinist, father of **August Labitzky;** b. Schönfeld, Eger, July 5, 1802; d. Karlsbad, Aug. 19, 1881. He studied with Veit in Bečov (Petschau); in 1820, joined the orch. in Marienbad as first violinist; then occupied a similar post in Karlsbad; organized his own orch. and toured southern Germany. He studied with Winter in Munich, where he publ. his first dances (1827); returning to Karlsbad in 1835, he organized an orch. and toured Europe. Many of his waltzes, galops, quadrilles, etc. (about 300 opus numbers) enjoyed a great vogue.

Lablache, Luigi, famous Italian bass of French and Irish descent; b. Naples, Dec. 6, 1794; d. there, Jan. 23, 1858. He studied voice with Valesi at the Naples Cons. della Pietà dei Turchini; at 18 he commenced his career there as a *basso buffo.* In 1812 he married Teresa Pinotti, the daughter of an actor. In 1813 he

went to Palermo as *primo basso cantante;* then appeared at La Scala in Milan; made his debut in London as Geronimo in *Il matrimonio segreto* (March 30, 1830), with instantaneous success; appeared in Paris in the same role on Nov. 4, 1830. In 1836–37 Lablache lived in England as singing master to Queen Victoria. He also sang in Naples, Vienna, and St. Petersburg, always winning acclaim. He was greatly esteemed by his contemporaries; Schubert dedicated to him his 3 Italian songs (1827).

Labor, Josef, Austrian pianist, organist, and composer; b. Horowitz, June 29, 1842; d. Vienna, April 26, 1924. He lost his sight as a youth; studied with Sechter at the Vienna Cons.; in 1863 was tutor to the princesses of Hannover, who were then living in exile with their family in Vienna. He played in London (1865), Paris, and in Russia; in 1868 returned to Vienna, where he settled as a teacher; among his students were Julius Bittner and Arnold Schoenberg. Labor wrote several sonatas; a Piano Quartet; pieces for organ and for piano; church music; songs, etc.; also edited Biber's violin sonatas for Denkmäler der Tonkunst in Österreich.

Laborde, Jean Benjamin de, French violinist and composer; b. Paris, Sept. 5, 1734; d. there (on the guillotine), July 22, 1794. He studied violin with Dauvergne and composition with Rameau; was chamberlain to Louis XV, and a member of the Compagnie des Fermiers-Généraux; then withdrew from the court and devoted himself to composition. He wrote 32 operas, and songs; also an *Essai sur la musique ancienne et moderne,* containing an early study of folk songs (1780); *Recueils de chansons avec un accompagnement de violon et la basse continue; Choix de chansons mises en musique* (4 vols., 1773); *Mémoires historiques sur Raoul de Coucy* (1781).

Labroca, Mario, Italian composer; b. Rome, Nov. 22, 1896; d. there, July 1, 1973. He studied composition with Malipiero and Respighi and graduated from the Parma Cons. in 1921. He held numerous administrative and teaching posts; was music director of the Teatro La Fenice in Venice (from 1959); lectured at the Univ. of Perugia (from 1960). He was closely connected with the theater and the cinema in Italy and composed many scores for plays and films.

WORKS: 2 operas: *La Principessa di Perepepè* (Rome, Dec. 11, 1927) and *Le tre figliuole di Pinco Pallino* (Rome, Jan. 27, 1928); Stabat Mater for Soprano, Mixed Chorus, and Orch. (Rome, Dec. 15, 1935); Symph. (1934); *Sinfonia* for String Orch. (1927); 2 string quartets (1925, 1934); Piano Trio (1925); Suite for Viola and Piano (1926); *3 cantate dalla Passione secondo San Giovanni* (1950).

Labunski, Felix, Polish-American composer and teacher, brother of **Wiktor Labunski** (1895–1974); b. Ksawerynów, Dec. 27, 1892; d. Cincinnati, April 28, 1979. Brought up in a musical environment (his father, a civil engineer, was an amateur singer; his mother played the piano), he began studying piano as a child; then entered the Warsaw Cons., where he was a student of Marczewski and Maliszewski. He met Paderewski, who arranged for him a stipend at the Ecole Normale de Musique in Paris, where he studied with Nadia Boulanger and Paul Dukas. In 1927 he formed, with Czapski, Perkowski, and Wiechowicz, the Association of Young Polish Musicians in Paris. Returning to Poland, Labunski held the post of director of the dept. of classical music of the Polish Radio in Warsaw (1934–36). In 1936 he emigrated to America; became a naturalized citizen in 1941. He lived in N.Y. until 1945, when he joined the staff of the Cincinnati College of Music, continuing in this position when it merged with the Cincinnati Cons. of Music in 1955; he retired in 1964 as prof. emeritus in composition. In his music, Felix Labunski remains faithful to the legacy of Romanticism as cultivated in Poland and Russia.

Labunski, Wiktor, pianist and composer, brother of **Felix Labunski;** b. St. Petersburg, April 14, 1895; d. Kansas City, Jan. 26, 1974. He studied at the St. Petersburg Cons. with Nikolayev (piano), Kalafati and Vitols (composition); later, piano with Felix Blumenfeld and Safonov, and conducting with Emil Mlynarski. From 1919 till 1928 he was head of the piano dept. at the Cons. of Cracow; then came to the U.S.; made his debut in 1928 as a pianist at Carnegie Hall in N.Y.; was an instructor at the Nashville Cons. (1928–31); prof. and director of the Memphis (Tenn.) College of Music (1931–37); in 1937, was appointed prof. and director of the Cons. of Music of Kansas City. In 1920 he married Wanda Mlynarska, daughter of his teacher Emil Mlynarski.

Lacerda, Francisco de, Portuguese conductor and musicologist; b. Ribeira Seca, S. Jorge, Azores, May 11, 1869; d. Lisbon, July 18, 1934. He studied at the Lisbon Cons.; received a government stipend for study in Paris, where he took a course with Vincent d'Indy at the Schola Cantorum. In Paris he associated himself with Bourgault-Ducoudray and worked with him in the International Folklore Assoc.; also conducted concerts. At the outbreak of World War I he returned to Portugal; in 1913 he organized the Orquestra Filarmonica in Lisbon. He compiled the important *Cancioneiro musical portugues,* containing some 500 folk songs; wrote a number of original compositions, among them the symph. works *Adamastor, Almorol, Rapsodia insular,* etc.

Lach, Robert, Austrian musicologist and composer; b. Vienna, Jan. 29, 1874; d. Salzburg, Sept. 11, 1958. He was a pupil of R. Fuchs at the Cons. of the Gesellschaft der Musikfreunde in Vienna (1893–99); also studied philosophy and musicology there, with Wallaschek, Rietsch, and Adler; received a Dr.Phil. from the Univ. of Prague in 1902, with the dissertation *Studien zur Entwicklungsgeschichte der ornamentalen Melopöie* (publ. in Leipzig, 1913), viewing the entire field of musical history in the light of new discoveries of ethnographic investigation. From 1911 to 1920 he was chief of the music division of the Vienna State Library; in 1915, joined the faculty of the Univ. of Vienna. He recorded for the Phonogram Archives of Vienna the songs of Russian prisoners of World War I (with particular emphasis on Asian and Caucasian nationalities), and publ. numerous papers on these melodies. He was pensioned in 1939, and lived in Vienna in retirement, devoting his time to the compilation of oriental glossaries (Babylonian, Sumerian, Egyptian, etc.). In 1954 he became general editor of the new Denkmäler der Tonkunst in Österreich. The dedicatory brochure, *Robert Lach, Persönlichkeit und Werk, zum 80. Geburtstag* (Vienna, 1954), contains a complete list of his works and scholarly writings. His list of musical works attains 150 opus numbers, among them 10 symphs.; 25 string quartets; 14 string quintets; 7 string sextets; a Septet, Octet, Nonet, and Decet; trios; sonatas; cantatas; 8 masses; etc. He also wrote philosophical poems and mystical plays; contributed dozens of articles on various subjects to music periodicals.

Lachmann, Robert, noted German musicologist; b. Berlin, Nov. 28, 1892; d. Jerusalem, May 8, 1939. He studied languages in Berlin and London; served in the German army during World War I, when he began to collect folk melodies from African and Indian war prisoners; later studied musicology with Stumpf and Johannes Wolf, and Arabic with Mittwoch at the Univ. of Berlin; received his Ph.D. (1922) with the thesis *Die Musik in den tunesischen Städten,* publ. in the *Archiv für Musikwissenschaft* (1923). He was librarian of the music division of the Prussian State Library from 1927 until 1933, when he was ousted by the Nazi authorities as a Jew. In 1935 he went to Jerusalem, where he worked at the Hebrew Univ.

Lachmund, Carl Valentine, American pianist and teacher; b. Booneville, Mo., March 27, 1857; d. Yonkers, N.Y., Feb. 20, 1928. He studied at the Cologne Cons. with Hiller, and later with Liszt, of whom he was one of the last pupils (1881–84); taught at the Scharwenka Cons. in Berlin, and appeared as a pianist, touring America with August Wilhelmj in 1880. Settling in N.Y. in 1891, he established his own cons. He also founded the Women's String Orch., which he directed for 12 seasons.

Lachner, Franz, German composer and conductor, brother of **Ignaz** and **Vincenz Lachner;** b. Rain-am-Lech, April 2, 1803; d. Munich, Jan. 20, 1890. He studied with Sechter and Stadler in Vienna; became an intimate friend of Schubert; from 1827 to 1834 was conductor of the Kärntnertor Theater in Vienna; in 1834, became conductor of the Mannheim Opera; in 1836, court conductor in Munich, then Generalmusikdirektor (1852–65).

Lachner, Ignaz, German organist, conductor, and composer, brother of **Franz** and **Vincenz Lachner;** b. Rain-am-Lech, Sept. 11, 1807; d. Hannover, Feb. 24, 1895. He studied music with his father; in 1824 joined Franz in Vienna, where he became an assistant conductor at the Kärntnertor Theater (1825); in 1828 became assistant Kapellmeister at the Vienna Court Opera. In 1831 he went to Stuttgart as court music director; in 1842, occupied a similar post in Munich; became conductor at the theater in Hamburg (1853); in 1858, became court conductor in Stockholm; in 1861, settled in Frankfurt as a music director.

Lachner, Vincenz, German organist, conductor, and composer, brother of **Franz** and **Ignaz Lachner;** b. Rain-am-Lech, July 19, 1811; d. Karlsruhe, Jan. 22, 1893. He first studied with his father, and later in Vienna with his brothers, succeeding Ignaz as organist and Franz as conductor at the Kärnthnertor Theater there in 1834, and Franz as court Kapellmeister at Mannheim in 1836. He conducted the German opera in London in 1842, and the municipal opera in Frankfurt in 1848. In 1873 he received a pension and settled in Karlsruhe, joining the faculty of the Cons. there in 1884. His 4-part male choruses are celebrated, particularly his settings of nearly all of Scheffel's songs, among the best being *Alt Heidelberg, du feine; Im schwarzen Wallfisch; Nun grüss' dich Gott;* he also wrote symphs., overtures, string quartets, a Piano Quartet, and numerous songs.

Lachnith, Ludwig Wenzel, Bohemian composer; b. Prague, July 7, 1746; d. Paris, Oct. 3, 1820. He was a member of the court orch. in Pfalz-Zweibrücken; in 1773 went to Paris and studied with Rudolph (horn) and Philidor (composition). He is known chiefly for his pasticcios, works in which he combined the music of several different composers; an instance is his oratorio *Saul,* with music taken from scores by Mozart, Haydn, Cimarosa, Paisiello, Gossec, and Philidor. He also arranged the music of Mozart's *Zauberflöte,* to a libretto reworked by Etienne Morel de Chefdeville, and produced it under the title *Les Mystères d'Isis,* justly parodied as *Les Misères d'ici.* In several of his ventures he had the older Kalkbrenner as his collaborator. Original compositions by Lachnith include the operas *L'Heureuse Réconciliation* (1785), *L'Antiquaire* (1789), and *Eugénie et Linval* (1798); 3 piano concertos; chamber music.

Lack, Théodore, French pianist and composer; b. Quimper, Finistère, Sept. 3, 1846; d. Paris, Nov. 25, 1921. A precocious musician, Lack was appointed organist of his village church when he was only 10 years old. At 14 he entered the Paris Cons., where he studied piano with Marmontel, harmony with Bazin, and theory with Lefébure-Wély. Graduating from the Cons. at 18, he became a piano instructor there, and held this position for 57 years (1864–1921) until his death, without ever leaving Paris. He wrote a great many salon pieces for piano (*Tarentelle, Boléro, Etudes élégantes, Valse espagnole, Scènes enfantines, Souvenir d'Alsace, Polonaise de concert,* etc.).

Lacombe, Louis (Trouillon), French pianist and composer; b. Bourges, Nov. 26, 1818; d. Saint-Vaast-la-Hougue, Sept. 30, 1884. He studied at the Paris Cons. with Zimmermann, winning the first piano prize at the age of 13. After touring through France, Belgium, and Germany, he took courses with Czerny, Sechter, and Seyfried in Vienna. Following another concert tour, he settled in Paris (1839), concentrating on composition. WORKS: Melodrama, *L'Amour* (Paris, Dec. 2, 1859); one-act opera, *La Madone* (Paris, Jan. 16, 1861); 2-act comic opera, *Le Tonnelier* (produced as *Meister Martin und seine Gesellen* at Coblenz, March 7, 1897); 4-act grand opera, *Winkelried* (Geneva, Feb. 17, 1892); cantata, *Sapho* (1878; won a prize at the Paris Exhibition); grand *Epopée lyrique* for Orch.; 2 dramatic symphs. with Soli and Chorus: *Manfred* (1847) and *Arva ou Les Hongrois* (1850); *Lassan et Friss,* Hungarian fantasy for Orch.; *Au tombeau d'un héros,* elegy for Violin and Orch.; Quintet for Piano, Violin, Cello, Oboe, and Bassoon; 2 piano trios; numerous piano pieces (*Etudes en octaves; 6 romances sans paroles;* etc.); also choruses. His essay *Philosophie et musique* was publ. posthumously (Paris, 1895).

Lacombe, Paul, French composer; b. Carcassonne, Aude, July 11, 1837; d. there, June 5, 1927. He studied in Carcassonne with François Teysserre, an organist. He was a prolific composer; his works total more than 150, including *Ouverture symphonique* (1876); 3 symphs. (No. 3 won the prize of the Société des Compositeurs de Musique, 1886); *Suite pastorale* for Orch.; *Marche dernière* for Orch.; *Scène au camp* for Orch.; *Dialogue sentimental* for Flute, Bassoon, and Piano (1917); 3 violin sonatas; Cello Sonata; 3 trios; String Quartet; Mass; Requiem; songs; characteristic piano pieces (*Aubade aux mariés, Arabesques,* etc.).

Lacome, Paul (Paul-Jean-Jacques Lacome de l'Estalenx), French composer; b. Houga, Gers, March 4, 1838; d. there, Dec. 12, 1920. In 1860 he went to Paris; became known as a composer of operettas, including *Jeanne, Jeannette et Jeannot* (1876); *Le Beau Nicolas* (1880); *Madame Boniface* (1883); *Myrtille* (1885); *Ma mie Rosette* (1890); *Le Cadeau de noces* (1893); *La Bain de Monsieur* (1895); *Le Maréchal Chaudron* (1898); and *Les Quatre Filles Aymon* (1898); also the orch. suites *Clair de lune, Suite ancienne, La Verbena;* quartets; trios; Psalms; piano pieces (*Les Succès de famille,* etc.); over 200 songs (*L'Estudiantina,* etc.). He publ. *Introduction à la vie musicale* (1911).

Laderman, Ezra, American composer; b. New York, June 29, 1924. He studied at Brooklyn College and at Columbia Univ. with Otto Luening and Douglas Moore (composition) and Paul Henry Lang (musicology); received 3 Guggenheim grants. He taught at Sarah Lawrence College in 1960–61 and again in 1965–66; from 1971 taught at the State Univ. of N.Y. at Binghamton; in 1978 was appointed director of the music program of the National Endowment for the Arts. WORKS: Operas: *Jacob and the Indians* (Woodstock, N.Y., July 26, 1957); *Sarah,* television opera (N.Y., Nov. 30, 1958); *Goodbye to the Clown* (N.Y., May 22, 1960); *The Hunting of the Snark,* children's opera after Lewis Carroll (N.Y., March 25, 1961); *Galileo Galilei,* opera oratorio for television (N.Y., May 14, 1967); reworked into a stage opera, Binghamton, Feb. 4, 1979); *Magic Prison* for 2 Narrators and Orch. (N.Y., June 12, 1967); 4 symphs.: No. 1 (1945); No. 2 (1963–64); No. 3 (1968); No. 4 (1973); Concerto for Orch.; Violin Concerto; *Sonore* for Orch. (Denver, Nov. 10, 1983); *Celestial Bodies* for Flute and Strings; *Double Helix* for Flute, Oboe, and Strings; Nonet for Wind Instruments; Octet for Wind Instruments; 2 piano sonatas. He also wrote the score for the film *The Eleanor Roosevelt Story,* which won an Oscar. His cantata *And David Wept* was produced by CBS Television in N.Y. on April 10, 1971.

Ladmirault, Paul-Emile, French composer; b. Nantes, Dec. 8, 1877; d. Kerbili, near Penestin (Morbihan), Oct. 30, 1944. As a child, he studied piano, organ, and violin; entered the Nantes Cons. in 1892, winning first prize in 1893; he was only 15 when his 3-act opera *Gilles de Retz* was staged in Nantes (May 18, 1893); he entered the Paris Cons. in 1895, studying with Gédalge and Fauré; subsequently returned to Nantes, where he taught at the Cons. His *Suite bretonne* (1902–3) and symph. prelude *Brocéliande au matin* (Colonne concert, Nov. 28, 1909) were extracts from a 2nd opera, *Myrdhin* (1902–9), which was never performed; the ballet *La Prêtresse de Koridwen* was produced at the Paris Opéra (Dec. 17, 1926). Other works include the operetta *Glycère* (Paris, 1928); Symph. (1910); *La Brière* for Orch. (Paris, Nov. 20, 1926); *En forêt,* symph. poem (1932); incidental music to *Tristan et Iseult* (1929); *Valse triste* for Piano and Orch.; *Airs anciens* for Tenor, String Quartet, and Piano (1897); *Ballet bohémien* for Flute, Oboe, Double String Quartet, and Piano (1898); *Fantaisie* for Violin and Piano (1899); *Chanson grecque* for Flute and Piano (1900); Violin Sonata (1901); *De l'ombre à la clarté* for Violin and Piano (1936); piano pieces; songs; many arrangements of Breton folk songs. He contributed articles on music to various periodicals.

La Fage, Juste-Adrien-Lenoir de, eminent French writer on music; b. Paris, March 28, 1801; d. Charenton, March 8, 1862. He studied in Paris with Perne and Choron, and in Rome with Baini. Returning to Paris, he devoted himself to scholarly analysis of music theory. He ended his life at the Charenton Insane Asylum.

Lafont, Charles-Philippe, French violinist and composer; b. Paris, Dec. 1, 1781; d. Tarbes, Aug. 14, 1839. He received his first violin instruction from his mother; then studied in Paris with Kreutzer and Rode. In 1801–8 he toured Europe; then became Rode's successor at the Russian court in St. Petersburg (1808); returned to Paris in 1815 as solo violinist to Louis XVIII. He engaged in a violin-playing debate with Paganini in Milan (1816). During an

extended tour with the pianist Henri Herz beginning in 1831, Lafont was killed in a carriage accident in southern France. He wrote 7 violin concertos; fantasias, variations, etc., for violin with various instrumental groups; about 200 *romances* for voice; and 2 comic operas.

La Forge, Frank, American pianist, vocal teacher, and composer; b. Rockford, Ill., Oct. 22, 1879; d. New York, May 5, 1953. He studied piano with Leschetizky in Vienna; toured Germany, France, Russia, and the U.S. as accompanist to Marcella Sembrich (1908–18) and to Schumann-Heink (1919). In 1920 he settled in N.Y. as a voice teacher; among his students were Lawrence Tibbett, Marian Anderson, Lucrezia Bori, and Richard Crooks. He died while playing the piano at a dinner given by the Musicians Club in N.Y. He wrote many effective songs (*To a Violet, Retreat, Come unto these yellow sands, My love and I, To a Messenger, I came with a song, Before the crucifix,* etc.) and piano pieces (*Gavotte and Musette, Valse de concert, Improvisations,* etc.).

La Guerre, Elisabeth Jacquet de, French composer, organist, and clavecinist; b. Paris, 1659; d. there, June 27, 1729. A member of a family of professional musicians, she evinced talent at an exceptionally early age; was favored by the court of Louis XIV, completing her education under the patronage of Mme. de Montespan. She married Marin de La Guerre, organist of several Paris churches. Her works include an opera, *Céphale et Procris* (Paris, March 15, 1694); a ballet (1691); keyboard suites; a Violin Sonata; cantatas, mostly sacred; etc.

La Guerre, Michel, French organist and composer; b. Paris, c.1605; d. there, Nov. 13, 1679. He was organist at Sainte-Chapelle from 1633 until his death. His historical importance rests upon his being the author of the first French opera, a "comédie de chansons," *Le Triomphe de l'amour sur bergers et bergères* (Paris, Louvre, Jan. 22, 1655), to a libretto by Charles de Beys, court poet. At least, this is the claim made for La Guerre by H. Quittard, in his article "La Première Comédie Française en musique " (*Bulletin Français de la Société Internationale de Musique,* April–May, 1908). The claim is disputed by Romain Rolland and others.

Lahee, Henry, English pianist and composer, father of **Henry Charles Lahee;** b. Chelsea, April 11, 1826; d. London, April 29, 1912. He studied with Sterndale Bennett, C. Potter (piano), and J. Goss (composition). He was organist at Holy Trinity Church, Brompton (1847–74); also a concert pianist; was a member of the Phil. Society. He wrote madrigals and glees: *Hark, how the birds* (1869); *Hence, loathed melancholy* (1878); *Away to the hunt* (1879); *Love in my Bosom* (1880); etc.

Lahee, Henry Charles, American writer on music, son of **Henry Lahee;** b. England, July 2, 1856; d. Hingham, Mass., April 11, 1953, as a result of injuries sustained in an automobile accident. He served in the British mercantile marine (1871–79); in 1880, settled in Boston; was secretary of the New England Cons. (1891–99); then established a musical agency (1899); retired in 1951.

WRITINGS: (all publ. in Boston): *Famous Singers of Today and Yesterday* (1898; new ed., 1936); *Famous Violinists of Today and Yesterday* (1899; 2nd ed., 1912); *Famous Pianists of Today and Yesterday* (1901); *Grand Opera in America* (1902); *The Organ and Its Masters* (1903; new revised ed., 1927); *The Grand Opera Singers of Today* (1922); *Annals of Music in America* (1922; very valuable; contains a chronology of performances of major works); *The Orchestra: A Brief Outline of Its Development in Europe and America* (1925).

La Hèle, George de, composer; b. Antwerp, 1547; d. Madrid, Aug. 27, 1586. After early training as a chorister, he was sent to Madrid to join the royal chapel of Philip II in 1560, remaining in Spain for 10 years. In 1571, he entered the Univ. of Louvain; in 1572, became choirmaster at the church of Saint-Rombaud in Malines, remaining there until 1574, when he accepted a similar post at the Tournai Cathedral; he returned to Madrid in 1582 to take charge of music in the royal chapel. In 1576 he won prizes in the competition at Evreux for his motet *Nonne Deo subjecta* and his chanson *Mais voyez mon cher esmoy.* His 8 masses (1577; printed by Plantin, Antwerp, 1578), dedicated to Philip II, are all parody masses and are modeled on works by Josquin, Lassus, Rore, and Crecquillon; he also wrote other sacred works. A modern edition of his works was compiled by L. Wagner: *Collected Works of George de la Hèle,* in Corpus Mensurabilis Musicae, LVI (1972).

Laidlaw, Anna Robena, English pianist; b. Bretton, Yorkshire, April 30, 1819; d. London, May 29, 1901. She studied in Edinburgh with Robert Müller, in Königsberg, and in London with Henry Herz. In 1837 she played with the Gewandhaus Orch. in Leipzig; continued her successful career as a concert pianist until her marriage in 1855. She was an acquaintance of Schumann, whose *Fantasiestücke* are inscribed to her.

Lajarte, Théodore-Edouard Dufaure de, French writer on music and composer; b. Bordeaux, July 10, 1826; d. Paris, June 20, 1890. He studied at the Paris Cons. with Leborne; was archivist of the Grand Opéra (1873–90). He is best known for his writings on music: *Bibliothèque musicale du Théâtre l'Opéra* (2 vols., 1876–78; reprint, Geneva, 1969); *Instruments Sax et fanfares civiles* (1867); *Traité de composition musicale* (with Bisson; 1880); *Grammaire de la musique* (1880); *Petite encyclopédie musicale* (1881–84); *Curiosités de l'Opéra* (1883); also publ. a collection of *Airs à danser de Lulli à Méhul;* and the series Chefs-d'œuvre Classiques de l'Opéra Français. Early in his career Lajarte wrote the operettas *Monsieur de Floridor* (Paris, Oct. 11, 1880); *Mam-*

zelle Pénélope; Duel du Commandeur; Portrait; Roi de Carreau; the ballet *Les Deux Jumeaux de Bergame* (Paris, Jan. 26, 1886); also marches and dances for military band.

Lajeunesse, Marie Louise Cecilia Emma. See **Albani, Emma.**

Lajtha, László, significant Hungarian composer; b. Budapest, June 30, 1892; d. there, Feb. 16, 1963. He studied piano with Arpád Szendy and theory with Victor von Herzfeld at the Budapest Academy of Music; traveled to Leipzig, Geneva, and Paris; returned to Budapest in 1913 to become an associate of the Ethnographical Dept. of the Hungarian National Museum. From 1919 to 1949 he was a prof. at the National Cons., and after 1952 was prof. of musical folklore at the Academy of Music in Budapest. In 1951 he was awarded the Kossuth Prize for his work on Hungarian folk music. He was a brilliant symphonist; his instrumental music is distinguished by consummate mastery of contrapuntal writing.

WORKS: 3 ballets: *Lysistrata* (1933; Budapest, Feb. 25, 1937); *Le Bosquet des quatre dieux* (1943); *Capriccio* (1944); 10 symphs.: No. 1 (1936); No. 2 (1938); *Les Soli,* symph. for String Orch., Harp, and Percussion (1941); No. 3 (1947–48); No. 4, *Le Printemps* (*The Spring;* 1951); No. 5 (1952; Paris, Oct. 23, 1954); No. 6 (1955; Brussels, Dec. 12, 1960); No. 7 (1957; Paris, April 26, 1958); No. 8 (1959; Budapest, May 21, 1960); No. 9 (1961; posthumous, Paris, May 2, 1963); *Hortobágy Suite* for Orch. (1935); 2 divertissements for Orch. (1936, 1939); *3 Nocturnes* for Chorus and Orch. (1941); *In Memoriam* for Orch. (1941); 2 sinfoniettas for String Orch. (1946, 1956); *11 Variations* for Orch. (1947); *Missa in tono phrygio* for Chorus and Orch. (1949–50); *Dramma per musica,* piano quintet (1922); 10 string quartets (1923; 1926; 1929; 1930; 5 *études,* 1934; 4 *études,* 1942; 1950; 1951; 1953; *Suite Transylvaine,* 1953); Piano Quartet (1925); 3 string trios (1927, 1932, 1945); Piano Trio (1928); Violin Sonatina (1930); Cello Sonata (1932); 2 trios for Harp, Flute, and Cello (1935, 1949); 2 quintets for Flute, Violin, Viola, Cello, and Harp (*Marionettes,* 1937; 1948); *Sonata en concert* for Cello and Piano (1940); *Sonata en concert* for Flute and Piano (1958); *Sonata en concert* for Violin and Piano (1962); *Des esquisses d'un musicien* for Piano (1913); *Contes I* for Piano (1913); Piano Sonata (1914); *Scherzo and Toccata* for Piano (1930); Mass for Chorus and Organ (1951–52).

Lalande, Michel-Richard de. See **Delalande.**

La Laurencie, Lionel de, important French musicologist; b. Nantes, July 24, 1861; d. Paris, Nov. 21, 1933. After studying law and science, he became a pupil of Léon Reynier (violin) and Alphonse Weingartner (harmony), and of Bourgault-Ducoudray at the Paris Cons. In 1898 he became a lecturer at the Ecole des Hautes Etudes Sociales; he contributed regularly to several musical journals.

WRITINGS: *La Légende de Parsifal et le drame*

musical de R. Wagner (1888–94); España (1890); Le Goût musical en France (1905); L'Académie de musique et le concert de Nantes (1906); "Rameau," in Musiciens célèbres (1908); "Lully," in Les Maîtres de la Musique (1911); "Contribution à l'histoire de la symphonie française vers 1750," L'Année Musicale (with G. de Saint-Foix; 1911); Les Créateurs de l'opéra français (1920; 2nd ed., 1930); L'Ecole française de violon, de Lully à Viotti (3 vols., 1922–24); Les Luthistes, in Musiciens célèbres (1928); La Chanson royale en France (1928); Inventaire critique du fonds Blancheton à la Bibliothèque du Conservatoire (2 vols., 1930–31); Chansons au luth et airs du XVIᵉ siècle (with Thibault and Mairy; 1931); Orfée de Gluck (1934). In 1916 La Laurencie became editor of Lavignac's Encyclopédie de la musique et dictionnaire du Conservatoire, to which he contributed articles on French music of the 17th and 18th centuries. The Catalogue des livres de musiciens de la bibliothèque de l'Arsénal à Paris, ed. by La Laurencie and A. Gastoué, was publ. in 1936.

Lalewicz, Georg, Russian pianist; b. Suwalki, Poland, Aug. 21, 1875; d. Buenos Aires, Dec. 1, 1951. He studied piano with Annette Essipov and composition with Liadov and Rimsky-Korsakov at the St. Petersburg Cons. Upon graduation, he taught piano at the Odessa Cons. (1902–5), the Cracow Cons. (1905–12), and the Vienna Imperial Academy (1912–19). In 1921 he went to Argentina, settling in Buenos Aires as a prof. at the Cons. Nacional; changed his name to **Jorge Lalewicz.** An international prize for piano performance was established in his memory in 1952.

Laliberté, Alfred (full Christian name, **Joseph François Alfred**), Canadian pianist and composer; b. St. Jean, Quebec, Feb. 10, 1882; d. Montreal, May 7, 1952. He studied in Berlin (1900–1905) with Lutzenko (piano) and Klatte (theory); later took lessons with Teresa Carreño. In 1906 he formed a friendship with Scriabin and became an ardent propagandist of his music. Laliberté wrote an opera, Sœur Béatrice (after Maeterlinck), 2 string quartets, several piano pieces (some on Canadian themes); also made arrangements of some 800 Canadian songs. Most of his music remains in MS; a few original songs have been publ.

Lalo, Edouard (-Victoire-Antoine), distinguished French composer (of Spanish descent); b. Lille, Jan. 27, 1823; d. Paris, April 22, 1892. He studied with Baumann at the Lille branch of the Paris Cons.; then at the Paris Cons. with Habeneck (violin) and Schulhoff and Crèvecœur (composition); he played with equal skill on the violin and viola, and was violist of the Armingaud-Jacquard Quartet, a group organized in Paris for the purpose of spreading the works of the German masters. In 1848–49 he publ. his first songs (L'Adieu au désert, L'Ombre de Dieu, Le Novice, 6 Romances populaires de Béranger) and subsequently some chamber music. All of this music met with indifference, and Lalo was discouraged to the point of abandoning composition

for several years; his ambition, however, was stimulated again by his marriage (in 1865) to **Mlle. Bernier de Maligny,** a fine contralto singer, who performed many of his songs. He wrote a 3-act opera, Fiesque, and sent the score to the competition established in 1867 by the Théâtre-Lyrique; it was ranked 3rd, and failed to reach production; the ballet music from it was performed under the title Divertissement at the Concert Populaire (Dec. 8, 1872), with excellent success. His next signal success was the performance of his Violin Concerto, played by Sarasate (Jan. 18, 1874) at a Châtelet concert; then came his most famous work, Symphonie espagnole, also performed by Sarasate (Feb. 7, 1875). This work, a true virtuoso piece with vibrant Spanish rhythms, became one of the greatest favorites in the violin repertoire, and secured for Lalo international fame. His Fantaisie norvégienne for Violin and Orch. followed; it was subsequently rearranged for orch. alone, and performed as Rapsodie norvégienne (Colonne Concerts, Oct. 26, 1879). He had not, however, abandoned his efforts at writing for the stage. As early as 1875 he began work on the opera Le Roi d'Ys; after several revisions, the work was produced at the Opéra-Comique (May 7, 1888), obtaining enormous success; repeated performances followed, in France and elsewhere in Europe; the American premiere took place at New Orleans, Jan. 23, 1890. In 1888 Lalo was made an officer of the Legion of Honor; also was awarded the Prix Monbinne by the Académie des Beaux-Arts. Besides the works already mentioned, there were the following: one act from an unfinished opera, La Jacquerie (completed by Artur Coquard; posthumously produced in Monte Carlo, March 9, 1895); ballets: Namouna (Paris, March 6, 1882) and Néron (Paris, March 28, 1891); 3 symphs., 2 of them unpubl.; Cello Concerto (Paris, Dec. 9, 1877); Piano Concerto (1889); 3 piano trios; String Quartet; Violin Sonata; 4 impromptus for Violin and Piano; Soirées parisiennes for Violin and Piano; Guitare for Violin and Piano; Cello Sonata; songs.

Laloy, Louis, French musicologist and critic; b. Grey, Haute-Saône, Feb. 18, 1874; d. Dôle, March 3, 1944. He studied philosophy in Paris, receiving the degree of docteur ès lettres in 1904; in 1899–1905, was also a pupil of Breéille and d'Indy at the Schola Cantorum. He was co-founder (1901) of the Revue d'Histoire et de Critique Musicale; in 1905 he founded, with J. Marnold, the Mercure Musical; contributed articles to Revue de Paris, Grande Revue, Mercure de France, and Gazette des Beaux-Arts. He publ. Aristoxène de Tarente et la musique de l'antiquité (1904); Rameau (1908); Debussy (1909; new ed., 1944); Notes sur la musique cambodgienne (in the Bericht über den zweiten Kongress of the Internationale Musik-Gesellschaft at Basel, 1906; publ. in Leipzig, 1907); La Musique chinoise (1910); The Future of Music (London, 1910); "L'Opéra," in Cinquante ans de musique française, 1874–1923 (1924); La Musique retrouvée, 1902–27 (1928); Une Heure de musique avec Beethoven (1930). He also provided the poem for Roussel's opera-ballet *Padmâvati* and for Debussy's *Ode à la France;* publ. a vol. of transcriptions of Chinese compositions; and supplied the French versions of a number of Russian opera librettos.

La Mara. See **Lipsius, Marie.**

LaMarchina, Robert, American cellist and conductor; b. New York, Sept. 3, 1928. He studied cello with his father; appeared as a *wunderkind* in public; continued his studies with Gregor Piatigorsky and Emanuel Feuermann; in 1944 played in the NBC Symph. under Toscanini; later joined the Los Angeles Phil.; sporadically conducted orchs. near and around Los Angeles; ultimately became primarily a conductor. From 1967 to 1979 he conducted the Honolulu Symph. Orch.

La Marre (Lamare), Jacques-Michel-Hurel de, French cellist; b. Paris, May 1, 1772; d. Caen, March 27, 1823. He toured Europe, including Russia, with great success; Clementi called him "the Rode of the violoncello." Four cello concertos and an *air varié* publ. under La Marre's name are actually by Auber.

Lambert, Constant, English composer, conductor, and writer on music; b. London, Aug. 23, 1905; d. there, Aug. 21, 1951. He was a member of an artistic family; studied at the Royal College of Music with R.O. Morris and Vaughan Williams. While he was still a student, Diaghilev commissioned a ballet from him (*Romeo and Juliet;* Monte Carlo, May 4, 1926). This early association with the dance proved decisive, for Lambert spent most of his life as a composer and conductor of ballets. His compositions are notable for the assimilation of a jazz idiom: in his *Elegiac Blues* (1927), in his very successful *Rio Grande* (on a poem of Sacheverell Sitwell) for Solo Piano, Chorus, and Orch. (Manchester, Dec. 12, 1929), and in his Piano Sonata (1928–29) and Piano Concerto with Small Orch. (1931). He wrote the ballets *Pomona* (Buenos Aires, Sept. 9, 1927) and *Horoscope* (London, Jan. 27, 1938); *The Bird Actors,* overture for Orch. (1925); *Summer's Last Will and Testament,* masque for Chorus and Orch. (after Thomas Nashe; London, Jan. 29, 1936); *King Pest* for Orch. (London, 1937); *Aubade héroïque* for Orch. (1942); *Prizefight* for Band (1923); *8 Chinese Songs* (on poems by Li-Po). Lambert also transcribed and edited works by Boyce, Handel, Roseingrave, etc.; rescored Vaughan Williams's *Job* for theater orch. (1931). He was music critic of the *Sunday Referee,* and publ. a provocative book, *Music Ho! A Study of Music in Decline* (London, 1934).

Lambert, Herbert, English clavichord and harpsichord maker; b. Bath, Dec. 22, 1881; d. there, March 7, 1936. Originally a professional photographer, he turned his craftsmanship and research activity to the building of old keyboard instruments, especially clavichords. His name is perpetuated in *Lambert's Clavichord* (1928), a small book of compositions for this instrument by Herbert Howells.

Lambert, Lucien, French composer and pianist; b. Paris, Jan. 5, 1858; d. Oporto, Portugal, Jan. 21, 1945. He studied first with his father; after a tour of America and Europe, returned to Paris to study at the Cons. with Dubois and Massenet, taking the Prix Rossini in 1885 with his cantata *Prométhée enchaîné.* He settled in Portugal in 1914; was a prof. of composition at the Oporto Cons. (1922–37).
  WORKS: Operas: *Brocéliande* (Rouen, Feb. 25, 1893); *Le Spahi* (Paris, Oct. 18, 1897); *La Marseillaise* (Paris, July 14, 1900); *La Flamenca* (Paris, Oct. 31, 1903); *Harald* (1937); *Penticosa; La Sorcière;* ballets: *La Roussalka* (Paris, Dec. 8, 1911) and *Les Cloches de Porto* (1937); *Florette,* lyric comedy (1921); *Légende roumaine,* symph. poem; *Fantaisie monothématique* for Orch., on an oriental theme (Paris, March 19, 1933); *Tanger le soir,* Moorish rhapsody for Orch.; *Esquisses créoles,* orch. suite, on themes by Gottschalk; *Andante et fantaisie tzigane* for Piano and Orch.; String Quartet; String Sextet; Mass; piano pieces; songs.

Lambert, Michel, French lutenist and singer; b. Champigny-sur-Veude, near Chinon (Indre-et-Loire), 1610; d. Paris, June 29, 1696. He was master of chamber music at the court of Louis XIV; also a celebrated singing teacher. His daughter married Lully. He publ. *Airs et brunettes* (1666; 2nd ed., 1689) and *Airs et dialogues* (1698; posthumous).

Lamond, Frederic Archibald, Scottish pianist; b. Glasgow, Jan. 28, 1868; d. Stirling, Feb. 21, 1948. He played organ as a boy in a local church; also studied oboe and violin; in 1882, entered the Raff Cons. in Frankfurt, studying with Heermann (violin), Max Schwarz (piano), and Urspruch (composition); then piano with Hans von Bülow, Clara Schumann, and Liszt. A brilliant concert pianist, Lamond appeared in Berlin, Vienna, London, N.Y., and in Russia. He became renowned for his skillful interpretation of Beethoven; publ. an edition of Beethoven's sonatas (1923). He married Irene Triesch, a German actress, in 1904 and settled in Berlin, until the outbreak of World War II, when he moved to London. He was also a composer; wrote a Symph. (Glasgow, Dec. 23, 1889), some chamber music, and numerous piano pieces. He publ. an interesting vol. of reminiscences about Liszt and others, entitled *Memoirs* (Glasgow, 1949).

La Montaine, John, American composer; b. Oak Park, Ill., March 17, 1920. He studied piano in Chicago with Rudolph Ganz, and in Rochester at the Eastman School of Music, with Howard Hanson and Bernard Rogers; at the Juilliard School in N.Y. with Bernard Wagenaar; and with Nadia Boulanger. He received 2 Guggenheim fellowships in composition (1959, 1960); in 1962 served as composer-in-residence at the American Academy in Rome; was a visiting prof. at the Eastman School of Music in 1964–65. He received the Pulitzer Prize for his Piano Concerto in 1959. In 1977 he became holder of the Nixon Chair as a Nixon Distinguished Scholar at Nixon's alma mater, Whittier College, in California.

WORKS: Piano Concerto (Washington, D.C., Nov. 25, 1958); *Jubilant Overture; Colloquy* for String Orch.; Symph. No. 1; *From Sea to Shining Sea* for Orch.; *Novellis, Novellis,* Christmas pageant opera (Washington Cathedral, Dec. 24, 1961); *The Shepherdes Playe,* opera television production (Washington, Dec. 24, 1967); *Erode the Great,* cantata (Washington, Dec. 30, 1969); *Be Glad, Then, America,* Bicentennial opera (Univ. Park, Pa., Feb. 6, 1976); *Birds of Paradise* for Piano and Orch.; Te Deum; *Songs of the Rose of Sharon* for Soprano and Orch.; Cello Sonata; String Quartet; Flute Concerto (1981); organ pieces; songs.

Lamote de Grignon, Juan, Catalan conductor and composer; b. Barcelona, July 7, 1872; d. there, March 11, 1949. He studied at the Cons. of Barcelona, and upon graduation, taught piano there; made his debut as a conductor in Barcelona (April 26, 1902). In 1910 he founded the Orquesta Sinfónica of Barcelona, which carried on its activity until 1924; also led the municipal band (from 1914).

WORKS: One-act opera, *Hesperia* (Barcelona, Jan. 25, 1907); for Orch.: *Andalucía; Hispanicas; Scherzo; Cantos populares españoles; Poema romántico;* oratorio, *La Nit de Nadal;* numerous songs: *12 chansons catalanes; Violetas; 3 motetes; 3 cantos espirituales; Passioneras;* etc. He publ. *Musique et musiciens français à Barcelona, catalans à Paris* (Barcelona, 1935).

Lamoureux, Charles, noted French conductor and violinist; b. Bordeaux, Sept. 28, 1834; d. Paris, Dec. 21, 1899. He studied at the Paris Cons. with Girard (violin), taking first prize in 1854; also studied with Tolbecque (harmony), Leborne (counterpoint), and Alexis Chauvet (theory). In 1850 he became solo violinist in the Théâtre du Gymnase orch.; then became a member of the Paris Opéra orch. In 1860 he and Colonne, Adam, and A. Pilet founded a society for chamber music; in 1873, he organized the Société de l'Harmonie Sacrée; he became known as conductor of the Cons. Concerts (1872–73); was conductor of the Paris Opéra (1877–79). He founded the celebrated Concerts Lamoureux (Nouveaux Concerts) on Oct. 23, 1881; retired as its conductor in 1897, and was succeeded by his son-in-law, Chevillard. More than any other French musician, Lamoureux educated Parisians to appreciate Wagner; he was responsible not only for highly competent performances of classical masterpieces, but also for presentation of compositions of his contemporaries.

Lampe, Walther, German pianist, composer and pedagogue; b. Leipzig, April 28, 1872; d. Munich, Jan. 23, 1964. He studied piano with Clara Schumann; composition with Knorr in Frankfurt and with Humperdinck in Berlin; was a prof. of piano at the Munich Academy of Music from 1920 to 1937. His edition of Mozart piano sonatas (2 vols., Munich, 1954), based on the original MSS, is valuable. Among his works are piano pieces and songs.

Lamperti, Francesco, Italian singing teacher; b. Savona, March 11, 1811; d. Cernobbio, May 1, 1892. He studied at the Milan Cons.; was director at the Teatro Filodrammatico in Lodi; tutored many distinguished singers, including Albani, Mme. Artôt, both Cruvelis, Campanini, Collini, and Mme. Lagrange; taught at the Milan Cons. (1850–75). He publ. *Guida teorico-pratico-elementare per lo studi del canto; Studi di bravura per soprano; Esercizi giornalieri per soprano o mezzo-soprano; L'arte del canto; Osservazioni e consigli sul trillo; Solfeggi;* etc. His methods and studies in voice production have also appeared in Eng. trans.: *Studies in Bravura Singing for the Soprano Voice* (N.Y., 1875); *A Treatise on the Art of Singing* (London, 1877; revised ed., N.Y., 1890).

Lamperti, Giovanni Battista, Italian singing teacher, son of **Francesco Lamperti;** b. Milan, June 24, 1839; d. Berlin, March 18, 1910. At the age of 9 he was a choirboy at the Milan Cathedral; studied piano and voice at the Milan Cons.; served as accompanist in his father's class there. He taught first in Milan; subsequently in Dresden for 20 years; then in Berlin. Among his pupils were Sembrich, Schumann-Heink, Bulss, Stagno, etc. He publ. *Die Technik des Bel Canto* (1905; Eng. trans. by T. Baker; N.Y., 1905); *Scuola di canto* (8 vols. of solfeggi and vocalises); other technical exercises. His pupil W.E. Brown publ. *Vocal Wisdom; Maxims of G.B. Lamperti* (N.Y., 1931; new ed., 1957).

Lanchbery, John, English conductor; b. London, May 15, 1923. He studied at the Royal Academy of Music in London; was then music director of the Metropolitan Ballet (1948–50) and the Sadler's Wells Theatre Ballet (1951–60); subsequently occupied a similar post with the Royal Ballet at Covent Garden (1960–72). In 1972 he was named music director of the Australian Ballet.

Land, Jan Pieter Nicholaas, Dutch orientalist and musicologist; b. Delft, April 23, 1834; d. Arnhem, April 30, 1897. In 1864 he was prof. of classical and oriental languages and of philosophy at the Amsterdam Academy; then was prof. of philosophy at Leyden Univ. (1872–94). He was an accomplished linguist, specializing in Semitic philology; was deeply interested in musico-historical research, to which he made most valuable contributions.

WRITINGS: *Noord Nederlands muziekgeschiedenis* (1874–81); *Over de toonladders der arabische muziek* (1880); *Musique et musiciens au XVIIᵉ siècle. Correspondance et œuvres musicales de Constantijn Huygens* (with Jonckbloet; Leyden, 1882); *Recherches sur l'histoire de la gamme arabe* (Leyden, 1884); *Essai de notation musicale chez les arabes et les persans* (1885); *Over onze kennis der javaansche muziek* (Amsterdam, 1891).

Landi, Stefano, Italian singer and composer; b. Rome, c.1586; d. there, Oct. 28, 1639. He studied at the Collegio Germanico in Rome; attended the Seminario Romano from 1602 to 1607. In 1618–20 he was maestro di cappella to Bishop Cornaro of Padua; returned to Rome in 1620, and was appointed to a similar post at Santa Maria dei Monti (1624); in 1629, became contralto singer at the Cappella Giulia, St. Peter's. He was one of the most eminent contrapuntists of the Roman school; was a pupil of the 2 Naninis; was one of the creators of the cantata, and one of the earliest operatic composers in Rome.

WORKS: *La morte d'Orfeo,* pastoral opera (Venice, 1619); *Il Sant' Alessio,* sacred opera (Rome, Feb. 23, 1632); also *Missa in benedictione nuptiarum* for 6 Voices (1628); a book of masses a cappella for 4–5 Voices; madrigals for 4–5 Voices (1619 and 1624); arias for one to 2 Voices (5 vols., 1620–38); etc.

Landini (Landino), Francesco, Italian instrumentalist and composer; b. Fiesole, 1325; d. Florence, Sept. 2, 1397. Blinded by smallpox as a youth, he turned early to music, becoming proficient in the art of playing the lute, guitar, flute, and organ. He was one of the most celebrated organ virtuosos of his time; was known as "Francesco degli organi." He studied with Giovanni da Cascia and Jacopo da Bologna; was organist at the monastery of Santa Trinità in 1361; from 1365 until his death was "cappellanus" at the church of San Lorenzo in Florence. Although not the first, he was probably the most famous master of the Florentine "Ars nova" of the 14th century; his works, of which more than 150 are preserved in the libraries of Italy and southern Germany, represent about a quarter of extant Italian 14th-century music; he wrote madrigals, *cacce, ballate,* etc. Modern reprints: *The Works of Francesco Landini,* ed. by L. Ellinwood (Medieval Academy of America Publication 36; Cambridge, Mass., 1939); *The Works of Francesco Landini,* ed. by L. Schrade (Polyphonic Music of the 14th Century, vol. 4; Monaco, 1958).

Landon, H(arold) C(handler) Robbins, eminent American musicologist; b. Boston, March 6, 1926. He studied music history and theory with Alfred J. Swan at Swarthmore College, and composition there with Harl McDonald; he also took a course in English literature with W.H. Auden (1943–45); then went to Boston, where he enrolled in the musicology class of Karl Geiringer at Boston Univ. (B.Mus., 1947). In 1948 he traveled to Europe and settled in Vienna; in 1949 he founded the Haydn Society, with a view to preparing a complete edition of Haydn's works. He also instituted an energetic campaign to locate music MSS which had disappeared or been removed; thus, he succeeded in finding the MS of Haydn's Mass No. 13; he also found the MS of the so-called Jena Symph., erroneously ascribed to Beethoven, and proved that it had actually been composed by Friedrich Witt. In 1983 Landon discovered and edited for performance Handel's *Roman Vespers.* In *The Symphonies of Joseph Haydn* (London, 1955; supplement, 1961), he analyzes each symph. and suggests solutions for numerous problems of authenticity; in his new edition of the symphs. (Vienna, 1965–68), he carefully establishes the version nearest to the original authentic text. He subsequently publ. his massive study *Haydn: Chronicle and Works* in 5 vols. (Bloomington, Ind., and London): Vol. I, *Haydn: The Early Years, 1732–1765* (1980); Vol. II, *Hadyn at Esterháza, 1766–1790* (1978); Vol. III, *Haydn in England, 1791–1795* (1976); Vol. IV, *Haydn: The Years of "The Creation," 1796–1800* (1977); Vol. V, *Haydn: The Late Years, 1801–1809* (1977). His other publications include *The Mozart Companion* (ed. with Donald Mitchell; London, 1956; 2nd ed., revised, 1965); *The Collected Correspondence and London Notebooks of Joseph Haydn* (London, 1959); a foreword with many emendations to C.S. Terry's *John Christian Bach* (London, 1929; 2nd ed., revised, 1967); *Beethoven: A Documentary Study* (London, 1970); *Essays on the Viennese Classical Style: Gluck, Haydn, Mozart, Beethoven* (London and N.Y., 1970); *Haydn: A Documentary Study* (London, 1981); *Mozart and the Masons* (London, 1983). During Landon's early years in Europe, his wife, Christa Landon (1922–77), joined him as a research partner in the search for rare MSS in libraries, churches, and monasteries. She publ. editions of works by Haydn, Mozart, and Bach; her edition of Haydn's piano sonatas (Vienna, 1963) supersedes the one by Hoboken. In 1983 Landon was named Distinguished Prof. of the Humanities at Middlebury College in Vermont.

Landormy, Paul (Charles-René), French musicologist and critic; b. Issy, Jan. 3, 1869; d. Paris, Nov. 17, 1943. For a number of years he taught philosophy in the provinces; going to Paris in 1892, he studied singing with Sbriglia and Pol Plançon. With Romain Rolland he organized a series of lectures on music history at the Ecole des Hautes Etudes Sociales; established an acoustic laboratory there; was music critic of *La Victoire* (1918); also contributed articles to *Le Temps* and various other journals. He publ. *Histoire de la musique* (Paris, 1910; augmented ed., 1923; Eng. trans., N.Y., 1923); *Brahms* (1920) and *Bizet* (1924) in the series Les Maîtres de la Musique; *La Vie de Schubert* (Paris, 1928); *Gluck* (Paris, 1941); *Gounod* (Paris, 1942); *La Musique française de Franck à Debussy* (Paris, 1943).

Landowska, Wanda (Alexandra), celebrated harpsichordist and authority on old music; b. Warsaw, July 5, 1879; d. Lakeville, Conn., Aug. 16, 1959. She studied piano at the Warsaw Cons. with Michalowski and in Berlin with Moszkowski. In 1900 she went to Paris, where she married Henry Lew, a writer. She traveled widely in Europe as a pianist; in 1909 made a tour of Russia, and played for Tolstoy, who showed great interest in her ideas on classical music. Subsequently, she devoted her efforts principally to reviving the art of playing upon the harpsichord. In 1912 she commissioned the Pleyel firm of Paris to construct a harpsichord for her; this was the first of the many keyboard instruments built for her in subsequent years. In 1913 she was invited by Kretzschmar to give a special course in harpsichord playing at the Berlin Hochschule für Musik. The outbreak of World War I found her in

Germany, and she was interned there until the Armistice; in 1918 her husband was killed in an automobile accident in Berlin. In 1919 she gave master classes of harpsichord playing at the Basel Cons.; then returned to Paris. In 1925 she bought a villa in St.-Leu-la-Forêt, near Paris, and established there a school for the study of early music. A concert hall was built there in 1927; she presented regular concerts of early music, and gave lessons on the subject; also assembled a large collection of harpsichords. Her school attracted students from all over the world; she also taught at the Cons. of Fontainebleau, and frequently appeared at concerts in Paris, both as a pianist and as a harpsichordist. She commissioned Manuel de Falla to compose a Chamber Concerto for Harpsichord, and played the solo part in its first performance in Barcelona (Nov. 5, 1926); another commission was Poulenc's *Concert champêtre* for Harpsichord and Small Orch. (Paris, May 3, 1929). She appeared for the first time in America on Nov. 20, 1923, as soloist with the Philadelphia Orch., under Stokowski; then returned to France. When the Germans invaded France in 1940, Landowska fled to Switzerland, abandoning her villa, her library, and her instruments. In 1941 she reached N.Y.; presented a concert of harpsichord music there on Feb. 21, 1942; then devoted herself mainly to teaching; also made recordings; settled in her new home at Lakeville, Conn. She is acknowledged as one of the greatest performers on the modern harpsichord; her interpretations of Baroque music are notable in their balance between Classical precision and freedom from rigidity, particularly in the treatment of ornamentation. She wrote *Bach et ses interprètes* (Paris, 1906); *Musique ancienne* (Paris, 1909; 7th ed., 1921; Eng. trans., N.Y., 1924); many articles in various French and German magazines (on Bach, Chopin, harpsichord playing, etc.). A collection of her articles was publ. posthumously under the title *Landowska on Music,* edited and trans. by Denise Restout and Robert Hawkins (N.Y., 1964). She also wrote cadenzas for Mozart's concertos.

Landowski, Marcel, French composer; b. Prêt L'Abbé (Finistère), Feb. 18, 1915. He studied with Büsser, Gaubert, and Munch; has been active as a conductor as well as a composer. His works include the opera *Le Rire de Nils Halerius* (Mulhouse, Jan. 19, 1951); oratorio, *Rythmes du monde* (1941); *Clairs-Obscurs,* suite for Orch. (Paris, 1938); *Edina,* symph. poem (1946); *Le Petit Poucet,* symph. suite (Paris, 1947); Symph. (Paris, 1949); Piano Concerto (Paris, March 1, 1942); Cello Concerto (Paris, 1946); *Le Ventriloque,* lyric comedy (Paris, Feb. 8, 1957); *Les Adieux,* one-act lyric drama (Paris, Oct. 8, 1960); *L'Orage,* symph. poem (1961); *L'Opéra de poussière,* opera in 2 acts (Avignon, Oct. 25, 1962); *Les Notes de nuit* for Narrator and Orch. (Boulogne, Dec. 16, 1962); Piano Concerto No. 2 (Paris, Feb. 28, 1964); Symph. No. 2 (Strasbourg, June 24, 1965); Symph. No. 3 (1965); Concerto for Flute and String Orch. (1968); also music for films.

Landowski, Mme. W.-L. (Alice-Wanda), French writer on music; b. Paris, Nov. 28, 1899; d. there, April 18, 1959. She studied piano in Paris at the Marguerite Long School; theory with Gustave Bret. She taught music history at the Cons. of Clermont; in 1945, became a prof. at the Rouen Cons., a branch of the Paris Cons.; also was engaged as music critic of *Le Parisien.* She adopted the initials W.-L. (L. for Ladislas, her father's name) to avoid confusion with Wanda Landowska, who was not a relation.

Landré, Guillaume (Louis Frédéric), important Dutch composer, son of **Willem Landré;** b. The Hague, Feb. 24, 1905; d. Amsterdam, Nov. 6, 1968. He took music lessons from Zagwijn and Pijper (1924–29); studied jurisprudence at Utrecht Univ., receiving a master's degree in 1929; then was a teacher of economics in Amsterdam (1930–47). He was general secretary of the Netherlands Arts Council (1947–58) and president of the Society of Netherlands Composers (1950–62). As a composer, he endeavored to revive the spirit and the polyphonic technique of the national Flemish School of the Renaissance in a 20th-century guise, with euphonious dissonances and impressionistic dynamics creating the modern aura. In his later works he experimented with serial devices.

Landré, Willem, Dutch writer on music and composer, father of **Guillaume Landré;** b. Amsterdam, June 12, 1874; d. Eindhoven, Jan. 1, 1948. He was a pupil of Bernard Zweers. In 1901 he became music critic of the *Oprechte Haarlemsche Courant* in Haarlem; was music editor of the *Nieuwe Courant* in The Hague (1901–5), then of the *Nieuwe Rotterdamsche Courant* in Rotterdam (1905–37); taught theory, composition, and the history of music at the Rotterdam Cons.; was editor of *Caecilia, Het Muziekcollege.*

Lane, Eastwood, American composer; b. Brewerton, N.Y., May 22, 1879; d. Central Square, Oswego County, N.Y., Jan. 22, 1951. He attended Syracuse Univ.; then devoted himself to composition. His works are mostly in a light, descriptive vein, for piano; 2 of his piano sketches, *Sea Burial* and *Persimmon Pucker,* were orchestrated by Ferde Grofé for performance by Paul Whiteman; other works are piano suites: *Sleepy Hollow, Adirondack Sketches,* and *5 American Dances;* he also wrote 2 ballets: *Abelard and Heloise* and *A Caravan from China Comes.*

Lane, Louis, American conductor; b. Eagle Pass, Texas, Dec. 25, 1923. He studied at the Univ. of Texas, at the Eastman School of Music in Rochester, N.Y., and at the Berkshire at Music Center in Tanglewood. In 1947 he won a competition to become apprentice conductor to George Szell, the music director of the Cleveland Orch.; in 1956 he was appointed assistant conductor to Szell. In 1959 he was appointed regular conductor of the Akron (Ohio) Symph. Orch. In addition, he appeared as guest conductor with the Chicago Symph. Orch. and with the Detroit Symph. Orch. He conducted several Cleveland Orch. concerts during its 1965 European (and Russian) tour. From 1970 to 1973 he was resident conductor of the Cleveland Orch.; in 1968–73 was associate director of the Blossom Festival School; in 1973 was named principal guest conductor, and in 1974–77 co-principal conductor, of the Dallas Symph. In 1971 he was awarded the prestigious Mahler Medal. In 1983 he became principal conductor of the National Symph. Orch. of the South African Broadcasting Corp. and also principal guest conductor of the Atlanta Symph. Orch.

Lang, Benjamin Johnson, American pianist and conductor; b. Salem, Mass., Dec. 28, 1837; d. Boston, April 3, 1909. He studied with his father and with Alfred Jaëll. In 1855 he went to Berlin for advanced studies; for a time took piano lessons with Liszt. Returning to America, he was engaged as a church organist; was also organist of the Handel and Haydn Society in Boston for many years (1859–95); then was its conductor (1895–97); directed the Apollo Club and the Cecilia Society from their foundation (1868 and 1874, respectively); gave numerous concerts of orchestral, choral, and chamber music on his own account. As a pianist, teacher, conductor, and organizer, he was in the first rank of Boston musicians for a third of a century, and brought out a long list of important works by European and American composers. Among his pupils were Arthur Foote and Ethelbert Nevin. He was also a composer; wrote an oratorio, *David,* and a great many sacred works; also songs and piano pieces.

Lang, Josephine, German composer of art songs, daughter of the German singer **Sabina Hitzelberger;** b. Munich, March 14, 1815; d. Tübingen, Dec. 2, 1880. She studied music with her mother and also took lessons with Mendelssohn; composed and publ. a considerable number of surprisingly competent lieder in an amiably songful, Germanically Romantic vein, in addition to some very playable piano pieces. She was married to a poet who wrote under the nom de plume Christian Reinhold.

Lang, Margaret Ruthven, American composer, daughter of **Benjamin J. Lang;** b. Boston, Nov. 27, 1867; d. Boston, May 29, 1972, at the age of 104(!). She studied in Boston with her father and later in Munich; also with Chadwick and MacDowell. Her works include the overture *Witichis* (1893); *Dramatic Overture* (1893); the overture *Totila; Ballade* for Orch. (1901); *Sappho's Prayer to Aphrodite,* aria for Contralto, with Orch. (1895); *Phoebus,* aria for Baritone and Orch.; *In the Manger* for Mixed Choir; *The Heavenly Noël* for Solo, Women's Chorus, Piano, and String Orch.; *Christmas Cycle* for Vocal Quartet; piano pieces; some 200 songs. She stopped composing about 1930. She attended Boston Symph. concerts from their foundation; was present at a concert 3 days before her 100th birthday, at which Erich Leinsdorf included in the program the psalm tune *Old Hundredth* in her honor.

Lang, Paul Henry, eminent American musicologist and teacher; b. Budapest, Aug. 28, 1901. He studied bassoon and piano; took courses in composition at the Budapest Music Academy with Kodály and Leo Weiner; played bassoon in various orch. groups in Budapest; also appeared as a pianist in chamber music recitals; was chorus répétiteur at the Royal Opera in Budapest (1923–24); then attended the Univ. of Heidelberg, and the Sorbonne in Paris, where he studied musicology with André Pirro (1924–28); in 1928 he went to the U.S., where he enrolled in Cornell Univ., in the class of Otto Kinkeldey; obtained his Ph.D. in 1934 with the dissertation *A Literary History of French Opera.* He was an assistant prof. at Vassar College (1930–31); associate prof., Wells College (1931–33); visiting lecturer, Wellesley College (1934–35); associate prof. of musicology, Columbia Univ. (1933–39); full prof., 1939; emeritus, 1970. He was vice-president of the American Musicological Society (1947–49) and president of the International Musicological Society (1955–58). From 1945 to 1972 he was editor of the *Musical Quarterly;* from 1954 to 1963, music editor of the *N.Y. Herald Tribune.* He publ. a valuable and very popular vol., *Music in Western Civilization* (N.Y., 1941; many subsequent reprints); an important biography, *George Frideric Handel* (N.Y., 1966); *Critic at the Opera* (N.Y., 1971); further brought out *A Pictorial History of Music* (with O. Bettman, N.Y., 1963); edited *One Hundred Years of Music,* a collection of articles marking the centennial of the G. Schirmer, Inc., music publishing house (N.Y., 1961); *Problems of Modern Music* (N.Y., 1962; separate publication of articles from the *Musical Quarterly,* 1960); *Stravinsky. A New Appraisal of His Work* (N.Y., 1963); *The Creative World of Mozart* (N.Y., 1963); *Contemporary Music in Europe. A Comprehensive Survey* (with Nathan Broder; N.Y., 1965; a reprint of the semicentennial issue of the *Musical Quarterly*).

Lang, Walter, Swiss pianist and composer; b. Basel, Aug. 19, 1896; d. Baden, Switzerland, March 17, 1966. He was a pupil of Jaques-Dalcroze; taught at the Dalcroze School in Geneva; then studied in Munich with Klose, and in Zürich with Andreae and W. Frey; appeared as a concert pianist and as an accompanist; then taught theory in Basel (1920–22); was a prof. of piano at the Zürich Cons. (1922–41); music director of Monte Ceneri Radio (1942–48); in 1948, he became an instructor at the Basel Cons. He was married to the coloratura soprano **Mimi Lang-Seiber.**

Langdon, Michael, English bass; b. Wolverhampton, Nov. 12, 1920. He studied at the Guildhall School of Music in London; subsequently took voice lessons with Alfred Jerger in Vienna, Maria Carpi in Geneva, and Otakar Kraus in London. In 1948 he joined the chorus at the Royal Opera House, Covent Garden; made his operatic debut there in 1950. He created several bass roles in operas by Benjamin Britten; was also noted for his command of the standard operatic repertoire. In 1978 he became director of the National Opera Studio. He was made a Commander of the Order of the British Empire in 1973.

Lange, Daniel de, Dutch cellist and composer, brother of **Samuel de Lange;** b. Rotterdam, July 11, 1841; d. Point Loma, Calif., Jan. 31, 1918. He studied cello with Servais and composition with Verhulst. As a young man he taught at the Lwow Cons. (1860–63); returning to Amsterdam, he occupied various teaching posts; in 1895 became director of the Amsterdam Cons., remaining in that post until 1913; gave numerous choral concerts of old Dutch music; also wrote music criticism. In 1913 he went to California, where he lived at the headquarters of the Universal Brotherhood and Theosophical Society at Point Loma. He wrote an opera, *De val van Kuilenburg;* 2 symphs.; Cello Concerto; chamber music; sacred works; also publ. *Exposé d'une théorie de la musique.*

Lange, Francisco Curt, German musicologist; b. Eilenburg, Dec. 12, 1903. He studied music with Abert, Bekker, Bücken, and Sandberger. He received his Ph.D. in 1929 from the Univ. of Bonn with the dissertation *Über die Mehrstimmigkeit der Niederländischen Motetten.* In 1930 he went to Uruguay; established the Instituto Interamericano de Música, and Editorial Cooperativo Interamericano de Compositores, which publ. a long series of works by Latin American composers. Beginning in 1935, he edited the *Boletín Latino-Americano de Música,* a series of bulky vols. containing documentary data on Latin American music and composers; separate vols. appeared in Montevideo, Lima, Bogota, Caracas, Rio de Janeiro, etc. He also publ. numerous essays and pamphlets dealing with literature, philosophy, pedagogy, and sociology (all in Spanish); brought out an anthology, *Latin-American Art Music for the Piano* (G. Schirmer, Inc., N.Y., 1942), with biographical sketches of 12 composers; also publ. a collection of Brazilian church music of the 18th century. In 1948 he founded the musicology dept. of the National Univ. of Cuzo in Mendoza, Argentina.

Lange, Hans, German-American violinist and conductor; b. Constantinople, Feb. 17, 1884 (of German parents); d. Albuquerque, N.Mex., Aug. 13, 1960. He studied the violin as a child, then at the Prague Cons. with Ševčik, graduating in 1902 with highest honors. In 1903 he joined the Berlin Phil.; later played in the orch. of the Frankfurt Opera; settled in the U.S. in 1923; was assistant conductor of the N.Y. Phil. (1923–33) and later an associate conductor (1933–36); then associate conductor of the Chicago Symph. Orch. (1936–46). He was conductor of the Albuquerque Symph. Orch. from 1951 to 1958.

Lange, Samuel de, Dutch organist and composer, brother of **Daniel de Lange;** b. Rotterdam, Feb. 22, 1840; d. Stuttgart, July 7, 1911. He studied with Verhulst in the Netherlands and with Winterberger in Vienna. He was with his brother in Lwow (1859–63); then taught successively at the Rotterdam Music School (1863–74), the Basel Music School (1874–76), and the Cologne Cons. (1876–85); then was conductor of the Oratorio Society at The Hague (1885–93); finally was a prof. of organ and composition at the Stuttgart Cons. (1894); became its director in 1900. He wrote a Piano Concerto; 3 symphs.; 4 string quartets; 2 piano trios; 4 violin sonatas; 2 cello sonatas; 8 sonatas for organ; an oratorio, *Moses;* 3 cantatas: *De Opstanding, Die Totenklage,* and *Eines Königs Tränen;* male choruses; songs.

Langer, Victor, Hungarian composer; b. Budapest, Oct. 14, 1842; d. there, March 19, 1902. He studied in Budapest with R. Volkmann, and later at the Leipzig Cons. Returning to Budapest, he was active as a teacher, theater conductor, and editor of a Hungarian music journal. His songs *Ögyek dalai,* Hungarian dances, arrangements, etc., publ. under the pen name of **Aladar Tisza,** are in the genuine national vein; they enjoyed great popularity.

Langgaard, Rued, Danish composer and organist; b. Copenhagen, July 28, 1893; d. Ribe, July 10, 1952. His father, **Siegfried Langgaard** (1852–1914), was a pupil of Liszt and an accomplished pianist. Rued Langgaard studied organ with Gustav Helsted; from his early youth he was occupied mainly as a church organist. As a composer, he followed neo-Romantic trends, in the manner of Bruckner and Mahler, scaling heights and plumbing depths of grandiose designs.
WORKS: Biblical opera, *Antichrist* (1921–30); 16 symphs.: No. 1, *Klippepastoraler* (1908–11; Berlin, 1913); No. 2, *Vaarbrud (Spring Song),* with Solo Soprano (1912–13; Copenhagen, 1914; revised and perf. on Danish Radio, 1948); No. 3, *Ungdomsbrus (The Sound of Youth),* with Piano, Chorus, and Ad Libitum (1915; Copenhagen, 1918; revised 1926); No. 4, *Løvfald (The Fall of the Leaf;* 1916; Copenhagen, 1917); No. 5, *Steppenatur* (1918; Copenhagen, 1926; revised, Danish Radio, 1938); No. 6, *Det Himmelrivende (The Heaven Rending;* 1919); No. 7, *Ved Tordenskjold i Holmens Kirke* (1925–26; Copenhagen, 1926; revised, Danish Radio, 1935); No. 8, *Minder om Amalienborg* (1928); No. 9, *Dronning Dagmar* (1942; Danish Radio, 1943); No. 10, *Hin Tordenbolig* (1944); No. 11, *Ixion* (1945; Danish Radio, July 29, 1968); No. 12, *Helsingeborg* (1946); No. 13, *Undertro (Belief in Miracles;* 1947); No. 14, *Morgenen (Morning),* suite for Chorus and Orch. (1948); No. 15, *Søstormen (The Storm at Sea;* 1948); No. 16, *Syndflod af Sol (Flood of Sun;* 1951; Copenhagen, March 17, 1966); for Voices, with Orch.: *Musae triumphantes* (1906); *Angelus (The Gold Legend;* 1915–37); *Sfaerernes Musik (Music of the Spheres;* 1916–18; his most interesting work; perf. in Karlsruhe, 1921); *Endens Tid (The End of Time;* 1921–39); 2 church cantatas: *Krematio* (1928–36) and *Jephta* (1948); *Højsangen (Song of Solomon;* 1949; Danish Radio, Feb. 24, 1969); *Heltedød (Death of a Hero)* for Orch. (1907); *Drapa* for Orch. (1907); *Sfinx,* overture (1909); *Saga blot* for Orch. (1917); Violin Concerto (1943–44; Danish Radio, July 29, 1968); dedicatory overture, *Carl Nielsen vor store Komponist (Carl*

Nielsen Our Great Composer), for Orch. (1948); 6 string quartets (1914–31); 5 violin sonatas (1915–49); *Dies irae* for Tuba and Piano (1948); many minor organ pieces, motets, and songs.

Langlotz, Karl A., German-American composer; b. Saxe-Meiningen, June 20, 1834; d. Trenton, N.J., Nov. 25, 1915. He was a member of the Liszt circle in Weimar; in 1853, came to America; lived in Philadelphia as a music teacher; in 1857–68 was an instructor of German at Princeton; in 1868, entered the Theological Seminary there, graduating in 1871; in 1874, moved to Trenton, where he taught music. He is known for composing the famous Princeton song *Old Nassau* (1859), at the suggestion of Princeton students and teachers who gathered regularly to sing college songs; the song was first publ. in the earliest Princeton songbook, *Songs of Old Nassau* (N.Y., 1859).

Lanier (Laniere), Nicholas, English composer, lutenist, and painter; b. Greenwich (baptized, Sept. 10), 1588; d. London, Feb. 24, 1666. He is important as having been probably the first to introduce the Italian recitative style into England, in his music to masques, of which the first was Ben Jonson's *Lovers Made Men* (London, Feb. 22, 1617). He was Master of the King's Musick under Charles I and Charles II. He wrote a pastoral on the birth of Prince Charles; a funeral hymn for Charles I; a cantata, *Hero and Leander;* and some New Year's songs; his songs are found in MS in the British Museum, Bodleian Music School, Christ Church, and Fitzwilliam Museum; also in the publ. collections *Select Musicall Ayres and Dialogues* (1653, 1659); *The Musical Companion* (1667); *The Treasury of Musick* (1669); *Choice Ayres and Songs* (1685); and J.S. Smith's *Musica Antiqua* (1812).

Lanier, Sidney, American poet and musician; b. Macon, Ga., Feb. 3, 1842; d. Lynn, N.C., Sept. 7, 1881. Best known for his poetry, Lanier learned as a child to play the piano, flute, guitar, violin, and organ. After serving in the Civil War, he was organist and choirmaster for a short period at a church in Montgomery, Ala. In 1873 he became first flutist of the Peabody Symph. Orch. in Baltimore. He wrote a number of articles on music (collected in *Music and Poetry: Essays upon Some Aspects and Interpretations of the Two Arts,* 1898; reprinted, N.Y., 1969) and composed songs and flute pieces.

Lanner, Joseph (Franz Karl), historically significant Austrian violinist and dance composer; b. Vienna, April 12, 1801; d. Oberdöbling, near Vienna, April 14, 1843. A self-taught violinist and composer, he joined Pamer's dance orch. when he was 12. In 1818 he formed a trio; Johann Strauss, Sr., joined it, making it a quartet. The group grew in size, and by 1824 it was a full-sized classical orch. which became famous and performed in coffeehouses, taverns, at balls, etc. The orch. was subsequently divided into 2 ensembles, with Lanner leading one, and Strauss the other. Lanner and Strauss are credited with the creation of the mid-19th-century Viennese waltz. Lanner's output totals 207 popular pieces, including 112 waltzes, 25 Ländler, 10 quadrilles, 3 polkas, 28 galops, and 6 marches; overture to *Der Preis einer Lebensstunde; Banquet-Polonaise; Tarantella;* and *Bolero.* His complete works in 8 vols., ed. by E. Kremser, were publ. by Breitkopf & Härtel in 1889 (reprinted N.Y., 1971); selections were brought out by Oskar Bie (Munich, 1920) and Alfred Orel, in Denkmäler der Tonkunst in Österreich, 65 (33.ii).

Lantins, Arnold de, Netherlandish composer; b. probably at Lantin, near Liège, c.1400; date of death unknown. He traveled in Italy about 1427; was a singer in the Papal Chapel in Rome between Nov. 1431 and July 1432. His employment of carefully connected chords suggesting purely harmonic procedures is of historical interest. Two motets, *Tota pulchra es* and *O pulcherrima mulierum* (from the Song of Solomon), are reproduced in Charles Van den Borren's *Polyphonia Sacra: A Continental Miscellany of the 15th Century* (1932). Other works are found in J. Stainer, *Dufay and His Contemporaries* (London, 1898); in J. Wolf, *Geschichte der Mensural-Notation;* and in vol. 61 (31) of Denkmäler der Tonkunst in Österreich.

Lanza, Mario (real name, **Alfredo Arnold Cocozza**), American singer of Italian descent; b. Philadelphia, Jan. 31, 1921; d. Rome, Oct. 7, 1959. He studied singing with Enrico Rosati; appeared in recitals and opera. In 1951 he starred in the title role of a highly successful film, *The Great Caruso.*

Laparra, Raoul, French composer; b. Bordeaux, May 13, 1876; killed during an air raid near Paris, April 4, 1943. He studied at the Paris Cons. with Gédalge, Massenet, and Fauré; won the Grand Prix de Rome with his cantata *Ulysse* (June 27, 1903). He was music critic of *Le Matin,* resigning in 1937 to dedicate himself entirely to composition. He was at his best in music inspired by Spanish subjects.

WORKS: Operas: *Peau d'âne* (Bordeaux, 1899); *La Habanera* (Paris, Feb. 26, 1908; his best-known work); *La Jota* (Paris, April 26, 1911); *Le Joueur de viole* (Paris, Dec. 24, 1925); *Las toreras* (Lille, Feb. 1929); *L'Illustre Fregona* (Paris, Feb. 16, 1931); incidental music to *El Conquistador; Un Dimanche basque,* suite for Orch. and Piano; etc.

La Pouplinière, Alexandre-Jean-Joseph Le Riche de, French musical amateur; b. Chinon, July 26, 1693; d. there, Dec. 5, 1762. A wealthy member of the nobility and a statesman, he was a patron of music and a pupil of Rameau. The musical soirées he gave in his private theater were famous; he engaged Gossec as music director (1751); introduced Johann Stamitz to the Parisian public; upon Stamitz's advice, he added horns, clarinets, and a harp to his orch., instruments seldom heard in a concert orch. before that time. La Pouplinière wrote a number of arias, some of which Rameau incorporated into his own works.

Lara, Agustín, Mexican composer of popular songs; b. Tlacotalpán, Oct. 14, 1900; d. Mexico City, Nov. 5, 1970. He learned to play piano by ear; earned his living as an entertainer in a Mexican house of tolerance, where he wrote his first successful song, *Rosa;* an encounter with a woman who impulsively slashed his face during an altercation inspired him to write a paean to womanhood, *Morucha,* which acquired great popularity. His other songs that became famous are *Tus pupilas, Gotas de amor,* and the most famous, *Mujer.*

Lara, Isidore de. See **De Lara, Isidore.**

Laredo, Jaime, Bolivian violinist; b. Cochabamba, June 7, 1941. He was brought to the U.S. as a child; studied violin with Antonio de Grassi and Frank Houser in San Francisco, Josef Gingold in Cleveland, and Ivan Galamian at the Curtis Inst. of Music in Philadelphia. In 1959, a week before his 18th birthday, he won the Queen Elisabeth of Belgium Competition in Brussels, and subsequently appeared with great success in America and Europe as a soloist with leading orchs. The proud Bolivian government issued a series of airmail stamps with Laredo's picture and a musical example with the notes A, D, C in the treble clef, spelling his name in Latin notation (La-Re-Do). In 1960 he married the pianist **Ruth Meckler** (divorced in 1974); his second wife, **Sharon Robinson,** was a cellist. With her and the pianist Joseph Kalichstein, he formed a trio which gave successful concerts.

Laredo, Ruth (née **Meckler**), American pianist; b. Detroit, Nov. 20, 1937. She studied with Rudolf Serkin at the Curtis Inst. of Music in Philadelphia; in 1962 made her debut with Leopold Stokowski and the American Symph. in N.Y. In 1965 she played in Europe with Rudolf Serkin and his son Peter Serkin; in 1977 she toured Japan. In 1960 she married the Bolivian violinist **Jaime Laredo,** with whom she played numerous recitals; but they were divorced in 1974. She is particularly fond of Russian music, and plays piano works of Rachmaninoff and Scriabin with passionate devotion.

La Rotella, Pasquale, Italian composer and conductor; b. Bitonto, Feb. 26, 1880; d. Bari, March 20, 1963. He studied in Naples; was choral conductor at the Bari Cathedral (1902–13); in 1934–49, taught at the Liceo Musicale there; toured Italy as an opera conductor. His works include the operas *Ivan* (Bari, Jan. 20, 1900); *Dea* (Bari, April 11, 1903); *Fasma* (Milan, Nov. 28, 1908); *Corsaresca* (Rome, Nov. 13, 1933); *Manuela* (Nice, March 4, 1948); much sacred music.

Larrivée, Henri, French bass-baritone; b. Lyons, Jan. 9, 1737; d. Vincennes, Aug. 7, 1802. He sang in the chorus of the Paris Opéra; made his debut there in Rameau's *Castor et Pollux* in 1755; he subsequently distinguished himself in the operas of Gluck, creating the roles of Agamemnon in *Iphigénie en Aulide* (1774) and Orestes in *Iphigénie en Tauride* (1779). His wife, **Marie Jeanne Larrivée** (née **Le Mière;** b. Sedan, Nov. 29, 1733; d. Paris, Oct. 1786), was a soprano who sang minor roles at the Paris Opéra (1750–77); she created the title role of Ernelinde in Philidor's opera of 1767, and also the role of Eponine in *Sabinus* (1773) by Gossec.

Larrocha, Alicia de, brilliant Spanish pianist; b. Barcelona, May 23, 1923. She studied piano with Frank Marshall and theory with Ricardo Lamote de Grignon. She made her first public appearance at the age of 5; was soloist with the Orquesta Sinfónica of Madrid at the age of 11. In 1940 she launched her career in earnest; from 1947 made extensive concert tours in Europe and America. Her interpretations of Spanish music have evoked universal admiration for their authentic quality, but she has also been exuberantly praised by sober-minded critics for her impeccable taste and exquisitely polished technique in classical works.

Larsen, Jens Peter, distinguished Danish musicologist; b. Copenhagen, June 14, 1902. He studied mathematics and musicology at the Univ. of Copenhagen; also took private organ lessons with Wöldike. He received his M.A. in 1928 from the Univ. of Copenhagen; then joined its staff; obtained his Ph.D. there in 1939 with the dissertation *Die Haydn-Überlieferung* (publ. in Copenhagen, 1939); he retired in 1970. A leading authority on the music of Haydn, he served as general editor of the critical edition sponsored by the Joseph Haydn Inst. of Cologne from 1955 to 1960; his studies on the music of Handel are also of value.

Larsén-Todsen, Nanny, Swedish soprano; b. Hagby, Kalmar county, Aug. 2, 1884; d. Stockholm, May 26, 1982. She studied at the Stockholm Cons. and in Germany and Italy. In 1906 she made her debut at the Royal Theater in Stockholm as Agathe in *Der Freischütz;* was a member of the Royal Theater (1907–22), specializing in Wagnerian roles; sang at La Scala in Milan (1923–24), at the Metropolitan Opera House in N.Y. (1925–27; debut there Jan. 31, 1925, as Brünnhilde in *Götterdämmerung*), and at Bayreuth (1927–31); made guest appearances at most of the European opera houses. Her principal roles were the 3 Brünnhildes, Isolde, Fricka, and Leonore. She married H. Todsen in 1916; following her retirement from the stage, she became a teacher in Stockholm.

Larsson, Lars-Erik, important Swedish composer; b. Åkarp, near Lund, May 15, 1908. He studied composition (with Ellberg) and conducting (with Olallo Morales) at the Royal Academy of Music in Stockholm (1925–29); then went to Vienna, where he took lessons with Alban Berg (1929–30); upon returning to Sweden, he was choirmaster of the Royal Opera in Stockholm (1930–31) and conducted the Swedish Radio orch. (1937–54); taught at the Royal Academy (1947–59) and was music director of Uppsala Univ. (1961–65). His early compositions were in a classical spirit, but with time his idiom became increasingly complex; there are also some instances of the application of dodecaphonic procedures in his later compositions.

WORKS: For the stage: Opera, *Prinsessan av Cypern (The Princess of Cyprus;* 1930–36; Stockholm, April 29, 1937); opera-buffa, *Arresten på Bohus (The Arrest at Bohus;* 1938–39); ballet, *Linden* (1958). For orch.: 3 symphs. (1927–28, 1936–37, 1945); 3 concert overtures (1929, 1934, 1945); *Symphonic Sketch* (1930); *Sinfonietta* for Strings (1932); *Little Serenade* for Strings (1934); Saxophone Concerto (1934); *Divertimento* for Chamber Orch. (1935); *Little March* (1936); *Ostinato* (Stockholm, Nov. 24, 1937); *En vintersaga (A Winter Tale),* suite (1937); *Pastoral Suite* (1938); *The Earth Sings,* symph. poem (1940); *The Land of Sweden,* suite (1941); *Gustavian Suite* for Flute, Harpsichord, and Strings (1943); Cello Concerto (1947); *Music for Orchestra* (1948-49); Violin Concerto (1952); 12 concertinos, with String Orch., for solo instruments: Flute, Oboe, Clarinet, Bassoon, Horn, Trumpet, Trombone, Violin, Viola, Cello, Double Bass, and Piano (1953-57); *Adagio* for Strings (1960); *3 Pieces* (1960); *Orchestral Variations* (1962); *Lyric Fantasy* for Small Orch. (1967); *2 auguri* (1971); *Barococo,* suite (1973). Vocal music: *Förklädd gud (The Disguised God),* lyric suite for Narrator, Soprano, Baritone, Chorus, and Orch. (1940); *Väktarsånger (Watchman's Songs)* for Narrator, Baritone, Male Chorus, and Orch. (1940); *Missa brevis* for a cappella Chorus (1954); *Intrada Solemnis* for 2 Choruses, Boys' Chorus, Winds, and Organ (1964); *Soluret och urnan (The Sundial and the Urn),* cantata (1965–66). Chamber music: Violin Sonatina (1928); *Duo* for Violin and Viola (1931); *Intimate Miniatures* for String Quartet (1938); 3 string quartets (1944, 1955, 1975); *4 tempi,* divertimento for Wind Quintet (1968); Cello Sonatina (1969); *3 Pieces* for Clarinet and Piano (1970); *Aubade* for Oboe, Violin, and Cello (1972). Piano music: 3 sonatinas (1936, 1947, 1950); *Croquiser* (1947); *7 Little Preludes and Fugues* (1969).

La Rue, Jan (full Christian name, **Adrian Jan Pieters**), eminent American musicologist; b. Kisaran, Sumatra, July 31, 1918, of American parents (his ancestor was a French Huguenot who fled first to the Palatinate and then came to America, landing in Massachusetts in 1670; LaRue's parents spent 3 years in Indonesia, where his father served as a botanist and developed a basic budding process used on rubber trees). He studied at Harvard Univ. (Ph.D., 1952) and at Princeton Univ.; taught at Wellesley College; in 1957 became a prof. at N.Y. Univ. His dual specialties are 18th-century music and style analysis. He prepared a thematic catalogue of about 10,000 entries on symphs. and instrumental concertos of the Classical period; contributed to various publications a number of original articles bringing informing light on obscure subjects. His most important papers include: "Native Music in Okinawa," *Musical Quarterly* (April 1946); "The Okinawan Notation System," *Journal of the American Musicological Society* (1951); "Die Datierung von Wasserzeichen im 18. Jahrhundert," *Kon-*

gress-Bericht, Mozart-Jahr, 1956 (also in Eng., "Watermarks and Musicology," *Acta Musicologica,* 1961). He publ. *Guidelines for Style Analysis* (N.Y., 1970); was editor of the *Report of the Eighth Congress of the International Musicological Society, New York 1961* (Kassel, 1961); co-editor of the Festschrift for Otto Erich Deutsch (Kassel, 1963) and of the Festschrift for Gustave Reese (N.Y., 1965). In 1966–68 he was president of the American Musicological Society.

La Rue, Pierre de (Petrus Platensis, Pierchon, Pierson, Pierzon, Perisone, Pierazon de la Ruellien), eminent Netherlandish contrapuntist and composer; b. in all probability between 1455 and 1460, in Tournai, where his family is known to have resided; d. Courtrai, Nov. 20, 1518. He was at the court of Burgundy (1477); a singer at the Cathedral of Siena intermittently from 1482 to 1485; was attached to the chapel of Archduke Maximilian of Austria (April 1485) and the chapel of Notre-Dame in Bois-le-Duc (1490–91); was a chapel singer at the court of Burgundy (1492–1510); canon at the court of Philippe le Beau in Malines (1501); prebend at Courtrai, Namur, and Termonde (from 1501); *cantor principis* at Courtrai (1502). He returned to the Netherlands about 1508; was a singer at the court of Margaret of Austria at Mechelen; then served Archduke Karl (1514–16). He wrote about 50 masses, of which many were publ.; others are in MS in libraries in Brussels, Malines, Rome, Vienna, Berlin, etc. One of Petrucci's early publications using movable type was 7 "Misse Petri de La Rue," issued at Venice in 1503. Motets and chansons were printed in collections of the time. A motet was scored by Dreher in his *Cantiones sacrae* (1872); the mass *Ave Maria* was publ. by H. Expert in *Les Maîtres-Musiciens de la renaissance française* (1890); a Kyrie in A. Schering, *Geschichte der Musik in Beispielen* (no. 65); some motets in R.J. van Maldeghem, *Trésor musical* (1865–93); motets and a Requiem in F. Blume, *Das Chorwerk* (vols. 11 and 91); 3 masses in *Monumenta musicae belgicae,* 8.

Las Infantas, Fernando de. See **Infantas, Fernando de las.**

Lassen, Eduard, eminent Danish conductor and composer; b. Copenhagen, April 13, 1830; d. Weimar, Jan. 15, 1904. His family moved to Brussels when he was a child; he entered the Brussels Cons., taking the Belgian Prix de Rome (1851). Following a tour through Germany and Italy, he went to Weimar, where Liszt fostered the presentation of his 5-act opera *Landgraf Ludwigs Brautfahrt* (1857). He became court music director in Weimar (1858); then was conductor of the Weimar Opera (1860–95); led the world premiere of Saint-Saëns's opera *Samson et Dalila* (Weimar, Dec. 2, 1877). He also wrote the operas *Frauenlob* (Weimar, 1860) and *Le Captif* (Brussels, April 24, 1865); a ballet, *Diana;* 2 symphs.; *Fest-Cantate;* 2 overtures; Te Deum; a set of *Biblische Bilder* for Chorus and Orch.; songs; etc.; also incidental music to *Oedipus* (1874); Hebbel's *Nibe-*

lungen; Goethe's *Faust* (parts 1 and 2; 1876); Scheffel's *Die Linde um Ettersberg* (1878); *Circe* (1881); Goethe's *Pandora* (1886).

Lassus, Ferdinand de, eldest son of **Roland de Lassus;** b. Munich, c.1560; d. Aug. 27, 1609. He was a musician at the Munich court (1584–85); court conductor at Sigmaringen (1585–90); a tenor singer in Munich (1590); went with the court to Landshut (1595) and later became court conductor there (1602). He brought out a book of *Cantiones sacrae suavissimae* (1587; motets); edited, with his brother **Rudolph,** his father's *Magnum opus musicum.*

Lassus, Ferdinand de, son of **Ferdinand** and grandson of **Roland de Lassus;** d. c.1635. He studied in Rome (1609); was court conductor (1616) and official (1629) under the Duke of Bavaria. Of his works, written for 8- to 16-voiced double choruses in the style made popular by the Venetian school, few remain. He publ. *Apparatus musicus* (motets, Mass, Magnificat, Litany, etc.; 8 voices; 1622).

Lassus, Roland de (Latin, **Orlandus Lassus;** Italian, **Orlando di Lasso;** French, **Roland Delattre**), one of the greatest of the Netherlandish composers and one of the foremost contrapuntists of the Renaissance; b. Mons, 1532; d. Munich, June 14, 1594. At the age of 18, he was placed in the service of Constantino Castrioto of Naples (1550). From April 1553 to Dec. 1554 he was chorus master at St. John Lateran in Rome. His parents died in 1554; Lassus subsequently joined J. Cesare Brancaccio, a music lover from Naples; with him he supposedly visited England and France; this visit was of brief duration, if it took place at all. In 1555 he settled in Antwerp. Both socially and artistically, he enjoyed a fine reputation in Antwerp, despite his youth; he had his first works printed in Venice (1555), containing 22 madrigals to poems of Petrarch; in the same year he publ. in Antwerp a collection of madrigals and motets to words in Italian, French, and Latin. In 1556 he was offered a highly desirable post at the court of Duke Albrecht V of Bavaria, and settled in Munich; in 1558 he married an aristocratic lady, Regina Wechinger (Wäckinger). He remained in Munich for most of the next 38 years, until his death. He did make occasional trips, including to Flanders to recruit singers (1560); to Frankfurt for the coronation of Emperor Maximilian II in 1562; to Northern Italy in 1567; and to the French court in 1571, 1573, and 1574. He brought Giovanni Gabrieli to Munich in 1575. On Dec. 7, 1570, he received from the Emperor Maximilian a hereditary rank of nobility. His last journey was to Regensburg, a year before his death. Lassus represents the culmination of the great era of Franco-Flemish polyphony; his superlative mastery in sacred as well as secular music renders him one of the most versatile composers of his time; he was equally capable of writing in the most elevated style and in the popular idiom; his art was supranational; he wrote Italian madrigals, German lieder, French chansons, and Latin motets. Musicians of his time described him variously as the "Belgian

Orpheus" and the "Prince of Music." The sheer scope of his production is amazing; he left more than 2,000 works in various genres. The Patrocinium Musices (1573–98), a 12-vol. series publ. in Munich by Adam Berg, under ducal patronage, contains 7 vols. of Lassus's works: vol. I, 21 motets; vol. II, 5 masses; vol. III, Offices; vol. IV, a Passion, vigils, etc.; vol. V, 10 Magnificats; vol. VI, 13 Magnificats; vol. VII, 6 masses. Lassus's sons publ. 516 of his motets under the title *Magnum opus musicum* (1604). Eitner publ. *Chronologisches Verzeichnis der Druckwerke des Orlando di Lassus* (Berlin, 1874). His collected works (21 vols., 1894–1926), were issued by Breitkopf & Härtel of Leipzig under the editorship of Haberl and Sandberger; a new series was begun in 1956 (12 vols. completed as of 1977) by the Bärenreiter Verlag under the editorship of W. Boetticher, who also publ. a complete catalogue of works (Berlin, 1956). Various works are contained in vols. 13, 34, 37, 41, and 48 of *Das Chorwerk,* and there are a considerable number in the catalogues of leading publishers.

Lassus, Rudolph de, organist and composer, son of **Roland de Lassus;** b. Munich, c.1563; d. there, 1625. He was a musician in the court orch. at Munich from 1585 until his death; was an organist and composer of merit and repute; from 1609 was court composer to the Duke; various works by him were publ.; 3 masses and 3 Magnificats are in MS in Munich; 2 motets are included in Proske's *Musica divina* (vol. I). With his brother Ferdinand he edited his father's *Magnum opus musicum.*

László, Alexander, Hungarian composer; b. Budapest, Nov. 22, 1895. He studied at the Budapest Academy with A. Szendy (piano) and Herzfeld (composition); in 1915 he went to Berlin; was active as a pianist; also worked on the radio and in film enterprises. In 1938 he emigrated to the U.S.; in 1945, settled in Hollywood. He cultivated the idea of music expressed through colors; introduced a specially constructed "color pianoforte" (*Farblichtklavier*) at the Kiel music festival (June 14, 1925); for the projection of the colors corresponding to music in proportional wavelengths he invented the Sonchromatoscope and a new system of notation called Sonchromography. His book *Die Farblichtmusik* (1925) discusses this new technique. His works include, besides special compositions for color lights, the pantomimes *Marionetten* (Budapest, 1916); *Die schöne O-sang* (Hamburg, 1919); *Panoptikum;* etc.; for Piano: *News of the Day, Hungarian Dance Suite,* and *Fantasy of Colors; Mechanized Forces* for Orch.; *Hollywood Concerto* and *The Ghost Train of Marshall Pass* for Piano and Orch.; arrangements for piano of various works by classical composers; film music. His sophisticated ideas about music and color found a fertile ground in Hollywood, where he supplied many musical scores to television; also wrote a musical, *Wanted: Sexperts and Serpents for Our Garden of Maidens* (1968); *Pacific Triptych* for Orch. (1962); symph. fantasy, *Roulette hématologique* (1969).

Lateiner, Jacob, American pianist; b. Havana, May 31, 1928. He studied piano with Jascha Fischermann in Havana, and with Isabelle Vengerova at the Curtis Inst. of Music in Philadelphia; also attended the chamber music classes given by Piatigorsky and Primrose. He made his debut with the Philadelphia Orch. in 1945; subsequently performed throughout America and in Europe. He appeared regularly in chamber music recitals with Heifetz and Piatigorsky. From 1963–70 he taught at the Mannes College of Music in N.Y.; in 1966 was appointed to the faculty of the Juilliard School of Music in N.Y.

Latilla, Gaetano, Italian composer; b. Bari, Jan. 21, 1711; d. Naples, Jan. 15, 1788. As a child, he sang in the choir of the Cathedral in Bari; then studied at the Cons. di Sant' Onofrio in Naples. He was 2nd maestro di cappella at Santa Maria Maggiore in Rome from 1738 to 1741, when illness forced him to return to Naples; in 1756 he became chorus master at the Cons. della Pietà in Venice; in 1762, 2nd maestro di cappella at St. Mark's in Venice. In 1772 Latilla again returned to Naples, where he remained until his death. He wrote about 50 operas, including *Li Mariti a forza* (Naples, 1732); *Angelica ed Orlando* (Naples, 1735); *Gismòndo* (Naples, 1737; also known as *La finta giardiniera;* perf. as *Don Colascione* in London, 1749); *Madama Ciana* (Rome, 1738; perf. as *Gli Artigiani arrichiti* in London, 1750, and in Paris, 1753); *I Sposi incogniti* (Naples, 1779); also the oratorio *L'onnipotenza e la misericordia divina;* 6 string quartets; church music; etc.

Laub, Ferdinand, Austrian violinist and composer; b. Prague, Jan. 19, 1832; d. Gries, near Bozen, Tyrol, March 18, 1875. A precocious violinist, he entered the Prague Cons. as a child; under the patronage of the Grand Duke Stephen, he went to Vienna for further study (1847); then made a German tour, visited Paris, and played in London; in 1853, became concertmaster at Weimar; in 1855, leader of the court orch. in Berlin; in 1855–57, taught at the Stern Cons. there. After spending some time in Vienna (1862–65), he went on a Russian tour, after which he became a prof. of violin at the Moscow Cons. (1866). He spent his last years in Karlsbad and Tyrol. He wrote an opera, *Die Griesbäcker;* brought out 2 collections of Czech melodies; publ. violin pieces.

Lauber, Joseph, Swiss composer; b. Ruswil, Lucerne canton, Dec. 27, 1864; d. Geneva, May 28, 1952. He studied in Zürich with Hegar, in Munich with Rheinberger, and in Paris with Massenet and Diémer. Returning to Switzerland, he taught at the Zürich Cons.; then conducted a theater orch. in Geneva (1905–7). He wrote more than 200 compositions, including the opera *Die Hexe;* an oratorio, *Ad gloriam Dei;* 6 symphs. and other orch. works; 5 concertos (including one for Double Bass, with Orch.); chamber works; choral music; piano pieces; songs; etc.

Laurencie, Lionel de la. See **La Laurencie, Lionel de.**

Lauri-Volpi, Giacomo, Italian tenor; b. Lanuvio, near Rome, Dec. 11, 1892; d. Valencia, Spain, March 17, 1979. He studied law; then went to Rome, where he took singing lessons with Enrico Rosati. He made his debut in Viterbo in 1919; then sang in the opera houses in Florence and at La Scala in Milan. He made his first American appearance at the Metropolitan Opera House in N.Y., on Jan. 26, 1923, as the Duke in *Rigoletto;* remained a member of the Metropolitan until 1933, while filling guest engagements at Covent Garden in London, at the Paris Opéra, and at the Teatro Colón in Buenos Aires. In 1934 he returned to Europe, and lived mostly in Burjasot, near Valencia. During World War II he continued to sing in Spain in concert and in opera, and in a remarkable demonstration of his tenorial vim and vigor, he sang an aria of Calaf from Puccini's opera *Turandot* at the Teatro Liceo in Barcelona in 1972, at the age of 80. He publ. several books of reminiscences, among them *L'equivoco* (Milan, 1939); *Cristalli viventi* (Rome, 1948); *A visa aperto* (Milan, 1953); 2 books on voices of the present and past, *Voci paralele* (Milan, 1955) and *Misteri della voce umana* (Milan, 1957).

Lauska, Franz (Seraphinus Ignatius), Bohemian pianist and composer; b. Brünn, Jan. 13, 1764; d. Berlin, April 18, 1825. He studied in Vienna with Albrechtsberger; was a chamber musician in Munich; in 1794–98, taught in Copenhagen; settled in Berlin in 1798; became a teacher at court; among his pupils was Meyerbeer. He wrote 24 sonatas (*Grande sonate, Sonate pathétique,* etc.); Cello Sonata; pieces for Piano, 4-hands (*6 Easy and Agreeable Pieces, Polonaise,* etc.); and variations for 2-hands; rondos; etc.

Laux, Karl, German writer on music; b. Ludwigshafen, Aug. 26, 1896; d. Dresden, June 27, 1978. He studied at the Univ. of Heidelberg; later taught at the Hochschule für Musik in Dresden, retiring in 1963; was active as a music critic. He publ. a biography of Anton Bruckner (Leipzig, 1940; revised ed., 1947); *Musik und Musiker der Gegenwart* (Essen, 1949); *Die Musik in Russland und in der Sowjetunion* (Berlin, 1958), and a number of valuable monographs and special articles on music in the German Democratic Republic.

Lavallée, Calixa, Canadian pianist and composer; b. Verchères, Quebec, Dec. 28, 1842; d. Boston, Jan. 21, 1891. He first studied with his father; then at the Paris Cons. with Marmontel (piano), and Bazin and Boieldieu *fils* (composition). Returning to Canada, he made tours of his native country and the U.S.; took part in the Civil War; in 1881, became soloist in the company of Mme. Gerster, the German singer. He wrote the music to the Canadian national song *O Canada* (first perf. in Montreal, June 24, 1880; poem by Judge Routhier). He subsequently settled in Boston, where he became an instructor at the Petersilea Academy; wrote a comic opera, *The Wid-*

ow (Springfield, Ill., March 25, 1882).

Lavigna, Vincenzo, Italian composer and eminent music teacher; b. Altamura, Feb. 21, 1776; d. Milan, Sept. 14, 1836. He studied at the Cons. di Santa Maria di Loreto in Naples; subsequently went to Milan, where he was "maestro al cembalo" at La Scala until 1832; also was prof. of solfeggio at the Milan Cons.; he was a teacher of Verdi. He wrote 10 operas, of which his first, *La muta per amore, ossia Il Medico per forza* (Milan, 1803), was his best; also 2 ballets.

Lavignac, (Alexandre Jean) Albert, eminent French musicologist and pedagogue; b. Paris, Jan. 21, 1846; d. there, May 28, 1916. He studied at the Paris Cons. with Marmontel (piano), Bazin and Benoist (harmony), and A. Thomas (composition), winning first prize for *solfège* in 1857, for piano in 1861, for harmony and accompaniment in 1863, and for counterpoint and fugue in 1864; he won 2nd prize for organ in 1865; was appointed assistant prof. of *solfège* (1871), prof. of *solfège* (1875), and then prof. of harmony (1891) there.
WRITINGS: His *Cours complet théorique de dictée musicale* (6 vols., 1882) attracted considerable attention and led to the introduction of musical dictation as a regular subject in all the important European conservatories; it was followed by *Dictées musicales* (additional exercises) in 1900. His magnum opus was the famous *Encyclopédie de la musique et Dictionnaire du Conservatoire,* which he edited from 1913 until his death. Other works: *Solfèges manuscrits* (6 vols.); *50 leçons d'harmonie; Ecole de la pédale du piano* (1889); *La Musique et les musiciens* (1895; 8th ed., 1910; entirely revised, 1950; Eng. trans. with additions on American music by H.E. Krehbiel, 1899); *Le Voyage artistique à Bayreuth* (1897; Eng. trans. as *The Music Dramas of Richard Wagner,* 1898); *Les Gaîtés du Conservatoire* (1900); *L'Education musicale* (1902; Eng. trans., 1903); *Notions scolaires de musique* (1905; Spanish trans., 1906); *Théorie complète des principes fondamentaux de la musique moderne* (1909). Lavignac's compositions (chiefly for the piano) are of little importance; together with T. Lack, he publ. arrangements for 2 pianos of Beethoven's First and 2nd Symphs.

La Violette, Wesley, American composer; b. St. James, Minn., Jan. 4, 1894; d. Escondido, Calif., July 29, 1978. He studied at Northwestern Univ. and at Chicago Musical College (M.M.; Mus.Doc., 1925); taught at Chicago Musical College (1923–33); in 1940 he went to California and lived in La Jolla.
WORKS: Opera, *Shylock* (1927; awarded the David Bispham Memorial Medal, 1930; excerpts perf., Chicago, Feb. 9, 1930); opera on the life of Buddha, *The Enlightened One* (1955); Symph. No. 1 (Rochester, N.Y., Oct. 19, 1938); Symph. No. 2, subtitled *Miniature,* or *Tom Thumb Symphony* (Chicago, May 25, 1942); *The Song of the Angels,* choral symph. (1952); cantata, *The Road to Calvary* (1952); 2 violin concertos (1929, 1938); *Penetrella* for Divid-

ed Strings, 18 parts (Chicago, Nov. 30, 1928); *Osiris,* Egyptian tone poem (1929); *Chorale* for Large Orch. (Chicago, July 31, 1936); *Music from the High Sierras* (San Francisco, March 4, 1941); Symph. No. 4 for Band (1942); Concertino for Flute and Orch. (1943); 3 string quartets; Piano Quintet (1927); Octet (1937); Sextet for Piano, Flute, Oboe, Clarinet, Bassoon, and Horn (1940); Flute Quintet (1943); Flute Sonata; 2 violin sonatas; Viola Sonata; Piano Sonata; etc. He is the author of several publications on philosophy and religion: *The Creative Light* (N.Y., 1947); *The Wayfarer* (Los Angeles, 1956); etc. He publ. a book, *The Crown of Wisdom* (Bombay, 1960).

Lavrangas, Denis, Greek conductor and composer; b. Argostoli, Cephalonia, Oct. 17, 1864; d. Razata, Cephalonia, July 30, 1941. He studied first in Argostoli with N. Serao (violin) and N. Tzanis (theory); then at the Cons. of San Pietro a Majella in Naples; and at the Paris Cons. with Delibes, Massenet, and Dubois; conducted an opera company touring through France; went to Italy and conducted theater orchs. in Turin, Venice, etc. Returning to Greece in 1894, he became artistic director of the Phil. Society of Athens.
WORKS: Operas: *Elda di Vorn* (Naples, 1890); *The 2 Brothers* (Athens, July 22, 1900); *The Sorceress* (Athens, 1901); *Dido* (Athens, April 19, 1909; his best work); *Black Butterfly* (Athens, 1928); *Redeemer* (Corfu, 1935); *Facanapas* (1935; perf. posthumously, Athens, Dec. 2, 1950); operettas: *White Hair* (Athens, 1915) and *Sporting Club* (Athens, 1919); *Ouverture grecque, Suites grecque,* and other works for Orch.; 2 masses; choruses; piano pieces; songs. He also publ. teaching manuals.

Lavry, Marc, significant Israeli composer; b. Riga, Dec. 22, 1903; d. Haifa, March 20, 1967. He studied with Teichmüller at the Leipzig Cons.; then was active as a conductor in Germany and in Sweden. In 1935 he went to Palestine; in 1951 he was appointed head of the music section of the Jerusalem Broadcasting Service. In 1952 he visited the U.S. His music is imbued with intense feeling for Jewish folk motifs. Among his works prior to his going to Palestine, the most notable is *Fantastische Suite* for Orch. (1932). He was the composer of the first Palestinian opera in Hebrew to receive a stage performance, *Dan Hashomer (Dan the Guard),* which he conducted in Tel Aviv on Feb. 17, 1945; another opera, *Tamar and Judah,* in the form of a series of cantillations with homophonic instrumental accompaniment, composed in 1958, was first performed in concert form, at the Jewish Arts Festival of Congregation Rodeph Sholom in N.Y., posthumously, March 22, 1970; he further composed *Israeliana I* for Orch. (1966); symph. poems: *Stalingrad* and *Emek (The Valley);* 2 piano concertos; many songs *(The Song of Emek* appearing in numerous eds.) and smaller works.

Law, Andrew, American singing teacher and composer; b. Milford, Conn., March 21, 1749; d. Cheshire, Conn., July 13, 1821. He graduated from Rhode Island College, receiving his M.A. in 1778; then studied theology and was ordained in Hartford (1787); subsequently he was active as a preacher in Philadelphia and Baltimore; later as a pioneer singing teacher in New England. He invented a new system of notation, patented in 1802, which employed 4 (later increased to 7) different shapes of notes without the staff; it was not successful and was used in only a few of his own books. A 2nd innovation (at least as far as American usages were concerned) was his setting of the melody in the soprano instead of in the tenor. In 1786 he received an honorary M.A. degree from Yale; in 1821, an LL.D. from Allegheny College in Meadville, Pa. He compiled *A Select Number of Plain Tunes Adapted to Congregational Worship* (1775); *Select Harmony* (Cheshire, 1778); *A Collection of Hymns for Social Worship* (Cheshire, 1782); *The Rudiments of Music* (Cheshire, 1783); *The Art of Singing*, in 3 parts, each separately paged: I. *The Musical Primer;* II. *The Christian Harmony;* III. *The Musical Magazine* (Cheshire, 1792–93; 4th ed., Windsor, Vt., 1803; part III contains 6 books of tunes); *Harmonic Companion, and Guide to Social Worship: Being a Choice Selection of Tunes Adapted to the Various Psalms and Hymns* (Philadelphia, 1807); *The Art of Playing the Organ and Pianoforte* (Philadelphia, 1809); *Essays on Music* (Philadelphia, 1814). Only one of his hymn tunes, *Archdale,* acquired some popularity; but his teaching books, quaintly but clearly written, contributed considerably to early music education in America.

Lawes, Henry, English composer, brother of **William Lawes;** b. Dinton, Wiltshire, Jan. 5, 1596; d. London, Oct. 21, 1662. He studied in London with Coperario; in 1626, became Epistler and Gentleman of the Chapel Royal, then clerk; was a member of the King's private band; also music master to the Earl of Bridgewater; lost these appointments during the Protectorate, but was reinstated in 1660. He is interred in the cloisters of Westminster Abbey. Lawes is historically important because his infinite care in setting texts with proper note and accent marked a step in the development of vocal composition which culminated in Purcell.

WORKS: *Coelum Britannicum,* masque (London, Feb. 17, 1634); *Comus,* masque (Sept. 29, 1634); *The Triumphs of Peace,* masque; *A Paraphrase upon the Psalmes of David* (1637); *Choice Psalmes put into Musick for 3 Voices* (1648; includes many compositions by his brother **William Lawes**); *Ayres and Dialogues for 1, 2, and 3 Voices* (3 vols., 1653, 1655, 1658); music to poems by Milton, Herrick, W. Cartwright, Davenant, etc.; songs and anthems in contemporary collections: *The Treasury of Musick* (1669); Clifford's *Divine Services and Anthems* (1664); MSS are in the libraries of the British Museum and Christ Church, Oxford.

Lawes, William, English composer, brother of **Henry Lawes;** b. Salisbury (baptized, May 1), 1602; d. Chester, Sept. 24, 1645. He studied with Coperario in London; was "musician in ordinary" to Charles I. He was killed in the service of the Royalist army during the Civil War. He is best known for his part-song *Gather ye rosebuds while ye may;* other works include music to Shirley's *The Triumph of Peace* (with Simon Ives; 1633); *The Triumph of Prince d'Amour* (1635); one of his anthems appears in Boyce's *Cathedral Music;* songs and vocal works in *Select Musicall Ayres and Dialogues* (1653 and 1659); *Catch that catch can* (1652); *The Treasury of Musick* (1669), *Choice Psalms* (1648); instrumental music in *Courtly Masquing Ayres* (1662); *The Royal Consort* (66 short pieces for viols, lutes, etc.) and some *Airs* for violin and bass can be found in the British Museum; his *Great Consort* (6 suites for 2 Treble Viols, 2 Theorbos, and 2 Bass Viols) is in the library of Christ Church, Oxford; other MSS of his anthems and canons are in the British Museum and the library of Christ Church, Oxford; *Select Consort Music of William Lawes* is publ. in *Musica Britannica,* 21.

Lawrence, Marjorie, Australian soprano; b. Dean's Marsh, Victoria, Feb. 17, 1907; d. Little Rock, Ark., Jan. 13, 1979. She studied in Melbourne with Ivor Boustead; then in Paris with Cécile Gilly. She made her American debut at the Metropolitan Opera House on Dec. 18, 1935, as Brünnhilde in *Die Walküre;* remained on its roster until 1941; made guest appearances with the Chicago, San Francisco, St. Louis, and Cincinnati operas. An attack of poliomyelitis while she was in Mexico (1941) interrupted her career. However, she staged a remarkable return at a concert in N.Y. on Nov. 9, 1942, when she sang reclining upon a couch. Her last appearance as an opera singer took place on Dec. 18, 1943, as Venus in *Tannhäuser.* She subsequently devoted herself to teaching. She publ. an autobiography, *Interrupted Melody, The Story of My Life* (N.Y., 1949), which was made into a motion picture in 1955.

Lawrence, Vera Brodsky, American pianist and music editor; b. Norfolk, Va., July 1, 1909. She studied with Josef and Rosina Lhévinne at the Juilliard School of Music in N.Y. (1929–32); gave duo-piano concerts with Harold Triggs, and appeared as a soloist with American orchs. In a radical change of direction, she abandoned her concert career in 1965 to become a historian of American music. In 1967 she was appointed administrator of publications for the Contemporary Music Project, and supervised publication of numerous works by American composers. In 1969 she brought out the collected piano works of Louis Moreau Gottschalk, in 5 vols.; in 1970 she compiled, edited, and produced the collected works of Scott Joplin, in 2 vols., and in 1975 publ. the valuable vol. *Music for Patriots, Politicians, and Presidents,* tracing American history as reflected in popular music, profusely illustrated with title pages and musical excerpts from publ. songs and dances celebrating historical events, and campaign ballads written during presidential elections; this work received the ASCAP–Deems Taylor award in 1976.

Layton, Robert, English musicologist; b. London, May 2, 1930. He was educated at Worcester College, Oxford (B.A., 1953); then went to Sweden, learned the language, and took courses at the univs. of Uppsala and Stockholm; in 1959 he joined the staff of the BBC in London, where he prepared music seminars. He became an authority on Scandinavian music; his books include *Franz Berwald* (in Swedish, Stockholm, 1956; in Eng., London, 1959); *Sibelius and His World* (London, 1970; 3rd revised ed., 1983). He also contributed the majority of the articles on Scandinavian composers to *The New Grove,* and in a spirit of mischievous fun also inserted a biography of a nonexistent Danish composer, making up his name from the stations of the Copenhagen subway. The editor was not amused, and the phony entry had to be painfully gouged in the galleys for the new printing.

Lazar, Filip, Rumanian composer; b. Craiova, May 18, 1894; d. Paris, Nov. 3, 1936. He studied with Kiriac and Castaldi at the Bucharest Cons. (1907–12) and with Teichmüller and Krehl at the Leipzig Cons. (1913–14). In 1915 he went to Paris; was a founding member of the modern musical society Triton (1928). His music is brilliantly hedonistic, with the ethnic Rumanian element furnishing an exotic element *à la moderne.*

Lazarof, Henri, brilliant Bulgarian-American composer; b. Sofia, April 12, 1932. He left Bulgaria in 1948 for Palestine, and studied composition with Paul Ben-Haim in Jerusalem; then took courses with Goffredo Petrassi at the Santa Cecilia Academy in Rome (1955–57). He received a study fellowship from Brandeis Univ., where he studied with Harold Shapero (1957–59); in 1962 he joined the music faculty at the Univ. of Calif., Los Angeles; in 1970–71 he was named artist-in-residence at the Univ. in West Berlin; then returned to U.C.L.A. His music is marked by inventive originality in its thematic structure and subtle "sonorism" in instrumentation, without imperiling the pragmatic quality of the basic design; instances of serial procedures are unobtrusive.
WORKS: Piano Concerto (1957); *Piccola serenata* for Orch. (Boston, June 14, 1959); Viola Concerto (Monaco, Feb. 20, 1962; first prize at the International Competition of Monaco); Concerto for Piano and 20 Instruments (Milan Radio, May 28, 1963); *Odes* for Orch. (1963); *Concertino da camera* for Woodwind Quintet (1959); *Tempi concertati,* double concerto for Violin, Viola, and Chamber Orch. (1964); 2 string quartets (1956, 1962); String Trio (1957); Sonata for Violin Solo (1958); *Inventions* for Viola and Piano (1962); *Asymptotes* for Flute and Vibraphone (1963); *Quantetti* (a telescoped title for "Quattro canti per quartetto di pianoforte"), scored for 4 Pianos (1964); *Structures sonores* for Orch. (1966; received first International Prize of the City of Milan, La Scala Award); *Rhapsody* for Violin and Piano (1966); *Espaces* for 10 Instruments (1966); Octet for Wind Instruments (1967); *Mutazione* for Orch. (1967); Concerto for Cello and Orch. (1968;

Oslo, Sept. 12, 1969); *Omaggio,* chamber concerto for 19 Players (1968); *Divertimenti* for 5 Players (1969); *Textures* for Piano and 5 Ensembles (1970); *Continuum* for Strings (1970); *Events,* ballet (1973); *Partita* for Brass Quintet (1973); *Concertazioni* for Orch. (1973); Chamber Concerto No. 3 (1974); *Duo-1973* for Piano and Cello (1974)); *Spectrum* for Trumpet, Orch., and Tape (Salt Lake City, Jan. 17, 1975); *Volo* for Solo Viola and 2 String Ensembles (1976); *Chamber Symphony* (1977); Concerto for Orch. (1977); *Canti,* ballet (1980); *Mirrors, Mirrors,* ballet (1981).

Lazarus, Daniel, French composer; b. Paris, Dec. 13, 1898; d. there, June 27, 1964. He studied at the Paris Cons., taking first prize in composition (1915). His works include the ballet *Le Roseau* (Paris, Nov. 15, 1924); *Symphonie avec Hymne,* a large work in 5 parts for Chorus and Orch. portraying the destiny of the Jewish people; an "épopée lyrique," *Trumpeldor* (Paris, April 30, 1946; perf. in concert form); *Fantaisie* for Cello and Orch.; Violin Sonata; piano pieces; etc.

Lazzari, Sylvio, French composer; b. Bozen, Dec. 30, 1857; d. Paris, June 18, 1944. He entered the Paris Cons. in 1883, studying with César Franck and Guiraud; became a naturalized French citizen, settling in Paris. Up to 1894 he was an active propagandist for the works of Wagner, contributing essays to various journals; then he devoted himself entirely to composition, adopting the principles of Impressionism. He visited the U.S. to conduct the world premiere of his opera *Le Sautériot* (Chicago, Jan. 19, 1918). He also wrote the operas *Armor* (Prague, Nov. 7, 1898); *La Lépreuse* (Paris, Feb. 7, 1912); *Melaenis* (Mulhouse, 1927); *La Tour de feu* (Paris, Jan. 16, 1928); a pantomime, *Lulu* (1887); orch. works: Symph.; *Rapsodie espagnole; Ophélie,* symph. poem; *Impressions d'Adriatique; Effet de nuit,* symph. poem (1904); *Marche pour une fête joyeuse; Tableau symphonique d'après Verlaine; Chanson de Moulin; Au bois de Misène; Cortège nocturne; Fête bretonne; Et la jeune fille parla; Perdu en mer; Rapsodie* for Violin and Orch.; *Le Nouveau Christ* for Baritone and Orch.; *Des choses des choses* for Soprano and Orch.; *Apparitions* for Soprano and Orch.; incidental music to *Faust;* Piano Trio; String Quartet; Octet for Wind Instruments; Violin Sonata; piano works; songs; etc.

Lear, Evelyn, outstanding American soprano; b. Brooklyn, Jan. 8, 1926. Her maiden name was **Evelyn Shulman.** Her grandfather, Zavel Kwartin, was a synagogue cantor; her mother was a professional singer; her father, a lawyer, was an amateur musician. She studied piano and also practiced on the French horn, and played it in a student orch. at the Berkshire Music Center in Tanglewood. She married Dr. Walter Lear at 17, and assumed his name in her professional career, keeping it after her divorce. She began to take voice lessons in Washington, D.C., with the baritone John Yard and sang in musicals. Realizing her inadequacies in vocal technique, she enrolled in the class of Sergius Kagen at the Juilliard School of Music in N.Y. There she met the baritone **Thomas Stewart,** who in 1955 became her second husband. They obtained Fulbright grants and went to Berlin for further study; she took voice with Maria Ivogün at the Berlin Hochschule für Musik. Soon both she and Stewart received a contract to sing at the Städtische Oper in Berlin. She made her debut there in 1959. An extraordinary opportunity to show her expertise was presented to her when she was asked to sing the challenging title role in a concert performance of Alban Berg's opera *Lulu* in Vienna on May 24, 1960. She acquitted herself brilliantly, and was engaged to sing Lulu in the stage performance in Vienna in 1962. She was then invited to sing parts in other modern operas; she also gave fine performances of Baroque operas. She made her debut at the Metropolitan Opera in N.Y. on March 17, 1967, as Lavinia in David Levy's opera *Mourning Becomes Electra.* Later she sang at the Metropolitan the parts of the Countess in *Le nozze di Figaro,* Donna Elvira in *Don Giovanni,* and the Marschallin in *Der Rosenkavalier.* On April 2, 1969, she scored a signal success at the Metropolitan in the role of Marie in *Wozzeck.* She often appeared with her husband in the same opera, for instance as Count Almaviva and Cherubino in *Le nozze di Figaro,* as Donna Elvira and Don Giovanni, as Desdemona and Iago in *Otello,* and as Tosca and Scarpia.

Leborne, Aimé-Ambroise-Simon, French composer; b. Brussels, Dec. 29, 1797; d. Paris, April 2, 1866. He went to France as a child; studied at the Paris Cons. with Berton and Cherubini; won the 2nd Prix de Rome (1818) and then the First Prix de Rome (1820); joined the faculty of the Paris Cons., as a prof. first of counterpoint, then of fugue, and finally of composition; retained this post until his death; was also librarian of the Paris Opéra and of the Royal Chapel. He wrote the operas *Le Camp du drap d'or* (Paris, Feb. 28, 1828); *Cinq ans d'entr'acte,* and *Lequel* (Paris, March 21, 1838); adapted Carafa's *Les Deux Figaros;* also edited a new edition of Catel's *Traité d'harmonie,* making numerous additions to the practical part (1848).

Lebrun, Franziska (neé **Danzi**), renowned German soprano, wife of **Ludwig August Lebrun;** b. Mannheim, March 24, 1756; d. Berlin, May 14, 1791. She made her debut in Schwetzingen on Aug. 9, 1772, as Sandrina in Sacchini's *La Contadina in corte;* her London debut was on Nov. 8, 1777, as Ariene in Sacchini's *Creso.* She sang in Paris at the Concert Spirituel, and in Milan during the first season of the Teatro alla Scala; also appeared in Naples and Berlin. She was also a composer; publ. 36 sonatas for violin and piano.

Lebrun, Jean, French horn player; b. Lyons, April 6, 1759; d. Paris, c.1809. He studied in Paris with Punto. His playing was remarkable for its purity of tone and for the ease with which he took the high notes. He played first horn in the Paris Opéra orch.

(1786–92); after a visit to England, he entered the court orch. at Berlin; following extended tours, returned to Paris in 1806, but found no employment, and in despair, committed suicide. The mute for the horn is his innovation.

Lebrun, Louis-Sébastien, French tenor and composer; b. Paris, Dec. 10, 1764; d. there, June 27, 1829. Unsuccessful as a singer in the Paris Opéra and Opéra-Comique, he became one of the 4 "maîtres de chant" at the Opéra; in 1807, became a tenor in Napoleon's chapelle, and in 1810, "chef du chant" there. He wrote 16 operas, the most successful being *Marcelin* (Paris, March 22, 1800) and *Le Rossignol* (Paris, April 23, 1816); also a Te Deum (1809); *Missa solemnis* (1815); and a collection of *romances.*

Lebrun, Ludwig August, German oboe player, one of the greatest of his time; b. Mannheim (baptized, May 2), 1752; d. Berlin, Dec. 16, 1790. He studied with his father; was a member of the court orch. at Mannheim (1764–78); then toured with his wife, the singer **Franziska Lebrun,** in Germany, Italy, Austria, France, and England; his concerts in London (1781) and Paris (1784), both solo and with his wife, created a sensational success. He composed the ballets *Armida* and *Agus;* also 7 oboe concertos; 12 trios for Oboe, Violin, and Cello; duos for flutes.

Le Carpentier, Adolphe-Clair, French pianist and composer; b. Paris, Feb. 17, 1809; d. there, July 14, 1869. He was a pupil of Lesueur and Fétis at the Paris Cons. (1818), winning several prizes. He publ. an excellent *Méthode de piano pour les enfants;* also 25 *Etudes élémentaires* (op. 59), and a collection of 24 études, *Le Progrès;* also nearly 300 fantasias on operatic and national airs, well arranged and of moderate difficulty.

Lechner, Leonhard (Leonardus Lechner Athesinus), composer; b. in the valley of Adige (Athesinus; hence his surname) in the Austrian Tyrol, c.1550; d. Stuttgart, Sept. 9, 1606. He was a boy chorister under Roland de Lassus in Munich and Ivo de Vento in Landshut; then a teacher in Nuremberg (1570); was Kapellmeister in Hechingen (1584); from 1585 lived in Tübingen; became a tenor at the Hofkapelle in Stuttgart in 1585, and in 1595 was made Kapellmeister there. His later works, as illustrated by his *Johannispassion, Hohelied Salomonis,* and *Deutsche Sprüche vom Leben und Tod,* show him to be one of the most gifted of the German composers in the period immediately preceding Heinrich Schütz. He publ. *Motectaesacrae* (in 4–6 voices; 2 vols., 1575, 1581, the latter vol. bearing the title *Sacrae cantiones,* partly reprinted by Commer); *Newe teutsche Lieder* (3-voiced villanelles; 2 vols., 1576, 1577; collected ed., 1586, 1590); *Newe teutsche Lieder* (in 4–5 voices; 1577); *Newe teutsche Lieder* (in 4–5 voices; 1582; reprinted by E. Fritz Schmid, 1926); 8 Magnificats (in 4 voices; 1578); 3 masses (in 5–6 voices; 1584); 10 introits (in 5–6 voices; 1584); *Newe lustige teutsche Lieder, nach Art der welschen Canzonen* (in 4 voices; 1586, 1588);

7 *Psalmi Poenitentiales* (in 6 voices; 1587); *Harmoniae miscellae,* collection (1583); *Johannispassion* (1594; reprinted by Ameln, 1926); *Hohelied Salomonis* (in 4 voices; 1606; ed. by Ameln and Lipphardt, 1927); *Deutsche Sprüche vom Leben und Tod* (in 4 voices; 1606; ed. by Ameln and Lipphardt, 1927); other Psalms and motets for 4–18 voices (1575–1604). He also made arrangements for 5 voices of 3-part villanelles by Regnart (1579; partly reprinted in *Monatshefte für Musikgeschichte,* vol. 19, ed. by Eitner); publ. works of Lassus. A complete ed. of Lechner's works was begun in 1954 under the general editorship of Konrad Ameln; by 1977, vols. 1–5, 7–9, 12, and 13 were issued.

Leclair, Jean Marie (l'aîné), celebrated French violinist; b. Lyons, May 10, 1697; d. Paris, Oct. 22, 1764. At first he was a dancer; was a ballet master at Turin, where the violinist Somis was attracted by dance music he wrote, and gave him further instruction. In 1729–31, he played the violin in the orch. of the Paris Opéra; was a frequent performer at the Concert Spirituel (1728–34). Thenceforth he lived in Paris as a composer and teacher; made brief visits to the Netherlands and Spain in 1743–44. He was assassinated in his own house; the circumstances that no robbery was attempted and that he was stabbed 3 times, in the front part of his body, suggest that the murderer was known to him; it may have been his estranged wife, who was also his publisher and engraver of his music. (See "The Murder of Leclair" in N. Slonimsky's *A Thing or Two about Music;* N.Y., 1948; pp. 86–90.) Leclair was one of the best composers for the violin in the 18th century; although he followed the Italian school in his early works, he developed a distinct style in his later music; he used technical devices in the virtuoso category.

Lecocq, Charles, French composer of light opera; b. Paris, June 3, 1832; d. there, Oct. 24, 1918. He studied at the Paris Cons. under Bazin (harmony), Halévy (composition), and Benoist (organ); obtained first prize for harmony (1850) and 2nd prize for fugue (1852). In 1857 he shared with Bizet a prize offered by Offenbach for the best opera buffa, with his *Le Docteur Miracle* (Paris, April 8, 1857). From that time on, he composed industriously for the stage; after several transient successes he produced an operetta, *Fleur de thé* (1868), which had a run of a hundred nights in Paris, and was also well received in England and Germany. He produced 9 more operettas before *La Fille de Mme. Angot* (Brussels, Dec. 4, 1872; Paris, Feb. 21, 1873), which brought him fame. In Paris alone it enjoyed an uninterrupted series of performances for over a year. It was closely followed by its rival in popularity, *Giroflé-Girofla* (Brussels, March 21, 1874). Altogether, he produced some 40 operettas and comic operas, distinguished by melodic grace, instrumental finish, and dramatic acumen, not inferior to the productions of Offenbach and Hervé. His serious opera *Plutus* (Opéra-Comique, March 31, 1886) was unsuccessful. He publ. a ballet pantomime for Piano, *Les Fantoccini;* 24 "morceaux de genre," *Les Mielles;* and a gavotte; also an aubade; melodies and chansons for voice with piano; sacred songs for women's voices (*La Chapelle au couvent*); etc.

Lecuna, Juan Vicente, Venezuelan composer; b. Valencia, Nov. 20, 1891; d. Rome, Italy, April 15, 1954. He studied at the Escuela Normal, graduating in 1906; then went to Caracas and studied music theory with Juan Vicente at the Caracas Cons.; also took piano lessons with Salvador Llamozas. In 1918 he went to N.Y., where he earned a living by playing at hotels and restaurants. He then returned to Caracas and entered the diplomatic service. In 1936 he was appointed a civil employee at the Venezuelan embassy in Washington, D.C. Concurrently, he took courses in orchestration with Gustav Strube in Baltimore. In 1943 he was sent by the Venezuelan dept. of education to study musical education in Brazil, Uruguay, Argentina, and Chile. In 1947 he was named Secretary of the Legation of Venezuela in Rome, and later was appointed a member of the Venezuelan legation at the Vatican. He composed a Piano Concerto; *Suite venezolana* for 4 Guitars; a String Quartet; and a suite of 4 Venezuelan dances for Piano.

Lecuona, Ernesto, Cuban composer of popular music; b. Havana, Aug. 7, 1896; d. Santa Cruz de Tenerife, Canary Islands, Nov. 29, 1963. He played piano as a child, and wrote his first song when he was 11 years old. He graduated from the National Cons. of Havana (1911); toured South America and Europe as leader of a Cuban dance band. Among his melodies, the most successful are *Malagueña, Andalucía,* and *Siboney.*

Ledbetter, Huddie (Leadbelly), black American folksinger and guitarist; b. Mooringsport, La., Jan. 21, 1885; d. New York, Dec. 6, 1949. He never had an education but possessed a genuine talent for folksong singing. He was jailed for murder in 1918; released in 1925; served another term for attempted homicide (1930–34) and another for assault (1939–40). It was during this last incarceration that he was discovered by folk researchers John and Alan Lomax, and they were instrumental in obtaining his early release and starting him on a career as a professional and renowned performer. The recordings of prison songs he made for the Lomaxes are now on deposit at the Library of Congress. After his release, he played and sang in nightclubs. The authenticity of his performance gives him a historic niche in folk-song history. A cult arose around his name after his death; the "hootenanny" movement was much influenced by his style. He is the composer of the song *Good Night, Irene,* but it did not become popular until after his death.

Ledger, Philip, English conductor, organist, harpsichordist, pianist, editor, and arranger; b. Bexhill-on-Sea, Sussex, Dec. 12, 1937. He was educated at King's College, Cambridge, and at the Royal College of Music, London. He served as Master of the Music at Chelmsford Cathedral (1962–65), as director of music at the Univ. of East Anglia (1965–73), and as dean of the School of Fine Arts and Music (1968–71). In 1968 he was named an artistic director of the Aldeburgh Festival; subsequently was engaged as conductor of the Cambridge Univ. Musical Society (1973) and director of music and organist at King's College (1974). In 1982 he was appointed principal of the Royal Scottish Academy of Music and Drama in Glasgow. He edited *The Oxford Book of English Madrigals* (1978) and works of Byrd, Purcell, and Handel. A versatile musician, he is renowned as an elegant performer of early English music.

Leduc, Alphonse, French music publisher; b. Nantes, March 9, 1804; d. Paris, June 17, 1868. He studied with Reicha at the Paris Cons.; played piano and bassoon. In 1841 he founded a music business in Paris; after his death, his son **Alphonse II** (1844–92) inherited the business; at the death of the latter, his widow directed the firm until 1904, when their son **Emile Alphonse III** (b. Nov. 14, 1878; d. Paris, May 24, 1951) became the next owner; his sons **Claude** and **Gilbert Leduc** (partners with their father from 1938) continued the business. From 1860 to 1895 the firm publ. *L'Art Musical,* which was then assimilated with the *Guide Musical.*

Le Duc, Simon, French composer; b. Jan. 15, 1742; d. Paris, Jan. 20, 1777. He studied violin with Gaviniès; made his debut as a soloist on Sept. 8, 1763, at the Concert Spirituel in Paris. He subsequently became active as a composer of instrumental music and a publisher. His works comprise 3 symphs., *Symphonie concertante,* and concertante string trios, with orch.

Leedy, Douglas, American composer, pianist, and conductor; b. Portland, Oreg., March 3, 1938. He studied at Pomona College (B.A., 1959) and at the Univ. of Calif. at Berkeley (M.A., 1962). He played the French horn in the Oakland (Calif.) Symph. Orch. and in the San Francisco Opera and Ballet orchs. (1960–65); in 1965–66 he held a joint U.S.-Polish government grant for study in Poland; from 1967 to 1970 was on the faculty of the Univ. of Calif., Los Angeles; from 1973 to 1978 he taught at Reed College in Portland, Oreg. His early works cultivated avant-garde methods of electronic application to mixed media, but later he sought to overcome the restrictions of Western music and its equal temperament; for this purpose, he began in 1979 to work with the Carnatic vocalist K.V. Nārāyanaswāmy in Madras, India. Parallel to that, he evinced an interest in early Western music; edited *Chansons from Petrucci in Original Notation . . .* in the Musica Sacra et Profana series (1983), and also led the Oregon Telemann Ensemble (later known as the Harmonie Universelle).

Lees, Benjamin, outstanding American composer; b. Harbin, Manchuria, Jan. 8, 1924, of Russian parents (his family name was **Lysniansky**). He was brought to the U.S. in infancy; studied piano in San Francisco and Los Angeles; served in the U.S. Army (1942–45); then enrolled at the Univ. of Southern Calif., Los Angeles, as a student in theory of composition with Halsey Stevens, Ingolf Dahl, and Ernst Kanitz; also took private lessons with George Antheil. He held a Guggenheim fellowship in 1955. In 1956 he went to Finland on a Fulbright fellowship, returning to America in 1962, after several years in Europe; in 1967 he visited Russia under the auspices of the State Dept. He taught composition at the Peabody Cons. in Baltimore, and at Queens College and the Manhattan School of Music in N.Y. Eventually he made his home in Great Neck, Long Island, N.Y., and devoted himself mainly to composition. He writes mostly for instruments; his music possesses an ingratiating quality, modern but not arrogantly so; his harmonies are lucid and are couched in euphonious dissonances; he favors rhythmic asymmetry; the formal design of his works is classical in its clarity. An interesting idiosyncrasy is the use of introductory instrumental solos in most of his symphs. and concertos. The accessibility of his musical expression makes his music attractive to conductors and soloists.

WORKS: 4 piano sonatas (1949, 1950, 1951, 1963); Sonata for 2 Pianos (1951); *Profile* for Orch. (1952; NBC Symph. Orch., N.Y., Milton Katims conducting, April 18, 1954); String Quartet No. 1 (1952); Sonata for Horn and Piano (1952); *Declamations* for String Orch. and Piano (1953; Oklahoma City, Feb. 15, 1956); Toccata for Piano (1953); Symph. No. 1 (1953); *Fantasia* for Piano (1954); Violin Sonata No. 1 (1954); *10 Kaleidoscopes* for Piano (1954); *3 Variables* for Wind Quartet and Piano (1955); *The Oracle,* music drama, libretto by the composer (1955); String Quartet No. 2 (1955); Piano Concerto No. 1 (Vienna, April 26, 1956); *Divertimento burlesca* for Orch. (1957); Symph. No. 2 (Louisville, Dec. 3, 1958); Violin Concerto (1958; Boston, Feb. 8, 1963); *Concertante breve* for Oboe, 2 Horns, Piano, and Strings (1959); *Prologue, Capriccio, and Epilogue* (Portland, April 9, 1959); *Concerto for Orchestra* No. 1 (1959; Rochester, N.Y., Feb. 22, 1962); *Epigrams* for Piano (1960); *Visions of Poets,* dramatic cantata to texts of Walt Whitman's words (Seattle, May 15, 1962); Concerto for Oboe and Orch. (1963); *Spectrum* for Orch. (1964); *The Gilded Cage,* opera (N.Y., 1964); Concerto for String Quartet and Orch. (Kansas City, Jan. 19, 1965); *Invenzione* for Solo Violin (1965); Concerto for Chamber Orch. (1966); Piano Concerto No. 2 (Boston, March 15, 1968); *Silhouettes* for Wind Instruments and Percussion (1967); *Medea of Corinth* for Vocal Soloists, Wind Quintet, and Timpani (London, Jan. 10, 1971); *Odyssey* for Piano (1970); *Study No. 1* for Cello Solo (1970); *The Trumpet of the Swan* for Narrator and Orch. (Philadelphia, May 13, 1972); *Collage* for String Quartet, Woodwind Quintet, and Percussion (Milwaukee, May 8, 1973); Violin Sonata No. 2 (1972); *Etudes* for Piano and Orch. (Houston, Oct. 28, 1974); *Labyrinths* for Wind Ensemble (Bloomington, Ind., Nov. 18, 1975); Variations for Piano and Orch. (Dallas, March 31, 1976); *Passacaglia* for Orch. (Washington, D.C., April 13, 1976); Concerto for Woodwind Quintet and Orch. (Detroit, Oct. 7, 1976); *Dialogue* for

Cello and Piano (N.Y., March 2, 1977); *Scarlatti Portfolio*, ballet (San Francisco, March 15, 1979); *Mobiles* for Orch. (N.Y., April 13, 1979); String Quartet No. 3 (1980); Double Concerto for Piano, Cello, and Orch. (N.Y., Nov. 7, 1982); Concerto for Brass and Orch. (Dallas, March 18, 1983).

Leeuw, Reinbert de, Dutch composer and pianist; b. Amsterdam, Sept. 8, 1938. He studied at the Amsterdam Cons.; in 1963 was appointed to the faculty of the Cons. of The Hague. Apart from his professional occupations, he became a political activist; collaborated with Louis Andriessen, Mischa Mengelberg, Peter Schat, and Jan van Viljmen on the anti-American multimedia spectacle *Reconstructie,* produced during the Holland Festival in Amsterdam on June 29, 1969. He further wrote an opera, *Axel* (with Vlijmen; 1975–76); *Solo I* for Solo Cello (1961); *3 Positions* for Solo Violin (1963); String Quartet (1963); *Interplay* for Orch. (1965); *Hymns and Chorals* for 15 Winds, 2 Electric Guitars, and Electric Organ (Amsterdam, July 5, 1970); *Duets* for Solo Recorder (1971); *Abschied (Farewell),* symph. poem, a stylistically historical recapitulation of the late Romantic period of German music between 1890 and 1910, culminating with the emergence of Schoenberg (1971–73; Rotterdam, May 11, 1974). Leeuw publ. a book about Ives (in collaboration with J. Bemlef; Amsterdam, 1969) and a collection of 17 articles, *Muzikale anarchie* (Amsterdam, 1973).

Leeuw, Ton de, Dutch composer; b. Rotterdam, Nov. 16, 1926. He studied piano and theory with Louis Toebosch in Breda (1947–49), composition with Badings in Amsterdam (1947–49) and with Messiaen and Thomas de Hartmann in Paris (1949–50); also took courses in ethnomusicology with Jaap Kunst in Amsterdam (1950–54). He was director of sound for the Netherlands Radio Union in Hilversum (1954–59); then was engaged as a teacher of music in Utrecht and Amsterdam. In his works he explores all thinkable, and some unthinkable but conceptually plausible, ways, pathways, and byways of musical techniques. A government grant enabled him to make a tour of Iran and India in 1961, to study non-European systems of composition.
WORKS: Television opera, *Alceste* (Dutch Television, March 13, 1963); opera, *De droom (The Dream),* based on 14 haiku (Holland Festival, June 16, 1965); radio oratorio, *Hiob (Job),* for Soloists, Chorus, Orch., and Tape (1956); television play, *Litany of Our Time,* for Soprano, Chorus, Instruments, and Electronic Sound (1969; Dutch Television, Jan. 1, 1971); 2 ballets: *De bijen (The Bees;* Arnhem, Sept. 15, 1965) and *Krishna and Radha* for Flute, Harp, and Percussion (1964); Concerto Grosso for String Orch. (1946); *Treurmuziek in memoriam Willem Pijper* for Chamber Orch. (1948); Symph. for Strings and Percussion (1950); Symph. for String Orch. (1951); *Plutos-Suite* for Chamber Orch. (1952); 2 violin concertos (1953, 1961); *Suite* for Youth Orch. (1954); *10 mouvements rétrogrades* for Orch. (1957);

Brabant, symph. song for Middle Voice and Orch. (1959); *Nritta,* orch. dance (1961); *Ombres* for Orch. (1961); *Symphonies for Winds,* an homage to Stravinsky, for 29 Winds (1962–63); *Haiku I* for Voice and Piano (1963); *Haiku II* for Soprano and Orch. (Rotterdam, July 5, 1968); *Spatial Music I* for 32–48 Players (1965–66); *Spatial Music II* for Percussion (1971); *Spatial Music III* for Orch. in 4 groups (1967); *Spatial Music IV (Homage to Stravinsky)* for 12 Players (1968); *Syntaxis I* for Tape (1966) and *II* for Orch. (1966; Utrecht, May 16, 1966); *Lamento pacis* for Chorus and 16 Instruments (1969); *Music* for 12 Strings (1970); *Music* for Organ and 12 Players (Zwolle, June 29, 1972); *Gending* for Javanese Gamelan Orch. (Hilversum, Oct. 11, 1975); String Trio (1948); Flute Sonata (1949); Violin Sonata (1951); Trio for Flute, Clarinet, and Piano (1952); *5 Sketches* for Oboe, Clarinet, Bassoon, Violin, Viola, and Cello (1952); 2 string quartets (1958; with Tape, 1964); *Antiphony* for Wind Quintet and 4 Electronic Tracks (1960); *Schelp* for Flute, Viola, and Guitar (1964); *The 4 Seasons* for Harp (1964); *Night Music* for one Performer on 3 different Flutes (1966); *Music* for one or 2 Violins (1967); *Music* for Solo Oboe (1969); *Reversed Night* for Solo Flute (1971); *Midare* for Solo Marimba (1972); *Music* for Solo Trombone (1973–74); *Canzone* for 4 Horns, 3 Trumpets, and 3 Trombones (1973–74); *Rime* for Flute and Harp (1974); *Mo-Do* for Amplified Harpsichord (1974); *Modal Music* for Accordion (1978–79); Piano Sonatina (1949); *Introduzione e Passacaglia* for Organ (1949); 2-piano Sonata (1950); *5 Etudes* for Piano (1951); *4 Rhythmic Etudes* for Piano (1952); *Lydische Suite* for Piano (1954); *3 African Studies* for Piano (1954); *Men Go Their Ways* for Piano (1964); *Sweelinck Variations* for Organ (1972–73); *De Toverfluit,* 4 songs for Soprano, Flute, Cello, and Piano (1954); *Car nos vignes sont en fleur* for 12 Mixed Voices (1981); *And They Shall Reign Forever* for Mezzo-soprano, Clarinet, Horn, Piano, and Percussion (1981); *Electronic Suite* for Tape (1958); *Clair-Obscur* for Electronic Sounds (1982); solo songs; choruses. He publ. a book, *Muziek van de twintigate eeuw (Music of the Twentieth Century;* Utrecht, 1964). See *Key Notes,* 3 (1976; pp. 67–74).

LeFanu, Nicola, British composer, daughter of **Elizabeth Maconchy;** b. Wickham Bishops, Essex, April 28, 1947. She studied music at St. Hilda's College, Oxford (B.A., 1968); also took private lessons with Goffredo Petrassi in Italy and with Thea Musgrave and Peter Maxwell Davies in England. Although she scrutinized her mother's works with great care and interest, she never engaged in a course of formal instruction with her. Brought up in an extremely cultured and sophisticated environment (her father, William LeFanu, made a mark in the British literary world), she absorbed the seemingly conflicting musical influences in the modern world with elegance and ease; her own style of composition represents a median line of modernism which she developed *sine ira et studio,* without discrimination even against such obsolescent resources as major triads. As a result, her music pleased the public and appealed to unprejudiced judges of musical competitions. Thus, in 1970, she won first prize at the BBC National Competition for her Variations for Oboe Quartet (1968). Most of her compositions are set for distinctive chamber music groups.

WORKS: *Soliloquy* for Oboe Solo (1965); *Preludio* for Chamber Orch. (1967); *Chiaroscuro* for Piano (1969); *Quartettsatz* for String Quartet (1970); Quintet for Clarinet and Strings (1970); *The Hidden Landscape* for Orch. (London, Aug. 7, 1973); *Columbia Falls* for Percussion, Harp, and Strings (Birmingham, Nov. 20, 1975); *Farne* for Orch. (Bradford, March 28, 1980); *Collana* for Solo Percussion and Ensemble (Boston, April 25, 1976); *Deva* for Solo Cello and 7 Players (London, March 23, 1979) *Christ Calls Man Home*, music for church service (1971); *The Valleys Shall Sing* for Chorus and Winds (1973); *The Same Day Dawns* for Soprano and 5 Players (1974; Boston, Nov. 1974); *For We Are the Stars* for 16 Solo Voices, to a text based on an American Indian poem (1978); *Like a Wave of the Sea* for Mixed Choir and Ensemble of Early Instruments (1981); *The Old Woman of Beare* for Soprano and 13 Players (1981); *Anti-World* for Dancer, Soprano, Baritone, and Ensemble (1972); *The Last Laugh* for Soprano, Tape, and Instrumental Ensemble (1972); *Dawnpath*, chamber opera (London, Sept. 29, 1977).

Leffler-Burckard, Martha, German soprano; b. Berlin, June 16, 1865; d. Wiesbaden, May 14, 1954. She made her debut as a coloratura soprano in Strasbourg (1890); then sang at Breslau, Cologne, and Bremen; in 1898–1900, was at the court theater in Weimar; in 1900–1902, was at Wiesbaden; after that, at the principal German opera houses; in 1906, at Bayreuth; in 1908, at the Metropolitan Opera House in Wagner roles; in 1912–19, was a member of the Berlin Opera. Her best roles were Fidelio, Isolde, and the 3 Brünnhildes.

Le Flem, Paul, French composer and music critic; b. Lézardrieux, Côtes-du-Nord, March 18, 1881; still verifiably alive, albeit nearly blind, in Paris in October 1983, in his 103rd year of an active long life. He studied philosophy at the Sorbonne in Paris; in 1901 traveled to Russia; then studied music with Lavignac at the Paris Cons. and later with Vincent d'Indy and Albert Roussel at the Schola Cantorum. He subsequently taught a course in counterpoint at the Schola Cantorum; was engaged as a chorus conductor at the Opéra-Comique in 1924; then devoted himself mainly to music criticism; was for 17 years principal music critic of *Comœida;* was one of the founders of the modern concert series *La Spirale* in Paris in 1935. He received the Grand Prix Musical of the City of Paris in 1951 in appreciation of his work as a writer, scholar, and composer. In his writings he energetically promoted the cause of modern music. His own compositions followed the musical methods of the French neo-Classical school; in several of his works he employed the melodic patterns of his native Brittany.

WORKS: For the stage: *Aucassin et Nicolette,*

fairy tale (Paris, July 20, 1923); *Le Rossignol de St. Malo* (Paris, Opéra-Comique, May 5, 1942); *La Clairière des fées,* lyric fantasy (1943; Paris Radio, Nov. 29, 1968); *La Magicienne de la mer,* lyric opera (Paris, Oct. 29, 1954). For Orch.: 4 symphs. (1908, 1958, 1967, 1977–78); *Konzertstück* for Violin and Orch. (1965); *La Maudite,* dramatic legend for Voices and Orch. (1967; new version, 1971); chamber music; piano pieces; choruses; songs.

Legge, Walter, British record producer; b. London, June 1, 1906; d. St. Jean-Cap Ferrat, France, March 22, 1979. Although not a professional musician by education or training, he became an ardent promoter of high-grade recordings of classical music; artists who appeared in recording sessions with him described him as a rigorous taskmaster who was willing to work endless hours until satisfactory results were achieved. Among the singers who performed for him was **Elisabeth Schwarzkopf,** whom he married in 1953. He also supervised records by Artur Schnabel and Wanda Landowska. In 1945 he sponsored the Philharmonia of London, conducted by Sir Thomas Beecham and later by Otto Klemperer. An important contribution to the auditory preservation of great performances was Legge's recordings of the piano performances by Dinu Lipatti, the brilliant Rumanian musician who died at an early age. Elisabeth Schwarzkopf edited a memorial publication, *On and Off the Record: A Memoir of Walter Legge* (N.Y., 1982). Incidentally, Legge pronounced his name "leg," as in a leg of lamb.

Leginska, Ethel (real name, **Liggins**), English pianist, teacher, and composer; b. Hull, April 13, 1886; d. Los Angeles, Feb. 26, 1970. She showed a natural talent for music at an early age; the pseudonym Leginska was given to her by Lady Maud Warrender, under the illusion that a Polish-looking name might help her artistic career. She studied piano at the Hoch Cons. in Frankfurt, and later in Vienna with Leschetizky. She made her debut as a pianist in London; also toured Europe; on Jan. 20, 1913, she appeared for the first time in America, at a recital in N.Y. Her playing was described as having masculine vigor, dashing brilliance, and great variety of tonal color; however, criticism was also voiced against an individualistic treatment of classical works. In the midst of her career as a pianist, she developed a great interest in conducting; she organized the Boston Phil. Orch. (100 players), later the Women's Symph. Orch. of Boston; appeared as a guest conductor with various orchs. in America and in Europe. In this field of activity she also elicited interest, leading to a discussion in the press of a woman's capability of conducting an orch. While in the U.S., she took courses in composition with Rubin Goldmark and Ernest Bloch; wrote music in various genres, distinguished by rhythmic display and a certain measure of modernism. She married the composer **Emerson Whithorne** in 1907 (divorced in 1916). In 1939 she settled in Los Angeles as a piano teacher.

WORKS: Operas: *Gale* (Chicago Civic Opera Co.,

Nov. 23, 1935, composer conducting) and *The Rose and the Ring* (1932; perf. for the first time, Los Angeles, Feb. 23, 1957, composer conducting); *From a Life* for 13 Instruments (N.Y., Jan. 9, 1922); *Beyond the Fields We Know,* symph. poem (N.Y., Feb. 12, 1922); *2 Short Pieces* for Orch. (Boston Symph., Feb. 29, 1924, Monteux conducting); *Quatre sujets barbares,* inspired by Gauguin, suite for Orch. (Munich, Dec. 13, 1924, composer conducting); *Fantasy* for Orch. and Piano (N.Y., Jan. 3, 1926); *Triptych* for 11 Instruments (Chicago, April 29, 1928); String Quartet, after 4 poems by Tagore (Boston, April 25, 1921); *6 Nursery Rhymes* for Soprano and Chamber Orch.; piano pieces; songs.

Legley, Victor, outstanding Belgian composer; b. Hazebrouck, French Flanders, June 18, 1915. He studied viola and music theory at the Brussels Cons. (1933–35); also took private lessons in composition with Jean Absil (1941), who was mainly influential in shaping Legley's style; in 1947 he became a programmer for the Flemish broadcasts of Belgian Radio; from 1949 taught at the Brussels Cons. In his works he adheres to the pragmatic tenets of modern music, structurally diversified and unconstricted by inhibitions against dissonance.

WORKS: Opera, *La Farce des deux nus* (Antwerp, Dec. 10, 1966); ballet, *Le Bal des halles* (1954); *Symphonic Variations on an Old Flemish Folk Song* (1941); 5 symphs. (1942, 1947, 1953, 1964, 1965); *Concert à 13,* chamber symph. (1944); *Suite* for Orch. (1944); *Music for a Greek Tragedy* for Orch. (1946); *Symphonie miniature* for Chamber Orch. (1946); 2 violin concertos: No. 1 (1947) and No. 2 (1966; Brussels, May 22, 1967; mandatory work of the 1967 Queen Elisabeth violin competition finals); *The Golden River,* symph. sketch (1948); Piano Concerto (1952); *Divertimento* for Orch. (1952); *Little Carnaval Overture* (1954); Concertino for Timpani and Orch. (1956); *Serenade* for String Orch. (1957); *La Cathédrale d'acier (The Steel Cathedral),* symph. sketch after a painting by Fernand Steven (1958); *Overture to a Comedy by Goldoni* (1958); *3 Pieces* for Chamber Orch. (1960); *Dyptiek* for Orch. (1964); *Harp Concerto* (1966); *Paradise Regained* for Orch. (1967); *Prélude for a Ballet* (1969); *3 Movements* for Brass and Percussion (1969); *Espaces* for String Orch. (1970); Viola Concerto (1971); 5 string quartets (1941; 1947; 1956; 1963; *Esquisses,* 1970); Trio for Oboe, Clarinet, and Bassoon (1942); Quartet for 4 Flutes (1943); Violin Sonata (1943); Viola Sonata (1943); Sextet for Piano and Wind Quintet (1945); Cello Sonata (1945); *Musique de midi,* nonet (1948); Clarinet Sonata (1952); Trumpet Sonata (1953); *Serenade* for 2 Violins and Piano (1954); *Burlesque* for Violin and Piano (1956); *Poème d'été* for Violin and Piano (1957); *Serenade* for Flute, Violin, and Cello (1957); *5 Miniatures* for 4 Saxophones (1958); Trio for Flute, Viola, and Guitar (1959); Wind Quintet (1961); *4 Pieces* for Guitar (1961); *Rhapsodie* for Trumpet and Piano (1967); Piano Quartet (1973); Piano Trio (1973); String Trio (1973); *4 Ballades* for either Violin, Viola, Cello, or Double Bass, each with Piano (1975); 2 piano sonatas (1946, 1974); *4 Portraits* for Piano (1954–55); *Music* for 2 Pianos (1966); *3 Marches* for Piano (1968); *Brindilles* for Piano (1974); *Brieven uit Portugal* for Voice and Piano (1955); *Zeng* for Soprano, and String Quartet or String Orch. (1965); other works for voice.

Legrenzi, Giovanni, celebrated Italian composer; b. Clusone, near Bergamo (baptized, Aug. 12), 1626; d. Venice, May 27, 1690. He was the son of a violinist and composer named **Giovanni Maria Legrenzi.** In 1645 he became organist at S. Maria Maggiore in Bergamo; in 1651 he was ordained and made resident chaplain there; in 1653 became first organist. In 1656 he was named maestro di cappella of the Accademia dello Spirito Santo in Ferrara; his first opera, *Nino il giusto,* was given in Ferrara in 1662. He left Ferrara in 1665; in 1671 he settled in Venice, where he served as an instructor at the Conservatorio dei Mendicanti; in 1683 was its maestro di coro. In 1677 he was maestro of the Oratorio at S. Maria della Fava. In 1681 he became vice-maestro of San Marco; in 1685 was elected maestro there; under his regimen the orch. was increased to 34 instrumental parts (8 violins, 11 violettas, 2 viole da braccio, 3 violones, 4 theorbos, 2 cornets, one bassoon, and 3 trombones). Legrenzi was a noted teacher; among his pupils were Gasparini, Lotti, and Caldara, as well as his own nephew, **Giovanni Varischino.** Legrenzi's sonatas are noteworthy, since they served as models of Baroque forms as later practiced by Vivaldi and Bach. His operas and oratorios were marked by a development of the *da capo* form in arias, and his carefully wrought orch. support of the vocal parts was of historic significance as presaging the development of opera.

Legros, Joseph, French tenor; b. Monampteuil, Sept. 7, 1739; d. La Rochelle, Dec. 20, 1793. He was a choirboy in Laon; made his debut at the Paris Opéra in 1764 as Titon in Mondonville's *Titon et l'Aurore;* subsequently created several roles in operas by Gluck, including Achilles in *Iphigénie en Aulide* (1774) and Pylades in *Iphigénie en Tauride* (1779); he also sang in operas by Piccinni, Grétry, and others; he retired from the stage in 1783. He served as director of the Concert Spirituel (1777–90). He also was a composer; he wrote several operas and a number of songs.

Lehár, Franz, celebrated Austrian operetta composer; b. Komorn, Hungary, April 30, 1870; d. Bad Ischl, Oct. 24, 1948. He was first instructed in music by his father, Franz Lehár (1838–98), a military bandmaster; entered the Prague Cons. at 12 and studied violin with A. Bennewitz and theory with J. Foerster. In 1885 he was brought to the attention of Fibich, who gave him lessons in composition independently from his studies at the Cons. In 1887 Lehár submitted 2 piano sonatas to Dvořák, who encouraged him in his musical career. In 1888 he became a violinist in a theater orch. in Elberfeld; in 1889, entered his father's band (50th Infantry) in Vienna, and assisted him as conductor; after 1890 he led various military bands in Pola, Trieste, Budapest, and Vienna. His first success as a stage composer came with the production of his opera *Kukuschka* (Leipzig, Nov. 28, 1896); most of his subsequent productions took place in Vienna. His most celebrated operetta is *Die lustige Witwe (The Merry Widow)*; the first production, in Vienna in 1905, was followed by innumerable performances throughout the world; in Buenos Aires it was played simultaneously in 5 languages (1907); other operettas that achieved tremendous success were *Der Graf von Luxemburg* (1909) and *Zigeunerliebe* (1910). Lehár's music exemplifies the spirit of gaiety and frivolity that was the mark of Vienna early in the century; his superlative gift of facile melody and infectious rhythms is combined with genuine wit and irony; a blend of nostalgia and sophisticated humor made a lasting appeal to audiences, undiminished by the upheavals of wars and revolutions.

WORKS: Opera, *Kukuschka* (Leipzig, Nov. 28, 1896; rewritten as *Tatjana*, Brünn, Feb. 24, 1905); operettas: *Wiener Frauen* (Vienna, Nov. 25, 1902; in Berlin as *Der Klavierstimmer;* rewritten as *Der Schlüssel zum Paradiese*, Leipzig, 1906); *Der Rastelbinder* (Vienna, Dec. 20, 1902); *Der Göttergatte* (Vienna, Jan. 20, 1904); *Die Juxheirat* (Vienna, Dec. 22, 1904); *Die lustige Witwe* (Vienna, Dec. 28, 1905); *Mitislaw der Moderne* (Vienna, Jan. 5, 1907); *Der Mann mit den drei Frauen* (Vienna, Jan. 21, 1908); *Das Fürstenkind* (Vienna, Oct. 7, 1909); *Der Graf von Luxemburg* (Vienna, Nov. 12, 1909); *Zigeunerliebe (Gypsy Love;* Vienna, Jan. 8, 1910); *Eva* (Vienna, Nov. 24, 1911); *Endlich allein* (Vienna, Feb. 10, 1914; revised and produced as *Schön ist die Welt*, Vienna, Dec. 21, 1934); *Der Sterngucker* (Vienna, Jan. 14, 1916; revised and produced in Milan as *La danza delle libellule*, Sept. 27, 1922); *Wo die Lerche singt* (Budapest, Feb. 1, 1918); *Die blaue Mazur* (Vienna, May 28, 1920); *Die Tangokönigin* (Vienna, Sept. 9, 1921); *Frasquita* (Vienna, May 12, 1922); *Die gelbe Jacke* (Vienna, Feb. 9, 1923; revised and produced as *Das Land des Lächelns*, Berlin, Oct. 10, 1929); *Clo-Clo* (Vienna, March 8, 1924); *Paganini* (Vienna, Oct. 30, 1925); *Der Zarewitsch* (Vienna, Feb. 21, 1927); *Friederike* (Berlin, Oct. 4, 1928); *Giuditta* (Vienna, Jan. 20, 1934). Besides his operettas, Lehár wrote an *Ungarische Fantasie* for Violin and Small Orch.; *Huldigungsouvertüre; Ein Märchen aus 1001 Nacht; Il guado,* symph. poem for Orch. and Piano; *Eine Vision,* overture; symph. poem, *Fieber;* song cycle, *Musikalischer Roman* (1936); numerous marches and dances for orch.

Lehmann, Fritz, German conductor; b. Mannheim, May 17, 1904; d. Munich, March 30, 1956. He studied at the univs. of Heidelberg and Göttingen; was a conductor in Göttingen (1923–27) and taught conducting at the Folkwangschule in Essen (1927–29); also conducted in Hildesheim and Hannover. In 1934 he became conductor of the Handel Festival in Göttingen; also Generalmusikdirektor in Bad Pyrmont (1935–38), in Wuppertal (1938–47), and at the Göttingen Opera (1946–50); subsequently was a teacher at the Hochschule für Musik in Munich. He was particularly distinguished as an interpreter of Handel, Bach, and other Baroque composers.

Lehmann, Lilli, celebrated German soprano; b. Würzburg, Nov. 24, 1848; d. Berlin, May 16, 1929. Her mother, **Marie Loew** (1807–83), who had sung leading soprano roles and had also appeared as a harpist at the Kassel Opera under Spohr, became harpist at the National Theater in Prague in 1853, and there Lilli Lehmann spent her girlhood. At the age of 6 she began to study piano with Cölestin Müller, and at 12 progressed so far that she was able to act as accompanist to her mother, who was the only singing teacher she ever had. She made her professional debut in Prague on Oct. 20, 1865, as the First Page in *Die Zauberflöte;* then sang in Danzig (1868) and Leipzig (1869–70). In 1870 she became a member of the Berlin Opera, and soon established a reputation as a brilliant coloratura singer. During the summer of 1875 she was in Bayreuth, and was coached by Wagner himself in the parts of Wöglinde (*Rheingold* and *Götterdämmerung*), Helmwige, and the Forest Bird; these roles she created at the Bayreuth Festival the following summer. She then returned to Berlin under a life contract with the Berlin Opera; she was given limited leaves of absence, which enabled her to appear in the principal German cities, in Stockholm (1878), and in London (debut as Violetta, June 3, 1880; as Isolde, July 2, 1884; as Fidelio in 1887). She made her American debut at the Metropolitan Opera in N.Y. on Nov. 25, 1885, as Carmen; 5 days later she sang Brünnhilde in *Die Walküre;* then sang virtually all the Wagner roles through subsequent seasons until 1890; her last season there was 1898–99; also appeared as Norma, Aida, Donna Anna, Fidelio, etc. She sang Isolde at the American premiere of *Tristan* (Dec. 1, 1886), and appeared in Italian opera with the De Reszkes and Lassalle during the season of 1891–92. In the meantime her contract with the Berlin Opera was canceled (1889), owing to her protracted absence, and it required the intervention of Wilhelm II to reinstate her (1891). In 1896 she sang the 3 Brünnhildes at the Bayreuth Festival. Her great admiration for Mozart caused her to take an active part in the annual Mozart Festivals held at Salzburg, and from 1905 she was practically the chief organizer of these festivals. In 1909 she still sang Isolde in Vienna. Her operatic repertoire comprised 170 roles in 114 operas (German, Italian, and French). She possessed in the highest degree all the requisite qualities of a great interpreter; she had a boundless capacity for work, a glorious voice, and impeccable technique; she knew how to subordinate her fiery temperament to artistic taste; on the stage she had plasticity of pose, grace of movement, and regal presence; her ability to project her interpretation with conviction to audiences in different countries was not the least factor in her universal success. Although she was celebrated chiefly as an opera singer, she was equally fine as an interpreter of German lieder; she gave recitals concurrently with her operatic appearances, and continued them long after she had abandoned the stage; her repertoire of songs exceeded 600. She was also a successful teacher; among her pupils were Geraldine Farrar and Olive Fremstad. On Feb. 24, 1888, she married the tenor **Paul Kalisch** in N.Y.; they appeared together as Tristan and Isolde; some years later, they were legally separated (but not actually divorced). After Lilli Lehmann's death, Paul Kalisch inherited her manor at Salzkammergut, and remained there until his death in 1946, at the age of 90.

Lilli Lehmann was the author of the books *Meine Gesangskunst* (1902; Eng. trans. by Richard Aldrich, under the title *How to Sing,* N.Y., 1902; 3rd revised and supplemented ed., trans. by Clara Willenbücher, N.Y., 1924; reprint, 1949); *Studie zu Fidelio* (1904); *Mein Weg,* an autobiography (1913; 2nd ed., 1920; in Eng. as *My Path through Life,* 1914). She also edited arias of Mozart and many classical songs for the Peters Edition.

Lehmann, Liza (Elizabetha Nina Mary Frederica), English soprano and composer; b. London, July 11, 1862; d. Pinner, Middlesex, Sept. 19, 1918. She was of German-Scotch parentage; grew up in an intellectual and artistic atmosphere: her grandfather was a publisher, her father a painter, her mother a singer. From her childhood she lived in Germany, France, and Italy; among the guests at her house in Rome was Liszt. She studied voice with Alberto Randegger in London, and composition with Wilhelm Freudenberg in Wiesbaden. She made her professional debut as a singer at a Monday Popular Concert in London (Nov. 23, 1885), and subsequently appeared at various festivals in England. On Oct. 10, 1894, she married the English painter and composer **Herbert Bedford,** and retired from the stage; she then applied herself with great earnestness to composition, with remarkable results, for she was able to produce a number of works (mostly vocal) of undeniable merit, and was the first English woman composer to enjoy success with a large public, in England and in America. Her best-known work, which has become a perennial favorite, is *In a Persian Garden,* to words from Omar Khayyám's *Rubaiyát,* in Fitzgerald's version; it is a song cycle, with recitatives, scored for 4 voices, with piano accompaniment; while the music itself is entirely conventional, the vocal parts are eminently effective, both in dramatic and in lyrical passages. In 1910 Liza Lehmann made a tour in the U.S., presenting concerts of her songs, with herself at the piano.

WORKS: *Sergeant Brue,* musical farce (London, June 14, 1904); *The Vicar of Wakefield,* "romantic light opera" (Manchester, Nov. 12, 1906); *Everyman,* one-act opera (London, Dec. 28, 1915); *Once upon a Time,* "fairy cantata" (London, Feb. 22, 1903); *Young Lochinvar* for Baritone Solo, Chorus, and Orch., *Endymion* for Soprano and Orch., *Romantic Suite* for Violin and Piano; *In a Persian Garden* for Vocal Quartet and Piano (London, Jan. 10, 1897, first American perf., Boston, Jan. 5, 1910); song cycles (several of a humorous nature): *The Daisy Chain* (12 songs of childhood); *More Daisies; Prairie Pictures; In Memoriam* (after Tennyson); *Nonsense Songs* (from *Alice in Wonderland*); *The Caution-*

ary Tales and a Moral (after Hilaire Belloc); also piano pieces (*Cobweb Castles,* etc.). Her memoirs, *The Life of Liza Lehmann, by Herself,* were publ. shortly after her death (London, 1919).

Lehmann, Lotte, celebrated German soprano; b. Perleberg, Feb. 27, 1888; d. Santa Barbara, Calif., Aug. 26, 1976. She studied in Berlin with Erna Tiedke, Eva Reinhold, and Mathilde Mallinger. She made her debut on Sept. 2, 1910, as the 2nd Boy in *Die Zauberflöte* at the Hamburg Opera, but soon was given important parts in Wagner's operas, establishing herself as one of the finest Wagnerian singers. In 1916 she was engaged at the Vienna Opera. Richard Strauss selected her to sing the Young Composer in *Ariadne auf Naxos* when it was first performed in Vienna; then she appeared as Octavian in *Der Rosenkavalier,* and later as the Marschallin, which became one of her most famous roles. In 1922 she toured in South America. On Oct. 28, 1930, she made her U.S. debut as Sieglinde with the Chicago Opera, and on Jan. 11, 1934, sang Sieglinde at the Metropolitan Opera in N.Y. She continued to appear at the Metropolitan, with mounting success, in the roles of Elisabeth in *Tannhäuser,* Tosca, and the Marschallin in *Der Rosenkavalier.* In 1939 she toured Australia. In 1945 she became an American citizen; she eventually settled in Santa Barbara, Calif. She publ. a novel, *Orplid mein Land* (1937; in Eng. as *Eternal Flight,* 1938), and an autobiography, *Anfang und Aufstieg* (Vienna, 1937; London, as *Wings of Song,* and N.Y., as *Midway in My Song,* 1938); *More Than Singing* (N.Y., 1945); *My Many Lives* (N.Y., 1948; a sequel to the previous vol.); she also publ. a book of reminiscences, *Five Operas and Richard Strauss* (N.Y., 1964).

Lehmann, Marie, dramatic soprano, sister of **Lilli Lehmann;** b. Hamburg, May 15, 1851; d. Berlin, Dec. 9, 1931. She was a pupil of her mother, and later of her sister; made her debut in Leipzig (May 1, 1867); in 1876 she created the parts of Wellgunde (*Rheingold*) and Ortlinde (*Walküre*) at Bayreuth; from 1881 until her retirement in 1902 she was a member of the Vienna Court Opera; then lived in Berlin as a teacher.

Leibowitz, René, Polish-French composer and theorist; b. Warsaw, Feb. 17, 1913; d. Paris, Aug. 28, 1972. His family settled in Paris in 1926; from 1930 till 1933 he studied in Berlin with Schoenberg and in Vienna with Anton von Webern; under their influence he adopted the 12-tone method of composition; upon his return to France he became the foremost exponent of the 12-tone method in France; he had numerous private students, among them Boulez. He publ. *Schoenberg et son école* (Paris, 1947; in Eng., N.Y., 1949); *Introduction à la musique de douze sons* (Paris, 1949); a manual of orchestration, *Thinking for Orchestra* (with Jan Maguire; N.Y., 1958); *Histoire de l'Opéra* (Paris, 1957); *Erich Itor Kahn, Un Grand Représentant de la musique contemporaine* (with Konrad Wolff; Paris, 1958; in Eng., N.Y. 1958).

WORKS: Operas: *La Nuit close* (1949); *La Rumeur de l'espace* (1950); *Ricardo Gonfolano* (1953); *Les Espagnols à Venise*, opera buffa (1963; Grenoble, Jan. 27, 1970); *Labyrinthe*, after Baudelaire (1969); *Todos caerán*, to Leibowitz's own libretto (1970–72); for Orch.: *Fantaisie symphonique* (1956); Violin Concerto (1959); *3 Bagatelles* for String Orch. (1959); Concertino for Trombone (1960); Cello Concerto (1962); *Rapsodie symphonique* (1964–65); chamber music: *Marijuana* for Violin, Trombone, Vibraphone, and Piano (1960); *Sinfonietta da camera* (1961); *Capriccio* for Flute and Strings (1967); *Suite* for 9 Instruments (1967); Saxophone Quartet (1969); *Petite suite* for Clarinet Sextet (1970); 8 string quartets (1940, 1950, 1952, 1958, 1963, 1965, 1966, 1968); vocal works: *Tourist Death* for Soprano and Chamber Orch. (1943); *L'Explication des métaphores* for Speaker, 2 Pianos, Harp, and Percussion (1947); *Chanson Dada* for Children's Chorus and Instruments (1968); *Laboratoire central* for Speaker and Chorus (1970); numerous solo songs.

Leichtentritt, Hugo, eminent German-American music scholar; b. Pleschen, Posen, Jan. 1, 1874; d. Cambridge, Mass., Nov. 13, 1951. He was educated at Harvard Univ. (1891–94) and took a music course with Prof. Paine; went to Berlin in 1895 to complete his musical studies; obtained the degree of Dr.Phil. at Berlin Univ. with the dissertation *Reinhard Keiser in seinen Opern* (1901); he subsequently taught at the Klindworth–Scharwenka Cons. and wrote music criticism for German and American publications. In 1933 he left Germany and became a lecturer on music at Harvard Univ.; retired from Harvard in 1940. Although known chiefly as a scholar, Leichtentritt was also a composer; he wrote a Symph.; Violin Concerto; Cello Concerto; Piano Concerto; much chamber music; several song cycles; numerous piano pieces. He also wrote a comic opera, *Der Sizilianer*, which was produced in Freiburg on May 28, 1920. All his music MSS were donated after his death to the Library of Congress in Washington, D.C.
WRITINGS: *Chopin* (1905); *Geschichte der Motette* (Leipzig, 1908; a fundamental source on the subject); *Musikalische Formenlehre* (Leipzig, 1911; 5th ed., 1952; in Eng. as *Musical Form*, Cambridge, Mass., 1951); *Erwin Lendvai* (Berlin, 1912); *Ferruccio Busoni* (Leipzig, 1916); *Analyse der Chopinschen Klavierwerke* (2 vols., Berlin, 1920, 1922); *Händel* (Berlin, 1924; very valuable); *The Complete Piano Sonatas of Beethoven* (analytical notes; N.Y., 1936); *Everybody's Little History of Music* (N.Y., 1938); *Music, History, and Ideas* (Cambridge, Mass., 1938; very successful; 14 printings); *The Boston Symphony Orchestra and the New American Music* (Cambridge, Mass., 1946); *Music of the Western Nations* (posthumous; ed. and amplified by N. Slonimsky; Cambridge, Mass., 1956).

Leider, Frida, German opera soprano; b. Berlin, April 18, 1888; d. there, June 3, 1975. She was employed as a bank clerk in Berlin, and studied voice with Otto Schwarz on the side. She made her debut in Halle in 1915 as Venus in *Tannhäuser;* then sang at Rostock, Königsberg, and Hamburg. She was engaged by the Berlin State Opera in 1923, and remained on its roster until 1940; she also made guest appearances at La Scala in Milan, at the Paris Opéra, and in Vienna, Munich, Stockholm, Amsterdam, and Brussels. In 1928 she made her American debut at the Chicago Opera Co. as Brünnhilde in *Die Walküre;* appeared at the Metropolitan Opera in N.Y. on Jan. 16, 1933, as Isolde. In 1934 she returned to Germany; she encountered difficulties because her husband, a violinist named **Rudolf Deman,** was Jewish. She was confronted by the Nazis with the demand to divorce him, but refused; he succeeded in going to Switzerland. After the war and the collapse of the Nazi regime, she maintained a vocal studio at the Berlin State Opera until 1952; then taught at the Hochschule für Musik in Berlin until 1958. She publ. a memoir, *Das war mein Teil, Erinnerungen einer Opernsängerin* (Berlin, 1959; publ. in Eng. as *Playing My Part,* N.Y., 1966).

Leifs, Jón, foremost Icelandic composer and writer; b. Sólheimar, May 1, 1899; d. Reykjavik, July 30, 1968. After completing his primary education at Reykjavik, he went to Germany, where he studied at the Leipzig Cons. with Teichmüller, Szendrei, Scherchen, Lohse, and Graener; then conducted concerts in various German towns; in 1926 led the Hamburg Phil. when it visited Iceland; in 1934–37, was music director of Icelandic Radio; also president of the Council of Northern Composers (1951) and other musical societies in Iceland and Scandinavia. His music is technically derived from the German Romantic tradition; but in several of his works he makes use of Icelandic melodies and rhythms; often he abandons opulent harmonic accoutrements to portray Arctic nature in bleak, organum-like diaphony.
WORKS: Wordless music dramas: *Loftr* (Copenhagen, Sept. 3, 1938) and *Baldr* (1950); *Hljomkvida,* symph. trilogy (Karlsbad, 1925); *Icelandic Overture* (Oslo, 1926; his most successful work); *Kyrie on Icelandic Themes* for a cappella Chorus; *Island-Kantate* (Greifswald, 1930); *Saga-symfoni* (Helsinki, Sept. 18, 1950); 2 string quartets; several piano cycles based on Icelandic dance tunes; songs. He publ. (in Icelandic) a manual on musical forms; in German, *Islands künstlerische Anregung* (Reykjavik, 1951); contributed articles on Icelandic music to *Die Musik* (Oct. 1923), *Volk und Rasse* (Munich, 1932), and other publications.

Leigh, Walter, English composer; b. London, June 22, 1905; killed in action near Tobruk, Libya, June 12, 1942. He was a student of Edward Dent at Cambridge; also took lessons with Harold Darke and later with Paul Hindemith at the Hochschule für Musik in Berlin (1927–29). He was particularly adept in his writing for the theater.
WORKS: 2 light operas: *The Pride of the Regiment, or Cashiered for His Country* (Midhurst, England, Sept. 19, 1931) and *The Jolly Roger, or The Admiral's Daughter* (Manchester, Feb. 13, 1933);

musical revue, *9 Sharp* (London, 1938); several pieces designated for amateur orch.; Sonatina for Viola and Piano (perf. at the Festival of the International Society for Contemporary Music, Vienna, June 17, 1932); Trio for 3 Pianos (1934); Trio for Flute, Oboe, and Piano (1935); several scores of incidental music for the theater; piano pieces and songs.

Leighton, Kenneth, English composer; b. Wakefield, Yorkshire, Oct. 2, 1929. He enrolled at Queen's College, Oxford, to study classics and music (B.Mus., 1951); later took courses with Goffredo Petrassi in Rome. In 1956–68 he was a lecturer in composition at the Univ. of Edinburgh; then a lecturer in music at Worcester College, Oxford (1968–70), and from 1970 again at the Univ. of Edinburgh.

WORKS: FOR ORCH.: Symph. for Strings (1948); *Primavera romana*, overture (1951); Piano Concerto No. 1 (1951); Concerto for Viola, Harp, Timpani, and Strings (1952); Violin Concerto (1952); Concerto for Oboe and Strings (1953); Concerto for 2 Pianos, Timpani, and Strings (1953); Cello Concerto (1956); Piano Concerto No. 2 (1960); Concerto for String Orch. (1961); Symph. No. 1 (1964); *Dance Suite* No. 1 (1968); *Dance Suite* No. 2 (1970); Piano Concerto No. 3 (1969); Organ Concerto (1970); Symph. No. 2, *Sinfonia Mistica*, for Soprano, Chorus, and Orch. (1977); *The Birds*, choral suite for Soprano, Tenor, Chorus, and Orch. (1954); *Laudes Montium*, psalm with orch. (1975); *Columba*, opera (Glasgow, June 16, 1981). CHAMBER MUSIC: Piano Quintet (1959); 2 violin sonatas (1951, 1956); 2 string quartets (1956, 1957); *Fantasy on a Chorale* for Violin and Organ (Washington, D.C., May 4, 1980); *Animal Heaven* for Soprano and Instruments, to texts by Walt Whitman and James Dickey (1980); Fantasy-Octet, "Homage to Percy Grainger" (1982). FOR CHORUS: *Sinfonia sacra, The Light Invisible* for Tenor, Chorus, and Orch., to texts from the Bible and poems by T.S. Eliot (1958). FOR KEYBOARD: *Fantasia contrapuntistica* for Piano (1956); organ pieces.

Leighton, Sir William, English musician, "gentleman pensioner"; b. Plash, Shropshire(?), c.1565; d. (buried, London, July 31) 1622. He publ. *The Teares or Lamentacions of a Sorrowfull Soule Composed with Musicall Ayres and Songs both for Voyces and Divers Instruments* (1614), containing 54 metrical Psalms and hymns, 17 being for 4 voices with accompaniments in tablature for the lute, bandora, and cittern, and 13 for 4 voices and 24 for 5 voices without accompaniment. The first 8 are by Leighton himself; the others are by Bull, Byrd, Dowland, Gibbons, Coperario, Weelkes, Wilbye, etc. A complete modern edition of his works was edited by C. Hill in *Early English Church Music*, XI (London, 1970).

Leimer, Kurt, German pianist and composer; b. Wiesbaden, Sept. 7, 1920; d. Vaduz, Liechtenstein, Nov. 20, 1974. He studied piano with his great-uncle Karl Leimer (1858–1944), who was the teacher of Gieseking. After a brief concert career, Leimer took lessons in composition with Kurt von Wolfurt; made

rapid progress as a composer, and produced 4 piano concertos (one for left hand), all very effective in their high-flown Romantic style; he was soloist in his 4th Piano Concerto in N.Y., on Oct. 14, 1956, with Stokowski conducting; Karajan also conducted some of his works. Leimer became an Austrian citizen in 1956, but lived in Vaduz.

Leinsdorf, Erich, eminent Austrian-born American conductor; b. Vienna, Feb. 4, 1912. He was a scion of a cultural Jewish family; his real last name was **Landauer.** His mother gave him his first music lessons; later he studied piano with Paul Emerich and Hedwig Kammer-Rosenthal; at 13 he began to study cello with Lilly Kosz. He also had private lessons in composition with Paul Pisk. In 1930 he took a master class in conducting at the Mozarteum in Salzburg, and then studied for a short time in the music dept. of the Univ. of Vienna; from 1931 to 1933 he took courses at the State Academy of Music, making his debut as a conductor at the Musikvereinsaal upon his graduation. In 1933 he served as assistant conductor of the Workers' Chorus in Vienna; in 1934 he went to Salzburg, where he had a successful audition with Bruno Walter and Toscanini at the Salzburg Festivals, and was appointed their assistant. In 1937 he was engaged as a conductor of the Metropolitan Opera in N.Y.; he made his American debut there conducting *Die Walküre* on Jan. 21, 1938, with notable success; he then conducted other Wagnerian operas, ultimately succeeding Bodanzky as head of the German repertoire there in 1939. In 1942 he became an American citizen. In 1943 he was appointed music director of the Cleveland Orch.; however, his induction into the U.S. Army in Dec. 1943 interrupted his term there. After his discharge in 1944, he once again conducted at the Metropolitan in 1944–45; also conducted several concerts with the Cleveland Orch. in 1945 and 1946, and made appearances in Europe. From 1947 to 1955 he was music director of the Rochester (N.Y.) Phil. Orch. In the fall of 1956 he was briefly music director of the N.Y. City Opera; then returned to the Metropolitan as a conductor and musical consultant in 1957. He also appeared as a guest conductor in the U.S. and Europe. In 1962 he received the prestigious appointment of music director of the Boston Symph. Orch., a post he retained until 1969; then he conducted opera and symph. concerts in many of the major music centers of America and in Europe; from 1977 to 1980 he held the post of principal conductor of the (West) Berlin Radio Symph. Orch. He publ. a semiautobiographical and rather candid book of sharp comments, *Cadenza: A Musical Career* (Boston, 1976); also *The Composer's Advocate: A Radical Orthodoxy for Musicians* (New Haven, 1981).

Leitner, Ferdinand, eminent German conductor, b. Berlin, March 4, 1912. He studied at the State Academy of Music in Berlin; then served as Generalmusikdirektor of the Hamburg State Opera (1945–46) and of the Bavarian State Opera in Munich (1946–47). In 1947 he became Generalmusikdirektor of the Württemberg State Theater in Stuttgart.

He left Stuttgart in 1969 to become chief conductor of the Zürich Opera, retiring from this post in 1984. He also was named chief conductor of the Residentie Orch. at The Hague (1976–80).

Le Jeune, Claude (or **Claudin**), French composer; b. Valenciennes, 1528; d. Paris, Sept. 25, 1600. He was active chiefly in Paris, where he appears to have been for some time associated with the poet Antoine de Baïf in the Académie de Musique, founded to encourage the growth of a new style of musical composition known as "musique mesurée," in which the music is made to follow the metrical rhythm of the text in conformity with the rules of classical prosody. The type of poetry set to music in this manner was called "vers mesurez," and 33 examples of such settings by Le Jeune are to be found in the work entitled *Le Printemps,* publ. posthumously at Paris in 1603 by his sister Cécile Le Jeune. The metrical scanning is given at the head of each song. In the preface to this work Le Jeune is given credit for having been the first to achieve the "mating of ancient rhythm and modern harmony"; if not the first, he was at least, together with his contemporary and friend Jacques Mauduit, one of the earliest and most notable cultivators of this new and significant style. Le Jeune also cultivated every other variety of vocal music known in his time, such as French chansons in "vers rimez," Italian madrigals, Latin motets, etc. Special mention must be made of his settings of the Psalms, of which several collections appeared in 1564–1606. So great was his renown even during his lifetime that a wood engraving dated 1598 bore the legend: "Le Phénix des Musiciens." His best-known work is his setting of the Genevan Psalter *a* 4 and 5, publ. by Cécile Le Jeune in 1613. This simple contrapuntal setting of the Psalms was widely used in the Reformed churches of France and the Netherlands, and it was also publ. in a German trans. Some of these harmonizations even found their way into early New England psalmbooks, such as *The Ainsworth Psalter* (cf. *Early Psalmody in America,* ed. by C.S. Smith for the N.Y. Public Library, 1939). A more elaborate setting of some Psalms, *12 psaumes de David,* in motet style for 2 to 7 voices, was contained in the work entitled *Dodecacorde,* publ. at La Rochelle in 1598. On the title page of this work, Le Jeune is described as "compositeur de la musique de la chambre du roy," showing that he was then attached to the court of Henri IV. It is known that he had espoused the Huguenot cause during the wars of the Catholic League, and it is said that his MSS narrowly escaped destruction during the siege of Paris in 1588, having been saved only by the intervention of his Catholic colleague Mauduit. In 1612 a nephew of Le Jeune publ. a *Second livre de meslanges à 4–10,* containing miscellaneous vocal pieces and 2 instrumental fantasias. The most important works of Le Jeune have been reprinted by H. Expert in his *Maîtres musiciens de la renaissance française,* as follows: *Dodecacorde* (vol. 11); *Le Printemps* (vols. 12–14); one part of the *Livre de meslanges* (vol. 16); *Psaumes en vers mesurez* (vols.

20–22); also, in *Monuments de la musique française* (vols. 1 and 8) are *Octonaires de la vanité et inconstance du monde* and other works; *Missa ad placitum* is in Le Pupitre, 2; chansons in *Florilège du concert vocal de la renaissance,* 6; the *Airs* (1608) are publ. in 4 vols. by D.P. Walker in the Miscellenea series of the American Inst. of Musicology.

Lekeu, Guillaume, talented Belgian composer; b. Heusy, near Verviers, Jan. 20, 1870; d. Angers, Jan. 21, 1894. He went to school in Poitiers; after graduation, followed his family to Paris, where he studied with Gaston Vallin; he also received some advice from César Franck and took a course with Vincent d'Indy. He subsequently went to Brussels to compete for the Belgian Prix de Rome; won 2nd prize with his cantata *Andromède* (1891). Returning to Paris, he wrote several works of excellent quality, but death (of typhoid fever) intervened when he was barely 24 years old. His style of composition was influenced mainly by César Franck; his most durable work, a Violin Sonata with modal inflections and chromatic progressions, closely follows the procedures of Franck's Violin Sonata.

WORKS: The list of his works is necessarily small: Cello Sonata (1888); *Adagio* for Strings (1888); *Chant de triomphale délivrance* for Orch. (1889); *Hamlet* for Orch. (1890); *Fantaisie sur un cramignon liégois* for Orch. (1890); *Chant lyrique* for Chorus and Orch. (1891); *Introduction et Adagio* for Tuba and Wind Orch. (1891); Piano Trio (1891); Violin Sonata (1891; his most frequently perf. work); Piano Sonata (1891); *Fantaisie sur 2 airs angevins* for Orch. (1892); *Suite* for Voice and Orch (1892); *Barberine* (fragments for an opera); *Chanson de mai* for Chorus and Orch.; *Adagio* for String Quartet; *Epithalame* for Strings, Trombones, and Organ; String Quartet; *Meditation* and *Minuet* for String Quartet; *Noël* for Soprano, String Quartet, and Piano; Piano Quartet (unfinished; completed by Vincent d'Indy); Piano Sonata; *Tempo di mazurka* for Piano; a group of songs.

Lemacher, Heinrich, German composer; b. Solingen, June 26, 1891; d. Cologne, March 16, 1966. He studied at the Cons. of Cologne; in 1928, he became a teacher at the Cologne Hochschule für Musik. A disciple of the German Romantic school, he elaborated its principles in a number of choral and instrumental works; the chief influences are Bruckner and Reger. He wrote several symph. suites; chamber music; piano pieces. More important than these are his compositions for the Catholic service: several masses, offertories, motets, cantatas with organ accompaniment, etc., in which he succeeded in establishing a practical style of modern polyphony. Written shortly before his death, his last work, Sextet for 3 Trumpets, 2 Trombones, and Tuba, bears the opus number 208. He publ. several books on music theory: *Lehrbuch des Kontrapunktes* (Mainz, 1950; 4th ed., 1962); *Harmonielehre* (Cologne, 1958; 5th ed., 1967); *Formenlehre der Musik* (with H. Schroeder, Cologne, 1962; in Eng. as *Musical Form,* 1967).

Lemaire (or **Le Maire**), **Jean,** French musician; b. Chaumont en Bassigny, 1581; d. c.1650. He is said to have proposed the adoption of a 7th solmisation syllable *si* (so asserted by Rousseau in his *Dictionnaire de musique; za,* according to Mersenne's *Harmonie universalle*). However, the designation *si* seems to have been proposed even earlier, so the question of priority remains moot. Lemaire constructed a lute which he called the "Almérie" (anagram of Lemaire).

Lemaire, Jean Eugène Gaston, French composer; b. Château d'Amblainvilliers, Seine-et-Oise, Sept. 9, 1854; d. (suicide; body found in the Seine) Paris, Jan. 9, 1928. He studied at the Ecole Niedermeyer; was a prolific composer of light music (operettas, piano pieces, and characteristic pieces for orch.).
    WORKS: *Pierrette et le pot au lait,* pantomime (Paris, Feb. 11, 1891); *Conte de printemps,* pantomime (Paris, May 18, 1892); *La Belle Tunisienne,* opera in one act (Paris, Aug. 26, 1892); operettas: *Les Maris de Juanita, Le Supplice de Jeannot, Le Rêve de Manette; Rose,* lyric fairy tale (Paris, March 14, 1895); ballets: *Feminissima* (1902) and *Pierrot venge son rival* (1917). He also wrote a number of fox-trots, one of which, *La Grenouille,* became popular; and songs, of which *Vous dansez, marquise,* was a great favorite.

Le Maistre (or **Le Maître**), **Mattheus,** Flemish composer; b. near Liège, c.1505; d. Dresden, 1577. In 1554 he succeeded J. Walter as Kapellmeister at the court in Dresden; retired on a pension, Feb. 12, 1568. Fétis and Otto Kade wrongly identified him with Hermann Matthias Werrekoren, choirmaster in Milan.
    WORKS: *Magnificat octo tonorum* (1577); *Catechesis numeris musicis inclusa* (1563; for the choirboys of the Dresden Chapel); *Geistliche und weltliche teutsche Gesänge* for 4–5 Voices (1566); motets for 5 Voices (1570); *Officia de nativitate et Ascensione Christi* for 5 Voices (1574); *Schöne und auserlesene teutsche und lateinische geistliche Lieder* (1577). A motet for 4 Voices, *Estote prudentes,* is in Commer's *Collectio* (vol. 8); 2 lieder for 4 Voices are in Ambros's *Geschichte der Musik* (vol. 5, *Beispielband,* ed. by O. Kade, 1882).

Lemare, Edwin Henry, British-American organist; b. Ventnor, Isle of Wight, Sept. 9, 1865; d. Los Angeles, Sept. 24, 1934. He received his early training from his father, an organist; then studied at the Royal Academy of Music in London; at the age of 19 he played at the Inventions Exhibition in London; in 1892 he began a series of weekly organ recitals at Holy Trinity Church in London; from 1897 to 1902 he was organist at St. Margaret's, Westminster. In 1901 he made a concert tour through the U.S. and Canada; from 1902 to 1905 he was organist at the Carnegie Inst. in Pittsburgh; then held the post of municipal organist in San Francisco (1917–21), Portland, Maine (1921–23), and Chattanooga, Tenn. (1924–29). He publ. about 200 organ works and made many arrangements. His *Andantino in D-flat* acquired wide popularity when it was used for the American ballad *Moonlight and Roses.* His booklet of reminiscences, *Organs I Have Met,* was publ. posthumously in 1957.

Lemeshev, Sergei, Russian tenor; b. Knyazevo, near Tver, July 10, 1902; d. Moscow, June 26, 1977. In his youth he worked at a cobbler's shop in Petrograd; then went to Moscow, where he studied at the Moscow Cons. with Raysky, graduating in 1925. He made his operatic debut at Sverdlovsk in 1926; then was a member of the Kharbin Opera in Manchuria (1927–29) and at the Tiflis Opera (1929–31). In 1931 he joined the Bolshoi Theater in Moscow, and gradually created an enthusiastic following; he was particularly admired for his performance of the role of Lensky in *Eugene Onegin;* in 1972, on his 70th birthday, he sang it again at the Bolshoi Theater. Other roles in which he shone, apart from the Russian repertoire, included Faust, Romeo, and Werther. He also made numerous appearances in solo recitals; was the first to present an entire cycle of Tchaikovsky's songs in 5 concerts.

Lemoine, Antoine-Marcel, French music publisher, violinist, and guitar player, father of **Henry Lemoine;** b. Paris, Nov. 3, 1753; d. there, April 10, 1816. A self-taught musician, he played viola at the Théâtre de Monsieur, conducted at minor Parisian theaters, and finally founded a music publishing firm.

Lemoine, Henry, French music publisher, son of **Antoine-Marcel Lemoine;** b. Paris, Oct. 21, 1786; d. there, May 18, 1854. He studied at the Paris Cons. (1798–1809); in 1821 he also had harmony lessons from Reicha; taught piano; at his father's death, succeeded to the latter's music publishing business. He publ. methods for harmony, piano, and solfeggio; *Tablettes du pianiste: Memento du professeur de piano*; sonatas, variations, dances, etc., for piano.

Lemoyne, Jean Baptiste, French conductor and composer; b. Eymet, Périgord, April 3, 1751; d. Paris, Dec. 30, 1796. He studied with Graun and Kirnberger at Berlin, where he became 2nd Kapellmeister to Frederick the Great. Returning to Paris, he brought out an opera, *Electre* (July 2, 1782), pretending to be a pupil of Gluck, an imposture that Gluck did not see fit to expose until the failure of Lemoyne's piece. In his next operas, Lemoyne abandoned Gluck's ideas, copied the style of Piccinni and Sacchini, and produced several successful works, including *Phèdre* (Fountainebleau, Oct. 26, 1786) and *Nephté* (Paris, Dec. 15, 1789).

Lendvay, Kamilló, Hungarian composer; b. Budapest, Dec. 28, 1928. He studied composition with Viski at the Budapest Academy of Music; devoted himself mainly to the musical theater, as a composer and a conductor; in 1973 was appointed conductor of the Capitol Operetta Theater; also taught at the

Budapest Academy.

WORKS: Television opera buffa, *Abüvös szék* (*The Magic Chair;* 1972); 4 musicals: *The 3 Musketeers* (1962); *10 Days That Shook the World* (1967); *Ex* (1968); *Knock Out* (1968); 2 ballets: *Eszmélés* (*Awakening;* 1964) and *Musica leggiera* (jazz ballet; 1965); oratorio, *Orogenesis* (1969); *Tragic Overture* (1958); *Mauthausen* for Orch. (1958); Concertino for Piano, Wind Instruments, Percussion, and Harp (1959); *The Indomitable Tin Soldier,* orch. suite, with Narrator (1961); Violin Concerto (1961–62); *4 Invocations* for Orch. (1966); *Chamber Concerto* for 13 Instruments (1969); *Kifejezések* (*Expressions)* for 11 Strings or String Orch. (1974); *Pezzo concertato* for Cello and Orch. (Trieste, Oct. 18, 1975); *Fantasy* for Violin and Piano (1951); *Rhapsody* for Violin and Piano (1955); String Quartet (1962); *4 Duos* for Flute and Piano (1965); *Disposizioni* for Solo Cimbalom (1975); choruses; songs.

Lenepveu, Charles (Ferdinand), French composer and pedagogue; b. Rouen, Oct. 4, 1840; d. Paris, Aug. 16, 1910. While a law student, he took music lessons from Servais; won first prize at Caen in 1861 for a cantata; entered Ambroise Thomas's class at the Paris Cons. in 1863, and in 1865 took the Grand Prix de Rome with the cantata *Renaud dans les jardins d'Armide* (Paris, Jan. 3, 1866). His comic opera *Le Florentin* also won a prize, offered by the Ministry of Fine Arts (1867), and was performed at the Opéra-Comique (Feb. 26, 1874). The grand opera *Velléda* was produced at Covent Garden in London (July 4, 1882), with Adelina Patti in the title role. In 1891 Lenepveu succeeded Guiraud as prof. of harmony at the Cons., and in 1893 again succeeded him as prof. of composition, taking an advanced class in 1894. In 1896 he was elected to Ambroise Thomas's chair in the Académie des Beaux-Arts; was a Chevalier of the Legion of Honor, and an Officer of Public Instruction.

Léner, Jenö, Hungarian violinist; b. Szabadka, April 7, 1894; d. New York, Nov. 4, 1948. He studied at the Hungarian Music Academy in Budapest; worked as a violinist in theater orchs.; in 1918 organized the Léner String Quartet (with Joseph Smilovits, Sándor Roth, and Imre Hartmann), which became one of the most renowned string quartets of modern times; it was particularly noted for its interpretation of Beethoven's quartets. In 1925 Léner took his quartet to London, and in 1929 to the U.S.; it was disbanded in 1942, but reorganized, with a partly new membership, in 1945. The fame enjoyed by the Léner quartet can be judged by Aldous Huxley's discussion of its performance of Beethoven's last quartets in his novel *Point Counterpoint* (1928).

Leng, Alfonso, Chilean composer; b. Santiago, Feb. 11, 1884; d. there, Nov. 7, 1974. He was of mixed German and English descent; studied dentistry, and became a professional dentist in Santiago; also took music lessons with Enrique Soro. In his leisure time, he composed short symph. sketches in a Romantic vein, songs, and evocative piano pieces.

WORKS: *5 dolores* for Orch. (1920); *La muerte de Alsino,* symph. poem (1920; Santiago, May 30, 1931); *Canto de Invierno* for Orch. (1932); *Fantasia* for Piano and Orch. (Santiago, August. 28, 1936); *Psalm 77* for Soloists, Chorus, and Orch. (1941); *Fantasia quasi Sonata* for Piano (1909); *10 Preludes* for Piano (1919–32); *Andante* for Piano and String Quartet (1922); *2 Otoñales* for Piano (1932); 2 piano sonatas (1927, 1950); many songs. A special issue of the *Revista Musical Chilena* (Aug./Sept. 1957) was publ. in his honor, with articles by Domingo Santa Cruz, Alfonso Letelier, and others.

Lennon, John (Winston), English rock-'n'-roll singer, guitarist, poet, and instinctive composer, member of the celebrated rock group The Beatles; b. Liverpool, Oct. 9, 1940, during a German air raid on the city; d. Dec. 8, 1980, gunned down by a wacko in front of his apartment in New York. He was educated by an aunt after his parents separated; played the mouth organ as a child; later learned the guitar; was encouraged to become a musician by the conductor of a Liverpool-Edinburgh bus. Emotionally rocked over by Elvis Presley's animal magnetism, he became infatuated with American popular music. With 3 other rock-crazed Liverpudlians, Paul McCartney, George Harrison, and Stuart Sutcliffe, he formed a pop combo. Inspired by the success of a local group, The Crickets, Lennon hit upon the name The Beatles, which possessed the acoustical ring of the coleopterous insect *beetle* and the rock-associated *beat.* The Beatles opened at the pseudo-exotic Casbah Club in Liverpool in 1959; soon moved to the more prestigious Cavern Club, where they co-opted Pete Best as a drummer. In 1960 they played in Hamburg, scoring a gratifyingly vulgar success with the beer-sodden customers by their loud, electrically amplified sound. Back in England, The Beatles crept on to fame. In 1961 they were taken up by the perspicacious promoter Brian Epstein, who launched an extensive publicity campaign to put them over the footlights. Sutcliffe died of a brain hemorrhage in 1962. Pete Best left the group and was replaced by Richard Starkey, whose "nom-de-beatle" became Ringo Starr. The quartet opened at the London Palladium in 1963 and drove the youthful audience to a frenzy, a scene that was to be repeated elsewhere in Europe, in America, in Japan, and in Australia. After a period of shocked recoil, the British establishment acknowledged the beneficial contribution of The Beatles to British art and the Exchequer. In 1965 each beatle was made a Member of the Order of the British Empire. Although American in origin, the type of popular music plied by John Lennon and The Beatles as a group has an indefinably British lilt. The meter is square; the main beat is accentuated; syncopation is at a minimum; the harmony is modal, with a lowered submediant in major keys as a constantly present feature; a propensity for plagal cadences and a proclivity for consecutive triadic progressions create at times a curiously hymnal mood. But professional arrangers employed by The Beatles invested their bland melodies in raucous dissonance; electronic amplification made the music of The Beatles the loudest in the world for their time. The lyrics, most of them written by John Lennon and Paul McCartney, are distinguished by suggestive allusions, sensuous but not flagrantly erotic, anarchistic but not destructive, cynical but also humane. There are covert references to psychedelic drugs. The Beatles produced the highly original films *A Hard Day's Night, Help!, Yellow Submarine,* and *Let It Be.* The most successful individual songs in the Beatles' repertoire were *Love Me Do, I Want to Hold Your Hand, Can't Buy Me Love, Ticket to Ride, Day Tripper, All My Loving, I Wanna Be Your Man, And I Love Her, Eight Days a Week, Yesterday, Michelle, Eleanor Rigby, With a Little Help from My Friends, Sergeant Pepper's Lonely Hearts Club Band, Magical Mystery Tour, Lady Madonna, You're Gonna Lose That Girl, Norwegian Wood, Good Day Sunshine, Hey Jude;* also title songs of the films. Lennon's 2nd wife, the Japanese-American artist Yoko Ono, greatly influenced the development of his social consciousness; they collaborated on his last album, *Double Fantasy,* which achieved great popularity. The shock waves produced by Lennon's murder reverberated throughout the world; crowds in deep mourning marched in N.Y., Liverpool, and Tokyo; Yoko Ono issued a number of declarations urging Lennon's fans not to give way to despair. Not even the death of Elvis Presley generated such outbursts of grief. A photograph taken on the afternoon before his murder, of John in the nude, embracing a fully dressed Yoko Ono, was featured on the cover of a special issue of *Rolling Stone* magazine (Jan. 22, 1981).

Lenormand, René, French composer; b. Elbeuf, Aug. 5, 1846; d. Paris, Dec. 3, 1932. He received his musical training from his mother, who was an excellent pianist; in 1868 he went to Paris, where he studied with Damcke. Lenormand's main interest was in the creation of an international type of the German lied, and for that purpose he organized in Paris a society which he called Le Lied en Tous Pays. Besides his songs, Lenormand wrote an opera, *Le Cachet rouge* (Le Havre, 1925); Piano Concerto; *Le Lahn de Mabed* (on an old Arabian theme) for Violin and Orch.; *Le Voyage imaginaire,* symph. tableaux after Loti; *2 esquisses sur des thèmes malais* for Orch.; piano pieces (*Une Journée à la campagne, Le Nuage vivant, Valses sérieuses, Pièces exotiques,* etc.); for 4-hands: *Divertissement américain, La Nouba Medjenneba,* etc.); also publ. a valuable manual on harmony, *Etude sur l'harmonie moderne* (Paris, 1912; Eng. trans. as *A Study of Modern Harmony,* London, 1915).

Lentz, Daniel, American composer of the avantgarde; b. Latrobe, Pa., March 10, 1942. He began his career as a follower of the medieval troubadours and goliards; like them, he traveled far and wide; like them, he was the recipient of bounties from foundations and individuals in power. He received 2 grants from the National Endowment for the Arts,

a Fulbright grant, and a Tanglewood Composition fellowship. He traveled in the Netherlands in 1970 and in Germany in 1973, and presented concerts and multimedia exhibitions in California and other receptive regions of the U.S. The titles of some of his works are inscrutable, as *Fermentation Notebooks, North American Eclipse;* or alliterative, as *The Iridescence of Eurydice.* Perhaps his most startling composition is *Love and Conception,* in sonata form, in which 2 naked young people, one of each gender, are told to crawl under the lid of a grand piano and simulate sexual intercourse; the piece was actually performed at the Univ. of Calif., Santa Barbara, on Feb. 26, 1969, but as a result, the composer was fired from his teaching job there. A similarly audacious work was his *Kissing Song* for 24 amplified Unisex Voices, performing vocalized osculations, with each kissing pair sliding their respective tongues into his (or her) mouth (1971); it was scheduled for public performance at the Metamusik Festival in Berlin in 1978 but was canceled because of the reluctance of the kissers to sing between someone else's lips.

Lenya, Lotte, Austrian actress and singer; b. Vienna, Oct. 18, 1898; d. New York, Nov. 27, 1981. She began her stage career as a dancer in Zürich, where she went at the outbreak of World War I in 1914; after the end of the war she went to Berlin. There she met **Kurt Weill,** whom she married in 1926; in 1927 she made her debut as a singer in the Brecht-Weill scenic cantata *Mahagonny;* in 1928 she sang in the production of the Brecht-Weill *Die Dreigroschenoper* in Berlin; from then on she identified herself with practically all of Weill's musicals. She and Weill fled Nazified Berlin in 1933, and after a couple of years in Paris and London, went to America. Although not a singer of a professional caliber, Lotte Lenya adapted herself to the peculiar type of half-spoken, half-sung roles in Weill's works with total dedication.

Lenz, Wilhelm von, Russian writer on music; b. Riga, June 1, 1809; d. St. Petersburg, Jan. 31, 1883. He traveled in Europe; studied piano in Paris with Liszt and Chopin (1842); returning to Russia, he became a government councillor in St. Petersburg. His writings are historically valuable because of the intimate personal experience that they reflect. His most notable book is *Beethoven et ses trois styles* (2 vols., St. Petersburg, 1852; new ed., by Calvocoressi, Paris, 1909), in which he proposed for the first time the division of Beethoven's works into 3 chronological periods: the first (opp. 1–21) entirely Classical; the 2nd (opp. 22–95), and to Lenz the best, truly Beethovenian in its nobility and individuality; and the 3rd (from op. 96) marking partly a decline, partly an attempt to scale unattainable heights. Lenz further publ. *Beethoven: Eine Kunststudie* (6 vols., 1855–60); vols. 4–6 were separately publ. as *Kritischer Katalog der sämmtlichen Werke nebst Analysen derselben* (Hamburg, 1860), and vol. 1 as *Beethoven: Eine Biographie* (2nd ed., 1879; reprinted, with additions by A. Kalischer, 1908); *Die grossen Piano-*

forte-Virtuosen unserer Zeit (brief character sketches of Liszt, Chopin, Tausig, and Henselt; 1872; Eng. trans., N.Y., 1899).

Leo, Leonardo (Lionardo Ortensio Salvatore de Leo), important Italian composer; b. San Vito degli Schiavi, near Brindisi, Aug. 5, 1694; d. Naples, Oct. 31, 1744. In 1709 he went to Naples, where he studied with Fago at the Conservatorio S. Maria della Pietà dei Turchini; his sacred drama *S. Chiara, o L'infedeltà abbattuta* was given there in 1712. In 1713 he was made supernumerary organist in the Viceroy's Chapel; also served as maestro di cappella to the Marchese Stella. His first opera, *Il Pisistrato,* was performed in Naples on May 13, 1714. His first comic opera, *La 'mpeca scoperta* in the Neapolitan dialect, was given in Naples on Dec. 13, 1723. In all, he wrote some 50 operas, most of them for Naples. Following Alessandro Scarlatti's death in 1725, he was elevated to the position of first organist at the viceregal chapel. In 1730 he became provicemaestro of the Royal Chapel; in 1737 vicemaestro. He taught as vicemaestro at the Conservatorio S. Maria della Pietà dei Turchini from 1734 to 1737; from 1741 was primo maestro in succession to his teacher, Fago; also was primo maestro at the Conservatorio S. Onofrio from 1739. In Jan. 1744 he became maestro di cappella of the Royal Chapel, but died that same year. Among his famous pupils were Piccinni and Jommelli. Leo's music for the theater (especially his comic operas) is noteworthy; of no less significance were his theoretical works, *Istituzioni o regole del contrappunto* and *Lezione di canto fermo.*

WORKS: OPERAS: All premiered in Naples unless otherwise given: *Il Pisistrato* (May 13, 1714); *Sofonisba* (Jan. 22, 1718); *Caio Gracco* (April 19, 1720); *Arianna e Teseo* (Nov. 26, 1721); *Baiazete, imperator dei Turchi* (Aug. 28, 1722); *Timocrate* (Venice, 1723); *La' mpeca scoperta* (comic opera; Dec. 13, 1723); *Il Turno Aricino* (with L. Vinci; 1724); *L'amore fedele* (comic opera; April 25, 1724); *Lo pazzo apposta* (comic opera; Aug. 26, 1724); *Zenobia in Palmira* (May 13, 1725); *Il trionfo di Camilla, regina dei Volsci* (Rome, Jan. 8, 1726); *Orismene, ovvero Dalli sdegni l'amore* (comic opera; Jan. 19, 1726); *La semmeglianza de chi l'ha fatta* (comic opera; Fall 1726); *Lo matrimonio annascuso* (comic opera; 1727); *Il Cid* (Rome, Feb. 10, 1727); *La pastorella commattuta* (comic opera; Fall 1727); *Argene* (Venice, Jan. 17, 1728); *Catone in Utica* (Venice, 1729); *La schiava per amore* (comic opera; 1729); *Semiramide* (Feb. 2, 1730); *Rosmene* (comic opera; Summer 1730); *Evergete* (Rome, 1731); *Demetrio* (Oct. 1, 1732); *Amor da' senno* (comic opera; 1733); *Nitocri, regina d'Egitto* (Nov. 4, 1733); *Il castello d'Atlante* (July 4, 1734); *Demofoonte* (Jan. 20, 1735; Act 1 by D. Sarro, Act 2 by F. Mancini, Act 3 by Leo, and intermezzos by G. Sellitti); *La clemenza di Tito* (Venice, 1735); *Emira* (July 12, 1735; intermezzos by I Prota); *Demetrio* (Dec. 10, 1735; different setting from earlier opera of 1732); *Onore vince amore* (comic opera; 1736); *Farnace* (Dec. 19, 1736); *L'amico traditore* (comic opera; 1737); *Siface* (Bologna, May 11,

1737; revised version as *Viriate,* Pistoia, 1740); *La simpatia del sangue* (comic opera; Fall 1737); *Olimpiade* (Dec. 19, 1737); *Il conte* (comic opera; 1738); *Il Ciro riconosciuto* (Turin, 1739); *Amor vuol sofferenze* (comic opera; Fall 1739; revised version as *La finta frascatana,* Nov. 1744); *Achille in Sciro* (Turin, 1740); *Scipione nelle Spagne* (Milan, 1740); *L'Alidoro* (comic opera; Summer 1740); *Demetrio* (Dec 19, 1741; different setting from the earlier operas of 1732 and 1735); *L'ambizione delusa* (comic opera; 1742); *Andromaca* (Nov. 4, 1742); *Il fantastico, od Il nuovo Chisciotte* (comic opera; 1743; revised version, Fall 1748); *Vologeso, re dei Parti* (Turin, 1744); *La fedeltà odiata* (comic opera; 1744); he also contributed to a pasticcio setting of *Demetrio* (June 30, 1738); he likewise composed prologues, arias, etc., to operas by other composers. A number of operas long attributed to Leo are now considered doubtful.

Leo also composed serenatas, feste teatrali, chamber cantatas, etc. He wrote the following sacred dramas and oratorios: *S. Chiara, o L'infedeltà abbattuta* (Naples, 1712); *Il trionfo della castità di S. Alessio* (Naples, Jan. 4, 1713); *Dalla morte alla vita di S. Maria Maddalena* (Atrani, July 22, 1722); *Oratorio per la Ss. vergine del rosario* (Naples, Oct. 1, 1730); *S. Elena al Calvario* (Bologna, 1734); *La morte di Abele* (Bologna, 1738); *S. Francesco di Paola nel deserto* (Lecce, 1738); *Il verbo eterno e la religione* (Florence, 1741); he also composed 6 Neapolitan masses, various mass movements, 2 Magnificats, offertories, antiphons, motets, etc.; most notable is his *Miserere* for Double Choir and Organ (1739), publ. in a modern ed. by H. Wiley Hitchcock (St. Louis, 1961). His instrumental works include 6 concerti for Cello, String Orch., and Basso Continuo (1737–38); of these, one in D major has been ed. by F. Cilea (Milan, 1934), one in A major by E. Rapp (Mainz, 1938), and 3 in the Series of Early Music, VII (1973); Concerto in D major for 4 Violins and Basso Continuo (publ. in *Musikschätze der Vergangenheit,* XXIV, Berlin, 1952); works for harpsichord; etc.

Leoncavallo, Ruggero, Italian dramatic composer; b. Naples, April 23, 1857; d. Montecatini, Aug. 9, 1919. He attended the Naples Cons., where his teachers were B. Cesi (piano) and M. Ruta and L. Rossi (composition), and at 16 made a pianistic tour. His first opera, *Tommaso Chatterton,* was about to be produced in Bologna (1878) when the manager disappeared, and the production was called off. Leoncavallo earned his living as a young man by playing piano in cafés; this life he continued for many years, traveling through Egypt, Greece, Turkey, Germany, Belgium, and the Netherlands before settling in Paris. There he found congenial company; composed chansonettes and other popular songs; wrote an opera, *Songe d'une nuit d'été* (*Midsummer Night's Dream,* after Shakespeare), which was privately sung in a salon. He began to study Wagner's scores, and became an ardent Wagnerian; he resolved to emulate the master by producing a trilogy, *Crepusculum,* depicting in epical traits the Italian Renaissance; the separate parts were to be *I Medici, Girolamo Savonarola,* and *Cesare Borgia.* He spent 6 years on the basic historical research; having completed the first part, and with the scenario of the entire trilogy sketched, he returned to Italy in 1887. There, the publisher Ricordi became interested in the project, but kept delaying the publication and production of the work. Annoyed, Leoncavallo turned to Sonzogno, the publisher of Mascagni, whose opera *Cavalleria rusticana* had just obtained a tremendous vogue. Leoncavallo submitted a short opera in a similarly realistic vein; he wrote his own libretto based on a factual story of passion and murder in a Calabrian village, and named it *Pagliacci.* The opera was given with sensational success at the Teatro dal Verme in Milan under the direction of Toscanini (May 21, 1892), and rapidly took possession of operatic stages throughout the world; it is often played on the same evening with Mascagni's opera, both works being of brief duration. Historically, these 2 operas signalized the important development of Italian operatic *verismo,* which influenced composers of other countries also. The holograph score of *Pagliacci* is in the Library of Congress.

The enormous success of *Pagliacci* did not deter Leoncavallo from carrying on his more ambitious projects. The first part of his unfinished trilogy, *I Medici,* was finally brought out at La Scala in Milan on Nov. 9, 1893, but the reception was so indifferent that Leoncavallo turned to other subjects; the same fate befell his youthful *Tommaso Chatterton* at its production in Rome (March 10, 1896). His next opera, *La Bohème* (Venice, May 6, 1897), won considerable success, but had the ill fortune of coming a year after Puccini's masterpiece on the same story, and was dwarfed by comparison. There followed a light opera, *Zazà* (Milan, Nov. 10, 1900), which was fairly successful, and was produced repeatedly on world stages. In 1904 Leoncavallo was commissioned by the German Emperor Wilhelm II to write an opera for Berlin; this was *Der Roland von Berlin,* on a German historic theme; it was produced in Berlin on Dec. 13, 1904, but despite the high patronage it proved a fiasco. In 1906 Leoncavallo made a tour of the U.S. and Canada, conducting his *Pagliacci* and a new opera, *La Jeunesse de Figaro,* specially written for his American tour; it was so unsuccessful that Leoncavallo never attempted to stage it in Europe. Back in Italy he resumed his industrious production; 2 new operas, *Maia* (Rome, Jan. 15, 1910) and *Malbruk* (Rome, Jan. 19, 1910), were produced within the same week; another opera, *La Reginetta delle rose,* was staged simultaneously in Rome and in Naples (June 24, 1912). In the autumn of that year, Leoncavallo visited London, where he presented the premiere of his *Gli Zingari* (Sept. 16, 1912); a year later, he revisited the U.S., conducting in San Francisco. He wrote several more operas, but they made no impression; 3 of them were produced during his lifetime: *La Candidata* (Rome, Feb. 6, 1915), *Goffredo Mameli* (Genoa, April 27, 1916), and *Prestami tua moglie* (Montecatini, Sept. 2, 1916); the following were produced posthumously: *A chi la giarettiera?* (Rome, Oct. 16, 1919), *Edipo re*

(Chicago, Dec. 13, 1920), and *Il primo bacio* (Montecatini, April 29, 1923); yet another opera, *Tormenta,* remained unfinished. Salvatore Allegra collected various sketches by Leoncavallo and arranged from them a 3-act operetta, *La maschera nuda,* which was produced in Naples on June 26, 1925.

Leonhard, Julius Emil, German composer; b. Lauban, June 13, 1810; d. Dresden, June 23, 1883. He became a prof. of piano at the Munich Cons. in 1852, and at the Dresden Cons. in 1859. He wrote an oratorio, *Johannes der Täufer;* 3 cantatas for Soli, Chorus, and Orch.; Symph.; overture to Oehlenschläger's *Axel und Walpurg;* Piano Sonata; 2 violin sonatas; 3 string trios; Piano Quartet; etc.

Leonhardt, Gustav, eminent Dutch organist and harpsichord player; b. 's Graveland, May 30, 1928. He studied in the Netherlands and Switzerland; toured widely in Europe; made 6 tours in America as a performer and lecturer. He edited collections of keyboard music; publ. *The Art of Fugue, Bach's Last Harpsichord Work* (The Hague, 1952).

Leoni, Franco, Italian composer; b. Milan, Oct. 24, 1864; d. London, Feb. 8, 1949. He studied at the Milan Cons. with Dominiceti and Ponchielli; in 1892 went to London, where he remained for 25 years, until 1917; then lived in France and Italy, eventually returning to England.

WORKS: Operas: *Raggio di luna* (Milan, June 5, 1890); *Rip van Winkle* (London, Sept. 4, 1897); *Ib and Little Christina,* "a picture in 3 panels" (London, Nov. 14, 1901); *The Oracle* (London, June 28, 1905; Metropolitan Opera, N.Y., Feb. 4, 1915; his most successful opera); *Tzigana* (Genoa, Feb. 3, 1910); *Le baruffe chiozzotte* (Milan, Jan. 2, 1920); *La terra del sogno* (Milan, Jan. 10, 1920); cantatas: *Sardanapalus* (1896) and *Golgotha* (1911); oratorio, *The Gate of Life* (London, March 16, 1898); songs.

Leoni, Leone, Italian composer; b. Verona, c.1560; d. Vicenza, June 24, 1627. He studied at the "academy" maintained by Count Mario Bevilacqua in Verona; was maestro di cappella in Vicenza from Oct. 4, 1588, until his death. He was a disciple of the Venetian school; his works are characteristic for their application of chromatic devices in harmony, and antiphonal choral usages. He publ. 5 books of madrigals for 5 Voices (Venice, 1588–1602); 4 books of motets, with Organ, under the title *Sacri fiori* (1606–22); *Aurea corona* for 4 Voices accompanied by 6 Instruments (1618). His motets are particularly fine.

Leonin (Leoninus), great master of the Notre Dame School and of the Ars Antiqua; flourished probably before the cornerstone of Notre Dame de Paris was laid in 1163; was theretofore active at the earlier church, Beatae Mariae Virginis. According to the treatise of Anonymus IV (Coussemaker, *Scriptores,* I, 342), he complied the *Magnus Liber organi de graduali et antiphonario pro servitio* *divino multiplicando*, a cycle of 2-part liturgical settings for the whole church year, a work later revised by Leonin's successor, Perotin. The original of this collection has not been preserved, but there are 4 extant MSS containing music from it; of these, MS Wolfenbüttel 677 (formerly Helmstedt 628), dating from the 14th century (facsimile reprint in J.H. Baxter, *An Old St. Andrews Music Book*, 1931), though not the oldest, appears to preserve music from the *Magnus Liber* in purest form; the other 3 MSS are Pluteus 29.1 in the Biblioteca Medicea-Laurenziana of Florence, Wolfenbüttel 1206, and Madrid Biblioteca Nacional 20486. Leonin was the chief figure of his period, standing midway between the St. Martial school and Perotin; his technique is characterized by the juxtaposition in individual pieces of the note-against-note style, and the style in which, over a lower part characterized by long sustained notes, an upper part moves in freely flowing rhythm. (Both styles had already been used at St. Martial.)

Leonova, Darya, Russian contralto; b. Vyshny-Volochok, March 9, 1829; d. St. Petersburg, Feb. 6, 1896. She studied singing in St. Petersburg; in 1852 sang the part of Vanya in Glinka's *A Life for the Tsar*, and was greatly praised by Glinka himself. In 1875 she went on a concert tour around the world, through Siberia, China, Japan, and America. In 1879 she traveled in southern Russia and the Crimea with Mussorgsky as accompanist; sang arias from Mussorgsky's operas and his songs; in 1880 opened a singing school in St. Petersburg, with Mussorgsky acting as coach.

Leopold I, Austrian emperor who reigned from 1658 till 1705; b. Vienna, June 9, 1640; d. there, May 5, 1705. During his reign Vienna became the center of the world's operatic activity, no fewer than 400 new operas having been produced in that time; he was not only an enthusiastic patron but also a practically trained musician and diligent composer. His complete works are in MS in the State Library at Vienna: 15 oratorios, 7 operas, 17 ballet suites, 155 arias, 79 sacred compositions (2 masses, 5 Offices for the Dead, 4-part Miserere with Instruments, etc.).

Leppard, Raymond, English conductor and harpsichordist; b. London, Aug. 11, 1927. He studied at Trinity College, Cambridge; was a lecturer in music at Cambridge Univ. (1958–68). In 1963 he organized the English Chamber Orch. and traveled with it to Japan in 1970. In 1973 he became principal conductor of the Northern Symph. Orch. in England, resigning in 1980; then lived in N.Y. In 1978 he was guest conductor of the N.Y. Phil.; in 1983 he was made a Commander of the Order of the British Empire; in 1984 he became principal guest conductor of the St. Louis Symph. Orch. He took particular interest in early Baroque music; gave harpsichord recitals.

Leps, Wassili, Russian conductor and composer; b. St. Petersburg, May 12, 1870; d. Toronto, Dec. 22, 1943. He went to Germany, where he studied at the Dresden Cons. with Draeseke, Wüllner, and Theodor Kirchner. In 1894 he settled in America; taught at the Philadelphia Music Academy; then became conductor of the Philadelphia Operatic Society, which he led until 1923, producing 47 operas. In 1932 he organized the Providence Symph. Orch.; was its conductor until 1941, when he retired and went to Toronto to reside with a daughter. He wrote an opera on a Japanese subject, *Hoshi-San*, which he conducted with the Philadelphia Operatic Society on May 21, 1909; a cantata, *Yo-Nennen*, and some symph. music.

Leroux, Xavier, French composer; b. Velletri, Papal States, Oct. 11, 1863; d. Paris, Feb. 2, 1919. He was a pupil of Dubois and Massenet at the Paris Cons.; won first Grand Prix de Rome in 1885; was appointed a prof. at the Cons. in 1896.
WORKS: Operas: *Cléopâtre* (Paris, Oct. 23, 1890); *Evangeline* (Brussels, 1895); *Astarté* (Paris, Feb. 15, 1901); *La Reine Fiammette* (Paris, Dec. 23, 1903; Metropolitan Opera, N.Y., Jan. 24, 1919); *Vénus et Adonis* (Nîmes, 1905); *William Ratcliff* (Nice, Jan. 26, 1906); *Théodora* (Monte Carlo, March 19, 1907); *Le Chemineau* (Paris, Nov. 6, 1907; Metropolitan Opera, Jan. 31, 1919); *Le Carillonneur* (Paris, March 20, 1913); *La Fille de Figaro* (Paris, March 11, 1914); *Les Cadeaux de Noël* (Paris, Dec. 25, 1915); *1814* (Monte Carlo, April 6, 1918); *Nausithoé* (posthumous; Nice, April 9, 1920); *La Plus Forte* (posthumous; Paris, Jan. 11, 1924); *L'Ingénu* (Bordeaux, Feb. 13, 1931); songs; piano pieces.

Lert, Ernst Josef Maria, Austrian opera Intendant and writer; b. Vienna, May 12, 1883; d. Baltimore, Jan. 30, 1955. He studied at the Univ. of Vienna with G. Adler; in 1908 received his Dr.Phil.; was dramatic coach at the Municipal Theater in Breslau and in Leipzig; in 1920–23, opera director of the Municipal Theater and teacher at the Hoch Cons. in Frankfurt; in 1923–29, stage director at La Scala in Milan (with Toscanini); in 1929–31, stage director at the Metropolitan Opera House in N.Y.; in 1936–38, head of the opera dept. of the Curtis Inst. of Music in Philadelphia; after 1938, head of the opera dept. of the Peabody Cons., in Baltimore. He publ. *Mozart auf dem Theater* (Berlin, 1918; 4th ed., 1922); *Otto Lohse*, a biography (Leipzig, 1918).

Lert, Richard Johanes, Austrian conductor, brother of **Ernst Lert;** b. Vienna, Sept. 19, 1885; d. Los Angeles, April 25, 1980. He studied with Heuberger; then served as a conductor in Düsseldorf, Darmstadt, Frankfurt, Hannover, and Mannheim; later was guest conductor with the Staatsoper in Berlin. He emigrated to the U.S. in 1934 and settled in Pasadena, Calif., as a conductor and teacher. In 1916 he married the novelist Vicki Baum. He celebrated his 90th birthday in 1975, but continued to be active, conducting summer concerts at Orkney Springs, Va.; also gave courses in conducting.

731

Leschetizky, Theodor, great Austrain pianist and famous pedagogue; b. Lancut, Austrian Poland, June 22, 1830; d. Dresden, Nov. 14, 1915. He first studied with his father, who took him to Vienna, where he became a pupil of Czerny. He acquired a mastery of the piano in an amazingly short time, and was only 15 when he himself began to teach. He also attended the Univ. of Vienna as a student of philosophy, until its closure in the wake of the 1848 revolution. In 1852 he went to Russia; his initial concerts in St. Petersburg were extremely successful, and gradually he attracted many pupils. He was also active as music director to the Grand Duchess Helen. In 1862 Anton Rubinstein, director of the newly opened St. Petersburg Cons., engaged him as a teacher. After 16 years in Russia, Leschetizky returned to Vienna; there he married his former pupil Anna Essipova (she was his 2nd wife); they were divorced in 1892; Leschetizky contracted 2 more marriages after that. He continued to make occasional concert tours, but concentrated mainly on teaching; his fame grew, and pupils flocked from all over the world to his studio in Vienna. His most celebrated pupil was Paderewski; other pupils were Gabrilowitsch, Schnabel, Isabelle Vengerova, etc., as well as his 3rd and 4th wives, Dominirska Benislavska and Marie Rozborska. His method of playing with the "Kugelhand" (arched hand) was to secure fullness of tone and finger dexterity, with the flexible wrist reserved for octave playing and chord passages. A Leschetizky Society, composed of his pupils, was organized after his death; a branch was established in the U.S.

Leschetizky was also a composer; he wrote an opera, *Die erste Falte* (Prague, Oct. 9, 1867), and some chamber music; but it is his piano pieces that still remain of interest and value; of these, the following are the most effective: *Les 2 Alouettes; Grand polka de caprice; La Cascade; Perpetuum mobile; Valse chromatique; Souvenirs d'Italie; A la campagne,* and *3 études caractéristiques.*

Le Sueur (or **Lesueur**), **Jean François,** French composer; b. Drucat–Plessiel, near Abbeville, Feb. 15, 1760; d. Paris, Oct. 6, 1837. At 7 he was a choirboy at Abbeville; at 14, in Amiens, where he took a course of studies; interrupting his academic education, he became maître de musique at the Cathedral of Séez; then an assistant at the Church of the Innocents in Paris. Abbé Roze gave him some instruction in harmony; this constituted practically all of his musical training; he developed his musical talent without teachers. His subsequent positions were as maître de musique at the Cathedral of Dijon (1781), at Le Mans (1783), and at Tours (1784). He then returned to Paris, now serving (upon the recommendation of Grétry) as maître de chapelle at the Innocents. When the competition for the post of maître de chapelle at Notre Dame was announced in 1786, Le Sueur entered it, and won. He organized an orch. for the chief festive days, and brought out masses, motets, services, etc., using a full orch., thus completely transforming the character of the services; he was greatly successful with the congregation, but the conservative clergy strongly objected to his innovations; other critics called his type of musical productions "opéra des gueux" (beggars' opera). He expounded his ideas of effective and descriptive music in a pamphlet, *Essai de musique sacrée ou musique motivée et méthodique, pour la fête de Noël, à la messe de jour* (1787); this evoked an anonymous attack, to which he replied with another publication, *Exposé d'une musique unie, imitative, et particulière à chaque solennité* (1787), reasserting his aim of making church music dramatic and descriptive. He retired temporarily in 1788, and spent 4 years in the country. Upon his return to Paris, he brought out at the Théâtre Feydeau 3 operas: *La Caverne* (Feb. 16, 1793), which had a popular success, *Paul et Virginie* (Jan. 13, 1794), and *Télémaque* (May 11, 1796). When the Paris Cons. was organized in 1795, Le Sueur was appointed inspector, and a member of the Committee on Instruction; with Méhul, Langlé, Gossec, and Catel, he wrote the *Principes élémentaires de la musique* and the *Solfèges du Conservatoire.* Le Sueur was dismissed in 1802 because of an altercation that occurred following the rejection, by the Opéra, of 2 of his operas in favor of *Sémiramis,* written by Catel. For 2 years he lived in poverty and suffering, until Napoleon, in 1804, raised him to the highest position attainable by a musician in Paris by appointing him as maître de chapelle, succeeding Paisiello. His rejected opera, *Les Bardes,* was then produced (Paris, July 10, 1804) with great applause, and *La Mort d'Adam,* the other rejected work, was also staged (Paris, March 21, 1809). After the restoration of the monarchy, and despite Le Sueur's avowed veneration of Napoleon, the government of Louis XVIII appointed him superintendent and composer to the Chapelle du Roi; from 1818 he was also prof. of composition at the Paris Cons.; he had several celebrated pupils, among them Berlioz, Gounod, and Ambroise Thomas. He taught at the Cons. until his death; was a member of the Institut (1813), and held several other honorary positions. His last 3 operas were accepted for performance, but were not produced; these were *Tyrtée* (1794), *Artaxerse* (1797), and *Alexandre à Babylone;* other works were 2 secular cantatas: *L'Inauguration du temple de la Victoire* (Paris, Jan. 2, 1807) and *Le Triomphe de Trajan* (Paris, Oct. 23, 1807); several sacred oratorios (*Debora, Rachel, Ruth et Noémi, Ruth et Booz*); Solemn Mass for 4 Voices, Chorus, and Orch.; cantata, *L'Ombre de Sacchini;* 3 Te Deums; 2 Passions; *Stabat Mater;* these, and some other works, were publ.; he left many more (over 30 masses, etc.) in MS. He publ. *Notice sur la mélopée, la rythmopée, et les grands caractères de la musique ancienne* (Paris, 1793); a sketch of Paisiello (1816); and some pamphlets. In 1980 J. Mongredien publ. *Jean-François Le Sueur: A Thematic Catalogue of his Complete Works* (N.Y.).

Lesur, Daniel, French composer, pianist, and organist; b. Paris, Nov. 19, 1908. He studied at the Paris Cons. with Tournemire, Caussade, and Ferté; was assistant organist at Ste.-Clothilde (1927–37) and prof. of counterpoint at the Schola Cantorum (1935–39). In 1936 he and Yves Baudrier, O. Messiaen, and Jolivet organized "La Jeune France." His works include the ballet *L'Infante et le monstre* (with A. Jolivet; 1938); *Ave Maria sur un Noël* for Soprano, Contralto, Women's Chorus, and Organ (1938); *Andrea del Sarto*, symph. poem (Paris, June 21, 1949); *Andrea del Sarto*, opera (Marseille, Jan. 24, 1969); *Suite française* for Orch. (1935); *Pastorale* for Chamber Orch. (1938); *Ricercare* for Orch. (1939); *Passacaille* for Piano and Orch. (1937); *L'Etoile de Séville,* suite for Chamber Orch. (1941); *Chansons cambodgiennes* for Voice and Chamber Orch. (1947); Suite for Piano and String Trio (1943); *Suite médiévale* for Flute, Violin, Viola, Cello, and Harp (1946); *Le Village imaginaire* for 2 Pianos (1947); piano pieces (*Soirs, Les Carillons, Bagatelle, Pavane, 2 Noëls, Pastorale variée, Ballade,* etc.); organ music; songs (*Les Harmonies intimes, La Mort des voiles, 3 poèmes de Cécile Sauvage, L'Enfance de l'art, Clair comme le jour,* etc.).

Lesure, François, French music librarian, musicologist, and writer; b. Paris, May 23, 1923. He studied at the Ecole des Chartres, then at the Ecole Pratique des Hautes Etudes and the Sorbonne, and musicology at the Paris Cons. A member of the music dept. at the Bibliotheque Nationale since 1950, he was made its chief curator in 1970. From 1953 to 1967 he headed the Paris office (responsible for Series B) of the Répertoire International des Sources Musicales (RISM), for which he himself edited 3 vols.: *Recueils imprimés: XVIe–XVIIe siècles* (Munich, 1960); *Recueils imprimés: XVIIIe siècle* (Munich, 1964; supplement in *Notes*, March 1972, vol. XXVIII, pp. 397–418, and the 2 vols. of *Ecrits imprimés concernant la musique* (Munich, 1971). His other posts have included a professorship at the Free Univ. of Brussels and editorship, since 1967, of the series reprinting early music known as Le Pupitre. He has also edited such non-serial works as the report of the 1954 Arras Conference, *La Renaissance dans les provinces du Nord* (Paris, 1956); *Anthologie de la chanson parisienne au XVIe siècle* (Monaco, 1953); 6 vols. of *Chansons polyphoniques* (Monaco, 1967–72; with A.T. Merritt; the first 5 vols. constitute the collected works of C. Janequin); P. Trichet's *Traité des instruments de musique (vers 1640)* (Neuilly, 1957); and a collected edition of Debussy's writings on music, *Monsieur Croche et autres écrits* (Paris, 1971; in Eng., N.Y., 1977). In 1971 he became president of the Société Française de Musicologie and in 1973 director of the published *Archives* of the Ecole Pratique des Hautes Etudes. His own publications include a *Bibliographie des éditions d'Adrian Le Roy et Robert Ballard, 1551–1598* (with G. Thibault, Paris, 1955; supplement in *Revue de Musicologie,* 1957); *Musicians and Poets of the French Renaissance* (N.Y., 1955); *Mozart en France* (Paris, 1956); *Collection musicale A. Meyer* (with N. Bridgman, Abbeville, 1961); *Musica e società* (Milan, 1966; German version as *Musik und Gesellschaft im Bild: Zeugnisse der Malerei aus sechs Jahrhunderten,* Kassel, 1966; in Eng. as *Music and Art in Society,* Univ. Park, Pa., 1968); *Bibliographie des éditions musicales publiées par Estienne Roger et Michel-Charles Le Cene, Amsterdam, 1696–1743* (Paris, 1969); and *Musique et musiciens français du XVIe siècle* (Geneva, 1976, a reprinting in book form of 24 of Lesure's many articles originally publ. 1950–69). He contributed *L'Opéra classique français: 17e et 18e siècles* (Geneva, 1972) and *Claude Debussy* (Geneva, 1975) to the series Iconographie Musicale. For the Bibliothèque Nationale he prepared a series of exhibition catalogs, most notably one on Berlioz (Paris, 1969). The culmination of his Debussy studies is a *Catalogue de l'œuvre de Claude Debussy* (Geneva, 1977).

Letz, Hans, German violinist; b. Ittenheim, Alsace, March 18, 1887; d. Hackensack, N.J., Nov. 14, 1969. He studied violin with H. Schuster at the Strasbourg Cons., and later with Joachim at the Hochschule für Musik in Berlin. In 1908 he emigrated to the U.S.; made his debut in N.Y. on Nov. 3, 1908; subsequently was concertmaster of the Chicago Symph. Orch. (1909–12), and 2nd violinist of the Kneisel Quartet (1912–17). In 1917 he settled in N.Y. as a teacher at the Inst. of Musical Art; also formed his own string quartet. He publ. a guide, *Music for the Violin and Viola* (N.Y., 1949).

Leuckart, F. Ernst Christoph, German music publisher; b. Halberstadt, March 21, 1748; d. Breslau, Feb. 2, 1817. He established a music business at Breslau in 1782; it was acquired in 1856 by Constantin Sander, who removed it to Leipzig in 1870, and added to it by buying out the firms of Weinhold & Förster (Breslau), Damköhler (Berlin), and Witzendorf (Vienna). The new firm, Constantin Sander, vormals F.E.C. Leuckart, publ. many learned works (e.g., by Ambros, Lussy, Westphal, Niecks, Molitor, etc.) and compositions of R. Franz, Rheinberger, Draeseke, Bossi, Hausegger, Huber, Klose, Duparc, Richard Strauss, Max Reger, Atterberg, Bantock, Ernest Bloch, Johan Wagenaar, Schjelderup, and others. Constantin Sander's son Martin (b. Breslau, Nov. 11, 1859; d. Leipzig, March 14, 1930) was head of the firm until his death.

Levant, Oscar, American pianist and composer; b. Pittsburgh, Dec. 27, 1906; d. Beverly Hills, Aug. 14, 1972. He studied piano with Stojowski; also took a few composition lessons with Schoenberg and Schillinger. As a pianist, he established himself by his authentic performances of Gershwin's music (*Rhapsody in Blue, Concerto in F*); also emerged as a professional wit on the radio; publ. a brilliant book, *A Smattering of Ignorance* (N.Y., 1940). He wrote music of considerable complexity, in the modern vein; was soloist in his Piano Concerto (NBC Symph. Orch., Feb. 17, 1942); other works are *Nocturne* for Orch. (Los Angeles, April 14, 1937); String Quartet (1937); piano pieces; film scores.

Levasseur, Nicolas-Prosper, French bass; b. Bresles, March 9, 1791; d. Paris, Dec 7, 1871. He was admitted to the Paris Cons. in 1807, and he entered

Garat's singing class in 1811; made his debut at the Paris Opéra (Oct. 14, 1813); sang subordinate roles until 1820, when his success at Milan in Meyerbeer's *Marguerite d'Anjou* (Nov. 14, 1820) attracted attention, and he was engaged for 5 years at the Théâtre Italien in Paris; later took leading bass roles at the Opéra. He was also a prof. at the Paris Cons. (1841–69).

Levasseur, Rosalie (real Christian names, **Marie Claude Josèphe**), French soprano; b. Valenciennes, Oct. 8, 1749; d. Neuwied-on-Rhine, May 6, 1826. She was born out of wedlock to Jean-Baptiste Levasseur and Marie-Catherine Tournay; the parents were married when she was 11. She was described by contemporaries as being not at all attractive; still, she must have possessed a fine voice and musical ability, for she was a formidable rival of Sophie Arnould. She first appeared on the stage under the name of **Mlle. Rosalie;** in 1775 she assumed the name Levasseur. The Austrian ambassador in Paris used his influence to promote her career; they lived as husband and wife.

Levi, Hermann, eminent German conductor; b. Giessen, Nov. 7, 1839; d. Munich, May 13, 1900. He was a pupil of Vincenz Lachner in Mannheim (1852–55) and at the Leipzig Cons. (1855–58). He conducted at Saarbrücken (1859–61) and at the German Opera in Rotterdam (1861–64). He became court conductor at Karlsruhe in 1864, and in 1872 he received his most important appointment, at the court theater in Munich; became its Generalmusikdirektor in 1894; retired in 1896. He enjoyed great respect among German musicians, and was influential in spreading the Wagnerian gospel. He conducted the first performance of *Parsifal* at Bayreuth (July 26, 1882), and his interpretation received complete approval from Wagner himself, who, for the nonce, repressed his opposition to Jews. Levi conducted the musical program at Wagner's funeral. He was also a friend of Brahms; his correspondence with Brahms was publ. in vol. 7 of *Brahms Briefwechsel* (Berlin, 1912). He wrote *Gedanken aus Goethes Werken* (1901; 3rd ed., 1911).

Levidis, Dimitri, Greek composer; b. Athens, April 8, 1886; d. there, May 30, 1951. He studied at the Athens Cons., then with A. Denéréaz in Switzerland; in 1910, settled in Paris; from 1939 till his death, was again in Greece. He was the first to write works for the Martenot "Ondes Musicales," including *Poème symphonique pour solo d'Ondes Musicales et Orchestre* (Paris, Dec. 23, 1928) and *De profundis* for Voice and 2 Soli of Ondes Musicales (Paris, Jan. 5, 1930). Other works include a ballet, *Le Pâtre et la nymphe* (Paris, April 24, 1924); *Divertissement* for English Horn, Harps, Strings, Celesta, and Percussion (Paris, April 9, 1927); oratorio, *The Iliad; Poem* for Violin and Orch. (1927); *Chant payen* for Oboe and Strings; compositions for the "Dixtuor æolien d'orchestre"; pieces for chamber ensembles; song cycles; piano pieces.

Levine, James (Lawrence), brilliant American pianist and conductor; b. Cincinnati, June 23, 1943. His maternal grandfather was a cantor in a synagogue; his father was a violinist who led a dance band; his mother was an actress. He absorbed music by osmosis and began playing the piano as a small child. At the age of 10 he was soloist in Mendelssohn's 2nd Piano Concerto at a youth concert of the Cincinnati Symph. Orch.; he then studied music theory with Walter Levin, first violinist in the La Salle Quartet; in 1956 he took piano lessons with Rudolf Serkin at the Marlboro School of Music; in 1957 he began piano studies with Rosina Lhévinne at the Aspen Music School. In 1961 he entered the Juilliard School of Music in N.Y., and took courses in conducting with Jean Morel; he also had conducting sessions with Wolfgang Vacano in Aspen. In 1964 he graduated from the Juilliard School and joined the American Conductors Project connected with the Baltimore Symph. Orch., where he had occasion to practice conducting with Alfred Wallenstein, Max Rudolf, and Fausto Cleva. In 1964–65 he served as an apprentice to George Szell with the Cleveland Orch.; then became a regular assistant conductor with it (1965–70). In 1966 he organized the Univ. Circle Orch. of the Cleveland Inst. of Music; also led the student orch. of the summer music institute of Oakland Univ. in Meadow Brook, Mich. (1967–69). In 1970 he made a successful appearance as guest conductor with the Philadelphia Orch. at its summer home at Robin Hood Dell; subsequently appeared with other American orchs. In 1970 he also conducted the Welsh National Opera and the San Francisco Opera. He made his Metropolitan Opera debut in N.Y. on June 5, 1971, in a festival performance of *Tosca;* his success led to further appearances and appointment as principal conductor in 1973; he was named music director in 1975. In 1973 he also became music director of the Ravinia Festival, the summer home of the Chicago Symph. Orch.; in addition, he was music director of the Cincinnati May Festival from 1974 to 1978. In 1975 he began to conduct at the Salzburg Festivals; in 1982 he conducted at the Bayreuth Festival for the first time. He continued to make appearances as a pianist, playing chamber music with impeccable technical precision. But it is as a conductor and an indefatigable planner of the seasons at the Metropolitan Opera that he inspired respect. Unconcerned with egotistical projections of his own personality, he presided over the singers and the orch. with concentrated efficiency.

Levitzki, Mischa, Russian pianist; b. Kremenchug, May 25, 1898; d. Avon-by-the-Sea, N.J., Jan. 2, 1941. When he was 8 years old, his parents, who were naturalized American citizens, returned to the U.S. He studied at the Inst. of Musical Art in N.Y. with Stojowski (1906–11). In 1911 he went to Germany, where he studied with Dohnányi at the Hochschule für Musik in Berlin; won the Mendelssohn Prize. In 1915 he returned to America; appeared in a N.Y. recital on Oct. 17, 1916; subsequently made numerous tours in the U.S. and in the Orient. He publ. a number of attractive piano pieces (*Valse in A, Arabesque valsante, Valse tzigane, Gavotte, The Enchanted Nymph*, etc.).

Lévy, Alexandre, Brazilian composer; b. São Paulo, Nov. 10, 1864; d. there, Jan. 17, 1892. He studied with Emile Durand in Paris. His compositions include a Symph., which received a Columbus Celebration prize in 1892; *Comala*, symph. poem; *Suite brasileira* for Orch.; chamber music and piano works (*Schumanniana*, suite; *Allegro appassionato*; etc.). Although his music is steeped in the European Romantic tradition and his technique is limited, he appears an important figure in Brazilian music because of his contribution to the nationalist movement in music; he was one of the earliest Brazilian composers to use native folk material in instrumental works.

Lévy, Ernst, distinguished Swiss pianist and composer; b. Basel, Nov. 18, 1895; d. Morges, Switzerland, April 19, 1981. He studied in Basel with Huber and Petri, and in Paris with Pugno. In 1941 he came to the U.S.; taught at the New England Cons. in Boston (1941–45), Bennington College in Vermont (1946–51), the Univ. of Chicago (1951–54), the Mass. Inst. of Technology in Boston (1954–59), and Brooklyn College of the City Univ. of N.Y. (1959–66). In 1966 he went to Switzerland and lived in Morges. A man of profound culture, he was also a virtuoso pianist. Besides his musical accomplishments, he was an alpinist and a master carpenter; his writings on philosophical subjects remain unpubl. He composed 15 symphs. between 1920 and 1967; much chamber music and many choral works; pieces for solo cello, solo viola, solo violin; *Soliloquy* for Solo Clarinet; 55 pieces for clavichord; a study on wholetone scales for piano; organ pieces; etc. He publ. a theoretical study (with S. Levarie), *Tone: A Study in Musical Acoustics* (Kent, Ohio, 1968).

Lévy, Heniot, Polish-American pianist and composer; b. Warsaw, July 19, 1879; d. Chicago, June 16, 1946. He was a pupil at the Hochschule für Musik in Berlin, and of Max Bruch (composition); made his debut as a pianist with the Berlin Phil. Orch. (1899); in 1900 he emigrated to America, and became a piano teacher at the American Cons. in Chicago. Among his works are *24 Variations on an Original Theme* for Orch. (Chicago, April 9, 1942); Piano Concerto; String Sextet; String Quintet; 2 piano quintets; 4 string quartets; 2 piano trios; Cello Sonata; numerous piano pieces; songs.

Lévy, Lazare, distinguished French pianist and pedagogue; b. (of French parents) Brussels, Jan. 18, 1882; d. Paris, Sept. 20, 1964. He studied with Diémer at the Paris Cons. (1894–98), where he was awarded first prize for piano; also studied harmony with Lavignac and composition with Gédalge; gave concerts with the principal orchs. of Europe; in 1920, succeeded Alfred Cortot as a prof. at the Paris Cons. He publ. numerous piano pieces.

Levy, Marvin David, American composer; b. Passaic, N.J., Aug. 2, 1932. He studied composition with Philip James at N.Y. Univ., and with Otto Luening at Columbia Univ.; was awarded an American Prix de Rome and a Guggenheim fellowship. He showed a particular disposition toward the musical theater. In his vocal and instrumental writing Levy adopts an expressionistic mode along atonal lines, in an ambience of cautiously dissonant harmonies vivified by a nervously asymmetric rhythmic pulse.

WORKS: One-act operas: *Sotoba Komachi* (N.Y., April 7, 1957); *The Tower* (Sante Fe, Aug. 2, 1957); *Escorial* (N.Y., May 4, 1958). In 1961 he was commissioned to write an opera for the Metropolitan Opera at Lincoln Center, N.Y., to a libretto from O'Neill's play *Mourning Becomes Electra*. It was produced at the Metropolitan on March 17, 1967; although critical reception was indecisive, the opera was retained in the repertoire for several seasons, a signal honor to an American composer; he also wrote the opera *The Balcony* (1978). His other works include String Quartet (1955); *Rhapsody* for Violin, Clarinet, and Harp (1956); *Chassidic Suite* for French Horn and Piano (1956); Christmas oratorio, *For the Time Being* (1959); *Caramoor Festival Overture* (1959); Symph. (1960); *Sacred Service* for the Park Avenue Synagogue in N.Y. (1964); Piano Concerto (Chicago, Dec. 3, 1970).

Lévy, Michel-Maurice, French composer; b. Ville-d'Avray, June 28, 1883; d. Paris, Jan. 24, 1965. He studied at the Paris Cons. with Lavignac and Leroux. In 1920–32 he was popular as a musical parodist in vaudeville under the name of **Bétove** (i.e., Beethoven); wrote operettas under that name: *Pom-Pom* (1928); *Les Exploits galants du Baron de Crac* (1932); *D'Artagnan* (1945). Under his own name he wrote the operas *Le Cloître* (Lyons, 1932) and *Dolorés* (Paris, 1952); operettas: *Lydia* (Brussels, 1936) and *La Demoiselle de Carentan* (Paris, 1951); *Les Trois Pantins de bois*, ballet suite for Orch.; *Le Chant de la terre*, symph. poem (1945); *Moïse*, "fresque lyrique" (Mulhouse, 1955); film music; choral works; songs.

Lewandowski, Louis, eminent Jewish scholar; b. Wreschen, near Posen, April 3, 1821; d. Berlin, Feb. 3, 1894. He studied at the Academy of Music in Berlin; became music director of the Berlin Synagogue from 1840; established himself as a voice teacher. His greatest accomplishment is the compilation of the Jewish service music for use by Berlin's Jewish community; in his arrangements of the traditional tunes, Lewandowski applied the technique of German Romantic music, and often reduced the exotic and asymmetrical pattern of the Jewish cantilena to simple song meters; his compositions for organ also employed ordinary 19th-century harmonies. This treatment contributed to the popularity of Lewandowski's service music, but at the same time traduced the true spirit of Jewish cantillation, so that the more nationalistic Jewish scholars refused to accept it.

Lewenthal, Raymond, American pianist; b. San Antonio, Texas, Aug. 29, 1926. He was taken to Hollywood as a child; studied piano with local teachers. He then enrolled at the Juilliard School of Music in N.Y., as a student of Olga Samaroff; continued his studies in Europe with Alfred Cortot; spent a year in Rio de Janeiro as a piano teacher. Returning to the U.S., he devoted himself to promoting the piano music of neglected Romantic composers, among them Thalberg, Hummel, and Henselt, whose works he performed at his recitals. Particularly meritorious is his redemption from undeserved oblivion of the voluminous output of Charles-Valentin Alkan. He edited a collection of Alkan's piano works for G. Schirmer, Inc.

Lewis, Sir Anthony, renowned English musicologist, conductor, and composer; b. Bermuda, March 2, 1915; d. Haslemere, England, June 5, 1983. He was educated at Wellington College and Cambridge Univ.; also took courses with Nadia Boulanger in Paris. From 1947–68 he was a prof. of music at the Univ. of Birmingham; then was dean of the faculty of fine arts there (1961–64). From 1968–82 he served as principal of the Royal Academy of Music in London. He was knighted in 1972. His specialty was the music of the Baroque period; he edited, conducted, and recorded works by Purcell, Rameau, and Handel. His own works reveal his devotion to Baroque formulas. He wrote *Elegy and Capriccio* for Trumpet and Orch. (1947); *A Tribute of Praise* for Voices a cappella (1951); Concerto for Horn and Orch. (1956). He was one of the founders of the prestigious collection *Musica Britannica* (1951; 42 vols. to date).

Lewis, Daniel, American conductor; b. Flagstaff, Ariz., May 10, 1925. He studied composition with Nino Marcelli in San Diego, Calif. (1939–41); also took violin lessons in Boston; graduated from San Diego State College (B.M., 1949); attended the Claremont (Calif.) Graduate School (M.A., 1950). In 1959 he went to Germany, where he attended the Munich Hochschule für Musik and studied conducting with Eugen Jochum; also participated in a conducting seminar with Herbert von Karajan in Salzburg (1959–60). Returning to the U.S., he served as associate conductor with the San Diego Symph.; was also a conductor at the Alaska Music Festival in Anchorage. His other conducting engagements were at La Jolla, Calif. (1961–69), and with the Orange County (Calif.) Symph. (1966–70). In 1972 he was appointed music director and conductor of the Pasadena Symph., which he brought to a high degree of excellence, presenting programs of Classical, Romantic, and modern music. He also served as guest conductor with the Phoenix Symph. and Atlanta Symph. (1975–76), with the Philharmonia in the Aspen Music Festival (1975–77), with the Los Angeles Phil. (1974–76), with the Oakland Symph. (1978), and with the Minnesota Orch. (1979). He gave summer classes in Anchorage, Alaska (1958–65); he also taught at Calif. State Univ. at Fullerton (1963–70) and the Univ. of Southern Calif. (from 1970).

Lewis, Henry, black American conductor; b. Los Angeles, Oct. 16, 1932. He learned to play piano and string instruments as a child; at the age of 16 was engaged as a double-bass player in the Los Angeles Phil.; in 1955–59 played double bass in the 7th Army Symph. Orch. overseas, and also conducted it in Germany and the Netherlands. Returning to the U.S., he founded the Los Angeles Chamber Orch.; in 1963 traveled with it in Europe under the auspices of the State Dept. From 1968 to 1976 he was conductor and musical director of the New Jersey Symph. Orch. in Newark; subsequently conducted opera and orch. guest engagements. He married **Marilyn Horne** on July 2, 1960, but they were eventually separated.

Lewis, Richard, noted English tenor; b. Manchester, May 10, 1914. He studied at the Royal Manchester College of Music; then took courses with Norman Allin at the Royal Academy of Music in London; made his operatic debut with the Carl Rosa Opera Co. in 1939; in 1947 he sang at the Glyndebourne Festival and at Covent Garden. In 1955 he appeared with the San Francisco Opera; also sang with it as a guest artist between 1962 and 1968. In 1963 he was named a Commander of the Order of the British Empire. His repertoire was extensive, including roles in operas ranging from Monteverdi and Mozart to Schoenberg, Britten, and Tippett.

Lewisohn, Adolph, German-American musical philanthropist; b. Hamburg, May 27, 1849; d. Saranac Lake, N.Y., Aug. 17, 1938. The principal services to music and education performed by this prominent industrialist were the erection in 1914 of the Lewisohn Stadium, which he donated to the College of the City of N.Y., and the inauguration of summer concerts by the N.Y. Phil. there. He also founded the Lewisohn chamber music education courses at Hunter College in N.Y.

Lewkowitch, Bernhard, Danish organist and composer; b. Copenhagen, May 28, 1927 (of Russian parents). He studied organ and composition at the Copenhagen Cons. (1946–50) with Schierbeck and Jersild. From 1947 to 1963 he served as organist and choirmaster at the Catholic Church of St. Ansgar, in Copenhagen. In 1953 he founded in Copenhagen a choral society, Schola Cantorum, with which he performed medieval and Renaissance music. In 1963 he was awarded the prestigious Carl Nielsen Prize; in 1966 he was given a lifetime Danish government pension. His own music is primarily choral, to Latin texts, and is derived essentially from the Renaissance paradigms of modal counterpoint; it has an affinity with sacred works of Stravinsky, but is otherwise sui generis in its stylized archaisms; several of these works have become repertoire pieces in Denmark, and were also performed at the international festivals of contemporary music in Haifa (1954), Cologne (1960), Amsterdam (1963), and Copenhagen (1964).

Leybach, Ignace, Alsatian pianist and composer;

b. Gambsheim, July 17, 1817; d. Toulouse, May 23, 1891. He studied in Paris with Pixis, Kalkbrenner, and Chopin; in 1844, became organist at the Cathedral of Toulouse. He publ. some 225 piano pieces, in a facile and pleasing manner. His 5th Nocturne, op. 52, became famous, and its popularity continued among succeeding generations of piano students; it was reprinted in countless anthologies of piano music. Other piano compositions are: *Boléro brillant; Ballade; Valse poétique; Les Batelières de Naples;* etc.; he also publ. an extensive organ method (3 vols.; 350 pieces).

Lhévinne, Josef, celebrated Russian pianist; b. Orel, Dec. 13, 1874; d. New York, Dec. 2, 1944. After some preliminary study in his native town, he was taken to Moscow, and entered Safonov's piano class at the Moscow Cons.; at the age of 15 he played the *Emperor Concerto,* with Anton Rubinstein conducting; he graduated in 1891; won the Rubinstein Prize in 1895. In 1900 he traveled to the Caucasus; taught piano at the Cons. of Tiflis; in 1902–6, taught at the Moscow Cons. In 1906 he went to the U.S.; made his American debut in N.Y. with the Russian Symph. Orch., conducted by Safonov (Jan. 27, 1906); afterward he made numerous concert tours in America. He lived mostly in Berlin from 1907 till 1919; was interned during World War I, but was able to continue his professional activities. In 1919 he returned to the U.S.; appeared in recitals, and with major American orchs.; also in duo recitals with his wife, **Rosina.** They established a music studio, where they taught numerous pupils; also taught at the Juilliard Graduate School. Lhévinne's playing was distinguished not only by its virtuoso quality, but by an intimate understanding of the music, impeccable phrasing, and fine gradations of singing tone. He was at his best in the works of the Romantic school; his performances of the concertos of Chopin and Tchaikovsky were particularly notable.

Lhévinne, Rosina, Russian pianist and teacher, wife of **Josef Lhévinne;** b. Kiev, March 28, 1880; d. (at the age of 96) Glendale, Calif., Nov. 9, 1976. She graduated from the Kiev Cons. in 1898, winning the gold medal; in 1899 she married Josef Lhévinne in Moscow; appeared as a soloist in Vienna (1910), St. Petersburg (1911), and Berlin (1912); remained in Berlin with her husband through World War I; in 1919, came to the U.S.; taught at the Juilliard Graduate School; also privately in N.Y., establishing a reputation as a fine pedagogue. Among her many pupils was Van Cliburn.

Lhotka-Kalinski, Ivo, Croatian composer, son of **Fran Lhotka;** b. Zagreb, July 30, 1913. He studied with Pizzetti in Rome; after the end of World War II he taught singing at the Music Academy of Zagreb; in 1967 became its regional director. He has a natural flair for stage composition in the folk style; he wrote several brilliant musical burlesques, among them *Analfabeta (The Illiterate;* Belgrade, Oct. 19, 1954); *Putovanje (The Journey),* first television opera in Yugoslavia (Zagreb, June 10, 1957); *Dugme*

(The Button; Zagreb, April 21, 1958); *Vlast (Authority;* Zagreb Television, Oct. 18, 1959); *Svjetleći grad (The Town of Light;* Zagreb, Dec. 26, 1967); also a children's opera, *Velika coprarija (The Great Sorcerer;* 1952); *Misli (Thoughts)* for Clarinet and Strings (1965); a number of choral works, songs, and piano pieces.

Liadov, Anatoli, significant Russian composer, son of **Konstantin Liadov;** b. St. Petersburg, May 10, 1855; d. on his estate of Polynovka, in the district of Novgorod, Aug. 28, 1914. He was a member of an exceptionally gifted musical family. His father was an outstanding opera conductor; his grandfather was conductor of the St. Petersburg Phil. Society; Liadov's uncles were also professional musicians. After his primary education at home, Liadov entered the St. Petersburg Cons. (1870); studied piano with G.G. Kross, theory with J. Johannsen, composition with Rimsky-Korsakov; he was expelled from the school for failing to attend classes (1876), but was allowed to compete for a diploma in 1878, and passed the final examination brilliantly. He was immediately engaged as an instructor of theory and harmony at the Cons., and held this post until his death. Among his students were Prokofiev, Miaskovsky, Asafiev, and other notable Russian composers. From his first attempts at composition, Liadov was fascinated by Russian folklore, and most of his works possess the imaginative quality of Russian fairy tales. He was not a prolific composer; he was at his best in miniatures, which he worked out with a fine artistic sense; of these, the piano cycle *Birulki* (1876) and *Tabatière à musique (Music Box;* 1893) are particularly popular; for orch. he wrote the symph. tableaux *Baba Yaga, Enchanted Lake,* and *Kikimora,* which are still in the permanent repertoire of Russian orchs.; his arrangements of Russian songs are valuable for their authentic harmonization.

WORKS: For Orch.: *Scherzo* (1887); *Mazurka* (1888); *Polonaise* (1900); *Baba Yaga* (St. Petersburg, March 18, 1904); *8 Russian Folk Songs* (1906); *Enchanted Lake* (St. Petersburg, Feb. 21, 1909); *Kikimora* (St. Petersburg, Dec. 12, 1909); *Fragments from Apocalypse* (St. Petersburg, Dec. 8, 1912); *Nenie,* threnody (1914). For Piano: *Birulki* (1876); *4 Arabesques* (1879); *4 Intermezzos* (1882–83); *2 Mazurkas* (1887); *Novelette* (1889); *Ballade* (1890); *Marionnettes* (1892); *Bagatelle* (1892); *Tabatière à musique* (1893; also for Small Orch.); *Variations on a Polish Theme* (1901); 4 pieces: *Grimaces, Twilight, Temptation, Recollection* (1910); several sets of preludes and études; etc. Vocal works: 120 Russian folk songs for Voice and Piano (1903); other Russian song arrangements and harmonizations. Liadov contributed a movement to a string quartet on the theme B-La-F, in honor of the publisher Belaiev (1895), and a polka for string orch. to the collection *Fridays* (1899).

Liadov, Konstantin, Russian conductor, father of **Anatoli Liadov;** b. St. Petersburg, May 10, 1820; d. there, Dec. 19, 1868. He studied at the Theatrical

School; in 1850 became conductor of the Imperial Opera; resigned shortly before his death, and was succeeded by Napravnik. He was an efficient drill-master, and did much to raise the standard of performance; produced several Russian operas for the first time, and was instrumental in encouraging Russian music; he was greatly appreciated by his co-workers; Glinka often sought his advice on details of production of his operas.

Liapunov, Sergei, important Russian pianist and composer; b. Yaroslavl, Nov. 30, 1859; d. Paris, Nov. 8, 1924. He studied piano at the Moscow Cons. with Pabst and Klindworth, and composition with Hubert and Taneyev. From 1894 to 1902 he was subdirector of the Imperial Choir at St. Petersburg; from 1902 to 1910, inspector of music at St. Helen's Inst.; in 1910 became a prof. at the St. Petersburg Cons.; following the Russian Revolution, he lived in Paris. He was a member of the Imperial Geographic Society, which commissioned him to collect the folk songs of the regions of Vologda, Viatka, and Kostroma (publ. with piano accompaniments in 1897). As a composer, he followed the tradition of the Russian national school, but was also willing to experiment with harmonic innovations; his writing for piano possesses excellent expertise; his First Piano Concerto is still in the repertoire of Russian pianists.

WORKS: Symph. No. 1 (1887; St. Petersburg, April 23, 1888; also perf. in Berlin, Jan. 15, 1907); *Ouverture solennelle*, on Russian themes (St. Petersburg, May 6, 1896); *Zelazova Vola*, named after Chopin's birthplace and composed for Chopin's centennial (1910); *Hashish*, oriental symph. poem (1914); Symph. No. 2 (1910–17; Leningrad, Dec. 28, 1950); Violin Concerto; 2 piano concertos (1890, 1909); *Ukrainian Rhapsody* for Piano and Orch. (Berlin, March 23, 1908; Busoni, soloist); numerous piano compositions, of which *12 études d'exécution transcendante*, all in sharp keys, were written in emulation of Liszt's similarly titled piano studies in flat keys.

Liatoshinsky, Boris, Ukrainian composer; b. Zhitomir, Jan. 3, 1895; d. Kiev, April 15, 1968. He studied jurisprudence at the Univ. of Kiev, simultaneously taking lessons in composition at the Kiev Cons. with Glière, graduating in 1919. In 1920 he was appointed a prof. at the Kiev Cons.; also taught at the Moscow Cons. (1935–38 and 1941–43). His style of composition follows the broad outlines of national music, with numerous thematic allusions to folk songs.

WORKS: Operas: *The Golden Hoop* (Odessa, March 26, 1930); *Shchors* (Kiev, Sept. 1, 1938; glorifying the exploits of the Soviet partisan leader Nicolai Shchors); *Grazina*, symph. ballad (Kiev, Nov. 26, 1955); 5 symphs. (1918–67); *Reunion*, symph. poem (1949); *Slavonic Concerto* for Piano and Orch. (1953); 4 string quartets (1915–43); 2 piano trios (1925, 1942); Ukrainian Quintet for Piano (1946); numerous arrangements for chorus of Ukrainian folk songs; piano pieces; etc.

Liberace, Walter (Wladziu Valentino), popular American pianist of Italian-Polish parentage; b. West Allis, Wis., May 16, 1919. He received rudimentary musical training from his father, a French-horn player. Encouraged by Paderewski, he began to study piano; played at nightclubs, billed as **Walter Busterkeys.** In 1940 he moved to N.Y.; evolved a facile repertoire of semiclassical arrangements; made a synthesis of the first movement of Beethoven's *Sonata quasi una fantasia* and Rachmaninoff's Prelude in C-sharp minor, taking advantage of the fact that both works are in the same key. He prospered; made lucrative inroads on television; built a home in California with a piano-shaped swimming pool. Inspired by a movie on Chopin, he placed a candelabrum on the piano at his concerts; this decorative object identified him as a Romantic pianist, an impression enhanced by the dress suit of white silk mohair he habitually wears. In 1959 he won a suit for defamation of character against the London *Daily Mirror* and its columnist W. Connor (Cassandra), who suggested in print that Liberace was a deviate. In 1982 his chauffeur-bodyguard-companion brought a lawsuit against Liberace for $380 million for services rendered in "an exclusive non-marital relationship," but lost.

Licad, Cecile, pianist; b. Manila, Philippines, May 11, 1961. She studied piano with Rosario Picazo; made her public concert debut at the age of 7; then went to the U.S.; enrolled at the Curtis Inst. of Music in Philadelphia in the classes of Rudolf Serkin, Seymour Lipkin, and Mieczyslaw Horszowski. In 1979 she was soloist with the Boston Symph. Orch. at the Berkshire Music Center in Tanglewood; in 1981 she won the Leventritt Gold Medal, which launched her on a fine career; she was a soloist with the N.Y. Phil., Chicago Symph., London Symph., Pittsburgh Symph., Cleveland Orch., and Philadelphia Orch.; also gave recitals.

Lichnowsky, Prince Carl, nobleman of Polish origin, friend of Mozart and Beethoven; b. Vienna, June 21, 1761; d. there, April 15, 1814. He received the title of nobility from the Russian government in 1773, but spent most of his life in Vienna. He was a pupil of Mozart, who accompanied him on a visit to the Prussian court in 1789. Beethoven's opp. 1, 13, 26, and 36 are dedicated to Lichnowsky. In his home, Lichnowsky presented regular chamber music concerts with a quartet composed of Schuppanzigh, Sina, Weiss, and Kraft. Lichnowsky's younger brother, Count Moritz (1771–1837), was also a friend of Beethoven, who dedicated his opp. 35, 51, and 90 to the Count and his wife.

Lichtenwanger, William, learned American librarian; b. Asheville, N.C., Feb. 28, 1915. He studied at the Univ. of Michigan at Ann Arbor (B.Mus., 1937; M.Mus., 1940); played double bass, oboe, and other instruments in the band and orch.; wrote pieces with whimsical titles, e.g., *Phrygidair* (in Phrygian mode, naturally). He served as assistant reference librarian of the Music Division at the Library of

Congress in Washington, D.C. (1940–53, except for service in the U.S. Army, 1941–45); assistant head (1953–60) and head (1960–74) of the music reference section there; was associate editor of *Notes* of the Music Library Assoc. (1946–60), then its editor (1960–63); in 1975 he was made a member emeritus of the Music Library Assoc. In addition, he was music editor of Collier's Encyclopedia (1947–50) and consultant for the biographical dictionary *Notable American Women* (1971); also was a contributor to supplements II and III of the *Dictionary of American Biography;* was chairman and compiler of *A Survey of Musical Instrument Collections in the U.S. and Canada,* publ. by the Music Library Assoc. (1974). A polyglot and a polymath, he is fluent in German, French, and Turkish; nearly fluent in Japanese, and fairly fluent in personalized Russian. With his excellent wife, Carolyn, he edited an analytic index to *Modern Music* (N.Y., 1976). Among his scholarly achievements, perhaps the highest is his incandescent essay "The Music of *The Star-Spangled Banner*—From Ludgate Hill to Capitol Hill," in the *Quarterly Journal of the Library of Congress* (July 1977), in which he furnishes documentary proof that the tune of the American national anthem was indeed composed by John Stafford Smith, all demurrings by various estimable historians to the contrary notwithstanding. To the 6th edition of *Baker's Biographical Dictionary of Musicians* he contributed incalculably precious verifications, clarifications, rectifications, and refutations of previous inadvertent and/or ignorant fabrications and unintentional prevarications; he also edited *Oscar Sonneck and American Music* (Urbana, Ill., 1984).

Lidholm, Ingvar, Swedish composer; b. Jönköping, Feb. 24, 1921. He studied violin and music theory at the Royal College of Music in Stockholm (1940–45) with Charles Barkel, Hilding Rosenberg, and Tor Mann; was a stipendiary of the Jenny Lind Foundation for studies in France, Switzerland, and Italy; then had private lessons with Mátyás Seiber in England. He played viola; then was engaged as conductor of the municipal orch. in Örebro (1947–56) and director of chamber music at the Swedish Broadcasting Corp. (1956–65); from 1965 to 1971 he taught at the Royal College of Music in Stockholm, and in 1974 became head of planning at the music dept. of the Swedish Radio. He became associated with the cosmopolitan avant-garde active in Sweden; contributed greatly to the formulation of methods and aims of modern music; with Ligeti and Lutoslawski he compiled the brochure *Three Aspects of New Music. From the Composition Seminar in Stockholm,* publ. in Eng. (Stockholm, 1968). In his own works he applies constructivist methods with various serial algorithms.

Lie (Lie-Nissen), Erika, Norwegian pianist; b. Kongsvinger, Jan. 17, 1845; d. Christiania, Oct. 27, 1903. She studied with Kjerulf in Christiania and with Theodor Kullak in Berlin; later taught at Kullak's Academy there. She made concert tours throughout Europe; was particularly noted for her interpretation of Chopin. In 1870 she joined the faculty of the Copenhagen Cons. Returning to Norway, she married Dr. Oscar Nissen in 1874, and settled in Christiania.

Liebermann, Rolf, Swiss composer and opera director; b. Zürich, Sept. 14, 1910. He studied composition with Wladimir Vogel, then resident in Switzerland; most of his works were in an experimental idiom, sharing the influence of hedonistic eclecticism, French neo-Classicism, and Viennese dodecaphony; he became particularly attracted to theatrical applications of modernistic procedures. He soon veered away from composition and made an extremely successful career as an opera administrator. In 1959 he became Intendant of the Hamburg State Opera, and in 1962 its artistic director; in this post he instituted an audacious program of commissioned works from avant-garde composers (among them Krenek, Schuller, and Penderecki). Concurrently he was program director of the North German Radio and the West Berlin Radio. In 1973 he was named director of the Paris Opéra. WORKS: Operas: *Leonore 40/45* (Basel, March 25, 1952); *Penelope* (Salzburg, Aug. 17, 1954); *The School for Wives* (Louisville, Dec. 3, 1955; revised as a 3-act opera, *Die Schule der Frauen,* and produced in Salzburg in 1957); *Volkslieder Suite* (BBC broadcast, Jan. 10, 1947); *Furioso* for Orch. (1947; Dallas, Dec. 9, 1950); *Concerto for Jazzband and Orchestra* (Donaueschingen Festival, Oct. 17, 1954); cantatas: *Streitlied zwischen Leben und Tod* and *Une des fins du monde; Les Echanges* for 52 Industrial Machines recorded on tape (composed for an exhibition in Lausanne, where it was perf. on April 24, 1964); several piano pieces and songs. A Festschrift in his honor was presented to him on his 60th birthday (Hamburg, 1970).

Lieberson, Goddard, American composer and music executive; b. Hanley, Staffordshire, England, April 5, 1911; d. New York, May 29, 1977. He was brought to the U.S. as a child; studied at the Eastman School of Music in Rochester, N.Y.; settled in N.Y. in 1936. In 1939 he became a member of the staff of Columbia Records, Inc., and rapidly progressed in business; was president of Columbia Records (1955–66, 1973–75); in 1964 he was named president of the Record Industry Assoc. of America while continuing as head of Columbia Records. In this latter position he was the chief catalyst in promoting long-playing records since their introduction in 1948, and was also responsible for Columbia Records' liberal policy in recording modern works. He composed the orch. suites *5 Modern Painters* (1929); *Piano Pieces for Advanced Children or Retarded Adults;* edited *Columbia Book of Musical Masterpieces* (N.Y., 1950).

Liebling, Emil, German-American pianist, brother of **Georg Liebling;** b. Pless, Silesia, April 12, 1851; d. Chicago, Jan. 20, 1914. He studied piano with Theodor Kullak in Berlin, Dachs in Vienna, and Liszt in Weimar; composition with Dorn in Berlin. In 1867 he came to America and lived in Chicago from 1872, actively engaged as a concert pianist and teacher. He wrote a number of effective piano pieces in a light vein (*Florence Valse, Feu follet, Albumblatt, 2 Romances, Cradle Song, Canzonetta, Menuetto scherzoso, Mazurka de concert, Spring Song.*) He edited *The American History and Encyclopedia of Music* and co-edited a *Dictionary of Musical Terms.*

Liebling, Estelle, American singer and vocal pedagogue, sister of **Leonard Liebling,** niece of **Emil** and **Georg Liebling;** b. New York, April 21, 1880; d. New York, Sept. 25, 1970. She studied with Mathilde Marchesi in Paris and S. Nicklass-Kempner in Berlin; made her debut as Lucia at the Dresden Royal Opera; also appeared at the Stuttgart Opera, the Opéra-Comique in Paris, and the Metropolitan Opera House in N.Y. (1902–3); was a soloist with leading symph. orchs. in the U.S., France, and Germany; also with Sousa; in 1936–38 was a prof. at the Curtis Inst. of Music in Philadelphia; then settled in N.Y. as a vocal teacher. She publ. *The Estelle Liebling Coloratura Digest* (N.Y., 1943).

Liebling, Georg, German-American pianist and composer, brother of **Emil Liebling;** b. Berlin, Jan. 22, 1865; d. New York, Feb. 7, 1946. He studied piano with Theodor and Franz Kullak, and Liszt; composition with Urban and Dorn; toured Europe (1885–89); was court pianist to the Duke of Coburg (1890). In 1894–97 he directed his own music school in Berlin; in 1898–1908, was a prof. at the Guildhall School of Music in London. He came to the U.S. in 1924; made his N.Y. concert debut on Nov. 19, 1924. He used the pseudonym **André Myrot.**
   WORKS: *Great Mass* for Soli, Chorus, Orch., and Organ (Los Angeles, 1931); *Concerto eroico* for Piano and Orch. (1925); 2 violin concertos; 2 violin sonatas; 3 Preludes for Violin and Piano; *Aria e Tarantella* for Cello and Piano; *Légende* for Violin and Piano; etc.; piano pieces; songs.

Liebling, Leonard, American music critic and editor, nephew of **Georg** and **Emil Liebling** and brother of **Estelle Liebling;** b. New York, Feb. 7, 1874; d. there, Oct. 28, 1945. He studied at City College in N.Y., and privately with Leopold Godowsky (piano); then in Berlin with Kullak and Barth (piano) and Urban (composition); toured Europe and America as a pianist. In 1902 he joined the staff of the *Musical Courier* in N.Y., and in 1911 became its editor in chief; his weekly columns on topical subjects were both entertaining and instructive. He also served as music critic of the *N.Y. American* (1923–34, 1936–37). He wrote some chamber music, piano pieces, and songs, as well as librettos of several light operas, including Sousa's *The American Maid.*

Lieurance, Thurlow, American composer; b. Oskaloosa, Iowa, March 21, 1878; d. Boulder, Colo., Oct. 9, 1963. He studied at the Cincinnati College of Music; served as an army bandmaster during the Spanish-American War. He became interested in American Indian music, and lived on various reservations, studying the culture of Indian tribes; this research resulted in the composition of music showing the influence of Indian melodies; one of the songs, *By the Waters of Minnetonka,* achieved tremendous popularity; he further publ. *9 Indian Songs* (1919); *Songs of the North American Indian* (1921); *8 Songs from the Green Timber* (1922); *Forgotten Trails* (1923); wrote several symph. pieces: *Medicine Dance, Colonial Exposition Sketches, Scenes Southwest, Prairie Sketches, Water Moon Maiden,* etc. In 1940 he was appointed dean of the music dept. of Municipal Univ. of Wichita, Kans.; in 1957, was named dean emeritus.

Ligeti, György, innovative Hungarian composer of the avant-garde; b. Dicsöszentmartin, Transylvania, May 28, 1923. He studied composition with Sándor Veress and Ferenc Farkas at the Budapest Music Academy (1945–49) and became an instructor there (1950–56). In 1956 he left Budapest; worked in the Studio for Electronic Music in Cologne (1957–59); then lived mostly in Vienna (1959–69) and in Berlin (1969–73); in summers he lectured at the International Courses for New Music in Darmstadt; from 1961 was a guest prof. of composition at the Musical High School in Stockholm; in addition, he gave lectures in Spain, the Netherlands, Germany, and Finland, and at Tanglewood in the U.S.; in 1972 was composer-in-residence at Stanford Univ.; in 1973 was appointed prof. of composition at the Hochschule für Musik in Hamburg. In his bold and imaginative experimentation with musical materials and parameters, Ligeti endeavors to bring together all aural and visual elements in a synthetic entity, making use of all conceivable effects, employing homely kitchen utensils and plebeian noisemakers or grandiose electronic blasts, alternating tremendous sonorous upheavals with static chordal masses and shifting dynamic colors.
   WORKS: *Rumanian Concerto* for Orch. (1951); *Glissandi* for Electronic Sound (1957); *Articulation* for Electronics (1958); *Apparitions* for Orch. (1959); *Atmospheres* for Orch. (1961); *Volumina* for Organ (1962); *Aventures* for 3 Singers and 7 Instruments (1962); *Nouvelles aventures* for Soprano and 7 Instruments (1962–65); *Requiem* for Soprano, Mezzosoprano, 2 Choruses, and Orch. (1963–65; Stockholm, March 14, 1965; the *Kyrie* from it was used in the film score for *2001: A Space Odyssey*); Cello Concerto (Berlin, April 19, 1967); *Lontano* for Orch. (Donaueschingen, Oct. 22, 1967); *10 Pieces* for Wind Quintet (Malmö, Jan. 19, 1969); *Ramifications* for String Orch. (1969); *Chamber Concerto* for 13 Instruments (Ottawa, April 2, 1970); Double Concerto for Flute, Oboe, and Orch. (1972); *Clocks and Clouds* for Female Chorus and Orch. (1973); *San Francisco Polyphony* for Orch. (1974); *Monument-Selbstporträt-Bewegung* for 2 Pianos (1976); opera, *Le Grand Macabre,* after Ghelderode's play (Stockholm, April 12, 1978); Trio for Violin, Horn, and Piano (1981); also 2 string quartets (1954, 1968). Ligeti's *Poème symphonique* for 100 Metronomes, all running at different speeds, was performed at the Buffalo Fes-

tival of the Arts Today (March 4, 1965), causing a sensation.

Lilburn, Douglas, New Zealand composer; b. Wanganui, Nov. 2, 1915. He studied with Vaughan Williams at the Royal College of Music in London; then returned to New Zealand, where he became a prof. of music at Victoria Univ. in Wellington. Among his works are *Forest,* symph. poem (1937); *Aoteroa,* overture (London, April 16, 1940); *Song of the Antipodes* for Orch. (Wellington, Aug. 20, 1947); *Diversions* for String Orch. (London, June 28, 1947); 3 symphs.: No. 1 (first full-fledged symph. by a New Zealand composer; Wellington, May 12, 1951); No. 2 (1955); No. 3 (1961); 2 string quartets; 3 violin sonatas; String Trio; Clarinet Sonata; Piano Sonata; other piano pieces; songs.

Liljeblad, Ingeborg, Finnish soprano; b. Helsinki, Oct. 17, 1887; d. there, Feb. 28, 1942. She studied in Berlin with Etelka Gerster, and in Paris with Félia Litvinne; was engaged at the Mannheim Opera (1911–13) and in Hamburg for the season of 1913–14. Returning to Helsinki in 1927, she taught at the Sibelius Academy. She was married to the conductor **Leo Funtek.**

Liljefors, Ingemar, Swedish composer, son of **Ruben Liljefors;** b. Göteborg, Dec. 13, 1906; d. Stockholm, Oct. 14, 1981. He studied at the Royal Academy of Music in Stockholm (1923–27 and 1929–31); in 1938 was appointed to its staff. From 1947 to 1963 he was chairman of the Assoc. of Swedish Composers. He publ. a manual on harmony from the functional point of view (1937) and one on harmonic analysis along similar lines (1951). His compositions frequently employ elements of Swedish folk music.

Liljefors, Ruben, Swedish composer and conductor; b. Uppsala, Sept. 30, 1871; d. there, March 4, 1936. He studied in Uppsala; then with Jadassohn at the Leipzig Cons.; later in Dresden with Draeseke; and with Max Reger in Leipzig. Returning to Sweden, he was active as a choral conductor in Uppsala (1902) and in Göteborg (1903–11); in 1912 he went to Gävle as conductor of the Orchestral Society.

Lill, John, English pianist; b. London, March 17, 1944. He studied at the Royal College of Music in London; made his debut at a concert in the Royal Festival Hall in 1963. In 1970 he won first prize in the International Tchaikovsky Competition in Moscow, which was the beginning of his successful international career. In 1978 he received the Order of the British Empire.

Lin, Cho-Liang, Chinese violinist; b. Taiwan, Jan. 29, 1960. He began to study the violin as a child; when he was 10 he won the Taiwan National Youth Competition. He then studied with Robert Pikler at the New South Wales State Conservatorium of Music in Sydney; at 15 he came to the U.S., where he enrolled at the Juilliard School of Music in N.Y. as a scholarship student of Dorothy DeLay. In 1977 he won first prize in the Queen Sofia International Competition in Madrid, and subsequently appeared as a soloist with the N.Y. Phil., Philadelphia Orch., Chicago Symph., Pittsburgh Symph., Cleveland Orch., Los Angeles Phil., London Symph., Royal Phil. of London, London Phil., Bavarian Radio Symph., and Royal Danish Orch. In 1981 he toured the People's Republic of China; he also played in Hong Kong, New Zealand, and Japan.

Lincke, Paul, German composer of light music; b. Berlin, Nov. 7, 1866; d. Klausthal-Zellerfeld, near Göttingen, Sept. 3, 1946. He was active in many fields; played violin and bassoon; conducted theater orchs.; engaged in music publishing; after World War I he conducted revues at the Folies-Bergère in Paris (1918–20). His chief fame comes from his operettas; he is generally credited as being the progenitor of a special type of "Berlin operetta," as distinguished from the Vienna genre. The best known of these are *Venus auf Erden* (1897); *Im Reiche des Indra* (Berlin, Dec. 17, 1899); *Frau Luna* (Berlin, Dec. 31, 1899); *Fräulein Loreley* (Berlin, 1900); *Lysistrata* (Berlin, 1902), which contains the famous tune *Glühwürmchen-Idyll (Glowworm); Prinzessin Rosine* (1905); *Grigri* (1911); *Casanova* (1913). His last operetta was *Ein Liebestraum,* which was produced in Hamburg in 1940; a postage stamp in Lincke's honor, with a musical example showing the melody *Berliner Luft* from *Frau Luna,* was issued by the West German government in 1957.

Lind, Jenny, famous soprano, called "the Swedish Nightingale"; b. Stockholm, Oct. 6, 1820; d. at her villa, Wynd's Point, Malvern Wells, England, Nov. 2, 1887. At the age of 10 she entered the Royal Opera School in Stockholm; her early teachers there were C.M. Craelius and I. Berg; she later studied with A.F. Lindblad and J.A. Josephson. She made her professional debut as Agathe in *Der Freischütz* at the Stockholm Opera on March 7, 1838; she then sang Euryanthe in Weber's opera, and several parts in French operas. In 1840 she was appointed a regular member of the Royal Swedish Academy of Music, and was also given the rank of court singer. However, she felt the necessity of improving her voice, and in 1841 went to Paris, where she studied for about a year with Manuel García, who gave her a thorough training according to his well-known "scientific" method. In Paris Meyerbeer heard her, and was so impressed that he wrote for her the part of Vielka in his opera *Ein Feldlager in Schlesien.* Jenny Lind returned to Stockholm in 1842; in 1844 she went to Berlin; sang there, and also in Hannover, Hamburg, Cologne, and Coblenz; then appeared in Frankfurt, Darmstadt, Copenhagen, and again in Berlin; her other important engagements were at the Gewandhaus in Leipzig (Dec. 6, 1845), and at the Vienna Opera (April 18, 1846). By this time, her fame became legendary in Europe; she was engaged to sing in London, and her appearance there was preceded by an extraordinary publicity campaign. She made her London debut as Alice in *Robert le Diable* on May 4, 1847, with sensational success; as Chorley reported, the town "went mad about the Swedish Nightingale." If her success in England was great, her American tour exceeded all expectations in public agitation and monetary reward. She arrived in America in 1850, under the sponsorship of P.T. Barnum, the circus manager, who presented Jenny Lind as a natural phenomenon rather than as an artist; nonetheless, she made a fine impression on the musical public as well; she sang recitals in N.Y., Boston, St. Louis, and other cities; a 4-page broadside in folio format with golden type was issued in anticipation of her Boston appearance by the F. Gleason Publishing Co. (1850); poems were written in her honor, and accounts of her concerts were publ. in hundreds of newspapers. She earned fantastic fees, and made generous donations to various charitable institutions in Sweden. On Feb. 5, 1852, she married, in Boston, her accompanist, **Otto Goldschmidt;** with him she returned to Europe; remained for some time in Dresden; in 1856 she went to London, and remained in England for the rest of her life, with the exception of a few appearances in Europe. She had left the operatic stage in 1849, before her American tour; in England she sang with her husband's Bach Choir; her final public appearance was at the Rhenish Music Festival in 1870, when she sang the principal part in her husband's oratorio *Ruth;* in 1883 she joined the faculty of the Royal College of Music in London. Unlike many other celebrated singers of her era, Jenny Lind was a paragon of domestic virtue, and was distinguished by her lack of vanity; even her most ardent worshipers did not claim that she was beautiful, but there was no disagreement as to the quality of her voice and her musicianship. She possessed a fine coloratura, with a compass reaching high G; never striving for dramatic effect, she was able to maintain a perfect phrase. Among her best operatic parts were La Sonnambula and Lucia. A bust of Jenny Lind was unveiled in Westminster Abbey on April 20, 1894. A Jenny Lind Association was formed in N.Y. in 1922, and a Jenny Lind Society was organized in Stockholm in 1943.

Lindblad, Adolf Fredrik, Swedish composer; b. Skänninge, near Stockholm, Feb. 1, 1801; d. Linköping, Aug. 23, 1878. He studied in Berlin with Zelter. His numerous songs, tinged with national color, won deserved popularity, especially after Jenny Lind, his pupil, sang them in public; he was called the "Schubert of the North."
WORKS: Opera, *Frondörerna* (*The Frondists;* Stockholm, May 11, 1835); 2 symphs.; 7 string quartets; Piano Trio; Duo for Piano and Violin; songs (*The Song of the Dalecarlian Maiden, Lament, The Wood by the Aren Lake, A Day in Spring, A Summer's Day, Autumn Evening,* etc.).

Linde, Bo, Swedish composer; b. Gävle, Jan. 1, 1933; d. there, Oct. 2, 1970. He studied composition with Lars-Erik Larsson at the Royal Academy of Music in Stockholm; then took courses in conducting in Vienna (1953–54). In 1960 he returned to Gävle. In his music he follows a healthy Scandinavian style of composition, liberally diversified with cosmopolitan neo-Classical techniques, bordering on polytonality.

Lindeman, Ludvig Mathias, Norwegian organist and folk-song collector; b. Trondheim, Nov. 28, 1812; d. Christiania, May 23, 1887. He turned from theology to the study of music; in 1839, became organist at Our Saviour's Church in Christiania; in 1849, a teacher of church singing at the Theological Seminary of Christiania Univ.; in 1883 he and his son Peter Lindeman (1858–1930) founded a music school, which later developed into the Christiania Cons. He was one of the earliest and most active collectors of Norwegian folk songs; publ. nearly 600 folk melodies in the collection *Older and Newer Norwegian Mountain Melodies* (3 vols., 1853–67); also *68 Norwegian Mountain Melodies* (1841); *50 Norwegian Melodies* (1862); and *30 Norwegian Ballads* (1863). His *Chorale Book for the Norwegian Church* (1877) remains a standard work; it contains some melodies by Lindeman, including *Kirken den er et gammelt hus,* one of the best-known Norwegian hymn tunes; he also composed *Draumkvoedet (Dream Chant)* for Chorus; organ fugues; etc.

Lindholm, Berit, Swedish soprano, b. Stockholm, Oct. 18, 1934. She studied music in Stockholm and made her professional debut at the Royal Opera there in 1963. In 1966 she sang at Covent Garden in London; later also appeared at Bayreuth. In 1972 she sang at the San Francisco Opera; on Feb. 20, 1975, she made her debut at the Metropolitan Opera in N.Y. as Brünnhilde in *Die Walküre.* Her effective performances of Wagnerian roles established her reputation as an opera singer.

Lindpaintner, Peter Joseph von, German conductor and composer; b. Coblenz, Dec. 9, 1791; d. Nonnenhorn, Lake Constance, Aug. 21, 1856. He studied violin and piano in Augsburg; theory in Munich with Winter and Joseph Grätz; in 1812, became music director of the Isarthor Theater in Munich; from 1819 until his death, was conductor of the court orch. at Stuttgart, where his ability made the orch. famous.
WORKS: 28 operas, including *Der Bergkönig* (Stuttgart, Jan. 30, 1825); *Der Vampyr* (Stuttgart, Nov. 21, 1828); *Die Genueserin* (Vienna, Feb. 8, 1839); *Lichtenstein* (Stuttgart, Aug. 26, 1846); 3 ballets (*Joko,* etc.); 5 melodramas; 5 oratorios; symphs.; overture to *Faust;* incidental music to *Lied von der Glocke;* 6 masses; *Stabat Mater;* songs (*Die Fahnenwacht, Roland,* etc.).

Linley, Thomas, Jr., English violinist and composer; eldest son of **Thomas Linley, Sr.;** b. Bath, May 7, 1756; d. Grimsthorpe, Aug. 5, 1778. He was extremely gifted as a child, and played a violin concerto in public at the age of 8. He studied music in London with his father and with Boyce; was then sent to Florence, where he studied violin with Nardini, and while there, met Mozart, with whom he subsequently formed a close friendship. Returning to England, he played at his father's concerts at Bath and in London. He wrote incidental music for various plays in London. He lost his life by drowning at the early age of 22. Some of his vocal pieces were included in the posthumous collection of his father's music.

Linley, Thomas, Sr., English composer; b. Badminton, Jan. 17, 1733; d. London, Nov. 19, 1795. He first studied with a church organist in Bath; then with Paradisi. He organized performances of oratorios in Bath; in 1774 he went to London, where he produced several oratorios, and various stage works, to which he contributed an occasional song; also arranged and orchestrated ballets, comic operas, etc., by other composers. He publ. *6 Elegies* for 3 Voices (his finest work) and *12 Ballads;* 2 vols. of miscellaneous vocal pieces by him were publ. posthumously. The writer Sheridan was his son-in-law; Linley wrote 7 numbers for the production of Sheridan's *The Duenna,* and arranged the other musical works for the opera; it was produced at Covent Garden in London on Nov. 21, 1775, and became one of the most successful comic operas in England of the 18th century (about 75 perfs. during the season). Linley's 3 sons and 3 daughters were also professional musicians.

Lioncourt, Guy de, French composer; b. Caen, Dec. 1, 1885; d. Paris, Dec. 24, 1961. He studied at the Schola Cantorum with Vincent d'Indy, who was his uncle by marriage; in 1918 he won the Grand Prix Lasserre with his fairy-tale opera *La Belle au bois dormant* (1912). In 1935 he was co-founder, with L. de Serres, of the Ecole César Franck in Paris.
WORKS: Dramatic: *Le Petit Faune aux yeux bleus* (1911); *Les Dix Lépreux* (1920); *Jean de la lune* (1921); *Le Mystère de l'Emmanuel* (Liège, 1924); *Le Mystère de l'Alléluia* (1927); *Le Réniement de St.-Pierre* (1928); *Le Dict de Mme. Sante-Barbe* (1937); *Le Navrement de Notre Dame* (1944); *Le Mystère de l'Esprit* (1946); String Quartet; Piano Quartet; 3 *Mélodies grégoriennes* for Organ; *Elevations liturgiques* for Organ; 3 masses; motets. He publ. *Un Témoignage sur la musique et sur la vie au XXe siècle* (Reims, 1956).

Lipatti, Dinu, outstanding Rumanian pianist and composer; b. Bucharest, April 1, 1917; d. Chêne-Bourg, near Geneva, Dec. 2, 1950. His father was a violinist who had studied with Sarasate, and his mother, a pianist. He received his early training from his parents; then studied with Florica Musicescu at the Bucharest Cons. (1928–32). He received a 2nd prize at the International Competition at Vienna in 1934; then studied piano with Cortot, conducting with Munch, and composition with Paul Dukas and Nadia Boulanger in Paris (1934–39). He gave concerts in Germany and Italy, returning to Rumania at the outbreak of World War II. In 1943 he made his way to Stockholm, and then to Geneva, where he taught piano at the Geneva Cons. He visit-

ed England 4 times between 1946 and 1950; projected tours in America and Australia had to be canceled owing to his illness (lymphogranulomatosis), which led to his early death. He was generally regarded as one of the most sensitive interpreters of Chopin, and was also praised for his deep understanding of the Baroque masters. Lipatti was married to **Madeleine Cantacuzene,** herself a concert pianist. He was also a fine composer.

Lipawsky, Josef, Austrian composer; b. Hohenmauth, Bohemia, Feb. 22, 1769; d. Vienna, Jan. 7, 1810. He studied philosophy in Prague; then settled in Vienna, where he enjoyed the friendship of Mozart, who gave him some instruction; was house musician for Count Adam Teleky; also gave public piano concerts. He wrote a Symph.; *Grande sonate pathétique* for Piano; songs. His music was highly regarded by his contemporaries.

Lipinsky, Carl, Polish violinist and composer; b. Radzyn, Oct. 30, 1790; d. near Lwow, Dec. 16, 1861. His father was a professional musician and gave him his primary education. He met Paganini, who agreed to teach him the violin; in 1835 he visited Leipzig; Schumann was greatly impressed by his playing and dedicated *Carnaval* to him. Lipinsky appeared in London on April 25, 1836, as soloist in his *Military Concerto* for Violin and Orch.; in 1839 he settled in Dresden as concertmaster of the Dresden Orch.; Liszt once played at the same concert with him. Lipinsky wrote a comic opera, *Klótnia przez zaklad* (Lwow, May 27, 1814), and other stage pieces; polonaises and *Rondos alla polacca* for violin and piano; numerous technical violin studies.

Lipkovska, Lydia, Russian soprano; b. Babino, Khotin district, Bessarabia, May 10, 1884; d. Beirut, Jan. 22, 1955. She studied voice with Madame Iretzkaya in St. Petersburg, and made her professional debut there in the spring of 1909. She sang in Paris with great success, and received a contract for an American tour. Her American debut took place with the Boston Opera on Nov. 12, 1909, when she sang *Lakmé;* on Nov. 18, 1909, she appeared at the Metropolitan Opera House in *La Traviata* with Caruso. She was reengaged for the following season in the U.S.; also appeared in London (July 11, 1911). During World War I she was in Russia; after the Revolution she went to France; in 1919 she married Pierre Bodin, a lieutenant in the French army; toured the U.S. again in 1920. She then lived in France and her native Bessarabia; during the Rumanian occupation of Odessa (1941–44) she appeared at the Odessa Opera in her favorite role of Violetta; also acted in drama. In 1944 she went to Paris; then accepted a teaching position in Beirut; during her last years of life she was supported by the Tolstoy Foundation of America.

Lipowsky, Felix Joseph, German music lexicographer and composer, son of **Thaddäus Ferdinand Lipowsky;** b. Wiesensteig, Jan. 25, 1764; d. Munich, March 21, 1842. He was engaged in many scholarly pursuits, as a legal scientist, politician, art historian, etc. He was active as a church organist and choir leader; in 1787 he obtained his Dr.Jur. degree; then served as a municipal officer in Bavaria. He publ. *Bairische Musiklexikon* (Munich, 1811), which contains valuable material despite many faults of commission and omission. He wrote several sacred choral works and some instrumental music.

Lipowsky, Thaddäus Ferdinand, German composer; b. St. Martin, Bavaria, Dec. 28, 1738; d. Wiesensteig, March 18, 1767. He studied with Leopold Mozart in Salzburg; obtained a law degree in Wiesensteig (1763); composed many violin pieces. A lengthy account of his career is found in the *Baierisches Musik-Lexikon* compiled by his son, **Felix Joseph Lipowsky.**

Lipp, Wilma, Austrian soprano; b. Vienna, April 26, 1925. She studied at the Vienna Cons. and with Toti Dal Monte in Milan. In 1945 she joined the Vienna State Opera; then sang in Milan (La Scala), London (Covent Garden), Hamburg, Paris, Munich, and Berlin; took part at the music festivals in Salzburg, Bayreuth, and Edinburgh. She was equally distinguished as a coloratura and as a lyric soprano.

Lipsius, Marie (pen name, **La Mara**), German writer on music; b. Leipzig, Dec. 30, 1837; d. Schmölen, near Wurzen, March 2, 1927. She received her entire education from her father, Dr. Adalbert Lipsius, rector of the Thomasschule in Leipzig; through R. Pohl, she was introduced to Liszt; in Liszt's circle at Weimar she had the happy fortune of meeting the foremost musicians of the time. Her writings on Liszt and Wagner, and on other German composers of the Romantic school, possess a stamp of authority and intimate understanding.

Lisinski, Vatroslav, important Croatian composer; b. Zagreb, July 8, 1819; d. there, May 31, 1854. He was a student of Sojka and Wiesner von Morgenstern in Zagreb; as late as 1847, he went to Prague to study with Pitsch and Kittl. Although he never acquired a solid technique of composition, he was notable in that he tried to establish a national style in dramatic writing. He was the composer of the first Croatian opera, *Ljubav i zloba (Love and Malice),* for which he wrote only the vocal score; it was orchestrated by his teacher Wiesner von Morgenstern, and performed in Zagreb on March 28, 1846. His 2nd opera, *Porin,* also in Croatian, was given many years after his death, in Zagreb, on Oct. 2, 1897. He further wrote 7 overtures and a number of choruses and songs.

Lissa, Zofia, outstanding Polish musicologist; b. Lwow, Oct. 19, 1908; d. Warsaw, March 26, 1980. She studied with Chybinski. The outbreak of the war interrupted her further studies; in 1947–54 she was vice-president of the Union of Polish Composers; in 1957 was appointed a prof. of musicology at Warsaw Univ.; she also served as a member-correspondent

with the Berlin Academy of Fine Arts (from 1957) and of the Academy of Sciences and Literature of Mainz (1972). She wrote voluminously on a variety of subjects connected with music history, education, broadcasting, film music, psychology of music, and social implications of music; publ. *The Outlines of Musical Science* (Lwow, 1934; new ed., 1948); *Some Problems of Musical Esthetics* (Cracow, 1952; in Japanese, 1956; in Chinese, 1962); *Essays on Musical Esthetics* (Cracow, 1964; in German, Berlin, 1969; in Hungarian, Budapest, 1973; in Serbian, Belgrade, 1973); of peculiar interest is her publication *The Marxist Method in Musicology* (Cracow, 1951) in which she propounds the interpretation of socialist realism and other doctrines of Marxist science as applied to both musical composition and musical evaluation. She contributed numerous articles on Polish music to *Die Musik in Geschichte und Gegenwart.*

Lissenko, Nicolai, significant Ukrainian composer; b. Grinki, near Kremenchug, March 22, 1842; d. Kiev, Nov. 6, 1912. He was the son of a landowner; grew up in a musical atmosphere; the singing of Ukrainian songs by local peasants produced a lasting impression on him, and determined his future as a national composer. He studied natural sciences at the Univ. of Kiev, graduating in 1864; was a justice of the peace in the Kiev district (1864–66); then abandoned his nonmusical pursuits and went to Leipzig, where he entered the Cons., and took courses with Richter (theory), Reinecke (piano), and Papperitz (organ). Returning to Russia in 1868, he taught piano at the Kiev Inst. of the Daughters of Nobility; in 1874–76 he studied orchestration with Rimsky-Korsakov in St. Petersburg. As early as 1868 he publ. his first collection of Ukrainian songs (printed in Leipzig); subsequent issues comprised 240 songs in 5 books, arranged according to their categories (Spring Songs, Midsummer Night Songs, Christmas Songs, etc.); he set to music a great number of poems from *Kobzar* by the Ukrainian poet Shevchenko (5 albums for 2, 3, and 4 voices; publ. in Kiev, 1870–97). In 1903, on the occasion of the 35th anniversary of the publication of his first collection of Ukrainian songs, Lissenko received a gift of 5,000 rubles from his admirers.

In his pamphlet *The Characteristics of the Ukrainian Dumki* (1874), Lissenko presents a theory that Ukrainian modes are derived from Greek music, and that antiphonal construction is one of the main features of Ukrainian songs, while the persistence of symmetrical rhythms distinguishes them from Russian songs. In his original compositions, Lissenko asserted himself as an ardent Ukrainian nationalist; he wrote several operas to Ukrainian librettos: *Chernomortsy* (1870); *Rizdviana Nitch,* after Gogol's *Christmas Eve Night* (1870); *Winter and Spring* (1880); *Utoplena,* after Gogol's *May Night* (1885); *Taras Bulba,* after Gogol's novel of the same name (1890; Kiev, Dec. 20, 1903; revised by Liatoshinsky and produced in Kiev in 1937); and his most popular stage work, after Kotlarevsky's play, *Natalka-Poltavka (Natalie from Poltava),* originally in the form of incidental music, then expanded into a 3-act opera (1890). He further wrote the opera *Sappho,* with a Ukrainian text, which was unsuccessful; and 2. children's operas, *Pan Kotsky (Puss-in-Boots;* 1891) and *Koza-Dereza* (Kiev, April 20, 1901). Other works include 2 cantatas: *The Torrents Roar* (1877) and *Rejoice, Field Unplowed* (1883); also *Cossack Scherzo* for Orch. (1872); *Capriccio elegiaco* for Violin and Orch. (1894); 2 rhapsodies on Ukrainian themes for Piano; vocal pieces.

List, Emanuel, Austrian bass; b. Vienna, March 22, 1888; d. there, June 21, 1967. He was a chorister at the Theater-an-der-Wien; studied voice in Vienna, and made his debut at the Volksoper there in 1922 as Méphistophélès in *Faust;* in 1923, was engaged at the Berlin State Opera, remaining there until 1933; specialized in Wagnerian roles. On Dec. 27, 1933, he made his first American appearance at the Metropolitan Opera in N.Y., as the Landgraf in *Tannhäuser;* in subsequent seasons, sang almost all Wagnerian bass roles; remained with the company until 1948; sang at Bayreuth and Salzburg; also appeared as a singer of German lieder.

List, Eugene, American pianist; b. Philadelphia, July 6, 1918. He was taken to Los Angeles when a year old; studied there at the Sutro-Seyler Studios and made his debut with the Los Angeles Phil. at the age of 12; later studied in Philadelphia with Olga Samaroff, and at the Juilliard Graduate School in N.Y.; made his N.Y. debut playing the solo part in the American premiere of Shostakovich's Piano Concerto No. 1 with the Philadelphia Orch. (Dec. 12, 1934). As a sergeant in the U.S. Army, he was called upon to play the piano at the Potsdam Conference in July 1945, in the presence of Truman, Churchill, and Stalin. In 1964 he was appointed a prof. of piano at the Eastman School of Music in Rochester, N.Y.; left there in 1975; then joined the faculty of N.Y. Univ.

Listemann, Bernhard, German-American violinist and conductor; b. Schlotheim, Aug. 28, 1841; d. Chicago, Feb. 11, 1917. He studied with Ferdinand David in Leipzig, with Vieuxtemps in Brussels, and with Joachim in Hannover; became concertmaster of the court orch. in Rudolstadt (1859–67); then went with his brother **Fritz Listemann** to America; in 1871–74, was concertmaster of the Thomas Orch. in N.Y.; in 1874 he went to Boston, where he founded the Phil. Club, and later the Phil. Orch., which he conducted until 1881, when he became concertmaster of the newly established Boston Symph. Orch.; meanwhile, he started the Listemann Quartet; also was director of the Listemann Concert Co. (1885–93). In 1893 he went to Chicago, where he taught violin at the Chicago College of Music.

Listemann, Franz, American cellist, son of **Bernhard Listemann;** b. New York, Dec. 17, 1873; d. Chicago, March 11, 1930. He studied with Fries in Boston, with Julius Klengel in Leipzig, and with Hauss-

mann in Berlin. After a year as first cellist in the Pittsburgh Orch., he settled in N.Y.; he was soloist at the American premiere of Dvořák's Cello Concerto (1896).

Listemann, Fritz, German violinist, brother of **Bernhard Listemann;** b. Schlotheim, March 25, 1839; d. Boston, Dec. 28, 1909. Like his brother, he studied with Ferdinand David at the Leipzig Cons.; was a member of the court orch. at Rudolstadt (1858–67); he went with his brother to America; played violin in the Thomas Orch. in N.Y. (1871–74); then was in Boston, where he played in various chamber music organizations, and (from 1878) in his brother's Phil. Orch.; in 1881–85, was a violinist in the Boston Symph. Orch.; then played in the Listemann Concert Co. directed by his brother. He wrote 2 violin concertos; violin pieces.

Listemann, Paul, American violinist, son of **Bernhard Listemann;** b. Boston, Oct. 24, 1871; d. Chicago, Sept. 20, 1950. He was taught by his uncle **Fritz Listemann,** and also by his father; as a boy, participated in the various organizations directed by his father; then went to Germany, where he studied in Leipzig with Brodsky and in Berlin with Joachim; he was subsequently engaged as an orch. violinist in Pittsburgh, N.Y., etc.; was a member of the Metropolitan Opera Orch. from 1903 to 1920. In 1930 he moved to Chicago.

Liszt, Franz (Ferencz), greatly celebrated Hungarian pianist and composer, creator of the symphonic poem and a reformer of modern piano technique; b. Raiding, near Ödenburg, Oct. 22, 1811; d. Bayreuth, July 31, 1886. His father was an excellent amateur musician and trained him in music from earliest childhood; at the age of 9 young Liszt played the difficult Piano Concerto in E-flat major by Ries. A group of Hungarian aristocrats provided sufficient funds (600 florins annually) to finance his musical education for 6 years. In 1822 the family moved to Vienna, where Liszt became a pupil of Czerny in piano and studied music theory with Salieri. Liszt's ambitious father was eager to introduce him to Beethoven, and as a legend (supported by Liszt himself in his later years) had it, Beethoven kissed him on the brow after Liszt played an arrangement of Beethoven's Trio, op. 97, for him entirely from memory. Beethoven's factotum, Schindler, made an earnest effort to persuade Beethoven to come to Liszt's concert in Vienna on April 13, 1823, but Beethoven did not acquiesce. After concerts in Munich and Stuttgart, young Liszt proceeded to Paris, where he applied for admission to the Cons.; but Cherubini, then director of the Paris Cons., who was opposed to infant prodigies, refused to accept him as a student, using as an excuse a rule forbidding the entrance of foreigners. As a consequence, Liszt took no more piano lessons; he studied composition for a short time with Paër and then with Reicha. At the age of 13 Liszt composed an operetta, *Don Sanche, ou Le Château d'Amour,* which was performed 4 times at the Académie

Liszt

Royale de Musique in 1825. Liszt's father died in 1827, and he settled in Paris. He was already well-known as a virtuoso pianist, and in Paris he moved in the highest circles of letters and arts; he was fascinated by the new Romantic spirit of the age; the socialistic ideas of St.-Simon, the revolutionary rumblings of 1830, greatly affected him. Paganini's spectacular performances on the violin inspired Liszt to emulate him in creating a new pianistic technique that exploited all possible sonorities of the instrument; the corresponding ideas of Berlioz in enlarging orch. sonorities found in Liszt an enthusiastic supporter. At the same time Liszt never abandoned the basic Romantic feeling for music as an expressive art, the voice of the human soul translated into musical tones; in this he was an ardent companion of Chopin, his close contemporary. He formed a liaison with the Countess d'Agoult, who wrote literary works under the nom de plume of Daniel Stern, and went to live with her in Geneva (1835–36). Three children were born to them: Cosima, the younger of 2 daughters, eventually became the wife of Richard Wagner. After his Geneva sojourn Liszt set out on a concert tour through Europe, which proved to be a series of triumphs. To underline the narrative Romantic quality of his playing and his compositions, he accepted the suggestion of his London friend Frederick Beale to use the word "recital," and the term became universally accepted. Since Liszt himself acknowledged that in his piano works he set Paganini as a model, it was only natural that he was often described as the "Paganini of the piano." But he maintained that his virtuosity was but a means of re-creating great music, and held that the interpreter's duty was to reveal the composer's innermost intentions. His spiritual affinity with Beethoven moved him to superlative renditions of the master's piano sonatas; but he was also able to give intimate interpretations of Chopin. Withal, Liszt was a man of the world, a practical musician who was willing to give to his public what was expected of him. On stage he was often an actor; he wore white gloves, as was the custom of the day, and took them off ceremoniously in front of the audience; at some concerts he had 2 pianos on the stage, and played a group of pieces on each in alternation so that his hands could be seen from every area of the audience. He included in some of his programs free improvisations on themes proffered to him by musical amateurs. His private life underwent another upheaval when he formed a new liaison with the Polish Princess Carolyne Sayn-Wittgenstein, who took up residence with Liszt; she was very influential in turning him toward established religion. Liszt became a Freemason in 1841; a tertiary of St. Francis in 1857. In 1865 Pope Pius IX conferred on him the dignity of Abbé. In 1879 he received the tonsure and the 4 minor orders (ostuary, lector, exorcist, and acolyte) and an honorary canonry; however, he was never ordained a priest, and could not say Mass, or hear confession. But he could discard his cassock and even marry if he so wished. He practically abandoned his concert career in 1842, when he accepted the position of court Kapellmeister at Weimar. When Wagner was exiled from Saxony, Liszt arranged the production of his opera *Lohengrin* in Weimar on Aug. 28, 1850; he also was instrumental in supervising performances of Wagner's *Der fliegende Holländer* and *Tannhäuser* and the music of Berlioz. In 1861 he left Weimar and lived for the most part in Rome. In 1870 he returned to Weimar to conduct a centennial Beethoven festival there. In 1875 he was made president of the New Hungarian Academy of Music in Budapest; the last years of his life were spent in Weimar, Budapest, and Rome. In Weimar he formed a faithful retinue of loyal and admiring students, and he displayed great interest in new movements in musical composition. He was an eager correspondent; his letters, many of them still unpubl., number in the thousands, written in French and German, in longhand; he did not employ a secretary. According to a will he made in 1860, Liszt's MSS passed into the possession of the Princess Carolyne Sayn-Wittgenstein; after her death in 1887, they were inherited by her daughter Marie Hohenlohe-Schillingsfürst. She in turn left these materials to the Weimar court; eventually they became part of the Liszt Museum.

Liszt's achievement as a composer is of revolutionary significance. He created the transcendental style of piano playing and introduced a new concept of the spiritual relationship between music and literature; he was allied with Wagner in the movement that was called, both in derision and admiration, *Zukunftsmusik*, the music of the future. The term applied to a mystical synthesis of the arts, which for Liszt implied the adoption of a programmatic design in a musical composition and a liberation from the classical rules of musical form. Such a synthesis was accomplished by Liszt in the creation of the symph. poem, explicitly descriptive and connected with a literary work or a philosophical idea. "Music of the future" also embraced the field of harmony, modulation, and melody. Both Liszt and Wagner greatly enhanced the type of chromatic harmony resulting from instant modulation into unrelated keys. In the last years of his life, Liszt experimented with melodic patterns, such as those derived from the whole-tone scale, which tend to obscure tonality, and with harmonic combinations rich in dissonance produced by long-delayed resolutions. Liszt defied tradition when he boldly outlined the main subject of his *Faust Symphony*, formed of 4 arpeggiated, chromatically descending, augmented triads, the whole aggregating into 12 different notes. In his orchestration he summoned large sonorities following the precedent of Berlioz. It was this unremitting flow of sound that outraged the music critics of Liszt's day and moved them to denounce Liszt as a purveyor of noise in the guise of music. But Liszt was also capable of writing music of intimate lyric quality; his songs to German or French words possess the deepest lyrical expressiveness; his piano pieces distill the poetry and the drama of the literary program to the finest gradation of sentiment. His B-minor Piano Sonata introduces a new dimension into this classical form: in place of an orderly succession and development of basic themes, Liszt cultivates here an association of motifs, thus transforming the work into a musical narrative. His 3 albums of *Années de pèlerinage* for piano are tone paintings, evoking the scene with pictorial vividness. His 2 piano concertos, his brilliant *Hungarian Rhapsodies*, his *Mephisto-Waltz*, and particularly his *Études d'exécution transcendante*, are unsurpassed in their sonorous grandeur and authentic virtuosity. In his transcriptions of Schubert's and Schumann's songs, he transmutes their vocal lines and accompanying harmonies into new tonal creations. Finally, his flamboyant arrangements of operatic arias by Auber, Donizetti, Gounod, Meyerbeer, Mozart, Rossini, Verdi, and Wagner are exhibitions of the highest art of transmutation from one medium into another. Liszt never wrote a full-fledged opera, but he composed oratorios that are operatic in substance and presentation. His many sacred works enhance the originality of his secular harmonies without losing their devotional character. Liszt was deeply conscious of his Hungarian heritage, but he spent most of his life in France, Germany, and Italy. Contrary to the natural assumption that Liszt, being the greatest Hungarian composer, spoke the language, it appears that his mother tongue was German, and that he could not converse in Hungarian at all; in later years he took lessons in Hungarian with Father Zsigmond Vadász, but abandoned the attempt after a few sessions. He never went into the countryside in quest of the folk origins of Hungarian music, as the 2 modern Hungarians Kodály and Bartók did; rather, he gathered the ethnic materials that he so brilliantly used in his *Hungarian Rhapsodies* and other works of Hungarian inspiration from Gypsy bands he frequently heard in public places in Budapest; in one extraordinary instance, he borrowed the theme for the most famous of these, No. 2, from an unpubl. work by an obscure Austrian musician named Heinrich Ehrlich, who had sent him his MS on approval; Ehrlich recounted this episode in his *30 Jahre Künstlerleben* (1893).

WORKS: FOR THE STAGE: *Don Sanche, ou Le Château d'Amour,* one-act operetta, a juvenile work (1825; the score, believed to have been lost, was discovered in 1903; the overture and an aria from it were publ. in the May 1904 issue of *Die Musik*). FOR ORCH.: Symph. poems (all conducted for the first time by Liszt himself, except where otherwise noted): *Ce qu'on entend sur la montagne,* after Victor Hugo (Weimar, Jan. 7, 1857); *Tasso, Lamento e Trionfo* (Weimar, Aug. 28, 1849; revised version, Weimar, April 19, 1854); *Les Préludes,* after Lamartine's "Méditations poétiques" (Weimar, Feb. 23, 1854); *Orpheus* (Weimar, Feb. 16, 1854); *Prometheus* (Weimar, Aug. 24, 1850); *Mazeppa,* after Victor Hugo (Weimar, April 16, 1854); *Festklänge* (Weimar, Nov. 9, 1854); *Héroïde funèbre* (sketched in 1830 as *Symphonie révolutionnaire;* revised and orchestrated in 1850; Breslau, Nov. 10, 1857, Moritz Schön conducting); *Hungaria* (sketched in 1848; revised in 1856; first perf., Budapest, Sept. 8, 1856); *Hamlet* (1858; Sondershausen, July 2, 1876, Max Erdmannsdörfer conducting); *Hunnenschlacht,* after Kaulbach's painting (Weimar, Dec. 29, 1857); *Die Ideale,* after Schiller (Weimar, Sept. 5, 1857); *Eine Faust-Symphonie,* in 3 characteristic pictures, after Goe-

the, with a choral finale (Weimar, Sept. 5, 1857); a *Symphony* to Dante's *Divina commedia,* with a Female Chorus (Dresden, Nov. 7, 1867); 2 *Episodes* from Lenau's "Faust" (1860–61); 2 *Mephisto Waltzes* (1860, 1880); 3 *odes funèbres,* with Male Chorus (1860–66); *Salve Polonia* (1863); *Festival March* for Goethe's jubilee (1849); for Piano and Orch.: Concerto No. 1, in E-flat, nicknamed the "Triangle Concerto" because of the prominent use of a triangle solo (1849; revised 1853; Weimar, Feb. 16, 1855; Berlioz conducting, composer at the piano); Concerto No. 2, in A major (1848; revised 1856–61; Weimar, Jan. 7, 1857; Hans von Bronsart, soloist, composer conducting; *Fantasie* on motifs from Beethoven's *Ruins of Athens* (Budapest, June 1, 1853); *Totentanz,* paraphrase on *Dies irae* (1849; revised 1853–59; The Hague, April 15, 1865, Hans von Bülow, soloist).

FOR PIANO SOLO: *Album d'un voyageur* (3 books); *3 apparitions; Rondo sur un thème espagnol (El Contrabandista); Napolitana; Rhapsodie espagnole* (arranged for Piano and Orch. by Busoni); *3 études de concert; 2 études de concert (Waldesrauschen, Gnomenreigen); Harmonies poétiques et religeuses* (10 pieces); *Liebesträume,* 3 nocturnes (originally they were songs); *3 sonetti del Petrarca; Valse impromptu; Mazurka brillante; 2 Polonaises; Scherzo and March; Grand solo de concert* (also for 2 Pianos); *Grand galop chromatique; 12 grandes études* (originally publ. as *Etudes en forme de 12 exercices pour piano); Ab irato, étude de perfectionnement; Sonata* in B minor (1854); *Berceuse; 2 ballades; 3 valses-caprices; 6 consolations; 20 Hungarian Rhapsodies* (No. 3 is the *Héroïde funèbre;* No. 9, the *Carnaval de Pest;* No. 15, the *Rákoczy March;* No. 20 is unpubl.; the MS is in the Liszt Museum at Weimar); *3 airs suisses; Années de pèlerinage* (3 series; contains such famous pieces as *Au bord d'une source, Venezia e Napoli,* and *Les Jeux d'eau à la Villa d'Este;* Book I is a revised version of Book I of the *Album d'un voyageur); Ave Maria; 3 élégies; 12 études d'exécution transcendante; Mephisto-Waltz* (originally for Orch.); 3 versions for Piano Solo; No. 4, unpubl., subtitled "Bagatelle sans tonalité"); *Via Crucis; Epithalamium; Bülow March; 3 valses oubliées; valse élégiaque; Weihnachtsbaum* (12 pieces); *Mosonyi's Grabgeleit; Mephisto-Polka; Impromptu* in F-sharp; *2 légendes: St. François d'Assise prédicant aux oiseaux* and *St. François de Paule marchant sur les flots; La Lugubre Gondole; Heroischer Marsch im ungarischen Stil; 2 arabesques; Czardas obstiné; Czardas macabre; Hymne du Pape; 7 Ungarische Bildnisse; Rhapsody, nach Siebenbürgischen und Walachischen Motiven; Phantasy and Fugue on B-A-C-H;* Variations on a theme from Bach's B-minor Mass; Variations on Bach's prelude *Weinen, Klagen; Technische Studien* (12 books); transcriptions of Beethoven's symphs., of Berlioz's *Symphonie fantastique, Harold en Italie,* and overtures to *Les Francs-juges* and *King Lear,* of Wagner's overture to *Tannhäuser,* of 6 of Chopin's *Chants polonais,* of 10 songs by Robert Franz, 7 songs by Mendelssohn, songs from several cycles by Schubert (*Schwanengesang, Winterreise, Geistliche Lieder,*

Müllerlieder, also *Die Forelle,* etc.), Schumann's *Liebeslied,* and other songs, etc.

VOCAL WORKS: *Missa solemnis* (the *Gran* festival Mass); *Hungarian Coronation Mass*; Mass in C minor, with Organ; *Missa choralis* in A minor, with Organ; Requiem; 3 oratorios: *Die Legende von der Heiligen Elisabeth; Christus; Stanislaus* (unfinished); 9 choruses, with Organ; *Die Seligkeiten* for Baritone Solo, Chorus, and Organ; *Pater noster* for Mixed Chorus and Organ; *Pater noster* and *Ave Maria* for Men's Voices and Organ; *Psalm 13* for Tenor Solo, Chorus, and Orch.; *Psalm 18* for Men's Chorus, Orch., and Organ; *Psalm 23* for Tenor (or Soprano) Solo, with Harp (or Piano) and Organ (or Harmonium); *Psalm 116* for Soli, Men's (or Mixed) Chorus, Organ, and Orch.; *Psalm 137* for Solo, Women's Chorus, Violin, Harp, Piano, and Organ; *Christus ist geboren* for Chorus, with Organ; *An den heiligen Franziskus* for Men's Voices, Organ, Trombones, and Drums; *Les Morts* for Men's Chorus and Orch.; numerous minor sacred compositions; cantatas: *Die Glocken des Strassburger Münsters, Die heilige Cäcile, An die Künstler* (for Soli, Men's Chorus, and Orch.), *Hungaria* (for Soli, Mixed Chorus, and Orch.; has nothing in common with the symph. poem bearing the same title; score lost for many years, discovered by P. Raabe in 1912); *Zur Säcular-Feier Beethovens; Festalbum* (for Goethe's 100th birthday); *Festchor* (for the unveiling of the Herder monument, Weimar, 1850); numerous 4-part men's choruses (*Das Lied der Begeisterung; Weimars Volkslied; Was ist das Deutsche Vaterland?,* with Piano; *Festgesang,* with Organ); about 60 songs with Piano, many strikingly beautiful (*Du bist wie eine Blume, Es muss ein wunderbares sein, Die Macht der Musik, Jeanne d'Arc au bûcher*). Vol. 2 of Peter Raabe's biography (1931) includes a complete catalogue of works. Thematic catalogues of Liszt's works were publ. by Breitkopf & Härtel in 1855 and 1876; a complete catalogue of the publ. works, by A. Göllerich, appeared in the *Neue Zeitschrift für Musik* (1887–88); a *Chronologisch-systematisches Verzeichnis* by L. Friwitzer was publ. in the *Wiener Musikalische Chronik* (Nov. 1887–March 1888).

In 1905 plans were made to publ. Liszt's complete works, to be issued periodically by Breitkopf & Härtel of Leipzig. Vol. I appeared in 1907; by 1936 Breitkopf & Härtel had issued 34 vols., but world conditions put an end to the project. In 1950 the Liszt Society of London, with E.J. Dent as president, began to issue a new series, but by 1968 only 56 vols. had appeared, 5 of them devoted to Liszt's lesser-known piano works, one to selected songs. A Neue Liszt-Ausgabe was begun in 1970 under the editorial direction of Zoltán Gárdonyi and István Szelényi, and by 1977, 8 vols. had been issued jointly by the Bärenreiter Verlag of Kassel and Editio Musica of Budapest.

Litinsky, Genrik (Heinrich), distinguished Russian composer; b. Lipovetz, March 17, 1901. He studied composition with Glière at the Moscow Cons., graduating in 1928; subsequently taught there

(1928–43); among his students were Khrennikov, Zhiganov, Arutiunian, and other Soviet composers. In 1945 he went to Yakutsk as an ethnomusicologist; in collaboration with native Siberian composers he produced the first national Yakut operas, based on authentic folk melorhythms and arranged in contemporary harmonies according to the precepts of socialist realism: *Nurgun Botur* (Yakutsk, June 29, 1947); *Sygy Kyrynastyr* (Yakutsk, July 4, 1947); *Red Shaman* (Yakutsk, Dec. 9, 1967). He wrote 3 Yakut ballets: *Altan's Joy* (Yakutsk, June 19, 1963); *Field Flower* (Yakutsk, July 2, 1947); *Crimson Kerchief* (Yakutsk, Jan. 9, 1968). Other works include: Symph. (1928); *Dagestan Suite* for Orch. (1931); Trumpet Concerto (1934); *Festive Rhapsody* for Orch. (1966); 12 string quartets (1923–61); String Octet (1944); 12 concert studies for Cello (1967); 12 concert studies for Trumpet and Piano (1968); 15 concert studies for Oboe and Piano (1969). He publ. the valuable manuals *Problems of Polyphony* (3 vols., 1965, 1966, 1967), ranging from pentatonic to dodecaphonic patterns and from elementary harmonization to polytonality; also *Formation of Imitation in the Strict Style* (1970). In 1964 he was named a People's Artist of the Yakut Soviet Socialist Republic and of the Tatar Autonomous Soviet Socialist Republic.

Litolff, Henry Charles, pianist, composer, and publisher; b. London (of an Alsatian father and English mother), Feb. 6, 1818; d. Colombes, near Paris, Aug. 6, 1891. A precocious pianist, he studied with Moscheles; made his professional debut in London on July 24, 1832, at the age of 14. An early marriage (at 17) forced him to seek a livelihood in Paris, where he attracted attention by his brilliant concerts; then he became an itinerant musician, traveling in Poland, Germany, and the Netherlands; was in Vienna during the Revolution of 1848, and became involved, so that he was compelled to flee. He then settled in Braunschweig; after the termination of his first marriage, he married the widow of the music publisher Meyer, acquiring the business. Litolff was one of the pioneers in the publication of cheap editions of classical music (Collections Litolff). In 1860 he turned over the firm to his adopted son, **Theodor Litolff** (1839–1912). Then he went to Paris, marrying for a 3rd time (the Comtesse de Larochefoucauld); after her death (1870) he married a 15-year-old girl.

WORKS: Besides his business pursuits, he was a prolific composer; 115 of his works were publ.; of these, the most famous is the overture *Robespierre* (Paris, Feb. 2, 1870), which carries the idea of programmatic music to its utmost limit, with a vivid description of Robespierre's execution (drumbeats, etc.); operas: *Die Braut von Kynast* (Braunschweig, 1847); *Les Templiers* (Brussels, Jan. 25, 1886); *Héloïse et Abélard* (Paris, Oct. 17, 1872); oratorio, *Ruth et Booz* (1869); *Szenen aus Goethes Faust* for Soli, Chorus, and Orch.; 5 *Concertos-Symphonies* for piano and Orch., of which the 4th contains a brilliant scherzo which became a perennial favorite; *Eroica,* violin concerto; a funeral march for Meyerbeer; 3 piano trios; 6 *études de concert* for

Piano; many character pieces for piano, of which *Chant de la fileuse* became popular.

Litvinne, Félia (real name, **Françoise-Jeanne Schütz**), Russian soprano; b. St. Petersburg, 1861; d. Paris, Oct. 12, 1936. She studied in Paris with Mme. Barth-Banderoli and Victor Maurel; made her debut there in 1885 at the Théâtre des Italiens; then sang at the Academy of Music in N.Y. with Mapleson's company; made successful appearances in St. Petersburg, Moscow, and Italy; returned to Paris, where she sang at the Opéra-Comique and the Théâtre Lyrique de la Gaîté; also sang at Monte Carlo, La Scala, Covent Garden, and the Metropolitan Opera House; made a tour of South America. In 1927 she was appointed prof. of singing at the American Cons. of Fontainebleau. She publ. her memoirs, *Ma vie et mon art* (Paris, 1933).

Llobet, Miguel, Catalan guitar virtuoso; b. Barcelona, Oct. 18, 1875; d. there, Feb. 22, 1938. He began his career as a painter; then turned to music and studied with Tarrega; lived in Paris (1904–14); toured in Argentina (1910), Chile (1912), the U.S. (1915–17), and throughout Europe. Manuel de Falla composed his *Homenaje* (for the *Tombeau de Debussy*) for him, and Llobet himself made many arrangements for the guitar.

Lloyd, Albert Lancaster, noted English ethnomusicologist and folk singer; b. London, Feb. 29, 1908; d. Greenwich, Sept. 29, 1982. His early commitment to the Socialist cause contributed to his interest in folk-song research; he collected folk songs in Australia, and in later years in Eastern Europe; he lectured widely in England and the U.S., and also produced radio programs and documentary films. He publ. the valuable books *Come All Ye Bold Miners: Songs and Ballads of the Coalfields* (1952), *The Penguin Book of English Folk Song* (with Vaughan Williams; 1959), and the standard text *Folk Song in England* (1967).

Lloyd, Charles Harford, English organist and composer; b. Thornbury, Gloucestershire, Oct. 16, 1849; d. Slough, Oct. 16, 1919. He attended Magdalen Hall, Oxford (Mus.Bac., 1871; B.A., 1872; M.A., 1875; Mus.Doc., 1892); in 1887–92 was a teacher of organ and composition at the Royal College of Music; in 1892, an instructor at Eton College; from 1914 until his death, organist at the Chapel Royal, St. James'.

Lloyd, George, English composer; b. St. Ives, June 28, 1913. He learned to play piano and violin at home; then studied composition with Harry Farjeon. He was in the Royal Marines during World War II; served in the Arctic on convoys to Russia, and nearly lost his life when his ship was sunk. He composed mainly for the theater; among his works are the operas *Iernin* (Penzance, Nov. 6, 1934); *The Serf* (London, Oct. 20, 1938); *John Socman* (Bristol, May 15, 1951); he also wrote 9 symphs.; 4 piano concertos; Violin Concerto; pieces of chamber music. In 1970

he was made an Officer of the Order of the British Empire.

Lloyd, Norman, American composer and music theorist; b. Pottsville, Pa., Nov. 8, 1909; d. Greenwich, Conn., July 31, 1980. He studied at N.Y. Univ.; received a D.Mus. from the Philadelphia Cons. in 1963, and was engaged as a teacher there and at other music schools. He served as director of the Juilliard School of Music in N.Y. (1946–49) and remained on its faculty until 1963. He became greatly interested in rural and urban folk music, including ragtime; also worked with choreographers on musical arrangements for modern dances. In 1952 he publ. *The Fireside Book of Favorite American Songs;* also edited *The Fireside Book of Folk Songs* and *The Golden Encyclopedia of Music.* With his wife, the pianist **Ruth Dorothy Lloyd,** he compiled *The Complete Sight Singer.*

Lloyd Webber, Andrew, highly successful British composer of musicals; b. London, March 22, 1948. His father, **William Southcombe Lloyd Webber,** was the director of the London College of Music; his mother was a piano teacher; his brother was a cellist. Conditioned by such an environment, Lloyd Webber learned to play piano, violin, and French horn, and soon began to improvise music, mostly in the form of American musicals. He attended Westminster School in London, then went to Magdalen College, Oxford, and to the Royal College of Music. In college he wrote his first musical, *The Likes of Us,* dealing with a philanthropist. At the age of 19, in 1967, he composed the theatrical show *Joseph and the Amazing Technicolor Dreamcoat,* which was performed at St. Paul's Junior School in London in 1968; it was later expanded to a full-scale production, and achieved considerable success for its amalgam of a biblical subject with rock music, French chansonnettes, and country-western songs. In 1970 it was produced in America and in 1972 was shown on television. Lloyd Webber achieved his first commercial success with *Jesus Christ Superstar,* an audacious treatment of the religious theme in terms of jazz and rock. It was produced in London on Aug. 9, 1972, and ran for 3,357 performances; it was as successful in America. Interestingly enough, the "rock opera," as it was called, was first released as a record album, which eventually sold 3 million copies. *Jesus Christ Superstar* opened on Broadway on Oct. 12, 1971, even before the London production. There were protests by religious groups against the irreverent treatment of a sacred subject; particularly offensive was the suggestion in the play of a carnal relationship between Jesus and Mary Magdalen; Jewish organizations, on the other hand, protested against the implied portrayal of the Jews as guilty of the death of Christ. The musical closed on Broadway on June 30, 1973, after 720 performances; it received 7 Tony awards. In 1981 the recording of *Jesus Christ Superstar* was given the Grammy award for best cast show album of the year. The great hullabaloo about the musical made a certainty of Lloyd Webber's further successes. His early musical *Joseph and the Amazing Technicolor Dreamcoat* was revived at the off-Broadway Entermedia Theatre in N.Y.'s East Village on Nov. 18, 1981, and from there moved to the Royale Theater on Broadway. In the meantime Lloyd Webber produced a musical with a totally different chief character, *Evita*, a semi-fictional account of the career of Mrs. Perón of Argentina; it was staged in London on June 21, 1978; a N.Y. performance soon followed, with splendid success. But perhaps the most spectacular production of Lloyd Webber's was *Cats*, inspired by T.S. Eliot's *Old Possum's Book of Practical Cats;* it was produced in London on May 11, 1981, and was brought out in N.Y. in Oct. 1982 with fantastic success; *Evita* and *Joseph and the Amazing Technicolor Dreamcoat* were still playing on Broadway, so that Lloyd Webber had the satisfaction of having 3 of his shows running at the same time. Apart from his popular shows, Lloyd Webber wrote a mini-opera, *Tell Me on a Sunday,* about an English girl living in N.Y., which was produced by BBC Television in 1980; he also composed *Variations* for Cello for his cellist brother **Julian Lloyd Webber;** the work is derived from Paganini.

Lloyd-Webber, Julian, English cellist; b. London, April 14, 1951. He studied at the Royal College of Music; his principal teacher was Douglas Cameron; he also studied with Pierre Fournier in Geneva. He made his concert debut at London's Queen Elizabeth Hall in 1972; subsequently played many engagements as a soloist with English orchs. He made his American debut in N.Y. in 1980. In 1978 he became prof. of cello at the Guildhall School of Music in London. He is the brother of the composer **Andrew Lloyd Webber.**

Lobe, Johann Christian, German flutist, writer on music, and composer; b. Weimar, May 30, 1797; d. Leipzig, July 27, 1881. He studied with A.E. Müller; played a flute solo with the Gewandhaus Orch. in Leipzig (1811); then was a flutist, later a viola player, in the Weimar Court Orch. until 1842; founded a music school; in 1846–48 was in Leipzig as editor of the *Allgemeine Musikzeitung;* in 1853 publ. the periodical *Fliegende Blätter für Musik;* was music editor of *Illustrierte Zeitung;* also contributed articles to various journals.

Lobkowitz, Prince Franz Joseph (Maximilian Ferdinand) von, Austrian art patron; b. Vienna, Dec. 7, 1772; d. Raudnitz an der Elbe, Dec. 16, 1816. Beethoven dedicated to him the quartet op. 18; the 3rd, 5th, and 6th symphs.; the Triple Concerto; the quartet op. 74; and the song cycle *An die ferne Geliebte.*

Lobo, Duarte (also Latinized as **Eduardus Lupus**), Portuguese composer; b. Alcáçovas, c.1565 (he was not identical with the person of the same name baptized on Sept. 19, 1565; his date of birth must therefore remain uncertain); d. Lisbon, Sept. 24, 1646. He was a pupil of Manuel Mendes at Evora; served as choirmaster there before moving to Lisbon; in 1594,

became master of the chapel at the Cathedral. As a composer of church music, he enjoyed considerable renown; his mastery of polyphony inspired respect, but comparisons with Victoria Benevoli and other great composers of his time are exaggerations. The following works were printed in his lifetime: *Natalitiae noctis responsoria, a* 4–8; *Antiphonae, a* 8; *Salve, a* 3–11 (Antwerp, 1602); *Officium defunctorum* (Lisbon, 1603); *Magnificat, a* 4 (Antwerp, 1605); 2 books of masses, *a* 4–8 (Antwerp, 1621, 1639); MSS are in the British Museum, in the Fitzwilliam Collection in Cambridge, and at the cathedrals of Granada and Toledo. An antiphon and 2 masses are reprinted in J.E. dos Santos, *A polifonia clássica portuguêsa* (Lisbon, 1937); 16 Magnificats for 4 Voices, transcribed by M. Joaquim (Lisbon, 1945).

Locatelli, Pietro, Italian violinist and composer; b. Bergamo, Sept. 3, 1695; d. Amsterdam, March 30, 1764. As a youth he was appointed violinist at S. Maria Maggiore in Rome; played violin at the basilica of S. Lorenzo in Damaso (1717–23); subsequently made long professional tours, including appearances outside Italy; in 1729 he settled in Amsterdam, establishing regular public concerts, and enjoying fame there. His technical feats, particularly in double stops, were considered marvelous at the time; by changing the tuning of his violin, he produced apparently impossible effects; Paganini is said to have profited by Locatelli's innovations. A modern edition of his works was publ. by A. Koole, *Pietro Antonio Locatelli: Gesamtausgabe,* in Monumenta Musicae Neerlandicae, IV (1961).

Locke, Matthew, English composer; b. Exeter, c.1620; d. London, Aug. 1677. He was a chorister at Exeter Cathedral, studying under Edward Gibbons and William Wake; then was composer to Charles II (1660); became a Roman Catholic, and was appointed organist to Queen Catherine. Prominent among English composers of his era, he wrote music to *The Tempest* and *Macbeth,* and to Shadwell's *Psyche* (London, March 9, 1675; the music for *The Tempest* and *Psyche* were publ. in 1675 as *The English Opera*), to Shirley's masque *Cupid and Death,* and to Stapleton's comedy *The Stepmother;* also 6 suites, anthems, etc. He also wrote the first English work on thoroughbass, *Melothesia, or Certain General Rules for Playing upon a Continued Bass* (1673); and pamphlets versus Salmon's attempt at reducing music notation to one universal character. P. Warlock and A. Mangeot publ. 6 *Consorts a 4* (London, 1932). Chamber music is reprinted in vols. 31–32 of *Musica Brittanica,* anthems and motets in vol. 38. R.E.M. Harding compiled *A Thematic Catalogue of the Works of Matthew Locke* (1971).

Lockspeiser, Edward, English writer on music; b. London, May 21, 1905; d. there, Feb. 3, 1973. He studied in Paris with Alexandre Tansman and Nadia Boulanger; then attended the classes of C.H. Kitson and Malcolm Sargent at the Royal College of Music in London. He dedicated himself to musical journalism, particularly to the cause of French music; publ.

valuable monographs on Debussy (London, 1936; revised ed., 1951), Berlioz (1940), and Bizet (1947), and an exhaustive biography, *Debussy: His Life and Mind* (2 vols., London, 1962, 1965). He also edited *Claude Debussy: Lettres inédites à André Caplet, 1908–1914* (Monaco, 1957).

Lockwood, Anna, composeress of the militant avant-garde; b. Christchurch, New Zealand, July 29, 1939. She studied at Canterbury Univ. in New Zealand; then went to London, where she took courses with Peter Racine Fricker at the Royal College of Music; subsequently attended classes at the Hochschule für Musik in Cologne and at the Electronic Music Center in Bilthoven, the Netherlands. In 1968 she gave non-lectures at the Anti-University of London. With her husband, Harvey Matusow, she undertook a series of experiments in total art, including aural, oral, visual, tactile, gustatory, and olfactory demonstrations and sporadic transcendental manifestations; of these, the most remarkable was the summoning (in German) of Beethoven's ghost at a séance held in London on Oct. 3, 1968, with sound recorded on magnetic tape, which in playback revealed some surprisingly dissonant music of apparently metapsychic origin, tending to indicate that Beethoven was a posthumous avant-garde composer (the tape was not released in order to avoid unanswerable controversy); the séance was preceded by the burning of a combustible piano and of an inflammable microphone. Not content with setting the piano afire, she also demonstrated the drowning of an upright piano in a lake in Amarillo, Texas (Dec. 27, 1972). Anna Lockwood also experimented with surgical piano transplants. Her other works, some of them consisting of controlled glossolalia and notated optically on graphic paper, are *A Abélard, Héloïse* for Mezzo-soprano and 10 Instruments (1962); *Aspects of a Parable* for Baritone and 12 Instruments (1963); *Love Field* for Tape, a lament for John F. Kennedy, with reference to the name of the Dallas Airport (1964); *Glass Concert I* (1967); *Glass Concert II,* scored for Sheets of Armor-plate Glass, Spotlight Bulbs, Wineglasses, Milk Bottles, Glass Curtains, Fluorescent Tubes, Glass Mobiles, and other vitreous objects (1969; blueprint and directions publ. in *Source, 5); Dark Touch* for Tactile-Aural Equipment (1970); *Gentle Grass,* a ritual for 6 Players (1970); *Humm* for 70 or more Hummers (1971); *Bus Trip,* a moving event with Food, Free Love, and Realistic Sound Effects (1971); *River Archives,* an anthology of Sounds from world rivers (1971); *World Rhythms,* incorporating Ambient Recorded Sounds, inspired by long sessions of transcendental meditation (1975).

Lockwood, Lewis (Henry), distinguished American musicologist; b. New York, Dec. 16, 1930. He studied musicology with Lowinsky at Queens College in N.Y. (B.A., 1952) and with Strunk and Mendel at Princeton Univ. (M.F.A., 1955; Ph.D., 1960, with the dissertation *The Counter-Reformation and the Sacred Music of Vincenzo Ruffo,* publ. in Venice, 1970). In 1958 he joined the faculty of Princeton

Univ. In 1980 he was appointed prof. at Harvard Univ. He is regarded as a prime authority on Renaissance music; his studies on music in Italy in the 15th and 16th centuries are especially thorough; he publ. a valuable book, *Music in Renaissance Ferrara, 1400–1505* (London, 1984). He was a senior consulting editor of *The New Grove Dictionary of Music and Musicians* (London, 1980).

Lockwood, Normand, American composer; b. New York, March 19, 1906. He studied at the Univ. of Michigan; in 1925 went to Europe and took lessons with Respighi in Rome and Nadia Boulanger in Paris; he was a Fellow at the American Academy in Rome (1929–31); upon his return to America he was an instructor in music at the Oberlin (Ohio) Cons. (1932–43); from 1945 to 1953, was a lecturer at Columbia Univ.; then at Trinity Univ. in San Antonio, Texas (1953–55); also taught at the Univ. of Hawaii and at the Univ. of Oregon. In 1961 he was appointed a member of the faculty of the Univ. of Denver; became prof. emeritus in 1974.
  WORKS: Operas: *Scarecrow* (Columbia Univ., N.Y., May 19, 1945); *Early Dawn* (Denver, Aug. 7, 1961); *The Wizards of Balizar* (Denver, Aug. 1, 1962); *The Hanging Judge* (Denver, March 1964); *Requiem for a Rich Young Man* (Denver, Nov. 24, 1964); *Moby Dick* for Chamber Orch. (1946); Oboe Concerto (1966); *Symphonic Sequences* (1966); *From an Opening to a Close* for Wind Instruments and Percussion (1967); 2 concertos for Organ and Brass (1950, 1970); Clarinet Quintet (1960); Mass for Children and Orch.; 8 duets for 2 Trumpets; Flute Sonata; *Sonata-Fantasia* for Accordion; *Valley Suite* for Violin and Piano; *4 Excursions* for 4 String Basses; 4 *Songs from James Joyce's "Chamber Music"* for Medium Voice and String Quartet (N.Y., March 28, 1948); oratorios: *Light out of Darkness* (1956) and *Children of God* (Cincinnati, Feb. 1, 1957); numerous other sacred works.

Loeffler, Charles Martin (Tornow), outstanding American composer; b. Mulhouse, Alsace, Jan. 30, 1861; d. Medfield, Mass., May 19, 1935. His father was a writer who sometimes used the nom de plume Tornow, which Loeffler later added to his name. When he was a child, the family moved to Russia, where his father was engaged in government work in the Kiev district; later they lived in Debrecen in Hungary, and in Switzerland. In 1875 Loeffler began taking violin lessons in Berlin with Rappoldi, who prepared him for study with Joachim; he studied harmony with Kiel; also took lessons with Bargiel. He then went to Paris, where he continued his musical education with Massart (violin) and Guiraud (composition). He was engaged briefly as a violinist in the Pasdeloup Orch.; then was a member of the private orch. of the Russian Baron Paul von Derwies at his sumptuous residences near Lugano and in Nice (1879–81). When Derwies died in 1881, Loeffler went to America, with letters of recommendation from Joachim. He played in the orch. of Leopold Damrosch in N.Y. In 1882 he became 2nd concertmaster of the newly organized Boston Symph.

Orch., but was able to accept other engagements during late spring and summer months; in the spring of 1883, he traveled with the Thomas Orch. on a transcontinental tour; the summers of 1883 and 1884 he spent in Paris, where he took violin lessons with Hubert Léonard. He resigned from the Boston Symph. in 1903, and devoted himself to teaching and composition, living in Boston and suburban Medfield. He was married to Elise Burnett Fay (1910). After his death, she donated to the Library of Congress all of his MSS, correspondence, etc.; by his will, he left the material assets of his not inconsiderable estate to the French Academy and the Paris Cons. He was an officer of the French Academy (1906); a Chevalier in the French Legion of Honor (1919); a member of the American Academy of Arts and Letters; Mus.Doc. (*honoris causa*), Yale Univ. (1926).

Loeffler's position in American music is unique, brought up as he was under many different national influences, Alsatian, French, German, Russian, and Ukrainian. One of his most vivid scores, *Memories of My Childhood*, written as late as 1924, reflects the modal feeling of Russian and Ukrainian folk songs. But his esthetic code was entirely French, with definite leanings toward Impressionism; the archaic constructions that he sometimes affected, and the stylized evocations of "ars antiqua," are also in keeping with the French manner. His most enduring work, *A Pagan Poem*, is cast in such a neo-archaic vein. He was a master of colorful orchestration; his harmonies are opulent without saturation; his rhapsodic forms are peculiarly suited to the evocative moods of his music. His only excursion into the American idiom was the employment of jazz rhythms in a few of his lesser pieces.

WORKS: *The Nights in the Ukraine,* after Gogol, suite for Violin and Orch. (Boston, Nov. 20, 1891); *Fantastic Concerto* for Cello and Orch. (Boston, Feb. 2, 1894); *Divertimento* for Violin and Orch. (Boston, Jan. 4, 1895); *La Mort de Tintagiles,* after Maeterlinck, dramatic poem for 2 Viole d'Amore and Orch. (revised for Orch. and Viola d'Amore, 1900; first perf., Boston, Feb. 16, 1901); *Divertissement espagnol* for Orch. and Saxophone (1901); *La Villanelle du Diable,* symph. fantasy for Orch. and Organ (Boston, April 11, 1902); *Poem* for Orch., inspired by Verlaine's *La Bonne Chanson* (Boston, April 11, 1902; reorchestrated, and perf. by the Boston Symph., Nov. 1, 1918); *A Pagan Poem,* after Virgil, for Orch., with Piano, English Horn, and 3 Trumpets obbligati (originally as chamber music, 1901; revised for Orch. and Piano, 1906; first perf., Boston Symph., Nov. 22, 1907, Karl Muck conducting); *Hora mystica* for Orch. and Men's Chorus (Boston Symph., March 2, 1917, Karl Muck conducting); *5 Irish Fantasies* for Voice and Orch. (3 numbers perf., Boston, March 10, 1922); *Memories of My Childhood (Life in a Russian Village)* for Orch. (awarded the Chicago North Shore Festival Assoc. prize, 1924; Chicago Symph., Evanston, Ill., May 30, 1924); *Canticum fratris solis (The Canticle of the Sun)* for Solo Voice and Chamber Orch. (commissioned by the E.S. Coolidge Foundation; first perf. at the Library of Congress Festival of Chamber Music,

Oct. 28, 1925); *Evocation* for Women's Voices and Orch. (on lines from the *Select Epigrams of Greek Anthology* by J.W. Machail; commissioned for the opening of Severance Hall, Cleveland; perf. there, Feb. 5, 1931); Psalm 137, *By the Rivers of Babylon,* for 4-part Women's Chorus, with Organ, Harp, 2 Flutes, and Cello obbligato (1907); *For one who fell in battle* for 8-part Mixed Chorus a cappella (1911); *Beat! Beat! Drums!,* after Whitman, for Men's Chorus in unison, 6 Piccolos, 3 Saxophones, Brass, Drums, and 2 Pianos (1917; Cleveland, Nov. 17, 1932); 2 rhapsodies for Oboe, Viola, and Piano (*L'Etang* and *La Cornemuse,* after poems by Maurice Rollinat; 1905); Octet for 2 Clarinets, 2 Violins, Viola, Cello, Double Bass, and Harp; String Sextet; *Music for 4 Stringed Instruments* (in memory of the American aviator Victor Chapman; 1917); Quintet for 3 Violins, Viola, and Cello; *4 Melodies* for Voice and Piano, to poems by G. Kahn (1903); *4 Poems* for Voice, Viola, and Piano (1904); *4 Poems* for Voice and Piano (1906); *The wind among the reeds* for Voice and Piano to poems by Yeats (1908); *The Reveller* for Solo Voice, Violin, and Piano (1925); *Partita* for Violin and Piano (1930). In MS, a 4-act Chinese opera, *Life Is but a Dream;* and an opera based on a short play by Cecil Sharp. He also wrote *Violin Studies for the Development of the Left Hand* (publ. 1936).

Loeillet, Jacques, oboe player, brother of **Jean-Baptiste Loeillet;** b. Ghent, July 7, 1685; d. there, Nov. 28, 1748. He played in court orchs. in Brussels and Munich. In 1727 he went to France; demonstrated his virtuosity, performing on several wind instruments and on the violin, at the Versailles court, and was appointed chamber musician to Louis XV. He publ. 6 sonatas for 2 flutes; 6 sonatas for solo flute, with continuo.

Loeillet, Jean-Baptiste (known in England as **John Loeillet**), notable harpsichordist and flutist, brother of **Jacques Loeillet;** b. Ghent, Nov. 18, 1680; d. London, July 19, 1730. The family name has been variously spelled **L'Oeillet, Luly, Lulli, Lullie,** and even **Lully,** which form led to a great deal of confusion, so that Loeillet's Minuet in A has been misattributed in some editions to the great Lully. Locillet studied in Ghent and in Paris. In 1705 he went to London, where he played the oboe and the flute at the Queen's Theatre (until 1710). He became extremely successful as a teacher, harpsichord player, and collector of musical instruments. He popularized the German transverse flute in England. In his music he followed the Italian tradition; his writing for the flute shows a thorough understanding of the virtuoso possibilities of the instrument.

WORKS: He publ. in London, under the name of John Loeillet, the following works: 6 suites of lessons for the harpsichord; 6 sonatas for various instruments; 12 sonatas for violins, German flutes, and common flutes; 12 solos for a German flute, common flute, and violin; the following were publ. under the name of **Jean-Baptiste Loeillet de Gand:** 4 books of solos for a flute and a bass; 6 sonatas for

2 flutes; and 6 sonatas for 2 German flutes. There are 2 different sets of opus numbers, which suggests that there was another Loeillet, possibly identifiable with John Loeillet's cousin, also named Jean-Baptiste, and active in Lyons. Reprints of authentic and putative works by John Loeillet include a set of sonatas ed. by Béon (Paris, 1911); a sonata ed. by Moffat; harpsichord pieces ed. by J. Watelet (Antwerp, 1932); 2 sonatas for flute and piano ed. by J. van Etsen (Antwerp, 1938); etc.

Loeillet, John. See **Loeillet, Jean-Baptiste.**

Loeschhorn, Albert. See **Löschhorn, Albert.**

Loesser, Arthur, brilliant American pianist and imaginative writer on music, brother of **Frank Loesser;** b. New York, Aug. 26, 1894; d. Cleveland, Jan. 4, 1969. He studied with Stojowski and Goetschius at the Inst. of Musical Art in N.Y.; began an auspicious concert career in 1913; toured Australia and the Orient in 1920–21. In 1926 he was appointed a prof. of piano at the Cleveland Inst. of Music. In 1943 he was commissioned in the U.S. Army as an officer in the Japanese intelligence dept.; mastered the language and, after the war, gave lectures in Japanese in Tokyo; was the first American musician in uniform to play for a Japanese audience (1946). He publ. *Humor in American Song* (N.Y., 1943) and an entertaining vol., *Men, Women and Pianos: A Social History* (N.Y., 1954).

Loesser, Frank, American composer of popular music, brother of **Arthur Loesser;** b. New York, June 29, 1910; d. there, July 28, 1969. He was educated at City College in N.Y., where he began writing songs for college activities; he subsequently was active as a reporter, singer, and vaudeville performer. In 1931 he settled in Hollywood and devoted himself mainly to writing musical comedies. During World War II he was in the U.S. Army, and wrote several Army songs (*What Do You Do in the Infantry?; Salute to the Army Service Forces; Praise the Lord and Pass the Ammunition; They're Either Too Young or Too Old;* etc.); continued to produce popular songs after the war (*On a Slow Boat to China; Small Fry; The Moon of Manakoora; Dolores; How Sweet You Are; Now That I Need You; Roger Young; Just Another Polka; Two Sleepy People; Spring Will Be a Little Late This Year; A Touch of Texas; Jingle Jangle Jingle; I Wish I Didn't Love You So; My Darling, My Darling; Baby, It's Cold Outside;* etc.); also wrote music for several highly successful Broadway plays: *Where's Charley?, Guys and Dolls, The Most Happy Fella,* etc.

Loewe, (Johann) Carl (Gottfried), outstanding German composer of lieder; b. Löbejün, near Halle, Nov. 30, 1796; d. Kiel, April 20, 1869. His father, a schoolmaster and cantor, taught him the rudiments of music; when he was 12 he was sent to the Francke Inst. in Halle, where his attractive manner, excellent high voice, and early ability to improvise brought him to the attention of Jerome Bonaparte, who granted him a stipend of 300 thalers annually until 1813. His teacher was Türk, the head of the Francke Inst.; after Türk's death in 1813, Loewe joined the Singakademie founded by Naue. He also studied theology at the Univ. of Halle, but soon devoted himself entirely to music. He had begun to compose as a boy; under the influence of Zelter, he wrote German ballades, and developed an individual style of great dramatic force and lyrical inspiration; he perfected the genre, and was regarded by many musicians as the greatest song composer after Schubert and before Brahms. His setting of Goethe's poem *Erlkönig* (1818), which came before the publication of Schubert's great song to the same poem, is one of Loewe's finest creations; other songs that rank among his best are *Edward, Der Wirthin Töchterlein, Der Nöck, Archibald Douglas, Tom der Reimer, Heinrich der Vogler, Oluf, Die verfallene Mühle,* etc. Loewe was personally acquainted with Goethe, and also met Weber. In 1820 he became a schoolmaster at Stettin, and organist at St. Jacobus there. He lived in Stettin, except for frequent travels, until 1866, when he settled in Kiel. He visited Vienna (1844), London (1847), Sweden and Norway (1851), and Paris (1857), among other places. Loewe was an excellent vocalist, and was able to perform his ballades in public.

WORKS: 5 operas, only one of which, *Die drei Wünsche,* was performed (Berlin, Feb. 18, 1834); 17 oratorios; cantata; *Die Hochzeit der Thetis; Die erste Walpurgisnacht,* after Goethe, ballade for Soli, Chorus, and Orch.; 368 ballades for voice and piano, publ. in his collected ed. and in numerous anthologies (Peters and Schlesinger publ. "Loewe-Albums" containing 20 and 16 numbers, respectively). Loewe's instrumental works (symphs., overtures, 3 string quartets, Piano Trio, several piano sonatas, etc.) are mostly in MS. He publ. several pedagogic works: *Gesanglehre für Gymnasien, Seminarien und Bürgerschulen* (Stettin, 1826; 5th ed., 1854); *Musikalischer Gottesdienst; Methodische Anweisung zum Kirchengesang und Orgelspiel* (1851, and subsequent eds.); *Klavier- und Generalbass-Schule* (2nd ed., 1851). A *Gesamtausgabe der Balladen, Legenden, Lieder und Gesänge,* in 17 vols., ed. by Max Runze, was publ. by Breitkopf & Härtel (1899–1905). A Loewe-Verein was founded in Berlin in 1882.

Loewe, Ferdinand. See **Löwe, Ferdinand.**

Loewe, Frederick, Austrian-American composer of popular music; b. Vienna, June 10, 1904. He studied piano in Berlin with Busoni and Eugène d'Albert; composition with Reznicek. In 1924 he emigrated to the U.S.; was active as a concert pianist; then devoted himself chiefly to production of popular music. Adapting himself adroitly to the American idiom, he became one of the most successful writers of musical comedies; among them are *Salute to Spring; Great Lady; The Life of the Party; What's Up?; The Day before Spring; Brigadoon; Paint Your Wagon;* and (the most spectacularly successful of them all) *My Fair Lady,* after Shaw's *Pygmalion* (1956; 2,717 perfs.); this was followed by another hit, *Camelot* (1960); in all these his lyricist was Alan Jay Lerner.

Loewe, Sophie, German soprano; b. Oldenburg, March 24, 1815; d. Budapest, Nov. 28, 1866. She studied in Vienna with Ciccimarra and in Milan with Lamperti; made her debut in Vienna in 1832; sang in London in 1841; also in 1841, appeared at La Scala in Milan, where she created Donizetti's Maria Padilla; also created Verdi's Elvira in *Ernani* and Odabella in *Attila* at the Teatro La Fenice in Venice. She retired from the stage in 1848.

Loewenberg, Alfred, German musicologist; b. Berlin, May 14, 1902; d. London, Dec. 29, 1949. He studied at Jena Univ. (Ph.D., 1925); settled in London in 1935. His unique achievement is the compilation of *Annals of Opera: 1597-1940* (Cambridge, 1943; new ed., Geneva, 1955; revised and corrected, 1978), tabulating in chronological order the exact dates of first performances and important revivals of some 4,000 operas, with illuminating comments of a bibliographical nature. He also publ. *Early Dutch Librettos and Plays with Music in the British Museum* (London, 1947), and a number of articles.

Logan, Frederick Knight, American composer of popular songs; b. Oskaloosa, Iowa, Oct. 15, 1871; d. June 11, 1928. He wrote a number of sentimental ballads in collaboration with his mother, **Virginia Logan.** He was the composer of the celebrated *Missouri Waltz,* which he publ. as a piano solo in 1914 with his name on the cover of the sheet music as an "arranger," for he was reluctant to admit the authorship of the tune that seemed beneath his estimate of himself as a composer. But when the words were added in 1916, the thing became a sensational hit. The state of Missouri accepted it as its official song. Harry Truman loved to play it on the piano and, for better or for worse, the *Missouri Waltz* became associated with his (Truman's) political deeds and misdeeds.

Logier, Johann Bernhard, German pianist, teacher, and composer; b. Kassel, Feb. 9, 1777; d. Dublin, July 27, 1846. He received his early musical training at home; as a youth he went to England and played the flute in a regimental band; he was employed as an organist in Westport, Ireland, where he perfected his invention of the "chiroplast," for holding the hands in the most convenient positions during piano practice; he patented it in 1814 and promoted it with fanatic persistence. Amazingly enough, it obtained great vogue in England, and was equally successful in Germany; in 1821 he was invited to Berlin, where he taught his method from 1822 to 1826; then returned to Ireland, and settled in Dublin in 1829. In reply to numerous polemical attacks on his invention Logier publ. equally bitter assaults on his detractors, among them the pamphlets *An Explanation and Description of the Royal Patent Chiroplast, or Hand-Director for Pianoforte* (London, 1816) and *An Authentic Account of the Examination of Pupils Instructed on the New System of Musical Education, by J.B. Logier* (London, 1818). He further publ. *The First Companion to the Royal Patent Chiroplast* (London, 1818; it went through numerous eds.) and *Logier's Practical Thorough-Bass,* and in German, *System der Musikwissenschaft und der musikalischen Komposition* (Berlin, 1827). He also introduced a method of simultaneous practice on different pianos, which for a time was adopted even in such a bastion of traditional music instruction as the Paris Cons. In the end, Logier's "chiroplast" joined a number of other equally futile pseudo-scientific inventions in the repository of musical curiosities.

Logothetis, Anestis, Bulgarian-born avant-garde composer of Greek extraction; b. Burgas, Oct. 27, 1921. He was trained in mechanical engineering in Vienna (1942–45); then took lessons in composition there with Ratz and Uhl (1945–51); exhibited in Vienna galleries a series of polymorphic graphs capable of being performed as music by optional instrumental groups. He employs a highly personalized "integrating" musical notation, making use of symbols, signs, and suggestive images, playing on a performer's psychological associations.

Logroscino, Nicola, Italian composer; b. Bitonto (baptized, Oct. 22), 1698; d. Palermo, after 1765. He was a pupil of Veneziano and Perugino (1714–27) at the Cons. di Santa Maria di Loreto in Naples; in 1728–31, was organist at Conza (Avellino); in 1731, was again in Naples. In 1747 he became first prof. of counterpoint at the Cons. dei Figliuoli Dispersi in Palermo; then went to Naples, where he produced his most successful operas; he is regarded as the creator of Neapolitan opera buffa in the local dialect, among them *Il Governatore, Il vecchio marito,* and *Tanto bene che male.* Of his serious operas, *Giunio Bruto* (1748) and *Olimpiade* (1753) were the most notable.

Löhlein, Georg Simon, German composer; b. Neustadt, near Coburg, July (baptized, July 16) 1725; d. Danzig, Dec. 16, 1781. On account of his tall stature (6 feet 2 inches), he was seized on a journey and forced into the Prussian Guard; he was stationed at Potsdam and served at the palace of Frederick the Great. He was severely wounded at the battle of Collin during the Seven Years' War, but recovered and went to Jena, where he completed his interrupted musical education; at the age of 38 he enrolled at the Univ. of Leipzig; there he was active as both a violinist and a pianist. In 1781 he received a post as organist at the St. Mary Church in Danzig, but suffered from the rigors of the climate, and died a few months after arrival there. Löhlein wrote a singspiel, *Zemire und Azor* (Leipzig, 1775); several instrumental concertos; chamber music; etc.; but he became known mainly through his pedagogical work, *Clavier-Schule* (2 vols., 1765 and 1781), which passed through many editions and was revised by

Czerny; he also publ. *Violinschule* (1774).

Lohse, Otto, German conductor and composer; b. Dresden, Sept. 21, 1858; d. Baden-Baden, May 5, 1925. He was a pupil at the Dresden Cons. of Richter (piano), Grützmacher (cello), Draeseke and Wüllner (composition). In 1880 he went to Russia and conducted theater music in Riga; in 1893 he was in Hamburg; there he married the famous singer **Katharina Klafsky,** and in the spring of 1896 both artists were members of the Damrosch Opera Co. in N.Y., with Lohse as conductor. From 1897 to 1904, Lohse conducted opera in Strasbourg; in 1904–11, in Cologne; in 1911–12, at the Théâtre de la Monnaie in Brussels; in 1912–23, at the Leipzig Stadttheater. He composed an opera, *Der Prinz wider Willen* (Riga, 1890), and songs.

Lolli, Antonio, Italian violinist and composer; b. Bergamo, c.1730; d. Palermo, Aug. 10, 1802. Little is known of his early life; he was in Stuttgart at the court of the Duke of Württemberg from 1758 till 1772; asked for a leave of absence, but did not return to Stuttgart; however, he drew his salary until 1774. He gave violin concerts in Hamburg, Lübeck, and Stettin in 1773–74; then proceeded to St. Petersburg, where he became a special favorite of Catherine II, and also ingratiated himself with Potemkin. He received 4,000 rubles annually as violinist to the Empress and chapel master of the court. In Dec. 1777 he visited Stockholm, and then went to Germany. An incorrigible gambler, he dissipated the fortune of 10,000 florins he had accumulated from the Russian emoluments, and in 1780, after protracted journeys through Europe, went back to St. Petersburg; there he was able to regain his social and artistic position; gave concerts at Potemkin's palace in St. Petersburg, and also played in Moscow. Despite his frequent derelictions of duty, he was retained at the court until 1783, when his contract was canceled and he was succeeded as chapel master by Paisiello. However, he continued to give some public concerts, and also lessons, before leaving Russia in 1784. In 1785 he appeared in London; then was in Paris and in Naples, finally settling in Palermo. Contemporary accounts indicate that Lolli was a violinist of great ability, but also addicted to eccentricities in playing technical passages. He composed and publ. several sets of violin works, among them *5 Sonates et Divertissement* for Violin, with Continuo (1776; dedicated to Potemkin); other violin pieces (concertos, sonatas, etc.); also an *Ecole du violon en Quatuor* (Berlin, 1776; many reprints by various German and French publishers).

Lomax, Alan, American ethnomusicologist; b. Austin, Texas, Jan. 31, 1915. He acquired his métier from his father, **John Avery Lomax;** studied at the Univ. of Texas in Austin (B.A., 1936) and at Columbia Univ. During the years 1933–42 he undertook the task of collecting folk songs of the Southwestern and Midwestern regions of the U.S.; in 1963 was appointed head of the Bureau of Applied Social Research. With his father he brought out several collections of unknown American folk songs, among them *The Folk Songs of North America in the English Language* (N.Y., 1960); *Hard-Hitting Songs for Hard-Hit People* (N.Y., 1967); *Folk Song Style and Culture* (Washington, D.C., 1968). They also supervised field recordings of rural and prison work songs, and it was on one such occasion that they discovered Leadbelly. Another "discovery" was "Jelly Roll" Morton, and their recorded interviews, made at the Library of Congress in 1938, resulted in the book *Mr. Jelly Roll* (N.Y., 1950; 2nd ed., Berkeley, 1973).

Lomax, John Avery, American ethnomusicologist; b. Goodman, Miss., Sept. 23, 1867; d. Greenville, Miss., Jan. 26, 1948. He began collecting and notating American folk songs in his early youth; studied music at the Univ. of Texas in Austin; founded the Texas Folklore Society. In 1933 his son **Alan Lomax** joined him in his research.

WRITINGS: *American Ballads and Folk Songs* (N.Y., 1934); *Cowboy Songs and Other Frontier Ballads* (with Alan Lomax; N.Y., 1938; enlarged ed.; 1945); *Our Singing Country* (with Alan Lomax; N.Y., 1941); *Best Songs from the Lomax Collections for Pickers and Singers* (posthumous, ed. by Alan Lomax; N.Y., 1966). He also publ. an autobiography, *Adventures of a Ballad Hunter* (N.Y., 1947).

Lombard, Alain, French conductor; b. Paris, Oct. 4, 1940. He studied with Gaston Poulet and Suzanne Desmarques in Paris. In 1961 he became a conductor at the Lyons Opera. From 1966–74 he was conductor and music director of the Miami Phil. Orch. In 1971 he was named chief conductor of the Strasbourg Phil. Orch., resigning this post in 1983.

Lombardo, Carmen, Canadian-born American songwriter and saxophone player; b. London, Ontario, July 16, 1903; d. North Miami, Fla., April 17, 1971. He was a brother of **Guy Lombardo** and played the saxophone in his band from 1929 until the year of his death. Carmen Lombardo's lush saxophone tone contributed greatly to the emotional euphony of the Lombardo sound, and his vibrato was most ingratiating. He was also a composer; among his popular hits are such tunes as *Sailboat in the Moonlight, Powder Your Face with Sunshine,* and the lachrymose classic *Boo Hoo,* which he composed in collaboration with John Jacob Loeb.

Lombardo, Guy, Canadian-born American bandleader; b. London, Ontario, June 19, 1902 (of Italian parents); d. Houston, Nov. 5, 1977. With his brother **Carmen Lombardo,** the saxophone player, he organized a dance band, The Royal Canadians, and took it to the U.S. in 1924; 2 other brothers, **Lebert** and **Victor,** were also members of the band. The band rapidly rose to success on the commercial wave of pervasive sentimentality; in 1928 it was publicized as the purveyor of "the sweetest music this side of Heaven." The rendition of *Auld Lang Syne* by the Guy Lombardo Band at the Waldorf-Astoria Hotel in N.Y. at New Year's Eve celebrations every winter from 1929 to 1977 (with the exception of 1959) became a nostalgic feature. In his arrangements, Guy Lombardo cultivated unabashed emotionalism; in his orchestrations, all intervallic interstices are well filled and saxophones are tremulous with vibrato. The result is a velvety, creamy, but not necessarily oleaginous harmoniousness, which possesses an irresistible appeal to the obsolescent members of the superannuated generation of the 1920s. His preferred dynamics was *mezzo-forte,* and his favorite tempo, *andante moderato;* he never allowed the sound of his band to rise to a disturbing *forte* or to descend to a squeaking *pianissimo.* He was a wizard of the golden mean, and his public loved it.

London, George, American bass-baritone; b. Montreal, May 5, 1919, of Russian-Jewish parents. His real name was **Burnstein.** The family moved to Los Angeles in 1935; there he took lessons in operatic interpretations with Richard Lert; also studied voice with Hugo Strelitzer and Nathan Stewart; made his public debut in the opera *Gainsborough's Duchess* by Albert Coates in a concert performance in Los Angeles on April 20, 1941. He appeared as Dr. Grenvil in Verdi's *La Traviata* on Aug. 5, 1941, at the Hollywood Bowl; also sang with the San Francisco Opera on Oct. 24, 1943, in the role of Monterone in *Rigoletto.* He took further vocal lessons with Enrico Rosati and Paola Novikova in N.Y.; then, anticipating a serious professional career, he changed his name from the supposedly plebeian and ethnically confining Burnstein to a resounding and patrician London. In 1947 he toured the U.S. and Europe as a member of the Bel Canto Trio, with Frances Yeend, soprano, and Mario Lanza, tenor. His European operatic debut took place, as Amonasro, at the Vienna State Opera on Sept. 3, 1949; he made his Metropolitan Opera debut in N.Y. in the same role on Nov. 13, 1951; this was also the role he sang at his last Metropolitan appearance on March 10, 1966. Altogether he sang with the Metropolitan 249 times in N.Y. and 54 times on tour. On Sept. 16, 1960, he became the first American to sing Boris Godunov (in Russian) at the Bolshoi Theater in Moscow. In 1967 he was stricken with a partial paralysis of the larynx, but recovered sufficiently to be able to perform administrative duties. From 1968–71 he was artistic administrator of the John F. Kennedy Center for the Performing Arts in Washington, D.C.; was also executive director of the National Opera Inst. from 1971–77. He was general director of the Opera Society of Washington, D.C., from 1975–77, when he suffered a cardiac arrest that precluded any further public activities. Among his best roles were Wotan, Don Giovanni, Scarpia, Escamillo, and Boris Godunov.

Long, Marguerite, notable French pianist and pedagogue; b. Nîmes, Nov. 13, 1874; d. Paris, Feb. 13, 1966. She studied piano with Marmontel at the Paris Cons.; was appointed an instructor there in 1906, her tenure running until 1940; in 1920 she founded her own music school; in 1940 Jacques Thibaud, the violinist, joined her; with him she gave numerous recitals and established the Long-Thibaud Competitions. She played an important role in promoting French music; in 1931 gave the first performance of the Piano Concerto by Ravel, dedicated to her. She was married to Joseph de Marliave. She publ. *Au piano avec Claude Debussy* (Paris, 1960); *Au piano avec Gabriel Fauré* (Paris, 1963).

Longas, Federico, Spanish pianist and composer; b. Barcelona, July 18, 1893; d. Santiago, Chile, June 17, 1968. He was a pupil of Granados and Malats; toured widely in the U.S., South America, and Europe as accompanist to Tito Schipa and as a soloist. He founded a piano school, the Longas Academy, in Barcelona; later he went to Paris; then to the U.S., settling in N.Y. His works include effective piano pieces (*Jota, Aragon,* etc.) and over 100 songs (*Castilian Moonlight, La guinda, Muñequita,* etc.).

Longo, Alessandro, Italian pianist and music editor; b. Amantea, Dec. 30, 1864; d. Naples, Nov. 3, 1945. He studied with Cesi (piano) and Serrao (composition); in 1887, was appointed prof. of piano at the Naples Cons. In 1892 he founded the Circolo Scarlatti to promote the works of Domenico Scarlatti; from 1914, edited the periodical *L'Arte Pianistica.* His most important achievement is the complete edition of Domenico Scarlatti's harpsichord works (10 vols. and a supplement; the order of sonatas was partly superseded by Kirkpatrick's catalogue). He was also a prolific composer; publ. numerous pieces for piano solo and piano, 4-hands; Piano Quintet; *Tema con variazioni* for Harp; Suite for Clarinet and Piano; songs.

Longy, Georges, French oboe virtuoso; b. Abbeville, Aug. 29, 1868; d. Mareuil (Dordogne), March 29, 1930. He studied at the Paris Cons. (first prize, 1886); was a member of the Lamoureux Orch. (1886–88) and of the Colonne Orch. (1888–98). In 1898 he was engaged as first oboe player of the Boston Symph. Orch., and remained there until 1925. From 1899 to 1913 he conducted the Boston Orchestral Club. In 1900 he founded the Longy Club for chamber music; in 1916 he established his own music school in Boston (later the Longy School of Music in Cambridge, Mass.).

Loomis, Clarence, American pianist and composer; b. Sioux Falls, S.Dak., Dec. 13, 1889; d. Aptos, Calif., July 3, 1965. He studied at the American Cons. of Chicago with Heniot Levy (piano) and Adolph Weidig (composition); subsequently took lessons with Leopold Godowsky in Vienna. Returning to the U.S., he held various positions as a music teacher; taught piano and organ at Highland Univ. in New Mexico (1945–55); in 1960 he settled in Aptos, Calif..

Loomis, Harvey Worthington, American composer; b. Brooklyn, Feb. 5, 1865; d. Boston, Dec. 25, 1930. He was a pupil in composition of Dvořák at the National Cons. in N.Y. (1891–93) when Dvořák was director there; later lived mostly in Boston; became interested in Indian music, and publ. many arrangements of Indian melodies; also original works in that style (*Lyrics of the Red Man,* etc.).

Lopatnikoff, Nicolai, outstanding Russian-American composer; b. Reval, Estonia, March 16, 1903; d. Pittsburgh, Oct. 7, 1976. He studied at the St. Petersburg Cons. (1914–17); after the Revolution, continued his musical training at the Helsinki Cons. with Furuhjelm (1918–20); then went to Germany, where he studied with Hermann Grabner in Heidelberg (1920) and Ernst Toch and Willy Rehberg in Mannheim (1921); concurrently took civil engineering at the Technological College in Karlsruhe (1921–27). He lived in Berlin (1929–33) and London (1933–39); came to the U.S. in 1939; became a naturalized citizen in 1944. He taught in N.Y. and Connecticut; in 1945 became a prof. of composition at the Carnegie Inst. of Technology (now Carnegie-Mellon Univ.) in Pittsburgh, retiring in 1969. In 1951 he married the poet Sara Henderson Hay. He was elected to the National Inst. of Arts and Letters in 1963. His music is cast in a neo-Classical manner, distinguished by a vigorous rhythmic pulse, a clear melodic line, and a wholesome harmonic investment. A prolific composer, he wrote music in all genres; being a professional pianist, he often performed his own piano concertos with orchs.
WORKS: FOR THE STAGE: Opera, *Danton* (1930–32, unperf.; a *Danton Suite* for Orch., excerpted from the opera, was first perf. in Pittsburgh, March 25, 1967; a ballet in 6 scenes, *Melting Pot* (1975; Indianapolis, March 26, 1976).
FOR ORCH.: *Prelude to a Drama* (1920; lost); 2 piano concertos: No. 1 (1921; Cologne, Nov. 3, 1925) and No. 2 (1930; Düsseldorf, Oct. 16, 1930); *Introduction and Scherzo* (1927–29; first complete perf., N.Y., Oct. 23, 1930); 4 symphs.: No. 1 (1928; Karlsruhe, Jan. 9, 1929); No. 2 (1938–39; 4-movement version, Boston, Dec. 22, 1939; withdrawn and revised in 3 movements); No. 3 (1953–54; Pittsburgh, Dec. 10, 1954); No. 4 (1970–71; Pittsburgh, Jan. 21, 1972); *Short Overture* (1932; lost); *Opus Sinfonicum* (1933; revised 1942; first prize of the Cleveland Orch.; Cleveland, Dec. 9, 1943); *2 Russian Nocturnes* (1939; originally the 2 middle movements of the 2nd Symph.); Violin Concerto (1941; Boston, April 17, 1942); Sinfonietta (1942; first public perf., Festival of International Society for Contemporary Music, Berkeley, Calif., Aug. 2, 1942); Concertino for Orch. (1944; Boston, March 2, 1945); Concerto for 2 Pianos and Orch. (1950–51; Pittsburgh, Dec. 7, 1951); Divertimento (1951; La Jolla, Calif., Aug. 19, 1951); *Variazioni concertanti* (1958; Pittsburgh, Nov. 7, 1958); *Music for Orchestra* (1958; Louisville, Ky., Jan. 14, 1959); *Festival Overture* (1960; Detroit, Oct. 12, 1960); Concerto for Orch. (1964; Pittsburgh, April 3, 1964; orch. version of Concerto for Wind Orch.); *Partita concertante* for Chamber Orch. (1966); *Variations and Epilogue* for Cello and Orch. (1973; Pittsburgh, Dec. 14, 1973; orchestration of 1946 chamber piece).

Lopes-Graça, Fernando, eminent Portuguese pia-
nist, composer, and musicologist; b. Tomar, Dec. 17, 1906. He took piano lessons at home; studied composition with Tomás Borba and musicology with Luís de Freitas Branco at the Lisbon Cons. (1923–31); subsequently was an instructor at the Instituto de Música in Coimbra (1932–36); was compelled to leave Portugal in 1937 for political reasons, and went to Paris, where he studied composition with Charles Koechlin. After the outbreak of World War II he returned to Lisbon and became active in the modern musical movement; taught at the Academia de Amadores de Música there (1940–54); in 1958 went to Brazil as a pianist; in 1959 made a concert tour in Angola, a Portuguese colony at the time; and in 1977 toured the Soviet Union with the Portuguese tenor Fernando Serafim. His music is inspired by nationalistic themes, and is inherently lyrical.
WORKS: FOR THE STAGE: Cantata-melodrama in 2 parts, *D. Duardos e Flérida,* for Narrator, 3 Soloists, Chorus, and Orch. (1964–69; Lisbon, Nov. 28, 1970); revue-ballet, *La Fièvre du temps,* for 2 Pianos (1938).
FOR ORCH.: *Poemeto* for Strings (1928); *Prelúdio, Pastoral e Dança* (1929); 2 piano concertos (1940, 1942); *3 Portuguese Dances* (1941); Sinfonia (1944); *5 estelas funerárias* (1948); *Scherzo heróico* (1949); *Suite rústica No. 1* (1950–51); *Marcha festiva* (1954); Concertino for Piano, Strings, Brass, and Percussion (1954); *5 Old Portuguese Romances* (1951–55); *Divertimento* for Winds, Kettledrums, Percussion, Cellos, and Double Basses (1957); *Poema de Dezembro* (1961); Viola Concertino (1962); *4 bosquejos (4 Sketches)* for Strings (1965); *Concerto da camera,* with Cello obbligato (Moscow, Oct. 6, 1967, Rostropovich, soloist); *Viagens na minha terra (Travels in My Country;* 1969–70); *Fantasia* for Piano and Orch., on a religious song from Beira-Baixa (1974).
FOR VOICE: *Pequeno cancioneiro do Menino Jesus (Little Songbook of the Child Jesus)* for Women's Chorus, 2 Flutes, String Quartet, Celesta, and Harp (1936–59); *História trágico-marítima* for Baritone, Contralto, Chorus, and Orch. (1942–59); *9 Portuguese Folk Songs* for Voice and Orch. (1948–49); *4 Songs of Federico García Lorca* for Baritone, 2 Clarinets, Violin, Viola, Cello, Harp, and Percussion (1953–54); *Cantos do Natal (Christmas Carols)* for Female Voices and Instrumental Ensemble (1958); *9 cantigas de amigo* for Voice and Chamber Ensemble (1964); *6 cantos sefardins (Sephardite Songs)* for Voice and Orch. (1971); choruses; songs.

López-Buchardo, Carlos, Argentine composer; b. Buenos Aires, Oct. 12, 1881; d. there, April 21, 1948. He studied piano and harmony in Buenos Aires; composition with Albert Roussel in Paris; became director of the National Cons. in Buenos Aires. His music is set in a vivid style, rooted in national folk song; particularly successful in this respect is his symph. suite *Escenas argentinas* (Buenos Aires, Aug. 12, 1922, under Felix Weingartner). Other works are the opera *El sueño de alma* (Buenos Aires, Aug. 4, 1914; won the Municipal Prize); lyric comedies: *Madame Lynch* (1932); *La perichona*

(1933); *Amalia* (1935); several piano pieces in an Argentine folk manner; songs.

Lopez-Cobos, Jesús, Spanish conductor; b. Toro, Feb. 25, 1940. He studied philosophy at Madrid Univ.; at the same time he took courses in music; then went to Vienna to study conducting with Hans Swarowsky. In 1969 he won first prize in the International Conductors' Competition in Besançon. He then conducted in Italy and West Germany. In 1972 he made his American debut with the San Francisco Opera. In 1980 he was named Generalmusikdirektor of the Deutsche Oper in West Berlin.

Lorentz, Alfred, German composer and conductor; b. Strasbourg, March 7, 1872; d. Karlsruhe, April 23, 1931. He studied with Rheinberger in Munich (composition), and with Mottl at Karlsruhe (conducting). He was chorus master, and later conductor, at the Municipal Theater in Strasbourg; from 1899 to 1925, was court conductor in Karlsruhe. He wrote the operas *Der Mönch von Sendomir* (Karlsruhe, 1907); *Die beiden Automaten* (Karlsruhe, 1913); *Liebesmacht* (Karlsruhe, 1922); *Schneider Fips* (Coburg, 1928); an operetta, *Die Mondscheindame* (Karlsruhe, 1919); some orch. works.

Lorentzen, Bent, Danish composer; b. Stenvad, Feb. 11, 1935. He studied with Jeppesen at the Aarhus Cons., and with Hjelmborg, Halmboe, Jersild, and Hoffding at the Royal Cons. in Copenhagen; had training in electronic music in Stockholm (1967–68). He subsequently taught at the Jutland Cons. in Aarhus. In his music he employs a variety of quaquaversal techniques, often utilizing purely sonoristic effects.
WORKS: 6 operas: *Stalten Mettelil (Haughty Little Mette;* 1963; Aarhus, Nov. 20, 1963; revised 1972); *Dissonances* (1964); *Eurydice,* radio opera (1965; Danish Radio, Dec. 16, 1969; first stage production, Aarhus, Sept. 1973; Prix Italia, 1970); *Tärnet (The Tower),* a film opera (1966); *Tristan Variations* for 3 Voices and Tape (1969); *This Music Seems Very Familiar,* comic skit based on Mozart's operas, for 4 Singers and Tape (1973–74; Kiel, Germany, May 3, 1974); 2 ballets: *Jomfru i fugleham (Young Maiden as a Bird)* for Orch. and Tape (1967) and *Afgrundens Brønd (The Bottomless Pit)* for Tape (1972); *The Night* for Soprano, Chorus, and Orch. (1965; Aarhus, April 4, 1979); *Shiftings* for Orch. (1966–67); *Cyclus 4* for String Orch. and Percussion (1966); *Music for Mozart Orchestra* (1966–67); *The Unconscious* for Orch. (1967); *Tide* for Orch. (1971; revised 1977); *My Bride Is an Enclosed Garden* for Solo Voice, Tape, and Orch. (1972); *Quadrata* for String Quartet (1963); *Cyclus 1* for Violin, Cello, and Double Bass (1966); *Cyclus 2* for 3 Percussionists (1966); *Cyclus 3* for Cello and Triple Playback (1966); *Studie fur 2* for Cello and Percussion (1967); *Music Theater for 3* for Soprano, Cello, and Percussion (1968); *The End* for Solo Cello (1969); *Danish Wind* for Wind Quintet (1970); *Intersection* for Organ (1970); *Syncretism* for Clarinet, Trombone, Cello, and Piano (1970); *3 Mobiles* for Accordion, Guitar, and Percussion (1971); *Quartetto Rustico* for String Quartet (1971); *Quartz* for Solo Violin (1971); *Granite* for Solo Cello (1971); *Puncta* for Organ (1973); *Triplex* for Organ (1973); *Groppe* for Organ (1974); *Carnaval* for 3 Voices and Tape (1976); choruses.

Lorenz, Alfred Ottokar, Austrian musicologist, composer, and conductor; b. Vienna, July 11, 1868; d. Munich, Nov. 20, 1939. He studied at the Univ. of Vienna with Spitta; conducted opera at Königsberg and Elberfeld (1894–97), and at Coburg-Gotha (1898–1916); from 1920, lived in Munich; lectured at Munich Univ. from 1923. He made a specialty of Wagnerian research; publ. the comprehensive work *Das Geheimnis der Form bei Richard Wagner,* in 4 vols.: *Die musikalische Formgebung in Richard Wagners Ring des Nibelungen* (1924), *Der musikalische Aufbau von Tristan und Isolde* (1926), *Die Meistersinger* (1930), and *Parsifal* (1933); the musical architecture and form of the operas are here analyzed in minute detail. He further publ. *Alessandro Scarlattis Jugendoper* (1927); *Abendländische Musikgeschichte im Rhythmus der Generationen* (1928); and numerous smaller essays in various music magazines, on Bach, Mozart, Beethoven, Weber, Wagner, Richard Strauss, etc. He composed an opera, *Helges Erwachen* (Schwerin, 1896); incidental music to various plays; the symph. poems *Bergfahrt* and *Columbus;* some chamber music; and songs.

Lorenz, Max, German tenor; b. Düsseldorf, May 17, 1901; d. Salzburg, Jan. 11, 1975. He studied with Grenzebach; sang with the Dresden Opera; made his American debut with the Metropolitan Opera Co. in N.Y. as Walther in *Die Meistersinger* (N.Y., Nov. 12, 1931); appeared there again in 1933–34. From 1934 to 1939 he sang in Berlin and in Vienna; joined the Chicago Opera for one season; also made appearances in London, at La Scala in Milan, and at the Paris Opéra. He sang the roles of Tristan and Siegfried at the Bayreuth Festival (1933, 1942, 1952).

Lorenzani, Paolo, Italian composer; b. Rome, 1640; d. there, Oct. 28, 1713. He was a pupil of Orazio Benevoli at the Vatican; having failed to obtain Benevoli's position after the latter's death in 1672, he was given the post of maestro di cappella at the Jesuit College and at the Seminario Romano in Rome in 1675; in 1675–76 held a similar position at the Cathedral of Messina; when Sicily was captured by the French, the Duc de Vivonne, who was the French viceroy, induced Lorenzani to go to Paris (1678); he found favor with Louis XIV, and became court musician; in 1679 he was sent to Italy to recruit singers for the French court; he produced his Italian pastoral, *Nicandro e Fileno,* at Fontainebleau (1681); in 1679–83 he was "surintendant" of music to the Queen; after the Queen died he became choirmaster at the Italian religious order of Théatins in Paris (1685). For several years Lorenzani was supported by the Paris faction opposed to Lully; after Lully's death, Lorenzani produced an opera with a French libretto, *Orontée* (Paris, Aug. 23, 1687). This having failed, Lorenzani turned to the composition of motets, which proved his best works; the famous Paris publisher Ballard brought them out in an impressively printed edition; Ballard also publ. a book of Italian airs by Lorenzani. In 1694 Lorenzani returned to Italy, and was appointed maestro of the Cappella Giulia at St. Peter's, the post he had tried unsuccessfully to secure in 1672; there he remained until his death. His printed works include 25 motets for one to 5 voices (Paris, 1693); 6 Italian airs (Paris, 1690); and several separate vocal numbers; Henry Prunières reproduced a scene from Lorenzani's opera *Nicandro e Fileno* in the *Revue Musicale* (Aug. 1922).

Lorenzo, Leonardo de, Italian flutist; b. Viggiano, Aug. 29, 1875; d. Santa Barbara, Calif., July 27, 1962. He studied at the Naples Cons.; from 1897 to 1907, was a flutist in various traveling orchs. In 1910 he emigrated to the U.S.; was first flutist of the N.Y. Phil. (1910–12); later, with the Minneapolis Symph. Orch., the Los Angeles Phil., and the Rochester Phil.; taught flute at the Eastman School of Music in Rochester, N.Y.; in 1935, settled in California. He publ. several books of flute studies and some solo pieces, and an informative book on flute playing and flute players, *My Complete Story of the Flute* (N.Y., 1951).

Loriod, Yvonne, French pianist; b. Houilles, Jan. 20, 1924. She studied at the Paris Cons. with Lazar Lévy and composition with Messiaen and Milhaud. She toured as a concert pianist in Germany and Austria; made her American debut in 1949 as piano soloist in Messiaen's work *Turangalila;* subsequently joined the faculty of the Paris Cons. She was the 2nd wife of **Olivier Messiaen.**

Lortzing, (Gustav) Albert, celebrated German opera composer; b. Berlin, Oct. 23, 1801; d. there, Jan. 21, 1851. His parents were actors, and the wandering life led by the family did not allow him to pursue a methodical course of study. He learned acting from his father, and music from his mother at an early age. After some lessons in piano with Griebel and in theory with Rungenhagen in Berlin, he continued his own studies, and soon began to compose. On Jan. 30, 1823, he married the actress Rosina Regina Ahles in Cologne; they had 11 children. In 1824 he wrote his first opera (to his own libretto), *Ali Pascha von Janina,* which, however, was not produced until 4 years later (Münster, Feb. 1, 1828). In 1832 he brought out the liederspiel *Der Pole und sein Kind* and the singspiel *Scenen aus Mozarts Leben,* which were well received on several German stages. From 1833 to 1844 he was engaged at the Municipal Theater of Leipzig as a tenor; there he launched a light opera, *Die beiden Schützen* (Feb. 20, 1837), which became instantly popular; on the same stage he produced, on Dec. 22, 1837, his undoubted masterpiece, *Czaar und Zimmermann* (later spelling, *Zar und Zimmermann*), to his own libretto derived from various French plays, and based on the true history of Peter the Great of Russia, who worked as a carpenter in the

Netherlands. The opera was produced in Berlin in 1839, and from then on its success was assured; after a few years it became a favorite on most European stages. Lortzing's next opera, *Caramo, oder Das Fischerstechen* (Leipzig, Sept. 20, 1839), was a failure; there followed *Hans Sachs* (Leipzig, June 23, 1840) and *Casanova* (Leipzig, Dec. 31, 1841), which passed without much notice; subsequent comparisons showed some similarities between *Hans Sachs* and *Die Meistersinger,* not only in subject matter, which was derived from the same source, but also in some melodic patterns; however, no one seriously suggested that Wagner was influenced by Lortzing's inferior work. There followed a Romantic opera, *Der Wildschütz* (Leipzig, Dec. 31, 1842), which was in many respects the best that Lortzing wrote, but its success, although impressive, never equaled that of *Zar und Zimmermann.* At about the same time, Lortzing attempted still another career, that of opera impresario, but it was short-lived; his brief conductorship at the Leipzig Opera was similarly ephemeral. Composing remained his chief occupation; he produced *Undine* in Magdeburg (April 21, 1845) and *Der Waffenschmied* in Vienna (May 31, 1846). In Vienna he also acted as a conductor; after a season or two at the Theater an der Wien, he returned to Leipzig, where he produced the light opera *Zum Grossadmiral* (Dec. 13, 1847), which was only moderately successful. The revolutionary events of 1848 seriously affected his position in both Leipzig and Vienna; after the political situation became settled, he produced in Leipzig an opera of a Romantic nature, *Rolands Knappen* (May 25, 1849). Although at least 4 of his operas were played at various German theaters, Lortzing received no honorarium, owing to a flaw in the regulations protecting the rights of composers. He was compelled to travel again as an actor, but could not earn enough money to support his large family, left behind in Vienna. In the spring of 1850 he was engaged as music director at a small theater in Berlin; on Jan. 20, 1851, his last opera, *Die Opernprobe,* was produced in Frankfurt while he was on his deathbed in Berlin; he died the next day. His opera *Regina, oder Die Marodeure,* written in 1848, was edited by Richard Kleinmichel, with the composer's libretto revised by Adolf L'Arronge, and performed in Berlin on March 21, 1899; another opera, *Der Weihnachtsabend,* was not produced. Lortzing also wrote an oratorio, *Die Himmelfahrt Christi;* some incidental music to various plays; and songs. But it is as a composer of characteristically German Romantic operas that Lortzing holds a distinguished, if minor, place in the history of dramatic music. He was a follower of Weber, without Weber's imaginative projection; in his lighter works, he approached the type of French operetta; in his best creations he exhibited a fine sense of facile melody, and infectious rhythm; his harmonies, though unassuming, were always proper and pleasing; his orchestration, competent and effective.

Löschhorn, (Carl) Albert, German pianist, composer, and pedagogue; b. Berlin, June 27, 1819; d.

there, June 4, 1905. He studied at the Royal Inst. for Church Music with L. Berger, Killitschgy, Grell, and A.W. Bach; became a piano teacher there in 1851. He publ. a series of excellent piano studies, including *Melodious Studies, La Vélocité, Universal Studies, Le Trille,* and *School of Octaves,* which became standard pedagogical works; also wrote attractive piano solos: *La Belle Amazone, 4 pièces élégantes, Tarentelle; 2 valses,* the barcarolle *A Venise,* and *3 mazurkas;* suites, sonatas, sonatinas, etc. With J. Weiss he publ. a *Wegweiser in die Pianoforte-Literatur* (1862; 2nd ed., 1885, as *Führer durch die Klavierliteratur*).

Lott, Felicity, English soprano; b. Cheltenham, May 8, 1947. She studied at the Royal Academy of Music in London; in 1976 she sang at Covent Garden in the world premiere of Henze's *We Come to the River;* she also appeared there as Anne Trulove in Stravinsky's *The Rake's Progress,* as Octavian in *Der Rosenkavalier,* and in various other roles. She appeared in Paris for the first time in 1976; made her Vienna debut in 1982 singing the *4 Letze Lieder* of Strauss; in 1984 was engaged as soloist with the Chicago Symph. Orch.

Lotti, Antonio, Italian organist and composer; b. Venice, c.1667; d. there, Jan. 5, 1740. He was a pupil of Legrenzi in Venice; in 1687 he became chorister at San Marco; in 1690, assistant organist there, and in 1692, 2nd organist. On Aug. 17, 1704, he was appointed first organist; in 1736 he was elected primo maestro di cappella. While at San Marco, he industriously composed church music, masses, anthems, etc.; he also wrote dramatic music. As a teacher, he was highly renowned; among his pupils were Alberti, Gasparini, Galuppi, and Marcello. He absented himself from Venice but once (1717–19), when he went to Dresden at the Crown Prince's invitation.

WORKS: 21 operas, including *Alessandro Severo* (Venice, Dec. 26, 1716); *Giove in Argo* (Dresden, Oct. 25, 1717); *Teofane* (Dresden, Nov. 13, 1719); *Costantino* (Vienna, Nov. 19, 1716; in collaboration with Fux and Caldara); 7 oratorios, including *Il voto crudele, L'umiltà coronata, Gioa re di Giuda,* and *Giuditta;* many masses, motets, etc., none of which were publ. by him. Lück's *Sammlung ausgezeichneter Compositionen* contains 4 masses and other numbers; Rochlitz, Proske, Trautwein, Commer, Schlesinger, and others have printed Misereres and other sacred music by Lotti; 8 masses were ed. by H. Müller in Denkmäler Deutscher Tonkunst, 60. During Lotti's lifetime his only work publ. was *Duetti, Terzetti e Madrigali a più voci* (Venice, 1705, dedicated to Joseph I; includes the madrigal *In una siepe ombrosa,* the appropriation of which caused Bononcini's downfall).

Loucheur, Raymond, French composer; b. Tourcoing, Jan. 1, 1899; d. Nogent-sur-Marne, Sept. 14, 1979. He studied music with Henry Woollett at Le Havre (1915–18) and with Nadia Boulanger, Gédalge, d'Indy, Fauchet, and Paul Vidal at the Paris Cons. (1920–23). In 1928 he won the Premier Grand

Prix de Rome for his cantata *Héracles à Delphe.* From 1925 to 1940 he was a teacher in Paris; in 1941, became the principal inspector of musical education in the Paris city schools and later was director of the Paris Cons. (1956–62). His music is chromatically lyrical and displays rhythmic spontaneity.

Loughran, James, Scottish conductor; b. Glasgow, June 30, 1931. He began his conducting career as an assistant conductor at the Bonn Opera; also held similar posts in Amsterdam and Milan. In 1962 became associate conductor of the Bournemouth Symph. In 1965 he was named principal conductor of the BBC Scottish Symph. in Glasgow. In 1971 he was appointed principal conductor of the Hallé Orch. of Manchester, succeeding the late Sir John Barbirolli. In 1979 he became principal conductor of the Bamberg Symph. in West Germany.

Louis Ferdinand, Prince of Prussia, nephew of **Frederick the Great;** b. Friedrichsfelde, near Berlin, Nov. 18, 1772; fell at Saalfeld, Oct. 10, 1806. He was an excellent amateur musician. While traveling in 1804, he met Beethoven, and showed great interest in the master's music. Beethoven's 3rd Piano Concerto in C minor is dedicated to Louis Ferdinand, which testifies to their mutual esteem. However, the statement sometimes made that Louis Ferdinand imitated Beethoven in his own works is untenable inasmuch as the Prince fell in battle 2 years after his first acquaintance with Beethoven's music. The following compositions by Louis Ferdinand are publ.: 2 piano quintets; 2 piano quartets; 4 piano trios; Octet for Clarinet, 2 Horns, 2 Violins, 2 Cellos, and Piano; *Notturno* for Flute, Violin, Cello, and Piano; *Andante and Variations* for Viola, Cello, and Piano; *Rondo* for Piano and Orch.; *Rondo* for Piano Solo. H. Kretzschmar edited his collected works (Leipzig, 1915–17).

Louis XIII, King of France from 1610 to 1643; b. Paris, Sept. 27, 1601; d. there, May 14, 1643. He was an amateur musician, and wrote madrigals. The well-known *Amaryllis,* arranged by Henri Ghis and widely publ. as "Air of Louis XIII," is a misattribution; the melody first appears in print as "La Clochette" in the *Ballet-Comique de la Reine* by Balthazar de Beaujoyeux, produced in 1582, long before Louis XIII was born. A gavotte, also entitled *Amaryllis,* with a melody totally different from the apocryphal "Air of Louis XIII" and dated 1620, may be an authentic composition of Louis XIII.

Loulié, Etienne, 17th-century French writer on music and inventor of the "chronomètre," the precursor of the metronome; b. Paris c.1655; d. there, c.1707. He studied with Gehenault and Ouvrard under the patronage of Mlle. de Guise; was at the Saint-Chapelle in Paris in 1663–73. He publ. *Eléments ou principes de musique dans un nouvel ordre . . . avec l'estampe et l'usage du chronomètre* (Paris, 1696; Eng. trans., 1965), which describes and illustrates his invention, an unwieldy device 6 feet tall; and a *Nouveau système de musique* (1698), describing the "sonomètre" (a monochord to aid in tuning), which he also invented.

Lourié, Arthur (Vincent), Russian composer; b. St. Petersburg, May 14, 1892; d. Princeton, N.J., Oct. 13, 1966. He studied at the St. Petersburg Cons.; participated in various modernistic groups, and wrote piano music, much influenced by Scriabin (*Préludes fragiles, Synthèses,* etc.); experimented in futuristic composition (e.g., *Formes en l'air,* dedicated to Picasso, and graphically imitating a cubist design by omitting the staves instead of using rests); also composed religious music (*Lamentations de la Vierge,* etc.). After the Soviet Revolution, he was appointed chief of the music dept. of the Commissariat for Public Instruction; in 1921 he left Russia, and lived in Paris; in 1941, emigrated to the U.S., and became an American citizen. In his music written after 1920 he followed mainly Stravinsky's practice of stylizing old forms, secular and sacred.

Lover, Samuel, Irish novelist, poet, painter, and composer; b. Dublin, Feb. 24, 1797; d. St. Heliers, Jersey, July 6, 1868. He wrote music to several Irish plays, and to many songs; publ. *Songs and Ballads* (London, 1859). Among his most popular songs (some of which are set to old Irish tunes) are *The Angel's Whisper, Molly Bawn,* and *the Low-Backed Car.* He wrote an opera, *Grana Uile, or The Island Queen* (Dublin, Feb. 9, 1832). He devised a very successful musical entertainment, *Irish Evenings* (1844), with which he toured the British Isles and the U.S. (1846). He was **Victor Herbert**'s grandfather.

Löwe, Ferdinand, Austrian conductor; b. Vienna, Feb. 19, 1865; d. there, Jan. 6, 1925. He studied with Dachs, Krenn, and Bruckner at the Vienna Cons.; then taught piano and choral singing there (1883–96). In 1897 he became conductor of the Kaim Orch. in Munich; then of the court opera in Vienna (1898–1900); of the Gesellschaftskonzerte (1900–1904); in 1904 he became conductor of the newly organized Vienna Konzertverein Orch., which he made one of the finest instrumental bodies in Europe; returned to Munich as conductor of the Konzertverein (1908–14), which comprised members of the former Kaim Orch.; also conducted in Budapest and Berlin; from 1918 to 1922 was head of the Vienna Staatsakademie für Musik. He was a friend and trusted disciple of Bruckner; edited (somewhat liberally) several of Bruckner's works even during the master's lifetime; conducted the 3 finished movements of Bruckner's posthumous 9th Symph. (Vienna, Feb. 11, 1903), with considerable cuts and alterations, adding Bruckner's Te Deum in lieu of the unfinished finale.

Löwe, Karl. See **Loewe, Carl.**

Lowens, Irving, eminent American musicologist, music critic, and librarian; b. New York, Aug. 19, 1916; d. Baltimore, Nov. 14, 1983. He studied at Teachers College, Columbia Univ. (B.S. in Music, 1939). During World War II he served as an air-traffic controller for the Civil Aeronautics Administration; he continued in this capacity at the National Airport in Washington, D.C.; then took special courses in American civilization at the Univ. of Maryland (M.A., 1957; Ph.D., 1965). In 1953 he began to write music criticism for the *Washington Star;* from 1960–78 he was its chief music critic; received the ASCAP Deems Taylor Award for the best articles on music in 1972 and 1977. From 1960–66 he was a librarian in the Music Division of the Library of Congress in Washington, D.C. From 1978–81 he was dean of the Peabody Inst. of the Johns Hopkins Univ. in Baltimore; also wrote music criticism for the *Baltimore News American.* A linguist, he traveled widely on numerous research grants in Europe; in 1970 he was the sole American representative at the Enesco Festival in Bucharest. He was a founding member of the Music Critics' Assoc., and from 1971–75 served as its president.

Lowenthal, Jerome, American pianist; b. Philadelphia, Feb. 11, 1932. He studied piano at an early age; made his debut in Philadelphia at the age of 13; then took lessons with William Kapell and with Eduard Steuermann at the Juilliard School of Music in N.Y.; received a Fulbright grant and went to Paris to study with Alfred Cortot at the Ecole Normale de Musique. He then traveled to Israel, where he gave concerts and taught at the Jerusalem Academy of Music; returned to the U.S. in 1961. His repertoire embraced the standard piano literature as well as contemporary works; among composers who wrote special works for him were George Rochberg and Ned Rorem.

Lowinsky, Edward, eminent German-born American musicologist; b. Stuttgart, Jan. 12, 1908. He studied at the Hochschule für Musik in Stuttgart (1923–28); took his Ph.D. at the Univ. of Heidelberg in 1933 with the dissertation *Das Antwerpener Motettenbuch Orlando di Lassos und seine Beziehungen zum Motettenschaffen der niederländischen Zeitgenössen* (publ. in The Hague, 1937). When the Nazis came to power, he went to the Netherlands; in 1940 he emigrated to the U.S.; became an American citizen in 1947. He held the positions of assistant prof. of music at Black Mountain College (1942–47), associate prof. of music at Queens College, N.Y. (1948–56); prof. of music at the Univ. of Calif., Berkeley (1956–61); and prof. of music at the Univ. of Chicago (1961–76), where he also held a postretirement professorship until 1978. He held Guggenheim fellowships in 1947–48 and 1976–77; was a Fellow at the Inst. for Advanced Study at Princeton Univ. from 1952 to 1954; was made a Fellow of the American Academy of Arts and Sciences in 1973; was named Albert A. Bauman Distinguished Research Fellow of the Newberry Library in 1982. He was general editor of the Monuments of Renaissance Music series; publ. the valuable studies *Secret Chromatic Art in the Netherlands Motet* (N.Y., 1946) and *Tonality and Atonality in Sixteenth-Century Music* (Berkeley and Los Angeles, 1961; 2nd revised printing, 1962). He also prepared the vol. *Josquin des Prez. Proceedings of the International Josquin Festival-Conference* (London, 1976). He was married to the musicologist **Bonnie Blackburn.**

Lualdi, Adriano, Italian composer, conductor, and critic; b. Larino, Campobasso, March 22, 1885; d. Milan, Jan. 8, 1971. He studied composition with Falchi in Rome and Wolf-Ferrari in Venice; began his musical career as an opera conductor; in 1918 went to Milan, where he was active as a music critic and government administrator on musical affairs; from 1936 to 1943 he was director of the Cons. of San Pietro a Majella in Naples; then was appointed director of the Florence Cons. (1947–56). He was a voluminous composer, excelling particularly in opera. His opera *Le nozze di Haura,* written in 1908, had a concert performance by the Radio Italiano on Oct. 15, 1939, and its first stage production in Rome on April 17, 1943. His subsequent operas were *La Figlia del re,* after the *Antigone* of Sophocles (Turin, March 18, 1922); *Le furie d'Arlecchino* (Milan, May 10, 1915); *Il Diavolo nel campanile* (La Scala, Milan, April 22, 1925); *La granceola* (Venice, Sept. 10, 1932); *La luna dei Caraibi,* one-act opera after O'Neill (Rome, Jan. 29, 1953); mimodrama, *Lumawig e la saetta* (Rome, Jan. 23, 1937); *Il testamento di Euridice,* lyric tragedy (1939–52); satiric radio comedy, *Tre alla radarstratotropojonosferaphonotheca del Luna Park* (1953–58); cantata, *La rosa di Saron* (1915; also titled *Il cantico;* Milan, May 10, 1915); symph. poems: *La leggenda del vecchio marinaio* (1910) and *L'interludio del sogno* (1917); *Suite adriatica* for Orch. (1932); *Africa,* rhapsody for Orch. (1936); *Divertimento* for Orch. (1941); numerous choruses and minor pieces for various instruments. Lualdi was also an industrious writer on musical subjects. He publ. several vols. of reminiscences of his "musical voyages": *Viaggio musicale italiano* (1931); *Viaggio musicale in Europa* (1928); *Viaggio musicale nel Sud-America* (Milan, 1934); *Viaggio musicale nel l'U.R.S.S.* (1941); also *L'arte di dirigere l'orchestra* (1940) and *Tutti vivi,* a collection of miscellaneous articles (Milan, 1955).

Lübeck, Ernst, Dutch pianist and composer, son of **Johann Heinrich Lübeck;** b. The Hague, Aug. 24, 1829; d. Paris, Sept. 17, 1876. He was trained as a pianist by his father; as a youth, he made a voyage to America, playing concerts in the U.S., Mexico, and Peru (1849–54); then returned to Europe and settled in Paris, where he acquired the reputation of a virtuoso; Berlioz wrote enthusiastically about his playing. He became mentally unbalanced following the events of the Paris Commune of 1871; there his career ended. He wrote some pleasing salon pieces for piano, among them *Berceuse; Tarentelle; Polonaise; Trilby the Sprite; Rêverie caractéristique.*

Lübeck, Johann Heinrich, Dutch violinist and composer; b. Alphen, Feb. 11, 1799; d. The Hague, Feb. 7, 1865. He was a Prussian regimental musician (1813–15); studied music in Potsdam; then was a player in theater orchs. in Riga and Stettin; in 1823, settled in the Netherlands, giving violin concerts. From 1827 until his death he was director of the Cons. of The Hague; was also conductor of the "Diligentia" concerts there, and in 1829, became court conductor.

Lübeck, Louis, Dutch cellist, son of **Johann Heinrich Lübeck;** b. The Hague, Feb. 14, 1838; d. Berlin, March 8, 1904. He studied with Jacquard in Paris; in 1863–68, taught cello at the Leipzig Cons.; toured Germany, the Netherlands, England, and the U.S. (1875–81); in 1881 he settled in Berlin as a cellist in the court orch. He wrote 2 concertos for cello, and solo pieces.

Lübeck, Vincentius (Vincenz), German organist and composer; b. Padingbüttel, Sept. 1654; d. Hamburg, Feb. 9, 1740. He studied with his father; from 1675 to 1702 was an organist at Stade; in 1702, became organist at the Nicolaikirche in Hamburg, remaining in that post until his death. Lübeck's works, including 3 cantatas, chorale preludes for organ, etc., were publ. by Gottlieb Harms (Klecken, 1921). An edition of the complete organ works was publ. by K. Beckmann (Wiesbaden, 1973).

Lubin, Germaine, French soprano; b. Paris, Feb. 1, 1890; d. there, Oct. 27, 1979. She studied at the Paris Cons.; made her debut at the Opéra-Comique in 1912; in 1914 she joined the Paris Opéra, remaining on its roster until 1944. In 1931 she sang at Salzburg, in 1937 at Covent Garden in London; in 1938 she became the first French singer to appear at Bayreuth, gaining considerable acclaim for her Wagnerian roles. She continued her career in Paris during the German occupation and was briefly under arrest after the liberation of Paris, charged with collaboration with the enemy. She was later absolved of this charge, and upon retirement from the stage gave private voice lessons, dying in her 90th year.

Luboshutz (real name, **Luboshits**), **Léa,** Russian violinist; b. Odessa, Feb. 22, 1885; d. Philadelphia, March 18, 1965. She studied violin with her father; played in public at the age of 7; after study at the Odessa Music School, she went to the Moscow Cons., graduating with a gold medal (1903); gave concerts in Germany and France, and also took additional lessons from Eugène Ysaÿe in Belgium; returned to Russia, and organized a trio with her brother **Pierre** (piano) and sister **Anna** (cello); left Russia after the Revolution and lived in Berlin and Paris (1921–25). In 1925 she settled in N.Y.; played the American premiere of Prokofiev's First Violin Concerto (Nov. 14, 1925); made several appearances in joint recitals with her son, **Boris Goldovsky,** a pianist. From 1927, she was on the faculty of the Curtis Inst. of Music.

Luboshutz, Pierre, Russian pianist, brother of **Léa Luboshutz;** b. Odessa, June 17, 1891; d. Rockport, Maine, April 17, 1971. He studied violin with his father; then turned to the piano, and entered the Moscow Cons. as a pupil of Igumnov, graduating in 1912; also studied in Paris with Edouard Risler; returning to Russia, he played in a trio with his 2 sisters, **Léa** (violin) and **Anna** (cello); in 1926 went to America as accompanist to Zimbalist, Piatigorsky, and others. In 1931 he married **Genia Nemenoff** (b. Paris, Oct. 23, 1905); with her he formed a piano duo (N.Y. debut, Jan. 18, 1937); as Luboshutz-Nemenoff, they gave annual concerts with considerable success. From 1962 to 1968, they headed the piano dept. at Michigan State Univ.; then returned to N.Y.

Lucas, Mary Anderson, English composer; b. London, May 24, 1882; d. there, Jan. 14, 1952. She studied piano at the Dresden Cons.; later took lessons in composition with R.O. Morris and Herbert Howells. She adopted an advanced harmonic style of composition; her works include a ballet, *Sawdust* (1941), which had considerable success; 6 string quartets; Trio for Clarinet, Viola, and Piano; *Rhapsody* for Flute, Cello, and Piano; many songs.

Lucca, Pauline, Austrian soprano; b. Vienna, April 25, 1841; d. there, Feb. 28, 1908. She was a daughter of an Italian father and a German mother; she studied singing in Vienna and sang in the chorus of the Vienna Opera. Her professional debut took place in Olmütz as Elvira in *Ernani* on Sept. 4, 1859. Her appearance in Prague as Norma attracted the attention of Meyerbeer, who arranged her engagements in Berlin. In 1863 she sang in London with excellent success; in 1872 she made her first appearance in the U.S. Returning to Europe, she joined the staff of the Vienna Opera (1874–89); then retired from the stage. In her prime she was regarded as "prima donna assoluta," and her private life and recurring marriages and divorces were favorite subjects of sensational press stories; a curious promotional pamphlet, entitled *Bellicose Adventures of a Peaceable Prima Donna,* was publ. in N.Y. in 1872, presumably to whip up interest in her public appearances, but it concerned itself mainly with a melodramatic account of her supposed experiences during the Franco-Prussian War.

Lucier, Alvin, American composer; b. Nashua, N.H., May 14, 1931. He studied theory with Quincy Porter at Yale Univ. and with Arthur Berger, Irving Fine, and Harold Shapero at Brandeis Univ.; also took a course with Lukas Foss at Tanglewood. He spent 2 years in Rome on a Fulbright scholarship. Returning to America in 1962, he was appointed to the faculty at Brandeis Univ.
WORKS: In his works he exploits serial and electronic techniques. Among them are *Music for Solo Performer* (1965), derived from amplified electroencephalographic waves, which activate percussion instruments; *Whistlers,* depicting magnetic disturbances in the ionosphere; *Shelter 999,* amplifications of mini-sounds in the immediate environment with parietal filters; *Music for High Structures; Chambers,* derived from the noises of displaced objects; *Vespers,* produced by acoustic orientation by means of echolocation; *The Only Talking Machine of Its Kind in the World* for Mixed Media, featuring electronic ventriloquy (1969); *Reflections of Sounds from the Wall.* He wrote a computer-controlled environmental work for the Pepsi-Cola pavilion at Expo '70 in Osaka, Japan, a sound mosaic with hundreds of tape recorders; also a biographical composition for oboe, accompanied by the Atlantic Ocean, a chest of drawers, and the Federal Bureau of Investigation (1970); also produced an experimental composition, *Still and Moving Lines of Silence in Families of Hyperbolas* (N.Y., Feb. 21, 1975); and 4 pieces for multimedia (1975–77), involving electronic sound and a modified birdcall. In 1970 he resigned from Brandeis Univ. and joined the staff of Wesleyan Univ. In 1977 he was teaching at Wesleyan Univ.; was music director of the Viola Farber Dance Co. and a member of the Sonic Arts Union.

Lucký, Štěpán, Czech composer; b. Žilina, Jan. 20, 1919. He studied quarter-tone composition with Alois Hába at the Prague Cons. (1936–39). During the occupation of Czechoslovakia he was interned in concentration camps at Bucharest, Auschwitz, and Buchenwald, but survived; after the war he enrolled in the Prague Cons., where he studied with Řídký, graduating in 1947. His music is couched in a pragmatic modernistic manner without circumscription by any particular doctrine or technique.
WORKS: Opera, *Půlnoční překvapení (Midnight Surprise;* 1958; Prague, 1959); *Divertimento* for 3 Trombones and String Ensemble (1946); Cello Concerto (1946); Piano Concerto (1947); Violin Concerto (1963–65); Octet for Strings (1970); *Double Concerto* for Violin, Piano, and Orch. (1971); Wind Quintet (1946); *Sonata brevis* for Violin and Piano (1947); *Elegy* for Cello and Piano (1948); Brass Quartet (1949); *Elegy* for Horn and Piano (1965); Sonata for Solo Violin (1967–69); *3 Pieces for Due Boemi* for Bass Clarinet and Piano (1969–70; Due Boemi is a Czech duo); *Sonata doppia* for 2 Violins (1971); Flute Sonata (1973); *Divertimento* for Wind Quintet (1974); Piano Sonata (1940); Piano Sonatina (1945); *3 Etudes* for Quarter-tone Piano (1946); *Little Suite* for Piano (1971); songs.

Ludikar, Pavel, Austrian bass; b. Prague, March 3, 1882; d. Vienna, Feb. 19, 1970. He studied law in Prague; then took piano lessons, acquiring sufficient proficiency to be able to play accompaniment to singers; then finally devoted himself to his real profession, that of opera singing. He appeared in Vienna, Dresden, Milan, and Buenos Aires; was a member of the Boston Civic Opera (1913–14); from 1926 to 1932 he was on the staff of the Metropolitan Opera Co.; his most successful role was that of Figaro in *Il Barbiere di Siviglia,* which he sang more than 100 times in the U.S.; he was also renowned for bass parts in Russian operas, and sang the title role of Krenek's opera *Karl V* in Prague on June 22, 1938. His repertoire included about 18 operatic roles in 4 languages.

Ludkewycz, Stanislaus, significant Polish composer; b. Jaroslav, Austrian Galicia, Jan. 24, 1879; d. Lwow, Sept. 10, 1979, at the age of 100. He studied philosophy in Lemberg (Lwow), graduating in 1901; then went to Vienna, where he studied musical composition with Grädener and Zemlinsky at the Vienna Cons.; received his Dr.Phil. in 1908. He then settled in Lemberg. From 1910 to 1914 he served as director of the Inst. of Music there; then was recruited in the Austrian army, and was taken prisoner by the Russians (1915). After the Russian Revolution he was evacuated to Tashkent; liberated in 1918, he returned to Lwow; from 1939 to 1972, until the age of 93, he was a prof. of composition at the Cons. there. When the city was incorporated in the Ukrainian Soviet Republic after World War II, Ludkewycz was awarded the Order of the Red Banner by the Soviet government (1949). On the occasion of his 100th birthday in 1979 he received the Order of Hero of Socialist Labor. His music followed the precepts of European Romanticism, with the representational, geographic, and folkloric aspects in evidence. Stylistically, the influence of Tchaikovsky was paramount in his vocal and instrumental compositions.

Ludwig, August, German composer and musical journalist; b. Waldheim, Jan. 15, 1865; d. Dresden, April 9, 1946. He studied at the Cons. of Cologne, and later in Munich; brought out a number of orch. compositions, notably the overtures *Ad astra* and *Luther-Ouvertüre;* also a comic opera, *Kunst und Schein* (1906). From 1894 till 1903 he was editor of the *Neue Berliner Musikzeitung.* He publ. *Geharnischte Aufsätze über Musik* (a collection of essays); *Der Konzertagent* (1894); *Stachel und Lorbeer* (1897); *Zur Wertschätzung der Musik* (1898); *Tannhäuser redivivus* (1908). He attracted unfavorable attention by his abortive attempt to "complete" Schubert's "Unfinished" Symph., adding 2 movements, a *Philosophen-Scherzo,* and a *Schicksalsmarsch.*

Ludwig, Christa, remarkable German soprano; b. Berlin, March 16, 1928. She stemmed from a musical family; her father managed an opera; her mother sang. Christa Ludwig studied at the Hochschule für Musik in Frankfurt; in 1946 she made her opera debut in Frankfurt, in the role of Orlofsky in *Die Fledermaus.* In 1954 she sang the roles of Cherubino and Octavian at the Salzburg Festival; in 1955 was engaged by the Vienna State Opera. She made her artistic impact as a Wagnerian singer, and was equally successful in such disparate roles as Kundry in *Parsifal,* Fricka in *Das Rheingold,* Venus in *Tannhäuser,* and Magdalene in *Die Meistersinger.* She obtained brilliant success as the Marschallin in *Der Rosenkavalier,* and in other operas by Richard Strauss. In the Italian repertoire she gave fine interpretations of the roles of Amneris in *Aida,* Rosina in *The Barber of Seville,* and Lady Macbeth in Verdi's opera. Her career took her to opera theaters all over the world; she sang at La Scala in Milan, Covent Garden in London, the Teatro Colón in Buenos Aires, and the Nissei Theater in Tokyo. Sober-minded, skeptical music critics in Europe and America exerted their vocabularies to extol Christa Ludwig as a superb singer not only in opera but also in the art of German lieder; some even praised her physical attributes. In 1962 she was named Kammersängerin of Austria, and in 1969 she received the Cross of Merit, First Class, of the Republic of Austria. On Sept. 29, 1957 she married **Walter Berry,** the Austrian baritone; they frequently appeared in the same opera together; when she sang Carmen, Walter Berry was her conquering torero, Escamillo; they separated and in 1970 were divorced; in 1972 she married the French actor Paul-Emile Deiber, and became a French citizen.

Ludwig, Leopold, Austrian conductor; b. Witkowitz (Ostrava), Jan. 12, 1908; d. Lüneburg, April 25, 1979. He studied piano in Vienna; then conducted provincial theater orchs. in Austria and Germany, in Oldenburg (1936–39), at the Vienna Staatsoper (1939–43), and at the Städtische Oper in Berlin (1943–50). In 1951 he was appointed Generalmusikdirecktor of the Hamburg Staatsoper, and remained at this post until 1970; during his tenure there he introduced a number of new German operas, among them Krenek's *Pallas Athene weint* (1955) and Henze's *Der Prinz von Homburg* (1960). As guest conductor, Ludwig made special appearances in Edinburgh (1956) and San Francisco (1959). From 1968 until his death he taught at the Univ. of Hamburg.

Ludwig II, Bavarian king, royal patron of Wagner; b. in the Nymphenburg castle in Munich, Aug. 25, 1845; d. insane, by suicide, in the Starnberg Lake, June 13, 1886. As a crown prince he conceived an extreme adulation for Wagner, and when he became King, at 19, he declared his intention to sponsor all of Wagner's productions, an event that came at the most difficult time of Wagner's life, beset as he was by personal and financial problems. In sincere gratitude, Wagner spoke of his future plans of composition as "a program for the King." In his total devotion to Wagner, Ludwig converted his castle Neuschwanstein into a "worthy temple for my divine friend," installing in it architectural representations of scenes from Wagner's operas. His bizarre behavior caused the government of Bavaria to order a psychiatric examination of Ludwig, and he was eventually committed to an asylum near the Starnberg Lake. During a walk, he overpowered the psychiatrist escorting him, and apparently dragged him to his death in the lake, and drowned himself, too. Much material on Ludwig II is found in Wagner's bibliography; for a detailed account of his life see Wilfrid Blunt, *The Dream King, Ludwig II of Bavaria* (London, 1970).

Luening, Otto (Clarence), multifaceted American musician, composer, conductor, flutist, educator, and pioneer of electronic music; b. Milwaukee, June 15, 1900, of deeply rooted German ancestry, traceable to one Manfried von Lüninck, who flourished in 1350; one of Luening's maternal ancestors was said to be a descendant of Martin Luther's sister. Luening's great-grandfather emigrated to the U.S. in 1839 and settled in Wisconsin; he made the first barley beer in Milwaukee. Luening's paternal grandfather was American-born; he became active in bilingual culture in Wisconsin and was an organizer of the German-English Academy. Luening's father was an educated musician who received his training at the Leipzig Cons.; he had met Wagner and sung in performances of Beethoven's 9th Symph., with Wagner conducting; returning to Milwaukee, he became active in German-American music; he kept his cultural associations with Germany, and in 1912 took his family to Munich. There Otto Luening enrolled in the Akademie der Tonkunst; he studied flute with Alois Schellhorn, piano with Josif Becht, and composition with Beer-Walbrunn. He gave his first concert as a flutist in Munich on March 27, 1916. When America entered the war in 1917, Luening went to Switzerland, where he continued his musical education, studying with Philip Jarnach and Volkmar Andreae at the Zürich Cons.; he also had an opportunity to take private lessons with Busoni; pursuing his scientific interests, he attended a seminar in abnormal psychology at the Univ. of Zürich, and also appeared as an actor in the English Players Co. in Switzerland. He began to compose; his violin sonata and a sextet were performed at the Zürich Cons. Luening returned to the U.S. in 1920; he earned a living playing the flute in theater orchs. In 1925 he moved to Rochester, N.Y., where he served as coach and executive director of the opera dept. at the Eastman School of Music; in 1928 he went to Cologne; in 1930–31 he held a Guggenheim fellowship; in 1932–34 he was on the faculty of the Univ. of Arizona in Tucson. In 1934 he became chairman of the music dept. at Bennington College in Vermont, keeping this position until 1964; concurrently he also taught at Barnard College in N.Y.; in 1949 he joined the philosophy faculty at Columbia Univ., holding seminars in composition; retired in 1968 as prof. emeritus. While thus occupied, he continued to compose. His opera *Evangeline*, to his own libretto after Longfellow, which he completed in 1932 but revised numerous times, finally achieved production at Columbia Univ. on May 5, 1948, with Luening conducting; the opera received what is usually described as mixed reviews. As an inveterate flute blower, Luening used flutes in a number of his works; of these, the most self-indulgent was *Sonority Canon*, projecting a murmuration of innumerable flutes, written in 1962. He also was active as a conductor; he led the premiere of Menotti's opera *The Medium* in N.Y. on May 8, 1946, and of Virgil Thomson's *The Mother of Us All* in N.Y. on May 12, 1947.

An important development in Luening's career as a composer took place in 1952, when he began to experiment with the resources of the magnetic tape; he composed a strikingly novel piece, *Fantasy in Space*, in which he played the flute with its accompaniment electronically transmuted on tape; Stokowski conducted it in N.Y. on Oct. 28, 1952, along with Luening's 2 other electronic pieces, *Low

Speed* and *Invention*. He found a partner in Vladimir Ussachevsky, who was also interested in musical electronics. Together, they produced the first work that combined real sounds superinduced on an electronic background, *Rhapsodic Variations* for tape recorder and orch., performed by the Louisville Orch. on March 30, 1954; its performance anticipated by a few months the production of Varèse's similarly constructed work, *Déserts*. Another electronic work by Luening and Ussachevsky, *A Poem in Cycles and Bells* for tape recorder and orch., was played by the Los Angeles Phil. on Nov. 18, 1954; on March 31, 1960, Leonard Bernstein gave the first performance with the N.Y. Phil. of still another collaborative composition by Luening and Ussachevsky, *Concerted Piece* for tape recorder and orch. Thenceforth, Luening devoted a major part of his creative effort to an integration of electronic sound into the fabric of a traditional orch., without abondoning the fundamental scales and intervals; most, but not all, of these works were in collaboration with Ussachevsky. Unaided, he produced *Synthesis* for electronic tape and orch. (1960) and *Sonority Canon* (1962). He also wrote straightforward pieces without electronics; of these the most important is *A Wisconsin Symphony*, a sort of musical memoir of a Wisconsin-born composer; it was performed in Milwaukee, Luening's birthplace, on Jan. 4, 1976. His native state reciprocated proudly, awarding Luening an hononary doctorate from the Univ. of Wisconsin in Madison, a medal from the Wisconsin Academy of Sciences, Arts and Letters, and a citation from the Wisconsin State Assembly. Luening described his career, with its triumphs and disappointments, in an autobiography, *The Odyssey of an American Composer*, publ. in 1980.

WORKS: OPERA: *Evangeline*, to Luening's libretto after Longfellow's peom (1928–33; revised 1947; produced at Columbia Univ., N.Y., May 5, 1948, composer conducting). FOR ORCH.: Concertino for Flute and Chamber Orch. (1923; Philadelphia, Jan. 30, 1935); *First Symphonic Fantasia* (Rochester, N.Y., Nov. 25, 1925); *2 Symphonic Interludes* (1935; N.Y., April 11, 1936); *Preludes to a Hymn Tune*, after William Billings (N.Y., Feb. 1, 1937); *Kentucky Concerto* (1951); *Pilgrim's Hymn* (N.Y., Oct. 12, 1952); *Wisconsin Suite: Of Childhood Tunes Remembered* (1955); *2nd Symphonic Fantasia* (N.Y., Oct. 18, 1957); *Fantasia* for String Quartet and Orch. (1961); *Sonority Forms* (1973); *A Wisconsin Symphony* (Milwaukee, Jan. 4, 1976). CHAMBER MUSIC: Violin Sonata No. 1 (1917); Sextet for Flute, Clarinet, Horn, Violin, Viola, and Cello (1918); String Quartet No. 1 (1919–20); Sonatina for Flute and Piano (1919); Piano Trio (1921); Violin Sonata No. 2 (1922); String Quartet No. 2 (1923); Sonata No. 1 for Cello Solo (1924); *Serenade* for 3 Horns and Strings (1927); String Quartet No. 3 (1928); *Fantasia brevis* for Flute and Piano (1929); *Short Fantasy* for Violin and Horn (1930); *Mañana* for Violin and Piano (1933); *Fantasia brevis* for Violin, Viola, and Cello (1936); *Fantasia brevis* for Clarinet and Piano (1936); *Short Sonata* for Flute and Piano No. 1 (1937); *Short Fantasy* for Violin and Piano (1938);

Fuguing Tune for Woodwind Quintet (1938); *The Bass with the Delicate Air* for Flute, Oboe, Clarinet, and Bassoon (1940); Violin Sonata No. 2 (1943); Suite for Cello and Piano (1946); Suite for Flute Solo No. 1 (1947); *3 Nocturnes* for Oboe and Piano (1951); *Legend* for Oboe and Strings (1952); Trio for Flute, Violin, and Piano (1952); Sonata for Bassoon and Piano (1952); Suite for Flute Solo No. 2 (1953); Sonata for Trombone and Piano (1953); *Song, Poem and Dance* for Flute and Strings (1957); Sonata for Viola Solo (1958); Sonata No. 2 for Solo Cello (1958); Sonata No. 1 for Violin Solo (1958); *Lyric Scene* for Flute and Strings (1958); *3 Fantasias* for Guitar Solo (1960); Suite for Flute Solo No. 3 (1961); Trio for Flute, Cello, and Piano (1962); *Sonority Canon* for 2 to 37 Flutes (1962); 3 Duets for 2 Flutes (1962); Suite for Flute Solo No. 4 (1963); Duo for Violin and Viola (1963); *Short Sonata* for Flute and Piano No. 2 (1966); *Fantasia* for Cello Solo (1966); Trio for 3 Flutes (1966); Violin Sonata No. 3 (1966); *14 Easy Duets* for Recorders (1967); Sonata No. 2 for Violin Solo (1968); Suite for Flute Solo No. 5 (1969); Trio for Trumpet, Horn, and Trombone (1969); Sonata No. 3 for Violin Solo (1970); *8 Tone Poems* for 2 Violas (1971); *Short Sonata* No. 2 for Flute and Piano (1971); *Elegy for the Lonesome Ones* for 2 Clarinets and Strings (1974); *Prelude* for Flute, Clarinet, and Bassoon (1974); *Mexican Serenades* for Wind Instruments, Double Bass, and Percussion (1974); Suite for 2 Flutes and Piano (1976); *Canons* for 2 Violins and Flute (1976); *Fantasias on Indian Motives* for Flute Solo. FOR PIANO: *6 Short and Easy Piano Pieces* (1928); Dance Sonata (1929); *5 Intermezzi* (1932); 6 Piano Preludes (1935); 8 Preludes (1936); 8 Inventions (1938); *Short Sonata* No. 1 (1940); 10 Pieces for 5 Fingers (1946); *Gay Picture* (1957); *Short Sonata* No. 2 (1958); *Short Sonata* No. 3 (1958); *Short Sonata* No. 4 (1967); *Short Sonatas* Nos. 5, 6, 7 (1979). VOCAL MUSIC: *The Soundless Song* for Soprano, Instruments, Dancers, Light Projections (1923); *Alleluia* for Chorus (1944). ELECTRONIC MUSIC: *Fantasy in Space* for Flute and Electronic Tape (1952; N.Y., Oct. 28, 1952, Stokowski conducting); *Low Speed* for Flute and Electronic Tape (1952); *Invention in 12 Tones* for Flute and Tape (1952); electronic background music for *King Lear*, produced by Orson Welles (N.Y., Jan. 12, 1956); *Theatre Piece No. 2* for Electronic Tape, Voice, Brass, Percussion, and Narrator (choreographed by Doris Humphrey and José Limon; N.Y., April 20, 1956, composer conducting); also incidental music in electronics for a production of G.B. Shaw's *Back to Methuselah* (N.Y., March 5, 1958); *Gargoyles* for Violin Solo and Synthesized Sound (1960); *Synthesis* for Electronic Sound and Orch. (1960; Erie, Pa., Oct. 22, 1963); *Electronic Doubles of Choral Fantasy and Fugue* (1973). The following were produced in collaboration with Vladimir Ussachevsky: *Rhapsodic Variations* for Orch. and Electronic Tape, the first score ever composed which combined electronic sound with human musicians (Louisville, Ky., March 30, 1954; numerous subsequent perfs. in the U.S. and in Europe); *A Poem in Cycles and Bells* for Tape and Orch. (Los Angeles, Nov. 18, 1954); *Concerted Piece* for Tape Recorder and Orch. (N.Y., March 31, 1960).

Luigini, Alexandre (-Clément-Léon-Joseph), French composer; b. Lyons, March 9, 1850; d. Paris, July 29, 1906. He was the son of the Italian musician Giuseppe Luigini (1820–98), who conducted at the Théâtre-Italien in Paris; studied at the Paris Cons. with Massart (violin) and Massenet (composition); then entered his father's orch. at Lyons (1869) as a violinist, and began his very successful career as a ballet composer with the production of his first stage work, *Le Rêve de Nicette* (Lyons, 1870); in 1877 he became conductor at the Grand Théâtre at Lyons and a prof. of harmony at the Lyons Cons.; after 20 years there, went to Paris as conductor at the Opéra-Comique, where he remained till his death, except during 1903, when he conducted the orch. at the Théâtre-Lyrique. His greatest success as a composer came with the production of *Ballet égyptien* (Lyons, Jan. 13, 1875), still one of the most popular ballet scores; it was inserted, with Verdi's permission, in the 2nd act of *Aida* at its performance in Lyons in 1886. Other works: comic operas: *Les Caprices de Margot* (Lyons, 1877); *La Reine des fleurs* (Lyons, 1878); *Faublas* (Paris, 1881); ballets: *Ballet égyptien* (Lyons, 1875); *Anges et démons* (1876); *Les Noces d'Ivanovna* (1883); *Le Bivouac* (1889); *Les Echarpes* (1891); *Rayon d'or* (1891); *Rose et Papillon* (1891); *Le Meunier* (1892); *Arlequin écolier* (1894); *Dauritha* (1894); also *Romance symphonique* for Orch.; 3 string quartets (all won prizes); marches for orch.; numerous piano pieces.

Lully (or Lulli), Jean-Baptiste, celebrated Italian-born French composer; b. Florence, Nov. 28, 1632; d. Paris, March 22, 1687. The son of a poor Florentine miller, he was taught the elements of music by a Franciscan monk, and also learned to play the guitar, and later the violin. Attracted by his vivacious temperament and a talent for singing, the Chevalier de Guise took him to Paris in 1646 as a page to Mademoiselle d'Orléans, a young cousin of Louis XIV. He soon adapted himself to the ways and manners of the French court, and quickly mastered the language, although he could never rid himself of a pronounced Italian accent. The story that he was once a scullery boy is apocryphal, but he kept company with the domestic servants, and his talent as a violin player was first revealed by his improvisations in the royal kitchen; the Count de Nogent heard him, and secured for him a position in the private band of Mademoiselle d'Orléans. When he set to music a satirical poem reflecting on his patroness, he lost favor with her, but entered the service of young Louis XIV (1652), winning his first success as a ballet dancer. He contrived to obtain instruction on the harpsichord and in composition from Nicolas Métru, organist of St. Nicolas-des-Champs, and François Roberday, organist at the Eglise des Petits-Pères. He attended opera and concerts at the court, led by his compatriot Luigi Rossi, and conceived a passion for the theater, which became the determining factor of his entire career. After a brief association with the King's private orch., "les 24 violons du roi," he organized his own band of 17 instruments (later 21), "les petits violons," which he developed into a fine ensemble. He rose fast in royal favor; became a favorite composer of court ballets for various occasions; in several of these productions Louis XIV himself took part next to Lully, who danced and acted as "M. Baptiste." In 1661 he received the lucrative post of composer to the king, and in 1662, a further appointment as maître de musique of the royal family. In 1662 he married Madeleine Lambert, daughter of the court musician Michel Lambert. From 1663 to 1671 he wrote music for several comic ballets by Molière, including *Le Mariage forcé, L'Amour médecin,* and *Le Bourgeois Gentilhomme,* which foreshadowed the development of opéra-comique. In 1672 he obtained letters patent for the establishment of the Académie Royale de Musique (which eventually became the Grand Opéra), taking the privilege from Perrin and Cambert, who originally launched the enterprise in 1668. With the formation of a national opera house, Lully found his true calling, that of creating French operatic art, setting French texts to music with sensitivity to the genius of the language, and abandoning the conventional Italian type of opera, with its repetitive extensions of arias, endless fiorituras, etc. In the theater, Lully did not confine himself to the composer's functions, but also acted as director, stage manager, conductor, and even, upon occasion, machinist. From 1672 he worked in close cooperation with a congenial librettist, Quinault, who followed Lully's ideas with rare understanding. Lully developed a type of overture which became known as the "Lully overture" or "French overture" and of which the earliest example occurs in his ballet *Alcidiane* (1658); this type of overture opens with a slow, solemn, homophonic section with sharply dotted rhythms, followed by a fast section with some elements of imitation; frequently the overture ends with a return to the tempo and rhythm of the opening. In vocal writing, Lully demonstrated his mastery of both dramatic recitative and songful arias; he imparted dramatic interest to his choral ensembles; the instrumental parts were also given more prominence than in early Italian opera. That an Italian-born musician should have become the founder of French opera is one of the many paradoxes of music history. As a man, Lully was haughty, arrogant, and irascible, tolerating no opposition; his ambition was his prime counsellor; considerations of morality played a small part in his actions. With those in power, he knew how to be submissive; a shrewd courtier, he often gained his aims by flattery and obsequiousness; the manner in which he secured for himself the directorship of the Académie Royale de Musique, through the royal favorite Mme. de Montespan, moved some of his critics to berate him savagely. Yet, thanks to his volcanic energy and his disregard of all obstacles, he was able to accomplish an epoch-making task. His death resulted from a symbolic accident: while conducting, he vehemently struck his foot with a sharp-pointed cane used to pound out the beat; gangrene set in, and he died of blood poisoning.

WORKS: BALLETS (produced at court in Paris, Versailles, Saint-Germain, and Fontainebleau): *La Nuit* (Feb. 23, 1653); *Alcidiane* (Feb. 14, 1658); *La Raillerie* (Feb. 19, 1659); *L'Impatience* (Feb. 19, 1661); *Les Saisons* (July 30, 1661); *Hercule amoureux* (ballet music for Cavalli's opera *Ercole amante;* Feb. 7, 1662); *Les Arts* (Jan. 8, 1663); *Les Noces de village* (Oct. 3, 1663); *Le Mariage forcé* (Jan. 29, 1664); *Les Amours déguisés* (Feb. 15, 1664); *Les Plaisirs de l'isle enchantée* (May 8, 1664); *La Naissance de Vénus* (Jan. 26, 1665); *L'Amour médecin* (Sept. 15, 1665); *Les Muses* (Dec. 2, 1666); *Le Sicilien, ou L'Amour peintre* (Feb. 10, 1667); *Le Carnaval* (Jan. 18, 1668); *Georges Dandin* (July 18, 1668); *Flore* (Feb. 13, 1669); *Monsieur de Pourceaugnac* (Oct. 6, 1669); *Les Amants magnifiques* (Feb. 4, 1670); *Le Bourgeois Gentilhomme* (Oct. 14, 1670); *Psyché* (Jan. 17, 1671); *Le Triomphe de l'Amour* (Jan. 21, 1681).

OPERAS: *Les Fêtes de l'Amour et de Bacchus* (1672); *Cadmus et Hermione* (April 27, 1673); *Alceste, ou Le Triomphe d'Alcide* (Jan. 19, 1674); *Thésée* (Jan. 12, 1675); *Atys* (Jan. 10, 1676); *Isis* (Jan. 5, 1677); *Psyché* (a different work from the similarly named ballet; April 19, 1678); *Bellérophon* (Jan. 31, 1679); *Proserpine* (Feb. 3, 1680); *Persée* (April 18, 1682); *Phaéton* (Jan. 9, 1683); *Amadis de Gaule* (Jan. 18, 1684); *Roland* (Jan. 8, 1685); *Idylle sur la paix* (July 16, 1685); *Le Temple de la paix* (Oct. 20, 1685); *Armide et Renaud* (Feb. 15, 1686); *Acis et Galatée* (Sept. 17, 1686); *Achille et Polyxène* (Nov. 7, 1687). For further details about productions and revivals of Lully's operas, see A. Loewenberg, *Annals of Opera* (1943; new ed., 1955). Ten stage works produced at the French court between 1653 and 1657 had several numbers contributed by Lully. Most of Lully's operas have been publ. by Breitkopf & Härtel, in *Chefs-d'œuvre classiques de l'opéra français; Armide et Renaud* in Eitner's *Publikationen älterer Musikwerke* (vol. 14; full score, and a piano score). Besides his stage works, Lully wrote a Te Deum, a Miserere, a 4-part Mass a cappella, many motets; instrumental works (string trios, airs for violin, etc.). Henry Prunières undertook a complete ed. of Lully's works (9 vols., publ. 1930–39).

Lumbye, Hans Christian, Danish composer of light music; b. Copenhagen, May 2, 1810; d. there, March 20, 1874. He played in military bands as a youth; in 1839 formed his own orch., soon achieving fame as a conductor and composer of dance music, especially with his concerts in the Tivoli amusement park in Copenhagen. He composed about 400 pieces of dance music (waltzes, galops, polkas, marches, etc.), which earned him the sobriquet of "the Johann Strauss of the North." His 2 sons were also musicians; the elder, **Carl Lumbye** (b. Copenhagen, July 9, 1841; d. there, Aug. 10, 1911), was a violinist, conductor, and composer of dance music; the younger son, **Georg Lumbye** (b. Copenhagen, Aug. 26, 1843; d. there, Oct. 30, 1922), studied at the Paris Cons., conducted dance music in Copenhagen, wrote the operetta *Heksefløtjen* (*The Witch's Flute;* 1869) and numerous vaudevilles.

Lund, Signe, Norwegian composer; b. Oslo, April

15, 1868; d. there, April 6, 1950. She studied in Berlin, Copenhagen, and Paris; spent several years in America. As a composer, she was completely under the lyrical domination of Grieg's music, and her works are eminently perishable. She wrote a ceremonial overture, *The Road to France*, on the occasion of America's entry into World War I in 1917; also various instrumental pieces and songs. She publ. an autobiography, *Sol gjennem skyer* (Oslo, 1944).

Lundquist, Torbjörn, Swedish composer; b. Stockholm, Sept. 30, 1920. He studied composition with Dag Wirén; acquired proficiency on the accordion, and wrote many works for this popular instrument. In his music he followed the Romantic "Scandinavian" tradition; during his travels in the North he collected songs of Lapland, which he used in heterophonic counterpoint in some of his works. He also experimented with ultramodern techniques of "organized spontaneity."

Lunetta, Stanley G., American avant-garde composer; b. Sacramento, Calif., June 5, 1937. He received his B.A. at Sacramento State College and completed graduate work at the Univ. of Calif., Davis, where he studied composition with Larry Austin, Jerome Rosen, and Richard Swift; also took a course with Karlheinz Stockhausen when the latter lectured at Davis. In 1963 Lunetta formed the New Music Ensemble, devoted to contemporary music. His works explore the potentialities of electronic media; a major project is to build a computer capable of independent creative composition, both in ultramodern and infra-classical fields.

WORKS: His pieces, most of them for mixed media characterized by disestablishmentarian latitudinarianism, include *A Piece for Bandoneon and Strings* (1966); *Funkart* for Mixers, Lights, and Audiovisual Input Material (1967); *TA-TA* for Chorus, with Mailing Tubes (Santa Barbara, May 15, 1969); *I Am Definitely Not Running for Vice President* for Photocells, Modulators, and 4 Governors (1967); *TWOMANSHOW*, an evening of environmental theater (1968); *Spider-Song*, a comic book and a situation (in collaboration with Larry Austin, first demonstrated in N.Y., Dec. 17, 1968); *Mr. Machine* for Flute and Electronics (1969); an epithalamium for a married percussionist couple (1970). He was one of the editors of the fantastically screwed-up hyper-modern music magazine *Source,* publ. (where else?) in California.

Lunssens, Martin, Belgian conductor and composer; b. Molenbeek-Saint-Jean, April 16, 1871; d. Etterbeek, Feb. 1, 1944. He studied with Gevaert, Jehin, and Kufferath at the Brussels Cons., gaining the First Belgian Prix de Rome in 1895 with the cantata *Callirhoé;* then became a prof. at the Brussels Cons.; subsequently was director of the Music Academy at Courtrai (1905–16); at Charleroi (1916–21); at the Cons. of Louvain (1921–24); and finally at Ghent (from 1924). He was also known as an excellent conductor; was in charge of the Flemish Opera

in Antwerp, where he conducted many Wagner operas.

Lupu, Radu, Rumanian pianist; b. Galati, Nov. 30, 1945. After studies in his native country he was awarded a scholarship to continue his education at the Moscow Cons.; his teachers there included Heinrich Neuhaus and his son Sviatoslav. In quick succession he won first prize in the Van Cliburn (1966), Enesco (1967), and Leeds (1969) competitions. In 1972 he made his American debut as soloist with the Cleveland Orch., and subsequently played with the Chicago, Los Angeles, N.Y., and Boston orchs. In Europe he made successful appearances in Berlin, Paris, and Amsterdam in varied programs ranging from classical to modern works.

Lupus, Eduardus. See **Lobo, Duarte.**

Lupus (Latinized name of **De Wolf**), **Michael,** Flemish composer; b. c.1500; d. Lierre, July 15, 1567. Biographical data are scant, and identity uncertain. He had a prebend at Soignies in 1535; in the same year was named chaplain to the court of Charles V at Naples. Upon his return to the Netherlands, he received a new prebend at Lierre. He traveled with Charles V in Germany (1547–48); when the Emperor abdicated in 1555, Lupus lost his positions. Four motets by Lupus are found in Fuenllana's collection of 1554, and in Petrucci's *Motetti de la Corona* (1526).

Luther, Martin, great religious reformer; b. Eisleben, Nov. 10, 1483; d. there, Feb. 18, 1546. His reform of the church extended to the musical services, in which he took the deepest interest. After leaving the Wartburg, near Eisenach (March 22, 1522), he gave his ideas practical shape; his *Formula missae* (1523) and *Deutsche Messe* ("German Mass"; 1526; facsimile ed. by J. Wolf, Kassel, 1934) established the new service. He changed the order of the Mass; a German psalm took the place of the introit; the German Creed was substituted for the Latin Credo. The German Mass was sung for the first time in the Parish Church at Wittenberg on Christmas Day, 1524. Kapellmeister Conrad Rupsch and cantor Johann Walter aided Luther in organizing the musical part of the Mass. Walter states that Luther invented chorale melodies on the flute (he was an excellent flutist), and that these were noted down by Walter and Rupsch. It is impossible to establish with certainty which hymn tunes ascribed to Luther are really his; *Jesaia dem Propheten das geschah* is definitely Luther's; and the celebrated hymn tune *Ein' feste Burg ist unser Gott* is most probably authentic. Most important, the words of many chorales were written, arranged, or translated from Latin by Luther. In *Geschichte des Kirchenlieds* Koch gives a list of 36.

Lutoslawski, Witold, outstanding Polish composer; b. Warsaw, Jan. 25, 1913. He played piano and violin as a child; then took formal piano lessons with Lefeld (1932–36) and composition with Maliszewski (1932–37) at the Warsaw Cons. At the beginning of World War II he was in the Polish army; became a German prisoner of war, but got back to Warsaw; earned a living by playing piano in cafés and cabarets. After the war he dedicated himself to composition and teaching. His *renommée* soon reached the outside world; he received invitations to give seminars and to lecture in England, West Germany, Denmark, and Sweden; he gave a seminar at the Berkshire Music Center in Tanglewood in 1962; was composer-in-residence at Dartmouth College in Hanover, N.H., in 1966. He received numerous awards: 3 first mentions in the International Rostrum of Composers, UNESCO (1958, 1964, 1968); Grand Prix du Disque, Paris (1965); Ravel Prize, Paris (1971); Sibelius Prize, Helsinki (1973); was made an honorary member of the Free Academy of Arts in Hamburg (1966); extraordinary member of the Academy of Arts in West Berlin (1968); honorary member of the International Society for Contemporary Music (1969); associate member of the German Academy of Arts in East Germany (1970); corresponding member of the American Academy of Arts and Letters (1975) and Royal Academy of Music in London (1976). He received honorary D.Mus. degrees from the Cleveland Inst. of Music (1971) and the Univ. of Warsaw (1973), and an honorary degree of D.F.A. from Northwestern Univ. (1974). His early works are marked by a neo-Classical tendency, with an influx of national Polish motifs; gradually he turned to a more structural type of composition in which the melodic and rhythmic elements are organized into a strong unifying network, with occasional incursions of dodecaphonic and aleatory practices; the influence of Béla Bartók is felt in the constantly changing colors, angular intervallic progressions, and asymmetrical rhythms. In this respect, Lutoslawski's *Musique funèbre* for String Orch., dedicated to the memory of Béla Bartók, thematically built on a concatenation of upward tritones and downward semitones, is stylistically significant.

WORKS: For ORCH.: *Symphonic Variations* (1936–38; Cracow, June 17, 1939); 3 symphs.: No. 1 (1941–47; Katowice, April 6, 1948); No. 2 (1966–67; Katowice, June 9, 1967); No. 3 (1972–83; Chicago, Sept. 29, 1983); *Overture* for Strings (1949; Prague, Nov. 9, 1949); *Little Suite* for Chamber Orch. (1950; Warsaw, April 20, 1951); Concerto for Orch. (1950–54; Warsaw, Nov. 26, 1954); *5 Dance Preludes* for Clarinet, Harp, Piano, Percussion, and Strings (1955; a version for Nonet, 1959); *Musique funèbre* for String Orch., in memory of Béla Bartók (1958; Katowice, March 26, 1958); *3 Postludes:* No. 1 for the centennial of the International Red Cross (1958); No. 2 (1960); No. 3 (1960); *Jeux vénitiens* (1961; Venice, April 24, 1961); *Livre* (The Hague, Nov. 18, 1968; individual movements are called Chapters); Cello Concerto (1970; London, Oct. 14, 1970; Rostropovich, soloist); *Mi-parti* (Rotterdam, Oct. 22, 1976); *Novelette* for Orch. (1979; Washington, D.C., Jan. 29, 1980); Double Concerto for Oboe, Harp, and Chamber Orch. (Lucerne Festival, Aug. 24, 1980). CHAMBER MUSIC: Trio for Oboe, Clarinet, and Bassoon (1945); *Recitativo e Arioso* for Violin and Piano (1951); 5

Folk Melodies for Strings (1952); *Bucoliche,* 5 pieces for Viola and Piano (1952); *Preludia taneczne* for Clarinet and Piano (1954); String Quartet (1964); *Preludes and Fugue* for 13 Solo Strings (1971; Festival of the International Society for Contemporary Music, Graz, Oct. 22, 1972). VOCAL WORKS: *Belated Nightingale* and *Mr. Tralala,* 2 songs for Voice and Orch. (1947); *A Straw Chain* for Soprano, Mezzo-soprano, Flute, Oboe, 2 Clarinets, and Bassoon (1951); *Silesian Triptych* for Soprano and Orch. (Warsaw, Dec. 2, 1951); *5 Songs* for Female Voice and 30 Solo Instruments (1958); *3 poèmes d'Henri Michaux* for Choir, Wind Instruments, Percussion, 2 Pianos, and Harp (Zagreb, May 9, 1963; perf. requires 2 conductors reading from separate scores); *Paroles tissées* for Tenor, String Ensemble, Harp, Piano, and Percussion (Aldeburgh [England] Festival, June 20, 1965); *Les Espaces du sommeil* for Baritone and Orch. (1975; Berlin, March 12, 1978); piano pieces.

Lutyens, Elisabeth, important and remarkably prolific English composer; b. London, July 9, 1906; d. Hampstead, April 14, 1983. She was a daughter of the noted architect Sir Edwin Lutyens, and was brought up in an atmosphere of cultural enlightenment. She studied composition with Harold Darke and viola with Ernest Tomlinson at the Royal College of Music in London (1926–30); then went to Paris and took lessons with Caussade. In her vivid autobiography, *A Goldfish Bowl* (London, 1972), she recounted her search for a congenial idiom of musical expression, beginning with the erstwhile fashionable Romantic manner and progressing toward a more individual, psychologically tense writing in an atonal technique using a sui generis dodecaphonic method of composition. In 1969 she received the honorary title of Commander of the Order of the British Empire.

WORKS: FOR THE STAGE: *The Pit,* dramatic scene for Tenor, Bass, Women's Chorus, and Orch. (Palermo, April 24, 1949); *Penelope,* radio opera (1950); *Infidelio,* chamber opera (1956; London, April 17, 1973); *The Numbered,* an opera (1965–67); "a charade in 4 acts and 3 interruptions," *Time Off? Not a Ghost of a Chance* (1967–68; Sadler's Wells, London, March 1, 1972); *Isis and Osiris,* lyric drama for 8 Voices and Chamber Orch. (1969); *The Linnet from the Leaf,* musical theater for 5 Singers and 2 Instrumental Groups (1972); *The Waiting Game,* 5 scenes for Mezzo-soprano, Baritone, and Chamber Orch. (1973); *One and the Same,* scena for Soprano, Speaker, and Mimes (1973); *The Goldfish Bowl,* ballad opera (1975); *Like a Window,* extracts from letters of Van Gogh (1976); ballet, *The Birthday of the Infanta* (London, 1932).

FOR ORCH.: *3 Pieces* (1939); 6 chamber concertos, some with Solo Instruments (1939–48); *3 Symphonic Preludes* (1942); Viola Concerto (1947); *Music I* (1954); *Music II* (1962); *Music III* (1964); *Quincunx* (1960); *En voyage,* symph. suite (London, July 2, 1960); *Symphonies* for Piano, Wind Instruments, Harps, and Percussion (London, July 28, 1961); *Music* for Piano and Orch. (1964); *Novenaria* (1967);

Plenum II for Oboe and Chamber Orch. (London, June 14, 1974); *The Winter of the World* for Cello and Chamber Ensemble (London, May 5, 1974); *Eos* for Chamber Orch. (1975); *Rondel* (1976); *6 Bagatelles* for Chamber Orch. (1976); *Nox* for Piano and 2 Chamber Orchs. (1977); *Wild Decembers* (1980); *Music for Orchestra IV* (1981).

Luxon, Benjamin, English baritone; b. Redruth, March 24, 1937. He was educated at the Guildhall School of Music in London; made his debut with the English Opera Group in 1963. He gained wide recognition for his performance of the title role in Britten's television opera *Owen Wingrave,* produced in London by the BBC on May 16, 1971. From 1972 he sang at Covent Garden; also appeared at the Glyndebourne and Edinburgh festivals. On Feb. 2, 1980, he sang the title role in Tchaikovsky's *Eugene Onegin* at his Metropolitan Opera debut in N.Y.

Luython, Charles, Flemish composer; b. Antwerp, c.1556; d. Prague, 1620. After receiving elementary training as a chorister in his native land, he was sent, at the age of 10, to the Imperial Chapel in Vienna, where he remained until he was 15. He wrote 2 masses for Emperor Maximilian II; in 1582 was appointed court organist by Rudolph II, for whom he wrote a book of madrigals (publ. by Gardano in Venice). He remained with Rudolph II at his residence in Prague; in 1603 became successor to Philippe de Monte as court composer while continuing to hold his post as court organist. He retired from the service in 1611. Apart from his book of madrigals (Venice, 1582), he publ. *Sacrae cantiones* for 6 Voices (Prague, 1603); *Lamentationes* for 6 Voices (Prague, 1604); 9 masses for 3–7 Voices (Prague, 1609). Among his extant works for instruments, there is a *Fuga suavissima* (publ. in Woltz's *Tabulatur-Buch,* 1617). Luython was a composer of considerable ingenuity; Michael Praetorius recounts in his *Syntagma musicum* that Luython owned a keyboard instrument with 3 manuals, representing the diatonic, chromatic, and enharmonic intervals (18 notes to the octave), thus securing theoretically correct modulations through sharps or flats.

Luzzaschi, Luzzasco, Italian composer; b. Ferrara, 1545; d. there, Sept. 11, 1607. He studied with Cypriano de Rore as a child (until 1558); became a singer at the Este court in 1561; was first organist there from 1564; also directed one of the orchs., composed, and taught there; was also organist at the Ferrara Cathedral and at the Accademia della Morte; later was director of Duke Alfonso's private musica da camera. He attained great renown as a teacher; Frescobaldi was one of his many pupils.
  WORKS: 7 books of madrigals for 5 Voices, of which 5 are extant (1571–1604); *Sacrae cantiones* for 5 Voices (1598); madrigals for one to 3 sopranos, with keyboard accompaniment (1601). Diruta's collection *Il Transilvano* contains an organ toccata and 2 ricercari by Luzzaschi; the toccata is reprinted in Ritter's *Zur Geschichte des Orgelspiels;* a 4-part *Canzon da sonar* is given in Rauerij's collection (1608); the accompanied madrigal *Ch'io non t'ami,* in Otto Kinkeldey's *Orgel und Klavier in der Musik des 16. Jahrhunderts* (Leipzig, 1910; p. 291). Other reprints are found in L. Torchi's *L'arte musicale in Italia* (vol. 4), in Riemann's *Musikgeschichte in Beispielen* (no. 73), and in Schering's *Geschichte der Musik in Beispielen* (no. 166).

Lvov, Alexei, Russian violinist and composer, author of the Russian national anthem under the Czars; b. Reval, June 5, 1798; d. Romano, near Kovno, Dec. 28, 1870. He was the son of the director of the Imperial Court Chapel in St. Petersburg; received his primary education at home; attended the Inst. of Road Engineering (graduated in 1818); at the same time studied violin. In 1827 he was sent to the Turkish front in Bulgaria; then was attached to the court. He wrote the national anthem *God Save the Czar* in 1833, and it was first performed in Moscow on the name day of Czar Nicholas I, on Dec. 6 (18), 1833; it remained the official anthem until the Revolution of 1917. In 1837 he succeeded his father as director of the Imperial Chapel (until 1861); in 1839 he organized instrumental classes there; edited a collection of services for the entire ecclesiastical year of the Greek Orthodox Church. In 1840 he traveled in Europe; played his Violin Concerto with the Gewandhaus Orch. in Leipzig (Nov. 8, 1840); Schumann greatly praised his playing. Returning to Russia, he established a series of orch. concerts in St. Petersburg, presenting classical programs. Growing deafness forced him to abandon his activities in 1867. As a composer, he slavishly followed the Italian school.

Lyford, Ralph, American composer; b. Worcester, Mass., Feb. 22, 1882; d. Cincinnati, Sept. 3, 1927. He began to study piano and violin as a child; entered the New England Cons. in Boston at 12, studying piano with Helen Hopekirk, organ with Goodrich, and composition with Chadwick; then went to Leipzig to study conducting with Artur Nikisch (1906). Returning to America, he became assistant conductor of the San Carlo Opera Co. (1907–8); then was with the Boston Opera Co. (1908–14). In 1916 he settled in Cincinnati, where he taught at the Cons., and also conducted the summer seasons of opera at the Zoölogical Gardens there; in 1925 he became associate conductor of the Cincinnati Symph. Orch.
  WORKS: Opera, *Castle Agrazant* (Cincinnati, April 29, 1926; won the David Bispham Medal); Piano Concerto (1917); chamber music; songs.

Lyman, Howard Wilder, American voice teacher; b. Lancaster, Mass., Feb. 2, 1879; d. Herkimer, N.Y., Feb. 27, 1980, at the age of 101. He studied at the New England Cons., graduating in 1909; was for many years on the music faculty at the Univ. of Syracuse (1912–45) and concurrently director of music at the Methodist church there (1926–53). In his extreme old age he took shelter at the Folts Home in Herkimer.

Lympany, Moura, English pianist; b. Saltash, Aug. 18, 1916. She was educated at the Royal Academy of Music in London; also studied in Vienna with Paul Weingarten; then returned to England for further training with Mathilda Verne and Tobias Matthay. In 1938 she won second prize in the Ysaÿe Competition in Brussels; subsequently she developed an international career; made her American debut in 1948. In her programs she championed works by British composers; in 1969 she performed the Piano Concerto by Cyril Scott on the occasion of his 90th birthday, with the composer himself present and joining in appreciative applause. In 1979 she was made a Commander of the Order of the British Empire.

Lyne, Felice, American soprano; b. Slater, Mo., March 28, 1887; d. Allentown, Pa., Sept. 1, 1935. Her family moved to Allentown when she was a child; she studied there with F.S. Hardman; then in Paris with Mme. Marchesi, J. de Reszke, and L. d'Aubigne. She made a successful debut as Gilda in *Rigoletto* at Hammerstein's London Opera (Nov. 25, 1911), and appeared there 36 times that season, creating the principal soprano parts in the English premieres of Massenet's *Don Quichotte* and *Jongleur de Notre-Dame,* and Holbrooke's *Children of Don;* toured with the Quinlan Opera Co. Returning to the U.S., she became a member of the Boston Opera Co.; also appeared in concerts.

Lyon, James, early American composer; b. Newark, N.J., July 1, 1735; d. Machias, Maine, Oct. 12, 1794. He graduated from the College of New Jersey at Princeton in 1759; in 1764, accepted a pastorate in Nova Scotia; then in Machias, Maine (1772 until his death). The *N.Y. Mercury* of Oct. 1, 1759, speaks of an ode composed by Lyon, a member of the graduating class of Princeton, and mentions its performance at the graduation exercises on Sept. 26; but the music of this work, written in the same year that Hopkinson wrote his first songs, is lost. The first known compositions of Lyon are 6 psalm tunes publ. by him in the collection *Urania* (Philadelphia, 1761; facsimile reproduction, with introduction by R. Crawford, N.Y., 1973); he also wrote settings of 2 poems by Watts, *A Marriage Hymn* and *Friendship,* and of Psalms 8, 17, 19, 23, 95, 104, and 150.

Lyra, Justus Wilhelm, German cleric and song composer; b. Osnabrück, March 23, 1822; d. Gehrden, Dec. 30, 1882. He studied philosophy and theology in Berlin; filled various church offices in Germany; eventually became "pastor primarious" at Gehrden and Hannover. As a student, he wrote many scholastic songs, which became very popular in German univs. (e.g., *Der Mai ist gekommen, Durch Feld und Buchenhallen, Zwischen Frankreich und dem Böhmerwald, Meine Mus' ist gegangen*); he also wrote church music (Christmas cantata, 1872); publ. 5 books of songs, ranging from one voice to mixed chorus; *Die liturgischen Altarweisen des lutherischen Hauptgottesdienstes* (1873); *Andreas Ornithoparchus und dessen Lehre von den Kirchenakzenten* (Gütersloh, 1877); *Luthers Deutsche Messe* (posthumously publ., 1904).

Lysberg, Charles-Samuel. See **Bovy-Lysberg, Charles-Samuel.**

M

Ma, Yo-Yo, remarkable Chinese cellist; b. Paris, Oct. 7, 1955. He first studied with his father; then came to America to study with Leonard Rose at the Juilliard School of Music in N.Y. His rise on the violoncellistic firmament was spectacular; he was unreservedly praised for his unostentatious musicianship, for the freedom of his technical resources, and for the unforced tone of his melodious lyricism. He appeared with equal success as a soloist with American and European orchs. and as a chamber music player, commending himself as a foremost cello virtuoso.

Maag, Peter, distinguished Swiss conductor; b. St. Gallen, May 10, 1919. His father was the Lutheran minister and educated musician Otto Maag; his mother played violin in the Capet Quartet. After studying music at home, he went to the univs. of Zürich, Basel, and Geneva; among his teachers were Karl Barth in theology and Karl Jaspers in philosophy. He studied piano and music theory with Czeslaw Marek in Zürich; then went to Paris, where he had private lessons with Cortot; he studied conducting with Franz von Hoesslin and Ernest Ansermet in Geneva. He began his professional career as répétiteur and chorus master at the town theater in Biel-Solothurn. In 1952 he was appointed first con-

ductor of the Düsseldorf Opera under the directorship of Eugen Szenkar; from 1955–59 he was Generalmusikdirektor of the Bonn Opera; from 1964–68, chief conductor of the Vienna Volksoper; in 1972–74, artistic director of the Teatro Regio in Parma; held a similar post with the Teatro Regio in Turin from 1974–76. He conducted at Covent Garden in London in 1958. He made his U.S. debut in 1959 as a guest conductor of the Cincinnati Symph. Orch.; in 1961 conducted at the Chicago Lyric Opera. On Sept. 23, 1972, he made his Metropolitan Opera debut in N.Y. conducting *Don Giovanni;* was guest conductor with the Boston Symph., Detroit Symph., and National Symph. of Washington, D.C. He also toured South America and Japan.

Maas, Louis (Philipp Otto), composer and pianist; b. Wiesbaden, Germany, June 21, 1852; d. Boston, Sept. 17, 1889. He studied with Reinecke and Papperitz at the Leipzig Cons. (1867–71), and for 3 summers with Liszt. From 1875–80 he taught at the Leipzig Cons.; in 1880 he emigrated to the U.S., settling in Boston; conducted the Boston Phil. Concerts (1881–82). As a token of gratitude to his adoptive country, he wrote an "American Symphony," *On the Prairies,* dedicated to President Chester A. Arthur, which he conducted in Boston, Dec. 14, 1882.

This symph., Germanic in form and harmonic language, contained some Indian themes. Maas further wrote overtures, suites, marches, fantasias, etc., for orch.; a String Quartet; a Piano Concerto; 3 sonatas, 3 impromptus, and 12 *Phantasiestücke* for Piano; violin sonatas; and songs.

Maazel, Lorin, brilliant American conductor; b. Neuilly, France, March 6, 1930, of American parents. They took him to Los Angeles when he was an infant. At a very early age he showed innate musical ability; he had perfect pitch and could assimilate music osmotically; he began to study violin at age 5 with Karl Moldrem, and then piano at age 7 with Fanchon Armitage. Fascinated by the mysterious art of conducting, he went to symph. concerts and soon began to take lessons in conducting with Vladimir Bakaleinikov, who was an associate conductor of the Los Angeles Phil.; on July 13, 1938, at the age of 8, he was given a chance to conduct a performance of Schubert's *Unfinished Symphony* with the visiting Univ. of Idaho orch. In 1938 Bakaleinikov was appointed assistant conductor of the Pittsburgh Symph. Orch., and the Maazel family followed him to Pittsburgh. From Bakaleinikov, Lorin Maazel quickly learned to speak Russian. On Aug. 18, 1939, he made a sensational appearance in N.Y. conducting the National Music Camp Orch. of Interlochen at the World's Fair, eliciting the inevitable jocular comments (he was compared to a trained seal). Maazel was 11 when he conducted the NBC Symph. Orch. (1941) and 12 when he led an entire program with the N.Y. Phil. (1942). He survived these traumatic exhibitions, and took academic courses at the Univ. of Pittsburgh; in 1948 he joined the Pittsburgh Symph. Orch. as a violinist, and at the same time was appointed its apprentice conductor. In 1952 he received a Fulbright fellowship for travel in Italy, where he undertook a serious study of Baroque music; he also made his adult debut as a conductor in Catania on Dec. 24, 1953. On Feb. 20, 1955, he conducted at the Florence Music Festival; in 1956 he was guest conductor in Argentina; in 1957 he led the Vienna Festival; in 1958 he conducted at the Edinburgh Festival. In 1960 he became the first American to conduct at the Bayreuth Festival, where he led 8 performances of *Lohengrin.* In 1962 he toured the U.S. with the Orchestre National de France; on Nov. 1, 1962, he made his Metropolitan Opera debut in N.Y. in *Don Giovanni*, conducting it from memory. In the summer of 1963 he made a tour of Russia, conducting concerts in Moscow and Leningrad. From 1965 to 1971 he was artistic director of the Deutsche Oper in West Berlin; from 1965 to 1975 also served as chief conductor of the West Berlin Radio Symph. Orch. He was associate principal conductor of the New Philharmonia Orch. of London from 1970 to 1972, and its principal guest conductor from 1976 to 1980. In 1972 he became music director of the Cleveland Orch., a position he held with great distinction until 1982; was then made conductor emeritus. He led the Cleveland Orch. on 10 major tours abroad, including Australia and New Zealand (1973), Japan (1974),

twice in Latin America, and twice in Europe, and maintained its stature as one of the world's foremost orchs. He was also chief conductor of the Orchestre National de France from 1977 to 1982; then became its principal guest conductor. In 1980 he became conductor of the famous Vienna Phil. New Year's Day Concerts. In 1982 he assumed the positions of artistic director and general manager of the Vienna State Opera, the first American to be so honored.

Maazel is equally adept as an interpreter of operatic and symph. scores; he is blessed with a phenomenal memory, and possesses an extraordinary baton technique. He also maintains an avid interest in nonmusical pursuits; a polyglot, he is fluent in French, German, Italian, Spanish, Portuguese, and Russian. He was married twice; first in 1952, to the Brazilian-American pianist Miriam Sandbank, and, after their divorce in 1969, to the Israeli pianist Israela Margit. Maazel was the recipient of many awards; he received an honorary doctorate from the Univ. of Pittsburgh in 1965, the Sibelius Prize in Finland, the Commander's Cross of the Order of Merit from West Germany, and, for his numerous recordings, the Grand Prix de Disque in Paris and the Edison Prize in the Netherlands.

Mabellini, Teodulo, Italian composer; b. Pistoia, April 2, 1817; d. Florence, March 10, 1897. He studied with Pilotti in his native town, and then at the Istituto Reale Musicale at Florence; at the age of 19, he produced there an opera, *Matilda a Toledo* (Aug. 27, 1836), which made so favorable an impression that Grand Duke Leopold II gave him a stipend to study with Mercadante at Novara. His 2nd opera, *Rolla* (Turin, Nov. 12, 1840), was no less successful; thereupon he wrote many more operas, among them *Ginevra degli Almieri* (Turin, Nov. 13, 1841), *Il Conte di Lavagna* (Florence, June 4, 1843), *I Veneziani a Costantinopoli* (Rome, 1844), *Maria di Francia* (Florence, March 14, 1846), and *Fiammetta* (Florence, Feb. 12, 1857). He also wrote several effective oratorios and cantatas: *Eudossia e Paolo* (Florence, 1845), *Etruria* (Florence, August 5, 1849), *Lo spirito di Dante* (Florence, May 15, 1865), and a patriotic hymn, *Italia risorta* (Florence, Sept. 12, 1847); *Grande fantasia* for Flute, Clarinet, Horn, Trumpet, and Trombone; sacred works for chorus and orch. He lived in Florence from 1843 until his death; conducted the concerts of the Società Filarmonica (1843–59); taught composition at the Istituto Reale Musicale (1859–87).

Macbeth, Florence, American coloratura soprano; b. Mankato, Minn., Jan. 12, 1891; d. Hyattsville, Md., May 5, 1966. She studied in Europe; in 1913 made her operatic debut as Rosina in *Il Barbiere di Siviglia* in Braunschweig, Germany. On Jan. 14, 1914, she made her American debut with the Chicago Opera Co. and remained on its staff as prima coloratura soprano until 1930; for a season she undertook an American tour with the Commonwealth Opera Co., singing in Gilbert and Sullivan operettas. So melodious and mellifluous were her fiorituras that she was dubbed the "Minnesota Nightingale." In 1947 she married the novelist James M. Cain and settled in Maryland.

MacCunn, Hamish, Scottish composer and conductor; b. Greenock, March 22, 1868; d. London, Aug. 2, 1916. He studied at the Royal College of Music (1883–86) with Parry; then taught at the Royal Academy of Music (1888–94); in 1898, became conductor of the Carl Rosa Opera Co.; from 1900 to 1905 conducted at the Savoy Theatre; later he toured with various troupes, conducting light opera.

WORKS: Operas: *Jeanie Deans,* after Scott's *The Heart of Midlothian* (Edinburgh, Nov. 15, 1894); *Diarmid* (London, Oct. 23, 1897); *The Masque of War and Peace* (London, Feb. 13, 1900); *The Golden Girl,* musical comedy (Birmingham, Aug. 5, 1905); cantatas: *Lord Ullin's Daughter,* after Walter Scott (London, Feb. 18, 1888); *Bonny Kilmeny* (Edinburgh, Dec. 15, 1888); *The Lay of the Last Minstrel* (Glasgow, Dec. 18, 1888); *The Cameronian's Dream* (Edinburgh, Jan. 27, 1890); *Queen Hynde of Caledon* (Glasgow, Jan. 28, 1892); *The Wreck of the Hesperus,* after Longfellow (London, Aug. 28, 1905); overtures: *Cior Mhor* (London, Oct. 27, 1885); *The Land of the Mountain and the Flood,* after Scott (London, Nov. 5, 1887); *The Ship o' the Fiend* (London, Feb. 21, 1888); *The Dowie Dens o' Yarrow* (London, Oct. 13, 1888); *Highland Memories,* orch. sketch (London, March 13, 1897); *Scotch Dances* for Piano; songs; etc.

MacDermid, James G., American pianist, vocalist, and composer; b. Utica, Ontario, June 10, 1875; d. Brooklyn, Aug. 16, 1960. He studied in London, Ontario; in 1893 went to Chicago for further studies, and remained in the U.S.; became an American citizen in 1906; for several seasons toured as accompanist to his wife, **Sibyl Sammis MacDermid,** soprano (b. Foreston, Ill., May 15, 1876; d. New York, Nov. 2, 1940). He publ. about 75 sacred and secular songs.

MacDonald, Hugh, English musicologist; b. Newbury, Berkshire, Jan. 31, 1940. He was educated at Pembroke College, Cambridge (B.A., 1961; M.A., 1965; Ph.D., 1969); in 1966 he became a lecturer at Cambridge Univ., then at Oxford Univ. in 1971; in 1979 he was a visiting prof. at Indiana Univ. in Bloomington; in 1980 he was named Gardiner Prof. of Music at Glasgow Univ. His special field of interest is 19th-century music; he is particularly noted for his studies in French music, and is a leading authority on the life and works of Berlioz; in 1965 he became general editor of the *New Berlioz Edition.* He publ. *Berlioz: Orchestral Music* (London, 1969) and *Skryabin* (London, 1978).

MacDowell, Edward Alexander, greatly significant national American composer; b. New York, Dec. 18, 1860; d. (insane) there, Jan. 23, 1908. His father was a Scotch-Irish tradesman; his mother, an artistically inclined woman who encouraged MacDowell's musical studies. He took piano lessons with one Juan Buitrago and later with Paul Desver-

nine. In 1876, after traveling in Europe with his mother, MacDowell enrolled as an auditor in Augustin Savard's elementary class at the Paris Cons.; on Feb. 8, 1877, he was admitted as a regular student; also studied piano with Antoine-François Marmontel, and solfège with Marmontel's son. Somewhat disappointed with his progress, he withdrew from the Cons. on Sept. 30, 1878, and went to Germany for further study; there he took private lessons with Louis Ehlert, a pupil of Mendelssohn, in Wiesbaden; in 1879 he enrolled at the newly founded but already prestigious Hoch Cons. in Frankfurt as a student of Carl Heymann in piano, and in composition with the director of the school, the illustrious teacher and composer Joachim Raff. During MacDowell's stay there, Raff's class had a visit from Liszt, and MacDowell performed the piano part in Schumann's Quintet, op. 44, in Liszt's presence. At another visit, MacDowell played Liszt's *Hungarian Rhapsody* No. 14 for him; 2 years later MacDowell visited Liszt in Weimar, and played his own First Piano Concerto for him, accompanied by Eugène d'Albert at the 2nd piano. Encouraged by Liszt's interest, MacDowell sent him the MS of his *Modern Suite,* op. 10, for piano solo; Liszt recommended the piece for performance at the meeting of the Allgemeiner Deutscher Musikverein held in Zürich on July 11, 1882; Liszt also recommended MacDowell to the publishers Breitkopf & Härtel, and the firm brought out the first works of MacDowell to appear in print, the *Modern Suites* for piano, opp. 10 and 14. Despite his youth, MacDowell was given a teaching position at the Darmstadt Cons.; he also accepted private pupils; among them was Marian Nevins of Connecticut; they were married on July 9, 1884. During the early years of their marriage, the MacDowells made their 2nd home in Wiesbaden, where MacDowell composed industriously; his works were performed in neighboring communities; the famous pianist Teresa Carreño put several of his piano pieces on her concert programs. There were also performances in America. However, the MacDowells were beset by financial difficulties; his mother offered him help, but he declined her proposed plan for him and his wife to live on the family property. MacDowell also declined an offer to teach at the National Cons. in N.Y. at a munificent fee of $5 an hour. Similarly, he rejected an offer to take a clerical position at the American Consulate in Crefeld, Germany. In 1888 he finally returned to the U.S. for good, and was welcomed in artistic circles as a famous composer and pianist; musical America at the time was virtually a German colony, and MacDowell's German training was a certificate of his worth. The Boston Symph. conductors Gericke, Nikisch, and Paur, all Germans, played his orch. works. On Nov. 19, 1888, MacDowell made his American debut as a composer and pianist at a N.Y. concert of the Kneisel String Quartet, featuring his *Modern Suite,* op. 10. On March 5, 1889, he was the soloist with the N.Y. Phil. in his 2nd Piano Concerto, under the direction of the famous German musician Theodore Thomas, in its world premiere. Then Frank van den Stucken invited MacDowell to play his concerto at the spectacular Paris Exposition on July 12, 1889. MacDowell had no difficulty having his works publ., although for some reason he preferred to have his early piano pieces printed under the pseudonym **Edgar Thorn.** When Columbia Univ. established its music dept. in 1896, MacDowell was offered a position as the first incumbent, being cited as "the greatest musical genius America has produced." Unfortunately, mutual disenchantment soon developed between MacDowell and the univ. authorities, and in 1904 he resigned his post. It is idle to speculate as to whether this event was a contributing cause of MacDowell's mental deterioration; he was already showing signs of depression: extreme irritability and gradual loss of vital functions; he eventually lapsed into total insanity. He spent the last years of his life in a childlike state, unaware of his surroundings. In 1906 a public appeal was launched to raise funds for MacDowell's care; among the signers were Horatio Parker, Victor Herbert, Arthur Foote, George Chadwick, Frederick Converse, Andrew Carnegie, J. Pierpont Morgan, and former President Grover Cleveland. MacDowell was only 47 years old when he died. The sum of $50,000 was raised for the organization of the MacDowell Memorial Assoc. Mrs. MacDowell, who outlived her husband by nearly half a century (she died at the age of 99, in 1956), deeded to the association her husband's summer residence at Peterborough, N.H. This property became a pastoral retreat, under the name of the MacDowell Colony, for American composers and writers, who could spend summers working undisturbed in separate cottages, paying a minimum rent for lodgings and food. During the summer of 1910, Mrs. MacDowell arranged an elaborate pageant with music from MacDowell's works; the success of this project led to the establishment of a series of MacDowell Festivals at Peterborough.

Among American composers, MacDowell occupies a historically important place as the first American whose works were accepted as comparable in quality and technique with those of the average German composers of his time. His music adhered to the prevalent representative Romantic art. Virtually all of his works bear titles borrowed from mythical history, literature, or painting; even his piano sonatas, set in Classical forms, carry descriptive titles—Tragica, Eroica, Norse, Keltic—indicative of the mood of melodic resources, or as an ethnic reference. MacDowell lived in Germany during his formative years, and German musical culture was decisive in shaping his musical development; even the American rhythms and melodies in his music seem to be European reflections of an exotic art. A parallel with Grieg is plausible, for Grieg was also a regional composer trained in Germany. But Grieg possessed a much more vigorous personality, and he succeeded in communicating the true spirit of Norwegian song modalities in his works. Lack of musical strength and originality accounts for MacDowell's gradual decline in the estimation of succeeding generations; MacDowell's romanticism was apt to lapse into salon sentimentality. The frequency of performance of his works in concert (he

never wrote for the stage) declined in the decades following his death, and his influence on succeeding generations of American composers receded to a faint recognition of an evanescent artistic period.

WORKS (opp. 1–7 were publ. under the pseudonym Edgar Thorn): FOR ORCH.: *Hamlet and Ophelia,* symph. poem, op. 22 (1885; Boston Symph., Jan. 27, 1893); *Lancelot and Elaine,* symph. poem, op. 25 (1888; Boston Symph., Jan. 10, 1890); *Lamia,* symph. poem, op. 29 (1889; Boston Symph., Oct. 23, 1908); *The Saracens* and *The Lovely Alda,* 2 symph. poems, op. 30 (Boston Phil., Nov. 5, 1891); Suite No. 1 for Orch., op. 42 (Worcester Festival, Sept. 24, 1891); Suite No. 2, *Indian Suite* (N.Y., Jan. 23, 1895; Boston Symph. Orch., Jan. 31, 1895); Piano Concerto No. 1, in A minor, op. 15 (1882; Vienna, April 17, 1898); Piano Concerto No. 2, in D minor, op. 23 (N.Y., March 5, 1889, composer soloist); *Romance* for Cello and Orch., op. 35 (1888).

FOR CHORUS: 2 choruses for Men's Voices, op. 3: *Love and Time* and *The Rose and the Gardener* (1897); *The Witch* for Men's Chorus, op. 5 (1898); *War Song* for Men's Chorus, op. 6 (1898); 3 songs for Men's Chorus, op. 27 (1887); 2 songs for Men's Chorus, op. 41 (1890); *2 Northern Songs* for Mixed Voices, op. 43 (1891); 3 choruses for Men's Voices, op. 52 (1897); *2 Songs from the 13th Century* for Men's Chorus (1897); 2 choruses for Men's Voices, op. 53 (1898); 2 choruses for Men's Voices, op. 54 (1898); *College Songs* for Men's Voices (1901); *Summer Wind* for Women's Chorus (1902).

FOR VOICE AND PIANO: *2 Old Songs,* op. 9 (1894); 3 songs, op. 11 (1883); 2 songs, op. 12 (1883); *From an Old Garden* (6 songs), op. 26 (1887); 3 songs, op. 33 (1888; revised 1894); 2 songs, op. 34 (1888); *6 Love Songs,* op. 40 (1890); 8 songs, op. 47 (1893); 4 songs, op. 56 (1898); 3 songs, op. 58 (1899); 3 songs, op. 60 (1902).

FOR PIANO: *Amourette,* op. 1 (1896); *In Lilting Rhythm,* op. 2 (1897); *Forgotten Fairy Tales (Sung outside the Prince's Door, Of a Tailor and a Bear, Beauty in the Rose Garden, From Dwarfland),* op. 4 (1898); *6 Fancies (A Tin Soldier's Love, To a Humming Bird, Summer Song, Across Fields, Bluette, An Elfin Round),* op. 7 (1898); *Waltz,* op. 8 (1895); *First Modern Suite,* op. 10 (1880); *Prelude and Fugue,* op. 13 (1883); *2nd Modern Suite,* op. 14 (1881); *Serenata,* op. 16 (1883); *2 Fantastic Pieces (Legend, Witches' Dance),* op. 17 (1884); *2 Pieces (Barcarolle, Humoresque),* op. 18 (1884); *Forest Idyls (Forest Stillness, Play of the Nymphs, Reverie, Dance of the Dryads),* op. 19 (1884); *4 Pieces (Humoresque, March, Cradle Song, Czardas),* op. 24 (1887); *6 Idyls after Goethe (In the Woods, Siesta, To the Moonlight, Silver Clouds, Flute Idyl, The Bluebell),* op. 28 (1887); *6 Poems after Heine (From a Fisherman's Hut, Scotch Poem, From Long Ago, The Post Wagon, The Shepherd Boy, Monologue),* op. 31 (1887); *4 Little Poems (The Eagle, The Brook, Moonshine, Winter),* op. 32 (1888); *Etude de concert* in F-sharp, op. 36 (1889); *Les Orientales,* after Victor Hugo (*Clair de lune, Danse le Hamac, Danse Andalouse),* op. 37 (1889); *Marionnettes,* 8 Little Pieces (*Prologue, Soubrette, Lover, Witch, Clown, Villain, Sweetheart, Epilogue),* op. 38 (1888; originally only 6 pieces; *Prologue* and *Epilogue* were added in

1901); 12 Studies, Book I (*Hunting Song, Alla Tarantella, Romance, Arabesque, In the Forest, Dance of the Gnomes*); Book II (*Idyl, Shadow Dance, Intermezzo, Melody, Scherzino, Hungarian*), op. 39 (1890); Sonata No. 1, *Tragica*, op. 45 (1893); 12 Virtuoso Studies (*Novelette, Moto perpetuo, Wild Chase, Improvisation, Elfin Dance, Valse triste, Burleske, Bluette, Träumerei, March Wind, Impromptu, Polonaise*), op. 46 (1894); *Air* and *Rigaudon*, op. 49 (1894); Sonata No. 2, *Eroica*, op. 50 (1895); *Woodland Sketches*, 10 pieces (*To a Wild Rose, Will o' the Wisp, At an Old Trysting Place, In Autumn, From an Indian Lodge, To a Water Lily, From Uncle Remus, A Desert Farm, By a Meadow Brook, Told at Sunset*), op. 51 (1896); *Sea Pieces (To the Sea, From a Wandering Iceberg, A.D. 1620, Star-light, Song, From the Depths, Nautilus, In Mid-Ocean)*, op. 55 (1898); Sonata No. 3, *Norse*, op. 57 (1900); Sonata No. 4, *Keltic*, op. 59 (1901); *Fireside Tales (An Old Love Story, Of Br'er Rabbit, From a German Forest, Of Salamanders, A Haunted House, By Smouldering Embers)*, op. 61 (1902); *New England Idyls*, 10 pieces (*An Old Garden, Midsummer, Midwinter, With Sweet Lavender, In Deep Woods, Indian Idyl, To an Old White Pine, From Puritan Days, From a Log Cabin, The Joy of Autumn*), op. 62 (1902); 6 Little Pieces on Sketches by J.S. Bach (1890); Technical Exercises, 2 Books (1893, 1895). MacDowell's writings were collected by W.J. Baltzell and publ. as *Critical and Historical Essays* (1912; reprinted, with new introduction by I. Lowens, N.Y., 1969).

Macfarlane, William Charles, English-born American organist and composer; b. London, Oct. 2, 1870; d. North Conway, N.H., May 12, 1945. In 1874 he was taken to N.Y.; was taught by his father, Duncan Macfarlane (1836–1916), and by S.P. Warren. He made his debut as an organist in N.Y. on March 22, 1886; from 1898 to 1919 held various positions as an organist and a choral conductor; in 1941, retired to North Conway. He wrote *America First, A Boy Scout Operetta* (1917); light operas: *Little Almond Eyes* (Portland, 1916) and *Sword and Scissors* (1918); cantata, *The Message from the Cross* (1907); *The Church Service Book* (N.Y., 1912); numerous anthems and other sacred music; organ pieces (*Lullaby, Serenade, Scherzo, Romanza*, etc.).

Macfarren, Sir George Alexander, eminent English composer and pedagogue; b. London, March 2, 1813; d. there, Oct. 31, 1887. He received general education from his father, George Macfarren, the dramatist, and studied at the Royal Academy of Music; after graduation, he joined its faculty as a tutor in 1834. After many years as a prof. there, in 1875 he was appointed a prof. of music at Cambridge Univ., as successor to Sterndale Bennett. He was knighted in 1883. He had the great satisfaction of having his early overture *Chevy Chace* performed by Mendelssohn in Leipzig (1843) and by Wagner in London (1855). Macfarren's greatest ambition was to write an opera that would reflect the spirit of England, as the operas of Weber were redolent of the mythical lyricism of German folklore, but he signally failed

in this endeavor. His 9 symphs. enjoyed some transient favor, but attempts at their revival foundered in future years. His wife, **Natalie Macfarren** (née Clarina Thalia Andrae; b. Lübeck, Dec. 14, 1826; d. Bakewell, April 9, 1916), a singer, studied music with Macfarren, whom she married in 1844; she dutifully sang her husband's operas in England. She publ. a *Vocal Method* and an *Elementary Course of Vocalising and Pronouncing the English Language.*

WORKS: OPERAS: *An Adventure of Don Quixote* (London, Feb. 3, 1846); *King Charles II* (London, Oct. 27, 1849); *Robin Hood* (London, Oct. 11, 1860); *Helvellyn* (London, Nov. 3, 1864). FOR ORCH.: 9 symphs. (1828, 1831, 1832, 1833, 1833, 1836, 1840, 1845, 1874); Piano Concerto (1835); Flute Concerto (1863); Violin Concerto (1871–74); overtures: *The Merchant of Venice* (1834); *Romeo and Juliet* (1836); *Chevy Chace* (1836); *Don Carlos* (1842); *Hamlet* (1856); *Festival Overture* (1874). FOR VOICE: Oratorios and cantatas: *The Sleeper Awakened* (London, Nov. 15, 1850); *Lenora* (London, April 25, 1853); *Christmas* (London, May 9, 1860); *St. John the Baptist* (Bristol, Oct. 23, 1873); *The Resurrection* (Birmingham, 1876); *Joseph* (Leeds, 1877); *King David* (Leeds, 1883); numerous sacred and secular vocal works; part-songs; trios; duets; and some 160 solo songs. CHAMBER MUSIC: 5 string quartets (1834, 1842, 1846, 1849, 1878); Quintet for Violin, Viola, Cello, Double Bass, and Piano (1844); Violin Sonata (1887); 3 piano sonatas; various piano and organ pieces. ARRANGEMENTS: *Popular Music of the Olden Time* (1859); *Popular Songs of Scotland* (1874). EDUCATIONAL WORKS: *Rudiments of Harmony* (1860; 14 eds.); *Six Lectures on Harmony* (London, 1867).

Macfarren, Walter Cecil, English pianist and composer, brother of **George Alexander Macfarren;** b. London, Aug. 28, 1826; d. there, Sept. 2, 1905. He was a chorister at Westminster Abbey; then studied at the Royal Academy of Music, with Holmes (piano) and with his brother (composition). From 1846 until 1903 he was a prof. of piano at the Royal Academy of Music; conducted its concerts from 1873 till 1880. He composed a number of overtures on Shakespearean subjects; a Piano Concerto; many piano pieces; edited Beethoven's sonatas, and several albums of piano pieces under the title *Popular Classics*. He publ. *Memories; An Autobiography* (London, 1905).

Mach, Ernst, eminent German acoustician; b. Turas, Moravia, Feb. 18, 1838; d. Vaterstetten, near Munich, Feb. 19, 1916. He was a prof. of physics in Prague (1864) and in Vienna (1895). Besides his scientific works of far-reaching importance, he publ. a number of books and studies dealing with musical acoustics: *Zwei populäre Vorträäge uüber musikalische Akustik* (1865); *Einleitung in die Helmholtz'sche Musiktheorie* (1866); *Zur Theorie des Gehöörorgans* (1872); *Beitrag zur Geschichte der Musik* (1892); *Die Analyse der Empfindungen und das Verhäältnis des Physischen zum Psychischen* (5th ed., 1906); "Zur Geschichte der Theorie der Konsonanz," in *Populärwissenschaftliche Vorträge* (3rd ed., 1903). The unit of velocity of sound "Mach" is named after him.

Machabey, Armand, French musicologist; b. Pont-de-Roide, Doubs, May 7, 1886; d. Paris, Aug. 31, 1966. He studied with Vincent d'Indy and André Pirro; received his doctorat ès lettres from the Univ. of Paris in 1928 with the dissertation *Essai sur les formules usuelles de la musique occidentale des origines à la fin du XVᵉ siècle* (publ. in Paris, in a revised ed. in 1955, as *Genèse de la tonalité musicale classique);* subsequently was active as a music historian and essayist; also was one of the editors of *Larousse de la musique* (Paris, 1957). His writings include *Sommaire de la méthode en musicologie* (Paris, 1930); *Précis-manuel d'histoire de la musique* (Paris, 1942; 2nd ed., 1947); *La Vie et Maurice Ravel* (Paris, 1947); *Traité de la critique musicale* (Paris, 1947); *L'Œuvre d' Anton Bruckner* (Paris, 1947); *Le "bel canto"* (Paris, 1948); *Portraits de trente compositeurs français* (Paris, 1950); *Gerolamo Frescobaldi Ferrarensis* (Paris, 1952); *La Musique et la médicine* (Paris, 1952); *La Notation musicale* (Paris, 1952; 3rd ed., revised, 1971); *Guillaume de Machaut: La vie et l'œuvre musicale* (Paris, 1955); *Problèmes de notation musicale* (Paris, 1958); *La Musicologie* (Paris, 1962; 2nd ed., 1969); *Embryologie de la musique occidentale* (Paris, 1963); *La Musique de danse* (Paris, 1966).

Machado, Augusto, Portuguese composer; b. Lisbon, Dec. 27, 1845; d. there, March 26, 1924. He was a pupil of Junior, Lami, and D'Almeide in Lisbon, and of Lavignac and Danhauser in Paris; in 1892–1908, was director of the San Carlos Theater in Lisbon; in 1894–1910, director of the Cons. there. Besides numerous operettas, he wrote the operas *A Cruz de oiro* (Lisbon, 1873); *A Maria da Fonte* (Lisbon, 1879); *Lauriane* (Marseilles, Jan. 9, 1883; his most successful work); *Os Dorias* (Lisbon, 1887); *Mario Wetter* (Lisbon, 1898); *Venere* (Lisbon, 1905); *La Borghesina* (Lisbon, 1909). For the 3rd centenary of the death of Camoëns he wrote the symph. ode *Camões es os Luziadas* (1880); also wrote organ and piano pieces.

Machaut (or **Machault, Machaud**), **Guillaume de (Guillelmus de Mascaudio),** important French composer and poet, probably a native of Machaut in the Champagne; b. c.1300; d. Rheims, 1377. He studied theology; took Holy Orders; in 1323–40 was in the service of King John of Bohemia (Duke of Luxembourg) as almoner (1330), notary (1332), and secretary (1335), traveling widely with that prince (their visits extended to Russia). Later he was at the court of Charles V of France. He held various ecclesiastical benefices (Houdain, Arras, Verdun), and from 1337 was canon of Rheims, where he resided from 1340 until his death (he visited Paris in 1363). His works include ballades, rondeaux, virelais, and motets. He wrote the earliest polyphonic (4 voices) setting of the complete Mass by a single composer. A complete ed. of Machaut's musical works was pre-

pared by Friedrich Ludwig for the *Publikationen älterer Musik* (vols. I, 1; III, 1; IV, 2; 1926–34, containing about two-thirds of his *opera omnia* and a commentary); the Mass, lais, and hocket, not included in Ludwig's collection, were brought out for the *Publikationen* by H. Besseler in 1943, but the printed copies were destroyed in an air raid. After the war, several editions of the Mass were publ. (by Chailley, Paris, 1948; by Machabey, Liège, 1948; by de Van, Rome, 1949; by Hübsch, Heidelberg, 1953; and Besseler's again, Leipzig, 1954). The complete works are publ. in L. Schrade, ed., *Polyphonic Music of the 14th Century* (vols. 2 and 3, Monaco, 1956); 14 works (including parts of the Mass) are found in J. Wolf's *Geschichte der Mensuralnotation von 1250–1450* (Leipzig, 1904); 2 pieces in Schering's *Geschichte der Musik in Beispielen;* other pieces in Davison and Apel, *Historical Anthology of Music* (Cambridge, Mass., 1946). *La Louange des dames,* lyric poems, was ed. by N. Wilkins (Edinburgh, 1972).

Machavariani, Alexei, Georgian composer; b. Gory, Sept. 23, 1913. He studied at the Cons. of Tiflis, graduating in 1936; in 1940 became an instructor in music theory there. His music is profoundly infused with Caucasian melorhythms. He wrote the operas *Deda da shvili (Mother and Son;* Tiflis, May 1, 1945), on a patriotic subject connected with the struggle for independence in the Caucasus, and *Hamlet* (1964); ballet, *Knight in a Tiger's Skin* (1965); symph. poems: *Mumly Muhasa* (1939); *Satchidao* (1940); *On the Death of a Hero* (1948); overture, *The People's Choice* (1950); cantata, *For Peace, for Fatherland* (1951); Piano Concerto (1944); Violin Concerto (1950); oratorio, *The Day of My Fatherland* (1954); many songs, of which *Blue Light* (1949) achieved great popularity in Russia; *Khorumy,* a Georgian military dance, for Piano (1941; very popular); 2 symphs. (1947, 1973).

Mâche, François-Bernard, remarkable French composer and classical scholar; b. Clermont-Ferrand, April 4, 1935. Of a musical family, he studied piano locally; in 1955 entered L'Ecole Normale Supérieure in Paris, studying classical languages and literature; received his diploma in 1958; then enrolled at the Paris Cons., in the composition class of Olivier Messiaen; continued his classical studies, and in 1962 was given a professorship in classical literature. He also learned modern Greek, and translated contemporary Greek poetry and prose into English; several of his works are inspired by Greek mythology. In musical composition, Mâche became an adherent of experimental methods; in 1980 he received a national doctorate for his thesis on models of new music. He adopted the ideal of "organized sound" as enunciated by Varèse; but he also annexed sounds of nature; for resources he studied ornithology, but rather than translate the intonations of bird songs into human melorhythms performable on instruments, as his teacher Messiaen professed to do, Mâche transmutes the natural material into suggestive images of sound; in one of his works, *Amorgos,* named after an island in the

Aegean Sea, he uses as a background the actual sound of the sea waves recorded on magnetic tape. In one score, *Naluan,* he used recorded animal sounds. He also publ. an essay, *Musique, mythe, nature ou Les Dauphins d'Arion* (1982).

WORKS: *La Peau du silence* for Orch. (1962); *Rituel d'Oubli* for Orch. and Concert Band (1969); *Danae* for 12 Solo Voices and Percussion (1970); *Naluan* for 8 Instruments and Animal Sounds (1974); *Marae* for 6 Percussionists and Sounds of Nature (1974); *Kassandra* for 14 Instruments and Band (1977; Paris Radio, Oct. 16, 1977); *Andromède* for Orch., Double Chorus, and 3 Pianos (1979); *Amorgos* for 12 Instruments and Recorded Sea Waves (1979; Metz Festival, Nov. 16, 1979); *Sopiana* for Flute, Piano, and Magnetic Tape (1980; Pecs, Hungary, July 12, 1980); *Temboctou,* musical spectacle (1982).

Machlis, Joseph, American music historian and pedagogue; b. Riga, Latvia, Aug. 11, 1906. He was brought to the U.S. as an infant. He studied at the College of the City of N.Y. (B.A., 1927), and at the Inst. of Musical Art of the Juilliard School (Teachers Diploma, 1927); also took an M.A. in English literature from Columbia Univ. (1938). In 1938 he was appointed to the music faculty at Queens College of the City Univ. of N.Y. He publ. several well-written texts: the immensely popular *The Enjoyment of Music* (N.Y., 1955; 3rd ed., 1970); *Introduction to Contemporary Music* (N.Y., 1961); *American Composers of Our Time* for young people (N.Y., 1963); *Getting to Know Music* for high school students (N.Y., 1966). He trans. a number of operatic librettos for the NBC Opera Co. (*Rigoletto, La Traviata, Fidelio, La Bohème, Cavalleria rusticana,* Prokofiev's *War and Peace,* etc.); *Boris Godunov, Tosca,* and Manuel de Falla's *Atlántida* for other opera companies. He is the author of 2 novels: *57th Street,* about the "concert industry" (N.Y., 1970), and *Lisa's Boy* (N.Y., 1982), publ. under the phonetically palindromic pseudonym **George Selcamm.**

Mackenzie, Sir Alexander Campbell, distinguished British composer and educator; b. Edinburgh, Aug. 22, 1847; d. London, April 28, 1935. A scion of a musical family (there were 4 generations of musicians in his paternal line), he showed musical aptitude as a child; was sent to Germany, where he studied violin with K.W. Ulrich and theory with Eduard Stein, at the Sondershausen Cons. (1857–62); returning to England, he studied violin with Sainton, piano with Jewson, and music theory with Charles Lucas at the Royal Academy of Music; subsequently was active in Edinburgh as a violinist and teacher (1865–79). Between 1879 and 1888 he spent part of each year in Florence. In 1888 he was elected principal of the Royal Academy of Music in London, holding this post until 1924. From 1892 to 1899 he conducted the concerts of the Phil. Society of London. His reputation as an educator and composer was very high among musicians. He was knighted in 1895. As a composer, he was a staunch believer in programmatic music; he introduced national Scottish elements in many of his works; his *Pibroch Suite* for Violin and Orch., first introduced by Sarasate at the Leeds Festival (1889), acquired considerable popularity; Paderewski gave the first performance of his *Scottish Concerto* with the Phil. Society of London (1897). In 1922 he was made a Knight Commander of the Royal Victorian Order.

WORKS: OPERAS (all first perf. in London): *Colomba* (April 9, 1883); *The Troubadour* (June 8, 1886); *His Majesty* (Feb. 20, 1897); *The Cricket on the Hearth* (composed 1900; perf. June 6, 1914); *The Knights of the Road* (Feb. 27, 1905). CANTATAS: *Jason* (1882); *The Rose of Sharon* (Norwich Festival, Oct. 16, 1884); *The Story of Sayid* (1886); *The Witches' Daughter* (1904); *The Sun-God's Return* (1910). FOR ORCH.: *Cervantes,* overture (1877); *Scottish Rhapsody* No. 1 (1880); *Burns* (*Scottish Rhapsody* No. 2; 1881); *La Belle Dame sans merci,* after Keats (1883); *Twelfth Night,* after Shakespeare (1888); *Coriolanus,* suite (1901); *London Day by Day,* suite (1902); *Canadian Rhapsody* (1905); *Tam o' Shanter* (*Scottish Rhapsody* No. 3; 1911); *Youth, Sport and Loyalty,* overture (1922); Violin Concerto (1885); *Pibroch Suite* for Violin and Orch. (Leeds, Oct. 10, 1889); Suite No. 2 for Violin and Orch. (London, Feb. 18, 1897); *Scottish Concerto* for Piano and Orch. (London, March 24, 1897). CHAMBER MUSIC: Piano Trio (1874); String Quartet (1875); Piano Quartet (1875); *From the North,* 9 pieces for Violin and Piano (1895); *4 Dance Measures* for Violin and Piano (1915); several characteristic piano suites (*Rustic Suite, In the Scottish Highlands, Odds and Ends, Jottings, In Varying Moods*); a number of songs; arrangements of Scottish songs; etc. He publ. an autobiography, *A Musician's Narrative* (London, 1927).

Mackerras, Sir Charles, eminent Australian conductor; b. Schenectady, N.Y., of Australian parents, Nov. 17, 1925. He was taken to Sydney, Australia, as an infant; studied oboe, piano, and composition at the New South Wales Conservatorium there; then played oboe in the Sydney Symph. Orch. He won a British Council scholarship in 1947, and went to Prague to study conducting with Vaclav Talich at the Prague Academy of Music. Returning to London in 1948, he joined the conducting staff at the Sadler's Wells Opera; then was engaged as principal conductor of the BBC Concert Orch. (1954–56); subsequently appeared as a guest conductor with British orchs.; also had engagements on the Continent. From 1966 to 1970 he held the post of first conductor at the Hamburg State Opera. In 1970 he became music director at the Sadler's Wells Opera (it was renamed the English National Opera in 1974), a position he held until 1977. He further served as chief guest conductor of the BBC Symph. (1978–79). In 1978 he was named principal guest conductor of the English National Opera. In 1979 he visited the U.S.; was a guest conductor with the Metropolitan Opera and the N.Y. Phil. Returning to Europe, he made an appearance with the Vienna Phil. on Nov. 24, 1979. He was made a Commander of the Order of the British Empire in 1974, and was knighted in 1979. In 1982 he was named chief conductor of the Sydney (Australia) Symph. Orch. His conducting method is marked by carefully delineated instrumental and vocal parts, with a scrupulously high regard for the stylistic characteristics of each work.

Maclean, Alexander Morvaren (Alick), English composer and conductor, son of **Charles Donald Maclean;** b. Eton, near Windsor, July 20, 1872; d. London, May 18, 1936. He studied with Sir Joseph Barnby; later conducted the Spa Orch. at Scarborough (from 1911) and the New Queen's Hall Light Orch. (1915–23). He wrote several operas; of these, 2 were produced in German, in Mainz: *Die Liebesgeige* (April 15, 1906) and *Waldidyll* (March 23, 1913); and 3 in London: *Petruccio* (June 29, 1895), *The King's Price* (April 29, 1904), and *Maître Seiler* (Aug. 20, 1909). His most successful opera, *Quentin Durward* (after Walter Scott), written in 1892, was not produced until many years later, at Newcastle upon Tyne (Jan. 13, 1920). He also wrote an oratorio, *The Annunciation* (London, 1910); *Rapsodie monégasque* for Orch. (1935); choral works.

Maclean, Charles Donald, English organist; b. Cambridge, March 27, 1843; d. London, June 23, 1916. He studied theory with Ferdinand Hiller in Cologne; later at Oxford Univ. (D.Mus., 1865). He was music director at Eton College (1871–75); then entered the Indian Civil Service, returning to London in 1898. He was the English editor of the International Musical Society.

MacMillan, Sir Ernest (Alexander Campbell), eminent Canadian conductor and composer; b. Mimico, Ontario, Aug. 18, 1893; d. Toronto, May 6, 1973. He studied organ in Toronto and then at Edinburgh Univ. with Alfred Hollins and Frederick Niecks; in the summer of 1914 he went to Bayreuth to attend the Wagner Festival and was interned as an enemy alien at the outbreak of World War I; after the Armistice he returned to Canada and settled in Toronto; was director of the Toronto Cons. (1926–42) and dean of the faculty of music at the Univ. of Toronto (1927–52); was also conductor of the Toronto Symph. Orch. (1931–56) and the Mendelssohn Choir in Toronto (1942–57); filled in engagements as guest conductor in the U.S., England, Australia, and South America. He held several important administrative posts, including the presidency of the Canadian Music Council (1947–66), and of the Canadian Music Centre (1959–70). He was knighted by King George V in 1935 and received 9 honorary doctorates from Canadian and American univs.

Macmillen, Francis, American violinist; b. Marietta, Ohio, Oct. 14, 1885; d. Lausanne, Switzerland, July 14, 1973. A precocious child, he was sent to Germany at the age of 10 and was accepted by Joachim as a pupil; later he studied with César Thomson at the Brussels Cons., winning the first prize in 1901; continued his studies with Carl Flesch in Berlin and Leopold Auer in St. Petersburg. He made his professional debut as a concert violinist at the age of 17 in Brussels (March 30, 1903); appeared with the N.Y. Symph. Orch. on Dec. 7, 1906; then embarked on a concert tour of Europe; after the outbreak of World War I in 1914 he returned to the U.S. and taught violin at Ithaca, N.Y.; resumed his European tours in 1929; then lived in N.Y., Florence, Italy, and lastly, Switzerland.

MacNeil, Cornell, American opera baritone; b. Minneapolis, Sept. 24, 1922. He began to earn his living as a machinist, and simultaneously made appearances as a radio actor and operetta singer. His professional singing debut was in the baritone role in Menotti's opera *The Consul* in N.Y. on March 1, 1950. He joined the N.Y. City Opera in 1953; also made guest appearances in San Francisco, Chicago, and Mexico City. On March 5, 1959, he sang the role of Charles V in Verdi's opera *Ernani* at La Scala in Milan. On March 21, 1959, he sang Rigoletto at the Metropolitan Opera in N.Y. and became a regular member of the company; also sang in Europe. He attracted unexpected notoriety when he walked off the stage during the 3rd act of Verdi's opera *Un ballo in maschera* on Dec. 27, 1964, in Parma, Italy, in protest against the offensive attitude of the audience, and engaged in a fistfight with the opera manager. Pacified, he resumed his career in America, but also became active in labor union affairs; in 1969 he was elected president of the American Guild of Musical Artists.

Maconchy, Elizabeth, significant English composer of Irish extraction; b. Broxbourne, Hertfordshire, March 19, 1907. She studied with Vaughan Williams and Charles Wood at the Royal College of Music in London (1923–29); in 1930 went to Prague, where she absorbed the styles and techniques of Expressionism; upon returning to England, she composed prolifically in all genres; developed a style peculiarly her own: tonally tense, contrapuntally dissonant, and coloristically sharp in instrumentation. In 1977 she was made a Dame Commander of the Order of the British Empire.

WORKS: FOR THE STAGE: 3 one-act operas: *The Sofa,* to a libretto by Ursula Vaughan Williams (London, Dec. 13, 1959); *The Departure* (London, Dec. 16, 1962); *The 3 Strangers,* after Thomas Hardy (London, June 5, 1968); *The Birds,* operatic extravaganza, after Aristophanes (London, June 5, 1968, on the same day with *The 3 Strangers*); church masque, *The Jesse Tree* (Dorchester Abbey, Oct. 7, 1970); ballets: *Great Agrippa* (1933); *The Little Red Shoes* (1935); *Puck Fair* (1940). FOR ORCH.: *The Land,* symph. suite (1929); Piano Concerto (1930); *Theme and Variations* for Strings (1942); Symph. (1945–48); Viola Concerto (1937); *Dialogue* for Piano and Orch. (1940); Concertino for Clarinet and Strings (Copenhagen Festival of the International Society for Contemporary Music, June 2, 1947); Symph. for Double String Orch. (1953); *Proud Thames,* overture (1953); *Serenata concertante* for Violin and Orch.

(1962); *An Essex Overture* (1966); *3 Cloudscapes* for Orch. (1968); *Sinfonietta* (1975–76); *Epyllion* for Cello and 14 Strings (1975); *Romanza* for Viola and Chamber Orch. (London, March 12, 1979); Little Symph. (1980; Norwich, July 28, 1981); *Music for Strings* (Proms concert, London, July 26, 1983). CHAMBER MUSIC: 12 string quartets (1933, 1936, 1938, 1943, 1948, 1951, 1956, 1966, 1967, 1970, 1978, 1979); Quintet for Oboe and Strings (1932); *Prelude, Interlude and Fugue* for 2 Violins (Prague Festival of the International Society for Contemporary Music, Sept. 4, 1935); Viola Sonata (1938); Violin Sonata (1944); Concertino for Piano and Strings (1951); Concertino for Bassoon and Strings (1954); String Trio (1957); Double Concerto for Oboe, Clarinet, Viola, and Harp (1960); Clarinet Quintet (1963); *Music* for Double Bass and Piano (1970); *3 Bagatelles* for Oboe and Harp (1972); *Contemplation* for Cello and Piano (1978); *Colloquy* for Flute and Piano (1979); *Fantasia* for Clarinet and Piano (1979); *Piccola musica* for String Trio (Cheltenham, July 13, 1981); *Trittico* for 2 Oboes, Bassoon, and Harpsichord (1981); Wind Quintet (1982); *Tribute* for Violin and 8 Wind Instruments (1983). VOCAL WORKS: *Samson at the Gates of Gaza* for Chorus and Orch. (1963); *The Starlight Night and Peace* for Soprano and Chamber Orch. (1964); *Witnesses* for 2 Sopranos, Flute, Oboe, Clarinet, Horn, Cello, Percussion, and Ukelele (1966); *3 Donne Songs* for Tenor and Piano (1966); *The Leaden Echo and the Golden Echo* for Chorus, Flute, Viola, and Harp (1978); *Creatures* for Chorus (1979); 3 settings of poems by Gerard Manley Hopkins for Soprano and Orch. (1964–70); *Ariadne* for Soprano and Orch. (1970); *Heloise and Abelard*, cantata for Soloists, Chorus, and Orch. (1978); *My Dark Heart*, after Petrarch, for Soprano and Instrumental Ensemble (1982); *L'Horloge* for Soprano, Clarinet, and Piano (1983); piano pieces.

Macque, Giovanni (Jean) de, Flemish composer; b. Valenciennes, c.1550; d. Naples, Sept. 1614. On his marriage certificate (1592) he is named "Fiammingo della città de Valencena"; a book of motets (Rome, 1596) describes him as a Belgian from Valenciennes. He studied with Philippe de Monte; then went to Rome (c.1570), where he became a member of the Compagnia dei Musici di Roma (organized in 1584); other members were Palestrina and Marenzio. In 1586 Macque went to Naples and entered the service of Don Fabrizio Gesualdo da Venosa, father of the composer Carlo Gesualdo. On May 20, 1590, Macque was appointed 2nd organist of the Church of the Annunciation in Naples. In 1594 he was appointed organist of the viceregal chapel, and in Dec. 1599 became its choir director. Among his pupils in Naples were Ascanio Mayone, Giovanni Maria Trabaci, Luigi Rossi, and Falconieri. Several of Macque's madrigals are found in Younge's *Musica transalpina* (1588) and in Morley's collection of Italian works (1598); extant keyboard pieces are reproduced in the *Monumenta musicae belgicae* (Antwerp, 1938; with a list of sources and a biographical sketch). Macque was one of the first to employ rhythmic transformations of a single theme (in canzonas), which were later used extensively by Frescobaldi; Macque also applied the keyboard technique of Cabezón's "diferencias" (variations).

Maderna, Bruno, remarkable Italian conductor and composer of modern propensities; b. Venice, April 21, 1920; d. Darmstadt, Germany, Nov. 13, 1973. He played violin as a child, instructed by his grandfather; his father was also a musician. He entered the Cons. of Milan, but his musical education was interrupted when he was drafted into the Alpine Regiment and was sent to fight on the Russian front. After the war, he studied in Milan and in Rome; then attended master classes in composition in Venice with Malipiero. In 1949 he went to Darmstadt, where he took conducting lessons with Scherchen. In his own conducting career Maderna promoted the most advanced works of the modern avant-garde. In 1955 he founded, with Luciano Berio, the electronic music studio at Milan Radio; from 1954 to 1967 he lectured at the summer courses in new music at Darmstadt, and after 1961 led the International Chamber Ensemble there; later taught at the Cons. of Rotterdam; in 1971 and 1972 he gave summer courses at the Berkshire Music Center in Tanglewood. He lived mostly in West Germany; became a naturalized German citizen in 1963. Stricken with cancer, he continued to conduct concerts as long as it was physically possible. Maderna was held in great esteem by composers of the international avant-garde, several of whom wrote special works for him. He was also a significant composer in his own right. WORKS: FOR THE STAGE: *Don Perlimplin,* radio opera after Lorca (1961; RAI Radio, Aug. 12, 1962); *Hyperion,* a "Lirica in forma di spettacolo" (1964; Venice Festival, Sept. 6, 1964; a composite of *Dimensioni III, Aria de Hyperion,* and tape); *Von A bis Z,* opera (1969; Darmstadt, Feb. 22, 1970); *Oedipe-Roi,* electronic ballet (Monte Carlo, Dec. 31, 1970); *Satyrikon,* opera after Petronius (1972; Scheveningen, the Netherlands, March 16, 1973; U.S. premiere, Tanglewood, Aug. 6, 1973). FOR ORCH.: *Introduzione e passacaglia* (1947); Concerto for 2 Pianos, Percussion, and 2 Harps (1948; Venice, Sept. 17, 1948); *Composizioni No. 1* (1949); *Composizioni No. 2* for Chamber Orch. (1950); *Improvvisazione I* and *II* (1951, 1952); *Composizioni in 3 tempi* (1954; Hamburg Radio, Dec. 8, 1954); Flute Concerto (1954); *Dark Rapture Crawl* (1957); Piano Concerto (1959; Darmstadt, Sept. 2, 1959); 3 oboe concertos: No. 1, with 23 Instruments (1962; revised 1965); No. 2 (1967; Cologne Radio, Nov. 10, 1967); No. 3 (1973; Amsterdam, July 6, 1973); *Dimensioni III* for Flute and Orch. (1963; Paris Radio, Dec. 12, 1963); *Stele per Diotima* for Orch., with cadenzas for Violin, Clarinet, Bass Clarinet, and Horn (1965; Cologne Radio, Jan. 19, 1966); *Dimensioni IV* (combination of *Dimensioni III* and *Stele per Diotima*); *Amanda* for Chamber Orch. (1966; Naples, Nov. 22, 1966); *Quadrivium* for 4 Percussionists and 4 Orch. Groups (1969); Violin Concerto (1969; Venice, Sept. 12, 1969); *Grande aulodia* for

Flute, Oboe, and Orch. (1969; Rome, Feb. 7, 1970); *Juilliard Serenade (Free Time I)* for Chamber Orch. and Tape Sounds (1970; N.Y., Jan. 31, 1971); *Music of Gaiety* for Solo Violin, Oboe, and Chamber Orch., based on pieces in the "Fitzwilliam Virginal Book" (1970); *Aura* (1971; Chicago Symph., March 23, 1972); *Biogramma* (1972); *Giardino religioso* for Chamber Ensemble (1972; Tanglewood, Aug. 8, 1972).

FOR VOICE: *3 Greek Lyrics* for Soprano, Chorus, and Instruments (1948); *Studi per "Il Processo" di Kafka* for Narrator, Soprano, and Small Orch. (1949); *4 Briefe* for Soprano, Bass, and Chamber Orch. (1953); *Aria de "Hyperion"* for Soprano, Flute, and Orch. (1964); *Hyperion II* (combination of *Dimensioni III, Cadenza* for Flute, and *Aria da "Hyperion"*); *Hyperion III* (combination of *Hyperion* and *Stele per Diotima*); *Ausstrahlung* for Soprano, Chorus, and Orch. (1971); *Boswell's Journal* for Tenor and Chamber Orch. (N.Y., March 12, 1972).

ELECTRONIC MUSIC: *Notturno* (1955); *Syntaxis* for 4 different but unspecified timbres produced electronically (1956); *Continuo* (1958); *Dimensioni II,* "Invenzioni sue una voce" (1960); *Serenata No. 3* (1962); *Le Rire* (1964); *Ages* (with G. Pressburger, 1972).

Madetoja, Leevi, outstanding Finnish composer; b. Oulu (Uleaborg), Feb. 17, 1887; d. Helsinki, Oct. 6, 1947. He studied in Helsinki with Järnefelt and Sibelius (1906–10); took lessons in Paris with Vincent d'Indy (1910–11) and in Vienna with Robert Fuchs (1911–12). Returning to Finland, he conducted the Helsinki Phil. (1912–14) and the Viipuri (Vyborg) Orch. (1914–16); taught at the Helsinki Cons. (1916–39); was also active as a music critic. Madetoja's music is inspired by Finnish melos; he is held in great esteem in Finland as a worthy continuator of the national Finnish school of composition, according to precepts established by Sibelius.

WORKS: 2 operas: *Pohjalaisia (The Ostrobothnians;* Helsinki, Oct. 25, 1924) and *Juha* (Helsinki, Feb. 17, 1935); *Symphonic Suite* (1910); *Concert Overture* (1911); *Tanssináky* for Orch. (*Dance Vision;* 1911–12); *Kullervo,* symph. poem (1913); 3 symphs. (1916, 1918, 1926); *Comedy Overture* (1923); ballet-pantomime, *Okon Fuoko* (Helsinki, Dec. 2, 1930); Piano Trio (1909); Violin Sonatina (1914); *Lyric Suite* for Cello and Piano (1922); many cantatas and solo songs; 40 a cappella works for male chorus; incidental music for plays; film music.

Madge, Geoffrey Douglas, extraordinary Australian pianist; b. Adelaide, Oct. 3, 1941. He studied piano with Clemens Leski at the Elder Cons. of the Univ. of Adelaide, graduating in 1959; toured Australia as a pianist in a piano trio (1959–63). In 1963 he went to Europe; studied piano with Géza Anda in Switzerland (1964) and with Peter Solymos in Hungary (1967). In 1971 he was appointed senior lecturer of classical and contemporary piano repertoire at the Royal Cons. of The Hague. As a pianist, he became known chiefly by his propaganda of ultra-

modern music; his repertoire includes works by Ives, Sorabji, Xenakis, Boulez, Cage, Stockhausen, Wolpe, Barraqué, and Bussotti; a specialty is rarely played music of the Russian modernists, Mossolov, Obouhov, Roslavetz, Lourié, Alexandrov, and Wyschnegradsky. On June 11, 1982, at Utrecht, during the annual Holland Festival, he gave the 2nd complete performance (after 50 years) of Kaikhosru Sorabji's mammoth *Opus Clavicembalisticum;* he began it at 8:16 P.M. and finished at 12:47 the next morning. On April 24, 1983, he gave another performance of the work at the Univ. of Chicago; then repeated the feat at Bonn, Germany, on May 10, 1983. On Sept. 19, 1979, as part of that year's International Society for Contemporary Music Festival in Athens, he gave the first complete performance of Nikos Skalkottas's 2-hour set of *32 Piano Pieces,* as well as his *4 Etudes.* His technical powers as a pianist are astonishing, and possibly without equal; certainly no other pianist has assembled such a repertoire of formidable modern works. Madge is a self-taught composer; he wrote a Viola Sonata (1963); a String Quartet (1965); a Violin Sonatina (1966); *Monkeys in a Cage,* a ballet for 12 Instruments (1976; Sydney Opera House, 1977); *Tendrils of the Rock,* 3 movements for Piano (1979); and a Piano Concerto (1979; Amsterdam, 1980).

Maegaard, Jan, Danish composer; b. Copenhagen, April 14, 1926. He studied music theory with Poul Schierbeck and B. Hjelmborg; counterpoint with Knud Jeppesen and orchestration with J. Jersild at the Royal Cons. in Copenhagen (1945–50), and at the Univ. of Copenhagen, where he took a course in musicology with Jens Peter Larsen (*magister artis,* 1957). He then went to the U.S., where he studied musicography with Robert Nelson at the Univ. of Calif., Los Angeles (1958–59). Returning to Denmark, he taught at the Copenhagen Cons.; was appointed prof. at the Musicological Inst. of the Univ. of Copenhagen in 1971; received his D.Phil. for a 3-vol. dissertation, *Studies of the Evolution of Schoenberg's Dodecaphonic Method* (Copenhagen, 1972). Once more in America, he was guest lecturer at the State Univ. of N.Y. at Stony Brook (1974) and at the Univ. of Calif., Los Angeles (1978). He served on the board of the Society for Publishing Danish Music (1958–78).

WORKS: *Chamber Concerto No. 1* (1949); *Chamber Concerto No. 2* (1961–62); *Gaa udenom sletterne (Avoid the Plains)* for Chorus and Orch. (1953; Copenhagen, March 21, 1957); *Due tempi* for Orch. (Copenhagen, Aug. 31, 1961); music for a television production of *Antigone* for Chorus, Orch., and Tape (1966); *Suite* for Violin and Piano (1949); Trio for Oboe, Clarinet, and Bassoon (1950); Wind Quintet (1951); *Suite* for 2 Violins (1951); *Den gyldne harpe (The Golden Harp)* for Mezzo-soprano, Oboe, Cello, and Piano (1951); *Quasi una sonata* for Viola and Piano (1952); Bassoon Sonata (1952); *Variations impromptus* for Violin, Viola, Cello, and Piano (1953); *Jaevndøgnselegi (Equinox Elegy)* for Soprano, Cello, and Organ (1955); *Alter Duft aus Märchenzeit* for Piano Trio (1960); *Movimento* for Clarinet,

Horn, Hammond Organ, String Quartet, and Percussion (1967); *Musica riservata No. 1* for String Quartet (1970); *Musica riservata No. 2* for Oboe, Clarinet, Saxophone, and Bassoon (1976); *Pastorale* for 2 Clarinets (1976); Piano Sonata (1955); choruses; songs; cadenzas; transcriptions of Bach, Mozart, and Schoenberg. He publ. a textbook on new music, *Musikalsk modernisme 1945–62* (Copenhagen, 1964; 2nd ed., 1971).

Maelzel, Johannes Nepomuk, German inventor of the metronome; b. Regensburg, Aug. 15, 1772; d. on board the brig *Otis* in the harbor of La Guiara, Venezuela, en route to Philadelphia, July 21, 1838. He studied music with his father, an organ manufacturer. In 1972 he went to Vienna, where he began constructing mechanical instruments, which attracted great attention in Vienna and subsequently in other European cities; of these the Panharmonicon was particularly effective; in 1812 he inaugurated an Art Cabinet, where he exhibited his inventions, including an automatic trumpeter. In 1816 he constructed the metronome, the idea for which he obtained from Winkel of Amsterdam (who had exhibited similar instruments, but without the scale divisions indicating the number of beats per minute). Maelzel put the metronome on the market, despite a lawsuit brought by Winkel, and the initial of his last name was thenceforth added to the indication of tempo in musical compositions (M.M., Maelzel's metronome). Beethoven wrote a piece for Maelzel's Panharmonicon, which he subsequently orchestrated and publ. as *Wellington's Victory.* Maelzel also exhibited an "automatic chess player." Though he claimed it as his invention, it was really designed and built by Wolfgang von Kempelen. He was able to impress the public by his "scientific" miracle, but it was soon exposed by skeptical observers, among them Edgar Allan Poe, as an ingenious mechanical contrivance concealing a diminutive chess master behind its gears. (In this connection, see C.M. Carroll, *The Great Chess Automaton,* N.Y., 1975.)

Magaloff, Nikita, Russian-Swiss pianist; b. St. Petersburg, Feb. 21, 1912. His family left Russia after the Revolution; he enrolled in the Paris Cons. as a student of Isidor Philipp; graduated with the Premier Prix at the age of 17. In 1939 he settled in Switzerland; in 1947 made his first American tour; also toured South America, South Africa, etc. From 1949 to 1960 he conducted a school of piano virtuosity at the Geneva Cons.; then gave summer courses at Taormina, Sicily, and at the Accademia Musicale Chigiana in Siena. In 1956 he became a Swiss citizen, living mostly in Coppet (Vaud). He is renowned for his lyrico-dramatic interpretations of Chopin, with lapidary attention to detail. He is also a composer; he wrote a Piano Toccata; Sonatina for Violin and Piano; songs; cadenzas for Mozart's piano concertos.

Maganini, Quinto, American flutist, conductor, arranger, and composer; b. Fairfield, Calif., Nov. 30, 1897; d. Greenwich, Conn., March 10, 1974. He played the flute in the San Francisco Symph. Orch. (1917) and in the N.Y. Symph. (1919–28); studied flute playing with Barrère in N.Y. and composition with Nadia Boulanger in France, at the American Cons. in Fontainebleau; in 1927, won a Pulitzer scholarship; in 1928–29, was awarded a Guggenheim fellowship; in 1930, became conductor of the N.Y. Sinfonietta; in 1932 he organized his own orch., the Maganini Chamber Symph., with which he toured widely. From 1939 till 1970 he was conductor of the Norwalk (Conn.) Symph.
WORKS: *Toulumne,* "a Californian Rhapsody," for Orch., with Trumpet obbligato (N.Y., Aug. 9, 1924); *South Wind,* orch. fantasy (N.Y., April 7, 1931); *Sylvan Symphony* (N.Y., Nov. 30, 1932); *Napoleon,* an orch. portrait (N.Y., Nov. 10, 1935); *The Royal Ladies,* orch. suite on airs ascribed to Marie Antoinette (Greenwich, Conn., Feb. 3, 1940); opera, *Tennessee's Partner* (American Opera Festival, Radio Station WOR, N.Y., May 28, 1942); numerous arrangements for small orch. of classical and modern works.

Mager, Jörg, German music theorist and pioneer in electronic music; b. Eichstätt, Nov. 6, 1880; d. Aschaffenburg, April 5, 1939. After completing his univ. studies, he became interested in electronic reproduction of sounds; constructed several instruments capable of producing microtonal intervals by electronic means, which he named Sphärophon, Elektrophon, and Partiturophon; he was also active in visual music for film. He publ. *Vierteltonmusik* (Aschaffenburg, 1916) and *Eine neue Epoche der Musik durch Radio* (Berlin, 1924).

Maggini, Giovanni Paolo, Italian violin maker; b. Brescia, Nov. (baptized, Nov. 29) 1579; d. there, c.1630. He worked in the shop of Gasparo da Salò; after his marriage in 1615, he set up his own workshop and became prosperous, thanks to the excellence of his manufacture; about 50 violins and 20 violas and cellos are extant; his instruments are prized particularly because of the softness of their tone in deep registers. His label reads: Gio. Paolo Maggini, Brescia.

Magnard, (Lucien-Denis-Gabriel-) Albéric, French composer; b. Paris, June 9, 1865; d. Baron, Oise, Sept. 3, 1914 (killed by German soldiers in his house). He was brought up in an intellectual family; his father was editor of *Le Figaro.* He studied at the Paris Cons. with Dubois and Massenet, and later with Vincent d'Indy. He fell under the influence of Wagner, but succeeded in generating an element of national French music in his works; his mastery of instrumentation is incontestable, and the rhapsodic sweep of his symphs. is impressive. Despite these qualities, Magnard's symph. music never gained a stable place in the orch. repertoire; his operas were even less successful.
WORKS: Operas: *Yolande* (Brussels, Dec. 27, 1892); *Guercœur* (1900; revised by Guy-Ropartz, and produced at the Paris Opéra, April 24, 1931); *Béré-*

nice (Opéra-Comique, Paris, Dec. 15, 1911); 4 symphs. (1894, 1899, 1902, 1913); *Suite dans le style ancien* for Orch. (1892); *Hymne à la Justice* (1903); *Hymne à Vénus* (1906); Quintet for Wind Instruments and Piano (1904); String Quartet (1904); Piano Trio (1906); Violin Sonata; Cello Sonata; songs.

Magne, Michel, French composer; b. Lisieux, March 20, 1930. He began to compose as a very young man, adopting at once an ultramodern method; his film score *Le Pain vivant* (1955) received critical acclaim; he has also experimented with electronic music; on May 26, 1955, he conducted in Paris his *Symphonie humaine* for 150 Performers, making use of inaudible "infrasounds" to produce a physiological reaction by powerful low frequencies. He wrote the musical score for Françoise Sagan's ballet *Le Rendez-vous manqué* (1957).

Mahler, Fritz, Austrian-American conductor, nephew of **Gustav Mahler;** b. Vienna, July 16, 1901; d. Winston-Salem, N.C., June 18, 1973. He studied composition in Vienna with Schoenberg, Anton von Webern, and Alban Berg; musicology with Guido Adler at the Univ. of Vienna (1920–24); conducting with Leopold Reichwein. He conducted summer orchs. in Bad Hall (1924–26); light opera at the Volksoper in Vienna; in 1930–35, was conductor of the radio orch. in Copenhagen; in 1936 emigrated to America, where he taught at the Juilliard Summer School; was conductor of the Erie (Pa.) Phil. Orch. (1947–53); in 1953–64, conductor of the Hartford (Conn.) Symph. Orch.

Mahler, Gustav, great Austrian composer and conductor; b. Kalischt, Bohemia, July 7, 1860; d. Vienna, May 18, 1911. He attended school in Iglau; in 1875 entered the Vienna Cons. where he studied piano with Julius Epstein, harmony with Robert Fuchs, and composition with Franz Krenn. He also took academic courses in history and philosophy at the Univ. of Vienna (1877–80). In the summer of 1880 he received his first engagement as a conductor, at the operetta theater in the town of Hall in Upper Austria; subsequently he held posts as theater conductor at Ljubljana (1881), Olmütz (1882), Vienna (1883), and Kassel (1883-85). In 1885 he served as 2nd Kapellmeister to Anton Seidl at the Prague Opera, where he gave several performances of Wagner's operas. From 1886 to 1888 he was assistant to Arthur Nikisch in Leipzig; in 1888 he received the important appointment of music director of the Royal Opera in Budapest. In 1891 he was engaged as conductor at the Hamburg Opera; during his tenure there he developed a consummate technique for conducting. In 1897 he received a tentative offer as music director of the Vienna court opera, but there was an obstacle to overcome. Mahler was Jewish, and although there was no overt anti-Semitism in the Austrian government, an Imperial appointment could not be given to a Jew. Mahler was never orthodox in his religion, and had no difficulty in converting to Catholicism, which was the prevailing faith in Austria. He held this position at the Vienna court opera for 10 years; under his guidance it reached the highest standards of artistic excellence. Mahler became an undisputed dictator of music in Vienna. Even the imperial Cosima Wagner adopted a deferential tone in her requests for Mahler's favors, especially when it concerned Siegfried Wagner's operas, which Mahler reluctantly accepted for performances. In 1898 Mahler was engaged to succeed Hans Richter as director of the Vienna Phil. Concerts. Here, as in his direction of opera, he proved a great interpreter, but he also allowed himself considerable freedom in rearranging the orchestration of classical scores when he felt it would redound to greater effect. He also aroused antagonism among the players by his autocratic behavior toward them. He resigned from the Vienna Phil. in 1901; in 1907 he also resigned from the Vienna court opera. In the meantime, he became immersed in strenuous work as a composer; he confined himself exclusively to composition of symph. music, sometimes with vocal parts; because of his busy schedule as conductor, he could compose only in the summer months, in a villa on the Wörthersee in Carinthia. In 1902 he married Alma Schindler; they had 2 daughters. The younger daughter, Anna Mahler, was briefly married to Ernst Krenek; the elder daughter died in infancy. Alma Mahler studied music with Zemlinsky, who was the brother-in-law of Arnold Schoenberg.

Having exhausted his opportunities in Vienna, Mahler accepted the post of principal conductor of the Metropolitan Opera in N.Y. in 1907. He made his American debut there on Jan. 1, 1908, conducting *Tristan und Isolde*. In 1909 he was appointed conductor of the N.Y. Phil. Society. His performances both at the Metropolitan and with the N.Y. Phil. were enormously successful with the audiences and the N.Y. music critics, but inevitably he had conflicts with the board of trustees in both organizations, which were mostly commanded by rich women. He resigned from the Metropolitan Opera; on Feb. 21, 1911, he conducted his last concert with the N.Y. Phil. and then returned to Vienna; he died there of pneumonia on May 18, 1911, at the age of 50. The N.Y. newspapers published lurid accounts of his struggle for artistic command with the regimen of the women of the governing committee. Alma Mahler was quoted as saying that although in Vienna even the Emperor himself did not dare to order Mahler about, in N.Y. he had to submit to the whims of 10 ignorant women. The newspaper editorials mourned Mahler's death, but sadly noted that his N.Y. tenure was a failure. As to Mahler's own compositions, the *N.Y. Tribune* said bluntly, "We cannot see how any of his music can long survive him." His symphs. were sharply condemned in the press as being too long, too loud, and too discordant. It was not until the 2nd half of the 20th century that Mahler became fully recognized as a composer, the last great Romantic symphonist. Mahler's symphs. were drawn on the grandest scale, and the technical means employed for the realization of his ideas was correspondingly elaborate. The sources of his inspiration were twofold: the lofty concepts of universal art, akin to those of Bruckner, and ultimately stemming from Wagner; and the simple folk melos of the Austrian countryside, in pastoral moods recalling the intimate episodes in Beethoven's symphs. True to his Romantic nature, Mahler attached descriptive titles to his symphs.; the first was surnamed *Titan;* the 2nd, *Resurrection;* the 3rd, *Ein Sommermorgentraum;* and the 5th, *The Giant.* The great 8th became known as "symph. of a thousand," because it required about 1,000 instrumentalists, vocalists, and soloists for performance; however, this sobriquet was the inspiration of Mahler's agent, not of Mahler himself. Later in life Mahler tried to disassociate his music from their programmatic titles; he even claimed that he never used them in the first place, contradicting the evidence of the MSS, in which the titles appear in Mahler's own handwriting. Mahler was not an innovator in his harmonic writing; rather, he brought the Romantic era to a culmination by virtue of the expansiveness of his emotional expression and the grandiose design of his musical structures. Morbid by nature, Mahler brooded upon the inevitability of death; one of his most poignant compositions was the cycle for voice and orch. *Kindertotenlieder (Songs of the Death of Children);* he wrote it shortly before the death of his little daughter, and somehow he blamed himself for this seeming anticipation of his personal tragedy. In 1910 he consulted Sigmund Freud in Vienna, but the treatment was brief and apparently did not help Mahler to resolve his psychological problems. Unquestionably, Mahler suffered from an irrational feeling of guilt. In the 2nd movement of his unfinished 10th Symph., significantly titled *Purgatorio,* he wrote on the margin, "Madness seizes me, annihilates me," and appealed to the Devil to take possession of his soul. But he never was clinically insane.

Mahler's importance to the evolution of modern music is very great; the early works of Schoenberg and Alban Berg show the influence of Mahler's concepts. A society was formed in the U.S. in 1941 "to develop in the public an appreciation of the music of Bruckner, Mahler and other moderns." An International Gustav Mahler Society was formed in Vienna in 1955, with Bruno Walter as honorary president. On Mahler's centennial, July 7, 1960, the government of Austria issued a memorial postage stamp of one-and-a-half shillings, with Mahler's portrait.

WORKS: SYMPHS.: No. 1, in D, *Titan* (1883–88; Budapest, Nov. 20, 1889, composer conducting; U.S. premiere, N.Y., Dec. 16, 1909, composer conducting; a rejected movement, entitled *Blumine,* was reincorporated and per. separately by Benjamin Britten at the Aldeburgh Music Festival on June 18, 1967); No. 2, in C minor, *Resurrection,* with Soprano, Contralto, and Chorus (1887–94; Berlin, Dec. 13, 1895, composer conducting; American premiere, N.Y., Dec. 8, 1908, composer conducting); No. 3, in D minor, *Ein Sommermorgentraum* (1893–96; Krefeld, June 9, 1902, composer conducting; American premiere, N.Y., Feb. 8, 1922, Mengelberg conducting); No. 4, in G (1899–1901; Munich, Nov. 25, 1901, composer conducting; American premiere, N.Y., Nov. 6, 1904); No. 5, in C-sharp minor, *The Giant* (1901–2;

Cologne, Oct. 18, 1904, composer conducting; American premiere, Cincinnati, March 24, 1905); No. 6, in A minor (1903–5; Essen, May 27, 1906, composer conducting; American premiere, N.Y., Dec. 11, 1946, Mitropoulos conducting); No. 7, in E minor (1904–6; Prague, Sept. 19, 1908, composer conducting; American premiere, Chicago, April 15, 1921); No. 8, in E-flat, "Symphony of a Thousand," with 8 Solo Voices, Adult and Children's Choruses (1906–7; Munich, Sept. 12, 1910, composer conducting; American premiere, Philadelphia, March 2, 1916, Stokowski conducting); No. 9, in D (1909–10; posthumous premiere, Vienna, June 26, 1912, Bruno Walter conducting; American premiere, Boston, Oct. 16, 1931, Koussevitzky conducting); No. 10, in F-sharp minor (sketched 1909–10, unfinished; 2 movements, *Adagio* and *Purgatorio,* perf. in Vienna, Oct. 12, 1924, Franz Schalk conducting; publ. in facsimile, 1924, by Alma Mahler; a performing version of the 10th Symph., using the sketches then available and leaving the 2 scherzo movements in fragmentary form, was made by Deryck Cooke; it was broadcast by the BBC from London for the first time on Dec. 19, 1960; Alma Mahler approved of Cooke's realization; further sketches were made available, and a full performing version was premiered in London, Aug. 13, 1964; the U.S. premiere followed in Philadelphia on Nov. 5, 1965; a final revision of the score was made in 1972).

FOR VOICE: *Das klagende Lied* for Soprano, Contralto, Tenor, Chorus, and Orch. (1878–80; revised 1896–98; Vienna, Feb. 17, 1901, composer conducting); *Lieder und Gesänge aus der Jugendzeit,* 14 songs for Voice and Piano (1880–91); *Lieder eines fahrenden Gesellen,* 4 songs with Orch. (1883–85; Berlin, March 16, 1896, Mahler conducting); 14 Lieder from *Das Knaben Wunderhorn* for Voice and Orch. (1892–1901); 5 songs, to poems by Rückert (1901–3); *Kindertotenlieder,* 5 songs, with Piano or Orch., to poems by Rückert (1901–4; Vienna, Jan. 29, 1905, composer conducting); *Das Lied von der Erde,* symph. for Contralto or Baritone, Tenor, and Orch. (1907–9; Munich, Nov. 20, 1911, Bruno Walter conducting; Philadelphia, Dec. 14, 1916, Stokowski conducting).

Mahler destroyed the MSS of several of his early works, among them a piano quintet, performed in Vienna on July 11, 1878, with the composer at the piano, and 3 unfinished operas: *Herzog Ernst von Schwaben,* to a drama by Uhland; *Die Argonauten,* from a trilogy by Grillparzer, and *Rübezahl,* after Grimm's fairy tales. He further made an arrangement of Weber's *Die drei Pintos* (Leipzig, Jan. 20, 1888, composer conducting) and *Oberon* (c.1907); also arranged Bruckner's 3rd Symph. for 2 Pianos (1878). Mahler made controversial reorchestrations of symphs. by Beethoven, Schumann, and Bruckner, and a version for String Orch. of Beethoven's String Quartet in C-sharp minor, op. 131.

Maier, Guy, American pianist; b. Buffalo, Aug. 15, 1891; d. Santa Monica, Calif., Sept. 24, 1956. He studied at the New England Cons. in Boston, and privately with Schnabel. After a series of solo appearances in the U.S., he formed, with Lee Pattison, a partnership as duo-pianists, and gave numerous concerts with him (until 1931). From 1933 till 1946 he taught at the Juilliard School of Music in N.Y.; in 1946 he went to California. He made numerous transcriptions of various classical works for piano.

Mainardi, Enrico, Italian cellist and composer; b. Milan, May 19, 1897; d. Munich, April 10, 1976. He studied cello and composition at the Milan Cons., graduating in 1920; then went to Berlin, where he was a student of Hugo Becker. He played chamber music; appeared in concerts with Dohnányi; then formed a trio with the flutist Gazzelloni and the pianist Agosti; taught cello at the Santa Cecilia Academy in Rome, beginning in 1933; later went to live in Germany.
WORKS: 3 cello concertos: No. 1 (1943; Rome, May 13, 1947; composer soloist) No. 2 (1960); No. 3, with String Orch. (1966); *Musica per archi; Elegie* for Cello and String Orch. (1957); Concerto for 2 Cellos and Orch. (1969; Freiburg, West Germany, Oct. 12, 1970); *Divertimento* for Cello and String Orch. (1972); 2 unnumbered string trios (1939, 1954); *Suite* for Cello and Piano (1940); Cello Sonatina (1943); *Notturno* for Piano Trio (1947); String Quartet (1951); Cello Sonata (1955); Sonata and *Sonata breve* for Solo Cello; *7 studi brevi* for Solo Cello (1961); *Sonata quasi fantasia* for Cello and Piano (1962); Violin Sonata; Piano Quartet (1968); Viola Sonata (1968); *Burattini,* suite of 12 pieces for Cello and Piano (1968); Trio for Clarinet, Cello, and Piano (1969); String Quintet (1970); Piano Sonatina (1941); other piano pieces.

Maine, Basil Stephen, English writer on music; b. Norwich, March 4, 1894; d. Sheringham, Norfolk, Oct. 13, 1972. He studied with Stanford, Rootham, and Dent at Queen's College in Cambridge; was active after graduation as a schoolteacher and occasionally an actor; in 1921 he became a music director in London; was music critic there in 1925–37; was ordained a priest in 1939. He publ. a number of monographs about music, among them biographies of *Elgar* (2 vols., London, 1933); *Chopin* (London 1933; 2nd ed., 1948); also collections of essays: *The Glory of English Music* (1937); *The Best of Me; A Study in Autobiography* (London, 1937); *Basil Maine on Music* (1945); *Twang with Our Music, Being a Set of Variants to Mark the Completion of Thirty Years' Practice in the Uncertain Science of Music Criticism* (London, 1957). He also composed some choral works and organ pieces.

Mainwaring, John, English churchman and first biographer of Handel; b. Drayton Manor, Staffordshire, c.1724; d. Church Stetton, April 15, 1807. He was educated at St. John's College, Cambridge; was ordained in 1748; in 1749 became rector of Church Stetton, Shropshire; was a Fellow of St. John's College, 1748–88; then became Lady Margaret Prof. of Divinity at Cambridge Univ. His biography of Handel, which utilized material provided by John Christopher Smith, appeared under the title *Memoirs of the Life of the Late George Frederic Handel* (London, 1760); a portion of the biography was written by Robert Price; it was trans. into German by J. Mattheson (Hamburg, 1761).

Mainzer, Joseph, German singing teacher and musical journalist; b. Trier, Oct. 21, 1801; d. Salford, Lancashire, Nov. 10, 1851. He was a chorister at the Trier Cathedral; then studied music in Darmstadt, Munich, and Vienna; returning to his native town, he was ordained a priest; taught at the seminary there, and publ. a sight-singing method, *Singschule* (1831). He then abandoned the priesthood; moved to Brussels (1833), and then to Paris (1834), where he started the short-lived *Chronique Musicale de Paris* (1838). In 1841 he went to England; lived for a time in London, and finally established himself in Manchester as a singing teacher. In 1844 he began publication of the monthly *Mainzer's Musical Times and Singing Circular,* which in 1846 became the *Musical Times* (publ. without interruption through nearly one and a half centuries). Mainzer mastered the English language to such an extent that he was able to engage in aggressive musical journalism. His methods of self-advertising were quite uninhibited; he arranged singing courses in open-air gatherings, and had pamphlets printed with flamboyant accounts of receptions tendered him.

Maitland, John Alexander Fuller. See **Fuller-Maitland, John Alexander.**

Maizel, Boris, significant Russian composer; b. St. Petersburg, July 17, 1907. He graduated from the Leningrad Cons. in 1936, in the composition class of Riazanov; during the siege of Leningrad by the Germans in 1942 he was evacuated to Sverdlovsk; in 1944 he settled in Moscow.
WORKS: For Orch.: 9 symphs.: No. 1 (1940); No. 2, subtitled *Ural Symphony* (1944); No. 3, *Victoriously Triumphant,* written in celebration of the victory over Germany (1945); No. 4 (1947); No. 5 (1962); No. 6 (1967); No. 7 (1970); No. 8 (1973); No. 9 (1976); Double Concerto for Violin, Piano, and Orch. (1949); Double Concerto for Flute, Horn, Strings, and Percussion (1971); Concerto for 10 Instruments (1977); Concerto for 2 Pianos and String Orch. (1978); 3 symph. poems: *Distant Planet* (1961; also as a ballet, 1962); *Leningrad Novella* (1969); *Along Old Russian Towns* (1975). For the stage: *The Shadow of the Past,* opera (1964); *Snow Queen,* ballet (1940; also a symph. suite, 1944); *Sombrero,* children's ballet (1959). Chamber music: Cello Sonata (1936); Piano Trio (1951); 2 string quartets (1937, 1974). Also, song cycles; piano pieces; various theatrical compositions based on the themes of the Buryat Soviet Republic; film music.

Major (real name, **Mayer**), **Jakab Gyula,** Hungarian pianist, conductor, and composer; b. Kosice, Dec. 13, 1858; d. Budapest, Jan. 30, 1925. He studied with Robert Volkmann; graduating from the Budapest Cons. in 1882, he became a teacher in Hungarian schools. He toured in Europe as a pianist; then returned to Budapest. His music follows the Romantic tradition of the German school. He wrote the operas *Erzsike* (Budapest, Sept. 24, 1901), *Széchy Mária* (1906), and *Mila* (1913); 5 symphs.; Piano Concerto; Violin Concerto; Cello Concerto; 4 string quartets; Piano Quintet; 2 violin sonatas; much piano music.

Makarova, Nina, Russian composer; b. Yurino, Aug. 12, 1908; d. Moscow, Jan. 15, 1976. She studied with Miaskovsky at the Moscow Cons., graduating in 1936. Her early works show a Romantic flair, not without some coloristic touches of French Impressionism. She wrote an opera, *Zoya* (1955); a Symph. (1938), which she conducted herself in Moscow on June 12, 1947; a number of violin pieces; a Sonatina and 6 études for piano; several song cycles; a cantata, *The Saga of Lenin* (1970). She was married to **Aram Khachaturian.**

Makedonski, Kiril, Macedonian composer; b. Bitol, Jan. 19, 1925. After completing his academic schooling in Skoplje, he studied with Krso Odak at the Music Academy in Zagreb; later continued his composition studies with Brkanović in Sarajevo, and in Ljubljana with Škerjanc. He is the composer of the first national Macedonian opera, *Goce* (Skoplje, May 24, 1954); his 2nd opera was *Tsar Samuil* (Skoplje, Nov. 5, 1968). He also wrote 4 symphs., chamber music, and a number of choruses. His idiom follows the fundamental vocal and harmonic usages of the Russian national school.

Malcolm, George, English harpsichordist, pianist, and conductor; b. London, Feb. 28, 1917. He studied at Balliol College, Oxford, and at the Royal College of Music, London. He was Master of Music at Westminster Cathedral (1947–59) and artistic director of the Philomusica of London (1962–66), which gave performances of Baroque music. In 1965 he was made a Commander of the Order of the British Empire.

Malcuzynski, Witold, outstanding Polish pianist; b. Warsaw, Aug. 10, 1914; d. Palma, Majorca, July 17, 1977. He studied with Turczynski at the Warsaw Cons.; graduated in 1936; then took lessons with Paderewski in Switzerland. After his marriage to the French pianist **Colette Gaveau,** he went to Paris (1939); then toured in South America (1940–42); made his American debut in 1942; gave concerts in Australia in 1950. He made in all 14 U.S. tours, 9 South American tours, and 2 world tours (1949; 1956). He was particularly distinguished as an interpreter of Chopin.

Maldere (Malderre), Pierre van, Belgian violinist and composer; b. Brussels, Oct. 16, 1729; d. there, Nov. 1, 1768. In 1746 he became a member of the ensemble of the Royal Chapel of Brussels. From 1751 to 1753 he was in Dublin as a violinist, conductor, and composer. He then traveled to Paris (1754) and Austria (1757–58); returning to Brussels, he became conductor of the Opera, and also wrote stage works for production there; in 1762–67 was director of the Grand Théâtre in Brussels. Three of his brothers were also violinists.

Maleingreau (or **Malengreau**), **Paul de,** Belgian composer and organist; b. Trélon-en-Thiérache, Nov. 23, 1887; d. Brussels, Jan. 9, 1956. He studied with Edgar Tinel at the Brussels Cons.; in 1913, became a prof. of harmony there; in 1919, was appointed instructor of organ; in 1946 he was elected president of the Froissart Academy. His performances of Bach organ works were highly regarded in Belgium. Among his compositions are 2 symphs.; *Légende de St. Augustin* for Solo Voices, Chorus, and Orch. (1934); Easter Mass (1925); 2 diptychs for Orch. (1947); organ works; piano pieces.

Malherbe, Charles-Théodore, French writer on music and conductor; b. Paris, April 21, 1853; d. Cormeilles, Eure, Oct. 5, 1911. First he studied law, and was admitted to the bar; but then took up music under A. Danhauser, A. Wormser, and J. Massenet. After a tour (as Danhauser's secretary) through Belgium, the Netherlands, and Switzerland in 1880–81, to inspect the music in the public schools, he settled in Paris; in 1896, was appointed assistant archivist to the Grand Opéra, succeeding Nuitter as archivist in 1899. He edited *Le Ménestrel,* and contributed to many leading reviews and musical journals. His collection of musical autographs, which he left to the Paris Cons., was probably one of the finest private collections in the world.

Malherbe, Edmond Paul Henri, French composer; b. Paris, Aug. 21, 1870; d. Corbeil-Essonnes (Seine-et-Oise), March 7, 1963. He studied at the Paris Cons. with Massenet and Fauré; in 1898, won the Premier Second Prix de Rome, and in 1899, the Deuxième Premier Grand Prix; 3 times winner of the Prix Trémont of the Académie des Beaux-Arts (1907, 1913, 1921); in 1950 received the Grand Prix Musical of the City of Paris for the total of his works. A productive composer, he continued to write music in his 80s, but very few of his larger compositions were performed, and virtually none publ.

Malibran, María Felicità (née **García**), famous contralto, daughter of **Manuel García;** b. Paris, March 24, 1808; d. Manchester, Sept. 23, 1836. Taken to Naples, she played a child's part in Paër's opera *Agnese;* later she studied solfeggio with Panseron; from the age of 15, however, she was her father's pupil in singing. Her debut in London (June 7, 1825), as Rosina in the *Barbiere,* procured her engagement for the season. The family then voyaged to N.Y., where for 2 years she was the popular favorite, singing in *Otello, Romeo, Don Giovanni, Tancredi, Cenerentola,* and the 2 operas which her father wrote for her, *L'Amante astuto* and *La Figlia dell'aria.* In N.Y. she married the French merchant Malibran; he soon became bankrupt, and they separated. Returning to Paris, her immense success led to an engagement at a salary of 50,000 francs; after

1829 she sang every season at London; also appeared at Rome, Naples, Bologna, and Milan. She married the violinist **Bériot** in 1836, only a few months before her death, which was caused by overexertion after a severe fall from her horse. As a singer and actress, she exercised over her audiences the fascination of a highly endowed personality. Her voice was of extraordinary compass, but the medium register had several "dead" tones. She was also a good pianist, and composed numerous nocturnes, romances, and chansonnettes, publ. in album form as *Dernières pensées.*

Malipiero, Francesco, Italian composer, grandfather of **Gian Francesco Malipiero;** b. Rovigio, Jan. 9, 1824; d. Venice, May 12, 1887. He studied with Melchiore Balbi at the Liceo Musicale in Venice. At the age of 18 he wrote an opera, *Giovanna di Napoli,* which was produced with signal success; Rossini praised it. Other operas by Malipiero were *Attila* (Venice, Nov. 15, 1845; renamed later *Ildegonda di Borgogna*); *Alberigo da Romano* (Venice, Dec. 26, 1846; his best); *Fernando Cortez* (Venice, Feb. 18, 1851).

Malipiero, Gian Francesco, greatly distinguished Italian composer; b. Venice, March 18, 1882; d. Treviso, near Venice, Aug. 1, 1973. He was reared in a musical environment: his grandfather, Francesco Malipiero, wrote operas; his father, Luigi Malipiero, was also a musician. In 1898 Malipiero enrolled at the Vienna Cons. as a violin student; in 1899 he returned to Venice, where he studied at the Liceo Musicale Benedetto Marcello with Marco Bossi, whom he followed to Bologna in 1902; he took a diploma in composition at the Liceo Musicale G.B. Martini in Bologna in 1904. In 1913 he went to Paris, where he absorbed the techniques of musical Impressionism, cultivating parallel chord formations and amplified tonal harmonies with characteristic added sixths, ninths, and elevenths. However, his own style of composition was determined by the polyphonic practices of the Italian Baroque. In 1921 Malipiero returned to Italy; taught composition at the Univ. of Parma (1921–23); afterwards lived mostly in Asolo, near Venice. He became director of the Liceo Musicale Benedetto Marcello in Venice in 1939; was named a member of the National Inst. of Arts and Letters in N.Y. in 1949, of the Royal Flemish Academy in Brussels in 1952, of the Institut de France in 1954, and of the Akademie der Künste in West Berlin in 1967. Apart from his activities as composer and educator, Malipiero was the erudite and devoted editor of collected works of Monteverdi and Vivaldi.
WORKS: OPERAS: *Canossa* (1911; Rome, Jan. 24, 1914; destroyed); *Sogno d'un tramonto d'autunno* (1914; not perf. until nearly half a century later, when it was brought out in concert production on the Milan Radio, Oct. 4, 1963); *L'Orfeide,* in 3 parts: *La morte della maschere, 7 canzoni,* and *Orfeo* (1919–22; first complete perf., Düsseldorf, Nov. 5, 1925), the 2nd part, *7 canzoni* (Paris, July 10, 1920), often being perf. separately; the trilogy *3 commedie*

goldoniane (1920–22; consisting of *La bottega da caffè, Sior Todaro Brontolon,* and *Le baruffe chiozzotte,* first perf. in its entirety, Darmstadt, March 24, 1926); *Filomela e l'Infatuato* (1924–25; Prague, March 31, 1928); *Merlino, Maestro d'organi* (1927; Rome Radio, Aug. 4, 1934); *Il mistero di Venezia,* in 3 parts: *Le aquile di aquileia, Il finto Arlecchino,* and *I corvi di San Marco* (1925–28; first perf. in its entirety, Coburg, Germany, Dec. 15, 1932); *Torneo notturno* (1929; Munich, May 15, 1931); *Il festino* (1930; Turin Radio, Nov. 6, 1937); *La favola del figlio cambiato* (1933; Braunschweig, Germany, in a German version, Jan. 13, 1934); *Giulio Cesare* (1935; Genoa, Feb. 8, 1936); *Antonio e Cleopatra* (1937; Florence, May 4, 1938); *Ecuba* (1939; Rome, Jan. 11, 1941); *La vita è sogno* (1940; Breslau, Poland, June 30, 1943); *I capricci di Callot* (1941–42; Rome, Oct. 24, 1942); *L'allegra brigata* (1943; Milan, May 4, 1950); *Mondi celesti e infernali* (1948–49; concert version, Turin Radio, Jan. 12, 1950); *Il Figliuol prodigo* (1952; first stage perf., Florence May Festival, May 14, 1957); *Donna Urraca* (1953; Bergamo, Oct. 2, 1954); *Venere prigioniera* (1955; Florence May Festival, May 14, 1957); *Il Capitan Spavento* (1955; Naples, March 16, 1963); *Il Marescalco* (1960; Treviso, Oct. 1969); *Rappresentazione e festa del Carnasciale e della Quaresima* (1961; Venice, Jan. 20, 1970); *Don Giovanni,* after Pushkin (1962; Naples, Sept. 22, 1963); *Le metamorfosi di Bonaventura* (1963–65; Venice, Sept. 5, 1966); *Don Tartufo bacchettone* (1966; Venice, Jan. 20, 1970); *Gli Eroi di Bonaventura* (1968; Milan, Feb. 5, 1969); *L'Iscariota* (1970; Siena, Aug. 28, 1971); *Uno dei dieci* (1970; Siena, Aug. 28, 1971).
BALLETS: *Pantea* (1918–19; Venice, Sept. 6, 1932); *La mascherata delle principesse prigioniere* (1919; Brussels, Oct. 19, 1924); *Stradivario* (1947–48; Florence, June 20, 1949); *Il mondo novo* (1951; Rome, Dec. 16, 1951; revised as *La lanterna magica,* 1955).
DIALOGHI: No. 1, *con M. de Falla,* for Orch.; No. 2 for 2 Pianos; No. 3, *con Jacopone da Todi,* for Voice and 2 Pianos; No. 4 for Wind Quintet; No. 5 for Viola and Orch.; No. 6 for Harpsichord and Orch.; No. 7 for 2 Pianos and Orch.; No. 8, *La morte di Socrate,* for Baritone and Small Orch. (all 1956–57).
OTHER WORKS FOR ORCH.: *Sinfonia degli eroi* (1905; lost); *Sinfonia del mare* (1906); *Sinfonie del silenzio e della morte* (1908); *Impressioni dal vero* in 3 parts (first part, Milan, May 15, 1913; 2nd part, Rome, March 11, 1917; 3rd part, Amsterdam, Oct. 25, 1923); *Armenia,* on Armenian folk songs (1917); *Ditirambo tragico* (1917; London, Oct. 11, 1919); *Pause del silenzio* in 2 parts (first part, his most famous orch. work, Rome, Jan. 27, 1918; 2nd part, Philadelphia, April 1, 1927); *Per una favola cavalleresca* (1920; Rome, Feb. 13, 1921); *Oriente immaginario* for Chamber Orch. (Paris, Dec. 23, 1920); *Variazioni senza tema* for Piano and Orch. (1923; Prague, May 19, 1925); *L'esilo dell'eroe,* symph. suite (1930); *Concerti per orchestra* (1931; Philadelphia, Jan. 29, 1932); *Inni* (Rome, April 6, 1933); 2 violin concertos: No. 1 (1932; Amsterdam, March 5, 1933) and No. 2 (1963; Venice, Sept. 14, 1965); *7 invenzioni* (1932; Rome, Dec. 24, 1933); *4 invenzioni* (1932; Dresden, Nov. 11, 1936); 11 numbered symphs.: No.

Malipiero

1 (1933; Florence, April 2, 1934); No. 2, *Elegiaca* (1936; Seattle, Jan. 25, 1937); No. 3, *Delle campane* (1944; Florence, Nov. 4, 1945); No. 4, *In Memoriam* (1946; Boston, Feb. 27, 1948; dedicated to the memory of Natalie Koussevitzky); No. 5, *Concertante, in eco,* for 2 Pianos and Orch. (London, Nov. 3, 1947); No. 6, *Degli archi,* for Strings (1947; Basel, Feb. 11, 1949); No. 7, *Delle canzoni* (1948; Milan, Nov. 3, 1949); No. 8, *Symphonia brevis* (1964); No. 9, *Dell'ahimè* (1966; Warsaw, Sept. 21, 1966); No. 10, *Atropo* (1967); No. 11, *Delle cornamuse* (1969); 6 piano concertos: No. 1 (1934; Rome, April 3, 1935); No. 2 (1937; Duisburg, Germany, March 6, 1939); No. 3 (1948; Louisville, Ky., March 8, 1949); No. 4 (1950; Turin Radio, Jan. 28, 1951); No. 5 (1958); No. 6, *Delle macchine* (1964; Rome, Feb. 5, 1966); Cello Concerto (1937; Belgrade, Jan. 31, 1939); *Concerto a 3* for Violin, Cello, Piano, and Orch. (1938; Florence, April 9, 1939); *Sinfonia in un tempo* (1950; Rome, March 21, 1951); *Sinfonia dello zodiaco* (1951; Lausanne, Jan. 23, 1952); *Passacaglie* (1952); *Fantasie di ogni giorni (Fantasies of Every Day;* 1953; Louisville, Nov. 17, 1954); *Elegy-Capriccio* (1953); 4 *Fantasie concertanti* (all 1954): No. 1 for String Orch.; No. 2 for Violin and Orch.; No. 3 for Cello and Orch.; No. 4 for Piano and Orch.; Concerto for 2 Pianos and Orch. (Besançon Festival, Sept. 11, 1957); *Notturno di canti e ballo* (1957); *Serenissima* for Saxophone and Orch. (1961); *Sinfonia per Antigenida* (1962); Flute Concerto (1968).
OTHER VOCAL WORKS: *San Francesco d'Assisi,* mystery for Soli, Chorus, and Orch. (1920; N.Y., March 29, 1922); *La Principessa Ulalia,* cantata (1924; N.Y., Feb. 19, 1927); *La cena* for Soli, Chorus, and Orch. (1927; Rochester, N.Y., April 25, 1929); *Il commiato* for Baritone and Orch. (1934); *La Passione* for Soli, Chorus, and Orch. (Rome, Dec. 15, 1935); *De Profundis* for Solo Voice, Viola, Bass Drum, and Piano (1937); *Missa pro mortuis* for Solo Baritone, Chorus, and Orch. (Rome, Dec. 18, 1938); 4 *vecchie canzoni* for Solo Voice and 7 Instruments (1940; Washington, D.C., April 12, 1941); *Santa Eufrosina,* mystery for Soli, Chorus, and Orch. (Rome, Dec. 6, 1942); *Universa Universis* for Male Chorus and Chamber Orch. (1942; Liviano, April 11, 1943); *Vergilii Aeneis,* heroic symph. for 7 Soli, Chorus, and Orch. (1943–44; Turin, June 21, 1946; scenic version, Venice, Jan. 6, 1958); *Le 7 allegrezze d'amore* for Solo Voice and 14 Instruments (Milan, Dec. 4, 1945); *La Terra* for Chorus and Orch. (1946; Cambridge, Mass., May 2, 1947, with Organ); *I 7 peccati mortali* for Chorus and Orch. (1946; Montecenери, Nov. 20, 1949); *Mondi celesti* for Solo Voice and 10 Instruments (1948; Capri, Feb. 3, 1949); *La festa de la Sensa* for Baritone, Chorus, and Orch. (1948; Brussels Radio, July 2, 1954); 5 *favole* for Solo Voice and Small Orch. (Washington, Oct. 30, 1950); *Passer mortuus est* for a cappella Chorus (Pittsburgh, Nov. 24, 1952); *Magister Josephus* for 4 Voices and Small Orch. (1957); *Preludio e Morte di Macbeth* for Baritone and Orch. (1958); *L'asino d'oro* for Baritone and Orch., after Apuleius (1959); *Concerto di concerti ovvero Dell'-uom malcontento* for Baritone, Concertante Violin, and Orch. (1960); *Abracadabra* for Baritone and Orch. (1962); *Ave Phoebe, dum queror* for Chorus and 20 Instruments (1964); *L'Aredodese* for Reciter, Chorus, and Orch. (1967).
OTHER CHAMBER MUSIC: 8 string quartets: No. 1, *Rispetti e Strombotti* (1920); No. 2, *Stornelli e Ballate* (1923); No. 3, *Cantari alla madrigalesca* (1930; also for String Orch.); No. 4 (1934); No. 5, *Dei capricci* (1940); No. 6, *L'arca di Noè* (1947); No. 7 (1950); No. 8, *Per Elisabetta* (1964); *Ricercari* for 11 Instruments (Washington, Oct. 7, 1926); *Ritrovari* for 11 Instruments (1926; Gardone, Italy, Oct. 26, 1929); *Sonata a 3* for Piano Trio (1927); *Epodi e giambi* for Violin, Viola, Oboe, and Bassoon (1932); *Sonata a 5* for Flute, Violin, Viola, Cello, and Harp (1934); Cello Sonatina (1942); *Sonata a 4* for 4 Winds (1954); *Serenata mattutini* for 10 Instruments (1959); *Serenata* for Bassoon and 10 Instruments (1961); *Macchine* for 14 Instruments (1963); *Endecatode,* chamber symph. for 14 Instruments and Percussion (1966; Dartmouth College, Hanover, N.H., July 2, 1967).
OTHER WORKS FOR PIANO: 6 *morceaux* (1905); *Bizzarrie luminose dell' alba, del meriggio e della notte* (1908); *Poemetti lunari* (1910); *Preludi autunnali* (1914); *Poemi asolani* (1916); *Barlumi* (1917); *Risonanze* (1918); *Maschere che passano* (1918); 3 *omaggi* (1920); *Omaggio a Claude Debussy* (1920); *Cavalcate* (1921); *La siesta* (1921); *Il tarlo* (1922); *Pasqua di Risurrezione* (1924); *Preludi a una fuga* (1926); *Epitaffio* (1931); *Omaggio a Bach* (1932); *Preludi, ritmi e canti gregoriani* (1937); *Preludio e fuga* (1941); *Hortus conclusus* (1946); 5 *studi per domani* (1959).

Malipiero, Riccardo, Italian composer, nephew of **Gian Francesco Malipiero;** b. Milan, July 24, 1914. He studied piano and composition at the Milan and Turin conservatories (1930–37); completed studies with his uncle at the Benedetto Marcello Cons. in Venice (1937–39); traveled as a lecturer and pianist in Europe, South America, and the U.S. As a composer, he followed the Italian neo-Baroque, but about 1950 he adopted a fairly consistent method of 12-tone composition. WORKS: FOR THE STAGE: 3 operas: *Minnie la Candida* (Parma, Nov. 19, 1942); *La Donna è mobile,* opera buffa (1954; Milan, Feb. 22, 1957); television opera, *Battono alla Porta* (Italian Television, Feb. 12, 1962; stage version, Genoa, May 24, 1963). FOR ORCH.: Piano Concerto (1937); 3 *Dances* for Orch. (1937); 2 cello concertos (1938, 1957); *Balleto* for Orch. (1939); *Piccolo concerto* for Piano and Orch. (1945); *Antico sole* for Soprano and Orch. (1947); *Cantata sacra* for Soprano, Chorus, and Orch. (1947); 3 symphs.: No. 1 (1949); No. 2, *Sinfonia Cantata,* for Baritone and Orch. (1956; N.Y., March 19, 1957); No. 3 (1959; Univ. of Florida, Miami, April 10, 1960); Violin Concerto (1952; Milan, Jan. 31, 1953); *Studi* for Orch. (1953; Venice Festival, Sept. 11, 1953); *Ouverture-Divertimento "del Ritorno"* (1953); Concerto for Piano and Chamber Orch. (1955); *Concerto breve* for Ballerina and Chamber Orch. (1956; Venice Festival, Sept. 11, 1956); *Cantata di natale* for Soprano, Chorus, and Orch. (1959; Milan, Dec. 21, 1959); Sonata for Oboe and Strings (1960); *Concerto per Dimitri* for Piano and Orch.

(1961; Venice Festival, April 27, 1961); *Nykteghersia* for Orch. (1962); *Cadencias* for Orch. (1964; Geneva ·Radio, Jan. 13, 1965); *Muttermusik* for Orch. (1965–66; Milan, Feb. 28, 1966); *Mirages* for Orch. (1966; Milan, Feb. 6, 1970); *Carnet de notes* for Chamber Orch. (1967); *Rapsodia* for Violin and Orch. (1967); *Serenata per Alice Tully* for Chamber Orch. (1969; N.Y., March 10, 1970); *Monologo* for Female Voice and Strings (1969); Concerto for Piano Trio and Orch. (1971; Milan, Jan. 16, 1976); *Requiem 1975* for Orch. (Florence, Nov. 6, 1976); *Go Placidly* for Baritone and Chamber Orch. (1976; N.Y., Nov. 10, 1976). CHAMBER MUSIC: *Musik I* for Cello and 9 Instruments (1938); 3 string quartets (1941, 1954, 1960); Violin Sonata (1956); Piano Quintet (1957); *Musica da camera* for Wind Quintet (1959); Oboe Sonata (1959); *6 poesie di Dylan Thomas* for Soprano and 10 Instruments (1959); *Mosaico* for Wind and String Quintets (1961); *Preludio Adagio e Finale* for Soprano, 5 Percussionists, and Piano (1963); *In Time of Daffodils*, to poems by e.e. cummings, for Soprano, Baritone, and 7 Instrumentalists (Washington, D.C., Oct. 30, 1964); *Nuclei* for 2 Pianos and Percussion (1966); *Cassazione* for String Sextet (1967); Piano Trio (1968); *Ciaccona di Davide* for Viola and Piano (1970); *Memoria* for Flute and Piano (1973); *Giber Folia* for Clarinet and Piano (1973). FOR PIANO: *14 Inventions* (1938); *Musik* for 2 Pianos (1939); *Piccolo musica* (1941); *Invenzioni* (1949); *Costellazioni* (1965); *Le Rondini de Alessandro* (1971). He publ. several monographs: *J.S. Bach* (Brescia, 1948); *Debussy* (Brescia, 1948); *Guida alla dodecafonia* (Milan, 1961); *Musica ieri e oggi* (with E. Radius and G. Severi; 6 vols., Rome, 1970).

Maliponte, Adriana, Italian soprano; b. Brescia, Dec. 26, 1938. Her family moved to Mulhouse, and she studied at the Cons. there. She made her operatic debut as Mimi in *La Bohème* at the Teatro Nuovo, Milan, in 1958; also sang minor roles at La Scala; subsequently had engagements at the Paris Opéra and the Opéra-Comique. She made her American debut in Philadelphia in 1963; then sang in Chicago and Cincinnati. On March 19, 1971, she made her Metropolitan Opera debut in N.Y. as Mimi.

Maliszewski, Witold, Polish composer; b. Mohylev-Podolsk, July 20, 1873; d. Zalesie, July 18, 1939. He studied piano in Warsaw and violin in Tiflis; then enrolled in the St. Petersburg Cons., in the class of Rimsky-Korsakov. He became director of the Odessa Cons. in 1908; went to Poland in 1921, and was active there mainly as a teacher; in 1932 he joined the staff of the Warsaw Cons. As a composer, he followed the Russian Romantic tradition; some of his symph. works had a modicum of success. He wrote the operas *The Mermaid* (Warsaw, 1928) and *Boruta* (1930); 4 symphs.; Piano Concerto (1932); 4 string quartets; Violin Sonata; Cello Sonata; many piano pieces; songs.

Malko, Nicolai, eminent Russian conductor; b. Brailov, May 4, 1883; d. Sydney, Australia, June 23, 1961. He studied philology at the Univ. of St. Peters-

burg, graduating in 1906; also studied composition and orchestration with Rimsky-Korsakov, Liadov, and Glazunov; conducting with Tcherepnin. After graduation he went to Munich, where he took a conducting course with Mottl. Returning to Russia, he conducted opera in St. Petersburg; was conductor of the Leningrad Phil. (1926–28), with which he performed many new works by Soviet composers, including the premiere of Shostakovich's First Symph. In 1928 he left Russia; conducted orchs. in Vienna, Buenos Aires, Prague, etc.; was particularly successful in Denmark, where he made frequent appearances, and established a conducting class; many Danish musicians became his pupils, including the King of Denmark, who was a talented amateur. In 1938 he visited the U.S. as a lecturer; also appeared as guest conductor with several American orchs.; became an American citizen on May 7, 1946. He subsequently conducted the Yorkshire Symph. Orch. in England (1954–56). In 1956 he was appointed resident conductor of the Sydney Symph. Orch. in Australia, where he established a fine tradition of orch. performance, striving above all for clarity and balance of sonorities. He publ. a manual, *The Conductor and His Baton* (Copenhagen, 1950), and his memoir, *A Certain Age* (N.Y., 1966); also composed various works, among them a Clarinet Concerto (Copenhagen, Sept. 27, 1952). The Danish Radio inaugurated in his honor a triennial Malko International Contest for conductors.

Malling, Otto (Valdemar), Danish composer; b. Copenhagen, June 1, 1848; d. there, Oct. 5, 1915. He studied with Gade and J.P.E. Hartmann at the Copenhagen Cons.; conducted the Student's Choral Society (1872–84); was an organist at various churches in Copenhagen (1878–1910); became conductor of the Concert Society there (1874–93); in 1885 was appointed instructor of music theory at the Copenhagen Cons.; in 1899 became its director. WORKS: His publ. works, comprising about 100 opus numbers, include a Symph.; Fantasia for Violin and Orch.; *Oriental Suite, Musique de ballet;* Piano Concerto; several cantatas; works for organ; numerous songs; characteristic pieces for piano; ballet, *Askepot (Cinderella;* Copenhagen, Sept. 25, 1910); and a treatise on instrumentation.

Malotte, Albert Hay, American organist and song composer; b. Philadelphia, May 19, 1895; d. Los Angeles, Nov. 16, 1964. He was a chorister at St. James Episcopal Church; studied with W.S. Stansfield, and later in Paris with Georges Jacob; then moved to Hollywood, where he became a member of the music staff of the Walt Disney Studios; composed the scores for some of Disney's "Silly Symphonies" and "Ferdinand, the Bull." He was the composer of the enormously popular setting *The Lord's Prayer* (1935); he also set to music the 23rd Psalm and other religious texts.

Mamangakis, Nikos, Greek composer; b. Rethymnon, Crete, March 3, 1929. He studied music at the Hellikon Cons. in Athens (1947–53); then composition with Carl Orff and Harald Genzmer at the Hochschule für Musik in Munich (1957–61) and electronic music at the Siemens Studio in Munich (1961–62); subsequently divided his time between Athens and Berlin. His works reflect modern quasi-mathematical procedures, with numerical transformations determining pitch, rhythm, and form.

WORKS: *Music for 4 Protagonists* for 4 Voices and 10 Instrumentalists, on a text by Kazantzakis (1959–60); *Constructions* for Flute and Percussion (1959–60); *Combinations* for Solo Percussionist and Orch. (1961); *Speech Symbols* for Soprano, Bass, and Orch. (1961–62); "Cycle of Numbers": No. 1, *Monologue*, for Solo Cello (1962); No. 2, *Antagonisms*, for Cello and One Percussionist moving in an arc along the stage (1963); No. 3, *Trittys (Triad)*, for Guitar, 2 Double Basses, Santouri, and Percussion (1966); and No. 4, *Tetraktys*, for String Quartet (1963–66); *Kassandra* for Soprano and 6 Performers (1963); *Erotokritos*, ballad for 3 Voices and 5 Instruments in an old style (1964); *Ploutos*, popular opera after Aristophanes (1966); *Theama-Akroama*, visual-auditive event (happening) for Actor, Dancer, Painter, Singer, and 8 Instruments (Athens, April 3, 1967); *Scenario for 2 Improvised Art Critics* for Voice, Instruments, and Tape (1968); *Antinomies* for Solo Voice, Flute, Electric Double Bass, 2 Harps, 4 Cellos, 2 Percussionists, Hammond Organ, 4 Basses, and 4 Sopranos (Athens, Dec. 18, 1968); *Bolivar*, folk cantata in pop-art style (1968); *The Bacchants*, electronic ballet (1969); *Parastasis* for various Flutes, Voice, and Tape (1969); *Askesis* for Solo Cello (1969-70); *Perilepsis* for Solo Flute (1970); *Erophili*, popular opera (1970); *Anarchia* for Solo Percussion and Orch. (Donaueschingen, Oct. 16, 1971); *Penthima*, in memory of Jani Christou, for Solo Guitar (1970–71); *Monologue II* for Violin and Tape (1971); *Kykeon* for several Solo Instruments (1972); *Olophyrmos* for Magnetic Tape (1973).

Mamiya, Michio, brilliant Japanese composer; b. Asahikawa, Hokkaido, June 29, 1929. He studied with Ikenouchi at the State Music School in Tokyo; upon graduation he devoted himself mainly to the cultivation of national Japanese music in modern forms, with inventive uses of dissonant counterpoint and coloristic instrumentation.

WORKS: Opera, *Mukashi banashi hitokai Tarobê* (*A Fable from Olden Times about Tarobê, the Slavedealer;* 1959); oratorio, *15 June 1960,* an homage to an activist Japanese student killed during the demonstration against the renewal of the Japanese-American defense treaty (1961); a musical, *Elmer's Adventure* (Tokyo Radio, Aug. 28, 1967); 2 piano concertos (1954, 1970); Sonata for Violin, Piano, Percussion, and Double Bass (1966); Violin Concerto (Tokyo, June 24, 1959); Quartet for Japanese Instruments (1962); Sonata for Violin Solo (1971); Nonet (1972); a number of choral works.

Mana-Zucca (real name, **Augusta Zuckermann**), American pianist and composer; b. New York, Dec. 25, 1887; d. Miami Beach, March 8, 1981. She studied piano with Alexander Lambert in N.Y.; then went to

Europe, where she took some lessons with Leopold Godowsky and Busoni in Berlin. Upon her return to the U.S., she was exhibited as a piano prodigy. In 1916 she changed her name by juggling around the syllables of her real last name and dropping her first name altogether. She was soloist in her own Piano Concerto in N.Y. on Aug. 20, 1919; her Violin Concerto, op. 224, was performed in N.Y. on Dec. 9, 1955. She further wrote 2 operas, *Hypatia* and *The Queue of Ki-Lu;* a ballet, *The Wedding of the Butterflies;* and a number of unpretentious orch. pieces, such as *Frolic for Strings, Fugato Humoresque, Bickerings,* and *Havana Nights.* She publ., under the title *My Musical Calendar,* a collection of 366 piano pieces, one to be played every day, with the supernumerary opus to account for leap years. But she attained real success with her lyrically soaring songs, most of them to her own words, with such appealing titles as *I Love Life* and *There's Joy in My Heart.* In 1940 she settled in Florida.

Mancinelli, Luigi, distinguished Italian conductor and composer; b. Orvieto, Feb. 5, 1848; d. Rome, Feb. 2, 1921. He studied organ and cello with his brother, Marino; then was a cellist in the Orvieto cappella and the orch. of the Teatro della Pergola in Florence; he also studied cello with Sbolà and composition with Mabellini in Florence; then was first cellist and maestro concertatore at the Teatro Morlacchi in Perugia; in 1874 he made his conducting debut there in *Aida* after the regular conductor was unable to lead the performance owing to a temporarily inebriated condition. He then was called to Rome, where he was conductor of the Teatro Apollo from 1874 to 1881; subsequently he served as director of the Cons. in Bologna. On June 18, 1886, he made his London debut conducting a concert performance; in 1887 he conducted at Drury Lane; from 1888 to 1905 he was chief conductor at Covent Garden; from 1887 to 1893 conducted opera in Madrid. He joined the roster of the Metropolitan Opera in N.Y. in 1893, and continued to conduct there until 1903. On May 25, 1908, he led the first performance at the newly opened Teatro Colón in Buenos Aires; he returned there in 1909, 1910, and 1913. He enjoyed a fine reputation as a competent, dependable, and resourceful opera conductor; naturally, he excelled in the Italian repertoire, but he also conducted Wagner's operas, albeit in dubious Italian translation. From his experience as an opera conductor, he learned the art of composing for the theater; his operas are indeed most effective; of these, *Ero e Leandro* became a favorite.

Mancini, Henry, American composer of film and television music; b. Cleveland, April 16, 1924, of Italian parents. He took piccolo lessons from his father, a member of the Sons of Italy band in Aliquippa, Pa. After playing in dance bands, he studied at Carnegie Inst. in Pittsburgh and at the Juilliard School of Music in N.Y. He further studied composition in Los Angeles with Castelnuovo-Tedesco, Ernst Krenek, and Alfred Sendrey. In 1952 he became a composer for Universal-International film studios and in 1958 began writing background music for television. His jazzy theme for the Peter Gunn series placed him at once as one of the most adroit composers of melodramatic music; he won 5 television awards and several Academy Awards for film scores.

Mandel, Alan, brilliant American pianist; b. New York, July 17, 1935. He began taking piano lessons with Hedy Spielter at the incredible underage of 3½, and continued under her pianistic care until he was 17. In 1953 he entered the class of Rosina Lhévinne at the Juilliard School of Music in N.Y. (B.S., 1956; M.S., 1957); later took private lessons with Leonard Sure (1957–60). In 1961 he obtained a Fulbright fellowship; went to Salzburg, where he studied advanced composition with Hans Werner Henze (1961–63). Returning to the U.S., he taught piano at Pa. State College (1963–66). In 1966 he was appointed head of the piano division at the American Univ. in Washington, D.C. In 1980 he founded the Washington Music Ensemble with the aim of presenting modern music of different nations. As a pianist, he made 24 tours in 45 countries, not counting islands, north and south; toured Australia twice. One of Mandel's chief accomplishments was the recording of the complete piano works of Charles Ives; he also recorded 40 piano works of Gottschalk and all the piano sonatas of **Elie Siegmeister** (his father-in-law). Mandel's own compositions include a Piano Concerto (1950), a Symph. (1961), and a number of pieces for piano solo.

Mandyczewski, Eusebius, eminent Austrian musicologist; b. Czernowitz, Aug. 17, 1857; d. Vienna, July 13, 1929. He studied with Robert Fuchs and Nottebohm in Vienna; in 1880 he became choirmaster of the Vienna Singakademie, and archivist to the Gesellschaft der Musikfreunde; in 1896 he joined the faculty of the Vienna Cons., where he taught music history and composition. He was subsequently engaged as one of the editors of the great edition of Haydn's works undertaken by Breitkopf & Härtel; collaborated in many other scholarly editions, including the complete works of Brahms, who was a friend of his; his correspondence with Brahms was publ. by Karl Geiringer in the *Zeitschrift für Musikwissenschaft* (May 1933).

Manfredini, Francesco, Italian violinist and composer; b. Pistoia (baptized, June 22), 1684; d. there, Oct. 6, 1762. He was engaged as a violinist in Ferrara and Bologna (1704–11); was maestro di cappella at the Cathedral of Pistoia from 1727. He publ. *Concertini per camera* (1704); *12 sinfonie da chiesa* (1709); *12 concerti grossi* (1718). His *Concerto grosso per il santissimo natale* (which includes a fine *Pastorale*) was publ. for 2 Violins, String Quartet, and Piano (Leipzig, 1906); his 6 sonatas for 2 Violins and Cello appeared in London (c.1764); his Sinfonia No. 10, in Vienna (1935); the Concerto Grosso No. 9 was edited for string orch. by E. Bonelli (Padua, 1948); the Sinfonia No. 12, was edited by R. Nielsen (Rome, 1949).

Manfredini, Vincenzo, Italian composer, son of **Francesco Manfredini;** b. Pistoia, Oct. 22, 1737; d. St. Petersburg, Aug. 16, 1799. He was a pupil of his father; later studied with Perti in Bologna and with Fioroni in Milan. In 1758 he went to Russia, where he was attached to the court (until 1769); then returned to Italy; lived in Bologna and Venice; in 1798 was engaged by Paul I (who was his former pupil) to come to Russia again; he died there the following year. During his first visit to Russia he produced the following works: *Amour et Psyché,* ballet (Moscow, Oct. 20, 1762); *L'Olimpiade,* opera (Moscow, Nov. 24, 1762); *Pygmalion,* ballet (St. Petersburg, Sept. 26, 1763); *Carlo Magno,* opera (St. Petersburg, Nov. 24, 1763); wrote 6 clavecin sonatas for Catherine the Great (1765).

Mangold, Karl (Ludwig Amand), German composer, brother of **Wilhelm Mangold;** b. Darmstadt, Oct. 8, 1813; d. Oberstdorf, Aug. 5, 1889. He studied at the Paris Cons. with Berton and Bordogni; returning to Darmstadt, became a violinist in the court orch.; from 1848–69, was court music director; also conducted various choral societies there. He wrote an opera, *Tannhäuser,* which was produced in Darmstadt on May 17, 1846, only a few months after the premiere of Wagner's great work; in order to escape disastrous comparisons, the title was changed to *Der getreue Eckart,* and the libretto revised; the new version was produced posthumously in Darmstadt on Jan. 17, 1892. Mangold wrote 2 more operas, *Gudrun* and *Dornröschen;* several "concert dramas" (*Frithjof, Hermanns Tod, Ein Morgen am Rhein, Barbarossas Erwachen*); also oratorios (*Abraham, Wittekind, Israel in der Wüste*); chamber music; and a number of male quartets, which attained great popularity in Germany.

Mangold, (Johann) Wilhelm, German composer and violinist, brother of **Karl Mangold;** b. Darmstadt, Nov. 19, 1796; d. there, May 23, 1875. He studied with Rinck and Abbé Vogler; then went to Paris for lessons with Cherubini at the Paris Cons.; in 1825, became court conductor at Darmstadt; was pensioned in 1858. He wrote 3 operas, chamber music, and melodies for clarinet with piano, which were popular for a time.

Mann, Robert, American violinist, composer, and conductor; b. Portland, Oreg., July 19, 1920. He studied violin with Edouard Déthier at the Juilliard Graduate School in N.Y., and had instruction in chamber music with Adolfo Betti, Felix Salmond, and Hans Letz; also took courses with Edgar Schenkman in conducting, and Bernard Wagenaar and Stefan Wolpe in composition. In 1941 he won the Naumburg Competition, and made his N.Y. debut as a violinist. From 1943 to 1946 he was in the U.S. Army; then joined the faculty of the Juilliard School and in 1948 founded the Juilliard String Quartet, in which he plays first violin, and which was to become one of the most highly regarded chamber music groups; in 1962 it was established as the quartet in residence under the Whittall Foundation at the Library of Congress, without suspending its concert tours in America and abroad. As a conductor, Robert Mann specializes in contemporary music; was associated as a performer and lecturer with the Music Festival and Inst. at Aspen, Colo., and also served with the National Endowment for the Arts; in 1971 he was appointed president of the Walter W. Naumburg Foundation, with his wife, Lucy Rowan, as secretary and executive administrator. He has composed a String Quartet (1952); *Suite* for String Orch. (1965); several "lyric trios" for violin, piano, and narrator.

Mannes, Clara Damrosch, pianist, daughter of **Leopold Damrosch;** b. Breslau, Dec. 12, 1869; d. New York, March 16, 1948. At the age of 6 she began to study piano in N.Y.; then went to Dresden, where she took lessons with H. Scholtz; later also was a pupil of Busoni in Berlin (1897). On June 4, 1898, she married the violinist **David Mannes,** with whom she toured the U.S. and England for 20 years in joint recitals; was co-director of the Mannes School in N.Y.

Mannes, David, American violinist and conductor; b. New York, Feb. 16, 1866; d. there, April 25, 1959. He studied violin in Berlin, and was briefly a student of Ysaÿe in Brussels (1903). He was a member of the N.Y. Symph. Orch. conducted by Walter Damrosch, beginning in 1891, and was its concertmaster from 1898 to 1912; married **Clara Damrosch,** June 4, 1898. In 1912 he founded in N.Y. the Music School Settlement for Colored People; conducted a series of free symph. concerts at the Metropolitan Museum in N.Y. (1919–47). In 1916 he opened his own music school in N.Y., known as the David Mannes School of Music; continued to be active until a very advanced age; on his 90th birthday, in 1956, a special concert was organized in his honor at the Metropolitan Museum. He publ. an autobiography, *Music Is My Faith* (N.Y., 1938).

Mannes, Leopold Damrosch, American pianist, son of **David Mannes** and **Clara Damrosch Mannes;** b. New York, Dec. 26, 1899; d. Martha's Vineyard, Cape Cod, Mass., Aug. 11, 1964. He graduated from Harvard Univ. (B.A., 1920); studied at the David Mannes School and at the Inst. of Musical Art in N.Y.; was a pupil of Elizabeth Quaile, Guy Maier, and Alfred Cortot (piano), and Schreyer, Scalero, and Goetschius (theory); won a Pulitzer scholarship (1925) and a Guggenheim fellowship (1926); subsequently taught composition and piano at the Inst. of Musical Art and at the Mannes School; succeeded his father as director of the latter. He temporarily abandoned music as a profession to enter the research laboratory of the Eastman Kodak Co. at Rochester, N.Y., and was a co-inventor, with Leopold Godowsky (son of the pianist), of the Kodachrome process of color photography. Among his works are: Suite for 2 Pianos (1924); String Quartet (1928; perf. many times by the Kneisel Quartet); *3 Short Pieces* for Orch. (1926); incidental music to Shakespeare's *Tempest* (1930).

Mannino, Franco, Italian pianist, conductor, and composer; b. Palermo, April 25, 1924. He studied piano with R. Silvestri and composition with V. Mortari at the Santa Cecilia Academy in Rome; made his debut as a pianist at the age of 16; subsequently toured as a pianist in Europe and America. In 1957 he conducted the orch. of the Maggio Musicale of Florence on a tour of the U.S. He subsequently conducted in Europe, South America, and the Far East; was a frequent guest conductor in the Soviet Union, where he regularly appeared with the Leningrad Phil. In 1969 he became artistic director of the Teatro San Carlo in Naples; from 1974 was its artistic adviser. In 1982 he was appointed principal conductor and artistic adviser of the National Arts Centre Orch. in Ottawa. He was a prolific composer; his operas and other works are written in traditional melodramatic Italian style, diversified by occasional modernistic procedures.

WORKS: OPERAS: *Mario e il mago* (1952; Milan, Feb. 23, 1956); *Vivi* (1955; Naples, March 28, 1957; many subsequent perfs.); *La speranza* (1956; Trieste, Feb. 14, 1970); *La stirpe di davide* (1958; Rome, April 19, 1962); *Le notti della paura* (1960; RAI, Rome, May 24, 1963); *Il Diavolo in giardino* (1962; Palermo, Feb. 28, 1963); *Luisella* (1969; Palermo, Feb. 28, 1963); *Il quadro delle meraviglie* (1963; Rome, April 24, 1963); *Il ritratto di Dorian Gray* (1973; Catania, Jan. 12, 1982); *Il Principe Felice* (1981). FOR ORCH.: Piano Concerto (1954; Remschied, Dec. 1, 1954); *Sinfonia Americana* (1954; Florence, Nov. 11, 1956); *Sinfonia* (1958); *Demoniaca,* overture (1963); Concerto for 3 Violins (1965; Moscow, March 21, 1966); *Laocoonte* for Orch. (1966; Trieste, May 8, 1968); Concerto for Piano, 3 Violins, and Orch. (1969); *Notturno Napoletano* (1969; Naples, March 13, 1970); *Concerto grosso* (1970); Violin Concerto (1970; Milan, May 14, 1971); Concerto No. 2 for Piano (1974; Cagliari, April 22, 1980); Cello Concerto (1974; Naples, July 14, 1975); *Supreme Love,* cantata for Solo Voices, Chorus, and Orch. (1977; Naples, Sept. 30, 1978); *Settecento* for Orch. (1979); *Olympic Concert* for 6 Violins, 2 Pianos, and Orch. (1979); *Nirvana,* poem for Orch. (1980; Cagliari, April 22, 1980); Concerto for 6 Violins, 2 Pianos, and Orch. (1980); Symph. No. 4, *Leningrad* (1981; Lecce, May 11, 1982).

Manns, Sir August, German-English conductor; b. Stolzenberg, near Stettin, March 12, 1825; d. London, March 1, 1907. He learned to play the violin, clarinet, and flute; was a member of various bands in Danzig and Berlin; then conducted bands in Königsberg and Cologne. In 1854 he went to London, where he became a conductor at the Crystal Palace; in 1855 he inaugurated the famous Saturday Concerts at the Crystal Palace, which he conducted for 45 seasons, until 1901, presenting about 14,000 concerts in all, in programs of a regular symph. repertoire. He became a celebrated musical and social figure in London, and was knighted in 1903. Besides the Saturday Concerts, he conducted 6 Triennial Handel Festivals (1883–1900) and the orch. concerts of the Glasgow Choral Union (1879–92).

Manschinger, Kurt, Austrian composer; b. Zeil-Wieselburg, in a castle of which his father was an administrator, July 25, 1902; d. New York, Feb. 23, 1968. He studied musicology at the Univ. of Vienna, and at the same time took private lessons with Anton von Webern (1919–26). After graduation he was mainly active as a theatrical conductor in Austria and Germany. His practical acquaintance with operatic production led to his decision to write operas, for which his wife, the singer **Greta Hartwig,** wrote librettos. Of these, his first opera, *Madame Dorette,* was to be performed by the Vienna State Opera, but the invasion of Austria by the Nazi troops in 1938 made this impossible. Manschinger and his wife fled to London, where they organized an émigré theater, The Lantern. In 1940 they emigrated to America; Manschinger changed his name to **Ashley Vernon** and continued to compose; earned his living as a musical autographer by producing calligraphic copies of music scores for publishers.
WORKS: Operas: *The Barber of New York* (N.Y., May 26, 1953); *Grand Slam* (Stamford, Conn., June 25, 1955); *Cupid and Psyche* (Woodstock, N.Y., July 27, 1956); *The Triumph of Punch* (Brooklyn, Jan. 25, 1969); *Der Talisman* for Voices, Violin, Viola, Cello, and Piano (London, Feb. 24, 1940); Sinfonietta (1964); Symph. (1967); chamber music.

Manski, Dorothée, American soprano; b. New York, March 11, 1895; d. Atlanta, Feb. 24, 1967. She went to Germany as a child; appeared at Berlin in Max Reinhardt's productions; made her first American appearance with the Metropolitan Opera in N.Y., on Nov. 5, 1927, as the Witch in *Hänsel und Gretel;* remained with the Metropolitan Opera until 1941; then joined the faculty of the School of Music at Indiana Univ. as a vocal teacher.

Mantovani, Annunzio Paolo, Italian conductor of popular music; b. Venice, Nov. 15, 1905; d. Tunbridge Wells, England, March 29, 1980. He went to London as a youth; studied at the Trinity College of Music there; became a British subject in 1933. He formed an orch. of his own in Birmingham at the age of 18; then led bands in hotels and in theaters. His ingratiatingly harmonious orch. arrangements made his name famous; the "Mantovani sound" became a byword with sedentary music-lovers seeking relaxation and listening pleasure as an antidote to the dramatic enervation of hazardous modern living and raucous popular music.

Manuel, Roland. See **Roland-Manuel, Alexis.**

Manzoni, Giacomo, Italian composer; b. Milan, Sept. 26, 1932. He studied music in Messina and Milan; taught composition at the Milan Cons. (1962–64) and at the Bologna Cons. (1965–75). His opera *Atomtod* (*Atom Death*), descriptive in apocalyptic sounds of the ultimate atomic war, attracted a great deal of attention at its production (Milan, March 17, 1965). Other works: opera, *La sentenza* (Bergamo, Oct. 13, 1960); *5 Vicariote* for Chorus and Orch. (Radio Turin, Nov. 29, 1968); *Don Chisciotte* for So-prano, Small Chorus, and Chamber Orch. (1961; Venice Festival, Sept. 14, 1964); *4 poesie spagnole* for Baritone, Clarinet, Viola, and Guitar (1961); *Studio per 24* for Chamber Orch. (1962); *Studio No. 2* for Orch. (Milan, April 20, 1963); *Studio No. 3* for Tape (1964); *Musica notturna* for 5 Wind Instruments, Piano, and Percussion (1966); *Insiemi* for Orch. (Milan, Oct. 30, 1969); *Spiel* for 11 Strings (1969); *Parafrasi con finale* for 10 Instruments (1969); *Variabili* for Orch. (1973); *Percorso C* for Bassoon and String Orch. (1976).

Mapleson, Col. James Henry, English impresario; b. London, May 4, 1830; d. there, Nov. 14, 1901. He studied at the Royal Academy of Music in London; subsequently was engaged as a singer and a viola player; sang in Italy under the name of **Enrico Mariani.** In 1861 he became the manager of the Italian Opera at the Lyceum Theatre in London; then of Her Majesty's Theatre (1862–67); at Drury Lane (1868–69); in partnership with Gye at Covent Garden (1869–70); again at Drury Lane (1871–76); at the reconstructed (after the fire of 1868) Her Majesty's Theatre (from 1877). He gave several seasons of opera in the U.S. (during intervals of his London enterprises); his American ventures fluctuated between success and disaster; his last season was 1896–97 at the N.Y. Academy of Music. On March 17, 1890, he married the American singer **Laura Schirmer.** An exuberant personality, he dominated the operatic news in both England and America by his recurrent professional troubles and his conflicts with, and attachments to, prima donnas. He was known as "Colonel" Mapleson by his intimates, but held no such rank. He publ. *The Mapleson Memoirs* (2 vols., London, 1888). His nephew, **Lionel S. Mapleson** (b. London, Oct. 23, 1865; d. New York, Dec. 21, 1937), came to the U.S. as a violinist; in 1889 joined the orch. of the Metropolitan Opera in N.Y.; then, for a half century, was librarian there; left his own valuable library to the Metropolitan Opera, including the first recordings, made by himself, ever taken of actual performances, with the voices of de Reszke, Calvé, and others.

Mara, Gertrud Elisabeth (née **Schmeling**), German soprano; b. Kassel, Feb. 23, 1749; d. Reval, Russia, Jan. 20, 1833. She learned to play the violin as a child; gave concerts in Vienna and London; returning to Germany, she studied voice and developed an extraordinary range, reaching high E; she sang in Hiller's concerts in Leipzig in 1766; then sang with the Dresden Opera (1767–71) and was engaged by the Berlin Opera (1771–79). She married the cello player Mara, and appeared under her married name. From 1784 to 1802 she lived mostly in London; in 1799 she separated from her husband; then went to Russia, where she supported herself as a singing teacher; she lived in Moscow until 1812, when Napoleon's invasion forced her to seek refuge elsewhere; from 1813 she was a singing teacher in Reval, where she remained until the end of her life. She was a famous prima donna in her time, and there was much literature written about her.

Marais, Marin, great French player of the viola da gamba and composer; b. Paris, May 31, 1656; d. there, Aug. 15, 1728. He was apprenticed as a choirboy at the Sainte-Chapelle; studied bass viol with Sainte-Colombe and composition with Lully (whom he addresses as teacher in a letter publ. in his first book of pieces for his instrument). He then became "joueur de viole du roi" (Aug. 1, 1679). In 1686 he presented at Versailles an *Idylle dramatique;* in 1701 he was called upon to write a Te Deum for the convalescence of the Dauphin. He retired in 1725. Marais possessed matchless skill as a virtuoso on the viola da gamba, and set a new standard of excellence by enhancing the sonority of the instrument. He also established a new method of fingering, which had a decisive influence on the technique of performance. As a composer, he followed Lully's French manner; his recitatives comport with the rhythm of French verse and the inflection of the rhyme. The purely instrumental parts in his operas were quite extensive; in *Alcione* (Paris, Feb. 18, 1706) he introduced a "tempeste," which is one of the earliest attempts at stage realism in operatic music. His other operas are *Alcide* (1693), *Ariane et Bacchus* (1696), and *Sémélé* (1709). He publ. 5 books of pieces for gamba (1686–1725); trios (or "symphonies") for violin, flute, and viola da gamba (1692); a book of trios for violin, viola da gamba, and harpsichord under the title *La Gamme* (1723). An edition of his instrumental works, edited by J. Hsu, began publication in N.Y. in 1980. He was married on Sept. 21, 1676, and had 19 children; in 1709 he played a concert with 3 of them for Louis XIV. His son **Roland** was also a talented gambist; he publ. 2 books of pieces for the instrument with a basso continuo and a *Nouvelle méthode de musique pour servir d'introduction aux acteurs modernes* (1711).

Marazzoli, Marco, significant Italian composer; b. Parma, between 1602 and 1608; d. Rome, Jan. 26, 1662. In 1631 he gained the patronage of Cardinal Antonio Barberini in Rome; in 1637 he settled in Rome in the cardinal's service and became a tenor in the Papal Chapel, a position he held until his death; he also was engaged by Cardinal Mazarin in Paris in 1643; returned to Rome in 1645; in 1656 he became virtuoso di camera to Queen Christina of Sweden, who held her court in Rome at the time. Marazzoli was a prolific composer of choral music; about 375 of his cantatas and oratorios are extant. His name is also associated with that of Virgilio Mazzocchi; they collaborated on the first comic opera, *Chi soffre, speri* (Rome, Feb. 27, 1639), which was a revision of *Il facone* (Rome, Feb. 1637). His other operas include *L'amore trionfante dello sdegno* (also known as *L'Armida;* Ferrara, Feb. 1641); *Gli amori di Giasone e d'Issifile* (Venice, 1642; not extant); *Le pretensioni del Tebro e del Po* (Ferrara, March 4, 1642); *Il capriccio* or *Il giudizio della ragione fra la Beltà e l'Affetto* (Rome, 1643); *Dal male il bene* (with A.M. Abbatini; Rome, 1653); *Le armi e gli amori* (Rome, 1654); *La vita humana, ovvero Il trionfo della pietà* (Rome, Jan. 31, 1656).

Marbeck (Merbecke), John, English composer and theologian; b. Windsor, c.1510; d. there, c.1585. He was a chorister in St. George's Chapel, Windsor (1531); narrowly escaped burning as a heretic in 1544; was imprisoned, but pardoned by Henry VIII; Mus.Bac., Oxford, 1550; lay clerk and organist of St. George's Chapel. His chief work is *The Booke of Common Praier noted* (1550), an adaptation of the plainchant of earlier rituals to the first ritual of Edward VI; reprinted in facsimile, 1939: republ. in Jebb's *Choral Responses and Litanies* (1857; vol. II). One of his hymns appears in Hawkins's *General History of the Science and Practice of Music.* Marbeck was also the compiler of a concordance of the English Bible (1550).

Marcel (real name, **Wasself**), **Lucille,** American soprano; b. New York, 1885; d. Vienna, June 22, 1921. She studied in Paris with Jean de Reszke, who recommended her for the role of Elektra at the Vienna premiere of Strauss's opera; she made her debut in this very difficult part on March 24, 1908, under the direction of **Felix Weingartner,** whom she married in 1907; she was the principal soprano when Weingartner became conductor of the Hamburg Opera (1912–14). She sang with the Boston Opera Co., making her American debut as Tosca on Feb. 14, 1912; later she returned to Vienna, where she remained until her death.

Marcello, Alessandro, Italian scholar and composer, brother of **Benedetto Marcello;** b. Venice, Aug. 24, 1669; d. Padua, June 19, 1747. He publ. his works under the name of **Eterico Stinfalico;** extant are *Concerti a cinque con violino solo e violoncello obbligato* (op. 1); various pieces for flutes and oboes with strings, etc. Alessandro Marcello seems to have been the composer of the Oboe Concerto transcribed by Bach, which is usually attributed to Benedetto Marcello.

Marcello, Benedetto, famous Italian composer and poet; b. Venice, Aug. 9, 1686; d. Brescia, July 24, 1739. He received an excellent education; studied jurisprudence as well as music; studied violin with his father; then singing and counterpoint with Gasparini and Lotti; had a political career: was a member of the Council of Forty for 14 years, "Provveditore" at Pola for 8 years, and finally papal chamberlain at Brescia, a position he retained from 1738 until his death. His masterwork is the settings of Giustiniani's paraphrases of the first 50 Psalms (*Estro poetico-armonico; Parafrasi sopra i cinquanta primi Salmi;* Venice, publ. by D. Lovisa, 1724–26, in 8 vols. folio); they are for one, 2, 3, and 4 voices, with basso continuo for organ or clavicembalo; a few with cello obbligato or 2 violas; they have been often republ. (by Carli in Paris, etc.). He also publ. *Concerti grossi* for 5 parts (1701); *Sonate per cembalo, Sonate a cinque, e flauto solo con basso continuo* (1712), *Canzoni madrigaleschi ed Arie per camera a 2–4* (1717); a satire on operatic manners, *Il teatro alla moda, o sia Metodo sicuro e facile per ben comporre ed eseguire opere italiane in* *musica* (1720; 2nd ed., 1722; modern ed. by E. Fondi, Lanciano, 1913; Eng. trans. by R.G. Pauly in the *Musical Quarterly,* July 1948, and January 1949; German trans. by A. Einstein in *Perlen älterer romanischer Prosa,* 24); the pamphlet *Lettera famigliare* (1705), a rather captious critique of Lotti, was printed incomplete, with a statement that it no longer corresponded to the views of the author. Both *Il teatro alla moda* and *Lettera famigliare* were publ. anonymously, but Marcello's authorship was never in dispute. Besides the works named above, Marcello composed oratorios and over 400 secular cantatas, preserved in MS in the libraries of Dresden and Vienna, and sacred works.

Marchand, Louis, French organist, harpsichordist, and composer; b. Lyons, Feb. 2, 1669; d. Paris, Feb. 17, 1732. He went to Paris as a youth; in 1691 he received the post of organist of the Jesuit church in the rue St. Jacques there; he was also organist at other Parisian churches; in 1708 he was named an organiste du roi, in which capacity he earned a considerable reputation; in 1713 he made a major tour of Germany. Marchand's name is historically connected with that of Bach because both were scheduled to meet in open competition in Dresden in 1717; however, Marchand failed to appear and Bach was deemed the superior virtuoso by default. Marchand composed 3 books for clavecin (1–2, Paris, 1702; 3, Paris, 1707). A number of his organ works are included in Guilmant's *Archives de maîtres de l'orgue;* his *Plein jeu* (in 6 parts) is reproduced in J. Bonnet's *Historical Organ Recitals* (vol. 1). See also T. Dart, ed., *Louis Marchand: Pièces de clavecin* (Paris, 1960).

Marchesi, Blanche (Baroness André Caccamisi), famous dramatic soprano, daughter of **Salvatore** and **Mathilde Marchesi;** b. Paris, April 4, 1863; d. London, Dec. 15, 1940. She was first trained as a violinist; took lessons with Nikisch in Germany and with Colonne in Paris. In 1881 she began to study singing with her mother, and, until her marriage to Baron Caccamisi, acted as her mother's assistant. She made her concert debut in Berlin (1895); when she sang in London (1896), the reception was so enthusiastic that she made England her home; her operatic debut followed in Prague in 1900 as Brünnhilde in *Die Walküre;* then she sang with the Moody-Manners company in London; from 1902 sang the Wagner roles at Covent Garden; made tours of Russia and Central Europe; also made 2 concert tours of the U.S. (1899, 1909); gave her farewell concert in 1938. In her last years, she established herself as a highly esteemed teacher in London. She publ. her memoirs under the title *A Singer's Pilgrimage* (London, 1923).

Marchesi, Luigi, celebrated male soprano, known as **"Marchesini,"** b. Milan, Aug. 8, 1754; d. Inzago, Dec. 14, 1829. He was a chorister in Milan; made his debut at Rome at age 17, scoring an immediate success. His fame as a sopranist grew rapidly after his visits to other Italian cities. In 1785 he was engaged

as a singer at the court of Catherine the Great; on his way to St. Petersburg, he stopped over in Vienna, where he sang at the Imperial court of Joseph II. He made his Russian debut in St. Petersburg, early in 1786, as Rinaldo in Sarti's opera *Armida e Rinaldo;* the Italian female soprano Luiza-Rosa Todi intrigued against him, and despite his successes, he left Russia before the expiration of his contract. On March 9, 1787, he sang in Berlin, winning great acclaim; then toured through Switzerland and Italy. He sang for the last time at the age of 66 in Naples; then returned to Milan.

Marchesi de Castrone, Mathilde (née **Graumann**), famous German vocal teacher; b. Frankfurt, March 24, 1821; d. London, Nov. 17, 1913. She studied singing in Frankfurt with Felice Ronconi, in Vienna with Nicolai, and in Paris with Manuel García; made her concert debut in Frankfurt on Aug. 31, 1844. In 1849 she went to London; in 1852 she married the Italian baritone **Salvatore Marchesi de Castrone.** Later in life she devoted herself mainly to teaching; had classes at the Vienna Cons. (1854–61 and 1869–78); also taught privately in Paris. Among her famous pupils were Murska, Gerster, Melba, Eames, Calvé, and Sanderson. She wrote an autobiography, *Erinnerungen aus meinem Leben* (Vienna, 1877), which was publ. in a revised and amplified edition under the title *Marchesi and Music: Passages from the Life of a Famous Singing Teacher* (N.Y., 1897). She further publ. a vocal manual, *10 Singing Lessons* (N.Y., 1910), which was reprinted under a new title, *Theoretical and Practical Vocal Method* (N.Y., 1970, with an introduction by Philip L. Miller).

Marchesi de Castrone, Salvatore (complete name and title, **Cavaliere Salvatore de Castrone, Marchese della Rajata**), baritone and famous teacher; b. Palermo, Jan. 15, 1822; d. Paris, Feb. 20, 1908. Of a noble family, he was destined for a government career and studied law in Palermo; however, he turned to music, and took lessons in singing and theory with Raimondi in Palermo, and with Lamperti in Milan. He was involved in the revolutionary events of 1848, and was compelled to leave Italy; went to N.Y., where he made his operatic debut in Verdi's *Ernani.* He then studied with García in London; married **Mathilde Graumann (Mathilde Marchesi de Castrone)** in 1852, and sang with her in opera on the Continent. From 1854 till 1861, they both taught at the Vienna Cons.; later at the Cologne Cons. (1865–68), and again in Vienna (1869–78); after that they resided in Paris.

Marchetti, Filippo, Italian opera composer; b. Bolognola, near Camerino, Feb. 26, 1831; d. Rome, Jan. 18, 1902. He was a pupil of Lillo and Conti at the Royal Cons. in Naples. His first opera, *Gentile da Varano* (Turin, Feb. 1856), was extremely well received, and he repeated his success with another opera, *La Demente,* for Turin (Nov. 27, 1856); however, his next opera, *Il Paria,* never reached the stage. He was not discouraged by this and wrote his

Romeo e Giulietta (Trieste, Oct. 25, 1865), which had a pronounced success in performances at La Scala in Milan and other Italian theaters. He achieved his greatest success with *Ruy-Blas* (La Scala, April 3, 1869), which was produced also in Germany and England; the remaining operas were *Gustavo Wasa* (La Scala, Feb. 7, 1875) and *Don Giovanni d'Austria* (Turin, March 11, 1880). In 1881 he was appointed president of the Santa Cecilia Academy in Rome; then was director of the Liceo Musicale (1886–1901).

Marchetto da Padua, an early proponent of *Ars Nova* who flourished in the 14th century and worked in Florence; author of the important treatises *Lucidarium in arte musicae planae* (on plainsong, early 14th century) and *Pomerium artis musicae mensurabilis* (on mensural music, 1318); the latter is included (in part) in Strunk's *Source Readings in Music History* (N.Y., 1950); a modern edition is found in *Corpus scriptorum de musica*, VI (1961). He also wrote *Brevis compilatio in arte musicae mensuratae,* which has been edited by G. Vecchi, "Su la composizione del *Pomerium* di Marchetto de Padova e la *Brevis compilatio,*" in *Quadrivium*, i (1956).

Marcoux, Vanni (full name, **Jean Emile Diogène Marcoux**), dramatic baritone; b. (of French parents) Turin, June 12, 1877; d. Paris, Oct. 21, 1962. He was a law student at the Univ. of Turin; then went to France, where he enrolled at the Paris Cons. He made his debut in Turin in 1894 as Sparafucile in *Rigoletto;* subsequently obtained considerable success at his debut at the Paris Opéra as Colonna in the premiere of Février's *Monna Vanna* (Jan. 13, 1909). Massenet entrusted to him the part of Don Quichotte in the premiere of his opera of that name (Monte Carlo, Feb. 19, 1910). In 1912 he sang with the Boston Opera Co., and later with the Chicago Opera Co. His repertoire included more than 200 roles in several languages. He eventually returned to Paris and was instructor in lyric declamation at the Paris Cons.; sang at the Paris Opéra for nearly 40 years; was also director of the Grand Theater in Bordeaux (1948–51). In professional appearances, he used the hyphenated name **Vanni-Marcoux.**

Maréchal, Adolphe, Belgian tenor; b. Liège, Sept. 26, 1867; d. Brussels, Feb. 1, 1935. He studied at the Liège Cons.; made his debut in Tournai in 1891; then sang in Rheims, Bordeaux, and Nice; in 1895 he became a member of the Opéra-Comique in Paris, where he remained until 1907; during that time, he created the roles of Julien in *Louise,* Alain in *Grisélidis,* and Danielo in *La Reine fiammette;* also Jean in *Le Jongleur de Notre-Dame* at Monte Carlo. He retired in 1907 after the loss of his singing voice.

Maréchal, Henri-Charles, French composer; b. Paris, Jan. 22, 1842; d. there, May 12, 1924. He studied piano and theory at the Paris Cons.; composition with Victor Massé; won the Grand Prix de Rome (1870) with the cantata *Le Jugement de Dieu.* After

his return from Rome he produced an oratorio, *La Nativité* (1875), and several operas: *Les Amoureux de Catherine* (Paris, May 8, 1876), *La Taverne des Trabans* (1881), *Calendal* (Rouen, Dec. 21, 1894), *Ping-Sin* (Paris, Jan. 25, 1918), etc.; also wrote several orch. suites, choral works, etc. He publ. 2 vols. of reminiscences: *Rome: Souvenirs d'un musicien* (Paris, 1904; 2nd ed., 1913) and *Paris: Souvenirs* (Paris, 1907); also *Monographie universelle de l'Orphéon* (Paris, 1910; on singing societies) and *Lettres et Souvenirs, 1871–1874* (Paris, 1920).

Marenco, Romualdo, Italian composer; b. Novi Ligure, March 1, 1841; d. Milan, Oct. 9, 1907. He played the violin, then the bassoon at the Doria Theater in Genoa, for which he wrote his first ballet, *Lo sbarco di Garibaldi a Marsala.* He studied counterpoint under Fenaroli and Mattei; traveled; and became in 1873 director of ballet at La Scala in Milan. He composed over 20 ballets (*Sieba, Excelsior, Sport,* etc.); operas: *Lorenzio de' Medici* (Lodi, 1874); *I Moncada* (Milan, 1880); *Le Diable au corps* (Paris, 1884); and the "idilio giocoso" *Strategia d'amore* (Milan, 1896). A posthumous opera, *Federico Struensea,* was produced in Milan in 1908.

Marenzio, Luca, important Italian composer; b. Coccaglio, near Brescia, 1553 or 1554; d. Rome, Aug. 22, 1599. Little is known of his early life; he may have studied with Giovanni Contino in Brescia; about 1574 he entered the service of Cardinal Cristoforo Madruzzo in Rome; following Madruzzo's death in 1578, he entered the service of Cardinal Luigi d'Este; he made an extended visit with the cardinal to the court of Duke Alfonso II d'Este in Ferrara, where he spent the months of Nov. 1580 to May 1581; he dedicated 2 volumes of madrigals to the duke and his sister Lucrezia. After the death of the cardinal in 1586, he entered the service of Ferdinando de' Medici, the grand duke of Florence (1588); in 1589 he returned to Rome, where he apparently received the patronage of several cardinals; about 1593 he entered the service of Cardinal Cinzio Aldobrandini; he subsequently served at the court of Sigismund III of Poland (1596–98); he then returned to Rome, where he died the following year. Marenzio was one of the foremost madrigalists of his time; his later works in the genre are historically significant for their advanced harmonic procedures. He also composed about 75 motets. He was called by his contemporaries "il più dolce cigno d'Italia" and "divino compositore."
WORKS: His secular works were publ. as follows: *Il primo libro de madrigali* for 5 Voices (Venice, 1580); *Il primo libro de madrigali* for 6 Voices (Venice, 1581); *Il secondo libro de madrigali* for 5 Voices (Venice, 1581); *Il terzo libro de madrigali* for 5 Voices (Venice, 1582); *Il secondo libro de madrigali* for 6 Voices (Venice, 1584); *Madrigali spirituali* for 5 Voices (Rome, 1584; enlarged ed., 1610); *Il quarto libro de madrigali* for 5 Voices (Venice, 1584); *Il primo libro delle villanelle* for 3 Voices (Venice, 1584); *Il quinto libro de madrigali* for 5 Voices (Venice, 1585); *Il terzo libro de madrigali* for 6

Voices (Venice, 1585); *Il secondo libro delle canzonette alla napolitana* for 3 Voices (Venice, 1585); *Madrigali . . . libro primo* for 4 Voices (Rome, 1585); *Il terzo libro delle villanelle* for 3 Voices (Venice, 1585; 4th ed., enlarged, 1600); *Il quarto libro de madrigali* for 6 Voices (Venice, 1587; 3rd ed., revised, 1593); *Il quarto libro delle villanelle* for 3 Voices (Venice, 1587; 4th ed., revised, 1600); *Il quinto libro delle villanelle* for 3 Voices (Venice, 1587); *Madrigali . . . libro primo* for 4, 5, and 6 Voices (Venice, 1588); *Il quinto libro de madrigali* for 6 Voices (Venice, 1591); *Il sesto libro de madrigali* for 5 Voices (Venice, 1594); *Il sesto libro de madrigali* for 6 Voices (Venice, 1595); *Il settimo libro de madrigali* for 5 Voices (Venice, 1595); *L'ottavo libro de madrigali* for 5 Voices (Venice, 1598); *Il nono libro de madrigali* for 5 Voices (Venice, 1599); also *Il secondo libro de madrigali* for 4 Voices, which is not extant. His sacred works were publ. as follows: *Motectorum pro festis totius anni cum Communi Sanctorum* for 4 Voices (Venice, 1585); *Completorium et antiphonae* for 6 Voices (Venice, 1595; not extant); *Motetti* for 12 Voices (Venice, 1614); *Sacrae cantiones* for 5, 6, and 7 Voices (Venice, 1616). B. Meier and R. Jackson are editing the *Opera omnia* in Corpus Mensurabilis Musicae (1976—); S. Ledbetter and P. Myers are also editing *The Secular Works* (N.Y., 1977—).

Maresch, Johann Anton, inventor of the Russian "hunting-horn music," in which each player has a horn producing a single tone; b. Chotěboř, Bohemia, 1719; d. St. Petersburg, June 10, 1794. He studied horn with Hampel in Dresden, and cello in Berlin. In 1748 he was engaged by the Russian Chancellor Bestuzhev as horn player in his private orch. in St. Petersburg, and later became chamber musician to the Russian court. In 1751 he was commissioned to organize an ensemble of hunting horns for the court; he formed a group comprising 2 complete octaves tuned chromatically, adding large drums with church bells suspended within them; also constructed wooden horns for soft accompaniment to operas. The vogue of horn orchs. in Russia continued for about 50 years after Maresch's death; the players were recruited usually from among serfs. After the emancipation of serfs in Russia in 1861, the horn orchs. gradually disappeared.

Mareschall, Samuel, Flemish composer; b. Tournai, May 22, 1554; d. Basel, 1640. He studied at the Univ. of Basel. In 1577 became a prof. of music there and organist at the Basel Cathedral; in 1576 was appointed prof. at the Univ. there. His collection of 4-part vocal settings of the Psalms (1606) became a traditional Lutheran hymnbook; another book of Psalms (including hymns by Luther) appeared in 1616. He also compiled *Melodiae suaves* (1622); much earlier he publ. a disquisition, *Porta Musica, mit einem kurtzen Bericht und Anleitung zu den Violen* (Basel, 1589).

Maretzek, Max, operatic impresario; b. Brünn, Moravia, June 28, 1821; d. Staten Island, N.Y., May 14, 1897. He studied medicine and law at the Univ. of Vienna; music with Ignaz von Seyfried (a pupil of Mozart and Haydn). He progressed rapidly, and at the age of 22 conducted his first opera, *Hamlet* (Brünn, 1843). He then traveled in France and England as a theater conductor and composer of ballet music. In 1848 he arrived in N.Y. as conductor and manager of the Italian Opera Co. He presented Adelina Patti for the first time in opera (as Lucia, 1859); in 1876 he staged his own play with music, *Baba;* conducted his pastoral opera *Sleepy Hollow; or, The Headless Horseman,* after Washington Irving (N.Y., Sept. 25, 1879). As a worldly impresario, he was extremely successful; traveled to Mexico and Cuba, but lived mostly in N.Y., and became an American citizen. He publ. a book of reminiscences, *Crotchets and Quavers, or Revelations of an Opera Manager in America* (N.Y., 1855); and a sequel, *Sharps and Flats* (N.Y., 1870).

Maria Antonia Walpurgis, Electress of Saxony, daughter of the Elector of Bavaria (Emperor Charles VII); b. Munich, July 18, 1724; d. Dresden, April 23, 1780. She was not only a generous patroness of the fine arts, but a trained musician, pupil of Hasse and Porpora (1747–52); under the pseudonym **E.T.P.A. (Ermelinda Talea Pastorella Arcada,** her name as member of the Academy of Arcadians) she produced and publ. 2 Italian operas to her own librettos, *Il trionfo della Fedeltà* (Dresden, 1754) and *Talestri* (Nymphenburg, near Munich, Feb. 6, 1760; Dresden, Aug. 24, 1763); the former was one of the earliest publications of Breitkopf & Härtel printed from their new types (1765); she also wrote texts of oratorios and cantatas for Hasse and Ristori.

Mariani, Angelo, Italian conductor and composer; b. Ravenna, Oct. 11, 1821; d. Genoa, June 13, 1873. He studied violin and composition; had some lessons with Rossini in Bologna; made his principal career as an opera conductor, first in Italy (1844–47), then in Denmark (1847–48). He took part in the Italian war of independence of 1848; then was compelled to leave Italy, and spent 4 years in Istanbul. In 1852 he returned to Italy as opera conductor and director of the Teatro Carlo Felice in Genoa, a post he held until his death; introduced Wagner's *Lohengrin* in Bologna, where he was also music director of the Teatro Comunale from 1860 until his death. He was also favorably known as a composer; wrote several attractive songs (*Liete e tristi rimembranze, Il Trovatore nella Liguria, Rimembranze del Bosforo,* etc.); also some orch. music. He arranged 3 operas by Verdi (in their entirety) for string quartet: *Macbeth, I vespri Siciliani,* and *Un ballo in maschera.*

Marić, Ljubica, remarkable Serbian composer; b. Kragujevac, March 18, 1909. She studied with Josip Slavenski in Belgrade; then went to Prague, where she took composition courses with J. Suk and Alois Hába; also studied conducting with Malko in Prague (1929–32) and with Scherchen in Strasbourg (1933); she returned to Prague for more study with Hába in his special quarter-tone classes (1936–37). She subsequently taught at a music school in Belgrade. During the period of Nazi occupation of Serbia she was an active participant in the resistance. After the war she was a member of the teaching staff of the Belgrade Music Academy (1945–67). In her music she adopted a global type of modern technique, utilizing variable tonal configurations, atonal melodic progressions, and microtonal structures while adhering to traditional forms of composition.

WORKS: String Quartet (1931); Wind Quintet (1932); Trio for Clarinet, Trombone, and Double Bass in quarter-tones (1937); Violin Sonata (1948); *Passacaglia* for Orch. (Belgrade, April 21, 1958); cantatas: *Pesme prostora (Songs of Space)*, based on inscriptions on the graves of Bogomils, a heretical religious sect of the Middle Ages (Belgrade, Dec. 8, 1956; her most acclaimed work); *Slovo svetlosti (Sound of Light)*, oratorio to texts from medieval Serbian poetry (1966); *Prag sna (Threshold of Dream)*, chamber cantata for Narrator, Soprano, Alto, and Instrumental Ensemble (1961; Opatija, Oct. 30, 1965); numerous piano pieces and songs. Apart from her experimental works, Ljubica Marić became deeply immersed in the study of ancient Byzantine chants, and wrote several modern realizations of the Serbian Octoichos; to this category belong her *Muzika Oktoiha No. 1* for Orch. (Belgrade, Feb. 28, 1959); *Vizantijski koncert (Byzantine Concerto)* for Piano and Orch. (Belgrade, June 4, 1963); *Ostinato super thema octoicha* for String Quintet, Harp, and Piano (Warsaw, Sept. 27, 1963); and *Simfonija oktoiha*, begun in 1964.

Marie, Gabriel, French composer of light music; b. Paris, Jan. 8, 1852; d. Puigcerda, Catalonia, Aug. 29, 1928. He studied at the Paris Cons.; was chorus master of the Lamoureux Concerts (1881–87); conductor of the orch. concerts of the Société Nationale de Musique (1887–94); of Ste.-Cécile in Bordeaux; at Marseilles and (during the summer months) at the Casino in Vichy. He wrote a number of melodious pieces for orch., of which *La Cinquantaine* (in arrangements for violin or cello, with piano) became immensely popular. He also wrote music criticism, collected in *Pour la musique* (Paris, 1930).

Marini, Biagio, Italian violinist and composer; b. Brescia, c.1587; d. Venice, March 20, 1665. He was a violinist under Monteverdi at San Marco in Venice (1615–18); then was music director of the Accademia degli Erranti in Brescia (1620); subsequently was a violinist in the Farnese court in Parma (1621); then went to Germany and served at the courts in Neuberg and Düsseldorf (1623–49). In 1649 he was appointed maestro di cappella at S. Maria della Scala in Milan; in 1652 he was director of the Accademia della Morte in Ferrara. He publ. about 25 opus numbers of vocal and instrumental music. His op. 1, *Affetti musicali* (1617), contains the earliest specimen of the Italian solo violin sonata, entitled *La Gardana* (reprinted in Schering's "Zur Geschichte der Solosonate in Der ersten Hälfte des 17. Jahrhunderts," in *Riemann-Festschrift* (Leipzig,

1909); other reprints are in J. von Wasielewski, *Die Violine im 17. Jahrhundert* and in L. Torchi, *L'arte musicale in Italia* (vol. 8).

Marini, Ignazio, noted Italian bass; b. Tagliuno, Nov. 28, 1811; d. Milan, April 29, 1873. In 1833 he joined La Scala in Milan, where he sang until 1847; then appeared at London (1847–49) and N.Y. (1850–52); in 1856 he went to St. Petersburg, where he remained until 1863. He was one of the leading bass singers of his day; created the title roles in Verdi's *Oberto* and *Attila;* was a distinguished interpreter of bass parts in Rossini's operas.

Marinuzzi, Gino, Italian conductor and composer, son of **Giuseppe Marinuzzi;** b. New York, April 7, 1920. He studied at the Milan Cons. with Renzo Bossi, graduating as a pianist and composer in 1941. He began his career as conductor at the Rome Opera in 1946. He was one of the first Italian composers to explore the potentialities of electronic music; in collaboration with Ketoff he developed an electronic synthesizer, the "Fonosynth," and was a founder of an electronic studio in Rome. His compositions include a Violin Concerto, a Piano Concerto, and several other works for various instrumental combinations; also a radio opera, *La Signora Paulatim* (Naples, 1966), as well as a number of pieces specially adapted for electronic tape.

Marinuzzi, Giuseppe (Gino), Italian conductor and composer; b. Palermo, March 24, 1882; d. Milan, Aug. 17, 1945. He studied with Zuelli at the Palermo Cons.; began his career as a conductor in Catania; conducted in Italy and Spain; went to South America on tour with the Teatral Opera Co.; then was director of the Liceo Musicale in Bologna (1915–18); in 1919 conducted in Rome; in 1920 came to the U.S. as artistic director of the Chicago Opera Association; returned to Italy in 1921; was chief conductor of the Rome Opera in 1928–34, and of La Scala from 1934 to his death. False dispatches about his assassination at the hands of the Italian anti-Fascists found their way into periodicals and eventually into reputable reference works, but upon verification, it appears that he died peacefully in a hospital, a victim not of a bullet but of hepatic anemia. He wrote 3 operas: *Barberina* (Palermo, 1903); *Jacquerie* (Buenos Aires, Aug. 11, 1918); *Palla de' Mozzi* (La Scala, Milan, April 5, 1932); and several works for orch., on Italian themes.

Mario, Giovanni, celebrated tenor; b. Cagliari, Sardinia, Oct. 17, 1810; d. Rome, Dec. 11, 1883. He was of noble birth (his real name was **Mario Cavaliere di Candia**), and was destined for a military career; after a period of training at the Turin Military Academy, he joined the regiment of which his father was the colonel, but eloped to Paris with a ballerina in 1836; there he studied with Bordogni and Poncharde at the Cons., and made his debut at the Opéra in *Robert le Diable* (Nov. 30, 1838); in 1840 he joined the roster of the Italian Opera in Paris, and won triumphs by the freshness and power of his voice and his exquisite vocal style; this was combined with a handsome figure, which made him the idol of the pleasure-loving women of Paris. In order not to embarrass his aristocratic relatives, he appeared under his Christian name, Mario, without a surname, achieving fame not only in opera, but also in concerts; he was as successful in London and St. Petersburg as in France. For some years, he, Tamburini, Lablache, and **Giulia Grisi** formed a celebrated vocal quartet; he married Grisi; retired in 1867, and lived in Paris and Rome.

Mario, Queena (real name, **Tillotson**), American soprano; b. Akron, Ohio, Aug. 21, 1896; d. New York, May 28, 1951. She was a practicing journalist in N.Y. before she began to study music; took voice lessons with Oscar Saenger and Marcella Sembrich; made her debut with the San Carlo Opera in N.Y. (Sept. 4, 1918); then joined the staff of the Metropolitan Opera; her first appearance there was as Micaela in *Carmen* (Nov. 30, 1922); retired from the opera stage in 1938, but continued to give concerts; taught at the Curtis Inst. of Music in Philadelphia from 1931 as successor to Marcella Sembrich. She married the conductor **Wilfred Pelletier** in 1925; they divorced in 1936. She was the author of several mystery novels (*Murder in the Opera House*, etc.).

Mariotte, Antoine, French opera composer; b. Avignon, Dec. 22, 1875; d. Izieux (Loire), Nov. 30, 1944. He was trained at the Naval Academy; in 1897 he became a pupil of Vincent d'Indy at the Schola Cantorum; in 1899 was appointed conductor of the symph. concerts at St.-Etienne, Loire; from 1902 until 1919 he taught at the Cons. of Orléans; in 1920 was appointed its director; from 1936 to 1938 he was director of the Paris Opéra-Comique.

WORKS: Operas: *Salomé* (Lyons, Oct. 30, 1908); *Le Vieux Roi* (Lyons, 1911); *Léontine Sœurs* (Paris, May 21, 1924); *Esther, Princesse d'Israël* (Paris, May 5, 1925); *Gargantua* (Paris, Feb. 13, 1935); also a symph. suite, *Impressions urbaines;* numerous teaching pieces for piano; and songs.

Mariz, Vasco, Brazilian musicologist, diplomat, and bass; b. Rio de Janeiro, Jan. 22, 1921. He studied composition with Oscar Lorenzo Fernandez and voice with Vera Janacopoulos; also took courses in law at the Univ. of Rio de Janeiro, obtaining his D.J. degree in 1943. He sang minor roles in opera at Rio de Janiero, São Paulo, and Porto Alegre, and gave solo recitals as a lieder singer; also recorded Brazilian songs. In 1945 he entered the diplomatic service; was vice-consul at Oporto, Portugal (1948–49); attaché in Belgrade (1950–51); consul in Rosario, Argentina (1952–53); consul in Naples (1956–58); counselor of the Brazilian embassy in Washington, D.C. (1959–60); counselor of the Brazilian mission to the U.N. (1961–62); Brazilian envoy to the Organization of American States in Washington, D.C. (1967–69); head of the Cultural Dept. of the Brazilian Ministry of Foreign Affairs (1970); Brazilian ambassador to Ecuador (1971–74); assistant secretary of state for legislative affairs in Brasilia (1975–76);

Brazilian ambassador to Israel (1977–82); Brazilian ambassador to Peru (1983–84).

PUBLICATIONS: *Figuras da musica brasileira contemporánea* (Oporto, 1948; 2nd ed., Brasilia, 1970); *Dicionário biográfico musical* (Rio de Janeiro, 1948; 2nd ed., 1984); *Hector Villa-Lobos, Compositor brasileiro* (Rio de Janeiro, 1949; 6th ed., 1983); *Canção brasileira* (Oporto, 1948; 4th ed., Rio de Janeiro, 1980); *Alberto Ginastera* (Rosario, 1954); *Vida musical I* (Oporto, 1950); *Vida musical II* (Rio de Janeiro, 1970); *Historia de musica no Brasil* (Rio de Janeiro, 1981; 2nd ed., 1983); *Tres musicologos brasileiros* (Rio de Janeiro, 1983).

Markevitch, Igor, greatly talented Russian-born composer and conductor; b. Kiev, July 27, 1912; d. Antibes, France, March 7, 1983. He was taken to Paris in his infancy; in 1916 the family settled in Vevey, Switzerland, which remained Markevitch's home for the next decade. He began to study piano with his father, subsequently took piano lessons with Paul Loyonnet; he also took academic courses at Vevey College. In 1925 he joined the piano class of Alfred Cortot in Paris at the Ecole Normale de Musique, and studied harmony, counterpoint, and composition with Nadia Boulanger. He attracted the attention of Serge Diaghilev, who commissioned him to write a piano concerto and also to collaborate with Boris Kochno on a ballet. Markevitch was soloist in his Piano Concerto at Covent Garden in London on July 15, 1929. Diaghilev died on Aug 19, 1929, and Markevitch interrupted his work on the ballet for him; he used the musical materials from it in his cantata to a text by Jean Cocteau; it was produced in Paris on June 4, 1930, achieving extraordinary success. On December 8, 1930, Markevitch's Concerto Grosso was performed for the first time in Paris with even a greater acclaim. Finally, his ballet, *Rebus,* was produced in Paris on Dec. 15, 1932, to enthusiastic press reviews. Markevitch was hailed, only half-facetiously, as "Igor II" (the first Igor being, of course, Igor Stravinsky). In 1933 Markevitch also began his career as a conductor, with a concert in Amsterdam. On June 26, 1933, his new ballet, *L'Envol d'Icare,* was given for the first time in Paris; Darius Milhaud opined that the occasion would probably "mark a date in the evolution of music." But swift as was Markevitch's Icarus-like ascent as a composer, even more precipitous was his decline. He began to be sharply criticized for his penchant toward unrelieved dissonance. When he conducted the world premiere of his oratorio, *Le Paradis perdu,* in London on Dec. 20, 1935, it was roundly condemned for sins of dissonance. Although Markevitch continued to compose, his main activities turned toward conducting. In 1934–36 he took conducting lessons in Switzerland with Hermann Scherchen. On Jan. 31, 1938, Markevitch conducted in Warsaw his new symph. work, *Le Nouvel Age,* for the first time anywhere. In 1940, with the war already raging in Europe, Markevitch stayed in Florence, where he composed his sinfonia concertante *Lorenzo il magnifico.* In 1941 he completed his last original work, the *Variations, Fugue and Envoi on a Theme of Handel,* and devoted himself almost exclusively to conducting; he held permanent conducting posts in Stockholm, Montreal, Madrid, Monte Carlo, and Rome; was principal guest conductor of the Lamoureux Orch. in Paris; also made successful tours of Russia. For several years he led seminars in conducting in Salzburg. He settled in southern France.

WORKS: *Noces,* suite for Piano (1925); *A la foire* (1926); *Sinfonietta in F* (Brussels, Nov. 30, 1929); Piano Concerto (London, July 15, 1929, composer soloist); *Cantate,* to a text by Jean Cocteau (Paris, June 4, 1930); Concerto Grosso (Paris, Dec. 8, 1930); Partita (Paris, May 13, 1932); *Serenade* for Violin, Clarinet, and Bassoon (Wiesbaden, Aug. 5, 1931); *Ouverture Symphonique* (1931); *Rébus,* ballet, dedicated to the memory of Serge Diaghilev (Paris, Dec. 15, 1931); *Galop* for 8 Players (1932); *L'Envol d'Icare,* ballet (Paris, June 26, 1933; also arranged for Piano Solo under the title *La Mort d'Icare); Hymnes* for Orch. (Paris, June 26, 1933, composer conducting); *Petite suite d'après Schumann* for Orch. (1933); *Psaume* for Soprano and Chamber Orch. (Amsterdam, Dec. 3, 1933, composer conducting); *Le Paradis perdu,* oratorio after Milton (London, Dec. 20, 1935, composer conducting); *3 poèmes* for Voice and Piano (1935); *Hymne à la mort* for Chamber Orch. (1936); *Cantique d'amour* for Chamber Orch. (Rome, May 14, 1937); *Le Nouvel Age,* sinfonia concertante for Orch. (Warsaw, Jan. 21, 1938, composer conducting); *La Taille de l'homme* for Soprano and 12 Instruments; unfinished; first perf. as *Oraison musicale* (1939; Maastricht, Feb. 7, 1982); *Duo* for Flute and Bassoon (1939); *Stefan le poète* for Piano (1939–40); *Lorenzo il magnifico,* sinfonia concertante for Soprano and Orch. (Florence, Jan. 12, 1941); *Variations, Fugue and Envoi on a Theme of Handel* for Piano (Rome, Dec. 14, 1941); *Inno della liberazione nazionale,* songs for the Italian underground resistance (1943–44); *Le Bleu Danube* for Chamber Orch. (Florence, May 24, 1946, composer conducting).

Marliani, Marco Aurelio, Italian composer; b. Milan, Aug. 1805; d. Bologna, May 8, 1849. He studied philosophy; took some lessons with Rossini in Paris, where he went in 1830; under Rossini's influence, he wrote several operas, which reached the stage in Paris: *Il Bravo* (Feb. 1, 1834); *Ildegonda* (March 7, 1837); *Xacarilla* (Oct. 28, 1839); a ballet, *La Gypsy* (with A. Thomas; Jan. 28, 1839). He returned to Italy in 1847; produced another opera in Bologna, *Gusmano il Buono* (Nov. 7, 1847). He was involved in the revolutionary struggle of 1848; was wounded in a skirmish near Bologna, and died as a result of his injuries.

Marliave, Joseph de, French writer on music; b. Toulouse, Nov. 16, 1873; d. (killed in battle at Verdun) Aug. 24, 1914. He wrote a valuable monograph, *Les Quatuors de Beethoven,* which was publ. posthumously in Paris in 1917 and reprinted, with preface by Gabriel Fauré, in 1925. He was the husband of the pianist **Marguerite Long.**

Marlowe, Sylvia (original name, **Sylvia Sapira**), American harpsichordist; b. New York, Sept. 26, 1908; d. there, Dec. 11, 1981. She studied piano; went to Paris to take courses with Nadia Boulanger at the Ecole Normale de Musique; later became a student of Wanda Landowska in harpsichord playing. In 1953 she joined the faculty of the Mannes School of Music in N.Y. In 1957 she founded the Harpsichord Music Society, which commissioned works by Elliott Carter, Ned Rorem, Vittorio Rieti, Henri Sauguet, and others. Although her primary devotion was to the Baroque style of composition, she adventurously espoused the cause of popular American music; she was a member of the pop group called Chamber Music Society of Lower Basin Street and even performed in nightclubs, ostentatiously proclaiming her belief in music as an art in flux. She was married to a landscape painter named Leonid Berman, who died in 1976.

Marmontel, Antoine-François, celebrated French pedagogue and pianist; b. Clermont-Ferrand, July 16, 1816; d. Paris, Jan. 17, 1898. He studied at the Paris Cons. with Zimmermann (piano), Dourlen (harmony), Halévy (fugue), and Lesueur (composition); won first prize for piano playing in 1832. In 1837 he became instructor in solfeggio at the Cons.; in 1848 he succeeded Zimmermann as head of a piano class, and won enduring fame as an imaginative and efficient teacher; among his pupils were Bizet, Vincent d'Indy, Th. Dubois, E. Guiraud, Paladilhe, Diémer, Planté, and Debussy. He continued to teach until 1887. He publ. numerous didactic works: *L'Art de déchiffrer* (100 easy studies); *Ecole élémentaire de mécanisme et de style* (24 studies); *Ecole de mécanisme; 5 Etudes de salon; L'Art de déchiffrer à 4 mains;* also sonatas, serenades, characteristic pieces, salon music, dances, etc.

Maros, Rudolf, Hungarian composer; b. Stachy, Jan. 19, 1917; d. Budapest, Aug. 2, 1982. He studied composition with Kodály and Siklós and viola at the Budapest Academy of Music (1938–42); played viola in the Budapest Concert Orch. (1942–49); from 1949–78 he was on the faculty of the Budapest Academy of Music. The early period of his music is marked by nationalistic tendencies; later he adopted serial techniques and began to explore the field of "sonorism," or sound for sound's sake, making use of all available sonorous resources, such as tone clusters and microtones.

WORKS: BALLETS: *The Wedding at Ecser* (1950); *Bányászballada (Miner's Ballad;* 1961); *Cinque studi* (1967; after the orch. set of the same title); *Quadros soltos (Musica da ballo)* (1968); *Reflexionen* (1970); *Dance Pictures* (1971); *Metropolis* (1972); *The Poltroon* (1972). FOR ORCH.: *Puppet Show Overture* (1944); 2 sinfoniettas (1944, 1948); Bassoon Concertino (1954); *Symphony for Strings* (1956); *Ricercare* (1959); *Musica da ballo,* suite (1962; based on the ballet *Miner's Ballad*); *Cinque studi* (1960; as a ballet, 1967); *3 Eufonias: I* for Strings, 2 Harps, and Percussion (1963); *II* for 24 Winds, 2 Harps, and Percussion (1964); *III* for Orch. (1965); *Gemma (In Memoriam Kodály)* (1968); *Monumentum* (1969); *Nòtices* for Strings (1972); *Landscapes* for Strings (1974); *Fragment* (1977). CHAMBER MUSIC: String Quartet (1948); *Serenade* for Oboe, Clarinet, and Bassoon (1952); *Musica leggiera* for Wind Quintet (1956); String Trio (1957); *Musica da camera per 11* (1966; Dartmouth College, Hanover, N.H., July 12, 1967); Trio for Violin, Viola, and Harp (1967); *Consort* for Wind Quintet (1970); *Albumblätter* for Double-bass Solo (1973); *Kaleidoscope* for 15 Instruments (1976); *4 Studies* for 4 Percussionists (1977); *Contrasts* for Chamber Ensemble (1979); FOR VOICE: *2 Laments* for Soprano, Alto Flute, Harp, Piano, and Percussion (1962); *Lament* for Soprano and Chamber Ensemble (1967); *Messzeségek (Remoteness)* for Chorus a cappella (1975); *Strophen* for Soprano, Harp, and Percussion (1975); *Nyúlfarkkantáta (Tiny Cantata)* for Voices, Strings, and Piano (1976); *Cheremiss Folksongs* for Chorus a cappella (1977).

Marpurg, Friedrich, German opera composer, great-grandson of **Friedrich Wilhelm Marpurg;** b. Paderborn, April 4, 1825; d. Wiesbaden, Dec. 2, 1884. He played the violin and piano as a child; studied composition later with Mendelssohn and Hauptmann at Leipzig. He became conductor at the Königsberg Theater, then at Sondershausen (1864); succeeded Mangold as court music director at Darmstadt (1868); then was at Freiburg (1873), Laibach (1875), and Wiesbaden, where he became conductor of the Cäcilienverein.
WORKS: Operas: *Musa, der letzte Maurenkönig* (Königsberg, 1855); *Agnes von Hohenstaufen* (Freiburg, 1874); *Die Lichtensteiner* (not perf.).

Marpurg, Friedrich Wilhelm, German theorist; b. Seehof bei Seehausen, Brandenburg, Nov. 21, 1718; d. Berlin, May 22, 1795. While secretary to General von Rothenburg at Paris (1746–49), he became acquainted with Rameau and his theories; after a short stay in Berlin, and a prolonged sojourn in Hamburg, he joined the Prussian lottery at Berlin (1763), and was its director from 1766 until his death.

Marqués y García, Pedro Miguel, Spanish composer of light opera; b. Palma de Mallorca, May 20, 1843; d. there, Feb. 25, 1918. He studied in Paris with Alard and Armingaud, then at the Paris Cons. with Massart (violin) and Bazin (composition); also studied privately with Berlioz, and in 1867 at Madrid with Monasterio. From 1870–96 he was one of the most successful of the "zarzuela" composers, his most popular works being *El anillo de hierro* (1878), *El reloj de Lucerna, La monja alférez, El plato de dia,* etc. He wrote orch. variations, and was the author of a number of books (mostly on philosophy).

Marriner, Neville, outstanding English violinist and conductor; b. Lincoln, April 15, 1924. He studied at the Royal College of Music in London and at the Paris Cons.; was a member of the Martin String Quartet (1946–53); then was assistant concertmaster with the London Symph. Orch. (1956–68); Monteux, who conducted same, encouraged Marriner to become a symph. conductor. Following this advice, Marriner joined a summer class in conducting which Monteux had maintained at Hancock, Maine. In 1959 Marriner organized the Academy of St.-Martin-in-the-Fields in a London church of that name, this being an "academy" in the old German nomenclature descriptive of concert activity. In 1968 he was invited to Los Angeles to organize a local chamber orch.; as at his London "academy," so with the Los Angeles Chamber Orch., Marriner presented programs of Baroque music; he made a European tour with it in 1974. He founded, concurrently, a similar organization in Australia. In 1977 he was named artistic director of the Meadow Brook Music Festival in Rochester, Mich. In 1978 he accepted the prestigious appointment of conductor and music director of the Minnesota Orch. in Minneapolis; in 1981 he became principal guest conductor of the Stuttgart Radio Symph. Orch. In 1979 he was made a Commander of the Order of the British Empire.

Marsalis, Wynton, outstanding black American trumpet virtuoso; b. New Orleans, Oct. 18, 1961. He attended the Berkshire Music Center at Tanglewood, where, at the age of 17, he was singled out as the most gifted trumpet player; continued his studies at the Juilliard School of Music in N.Y. He subsequently joined Art Blakey's big band, and played with it at the Jazz Festival at Montreux, Switzerland, in 1980; then toured with his own quintet, which included his brother, Branford, a fine saxophonist; he also worked with Miles Davis. Concurrently he showed interest in the classical repertoire, and proceeded to perform trumpet concertos of the Baroque period with great aplomb. In 1983 he achieved unprecedented success when he won Grammy Awards in both the jazz and classical categories for his recordings.

Marschner, Heinrich (August), important German opera composer; b. Zittau, Saxony, Aug. 16, 1795; d. Hannover, Dec. 14, 1861. He sang in the school choir at the Zittau Gymnasium, and also studied music with Karl Hering. In 1813 he went to Leipzig, where he studied jurisprudence at the Univ.; encouraged by the cantor of the Thomasschule, J.C. Schicht, he turned to music as his main vocation. In 1816 he became a music tutor in Count Zichy's household in Pressburg, and also served as Kapellmeister to Prince Krasatkowitz. In his leisure hours he began to compose light operas; his first opera, *Titus* (1816), did not achieve a performance, but soon he had 2 more operas and a singspiel produced in Dresden. His first signal success was the historical opera *Heinrich IV und d'Aubigné,* which was accepted by Weber, who was then music director at the Dresden Opera, and was produced there on July 19, 1820. In 1817 he was in Vienna, where he was fortunate enough to meet Beethoven. In 1821 Marschner moved to Dresden and had his singspiel *Der Holzdieb* staged at the Dresden Opera (Feb. 22, 1825). He expected to succeed Weber as music director at the Dresden Opera after Weber died suddenly in London, but failed to obtain the post. He went to Leipzig, where he became Kapellmeister of the Stadttheater, and wrote for it 2 Romantic operas, in the manner of Weber: *Der Vampyr,* performed there on March 29, 1828, and *Der Templer und die Jüdin,* after the famous novel *Ivanhoe* by Sir Walter Scott (Dec. 22, 1829). In 1830 he was offered the position of Kapellmeister of the Hannover Hoftheater, and there he produced his most successful opera, *Hans Heiling,* which exhibited the most attractive Romantic traits of his music: a flowing melody, sonorous harmony, and nervous rhythmic pulse; the opera formed a natural transition to the exotic melodrama of Meyerbeer's great stage epics and to Wagner's early lyrical music dramas. Historically important was Marschner's bold projection of a continuous dramatic development, without the conventional type of distinct arias separated by recitative. In this respect Marschner was the heir of Weber and a precursor of Wagner. WORKS: For the stage: *Titus,* opera (1816; not perf.); *Der Kyffhäuserberg,* singspiel (1816; Zittau, Jan. 2, 1822); *Heinrich IV und d'Aubigné,* opera (1817–18; Dresden, July 19, 1820); *Saidar und Zulima,* romantic opera (Pressburg, Nov. 26, 1818); *Der Holzdieb,* singspiel (1823; Dresden, Feb. 22, 1825; revised in 1853 as *Geborgt*); *Lukretia,* opera (1820–26; Danzig, Jan 17, 1827); *Der Vampyr,* romantic opera (1827; Leipzig, March 29, 1828); *Der Templer und die Jüdin,* romantic opera (Leipzig, Dec. 22, 1829); *Des Falkners Braut,* comic opera (1830; Leipzig, March 10, 1832); *Hans Heiling,* romantic opera (1831–32; Berlin, May 24, 1833); *Das Schloss am Ätna,* romantic opera (1830–35; Leipzig, Jan. 29, 1836); *Der Bäbu,* comic opera (1836–37; Hannover, Feb. 19, 1838); *Kaiser Adolf von Nassau,* romantic opera (Dresden, Jan 5, 1845); *Austin,* romantic opera (1850–51; Hannover, Jan. 25, 1852); *Sangeskönig Hiarne, oder Das Tyringsschwert,* romantic opera (1857–58; Frankfurt, Sept. 13, 1863); ballet, *Die stolze Bäuerin* (Zittau, 1810); incidental music. Apart from his stage productions, he wrote a number of choral works, but his attempts to compose instrumental music were not successful; his 2 symphs. remained unfinished.

Marshall, Margaret, Scottish soprano; b. Stirling, Jan. 4, 1949. She studied at the Royal Scottish Academy of Music in Glasgow; also took voice lessons with Hans Hotter. In 1974 she won first prize at the International Competition in Munich; made her London debut in 1975; in 1978 she made her operatic debut in Florence as Euridice in *Orfeo;* she then sang the role of the Countess in the 1979 Florence production of *Le nozze di Figaro,* and made her Covent Garden debut in the same role in 1980. In 1982 she appeared in Milan and at the Salzburg Festival. She made her first appearances in the U.S. in 1980 as a soloist with the Boston Symph. and N.Y. Phil.; subsequently made several American tours as a concert artist.

Marsick, Armand, eminent Belgian composer, nephew of **Martin-Pierre-Joseph Marsick;** b. Liège, Sept. 20, 1877; d. Haine-Saint-Paul, April 30, 1959. He studied with his father, Louis Marsick; then took a course in composition with Sylvain Dupuis at the Liège Cons.; became first violinist in the Théâtre Municipal in Nancy; completed composition studies with Guy Ropartz at the Cons. there. In 1898 he became concertmaster at the Concerts Colonne in Paris. In 1908 he obtained the position of instructor at the Cons. of Athens; he remained in Greece until 1921; was appointed conductor at the Music Academy of Bilbao, Spain, in 1922. He returned to Belgium in 1927; was a prof. at the Liège Cons. (1927–42) and conductor of the Société des Concerts Symphoniques (1927–39). WORKS: 3 operas: *La Jane* (1903; first produced as *Vendetta corsa* in Rome, 1913; then at Liège, March 29, 1921); *Lara* (1913; Antwerp, Dec. 3, 1929); *L'Anneau nuptial* (1920; Brussels, March 3, 1928); radio play, *Le Visage de la Wallonie* (1937); symph. poems: *Stèle funéraire* (1902) and *La Source* (1908); *Improvisation et Final* for Cello and Orch. (1904); 2 suites: *Scènes de montagnes* (1910) and *Tableaux grecs* (1912); *Tableaux de voyage* for Small Orch. (1939); *Loustics en fête* for Small Orch. (1939); *3 morceaux symphoniques* (1950); Violin Sonata (1900); Quartet for 4 Horns (1950); *4 pièces* for Piano (1912); several sets of songs; choruses. A catalogue of his works was publ. by the Centre Belge de Documentation Musicale (Brussels, 1955).

Marsick, Martin-Pierre-Joseph, distinguished violinist; b. Jupille, near Liège, Belgium, March 9, 1848; d. Paris, Oct. 21, 1924. He studied at the Liège Cons.; at the age of 12, played the organ at the Cathedral; then studied violin with Léonard at the Brussels Cons. and with Massart at the Paris Cons., taking first prize there. In 1870 he became a pupil of Joachim in Berlin. After a brilliant debut at Paris in the Concerts Populaires (1873), he undertook long tours in Europe; also played in the U.S. (1895–96). In 1892 he was appointed prof. of violin at the Paris Cons. Among his pupils were Carl Flesch and Jacques Thibaud. He wrote 3 violin concertos and numerous solo pieces for the violin (*Adagio scherzando; 2 Reveries; Songe; Romance; Tarentelle; Agitato; Intermezzo; Berceuse;* etc.).

Marteau, Henri, famous French violinist; b. Reims, March 31, 1874; d. Lichtenberg, Bavaria, Oct. 3, 1934. He studied violin with Léonard at the Paris Cons. and began his concert career as a youth; was soloist with the Vienna Phil. at the age of 10, and played a concert in London at 14. In 1892, 1893, 1894, 1898, and 1906 he also toured the U.S.; gave concerts in Scandinavia, Russia, France, and Germany. In 1900 he was appointed prof. of violin at the Geneva Cons., and in 1908 succeeded Joachim as violin teacher at the Hochschule für Musik in Berlin. In 1915 he left Germany and went to Sweden, becoming a Swedish citizen in 1920; then taught at the German Music Academy in Prague (1921–24), at the Leipzig Cons. (1926–27), and (from 1928) at the Dresden Cons. He was greatly appreciated by musicians of Europe; Max Reger, who was a personal friend, wrote a violin concerto for him, as did Massenet; his teacher Léonard bequeathed to him his magnificent Maggini violin, formerly owned by the Empress Maria Theresa. Marteau was also a competent composer; he wrote an opera, *Meister Schwable* (Plauen, 1921); a symph. work, *Gloria naturae* (Stockholm, 1918); 2 violin concertos; Cello Concerto; *Sonata fantastica* for Violin alone; 3 string quartets; String Quintet; Clarinet Quintet; numerous violin pieces and arrangements of classical works.

Martelli, Henri, French composer; b. Santa Fe, Argentina, Feb. 25, 1895; d. Paris, July 15, 1980. He studied law at the Univ. of Paris; simultaneously took courses in composition with Widor and Caussade. He was secretary of the Société Nationale de Musique (1945–67) and director of programs there from 1968; from 1953 to 1973 was president of the French section of the International Society for Contemporary Music. In his compositions he attempted to re-create the spirit of old French music in modern techniques.

WORKS: Opera, *La Chanson de Roland* (1921–23; revised 1962–64; Paris, April 13, 1967); opera buffa, *Le Major Cravachon* (1958; French Radio, June 14, 1959); 2 ballets: *La Bouteille de Panurge* (1930; Paris, Feb. 24, 1937) and *Les Hommes de sable* (1951); *Rondo* for Orch. (1921); *Sarabande, Scherzo et Final* for Orch. (1922); *Divertissement sarrasin* for Orch. (1922); *Sur la vie de Jeanne d'Arc* for Orch. (1923); *Scherzo* for Violin and Orch. (1925); *Mors et Juventas* for Orch. (1927); *Bas-reliefs assyriens* for Orch. (1928; Boston, March 14, 1930); *Passacaille sur un thème russe* for Orch. (1928); Concerto for Orch. (1931; Boston, April 22, 1932); 3 suites for Orch.: No. 1, *Suite sur un thème corse* (1936); No. 2 (1950); No. 3 (1971); Concerto No. 1 for Violin and Chamber Orch. (1938); *Ouverture pour un conte de Boccace* (1942); *Suite concertante* for Wind Quintet and Orch. (1943); *Divertimento* for Wind Orch. (1945); *Fantaisie* for Piano and Orch. (1945); Sinfonietta (1948); 3 symphs.: No. 1 for Strings (1953; French Radio, March 13, 1955); No. 2 for Strings (1956; Paris, July 17, 1958); No. 3 (1957; Paris, March 8, 1960); Concertino No. 2 for Violin and Chamber Orch. (1954); Concertino for Oboe, Clarinet, Horn, Bassoon, and String Orch. (1955); Double Concerto for Clarinet, Bassoon, and Orch. (1956); *Le Radeau de la Méduse*, symph. poem (1957); *Variations* for String Orch. (1959); *Scènes à danser* for Orch. (1963); *Rapsodie* for Cello and Orch. (1966); Oboe Concerto (1971); *Le Temps*, cantata for Voice and 8 Instruments (1945); *Chrestomathie* for a cappella Chorus (1949); *Invention* for Cello and Piano (1925); Duo for Oboe and English Horn (1925); 2 string quartets (1932–33, 1944); Piano Trio (1935); Violin Sonata (1936); *Suite* for 4 Clarinets (1936); *Introduction et Final* for Violin and Piano (1937); Wind Octet (1941); *Scherzetto, Berceuse et Final* for Cello and Piano (1941); Bassoon Sonata (1941); Cello Sonatina (1941); Flute Sonata (1942); *3 esquisses* for Saxophone and Piano (1943); *Préambule et Scherzo* for Clarinet and Piano (1944); *7 Duos* for Violin and

Harp (1946); *Fantaisiestück* for Flute and Piano (1946); Wind Quintet (1974); Cornet Sonatina (1948); *Adagio, Cadence et Final* for Oboe and Piano (1949); 2 quintets for Flute, Harp, and String Trio (1950, 1952); Trio for Flute, Cello, and Piano (1951); *Cadence, Interlude et Rondo* for Saxophone and Piano (1952); *15 études* for Solo Bassoon (1953); Bass Trombone Sonata (1956); Viola Sonata (1959); *Suite* for Solo Guitar (1960); *Concertstück* for Viola and Piano (1962); Concertino for Cornet and Piano (1964); *Dialogue* for Trombone, Tuba or Bass Saxophone, and Piano (1966); Oboe Sonata (1972); String Trio (1973–74); Trio for Flute, Cello, and Harp (1976); *Suite galante* for Piano (1924); *Guitare* for Piano (1931); 3 *Petites suites* for Piano (1935, 1943, 1950); *Suite* for Piano (1939); 2-piano Sonata (1946); *Sonorités* for Piano, left-hand (1974); 17 radiophonic works (1940–62); songs.

Martenot, Maurice, French inventor of the electronic instrument "Ondes musicales," a.k.a. "Ondes Martenot"; b. Paris, Oct. 14, 1898; d. there, Oct. 10, 1980, as a result of a velocipede accident. He studied composition at the Paris Cons. with Gédalge; began to work on the construction of an electronic musical instrument with a keyboard, which he called Ondes musicales. He gave its first demonstration in Paris on April 20, 1928, and on Dec. 23, 1928, the first musical work for the instrument, *Poème symphonique pour solo d'Ondes musicales et orchestre*, by Dimitri Levidis, was presented in Paris. Martenot publ. *Méthode pour l'enseignement des Ondes musicales* (Paris, 1931). The instrument became popular, especially among French composers: it is included in the score of Honegger's *Jeanne d'Arc au bûcher* (1935); Koechlin's *Le Buisson ardent*, part 1 (1938); Martinot's 2nd Symph., subtitled *Hymne à la vie* (1944); and Messiaen's *Turangalîla-Symphonie* (1946–48). It was used as a solo instrument in Koechlin's *Hymne* (1929), Jolivet's *Concerto* (1947), Landowski's *Concerto* (1954), Bondon's *Kaleidoscope* (1957), and Charpentier's *Concertino "alla francese"* (1961); Milhaud, Jolivet, Rivier, Koechlin, Chaynes, Eloy, Tessier, Louvier, Bussotti, Goeyvaerts, Schibler, Mestres-Quadreny, and Calvin Hampton contributed to the growing literature of symph. and chamber music works that include the Ondes Martenot. Of all the early electronic instruments—Ondes Martenot, Trautonium, and Theremin—only Martenot's has proved a viable musical instrument. When Varèse's *Ecuatorial*, written in 1934 for a brass ensemble and including a Theremin, was publ. in 1961, the publ. score substituted an Ondes Martenot for the obsolescent Theremin. Martenot's sister, **Ginette Martenot** (b. Paris, Jan. 27, 1902), became the chief exponent of the Ondes Martenot in concert performances in Europe and America.

Martin, Frank, greatly renowned Swiss composer; b. Geneva, Sept. 15, 1890; d. Naarden, the Netherlands, Nov. 21, 1974. He studied with Joseph Lauber in Geneva (1906–14); then took courses in Zürich (1918–20), Rome (1921–23), and Paris (1923–25). He returned to Geneva in 1926 as a pianist and harpsichordist; taught at the Inst. Jaques-Dalcroze (1927–38); was founder and director of the Technicum Moderne de Musique (1933–39); president of the Assoc. of Swiss Musicians (1942–46). He moved to the Netherlands in 1946 and while living there taught classes in composition at the Cologne Hochschule für Musik (1950–57). His early music showed the influence of César Franck and French impressionists, but soon he succeeded in creating a distinctive style supported by a consummate mastery of contrapuntal and harmonic writing, and a profound feeling for emotional consistency and continuity. Still later he became fascinated by the logic and self-consistency of Schoenberg's method of composition with 12 tones, and adopted it in a modified form in several of his works. He also demonstrated an ability to stylize folk-song materials in modern techniques. In 1944, the director of Radio Geneva asked Martin to compose an oratorio to be broadcast immediately upon the conclusion of World War II. He responded with *In terra pax* for 5 Soli, Double Chorus, and Orch., which was given its broadcast premiere from Geneva at the end of the war in Europe, May 7, 1945; a public performance followed in Geneva 24 days later.

WORKS: FOR THE STAGE: Operas: *Der Sturm (The Tempest)*, after Shakespeare (1952–54; Vienna, June 17, 1956), and *Monsieur de Pourceaugnac*, after Molière (1960–62; Geneva, April 23, 1963). Ballets: *Das Märchen vom Aschenbrödel*, after the Cinderella legend (1941; Basel, March 12, 1942), and *Ein Totentanz zu Basel im Jahre 1943* (Basel, May 27, 1943); play with music, *La Nique à Satan*, for Baritone, Male and Female and Children's Choruses, Winds, Percussion, 2 Pianos, and Double Bass (1930–31; Geneva, Feb. 25, 1933); incidental music to *Oedipus Rex* (1923), *Oedipus Coloneus* (1924), *Le Divorce* (1928), *Romeo and Juliet* (1929), and *Athalic* (1946).

VOCAL WORKS: In addition to *In terra pax, 3 poèmes païens* for Baritone and Orch. (1910); *Les Dithyrambes* for 4 Soli, Mixed Chorus, Children's Chorus, and Orch. (1918); *4 sonnets à Cassandre* for Mezzo-soprano, Flute, Viola, and Cello (1921); *Messe* for Double Chorus a cappella (1922); *Musique pour les Fêtes du Rhône* for Chorus and Winds (1929); *Cantate sur la Nativité* for Soli, Chorus, String Orch., and Piano (1929; unfinished); *Chanson en canon* for Chorus a cappella (1930); *Le Vin herbé*, oratorio after the Tristan legend, for 12 Solo Voices, 7 Strings, and Piano (1938–41); first complete production, Zürich, March 26, 1942); *Cantate pour le 1er août* for Chorus, and Organ or Piano (1941); *Der Cornet* or *Die Weise von Liebe und Tod des Cornets Christoph Rilke*, after Rilke, cycle for Alto and Orch. (1942–43; Basel, Feb. 9, 1945); *Sechs Monologe aus "Jedermann" (6 Monologues from "Everyman")*, after Hofmannsthal, for Baritone or Alto, and Piano (1943; orchestrated 1949); *Dédicace* for Tenor and Piano (1945); *3 Chants de Noël* for Soprano, Flute and Piano (1974); *Golgotha*, oratorio for 5 Soli, Chorus, Orch., and Organ (1945–48; Geneva, April 29, 1949); *5 chansons d'Ariel* for Small Chorus a cappella (1950); *Psaumes de Genève*, psalm cantata for Chorus, Children's Chorus, Orch.,

and Organ (1958); *Le Mystère de la Nativité*, oratorio (1957–59; Geneva, Dec. 24, 1959); *3 Minnelieder* for Soprano and Piano (1960); *Ode à la musique* for Chorus, Trumpet, 2 Horns, 3 Trombones, Double Bass, and Piano (1961); *Verse à boire* for Chorus a cappella (1961); *Pilate*, short oratorio (Rome, Nov. 14, 1964); *Maria Triptychon* for Soprano, Violin, and Orch. (consists of the separate works *Ave Maria, Magnificat*, and *Stabat Mater*, 1967–69; Rotterdam, Nov. 13, 1969); *Poèmes de la Mort* for 3 Male Voices and 3 Electric Guitars (1969–71); *Requiem* (1971–72; Lausanne, May 4, 1973); *Et la vie l'emporta*, chamber cantata for Small Vocal and Instrumental Ensembles (1974; his last work; orchestration completed by Bernard Reichel in 1975).

INSTRUMENTAL WORKS: Suite for Orch. (1913); 2 violin sonatas (1913, 1931–32); *Symphonie pour orchestre burlesque sur des thèmes savoyards*, with Children's Instruments (1915); Piano Quintet (1919); *Esquisses* for Small Orch. (1920); *Pavane couleur de temps* for String Quintet or String Orch. or Small Orch. (1920); *Foxtrot*, overture for 2 Pianos (1924; also for Orch.); Piano Trio on popular Irish themes (1924); *Rythmes*, 3 symph. movements (1926; International Society for Contemporary Music Festival, Geneva, April 6, 1929); *Guitare*, 4 small pieces for Guitar (1933; versions for Piano and Orch.); 2 piano concertos: No. 1 (1933–34; Geneva, Jan. 22, 1936) and No. 2 (1968–69; The Hague, June 27, 1970); *Rhapsodie* for String Quintet (1935); *Danse de la peur* for 2 Pianos and Small Orch. (1936; music from an uncompleted ballet, *Die blaue Blume*); String Trio (1936); Symph., with Jazz Instruments (1937; Geneva, March 10, 1938); *Ballade* for Saxophone, Strings, Piano, and Percussion (1938); *Sonata da chiesa* for Viola d'Amore or Flute, and Organ or Orch. or String Orch. (1938); *Ballade* for Flute, and Orch. or String Orch. (1939); *Ballade* for Piano and Orch. (1939); *Ballade* for Trombone or Saxophone, and Piano or Orch. (1940); *Passacaille* for Organ (1944; versions for String Orch., 1952, and for Full Orch., 1962); *Petite symphonie concertante* for Harp, Harpsichord, Piano, and Double String Orch. (1944–45; Zürich, May 17, 1946; an alternate version, retitled *Symphonie concertante*, was created in 1946 for Full Orch., eliminating the solo instruments); *8 Preludes* for Piano (1947–48); Concerto for 7 Winds, Strings, and Percussion (1949; Bern, Oct. 25, 1949); *Ballade* for Cello, and Piano or Small Orch. (1949); Violin Concerto (1950–51; Basel, Jan. 24, 1952); Concerto for Harpsichord and Small Orch. (Venice, Sept. 14, 1952); *Clair de lune* for Piano (1953); *Etudes* for String Orch. or 2 Pianos (1955–56); *Ouverture en hommage à Mozart* (1956); *Pièce brève* for Flute, Oboe, and Harp (1957); *Ouverture en rondeau* (1958); *Inter arma caritas* for Orch. (1963); *Les Quatre Eléments* for Orch. (1963–64; Geneva, Oct. 7, 1964); *Etude rythmique* and *Etude de déchiffrage* for Piano (both 1965); Cello Concerto (1965–66; Basel, Jan. 26, 1967); String Quartet (1966–67); *Erasmi monumentum* for Orch. and Organ (Rotterdam, Sept. 24, 1969); *3 danses* for Oboe, Harp, and String Orch. (Zürich, Oct. 9, 1970); *Ballade* for Viola, Winds, Harp, and Harpsichord (1972); *Polyptyque*, 6 images of the Passion of Christ, for Violin and 2

String Orchs. (1972–73; Lausanne, Sept. 9, 1973); *Fantaisie sur des rythmes flamenco* for Piano (1973).

Martin, (Nicolas-) Jean-Blaise, famous French baritone; b. Paris, Feb. 24, 1768; d. Ronzières, Rhône, Oct. 28, 1837. He made his debut at the Théâtre de Monsieur in 1789 in *Le Marquis de Tulipano;* sang at the Théâtre Feydeau and the Théâtre Favart from 1794 until they were united as the Opéra-Comique in 1801, and there until 1823. In 1816–18 and again in 1832–37, he was a prof. at the Paris Cons. His voice, while essentially baritone in quality, had the extraordinary range of 3 full octaves, reaching high C.

Martin, Riccardo (real name, **Hugh Whitfield Martin**), American tenor; b. Hopkinsville, Ky., Nov. 18, 1874; d. New York, Aug. 11, 1952. He studied violin in Nashville and singing in N.Y.; was a pupil in composition of MacDowell at Columbia Univ.; in 1901 went to Paris, where he took singing lessons with Sbriglia; made his debut as Faust in Nantes (1904) and his American debut as Canio (in *Pagliacci*) with the San Carlo Opera Co. in New Orleans (1906); was a member of the Metropolitan Opera Co. from 1907 to 1915; then was with the Boston Grand Opera Co. (1916–17); again with the Metropolitan (1917–18); then with the Chicago Opera Co. (1920–22); subsequently settled in N.Y. and taught singing.

Martinelli, Giovanni, famous Italian tenor; b. Montagnana, near Padua, Oct. 22, 1885; d. New York, Feb. 2, 1969. One of the 14 children of a fertile Italian family, he played clarinet in the town band; then went to Milan and studied voice there with Mandolini. On Dec. 3, 1910, he made his debut in Milan singing in Rossini's *Stabat Mater;* he made his operatic debut at the Teatro del Varme in Milan as Ernani; Puccini heard him and invited him to sing in the European premiere of *La Fanciulla del West* (Rome, June 12, 1911); he sang for the first time at London's Covent Garden on April 22, 1912. He made his American debut on Nov. 3, 1913, in Philadelphia as Cavaradossi in *Tosca.* On Nov. 20, 1913, he appeared at the Metropolitan Opera in N.Y. as Rodolfo in *La Bohème,* scoring an immediate success with the public and the press; he remained with the Metropolitan for 30 years, until 1943; he returned in 1944, giving his farewell on March 8, 1945; during his final season there (1945–46), he appeared as a concert artist. He then taught voice in N.Y. while making occasional appearances as a singer; he made his last appearance in a production of *Turandot* in Seattle in 1967 in his 82nd year. At the Metropolitan, he sang Radames in *Aida* 126 times, Don José in *Carmen* 75 times, Canio in *Pagliacci* 68 times, and Manrico in *Il Trovatore* 70 times; other parts in his rich repertoire were the title roles in *Faust, Samson and Delilah, Andrea Chénier,* and *Otello.* However, he shunned the Wagnerian characters in opera.

Martinet, Jean-Louis, French composer; b. Ste.-Bazeille, Nov. 8, 1912. He studied music theory with Charles Koechlin, Roger-Ducasse, and Messiaen; also took lessons in conducting with Charles Munch and Roger Desormière. He naturally absorbed the harmonic essence of French Impressionism and the contrapuntal rigor of the neo-Classical style as practiced by Stravinsky and Béla Bartók; in later works he succumbed to the fashionable temptation of dodecaphony *à la française.* Among his works are a symph. poem, *Orphée* (1945); 6 pieces, each entitled *Mouvement symphonique* (1953–59); *Variations* for String Quartet (1946, in dodecaphonic technique); cantatas: *Episodes* (1950); *Elsa* (1959); *Les Amours* for Chorus a cappella (1960); *Les Douze* for Narrator, Chorus, and Orch., after a revolutionary poem by Alexander Blok (1961); symph., *In memoriam* (1963); *Divertissement pastoral* for Piano and Orch. (1966); *2 images* for Orch. (1966).

Martini, Giovanni Battista, known as **Padre Martini;** illustrious Italian pedagogue, writer on music, and composer; b. Bologna, April 24, 1706; d. there, Aug. 3, 1784. He received the rudiments of musical knowledge from his father, a violinist; then took courses with Angelo Predieri, Giovanni Antonio Ricieri, and Francesco Antonio Pistocchi. A man of unquenchable intellectual curiosity, he studied mathematics with Zanotti, and took a seminar in ecclesiastical music with Giacomo Perti. In 1721 he entered the Franciscan conventual monastery in Lugo di Romagna, but abandoned monastic aspirations and returned to Bologna in 1722; there he became organist, and later maestro di cappella, at S. Francesco in 1725, and was ordained a priest in 1729. He was a prolific composer and a learned scholar; his *Storia della musica* (3 vols., Bologna, 1757, 1770, and 1781; reprinted 1967) gives an extensive survey of music in ancient Greece. But it is as a pedagogue that Padre Martini achieved lasting fame. His magnum opus in music theory was *Esemplare ossia Saggio fondamentale practico di contrappunto* (2 vols., Bologna, 1774 and 1775). J.C. Bach, Jommelli, Grétry, and Mozart were his students. A by-product of his various activities was the accumulation of a magnificent library, which Burney estimated at nearly 17,000 vols.; after Martini's death, it became the foundation of the collection in the library of the Liceo Musicale (later the Civico Museo Bibliografico Musicale). He received many honors during his long life; in 1758 he became a member of the Accademia dell' Istituto delle Scienze di Bologna and of the Accademia dei Filarmonici di Bologna. In 1776 he was elected to membership in the Arcadi di Roma, where his Arcadian title was "Aristosseno Anfioneo" ("Aristoxenos Amphion"). He conducted a voluminous correspondence; about 6,000 letters are extant; it included communications with scholars, kings, and popes.

Martini (real name, **Schwarzendorf**), **Jean Paul Egide** (properly, **Johann Paul Ágid**), German organist and composer; b. Freystadt in the Palatinate (baptized, Aug. 31), 1741; d. Paris, Feb. 10, 1816. At the age of 10 he enrolled in the Jesuit Seminary in

Neuburg an der Donau, becoming organist there. In 1760, having studied organ, he settled in Nancy, and Italianized his name; then was attached to the retinue of King Stanislas at Lunéville (1761–66). In 1766 he went to Paris, where he won a prize for a military march for the Swiss Guard; this introduced him into army circles in France; he enlisted as an officer of a Hussar regiment, and wrote more band music; also composed an opera, *L'Amoureux de quinze ans,* which was produced with extraordinary success at the Italian Opera in Paris (April 18, 1771). Leaving the army, he became music director to the Prince of Condé, and later to the Comte d'Artois. He purchased the reversion of the office of First Intendant of the King's Music, a speculation brought to naught by the Revolution, which caused him to resign in haste his position as conductor at the Théâtre Feydeau, and flee to Lyons in 1792. He returned to Paris in 1794, and was appointed Inspector of the Paris Cons. in 1798; also taught composition there until 1802. In appreciation of his royalist record, he was given the post of Royal Intendant at the Restoration in 1814, but died 2 years later. He wrote 13 operas, a Requiem for Louis XVI, Psalms, and other church music, but he is chiefly remembered as the composer of the popular air *Plaisir d'amour,* which was arranged by Berlioz for voice and orch.

Martino, Donald, American composer; b. Plainfield, N.J., May 16, 1931. He learned to play the clarinet, oboe, and saxophone in his youth; then studied composition with Ernst Bacon at Syracuse Univ. (B.M., 1952) and with Milton Babbitt and Roger Sessions at Princeton Univ. (M.F.A., 1954); continued his studies with Luigi Dallapiccola in Florence, Italy, on a Fulbright scholarship (1954–56). In 1958–59 he was an instructor at Princeton Univ.; from 1959 to 1969 taught theory and composition at Yale Univ.; then was a prof. of composition at the New England Cons. of Music (1970–80), where he served as chairman of the composition dept. He was Irving Fine Prof. of Music at Brandeis Univ. (1980–83); in 1983 became a prof. of music at Harvard Univ. He received 3 Guggenheim fellowships (1967, 1973, 1982); was awarded the Pulitzer Prize in Music in 1974 for his chamber music piece *Notturno;* in 1981 was made a member of the American Academy and Inst. of Arts and Letters. In his music he adopts a quasi-mathematical method of composition based on arithmetical permutations of tonal and rhythmic ingredients.

WORKS: *Quodlibets* for Flute (1954); *A Set for Clarinet* (1954); *Portraits,* secular cantata for Mezzo-soprano, Bass-baritone, Mixed Chorus, and Orch., to texts by Walt Whitman, Edna St. Vincent Millay, and e.e. cummings (1955); *7 canoni enigmatici* for String Quartet or other instrumental combinations (1955); *Composition* for Orch. (retitled *Contemplations;* 1957); Quartet for Clarinet, Violin, Viola, and Cello (1957); *Piano Fantasy* (1958); Trio for Violin, Cello, and Piano (1959); *5 frammenti* for Oboe and Double Bass (1961); *Fantasy-Variations* for Violin (1962); Concerto for Wind Quintet (1964); *Parisonatina al'dodecafonia* for Cello (1964); Piano Concerto (1965); *B,A,B,B,IT,T* for Clarinet (1966); *Strata* for Bass Clarinet (1966); *Mosaic for Grand Orchestra* (1967); *Pianissimo,* piano sonata (1970); *7 Pious Pieces* for Chorus, to a text by Robert Herrick (1971); Cello Concerto (1972); *Augenmusik: A Mixed Mediacritique* for "actress, danseuse or uninhibited female percussionist and electronic tape" (1972); *Notturno* for Flute, Clarinet, Violin, Cello, Percussion, and Piano (1973); *Paradiso Choruses,* oratorio for 12 Soloists, Mixed Chorus, Children's Chorus ad libitum, Orch., and Tape, after Dante's *Divine Comedy* (1974); *Ritorno* for Orch. (1975); Triple Concerto for Clarinet, Bass Clarinet, Contrabass Clarinet, and Chamber Orch. (1977); *Fantasies and Impromptus* for Piano (1980); *Parody Suite* for Piano (1982); String Quartet (1983).

Martinon, Jean, significant French conductor and composer; b. Lyons, Jan. 10, 1910; d. Paris, March 1, 1976. He studied violin at the Paris Cons. (1926–29), winning a premier prix; then took lessons in composition with Albert Roussel and Vincent d'Indy and in conducting with Charles Munch. He was in the French army during World War II; was taken prisoner in 1940 and spent 2 years in a German prison camp (Stalag IX); during imprisonment he wrote several works of a religious nature, among them *Psalm 136, Musique d'exil ou Stalag IX,* and *Absolve Domine,* in memory of French musicians killed in the war. After the war he conducted the Concerts du Conservatoire de Paris; in 1946 he was appointed conductor of the Bordeaux Symph. Orch.; later had guest engagements as a conductor in England and South America. From 1947 to 1950 he served as associate conductor of the London Phil.; made his American debut with the Boston Symph. Orch., March 29, 1957, conducting the American premiere of his 2nd Symph. His other engagements were as principal conductor of the Lamoureux Orch. in Paris (1950–57), the Israel Phil. (1958–60), and the Düsseldorf Symph. (1960–66). In 1963 he was appointed conductor of the Chicago Symph. Orch.; during the 5 years of his tenure he conducted about 60 works by modern American and European composers of the modern school; this progressive policy met opposition from some influential people in Chicago society and in the press, and he resigned in 1968. He returned to France and led the Orch. National of Paris Radio; also conducted the Residente Orch. in The Hague. His own compositions follow the spirit of French neo-Classicism, euphonious in their modernity and expansive in their Romantic élan.

Martinů, Bohuslav, remarkable Czech composer; b. Polička, Dec. 8, 1890; d. Liestal, near Basel, Switzerland, Aug. 28, 1959. He studied violin at home; in 1907–9 he was enrolled at the Prague Cons.; then entered the Prague Organ School, where he studied organ and theory, but was expelled in 1910 for lack of application; played in the 2nd violin section in the Czech Phil. in Prague (1913–14), returning to Polička (1914–18) to avoid service in the Austrian army; after World War I he reentered the Prague Cons. as a pupil of Suk, but again failed to graduate. In 1923 he went to Paris and participated in the progressive musical circles there; took private lessons with Albert Roussel. In a relatively short time his name became known in Europe through increasingly frequent performances of his chamber works, ballets, and symph. pieces; several of his works were performed at the festivals of the International Society for Contemporary Music. In 1932 his String Sextet won the Elizabeth Sprague Coolidge Award. He remained in Paris until June 1940, when he fled the German invasion and went to Portugal and finally to America in 1941; settled in N.Y.; was a visiting prof. of music at Princeton (1948–51); spent the last 2 years of his life in Switzerland. On Aug. 27, 1979, his remains were taken from Schönenberg, Switzerland, to Polička, Czechoslovakia, where they were placed in the family mausoleum. His music is characterized by a strong feeling for Bohemian melorhythms; his stylizations of Czech dances are set in a modern idiom without losing their simplicity. In his large works he followed the neo-Classical trend, with some impressionistic undertones; his mastery of modern counterpoint was extraordinary. In his music for the stage, his predilections were for chamber forms; his sense of operatic comedy was very strong, but he was also capable of poignant lyricism.

WORKS: OPERAS: *Voják a tanečnice (The Soldier and the Dancer)*, in 3 acts (1926–27; Brno, May 5, 1928); *Les Larmes du couteau (The Knife's Tears)*, in one act (1928); *Trois souhaits, ou Les Vicissitudes de la vie (3 Wishes, or The Fickleness of Life)*, "opera-film in 3 acts" (1929; perf. posthumously, Brno, June 16, 1971; the normal orch. is augmented by a Jazz Flute, Saxophones, Flexatone, Banjo, and Accordion); *La Semaine de bonté*, in 3 acts (1929; unfinished); *Hry o Marii (The Miracle of Our Lady)*, in 4 parts (1933–34; Brno, Feb. 23, 1935); *Hlas lesa (The Voice of the Forest)*, radio opera in one act (1935; Czech Radio, Oct. 6, 1935); *Divadlo za bránou (The Suburban Theater)*, opera buffa in 3 acts (1935–36; Brno, Sept. 20, 1936); *Veselohra na mostě (Comedy on a Bridge)*, radio opera in one act (1935; revised 1950; Czech Radio, March 18, 1937); *Julietta, or The Key to Dreams*, lyric opera in 3 acts (1936–37; Prague, March 16, 1938); *Alexandre bis*, opera buffa in one act (1937; Mannheim, Feb. 18, 1964); *What Men Live By (Čím člověk žije)*, pastoral opera after Tolstoy, in one act (1951–52; N.Y., May 20, 1955); *The Marriage (Ženitba)*, television opera after Gogol, in 2 acts (1952; NBC television, N.Y., Feb. 7, 1953); *La Plainte contre inconnu*, in 3 acts (1953; unfinished); *Mirandolina*, comic opera in 3 acts (1954; Prague, May 17, 1959); *Ariadne*, lyric opera in one act (1958; Gelsenkirchen, West Germany, March 2, 1961); *Greek Passion (Řecké pašije)*, musical drama after Kazantzakis, in 4 acts (1955–59; Zürich, June 9, 1961).

BALLETS: *Noc (Night)*, a "meloplastic scene" in one act (1913–14); *Stín (The Shadow)*, in one act (1916); *Istar*, in 3 acts (1918–22; Prague, Sept. 11, 1924); *Who Is the Most Powerful in the World? (Kdo je na světě nejmocnější)*, ballet comedy, after an English fairy tale (1922; Brno, Jan. 31, 1925); *The Revolt (Vzpoura)*, ballet sketch in one act (1922–23; Brno, Feb. 11, 1928); *The Butterfly That Stamped (Motýl, ktery dupal)*, after Kipling, in one act (1926); *La Revue de cuisine (The Kitchen Revue;* Prague, 1927); *On tourne (Natáčí se)*, for a cartoon and puppet film (1927); *Le Raid merveilleux (Báječný let)*, "ballet mechanique" for 2 Clarinets, Trumpet, and Strings (1927); *Echec au roi (Checkmating the King)*, jazz ballet in one act (1930); *Špalíček (The Chap Book)*, with Vocal Soloists and Chorus (1931; revised 1940; Prague, Sept. 19, 1933; revision, Prague, April 2, 1949); *Le Jugement de Paris* (1935); *The Strangler (Uškreovač)*, for 3 Dancers (1948; New London, Conn., Aug. 15, 1948).

FOR ORCH.: 6 symphs.: No. 1 (1942; Boston, Nov. 13, 1942); No. 2 (1943; Cleveland, Oct. 28, 1943); No. 3 (1944; Boston, Oct. 12, 1945); No. 4 (1945; Philadelphia, Nov. 30, 1945); No. 5 (1946; Prague, May 27, 1947); and No. 6, *Fantaisies symphoniques* (1951–53; Boston, Jan. 7, 1955); Concertino for Cello, Wind Instruments, and Piano (1924); 5 piano concertos: No. 1 (1925; Prague, Nov. 21, 1926); No. 2 (1934; rescored 1944; Prague, 1935); No. 3 (1947–48; Dallas, Nov. 20, 1949); No. 4, *Incantation* (1955–56; N.Y., Oct. 4, 1956); No. 5 *Fantasia concertante* (1957; Berlin, Jan. 31, 1959); Concertino for Piano, left hand, and Chamber Orch. (1926; Prague, Feb. 26, 1947; originally titled *Divertimento*); 2 cello concertos: No. 1 for Cello and Chamber Orch. (1930; revised for Full Orch., 1939, and rescored in 1955) and No. 2 (1944–45); Concerto for String Quartet and Orch. (1931; also known as String Quartet with Orch.); 2 violin concertos: No. 1 (1931–32; Chicago, Oct. 25, 1973) and No. 2 (1943; Boston, Dec. 31, 1943); *Divertimento (Serenade No. 4)* for Violin, Viola, Oboe, Piano, and String Orch. (1932); Concertino for Piano Trio and Orch. (1933; Basel, Oct. 16, 1936); Concerto for Harpsichord and Chamber Orch. (1935); Concerto for Flute, Violin, and Chamber Orch. (1936); *Duo concertante* for 2 Violins and Orch. (1937); *Suite concertante* for Violin and Orch. (1937; revised 1945); Piano Concertino (1938; London, Aug. 5, 1948); *Sonata da camera* for Cello and Chamber Orch. (1940); *Sinfonietta giocosa* for Piano and Chamber Orch. (1940; revised 1941; N.Y., March 16, 1942); *Concerto da camera* for Violin, String Orch., Piano, and Timpani (1941; Basel, Jan. 23, 1942); 2-Piano Concerto (1943; Philadelphia, Nov. 5, 1943); *Sinfonia concertante* for Oboe, Bassoon, Violin, Cello, and Small Orch. (1949; Basel, Dec. 8, 1950); 2-Violin Concerto (1950; Dallas, Jan. 8, 1951); *Rhapsody-Concerto* for Viola and Orch. (1952; Cleveland, Feb. 19, 1953); Concerto for Violin, Piano, and Orch. (1953); Oboe Concerto (1955); *Smrt Tintagilova (The Death of Tintagile)*, music for the Maeterlinck drama (1910); *Anděl smrti (Angel of Death)*, symph. poem (1910; also for Piano); *Nocturno No. 1* (1914); *Ballada* (1915); *Mijející půlnoc (Vanishing Midnight;* 1921–22); *Half-Time*, rondo (1924; Prague, Dec. 7, 1924); *La Bagarre (The Tumult)*, rondo (1926; Boston, Nov. 18, 1927); *Jazz Suite* (1928); *La Rhapsodie* (1928; Boston, Dec. 14, 1928); *Praeludium*, in the form of a scherzo (1930); *Serenade* for Chamber Orch. (1930); *Sinfonia concertante* for 2 Orchs. (1932); *Partita*

Martín y Soler

(Suite No. 1) (1932); *Invence* (*Inventions;* 1934); Concerto Grosso for Small Orch. (1938; Boston, Nov. 14, 1941); *3 ricercari* for Chamber Orch. (1938; Venice, 1938); Double Concerto for 2 String Orchs., Piano, and Timpani (1938; Basel, Feb. 9, 1940); *Memorial to Lidice* (1943; N.Y., Oct. 28, 1943); *Thunderbolt P-47,* scherzo (1945; Washington, D.C., Dec. 19, 1945); *Toccata e due canzone* for Small Orch. (1946; Basel, Jan. 21, 1947); *Sinfonietta La Jolla* for Chamber Orch. and Piano (1950); *Intermezzo* for Orch. (1950; Louisville Orch., Carnegie Hall, N.Y., Dec. 29, 1950); *Les Fresques de Piero della Francesca,* impressions of 3 frescoes (1955; Salzburg Festival, Aug. 28, 1956); *The Rock,* symph. prelude (1957; Cleveland, April 17, 1958); *Parables* (1957–58; Boston, Feb. 13, 1959); *Estampes,* symph. suite (1958; Louisville, Feb. 4, 1959).

FOR VOICE: *Nipponari,* 7 songs for Female Voice and Chamber Ensemble (1912); cantata, *Česká rapsódie* (1918; Prague, Jan. 12, 1919); *Kouzelné noci (Magic Nights),* 3 songs for Soprano and Orch. (1918); *Le Jazz,* movement for Voice and Orch. (1928); a cantata on Czech folk poetry, *Kytice (Bouquet of Flowers;* 1937; Czech Radio, May 1938); *Polní mše (Field Mass)* for Male Chorus, Baritone, and Orch. (1939; Prague, Feb. 28, 1946); *Hora tři světel (The Hill of 3 Lights),* small oratorio for Soloists, Chorus, and Organ (1954; Bern, Oct. 3, 1955); *Hymnus k sv. Jakubu (Hymn to St. James)* for Narrator, Soloists, Chorus, Organ, and Orch. (1954; Polička, July 31, 1955); *Gilgameš (The Epic of Gilgamesh)* for Narrator, Soloists, Chorus, and Orch. (1954–55; Basel, Jan. 24, 1958); *Otvírání studánek (The Opening of the Wells)* for Narrator, Soloists, Female Chorus, 2 Violins, Viola, and Piano (1955); *Legend from the Smoke of Potato Fires* for Soloists, Chorus, and Chamber Ensemble (1957); *Mikeš z hor (Mikesh from the Mountains)* for Soloists, Chorus, 2 Violins, Viola, and Piano (1959); *The Prophesy of Isaiah (Proroctví Izaiášovo)* for Male Chorus, Soloists, Viola, Trumpet, Piano, and Timpani (1959; Jerusalem, April 2, 1963; his last work; posthumous perf.); numerous part-songs and a cappella choruses.

CHAMBER MUSIC: 7 string quartets: No. 1 (1918; reconstructed, with the addition of a newly discovered 4th movement, by Jan Hanuš in 1972); No. 2 (1925); No. 3 (1929); No. 4 (1937); No. 5 (1938); No. 6 (1946); No. 7, *Concerto da camera* (1947); 5 violin sonatas: in C major (1919); in D minor (1926); No. 1 (1929); No. 2 (1931); No. 3 (1944); 2 string trios (1923, 1934); Quartet for Clarinet, Horn, Cello, and Drum (1924); 2 unnumbered nonets: for Violin, Viola, Cello, Flute, Clarinet, Oboe, Horn, Bassoon, and Piano (1924–25), and for Violin, Viola, Cello, Double Bass, Flute, Clarinet, Oboe, Horn, and Bassoon (1959); 2 duos for Violin and Cello (1927, 1957); *Impromptu* for Violin and Piano (1927); String Quintet (1927); Sextet for Winds and Piano (1929); *5 Short Pieces* for Violin and Piano (1929); Wind Quintet (1930); *Les Rondes,* 6 pieces for 7 Instruments (1930); 3 piano trios (*5 Brief Pieces,* 1930; 1950; 1951); Sonatina for 2 Violins and Piano (1930); *Etudes rythmiques* for Violin and Piano (1931); *Pastorales* and *Nocturnes* for Cello and Piano (both 1931); *Arabesques* for Violin or Cello, and Piano (1931); String Sextet (1932);

Sonata for 2 Violins and Piano (1932); *Serenade* No. 1 for 6 Instruments; No. 2 for 2 Violins and Viola; No. 3 for 7 Instruments (all 1932; No. 4 is the *Divertimento* for Violin, Viola, Oboe, Piano, and String Orch.); 2 piano quintets (1933, 1944); Sonata for Flute, Violin, and Piano (1936); *4 Madrigals* for Oboe, Clarinet, and Bassoon (1937); Violin Sonatina (1937); *Intermezzo,* 4 pieces for Violin and Piano (1937); Trio for Flute, Violin, and Bassoon (1937); 3 cello sonatas (1939, 1944, 1952); *Bergerettes* for Piano Trio (1940); *Promenades* for Flute, Violin, and Harpsichord (1940); Piano Quartet (1942); *Madrigal Sonata* for Flute, Violin, and Piano (1942); *Variations on a Theme of Rossini* for Cello and Piano (1942); *Madrigal Stanzas,* 5 pieces for Violin and Piano (1943); Trio for Flute, Cello, and Piano (1944); Flute Sonata (1945); *Czech Rhapsody* for Violin and Piano (1945); *Fantasia* for Theremin, Oboe, String Quartet, and Piano (1945); 2 duos for Violin and Viola (*3 Madrigals,* 1947; 1950); Quartet for Oboe, Violin, Cello, and Piano (1947); *Mazurka-Nocturne* for Oboe, 2 Violins, and Cello (1949); *Serenade* for Violin, Viola, Cello, and 2 Clarinets (1951); Viola Sonata (1955); Clarinet Sonatina (1956); Trumpet Sonatina (1956); *Divertimento* for 2 Flutes-à-bec (1957); *Les Fêtes nocturnes* for Violin, Viola, Cello, Clarinet, Harp, and Piano (1959); *Variations on a Slovak Theme* for Cello and Piano (1959).

FOR PIANO: *Puppets,* small pieces for children (in 3 sets, 1914–24); *Scherzo* (1924; discovered 1971); *Fables* (1924); *Film en miniature* (1925); *3 Czech Dances* (1926); *Le Noël* (1927); *4 Movements* (1928); *Borová,* 7 Czech dances (1929; also for Orch.); *Préludes (en forme de . . .)* (1929); *Fantaisie* for 2 Pianos (1929); *A trois mains* (1930); *Esquisses de danse,* 5 pieces (1932); *Les Ritournelles* (1932); *Dumka* (1936); *Fenêtre sur le jardin (Window in the Garden),* 4 pieces (1938); *Fantasia and Toccata* (1940); *Mazurka* (1941); *Etudes and Polkas* (in 3 books, 1945); *The 5th Day of the 5th Moon* (1948); *3 Czech Dances* for 2 Pianos (1949); Sonata (1954); *Reminiscences* (1957). FOR HARPSICHORD: *2 Pieces* (1935); Sonata (1958); *Impromptus* (1959). FOR ORGAN: *Vigilie* (1959).

Martín y Soler, Vicente, Spanish opera composer; b. Valencia, June 18, 1754; d. St. Petersburg, Jan. 30, 1806. He was church organist at Alicante as a youth, before going to Madrid, where he produced his first opera, *I due avari* (1776). He then went to Italy, where he was known as Martini lo Spagnuolo (the Spaniard); wrote operas for Naples, Turin, and Lucca. He secured the services of Da Ponte as librettist, and produced with him the operas *Il Burbero di buon cuore (The Grumbler with a Good Heart;* Vienna, Jan. 4, 1786; much acclaimed; revived there, Nov. 9, 1789, with 2 additional airs written expressly for it by Mozart); *Una cosa rara* (his undoubted masterpiece; Vienna, Nov. 17, 1786; numerous productions in other European capitals; Mozart borrowed a theme from this opera for his *Don Giovanni*); *L'arbore di Diana* (Vienna, Oct. 1, 1787). Having achieved fame in Italy, where he was favorably compared with Cimarosa and Paisiello, Martín y

Soler was engaged as court composer by Catherine the Great (1788). In St. Petersburg, he produced the operas *Gorye Bogatyr Kosometovitch* (libretto by Catherine II; Feb. 9, 1789); *La melomania* (Jan. 7, 1790); *Fedul and His Children* (Jan. 16, 1791); *La Festa del villaggio* (Jan. 26, 1798); ballets: *Didon abandonnée* (1792); *L'Oracle* (1793); *Amour et Psyché* (1793); *Tancrède* (1799). In 1795 he went to London; his operas *La scola de' maritati* (Jan. 27, 1795) and *L'isola del piacere* (May 26, 1795), both to librettos by Da Ponte, were presented there with excellent success. In 1796 he returned to Russia, and remained there until his death.

Martirano, Salvatore, American composer; b. Yonkers, N.Y., Jan. 12, 1927. He studied piano and composition at the Oberlin Cons. of Music (B.M., 1951); then at the Eastman School of Music in Rochester, N.Y., with Bernard Rogers (M.M., 1952); later went to Italy, where he took courses with Luigi Dallapiccola at the Cherubini Cons. of Music in Florence (1952–54). He served in the U.S. Marine Corps; played clarinet and cornet with the Parris Island Marine Band; in 1956–59 he held a fellowship to the American Academy in Rome, and in 1960 received a Guggenheim fellowship and the American Academy of Arts and Letters Award. In 1963 he joined the faculty of the Univ. of Illinois at Urbana. He writes in a progressive avant-garde idiom, applying the quaquaversal techniques of unmitigated radical modernism, free from any inhibitions. WORKS: Sextet for Wind Instruments (1949); Prelude for Orch. (1950); Variations for Flute and Piano (1950); String Quartet No. 1 (1951); *The Magic Stones,* chamber opera after the *Decameron* (Oberlin Cons., April 24, 1952); *Piece for Orchestra* (1952); Violin Sonata (1952); *Contrasto* for Orch. (1954); *Chansons innocentes* for Soprano and Piano (1957); *O, O, O, O, That Shakespeherian Rag* for Mixed Chorus and Instrumental Ensemble (1958); *Cocktail Music* for Piano (1962); *Octet* (1963); *Underworld* for 4 Actors, 4 Percussion Instruments, 2 Double Basses, Tenor Saxophone, and Tape (1965); *Ballad* for amplified nightclub Singer and Instrumental Ensemble (1966); *L's.G.A.* for a gas-masked Politico, Helium Bomb, 3 16mm Movie Projectors, and Tape (1968); *The Proposal* for Tapes and Slides (1968); *Action Analysis* for 12 People, Bunny, and Controller (1968); *Selections* for Alto Flute, Bass Clarinet, Viola, and Cello (1970).

Marttinen, Tauno, Finnish composer; b. Helsinki, Sept. 27, 1912. He studied piano, composition, and conducting at the Viipuri (Vyborg) Inst. of Music and the Sibelius Academy in Helsinki; conducted the Hameenlinna (Tavastehus) City Orch.; was director of the Hameenlinna Music Inst. from 1950 to 1975. A remarkably prolific composer, he began writing music in a traditional "Scandinavian" manner; about 1955 he adopted a serial technique. His adventurous style, marked by a sense of enlightened eclecticism and drawing its inspiration from national sources, caused some enthusiastic Finnish commentators to compare him to Charles Ives.

WORKS: FOR THE STAGE: *Neiti Gamardin talo (The House of Lady Gamard),* opera after Balzac (1960–71); *Päällysviitta (The Cloak),* TV opera after Gogol's story (1962–63); *Kihlaus (The Engagement),* opera after Aleksis Kivi (1964); *Apotti ja ikäneito (The Abbot and the Old Maid),* opera based on Balzac (1965); *Hymy tikkaiden juurella (The Smile at the Foot of the Ladder),* ballet after Henry Miller (1965); *Tulitik uja lainaamassa (Borrowing Matches),* opera after Maiju Lassila (1965); *Lea,* opera after Aleksis Kivi (1967); *Poltettu oranssi (Burnt Orange),* TV opera after Eva-Liisa Manner (1968); *Dorian Grayn muotokuva (The Portrait of Dorian Gray),* ballet after Oscar Wilde (1969); *Lumikuningatar (The Snow Queen),* children's ballet after H.C. Andersen (1970); *Beatrice,* ballet from the play after Dante's *Divine Comedy* (1970; Helsinki, Feb. 24, 1972); *Mestari Patelin (Master Patelin),* chamber opera (1969–72); *Laestadiuksen saarna (Laestadius's Sermon),* opera (1974–76); *Psykiatri (The Psychiatrist),* opera (1974); *Meedio (The Medium),* a cappella opera (1975–76); *Jaarlin sisar (The Earl's Sister),* ballad opera (1977); *Faaraon kirje (The Pharaoh's Letter),* opera (1978–80); *The Sun out of the Moon,* ballet (1975–77).

FOR ORCH.: 7 symphs.: No. 1 (1957–58); No. 2 (1959); No. 3 (1963); No. 4 (1965; co-winner of first prize in the orch. section of the 1967 Camden Festival of Finnish music held in London); No. 5, *The Shaman* (1967; revised 1972); No. 6 (1974–75); No. 7 (1977); *Suite* (1960); *Linnunrata (The Milky Way),* variations (1960–61); *Rembrandt* for Cello and Orch. (1962); Violin Concerto (1958–62); *Panu, tulen jumala (Panu, God of Fire;* 1963); *Manalan linnut (Birds of the Underworld;* 1964); 2 piano concertos (1964, 1973); *Fauni,* fantasy (1965); cello concerto, *Dalai Lama* (1964–66); *Maailman luominen (The Creation of the World),* symph. poem (1966); *Intrada* for Wind Ensemble (1967); Bassoon Concerto (1966–68); *Mont Saint Michel* (1969); *Vanha linna (An Old Castle;* 1969); *Pentalia* (1969); *Harmonia* (1970; Hämeenlinna, Sept. 27, 1972); *Concert Piece for Trumpet and Chamber Orch.* (1971); *Pohjola (The North)* for Wind Orch. (1972; Helsinki, Nov. 22, 1972); Flute Concerto (1974); *Hirvenhiihto (On the Tracks of the Winter Moose),* concerto for Clarinet and Orch. (1974).

Martucci, Giuseppe, eminent Italian composer and conductor; b. Capua, Jan. 6, 1856; d. Naples, June 1, 1909. A pupil of his father (a trumpet player), he made his debut as a child pianist at the age of 7; at 11 he was admitted to the Cons. di San Pietro a Majella in Naples; there he studied piano with B. Cesi, and composition with P. Serrao, but left in 1871. Subsequently he traveled as a pianist in Italy, France, Germany, and England; in 1880 he became a prof. of piano at the Naples Cons.; conducted symph. concerts established by Prince d'Ardore, and was the director of the Neapolitan Società del Quartetto. From 1886 until 1902 he was director of the Bologna Cons.; in 1902 he returned to Naples, and became director of the Cons. there, a post he held until his death. His activities as a fine symph.

conductor contributed much to Italian musical culture, and he was greatly esteemed by his colleagues and the public; an ardent admirer of Wagner, he conducted the Italian premiere of *Tristan und Isolde* (Bologna, June 2, 1888); also led performances of other operas by Wagner. In his own works, he followed the ideals of the German school; the influences of Wagner and Liszt are particularly pronounced. As a composer, he was greatly admired by Toscanini, who repeatedly performed his orch. music.

Marx, Adolf Bernhard, eminent German music theorist and writer; b. Halle, May 15, 1795; d. Berlin, May 17, 1866. Intended for the law, he matriculated at the Univ. of Halle, but also studied music with Türk, and gave up a subsequent legal appointment at Naumburg to gratify his love for art. He continued the study of composition in Berlin with Zelter; in 1824 he founded the *Berliner Allgemeine Musikalische Zeitung* (with the publisher Schlesinger); he edited this publication with ability, and proved himself a conspicuous advocate of German music; however, the publication ceased in 1830. After taking the degree of Dr.Phil at Marburg (1827), Marx lectured on music at the Berlin Univ.; was appointed a prof. in 1830; became music director of the scholastic choir there in 1832. He was co-founder (with Kullak and Stern) of the Berlin Cons. (1850), retiring in 1856 to devote himself to literary and univ. work. He was an intimate friend of the Mendelssohn family, and advised young Mendelssohn in musical matters.

Marx, Joseph, Austrian composer and pedagogue; b. Graz, May 11, 1882; d. there, Sept. 3, 1964. He studied musicology with Degner at the Univ. of Graz, taking the degree of Dr.Phil. with the dissertation *Über die Funktionen von Intervallen, Harmonie und Melodie beim Erfassen von Tonkomplexen.* In 1914 he went to Vienna, where he taught at the State Academy; was its director (1922–24); then rector of the Hochschule für Musik in Vienna (1924–27); for 3 years was adviser to the Turkish government on music education, traveling to Ankara in that capacity; later resumed his teaching in Vienna until 1952; taught at the Univ. of Graz (1947–57). As a composer, he styled himself a "Romantic realist."

Marx, Karl, German composer and pedagogue; b. Munich, Nov. 12, 1897. He served in the German army during World War I and was a prisoner of war in England; after the Armistice, studied with Carl Orff, Hausegger, Beer-Walbrunn, and Schwickerath. In 1924 he was appointed to the faculty of the Akademie der Tonkunst in Munich; in 1928 became the conductor of the Bach Society in Munich; from 1939 to 1946 was instructor at the Hochschule für Musikerziehung in Graz; subsequently taught at the Hochschule für Musik in Stuttgart (1946–66). A master of German polyphony, Marx excels in choral composition, both sacred and secular; he is greatly esteemed as a pedagogue.
WORKS: FOR ORCH.: Concerto for 2 Violins and

Orch. (1926); Piano Concerto (1929; revised 1959); Viola Concerto (1929); *Passacaglia* (1932); Violin Concerto (1935); Concerto for Flute and Strings (1937); *15 Variations on a German Folk Song* (1938); *Musik nach alpenländischen Volksliedern* for Strings (1940); *Festival Prelude* (1956); Concerto for String Orch. (1964; a reworking of his 1932 *Passacaglia*); *Fantasia sinfonica* (1967; revised 1969); *Fantasia concertante* for Violin, Cello, and Orch. (1972).
VOCAL MUSIC: Several large cantatas, including *Die heiligen drei Könige* (1936); *Rilke-Kantate* (1942); *Und endet doch alles mit Frieden* (1952); *Raube das Licht aus dem Rachen der Schlange* (1957); *Auftrag und Besinnung* (1961); chamber cantatas; including *Die unendliche Woge* (1930); also cantatas for special seasons, children's cantatas, and the like; a cappella pieces; songs, many with Orch., including *Rilke-Kreis* for Voice and Piano (1927; version for Mezzo-soprano and Chamber Orch., 1952) and *3 Songs,* to texts by Stefan George, for Baritone and Chamber Orch. (1934). Also, *Fantasy and Fugue* for String Quartet (1927); *Variations* for Organ (1933); *Divertimento* for 16 Winds (1934); *Turmmusik* for 3 Trumpets and 3 Trombones (1938); *Divertimento* for Flute, Violin, Viola, Cello, and Piano (1942); 6 sonatinas for various instrumental combinations (1948–51); *Kammermusik* for 7 Instruments (1955); Trio for Piano, Flute, and Cello (1962); Cello Sonata (1964); *Fantasy* for Solo Violin (1966); *Partita über "Ein' feste Burg"* for String Quartet or String Orch. (1967); Wind Quintet (1973).

Maryon, Edward (full name, **John Edward Maryon-d'Aulby**), English composer; b. London, April 3, 1867; d. there, Jan. 31, 1954. He began to compose early in life; went to Paris, where his first opera, *L'Odalisque,* won the Gold Medal at the Exposition of 1889; however, he regarded the work as immature and destroyed the score. In 1891 he studied with Max Pauer in Dresden; later took lessons with F. Wüllner in Cologne; then lived in France; in 1914–19 he was in Montclair, N.J., where he established a cons. with a fund for exchange of music students between England and America; in 1933 he returned to London. Besides *L'Odalisque,* Maryon wrote the following operas: *Paolo and Francesca; La Robe de plume; The Smelting Pot; The Prodigal Son; Werewolf; Rembrandt; Greater Love;* and *Abelard and Heloise.* In his opera *Werewolf* he applied a curious system of musical symbolism, in which the human part was characterized by the diatonic scale and the lupine self by the whole-tone scale; Maryon made a claim of priority in using the whole-tone scale consistently as a leading motive in an opera. His magnum opus was a grandiose operatic heptalogy under the title *The Cycle of Life,* comprising 7 mystical dramas: *Lucifer, Cain, Krishna, Magdalen, Sangraal, Psyche,* and *Nirvana.* He further wrote a symph. poem, *The Feather Robe,* subtitled *A Legend of Fujiyama* (1905), which he dedicated to the Emperor of Japan; and *Armageddon Requiem* (1916), dedicated to the dead of World War I. Of his works, only the following were publ.: *Beatitudes* for Baritone, Double Chorus, and Orch. (1907); *6 Melodies* for Voice and Piano (1907); *The Paean of Asaph*, a festival cantata (1931). After Maryon's death, his complete MSS were donated by his heirs to the Boston Public Library. Maryon developed a theory of universal art, in which colors were associated with sounds; an outline of this theory was publ. in his pamphlet *Marcotone* (N.Y., 1919).

Mascagni, Pietro, famous Italian opera composer; b. Livorno, Dec. 7, 1863; d. Rome, Aug. 2, 1945. His father was a baker who wished him to continue in that trade, but yielded to his son's determination to study music. He took lessons with Alfredo Soffredini in his native town until he was enabled, by the aid of an interested patron, to enter the Cons. of Milan, where he studied with Ponchielli and Saladino (1882). However, he became impatient with school discipline, and was dismissed from the Cons. in 1884. The following year he obtained a post as conductor of the municipal band in the small town of Cerignola. He composed industriously; in 1888 he sent the MS of his one-act opera *Cavalleria rusticana* to the music publisher Sonzogno for a competition, and won first prize. The opera was performed at the Costanzi Theater in Rome on May 17, 1890, with sensational success; the dramatic story of village passion, and Mascagni's emotional score, laden with luscious music, combined to produce an extraordinary appeal to opera lovers. The short opera made the tour of the world stages with amazing rapidity, productions being staged all over Europe and America with never-failing success; the opera was usually presented in 2 parts, separated by an "intermezzo sinfonico" (which became a popular orch. number performed separately). *Cavalleria rusticana* marked the advent of the operatic style known as *verismo,* in which stark realism was the chief aim and the dramatic development was condensed to enhance the impressions. When, 2 years later, another "veristic" opera, Leoncavallo's *Pagliacci,* was taken by Sonzogno, the 2 operas became twin attractions on a single bill. Ironically, Mascagni could never duplicate or even remotely approach the success of his first production, although he continued to compose industriously and opera houses all over the world were only too eager to stage his successive operas. Thus, his opera *Le Maschere* was produced on Jan. 17, 1901, at 6 of the most important Italian opera houses simultaneously (Rome, Milan, Turin, Genoa, Venice, Verona); it was produced 2 days later in Naples. Mascagni himself conducted the premiere in Rome, but the opera failed to fire the imagination of the public; it was produced in a revised form in Turin 15 years later (June 7, 1916), but was not established in the repertoire even in Italy. In 1902 Mascagni made a tour of the U.S., conducting his *Cavalleria rusticana* and other operas, but owing to mismanagement, the visit proved a fiasco; a South American tour in 1911 was more successful. Mascagni also appeared frequently as a conductor of symph. concerts. In 1890 he was made a Knight of the Crown of Italy; in 1929 he was elect-

ed a member of the Academy. At various times he also was engaged in teaching; from 1895 until 1902 he was director of the Rossini Cons. in Pesaro. His last years were darkened by the inglorious role that Mascagni assumed in his ardent support of the Fascist regime, so that he was rejected by many of his old friends. It was only after his death that his errors of moral judgment were forgiven; his centennial was widely celebrated in Italy in 1963.

WORKS: Operas: *Pinotta* (written in 1880; score recovered after 50 years, and first produced in San Remo, March 23, 1932); *Guglielmo Ratcliff* (c.1885; Milan, Feb. 16, 1895); *Cavalleria rusticana* (Rome, May 17, 1890); *L'Amico Fritz* (Rome, Oct. 31, 1891; the only fairly successful opera by Mascagni after *Cavalleria rusticana;* still perf. in Italy); *I Rantzau* (Florence, Nov. 10, 1892); *Silvano* (Milan, March 25, 1895); *Zanetto* (Pesaro, March 2, 1896); *Iris* (Rome, Nov. 22, 1898); *Le Maschere* (premiere in 6 cities, Jan. 17, 1901); *Amica* (Monte Carlo, March 16, 1905); *Isabeau* (Buenos Aires, June 2, 1911); *Parisina* (Milan, Dec. 15, 1913); *Lodoletta* (Rome, April 30, 1917); *Scampolo* (1921); *Il piccolo Marat* (Rome, May 2, 1921); *Nerone* (Milan, Jan. 16, 1935); *I Bianchi ed i Neri* (1940). Other works include 2 symphs.: No. 1 (1879) and No. 2 (1881); *Poema Leopardiano* (for the centenary of G. Leopardi, 1898); Hymn in honor of Admiral Dewey (July 1899); *Rapsodia satanica* for Orch. (music for a film, Rome, July 2, 1917); *Davanti Santa Teresa* (Rome, Aug. 1923); chamber music.

Maschera, Fiorenzo or **Florentio,** Italian organist and composer; b. probably in Brescia, c.1540; d. there, c.1584. He first studied with his father; then was a pupil of Merulo; served as organist at Santo Spirito in Venice; on Aug. 22, 1557, he succeded Merulo as organist at the Cathedral in Brescia. Of his compositions, 23 are extant; all are 4-part instrumental canzonas. He published *Libro primo de canzoni da sonare a quattro voci* (Brescia, 1584), which has been edited by W. McKee in *The Music of Florentio Maschera (1540–1584)* (Diss., North Texas State Univ., 1958).

Mascheroni, Edoardo, Italian conductor and composer; b. Milan, Sept. 4, 1852; d. Ghirla, near Varese, March 4, 1941. As a boy, he showed special interest in mathematics and literature; wrote literary essays for the journal *La Vita Nuova* before he decided to study music seriously; took lessons with Boucheron in Milan, and composed various pieces. In 1880 he began a career in Brescia as a conductor, and it was in that capacity that he distinguished himself. He was first a theater conductor in Livorno; then went to Rome, where he established his reputation as an opera conductor (1884). Upon Verdi's explicit request, he was selected to conduct the premiere of *Falstaff* at La Scala in Milan (1893); he remained on the staff of La Scala until 1897; then conducted in Germany, Spain, and South America; also was successful as a symph. conductor. He wrote 2 operas: *Lorenza* (Rome, April 13, 1901) and *La Perugina* (Naples, April 24, 1909).

Mason, Colin, English music critic; b. Northampton, Jan. 26, 1924; d. London, Feb. 6, 1971. He studied at the Trinity College of Music in London; after the war he received a Hungarian state scholarship for the purpose of writing a book on Béla Bartók and entered as a student at the Budapest Academy of Music (1947–49). Returning to England, he was the music critic of the *Manchester Guardian* (1951–64) and of the *Daily Telegraph* (from 1964); also edited the music magazine *Tempo* (from 1962); was editor of the revised printing of Cobbett's *Cyclopedic Survey of Chamber Music* (London, 1963; with a supplementary 3rd vol.); publ. *Music in Britain, 1951–61* (London, 1963).

Mason, Daniel Gregory, eminent American composer and educator; b. Brookline, Mass., Nov. 20, 1873; d. Greenwich, Conn., Dec. 4, 1953. He was a scion of a famous family of American musicians; grandson of **Lowell Mason** and nephew of **William Mason;** his father, **Henry Mason,** was a co-founder of the piano manufacturing firm Mason & Hamlin. He entered Harvard Univ., where he studied with John K. Paine (B.A., 1895); after graduation he continued his studies with Arthur Whiting (piano), P. Goetschius (theory), and Chadwick (orchestration). Still feeling the necessity for improvement of his technique as a composer, he went to Paris, where he took courses with Vincent d'Indy. Returning to America, he became active as a teacher and composer. In 1905 he became a member of the faculty of Columbia Univ.; in 1929, was appointed MacDowell Professor of Music; he was chairman of the music dept. until 1940, and continued to teach there until 1942, when he retired. As a teacher, he developed a high degree of technical ability in his students; as a composer, he represented a conservative trend in American music; while an adherent to the idea of an American national style, his conception was racially and regionally narrow, accepting only the music of Anglo-Saxon New England and "the old South"; he was an outspoken opponent of the "corrupting" and "foreign" influences of 20th-century Afro-American and Jewish-American music. His ideals were the German masters of the Romantic school; but there is an admixture of impressionistic colors in his orchestration; his harmonies are full and opulent, his melodic writing expressive and songful. The lack of strong individuality, however, has resulted in the virtual disappearance of his music from the active repertoire, with the exception of the overture *Chanticleer* and the Clarinet Sonata.
WORKS: For orch.: Symph. No. 1, in C minor (Philadelphia, Feb. 18, 1916; revised radically, and perf. in a new version, N.Y., Dec. 1, 1922); *Chanticleer,* a festival overture (Cincinnati, Nov. 23, 1928); Symph. No. 2, in A (Cincinnati, Nov. 7, 1930); Symph. No. 3, *Lincoln* (N.Y., Nov. 17, 1937); *Prelude and Fugue* for Piano and Orch. (Chicago, March 4, 1921); *Scherzo-Caprice* for Chamber Orch. (N.Y., Jan. 2, 1917); *Suite after English Folksongs* (1934); *Russians* for Baritone and Orch. (1918). Chamber music: Quartet for Piano and Strings (1912); *Pastorale* for Violin, Clarinet, and Piano (1913); Sonata for Clarinet and Piano (1915); *String Quartet on Negro Themes* (1919); 3 pieces for Flute, Harp, and String Quartet (1922); *Variations on a Theme of John Powell* for String Quartet (1926); *Divertimento* for Flute, Oboe, Clarinet, Horn, and Bassoon (1927); *Fanny Blair,* folk-song fantasy for String Quartet (1929); *Serenade* for String Quartet (1932); *Sentimental Sketches,* 4 short pieces for Violin, Cello, and Piano (1935); *Variations on a Quiet Theme* (1939); a choral work, *Songs of the Countryside* (1926).

Mason, Lowell, American composer, organist, and conductor; b. Medfield, Mass., Jan. 8, 1792; d. Orange, N.J., Aug. 11, 1872. As a youth he studied singing with Amos Albee and Oliver Shaw; at 16 he directed the church choir at Medfield; from 1812–19 worked in a dry-goods store, then as a bank clerk in Savannah, Ga., also teaching and conducting; in 1827 went to Boston, becoming a church organist; was president of the Handel and Haydn Society (1827–32); established classes on Pestalozzi's system, teaching it privately from 1829 and in the public schools from 1838. He founded the Boston Academy of Music in 1833, with George J. Webb; in 1855, was made honorary Mus.Doc. by N.Y. Univ. (one of the first instances of the conferring of that degree in America); studied pedagogic methods in Zürich in 1837; publ. his experiences in *Musical Letters from Abroad* (N.Y., 1853); in 1851, went to N.Y.; after 1854, resided in Orange, N.J. He became wealthy through the sale of his many collections of music: *Handel and Haydn Society's Collection of Church Music* (1822; 16 later eds.); *Juvenile Psalmist* (1829); *Juvenile Lyre* (1830); *Lyra Sacra* (1832); *Sabbath School Songs* (1836); *Boston Academy Collection of Church Music* (1836); *Boston Anthem Book* (1839); *The Psaltery* (1845); *Cantica Laudis* (1850); *New Carmina Sacra* (1852); *Normal Singer* (1856); *Song Garden* (3 parts; 1864–65); etc. Many of his own hymn tunes, including *Missionary Hymn (From Greenland's Icy Mountains), Olivet, Boylston, Bethany, Hebron,* and *Olmutz,* are still found in hymnals. His valuable library, including 830 MSS and 700 vols. of hymnology, was given to Yale College after his death.

Mason, William, American pianist and pedagogue; b. Boston, Jan. 24, 1829; d. New York, July 14, 1908. The son of **Lowell Mason,** he had excellent opportunities for study; after piano lessons from Henry Schmidt in Boston, and frequent public appearances (first in Boston, March 7, 1846, at an Academy of Music concert), he studied in Leipzig (1849) under Moscheles, Hauptmann, and Richter; in Prague under Dreyschock; and under Liszt at Weimar. He played in Weimar, Prague, and Frankfurt; in 1853, in London; in 1854–55, in various American towns, settling in 1855 in N.Y. With Theodore Thomas, Bergmann, and Matzka, he founded the Mason and Thomas Soirées of Chamber Music, a series of classic concerts continued until 1868; thereafter he won wide celebrity as a composer and teacher. In 1872 Yale College conferred on him the degree of Mus.Doc. His principal textbook for piano playing is *Touch and Technic* (op. 44); others are *A Method for the Piano,* with E.S. Hoadley (1867); *System for Beginners* (1871); and *Mason's Pianoforte-Technics* (1878). His compositions, classical in form and refined in style and treatment, include a *Serenata* for Cello and Piano; some 40 numbers for piano solo, including *Amitié pour moi, Silver Spring, Monody, Rêverie poétique,* etc.; publ. *Memories of a Musical Life* (1901).

Mason & Hamlin Co., celebrated firm of piano manufacturers. The house was founded as the M. & H. Organ Co. in Boston in 1854 by **Henry Mason,** a son of **Dr. Lowell Mason,** and **Emmons Hamlin.** The latter, a brilliant mechanic, turned his attention to improving the quality of the reeds and obtaining great variety of tonal color, with the result that in 1861 the firm introduced the American Cabinet Organ. The firm became internationally famous, when at the Paris Exposition of 1867 its organs were awarded first prize over numerous European competitors; since then the firm has exhibited at every important exposition in Europe and America. In 1882 it began the construction of pianofortes, introducing a new system of stringing which found immediate favor; of several improvements patented by Mason & Hamlin, the most important is the Tension-Resonator (1902; described in *Scientific American,* Oct. 11, 1902), a device for preserving the tension of the sounding board. The firm subsequently became a subsidiary of the Aeolian American Corp. and eventually of the American Piano Corp. **Henry Lowell Mason,** son of the founder, was president of the firm until 1929. He died in Boston on Oct. 18, 1957, at the age of 93.

Massart, Lambert-Joseph, eminent violinist; b. Liège, July 19, 1811; d. Paris, Feb. 13, 1892. He was a pupil of R. Kreutzer at Paris, where, as a foreigner, he was refused admission to the Cons. by Cherubini; but he became so celebrated as a teacher that he was appointed prof. of violin there (1843–90). Wieniawski, Marsick, Sarasate, and Teresina Tua were his pupils. His wife, **Louise-Aglaë Massart** (b. Paris, June 10, 1827; d. there, July 26, 1887), was a pianist and teacher. In 1875 she succeeded Farrenc as teacher at the Paris Cons.

Massart, Nestor-Henri-Joseph, Belgian tenor; b. Ciney, Oct. 20, 1849; d. Ostend, Dec. 19, 1899. He was an officer in the Belgian army when his remarkable voice attracted the attention of the royal family, through whose influence he was granted a leave of absence for study. He sang with success in Brussels, Lyons, Cairo, New Orleans, San Francisco, and Mexico.

Massé, Victor (real name, **Félix-Marie**), French opera composer; b. Lorient, Morbihan, March 7, 1822; d. Paris, July 5, 1884. He was a child prodigy; was accepted at the Paris Cons. at the age of 12, and studied with Zimmerman (piano) and Halévy (composition); in 1844 he won the Grand Prix de Rome

with the cantata *Le Renégat de Tanger.* While in Rome he sent home an Italian opera, *La Favorita e la schiava.* After his return, his *romances* had great vogue, and his first French opera, *La Chambre gothique* (Paris, 1849), was fairly successful. In 1866 he succeeded Leborne as prof. of counterpoint at the Paris Cons.; and in 1872 he was elected member of the Institut de France, as successor to Auber. His most successful light opera was *Les Noces de Jeannette* (Paris, Feb. 4, 1853); the list of his other operas, performed in Paris, includes: *La Chanteuse voilée* (Nov. 26, 1850); *Galathée* (April 14, 1852); *La Fiancée du Diable* (June 3, 1854); *Miss Fauvette* (Feb. 13, 1855); *Les Saisons* (Dec. 22, 1855); *La Reine Topaze* (Dec. 27, 1856); *Fior d'Aliza* (Feb. 5, 1866); and *Le Fils du Brigadier* (Feb. 25, 1867); his last opera, *Une Nuit de Cléopatre,* was performed posthumously (April 25, 1885).

Masselos, William, American pianist; b. Niagara Falls, N.Y., Aug. 11, 1920. He studied piano with Carl Friedberg at the Juilliard School of Music in N.Y. (1932–42) and ensemble playing with Felix Salmond and Louis Persinger; music theory with Bernard Wagenaar. He made his professional debut in N.Y. in 1939; was a soloist with the N.Y. Phil. in 1952 under Mitropoulos; then played with Monteux in 1959 and with Bernstein in 1973. He served as pianist-in-residence at Indiana Univ. (1955–57); at Catholic Univ. of America in Washington, D.C. (1965–71); and at Georgia State Univ. in Atlanta (1972–75); in 1976 he was appointed to the piano faculty at Juilliard.

Massenet, Jules (-Emile-Frédéric), illustrious French composer; b. Montaud, near St.-Etienne, Loire, May 12, 1842; d. Paris, Aug. 13, 1912. At the age of 9 he was admitted to the Paris Cons.; studied with Laurent (piano), Reber (harmony), Savard and Ambroise Thomas (composition); after taking first prizes for piano playing and fugue (1859), he carried off the Grand Prix de Rome with the cantata *David Rizzio* (1863). In 1878 he was appointed prof. of composition at the Paris Cons., and at the same time was elected a member of the Académie des Beaux-Arts; he continued to teach at the Paris Cons. until his death; among his students were Alfred Bruneau, Gabriel Pierné, and Gustave Charpentier. As a pedagogue, he exercised a profound influence on French opera. After Gounod, Massenet was the most popular French opera composer; he possessed a natural sense of graceful melody in a distinctive French style; his best operas, *Manon, Werther,* and *Thaïs,* enjoy tremendous popularity in France; the celebrated *Meditation* for Violin and Orch. from *Thaïs* is a regular repertoire number among violinists.

WORKS: OPERAS: *La Grand'-Tante* (Paris, April 3, 1867); *Don César de Bazan* (Paris, Nov. 30, 1872); *Le Roi de Lahore* (Paris, April 27, 1877); *Hérodiade* (Brussels, Dec. 19, 1881); *Manon* (Paris, Jan. 19, 1884); *Le Cid* (Paris, Nov. 30, 1885); *Esclarmonde* (Paris, May 14, 1889); *Le Mage* (Paris, March 16, 1891); *Werther* (Vienna, Feb. 16, 1892); *Thaïs* (Paris,

March 16, 1894); *Le Portrait de Manon* (Paris, May 8, 1894); *La Navarraise* (London, June 20, 1894); *Sapho* (Paris, Nov. 27, 1897); *Cendrillon* (Paris, May 24, 1899); *Grisélidis* (Paris, Nov. 20, 1901); *Le Jongleur de Notre Dame* (Monte Carlo, Feb. 18, 1902); *Chérubin* (Monte Carlo, Feb. 14, 1905); *Ariane* (Paris, Oct. 31, 1906); *Thérèse* (Monte Carlo, Feb. 7, 1907); *Bacchus* (Paris, May 5, 1909); *Don Quichotte* (Monte Carlo, Feb. 19, 1910); *Roma* (Monte Carlo, Feb. 7, 1912); posthumous: *Panurge* (Paris, April 25, 1913); *Cléopatre* (Monte Carlo, Feb. 23, 1914); *Amadis* (Monte Carlo, April 1, 1922). INCIDENTAL MUSIC: *Les Erynnies* (1873); *Un Drame sous Philippe II* (1875); *Nana-Sahib* (1883); *Théodora* (1884); *Le Crocodile* (1886); *Phèdre* (1900); *Le Grillon du foyer* (1904); *Le Manteau du Roi* (1907); *Perce-Neige et les sept gnomes* (1909). BALLETS: *Le Carillon* (1892); *La Cigale* (1904); *Espada* (1908). ORATORIOS: *Marie-Magdeleine* (1873); *Eve* (1875); *La Terre promise* (1900). OTHER CHORAL WORKS: *Narcisse; La Vierge; Biblis.* FOR ORCH.: 7 suites: No. 1 (1865); No. 2, *Scènes hongroises* (1871); No. 3, *Scènes dramatiques* (1873); No. 4, *Scènes pittoresques* (1874); No. 5, *Scènes napolitaines* (1876); No. 6, *Scènes de féerie* (1879); No. 7, *Scènes alsaciennes* (1881); 3 overtures: *Ouverture de concert* (1863); *Phèdre* (1873); *Brumaire* (1899); symph. poem, *Visions* (1890); *Parade militaire* (1887); *Devant la Madone* (1897); *Marche solennelle* (1897); *Les Rosati* (1902); *Fantasie* for Cello and Orch. (1897); Concerto for Piano and Orch. (1903); about 200 songs; 12 vocal duets; piano pieces for 2- and 4-hands. Massenet completed and orchestrated Delibes's opera *Kassya* (1893).

Masson, Paul-Marie, eminent French musicologist; b. Sète, Hérault, Sept. 19, 1882; d. Paris, Jan. 27, 1954. He studied music history with Romain Rolland at the Sorbonne; received his degree with the dissertation *La Musique mesurée à l'Antique au XVIe siècle* (1907); subsequently enrolled in the Schola Cantorum as a pupil of Vincent d'Indy; also took lessons with Koechlin. In 1910 he was appointed prof. of the history of music at the Univ. of Grenoble, and entrusted with the organization of the Institut Français de Florence, with the aim of publishing complete editions of works of the early Italian masters. He taught music history at the Sorbonne (1931–52); in 1937 he was elected vice-president of the Société Française de Musicologie, and in 1949, its president. He publ. valuable books: *Lullistes et Ramistes* (1912); *Musique italienne et musique française* (1912); *Berlioz* (1923); *L'Opéra de Rameau* (1930); ed. *Chants de carnaval florentins* (vol. I) and 5-part madrigals by Gesualdo; contributed numerous articles to European music magazines, etc. He was also a competent composer; his works include a cantata to his own words, *Chant des peuples unis; Suite pastorale* for Wind Quintet; songs and piano pieces. A 2-vol. offering, *Mélanges d'histoire et d'esthétique musicale offertes à Paul-Marie Masson* (containing a brief biographical sketch and bibliography), was presented to him by his colleagues, friends, and pupils on his retirement from the Sorbonne in 1952; it was publ. posthumous-

ly (Paris, 1955).

Masur, Kurt eminent German conductor; b. Brieg, Silesia, July 18, 1927. He studied in Breslau and at the Hochschule fü r Musik in Leipzig; then was a theater conductor in Halle, Erfurt, and Leipzig (1948–55); conducted the Dresden Phil. (1955–58); was Generalmusikdirektor of the Mechlenburg State Theater in Schwerin (1958–60) and then principal music director of the Komische Oper in East Berlin (1960–64). He was chief conductor of the Dresden Phil. (1967–72); in 1970 became conductor of the Leipzig Gewandhaus Orch., with which he toured widely in Europe and the U.S. He made his U.S. debut with Cleveland Orch. in 1974.

Mata, Eduardo, noted Mexican conductor and composer; b. Mexico City, Sept. 5, 1942. He studied composition with Rodolfo Halffter at the National Cons. of Mexico (1954–60); then took lessons in composition and conducting with Carlos Chávez (1960–65) and Julian Orbón (1960–63); in 1964 went to the Berkshire Center in Tanglewood, Mass., where he attended conducting seminars led by Max Rudolf, Gunther Schuller, and Erich Leinsdorf. He was conductor of the Symph. Orch. of Guadalajara (1964–66); in 1970–78 he was principal conductor of the Phoenix (Ariz.) Symph. Orch.; in 1977 was appointed conductor and music director of the Dallas Symph. Orch. He proved his excellence as an interpreter of Classical and Romantic music to the satisfaction and even delectation of audiences that expect to be pleased by beautiful music, and his success with the public made it possible for him to introduce into his programs some decidedly unpleasing pieces by such un-Romantic composers as Boulez and Berio and by such forbidding representatives of the uncompromising avant-garde as Stockhausen and Cage. Eduardo Mata's own music finds the golden mean between neo-Classicism and ultramodernism; however, during the most hectic period of his activities as a conductor, beginning with 1970, he practically abandoned composition.

WORKS: *Trio a Vaughan Williams* for Clarinet, Snare Drum, and Cello (1957); Piano Sonata (1960); incidental music for Shakespeare's *Twelfth Night* for Soprano Recorder, Viola, and Guitar (1961); *Improvisaciones* for Clarinet and Piano (1961); 3 symphs.: No. 1, *Clásica* (Mexico City, March 24, 1962); No. 2, *Romántica* (Mexico City, Nov. 29, 1963); No. 3 for Horn obbligato and Wind Orch. (1966–67); *Débora*, ballet music (1963); *La venganza del pescador,* suite for 2 Flutes, Trombone, Violin, Guitar, and Percussion (1964); *Improvisaciones No. 1* for String Quartet and Piano, 4-hands (1964), *No. 2* for Strings and 2 Pianos (1965), and *No. 3* for Violin and Piano (1965); *Aires sobre un tema del siglo XVI* for Mezzo-soprano, 2 Flutes, Oboe, Bassoon, 2 Violas, Cello, and Double Bass (1964); Cello Sonata (1966).

Materna, Amalie, Austrian soprano; b. St. Georgen, Styria, July 10, 1844; d. Vienna, Jan. 18, 1918. She was a church singer; married the actor Karl

Friedrich; together they sang in light opera. She made her debut in Graz in 1865; in 1869 she first sang at the Vienna Court Opera, and remained on its staff until 1894. Her dramatic talent, powerful voice, and beauteous features attracted the notice of Wagner, who selected her for the role of Brünnhilde in the first Bayreuth Festival of 1876; the following year she sang at Wagner festival in London, under the composer's own direction, and also sang in Wagner festivals in N.Y., Chicago, and Cincinnati. Her American opera debut took place on Jan. 5, 1885, as Elisabeth in *Tannhäuser* during the first season of German opera at the Metropolitan Opera House; in 1894 she became a member of Walter Damrosch's German company in N.Y. In 1902 she returned to Vienna and opened a singing studio there.

Mather, Bruce, Canadian composer and pianist; b. Toronto, May 9, 1939. He studied composition with Ridout, Morawetz, and Weinzweig at the Toronto Cons. (1952–59); took summer courses in piano with Alexandre Uninsky at the Aspen School of Music in Colorado (1957–58); then went to Paris and studied with Simone Plé-Caussade, Messiaen, and Milhaud (1959–61); returning to America, he continued his musical education with Leland Smith at Stanford Univ. (M.A., 1964) and studied for his doctorate at the Univ. of Toronto (Ph.D., 1967). In 1966 he joined the faculty of McGill Univ. in Montreal; in 1970 became a prof. at the Univ. of Montreal. Mather's own music follows the path of unprejudiced modernism, extending from neo-Classicism to Expressionism and comprising elements of serialism and microtonality.
WORKS: Violin Sonata (1956); *2 Songs,* after Thomas Hardy, for Bass-baritone and Small Orch. (1956); *Venice,* after Byron, for Soprano, Clarinet, Cello, and Piano (1957); *3 Songs,* to poems of Robert Graves, for Soprano and String Orch. (1957–58); Concerto for Piano and Chamber Orch. of Wind Quintet and String Quartet (Aspen, Aug. 20, 1958; composer, soloist); *Elegy* for Saxophone and Strings (1959); *Cycle Rilke* for Voice and Guitar (1959–60); *Etude* for Solo Clarinet (1962); *Orphée* for Soprano, Piano, and Percussion (1963); *Symphonic Ode* for Orch. (Toronto, March 28, 1965); *Orchestra Piece 1967* (Toronto, Jan. 11, 1967); *Ombres* for Orch. (Montreal, May 1, 1968); 5 *Madrigals: I* for Soprano, Alto, Flute, Mandolin, Harp, Violin, and Cello (1967); *II* for Soprano, Alto, Flute, Harp, Violin, Viola, and Cello (1968); *III* for Alto, Marimba, Harp, and Piano (1971); *IV* for Soprano, Flute, Piano, and Tape (1972); *V* for Soprano, Alto, and 17 Instrumentalists (1972–73); *Music for Vancouver* for Small Orch. (1969); 2-Piano Sonata (1970); *Musique pour Rouen* for String Orch. (1970–71); *Mandola* for Mandolin and Piano (1971); *Music for Organ, Horn and Gongs* (1973); *In memoriam Alexandre Uninsky* for Piano (1974); *Eine kleine Bläsermusik* for Wind Quintet 1975); *Au Château de Pompairain* for Mezzo-soprano and Orch. (Ottawa, May 4, 1977); *Clos de Vougeot* for 4 Percussionists (1977).

Mathews, William Smythe Babcock, American organist and writer on music; b. London, N.H., May 8, 1837; d. Denver, April 1, 1912. He studied music in Boston; occupied various teaching posts in Georgia, North Carolina, Alabama, Chicago, and Denver; was organist in Chicago churches; edited the *Musical Independent* (1868–72); was music critic of the *Chicago Tribune* (1878–86); in 1891, founded and edited the monthly magazine *Music.* He publ. *Outlines of Musical Form* (1867); *Emerson Organ-Method,* with L.O. Emerson (1870); *Mason's Piano Techniques,* with William Mason (1876); *How to Understand Music* (2 vols., 1880 and 1888); *100 Years of Music in America* (1889); *Popular History of Music* (1889; 2nd ed., 1906); *Pronouncing and Defining Dictionary of Music* (1896); *Music, Its Ideals and Methods* (1897); *The Masters and Their Music* (1898); *The Great in Music* (3 vols., 1900–1903).

Mathias, Franz Xaver, Alsatian church musician; b. Dinsheim, July 16, 1871; d. Strasbourg, Feb. 2, 1939. He studied in Germany with Hugo Riemann; was organist at the Strasbourg Cathedral (1898–1908); then a prof. of sacred music at the Univ. of Strasbourg. Among his works the best known is the oratorio *Mystère de Joseph,* containing an instrumental *Ballet égyptien.* He also wrote an oratorio of gigantic dimensions, *Urbem Virgo tuam serva* for 2 choruses (with the assistance of a "crowd" of many voices); 28 cantatas; several masses; Psalms; motets; many organ pieces; publ. a manual of accompaniment of Gregorian chant.

Mathias, Georges (-Amédée-Saint-Clair), French composer; b. Paris, Oct. 14, 1826; d. there, Oct. 14, 1910. As a youth he had the privilege of taking piano lessons with Chopin; studied composition with Halévy and others at the Paris Cons.; in 1862 was appointed prof. of piano there, and taught until 1893. He composed 2 piano concertos; 6 piano trios; *5 morceaux symphoniques* for Piano and Strings; and a number of studies, under the promising titles *Etudes de style et de mécanisme* and *Etudes de genre.* He also publ. a collection of attractive piano pieces for 2- and 4-hands; his overtures and other symph. works are less interesting.

Mathias, William, Welsh composer; b. Whitland, Dyfed, Nov. 1, 1934. He studied at the Univ. College of Wales, Aberystwyth (B.Mus., 1956); then at the Royal Academy of Music with Lennox Berkeley (composition) and Peter Katin (piano). In 1965 he was elected a Fellow of the Royal Academy of Music; was awarded the D.Mus. degree by the Univ. of Wales in 1966; in 1968 he received the Bax Society Prize for composition. In 1969 he became a lecturer in music at the Univ. College of North Wales; in 1970 was appointed prof. and head of the dept. of music at the Univ. College of North Wales, Bangor. He was commissioned by Prince Charles to write a choral work for the royal bride at Westminster in July 1981. His style of composition may be described as civilized modernism, sophisticated but free of exhibitionistic affectation, optimistically tonal but occasionally somber, brilliantly idiomatic in instrumentation, and unequivocally populist in its euphonious appeal.

WORKS: FOR ORCH.: *Divertimento* for String Orch. (1958); *Dance Overture* (London, Aug. 10, 1962); *Invocation and Dance* (Cardiff Festival, March 1, 1962); *Serenade* for Chamber Orch. (1962); Concerto for Orch. (Liverpool, March 29, 1966); Symph. No. 1 (Birmingham, June 23, 1966); Sinfonietta (1967); *Litanies* (1968); *Festival Overture* (1970); *Holiday Overture* (BBC radio broadcast, Sept. 30, 1971); *Vistas* (Swansea Festival, Oct. 25, 1975); Piano Concerto No. 1 (1955); Piano Concerto No. 2 (1960); Piano Concerto No. 3 (Swansea, Oct. 15, 1968); Harp Concerto (Bournemouth, June 1, 1970); Concerto for Harpsichord, Strings, and Percussion (1971); Clarinet Concerto (North Wales Music Festival, Sept. 22, 1975); Symph. No. 2, *Summer Music* (Liverpool, May 14, 1983). CHAMBER MUSIC: Violin Sonata (1961); Quintet for Flute, Oboe, Clarinet, Horn, and Bassoon (1963); *Divertimento* for Flute, Oboe, and Piano (1963); Concertino for Flute, Oboe, Bassoon, and Harpsichord (1964); String Quartet (1967); several organ pieces; choruses; songs; anthems; carols and Psalms, with organ or a cappella; piano pieces.

Mathieu, Emile (-Louis-Victor), Belgian composer and pedagogue; b. Lille, France (of Belgian parentage), Oct. 18, 1844; d. Ghent, Aug. 20, 1932. He studied at the Brussels Cons. with Fétis and Auguste Dupont; taught at Louvain (1867–73); then was in Paris as a theater conductor; returning to Louvain, he became director of the music school there (1881–98); in 1898 was appointed director of the Ghent Cons. In 1869, in 1871, and for a 3rd time in 1873, he won the 2nd Grand Prix de Rome in Brussels; retired in 1924.

Matsudaira, Yori-aki, Japanese composer of the avant-garde, son of **Yoritsuné Matsudaira;** b. Tokyo, March 27, 1931. He studied biology in Tokyo (1948–57); then formed a composing collective, "Group 20.5," with which he produced *Variation on the Theme of Noh* for Flute, Clarinet, 3 Percussionists, Piano, Violin, Viola, and Cello (1960). His own works include: *Variations* for Piano Trio (1957); *Speed Coefficient* for Flute, Piano, and Keyboard Percussion (1958); *Orbits I–III* for Flute, Clarinet, and Piano (1960); *Instruction* for Piano (1961); *Configuration* for Chamber Orch. (1961–63; Tokyo, March 29, 1967); *Co-Action I & II* for Cello and Piano (1962); *Parallax* for Flute, Oboe, Clarinet, Bassoon, and Saxophone (1963); *Tangent '64* for Tape (1964); *Rhymes for Gazelloni* for Solo Flute (1965–66); *Distribution* for String Quartet and Ring Modular (1966–67); *What's Next!* for Soprano and 2 Noisemakers (1967; revised 1971); *Alternation for Combo* for Trumpet, Percussion, Piano, Double Bass, and Ring Modulator (1967); *Assemblage* for Tape (1968); *Assemblage* for Female Voice and Ring Modulator (1968); *Wand Waves* for Narrator and Tape (1970); *Allotropy* for Piano (1970); *Why Not?* for 4–5 Operators with Live Electronics (1970); *"The Symphony"* for 14 Players (1971); *Gradation* for Violin, Viola, and Oscillator (1971); *Substitution* for Soprano and Piano (1972); *Messages* for Wind Orch. and Tape (1972).

Matsudaira, Yoritsuné, Japanese composer; b. Tokyo, May 5, 1907. He studied composition with Alexander Tcherepnin when the latter was in Japan; won the Weingartner Prize in 1937 and the International Composition Competition Prize in Rome in 1962. His music amalgamates old Japanese modalities with modern harmonies.

WORKS: *Theme and Variations* on popular Japanese songs, for Orch. (Tokyo, Dec. 17, 1939); *Ancient Japanese Dance* for Orch. (Berlin, Oct. 9, 1953); *Negative and Positive Figures* for Orch. (Tokyo, May 28, 1954); *Metamorphoses on "Saibara"* (an old Japanese melody) for Soprano and 18 Instruments (Haifa Festival, June 3, 1954); *Koromogae (Love Song)* for Soprano and 19 Instruments (1954; Venice, Dec. 11, 1968); *Figures sonores* for Orch. (1956; Zürich Festival, June 1, 1957); *U-Mai*, ancient dance for Orch. (Darmstadt, Sept. 11, 1958); *Samai* for Chamber Orch. (Rome Festival, June 15, 1959); *Dance Suite* for 3 Orchs. (Donaueschingen, Oct. 18, 1959); *Bugaku* for Chamber Orch. (Palermo, Oct. 6, 1962); *3 Movements* for Piano and Orch. (Stockholm, March 20, 1964); *Ritual Dance and Finale* for Orch. (1963); *Serenata* for Flute and 10 Instruments (1963); Piano Concerto (Madrid Festival, May 20, 1965); *Concerto da camera* for Harpsichord, Harp, and Instrumental Ensemble (1964); *Dialogo coreografico* for 2 Pianos and Chamber Ensemble (1966; Royan, France, April 3, 1967); *Roei "Jisei" (2 Stars in Vega)* for Voice and Instrumental Ensemble (1967); *Music* for 17 Instruments (1967); *Mouvements circulatoires* for 2 Chamber Orchs. (Graz Festival, Oct. 10, 1972); *Prelude, Interlude and Aprèslude* for Orch. (1973); Sonatina for Flute and Clarinet (1940); Cello Sonata (1942); Concerto for 2 Solo Pianos (1946); Piano Trio (1948); 2 string quartets (1948, 1951); 2 violin sonatas (1948, 1952); *Suite* for Flute, Bassoon, and Piano (1950); Piano Sonata (1953); *Katsura* for Soprano, Harp, Harpsichord, Guitar, and Percussion (1957; revised 1967); *Somaksah* for Solo Flute (1961); *Portrait B* for 2 Pianos and 2 Percussionists (1967–68); *12 pezzi facili* for Piano (1968–69).

Matsushita, Shin-ichi, Japanese composer; b. Osaka, Oct. 1, 1922. He graduated in mathematics from the Kyushu Univ. in Fukuoka in 1947; concurrently studied music. In 1958 he went to work in an electronic-music studio in Osaka; taught both mathematics and music at the Univ. of Osaka City. In his music he follows cosmopolitan modernistic techniques, mostly of a functional, pragmatic nature.

WORKS: *Ouvrage symphonique* for Piano and Orch. (1957); *Correlazioni per 3 gruppi* for 12 Players (1958); *Composizione da camera per 8* (1958); *Isomorfismi* for Orch. (1958); *5 tempi per undici* for 11 Instruments (1958–59); *Le Croître noir* for Chorus, Electronic, and Musique Concrète Sounds,

Piano, Harp, and Percussion (1959; Osaka, Nov. 14, 1959); *Faisceaux* for Flute, Cello, and Piano (1959); *Jet Pilot* for Narrator, Orch., String Quartet, and Female Chorus (1960); 2 radio operas: *Comparing Notes on a Rainy Night* and *Amayo* (both 1960); *Sinfonia "Le Dimensioni"* (1961); *Cube for 3 Players* for Flute, Celesta, and Viola (1961); *Successioni* for Chamber Orch. (Radio Palermo, Oct. 1, 1962); *Meta-Musique* No. 1 for Piano, Horn, and Percussion (1962); *Uro* for Chamber Ensemble (1962); *Sinfonia "Vita"* (1963); *Musique* for Soprano and Chamber Ensemble (Osaka, Sept. 14, 1964); *Fresque sonore* for 7 Instruments (1964); *Hexahedra A, B* and *C* for Piano and Percussion (1964–65); *Spectra 1–4* for Piano (1964; 1967; for 2 Players, 1971; 1971); *Kristalle* for Piano Quartet (1966); *Alleluja in der Einsamkeit* for Guitar, Piccolo, and 2 Percussionists (1967); *Serenade* for Flute and Orch. (1967); *Subject 17* for Piano, Percussion, Horn, Trumpet, and Trombone (San Francisco, Oct. 31, 1967); *Sinfonie Pol* for Orch., Harp, and Piano (1968); *Haleines astrales* for Chamber Ensemble (1968); *Astrate Atem* for Orch., Harp, and Piano (1969–70); *Requiem on the Place of Execution* for 4 Soloists, Chorus, Orch., and Tape (1970); *Musik von der Liebe* for Flute, Vibraphone, Harp, Piano, Electone, and Tape (1970); *Musik der Steinzeit* for Violin, Ondes Martenot, Tape, and the sound of Cracking Stone (1970); *Ostinato obbligato* for Piano (1972).

Matteis, Nicola, Italian violinist, who settled in London in 1672, and publ. there 4 books of violin pieces (airs, preludes, fugues, allemandes, sarabands, etc.) under varying Italian and English titles; also *The False Consonances of Musick, or, Instructions for playing a true Base upon the Guitarre, with Choice Examples and Clear Directions to enable any man in a short time to play all Musicall Ayres*, etc. In addition, he wrote *A Collection of New Songs* (2 vols., London, 1696). His son, also named **Nicola** (d. 1749), lived in Vienna, and in Shrewsbury, England. He was Burney's teacher.

Matteo da Perugia, Italian church composer; b. Perugia in the 2nd half of the 14th century; date of death unknown. He was principal maestro di cappella of the Milan Cathedral; occupied this post from 1402 to 1416. He wrote 4 Glorias in 3 parts; one Gloria in 4 parts; a number of motets and other sacred works for services at the Milan Cathedral. The first vol. of the new series of the Istituzioni e Monumenti dell'Arte Musicale Italiana (1957) is devoted to music by Matteo, ed. by F. Fano; 22 pieces are transcribed in modern notation by Willi Apel in his anthology *French Secular Music of the Late 14th Century* (Cambridge, Mass., 1950).

Matthay, Tobias (Augustus), eminent English pianist and pedagogue; b. London, Feb. 19, 1858; d. High Marley, near Haslemere, Surrey, Dec. 14, 1945. He began to play the piano at the age of 6; was taught by private teachers; in 1871 he entered the Royal Academy of Music as a pupil of Dorrell (piano); won the Sterndale Bennett scholarship, and continued to study piano (with Macfarren); took courses with Sterndale Bennett, and after the latter's death (1875) completed his studies with Ebenezer Prout and Arthur Sullivan; was appointed sub-prof. of piano at the Royal Academy of Music in 1876; sub-prof. of harmony in 1878, and full prof. of piano in 1880. In that year he gave his first public recital, and for the next 15 years he appeared frequently on the concert platform; but his interest in teaching gradually engrossed his attention, so that in 1895 he gave up his career as a concert pianist, and in 1900 established his own piano school in London. The Matthay System, as his teaching method was known, became famous not only in England but on the Continent and in America. Students flocked to him and carried his method abroad. Matthay wrote about 100 piano pieces, a *Konzertstück* for Piano and Orch., a Piano Quartet, and some other works. His didactic publications include: *The Art of Touch* (1903); *The First Principles of Pianoforte Playing* (1905); *Relaxation Studies* (1908); *Commentaries on the Teaching of Pianoforte Technique* (1911); *The Rotation Principle* (1912); *The Child's First Steps in Piano Playing* (1912); *Musical Interpretation* (1913); *Pianist's First Music Making* (3 books); *The Nine Steps towards Finger-individualization; On Memorizing;* etc.

Mattheson, Johann, famous German composer, theorist, and lexicographer; b. Hamburg, Sept. 28, 1681; d. there, April 17, 1764. He received a thorough education in the liberal arts at the Johanneum; acquired proficiency in English, Italian, and French; studied music there with the Kantor, Joachim Gerstenbüttel. He received private musical instruction studying keyboard music and composition with J.N. Hanff; also took singing lessons and learned to play the violin, gamba, oboe, flute, and lute. At a very early age he began to perform as an organist in the churches of Hamburg; also sang in the chorus at the Hamburg Opera. He graduated from the Johanneum in 1693; concurrently took courses in jurisprudence. He then served as a page at the Hamburg court of Graf von Güldenlöw, who held the title of Vice-König of Norway. He made his debut as a singer in a female role with the Hamburg Opera during its visit to Kiel in 1696; from 1697 to 1705 he was a tenor with the Hamburg Opera, conducted rehearsals, and also composed works for it. He befriended Handel in 1703; together they journeyed to Lübeck to visit Buxtehude, who was about to retire as organist, and to apply for his post. The unwritten requirement for the job was marriage to one of Buxtehude's five daughters, whose attractions seemed dubious; both Mattheson and Handel declined the opportunity. In 1704 a violent quarrel broke out between Mattheson and Handel during a performance of Mattheson's opera *Cleopatra* at the Hamburg Opera. Mattheson sang the principal male role of Antonius while Handel acted as conductor from the keyboard in the capcity of maestro al cembalo. Upon the conclusion of his role on stage, Mattheson asked Handel to let him assume the position at the keyboard, since he was the composer. Handel refused and an altercation ensued. The dispute was finally decided by a duel, during which Mattheson broke his sword on a metal button of Handel's coat, or so at least the most credible report of the episode went. They were, however, soon reconciled and remained friends. In 1704 Mattheson became the tutor of Cyrill Wich, the son of Sir John Wich, British envoy at Hamburg. In 1706 he became secretary to Sir John; when the younger Wich became ambassador in 1715, he retained Mattheson as secretary, a position he held for most of his life. During this period Mattheson diligently studied English politics, law, and economics, thereby adding to his many other accomplishments. In 1715 he assumed the post of music director of the Hamburg Cathedral. He composed much sacred music for performance there, including many oratorios. In 1719 he also became Kapellmeister to the court of the Duke of Holstein. Growing deafness compelled him to resign his post at the Cathedral in 1728. In 1741 he was given the title of Legation Secretary to the Duke of Holstein, and was made counsel in 1744. Mattheson's output as a composer was substantial, but little of his music has survived. Of his major compositions, only the MSS of one of his operas, *Cleopatra* (modern ed., by G. Buelow in *Das Erbe deutscher Musik*, LXIX, 1975), and one of his oratorios, *Das Lied des Lammes* (modern ed. by B. Cannon, Madison, Wis.), are extant; the bulk of his MSS kept in the Hamburg Stadtbibliothek were destroyed during the hideous "fire-storm" bombing of Hamburg during World War II. However, most of his numerous literary writings are preserved. Outstanding among his books is *Der vollkommene Capellmeister* (1739), an original theoretical treatise on the state of music in his era. Also valuable is his *Grosse General-Bass-Schule* (1731; based on his earlier work *Exemplarische Organisten-Probe*, 1719) and the *Kleine General-Bass-Schule* (1735). Of great historical value is his biographical dictionary, *Grundlage einer Ehren-Pforte ...* (1740), which contains 149 entries. Many of the entries on musicians of his own time were compiled from information provided by the subjects themselves, and several prepared complete autobiographical accounts for his lexicon.

WORKS: All of the following were first perf. in Hamburg unless otherwise stated: OPERAS: *Die Plejades oder Das Sieben-Gestirne* (1699); *Der edelmüthige Porsenna* (1702); *Victor, Hertzog der Normannen* (pasticcio; Act 1 by Schiefferdecker; Act 2 by Mattheson; Act 3 by Bronner; 1702); *Die unglückselige Cleopatra* (1704); *Le Retour du siècle d'or* (Holstein, 1705); *Boris Goudenow* (1710); *Die geheimen Begebenheiten Henrico IV* (1711); he also prepared a German version of Orlandini's *Nero* (1723), with additions.

ORATORIOS: *heylsame Geburth und Menschwerdung unsers Herrn und Heylandes Jesu Christi* (1715); *Die gnädige Sendung Gottes des Heiligen Geistes* (1716); *Chera, oder Die Leidtragende und getröstete Wittwe zu Nain* (1716); *Der verlangte und erlangte Heiland* (1716); *Der Altonaische Hirten-Segen, nebst einer Passions-Andacht über den verlassenen Jesum* (1717); *Der reformirende Johannes* (1717); *Der für die Sünde der Welt gemar-*

tete und sterbende Jesus (1718); *Der aller-erfreulichste Triumph oder Der überwindende Immanuel* (1718); *Die glücklich-streitende Kirche* (1718); *Die göttliche Vorsorge über alle Creaturen* (1718); *Die Frucht des Geistes* (1719); *Christi Wunder-Wercke bey den Schwachgläubigen* (1719); *Die durch Christi Auferstehung bestägte Auferstehung aller Todten* (1720); *Das gröste Kind* (1720); *Der Blut-rünstige Kelter-Treter und von der Erden erhöhete Menschen-Sohn* (1721); *Das irrende und wieder zu recht gebrachte Sünde-Schaaf* (1721); *Die Freuden-reiche Geburt und Menschwerdung unsers Herrn und Heilandes Jesu Christi* (1721); *Der unter den Todten gesuchte, und unter den lebendigen gefundene Sieges-Fürst* (1722); *Das Grosse in dem Kleinen, oder Gott in den Herzen eines gläubigen Christen* (1722); *Das Lied des Lammes* (1723); *Der liebreiche und gedultige David* (1723); *Der aus dem Löwen-Graben befreyte, himmlische Daniel* (1725); *Das gottseelige Geheimnis* (1725); *Der undanckbare Jerobeam* (1726); *Der gegen seine Brüder barmherzige Joseph* (1727); *Das durch die Fleischwerdung des ewigen Wortes erfüllte Wort der Verheissung* (1727). Additional vocal works include many secular wedding cantatas, 18 Italian secular cantatas, serenades, etc. He also composed his own funeral oratorio, *Das fröhliche Sterbelied*.

INSTRUMENTAL MUSIC: *Sonate à due cembali per il Signore Cyrillo Wich gran virtuoso* (1705; ed. by B. Cannon, London, 1960); *Suite für 2 Cembali* (1705; ed. by B. Cannon, London, 1960); *XII sonates à deux et trois flûtes sans basse* (publ. in Amsterdam, 1708); Sonate for Harpsichord (1713); *Pièces de clavecin en deux volumes* (publ. in London, 1714; German ed. as *Matthesons Harmonisches Denkmahl, aus zwölff erwählten Clavier-Suiten*, publ. in London, 1714; reprint, 1965); *Der brauchbare Virtuoso, welcher sich ... mit zwölff neuen Kammer-Sonaten* for Flute, Violin, and Harpsichord (1720); *Die wol-klingende Finger-Sprache, in zwölff Fugen, mit zwey bis drey Subjecten* (first part, 1735; 2nd part, 1737; ed. by L. Hoffmann-Erbrecht, Leipzig, 1954).

Matthus, Siegfried, German composer; b. Mallenuppen, East Prussia, April 13, 1934. He studied composition with Wagner-Régeny at the Deutsche Hochschule für Musik in East Berlin (1952–58) and with Eisler at the Deutsche Akademie der Künste (1958–60); in 1964 he was appointed a composer and dramatist at the East Berlin Komische Oper; in 1972 became a member of the presidium of the Deutsche Akademie der Künste.

WORKS: FOR THE STAGE: 4 operas: *Lazarillo vom Tormes* (1960–63); *Der letzte Schuss* (1966–67); *Noch ein Löffel Gift, Liebling* (1971–72); *Omphale* (1972–73). FOR ORCH.: *Concerto for Orchestra* for 2 Flutes, 3 Trombones, Harp, Piano, Percussion, and Strings (1963); *Inventions* (1964); *Tua res agitur* for 15 Instruments and Percussion (1965); Violin Concerto (1968; East Berlin, Feb. 24, 1969); 2 symphs.: No. 1, *Dresdener Sinfonie* (1969), and No. 2 (1976); Piano Concerto (1970; East Berlin, Feb. 18, 1971); *Orchesterserenade* (1974); Cello Concerto (1975); *Werther*, "musical metaphor" (1976); *Responso*, concerto for

Orch. (1977); *Visions* for Strings (1978); Flute Concerto (1978); *Kammerkonzert* for Solo Flute, Harpsichord, and Strings (1980–81). FOR VOICE: *Es wird ein grosser Stern in meinen Schoss fallen,* 5 love songs for Soprano and Orch. (1961–62; East Berlin, Oct. 5, 1962); *Das Manifest,* cantata (1965); *Kammermusik* for Alto, 3 Female Voices, and 10 Instruments (1965); *Galileo* for Voice, 5 Instruments, and Tape (1966); *Vokalsinfonie* for Soprano, Baritone, 2 Choruses, and Orch. (1967; from the opera *Der letzte Schuss*); *Kantate von den Beiden* for Narrator, Soprano, Baritone, and Orch. (1968); *Vokalisen* for Soprano, Flute, Double Bass, and Percussion (1969); *Laudate pacem,* oratorio (1974); *Unter dem Holunderstrauch,* scene after Kleist for Soprano, Tenor, and Orch. (1976); *Holofernes-Portrait* for Baritone and Orch. (1981); choruses; songs. CHAMBER MUSIC: Sonatina for Piano and Percussion (1960); Sonata for Brasses, Piano, and Kettledrums (1968); Music for 4 Oboes and Piano (1968); Octet (1970); String Quartet (1971); Harp Trio for Flute, Viola, and Harp (1971). FOR PIANO: *Variations* (1958); *Konzertstück* (1958).

Matzenauer, Margarete, celebrated Hungarian-born singer; b. Temesvar, June 1, 1881; d. Van Nuys, Calif., May 19, 1963. Her father was a symph. conductor, and her mother a dramatic soprano; she grew up in favorable musical surroundings, and began to study singing at an early age, first in Graz, then in Berlin, and finally in Munich. In 1901 she joined the staff of the Strasbourg Opera; then sang contralto roles at the Munich Court Opera (1904–11); also sang at Bayreuth in 1911. She made her American debut as Amneris in *Aida* at the Metropolitan Opera House in N.Y. (Nov. 13, 1911) and remained one of its leading members until 1930; in the interim she sang in opera in Germany and South America. She began her operatic career as a contralto, but also sang soprano parts; from 1914 on she called herself a soprano singer. After a farewell concert recital in Carnegie Hall, N.Y., in 1938, she retired from the stage and lived in California.

Mauceri, John, American conductor; b. New York, Sept. 12, 1945. He studied at Yale Univ. (B.A., 1967); served as conductor of the Yale Symph. Orch. (1968–74), with which he toured France and Austria. In 1976–77 he conducted the Israel Phil. on its tour of Germany and Austria, as well as in Tel Aviv and Jerusalem. He also was guest conductor of the Los Angeles Phil. (1974), San Francisco Symph. (1974), National Symph. Orch. in Wolf Trap Farm Park (1975), L'Orchestre National de France in Paris (1975), Scottish National Orch. (Edinburgh, 1976) and Philadelphia Orch. at Robin Hood Dell (1976).

Mauduit, Jacques, French composer; b. Paris, Sept. 16, 1557; d. there, Aug. 21, 1627. He served as registrar in a Paris court, and studied music by himself, progressing so well that at the age of 24 he won the first prize for a motet at a competition. When the poet Antoine Baïf established in Paris the Académie Française de Musique et de Poésie (1570),

Mauduit became associated with him, and made several settings of Baïf's poems (Paris, 1586; reprinted by Henry Expert in *Les Maîtres-Musiciens de la Renaissance française*). He is reputed to have saved the musical MSS of Le Jeune when the latter was arrested for his Huguenot sympathies. Mauduit's 5-part Requiem, included in Mersenne's *Harmonie Universelle,* is reprinted in R.E. Chapman's Eng. trans. of Mersenne's books on instruments (The Hague, 1957).

Mauersberger, Rudolf, German choral conductor; b. Mauersberg, Erzgebirge, Jan. 29, 1889; d. Dresden, Feb. 22, 1971. He studied piano and organ at the Leipzig Cons.; won the Nikisch Prize for composition in 1914; served as organist and choirmaster in Aachen (1919–25); then was in charge of church music in Thuringia (1925–30), directing the choir at Eisenach's Georgenkirche. In 1930 he became choirmaster of the Kreuzkirche in Dresden; directed its famous boys' choir, taking it on numerous tours in Europe and abroad. He composed a number of choral works, including the *Dresdner Requiem* (1948), written in memory of those who lost their lives during the barbarous bombing of the beautiful porcelaneous city just a few weeks before the end of the war.

Maunder, John Henry, British composer of hymns; b. London, Feb. 21, 1858; d. there, Jan 25, 1920. He studied at the Royal Academy of Music in London; served as organist in several London churches. He began his career as a theater composer; wrote an operetta, *Daisy Dingle* (1885); later devoted himself exclusively to sacred music; his oratorio *The Martyrs* (Oxford, May 25, 1894) became a perennial favorite; even more successful was his oratorio *From Olivet to Calvary;* he further wrote sacred works for chorus a cappella (*Praise the Lord, Blessed be Thy Name, Christ Awake, Conquering Kings, This Is the Day, Worship the King, Sing of Heaven);* other choral works are *Bethlehem, Song of Thanksgiving,* and *Christ Is Risen* for Voice, with Orch. Accompaniment.

Maurel, Victor, famous French baritone; b. Marseilles, June 17, 1848; d. New York, Oct. 22, 1923. He studied singing at the Paris Cons.; made his debut at the Paris Opéra in 1868; then sang in Italy, Spain, England, and Russia; in 1873 he made an American tour. Returning to Paris, he was on the staff of the Opéra (1879–94). He made his debut at the Metropolitan Opera House in N.Y. on Dec. 3, 1894, as Iago in *Otello;* sang there until 1896; then was a member of the Opéra-Comique in Paris until 1904. In 1909 he emigrated to the U.S., where he remained until his death; in his last years he was active as stage designer in N.Y. He created the role of Iago in Verdi's *Otello* (Milan, Feb. 5, 1887) and the title role in *Falstaff* (Milan, Feb. 9, 1893); also distinguished himself in Wagnerian roles. He publ. several monographs on the esthetics of singing and also autobiographical reminiscences, among them *Le Chant renové par la science* (1892); *Un Problème d'art*

(1893); *L'Art du chant* (1897); *Dix ans de carrière* (1898).

Maurer, Ludwig (Wilhelm), German violinist and composer; b. Potsdam, Feb. 8, 1789; d. St. Petersburg, Oct. 25, 1878. A precocious child musician, he appeared in concerts at the age of 13; at 17 he went to Russia, remaining there for 10 years, giving concerts and serving as house musician to Russian aristocrats. From 1817 until 1832 he traveled in Europe, and was successful as a violinist in Berlin and in Paris. He was in Russia again (1832–45), then lived in Dresden, eventually returning to St. Petersburg. He produced 2 operas in Hannover, *Der neue Paris* (Jan. 27, 1826) and *Aloise* (Jan. 16, 1828); also wrote many stage pieces in Russia; with Aliabiev and Verstovsky, he contributed the music to Chmelnitsky's comedy *A Novel Prank, or Theatrical Combat* (1822). In addition, he wrote a curious quadruple concerto, *Symphonie concertante,* for 4 Violins with Orch. (1838); 3 violin concertos; string quartets, and other chamber music. His 2 sons **Vsevolod** (1819–92), a violinist, and **Alexis,** a cellist, remained in Russia.

Maw, Nicholas, remarkable English composer; b. Grantham, Lincolnshire, Nov. 5, 1935. He played clarinet and piano; studied composition with Lennox Berkeley and Paul Steinitz at the Royal Academy of Music in London (1955–58) and with Nadia Boulanger and Max Deutsch in Paris (1958–59). From 1966 to 1970 he was composer-in-residence at Trinity College, Cambridge. In his music he makes use of serial methods of composition without abandoning the principle of tonality. WORKS: FOR THE STAGE: *One Man Show,* comic opera (London, Nov. 12, 1964); *The Rising of the Moon,* opera (1967–70; Glyndebourne, July 19, 1970). FOR ORCH.: *Scenes and Arias* for Solo Voices and Orch. (London, Aug. 31, 1962); *Sinfonia* for Chamber Orch. (Newcastle upon Tyne, May 30, 1966); *Severn Bridge Variations* (1967); Sonata for String Orch. and 2 Horns (Bath, June 7, 1967); *Serenade* (Singapore, March 31, 1973); *Summer Dances* for Youth Orch. (Aldeburgh, July 27, 1981); *Toccata* (Norwich, Oct. 15, 1982). VOCAL MUSIC: *Nocturne* for Mezzo-soprano and Chamber Orch. (1957–58); *5 Epigrams* for Mixed Voices a cappella (1960); *Our Lady's Song* for Mixed Voices a cappella (1961); *The Angel Gabriel* for Mixed Chorus (1963); *Round* for Children's Chorus, Mixed Chorus, and Piano (1963); *6 Interiors* for High Voice and Guitar (1966); *The Voice of Love* for Mezzo-soprano and Piano (1966); *5 Irish Songs* for Mixed Chorus (Cork, May 4, 1973); *Reverdie,* 5 songs for Male Voices (Glasgow, Oct. 29, 1975); Te Deum for Soprano, Tenor, Mixed Chorus, and Organ (Bruton, May 29, 1975); *20 Nonsense Rhymes* for Voices and Piano (1976); *Anncs!* for Mixed Chorus (1976); *La vita nuova* for Soprano and Chamber Ensemble (London, Sept. 2, 1979); *The Ruin* for Double Chorus and Solo Horn (Edinburgh, Aug. 27, 1980). CHAMBER MUSIC: Sonatina for Flute and Piano (1957); *Essays* for Organ (1961); *Chamber Music* for Oboe, Clarinet, Horn, Bassoon, and Piano

(1962); 2 string quartets (1965, 1982); *Personae* for Piano (1973); *Life Studies* for 15 Solo Strings (1973); Quartet for Flute and Strings (1981); *Night Thoughts* for Solo Flute (1982).

Maxfield, Richard (Vance), American avant-garde composer; b. Seattle, Wash., Feb. 2, 1927; d. (by self-defenestration from a hotel room) Los Angeles, June 27, 1969. He studied at the Univ. of Calif., Berkeley, with Roger Sessions, and at Princeton Univ. with Milton Babbitt; also took courses with Ernst Krenek and Luigi Dallapiccola. He became deeply engaged in acoustical electronics; taught experimental music at the New School for Social Research in N.Y. and at San Francisco State College; contributed essays to avant-garde publications; 2 of them, in free verse, were publ. in *Contemporary Composers on Contemporary Music,* edited by Elliot Schwartz and Barney Childs (N.Y., 1967). He acquired an excellent technique of composition in the traditional idiom before adopting an extreme avant-garde style. WORKS: *Classical Overture* (1942); Trio for Clarinet, Cello, and Piano (1943); Septet for 2 Flutes, 3 Clarinets, French Horn, and Bassoon (1947); Sonata for Unaccompanied Violin (1949); Violin Sonata (1950); String Trio (1951); Sonata for Unaccompanied Flute (1951); *Structures* for 10 Wind Instruments (1951); *11 Variations* for String Quartet (1952); *5 Movements* for Orch. (1956); Chamber Concerto for 7 Instruments (1957); *Structures* for Orch. (1958); *Sine Music* (1959); *Stacked Deck,* opera for Tape, Actors, and Lighting (1959); *Perspectives* for Violin and Tape (1960); *Peripeteia* for Violin, Saxophone, Piano, and Tape (1960); *Clarinet Music* for 5 Clarinets and Tape (1961); *Cough Music,* with sonic materials obtained from coughs and other bronchial sound effects recorded during a modern dance recital and electronically arranged in a piece of tussive polyphony (perf. for the first time as the opening number in an audiovisual spectacle, "Musical Essays in Time, Space and Sound," by the Division of Adult Education of the Cooper Union for the Advancement of Science and Art in N.Y. on Jan. 13, 1961); *Toy Symphony* for Flute, Violin, Wooden Boxes, Ceramic Vase, and Tape (1962); *African Symphony* (1964); *Venus Impulses* for Electronic Sound (1967).

May, Florence, English pianist and writer, daughter of **Edward Collett May;** b. London, Feb. 6, 1845; d. there, June 29, 1923. She studied music with her father and with an uncle, Oliver May; began a promising career as a pianist in London; in 1871 went to Germany; took lessons with Clara Schumann in Baden-Baden; there she made the acquaintance of Brahms, who gave her some lessons. She became his enthusiastic admirer; upon her return to England, she started a vigorous campaign for performances of the music of Brahms; she herself gave many first performances of his works in London. The important result of her dedication to Brahms was her comprehensive work *The Life of Johannes Brahms* (2 vols., London, 1905; revised ed., publ. posthumously, 1948); she also publ. *The Girl-hood of Clara Schumann* (London, 1912).

Mayer, Frederick Christian, American organist; b. Columbus, Ohio, March 4, 1882; d. Amarillo, Texas, Oct. 20, 1973, in consequence of an automobile accident, while driving alone, at the age of 91, across the continent from a visit in California to his retirement home in Florida. He studied at the Cincinnati Cons., graduating in 1905; then went to Europe for further study of organ playing, at the Stern Cons. in Berlin and at the Cons. of Fountainebleau. Returning to the U.S., he taught at the Cincinnati Cons.; in 1911 was appointed organist of Cadet Chapel, West Point Military Academy; although he reached the mandatory retirement age of three-score and ten in 1952, he was allowed to carry on for another couple of years. He was reputed as a fine carillon builder; inspected and supervised dozens of carillons in the U.S., Canada and Belgium.

Mayer, Wilhelm (pseudonym, **W.A. Rémy**), Austrian pianist and pedagogue; b. Prague, June 10, 1831; d. Graz, Jan. 22, 1898. He studied with C.F. Pietsch; also took a course in law; received a Dr.Jur. (1856). In 1862 he became conductor of the Graz Musical Society, resigning in 1870 to apply himself to pedagogy; he taught both piano and composition, and achieved great renown; among his pupils were Busoni, Kienzl, Rezniček, and Weingartner.

Mayer-Serra, Otto, eminent Spanish musicologist; b. Barcelona, July 12, 1904, of German-Catalan parentage; d. Mexico City, March 19, 1968. He studied in Germany with H. Abert, Curt Sachs, J. Wolf, and E. von Hornbostel; received his Ph.D. in 1929 with the dissertation *Die romantische Klaviersonaten,* from the Univ. of Greifswald. He returned to Spain in 1933, and was music critic of the Catalan weekly *Mirador.* In 1936, at the outbreak of the Spanish Civil War, he was appointed head of the music division of the propaganda ministry of the Catalan government; served in the Loyalist Army in 1938–39; after its defeat, he fled to France. In 1940 he reached Mexico, where he became active as a writer, editor, lecturer, and manager.

Mayr, Richard, Austrian bass; b. Henndorf, near Salzburg, Nov. 18, 1877; d. Vienna, Dec. 1, 1935. He was a student of medicine in Vienna. At the age of 21, he enrolled in the Vienna Cons.; studied voice; and in 1902 made his operatic debut at Bayreuth as Hagen. He was then engaged by Gustav Mahler at the Vienna Opera, of which he remained a member until his death. He made his American debut on Nov. 2, 1927, with the Metropolitan Opera Co. as Pogner; sang there until 1930. He possessed a rich and powerful voice, equally suited for tragic and comic parts; was particularly distinguished as Wotan; his performance of Baron Ochs in *Der Rosenkavalier* was also notable.

Mayr (Mayer), (Johannes) Simon (Giovanni Simone), outstanding German opera composer; b. Mendorf, Bavaria, of Italian parentage, June 14, 1763; d. Bergamo, Dec. 2, 1845. He first studied music with his father, a schoolteacher and organist; he sang in a church choir, and played organ. In 1774 he entered the Jesuit college in Ingolstadt; in 1781 he began a study of theology at the Univ. of Ingolstadt. In 1787 a Swiss Freiherr, Thomas von Bassus, took him to Italy to further his musical education; in 1789 he commenced studies with Carlo Lenzi in Bergamo; he then was sent to Ferdinando Bertoni in Venice. He began his career as a composer of sacred music; his oratorios were performed in Venice. After the death of his patron, Count Presenti, in 1793, he was encouraged by Piccinni and Peter von Winter to compose operas. His first opera, *Saffo o sia I riti d'Apollo Leucadio,* was performed in Venice in 1794. He gained renown with his opera *Ginevra di Scozia* (Trieste, April 21, 1801), and it remained a favorite with audiences; also successful were his operas *La rosa bianca e la rosa rossa* (Genoa, Feb. 21, 1813) and *Medea in Corinto* (Naples, Nov. 28, 1813). In 1802 he became maestro di cappella at S. Maria Maggiore in Bergamo; in 1805 he reorganized the choir school of the Cathedral as the Lezioni Caritatevoli di Musica and assumed its directorship; intractable cataracts, which led to total blindness in 1826, forced him to limit his activities to organ playing. In 1822 he founded the Società Filarmonica of Bergamo. Mayr's operas, while reflecting the late Neapolitan school, are noteworthy for their harmonization and orchestration, which are derived from the German tradition. After 1815 he devoted most of his time to composing sacred music, which totals some 600 works in all. He was also an eminent pedagogue. Donizetti was his pupil.

WORKS: OPERAS: *Saffo o sia I riti d'Apollo Leucadio,* dramma per musica (Venice, Feb. 17, 1794); *La Lodoiska,* dramma per musica (Venice, Jan. 26, 1796; revised for Milan, Dec. 26, 1799); *Un pazzo ne fa cento [I Rivali delusi; La Contessa immaginaria],* dramma giocoso (Venice, Oct. 8, 1796); *Telemaco nell'isola di Calipso,* dramma per musica (Venice, Jan. 16, 1797); *Il segreto,* farsa (Venice, Sept. 24, 1797); *L'intrigo della lettera [Il pittore astratto],* farsa (Venice, Fall 1797); *Avviso ai maritati,* dramma giocoso (Venice, Jan. 15, 1798); *Lauso e Lidia,* dramma per musica (Venice, Feb. 14, 1798); *Adriano in Siria,* dramma per musica (Venice, April 23, 1798); *Che originali [Il trionfo della musica; Il fanatico per la musica: La musicomania],* farsa (Venice, Oct. 18, 1798); *Amor ingegnoso,* farsa (Venice, Dec. 27, 1798); *L'ubbidienza per astuzia,* farsa (Venice, Dec. 27, 1798); *Adelaide di Gueselino,* dramma per musica (Venice, May 1, 1799); *Labino e Carlotta,* farsa (Venice, Oct. 9, 1799); *L'Avaro,* farsa (Venice, Nov. 1799); *L'accademia di musica,* farsa (Venice, Fall 1799); *Gli sciti,* dramma per musica (Venice, Feb. 1800); *La Locandiera,* farsa (Vicenza, Spring 1800); *Il carretto del venditore d'aceto,* farsa (Venice, June 28, 1800); *L'Imbroglione e il castigamatti,* farsa (Venice, Fall 1800); *L'equivoco, ovvero Le bizzarie dell'amore,* dramma giocoso (Milan, Nov. 5, 1800); *Ginevra di Scozia [Ariodante],* dramma serio eroico per musica (Trieste, April 21, 1801;

inaugural perf. at the Teatro Nuovo there); *Le due giornate [Il Portatore d'acqua]*, dramma eroicomico per musica (Milan, Aug. 18, 1801); *I Virtuosi [I Virtuosi a teatro]*, farsa (Venice, Dec. 26, 1801); *Argene*, dramma eroico per musica (Venice, Dec. 28, 1801); *Elisa, ossia Il monte S. Bernardo*, dramma sentimentale per musica (Malta, 1801); *I misteri eleusini*, dramma per musica (Milan, Jan. 6, 1802); *I castelli in aria, ossia Gli Amanti per accidente*, farsa (Venice, May 1802); *Ercole in Lidia*, dramma per musica (Vienna, Jan. 29, 1803); *Gl'intrighi amorosi*, dramma giocoso (Parma, Carnival 1803); *Le finte rivali*, melodramma giocoso (Aug. 20, 1803); *Alonso e Cora*, dramma per musica (Milan, Dec. 26, 1803; revised as *Cora* for Naples, 1815); *Amor non ha ritegno [La fedeltà delle vedove]*, melodramma eroicomico (Milan, May 18, 1804); *I due viaggiatori*, dramma giocoso (Florence, Summer 1804); *Zamori, ossia L'Eroe dell'Indie*, dramma per musica (Piacenza, Aug. 10, 1804; inaugural perf. at the Nuovo Teatro Communale); *Eraldo ed Emma*, dramma eroico per musica (Milan, Jan. 8, 1805); *Di locanda in locanda e sempre in sala*, farsa (June 5, 1805); *L'amor coniugale [Il custode di buon cuore]*, dramma giocoso (Padua, July 26, 1805); *La rocca di Frauenstein*, melodramma eroicomico (Venice, Oct. 26, 1805); *Gli Americani [Idalide]*, melodramma eroico (Venice, Carnival 1806); *Palmira, o sia Il trionfo della virtù e dell'amore*, dramma per musica (Florence, Fall 1806); *Il piccolo compositore di musica*, farsa (Venice, 1806); *Nè l'un, nè l'altro*, dramma giocoso (Milan, Aug. 17, 1807); *Belle ciarle e tristi fatti [L'imbroglio contro l'imbroglio]*, dramma giocoso (Venice, Nov. 1807); *Adelasia e Aleramo*, melodramma serio (Milan, Dec. 25, 1807); *I cherusci*, dramma per musica (Rome, Carnival 1808); *Il vero originale*, burletta per musica (Rome, Carnival 1808); *La finta sposa, ossia Il Barone burlato*, dramma giocoso (Rome, Spring 1808); *Il matrimonio per concorso*, dramma giocoso (Bologna, Carnival 1809); *Il ritorno di Ulisse*, azione eroica per musica (Venice, Carnival 1809); *Amor non soffre opposizione*, dramma giocoso (Venice, Carnival 1810); *Raùl di Créqui*, melodramma serio (Milan, Dec. 26, 1810); *Il sacrifizio d'Ifigenia [Ifigenia in Aulide]*, azione seria drammatica per musica (Brescia, Carnival 1811); *L'amor figliale [Il Disertore]*, farsa sentimentale (Venice, Carnival 1811); *La rosa bianca e la rosa rossa [Il trionfo dell'amicizia]*, melodramma eroica (Genoa, Feb. 21, 1813); *Medea in Corinto*, melodramma tragico (Naples, Nov. 28, 1813); *Tamerlano*, melodramma serio (Milan, Carnival 1813); *Elena [Elena e Costantino]*, dramma eroicomico per musica (Naples, Carnival 1814); *Atar, o sia Il serraglio d'Ormus*, melodramma serio (Genoa, June 1814); *Le due duchesse, ossia La caccia dei lupi [Le due amiche]*, dramma semiserio per musica (Milan, Nov. 7, 1814); *La Figlia dell'aria, ossia La vendetta di Giunone*, dramma per musica (Naples, Lent 1817); *Nennone e Zemira*, dramma per musica (Naples, March 22, 1817); *Amor avvocato*, commedia per musica (Naples, Spring 1817); *Lanassa*, melodramma eroico (Venice, Carnival 1818); *Alfredo il grande*, melodramma serio (Rome, Feb. 1818); *Le Danaide [Danao]*, melodramma serio (Rome, Carnival 1819); *Fedra*, melodramma serio (Milan, Dec. 26, 1820); *Demetrio*, dramma per musica (Turin, Carnival 1824).

Mayseder, Joseph, Austrian violinist and composer; b. Vienna, Oct. 26, 1789; d. there, Nov. 21, 1863. He was a pupil of Suche and Wranitzky (violin); and of E. Förster (piano and composition). He joined the famous Schuppanzigh Quartet as 2nd violin; became concertmaster of the court theater in 1810; entered the court orch. in 1816; became solo violinist at the court opera in 1820 and chamber violinist to the Emperor in 1835; music director of the court chapel in 1836; retired in 1837. He never went on tours, and rarely gave concerts; yet he was a finished virtuoso, admired even by Paganini. In Vienna he was very successful as a teacher. His works include several violin concertos, 5 string quintets, 8 string quartets, trios, and solo violin pieces, all effectively written.

Mayuzumi, Toshirō, eminent Japanese composer; b. Yokohama, Feb. 20, 1929. He studied at the National Music Academy in Tokyo (1945–51); then took courses at the Paris Cons. with Aubin. Returning to Japan, he organized the modern group Ars Nova Japonica and also worked at the electronic studio in Tokyo. He became known in Europe with the production of his *Sphenogramme*, a modernistic piece for Voice and Instruments (Frankfurt Festival of the International Society for Contemporary Music, June 25, 1951), and *Ectoplasme* for Electronic Instruments, Percussion, and Strings (Stockholm Festival of the International Society for Contemporary Music, June 5, 1956). His style of composition embodies sonorous elements from old Japanese music, serial techniques, and electronic sound, all amalgamated in a remarkably effective manner; he was quite successful in writing film scores, and spent several years in Hollywood.

WORKS: Violin Sonata (1946); *Divertimento* for 10 Instruments (1948); *Symphonic Mood* (1950); *Mikrokosmos* for 7 Instruments (Modern Music Festival, Karuizawa, Japan, Aug. 12, 1957); *Phonologie symphonique* (Tokyo, May 28, 1957); *Nirvana Symphony* (Tokyo, April 2, 1958); *U-So-Ri*, oratorio (Tokyo, June 12, 1959); *Mandala-Symphonie* (Tokyo, March 27, 1960); *Bunraku* for Cello Solo (1960); *Music with Sculpture* for Winds (Pittsburgh, June 29, 1961); *Prelude* for String Quartet (1961); *Bugaku*, ballet (N.Y., March 20, 1963); *Samsara*, symph. poem (Tokyo, June 12, 1962); *Texture* for Band (Pittsburgh, June 10, 1962); *Essay in Sonorities* (Osaka, Jan. 21, 1963); *Fireworks* for Band (Pittsburgh, June 13, 1963); *Pratidesana*, Buddhist cantata (Kyoto, Sept. 5, 1963); *The Ritual Overture* for Band (Pittsburgh, July 2, 1964); *The Birth of Music*, symph. poem (Tokyo, Oct. 10, 1964); symph. poem, *Showa Tempyo Raku* (Old and Present Music; Tokyo, Oct. 31, 1970); opera, *Kinkakuji* (*The Temple of the Golden Pavilion*; Berlin, June 23, 1976).

Mazas, Jacques-Féréol, French violinist; b. Lavaur (Tarn), Sept. 23, 1782; d. Bordeaux, Aug. 25, 1849. He was a pupil of Baillot at the Paris Con., winning first prize as violinist (1805); then played in the orch. of the Italian Opera in Paris; toured Europe (1811–29); then was a teacher in Orléans, and director of a music school in Cambrai (1837–41). He spent the last years of his life in Bordeaux. He wrote a method for violin (new ed. by J. Hrímalý) and numerous valuable studies; also a method for viola; concertos, string quartets, trios, violin duets, fantasias, variations, romances, etc.; also 3 operas, one of which, *Le Kiosque,* was performed at Paris in 1842. A set of 6 études was publ. in a new ed. by Hubay.

Mazzocchi, Domenico, Italian composer; b. Veja, near Città Castellana (baptized, Nov. 8), 1592; d. Rome, Jan. 21, 1665. A learned Roman lawyer, he studied music with Nanini; in 1621 entered the service of Cardinal Ippolito Aldobrandini; publ. a book, *Madrigali a 5 voci in partitura* (1638), in which appear, for the first time, the conventional symbols for *crescendo* (\`) and *decrescendo* (>), *piano* (*p*), *forte* (*f*), and *trillo* (*tr*), which he explains in a preface. He also composed the operas *La catena d'Adone* (Rome, 1626) and *L'innocenza difesa,* several oratorios, and various pieces of church music.

Mazzocchi, Virgilio, Italian composer, brother of **Domenico Mazzocchi**; b. Veja (baptized, July 22), 1597; d. there, Oct. 3, 1646. He studied music with his brother in Rome; served as maestro di cappella at the Chiesa del Gesù; then was at St. John Lateran (1628–29). In 1629 he was engaged at Cappella Giulia, at St. Peter's, and served there until his death. His opera, *Chi soffre, speri,* was produced in Rome on Feb. 27, 1639; excerpts from it were publ. by H. Goldschmidt; an *Argomento et allegoria* relating to it was publ. at the time of its first performance; a copy is in the Library of Congress in Washington, D.C.

Mazzucato, Alberto, Italian violinist, composer, and writer on music; b. Udine, July 28, 1813; d. Milan, Dec. 31, 1877. He first studied mathematics; then turned to music, his teacher being Bresciano in Padua, where his first opera, *La Fidanzata di Lammermoor,* was given (Feb. 24, 1834); he wrote 8 more operas: *Don Chisciotte* (Milan, April 26, 1836), *Esmeralda* (Mantua, Feb. 10, 1838; his most successful stage work), *I Corsari* (Milan, Feb. 15, 1840), *I due sergenti* (Milan, Feb. 27, 1841), *Luigi V* (Milan, Feb. 25, 1843), *Hernani* (Genoa, Dec. 26, 1843); *Alberico da Romano* (Padua, 1847) and *Fede* (not perf.). Verdi's ascendance soon put him into the shade. He joined the faculty of the Milan Cons. in 1839, and from 1872 until his death was its director. From 1859 till 1869 he was concertmaster in the orch. of La Scala, Milan; for several years was editor of the influential *Gazzetta Musicale*; publ. *Trattato d'estetica musicale.*

McCabe, John, English pianist and composer of considerable attainments; b. Liverpool, April 21, 1939, of mixed Scottish-Irish stock on his father's side and of German-Scandinavian-Spanish ancestry on his mother's. He played piano, violin, and cello as a child and, according to family lore, composed 13 symphs. and an opera before the advent of puberty. He studied composition with Thomas Pitfield at Manchester Univ. (Mus.B., 1960), at the Royal Manchester College of Music, and in Munich with Harald Genzmer; was pianist-in-residence at Univ. College in Cardiff (1965–68); then settled in London. In 1978 he made a tour of the U.S. as a pianist-composer.

WORKS: FOR THE STAGE: *This Town's a Corporation Full of Crooked Streets,* an entertainment for Speaker, Tenor, Children's Chorus, Mixed Chorus, and Instrumental Ensemble (1969); *The Lion, the Witch, and the Wardrobe,* children's opera (1969); *The Teachings of Don Juan,* ballet (1973); *The Play of Mother Courage,* chamber opera (1974); *Mary Queen of Scots,* ballet (Glasgow, March 3, 1976). FOR ORCH.: 3 piano concertos: No. 1 (1966); No. 2 (1970); No. 3 (1977); 2 violin concertos: No. 1 (1959) and No. 2 (1980); 3 Symphs.: No. 1 (1965); No. 2 (1970); No. 3 (1978); *Concertante Music* (1968); *Metamorphoses* for Harpsichord and Orch. (1968); *Concerto funèbre* for Viola and Chamber Orch. (1962); Chamber Concerto for Viola, Cello, and Orch. (1965); Concerto for Chamber Orch. (1962; revised 1968); *Notturni ed Alba* for Soprano and Orch. (1970); *Concertante Variations* on a theme of Nicholas Maw, for Strings (1970); Concerto for Oboe d'Amore and Orch. (1972); *The Chagall Windows* (1974); Clarinet Concerto (1977); *The Shadow of Light* (1979); Concerto for Orch. (London, Feb. 10, 1983). VOCAL WORKS: *Aspects of Whiteness,* cantata for Mixed Chorus and Piano (1967); *Voyage Cantata* for Soloists, Chorus, and Orch. (1972); *Stabat Mater* for Soprano, Chorus, and Orch. (1976); *Reflections on a Summer Night,* cantata for Mixed Chorus and Orch. (1977); many choruses. CHAMBER MUSIC: *Movements* for Clarinet, Violin, and Cello (1964); *Concertante* for Harpsichord and Chamber Ensemble (1965); String Trio (1966); *Nocturnal* for Piano Quintet (1966); *Miniconcerto* for Organ, Percussion, and 485 Penny-whistles (1966); *Dance Movements* for Horn, Violin, and Piano (1967); *Rounds* for Brass Quintet (1967); Sonata for Clarinet, Cello, and Piano (1969); 3 string quartets: No. 1 (1960); No. 2 (1972); No. 3 (1979); many piano pieces and organ works.

McCartney, John Paul, English rock-'n'-roll singer and composer; member of the famous Liverpudlian quartet The Beatles; b. Liverpool, June 18, 1942. He picked out chords on a family piano (his father was an amateur ragtime player), and at puberty began playing a left-handed guitar. He is the only Beatle who attended college, and studied English literature. Fascinated by Elvis Presley, he tried to emulate the spirit of American rock 'n' roll *à l'anglaise.* He joined John Lennon and George Harrison in the Casbah Club in Liverpool in 1959; this fruitful and fantastically lucrative association with them, and later with Ringo Starr, continued until the breakup of the group in 1970, when McCartney went to High Court to end the partnership and asked for an accounting of assets and income. Endowed with an authentic poetic gift, McCartney infused a literary quality into the lyrics used by The Beatles, fashioning them in archaic English prosody, which in combination with the modal harmony of the arrangements imparted a somewhat distant quality to their products. Like his co-Beatles, McCartney went through a period of transcendental meditation when he sat at the feet of a hirsute Indian guru, but his British common sense soon overrode this metaphysical infatuation.

McCormack, John, famous Irish tenor; b. Athlone, June 14, 1884; d. Glena, Booterstown, Sept. 16, 1945. Without previous training, he took part in the National Irish Festival at Dublin in 1903, and carried off the gold medal; in 1903 he became a member of the Dublin Cathedral Choir and began to study seriously with the organist and choirmaster, Vincent O'Brien; he made his operatic debut at Savona on Jan. 13, 1906, and his debut as a concert singer at a concert of the Sunday League in London (Feb. 17, 1907); in 1909 he sang at the San Carlo Opera in Naples, and was engaged by Hammerstein for the Manhattan Opera House in N.Y., where he made his American debut on Nov. 10, 1909, as Alfredo Germont in *La Traviata;* he made his debut at the Metropolitan Opera House in N.Y. on Nov. 29, 1910; also appeared there in 1912–14 and in 1917–19; during the 1910–11 season he was with the Chicago Opera Co.; after that, he appeared seldom in opera, but became tremendously successful as a concert tenor. He was naturalized as an American citizen in 1919; was given the title of Count by Pope Pius XI in 1928 and named Papal Chamberlain. Postage stamps in his honor were issued in June 1984 to mark his centennial of birth: a 22-pence Irish stamp, and a 20-cent denomination in the U.S.

McCracken, James, remarkable American tenor; b. Gary, Ind., Dec. 16, 1926. His father was a singing fireman; his mother played the piano, although she could not read music. This created a musical environment, and McCracken began to play the clarinet. When he graduated from Horace Mann High School he was voted the most likely to succeed in music among his classmates, who matriculated mostly in baseball. He also married a school sweetheart, but then came the war and he joined the navy. After the war he enrolled at Columbia Univ. and began to study singing in earnest. He obtained engagements to sing secondary and tertiary roles in Broadway musicals, and held a regular job as a vocalist at the Roxy Theater in N.Y. In 1952 he made his opera debut as Rodolfo in *La Bohème* with the Central City Opera Co. in Colorado. He successfully auditioned for the Metropolitan Opera and was given a chance to sing minor roles there. In the meantime he was divorced and remarried. With his new wife, he went to Europe, and succeeded in making a number of respectable appearances with various European opera houses. He took an intensive course in Italian singing with Marcello Conati in Milan.

Upon his return to the U.S., he was engaged to sing the title role in Verdi's *Otello* with the Opera Society in Washington, D.C., on Jan. 22, 1960. He sang Otello at the Zürich Festival on June 15, 1961, and with the San Francisco Opera on Oct. 2, 1962, with excellent success. On March 10, 1963, he sang this role at the Metropolitan Opera in N.Y. His career was now assured. In 1964 he sang Otello at Covent Garden in London. Other roles in which he excelled were Canio in *Pagliacci,* Manrico in *Il Trovatore,* Don José in *Carmen,* Radames in *Aida,* Don Alvaro in *La forza del destino,* and Tannhäuser in Wagner's opera.

McDonald, Harl, American composer and music administrator; b. near Boulder, Colo., July 27, 1899; d. Princeton, N.J., March 30, 1955. He studied at the Univ. of Southern Calif.; became a professional pianist; also did research in the measurement of instrumental and vocal tones; publ. its results in *New Methods of Measuring Sound* (Philadelphia, 1935). In 1939 he was appointed business manager of the Philadelphia Orch., but continued to compose. His music gained performance almost exclusively by courtesy of the Philadelphia Orch., conducted by Stokowski and Ormandy.

McEwen, Sir John Blackwood, Scottish composer and pedagogue; b. Hawick, April 13, 1868; d. London, June 14, 1948. He studied at Glasgow Univ. (M.A., 1888) and at the Royal Academy of Music in London, with Corder, Matthay, and Prout; taught piano in Glasgow (1895–98) and composition at the Royal Academy of Music in London (1898–1936); in 1924 he succeeded Alexander Mackenzie as principal, retiring in 1936. He was knighted in 1931. He continued to compose until his last years.

McHugh, Jimmy, American composer of popular songs; b. Boston, July 10, 1894; d. Beverly Hills, May 22, 1969. He was a rehearsal accompanist for the Boston Opera Co. before embarking on composition. He moved to N.Y. in 1921. His first Broadway show was *Blackbirds of 1928,* which included his greatest hit song, *I Can't Give You Anything but Love, Baby.* In 1930 he went to Hollywood and began to write for films; one of his most famous songs of the period was *South American Way.* During the war he wrote the inspirational song *Comin' in on a Wing and a Prayer.* He was awarded a Presidential Certificate of Merit for his work on war bonds. He also received honorary doctor's degrees from Harvard Univ., Georgetown Univ. and Holy Cross College.

McIntyre, Donald, New Zealand bass-baritone; b. Auckland, Oct. 22, 1934. He went to London and studied at the Guildhall School of Music; in 1959 he made his debut with the Welsh National Opera; from 1960 was a member of the Sadler's Wells Opera; in 1967 he made his debut at Covent Garden; beginning in 1967, he sang at the Bayreuth Festivals. On Feb. 15, 1975, he made his Metropolitan Opera debut as Wotan in *Das Rheingold;* also sang in Hamburg, Paris, and Milan. He was particularly distinguished in Wagnerian roles.

McPhee, Colin, outstanding American composer; b. Montreal, Canada, March 15, 1901; d. Los Angeles, Jan. 7, 1964. He studied at the Peabody Cons. with Gustav Strube, graduating in 1921; then took piano lessons with Arthur Friedheim in Toronto and with Isidor Philipp in Paris. Returning to America in 1926, he joined the modern movement in N.Y.; wrote a Concerto for Piano and Wind Octet (1928; Boston, March 11, 1929) and also scores for the experimental films *H₂O* and *Mechanical Principles*. In 1934 he went to live on the island of Bali in Indonesia; in 1936 he was in Mexico, where he wrote his major work, *Tabuh-Tabuhan*, for 2 Pianos and Orch.; then was again in Bali, until 1939. From 1958 until his death he was at the Inst. of Ethnomusicology at the Univ. of Calif. in Los Angeles. He wrote *Balinese Ceremonial Music* for Flute and 2 Pianos (1942); *Transitions* for Orch. (1951); 3 symphs. (1955, 1957, 1962); *4 Iroquois Dances* for Orch.; *Invention and Kinesis* for Piano; publ. *A House in Bali* (N.Y., 1946) and *Music in Bali* (posthumous, New Haven, Conn., 1966).

Meale, Richard, Australian composer; b. Sydney, Aug. 24, 1932. He studied piano, harp, and clarinet at the New South Wales Cons. of Music (1947–55); in 1960 he took a course in Asian music at the Ethnomusicological Inst. at the Univ. of Calif. in Los Angeles; traveled to France and Spain before returning to Australia in 1961; was program planning officer of the Australian Broadcasting Commission (1962–69); then was on the faculty of the Univ. of Adelaide (1969–73). In his music he followed the precepts of ethnomusicology, seeking to create a synthesis of primitive natural melorhythms with modernistic counterpoints.

WORKS: *Stonehenge* for Piano (1945); *Rhapsody* for Violin and Piano (1952); Quintet for Oboe and Strings (1952); *Rhapsody* for Cello and Piano (1953); Horn Sonata (1954); ballet, *The Hypnotist* (1956); Solo Flute Sonata (1957); *Divertimento* for Piano Trio (1959); Flute Concerto (1959); *Sinfonia* for Piano, 4-hands and Strings (1959); *Orenda* for Piano (1959, revised 1968); Flute Sonata (1960); ballet, *At Five in the Afternoon* (1961); *Las Alboradas* for Flute, Violin, Horn, and Piano (1963); *Homage to García Lorca* for Double String Orch. (1964); *Intersections* and *Cyphers* for Flute, Viola, Vibraphone, and Piano (both 1965; graphic scores); *Images (Nagauta)* for Orch. (1966); *Nocturnes* for Solo Vibraphone, Harp, Celesta, and Orch. (1965–67); *Very High Kings* for Orch., Organ, 2 Amplified Pianos, and 6 Spatially Positioned Trumpets (1968); *Clouds Now and Then* for Orch. (1969); *Soon It Will Die* for Orch. (1969); *Interiors/Exteriors* for 2 Pianos and 3 Percussionists (1970); *Variations* for Orch. (1970); Wind Quintet (1970); *Coruscations* for Piano (1971); *Incredible Floridas*, an homage to Rimbaud, for Flute, Guitar, Violin, Cello, Piano, and Percussion (1971); *Plateau* for Wind Quintet (1971); *Evocations* for Oboe, Chamber Orch., and Obbligato Violin (1972); String Quartet (1974).

Meck, Nadezhda von, friend and benefactress of Tchaikovsky; b. Znamenskoye, near Smolensk, Feb. 10, 1831; d. Wiesbaden, Jan. 13, 1894. She became interested in Tchaikovsky's music through Nicholas Rubinstein, director of the Moscow Cons., of which she was a patroness. At first offering Tchaikovsky commissions, she later granted him a yearly allowance of 6,000 rubles in order that he might compose undisturbed by finanical considerations. He lived for long periods in close proximity to her, at Brailov (near Kiev) and in Florence, Italy, but although they carried on an extensive and intimate correspondence (publ. in 3 vols., Moscow, 1934–36), they never met face to face. Tchaikovsky's allowance was abruptly cut off in 1890 on the pretext of financial difficulties, leading to a complete break between him and Mme. von Meck in 1891. She employed the youthful Debussy as a pianist in her household.

Medinš, Jānis, foremost Latvian composer; b. Riga, Oct. 9, 1890; d. Stockholm, March 4, 1966. He graduated from the First Riga Musical Inst. in 1909; was violist and conductor of the Latvian Opera in 1913–15; In 1914–16 he was head of the piano dept. of the firm of A. Diederichs in St. Petersburg; in 1916–20, was military bandmaster there. In 1920 he returned to Riga; conducted opera at the Latvian National Theater (1920–28); was chief conductor of the Latvian Radio Symph. Orch. (1928–44); in 1929–44 was also a prof. at the Riga Cons. In 1944, as the Soviet armies approached Latvia, Medinš went to Germany, and in 1948 went to Stockholm. He wrote the operas *Uguns un nakts* (*Fire and Night;* Riga, May 26, 1921) and *Deevi un cilveki* (Riga, May 23, 1922); symph. and chamber music; choruses.

Medtner, Nicolai, notable Russian composer; b. (of German parents) Moscow, Jan. 5, 1880; d. London, Nov. 13, 1951. He first studied with his uncle, Theodore Goedicke; in 1892 entered Moscow Cons., where he took courses with Sapelnikov and Safonov (piano), and with Taneyev (composition); he graduated in 1900, winning the gold medal; in the same year he won the Rubinstein prize in Vienna; for the next 2 years he appeared with much success as a pianist in the European capitals; returning to Russia, he taught at the Moscow Cons. for one academic year (1902–3); was again prof. there from 1918 till 1921, when he left Russia; he lived in Berlin and Paris; eventually settled in London; made U.S. tours in 1924–25 and in 1929–30. In Russian music he was a solitary figure; he never followed the nationalist trend, but endeavored to create a new type of composition, rooted both in the Classical and the Romantic tradition; his sets of fairy tales in sonata form are unique examples of his favorite genre. He wrote his best compositions before he left Russia; although he continued to compose during his residence abroad, his late music lacks the verve and Romantic sincerity that distinguish his earlier works. He wrote almost exclusively for the piano and for the voice. A revival of his music was begun in Russia after his death.

WORKS: 3 piano concertos: No. 1 (1916–18); No. 2 (Moscow, March 13, 1927); No. 3 (London, Feb. 19, 1944, composer soloist); Piano Quintet (1950). For Piano: *3 Mood Pictures* (1902); *3 Improvisations* (1902); *3 Arabesques* (1905); *34 Fairy Tales* (1905–29); *3 Dithyrambs* (1906); *Sonata-Triad* (1907); *3 Novels* (1909); *4 Sonatas* (1909–14); *Fairy-tale Sonata* (1912); *Sonata-Ballade* (1913); *Sonata romantica* (1930); *Sonata minacciosa* (1931); *Sonata idillica* (1935); *4 Lyric Fragments* (1912); 3 sets of *Forgotten Melodies* (1919–20); 4 sets of *Romantic Sketches* (1933); *2 Elegies* (1945). Vocal works: 104 songs; *Sonata-Vocalise*, for Voice and Piano, without words (1921); *Suite-Vocalise* (1923). Chamber music: 2 violin sonatas; various pieces for Violin and Piano. A collection of Medtner's literary essays was publ. in an Eng. trans. by Alfred Swan, as *The Muse and the Fashion* (Haverford, Pa., 1951).

Méfano, Paul, French composer; b. Basra, Iraq, March 6, 1937. He studied at the Paris Cons. with Dandelot, Messiaen, Martenot, and Milhaud; attended seminars of Boulez, Stockhausen and Pousseur in Basel. He received a grant from the Harkness Foundation for residence in the U.S. (1966–68) and in Berlin (1968–69). In his music he pursues a constructivist style, with an emphasis on rhythmic percussion and electronic sound; the influences of Stravinsky and Varèse are particularly in evidence.

WORKS: *Incidences* for Orch. and Piano (1960); *Paraboles* for Soprano and Chamber Ensemble (Paris, Jan. 20, 1965); *Interférences* for a Chamber Group (1966); *Lignes* for Bass Voice, Brass, Percussion, Bassoon, and Amplified Double Bass (1968); *Aurélia* for 3 Choruses, 3 Orchs., and 3 Conductors (1968); *La Cérémonie* for Voices, Instrumental Groups, and Speaking Choruses (1970); *Intersection*, electronic piece for 2 Generators and Ring Modulator (1971).

Mehta, Mehli, Indian violinist and conductor, father of **Zubin Mehta;** b. Bombay, Sept. 25, 1908. He studied violin in Bombay and at Trinity College in London, obtaining his licentiate there in 1929. In 1935 he founded the Bombay Symph. Orch.; in 1942 organized the Bombay String Quartet. He was assistant concertmaster of the Hallé Orch. in Manchester from 1955 to 1959; then settled in the U.S. In 1964 he became conductor of the orch. of the Univ. of Calif., Los Angeles, which he brought up to a high degree of excellence.

Mehta, Zubin, exuberant, effulgent, and eloquent Indian conductor; b. Bombay, April 29, 1936. The family belonged to the historic tribe of Parsi nobles, the fire-worshiping followers of Zarathustra who fled en masse from the turbulence of Persia 13 centuries before Zubin Mehta's birth. He was tutored in music by his father, Mehli Mehta, who played violin in a hotel and also conducted a local orch.; he learned to play violin and piano; when he was 16 he successfully conducted a rehearsal of the Bombay Symph. Orch. Before deciding on a musical career, he took a course in medicine at St. Xavier College in Bombay; but he turned away from the unesthetic training in dissection, and instead went to Vienna, where he practiced to play the double bass at the Vienna Academy of Music and took conducting lessons with Hans Swarowsky. During the summers of 1956 and 1957 he attended conducting classes at the Accademia Chigiana in Siena with Carlo Zecchi and Alceo Galliera. In 1957 he graduated from the Vienna Academy of Music, and made his professional debut conducting the Tonkünstler Orch. in the Musikverein. In 1958 he married the Canadian singer **Carmen Lasky;** they had 2 children, but were divorced in 1964; she married Zubin Mehta's brother Zarin in 1966, thus making Zubin an uncle by marriage of his own children. On July 20, 1969, he married the actress Nancy Kovack in a dual ceremony, Methodist and Zoroastrian. In the meantime his career progressed by great strides; he won the competition of the Royal Liverpool Phil. in 1958, and conducted it for a season as an assistant; later he obtained guest engagements in Austria and Yugoslavia. When Eugene Ormandy needed a surrogate conductor on a date with the Vienna Phil. he was unable to fill in, Mehta became a successful substitute. In 1959 he competed in a conducting test in Tanglewood, and won 2nd prize. In 1960 he received a bona fide engagement to conduct the Vienna Symph. Orch. In July 1960 he made his formal American conducting debut at Lewisohn Stadium; later in 1960 he conducted 2 concerts of the Montreal Symph. and produced such a fine impression that he was appointed its music director. In 1962 Mehta took the Montreal Symph. to Russia, where he gave 8 concerts; then conducted 2 concerts with it in Paris and one in Vienna, where he took 14 bows in response to a vociferous ovation. In the meantime he received a contract to conduct the Los Angeles Phil., thus becoming the holder of 2 major conducting jobs, in Montreal and Los Angeles, a feat he was able to accomplish by commuting on newfangled jet airplanes; he was also the youngest conductor to function in this dual capacity. His career was now assuming the allure of a gallop, aided by his ability, rare among conductors, to maintain his self-control under trying circumstances. He has the reputation of a bon vivant; his joy of life is limitless. Professionally, he maintains an almost infallible reliability; he conducts all of his scores, even the most mind-boggling modern productions, and operas as well, from memory. He is also a polyglot; not only is he eloquent in English and Hindi, but he is fluent in German, French, and Spanish; he even speaks understandable Russian. He made his debut at the Metropolitan Opera in N.Y. on Dec. 29, 1965, conducting *Aida*. His performances of *Carmen* and *Turandot* were highly praised. In 1967 he resigned his post in Montreal; in 1968 he was named music adviser of the Israel Phil.; in 1977 he became its music director. In 1978 he left the Los Angeles Phil. after he received an offer he could not refuse, the musical directorship of the N.Y. Phil.; in 1980 he toured with it in Europe. His association with the Israel Phil. was particularly affectionate; he conducted it during the Six-Day War and at the 25th anniversary of Israel's independence; in 1974 he was given an honorary Ph.D. by Tel Aviv Univ. No Jew could be more Israeli than the Parsi Mehta. *Time* glorified him with a cover story in its issue of Jan. 19, 1968.

Mehul, Etienne-Nicolas Méhul, Etienne-Nicholas, famous French composer; b. Givet, Ardennes, June 22, 1763; d. Paris, Oct. 18, 1817. His father apprenticed him to the old blind organist of the Couvent des Récollets in Givet; he then went to Lavaldieu, where he studied with the German organist Wilhelm Hansen, director of music at the monastery there. In 1778 he went to Paris, where he continued his musical studies with the composer Jean-Frédéric Edelmann. His first opera to receive a performance was *Euphrosine, ou Le Tyran corrigé* (Théâtre Favart, Paris, Sept. 4, 1790); another opera, *Alonso et Cora* (later known as *Cora*), was staged at the Paris Opéra on Feb. 15, 1791. His next opera, *Adrien,* was in rehearsal by the end of 1791, but the revolutionary turmoil prevented a performance; it finally received its premiere at the Paris Opéra on June 4, 1799. His opera *Stratonice* was given at the Théâtre Favart in Paris on May 3, 1792, and was highly successful. Then followed his opera *Le Jeune Sage et le vieux fou,* which was performed at the same theater on March 28, 1793. In 1793 Méhul became a member of the Institut National de Musique, which had been organized by the National Convention under the revolutionary regime. He composed a number of patriotic works during these turbulent years of French history, including the popular *Chant du départ* (first perf. publicly on July 4, 1794). He also continued to compose for the theater, shrewdly selecting subjects for his operas allegorically suitable to the times. In 1794 he was awarded an annual pension of 1,000 francs by the Comédie-Italienne. In 1795 he became one of the 5 inspectors of the newly established Cons., and was also elected to the Institut. He became a member of the Légion d'Honneur in 1804. Between 1795 and 1807 Méhul composed 18 operas, some of which were written in collaboration with other composers. His greatest opera from this period is the biblical *Joseph* (Opéra-Comique, Feb. 17, 1807); its success in Paris led to performances in Germany, Austria, Hungary, Russia, the Netherlands, Belgium, Switzerland, England, Italy, and America. Also noteworthy is his *Chant national du 14 juillet 1800,* an extensive work calling for 2 choirs with an additional group of high voices and orchestral forces. Apart from operas, he composed several symphs. In spite of his poor health, he nevertheless continued to teach classes at the Paris Cons.; among his students was the opera composer Hérold. Méhul's last opera was *La Journée aux aventures,* which was given at the Opéra-Comique on Nov. 16, 1816. Although Méhul's operas practically disappeared from the active repertoire, his contribution to the operatic art remains of considerable historical importance. Beethoven, Weber, and Mendelssohn were cognizant of some of his symph. works. WORKS: OPERAS: *Euphrosine, ou Le Tyran corrigé* (Théâtre Favart, Paris, Sept. 4, 1790; revised as

Euphrosine et Coradin); *Alonso et Cora* (Paris Opéra, Feb. 15, 1791; later known as *Cora*); *Stratonice* (Théâtre Favart, Paris, May 3, 1792); *Le Jeune Sage et le vieux fou* (Théâtre Favart, Paris, March 28, 1793); *Horatius Coclès* (Paris Opéra, Feb. 18, 1794); *Le Congrès des rois* (Théâtre Favart, Paris, Feb. 26, 1794; in collaboration with 11 other composers); *Mélidore et Phrosine* (Théâtre Favart, Paris, May 6, 1794); *Doria, ou La Tyrannie détruite* (Théâtre Favart, Paris, March 12, 1795); *La Caverne* (Théâtre Favart, Paris, Dec. 5, 1795); *La Jeunesse d'Henri IV* (Théâtre Favart, Paris, May 1, 1797; later known as *Le Jeune Henri*); *La Prise du pont de Lodi* (Feydeau, Paris, Dec. 15, 1797); *Adrien, empéreur de Rome* (Paris Opéra, June 4, 1799, later known as *Adrien*); *Ariodant* (Théâtre Favart, Paris, Oct. 11, 1799); *Épicure* (Théâtre Favart, Paris, March 14, 1800; in collaboration with Cherubini); *Bion* (Théâtre Favart, Paris, Dec. 27, 1800); *L'Irato, ou L'Emporté* (Opéra-Comique, Paris, Feb. 17, 1801); *Une folie* (Opéra-Comique, Paris, April 5, 1802); *Le Trésor supposé, ou Le Danger d'écouter aux portes* (Opéra-Comique, Paris, July 29, 1802); *Joanna* (Opéra-Comique, Paris, Nov. 23, 1802); *Héléna* (Opéra-Comique, Paris, March 1, 1803); *Le Baiser et la quittance, ou Une Aventure de garnison* (Opéra-Comique, Paris, June 18, 1803; in collaboration with Boieldieu, R. Kreutzer, and Nicolo); *L'Heureux malgré lui* (Opéra-Comique, Paris, Dec. 29, 1803); *Les 2 Aveugles de Tolède* (Opéra-Comique, Paris, Jan. 28, 1806); *Uthal* (Opéra-Comique, Paris, May 17, 1806); *Gabrielle d'Estrées, ou Les Amours d'Henri IV* (Opéra-Comique, Paris, June 25, 1806); *Joseph* (Opéra-Comique, Paris, Feb. 17, 1807); *Amphion, ou Les Amazones* (Paris Opéra, Dec. 17, 1811; later known as *Les Amazones, ou La Fondation de Thèbes*); *Le Prince troubadour* (Opéra-Comique, Paris, May 24, 1813); *L'Oriflamme* (Paris Opéra, Feb. 1, 1814; overture by Méhul; remainder in collaboration with H.-M. Berton, R. Kreutzer, and Paer); *La Journée aux aventures* (Opéra-Comique, Paris, Nov. 16, 1816); *Valentine de Milan* (Opéra-Comique, Paris, Nov. 28, 1822); the opera *Lausus* and the opera-ballet *L'Amour et Psyché* are considered doubtful works in the Méhul canon. BALLETS: *Le Jugement de Paris* (Paris Opéra, March 5, 1793; with music by Gluck, Haydn, and others); *La Dansomanie* (Paris Opéra, June 14, 1800; with music by Mozart and others); *Daphnis et Pandrose* (Paris Opéra, Jan. 14, 1803; with music by Gluck, Haydn, and others); *Persée et Andromède* (Paris Opéra, June 8, 1810; with music by Haydn, Paer, and Steibelt). He also composed several pieces of incidental music, many choral works (including the *Chant national du 14 juillet 1800*), numerous songs and patriotic works, etc. FOR ORCH.: Several symphs. including those numbered by Méhul as No. 1 in G minor (1809), No. 2 in D major (1809), No. 3 in C major (1809), and No. 4 in E major (1810). He also composed 2 books of keyboard sonatas: *3 sonates,* book 1 (1783), and *3 sonates,* book 2 (1788); in addition, a chamber music work entitled *Ouverture burlesque,* for Piano, Violin, 3 Mirlitons, Trumpet, and Percussion.

Meibom (or **Meibomius, Meiboom, Meybom**),

Marcus, erudite scholar; b. Tönning, Schleswig, c.1620; d. Utrecht, Feb. 15, 1710. He was for some years prof. at the Univ. of Uppsala; in 1674 visited England; lived thereafter principally in Utrecht. His chief work is *Antiquae musicae auctores septem, graece et latine, Marcus Meibomius restituit ac notis explicavit* (Amsterdam, 1652; 2 vols.); it contains treatises on music by Aristoxenos, Euclid (*Introductio harmonica*), Nicomachos, Gaudentius Philosophos, Bacchius Senior, Aristides Quintilianus, and M. Capella (Book IX of the *Satyricon*); until the publication of the new ed. of those authors by Karl Jan, Meibom's work was the only accessible source of information.

Meier, Johanna, American soprano; b. Chicago, Feb. 13, 1938. She was a scholarship student at the Manhattan School of Music in N.Y. She made her debut with the N.Y. City Opera in 1969 as the Countess in Strauss's *Capriccio;* during the next 10 years she sang the roles of the Marschallin, Tosca, Senta, Rosalinda, etc., with the N.Y. City Opera. In 1979 she made her Metropolitan Opera debut in N.Y. as Ariadne, and subsequently appeared there as the Marschallin, Senta, and Marguerite; also sang with the opera companies of Chicago, Cincinnati, Pittsburgh, Seattle, and Baltimore. In Europe, she had guest engagements in opera in Zürich, Vienna, Hamburg, and Berlin; made her Bayreuth debut as Isolde in 1981.

Melani, Jacopo, Italian opera composer; b. Pistoia, July 6, 1623; d. there, Aug. 19, 1676. He was a member of an exceptionally gifted family of Italian musicians; his 7 brothers were singers and composers. He became organist of the Pistoia Cathedral in 1645, and maestro di cappella there in 1657. He specialized in comic operas, of which the following, performed in Florence, are the most important: *Il Podestà di Colognole* (Dec. 1656), *Ercole in Tebe* (July 8, 1661), and *Il Girello* (Jan. 20, 1670); regarding the last, see the discussion by R. Weaver, "*Il Girello*, a 17th-century Burlesque Opera," in *Quadrivium*, XII/2 (1971).

Melartin, Erkki Gustaf, Finnish composer; b. Käkisälmi (Kexholm), Feb. 7, 1875; d. Pukinmäki (near Helsinki), Feb. 14, 1937. He was a pupil of Wegelius at the Cons. in Helsinki and of Robert Fuchs in Vienna; taught theory at the Helsinki Cons. (1898; 1901–7); succeeded Wegelius as director in 1911, and remained at this post until 1936. His compositions are marked by a lyrical strain, with thematic materials often drawn from Finnish folk songs.

Melba, Dame Nellie (stage name of **Mrs. Helen Porter Armstrong,** née **Mitchell**), famous Australian coloratura soprano; b. Burnley, near Richmond, May 19, 1861; d. Sydney, Feb. 23, 1931. Her father, who had decided objections to anything connected with the stage, was nevertheless fond of music and proud of his daughter's talent. When she was only 6 years old he allowed her to sing at a concert in the Melbourne Town Hall, but would not consent to her having singing lessons; instead, she was taught piano, violin, and harp, and even had instruction in harmony and composition. As she grew older she frequently played the organ in a local church, and was known among her friends as an excellent pianist, while all the time her chief desire was to study singing. Not until after her marriage in 1882 to Captain Charles Armstrong was she able to gratify her ambition, when she began to study with a local teacher, Cecchi; her first public appearance as a singer was on May 17, 1884, in a benefit concert in Melbourne. The next year her father received a government appointment in London, and she accompanied him, determined to begin an operatic career. Her first concert in London (June 1, 1886) convinced her of the necessity of further study, and she went to Mme. Marchesi in Paris. Her debut as Gilda at the Théâtre de La Monnaie in Brussels (Oct. 13, 1887) created a veritable sensation; the famous impresario Sir Augustus Harris immediately engaged her for the spring season at Covent Garden, where she appeared on May 24, 1888, as Lucia, arousing great enthusiasim; a similar success attended her appearance in Paris, where she sang Ophelia in Ambroise Thomas's *Hamlet* (May 8, 1889); St. Petersburg (1891); Milan (La Scala, 1893; immense triumph over a carefully planned opposition); Stockholm and Copenhagen (Oct. 1893); N.Y. (Metropolitan Opera, as Lucia, Dec. 4, 1893); Melbourne (Sept. 27, 1902). From her first appearance at Covent Garden she sang there off and on until 1914; besides being one of the most brilliant stars of several seasons at the Metropolitan Opera, she also sang with Walter Damrosch's Opera Co. (1898) and at Hammerstein's Manhattan Opera (1906–7 and 1908–9), and made several transcontinental concert tours of the U.S. Bemberg wrote for her *Elaine,* (1892), and Saint-Saëns, *Hélène* (1904), in both of which she created the title roles. In 1915 she began teaching at the Albert Street Conservatorium in Melbourne; returned to Covent Garden for appearances in 1919, 1923, and a farewell performance on June 8, 1926. Then she returned to Australia and retired from the stage. Melba was by nature gifted with a voice of extraordinary beauty and bell-like purity; through her art she made this fine instrument perfectly even throughout its entire compass (*b*-flat–*f*³) and wonderfully flexible, so that she executed the most difficult *fioriture* without the least effort. As an actress she did not rise above the conventional, and for this reason she was at her best in parts demanding brilliant coloratura (Gilda, Lucia, Violetta, Rosina, Lakmé, etc.). On a single occasion she attempted the dramatic role of Brünnhilde in *Siegfried* (Metropolitan Opera, N.Y., Dec. 30, 1896), and met with disaster. In 1918 she was created a Dame of the British Empire. She was a typical representative of the golden era of opera; a prima donna *assoluta,* she exercised her powers over the public with perfect self-assurance and a fine command of her singing voice. As a measure of Melba's universal popularity, it may be mentioned that her name was attached to a delicious dessert (Peach Melba) consisting of half a cooked peach served with vanilla ice cream and a clear raspberry sauce (Melba sauce); and also to Melba toast, a crisp, thinly sliced toasted bread, patented in 1929 by Bert Weil (1890–1965), president of the Devonsheer Melba Corp. A motion picture based on her life was produced in 1953, with Patrice Munsel as Melba. She wrote an autobiography, *Melodies and Memories* (London, 1925).

Melchior, Lauritz, celebrated tenor; b. Copenhagen, March 20, 1890; d. Santa Monica, Calif., March 18, 1973. He studied with Paul Bang at the Royal Opera School, Copenhagen; in 1913, made his operatic debut in *Pagliacci* (as a baritone) at the Royal Opera, where he was engaged from 1914–21; studied at the same time with Wilhelm Herold, and in 1918 appeared as a tenor; in 1921–23, he studied with Beigel in London, then with Grenzebach in Berlin and Anna Bahr-Mildenburg in Munich; made his London debut at Covent Garden on May 14, 1924; he studied the Bayreuth traditions under Kittel, at the invitation of Cosima and Siegfried Wagner, and made his first appearance at the Festspielhaus there on July 23, 1924, as Siegfried; he sang at Bayreuth regularly till 1931, and acquired the reputation of being one of the finest Wagnerian tenors. He sang Tannhäuser at his first appearance with the Metropolitan Opera, N.Y. (Feb. 17, 1926); remained on its roster until 1950, the 1927–28 season excepted; then settled in California. He became an American citizen on June 13, 1947.

Melkus, Eduard, Austrian violinist; b. Baden-bei-Wien, Sept. 1, 1928. He was educated at the Vienna Academy of Music and the Univ. of Vienna; also studied in Paris, Zürich, and Winterthur. He then played in several Swiss orchs. In 1965 he founded the Cappella Academica of Vienna, an ensemble devoted to performances of Baroque music on original instruments.

Mellers, Wilfrid (Howard), English musicologist and composer; b. Leamington, April 26, 1914. He enrolled in Leamington College and at Cambridge Univ. (1933–38); studied composition with Wellesz and Rubbra; then taught at Dartington Hall (1938–40) and Downing College, Cambridge (1945–48); subsequently was on the faculty of the Univ. of Birmingham (1948–59) and served as Andrew W. Mellon Professor of Music at the Univ. of Pittsburgh (1960–63). In 1964 he was appointed to the music faculty of York Univ.
WRITINGS: *Music and Society: England and the European Tradition* (London, 1946); *Studies in Contemporary Music* (London, 1947); *François Couperin and the French Classical Tradition* (London, 1950); *Music in the Making* (London, 1952); *Romanticism and the 20th Century* (London, 1957); *The Sonata Principle* (London, 1957); *Music in a New Found Land: Themes and Developments in the History of American Music* (London, 1964); *Harmonious Meeting: A Study of the Relationship between English Music, Poetry and Theatre, c.1600–1900* (London, 1965); *Caliban Reborn:*

Renewal in Twentieth-Century Music (N.Y., 1967); *Twilight of the Gods: The Music of the Beatles* (N.Y., 1973) *Bach and the Dance of God* (N.Y., 1980); *Beethoven and the Voice of God* (London, 1983).
WORKS: Operas: *The Tragical History of Christopher Marlowe* (1952); *The Ancient Wound* (Univ. of Victoria, British Columbia, July 27, 1970). Instrumental and vocal music: *Sinfonia ricercata* (1947); *Alba, in 9 Metamorphoses* for Flute and Orch. (1961); *Noctambule and Sun-Dance* for Wind Instruments (1962); *Voices and Creatures* for Speaker, Flute, and Percussion (1962); *De Vegetalibus et Animalibus* for Soprano, Clarinet, Violin, Cello, and Harp (1971); *Venery for 6 Plus* for Dancing Singers and Instruments (1972); *The Gates of the Dream* for Soloists, Chorus, and Orch. (York, May 8, 1974).

Menasce, Jacques de, Austrian pianist and composer; b. Bad Ischl, Austria, Aug. 19, 1905, of a French-Egyptian father and a German mother; d. Gstaad, Switzerland, Jan. 28, 1960. He studied in Vienna with Sauer (piano) and with J. Marx, Paul Pisk, and Alban Berg (composition). From 1932 until 1940 he gave concerts in Europe as a pianist; in 1941 he came to America, living mostly in N.Y., but continued his concert career in Europe.

Menchaca, Angel, Paraguayan music theorist; b. Asunción, March 1, 1855; d. Buenos Aires, May 8, 1924. He was trained as a jurist; also taught history and literature at the National College in Buenos Aires. In 1914 he publ. a provocative book, *Sistema teórico-gráfico de la música*, in which he proposed a new system of notation, employing a basic alphabet of 12 notes and dispensing with the established signatures, staff, etc. He toured Europe for the purpose of lecturing on this device; invented a special keyboard to facilitate its application. He was also a composer; his compositions include songs and school choruses.

Mendel, Arthur, eminent American music scholar; b. Boston, June 6, 1905; d. Newark, N.J., Oct. 14, 1979. He studied at Harvard Univ. (A.B., 1925); also took courses in theory with Nadia Boulanger in Paris (1925–27); returning to America, he was literary editor of G. Schirmer, Inc. (1930–38); also wrote music criticism in the *Nation* (1930–33); from 1936 to 1953 he conducted in N.Y. a chorus, The Cantata Singers, specializing in Baroque music; taught at the Dalcroze School of Music from 1938; was its president in 1947–50; also lectured at Columbia Univ. (1949) and the Univ. of Calif., Berkeley (1951); he was then prof. of music and chairman of the music dept. at Princeton Univ. (1952–67); held the Henry Putnam Univ. Professorship there from 1969 to 1973. He edited (with H.T. David) the valuable "documentary biography" *The Bach Reader* (N.Y., 1945; revised N.Y., 1966); edited Bach's *St. John Passion* (1951), Schütz's *Christmas Story* (1949) and *Musicalische Exequien* (1957), and other works of the Baroque period. He publ. numerous important articles on the history of pitch, reprinted in *Studies* *in the History of Musical Pitch* (Amsterdam, 1969) and also promoted the possibility of music analysis with the aid of a computer, publ. in *Computers and the Humanities* (1969–70). A Festschrift, *Studies in Renaissance and Baroque Music in Honor of Arthur Mendel*, ed. by R. Marshall, was publ. in Kassel in 1974.

Mendel, Hermann, German music lexicographer; b. Halle, Aug. 6, 1834; d. Berlin, Oct. 26, 1876. He was a pupil of Mendelssohn and Moscheles in Leipzig, and of Wieprecht in Berlin. In 1870 he founded and edited the *Deutsche Musiker-Zeitung;* also edited *Mode's Opernbibliothek* (about 90 librettos, with commentaries and biographies of composers) and a *Volksliederbuch.* He publ. 2 small books on Meyerbeer (1868, 1869). His great work was the *Musikalisches Conversations-Lexikon,* which he began to publ. in 1870, but was able to continue only to the letter M; the rest was completed by August Reissmann; the entire edition was in 11 vols.; a supplementary vol. was publ. in 1883.

Mendelsohn, Alfred, Rumanian composer; b. Bucharest, Feb. 17, 1910; d. there, May 9, 1966. He studied in Vienna with Joseph Marx, Franz Schmidt, Egon Wellesz and others (1927–31), and at the Bucharest Cons. with Jora (1931–32). From 1946 to 1954 he was conductor of the Rumanian Opera in Bucharest; in 1949 was prof. at the Bucharest Cons., remaining there until his death. An exceptionally prolific composer, he produced a great amount of highly competent, technically accomplished music. Influenced primarily by the programmatic Romanticism of the Vienna School, he also probed the potentialities of motivic structures, suggesting the serial concepts of modern constructivists while remaining faithful to basic tonalitarianism.

Mendelssohn, Arnold, German composer; son of a cousin of **Felix Mendelssohn**; b. Ratibor, Dec. 26, 1855; d. Darmstadt, Feb. 19, 1933. He studied law at the Univ. of Tübingen; then entered the Hochschule für Musik in Berlin, where he studied with Löschhorn (piano), Haupt (organ), Grell, Kiel, and Taubert (composition). He was subsequently an instructor in Bielefeld (1883–85); a prof. at the Cologne Cons. (1885–90); then director of church music in Darmstadt. In 1912 he was appointed a prof. at the Hoch Cons. in Frankfurt; among his pupils there was Hindemith. He wrote 3 operas: *Elsi, die seltsame Magd* (Cologne, 1896), *Der Bärenhäuter* (Berlin, Feb. 9, 1900), and *Die Minneburg* (Mannheim, 1909); 2 cantatas: *Aus tiefer Not* and *Auf meinen lieben Gott;* a German Mass for 8-part Chorus a cappella; 3 symphs.; a Violin Concerto; 2 string quartets; a Cello Sonata; 2 piano sonatas; several sets of songs. He edited Schütz's oratorios and some of Monteverdi's madrigals. His book on esthetics, *Gott, Welt und Kunst,* was brought out by W. Ewald (Wiesbaden, 1949).

Mendelssohn, Fanny. See **Hensel, Fanny Cäcilia.**

Mendelssohn, Felix (full name, **Jacob Ludwig Felix Mendelssohn-Bartholdy**), illustrious German composer; b. Hamburg, Feb. 3, 1809; d. Leipzig, Nov. 4, 1847. He was a grandson of the philosopher Moses Mendelssohn and the son of the banker Abraham Mendelssohn; his mother was Lea Salomon; the family was Jewish, but upon its settlement in Berlin the father decided to become a Protestant and added Bartholdy to his surname. Mendelssohn received his first piano lessons from his mother; subsequently studied piano with Ludwig Berger and violin with Carl Wilhelm Henning and Eduard Rietz; he also had regular lessons in foreign languages and in painting (he showed considerable talent in drawing with pastels); he also had piano lessons with Marie Bigot in Paris, where he went with his father for a brief stay in 1816. His most important teacher in his early youth was Carl Friedrich Zelter, who understood the magnitude of Mendelssohn's talent; in 1821 Zelter took him to Weimar and introduced him to Goethe, who took considerable interest in the boy Mendelssohn after hearing him play. Zelter arranged for Mendelssohn to become a member of the Singakademie in Berlin in 1819 as an alto singer; on Sept. 18, 1819, Mendelssohn's *19th Psalm* was performed by the Akademie. In 1825 Mendelssohn's father took him again to Paris to consult Cherubini on Mendelssohn's prospects in music; however, he returned to Berlin, where he had better opportunities for development. Mendelssohn was not only a precocious musician, both in performing and in composition; what is perhaps without a parallel in music history is the extraordinary perfection of his works written during adolescence. He played in public for the first time at the age of 9, on Oct. 28, 1818, in Berlin, performing the piano part of a trio by Wölffl. He wrote a remarkable octet at the age of 16; at 17 he composed the overture for the incidental music to Shakespeare's *A Midsummer Night's Dream,* an extraordinary manifestation of his artistic maturity, showing a mastery of form equal to that of the remaining numbers of the work, which were composed 15 years later. Mendelssohn proved his great musicianship when he conducted Bach's *St. Matthew Passion* in the Berlin Singakademie on March 11, 1829, an event that gave an impulse to the revival of Bach's vocal music. In the spring of 1829 Mendelssohn made his first journey to England, where he conducted his Symph. in C minor (seated, after the fashion of the time, at the keyboard); later he performed in London the solo part in Beethoven's "Emperor" Concerto; he then traveled through Scotland, where he found inspiration for the composition of his overture *Fingal's Cave (Hebrides),* which he conducted for the first time during his 2nd visit to London, on May 14, 1832; 10 days later he played in London the solo part of his G minor Concerto and his *Capriccio brillante.* He became a favorite of the English public; Queen Victoria was one of his most fervent admirers; altogether he made 10 trips to England as a pianist, conductor, and composer. In 1830–32 he traveled in Germany, Austria, Italy, and Switzerland, and also went to Paris. In May 1833 he led the Lower-Rhine Music Festival in Düsseldorf; then conducted at Cologne in June 1835. He was still a very young man when, in 1835, he was offered the conductorship of the celebrated Gewandhaus Orch. in Leipzig; the Univ. of Leipzig bestowed upon him an honorary degree of Dr.Phil. Mendelssohn's leadership of the Gewandhaus Orch. was of the greatest significance for the development of German musical culture; he engaged the violin virtuoso Ferdinand David as concertmaster of the orch., which soon became the most prestigious symph. organization in Germany. On March 28, 1837, Mendelssohn married Cécile Charlotte Sophie Jeanrenaud of Frankfurt, the daughter of a French Protestant clergyman. Five children (Carl, Marie, Paul, Felix, and Elisabeth) were born to them, and their marriage was exceptionally happy. At the invitation of King Friedrich Wilhelm IV, Mendelssohn went in 1841 to Berlin to take charge of the music of the court and in the Cathedral; Mendelssohn received the title of Royal Generalmusikdirektor, but residence in Berlin was not required. Returning to Leipzig in 1842, Mendelssohn organized the famous "Conservatorium." Its splendid faculty comprised—besides Mendelssohn himself, who taught piano—ensemble playing, and later composition—Schumann, who taught classes in piano and composition; Hauptmann, in music theory; David, in violin; Becker, in organ; and Plaidy and Wenzel, in piano. The Conservatorium was officially opened on April 3, 1843. The financial nucleus of the foundation was a bequest from Blümner of 20,000 thaler, left at the disposal of the King of Saxony for the promotion of the fine arts, and Mendelssohn made a special journey to Dresden to petition the King on behalf of the Leipzig Cons. During Mendelssohn's frequent absences, the Gewandhaus Concerts were conducted by Hiller (1843–44) and Gade (1844–45). In the summer of 1844 Mendelssohn conducted the Phil. Concerts in London; this was his 8th visit to England; during his 9th visit he conducted the first performance of his oratorio *Elijah* in Birmingham, on Aug. 26, 1846. It was in England that the "Wedding March" from Mendelssohn's music to *A Midsummer Night's Dream* began to be used to accompany the bridal procession; it became particularly fashionable when it was played at the wedding of the Princess Royal in 1858. Mendelssohn made his 10th and last visit to England in the spring of 1847; this was a sad period of his life, for his favorite sister, Fanny, died on May 14, 1847. Mendelssohn's own health began to deteriorate, and he died in Leipzig at the age of 38. The exact cause of his early death is not determined; he suffered from severe migraines and chills before he died, but no evidence could be produced by the resident physicians for either a stroke or heart failure. A detailed account of Mendelssohn's illness and death is found in Dieter Kerner's *Krankheiten grosser Musiker* (Stuttgart, 1969; vol. 2, pp. 23–44). The news of Mendelssohn's death produced a profound shock in the world of music; not only in Germany and England, where he was personally known and beloved, but in distant America and Russia as well, there was genuine sorrow among musicians. Mendelssohn societies were formed all over the world; in America the Mendelssohn Quintette Club was founded in 1849. A Mendelssohn Scholarship was established in England in 1856; its first recipient was Arthur Sullivan.

Mendelssohn's influence on German, English, American, and Russian music was great and undiminishing through the years; his symphs., concertos, chamber music, piano pieces, and songs became perennial favorites in concerts and at home, the most popular works being the overture *Hebrides,* the ubiquitously played Violin Concerto, the *Songs without Words* for Piano, and the "Wedding March" from incidental music to *A Midsummer Night's Dream.* Professional music historians are apt to place Mendelssohn below the ranks of his great contemporaries, Schumann, Chopin, and Liszt; in this exalted company Mendelssohn is often regarded as a phenomenon of Biedermeier culture. A barbaric ruling was made by the Nazi regime to forbid performances of Mendelssohn's music as that of a Jew; his very name was removed from music history books and encyclopedias publ. in Germany during that time. This shameful episode was of but a transitory nature, however; if anything, it served to create a greater appreciation of Mendelssohn's genius.

WORKS: For the stage: *Ich, J. Mendelssohn . . . ,* Lustspiel (1820); *Die Soldatenliebschaft,* comic opera (1820; Wittenberg, April 28, 1962); *Die beiden Pädagogen,* singspiel (1821; Berlin, May 27, 1962); *Die wandernden Komödianten,* comic opera (1822; dialogue not extant); *Der Onkel aus Boston oder Die beiden Neffen,* comic opera (1823; Berlin, Feb. 3, 1824; dialogue not extant); *Die Hochzeit des Camacho,* op. 10, opera (1825; Berlin, April 29, 1827; dialogue not extant); *Die Heimkehr aus der Fremde,* op. 89, Liederspiel (1829, written for the silver wedding anniversary of Mendelssohn's parents, perf. at their home, Berlin, Dec. 26, 1829); *Der standhafte,* incidental music to Calderón's play (1833); *Trala. A frischer Bua bin i* (1833); *Ruy Blas,* incidental music to Hugo's play (1839); *Antigone,* op. 55, incidental music to Sophocles' play (Potsdam, Oct. 28, 1841); *A Midsummer Night's Dream,* op. 61, incidental music to Shakespeare's play (1842; Potsdam, Oct. 14, 1843); *Oedipus at Colonos,* op. 93, incidental music to Sophocles' play (Potsdam, Nov. 1, 1845); *Athalie,* op. 74, incidental music to Racine's play (Berlin-Charlottenburg, Dec. 1, 1845); *Lorelei,* op. 98, opera (begun in childhood but unfinished; *Ave Maria,* a vintage chorus, and finale to Act I only; Birmingham, Sept. 8, 1852).

Oratorios: *St. Paul,* op. 36 (1834–36; Düsseldorf, May 22, 1836, composer conducting); *Elijah,* op. 70 (1846; Birmingham, Aug. 26, 1846, composer conducting); *Christus,* op. 97 (unfinished).

Other sacred music: *Die Himmel erzählen* for 5 Voices (1820); *Gott, du bist unsre Zuversicht* for 5 Voices (1820); *Ich will den Herrn nach seiner Gerechtigkeit preisen* for 4 Voices (1820); *Tag für Tag sei Gott gepriesen* for 5 Voices (1820); *Das Gesetz des Herrn ist ohne Wandel* for 5 Voices (1821–22); *Er hat der Sonne eine Hütte gemacht* for 5 Voices (1821–22); *Jube Domine* for Solo Voices and Double Chorus (1822); *Psalm LXVI* for Double Female Chorus and Basso Continuo (1822); Magnificat in D major for Chorus and Orch. (1822); *Kyrie* in C minor for Solo Voices and Chorus (1823); *Jesus, meine Zuversicht* for Solo Voices and Chorus (1824); *Salve Regina* in E-flat major for Soprano and Strings (1824); 2 sacred pieces for Chorus: *Wie gross ist des Allmächt'gen Güte* (1824) and *Allein Gott in der Höh' sey Ehr* (1824); *Te Deum* in D major for Double Chorus and Basso Continuo (1826); *Jesu, meine Freude,* chorale cantata for Double Chorus and Strings; *Tu es Petrus* for Chorus and Orch., op. 111 (1827); *Ave Maria Stella* for Soprano and Orch. (1828); *Hora est* for 16 Voices and Organ (1828); 3 sacred pieces for Tenor, Chorus, and Organ, op. 23: *Aus tiefer Not, Ave Maria,* and *Mitten; Psalm CXV* for Solo Voices, Chorus, and Orch., op. 31 (1830); *Zum Feste der Dreieinigkeit (O beata et benedicta)* for 3 Sopranos and Organ (1830); 3 motets for Female Chorus and Organ, op. 39 (1830): *Hear my prayer, O Lord (Veni, Domine), O praise the Lord (Laudate pueri),* and *O Lord, thou hast searched me out (Surrexit Pastor); Verleih uns Frieden* for Chorus and Orch. (1831); *Te Deum* in A major for Solo Voices, Chorus, and Organ (1832); *Lord have mercy upon us* for Chorus (1833); 2 sacred choruses for Male Chorus, op. 115 (1833); *Responsorium et hymnus* for Male Voices, Cello, and Organ, op. 121 (1833); *Psalm XLII* for Solo Voices, Chorus, and Orch., op. 42 (1837); *Psalm XCV* for Tenor, Chorus, and Orch., op. 46 (1838); *Psalm V, Lord hear the voice* for Chorus (1839); *Psalm XXXI, Defend me, Lord* for Chorus (1839); *Hymn* in A major for Solo Voice, Chorus, and Orch., op. 96 (1840); *Psalm CXIV* for Double Chorus and Orch., op. 51 (1839); *Geistliches Lied* in E-flat major for Solo Voice, Chorus, and Organ (1840); *Psalm C, Jauchzet den Herrn* for Chorus (1842); *Herr Gott, dich loben wir* for Solo Voices, Chorus, Organ, and Orch. (1843); *Psalm XCVIII* for Double Chorus and Orch., op. 91 (1843); *Ehre sei dem Vater* for 8 Voices (1844); *Hear my prayer,* hymn for Soprano, Chorus, and Organ (1844); *Ehre sei dem Vater* in C major for 4 Voices (1845); *Er kommt aus dem kindlichen Alter der Welt* for 6 Voices (1846); *Lauda Sion* for Chorus and Orch., op. 73 (1846; Liège, June 11, 1846); *Die deutsche Liturgie* for 8 Voices (1846); *3 English Church Pieces* for Solo Voices and Chorus, op. 69 (1847): *Nunc dimittis, Jubilate,* and *Magnificat;* 3 Psalms for Solo Voices and Double Chorus, op. 78: *Psalm II* (1843), *Psalm XLIII* (1844), and *Psalm XXII* (1844); 6 *Anthems* for Double Chorus, op. 79: *Rejoice, O ye people; Thou, Lord, our refuge hast been* (1843); *Above all praises* (1846); *Lord, on our offences* (1844); *Let our hearts be joyful* (1846); *For our offences* (1844). Other works include: *Ach Gott vom Himmel sieh darein,* chorale cantata for Solo Voices, Chorus, and Orch.; *Cantique pour l'Eglise wallonne de Francfort (Venez chantez)* for 4 Voices; *Christe, du Lamm Gottes,* chorale cantata for Chorus and Orch.; *Gloria patri (Ehre sei dem Vater)* for 4 Voices; *Glory be to the Father* for 4 Voices; *Gloria* in E-flat major for Solo Voices, Chorus, and Orch. (unfinished); *Kyrie* for Chorus and Orch.; *Kyrie* in A major for 8 Voices; *Vom Himmel hoch,* chorale cantata for Solo Voices, Chorus, and Orch.; etc.

SECULAR CANTATAS: *In feierlichen Tönen,* wedding cantata for Soprano, Alto, Tenor, Chorus, and Piano (1820); *Grosse Festmusik zum Dürerfest* for Solo Voices, Chorus, and Orch. (Berlin, April 18, 1828); *Begrüssung (Humboldt Cantata),* festival music for Solo Male Voices, Male Chorus, and Wind (Berlin, Sept. 18, 1828); *Die erste Walpurgisnacht* for Chorus and Orch., op. 60 (1832; Berlin, Jan. 1833; revised 1843; Leipzig, Feb. 2, 1843); *Gott segne Sachsenland* for Male Voices and Wind (Dresden, June 7, 1843); *An die Künstler,* festival song for Male Voices and Brass, op. 68 (Cologne, June 1846).

CHORAL SONGS: *Einst ins Schlaraffenland zogen* for 4 Male Voices (1820); *Lieb und Hoffnung* for Male Voices (1820); *Jägerlied (Kein bess're Lust in dieser Zeit)* for 4 Male Voices (1822); *Lob des Weines (Seht, Freunde, die Gläser)* for Solo Male Voices and Male Chorus (1822); *Lass es heut am edlen Ort* for 4 Male Voices (1828); *Worauf kommt es überall an* for 4 Male Voices (1837); *Im Freien zu singen* for Mixed Voices, op. 41: 1, *Im Walde* (1838); 2, *Entflieh mit mir* (1838); 3, *Es fiel ein Reif* (1838); 4, *Auf ihrem Grab* (1838); 5, *Mailied* (1838); 6, *Auf dem See* (1838); *Der erste Frühlingstag* for Mixed Voices, op. 48 (1839): 1, *Frühlingsahnung;* 2, *Die Primel;* 3, *Frühlingsfeier;* 4, *Lerchengesang;* 5, *Morgengebet;* 6, *Herbstlied; Ersatz für Unbestand* for 4 Male Voices (1839); *Festgesang* for Male Voices (Leipzig, June 25, 1840; No. 2 adapted by W.H. Cummings for *Hark! the Herald Angels Sing);* 6 male choruses, op. 50: 1, *Türkisches Schenkenlied* (1839–40); 2, *Der Jäger Abschied* (1840); 3, *Sommerlied* (1839–40); 4, *Wasserfahrt* (1839–40); 5, *Liebe und Wein* (1839); 6, *Wanderlied* (1842); *Nachtgesang* for 4 Male Voices (1842); *Die Stiftungsfeier* for 4 Male Voices (1842); *Im Grünen* for Mixed Voices, op. 59: 1, *Im Grünen* (1837); 2, *Frühzeitiger Frühling* (1843); 3, *Abschied vom Wald* (1843); 4, *Die Nachtigall* (1843); 5, *Ruhetal* (1843); 6, *Jagdlied* (1843); *Sahst du ihn herniederschweben,* funeral song for Mixed Voices, op. 116 (1845); *Der Sänger* (1845; Leipzig, Nov. 10, 1846); *Wandersmann* for Male Voices, op. 75: 1, *Der frohe Wandersmann* (1844); 2, *Abendständchen* (1839); 3, *Trinklied;* 4, *Abschiedstafel* (1844); 4 male choruses, op. 76: 1, *Das Lied vom braven Mann;* 2, *Rheinweinlied* (1844); 3, *Lied für die Deutschen in Lyon* (1846); 4, *Comitat;* 6 choruses for Mixed Voices, op. 88: 1, *Neujahrslied* (1844); 2, *Der Glückliche* (1843); 3, *Hirtenlied* (1839); 4, *Die Waldvögelein* (1843); 5, *Deutschland* (1839–43); 6, *Der wandernde Musikant* (1840); 4 choruses for Mixed Voices, op. 100: 1, *Andenken* (1844); 2, *Lob des Frühlings* (1843); 3, *Frühlingslied* (1843–44); 4, *Im Wald* (1839); 4 male choruses, op. 120: 1, *Jagdlied* (1837); 2, *Morgengruss des Thüringischen Sängerbundes* (1847); 3, *Im Süden;* 4, *Zigeunerlied; Lob der Trunkenheit (Trunken müssen wir alle sein)* for 4 Male Voices; *Musikantenprügelei (Seht doch diese Fiedlerbanden)* for 2 Male Voices.—Also concert arias: *Che vuoi mio cor?* for Mezzo-soprano and Strings, and *Infelice* for Soprano and Orch., op. 94 (1834; revised 1843).

SONGS: *Ave Maria* (1820); *Raste Krieger, Krieg ist aus* (1820); *Die Nachtigall (Da ging ich hin)* (1821–22); *Der Verlassene (Nacht ist um mich her)* (1821–

22); *Von allen deinen zarten Gaben* (1822); *Wiegenlied (Schlummre sanft)* (1822); *Sanft weh'n im Hauch der Abendluft* (1822); *Der Wasserfall (Rieselt hernieder)* (1823); 12 songs, op. 8 (1828): 1, *Minnelied;* 2, *Das Heimweh* (by Fanny Mendelssohn); 3, *Italien* (by Fanny Mendelssohn); 4, *Erntelied;* 5, *Pilgerspruch;* 6, *Frühlingslied;* 7, *Maienlied;* 8, *Andres Maienlied (Hexenlied);* 9, *Abendlied;* 10, *Romanze;* 11, *Im Grünen;* 12, *Suleika und Hatem* (by Fanny Mendelssohn); *The Garland (Der Blumenkranz)* (1829); 12 songs, op. 9 (1829–30): 1, *Frage;* 2, *Geständnis;* 3, *Wartend;* 4, *Im Frühling;* 5, *Im Herbst;* 6, *Scheidend;* 7, *Sehnsucht* (by Fanny Mendelssohn); 8, *Frühlingsglaube;* 9, *Ferne;* 10, *Verlust* (by Fanny Mendelssohn); 11, *Entsagung;* 12, *Die Nonne* (by Fanny Mendelssohn); 4 songs (1830): 1, *Der Tag (Sanft entschwanden mir);* 2, *Reiterlied (Immer fort);* 3, *Abschied (Leb wohl mein Lieb);* 4, *Der Bettler (Ich danke Gott dir); Seemanns Scheidelied* (1831); *Weihnachtslied (Auf schicke dich recht feierlich)* (1832); 6 songs, op. 19a (1830–34): 1, *Frühlingslied;* 2, *Das erste Veilchen;* 3, *Winterlied;* 4, *Neue Liebe;* 5, *Gruss;* 6, *Reiselied; Mailied (Ich weiss mir'n Mädchen)* (1834); 2 romances: *There be none of beauty's daughters* (1833) and *Sun of the Sleepless* (1834); 2 songs: *Das Waldschloss* (1835) and *Pagenlied* (1835); 6 songs, op. 34 (1834–36): 1, *Minnelied;* 2, *Auf Flügeln des Gesanges;* 3, *Frühlingslied;* 4, *Suleika;* 5, *Sonntagslied;* 6, *Reiselied; Lied einer Freundin (Zarter Blumen leicht Gewinde)* (1837); *Im Kahn* (1837); *O könnt ich zu dir fliegen* (1838); 6 songs, op. 47 (1832–39): 1, *Minnelied;* 2, *Morgengruss;* 3, *Frühlingslied;* 4, *Volkslied;* 5, *Der Blumenstrauss;* 6, *Bei der Wiege;* 2 songs: *Todeslied der Bojaren* (1840) and *Ich hör ein Vöglein* (1841); 6 songs, op. 57 (1839–43): 1, *Altdeutsches Lied;* 2, *Hirtenlied;* 3, *Suleika;* 4, *O Jugend;* 5, *Venetianisches Gondellied;* 6, *Wanderlied;* 6 songs, op. 71 (1842–47): 1, *Tröstung;* 2, *Frühlingslied;* 3, *An die Entferne;* 4, *Schilflied;* 5, *Auf der Wanderschaft;* 6, *Nachtlied;* 3 songs, op. 84 (1831–39): 1, *Da lieg' ich unter den Bäumen;* 2, *Herbstlied;* 3, *Jagdlied;* 6 songs, op. 86 (1831–51): 1, *Es lauschte des Laub;* 2, *Morgenlied;* 3, *Die Liebende schreibt;* 4, *Allnächtlich im Traume;* 5, *Der Mond;* 6, *Altdeutsches Frühlingslied;* 6 songs, op. 99: 1, *Erster Verlust;* 2, *Die Sterne schau'n;* 3, *Lieblingsplätzchen;* 4, *Das Schifflein;* 5, *Wenn sich zwei Herzen scheiden;* 6, *Es weiss und rät es doch keiner;* 2 sacred songs, op. 112: *Doch der Herr, er leitet die Irrenden recht* and *Der du die Menschen lässest sterben;* also *Des Mädchens Klage; Warnung vor dem Rhein; Der Abendsegen (The Evening Service); Gretchen (Meine Ruh ist hin); Lieben und Schweigen (Ich flocht ein Kränzlein schöner Lieder); Es rauscht der Wald; Vier trübe Monden sind entfloh'n; Weinend seh' ich in die Nacht; Weiter, rastlos atemlos vorüber.*—Vocal duets: *Ein Tag sagt es dem andern* for Soprano and Alto (1821); 6 duets, op. 63 (1836–45): 1, *Ich wollt' meine Lieb';* 2, *Abschiedslied der Zugvögel;* 3, *Gruss;* 4, *Herbstlied;* 5, *Volkslied;* 6, *Maiglöckchen und die Blümelein;* 3 duets, op. 77 (1836–47): 1, *Sonntagsmorgen;* 2, *Das Aehrenfeld;* 3, *Lied aus "Ruy Blas";* 3 folk songs: 1, *Wie kann ich froh und lustig sein;* 2, *Abendlied;* 3, *Wasserfahrt;* also

various canons.

FOR ORCH.: 13 youthful sinfonias for Strings: No. 1, in C major (1821); No. 2, in D major (1821); No. 3, in E minor (1821); No. 4, in C minor (1821); No. 5, in B-flat major (1821); No. 6, in E-flat major (1821); No. 7, in D minor (1821–22); No. 8, in D major (1822); No. 9, in C major (1823); No. 10, in B minor (1823); No. 11, in F major (1823); No. 12, in G minor (1823); No. 13, in C minor (1823; one movement only); symphs.: No. 1, in C minor, op. 11 (1824); No. 2, in B-flat major, a symph.-cantata for Solo Voices, Chorus, and Orch., *Lobgesang* or *Hymn of Praise,* op. 52 (Leipzig, June 25, 1840, composer conducting); No. 3, in A minor, *Scottish,* op. 56 (1830–42; Leipzig, March 3, 1842, composer conducting); No. 4, in A major, *Italian,* op. 90 (London, May 13, 1833, composer conducting); No. 5, in D major, *Reformation,* op. 107 (1830–32; Berlin, Nov. 15, 1832, composer conducting); Violin Concerto in D minor for Strings (1822; Yehudi Menuhin gave its first perf. from the MS, N.Y., Feb. 4, 1952); Piano Concerto in A minor for Strings (1822); Concerto in D minor for Violin, Piano, and Strings (1823); Concerto in E major for 2 Pianos and Orch. (1823; Berlin, Nov. 14, 1824); Concerto in A-flat major for 2 Pianos and Orch. (1824; Stettin, Feb. 20, 1827); Overture in C major for Wind Instruments, op. 24 (1824); *Capriccio brillant* in B minor for Piano and Orch., op. 22 (1825–26; London, May 25, 1832); Overture (*Trumpet* Overture) in C major, op. 101 (1826; revised 1833); *Ein Sommernachtstraum,* overture for Shakespeare's *A Midsummer Night's Dream,* op. 21 (1826; Stettin, April 29, 1827); *Meeresstille und glückliche Fahrt (Calm Sea and Prosperous Voyage),* overture after Goethe, op. 27 (Berlin, April 18, 1828); *Die Hebriden or Fingals Höhle (The Hebrides or Fingal's Cave),* overture, op. 26 (1830; London, May 14, 1832); Piano Concerto No. 1, in G minor, op. 25 (Munich, Oct. 17, 1831, composer soloist); *Die schöne Melusine (The Fair Melusina),* overture after Grillparzer, op. 32 (1833; London, April 7, 1834); *Rondo brillant* in E-flat major for Piano and Orch., op. 29 (1834); *Trauermarsch* in A minor for Wind, op. 103 (1836); Piano Concerto No. 2, in D minor, op. 40 (Birmingham, Sept. 1837, composer soloist); *Serenade* and *Allegro giocoso,* in B minor, for Piano and Orch., op. 43 (1838); *Ruy Blas,* overture after Hugo, op. 95 (Leipzig, March 1839); March in D major, op. 108 (1841); Violin Concerto in E minor, op. 64 (1844; Leipzig, March 13, 1845; Ferdinand David, soloist; composer conducting).

CHAMBER MUSIC: Trio in C minor for Violin, Viola, and Piano (1820); Presto in F major for Violin and Piano (1820); Violin Sonata in F major (1820); 15 fugues for String Quartet (1821); Piano Quartet in D minor (1822); Piano Quartet No. 1, in C minor, op. 1 (1822); String Quartet in E-flat major (1823); Piano Quartet No. 2, in F minor, op. 2 (1823); Viola Sonata in C minor (1824); Sextet in D major for Violin, 2 Violas, Cello, Double Bass, and Piano, op. 110 (1824); Clarinet Sonata in E-flat major (1824); Piano Quartet No. 3, in B minor, op. 3 (1825); Violin Sonata in F minor, op. 4 (1825); Octet in E-flat major for 4 Violins, 2 Violas, and 2 Cellos, op. 20 (1825); Quintet No. 1, in A major, for 2 Violins, 2 Violas, and Cello, op. 18 (1826; revised 1832); String Quartet No. 2, in

A major, op. 13 (1827); Fugue in E-flat major for String Quartet (1827); Fugue in E-flat major for String Quartet, op. 81/4 (1827); *Variations concertantes* for Cello and Piano, op. 17 (1829); String Quartet No. 1, in E-flat major, op. 12 (1829); *The Evening Bell* for Harp and Piano (1829); Concert Piece in F major for Clarinet, Basset Horn, and Piano or Orch., op. 113 (1833); Concert Piece in D minor for Clarinet and Basset Horn, op. 114 (1833); string quartets: Nos. 3–5, op. 44 (1837–38); Violin Sonata in F major (1838); Cello Sonata No. 1, in B-flat major, op. 45 (1838); Piano Trio No. 1, in D minor, op. 49 (1839); *Capriccio* in E minor for String Quartet, op. 81/3 (1843); Cello Sonata No. 2, in D major, op. 58 (1843); Quintet No. 2, in B-flat major, op. 87 (1845); Piano Trio No. 2, in C minor, op. 66 (1845); *Lied ohne Worte* in D major for Cello and Piano, op. 109 (1845); String Quartet No. 6, in F minor, op. 80 (1847); *Andante* in E major for String Quartet, op. 81/1 (1847); *Scherzo* in A minor for String Quartet, op. 8½ (1847).

For piano: *Andante* in F major (1820); piano piece in E minor (1820); 2 little pieces (1820); 2 little pieces (1820); 5 little pieces (1820); *Largo-Allegro* in C minor (1820); *Recitativo (Largo)* in D minor (1820); Sonata in F minor (1820); Sonata in A minor (1820); *Presto* in C minor (1820); Sonata in E minor (1820); 2 studies (1820); *Allegro* in A minor (1821); Study in C major (1821); Sonata in G minor, op. 105 (1821); *Largo-Allegro molto* in C minor/major (1821–22); 3 fugues: D minor, D minor, and B minor (1822); *Allegro* in D minor (1823); *Fantasia (Adagio)* in C minor (1823); *Rondo capriccioso* in E major, op. 14 (1824); *Capriccio* in F-sharp minor, op. 5 (1825); Fugue in C-sharp minor (1826); Sonata in E major, op. 6 (1826); *7 charakteristische Stücke*, op. 7 (1827); *Fantasia* in E major, on "The Last Rose of Summer," op. 15 (1827); Sonata in B-flat major, op. 106 (1827); Fugue in E minor (1827); *Scherzo* in B minor (1829); *3 fantaisies ou caprices*, op. 16 (1829); *Andante* in A major (1830); *Lieder ohne Worte (Songs without Words)*: 8 books, opp. 19 (1829–30), 30 (1833–34), 38 (1836–37), 53 (1839–41), 62 (1842–44), 67 (1843–45), 85 (1834–45), 102 (1842–45); *Fantasia (Sonate écossaise)* in F-sharp minor, op. 28 (1833); *3 Caprices*, op. 33 (1833–35); *Scherzo a capriccio* in F-sharp minor (1835–36); Study in F minor (1836); *Andante* in A-flat major (1836); *Lied* in F-sharp minor (1836); *Prelude* in F minor (1836); *3 Preludes*, op. 104a (1836); 6 *Preludes* and *Fugues*, op. 35 (1832–37); *Gondellied (Barcarole)* in A major (1837); *Capriccio* in E major, op. 118 (1837); *Albumblatt (Lied ohne Worte)* in E minor, op. 117 (1837); *Andante cantabile* and *Presto agitato*, in B major (1838); 3 Studies, op. 104b (1834–38); *Prelude* and *Fugue* in E minor (1827–41); *Variations sérieuses* in D minor, op. 54 (1841); *Variations* in E-flat major, op. 82 (1841); *Variations* in B-flat major, op. 83 (1841); *Kinderstücke (Christmas Pieces)*, op. 72 (1842–47); *Perpetuum mobile* in C major, op. 119; etc.—For Piano Duet: *Lento-Vivace* in G minor (1820); *Fantasia* in D minor (1824); *Allegro brillant* in A major, op. 92 (1841); *Variations* in B-flat major, op. 83a (1841).— For 2 Pianos: *Duo concertant:* Variations on the march from Weber's *Preciosa* (1833; with Mos-

cheles).—Also several works for organ, including 3 *Preludes* and *Fugues*, op. 37 (1837), and 6 sonatas, op. 65 (1844–45).

Mendelssohn, Felix Robert, German cellist, great-grandnephew of the famous composer; b. Berlin, Sept. 27, 1896; d. Baltimore, May 15, 1951. He studied at the Stern Cons.; later taught cello there. In 1936 he settled in the U.S.; taught in N.Y.; in 1941 joined the Baltimore Symph. Orch. He died in Cadoa Hall, Baltimore, while playing Dohnányi's *Konzertstück*.

Mengelberg, Karel, Dutch composer and conductor; nephew of **Willem Mengelberg;** b. Utrecht, July 18, 1902. He studied with Pijper and later took a course at the Hochschule für Musik in Berlin. He conducted theater orchs. in provincial German towns and was a musician with Berlin Radio (1930–33); subsequently was conductor of the municipal band in Barcelona (1933); then went to Kiev, Russia, where he was in charge of the music dept. in the Ukrainian film studio. He returned to Amsterdam in 1938. WORKS: 2 ballets: *Bataille* (1922) and *Parfait Amour* (1945); *3 songs from Tagore's "The Gardener"* for Soprano and Orch. (1925); String Quartet (1938); Sonata for Solo Oboe (1939); Trio for Flute, Oboe, and Bassoon (1940); a short *Requiem* for Orch. (1946); *Divertimento* for Small Orch. (1948); Horn Concerto (1950); *Toccata* for Piano (1950); *Jan Hinnerik* for a cappella Chorus (1950); *Anion,* symph. sketch (1950); *Soliloquio* for Solo Flute (1951); *Ballade* for Flute, Clarinet, Harp, and String Quartet (1952); *Serenade* for String Orch. (1952); *Recitatief* for Baritone, Viola da Gamba, and Harpsichord (1953); *Suite* for Small Orch. (1954); *Roland Holst,* cantata for Chorus and Small Orch. (1955); *Soneria, Romanza e Mazurca* for Harp (1958). In 1961 he completed the revision, with a simplified orchestration, of Willem Pijper's 2nd Symph. (Pijper's own revised score was destroyed during a Nazi air raid on Rotterdam in May 1940).

Mengelberg, Kurt Rudolf, German-born musicologist and composer of Dutch descent, nephew of the conductor **Willem Mengelberg;** b. Krefeld, Feb. 1, 1892; d. Beausoleil, near Monte Carlo, Oct. 13, 1959. He studied piano with Neitzel in Cologne and musicology with Hugo Riemann at the Univ. of Leipzig, receiving his doctorate in 1915. He then went to Amsterdam, where he studied music theory with his uncle; in 1917, through his uncle's intervention, he became artistic assistant of the Concertgebouw Orch. in Amsterdam; then was artistic manager there in 1925–35, and finally director in 1935–54. Among his publications are the valuable program book *Das Mahler-Fest, Amsterdam Mai 1920* (Vienna, 1920); a biography of Mahler (Leipzig, 1923); *Nederland, spiegeleener beschaving (The Netherlands, Mirror of a Culture*; Amsterdam, 1929); a commemorative publication on the semicentennial of the Concertgebouw (Amsterdam, 1938); *Muziek, spiegel des tijds (Music, Mirror of*

Time, Amsterdam, 1948); and a biography of Willem Mengelberg. His own compositions are mainly liturgical; among them are *Missa pro pace* (1932); *Stabat Mater* (1940), and *Victimae Paschali laudes* (1946); he also wrote *Symphonic Variations* for Cello and Orch. (1927); Violin Concerto (1930); *Capriccio* for Piano and Orch. (1936); Concertino for Flute and Chamber Orch. (1943); solo songs and piano pieces.

Mengelberg, Misha, Dutch composer, son of **Karel Mengelberg;** b. Kiev, June 5, 1935. He was born in Kiev while his father was working in the U.S.S.R.; came in 1938 to the Netherlands, where he studied with Kees van Baaren at the Royal Cons. in The Hague, graduating in 1964. He was a co-founder of the Instant Composers Pool in 1967; in 1972 became president of the Guild of Improvising Musicians, a jazz organization.

WORKS: *Musica* for 17 Instruments (1959); *Medusa* for String Quartet (1962); *Commentary* for Orch. (1965); *Exercise* for Solo Flute (1966); *Omtrent een componistenactie (Concerning a Composer's Action)* for Wind Quintet (1966); *3 Piano Pieces + Piano Piece 4* (1966); *Amaga* for 3 Different Guitars and Electronic Equipment (1968); *Anatoloose* for Orch. and Tape (1968; Holland Festival, July 8, 1971); *Hello Windy Boys* for Double Wind Quintet (1968); *Met welbeleefde groet van de kameel (With the Very Polite Greetings of the Camel)* for Orch. with Electronic Sawing and Excavating Drills (1971–73); *Onderweg (On the Way)* for Orch. (1973; Bergen, Norway, Jan. 13, 1974). He participated in creating an anti-imperialistic collective opera, *Reconstructie* (1968–69; Holland Festival, June 29, 1969; in collaboration with Louis Andriessen, Reinbert de Leeuw, Peter Schat, and Jan van Vlijmen).

Mengelberg, Willem, celebrated Dutch conductor; b. Utrecht, March 28, 1871; d. Chur, Switzerland, March 21, 1951. He studied at the Cons. of Utrecht, and later at the Cologne Cons. with Seiss, Jensen, and Wüllner. He was appointed municipal music director in Lucerne in 1891, and his work there attracted so much attention that in 1895 he was placed at the head of the famous Concertgebouw Orch. in Amsterdam, holding this post for 50 years (resigning in 1945), a record tenure for any conductor; during his directorship, he elevated that orch. to a lofty position in the world of music. In addition, he became conductor of the Toonkunst choral society in Amsterdam (1898); appeared frequently as guest conductor in all the European countries; in England was an annual visitor from 1913 until World War II; appeared with the N.Y. Phil. in 1905; in 1908 was appointed conductor in Frankfurt; left in 1921 and accepted an invitation to conduct the National Symph. Orch. in N.Y., which was absorbed at his suggestion by the Phil. Society Orch.; he led the N.Y. Phil. at various intervals from 1922 till 1930; in 1928 he received the degree of Mus.Doc. at Columbia Univ. (*honoris causa*); in 1933 was appointed prof. of music at Utrecht Univ. During the occupation of

the Netherlands by the Germans, Mengelberg openly expressed his sympathies with the Nazi cause, and lost the high respect and admiration that his compatriots had felt for him; after the country's liberation he was barred from professional activities there, the ban to be continued until 1951, but he died in that year in exile in Switzerland. Mengelberg was one of the finest representatives of the Romantic tradition in symph. conducting; his interpretations extracted the full emotional power from the music, and yet he never transgressed the limits imposed by the structural forms of classical music; his renditions of Beethoven's symphs. were inspiring. He was a great admirer of Mahler and conducted a festival of Mahler's music in Amsterdam in May 1920; he was also a champion of works by Richard Strauss (who dedicated the score of *Ein Heldenleben* to him), Max Reger, and Debussy.

Mennin, Peter, eminent American composer and educator; b. Erie, Pa., May 17, 1923; d. New York, June 17, 1983. His family stemmed from Italy; Mennin's real name was **Mennini;** his brother, **Louis Mennini,** also a composer, did not cut off the last letter of his name as Peter did. His early environment was infused with music, mostly from phonograph recordings; he studied piano with Tito Spampani. In 1940 he enrolled in the Oberlin Cons. in Ohio, where he took courses in harmony with Normand Lockwood. He quickly learned the basics of composition, and at the age of 18 wrote a symph. and a string quartet. In 1942 he enlisted in the U.S. Army Air Force; was discharged in 1943, and resumed his musical studies at the Eastman School of Music in Rochester, N.Y., where his teachers were Howard Hanson and Bernard Rogers. He worked productively; wrote another symph. in 1944; a movement from it, entitled *Symphonic Allegro,* was performed by the N.Y. Phil., Leonard Bernstein conducting, on March 27, 1945. His 3rd Symph. was performed by Walter Hendl with the N.Y. Phil. on Feb. 27, 1947. Mennin progressed academically as well; he obtained his Ph.D. from the Eastman School of Music in 1947. He received a Guggenheim fellowship grant in 1948; a 2nd Guggenheim grant followed in 1956. From 1947 to 1958 he taught composition at the Juilliard School of Music; in 1958 he assumed the post of director of the Peabody Cons. in Baltimore. In 1962 he received his most prestigious appointment, that of president of the Juilliard School of Music, serving in that capacity until his death. Despite his academic preoccupations, he never slackened the tempo of his activities as a composer; he diversified his symphs. by adding descriptive titles; thus his 4th Symph. was subtitled *The Cycle* and was scored for chorus and orch.; his 7th Symph. was called *Variations Symphony;* the 4 movements of his 8th Symph. bore biblical titles. Increasingly also, he began attaching descriptive titles to his other works; his Concertato for Orch. was surnamed *Moby Dick;* there followed a *Canto for Orchestra,* a *Sinfonia capricciosa,* a *Cantata de Virtute, Voices,* and *Reflections of Emily,* to texts by Emily Dickinson. It is remarkable that Mennin never wrote operas, ballets, or any other works for the stage; his musical mind was directed toward pure structural forms; his music is characterized by an integrity of purpose and teleological development of thematic materials, all this despite the bold infusion of dissonant sonorities in contrapuntal passages. Mennin held honorary doctorates from the Univ. of Chicago, the Univ. of Wisconsin, Temple Univ., and the Univ. of Heidelberg in Germany.

WORKS: 9 symphs.: No. 1 (1942); No. 2 (Rochester, March 27, 1945); No. 3 (N.Y., Feb. 27, 1947); No. 4, *The Cycle,* for Chorus and Orch. (N.Y., March 18, 1949); No. 5 (Dallas, April 2, 1950); No. 6 (Louisville, Ky., Nov. 18, 1953); No. 7, *Variations Symphony* (Cleveland, Jan. 23, 1964); No. 8, in 4 movements, titled *In Principio, Dies Irae, De Profundis, Laudate Dominum* (N.Y., Nov. 21, 1974); No. 9 (Washington, D.C., March 10, 1981); *Sinfonia* for Chamber Orch. (Rochester, May 24, 1947); *Fantasia* for String Orch. (N.Y., Jan. 11, 1948); *Folk Overture* (Washington, D.C., Dec. 19, 1945); Violin Concerto (1950); Concertato, *Moby Dick,* for Orch. (Erie, Pa., Oct. 20, 1952); Cello Concerto (Juilliard School, Leonard Rose, soloist, Feb. 19, 1956); Piano Concerto (Cleveland, Feb. 27, 1958); Concertino for Flute, Strings, and Percussion (1945); *Canto for Orchestra* (San Antonio, Texas, March 4, 1963); *Sinfonia capricciosa* (Washington, D.C., March 10, 1981); *Cantata de Virtute* for Tenor, Baritone, Narrator, Chorus, Children's Chorus, and Orch., originally planned as a setting of Robert Browning's poem *The Pied Piper of Hamelin* (Cincinnati, May 2, 1969); *Symphonic Movements* (Minneapolis, Jan. 21, 1971; later perf. under the title *Sinfonia*); *Voices* for Mezzo-soprano, Percussion, Piano, Harp, and Harpsichord, to texts from Thoreau, Melville, Whitman, and Emily Dickinson (N.Y., March 28, 1976); *Reflections of Emily* for Treble Voices, Piano, Harp, and Percussion, to texts from poems by Emily Dickinson (N.Y., Jan. 18, 1979); Flute Concerto (N.Y., May 5, 1983); 2 string quartets (1941, 1951); *Sonata concertante* for Violin and Piano (Washington, D.C., Oct. 19, 1956); Piano Sonata (1963).

Mennini, Louis, American composer; brother of **Peter Mennin** (whose real name was **Mennini**); b. Erie, Pa., Nov. 18, 1920. He studied at the Oberlin Cons. (1939–42); then served in the U.S. Army Air Force (1942–45); subsequently studied composition with Bernard Rogers and Howard Hanson at the Eastman School of Music, Rochester, N.Y. (B.M., 1947; M.M., 1948); was on its faculty from 1949 to 1965; then served as dean of the School of Music, North Carolina School of the Arts at Winston-Salem (1965–71); in 1973 was appointed chairman of the dept. of music of Mercyhurst College in Erie, Pa. His music is pragmatic and functional, with occasional modernistic touches.

Menotti, Gian Carlo, remarkable composer; b. Cadegliano, Italy, July 7, 1911; was the 6th of 10 children. He learned the rudiments of music from his mother, and began to compose as a child, making his first attempt at an opera, entitled *The Death*

of Pierrot, at the age of 10. He studied for several years (1923–27) at the Milan Cons.; then came to the U.S., and entered the Curtis Inst. in Philadelphia (1927–33), where he studied with Rosario Scalero; subsequently taught composition at the Curtis Inst.; traveled often to Europe; made his home at Mt. Kisco, N.Y. Although Menotti has associated himself with the cause of American music, and spends most of his time in the U.S., he has retained his Italian citizenship. As a composer, he is unique on the American scene, being the first to create American opera possessing such an appeal to audiences as to become established in the permanent repertoire. Inheriting the natural Italian gift for operatic drama and an expressive singing line, he has adapted these qualities to the peculiar requirements of the American stage and to the changing fashions of the period; his serious operas have a strong dramatic content in the realistic style stemming from the Italian *verismo.* He writes his own librettos, marked by an extraordinary flair for drama and for the communicative power of the English language; with this is combined a fine, though subdued, sense of musical humor. Menotti makes no pretensions at extreme modernism, and does not fear to approximate the successful formulas developed by Verdi and Puccini; the influence of Mussorgsky's realistic prosody is also in evidence, particularly in recitative. When dramatic tension requires a greater impact, Menotti resorts to atonal and polytonal writing, leading to climaxes accompanied by massive dissonances. His first successful stage work was *Amelia Goes to the Ball,* an opera buffa in one act (originally to an Italian libretto by the composer, as *Amelia al ballo*), staged at the Academy of Music, Philadelphia, on April 1, 1937. This was followed by another comic opera, *The Old Maid and the Thief*, commissioned by the National Broadcasting Co., first performed on the radio, April 22, 1939, and on the stage, by the Philadelphia Opera Co., on Feb. 11, 1941. Menotti's next operatic work was *The Island God,* produced by the Metropolitan Opera, N.Y., on Feb. 20, 1942, with indifferent success; but with the production of *The Medium* (N.Y., May 8, 1946), Menotti established himself as the foremost composer-librettist of modern opera. The imaginative libretto, dealing with a fraudulent spiritualist who falls victim to her own practices when she imagines that ghostly voices are real, suited Menotti's musical talent to perfection; the opera had a long and successful run in N.Y., an unprecedented occurrence in the history of the American lyric theater. A short humorous opera, *The Telephone,* was first produced by the N.Y. Ballet Society, Feb. 18, 1947, on the same bill with *The Medium;* these 2 contrasting works were subsequently staged all over the U.S. and in Europe, often on the same evening. Menotti then produced *The Consul* (N.Y., March 1, 1950), his best tragic work, describing the plight of political fugitives vainly trying to escape from an unnamed country but failing to obtain the necessary visa from the consul of an anonymous power; very ingeniously, the author does not include the title character in the cast, since the consul never appears on the stage but remains a shadowy presence. *The*

Consul exceeded Menotti's previous operas in popular success; it had a long run in N.Y., and received the Pulitzer Prize. On Christmas Eve, 1951, the National Broadcasting Co. presented Menotti's television opera *Amahl and the Night Visitors,* a Christmas story of undeniable poetry and appeal; it became an annual television production every Christmas in subsequent years. His next opera was *The Saint of Bleecker Street,* set in a N.Y. locale (N.Y., Dec. 27, 1954); it won the Drama Critics' Circle Award for the best musical play of 1954, and the Pulitzer Prize for 1955. A madrigal ballet, *The Unicorn, the Gorgon and the Manticore,* commissioned by the Elizabeth Sprague Coolidge Foundation, was first presented at the Library of Congress, Washington, Oct. 21, 1956. His opera *Maria Golovin,* written expressly for the International Exposition at Brussels, was staged there on Aug. 20, 1958. In 1958 he organized the Festival of 2 Worlds in Spoleto, Italy, staging old and new works; in 1977 he inaugurated an American counterpart of the festival in Charleston, S.C. In many of the festival productions Menotti also acted as stage director. In the meantime he continued to compose; he produced in quick succession *Labyrinth,* a television opera to his own libretto (N.Y., March 3, 1963); *Death of the Bishop of Brindisi,* dramatic cantata with the text by the composer (Cincinnati, May 18, 1963); *Le Dernier Sauvage,* opera buffa, originally with an Italian libretto by Menotti, produced at the Opéra-Comique in Paris in a French trans. (Oct. 21, 1963; produced in Eng. at the Metropolitan Opera, N.Y., Jan. 23, 1964); *Martin's Lie,* chamber opera to Menotti's text (Bath, England, June 3, 1964); *Help, Help, the Globolinks!,* "an opera in one act for children and those who like children" to words by Menotti, with electronic effects (Hamburg, Dec. 19, 1968); *The Most Important Man,* opera to his own libretto (N.Y., March 12, 1971); *The Hero,* comic opera (Philadelphia, June 1, 1976); *The Egg,* a church opera to Menotti's own libretto (Washington Cathedral, June 17, 1976); *The Trial of the Gypsy* for Treble Voices and Piano (N.Y., May 24, 1978); *Miracles* for Boys' Choir (Fort Worth, Texas, April 22, 1979); *La loca,* opera to Menotti's own libretto dealing with a mad daughter of Ferdinand and Isabella (San Diego, June 3, 1979); *A Bride from Pluto,* opera (Washington, D.C., April 14, 1982). Among Menotti's non-operatic works are the ballets *Sebastian* (1944) and *Errand into the Maze* (N.Y., Feb. 2, 1947); Piano Concerto No. 1 (Boston, Nov. 2, 1945); *Apocalypse,* symph. poem (Pittsburgh, Oct. 19, 1951); Violin Concerto (Philadelphia, Dec. 5, 1952, Zimbalist soloist); *Triplo Concerto a Tre,* triple concerto in 3 movements (N.Y., Oct. 6, 1970); *Landscapes and Remembrances,* cantata to his own autobiographical words (Milwaukee, May 14, 1976); *First Symphony,* subtitled *The Halcyon* (Philadelphia, Aug. 4, 1976); Piano Concerto No. 2 (Miami, Fla., June 23, 1982); *Nocturne* for Soprano, String Quartet, and Harp (N.Y., Oct. 24, 1982); Double-bass Concerto (N.Y. Phil., Oct. 20, 1983, James VanDemark, soloist; Zubin Mehta conducting). He also wrote a number of *pièces d'occasion* such as *Trio for a House-Warming Party* for Piano, Cello, and Flute (1936); *Variations on a Theme by Schumann; Pastorale* for Piano and String Orch.; *Poemetti per Maria Rosa* (piano pieces for children); etc. Menotti is the author of the librettos for Samuel Barber's operas *Vanessa* (Metropolitan Opera, N.Y., Jan. 15, 1958) and *A Hand of Bridge* (1959), and wrote a play without music, *The Leper* (Tallahassee, Fla., April 22, 1970).

After many years in America, he bought an estate, Yester House, in Scotland, and made it his permanent abode in 1974 with his legally adopted son, Francis Phelan, who thenceforth bore his name.

Menter, Joseph, German cellist; b. Teisbach, Bavaria, Jan. 23, 1808; d. Munich, April 18, 1856. He began his career as a violinist; then studied cello with Moralt in Munich, and became a member of the orch. of the Bavarian Royal Opera (1833). His daughter, **Sophie Menter,** was a celebrated pianist.

Menter, Sophie, German pianist and teacher; daughter of **Joseph Menter;** b. Munich, July 29, 1846; d. there, Feb. 23, 1918. She studied piano with Niest in Munich and with Lebert in Stuttgart; made her professional debut in 1867 at the Gewandhaus Concerts in Leipzig, and later took lessons with Tausig and Liszt. In 1872 she married the cellist **David Popper** (divorced, 1886). From 1883 to 1887 she taught piano at the St. Petersburg Cons.; then lived mostly in the Tyrol. She composed a number of attractive pieces. Tchaikovsky orchestrated her work *Ungarische Zigeunerweisen* for piano and orch., and she played it under his direction in Odessa, on Feb. 4, 1893.

Menuhin, Hephzibah, American pianist; b. San Francisco, May 20, 1920; d. London, Jan. 1, 1981. Like her brother, **Yehudi Menuhin,** she appeared in public at a very early age. In her concert career she devoted herself exclusively to chamber music; played numerous sonata recitals with her brother.

Menuhin, Yehudi, celebrated American violinist; b. New York, April 22, 1916, of Russian-Jewish parents (the family surname was originally Mnuhin). As a child, he was taken to San Francisco, where he began to study violin with Sigmund Anker; in 1923 he began taking lessons with Louis Persinger, who was then concertmaster of the San Francisco Symph. Orch. On Feb. 29, 1924, he made his public debut in Oakland playing Bériot's *Scène de ballet* with Persinger as accompanist; Menuhin was only 7 at the time. On Jan. 17, 1926, when he was 9 years old, he played a recital in N.Y. He made his European debut in Paris on Feb. 6, 1927, with Paul Paray and the Lamoureux Orch. In Paris he began to study with Georges Enesco, who became his most influential teacher, and who guided his future career. Returning to America, Menuhin played the Beethoven Concerto with Fritz Busch and the N.Y. Symph. Orch. on Nov. 25, 1927, winning unanimous acclaim from the public and the press. He subsequently made tours throughout America and Europe; on April 12, 1929, he appeared with Bruno Walter and the Berlin Phil., playing concertos by Bach, Beethoven, and Brahms on the same program; on Nov. 4, 1929, he made his London debut. He continued to pursue his studies with Enesco, and also received additional instruction from Adolf Busch. On the sesquicentennial of the first concert given at the Gewandhaus in Leipzig, he appeared as soloist with the Gewandhaus Orch. in the Mendelssohn Concerto (Nov. 12, 1931). In 1935 he completed his first world tour, giving concerts in 73 cities in 13 countries, including Australia. He also became active in organizing music festivals; in 1956 he established the Gstaad Festival in Switzerland. In 1959 he made his home in London, and founded the Bath Festival, which he directed until 1968; he also founded the Windsor Festival and directed it from 1969 to 1972. He toured as soloist with his own chamber orch.; later he devoted much time to conducting and musical education. He toured Japan in 1951 and Russia in 1956. In 1963 he founded his own boarding school for musically gifted children at Stoke d'Abernon, Surrey. In 1965 he received an honorary knighthood from Queen Elizabeth II. In 1970 he received honorary citizenship from the community of Saanen, Switzerland, and assumed Swiss national allegiance while preserving his American citizenship. In 1971 he succeeded Barbirolli as president of Trinity College of Music in London. In 1976 he was awarded an honorary doctorate by the Sorbonne of Paris, the first musician to be so honored during its entire history. On Sept. 10, 1981, he celebrated the 50th anniversary of his first appearance in Leipzig by performing the Brahms Concerto with Kurt Masur and the Gewandhaus Orch.

Apart from his musical activities, he became deeply interested in art, politics, and above all, psychology and philosophy. He embraced the cause of oriental religions, practiced yoga exercises, and even lectured on these abstruse subjects. In 1963 he appeared over BBC in London in a discussion entitled "Yehudi Menuhin and His Guru." He also adopted a health diet eschewing carbohydrates and some other foods. In his political utterances he antagonized many factions in many lands. He was enthusiastically received in Israel during his tours in 1950, 1951, 1952, and 1953, but aroused Israeli animosity when he gave benefit concerts for Palestinian refugees. He embarrassed the Russians at a music congress in Moscow in 1971 when in his speech, which he read in understandable Russian, he appealed to them on behalf of human rights; he was never invited to Russia again. In the meantime, his artistry suffered somewhat; critics began to notice a certain unsteadiness in his intonation and technique; as a conductor he performed not more than satisfactorily. Still, he never slackened his energetic activities; on July 3, 1976, at a concert at Wolf Trap near Washington, D.C., he introduced a new violin concerto by Alan Hovhaness. He publ. a collection of essays under the title *Theme and Variations* (London, 1972); an autobiography, *Unfinished Journey* (N.Y., 1977); and, with Curtis W. Davis, *The Music of Man* (London, 1980), based on the television series of the same title.

Mercadante, (Giuseppe) Saverio (Raffaele), important Italian opera composer and teacher; b. Altamura, near Bari (baptized, Sept. 17), 1795; d. Naples, Dec. 17, 1870. He was born out of wedlock; was taken to Naples when he was about 11. In 1808 he was enrolled in the Collegio di San Sebastiano; he had no means to pay for his tuition; besides, he was over the age limit for entrance, and was not a Neapolitan; to gain admission he had to change his first Christian name and adjust his place and date of birth. He studied solfeggio, violin, and flute; also took classes in figured bass and harmony with Furno and counterpoint with Tritto; subsequently studied composition with the Collegio's director, Zingarelli (1816–20). He began to compose while still a student, writing marches, concertos, sinfonias, trios, quartets, and other works. In 1818 he composed 3 ballets; the success of the 3rd, *Il flauto incantato*, encouraged him to try his hand at an opera. His first opera, *L'apoteosi d'Ercole,* had a successful premiere at Naples on Jan. 4, 1819. He wrote 5 more operas before *Elisa e Claudio,* produced at La Scala in Milan on Oct. 30, 1821, which established his reputation. Other important operas were *Caritea, regina di Spagna* (Venice, Feb. 21, 1826); *Gabriella di Vergy* (Lisbon, Aug. 8, 1828); *I Normanni a Parigi* (Turin, Feb. 7, 1832); *I Briganti* (Paris, March 22, 1836); *Il giuramento* (Milan, March 10, 1837; considered his masterpiece); *Le due illustri rivali* (Venice, March 10, 1838); *Elena da Feltre* (Naples, Dec. 26, 1838); *Il Bravo* (Milan, March 9, 1839); *La Vestale* (Naples, March 10, 1840; one of his finest operas); *Il Reggente* (Turin, Feb. 2, 1843); *Leonora* (Naples, Dec. 5, 1844); *Orazi e Curiazi* (Naples, Nov. 10, 1846; a major success in Italy); and *Virginia* (Naples, April 7, 1866; his last opera to be perf. although composed as early as 1845; its premiere was delayed for political reasons). Mercadante wrote about 60 operas in all, for different opera houses, often residing in the city where they were produced; thus he lived in Rome, Bologna, and Milan; he also spent some time in Vienna (where he composed 3 operas in 1824) and in Spain and Portugal (1826–31). From 1833 to 1840 he was maestro di cappella at the Cathedral of Novara; about that time he suffered the loss of sight in one eye, and in 1862 he became totally blind. In 1839 Rossini offered him the directorate of the Licco Musicale in Bologna, but he served in that post only a short time; in 1840 he was named director of the Naples Cons. in succession to his teacher Zingarelli. Mercadante's operas are no longer in the active repertoire, but they are historically important, and objectively can stand comparison with those of his great compatriots Rossini, Bellini, and Donizetti.

Mercer, Johnny, American lyricist and composer of popular songs; b. Savannah, Ga., Nov. 18, 1909; d. Los Angeles, June 25, 1976. He went to N.Y. as a youth, and attracted the attention of Paul Whiteman; subsequently wrote songs for him, Benny Goodman, and Bob Crosby. In 1940 he went to Hollywood, where he founded Capitol Records. His first success as a lyric writer was *Lazybones*, with music by Hoagy Carmichael; another great success was

Accentuate the Positive, which he wrote for his psychoanalyst. He wrote both words and music for *Something's Gotta Give*, and other hits. He received 4 Academy Awards ("Oscars") for his lyrics.

Mercure, Pierre, Canadian composer; b. Montreal, Feb. 21, 1927; d. in an ambulance between Avallon and Auxerres, France, on Jan. 29, 1966, after an automobile crash while driving from Paris to Lyons. He studied composition with Claude Champagne at the Montreal Cons. (1944–49) and in Paris with Nadia Boulanger (1949–50); also took courses with Dallapiccola at the Berkshire Music Center in Tanglewood, and at Darmstadt and Dartington with Pousseur, Nono, and Berio. He played bassoon with the Montreal Symph. (1947–52); then became producer of musical broadcasts on the French radio network in Montreal. In his music he explored electronic sonorities in combinations with traditional instrumentation.

Méric-Lalande Henriette, French soprano; b. Dunkirk, 1798; d. Chantilly, Sept. 7, 1867. She studied with her father, who was the director of a provincial opera company; she made her debut in Nantes in 1814; her first appearance in Paris came in 1823 in a pasticcio. On March 7, 1824, she took part in the Venice premiere of Meyerbeer's *Il Crociatto in Egitto;* after further study in Italy, she created Bianca in Bellini's *Bianca e Gernando* (Naples, May 30, 1826), Imogene in *Il Pirata* (Milan, Oct. 27, 1827), and Alaide in *La Straniera* (Milan, Feb. 14, 1829), even though Bellini himself declared that she was "incapable of delicate sentiment." She appeared in London at the King's Theatre in 1830 as Imogene and sang in 1831 as Rossini's *Semiramis;* she retired shortly after creating the title role in Donizetti's *Lucrezia Borgia* (Milan, Dec. 26, 1833).

Merikanto, Aarre, Finnish composer, son of **Oskar Merikanto;** b. Helsinki, June 29, 1893; d. there, Sept. 29, 1958. He studied in Leipzig with Max Reger (1912–14) and with Vasilenko in Moscow (1916–17). In 1936 he joined the faculty at the Sibelius Academy in Helsinki, and in 1951 he succeeded Palmgren as head of the dept. of composition there; he held this post until his death. Like his father, he wrote on themes of Finnish folklore, but he also produced a few pieces that had elements of French Impressionism.

Merikanto, Oskar, Finnish composer; b. Helsinki, Aug. 5, 1868; d. Hausjärvi-Oiti, Feb. 17, 1924. After preliminary study in his native city, he went to Leipzig and Berlin to continue his musical education (1887). Returning to Finland, he became organist of St. John's Church, and from 1911 till 1922 was conductor of the National Opera in Helsinki. He wrote a great number of songs, which became very popular in Finland; organ works and manuals for organ playing; various instrumental pieces; and 3 operas: *Pohjan Neiti* (*The Maid of Bothnia;* Viborg, June 18, 1908), *Elinan surma* (*Elina's Death;* Helsinki, Nov. 17, 1910), and *Regina von Emmeritz*

(Helsinki, Jan. 30, 1920).

Merklin, Joseph, German organ builder; b. Oberhausen, Baden, Jan. 17, 1819; d. Nancy, France, June 10, 1905. He worked in his father's workshop in Freiburg; in 1843 went to Brussels; in 1853 took his brother-in-law, **F. Schütze,** into partnership, changing the name of his firm to Merklin, Schütze & Cie. In 1855 he bought out the Ducroquet firm in Paris; in 1858 he reorganized his partnership as the Société Anonyme pour la Fabrication des Orgues, Etablissement Merklin-Schütze. The firm supplied organs to several cathedrals in Europe. Merklin publ. an interesting technical paper, *Notice sur l'électricité appliquée aux grandes orgues* (Paris, 1887), containing some surprising insights on the possible manufacture of electric organs. His nephew **Albert Merklin** (1892–1925) went to Madrid at the outbreak of World War I in 1914 and established a Spanish branch of the firm. Merklin's Paris factory was acquired by Guttschenritter in 1899, and his branch in Lyons was bought in 1906 by the Swiss organ builder Theodor Kuhn; it was incorporated in 1926 as Société Anonyme des Anciens Établissements Michel, Merklin & Kuhn. After several further changes of ownership, the firm was taken over in 1967 by Fredrich Jakob in Zürich.

Merriam, Alan P(arkhurst), American anthropologist and ethnomusicologist; b. Missoula, Mont., Nov. 1, 1923; d. near Warsaw in a plane crash, March 14, 1980. He studied at the Univ. of Montana (B.A., 1947); took courses in anthropology from Melville Herskovits and Richard Waterman at Northwestern Univ. (M.M., 1948; Ph.D., 1951); taught anthropology there in 1953–54 and again from 1956–62, and at the Univ. of Wisconsin (1954–56); in 1962 became a prof. of anthropology at Indiana Univ. in Bloomington; was chairman of the dept. there in 1966–69. In 1976 he was engaged as a senior scholar in anthropology at the Univ. of Sydney. He was involved in field research among the Flathead Indians and the tribes in Zaïre.

Merrill, Robert, noted American baritone; b. Brooklyn, June 4, 1917. He first studied voice with his mother, Lillian Miller Merrill, a concert singer; subsequently took lessons with Samuel Margolis. He began his career as a popular singer on the radio; then made his operatic debut as Amonasro in *Aida* in Trenton, N.J., in 1944. After winning the Metropolitan Opera Auditions of the Air in N.Y., he made his debut with the Metropolitan on Dec. 15, 1945, as Germont in *La Traviata.* He remained on the roster of the Metropolitan Opera for 30 years; also gave solo recitals. He was briefly married to the American soprano **Roberta Peters.** He publ. 2 autobiographical books, *Once More from the Beginning* (N.Y., 1965) and *Between Acts* (N.Y., 1977).

Merritt, A(rthur) Tillman, American musicologist and pedagogue; b. Calhoun, Mo., Feb. 15, 1902. He studied at the Univ. of Missouri (B.A., 1924; B.F.A., 1926) and Harvard Univ. (M.A., 1927); then went to

Europe on a J.K. Paine traveling scholarship from Harvard, and studied in Paris with Nadia Boulanger and Paul Dukas; upon his return to America, he taught at Trinity College in Hartford, Conn. (1930–32). In 1932 he joined the faculty of the music dept. of Harvard Univ.; was its chairman from 1942–52 and from 1968 to 1972, when he retired. He publ. the valuable treatise *Sixteenth-century Polyphony: A Basis for the Study of Counterpoint* (Cambridge, Mass., 1939); also edited works by Janequin. On his retirement he was honored with a Festschrift, *Words and Music: The Scholar's View* (Cambridge, Mass., 1972).

Mersenne, Marin, important French theorist; b. La Soultière (Maine), Sept. 8, 1588; d. Paris, Sept. 1, 1648. He studied at the college of Le Mans; then at the Jesuit School at La Flèche (from 1604); then at the Collège Royal and the Sorbonne in Paris from 1609; in 1611 he joined the Order of Minims; between 1640 and 1645 made 3 trips to Italy; maintained a correspondence with the leading philosophers and scientists of his time. His writings provide souce material of fundamental importance for the history of 17th-century music.

Mersmann, Hans, German musicologist; b. Potsdam, Oct. 6, 1891; d. Cologne, June 24, 1971. He studied in Munich with Sandberger and Kroyer, in Leipzig with Riemann and Schering, and at the Univ. of Berlin with Wolf and Kretzschmar; received a Dr.Phil. with the dissertation *Christian Ludwig Boxberg und seine Oper "Sardanapalus" (Ansbach 1698), mit Beiträgen zur Ansbacher Musikgeschichte* (1914). He subsequently occupied various teaching positions: at the Stern Cons. in Berlin, and at the Technische Hochschule there, until 1933; was in charge of the folk-song archives of the Prussian Volksliederkommission (1917–33); also organized numerous seminars on musicology and modern music; from 1924 edited the periodical *Melos*; wrote music criticism. In 1946–47 he taught at the Hochschule für Musik in Munich; from 1947 to 1958 was director of the Hochschule für Musik in Cologne. As a historian and analyst of modern music, Mersmann occupies an important position in contemporary research.

Mertens, Joseph, Belgian composer; b. Antwerp, Feb. 17, 1834; d. Brussels, June 30, 1901. He was the first violinist at the Opéra in Brussels; was a violin teacher at the Cons.; was conductor of the Flemish Opera there (1878–89); then inspector of the Belgian music schools, and finally director of the Royal Theater at The Hague. He composed a number of Flemish and French operettas and operas which had local success: *De zwaarte Kapitein* (The Hague, 1877); *De Vrijer in de strop* (1866); *La Méprise* (1869); *L'Egoïsa* (1873); *Thécla* (1874); *Liederik l'intendent* (1875); *Les Trois Etudiants; Le Vin, le jeu et le tabac; Le Capitaine Robert; Les Evincés;* etc.

Merula, Tarquinio, significant Italian organist and composer; b. Cremona, c.1594; d. there, Dec. 10, 1665. In 1616 he received an appointment as organist of S. Maria Incoronata in Lodi. In 1621 he went to Poland, where he served as court organist. Returning to Italy, he became maestro di cappella at the Cathedral in Cremona in 1627; in 1631 he was engaged as maestro di cappella of S. Maria Maggiore in Bergamo; these positions he held until his death; from 1633 to 1635 he was also maestro di cappella for the Laudi della Madonna. He was a versatile composer and wrote both secular and sacred music; remarkably enough for a church organist, he also wrote instrumental music in a concertante style; his ensemble canzonas are especially fine.

Merulo (real name, **Merlotti**), **Claudio** (called **da Correggio**), Italian composer, organist, and music publisher; b. Correggio, April 8, 1533; d. Parma, May 4, 1604. He studied with Tuttovale Menon and Girolamo Donato. On Oct. 21, 1556, he became organist at the Cathedral in Brescia, succeeding Vincenzo Parabosco; on July 2, 1557, was chosen as 2nd organist at San Marco in Venice; in 1566 he succeeded Padovano as first organist, a position he held until 1584. He composed a number of works for state occasions, including intermedi to Frangipane's *Tragedia* for the visit of Henry III of France in 1574. Active as a music publisher between 1566 and 1570, he brought out several first editions of his own works, as well as of works by Primavera, Porta, and Wert. In 1586 he was appointed organist at the court of the Duke of Parma; in 1591 became organist to the company of the Steccata, a position he retained until his death. Merulo was reputed to be one of the greatest organists of his time; as a composer, he was an important representative of the Venetian school. His organ music is of especial merit; he also composed church music and madrigals.

Messager, André (-Charles-Prosper), celebrated French composer and conductor; b. Montluçon, Allier, Dec. 30, 1853; d. Paris, Feb. 24, 1929. He studied at the Ecole Niedermeyer in Paris with Gigout (composition), A. Laussel (piano), and C. Loret (organ); then took lessons with Saint-Saëns. In 1874 he became organist at St.-Sulpice; subsequently was choir director at Sainte-Marie des Batignoles (1882–84). He began his career as conductor at the Folies-Bergère; then conducted at the Eden-Theatre in Brussels in 1880; was music director at the Opéra-Comique (1898–1908); also directed the opera at Covent Garden, London (1901–7). From 1907 till 1915 he was the regular conductor of the Paris Opéra; was in charge of the Société des Concerts du Conservatoire from 1908 until his death; under the auspices of the French government he visited the U.S. with that orch., giving concerts in 50 American cities (1918). Returning to Paris, he again conducted at the Opéra-Comique; led a season of Diaghilev's Ballets Russes in 1924. As a conductor, he played an important role in Paris concert life; he directed the première of *Pelléas et Mélisande* (1902, with 21 rehearsals), the score of which Debussy dedicated to him. His initial steps as a composer were auspicious; his symph. (1875) was awarded the gold medal of the Société des Compositeurs and performed at the Concerts Colonne (Jan. 20, 1878); his dramatic scene *Don Juan et Haydée* (1876) was awarded a gold medal by the Academy of St. Quentin. He wrote several other works for orch. (*Impressions orientals, Suite funambulesque,* etc.) and some chamber music, but he was primarily a man of the theater. His style may be described as enlightened eclecticism; his music is characteristically French, and more specifically, Parisian, in its elegance and gaiety. He was honored in France; in 1926 he was elected to the Académie des Beaux Arts. He was married to **Hope Temple** (real name, **Dotie Davis,** 1858–1938), who was the author of numerous songs. His operas (first perf. in Paris except where otherwise indicated) include *François les-bas-bleus* (Jan. 20, 1878; score begun by F. Bernicat and completed after his death by Messager); *La Fauvette du temple* (Nov. 17, 1885); *La Béarnaise* (Dec. 12, 1885); *Le Bourgeois de Calais* (April 6, 1887); fairy tale, *Isoline* (Dec. 26, 1888; the ballet suite from it is popular); *La Basoche* (May 30, 1890; greatly acclaimed); *Madame Chrysanthème* (after Loti; Jan. 26, 1893; to a story similar to Puccini's *Madame Butterfly,* produced 11 years later; but Puccini's dramatic treatment eclipsed Messager's lyric setting); *Le Chevalier d'Harmental* (May 5, 1896); *Véronique* (Dec. 10, 1898; successful); *Les Dragons de l'Impératrice* (Feb. 13, 1905); *Fortunio* (June 5, 1907); *Béatrice* (Monte Carlo, March 21, 1914); *Monsieur Beaucaire* (Birmingham, April 7, 1919). Among his successful operettas were *Le Mari de la Reine* (Dec. 18, 1889); *Miss Dollar* (Jan. 22, 1893); *La Fiancée en loterie* (Feb. 15, 1896); *Les P'tites Michu* (Paris, Nov. 16, 1897; many subsequent perfs.); *La Petite Fonctionnaire,* dance-hall operetta (Paris, May 14, 1921); *Passionnément* (Paris, Jan. 15, 1926). His ballets include *Fleur d'oranger* (1878); *Les Vins de France* (1879); *Mignons et vilains* (1879); *Les Deux Pigeons* (1886); *Scaramouche* (1891); *Amants éternels* (1893); *Le Chevalier aux fleurs,* in collaboration with Pugno (1897); *Le Procès des roses* (1897); *Une Aventure de la Guimard* (1900); *Passconnement* (Jan. 19, 1926). He also wrote incidental music to Delair's *Hélène* (1891) and Moreau and Carré's *La Montagne enchantée,* in collaboration with Leroux (1897).

Messiaen, Olivier, outstanding French composer; b. Avignon, Dec. 10, 1908. A scion of an intellectual family (his father was a translator of English literature; his mother, Cécile Sauvage, a poet), he absorbed the atmosphere of culture and art as a child. A mystical quality was imparted by his mother's book of verses *L'Ame en bourgeon (The Burgeoning Soul),* dedicated to her as yet unborn child. He learned to play piano; at the age of 8 composed a song, *La Dame de Shalott,* to a poem by Tennyson. At the age of 11 he entered the Paris Cons., where he attended the classes of Jean and Noël Gallon, Marcel Dupré, Maurice Emmanuel, and Paul Dukas, specializing in organ, improvisation, and composition; he carried first prizes in all these departments. After graduation in 1930 he became or-

ganist at the Trinity Church in Paris. That same year he began teaching at the Ecole Normale de Musique and at the Schola Cantorum. That same year he organized, with André Jolivet, Ives Baudrier, and Daniel-Lesur, the group La Jeune France, with the aim of promoting modern French music. He was in the French army at the outbreak of World War II in 1939; was taken prisoner; spent 2 years in a German prison camp in Görlitz, Silesia; he composed there his *Quatuor pour la fin du temps;* was repatriated in 1942 and resumed his post as organist at the Trinity Church in Paris; was also appointed to the faculty of the Paris Cons., where he taught harmony and musical analysis. After the war he gave courses at the Berkshire Music Center in Tanglewood (1948) and at Darmstadt (1950–53). Young composers seeking instruction in new music became his eager pupils; among them were Pierre Boulez, Jean-Louis Martinet, Stockhausen, Xenakis, and others who were to become important composers in their own right. He received numerous honors; was made a Grand Officier de la Légion d'Honneur; was elected a member of the Inst. de France, of the Bavarian Academy of the Fine Arts, of the Santa Cecilia Academy in Rome, of the American Academy of Arts and Letters, and of other organizations. He is married to the pianist **Yvonne Loriod.** Messiaen is one of the most original of modern composers; in his music he makes use of a wide range of resources, from Gregorian chant to oriental rhythms. A mystic by nature and Catholic by religion, he strives to find a relationship between progressions of musical sounds and religious concepts; in his theoretical writing he strives to postulate an interdependence of modes, rhythms, and harmonic structures. Ever in quest of new musical resources, he employs in his scores the "Ondes Martenot" and exotic percussion instruments; a synthesis of these disparate tonal elements finds its culmination in his grandiose orch. work *Turangalîla-Symphonie.* One of the most fascinating aspects of Messiaen's innovative musical vocabulary is the phonetic emulation of bird song in several of his works; in order to attain ornithological fidelity, he made a detailed study notating the rhythms and pitches of singing birds in many regions of several countries. The municipal council of Parowan, Utah, where Messiaen wrote his work *Des canyons aux étoiles,* glorifying the natural beauties of the state of Utah, resolved to name a local mountain Mt. Messiaen on Aug. 5, 1978. On Nov. 28, 1983, his first opera, *St. François d'Assise,* was produced, with international acclaim, at the Paris Opéra.

WORKS: Opera, *St. François d'Assise* (Paris Opéra, Nov. 28, 1983). For Orch.: Fugue in D minor (1928); *Le Banquet eucharistique* (1928); *Simple chant d'une âme* (1930); *Les Offrandes oubliées* (1930; Paris, Feb. 19, 1931); *Le Tombeau resplendissant* (1931; Paris, Feb. 12, 1933); *Hymne au Saint Sacrement* (1932; Paris, March 23, 1933; N.Y., March 13, 1947, Stokowski conducting); *L'Ascension* (1933; Paris, Feb. 1935); *3 Talas* for Piano and Orch. (Paris, Feb. 14, 1948); *Turangalila-Symphonie* (1946–48; Boston, Dec. 2, 1949); *Réveil des oiseaux* for Piano and Orch. (Donaueschingen, Oct. 11, 1953); *Oiseaux exotiques* for Piano, 2 Wind Instruments, Xylophone, Glockenspiel, and Percussion (Paris, March 10, 1956); *Chronochromie* (Donaueschingen, Oct. 16, 1960); *7 Haï-kaï* for Piano, 13 Wind Instruments, Xylophone, Marimba, 4 Percussion Instruments, and 8 Violins (1962; Paris, Oct. 30, 1963); *Couleurs de la cité céleste* for Large Orch., with imitations of 2 New Zealand birds and one from Brazil (Donaueschingen, Oct. 17, 1964, Boulez conducting); *Et expecto resurrectionem mortuorum* for 18 Woodwinds, 16 Brass Instruments, and 3 Percussion Instruments (1964; Paris, May 7, 1965); *Des canyons aux étoiles* (1970–74; N.Y., Nov. 20, 1974). Chamber music: *Thème et variations* for Violin and Piano (1932); *Quatuor pour la fin du temps* for Violin, Clarinet, Cello, and Piano (perf. in Stalag 8A, Görlitz, Silesia, with the composer at the piano, Jan. 15, 1941); *Le Merle noir* for Flute and Piano (1951); *Le Tombeau de Jean-Pierre Guézec* for Horn (1971). Vocal works: *2 ballades de Villon* (1921); *3 mélodies* (1930); *La Mort du nombre* for Soprano, Tenor, Violin, and Piano (1930; Paris, March 25, 1931); Mass for 8 Sopranos and 4 Violins (1933); *Poèmes pour Mi* for Soprano and Piano (1936; Paris, April 28, 1937; orch. version, 1937; Paris, 1946); *O sacrum convivium!* for Chorus and Organ (1937); *Chants de terre et de ciel*, song cycle for Soprano and Piano to texts by the composer (1938); *Chœurs pour une Jeanne d'Arc* for Chorus a cappella (1941); *3 petites liturgies de la Présence Divine* for 18 Sopranos, Piano, Ondes Martenot, and Orch. (1944; Paris, April 21, 1945); *Harawi*, "chant d'amour et de mort," for Dramatic Soprano and Piano (1945); *5 rechants* for 12-voice Chorus (1949); *La Transfiguration de Notre Seigneur Jésus-Christ*, in 14 sections, for Chorus and Orch. (Lisbon, June 7, 1969). For Piano: *8 Preludes* (1929); *Pièce pour le tombeau de Paul Dukas* (1935); *Visions de l'Amen* for 2 Pianos (1942); *20 regards sur l'enfant Jésus* (1944); *Cantéyodjayâ* (1948); *4 études de rythme* (1949); *Catalogue d'oiseaux* (1956–58). For Organ: *Variations écossaises* (1928); *Le Banquet céleste* (1928); *Diptyque* (1929); *Apparition de l'église éternelle* (1932); *L'Ascension*, version of orch. work of 1933 with new 3rd movement (1934); *La Nativité du Seigneur* (1935); *Les Corps glorieux* (1939); *Messe de la Pentecôte* (1950); *Livre d'orgue* (1951); *Verset pour la fête de la dédicace* (1960); *Méditations sur le mystère de la Sainte Trinité* (1969).

Mester, Jorge, talented American conductor; b. Mexico City, April 10, 1935, of Hungarian parents. He began to play the violin and viola as a youth. He attended an American school in Mexico City and later a military academy in Hollywood. In 1952 he enrolled at the Juilliard School of Music in N.Y., where he studied conducting with Jean Morel; he received a master's degree there in 1957; also attended conducting classes with Leonard Bernstein in Tanglewood (1955). He made his orch. debut as a conductor in Mexico City in 1955. From 1957 to 1967 he taught conducting at the Juilliard School of Music. In 1964 he led a few exhibitionistic concerts of the parodistic P.D.Q. Bach series in N.Y. inaugurated with a great thud by Peter Schickele. In 1967 he was appointed conductor and music director of the Louisville (Ky.) Orch., holding this post until 1979. Following the Louisville Orch.'s unique policy of commissioning new works and then giving their premieres, Mester conducted, during his tenure, something like 200 first performances, and made about 70 recordings of some of them. Concurrently, he served as principal conductor of the Kansas City Phil. (1971–74). In 1970 he assumed the post of music director of the Aspen Music Festival; in 1980 he was charged with the task of reorganizing the Casals Festival in Puerto Rico. In 1982 he resumed his teaching duties at the Juilliard School of Music in N.Y. Equally at home in the classical and modern repertoire, in symph. music and in opera, Mester knows how to impart a sense of color with a precision of technical detail.

Mestres-Quadreny, Josep Maria, Spanish composer; b. Manresa, March 4, 1929. He studied composition with Cristòfor Taltabull at the Univ. of Barcelona (1950–56); in 1960 collaborated in the founding of Música Abierta, an organization of avant-garde musical activity; later he joined composers Xavier Benguerel, Joaquim Homs, and Josep Soler in founding the Conjunt Català de Música Contemporània, for the propagation of Catalan music. In 1968 he went to work in an electronic music studio. In his music he consciously attempts to find a counterpart to Abstract Expressionism in art, as exemplified by the paintings of Miró; for this purpose he applies serial techniques and aleatory procedures.

Metastasio, Pietro Antonio Domenico Bonaventura, famous Italian poet and opera librettist; b. Rome, Jan. 3, 1698; d. Vienna, April 12, 1782. He was the son of a papal soldier named Trapassi, but in his professional career assumed the Greek trans. of the name, both Trapassi (or Trapassamento) and Metastasio, meaning transition. He was a learned classicist; began to write plays as a young boy; studied music with Porpora; he achieved great fame in Italy as a playwright; in 1730 was appointed court poet at Vienna by Emperor Charles VI. He wrote about 35 opera texts, which were set to music by Handel, Gluck, Mozart, Hasse, Porpora, Jommelli, and many other celebrated composers; some of them were set to music 60 or more times. His librettos were remarkable for their melodious verse, which naturally suggested musical associations; the libretto to the opera by Niccolo Conforto, *La Nitteti* (1754; first perf. in Madrid, Sept. 23, 1756), was on the same subject as *Aida*, anticipating the latter by more than a century. Metastasio's complete works were publ. in Paris (1780–82; 12 vols.), Mantua (1816–20; 20 vols.); ed. by F. Gazzani (Torino, 1968); ed. by M. Fubino (Milano, 1968); see also A. Wotquenne, *Verzeichnis der Stücke in Versen . . . von Zeno, Metastasio und Goldoni* (Leipzig, 1905).

Metner, Nicolai. See **Medtner, Nicolai.**

Métra, (Jules-Louis-) Olivier, French composer of light music; b. Le Mans, June 2, 1830; d. Paris, Oct. 22, 1889. An actor's son, he became an actor himself as a boy; was first taught music by E. Roche; then was a pupil of Elwart at the Paris Cons. (1849–54). He played violin, cello, and double bass at Paris theaters; then conducted at various dance halls; the masked balls at the Opéra-Comique (1871); the orch. at the Folies-Bergère (1872–77); the balls at the Théâtre de la Monnaie, Brussels (1874–76); finally, the balls at the Paris Opéra. His waltzes, mazurkas, polkas, quadrilles, etc. were extremely popular; at the Folies-Bergère he produced 19 operettas and ballet divertissements; and at the Opéra, the ballet *Yedda* (1879).

Meulemans, Arthur, Belgian composer; b. Aarschot, May 19, 1884; d. Brussels, June 29, 1966. He studied with Edgar Tinel in Mechelen; in 1916 founded the Limburg School for organ at Hasselt; he then moved to Brussels; conducted the radio orch. there (1930–42); in 1954 was elected president of the Royal Flemish Academy of Fine Arts. He produced a prodigious amount of highly competent works in all genres.

Meybom, Marcus. See **Meibom, Marcus.**

Meyer, Ernst Hermann, German musicologist and composer; b. Berlin, Dec. 8, 1905. His father was a medical doctor of artistic interests who encouraged him to study music; he took piano lessons with Walter Hirschberg and played in chamber music groups. During the economic disarray in Germany in the 1920s Meyer was obliged to do manual labor in order to earn a living. In 1926 he was able to enroll in the Univ. of Berlin, where he studied musicology with Johannes Wolf, Arnold Schering, Friedrich Blume, Erich Hornbostel, and Curt Sachs; in 1928 he had additional studies with Heinrich Besseler at the Univ. of Heidelberg, obtaining his Ph.D. with the dissertation *Die mehrstimmige Spielmusik des 17. Jahrhunderts in Nord- und Mitteleuropa* (publ. in 1934 in Kassel). In 1929 he met Hanns Eisler, who influenced him in the political aspect of music. In 1930 he joined the German Communist Party. He conducted workers' choruses in Berlin and composed music for the proletarian revue *Der rote Stern (The Red Star)*. He also attended classes on film music given by Paul Hindemith. In 1931 he took a course in Marxism-Leninism with Hermann Duncker at the Marxist Workers' School in Berlin. He also began a detailed study of works by modern composers; in his own works, mostly for voices, he developed a style characteristic of the proletarian music of the time, full of affirmative action in march time adorned by corrosive discords, and yet eminently singable. When the Nazis bore down on his world with a different march, he fled to London, where, with the help of the English progressive musician Alan Bush, he conducted the Labour Choral Union. During the war he participated in the Chorus of the Free German Cultural Union in London and wrote propaganda songs; of

these, *Radio Moskau ruft Frau Krämer* was widely broadcast to Germany. He returned to Germany in 1948 and became engaged in pedagogical activities; taught music history at Humboldt Univ. in East Berlin, retiring in 1970. He was acknowledged as one of the most persuasive theoreticians of socialist realism in music; he founded the periodical *Music und Gesellschaft,* which pursued the orthodox Marxist line. He publ. *English Chamber Music: The History of a Great Art from the Middle Ages to Purcell* (London, 1946; in German as *Die Kammermusik Alt-Englands,* East Berlin, 1958); *Das Werk Beethovens und seine Bedeutung für das sozialistisch-realistische Gegenwartsschaffen* (East Berlin, 1970). A Festschrift was publ. in his honor in Leipzig in 1973.

Meyer, Kerstin, Swedish mezzo-soprano; b. Stockholm, April 3, 1928. She studied at the Royal Academy of Music in Stockholm; made her debut at the Royal Theater in Stockholm in 1952; also sang in Rome, Hamburg, Milan, Vienna, Salzburg, and other European music centers. On Oct. 29, 1960, she made her Metropolitan Opera debut as Carmen. She subsequently sang in South America and Japan. In 1963 she was named Swedish court soloist.

Meyer, Krzysztof, remarkable Polish composer; b. Cracow, Aug. 11, 1943. He played piano as a child; then took lessons in composition with Stanislaw Wiechowicz; subsequently undertook formal studies at the State College of Music in Cracow, where he obtained 2 diplomas: in 1965 in composition with Krzysztof Penderecki, and in 1966 in general music theory with Aleksander Frączkiewicz. In 1964, 1966, and 1968 he went to Paris, where he took courses with Nadia Boulanger; won several prizes at various competitions in France and in Poland. In 1970 he won the Grand Prix of the Prince Rainier III Competition in Monaco for his opera *Cyberiada.* In 1965–67 he appeared as a pianist with the contemporary music group MW-2; in 1966 he was appointed to the faculty of the State College of Music in Cracow. In 1981 he lived in Hamburg; then returned to Poland. Among his honors was the Award of the Minister of Culture and Arts in Poland (1975) and the Medal of the Government of Brazil (1975). Apart from his activities as a pianist and a composer, he has also contributed to Polish music journals, and publ. the first Polish-language monograph on Shostakovich, which was also trans. into German. His musical intelligence and acoustical acuity are of the rarest quality. As a composer, he adopts an advanced idiom without ever transcending the practical limits of instrumental and vocal techniques or of aural perception. As a demonstration of his talent for sophisticated mimicry, he composed a Mozartean symph. that is apt to confuse and seduce the most solemn Mozartologist. (It was, perhaps coincidentally, first performed on April Fools' Day in 1977.) Nadia Boulanger wrote of Meyer: "Il est un musicien tout à fait exceptionnel" (*Le Figaro,* Paris, May 7, 1970).
    WORKS: Fantastic comic opera, *Cyberiada,* libretto by composer after the novel by Stanislaw

Lem (Grand Prix at the Prince Rainier III Competition, Monaco, 1970); 5 symphs.: No. 1 (Cracow, June 12, 1964); No. 2, with Mixed Chorus, *Epitaphium Stanislaw Wiechowicz in memoriam* (1967; Katowice, Feb. 15, 1969); No. 3, *Symphonie d'Orphée*, with Mixed Choir, to words by Paul Valéry (1968; Warsaw, Sept. 1972); No. 4 (1973; Zagreb, May 14, 1975); No. 5 for String Orch. (Bialystok, Sept. 17, 1979); Symph. in D major, in the style of Mozart (1976; Poznan, April 1, 1977); Chamber Concerto for Oboe, Percussion, and String Orch. (1964; Cracow, June 25, 1965); Violin Concerto (1965; Poznan, March 22, 1969); Cello Concerto (Poznan, April 1975); Chamber Concerto for Oboe, Percussion, and String Orch. (Katowice, April 1975); Trumpet Concerto (1975; Poznan, April 2, 1976); *Fireballs* for Orch. (1976; Warsaw, April 20, 1978); *Polish Chants* for Soprano and Orch. (1977; Bydgoszcz, Sept. 9, 1979); *Lyric Triptych* for Tenor and Chamber Orch., to words by W.H. Auden (1976; Aldeburgh, June 22, 1978).

Meyer, Leonard B., American musicologist and writer on esthetics; b. New York, Jan. 12, 1918. He studied philosophy and composition at Columbia Univ. (M.A. in music, 1948) and humanities at the Univ. of Chicago (Ph.D., 1954); also took private lessons in composition with Stefan Wolpe and Aaron Copland. In 1946 he was appointed to the staff of the Univ. of Chicago; in 1961, became chairman of the music dept.; was prof. there until 1975; was prof. of music and humanities at the Univ. of Pa. from 1975. He publ. an important book dealing with the problems of communication and cultural contexts in the human response to music, *Emotion and Meaning in Music* (Chicago, 1956); *The Rhythmic Structure of Music* (with Grosvenor Cooper; Chicago, 1960); *Music, the Arts, and Ideas: Patterns and Predictions in Twentieth Century Culture* (Chicago, 1967); *Explaining Music: Essays and Explorations* (Berkeley, 1973); with E. Zonis, *Improvisation in Music: East and West* (Chicago, 1973). He also contributed valuable articles to various scholarly journals.

Meyer, Leopold von (called **Leopold de Meyer**), celebrated piano virtuoso; b. Baden, near Vienna, Dec. 20, 1816; d. Dresden, March 5, 1883. He studied with Czerny and Fischhof; at the age of 19, embarked on a series of pianistic tours in Europe; also toured in America (1845–47). At his concerts he invariably included his own compositions, written in a characteristic salon style; his agents spread sensational publicity about him in order to arouse interest. A *Biography of Leopold de Meyer* was publ. in London in 1845.

Meyerbeer, Giacomo, famous German opera composer; b. Vogelsdorf, near Berlin, Sept. 5, 1791; d. Paris, May 2, 1864. He was a scion of a prosperous Jewish family; his real name was **Jakob Liebmann Beer;** he added the name Meyer to his surname, forming the plausible compound Meyerbeer, and, following the Italian fashion in musical affairs,

changed his German first name, Jakob, to Giacomo. He studied piano with Lauska, and also had a chance to have some instruction in piano from Clementi, who was for a while a guest at Meyerbeer's house in Berlin. He began to study music theory with Zelter, and later took additional courses with Anselm Weber. From 1810 to 1812 he studied with the renowned musician Abbé Vogler at Darmstadt; Carl Maria von Weber was one of his fellow pupils. In Darmstadt he wrote the oratorio *Gott und die Natur*, which was performed in Berlin on May 8, 1811, when Meyerbeer was only 19 years old; there followed the composition of 2 operas, *Jephthas Gelübde*, produced in Munich on Dec. 23, 1812, and *Wirth und Gast, oder Aus Scherz Ernst*, staged at Stuttgart on Jan. 6, 1813; the 2nd of these operas was accepted for production in Vienna under the alternative title *Alimelik*. Meyerbeer knew Salieri, who advised him to enliven the heavily contrapuntal and somewhat Germanic style of his music by the infusion of a free-flowing Italian melos; Meyerbeer followed Salieri's advice, to his great profit. In 1815 he went to Venice, where he wrote several operas in the Italian vein: *Romilda e Costanza*, produced in Padua on July 19, 1817; *Semiramide riconosciuta*, staged in Turin early in 1819; and *Emma di Resburgo*, presented in Venice on June 26, 1819, in an Italian version, and later in German as *Emma von Leicester*. There followed *Margherita d'Angiù* (Milan, Nov. 14, 1820), which attained moderate success. In his next opera, *Il Crociato in Egitto*, produced in Venice on March 7, 1824, Meyerbeer displayed his great talent for dramatic action and Italianate melodic invention. It had a successful production in London on July 23, 1825, followed by a Paris performance on Sept. 25, 1825. He also arranged his opera *Margherita d'Angiù* for the French stage under the title *Margherita d'Anjou;* it was produced in Paris on March 11, 1826. In 1827 Meyerbeer began his long and fruitful association with the famous French writer and librettist Eugène Scribe, with whom he wrote his opera to the French text *Robert le diable*, produced at the Paris Opéra on Nov. 21, 1831, with extraordinary success. Personal events, both tragic and happy, intervened. His father died on Oct. 27, 1825. On May 25, 1826, he married his cousin Minna Mosson; 2 children, Eugénie and Alfred, were born to them but died in their infancy. He received the order of Chevalier of the Légion d'Honneur, and in 1834 was elected a member of the French Institut. From then on Meyerbeer took permanent residence in Paris. In 1832 he began work on his greatest opera, *Les Huguenots*, to a libretto mainly by Scribe; it was staged with enormous success at the Paris Opéra on Feb. 29, 1836, and eventually entered the repertoire of all major European opera houses. In 1836 Meyerbeer and Scribe began their collaboration on a new opera, *Le Prophète*, and in 1837 they completed the text and score of *L'Africaine;* both operas confirmed Meyerbeer's fame as a composer of tremendous power, capable of moving large audiences by their melodramatic effects, and at the same time impressing critics by the purely musical quality of the work. Meyerbeer became an undisputed king of the French opera establishment; indeed, it is said that Rossini, disgusted by the Meyerbeer cult in Paris, decided not to write anymore for the Paris Opéra. It was only in the early years of the 20th century that music historians began to question the gaudy brilliance of Meyerbeer's stellar flamboyance. After the production of *Les Huguenots* in Berlin in 1842, Meyerbeer was asked by King Friedrich Wilhelm IV to accept the position of Generalmusikdirektor at the capital. Meyerbeer accepted the flattering invitation and produced in Berlin his opera *Ein Feldlager Schlesien;* Jenny Lind lent her illustrious presence in a later performance of the opera, in the role of Vielka. A curious chapter in Meyerbeer's life was his association with Wagner, whom Meyerbeer, many years his senior, helped financially; Meyerbeer also conducted Wagner's opera *Rienzi* in Berlin. Wagner repaid Meyerbeer with ingratitude, attacking his operas as a harmful artistic influence and denigrating him as a Jew. The composition of *Le Prophète* proceeded slowly, but the work eventually received a brilliant stage performance at the Paris Opéra on April 16, 1849, with the celebrated prima donna Pauline Viardot-García in the role of Fidès. Meyerbeer's next opera was *L'Etoile du nord,* which utilized some musical material from *Ein Feldlager in Schlesien;* it was produced at the Opéra-Comique on Feb. 16, 1854; this was followed by the premiere, also at the Opéra-Comique, of Meyerbeer's next opera, *Le Pardon de Ploërmel,* on April 4, 1859. In 1862 Meyerbeer visited England to attend the first performance of a work he wrote for the World Exhibition in London, the *Fest-Ouverture im Marschstyl (Festive Overture in a March Style).* In the meantime, he continued work on a revision of his opera *L'Africaine;* this was greatly handicapped by Scribe's death in 1861. Meyerbeer supervised the rehearsals of the opera, but death supervened with dramatic suddenness on the night of May 2, 1864. Meyerbeer's body was taken to Berlin, where it was laid to earth in official ceremonies attended by the Prussian court and prominent dignitaries in the arts. Fétis was subsequently charged with making the final preparations for the first performance of *L'Africaine,* which was given at the Paris Opéra on April 28, 1865, with great acclaim. This opera, too, entered the general repertoire.

WORKS: OPERAS: *Jephthas Gelübde* (Munich, Dec. 23, 1812); *Wirth und Gast, oder Aus Scherz Ernst,* Lustspiel (Stuttgart, Jan. 6, 1813; revised as *Die beyden Kalifen,* Vienna, Oct. 20, 1814; later known as *Alimelek*); *Das Brandenburger Tor,* singspiel (composed 1814 but not perf.); *Romilda e Costanza,* melodramma semiserio (Padua, July 19, 1817); *Semiramide riconosciuta,* dramma per musica (Turin, March 1819); *Emma di Resburgo,* melodramma eroico (Venice, June 26, 1819); *Margherita d'Angiù,* melodramma semiserio (Teatro alla Scala, Milan, Nov. 14, 1820; revised as *Margherita d'Anjou,* Odéon, Paris, March 11, 1826); *L'Almanzore* (composed 1821 but not perf.); *L'Esule di Granata,* melodramma serio (Teatro alla Scala, Milan, March 12, 1821); *Il Crociato in Egitto,* melodramma eroico (Venice, March 7, 1824); *Robert le*

diable, grand opéra (Opéra, Paris, Nov. 21, 1831); *Les Huguenots,* grand opéra (Opéra, Paris, Feb. 29, 1836); *Ein Feldlager in Schlesien,* singspiel (Berlin, Dec. 7, 1844; later known as *Vielka*); *Le Prophète,* grand opéra (Opéra, Paris, April 16, 1849); *L'Etoile du nord,* opéra comique (Opéra-Comique, Paris, Feb. 16, 1854; much of the music based on *Ein Feldlager in Schlesien*); *Le Pardon de Ploërmel,* opéra comique (Opéra-Comique, Paris, April 4, 1859; also known as *Le Chercheur du trésor* and as *Dinorah, oder Die Wallfahrt nach Ploërmel*); *L'Africaine,* grand opéra (Opéra, Paris, April 28, 1865; originally known as *Vasco da Gama*); Meyerbeer also left a number of unfinished operas in various stages of development. Other stage works include *Der Fischer und das Milchmädchen, oder Viel Lärm um einen Kuss (Le Passage de la rivière, ou La Femme jalouse; Le Pêcheur et la laitière),* ballet-pantomime (Berlin, March 26, 1810); *Gli amori di Teolinda (Thecelindens Liebschaften),* monodrama (Genoa, 1816); *Das Hoffest von Ferrara,* masque (Berlin, Feb. 28, 1843); *Struensee,* incidental music for a drama by Michael Beer, Meyerbeer's brother (Berlin, Sept. 19, 1846); etc.

OCCASIONAL AND SECULAR CHORAL WORKS: *Festgesang zur Errichtung des Guttenbergischen Denkmals in Mainz* for 2 Tenors, 2 Basses, Men's Voices, and Piano ad libitum (Mainz, 1835); *Dem Vaterland* for Men's Voices (Berlin, 1842); *Le Voyageur au tombeau de Beethoven* for Bass Solo and Women's Voices a cappella (composed 1845); *Festhymne* for Solo Voices, Chorus, and Piano ad libitum (for the silver wedding anniversary of the King and Queen of Prussia, 1848); *Ode an Rauch* for Solo Voices, Chorus, and Orch. (in honor of the sculptor Christian Rauch; Berlin, 1851); *Maria und ihr Genius,* cantata for Soprano, Tenor, Chorus, and Piano (for the silver wedding anniversary of Prince and Princess Carl, 1852); *Brautgeleite aus der Heimat,* serenade for Chorus a cappella (for the wedding of Princess Luise, 1856); *Festgesang zur Feier des 100 jährigen Geburtsfestes von Friedrich Schiller* for Soprano, Alto, Tenor, Bass, Chorus, and Orch. (composed 1859); *Festhymnus* for Solo Voices, Chorus, and Piano ad libitum (for the coronation of Wilhelm I, 1861); etc.

Meyerowitz, Jan, German-American composer; b. Breslau, April 23, 1913. In 1927 he went to Berlin, where he studied with Gmeindl and Zemlinsky at the Hochschule für Musik. Compelled to leave Germany in 1933, he went to Rome, where he took lessons in advanced composition with Respighi and Casella, and in conducting with Molinari. In 1938 he moved to Belgium and later to southern France, where he remained until 1946; he then emigrated to the U.S., becoming a naturalized citizen in 1951. He married the French singer **Marguerite Fricker** in 1946. He held a Guggenheim fellowship twice (1956, 1958). In the U.S. he taught at the Berkshire Music Center in Tanglewood and at Brooklyn College; in 1962 was appointed to the faculty of the City College of N.Y. In 1977 he received a grant from the National Endowment for the Arts. His music is imbued with expansive emotionalism akin to that of Mahler; in his works for the theater there is a marked influence of the tradition of 19th-century grand opera. His technical idiom is modern, enlivened by a liberal infusion of euphonious dissonance, and he often applies the rigorous and vigorous devices of linear counterpoint.

WORKS: OPERAS: *The Barrier,* to a libretto by Langston Hughes (N.Y., Jan. 10, 1950); *Eastward in Eden* (title changed later to *Emily Dickinson;* Detroit, Nov. 16, 1951); *Simoon* (Tanglewood, Aug. 2, 1950); *Bad Boys in School* (Tanglewood, Aug. 17, 1953); *Esther,* libretto by Langston Hughes (Univ. of Illinois, Urbana, May 17, 1957); *Port Town,* libretto by Langston Hughes (Tanglewood, Aug. 4, 1960); *Godfather Death* (Brooklyn, June 2, 1961); *Die Doppelgängerin,* after Gerhart Hauptmann (title changed later to conform with the original title of Hauptmann's play, *Winterballade;* Hannover, Germany, Jan. 29, 1967). FOR ORCH.: *Silesian Symphony* (1957); *Symphony Midrash Esther* (N.Y. Phil., Jan. 31, 1957); *Flemish Overture* (Cleveland, 1959); Flute Concerto (1962); Oboe Concerto (1963); *Sinfonia brevissima* (Corpus Christi, Texas, 1965); *6 Pieces for Orchestra* (Pittsburgh, May 27, 1967); *7 Pieces for Orchestra* (Turin, 1972). CANTATAS: *Music for Christmas* (N.Y., 1954); *The Glory around His Head* (N.Y. Phil., April 14, 1955); *Missa Rachel Plorans* (N.Y., Nov. 5, 1955); *The Rabbis* (text from the Talmud; Turin, 1965); several solo cantatas, among them *Emily Dickinson Cantata; 6 Songs* to poems by August von Platen for Soprano and Orch. (Cologne, Feb. 12, 1977). CHAMBER MUSIC: Woodwind Quintet (1954); String Quartet (1955); Cello Sonata (1946); Trio for Flute, Cello, and Piano (1946); Violin Sonata (1960); Flute Sonata (1961); Piano Sonata (1958); *Homage to Hieronymus Bosch* for 2 Pianos, 4–hands (1945); songs to German, French and Eng. texts. Meyerowitz publ. a monograph on Schoenberg (Berlin, 1967); also a booklet, *Der echte jüdische Witz* (Berlin, 1971).

Miaskovsky, Nicolai, eminent Russian composer; b. Novogeorgievsk, near Warsaw, April 20, 1881; d. Moscow, Aug. 8, 1950. His father was an officer of the dept. of military fortification; the family lived in Orenburg (1888) and in Kazan (1889–93). In 1893 he was sent to a military school in Nizhny-Novgorod; in 1895 he went to a military school in St. Petersburg, graduating in 1899. At that time he developed an interest in music, and tried to compose; took lessons with the composer Kazanli; his first influences were Chopin and Tchaikovsky. In 1902–3 he was in Moscow, where he studied harmony with Glière. Returning to St. Petersburg in 1903, he took lessons with Kryzhanovsky, from whom he acquired a taste for modernistic composition in the impressionist style. In 1906, at the age of 25, he entered the St. Petersburg Cons. as a pupil of Liadov and Rimsky-Korsakov, graduating in 1911. At the outbreak of World War I in 1914, Miaskovsky was called into active service in the Russian army; in 1916 he was removed to Reval to work on military fortifications; he remained in the army after the

Bolshevik Revolution of 1917; in 1918 he became a functionary in the Maritime Headquarters in Moscow; was finally demobilized in 1921. In that year he became prof. of composition at the Moscow Cons., remaining at that post to the end of his life. A composer of extraordinary ability, a master of his craft, Miaskovsky wrote 27 symphs., much chamber music, piano pieces, and songs; his music is marked by structural strength and emotional élan; he never embraced extreme forms of modernism, but adopted workable devices of tonal expansion short of polytonality, and freely modulating melody short of atonality. His style was cosmopolitan; only in a few works did he inject his style folkloric elements.

WORKS: Symphs. (all first perf. in Moscow, unless otherwise indicated): No. 1, C minor (1908; Pavlovsk, June 2, 1914); No. 2, C-sharp minor (July 24, 1912); No. 3, A minor (Feb. 27, 1915); No. 4, E minor (Feb. 8, 1925); No. 5, D major (July 18, 1920); No. 6, E-flat minor (May 4, 1924); No. 7, B minor (Feb. 8, 1925); No. 8, A major (May 23, 1926); No. 9, E minor (April 29, 1928); No. 10, F minor (April 7, 1928); No. 11, B-flat minor (Jan. 16, 1933); No. 12, G minor (June 1, 1932); No. 13, B minor (world premiere, Winterthur, Switzerland, Oct. 16, 1934); No. 14, C major (Feb. 24, 1935); No. 15, D minor (Oct. 28, 1935); No. 16, F major (Oct. 24, 1936); No. 17, G-sharp minor (Dec. 17, 1937); No. 18, C major (Oct. 1, 1937); No. 19, E-flat (Feb. 15, 1939); No. 20, E major (Nov. 28, 1940); No. 21, F-sharp minor (Nov. 16, 1940; perf. by the Chicago Orch. as a commissioned work on Dec. 26, 1940, under the title *Symphonie Fantaisie*); No. 22, subtitled *Symphonie Ballade* (Tiflis, Jan. 12, 1942); No. 23, A minor, *Symphony-Suite* (July 20, 1942); No. 24, F minor (Dec. 8, 1943); No. 25, D-flat (March 6, 1947); No. 26, C major (1948; on old Russian themes; Dec. 28, 1948); No. 27, C minor (perf. posthumously, Dec. 9, 1950). Other orch. works: *Silence,* symph. poem after Edgar Allan Poe (Moscow, June 13, 1911); *Alastor,* symph. poem after Shelley (Moscow, Nov. 18, 1914); Serenade for Small Orch. (Moscow, Oct. 7, 1929); *Lyric Concertino* for Small Orch. (Moscow, Oct. 7, 1929); Sinfonietta for String Orch. (Moscow, May 1930); Violin Concerto (Leningrad, Nov. 14, 1938); *Salutatory Overture,* on Stalin's 60th birthday (Moscow, Dec. 21, 1939); Cello Concerto (Moscow, March 17, 1945). Also a cantata, *Kirov Is With Us* (1942); marches for military band; choruses; 13 string quartets; 2 cello sonatas; Violin Sonata; 9 piano sonatas; several sets of piano pieces; song cycles; etc. His collected works were issued in 12 vols. in Moscow in 1953–56.

Michael, David Moritz, German wind instrument player, violinist, and composer; b. Künhausen, near Erfurt, Oct. 27, 1751; d. Neuwied, on the Rhine, 1825. He spent some years as a Hessian army musician; in 1781 joined the Moravian church; from 1795 till 1815 he lived in the Moravian settlements at Nazareth and Bethlehem, Pa., and was the leading spirit in the musical performances in both towns; he played violin and most winds, and as a novelty, would amuse his audience by performing simultaneously on 2 French horns. A list of programs of the Collegium Musicum at Nazareth, beginning with 1796, is preserved in the Moravian Historical Society at Nazareth. Michael's compositions are listed in *A Catalogue of Music by American Moravians,* compiled by A.G. Rau and H.T. David (Bethlehem, 1938). They include a dozen choral works and 16 *Partien,* or suites, for 5, 6, and 7 Wind Instruments, among them one, a programmatic work, written for a boat ride on the Lehigh River.

Michaelides, Solon, Greek musicologist, conductor, and composer; b. Nicosia, Cyprus, Nov. 25, 1905; d. Athens, Sept. 9, 1979. He studied first at the Trinity College of Music in London; then took courses in composition at the Ecole Normale de Musique in Paris with Nadia Boulanger, and later in conducting with Marcel Labey at the Schola Cantorum. Upon his return to Cyprus, he founded ahe Schola cons. at Limassol in 1934 and was its director until 1956; subsequently was director of the Salonika State Cons. (1957–70) and permanent conductor of the Symph. Orch. of Northern Greece (1959–70). In 1970 he was pensioned and he moved to Athens. He publ. *Modern British Music* (Nicosia, 1939), *Cyprus Folk Music* (ibid., 1944; 2nd ed., 1956), *Modern Greek Music* (ibid., 1945; 2nd ed., 1952), the 2–vol. *Harmony of Contemporary Music* (Limassol, 1945), *The Neo-Hellenic Folk Music* (ibid., 1948) and *A Dictionary of Ancient Greek Music* (London, 1977). Among his compositions are an opera to his own libretto, *Ulysses* (1951); a ballet, *Nausicaa* (1961); *At the Cypriot Marriage,* symph. sketch for Flute and Strings (1934); *2 Byzantine Sketches* for Strings (1936); *2 Greek Symphonic Pictures* (1936); 2 cantatas: *The Tomb* (1936) and *Free Besieged* (1955); *Byzantine Offering* for Strings (1944); *Archaic Suite* for Flute, Oboe, Harp, and Strings (1962); Piano Concerto (1966); String Quartet (1934); Piano Trio (1946); *Suite* for Cello and Piano (1966); *Suite* for Piano (1966); *Hymn and Lament for Cyprus* for a cappella Chorus (1975).

Michalak, Thomas, Polish conductor; b. Cracow, Dec. 21, 1940. He studied violin in Warsaw; made his debut as a soloist with the Warsaw Phil. Orch. at the age of 16. His conducting debut was with the Ballets Russes de Monte Carlo during its tour of the U.S. in 1964. In 1967 he became a member of the faculty at Ithaca College. In 1972 he won first prize in the Koussevitzky awards at the Berkshire Music Center. He subsequently served on the conducting staff of the Pittsburgh Symph. Orch. (1974); later became music director of the Canton (Ohio) Symph. Orch. (1976–77). In 1977 he was appointed music director of the N.J. Symph. Orch. of Newark, retaining this post until 1983; in 1981–82 he served as music adviser of the Kansas City Phil.

Michalsky, Donal, American composer; b. Pasadena, Calif., July 13, 1928; d. (asphyxiated in a fire and burned to death with his wife, 2 small children, a house guest, and her daughter), Newport Beach, Calif., Jan. 1, 1976. He studied clarinet as a youth; then attended the Univ. of Southern Calif. at Los Angeles as a student in theory with Halsey Stevens and in orchestration with Ingolf Dahl, obtaining his doctorate in 1965. In 1958 he went to Germany, where he took a course with Wolfgang Fortner in Freiburg im Breisgau. In 1960 he was appointed prof. of composition at the Calif. State College at Fullerton, holding this position until his tragic death. In his music he adopted a powerful modern idiom in robust dissonant counterpoint, often written in dodecaphonic technique, and yet permeated with a lyric and almost Romantic sentiment.

Michelangeli, Arturo Benedetti, celebrated Italian pianist; b. Brescia, Jan. 5, 1920. He received his formal music training at the Venturi Inst. in Brescia, where he took violin lessons with Paolo Chiuieri; at the age of 10 he entered the Milan Cons. as a piano pupil of Giuseppe Anfossi, obtaining his diploma at the age of 13. In 1939 he won the Concours International de Piano in Geneva; later joined the piano faculty at the Martini Cons. in Bologna. He was a lieutenant in the Italian air force; after the formal surrender of Italy to the Allies and the German occupation, he was active in the country's anti-Fascist underground; he was taken prisoner by the Germans, but escaped after a few months. Despite these peripeteias he somehow managed to practice, acquiring a formidable virtuoso technique. However, he also developed idiosyncrasies, often canceling scheduled performances, and engaged in such distracting (and dangerous) activities as automobile racing, skiing, and mountain climbing. Both his virtuosity and his eccentricities contributed to his legend, and his rare concerts were invariably public successes. He toured the U.S. in 1950 and in 1966; played in the Soviet Union in 1964; also gave concerts in South America. Eventually he returned to Italy and dedicated himself to teaching; organized an International Academy for pianists in a rented palazzo in Brescia with a multitude of pianos in soundproof studios; among his pupils was Maurizio Pollini, who in time became himself a pianistic celebrity.

Michi, Orazio, called **della Arpa** (because of his virtuosity on the harp), Italian composer; b. Alifa Caserta, c.1595; d. Rome, Oct. 26, 1641. From 1614 till 1623 he was in Rome; after that, with Cardinal Maurizio of Savoy. Until 1914 his works were unknown except for 5 arias publ. in Bianchi's *Raccolta d'arie* (Rome, 1640) and a 6th one publ. by Torchi in vol. 5 of *L'arte musicale in Italia.* Then, A. Cametti publ., in the *Rivista Musicale Italiana* (April 1914), a full description and complete thematic catalogue of 43 pieces for one to 3 voices with continuo (chiefly arias) by Michi which he had discovered in various Italian libraries, and which prove that Michi was one of the earliest and most important Roman masters of the monodic style.

Middelschulte, Wilhelm, eminent German organist; b. Werne, near Dortmund, April 3, 1863; d. there, May 4, 1943. He studied at the Inst. für Kirchenmusik in Berlin with Löschhorn (piano), Haupt (organ), and Commer and Schröder (composition). After serving as organist at the Church of St. Luke in Berlin (1888–91), he went to America and settled in Chicago; was organist there at the Cathedral of the Holy Name (1891–95); also prof. of organ at the Wisconsin Cons. of Music in Milwaukee. He was greatly distinguished as a Bach player and pedagogue; in 1935 he became instructor of theory and organ at the Detroit Foundation Music School; in 1939 he returned to Germany.

Miedél, Rainer, German-American conductor; b. Regensburg, June 1, 1937; d. Seattle, March 25, 1983. He studied cello with André Navarra in Paris, and conducting with Istvan Kertesz and Carl Mellisz; also took conducting lessons with Franco Ferrara. In 1965 he was engaged as a cellist with the Stockholm Phil. Orch.; made his conducting debut with it in 1967. From 1969 to 1976 he was music director of the Gavleborgs Orch. in Sweden; concurrently served as assistant conductor of the Baltimore Symph. Orch. (1969–72) and then associate conductor (1972–73). In 1976 he was appointed music director and conductor of the Seattle Symph. Orch.; in 1980 he traveled with it on its first European tour. From 1980 to 1982 he served as interim music director of the Florida Phil.; he also had numerous guest conducting engagements in Berlin, Vienna, Leningrad, Bucharest, Hong Kong, Guadalajara, Copenhagen, Hamburg, Alaska, Chicago, Dallas, Toronto, Vancouver, Quebec, Indianapolis, Honolulu, etc. His career was ended when he was stricken with a peculiarly deadly form of cancer. He conducted his last concert in Seattle on Jan. 13, 1983.

Mielck, Ernst, Finnish composer; b. Viipuri (Vyborg), Oct. 24, 1877; d. Locarno, Italy, Oct. 22, 1899 (2 days before his 22nd birthday). He studied piano in St. Petersburg, and composition with Max Bruch in Berlin. His early death deprived Finland of a major musical talent. He left several works showing considerable technical skill and inventive power; among these are String Quartet (1895); *Macbeth Overture* (1895); String Quintet (1896–97); *Finnish Symphony* (1897); *Dramatic Overture* (1898); two piano concertos (1895, 1898); *Finnish Suite* for Orch. (1899). A monograph on Mielck was publ. by W. Mauke (Leipzig, 1901).

Miersch, Paul Friedrich Theodor, cellist and composer; b. Dresden, Jan. 18, 1868; d. New York, March 1, 1956. He studied at the Munich Academy with Werner (cello) and Rheinberger (composition); came to the U.S. in 1886, and lived in Washington, D.C.; during Tchaikovsky's American tour in 1891, he played the cello part in Tchaikovsky's trio in Washington, in the composer's presence. In 1892 he moved to N.Y.; was first cellist of the N.Y. Symph. Orch. (1893–98); then held a similar post at the Metropolitan Opera (1898–1912). After retirement from concert life, he remained in N.Y. as a teacher. He wrote a number of compositions, 46 of which have been publ.

Mies, Paul, noted German musicologist and pedagogue; b. Cologne, Oct. 22, 1889; d. there, May 15, 1976. He studied musicology, mathematics, and physics at the Univ. of Bonn, receiving his Ph.D. there in 1912 with the dissertation *Über die Tonmalerei;* then was active as a teacher of mathematics in Cologne (1919–39) while continuing his musicological work; in 1946 he became director of the Institut für Schulmusik at the Cologne Staatliche Hochschule für Musik, retaining this post until 1954.

Miessner, Benjamin Franklin, American inventor of electronic instruments; b. Huntingburg, Ind., July 27, 1890; d. Miami, Fla., March 25, 1976. He studied electrical engineering at Purdue Univ. (1913–16). About 1925 he organized his own company, Miessner Inventions, Inc. He perfected the Wurlitzer organ and electronic pianos before his retirement in 1959.

Mignone, Francisco, eminent Brazilian composer; b. São Paulo, Sept. 3, 1897. He studied music with his father; then took courses in piano, flute, and composition at the São Paulo Cons.; then studied with Ferroni at the Milan Cons. (1920); returning to Brazil, he was appointed to the faculty of the Escola Nacional de Música in Rio de Janeiro (1933), and taught there until 1967. His music shows the influence of the modern Italian school of composition; his piano pieces are of virtuoso character; his orchestration shows consummate skill. In many of his works he employs indigenous Brazilian motifs, investing them in sonorous modernistic harmonies not without a liberal application of euphonious dissonances.

WORKS: OPERAS: *O Contractador dos diamantes* (Rio de Janeiro, Sept. 20, 1924); *O inocente* (Rio de Janeiro, Sept. 5, 1928); *O Chalaça* (1972); operetta, *Mizú* (1937). BALLETS: *Maracatú de Chico-Rei* (Rio de Janeiro, Oct. 29, 1934), *Quadros amazónicos* (Rio de Janeiro, July 15, 1949), *O guarda chuva* (São Paulo, 1954). FOR ORCH.: *Suite campestre* (Rio de Janeiro, Dec. 16, 1918); *Congada*, from the opera *O Contractador dos diamantes* (São Paulo, Sept. 10, 1922; his most popular piece); *Scenas da Roda*, symph. dance (São Paulo, Aug. 15, 1923); *Festa dionisiaca* (Rome, Oct. 24, 1923); *Intermezzo lirico* (São Paulo, May 13, 1925); *Momus*, symph. poem (Rio de Janeiro, April 24, 1933); *Suite brasileira* (Rio de Janeiro, Dec. 9, 1933); *Sonho de um Menino Travesso* (São Paulo, Oct. 30, 1937); *4 fantasias brasileiras* for Piano and Orch. (1931–37); *Seresta* for Cello and Orch. (Rio de Janeiro, March 31, 1939); *Miudinho*, symph. dance (São Paulo, June 28, 1941); *Festa das Igrejas* (N.Y., April 22, 1942); *Sinfonia tropical* (1958); Piano Concerto (1958); Violin Concerto (1961); Concerto for Violin, Piano, and Orch. (1966); Concertino for Clarinet and Small Orch. (1957); Bassoon Concertino (1957); Concerto for Violin and Chamber Orch. (1975).

Migot, Georges, significant French composer; b. Paris, Feb. 27, 1891; d. Levallois, near Paris, Jan. 5,

1976. He began taking piano lessons at the age of 6; entered the Paris Cons. in 1909; after preliminary courses in harmony, he studied composition with Widor, counterpoint with André Gedalge, and music history with Maurice Emmanuel; orchestration with Vincent d'Indy, and organ with Gigout and Guilmant. Before completing his studies at the Paris Cons., he was mobilized into the French army, was wounded at Longuyon in 1914, and was released from military service. In 1917 he presented in Paris a concert of his own works; received the Lily Boulanger Prize in 1918. He competed twice for the Prix de Rome in 1919 and 1920, but failed to win and abandoned further in 1919 and attempts. In the meantime he engaged in a serious study of painting; in fact, he was more successful as a painter than as a composer in the early years of his career; he exhibited his paintings in Paris art galleries in 1917, 1919, 1923, and in subsequent years. He also wrote poetry; virtually all of his vocal works are written to his own words. In his musical compositions he endeavored to recapture the spirit of old French polyphony, thus emphasizing the continuity of national art in history. His melodic writing is modal, often with archaic inflections, while his harmonic idiom is diatonically translucid; he obtains subtle coloristic effects through unusual instrumental registration. Profoundly interested in the preservation and classification of old musical instruments, Migot served as curator of the Instrumental Museum of the Paris Cons. (1949–61).

WORKS: *Hagoromo*, "symphonie lyrique et chorégraphique" for Baritone, Chorus, and Orch., to a text by Migot and Laloy (Monte Carlo, May 9, 1922); *Le Rossignol en amour*, chamber opera to a text by Migot (1926–28; Geneva, March 2, 1937); *La Sulamite*, concert opera to a libretto by Migot (1969–70); *L'Arche*, "polyphonie spatiale" for Soprano, Female Chorus, and Orch., to a poem by Migot (1971; Marseilles, May 3, 1974); 13 symphs. (some of their material was derived from earlier pieces of chamber music, and their numeration does not follow chronological order): No. 1, *Les Agrestides* (1919–20; Paris, April 29, 1922); No. 2 (1927; Festival of Besançon, Sept. 7, 1961); No. 3 (1943–49); No. 4 (1946–47); No. 5, *Sinfonia da chiesa,* for Wind Instruments (1955; Roubaix, Dec. 4, 1955); No. 6 for Strings (1944–51; Strasbourg, June 22, 1960); No. 7 for Chamber Orch. (1948–52); No. 8 for 15 Wind Instruments and 2 Double Basses (1953); No. 9 for Strings (incomplete); No. 10 (1962); No. 11 for Wind Instruments (1963); No. 12 (1954–64; Lille, May 29, 1972); No. 13 (1967); also *Petite Symphonie en trois mouvements enchaînés* for String Orch. (1970; Béziers, July 23, 1971). OTHER ORCH. WORKS: *Le Paravent de laque aux cinq images* (1920; Paris, Jan. 21, 1923); *Trois ciné-ambiances* (1922); *La Fête de la bergère* (1921; Paris, Nov. 21, 1925); *Prélude pour un poète* (Paris, June 7, 1929); *Le Livre des danceries*, orch. suite (Paris, Dec. 12, 1931); *Le Zodiaque* (1931–39); *Phonie sous-marine* (1962); *Dialogue* for Piano and Orch. (1922–25; Paris, March 25, 1926); *Dialogue* for Cello and Orch. (1922–26; Paris, Feb. 7, 1927); *Suite* for Violin and Orch. (1924; Paris, Nov. 14, 1925); *Suite* for Piano and Orch. (Paris, March 12,

1927); *Suite en concert* for Harp and Orch. (Paris, Jan. 15, 1928); *La Jungle*, "polyphonie" for Organ and Orch. (1928; Paris, Jan. 9, 1932); Piano Concerto (1962; Paris, June 26, 1964); Concerto for Harpsichord and Chamber Orch. (Paris, Dec. 12, 1967). CHAMBER MUSIC: *Les Parques* for 2 Violins, Viola, and Piano (1909); 3 string quartets (1921, 1957, 1966); Quartet for Flute, Violin, Cello, and Piano (1960); Quartet for Violin, Viola, Cello, and Piano (1961); Quartet for 2 Clarinets, Corno di Bassetto, and Bass Clarinet (1925); Quartet for Saxophones (1955); Quartet for 2 Violins and 2 Cellos (1955); Quintet for Flute, Oboe, Clarinet, Horn, and Bassoon (1954); *Introduction pour un concert de chambre* for 5 Strings and 5 Wind Instruments (1964); Trio for Oboe, Violin, and Piano (1906); Trio for Violin, Viola, and Piano (1918); Piano Trio (1935); Trio for Oboe, Clarinet, and Bassoon (1944); String Trio (1944–45); Trio for Flute, Cello, and Harp (1965); Guitar Sonata (1960); *Sonate luthée* for Harp Solo (1949); 2 sonatas for Violin Solo (1951, 1959); Violin Sonata (1911); *Dialogue No. 1* for Violin and Piano (1923); *Dialogue No. 2* for Violin and Piano (1925); Sonata for Viola Solo (1958); Sonata for Cello Solo (1954); *Dialogue No. 1* for Cello and Piano (1922); *Dialogue No. 2* for Cello and Piano (1929); Sonata for Cello and Piano (1958); *Suite* for 2 Cellos (1962); *Suite* for Flute Solo (1931); Flute Sonata (1945); *Pastorale* for 2 Flutes (1950); *Suite* for English Horn and Piano (1963); Sonata for Clarinet Solo (1953); Sonata for Bassoon Solo (1953). VOCAL WORKS: *6 tétraphonies* for Baritone, Flute, Violin, and Cello, to words by Migot (1945); *7 petites images du Japon* for Voice and Piano (1917); *Vini vinoque amor* for 2 Voices, Flute, Cello, and Piano (1937); numerous unaccompanied vocal trios and quartets; sacred choruses a cappella; double and triple choruses a cappella; *Liturgie œcuménique* for 3 Voices and Organ (1958); oratorio, *La Mise au tombeau* to Migot's text (1948–49); "lyric mystery," *La Nativité de Notre Seigneur* for Soloists, Chorus, and Instruments, to text by Migot (1954); *La Passion*, oratorio (1939–46; Paris, July 25, 1957); *L'Annonciation*, oratorio (1943–46); *Mystère orphique* for Voice and Orch. (1951; Strasbourg, March 18, 1964); *Cantate d'amour*, concert opera, to texts by Migot (1949–50); *La Résurrection*, oratorio (1953; Strasbourg, March 28, 1969); *Du ciel et de la terre*, "space symphony" for a film (1957); *Le Zodiaque*, "chorégraphie lyrique" with libretto by Migot (1958–60); *La plate, vaste savane* for Soprano and Instruments (1967); *3 chansons de joie et de souci* for Voice and Guitar (1969); *3 Dialogues* for Voice and Cello (1972); *5 Chants initiatiques* for Voice and Piano (1973); also much liturgical music; a group of albums of character pieces for piano; numerous works for organ. Migot publ. an autobiography, *Kaléidoscope et Miroirs* (Toulouse, 1970); *Essais pour une esthétique générale* (Paris, 1920); *Jean-Philippe Rameau et le génie de la musique française* (Paris, 1930); *Lexique de quelques termes utilisés en musique* (Paris, 1947); 2 vols. of poems (Paris, 1950, 1951).

Mihalovich, Edmund (Ödön) von, Hungarian

composer; b. Fericsancze, Sept. 13, 1842; d. Budapest, April 22, 1929. He studied with Mosonyi in Budapest, and with Hauptmann in Leipzig; also took lessons with Peter Cornelius in Munich. From 1887 to 1919 he taught at the Hungarian Academy of Music in Budapest. He was an ardent Wagnerite and opposed Hungarian musical nationalism; the melodic materials of his own works are entirely Germanic.

WORKS: OPERAS: *Hagbart und Signe* (Dresden, March 12, 1882); *Eliane* (Budapest, Feb. 16, 1908); *Toldi szerelme* (*Toldi's Love*; Budapest, March 18, 1893); 4 symphs. (1879, 1892, 1900, 1902); *Hero and Leander*, symph. poem (1875); *Faust*, fantasy for Orch. (1880); Violin Sonata; piano pieces; songs.

Mihalovici, Marcel, significant Rumanian-French composer; b. Bucharest, Oct. 22, 1898. He studied composition privately with Cuclin in Bucharest; in 1919 went to Paris, where he settled; became a French citizen in 1955. He studied violin with Nestor Lejeune, Gregorian chant with Amédée Gastoué, and composition with Vincent d'Indy at the Schola Cantorum (1919–25). With Martinu, Conrad Beck, and Tibor Harsányi, he formed a freely associated "Ecole de Paris," consisting of emigrants, which later attracted several other Parisian composers, among them Alexandre Tcherepnin of Russia, Alexandre Tansman of Poland, and Alexander Spitzmueller of Austria. Mihalovici was a founding member of the modern music society "Triton" (1932); was elected a member of the Inst. de France in 1964. He married the noted pianist **Monique Haas.** Mihalovici's music presents a felicitous synthesis of French and Eastern European elements, tinted with a roseate impressionistic patina and couched in euphoniously dissonant harmonies.

WORKS: OPERAS: *L'Intransigeant Pluton* (1928; Paris, April 3, 1939); *Phèdre* (1949; Stuttgart, June 9, 1951); *Die Heimkehr* (Frankfurt, June 17, 1954); *Krapp ou La Dernière Bande*, libretto by Samuel Beckett (1959–60; Bielefeld, Germany, Feb. 25, 1961); opera-buffa, *Les Jumeaux* (1962; Braunschweig, Germany, Jan. 23, 1963). BALLETS: *Une Vie de Polichinelle* (Paris, 1923); *Le Postillon du Roy* (Paris, 1924); *Divertimento* (Paris, 1925); *Karagueuz*, ballet for marionettes (Paris, 1926; Chicago, 1926); *Thésée au labyrinthe* (1956; Braunschweig, April 4, 1957; revised version as *Scènes de Thésée*, Cologne, Oct. 15, 1958); *Alternamenti* (1957; Braunschweig, Feb. 28, 1958); *Variations* (Bielefeld, March 28, 1960). FOR ORCH.: *Notturno* (1923); *Introduction au mouvement symphonique* (1923; Bucharest, Oct. 17, 1926); *Fantaisie* (1927; Liège Festival, Sept. 6, 1930); *Cortège des divinites infernales* (1928; Bucharest, Dec. 7, 1930); *Chindia* for 13 Wind Instruments and Piano (1929); *Concerto quasi una Fantasia* for Violin and Orch. (1930; Barcelona Festival, April 22, 1936); *Divertissement* (1934); *Capriccio roumain* (1936); *Prélude et Invention* for String Orch. (1937; Warsaw Festival, April 21, 1939); *Toccata* for Piano and Orch. (1938, revised 1940); *Symphonies pour le temps présent* (1944); *Variations* for Brass and Strings (1946); *Séquences* (1947); *Ritournelles* (1951); 5 symphs.: *Sinfonia giocosa* (Basel, Dec. 14,

1951); *Sinfonia partita* for Strings (1952); *Sinfonia variata* (1960); *Sinfonia cantata* for Baritone, Chorus, and Orch. (1953–63); and No. 5 for Dramatic Soprano and Orch. (in memory of Hans Rosbaud, 1966–69; Paris, Dec. 14, 1971); *Etude en 2 parties* for Piano Concertante, 7 Wind Instruments, Celesta, and Percussion (Donaueschingen, Oct. 6, 1951); *Elegie* (1955); *Ouverture tragique* (1957); *Esercizio* for Strings (1959); *Musique nocturne* for Clarinet, String Orch., Harpsichord, and Celesta (1963); *Aubade* for Strings (1964); *Périples* for Orch. with Piano Concertante (1967; Paris, March 22, 1970); *Prétextes* for Oboe, Bass Clarinet, and Chamber Orch. (1968); *Variantes* for Horn, and Orch. or Piano (1969); *Borne* (1970); *Rondo* (1970); *Chant Premier* for Saxophone and Orch. (1973–74); *Follia*, paraphrases for Orch. (1976–77). VOCAL MUSIC: Cantata, *La Genèse* (1935–40); *Cantilène* for Mezzo-soprano and Chamber Orch. (1972); *Cascando*, invention for Music and Voice (1962); *Mémorial*, 5 a cappella motets, each dedicated to a different deceased composer (1952); songs, *Abendgesang* (1957), *Stances* (1967), and *Textes* (1974).

Mihály, András, Hungarian composer and conductor; b. Budapest, Nov. 7, 1917. He studied cello with Adolf Schiffer and chamber music with Leo Weiner and Imre Waldbauer at the Budapest Academy of Music (1934–38); took private composition lessons from Paul Kadosa and István Strasser. He played cello in the orch. of the Budapest Opera House (1948–50); in 1950 was appointed prof. of the Budapest Academy of Music. In 1968 he organized the Budapest Chamber Ensemble and conducted it in a series of concerts with programs of new music. As a composer, he writes in a compact contrapuntal style oxygenated by a breath of lyricism. He won the Kossuth Prize in 1955 and the Erkel Prize 3 times (1952, 1954, 1964).

Mikhashoff, Ivar, American pianist; b. Albany, N.Y., March 8, 1944. He studied at the Eastman School of Music; then enrolled at the Juilliard School of Music in N.Y. as a student of Beveridge Webster; subsequently traveled to Paris to take a course with Nadia Boulanger (1968–69). In 1973 he received a D.M.A. in composition from the Univ. of Texas; taught at the State Univ. of New York in Buffalo; in 1981 joined the faculty of the Boston Univ. Tanglewood Inst. He included in his repertoire a variety of works by modern composers, among them Aaron Copland, Lukas Foss, Charles Ives, and Dane Rudhyar. He also appeared as a multimedia performer. In 1980 he played the principal acting role in the La Scala premiere of Bussotti's opera *La Racine.* In 1982 he organized the Holland Festival's 2-week-long celebration of 200 years of Dutch-American friendship through a series of 9 thematic concerts covering 250 years of American music. He also composed some chamber music and a Piano Concerto.

Mikorey, Franz, German composer and conductor; b. Munich, June 3, 1873; d. there, May 11, 1947. He studied in Munich with Thuille and H. Levi; later in Berlin with H. von Herzogenberg; conducted in Bayreuth (1894); then in Prague, Regensburg, Elberfeld, and Vienna; in 1902 was engaged as court conductor in Dessau; was appointed music director there in 1912. He conducted opera at Helsinki from 1919 to 1924; then returned to Germany.

Milán, Luis, Spanish musician, courtier, and poet; b. Valencia, c.1500; d. after 1561. He was a favorite at the viceregal court of Valencia under Germaine de Foix and her 3rd husband, Don Fernando of Aragón. In 1535–36 he brought out his most important work, *Libro de música de vihuela de mano intitulado El Maestro* (Valencia), intended as an instruction book for learning to play the vihuela (a large 6-stringed guitar). This was the first book of its kind to be publ. in Spain, and it is valuable for its many musical examples (*tientos,* fantasias, pavanes, and solo songs with guitar accompaniment: *villancicos,* romances, and *sonetos*), which reveal Milán's high qualities as a composer. Milán also publ. *El cortesano* (1561), giving a description of courtly life at Valencia in his day. *El Maestro,* with the original tablature and transcription into modern notation, was edited by Leo Schrade in *Publikationen älterer Musik, 2* (Leipzig, 1927); modern eds. have been publ. by R. Chiesa (Milan, 1965) and C. Jacobs (University Park, Pa., 1971).

Milanov, Zinka (née **Kunc**), famous soprano; b. Zagreb, Yugoslavia, May 17, 1906. She studied with Milka Ternina in Zagreb, and made her professional debut with the Ljubljana Opera (1927); then sang opera in Hamburg and Vienna; in 1937 was soloist in Verdi's Requiem, under the direction of Toscanini in Salzburg. She made her American debut at the Metropolitan Opera House, N.Y., on Dec. 17, 1937, in *Il Trovatore;* remained on its staff, off and on, until 1966; then taught at the Indiana Univ. School of Music in Bloomington (1966–67). In 1937 she married Predrag Milanov; they were divorced in 1946; she married Ljubomir Ilic in 1947.

Mildenberg, Albert, American composer; b. Brooklyn, N.Y., Jan. 13, 1878; d. there, July 3, 1918. He was a member of a musical family; studied piano with his mother; then took lessons with Rafael Joseffy (piano) and Bruno Oscar Klein (composition). In 1905 he went to Rome, where he studied with Sgambati; later studied in Paris with Massenet; in 1907 he made a public appearance in Paris as a conductor. Returning to America, he became dean of the music dept. of Meredith College at Raleigh, N.C. He wrote a number of songs, many of them to his own texts; also wrote his own opera librettos. His style was in the Italian tradition; Massenet commended his gift of melody. His light opera *The Wood Witch* was produced in N.Y. on May 25, 1903; another comic opera, *Love's Locksmith,* was given in N.Y. in 1912.

Mildenburg, Anna von, famous dramatic soprano; b. Vienna, Nov. 29, 1872; d. there, Jan. 27, 1947. She studied at the Vienna Cons. with Rosa Papier and Pollini; made her opera debut in Hamburg, where her fine voice and acting ability attracted a great deal of attention; in 1897 she was engaged to sing in Bayreuth; in 1898 she became a member of the Vienna Opera; retired from the stage in 1917; went to Munich, where she taught singing at the State Academy; later taught in Berlin; eventually returned to Vienna. Her repertoire included all the great Wagnerian roles. In 1909 she married the playwright Hermann Bahr, with whom she wrote *Bayreuth und das Wagner Theater* (Leipzig, 1910; Eng. trans., London, 1912); she also publ. *Erinnerungen* (1921) and *Darstellung der Werke Richard Wagner aus dem Geiste ser Dichtung und Musik* (vol. 1, *Tristan und Isolde*; Leipzig, 1936). Bahr alone wrote *Parsifalschutz ohne Ausnahmegesetz* (Berlin, 1912).

Milder-Hauptmann, Pauline Anna, soprano; b. Constantinople, Dec. 13, 1785; d. Berlin, May 29, 1838. She was the daughter of an Austrian diplomatic official; in Vienna she attracted the notice of Schikaneder. He recommended her to Tomaselli and Salieri, who taught her opera singing. She made her debut at the Vienna Opera on April 9, 1803, and soon became so well regarded as an artist and singer that Beethoven wrote the role of Fidelio for her. Her voice was so powerful that Haydn reportedly said to her: "Dear child, you have a voice like a house." In 1810 she married a Vienna merchant, Hauptmann. In 1812 she went to Berlin, where she created a sensation, particularly as Gluck's heroines (in *Iphigenia, Alcestis,* and *Armida*); she left Berlin in 1829; then sang in Russia, Sweden, and Austria; retired in 1836.

Milford, Robin, English composer; b. Oxford, Jan. 22, 1903; d. Lyme Regis, Dec. 29, 1959. He studied with Holst, Vaughan Williams, and R.O. Morris, at the Royal College of Music in London. While still a student, he composed a number of works, mostly in small forms, in a clear rhythmic manner, with thematic materials suggesting English folk music. WORKS: Ballet, *The Snow Queen,* after Hans Christian Andersen (1946); oratorio, *The Pilgrim's Progress,* after John Bunyan (1932); *The Forsaken Merman,* after Matthew Arnold, for Tenor, Women's Chorus, Strings, and Piano (1938–50); *A Litany to the Holy Spirit,* after Robert Herrick (1947); Suite for Chamber Orch. (1924); *Miniature Concerto* for Strings (1933); *Ariel* for Small Orch. (1940); *Miniature Concerto* for Harpsichord and Chamber Orch. (1927); Violin Concerto (1937); *Elegiac Meditation* for Viola and Strings (1947); *Fantasia* for String Quartet (1945); Trio for Clarinet, Cello, and Piano (1948); Trio for 2 Violins and Piano (1949); Flute Sonata (1944); Violin Sonata (1945); *A Festival* for Strings (1951); *Fishing by Moonlight* for Piano and Strings (1952); opera, *The Scarlet Letter* (1959); piano pieces; songs; other works in various forms.

Milhaud, Darius, eminent French composer; b. Aix-en-Provence, Sept. 4, 1892; d. Geneva, June 22,

1974. He was the descendant of an old Jewish family, settled in Provence for many centuries. His father was a merchant of almonds; there was a piano in the house, and Milhaud improvised melodies as a child; then began to take violin lessons. He entered the Paris Cons. in 1909, almost at the age limit for enrollment; studied with Berthelier (violin), Lefèvre (ensemble), Leroux (harmony), Gédalge (counterpoint), Widor (composition and fugue), and Vincent d'Indy (conducting); he played violin in the student orch. of the Cons. under the direction of Paul Dukas. He received first "accessit" in violin and counterpoint, and 2nd in fugue; won the Prix Lepaulle for composition. While still a student, he wrote music in a bold modernistic manner; became associated with Erik Satie, Jean Cocteau, and Paul Claudel. When Claudel was appointed French minister to Brazil, he engaged Milhaud as his secretary; they sailed for Rio de Janeiro early in 1917; returned to Paris (via the West Indies and N.Y.) shortly after the Armistice of Nov. 1918. Milhaud's name became known to a larger public as a result of a newspaper article by Henri Collet in Comœdia (Jan. 16, 1920), grouping him with 5 other French composers of modern tendencies (Auric, Durey, Honegger, Poulenc, and Germaine Tailleferre) under the sobriquet Les Six, even though the association was stylistically fortuitous. In 1922 Milhaud visited the U.S.; he lectured at Harvard Univ., Princeton, and Columbia; appeared as pianist and composer in his own works; in 1925, he traveled in Italy, Germany, Austria, and Russia; returning to France, he devoted himself mainly to composition and teaching. At the outbreak of World War II, he was in Aix-en-Provence; in July 1940 he came to the U.S.; taught for several years at Mills College in Oakland, Calif. In 1947 he returned to France; was appointed prof. at the Paris Cons., but continued to visit the U.S. as conductor and teacher almost annually, despite his illness (arthritis), which compelled him to conduct while seated; he retained his post at Mills College until 1971; then settled in Geneva. Exceptionally prolific since his student days, he wrote a great number of works in every genre; introduced a modernistic type of music drama, "opéra à la minute," and also the "miniature symphony." He experimented with new stage techniques, incorporating cinematic interludes; has also successfully revived the Greek type of tragedy with vocal accompaniment. He has composed works for electronic instruments, and has demonstrated his contrapuntal skill in such compositions as his 2 string quartets (No. 14 and No. 15), which can be played together as a string octet. He was the first to exploit polytonality in a consistent and deliberate manner; has applied the exotic rhythms of Latin America and the West Indies in many of his lighter works; of these, his Saudades do Brasil are particularly popular; Brazilian movements are also found in his Scaramouche and Le Bœuf sur le toit; in some of his works he has drawn upon the resources of jazz. His ballet La Création du monde, produced in 1923, portraying the Creation in terms of Negro cosmology, constitutes the earliest example of the use of the blues and jazz in a symph. score, anticipating Gershwin

in this respect. Despite this variety of means and versatility of forms, Milhaud has succeeded in establishing a style that is distinctly and identifiably his own; his melodies are nostalgically lyrical or vivaciously rhythmical, according to mood; his instrumental writing is of great complexity and difficulty, and yet entirely within the capacities of modern virtuoso technique; he has arranged many of his works in several versions each.

WORKS: OPERAS: *La Brebis égarée*, "roman musical" (1910–15; Paris, Dec. 10, 1923); *Agamemnon* (1913; Paris, April 16, 1927); *Le Pauvre Matelot*, "complainte en trois actes" (1926; Paris, Dec. 12, 1927); *Les Choéphores* (Paris, June 15, 1919, in concert form; stage perf., Brussels, March 27, 1935); *Les Euménides* (1922; Antwerp, Nov. 27, 1927); *Les Malheurs d'Orphée* (Brussels, May 7, 1926); *Esther de Carpentras*, opéra-bouffe (1925; Paris, Feb. 1, 1938); 3 "minute operas": *L'Enlèvement d'Europe* (Baden-Baden, July 17, 1927), *L'Abandon d'Ariane*, and *La Délivrance de Thésée* (Wiesbaden, April 20, 1928); *Christophe Colomb*, grand opera in 26 scenes, to a book by Paul Claudel (Berlin, May 5, 1930); *Maximilien* (Paris, Jan. 4, 1932); *Médée* (Antwerp, Oct. 7, 1939); *Bolivar* (1943; Paris, May 12, 1950); *Le Jeu de Robin et Marion*, mystery play after Adam de la Halle (Wiesbaden, Oct. 28, 1951); *David*, opera in 5 acts and 12 scenes (Jerusalem, June 1, 1954, to celebrate the establishment of Jerusalem as the capital of Judea); *La Mère coupable*, to a libretto by Madeleine Milhaud, after Beaumarchais (Geneva, June 13, 1966); *Saint Louis, Roi de France*, opera-oratorio to the poem by Paul Claudel (1970–71; Rio de Janeiro, April 14, 1972); *Jeux d'enfants* (short plays for children for voice and instruments); *A propos de bottes* (1932), *Un Petit Peu de musique* (1933), *Un Petit Peu d'exercise* (1937).

BALLETS: *L'Homme et son désir* (Paris, June 6, 1921); *Le Bœuf sur le toit* (Paris, Feb. 21, 1920); *Les Mariés de la Tour Eiffel* (Paris, June 19, 1921; with Honegger, Auric, Poulenc, and Tailleferre); *La Création du monde* (Paris, Oct. 25, 1923); *Salade*, "ballet chanté" (Paris, May 17, 1924); *Le Train bleu*, "danced operetta" (Paris, June 20, 1924); *Polka* for a ballet, *L'Éventail de Jeanne*, homage to Jeanne Dubost, patroness of music (other numbers contributed by Ravel, Ibert, Roussel, and others; Paris, June 16, 1927); *'adame Miroir* (Paris, May 31, 1948); *Jeux de printemps* (Washington, D.C., Martha Graham, choreographer, Oct. 30, 1944); *The Bells*, after Poe (Chicago, April 26, 1946); *Vendange* (1952; produced 20 years later, Nice, April 17, 1972); *La Rose des vents* (Paris, 1958); *La Branche des oiseaux* (Nice, 1965).

FOR ORCH: *Suite symphonique* No. 1 (Paris, May 26, 1914); *Suite symphonique* No. 2 (from incidental music to Paul Claudel's *Protée*; Paris, Oct. 24, 1920); 5 symphs. for Small Orch.: No. 1, *Le Printemps* (1917), No. 2, *Pastorale* (1918), No. 3, *Sérénade* (1921), No. 4, *Dixtuor à cordes* (1921), No. 5, *Dixtuor d'instruments à vent* (1922); 12 symphs. for Large Orch.: No. 1 (Chicago, Oct. 17, 1940, composer conducting); No. 2 (Boston, Dec. 20, 1946, composer conducting); No. 3, *Hymnus ambrosianus*, with Chorus (Paris, Oct. 30, 1947); No. 4 (Paris, May 20, 1948, composer conducting); No. 5 (Turin, Oct. 16, 1953); No. 6 (Boston, Oct. 7, 1955; composer conducting); No. 7 (Chicago, March 3, 1956); No. 8, subtitled *Rhodanienne* (Univ. of Calif., Berkeley, Festival, April 22, 1958); No. 9, (Fort Lauderdale, Fla., March 29, 1960); No. 10 (Portland, Oreg., April 4, 1961); No. 11, *Romantique* (1960; Dallas, Texas, Dec. 12, 1960); No. 12, *Rural* (Davis, Calif., Feb. 16, 1962); *Cinéma-Fantaisie sur Le Bœuf sur le toit* for Violin and Orch. (Paris, Dec. 4, 1920); *Caramel mou,* a shimmy, for Jazz Band (1920); *5 études* for Piano and Orch. (Paris, Jan. 20, 1921); *Saudades do Brasil,* suite of dances (also for Piano; 12 numbers; 1920–21); *Ballade* for Piano and Orch. (1921); *3 Rag Caprices* (Paris, Nov. 23, 1923); *Le Carnaval d'Aix,* for Piano and Orch. (N.Y., Dec. 9, 1926, composer soloist); *2 hymnes* (1927); Violin Concerto No. 1 (1927); Viola Concerto (Amsterdam, Dec. 15, 1929); Concerto for Percussion and Small Orch. (Paris, Dec. 5, 1930); Piano Concerto No. 1 (Paris, Nov. 23, 1934); *Concertino de printemps,* for Violin and Orch. (Paris, March 21, 1935); Cello Concerto No. 1 (Paris, June 28, 1935); *Suite provençale* (Venice Festival, Sept. 12, 1937); *L'Oiseau* (Paris, Jan. 30, 1938); *Cortège funèbre* (N.Y., Aug. 4, 1940); Piano Concerto No. 2 (Chicago, Dec. 18, 1941, composer soloist); Concerto for 2 Pianos and Orch. (Pittsburgh, Nov. 13, 1942); *Opus Americanum* (San Francisco, Dec. 6, 1943); Clarinet Concerto (1941; Washington, Jan. 30, 1946); *Suite française* (Goldman Band, N.Y., June 13, 1945; for Orch., N.Y. Phil., July 29, 1945); *Cain and Abel* for Narrator and Orch. (Hollywood, Oct. 21, 1945); *Le Bal martiniquais* (N.Y., Dec. 6, 1945, composer conducting); *2 Marches* (CBS, N.Y., Dec. 12, 1945); *Fête de la Victoire* (1945); Cello Concerto No. 2 (N.Y., Nov. 28, 1946); *Suite* for Harmonica and Orch. (1942; Paris, May 28, 1947, Larry Adler, soloist; also for Violin and Orch., Philadelphia, Nov. 16, 1945, Zino Francescatti, soloist); Concerto No. 3 for Piano and Orch. (Prague, May 26, 1946); Violin Concerto No. 2 (Paris, Nov. 7, 1948); *L'Apothéose de Molière* for Harpsichord and Strings (Capri, Sept. 15, 1948); *Kentuckiana* (Louisville, Jan. 4, 1949); Concerto for Marimba, Vibraphone, and Orch. (St. Louis, Feb. 12, 1949); Piano Concerto No. 4 (Boston, March 3, 1950); Piano Concerto No. 5 (N.Y., June 25, 1956); *West Point Suite* for Band (West Point, May 30, 1952); *Concertino d'hiver* for Trombone and String Orch. (1953); *Ouverture méditerranéenne* (Louisville, May 22, 1954); Harp Concerto (Venice, Sept. 17, 1954); Oboe Concerto (1957); Concerto No. 3 for Violin and Orch. (*Concerto royal,* 1958); *Aubade* (Oakland; Calif., March 14, 1961); *Ouverture philharmonique* (N.Y., Nov. 30, 1962); *A Frenchman in New York* (Boston, June 25, 1963); *Odes pour les morts des guerres* (1963); *Murder of a Great Chief of State,* in memory of John F. Kennedy (Oakland, Calif., Dec. 3, 1963); *Pacem in terris,* choral symph. (Paris, Dec. 20, 1963); *Music for Boston* for Violin and Orch. (1965); *Musique pour Prague* (Prague, May 20, 1966); *Musique pour l'Indiana* (Indianapolis, Oct. 29, 1966); *Musique pour Lisbonne* (1966); *Musique pour Nouvelle Orléans* (commissioned by the New Orleans Symph. Orch., but unaccountably canceled, and perf. for the first time instead in As-

pen, Colo., Aug. 11, 1968, with Milhaud conducting); *Musique pour l'Univers Claudelien* (Aix-en-Provence, July 30, 1968); *Musique pour Graz* (Graz, Nov. 24, 1970); *Musique pour San Francisco,* "with the participation of the audience"(1971); *Suite in G* (San Rafael, Calif., Sept. 25, 1971); *Ode pour Jerusalem* (1972).

CHAMBER MUSIC: 18 string quartets (1912–51), of which No. 14 and No. 15 are playable together, forming an octet; first perf. in this form at Mills College, Oakland, Calif., Aug. 10, 1949); 2 violin sonatas (1911, 1917); Sonata for Piano and 2 Violins (1914); *Le Printemps* for Piano and Violin (1914); Sonata for Piano, Flute, Clarinet, and Oboe (1918); Sonatina for Flute and Piano (1922); *Impromptu* for Violin and Piano (1926); *3 Caprices de Paganini* for Violin and Piano (1927); Sonatina for Clarinet and Piano (1927); *Pastorale* for Oboe, Clarinet, and Bassoon (1935); *Suite* for Oboe, Clarinet, and Bassoon (1937); *La Cheminée du Roi René,* suite for Flute, Oboe, Clarinet, Horn, and Bassoon (1939); Sonatina for 2 Violins (1940); *Sonatine à trois* for Violin, Viola, and Cello (1940); Sonatina for Violin and Viola (1941); *Quatre visages* for Viola and Piano (1943); 2 viola sonatas (1944); *Elegie* for Cello and Piano (1945); *Danses de Jacarémirim* for Violin and Piano (1945); Sonata for Violin and Harpsichord (1945); Duo for 2 Violins (1945); String Trio (1947); *Aspen Serenade* for 9 Instruments (1957); String Sextet (1958); Chamber Concerto for Piano, Wind Instruments, and String Quintet (1961); String Septet (1964); Piano Quartet (1966); Piano Trio (1968); *Stanford Serenade* for Oboe and 11 Instruments (Stanford, Calif., May 24, 1970); *Musique pour Ars nova* for 13 Instruments, with aleatory episodes (1969); Wind Quintet (1973).

VOCAL WORKS: 3 albums of songs to words of Francis Jammes (1910–12); *7 Poèmes de la Connaissance de l'Est,* to words by Paul Claudel (1913); *3 Poèmes romantiques* for Voice and Piano (1914); *Le Château,* song cycle (1914); *4 Poèmes* for Baritone, to words by Paul Claudel (1915–17); *8 Poèmes juifs* (1916); *Child poems,* to Tagore's words (1916); *3 poèmes,* to words by Christina Rossetti (1916); *Le Retour de l'enfant prodigue,* cantata for 5 Voices and Orch. (1917; Paris, Nov. 23, 1922, composer conducting); *Chansons bas,* to Mallarmé's words, for Voice and Piano (1917); *2 Poèmes de Rimbaud* for Voice and Piano (1917); *Psalm 136* for Baritone, Chorus, and Orch. (1918); *Psalm 129* for Baritone and Orch. (1919); *Les Soirées de Pétrograd,* in 2 albums: *L'Ancien Régime* and *La Révolution* (1919); *Machines agricoles* for Voice and 7 Instruments, to words from a commercial catalogue (1919); *3 Poèmes de Jean Cocteau* for Voice and Piano (1920); *Catalogue de fleurs* for Voice with Piano or 7 Instruments (1920); *Feuilles de température* for Voice and Piano (1920); *Cocktail* for Voice and 3 Clarinets (1921); *Psalm 126* for Chorus a cappella (1921); *4 Poèmes de Catulle* for Voice and Violin (1923); *6 Chants populaires hébraïques* for Voice and Piano (1925); *Hymne de Sion* for Voice and Piano (1925); *Pièce de circonstance,* to words by Jean Cocteau, for Voice and Piano (1926); *Cantate pour louer le Seigneur* for Soli, Choruses, and Orch. (1928); *Pan et Syrinx,* cantata (1934); *Les Amours de Ronsard* for Chorus and Small Orch. (1934); *Le Cygne* for Voice and Piano, to words by Paul Claudel (1935); *La Sagesse,* for Voices and Small Orch., to words by Paul Claudel (1935; Paris Radio, Nov. 8, 1945); *Cantate de la Paix,* to words by Paul Claudel (1937); *Cantate nuptiale,* after *Song of Songs* (Marseilles, Aug. 31, 1937); *Les Deux Cités,* cantata a cappella (1937); *Chanson du capitaine* for Voice and Piano (1937); *Les Quatre Eléments* for Soprano, Tenor, and Orch. (1938); *Récréation,* children's songs (1938); *3 élégies* for Soprano, Tenor, and Strings (1939); *Incantations* for Male Chorus (1939); *Quatrains valaisans* for Chorus a cappella, to Rilke's words (1939); *Cantate de la guerre* for Chorus a cappella, to Paul Claudel's words (1940); *Le Voyage d'été,* suite for Voice and Piano (1940); *4 chansons de Ronsard* for Voice and Orch. (1941); *Rêves,* song cycle (1942); *La Libération des Antilles* for Voice and Piano (1944); *Kaddisch* for Voice, Chorus, and Organ (1945); *Sabbath Morning Service* for Baritone, Chorus, and Organ (1947); *Naissance de Vénus,* cantata for Mixed Chorus a cappella (Paris Radio, Nov. 30, 1949); *Ballade-Nocturne* for Voice and Piano (1949); *Barba Garibo,* 10 French folk songs, with Orch. (for the celebration of the wine harvest in Menton, 1953); *Cantate de l'initiation* for Chorus and Orch. (1960); *Cantate de la croix de charité* (1960); *Invocation à l'ange Raphael* for 2 Women's Choruses and Orch. (1962); *Adam* for Vocal Quintet (1964); *Cantate de Psaumes* (Paris, May 2, 1968); choral comedy, *Les Momies d'Egypte* (1972).

FOR PIANO: *Le Printemps,* suite (1915–19); 2 sonatas (1916 and 1949); *Saudades do Brasil,* 12 numbers in 2 books (1921); *3 Rag Caprices* (1922; also for Small Orch.); *L'Automne,* suite of 3 pieces (1932); *4 romances sans paroles* (1933); 2 sets of children's pieces: *Touches noires; Touches blanches* (1941); *La Muse ménagère,* suite of 15 pieces (1944; also for Orch.); *Une Journée,* suite of 5 pieces (1946); *L'Enfant aimé,* suite of 5 pieces (also for Orch.; 1948); *Le Candélabre à sept branches,* piano suite (Ein Gev Festival, Israel, April 10, 1952); *Scaramouche,* version for 2 Pianos (1939); *Le Bal martiniquais,* version for 2 Pianos (1944); etc. *Paris,* suite of 6 pieces for 4 Pianos (1948); *6 Danses en 3 mouvements* for 2 Pianos (Paris, Dec. 17, 1970). Also film music; incidental music for plays by Claudel, Romain Rolland, etc. Milhaud publ. a collection of essays, *Etudes* (Paris, 1926), and an autobiography, *Notes sans musique* (Paris, 1949; in Eng. as *Notes without Music,* London, 1952); also *Entretiens avec Claude Rostand* (Paris, 1952), *Ma vie heureuse* (Paris, 1973).

Miller, Dayton Clarence, American physicist and flutist; b. Strongsville, Ohio, March 13, 1866; d. Cleveland, Feb. 22, 1941. After graduation from Baldwin Univ. and Princeton (D.Sc., 1890), he became prof. of physics at the Case School of Applied Science (from 1893). An early interest in the flute led to his experimentation with various versions of the instrument (including a double-bass flute); he accumulated an extensive collection of flutes and various materials relating to the flute,

which he left to the Library of Congress Washington, D.C. A leading authority in the field of acoustics and light, he was president of the American Physical Society (1925–26) and of the Acoustical Society of America (1931–32), and vice-president of the American Musicological Society (1939). He publ. *The Science of Musical Sounds* (1916; revised 1926; reprinted 1934); *Catalogue of Books and Literary Material Relating to the Flute and Other Musical Instruments* (1935); *Anecdotal History of the Science of Sound to the Beginning of the 20th Century* (1935); *Sound Waves, Their Shape and Speed* (1937); etc. He also trans. and annotated Böhm's *The Flute and Flute Playing* (Cleveland, 1908; revised ed., 1922).

Miller, Glenn, American trombonist and band leader; b. Clarinda, Iowa, March 1, 1904; perished in a plane during World War II on a flight from England to France, Dec. 16, 1944. He studied at the Univ. of Colorado; went to N.Y. in 1930; in 1935 joined Ray Noble's band. He then went to Joseph Schillinger to study orchestration; began experimenting with special effects, combining clarinets with saxophones in the same register; the resultant sound became the Glenn Miller hallmark. At the outbreak of World War II, he assembled a large band and flew to England, where he played for the U.S. Air Force. A motion picture, *The Glenn Miller Story,* was produced in 1953.

Miller, Mitch(ell William), American oboist, recording executive, and conductor; b. Rochester, N.Y., July 4, 1911. He studied at the Eastman School of Music (B.Mus., 1932); played oboe in the Rochester Phil. Orch. (1930–33) and in the CBS Symph. Orch. (1935–47); was director of artists and repertoire for the classical division of Mercury Records (1947–50); then was in charge of the popular division of Columbia Records (1950–61); ultimately starred in his own television program, "Sing-Along with Mitch" (1960–65), which became extremely popular.

Miller, Philip Lieson, American librarian and musicologist; b. Woodland, N.Y., April 23, 1906. He studied at the Manhattan Music School and the Juilliard School of Music in N.Y.; from 1927, he worked in the Music Division of the N.Y. Public Library; was assistant chief (1946–59); chief (1959–1966). He was one of the principal founders and first president (1966–68) of the Assoc. for Recorded Sound Collections; in 1963–64, was president of the Music Library Assoc. He publ. many articles and reviews, dealing especially with singers and singing, and the books *Vocal Music* (N.Y., 1955) and *The Ring of Words. An Anthology of Song Texts* (very valuable; N.Y., 1963).

Millöcker, Karl, Austrian operetta composer; b. Vienna, April 29, 1842; d. Baden, near Vienna, Dec. 31, 1899. His father was a jeweler, and Millöcker was destined for that trade, but showed irrepressible musical inclinations and learned music as a child; played the flute in a theater orch. at 16; later took courses at the Cons. of the Gesellschaft der Musikfreunde in Vienna. Upon the recommendation of Franz von Suppé, he received a post as theater conductor in Graz (1864); produced his operettas *Der tote Gast* and *Die beiden Binder* there (both on Dec. 21, 1865). In 1866 he returned to Vienna; from 1869 to 1883 was conductor of the Theater an der Wien; there he presented a number of his operettas, among them *Drei Paar Schuhe* (Jan. 5, 1871); *Wechselbrief und Briefwechsel,* or *Ein nagender Wurm* (Aug. 10, 1872); *Ein Abenteuer in Wien* (Jan. 20, 1873); *Gräfin Dubarry* (Oct. 31, 1879), *Apajune der Wassermann* (Dec. 18, 1880); *Die Jungfrau von Belleville* (Oct. 29, 1881); *Der Bettelstudent* (Dec. 6, 1882; his most successful work; popular also in England and America as *Student Beggar;* N.Y., Oct. 29, 1883); *Gasparone* (Jan. 26, 1884); *Der Vice-Admiral* (Oct. 9, 1886); *Die sieben Schwaben* (Oct. 29, 1887); *Der arme Jonathan* (Jan. 4, 1890; new version by Hentschke and Rixner, 1939; quite successful); *Das Sonntagskind* (Jan. 16, 1892); *Der Probekuss* (Dec. 22, 1894); *Das Nordlicht* (Dec. 22, 1896). Millöcker possessed a natural gift for melodious music; although his popularity was never as great as that of Johann Strauss or Lehár, his operettas captured the spirit of Viennese life.

Mills, Charles, American composer; b. Asheville, N.C., Jan. 8, 1914; d. New York, March 7, 1982. A scion of a long line of English settlers in the Carolinas, Mills spent his formative period of life in a rural environment; was active in sports, but at the same time played in dance bands. In 1933 he went to N.Y. and engaged in serious study of composition, first with Max Garfield and then with Aaron Copland (1935–37), Roger Sessions (1937–39), and Roy Harris (1939–41). He enjoyed composing; wrote mostly in a severe but eloquent contrapuntal style; in virtually his entire career as a composer he pursued the ideal of formal cohesion; his style of composition may be described as *Baroque à l'Américaine.* His quest for artistic self-discipline led him to the decision to become a Catholic, a faith in which no uncertainty exists. He was baptized according to the Roman Catholic rite on May 14, 1944. In 1952 he was awarded a Guggenheim fellowship; he also engaged in teaching. In his last works Mills gradually adopted the serial method of composition, which seemed to respond to his need of strong discipline.

Mills, Frederick Allen ("Kerry"), American composer and music publisher (composed as Kerry Mills; his publishing house was called F.A. Mills); b. Philadelphia, Feb. 1, 1869; d. Hawthorne, Calif., Dec. 5, 1948. In 1892–93 he taught violin at the Univ. of Michigan; in 1895 he publ. in Detroit his own cakewalk march, *Rastus on Parade;* encouraged by favorable sales, he moved to N.Y., where he became one of the most important publishers of minstrel songs, cakewalks, early ragtime, and other popular music. His own compositions were particularly successful; *At a Georgia Campmeeting* (1897) became the standard against which all other cakewalks were measured; performed in Europe by John Philip Sousa, it became popular there as well; it was roundly denounced in the Leipzig *Illustrierte Zeitung* (Feb. 5, 1903), and could well have been the inspiration for Debussy's *Golliwog's Cakewalk.* Some of his other hits also reached Europe; his *Whistling Rufus* (1899) was publ. in Berlin as *Rufus das Pfeifergigerl.*

Milner, Anthony, English composer; b. Bristol, May 13, 1925. He studied with Herbert Fryer and R.O. Morris at the Royal College of Music in London and privately with Mátyás Seiber. He taught at Morley College in London (1947–62); was appointed to the staff of the Royal College of Music in London in 1962. In 1965 he was named lecturer at the Univ. of London, King's College. He publ. *Harmony for Class Teaching* (2 vols.; 1950).

Milnes, Sherrill, American baritone; b. Hinsdale, Ill., Jan. 10, 1935. His father managed a spacious farm at Downers Grove, some distance from Chicago; his mother sang and directed the Congregational church choir at Downers Grove. Sherrill Milnes helped his parents with daily chores, milking cows and removing fecal matter; after cleaning up, he would play piano and violin, which he had learned at home. He honked the tuba in a school band; then enrolled as a medical student in North Central College in Naperville. He finally turned to music, studied voice at Drake Univ. in Des Moines, and also played in jazz groups to earn a living. He transferred to Northwestern Univ. for further musical education, then joined the chorus of the Chicago Symph.; in 1960 he was induced by Boris Goldovsky to join his New England Opera Co., and Milnes traveled with it far and wide in the U.S., performing such prestigious roles as Figaro, Rigoletto, and Escamillo. In 1961 he met Rosa Ponselle in Baltimore, where she resided at the time, and she coached him in some of his roles. He won an award in the competition of the American Opera Auditions in 1964; subsequently made his European debut as Figaro in *The Barber of Seville* at the Teatro Nuovo in Milan on Sept. 23, 1964. Returning to the U.S., he sang, on Oct. 18, 1964, the part of Valentin in *Faust* with the N.Y. City Opera. On Dec. 22, 1965, he made his debut with the Metropolitan Opera in N.Y. as Valentin; he gradually rose to a stellar position with the Metropolitan, scoring acclaim in virtually all the baritone parts of the standard repertoire: Escamillo, Figaro, the Count di Luna, Tonio, Iago, Don Carlo, Rigoletto, and Scarpia; his greatest role was Don Giovanni. He also took time off for guest appearances in Europe. Among his avocations was conducting; he actually led the Milwaukee Symph. Orch. at two weekend concerts in 1975, acquitting himself with surprising allure.

Milojević, Miloje, Serbian composer and writer on music; b. Belgrade, Oct. 27, 1884; d. there, June 16, 1946. He was taught piano by his mother; then entered the Serbian school at Novi Sad. Returning to

Belgrade after graduation (1904), he became a student of literature at Belgrade Univ. and a pupil at the Serbian School of Music. In 1907 he married the singer **Ivanka Milutinović;** they settled in Munich until 1910; Milojević served at the headquarters of the Serbian army in 1914. In 1917–19 he was in France; from 1919, was again in Belgrade. He publ. a school manual, *Elements of the Art of Music* (1922). As a composer, he wrote mostly in small forms; was influenced successively by Grieg, Strauss, Debussy, and Russian modernists; his music contains an original treatment of Balkan folk songs. His piano suite, *Grimaces rythmiques* (in a modern vein), was performed at the Paris Festival on June 26, 1937. His list of works contains 89 opus numbers.

Milstein, Nathan, celebrated Russian-born American violinist; b. Odessa, Dec. 31, 1904. His father was a well-to-do merchant in woolen goods; his mother was an amateur violinist who gave him his first lessons. He then began to study with the well-known Odessa violinist Pyotr Stolyarsky, remaining under his tutelage until 1914; then went to St. Petersburg, where he entered the class of the great teacher Leopold Auer at the St. Petersburg Cons. He began his concert career in 1919, with his sister as piano accompanist. In Kiev he met Vladimir Horowitz, and they began giving duo recitals; later they were joined by Gregor Piatigorsky, and organized a trio. Russia was just emerging from a devastating civil war, and communications with Western Europe were not established until much later. In 1925 Milstein was able to leave Russia; he went to Berlin and then to Brussels, where he met Eugène Ysaÿe, who encouraged him in his career. He gave several recitals in Paris, then proceeded to South America. On Oct. 28, 1929, he made his American debut with the Philadelphia Orch. conducted by Stokowski. In 1942 he became an American citizen. He celebrated the 50th anniversary of his American debut in 1979 by giving a number of solo recitals and appearing as soloist with American orchs. As an avocation, he began painting and drawing, arts in which he achieved a certain degree of self-satisfaction. He also engaged in teaching; held master classes at the Juilliard School of Music in N.Y., and also in Zürich. He composed a number of violin pieces, and wrote cadenzas for the violin concertos of Beethoven, Brahms, and Paganini.

Mimaroglu, Ilhan Kemaleddin, Turkish-American composer and writer on music; b. Istanbul, March 11, 1926. He studied law at the Univ. of Ankara; in 1955 traveled to the U.S. on a Rockefeller fellowship, and settled in N.Y., where he studied theory with Jack Beeson and Chou Wen-Chung, musicology with Paul Henry Lang, and electronic music with Vladimir Ussachevsky at Columbia Univ.; he took lessons in modern composition with Stefan Wolpe, and also received inspiring advice from Edgar Varèse. He was subsequently a recipient of a Guggenheim fellowship (1971–72). He publ. several books in Turkish (*Sounds of America, Jazz as an Art, 11 Contemporary Composers, A History of Music, Little Encyclopedia of Western Music,* etc.). In 1963 he began his association with the Columbia-Princeton Electronic Music Center, where he composed most of his electronic works, among them *Le Tombeau d'Edgar Poe* (1964), *Anacolutha* (1965), *Wings of the Delirious Demon* (1969), and music for Jean Dubuffet's *Coucou Bazar* (1973). He developed compositional methods viewing electronic music in a parallel to cinema, resulting in works for tape in which recorded performance dominates individual rendition. Concurrently, he displayed a growing political awareness in his choice of texts, conveying messages of New Left persuasion in such works as *Sing Me a Song of Songmy,* a protest chant against the war in Vietnam (1971) and *To Kill a Sunrise* (1974). Other works include *Parodie sérieuse* for String Quartet (1947); Clarinet Concerto (1950); *Metropolis* for Orch. (1955); *Pièces futiles* for Clarinet and Cello (1958); *Epicedium* for Voice and Chamber Ensemble (1961); *2 × e.e.* for Vocal Quartet, on poems of e.e. cummings (1963); *September Moon* for Orch. (1967); *Music Plus One* for Violin and Tape (1970); *Cristal de Bohème* for Percussion Ensemble (1971); various piano pieces and songs.

Mingus, Charles, black American jazz musician; b. Nogales, Ariz., April 22, 1922; d. Cuernavaca, Mexico, Jan. 5, 1979. His signal achievement was to elevate the role of the double bass in the rhythm section of the jazz band to that of a melody carrier; by so doing, he created a peculiar type of black instrumentation. He worked in California before moving to N.Y., where he played with Duke Ellington and other famous jazz bandleaders. A highly explosive individual, he became known as the "angry man of jazz." He even expressed his disgust with the very term "jazz": "The word means nigger, second-class citizen." In his own groups he insisted on including white players. He toured Europe in 1972 and 1975, but later sank into depression and retired to Mexico, where he hoped to find a cure for his illness, an amyotrophic lateral sclerosis. A convert to Hinduism, he instructed his last wife to scatter his ashes over the Ganges River. He improvised a number of jazz pieces with sophisticated titles such as *Pithecanthropus Erectus,* which were eventually notated and publ. He also left an autobiography, dictated to a collaborator under the title *Beneath the Underdog: His World as Composed by Mingus* (N.Y., 1971).

Minkus, Alois (Louis), Austrian composer of ballet music; b. Vienna, March 23, 1826; d. there, Dec. 7, 1917. (The exact date of his death was established in 1976 from documentation available in the parish register and the burial records of the city of Vienna.) He was a violinist by profession; as a young man went to Russia, where he was engaged by Prince Yusupov as leader of his serf orch. in St. Petersburg (1853–55). From 1862 to 1872 he was concertmaster of the Bolshoi Theater in Moscow. In 1869 the Bolshoi Theater produced his ballet *Don*

Quixote to the choreography of the famous Russian ballet master Petipa; its success was extraordinary, and its appeal to the Russian audiences so durable that the work retained its place in the repertoire of Russian ballet companies for more than a century, showing no signs of diminishing popularity. Equally popular was his ballet *La Bayadère*, produced by Petipa in St. Petersburg in 1877; another successful ballet by Minkus was *La Fiametta or The Triumph of Love*, originally produced in Paris in 1864. From 1872 to 1885 Minkus held the post of court composer of ballet music for the Imperial theaters in St. Petersburg; he remained in Russia until 1891; then returned to Vienna, where he lived in semi-retirement until his death at the age of 91. The ballets of Minkus never took root outside Russia, but their cursive melodies and bland rhythmic formulas suit old-fashioned Russian choreography to the airiest *entrechat.*

Mirovitch, Alfred, Russian-American pianist; b. St. Petersburg, May 4, 1884; d. Whitefield, N.Mex., Aug. 3, 1959. He graduated from the St. Petersburg Cons. with the first prize in piano as a student of Anna Essipova in 1909; began his concert career in 1911; made 9 world tours; made his American debut in 1921. He conducted master classes in piano at the Juilliard School of Music in N.Y. (1944–52); then joined the faculty of Boston Univ. He edited, for G. Schirmer, Inc., a number of collections of classical piano music for students: *Early Classics for the Piano; Introduction to Piano Classics* (3 vols. for different grades); *Introduction to the Romantics; Introduction to the Study of Bach* (2 vols.); *Introduction to Chopin* (2 vols.); he also edited piano pieces by Russian composers; wrote original piano compositions (*Spring Song, Toccata,* etc.).

Mirzoyan, Edvard, Armenian composer; b. Gori, Georgia, May 12, 1921. He studied at the Erevan Cons., graduating in 1941; then went to Moscow and entered the composition class of Litinsky at the Moscow Cons. In 1948 he was appointed instructor at the Erevan Cons.; in 1965 became a prof. there. In his music he follows a lucid neo-Classical style, while his thematic materials are of native Armenian provenance. He wrote a String Quartet (1947); the cantatas *Soviet Armenia* (1948) and *Lenin* (in collaboration with Arutyunian, 1950); a Symph. for Strings (1962, his strongest composition); songs.

Mischakoff, Mischa, Russian-American violinist; b. Proskurov, April 3, 1895; d. Petoskey, Mich., Feb. 1, 1981. His original name was **Mischa Fischberg;** owing to a plethora of Russian-Jewish violinists named Fischberg, he decided to change his name to Mischakoff, formed by adding the Russian ending *-koff* to his first name, which itself is a Russian diminutive for Michael. He studied with Leopold Auer at the St. Petersburg Cons., graduating in 1912 with a gold medal for excellence; then taught at the Cons. of Nizhny-Novgorod (1918–20); emigrated to the U.S. in 1921 and became a naturalized citizen in 1927. He was concertmaster of the N.Y. Symph.

Orch. (1924–27), the Philadelphia Orch. (1927–29), the Chicago Symph. Orch. (1930–36), the NBC Symph. Orch. under Toscanini (1937–51), and the Detroit Symph. Orch. (1951–68). He was a member of the faculty of the Juilliard School of Music in N.Y. (1940–52); then taught at Oakland Univ. (1965–68) and the Peabody Cons. (1969–70), and was a guest prof. at the Aspen (Colo.) Music Festival (1970–73). At the time of his death, he was teaching at Wayne State Univ. in Detroit.

Mitchell, Donald, eminent English music scholar and publishing executive; b. London, Feb. 6, 1925. He studied at Dulwich College in London (1939–42); after noncombatant wartime service (1942–45), he founded (1947) and then became co-editor (with Hans Keller) of *Music Survey* (1949–52); in 1953–57 he was London music critic of the *Musical Times.* In 1958 he was appointed music editor and adviser of Faber & Faber Ltd., book publishers; in 1965 he became business manager, and in 1973 director, of the firm. He edited *Tempo* (1958–62); was on the music staff of the *Daily Telegraph* (1959–64); in 1963–64 served as music adviser to Boosey & Hawkes Ltd.; in 1967 was a member of the BBC Central Music Advisory Council; in 1971–76 was prof. of music, and from 1976 visiting prof. of music, at the Univ. of Sussex; in 1973 was awarded by it an honorary M.A. degree; received his doctorate in 1977 from Southampton Univ., with a dissertation on Mahler. He lectured widely on musical subjects in the United Kingdom, U.S., and Australia; contributed articles to the *Encyclopædia Britannica* and other reference publications; was active in broadcasting plans for BBC dealing with musical subjects. As a music scholar, Mitchell made a profound study, in Vienna and elsewhere, of the life and works of Gustav Mahler; was awarded in 1961 the Mahler Medal of Honor by the Bruckner Society of America. His major work is a Mahler biography: vol. 1, *Gustav Mahler: The Early Years* (London, 1958; revised ed., 1980); vol. 2, *The Wunderhorn Years* (London, 1976); other publications are *The Language of Modern Music* (London, 1963; 3rd ed., 1970), *The Faber Book of Nursery Songs* (London, 1968) and *The Faber Book of Children's Songs* (London, 1970). He ed. and annotated Alma Mahler's *Gustav Mahler: Memories and Letters* (1968; 3rd revised ed., 1973); also publ. *W.A. Mozart: A Short Biography* (London, 1956). With Hans Keller he compiled the symposium *Benjamin Britten: A Commentary on All His Works from a Group of Specialists* (London, 1952); with H.C. Robbins Landon, *The Mozart Companion* (N.Y., 1956); with J. Evans, he ed. *Benjamin Britten, 1913–1976: Pictures from a Life* (London, 1978).

Mitchell, Leona, talented black American soprano; b. Enid, Okla., Oct. 13, 1948. She was one of 15 children; her father, a Pentecostal minister, played several instruments by ear; her mother was a good amateur pianist. Leona Mitchell sang in local church choirs; then received a scholarship to Oklahoma City Univ., where she obtained her B.Mus. degree in 1971. She made her operatic debut in 1973 as Micaëla in *Carmen* with the San Francisco Spring Opera Theater. She then received the $10,000 Opera America grant, which enabled her to take voice lessons with Ernest St. John Metz in Los Angeles. On Dec. 15, 1975, she made her Metropolitan Opera debut in N.Y. as Micaëla; subsequently sang there the roles of Pamina in *Die Zauberflöte* and Musetta in *La Bohème;* she won critical acclaim for her portrayal of Leonora in *La forza del destino* in 1982.

Mitchell, William John, American musicologist; b. New York, Nov. 21, 1906; d. Binghamton, N.Y., Aug. 17, 1971. He studied at the Inst. of Musical Arts in N.Y. (1925–29); then at Columbia Univ. (B.A., 1930); went to Vienna for further studies (1930–32). Upon his return to N.Y. he was on the staff at Columbia Univ.; received his M.A. there in 1938; became a full prof. in 1952, then served as chairman of the music dept. from 1962 to 1967; concurrently he taught at the Mannes College of Music in N.Y. (1957–68); he subsequently joined the faculty of the State Univ. of N.Y. in Binghamton. Among his publications are *Elementary Harmony* (N.Y., 1939; 3rd ed., revised, 1965); he trans. C.P.E. Bach's *Versuch über die wahre Art das Clavier zu spielen,* publ. in N.Y., 1949, as *Essay on the True Art of Playing Keyboard Instruments*; with F. Salzer, he ed. the *Music Forum* (a hard-cover, unperiodical periodical emphasizing Schenkerian analysis; 1967—); contributed articles on the *Tristan Prelude* and a work of Orlando di Lasso. He also wrote valuable articles dealing with the evolution of chromaticism and chord symbolism.

Mitjana y Gordón, Rafael, eminent Spanish music historian; b. Málaga, Dec. 6, 1869; d. Stockholm, Aug. 15, 1921. He studied music with Eduardo Ocón in Málaga, Felipe Pedrell in Madrid, and Saint-Saëns in Paris; was employed in the Spanish diplomatic service in Russia, Turkey, Morocco, and Sweden.

Mitropoulos, Dimitri, celebrated Greek conductor and composer; b. Athens, March 1, 1896; d. while on the podium conducting a La Scala rehearsal of Mahler's 3rd Symph., Milan, Nov. 2, 1960. He studied composition with Armand Marsick, the Belgian musician who spent many years in Greece, at the Odeon in Athens; wrote an opera after Maeterlinck, *Sœur Béatrice* (1918), performed at the Odeon (May 20, 1919); in 1920, after graduation from the Odeon, he went to Brussels, where he studied composition with Paul Gilson; in 1921 he went to Berlin, where he took piano lessons with Busoni; served as an assistant conductor at the Berlin Opera (1921–24); then returned to Greece, where he became conductor of the municipal orch. in Athens. In 1930 he was invited to conduct a concert of the Berlin Phil.; when the soloist Egon Petri became suddenly indisposed, Mitropoulos substituted for him as soloist in Prokofiev's Piano Concerto No. 3, conducting from the keyboard (Feb. 27, 1930). He played the same concerto in Paris in 1932, as a pianist-conductor,

and later in the U.S. His Paris debut as a conductor (1932) obtained a spontaneous success; he conducted the most difficult works from memory, which was a novelty at the time; also led rehearsals without a score. He made his American debut with the Boston Symph. on Jan. 24, 1937, with immediate acclaim; that same year he was engaged as permanent conductor of the Minneapolis Symph. Orch.; there he frequently performed modern music, including works by Schoenberg, Alban Berg, and other representatives of the atonal school; the opposition that naturally arose was not sufficient to offset his hold on the public as a conductor of great emotional power. He resigned from the Minneapolis Symph. in 1949 to accept the post of conductor of the N.Y. Phil.; shared the podium with Stokowski for a few weeks, and in 1950 became music director. In 1956 Leonard Bernstein was engaged as associate conductor with Mitropoulos, and in 1958 succeeded him as music director. With the N.Y. Phil., Mitropoulos continued his policy of bringing out important works by European and American modernists; he also introduced the innovation of programming modern operas (*Elektra, Wozzeck*) in concert form. A musician of astounding technical ability, Mitropoulos became very successful with the general public as well as with the musical vanguard whose cause he so boldly espoused. While his time was engaged mainly in the U.S., Mitropoulos continued to appear as guest conductor in Europe; he also appeared on numerous occasions as conductor at the Metropolitan Opera House and at various European opera theaters. He became an American citizen in 1946. Mitropoulos was one of the earliest among Greek composers to write in a distinctly modern idiom.

Miyagi, Michio, Japanese virtuoso on the koto and composer; b. Kobe, April 7, 1894; d. near Tokyo (in a railroad accident), June 25, 1956. He lost his eyesight at the age of 7; was instructed in koto playing by a blind musician named Nakajima; in 1908 he went to Korea; in 1917 moved to Tokyo, where he remained most of his life. In 1918 he introduced a koto with 17 strings. He was named a member of the Academy of Fine Arts in Tokyo in 1948; was the Japanese delegate at the Folk Music and Dance Festival in Europe in 1953. He composed more than 1,000 works for the koto and for other Japanese instruments; all of these are descriptive of poetic moods, or suggest a landscape. His Concerto for Koto, Flute, and Orch. entitled *Haru no Umi (Sea at Springtime)* was presented by André Kostelanetz with the N.Y. Phil. on Dec. 31, 1955, with Shinichi Yuize, a member of the Kabuki Dance Group, as soloist on the koto. Other works are *Variations on Etenkagu* for Koto and Orch. (1925); *Ochiba no Odori (Dance of Falling Leaves)* for Koto Solo; etc. He also publ. a book, *Ame no Nembutsu (Prayers for Rain)*.

Miyoshi, Akira, Japanese composer; b. Tokyo, Jan. 10, 1933. He joined the Jiyû-Gakuen children's piano group at the age of 3, graduating at the age of 6. He studied French literature; in 1951 began to study music with Hirai, Ikenouchi, and the French musician Raymond Gallois-Montbrun, who was in Tokyo at that time. He obtained a stipend to travel to France and took lessons in composition with Henri Challan and again with Gallois-Montbrun (1955–57); upon his return to Japan, he resumed his studies in French literature at the Univ. of Tokyo, obtaining a degree in 1961. In 1965 he was appointed instructor at the Toho Gakuen School of Music in Tokyo.

Mizler, Lorenz Christoph, learned German music scholar; b. Heidenheim, Franconia, July 25, 1711; d. Warsaw, March 1778. He entered the Ansbach Gymnasium when he was 13; also took music lessons from Ehrmann in Ansbach, and learned to play the violin and flute. In 1731 he enrolled as a theology student at the Univ. of Leipzig; he received his bachelor's degree in 1733, and his master's degree in 1734 with his *Dissertatio, Quod musica ars sit pars eruditionis philosophicae* (2nd ed., 1736; 3rd ed., 1740). He was a friend of J.S. Bach. In 1735 he went to Wittenberg, where he studied law and medicine. Returning to Leipzig in 1736, he gave his disputation *De usu atque praestantia philosophiae in theologia, jurisprudentia, medicina* (Leipzig, 1736; 2nd ed., 1740). In May 1737 he joined the faculty of the Univ. of Leipzig, where he lectured on Mattheson's *Neu-eröffnete Orchester* and music history. In 1738 he also established the Korrespondierende Sozietät der Musicalischen Wissenschaften. He likewise publ. the valuable music periodical *Neu eröffnete musikalische Bibliothek* (1739–54). In 1743 he entered the service of the Polish Count Malachowski of Konshie, working as a secretary, teacher, librarian, and mathematician; he learned the Polish language and devoted much time to the study of Polish culture. In 1747 he took his doctorate in medicine at the Univ. of Erfurt; that same year he went to Warsaw, where he was made physician to the court in 1752. He was ennobled by the Polish court as Mizler von Kolof in 1768. His vast erudition in many branches of knowledge impelled him to publish polemical works in which he, much in the prevalent manner of 18th-century philosophers, professed omniscience. Thus he publ. the pamphlet *Lusus ingenii de praesenti bello* (Wittenberg, 1735), in which he proposed, by means of a musical game, to advise the German emperor Karl VII on the proper conduct of the war waged at the time. Pugnacious by nature, he derided "the stupidities of conceited self-grown so-called composers making themselves ridiculous" in a lampoon entitled "Musical Stabber" (*Musikalischer Starstecher, in welchem rechtschaffener musikverständigen Fehler bescheiden angemerket, eingebildeter und selbst gewachsener sogenannter Componisten Thorheiten aber lächerlich gemachet werden,* Leipzig, 1739–40). His theoretical writings include *Anfangs-Gründe des General-Basses nach mathematischer Lehr-Art abgehandelt* (an attempt to instruct figured bass by mathematical rules), publ. in Leipzig in 1739. He also translated into German Fux's *Gradus ad Parnassum,* with annotations (Leipzig, 1742). He prepared an autobiography for Mattheson's basic biographical music dictionary, *Grundlage einer Ehren-Pforte* (Hamburg, 1749; new ed. by M. Schneider, Berlin, 1910; reprint, 1969).

Mlynarski, Emil, Polish conductor and composer; b. Kibarty, July 18, 1870; d. Warsaw, April 5, 1935. He studied at the St. Petersburg Cons. (1880–89), taking up both the violin, with Leopold Auer, and piano, with Anton Rubinstein; also took a course in composition with Liadov. He embarked on a career as a conductor; in 1897 he was appointed principal conductor of the Warsaw Opera, and concurrently conducted the concerts of the Warsaw Phil. (1901–5); from 1904 to 1907 he was director of the Warsaw Cons. He achieved considerable success as a conductor in Scotland, where he appeared with Scottish Orch. in Glasgow and Edinburgh (1910–16). He was director of the Warsaw Cons. in 1919–22, and of the Warsaw Opera in 1918–29. From 1929 to 1931 he taught conducting at the Curtis Inst. of Music in Philadelphia; in 1931 returned to Warsaw. He composed some effective violin music, including 2 concertos, of which the first won the Paderewski prize (1898). He also composed a comic opera, *Noc letnia* (*Summer Night;* Warsaw, March 29, 1924).

Mocquereau, Dom André, distinguished French scholar; authority on Gregorian chant; b. La Tessoualle, near Cholet (Maine-et-Loire), June 6, 1849; d. Solesmes, Jan. 18, 1930. In 1875 he joined the Order of Benedictines at the Abbey of Solesmes, devoted himself to the study of Gregorian chant under the direction of Dom Pothier, and became teacher of choral singing in the abbey. After the expulsion, in 1903, of the Order from France, they found a refuge of the Isle of Wight (Quarr Abbey, Ryde), where Mocquereau then became prior; later he returned to Solesmes. He was the founder and editor of the capital work *Paléographie musicale,* of which 17 vols. appeared between 1889 and 1958. Works by Mocquereau include *Le Nombre musical grégorien ou Rythmique grégorienne* (very valuable; 1908–27); *L'Art grégorien, Son but, ses procédés, ses caractères; Petit traité de psalmodie; La Psalmodie romaine et l'accent tonique latin* (1895); *Notes sur l'influence de l'accent et du cursus tonique latins dans le chant ambrosien* (1897); *Méthode de chant grégorien* (1899).

Mödl, Martha, German soprano; b. Nuremberg, March 22, 1912. She studied at the Nuremberg Cons. and in Milan; made her debut as a mezzo-soprano in Remscheid in 1942; later sang in Düsseldorf; in 1948 she joined the Hamburg State Opera. After 1950 she sang dramatic soprano roles with notable success; made many appearances at Bayreuth from 1951 to 1967; in 1955 she took part in the reopening celebrations at the Vienna State Opera. On March 2, 1957, she made her Metropolitan Opera debut as Brünnhilde in *Die Gotterdämmerung;* remained on its roster until 1960. She was made both an Austrian and German Kammersängerin. She was particularly distinguished in Wagnerian parts.

Moeck, Hermann, German music publisher and instrument maker; b. Elbing, July 9, 1896; d. Celle, Oct. 9, 1982. He established his publishing business in Celle in 1930; in 1960 he handed it over to his son **Hermann Moeck, Jr.** (b. Lüneburg, Aug. 16, 1922). The firm was influential in the revival of the manufacture of the vertical flute (recorder) and other Renaissance and early Baroque instruments; Moeck also publ. arrangements and authentic pieces for recorders and the theretofore obsolete fidels. Hermann Moeck, Jr. wrote a valuable monograph, *Ursprung und Tradition der Kernspaltflöten* (2 vols., 1951), also publ. in an abridged form as *Typen europäischer Blockflöten* (Celle, 1967).

Moeran, E(rnest) J(ohn), English composer of Irish descent; b. Heston, Middlesex, Dec. 31, 1894; d. Kenmare, County Kerry, Ireland, Dec. 1, 1950. His father was a clergyman, and he learned music from hymnbooks; then studied at the Royal College of Music; was an officer in the British army in World War I, and was wounded. Returning to London, he took lessons in composition with John Ireland (1920–23); also became interested in folk music; he collected numerous folk songs in Norfolk, some of which were publ. by the Folksong Society (1922). Most of his compositions were inspired by simple folk patterns; his folk-song arrangements are aptly made and are authentic in feeling.

Moevs, Robert W., American composer; b. La Crosse, Wis., Dec. 2, 1921. He studied at Harvard Univ. (A.B., 1942); after service as a pilot in the U.S. Air Force, he took courses in Paris with Nadia Boulanger (1946–51); was a Fellow at the American Academy in Rome (1952–55); returning to the U.S., he was on the music faculty at Harvard Univ. (1955–63); from 1963, was prof. of music at Rutgers Univ. in New Brunswick, N.J. His music is marked by sonorous exuberance and rhythmic impulsiveness; his use of percussion is plangent. He favors ornamental variation forms.

Moffat, Alfred Edward, Scottish music editor and arranger; b. Edinburgh, Dec. 4, 1863; d. London, June 9, 1950. He studied with L. Bussler in Berlin (1882–88); then went to London, where he became active as an editor of violin music by old English composers; he publ. the series Old English Violin Music (London) and Meisterschule der Alten Zeit (Berlin); also publ. numerous arrangements: *The Minstrelsy of Scotland* (200 Scottish songs); *The Minstrelsy of Ireland*; *40 Highland Reels and Strathspeys*; *Songs and Dances of All Nations* (with J.D. Brown); various other eds. of string and vocal music; etc.

Moffo, Anna, American soprano; b. Wayne, Pa., June 27, 1932, of Italian parentage. She studied voice at the Curtis Inst. of Music in Philadelphia; later went to Italy on a Fulbright fellowship and studied at the Santa Cecilia Academy in Rome. She made her debut in Spoleto in 1955, and, progressing rapidly in her career, was engaged at La Scala in Milan, at the Vienna State Opera, and in Paris. Returning to America, she sang with the Chicago Lyric Opera; on Nov. 14, 1959, she made her debut at the Metropolitan Opera in N.Y. as Violetta, obtaining a gratifying success; she continued to sing regularly at the Metropolitan, earning a stellar reputation for both her singing and acting ability.

Mohaupt, Richard, German composer; b. Breslau, Sept. 14, 1904; d. Reichenau, Austria, July 3, 1957. He studied with J. Prüwer and R. Bilke; began his musical career as an opera conductor; also gave concerts as pianist. After the advent of the Nazi regime in 1933, he was compelled to leave Germany because his wife was Jewish; he settled in N.Y. in 1939, and continued to compose; was also active as a teacher. In 1955 he returned to Europe.

WORKS: Operas: *Die Wirtin von Pinsk* (Dresden, Feb. 10, 1938); *Die Bremer Stadtmusikanten* (Bremen, June 15, 1949); *Double Trouble* (Louisville, Dec. 4, 1954); *Der grüne Kakadu* (Hamburg, Sept. 16, 1958). Ballets: *Die Gaunerstreiche der Courasche* (Berlin, Aug. 5, 1936); *Lysistrata* (1946); *The Legend of the Charlatan,* pantomime (1949); *Max und Moritz,* dance-burlesque, after Wilhelm Busch (Karlsruhe, Dec. 18, 1950). For Orch.: Symph. (N.Y. Phil., March 5, 1942); *Stadtpfeifermusik* (London Festival of the International Society for Contemporary Music, July 7, 1946); *Bucolica* for Double Chorus and Orch. (1948); *Trilogy* for Contralto Solo and Orch. (1951); Violin Concerto (N.Y. Phil., April 29, 1954); chamber music; songs; piano pieces.

Moiseiwitsch, Benno, pianist; b. Odessa, Feb. 22, 1890; d. London, April 9, 1963. He studied in Odessa, and won the Anton Rubinstein prize at the age of 9; then went to Vienna, where he studied with Leschetizky. He made his debut in Reading, England, on Oct. 1, 1908, and subsequently made London his home; made his American debut in N.Y. on Nov. 29, 1919, and toured many times in Australia, India, Japan, etc. He represented the traditional school of piano playing, excelling mostly in Romantic music.

Mojsisovics, Roderich von, Austrian composer; b. Graz, May 10, 1877; d. there, March 30, 1953. He studied with Degner in Graz, with Wüllner and Klauwell at the Cologne Cons., and with Thuille in Munich. He conducted a choral group in Brno (1903–7); then taught in various Austrian towns. He became director of the Steiermärkische Musikverein in 1912; it became the Graz Cons. in 1920, and he remained as director until 1931; in 1932–35 he taught music history at the Univ. of Graz; then lectured in Munich and Mannheim; he returned to teach at the Graz Cons. from 1945 to 1948. In his music he was a decided follower of Wagnerian precepts. He wrote 8 operas; 5 symphs.; a symph. poem, *Stella;* 2 overtures; a Violin Concerto; numerous chamber works; songs; publ. the biographies *Max Reger* (1911) and *E.W. Degner* (1919); also *Bachprobleme* (1930); etc.

Mokranjac, Stevan, Serbian composer; b. Negotin, Jan. 9, 1856; d. Skoplje, Sept. 28, 1914. He studied in Munich with Rheinberger, and in Leipzig with Jadassohn and Reinecke; in 1887 he became director of the Serbian Choral Society in Belgrade, with which he also toured. In 1899 he founded the Serbian Music School in Belgrade, and remained its director until his death. He wrote 15 choral rhapsodies on Serbian and Macedonian melodies; a Liturgy of St. John Chrysostomos (publ. in Leipzig, 1901; also with an Eng. trans. as *Serbian Liturgy,* London, 1919); a Funeral Service ("Opelo"); he compiled a large collection of church anthems according to the Serbian usage and derived from old Byzantine modes; wrote a collection of songs for Mixed Chorus, *Rukoveti (Bouquets).*

Mokranjac, Vasilije, Serbian composer; b. Belgrade, Sept. 11, 1923. He was brought up in a musical enviroment (his father was a cellist, a nephew of the famous Serbian composer **Stevan Mokranjac**). He studied piano and composition at the Belgrade Academy of Music. His early works are Romantic in style, but he gradually began experimenting with serial techniques, while safeguarding the basic tonal connotations.
WORKS: Symph. No. 1 (Belgrade, Feb. 2, 1962); Symph. No. 2 (Belgrade, April 1, 1966); Symph. No. 3 (Belgrade, Oct. 25, 1968); *Dramatic Overture* (1950); *Concertino* for Piano, String Orch., and 2 Harps (Belgrade, March 15, 1960); chamber music; piano pieces; incidental music for dramatic plays.

Mokrejs, John, American pianist, composer, and teacher of Czech descent; b. Cedar Rapids, Iowa, Feb. 10, 1875; d. there, Nov. 22, 1968. He studied piano with Leopold Godowsky and theory with Adolph Weidig at the American Cons. of Music in Chicago; was active as a piano teacher in N.Y.; from 1945 to 1966 lived in Los Angeles; then returned to Cedar Rapids.
WORKS: Opera, *Sohrab and Rustum*; operetta, *The Mayflower*; *American Cantata* (on the life of Abraham Lincoln); Piano Trio; String Quartet; songs. He is best known, however, for his teaching pieces for piano: *Valcik (Little Waltz), Boutade, Bird Rondo, Day in Summer, Indian Dance, Harvest Moon, Military Nocturne, Moravian Lullaby, Carillon,* and *Rainbow Pieces.* He also publ. instruction books: *Lessons in Sight Reading* (Chicago, 1909); *Lessons in Harmony* (N.Y., 1913); *Natural Counterpoint* (Chicago, 1941).

Molchanov, Kirill, Soviet composer; b. Moscow, Sept. 7, 1922; d. there, March 14, 1982. He was attached to the Red Army Ensemble of Song and Dance during World War II; after demobilization, he studied composition with Anatoly Alexandrov at the Moscow Cons., graduating in 1949. From 1973 to 1975 he served as director of the Bolshoi Theater and accompanied it on its American tour in 1975. He was primarily an opera composer; his music style faithfully follows the precepts of socialist realism.

Moldenhauer, Hans, German-American musicologist; b. Mainz, Dec. 13, 1906. He studied music with Dressel, Zuckmayer, and Rosbaud in Mainz; was active as a pianist and choral conductor there. In 1938 he went to the U.S., and settled in Spokane, Wash.; as an expert alpinist, he served in the U.S. Mountain Troops during World War II. After the war he organized the Spokane Cons. (founded by him in 1942), incorporated as an educational inst. in 1946. With his wife, the pianist **Rosaleen Moldenhauer** (1926–82), he inaugurated a series of radio broadcasts of 2-piano music; the outgrowth of this was the publ. of his valuable book *Duo-Pianism* (Chicago, 1950). As a music reseacher, he became profoundly interested in the life and works of Anton von Webern; he organized 6 international Webern festivals, in Seattle (1962), Salzburg (1965), Buffalo (1966), at Dartmouth College, Hanover, N.H. (1968), in Vienna (1972), and at Louisiana State Univ., Baton Rouge (1976). His major achievement in research was the formation of the Moldenhauer Archives ("Music History from Primary Sources") embodying a collection of some 10,000 musical autographs, original MSS, correspondence, etc., of unique importance to musical biography. Particularly rich is the MS collection of works of Webern, including some newly discovered works; for this accomplishment, Moldenhauer was awarded in 1970 the Austrian Cross of Honor for Science and Art. Moldenhauer's publications concerning Anton von Webern include *The Death of Anton Webern. A Drama in Documents* (N.Y., 1961); establishes for the first time the circumstances of Webern's tragic death in 1945; *Anton von Webern: Perspectives* (Seattle, 1966): *Anton von Webern, Sketches 1926–1945* (N.Y., 1968) and *Anton von Webern: Chronicle of His Life and Work* (in collaboration with Rosaleen Moldenhauer, N.Y., 1978). Moldenhauer suffered from a hereditary eye disease, Retinitis pigmentosa, and became totally blind in 1980. He remarried in 1982, a few months after his first wife's death.

Molina, Antonio J., Philippine composer and conductor; b. Quiapo, Manila, Dec. 26, 1894; received his primary education at the Boy's Catholic School in his native town; then studied with Bibiano Morales in Manila; founded and directed a string group, Rondalla Ideal; also was engaged as conductor of various theater and cinema orchs. in Manila; wrote popular waltzes; then began to compose more ambitious theater music; conducted at Manila the premiere of his lyric drama *Ritorna Vincitor* (March 10, 1918) and his zarzuelas *Panibuglo (Jealousy;* April 16, 1918) and *Ang Ilaw* (Nov. 23, 1918). In 1925 he became a teacher of harmony at the Univ. of the Philippines; in 1934 he joined the staff of the President's Committee on Filipino Folksongs and Dances. He wrote a Christmas carol for Mixed Chorus and Orch., *The Living Word* (Manila, Dec. 18, 1936); a Quintet for Piano and Strings, based on native folk songs (Manila, Jan 21, 1950); also numerous piano pieces and songs.

Molinari, Bernardino, eminent Italian conductor; b. Rome, April 11, 1880; d. there, Dec. 25, 1952. He studied with Falchi and Renzi at the Santa Cecilia Academy in Rome; in 1912, became conductor of the Augusteo orch. in Rome; also conducted throughout Europe and South America. In 1928 he made his American debut with the N.Y. Phil., which he conducted again during the 1929–30 and 1930–31 seasons; he also appeared with other American orchs. He was a champion of the modern Italian school, and brought out many works by Respighi, Malipiero, and other outstanding Italian composers; publ. a new ed. of Monteverdi's *Sonata sopra Sonata Maria* (1919) and concert transcriptions of Carissimi's oratorio *Giona*, Vivaldi's *Le quattro stagioni*, etc.; also orchestrated Debussy's *L'Isle joyeuse*.

Molinari-Pradelli, Francesco, Italian conductor; b. Bologna, July 4, 1911. He studied in Bologna and in Rome. In 1946 he conducted at La Scala in Milan; in 1951 he was guest conductor in London; also conducted opera at San Carlo, Naples; from 1957 he led successful opera performances in San Francisco and Los Angeles. He is particularly renowned for his interpretations of Wagner and Puccini.

Molique, Wilhelm Bernhard, German violinist and composer; b. Nuremburg, Oct. 7, 1802; d. Cannstadt, near Stuttgart, May 10, 1869. He first studied with his father; King Maximilian I, hearing of his uncommon gifts, sent him to Munich (1816) to study with Rovelli, concertmaster of the Munich Court Orch.; he succeeded Rovelli in that post in 1820; in 1826 he became concertmaster of the Stuttgart orch., with the title of Musikdirektor. He won fame abroad with extended tours in the Netherlands, Russia, England, and France. The political crisis of 1849 caused him to settle in London, where he remained until 1866; he then returned to Germany. His works include 6 violin concertos; 8 string quartets; pieces for violin and piano, and for violin and flute; fantasias, rondos, and other works for solo violin; etc.

Mollenhauer, Eduard, German violinist; b. Erfurt, April 12, 1827; d. Owatoma, Minn., May 7, 1914. He was a violin pupil of Ernst (1841) and Spohr (1843); after a brief concert career in Germany, he went to London, where he joined Jullien's Orch., of which an older brother, **Friedrich Mollenhauer** (1818–85), also a violinist, was a member; after a tour with Jullien's Orch. in the U.S. (1853), the brothers settled in New York as teachers; Eduard Mollenhauer also appeared as a soloist with the N.Y. Phil. Society. He wrote the operas *The Corsican Bride* (N.Y., 1861) and *Breakers* (N.Y., 1881); 3 symphs.; a Violin Concerto; solo pieces for violin (*La Sylphide*, etc.); songs.

Mollenhauer, Emil, American violinist and conductor; son of **Friedrich Mollenhauer;** b. Brooklyn, Aug. 4, 1855; d. Boston, Dec. 10, 1927. He studied violin with his father; in 1872 entered Theodore Thomas's orch.; then joined the Damrosch Orch.; from 1885 to 1888 was a member of the Boston Symph. Orch.; then assumed the conductorship of the Boston Festival Orch., and toured the U.S. with it, featuring many celebrated soloists (Calvé, Nordica, Melba, Campanari, Joseffy, Ysaÿe, Marteau, etc.). In 1899 he was elected conductor of the Boston Handel and Haydn Society, which he led until 1927.

Mollenhauer, Henry, German cellist; brother of **Friedrich** and **Eduard Mollenhauer;** b. Erfurt, Sept. 10, 1825; d. Brooklyn, N.Y., Dec. 28, 1889. In 1853 he was a member of the Royal Orch. in Stockholm; toured the U.S. (1856–58) with Thalberg, Gottschalk, and Carlotta Patti; then settled in Brooklyn as a teacher; founded the Henry Mollenhauer Cons., which later flourished under the direction of his sons **Louis, Henry,** and **Adolph.**

Mollenhauer, Louis, American violinist; son of **Henry Mollenhauer;** b. Brooklyn, Dec. 17, 1863; d. there, Feb. 9, 1926. He studied with his uncle, **Eduard Mollenhauer;** was a member of the Mollenhauer Quintet Club; after his father's death, was director of his cons. (1889–91); then founded his own cons. in Brooklyn.

Moller (or **Möller**), **Joachim.** See **Burck, Joachim.**

Moller, John Christopher, German composer and organist; b. 1755; d. New York, Sept. 21, 1803. In 1790 he appeared in N.Y. as a harpsichordist, but left immediately after his concerts for Philadelphia, where he became organist and composer for the Zion German Lutheran Church (appointed, Oct. 11, 1790). From 1791–92 he took part in the City Concerts (with Reinagle, and later Henri Capron) both as manager and performer. Apparently he was also proficient as a pianist, violinist, and performer on the glass harmonica. In 1793 he was joint proprietor, with Capron, of a music store, which he also used as a music school. Because of the destruction of the Zion Church by fire on Dec. 26, 1794, Moller's income was severely reduced, and in Nov. 1795 he returned to N.Y. In 1796 he succeeded Hewitt in the management of the N.Y. City Concerts with the Van Hagens. His attempt to continue this subscription series by himself, when Van Hagen later left for Boston, was unsuccessful.

Molloy, James Lyman, Irish composer of light music; b. Cornalaur, King's County, Aug. 19, 1837; d. Wooleys, Bucks, Feb. 4, 1909. His operettas (*Students' Frolic, My Aunt's Secret, Very Catching*), numerous songs (*Love's Old Sweet Song, London Bridge, The Kerry-dance, The Postilion, Punchinello*, etc.), and Irish melodies with new accompaniments enjoyed great popularity.

Momigny, Jérôme Joseph de, French music theorist; b. Philippeville, Namur, Jan. 20, 1762; d. in an insane asylum in Charenton, near Paris, Aug. 25, 1842. He studied music early in life, and at the age of 12 was already engaged as a church organist in

St. Omer; in 1785 he went to Lyons. He became involved in the political struggle against the Jacobins in 1793; after their ouster he was appointed provisional municipal officer, and took part in the resistance against the troops of the National Convention; when that enterprise failed, he fled to Switzerland. After the fall of Robespierre he returned to Lyons; then went to Paris, where he remained under Napoleon and the restoration of the monarchy. He opened there a successful music publishing business which flourished for 28 years (1800–28) and which publ. about 750 works by 153 composers, including a number of his own compositions and treatises on music, in which he claimed to have invented a new and unfailing system of theory and harmony; the titles alone, containing such immoderate asseverations as "théorie neuve et générale," "seul système musical qui soit vraiment fondé et complet," "la seule vraie théorie de la musique," etc., reveal his uncommon faith in himself. He bolstered his self-assurance by such declarations as: there can exist only one true art of music; there is one and only one code of morals; there must be a sharp distinction between good and bad combinations of sounds, as there is between right and wrong in morality. By false analogy with order in music, he extolled monarchical rule and publ. numerous pamphlets in support of his reactionary convictions. Not finding a ready response from the authorities, he gradually sank into pathetic solitude and ended his days in an asylum. His tracts, both on music and on politics, are of interest only to investigators of material on depraved mental states, and his own compositions fell into utter desuetude during his lifetime. Riemann publ. a devastating review of Momigny's theories which drove a mortuary nail into his hopes for recognition.

Mompou, Federico, significant Spanish composer; b. Barcelona, April 10, 1893. After preliminary studies at the Cons. of Barcelona he went to Paris, where he studied piano with Isidor Philipp and composition with S.S. Rousseau. He returned to Barcelona during World War I; then was again in Paris until 1941, when he once more went back to Spain. He visited N.Y. in 1970, 1973, and 1978. His music is inspired by Spanish and Catalan melos, but its harmonic and instrumental treatment is entirely modern. He wrote mostly for piano: *6 impressions intimes* (1911–14); *Scènes d'enfants* (1915); *Suburbis* (1916–17); *3 pessebres* (1918); *Cants magics* (1919); *Festes Llunyanes* (1920); *6 charmes* (1921); *3 variations* (1921); *Dialogues* (1923); a series, *Canción y danza* (1918–53); *10 preludes* (1927–51); *3 paisajes* (1942, 1947, 1960); *Música callada* (4 albums, 1959–67); *Suite compostelana* for guitar (1963); choral works and songs.

Monaco, Mario del. See **Del Monaco, Mario.**

Monasterio, Jesús de, famous Spanish violinist and pedagogue; b. Potes, near Santander, March 21, 1836; d. Casar del Periedo, Sept. 28, 1903. He played for the Queen in 1843, and she became his patroness; he made his debut in 1845 in Madrid, as an infant prodigy; studied at the Brussels Cons. with Bériot (violin) and with Fétis (theory). In 1857 he returned to Madrid as honorary violinist of the Royal Chapel; was appointed prof. of violin at the Madrid Cons., and taught there for many years; was its director from 1894 to 1897; conducted the Sociedad de Conciertos (1869–76), and was influential in forming a taste for classical music in Spain. He publ. a number of violin pieces, some of which (e.g., *Adíos a la Alhambra*) were very popular.

Moncayo García, José Pablo, Mexican composer; b. Guadalajara, June 29, 1912; d. Mexico City, June 16, 1958. He studied with Chávez; from 1932 was a member of the Mexican Symph. Orch.; was conductor of the National Symph. Orch. in 1949–52; in company with Ayala, Contreras, and Galindo (also pupils of Chávez), he formed the so-called Grupo de Los Cuatro for the purpose of furthering the cause of Mexican music.

WORKS: Opera, *La mulata de Córdoba* (Mexico City, Oct. 23, 1948); *Huapango* for Orch. (1941), *Homenaje a Cervantes* for 2 Oboes and Strings (Mexico City, Oct. 27, 1947), *Cumbres* for Orch. (Louisville, Ky., June 12, 1954); piano pieces, choruses.

Mondonville, Jean-Joseph Cassanea de (de Mondonville was his wife's maiden name), French violinist and composer; b. Narbonne (baptized, Dec. 25), 1711; d. Belleville, near Paris, Oct. 8, 1772. He appeared as a violinist in the Concert Spirituel in Paris (1734); wrote numerous motets for that organization; succeeded Gervais in 1744 as intendant of the "musique de la chapelle" at Versailles; was music director of the Concert Spirituel from 1755 till 1762. He produced several operas and pastorales: *Isbé* (Paris, April 10, 1742); *Le Carnaval du Parnasse* (Sept. 23, 1749; included ballet scenes); *Titon et l'Aurore* (Paris, Jan. 9, 1753); *Daphnis et Alcimadure* (Fontainebleau, Oct. 29, 1754); also wrote some instrumental music: *Pièces de clavecin en sonates* (with Violin; 1734); *Les Sons harmoniques* for Violin and Continuo (1736); and various other works.

Monestel, Alejandro, Costa Rican composer; b. San José, April 26, 1865; d. there, Nov. 3, 1950. He studied music at the Brussels Cons.; returning to Costa Rica in 1884, he was organist at the San José Cathedral (1884–1902); then lived in N.Y. (1902–37), where he was active as a church organist and composer. He wrote 14 masses, 4 Requiems, 5 cantatas on the life of Jesus; also *Rapsodia costarricense* for Orch. (San José, Aug. 28, 1935); he publ. arrangements of Costa Rican songs.

Moniuszko, Stanislaw, famous Polish composer; b. Ubiel, province of Minsk, Russia, May 5, 1819; d. Warsaw, June 4, 1872. He studied with August Freyer in Warsaw (1827–30) and with Rungenhagen in Berlin (1837–39); served as church organist in Vilna (1840–58), where he also produced a number of his operas. In 1858 he settled in Warsaw; was prof. at the Warsaw Cons. He wrote about 20 operas and operettas; his masterpiece was *Halka,* the first genuinely national Polish opera, which attained a lasting success in Poland, in Russia, and to some extent in Germany. It was first presented in 2 acts in Vilna, by an amateur group (Jan. 1, 1848); then was expanded to 4 acts, and produced 10 years later in Warsaw (Jan. 1, 1858). Other operas are: *Loterya* (Warsaw, Sept. 12, 1846), *Jawnuta* (Vilna, May 20, 1852), *Flis (The Raftsman;* Warsaw, Sept. 24, 1858), *Hrabina (The Countess;* Warsaw, Feb. 7, 1860), *Verbum nobile* (Warsaw, Jan. 1, 1861), *Straszny dwór* (The Haunted Castle; Warsaw, Sept. 28, 1865), *Paria* (Warsaw, Dec. 11, 1869), *Beata* (Warsaw, Feb. 2, 1872), he also wrote about 270 songs (some of which are very popular in Poland); choral works; a symph. poem, *Bajka (Fairy Tale);* etc. Several biographies of Moniuszko have been publ. in Polish: by A. Walicki (1873); J. Karlowicz (1885); B. Wilczynski (1900); A. Koehler (1919); Z. Jachimecki (1924; revised 1961); H. Opienski (1924); S. Niewiadomski (1928); E. Wrocki (1930); T. Joteyko (1932); W. Hulewicz (1933); K. Stromenger (1946). Witold Rudzinski publ. a comprehensive biography with a complete list of works (Warsaw, 1954; 4th ed., 1972) and also brought out an *Almanach moniuszkowski 1872–1952,* on the 50th anniversary of Moniuszko's death (Warsaw, 1952).

Monk, Thelonious ("Sphere"), black American jazz pianist; b. Rocky Mount, N.C., Oct. 10, 1918; d. Englewood, N.J., Feb. 17, 1982. He spent most of his life in Harlem, where he played in nightclubs; gradually surfaced as a practitioner of bebop, set in angular rhythms within asymmetrical bar sequences. His eccentric behavior was signalized by his external appearance; he wore skullcaps and dark sunglasses; time and again he would rise from the keyboard and perform a tap dance. Although not educated in the formal sense, he experimented with discordant harmonies, searching for new combinations of sounds. Paradoxically, he elevated his ostentatious ineptitude to a weirdly cogent modern idiom, so that even deep-thinking jazz critics could not decide whether he was simply inept or prophetically innovative. Monk's own tunes, on the other hand, seemed surprisingly sophisticated, and he gave them impressionistic titles, such as *Crepuscule with Nellie* (Nellie was the name of his wife) and *Epistrophy,* or else ethnically suggestive ones, as in *Rhythm-a-ning.* A profoundly introspective neurotic, he would drop out of the music scene for years, withdrawing into his inner self. During the period between 1973 and 1976 he stayed with an admirer, the Baroness Nica de Koenigswarter, in her mansion in Weehawken, N.J., but was visited daily by his wife, Nellie. He made his last public appearance at the Newport Jazz Festival in 1976, but seemed a faint shadow, a weak echo of his former exuberant personality. His song *Criss-Cross* was used by Gunther Schuller for his *Variations on a Theme of Thelonious Monk.*

Monleone, Domenico, Italian opera composer; b. Genoa, Jan. 4, 1875; d. there, Jan. 15, 1942. He studied at the Cons. of Milan; from 1895 to 1901 was active as a theater conductor in Amsterdam and in Vienna. He attracted attention by producing in Amsterdam (Feb. 5, 1907) an opera, *Cavalleria Rusticana,* to a libretto by his brother **Giovanni,** on the same subject as Mascagni's celebrated work; after its first Italian performance (Turin, July 10, 1907), Mascagni's publisher, Sonzogno, brought a lawsuit against Monleone for infringement of copyright. Monleone was forced to change the title; his brother rewrote the libretto, and the opera was produced as *La Giostra dei falchi* (Florence, Feb. 18, 1914). Other operas were: *Una novella di Boccaccio* (Genoa, May 26, 1909); *Alba eroica* (Genoa, May 5, 1910); *Arabesca* (Rome, March 11, 1913; won first prize at the competition of the City of Rome); *Suona la ritrata* (Milan, May 23, 1916); *Il mistero* (Venice, May 7, 1921); *Fauvette* (Genoa, March 2, 1926); *La ronda di notte* (Genoa, March 6, 1933); also an opera in Genovese dialect, *Scheüggio Campann-a* (Genoa, March 12, 1928). For some of his works he used the pseudonym **W. di Stolzing.**

Monn, Georg Matthias, Austrian composer; b. Lower Austria, April 9, 1717; d. Vienna, Oct. 3, 1750. For many years he was organist of the Karlskirche there. He wrote instrumental works marking a transition from the Baroque to the new style perfected by Johann Stamitz. A selection of his extant works appears in Denkmäler der Tonkunst in Österreich, 31 (15.ii), ed. by Horwitz and Riedel: 3 symphs. of which one, in E-flat, may possibly be by a younger relative, **Johann Christoph Monn** or **Mann** (1726–1782), and a trio sonata; in vol. 39 (19.ii), ed. by W. Fischer and Arnold Schoenberg: 5 symphs., Cello Concerto in G minor, and Harpsichord Concerto in D (together with thematic catalogue of instrumental works of Georg Matthias Monn and Johann Christoph Monn). He wrote several symphs.; one, in E-flat major, formerly ascribed to him, has been proved to be a work by F.X. Pokorný (see *Notes,* Summer 1966, p. 1179). The Quartet Fugues reprinted by Albrechtsberger are by Johann Christoph Monn. G.M. Monn's Harpsichord Concerto was transcribed by Schoenberg for cello and orch. (1933).

Monrad Johansen, David. See **Johansen, David Monrad.**

Monsigny, Pierre-Alexandre, French opera composer; b. Fauquembergues, near St.-Omer, Oct. 17, 1729; d. Paris, Jan. 14, 1817. He was forced at an early age, by his father's death, to support his family; he abandoned his study of music and took a position as clerk in the Bureaux des Comptes du Clergé (1749); then became maître d'hôtel (majordomo) to the Duke of Orléans; in 1754, a performance of Pergolesi's *Serva padrona* so fired his imagination that he decided to try his own skill at comic opera. He took a rapid course of harmony with the double-bass player Gianotti, and soon completed his first stage work, *Les Aveux indiscrets,* produced at the Théâtre de la Foire Saint-Germain (Feb. 7, 1759). In quick succession, and with increasing success, the same theater brought out 3 more of Monsigny's operas: *Le Maître en droit* (Feb. 13, 1760), *Le Cadi dupé* (Feb. 4, 1761), and *On ne s'avise jamais de tout* (Sept. 14, 1761). The members of the Comédie-Italienne, alarmed at the rising prestige of the rival enterprise, succeeded in closing it, by exercise of vested privilege, and took over its best actors. Monsigny thereafter wrote exclusively for the Comédie-Italienne; a few of his operas, however, were first presented at the private theater of the Duke of Orléans, at Bagnolet. The operas produced at the Comédie-Italienne in Paris were *Le Roi et le fermier* (Nov. 22, 1762), *Rose et Colas* (March 8, 1764), *Aline, reine de Golconde* (April 15, 1766), *L'Ile sonnante* (Bagnolet, June 5, 1767), *Le Déserteur* (March 6, 1769), *Le Faucon* (Fontainebleau, Nov. 2, 1771), *La Belle Arsène* (Fountainebleau, Nov. 6, 1773), and *Félix, ou L'Enfant trouvé* (Fountainebleau, Nov. 10, 1777). Here Monsigny stopped abruptly, perhaps (as he himself modestly explained it) for lack of ideas. After the Revolution, he lost the stewardship of the estates of the Duke of Orléans, but the Opéra-Comique allowed him a pension of 2,400 francs; in 1800 he was made Inspector of Instruction at the Cons. (resigning in 1802). In 1813 he was elected to Grétry's chair in the Institut de France. Monsigny possessed an uncommon and natural melodic invention, and sensibility in dramatic expression, but his theoretical training was deficient; still, his works attained the foremost rank among the precursors of the French comic operas.

Montagu-Nathan, Montagu, English writer on music; b. Banbury, Sept. 17, 1877; d. London, Nov. 15, 1958. His original name was **Montagu Nathan;** he changed it legally to Montagu Montagu-Nathan on March 17, 1909. He studied in Birmingham; then took violin lessons with Ysaÿe in Brussels, with Heermann in Frankfurt, and with Wilhelmj in London. He appeared as a violinist in Belfast and Leeds, but soon abandoned concerts in favor of music journalism. He learned the Russian language and wrote several books on Russian music: *A History of Russian Music* (1914), *Handbook to the Piano Works of A. Scriabin* (1916; reprinted 1922); *Contemporary Russian Composers* (1917); and monographs on Glinka, Mussorgsky, and Rimsky-Korsakov.

Monte, Philippe de (**Filippo di Monte** or **Philippus de Monte**), great Belgian composer; b. Mechlin, 1521; d. Prague, July 4, 1603. He went to Italy in his youth and was active there as a singer and teacher. From 1542 to 1551 he was in Naples in the service of the Pinelli family; then went to Rome, where he publ. his first book of madrigals (1554); from Rome he proceeded to Antwerp in 1554, and then to England, where he served as chorus praefectus in the private chapel of Philip II of Spain, the husband of the Queen, Mary Tudor. In Sept. 1555 he left England and went to Italy again; in 1567 he was in Rome. On May 1, 1568, he became Imperial Court Kapellmeister to the Emperor Maximilian II in Vienna; he held this position until his death, which occurred while the court was at Prague during the summer of 1603. In 1572 he was appointed treasurer of Cambrai Cathedral, and in 1577, also a canon (residence was not required for either position there). He was greatly esteemed as a composer; he wrote some 1,000 madrigals, about 40 masses, and many other works of sacred music.

WORKS: MASSES: *Missa ad modulum "Benedicta es"* for 6 Voices (Antwerp, 1579); *Liber primus* (7) *missarum* for 5, 6, and 8 Voices (Antwerp, 1587); Mass for 5 Voices (Venice, 1590); none of his other masses were publ. in his lifetime, and most of these remain in MS. MOTETS: *Sacrarum cantionum ... liber primus* for 5 Voices (Venice, 1572); *Sacrarum cantionum ... liber secundus* for 5 Voices (Venice, 1573); *Sacrarum cantionum ... liber tertius* for 5 Voices (Venice, 1574); *Libro quarto de motetti* for 5 Voices (Venice, 1575); *Sacrarum cantionum ... liber quintus* for 5 Voices (Venice, 1579); *Sacrarum cantionum ... liber sextus* for 5 Voices (Venice, 1584; not extant); *Sacrarum cantionum ... liber primus* for 6 and 12 Voices (Venice, 1585); *Sacrarum cantionum ... liber secundus* for 6 Voices (Venice, 1587); *Sacrarum cantionum ... liber primus* for 4 Voices (Venice, 1596); *Sacrarum cantionum ... liber septimus* for 5 Voices (Venice, 1600); etc.

MADRIGALI SPIRITUALI: *Il primo libro de madrigali spirituali* for 5 Voices (Venice, 1581); *Il primo libro de madrigali spirituali* for 6 Voices (Venice, 1583); *Il secondo libro de madrigali spirituali* for 6 and 7 Voices (Venice, 1589); *Il terzo libro de madrigali spirituali* for 6 Voices (Venice, 1590); *Eccellenze di Maria vergine* for 5 Voices (Venice, 1593).

MADRIGALS: *Madrigali ... libro primo* for 5 Voices (Rome, 1554); *Il primo libro de madrigali* for 4 Voices (Venice, 1562); *Il secondo libro de madrigali* for 5 Voices (Venice, 1567); *Il primo libro de' madrigali* for 6 Voices (c.1568; not extant; 2nd ed., Venice, 1569); *Il secondo libro delli madrigali* for 6 Voices (Venice, 1569); *Il secondo libro delli madrigali* for 4 Voices (Venice, 1569); *Il terzo libro delli madrigali* for 5 Voices (Venice, 1570); *Il quarto libro delli madrigali* for 5 Voices (Venice, 1571); *Madrigali ... libro quinto* for 5 Voices (Venice, 1574); *Il sesto libro delli madrigali* for 5 Voices (Venice, 1575); *Il terzo libro de madrigali* for 6 Voices (Venice, 1576); *Il settimo libro delli madrigali* for 5 Voices (Venice, 1578); *Il quarto libro de madrigali* for 6 Voices (Venice, 1580); *L'ottavo libro delli madrigali* for 5 Voices (Venice, 1580); *Il nono libro de madrigali* for 5 Voices (Venice, 1580); *Il terzo libro de madrigali* for 4 Voices (c.1580; not extant; 2nd ed., Venice, 1585); *Il decimo libro delli madrigali* for 5 Voices (Venice, 1581); *Il quarto libro de madrigali* for 4 Voices (Venice, 1581); *Il primo libro de madrigali* for 3 Voices (Venice, 1582); *Il quinto libro de madrigali* for 6 Voices (Venice, 1584); *L'undecimo libro delli madrigali* for 5 Voices (Venice, 1586); *Il duodecimo libro delli madrigali* for 5 Voices (Venice, 1587); *Il terzodecimo libro delli madrigali* for 5 Voices (Venice, 1588); *Il quartodecimo libro delli madrigali* for 5 Voices (Venice, 1590); *Il sesto libro de madrigali* for 6 Voices (Venice, 1591); *Il settimo libro de madrigali* for 6 Voices (Venice, 1591); *Il quintodecimo libro de madrigali* for 5 Voices (Venice, 1592); *Il sestodecimo libro de madrigali* for 5 Voices (Venice, 1593); *L'ottavo libro de madrigali* for 6 Voices (Venice, 1594); *Il decimosettimo libro delli madrigali* for 5 Voices (Venice, 1595); *Il decimottavo libro de madrigali* for 5 Voices (Venice, 1597); *Il decimonono libro delli madrigali* for 5 Voices (Venice, 1598); *La fiammetta ... libro primo* for 7 Voices (Venice, 1599); *Musica sopra Il pastor fido ... libro secondo* for 7 Voices (Venice, 1600); etc. A complete ed. of his works was edited by C. van den Borren and G. van Doorslaer as *Philippe de Monte: Opera* (31 vols., Bruges, 1927–39; reprint, 1965). R. Lenaerts and others are editing *Philippe de Monte: New Complete Edition* (Louvain, 1975—).

Monte, Toti dal. See **Dal Monte, Toti.**

Montéclair, Michel Pignolet de, French composer; b. Andelot (baptized, Dec. 4), 1667; d. near St.-Denis, Sept. 22, 1737. He was one of the early players of the modern double bass; from 1699 to his death he played in the orch. of the Académie Royale de Musique; there he produced his ballet-opera *Les Fêtes de l'été* (June 12, 1716) and a lyric tragedy, *Jephté,* in 5 acts (Feb. 28, 1732), the first stage work on a biblical subject to be presented at the Académie. He also wrote a Requiem, 6 trio sonatas, flute duets, and "brunettes" (French love songs); publ. a *Nouvelle méthode pour apprendre la musique* (Paris, 1700; revised eds., 1709, 1736), a *Méthode facile pour apprendre à jouer du violon* (Paris, 1712; a pioneer violin method); and *Principes de musique* (Paris, 1736).

Montemezzi, Italo, eminent Italian opera composer; b. Vigasio, near Verona, Aug. 4, 1875; d. there, May 15, 1952. He was a pupil of Saladino and Ferroni at the Milan Cons., and graduated in 1900; his graduation piece, conducted by Toscanini, was *Cantico dei Cantici,* for chorus and orch. He then devoted himself almost exclusively to opera. In 1939 he went to the U.S.; lived mostly in California; in 1949 he returned to Italy. Montemezzi's chief accomplishment is the maintenance of the best traditions of Italian dramatic music, without striving for realism or overelaboration of technical means. His masterpiece in this genre is the opera *L'amore dei tre re* (Milan, La Scala, April 10, 1913), which has become a standard work in the repertoire of opera houses all over the world. Other operas are: *Giovanni Gallurese* (Turin, Jan. 28, 1905); *Hellera* (Turin, March 17, 1909); *La nave* (libretto by Gabriele d'Annunzio; Milan, Nov. 1, 1918); *La notte di Zoraima* (Milan, Jan. 31, 1931); *L'incantesimo* (radio premiere, NBC, Oct. 9, 1943, composer conducting); he also wrote the symph. poems *Paolo e Virginia* (Rome, 1930) and *Italia mia!* (1944), etc.

Monteux, Claude, American flutist and conductor, son of **Pierre Monteux;** b. Brookline, Mass., Oct. 15, 1920. He studied flute with Georges Laurent; then played in the Kansas City Phil. (1946–49); subsequently began a career as a conductor; was music director of the Columbus (Ohio) Symph. Orch. from 1951 to 1956. He then was music director of the Hudson Valley Phil. in Poughkeepsie, N.Y., from 1959 to 1975. He also appeared as a guest conductor in the U.S. and Europe.

Monteux, Pierre, celebrated French conductor; b. Paris, April 4, 1875; d. Hancock, Maine, July 1, 1964. He studied at the Paris Cons. with Berthelier (violin), Lavignac (harmony), and Lenepveu (composition); received first prize for violin (1896); then was a viola player in the Colonne Orch., and later chorus master there; also played viola in the orch. of the Opéra-Comique. He then organized his own series, the Concerts Berlioz, at the Casino de Paris. In 1911 he became conductor for Diaghilev's Ballets Russes; his performances of modern ballet scores established him as one of the finest technicians of the baton. He led the world premieres of Stravinsky's *Petrouchka, Le Sacre du printemps,* and *Le Rossignol;* Ravel's *Daphnis et Chloé;* and Debussy's *Jeux;* conducted at the Paris Opéra (1913–14); founded the Société des Concerts Populaires in Paris (1914); appeared as guest conductor in London, Berlin, Vienna, Budapest, etc. In 1916–17 he toured the U.S. with the Ballets Russes; in 1917, conducted the Civic Orch. Society, N.Y.; in 1917–19, at the Metropolitan Opera House. In 1919 he was engaged as conductor of the Boston Symph. Orch., and held this post until 1924 (succeeded by Koussevitzky); from 1924 to 1934 he was associate conductor of the Concertgebouw Orch. in Amsterdam; in 1929–38 was principal conductor of the newly founded Orch. Symphonique de Paris. From 1936 until 1952 he was conductor of the reorganized San Francisco Symph. Orch.; then continued to conduct in Europe and America; was a frequent guest conductor with the Boston Symph. (conducted it on his 80th birthday, April 4, 1955); also led its concerts at Tanglewood; shared the podium with Munch during the European tour of the Boston Symph. in 1956 (which included Russia). In 1961 (at the age of 86) he became principal conductor of the London Symph. Orch., retaining this post until his death. He was married in 1927 to **Doris Hodgkins,** an American singer (b. Salisbury, Maine, 1895; d. Hancock, Maine, March 13, 1984) who co-founded in 1941 the Domaine School for Conductors and Orchestral Players in Hancock, Maine, of which Monteux was director. She publ. 2 books of memoirs, *Everyone Is Someone* and *It's All in the Music* (N.Y., 1965). After Monteux's death she established the Pierre Monteux Memorial Foundation. As an interpreter, Monteux endeavored to bring out the inherent essence of the music, without imposing his own artistic personality; unemotional and restrained in his podium manner, he nonetheless succeeded in producing brilliant performances.

Monteverdi, Claudio (Giovanni Antonio), great Italian composer; b. Cremona, (baptized, May 15) 1567; d. Venice, Nov. 29, 1643. His surname is also rendered as **Monteverde.** He was the son of a chemist who practiced medicine as a barber-surgeon;

studied singing and theory with Marc' Antonio Ingegneri, maestro di cappella at the Cathedral of Cremona; he also learned to play the organ. He acquired the mastery of composition at a very early age; he was only 15 when a collection of his 3-part motets was publ. in Venice; there followed several sacred madrigals (1583) and canzonettas (1584). In 1589 he visited Milan, and made an appearance at the court of the Duke of Mantua; by 1592 he had obtained a position at the court in the service of Vincenzo I as "suonatore" on the viol (viola da gamba) and violin (viola da braccio). He came into contact with the Flemish composer Giaches de Wert, maestro di cappella at the Mantuan court, whose contrapuntal art greatly influenced Monteverdi. In 1592 Monteverdi publ. his 3rd book of madrigals, a collection marked by a considerable extension of harmonic dissonance. In 1595 he accompanied the retinue of the Duke of Mantua on forays against the Turks in Austria and Hungary, and also went with him to Flanders in 1599. He married Claudia de Cattaneis, one of the Mantuan court singers, on May 20, 1599; they had 2 sons; a daughter died in infancy. In 1601 he was appointed maestro di cappella in Mantua following the death of Pallavicino. The publication of 2 books of madrigals in 1603 and 1605 further confirmed his mastery of the genre. Having already composed some music for the stage, he now turned to the new form of the opera. *L'Orfeo,* his first opera, was given before the Accademia degli Invaghiti in Mantua in Feb. 1607. In this pastoral, he effectively moved beyond the Florentine model of recitative-dominated drama by creating a more flexible means of expression; the score is an amalgam of monody, madrigal, and instrumental music of diverse kinds. In 1607 Monteverdi was made a member of the Accademia degli Animori of Cremona. He suffered a grievous loss in the death of his wife in Cremona on Sept. 10, 1607. Although greatly depressed, he accepted a commission to compose an opera to celebrate the marriage of the heir-apparent to the court of Mantua, Francesco Gonzaga, to Margaret of Savoy. The result was *L'Arianna,* to a text by Rinuccini, presented in Mantua on May 28, 1608. Although the complete MS has been lost, the extant versions of the Lamento d'Arianna from the score testify to Monteverdi's genius in expressing human emotion in moving melodies. In 1614 Monteverdi prepared a 5-part arrangement of his 6th book of madrigals, also publ. separately (Venice, 1623). He further wrote 2 more works for wedding celebrations, the prologue to the pastoral play *L'Idropica* (not extant), and the French-style ballet *Il ballo delle ingrate.* His patron, Duke Vincenzo of Mantua, died in 1612; and his successor, Francesco, did not retain Monteverdi's services. However, Monteverdi had the good fortune of being called to Venice in 1613 to occupy the vacant post of maestro di cappella at San Marco, at a salary of 300 ducats, which was raised to 400 ducats in 1616. His post at San Marco proved to be the most auspicious of his career, and he retained it for the rest of his life. He composed mostly church music, but did not neglect the secular madrigal forms. He accepted important commissions from Duke Ferdinando of Mantua.

His ballet, *Tirsi e Clori,* was given in Mantua in 1616. In 1619 he publ. his 7th book of madrigals, significant in its bold harmonic innovations. In 1624 his dramatic cantata, *Il combattimento di Tancredi e Clorinda,* after Tasso's *Gerusalemme liberata,* was performed at the home of Girolamo Mocenigo, a Venetian nobleman. The score is noteworthy for the effective role played by the string orch. Other works comprised intermedi for the Farnese court in Parma. A great inconvenience was caused to Monteverdi in 1627 when his son Massimiliano, a medical student, was arrested by the Inquisition for consulting books on the Index Librorum Prohibitorum; he was acquitted. In 1630 Monteverdi composed the opera *Proserpina rapita* for Venice; of it only one trio has survived. Following the plague of 1630–31, he wrote a mass of thanksgiving for performance at San Marco (the *Gloria* is extant); in 1632 he took Holy Orders. His *Scherzi musicali* for One and 2 Voices was publ. in 1632. Then followed his *Madrigali guerrieri et amorosi,* an extensive retrospective collection covering some 30 years, which was publ. in 1638. In 1637 the first public opera houses were opened in Venice, and Monteverdi found a new outlet there for his productions. His operas *Il ritorno d'Ulisse in patria* (1640), *Le nozze d'Enea con Lavinia* (1641; not extant), and *L'incoronazione di Poppea* (1642) were all given in Venice. The 2 extant operas may be considered the first truly modern operas in terms of dramatic viability. Monteverdi died at the age of 76 and was accorded burial in the church of the Fratri in Venice. A commemorative plaque was erected in his honor, and a copy remains in the church to this day.

Monteverdi's place in the history of music is of great magnitude. He established the foundations of modern opera conceived as a drama in music. For greater dynamic expression, he enlarged the orch., in which he selected and skillfully combined the instruments accompanying the voices. He was one of the earliest, if not the first, to employ such coloristic effects as string tremolo and pizzicato; his recitative assumes dramatic power, at times approaching the dimensions of an arioso. In harmonic usage he introduced audacious innovations, such as the use of the dominant seventh-chord and other dissonant chords without preparation. He is widely regarded as having popularized the terms "prima prattica" and "secunda prattica" to demarcate the polyphonic style of the 16th century from the largely monodic style of the 17th century, corresponding also to the distinction between "stile antico" and "stile moderno." For this he was severely criticized by the Bologna theorist Giovanni Maria Artusi, who publ. in 1600 a vitriolic pamphlet against Monteverdi, attacking the "musica moderna" which allowed chromatic usages in order to achieve a more adequate expression.

WORKS: In addition to various eds. of his works in separate format, G.F. Malipiero edited a complete ed. as *Claudio Monteverdi: Tutte le opere* (16 vols., Asolo, 1926–42; 2nd ed., revised, 1954; vol. 17, supplement, 1966). All of these are now being superseded by 2 new complete eds.: one, by the Fondazione Claudio Monteverdi, began publication in 1970; the other, ed. by B.B. de Surcy, began issuing simultaneously critical and facsimile eds. in 1972. A list of his works follows:

DRAMATIC: *L'Orfeo,* opera, designated "favola in musica" (Mantua, Feb. 1607; publ. in Venice, 1609); *L'Arianna,* opera (Mantua, May 28, 1608; not extant except for various versions of the Lament); *In ballo delle ingrate,* ballet (Mantua, 1608; publ. in *Madrigali guerrieri et amorosi,* Venice, 1638); Prologue to *L'Idropica,* comedy with music (Mantua, June 2, 1608; not extant); *Tirsi e Clori,* ballet (Mantua, 1616; publ. in *Concerto: Settimo libro,* Venice, 1619); *Le nozze di Tetide,* favola marittima (begun 1616 but unfinished; not extant); *Andromeda,* opera (begun c.1618 but unfinished; not extant); *Apollo,* dramatic cantata (unfinished; not extant); *Il combattimento di Tancredi e Clorinda* (Venice, 1624; publ. in *Madrigali guerrieri et amorosi,* Venice, 1638), *La finta pazza Licori* (composed for Mantua, 1627; never perf.; not extant); *Gli amori di Diana e di Endimione* (Parma, 1628; not extant); *Mercurio e Marte,* torneo (Parma, 1628; not extant); *Proserpina rapita,* opera (Venice, 1630; only one trio extant); *Volgendo il ciel,* ballet (Vienna, c.1636; publ. in *Madrigali guerrieri et amorosi,* Venice, 1638); *Il ritorno d'Ulisse in patria,* opera (Venice, 1640); *Le nozze d'Enea con Lavinia,* opera (Venice, 1641; not extant); *La vittoria d'Amore,* ballet (Piacenza, 1641; not extant); *L'incoronazione di Poppea,* opera (Venice, 1642).

SECULAR VOCAL: Places and dates of publication are included: *Canzonette* for 3 Voices (Venice, 1584); *Il primo libro de madrigali* for 5 Voices (Venice, 1587); *Il secondo libro de madrigali* for 5 Voices (Venice, 1590); *Il terzo libro de madrigali* for 5 Voices (Venice, 1592); *Il quarto libro de madrigali* for 5 Voices (Venice, 1603); *Il quinto libro de madrigali* for 5 Voices (Venice, 1605); *Musica tolta da i madrigali di Claudio Monteverde e d'altri autori, e fatta spirituale da Aquilino Coppini* for 5 and 6 Voices (Milan, 1607); *Scherzi musicali di Claudio Monteverde, raccolti da Giulio Cesare Monteverde suo fratello* for 3 Voices (Venice, 1607); *Il secondo libro della musica di Claudio Monteverde e d'altri autori, fatta spirituale da Aquilino Coppini* for 5 Voices (Milan, 1608); *Il terzo libro della musica di Claudio Monteverde e d'altri autori, fatta spirituale da Aquilino Coppini* for 5 Voices (Milan, 1609); *Il sesto libro de madrigali* for 5 Voices, "con uno dialogo," and 7 Voices, with Basso Continuo (Venice, 1614); *Concerto: Settimo libro de madrigali, con altri generi de canti* for One to 4 and 6 Voices, with Basso Continuo (Venice, 1619); *Scherzi musicali cioè arie, et madrigali in stil recitativo, con una ciaccona . . . raccolti da Bartholomeo Magni* for One and 2 Voices, with Basso Continuo (Venice, 1632); *Madrigali guerrieri et amorosi con alcuni opuscoli in genere rappresentativo, che saranno per brevi episodii frà i canti senza gesto: libro ottavo* for One to 8 Voices and Instruments, with Basso Continuo (Venice, 1638); *Madrigali e canzonette . . . libro nono* for 2 and 3 Voices, with Basso Continuo (Venice, 1651).

SACRED VOCAL: *Sacrae cantiunculae . . . liber primus* for 3 Voices (Venice, 1582); *Madrigali spirituali* for 4 Voices (Brescia, 1583); *Musica tolta da i madrigali di Claudio Monteverde e d'altri autori, e fatta spirituale da Aquilino Coppini* for 5 and 6 Voices (Milan, 1607); *Il secondo libro della musica di Claudio Monteverde e d'altri autori, fatta spirituale da Aquilino Coppini* for 5 Voices (Milan, 1608); *Il terzo libro della musica di Claudio Monteverdi e d'altri autori, fatta spirituale da Aquilino Coppini* for 5 Voices (Milan, 1609); *Sanctissimae virgini missa senis vocibus ad ecclesiarum choros ac Vespere pluribus decantandae —cum nonnullis sacris concentibus ad sacella sive principum cubicula accommodata* for One to 3, 6 to 8, and 10 Voices and Instruments, with Basso Continuo (Venice, 1610); *Selva morale e spirituale* for One to 8 Voices and Instruments (Venice, 1641); *Messa* for 4 Voices, *et salmi* for One to 8 Voices, and *concertati, e parte da cappella, et con le letanie della beata vergine* for 6 Voices (Venice, 1650).

Monteverdi, Giulio Cesare, Italian organist, composer, and writer on music, brother of **Claudio Monteverdi;** b. Cremona, (baptized, Jan. 31) 1573; d. Salò, Lake Garda, during the plague of 1630–31. In 1602 he entered the service of the Duke of Mantua, where his famous brother was maestro di cappella. He composed the music for the 4th intermedio in Guarini's play *L'Idropica,* which was performed for the wedding celebration of the Mantuan heir-apparent, Francesco Gonzaga, with Margaret of Savoy in 1608. His opera *Il rapimento di Proserpina* was given in Casale Monferrato in 1611. In 1620 he was named maestro di cappella of the Cathedral in Salò. He publ. a collection of 25 motets under the title *Affetti musici, ne quali si contengono motetti a 1–4 et 6 voci, per concertarli nel basso per l'organo* (Venice, 1620). A madrigal for 3 Voices and Continuo (1605) and 2 pieces in his brother's *Scherzi musicali* (Venice, 1607) are extant. He contributed to the collection *Scherzi musicali* an important *Dichiaratione,* in which he expounded at length the musical ideas of his brother and gave a vigorous reply to the attacks on Monteverdi by Artusi; an Eng. trans. is found in O. Strunk, *Source Readings in Music History* (N.Y., 1950).

Montgomery, Wes, black American jazz guitarist; b. Indianapolis, March 6, 1925; d. there, June 15, 1968. He played in a local club before joining Lionel Hampton's band in 1948; returned to Indianapolis in 1950, and then established himself as a leading jazz artist in the Midwest; after 1959 he made many tours in the company of his brothers or other small jazz groups. He gained wide recognition with his first record album, *Movin' Wes* (1965), which was followed by *Bumpin'* (1965), *Goin' Out of My Head* (1966), and *A Day in the Life* (1967). He was regarded as one of the great jazz guitarists of his time; his unique style resulted from his use of the thumb as a plectrum.

Montoya, Carlos, popular flamenco guitarist; b. Madrid, Dec. 13, 1903. He began to play the guitar when he was 8; within a few years he performed professionally with various dance groups, and later gave solo recitals which attracted faithful aficionados; he traveled in the U.S., in South America, in Spain, in Japan, and in South Vietnam. He also improvised a number of attractive pieces, among them a *Suite flamenca* for Guitar and Orch. (1966); they were notated by helpers, since Montoya himself never learned to read music.

Moog (pronounced Mohg), **Robert A.,** American electric engineer, inventor of the Moog music synthesizer; b. Flushing, N.Y., May 23, 1934. He attended the Bronx High School of Science (1948–52), Queens College (1952–55), Columbia Univ. (1955–57) and Cornell Univ. (1957–65); received his B.S. in physics from Queens College (1957); B.S. in electrical engineering from Columbia Univ. (1957); Ph.D. in engineering physics from Cornell Univ. (1965). He established the R.A. Moog Co. in 1954 for the purpose of perfecting electronic musical instruments; introduced components of electronic music synthesizers in 1964; the company was incorporated in 1968, with its office at Trumansburg, N.Y. His synthesizer, which has colloquially been dubbed as "The Moog," rapidly acquired popularity. Although even pre-Moog electronic generators could synthesize tone colors, the Moog has achieved a high degree of vitality, which made it an artistic musical medium. The 1969 Moog has a manual of 5½ octaves, with the keys responding to the touch of the fingers, enabling the player to secure an extended spectrum of dynamic gradations. As the technology of the Moog continued to improve, there arose a whole generation of Moog virtuosos; among these, Walter Carlos earned enviable fame for his colorful renditions of Bach's keyboard music in a manner which was popularized as "switched-on Bach."

Moór, Emanuel, Hungarian pianist and inventor; b. Kecskemét, Feb. 19, 1863; d. Mont Pèlerin, near Montreux, Switzerland, Oct. 20, 1931. He studied in Budapest and Vienna; toured the U.S. from 1885 to 1887, as director of the Concerts Artistiques, for which he engaged Lilli Lehmann, Ovide Musin, and other celebrated artists, and also acted as their accompanist. He then lived in London, Lausanne, and Munich. He invented the Moór-Duplex piano, consisting of a double keyboard with a coupler between the two manuals (an octave apart). With the introduction of this piano a new technique was made possible, facilitating the playing of octaves, tenths, and even chromatic glissandos. Some piano manufacturers (Steinway, Bechstein, Bösendorfer) have put the Moór mechanism into their instruments. Moór's 2nd wife, **Winifred Christie** (b. Stirling, Feb. 26, 1882; d. London, Feb. 8, 1965), an English pianist, aided him in promoting the Moór keyboard, and gave many performances on it in Europe and America. She publ. (in collaboration with her husband) a manual of technical exercises for the Moór piano. Needless to say, Moór's invention sank into innocuous desuetude along with phonetic alphabets, Volapük, and similar elucubrations of earnest but impractical innovators. Moór was also a composer; his works include 5 operas: *La Pompadour* (Cologne, Feb. 22, 1902), *Andreas Hofer* (Cologne, Nov. 9, 1902), *Hochzeitsglocken* (Kassel, Aug. 2, 1908; in London, under the title *Wedding Bells,* Jan. 26, 1911), *Der Goldschmied von Paris,* and *Hertha;* 8 symphs. and other orch. works; 4 piano concertos; 3 violin concertos; 2 cello concertos; Triple Concerto for Violin, Cello, and Piano; Concerto for 2 Cellos and Orch.; 2 piano quintets; 2 string quartets; 2 piano trios; *Suite* for 4 Cellos; 12 violin sonatas; 7 cello sonatas; 3 piano sonatas; Hungarian Dances for Piano; Harp Sonata; Sonata for 4 Harps; a great number of songs.

Moor, Karel, Czech composer; b. Bělohrad, Dec. 26, 1873; d. Prague, March 30, 1945. His real name was **Mohr.** He studied at the Cons. of Prague; then went for further study to Vienna. From 1900 to 1923 he was active as a theatrical director and conductor in Bohemia and Serbia; then lived mainly in Prague. He achieved his first success as a composer with the operetta *Pan profesor v pekle (Professor in Hell),* produced in Brno in 1908; his other operas, *Viy,* after Gogol's fantastic tale (Prague, July 14, 1903), and *Hjoerdis* (Prague, Oct. 22, 1905), were also successful. A facile writer, he publ. an autobiography in the form of a novel (Prague, 1906), a vol. of reminiscences (Pilsen, 1917) and a semi-fictional book, *V dlani osudu (In the Hand of Destiny;* publ. posthumously in 1947).

Moore, Douglas Stuart, distinguished American composer and music educator; b. Cutchogue, N.Y., Aug. 10, 1893; d. Greenport, Long Island, N.Y., July 25, 1969. He studied at Yale Univ. with D.S. Smith and Horatio Parker; wrote several univ. songs, among them the football song *Good Night, Harvard,* which became popular among Yale students; after obtaining his B.A. (1915) and Mus.Bac. (1917), he joined the U.S. Navy; following the Armistice of 1918, he attended classes of Vincent d'Indy at the Schola Cantorum in Paris and also took lessons in organ playing with Tournemire and in composition with Nadia Boulanger, and with Ernest Bloch in Cleveland. Returning to the U.S., he served as organist at the Cleveland Museum of Art (1921–23) and at Adelbert College, Western Reserve Univ. (1923–25); in 1925 he received a Pulitzer traveling scholarship in music and spent a year in Europe. In 1926 he was appointed to the faculty of Columbia Univ.; in 1940 he succeeded Daniel Gregory Mason as the head of the music dept. there; many American composers were his students. He retired in 1962. A fine musical craftsman, Moore applied his technical mastery to American subjects in his operas and symph. works. He achieved popular success with his "folk opera" *Ballad of Baby Doe,* dealing with the true story of an actual historic figure during the era of intensive silver mining; the opera was staged on July 7, 1956, at Central City, Colo., where its action took place; the opera had numerous revivals in America, and also in Europe. His other operas were *The Headless Horseman* (1936); *The Devil and Dan-*

iel Webster (N.Y., May 18, 1939); *White Wings,* chamber opera (Hartford, Feb. 2, 1949); *The Emperor's New Clothes* (N.Y., Feb. 19, 1949); *Giants in the Earth* (N.Y., March 28, 1951; awarded the Pulitzer Prize); *Gallantry, a "Soap Opera"* (N.Y., March 15, 1958); *The Wings of the Dove* (N.Y., Oct. 12, 1961); *The Greenfield Christmas Tree* (Baltimore, Dec. 8, 1962); and *Carrie Nation,* to the story of a notorious temperance fighter (Lawrence, Kans., April 28, 1966); he wrote for orch. *Pageant of P.T. Barnum* (Cleveland, April 15, 1926); *Moby Dick,* symph. poem (1927); *A Symphony of Autumn* (1930); *Overture on an American Tune* (N.Y., Dec. 11, 1932); *Village Music* (N.Y., Dec. 18, 1941); *In Memoriam* (Rochester, N.Y., April 27, 1944); Symph. in A (Paris, May 5, 1946; received honorable mention by the N.Y. Music Critics' Circle, 1947); *Farm Journal* for Chamber Orch. (N.Y., Jan. 19, 1948); Violin Sonata (1929); String Quartet (1933); Wind Quintet (1942); Quintet for Clarinet, 2 Violins, Viola, and Cello (1946); Piano Trio (1953). He publ. *Listening to Music* (N.Y., 1932; revised 1963) and *From Madrigal to Modern Music: A Guide to Musical Styles* (N.Y., 1942).

Moore, Gerald, English pianist and preeminent accompanist; b. Watford, July 30, 1899. He studied at the Univ. of Toronto. After a brief career as a concert pianist, he devoted himself almost exclusively to the art of accompaniment, in which he attained the foremost rank and a well-nigh legendary fame. As a witty account of his experiences at the piano he publ. a sort of autobiography, *The Unashamed Accompanist* (London, 1943; revised ed., 1957), followed by an even more unzipped opus, *Am I Too Loud?* (N.Y., 1962), and concluding with a somewhat nostalgic vol., *Farewell Recital: Further Memoirs* (London, 1978), and a rip-roaring sequel, *Furthermoore [sic]: Interludes in an Accompanist's Life* (London, 1983). Of a purely didactic nature are his books *Singer and Accompanist: The Performance of 50 Songs* (London, 1953), *The Schubert Song Cycles* (London, 1975), and *"Poet's Lore" and Other Schumann Cycles and Songs* (London, 1984).

Moore, Grace, American Soprano; b. Nough, Tenn., Dec. 5, 1898; d. Copenhagen, Jan. 26, 1947. She studied at the Wilson Greene School of Music in Chevy Chase, Md., and with Marafioti; first appeared in musical comedy in N.Y. (1921–26); then studied in France. Upon returning to America, she made her operatic debut as Mimi at the Metropolitan Opera House (Feb. 7, 1928), and sang there off and on until 1946; made successful appearances also at the Paris Opéra-Comique (1928); at Covent Garden, London (1935); and at other European centers; also sang with the Chicago City Opera (1937); appeared in several motion pictures. She was killed in an airplane accident, on a flight from Copenhagen to Stockholm. She publ. an autobiography, *You're Only Human Once* (1944).

Moore, John Weeks, pioneer American musicologist and lexicographer; b. Andover, N.H.,

April 11, 1807; d. Manchester, N.H., March 23, 1889. He was a newspaper publisher and editor at Bellows Falls, Vt., where he publ. the *Bellows Falls Gazette* (1838–55); also was for a time editor of the musical journals *World of Music* and *Musical Library.* His magnum opus is the *Complete Encyclopedia of Music, Elementary, Technical, Historical, Biographical, Vocal, and Instrumental* (Boston, 1854; 1004 pages; Appendix, 1875); also the *Dictionary of Musical Information* (1876); he publ. the collections *Sacred Minstrel* (1842), *American Collection of Instrumental Music* (1856), and *The Star Collection of Instrumental Music* (1858); also *Puritanism of Music in America* (18 numbers), *Musical Record* (5 vols.; 1867–70), *Song and Song Writers of America* (200 numbers; 1859–80), etc.

Moore, Mary Carr, American composer; b. Memphis, Tenn., Aug. 6, 1873; d. Inglewood, Calif., Jan. 9, 1957. Her father was a cavalry officer in the U.S. Army, who sang; her mother authored several theater dramas; her uncle, **John Harraden Pratt,** was an organist. The family moved to California in 1885. Mary Moore studied theory with her uncle, and singing with H.B. Pasmore. In 1894 she wrote, to her own libretto, an operetta, *The Oracle,* which was produced in San Francisco in 1894, and she sang the leading part in it. In 1926 she settled in Los Angeles, where she taught at a private piano school. She dedicated herself to the composition of operas. On March 27, 1922, she herself conducted a performance in San Francisco of her "Indian Intermezzo" in one act, *The Flaming Arrow,* to a libretto by her mother. There followed a one-act musical tragedy, *The Leper,* never produced. In 1912 she wrote a "grand opera," *Narcissa,* to a book by her mother, dealing with missionaries and Indians; it was produced in Seattle on April 22, 1912, and revived in San Francisco, when Mary Moore conducted 9 performances of it during the week of Sept. 7, 1925. The next opera was *Rizzio,* based on the tragic fate of Mary Stuart's Italian lute instructor; it was produced in Los Angeles, on May 26, 1932. Her last opera to enjoy a production was *Los Rubios,* depicting the early history of Los Angeles; it was produced in Los Angeles on Sept. 10, 1931. Mary Moore also wrote a Piano Concerto, 2 string quartets, a String Trio, 3 piano trios, 67 piano pieces, 54 choruses, and 220 songs. She made no pretense at musical sophistication in her productions. Her integrity was total.

Moore, Thomas, famous Irish poet, ballad singer, and song composer; b. Dublin, May 28, 1779; d. near Devizes, Wilts, Feb. 25, 1852. He had no regular musical training, but learned to play the piano with the aid of the organist William Warren. He was in London from 1799 to 1803; then received a position as a government functionary in Bermuda; however, he stayed there only a few months; then returned to London by way of the U.S. and Canada. In London he became extremely popular as a ballad singer in the houses of the aristocracy; in 1807 he publ. a volume of poetry, *Irish Melodies,* set to music by Sir John Stevenson. In 1817 he issued his celebrated poem *Lalla Rookh*. An ardent Irish nationalist, he played an important role in the creation and revival of Irish poetry and music. Among his own melodies are *Love thee, dearest*, *When midst the gay*, *One dear smile*, and *The Canadian Boat-Song*. He freely borrowed his musical materials from popular Irish tunes and in some cases modified them sufficiently to produce apparently new songs. He also composed short concerted vocal pieces; the terzetto *O lady fair* and the 3-part glee *The Watchman* won wide popularity. In 1895 Sir Charles Stanford publ. *The Irish Melodies of Thomas Moore: The Original Airs Restored*.

Mooser, Aloys, Swiss organ manufacturer; b. Niederhelfenschwyl, June 27, 1770; d. Fribourg, Dec. 19, 1839. He studied with his father, an Alsatian organist; attained fame as one of the greatest masters in organ building; the quality of the "vox humana" in his organs was particularly admired.

Mooser, R(obert) Aloys, Swiss writer on music; great-grandson of the preceding; b. Geneva, Sept. 20, 1876; d. there, Aug. 24, 1969. His mother was a Russian, and he acquired the knowledge of the Russian language in childhood. He studied with his father and Otto Barblan in Geneva. In 1896 he went to St. Petersburg, where he served as organist at the French church, wrote music criticism for the *Journal de St. Petersbourg*, and made an extensive study of Russian music in the archives. He took courses with Balakirev and Rimsky-Korsakov. In 1909 he returned to Geneva and became active as a music critic there. His reviews were collected in the vols.: *Regards sur la musique contemporaine: 1921–46* (Lausanne, 1946); *Panorama de la musique contemporaine: 1947–1953* (Geneva, 1953); *Aspects de la musique contemporaine: 1953–1957* (Geneva, 1957) *Visage de la musique contemporaine, 1957–1961* (Paris, 1962). He wrote the following books on Russian music: *L'Opéra-comique français en Russie au XVIIIᵉ siècle* (Geneva, 1932; 2nd ed., 1954); *Violonistes-compositeurs italiens en Russie au XVIIIᵉ siècle* (Milan, 1938–50); *Opéras, intermezzos, ballets, cantates, oratorios joués en Russie durant le XVIIIᵉ siècle* (Geneva, 1945; 2nd ed., 1955); *Annales de la musique et des musiciens en Russie au XVIIIᵉ siècle* (of prime importance for new, detailed, and accurate documentation; 3 vols.; Geneva, 1948–51); also wrote *Deux violonistes genevois, G. Fritz et Chr. Haensel* (Geneva, 1968).

Morales, Cristóbal de, eminent Spanish composer; b. Seville, c.1500; d. Málaga, 1553 (between Sept. 4 and Oct. 7). He was a pupil of Fernández de Castilleja, who was chapel master at the Seville Cathedral. From 1526 to 1528, Morales was choirmaster of the Avila Cathedral; then was in Plasencia until 1531. In 1535 he entered the papal choir in Rome (until 1540, and again in 1541–45); he composed much sacred music during this period. After a brief journey to Spain, he returned to Rome and increased his productivity as a composer; he also traveled in the retinue of the Pope to various towns in Italy. From 1545 to 1547 he was choirmaster at the cathedral of Toledo; in 1551 he obtained a similar post at Málaga, where he remained until his death. Morales was one of the outstanding masters of the polyphonic style; he was greatly esteemed by contemporary musicians; Bermudo described him as "the light of Spain in music." 2 books of masses, many motets, Magnificats, and Lamentations were publ. during his lifetime. Modern reprints are in Eslava's *Lira sacro-hispana;* Pedrell's *Hispaniae Schola musica sacra;* Martini's *Esemplare;* Rochlitz's *Sammlung;* etc. The *Opera omnia* are appearing in Monumentos de la Música Española, vols. 11, 13, 15, 17, 20, 21, 24, 34 (Madrid, 1952—).

Morales, Melesio, Mexican composer; b. Mexico City, Dec. 4, 1838; d. San Petro de los Pinos, May 12, 1908. He began to compose salon music for piano and soon acquired sufficient technique to write for the stage; produced 2 operas, *Romeo y Julieta* (Mexico City, Jan. 27, 1863) and *Ildegonda* (Mexico City, Jan. 27, 1866); then went to France and Italy for additional study. Returning to Mexico after 4 years abroad, he presented 2 more operas: *Gino Corsini* (Mexico City, July 14, 1877) and *Cleopatra* (Mexico City, Nov. 14, 1891). Despite his passionate advocacy of national music, he followed conventional Italian models in his own works.

Morales, Olallo Juan Magnus, writer and composer; b. (of a Spanish father and Swedish mother) Almería, Spain, Oct. 15, 1874; d. Tällberg, April 29, 1957. Taken to Sweden as a child, he received his education there, first at Göteborg, then at the Stockholm Cons., with W. Stenhammar and others (1891–99), and in Berlin with H. Urban (composition) and Teresa Carreño (piano). In 1901 he returned to Sweden; was conductor of the Göteborg Symph. Orch. (1905–9). From 1909 he lived in Stockholm; was a prof. at the Stockholm Cons. (1917–39); was secretary of the Academy of Music (1918–40). With T. Norlind, he compiled a history of the Royal Academy of Music on its sesquicentennial (1921); also publ. a handbook of conducting (Stockholm, 1946). His works include a Symph.; several overtures; Violin Concerto (1943); String Quartet; Piano Sonata; *Balada andaluza* for Piano (1946); *Nostalgia* and other character pieces for Piano; choral works; songs.

Moralt, Joseph, eldest brother and first violin in a famous Munich string quartet of brothers; b. Schwetzingen, Aug. 5, 1775; d. Munich, Nov. 13, 1855. **Johann Baptist Moralt,** the 2nd violin (b. Mannheim, March 10, 1777; d. Munich, Oct. 7, 1825), wrote symphs. and string quartets; **Philipp Moralt,** the cellist (b. Munich, Dec. 29, 1780; d. there, Jan. 10, 1830), also played in the Munich municipal band; **Georg Moralt,** the viola player (b. Munich, 1781; d. there, 1818), was a member of the quartet until his death.

Moralt, Rudolf, German conductor; b. Munich, Feb. 26, 1902; d. Vienna, Dec. 16, 1958. He was educated at the Academy of Music in Munich. He then conducted opera in Kaiserslautern (1923–28, 1932–34), Braunschweig (1934–36), and Graz (1937–40). In 1940 he became one of the principal conductors of the Vienna State Opera, continuing there until his death.

Moran, Robert Leonard, American composer of the avant-garde; b. Denver, Jan. 8, 1937. He studied piano; went to Vienna in 1958, where he took lessons in 12-tone composition with Hans Erich Apostel. Returning to America, he enrolled at Mills College, where he attended seminars of Luciano Berio and Darius Milhaud (M.A., 1963). At the same time he painted in the manner of Abstract Expressionism. In 1959 he toured Sweden as a pianist in programs of hyper-modernistic compositions. His music is written in graphic notation, and is animated by surrealistic imagination.

WORKS: *Eclectic Boogies* for 13 Percussionists (N.Y., Jan. 14, 1965); *Interiors* for Any Instrumental Ensemble (San Francisco, April 12, 1965); *Within the Momentary Illumination* for 2 Harps, Electric Guitar, Timpani, and Brass (Tokyo, Dec. 1, 1965); *L'Après-midi du Dracoula* for Any Group of Instruments capable of producing Any Kind of Sound (1966); *Elegant Journey with Stopping Points of Interest* for Orch. (1967); *Smell Piece for Mills College* for Frying Pans and Foods (Mills College, Nov. 20, 1967; originally intended to produce a conflagration sufficiently thermal to burn down the college); *Scream Kiss No. 1* for Harpsichord and Stereophonic Tape (1968); *Let's Build a Nut House,* opera in memory of Paul Hindemith (San Jose, April 19, 1969); *Titus* for Amplified Automobile and Players (1969); *39 Minutes for 39 Autos,* environmental work for 30 Skyscrapers, 39 Auto Horns, Moog Synthesizer, and Players, employing 100,000 Persons, directed from atop Twin Peaks in San Francisco, and making use of Autos, Airplanes, Searchlights and local Radio and Television Stations (San Francisco, Aug. 20, 1969); *Silver and the Circle of Messages* for Chamber Orch. (San Francisco, April 24, 1970); *Hallelujah,* "a joyous phenomenon with fanfares" for Marching Bands, Drum and Bugle Corps, Church Choirs, Organs, Carillons, Rock-'n'-Roll Bands, Television Stations, Automobile Horns, and any other sounding implements, commissioned by Lehigh Univ. for the city of Bethlehem, Pa., with the participation of its entire population of 72,320 inhabitants (staged in Bethlehem, April 23, 1971); *Divertissement No. 3,* a "street opera" (BBC Television, London, 1971); *Evening Psalm of Dr. Dracula* for Prepared Piano and Tape (1973).

Morawetz, Oskar, significant Czech-born Canadian composer; b. Svetla, Jan. 17, 1917. He studied with Jaroslav Křička at Prague Univ. (1933–36); after the invasion of Czechoslovakia by the Nazis in 1939 he went to Paris; then proceeded to Canada by way of Italy and the Dominican Republic; entered the Univ. of Toronto (B.M., 1944; D.Mus., 1953). He taught at the Royal Cons. of Music in Toronto (1946–51) and from 1951 at the Univ. of Toronto. His music is Classical in format, Romantic in spirit, impressionistic in coloring, and modernistic in harmonic usage.

Moreau, Jean-Baptiste, French composer; b. Angers, 1656; d. Paris, Aug. 24, 1733. He was a chorister at the Cathedral of Angers; then was choirmaster at the Cathedral of Langres. After a year in Dijon, he went to Paris in 1686; was introduced at the French court by the Dauphine, and was commissioned by Louis XIV to write several divertissements, among them *Les Bergers de Marly* (1687). He won great success with his musical interludes (recitatives and choruses) for Racine's *Esther* (1698) and *Athalie* (1691), performed at the royal school of St.-Cyr, where Moreau was maître de chapelle; he also wrote music for Racine's *Cantiques spirituels,* for performance at St.-Cyr. His success at court was marred by his dissolute habits; however, he was greatly esteemed as a teacher of singing and composition; among his pupils were Montéclair, J.F. Dandrieu, Clérambault, and the singers Louise Couperin and his own daughter Marie-Claude Moreau. The music to *Esther* and *Athalie,* and the *Cantiques spirituels,* were publ. in the music supplement to P. Mesnard's *Œuvres de J. Racine* (Paris, 1873).

Morel, François d'Assise, Canadian composer; b. Montreal, March 14, 1926. He studied piano with Trudel and composition with Claude Champagne, Isabelle Delorme, and Germaine Malépart at the Quebec Provincial Cons. in Montreal (1944–53); in 1958 was a founding member (along with Joachim, Garant, and Geanne Landry) of Musique de Notre Temps, an organization specializing in performances of new music; then joined the faculty of the Institut Nazareth in Montreal. His music parallels the esthetic fashions of the modern times, from Debussyan coloristic imagism to motoric neo-Classicism to the organized sound of Varèse to the stern serialism of the cosmopolitan avant-garde.

Morel, Jean, French conductor; b. Abbeville, Jan. 10, 1903; d. New York, April 14, 1975. He studied piano with Isidor Philipp, music theory with Noel Gallon, music theory with Maurice Emmanuel, opera conducting with Reynaldo Hahn, and composition with Pierné; subsequently taught at the American Cons. in Fountainebleau (1921–36). At the outbreak of war in 1939 he emigrated to the U.S.; taught at Brooklyn College (1940–43); then conducted opera in Brazil and Mexico. In 1949 he was appointed to the faculty of the Juilliard School of Music in N.Y., and became conductor of the Juilliard Orch. He also conducted at the Metropolitan Opera House in 1956–1962, 1967–68, and 1969–71. He gained wide recognition as a teacher of conducting; retired from Juilliard in 1971.

Morena (real name, **Meyer**), **Berta,** German soprano; b. Mannheim, Jan. 27, 1878; d. Rottach-Egern, Oct. 7, 1952. Her buxom beauty attracted the attention of the famous painter von Lenbach; at his behest, she was engaged (after brief training under

Sophie Röhr-Brajnin in Munich) to sing Agathe in *Der Freischütz* at the Munich Opera (1898), and was immediately successful. She remained at the Munich Opera until 1923; made her American debut with the Metropolitan Opera, N.Y., as Sieglinde (March 4, 1908), and returned to sing in 1910–12 and 1924–25. Her talent as an actress greatly helped her in her career; she was regarded in Germany as one of the most intelligent and musicianly singers; she excelled particularly in the Wagnerian parts (Elisabeth, Elsa, Eva, Isolde, the three Brünnhildes, etc.).

Moreno, Segundo Luis, Ecuadorian composer; b. Cotacachi, Aug. 3, 1882; d. Quito, Nov. 18, 1972. He played the clarinet in a civil band in Quito. He studied at the Quito Cons.; then was active as a military band leader in various localities in Ecuador; in 1937, took over the newly established Cons. Nacional de Música in Cuenca; later was director of the Cons. of Guayaquil. He composed mostly for military band; many of his pieces celebrate various patriotic events in Ecuador, as the cantata *La emancipación* (1920); the overture *9 de Julio* (1925), and various pieces on native motifs, among them *3 suites ecuatorianas* for Orch. (1921, 1944, 1945). He publ. the valuable ethnomusicological treatises *Música y danzas del Ecuador* (1949, in Spanish and Eng.) and *La música de los Incas* (1957).

Morera, Enrique, Spanish composer; b. Barcelona, May 22, 1865; d. there, March 11, 1942. As a child, he was taken to Argentina, and studied in Buenos Aires; then took courses at the Cons. of Brussels. Returning to Barcelona, he studied piano with Albéniz and harmony with Felipe Pedrell. In 1896 he founded the choral society Catalunya Nova, which he conducted for several years; taught at the Escuela Municipal de Música in Barcelona (1910–28). He was an ardent propagandist of Catalan music, and wrote a number of songs to Catalan words; also collected 193 melodies of popular origin. His opera *Emporium*, originally to a Catalan text, was performed first in Italian (Barcelona, Jan. 20, 1906); he wrote more than 50 other stage works (lyric comedies, zarzuelas, operettas, intermezzos, etc.); several symph. poems (*Atlántida, Traidoría*, etc.); a Cello Concerto; some chamber music; a set of 5 sardanas (national dances of Catalonia) for Piano, etc.

Moreschi, Alessandro, the last of the artificial male sopranos; b. Montecompatri, near Rome, Nov. 11, 1858; d. Rome, April 21, 1922. He studied with Capocci in Rome; from 1883 to 1913 was sopranist at the Sistine Chapel in the Vatican. His voice was of such purity and beauty that he was nicknamed "l'angelo di Roma."

Moriani, Napoleone, outstanding Italian tenor; b. Florence, March 10, 1806; d. there, March 4, 1878. He studied with C. Ruga; made his operatic debut in Pacini's *Gli Arabi delle Gallie* in Pavia in 1833; then sang throughout Italy, garnering great praise for his interpretations of Bellini, Donizetti, and Verdi; he created the role of Enrico in Donizetti's *Maria di Rudenz* in Venice in 1838, and that of Carlo in *Linda di Chamounix* in Vienna in 1842; he also sang in London (1844–45). He was forced to retire from the stage in 1847 as a result of the deterioration of his vocal cords.

Morini, Erica (originally **Erika**), violinist; b. Vienna, Jan. 5, 1904. Her father was Italian, her mother Viennese. She studied at her father's school of music in Vienna; then with Ševčík; made her professional debut as a child prodigy, at the age of 12; played with the Gewandhaus Orch. in Leipzig, under the direction of Nikisch (1918). She made her U.S. debut in N.Y. on Jan. 26, 1921; in subsequent years played with virtually all major American orchs.; also toured South America, Australia, and the Orient; eventually settled in N.Y.

Morison, Elsie, Australian soprano; b. Ballarat, Aug. 15, 1924. She studied with Olive Carey at the Melbourne Cons.; made her debut at the Royal Albert Hall in London in 1948; then sang with the Sadler's Wells Opera (1948–54) and at Covent Garden (1953–62). She married the Czech conductor **Rafael Kubelik.**

Morlacchi, Francesco, Italian composer; b. Perugia, June 14, 1784; d. Innsbruck, Oct. 28, 1841. He was a pupil of Caruso in Perugia, and of Zingarelli at Loreto; received the diploma of "maestro compositore" from the Liceo Filarmonico of Bologna (1805). At the time of graduation, he wrote a cantata for the coronation of Napoleon as King of Italy (1805); even earlier he wrote church music and an opera. His first stage work to be performed was an operetta, *Il Poeta spiantata, o Il Poeta in campagna* (Florence, 1807); he showed his contrapuntal skill in the composition of a Miserere in 16 parts; then produced a comic opera, *Il ritratto* (Verona, April 1807), and a melodrama, *Il Corradino* (Parma, Feb. 25, 1808). His first signal success as an opera composer was the production of *Le Danaide* in Rome (Feb. 11, 1810). He was engaged as music director of the Italian Opera in Dresden in 1811; wrote there several operas and, in 1814, a Mass in celebration of the return of the King of Saxony to Dresden; also wrote music for the Russian governor of Dresden during the occupation, and other occasional pieces. He continued to compose operas, for Naples, Milan, Venice, and Genoa, among them *Gianni di Parigi* (Milan, May 30, 1818), *Tebaldo ed Isolina* (Venice, Feb. 4, 1822; his most famous work; produced also in London, Paris, Leipzig, Prague, etc.), and *Colombo* (Genoa, June 21, 1828). When the King of Saxony died in 1827, Morlacchi wrote a Requiem, one of his finest works. He spent the last years of his life partly in Dresden and partly in Italy; he died on his way to Italy, at Innsbruck.

Morley, Thomas, famous English composer; b. Norwich, 1557 or 1558; d. London, Oct. 1602. He studied with William Byrd. From 1583 to 1587 he was organist and master of the choristers at Norwich Cathedral. In 1588 he received his B.Mus. from Oxford. About this time he became organist at St. Paul's Cathedral. By 1591 he had turned spy for the government of Queen Elizabeth I. In 1592 he was sworn in as a Gentleman of the Chapel Royal and was made Epistler and then Gospeller. He was also active as a printer, holding a monopoly on all music publishing under a patent granted to him by the government in 1598. In addition to publishing his own works, he acted as editor, arranger, translator, and publisher of music by other composers. Notable among his editions was *The Triumphes of Oriana* (1601), a collection of madrigals by 23 composers. He gained distinction as a music theorist; his *A Plaine and Easie Introduction to Practicall Musicke* (1597) became famous as an exposition of British musical schooling of his time.

WORKS: MADRIGALS: *Canzonets, or Little Short Songs to Three Voyces* (London, 1593; 3rd ed., enlarged, 1602, as *Canzonets... with Some Songs added by the Author*); *Madrigalls to Foure Voyces: the First Booke* (London, 1594; 2nd ed., enlarged, 1600, as *Madrigalls... with Some Songs added by the Author*); *The First Booke of Balletts to Fiue Voyces* (London, 1595; 3rd ed., 1600); *The First Booke of Canzonets to Two Voyces* (London, 1595); *Canzonets or Little Short Aires to Fiue and Sixe Voyces* (London, 1597); he ed. the last 3 in Italian editions as well; he also ed. *Madrigales: The Triumphes of Oriana, to Fiue and Six Voyces Composed by Divers Seurall Aucthors* (London, 1601). SOLO SONGS: *The First Booke of Aires or Little Short Songs to Sing and Play to the Lute with the Base-Viol* (London, 1600; it contains the song *It was a lover and his lasse* from Shakespeare's *As You Like It*). Many of the preceding works were ed. by E.H. Fellowes in *The English Madrigal School* (4 vols., 1913 et seq.: I, *Canzonets to 2 Voices* [1595] and *Canzonets to 3 Voices* [1593], revised by T. Dart, 1956; II, *Madrigals to 4 Voices* [1594], revised by T. Dart, 1963; III, *Canzonets to 5 and 6 Voices* [1597], revised by T. Dart, 1966; IV *Ballets to 5 Voices* [1600], revised by T. Dart, 1966). *The Triumphes of Oriana* was ed. by E.H. Fellowes in *The English Madrigal School, A Guide to Its Practical Use* (London, 1926; revised by T. Dart, 1962, in *The English Madrigalists*). *The First Booke of Aires* was ed. by E.H. Fellowes in *The English School of Lutenist Song Writers* (London, 1920–32; revised by T. Dart, 1966, in *The English Lute-Songs*). Modern eds. of additional works by Morley include H. Andrews and T. Dart, *Collected Motets* (London, 1959), and T. Dart, ed., *Keyboard Works,* in *English Keyboard Music* (London, 1959). Morley ed. *The First Booke of Consort Lessons, made by divers exquisite Authors for sixe Instruments to play together, viz. the Treble Lute, the Pandora, the Citterne, the Base Violl, the Flute, and the Treble Violl* (London, 1599; 2nd ed., corrected and enlarged, 1611; modern ed. by S. Beck, N.Y., 1959). His treatise *A Plaine and Easie Introduction to Practicall Musicke* (London, 1597) was publ. in a facsimile ed. by E.H. Fellowes (London, 1937); a modernized ed. was publ. by R. Alec Harman (London, 1952; 2nd ed., 1963).

Mornington, Garrett Colley Wellesley, Earl of, father of the Duke of Wellington; b. Dangan, Ireland, July 19, 1735; d. London, May 22, 1781. He was a glee composer. In 1776 and 1777 the Catch Club awarded him prizes for catches; and in 1779 he won a prize for the glee *Here in a cool grot.* Sir Henry Bishop edited a complete collection of his glees and madrigals (1846). Mornington received a Mus.Doc. from the Univ. of Dublin, and was a prof. there from 1764 to 1774.

Moroi, Makoto, Japanese composer, son of **Saburo Moroi;** b. Tokyo, March 12, 1930. He studied composition with his father and Tomojiro Ikenouchi at the Tokyo Academy of Music (1948–52); later taught at the Osaka Univ. of Arts and Science. His music partakes of three different sources which sometimes fuse into a unified modality: ancient Japanese elements, serialism, and sonorism, i.e., organized sound with electronic instruments.

Moroi, Saburo, Japanese composer, father of **Makoto Moroi;** b. Tokyo, Aug. 7, 1903; d. there, March 24, 1977. He studied literature at Tokyo Univ. (1926–28), later took lessons in composition with Max Trapp, orchestration with Gmeindl, and piano with Robert Schmidt at the Hochschule für Musik in Berlin (1932–34). Upon returning to Japan, he was active as a music teacher; among his students who achieved a reputation as composers in their own right were Dan, Irino, and his son **Makoto Moroi.**

WORKS: 2 piano concertos (1933, 1977); 5 symphs.: No. 1 (Berlin, Oct. 2, 1934), No. 2 (Tokyo, Oct. 12, 1938), No. 3 with Organ (Tokyo, May 26, 1950), No. 4 (Tokyo, March 26, 1951), and No. 5 (Tokyo, 1971); Cello Concerto (1936); Bassoon Concerto (1937); Violin Concerto (1939); *2 Symphonic Movements* (1942); Sinfonietta (1943); *Allegro* for Piano and Orch. (1947); *2 Songs* for Soprano and Orch. (1935); fantasy-oratorio, *A Visit of the Sun* (Tokyo, June 30, 1969); Violin Sonata (1930); String Quartet (1933); Piano Quartet (1935); Viola Sonata (1935); Flute Sonata (1937); String Sextet (1939); String Trio (1940); 2 piano sonatas (1933, 1940); *Preludio ed Allegro giocoso* for Piano (1971). Among his numerous publications are a text, *Junsui talicho,* on strict counterpoint, and the 5-vol. *Historical Research of Musical Forms* (Tokyo, 1957–67).

Moross, Jerome, American composer; b. Brooklyn, Aug. 1, 1913; d. Miami, July 25, 1983. He studied music at the Juilliard School in N.Y.; became associated with various ballet groups and wrote a number of scores for the dance, most of them on American subjects, all of them in a vivid folklike manner. In 1940 he went to Hollywood as an arranger; collaborated with Aaron Copland on the score for *Our Town.* He held 2 Guggenheim fellowships, in 1947 and 1948. His first film score was *Close Up* (1948); his other film scores were for *The Cardinal, The Proud Rebel,* and *The Big Country.* For Broadway he wrote music for *Parade* (1935). His works for the dance included *Paul Bunyan* (1934); *American Patterns* (1937); *Frankie and Johnny* (1938); *Guns and*

Castanets (1939); *The Eccentricities of Davy Crockett* (1946); *Robin Hood* (1946). He also wrote ballets-operas: *Susanna and the Elders* (1940); *Willie the Weeper* (1945); *The Golden Apple* (1952); *Gentleman, Be Seated!* (N.Y., Oct. 10, 1963); a ballet suite, *The Last Judgment* (1953); several orch. works, including a Symph. (conducted by Sir Thomas Beecham in Seattle on Oct. 18, 1943); *Beguine* (N.Y., Nov. 21, 1934); and *A Tall Story* (N.Y., Sept. 25, 1938); chamber music, including Sonatina for Clarinet Choir (1966); Sonatina for Strings, Double Bass, and Piano (1967); Sonatina for Brass Quintet (1968); Sonatina for Woodwind Quintet (1970); Sonatina for Divers Instruments (1972); Sonata for Piano Duet and String Quartet (1975); and Concerto for Flute and String Quartet (1978). Shortly before his death he completed a one-act opera, *Sorry, Wrong Number.*

Morphy, Guillermo, Conde de, Spanish courtier and musician; b. Madrid, Feb. 29, 1836; d. Baden, Switzerland, Aug. 28, 1899. He was taken to Germany as a child; there he studied music; took courses with Fétis in Brussels, where he wrote an orch. *Serenata española,* which had several performances. In 1864 he was named "chamber gentleman" to the Prince of Asturias, the future Alfonso XII, and then became his secretary; received his nobiliary title in 1885. He spent much time in Vienna and Paris, and took up the study of Spanish tablature music of the 16th century. His transcriptions (marred by inaccuracies) were publ. posthumously, with an introduction by Gevaert, as *Les Luthistes espagnols du XVIᵉ siècle* (2 vols., Leipzig, 1902; German text by Riemann). In his influential position at the Spanish court, Morphy helped many talented musicians; he was instrumental in procuring a stipend for Albéniz to enable him to study in Brussels.

Morris, Harold, American composer and pianist; b. San Antonio, Texas, March 17, 1890; d. New York, May 6, 1964. He studied at the Univ. of Texas (B.A.) and the Cincinnati Cons.; lectured at the Rice Inst. of Houston, Texas (1933), at Duke Univ. (1939–40), etc.; was on the faculty of the Juilliard School of Music (1922–39); Teachers College, Columbia Univ. (1939–46); received many awards (National Federation of Music Clubs, Philadelphia Music Guild Award, etc.); was one of the principal founders of the American Music Guild in N.Y. (1921). In his music, he reveals himself as a Romanticist; in the main direction of his creative development, he was influenced by Scriabin. Many of his works are of programmatic content; some of them include American thematic material.

Morris, R(eginald) O(wen), English composer and eminent pedagogue; b. York, March 3, 1886; d. London, Dec. 14, 1948. He studied at the Royal College of Music, with Charles Wood; from 1920, taught at the Royal College of Music, with the exception of 2 years (1926–28), when he taught theory at the Curtis Inst. of Music in Philadelphia.

Morris, Wyn, Welsh conductor; b. Triech, Feb. 14, 1929. He studied at the Royal Academy of Music in London and the Salzburg Mozarteum; then was apprentice conductor with the Yorkshire Symph. Orch. (1950–51) and conductor of an army band (1951–53). In 1954 he founded the Welsh Symph. Orch.; in 1957 he went to the U.S., where he led the Cleveland Chamber Orch. and other groups. In 1960 he returned to Great Britain; served as conductor of the choir of the Royal National Eisteddfod of Wales (1960–62), of the Royal Choral Society of London (1968–70), and of the Huddersfield Choral Society (1969–74); then organized the Symphonica of London, with which he gave regular concerts in ambitious programs, particularly of Mahler's music.

Mortari, Virgilio, Italian composer and pianist; b. Passirana di Lainate, near Milan, Dec. 6, 1902. He studied at the Milan Cons. with Bossi and Pizzetti; after a few years as a concert pianist he became an instructor at the Cons. Benedetto Marcello in Venice (1933–40); in 1940 he was appointed prof. of music at the Santa Cecilia Academy in Rome, remaining at this post until 1973; in 1963 he became vice-president there. His music combines the traits of the Italian Baroque and the modern French school of composition. He wrote the operas *Secchi e Sberlecchi* (1927), *La scuola delle moglie* (1930), *La Figlia del diavolo* (Milan, March 24, 1954), and *Il contratto* (1962); he also completed Mozart's unfinished work *L'Oca del Cairo,* which was performed in his version in Salzburg, on Aug. 22, 1936. He further wrote the ballets *L'allegra piazetta* (1945), *Specchio a tre luci* (1973), and numerous orch. works, among them Fantasia for Piano and Orch. (1933), *Notturno incantato* (1940), Piano Concerto (1952), the overture *Eleonora d'Arborea* (1968), *Tripartita* (1972); concertos for solo instruments with orch.: Piano Concerto (1960), Viola Concerto (1966), Double-bass Concerto (1966), Violin Concerto (1967), Double Concerto for Violin and Piano (1968), Cello Concerto (1969), Harp Concerto (1972); also Concerto for String Quartet and Orch. (1937); Sonatina for Harp (1938), *Piccola serenata* for Cello Solo (1946), *Piccola serenata* for Violin Solo (1947), *Duettini concertati* for Violin and Double Bass (1966), *Capriccio* for Violin Solo (1967); vocal works: 2 *Funeral Psalms* in memory of Alfredo Casella for Voice and Instruments (1947); *Alfabeto a sorpresa* for 3 Voices and 2 Pianos (1959); songs with piano. He publ. *La tecnica dell'orchestra contemporanea* (in collaboration with Casella; Milan, 1947; 2nd ed., 1950); also arranged fragments from operas by Galuppi, Pergolesi, and Monteverdi.

Mortensen, Finn, Norwegian composer; b. Oslo, Jan. 6, 1922; d. there, May 21, 1983. He studied harmony with Thorlief Eken (1942), vocal polyphony with Egge (1943), and in the winter of 1956, composition with Niels Viggo Bentzon in Copenhagen. In 1970 he was appointed to the faculty of the Oslo Cons. (renamed the Norwegian State Academy of Music in 1973); succeeded Egge as chairman of the Norwegian Society of Composers (1972–74). In some compositions he adopted a modified 12-tone idiom, supplemented by the devices of permutation and thematic rotation.

WORKS: FOR ORCH.: Symph. (1953; first complete perf., Bergen, Jan. 21, 1963); *Pezzo orchestrale* (1957); *Evolution* (1961); *Tone Colors* (1961); Piano Concerto (1963; Oslo, Sept. 11, 1963); *Fantasia* for Piano and Orch. (1965–66; Oslo, May 6, 1966); *Per orchestra* (1967; Oslo, Nov. 27, 1967); *Hedda* (1974–75); *Fantasia* for Violin and Orch. (1977). CHAMBER MUSIC: String Trio (1950); Wind Quintet (1951); Solo Flute Sonata (1953); Duo for Soprano and Violin (1956); Sonatina for Clarinet Solo (1957); Sonatina for Balalaika and Piano (1957); *5 Studies* for Solo Flute (1957); Sonatina for Solo Viola (1959); Oboe Sonatina (1959); *Fantasia* for Solo Bassoon (1959); Violin Sonata (1959); Viola Sonatina (1959); Piano Quartet (1960); *3 Pieces* for Violin and Piano (1961–63); *Constellations* for Accordion, Guitar, and Percussion (1971); *Neoserialism I* for Flute and Clarinet (1971), *II* for Flute, Clarinet, and Bassoon (1972), and *III* for Violin, Viola, and Cello (1973); *Suite* for Wind Quintet (1972); *Serenade* for Cello and Piano (1972); *3 Pieces* for Solo Accordion (1973); *Construction* for Solo Horn (1974–75); *Adagio and Fugue* for 16 Horns (1976); Sonata for Oboe and Harpsichord (1976); *Fantasia* for Solo Trombone (1977); *Suite* for 5 Recorders and String Quintet (1978–79); String Quartet (1981). FOR PIANO: 2 sonatinas (1943, 1949); 2 sonatas (1956, 1977); *Fantasia and Fugue* (1957–58); 2-Piano Sonata (1964); *Drawing* (1966); *Impressions* for 2 Pianos (1971).

Morton, "Jelly Roll" (real Christian names, **Ferdinand Joseph La Menthe**), black American (actually, a "Creole-of-color," having mixed African and French-American ancestry) ragtime-blues-jazz pianist and composer; b. New Orleans, Sept. 20, 1885; d. Los Angeles, July 10, 1941. Born into a French-speaking family that proudly recalled its former days of wealth and position, Morton grew up surrounded by musical instruments and frequently attended performances at the New Orleans French Opera House. He played several instruments, but settled on the piano, and (against the wishes of his family) was playing professionally by the time he was 15; he worked with Bunk Johnson in 1900, and was particularly successful as a pianist in the local bordellos of "Storyville" (the red-light district of New Orleans). He left New Orleans in 1907 and traveled through much of the U.S., both spreading his concept of ragtime and jazz and learning the various regional styles; he was in N.Y. in 1911, Tulsa in 1912, San Francisco and Chicago in 1915, etc.; also traveled in Mexico and Canada. He was a colorful and flamboyant figure, given to extravagant boasting and flashy living; in addition to his being a musician, he was a professional gambler (cards and billiards), nightclub owner, and producer; he made and lost several fortunes. His early compositions (*King Porter Stomp*, composed 1902, publ. 1924; *Jelly Roll Blues*, composed 1905, publ. 1915) are important samples of the styles of the period. Around 1922 he made his first piano rolls, and in 1923 began re-

cording, both solo and with the New Orleans Rhythm Kings (unusual, for this was a white group); his own band, the Red Hot Peppers, recorded during the years 1926–30 and produced some of the finest samples ever made of the New Orleans Dixieland style. In 1938 he recorded for the Library of Congress, playing piano, singing, demonstrating styles, relating anecdotes and stories, and creating, in sound, his view of the history of jazz; a major outgrowth of these recordings is his biography, Alan Lomax's *Mister Jelly Roll. The Fortunes of Jelly Roll Morton, New Orleans Creole and "Inventor of Jazz"* (N.Y., 1950; 2nd ed., Berkeley, 1973).

Morton, Robert, English composer; b. c.1440; d. 1475. He was clerk and *chappellain* of the chapel of Philip the Good and Charles the Bold of Burgundy (1457–76); was possibly identical with **Robertus Anglicus** (d. 1485), a singer at St. Peter's, Rome. Some of his compositions are preserved in the *Kopenhagener chansonnier*, publ. by K. Jeppesen (1927); several MSS are in Belgian archives. A modern ed. of his works, edited by A. Atlas, is in progress.

Moscheles, Ignaz, eminent pianist, pedagogue, and composer; b. Prague, May 23, 1794; d. Leipzig, March 10, 1870. Of a well-to-do family (his father was a Jewish merchant), he was trained in music as soon as his ability was discovered; his first piano teacher was Dionys Weber at the Prague Cons.; at the age of 14, Moscheles performed publicly a concerto of his own composition. Soon afterward, following his father's death, he went to Vienna to study under Albrechtsberger and Salieri, at the same time earning his living as a teacher. His conspicuous talents won him access to the best circles; he prepared the piano score of Beethoven's *Fidelio*. At concerts in Munich, Dresden, and Leipzig (1816), and in Paris (1820), his remarkable playing was much applauded; he was a pioneer in developing various modifications of tone by touch, afterward exploited by Liszt. In 1821 Moscheles settled in London; made frequent trips to the Continent, and gave Mendelssohn piano lessons at Berlin in 1824. The teacher and the pupil became close friends; on July 13, 1829, they gave the first performance in London of Mendelssohn's Concerto for 2 pianos and orch. After the foundation of the Leipzig Cons. in 1846, Mendelssohn invited Moscheles to join its staff. There, a host of pupils from all quarters of the globe were trained by him with sympathetic consideration, and yet with unflinching discipline in musical matters. He was noted for his energetic, brilliant, and strongly rhythmical playing; his virtuosity equaled his emotional absorption in the music; his romantic pieces for piano expressed clearly his ideas of the extent and the limitations of the instrument.

Mosel, Ignaz Franz von, Austrian composer, conductor, and writer on music; b. Vienna, April 1, 1772; d. there, April 8, 1844. He began his career as an opera conductor, and was the first in Vienna to use a baton (1812). In 1816 he conducted the first concert of the Gesellschaft der Musikfreunde. In 1820 he was appointed vice-director of the court theaters in Vienna, and in 1829, custodian of the Imperial Library.

WORKS: Three of his operas were produced at the Vienna Court Opera: *Die Feuerprobe* (April 28, 1811), *Salem* (March 5, 1813), and *Cyrus und Astyages* (June 13, 1818); he also publ. 3 collections of songs.

WRITINGS: *Versuch einer Ästhetik des dramatischen Tonsatzes* (1813); *Die Tonkunst in Wien während der letzten fünf Dezennien* (1818, in the Vienna *Allgemeine Musikalische Zeitung;* separate reprint, 1840); *Über das Leben und die Werke des Anton Salieri* (1827); *Über die Originalpartitur des Requiems von W.A. Mozart* (1839); *Geschichte der kaiserl. königl. Hofbibliothek zu Wien* (1835).

Moser, Andreas, notable German violinist and music scholar; b. Semlin, Hungary, Nov. 29, 1859; d. Berlin, Oct. 7, 1925. He studied first in Zürich, with Hegar; also took courses in engineering and architecture in Stuttgart; in 1878 he became a violin pupil of Joachim in Berlin; in 1883 was concertmaster in Mannheim; in 1884 settled in Berlin. In 1888 he was appointed a teacher at the Hochschule für Musik, a post he held until his death. He publ. valuable studies on the history of the violin.

WRITINGS: *Joseph Joachim. Ein Lebensbild* (Berlin, 1898; revised and enlarged 4th ed., 1908; Eng. trans. 1900); *Methodik des Violinspiels* (2 parts; Leipzig, 1920); *Geschichte des Violinspiels* (Berlin, 1923; 2nd ed., revised and enlarged, 1966–67); *Technik des Violinspiels* (2 vols.; Leipzig, 1925); collaborated with Joachim on a 3-vol. *Violinschule* (Berlin, 1902–5; 2nd. ed., revised by M. Jacobsen, 1959; French trans. by Marteau; Eng. trans. by Moffat); ed. *Johannes Brahms im Briefwechsel mit Joseph Joachim* (1908; vols. V and VI of the Brahms correspondence) and, with Johannes Joachim, *Briefe von und an Joseph Joachim* (3 vols., 1911–13); ed. (with Joachim) Beethoven's string quartets and Bach's partitas for violin; also various other violin works.

Moser, Edda, German soprano, daughter of **Hans Joachim Moser;** b. Berlin, Oct. 27, 1938. She took vocal lessons in Berlin; made her professional debut at the Würzburg Opera in 1963, and in 1967 sang at the Deutsche Oper in West Berlin; in 1968–71 she was a member of municipal opera houses in Frankfurt; in 1971 joined the Vienna State Opera. She also sang at Easter Festivals in Salzburg. She made her American debut at the Metropolitan Opera in N.Y. on Nov. 22, 1968. She maintains an extensive repertoire, both in coloratura soprano and lyrico-dramatic roles, being equally successful in traditional and modern works.

Moser, Hans Joachim, eminent German musicologist, son of **Andreas Moser** and father of **Edda Moser;** b. Berlin, May 25, 1889; d. there, Aug. 14, 1967. He studied violin with his father; then took courses in musicology with Kretzschmar and Wolf at the

Univ. of Berlin, with Schiedermair at the Univ. of Marburg, and with Riemann and Schering at the Univ. of Leipzig; also studied voice with Oskar Noë and Felix Schmidt, and took courses in composition with H. van Eyken, Robert Kahn, and G. Jenner; he received his Ph.D. from the Univ. of Rostock in 1910 with the dissertation *Die Musikergenossenschaften im deutschen Mittelalter.* Returning to Berlin, he was active as a concert singer (bass-baritone); then served in the German army during World War I. He subsequently completed his Habilitation at the Univ. of Halle in 1919 with his *Das Streichinstrumentenspiel im Mittelalter* (publ. in A. Moser's *Geschichte des Violinspiels,* Berlin, 1923; 2nd ed., revised and enlarged, 1966–67). In 1919 he joined the faculty of the Univ. of Halle as a Privatdozent of musicology, and then became a reader there in 1922; he then was a reader at the Univ. of Heidelberg from 1925 to 1927; he was honorary prof. at the Univ. of Berlin from 1927 to 1934, and also served as director of the State Academy for Church and School Music in Berlin from 1927 to 1933; he received the degree of doctor of theology at Königsberg in 1931. He retired from his public positions in 1934 but continued his musicological pursuits in Berlin; he later served as head of the Reichsstelle für Musik-Bearbeitungen from 1940 to 1945. After World War II, he resumed teaching by accepting appointments as a prof. at the Univ. of Jena and the Hochschule für Musik in Weimar in 1947; he then served as director of the Berlin Cons. from 1950 until 1960. He was an outstanding music historian and lexicographer; his numerous writings are notable for their erudition. However, his unquestionable scholarship was marred by his ardent espousal of the Nazi racial philosophy; so ferocious was his anti-Semitism that he excluded Mendelssohn from his books publ. during the Third Reich. He also composed a number of songs and choruses, as well as the school opera *Der Reisekamerad,* after Andersen; in addition, he wrote novels, short stories, and a comedy. He arranged operas by Handel and Weber; wrote an entirely new libretto for Weber's *Euryanthe* and produced it under the title *Die sieben Raben* (Berlin, March 5, 1915). He served as editor of a projected complete edition of Weber's works (Augsburg and Leipzig, 1926–33), but it remains unfinished. Other works he edited include *Luthers Lieder, Werke,* XXXV (Weimar, 1923; with O. Albrecht and H. Lucke); *Minnesang und Volkslied* (Leipzig, 1925; 2nd ed., enlarged, 1933); *Das Liederbuch des Arnt von Aich* (Kassel, 1930; with E. Bernoulli); *Das deutsche Sololied und die Ballade, Das Musikwerk,* XIV (1957; Eng. trans., 1958); *Heinrich Schütz: Italienische Madrigale, Neue Ausgabe sämtlicher Werke,* XXII (Kassel, 1962); etc.

Moser, Rudolf, Swiss composer; b. Niederuzwyl, St. Gall, Jan. 7, 1892; d. in a fall, while mountain climbing in Silvaplana (Graubünden), Aug. 20, 1960. He studied theology at Basel Univ. and musicology with Nef; then studied at the Leipzig Cons. (1912–14) with Max Reger, Sitt, and Klengel; further with Huber in Basel and Lauber in Geneva. He became conductor of the cathedral choir in Basel; was also active as a pedagogue.

Moskowa, Prince de la, Joseph Napoléon, eldest son of Marshal Ney; French musician; b. Paris, May 8, 1803; d. St.-Germain-en-Laye, July 25, 1857. A senator, and brigadier general under Napoleon III, he was also a talented musician. In 1843 he established the Société de Musique Vocale, Religieuse et Classique (for the perf. of works of the 16th–17th centuries), himself conducting the concerts in his palace; the society publ. 11 vols. of these works as *Recueil des morceaux de musique ancienne,* which included works by Allegri, Arcadelt, Bach, Bononcini, Carissimi, the 2 Gabrielis, Gesualdo, Orlando Gibbons, Gluck, Handel, Haydn, Janequin, Josquin Des Prez, Lotti, Marcello, Orlando Lasso, Palestrina, Scarlatti, Stradella, Victoria, etc. He composed 2 comic operas, *Le Cent-Suisse* (Paris, June 7, 1840) and *Yvonne* (Paris, March 16, 1855); also a Mass with Orch. in 1831.

Mosolov, Alexander, Russian composer of avant-garde tendencies; b. Kiev, Aug. 11, 1900; d. Moscow, July 12, 1973. He fought in the Civil War in Russia (1918–20); was wounded and decorated twice with the Order of the Red Banner for heroism. After the war, he studied composition with Glière in Kiev; also privately with Miaskovsky in Moscow; took piano lessons with Igumnov at the Moscow Cons., graduating in 1925. He played his First Piano Concerto in Leningrad on Feb. 12, 1928. In his earliest works he adopted modernistic devices; wrote songs to texts of newspaper advertisements. His ballet *Zavod (Iron Foundry;* Moscow, Dec. 4, 1927) attracted attention because of the attempt to imitate the sound of a factory at work by shaking a large sheet of metal. However, Mosolov's attempt to produce "proletarian" music by such means elicited a sharp rebuke from the official arbiters of Soviet music. On Feb. 4, 1936, he was expelled from the Union of Soviet Composers for staging drunken brawls and behaving rudely to waiters in restaurants. He was sent to Turkestan to collect folk songs as a move toward his rehabilitation.

Mosonyi, Mihály (real name, **Michael Brandt**), Hungarian composer; b. Frauenkirchen, Sept. 2, 1814; d. Budapest, Oct. 31, 1870. He learned to play violin, double bass, and organ as a child; then took some lessons with Karl Turányi in Pressburg; subsequently earned his living as a private tutor in aristocratic families in Hungary and Vienna; he also played double bass in various orchs. Although he was a product of the Classical school of composition, he became enamored of Hungarian national music; began to write in the Hungarian idiom, while his harmonies remained Germanic. Liszt took great interest in his works, and proposed to bring out Mosonyi's German opera *Kaiser Max auf der Martinswand* (1857), but Mosonyi delayed the final revision of the work, and it never reached performance. His 2nd opera, *Szêp Llon (Pretty Helen),* was produced at Budapest on Dec. 19, 1861; another

opera, *Almos,* was not staged until Dec. 6, 1934, 64 years after Mosonyi's death. He further wrote 5 masses and other church music; 2 symphs.: No.1 (Pest, March 1844); No. 2 (Pest, March 30, 1856); 6 string quartets; several choruses for men's voices; songs. His *Funeral Music for Széchenyi* employs the so-called Hungarian mode, and its strong national character established Mosonyi as one of the founders of the Hungarian School.

Moszkowski, Moritz, famous pianist, teacher, and composer; b. Breslau, Aug. 23, 1854; d. Paris, March 4, 1925. He studied at the Dresden Cons.; later at the Stern Cons. and at the Kullak Academy in Berlin; then became a teacher at the latter institution. He gave his first public concert in Berlin in 1873; then played elsewhere in Germany, and in Paris, where he established his reputation as a pianist; in 1897, he made Paris his headquarters. As a composer, he is most widely known by his pieces in the Spanish vein, particularly the 2 books of *Spanish Dances* for Piano Solo or Piano Duo; also popular were his études, concert waltzes, gavottes, *Skizzen,* a tarantella, a humoresque, etc. In larger forms he essayed an opera, *Boabdil der Maurenkönig* (Berlin, April 21, 1892), which contains a ballet number that became popular; he also wrote a ballet, *Laurin* (1896); a symph. poem, *Jeanne d'Arc; Phantastischer Zug* for Orch.; *Aus aller Herren Länder* for Orch.; Violin Concerto; Piano Concerto.

Motta, José Vianna da. See **Da Motta, José Vianna.**

Mottl, Felix, celebrated Austrian conductor; b. Unter-St. Veit, near Vienna, Aug. 24, 1856; d. Munich, July 2, 1911. After preliminary studies at a seminary, he entered the Vienna Cons., and studied there with Door (piano), Bruckner (theory), Dessoff (composition), and Hellmesberger (conducting), graduating with high honors. In 1876 he acted as one of the assistants at the first Wagner festival at Bayreuth. In 1881 he succeeded Dessoff as court conductor at Karlsruhe; in 1893 was appointed Generalmusikdirektor there. He conducted *Tristan und Isolde* at the Bayreuth Festival in 1886; led a Wagner concert in London in 1894; and gave the entire *Ring* tetralogy at Covent Garden in 1898. In 1903 he was engaged to conduct the projected performances of *Parsifal* at the Metropolitan Opera in N.Y., but withdrew owing to the protests of the Wagner family. Mottl secured recognition for Peter Cornelius's *Der Barbier von Bagdad* by re-orchestrating the score, and producing it first at Karlsruhe, on Feb. 1, 1884; additional changes were made by him with Hermann Levi, and in this form the work finally became established in the opera repertoire. In 1903 he became Generalmusikdirektor of the Munich Court Opera; was conductor of the Vienna Phil. from 1904 to 1907. In Dec. 1905 he conducted, also in Karlsruhe, the first complete performance of both parts of Berlioz's *Les Troyens* (in German); he orchestrated Wagner's 5 *Gedichte,* and edited Wagner's early overtures. Mottl composed 3 operas:

Agnes Bernauer (Weimar, 1880), *Rama,* and *Fürst und Sänger;* a String Quartet; numerous songs. Among his arrangements, that of Chabrier's *Bourrée fantasque* enjoys continued popularity in the concert hall.

Moulaert, Pierre, Belgian composer, son of **Raymond Moulaert;** b. Brussels, Sept. 24, 1907; d. there, Nov. 13, 1967. He studied at the Royal Cons. in Brussels with his father and Joseph Jongen, and taught there from 1927 until his death. He was not a prolific composer, and wrote mostly in small forms, but his music has a distinctive quality of fine craftsmanship.

Moulaert, Raymond, Belgian composer, father of **Pierre Moulaert;** b. Brussels, Feb. 4, 1875; d. there, Jan. 18, 1962. He studied at the Brussels Cons. with Arthur de Greef (piano) and Edgar Tinel (theory); then was appointed to its staff and taught composition (1939); concurrently was director of his own music school in St.-Gilles for 25 years (1913–38); also lectured at the Queen Elizabeth Chapel of Music in Brussels.

Mount-Edgcumbe, Richard, British nobleman (2nd Earl of Mount-Edgcumbe) and music amateur; b. Plymouth, Sept. 13, 1764; d. Richmond, Surrey, Sept. 26, 1839. He was the author of the book *Musical Reminiscences, containing an Account of the Italian Opera in England from 1773,* which he publ. anonymously in 1825. He also wrote an opera, *Zenobia* (in Italian), which was produced at London on May 22, 1800.

Mouret, Jean Joseph, French composer; b. Avignon, April 11, 1682; d. Charenton, Dec. 20, 1738. He was attached to the court in Paris; produced an opera-ballet, *Les fêtes ou Le Triomphe de Thalie* (Paris, Aug. 14, 1714); an opera, *Ariane* (Paris, April 6, 1717); *Les Amours des dieux,* opera-ballet (Paris, Sept. 14, 1727). He was director of the Concert Spirituel (1728–34); wrote motets for performances there; also divertissements for the Comédie-Italienne; about 50 of his chamber pieces were publ. during his lifetime.

Moussorgsky, Modest. See **Mussorgsky, Modest.**

Mouton, Jean, important French composer; b. Holluigue (now Haut-Wignes), near Samer, c.1459; d. St. Quentin, Oct. 30, 1522. In 1477 he became a singer and teacher of religion (écolâtre-chantre) at the collegiate church of Notre Dame in Nesle. He became maître de chapelle in Nesle in 1483, and also entered the priesthood. In 1500 he was in charge of the choirboys at the Cathedral of Amiens. In 1501 he was director of music at the collegiate church of St. André in Grenoble, but left his position without permission in 1502. He subsequently entered the service of Queen Anne; later served Louis XII and François I. He was made canon in absentia

at St. André in Grenoble, which conferred a benefice on him in 1510, and later was elected a canon at St. Quentin. Pope Leo X made him an apostolic notary. He was the teacher of Adrian Willaert. In his music he followed the precepts of Josquin Des Prez; he particularly excelled in the art of the canon. He composed more than 100 motets, some 15 masses, and over 20 chansons. About 50 of his works were publ. in his lifetime; several collections were publ. posthumously. His *Opera omnia,* edited by A. Minor, began publication in 1967 in the Corpus Mensurabilis Musicae series of the American Inst. of Musicology.

Moyse, Louis, French flutist, son of **Marcel Moyse;** b. Scheveningen, the Netherlands, July 14, 1912. He was taken to Paris as an infant; learned to play the piano and flute at home; later took private piano lessons with Isidore Philipp (1925–27); in 1930 he entered the Paris Cons., where he studied flute with Philippe Gaubert and composition with Eugène Bigot; he graduated in 1932, with the Premier Prix in flute; then was his father's teaching assistant at the Paris Cons., and filled in with various jobs playing at movie theaters and restaurants. He served in the French army during World War II; after the war he organized the Moyse Trio, with his father as flutist, his wife, **Blanche Honegger-Moyse,** as violinist, and himself as pianist. In 1948 he went with his wife to the U.S.; became an American citizen in 1959. He joined his father at Marlboro College in Vermont, where he taught until 1975; then was appointed prof. of flute and chamber music at the Univ. of Toronto. He publ. in N.Y. several educational collections of flute pieces, among them *Solos for Flute Players, 40 Little Pieces for Beginner Flutists, Album of Flute Duets, 30 Easy Duets for Flutes,* etc. WORKS: *Suite* for 2 Flutes and Viola (1957); *4 Dances* for Flute and Violin (1958); Woodwind Quintet (1961); *Divertimento* for Double Woodwind Quintet, 2 Cellos, Double Bass, and Timpani (1961); *4 Pieces* for 3 Flutes and Piano (1965); *3 Pieces* for Flute and Guitar (1968); *Marlborian Concerto* for Flute, English Horn, and Orch. (1969); *A Ballad for Vermont* for Narrator, Soloists, Chorus, and Orch. (1971–72); Flute Sonata (1975); *Serenade* for Piccolo, 4 Flutes, Alto Flute, Bass Flute, and Piano (1977); he also arranged for flute and various instrumental groups works by Bach, Telemann, Handel, Mozart, Beethoven, and Weber.

Moyse, Marcel, celebrated French flutist; b. Saint-Amour (Jura), May 17, 1889. He studied flute with Taffanel at the Paris Cons.; upon graduation was first flutist in several Paris orchs. (Lamoureux, Cologne, Pasdeloup, etc.). In 1932 he succeeded Philippe Gaubert as prof. of flute at the Paris Cons. In 1949 he went to the U.S.; in 1950 organized, with his son **Louis Moyse,** Rudolf Serkin, Adolf Busch, and Hermann Busch, the Marlboro School and Festival of Music in Brattleboro, Vt.; also conducted master classes in flute and chamber music in Switzerland; gave similar courses in Japan in 1973. At the age of 92 he conducted an instrumental ensemble in the music of Mozart and Dvořák, on Aug. 11, 1981, in N.Y. He publ. a series of excellent flute studies, among them *20 exercises et études*, *24 petites études mélodiques*, *25 études mélodiques*, *100 études faciles et progressives*, *25 études de virtuosité* (after Czerny), *12 études de grande virtuosité* (after Chopin), etc.; also wrote 50 variations on the Allemande from Bach's Flute Sonata in A minor and compiled a manual for flute, *Tone Developement through Interpretation*.

Mozart, (Johann Georg) Leopold, German-born Austrian composer, violinist, and theorist, father of **Wolfgang Amadeus Mozart;** b. Augsburg, Nov. 14, 1719; d. Salzburg, May 28, 1787. A bookbinder's son, he studied at the Augsburg Gymnasium (1727–35); continued his studies at the Lyceum attached to the Jesuit school of St. Salvator (1735–36). In 1737 he went to Salzburg, where he studied philosophy and law at the Benedictine Univ.; he received his bachelor of philosophy degree in 1738. Subsequently he entered the service of Johann Baptist, Count of Thurn-Valsassina and Taxis, the Salzburg canon and president of the consistory, as both valet and musician. In 1743 he became 4th violinist in the Prince-Archbishop's court orch.; also taught violin and keyboard to the choirboys of the Cathedral oratory. In 1757 he became composer to the court and chamber; in 1758 he was promoted to 2nd violinist in the court orch.; in 1762 he was appointed Vice-Kappellmeister. He married Anna Maria Pertl of Salzburg on Nov. 21, 1747; of their 7 children, only "Nannerl" and Wolfgang survived infancy. He dedicated himself to the musical education of his children, but his methods of presentation of their concerts at times approached frank exploitation, and his advertisements of their appearances were in poor taste. However, there is no denying his great role in fostering his son's career. Leopold Mozart was a thoroughly competent composer; the mutual influence between father and son was such that works long attributed to his son proved to be his. Leopold Mozart was also important as a theorist. He produced an influential violin method in his *Versuch einer gründlichen Violinschule* (Augsburg, 1756; 2nd ed., revised, 1769–70; 3rd ed., enlarged, 1787; facsimile of 1756 ed., Vienna, 1922; also various translations, including one in Eng., London, 1939; 2nd ed., 1951). His *Nannerl-Notenbuch* is a model of a child's music album; it was publ. in 1759; edited in part by E. Valentin (Munich, 1956; 2nd ed., 1969). M. Seiffert edited *Leopold Mozart: Ausgewählte Werke* in Denkmäler der Tonkunst in Bayern, XVII, Jg. IX/2 (Leipzig, 1908). Leopold Mozart's vocal works include sacred cantatas, masses, litanies, school dramas, and secular lieder. He also composed symphs.; the famous *Kindersinfonie (Toy Symphony)*, long attributed to Haydn, was in all probability a work by Leopold Mozart. On this, see E.F. Schmid, "Leopold Mozart und die Kindersinfonie," *Mozart Jahrbuch 1951*, and R. Münster, "Wer ist der Komponist der 'Kindersinfonie'?," *Acta Mozartiana*, XVI (1969). A.A. Abert attributes Wolfgang's Symph. in G major, K. Anh. 221; 45a, "Old

Lambach" (1768), to Leopold; see her "Methoden der Mozartforschung," *Mozart Jahrbuch 1964*, and "Stilistischer Befund und Quellenlage: Zu Mozarts Lambacher Sinfonie KV Anh. 221–45a," in *Festschrift Hans Engel* (Kassel, 1964). Other orch. works include several concertos, among them *Die musikalische Schlittenfahrt* (1755); dances; etc. He also composed chamber music and works for the keyboard.

Mozart, Maria Anna (Walburga Ignatia), nicknamed **"Nannerl,"** daughter of **Leopold Mozart** and sister of **Wolfgang Amadeus Mozart;** b. Salzburg, July 30, 1751; d. there. Oct. 29, 1829. She was taught music by her father from her earliest childhood, and appeared in public as a pianist with her brother; together they traveled to Vienna in 1768; upon her return to Salzburg, she devoted herself mainly to teaching. In 1784 she married Baron von Berchthold zu Sonnenburg, who died in 1801. She went blind in 1825. Although nearly 5 years older than Wolfgang Mozart, she survived him by 38 years, and lived long enough to survive also Beethoven and Schubert.

Mozart, Wolfgang Amadeus (baptismal names, **Johannes Chrysostomus Wolfgangus Theophilus**), supreme genius of music whose works in every genre are unsurpassed in lyric beauty, rhythmic variety, and effortless melodic invention; b. Salzburg, Jan. 27, 1756; d. Vienna, Dec. 5, 1791. He and his sister, tenderly nicknamed "Nannerl," were the only 2 among the 7 children of Anna Maria and **Leopold Mozart** to survive infancy. Mozart's sister was 4½ years older; she took harpsichord lessons from her father, and Mozart as a very young child eagerly absorbed the sounds of music. He soon began playing the harpsichord himself, and later studied the violin. Leopold Mozart was an excellent musician, but he also appreciated the theatrical validity of the performances that Wolfgang and Nannerl began giving in Salzburg. On Jan. 17, 1762, he took them to Munich, where they performed before the Elector of Bavaria. In Sept. 1762 they played for Emperor Francis I at his palace in Vienna. The family returned to Salzburg in Jan. 1763, and in June 1763 the children were taken to Frankfurt, where Wolfgang Mozart showed his skill in improvising at the keyboard. In Nov. 1763 they arrived in Paris, where they played before Louis XVI and Marie Antoinette; it was in Paris that Wolfgang's first compositions were printed (4 sonatas for harpsichord, with violin ad libitum). In April 1764 they proceeded to London; there Wolfgang played for King George III. In London he was befriended by Bach's son Johann Christian Bach, who gave exhibitions improvising 4-hands at the piano with the child Mozart. By that time Mozart had tried his ability in composing serious works; he wrote 2 symphs. for a London performance, and the MS of another very early symph., purportedly written by Mozart in London, was discovered in 1980. Leopold Mozart wrote home with undisguised pride: "Our great and mighty Wolfgang seems to know everything at the age of 7 that a man acquires at the age of 40." Knowing the power of publicity, he diminished Wolfgang's age, for at the time the child was fully 9 years old. In July 1765 they journeyed to the Netherlands, then set out for Salzburg, visiting Dijon, Lyons, Geneva, Bern, Zürich, Donaueschingen, and Munich on the way. Arriving in Salzburg in Nov. 1766, Wolfgang applied himself to serious study of counterpoint under the tutelage of his father. In Sept. 1767 the family proceeded to Vienna, where Wolfgang began work on an opera, *La finta semplice;* his 2nd theater work was a singspiel, *Bastien und Bastienne,* which was produced in Vienna at the home of Dr. Franz Mesmer, the protagonist of the famous method of therapy by "animal magnetism," which became known as Mesmerism. On Dec. 7, 1768, Mozart led a performance of his *Missa solemnis* in C minor before the royal family and court at the consecration of the Waisenhauskirche. Upon Mozart's return to Salzburg in Jan. 1769, Archbishop Sigismund von Schrattenbach named him his Konzertmeister; however, the position was without remuneration. Still determined to broaden Mozart's artistic contacts, his father took him on an Italian tour. The announcement for a concert in Mantua on Jan. 16, 1770, just a few days before Mozart's 14th birthday, was typical of the artistic mores of the time: "A Symphony of his own composition; a harpsichord concerto, which will be handed to him, and which he will immediately play *prima vista;* a Sonata handed him in like manner, which he will provide with variations, and afterwards repeat in another key; an Aria, the words for which will be handed to him and which he will immediately set to music and sing himself, accompanying himself on the harpsichord; a Sonata for harpsichord on a subject given him by the leader of the violins; a Strict Fugue on a theme to be selected, which he will improvise on the harpsichord; a Trio in which he will execute a violin part *all' improvviso;* and, finally, the latest Symphony by himself." Legends of Mozart's extraordinary musical ability grew; it was reported, for instance, that Mozart wrote out the entire score of *Miserere* by Allegri, which he had heard in the Sistine Chapel at the Vatican only twice. Young Mozart was subjected to numerous tests by famous Italian musicians, among them Giovanni Sammartini, Piccini, and Padre Martini; he was given a diploma as an elected member of the Accademia Filarmonica in Bologna after he had passed examinations in harmony and counterpoint. On Oct. 10, 1770, the Pope made him a Knight of the Golden Spur. He was commissioned to compose an opera; the result was *Mitradate, rè di Ponto,* which was performed in Milan on Dec. 26, 1770; Mozart himself conducted 22 performances of this opera from the harpsichord; also in Milan he composed a serenata for the wedding festivities of Archduke Ferdinand, which was produced there on Oct. 17, 1771. He returned to Salzburg late in 1771; his patron, Archbishop Schrattenbach, died about that time, and his successor seemed to be indifferent to Mozart as a musician. Once more Mozart went to Italy, where his newest opera, *Lucio Silla,* was performed in Milan on Dec. 26, 1772. In July 1773 he traveled to Vienna, where he became acquainted with the music of Haydn, who greatly influenced his instrumental style. Returning to Salzburg once more, he supervised the production of his opera *Il Rè pastore,* which was performed on April 23, 1775.

In March 1778 he visited Paris again for a performance of his "Paris" Symph. at a Concert Spirituel. Returning to Salzburg in Jan. 1779, he resumed his duties as Konzertmeister and also obtained the position of court organist at a salary of 450 gulden. In 1780 the Elector of Bavaria commissioned from him an opera seria, *Idomeneo,* which was successfully produced in Munich on Jan. 29, 1781. In May 1781 Mozart lost his position with the Archbishop in Salzburg and decided to move to Vienna, which became his permanent home. There he produced his operatic masterpiece *Die Entführung aus dem Serail,* staged at the Burgtheater on July 16, 1782, with excellent success. On August 4, 1782, he married Constanze Weber, the sister of Aloysia Weber, with whom Mozart had previously been infatuated. Two of his finest symphs. —No. 35 in D major, "Haffner," written for the Haffner family of Salzburg; and No. 36 in C major, the "Linz"— dated from 1782 and 1783, respectively. From this point forward Mozart's productivity reached extraordinary dimensions, but despite the abundance of commissions and concert appearances, he was unable to earn enough to sustain his growing family. Still, melodramatic stories of Mozart's abject poverty are gross exaggerations. He apparently felt no scruples in asking prosperous friends for financial assistance. Periodically he wrote to Michael Puchberg, a banker and a brother Mason (Mozart joined the Masonic Order in 1784), with requests for loans (which he never repaid); invariably Puchberg obliged, but usually granting smaller amounts than Mozart requested. (The market price of Mozart autographs has grown exponentially; a begging letter to Puchberg would fetch, some 2 centuries after it was written, a hundred times the sum requested.) In 1785 Mozart completed a set of 5 string quartets which he dedicated to Haydn; unquestionably the structure of these quartets owed much to Haydn's contrapuntal art. Haydn himself paid a tribute to Mozart's genius; Mozart's father quoted him as saying, "Before God and as an honest man I tell you that your son is the greatest composer known to me either in person or by name." On May 11, 1786, Mozart's great opera buffa, *Le nozze di Figaro,* was produced in Vienna, obtaining a real triumph with the audience; it was performed in Prague early in 1787 with Mozart in attendance. It was during that visit that Mozart wrote his 38th Symph., in D major, known as the "Prague" Symph.; it was in Prague, also, that Mozart's operatic masterpiece *Don Giovanni* was produced, on Oct. 29, 1787. It is interesting to note that at its Vienna performance the opera was staged under the title *Die sprechende Statue,* unquestionably with the intention of sensationalizing the story; the dramatic appearance of the statue of the Commendatore, introduced by the ominous sound of trombones, was a shuddering climax to the work. In Nov. 1787 Mozart was appointed Kammer-musicus in Vienna as a successor to Gluck, albeit at a smaller salary: Mozart received 800 gulden per annum as against Gluck's salary of 2,000 gulden. The year 1788 was a glorious one for Mozart and for music history; it was the year when Mozart composed his last 3 symphs.: No. 39 in E-flat major; No. 40 in G minor; and No. 41 in C major, known under the name "Jupiter" (the Jovian designation was apparently attached to the work for the first time in British concert programs; its earliest use was in the program of the Edinburgh Festival in Oct. 1819). In the spring of 1789 Mozart went to Berlin; on the way he appeared as soloist in one of his piano concertos before the Elector of Saxony in Dresden, and also played the organ at the Thomaskirche in Leipzig. His visits in Potsdam and Berlin were marked by his private concerts at the court of Friedrich Wilhelm II; the King commissioned from him a set of 6 string quartets and a set of 6 piano sonatas, but Mozart died before completing these commissions. Returning to Vienna, Mozart began work on his opera buffa *Così fan tutte* (an untranslatable sentence because *tutte* is the feminine plural, so that the full title would be "Thus do all women"). The opera was first performed in Vienna on Jan. 26, 1790. In Oct. 1790 Mozart went to Frankfurt for the coronation of Emperor Leopold II. Returning to Vienna, he saw Haydn, who was about to depart for London. In 1791, during his last years of life, he completed the score of *Die Zauberflöte*, with a German libretto by Emanuel Schikaneder. It was performed for the first time on Sept. 30, 1791, in Vienna. There followed a mysterious episode in Mozart's life; a stranger called on him with a request to compose a Requiem; the caller was an employee of Count Franz von Walsegg, who intended to have the work performed as his own in memory of his wife. Mozart was unable to finish the score, which was completed by his pupil Franz Xavier Süssmayr, who dutifully handed it over to Walsegg.

The immediate cause of Mozart's death at the age of 35 years, 10 months, and 9 days seems to have been acute nephritis. A detailed discussion of the clinical aspects of Mozart's illness is found in Dieter Kerner's *Krankheiten grosser Musiker* (Stuttgart, 1973; vol. I, pp. 9–87). Almost immediately after the sad event, myths and fantasies appeared in the press; the most persistent of them all was that Mozart had been poisoned by Salieri out of professional jealousy; this particularly morbid piece of invention gained circulation in European journals; the story was further elaborated upon by a report that Salieri confessed his unspeakable crime on his deathbed in 1825. Pushkin used the tale in his drama *Mozart and Salieri,* which Rimsky-Korsakov set to music in his opera of the same title; a fanciful dramatization of the Mozart-Salieri rivalry was made into a successful play, *Amadeus,* by Peter Shaffer, which was produced in London in 1979 and in N.Y. in 1980. A cheap attempt to cash in on the Mozart tragedy was made in a book publ. in 1983, which alleged that Mozart was poisoned by the husband of Mozart's putative mistress, but such repellent publications do not deserve bibliographic notice. The notion of Mozart's murder also appealed to the Nazis; in the ingenious version propagated by some German writers of the Hitlerian persuasion, Mozart was a victim of a double conspiracy of Masons and Jews who were determined to suppress the flowering of racial Germanic greatness; the Masons, in this interpretation, were outraged by Mozart's revealing of their secret rites in *Die Zauberflöte,* and allied themselves with plutocratic Jews to prevent further spread of Mozart's dangerous revelations. Another myth related to Mozart's death that found its way into the majority of Mozart biographies and even into respectable reference works was that a blizzard raged during Mozart's funeral and that none of his friends could follow his body to the cemetery; this story is easily refuted by the records of the Vienna weather bureau for the day (see in this connection N. Slonimsky, "The Weather at Mozart's Funeral," *Musical Quarterly,* Jan. 1960). It is also untrue that Mozart was buried in a pauper's grave; his body was removed from its original individual location because the family neglected to pay the mandatory dues.

The universal recognition of Mozart's genius during the 2 centuries since his death has never wavered among professional musicians, amateurs, and the general public. In his music, smiling simplicity was combined with somber drama; lofty inspiration was contrasted with playful diversion; profound meditation alternated with capricious moodiness; religious concentration was permeated with human tenderness. Devoted as Mozart was to his art and respectful as he was of the rules of composition, he was also capable of mocking the professional establishment. A delightful example of this persiflage is his little piece *Ein musikalischer Spass,* subtitled "Dorf Musikanten," a "musical joke" at the expense of "village musicians," in which Mozart all but anticipated developments of modern music, 2 centuries in the future; he deliberately used the forbidden consecutive fifths, allowed the violin to escape upward in a whole-tone scale, and finished the entire work in a welter of polytonal triads.

The variety of technical development in Mozart's works is all the more remarkable considering the limitations of instrumental means in his time; the topmost note on his keyboard was F above the 3rd ledger line, so that in the recapitulation in the first movement of Mozart's famous C major Piano Sonata, the subject had to be dropped an octave lower to accommodate the modulation. The vocal technique displayed in Mozart's operas is amazing in its perfection; to be sure, the human voice has not changed since Mozart's time, but Mozart knew how to exploit vocal resources to the utmost. This adaptability of his genius to all available means of sound production is the secret of the eternal validity of his music, and the explanation of the present popularity of Mozart mini-festivals, such as the N.Y. concert series advertised as "Mostly Mozart."

In the list of Mozart's works given below, the K. numbers represent the system of identification established by L. von Köchel in his *Chronologisch-thematisches Verzeichnis sämtlicher Tonwerke Wolfgang Amade Mozarts* (Leipzig, 1862; 6th ed., revised by F. Giegling, A. Weinmann, and G. Sievers, Wiesbaden, 1964); the revised K. numbers of the 6th edition are also included.

WORKS: OPERAS AND OTHER COMPOSITIONS FOR THE STAGE: *Apollo et Hyacinthus*, K. 38, Latin intermezzo (Salzburg Univ., May 13, 1767); *La finta semplice*, K. 51; 46a, opera buffa (Archbishop's palace, Salzburg, May 1?, 1769); *Bastien und Bastienne*, K. 50; 46b, singspiel (Franz Mesmer's residence, Vienna, Sept.?–Oct.? 1768); *Mitridate, Rè di Ponto*, K. 87; 74a, opera seria (Regio Ducal Teatro, Milan, Dec. 26, 1770); *Ascanio in Alba*, K. 111, festa teatrale (Regio Ducal Teatro, Milan, Oct. 17, 1771); *Il sogno di Scipione*, K. 126, serenata (Archbishop's palace, Salzburg, May? 1772); *Lucio Silla*, K. 135, opera seria (Regio Ducal Teatro, Milan, Dec. 26, 1772); *La finta giardiniera*, K. 196, opera buffa (Munich, Jan. 13, 1775; also produced as a singspiel, *Die verstellte Gärtnerin*, Augsburg, May 1, 1780); *Il Rè pastore*, K. 208, dramma per musica (Archbishop's palace, Salzburg, April 23, 1775); *Semiramis*, K. Anh. 11; 315e, duodrama (not extant); *Thamos, König in Ägypten*, K. 345; 336a, music for Gebler's play; *Zaide*, K. 344; 336b, singspiel (unfinished; dialogue rewritten and finished by Gollmick, with overture and finale added by Anton André, Frankfurt, Jan. 27, 1866); *Idomeneo, Rè di Creta*, K. 366, opera seria (Hoftheater, Munich, Jan. 29, 1781); *Die Entführung aus dem Serail*, K. 384, singspiel (Burgtheater, Vienna, July 16, 1782); *L'oca del Cairo*, K. 422, opera buffa (unfinished); *Lo Sposo deluso*, K. 430; 424a, opera buffa (unfinished); *Der Schauspieldirektor*, K. 486, singspiel (Schönbrunn Palace, Heitzing [suburb of Vienna], Feb. 7, 1786); *Le nozze di Figaro*, K. 492, opera buffa (Burgtheater, Vienna, May 1, 1786); *Il dissoluto punito, ossia Il Don Giovanni*, K. 527, opera buffa (National Theater, Prague, Oct. 29, 1787); *Così fan tutte, ossia La scuola degli amanti*, K. 588, opera buffa (Burgtheater, Vienna, Jan. 26, 1790); *Die Zauberflöte*, K. 620, singspiel (Theater auf der Wieden, Vienna, Sept. 30, 1791); *La clemenza di Tito*, K. 621, opera seria (National Theater, Prague, Sept. 6, 1791). —Arias and scenes for Voice and Orch.: 39 for Soprano (4 not extant); one for Alto; 11 for Tenor (one with only 48 bars extant); 8 for Bass. —Duets for Solo Voices and Orch.: One for 2 Tenors; one for Soprano and Tenor; 2 for Soprano and Bass. —Ensembles for Solo Voices and Orch.: one for Soprano, Tenor, and Bass; one for Tenor and 2 Basses; one for Soprano, Tenor, and 2 Basses; one for Soprano, Alto, Tenor, and Bass (not extant).—Ensembles for Solo Voices, and Piano or other Instruments: One for 2 Sopranos; 5 for 2 Sopranos and Bass; 2 for Soprano, Tenor, and Bass; one for 2 Sopranos and Bass; one for Soprano, 2 Tenors, and Bass.—34 songs for Solo Voices, with Piano (2 with Mandolin); 2 Masonic songs, with Male Chorus). —Numerous canons.

MASSES, ORATORIOS, CANTATAS, ETC.: Kyrie in F major, K. 33 (1766); *Die Schuldigkeit des ersten Gebots*, K. 35, sacred drama (1767; part one by Mozart, part 2 by Michael Haydn, part 3 by Adlgasser; Salzburg, March 12, 1767); *Grabmusik*, K. 42; 35a, cantata (1767; Salzburg Cathedral, April 7, 1767); *Missa solemnis* in C minor, K. 139; 47a, "Waisenhausmesse"

(1768; Vienna, Dec. 7, 1768); *Missa brevis* in G major, K. 49; 47d (1768; only fragments extant); *Missa brevis* in D minor, K. 65; 61a (1769; Collegiate Church, Salzburg, Feb. 5, 1769); *Missa* in C major, K. 66, "Dominicus" (1769; St. Peter, Salzburg, Oct. 15, 1769); *La Betulia liberata*, K. 118; 74c, oratorio (1771); *Missa brevis* in G major, K. 140; C 1.12 (1773; may not be by Mozart); *Missa* in C major, K. 167, "In honorem Ssmae Trinitatis" (1773); *Missa brevis* in F major, K. 192; 186f (1774); *Missa brevis* in D major, K. 194; 186h (1774); *Missa brevis* in G major, K. 220; 196b, "Spatzenmesse" (1775–76); *Missa* in C major, K. 262; 246a (1775); *Missa* in C major, K. 257, "Credo" (1776); *Missa brevis* in C major, K. 258, "Spaur" (1776); *Missa brevis* in C major, K. 259, "Organ Solo" (1776); *Missa brevis* in B-flat major, K. 275; 272b (1777; St. Peter, Salzburg, Dec. 21, 1777); *Missa* in C major, K. 317, "Coronation" (1779); *Missa solemnis* in C major, K. 337 (1780); Kyrie in D minor, K. 341; 368a (1780–81); *Missa* in C minor, K. 427; 417a (1782–83; unfinished; Kyrie and Gloria, St. Peter, Salzburg, Oct. 25, 1783); *Dir, Seele des Weltalls*, K. 429; 468a, cantata (1785; unfinished); *Davidde penitente*, K. 469, oratorio (1785; music from the *Missa* in C minor, K. 427; 417a, 2 arias excepted); *Die Maurerfreude*, K. 471, cantata (1785; "Zur gekronten Hoffnung" Lodge, Vienna, April 24, 1785); *Die ihr des unermesslichen Weltalls Schöpfer ehrt*, K. 619, cantata (1791); *Eine kleine Freimaurer-Kantate*, K. 623 (1791; "Zur neugekronten Hoffnung" Lodge, Vienna, Nov. 18, 1791); Requiem in D minor, K. 626 (1791; unfinished; completed by Franz Xavier Süssmayr). —Also the following: *God Is Our Refuge* in G minor, K. 20, motet (1765); *Stabat Mater*, K. 33c (1766; not extant); *Scande coeli limina* in C major, K. 34, offertory (1767); *Veni Sancte Spiritus* in C major, K. 47 (1768); *Benedictus sit Deus* in C major, K. 117; 66a, offertory (1768); *Te Deum* in C major, K. 141; 66b (1769); *Ergo interest* in G major, K. 143; 73a, motet (1773); *Miserere* in A minor, K. 85; 73s (1770); *Cibavit eos* in A minor, K. 44; 73u, antiphon (1770; may not be by Mozart); *Quaerite primum* in D minor, K. 86; 73v, antiphon (1770); *Regina coeli* in C major, K. 108; 74d (1771); *Inter natos mulierum* in G major, K. 72; 74f, offertory (1771); *Regina coeli* in B-flat major, K. 127 (1772); *Exultate, jubilate* in F major, K. 165; 158a, motet (1773; Milan, Jan. 17, 1773); *Tantum ergo* in D major, K. 197; C 3.05 (1774; may not be by Mozart); *Sub tuum praesidium* in F major, K. 198; C 3.08, offertory (1774; may not be by Mozart); *Misericordias Domini* in D minor, K. 222; 205a, offertory (1775); *Venite populi* in D major, K. 260; 248a (1776); *Alma Dei creatoris* in F major, K. 277; 272a, offertory (1777); *Sancta Maria, mater Dei* in F major, K. 273, gradual (1777); Miserere, K. Anh. 1; 297a (1778; not extant); *Kommet her, ihr frechen Sünder* in B-flat major, K. 146; 317b, aria (1779); *Regina coeli* in C major, K. 276; 321b (1779?); *O Gottes Lamm; Als aus Aegypten*, K. 343; 336c, 2 German sacred songs (1787?); *Ave verum corpus* in D major, K. 618, motet (1791). —Additional works: *Litaniae Lauretanae* in B-flat major, K. 109; 74e (1771); *Litaniae de venerabili altaris sacramento* in B-flat major, K. 125 (1772); *Litaniae Lauretanae* in D major, K. 195; 186d (1774); *Dixit Dominus, Magnificat* in C major,

Mozart

K. 193; 186g (1774); *Litaniae de venerabili altaris sacramento* in E-flat major, K. 243 (1776); *Vesperae de Dominica* in C major, K. 321 (1779); *Vesperae solennes de confessore* in C major, K. 339 (1780).

FOR ORCH.: SYMPHS.: No. 1, in E-flat major, K. 16 (1764–65); A minor, K. Anh. 220; 16a (1765; not extant); No. 4, in D major, K. 19 (1765); F major, K. Anh. 223; 19a (1765; considered lost until discovered in 1980); C major, K. Anh. 222; 19b (1765; not extant); No. 5, in B-flat major, K. 22 (1765); No. 43, in F major, K. 76; 42a (1767); No. 6, in F major, K. 43 (1767); No. 7, in D major, K. 45 (1767); G major, K. Anh. 221; 45a, "Old Lambach" (1768; may be by Leopold Mozart); G major, "New Lambach" (1768); B-flat major, K. Anh. 214; 45b (1768); No. 8, in D major, K. 48 (1768); D major, K. Anh. 215; 66c (1769; not extant); B-flat major, K. Anh. 217; 66d (1769; not extant); B-flat major, K. Anh. 218; 66e (1769; not extant); No. 9, in C major, K. 73 (1772); No. 44, in D major, K. 81; 731 (1770; may be by Leopold Mozart); No. 47, in D major, K. 97; 73m (1770); No. 45, in D major, K. 95; 73n (1770); No. 11, in D major, K. 84; 73q (1770; may not be by Mozart); No. 10, in G major, K. 74 (1770); B-flat major, K. Anh. 216; C 11.03 (1770–71; may not be by Mozart); No. 42, in F major, K. 75 (1771); No. 12, in G major, K. 110; 75b (1771); D major, K. 120; 111a (1771; finale only; perf. with the overture to *Ascanio in Alba*, K. 111, forming a symph.); No. 46, in C major, K. 96; 111b (1771); No. 13, in F major, K. 112 (1771); No. 14, in A major, K. 114 (1771); No. 15, in G major, K. 124 (1772); No. 16, in C major, K. 128 (1772); No. 17, in G major, K. 129 (1772); No. 18, in F major, K. 130 (1772); No. 19, in E-flat major, K. 132 (1772; with alternative slow movements); No. 20, in D major, K. 133 (1772); No. 21, in A major, K. 134 (1772); No. 50, in D major, K. 161, 163; 141a (1773–74); No. 26, in E-flat major, K. 184; 161a (1773); No. 27, in G major, K. 199; 161b (1773); No. 22, in C major, K. 162 (1773); No. 23, in D major, K. 181; 162b (1773); No. 24, in B-flat major, K. 182; 173dA (1773); No. 25, in G minor, K. 183; 173dB (1773); No. 29, in A major, K. 201; 186a (1774); No. 30, in D major, K. 202; 186b (1774); No. 28, in C major, K. 200; 189k (1774); D major, K. 121; 207a (1774–75; finale only; perf. with the overture to *La finta giardiniera*, K. 196, forming a symph.); D major (4 movements from the Serenade in D major, K. 204; 213a); C major, K. 102; 213c (1775; finale only; perf. with versions of the overture and first aria from *Il Rè pastore*, K. 208); D major (4 movements from the Serenade in D major, K. 250; 248b); No. 31, in D major, K. 297; 300a, "Paris" (1778: with 2 slow movements); No. 32, in G major, K. 318 (1779; in one movement); No. 33, in B-flat major, K. 319 (1779); D major (3 movements from the Serenade in D major, K. 320, "Posthorn"); No. 34, in C major, K. 338 (1780); C major, K. 409; 383f (1782; minuet only; may have been intended for the Symph. No. 34 in C major, K. 338); No. 35, in D major, K. 385, "Haffner" (1782; based on the Serenade in D major, K. 250; 248b, "Haffner"); No. 36, in C major, K. 425, "Linz" (1783); No. 37, in G major, K. 444; 425a (1783?; only the introduction is by Mozart; remainder by Michael Haydn; No. 38, in D major, K. 504, "Prague" (1786); No. 39, in E-flat major, K. 543 (1788); No. 40, in G minor, K. 550 (1788); No. 41, in C major, K. 551, "Jupiter" (1788). A symph.

listed as K. Anh. 8; 311A was never composed.

PIANO CONCERTOS: No. 5, in D major, K. 175 (1773); No. 6, in B-flat major, K. 238 (1776); No. 8, in C major, K. 246 (1776); No. 9, in E-flat major, K. 271 (1777); No. 12, in A major, K. 414; 385p (1782); No. 11, in F major, K. 413; 387a (1782–83); No. 13, in C major, K. 415; 387b (1782–83); No. 14, in E-flat major, K. 449 (1784); No. 15, in B-flat major, K. 450 (1784); No. 16, in D major, K. 451 (1784); No. 17, in G major, K. 453 (1784); No. 18, in B-flat major, K. 456 (1784); No. 19, in F major, K. 459 (1784); No. 20, in D minor, K. 466 (1785); No. 21, in C major, K. 467 (1785); No. 22, in E-flat major, K. 482 (1785); No. 23, in A major, K. 488 (1786); No. 24, in C minor, K. 491 (1786); No. 25, in C major, K. 503 (1786); No. 26, in D major, K. 537, "Coronation" (1788); No. 27, in B-flat major, K. 595 (1790–91).—Also No. 10, in E-flat major, for 2 Pianos, K. 365; 316a (1779); No. 7, in F major, for 3 Pianos, K. 242 (1776); Rondo in D major, K. 382 (1782; new finale for No. 5, in D major, K. 175); Rondo in A major, K. 386 (1782).

VIOLIN CONCERTOS: No. 1, in B-flat major, K. 207 (1775); No. 2, in D major, K. 211 (1775); No. 3, in G major, K. 216 (1775); No. 4, in D major, K. 218 (1775); No. 5, in A major, K. 219 (1775).—Also the following: Concertone in C major for 2 Violins, K. 190; 186e (1774); Adagio in E major for Violin, K. 261 (1776; for Violin Concerto No. 5, in A major, K. 219); Rondo in B-flat major for Violin, K. 269; 261a (1776); Sinfonia concertante in E-flat major for Violin and Viola, K. 364; 320d (1779); Rondo in C major for Violin, K. 373 (1781); Andante in A major for Violin, K. 470 (1785; not extant).

FOR WIND INSTRUMENTS: Concerto for Trumpet, K. 47c (1768; not extant); Concerto for Bassoon in B-flat major, K. 191; 186e (1774); Concerto for Oboe, K. 271k (1777; not extant; perhaps a version of K. 314; 285d below); Concerto for Flute in G major, K. 313; 285c (1778); Concerto for Oboe or Flute in C/D major, K. 314; 285d (1778; oboe version may be for K. 271k above); Andante for Flute in C major, K. 315; 285e (1779–80); Sinfonia concertante for Flute, Oboe, Bassoon, and Horn, K. Anh. 9; 297B (1778?; not extant; may not have been composed); Sinfonia concertante in E-flat major for Oboe, Clarinet, Bassoon, and Horn, K. Anh. 9; C 14.01 (doubtful); Concerto for Flute and Harp in C major, K. 299; 297c (1778); Sinfonia concertante in G major for 2 Flutes, 2 Oboes, and 2 Bassoons, K. 320 (movements 3 and 4 of the Serenade in D major, K. 320, "Posthorn"); Rondo for Horn in E-flat major, K. 371 (1781; unfinished); concertos for Horn: No. 1, in D major, K. 412; 386b (1782–87); No. 2, in E-flat major, K. 417 (1783); No. 3, in E-flat major, K. 447 (1783?); No. 4, in E-flat major, K. 495 (1786); Concerto for Clarinet in A major, K. 622 (1791).

SERENADES, DIVERTIMENTOS, CASSATIONS, ETC.: *Gallimathias musicum*, K. 32 (1766); 6 divertimentos, K. 41a (1767; not extant); Cassation in D major, K. 100; 62a (1769); Cassation in G major, K. 63 (1769); Cassation in C major (1769; not extant); Cassation in B-flat major, K. 99; 63a (1769); Divertimento in E-flat major, K. 113 (1771); Divertimento in D major, K. 131 (1772); Divertimento in D major, K. 205; 167a (1773?); Serenade in D major, K. 185; 167a (1773);

Serenade in D major, K. 203; 189b (1774); Serenade in D major, K. 204; 213a (1775); *Serenata notturna* in D major, K. 239 (1776); Divertimento in F major, K. 247 (1776); Serenade in D major, K. 250; 248b, "Haffner" (1776); Divertimento in D major, K. 251 (1776); *Notturno* in D major, K. 286; 269a (1776–77); Divertimento in B-flat major, K. 287; 271h (1777); Serenade in D major, K. 320, "Posthorn" (1779); Divertimento in D major, K. 334; 320b (1779–80); *Maurerische Trauermusik* in C minor, K. 477; 479a (1785); *Ein musikalischer Spass* in F major, K. 522 (1787; satirical; employs deliberate discords, consecutive fifths, etc.); *Eine kleine Nachtmusik* in G major, K. 525 (1787).—Also 14 divertimentos for Wind Ensemble; 15 marches (2 not extant); 10 German dances, *ländler;* 17 contredanses (several not extant); ballet, *Les Petits Riens,* K. Anh. 10; 299b (1778; Opéra, Paris, June 11, 1778); etc.

CHAMBER MUSIC: STRING QUARTETS: G major, K. 80; 73f (1770); Divertimento in D major, K. 136; 125a (1772); Divertimento in B-flat major, K. 137; 125b (1772); Divertimento in F major, K. 138; 125c (1772); D major, K. 155; 134a (1772); G major, K. 156; 134b (1772); C major, K. 157 (1772–73); F major, K. 158 (1772–73); B-flat major, K. 159 (1773); E-flat major, K. 160; 159a (1773); F major, K. 168 (1773); A major, K. 169 (1773); C major, K. 170 (1773); E-flat major, K. 171 (1773); B-flat major, K. 172 (1773); D minor, K. 173 (1773); G major, K. 387 (1782); D minor, K. 421; 417b (1783); E-flat major, K. 428; 421b (1783); B-flat major, K. 458, "Hunt" (1784); A major, K. 464 (1785); C major, K. 465, "Dissonance" (1785); D major, K. 499, "Hoffmeister" (1786); Adagio and Fugue in C minor, K. 546 (1788); D major, K. 575, "Prussian" (1789); B-flat major, K. 589, "Prussian" (1790); F major, K. 590, "Prussian" (1790).

STRING QUINTETS (2 Violins, 2 Violas, and Cello): B-flat major, K. 174 (1773); C major, K. 515 (1787); G minor, K. 516 (1787); C minor, K. 406; 516b (1788); D major, K. 593 (1790); E-flat major, K. 614 (1791).

FOR STRINGS AND WIND INSTRUMENTS: Duo in B-flat major for Bassoon and Cello, K. 292; 196c (1775); Quartet in D major for Flute, Violin, Viola, and Cello, K. 285 (1777); Quartet in G major for Flute, Violin, Viola, and Cello, K. 285a (1778); Quartet in C major for Flute, Violin, Viola, and Cello, K. Anh. 171; 285b (1781–82); Quartet in A major for Flute, Violin, Viola, and Cello, K. 298 (1786–87); Quartet in F major for Oboe, Violin, Viola, and Cello, K. 370; 368b (1781); Quintet in E-flat major for Horn, Violin, 2 Violas, and Cello, K. 407; 386c (1782); Quintet in A major for Clarinet, 2 Violins, Viola, and Cello, K. 581 (1789).

STRING SONATAS, DUOS, AND TRIOS: Solos for Cello and Bassoon, K. 33b (1766; not extant); *Nachtmusik* for 2 Violins and Bassoon, K. 41g (1767; not extant); Sonata in C major for Violin and Bassoon, K. 46d (1768); Sonata in F major for Violin and Bassoon, K. 46e (1768); Trio in B-flat major for 2 Violins and Bassoon, K. 266; 271f (1777); 4 preludes for Violin, Viola, and Cello, K. 404a (1782; may not be by Mozart); Duo in G major for Violin and Viola, K. 423 (1783); Duo in B-flat major for Violin and Viola, K. 424 (1783); Trio in E-flat major for Violin, Viola, and Cello, K. 563 (1788).

FOR KEYBOARD AND OTHER INSTRUMENTS: Divertimento in B-flat major for Piano, Violin, and Cello, K. 254 (1776); Trio in D minor for Piano, Violin, and Cello, K. 442 (1783?–90; unfinished; completed by M. Stadler); Quintet in E-flat major for Piano, Oboe, Clarinet, Bassoon, and Horn, K. 452 (1784); Quartet in G minor for Piano, Violin, Viola, and Cello, K. 478 (1785); Quartet in E-flat major for Piano, Violin, Viola, and Cello, K. 493 (1786); Trio in G major for Piano, Violin, and Cello, K. 496 (1786); Trio in E-flat major for Piano, Clarinet, and Viola, K. 498 (1786); Trio in B-flat major for Piano, Violin, and Cello, K. 502 (1786); Trio in E major for Piano, Violin, and Cello, K. 542 (1788); Trio in C major for Piano, Violin, and Cello, K. 548 (1788); Trio in G major for Piano, Violin, and Cello, K. 564 (1788); Adagio and Rondo in C minor for Glass Harmonica, Flute, Oboe, Viola, and Cello, K. 617 (1791).

FOR KEYBOARD AND VIOLIN: Sonata in C major, K. 6 (1762–64); Sonata in D major, K. 7 (1762–64); Sonata in B-flat major, K. 8 (1763–64); Sonata in G major, K. 9 (1763–64); Sonata in B-flat major, K. 10 (1764); Sonata in G major, K. 11 (1764); Sonata in A major, K. 12 (1764); Sonata in F major, K. 13 (1764); Sonata in C major, K. 14 (1764); Sonata in B-flat major, K. 15 (1764); Sonata in E-flat major, K. 26 (1766); Sonata in G major, K. 27 (1766); Sonata in C major, K. 28 (1766); Sonata in D major, K. 29 (1766); Sonata in F major, K. 30 (1766); Sonata in B-flat major, K. 31 (1766); Sonata in G major, K. 301; 293a (1778); Sonata in E-flat major, K. 302; 293b (1778); Sonata in C major, K. 303; 293c (1778); Sonata in A major, K. 305; 293d (1778); Sonata in C major, K. 296 (1778); Sonata in E minor, K. 304; 300c (1778); Sonata in D major, K. 306; 300l (1778); Sonata in B-flat major, K. 378; 317d (1779?); Sonata in B-flat major, K. 372 (1781; unfinished; completed by M. Stadler); Sonata in G major, K. 379; 373a (1781); Variations in G major, K. 359; 374a (1781); Variations in G minor, K. 360; 374b (1781); Sonata in F major, K. 376; 374d (1781); Sonata in F major, K. 377; 374e (1781); Sonata in E-flat major, K. 380; 374f (1781); Sonata in C major, K. 403; 385c (1782; unfinished; completed by M. Stadler); Sonata in C major, K. 404; 385d (1782?; unfinished); Sonata in A major, K. 402; 385e (1782; unfinished; completed by M. Stadler); Sonata in C minor, K. 396; 385f (1782; one movement only; completed by M. Stadler); Sonata in B-flat major, K. 454 (1784); Sonata in E-flat major, K. 481 (1785); Sonata in A major, K. 526 (1787); Sonata in F major, K. 547, "für Anfänger" (1788).

FOR KEYBOARD SOLO: Sonata in G major, K. Anh. 199; 33d (1766; not extant); Sonata in B-flat major, K. Anh. 200; 33e (1766; not extant); Sonata in C major, K. 201; 33f (1766; not extant); Sonata in F major, K. 202; 33g (1766; not extant); Sonata in C major, K. 279; 189d (1775); Sonata in F major, K. 280; 189e (1775); Sonata in B-flat major, K. 281; 189f (1775); Sonata in E-flat major, K. 282; 189g (1775); Sonata in G major, K. 283; 189h (1775); Sonata in D major, K. 284; 205b (1775); Sonata in C major, K. 309; 284b (1777); Sonata in D major, K. 311; 284c (1777); Sonata in A minor, K. 310; 300d (1778); Sonata in C major, K. 330; 300h (1781–83); Sonata in A major, K. 331; 300i (1781–83); Sonata in F major, K. 332; 300k (1781–83); Sonata in

B-flat major, K. 333; 315c (1783–84); Sonata in C minor, K. 457 (1784); Sonata in F major, K. 533 (1786); Sonata in C major, K. 545, "für Anfänger" (1788); Sonata in F major, K. Anh. 135; 547a (1788; may not be by Mozart); Sonata in B-flat major, K. 570 (1789); Sonata in D major, K. 576 (1789).

FOR KEYBOARD DUET: Sonata in C major, K. 19d (1765); Sonata in D major, K. 381; 123a (1772); Sonata in B-flat major, K. 358; 186c (1773–74); Sonata in F major, K. 497 (1786); Sonata in C major, K. 521 (1787).—Also: Sonata in D major for 2 Keyboards, K. 448; 375a (1781); 17 variations for Keyboard Solo (one not extant) and one for Piano Duet; many miscellaneous pieces; 17 sonatas for Organ, most with 2 Violins and Bassoon; etc.

Since the publication of the Breitkopf & Härtel edition of Mozart's works, the list of doubtful and spurious compositions has grown extensively. The pioneering research of Wyzewa and Saint-Foix has been followed by the important studies of Wolfgang Plath, Alan Tyson, and other scholars. For detailed information, see the bibliography below. A selected compilation of doubtful and spurious works follows (those noted in the list of works above are excluded):

Masses: F major, K. 116; 90a, by Leopold Mozart; E-flat major, K. Anh. 235f; C 1.02, by B. Schack; G major, K. Anh. 232; C 1.04, "Twelfth Mass"; G major, K. *deest*; C 1.18, "Missa solemnis pastorita"; D minor, K. Anh. 237; C 1.90, "Requiem brevis"; Kyrie in C major, K. 340; C 3.06; Kyrie in C major, K. 221; A1, by Eberlin.—Also: *Lacrimosa* in C minor, K. Anh. 21; A2, by Eberlin; *Justum deduxit Dominus,* hymn, K. 326; A4, by Eberlin; *Adoramus te,* hymn, K. 327; A10, by Q. Gasparini; *De profundis clamavi,* Psalm, K. 93; A22, by Reutter; *Salve Regina,* K. 92; C 3.01; *Tantum ergo* in B-flat major, K. 142; C 3.04; *Offertorium sub exposito venerabili,* K. 177 and 342; C 3.09, by Leopold Mozart.

Symphs.: No. 2, in B-flat major, K. 17; C 11.02; B-flat major, K. Anh. 216; C 11.03; No. 3, in E-flat major, K. 18; A51, by C.F. Abel; F major, K. 98; C 11.04; B-flat major, K. 311a; C 11.05, the so-called "2nd Paris" Symph.—Also: Fugue in D major, K. 291; A52, by M. Haydn, finished by S. Sechter.

Piano concertos: The first 4 piano concertos, K. 37, 39, 40, and 41, are arrangements of sonata movements by Raupach, Honauer, Schobert, Eckard, and C.P.E. Bach; the 5th Piano Concerto, K. 107, consists of arrangements of 3 sonatas by Johann Christian Bach.

Violin concertos: Two violin concertos, one in D major, K. 271a; 271i, the other in E-flat major, K. 268; C 14.04, may contain some music composed by Mozart. The Violin Concerto in D major, K. Anh. 294a; C 14.05, the so-called "Adelaide" Concerto, which was widely performed after its alleged discovery in 1931, was actually composed by the French violinist Marius Casadesus; it was supposedly dedicated to Princess Adelaide, the daughter of Louis XV, by the boy Mozart during his visit to Paris at the age of 10.—Also: *Sinfonia concertante* in A major for Violin, Viola, and Cello, K. Anh. 104; 320e.

Sonatas for Keyboard and Violin: K. 55–60; C 23.01–6 and K. 61, by Raupach.

Mozart, Wolfgang Amadeus (Franz Xaver), son of the great composer; b. Vienna, July 26, 1791; d. Karlsbad, July 29, 1844. He studied with Hummel and Salieri in Vienna; gave a concert as pianist at the age of 13; lived many years as a private tutor in Lwow, where he founded the Cecilia Society. He wrote 2 piano concertos; a String Quartet; Piano Trio; Violin Sonata; many pieces for piano.

Mraczek, Joseph Gustav, Czech composer; b. Brno, March 12, 1878; d. Dresden, Dec. 24, 1944. He received his first instruction from his father, the cellist **Franz Mraczek;** was a chorister in various churches in Brno before going to Vienna, where he studied with Hellmesberger, Stocker, and Löwe at the Cons.; from 1897 to 1902 was concertmaster at the Stadttheater in Brno; then taught violin in Brno (until 1918). In 1919, he went to Dresden to teach composition at the Cons. there; conducted the Dresden Phil. (1919–24); remained in Dresden to the end of his life. He wrote 6 operas: *The Glass Slipper* (Brno, 1902); *Der Traum* (Brno, Feb. 26, 1909); *Aebelö* (Breslau, 1915); *Ikdar* (Dresden, 1921); *Herrn Dürers Bild oder Madonna am Wiesenzaun* (Hannover, Jan. 29, 1927); *Der Liebesrat* (not produced); his most successful piece was a symph. burlesque, *Max und Moritz* (Brno, 1911; also widely played throughout Germany, and in the U.S.); other works include: *Oriental Sketches* for Small Orch. (1918); symph. poem, *Eva* (1922); *Oriental Dance Rhapsody* (1931); a Piano Quintet; a String Quartet; piano pieces; songs.

Mravina (original name, **Mravinskaya**), **Evgeniya,** noted Russian soprano; b. St. Petersburg, Feb. 16, 1864; d. Yalta, Oct. 25, 1914. She studied in St. Petersburg with Pryanishnikov, and later with Désirée d'Artôt in Berlin; then sang in Italy. After returning to Russia, she joined the Maryinsky Theater in St. Petersburg in 1886, remaining on its roster until 1900. In 1891–92 she toured in England, France, Belgium, and Germany. She had the privilege of going over the part of Marguerite in *Faust* with Gounod, and the part of Mignon in the opera of that name by Ambroise Thomas with the composer himself. She gave brilliant renditions of Italian soprano roles; was greatly praised in Russia for her performances of the Russian operatic parts. She retired from the operatic stage in 1900 but continued to appear in recital.

Mravinsky, Evgeni, eminent Russian conductor; b. St. Petersburg, June 4, 1903. He studied biology at St. Petersburg Univ.; then joined the Imperial Ballet as a pantomimist and rehearsal pianist; in 1924 he enrolled in the Leningrad Cons., where he studied conducting with Gauk, graduating in 1931; also took additional training with Malko; had courses in composition with Vladimir Shcherbachev; then was conductor of the Leningrad Theater of Opera and Ballet (1932–38). In 1938 he was appointed principal conductor of the Leningrad Phil. Mravinsky represents the best of the Soviet school of conducting, in which technical precision and fidelity to the music are combined with individual and even Romantic interpretations. He is especially noted for his fine performances of Tchaikovsky's operas, ballets, and symphs.; he gave first performances of several symphs. of Prokofiev and Shostakovich; also conducted works by Béla Bartók and Stravinsky. In 1973 he was awarded the order of Hero of Socialist Labor.

Muck, Karl, great German conductor; b. Darmstadt, Oct. 22, 1859; d. Stuttgart, March 3, 1940. He received his first musical instruction from his father; also studied piano with Kissner in Würzburg; later pursued academic studies (classical philology) at the Univ. of Heidelberg and at Leipzig; received his Dr.Phil. in 1880. He also attended the Leipzig Cons., and shortly before graduation made a successful debut as pianist with the Gewandhaus Orch. However, he did not choose to continue a pianistic career; he obtained a position as chorus master at the municipal opera in Zürich; his ability soon secured him the post of conductor there; in subsequent years he was theater conductor in Salzburg, Brünn, and Graz; there Angelo Neumann, impresario of a traveling opera company, heard him, and engaged him as conductor for the Landestheater in Prague (1886), and then as Seidl's successor for his traveling Wagner Co. It was during those years that Muck developed his extraordinary qualities as a masterful disciplinarian and faithful interpreter possessing impeccable taste. In 1889 he conducted the Wagner tetralogy in St. Petersburg, and in 1891, in Moscow. In 1892 he was engaged as first conductor at the Berlin Opera, and also frequently conducted symph. concerts of the Royal Chapel there. From 1894 to 1911 he led the Silesian Music Festivals; in 1899 he conducted the Wagner repertoire at Covent Garden; from 1904 to 1906, he conducted the concerts of the Vienna Phil. (alternating with Mottl); he also appeared, with outstanding success, in Paris, Rome, Brussels, Madrid, Copenhagen, and other European centers. In 1901 he was selected to conduct the performances of *Parsifal* at Bayreuth. In 1906 he was engaged as conductor of the Boston Symph. Orch., and led it for 2 seasons, returning to Berlin in 1908, as Generalmusikdirektor. He returned to America in the autumn of 1912 and assumed the post of permanent conductor of the Boston Symph. His farewell appearance at the Berlin Opera, conducting *Tristan und Isolde,* was made the occasion of a tumultuous demonstration. During the 20 years of his activity in Berlin he conducted 1,071 performances of 103 operas, of which 35 were novelties. With the entry of the U.S. into the war in the spring of 1917, Muck's position in Boston became ambiguous; he was known as a friend of Wilhelm II, and did not temper his intense German nationalism. Protests were made against the retention of Muck as conductor in Boston, and despite the defense offered by Major Higginson, the founder of the Boston Symph., Muck was arrested at his home on March 25, 1918, and interned as an enemy alien until the end of the war. In 1919 he returned to Germany; conducted the Hamburg Phil. from 1922 until 1933; then went to Stuttgart.

Mudarra, Alonso, Spanish lutenist; b. c.1508; d. Seville, April 1, 1580. He was appointed canon of the Seville Cathedral in 1566. His important work, *Tres libros de música en cifra para vihuela* (i.e., lute music in tablature), originally publ. in Seville in 1546, was printed in modern notation by Emilio Pujol (Barcelona, 1946); this edition contains 77 works by Mudarra and his contemporaries, a biographical sketch, and commentary.

Muffat, Georg, important organist and composer; b. Megève, Savoy (baptized, June 1), 1653; d. Passau, Feb. 23, 1704. He studied with Lully in Paris (1663–69); was named organist at the Molsheim Cathedral on March 31, 1671; in 1674, went to Ingolstadt to study law; then went to Vienna; in 1678, entered the service of the Archbishop of Salzburg. In 1681 he was in Italy; studied with Corelli and Pasquini in Rome; also spent several years in Paris. In 1687 he was appointed organist to the Bishop of Passau; in 1690, became Kapellmeister there. He was a significant composer; developed the German type of concerto grosso; publ. organ works, sonatas for various instruments, orch. suites, etc.

WORKS: *Armonico tributo,* polyphonic sonatas (1682; partly reprinted in Denkmäler der Tonkunst in Österreich, 89); *Florilegium,* orch. suites for Organ (1690; reprinted by Lange, 1888, and by Rietsch in Denkmäler der Tonkunst in Österreich, 2, 4 [1.ii, 2.ii]); *Apparatus musico-organisticus,* toccatas for Organ (1960; reprinted by Lange, 1888, and by Kaller-Valentin, 1933); 12 concerti grossi, publ. under the title *Auserlesener ... Instrumentalmusik erste Versamblung* (1701; reprinted in Denkmäler der Tonkunst in Österreich, 23 [11.ii]); a toccata is included in J. Bonnet's *Historical Organ Recitals* (vol. 1).

Muffat, Gottlieb (Theophil), Austrian organist and composer; son of **Georg Muffat;** b. Passau (baptized, April 25), 1690; d. Vienna, Dec. 9, 1770. In 1711 he went to Vienna, where he studied with J.J. Fux; from 1714, was in charge of the accompaniment of operas, church festivals, and chamber music at the Vienna court; became 2nd court organist in 1717; first organist, in 1741; retired on a pension in 1763.

WORKS: *72 Versetl sammt 12 Toccaten* for Organ (1726; reprinted by Guido Adler in Denkmäler der Tonkunst in Österreich, 58 [29.ii]); *Componimenti musicali* for Harpsichord (ibid., 7 [3.iii]; includes an essay on ornaments; Handel used this material for ornamental phrases in his oratorios).

Mugnone, Leopoldo, Italian conductor; b. Naples, Sept. 29, 1858; d. there, Dec. 22, 1941. He studied with Cesi and Serrao at the Naples Cons.; began to compose as a young student; when he was 16, he produced a comic opera, *Don Bizarro e le sue figlie* (Naples, April 20, 1875); other operas were *Il Biricchino* (Venice, Aug. 11, 1892; fairly successful) and *Vita Bretone* (Naples, March 14, 1905). He also composed an attractive Neapolitan song, *La Rosella,* and other light music. But it was as a fine opera conductor that Mugnone achieved fame; his performances of Italian stage works possessed the highest degree of authority and an intense musicianly ardor. He also brought out Wagner's music dramas in Italy; conducted the first performance of Mascagni's *Cavalleria rusticana* (Rome, in May 17, 1890).

Mühlfeld, Richard, famous German clarinetist; b. Salzungen, Feb. 28, 1856; d. Meiningen, June 1, 1907. He first studied the violin and played in the Meiningen Court Orch.; then practiced on the clarinet without a teacher, and in 1876, at the age of 20, became first clarinetist at Meiningen. From 1884 to 1896 he was first clarinetist at the Bayreuth Festivals. Brahms wrote for him the Trio, op. 114 (for Clarinet, Cello, and Piano), the Quintet, op. 115 (for Clarinet, 2 Violins, Viola, and Cello), and the 2 clarinet sonatas, op. 120.

Muldowney, Dominic, British composer; b. Southampton, July 19, 1952. He studied with Jonathan Harvey at Southampton Univ. and later with Birtwistle in London and with Bernard Rands and David Blake at York Univ.; in 1976 he was appointed composer-in-residence at the National Theatre in London. He belongs to a group of British composers who reject esoteric musical abstractions and doctrinaire methodology in favor of an art which is readily accessible to a wide range of listeners.
WORKS: *Driftwood to the Flow* for 18 Strings (1972); *Klavier-Hammer* for one or more Pianos (1973); *Music at Chartres* for 16 Instruments (1973); String Quartet No. 1 (1973); String Quartet No. 2 (1980); Cantata for Soloists, 2 Speakers, 2 Cellos, and Percussion (1974); *Lovemusic for Bathsheba Evergreen and Gabriel Oak* for Chamber Group (1974); Solo/Ensemble for Chamber Group (1974); *The Earl of Essex's Galliard* for 3 Actors, Dancer, and Instruments (1975–76); *Double Helix* for 8 Players (1977); *Garland of Chansons* for 6 Oboes and 3 Bassoons (1978); *3 Hymns to Agape* for Chamber Orch. (1978); *Macbeth,* ballet music, for Orch. (1979); 6 Psalms for Choir, Soprano, Tenor, and Instruments (1979; Horsham, Dec. 6, 1980); *5 Theatre Poems,* after Brecht, for Mezzo-soprano and Instruments (1980–81; London, April 26, 1982); Piano Trio (1980; Bath Festival, May 25, 1982); *In Dark Times* for 4 Soloists and Chamber Group, to 8 poems by Brecht (1981; London, Feb. 23, 1982); *Sports et Divertissements,* after Satie, for Reciter and Chamber Group (1981); *The Duration of Exile* and *A Second Show* for Mezzo-soprano and Chamber Group (1983; London, June 2, 1983); Piano Concerto (1983; London, July 27, 1983).

Mulè, Giuseppe, Italian composer; b. Termini, Sicily, June 28, 1885; d. Rome, Sept. 10, 1951. He studied at the Cons. of Palermo; graduated as a cellist as well as in composition. In 1922 he was engaged as director of the Cons. of Palermo (until 1925); in 1925 he succeeded Respighi as director of the Santa Cecilia Academy in Rome; remained there until 1943. He wrote mostly for the stage, and was par-

ticularly successful in providing suitable music for revivals of Greek plays. He composed numerous operas in the tradition of the Italian *verismo: La Baronessa di Carini* (Palermo, April 16, 1912), *La Monacella della fontana* (Trieste, Feb. 17, 1923), *Dafni* (Rome, March 14, 1928), *Liolà* (Naples, Feb. 2, 1935); the oratorio *Il Cieco di Gerico;* the symph. poems *Sicilia canora* (1924) and *Vendemmia* (1936); also *3 canti siciliani* for Voice and Orch. (1930); a String Quartet and other chamber music; songs.

Müller, August Eberhard, German organist and composer; b. Nordheim, Hannover, Dec. 13, 1767; d. Weimar, Dec. 3, 1817. He was an organist at various churches at Magdeburg and Leipzig; in 1800 became assistant to Johann Adam Hiller at the Thomasschule in Leipzig, and succeeded him as cantor there in 1804; also was music director of the Thomaskirche and Nikolaikirche. In 1810 he became court conductor in Weimar. He wrote 3 piano concertos and 18 piano sonatas; 11 flute concertos; 11 church cantatas; a practical piano method (1805; actually the 6th ed. of Löhlein's *Pianoforte-Schule,* revised by Müller; Kalkbrenner's method is based on it; Czerny publ. the 8th ed. in 1825); a method for the flute. He also publ. cadenzas for, and a guide to the interpretation of, Mozart's concertos; arranged piano scores of Mozart's operas (very popular in his time).

Müller, Georg Gottfried (also known as **George Godfrey**), American Moravian minister, violinist, and composer; b. Gross Hennersdorf, Saxony, May 22, 1762; d. Lititz, Pa., March 19, 1821. He came to America in 1784, and spent the major part of his life at Lititz, as a member of the culturally important group of Moravians in America. His works are listed by A.G. Rau and H.T. David in *A Catalogue of Music by American Moravians* (Bethlehem, 1938), and his music is represented in vol. I of the series Music by the Moravians in America, publ. by the N.Y. Public Library (1938).

Müller, Iwan, clarinetist and instrument maker; b. Reval, Estonia, Dec. 14, 1786; d. Bückeburg, Feb. 4, 1854. He developed the clarinet with 13 keys plus the "Altclarinet" (superseding the basset horn). In 1809 he went to Paris, where he established a clarinet workshop; although he faced the opposition of conservative instrument makers, his improved clarinet eventually won general popularity. He spent the last years of his life at Bückeburg as court musician; publ. a method for his new instruments; 6 clarinet concertos and 2 clarinet quartets.

Müller, Wenzel, Austrian composer; b. Tyrnau, Moravia, Sept. 26, 1767; d. Baden, near Vienna, Aug. 3, 1835. He studied with Dittersdorf; conducted theater orchs. in provincial towns; was director of the German Opera in Prague from 1807 to 1813; then went to Vienna as conductor at the Leopoldstadt Theater, a post he held almost to the end of his life. He wrote an enormous amount of stage music, and his singspiels were very popular in their day;

among them were the following, which he brought out at the Leopoldstadt Theater: *Das Sonnenfest der Braminen* (Sept. 9, 1790); *Kaspar der Fagottist, oder Die Zauberzither* (June 8, 1791); *Das Neusonntagskind* (Oct. 10, 1793); *Die Schwestern von Prag* (March 11, 1794); *Die Teufelsmühle am Weinerberg* (an Austrian fairy tale; Nov. 12, 1799; his most popular stage work). A full list of his operas is in the 2nd Supplement to Riemann's *Opernhandbuch* (Leipzig, 1887).

Müller-Hermann, Johanna, Austrian composer and pedagogue; b. Vienna, Jan. 15, 1878; d. there. April 19, 1941. She studied with Karl Nawratil, Josef Labor, Guido Adler, Zemlinsky, and J.B. Foerster; began to compose at an early age, in a Romantic vein, influenced chiefly by Mahler and Max Reger; was regarded as one of the foremost European women composers of orch. and chamber music. She wrote an oratorio, *In Memoriam*, to Walt Whitman's words; a Symph. for Voices with Orch.; a Symph. Fantasy on Ibsen's play *Brand*; String Quartet; String Quintet; Piano Quintet; Violin Sonata; Cello Sonata; Piano Sonata; several song cycles.

Müller von Asow, Erich Hermann, German musicologist; b. Dresden, Aug. 31, 1892; d. Berlin, June 4, 1964. He studied at the Univ. of Leipzig with Hugo Riemann (1912–15); during World War I was engaged as a military band conductor in the German army; then was in charge of the Pädagogium der Tonkunst in Dresden (1926–32); in 1936 he went to Austria; was briefly under arrest by the Gestapo in 1943; in 1945 returned to Germany, and lived mostly in Berlin. His publications include several valuable biographical studies, among them *Angelo und Pietro Mingotti* (Leipzig, 1917); *J.G. Mraczek* (Dresden, 1917); *Heinrich Schütz* (Dresden, 1922); *An die unsterbliche Geliebte: Liebesbriefe berühmter Musiker* (Dresden, 1934; 2nd ed., Vienna, 1942); *The Letters and Writings of G.F. Handel* (in Eng., London, 1935; in German, 1949); *J.S. Bach, Gesammelte Briefe und Schriften* (Regensburg, 1940; 2nd ed., 1950); *Egon Kornauth* (Leipzig, 1941); *Johannes Brahms und seine Welt* (Vienna, 1943); *Max Reger und seine Welt* (Berlin, 1944); numerous publications on Mozart. He began in 1955 a thematic catalogue of the works of Richard Strauss, which was completed by A. Ott and F. Trenner (3 vols.; Vienna, 1959–74). Anticipating the ominous zeitgeist, he regrettably publ. a *Handbuch der Judenfrage, Das Judentum in der Musik* (Leipzig, 1932). A Festschrift on the occasion of his 50th birthday was publ. in Salzburg (1942); and a compendium, *Epistolae et musica*, on his 60th birthday (Hamburg, 1952). A complete list of his writings is in *Kürschners deutscher Musiker-Kalender* (1954).

Mullings, Frank, distinguished English tenor; b. Walsall, March 10, 1881; d. Manchester, May 19, 1953. He studied voice in Birmingham; made his debut in Coventry in 1907 as Faust; then sang Tristan in London in 1913, and performed the role of Otello in Manchester in 1916. In 1919 he was the first to sing Parsifal in English, at Covent Garden in London. From 1922–29 he was the principal dramatic tenor of the British National Opera Co., and appeared with it as Apollo in the first performance, in 1924, of Rudland Boughton's *Alkestis.* His other roles include Siegfried, Tannhäuser, Canio, and Radames. From 1930–45 he appeared mainly in concerts.

Mumma, Gordon, American avant-garde composer; b. Framingham, Mass., March 30, 1935. He began experimenting with electronic music at the age of 19, composing music and sound effects for an experimental theater in Ann Arbor. In 1957 he joined Robert Ashley and the artist Milton Cohen in a revolutionary theatrical art based on projected images; this developed into an esthetic medium called "Manifestations: Light and Sound" and later "Space Theatre"; in 1964 Mumma, Cohen, and Ashley gave a memorable presentation of the Space Theatre at the Biennial Exhibition in Venice, becoming pioneers in the electronic light-show. With the development of transistor circuitry in electronics, Mumma began a serious study of its technology. In 1961 Mumma became a founder of the annual contemporary music festival in Ann Arbor called ONCE. Working at the Inst. of Science and Technology in Ann Arbor, he developed a skill in seismology; made a study of tape recordings of earthquakes and underground nuclear explosions. In 1966 he joined the Merce Cunningham Dance Co. and moved to N.Y.; formed an ensemble called the Sonic Arts Union, which made 2 European tours. He gave courses in electronic circuitry at Brandeis Univ. (1966–67) and at the Univ. of Illinois in Urbana (1969–70); designed the Sound Modifier Console for the Pepsi-Cola Pavilion at EXPO '70 in Osaka, Japan; developed a process of "cybersonic" control of acoustical and electronic media. He also applied computer techniques to composition.

Munch, Charles, eminent Alsatian conductor; b. Strasbourg, Sept. 26, 1891; d. Richmond, Va., Nov. 6, 1968. The original spelling of his name was **Münch;** he was a son of **Ernst Münch,** a choral conductor in Alsace. He studied violin at the Strasbourg Cons., then went to Paris, where he studied violin with Lucien Capet, and later took further violin lessons with Carl Flesch in Berlin and conducting with Furtwängler in Leipzig. He was sergeant of artillery in the German army during World War I; was gassed at Peronne, and wounded at Verdun. In 1918, as an Alsatian, he became a French citizen; was concertmaster of the municipal orch. of Strasbourg (1919–26); later joined the Gewandhaus Orch. in Leipzig as concertmaster. He made his professional debut as a symph. conductor in Paris with the Straram Orch. (Nov. 1, 1932); in order to perfect his conducting technique he took some instruction with Alfred Szendrei (Sendrey), a Hungarian conductor then living in Paris (1933–40). Although he began his career as a conductor at the age of 41, he quickly rose to eminence; organized his own orch. in Paris, the Orch. de la Société Philharmonique (1935–38), performing many French works. In 1938 he was engaged to conduct the Société des Concerts du Conservatoire de Paris, and remained with it during the difficult time of the German occupation. He was awarded the French Légion d'Honneur in 1945. He made his American debut with the Boston Symph. Orch. on Dec. 27, 1946; in 1948 he made a transcontinental tour of the U.S. with the French Radio Orch. In 1949 he was selected as permanent conductor of the Boston Symph., to succeed Koussevitzky. In 1952 he traveled with the Boston Symph. to Europe on its first European tour; in 1956 the Boston Symph., with Munch and Monteux as conductors, made another European tour, which included Russia. He retired as conductor of the Boston Symph. Orch. in 1962. Returning to Paris, he organized there the Orch. de Paris; it was during an American tour of this orch. that he collapsed and died in Richmond, Va. In his conducting Munch combined a distinct individuality with a fine sense of authentic color and stirring rhythms; in Classical works he continued the traditions of the German school, striving mainly for precision and fidelity to the music, while making allowances for appropriate Romantic effusions. Modern French music occupied a prominent place on his programs; he brought out new works by Albert Roussel, Milhaud, Honegger and others. He publ. a book, *Je suis chef d'orchestre* (Paris, 1954; in Eng., *I Am a Conductor,* N.Y., 1955).

Münch, Ernst, Alsatian organist and choral conductor; b. Niederbronn, Dec. 31, 1859; d. Strasbourg, April 1, 1928. He was appointed organist at St. Wilhelm (St. Guillaume) Church in Strasbourg in 1882, where he founded a choir which attained a great renown for its performance of Bach's cantatas and passions; Albert Schweitzer served as organist at these performances. His son, **Fritz Münch** (b. Strasbourg, June 2, 1890), succeeded him as conductor of the St. Wilhelm Choir in 1924; his second son, **Charles Münch (Munch),** became a celebrated conductor; his third son was **Hans Münch.**

Münch, Hans, Alsatian conductor; b. Mulhouse, March 9, 1893. He was a nephew of **Ernst Münch** and son of the organist **Eugen Münch** of Mulhouse. He studied organ, composition, and conducting at the Basel Cons. He conducted the choral society of Basel (1925–65) and also the subscription concerts of the Allgemeine Musikgesellschaft, from 1935 until 1966; was director of the Basel Music School in 1935–47. He composed several cantatas, a Symph. (1951), and *Symphonische Improvisationen* (1971).

Münchinger, Karl, German conductor; b. Stuttgart, May 29, 1915. He studied at the Hochschule für Musik in Stuttgart; then with Abendroth at the Leipzig Cons.; in 1941–43 he conducted symph. orchs. in Hannover, and in 1945 founded the Stuttgart Chamber Orch. From then on he pursued his conducting career mainly outside of Germany; toured America, Japan and Russia; made his U.S. debut in San Francisco in 1953, and during the following season made a U.S. tour with his Stuttgart

Chamber Orch.; he visited the U.S. again in 1977. In 1966 he organized the "Klassische Philharmonie" in Stuttgart, with which he gave regular performances.

Munrow, David, English recorder player; b. Birmingham, Aug. 12, 1942; d. Chesham Bois, Buckinghamshire, May 15, 1976. He read English at Pembroke College, Cambridge; during this period (1961–64) he founded an ensemble for the furtherance of early English music and organized a recorder consort. In 1967 he formed the Early Music Consort of London, which gave many successful concerts of medieval and Renaissance music. He wrote *Instruments of the Middle Ages and Renaissance* (London, 1976). He killed himself for obscure reasons in his early maturity.

Munz, Mieczyslaw, Polish-American pianist and pedagogue; b. Cracow, Oct. 31, 1900; d. New York, Aug. 25, 1976. He studied piano and composition at the Vienna Academy of Music, and later at the Hochschule für Musik in Berlin; his principal teacher there was Ferruccio Busoni. He made a brilliant debut in Berlin in 1920 as soloist in 3 works on the same program: the Brahms Piano Concerto in D minor, Liszt's Piano Concerto in A, and *Variations symphoniques* by César Franck. His American debut took place in a solo recital in N.Y. on Oct. 20, 1922; he subsequently was soloist with a number of orchs. in the U.S.; also toured Europe, South America, Australia, and Japan. He was on the faculty of the Curtis Inst. of Music in Philadelphia from 1941 to 1963, when he was engaged as a prof. of piano at the Juilliard School of Music in N.Y. In 1975 he gave courses in Tokyo. His piano playing was distinguished by a fine Romantic flair supported by an unobtrusive virtuoso technique. He was highly esteemed as a teacher.

Muradeli, Vano, Russian composer; b. Gori, Georgia, April 6, 1908; d. Tomsk, Siberia, Aug. 14, 1970. As a child he improvised songs, accompanying himself on the mandolin (there was no piano in his home); he did not learn to read music until he was 18, when he entered the Tiflis Cons.; after graduation (1934) he went to the Moscow Cons., where he studied first with Shekhter and then with Miaskovsky. His early compositions were influenced by his native folk music; he wrote a *Georgian Suite* for Piano (1935) and incidental music to plays on Caucasian subjects. His first important work was a symph. in memory of the assassinated Soviet dignitary Kirov (Moscow, Nov. 28, 1938); his 2nd Symph. (1946) received a Stalin prize. The performance of his opera *Great Friendship* (Moscow, Nov. 7, 1947) gave rise to an official condemnation of modernistic trends in Soviet music, culminating in the resolution of the Central Committee of the Communist Party of Feb. 10, 1948, which described the opera as "chaotic, inharmonious and alien to the normal human ear." Muradeli's reputation was rehabilitated by his subsequent works: *The Path of Victory* for Orch., a series of choruses (*Stalin's Will Has Led Us; Song of* the *Fighters for Peace; Hymn to Moscow,* which received a Stalin prize in 1951), and an opera, *October* (Moscow, April 22, 1964).

Muratore, Lucien, French tenor; b. Marseilles, Aug. 29, 1876; d. Paris, July 16, 1954. He studied at the Cons. of Marseilles, graduating with honors in 1897, but began his career as an actor. Later he studied opera at the Paris Cons.; made his opera debut at the Opéra–Comique on Dec. 16, 1902, in Hahn's *La Carmélite,* with extraordinary success. Muratore also sang in the premières of several operas by Massenet: *Ariane* (1906), *Bacchus* (1909), and *Roma* (1912); Février's *Monna Vanna* (1909) and Giordano's *Siberia* (1911); etc. In 1913 he made his American debut with the Boston Opera Co.; on Dec. 15, 1913, he sang Faust with the Chicago Opera Co. In 1914 he joined the French army; in 1917 he sang at the Teatro Colón in Buenos Aires; then returned to the Chicago Opera Co. In 1922 he went back to France; for 7 years he served as mayor of the town of Biot. He was married 3 times; his first 2 marriages (to **Marguerite Bériza,** a soprano, and to the famous prima donna **Lina Cavalieri**) ended in divorce; his 3rd wife was Marie Louise Brivaud.

Muris, Johannes de (original French rendering may have been **Jehan des Murs, de Murs, de Meurs,** etc.), important French music theorist, astronomer, and mathematician; b. in the diocese of Lisieux, Normandy; c.1300; d. c.1351. He was long confused with Julian des Murs, a Master of the Children of the Sainte-Chapelle of Paris (c.1350), who later served as secretary to Charles V of France; it seems most likely, however, that the 2 were close relatives. Johannes de Muris is listed as a baccalaureate student in the Faculty of Arts in Paris in 1318. During the next few years he was active in Evreux and Paris; was associated with the Collège de Sorbonne in Paris, where he achieved the academic degree of Magister. In 1326–27 he was at the monastery of Fontevrault (Maine-et-Loire); it is known that Julian des Murs was his clerk at this time. In 1332–33 he was in Evreux; then returned to Paris, where he was again associated with the Sorbonne (1336–37). In 1338–42 he was in service at the court of the King of Navarra, Philippe d'Evreux. In 1342 he was one of the 6 canons of the collegiate church in Mezières-en-Brenne (Indre); in 1344 he went, at the invitation of Pope Clement VI, to Avignon, where he participated in the conference on the reform of the calendar. There is extant a letter in verse which he wrote to Philippe de Vitry.

The writings by Johannes de Muris pose problems; titles and versions of the various works attributed to him are questionable. Those that appear authentic are as follows: *Ars novae musicae* or *Notitia artis musicae* (1321; although he gave it the title *Summa musicae,* the work is always known by the 2 preceding titles in order to avoid confusion with a spurious work of the same name); *Questiones super partes musicae* or *Compendium musicae practicae* (c.1322; apparently a condensed version of the 2nd book of the *Ars novae musicae*);

Musica speculativa secundum Boetium (June 1323). Some scholars also attribute to him *Libellus cantus mensurabilis (secundum Johannes de Muris)* (c.1340) and *Ars contrapuncti secundum Johannes de Muris* (after 1340). The *Speculum musicae* (c.1325), long attributed to Muris, has been proved to be a work by Jacques de Liège.

Muro, Bernardo de, Italian operatic tenor; b. Tempio Pausanio, Sardinia, 1881; d. Rome, Oct. 27, 1955. He studied at the Santa Cecilia Academy in Rome. He sang Turiddu in *Cavalleria rusticana* in 1911; in 1912 appeared in the title role of *Don Carlos* at La Scala in Milan; then sang major tenor roles in practically all the standard Italian operas; toured in South America, and briefly in the U.S., with the San Carlo Opera Co. He never became a star on the operatic firmament, yet knowledgeable critics regarded him as worthy of comparison with Caruso, both in the carrying force of his natural voice and in emotional appeal.

Murschhauser, Franz Xaver Anton, German music theorist; b. Zabern, near Strasbourg, June (baptized, July 1) 1663; d. Munich, Jan. 6, 1738. He studied with J.K. Kerll in Munich; from 1691 was music director of the Frauenkirche there. He wrote the theoretical treatise *Academia musico-poetica bipartita, oder Hohe Schule der musikalischen Composition,* the first part of which appeared in 1721, provocatively described as being intended "to give a little more light to the excellent Herr Mattheson." The latter retaliated with such devastating effect in his *Melopoetische Lichtscheere (Critica musica,* 1722; pp. 1–88) that Murschhauser refrained from publishing the 2nd part of his work. His compositions for organ are reprinted in Denkmäler der Tonkunst in Bayern, 30 (18), edited by M. Seiffert, with a biographical sketch.

Musard, Philippe, famous French dance composer; b. Tours, Nov. 8, 1792; d. Auteuil (Paris), March 30, 1859. He studied music privately with Reicha; first came into public view at the promenade concerts in Paris, begun in Nov. 1833, in a bazaar of the Rue St. Honoré; there he introduced Dufresne, a remarkable player on the cornet, and wrote special solo pieces for him which became a great attraction; he also conducted balls at the Paris Opéra (1835–36), at which his orch. of 70 musicians won great acclaim. His quadrilles and galops enjoyed immense popularity, and he earned the sobriquet "le roi des quadrilles." In London he conducted the promenade concerts at Drury Lane during the season of 1840–41; he appeared at other concerts in England. His son **Alfred Musard** (1828–81) was also a composer of quadrilles, and a bandleader.

Musgrave, Thea, remarkable Scottish composer; b. Barnton, Midlothian, May 27, 1928. She planned to study medicine and enrolled in the Univ. of Edinburgh for preliminary studies; concurrently she attended courses in musical analysis with Mary Grierson and advanced composition and counterpoint with a visiting Austrian composer, Hans Gál. She received her B.M. degree in 1950 and went to Paris to study with Nadia Boulanger. Her first compositions were in a cautiously impressionistic manner. She wrote a ballet, with a scenario based on Chaucer's subject from *The Pardoner's Tale,* and she received a prize for her work. In 1954 she wrote a cantata for the BBC of Scotland which was successfully performed. In 1955 she completed a chamber opera, *The Abbot of Drimock,* based on a Scottish story, and it was successfully performed, first as a concert work, and later as a stage production. From 1959–65 she served as a lecturer on music at London Univ. in Teddington. All these years she followed the acceptable modern style of composition, but soon the diatonic lyricism of the initial period of her creative evolution gave way to increasingly chromatic constructions, eventually systematized into serial organization. She herself described her theatrical works as "dramatic-abstracts" in form, because even in the absence of a programmatic design, they revealed some individual dramatic traits. From 1955–70 she was active mainly as a choral conductor and accompanist; from 1970–78 she was on the music faculty at the Univ. of Calif., Santa Barbara. There she met a congenial colleague, the American viola player **Peter Mark;** they were married in 1971. In 1974 she received a Guggenheim fellowship; this enabled her to compose music without concern for fiscal matters. During this period, her most important work was *Mary, Queen of Scots,* commissioned by the Scottish Opera for the Edinburgh Festival in 1977. Appreciated by critics and audiences alike, her compositions, in a variety of styles but invariably effective and technically accomplished, enjoyed numerous performances in Europe and America.

WORKS: *The Abbott of Drimock,* chamber opera (London, 1955); *The Decision* (1964; London, Nov. 30, 1967); *The Voice of Ariadne,* after *The Last of the Valerii* by Henry James (Aldeburgh [England] Festival, June 11, 1974); *Mary, Queen of Scots* (Edinburgh Festival, Sept. 6, 1977); *A Christmas Carol* (Norfolk, Va., Dec. 7, 1979); *An Occurrence at Owl Creek Bridge,* radio opera for Baritone, 3 Speakers, Tape, and Orch. (London, Dec. 20, 1981); *A Tale for Thieves,* ballet (1953); *Orfeo,* ballet for Dancer, Flute, and Tape (1975); *4 Madrigals* for Unaccompanied Chorus (1953); *A Suite o' Bairnsangs* for Voice and Piano (1953); *Cantata for a Summer's Day* for Vocal Quartet, Speaker, Flute, Clarinet, String Quartet, and Double Bass (1954); *Song of the Burn* for Unaccompanied Chorus (1954); *5 Love Songs* for Tenor and Guitar (1955); *Divertimento* for String Orch. (1957); String Quartet (1958); *Obliques* for Orch. (1958); *A Song for Christmas* for Voice and Piano (1958); *Scottish Dance Suite* for Orch. (1959); *Triptych* for Tenor and Orch. (1959); *Colloquy* for Violin and Piano (1960); Trio for Flute, Oboe, and Piano (1960); *Monologue* for Piano (1960); *Serenade* for Flute, Clarinet, Harp, Viola, and Cello (1961); *Perspectives* for Orch. (1961); Chamber Concerto No. 1 for 9 Instruments (1962); *Theme and Interludes* for Orch. (1962); *The Phoenix and the Turtle* for Chorus and Orch. (1962); *Marko the Mi-*

ser, "a tale for children to mime, sing and play" (1962); *Sinfonia* (1963); *The 5 Ages of Man* for Chorus and Orch. (1964); *Excursions* for Piano Duet (1965); *Festival Overture* (1965); Chamber Concerto No. 2 for 5 Instruments (1966); Chamber Concerto No. 3 for 8 Instruments (1966); *Nocturnes and Arias* for Orch. (1966); *Variations* for Brass Band (1966); *Sonata for 3* for Flute, Violin, and Guitar (1966); *Impromptu No. 1* for Flute and Oboe (1967); *Concerto for Orchestra* (1967); *Memento Creatoris* for Unaccompanied Chorus (1967); *Music* for Horn and Piano (1967); Clarinet Concerto (London, Feb. 5, 1969; a deft, chic virtuoso piece, requiring the soloist to promenade among members of the orch.); *Beauty and the Beast,* ballet for Chamber Orch. and Electronic Tape (1968–69; London, Nov. 19, 1969); *Soliloquy No. 1* for Guitar and Electronic Tape (1969); *Night Music* for Chamber Orch. (1969); *Memento Vitae* for Orch. (1969–70); *Elegy* for Viola and Cello (1970); *Impromptu No. 2* for Flute, Oboe, and Clarinet (1970); *From One to Another* for Viola and Electronic Tape (1970); Horn Concerto (1971); Viola Concerto (1973); *Space Play,* concerto for 9 Instruments (1974); *Rorate Coeli* for Mixed Chorus (1974); *Orfeo II,* orch. version of the ballet (1975; Los Angeles, March 28, 1976); *From One to Another* for Viola and Strings (1979–80; Minneapolis, March 1982); *The Last Twilight* for Chorus, Brass, and Percussion (Santa Fe, July 20, 1980); *Peripeteia* for Orch. (1981).

Musin, Ovide, Belgian violinist; b. Nandrin, near Liège, Sept. 22. 1854; d. Brooklyn, N.Y., Nov. 24, 1929. He studied with Heynberg and Léonard at the Liège Cons., taking first violin prize at the age of 13; he won the gold medal at 15; toured Europe from 1874 to 1882 with remarkable success. In 1883 he went to America; between 1892 and 1897 he made 2 world tours. From 1897 to 1908 he taught at the Cons. of Liège; in 1908 he established himself in N.Y., and opened his own school of music. He publ. a number of brilliant violin pieces; also the instructive works *System of Daily Practice* (1899) and *The Belgian School of the Violin* (4 vols.; 1916; a combination of his own methods with those of his teacher Léonard); also publ. a book, *My Memories* (1920). His wife, **Annie Louise Tanner-Musin** (b. Boston, Oct. 3, 1856; d. there, Feb. 28, 1921), was a well-known coloratura soprano.

Mussorgsky, Modest, great Russian composer; b. Karevo, Pskov district, March 21, 1839; d. St. Petersburg, March 28, 1881. He received his first instruction on the piano from his mother; at the age of 10 was taken to St. Petersburg, where he had piano lessons with Anton Herke. In 1852 he entered the cadet school of the Imperial Guard; composed a piano piece entitled *Porte enseigne Polka,* which was publ. (1852); after graduation, he joined the regiment of the Guard. In 1857, he met Dargomyzhsky, who introduced him to Cui and Balakirev; he also became friendly with the critic and chief champion of Russian national music, Vladimir Stasov. These associations prompted Mussorgsky's decision to become a professional composer. He played and analyzed piano arrangements of works by Beethoven and Schumann; Balakirev helped him to acquire a knowledge of form; he tried to write music in classical style, but without success; his inner drive was directed toward "new shores," as Mussorgsky himself expressed it. The liquidation of the family estate made it imperative for Mussorgsky to take a paying job; he became a clerk in the Ministry of Communications (1863), resigning 4 years later. During this time, he continued to compose, but his lack of technique compelled him time and again to leave his various pieces unfinished. He eagerly sought professional advice from his friends Stasov (for general esthetics) and Rimsky-Korsakov (for problems of harmony); to the very end of his life, he regarded himself as being only half-educated in music, and constantly acknowledged his inferiority as a craftsman. But he yielded to no one in his firm faith in the future of national Russian music. When a group of composers from Bohemia visited St. Petersburg in 1867, Stasov published an article in which he for the first time referred to the "mighty handful of Russian musicians" pursuing the ideal of national art. The expression was picked up derisively by some journalists, but it was accepted as a challenge by Mussorgsky and his comrades-in-arms, Balakirev, Borodin, Cui, and Rimsky-Korsakov, the "mighty five" of Russian music. In 1869, Mussorgsky once more entered government service, this time in the forestry dept. He became addicted to drink, and had epileptic fits; he died a week after his 42nd birthday. The significance of Mussorgsky's genius did not become apparent until some years after his death. Most of his works were prepared for publication by Rimsky-Korsakov, who corrected some of Mussorgsky's harmonic crudities, and reorchestrated the symph. works. Original versions of Mussorgsky's music were preserved in MS, and eventually publ. But despite the availability of the authentic scores, Mussorgsky's works continue to be performed in Rimsky-Korsakov's editions, made familiar to the whole musical world. In his dramatic works, and in his songs, Mussorgsky draws a boldly realistic vocal line, in which inflections of speech are translated into a natural melody. His first attempt in this genre was an unfinished opera, *The Marriage*, to Gogol's comedy; here Mussorgsky also demonstrated his penetrating sense of musical humor. His ability to depict tragic moods is revealed in his cycle *Songs and Dances of Death;* his understanding of intimate poetry is shown in the children's songs. His greatest work is the opera *Boris Godunov* (to Pushkin's tragedy), which has no equal in its stirring portrayal of personal destiny against a background of social upheaval. In it, Mussorgsky created a true national music drama, without a trace of the Italian conventions that had theretofore dominated the operatic works by Russian composers. Mussorgsky wrote no chamber music, perhaps because he lacked the requisite training in contrapuntal technique. Of his piano music, the set of pieces *Pictures at an Exhibition* (somewhat after the manner of Schumann's *Carnaval*) is remarkable for its

vivid representation of varied scenes (it was written to commemorate his friend, the painter Victor Hartmann, whose pictures were the subjects of the music); the work became famous in the brilliant orchestration of Ravel. Although Mussorgsky was a Russian national composer, his music influenced many composers outside Russia, and he came to be regarded as the most potent talent of the Russian national school.

WORKS: OPERAS: *The Marriage* (1868; only the first act completed; produced, St. Petersburg, April 1, 1909; completed and orchestrated by Alexander Tcherepnin; perf. in this form for the first time, Essen, Sept. 14, 1937); *Boris Godunov* (1868–69, with 7 scenes; Leningrad, Feb. 16, 1928; 2nd version, with prologue and 4 acts, St. Petersburg, Feb. 8, 1874; revised and reorchestrated by Rimsky-Korsakov in 1896; produced in this new form, St. Petersburg, Dec. 10, 1896, and subsequently all over the world; Mussorgsky's original score, ed. by Paul Lamm, publ. in 1928); *Khovanshchina* (on a historical subject from the time of Peter the Great; completed and orchestrated by Rimsky-Korsakov; first perf., St. Petersburg, Feb. 21, 1886); *The Fair at Sorochinsk* (unfinished, completed by Cui; Moscow, Oct. 21, 1913; also arranged and orchestrated by Nicolas Tcherepnin, and produced at Monte Carlo, March 17, 1923). CHORAL WORKS: *The Destruction of Sennacherib*, after Byron, for Chorus and Orch. (St. Petersburg, March 18, 1867) and *Joshua* for Contralto, Bass, Chorus, and Piano (1874–77). FOR ORCH.: *Scherzo* (St. Petersburg, Jan. 23, 1860); *Intermezzo in modo classico* (1867); *A Night on Bald Mountain* (1860–66; reorchestrated by Rimsky-Korsakov and perf. posthumously, St. Petersburg, Oct. 27, 1886). FOR PIANO: *Scherzo* (1858); *Jeux d'enfants–les quatre coins* (German subtitle *Ein Kinderscherz;* 1859); *Impromptu passionné* (1859); Sonata for Piano, 4-hands (1860); *Souvenirs d'enfance* (1865); *Rêverie* (1865); *La Capricieuse* (1865); *Intermezzo in modo classico* (piano version of the orch. piece; 1867); *Pictures at an Exhibition* (1874; *Promenade; Gnomus; Il vecchio castello; Tuileries; Bydlo; Ballet des poussins dans leurs coques; Deux juifs, l'un riche et l'autre pauvre; Promenade; Limoges—Le Marché; Catacombae; Cum mortuis in lingua mortua; La Cabane sur des pattes de poule; La Grande Porte de Kiev;* French titles by Mussorgsky); *En Crimée* (1880); *Méditation* (1880); *Une Larme* (1880); piano transcriptions of dances from the opera *The Fair at Sorochinsk;* many incomplete fragments of youthful works, etc. SONGS: *King Saul* (1863); *Cradle Song* (1865); *Darling Savishna* (1866); *The Seminarist* (1866); *Hopak* (1866); *On the Dnieper* (1879); *Hebrew Song* (1879); *The Classicist* (satirical; 1867); *The Garden by the Don* (1867); *The Nursery*, children's song cycle (1868–72); *Rayok* (*The Peep-show;* musical lampoon at assorted contemporaries; 1870); *Sunless*, song cycle (1874); *Forgotten* (1874); *Songs and Dances of Death*, cycle of 4 songs (1875–77); *Mephistopheles' Song of the Flea* (1879); a number of other songs. In 1928–34 the Soviet State Publishing House undertook, under the direction of Paul Lamm, the publication of his complete works, including variants, fragments, notations of folk songs, etc.

Mustel, Victor, celebrated French builder of harmoniums; inventor of the celesta; b. Le Havre, June 13, 1815; d. Paris, Jan. 26, 1890. He began as a carpenter; in 1844 went to Paris, where he worked in several shops, becoming foreman in Alexandre's harmonium factory; established himself in 1853; the following year invented "the double expression," which won the first prize at the Paris Exposition of 1855; from 1866 the firm became famous as V. Mustel et ses Fils. He also constructed an instrument consisting of graduated tuning forks in a resonance box, operated by a keyboard; this was patented in 1886 by his son **Auguste** (1842–1919) as the "Celesta." Tchaikovsky heard the celesta in Paris, and became so enchanted with it that he used it (for the first time in any score) in his ballet *The Nutcracker*

Müthel, Johann Gottfried, German organist and composer; b. Mölln, Jan. 17, 1728; d. Bienenhof, near Riga, July 14, 1788. He studied at Lübeck and became court organist at Schwerin in 1747. In 1750 he traveled to Leipzig to see Bach, and remained with him for a few days before Bach's death. He then journeyed to Potsdam, where he met Carl Philipp Emanuel Bach. In 1753 he went to Riga, where he became an organist at the Lutheran church. He composed a number of organ pieces, and also several piano works, including a duet, the title of which includes for the first time the word "Fortepiano."

Muti, Riccardo, greatly talented and multiply gifted Italian conductor; b. Naples, July 28, 1941. His father was a medical doctor who possessed a natural Neapolitan tenor voice; under his guidance Muti began to play the violin and piano; later enrolled at the Cons. of San Pietro a Maiella in Naples, where he studied composition with Jacopo Napoli and Nino Rota; there he also obtained a diploma in piano; then went to Milan to study conducting with Antonino Votto and composition with Bruno Bettinelli at the Verdi Cons.; in 1965 he attended a seminar in conducting with Franco Ferrara in Venice. In 1967 he won the prestigious Guido Cantelli competition for conductors and received several engagements as a symph. conductor, first at RAI (Radiotelevisione Italiana) in Milan and then at the Maggio Musicale Fiorentino in Florence. In 1968 he conducted opera at the Autunno Musicale Napoletano. In 1970 he was appointed principal conductor at the Teatro Comunale in Florence, where he produced a number of operas in the standard Italian repertoire; he also continued to conduct the orch. of the Maggio Musicale Fiorentino. Soon he expanded his activities beyond Italy. He conducted performances at the festivals of Salzburg, Lucerne, Montreux, and Prague; also had guest engagements with the Berlin Phil., the Vienna Phil., and orchs. in Amsterdam, Budapest, Milan, and Madrid. On Oct. 27, 1972, Muti made his first American appearance, conducting the Philadelphia Orch., and later had a guest engagement with it in N.Y.; the critics were impressed with his musicianship

and also with his handsome Roman profile. A cornucopia of engagements followed. In 1973 he succeeded Klemperer as principal conductor of the New Phil. Orch. of London (it restored its original name of Philharmonia Orch. in 1977); he was named its music director in 1979 and continued in that capacity until 1982; he also retained his post with the Maggio Musicale in Florence until 1982, when his main activities definitely shifted to America. He was a frequent guest conductor with the Philadelphia Orch. and formed an enthusiastic following in that city; in 1977 he was named the orch.'s principal guest conductor. Finally, after much discussion and speculation as to the inevitable succession to the energetic but aging Eugene Ormandy, Muti was announced in 1980 as his heir. In 1982 he took the Philadelphia Orch. on a tour of festivals in Europe. Muti's career was now firmly established on both sides of the Atlantic; if he follows the musical longevity of his Philadelphia predecessors, Stokowski and Ormandy, he will keep his symphonic aureole (he has a magnificent head of black hair, with no sign of incursive alopecia) until 2020 A.D.

Mutter, Anne-Sophie, talented German violinist; b. Rheinfeldin, June 29, 1963. At the age of 6 she won "First Prize with Special Distinction" at the "Jungen Musiziert" National Competition, the youngest winner in its annals. In 1976 she came to the notice of Herbert von Karajan during her appearance at the Lucerne Festival; in 1977 he invited her to be a soloist with him and the Berlin Phil. at the Salzburg Easter Festival; this was the beginning of an auspicious career. She subsequently appeared regularly with Karajan and the Berlin Phil., and also recorded standard violin concertos with him.

Muzio, Emanuele, Italian composer; b. Zibello, Aug. 25, 1825; d. Paris, Nov. 27, 1890. He studied piano with Margherita Barezzi (Verdi's first wife), and composition with Verdi himself; was one of the very few pupils Verdi ever had. In 1852 he was engaged as conductor of the Italian Opera in Brussels; he later traveled to England and America; settled in Paris in 1875 as a singing teacher. Carlotta Patti and Clara Louise Kellogg were his pupils. He wrote several operas: *Giovanna la pazza* (Brussels, April 8, 1851); *Claudia* (Milan, Feb. 7, 1853); *Le due regine* (Milan, May 17, 1856); *La Sorrentina* (Bologna, Nov. 14, 1857); also many songs and piano pieces.

Myers, Rollo, English writer on music; b. Chislehurst, Kent, Jan. 23, 1892. He studied briefly at the Royal College of Music in London; then was music correspondent for English newspapers in Paris (1919–34); was a member of the staff of the BBC in London (1935–44); was active as music journalist and editor; publ. the books *Modern Music: Its Aims and Tendencies* (London, 1923); *Music in the Modern World* (London, 1939); *Erik Satie* (London, 1948); *Debussy* (London, 1949; 2nd ed., revised, 1948); *Introduction to the Music of Stravinsky* (London, 1950); *Ravel: Life and Works* (London, 1960); *Em-*

manuel *Chabrier and His Circle* (London, 1969); *Modern French Music* (Oxford, 1971). He edited an anthology, *Twentieth Century Music* (London, 1960; 2nd ed., enlarged, 1968); wrote numerous articles on music.

Mysliveček (Mysliweczek; Mislíveček), Josef, famous Bohemian composer, called "Il divino Boemo" and "il Venatorini" in Italy; b. Ober-Sárka, near Prague, March 9, 1737; d. Rome, Feb. 4, 1781. His father was a miller. He was a pupil at the Normalschule of the Dominicans of St. Jilgi (1744–47) and the Jesuit Gymnasium (1748–53), where he received his first instruction in music; he also sang in the choir of St. Michal under Felix Benda. He then was apprenticed as a miller, being made a master miller in 1761. He also pursued his musical studies, taking courses in counterpoint with František Habermann and organ with Josef Seger. In 1760 he publ. anonymously a set of 6 sinfonias, named after the first 6 months of the year. Determined upon a career as a composer, he went to Venice in 1763 to study the art of operatic writing with Giovanni Pescetti. His first opera, *Medea,* was produced in Parma in 1764. While in Parma, he met the singer Lucrezia Aguiari, who became his mistress in the first of his many romantic liaisons. He was commissioned to write another opera, *Il Bellerofonte,* for the Teatro San Carlo in Naples, where it was performed with considerable success on Jan. 20, 1767. This led to other commissions from Italian theaters. His opera *Ezio* (Naples, June 5, 1775) and his oratorio *Isacco figura del Redentore* (Florence, March 10, 1776) were successfully performed in Munich in 1777; his career was blunted, however, by syphilis and disfiguring facial surgery. He returned to Italy but never regained his social standing. He succumbed at the age of 43. Mysliveček was one of the most significant Bohemian composers; his operas and oratorios were frequently performed and publ. in his lifetime. Mozart expressed admiration of his talent.

WORKS: OPERAS: *Medea* (Parma, 1764); *Il Bellerofonte* (Naples, Jan. 20, 1767); *Farnace* (Naples, Nov. 4, 1767); *Il trionfo di Clelia* (Turin, Dec. 26, 1767); *Il Demofoonte* (Venice, Jan. 1769); *L'Ipermestra* (Florence, March 28, 1769); *La Nitteti* (Bologna, Spring 1770); *Montezuma* (Florence, Jan. 23, 1771); *Il gran Tamerlano* (Milan, Dec. 26, 1771); *Il Demetrio* (Pavia, Jan. 25, 1773); *Erifile* (Munich, 1773); *Romolo ed Ersilia* (Naples, Aug. 13, 1773); *La clemenza di Tito* (Venice, Dec. 26, 1773); *Antigona* (Turin, Carnival 1774); *Atide* (Padua, June 1774); *Artaserse* (Naples, Aug. 13, 1774); *Ezio* (Naples, June 5, 1775); *Merope* (Naples, 1775); *Adriano in Siria* (Florence, Fall 1776); *Las Calliroe* (Naples, May 30, 1778); *L'Olimpiade* (Naples, Nov. 4, 1778); *La Circe* (Venice, May 1779); *Il Demetrio* (Naples, Aug. 13, 1779); *Armida* (Milan, Dec. 26, 1779); *Medonte* (Rome, Jan. 1780); *Antigono* (Rome, April 1780). ORATORIOS: *La famiglia di Tobia* (Padua, 1769); *Adamo ed Eva* (Florence, May 24, 1771); *Giuseppe riconosciuto* (Padua, 1771); *La Passione di Gesù Cristo* (Prague, 1773); *La liberazione d'Israele*

(1775); *Isacco figura del Redentore* (Florence, March 10, 1776); also sinfonias, overtures, keyboard concertos, sonatas for keyboard, string quartets, trios.

Mysz-Gmeiner, Lula, Hungarian contralto; b. Kronstadt, Transylvania, Aug. 16, 1876; d. Schwerin, Aug. 7, 1948. She studied violin in her native town, and singing in Berlin with Etelka Gerster and Lilli Lehmann; made her debut there in 1900; then traveled in Europe as a concert singer; was greatly praised for her interpretations of German lieder. She married an Austrian officer, Ernst Mysz (1900).

Myszuga, Aleksander, Polish tenor; b. Nowy Witkow, near Lwow, June 7, 1853; d. Schwarzwald, near Freiburg, March 9, 1922. He was of Ukrainian descent; studied voice in Lwow and Milan; later took lessons with Sbriglia in Paris, adopting the name **Filippi** for his stage appearances. He sang widely in Italy, Vienna, and Prague in both lyrical and dramatic roles in French and Italian operas; he was also noted for singing tenor parts in Polish operas. In later years he taught voice in Kiev and Stockholm.

N

Nabokov, Nicolas, distinguished Russian-American composer; b. near Lubcha, Novogrudok district, Minsk region, April 17, 1903; d. New York, April 6, 1978. He was a scion of a distinguished Russian family; his uncle was a liberal member of the short-lived Duma (Russian parliament); the famous writer Vladimir Nabokov was his first cousin. (The name is pronounced with stress on the 2nd syllable, Nabókov.) Nabokov received his early education in St. Petersburg; after the Revolution he went to Yalta in the Crimea, where he took composition lessons with Rebikov; then he proceeded to Berlin, where he became a student of Busoni; finally moved to Paris, where he was introduced to Diaghilev, who commissioned him to write a work for the Ballets Russes; this was an auspicious beginning to Nabokov's career. In 1933 he went to the U.S.; taught at Wells College (1936–41) and at the Peabody Cons. of Music, Baltimore (1947–52). From 1952 to 1963 he was secretary-general of the Congress for Cultural Freedom; then served as artistic director of the Berlin Music Festivals (1963–68); lectured on esthetics at the State Univ. of N.Y. at Buffalo (1970–71) and at N.Y. Univ. (1972–73). In his music he adopted a cosmopolitan style, with an astute infusion of fashionable bitonality; in works of Russian inspiration, he reverted to melorhythms of Russian folk songs.

WORKS: Operas: *The Holy Devil,* on the subject of Rasputin (Louisville, Ky., April 18, 1958; revised and expanded, produced in Cologne under the title *Der Tod des Grigori Rasputin,* Nov. 27, 1959); *Love's Labour's Lost,* to a libretto of W.H. Auden after Shakespeare (Brussels, 1973); ballets: *Union Pacific* (Philadelphia, April 6, 1934); *Vie de Polichinelle* (1934); *The Wanderer* (1966); *Don Quichotte* (N.Y., 1966); ballet-cantata, *Ode, or Meditation at Night on the Majesty of God, as Revealed by the Aurora Borealis* (Ballets Russes, Paris, June 6, 1928); Symph. No. 1, *Symphonie lyrique* (Paris, Feb. 16, 1930); Symph. No. 2, *Sinfonia biblica* (N.Y., Jan. 2, 1941); Symph. No. 3, *A Prayer* (N.Y., Jan. 4, 1968); incidental music to Milton's *Samson Agonistes* (Wells College, Aurora, N.Y., May 14, 1938); *The Return of Pushkin* for Voice and Orch. (Boston, Jan. 2, 1948); *Vita nuova* for Soprano, Tenor, and Orch. (Boston, March 2, 1951); Cello Concerto, subtitled *Les Hommages* (Philadelphia, Nov. 6, 1953); *America Was Promises,* cantata (N.Y., April 25, 1950); oratorio, *Job* (1933); *Collectionneur d'échos* for Soprano, Bass, and 9 Percussion Instruments (1933); *Symboli Chrestiani* for Baritone and Orch. (1953); *5 Poems by Anna Akhmatova* for Voice and Orch. (1964); *Studies in Solitude* (1961); String Quartet (1937); Sonata for Bassoon and Piano (1941); 2 piano sonatas (1926, 1940); Piano Concerto (1932); Flute Concerto (1948); piano pieces; songs.

Nägeli, Johann (Hans) Georg, Swiss publisher, writer, and composer; b. Wetzikon, near Zürich, May 26, 1773; d. there, Dec. 26, 1836. He was a music publisher at Wetzikon (established 1792); was founder and president of the Swiss Assoc. for the Cultivation of Music; was a singing teacher at a primary school, applying the Pestalozzian system. As a song composer he is best known by *Freut euch des Lebens* ("Life let us cherish"). He wrote *Gesangsbildungslehre nach Pestalozzischen Grundsätzen* (with M. Pfeiffer; 1810; popular ed., 1811); *Christliches Gesangbuch* (1828); *Vorlesungen über Musik mit Berücksichtigung der Dilettanten* (1826); *Musikalisches Tabellwerk für Volksschulen zur Herausbildung für den Figuralgesang* (1828); a polemical pamphlet against Thibaut; *Der Streit zwischen der alten und der neuen Musik* (1826); etc. Nägeli publ. (from 1803) a periodical, *Répertoire des Clavecinistes*, in which he brought out piano pieces by contemporary composers, including the first publication of Beethoven's sonatas, op. 31. With Beethoven he was on intimate terms, despite disagreements.

Nancarrow, Conlon, remarkable American composer, innovator in the technique of recording notes on a player-piano roll; b. Texarkana, Ark., Oct. 27, 1912. He played the trumpet in jazz orchs.; then took courses at the Cincinnati Cons.; subsequently traveled to Boston, where he became a private student of Nicolas Slonimsky, Walter Piston, and Roger Sessions. In 1937 he joined the Abraham Lincoln Brigade and went to Spain to fight in the ranks of the Republican Loyalists against the brutal assault of General Franco's armies. Classified as a premature anti-Fascist after the Republican defeat in Spain, Nancarrow was refused a U.S. passport and moved to Mexico City, where he remained for 40 years, eventually obtaining Mexican citizenship. In 1981, with political pressures defused in the U.S., Nancarrow was able to revisit his native land and to participate at the New American Music Festival in San Francisco. In 1982 he was a composer-in-residence at the Cabrillo Music Festival in Aptos, Calif.; also traveled to Europe, where he participated at festivals in Austria, Germany, and France. An extraordinary event occurred in his life in 1983, when he was awarded the "genius grant" of $300,000 by the MacArthur Foundation of Chicago, enabling him to continue his work without any concerns about finances. The unique quality of Nancarrow's compositions is that they can be notated only by perforating player-piano rolls to mark the notes and rhythms, and can be performed only by activating such piano rolls. This method of composition gives Nancarrow total freedom in conjuring up the most complex contrapuntal, harmonic, and rhythmic combinations that no human pianist or any number of human pianists could possibly perform. The method itself is extremely laborious; a bar containing a few dozen notes might require an hour to stamp out on the piano roll. Some of Nancarrow's studies were publ. in normal notation in Cowell's *New Music Quarterly*. Aaron Copland, Ligeti, and other contemporary composers expressed their appreciation of Nancarrow's originality in high terms of praise. On Jan. 30, 1984, Nancarrow gave a concert of his works in Los Angeles, in a program including his *Prelude and Blues for Acoustic Piano* and several of his studies. An audiovisual documentary on Nancarrow was presented on slides by Eva Soltes. A number of Nancarrow's *Studies for Player Piano* which could be adequately notated were publ. in *Soundings 4* (1977), accompanied with critical commentaries by Gordon Mumma, Charles Amirkhanian, John Cage, Roger Reynolds, and James Tenney.

Nanino (Nanini), Giovanni Bernardino, Italian composer and teacher, brother of **Giovanni Maria Nanino;** b. c.1550; d. Rome, 1623. He was a boy soprano at the Cathedral in Vallerano; studied music with his brother. From 1591 to 1608 he was maestro di cappella at S. Luigi dei Francesi in Rome. His brother lived with him in a home maintained by the church, and they boarded and taught the boy sopranos. He subsequently was maestro di cappella at S. Lorenzo in Damaso, the small church in the home of Cardinal Montalto. He was a significant composer and teacher in his day.

Nanino (Nanini), Giovanni Maria, important Italian composer and teacher, brother of **Giovanni Bernardino Nanino;** b. Tivoli, 1543; d. Rome, March 11, 1607. He was a boy soprano at the Cathedral in Vallerano, and was a pupil of Palestrina in Rome. Following Palestrina's resignation as maestro di cappella at S. Maria Maggiore in 1567, Nanino was named his successor. From 1575 to 1577 he was maestro di cappella at S. Luigi dei Francesi. In 1577 he became a tenor in the papal choir, remaining a member until his death; he also was elected to the position of maestro di cappella several times after 1586. He continued an association with S. Luigi dei Francesi; after his brother was made maestro di cappella there in 1591, he lived with his brother in a home maintained by the church, where they boarded and taught the boy sopranos. His pupils included Paolo Agostino, Felice Anerio, Antonio Brunelli, and other outstanding musicians. Nanino was one of the most significant composers and teachers of the Roman school. His sacred and secular works are of great merit.

Napravnik, Eduard, celebrated Russian conductor of Czech origin; b. Býšt, near Hradec Králové, Bohemia, Aug. 24, 1839; d. St. Petersburg (Petrograd), Nov. 23, 1916. He studied music at home and in Prague; also took lessons with J.B. Kittl. In 1861 he was engaged by the Russian nobleman Yussupov to lead his private orch. in St. Petersburg; in 1863 he became a répétiteur at the Imperial Opera; became 2nd conductor in 1867, and chief conductor in 1869. He held this post for 47 years, until his death, and became greatly renowned as a thorough musician, possessing a fabulous sense of pitch and rhythm, and exceptional ability as a disciplinarian. His reputation and influence were very great in Russian operatic affairs; Dostoyevsky in one of his novels uses Napravnik's name as a synonym for a guiding spirit. Napravnik conducted the premiere of *Boris Godunov* and of many other Russian operas; his interpretations of the Russian repertoire established a standard emulated by other Russian conductors; yet he was deficient in emotional inspiration; his performances of symph. works were regarded as competent but not profound. He was himself a composer of several operas in the Russian style, imitative of Tchaikovsky; one of them, *Dubrovsky* (St. Petersburg, Jan. 15, 1895), has become part of the active repertoire in Russia. Other operas were *Nizhegorotzy* (St. Petersburg, Jan. 8, 1869); *Harold* (St. Petersburg, Nov. 23, 1886); *Francesca da Rimini* (St. Petersburg, Dec. 9, 1902). He also wrote 4 symphs., some chamber music, piano pieces, etc.

Nardini, Pietro, Italian violinist; b. Livorno, April 12, 1722; d. Florence, May 7, 1793. He was a pupil of Tartini at Padua; in 1762–65 was solo violinist in the Stuttgart Court Orch.; lived with Tartini until the latter's death in 1770; then was maestro of the court music at Florence. Both Leopold Mozart and Schubart praised his playing. Among his works are 6 violin concertos; 6 sonatas for Violin and Bass; 6 violin solos; 6 violin duets; 6 string quartets; 6 flute trios. Some of his sonatas are in Alard's *Les Maîtres classiques* and David's *Hohe Schule des Violinspiels;* other works appear in Jensen's *Klassische Violinmusik;* also in numerous new eds.

Narváez, Luis de, Spanish guitar virtuoso of the 16th century. He was a native of Granada; was chamber musician to Philip II. He publ. *Los seys libros del Delphin de música de cifra para tañer vihuela* (Vallodolid, 1538; in tablature), containing the earliest examples of variation form publ. in Spain; it was reprinted in modern notation by E Pujol in *Monumentos de la música española* (vol. 3, Barcelona, 1945); some selections are in Morphy's *Les Luthistes espagnols du XVIᵉ siècle* (Leipzig, 1902); one is in A.T. Davison and W. Apel, *Historical Anthology of Music* (vol. 1, Cambridge, Mass., 1946); modern ed. by G. Tarragó (Madrid, 1971).

Nastasijević, Svetomir, Serbian composer; b. Gornje Milanovec, April 1, 1902. He studied engineering and architecture; at the same time he learned to play the violin; wrote music criticism and publ. 2 manuals on music theory. His works include the music drama *Medjuluško blago (The Treasure of the Medjuluzje;* Belgrade, March 4, 1937); *Durad Branković,* national opera from medieval Serbian history (Belgrade, June 12, 1940); several symph. poems and choruses. In his operas, he adopts the Wagnerian system of leitmotifs.

Nathan, Montagu. See **Montague-Nathan, Montagu.**

Naumann, Johann Gottlieb, distinguished German composer and conductor; b. Blasewitz, near Dresden, April 17, 1741; d. Dresden, Oct. 23, 1801. He received his first instruction in music at the Dresden Kreuzschule. In 1757 the Swedish violinist Anders Wesström took him to Italy, where he received valuable instruction from Tartini in Padua, Padre Martini in Bologna, and Hasse in Venice. His intermezzo *Il tesoro insidiato* was premiered in Venice on Dec. 28, 1762. In 1764 he returned to Dresden, where he was appointed 2nd church composer to the court; in 1765 he was named chamber composer. He made return trips to Italy (1765–68; 1772–74), where he brought out several operas. In 1776 he was appointed Kapellmeister in Dresden. In 1777 he visited Stockholm at the invitation of Gustavus III, and was charged with reorganizing the Hofkapelle. His most popular opera, *Cora och Alonzo,* received its first complete performance in Stockholm during the consecration of the New Opera House on Sept. 30, 1782. Another important opera, *Gustaf Wasa,* was premiered there on Jan. 19, 1786, and was considered the Swedish national opera for many years. In 1785–86 he visited Copenhagen, where he carried out some reforms at the Hofkapelle and court opera. He composed the opera *Orpheus og Eurydike* for the Danish king's birthday, and it was premiered in Copenhagen on Jan. 31, 1786. He was named Oberkapellmeister for life in Dresden in 1786. At the request of Friedrich Wilhelm II, he made several visits to Berlin, where his operas *Medea in Colchide* (Oct. 16, 1788) and *Protesilao* (Jan. 26, 1789) were premiered at the Royal Opera. He also wrote masses, cantatas, oratorios, and lieder.

WORKS: FOR THE STAGE: All first performed at the Kleines Kurfürstliches Theater in Dresden unless otherwise given: *Il tesoro insidiato,* intermezzo (Teatro San Samuele, Venice, Dec. 28, 1762); *Li creduti spiriti,* opera buffa (Teatro San Cassiano, Venice, Carnival 1764; in collaboration with 2 other composers); *L'Achille in Sciro,* opera seria (Teatro San Cecilia, Palermo, Sept. 5, 1767); *Alessandro nelle Indie,* opera seria (1768; unfinished); *La clemenza di Tito,* opera seria; (Feb. 1, 1769); *Il villano geloso,* opera buffa (1770); *Solimano,* opera seria (Teatro San Benedetto, Venice, Carnival 1773); *L'isola disabitata,* azione per musica (Venice, Feb. 1773); *Armida,* opera seria (Teatro Nuovo, Padua, June 13, 1773); *Ipermestra,* opera seria (Teatro San Benedetto, Venice, Feb. 1, 1774); *La villanella incostante,* opera buffa (Teatro San Benedetto, Venice, Fall 1773); *L'Ipocondriaco,* opera buffa (March 16, 1776); *Amphion,* prologue and opera-ballet (Royal Theater, Stockholm, Jan. 1, 1778); *Elisa,* opera seria (April 21, 1781); *Cora och Alonzo,* opera seria (New Opera House, Stockholm, Sept. 30, 1782); *Osiride,* opera seria (Oct. 27, 1781); *Tutto per amore,* opera buffa (March 5, 1785); *Gustaf Wasa,* lyric tragedy (New Opera House, Stockholm, Jan. 19, 1786); *Orpheus og Eurydike,* opera seria (Royal Theater, Copenhagen, Jan. 31, 1786); *La reggia d'Imeneo,* festa teatrale (Oct. 21, 1787); *Medea in Colchide,* opera seria with ballet (Royal Opera, Berlin, Oct. 16, 1788); *Protesilao,* opera seria with ballet and choruses (Royal Opera, Berlin, Jan. 26, 1789; in collaboration with J.F. Reichardt); *La dama soldato*, opera buffa (March 30, 1791); *Amore giustificato*, festa teatrale (May 12, 1792); *Aci e Galatea ossia I ciclopi amanti*, opera buffa (April 25, 1801). ORATORIOS: All performed in Dresden unless otherwise given: *La passione di Gesù Christo* (Padua, 1767); *Isacco, figura del Redentore* (1772); *S. Elena al calvario* (1775); *Giuseppe riconosciuto* (1777); *Il ritorno del figliolo prodigo* (1785); *La morte d'Abel* (1790); *Davide in Terebinto, Figura del Salvatore* (1794); *I pellegrini al sepolcro* (1798); *Il ritorno del figliolo prodigo* (1800); *Betulia liberata* (1805); also masses, including a *Missa solenne* in A-flat major (Vienna, 1804), and sacred cantatas. LIEDER: *Freimaurerlieder ... zum Besten der neuen Armenschule* (publ. in Leipzig, 1775); 40 *Freymäurerlieder zum Gebrauch der teutschen auch französischen Tafellogen* (publ. in Berlin, 1782; 2nd ed., 1784); *Sammlung von Liedern* (publ. in Pförten, 1784); 6 *neue Lieder* (publ. in Berlin, 1795); 25 *neue Lieder verschieden Inhalts* (publ. in Dresden, 1799); etc. His instrumental works include sinfonias, a Keyboard Concerto, quartets, sonatas for Keyboard and Violin, sonatas for Glass Harmonica, etc.

Navarra, André, noted French cellist; b. Biarritz, Oct. 13, 1911. He studied at the Cons. of Toulouse; also at the Paris Cons.; in 1949 he was appointed to its faculty. In 1954 he began teaching master classes in Siena; in 1958 became a prof. at the North West German Music Academy in Detmold. Despite his activity as a pedagogue, he never abandoned his career as a solo cellist; he also commissioned cello concertos to several French composers, and gave first performances of these works, among them the concertos by André Jolivet (1962) and Henri Tomasi (1970).

Navarrini, Francesco, distinguished Italian bass; b. Citadella, 1853; d. Milan, Feb. 23, 1923. He studied with Giuseppe Felix and Carlo Boroni in Milan; made his debut as Alfonso in *Lucrezia Borgia* in Ferrara in 1876. From 1883 to 1900 he was a member of La Scala in Milan; created the role of Lodovico in Verdi's *Otello* there (Feb. 5, 1887); then toured in England, France, and Russia. He made his first American appearance in 1902 as a member of Mascagni's traveling opera company. A giant of a man (he measured 6 and a half feet), he imposed his presence in heroic and buffo bass roles, including roles in Wagner's operas.

Navarro, García, Spanish conductor; b. Chiva, April 30, 1941. He was educated at the Valencia Cons., where he studied oboe; also took courses at the Cons. of Madrid. He then went to Vienna to study conducting with Hans Swarowsky, Karl Oesterreicher, and Reinhold Schmid; also took composition lessons with Alfred Uhl. In 1967 he won first prize at the conducting competition in Besançon, France. He was music director of the Valencia Symph. Orch. (1970–74); then was associate conductor of the North Hollywood Phil. (1974–78). In 1979 he made his debut as an opera conductor at Covent Garden, London. In 1980 he became music director of the National Opera at the São Carlos Theater in Lisbon; remained there until 1982. In 1980, he made his first appearances in America as a guest conductor, of the orchs. of St. Louis and Chicago.

Navarro, Juan, Spanish composer; b. Seville or Marchena, c.1530; d. Palencia, Sept. 25, 1580. He was a pupil of Fernández de Castilleja in Seville; sang as a tenor in the choir of the Duke of Arcos at Marchena in 1549; then sang at the Cathedral in Jaén; joined the choir at Málaga Cathedral in 1553; in 1554 applied unsuccessfully for the post of *maestro de capilla* there (F. Guerrero was the successful candidate); was *maestro de capilla* at Ávila (1563–66); then at Salamanca (1566–74); director of the choir at Ciudad Rodrigo (1574–78); from 1578 was *maestro de capilla* at the Cathedral in Palencia. Navarro's *Psalmi, Hymni ac Magnificat totius anni ... 4, 5 ac 6 v.* were publ. at Rome in 1590 (modern ed. by S. Rubio, Madrid, 1978). The book *Liber in quo 4 Passiones Christi Domini continentur ... 8 Lamentationes: Oratioque Hieremiae Prophetae* is by another Juan Navarro, a Franciscan monk born in Cádiz and serving in Mexico. Extant MSS: *Antifona a San Sebastian* (in Málaga); part of a Magnificat (in Seville); 8 pieces (in Toledo); *Recuerde el alma dormida*, madrigal *a* 5 (in the Collección del Patriarca, Valencia); madrigals: 7 for 4 voices; one for 5 voices (Biblioteca Medinaceli and Biblioteca Nacional, Madrid). The madrigal *Ay de mí, sin ventura* was printed by Pedrell in *Cancionero Musical Popular Español*, III; Eslava printed 3 Magnificats and 2 Psalms; several motets are in the *Antología Musical*, ed. by Elústiza and Castrillo Hernández (Barcelona, 1933; with biography).

Naylor, Bernard, English-born Canadian conductor and composer; b. Cambridge, Nov. 22, 1907. He studied composition with Vaughan Williams, Holst, and Ireland at the Royal College of Music in London (1924–26); then served as conductor of the Oxford Univ. Opera Club (1927–31). In 1932 he went to Canada, and was engaged to conduct the Winnipeg Symph. Orch.; returned to England in 1936 and was organist and director of music at Queen's College, Oxford, until 1939; once more in Canada, he conducted the Little Symph. Orch. in Montreal (1942–47); returned again to England and taught at Oxford (1950–52) and at Reading Univ. (1953–59). He moved permanently to Canada in 1959. As a composer, he specializes in sacred choral music.

Nazareth, Ernesto, Brazilian pianist and composer of dance music and songs; b. Rio de Janeiro, March 20, 1863; d. there, Feb. 4, 1934. He was a pioneer in fostering a national Brazilian type of composition, writing pieces in European forms with Brazilian melorhythmic inflections, pointedly entitled *Fado brasileiro, Tango brasileiro, Valsa brasileira, Marcha brasileira*, etc.; he also composed original dances in the rhythms of the samba and chôro. In his declining years he became totally deaf. A detailed list of his works is found in *Com-

posers of the Americas, vol. X (Washington, D.C., 1964).

Neate, Charles, English pianist and cellist; b. London, March 28, 1784; d. Brighton, March 30, 1877. He studied music with James Windsor and later took piano lessons with John Field; he further studied cello with W. Sharp and composition with Wölff. He started his career as a concert pianist in London; in 1813 became one of the founders of the London Phil. Society, with which he appeared as performer and conductor; in 1815 he went to Vienna, where he succeeded in entering into a friendly relationship with Beethoven. He composed 2 piano sonatas; a Quintet for Piano, Woodwinds, and Double Bass; 2 piano trios; also publ. *An Essay on Fingering* (1855). Literature on Beethoven frequently mentions Neate's relationship with him.

Neblett, Carol, American soprano; b. Modesto, Calif., June 1, 1946. She studied voice with William Vermond, and later with Lotte Lehmann and Pierre Bernac. In 1969 she joined the N.Y. City Opera; also made successful appearances with the Chicago Opera, the Dallas Opera, the Metropolitan Opera, and several opera houses in Europe.

Nebra (Blasco), José (Melchor de), Spanish composer; b. Catalayud, Zaragoza, 1702 (baptized, Jan. 6); d. Madrid, July 11, 1768. He was organist at the Convent of the Descalzas Reales in Madrid; was appointed 2nd organist to the Royal Chapel in 1724, and music director there in 1751. Together with Literes, he was engaged to reconstruct and compose new music when the archives of the Royal Chapel were destroyed in the fire of 1734. He was a prolific composer; wrote about 20 operas, a great deal of sacred music. His Requiem for Queen Barbara (1758) is reproduced in Eslava's *Lira Sacro-His-pana.*

Nedbal, Oskar, Czech composer and conductor; b. Tábor, Bohemia, March 26, 1874; d. (suicide) Zagreb, Dec. 24, 1930. He was a pupil of Bennewitz (violin), Knittl and Stecker (theory), and Dvořák (composition) at the Prague Cons., where he graduated in 1892. From 1891 to 1906 he played viola in the famous Bohemian String Quartet (Karl Hoffmann, Josef Suk, Nedbal, Hans Wihan); in 1896–1906 he conducted the Czech Phil.; in 1906–19, was conductor of the Tonkünstler-Orch. in Vienna; also of the Volksoper there for a time; from 1919, was a guest conductor in Czechoslovakia, Austria, and Yugoslavia; conducted the Sak Phil. in 1920–21. He later was director of the Slovak National Theater in Bratislava and head of Bratislava Radio.
WORKS: Ballets: *Der faule Hans* (1902); *Grossmütterchens Märchenschätze* (1908); *Prinzessin Hyazintha* (1911); *Des Teufels Grossmutter* (1912); *Andersen* (1914); operettas: *Die keusche Barbara* (Prague, 1910); *Polenblut* (Vienna, Oct. 25, 1913; successfully revived, Oct. 10, 1954); *Die Winzerbraut* (Vienna, Feb. 11, 1916); *Die schöne Saskia* (Vienna, Nov. 16, 1917); *Eriwan* (Vienna, Nov. 29, 1918); opera, *Sedlák Jakub (Farmer James;* Brno, Oct. 13, 1922); also instrumental works.

Neefe, Christian Gottlob, German composer and conductor; b. Chemnitz, Feb. 5, 1748; d. Dessau, Jan. 26, 1798. He studied music in Chemnitz with Wilhelmi, the city organist; also with C.G. Tag, the cantor of Hohenstein. He began to compose when he was 12, and he studied the textbooks of Marpurg and C.P.E. Bach. He studied law at the Univ. of Leipzig (1769–71); subsequently continued his studies in music with A. Hiller; then succeeded Hiller as conductor of Seyler's traveling opera troupe (1776). In 1779 he became conductor of the Grossmann-Hellmuth opera enterprise in Bonn. Neefe's name is especially honored in music history because about 1780 Beethoven was his pupil in piano, organ, figured-bass practice, and composition in Bonn; there is evidence that Neefe realized the greatness of Beethoven's gift even as a child. In 1782 Neefe was named court organist. After the Grossmann theater closed in 1784, Neefe devoted himself mainly to teaching as a means of support. The theater was reopened in 1789, and Neefe served as its stage director until 1794, when the French army occupied Bonn and the theater was closed again. He then moved to Dessau. In 1796 he became music director of the Dessau theater. Neefe's autobiography, *Lebenslauf von ihn selbst geschrieben,* dated 1782, was revised by F. Rochlitz for publication in the *Allgemeine musikalische Zeitung* (1798–99; Eng. trans. in Paul Nettl, *Forgotten Musicians,* N.Y., 1951).
WORKS: *Die Apotheke,* comic opera (Berlin, Dec. 13, 1771); *Amors Guckkasten,* operetta (Leipzig, May 10, 1772); *Die Einsprüche,* operetta (Leipzig, Oct. 16, 1772); *Zemire und Azor* (Leipzig, March 5, 1776; not extant); *Heinrich und Lyda,* singspiel (Berlin, March 26, 1776); *Die Zigeuner* (Frankfurt, Nov. 1777); *Sophonisbe,* monodrama (Mannheim, Nov. 3, 1778); *Adelheit von Veltheim,* opera (Frankfurt, Sept. 23, 1780); lieder; concertos; keyboard music.

Neel, Boyd, English conductor; b. Blackheath, Kent, July 19, 1905; d. Toronto, Canada, Sept. 30, 1981. He studied medicine and was trained as a medical doctor before taking up music. In 1933 he organized the Boyd Neel String Orch., originally counting 18 members, with a repertoire of Baroque music, supplemented by modern works for chamber orch. After a successful debut in London, he toured widely with his orch. all over the world, including the U.S., Australia, and New Zealand; he also conducted ballet and opera. From 1953 to 1971 he served as dean of the Royal Cons. of Music in Toronto. He publ. a book, *The Story of an Orchestra* (London, 1950), in which he recounted his musical adventures.

Neidhardt (Neidhart, Nithart) von Reuenthal, German Minnesänger; b. c.1180; d. c.1240. He was in all probability the earliest German musician whose songs are extant. These are found in MS collections of the late 14th century; a complete list of sources is in Hagen's *Minnesinger* (vol. 4; 1838). An edition of Neidhardt's songs, with facsimile reproductions and transcriptions in modern notation, was brought out by Wolfgang Schmieder in Denkmäler der Tonkunst in Österreich, 71 (1930; 37.i). Another collection, *Neidhardt-Lieder,* ed. by F. Gennrich, was publ. as no. 9 in the series Summa Musica Medii Aevi (Darmstadt, 1962).

Nejedlý, Vít, Czech composer, son of **Zdeněk Nejedlý;** b. Prague, June 22, 1912; d. Dukla, Slovakia, Jan. 1, 1945. He studied composition with Jeremiáš and conducting with Talich at the Charles Univ. in Prague, obtaining his Ph.D. in 1936; after the occupation of Czechoslovakia by the Nazis in 1939 he went to the Soviet Union, where he was an editor of Czech programs for Radio Moscow foreign broadcasts; in 1943 joined the Czechoslovak contingent of the Red Army, and moved with it to the borders of Czechoslovakia, when he died of typhoid fever.
WORKS: Opera, *Tkalci (The Weavers),* after Hauptmann (1938; completed by Jan Hanuš; Pilsen, May 7, 1961); melodrama, *The Dying* (1933); 3 symphs.: No. 1 (1931); No. 2, *Bídy a smrti (Poverty and Death,* 1934); No. 3, *Španělská (Spanish,* 1937–38; dedicated to the Spanish Loyalist Army fighting Franco); *Overture* to Verhaeren's *Dawn* (1932); *Commemoration* for Orch. (1933); Sinfonietta (1937); *Dramatic Overture* (1940); *Lidová suita (Popular Suite)* for Orch. (1940); 2 cantatas, *Den (The Day,* 1935) and *To You—the Red Army* (1943); 2 *Compositions* for Wind Quintet (1934); 2 *Compositions* for Nonet (1934); *Small Suite* for Violin and Piano (1935); String Quartet (1937); Concertino for Nonet (1940); *Fantasy* for Piano (1937); many songs, military marches and choruses.

Nejedlý, Zdeněk, Czech music scholar, historian, and socialist politician; b. Litomysl, Feb. 10, 1878; d. Prague, March 9, 1962. He studied music with Zdenko Fibich in Prague and musicology with Hostinský at Charles Univ. in Prague. From 1899 to 1909 he was employed as an archivist of the National Museum in Prague; in 1905 he joined the staff, and from 1919 to 1939 was a prof. at, Charles Univ., where he organized the dept. of musicology. Intensely involved in political activities, he joined the Communist Party of Czechoslovakia in 1929. After the Nazi invasion of 1939 he went to Russia, where he was a prof. in the history dept. at Moscow Univ. In 1945 he returned to Czechoslovakia; served as minister of education (1948–53) and deputy premier (1953). He publ. a number of books on the history of Czech music; of these the most original is a history of Bohemian music, in the form of a catechism, in 3 vols. (Prague, 1904, 1907, 1913); he further publ. several monographs on Czech composers and their works, among them *Smetana's Operas* (1908; 3rd ed., 1954), *The Modern Bohemian Opera since Smetana* (1911), and *Vitězslav Novák* (1921); also biographies of Mahler (1913; 2nd ed., 1958) and Wagner (1916; 2nd ed., 1961).

Nelhybel, Vaclav, Czech-American composer; b. Polanka, Sept. 24, 1919. He studied composition and conducting with Rídký at the Prague Cons. (1938–42) and musicology at the Univ. of Prague (also 1938–42); in 1942 went to Switzerland and took courses in medieval and Renaissance music at the Univ. of Fribourg; was affiliated with Swiss National Radio (1947–50); then was music director of Radio Free Europe in Munich (1950–57). In 1957 he settled in the U.S., becoming a citizen in 1962; subsequently evolved energetic activities as a lecturer and guest conductor at American colleges and high schools. As a composer, he is especially notable for his fine pieces for the symphonic band. His harmonic idiom is of a freely dissonant texture, with melorhythmic components gravitating toward tonal centers.

Nelson, John, American conductor; b. San José, Costa Rica (of American missionary parents), Dec. 6, 1941. He received his primary musical training with local teachers in Costa Rica; then went to N.Y., where he studied conducting with Jean Morel at the Juilliard School of Music (1963–67). He began making professional appearances while still a student; conducted the Pro Arte Chorale in N.Y., eliciting high praise for his performance of *Les Troyens* of Berlioz. He subsequently made guest appearances with major American and European orchs.; also led the Jerusalem Symph. Orch. He revisited Costa Rica to conduct the National Symph. Orch. in San José. In 1976 he was appointed conductor and music director of the Indianapolis Symph. Orch.; in 1979–80 was artistic consultant and principal guest conductor of the Louisville Orch.

Nelson, Judith, American soprano; b. Chicago, Sept. 10, 1939. She studied at St. Olaf College in Northfield, Minn.; then sang with music groups of the Univ. of Chicago and the Univ. of Calif. at Berkeley; made her operatic debut as Drusilla in Monteverdi's *L'incoronazione di Poppea* in Brussels in 1979. She is particularly noted for her performances of Baroque music.

Nelson, Oliver E., black American composer and arranger; b. St. Louis, June 4, 1932; d. Los Angeles, Oct. 27, 1975. He studied piano, saxophone, taxidermy, dermatology, and embalming. After serving in the Marines, he studied composition with Robert Wykes at Washington Univ. in St. Louis (1954–58); had private lessons with Elliott Carter in N.Y. and George Tremblay in Los Angeles; in the 1950s and early 1960s, he played saxophone in several jazz orchs., among them those led by Wild Bill Davis, Louis Bellison, Duke Ellington, and Count Basie; then moved to Hollywood.
WORKS: Saxophone Sonata (1957); *Songs* for Contralto and Piano (1957); Divertimento for 10 Woodwinds and Double Bass (1957); *Afro-American Sketches* for Jazz Ensemble (1960); *Blues and the Abstract Truth* for Jazz Ensemble (1960); Woodwind Quintet (1960); *Dirge* for Chamber Orch. (1961); *Soundpiece* for Contralto, String Quartet, and Piano (1963); *Soundpiece* for Jazz Orch. (1964);

Patterns for Jazz Ensemble (1965); *A Study in 5/4* for Wind Ensemble (1966); Concerto for Xylophone, Marimba, Vibes, and Wind Orch. (1967); *The Kennedy Dream Suite* for Jazz Ensemble (1967); *Jazzhattan Suite* for Jazz Orch. (1967; N.Y., Oct. 7, 1967); Septet for Wind Orch. (1968); *Piece* for Orch. and Jazz Soloists (1969); *A Black Suite* for Narrator, String Quartet, and Jazz Orch. (1970); *Berlin Dialogue* for Jazz Orch. (1970; Berlin, 1970); *Concert Piece* for Alto Saxophone and Studio Orch. (1972); *Fugue and Bossa* for Wind Orch. (1973). In 1966 he made a sterling jazz arrangement of Prokofiev's *Peter and the Wolf;* then wrote music for films (*Death of a Gunfighter, Skullduggery,* and *Zig Zag*) and television (*It Takes a Thief, Ironside, The Name of the Game, Longstreet, The Six Million Dollar Man,* etc.). He publ. a valuable improvisation saxophone book, *Patterns for Jazz* (Los Angeles, 1966; originally titled *Patterns for Saxophone*).

Nelsova, Zara, brilliant Canadian-born American cellist; b. Winnipeg, Dec. 23, 1918, of Russian extraction. Her father, a flutist, gave her music lessons; she later studied with Dezso Mahalek (1924–28). In 1929 she went to London, where she continued her studies with Herbert Walenn in London (1929–35). In 1931, at the age of 13, she appeared as soloist with the London Symph. Orch. With her 2 sisters, a pianist and a violinist, she organized a group billed as the Canadian Trio, and toured in England, Australia, and South Africa. Returning to Canada, she served as principal cellist of the Toronto Symph. Orch. (1940–43); she was also a member of another Canadian Trio, this time with Kathleen Parlow and Sir Ernest MacMillan (1941–44). In 1942 she made her U.S. debut at Town Hall in N.Y.; also continued her studies, receiving valuable instruction from Feuermann, Casals, and Piatigorsky. In 1962 she joined the faculty of the Juilliard School of Music in N.Y. In 1953 she became an American citizen. From 1963 to 1973 she was the wife of the American pianist **Grant Johannesen.** She received rather rapturous press reviews for her lyrical interpretations of classical and modern cello music in a purportedly "Russian" (i.e., wonderful) style.

Němeček, Franz Xaver. See **Niemtschek, Franz Xaver.**

Nemtin, Alexander, Soviet composer; b. Perm, July 13, 1936. He studied at the Moscow Cons., graduating in 1960. He writes music in different genres, but his most notable creation is an intimately plausible reification of Scriabin's *Acte préalable,* the "preliminary act" of the planned *Mysterium.* Nemtin put together the score from sketches left by Scriabin after his death, supplemented by materials from his late opus numbers, endeavoring to recreate Scriabin's symph. textures. The first part of this work was performed in Moscow on March 16, 1973.

Nenna, Pomponio, Italian madrigalist; b. Bari, near Naples, c. 1550; d. Rome, c. 1613. Held in high regard by his contemporaries, he was created a Knight of the Golden Spur in 1603. He publ. 6 books of madrigals for 5 voices from 1582 to 1618, and a book of madrigals *a* 4 (1613; 2nd ed., 1621). Several responds are printed in *Istituzione e monumenti dell'arte musicale italiana,* vol. 5 (pp. LIII–LX); his madrigals, ed. by E. Dagnino, in *Pubblicazioni dell'Istituto Italiano per la Storia della Musica* (Rome, 1942).

Nepomuceno, Alberto, important Brazilian composer; b. Fortaleza, July 6, 1864; d. Rio de Janeiro, Oct. 16, 1920. He studied in Rome, Berlin, and Paris, returning to Brazil in 1895. In 1902 he was appointed director of the Instituto Nacional de Musica in Rio de Janeiro, remaining only for a few months; he returned to this post in 1906, holding it until 1916. In 1910 he conducted Brazilian music at the International Exposition in Brussels. In some of his music he introduced thematic material from Brazilian folk music.

WORKS: Operas: *Artemis* (Rio de Janeiro, June 14, 1898); *O Garatuja* (Rio de Janeiro, Oct. 26, 1904); *Abul* (Buenos Aires, June 30, 1913); Symph. (an early work; publ. posthumously, 1937); *Suite brasileira* for Orch. (contains a popular *Batuque*); songs; piano pieces.

Neri, Saint Donna Filippo, one of the greatest spiritual leaders of the Renaissance; b. Florence, July 21, 1515; d. Rome, May 26, 1595. He was educated in Florence; by 1534 was in Rome; in 1548 he founded the Confraternità della Ss. Trinità; in 1551 took Holy Orders. He began by giving lectures on religious subjects and holding spiritual exercises in the oratory of the church of San Girolamo della Carità, and soon attracted a large following. These meetings invariably ended with the singing of hymns, or *laudi spirituali,* for which the poet Ancina wrote many of the texts, while Giovanni Animuccia, maestro di cappella at the Vatican and music director of the Oratory, set them to music. In 1575 the Congregation of the Oratory, as a seminary for secular priests, was officially recognized by Pope Gregory XIII, and in 1578 the Congregation transferred its headquarters to the church of Santa Maria in Vallicella. But the founder himself remained at S. Girolamo until 1583; from 1578 the great Spanish polyphonist Victoria lived with him there, as chaplain at this church. Another Spanish musician who was prominently associated with the Oratorio was Francisco Soto de Langa. S. Filippo was friendly with Palestrina, whose spiritual adviser he was, but there is no evidence that the latter succeeded Animuccia as music director of the Oratory. From the musical practice of the Oratory there eventually developed the form that we know as "oratorio." Contrary to general belief, this form did not make its first appearance in Cavalieri's *Rappresentazione di anima e di corpo,* performed at S. Maria in Vallicella in 1600, but in Giovanni Francesco Anerio's *Teatro Armonico spirituale di madrigali a 5, 6, 7 e 8 voci,* dating from 1619 and consisting of musical settings of the Gospels and of stories from the Bible. It was not until about 1635–40 that this form actually began to receive the title of oratorio, from the place where the performances were given. S. Filippo was beatified on May 25, 1615, and canonized on March 12, 1622.

Neruda, Franz Xaver, Bohemian cellist, brother of **Wilma Maria Francisca Neruda;** b. Brünn, Dec. 3, 1843; d. Copenhagen, March 20, 1915. At an early age he appeared in concerts with his father and sister; in 1864–76 was a member of the Royal Orch. in Copenhagen, where in 1868 he founded the Society for Chamber Music; he succeeded Gade in 1892 as conductor of a similar organization in Stockholm. He composed 5 cello concertos; *Aus dem Böhmerwald* and *Slovakische Märsche* for Orch.; string quartets; pieces for cello, for piano, and for organ; songs.

Neruda (Lady Hallé), Wilma Maria Francisca, Czech violinist; b. Brünn, March 21, 1839; d. Berlin, April 15, 1911. Her father was an organist; her brother, **Franz Xaver Neruda,** a cellist. She first played in public in Vienna when she was 7 years old, with her sister **Amalie,** a pianist; then made a tour with her father, sister, and brother through Germany. On June 11, 1849, she played at a Phil. Society concert in London; after prolonged travels on the Continent, including Russia, she married the Swedish conductor **Ludvig Norman,** from whom she was divorced in 1869; she returned to London the same year. On July 26, 1888, she married **Sir Charles Hallé,** and with him made tours to Europe, Australia, and South Africa until her husband's death in 1895. When she announced her intention of retiring, a number of admirers, headed by the Prince of Wales (Edward VII), raised a subscription and presented to her a palace at Asolo, near Venice. In 1899 she made an American tour. In 1901 Queen Alexandra conferred upon her the title of "Violinist to the Queen." Her instrument, a Stradivarius dated 1709, considered one of the finest in existence, was presented to her in 1876 jointly by the Duke of Saxe-Coburg and Gotha, Earl Dudley, and Earl Hardwicke.

Nessler, Victor E., Alsatian composer; b. Baldenheim, Jan. 28, 1841; d. Strasbourg, May 28, 1890. He studied in Strasbourg, where he produced his first opera, *Fleurette* (1864). In 1870 he became conductor of the Caroltheater in Leipzig and produced there his opera *Der Rattenfänger von Hameln* (Leipzig, March 19, 1879), which established his reputation as an opera composer. An even greater success was achieved by his opera *Der Trompeter von Säkkingen* (Leipzig, May 4, 1884), which entered the repertoire of many European opera houses. In both operas Nessler adroitly appealed to the Romantic tastes of the German audiences, even though from a purely musical standpoint these productions offered little originality. His other operas, none of which achieved a comparable success, included *Dornröschens Brautfahrt* (1867), *Irmingard* (1876), *Der wilde Jäger* (1881), *Otto der Schütz* (1886), and *Die Rose von Strassburg* (1890). He also wrote several operettas: *Die Hochzeitsreise* (1867), *Nachtwächter und Student* (1868), and *Am Alexandertag* (1869).

Nesterenko, Evgeni, Russian bass; b. Moscow, Jan. 8, 1938. He first studied architectural engineering; graduated from the Leningrad Structural Inst. in 1961; then enrolled in the Leningrad Cons., where he studied voice with Lukanin. He began his opera career at the Maly Theater in Leningrad (1963–67); then was a member of the Kirov Opera and Ballet Theater there (1967–71). In 1970 he won first prize at the International Tchaikovsky Competition in Moscow; in 1971 he joined the Bolshoi Theater. He then engaged on a European concert tour; also sang in the U.S. In 1975 he was appointed chairman of the voice dept. at the Moscow Cons. He excelled in such roles as Boris Godunov and Méphistophélès. In 1982 he was awarded the Lenin Prize.

Nestyev, Izrail, Russian musicologist; b. Kerch, April 17, 1911. He studied at the Moscow Cons., graduating in 1937; during World War II served as a military correspondent; subsequently was in charge of the programs of Moscow Radio (1945–48); in 1956, he joined the staff of the Moscow Cons., conducting seminars on European music. He is the author of the standard biography of Prokofiev (Moscow, 1946; in Eng., N.Y., 1946; new revised ed., Moscow, 1957; in Eng., Stanford, Calif., 1960, with a foreword by N. Slonimsky); other books are *Popular Song as Foundation of Musical Creativity* (Moscow, 1961); *How to Understand Music* (Moscow, 1962); *Hanns Eisler and His Songs* (Moscow, 1962); *Puccini* (Moscow, 1963); *Béla Bartók, Life and Works* (Moscow, 1969). He was a co-editor of the symposium *Sergei Prokofiev; Articles and Materials* (Moscow, 1962); and of *European Music of the 20th Century; Materials and Documents* (Moscow, 1975).

Nettl, Bruno, American musicologist, son of **Paul Nettl;** b. Prague, March 14, 1930. He was brought to the U.S. in 1939; studied at Indiana Univ. (A.B., 1950; M.A., 1951; Ph.D., 1953, with the dissertation *American Indian Music North of Mexico: Its Styles and Areas,* publ. as *North American Indian Musical Styles,* Philadelphia, 1954); he also received an M.A. degree in library science from the Univ. of Michigan in 1960. He taught at Wayne State Univ. (1953–64); in 1964 he joined the faculty of the Univ. of Illinois at Urbana, becoming a prof. of music and anthropology in 1967. His books include *Music in Primitive Culture* (Cambridge, Mass., 1956); *Cheremis Musical Styles* (Bloomington, Ind., 1960); *An Introduction to Folk Music in the United States* (Detroit, 1960; 3rd ed., revised and enlarged, 1976); *Reference Materials in Ethnomusicology* (Detroit, 1961; 2nd ed., 1967); *Theory and Method in Ethnomusicology* (N.Y., 1964); *Folk and Traditional Music of the Western Continents* (Englewood Cliffs, N.J., 1965; 2nd ed., 1973); etc.

Nettl, Paul, eminent American musicologist; b. Hohenelbe, Bohemia, Jan. 10, 1889; d. Bloomington,

Ind., Jan. 8, 1972. He studied jurisprudence (LL.D., 1913) and musicology (Ph.D., 1915) at the German Univ. of Prague; from 1920 to 1937 was on its faculty. In 1939 he emigrated to the U.S.; from 1946 to 1959 he taught at Indiana Univ. in Bloomington. His writings include *Über den Ursprung der Musik* (Prague, 1920); *Alte jüdische Spielleute und Musiker* (Prague, 1923); *Musik und Tanz bei Casanova* (Prague, 1924); *Musik-Barock in Böhmen und Mähren* (Brunn, 1927); *Der Prager Kaufruf* (Prague, 1930); *Das Wiener Lied im Zeitalter des Barock* (Vienna, 1934); *Mozart in Böhmen*, after Prochazka's *Mozart in Prag* (Prague, 1938); *The Story of Dance Music* (N.Y., 1947); *The Book of Musical Documents* (N.Y., 1948); *Luther and Music* (N.Y., 1948); *Casanova und seine Zeit* (Esslingen, 1949); *Goethe und Mozart: Eine Betrachtung* (Esslingen, 1949); *The Other Casanova* (N.Y., 1950); *Forgotten Musicians* (N.Y., 1951); *National Anthems* (N.Y., 1952; 2nd ed., enlarged, 1967); *Beethoven Encyclopedia* (N.Y., 1956; 2nd ed., revised, 1967, as *Beethoven Handbook*); *Mozart and Masonry* (N.Y., 1957); *Beethoven und seine Zeit* (Frankfurt, 1958); *Georg Friedrich Händel* (Berlin, 1958); *Mozart und der Tanz* (1960); *The Dance in Classical Music* (N.Y., 1963); R. Daniel, ed., *Paul Nettl: Selected Essays* (Bloomington, 1975). A bio-bibliographical brochure, *Ein Musikwissenschaftler in zwei Welten: Die musikwissenschaftlen und literarischen Arbeiten von Paul Nettl*, compiled by Thomas Atcherson, was publ. as part of a Festschrift in Vienna in 1962.

Neuendorff, Adolf, German conductor; b. Hamburg, June 13, 1843; d. New York, Dec. 4, 1897. He went to America in 1854 and studied violin with Matzka and Weinlich, and piano with Schilling. He appeared both as a concert violinist and pianist; gave violin concerts in Brazil in 1861. In 1863 he went to Milwaukee, then a center of German music, and served as music director of the German theater there; subsequently moved to N.Y., where he conducted German opera, including the first American performances of *Lohengrin* (April 3, 1871) and *Die Walküre* (April 2, 1877); in 1884 he moved to Boston and became the first conductor of the Music Hall Promenade Concerts (later Boston Pops); he then followed his wife, the singer **Georgine von Januschowsky,** to Vienna, where she was prima donna at the Imperial Opera (1893–95); he finally returned to N.Y., and in 1897 became conductor of the Metropolitan Permanent Orch., succeeding Seidl.

Neuhaus, Heinrich, eminent Russian pianist and pedagogue; b. Elizavetgrad, April 12, 1888; d. Moscow, Oct. 10, 1964. He studied piano with his father, **Gustav Neuhaus** (1847–1938); other musical members of the family were his uncle, the pianist and composer **Felix Blumenfeld,** and his first cousin, the Polish composer **Karol Szymanowski.** Neuhaus began giving concerts at the age of 9; he made a concert tour in Germany in 1904, then studied composition with Paul Juon in Berlin; in 1912–14 he took piano lessons with Leopold Godowsky in Vienna.

Returning to Russia, he taught piano at the Kiev Cons. (1918–22); then was a prof. from 1922 to his death at the Moscow Cons. Among his students were Gilels and Sviatoslav Richter. Neuhaus publ. *The Art of Piano Playing* (Moscow, 1958; in Eng., London, 1983).

Neukomm, Sigismund Ritter von, Austrian composer and conductor; b. Salzburg, July 10, 1778; d. Paris, April 3, 1858. He was a pupil of the organist Weissauer, and of Michael Haydn for composition; from 1798 to 1805 he studied in Vienna under Joseph Haydn, who showed him fatherly care. In 1804 he passed through Stockholm, where he was elected a member of the Academy, to St. Petersburg, there becoming conductor of the German Opera. The year 1809 found him in Paris, an intimate of Grétry and Cherubini, and pianist to Talleyrand after Dussek. For his Requiem in memory of Louis XVI (Vienna, 1814), Louis XVII ennobled him in 1815, decorating him with the cross of the Legion of Honor. In 1816 Neukomm went to Rio de Janeiro, and was appointed court music director by Emperor Dom Pedro, whom he accompanied to Lisbon on the outbreak of the revolution in 1821. He was in Talleyrand's service until 1826; then traveled for many years; and finally resided alternately in London and Paris. Despite his almost continuous travels, he was a most industrious composer; besides much church music, he produced several German operas; 2 symphs., 5 overtures, and 6 fantasias for orch.; chamber music; a Piano Concerto and many piano pieces; 57 organ pieces; about 200 French, English, Italian, and German songs; etc. His autobiography was publ. as *Esquisses biographiques de Sigismond Neukomm* (Paris, 1859).

Neumann, Angelo, Austrian tenor and opera administrator; b. Vienna, Aug. 18, 1838; d. Prague, Dec. 20, 1910. He began a mercantile career, but deserted it after taking vocal lessons from Stilke-Sessi, and after his debut as a lyric tenor in 1859; he sang at theaters in Cracow, Odenburg, Pressburg, Danzig, and the Vienna Court Opera (1862–76); in 1876–82 he was manager of the Leipzig opera under Förster; then gathered together a traveling company for producing Wagner operas, journeying as far as Italy; from 1882 to 1885 he was manager of the Bremen opera; then until his death, of the German opera in Prague (Landestheater). He publ. *Erinnerungen an Richard Wagner* (1907; Eng. trans. by E. Livermore, 1908).

Nevada, Emma, stage name of **Emma Wixom,** operatic soprano; b. Alpha, near Nevada City, Calif., Feb. 7, 1859; d. Liverpool, June 20, 1940. She studied from 1877 with Marchesi in Vienna; made her debut in London on May 17, 1880, in *La Sonnambula*; sang at Trieste in the autumn; then in Florence, Livorno, Naples, Rome, and Genoa, and at La Scala, Milan. Her first appearance in Paris was at the Opéra-Comique, May 17, 1883, as Zora in F. David's *Perle du Brésil*. During the season of 1884–85 she was a member of Col. Mapleson's company at the old

Academy of Music in N.Y., singing on alternate nights with Patti. She sang in Chicago at the Opera Festival in 1885, and again in 1889. She then sang mostly in Europe; retired in 1910.

Nevada, Mignon Mathilde Marie, daughter of **Emma Nevada;** operatic soprano; b. Paris, Aug. 14, 1886; d. Long Melford, England, June 25, 1971. She made her debut at the Costanzi Theater, Rome, as Rosina in *Il Barbiere di Siviglia* in 1907; then sang a season at the San Carlos in Lisbon; after a season at the Pergola Theater in Florence, she made her London debut at Covent Garden as Ophelia (Oct. 3, 1910), and sang there in subsequent seasons; also appeared at La Monnaie in Brussels, and (1923) at La Scala in Milan; during World War II she engaged in war work at Liverpool, England; from 1954, lived in London.

Neveu, Ginette, French violinist; b. Paris, Aug. 11, 1919; d. in an airplane disaster at the Azores Islands, Oct. 28, 1949. She was a grandniece of **Widor;** studied with her mother, and later with Carl Flesch; first played in public with the Colonne Orch. in Paris at the age of 7. After graduating from the Paris Cons. with a first prize, she won the Wieniawski Grand Prize at the International Contest in Warsaw in 1934. Her American debut took place with the Boston Symph., on Oct. 24, 1947; her success was immediate and unmistakable. She was at the height of her career when she perished on her way to the U.S. for her 3rd annual tour.

Nevin, Arthur Finley, American composer and pedagogue, brother of **Ethelbert Nevin;** b. Edgeworth, Pa., April 27, 1871; d. Sewickley, Pa., July 10, 1943. He received a musical training at home, mainly from his father; then studied at the New England Cons. in Boston; in 1893 went to Berlin, where he studied piano with Klindworth and composition with Boise. Returning to the U.S., he devoted himself to teaching and conducting; was a prof. of music at the Univ. of Kansas (1915–20) and director of the municipal music dept. of Memphis, Tenn. (1920–22); lived for a time on Montana Indian reservations studying Indian music. He was unable to secure a performance for his "Indian" opera *Poia*, but succeeded in making arrangements with the Berlin State Opera to produce it; it was staged on April 23, 1910, but only 4 performances were given; the composer attributed the failure to the hostile anti-American Berlin group; another opera, *A Daughter of the Forest*, was produced in Chicago, January 5, 1918; among his other works were 2 orch. suites, *Lorna Doone* and *Love Dreams;* some chamber music; and a number of piano pieces.

Nevin, Ethelbert Woodbridge, popular American composer; brother of **Arthur Finley Nevin;** b. Edgeworth, Pa., Nov. 25, 1862; d. New Haven, Conn., Feb. 17, 1901. After preliminary musical studies in America, he went to Germany, where he took lessons in singing and piano with Franz Böhme (1877–78); returning to the U.S., he studied piano with Ben-

jamin J. Lang and harmony with Stephen A. Emery in Boston. In 1884 he went again to Germany to study piano with Karl Klindworth (1884–86); then lived in Berlin, Paris, and Florence, before finally settling in New Haven. He had a natural talent for melodious songs and piano pieces in a semi-Classical manner. His *Narcissus* for Piano became a perennial favorite with sentimental piano teachers; his songs *The Rosary* and *Mighty Lak' a Rose* achieved tremendous popularity in women's clubs. His pantomime *Lady Floriane's Dream* was produced in N.Y. in 1898.

Neway, Patricia, American soprano; b. Brooklyn, Sept. 30, 1919. She studied at the Mannes College of Music in N.Y. After several appearances in minor roles, she achieved her first significant success as Magda in Menotti's opera *The Consul* (Philadelphia, March 1, 1950); appeared in another Menotti opera, *Maria Golovin*, at the Brussels World's Fair on Aug. 20, 1958. Her repertoire includes parts in operas by Alban Berg, Benjamin Britten, and Menotti.

Newlin, Dika, American writer on music and composer; b. Portland, Oreg., Nov. 22, 1923. She studied piano and theory at Michigan State Univ., East Lansing (B.A., 1939) and at the Univ. of Calif., Los Angeles (M.A., 1941); later took courses at Columbia Univ. in N.Y. (Ph.D., 1945); in the interim she attended the classes of Schoenberg in Los Angeles, acquiring a thorough knowledge of the method of composition with 12 tones; also had some sessions with Sessions, and took additional instruction in piano playing with Serkin and Schnabel. She taught at Western Maryland College (1945–49); at Syracuse Univ. (1949–51); at Drew Univ. in Madison, N.J. (1952–65); and at North Texas State Univ. in Denton (1965–75). In 1977 she joined the faculty of The New School for Social Research in N.Y. She publ. a valuable study on comparative musical styles, *Bruckner-Mahler-Schoenberg* (Diss., Columbia Univ., 1945; publ. in N.Y., 1947; totally revised ed., N.Y., 1978); she trans. into Eng. Leibowitz's *Schoenberg et son école* (N.Y., 1949), Schoenberg's *Style and Idea* (N.Y., 1951), and Rufer's *Das Werk A. Schönbergs* (London, 1962). Her compositions follow the Schoenbergian idiom; she wrote a *Sinfonia* for Piano (1947); Piano Trio (1948); Chamber Symph. (1949); *Fantasy on a Row* for Piano (1958); *Study in 12 Tones* for Viola d'Amore and Piano (1959); *Atone* for Chamber Ensemble (1976); *Second-Hand Rows* for Voice and Piano (1977–78).

Newman, Alfred, American film composer; b. New Haven, Conn., March 17, 1900; d. Hollywood, Feb. 17, 1970. He studied piano with Sigismund Stojowski and composition with Rubin Goldmark; also had private lessons with Schoenberg in Los Angeles. He began his career in vaudeville shows billed as "The Marvelous Boy Pianist"; later, when he led theater orchs. on Broadway, he was hailed as "The Boy Conductor" and "The Youngest Conductor in the U.S." In 1930 he went to Hollywood and devoted himself entirely to writing film music; he wrote about 230 film scores; 45 of this number were nominated for awards of the Motion Picture Academy, and 9 were winners. However, only his musical scores for *The Song of Bernadette* and *Love Is a Many-Splendored Thing* were complete scores; the rest were merely incidental to the action on the screen. Among his most successful scores were *All about Eve, The Egyptian* (partly written by the original assignee, Bernard Herrman), *The Prisoner of Zenda* (1937), *Wuthering Heights* (1939), *Captain from Castille* (1947), and *The Robe* (1953). Stylistically he followed an eclectic type of theatrical Romanticism, often mimicking, almost literally, the most popular works of Tchaikovsky, Rachmaninoff, Wagner, and Liszt, and amalgamating these elements in colorful free fantasia; in doing so, he created a category of composition that was to become known, with some disdain, as "movie music."

Newman, Anthony, American harpsichordist, pianist, organist, conductor, and composer; b. Los Angeles, May 12, 1941. He studied piano and organ; in 1959 went to Paris, where he took courses at the Ecole Normale de Musique with Pierre Cochereau and Nadia Boulanger; returning to the U.S., he studied organ at the Mannes College of Music in N.Y. (B.S., 1962) and composition with Leon Kirchner and Luciano Berio at Harvard Univ. (M.A., 1963); received his D.M.A. from Boston Univ. in 1966. He made his professional debut at Carnegie Hall in 1967, in a recital featuring the pedal harpsichord; subsequently toured widely as a harpsichordist, organist, pianist, and fortepianist. He served on the faculty of the Juilliard School of Music in N.Y. (1968–73), at the State Univ. of N.Y. at Purchase (1968–75), and at the Indiana Univ. School of Music in Bloomington (1978–81); also gave master classes. His own compositions are in a neo-Baroque style.
  WORKS: For Orch.: Orch. Cycle I (1975); Violin Concerto, composed for the 50th anniversary of the Indianapolis Symph. Orch. (Indianapolis, Oct. 26, 1979; Hidetaro Suzuki, soloist; John Nelson, conductor). Chamber music: Violin Sonata (1976); Cello Sonata (1977); Sonata for Double Bass and Piano (1981); Piano Trio (1980); Piano Quintet (1981). For Piano: Piano Cycle I (1976). For Organ: *Bhajeb* (1970); *Symphony in the French Manner* (1979); *Prelude and Contrapunctus* (1981). For Guitar: *Variations and Grand Contrapunctus* (1979); Suite for Guitar (1982).

Newman, Ernest, renowned English music critic; b. Liverpool, Nov. 30, 1868; d. Tadworth, Surrey, July 7, 1959. His real name was **William Roberts;** he assumed his *nom de plume* to symbolize an "earnest new man." He prepared himself for the Indian Civil Service, but entered business in Liverpool, pursuing his musical studies as a favorite avocation. In 1904 he accepted an instructorship in the Midland Inst., Birmingham, and took up music as a profession; in 1905, he was in Manchester as critic of the *Guardian;* in 1906–18, in Birmingham as critic for the *Daily Post;* in 1919–20, in London as critic for the

Observer; from March 1920 to 1958, was on the staff of the *London Sunday Times;* from 1923, was also a contributor to the *Glasgow Herald;* in 1924–25, was guest critic of the *N.Y. Evening Post.* One of the best equipped and most influential of the English music critics, he continued to write his regular column in the *Sunday Times* in his 90th year.

Newman, William S., distinguished American music scholar; b. Cleveland, April 6, 1912. He studied piano with Riemenschneider and Arthur Loesser; composition with Elwell and Shepherd, in Cleveland; received his Ph.D. at Western Reserve Univ. in 1939 with the dissertation *The Present Trend of the Sonata Idea;* then took courses in musicology with Paul Henry Lang at Columbia Univ. in 1940; during World War II served in the U.S. Army Air Force Intelligence. In 1945 he joined the staff of the Univ. of North Carolina at Chapel Hill; became prof. emeritus, 1976. He focused most of his research on the evolution of the instrumental sonata. His chief project was *A History of the Sonata Idea* in 3 vols.: *The Sonata in the Baroque Era* (Chapel Hill, 1959; 2nd ed., revised, 1966); *The Sonata in the Classic Era* (Chapel Hill, 1963; 2nd ed., revised, 1972); *The Sonata since Beethoven* (Chapel Hill, 1969; 2nd ed., revised, 1972). His other publications include 3 critical editions of works in sonata forms *(13 Keyboard Sonatas of the 18th and 19th Centuries; 6 Keyboard Sonatas from the Classic Era; 3 Keyboard Sonatas by the Sons of Bach);* he further contributed articles on the sonata to the *Enciclopedia della musica, Die Musik in Geschichte und Gegenwart,* and *Grove's Dictionary of Music and Musicians.* He publ. *Performance Practices in Beethoven's Piano Sonatas* (N.Y., 1971), and contributed numerous articles to American and European music magazines on various aspects of Classical sonata form. He began his musical career as a pianist, appearing in solo recitals and also with orchs. (until 1970); publ. a useful manual, *The Pianist's Problems* (N.Y., 1950; 4th ed., 1984). He composed an operetta, *Freddy and His Fiddle* (1936); *An American Tragedy,* concert overture (1941); several pieces for band; and some chamber music.

Newmarch, Rosa Harriet (née **Jeaffreson**), English writer on musical subjects; b. Leamington, Dec. 18, 1857; d. Worthing, April 9, 1940. Growing up in an artistic atmosphere, she entered the Hetherley School of Art to study painting, but after a time abandoned that career for literary pursuits; settled in London in 1880 as a contributor to various journals. There she married Henry Charles Newmarch, in 1883. She visited Russia in 1897 and many times afterward; established contact with the foremost musicians there; her enthusiasm for Russian music, particularily that of the Russian national school of composition, was unlimited, and she publ. several books on the subject which were of importance to the appreciation of Russian music in England, though her high-pitched literary manner was sometimes maintained to the detriment of factual material.

Newton, Ivor, English pianist; b. London, Dec. 15, 1892; d. there, April 21, 1981. He studied piano with Arthur Barclay; then went to Berlin, where he studied lieder with Zur Mühlen and the art of accompaniment with Conraad van Bos. An earnest student of the history of song and the proper role of accompaniment, he became one of the most appreciated piano accompanists of the time, playing at recitals with celebrated singers and instrumentalists, among them Dame Nellie Melba, John McCormack, Chaliapin, Kirsten Flagstad, Pablo Casals, Yehudi Menuhin, and Maria Callas. His career, which spanned more than 60 years, is chronicled in his interesting autobiography, *At the Piano —Ivor Newton* (London, 1966). In 1973 he was made a Commander of the Order of the British Empire.

Ney, Elly, German pianist; b. Düsseldorf, Sept. 27, 1882; d. Tutzing, March 31, 1968. She was a piano student of Leschetizky and Sauer in Vienna; made her debut in Vienna in 1905; gave successful recitals in Europe and America; then devoted herself mainly to teaching; lived mostly in Munich. She was married to Willem van Hoogstraten (1911–27); in 1928 she married P.F. Allais of Chicago. She publ. an autobiography, *Ein Leben für die Musik* (Darmstadt, 1952; 2nd ed. as *Erinnerungen und Betrachtungen; Mein Leben aus der Musik,* 1957).

Nezhdanova, Antonina, Russian soprano; b. Krivaya Balka, near Odessa, June 16, 1873; d. Moscow, June 26, 1950. She studied at the Moscow Cons.; in 1902 joined the staff of the Bolshoi Theater. She was equally successful as a lyric, dramatic, and coloratura soprano; her range extended to high G. In 1912 she made an appearance as Gilda in *Rigoletto* at the Grand Opéra in Paris. Her best roles were Tatiana in *Eugene Onegin,* Marguerite in *Faust,* and Elsa in *Lohengrin.* In 1943 she became a prof. of voice at the Moscow Cons.

Nichols, "Red" (Ernest Loring Nichols), American jazz cornetist and bandleader; b. Ogden, Utah, May 8, 1905; d. Las Vegas, June 28, 1965. His father taught him cornet, and he played in his father's brass band from the age of 12. He then cut a swath in the world of popular music with his own band, advertised as "Red Nichols and His Five Pennies" (actually, the number of "Pennies" was 10); among its members were such future celebrities as Jimmy Dorsey, Benny Goodman, and Glenn Miller. A maudlin motion picture, *The Five Pennies,* was manufactured in 1959, and catapulted "Red" Nichols into the stratosphere of jazzdom. Heuristic exegetes of European hermeneutics bemoaned the commercialization of his style, giving preference to his earlier, immaculate, jazzification.

Nicodé, Jean-Louis, German pianist and composer; b. Jerczik, near Posen, Aug. 12, 1853; d. Langebrück, near Dresden, Oct. 5, 1919. He was taught by his father and by the organist Hartkäs; in 1869 entered Kullak's Academy in Berlin, where he studied piano with Kullak, harmony with Wüerst, and counterpoint and composition with Kiel. He made a concert tour (1878) with Mme. Artôt through Galicia and Rumania; in 1878–85, was a piano teacher at the Dresden Cons.; till 1888, was conductor of the Phil. Concerts; established the Nicodé Concerts in 1893, and, in order to enlarge their scope by the production of larger choral works, formed the Nicodé Chorus in 1896. In 1900 he abandoned these concerts, retired to Langebrück, and devoted himself to composition. He wrote a Symph.; symph. poems; 2 sonatas for Cello and Piano; many piano pieces; songs.

Nicolai, (Carl) Otto (Ehrenfried), famous German opera composer and conductor; b. Königsberg, June 9, 1810; d. Berlin, May 11, 1849. He studied piano at home; in 1827 he went to Berlin, where he took lessons in theory with Zelter; he also took courses with Bernhard Klein at the Royal Inst. for Church Music. On April 13, 1833, he made a concert debut in Berlin as a pianist, singer, and composer. He then was engaged as organist to the embassy chapel in Rome by the Prussian ambassador, Bunsen. While in Italy he also studied counterpoint with Giuseppe Baini. In 1837 he proceeded to Vienna, where he became a singing teacher and Kapellmeister at the Kärnthnertortheater. In Oct. 1838 he returned to Italy; on Nov. 26, 1839, he presented in Trieste his first opera, *Rosmonda d'Inghilterra,* given under its new title as *Enrico II.* His 2nd opera, *Il Templario,* was staged in Turin on Feb. 11, 1840. In 1841 he moved to Vienna, where he as appointed court Kapellmeister in succession to Kreutzer. There Nicolai was instrumental in establishing symph. concerts utilizing the musicians of the orch. of the Imperial Court Opera Theater; on March 28, 1842, he conducted this ensemble featuring Beethoven's 7th Symph.; this became the inaugural concert of the celebrated Vienna Phil. Orch. In 1848 he was appointed Kapellmeister of the Royal Opera in Berlin. On March 9, 1849, his famous opera *Die lustigen Weiber von Windsor,* after Shakespeare, was given at the Berlin Royal Opera; it was to become his only enduring creation. Nicolai died suddenly 2 months after its production. In 1887 Hans Richter, then conductor of the Vienna Phil., inaugurated an annual "Nicolai-Konzert" in his memory, and it became a standard occasion. It was conducted by Gustav Mahler in 1899–1901; by Felix Weingartner in 1909–27; by Wilhelm Furtwängler in 1928–31, 1933–44, and 1948–54; by Karl Böhm in 1955–57 and 1964–80; and by Claudio Abbado in 1980 and 1983.

Nicolet, Aurèle, Swiss flutist; b. Neuchâtel, Jan. 22, 1926. He was educated in Zürich and Paris; then played flute in Swiss orchs.; later joined the Berlin Phil. (1950–59). He was a prof. at the Berlin Hochschule für Musik (1953–65); then taught at the Hochschule für Musik in Freiburg; also gave summer classes at the Salzburg Mozarteum. Apart from his activities as a pedagogue, he developed a wide international career giving worldwide flute recitals which took him to the U.S., Israel, and Japan.

Nicolini, stage name of **Ernest Nicolas,** French dramatic tenor; b. Saint-Malo, Feb. 23, 1834; d. Pau, Jan. 19, 1898. He studied at the Paris Cons.; made his debut in July 1857, in Halévy's *Mousquetaires de la Reine,* at the Opéra-Comique, where he was engaged till 1859; then went to Italy, and sang as "Nicolini" with moderate success. In 1862–70 he sang at the Salle Ventadour in Paris; in 1866 he visited London, where he made his debut at Covent Garden on May 29, 1866. In 1871 he sang opera at Drury Lane; from 1872 to 1884, at Covent Garden. After touring with **Adelina Patti,** he married her, on Aug. 10, 1886.

Niecks, Friedrich (Frederick), German pedagogue and writer on music; b. Düsseldorf, Feb. 3, 1845; d. Edinburgh, June 24, 1924. He studied the violin under Langhans, Grünewald, and Auer, and piano and composition with J. Tausch; made his debut (as a violinist) at Düsseldorf in 1857; until 1867 he was a member of the orch. there, the last years as concertmaster; in 1868, became organist at Dumfries, Scotland, and viola player in a quartet with A.C. Mackenzie. After 2 terms at Leipzig Univ. (1877) and travels in Italy, he won a position in London as critic for the *Monthly Musical Record* and *Musical Times*; in 1891, was appointed Reid Prof. of Music at Edinburgh Univ. In 1901 Niecks founded the Music Education Society. He was made a Mus.Doc. (*honoris causa*) by Dublin Univ. in 1898; LL.D. by Edinburgh Univ. After his retirement in 1914 he lived in Edinburgh.

Niedermeyer, Louis, Swiss composer; b. Nyon, April 27, 1802; d. Paris, March 14, 1861. He was a pupil in Vienna of Moscheles (piano) and Förster (composition); in 1819, of Fioravanti in Rome and Zingarelli in Naples. He lived in Geneva as an admired song composer, and settled in Paris in 1823; there he brought out 4 unsuccessful operas (*La casa nel bosco,* May 28, 1828; *Stradella,* March 3, 1837; *Marie Stuart,* Dec. 6, 1844; *La Fronde,* May 2, 1853). He then bent his energies to sacred composition, and reorganized Choron's Inst. for Church Music as the Ecole Niedermeyer, which eventually became a flourishing inst. with government subvention; he also founded (with d'Ortigue) a journal for church music, *La Maîtrise;* and publ. with him *Méthode d'accompagnement du plain-chant* (1856; 2nd ed., 1876; Eng. trans. by W. Goodrich, N.Y., 1905). Niedermeyer's masses, motets, hymns, etc. were well received; his romances (*Le Lac; Le Soir; La Mer; L'Automne;* etc.) are widely known; he also publ. organ preludes, piano pieces, etc.

Nielsen, Carl (August), greatly significant Danish composer; initiator of the modern Danish school of composition; b. Nørre-Lyndelse, near Odense, on the island of Fyn (Funen), June 9, 1865; d. Copenhagen, Oct. 3, 1931. As a boy, he received violin lessons from his father; then played 2nd violin in his village orch. and took trumpet lessons; at the age of 14 became a trumpeter in the Odense military band. While in Odense he made his first efforts at compos-

ing, producing a few chamber pieces; a string quartet he wrote qualified him for admission to the Royal Cons. in Copenhagen, where he studied composition with O. Rosenhoff, violin with V. Tofte, and music history with Gade (1884–86). He played violin in the Royal Chapel Orch. in Copenhagen (1889–1905); later conducted at the Royal Opera in Copenhagen (1908–14) and led the Musikföreningen (Music Society) in Copenhagen (1915–27); also conducted concerts in Germany, the Netherlands, Sweden, and Finland; a few months before his death he was appointed director of the Royal Cons. in Copenhagen. The early style of his music, Romantic in essence, was determined by the combined influences of Gade, Grieg, Brahms, and Liszt, but later on he experienced the powerful impact of modern music, particularly in harmony, which in his works grew more and more chromatic and dissonant; yet he reserved the simple diatonic progressions, often in a folk-song manner, for his major climaxes; in his orchestration he applied opulent sonorities and colorful instrumental counterpoint; there are instances of bold experimentation in some of his works, as, for example, the insertion of a snare-drum solo in his 5th Symph., playing independently of the rest of the orch.; he attached somewhat mysterious titles to his 3rd and 4th symphs. (*Expansive* and *Inextinguishable*). Nielsen is sometimes described as the Sibelius of Denmark, despite obvious dissimilarities in idiom and sources of inspiration; while the music of Sibelius is deeply rooted in national folklore, both in subject matter and melodic derivation, Nielsen seldom drew on Danish popular modalities; Sibelius remained true to the traditional style of composition, while Nielsen sought new ways of modern expression. It was only after his death that Nielsen's major works entered the world repertoire; festivals of his music were organized on his centennial in 1965, and his symphs. in particular were played and recorded in England and America, so that Nielsen finally emerged as one of the most important composers of his time.

WORKS: (all premieres in Copenhagen, except where otherwise noted): FOR THE STAGE: 2 operas: *Saul og David,* after E. Christiansen (*Saul and David,* 1898–1901; Nov. 28, 1902) and *Maskarade,* after V. Andersen (1904–6; Nov. 11, 1906); incidental music to 14 plays, including *Aladdin* (1918–19; Feb. 15, 1919) and *Moderen* (*The Mother,* 1920; Jan. 30, 1921). FOR ORCH.: 6 symphs.: No. 1 (1891–92; March 14, 1894); No. 2, *De fire temperamenter* (*The 4 Temperaments,* 1901–2; Dec. 1, 1902); No. 3, *Sinfonia espansiva* (1910–11; Feb. 28, 1912); No. 4, *Det uudslukkelige* (*The Inextinguishable,* 1915–16; Feb. 1, 1916); No. 5 (1921–22; Jan. 24, 1922); No. 6, *Sinfonia semplice* (1924–25; Dec. 11, 1925); *Little Suite* for Strings (1888; Sept. 8, 1888); *Symphonic Rhapsody* (1888; Feb. 24, 1893; lost); *Helios,* overture (1903; Oct. 8, 1903); *Saga-Drøm* (*Dream of Saga,* 1908; April 6, 1908); *Ved en ung kunstners baare* (*At the Bier of a Young Artist); Andante lamentoso* for String Orch. (1910); Violin Concerto (1911; Feb. 28, 1912); paraphrase on *"Naermere Gud til dig"* (*"Nearer My God to Thee"*) for Wind Orch. (1912; Aug. 22, 1915); *Pan og Syrinx,* pastorale (*Pan and Syrinx,* 1917–18; Feb.

11, 1918); Flute Concerto (1926; Paris, Oct. 21, 1926); *Rhapsodic Overture, En fantasirejse til Faerøerne* *(A Fantasy-Journey to the Faroe Islands,* 1927; Nov. 27, 1927); Clarinet Concerto (1928; Humlebaek, Sept. 14, 1928); *Bøhmisk-Dansk folketone (Bohemian and Danish Folktunes),* paraphrase for String Orch. (1928; Nov. 1, 1928). FOR VOICE: 10 cantatas for various ceremonial occasions; *Hymnus amoris* for Soprano, Tenor, Baritone, Bass, Chorus, and Orch. (1896–97; April 27, 1897); *Søvnen (Sleep)* for Chorus and Orch. (1903–4; March 21, 1905); *Fynsk foraar (Springtime in Funen),* lyrical humoresque for Soprano, Tenor, Bass-baritone, Chorus, and Orch. (1921; Odense, July 8, 1922); *3 Motets* for Chorus a cappella (1929; April 11, 1930); numerous original songs to Danish words; harmonizations of Danish folk songs. CHAMBER MUSIC: String Quintet (1888); 4 string quartets: No. 1 (op. 13, 1888; revised 1897), No. 2 (op. 5, 1890), No. 3 (op. 14, 1898), and No. 4 (op. 44, 1906; originally titled *Piacevolezza,* op. 19); *2 Fantasias* for Oboe and Piano (1889); 2 violin sonatas (1895, 1912); *Serenata in Vano* for Clarinet, Bassoon, Horn, Cello, and Bassoon (1914); from incidental music to *Moderen: Faith and Hope Are Playing* for Flute and Viola, *The Fog Is Lifting* for Flute and Harp, and *The Children Are Playing* for Solo Flute (all 1920); Wind Quintet (1922; Oct. 9, 1922); *Prelude and Theme with Variations* for Solo Violin (1923); *Praeludio e Presto* for Solo Violin (1928); *Canto serioso* for Horn or Cello, and Piano (1928); *Allegretto* for 2 Recorders (1931). FOR PIANO: *5 Pieces* (1890); *Symphonic Suite* (1894); 6 *Humoreske-Bagateller* (1894–97); *Festpraeludium* (1900); *Chaconne* (1916); *Theme with Variations* (1916); *Suite (Den Luciferiske) (Lucifer Suite,* 1919–20); *3 Pieces* (1928); *Klavermusik for smaa og store (Piano Music for Young and Old),* 24 short 5-tone pieces in all keys in 2 vols. (1930). FOR ORGAN: *29 Short Preludes* (1929); *2 Posthumous Preludes* (1929); *Commotio* (1930–31). Nielsen publ. the books *Levende musik* (Copenhagen, 1925; in Eng. as *Living Music,* London, 1953) and *Min Fynske barndom* (reminiscences of his childhood, Copenhagen, 1927; in Eng. under the title *My Childhood,* London, 1953).

Nielsen, Riccardo, Italian composer; b. Bologna, March 3, 1908. He studied with Alfredo Casella and Carlo Gatti; began composing in the Italian Baroque manner but eventually made a decisive turn toward the 12-tone technique of composition. He occupied various administrative and teaching positions; from 1946 to 1950 was director of the Teatro Communale in Bologna; in 1952 became director of the Liceo Frescobaldi in Ferrara, where he also taught composition.

Niemann, Albert, German opera tenor; b. Erxleben, near Magdeburg, Jan. 15, 1831; d. Berlin, Jan. 13, 1917. He began his career as an actor and dramatist; then sang in a chorus in Dessau; made his debut there in 1849; had lessons with F. Schneider and the baritone Nusch; sang in Halle in 1852–54; then in Hannover; then went to Paris, where he studied with Duprez. In 1866 he was engaged at the Royal Court Opera in Berlin, and remained on the staff until 1888. Wagner thought highly of him and asked him to create the role of Tannhäuser in Paris (March 13, 1861) and of Siegmund at the Bayreuth Festival in 1876. From 1886 to 1888 he was a member of the Metropolitan Opera Co. in N.Y.; his debut there was in his star role as Siegmund (Nov. 10, 1886); then he sang Tristan at the American premiere of *Tristan und Isolde* (Dec. 1, 1886) and Siegmund in *Götterdämmerung* (Jan. 25, 1888).

Niemann, Walter, German writer on music and composer; b. Hamburg, Oct. 10, 1876; d. Leipzig, June 17, 1953. He was a pupil of his father, Rudolph Niemann, and of Humperdinck (1897); in 1898–1901, studied at the Leipzig Cons. with Reinecke and von Bose, and at the Univ. with Riemann and Kretzschmar (musicology); received a Dr.Phil. in 1901, with the dissertation *Über die abweichende Bedeutung der Ligaturen in der Mensuraltheorie der Zeit vor Johannes de Garlandia* (publ. in Leipzig, 1902; reprint, Wiesbaden, 1971); in 1904–6, was editor of the *Neue Zeitschrift für Musik* in Leipzig; in 1906–7, was a teacher at the Hamburg Cons.; in 1907–17, was again in Leipzig as a writer and critic of the *Neueste Nachrichten,* then gave up this position to devote himself to composition. Besides a Violin Sonata and a few works for orch. and string orch., he wrote numerous piano pieces (over 150 opus numbers).

Niemtschek (Niemetschek, Němeček), Franz Xaver, Czech writer on music; b. Sadská, near Poděbrady, July 24, 1766; d. Vienna, March 19, 1849. He studied at the Prague Gymnasium (1776–82); then studied philosophy at Prague Univ. (Ph.D., 1800); was a prof. of philosophy at the Univ. of Prague from 1802 to 1820; is known in musical annals for his biography of Mozart, whom he greatly admired and evidently knew personally: *Leben des k. k. Kapellmeisters Wolfgang Gottlieb Mozart* (Prague, 1798; 2nd ed., 1808; in Eng., London, 1956).

Niessen-Stone, Matja von, American soprano; b. Moscow, Dec. 28, 1870; d. New York, June 8, 1948. At the age of 6 she was taken to Germany, where she studied singing in Dresden with Adolf Jansen and in Berlin with Lilli Lehmann and others; after a successful debut in Dresden in 1890 she toured Europe; in 1906 she went to the U.S. and sang at the Metropolitan Opera House in N.Y., during the season 1908–9. From 1910 to 1917 she taught voice at the Inst. of Musical Art in N.Y. In 1922 she went back to Europe and taught singing in Berlin until 1938, when she returned to N.Y.

Nietzsche, Friedrich, celebrated philosopher; b. Röcken, near Lützen, Oct. 15, 1844; d. Weimar, Aug. 25, 1900, after 11 years of insanity. He was prof. of classical philology at the Univ. of Basel (1869–79); was at first a warm partisan of Wagner, whom he championed in *Die Geburt der Tragödie aus dem Geiste der Musik* (1872; 2nd ed., 1874) and *Richard Wagner in Bayreuth* (1876). In *Der Fall Wagner* and *Nietzsche contra Wagner* (both 1888) and in *Götzendämmerung* (1889), he turned against his former idol and became a partisan of Bizet. Nietzsche was also a trained musician; he publ. 17 songs (1864) and *An das Leben* for Chorus and Orch. (1887); in MS are piano pieces (2- and 4-hands) and songs. His lieder have been edited by G. Göhler (Leipzig, 1924), and his *Complete Works,* by Curt Paul Jang (Basel, 1976).

Nigg, Serge, French composer; b. Paris, June 6, 1924. He studied composition with Messiaen and Simone Plé-Caussande at the Paris Cons. (1941–46) and privately with René Liebowitz (1946–48), mainly the Schoenbergian method of composition with 12 tones. Nigg became one of the earliest representatives of dodecaphony in France; however, under the influence of his political convictions, he later abandoned modern techniques and began writing in a manner accessible to a broad public. In 1959 he formed, with Durey and others, the Assoc. of Progressive Musicians, advocating socialist realism in music. WORKS: FOR ORCH.: *Timour,* symph. poem (1944); Concertino for Piano, Wind Instruments, and Percussion (1946); *3 mouvements symphoniques* (1947); *Pour un poète captif,* symph. poem appealing for the liberation of a radical poet imprisoned for political disturbances (1950); 2 piano concertos: No. 1 (1954; Paris, Jan. 10, 1955) and No. 2 (1970–71; Strasbourg, June 10, 1971); Violin Concerto (1957; Paris, May 27, 1960); *Musique funèbre* for Strings (1958); *Jérôme Bosch—Symphonie (Hieronymus Bosch Symphony;* 1960; Strasbourg, June 21, 1960); Concerto for Flute and Strings (1961); *Visages d'Axël,* suite in 2 parts (1967; Paris, Sept. 4, 1967); *Fulgar* for Band, Percussion, 2 Harps, Piano, Celesta, and Tubular Chimes (1969; Paris, Oct. 9, 1969); *Scènes concertantes* for Piano and Strings (1976; Paris Radio, March 26, 1976); *Millions d'oiseaux d'or* (1980–81; Toulouse Orch. on U.S. tour, Boston, March 20, 1981). cantata (1953); *Prière pour le premier jour Jérôme Bosch* (1958); 2 sonatas (1943, 1965).

Nikisch, Arthur, celebrated Hungarian conductor; b. Szent-Miklós, Oct. 12, 1855; d. Leipzig, Jan. 23, 1922. His father was head bookkeeper to Prince Lichtenstein. Nikisch attended the Vienna Cons., studying with Dessoff (composition) and Hellmesberger (violin), graduating in 1874. While still a student he had the honor of playing among the first violins under Wagner's direction at the laying of the cornerstone of the Bayreuth Theater (1872). He was at first engaged as a violinist in the Vienna Court Orch. (1874); then as 2nd conductor at the Leipzig Theater (1878). From 1882 to 1889 he was first conductor there. In 1889 he was engaged as conductor of the Boston Symph. Orch., with excellent success, remaining at this post until 1893. Returning to Europe, he was music director of the Budapest Opera (1893–95); also conducted the Phil. Concerts there; from 1895, was conductor of the Gewandhaus Concerts in Leipzig, succeeding Reinecke, and of

the Phil. Concerts in Berlin. From 1897 he was in constant demand as a visiting conductor, and made a number of extended tours with the Berlin Phil. Orch.; he directed many of the concerts of the London Phil. Society, and works of Wagner and Richard Strauss at Covent Garden; in 1912 he made a tour of the U.S. with the entire London Symph. Orch. (85 performers). In 1902–7, he was director of studies at the Leipzig Cons.; in 1905–6, general director of the Stadttheater. As a symph. conductor he possessed an extraordinary Romantic power of musical inspiration; he was the first of his profession to open the era of "the conductor as hero," exercising a peculiar magnetism on his audiences equal to that of virtuoso artists; his personal appearance, a poetic-looking beard and flowing hair, contributed to his success. His son **Mitja Nikisch** (b. Leipzig, May 21, 1899; d. Venice, Aug. 5, 1936) was an excellent pianist; he toured South America in 1921; made his U.S. debut in N.Y., Oct. 23, 1923.

Nikolaidi, Elena, contralto; b. Izmir, Turkey, of Greek parents, June 13, 1909. She studied voice with Thanos Mellos, whom she married on April 27, 1936; made her operatic debut at the Vienna State Opera, Dec. 16, 1936; later sang in Salzburg, London, Prague, and Cairo; made her American debut (in a concert) in N.Y., on Jan. 20, 1949.

Niles, John Jacob, American folksinger and authority on folk music; b. Louisville, Ky., April 28, 1892; d. at his Boot Hill farm, near Lexington, Ky., March 1, 1980. He studied at the Cincinnati Cons.; later devoted himself to collecting and arranging the songs of the Southern Appalachians; also composed choruses in a folk-song manner. Among his publications are *7 Kentucky Mountain Songs* (1929); *7 Negro Exultations* (1929); *Songs of the Hill Folk* (1934); *10 Christmas Carols* (1935); *More Songs of the Hill Folk* (1936); *Ballads and Tragic Legends* (1937); *The Anglo-American Ballad Study Book* (1945); *The Anglo-American Carol Study Book* (1948); and *The Shape-Note Study Book* (1950). He also publ. *Songs My Mother Never Taught Me* (with Douglas Moore, 1929).

Nilson, Leo, Swedish composer of electronic music; b. Malmö, Feb. 20, 1939. He studied organ and piano at the Music Academy in Stockholm; was briefly an organist of the Swedish church in Paris, where he was exposed to *musique concrète;* upon his return to Sweden began writing electronic music for films, television, and various avant-garde exhibitions. His works include *Skorpionen* (1965); *Skulpturmusik I, II,* and *III* (1966, 1967, 1968); *Satellitmusik* (1967); *That Experiment H_2S* (1968); *Sirrah* (1971); *Star-75,* multimedia work with Dancers and Sculptor (1975).

Nilsson, Birgit, celebrated Swedish dramatic soprano; b. near Karup, May 17, 1918. She studied singing in Stockholm. In 1947 she joined the Royal Opera; sang Elsa at the Bayreuth Festival in 1954, and Isolde in 1957 and 1959; she also appeared at La

Scala in Milan. She made her U.S. debut at the Hollywood Bowl on Aug. 9, 1956; sang Wagnerian roles with the San Francisco Opera and the Chicago Lyric Opera. In London she sang Brünnhilde in a complete cycle of Wagner's tetralogy in 1957. She made her long-delayed debut with the Metropolitan Opera in N.Y. as Isolde, on Dec. 18, 1959. At the peak of her career she was acclaimed as one of the greatest Wagnerian singers of all time. After an absence of 5 years from the Metropolitan she gave a gala concert there on Nov. 4, 1979; on Feb. l, 1980, she returned to the Met roster; on Feb. 16, 1980, at the age of 62, she sang the title role in *Elektra* by Richard Strauss; the performance was taped for television and broadcast on Jan. 28, 1981.

Nilsson, Bo, Swedish composer of ultramodern tendencies; b. Skellefteaa, May 1, 1937. Largely autodidact, he experimented with techniques of serial composition, the phonetic possibilities of vocal music, and electronic sonorities; attended seminars on modern techniques in Cologne and Darmstadt. His works are constructed on precise quasi-mathematical, serial principles, and are often given abstract titles in German. WORKS: *Frequenzen* for Piccolo, Flute, Percussion, Guitar, Xylophone, Vibraphone, and Double Bass (1955–56); *Bewegungen (Movements)* for Piano (1956); *Schlagfiguren* for Piano (1956); *Buch der Veränderungen (Book of Changes)* for Orch. (1957); *Zeiten im Umlauf (Times in Transit)* for 8 Woodwinds (1957); *Kreuzungen (Crossings)* for Flute, Vibraphone, Guitar, and Xylophone (1957); *Audiogramme* for Tape (1957–58); *Ett blocks timme (Stunde eines Blocks),* chamber cantata for Soprano and 6 Instrumentalists (1957–58); *20 Gruppen* for Piccolo, Oboe, and Clarinet, or any 3 instruments (1958); *Quantitäten* for Piano (1958); *Plexus* for Orch. (1959); *Stenogramm* for Percussion or Organ (1959); *Reaktionen* for 1–4 Percussionists (1960); *Szenes I–IV: I* for 2 Flutes, 2 Trumpets, Piano, Harp, and 2 Percussionists (1960); *II* for 6 Trumpets, 6 Violins, 4 Percussionists, Piano, Harp, Celesta, and Vibraphone (1961); *III* for Chamber Orch. (1961); *IV* for Saxophone, Orch., and Chorus (1974–75); *Versuchungen (Temptations)* for 3 Orch. Groups (1961); *La Bran* for Chorus and Orch. (1961); *Entrée* for Tape and Orch. (1963); *Litanei über das verlorene Schlagzeug (Litany for the Lost Drum)* for Orch. without Percussion, to conform to the title (1965); *Déjà-vu* for Wind Quartet (1967); *Revue* for Orch. (1967); *Attraktionen* for String Quartet (1968); *Design* for Violin, Clarinet, and Piano (1968); *Rendezvous* for Piano (1968); *Quartets* for 36 Winds, Percussion, and Tape (1969); *Caprice* for Orch. (1970); *Exit* for Tape and Orch. (1970); *Eurythmical Voyage* for Piano, Tape, and Orch. (1970); *Déjà-connu (Already Known)* for Wind Quintet (1973); *Nazm* for Speakers, Vocal Soloists, Chorus, Orch., and Tape (1972–73). He publ. an autobiography under the title *Spaderboken* (Stockholm, 1966).

Nilsson, Kristina (Christine), Swedish soprano; b. Sjöabol, near Växjö, Aug. 20, 1843; d. Stockholm, Nov. 22, 1921. Her teachers were Baroness Leuhausen, and F. Berwald in Stockholm; with him she continued study in Paris, and on Oct. 27, 1864, made her debut, as Violetta in *La Traviata*, at the Théâtre Lyrique, where she was engaged for 3 years. After successful visits to London, she was engaged in 1868–70 at the Paris Opéra; then made long tours with Strakosch in America (1870–72), and sang in the principal continental cities. In 1872 she married Auguste Rouzaud (d. 1882); her 2nd husband (married 1887) was the Spanish count Angel Vallejo y Miranda. She revisited America in the winters of 1873, 1874, and 1883, making her debut on the opening night of the Metropolitan Opera House in N.Y. on Oct. 22, 1883, as Marguerite in *Faust*. Her voice was not powerful, but it was brilliant. She excelled as Marguerite and Mignon.

Nin (y Castellanos), Joaquín, Spanish composer and pianist; b. Havana, Sept. 29, 1879; d. there, Oct. 24, 1949. He studied piano with Carlos Vidiella in Barcelona, and M. Moszkowski in Paris; composition with d'Indy at the Schola Cantorum; in 1906–8, was a prof. there; in 1908–10, was in Berlin; then briefly in Havana and Brussels; he lived for many years in Paris; was a member of the French Legion of Honor, the Spanish Academy, etc. He was especially noted as an interpreter of early piano music.

Nin-Culmell, Joaquín, Cuban-Spanish pianist and composer, son of **Joaquín Nin;** b. Berlin, Sept. 5, 1908. He studied piano in Paris at the Schola Cantorum; later took private lessons with Alfred Cortot, and composition at the Paris Cons. with Paul Dukas; in 1930–34 he had lessons in Granada with Manuel de Falla. He emigrated to the U.S. in 1936; was prof. of music and chairman of the music dept. of Williams College, Williamstown, Mass. (1940–49); in 1950 he was appointed to the faculty of the Univ. of Calif. at Berkeley; became prof. emeritus in 1974. His music retains its national Spanish element, the main influence being that of de Falla, but he employs modern harmonies and characteristic asymmetrical rhythms of the cosmopolitan modern school. He was soloist in his own Piano Concerto at a concert of the Rochester (N.Y.) Phil. in Williamstown, Mass. (Dec 5, 1946); other works are the opera *La Celestina;* Cello Concerto (1963); Piano Quintet (1938); *Tonadas* for Piano (4 books); *Dedication Mass* for Mixed Chorus and Organ; *Jorge Manrique* for Soprano and String Quartet (1963); *A Celebration for Julia,* one-movement string quartet in memory of Julia Hanes Hurley, a music patroness (N.Y., March 3, 1982); also several song cycles.

Nissen, Georg Nikolaus, Danish Councillor of State; b. Hadersleben, Jan. 22, 1761; d. Salzburg, March 24, 1826. He married Mozart's widow in 1809, and collected materials for a biography of Mozart, publ. by his widow in 1828 as *Biographie W.A. Mozarts nach Originalbriefen.*

Nixon, Roger, American composer; b. Tulare, Calif., Aug. 8, 1921. He studied clarinet with a local teacher; in 1940 attended a seminar in composition with Arthur Bliss at the Univ. of Calif. at Berkeley, and in 1941, with Ernest Bloch. In 1942–46 he was in the U.S. Army; he returned in 1947 to Berkeley, where he had fruitful sessions with Sessions (Ph.D., 1952); in the summer of 1948 he took private lessons with Schoenberg. In 1959 he joined the staff of San Francisco State College. A prolific composer, he writes in a consistent modern idiom anchored in fluctuating tonality and diversified by atonal protuberances. His music is marked by distinctly American melorhythms; his miniature opera, *The Bride Comes to Yellow Sky,* is an exemplar of adroit modernistic Westernism fashioned in a non-ethnomusicological manner.

Noble, Ray, English bandleader, composer, and arranger, nephew of **Thomas Tertius Noble;** b. Brighton, Dec. 17, 1903; d. London, April 2, 1978. He received a thorough musical training at Cambridge; formed a band in London, assembled mostly from hotel orch. groups. Most of his arrangements were of English folk tunes; then he began to compose; among his most popular songs was *Goodnight, Sweetheart,* which subsequently became his theme song on American radio shows. In 1934 he went to the U.S.; Glenn Miller helped him to assemble musicians for his band, and he opened at the Rainbow Room in N.Y. on June 1, 1935, seated at a white grand piano on a rotating platform, making tours among the guests at the floorside, and returning to the bandstand at the end of each number. He became extremely successful on network radio shows, appearing not only as a bandleader and composer but also as an actor, usually in the role of a comical Englishman. Besides his theme song— *Goodnight, Sweetheart*—he composed *The Very Thought of You, By the Fireside, The Touch of Your Lips,* and several other hit songs. His *Cherokee,* originally a section of his *American Indian Suite,* became a perennial favorite. Ray Noble demonstrated, in a chorus he wrote for 5 saxophones, his expertise in purely contrapuntal writing with a jazz flavor.

Noble, Thomas Tertius, English organist and composer; b. Bath, May 5, 1867; d. Rockport, Mass., May 4, 1953. He studied organ with Parratt at the Royal College of Music in London, where he also took courses in music theory with Bridge and Stanford. He was subsequently employed as a church organist in Colchester and Cambridge. In 1898 he organized the York Symph. Orch., which he conducted until 1912; he then emigrated to America and served as organist at St. Thomas's Episcopal Church in N.Y., until 1947; he gave his final organ recital, playing his own works, in N.Y. on Feb. 26, 1947. He publ. *The Training of the Boy Chorister* (N.Y., 1943).

Nobre, Marlos, Brazilian composer; b. Recife, Feb. 18, 1939. He studied piano and theory at the Pernambuco Cons. (1946–54); in 1960 went to Rio de Janeiro, where he took composition lessons with H.J. Koellreutter; later studied with Camargo Guarnieri at the São Paulo Cons. (1963–64) and with Alberto Ginastera in Buenos Aires (1963–64); took a course in electronic music with Ussachevsky at Columbia Univ. (1969); was music director of the National Symph. Orch. of Brazil (1971–76). Despite a somewhat quaquaversal efflux of styles and idioms to which he was exposed during his student days, he succeeded in forming a strongly individual manner of musical self-expression, in which sonorous and structural elements are effectively combined with impressionistic, pointillistic, and serial techniques, supplemented by restrained aleatory procedures. He is one of the few contemporary Latin-American composers who does not disdain to make use of native melorhythmic inflections, resulting in ingratiating harmoniousness.

Noda, Ken, fantastically precocious Japanese-American pianist and composer; b. New York, Oct. 5, 1962. He studied piano with Adele Marcus in N.Y.; made his professional debut at 14 as soloist with the Minnesota Orch. in Beethoven's 3rd Piano Concerto (Minneapolis, May 14, 1977); later played with the New York Phil., the St. Louis Symph., and the Baltimore Symph.; in the meantime he took composition lessons with Sylvia Rabinof and Thomas Pasatieri in N.Y. He was only 10 years old when his one-act opera, *The Canary,* was performed (to piano accompaniment) at the Music Festival in Brevard, N.C., on Aug. 18, 1973; the following year, it received first prize in the National Young Composers' Contest sponsored by the National Federation of Music Clubs; he wrote another one-act opera, *The Swing,* in 1974. So impressive were his achievements that in 1976 he was awarded a National Endowment of the Arts grant to write an opera, titled *The Rivalry,* to his own libretto based on a story of Andrew Jackson. He also composed *A Zoo Suite* for Piano (1973); Piano Sonatina (1974); *Prelude and Canon* for Piano (1974); *An Emily Dickinson Song Cycle, A Christina Rossetti Song Cycle,* and *A Cycle of German Poems* (all in 1977). With commendable modesty he acknowledges influences of Mozart, Verdi, Puccini, Rachmaninoff, Menotti, Barber, and Pasatieri.

Nono, Luigi, prominent Italian composer of the musical and political avant-garde; b. Venice, Jan. 29, 1924. He studied jurisprudence at the Univ. of Padua, graduating in 1946; then took lessons in composition with Malipiero at the Cons. of Venice; later studied advanced harmony and counterpoint with Bruno Maderna and Hermann Scherchen. During the final years of World War II he was a participant in the Italian Resistance movement against the Nazis. He became a member of the Italian Communist Party and in 1975 was elected to its Central Committee. In his compositions he adopted Schoenberg's 12-tone method; his devotion to Schoenberg's ideas was strengthened by his marriage to Schoenberg's daughter Nuria. As a resolutely "engaged" artist, Nono mitigates the antinomy between the modern idiom of his music and the conservative Soviet ideology of socialist realism by his militant political attitude and his emphasis on revolutionary subjects in his works, so that even extreme dissonances may be dialectically justified as representing the horrors of Fascism. Nono made 3 visits to the Soviet Union (1963, 1973, 1976), but his works are rarely, if ever, performed there. He makes use of a variety of techniques: serialism, "sonorism" (employment of sonorities for their own sake), aleatory and concrete music, electronics. Perhaps his most militant composition, both politically and musically, is *Intolleranza 1960,* to texts by Brecht, Eluard, Sartre, and Mayakovsky, a protest against imperialist policies and social inequities; at its production in Venice on April 13, 1961, a group of neo-Fascists showered the audience with leaflets denouncing Nono for his alleged contamination of Italian music by alien doctrines, and even making a facetious allusion to his name as representing a double negative.

WORKS: (besides *Intolleranza*): *Variazioni canoniche* for Orch., based on the 12-tone row of Schoenberg's *Ode to Napoleon Buonaparte* (Darmstadt, Aug. 27, 1950); *Polifonica, Monodia, Ritmica* for Flute, Clarinet, Bass Clarinet, Saxophone, Horn, Piano, and Percussion (Darmstadt, July 10, 1951); *España en el corazón* (to words by F.G. Lorca) for Voices and Instruments (Darmstadt, July 21, 1952); ballet, *Der rote Mantel* (Berlin, Sept. 20, 1954); *La Victoire de Guernica* for Voices and Orch. (1954); *Canti* for 13 Instruments (Paris, March 26, 1955); *Incontri* for 24 Instruments (Darmstadt, May 30, 1955); *Varianti* for Violin Solo, Strings, and Woodwinds (Donaueschingen, Oct. 20, 1957); *La terra e la compagna* for Soli, Chorus, and Instruments (Hamburg, Jan. 13, 1958); *Il canto sospeso* for Solo Voices, Chorus, and Orch., to texts from letters by young men and women condemned to death by the Fascists (Cologne, Oct. 24, 1956); *Sarà dolce tacere* for 8 Solo Voices, to texts from "La terra e la morte" by Cesare Pavese (Washington, D.C., Feb. 17, 1961); *La fabbrica illuminata* for Voice and Magnetic Tape (1964); music for the documentary play *Die Ermittlung* by Peter Weiss, dealing with the trial of Nazi guards (Frankfurt, Oct. 19, 1965); *Sul ponte di Hiroscima,* commemorating the victims of the atomic attack on Hiroshima, for Soloists and Orch. (1962); *A Floresta é jovem e cheja de vida,* oratorio to texts from declarations by the Vietnam guerrilla fighters (1966); *Per Bastiana* for Electronic Tape and 3 Orch. Groups (1967); *Non consumiano Marx* for Electronic Sound (1968); *Voci destroying Muros* for Women's Voices and Instruments in Mixed Media, featuring a machine gun pointed toward the audience (1970); *Y entonces comprendió* for Voices and Magnetic Tape, dedicated to Ché Guevara (1970); *Ein Gespenst geht um in der Welt (A Spectre Rises over Europe),* to words from the Communist Manifesto, for Voice and Orch. (Cologne, Feb. 11, 1971); *Como una ola de fuerza y luz* for Singer, Piano, Magnetic Tape, and Orch. (1972); 2 piano concertos (1972, 1975); an opera, *Al gran sole carico d'amore* (1974); *...sofferte onde serene...* for Piano and Tape (1976); *Con Luigi Dallapiccola* for 6 Percussionists and Live Electronics (1979); *Fragmente-Stille, an Diotima* for String Quartet (1979–80); *Das*

atmende Klarsein for Bass Flute, Choir, and Live Electronics (1980–81); *Quando stanno morendo...* for 4 Female Voices, Bass Flute, Cello, and Live Electronics (1982); *Omaggio a György Kurtág* for Trombone and Live Electronics.

Nordheim, Arne, significant Norwegian composer; b. Larvik, June 20, 1931. He studied at the Oslo Cons. (1948–52) with Karl Andersen and Bjarne Brustad; in 1955 took additional instruction with Holmboe in Copenhagen. Returning to Oslo, he joined the avant-garde circles; experimented in pointillistic tone color; adopted a motivic method of melorhythmic structures without formal development. He was a music critic for the Oslo daily *Dagbladet;* in 1968 he visited the U.S. as a lecturer and composer.

Nordica, Lillian (real name, **Lillian Norton**), distinguished American soprano; b. Farmington, Maine, Dec. 12, 1857; d. Batavia, Java, May 10, 1914. She studied with John O'Neill at the New England Cons. in Boston; made her concert debut in Boston in 1876, and toured with the Handel and Haydn Society. In 1878 she traveled to Europe as a soloist with Gilmore's band. She then studied operatic roles in Milan with Antonio Sangiovanni, who suggested the stage name Nordica, which she used for her operatic debut there on March 8, 1879, as Elvira in *Don Giovanni.* In St. Petersburg, she sang for Czar Alexander II a week before he was assassinated in March 1881. After making appearances in several German cities, she made her Paris debut on July 22, 1882, as Marguerite, at the Opéra; on Jan. 22, 1883, she married Frederick A. Gower. With him she returned to America and made her American debut with Colonel Mapleson's company in N.Y. on Nov. 23, 1883. In 1884 she began proceedings for divorce from her first husband, but he mysteriously disappeared while attempting to cross the English Channel in a balloon. She made her debut at Covent Garden in London on March 12, 1886. She first sang at the Metropolitan Opera House in N.Y. on Dec. 18, 1891, as Valentine in *Les Huguenots.* She was heard for the first time as Isolde at the Metropolitan on Nov. 27, 1895, scoring an overwhelming success. From then on she sang chiefly Wagnerian roles; she continued to appear off and on at the Metropolitan until 1909, when she began to make extended concert tours. Her farewell appearance was in Reno, Nev., on June 12, 1913. In 1896 she married the Hungarian tenor Zoltan Doeme, from whom she was divorced in 1904; in 1909 she married the banker George W. Young in London. She died while on a trip around the world.

Nordoff, Paul, American composer; b. Philadelphia, June 4, 1909; d. Herdecke, West Germany, Jan. 18, 1977. He studied piano with Olga Samaroff and composition with Rubin Goldmark at the Juilliard School of Music in N.Y. (1928–33). He subsequently taught composition classes at the Philadelphia Cons. (1937–42), Michigan State College (1945–49), and Bard College (1949–59); afterward devoted himself mainly to music therapy and work with mentally retarded children, in Germany, Finland, and England. He held two Guggenheim fellowships (1933, 1935).

Nordquist, Johan Conrad, Swedish conductor; b. Vänersborg, April 11, 1840; d. Charlottenlund, April 16, 1920. He was a pupil of the Music Academy in Stockholm (1856); joined the court orch. in 1859 as a viola player; in 1864 became regimental bandmaster; in 1876 became chorus master at the Royal Opera; in 1885, became court conductor; in 1888–92, was general director. From 1870 to 1872 and again from 1880 to 1900 he taught at the Stockholm Cons.; then occupied various posts as organist and conductor. He wrote a funeral march for the obsequies of Charles XV (1872) and a festival march for the golden wedding anniversary of Oscar II (1897), besides piano pieces and songs.

Nordraak, Rikard, composer of the Norwegian national hymn, *Ja, vi elsker;* b. Christiania, June 12, 1842; d. Berlin, March 20, 1866. He was a pupil of Kiel and Kullak in Berlin; was a composer with a strong Norwegian nationalist tendency; was a close friend of Grieg, upon whom he exerted a considerable influence, and who wrote a funeral march in his memory. His death at the age of 23 was a grievous loss to Norway's music. Besides the Norwegian national anthem, he wrote music to Björnson's *Mary Stuart in Scotland;* also songs and piano pieces.

Noren, Heinrich Gottlieb (real name, **Heinrich Suso Johannes Gottlieb**—in 1916 he added his wife's name, Noren, to his own), Austrian composer; b. Graz, Jan. 5, 1861; d. Rottach, Bavaria, June 6, 1928. He studied violin with Vieuxtemps in Brussels (1878) and with Massart in Paris (1883); music theory with Bussler in Berlin; in 1895 he settled in Krefeld, where he founded his own music school. He then taught at the Stern Cons. in Berlin (1902–7); in 1915 he moved to Rottach. His name attracted attention with the performance of his orch. variations, *Kaleidoskop* (Dresden, July 1, 1907), in which the last movement, dedicated to "a famous contemporary," was a variation on a theme from *Ein Heldenleben* by Richard Strauss. The publishers of Strauss instituted a lawsuit against Noren, which created a ripple of excitement in musical circles. Noren also composed an opera, *Der Schleier der Beatrice;* a Symph.; a Violin Concerto; and some chamber music.

Norena, Eide (real name, **Kaja Hansen Eide**), Norwegian soprano; b. Horten, April 26, 1884; d. Lausanne, Nov. 19, 1968. She studied voice in Oslo, then in Weimar, London, and Paris; was a pupil of Raimund von Zur Mühlen; began her career as a concert singer in Scandinavia, later joining the Oslo Opera Co.; sang at La Scala in Milan, then at Covent Garden; in 1926–32, she was a member of the Chicago Civic Opera; from 1932 to 1938, of the Metropolitan Opera Co. (made her debut as Mimi, on Feb. 9, 1933); from 1935, of the Paris Opéra; toured the U.S. in concert.

Nørgaard, Per, prominent Danish composer; b. Gentofte, near Copenhagen, July 13, 1932. He studied music theory at the Royal Danish Music Cons. in Copenhagen with Holmboe, Høffding, and Hjelmborg (1952–56) and also took courses with Nadia Boulanger in Paris (1956–57). Returning to Denmark, he taught at the Funen Cons. (1958–60), the Royal Cons. (1960–65), and from 1965, at the Aarhus Cons. After a period of adolescent emulation of Sibelius, he plunged into the mainstream of cosmopolitan music-making, exploring the quasi-mathematical serial techniques based on short tonal motifs, rhythmic displacement, metrical modulation, pointillism, graphic notation, and a "horizontal" invariant fixing certain notes to specific registers; then shifted to a pointillistically impressionistic colorism evolving in a tonal bradykinesis. WORKS: 4 operas: *The Labyrinth* (1963; Copenhagen, Sept. 2, 1967); *Gilgamesh* (1971–72; Aarhus, May 4, 1973); *Siddharta* (1977–79; Stockholm, March 18, 1983); *The Divine Tivoli,* chamber opera (1982); 3 ballets: *Le Jeune Homme à marier* (*The Young Man Is to Marry,* after Ionesco, 1964; Danish Television, April 2, 1965; first stage perf., Copenhagen, Oct. 15, 1967), *Tango Chicane* (Copenhagen, Oct. 15, 1967), and *Trio* for 3 Dancers and Percussion (Paris, Dec., 1972); 3 oratorios: *It Happened in Those Days,* Christmas oratorio for youth (1960); *Dommen (The Judgement),* Easter oratorio for youth (1962); *Babel* (1964; Stockholm, Sept. 15, 1966); *Metamorphose* for Strings (1952); 4 symphs.: No. 1, *Sinfonia austera* (1954; Danish Radio, Aug. 19, 1958); No. 2 (1970; Aarhus, April 13, 1970); No. 3, with Chorus and Organ (1972–75; Copenhagen, Sept. 2, 1976); No. 4, *Indian Rose Garden and Chinese Witch Lake* (Hamburg, Oct. 30, 1981); *Triptychon* for Mixed Voices, and Wind Instruments or Organ (1957); *Constellations,* concerto for 12 Solo Strings or 12 String Groups (Copenhagen, Nov. 3, 1958); *Lyse Danse* for Chamber Orch. (1959); *Fragment VI* for 6 Orch. Groups: Winds, Brass, Percussion, Harp, Pianos, Timpani (1959–61; Aarhus, Feb. 12, 1962); *Nocturnes,* suite for Soprano, and Piano or 19 Instruments (1961–62); *3 Love Songs* for Contralto and Orch. (1963); *Prism* for 3 Vocalists and Instrumental Ensemble (1964); *Composition* for Small Orch. (1966); *Iris* for Orch. (Copenhagen, May 19, 1967); *Luna, 4 Phases* for Orch. (Danish Radio, Sept. 5, 1968); *Recall* for Accordion and Orch. (1968); *Voyage into the Golden Screen* for Chamber Orch. (Copenhagen, March 24, 1969); *Mosaic* for 16 Winds (1969); *Doing* for Wind Orch. (1969); *Lilá* for 11 Instruments (1972); Quintet for Flute, Violin, Viola, Cello, and Piano (1951–52); *Suite* for Flute and Piano (1952); *Solo intimo* for Solo Cello (1953); *Diptychon* for Violin and Piano (1953); 2 trios for Clarinet, Cello, and Piano (1955, 1974); *Songs from Aftonland* for Contralto, Flute, Harp, Violin, Viola, and Cello (1956); 3 string quartets: No. 1, *Quartetto brioso* (1958); No. 2, *In 3 Spheres* (1965); No. 3, *Inscape* (1969); *Miniatures* for String Quartet (1959); 2 piano sonatas (1952, 1957);

Trifoglio for Piano (1953); *4 Sketches* and *9 Studies* for Piano (1959); *Travels* for Piano (1969); electronic pieces; incidental music; songs.

Norman, Jessye, black American soprano; b. Augusta, Ga., Sept. 15, 1945. She received a scholarship to study at Howard Univ. in Washington, D.C.; then continued her musical training at the Peabody Cons. of Music in Baltimore; also studied with Pierre Bernac at the Univ. of Michigan. She made her operatic debut at the Deutsche Oper in West Berlin in 1969; then sang in Rome and Florence. In 1972 she appeared at La Scala in Milan; she made her debut at the Metropolitan Opera in N.Y. on Sept. 26, 1983, in *Les Troyens.* In addition to opera, she became a successful as a solo performer in recital.

North, Alex, American composer and conductor; b. Chester, Pa., Dec. 4, 1910. He studied at the Curtis Inst. in Philadelphia and at the Juilliard School of Music in N.Y.; also took private lessons with Ernst Toch in Los Angeles. He began his career as a composer for documentary films and gradually established himself as a composer of imaginative cinema music; wrote the scores for *Death of a Salesman, Viva Zapata!, A Streetcar Named Desire, The Bad Seed, The Sound and the Fury, Spartacus, The Misfits, Cleopatra, The Agony and the Ecstasy,* and *Who's Afraid of Virginia Woolf?* His song *Unchained Melody* acquired great popularity. Apart from these lucrative tasks, he composed grand symphs., modernistic concertos, and unorthodox cantatas.
WORKS: *Rhapsody* for Piano and Orch. (N.Y., Nov. 11, 1941); *Revue* for Clarinet and Orch. (N.Y., Nov. 20, 1946, Benny Goodman, soloist; Leonard Bernstein conducting); Symph. No. 1 (1947); *Morning Star Cantata* (N.Y., May 18, 1947); *Little Indian Drum* for Narrator and Orch. (N.Y., Oct. 19, 1947); *Negro Mother Cantata* (N.Y., May 17, 1948); *Holiday Set* for Orch. (Saratoga, N.Y., July 10, 1948); Symph. No. 2 (1968); Symph. No. 3 (1971; incorporating parerga & paralipomena from the score originally written for the film *2001, A Space Odyssey,* which was not used in the actual production).

Noskowski, Sigismund (Zygmunt von), significant Polish conductor and composer; b. Warsaw, May 2, 1846; d. there, July 23, 1909. He studied at the Warsaw Music Inst.; then became an instructor in a school for the blind, and devised a music notation for the blind. He subsequently went to Germany, where he studied composition with Kiel in Berlin. After a brief period of professional activities in Western Europe, he returned to Warsaw and was director of the Music Society there (1881–92); in 1888 he was appointed a prof. at the Warsaw Cons.; later conducted at the Warsaw Opera and led some concerts of the Warsaw Phil. Society. He wrote the operas *Livia Quintilla* (Lwow, Feb. 1, 1898), *Wyrok* (Warsaw, Nov. 15, 1906), and *Zemsta* (Warsaw, 1909); 3 symphs. (1875, 1880, 1903); and several symph. poems, of which *Step* (1897) became quite popular in Poland; also chamber music and songs.

He publ. 2 collections of folk melodies and was co-author with M. Zawirski of a book on harmony and counterpoint (Warsaw, 1909).

Notker (Balbulus), a monk at the Monastery of St. Gall; b. Elgg, near Zürich (or Jonschwyl, near St. Gall), c.840; d. April 6, 912. He was one of the earliest and most important writers of sequences; his *Liber hymnorum* (sequence texts of the year 884) is of particular interest. Several short musical treatises in Latin and German are traditionally ascribed to him; but these should be more correctly attributed to a certain **Notker Labeo,** who was also a monk at St. Gall but who flourished about a century later than Notker "Balbulus" (a nickname meaning "the stammerer"). It has also been established that Notker Balbulus was not the author of the *Media in vita in morte sumus* (cf. P. Wagner, "Das Media vita," in *Schweizerisches Jahrbuch für Musikwissenschaft,* I). Gerbert (*Scriptores,* I) publ. 4 of the above-mentioned treatises, together with a commentary on the so-called "Romanian" letters (probably spurious). Two of these treatises, also a 5th one (presumably also by N. Labeo), are included in Riemann's *Studien zur Geschichte der Notenschrift.* All 5 treatises were publ. by Piper in 2 vols. as part of the projected collected edition of Notker Labeo's works.

Nottebohm, (Martin) Gustav, distinguished German musicologist; b. Lüdenscheid, Westphalia, Nov. 12, 1817; d. Graz, Oct. 29, 1882. He studied with Berger and Dehn in Berlin (1838–39); then with Mendelssohn and Schumann in Leipzig (1840–45); finally with Sechter in Vienna (1846), where he settled as a music teacher. He revised the Beethoven edition publ. by Breitkopf & Härtel, prepared thematic catalogues of the works of Beethoven and Schubert, and edited some of the works of Mozart. Of particular importance are his studies of Beethoven's sketchbooks.

Nouguès, Jean, French composer; b. Bordeaux, April 25, 1875; d. Auteuil, Aug. 28, 1932. He showed remarkable precocity as a composer, having completed an opera, *Le Roi du Papagey,* before he was 16. After regular study in Paris, he produced his opera *Yannha* at Bordeaux in 1897. The next 2 operas, *Thamyris* (Bordeaux, 1904) and *La Mort de Tintagiles* (Paris, 1905), were brought out without much success; but after the production of his spectacular *Quo Vadis* (text by H. Cain, after Sienkiewicz's famous novel; Nice, Feb. 9, 1909) he suddenly found himself famous. The work was given in Paris on Nov. 26, 1909, in N.Y on April 4, 1911; had numerous revivals in subsequent years. His later operas failed to measure up to *Quo Vadis;* they included *L'Auberge rouge* (Nice, Feb. 21, 1910), *La Vendetta* (Marseilles, 1911), *L'Aiglon* (Rouen, Feb. 2, 1912), and *Le Scarabée bleu* (1931).

Nourrit, Adolphe, celebrated French tenor; b. Montpellier, March 3, 1802; d. (suicide) Naples, March 8, 1839. His father, **Louis Nourrit** (1780–1831), was a leading opera tenor in France; Adolphe Nourrit studied voice with the famous teacher Manuel García; at the age of 19 he made his debut as Pylaides in Gluck's opera *Iphigénie en Tauride* at the Paris Opéra (Sept. 10, 1821), with excellent success. He soon became known in Paris as one of the finest tenors of his generation, and famous opera composers entrusted him with leading roles at the premieres of their works; thus, he appeared in the title role of Meyerbeer's *Robert le Diable* (Paris, Nov. 21, 1831) and as Raoul in *Les Huguenots* (Paris, Feb. 29, 1836); in the title role in Rossini's *Le Comte Ory* (Paris, Aug. 20, 1828) and as Arnold in his *Guillaume Tell* (Paris, Aug. 3, 1829); as Masaniello in Auber's *La Muette de Portici* (Paris, Feb. 29, 1828); as Eléazar in Halévy's *La Juive* (Paris, Feb. 23, 1835); and others. He then traveled in Italy in Dec. 1837, and was particularly successful in Naples. His career seemed to be assured, but despite all these successes, vocal problems and a liver ailment led to depression, and he killed himself by jumping from the roof of his lodging in Naples.

Nováček, Ottokar, American violinist and composer of Czech descent; b. Weisskirchen, Hungary, May 13, 1866; d. New York, Feb. 3, 1900. He studied violin with his father, Martin Joseph Nováček, and with Brodsky at the Leipzig Cons., graduating in 1885. In 1891 he was engaged by Nikisch to join the Boston Symph. Orch., of which Nikisch was the music director. In America, Nováček began to compose; his name became known chiefly through his brilliant violin piece *Perpetuum mobile;* he also wrote a Piano Concerto; 3 string quartets; *8 Concert-Caprices* for Violin and Piano; *Bulgarian Dances* for Violin and Piano; and songs.

Novães, Guiomar, extraordinary Brazilian pianist; b. São João da Bõa Vista, Feb. 28, 1895; d. São Paulo, March 7, 1979. She was the 17th of 19 offspring in a highly fecund family; studied piano with a local Italian teacher, Luigi Chiafarelli; soon began performing in public recitals. The Brazilian government sent her to France to take part in a competition for entering the Paris Cons.; she won first place among 388 contestants from a jury that included Debussy and Fauré; Debussy praised her for "the power of total inner concentration, rare among artists." She enrolled in the class of Isidor Philipp, who later described her as a true "force of nature." She graduated from the Paris Cons. in 1911, and made a successful concert tour in France, England, and Italy. She made her American debut at a N.Y. recital on Nov. 11, 1915, and subsequently made numerous tours of the U.S. Reviewing one of her concerts, James Huneker described her as "the Paderewska of the Pampas." In 1922 she married the Brazilian composer **Octavio Pinto.** She made her home in São Paulo, with frequent sojourns in N.Y. In 1956 the Brazilian government awarded her the Order of Merit as a goodwill ambassador to the U.S. She made her last American appearance in 1972. She was especially praised for her interpretations of the music of Chopin, Schumann, and other composers of the Romantic era; she also played pieces by South American composers, including some works written for her by her husband. Her playing was notable for its dynamic colors; she exuded a personal charm, while often disregarding the more pedantic aspects of the music.

Novák, Jan, Czech composer; b. Nová Říše, April 8, 1921. He studied piano with local teachers, and composition with Petrželka at the Brno Cons. (1940–46) and with Bořkovec at the Prague Academy of Musical Arts (1946–47); during the summer of 1947 he attended the composition classes of Aaron Copland at the Berkshire Music Center at Tanglewood, Mass., and also took lessons with Martinu in N.Y. (1947–48). Returning to Czechoslovakia, he lived in Brno; but left the country in the wake of the political events of 1968; he moved to Denmark (1968–70) and in 1970 settled in Rovereto, Italy, where he taught piano at the municipal music school.

Novák, Johann Baptist, Slovenian composer; b. Ljubljana, 1756; d. there, Jan. 29, 1833. He served as a government clerk and at the same time studied music; in 1799–1800 was conductor, and in 1808–25 music director, of the Phil. Society in Ljubljana; he gave concerts as a singer and violinist. A close contemporary of Mozart, he composed in a Mozartean manner. His historical importance lies in his incidental music to *Figaro,* a play in the Slovenian language based on the same comedy by Beaumarchais that served for Mozart's great opera. Novák's music forms a striking parallel to Mozart's procedures and yet contains some original traits.

Novák, Vítězslav, eminent Czech composer; b. Kamenitz, Dec. 5, 1870; d. Skuteč, July 18, 1949. He studied jurisprudence and philosophy at the Univ. of Prague, and music at the Cons. there, where his teachers were Jiránek, Stecker, and Dvořák. From 1909 to 1920 he taught at the Prague Cons., and from 1918 to 1939 was a prof. of composition at the Master School of the Czech State Cons. Brahms was the first to discover the extraordinary talent of Novák, and recommended him to his own publisher, Simrock. Novák's early works follow the general line of German Romantic composition, but in his operas and symph. poems he showed a profound feeling for national elements in Czech music. In 1946 he received the title of National Artist of the Republic of Czechoslovakia.

Novello, (Joseph) Alfred, English music publisher, son of **Vincent Novello;** b. London, Aug. 12, 1810; d. Genoa, July 16, 1896. He was also a bass singer, organist, and composer; was choirmaster at Lincoln's Inn Chapel. He entered his father's business at 19. He inaugurated an important innovation, the printing of separate vocal parts for choir use; did much to popularize classical music in England by publishing cheap oratorio scores. After his retirement he lived in Genoa.

Novello, Clara Anastasia, daughter of **Vincent**

Novello; English soprano; b. London, June 10, 1818; d. Rome, March 12, 1908. Having studied piano and singing in London, she entered the Paris Cons. in 1829, but returned home the following year because of the revolution. After a successful debut on Oct. 22, 1832, at Windsor, she was engaged for the Phil. Society, the Antient Concerts, and the principal festivals. In 1837 Mendelssohn engaged her for the Gewandhaus concerts; she then sang in Berlin, Vienna, and St. Petersburg. She made her operatic debut in Padua (July 6, 1841); sang with great success in the principal Italian cities. On Nov. 22, 1843, she married Count Gigliucci, withdrawing to private life for several years; she reappeared in 1850, singing in concert and opera (chiefly in England and Italy). After her farewell appearance in London in 1860, she retired to Rome. Schumann greatly admired Clara Novello, and coined the term Novelette for some of his pieces as an affectionate homage to her.

Novello, Vincent, English music publisher; b. London, Sept. 6, 1781; d. Nice, Aug. 9, 1861. He was a chorister in the Sardinian Chapel on Duke Street; later deputy organist to Webbe and Danby, and in 1797–1822, organist at the chapel of the Portuguese Embassy. He was pianist to the Italian Opera in 1812; was a founder of the Phil. Society in 1813, sometimes conducting its concerts; in 1840–43, was organist at the Roman Catholic Chapel in Moorfields. In 1811 he founded the great London music publishing firm of **Novello & Co.** Himself a composer of sacred music (masses, motets, anthems, Kyries, etc.), he gathered together and publ. excellent collections: *A Collection of Sacred Music* (1811; 2 vols.); *Purcell's Sacred Music* (1829; 5 vols.); *Croft's Anthems; Greene's Anthems; Boyce's Anthems;* masses by Haydn, Mozart, Beethoven; etc. He retired to Nice in 1849.

Novello & Co., prominent firm of music publishers, founded 1811 in London by **Vincent Novello.** Under the management of his eldest son, **(Joseph) Alfred Novello,** the business increased enormously, and after the latter's retirement in 1856, **Henry Littleton** (b. London, Jan. 2, 1823; d. there, May 11, 1888), who became a partner in 1861, assumed the general management, becoming sole proprietor in 1866. The following year he acquired the business of Ewer and Co., and in 1867 changed the name of the firm to **Novello, Ewer & Co.** On his retirement in 1887 he was succeeded by his sons, **Alfred H.** and **Augustus J. Littleton,** and his sons-in-law, **George T.S. Gill** and **Henry W. Brooke.** In 1898 the house was formed into a limited company, under the name of Novello & Co., Ltd. In 1846 they acquired *Mainzer's Musical Times* (established 1844), which they have publ. since then as the *Musical Times.* The N.Y. branch, established in 1850, was taken over in 1906 by H.W. Gray & Co.

Novello-Davies, Clara, Welsh singing teacher and choral conductor; b. Cardiff, April 7, 1861; d. London, March 1, 1943. Her real surname was Davies; her father (who was also her first teacher) called her "Clara Novello" after the celebrated singer of that name, and she adopted the combined name professionally. She sang at concerts; in 1881 she turned to choral conducting; organized a Royal Welsh Ladies' Choir, with which she traveled with fine success in Great Britain, France, America, and South Africa; at the World's Fair in Chicago (1893) and at the Paris Exposition of 1900 the chorus was awarded first prize. She was commended by Queen Victoria (1894) and by King George and Queen Mary (1928). She publ. a number of successful songs (*A Voice from the Spirit Land, The Vigil, Comfort,* etc.); was also author of the book *You Can Sing* and an autobiography, *The Life I Have Loved* (London, 1940). Her son, **Ivor Novello** (b. Cardiff, Jan. 15, 1893; d. London, March 6, 1951), wrote (at her request) the song *Keep the Home Fires Burning,* immensely popular during World War I.

Novotná, Jarmila, Czech soprano; b. Prague, Sept. 23, 1907. She studied with Emmy Destinn; made her debut in *La Traviata* (Prague, June 27, 1926); in 1928 joined the roster of the Berlin State Opera. She made her American debut at San Francisco, in *Madama Butterfly* (Oct. 18, 1939); first sang at the Metropolitan Opera in N.Y. in *La Bohème,* on Jan. 5, 1940; remained on its staff until 1951; again from 1952–56; then retired to Vienna.

Novotný, Václav Juda, Bohemian composer; b. Wesetz, near Počatek, Sept. 17, 1849; d. Prague, Aug. 1, 1922. He studied at the Prague Organ School with Skuherský; for many years was editor of the Bohemian musical paper *Dalibor;* composed pieces for violin and songs; compiled a large collection of Bohemian folk songs; trans. into Czech about 100 opera texts, among them all the dramatic works of Wagner.

Nowak, Leopold, eminent Austrian musicologist; b. Vienna, Aug. 17, 1904. He studied piano and organ with Louis Dité and counterpoint with Franz Schmidt at the Vienna Academy of Music; then took courses in musicology with Guido Adler and Robert Lach at the Univ. of Vienna; received his Ph.D. there in 1927 with the dissertation *Das deutsche Gesellschaftslied bei Heinrich Finck, Paul Hofhaymer und Heinrich Isaac;* completed his Habilitation with his *Grundzüge einer Geschichte des Basso ostinato* (publ. in Vienna, 1932). He lectured at the Univ. of Vienna from 1932 until 1973; in 1945 he became editor of the critical edition of Bruckner's works; from 1946 to 1969 he was director of the music division of the Nationalbibliothek in Vienna, where he compiled valuable catalogues for special exhibitions on Bruckner, Bach, Mozart, Haydn, and others. His exhaustive studies on the life and music of Bruckner are of prime value.

Nunó, Jaime, Spanish bandmaster; composer of the Mexican national anthem; b. San Juan de las Abadesas, Sept. 8, 1824; d. Auburndale, N.Y., July 18, 1908. He studied with Mercadante in Italy; in 1851 went to Cuba, and in 1854 to Mexico, where he was appointed chief of military bands; was commissioned to write a national anthem for Mexico; it was sung for the first time on Sept. 15, 1854. Subsequently he was active as an impresario for Italian opera companies in Cuba, Mexico, and the U.S.

Nyiregyházi, Erwin, remarkable Hungarian pianist; b. Budapest, Jan. 19, 1903. He absorbed music by a kind of domestic osmosis, from his father, a professional tenor, and his mother, an amateur pianist. An exceptionally gifted *wunderkind,* he had perfect pitch and a well-nigh phonographic memory as a very small child; played a Haydn sonata and pieces by Grieg, Chopin, and himself at a concert in Fiume at the age of 6. In 1910 he entered the Budapest Academy of Music, studying theory with Albert Siklós and Leo Weiner, and piano with István Tomán. In 1914 the family moved to Berlin, where he became a piano student of Ernst von Dohnányi. He made his debut in Germany playing Beethoven's 3rd Piano Concerto with the Berlin Phil. (Oct. 14, 1915). In 1916 he began studying with Frederic Lamond, a pupil of Liszt, who was instrumental in encouraging Nyiregyházi to study Liszt's music, which was to become the most important part of his concert repertoire. In 1920 he went to the U.S.; his American debut (Carnegie Hall, N.Y., Oct. 18, 1920) was sensationally successful; the word "genius" was freely applied to him by critics usually restrained in their verbal effusions. Inexplicably, his American career suffered a series of setbacks; he became involved in a lawsuit with his manager; he married his next manager, a Mrs. Mary Kelen, in 1926, but divorced her a year later. He then went to California, where he became gainfully employed as a studio pianist in Hollywood; in 1930 he made a European tour; then lived in N.Y. and in Los Angeles. Beset by personal problems, he fell into a state of abject poverty, but resolutely refused to resume his concert career; he did not even own a piano. He married frequently, and as frequently divorced his successive wives. In 1972 he married his 9th wife, a lady 10 years his senior; she died shortly afterward. Attempts were made in vain by friends and admirers in California to induce him to play in public; a semi-private recital was arranged for him in San Francisco in 1974; a recording of his playing of Liszt was issued in 1977; it was greeted with enthusiastic reviews, all expressing regret for his disappearance from the concert stage. Nyiregyházi composed several hundred works, mostly for piano; they remain in MS. As a child, Nyiregyházi was the object of a "scientific" study by Dr. Géza Révész, director of the Psychological Laboratory in Amsterdam, who made tests of his memory, sense of pitch, ability to transpose into different keys at sight, etc.; these findings were publ. in German as *Psychologische Analyse eines musikalisch hervorragenden Kindes* (Leipzig, 1916) and in Eng. as *The Psychology of a Musical Prodigy* (London, 1925), but the examples given and the tests detailed in the book proved to be no more unusual than the capacities of thousands of similarly gifted young musicians.

Nystroem, Gösta, Swedish composer; b. Silvberg, Oct. 13, 1890; d. Särö, near Göteborg, Aug. 9, 1966. He studied piano with his father and theory with Hallen. In 1919 he went to Paris, where he took courses with Vincent d'Indy, Chevillard, and the Russian musician Leonid Sabaneyev, at that time living in France. In 1932 Nystroem returned to Sweden. His music is marked with Romantic tendencies, tinged with Impressionism.

Oakeley, Sir Herbert Stanley, English composer; b. Ealing, Middlesex, July 22, 1830; d. London, Oct. 26, 1903. He studied at Oxford; later attended the Leipzig Cons.; also took organ lessons in Dresden and Bonn. In 1865 he was appointed a prof. of music at Edinburgh Univ., and held this post until 1891; was influential in the musical affairs of Scotland in general. He wrote a cantata, *Jubilee Lyric; Suite in the Olden Style* for Orch.; many pieces of church music; choruses; arrangements of Scottish national melodies; etc.

Obouhov, Nicolas, remarkable Russian composer; b. Moscow, April 22, 1892; d. Paris, June 13, 1954. He studied at the St. Petersburg Cons. with Nicolas Tcherepnin and Maximilian Steinberg; after the Revolution he emigrated to France and lived in Paris, where he had some instruction from Ravel. As early as 1914 he began experimenting with harmonic combinations containing 12 different notes without duplication (he called his system "absolute harmony"). In 1915 he devised a special notation for this type of harmony, entirely enharmonic, with crosses indicating sharps or flats; several composers, among them Honegger, wrote pieces in Obouhov's notation. He gave a demonstration of his works written and notated in this system in Petro-grad at a concert organized by the editors of the review *Muzykalnyi Sovremennik* on Feb. 3, 1916. He devoted his entire life to the composition of his magnum opus, *Le Livre de vie,* for Solo Voices, Chorus, 2 Pianos, and Orch. The MS score, some 2,000 pages long, was deposited after his death at the Bibliothèque Nationale in Paris. A mystic, Obouhov signed his name "Nicolas l'illuminé" and used his own blood to mark sections in the score; the finale represented the spiritual and religious apotheosis in which both the old and the new Russian societies and political factions become reunited. In this and some other scores Obouhov introduced shouting, screaming, sighing, and groaning sounds for the voice parts. A section of *Le Livre de vie* was performed by Koussevitzky in Paris on June 3, 1926. In quest of new sonorities, Obouhov devised an electronic instrument, the "croix sonore," in the form of a cross, and composed works for it, which were performed by Mme. Aussenac de Broglie. He publ. *Traité d'harmonie tonale, atonale et totale* (Paris, 1946), which presents an exposition of his system.

Oboussier, Robert, Swiss composer; b. Antwerp (of Swiss parents), July 9, 1900; d. (stabbed to death by his roommate), Zürich, June 9, 1957. He studied at the Cons. of Zürich, with Volkmar Andreae and

919

Philipp Jarnach (composition); then with Siegfried Ochs in Berlin (conducting). He then lived in Florence (1922–28); was music editor of the *Deutsche Allgemeine Zeitung;* but in 1938 political conditions in Germany impelled him to leave for Switzerland; in 1942 he became director of the Central Archive of Swiss Music. Of cosmopolitan background, he combined in his music the elements of both Germanic and Latin cultures. His collection of critical reviews, *Berliner Musik-Chronik 1930–38,* was publ. posthumously in 1969.

Obradović, Aleksandar, Serbian composer; b. Bled, Aug. 22, 1927. He studied composition with Logar at the Belgrade Academy of Music, graduating in 1952; had advanced studies with Lennox Berkeley in London (1959–60); traveled to Russia in 1963; spent a year in the U.S. studying at the Columbia Univ. electronic music center in N.Y. (1966–67); in 1969 he was appointed a prof. at the Belgrade Academy of Music. Formally, his music adheres to the architectonic Classical design with strongly discernible tonal centers, but he experiments with atonal thematics and polytonal harmonies; in some of his works he applies explicit dodecaphonic formulas.

Obraztsova, Elena, outstanding Russian mezzo-soprano; b. Leningrad, July 7, 1937. Her father was an engineer who played the violin. She studied voice at the Leningrad Cons., graduating in 1964; made her operatic debut at the Bolshoi Theater in Moscow during the 1964–65 season as Marina in *Boris Godunov;* won first prize at the International Tchaikovsky Competition in Moscow in 1970. She made her first tour of the U.S. with the Bolshoi troupe in June–July 1975; on Oct. 12, 1976, she made her Metropolitan Opera debut in N.Y. as Princess de Bouillon in Cilèa's *Adriana Lecouvreur.* She was awarded the Lenin prize in 1976. She possesses a remarkably even tessitura, brilliant in all registers; her roles include virtually the entire Russian operatic repertoire, and such parts of the standard operas as Norma, Amneris, and Carmen.

Obrecht (Hobrecht, Obreht, Obertus, Hobertus), Jacob, famous Netherlandish contrapuntist; b. Bergen-op-Zoom, Nov. 22, 1450 (or 1451); d. Ferrara, 1505 (of the pestilence). The son of a city trumpeter, he received his rudimentary musical training in his native town; he entered the Univ. of Louvain on Aug. 17, 1470; then returned to Bergen-op-Zoom; took Holy Orders, and said his first Mass as an ordained priest there on April 23, 1480. He was named *maître des enfants* at Cambrai on July 28, 1484; was in Bruges from 1485 to 1487; at the request of the Duke of Ferrara, he obtained a leave of absence for 6 months to travel to Italy; arrived in Ferrara in Dec. 1487; returned to Bruges in 1488, and remained there until 1491, when he became music director at Notre-Dame in Antwerp; he visited Bergen-op-Zoom in 1496–97, after which he went again to Bruges; at various times was also in Antwerp. In 1504 he once more entered the service of the ducal court at Ferrara, where he remained until his death. He was a prolific composer; his masses, motets, hymns, etc., are found in various collections of the period, and also in the Archives of the Papal Chapel. He was well known in Italy during his lifetime; Petrucci publ. the collection *Missae Obrecht* (1503), containing the masses *Je ne demande, Grecorum, Fortuna desperata, Malheur me bat,* and *Salve diva parens;* the collection *Missae diversorum* (vol. I) includes Obrecht's mass *Si dedero.* The extensive edition of Obrecht's works in 7 vols., edited by Johannes Wolf (1908–21, Amsterdam and Leipzig), contains 24 masses, 22 motets, chansons, and the famous 4-part Passion according to St. Matthew, the oldest known polyphonic setting of this text. Since the publication of this edition, additional works by Obrecht have been brought to light. On the other hand, some works formerly attributed to him have been proved to be spurious; thus another Passion, long thought to have been by Obrecht, was apparently by a chapel singer named Longueval, in the court of King Louis XII of France. A new *Opera omnia,* edited by A. Smijers, began publication in 1953 (Vereeniging voor Nederlandse Muziekgeschiedenis, Amsterdam).

Obukhova, Nadezhda, Russian mezzo-soprano; b. Moscow, March 6, 1886; d. Feodosiya, Aug. 14, 1961. She studied with Masetti at the Moscow Cons., graduating in 1912. She made her debut at the Bolshoi Theater there in 1916 as Pauline in *The Queen of Spades;* remained on its roster until 1943. In addition to the Russian repertoire, she was noted for her portrayals of Carmen, Dalila, Amneris, and others. She was greatly esteemed in Russia; in 1943 she was awarded the State Prize of the U.S.S.R.

Ockeghem (or **Okeghem, Okenghem, Ockenheim,** etc.), **Johannes** (or **Jean de**), great Flemish contrapuntist and teacher; b. East Flanders, c.1410; d. Tours, Feb. 6, 1496 (old-style calendar), according to an entry in the Archives Nationales, Paris. He was probably a pupil of Binchois; was a boy chorister at Antwerp Cathedral (1443–44); a chorister in the chapel of Duke Charles of Bourbon (1446–48); a pupil of Dufay in Cambrai (1449); a chorister in the royal chapel (1452–53); from 1454, was composer and first chaplain to 3 successive kings of France: Charles VII, Louis XI, and Charles VIII; was treasurer of the Abbey of St.-Martin at Tours; in 1465 was "maître de la chapelle du roy"; in 1469 he traveled to Spain, and in 1484 to Flanders, at the King's expense. Upon Ockeghem's death, Guillaume Crétin wrote a poetic "Déploration," and Josquin Des Prez (his greatest pupil) and Lupi composed musical epitaphs. Important both as a teacher and composer, Ockeghem was the leader of the 2nd generation of the great Franco-Flemish school of the 15th century (which includes Busnois, Regis, and Caron). His art expresses the mysticism of the Netherlands in the late Middle Ages; his technical skill in the development of purely formal resources, while very important, is not the most prominent characteristic of his style, as most historians have asserted. At the same time, Ockeghem's achievements in the art of imitative counterpoint unquestionably make his music a milestone on the way to the a cappella style of the coming generations.

WORKS: 16 masses and individual sections of masses; 9 motets; a ninefold canon-motet, *Deo gratias*, in 36 parts (of doubtful authenticity); about 20 chansons and one canon (*Fuga a 3 in epidiatessaron* = the chanson *Prenez sur moi*). Burney, Forkel, Kiesewetter, Schlecht, Ambros-Kade, Wooldridge, and P. Wagner have printed fragments of the mass *Cujusvis toni (ad omnem tonum); Bellermann (Die Mensuralnoten und Taktzeichen),* a fragment of the *Missa Prolationum;* Riemann, in *Musikgeschichte in Beispielen* (1912; no. 16) and in *Handbuch der Musikgeschichte* (II, 1), fragments of the mass *Pour quelque peine* (probably not by Ockeghem); the masses *Caput* and *Le Serviteur* (the latter probably a work of V. Faugues, according to Tinctoris [Coussemaker, *Scriptores*, IV, 146a]) are publ. in their entirety in Denkmäler der Tonkunst in Österreich, 38 (19.i); the mass *Mi mi* (ed. for practical use by H. Besseler) is in F. Blume's *Das Chorwerk,* #4 (1928); 2 sections of the mass *L'Homme armé* are in A.T. Davison and W. Apel, *Historical Anthology of Music* (Cambridge, Mass., 1947); a motet, *Alma redemptoris mater,* is in *Altniederländische Motetten* (Kassel, 1929), ed. by H. Besseler; another motet, *Ut heremita solus,* in Schering's *Geschichte der Musik in Beispielen* (1931; no. 52); the "Déploration" on the death of Binchois, *Mort tu as navré,* in J. Marix's *Les Musiciens de la cour de Bourgogne au XVᵉ siècle* (1937; no. 54); the motet *Intemerata Dei Mater,* in Smijers's *Muziekgeschiedenis in Voorbeelden,* I (1939); the canon-motet in 36 parts, in Riemann's *Handbuch der Musikgeschichte,* II, 1. Regarding the chansons, there are 4 in Ambros-Kade's *Geschichte,* V; 4 in O. Gombosi's *Jacob Obrecht* (1925); one in J. Wolf's *Sing- und Spielmusik aus älterer Zeit* (1926); 8 in *Trois chansonniers français du XVᵉ siècle,* I (1927), ed. by Droz-Rokseth-Thibault; 2 in K. Jeppesen's *Der Kopenhagener Chansonnier* (1927); and 2 in Davison and Apel, *Historical Anthology of Music.* A 3-part chanson, *O rosa bella,* by Hert, with a new discantus added to it by Ockeghem, is in Denkmäler der Tonkunst in Österreich, 14/15 (7). The *Fuga in epidiatessaron* has been discussed, reprinted, and solved with more or less success by innumerable writers; reprints are to be found in Jeppesen, Droz-Rokseth-Thibault, and J.S. Levitan (see below). A complete ed. of Ockeghem's works, edited by D. Plamenac, was begun in 1927 in the *Publikationen älterer Musik* of the Deutsche Musikgesellschaft, with a vol. containing 8 masses (new ed. of this vol., N.Y., 1958; vol. 2, containing 8 masses and Mass sections, N.Y., 1947; revised 1966).

Odak, Krsto, Croatian composer; b. Siverić, Dalmatia, March 20, 1888; d. Zagreb, Nov. 4, 1965. He studied composition with P. Hartmann in Munich (1911–13) and with Novák in Prague. Upon his return to Yugoslavia, he was prof. of composition at the Music Academy of Zagreb, retiring in 1961. He wrote 4 symphs. (1940, 1953, 1961, 1965); the operetta *Dorica pleše (Dorrit Dances;* 1934); the radio opera *Majka Margarita (Mother Margaret;* Zagreb, 1955); Piano Concerto (1963); 4 string quartets (1925, 1927, 1934, 1957); 2 masses in the old Slavonic language; other sacred works; song cycles.

Odington, Walter (Walter of Evesham), a Benedictine monk at the monastery of Evesham; he was at Oxford in 1316, and at Merton College there in 1330. He is one of the chief medieval writers on mensural notation; his *De speculatione musices* (MS in Corpus Christi College, Cambridge) was printed by Coussemaker in 1864 (*Scriptores,* I; modern ed. by F. Hammond, *Walteri Odington Summa de speculatione musicae,* in Corpus Scriptorum de Musica, XIV, 1970). This work is particularly valuable for the light it throws on musical rhythm as practiced in the late 13th century; it also discusses intervals, notation, musical instruments, and musical forms (rondellus, motet, etc.). His views on consonance and dissonance are interesting for their acceptance of thirds and sixths as legitimate consonances. He was also noted as an astronomer.

Odo de Cluny (Saint), important musical theorist of the 10th century; b. near Le Mans, 879; d. Tours, Nov. 18, 942. A pupil of Rémy d'Auxerre in Paris, he took Holy Orders at 19, and in 899 was canon and choir singer at Tours; in 909 he entered the Benedictine monastery at Baume, near Besançon, and then was successively abbot at Aurillac, Fleuri, and (from 927) Cluny. The famous medieval treatise *Dialogus de musica* (also known as *Enchiridion musices*) is attributed to him without foundation (it is printed in Gerbert's *Scriptores* and, in Eng. trans., in Oliver Strunk's *Source Readings in Music History,* N.Y., 1950). In the development of pitch notation through letter-names, he was the first to give a complete series (2 octaves and a fifth) of letter-names (G, A, B, C, D, E, F, G, etc.) corresponding to our modern series; but whereas we change from capital to lower-case letters at *c* to designate the pitches of the 2nd octave, in Odo's system the change was made at *a.* He was also the first to add the sign *gamma* (Greek "G") to designate the note corresponding to G on the first line of our bass clef. He distinguished between b flat and b natural (b *rotundum* and b *quadratum*), but only at one point in the gamut, namely, the note lying one degree below middle C in our system.

O'Dwyer, Robert, English-Irish composer and conductor; b. Bristol, Jan. 27, 1862; d. Dublin, Jan. 6, 1949. He was a conductor of the Carl Rosa Opera Co. in London and on tour (1891); then with the Arthur Rousbey Opera Co. in England and Ireland (1892–96); in 1899 became music director at the Univ. of Ireland in Dublin; from 1914 to 1939, was prof. of Irish music there; was music director (from 1901) of the Gaelic League choir, for which he arranged many Irish songs. He wrote one of the earliest operas with a Gaelic text, *Eithne,* produced in Dublin on May 16, 1910; also composed songs with Gaelic words; organ pieces. He left a book in MS, *Irish Music and Its Traditions.*

Oehl, Kurt, eminent German musicologist; b. Mainz, Feb. 24, 1923. He was educated at the Johannes Gutenberg Univ. in Mainz; obtained his Ph.D. (1952) with the dissertation *Beitrage zur Geschichte der deutschen Mozart-Übersetzungen.* After working as a dramaturge, he became a member of the editorial staff of the *Riemann Musiklexikon* in 1960. In this capacity, he helped to prepare the vol. on musical terms and historical subjects (*Sachteil*) for the 12th edition (Mainz, 1967); also served as a biographical editor for the *Supplement* (2 vols.; Mainz, 1972, 1975). He then became an editor for the *Brockhaus-Riemann Musiklexikon* (2 vols.; Mainz, 1979). In 1973 he joined the faculty of the Johannes Gutenberg Univ.

Oestvig, Karl, Norwegian tenor; b. Oslo, May 17, 1889; d. there, July 21, 1968. He studied in Cologne; made his debut at the Stuttgart Opera in 1914; remained on its roster until 1919; was then a member of the Vienna State Opera (1919–27), where he created the role of the Emperor in Strauss's *Die Frau ohne Schatten* in 1919; also sang at the Berlin State Opera and the Städtische Oper. He accepted the post of director of the Oslo Opera (1941) during the Nazi occupation of Norway, an action which brought him disgrace after the war. As an opera singer, he was at his best in the Wagnerian repertoire.

Offenbach, Jacques, the creator of French burlesque opera; b. Cologne, June 20, 1819; d. Paris, Oct. 5, 1880. He was the son of a Jewish cantor, whose original surname was Eberst; Offenbach was the town where his father lived. He went to Paris in Nov. 1833; studied cello with Vaslin at the Cons. (1833–34); then played the cello in the orch. of the Opéra-Comique; composed various pieces for his instrument. In 1850 he was engaged as conductor at the Théâtre Français; wrote *Chanson de Fortunio* for the production of Alfred de Musset's *Chandelier* (1850); the song proved tremendously popular; he then undertook the composition of operettas, a genre in which he became a master.
WORKS: He wrote a one-act operetta, *Pepito* (Théâtre des Variétés, Oct. 28, 1853); in 1855 he ventured to open a theater of his own, the old Théâtre Comte, in the Passage Choiseul, which under a new name, Bouffes-Parisiens, became celebrated; he carried on the enterprise until 1866, producing a number of his most popular pieces, among them *Les Deux Aveugles,* for the opening of the Bouffes-Parisiens (July 5, 1855), *Le Violuneux* (Aug. 31, 1855), *Madame Papillon* (Oct. 3, 1855), *Ba-ta-clan* (Dec. 29, 1855), *La Bonne d'enfants* (Oct. 14, 1856), *Les Trois Baisers au diable* (Jan. 15, 1857), *Le Mariage aux lanternes* (Oct. 10, 1857), *Mesdames de la Halle* (March 3, 1858), *Orphée aux enfers* (one of his most celebrated pieces; Oct. 21, 1858), *Geneviève de Brabant* (Nov. 19, 1859), *Daphnis et Chloé* (March 27, 1860), *Barkouf* (Dec. 24, 1860), *La Chanson de For-*

tunio (a new operetta to Musset's *Chandelier*), *Le Pont des soupirs* (March 23, 1861), *Monsieur et Madame Denis* (Jan. 11, 1862), etc. Having abandoned the management of the Bouffes-Parisiens, he produced several operettas in Ems, Germany, and an opera-ballet, *Die Rheinnixen,* in Vienna (Feb. 8, 1864); then returned to Paris, where he staged, at the Variétés, one of his most spectacular successes, *La Belle Hélène* (Dec. 17, 1864), an operetta that was soon taken over by theater enterprises all over the world; another fabulously successful operetta was *La Vie parisienne* (Palais Royal, Oct. 31, 1866); subsequent productions were *La Grande Duchesse de Gérolstein* (Variétés, April 12, 1867), *La Périchole* (Variétés, Oct. 6, 1868; one of the most enduringly popular operas of Offenbach; recurring revivals in many countries), and *Les Brigands* (Variétés, Dec. 10, 1869). In 1870, the Franco-Prussian War interrupted his activities in Paris; he resumed the production of operettas with *Boule-de-neige* (Bouffes-Parisiens, Dec. 14, 1871); in 1873 he took over the management of the Théâtre de la Gaîté, and produced there a new enlarged version of *Orphée aux enfers,* as an "opéra-féerique" (Feb. 7, 1874). In 1877 he undertook a tour in America, which was not wholly successful; he described his impressions in *Notes d'un musicien en voyage* (Paris, 1877) and in *Offenbach en Amérique* (Paris, 1877; in Eng., 1877, as *Offenbach in America;* republ. as *Orpheus in America* by the Indiana Univ. Press in Bloomington, 1957). His last operetta produced in his lifetime was *La Fille du tambour-major* (Paris, Folies-Dramatiques, Dec. 13, 1879). A posthumous work, *La Belle Lurette,* was revised by Delibes, and staged in Paris on Oct. 30, 1880. Offenbach's only grand opera, and his true masterpiece, *Les Contes d'Hoffmann,* remained unfinished at his death; recitatives were added by Ernest Guiraud. The famous barcarolle was taken from Offenbach's opera-ballet *Die Rheinnixen* (1864), where the tune was used for a ghost song. *Les Contes d'Hoffmann* was produced at the Opéra-Comique on Feb. 10, 1881, with immediate and decisive success; it was presented in N.Y. on Oct. 16, 1882; also all over Europe. Offenbach's music is characterized by an abundance of flowing, rollicking melodics, seasoned with ironic humor, suitable to the extravagant burlesque of the situations. His irreverent treatment of mythological characters gave Paris society a salutary shock; his art mirrored the atmosphere of precarious gaiety during the 2nd Empire.

Ogdon, John (Andrew Howard), English pianist; b. Manchester, Jan. 27, 1937. He studied at the Royal Manchester College of Music; made appearances in recitals and as a soloist with orchs. In 1962 he won the world's most prestigious contest, the Tchaikovsky Competition in Moscow (another first prize was awarded that year to Vladimir Ashkenazy); from 1976 to 1980 was on the faculty of Indiana Univ. in Bloomington. A man of massive physique, he handles the piano with masculine power, but is also capable of the finest quality of lyricism.

Oginski, Prince Michael Cleophas, Polish composer; b. Guzow, near Warsaw, Sept. 25, 1765; d. Florence, Oct. 15, 1833. He was a Polish nobleman of a musical family; his uncle, Michael Casimir Oginski (1731–1803), was an amateur composer of some talent. Oginski pursued the career of diplomacy; as a Polish patriot, he left Poland after its partition, and agitated in Turkey and France for the Polish cause. In 1799 he wrote an opera, *Zelis et Valcour ou Bonaparte au Caire,* to ingratiate himself with Napoleon; it was revived in a radio performance in Cracow on June 29, 1953. Of historical interest are his polonaises, many of which were publ.; the one in A minor, known as *Death Polonaise,* became extremely popular; he also wrote mazurkas and waltzes for piano, and a patriotic Polish march (1825).

O'Hara, Geoffrey, American song composer; b. Chatham, Ontario, Canada, Feb. 2, 1882; d. St. Petersburg, Fla., Jan. 31, 1967. He settled in the U.S. in 1904; became an American citizen in 1922. He studied with Homer Norris and J. Vogler; played organ in the Chatham Episcopal church; then acted in vaudeville as a pianist, singer, and composer; wrote the song *Your eyes have told me* for Caruso. In 1913 he was appointed an instructor in American Indian music as part of a program of the Dept. of the Interior; in 1917, became an army song leader; was instructor in community singing at Teachers College, Columbia Univ. (1936–37); charter member of the American Society of Composers, Authors and Publishers (1914).

Ohlsson, Garrick, American pianist; b. Bronxville, N.Y., April 3, 1948. He entered the preparatory division of the Juilliard School of Music in 1961 as a student of Sascha Gorodnitzki; in 1968 he enrolled in the master class of Rosina Lhévinne. He came to public notice in 1969, when he won the international Busoni competition in Bolzano and the Montreal contest for pianists. A giant leap in his career was made when he became the first American pianist to win the prestigious quinquennial Chopin International Piano Competition in Warsaw in 1970, contending against topnotch Polish and Russian performers. A Polish writer described Ohlsson as a "bear-butterfly" for his ability to traverse the entire spectrum of 18 dynamic degrees discernible on the modern pianoforte, from the thundering fortississimo to the finest pianississimo, with reference also to his height (6 foot, 4 inches), weight (225 lbs.), and stretch of hands (an octave and a fifth in the left hand and an octave and a fourth in the right hand). His interpretations are marked by a distinctive Americanism, technically flawless and free of Romantic mannerisms.

Oistrakh, David, famous Russian violinist; b. Odessa, Sept. 30, 1908; d. Amsterdam, Oct. 24, 1974. He studied violin as a child with Stolarsky in Odessa; then entered the Odessa music school, graduating in 1926; appeared as soloist in Glazunov's Violin Concerto under the composer's direction in Kiev in 1927. In 1928 he went to Moscow; in 1934 was appointed to the faculty of the Moscow Cons. His name attracted universal attention in 1937 when he won first prize at the International Competition in Brussels, in which 68 violinists from 21 countries took part. He played in Paris and London in 1953 with extraordinary success; made his first American appearances in 1955, as soloist with major American orchs. and in recitals, winning enthusiastic acclaim; his playing was marked, apart from a phenomenal technique, by stylistic fidelity to works by different composers of different historical periods. Soviet composers profited by his advice as to technical problems of violin playing; he collaborated with Prokofiev in making an arrangement for violin and piano of his Flute Sonata. (He also played a chess match with Prokofiev.) A whole generation of Soviet violinists numbered among his pupils, first and foremost his son **Igor Oistrakh** (b. Odessa, April 27, 1931), who has had a spectacular career in his own right; he won first prize at the International Festival of Democratic Youth in Budapest (1949) and the Wieniawski Contest in Poznan (1952); some critics regarded him as equal to his father in virtuosity.

Okeghem, Johannes. See **Ockeghem, Johannes.**

Olah, Tiberiu, Rumanian composer; b. Arpasel, Jan. 2, 1928. He studied at the Cons. in Cluj (1946–49); then went to Russia, where he studied at the Moscow Cons. (1949–54); in each of the years from 1966 to 1969, he attended the summer courses in new music at Darmstadt. In 1958 he was appointed to the staff of the Bucharest Cons. In his music Olah adopts a strong contrapuntal style, with some excursions into the atonal domain and dodecaphonic organization.

WORKS: Piano Sonatina (1950); String Quartet (1952); Trio for Violin, Clarinet, and Piano (1954); Symph. No. 1 (1955); Violin Sonatina (1955); 4 cantatas: *Cantata* for Female Chorus, 2 Flutes, Strings, and Percussion (1956); *Prind visele aripi* (*Dreams Become Reality,* 1959); *Lumina lui Lenin* (*The Light of Lenin,* 1959); *Constelaţia omului* (*The Galaxy of Man,* 1960); a cycle of 5 works inspired by the works of the Rumanian sculptor Constantin Brâncuşi: *Coloana fără sfîrşit* (*Endless Column*), symph. poem (1962); Sonata for Solo Clarinet (1963); *Spaţiu şi ritm* (*Space and Rhythm*), étude for 3 Percussion Groups (1964); *Poarta sărutului* (*Archway of the Kiss*), symph. poem (1966); *Masa tăcerii* (*The Table of Silence*), symph. poem (1967–68); 5 *Pieces* for Orch. (1966); *Echinocţii* (*Equinoxes*) for Voice, Clarinet, and Piano (1967); *Translations* for 16 Strings (1968); *Perspectives* for 13 Instruments (1969); Sonata for Solo Cello (1971); *Invocation* for 5 Instruments (1971); *Crescendo* for Orch. (1972); *Evenimente 1907* for Orch. (1972); *The Time of Memory* for Chamber Ensemble (1973; N.Y., Dec. 6, 1974); songs.

Olczewska, Maria (real name, **Marie Berchtenbreitner**), German mezzo-soprano; b. Augsburg, Aug.

12, 1892; d. Klagenfurt, Austria, May 17, 1969. She sang in operetta in Hamburg; then was engaged at the Leipzig Opera (1920–23); subsequently was a member of the Vienna State Opera (1923–36) and of Covent Garden in London (1924–32), where she sang Wagnerian operas with excellent success. She was then engaged at the Chicago Opera and at the Metropolitan Opera in N.Y., making her debut as Brangäne (Jan. 16, 1933) and remaining on its staff until 1935. In 1947 she returned to Vienna, where she taught at the Cons. She had a powerful voice, which made it possible for her to master the Wagner roles; but she was also excellent in dramatic parts, such as Carmen. Furthermore, she had a genuine talent as a stage actress.

Oldberg, Arne, American composer; b. Youngstown, Ohio, July 12, 1874; d. Evanston, Ill., Feb. 17, 1962. He studied composition with Middelschulte; then went to Vienna, where he was a piano pupil of Leschetizky (1893–95); also took courses with Rheinberger in Munich. Returning to America in 1899, he became head of the piano dept. at Northwestern Univ.; retired in 1941. Most of his orch. works were performed by the Chicago Symph. Orch., among them *Paolo and Francesca* (Jan. 17, 1908), *At Night* (April 13, 1917), Symph. No. 4 (Dec. 31, 1942), Symph. No. 5 (Jan. 19, 1950), and *St. Francis of Assisi* for Baritone and Orch. (Ravinia Festival, July 16, 1954). Other works are: *Academic Overture* (1909); *The Sea,* symph. poem (1934); 2 piano concertos, of which the 2nd won the Hollywood Bowl prize and was performed (Aug. 16, 1932); Violin Concerto (1933; Chicago, Nov. 7, 1946); 2 rhapsodies for Orch.; chamber music; piano pieces.

Olenin, Alexander, Russian composer, brother of the singer **Marie Olénine d'Alheim;** b. Istomino, Riazan district, June 13, 1865; d. Moscow, Feb. 15, 1944. He studied with P. Pabst and with Erdmannsdörfer; lived most of his life in Moscow. He wrote an opera in a folk style, *Kudeyar* (Moscow, Nov. 26, 1915); a symph. poem, *After the Battle; Préludes prairiales* for 2 Oboes, Violin, and Piano (1927); Piano Sonata; Violin Sonata; several song cycles (*The Street, The Peasant's Son, The Autumn, Home,* etc.); 52 songs to texts by Heine.

Olénine d'Alheim, Marie, Russian soprano; b. Istomino, Riazan district, Oct. 2, 1869; d. Moscow, Aug. 27, 1970, at the age of 100. She studied in Russia and later in Paris; made her debut in Paris in 1896. Through her brother, the composer **Alexander Olenin,** she met Stasov, Balakirev, and Cui, and became interested in Russian vocal music. In 1893 she married the French writer Pierre d'Alheim (1862–1922), translator of the text of *Boris Godunov;* together they organized, in Moscow and in Paris, numerous concerts and lectures on Russian music, particularly on Mussorgsky; she was an outstanding interpreter of Russian songs; publ. a book, *Le Legs de Mussorgsky* (Paris, 1908). In 1935 she settled in Paris as a voice teacher; in 1949 joined the French Communist Party; in 1959 she returned to Russia.

Oliveira, Elmar, American violinist; b. Waterbury, Conn., June 8, 1950. He studied violin at the Hartt College of Music in Hartford, Conn., and later at the Manhattan School of Music. In 1975 he won the Walter W. Naumburg Competition in N.Y. In 1978 he won the Gold Medal of the International Tchaikovsky Competition in Moscow, which catapulted him onto an international career.

Oliveira, Jocy de, Brazilian pianist and avant-garde composer; b. Curitiba-Parana, Brazil, April 11, 1936, of French and Portuguese origin. She studied piano in São Paulo with J. Kliass and in Paris with Marguerite Long; then traveled to the U.S.; obtained her M.A. at Washington Univ. in St. Louis in 1968. She appeared as a piano soloist with major orchs. in Europe and America, specializing in the modern repertoire; in 1966 she played the piano part in Stravinsky's *Capriccio* in St. Louis, under Stravinsky's direction. As a composer, she occupies the aphelion of ultra-modernism, experimenting in electronic, environmental, theatrical, cinematic, and television media, as exemplified by *Probabilistic Theater* I, II, and III for Musicians, Actors, Dancers, Television and Traffic Conductor, and other environmental manifestations. Her *Polinteracões I, II, III* present the culmination of "total music" involving the visual, aural, tactile, gustatory, and olfactory senses, with an anatomic chart serving as a score for guidance of the participants, supplemented by a phonemic table indicating the proper verbalization of vocal parts. (Complete score and illustrations were reproduced in *Source,* no. 7, Sacramento, Calif., 1970.) A performance of *Polinteracões* was attempted on the occasion of the Catalytic Celebration of the 10th Anniversary Festival of the New Music Circle in St. Louis on April 7, 1970, but was stopped by the management as a noisy, noisome nuisance. Jocy de Oliveira is also active in belles-lettres; she wrote a sociological fantasy, *O 3° Mundo (The Third World;* a utopian, optimistic vision of the future); a controversial play, *Apague meu (Spotlight),* first produced in São Paulo in 1961; poetical works; etc. She also composed a number of advanced sambas, precipitating the vogue of the Brazilian bossa nova. She is the wife of the Brazilian conductor **Eleazar de Carvalho.**

Oliver, Henry Kemble, American composer of hymn tunes; b. Beverly, Mass., Nov. 24, 1800; d. Salem, Aug. 12, 1885. He was a chorister at Park Street Church in Boston; graduated from Dartmouth College in 1818; played the organ in various churches in Salem and Boston; in 1826, founded and managed the Salem Mozart Association; subsequently went to Lawrence, Mass., where he was mayor in 1859; later was also mayor of Salem; in 1861–65, was treasurer of the State of Massachusetts. He was given B.A. and M.A. degrees by Harvard Univ. (1862) and was made a Mus.Doc. by Dartmouth College (1883). He wrote many well-known hymn tunes (*Federal Street, Morning, Harmony Grove, Beacon Street, Hudson*), motets, chants, and a *Te Deum;* publ. *The National Lyre*

(1848; with Tuckerman and Bancroft; contains many of his own compositions), *Oliver's Collection of Hymn and Psalm Tunes* (1860), and *Original Hymn Tunes* (1875).

Oliver, Joseph ("King"), black American jazz cornetist and bandleader; b. on a plantation near Abend, La., May 11, 1885; d. Savannah, Ga., April 8, 1938. In 1907 he was working in Storyville (the brothel district of New Orleans) with the Melrose Brass Band; in subsequent years he was with a number of other brass bands there, and in 1915 he formed his own group, eventually known as the Creole Jazz Band; in 1917 he acquired the nickname "King," traditionally reserved for the leading jazz musicians. Also in 1917, the government closed the bordellos in Storyville, putting most of the musicians (among others) out of work; the following year Oliver moved his band to Chicago, leading a migration of jazz musicians to the city that was largely responsible for the dispersion of the black New Orleans jazz style throughout the country. In 1922 Louis Armstrong, whom he had known in New Orleans, joined the band, helping to make it the most polished exponent of New Orleans collectively improvised jazz; the group's 1923 recordings were the most influential early jazz recordings ever made; they have been reissued by the Smithsonian Inst. Subsequent bands formed by Oliver remained a potent force in jazz until around 1928. Oliver is the uncle of the composer **Ulysses Kay.**

Olivero, Magda, Italian soprano; b. Saluzzo, near Turin, March 25, 1912. She studied at the Turin Cons.; made her debut in Turin in 1933; then sang in the Italian provinces. She temporarily retired from the stage when she married in 1941, but resumed her career in 1951; made successful appearances at La Scala in Milan, and in Paris and London. In 1966 she made her American debut in Dallas in the title role of Cherubini's *Medea;* she was 63 years old when she made her first appearance with the Metropolitan Opera, N.Y., on April 3, 1975, as Tosca, an unprecedented occurrence in the annals of opera; on Dec. 5, 1977, she gave a highly successful recital in a program of Italian art songs at Carnegie Hall, N.Y. Among her operatic roles were Violetta, Mimi, and Tosca; she was praised mainly for her dramatic penetration of each character and her fine command of dynamic nuances.

Oliveros, Pauline, American composer; b. Houston, Texas, May 30, 1932. She was of a musical family; her mother and grandmother were piano teachers from whom she learned the rudiments of music; she also took violin lessons with William Sydler and studied accordion playing with Marjorie Harrigan. From her earliest days she became sensitive to pleasing animal sounds, and was able aurally to suppress the rude noise of motorcars in her environment. She added to her practical musical knowledge by studying the French horn with J.M. Brandsetter. From 1949 to 1952 she studied composition with Paul Koepke at the Univ. of Houston; in 1954 she enrolled at San Francisco State College (B.A., 1958); also studied privately with Robert Erickson (1954–60), who initiated her into modern harmony, the art of asymmetrical rhythms, group improvisation, and acoustical sonorism. Gradually, she expanded her receptivity into the range of subliminal sounds, derived from the overtone series, differential tones, and sonic abstractions. In 1960 she composed a piano sextet which explored a variety of such elusive tonal elements; it received the Pacifica Foundation National Prize. Advancing further into the domain of new sonorities, she wrote a choral work, *Sound Patterns,* to wordless voices (1962), which received a prize in the Netherlands. With Morton Subotnick and others she organized the San Francisco Tape Music Center, and experimented with the resources of magnetic tape. On July 22, 1967, she presented in San Francisco a 12-hour marathon of recorded electronic music of her own composition. In 1967 she joined the music faculty of the Univ. of Calif. at San Diego, where she remained until 1981. There she was able to develop her ideas further afield. Taking advantage of her skill as a gardener, she arrayed garden hoses and lawn sprinklers as part of a musical ensemble accompanied by the sounds of alarm clocks and various domestic utensils. Occasionally, a musician was instructed to bark. To this enriched artistic vocabulary was soon added a physical and psychosomatic element; performers had to act the parts of a magician, a juggler, and a fortune-teller. Page turners, piano movers, and floor sweepers were listed as performing artists. In her later works she reduced such kinetic activities and gradually began to compose ceremonial works of sonic meditation, sotto voce murmuration, lingual lallation, and joyful ululation, with the purpose of inducing an altered state of consciousness or unconsciousness; sometimes an exotic but usually digestible meal was served at leisurely intervals. Pauline Oliveros often presided over such sessions, singing and playing her faithful accordion; sometimes this music was left to be unheard by ordinary ears, but it could be perceived mystically. In 1979 she took part in the Berlin Festival of Metamusic, to audible acclaim. In 1977 she obtained first prize from the city of Bonn for a work commemorating the sesquicentennial of Beethoven's death; the piece was verbally notated with the intention to subvert perception of the entire city so that it would become a perceptual theater. As she moved higher into the realm of cosmic consciousness, Pauline Oliveros introduced the psychic element into her works; in 1970 she drew an equation for an indefinite integral of the differential *psi* (for psychic unit), to create the state of Oneness. Apart from her metamusical activities, she became a karate expert, the holder of the third Kyu black belt in Shotokan-style karate.

WORKS: *Variations for Sextet* for Flute, Clarinet, Trumpet, Horn, Cello, and Piano (1960); *Sound Patterns* for Chorus (1961); Trio for Trumpet, Piano, and Page Turner (1961); Trio for Trumpet, Accordion, and Double Bass (1961); *7 Passages* for 2-channel Tape, Mobile, and Dancer (1963); *Five* for Trumpet and Dancer (1964); *Duo* for Accordion and

Bandoneon, with possible Mynah Bird Obbligato (1964); *Apple Box Orchestra* for 10 Performers, Amplified Apple Boxes, etc. (1964); *Pieces of Eight* for Wind Octet and a number of Props, including a Cash Register (1965); *7 Sets of Mnemonics,* multimedia piece (1965); *George Washington Slept Here* for Amplified Violin, Film Projections, and Tape (1965); *Bye Bye Butterfly* for Oscillators, Amplifiers, and Tapes (1965); *Winter Light* for Tape, Mobile, and Figure (1965); *Participle Dangling in Honor of Gertrude Stein* for Tape, Mobile, and Work Crew (1966); *Theater Piece for Trombone Player* for Garden Hose, Instruments, and Tape (1966); *Night Jar* for Viola d'Amore (1968); *Festival House* for Orch., Mimes, Light, and Film Projections (1968); *Double Basses at Twenty Paces* for 2 Double Basses, Tape, and Projections (1968); *The Dying Alchemist Preview* for Narrator, Violinist, Trumpet, Piccolo, Percussion, and Slides (1969); *The Wheel of Fortune,* suggested by the trump cards in the tarot deck, for Solo Clarinet (1969); *Aeolian Partitions* for Flute, Clarinet, Violin, Cello, and Piano (1969); *To Valerie Solanis and Marilyn Monroe, in Recognition of Their Desperation,* verbally notated score (1970; Solanis, the founder of SCUM, i.e. the Society to Cut Up Men, tried unsuccessfully to shoot the pop artist Andy Warhol; Marilyn Monroe destroyed her own beautiful and desirable body by feeding herself sleeping pills to mortal excess); *Meditation on the Points of the Compass* for Chorus and Percussion (1970); *Bonn Feier,* intended to convert the city of Bonn into an imagined total theater (1971); *Post Card Theater,* multimedia event (1972); *Phantom Fathom,* mixed-media event with an Exotic Potluck Dinner (1972); *1000 Acres* for String Quartet (1972); *Sonic Images,* subliminal auditory fantasy (1972); *Crow Two,* ceremonial opera (1974); *Rose Mountain Slow Runner* for Voice and Accordion (1975; renamed *Horse Sings from Cloud,* inspired by a dream image of a horse lifted to a cloud by birds); *Willow Brook Generations and Reflections* for Wind Instruments and Vocalists (1976); *The Yellow River Map,* ceremonial meditation for a lot of people (1977); *King Kong Sings Along* for Chorus (1977); *Rose Moon,* ceremonial for Chorus and Percussion (1977); *The Witness* for Virtuoso Instrumentalists (1978); *El relicario de los animales* for Soprano and 20 Instruments (1979); *Carol Plantamura* for Voice and 20 Instruments (1979); *Gone with The Wind, 1980* for Assorted Ensembles (1980); *Wheel of Times,* for String Quartet and Electonics (1982); *The Mandala* for 4 Clarinets, 8 Crystal Glasses, Bass Drum, and Finger Cymbals (timeless date of composition).

d'Ollone, Max (full name, **Maximilien-Paul-Marie-Félix**), French composer and writer on music; b. Besançon, June 13, 1875; d. Paris, May 15, 1959. He studied with Lavignac, Massenet, and Lenepveu at the Paris Cons.; received the Grand Prix de Rome in 1897 with his cantata *Frédégonde;* was active as an opera conductor in Paris and the French provinces. A prolific composer, he wrote 5 operas: *Le Retour* (Angers, Feb. 13, 1913), *Les Uns et les autres* (Paris,

Nov. 6, 1922), *L'Arlequin* (Paris, Dec. 24, 1924), *George Dandin,* after Molière (Paris, March 19, 1930), and *La Samaritaine* (Paris, June 25, 1937); also *Dans la cathédrale* for Orch. (1906); *Fantaisie* for Piano and Orch. (1899); chamber music; many songs; he contributed to French magazines on musical subjects; publ. a book, *Le Théâtre lyrique et le public* (Paris, 1955).

Olsen, Ole, Norwegian composer; b. Hammerfest, July 4, 1850; d. Oslo, Nov. 10, 1927. He studied with J. Lindeman; was active as an organist and theater conductor in Trondheim and other provincial towns; in 1870 went to Leipzig, where he studied with Richter and Reinecke. Returning to Norway in 1874, he became a piano teacher in Oslo; was conductor of the Music Society there (1878–81), instructor of music at the Military Academy (1887–1903), and inspector of military music (1899–1919). He wrote the operas *Stig Hvide* (1876), *Stallo* (1902), and *Klippeøerne* (1905), which were not produced, and *Lajla* (Oslo, Oct. 8, 1908); also some incidental music; a Symph. (1878); the symph. poems *Aasgaardsreien* (1878) and *Alfedans* (*Elf Dance;* 1880); Concerto for Horn and Orch. (Oslo, April 1, 1905); numerous choruses; songs; piano music.

Olsen, Poul Rovsing, Danish composer and ethnomusicologist; b. Copenhagen, Nov. 4, 1922; d. there, July 2, 1982. He studied law at the Univ. of Aarhus (1940–42) and at the Univ. of Copenhagen (1942–48); concurrently, took lessons in composition with Knud Jeppesen at the Royal Cons. of Music in Copenhagen (1943–46); later studied with Nadia Boulanger in Paris (1948–49). Between 1958 and 1963 he took part in ethnomusicological expeditions to Arabia, India, Greece, and eastern Greenland and wrote numerous valuable papers on the folklore and musical cultures of the areas he visited. He worked until 1960 for the Danish Ministry of Education as a legal expert on music copyright; served as chairman of the Danish Society of Composers (1962–67); taught ethnomusicology at the Univ. of Lund, Sweden (1967–69), and subsequently at the Univ. of Copenhagen. He was president of the International Council of Traditional Music (formerly the International Folk Music Council) from 1977 until his death. He was a music critic for the newspapers *Morgenbladet* (1945–46), *Information* (1949–54), and *Berlingske Tidende* (1954–74). Much of his music embodies materials of non-European cultures, reflecting the influence of his travels. His *Elegy* for Organ (1953) is the first piece in the serial system by a Danish composer. WORKS: FOR THE STAGE: 2 operas: *Belisa,* after García Lorca (1964; Copenhagen, Sept. 3, 1966) and *Usher,* after Poe (1980); 4 ballets: *Ragnarök (Twilight of the Gods;* 1948; Copenhagen, Sept. 12, 1960); *La Création* (1952; Copenhagen, March 10, 1961); *Brylluppet (The Wedding;* 1966; Copenhagen, Sept. 15, 1969); *Den Fremmede (The Stranger;* 1969; Copenhagen, July 17, 1972). FOR ORCH.: *Symphonic Variations* (1953); Piano Concerto (1953–54); *Sinfonia I* (1957–58; Copenhagen, April 13, 1959); *Sin-*

fonia II, Susudil, based on Arab and Turkish modes (1966; Copenhagen, Oct. 31, 1966); *Capriccio* (1961–62); *Et russisk bal (The Russian Ball),* 3 dances (1965); *Au Fond de la nuit* for Chamber Orch. (1968); *Randrussermarchen* (1977); *Lux Coelestis* (1978). FOR VOICE: *Schicksalslieder,* after 4 Hölderlin poems, for Soprano or Tenor, and 7 Instruments (1953); *Evening Songs* for Mezzo-soprano and Flute (1954); *Alapa-Tarana,* vocalise for Mezzo-soprano and Percussion (1959); *A l'inconnu* for Soprano or Tenor, and 13 Instruments (1962); *Kejseren (The Emperor)* for Tenor, Male Chorus, and Orch. (1963; Copenhagen, Sept. 5, 1964); *A Song of Mira Bai* for Chorus, 3 Trumpets, and Percussion (1971);

Ondříček, Emanuel, Czech violinist, son of **Jan Ondříček** and brother of **Franz Ondříček;** b. Pilsen, Dec. 6, 1882; d. Boston, Dec. 30, 1958. He studied with his father and with Ševčik at the Prague Cons.; after a series of concerts in Europe, he settled in the U.S. in 1912; became an eminent teacher in Boston and N.Y.; publ. a manual, *Mastery of Tone Production and Expression on the Violin.*

Ondříček, Franz, Czech violinist; b. Prague, April 29, 1857; d. Milan, April 12, 1922. He studied with his father, **Jan Ondříček,** and later with Bennewitz at the Prague Cons., winning first prize (1876–79); then with Massart at the Paris Cons., where he also won first prize (1879–81). He undertook extensive concert tours of Europe, America, Siberia, and the Far East before settling in Vienna (1907), where he founded the celebrated Ondříček Quartet (with Silbiger, Junck, and Jelinek); was a prof. at the New Vienna Cons. (1910–19); from 1919 taught at the Prague Cons. In 1885 he married **Anna Hlaváček,** a singer at the National Theater of Prague. As a concert player, he impressed his audiences with his fiery temperament, but in his later years developed a grand Classical style, marked by dignified repose. He publ. *Rapsodie bohème* for Violin and Orch.; a cadenza to the Violin Concerto of Brahms; numerous pieces for violin with piano. In collaboration with S. Mittelmann, he brought out *Neue Methode zur Erlangung der Meistertechnik des Violinspiels auf anatomisch-physiologischer Grundlage* (2 parts, 1909) with 15 of his own études.

Ondříček, Jan, Czech violinist; b. Běleč, near Bratronice, May 6, 1832; d. Prague, March 13, 1900. He was the son of a village violinist, and studied with him; played in various orchs., and also conducted; was a friend of Dvořák. He had 9 children, all of whom were musicians.

Onégin, Sigrid (neé **Hoffmann;** full name, **Elizabeth Elfriede Emilie Sigrid**), contralto; b. Stockholm (of a German father and a French mother), June 1, 1889; d. Magliaso, Switzerland, June 16, 1943. She studied in Frankfurt with Resz, in Munich with E.R. Weiss, and with di Ranieri in Milan. She made her first public appearance, using the name **Lilly Hoffmann,** in Wiesbaden, Sept. 16, 1911, in a recital, accompanied by the Russian pianist and composer **Eugene**

Onégin (b. St. Petersburg, Oct. 10, 1883; d. Stuttgart, Nov. 12, 1919; real name, Lvov; he was a grand-nephew of Alexis Lvov, author of the Russian Czarist hymn). She married him on May 25, 1913; after his death, she married a German doctor, Fritz Penzoldt (Nov. 20, 1920). She made her first appearance in opera as Carmen, in Stuttgart, on Oct. 10, 1912; made her American operatic debut at the Metropolitan Opera House, N.Y., as Amneris, on Nov. 22, 1922; revisited America several times, her last tour (in recitals) being in 1938. From 1931 she lived mostly in Switzerland.

O'Neill, Norman, English conductor and composer; b. London, March 14, 1875; d. there, March 3, 1934. He was a direct descendant of the notable English musician **John Wall Callcott;** his father was a painter. He studied in London with Arthur Somervell, and later with Knorr in Frankfurt. Returning to London in 1899, he married the pianist **Adine Rückert** (1875–1947). He wrote incidental music for the Haymarket Theatre, of which he was music director from 1908 to 1919; also produced the ballets *Before Dawn* (1917), *Punch and Judy* (1924), *Alice in Lumberland* (1926), etc.

Onslow, George (full name, **André Georges Louis Onslow**), noted French composer; b. Clermont-Ferrand, July 27, 1784; d. there, Oct. 3, 1853. He was the grandson of the first Lord Onslow; studied in London with Hüllmandel, Dussek, and Cramer (piano) and in Paris with Reicha (composition). He wrote 3 comic operas, produced in Paris: *L'Alcalde de la Vega* (Aug. 10, 1824), *Le Colporteur* (Nov. 22, 1827), and *Le Duc de Guise* (Sept. 8, 1837); 4 symphs.; and some other orch. music. However, these works failed to maintain interest; Onslow's real achievement was the composition of a great number of chamber works, in which he demonstrated an uncommon mastery of counterpoint; he wrote 34 string quintets; 36 string quartets; 6 piano trios; a Sextet for Flute, Clarinet, Horn, Bassoon, Double Bass, and Piano (the double-bass part was expressly written for the famous virtuoso Dragonetti); Nonet for Violin, Viola, Cello, Double Bass, Flute, Oboe, Clarinet, Bassoon, and Horn; Septet for Flute, Oboe, Clarinet, Horn, Bassoon, Double Bass, and Piano; violin sonatas; cello sonatas; piano sonatas, 4-hands; a number of piano pieces. As a result of a hunting accident in 1829, when a stray bullet injured him, he became deaf in one ear; his Quintet No. 15, subtitled *Le Quintette de la balle (Quintet of the Bullet),* was the musical rendering of this episode.

Opieński, Henryk, eminent Polish music scholar and composer; b. Cracow, Jan. 13, 1870; d. Morges, Switzerland, Jan. 21, 1942. He studied with Zelenski in Cracow, with Vincent d'Indy in Paris, and with H. Urban in Berlin; then went to Leipzig, where he studied musicology with Riemann and conducting with Nikisch. In 1907 he was appointed an instructor at the Warsaw Musical Society; from 1908 to 1912 he conducted the Warsaw Opera; in 1912 he went again to Germany, where he took his degree of Dr.Phil. (Leipzig, 1914). He spent the years of World War I at Morges, Switzerland; returning to Poland, he was director of the Poznan Cons. (1919–26); then settled again in Morges.

Oppens, Ursula, talented American pianist; b. New York, Feb. 2, 1944. She studied economics and English literature at Radcliffe College (B.A., 1965); then studied with Rosina Lhévinne and Leonard Shure at the Juilliard School of Music. She won first prize at the Busoni Competition in Italy in 1969; co-founded Speculum Musicae in N.Y., a chamber music ensemble devoted to performing contemporary music. In 1976 she was awarded the Avery Fisher Prize.

Orbón (de Soto), Julián, Spanish-born composer; b. Avilés, Aug. 7, 1925. He received the rudiments of a musical education from his father, a professional pianist. After the Spanish Civil War the family emigrated to Cuba; he studied music theory with José Ardevol, with whom he also formed the Grupo de Renovación Musical (1942–49); was director of his father's Orbón Cons. in Havana in 1946–60. After the revolution of 1959 in Cuba, Orbón went to Mexico; taught at the National Cons. in Mexico City in 1960–63; in 1964 he settled in N.Y. In his music he follows a neo-Classical mode of composition; among his works are: Symphony in C (1945); *Danzas sinfónicas* (1955); Concerto Grosso (1958); *Oficios de 3 días* for Chorus and Orch. (1970); String Quartet (1951); numerous piano pieces and choruses.

Orchard, William Arundel, Australian pianist, conductor, and composer; b. London, April 13, 1867; d. during a voyage in the South Atlantic, off the coast of South Africa (23°49′S; 9°33′E), April 17, 1961. He studied in London and Durham; in 1903 went to Australia and lived in Sydney, where he was active as a conductor and music educator; served as director of the New South Wales State Cons. (1923–34); later taught at the Univ. of Tasmania. He wrote an opera, *The Picture of Dorian Gray,* after Oscar Wilde; a Violin Concerto; String Quartet; String Quintet; choruses; songs. He publ. 2 books dealing with Australian music: *The Distant View* (Sydney, 1943) and *Music in Australia* (Melbourne, 1952).

Ordoñez, Carlos, Austrian composer of Spanish extraction; b. Vienna, April 19, 1734; d. there, Sept. 6, 1786. He was employed as a clerk, but studied violin and performed successfully at chamber music concerts. He wrote numerous singspiels and much instrumental music, some of which was publ. during his lifetime. His singspiel *Diesmal hat der Mann den Willen* was performed in Vienna on April 22, 1778; his marionette opera *Alceste* was introduced by Haydn in Esterház on Aug. 30, 1775. Ordoñez developed an excellent métier, and several of his symphs. possessed enough merit to be misattributed to Haydn.

Orff, Carl, outstanding German composer; b. Mu-

nich, July 10, 1895; d. there, March 29, 1982. He studied at the Academy of Music in Munich, and with Heinrich Kaminski; from 1950 to 1960, was a prof. at the Hochschule für Musik in Munich. In his music he sought to revive the old monodic forms and to adapt them to modern tastes by means of dissonant counterpoint, with lively rhythm in asymmetrical patterns. Apart from his compositions, Orff initiated a highly important method of musical education, which was adopted not only in Germany but in England, America, and Russia; it stemmed from the Günther School for gymnastics, dance, and music which Orff founded in 1924 with Dorothee Günther in Munich, with the aim of promoting instrumental playing and understanding of rhythm among children; he commissioned the piano manufacturer Karl Maendler to construct special percussion instruments that would be extremely easy to play; the "Orff instruments" became widely adopted in American schools. Orff's ideas of rhythmic training owe much to the eurhythmics of Jaques-Dalcroze, but he simplified them to reach the elementary level; as a manual, he compiled a set of musical exercises, *Schulwerk* (1930–35, revised 1950–54).

WORKS: His most famous work is the scenic oratorio, *Carmina Burana* (Frankfurt, June 8, 1937; numerous productions in Europe and America); the words (in Latin and German) are from 13th-century student poems found in the monastery of Benediktbeuren in Bavaria ("Burana" is the Latin adjective of the locality). Other works: *Der Mond,* opera, after a fairy tale by Grimm (Munich, Feb. 5, 1939; revised version, Munich, Nov. 26, 1950); *Die Kluge,* opera, also after a fairy tale by Grimm (Frankfurt, Feb. 20, 1943); *Catulli Carmina,* scenic cantata after Catullus (Leipzig, Nov. 6, 1943); *Die Bernauerin,* musical play (Stuttgart, June 15, 1947); *Antigonae,* musical play after Sophocles (Salzburg, Aug. 9, 1949); *Trionfo di Afrodite* (3rd part of a triology under the general title *Trionfi,* the first and 2nd parts being *Carmina Burana* and *Catulli Carmina;* Milan, Feb. 13, 1953); *Astutuli,* opera-ballet (Munich, Oct. 20, 1953); *Comoedia de Christi Resurrectione,* Easter cantata (Munich, March 31, 1956); *Oedipus der Tyrann,* musical play after Sophocles (Stuttgart, Dec. 11, 1959); *Ludus de nato infante mirificus,* Nativity play (Stuttgart, Dec. 11, 1960); *Prometheus,* opera (Stuttgart, March 24, 1968); *Rota* for Voices and Instruments, after the canon *Sumer is icumen in,* composed as a "salute to youth" for the opening ceremony of the Munich Olympics (1972); stage play *De temporum fine comoedia* (Salzburg, 1973). He further wrote a dance play, *Der Feuerfarbene* (1925); *Präludium* for Orch. (1925); Concertino for Wind Instruments and Harpsichord (1927); *Entrata* for Orch., based on melodies of William Byrd (1928; revised 1940); Festival Music for Chamber Orch. (1928); *Bayerische Musik* for Small Ensemble (1934); *Olympischer Reigen* for Various Instruments (1936); revised versions of Monteverdi's *Orfeo* (Mannheim, April 17, 1925; 2nd version, Munich, Oct. 13, 1929; 3rd version, Dresden, Oct. 4, 1940) and Monteverdi's *Ballo delle ingrate, Lamento d'Arianna,* and *L'incoronazione di Poppea.*

Orgeni, Aglaja (real name, **Görger St. Jorgen**), Hungarian coloratura soprano; b. Roma Szombat, Dec. 17, 1841; d. Vienna, March 15, 1926. She was a pupil of Mme. Viardot-García at Baden-Baden; made her debut on Sept. 28, 1865, as Amina, at the Berlin Opera; made her first appearance in London on April 7, 1866, as Violetta, at Covent Garden; she sang later in Vienna, Dresden, Berlin, Copenhagen, etc.; from 1886, taught singing at the Dresden Cons.; was made a Royal Professor in 1908 (the first case of the title being conferred on a woman). In 1914 she settled in Vienna. Among her distinguished pupils were Erika Wedekind and Edyth Walker.

Ormandy, Eugene (real name, **Blau**), outstanding conductor; b. Budapest, Nov. 18, 1899. He studied violin with his father; entered the Royal Academy of Music in Budapest at the age of 5; began studying with Hubay at 9; received an artist's diploma for violin in 1914; received a teacher's certificate at the Royal Academy in 1917; then was concertmaster of the Blüthner Orch. in Germany; also gave recitals and played with orchs. as soloist. In 1921, he came to the U.S.; obtained the position of concertmaster of the Capitol Theater Orch., N.Y., and remained there for 2½ years; made his debut as conductor with that orch. in Sept. 1924; in 1925, became its associate music director; in 1929, conducted the N.Y. Phil. at Lewisohn Stadium; in 1930, became guest conductor with the Robin Hood Dell Orch., Philadelphia; on Oct. 30, 1931, conducted the Philadelphia Orch. In 1931, he was appointed music director and permanent conductor of the Minncapolis Symph. Orch.; in 1936, was engaged as associate conductor of the Philadelphia Orch. (with Stokowski); on Sept. 28, 1938, became permanent conductor; traveled with it on transcontinental tours in 1937, 1946, 1948, 1957, 1962, 1964, 1971, 1974, and 1977; in 1949, made an extended tour in England; in the spring of 1955, presented concerts with the Philadelphia Orch. in 10 European countries; in the summer of 1958 he led it on another European tour (including Russia). He appeared on numerous occasions as guest conductor with European orchs.; in Australia (summer of 1944); South America (summer of 1946); Latin America (1966); the Far East (1967, 1978); and Japan (1972). In 1970 he received the Presidential Medal of Freedom. In 1973 he took the Philadelphia Orch. to China and led it in several cities there; this was the first appearance of an American symph. orch. in the People's Republic of China. Ormandy was made an officer of the French Legion of Honor (1952; was promoted to Commander in 1958); was made a Knight of the Order of the White Rose of Finland (1955); became a holder of the medal of the Bruckner Society (1936); received an honorary Mus.Doc. from the Univ. of Pa. In 1976 he was named an honorary Knight Commander of the British Empire by Queen Elizabeth in honor of the American Bicentennial; altogether, he has received 26 awards and 23 honorary doctorates. In his interpretations, Ormandy reveals himself as a Romanticist; he excels in the works of Beethoven, Schumann, and Richard Strauss; his renditions of music by Debussy and of the moderns are marked by color without extravagance; he conducts all his scores from memory. After 42 seasons as music director of the Philadelphia Orch., he retired at the close of the 1979–80 season, and was named Conductor Laureate.

Ornithoparchus (Greek form of his real name, **Vogelsang**), **Andreas,** German music scholar; b. Meiningen, c.1485; d. Münster, c.1535. He matriculated at the Univ. of Rostock (M.A., 1512) and at the Univ. of Tübingen (M.A., 1515); was rector of the parochial school in Münster in 1514; also matriculated at Wittenberg (1516), Leipzig (1516), and Greifswald (1518). He publ. a valuable theoretical treatise, *Musice active micrologus* (1517; 6th ed., 1540; Eng. trans. by Dowland, London, 1609; reprinted 1977).

Ornstein, Leo, remarkable Russian pianist and composer; b. Kremenchug, Dec. 11, 1892. The son of a synagogal cantor, he studied music at home; then with Vladimir Puchalski in Kiev; at the age of 10 he was accepted as a pupil at the St. Petersburg Cons. As a consequence of anti-Semitic disturbances in Russia, the family decided to emigrate to the U.S. in 1907. Ornstein studied piano with Mrs. Bertha Feiring Tapper at the New England Cons. in Boston, and with Percy Goetschius; also attended the Inst. of Musical Art in N.Y. He gave his first concert in N.Y., as a pianist, on March 5, 1911; then played in Philadelphia and other cities. About 1910 he began to compose; he experimented with percussive sonorities, in dissonant harmonies; made a European tour in 1913; played in Norway, Denmark, and in Paris; appeared in London on March 27, 1914, in a piano recital announced as "futuristic music" and featuring his Sonata and other works. Returning to the U.S. early in 1915, he gave a series of recitals at the Bandbox Theater in N.Y., comprising works by Debussy, Ravel, Schoenberg, Scriabin, and other modern composers; also his own music; his *Danse sauvage* excited his audiences by its declared wildness. Ornstein was hailed as the prophet of a new musical era, but soon ceased to attract attention. He continued to compose, although the titles of his works were no longer wild and provocative; in 1974 he completed his major work, *Biography in Sonata Form*. His 90th birthday was celebrated by a special concert of his works in N.Y. in 1982.

WORKS: For Orch.: *3 Moods: Anger, Peace, Joy* (1914); *The Fog,* symph. poem (1915); Piano Concerto (Philadelphia Orch., Feb. 13, 1925, composer soloist); *Lysistrata Suite* (1933); *Nocturne and Dance of Fates* (St. Louis, Feb. 12, 1937); *3 Russian Choruses* a cappella (1921); Piano Quintet; 3 String Quartets: No. 1; No. 2 (1975); No. 3 (1979); Violin Sonata; Cello Sonata; *Nocturne* for Clarinet and Piano; 4 piano sonatas; many pieces for piano: *A la chinoise; Suicide in an Airplane* (1913); *Danse sauvage* (1915); *Suite russe;* songs (*The Corpse,* etc.).

Orr, Robin, Scottish composer; b. Brechin, June 2, 1909. He studied organ, piano, and composition at the Royal College of Music in London (1926–29) and at Cambridge Univ. (1929–32); subsequently took courses with Edward J. Dent in London, Alfredo Casella in Siena, and Nadia Boulanger in Paris. From 1938 to 1950 he was active as an organist and music instructor at St. John's College, Cambridge; received his Mus.D. from Cambridge Univ. in 1951; taught there until 1956; then at the Univ. of Glasgow (1956–65); in 1965 was appointed a prof. of music at Cambridge Univ.; he retired in 1976. His works include *Symphony in One Movement* (London, Dec. 12, 1963); *Full Circle,* opera (Perth, Scotland, April 10, 1968); *Journeys and Places* for Mezzosoprano and String Quintet (1971); String Quartet; choral pieces. He edited *The Kelvin Series of Scots Songs.*

Orrego-Salas, Juan, Chilean composer and music educator; b. Santiago, Jan. 18, 1919. He studied at the School of Architecture of the Catholic Univ. of Santiago (1938–42); studied composition with Humberto Allende and Domingo Santa Cruz at the National Cons. of Music of the Univ. of Chile (1936–43); came to the U.S. and attended classes in musicology with Paul Henry Lang and George Herzog at Columbia Univ. in N.Y. (1944–45); subsequently studied composition with Randall Thompson at Princeton Univ. (1945–46) and with Aaron Copland at Tanglewood, Mass. (summer 1946); in 1953 received a diploma as Profesor Extraordinario de Composición (Ph.D.) from the Univ. of Chile; was awarded the honorary degree of Doctor Scientiae by the Catholic Univ. of Santiago (1971). From 1942 to 1961 he taught at the Univ. of Chile; in 1961 was engaged as prof. of composition and Latin-American music history at Indiana Univ. in Bloomington, and director of the Latin-American Music Center there.
WORKS· Opera-oratorio, *El retablo del rey pobre* for 3 Sopranos, Mezzo-soprano, Contralto, Tenor, Baritone, Chorus, and Small Orch. (1950–51); 3 ballets: *Juventud* (after Handel's *Solomon,* 1948); *Umbral del sueño* (1951); *The Tumbler's Prayer* (1960); oratorio, *The Days of God* (Washington, D.C., Nov. 2, 1976); 2 cantatas: *Cantata de Navidad* for Soprano and Orch. (1946) and *América, no en vano invocamos tu nombre* (1966); *Missa, in tempore discordiae* for Tenor, Chorus, and Orch. (1968–69); *Psalms* for Narrator and Wind Orch. (1962); *Songs,* in 3 movements, for Medium Voice and String Quartet (1945); *Canciones castellanas* for Soprano and 8 Instruments (1948); *Cantos de advenimiento* for Medium Voice, Cello, and Piano (1948); *Words of Don Quixote* for Baritone and Chamber Ensemble (Washington, Oct. 31, 1970); numerous songs and choruses. FOR ORCH.: *Escenas de Cortes y Pastores,* suite (1946); *Obertura festiva* (1948); 4 symphs.: No. 1 (1949; Santiago, July 1950); No. 2, *a la memoria de un vagabundo* (1954; Minneapolis, Feb. 17, 1956); No. 3 (1961; Washington, April 22, 1961); No. 4, *de la respuesta lejana* (Bloomington, Ind., 1967); Piano Concerto (1950); *Concerto da camera* for Woodwind Quartet, 2 Horns, Harp, and Strings (1952); *Serenata concertante* (1954–55; Louisville, May 3, 1955); *Jubileus musicus* (1956); *Concerto a tre* for Violin, Cel-

lo, Piano, and Orch. (Washington, May 7, 1965); concerto for Wind Orch. (1963–64); *Volte* for Piano, 15 Winds, Harp, and Percussion (1971); *Variaciones serenas* for String Orch. (1971).

Orth, John, American organist and composer; b. Annweiler, Bavaria, Dec. 2, 1850; d. Boston, May 3, 1932. His parents settled in Taunton, Mass., when he was a year old; he studied organ with his father; then went to Germany, where he took courses with Kullak and Deppe (piano); also had lessons with Liszt; studied composition with Faiszt, Weitzmann, Kiel, and P. Scharwenka. In 1875 he settled in Boston as a pianist and teacher; in lecture-recitals became a propagandist for Liszt's music in America. In 1883 he married his pupil Lizette E. Blood, known as **L.E. Orth** (d. Boston, Sept. 14, 1913), who was herself a composer of songs and piano pieces. Orth publ. a number of teaching pieces for piano.

d'Ortigue, Joseph-Louis, French musicologist; b. Cavaillon, Vaucluse, May 22, 1802; d. Paris, Nov. 20, 1866. He studied law in Aix-en-Provence; in 1829 settled in Paris, where he wrote articles on music for various journals. In 1857 he founded *La Maîtrise* (with Niedermeyer) and in 1862, the *Journal des Maîtrises* (with F. Clément), both periodicals for church music; in 1863 he became editor of *Le Ménestrel;* succeeded Berlioz as critic for the *Journal des Débats.* In his various positions he exercised considerable influence on musical life in Paris.
WRITINGS: *Le Balcon de l'opéra* (Paris, 1833; a book of essays); *De l'Ecole musicale italienne et de l'administration de l'Académie Royale de Musique* (1839; republ. 1840 as *Du Théâtre italien et de son influence* ...); *Abécédaire du plain chant* (1844); *Dictionnaire liturgique,* etc. (1854); *Introduction à l'étude comparée des tonalités, et principalement du chant grégorien et de la musique moderne* (1853); *La Musique à l'église* (1861), *Traité théorique et pratique de l'accompagnement du plainchant* (with Niedermeyer; 1856; Eng. trans. by W. Goodrich, N.Y., 1905).

Ortiz, Diego, Spanish composer; b. Toledo, c.1510; d. Naples, c.1570. He was in the service of the Duke of Alba as maestro de capilla at the vice-regal court in Naples from 1558 until 1565. He was one of the earliest masters of variations (divisions). His greatest work is *Trattado de glosas sobre clausulas y otros géneros de puntos en la música de violones* (Rome, 1553; modern ed. by M. Schneider, Berlin, 1913; 3rd ed., Kassel, 1967), containing early examples of instrumental variations and ornamental cadenzas (for viola da gamba alone with harpsichord). An Italian version of this work was also publ. at Rome in 1553 (*Il primo libro de Diego Ortiz Toletano,* etc.). In addition, Ortiz publ. a vol. of sacred music at Venice in 1565 (hymns, motets, Psalms, etc., for 4–7 voices). Some motets by him (in lute tablature) were included in Valderrábano's *Silva de Sirenas* (1547). Modern reprints of his sacred music are in the collections of Proske, Eslava, and Pedrell.

Orto, Marbriano (Marbrianus) de, Netherland-ish composer and singer; b. diocese of Tournai, c.1460; d. Nivelles, Feb. 1529. As a young man he was a singer in the papal choir at Rome (1484–99); was dean of the collegiate church of St. Gertrude in Nivelles (1489–96); in 1505 he was in the service of Philip the Fair of Burgundy; went to Spain with him in 1506, and was ennobled. In 1509–17 he was in the chapel of Archduke Charles (later Emperor Charles V). Petrucci publ. a book of 5 masses by him (1505), also 11 chansons for 4 voices in the *Odhecaton* (1500–1503), and a Lamentation in *Lamentationum Jeremias prophetae liber I* (1506); several MSS are in the Vienna Library and at the Univ. of Jena; Ambros reproduced an *Agnus* from the so-called "Mi-mi" Mass (based on the theme of 2 notes, E, A) in the supplement of his *Geschichte der Musik.*

Osborne, Nigel, English composer; b. Manchester, June 23, 1948. He studied at Oxford Univ. with Egon Wellesz and Kenneth Leighton; then traveled to Po-land and worked with Witold Rudziński and at the Polish Radio Experimental Studio in Warsaw (1970–71); in 1978 became a lecturer in music at the Univ. of Nottingham. In his compositions he strives to present the olden modalities of remote musical eras with the aid of modern techniques, including elec-tronic sound.
WORKS: *Beautiful Thing I* and *Beautiful Thing II* for Chamber Ensemble (1969–70); *Byzantine Epi-grams* for Chorus a cappella (1969); *7 Words,* can-tata (1969–71); *Charivari* for Orch. (1973); *Chanson-nier* for Chamber Ensemble (1975); *Passers By* for Bass Recorder, Cello, Electronic Synthesizer, and Diapositive (1976); *I am Goya* for Bass-baritone and 4 Instruments (1977); *Concert piece* for Cello and Orch. (1977); *Sinfonia* (London, Aug. 2, 1982).

Osthoff, Helmuth, distinguished German musi-cologist, father of **Wolfgang Osthoff;** b. Bielefeld, Aug. 13, 1896; d. Würzburg, Feb. 9, 1983. He studied music in Bielefeld and in Münster. He served in the German army during World War I; after the Armis-tice he resumed his studies at the Univ. of Münster (1919), and later (1920–22) took courses with Wolf, Kretzschmar, and Schünemann at the Univ. of Ber-lin, where he received his Ph.D. in 1922 with the dissertation *Der Lautenist Santino Garsi da Par-ma: Ein Beitrag zur Geschichte der oberitaliensi-schen Lautenmusik der Spätrenaissance* (publ. in Leipzig, 1926). He subsequently studied conducting with Brecher, composition with Klatte, and piano with Kwast at the Stern Cons. (1922–23). In 1923–26 he served as répétiteur at the Leipzig Opera; in 1926 he became assistant lecturer to Arnold Schering in the dept. of musicology at the Univ. of Halle; in 1928 he was appointed chief assistant to Schering in the dept. of music history at the Univ. of Berlin; com-pleted his Habilitation there in 1932 with his trea-tise *Die Niederländer und das deutsche Lied 1400–1640* (publ. in Berlin, 1938). In 1938 he became a prof. and director of the inst. of musicology at the Univ. of Frankfurt, positions he held until his retirement in 1964. He was especially noted for his

astute studies of Renaissance music. His other pub-lications include *Adam Krieger; Neue Beiträge zur Geschichte des deutschen Liedes in 17. Jahrhun-dert* (Leipzig, 1929; 2nd ed., 1970); *Johannes Brahms und seine Sendung* (Bonn, 1942); *Josquin Desprez* (2 vols., Tutzing, 1962–65). A Festschrift was publ. in Tutzing in 1961 to honor his 65th birthday, a 2nd in 1969 for his 70th birthday (contains a bibliography of his writings), and a 3rd in 1977 for his 80th birth-day.

Osthoff, Wolfgang, German musicologist, son of **Helmuth Osthoff;** b. Halle, March 17, 1927. He stud-ied piano and theory at the Frankfurt Staatliche Hochschule für Musik (1939–43); then took lessons in conducting with Kurt Thomas (1946–47). He subsequently studied musicology with his father at the Univ. of Frankfurt (1947–49) and with Georg-iades at the Univ. of Heidelberg (1949–54); re-ceived his Ph.D. there in 1954 with the dissertation *Das dramatische Spätwerk Claudio Monteverdis* (publ. in Tutzing, 1960). He taught at the Univ. of Munich (1957–64); completed his Habilitation there in 1965 with his *Theatergesang und darstellende Musik in der italienischen Renaissance* (publ. in Tutzing, 1969). He became a lecturer at the Univ. of Munich in 1966. In 1968 he was named a prof. of musicology at the Univ. of Würzburg. In addition to many scholarly articles dealing with music history from the 15th to the 19th century, he also contribut-ed to many music reference works.

Ostrčil, Otakar, eminent Czech conductor and composer; b. Smichov, near Prague, Feb. 25, 1879; d. Prague, Aug. 20, 1935. He studied languages at the Univ. of Prague, and then taught at a school in Prague (until 1920); at the same time took courses in piano with Adolf Mikeš (1893–95) and studied composition privately with Fibich (1895–1900). From 1909 till 1922 he conducted an amateur orch. in Prague; also conducted opera there (1914–19); in 1920 he succeeded Karel Kovařovic as principal con-ductor at the Prague National Theater. In his com-positions, Ostrčil continued the Romantic tradition of Czech music, with some modern elaborations re-vealing the influence of Mahler.
WORKS: Operas: *Vlasty skon* (*The Death of Vla-sta;* Prague, Dec. 14, 1904); *Kunálovy oči* (*Kunala's Eyes;* Prague, Nov. 25, 1908); *Poupě* (*The Bud;* Prague, Jan. 25, 1911); *Legenda z Erinu* (*The Legend of Erin;* Brno, June 16, 1921); *Honzovo královstvi* (*Johnny's Kingdom;* Brno, May 26, 1934); Symph. (1905); Sinfonietta (1921); *Summer,* 2 symph. move-ments (1926); *Calvary,* set of variations (1928); sev-eral cantatas; String Quartet; Trio for Violin, Viola, and Piano; several song cycles.

Othmayr, Caspar, German composer; b. Amberg, March 12, 1515; d. Nuremberg, Feb. 4, 1553. He stud-ied at the Univ. of Heidelberg; in 1536 became "magister," and in 1545 rector, of the monastery school at Heilsbronn, near Ansbach; in 1548 became provost in Ansbach. He was celebrated not only for his sacred works but also for his ingenious polyphonic settings of secular songs; of the latter, the most important are *Reuterische und jegerische Liedlein* for 4 and 5 Voices (1549). Sacred works include: *Cantilenae* (1546); *Epitaphium Lutheri* (1546); *Bicinia sacra* (1547); *Symbola principum* (1547; new ed. by H. Albrecht, 1941); *Trincina* (1549).

Otterloo, Willem van, Dutch conductor and composer; b. Winterswijk, Dec. 27, 1907; d. as a result of an automobile accident, Melbourne, Australia, July 27, 1978. He studied cello with Orobio de Castro and composition with Sem Dresden at the Amsterdam Cons.; after graduation he was engaged as cellist in the Utrecht Orch.; in 1933 became its assistant conductor, and in 1937, associate conductor. From 1949 to 1972 he conducted the Residentie Orch. at The Hague, bringing it to a state of excellence. In 1967 he went to Australia as conductor of the Melbourne Symph. Orch. until 1971. From 1973 until his death he was chief conductor of the Sydney Symph. Orch.; in the interim he served as Generalmusikdirektor of the Düsseldorf Symph. Orch. (1974–77).

Ottman, Robert W., American music theorist and pedagogue; b. Fulton, N.Y., May 3, 1914. He studied music theory with Bernard Rogers at the Eastman School of Music in Rochester, N.Y. (M.Mus., 1943). During and after World War II he served in the infantry in the U.S. Army (1943–46); then took lessons in composition with Alec Rowley at Trinity College of Music in London; in 1946 was engaged as a lecturer in music at North Texas State Univ., from which he also received his Ph.D. (1956). He publ. a number of excellent school manuals: *Music for Sight Singing* (N.Y., 1956); *Elementary Harmony, Theory and Practice* (N.Y., 1961; 3rd ed., 1983); *Advanced Harmony, Theory and Practice* (N.Y., 1961; new ed., 1972); *The 371 Chorales of J.S. Bach* (with Frank Mainous; very successful; N.Y., 1966); *Workbook for Elementary Harmony* (N.Y., 1974); *Programmed Rudiments of Music* (with Frank Mainous; N.Y., 1978).

Otto, Lisa, German soprano; b. Dresden, Nov. 14, 1919. She was educated at the Hochschule für Musik in Dresden; made her debut in 1941 at the Landestheater in Beuthen. She was a member of the Dresden State Opera (1945–50); then sang at the Deutsche Oper in West Berlin and at the Bayreuth Festival. She toured widely, visiting the U.S., South America, and Japan.

Oulibicheff, Alexander, Russian official and music amateur; b. Dresden, April 13, 1794; d. Nizhny-Novgorod, Feb. 5, 1858. He studied violin at home in Dresden, where his father was Russian ambassador; was educated in Germany. When the family returned to Russia after 1812, he was employed in the Ministry of Finance, and later in the Ministry of Foreign Affairs (1816–30). He was the editor of the French periodical *Journal de St. Petersbourg* (1812–30); retired to his estate in Nizhny-Novgorod in 1841. His greatest admiration was for Mozart; his magnum opus is *Nouvelle biographie de Mozart,*

suivie d'un aperçu sur l'histoire générale de la musique (3 vols., Moscow, 1843; 2nd German ed., 1859; Russian trans. by Modest Tchaikovsky, Moscow, 1890). By way of praising Mozart, he inserted deprecating remarks on Beethoven's later style; when he was taken to task for this lack of appreciation (by Lenz and others), he publ. *Beethoven, ses critiques et ses glossateurs* (Leipzig and Paris, 1857), in which he emphatically reiterated his sharp criticism of Beethoven's harmonic and formal procedures.

Oury, Anna Caroline (née **Belleville**), German pianist; b. Landshut, June 24, 1808; d. Munich, July 22, 1880. Her father, a French nobleman named Belleville, was director of the Munich Opera. She studied with Czerny in Vienna; made her debut there; then gave concerts in Munich and in Paris; settled for many years in London, where she married the violinist **Antonio James Oury** (b. London, c.1880; d. Norwich, July 25, 1883) in 1831; toured with him in Russia, Germany, Austria, and France. She wrote a number of piano pieces in the salon style, of which nearly 200 were publ.

Ouseley, Sir Frederick Arthur Gore, English composer and theorist; b. London, Aug. 12, 1825; d. Hereford, April 6, 1889. He was the son of Sir Gore Ouseley, ambassador to Persia; studied at Oxford Univ. (B.A., 1846; M.A., 1849; D.Mus., 1854). He was ordained a priest in 1849; was curate at St. Barnabas, Pimlico (1849–51). In 1855 he succeeded Sir Henry Bishop as prof. of music at Oxford Univ. He was a fine organist, and excelled in fugal improvisation.

Overton, Hall, American composer; b. Bangor, Mich., Feb. 23, 1920; d. New York, Nov. 24, 1972. He studied piano at the Chicago Musical College; served in the U.S. Army overseas (1942–45). After the war, he studied composition with Persichetti at the Juilliard School of Music, N.Y., graduating in 1951; also took private lessons with Wallingford Riegger and Darius Milhaud. At the same time, he filled professional engagements as a jazz pianist and contributed to the magazine *Jazz Today*.
WORKS: Operas: *The Enchanted Pear Tree,* after Boccaccio's *Decameron* (Juilliard School of Music, N.Y., Feb. 7, 1950); *Pietro's Petard* (N.Y., June 1963); *Huckleberry Finn,* after Mark Twain (Juilliard American Opera Center, N.Y., May 20, 1971); 2 symphs. (1955, 1962); 2 string quartets; String Trio; Viola Sonata; Cello Sonata; *Pulsations* for Chamber Ensemble (his last work; 1972).

Ozawa, Seiji, glamorous Japanese conductor of extraordinary accomplishments; b. Hoten, Manchuria, of Japanese parents, Sept. 1, 1935. His father was a Buddhist, his mother a Christian. The family went back to Japan in 1944, at the end of Japanese occupation of Manchuria. Ozawa began to study piano; at 16 he enrolled at the Toho School of Music in Tokyo, where he studied composition and conducting; one of his teachers, Hideo Saito, a professional cellist, profoundly influenced his development as a musician; he graduated in 1959 with first prizes in composition and conducting. By that time he had already conducted concerts with the NHK (Japan Broadcasting Corp.) Symph. Orch. and the Japan Phil.; upon Saito's advice, he went to Europe; to defray his expenses he became a motor-scooter salesman for a Japanese firm, and promoted the product in Italy and France. In 1959 he won first prize at the international competition for conductors in Besançon, and was befriended by Charles Munch and Eugène Bigot; he then studied conducting with Bigot in Paris. Munch arranged for Ozawa to come to the U.S. and to study conducting at the Berkshire Music Center in Tanglewood; in 1960 he won its Koussevitzky Prize, and was awarded a scholarship to work with Herbert von Karajan and the Berlin Phil. Leonard Bernstein heard him in Berlin and engaged him as an assistant conductor of the N.Y. Phil. On April 14, 1961, he made his first appearance with the orch. at Carnegie Hall; later that year, he accompanied Bernstein and the orch. on its tour of Japan. In 1962 he was invited to return as a guest conductor of the NHK Symph. Orch., but difficulties arose between him and the players, who objected to being commanded in an imperious manner by one of their own countrymen; still, he succeeded in obtaining engagements with other Japanese orchs., which he conducted on his periodic visits to his homeland.

In the meantime, Ozawa advanced significantly in his American career; from 1964 to 1968 he was music director of the Ravinia Festival, the summer home of the Chicago Symph. Orch.; in 1969 he served as its principal guest conductor; from 1965 to 1969 he also was music director of the Toronto Symph. Orch., which he took to England in 1965. From 1970 to 1976 he was music director of the San Francisco Symph. Orch., and then its music adviser in 1976–77. In the spring of 1977 Ozawa took the San Francisco Symph. on a tour of Europe, visiting 15 cities, some in Russia, where he was received with exceptional acclaim. Even before completing his tenure in San Francisco, he had begun a close association with the Boston Symph. Orch.; with Gunther Schuller, he became co-artistic director of its Berkshire Music Center in 1970; in 1972 he assumed the post of music adviser of the Boston Symph., and in 1973 he became its conductor and music director, and sole artistic director of the Berkshire Music Center, an astonishing event in American music annals, marking the first time an oriental musician was chosen solely by his merit to head the Boston Symph. Orch., which was for years since its foundation the exclusive preserve of German, and later French and Russian, conductors. In 1976 Ozawa took the Boston Symph. on a tour of Europe; in 1978 he escorted it to Japan, where those among Japanese musicians who had been skeptical about his abilities greeted his spectacular ascendance with national pride. Another unprecedented event took place in the spring of 1979, when Ozawa traveled with the Boston Symph. to the People's Republic of China on an official cultural visit; in August 1979 Ozawa and the orch. went on a tour of European music festivals. The centennial of the Boston Symph. Orch. in 1981 was marked by a series of concerts, under Ozawa's direction, which included appearances in 14 American cities and a tour of Japan, France, Germany, Austria, and England.

With dormant racial prejudices finally abandoned in American society, Ozawa's reputation rose to universal recognition of his remarkable talent. He proved himself a consummate master of orchestral playing, equally penetrating in the classical repertoire as in the works of modern times; his performances of such demanding scores as Mahler's 8th Symph. and Schoenberg's *Gurrelieder* constituted proofs of his commanding technical skill, affirmed *a fortiori* by his assured presentation of the rhythmically and contrapuntally intricate 4th Symph. of Charles Ives. All these challenging scores Ozawa consuetudinarily conducted from memory, an astonishing feat in itself. He was married twice: first to the Japanese pianist **Kyoko Edo,** and 2nd, to a Eurasian, Vera Ilyan. He received an honorary doctorate in music from the Univ. of San Francisco in 1971, and one from the New England Cons. of Music in 1982.

P

Paap, Wouter, eminent Dutch musicologist and composer; b. Utrecht, May 7, 1908; d. Lage Vuursche (Baarn), Oct. 7, 1981. He studied piano and music theory; devoted himself mainly to musicology; served as editor in chief of the Dutch music periodical *Mens en Melodie;* was also co-editor of the valuable music encyclopedia in the Dutch-language *Algemene Muziekencyclopedie* (6 vols., Amsterdam, 1957–63).

Pablo, Luis de, Spanish composer; b. Bilbao, Jan. 28, 1930. He studied jurisprudence at Madrid Univ., receiving a law degree in 1952. He attended the Cons. of Madrid; traveled to Paris, where he received musical advice from Messiaen and Boulez; also took courses at the summer seminars for new music at Darmstadt. Returning to Spain, he organized the modern performance groups Tiempo y Música and Alea. Like most Spanish composers, he followed in his youth the precepts of the national school, with the music of Manuel de Falla as principal influence, but soon he adopted hyperserial techniques, in which whole tonal complexes, chords, or groups of chords become thematic units; similarly, dynamic processes assume the role of compositional determinants, eventually attaining the ultimate libertarianism in promiscuous cross-fertilization of all media, all styles, and all techniques of musical composition.

Pacchiarotti, Gasparo, famous Italian male soprano; b. Fabriano, near Ancona, 1740 (baptized, May 21); d. Padua, Oct. 28, 1821. He studied under Bertoni at St. Mark's in Venice; was principal soloist in San Marco in 1765–68; from 1769, sang at the principal Italian theaters with brilliant success; in 1778, went to London with Bertoni, returning there in 1781–84 and 1791. In 1793 he retired and settled in Padua; sang for Napoleon when the latter passed through Padua in 1796. A. Calegari publ. *Modi generali del canto* (1836), based on Pacchiarotti's method.

Pachelbel, Carl Theodorus, son of **Johann Pachelbel;** b. Stuttgart, Nov. 24, 1690; d. Charleston, S.C., Sept. 14, 1750. He emigrated to Boston in the 1730s and in 1733 assisted in the erection of the organ of Trinity Church in Newport, R.I., of which he was organist for about a year. On Jan. 21, 1736, he advertised a concert in N.Y., the first there of which details have been recorded, and on March 8, a 2nd one. He then moved to Charleston, became organist of St. Philip's Church, and on Nov. 22, 1737, gave a public concert in his home. An 8-part Magnificat, the only known composition of Carl Pachelbel, is in the State Library in Berlin (publ. N.Y., 1937).

Pachelbel, Johann, great German composer and organist; b. Nuremberg (baptized, Sept. 1), 1653; d. there (buried, March 9), 1706. He studied music in Nuremberg with Heinrich Schwemmer; received instruction in composition and instrumental performance from G.C. Wecker; pursued his academic studies at the local St. Lorenz school; also attended the lectures at the Auditorium Aegidianum. He then took courses briefly at the Univ. of Altdorf (1669–70), and served as organist at the Lorenzkirche there. He subsequently was accepted as a scholarship student at the Gymnasium Poeticum in Regensburg, and took private music lessons with Kaspar Prentz. In 1673 he went to Vienna as deputy organist at St. Stephen's Cathedral. In 1677 he assumed the position of court organist in Eisenach. In 1678 he became organist at the Protestant Predigerkirche in Erfurt. It was in Erfurt that he established his reputation as a master organist, composer, and teacher. He was a friend of the Bach family, and was the teacher of Johann Christoph Bach, who in turn taught Johann Sebastian Bach. On Oct. 25, 1681, Pachelbel married Barbara Gabler; she and their infant son died during the plague of 1683. He then married Judith Drommer on Aug. 24, 1684; they had 5 sons and 2 daughters. Two of their sons, **Wilhelm Hieronymus** and **Carl Theodorus,** became musicians; another son, Johann Michael, became an instrument maker; a daughter, Amalie, became a painter. In 1690 he accepted an appointment as Württemberg court musician and organist in Stuttgart. However, with the French invasion in the fall of 1692 he fled to Nuremberg; in November of that year he became town organist in Gotha. In 1695 he succeeded his teacher Wecker as organist at St. Sebald in Nuremberg, a position he held until his death. Pachelbel was one of the most significant predecessors of Johann Sebastian Bach. His liturgical organ music was of the highest order, particularly his splendid organ chorales. His non-liturgical keyboard music was likewise noteworthy, especially his fugues and variations (of the latter, his *Hexachordum Apollinis* of 1699 is extraordinary). He was equally gifted as a composer of vocal music. His motets, sacred concertos, and concertato settings of the *Magnificat* are fine examples of German church music. Pachelbel was a pioneer in notational symbolism of intervals, scales, and pitch levels arranged to correspond to the meaning of the words. Thus, his setting of the motet *Durch Adams Fall* is accomplished by a falling figure in the bass; exaltation is expressed by a rising series of arpeggios in a major key; steadfast faith is conveyed by a repeated note; satanic evil is translated into an ominous figuration of a broken diminished-seventh-chord. Generally speaking, joyful moods are portrayed by major keys, mournful states of soul by minor keys, a practice which became a standard mode of expression through the centuries.

Pachelbel, Wilhelm Hieronymus, German organist and composer, son of **Johann Pachelbel;** b. Erfurt (baptized, Aug. 29), 1686; d. Nuremberg, 1764. His only known teacher was his father, who gave him instruction in both keyboard instruments and composition. He is believed to have begun his career as an organist in Fürth; then was organist of the Predigerkirche in Erfurt. In 1706 he became organist of the Jakobikirche in Nuremberg; that same year was named organist at St. Egidien there. In 1719 he became organist at St. Sebald, a post he held until his death. Little of his music is extant, all of it being for keyboard instruments. He publ. *Musicalisches Vergnügen bestehend in einem Praeludio, Fuga und Fantasia, sowohl auf die Orgel als auch auf das Clavier . . . vorgestellt und componiert* in D major (Nuremberg, 1725?) and *Praeludium und Fuga* in C major (Nuremberg, 1725?). He also composed *Fantasia super "Meine Seele, lass es gehen"; Fantasia* in B-flat major; *O Lamm Gottes unschuldig* for Clavier; *Toccata* in G major. See H.J. Moser and T. Fedtke, *Wilhelm Hieronymus Pachelbel: Gesamtausgabe der erhaltenen Werke für Orgel und Clavier* (Kassel, 1957).

Pachmann, Vladimir de, eccentric Russian pianist; b. Odessa, July 27, 1848; d. Rome, Jan. 6, 1933. He received his primary music education at home from his father, an Austrian violinist; then went to Vienna, where he enrolled in the piano class of Prof. Dachs at the Vienna Cons. He began his concert career with a tour of Russia in 1869; he was 40 years old before he made a decisive impact on the international scene; his first American tour, in 1891, was sensationally successful, and it was in America that he began exhibiting his curious eccentricities, some of them undoubtedly calculated to produce shock effect: he made grimaces when he did not like his own playing and shouted "Bravo!" when he played a number to his satisfaction; even more bizarre was his crawling under the grand piano after the concert, claiming that he was looking for the wrong notes he had accidentally hit; all this could be explained as idiosyncratic behavior; but he also allowed himself to mutilate the music itself, by inserting arpeggios between phrases and extra chords at the end of a piece. Most American critics were outraged by his shenanigans, but some, notably Philip Hale, found mitigation in the poetic quality of his interpretations. Pachmann was particularly emotional in playing Chopin, when his facial contortions became quite obnoxious; James Huneker dubbed him "Chopinzee." Pachmann did not lack official honors; in 1885, on his tour of Denmark, he was made a Knight of the Order of Danebrog; in 1916 the London Phil. Society awarded him the Beethoven Medal. His personal life was turbulent; he married frequently (the exact number of his wives is in dispute). His first wife was Maggie Oakey, whom he married in 1884; she edited several Chopin études, indicating Pachmann's own fingering; they were divorced in 1895.

Pacini, Giovanni, Italian composer; b. Catania, Feb. 17, 1796; d. Pescia, Dec. 6, 1867. He was a pupil of Marchesi and Padre Mattei at Bologna, and of Furlanetto at Venice; his first opera was *Don Pomponio* (1813; not perf.); then came *Annetta e Lucinda* (Milan, Oct. 17, 1813); up to 1835 he had produced over 40 operas on various Italian stages, when the failure of *Carlo di Borgogna* (Feb. 21, 1835) at Venice temporarily checked the flow of dramatic composition; he went to Viareggio, near Lucca, and established a very successful school of music there, for which he wrote several short treatises—*Corso teoretico-pratico di lezioni di armonia*), *Cenni storici sulla musica e trattato di contrappunto* (1864)—and built a private theater. Later he removed the school to Lucca. In 1840 Pacini, who prided himself on rapid work, wrote his dramatic masterpiece, *Saffo*, in 28 days (Naples, Nov. 29, 1840; enthusiastically received). Forty more operas followed up to 1867; the best were *Medea* (Palermo, Nov. 28, 1843), *La Regina di Cipro* (Turin, Feb. 7, 1846), and *Niccolò de' Lapi* (Florence, Oct. 29, 1873; posthumous production). Pacini also wrote numerous oratorios, cantatas, masses, etc.; a *Dante* symph.; an Octet; 6 string quartets; other chamber music, vocal duets, and arias. He was an active contributor to several musical papers; publ. memoirs, *Le mie memorie artistiche* (Florence, 1865; enlarged by Cicconetti, 1872; revised by F. Magnani, 1875). His brother, **Emilio Pacini** (b. 1810; d. Neuilly, near Paris, Dec. 2, 1898), was a distinguished librettist.

Pacius, Fredrik (Friedrich), German-born Finnish composer; b. Hamburg, March 19, 1809; d. Helsinki, Jan. 8, 1891. He studied violin with Spohr and composition with Hauptmann. He served as a violinist in the Royal Chapel in Stockholm (1828–34); then went to Helsinki, where he organized a choral society (1835) and later (1845) established regular symph. concerts there. Pacius wrote the first Finnish opera, *Kung Karls jakt* (to a Swedish libretto); it was staged in Helsinki on March 24, 1852. He was the author of the Finnish national anthem, *Maamme laulu*, set to the words of the Swedish poem *Vartland*, later trans. into Finnish (1848); he also wrote many other songs of a Swedish-Finnish inspiration. Among his other works are the opera *Lorelcy* (Helsinki, April 28, 1887); Violin Concerto (1845); numerous choral works and songs.

Paderewski, Ignacy (Ignace) Jan, celebrated Polish pianist and composer; b. Kurylowka, Podolia (Russian Poland), Nov. 18, 1860; d. New York, June 29, 1941. His father was an administrator of country estates; his mother died soon after his birth. From early childhood, Paderewski was attracted to piano music; he received some musical instruction from Peter Sowinski, who taught him 4-hands arrangements of operas. His first public appearance was in a charity concert at the age of 11, when he played piano with his sister. His playing aroused interest among wealthy patrons, who took him to Kiev. He was then sent to Warsaw, where he entered the Cons., learned to play trombone, and joined the school band. He also continued serious studies of

piano playing; his teachers at the Warsaw Cons. were Schlözer, Strobl, and Janotha. In 1875 and 1877 he toured to provincial Russian towns with the Polish violinist Cielewicz; in the interim periods he took courses in composition at the Warsaw Cons., and upon graduation in 1878 he was engaged as a member of the piano faculty there. In 1880 he married a young music student named Antonina Korsak, but she died 9 days after giving birth to a child, on Oct. 10, 1880. In 1882 he went to Berlin to study composition with Kiel; there he met Anton Rubinstein, who gave him encouraging advice and urged him to compose piano music. He resigned from his teaching job at the Warsaw Cons. and began to study orchestration in Berlin with Heinrich Urban. While on a vacation in the Tatra Mountains (which inspired his *Tatra Album* for piano) he met the celebrated Polish actress Modjeska, who proposed to finance his further piano studies with Leschetizky in Vienna. Paderewski followed this advice and spent several years as a Leschetizky student. He continued his career as a concert pianist. On March 3, 1888, he gave his first Paris recital, and on Nov. 10, 1888, played a concert in Vienna, both with excellent success. He also began receiving recognition as a composer. Anna Essipoff (who was married to Leschetizky) played his piano concerto in Vienna under the direction of Hans Richter. Paderewski made his London debut on May 9, 1890. On Nov. 17, 1891, he played for the first time in N.Y., and was acclaimed with an adulation rare for pianists; by some counts he gave 107 concerts in 117 days in N.Y. and other American cities and attended 86 dinner parties; his wit, already fully developed, made him a social lion in wealthy American salons. At one party, it was reported, the hostess confused him with a famous polo player who was also expected to be a guest, and greeted him effusively. "No," Paderewski is supposed to have replied, "he is a rich soul who plays polo, and I am a poor Pole who plays solo." American spinsters beseeched him for a lock of his luxurious mane of hair; he invariably obliged, and when his valet observed that at this rate he would soon be bald, he said, "Not I, my dog." There is even a story related by a gullible biographer that Paderewski could charm beasts by his art and that a spider used to come down from the ceiling in Paderewski's lodgings in Vienna and sit at the piano every time Paderewski played a certain Chopin étude. Paderewski eclipsed even Caruso as an idol of the masses. In 1890 he made a concert tour in Germany; also toured South America, South Africa, and Australia. In 1898 he purchased a beautiful home, the Villa Riond-Bosson on Lake Geneva, Switzerland; in 1899 he married Helena Gorska, Baroness von Rosen. In 1900, by a deed of trust, Paderewski established a fund of $10,000 (the original trustees were William Steinway, Major H.L. Higginson, and Dr. William Mason), the interest from which was to be used for triennial prizes given "to composers of American birth without distinction as to age or religion" for works in the following categories: symphonies, concertos, and chamber music. In 1910, on the occasion of the centennial of Chopin's birth, Paderewski donated $60,000 for the construction of the Chopin Memorial Hall in Warsaw; in the same year he contributed $100,000 for the erection of the statue of King Jagiello in Warsaw, on the quinquecentennial of his victory over the Teutonic Knights in 1410. In 1913 he purchased a ranch in Paso Robles in California.

Although cosmopolitan in his culture, Paderewski remained a great Polish patriot. During the First World War he donated the entire proceeds from his concerts to a fund for the Polish people caught in the war between Russia and Germany. After the establishment of the independent Polish state, Paderewski served as its representative in Washington; in 1919 he was named prime minister of the Polish Republic, the first musician to occupy such a post in any country at any period. He took part in the Versailles Treaty conference; it was then that Prime Minister Clemenceau of France welcomed Paderewski with the famous, if possibly apocryphal, remark: "You, a famous pianist, a prime minister! What a comedown!" Paderewski resigned his post on Dec. 10, 1919. He reentered politics in 1920 in the wake of the Russian invasion of Poland that year, when he became a delegate to the League of Nations; he resigned on May 7, 1921, and resumed his musical career. On Nov. 22, 1922, he gave his first concert after a hiatus of many years at Carnegie Hall in N.Y. In 1939 he made his last American tour. Once more during his lifetime Poland was invaded, this time by both Germany and Russia. Once more Paderewski was driven to political action. He joined the Polish government-in-exile in France and was named president of its parliament on Jan. 23, 1940. He returned to the U.S. on Nov. 6, 1940, a few months before his death. At the order of President Roosevelt, his body was given state burial in Arlington National Cemetery, pending the return of his remains to Free Poland. Paderewski received many honors. He held the following degrees: Ph.D. from the Univ. of Lemberg (Lwow, 1912); D.Mus. from Yale Univ. (1917); Ph.D. from the Univ. of Cracow (1919); D.C.L. from Oxford Univ. (1920); LL.D. from Columbia Univ. (1922); Ph.D. from the Univ. of Southern Calif. (1923); Ph.D. from the Univ. of Poznan (1924); and Ph.D. from the Univ. of Glasgow (1925). He also held the Grand Cross of the French Legion of Honor (1922). A postage stamp with his picture was issued in Poland in 1919, and 2 postage stamps honoring him in the series "Men of Liberty" were issued in the U.S. in 1960.

As an artist, Paderewski was a faithful follower of the Romantic school, which allowed free, well-nigh improvisatory declensions from the written notes, tempi, and dynamics; judged by 20th-century standards of precise rendering of the text, Paderewski's interpretations appear surprisingly free, but this very personal freedom of performance moved contemporary audiences to ecstasies of admiration. Also, Paderewski's virtuoso technique, which astonished his listeners, has been easily matched by any number of pianists of succeeding generations. Yet his position in the world of the performing arts remains undiminished by the later achievements of younger men and women pianists. As a composer,

Paderewski also belongs to the Romantic school. At least one of his piano pieces, the *Menuet in G* (which is a movement of his set of *6 Humoresques* for piano), achieved enormous popularity. His other compositions, however, never sustained a power of renewal and were eventually relegated to the archives of unperformed music. His opera *Manru*, composed in 1897–1900, dealing with folk life in the Tatra Mountains, was produced in Dresden on May 29, 1901, and was also performed by the Metropolitan Opera in N.Y. on Feb. 14, 1902. Another major work, a Symph. in B minor, was first performed by the Boston Symph. Orch. on Feb. 12, 1909. His other works included a Piano Concerto in A minor (1888); *Fantaisie polonaise* for Piano and Orch. (1893); Violin Sonata (1880); songs; and the following compositions for piano solo: *Prelude and Capriccio; 3 Pieces (Gavotte, Mélodie, Valse mélancholique); Krakowiak; Elégie; 3 Polish Dances; Introduction and Toccata; Chants du voyageur* (5 pieces); *6 Polish Dances; Album de mai* (5 pieces), *Variations and Fugue; Tatra Album* (also arranged for Piano, 4-hands); *6 Humoresques de concert* (which includes the famous *Menuet in G*); *Dans le désert; Miscellanea* (7 pieces); *Légende;* Sonata in E-flat minor (1903). A complete list of Paderewski's works was publ. in the *Bolletino bibliografico musicale* (Milan, 1932).

Padilla, Lola Artôt de, Spanish soprano, daughter of the baritone **Mariano Padilla y Ramos;** b. Sèvres, near Paris, Oct. 5, 1876; d. Berlin, April 12, 1933. She was trained solely by her mother, the singer **Désirée Artôt.** After singing in salons and concerts, she was engaged by Albert Carré for the Opéra-Comique in 1903. Later she toured as a concert singer through Europe; was engaged at the Komische Oper in Berlin in 1905–8 as prima donna; in 1909–27, was a member of the Royal (later State) Opera in Berlin; then retired.

Paër, Ferdinando, significant composer; b. Parma, June 1, 1771; d. Paris, May 3, 1839. He was a pupil of Fortunati and Ghiretti. His career as an opera composer began in 1792, when he produced the operas *Circe* (Venice) and *Le astuzie amorose* (Parma). In that year he was also appointed honorary maestro di cappella to the court of Parma. In Vienna, from 1797–1802, his style underwent a change, both harmony and orchestration showing increased variety and fullness; *Camilla, ossia Il sotterraneo* (Vienna, Feb. 23, 1799) is considered his best opera. Paër succeeded Naumann as court Kapellmeister at Dresden in 1802; *Leonara, ossia L'amore conjugale* (Dresden, Oct. 3, 1804) is identical in subject with Beethoven's *Fidelio*. In 1807 he went to Paris, becoming maître de chapelle to Napoleon and conductor of the Opéra-Comique; later (1812) he succeeded Spontini at the Italian Opera, where he remained, through the vicissitudes of Catalini's domination and the joint conductorship of Rossini (1824–26), his successful rival on the stage, until his forced resignation in 1827 (he was held to blame for the poor financial condition of the theater). In 1828 he received the cross of the Legion of Honor; was elected to the Institut in 1831; and in 1832 was appointed conductor of the royal chamber music. Although some of his 43 operas were successful—e.g., *Sargino* (Dresden, May 26, 1803) and *Agnese* (first perf. privately, near Parma, Oct. 1809)—they have all disappeared from the repertoire, except for *Le Maître de chapelle* (Paris, March 29, 1821), which is occasionally performed in France; he also wrote 2 oratorios and a Passion, 10 cantatas, and much other vocal music; a *Symphonie bacchante* and variations on *Vive Henri IV*, for Full Orch.; 4 grand military marches; many piano variations; etc.

Paganini, Niccolò, most famous of violin virtuosos; b. Genoa, Oct. 27, 1782; d. Nice, May 27, 1840. His father, a poor shopkeeper with little musical knowledge, but loving the art, taught him to play on the mandolin, and then procured abler teachers for his gifted son; under G. Servetto, and after him the maestro di cappella G. Costa, Niccolò's progress in violin playing was rapid; at 8 he composed a sonata for violin; in 1793 he appeared in public; from 1795 he studied with Ghiretti and began to compose seriously. His career as an independent virtuoso dates from 1798, when he ran away from his father after a concert at Lucca, and made a tour by himself to Pisa and other places. Though only 16, he was passionately fond of gambling, and addicted to all forms of dissipation; at Livorno he had to part with his violin to pay a gambling debt, but a French merchant named Levron lent him a fine Guarnerius violin, and was so charmed with his playing that he made him a present of it. In 1804 Paganini went home, and spent a year in assiduous practice; he set out again on his travels in 1805, arousing unbounded enthusiasm; was soon appointed court solo violinist at Lucca (where his novel performances on the G string began), and stayed there until 1808; then up to 1827 he traveled throughout Italy, his renown spreading from year to year and his vast technical resources maturing and augmenting so that victory over would-be rivals (Lafont at Milan, 1816, and Lipinski at Piacenza, 1817) was easy. When he left Italy for the first time in 1828, his opening concert, at Vienna, was a veritable triumph; from the municipality he received the great gold medal of St. Salvator; from the Emperor, the (honorary) title of court virtuoso. He reached Berlin in March 1829, Paris in March 1831; played for the first time in London on June 3, 1831. Within a year he accumulated a fortune in Britain. The winter of 1833–34 was passed in Paris; he then retired for a time to his villa at Parma, though often visiting Paris. He spent the winter of 1838 in Paris, where his chief disorder, laryngeal phthisis, was aggravated by the climate. In search of sun and fresh air he went to Nice, but soon died there.

Paganini's stupendous technique (in double stops, left-hand pizzicato, staccato, harmonics), great power, and perfect control of tone, the romantic passion and intense energy of his style, quite apart from mere tricks of virtuosity (such as tuning up the A string by a semitone or playing the *Witches'*

Dance on one string after severing the other 3 on stage, in sight of the audience, with a pair of scissors), made him the marvel of his time. He was an artist quite sui generis, whose dazzling genius held his audiences spellbound, and impressed musicians and amateurs alike.

WORKS: 24 *Capricci per violino solo,* op. 1; (piano transcriptions by Schumann and Liszt); 6 *Sonate per violino e chitarra,* op. 2; same, op. 3; 6 *Gran quartetti a violino, viola, chitarra e violoncello,* opp. 4, 5; Concerto in B minor, *La Campanella,* with rondo "à la clochette," op. 7; *Le Streghe,* variations on a theme by Süssmayr, op. 8; Variations on *God Save the King,* op. 9; *Il Carnevale di Venezia,* 20 variations, op. 10; *Concert allegro moto perpetuo,* op. 11; Variations on *Non più mesta,* op. 12; Variations on *Di tanti palpiti,* op. 13; *Variazioni di bravura* on airs from *Mosè;* 60 studies in 60 progressive variations on the air *Barucabà* (of these only opp. 1–5 were publ. during his life, the others posthumously). A number of works are still in MS. A piece for violin and guitar, written by Paganini in 1815, was publ. in 1977 as his Concerto No. 6, ed. by Ruggiero Ricci. His collected works are being publ. in an Edizione Nazionale, ed. by L. Ronga et al. (1976–).

Pahissa, Jaime, Catalan composer; b. Barcelona, Oct. 7, 1880; d. Buenos Aires, Oct. 27, 1969. He was a practicing architect for 4 years before turning to music as a profession; studied composition with Morera in Barcelona. He associated himself with the Catalan nationalist movement in art, obtaining his first important success in 1906 with the Romantic opera *La presó de Lleida (The Prison of Lérida),* which had 100 consecutive performances in Barcelona; it was later rewritten and produced in Barcelona on Feb. 8, 1928, under the title *La Princesa Margarita,* again obtaining a notable success. Other operas produced in Barcelona were *Gala Plácida* (Jan. 15, 1913) and *Marinela* (March 31, 1923). Among his orch. works the most remarkable is *Monodía,* written in unisons, octaves, double octaves, etc., without using any other intervals, and depending for its effect only on instrumental variety (Barcelona, Oct. 12, 1925); in a different vein is his *Suite Intertonal* (Barcelona, Oct. 24, 1926), based on his own method of free tonal and polytonal composition. In 1935 Pahissa emigrated to Argentina, settling in Buenos Aires, where he continued to compose; he also established himself as a teacher and writer there. He publ. in Buenos Aires several books: *Espíritu y cuerpo de la música* (1945); *Los grandes problemas de la música* (1945; new ed., 1954); *Vida y obra de Manuel de Falla* (Buenos Aires, 1947; also in Eng., London, 1954); *Sendas y cumbres de la música española* (1955). A detailed account of Pahissa's career in Barcelona is found in the *Diccionario de la música ilustrado* (1930).

Paik, Nam June, Korean-American avant-garde composer and experimenter in the visual arts; b. Seoul, July 20, 1932. He studied first at the Univ. of Tokyo; then went to Germany, where he took courses in music theory with Thrasybulos Georgiades in Munich and with Wolfgang Fortner in Freiburg im Breisgau. Turning toward electronics, he did experimental work at the Electronic Music Studio in Cologne (1958–60); attended the summer seminars for new music at Darmstadt (1957–61). In his showings he pursues the objective of total art as the sum of integrated synesthetic experiences, involving all sorts of actions—walking, talking, dressing, undressing, drinking, smoking, moving furniture, engaging in quaquaversal commotion—intended to demonstrate that any human or inhuman action becomes an artistic event through the power of volitional concentration of an ontological imperative. Paik attracted attention at his duo recitals with the topless cellist Charlotte Moorman, at which he acted as a surrogate cello, with his denuded spinal column serving as the fingerboard for Ms. Moorman's cello bow, while his bare skin provided an area for intermittent pizzicati. About 1963 Paik began experimenting with videotape as a medium for sounds and images; his initial experiment in this field was *Global Groove*, a high-velocity collage of intermingled television bits, which included instantaneous commercials, fragments from news telecasts, and subliminal extracts from regular programs, subjected to topological alterations. His list of works (some of them consisting solely of categorical imperatives) includes *Ommaggio a Cage* for piano demolition, breakage of raw eggs, spray painting of hands in jet black, etc. (Düsseldorf, Nov. 13, 1959); *Symphony for 20 Rooms* (1961); *Variations on a Theme of Saint-Saëns* for Cello and Piano, with the pianist playing *Le Cygne* while the cellist dives into an oil drum filled with water (N.Y., Aug. 25, 1965, composer at the keyboard, cellist Charlotte Moorman in the oil drum); *Performable Music*, wherein the performer is ordered to make with a razor an incision of no less than 10 centimeters on his left forearm (Los Angeles, Dec. 2, 1965); *Opéra sextronique* (1967); *Opéra électronique* (1968); *Creep into the Vagina of a Whale* (c.1969); *Young Penis Symphony*, a protrusion of 10 erectile phalluses through a paper curtain (c.1970; produced for the first time at "La Mamelle" in San Francisco, Sept. 21, 1975, under the direction of Ken Friedman, who also acted as one of the 10 performers). Of uncertain attribution is a symph. designated as No. 3, which Paik delegated to Ken Friedman, who worked on it in Saugus, Calif., the epicenter of the earthquake of Feb. 9, 1971, and of which the earthquake itself constituted the finale.

Pailliard, Jean-François, noted French conductor; b. Vitry-le-François, April 18, 1928. He received his musical training at the Paris Cons.; later took courses in conducting with Igor Markevitch at the Salzburg Mozarteum. In 1953 he founded the Jean-François Pailliard Chamber Orch., with which he toured widely. He also acted as a guest conductor in Europe and America. In 1970 he appeared with the Osaka Phil. in Japan. He was furthermore active as an editor of Baroque music, including works by Corelli, Torelli, and Delalande.

Paine, John Knowles, American composer and teacher; b. Portland, Maine, Jan. 9, 1839; d. Cambridge, Mass., April 25, 1906. His father kept a music store in Portland, and conducted the local band. Paine's first music teacher was H. Kotzschmar. He then went to Berlin and studied under Haupt (counterpoint), Fischer (singing), and Wieprecht (instrumentation) from 1858 to 1861. After organ concerts in Berlin and various American cities, he settled in Boston as organist of the West Church on Cambridge St. In 1862 he became a teacher of music at Harvard Univ., and organist at Appleton Chapel in Cambridge, Mass.; from 1875 until his death he occupied the newly created professorship of music at Harvard, the first in any American univ. In 1866–67 he toured Germany and conducted his Mass at Berlin. He was awarded the honorary degrees of M.A. (Harvard, 1869) and Mus.Doc. (Yale, 1890). He was one of the most notable pioneers in American musical development. Among his many pupils were J.A. Carpenter, A. Foote, E.B. Hill, F.S. Converse, H.T. Finck, and D.G. Mason.

WORKS: *Domine salvum fac* for Men's Chorus and Orch. (1863); Mass in D for Soli, Chorus, and Orch.; oratorio, *St. Peter; Centennial Hymn* for Chorus and Orch. (Philadelphia, 1876); music to *Œdipus tyrannus* (Sophocles) for Men's Voices and Orch.; *The Realm of Fancy,* cantata for Soprano Solo, Chorus, and Orch.; *Phœbus, arise; The Nativity,* cantata for Soli, Chorus, and Orch.; *Song of Promise,* cantata for Soprano, Chorus, and Orch.; incidental music to *The Birds* of Aristophanes; *Columbus March and Hymn,* for the Chicago Exposition (1893); *Hymn of the West,* for the St. Louis Exposition (1904); 2 symphs.: in C minor and in A (*Spring Symphony;* Cambridge, Mass., March 10, 1880); 2 symph. poems: *The Tempest* and *An Island Fantasy;* overture to *As You Like It; Duo concertante* for Violin and Cello, with Orch.; String Quartet; Piano Trio; Larghetto and Scherzo for Piano, Violin, and Cello; Romanza and Scherzo for Piano and Cello; Sonata for Piano and Violin; characteristic pieces for piano; variations and fantasias for organ; motets, part-songs, and songs. An opera, *Azara* (text by himself), was publ. in 1901, and had a concert performance in Boston in 1907. He wrote *The History of Music to the Death of Schubert* (posthumous, 1907). His *Lecture Notes* was publ. in 1885.

Paisible, Louis Henri, French violinist and composer; b. St. Cloud, near Paris, July 21, 1748; d. St. Petersburg, March 19, 1782 (suicide). He studied with Gaviniès; played in the orch. of the Concert Spirituel in Paris; then traveled through Europe; in 1778 was engaged at the Russian court in St. Petersburg. Although well received at first, he was unable to make headway with a series of concerts for which he solicited subscriptions; deprived of resources, he shot himself. Twelve of his string quartets and 2 violin concertos have been publ. in Paris and London.

Paisiello, Giovanni, famous Italian composer; b.

Taranto, May 9, 1740; d. Naples, June 5, 1816. From the age of 5 he studied at the Jesuit school in Taranto, where he was taught by a priest, Resta, and where his singing so delighted Guaducci, maestro at the Capuchin church, that he advised the boy's father to place him in the Cons. di S. Onofrio at Naples. There he studied under Durante, Cotumacci, and Abos, from 1754 to 1759, remaining 4 years longer as a teacher, and occupying himself with sacred composition (masses, oratorios, etc.). But a comic intermezzo performed at the Cons. in 1763 disclosed such dramatic talent that he was commissioned to write an opera for the Marsigli Theater at Bologna; here his first comic opera was produced, *La pupilla, ossia Il mondo alla rovescia* (1764). For 12 years, during which he brought out some 50 operas, his successes were many and reverses few, even in rivalry with Piccinni and Cimarosa. Important works of this period are *Le finte Contesse* (Rome, Feb. 1766), *L'idolo cinese* (Naples, Spring 1767), and *La Frascatana* (Venice, Nov. 1774). Invited to St. Petersburg by Empress Catherine II in 1776, he lived there 8 years on a princely salary; he produced several operas, including *Il Barbiere di Siviglia* (St. Petersburg, Sept. 26, 1782), which became so popular in Italy that it still stood as a rival to Rossini's masterpiece in 1816. During the next 15 years he acted as maestro di cappella to Ferdinand IV of Naples (1784–99); of his productions of this period, especially noteworthy are *Il Re Teodoro in Venezia* (Vienna, Aug. 23, 1784; perhaps his best opera), *Le Gare generose* (Naples, Spring 1786), *L'amor contrastato* (later called *La Molinara*; Naples, Summer 1788), *Nina, o La Pazza per amore* (Caserta, June 25, 1789; a charming "opera semiseria," a genre in which Paisiello excelled), and *I Zingari in fiera* (Naples, Nov. 21, 1789). During the revolutionary period of 1799–1801 Paisiello stood well with the republican government, but lost the favor of the King, together with his place and salary. In 1802–3 he was Napoleon's maître de chapelle at Paris. From 1803 until the Bourbon restoration of 1815, he held his former position at Naples, and other posts of importance, all of which later he lost on Ferdinand's return in 1815, being retained solely as maestro di cappella. Paisiello was an extraordinarily productive composer, and one of the most popular of his time; yet of his 100 or more operas, only a few are ever revived nowadays. His vein of melody was original, fresh, and natural; although he introduced instrumental effects that were novel in Italy, he carefully avoided the overelaborate numbers common to the period, obtaining his effect by the grace, beauty, and dramatic truthfulness of his melody.

Paladilhe, Emile, French composer; b. Montpellier, June 3, 1844; d. Paris, Jan. 6, 1926. He entered the Paris Cons. in 1853; was a pupil of Marmontel (piano), Benoist (organ), and Halévy (counterpoint); won first prize for piano and organ in 1857; won the Grand Prix de Rome in 1860 with the cantata *Le Czar Ivan IV* (Paris Opéra, 1860). He brought out the one-act comic opera *Le Passant* at the Opéra-Comique (April 24, 1872), followed by *L'Amour africain* (May 8, 1875); *Suzanne* (Dec. 30, 1878); *Diana* (Feb. 23, 1885); the 5-act opera *Patrie* (Opéra, Dec. 20, 1886); and *Les Saintes Maries de la mer*, a sacred lyric drama (Montpellier, 1892). He also produced 2 masses; Symph. in E-flat; some sacred music; numerous songs (*Mandolinata, Premières pensées, Mélodies écossaises*). In 1892 he succeeded Guiraud as member of the Institut de France.

Palau, Manuel, Spanish composer and conductor; b. Valencia, Jan. 4, 1893; d. there, Feb. 18, 1967. He studied first at the Cons. of Valencia; later in Paris, where he took lessons from Koechlin and Ravel. Returning to Valencia, he established himself as a teacher, conductor, and composer. Most of his thematic material is inspired by Catalan folk songs; his instrumental music usually bears programmatic content; his technique of composition follows the French impressionist procedures.
WORKS: Zarzuelas: *Beniflors, Amor torna,* etc.; *Gongoriana,* orch. suite (1927); 2 symphs.; *Concierto levantino* for Guitar and Orch.; *Homenaje a Debussy* for Orch.; Sonata for Guitar Solo; numerous songs of a popular nature; piano pieces: *Valencia, Levantina, Sonatina Valenciana, 3 impresiones fugaces, Campanas y paisaje balear, Danza hispalense, Danza iberica, Evocación de Andalucía,* etc.

Palester, Roman, Polish composer; b. Śniatyń, Dec. 28, 1907. He studied with Soltys at the Cons. of Lwow and with Sikorski at the Warsaw Cons.; he went to France in 1925, and after a brief visit in Poland, settled in Paris. In his music Palester adopted the modernistic devices of the French school, but preserved elements of Polish folk songs in the thematic structure of his works; harmonically he did not choose to transcend the limits of enhanced tonality. Several of his works were performed at festivals of the International Society for Contemporary Music: *Symphonic Music* (London, July 27, 1931); *Danse polonaise* for Orch. (Barcelona, April 22, 1936); Violin Concerto (London, July 14, 1946). Other works are: 5 symphs.: No. 1 (1935); No. 2 (1942); No. 3 for 2 Chamber Orchs. (1948); No. 4 (1951; revised 1971); No. 5 (1970–72); *Requiem* (1948); Sonatina for 3 Clarinets (1936); Concertino for Piano and Orch. (1942); *Serenade* for 2 Flutes and String Orch. (Cracow, Nov. 9, 1947); 2 string trios (1946, 1958); *Sonnets for Orpheus* for Voice and Chamber Orch. (1952); *Passacaglia* for Orch. (1953); *Variations* for Orch. (1955); Concertino for Harpsichord and Instrumental Ensemble (1955); one-act opera, *La Mort de Don Juan* (1959–60; Brussels, 1965); *Varianti* for 2 Pianos (1963); *Metamorphoses* for Orch. (1965–66); 2 piano sonatas (1968, 1975); Trio for Flute, Viola, and Harp (1969); Duo for 2 Violins (1972); *Suite à quatre* for Oboe and String Trio (1973); *Passacaglia and Variations* for Piano (1974); *Songs,* after Milosz, for Soprano and Chamber Orch. (1976); Viola Concerto (1977–78); *Te Deum* for 3 Choirs and Instruments (1978–79).

Palestrina (Giovanni Pierluigi, called **da Palestrina),** the greatest composer of the Catholic Church and of the Roman School; b. Palestrina, near Rome, c.1525; d. Rome, Feb. 2, 1594. He was a chorister at the Cathedral of his native town c.1532; in 1534, when Cardinal della Valle, Bishop of Palestrina, was made Archbishop of S. Maria Maggiore in Rome, he took Palestrina with him and entered him in the choir school of that church. In 1537 we find him listed as an elder choirboy; in 1539, his voice having broken, he left the choir and returned home. But by 1540, or soon after, he was back in Rome, studying music; his teacher may have been Firmin Le Bel, choirmaster of S. Maria Maggiore. In 1544 he was appointed organist and choirmaster at the Cathedral of St. Agapit in Palestrina; the bishop there was Cardinal del Monte, who in 1550 became Pope under the name of Julius III, and who in 1551 bestowed upon Palestrina the post of maestro of the Cappella Giulia. Meanwhile, Palestrina had married (June 12, 1547) and had become father of 2 sons. In 1554 he publ. his first book of masses, dedicated to Julius III, who rewarded him by making him a member of the Pontifical Choir (Jan. 1555); this aroused much resentment, for Palestrina was admitted without taking the entrance examination, and it is said that he had a poor voice. A few months later he was dismissed with a small pension by the new Pope, Paul V, on the ground that he was a married man. He then received the appointment of maestro of the church of St. John Lateran, for which he wrote his celebrated *Lamentations.* In 1560 he resigned this post, and in March of the following year he became maestro of S. Maria Maggiore. In 1563 his first book of motets was publ. About this time the Council of Trent concerned itself with the reform of church music, decreeing the exclusion of all profane and impure elements; contapuntal music, which lent itself to many abuses, might also have been forbidden, had it not been for the determined opposition of the Emperor Ferdinand I. Palestrina's role in influencing the decisions of the Council, especially as regards the proposed exclusion of contrapuntal music, has been grossly exaggerated and misrepresented by most historians, beginning with Baini. Palestrina's famous *Missa Papae Marcelli* is undoubtedly a model of the purest religious style; but there is no evidence that it played much part in shaping the fate of church music at that time. From 1565 to 1571 Palestrina was music director at the new Roman Seminary, where his elder sons were students. In 1567 he resigned his post at S. Maria Maggiore and entered the service of Cardinal Ippolito d'Este (d. 1572). In 1568 the Emperor Maximilian offered him the post of maestro at the court of Vienna, but Palestrina demanded so high a salary that the matter was dropped. In 1571 he resumed his old post as maestro of the Cappella Giulia, retaining this office until his death. In 1576 Pope Gregory XIII issued a decree for the revision of the Gradual, which was to be carried out by Palestrina and Annibale Zoilo; but the revised version, known as the "Medicean Gradual," was not printed until 20 years after Palestrina's death (1614). In 1580, having suffered several family bereavements, including the death of his wife, Palestrina decided to enter the priesthood; but soon he changed his mind, and on March 28, 1581, he married the widow of a prosperous furrier. He then took a partner and successfully carried on the fur business. In 1583 he was invited to become maestro at the court of Mantua, but again his terms were rejected as too high. In 1584 he brought out his settings of the Song of Solomon, and in 1589 his harmonized version of the Latin Hymnal was publ. At his death he was buried in the Cappella Nuova of old St. Peter's Church. In his music Palestrina aimed at technical smoothness and beauty of sound rather than at forceful expression and originality. In the "Motu Proprio" (1903) of Pope Pius X, on sacred music, Palestrina's works are recommended as "of excellent quality from a liturgical and musical standpoint."

Palisca, Claude Victor, American musicologist; b. Fiume, Yugoslavia, Nov. 24, 1921. He came to the U.S. in 1930; attended public schools in N.Y. and Florida; studied at Queens College (B.A., 1943) with Karol Rathaus (composition) and at Harvard Univ. with Walter Piston and Randall Thompson (composition) and with Otto Kinkeldey, Gombosi, and Davison (musicology); obtained his M.A. in 1948, and his Ph.D. in 1954 with the dissertation *The Beginnings of Baroque Music: Its Roots in Sixteenth-century Theory and Polemics.* He was a member of the faculty of the Univ. of Illinois at Urbana (1953–59); in 1959 joined the staff of Yale Univ. He held a John Knowles Paine Traveling Fellowship (1949–50), a Fulbright grant for Italy (1950–52), and a Guggenheim fellowship (1960–61).

Pallavicini, Carlo, Italian composer; b. Salò, near Brescia (date unknown); d. Dresden, Jan. 29, 1688. He served as an organist at S. Antonio in Padua in 1665–66, and in 1673–74 was maestro dei concerti there; then went to Venice; in 1687 he was appointed music director of the new Italian Opera at Dresden; wrote several operas for it. A scene from *Le Amazoni nell'isole fortunate* (Piazzola, near Padua, Nov. 11, 1679) was publ. in the *Sammelbände der Internationalen Musik-Gesellschaft* (vol. 2), and the complete score of *La Gerusalemme liberata* (Venice, Jan. 3, 1687) was edited by Abert in the Denkmäler Deutscher Tonkunst (vol. 55).

Pallavicino, Benedetto, Italian composer; b. Cremona, 1551; d. Mantua (date unknown). He was a court singer in Mantua from 1582 and maestro di cappella to the Duke from 1596. Monteverdi mentions Pallavicino's death in a letter applying for his post to the Duke of Mantua in Nov. 1601. Pallavicino publ. one book of madrigals *a* 4 (1579), 8 books *a* 5 (1581, ?, 1585, 1588, 1593, 1600, 1604, 1612), one book *a* 6 (1587), and other madrigals in collections; also a book of motets *a* 8, 12, and 16 (1595).

Palma, Athos, Argentine composer; b. Buenos Aires, June 7, 1891; d. Miramar, Jan. 10, 1951. He studied with C. Troiani (piano) and other teachers in Buenos Aires; in 1904, went to Europe, returning to Buenos Aires in 1914. There he was busily engaged as a teacher. His music follows the Italian tradition, although the subject matter is derived from South American history and literature. He wrote the operas *Nazdah* (Buenos Aires, June 19, 1924) and *Los Hijos del Sol (The Sons of the Sun,* after an Inca legend; Buenos Aires, Nov. 10, 1928); *Cantares de mi tierra* for Strings (1914); symph. poems: *Jardines* and *Los Hijos del Sol;* Violin Sonata; Cello Sonata; Piano Sonata; many songs; pedagogical works: *Teoría razonada de la música* and *Tratado completo de armonía.*

Palmer, Robert, American composer; b. Syracuse, N.Y., June 2, 1915. He studied at the Eastman School of Music in Rochester with Howard Hanson and Bernard Rogers (1934–38); then had lessons with Roy Harris and Aaron Copland (1939–40). In 1940–43 he was on the faculty at the Univ. of Kansas; in 1943 was appointed to the staff of Cornell Univ. In his music he adheres to the neo-Classical mold; in his melodic progressions he frequently employs a scale of alternating whole-tones and semitones, known as the "Rimsky-Korsakov scale," so called because Rimsky-Korsakov liked to use it for exotic effects in his operas.

Palmgren, Selim, eminent Finnish composer; b. Pori (Bjorneborg), Feb. 16, 1878; d. Helsinki, Dec. 13, 1951. He studied piano and composition at the Cons. of Helsinki (1895–99); then went to Berlin, where he continued his piano studies with Ansorge, Berger, and Busoni. Returning to Finland, he became active as a choral conductor in Helsinki (1902–4); in 1909–12 he was director of the Music Society in Turku. In 1921 he made a tour of the U.S. as a pianist; from 1923 to 1926 taught piano and composition at the Eastman School of Music in Rochester, N.Y.; then returned to Helsinki; became a prof. of harmony and composition at the Sibelius Academy in 1936, remaining there until his death. He was married to the Finnish soprano **Maikki Pakarinen** in 1910, after her divorce from Armas Järnefelt; after her death Palmgren married Minna Talwik. He excelled in piano compositions, often tinged with authentic Finnish colors; some of his pieces are marked by effective impressionistic devices, such as whole-tone scales and consecutive mild dissonances. Among his piano miniatures, *May Night* enjoys considerable popularity with music students and their teachers. WORKS: 5 piano concertos: No. 1 (1903); No. 2, *Virta (The Stream;* 1913); No. 3, *Metamorphoses* (1915); No. 4, *Huhtikuu (April;* 1924–26); No. 5 (1939–41); 2 operas: *Daniel Hjort* (April 15, 1910; revised version, Helsinki, 1938) and *Peter Schlemihl; Pastorale* for Orch. (1920); *Turun lilja (The Lily of Turku),* cantata (1929); *Ballet Music* for Orch. (1944); *Concert Fantasy* for Violin and Orch. (1945); for Piano: 2 sonatas; *Fantasia; 24 Preludes; Ballade* (in the form of a theme with variations); *Finnische Lyrik* (12 pieces); *Finnische Suite (The Seasons); Maskenball,* suite; *24 Etudes* (1921–22); etc.; songs

and men's choruses. He publ. a book, *Minusta Tuli Muusikko* (Helsinki, 1948).

Pálsson, Páll P., Austrian-born Icelandic composer and conductor; b. Graz, May 9, 1928. He studied with Michl, Mixa, and Brugger in Graz; settled in Iceland in 1949 and was first trumpet player in the Iceland Symph. Orch. In 1964 he was appointed director of the Reykjavik Male Choir and later became one of the conductors of the Icelandic Symph. Orch. and the Reykjavik Chamber Ensemble.

Panassié, Hugues, French music critic, expert on jazz; b. Paris, Feb. 27, 1912; d. Montauban, Dec. 8, 1974. He founded the Hot Club de France (1932); lectured on jazz at the Sorbonne in 1937, and in America in 1938; publ. *Le Jazz Hot* (basic treatise on the subject; Paris, 1934; in Eng. as *Hot Jazz,* N.Y., 1936); *The Real Jazz* (N.Y., 1942; in French, *La Véritable Musique de jazz,* Paris, 1946); *La Musique de jazz et le swing* (Paris, 1945); *Douze années de jazz (1927–1938)* (Paris, 1946); *Louis Armstrong* (Paris, 1947); *Jazz panorama* (Paris, 1950); *Discographie critique* (Paris, 1951); *Dictionnaire du jazz* (with Madeleine Gautier; Paris, 1954; in Eng. as *Dictionary of Jazz,* London, 1956; American ed., Boston, 1956, as *Guide to Jazz*).

Panizza, Ettore, Argentine conductor and composer of Italian extraction; b. Buenos Aires, Aug. 12, 1875; d. Milan, Nov. 27, 1967. He studied at the Cons. of Milan, graduating in 1898 with prizes for piano and composition; began his career as an operatic conductor in Italy in 1899, and continued successfully for more than half a century. From 1907 to 1914 he conducted Italian operas at Covent Garden in London; then at La Scala in Milan (1916–26) and at the Metropolitan Opera in N.Y. (1934–42). He publ. an autobiography, *Medio siglo de vida musical* (Buenos Aires, 1952). WORKS: Operas: *Il Fidanzato del mare* (Buenos Aires, Aug. 15, 1897); *Medio evo latino* (Genoa, Nov. 17, 1900); *Aurora* (Buenos Aires, Sept. 5, 1908); *Bisanzio* (Buenos Aires, July 25, 1939); also *Il Re della foresta* for Soli, Chorus, and Orch.; *Tema con variaciones* for Orch.; Violin Sonata; Cello Sonata; String Quartet; piano pieces; songs.

Pannain, Guido, distinguished Italian musicologist and composer; b. Naples, Nov. 17, 1891; d. there, Sept. 6, 1977. He studied composition with C. de Nardis at Naples; upon graduation, devoted himself mainly to research, into both old and new aspects of music.

Panofka, Heinrich, German singing teacher; b. Breslau, Oct. 3, 1807; d. Florence, Nov. 18, 1887. He began his career as a violinist; after playing some concerts in Germany, he went to Paris in 1832 and began taking singing lessons with Bordogni. With Bordogni he organized, in 1842, the Académie de Chant, which failed to prosper. In 1844 he went to London, where he became a fashionable singing teacher; eventually he went to Florence, spending his last days there. He publ. a manual, *L'Art de chanter* (Paris, 1853), which had a considerable vogue.

Panseron, Auguste-Mathieu, French singing teacher; b. Paris, April 26, 1795; d. there, July 29, 1859. His father, who orchestrated many operas for Grétry, taught him until he entered the Paris Cons. in 1804; he studied under Gossec, Levasseur, and Berton, winning the Prix de Rome in 1813. After study in Bologna, Rome, Naples, Vienna (with Salieri), and Munich, he returned to Paris in 1818, taught singing, was an accompanist at the Opéra-Comique, and wrote 3 one-act operas; became a prof. of solfeggio at the Cons. in 1826, of vocalization in 1831, and of singing in 1836. In 1825–40 he brought out some 200 *romances;* he also composed church music, but attained real eminence as a vocal teacher and as a writer of instructive works on singing.

Pantaleoni, Adriano, Italian baritone; b. Udine, Oct. 7, 1837; d. there, Dec. 18, 1908. He studied in Udine and Milan; was a principal member of La Scala in Milan (1871–77, 1896); also sang in London and the U.S.; after his retirement, he taught voice in Udine and Trieste. He was particularly noted for his roles in Verdi's operas. His sister, **Romilda Pantaleoni,** was well known as an operatic soprano.

Pantaleoni, Romilda, Italian soprano; b. Udine, 1847; d. Milan, May 20, 1917. She studied with Prati, Rossi, and Lamperti in Milan; made her debut at the Teatro Carcano in Milan in Foroni's *Margherita* in 1868; then sang in Turin and at La Scala in Milan, where she created the role of Desdemona in Verdi's *Otello* in 1887 and Tigrana in Puccini's *Edgar* in 1889. Her brother, **Adriano Pantaleoni,** was a noted baritone.

Panufnik, Andrzej, eminent Polish composer and conductor; b. Warsaw, Sept. 24, 1914. His mother was an Englishwoman who studied violin in Warsaw, his father a manufacturer of string instruments. Panufnik studied composition with Sikorski at the Warsaw Cons. (1932–36); then took lessons in conducting with Weingartner at the Vienna Academy (1937–38) and briefly with Philippe Gaubert in Paris. He returned to Warsaw in 1939, and remained there during the Nazi occupation of the city; had an underground performance in 1942 of his *Tragic Overture.* In 1945–46 he conducted the Cracow Phil., then conducted the Warsaw Orch. (1946–47). In 1954 he went to England, and in 1961 became a British subject. From 1957 to 1959 he was conductor and music director of the Birmingham Symph. Orch., and frequently a guest conductor in London. In his youth, before the war, he belonged to the vanguard group among Polish composers; he made use of advanced techniques, including quarter-tones, which he employed in the instrumental *Berceuse (Lullaby).* Even in the matter of notation he was an innovator; in several of the orch. scores he left blank spaces instead of rests in the inactive instrumental

parts. In his music of the later period he adopted a more circumspect idiom—expressive, direct, and communicative. He constantly revised his old scores for better effect.
WORKS: Piano Trio (1934; recomposed 1945 and revised 1967); *5 Polish Peasant Songs* for Treble Chorus, 2 Flutes, 2 Clarinets, and Bass Clarinet (1940; recomposed 1945; London Festival of the International Society for Contemporary Music, July 12, 1946; revised 1959); *Tragic Overture* (1942; score lost in Warsaw fires; recomposed 1945; first public perf., N.Y., March 24, 1949; revised 1955); *Lullaby* for 29 String Instruments, and 2 Harps (1947; Paris, April 26, 1948; revised 1955); *Nocturne* for Orch. (1947; revised 1955); *12 Miniature Studies* for Piano (1947; revised 1955); *Sinfonia rustica* (1948; Warsaw, May 13, 1949; revised 1955); *Hommage à Chopin* in 2 versions: for Soprano and Piano (1949) and for Flute and String Orch. (1966); *Old Polish Suite* for String Orch. (1950; revised 1955); *Concerto in modo antico (Gothic Concerto)* for Orch. (1951; revised 1955); *Symfonia pokoju (Symphony of Peace)* for Chorus and Orch. (Warsaw, May 25, 1951); *Heroic Overture* (1952; Helsinki Olympiad, July 27, 1952; revised 1965); *Rhapsody* for Orch. (1956; first public perf., London, Aug. 26, 1957); *Sinfonia elegiaca* (1957; revised 1966; first and 3rd sections arranged as a ballet, *Elegy,* N.Y., 1957); *Polonia,* suite for Orch. (1959; London, Aug. 21, 1959); *Autumn Music* for Orch. (1962); Piano Concerto (1962; revised 1972); *Sinfonia sacra* (1963; Monaco, Aug. 12, 1964; as a ballet, *Cain and Abel,* West Berlin, Nov. 1968); *Landscape* for String Orch. (London, Nov. 13, 1965); *Divertimento* for String Orch. (London, Sept. 24, 1966); *Jagiellonian Triptych* for Strings (London, Sept. 24, 1966); *Epitaph for the Victims of Katyń* for Woodwinds, Strings, and Timpani (N.Y., Nov. 17, 1968, Stokowski conducting); *Reflections* for Piano (1968); *Universal Prayer,* a setting of Alexander Pope's poem, for 4 Soloists, Chorus, 3 Harps, and Organ (Cathedral Church of St. John the Divine, N.Y., May 24, 1970, Stokowski conducting); *Thames Pageant,* cantata for Young Players and Singers (1969); ballet, *Miss Julie* (Stuttgart, March 8, 1970); Concerto for Violin and String Orch. (London, July 18, 1972); *Invocation for Peace* for Youth Chorus and Youth Orch. (Southampton, Nov. 28, 1972); *Winter Solstice* for Soprano, Baritone, Chorus, and Instruments (London, Dec. 16, 1972); *Sinfonia concertante* for Flute, Harp, and String Orch. (1973; London, May 20, 1974); *Sinfonia di sfere (Symphony of Spheres;* 1975; London, April 13, 1976); 2 string quartets: No. 1 (1976) and No. 2, *Messages* (1980); *Sinfonia mystica* (1977); *Metasinfonia* for Organ, Strings, and Timpani (1978); *Concerto festivo* for Orch. (1979); Concertino for Percussion, and Piano, 4-hands, or String Orch. (1980); *Sinfonia votiva* (1980–81; Boston, Jan 28, 1982); *A Procession for Peace* for Orch. (1982).

Papaioannou, Yannis, Greek composer; b. Kavala, Jan. 6, 1911. He studied piano and music theory at the Hellenic Odeon in Athens (1929–34); then had some composition lessons with Honegger in Paris

Papandopulo – Paray

(1949). In 1953 he was appointed to the staff of his alma mater; introduced into his courses a study of modern techniques of composition. His own music traversed from a fairly conservative neo-Classical idiom to dodecaphony and eventually integral serialism.

Papandopulo, Boris, Croatian conductor and composer; b. Bad Honneft am Rhein, Feb. 25, 1906. He studied in Zagreb and Vienna; in 1959 was appointed conductor of the National Theater in Zagreb; from 1964 to 1968 he conducted in Split and Rijeka; later filled engagements as a guest conductor in Yugoslavia. His operas and most of his instrumental works are written in a national Croatian idiom; but he also experimented with the 12-tone techniques, as exemplified by his pointedly titled *Dodekafonski concert* for 2 Pianos (1961).

Papier, Rosa, Austrian mezzo-soprano; b. Baden, near Vienna, Sept. 15, 1858; d. Vienna, Feb. 9, 1932. She sang at the Imperial Opera in Vienna; later taught at the Vienna Cons. In 1881 she married the pianist **Hans Paumgartner.**

Papineau-Couture, Jean, Canadian composer; b. Outremont (part of metropolitan Montreal), Nov. 12, 1916. He studied piano with Léo-Pol Morin (1939–40) and theory with Gabriel Cusson in Montreal (1937–40); then in the U.S. (1940–45) with Quincy Porter at the New England Cons. in Boston, with Nadia Boulanger at the Longy School in Cambridge, Mass., and in California. Upon returning to Montreal, he devoted himself to teaching and musical organization; was founding president of the Société de Musique Contemporaine du Québec (1966–73) and dean of the music faculty at the Univ. of Montreal (1968–73). His music underwent an evolution, common to many Canadian composers, from a neo-Baroque idiom to Expressionism, with judicious excursions into serial techniques.

Pâque, Désiré, remarkable Belgian composer; b. Liège, May 21, 1867; d. Bessancourt, France, Nov. 20, 1939. He began to compose as a child; wrote a Mass at the age of 12; studied at the Liège Cons.; lived in Sofia, Athens, Lisbon, and Geneva, settling in Paris in 1914. He wrote 144 opus numbers, among them the one-act opera *Vaima* (1903); 8 symphs. (1895, 1905, 1912, 1916, 1919, 1927, 1934, 1936); 2 piano concertos (1888, 1935); Cello Concerto (1893); *Ouverture sur 3 thèmes bulgares* (Ostende, Aug. 17, 1895); *Ouverture libre* (1899; Munich, Dec. 29, 1911); Requiem (1900); 10 string quartets (1892–1939); 3 piano quintets (1896, 1924, 1938); 2 sextets (1909, 1919); 5 suites for Piano, Violin, and Viola (1891–96); 3 piano trios (1903–30); 4 violin sonatas (1890–1934); 4 piano sonatas (1911); Viola Sonata (1915); 13 albums of piano pieces; choral works. His production falls into 3 periods: cosmopolitan and formal (1886–1908); freely episodic, in an *adjonction constante* of recurrent themes (1909–18); atonal and polytonal (1919–39). His last manner is exemplified by *10 pièces atonales pour la jeunesse* for Piano (1925).

Only a few of his works are publ.; the bulk of his music remains in MS.

Paradies (originally **Paradisi**), **Pietro Domenico,** Italian composer and harpsichordist; b. Naples, 1707; d. Venice, Aug. 25, 1791. He was a pupil of Porpora; brought out several operas in Italy; in 1747 went to London, where he earned a living mainly as a teacher of harpsichord playing, but also produced an opera, *Fetonte* (Jan. 17, 1747); publ. *12 sonate di gravicembalo* (London, 1754). Toward the end of his life he returned to Italy. Some of his MS works are preserved in the Fitzwilliam Museum at Cambridge; his sonatas were brought out by G. Benvenuti and D. Cipollini in Milan (1920).

Paradis, Maria Theresia von, Austrian pianist and composer; b. Vienna, May 15, 1759; d. there, Feb. 1, 1824. Blind from her 5th year, she was taught by Richter and Koželuh (piano), Salieri and Righini (singing), and Friberth and Abbé Vogler (composition), becoming an excellent pianist and organist; she played in Paris in 1784, and made a tour to London, Brussels, and German capitals in 1786. By the aid of a system of notation invented by a friend, she became a skillful composer, her chief works being a melodrama, *Ariadne und Bacchus* (Laxenburg, June 20, 1791; not extant); an operetta, *Der Schulkandidat* (Vienna, Dec. 5, 1792); the fairy opera *Rinaldo und Alcina* (Prague, June 30, 1797; not extant); a funeral cantata on the death of Louis XVI (1794); a Piano Trio; sonatas and variations for piano; songs; etc. In her last years she taught singing and piano playing.

Paray, Paul, distinguished French conductor and composer; b. Le Tréport, Normandy, May 24, 1886; d. Monte Carlo, Oct. 10, 1979. He received his musical education from his father, a church organist; in 1904 he entered the Paris Cons. as a composition student; studied there with Leroux, Caussade, Lenepveu, and Vidal; received the Premier Grand Prix de Rome with his cantata *Yanitza* (1911). He was drafted into the French army during World War I and was taken prisoner by the Germans; composed a string quartet while interned at Darmstadt; after the Armistice, he became conductor of the orch. of the Casino de Cauterets. Substituting for an ailing André Caplet, Paray made his Paris debut on Feb. 20, 1920, and soon became assistant conductor of the Lamoureux Orch., succeeding Chevillard as first conductor in 1923; was appointed conductor of symph. concerts in Monte Carlo in 1928, and in 1932 he succeeded Pierné as conductor of the Concerts Colonne, remaining until the orch. was disbanded by the Nazi occupiers of Paris in 1940; conducted briefly in Marseilles and, following the liberation of Paris, resumed duties with the Colonne Orch. (1944–52). Paray made his American debut in N.Y. on July 24, 1939, in a program of French music. In 1952 he was engaged to conduct the reorganized Detroit Symph. Orch., and on Oct. 18, 1956, inaugurated the new Ford Auditorium in Detroit in a program that included his own *Mass for the 500th Anniver-*

sary of the Death of Joan of Arc, a work first heard in the Cathedral in Rouen, France, in 1931; he resigned in 1963 and returned to France, though he continued to guest-conduct internationally. In July 1977, at the age of 91, he conducted an orch. concert in honor of Marc Chagall's 90th birthday celebration in Nice, and, at age 92, made his last conducting appearance in the U.S., leading the orch. of the Curtis Inst. of Music in Philadelphia; at the time of his death (in 1979), he had commitments through 1981. As a conductor, he concentrated on the Classics and Romantics, and French music. He was the composer of several highly competent works, including, besides *Yanitza* and his *Mass,* a ballet entitled *Artémis troublée* (Paris Opéra, April 28, 1922, perf. as a symph. poem, *Adonis troublé*); *Fantaisie* for Piano and Orch. (Paris, March 25, 1923); 2 full symphs., in C (1935) and in A (1940); Symph. for Strings; String Quartet (1918); Violin Sonata (1908); Cello Sonata (1919); piano pieces.

Parepa-Rosa (née **Parepa de Boyescu**), **Euphrosyne,** English soprano; b. Edinburgh, May 7, 1836; d. London, Jan. 21, 1874. Her father was a native of Bucharest; her mother, **Elizabeth Seguin,** was a well-known singer. She made her operatic debut at the age of 16 in Malta; then sang in principal Italian music centers, in Madrid, and in Lisbon. She made her first London appearance as Elvira in *I Puritani* on May 21, 1857, and became a great favorite of the English public. She married the impresario Carlo Rosa in 1867 during an American tour. She returned to England in 1873 and remained there until her death.

Parkening, Christopher, outstanding American guitarist; b. Los Angeles, Dec. 14, 1947. He began to play the guitar as a child; gave a public recital at the age of 12; subsequently engaged in a brilliant international career, touring throughout the U.S., Europe, and the Far East. He also publ. transcriptions of sacred music for the guitar and a valuable guitar method.

Parker, Charlie, nicknamed **"Yardbird"** or **"Bird"** (real Christian name, **Charles Christopher**), black American jazz saxophonist, the leading exponent of bebop; b. Kansas City, Aug. 29, 1920; d. New York, March 12, 1955. He was self-taught, on an alto saxophone given to him at age 11 by his mother; at 15 he left school and became a professional musician; in 1939 went to N.Y., and in 1941 was in the big band of Jay McShann, with which he made his first recordings. In 1943 he played tenor sax (his only extended period on that instrument) in Earl Hines's band; met Dizzy Gillespie and other young musicians dissatisfied with the prevailing big band swing style; after work they would meet in a club called Minton's, and there gradually evolved the new style of bebop. Parker became the acknowledged leader of this style as he developed an improvising technique characterized by virtuosic speed, intense tone, complex harmonies, and florid melodies having irregular rhythmic patterns and asymmetric phrase lengths. After the mid-1940s he usually worked in small combos led either by himself or by one of the other members of the small, close-knit circle of bopsters; occasionally he also worked with larger ensembles (including a string orch. for which he wrote the arrangements). As a composer, he usually worked with the 12-bar blues patterns (but always in an unstereotyped manner; he made 175 blues recordings, all markedly different) or with chord progressions of well-known "standard" tunes: his *Ornithology,* for instance, is based on the progressions of *How High the Moon.* He achieved a prominence that made him a living legend (a leading N.Y. club, Birdland, was named after him); his life, though, in addition to being tragically short, was plagued by the consequences of narcotics addiction (acquired when he was in his mid-teens) and alcoholism. He had a nervous breakdown in 1946 and was confined at Camarillo State Hospital in California for 6 months; because of suspected narcotics possession, the N.Y. City police rescinded his cabaret license in 1951, thereby denying him the right to work in N.Y. clubs; he attempted suicide twice in 1954, and subsequently entered Bellevue Hospital in N.Y. He died in the N.Y. apartment of a fervent admirer, Rothschild Baroness Pannonica de Konigswarter.

Parker, Horatio William, eminent American composer and pedagogue; b. Auburndale, Mass., Sept. 15, 1863; d. Cedarhurst, N.Y., Dec. 18, 1919. He studied piano with John Orth, theory with Emery, and composition with Chadwick in Boston; subsequently went to Germany, where he took courses in organ and composition with Rheinberger in Munich (1882–85); under his tutelage he wrote a cantata, *King Trojan* (1885). Returning to N.Y., he taught at the cathedral schools of St. Paul and St. Mary (1886–90), at the General Seminary (1892), and at the National Cons. of Music (1892–93); was organist and choirmaster at St. Luke's (1885–87), St. Andrew's (1887–88), and the Church of the Holy Trinity (1888–93); in 1893 went to Boston as organist and choirmaster at Trinity Church. He attracted attention with the first performance of his oratorio *Hora novissima* (N.Y., May 3, 1893), in which he demonstrated his mastery of choral writing, while his harmonic and contrapuntal style remained securely tied to German practices. In 1894 he was engaged as a prof. of theory School of Music, and remained there until his death. Many American composers received the benefit of his excellent instruction; among them was Charles Ives, who kept his sincere appreciation of Parker's teaching long after he renounced Parker's conservative traditions. Parker conducted performances of his works in England in 1900 and 1902; received an honorary degree of Mus.-Doc. at Cambridge Univ. in 1902. Returning to the U.S., he served as organist and choirmaster at the collegiate church of St. Nicholas in Boston in 1902–10. He continued to compose industriously, without making any concessions to the emerging modern schools of composition; his choral works are particularly notable. In 1911 his opera *Mona* won the

$10,000 prize offered by produced there on March 14, 1912; he also won a prize offered by the National Federation of Women's Clubs for his 2nd opera, *Fairyland,* which was produced in Los Angeles on July 1, 1915. Neither of the operas possessed enough power to survive in the repertoire. Besides the 2 operas and the oratorio *Hora novissima,* Parker wrote 2 symph. poems: *A Northern Ballad* and *Vatheil* (1903); a masque, *Cupid and Psyche,* for the 50th anniversary of the founding of the Yale Art School (New Haven, June 16, 1916); Concerto for Organ and Orch. (Boston, Dec. 26, 1902); 2 string quartets; Piano Trio and other pieces of chamber music; a great number of choral works, for which he is mainly distinguished: *The Lord Is My Shepherd; The Ballad of a Knight and His Daughter; King Trojan; Blow, Blow, Thou Winter Wind; The Norsemen's Raid; Morning and Evening Service; Harald Harfager; Dream-King and His Love; 6 Part-songs; The Holy Child; The Legend of St. Christopher; Adstant Angelorum Chori; A Wanderer's Psalm; Hymnos Andron; A Star Song; King Gorm the Grim; A Song of Times; Morven and the Grail; The Dream of Mary;* etc.; numerous songs, with orch. or piano accompaniments; patriotic odes, such as *Union and Liberty,* composed for the inauguration of Theodore Roosevelt in 1905, and the World War I song *The Red Cross Spirit Speaks;* he also wrote a Sonata for Organ and other organ pieces of various dimensions; publ. the educational vols. *The Progressive Music Series* (8 vols.) and *Music and Public Entertainment* (1911).

Parlow, Kathleen, Canadian violinist; b. Calgary, Sept. 20, 1890; d. Oakville, Ontario, Aug. 19, 1963. Her family moved to San Francisco when she was a child, and she had her early instruction in violin there; in 1906 she was sent to St. Petersburg, Russia, where she was accepted by Leopold Auer in his violin class at the St. Petersburg Cons. She subsequently developed an extensive concert career; played in England, Scandinavia, the U.S., and the Orient. In 1929–36 she was a violin instructor at Mills College in Oakland, Calif.; in 1941, joined the faculty of the Royal Cons. of Music in Toronto; there she organized in 1942 the Parlow String Quartet.

Parratt, Sir Walter, English organist; b. Huddersfield, Feb. 10, 1841; d. Windsor, March 27, 1924. He was a pupil of his father; at 7 played his first church service; at 11, was organist at Armitage Bridge, and passed through successive similar positions to Magdalen College, Oxford (1872), and St. George's Chapel, Windsor (1882), succeeding Elvey. He received a Mus.Bac. from Oxford in 1873; became a prof. of organ at the Royal College of Music in 1883; was knighted in 1892; was made Master of Music in Ordinary to the Queen (1893), to King Edward VII (1901), and to King George V (1910); from 1908 he was a prof. of music at Oxford (resigned on Jan. 1, 1918); from 1916, dean of music at London Univ.; in 1894 he received from Oxford a Mus.Doc. *honoris causa;* was named Commander of the Victorian Order; etc.

WORKS: Music to Aeschylus's *Agamemnon* and *Orestes; Elegy to Patroclus* (1883); anthems, songs, music for organ and piano.

Parris, Robert, American composer and pianist; b. Philadelphia, May 21, 1924. He studied piano as a youth; enrolled at the Univ. of Pa. (B.S., 1945; M.S., 1946); then studied composition with Peter Mennin at the Juilliard School of Music in N.Y. (B.S., 1948) and with Ibert and Copland at the Berkshire Music Center in Tanglewood (1950–51); in 1952–53 he received a Fulbright fellowship to study with Honegger at the Ecole Normale de Musique in Paris. He taught at several univs. before settling in Washington, D.C., where he joined the faculty of The George Washington Univ. in 1963. His music is distinguished by strong formal structure and tonal cohesion; when pragmatically justifiable, he applies serialistic techniques with deliberate circumspection.

Parrish, Carl, American musicologist and composer; b. Plymouth, Pa., Oct. 9, 1904; d. (as a result of injuries incurred in an automobile accident) Valhalla, N.Y., Nov. 27, 1965. After receiving his Ph.D at Harvard with the dissertation *The Early Piano and Its Influences on Keyboard Technique and composition in the Eighteenth Century* (1939), he taught at Wells College (1939–43), Fisk Univ. (1943–46), Westminster Choir College (1946–49), and Pomona College (1943–46); from 1953 he was a prof. at Vassar College. He publ. *The Notation of Medieval Music* (N.Y., 1957; 2nd ed., 1959) and *A Treasury of Early Music* (N.Y., 1958). In collaboration with John F. Ohl, he publ. *Masterpieces of Music before 1750* (N.Y., 1951); wrote choral settings of folk songs; a String Quartet; a song cycle; piano pieces.

Parrott, Andrew, English conductor; b. Walsall, March 10, 1947. He studied at Oxford Univ., where he pursued research into the performing practices of 16th- and 17th-century music. In 1973 he founded the Taverner Choir, and subsequently the Taverner Consort and Players. He conducted Monteverdi's *Vespers* at London's Promenade Concerts in 1977; gave the first performance in London of Bach's *B-minor Mass* with period instruments; also presented in authentic style the *St. Matthew Passion* and the *Brandenburg Concertos.* He appeared as a guest conductor with the English Chamber Orch., the London Bach Orch., and the Concerto Amsterdam.

Parrott, Ian, British composer; b. London, March 5, 1916. He studied at the Royal College of Music and at Oxford Univ., where he received his degrees of B.Mus. and D.Mus. During World War II he served in the Royal Corps of Signals in the Middle East and North Africa; after the war was a lecturer in music at Birmingham Univ. (1947–50) and from 1950 to 1983 at the Univ. College of Wales in Aberystwyth. He wrote the opera *The Black Ram* (in the Welsh language, Aberystwyth, March 9, 1966); ballet, *Maid in Birmingham* (1951); 3 symphs. (1946, 1960, 1966); symph. prelude, *El Alamein* (1944); symph. impression, *Luxor* (1948); Piano Concerto (1948); Wind Quintet (1948); *Fantasy Trio* for Piano, Violin, and Cello (1950); *Solemn Overture* (1956); Concerto for English Horn and Orch. (1956); Concerto for Trombone and Wind Instruments (1967); 4 string quartets. He publ. a number of useful manuals: *Pathway to Modern Music* (London, 1947); *A Guide to Musical Thought* (London, 1955); *Method in Orchestration* (London, 1957); and a monograph, *Elgar* (London, 1971).

Parry, Sir (Charles) Hubert (Hastings), eminent English composer and pedagogue; b. Bournemouth, Feb. 27, 1848; d. Knight's Croft, Rustington, Oct. 7, 1918. While at Eton, from 1861, he studied composition with G. Elvey; took part in the concerts of the Musical Society as pianist, organist, violinist, and composer. At 19, while still a student at Eton, he took the degree of Mus.Bac. at Oxford. He entered Exeter College, Oxford, in 1867. There he began to study music in earnest under Bennett and Macfarren, also taking piano lessons from Dannreuther (1872–79). His public career as a composer began with the production of an *Intermezzo religioso* for Strings at the Gloucester Festival of 1868. In 1883 Parry was appointed Choragus of Oxford Univ.; in that year Cambridge conferred on him the honorary degree of Mus.Doc., followed by Oxford (1884) and Dublin (1891) degrees. In 1894 he succeeded Sir George Grove as director of the Royal College of Music, which post he held until his death; in 1899–1908 he was a prof. of music at Oxford Univ.; in 1898 he was knighted.

Parry, Joseph, Welsh composer; b. Merthyr Tydfil, May 21, 1841; d. Penarth, near Cardiff, Feb. 17, 1903. His parents emigrated to America, but he returned to Britain, won Eisteddfod prizes for songs, and entered the Royal Academy of Music in 1868, studying under Bennett, Garcia, and Steggall; received his Mus.Bac. degree from Cambridge in 1871; then was appointed a prof. of music at the Univ. College in Aberystwyth.
WORKS: 5 operas: *Blodwen* (Aberdare, 1878); *Virginia* (Aberdare, 1883); *Arianwen* (Cardiff, 1890); *Sylvia* (Cardiff, 1895); *King Arthur* (finished 1897); oratorios: *Emmanuel* (1880) and *Saul of Tarsus* (1892); cantatas: *The Prodigal Son; Nebuchadnezzar; Cambria; The Maid of Cefu Idfa;* also, *Druids' Chorus;* an orch. ballade; overtures; String Quartet; piano music, anthems, songs.

Parsley (**Parseley, Persleye, Parcele,** etc.), **Osbert,** English church-music composer; b. 1511; d. Norwich, 1585. He was a lay clerk at Norwich Cathedral for about 50 years. *Tudor Church Music* (vol. 10) contains reprints of 5 of his works; MSS in the British Museum include several motets; *Perslis clocke* for 5 Voices; etc.

Pärt, Arvo, remarkably inventive Estonian composer; b. Paide, Sept. 11, 1935. He studied composition with Heino Eller at the Tallinn Cons., graduating in 1963; from 1958 to 1967 was attached to the music division of Estonian Radio. In 1980 he emigrated; in 1982 he settled in West Berlin. He began to compose in a traditional manner, writing instrumental pieces in a neo-Baroque idiom, strict to form, freely dissonant in harmony; under the influence of Western musical modernism he gradually levitated toward the empyreal emporium of empiric sonorism, without renouncing, however, the historic foundation of tonality. The spectrum of his musical vocabulary extends from abecedarian minimalism to quaquaversal polytonality, from impressionistic pointillism to austere serialism. One of his original specialities is a technique he calls "tintinnabuli," in which he applies shifting phases of a given chord. Pärt was the first Estonian composer to use the authentic Schoenbergian method of composition with 12 different tones related only to one another to form melodic and harmonic dodecaphonic structures. He applied it in his arresting *Nekrolog,* dedicated to the victims of the Holocaust. Extending the concept of integral dodecaphony, he makes use of pandiatonic and panpentatonic tone-clusters, culminating in the formation of a Brobdingnagian blob of "white noise." When at a loss for new ideas, he resorts to aleatory proceedings. He also harks upon occasion back to historic antecedents in applying the austere precepts of *ars antiqua.* In this, Pärt commends himself as a true *Homo ludens,* a musician playing a diversified game.
WORKS: FOR ORCH.: *Nekrolog,* dedicated to the victims of fascism (1960); 3 symphs.: No. 1, *Polyphonic* (1963); No. 2 (1966); No. 3 (1971); *Perpetuum mobile* (1963); *Collage on the Theme B-A-C-H* for Strings, Oboe, and Harpsichord (1964); *Pro et contra* for Cello and Orch. (1964); *Wenn Bach Bienen gezüchtet hätte (If Bach Had Raised Bees),* on the theme B-A-C-H, concertino for Harpsichord, Electric Bass Guitar, Electronic Tape, and Ensemble (1978; Graz, Oct. 7, 1983; version B for Harpsichord and 20 Strings, 1980); *Cantus in Memory of Benjamin Britten* for String Orch. and Glockenspiel (1977); *Tabula Rasa* ("scraped tablet," alluding to the epistemological philosophy propagated by John Locke asserting that the human mind possesses no innate notions), concerto for Violin, String Orch., and Prepared Piano (1977); *Fratres I,* version B, for String Orch. and Percussion (1977–82; Göteborg, Sweden, May 19, 1983); Concerto for Violin, Cello, and Chamber Orch. (1978–79; London, April 23, 1981); *Spiegel im Spiegel (Mirror in Mirror),* version B, for Violin, Piano, and Strings (1980); Cello Concerto (1983).
FOR VOICE: *Meie Aed (Our Garden),* cantata for Children's Chorus and Orch. (1959); *Maailma samm (The World's Stride),* oratorio (1961); *Solfeggio* for Mixed Chorus and String Quartet (1964); *Credo* for Solo Piano, Mixed Chorus, and Orch. (1968); *Laul armastatule (Song for the Beloved),* cantata-symph. to poems by Rustaveli (1973); *Calix (Dies irae)* for Chorus, Organ, Trumpet, Trombone, Glockenspiel, Tam-tam, 2 Electric Guitars, and Kettledrum (1976); *Modus (Tintinnabulum 2)* for Soprano and Instrumental Ensemble (1976); *Missa sillabica* for 4 Voices or Chamber Choir, and 6 In-

struments (1977); *Cantate Domino canticum novum (Psalm 95)* for 4 Voices and 4 Instruments (1977); *De profundis* for Male Chorus, Organ, and Percussion ad lib. (1970; *Summa* for Tenor, Baritone, and 6 Instruments (1978); *Passio Domini nostri Jesu Christi secundum Joannem* for Chorus and Ensemble (1981–82; Munich, Nov. 28, 1982).

CHAMBER MUSIC: String Quartet (1959); Quintettino for 5 Wind Instruments (1964); *Musica syllabica* for 12 Instruments (1964); *Kriips ja punkt (Dash and Dot)* for Ensemble (1967); *Fratres I*, version A, for String Quintet and Wind Quintet (1977), and version C, for Nonet (1977); *Fratres II* for Solo Violin (1980); *Fratres III* for Solo Cello (1980); *Arbos* for 7 Instruments (1977); *Spiegel im Spiegel*, version A, for Violin and Piano (1978); *Pari Intervallo*, version A, for 4 Instruments (1980); *Die Brüder* for Violin and Piano (1980).

FOR PIANO: 2 sonatinas (1958, 1959); *Partita* (1959); *Diagrams*, aleatory work (1964); *Für Alina* (1976); *Variationen zur Gesundung von Arinuschka (Variations for Arinuschka's Recuperation)* (1977); *Pari Intervallo*, version C (1980).

FOR ORGAN: *Trivium* (1976); *Annum per annum* (1980); *Pari intervallo*, version B (1980).

Partch, Harry, remarkable American composer; b. Oakland, Calif., June 24, 1901; d. San Diego, Sept. 3, 1974. Largely autodidact, he began experimenting with instruments capable of producing fractional intervals, which led him to the formulation of a 43-tone scale; he expounded his findings in his book, *Genesis of a Music* (1949). Among new instruments constructed by him are elongated violas, a chromelodeon, kitharas with 72 strings, harmonic canons with 44 strings, boos (made of giant Philippine bamboo reeds), cloud-chamber bowls, blow-boys (a pair of bellows with an attached automobile horn), etc. Seeking intimate contact with American life, he wandered across the country, collecting indigenous expressions of folkways, inscriptions on public walls, etc., for texts in his productions.

WORKS: *8 Hitchhiker Inscriptions from a California Highway Railing* and *U.S. Highball, A Musical Account of a Transcontinental Hobo Trip* for Chorus and Instruments (both perf. for the first time in Carnegie Chamber Hall, N.Y., April 22, 1944); *The Letter, A Depression Message from a Hobo Friend* for Voices and Instrumental Ensemble (1944); *Oedipus*, music drama (Mills College, Oakland, March 14, 1952); *The Bewitched*, dance satire (Univ. of Illinois, Urbana, March 26, 1957); *Revelation in the Courthouse Park*, musical tragedy (Univ. of Illinois, Urbana, April 11, 1961); *Water, Water*, an American ritual (Univ. of Illinois, March 9, 1962).

Partos, Oedoen, Hungarian-born Israeli composer and violist; b. Budapest, Oct. 1, 1907; d. Tel Aviv, July 6, 1977. He studied violin with Hubay and composition with Kodály at the Royal Academy of Music in Budapest (1918–24). In 1938 he went to Palestine; was first violist in the Palestine Symph. Orch. (later Israel Phil.) from 1938 to 1956. In 1951 he was appointed director of the Tel Aviv Academy of Music (later the Israel Rubin Academy of Tel Aviv Univ.); from 1961, he was a prof. there. He was the soloist for the premieres of his 3 viola concertos. His early works followed the rhythmical and melodic patterns of the oriental tradition, emphasized the chromatic melodic turns, and developed a free accumulation of variations on a theme that is never stated in its entirety. In 1971 Partos went to the Netherlands and experimented with the possibilities of 31-tone scales proposed by the 17th-century Dutch physicist and mathematician Christiaan Huygens.

Pasatieri, Thomas, talented American opera composer; b. New York, Oct. 20, 1945. He began to play the piano by spontaneous generation, and picked up elements of composition, particularly vocal, by a similar subliminal process; between the ages of 14 and 18 he wrote some 400 songs. He persuaded Nadia Boulanger to take him as a student by correspondence between Paris and N.Y. when he was 15; at 16 he entered the Juilliard School of Music, where he became a student of Vittorio Giannini and Vincent Persichetti; he also took a course with Darius Milhaud in Aspen, Colo., where his first opera, *The Women*, to his own libretto, was performed when he was only 19. It became clear to him that opera was his natural medium, and that the way to achieve the best results was by following the evolutionary line of Italian operatic productions characterized by the felicity of *bel canto*, facility of harmonic writing, and euphonious fidelity to the lyric and dramatic content of the subject. In striving to attain these objectives, Pasatieri ran the tide of mandatory inharmoniousness; while his productions were applauded by hoi polloi, they shocked music critics and other composers; one of them described Pasatieri's music as "a stream of perfumed urine." This attitude is akin to that taken by some toward Vittorio Giannini and Gian Carlo Menotti (interestingly, all 3 are of Italian genetic stock). From 1967 to 1969 Pasatieri taught at the Juilliard School; then was engaged at the Manhattan School of Music (1969–71); from 1980 was Distinguished Visiting Prof. at the Univ. of Cincinnati College-Cons. of Music.

WORKS: The list of Pasatieri's operas grows with every passing year: *The Women* (Aspen, Aug. 20, 1965); *La Divina* (N.Y., March 16, 1966); *Padrevia* (Brooklyn, Nov. 18, 1967); *Calvary* (Seattle, April 7, 1971); *The Trial of Mary Lincoln*, television opera (Boston, Feb. 14, 1972); *Black Widow* (Seattle, March 2, 1972); *The Seagull*, after Chekhov's play (Houston, March 5, 1974); *Signor Deluso*, after Molière's comedy *Sganarelle* (Greenway, Va., July 27, 1974); *The Penitentes* (Aspen, Aug. 3, 1974); *Ines de Castro* (Baltimore, March 30, 1976); *Washington Square*, after Henry James (Detroit, Oct. 3, 1976); *Before Breakfast* (1980); *Maria Elena* (Tucson, April 8, 1983). He further wrote *Héloïse and Abelard* for Soprano, Baritone, and Piano (1971); *Rites de passage* for Voice and Strings (1974); *3 Poems of James Agee* for Voice and Piano (1974); 2 piano sonatas and other piano pieces.

Pasdeloup, Jules-Etienne, famous French conductor; b. Paris, Sept. 15, 1819; d. Fontainebleau, Aug. 13, 1887. He studied piano at the Cons. with Laurent and Zimmerman; from 1841 he was répétiteur of a solfeggio class; in 1847–50, teacher of a piano class, which he gave up to organize the celebrated symph. concerts of the Société des Jeunes Elèves du Conservatoire (1853), developing (1861) into the Concerts Populaires de Musique Classique at the Cirque Napoléon, a pioneer series of good, inexpensive popular concerts which were a success from the start. Pasdeloup also taught a vocal ensemble class at the Cons. (1855–68). His popular concerts gradually lost ground in competition with Colonne and Lamoureux, ceasing in 1884; he revived them in 1886–87, just before his death. A grand popular music festival at the Trocadéro (1884), instituted for his benefit, netted him nearly 100,000 francs.

Pasero, Tancredi, Italian bass; b. Turin, Jan. 11, 1893; d. Milan, Feb. 17, 1983. He studied in Turin; made his debut in 1917 as Rodolfo in *La Sonnambula* in Vicenza; in 1926 he joined La Scala in Milan, remaining on its roster until 1952. He made his Metropolitan Opera debut in N.Y. on Nov. 1, 1929, as Alvise in *La Gioconda;* continued on its roster until 1933. He also had guest engagements in South America; his repertoire was extensive and included Italian, German, French, and Russian operas; he excelled in the bass roles in Verdi's operas, and made a distinctive appearance as Boris Godunov.

Pasquali (Pascale, Paschali), Francesco, Italian composer, one of the earliest musicians to write instrumental pieces with figured bass; b. Cosenza, c.1590; d. after 1633. He studied in Rome, and remained there for most of his life. Between 1615 and 1633 he brought out 3 books of madrigals for 4 and 5 voices, and several vols. of secular and sacred songs for one, 2, 3, 4, and 5 voices.

Pasquini, Bernardo, Italian organist and composer; b. Massa di Valdinievole, Tuscany, Dec. 7, 1637; d. Rome, Nov. 21, 1710. He came to Rome in 1650 and studied with Vittori and Cesti; was employed as a church organist at Chiesa Nuova (1661–63), at S. Maria Maggiore (1663), at Santa Maria in Aracoeli (1664 until his death), and at S. Luigi dei Francesi (1673–75); served as first organist at the Oratory of SS. Crocifisso (1664–85), and was at one time in the employ of Prince Giambattista Borghese as a chamber musician. He was renowned as a teacher; Durante, G. Muffat, and Della Ciaja were his pupils. He wrote about 17 oratorios, 14 operas (1672–92), and chamber cantatas, but was distinguished mainly for his keyboard composition; his toccatas and suites were publ. during his lifetime in the collection *Toccates et suites pour le clavecin de MM. Pasquini, Poglietti et Gaspard Kerle* (Paris, 1704). Other clavier works were brought out by L. Torchi in *L'arte musicale in Italia,* by Cesi, by Tagliapietra in *Antologia di musica antica e moderna per pianoforte,* and in other anthologies. His vocal pieces were publ. by F. Boghen (1923, 1930). His collected works for keyboard, edited by M.B. Haynes, were publ. in 7 vols. (Rome, 1964–68); a Sonata for 2 Claviers was brought out by W. Danckert (Kassel, 1971).

Pasquini, Ercole, Italian organist and composer; b. Ferrara; d. Rome, between 1608 and 1620. He studied with Alessandro Milleville; was an organist in Ferrara and later at St. Peter's in Rome (1597–1608). His set of *Canzone francese per cembalo* is reprinted by Torchi in *L'arte musicale in Italia* (vol. III); W. Shindle edited *Ercole Pasquini: Collected Keyboard Works,* in *Corpus of Early Keyboard Music,* XII (1966).

Pasta (née **Negri**), **Giuditta,** famous Italian dramatic soprano; b. Saronno, near Milan, Oct. 28, 1797; d. at her villa on Lake Como, April 1, 1865. She studied with Asioli at the Milan Cons. and made her debut in 1815; after indifferent appearances in London and Paris, she returned to Italy for further vocal study with Scappa. At her appearances in Paris in 1822 she was acclaimed as a vocal phenomenon; the range of her voice was from A in the low register to D in the high treble; but what contributed chiefly to her success was her extraordinary dramatic power, so that she won out with the audiences and critics against all possible rivals. So great was her fame at the peak of her career that renowned composers wrote into their operas roles to suit her voice; Bellini did so in *La Sonnambula* and *Norma,* Donizetti in *Anna Bolena,* and Pacini produced his *Niobe* for her.

Patanè, Giuseppe, talented Italian conductor; b. Naples, Jan. 1, 1932. He was a son of **Franco Patanè** (1908–68), a noted opera conductor; studied at the Cons. S. Pietro a Majella in Naples; made his debut as a conductor at the age of 19, when he led a performance of *La Traviata* at the Teatro Mercadante in Naples; he was subsequently 2nd conductor at the Teatro San Carlo in Naples (1951–56); became principal conductor of the Linz Opera in 1961, and in 1962 to 1968 was conductor of the Deutsche Oper in Berlin; he further filled engagements at La Scala in Milan, at the Vienna Opera, and in Copenhagen, with excellent acclaim; he also conducted the Radio Orch. of Berlin, the Orch. de la Suisse Romande in Switzerland, etc. In 1978 he conducted Italian opera at the Metropolitan Opera in N.Y.; in 1982 was appointed co-principal conductor of the American Symph. in N.Y., remaining at this post until 1984.

Patti, Adelina (Adela Juana Maria), one of the greatest coloratura singers of the 19th century, in both opera and concert; b. Madrid, Feb. 10, 1843; d. Brecknock, Wales, Sept. 27, 1919. The daughter of 2 Italian singers, she was taken to N.Y. at an early age; from 1851–55 she sang in many concerts there. She was taught piano by her sister **Carlotta,** and singing by her half-brother, Ettore Barili; her formal debut was made in N.Y. on Nov. 24, 1859, as Lucia (under the stage name of "the little Florinda"). In London she first appeared in *La Sonnambula* on May 14, 1861, at Covent Garden, her success rivaling that of Grisi; her Paris debut was in the same role, at the Théâtre Italien, on Nov. 19, 1862. In Paris in 1868 she married the Marquis de Caux, from whom she separated in 1877; they were divorced in 1885. She sang for the first time in Italy at La Scala in Milan on Nov. 3, 1877, Violetta in *La Traviata* being the role selected. She sang in all the chief cities of Europe, and was everywhere received with enthusiasm; made guest appearances at the Metropolitan Opera House in N.Y. in April 1892. She commanded very large fees. She retired from the stage in 1895, but continued to appear in concerts, giving an official "farewell" concert at Albert Hall in London on Dec. 1, 1906. Her last public appearance was at a benefit concert for the Red Cross in the same hall, on Oct. 20, 1914. Her 2nd husband, the tenor **Nicolini,** whom she married in 1886, died in 1898; she married a Swedish nobleman, Baron Cederström, in 1899. Although her voice was not powerful, it possessed a wide range (c^1–f^3), wonderful flexibility, and perfect evenness throughout; it probably excelled that of any other singer in voluptuous sweetness and bell-like purity. Her vocalization and technical skill were above all criticism, and the ease with which she took the highest notes was astonishing. But she was a poor actress, she lacked temperament, and her musical intelligence was ordinary. Her operatic repertoire included about 30 roles in the operas of Rossini, Bellini, Donizetti, Meyerbeer, Gounod, Auber, and Verdi (earlier works).

Patti, Carlotta, concert singer, sister of **Adelina Patti;** b. Florence, Oct. 30, 1835; d. Paris, June 27, 1889. Her father and mother were her first teachers in singing; she had piano lessons with Henri Herz in Paris. Her early youth was spent in N.Y. Lameness prevented success on the stage, but she was more fortunate as a concert singer, making her debut in N.Y. in 1861, followed by an American tour with the impresario Ullmann. Here, and in Europe, she became a favorite on the concert stage, more especially as a coloratura vocalist of exquisite technique united with great sentiment. In 1871 she married the cellist **De Munck.**

Pattison, Lee, American pianist; b. Grand Rapids, Mich., July 22, 1890; d. Claremont, Calif., Dec. 22, 1966. He first studied at the New England Cons. of Music; later in Berlin with Schnabel. In 1917 he formed a duo-piano team with Guy Maier; they gave a number of successful concerts until 1931, when the partnership was dissolved. From 1932 till 1937 he was head of the piano dept. at Sarah Lawrence College; also taught at the Juilliard Summer School; lived mostly in N.Y. His compositions include *Florentine Sketches* for Piano and a piano suite of 7 pieces, *Told in the Hills.*

Pauer, Ernst, Austrian pianist; b. Vienna, Dec. 21, 1826; d. Jugenheim, near Darmstadt, May 9, 1905. He studied piano with Mozart's son, W.A. Mozart, Jr.,

and composition with Sechter. In 1851 he went to London; taught at the Royal Academy of Music (1859–64); in 1861 he began a series of historical performances of harpsichord and piano music in chronological order, which attracted considerable attention. After a number of concerts in Germany and Austria he was appointed pianist to the Austrian court (1866). He continued his activities until 1896, when he retired and lived in Jugenheim. He publ. in English a number of educational works of some value, among them *The Art of Pianoforte-playing* (1877); *Musical Forms* (1878); *The Elements of the Beautiful in Music* (1877); also, *The Birthday Book of Musicians and Composers* (London, 1881) and *A Dictionary of Pianists and Composers for the Pianoforte* (1895); he further brought out collections for piano students: *The New Gradus ad Parnassum; Classical Companion: Celebrated Concert-studies;* and *Cultures of the Left Hand.* He made excellent arrangements of symphs. by Beethoven and Schumann, for piano solo, piano, 4-hands, and piano, 8-hands; also arranged Mendelssohn's orch. works for piano, 4-hands and 8-hands; these arrangements were widely used in the 19th century and were extremely useful for young pianists until the advent of the phonograph administered a lethal blow to this type of musical activity.

Pauer, Jiři, Czech composer; b. Libušín, near Kladno, central Bohemia, Feb. 22, 1919. He studied composition with Otakar Šín; then with Alois Hába at the Prague Cons. (1943–46) and with Borkovec at the Prague Academy of Music (1946–50). He occupied various administrative posts with the Ministry of Education and Culture and with Czech Radio; was artistic director of the Opera of the National Theater in Prague (1953–55, 1965–67); then taught at the Prague Academy. In 1979 he was appointed general manager of the Prague Opera; was director of the Czech Phil. from 1958 to 1980. His music follows the pragmatic precepts of socialist realism in its modern application, broadly lyrical and tensely dramatic by turns.

Pauer, Max, eminent English pianist and teacher, son of **Ernst Pauer;** b. London, Oct. 31, 1866; d. Jugenheim, May 12, 1945. He studied with his father; embarked on several successful concert tours in Germany; in 1887 was appointed prof. of piano at the Cologne Cons.; in 1897 became a prof. at the Stuttgart Cons.; was its director in 1908–20; in 1920 it became the Hochschule für Musik, which he directed until 1924; then he became director of the Leipzig Cons. (1924–32) and of the Mannheim Hochschule für Musik (1933–34); retired in 1934. He made an American tour in 1913–14. Following his father's excellent example in arranging Classical symphs. for piano, he made transcriptions of symphs. by Mozart and Haydn for piano solo and piano, 4-hands. He publ. an ironic autobiography, *Unser seltsames Ich* (Stuttgart, 1942).

Paul, Thomas, distinguished American bass; b. Chicago, Feb. 22, 1934. He studied with Howard

Swan and Robert Gross at Occidental College in Los Angeles (B.A., 1956); then took courses in conducting with Jean Morel and Frederic Waldman at the Juilliard School of Music in N.Y.; also studied voice privately in N.Y. He made his vocal debut in Handel's *Belshazzar* at Carnegie Hall on April 10, 1961. He sang with the N.Y. City Opera (1963–70), and with the opera companies of Philadelphia, Houston, Washington, D.C., Cincinnati, and New Orleans; was also a soloist with orchs., including the N.Y. Phil., Chicago Symph., Boston Symph., Cleveland Orch., Philadelphia Orch., Pittsburgh Symph., and Los Angeles Phil. He made his European debut in Zürich on April 3, 1976, in a performance of Bach's *St. Matthew Passion.* In 1971 he became a prof. of voice at the Eastman School of Music in Rochester, N.Y., and was also appointed to the faculty of the Aspen Music School. His finest roles include Boris Godunov, Figaro, and Méphistophélès.

Paulson, Gustaf, Swedish composer and organist; b. Hälsingborg, Jan. 22, 1898; d. there, Dec. 17, 1966. He studied composition in Copenhagen with Peder Gram; from 1929 until his death, served as church organist in Hälsingborg. He was an extraordinarily prolific composer; wrote 13 symphs. and 19 concertos for every instrument of the orch. His music reflected the type of Scandinavian Romanticism associated with Sibelius and Nielsen, pervaded by streaks of coherent polyphony.

Paulus, Olaf, Norwegian composer; b. Christiania, Jan. 25, 1859; d. Stavanger, June 29, 1912. He was a pupil of C. Cappelen and J. Svendsen; also studied at the Leipzig Cons.; from 1889 he was organist at the Cathedral in Stavanger; made a trip to the U.S. in 1902, directing choral concerts in Minneapolis and St. Paul. In his native country he is highly esteemed as a national composer; his men's choruses are in the repertoire of all Norwegian societies; he also wrote songs and piano pieces, and edited a collection of songs, *De 1,000 hjems sange* (*Home Songs;* 1888).

Pauly, Rosa, Hungarian dramatic soprano; b. Eperjes, March 15, 1894; d. Herzlia, Israel, Dec. 14, 1975. She studied voice with Rosa Papier-Paumgartner in Vienna, and made her operatic debut at the Vienna Opera as Desdemona in Verdi's *Otello* in 1918. She subsequently sang in Hamburg, Cologne, and Mannheim. In 1927–31 she was a member of the staff at the Kroll Opera in Berlin; she was also on the staff of the Vienna State Opera (1929–35); in 1934 she sang the challenging role of Elektra in Strauss's opera in Salzburg, gathering encomiums; in 1935 she appeared at La Scala in Milan. She made her American debut as Elektra in a concert performance with the N.Y. Phil. on March 21, 1937; sang it again at her first appearance with the Metropolitan Opera on Jan. 7, 1938; appeared there until 1940; also sang at the Teatro Colón in Buenos Aires in 1939. In 1946 she went to Palestine, and devoted herself to teaching in Tel Aviv. She was reputed to be one of the best dramatic sopranos of her era.

Paumann, Conrad, historically significant German organist and composer; b. Nuremberg, between 1410 and 1415; d. Munich, Jan. 24, 1473. He was blind from birth; through the patronage of Ulrich Grundherr, and later his son Paul Grundherr, he was able to obtain instruction in music. By 1446 he was appointed organist at St. Sebald in Nuremberg; in 1447 he became town organist. In 1450 he was called to Munich to serve as court organist to Duke Albrecht III of Bavaria. He won great renown as an organist, and traveled to Austria and Italy. He also achieved mastery as a player on the harp, the lute, and the recorder; he was particularly noted for his improvisations. Some of his extant works have been publ. in *Das Erbe deutscher Musik,* first series (1958); see also the *Fundamentum organisandi magistri Conradi Paumanns ceci de Nürenberga anno 1452* as ed. by W. Apel in *Keyboard Music of the Fourteenth and Fifteenth Centuries, Corpus of Early Keyboard Music,* I (1963).

Paumgartner, Bernhard, eminent Austrian musicologist and conductor; b. Vienna, Nov. 14, 1887; d. Salzburg, July 27, 1971. He was a son of **Hans Paumgartner** (1843–96), who was for many years a chorus master of the Vienna Court Opera, and of **Rosa Papier,** a well-known singer. He studied with Bruno Walter; in 1917 was engaged as director of the Mozarteum in Salzburg, which he headed until 1938, and again from 1945 to 1959. Shortly before his death he was elected an honorary president of the Salzburg Festival. A versatile musician, he was active as a conductor, composer, and writer on musical subjects. He wrote an opera, *Rossini in Neapel* (Zürich, March 27, 1936), and some other stage music, including ballets: *Pagoden* (Munich, 1927); *Ballo medico* (Vienna, 1943); *Salzburger divertimento* (Salzburg, 1955, using Mozart's music); *Ouvertüre zu einem ritterlichen Spiel* for Orch.; various instrumental pieces in a Baroque manner. Among his publications were *Mozart* (Berlin, 1927; 6th ed., enlarged, 1967); *Franz Schubert: Eine Biographie* (Zürich, 1943; 3rd ed., 1960); *J.S. Bach* (Zürich, 1950); he also contributed numerous articles on Mozart and on music to various publications in Salzburg. He publ. an autobiographical memoir, *Erinnerungen* (Salzburg, 1969). A collection of his articles and essays was publ. posthumously (Kassel, 1973).

Paur, Emil, Austrian conductor; b. Czernowitz, Bukovina, Aug. 29, 1855; d. Mistek, Bohemia, June 7, 1932. He was trained in the rudiments of music by his father, and played the violin and piano in public at the age of 8; at 11 he entered the Vienna Cons., where he studied violin with Hellmesberger and composition with Dessoff, graduating in 1870. He achieved an excellent reputation as a competent drillmaster, and in 1893 was engaged as conductor of the Boston Symph. Orch. to succeed Nikisch; he held this post for 5 seasons; from 1898 to 1902 he conducted the N.Y. Phil. Society; during the season of 1899–1900 he led the Wagner repertoire at the Metropolitan Opera in N.Y.; from 1899 to 1902 he served as director of the National Cons. in N.Y., succeeding Dvořák; from 1902 to 1904 he filled engagements in Europe; in 1904 he was again engaged in the U.S., as conductor of the Pittsburgh Symph. Orch. (until 1910). In 1912 he returned to Berlin, but failed to impress the fastidious concert audiences there; for the rest of his life he conducted occasional engagements. He was married to the pianist **Maria Bürger** (1862–99).

Pavarotti, Luciano, spectacularly popular silver-throated Italian tenor; b. Modena, Oct. 12, 1935. His father was a baker who liked to sing and wanted his son to sing, too; but his mother, who worked in a tobacco factory, hoped he would become a bank clerk. He followed the advice of neither, and earned his living by teaching school and selling insurance. He did not abandon his voice training, however, and took lessons with Arrigo Pola and Ettore Campogalliani. In 1961 he sang his first operatic role, that of Rodolfo in *La Bohème*, in Reggio Emilia; then received engagements in Venice and Palermo. There followed appearances in Amsterdam, Vienna, Dublin, and London. In 1963 he sang in Spain and in Poland. In 1965, he revisited London, and sang the role of Alfredo in *La Traviata* at Covent Garden. In 1966 he made his American debut in Miami; then went on a tour in Australia, with a troupe that included the famous soprano Joan Sutherland. Returning from this long tour, he made an important debut at La Scala in Milan. His repertoire now included most of the standard operas, and he received engagements all over Europe. In 1967 he sang with the San Francisco Opera. One of his major feats of sheer virtuosity was to perform the classical arias in Donizetti's operas in their original key, requiring repeated high C's, which he delivered with insouciant aplomb, fully conscious of the effect he was producing on the public and the critics. On Nov. 23, 1968, he made his debut with the Metropolitan Opera in N.Y., singing Rodolfo, with unqualified acclaim. His fame was established, and critics exhausted their vocabulary of superlatives to describe his renditions of the parts of the Duke in *Rigoletto*, Riccardo in *Un ballo in maschera*, Cavaradossi in *Tosca*, and other favorites of the Italian repertoire. (He carefully avoided singing Wagner.) Apart from opera, he appeared in recitals in the U.S., in Europe, and in Japan. Idolized by the public as no tenor had been since the days of Caruso, he plays the part of being Pavarotti with succulent delectation. Like Caruso, he is a gastronome. Unlike Caruso, he wears a substantial beard. Like Caruso, he is arrestingly corpulent (c.290 lbs.). Like Caruso, like Mario del Monaco, and like many other Italian tenors, he paints nicely. Like most tenors, he likes himself immensely. Unlike most tenors, he does not get involved in scandal, and ostentatiously projects himself in words and pictures as a family man. Like most successful artists, he plays tennis and swims for relaxation. In 1982 he agreed to appear in an American film with an idiotic title, *Yes, Giorgio!* It proved that he had no talent as a dramatic actor, outside of opera. He publ. an autobiography, *Pavarotti: My Own Story* (with W. Wright; Garden City, N.Y., 1981).

Pavlova, Anna, celebrated Russian dancer; b. St. Petersburg, Feb. 12, 1881; d. The Hague, Jan. 23, 1931. Of humble origin (her father was a soldier, her mother a domestic laundress), she joined the Imperial Ballet at a very early age, and in 1906 received the rank of prima ballerina. Her fame spread, and in 1914 she left Russia for a fabulously successful career abroad. In 1909 she took part in the season of the Ballets Russes in Paris; in 1910 she organized her own troupe, with which she toured in Europe, America, and Asia. She was celebrated for her performance of Giselle, but the greatest image she left for posterity was the solo dance *The Dying Swan,* to the music of Saint-Saëns, originally choreographed by Fokine. The correct pronunciation of her name is Páv-lo-va, (not Pav-ló-va, as is commonly heard).

Payne, John, American composer; b. New York, May 23, 1941. He studied psychology at Brown Univ. (B.A., 1962); played in jazz bands. Bypassing the traditional forms of conventional modernism, he devoted his energies to total environmental art. He collaborated with Carol Law and Charles Amirkhanian in producing a live-electronic theater event, *Ode to Gravity* (San Francisco, Sept. 21, 1968); staged the audience-participation happenings *Thursday Mix* (San Francisco, March 27, 1969, a Thursday) and *Friday Mix* (San Francisco, May 2, 1969, a Friday). He also programmed a number of electronic scores, among them *Elevator Music* and *Toot le fromage,* making use of inchoate concrete noises.

Paz, Juan Carlos, significant Argentine composer; b. Buenos Aires, Aug. 5, 1901; d. there, Aug. 25, 1972. He studied composition with Constantino Gaito in Argentina and later with Vincent d'Indy in Paris; in 1929, with several young composers of radical tendencies, he organized in Buenos Aires the "Grupo Renovación," and in 1937 inaugurated a series of concerts of new music; became a music critic and author of several books. His early works, after 1921, are marked by strong polyphony, in a neo-Classical style; about 1927, he adopted atonal and polytonal procedures; in 1934 he began to compose almost exclusively in the 12-tone idiom; after 1950 he modified his musical language, adopting a less rigid and more personal style of composition.
WORKS: FOR ORCH.: *Canto de Navidad* (1927; instrumented 1930); *Movimiento sinfónico* (1930); Suite for Ibsen's *Juliano Emperador* (1931); *3 Pieces* (1931); *Passacaglia* (1936; Paris Festival of the International Society for Contemporary Music, June 25, 1937; revised 1952–53); *Música (Preludio y fuga)* (1940); *Passacaglia* for String Orch. (1944; revised 1949); *Rítmica constante* (1952); *6 superposiciones* (1954); *Transformaciones canónicas* (1955–56); *Música* for Bassoon, Strings, and Percussion (1955–56); *Continuidad 1960* (1960–61; 3rd Festival of Music, Caracas, May 11, 1966); *Estructuras 1962* for Chamber Orch. (1962); *Música* for Piano and Orch.

(1964; 3rd Inter-American Music Festival, Washington, D.C., May 12, 1965). pieces for Solo transformaciones

Pears, Sir Peter, English tenor; b. Farnham, June 22, 1910. He studied at the Royal College of Music in London; during the season of 1936–37 toured the U.S. as a member of the New English Singers. In 1937 he joined Benjamin Britten in a series of recitals devoted mainly to contemporary English composers, with Britten acting as his accompanist. In 1948 he was a co-founder, with Britten, of the Aldeburgh Festival. Pears sang leading tenor parts in almost all of Britten's operas: *Peter Grimes, The Rape of Lucretia, Albert Herring, Billy Budd, Gloriana, The Turn of the Screw,* and *Death in Venice;* he also sang the tenor solo part in Britten's *War Requiem.* He made his debut at the Metropolitan Opera in N.Y. on Oct. 18, 1974, as Aschenbach in *Death in Venice.* He was made a Commander of the Order of the British Empire in 1957, and was knighted by Queen Elizabeth II in 1978.

Pearsall, Robert Lucas de, English composer; b. Clifton, March 14, 1795; d. Wartensee, on Lake Constance, Aug. 5, 1856. He studied law and music; as a boy of 13 wrote a cantata, *Saul and the Witch of Endor.* He lived many years in Germany, where he publ. many of his compositions; was in London on several extended visits; in 1842, purchased a castle on Lake Constance, and remained there for the rest of his life. As a composer, he was at his best in many ingenious madrigals; particularly popular were his part-songs, *Sir Patrick Spens, The Hardy Norseman,* and *O who will o'er the downs so free;* he edited old church music in Germany; publ. an *Essay on Consecutive Fifths and Octaves in Counterpoint.*

Pechner, Gerhard, German baritone; b. Berlin, April 15, 1903; d. New York, Oct. 21, 1969. He made his first appearance as an opera singer in Berlin in 1927; was compelled to leave Germany in 1933; from 1933 till 1939 he was on the staff of the German Opera House in Prague. In 1940 he was engaged by the San Francisco Opera, and on Nov. 27, 1941, made his debut at the Metropolitan Opera in N.Y.; remained there until 1947. He particularly distinguished himself in Wagnerian roles.

Pedrell, Carlos, Uruguayan composer; b. Minas, Uruguay, Oct. 16, 1878; d. Montrouge, near Paris, March 3, 1941. He studied in Madrid with his uncle, **Felipe Pedrell;** later went to Paris, where he took lessons with Vincent d'Indy and Bréville at the Schola Cantorum. Returning to South America, he was inspector of music in the Buenos Aires schools; lectured at the Univ. of Tucumán; in 1921 he went to Paris, where he remained for the rest of his life. His works are cast in the French style, but the rhythmic elements are related to Spanish and South American sources; his songs, with richly developed accompaniments, are the best among his works.

WORKS: Operas: *Ardid de Amor* (Buenos Aires, June 7, 1917); *Cuento de Abril; La Guitare* (Madrid, 1924); ballets: *La Rose et le gitan* (Antwerp, 1930) and *Alleluia* (Buenos Aires, 1936); for Orch.: *Une Nuit de Schéhérazade* (1908); *Danza y canción de Aixa* (1910); *En el estrado de Beatriz* (1910); *Fantasia Argentina* (1910); *Ouverture catalane* (1912); *Pastorales* for Voice and Orch. (Paris, 1928); choruses; songs.

Pedrell, Felipe, eminent Spanish musicologist and composer; b. Tortosa, Feb. 19, 1841; d. Barcelona, Aug. 19, 1922. A chorister in the Cathedral of Tortosa, he was guided in his musical studies by J.A. Nin y Serra. His prolific literary career began in 1867, with articles in various musical reviews; his first opera, *El último Abencerrage,* was produced at Barcelona in 1874. After a visit to Italy and a sojourn in Paris, he settled in Barcelona (1881), where he founded the *Salterio Sacro-Hispano* for the publication of contemporary religious music, and the weekly review *Notas Musicales y Literarias,* both of which ceased publication in 1883. In 1888 he founded the *Ilustración Musical Hispano-Americana,* which he edited until its demise in 1896. In 1889–91 he composed his great dramatic trilogy, *Los Pirineos,* and as a sort of introduction to this work he wrote his famous pamphlet *Por nuestra música,* a plea for the creation of a national lyric drama on the basis of the national folk song. In 1891–92, he was a critic for the *Diario de Barcelona;* in 1894 he went to Madrid, where he was made a member of the Royal Academy of Fine Arts; he also was a prof. at the Madrid Cons. (1895–1903) and a lecturer on music history at the Madrid Ateneo. He was invited to direct the reform of religious music in Spain; edited the review *Música Religiosa* in 1896–99. At the end of 1904 he returned to Barcelona as artistic director for the publishing firm of Vidal y Llimona, which revived the *Salterio Sacro-Hispano.* There he spent the rest of his life, writing, teaching, and composing. Among his pupils were Albéniz, Granados, Manuel de Falla, and Gerhard. Though Pedrell was highly praised by contemporary critics, his music has not obtained recognition outside Spain; but the importance of his achievement in bringing to light the treasures of Spain's musical past is universally recognized, and he is considered the leading spirit of the modern Spanish nationalist revival in music. On his 70th birthday he was honored by the publication of a Festschrift, *Al Maestro Pedrell: Escritos heortásticos,* with contributions from the foremost musical scholars throughout the world.

Pedrotti, Carlo, Italian composer and conductor; b. Verona, Nov. 12, 1817; d. there (suicide), Oct. 16, 1893. He studied with Domenico Foroni; obtained excellent success with his opera *Lina* (Verona, May 2, 1840); was then engaged as conductor of the Italian Opera at Amsterdam (1841–45), and wrote 2 operas there, *Mathilde* (Spring 1841) and *La Figlia del Arciere* (Feb. 29, 1844); returned to Verona in 1845 and presented there his operas *Romea di Monfort* (Feb. 19, 1846), *Fiorina* (Nov. 22, 1851), *Il Parruc-*

chiere della reggenza (May 5, 1852), and *Tutti in maschera* (Nov. 4, 1856; his principal work). The following operas were staged in Milan: *Gelmina* (Nov. 3, 1853), *Genoveffa del Brabante* (March 20, 1854), and *La guerra in quattro* (May 25, 1861). Other operas were *Isabella d'Arragona* (Turin, Feb. 7, 1859); *Mazeppa* (Bologna, Dec. 3, 1861); *Marion Delorme* (Trieste, Nov. 16, 1865); *Il Favorito* (Turin, March 15, 1870); *Olema la schiava* (Modena, May 4, 1872).

Peerce, Jan (real name, **Jacob Pincus Perelmuth**), American tenor; b. New York, June 3, 1904. He played the violin in dance bands, and sang at various entertainment places in N.Y. In 1933 he was engaged as a singer at Radio City Music Hall in N.Y.; made his operatic debut in Philadelphia as the Duke in *Rigoletto* (May 14, 1938), and gave his first solo recital in N.Y. on Nov. 7, 1939. His lyrical voice attracted attention, and he was engaged by the Metropolitan Opera Co.; made his debut there as Alfredo in *La Traviata* on Nov. 29, 1941; sang also the parts of Cavaradossi in *Tosca*, Rodolfo in *La Bohème*, and Faust in Gounod's opera; remained on the staff of the Metropolitan until 1966, appearing again in 1967–68.

Peeters, Flor, outstanding Belgian organist, pedagogue, and composer; b. Antwerp, July 4, 1903. He studied organ with Depuydt and Gregorian chant with van Nuffel at the Lemmens Inst. in Molines; he succeeded Depuydt as prof. of organ playing there in 1925, holding this position until 1952. He became a prof. of organ at the Antwerp Cons. in 1948, and was its director from 1952–68. He was elevated to the peerage as Baron Peeters by King Baudoin in 1971. He composed nearly 500 works for organ alone, and also wrote much sacred choral music. His works for organ include *Passacaglia and Fugue* (1938); *Sinfonia* (1940); *Organ Concerto* (1944); *Lied Symphony* (1948); *30 Short Chorale Preludes* (1959); *213 Hymn Preludes for the Liturgical Year* (in 24 installments, 1959–67); *6 Lyrical Pieces* (1966). He also publ. *Anthologia pro organo* (4 vols., Brussels, 1949–59); *Ars organi* (3 vols., Brussels, 1952–54); *Little Organ Book* (Boston, 1957); etc.

Pelissier, Victor, horn virtuoso and composer. His name appears first in 1792 on Philadelphia concert programs as "first horn of the Theatre in Cape François." In 1793 he went to N.Y., where he lived for many years, and became the principal horn player, also composer and arranger, of the Old American Co.
WORKS: Operas: *Edwin and Angelina or The Banditti* (John Street Theater, N.Y., Dec. 19, 1796); *Ariadne Abandoned by Theseus in the Isle of Naxos* (N.Y., 1797); *Sterne's Maria or The Vintage* (1799); incidental music to about 18 plays performed in N.Y. (mostly in 1794–96), including *Fourth of July or Temple of American Independence* (1799), *Castle of Otranto* (adaptation of *Sicilian Romance*), etc.; various pantomimes performed in Philadelphia; a quartet; and a few separate pieces. In 1811 he publ. the collection *Columbian Melodies,* which contains 3 songs from *Sterne's Maria.*

Pelletier, (Louis) Wilfred, noted Canadian conductor and music educator; b. Montreal, June 20, 1896; d. New York, April 9, 1982. His father, a baker by trade, was an amateur musician who gave Pelletier his primary instruction; at the age of 14 he played piano in the orch. of the National Theatre in Montreal; in 1915 he won the Prix d'Europe and went to Paris, where he studied piano with Isidor Philipp, composition with Charles-Marie Widor, and opera repertoire with Camille Bellaigue. In 1917 he returned to America and was engaged as rehearsal pianist at the Metropolitan Opera in N.Y.; in 1921 he was appointed an assistant conductor there; then directed its Sunday Night Concert series; from 1928–50 he was a principal conductor there, specializing in the French repertoire; in 1936 he founded the popular series Metropolitan Opera Auditions of the Air. He also was active as a conductor in Canada; from 1935–51 he was conductor of the Société des Concerts Symphoniques de Montréal, and from 1951–66, of the Orch. Symphonique de Québec. From 1943–61 he served as director of the Cons. de Musique in Montreal. In 1968 he was made a Companion of the Order of Canada. He was married consecutively to 2 sopranos: **Queena Mario** (1925–36) and (from 1937) **Rose Bampton.** He publ. an autobiographical sketch, *Une Symphonie inachevée* (Quebec, 1972).

Peñalosa, Francisco de, important Spanish composer; b. Talavera de la Reina, c.1470; d. Seville, April 1, 1528. In 1498 he became a singer in the chapel choir of Ferdinand V; the King obtained a canonry (in absentia) for him in 1505 at the Seville Cathedral; in 1506 the Cathedral authorities revoked the appointment, but by 1510 he was able to fulfill the residence requirement. In 1511 the King made him maestro de capilla to his grandson. In 1512 he went to the royal monastery of S. Pedro de Cardeña, near Burgos. In 1516 he returned to Seville, where he assumed administrative duties at the Cathedral. In 1517 he became chamberlain and singer at the papal chapel; in 1518 he resigned his canonry at Seville Cathedral to become archdeacon of Carmona. In 1521 he resumed his canonry at Seville Cathedral, where he remained until his death. Peñalosa was one of the most important composers of his era, a master of polyphonic sacred and secular music. His sacred works include masses, Magnificats, motets, and hymns. Some of them are found in H. Eslava y Elizondo, ed., *Lira sacro-hispaña* (first series, vol. I, Madrid, 1869).

Penderecki, Krzysztof, foremost Polish composer of the 20th-century avant-garde; b. Debica, Nov. 23, 1933. (His name is pronounced Kzhýshtov Penderétskee, not Penderekee.) He studied privately with F. Skolyszewski; then took courses in theory with Arthur Malawski and Stanislaw Wiechowicz at the Superior School of Music in Cracow (1955–58); after graduation he taught there (1958–66); went to West Germany and taught at the Folkwang Hochschule für Musik in Essen (1966–68); in 1973 became a part-time member of the faculty at Yale Univ.; also gave courses at Aspen, Colo. (1977). He rapidly acquired a reputation as one of the most original composers of his generation. In 1975 he was made an honorary member of the Royal Academy of Music in London, the Arts Academy of West Berlin, the Arts Academy of the German Democratic Republic, and the Royal Academy of Music in Stockholm. After a few works of an academic nature, he developed a hyper-modern technique of composition in a highly individual style, in which no demarcation line is drawn between consonances and dissonances, tonal or atonal melody, traditional or innovative instrumentation; an egalitarian attitude prevails toward all available resources of sound. While Penderecki's idiom is naturally complex, he does not disdain tonality, even in its overt triadic forms. In his creative evolution, he has bypassed orthodox serial procedures; his music follows an athematic course, in constantly varying metrical and rhythmic patterns. He utilizes an entire spectrum of modern sonorities, expanding the domain of tone to unpitched elements, making use of such effects as shouting, hissing, and verbal ejaculations in vocal parts, at times reaching a climax of aleatory glossolalia; tapping, rubbing, or snapping the fingers against the body of an instrument; striking the piano strings by mallets, etc. For this he designed an optical notation, with symbolic ideograms indicating the desired sound; thus a black isosceles triangle denotes the highest possible pitch; an inverted isosceles triangle, the lowest possible pitch; a black rectangle for a sonic complex of white noise within a given interval; vertical lines tied over by an arc for arpeggios below the bridge of a string instrument; wavy lines of varying amplitudes for extensive vibrato; curvilinear figures for aleatory passages; dots and dashes for repetitions of a pattern; sinusoidal oscillations for quaquaversal glissandos; etc. He applies these modern devices to religious music, including masses in the orthodox Roman Catholic ritual.

WORKS: *Psalmy Dawida (Psalms of David)* for Chorus, 2 Pianos, Celesta, Harp, 4 Double Basses, and Percussion (1958; Cracow, June 26, 1962); *Emanacje (Emanations)* for 2 Orchs. of String Instruments (1958–59); *Strofy (Strophes)* for Soprano, Narrator, and 10 Instruments (1959; Warsaw, Sept. 17, 1959); *3 Miniatures* for Violin and Piano (1959); *Anaklasis* for 42 Strings and Percussion (1959–60; Baden-Baden, Oct. 16, 1960); *Wymiary czasu i ciszy (Dimensions of Time and Silence)* for Wordless Chorus, Strings, and Percussion (1960; Warsaw, Sept. 18, 1960); *Tren pamieci ofiarom Hiroszimy (Threnody in Memory of Victims of Hiroshima)* for 52 String Instruments (1959–60; Warsaw Radio, May 31, 1961; Penderecki's most impressive and most frequently perf. work, rich in dynamic contrasts and ending on a tone cluster of 2 octavefuls of icositetraphonic harmony); String Quartet No. 1 (1960); *Fonogrammi* for 3 Flutes, Strings, and Percussion (1961); *Psalmus*, electronic music (1961); *Polymorphia* for 48 String Instruments (1961; Hamburg,

April 16, 1962; perf. as a ballet under the title *Noctiphobie,* Amsterdam, 1970); *Stabat Mater* for 3 Choruses a cappella (1962; an independent section of the *St. Luke Passion*); *Kanon* for 52 String Instruments and Tape (1962; Warsaw, Sept. 20, 1962); *Fluorescences* for Orch. (1962; Baden-Baden, Oct. 21, 1962); *Cantata in honorem almae matris Universitatis Jagellonicae* for Chorus and Orch. (1964); *Mensura Sortis* for 2 Pianos (1964); Sonata for Cello and Orch. (1964); *Capriccio* (No. 1) for Oboe and 11 Strings (1965); *Passio et mors Domini Nostri Jesu Christi secundum Lucam (Passion According to St. Luke)* for Narrator, Soprano, Baritone, Bass, Boys' Chorus, 3 Mixed Choruses, and Orch. (1962–65; Cathedral in Münster, West Germany, March 30, 1966; a specially commissioned work); *De natura sonoris* (No. 1) for Orch. (1965–66; Royan, France, April 7, 1966); *Dies irae,* oratorio for Soprano, Tenor, Bass, Chorus, and Orch. (1966–67; Cracow, April 14, 1967; also perf. 2 days later as a commemorative service at the site of the Nazi concentration camp at Oświecim-Brzezinka); Concerto for Violino Grande and Orch. (1967; Östersund, Sweden, July 1, 1967; revised version, Hanover, N.H., Aug. 4, 1968; the solo instrument is specially constructed with 5 strings); *Capriccio* (No. 2) for Violin and Orch. (1967; Donaueschingen, Oct. 22, 1967); *Pittsburgh Overture* for Wind Ensemble (1967; commissioned by the American Wind Symph. Orch. in Pittsburgh); *Capriccio per Siegfried Palm* for Solo Cello (1968); String Quartet No. 2 (1968); *De natura sonoris No. 2* for Winds, Percussion, and Strings (1968; Juilliard School of Music, N.Y., Dec. 3, 1971); a 3-act opera, *Die Teufel von Loudun (The Devils of Loudon),* dealing with a *furor uterinus* among nuns of Loudun struck by a multifutuent incubus personified by a neighboring monastic youth (1968–69; Hamburg, June 20, 1969); *Utrenja (Morning Prayer)* in 2 parts (1969–71); *Grablegung Christi (The Entombment of Christ)* for Soprano, Contralto, Tenor, Bass, Basso Profundo, 2 Choruses, and Orch., to a text in old Slavonic (Altenberg Cathedral, April 8, 1970), and *Auferstehung Christi (Resurrection of Christ)* for the same Soloists, Boys' Chorus, 2 Mixed Choruses, and Orch. (Münster Cathedral, May 28, 1971); *Kosmogonia* for Soprano, Tenor, Bass, Chorus, and Orch., commissioned by the United Nations and performed for the first time at its N.Y. headquarters building (1970; Oct. 24, 1970); *Actions* for Jazz Ensemble (1971; Donaueschingen, Oct. 17, 1971); *Prélude* for Winds, Percussion, and Double Basses (1971; Holland Festival, Amsterdam, July 4, 1971); *Partita,* concerto for Harpsichord, 4 other Electronically Amplified Solo Instruments, and Chamber Orch. (1971; Eastman School of Music, Rochester, N.Y., Feb. 11, 1972); Cello Concerto (1972; Baltimore, Md., March 8, 1972); *Ecloga VIII* for 6 Male Voices a cappella (1972; Edinburgh Festival, Aug. 21, 1972); *Ekecheireia* for Tape (1972); *Canticum canticorum Salomonis (Song of Songs)* for 16-voice Chorus, Chamber Orch., and ad libitum Dance Pair (1970–73; Lisbon, June 5, 1973); Symph. No. 1 (1973; London, July 19, 1973); *Intermezzo* for 24 Strings (1973); Magnificat for Bass Solo, Vocal Group, 2 Choruses, Boys' Chorus, and Orch. (1973–

74; Salzburg, Aug. 17, 1974); *Als Jakob erwachte* for Voices, Orch., and 12 Ocarinas (1974; Monte Carlo, Aug. 14, 1974); *Violin Concerto* (1976; Basel, April 27, 1977); opera, *Raj utracony (Paradise Lost),* after Milton (1976–78; Chicago, Nov. 29, 1978); *De profundis* for Chorus and Orch. (1977; Graz, Oct. 16, 1977); *Te Deum* for Soloists, Chorus, and Orch. (1980; Assisi, Italy, Sept. 27, 1980); Symph. No. 2, *Christmas Symphony* (1979–80; N.Y. Phil., May 1, 1980); *Cello Concerto No. 2* (1981–82; West Berlin, Jan. 11, 1983); *Viola Concerto* (1982–83).

Penna, Lorenzo, Italian composer; b. Bologna, 1613; d. there, Oct. 31, 1693. He studied at the Univ. of Ferrara. In 1630 he entered the Carmelite monastery of S. Martino in Bologna; became maestro di cappella at S. Illario in Casale Monferrato (1656); in 1665 received his doctorate in theology; was then maestro di cappella at S. Cassiano in Imola (1667–69); in 1669 entered the Carmelite Order in Mantua, remaining until 1672; subsequently was director of music at the Carmelite church in Parma (1672–73). In 1676 he became a member of the Accademia dei Filarmonici in Bologna, where he remained until his death.
WORKS: *Messe e salmi concertati* in 5 Voices (1656); *Psalmorum totius anni modulatio* in 4 and 5 Voices (1669); *Correnti francesi a quattro,* with String Instruments (1673; designated as "Sonate" in the dedication); *Il sacro Parnaso delli salmi festivi* for 4 to 8 Voices (1677); *Reggia del sacro Parnaso* for 4 to 8 Voices (1677); *Galeria del sacro Parnaso* for 4 to 8 Voices, with Instrumental Accompaniment ad libitum (1678); he also publ. didactic eds.: *Li primi albori musicali per li principianti della musica figurata* (1672); *Albori musicali per li studiosi della musica figurata* (1678); *Direttorio del canto fermo* (Modena, 1689).

Pennario, Leonard, brilliant American pianist; b. Buffalo, July 9, 1924. He was taken to California as a child and studied piano there; appeared in public at the age of 7, and was a soloist with the Los Angeles Phil. at 15. He then took piano lessons with Guy Maier; served in the U.S. Army Air Corps during World War II; then resumed his career; was the pianist with Heifetz and Piatigorsky in trio concerts; made several European tours; also was active as a teacher.

Pentland, Barbara, Canadian composer; b. Winnipeg, Jan. 2, 1912. After taking piano lessons at a Montreal boarding school, she went to N.Y., and studied with Frederick Jacobi and Bernard Wagenaar at the Juilliard School of Music (1936–39); also took summer courses with Aaron Copland at the Berkshire Music Center in Tanglewood (1941 and 1942). She was an instructor at the Toronto Cons. (1943–49) and with the music dept. of the Univ. of British Columbia in Vancouver (1949–63). In her compositions she adopts a pragmatic method of cosmopolitan modernism, employing dissonant linear counterpoint and dodecaphonic melodic structures within the framework of Classical forms.

Pépin, Clermont, Canadian composer; b. St.-Georges-de-Beauce, May 15, 1926. He studied piano in Quebec, and harmony in Montreal with Claude Champagne. In 1941 he went to Philadelphia, where he studied composition with Rosario Scalero. From 1949 to 1955 he lived in Paris and took composition lessons with Jolivet, Honegger, and Messiaen. Returning to Canada, he joined the staff of the Montreal Cons. (1955–64; director, 1967–72).

Pepping, Ernst, German composer; b. Duisburg, Sept. 12, 1901; d. Berlin, Feb. 1, 1981. He studied in Berlin with Gmeindl; became a teacher at the Church Music School in Berlin-Spandau in 1934, remaining there throughout his career; from 1953 to 1968 was a prof. of composition at the Berlin Hochschule für Musik. By virtue of his lifelong association with Lutheran Church culture, he acquired a profound understanding of German polyphonic music, both sacred and secular, and is generally regarded as the most significant representative of modern German choral writing; he also made arrangements of German folk songs. A Festschrift was publ. in his honor in 1971.

Pepusch, John Christopher (Johann Christoph), German-English opera composer; b. Berlin, 1667; d. London, July 20, 1752. He was taught by Klingenberg (theory) and Grosse (organ). He had a position at the Prussian court in 1681–97; then went to the Netherlands and (in 1700) to London; joined the Drury Lane orch. as a violinist; later as cembalist and composer, adapting Italian airs to English operas and adding recitatives and songs. In 1710 he founded (with Needler, Gates, Galliard, and others) the Academy of Ancient Music, famous for the revival of 16th-century compositions; in 1712, he was organist and composer to the Duke of Chandos, preceding Handel; in 1713, received his Mus.Doc. degree from Oxford. For many years he served as director of Lincoln's Inn Theatre, for which he wrote the masques *Venus and Adonis* (1715), *Apollo and Daphne* (1716), *The Death of Dido* (1716), and *The Union of the 3 Sister-Arts* (1723), and arranged music to the ballad-operas *The Beggar's Opera, Polly,* and *The Wedding.* In 1730 a fortune brought him by marriage with the singer **Marguerite de l'Epine** rendered him independent. From 1737 until his death he was organist of the Charterhouse. Pepusch was a learned, though conservative, musician who enjoyed high renown in England. He publ. a *Treatise on Harmony* (1731; reprinted Hildesheim, 1970); his various odes and cantatas, and his instrumental concertos and sonatas are of slight importance, and his name is preserved in music history mainly for his original music and some arranged numbers in *The Beggar's Opera.*

Peragallo, Mario, Italian composer; b. Rome, March 25, 1910. He was a student of Alfredo Casella, and in his early works followed the line of the Italian Baroque, characterized by modern but euphonious polyphony; later he adopted a radical quasi-dodecaphonic idiom, with frequent reversions to diatonic structures.

WORKS: Operas: *Ginevra degli Almieri* (Rome, Feb: 13, 1937); *Lo stendardo di S. Giorgio* (1941); *La Gita in campagna* (La Scala, Milan, March 24, 1954); scenic cantata, *La collina* (1947); Concerto for Orch. (1940); 2 piano concertos (1949, 1951); Violin Concerto (1954); *Forme sovrapposte* for Orch. (1959); *Vibrazioni* for Flute, "Tiptofono," and Piano (1960); 3 string quartets; Piano Quartet; numerous choral works and songs.

Perahia, Murray, outstanding American pianist of Spanish-Jewish parentage; b. New York, April 19, 1947. He studied piano with J. Haien (1953–64); then entered the Mannes College of Music, where he studied conducting and composition (B.S., 1969); he also continued his piano studies with Artur Balsam and Mieczyslaw Horszowski. In 1968 he made his Carnegie Hall debut; in 1972 he became the first American to win (by a unanimous vote of the jury) the Leeds International Pianoforte Competition; in 1975 he was awarded the first Avery Fisher Prize, sharing it with the cellist Lynn Harrell. He appeared as soloist with the leading orchs. of the U.S. and Europe; also gave many recitals in the U.S. and abroad. In 1982 he was appointed co-artistic director of the Aldeburgh Festival. He excels in classical music; mastered all of Mozart's concertos, often conducting from the keyboard; he is praised also for his congenial interpretation of the standard concert repertoire.

Peress, Maurice, American conductor; b. New York, March 18, 1930. He studied music at N.Y. Univ. (B.A., 1951) and at the Mannes College of Music, N.Y. (1955–57); was a member of the faculty of N.Y. Univ. (1957–61) and then assistant conductor of the N.Y. Phil. (1961–62). His other engagements were as music director of the Corpus Christi (Texas) Symph. Orch. (1962–75) and of the Austin (Texas) Symph. Orch. (1970–73). He was music director of the Kansas City Phil. from 1974–80. In 1981 he became president of the Conductors' Guild of the American Symph. Orch. League. In 1971 he conducted the world premiere of Leonard Bernstein's *Mass* at the Kennedy Center in Washington, D.C.; he also conducted the first European performance of the work at the Vienna State Opera in 1981.

Pérez, David, Italian composer of operas; b. Naples (of Spanish parents), 1711; d. Lisbon, Oct. 30, 1778. He was a pupil of Galli (violin) and Mancini (theory) at the Cons. di Loreto in Naples; presented his first opera, *La nemica amante,* at the Teatro San Carlo in Naples on Nov. 4, 1735, followed by *Li travestimenti amorosi* (Naples, July 10, 1740) and *Siroe* (Naples, Nov. 4, 1740); in 1741 went to Palermo as maestro of the court orch., remaining there until 1748. He then lived the life of a traveling composer, visiting various cities in Italy, until 1752, when he was engaged as maestro di cappella at the royal chapel in Lisbon. In 1755 he visited London. Among his best operas are *Alessandro nell'Indie* (Genoa, Carnival 1744); *Demetrio* (Venice, Spring 1751); and

Solimano (Lisbon, 1757; his most important dramatic work). As an opera composer, he was considered a worthy rival of Jommelli. He also wrote several masses; a Miserere for 5 Voices, with Bassoons obbligati and Organ; *Mattutino de' morti* for Chorus and Orch. (London, 1774); etc.

Perfall, Karl von, German composer and conductor; b. Munich, Jan. 29, 1824; d. there, Jan. 14, 1907. He took music lessons with Hauptmann in Leipzig (1848–49); became conductor of the Munich Liedertafel (1850); founded the Oratorio Society (1854); in 1864 was appointed Intendant of the court music and abandoned his activities as a conductor. From 1867 to 1893 he was Intendant of the Court Theater in Munich. Of his operas (all produced in Munich), *Raimondin* (March 27, 1881) and *Junker Heinz* (April 9, 1886) were successful. He publ. *25 Jahre Münchener Hoftheater-Geschichte* (1892; covering the period from 1867); *Ein Beitrag zur Geschichte des königlichen Theaters in München* (1894); *Die Entwickelung des modernen Theaters* (1899).

Pergament, Moses, Finnish-born Swedish composer and conductor; b. Helsinki, Sept. 21, 1893; d. Gustavsberg, near Stockholm, March 5, 1977. He studied violin at the St. Petersburg Cons. and conducting at Berlin. In 1915 he settled in Sweden; from 1923 to 1966 was active as a music critic in Swedish newspapers; he publ. 4 books on music. His musical style was initially circumscribed by Russian paradigms; later he was influenced by Sibelius; still later he adopted some modernistic procedures. Several of his compositions reflect an ancestral strain of Jewish melos.

Pergolesi, Giovanni Battista, remarkable Italian composer; b. Jesi, near Ancona, Jan. 4, 1710; d. Pozzuoli, March 16, 1736. The family's original name was **Draghi;** the surname Pergolesi was derived from the town of Pergola, where Pergolesi's ancestors lived. He was the only surviving child of his parents, 3 children having died in their infancy. He studied music with Francesco Santi, choir director at Jesi Cathedral; was given a stipend by the Marchese Cardolo Pianetti, which enabled him to enter the Cons. dei Poveri at Naples; there he was a pupil of Domenico de Matteis (violin) and Gaetano Greco (theory); later also studied with Durante and Feo. He became proficient as a violinist, and played on various occasions during the carnivals. His first performed work was an oratorio, *La conversione di S. Guglielmo d'Aquitania* (which included a comic section in the Neapolitan dialect), presented at the monastery of S. Agnello Maggiore in Naples in the summer of 1731; another oratorio, *La Fenice sul rogo,* was performed in the same year; this was followed by a serious opera, *Salustia,* and an opera buffa, *Lo Frate 'nnamorato* (Naples, Sept. 23, 1732). In Dec. 1732 he was commissioned by the municipal authorities of Naples to write a solemn Mass as a votive offering after a series of severe earthquakes. On Aug. 28, 1733, Pergolesi presented a serious opera, *Il Prigioniero superbo;* it contained a comic intermezzo, *La Serva padrona*, which was to become his most celebrated work. After a brief sojourn in Rome (May 1734) to conduct his Mass at the San Lorenzo Church, he returned to Naples; there his new opera, *Adriano in Siria*, was produced, on Oct. 25, 1734, with an intermezzo, *Livietta e Tracollo* (perf. at various times under different titles: *La Contadina astuta, La finta Polacca,* etc.). During another trip to Rome he performed his serious opera *L'Olimpiade* (Jan. 8, 1735), directing from the harpsichord, but it had little success. His last opera was a comic play, *Il Flaminio* (Naples, Autumn 1735). At that time his health was undermined by consumption; early in 1736 he went to Pozzuoli, where he died at the age of 26; he was buried in the common grave. His last completed work was a masterpiece of sacred music, *Stabat Mater*. Several dramatic works ascribed to Pergolesi and publ. under his name, notably *Il Maestro di musica* and *Il Geloso schernito,* are spurious. The revival of his comic intermezzo *La Serva padrona* in Paris in 1752 precipitated the so-called *querelle des bouffons* between the supporters of the Italian and the French factions. Pergolesi's instrumental music is less known, and there are grave doubts as to the authenticity of many of these works publ. under his name: 14 trio sonatas (of these, 3 were ed. by Riemann, Berlin, 1900); 6 concertini for Strings (publ. in London as works by Carlo Ricciotti; recently established as the works of Count Unico Wilhelm van Wassenaer); 3 "sinfonie" (string quartets); 2 concertos for Flute and Strings; Sonata for Violin and Strings; 5 harpsichord sonatas. Stravinsky used some of these instrumental works for his ballet *Pulcinella,* but most of the borrowed material is not by Pergolesi. *La Serva padrona* was publ. in new editions by Abert (1911), Karl Geiringer, and others; *Flaminio* was edited by Mortari (1942); the spurious *Il Maestro di musica* (which is in reality a pasticcio publ. in Paris in 1753) was orchestrated and edited by Schering (1924); the intermezzo *La finta Polacca* was issued by Radiciotti (1914); the *Stabat Mater* was publ. by Eulenburg in Alfred Einstein's edition. Among other extant works attributed to Pergolesi are the oratorios *Il Pentimento, La Morte d'Abel,* and *Septem verba;* 10 chamber cantatas; at least 5 masses; still doubtful is the authenticity of many arias, including the popular *Tre giorni son che Nina.* A complete edition of Pergolesi's works, *Opera omnia,* was brought out in Rome (1940–42) in 5 vols. (148 works, of which 129 publ. for the first time; many are spurious). The chaotic entanglement of spurious and authentic works is marvelously unraveled in M. Paymer's *Pergolesi: A Thematic Catalogue of the Opera Omnia* (N.Y., 1977).

Peri, Jacopo, Italian composer, called **"Il Zazzerino"** for his abundant hair; b. Rome, Aug. 20, 1561; d. Florence, Aug. 12, 1633. Of a noble family, he studied at Lucca under Cristoforo Malvezzi; was maestro at the court of Ferdinando I and Cosimo II de' Medici, and from 1601 at the court of Ferrara. A participant in the Florentine circle at the houses of Counts Bardi and Corsi, where the revival of an-

cient Greek musical declamation was planned, Peri set to music Rinuccini's text of *Dafne* (1597). It was first performed at Corsi's palace in Florence, and played again at Pitti's palace. Peri followed it with a setting of Rinuccini's *Euridice* for the wedding of Maria de' Medici with Henry IV of France (produced Oct. 6, 1600; publ. Florence, 1600; reprinted in *Monuments of Music and Music Literature in Facsimile,* I/8). *Dafne* was the first "opera" or drama set to music in monodic style (i.e., vocal soli supported by instruments); this style was termed *stile rappresentativo.* In 1608 Peri wrote for Mantua the recitatives of *Ariadne* (text by Rinuccini), while Monteverdi composed the arias. In the same year he submitted in Mantua the opera *Tetide* (text by Cini), which, however, was not produced. With Grazie, Signorini, and del Turco he wrote *Guerra d'amore* (Florence, 1615). No records are available showing that *Adone* (text by Cicognini), composed in 1620, ever had a public performance. *La precedenza delle dame* was produced at Florence in 1625, and Peri also collaborated with Gagliano on *La Flora* (Florence, Oct. 11, 1628). He publ. in 1609 *Le varie musiche* in one to 3 parts, some to be sung with harpsichord or chitarrone, others to be played on the organ. Kiesewetter printed 3 madrigals *a* 4 in *Schicksale und Beschaffenheit des weltlichen Gesanges* (1841). Fragments from *Euridice* are in several histories of music; a complete edition was publ. by Guidi in Florence, and by Torchi in vol. VI of *L'arte musicale in Italia;* a facsimile reprint was publ. in Milan in 1934; A. Schering's *Geschichte der Musik in Beispielen* contains 3 excerpts (nos. 171a–c).

Perle, George, American composer and theorist; b. Bayonne, N.J., May 6, 1915, of Russian-Jewish immigrant parents. He studied composition with Wesley La Violette at DePaul Univ. in Chicago (1935–38), and also took private lessons with Ernst Krenek (1939–41); obtained his degree of M.Mus. from the American Cons. of Music in Chicago in 1942; received his Ph.D. in 1956 from N.Y. Univ. with the dissertation *Serial Composition and Atonality* (publ. in Berkeley, 1962; 4th ed., 1977); also wrote *Twelve-Tone Tonality* (Berkeley, 1977). He held teaching posts at the Univ. of Louisville in Kentucky (1949–56) and at the Univ. of Calif. at Davis (1957–61); in 1961 he joined the faculty of Queens College in N.Y. He received Guggenheim fellowships in composition in 1966–67 and 1974–75, as well as several other grants. He contributed numerous analytic essays on the works of Schoenberg, Berg, and Webern. He is co-founder and director of the International Alban Berg Society at the City Univ. of N.Y.

WORKS: FOR ORCH.: 2 symphs.; *Rhapsody* (1953; Louisville, Jan. 16, 1954); *3 Movements* (1960; International Society for Contemporary Music Festival, Amsterdam, June 14, 1963); *6 Bagatelles* (1965; Long Island Symph., Nov. 18, 1977); Cello Concerto (1966); *Songs of Praise and Lamentation* for Solo Voices, Chorus, and Orch. (1974; N.Y., Feb. 18, 1975); Concertino for Piano, Winds, and Timpani (Chicago, April

27, 1979); *A Short Symphony* (Boston Symph., Tanglewood, Mass., Aug. 16, 1980); *Serenade III* for Piano and Chamber Orch. (N.Y., Dec. 14, 1983). CHAMBER MUSIC: 3 wind quintets (1959, 1960, 1967); 7 string quartets (1938–73); *Sonata quasi una fantasia* for Clarinet and Piano (1972); Sonata for Solo Viola (1942); Sonata for Solo Clarinet (1943); Sonata for Solo Cello (1947); 2 sonatas for Solo Violin (1959, 1963); *Monody I* for Solo Flute (1960); *Monody II* for Double Bass (1962); *Serenade I* for Viola and Chamber Ensemble (1962); *Serenade II* for Chamber Ensemble (1968); *Solo Partita* for Violin and Viola (1965). FOR PIANO: *Short Sonata* (1964); *Toccata* (1969); *Dodecatonal Suite* (1970); *6 Etudes* (1973–76); *Ballade* (1981). FOR VOICE: *2 Rilke Songs* for Voice and Piano; *13 Dickenson Songs* for Soprano and Piano (1978).

Perlea, Jonel, Rumanian-American conductor and composer; b. Ograda, Dec. 13, 1900; d. New York, July 29, 1970. He studied piano and composition in Munich (1918–20) and conducting in Leipzig (1920–23). He made his conducting debut in Bucharest in 1919; held posts as a conductor in Leipzig (1922–23) and Rostock (1923–25); then returned to Rumania and conducted the Bucharest Opera (1929–32, 1934–36) and the Bucharest Radio Orch. (1936–44), of which he was a founder. He led conducting classes at the Bucharest Cons. (1941–44); during the last year of World War II he was interned in a German concentration camp. After the war he conducted opera in Rome (1945–47); in 1950 conducted at La Scala in Milan. He made his American debut at the Metropolitan Opera in N.Y., on Dec. 1, 1949, conducting *Tristan und Isolde;* appeared at the San Francisco Opera and the Lyric Opera of Chicago; from 1955 to 1970 was conductor of the Conn. Symph. Orch. He taught conducting at the Manhattan School of Music from 1952 until shortly before his death; became a naturalized U.S. citizen in 1960. He suffered a heart attack in 1957 and a stroke in 1958, as a result of which he lost the use of his right arm, but he continued to conduct with his left hand.

Perlemuter, Vlado, pianist and teacher; b. Kaunas, Lithuania, May 26, 1904 (of Polish parents). He was taken to Paris as a child; studied at the Paris Cons. with Alfred Cortot. After graduation, he joined the faculty of the Cons.; later toured in England and Japan; also served as a visiting prof. at the Royal Northern College of Music in Manchester. He acquired a fine reputation as a congenial interpreter of French piano music.

Perlman, Itzhak, brilliant Israeli-American violinist; b. Tel Aviv, Aug. 31, 1945. He was stricken with polio when he was 4, which left his legs paralyzed; for the rest of his life he had to walk on crutches. Despite this ghastly handicap, he began to play the violin and gave regular recitals at Tel Aviv. In 1958 he was discovered in Israel by Ed Sullivan, the TV producer, and appeared on his show on Feb. 15, 1959. Perlman's courage and good humor endeared him to the public at once. He remained in N.Y., where

his parents soon joined him, and was accepted as a scholarship student in the classes of Ivan Galamian and Dorothy DeLay at the Juilliard School of Music. He made his professional American debut on March 5, 1963, playing with the National Orch. Assoc. in N.Y. In 1964 he won first prize in the Leventritt Competition, which carried, besides the modest purse ($1,000), a significant bonus—an appearance with the N.Y. Phil. It also brought about a lasting friendship with Isaac Stern, who promoted him with all the enthusiasm of a sincere admirer. Perlman's career was no longer a problem: he toured the U.S. from coast to coast in 1965–66 and toured Europe in 1966–67. He also began to teach, and in 1975 was appointed to the faculty of Brooklyn College. He seemed to be overflowing with a genuine love of life; he played not only so-called serious stuff but also rag music and jazz; with Isaac Stern and Pinchas Zukerman he indulged in public charivari on television to which he furnished enjoyable commentaries like a regular stand-up (but necessarily sit-down) comedian. And he became quite a habitué of the White House, being particularly popular with Ronald Reagan, who savored Perlman's show-biz savvy; his being a Jew and a handicapped person only added to the public appreciation of his TV appearances in the center of American power. On Jan. 5, 1967, Perlman married Toby Lynn Friedlander. They had children, too.

Perosi, Don Lorenzo, distinguished Italian composer of church music; b. Tortona, Dec. 21, 1872; d. Rome, Oct. 12, 1956. He studied at the Milan Cons. (1892–93); also took courses at Haberl's School for Church Music at Regensburg (1893); became maestro di cappella at Imola, and then at San Marco in Venice. He was ordained a priest in 1895; in 1898 became music director of the Sistine Chapel and leader of the papal choir; he resigned this post in 1915 owing to a severe mental disturbance; spent some time in a sanatorium (1922–23). Regaining his health after treatment, he returned to active service as a choral conductor and composer. Shortly after his 80th birthday, he led a performance of his oratorio *Il natale del Redentore* at the Vatican, before Pope Pius XII (Dec. 28, 1952). He was a self-denying and scholarly worker for the cause of the cultivation of a pure church style, both in composition and in performance, and was esteemed above all others as a church musician at the Vatican. His magnum opus, the sacred trilogy *La Passione di Cristo* (I, *La Cena del Signore;* II, *L'Orazione al monte;* III, *La morte del Redentore*), was produced in Milan, Dec. 2, 1897, at the Italian Congress for Sacred Music, and had numerous performances elsewhere in Europe and America. Other oratorios are *La Trasfigurazione del Nostro Signore Gesù Cristo* (Venice, March 20, 1898); *La Risurrezione di Lazaro* (Venice, July 27, 1898; in La Fenice Theater, by special permission); *La Risurrezione di Cristo* (Rome, Dec. 13, 1898); *Il natale del Redentore* (Como, Sept. 12, 1899); *L'entrata di Cristo in Gerusalemme* (Milan, April 25, 1900); *La strage degli innocenti* (Milan, May 18, 1900); *Mosè* (Milan,

Nov. 16, 1901); *Dies iste* (Rome, Dec. 9, 1904); *Transitus animae* (Rome, Dec. 18, 1907); *In patris memoriam* (Naples, May 15, 1919); *Giorni di tribulazione* (Milan, Oct. 1916). He wrote further some 40 masses, with Organ; a Requiem, with Instrumental Accompaniment; a *Stabat Mater* for Solo Voices, Chorus, and Orch.; *Vespertina oratio* for Solo Voices, Chorus, and Orch.; about 150 motets, Psalms, etc.; 2 symph. poems: *Dovrei non piangere* and *La festa del villaggio;* a series of 8 orch. pieces, each named after an Italian city: *Roma, Firenze, Milano, Venezia, Messina, Tortona, Genoa, Torina;* other orch. works; a Piano Concerto; a Violin Concerto; chamber music; many organ works.

Perotin (called **Perotinus Magnus**), celebrated composer of the 12th century; putative dates of life are: b. between 1155 and 1160; d. between 1200 and 1250. He was the greatest master (after Leonin) of the Notre Dame School, representing the flowering of the Ars Antiqua. He was maître de chapelle at Beatae Mariae Virginis (before the erection of Notre-Dame) in Paris. Among his extant works are organa in 2, 3, and 4 parts. His melodic writing differs from the practice of Leonin in that he employs triadic progressions; there is also a suggestion of rudimentary canonic procedures. His most famous quadruple organum, *Sederunt principes,* was publ. by R. Ficker in 1930, and appears in several collections of medieval music. Other works are in Coussemaker's *L'Art harmonique au XIIe et XIIIe siècles;* vol. I of *Oxford History of Music;* Y. Rokseth, *Motets du XIIIe siècle* (1936); Davison and Apel, *Historical Anthology of Music* (vol. 1, 1946). A complete edition is edited by E. Thurston (N.Y., 1970).

Perry, Julia, black American composer; b. Lexington, Ky., March 25, 1924; d. Akron, Ohio, April 29, 1979. After studying at the Westminster Choir College in Princeton, N.J. (1943–48), she took a course in composition with Dallapiccola at Tanglewood in the summer of 1951; then took composition lessons, intermittently, in Europe with Nadia Boulanger in Paris and again with Dallapiccola in Italy (1952–56); she also attended classes in conducting in Siena (1956–58). She received 2 Guggenheim fellowships and an award from the National Inst. of Arts and Letters.
WORKS: 3 operas: *The Cask of Amontillado* (Columbia Univ., Nov. 20, 1954); *The Selfish Giant* (1964); *The Bottle;* 12 symphs., some with Chorus and others for Band, many having subtitles, such as *Children's Symphony, Simple Symphony, Soul Symphony* (1959–73); *Stabat Mater* for Alto and String Orch. (1951); *Short Piece* for Orch. (1952; revised 1955 and 1965); *Homage to Vivaldi,* a Requiem for Orch. (N.Y., March 13, 1959); *Pastoral* for Flute and Strings (1959); *Homunculus, C.F.* for 10 Percussionists (1960); Violin Concerto (1963); *Frammenti dalle lettere de Santa Caterina* for Soprano, Chorus, and Orch.; *7 Contrasts* for Baritone and Chamber Ensemble; *Episode* for Orch.; *Venus Moon* for Band (1971); *Module* for Orch. (1975); 2 piano concertos; Violin Sonata and other chamber pieces; songs.

Persen, John, Norwegian composer; b. Porsanger, Norwegian Lapland, Nov. 9, 1941. He studied composition with Finn Mortensen at the Norwegian State Academy of Music in Oslo (1968–73); in 1974–76 was president of Ny Musikk, the Norwegian section of the International Society for Contemporary Music; in 1976–82 served as a member of the board of the Norwegian Music Information Center. His music follows the lines of the cosmopolitan avant-garde, with a mixture of jazz, rock, sonorism, and special effects (*CSV* requires 2 pistol shots to be heard at the end of the work). Persen is a nationalistic Lapp from the extreme Polar North; some titles of his compositions are political in their allusions.
WORKS: *Øre-Verk* for Orch. (1972; the title suggests both "earache" and "aural work"); *Orkesterwerk II* (1974; Oslo, May 4, 1974); *Sámesiidat—CSV* for Chorus a cappella (1976; based on a "joik," a Lapp folk song); *CSV* for Orch. (1976; Oslo, March 22, 1977; the ambiguous acronym of the title means either "Dare to show that you are a Lapp" or "the secret Lapp host"); *Stykket har ingen tittel* (i.e., *This Piece Has No Name*), subtitled *Dreietoner for Orchestra* (1976; Trondheim, Jan. 20, 1977); *Music for Resting Marching Band* for Brass Band (1977); *Under Kors og Krone (Under Cross and Crown),* opera (1978–82; based on a revolt of the Lapp population against the authorities in the late 19th century).

Persiani (née **Tacchinardi**), **Fanny,** Italian coloratura soprano; b. Rome, Oct. 4, 1812; d. Neuilly-sur-Seine, France, May 3, 1867. Her father, the tenor **Nicola Tacchinardi,** was her teacher. After a successful debut at Livorno in 1832, she sang in the principal cities of Italy; in 1837–47 she appeared in London and Paris with brilliant success; also visited the Netherlands and Russia, but returned to Paris in 1858. In 1830 she married the composer **Giuseppe Persiani.**

Persiani, Giuseppe, Italian opera composer; b. Recanati, Sept. 11, 1799; d. Paris, Aug. 13, 1869. As a youth he played violin in theater orchs. in Rome and Naples, where he studied with Zingarelli. In 1830 he married the singer **Fanny Tacchinardi,** who became known as "La Persiani"; her illustrious name completely eclipsed his; yet he was a notable composer whose dramatic opera *Ines de Castro,* produced in Naples on Jan. 27, 1835, scored great success and was performed all over Europe; the celebrated soprano Malibran sang the title role, and Czerny wrote a piano paraphrase on themes of the opera. Persiani's other operas are *Attila* (Parma, Jan. 31, 1827); *Il Solitario* (Milan, April 26, 1829); *Il Fantasma* (Paris, Dec. 14, 1843); *Eufemio di Messina* (Lucca, Sept. 20, 1829; perf. also under the alternative titles *La distruzione di Catania* and *I Saraceni a Catania*).

Persichetti, Vincent, outstanding American composer; b. Philadelphia, June 6, 1915. He studied piano, organ, double bass, tuba, theory, and composition as a youth; began his career as a professional musician when he was only 11 years old; became a church organist at 15. He took courses in composition with Russell King Miller at the Combs College of Music (Mus.B., 1935); then served as head of the theory and composition dept. there; concurrently studied conducting with Fritz Reiner at the Curtis Inst. of Music (diploma, 1938) and piano with Olga Samaroff at the Philadelphia Cons. (Mus.D., 1945); also studied composition with Roy Harris at Colorado College. From 1941 to 1947 he was head of the theory and composition dept. of the Philadelphia Cons.; in 1947 joined the faculty of the Juilliard School of Music in N.Y.; in 1963 was named chairman of the composition dept. there. In 1952 he became director of music publishing of Elkan-Vogel, Inc. With F. Schreiber, he wrote a biography of William Schumann (N.Y., 1954); publ. a valuable manual, *Twentieth Century Harmony: Creative Aspects and Practice* (N.Y., 1961). His music is remarkable for its polyphonic skill in fusing the ostensibly incompatible idioms of Classicism, Romanticism, and stark modernism, while the melodic lines maintain an almost Italianate diatonicism in a lyrical manner.

WORKS: Operas: *Parable XX,* in 2 acts (1976), and *Sibyl* (1984). For Orch.: 9 symphs.: No. 1 (1942; Rochester, N.Y., Oct. 21, 1947); No. 2 (1942); No. 3 (1946; Philadelphia, Nov. 21, 1947); No. 4 (1951; Philadelphia, Dec. 17, 1954); No. 5, *Symphony for Strings* (1953; Louisville, Ky., Aug. 28, 1954); No. 6, *Symphony for Band* (St. Louis, April 16, 1956); No. 7 (1958; St. Louis, Oct. 24, 1959); No. 8 (Berea, Ohio, Oct. 29, 1967); No. 9, *Sinfonia: Janiculum* (1970; Philadelphia, March 5, 1971); Concertino for Piano and Orch. (1941; Rochester, Oct. 23, 1945); *Dance Overture* (1942; Tokyo, Feb. 7, 1948); *Fables* for Narrator and Orch. (1943; Philadelphia, April 20, 1945); *The Hollow Men* for Trumpet and String Orch. (1944; Germantown, Pa., Dec. 12, 1946); *Divertimento* for Band (N.Y., June 16, 1950); *Fairy Tale* for Orch. (1950; Philadelphia, March 31, 1951); Concerto for Piano, 4-hands (Pittsburgh, Nov. 29, 1952); *Pageant* for Band (Miami, May 7, 1953); Piano Concerto (1962; Hanover, N.H., Aug. 2, 1964); *Introit* for Strings (1964; Kansas City, May 1, 1965); *Masquerade* for Band (1965; Berea, Ohio, Jan. 23, 1966); *Night Dances* for Orch. (Kiamesha Lake, N.Y., Dec. 9, 1970); *A Lincoln Address* for Narrator and Orch. (1972; based on excerpts from Lincoln's 2nd inaugural address; originally scheduled for perf. at President Richard Nixon's inaugural concert on Jan. 19, 1973, but canceled because of the ominous threat in the text of the "mighty scourge of war" to be brought down on the unyielding foe, which might have been misinterpreted in the light of the then-raging war in Vietnam; the work was eventually perf. by the St. Louis Symph. Orch. at Carnegie Hall in N.Y., on Jan. 25, 1973; also a version for Band, 1973); Concerto for English Horn and String Orch. (N.Y., Nov. 17, 1977); a series of works, each entitled *Serenade:* No. 1 for 10 Wind Instruments (1929); No. 2 for Piano (1929); No. 3 for Violin, Cello, and Piano (1941); No. 4 for Violin and Piano (1945); No. 5 for

Orch. (Louisville, Nov. 15, 1950); No. 6 for Trombone, Viola, and Cello (1950); No. 7 for Piano (1952); No. 8 for Piano, 4-hands (1954); No. 9 for Soprano and Alto Recorders (1956); No. 10 for Flute and Harp (1957); No. 11 for Band (1960; Ithaca, N.Y., April 19, 1961); No. 12 for Solo Tuba (1961); No. 13 for 2 Clarinets (1963); No. 14 for Solo Oboe (1984); a series of works, each entitled *Parable:* I for Solo Flute (1965); II for Brass Quintet (1968); III for Solo Oboe (1968); IV for Solo Bassoon (1969); V for Carillon (1969); VI for Organ (1971); VII for Solo Harp (1971); VIII for Solo Horn (1972); IX for Band (1972; Des Moines, Iowa, April 6, 1973); X actually his String Quartet No. 4 (1972); XI for Solo Alto Saxophone (1972); XII for Solo Piccolo (1973); XIII for Solo Clarinet (1973); XIV for Solo Trumpet (1973); XV for Solo English Horn (1973); XVI for Solo Viola (1974); XVII for Solo Double Bass (1974); XVIII for Solo Trombone (1975); XIX for Piano (1975); XX, an opera in 2 acts (1976); XXI for Solo Guitar (1978); XXII for Solo Tuba (1981); XXIII for Violin, Cello, and Piano (1981); XXIV for Harpsichord (1982); 4 string quartets (1939; 1944; 1959; 1972, also listed as *Parable X*); 12 piano sonatas (1939–80); 6 piano sonatinas (1950–54); 8 harpsichord sonatas (1951–84); Suite for Violin and Cello (1940); Sonata for Solo Violin (1940); Concertato for Piano and String Quartet (1940); Sonatine for Organ, Pedals Alone (1940); *Fantasy* for Violin and Piano (1941); *Pastoral* for Woodwind Quintet (1943; Philadelphia, April 20, 1945); *Vocalise* for Cello and Piano (1945); *King Lear,* septet for Woodwind Quintet, Timpani, and Piano (1948; perf. under the title *The Eye of Anguish* by the Martha Graham Dance Co., Montclair, N.J., Jan. 31, 1949); Sonata for Solo Cello (1952); Quintet for Piano and Strings (1954; Washington, D.C., Feb. 4, 1955); *Little Recorder Book* (1956); *Infanta Marina* for Viola and Piano (1960); *Shimah B'koli* (Psalm 130) for Organ (1962); *Masques* for Violin and Piano (1965); *Do Not Go Gentle* for Organ, Pedals Alone (1974); *Auden Variations for Organ* (1977); *Reflective Keyboard Studies* (1978); *Little Mirror Book for Piano* (1978); *4 Arabesques for Piano* (1978); *3 Toccatinas for Piano* (1979); *Mirror Etudes for Piano* (1979); *Dryden Liturgical Suite for Organ* (1980); *Song of David* for Organ (1981); *Little Harpsichord Book* (1983); many choral works, including *Proverb* for Mixed Chorus (1948); *Hymns and Responses for the Church Year* (1955; Philadelphia, Oct. 7, 1956); *Song of Peace* for Male Chorus and Piano (1959); *Mass for Mixed Chorus,* a cappella (1960; N.Y., April 20, 1961); *Stabat Mater* for Chorus and Orch. (1963; N.Y., May 1, 1964); *Te Deum* for Chorus and Orch. (1963; Philadelphia, March 15, 1964); *Spring Cantata* for Women's Chorus and Piano (1963; Boston, April 1, 1964); *Winter Cantata* for Women's Chorus, Flute, and Marimba (1964; Troy, N.Y., April 9, 1965); *Celebrations* for Chorus and Wind Ensemble (River Falls, Wis., Nov. 18, 1966); *The Pleiades* for Chorus, Trumpet, and String Orch. (1967; Potsdam, N.Y., May 10, 1968); *The Creation* for Soprano, Alto, Tenor, Baritone, Chorus, and Orch. (1969; N.Y., April 17, 1970); *Flower Songs* (Cantata No. 6) for Mixed Chorus and String Orch. (1983; Philadelphia, April 20, 1984); a number of songs, including the major cycle for Soprano and Piano entitled *Harmonium,* after poems of Wallace Stevens (1951; N.Y., Jan. 20, 1952).

Persinger, Louis, eminent American violinist and teacher; b. Rochester, Ill., Feb. 11, 1887; d. New York, Dec. 31, 1966. He was a student of Hans Becker at the Leipzig Cons., where he made his debut on March 23, 1904; then undertook further study with Ysaÿe in Brussels and Thibaud in Paris. He toured Germany, Austria, and Scandinavia as a concert violinist; served as concertmaster of the Berlin Phil. (1914–15); returning to the U.S., he was director of the Chamber Music Society of San Francisco (1916–28); then devoted himself mainly to teaching; in 1930 he joined the staff of the Juilliard School of Music in N.Y. He achieved a great reputation as a teacher who subordinated technical demands to the paramount considerations of formal balance and expressiveness of the melodic line. Among his pupils were Yehudi Menuhin, Ruggiero Ricci, and Isaac Stern.

Perti, Giacomo (Jacopo) Antonio, greatly significant Italian composer; b. Crevalcore, near Bologna, June 6, 1661; d. Bologna, April 10, 1756. He began to study music with his uncle, Lorenzo Perti, and with Rocco Laurenti; later took lessons in counterpoint with Petronio Franceschini. As early as 1678 he had a Mass performed at the church of S. Tomaso al Mercato. In 1679 he collaborated on the opera *Atide,* to which he contributed the score for the 3rd act. In 1681 he was elected a member of the Accademia Filarmonica, of which he was 5 times the *principe* (in 1719 was named *censor*). He then went to Parma, where he continued his studies with Giuseppe Corso. In 1689 he had his opera *Dionisio Siracusano* performed in Parma, and another opera, *La Rosaura,* in Venice. In 1690 he succeeded his uncle as maestro di cappella at the Cathedral of S. Pietro in Bologna. In 1696 he became maestro di cappella of S. Petronio, a position he held until his death. He also held similar positions at S. Domenico (1704–55; deputized for Alberti from 1734) and at S. Maria in Galliera (1706–50). Emperor Charles VI made him a royal councillor in 1740. His students included G.B. Martini and Giuseppe Torelli.

WORKS: OPERAS: *Atide* (Bologna, June 23, 1679; incomplete; in collaboration with others); *Marzio Coriolano* (Venice, Jan. 20, 1683; not extant); *Oreste in Argo* (Modena, Carnival 1685); *L'incoronazione di Dario* (Bologna, Jan. 13, 1686; not extant); *La Flavia* (Bologna, Feb. 16, 1686); *Dionisio Siracusano* (Parma, Carnival 1689; not extant); *La Rosaura* (Venice, 1689); *Brenno in Efeso* (Venice, 1690; not extant); *L'inganno scoperto per vendetta* (Venice, Carnival 1690 or 1691); *Il Pompeo* (Genoa, Carnival 1691; not extant); *Furio Camillo* (Venice, Carnival 1692); *Nerone fatto Cesare* (Venice, 1693); *La forza della virtù* (Bologna, May 25, 1694; not extant); *Laodicea e Berenice* (Venice, 1695; not extant); *Penelope la casta* (Rome, Jan. 25, 1696; not extant); *Fausta restituita all'impero* (Rome, Jan. 19, 1697; not extant); *Apollo geloso* (Bologna, Aug. 16, 1698; not extant); *Ariovisto* (Milan, Sept. 1699; in collabo-ration with others; not extant); *La prosperità di Elio Sejano* (Milan, Carnival 1699; in collaboration with others; not extant); *Dionisio rè di Portogallo* (Pratolino, Sept. 1707; not extant); *Il fratricida innocente* (Bologna, May 19, 1708; not extant); *Ginevra principessa di Scozia* (Pratolino, Fall 1708; not extant); *Berenice regina d'Egitto* (Pratolino, Sept. 1709; not extant); *Rodelinda regina de' Longobardi* (Pratolino, Fall 1710; not extant); *Lucio vero* (Bologna, Spring 1717; not extant); *Rosinde ed Emireno* (undated). ORATORIOS: *S. Serafina* [*I due gigli porporati nel martirio de S. Serafina e S. Sabina*] (Bologna, 1679); *Abramo vincitore* (Venice, 1683); *Mosè* (Modena, 1685); *Oratorio della passione di Cristo* (Bologna, 1685); *La beata Imelde Lambertini* (Bologna, 1686); *Agar* (Bologna, 1689); *La passione del Redentore* (Bologna, 1694); *S. Galgano* (Bologna, 1694); *Cristo al limbo* (Bologna, 1698); *La sepoltura di Cristo* (Bologna, 1704); *S. Giovanni* (Bologna, 1704); *Gesù al sepolcro* (Bologna, 1707); *S. Petronio* (Bologna, 1720); *L'amor divino* [*I conforti di Maria vergine addolorata*] (Bologna, 1723); also several undated oratorios. Additional sacred works include *Messa e salmi concertati* for 4 Voices, Instruments, and Chorus (Bologna, 1735) and *7 canzonette in aria marmoresca sopra le 7 principali feste di Nostra Signora* (Bologna, 1780); also 120 Psalms, 54 motets, 28 masses; about 150 secular cantatas; also *Cantate morali e spirituali* for One and 2 Voices, with Violin (Bologna, 1688).

Pessard, Emile-Louis-Fortuné, French composer; b. Paris, May 29, 1843; d. there, Feb. 10, 1917. He studied at the Paris Cons. with Bazin (harmony), Laurent (piano), Benoist (organ), and Carafa (composition); won the first harmony prize in 1862, and the Grand Prix de Rome in 1866 with the cantata *Dalila* (1867). In 1881 he was appointed prof. of harmony at the Paris Cons. He enjoyed considerable regard as a composer of fine songs. As a student, Debussy copied Pessard's song *Chanson d'un fou,* and the MS in Debussy's handwriting was publ. erroneously as Debussy's own.

WORKS: Operas (all produced in Paris): *La Cruche cassée* (Feb. 1870); *Don Quichotte* (Feb. 13, 1874); *Le Char* (Jan. 18, 1878); *Le Capitaine Fracasse* (July 2, 1878); *Tabarin* (Jan. 12, 1885); *Tartarin sur les Alpes* (Nov. 17, 1888); *Les Folies amoureuses* (April 15, 1891); *Une Nuit de Noël* (1893); *Mam'zelle Carabin* (Nov. 3, 1893); *L'Armée des vierges* (Oct. 15, 1902); *L'Epave* (Feb. 17, 1903).

Pestalozzi, Heinrich, Swiss composer; b. Wädenswil, near Zürich, Aug. 26, 1878; d. Zürich, Aug. 9, 1940. He studied theology and music in Berlin; was a singing teacher there (1902–12); then a pastor in Arosa, Switzerland; in 1917 was appointed voice teacher at the Zürich Cons. His many songs and choral works have enjoyed great popularity in Switzerland; a full list is found in Refardt's *Musikerlexikon der Schweiz.* Pestalozzi publ. several manuals on singing: *Individuelle Stimmbildung; Kehlkopfgymnastik; Die deutsche Bühnenaussprache im Gesang; Geheimnisse der Stimmbildung; Der Weg* *zu einer schönen Stimme.*

Peter, Johann Friedrich (John Frederick), American Moravian organist and composer; b. Heerendijk, the Netherlands (of German parentage), May 19, 1746; d. Bethlehem, Pa., July 13, 1813. He was educated in the Netherlands and Germany; came to America in 1770. He served the Moravian Church in various capacities in Nazareth, Bethlehem, and Lititz, Pa., and (from 1779–89) in Salem, N.C., where he married. He spent the rest of his life mostly in Bethlehem as organist of the church. He is widely considered the greatest of the American Moravian composers. His collection of copies of instrumental works by Stamitz, J.C.F. Bach, J.C. Bach, Abel, Boccherini, and Haydn (preserved in the Archives of the Moravian Church) proves his knowledge of contemporary music. He began to compose in 1770. While at Salem he wrote (in 1789) a set of 6 quintets for 2 Violins, 2 Violas, and Cello (his only secular works), which appear to be the oldest preserved examples of chamber music composed in America; they were publ., under the editorship of H.T. David, in 1955, for the N.Y. Public Library series Music of the Moravians in America. His solo arias and choral anthems (more than 100) for strings and organ, or with woodwinds, strings, and organ, are well written, often quite expressive, and evidently constitute the finest and most elaborate concerted church music written in America at that time. Those preserved in the Archives of the Moravian Church at Bethlehem are listed in A.G. Rau and H.T. David's *A Catalogue of Music by American Moravians* (Bethlehem, Pa., 1938).

Peter, Simon, American Moravian composer, brother of **Johann Friedrich Peter;** b. Heerendijk, the Netherlands (of German parentage), April 2, 1743; d. Salem, N.C., May 29, 1819. With his brother, he was educated at the Moravian Brethren's schools in the Netherlands and Germany; came to America in 1770. His ministry was spent in both the Northern and Southern Provinces of the Moravian Church (i.e., both Pennsylvania and North Carolina). From 1784 to 1819 he lived in North Carolina as pastor of several congregations, and was a member of the governing board of the Church. He composed only a few sacred anthems, but one of these, *O Anblick, der mirs Herze bricht,* may well be one of the most expressive of all Lenten songs written in America.

Peters, Carl Friedrich, German music publisher; b. Leipzig, March 30, 1779; d. Sonnenstein, Bavaria, Nov. 20, 1827. In 1814 Peters purchased Kühnel & Hoffmeister's Bureau de Musique (established in 1800; Hoffmeister left the firm in 1805; Kühnel was the sole owner from 1805 to his death in 1813). The firm was thenceforward known as C.F. Peters, Bureau de Musique. Its rich catalogue contained the first edition of collected works of J.S. Bach; it also included music by Beethoven, who entrusted to the Bureau de Musique the publication of his First Symph.; Piano Concerto, op. 19; Septet, op. 20; Piano Sonata, op. 22; and other works. Later C.F. Peters acquired works by Weber, Spohr, Czerny, Chopin, Schumann, Wagner, Liszt, and Brahms. In more recent times the works of Mahler, Grieg, Hugo Wolf, Max Reger, Richard Strauss (his 7 symph. poems), and others were publ. From 1868, classical works were publ. in the inexpensive and reliable Edition Peters. Its large and important musical library was opened to the public in 1893 as the Bibliothek Peters. Scholarly annual books (*Peters Jahrbuch*), containing articles by eminent musicologists, current bibliography, etc., were publ. until 1941. Dr. Max Abraham was sole proprietor from 1880 to 1900. After his death in 1900, his nephew Heinrich Hinrichsen (b. Hamburg, Feb. 5, 1868; d. Auschwitz concentration camp, Sept. 30, 1942) became head of the firm; from 1927 to 1932 he shared the ownership with his son Max Hinrichsen (b. Leipzig, July 6, 1901; d. London, Dec. 17, 1965); soon afterward, 2 other sons joined the firm—in 1933 Walter Hinrichsen (b. Leipzig, Sept. 23, 1907; d. New York, July 21, 1969), and in 1934 Hans Hinrichsen (b. Leipzig, Aug. 22, 1909; d. Perpignan (France) concentration camp, Sept. 18, 1940). The Litolff catalogue was acquired by Peters in 1938. Heinrich Hinrichsen was still in charge in 1939, when the Nazi regime finally forced him into exile, and Johannes Petschull was appointed manager in his stead. After World War II the firm was divided into 3 separate but closely affiliated companies: Peters Edition, London, under the direction of Max Hinrichsen; C.F. Peters Corp., N.Y., owned by Walter Hinrichsen; and the German firm, since 1950 in Frankfurt, under the management of Johannes Petschull. The original firm in Leipzig was taken over by the German Democratic Republic in 1949–50.

Peters (Petermann), Roberta, outstanding American soprano; b. New York, May 4, 1930. She studied voice with William Pierce Hermann; at the age of 20 she made her operatic debut with the Metropolitan Opera in N.Y. as Zerlina in *Don Giovanni* on Nov. 17, 1950, as a substitute on short notice; she subsequently remained on its roster for more than 30 years. She also sang with the opera companies of San Francisco and Chicago, at Covent Garden in London, at the Salzburg Festivals, and at the Vienna State Opera. She was briefly married to the American baritone **Robert Merrill.** With Louis Biancolli, she wrote *A Debut at the Met,* which was publ. in 1967.

Petersen, Wilhelm, German composer; b. Athens, March 15, 1890; d. Darmstadt, Dec. 18, 1957. He studied in Germany and worked as a theater conductor; served in the German army during World War I; in 1922 settled in Darmstadt as a teacher. He wrote the opera *Der goldne Topf* (Darmstadt, March 29, 1941); 5 symphs. (1921, 1923, 1934, 1941, 1957); 3 violin sonatas; 3 string quartets and other chamber music; several sacred choruses and songs. He was highly regarded in Darmstadt as a musician and pedagogue. In 1972 a Wilhelm Petersen Society was founded to memorialize his work.

Peterson, Oscar (Emmanuel), black Canadian jazz pianist; b. Montreal, Aug. 15, 1925. He studied piano; made appearances on Canadian radio; also played with the orch. of Johnny Holmes. In 1949 he went to N.Y., and soon established himself as one of the finest jazz pianists of the day. He made numerous tours, often appearing with a guitarist and bass player as fellow musicians (he later replaced the guitar with drums); he also was successful as a guest artist with American orchs.

Peterson-Berger, (Olof) Wilhelm, Swedish composer; b. Ullånger, Feb. 27, 1867; d. Frösön, Dec. 3, 1942. He studied with J. Dente and O. Bolander at the Stockholm Cons. (1886–89); then in Dresden with Scholtz (piano) and Kretschmar (composition); eventually settled in Stockholm, where he became active as a pedagogue and music critic of *Dagens Nyheter* (1896). A symposium of articles was publ. in Stockholm on the occasion of his 70th birthday (1937).

Petrassi, Goffredo, outstanding Italian composer; b. Zagarolo, near Rome, July 16, 1904. He worked as a clerk in a music store in Rome, studying musical compositions in his leisure time; began taking regular lessons in composition with Vincenzo di Donato and with Alessandro Bustini at the Santa Cecilia Academy in Rome; in 1939 was appointed to the faculty at the Santa Cecilia Cons. in 1939–59; then was a prof. at the Santa Cecilia Academy from 1959. In 1956 he conducted composition classes at the Berkshire Music Center in Tanglewood. Despite the late beginning, Petrassi acquired a solid technique of composition; the chief influence in his music was that of Casella; later he became interested in 12-tone procedures.
WORKS: OPERAS: *Il Cordovano* (1944–48; La Scala, Milan, May 12, 1949) and *La morte dell'aria* (1949–50; Rome, Oct. 24, 1950). BALLETS: *La follia di Orlando* (1942–43; La Scala, Milan, April 12, 1947) and *Il ritratto di Don Quixote* (1945; Paris, Nov. 21, 1947). FOR ORCH.: *Divertimento* (1930); *Ouverture da concerto* (1931); *Passacaglia* (1931); *Partita* (1932; Rome, April 2, 1933); 8 concertos for Orch.: No. 1 (1933–34; Rome, March 31, 1935); No. 2 (1951; Basel, Jan. 24, 1952); No. 3, *Récréation concertante* (1952–53; Aix-en-Provence Festival, July 23, 1953); No. 4, for String Orch. (1954; Rome, April 28, 1956); No. 5 (1955; Boston, Dec. 2, 1955); No. 6, *Invenzione concertata,* for Brass, Strings, and Percussion (1956–57; London, Sept. 9, 1957); No. 7 (1961–64; Bologna, March 18, 1965); No. 8 (1970–72; Chicago, Sept. 28, 1972); Piano Concerto (1936–39; Rome, Dec. 10, 1939, Walter Gieseking, soloist); Flute Concerto (1960; Hamburg, March 7, 1961); *Estri,* chamber symph. for 15 Performers (1966–67; Dartmouth College, Hanover, N.H., Aug. 2, 1967; as a ballet, Spoleto, July 11, 1968). VOCAL WORKS: *3 Choruses,* with Small Orch. (1932); *Psalm IX* for Chorus, Strings, Brass, 2 Pianos, and Percussion (1934–36); *Magnificat* for Soprano, Chorus, and Orch. (1939–40); *Coro di morti,* dramatic madrigal for Male Chorus, Brass, Double Basses, 3 Pianos, and Percussion (1940–41; Venice,

Sept. 28, 1941); *2 liriche di Saffo* for Voice, and Piano or 11 Instruments (1941); *Quattro inni sacri* for Tenor, Baritone, and Organ (1942; version with Orch., Rome, Feb. 22, 1950); *Noche oscura,* cantata (1950–51; Strasbourg, June 17, 1951); *Nonsense,* to words by Edward Lear, for Chorus a cappella (1952); *Propos d'Alain* for Baritone and 12 Performers (1960); *Sesto non-senso,* after Lear, for Chorus a cappella (1964); *Mottetti per la Passione* for Chorus a cappella (1966); *Beatitudines,* chamber oratorio in memory of Martin Luther King, Jr., for Baritone and 5 Instruments (1969; Fiuggi, July 17, 1969); *Orationes Christi* for Chorus, Brass, 8 Violins, and 8 Cellos (1974–75; Rome, Dec. 6, 1975). CHAMBER MUSIC: *Sinfonia, Siciliana e Fuga* for String Quartet (1929); *Siciliana e marcetta* for 2 Pianos (1930); *Introduzione e allegro* for Violin and Piano (1933; also with 11 Instruments); *Toccata* for Piano (1933); *Preludio, Aria e Finale* for Cello and Piano (1933); *Invenzioni* for 2 Pianos (1944); *Sonata da camera* for Harpsichord and 10 Instruments (1948); *Dialogo angelico* for 2 Flutes (1948); *Musica a 2* for 2 Cellos (1952); String Quartet (1958); *Serenata* for Flute, Viola, Double Bass, Harpsichord, and Percussion (1958); String Trio (1959); *Serenata II,* trio for Harp, Guitar, and Mandolin (1962); *Musica di Ottoni* for Brass and Timpani (1963); *3 per 7* for 3 Performers on 7 Wind Instruments (1966); *Ottetto di Ottoni* for 4 Trumpets and 4 Trombones (1968); *Souffle* for One Performer on 3 Flutes (1969); *Elogio per un'Ombra* for Solo Violin (1971); *Nunc* for Solo Guitar (1971); *Ala* for Flute and Harpsichord (1972); *4 odi* for String Quartet (1973–75); *Oh les beaux jours!* for Piano (1976); *Fanfare* for 3 Trumpets (1944–76); *Petite pièce* for Piano (1976).

Petrauskas, Kipras, Lithuanian tenor; b. Vilna, Nov. 23, 1885; d. there, Jan. 17, 1968. He studied with his brother, the composer **Mikas Petrauskas;** appeared in his brother's opera *Birute* (Vilna, Nov. 6, 1906); then became a singer at the Imperial Opera in St. Petersburg (1911–20); also appeared in Berlin, Paris, and Milan, and made a tour of the U.S. He returned to Lithuania before World War II, and remained there; in 1950 he received the Stalin Prize.

Petrauskas, Mikas, Lithuanian composer; b. Kaunas, Oct. 19, 1873; d. there, March 23, 1937. He studied organ with his father; was a church organist at the age of 15; then went to St. Petersburg, where he studied with Rimsky-Korsakov at the Cons. During the abortive revolution of 1905 he became implicated in various political activities and was imprisoned; he was briefly in Vilna, where he produced his opera *Birute* (Nov. 6, 1906); in 1907 he emigrated to America; settled in Boston in 1914, and founded the Lithuanian Cons. in South Boston; with the aid of a Lithuanian chorus there, he produced his operas *The Devil Inventor* (3 acts; South Boston, May 20, 1923) and *Egle, Queen of the Snakes* (6 acts; South Boston, May 30, 1924; Petrauskas himself sang the part of the King of the Snakes); cantatas; etc. The Lithuanian Cons. publ. the piano scores of his operas *The King of the Forest* (1918) and *Egle;* he also publ. arrangements of Lithuanian songs in the periodical *Kankles* (Boston, 1917–21); further publ. a brief dictionary of musical terms in Lithuanian (Boston, 1916) and an album of Lithuanian songs (Boston, 1922). In 1930 he went back to Lithuania.

Petri, Egon, distinguished pianist; b. Hannover, Germany, March 23, 1881; d. Berkeley, Calif., May 27, 1962. He was educated in a musical family; his father was the Dutch violinist **Henri Wilhelm Petri** (1856–1914). He studied violin before he began to take piano lessons with Teresa Carreño. As a boy he played 2nd violin in a string quartet organized by his father in Dresden. He then went to Berlin, where he became a pupil of Busoni, who influenced Petri's own conception of piano playing as the fullest representation, by a single instrument, of the sonorities of an orch.; he played with Busoni in London in 1921, in a concert for 2 pianos; made an extensive tour in Russia in 1923. He established himself as an eminent pedagogue in Europe; was a teacher of piano at the Hochschule für Musik in Berlin (1921–26); presented a series of concerts in the U.S. (American debut, N.Y., Jan. 11, 1932); then taught at Cornell Univ. (1940–46) and at Mills College in Oakland, Calif.

Petrić, Ivo, Slovenian composer; b. Ljubljana, June 16, 1931. He studied composition with Skerjanc and conducting with Švara at the Ljubljana Music Academy (1953–58). In 1962 he became the artistic leader of a group dedicated to the promotion of new music; in 1969 was appointed to the secretariat of the Union of Slovenian Composers. His compositions are Romantic in their inspiration, and agreeably modernistic in technical presentation.

Petridis, Petro, eminent Greek composer; b. Nigdé, Asia Minor, July 23, 1892; d. Athens, Aug. 17, 1977. He took courses at the American College in Constantinople and at the Univ. of Paris; took part in the Balkan war of 1911–12 as a member of the Greek army; then returned to Paris, where he took lessons in music theory with Albert Wolff and Albert Roussel; lived in Paris until 1939, when he returned to Athens. A man of great culture, he was conversant with classical literatures, and could recite Homer from memory. His own music reveals a similar cultural quality. He often used ancient modalities, adorned with modern harmonies.
WORKS: Opera, *Zemphyra* (1923–25); oratorio, *St. Paul* (Athens, June 29, 1951, composer conducting); *A Byzantine Requiem* (1952); 5 symphs. (1928, 1940, 1941, 1943, 1951); Concerto for 2 Pianos and Orch. (1972); Violin Concerto (1972); *Panighiri,* suite of Greek tableaux for Orch.; *Suite grecque; Suite ionienne;* Piano Concerto; chamber music; a number of songs.

Petrov, Osip, celebrated Russian basso; b. Elizavetgrad, Nov. 15, 1807; d. St. Petersburg, March 11, 1878. In 1830 the intendant of the Imperial Opera accidentally heard him singing with an inferior company at a fair in Kursk, and immediately engaged him. Petrov made his debut in St. Petersburg as Sarastro in *The Magic Flute.* The enormous compass of his voice, its extraordinary power and beautiful quality, combined with consummate histrionic skill, secured for him recognition as one of the greatest of Russian bassos; this place he held throughout his long career (he appeared on the stage for the last time March 10, 1878, on the eve of his death). He created the roles of Susanin in Glinka's *Life for the Tsar* (1836), Ruslan in *Ruslan and Ludmila* (1842), the Miller in Dargomyzhsky's *Rusalka* (1856), and Varlaam in Mussorgsky's *Boris Godunov* (1874).

Petrovics, Emil, Serbian-born Hungarian composer; b. Nagybecskerek (now Zrenjanin), Feb. 9, 1930. He lived in Belgrade until 1941; came to Budapest; studied at the Cons. there with Sugár (1949–51), Viski (1951–52), and Farkas (1952–57). He was music director of the Petöfi Theater in Budapest (1960–64); then taught at the Academy of Dramatic Arts.
WORKS: Satirical one-act opera, *C'est la guerre* (1961; Budapest Radio, Aug. 17, 1961; first stage perf., Budapest, March 11, 1962; highly successful; was awarded the Kossuth Prize in 1966; *Lysistrate,* comic opera after Aristophanes (1962); opera, *Bün és bünhödés (Crime and Punishment),* after Dostoyevsky (1969; Budapest, Oct. 26, 1969); 2 oratorios: *Jónás könyve (The Book of Jonah;* 1966), and *Ott essem el én (Let Me Die There)* for Male Chorus and Orch. (1972); Flute Concerto (1957); Symph. for String Orch. (1962); *Cassazione* for Brass (1953); String Quartet (1958); *4 Self-Portraits in Masks* for Harpsichord (1958); Wind Quintet (1964); *Passacaglia in Blues* for Bassoon and Piano (1964; as a ballet, Budapest, 1965).

Petrucci, Ottaviano dei, Italian music publisher, the first to print a complete collection of part-songs from movable type; b. Fossombrone, June 18, 1466; d. there, May 7, 1539. In 1498 he received from the Council of the Republic of Venice the privilege of printing music by this new method for 20 years, and worked there industriously from 1501–11, then ceding the business to A. Scotto and N. da Rafael, and removing to Fossombrone, with a 15-year privilege for printing within the Papal States. His editions, printed with great neatness, are rare and highly prized specimens of early presswork. In Fossombrone he labored from 1513–23. His publications appeared at the most flourishing epoch of the Netherlands School; his first work, *Odhecaton A* (1501; modern ed. by Helen Hewitt, Cambridge, Mass., 1942), contains 96 numbers by famous composers before 1501; *Canti B.* (1502) and *Canti C.* (1504), 49 and 137, respectively. Petrucci's last publications were 3 books of masses (1520–23), printed in folio as chorus books. Books I and IV of the 9 books of *frottole* publ. in Venice from 1504–8 by Petrucci were ed. by R. Schwartz in Jg. 8 of Th. Kroyer's *Publikationen älterer Musik* (Leipzig, 1933–35).

Petrželka, Vilém, noted Czech composer and music pedagogue; b. Královo Pole, near Brno, Sept. 10, 1889; d. Brno, Jan. 10, 1967. He studied with Janáček at the Brno Organ School (1905–8) and in 1910 became Janáček's assistant at the school; subsequently took private lessons in Prague with Vítězslav Novák; taught at the Phil. Society School in Brno (1914–19) and in 1919 became a prof. at the newly formed Brno Cons. In his compositions he continued the national tradition of modern Moravian music; he was mainly influenced by Janáček, but expanded his resources and on occasion made use of jazz rhythms, quarter-tones, and other modernistic procedures.

Pettersson, Gustaf Allan, remarkable sui generis Swedish composer; b. Västra Ryd, Sept. 19, 1911; d. Stockholm, June 20, 1980. His father was a blacksmith; his mother was a devout woman who could sing; the family moved to Stockholm, and lived in dire poverty. Pettersson sold Christmas cards and bought a violin from his meager returns. He also practiced keyboard playing on a church organ. In 1931 he entered the Stockholm Music Academy, studying violin and viola with J. Ruthström and music theory with H.M. Melchers. From 1940 to 1951 he played viola in the Stockholm Concert Society Orch., and also studied composition with Otto Olsson, Tor Mann, and Blomdahl. In his leisure hours he wrote poetry; he set 24 of his poems to music. In 1951 he went to Paris to study with Honegger and René Leibowitz. Returning to Sweden, he devoted himself to composition in large forms. His music is permeated with dark moods, and he supplied deeply pessimistic annotations to his symphs. and other works. In 1963 he began suffering from painful rheumatoid arthritis; he stubbornly continued to compose while compulsively proclaiming his misfortunes in private and in public print. He described himself as "a voice crying out, drowned in the noise of the times." The Stockholm Orch. played several of his symphs., but when his 7th Symph., originally scheduled for the American tour of the Stockholm Orch., was taken off the program, Pettersson, wrathful at this callous defection, forbade performance of any of his music in Sweden. Stylistically, Pettersson's music is related to Mahler's symph. manner, in the grandiosity of design and in the passionate, exclamatory dynamism of utterance. Most of his symphs. are cast in single movements, with diversity achieved by frequent changes of mood, tempo, meter, and rhythm. Characteristically, they all, except No. 10, are set in minor keys.
WORKS: 16 SYMPHS.: No. 1 (1950–51; withdrawn with instructions to perform it only posthumously); No. 2 (1952–53; Swedish Radio, Stockholm, May 9, 1954); No. 3 (1954 55; Göteborg, Nov. 21, 1956); No. 4 (1958–59; Stockholm, Jan. 27, 1961); No. 5 (1960–62; Stockholm, Nov. 8, 1963); No. 6 (1963–66; Stockholm, Jan. 21, 1968); No. 7 (1966–67; Stockholm, Oct. 13, 1968); No. 8 (1968–69; Stockholm, Feb. 23, 1972); No. 9 (1970; Göteborg, Feb. 18, 1971); No. 10 (1971–72; Swedish Television, filmed Dec. 16, 1973, for delayed broadcast of Jan. 14, 1974); No. 11 (1971–73; Bergen, Norway, Oct. 24, 1974); No. 12, *De döda på torget* (*The Dead on the Square*), with Mixed Chorus, to words by Pablo Neruda (1973–74; Stockholm, Sept. 29, 1977); No. 13 (1976; Bergen, June 7, 1978); No. 14 (1978; first perf. posthumously, Stockholm, Nov. 26, 1981); No 15 (1978; posthumous, Stockholm, Nov. 19, 1982); No. 16, originally designed as Concerto for Alto Saxophone and Orch., written for the American saxophonist Fred Hemke; posthumous, Stockholm, Feb. 24, 1983; Hemke, soloist); 3 concertos for String Orch.: No. 1 (1949–50; Stockholm, April 6, 1952); No. 2 (1956; Stockholm, Dec. 1, 1968); No. 3 (1956–57; Stockholm, March 14, 1958); Concerto No. 1 for Violin and String Quartet (1949; Stockholm, March 10, 1951); Concerto No. 2 for Violin and Orch. (1977–78; Stockholm, Jan. 25, 1980; Ida Haendel, soloist); *Symphonic Movement* (1976; as *Poem*, Swedish Television, Stockholm, Dec. 24, 1976).

Petyrek, Felix, Czech composer; b. Brno, May 14, 1892; d. Vienna, Dec. 1, 1951. He studied piano with Godowsky and Sauer; composition with Schreker at the Univ. of Vienna (graduated in 1919). He taught piano at the Salzburg Mozarteum (1919–21); then at the Berlin Hochschule für Musik (1921–23); lived in Italy (1923–26); taught composition at the Odeon Athenon in Athens (1926–30); from 1930 to 1939, taught at the Stuttgart Akademie für Musik; after 1945, he settled in Vienna. Among modern composers, he occupied a fairly advanced position; in his melodic writing, he adopted the scale of alternating whole tones and semitones as a compromise between tonality and atonality.

Petzel, Johann Christoph. See **Pezel, Johann Christoph.**

Peuerl (Peurl, Bäwerl, Bäurl, Beurlin), Paul, Austrian organist; b. Stuttgart (baptized, June 13), 1570; d. after 1625. He was an organist at Horn, Lower Austria (from 1602), and of the Protestant church school in Steyer (1609–25). He is generally acknowledged to be the originator of the German variation-suite; following the example of the lutenists, he expanded the earlier combination of pavane and galliard into a new 4-movement suite form for strings. He was also an organ builder. He edited the following (all publ. in Nuremberg): *Newe Padouan, Intrada, Däntz und Galliarda* (1611); *Weltspiegel, das ist: Neue teutsche Gesänge* (1613); *Ettliche lustige Padovanen, Intrada, Galliard, Couranten und Däntz sampt zweyen Canzon zu 4 Stimmen* (1620); *Gantz neue Padouanen, Auffzüg, Balletten, Couranten, Intraden und Däntz* (1625). Selections from his works, ed. by Karl Geiringer, appear in Denkmäler der Tonkunst in Österreich, 70 (36.ii).

Pevernage, Andries, Flemish composer; b. Harelbeke, near Courtrai, 1543; d. Antwerp, July 30, 1591. He was a boy chorister in Courtrai. On Feb. 11, 1563, he became choirmaster at St. Salvator in Bruges; on Oct. 17, 1563, he was appointed choirmaster of Notre Dame in Courtrai; due to religious upheavals, he fled to Antwerp in 1578; he returned to Courtrai to resume his post in 1584. On Oct. 29, 1585, he took the oath as choirmaster of Notre Dame in Antwerp. He was greatly honored there, and was buried in the Cathedral.

Peyser, Joan, American musicologist, editor, author, and journalist; b. New York, June 12, 1931. She played piano in public at 13; majored in music at Barnard College (B.A., 1951); studied musicology with Paul Henry Lang at Columbia Univ. (M.A., 1956); then devoted herself mainly to musical journalism; enlivened the music pages of the Sunday *N.Y. Times* with book reviews and breezy colloquies with composers; wrote scripts for the television series "The World of Music"; acted as musical adviser to the N.Y. City Board of Education. She publ. the popular book *The New Music: The Sense behind the Sound* (N.Y., 1971); created considerable excitement in the music world with her biography *Boulez: Composer, Conductor, Enigma* (N.Y., 1976); trying to penetrate the eponymous enigma, she undertook a journey to the interior of France, where she interviewed family and friends of her subject, with a fervor suggesting that Boulez was indeed the 4th B of music. From 1977 to 1983 she was editor of the *Musical Quarterly,* the first woman to occupy this position; during her tenure she attempted to veer away from the prevalent musicological sesquipedalianism toward plain diction.

Pezel (Petzold, Petzel, Pezelius, etc.), **Johann Christoph,** German musician; b. Calau, 1639; d. Bautzen, Oct. 13, 1694. He was made 4th Kunstgeiger in the Leipzig town band in 1664, and in 1670 was promoted to Stadtpfeifer. Because of the plague, he left Leipzig in 1681 for Bautzen, where he remained until his death. He publ. several collections of pieces for wind instruments: *Musica vespertina Lipsica* (1669); *Hora decima* (1670); *Intraden* (1676); *Deliciae musicales* (1678); etc. His most interesting work is *Fünffstimmigte blasende Musik* (Frankfurt, 1685; 3 pieces arranged for modern brass ensemble by Robert D. King, and publ. in Wakefield, Mass.). Selections from various of his works, ed. by A. Schering, are in Denkmäler Deutscher Tonkunst, 63.

Pfitzner, Hans Erich, eminent German composer; b. Moscow (of German parents), May 5, 1869; d. Salzburg, May 22, 1949. He studied piano with James Kwast and composition with Iwan Knorr at the Hoch Cons. in Frankfurt; in 1899 he abducted Kwast's daughter and took her to England, where he married her. In 1892–93 he taught piano and theory at the Cons. of Coblenz; then served as assistant conductor of the Municipal Theater in Mainz (1894–96); from 1897–1907 he was on the faculty of the Stern Cons. in Berlin; concurrently he conducted at the Theater Westens (1903–6). During the 1907–8 season he led the renowned Kaim Concerts in Munich. From 1908–18 he was in Strasbourg as municipal music director and also served as dean at the Strasbourg Cons.; from 1910–16 he conducted at the Strasbourg Opera. During the 1919–20 season he

filled conducting engagements at the Munich Konzertverein; from 1920–29 he led a master class at the Berlin Academy of Arts; from 1929–34 he taught composition at the Akademie der Tonkunst in Munich. Being of certified German stock, though born in Russia, he was favored by the Nazi authorities, and became an ardent supporter of the Third Reich; he reached the nadir of his moral degradation in dedicating an overture, *Krakauer Begrüssung,* to Hans Frank, the murderous Gauleiter of occupied Poland in 1944. After the collapse of Hitler's brief millennium, Pfitzner had to face the Denazification Court in Munich in 1948; owing to his miserable condition in body and soul, he was exonerated. He was taken to a home for the aged in Munich, and later was transferred to Salzburg, where he died in misery. Eventually, his dead body was honorably laid to rest in a Vienna cemetery.

In his better days, Pfitzner was hailed in Germany as a great national composer. He presented a concert of his works in Berlin on May 12, 1893, with excellent auguries. After the premiere of his opera *Der arme Heinrich* in Mainz on April 2, 1895, the critics, among them the prestigious Humperdinck, praised the work in extravagant terms. Even more successful was his opera *Palestrina,* making use of Palestrina's themes, written to his own libretto, which was conducted by Bruno Walter at its first performance on June 12, 1917, in Munich. The Pfitzner Society was formed in Munich as early as 1904, and a Hans Pfitzner Assoc. was established in Berlin in 1938, with Furtwängler as president. Althought Pfitzner's music is traditional in style and conservative in harmony, he was regarded as a follower of the modern school, a comrade-in-arms of his close contemporary Richard Strauss. Very soon, however, his fame began to dwindle; there were fewer performances of his operas and still fewer hearings of his instrumental works; he himself bitterly complained of this lack of appreciation of his art. It was a miserable end for a once important and capable musician.

WORKS: OPERAS: *Der arme Heinrich* (1891–93; Mainz, April 2, 1895); *Die Rose vom Liebesgarten* (1897–1900; Elberfeld, Nov. 9, 1901); *Das Christ-Elflein* (1906; Munich, Dec. 11, 1906); *Palestrina* (1911–15; Munich, June 12, 1917, conducted by Bruno Walter); *Das Herz* (1930–31; Berlin and Munich, Nov. 12, 1931). INCIDENTAL MUSIC: *Das Fest auf Solhaug,* after Ibsen (Mainz, Nov. 28, 1890); *Das Käthchen von Heilbronn,* after Kleist (1905; Berlin, Oct. 19, 1905). FOR ORCH.: Scherzo in C minor (1887; Frankfurt, Nov. 8, 1888); *3 Preludes,* symph. excerpts from the opera *Palestrina* (1917); Piano Concerto (1921; Dresden, March 16, 1921; Walter Gieseking, soloist); Violin Concerto (1923; Nuremberg, June 4, 1924, under Pfitzner's direction); Symph. in C-sharp minor, after the 2nd String Quartet (1932; Munich, March 23, 1933, composer conducting); Cello Concerto No. 1 (Frankfurt, 1935); *Duo* for Violin, Cello, and Chamber Orch. (1937; Frankfurt, Dec. 3, 1937, composer conducting); *Kleine Symphonie* (1939; Berlin, Nov. 19, 1939, Furtwängler conducting); Symphony in C (1940; Frankfurt, Oct. 11, 1940); *Elegie und Reigen* (1940; Salzburg, April 4, 1941); *Krakauer Begrüssung*

(1944; written in honor of Hans Frank, Nazi governor of Poland); Cello Concerto No. 2 (1944; Solingen, April 23, 1944, composer conducting); *Elegie* (1947). CHAMBER MUSIC: Cello Sonata (1890); Piano Trio (1896); 4 string quartets (1886, 1903, 1925, 1942); Piano Quintet (1908); Violin Sonata (1918); *5 Klavierstücke* (1941); *6 Studien* for Piano (1943); *Sextet* for Clarinet, Violin, Viola, Cello, Double Bass, and Piano (1945). VOCAL MUSIC: *Von deutscher Seele*, romantic cantata after J. von Eichendorff (1921; Berlin, Jan. 27, 1922); *Das dunkle Reich* for Solo Voices and Orch. (1929; Cologne, Oct. 21, 1930); *Fons salutatis* for Chorus and Orch. (1941); *Kantate*, after Goethe (1948–49; left unfinished; completed by R. Rehan); 106 lieder (1884–1931).

Phile (Fyles, Pfeil, Phyla), Philip, violinist and teacher; b. Germany, c.1734; d. Philadelphia, between Aug. 1 and Nov. 9, 1793, in a yellow-fever epidemic. He served in the Pa. German Regiment during the Revolutionary War; was transferred in July 1778 to the Invalid Regiment; was discharged on Jan. 4, 1783; a pension was granted to him on July 11, 1785. He was active in Philadelphia and N.Y.; gave concerts; played in theater orchs.; conducted the orch. of the Old American Co. of Comedians. He was probably the composer of the music of the *President's March*, to which Joseph Hopkinson (son of Francis Hopkinson) wrote the words *Hail Columbia*. He also wrote a piece entitled *Harmony Music* for the series of summer concerts at Gray's Gardens in Philadelphia.

Philidor (real name, **Danican**), famous family of French musicians. (1) **Jean Danican-Philidor;** b. c.1620; d. Paris, Sept. 8, 1679, as "Fifre de la Grande Ecurie" (piper in the King's military band). (2) **André Philidor** (*l'aîné*), son of Jean; d. Dreux, Aug. 11, 1730. As a youth he played the cromorne in the King's military band; later played the oboe, bassoon, and trompette marine, in addition to the cromorne, in the King's private band. He served as a librarian of the Royal Music Library at Versailles, and accumulated a collection of MSS of old instrumental pieces performed at the French court since the time of François I; the bulk of this collection, numbering some 350 MS vols., is at St. Michael's College, Tenbury, Worcester; 59 vols. are in the library of the Paris Cons., 35 vols. in the city library of Versailles, and 35 vols. in the collection of the Library of Congress in Washington, D.C. Among his publ. works are *Mascarade des Savoyards* (1700); *Mascarade du roi de la chine* (1700); *Suite de danses pour les violons et hautbois* (1699); *Pièces à 2 basses de viole, basse de violon et basson* (1700); *Marches et batteries de tambour avec les airs de fifres et de hautbois*. (3) **Jacques** (*le cadet*), brother of André (*l'aîné*); b. Paris, May 5, 1657; d. Versailles, May 27, 1708. He was a bassoonist in the Royal Chapel and later chamber musician to Louis XIV. (4) **Anne Danican-Philidor,** son of André (*l'aîné*); b. Paris, April 11, 1681; d. there, Oct. 8, 1728. A flute player, he composed pastoral operas (*L'Amour vainqueur,* 1697; *Diane et Endymion,* 1698; *Danaë,* 1701), and

music for flutes, violins, and oboes. He was the founder of the famous Paris concert series the Concert Spirituel (1725). (5) **Pierre Danican-Philidor,** son of Jacques (*le cadet*); b. Paris, Aug. 22, 1681; d. there, Sept. 1, 1731. He was a flute player; publ. 3 books of suites for 2 transverse flutes (1717, 1718), and flute trios. (6) **François André Danican-Philidor,** the last and greatest in the line of musicians in the family, the youngest son of André (*l'aîné*); b. Dreux, Sept. 7, 1726; d. London, Aug. 31, 1795. He achieved distinction not only in music but in chess; a famous chess opening was named after him. He defeated a number of celebrated chess masters of his time; brought out a fundamental treatise on chess, *L'Analyse des échecs* (London, 1749; new ed., under the title *Analyse du jeu des échecs,* 1777; altogether there were more than 100 eds. of this famous book). As a member of the London Chess Club, he was guaranteed a sum of money in exchange for his availability to play with other members of the club. In 1756 he began a surprisingly successful career as a composer for the stage. His first stage work was *Le Diable à 4,* a *comédie en vaudevilles,* which was the predecessor of opéra-comique; it was produced at the Opéra-Comique on Aug. 19, 1756. His next production was a ballet with music by Charpentier for which Philidor made some revisions, and which was produced under the title *Le Retour du printemps.* These were succeeded by several one-act pieces: *Blaise le savetier* (1759); *L'Huître et les plaideurs* (1759); *Le Quiproquo ou Le Volage fixé* (1760); *Le Soldat magicien* (1760); *Le Jardinier et son seigneur* (1761). But his most successful production of this period was *Le Maréchal ferrant,* in 2 acts (1761), which was performed more than 200 times; there followed a group of one-act pieces: *Sancho Pança* (1762); *Le Bûcheron, ou Les 3 Souhaits* (1763); *Le Sorcier,* in 2 acts (Jan. 2, 1764); and *Tom Jones,* in 3 acts (Feb. 27, 1765), which enjoyed great success, and incidentally contained an interesting novelty, a vocal quartet a cappella. Philidor's finest production, the grand opera *Ernelinde, Princesse de Norvège,* was staged on Nov. 24, 1767; it was revised in 1769 and produced under the title *Sandomir, Prince de Danemark,* but was revived in 1773 under its original title. Continuing his successful opera productions, Philidor staged *Le Jardinier de Sidon* (1768); *L'Amant déguisé* (1769); *La Nouvelle Ecole des femmes* (1770); *Le Bon Fils* (1773). His next opera, *Sémire et Mélide,* was given at Fontainebleau on Oct. 30, 1773, but it was publ. under the title *Mélide ou Le Navigateur.* There followed *Berthe* (Brussels, 1775); *Les Femmes vengées* (1775); and *Le Puits d'Amour* (1779), a play adapted from a novel originally publ. in 1765, for which Philidor composed 6 ariettes, which were publ. with the novel and then were used in the production of the play. Further works were *Persée* (1780); *L'Amitié au village* (1785); *Thémistocle* (first given at Fontainebleau on May 23, 1786, and then produced the following year at the Paris Opéra); *La Belle Esclave* (1787); and *Le Mari comme il les faudrait tous* (1788). A posthumous opera, *Bélisaire,* completed by Berton, was produced in 1796.

François André Philidor eclipsed his famous rivals Grétry and Monsigny in richness of harmony and skill in orchestration, but he yielded to Grétry, if not to Monsigny, in power of dramatic expression and melodic invention. Philidor was greatly admired by the Parisians, but his love for chess often distracted him from Paris in favor of frequent trips to London to play at the chess club there. Apart from his operas, he wrote church music and chamber pieces, among them quartets for 2 violins, oboe, and continuo. He set to music Horace's *Carmen saeculare,* a sort of secular oratorio that enjoyed notable success; in alternation with Jean-Claude Trial, he issued a series of publications, 12 Ariettes Périodiques.

Philipp, Isidor, eminent French pianist; b. Budapest, Sept. 2, 1863; d. Paris, Feb. 20, 1958 (as a result of injuries received from a fall in the Paris Métro). He was brought to Paris as an infant; studied piano with Georges Mathias at the Paris Cons., winning first prize in 1883; then took lessons with Saint-Saëns, Stephen Heller, and Ritter. His concert career was brief, but he found his true vocation in teaching; in 1903 he was appointed prof. of piano at the Paris Cons.; many famous musicians, among them Albert Schweitzer, were his pupils. In Paris he continued to perform, mostly in chamber music groups; formed a concert trio with Loeb and Berthelier, with which he gave a number of successful concerts. After the outbreak of World War II he went to the U.S.; arrived in N.Y. in 1941; despite his advanced age he accepted private students, not only in N.Y., but also in Montreal. At the age of 91, he played the piano part in Franck's Violin Sonata (N.Y., March 20, 1955); then returned to France. He publ. some technical studies for piano, among them *Exercises journaliers; Ecole d'octaves; Problèmes techniques; Etudes techniques basées sur une nouvelle manière de travailler; La Gamme chromatique;* made arrangements for 2 pianos of works by Bach, Mendelssohn, Saint-Saëns, and others; also brought out *La Technique de Liszt* (2 vols., Paris, 1932).

Philippe de Vitry. See **Vitry, Philippe de.**

Philips, Peter, important English composer and organist; b. 1561; d. Brussels, 1628. He belonged to a Catholic family; was probably a chorister at St. Paul's Cathedral; was befriended by a Catholic almoner, Sebastian Westcote, and received a bequest upon the latter's death in 1582. In that year, Philips left England; on Aug. 18, 1582, he arrived at Douai, where he presented himself at the English College; then proceeded to Rome, where he entered the service of Cardinal Alessandro Farnese; also was for 3 years organist at the English College in Rome (1582–85). In the autumn of 1585 Philips joined the household of Lord Thomas Paget in Rome, and subsequently traveled with him through Spain, France, and the Netherlands. From early 1587 until June 1588, Philips was with Paget in Paris; then went to Antwerp, remaining there until early 1589; also made visits to Brussels. After Paget's death in

1590, Philips settled in Antwerp, and was active there as a teacher of keyboard playing. In 1593 he went to Amsterdam, where he met Sweelinck. On his return trip to Antwerp, he was detained at Middelburgh, was charged with planning the assassination of Queen Elizabeth, and was alleged to have participated with Lord Paget in the act of burning the Queen in effigy in Paris. He stood trial in The Hague in Sept. 1593, but was released for lack of evidence. Late in 1593 he was back in Antwerp. In 1597 he moved to Brussels, entering the service of the Archduke Albert, as organist of the Royal Chapel. After Albert's marriage to Isabella of Spain (1599) Philips was officially designated as "Organist to Their Serene Highnesses the Archduke Albert and Isabella." On March 9, 1610, he received a canonry at Soignies, but continued to reside in Brussels. On Jan. 5, 1621, he exchanged his title at Soignies for a chaplainship at Tirlemont; in 1623 he is also described as canon of Béthune. However, he continued to be designated canon of Soignies for many years afterward, even in posthumous editions of his works, possibly because he was best known in that nominal post. Philips was highly esteemed in his day, and his works were printed in many collections; his music shows mixed Italian and Netherlandish characteristics; he excelled in madrigals and motets; his pieces for the virginal reveal a kinship with Sweelinck.

Phillips, Burrill, American composer; b. Omaha, Nov. 9, 1907. He studied music with Edwin Stringham in Denver; then with Howard Hanson and Bernard Rogers at the Eastman School of Music in Rochester, N.Y. After graduation he held numerous teaching posts: at the Eastman School of Music (1933–49, and again in 1965-66); at the Univ. of Illinois in Urbana (1949–64); and as guest lecturer at the Juilliard School of Music in N.Y. (1968–69) and at Cornell Univ. (1972–73). His music is cast in a neo-Classical style.

Phillips, Harvey, American tuba player; b. Aurora, Mo., Dec. 2, 1929. He played the sousaphone in high school; after attending the Univ. of Missouri (1947–48), he joined the Ringling Brothers and Barnum & Bailey Circus Band; then took general music courses at the Juilliard School of Music (1950–54) and at the Manhattan School of Music (1956–58); concurrently he played in various ensembles there, including the N.Y. City Ballet Orch., the N.Y. City Opera Orch., the Goldman Band, and the Symph. of the Air; he also was a founding member of the N.Y. Brass Quintet. From 1967–71 he held an administrative position at the New England Cons. of Music. In 1971 he became a prof. of music at the Indiana Univ. School of Music; was named a distinguished prof. of music there in 1979. He commissioned works for tuba from Gunther Schuller, Robert Russell Bennett, Alec Wilder, and Morton Gould.

Piaf, Edith, French chanteuse; b. Paris, Dec. 19, 1915; d. there, Oct. 11, 1963. Her real name was **Giovanna Gassion;** she took her first name from

Edith Cavell, a Belgian nurse shot by the Germans in World War I. Her childhood was tragic; she was abandoned by her mother, an Italian café singer and professional prostitute; traveled with her father, a circus contortionist, taking part in his act as a shill for his street-corner acrobatics. She then became a street singer in Paris, earning the nickname Piaf (Parisian argot for "sparrow") on account of her ragged and emaciated appearance. She was befriended by a cabaret owner; when he was murdered, she was held by the French police as a material witness. During the war and German occupation she entertained French prisoners in Germany; as a result, she was accused of collaboration, but was exonerated. In 1954 she made her first American tour. Although untutored, she developed a type of ballad singing that was infused with profound sentiment and expressive artistry, eliciting an enthusiastic response from nightclub audiences and sophisticated music critics alike. She composed chansonettes, among which *La Vie en rose* became popular; publ. a book of memoirs, *Au bal de la chance* (Paris, 1958; in Eng. as *The Wheel of Fortune*, 1965). A film on the early years of her life was produced in Paris in 1982.

Piatigorsky, Gregor, great Russian cellist; b. Ekaterinoslav, April 17, 1903; d. Los Angeles, Aug. 6, 1976. He received his first music lessons from his father, a violinist; then took cello lessons with Alfred von Glehn; played in various orchs. in Moscow. In 1921 he left Russia and proceeded to Berlin, where he took cello lessons with Julius Klengel. From 1924 to 1928 he was first cellist of the Berlin Phil.; then devoted himself entirely to his concert career. He played the solo part in *Don Quixote* by Richard Strauss under the composer's direction many times in Europe, and was probably unexcelled in this part; Strauss himself called him "mein Don Quixote." He went to America in 1929 and made his American debut at Oberlin, Ohio, on Nov. 5, 1929; played the Dvořák Concerto with the N.Y. Phil., eliciting great praise (Dec. 29, 1929). He was regarded as the world's finest cello player after Casals; continued giving solo recitals and appearing with major European and American orchs. for many years; gave first performances of several cello concertos commissioned by him to Hindemith, Dukelsky, Castelnuovo-Tedesco, and others. He taught advanced classes at the Curtis Inst. in Philadelphia and later at the Univ. of Southern Calif., Los Angeles; presented a series of trio concerts with Heifetz and Pennario. He was the recipient of honorary D.Mus. degrees from Temple Univ., Columbia Univ., the Univ. of Calif. at Los Angeles, etc. He publ. an autobiographical vol., *Cellist* (N.Y., 1965).

Piatti, Alfredo Carlo, Italian cellist and composer; b. Borgo Canale, near Bergamo, Jan. 8, 1822; d. Crocetto di Mozzo, July 18, 1901. He received his primary musical education from his father, the violinist **Antonio Piatti;** then studied cello at the Milan Cons.; began his concert career in 1838, and in 1843 played with Liszt in Munich; obtained excellent

success in England, where he gave annual concerts; from 1859 to 1898 he was a regular performer in the Saturday Popular Concerts of chamber music in London. He combined an excellent technical skill with profound musicianship; in the cello world he occupied a position of artistry and authority comparable with that of Joachim among violinists. He wrote 2 cello concertos, 6 cello sonatas, and a number of solo pieces for cello; also ed. 6 string sonatas by Boccherini and Locatelli and brought out editions of cello methods by Kummer and others.

Piccinni (Piccini), Niccolò, Italian opera composer; b. Bari, Jan. 16, 1728; d. Paris, May 7, 1800. Piccinni's father was a violinist at the Basilica di San Nicola in Bari, and his maternal uncle, **Gaetano Latilla** (1713–83), a well-known operatic composer. The innate ability of young Piccinni attracted the attention of the Archbishop of Bari, Muzio Gaeta, who arranged for him to enroll at the Cons. di Sant' Onofrio in Naples; there, at the age of 14, he began studying under the celebrated masters Leo and Durante; he continued as a student for 13 years, and then became an instructor at the same Cons. His first work, *Le Donne dispettose,* an opera buffa in the style made popular in Naples by Logroscino, was produced at the Teatro dei Fiorentini in 1754. He wrote 139 operas; in 1761 alone he produced 10 operas; 7 more followed in 1762. An instinct for the theater made him select librettos rich in dramatic content; his melodic invention was fresh, and his arias were written in a pleasing style eminently suitable to the voice; he elaborated the conventional climactic scenes so that dramatic interest was sustained to the end; he varied the tempos and the harmonies in the ensembles, which further contributed to the general effect. After modest successes in Naples with *Le Gelosie* (1755) and *Il Curioso del proprio danno* (1756), he went to Rome, where he produced his opera *Alessandro nelle Indie* (Jan. 21, 1758); later wrote another setting to the same subject (Naples, Jan. 12, 1774). Piccinni's greatest success in Rome was his comic opera *La bouna figliuola,* to Goldoni's libretto, based on Richardson's *Pamela* (Feb. 6, 1760; also produced in Italy as *La Cecchina nubile*); Piccinni wrote a sequel to it, *La buona figliuola maritata* (Bologna, June 10, 1761). Other operas produced in Rome were *Le Contadine bizarre* (Feb. 10, 1763); *Gli Stravaganti* (Jan. 1, 1764; also perf. under the title *La Schiava riconosciuta*); *Il Barone di Torreforte* (Jan. 10, 1765); *La Pescatrice* (Jan. 9, 1766); *Antigone* (1770); *Le finte gemelle* (Jan. 2, 1771). His fortunes declined with the rising popularity in Rome of a powerful rival, Anfossi; not wishing to compete, Piccinni returned to Naples, where he staged his opera *I Viaggiatori* with excellent success. Piccinni's historical role was destined to be played on the international scene in Paris, where he went with his family in Dec. 1776. His arrival in Paris precipitated one of the most famous controversies in music history, the "querelle célèbre," which was in essence a continuation of the "guerre des bouffons" of 1752. In the later case, the Parisian public was sharply divided into 2 warring factions, one supporting the Italian operatic art as practiced by Piccinni, and the other championing the operatic realism of Gluck. Piccinni himself had the highest regard for Gluck, and never encouraged the frenzied outbursts of the "Piccinnistes." Gluck left Paris in 1780; at his death in Vienna (1787) Piccinni made plans to organize annual concerts in Paris in Gluck's memory, but failed to find financial support for his project. Piccinni's first opera in French, *Roland* (Jan. 27, 1778), had considerable success; he continued to use French librettos, producing several operas in close succession, of which the following were fairly well received: *Le Fat méprisé* (Paris, May 16, 1779); *Atys* (Paris, Feb. 22, 1780); *Iphigénie* (Paris, Jan. 23, 1781; fairly successful, despite the fact that Gluck's masterpiece on the same subject was produced 2 years before); *Didon* (Fontainebleau, Oct. 16, 1783; his most enduring work; separate arias have been reprinted many times); *Le Dormeur éveillé* (Paris, Nov. 14, 1783); *Le Faux Lord* (Paris, Dec. 6, 1783); *Pénélope* (Fontainebleau, Nov. 2, 1785). In 1778 Piccinni became director of the Italian troupe in Paris; in 1784 he was appointed *maître de chant* at the newly founded Ecole Royale de Chant et de Déclamation Lyrique in Paris, but lost this position after the Revolution and returned to Naples, where he subsisted on a small pension granted him by the King of Naples; in 1798 went back to Paris, where he was received with public honors and given a purse of 5,000 francs for immediate necessities; an honorary position of 6th inspector was granted to him by the Paris Cons. (formerly the Ecole Royale de Chant). But Piccinni was too ill for active life; he retired to Passy, where he spent the last months of his life. *La Cecchina* was revived in Bari on his bicentenary, Feb. 7, 1928. A complete list of Piccinni's operas is given by A. Cametti under the title "Saggio cronologico delle opere teatrali di Niccolò Piccinni," in *Rivista Musicale Italiana,* 8 (also separately, Turin, 1901).

Pichl, Wenzel, Bohemian violinist and composer; b. Bechin, Sept. 23, 1741; d. Vienna, Jan. 23, 1805. He studied violin with Pokorny and composition with Seeger in Prague. In 1777 he was appointed chamber composer to Archduke Ferdinand at Milan; went with him to Vienna in 1796; also supplied musical entertainment to Viennese noblemen; he died during a concert at the palace of Prince Lobkowitz. He wrote about 700 works, including 13 operas; some 20 masses; 89 symphs. (of which 66 were publ.); 13 serenades (3 of which were publ.); a great number of concertos for violin and other instruments, with orch.; 7 octets; 7 septets; 6 sextets; 21 quintets; 172 string quartets (of which 163 were publ.); 148 works for baryton; piano pieces; etc. His 6 fugues with a fugal prelude for violin alone became fairly popular (reprint, ed. by Kocian and Gardavsky, Prague, 1951).

Pick-Mangiagalli, Riccardo, Italian composer; b. Strakonice, Bohemia, July 10, 1882; d. Milan, July 8, 1949. He was of mixed Italian and Bohemian par-

entage; studied at the Cons. Giuseppe Verdi in Milan with Appiani (piano) and Ferroni (composition). He began his career as a successful concert pianist, but later turned exclusively to composition. In 1936 he succeeded Pizzetti as director of the Cons. Giuseppe Verdi, and held this post until his death.

WORKS: OPERAS: *Basi e Bote* (Rome, March 3, 1927); *Casanova a Venezia* (La Scala, Milan, Jan. 19, 1929; an orch. suite from it, entitled *Scene carnevalesche,* was perf. in Milan, Feb. 6, 1931); *L'Ospite inatteso* (Milan-Turin-Genoa Radio network, Oct. 25, 1931; the first opera to be given a world premiere by radio anywhere); *Il notturno romantico* (Rome, April 25, 1936). FOR THE DANCE: *Il salice d'oro,* mimo-drama (Milan, Sept. 18, 1918); *Sumitra* (Frankfurt, 1922); *Mahit,* ballet-fable with singing (La Scala, Milan, March 20, 1923); *La Berceuse* (San Remo, Feb. 21, 1933); *Variazioni coreografiche* (San Remo, April 13, 1935). FOR ORCH.: *Sortilegi,* symph. poem for Piano and Orch. (Milan, Dec. 13, 1917); *Notturno e rondo fantastico* (Milan, May 6, 1919); *2 preludi* (Rome, March 1, 1921); *4 poemi* (Milan, April 24, 1925); *Piccola suite* (Milan, June 12, 1927); *Preludio e fuga* (Rome, March 11, 1928); *Preludio e scherzo sinfonico* (Milan, Oct. 22, 1938); Violin Sonata; String Quartet; piano pieces; songs.

Pierné, (Henri-Constant-) Gabriel, French composer, conductor, and organist; b. Metz, Aug. 16, 1863; d. Ploujean, near Morlaix, July 17, 1937. He studied at the Paris Cons. (1871-82), where his teachers were Marmontel (piano), César Franck (organ), and Massenet (composition); he won first piano prize (1879), first prize for counterpoint and fugue (1881), and first prize for organ (1882); was awarded the Grand Prix de Rome (1882) with the cantata *Edith;* succeeded César Franck as organist at Ste.-Clotilde (1890), where he remained until 1898. In 1903 he was appointed assistant conductor to Colonne, and in 1910 his successor (until 1934); was elected a member of the Académie des Beaux-Arts in 1925. He was a prolific composer, but of his many works only the oratorio *La Croisade des Enfants* and the piano piece *Marche des petits soldats de plomb* became popular.

WORKS: OPERAS: *La Coupe enchantée* (Royan, Aug. 24, 1895; revised version, Opéra-Comique, Paris, Dec. 26, 1905); *Vendée* (Lyons, March 11, 1897); *La Fille de Tabarin* (Opéra-Comique, Paris, Feb. 20, 1901); *On ne badine pas avec l'amour* (Opéra-Comique, Paris, May 30, 1910); *Sophie Arnould,* one-act lyric comedy, based on episodes from the life of the famous singer (Opéra-Comique, Feb. 21, 1927). BALLETS AND PANTOMIMES: *Le Collier de saphirs* (1891); *Les Joyeuses Commères de Paris* (1892); *Bouton d'or* (1893); *Le Docteur Blanc* (1893); *Salomé* (1895); *Cydalise et le chèvre-pied* (1919; Paris Opéra, Jan. 15, 1923; as an orch. suite, 1926); *Impressions de Music-Hall,* "ballet à l'Américaine" (Opéra, April 6, 1927); *Giration* (1934); *Fragonard* (1934); *Images,* "divertissement sur un thème pastoral" (Opéra, June 19, 1935); oratorios: *La Croisade des enfants* for Mixed Choir of Children and Adults (Paris, Jan. 18, 1905); *Les Enfants à Bethléem* for Soloists, Children's Chorus, and Orch. (Amsterdam, April 13, 1907); *Les Fioretti de St. François d'Assise* (1912). FOR ORCH.: *Suite de concert* (1883); *Première suite d'orchestre* (1883); *Ouverture symphonique* (1885); *Marche solonnelle* (1889); *Pantomime* (1889); *Ballet de cour* (1901); *Paysages franciscains* (1920); *Gulliver au pays de Lilliput* (Paris Festival of the International Society for Contemporary Music, June 23, 1937); Piano Concerto (1887); *Scherzo-Caprice* for Piano and Orch. (1890); *Poème symphonique* for Piano and Orch. (1901); *Konzertstück* for Harp and Orch. (1901); *L'An mil*, symph. poem, with Chorus (1897). CHAMBER MUSIC: *Pastorale variée dans le style ancien* for Wind Instruments (also for Piano); *Berceuse* for Violin and Piano; *Caprice* for Cello and Piano; *Canzonetta* for Clarinet and Piano; *Solo de concert* for Bassoon and Piano; *Variations libres et Finale* for Flute, Violin, Viola, Cello, and Harp. FOR PIANO: *15 pièces* (1883); *Etude de concert; Album pour mes petits amis* (containing the famous *Marche des petits soldats de plomb); Humoresque; Rêverie; Ariette dans le style ancien; Pastorale variée; Sérénade à Colombine; Sérénade vénitienne; Barcarolle* for 2 Pianos. SONG CYCLES: *Contes* (1897); *3 Adaptations musicales* (1902); *3 mélodies* (1904); 38 other songs; harp music; folksong arrangements; etc. He contributed the section "Histoire de l'instrumentation" to Lavignac's *Encyclopédie de la musique.*

Pierné, Paul, French composer, cousin of **Gabriel Pierné;** b. Metz, June 30, 1874; d. Paris, March 24, 1952. He studied at the Paris Cons. with Lenepveu and Caussade; wrote a number of works, which were occasionally performed in Paris: the operas *Le Diable galant* (1913), *Emilde,* and *Mademoiselle Don Quichotte;* a ballet, *Le Figurinai;* 2 symphs.; several symph. poems of a programmatic nature (*Jeanne d'Arc, Cléopâtre, De l'ombre à la lumière, Nuit évocatrice, Rapsodie Lorraine,* etc.); choral works; organ pieces; a song cycle, *Schéhérazade;* piano pieces.

Pierpont, James, American composer; b. Boston, 1822; d. Winter Haven, Fla., 1893. In 1857 he publ. a ballad entitled *One Horse Open Sleigh* (composed in 1850); in 1859 it was publ. under the title *Jingle Bells, or The One Horse Open Sleigh* (the original music is reprinted in facsimile in Richard Jackson's *Popular Songs of 19th-Century America,* N.Y., 1976); however, while the original words and the music to the verse are the same as those known today, the original music to the chorus is different. This song did not acquire its wide popularity as a Christmas song until the 20th century; during the 19th century, Pierpont's most popular works were *The Little White Cottage, or Gentle Nettie Moore* (1857); *We Conquer or Die* (1861); and *Strike for the South* (1863); the last 2 of these were rallying songs for the Confederacy during the Civil War (his father, in contrast, was a fiery abolitionist minister). He was the uncle of the millionaire financier John Pierpont Morgan.

Pierson (Pearson), Henry Hugh, English composer; b. Oxford, April 12, 1815; d. Leipzig, Jan. 28, 1873. He was educated at Cambridge; in 1839 went to Germany, where he studied music with Tomaschek and Reissiger; entered the circle of Mendelssohn in Leipzig; after a brief term as a prof. of music at the Univ. of Edinburgh (1844), he returned to Germany, where he remained for the rest of his life; married **Caroline Leonhardt,** who wrote the German librettos for his operas. He changed his name from the original form Pearson to Pierson in order to secure proper pronunciation by Germans; used the pen name **Edgar Mansfeldt** for his publ. music.
WORKS: Operas: *Leila* (Hamburg, Feb. 22, 1848) and *Contarini oder Die Verschwörung zu Padua* (Hamburg, April 16, 1872; revived in Dessau, April 24, 1883, under the title *Fenice*); oratorio, *Jerusalem* (Norwich Festival, Sept. 23, 1852); incidental music to the 2nd part of Goethe's *Faust;* overtures to Shakespeare's *Macbeth, As You Like It,* and *Romeo and Juliet.* His music was totally submerged in Mendelssohn's style.

Pijper, Willem, renowned Dutch composer; b. Zeist, Sept. 8, 1894; d. Leidschendam, March 18, 1947. He received a rudimentary education from his father, an amateur violinist; then went to the Toonkunst School of Music in Utrecht, where he studied composition with Johan Wagenaar and piano with Mme. H.J. van Lunteren-Hansen (1911–16); from 1918 to 1923, was music critic of *Utrecht Dagblad,* and from 1926 to 1929, co-editor of the monthly *De Muziek.* He taught theory at the Amsterdam Cons. (from 1918) and was a prof. of composition there from 1925 to 1930; served as director of the Rotterdam Cons. from 1930 until his death. In his music Pijper continued the Romantic tradition of Mahler, and also adopted the harmonic procedures of the modern French School. He postulated a "germ-cell theory," in which an opening chord or motif is the source of all succeeding harmonic and melodic development; he also cultivated the scale of alternating whole tones and semitones, regarding it as his own, not realizing that it was used abundantly by Rimsky-Korsakov (in Russian reference works it is termed the Rimsky-Korsakov scale); the "Pijper scale," as it became known in the Netherlands, was also used by Anton von der Horst and others. During the German bombardment of Rotterdam in May 1940, nearly all of Pijper's MSS were destroyed by fire, including the unpubl. reduced scoring of his large 2nd Symph. (restored in 1961 by Pijper's student Karel Mengelberg); also destroyed was the unpubl. *Divertimento* for Piano and String Orch.
WORKS: FOR THE STAGE: 2 operas ("symphonic dramas"): *Halewijn* (1932–33; Amsterdam, June 13, 1933; revised 1934) and *Merlijn* (1939–45; incomplete; produced posthumously, Rotterdam, June 7, 1952). INCIDENTAL MUSIC: To Sophocles' *Antigone* (1920; revised 1922 and 1926); Euripides' *Bacchantes* (1924) and *The Cyclops* (1925); Shakespeare's *The Tempest* (1930); Vondel's *Phaëton* (1937). FOR ORCH.:

3 symphs.: No. 1, *Pan* (1917; Amsterdam, April 23, 1918); No. 2, for Large Orch. (1921; Amsterdam, Nov. 2, 1922; reduced scoring accomplished by Karel Mengelberg, 1961); No. 3 (1926; Amsterdam, Oct. 28, 1926; his most frequently perf. work); *6 Symphonic Epigrams* (1928; Amsterdam, April 12, 1928); *6 Adagios* (1940; posthumous, Utrecht, Nov. 14, 1951); *Orchestral Piece with Piano* (1915; Utrecht, Dec. 11, 1915; Pijper originally titled this "Piano Concerto No. 1," which caused confusion with his later and only Piano Concerto [1927; Amsterdam, Dec. 22, 1927], which in turn was sometimes incorrectly referred to as "Piano Concerto No. 2" in some catalogues); Cello Concerto (1936; Amsterdam, Nov. 22, 1936; revised 1947); Violin Concerto (1938–39; Amsterdam, Jan. 7, 1940). CHAMBER MUSIC: 2 piano trios (1913–14, 1921); 5 string quartets (1914; 1920; 1923; 1928; 1946, unfinished); Septet for Wind Quintet, Double Bass, and Piano (1920); Sextet for Wind Quintet and Piano (1922-23); Trio for Flute, Clarinet, and Bassoon (1926–27); Wind Quintet (1928–29); 2 violin sonatas (1919, 1922); 2 cello sonatas (1919, 1924); Flute Sonata (1925); Sonata for Solo Violin (1931). FOR PIANO: *Theme with 5 Variations* (1913); *3 Aphorisms* (1915); 3 sonatinas (1917, 1925, 1925); *3 Old Dutch Dances* (1926); Sonata (1930); 2-piano Sonata (1935). FOR VOICE AND ORCH.: *Fêtes galantes*, after Verlaine, with Mezzo-soprano (1916; Schweningen, Aug. 2, 1917); *Romance sans paroles*, after Verlaine, with Mezzo-soprano (1919; Amsterdam, April 15, 1920); *Hymne*, after Boutens, with Bass-baritone (1941–43; Amsterdam, Nov. 1945). FOR VOICE AND PIANO: *8 vieilles chansons de France* (1918); *8 Noëls de France* (1919); *8 Old Dutch Love Songs* (1920; revised 1943); *8 Old Dutch Songs*, in 2 sets (1924, 1935). FOR A CAPPELLA CHORUS: *Heer Halewijn* (1920) and *Heer Danielken* (1925). He also wrote a *Passepied* for Carillon (1916) and made orchestrations and arrangements of Haydn, Mozart, etc.; publ. 2 collections of articles: *De Quinten-Cirkel* (Amsterdam, 1929) and *De Stemvork* (Amsterdam, 1930).

Pilarczyk, Helga, German soprano; b. Schöningen, March 12, 1925. She studied piano and aspired to a concert career; then took voice lessons and sang in operetta. She found her true vocation in opera; made her debut at Braunschweig in 1951; was a member of the Hamburg State Opera from 1953 until 1968. She made a specialty of modern music; sang Schoenberg's dramatic monologue *Erwartung*, and the leading parts in Alban Berg's *Wozzeck* and *Lulu* as well as in works by Stravinsky, Prokofiev, Dallapiccola, Honegger, Krenek, and others. She appeared as a guest artist at the Bavarian State Opera in Munich, the Vienna State Opera, La Scala in Milan, the Paris Opéra, Covent Garden in London, and the Metropolitan Opera in N.Y. (debut, Feb. 19, 1965, as Marie in *Wozzeck*); publ. an interesting essay, *Kann man die moderne Oper singen?* (Hamburg, 1964).

Pilkington, Francis, English composer; b. c.1570; d. Chester, 1638. He received a B.Mus. degree at Lincoln College, Oxford, in 1595. He became a lay clerk (or conduct) at Chester Cathedral in 1602, and then a minor canon in 1612. After taking Holy Orders, he was made a "full minister" on Dec. 18, 1614. He was active in the Cathedral choir, and was precentor there from 1623 until his death. He also held other curacies in Chester, including his principal charge at St. Bridget's from 1616. WORKS: *The First Booke of Songs or Ayres of 4. Parts: with tableture for the lute or orpherian, with the violl de gamba* (London, 1605; the versions for 4 voices with lute were publ. in *The Old English Edition*, XVIII–XX, London, 1897–98; the versions for voice and lute were publ. in E.H. Fellowes, ed., *The English School of Lutenist Song Writers*, London, 1920–32; revised by T. Dart, 1971, in *The English Lute-Songs*); *The First Set of Madrigals and Pastorals of 3. 4. and 5. parts* (London, 1613–14; ed. by E.H. Fellowes in *The English Madrigal School, A Guide to Its Practical Use*, London, 1926; revised by T. Dart, 1959, in *The English Madrigalists*); *The Second Set of Madrigals, and Pastorals, of 3. 4. 5. and 6. Parts: apt for violls and voyces* (London, 1624; ed. by E.H. Fellowes in *The English Madrigal School . . .*, London, 1926; revised by T. Dart, 1958, in *The English Madrigalists*). See also B. Jeffery, ed., *Francis Pilkington: Complete Works for Solo Lute* (London, 1970). He also contributed 2 songs to Sir William Leighton's collection *The Teares or Lamentacions of a Sorrowful Soule* (1614).

Pimsleur, Solomon, American pianist and composer; b. Paris (of Austrian-Jewish parents), Sept. 19, 1900; d. New York, April 22, 1962. He was taken to the U.S. as a child in 1903; studied piano privately; took music courses at Columbia Univ., but graduated in English literature (M.A., 1923); also studied with Rubin Goldmark. He gave numerous piano recitals in the U.S. His compositions, in a Romantically flavored and technically competent idiom, include *Ode to Intensity*, a "symphonic ballad" (N.Y., Aug. 14, 1933); *Overture to Disillusionment; Meditative Nocturne* for Orch.; 3 string quartets; Piano Trio; Piano Quintet; Violin Sonata; Cello Sonata; many piano pieces with imaginative titles (*Impulsive Sonata; Tranquil Sonata; Reflective Sonata; Mournful Prelude and Melodious Fugue;* etc.); *Shakespearean Sonnet Symphony* for Chorus and Orch. His projected opera, *Diary of Anne Frank,* remains unfinished.

Pincherle, Marc, noted French musicologist; b. Constantine, Algiers, June 13, 1888; d. Paris, June 20, 1974. He studied music in Paris with Pirro, Laloy, and Rolland; served in both world wars; was taken prisoner of war in June 1940 and was interned in Germany until March 1941. He taught the history of violin playing at the Ecole Normale; was artistic director of the Société Pleyel (1927–55) and president of the Société Française de Musicologie (1948–56). As a musicologist, he devoted his energy mainly to the history of violin music.

Pingoud, Ernest, Russian-born Finnish composer;

Pini-Corsi – Pipkov

b. St. Petersburg, Oct. 14, 1888; d. Helsinki, June 1, 1942. He studied piano in St. Petersburg with Siloti; then went to Leipzig, where he took courses in music history with Hugo Riemann and in composition with Max Reger. In 1918 he settled in Finland, where he served as managing director of the Helsinki Phil. Orch. (1924–42). In his music he was influenced by the Russian modern school, particularly by Scriabin, from whom he acquired his pre dilection for mystical titles, often in French (*La Flamme éternelle, Le Chant d'espace*, etc.).

Pini-Corsi, Antonio, Italian baritone; b. Zara, June 1858; d. Milan, April 22, 1918. He made his debut in Cremona in 1878; then sang throughout Italy; Verdi chose him to create the role of Ford in *Falstaff* at La Scala in Milan in 1893. He also sang at Covent Garden in London (1894–96, 1902–3). On Dec. 25, 1899, he made his N.Y. Metropolitan Opera debut as Dr. Bartolo in *Il Barbiere di Siviglia;* remained on its roster until 1901; returned for the 1909–14 seasons. He was one of the great buffo singers of his day, being famous for his portrayals of Dr. Bartolo, Leporello, Don Pasquale, and others.

Pinkham, Daniel, American composer; b. Lynn, Mass., June 5, 1923. He studied organ and music theory at Phillips Academy in Andover (1937–40) and at Harvard Univ. with A. Tillman Merritt, Walter Piston, and Archibald T. Davison (A.B., 1943; M.A., 1944); had harpsichord lessons with Putnam Aldrich and Wanda Landowska, and studied organ with E. Power Biggs; took summer courses in composition at the Berkshire Music Center in Tanglewood, with Aaron Copland, Arthur Honegger, and Nadia Boulanger; subsequently was music director of King's Chapel in Boston and a member of the faculty of the New England Cons. of Music. The formal design of his music is compact and contrapuntally cohesive; the rhythmic element is propulsive; now and then he astutely applies modernistic devices without disrupting the tonal fabric of the music. WORKS: FOR ORCH.: Piano Concertino (Cambridge, Mass., May 3, 1950); Concertante No. 1 for Violin and Harpsichord Soli, Strings, and Celesta (Boston, Dec. 16, 1954); Concerto for Celesta and Harpsichord Soli (N.Y., Nov. 19, 1955); Violin Concerto No. 1 (Falmouth, Mass., Sept. 8, 1956); Concertante No. 2 for Violin and Strings (Boston, May 9, 1958); Symph. No. 1 (1961); Symph. No. 2 (Lansing, Mich., Nov. 23, 1963); *Signs of the Zodiac* for Orch. and Optional Narrator (1965); Violin Concerto No. 2 (1968); Organ Concerto (1970); *Serenades* for Trumpet and Symphonic Wind Orch. (1979); also *Catacoustical Measures,* composed to test the acoustics at Lincoln Center's Phil. Hall in N.Y. (1962). FOR CHORUS AND ORCH.: *Wedding Cantata* (Cambridge, Mass., Sept. 22, 1956); *Easter Cantata* (1957); *Christmas Cantata (Sinfonia Sacra;* Boston, Dec. 10, 1957); Requiem (1963); Stabat Mater (1964); St. Mark Passion (1965); *Ascension Cantata* for Orch. of Winds and Percussion (1970); *The Passion of Judas* (1976); *The Descent into Hell* (1979); *When God

Arose (1979); *Hezekiah* (1979); *Before the Dust Returns* (1981); *The Conversion of Saul* (1981); various instrumental pieces for piano, organ, harpsichord, etc.; several dozens of adroit instrumental arrangements of Christmas songs.

Pinsuti, Ciro, celebrated Italian singing teacher and composer; b. Sinalunga, near Florence, May 9, 1829; d. Florence, March 10, 1888. His talent developed so rapidly that at 11 he was elected an honorary member of the Accademia Filarmonica of Rome. Taken to England soon after by Henry Drummond, he studied the piano under C. Potter, and the violin under Blagrove; returned to Bologna in 1845, and studied at the Liceo, also privately with Rossini, soon becoming assistant teacher of a piano class. In 1848 he went back to England; was appointed a prof. of singing at the Royal Academy of Music in 1856. He divided his time between London and Italy; brought out an opera, *Il Mercante di Venezia,* at Bologna (Nov. 9, 1873); another, *Mattia Corvino,* at Milan (1877); and a 3rd, *Margherita,* at Venice (1882). In 1871 he represented Italy at the opening of the London Exhibition, for which he composed the hymn *O people of this favoured land.* As a recipient of the order of the Italian Crown, he was styled "Cavaliere" Pinsuti. Besides his operas, he wrote some 200 songs to Eng. and Italian texts.

Pinto, Octavio, Brazilian composer; b. São Paulo, Nov. 3, 1890; d. there, Oct. 31, 1950. He was trained as an architect; built apartment houses in Brazil; also studied piano with Isidor Philipp. In 1922 he married the Brazilian pianist **Guiomar Novães;** Villa-Lobos wrote his suite *Prole do bébé* for their children. Pinto publ. a number of effective piano miniatures, of which *Scenas infantis* (1932) and *Children's Festival* (1939) are best known.

Pinza, Ezio (baptismal name, **Fortunio**), celebrated Italian bass; b. Rome, May 18, 1892; d. Stamford, Conn., May 9, 1957. The family moved to Ravenna when he was an infant; he studied engineering; also was active in sports. He began to study voice at the age of 18 with Ruzza and Vizzani, at the Cons. of Bologna; served in the Italian artillery during World War I; made his opera debut as Oroveso in *Norma* in Soncino (1914); then sang for 3 seasons at La Scala in Milan; was selected by Toscanini for the leading part in the world premiere of Boito's *Nerone* (May 1, 1924). He made his American debut at the Metropolitan Opera House as Pontifex Maximus in Spontini's *La Vestale* (Nov. 1, 1926) and remained on its staff until 1947; appeared also in San Francisco, Chicago, etc.; sang in Europe and in South America; his most celebrated roles were Méphistophélès in Gounod's *Faust,* Don Giovanni, and Boris Godunov. In 1949 he appeared as a musical comedy star in *South Pacific,* and immediately became successful in this new career; also appeared in films. R. Magidoff edited *Ezio Pinza: An Autobiography* (N.Y., 1958).

Pipkov, Lubomir, noted Bulgarian composer; b. Lovec, Sept. 19, 1904; d. Sofia, May 9, 1974. He studied piano at the Bulgarian State Cons. in Sofia (1923–26); then took courses in composition with Nadia Boulanger and Paul Dukas at the Ecole Normale de Musique in Paris (1926–32). Returning to Bulgaria, he occupied several administrative posts, including the directorship of the Sofia Opera Theater (1944–47). His style of composition is determined by the inherent asymmetry of Bulgarian folk songs; there is a similarity in his compositions with those of Bartók, resulting from common sources in Balkan and Macedonian music; his harmonic investiture is often polytonal or polymodal.

WORKS: 3 operas: *The 9 Brothers of Yanina* (1932; Sofia, Sept. 19, 1937); *Momchil* (1939–44; Sofia, April 24, 1948); *Antigone 43* (1961–62; Ruse, Dec. 23, 1963); *Oratorio for Our Time* (1959; Plovdiv, Dec. 18, 1959); 2 cantatas: *The Wedding* (1934) and *Cantata of Friendship* (1958); Concerto for Winds, Percussion, and Piano (1930); 4 symphs.: No. 1 (1939–40); No. 2 (1954); No. 3 for Strings, Trumpet, 2 Pianos, and Percussion (1965); No. 4 for String Orch. (1970); *Heroic Overture* (1950); *Journey through Albania*, variations for String Orch. (1950); Violin Concerto (1951); Piano Concerto (1954); *Symphony-Concerto* for Cello and Orch. (1963; Moscow, April 20, 1964); Concerto for Clarinet and Chamber Orch. (1966); *The Partisan's Grave* for Trombone and String Orch. (1970); 3 string quartets (1928, 1948, 1966); 2 violin sonatas (1929, 1969); Piano Trio (1930); Piano Quartet (1939); Sonata for Solo Violin (1969); *Tableaux et études métrorythmiques* for Piano (1972); *Suggestions printanières* for Piano (1972); choruses; songs.

Pirro, André, distinguished French musicologist; b. St.-Dizier, Haute-Marne, Feb. 12, 1869; d. Paris, Nov. 11, 1943. He was a pupil of his father, an organist; from 1896 he was a prof. at the Schola Cantorum; was also a member of its board of directors; from 1904 he was also a lecturer on the history of music theory at the Ecole des Hautes Etudes Sociales; in 1912 he succeeded R. Rolland as prof. of music history at the Sorbonne.

Pirrotta, Nino, eminent Italian musicologist; b. Palermo, June 13, 1908. He studied at the Cons. V. Bellini in Palermo and at the Univ. of Florence; served as librarian and lecturer in music history at the Cons. of Palermo (1936–48) and chief librarian at the Santa Cecilia Academy in Rome. He then went to the U.S.; was a visiting prof. at Princeton Univ. (1954–55), Columbia Univ. (1956), and Harvard Univ. (1956–72); was subsequently on the staff of the Univ. of Rome. His principal fields of research are Renaissance polyphony and Baroque opera; his publications include *Il Sacchetti e la tecnica musicale del trecento italiano* (with E. Li Gotti; Florence, 1935); *Il Codice Estense lat. 568 e la musica francese in Italia al principio dell '400* (Palermo, 1946); *Li due Orfei. Da Poliziano a Monteverdi* (Turin, 1969); "Gesualdo, Ferrara e Venezia" and "Monteverdi e i problemi dell'opera," in *Studi sul teatro veneto fra Rinascimento ed età*

barocca (Florence, 1971).

Pisador, Diego, Spanish lutenist; b. Salamanca, c.1509; d. after 1557. In 1526 he took minor orders; in 1552 he publ. in Salamanca *Libro de música de vihuela,* containing madrigals, a set of Spanish ballads, and transcriptions of secular and sacred works by Josquin Des Prez and others; the collection is reprinted by A. Morphy in *Les Luthistes espagnols du XVIe siècle.*

Pisari (Pizari), Pasquale, Italian composer; b. Rome, 1725; d. there, March 27, 1778. He was a pupil of Giovanni Biordi; in 1752 was taken into the papal chapel, being a fine bass singer; he wrote most of his sacred works for it, and the MSS are preserved in the archives of the papal chapel; they include several masses, motets, 2 Te Deums for 8 Voices, one Te Deum for 4 Voices (his most remarkable work); also a *Dixit* in 16 parts, for 4 Choirs, and a series of motets for the entire year, written for the Lisbon Court. Padre Martini called Pisari the "Palestrina of the 18th century."

Pischna, Josef, famous Bohemian pianist and pedagogue; b. Erdischowitz, June 15, 1826; d. Prague, Oct. 19, 1896. He was a pupil at the Prague Cons.; taught for many years in Moscow; then at the Prague Cons. His pedagogical work for piano, *60 Exercises,* became a standard method in Europe and has been reprinted in many editions.

Pisendel, Johann Georg, German violinist and composer; b. Kadolzburg, Dec. 26, 1687; d. Dresden, Nov. 25, 1755. He studied violin with Torelli at Ansbach, and music theory with Pistocchi; later (1716) took lessons in Venice from Vivaldi, who dedicated several works to him. In 1710 he succeeded Melchior Hoffmann as leader of the Collegium Musicum in Leipzig; then held the post of violinist in the Dresden court chapel orch. (1712); traveled with the Elector of Saxony to Paris, Berlin, Italy, and Vienna (1714–18); in 1728 became concertmaster in Dresden; in 1731 was appointed to a similar post in the orch. of the Dresden Opera. It seems certain that Bach wrote his partitas for unaccompanied violin for Pisendel. In his own works, Pisendel combined characteristics of German, French, and Italian music. Many of his MSS are extant in the Dresden archives, among them 8 violin concertos; 3 concertos for Oboes and String Orch.; 2 concerti grossi; a Symph.; 2 solo pieces for Violin, with Bass. A Violin Concerto is reprinted in Denkmäler Deutscher Tonkunst, 29/30.

Pisk, Paul Amadeus, Austrian-American composer, pedagogue, and musicologist; b. Vienna, May 16, 1893. He studied piano with J. Epstein, composition with Schoenberg, orchestration with Hellmesberger, musicology with Guido Adler; received his D.Mus. with the dissertation *Das Parodieverfahren in den Messen des Jacobus Gallus* (1916). From 1922 to 1934 he taught at the Volkshochschule Volksheim in Vienna; in 1925–26 was instructor in music theory at the New Vienna Cons.; in 1931–33 lectured at the Austro-American Cons. in Mondsee, near Salzburg. He also wrote music criticism for the Socialist newspaper *Wiener Arbeiterzeitung;* with Paul Stefan he founded the progressive music journal *Musikblätter des Anbruch.* He was closely associated with Schoenberg, Alban Berg, and Anton von Webern, and espoused the tenets of the New Vienna School, adopting in many of his own works the methods of composition with 12 tones related only to one another. As the dark cloud of ignorance and barbarity fell on Germany and approached Austria, Pisk left Vienna and emigrated to the U.S., in 1936. He occupied with great honor several teaching posts in America; at the Univ. of Redlands, Calif. (1937–51), the Univ. of Texas in Austin (1951–62), and Washington Univ. in St. Louis (1963–72); he also gave courses at summer sessions at the Univ. of Calif., Los Angeles (1966), the Univ. of Cincinnati (1969), and Dartmouth College (1972). In 1973 he settled in Los Angeles; his 90th birthday was celebrated by his many disciples and admirers in 1983. He continued to compose prolifically, accumulating an impressive catalogue of works, mostly for chamber music. He wrote (with Homer Ulrich) *History of Music and Musical Style* (N.Y., 1963); edited masses by Jacobus Gallus for Denkmäler der Tonkunst in Österreich. A Festschrift, *Paul A. Pisk, Essays in His Honor,* edited by J. Glowacki, was published by the Univ. of Texas Press, Austin, in 1966.

Pistocchi, Francesco Antonio, founder of the famous School of Singing at Bologna; b. Palermo, 1659; d. Bologna, May 13, 1726. Taken to Bologna while very young, he publ. his first work there in 1667, when he was but 8 years old: *Capricci puerili saviamente composti e passeggiati in 40 modi sopra un Basso da un balletto, per il clavicembalo ed altri instrumenti.* His teacher in theory was G.A. Perti; he studied singing under Padre Vastamigli and B. Monari. As a lad he became maestro at the church of San Giovanni in Monte; later a priest in the Oratorian order; was in the service of the Parma court (1686–95); in 1696–99 was Kapellmeister at the court of Ansbach; and returned to Bologna, via Vienna and Venice, about 1700. There he founded, soon after his return, the first school of music in which vocal instruction was given systematically in the several classes. In this school were trained many eminent singers (Bernacchi, Bertolino da Faenza, Minelli, Pio Fabri, etc.); similar institutions soon sprang up in other Italian cities. Pistocchi was twice elected president of the Accademia Filarmonica (1708, 1710).

Piston, Walter (Hamor), outstanding American composer; b. Rockland, Maine, Jan. 20, 1894; d. Belmont, Mass., Nov. 12, 1976. The family name was originally Pistone; his paternal grandfather was Italian. He received his primary education in Boston; studied painting at the Mass. Normal Art School, graduating in 1916; then took piano lessons with Harris Shaw and studied violin with Fiumara,

Theodorowicz, and Winternitz; played in restaurants and places of public entertainment as a youth. During World War I he was in the U.S. Navy; after the Armistice he entered Harvard Univ., graduating in musical subjects summa cum laude in 1924; while at Harvard he conducted concerts of the univ. orch., the Pierian Sodality. For a time he was employed as a draftsman for Boston Elevated Railway. In 1924 he went to Paris on a John Knowles Paine Fellowship, and became a student of Nadia Boulanger; also took courses with Paul Dukas at the Ecole Normale de Musique (1925); returning to the U.S. in 1926, he was appointed to the faculty of Harvard Univ.; in 1944 became a prof. of music; was named prof. emeritus in 1960. As a teacher he was greatly esteemed, not only because of his consummate knowledge of music and pedagogical ability, but also because of his immanent humanity in instructing students whose esthetics differed from his own; among his grateful disciples was Leonard Bernstein. As a composer, Piston followed a cosmopolitan course, adhering to classical forms while extending his harmonic structures toward a maximum of tonal saturation; he was particularly expert in contrapuntal writing. Beginning about 1965, Piston adopted, for the first time, a modified system of 12-tone composition, particularly in initial thematic statements; his Symph. No. 8 and *Variations* for Cello and Orch. are explicitly dodecaphonic. Piston rejected the narrow notion of ethnic Americanism in his music, and stated once that an artist could be as American working in the Library of the Boston Atheneum as roaming the Western prairie; yet he employed upon occasion the syncopated rhythms of jazz. He received Pulitzer Prizes for his Symph. No. 3 and Symph. No. 7, and N.Y. Music Critics Circle Awards for his Symph. No. 2, Viola Concerto, and String Quartet No. 5. He held the degree of D.Mus. *honoris causa* from Harvard Univ.; was elected a member of the National Inst. of Arts and Letters, the American Academy of Arts and Letters, and the American Academy of Arts and Sciences. He traveled little and declined invitations to go to South America and to Russia under the auspices of the State Dept., preferring to live in his house in suburban Belmont, near Boston. His working habits were remarkably methodical; he rarely altered or revised his music once it was put on paper, and his handwriting was calligraphic. With 2 exceptions, he never wrote for voices.

WORKS: FOR THE STAGE: Ballet, *The Incredible Flutist* (Boston Pops, May 30, 1938, Arthur Fiedler conducting; very popular as an orch. suite, first perf. in Pittsburgh, Nov. 22, 1940, Reiner conducting). FOR ORCH.: *Symphonic Piece* (1927; Boston, March 23, 1928, Koussevitzky conducting); 2 suites: No. 1 (1929; Boston, March 28, 1930, composer conducting) and No. 2 (1947–48; Dallas, Feb. 29, 1948, Dorati conducting); Concerto for Orch. (1933; Cambridge, Mass., March 8, 1934, composer conducting); *Prelude and Fugue* (1934; Cleveland, March 12, 1936); 8 symphs.: No. 1 (1937; Boston, April 8, 1938, composer conducting); No. 2 (1943; Washington, D.C., March 5, 1944; received the N.Y. Music Critics Circle Award, 1945); No. 3 (1947; Boston, Jan. 9, 1948, Koussevitzky conducting; received the Pulitzer Prize, 1948); No. 4 (1950; Minneapolis, March 30, 1951, Dorati conducting); No. 5 (1954; commissioned by the Juilliard School of Music in N.Y. for its 50th anniversary and perf. there, Feb. 24, 1956); No. 6 (1955; for the 75th anniversary of the Boston Symph. and perf. by it, Nov. 25, 1955, Munch conducting); No. 7 (1960; Philadelphia, Feb. 10, 1961, Ormandy conducting; won the Pulitzer Prize, 1961); No. 8 (1964–65; Boston, March 5, 1965, Leinsdorf conducting); Concertino for Piano and Chamber Orch. (CBS Radio, N.Y., June 20, 1937, composer conducting); 2 violin concertos: No. 1 (1939; N.Y., March 18, 1940) and No. 2 (Pittsburgh, Oct. 28, 1960); Sinfonietta (1940–41; Boston, Zighera Chamber Orch., March 10, 1941); *Fanfare for the Fighting French* for Brass Ensemble and Percussion (1942); *Prelude and Allegro* for Organ and Strings (CBS Radio, Boston, Aug. 8, 1943; E. Power Biggs, organist); *Fugue on a Victory Tune* (N.Y., Oct. 21, 1944); *Toccata* (Orch. National de France, Munch conducting, Bridgeport, Conn., Oct. 14, 1948); *Fantasy* for English Horn, Harp, and Strings (1952; Boston, Jan. 1, 1954, Munch conducting); *Serenata* (Louisville, Oct. 24, 1956); *Viola Concerto* (1957; Boston, March 7, 1958; received the N.Y. Music Critics Circle Award, 1959); Concerto for 2 Pianos and Orch. (1959; Dartmouth Community Orch., Hanover, N.H., July 4, 1964); *3 New England Sketches* (Detroit Symphony Orch. at the Worcester [Mass.] Music Festival, Oct. 23, 1959, Paray conducting); *Symphonic Prelude* (Cleveland, April 20, 1961, Szell conducting); *Lincoln Center Festival Overture* (Philadelphia Orch., inauguration week of Lincoln Center, N.Y., Sept. 25, 1962); *Capriccio* for Harp and String Orch. (1963; First Festival of American and Spanish Music, Madrid, Oct. 19, 1964; Zabaleta, soloist); *Variations on a Theme by E.B. Hill* (1963); *Pine Tree Fantasy* (Portland, Maine, Nov. 16, 1965); *Variations* for Cello and Orch. (1966; London Symph. Orch., N.Y., March 2, 1967; Rostropovich, soloist; Rozhdestvensky conducting); Clarinet Concerto (Dartmouth College, Hanover, N.H., Aug. 6, 1967); *Ricercare* (1967; N.Y., March 7, 1968); *Fantasia* for Violin and Orch. (1970; Dartmouth College, March 1973); Flute Concerto (1971; Boston, Sept. 21, 1972); *Bicentennial Fanfare* (1975); Concerto for String Quartet, Wind Ensemble, and Percussion (Portland, Oct. 26, 1976). FOR BAND: *Tunbridge Fair: Intermezzo* (1950). CHAMBER MUSIC: *3 Pieces for Flute, Clarinet, and Bassoon* (1926); Flute Sonata (1930); *Suite* for Oboe and Piano (1931); 5 string quartets (1933, 1935, 1947, 1951, 1962; No. 5 received the N.Y. Music Critics Circle Award, 1964); 2 piano trios (1935, 1966); Violin Sonata (1939); *Interlude* for Viola and Piano (1942); Quintet for Flute and Strings (1942); *Partita* for Violin, Viola, and Organ (1944); Sonatina for Violin, and Harpsichord or Piano (1945); *Divertimento* for 9 Instruments (N.Y., May 18, 1946); Duo for Viola and Cello (1949); Piano Quintet (1949); Wind Quintet (1956); Sextet for Strings (1964); Piano Quartet (1964); *Souvenir* for Flute, Viola, and Harp (1967); *Ceremonial Fanfare* for Brass Ensemble (1969; for the Metropolitan Museum of Art); Duo for Cello and Piano (1972); *3 Counterpoints* for Violin, Viola, and Cello (1973).

FOR VOICE: *Carnival Song* for Men's Chorus and 11 Brasses (1938; Harvard Glee Club, Cambridge, Mass., March 7, 1940); *Psalm and Prayer of David* for Chorus, Flute, Clarinet, Bassoon, Violin, Viola, Cello, and Double Bass (1958). FOR PIANO: Sonata (1926); *Passacaglia* (1943); *Improvisation* (1945). FOR ORGAN: *Chromatic Study on B.A.C.H.* (1940).

WRITINGS: *Principles of Harmonic Analysis* (Boston, 1933); *Harmony* (N.Y., 1944; 4th ed., 1978); *Counterpoint* (N.Y., 1947); *Orchestration* (N.Y., 1955).

Pitoni, Giuseppe Ottavio, Italian composer of church music; b. Rieti, March 18, 1657; d. Rome, Feb. 1, 1743. He began music studies at 5, under Pompeo Natale in Rome; at 8 was chorister at S. Giovanni de' Fiorentini, later at the SS. Apostoli, and studied counterpoint under Foggia. In 1673 he was maestro di cappella at Terra di Rotondo; in 1674, at Assisi; in 1676, at Rieti; finally, in 1677, he became maestro at the Collegio di S. Marco in Rome, retaining this post until death, though simultaneously engaged at S. Apollinare (1686), S. Lorenzo in Damaso (1686), S. Giovanni in Laterano (1708–19), and St. Peter's (1719); also in some minor Roman churches. He was an excellent teacher, and taught after the same method by which he himself rose to eminence as a composer, e.g., the writing out in score of Palestrina's works to study his style. Durante, Leo, and Feo were his greatest pupils. As a composer, he cultivated a distinct feature of the Roman school, the writing in many parts.

Pitt, Percy, English conductor and composer; b. London, Jan. 4, 1870; d. there, Nov. 23, 1932. He studied in Germany with Jadassohn and Reinecke at the Leipzig Cons. and with Rheinberger at the Akademie der Tonkunst in Munich. Returning to England in 1893, he became active primarily as a theater conductor; was conductor of the Beecham Opera Co. (1915–18), artistic director of the British National Opera Co. (1920–24), and music director of the British Broadcasting Corp. (1922–30). He wrote some instrumental music; his *Ballade* for Violin and Orch. (1900) was performed by Ysaÿe.

Pixis, Johann Peter, German pianist; b. Mannheim, Feb. 10, 1788; d. Baden-Baden, Dec. 22, 1874. Of a musical family (his father and his brother were good musicians), he received his primary education at home; went to Munich in 1809, and to Paris in 1823; established himself as a teacher, and was greatly esteemed in the Paris musical world. In 1840 he settled in Baden-Baden, where he continued to teach.

WORKS: Operas: *Almazinde, oder Die Höhle Sesam* (Vienna, April 11, 1820); *Bibiana, oder Die Kapelle im Walde* (Aachen, Oct. 8, 1829); etc.; Piano Concerto; Piano Quartet; Piano Quintet; String Quintet; 7 piano trios; sonatas, variations, transcriptions, etc., for piano solo; altogether about 150 opus numbers. Together with Liszt, Chopin, Thalberg, Czerny, and Herz, he wrote *Hexaméron* (a series of brilliant variations on the march from Bellini's opera *I Puritani*).

Pizzetti, Ildebrando, eminent Italian composer; b. Parma, Sept. 20, 1880; d. Rome, Feb. 13, 1968. He studied piano with his father, Odvardo Pizzetti, in Parma and composition with Tebaldini at the Cons. of Parma, graduating in 1901; then devoted himself to composition and teaching; was on the faculty of the Cons. of Parma (1907–8); then of the Cons. of Florence (1908–24), where he became director in 1917; in 1924–36 was director of the Milan Cons.; then taught at the Santa Cecilia Academy in Rome (1936–58); from 1947 to 1952 was also its president. In 1914 he founded (with G. Bastianelli) in Florence a modernistic periodical, pointedly named *Dissonanza,* to promote the cause of new music. In 1930 he made a trip to the U.S. to attend the performance of his *Rondo veneziano,* conducted by Toscanini with the N.Y. Phil.; in 1931 Pizzetti conducted his opera *Fra Gherardo* at the Teatro Colón in Buenos Aires. Pizzetti's music represents the Romantic trend in modern Italy; in his many works for the theater, he created the modern counterpart of medieval mystery plays; the mystical element is very strong in his own texts for his operas. He employed astringent chromatic harmony, but the mainstream of his melody flows along pure diatonic lines. WORKS: OPERAS: *Fedra* (Milan, March 20, 1915); *Debora e Jaele* (1915–21; Milan, Dec. 16, 1922); *Lo Straniero* (1922–25; Rome, April 29, 1930); *Fra Gherardo* (1925–27; Milan, May 16, 1928; Metropolitan Opera, N.Y., March 21, 1929; his most famous work); *Orsèolo* (Florence, May 5, 1935); *L'Oro* (1938–42; Milan, Jan. 2, 1947); *Vanna Lupa* (Florence, May 4, 1949); *Ifigenia* (1950; Turin Radio, Oct. 3, 1950; first stage perf., Florence, May 9, 1951); *Cagliostro* (La Scala, Milan, Jan. 24, 1953); *La Figlia di Jorio* (Naples, Dec. 4, 1954); *Assassinio nella cattedrale,* after T.S. Eliot's *Murder in the Cathedral* (La Scala, Milan, March 1, 1958; highly acclaimed); *Il calzare d'argento,* sacred play (La Scala, Milan, March 23, 1961); *Clitennestra,* music drama (La Scala, Milan, March 1, 1965). INCIDENTAL MUSIC: To Gabriele d'Annunzio's tragedy *La Nave* (1905) and *La Pisanella* (Paris, June 11, 1913); to *La sacra rappresentazione di Abram e d'Isaac,* mystery play (Florence, 1917; expanded and produced in Turin, March 11, 1926); to *Agamemnon* by Aeschylus (Greek Theater, Syracuse, 1930); to *The Trachiniae* by Sophocles (Greek Theater, Syracuse, 1936); to *As You Like It* by Shakespeare (Florence, May, 1938). CHORAL WORKS: *Requiem* (1922); *De profundis* (1938); *Cantico di gloria* for Treble Chorus, 24 Wind Instruments, 2 Pianos, and Percussion (1948). FOR ORCH.: *Ouverture per una farsa tragica* (1911); *Concerto dell'estate* (N.Y., Feb. 28, 1929, Toscanini conducting); *Rondo veneziano* (N.Y., Feb. 27, 1930; as a ballet, La Scala, Milan, Jan. 8, 1931); Cello Concerto (Venice, Sept. 11, 1934); Symph. in A (1940); Violin Concerto (Rome, Dec. 9, 1945); *Canzone di beni perduti* (Venice, Sept. 4, 1950). CHAMBER MUSIC: 2 string quartets (1906, 1933); Piano Trio (1925); Violin Sonata (1919); Cello Sonata (1921). FOR PIANO: *Da un autunno già lontano* (1911; 3 pieces); *Sonata 1942;* songs: *Tre*

liriche (1904); *Sera d'inverno* (1906); *I Pastori*, to a poem by Gabriele d'Annunzio (1908; his most remarkable song); *La Madre al figlio lontano* (1910); *Erotica* (1911); *2 canti popolari greci* (1912); *3 sonetti di Petrarca* (1922); *E il mio dolore io canto* (1940). Also, transcriptions of madrigals by Gesualdo, of Veracini's sonatas for violin and continuo, etc.

Pizzi, Emilio, Italian composer; b. Verona, Feb. 1, 1861; d. Milan, Nov. 27, 1940. He studied at the Instituto Musicale at Bergamo and at the Cons. of Milan (with Ponchielli and Bazzini); received first prize for his opera *Lina* (1885); in 1897, was appointed director of the Instituto Musicale at Bergamo; from 1900 lived for some time in London. WORKS: Operas: *Guglielmo Ratcliff* (Bologna, Oct. 31, 1889); *Gabriella* (world premiere, Boston, Nov. 25, 1893, with Adelina Patti in the title role); *La Rosalba* (Turin, May 31, 1899); *Vendetta* (in German, Cologne, Dec. 1, 1906; in Italian, as *Ivania,* Bergamo, Sept. 14, 1926); comic opera in Eng., *Bric-à-Brac Will* (London, 1895); *Messa solenne* for Soli, Chorus, and Orch.; Requiem; violin pieces; piano pieces; songs.

Plaidy, Louis, famous German piano teacher; b. Wermsdorf, Nov. 28, 1810; d. Grimma, March 3, 1874. He began his professional career as a violinist, and performed in public in Dresden and Leipzig; at the same time he took piano lessons from Agthe, and became greatly proficient as a pianist, so that Mendelssohn engaged him in 1843 as a piano teacher at the Leipzig Cons. Plaidy concentrated on the technical problems of piano pedagogy; taught at the Leipzig Cons. until 1865; then continued to give private lessons. He publ. a number of instructive piano studies which are still widely used; his *Technische Studien für das Pianoforte-Spiel* is a standard manual; he also publ. a booklet, *Der Klavierlehrer* (1874; British ed. as *The Pianoforte Teacher's Guide;* American ed., trans. by J.S. Dwight, as *The Piano-Teacher*).

Plamenac, Dragan, eminent Croatian-American musicologist; b. Zagreb, Feb. 8, 1895; d. Ede, the Netherlands, March 15, 1983. He studied jurisprudence at the Univ. of Zagreb and the Univ. of Vienna; then took courses in composition with Franz Schreker at the Vienna Academy of Music and with Vítězslav Novák in Prague. In 1919 he went to Paris and attended lectures at the Sorbonne given by André Pirro; then had a seminar with Guido Adler at the Univ. of Vienna, receiving his Ph.D. there in 1925 with the dissertation *Johannes Ockeghem als Motetten- und Chansonkomponist.* From 1928–39 he taught at the Univ. of Zagreb; after the outbreak of World War II, he came to the U.S., becoming a naturalized American citizen in 1946. In 1947 he received a Guggenheim fellowship; then taught at the Univ. of Illinois, Urbana (1955–63). Plamenac's chief accomplishment was his painstaking and fruitful research into the sources of the music of the Renaissance. He prepared a major edition of the works of Ockeghem in the *Publikationen älterer Musik,* Jg. I/2 (Leipzig, 1927); a 2nd ed., revised in 1959, was publ. in N.Y. as *Masses I–VIII* in the *Collected Works,* I; *Masses and Mass Sections IX–XVI* appeared as vol. II (N.Y., 1947; 2nd ed., 1966).

Plançon, Pol (-Henri), famous French bass; b. Fumay, June 12, 1851; d. Paris, Aug. 12, 1914. He was destined by his parents for a commercial career in Paris, but showed a natural vocal ability, and began to study singing with Sbriglia and Duprez; made his operatic debut in Lyons (1877); then appeared in Paris (Feb. 11, 1880); after a season in Monte Carlo, he made a highly successful appearance at the Paris Opéra as Méphistophélès in Gounod's *Faust* (June 25, 1883); sang that role more than 100 times during his 10 seasons at the Opéra, and was regarded as unrivaled in his dramatic delivery and vocal power. On June 3, 1891, he sang Méphistophélès in London; his American debut took place at the Metropolitan Opera House on Nov. 29, 1893, as Jupiter in Gounod's *Philemon et Baucis.* He then resigned from the Paris Opéra and remained a member of the Metropolitan Opera until his retirement in 1908. He had an imposing physique, mobile features, and an innate acting ability. His repertoire consisted of about 50 roles in French, Italian, German, and Eng. In some operas he sang more than one part, as in *Roméo et Juliette* (Capulet and Friar), *Aida* (Ramfis and the King), *Les Huguenots* (St.-Bris and Marcel), etc. Of Wagnerian roles, he sang the Landgrave, King Henry, and Pogner.

Planquette, Jean-Robert, French composer of operettas; b. Paris, July 31, 1848; d. there, Jan. 28, 1903. He studied at the Paris Cons. with Duprato; wrote chansonnettes and "saynètes" for cafés-concerts in Paris; then composed a one-act operetta, *Paille d'avoine* (March 12, 1874), and others. He achieved his first great success with the production of *Les Cloches de Corneville,* a comic opera in 3 acts, at the Folies-Dramatiques (April 19, 1877); it was performed for the 1,000th time there in 1886, and became one of the most popular works of its genre; in Eng., it was given as *The Chimes of Normandy* (N.Y., Oct. 22, 1877; London, Feb. 23, 1878). Other operettas were *Le Chevalier Gaston* (Monte Carlo, Feb. 8, 1879); *Rip Van Winkle* (London, Oct. 14, 1882; very successful); *Nell Gwynne* (London, Feb. 7, 1884); *Surcouf* (Oct. 6, 1887; in Eng. as *Paul Jones*); *La Cocarde tricolore* (Paris, Feb. 12, 1892); *Le Talisman* (Paris, Jan. 20, 1893); *Panurge* (Paris, Nov. 22, 1895); *Mam'zelle Quat'Sous* (Paris, Nov. 5, 1897). A posthumous operetta, *Le Paradis de Mahomet* (orchestrated by Louis Ganne), was produced at the Variétés in Paris on May 15, 1906.

Plantade, Charles-Henri, French composer; b. Pontoise, Oct. 14, 1764; d. Paris, Dec. 18, 1839. As a child, he studied singing and the cello in the Royal School for the "pages de musique"; afterward he took lessons with Honoré Langlé (theory), Hüllmandel (piano), and Petrini (harp). In 1797 he became a singing teacher at the Campan Inst. at St.-Denis,

where Hortense de Beauharnais, the future Queen of the Netherlands, was his pupil. He subsequently was in the service of Queen Hortense as her representative in Paris; was a prof. at the Paris Cons. from 1799 to 1807, and again in 1815–16 and 1818–28. From 1812 to 1815 he also held the post of maître de chambre at the Paris Opéra. He received the ribbon of the Legion of Honor from Louis XVIII (1814); from 1816 was music master of the Royal Chapel. Losing his various positions after the revolution of 1830, he retired to Batignolles. He wrote several operas, of which *Le Mari de circonstances* (Opéra-Comique, March 18, 1813) was the most successful; other operas include *Les 2 Sœurs* (May 22, 1792); *Les Souliers mordores* (May 18, 1793); *Au plus brave la plus belle* (Oct. 5, 1794); *Palma, ou Le Voyage en Grèce* (Aug. 22, 1797); *Romagnesi* (Sept. 3, 1799); *Le Roman* (Nov. 12, 1800); *Zoé, ou La Pauvre Petite* (July 3, 1800); *Lisez Plutarque* (Spring 1800); *Bayard à la ferté, ou Le Siège de Mezières* (Oct. 13, 1811). He further composed masses, motets, etc., for the Chapelle Royale; publ. 20 sets of *romances,* 3 books of vocal duets (nocturnes), and a Harp Sonata.

Planté, Francis, French pianist; b. Orthez, Basses-Pyrénées, March 2, 1839; d. St. Avit, near Mont-de-Marsan, Dec. 19, 1934. From 1849 he was a pupil of Marmontel at the Paris Cons.; won first prize after 7 months' tuition. After a course in harmony in Bazin's class (1853), he retired for private study for 10 years, and then reappeared as a pianist of finished technique and style. About 1900 he suddenly vanished from concert life, vowing that he would "never be seen again in public." He created a sensation in 1915 when he was heard again in several concerts in Paris; but, in order to keep his strange vow, he was hidden from the view of the audience by a screen.

Plaschke, Friedrich (original name, **Bedřich Plaška**), Czech bass-baritone; b. Jaroměř, Jan. 7, 1875; d. Prague, Feb. 4, 1952. He studied with Leontine von Dotscher and Ottilie Sklenář-Mala in Prague, and then with Karl Scheidemantel in Dresden; made his debut with the Dresden Court (later State) Opera as the Herald in *Lohengrin* in 1900; was on its roster until 1937; during his tenure there, he created the following roles in operas by Richard Strauss: Pöschel in *Feuersnot,* the first Nazarene in *Salome,* Altair in *Die aegyptische Helena,* Waldner in *Arabella,* and Sir Morosus in *Die schweigsame Frau.* He made many guest appearances at Vienna and Munich; also sang at Bayreuth, at Covent Garden in London, and in the U.S. with the German Opera Co. in 1923–24.

Plato, great Greek philosopher (427–347 B.C.). He formulated in his *Timaeus* a system of musical harmony, eruditely interpreted by Th.-Henri Martin in his *Etudes sur le Timée de Platon* (Paris, 1841). Also see R. von Westphal, in his *Harmonik und Melopöie der Griechen* (Leipzig, 1865); von Jan in "Die Harmonie der Sphären" (in *Philogus,* vol. LII); and H. Abert's *Die Lehre vom Ethos in der griechischen*

Musik (Leipzig, 1899). Plato's thoughts on music are collected in an essay by Deyk in Weber's *Cäcilia* (1828). Plato likened the movements of music to those of the soul, whose development may therefore be influenced by musical art.

Platti, Giovanni, Italian composer; b. Padua, July 9, 1697; d. Würzburg, Jan. 11, 1763. He was attached to the Würzburg court from 1724 to 1761; was active there as a tenor, violinist, composer, and teacher; was regarded by some music historians as the first composer to employ the classical sonata form, but this contention is debatable.

Playford, Henry, English music publisher, son of **John Playford;** b. London, May 5, 1657; d. there, c.1707. He continued his father's trade; his most important publications were *The Theatre of Musick* (with R. Carr; 4 books, 1685–87, described as "the newest and best songs"); *Banquet of Music* (6 books, 1688–92); Purcell's *Orpheus Britannicus* (1698–1702) and his *Ten Sonatas,* with a *Te Deum* and *Jubilate* for St. Cecilia's Day (1697); Blow's *Amphion Anglicus* (1700); and an ode on Purcell's death (1695).

Playford, John, English music publisher; b. Norfolk, 1623; d. London, Nov. 1686. He was in business for 37 years (1647–84); his publishing firm was responsible for the most important music editions of the 17th century; he publ. *The Dancing Master* (1651; 12th ed., 1703; modern ed. by M. Dean-Smith, London, 1958); Hilton's *Catch that catch can* (1652); *Musick's Recreation on the Lyra-Violl* (1652; facsimile ed. by N. Dolmetsch, London, 1960); *Select Musical Ayres and Dialogues* (1653); *Briefe Introduction to the Skill of Musick for Song and Violl* (1654; enlarged ed., 1655, with an essay on "The Art of Descant" by Dr. Thomas Campion, which was revised by Purcell in the 10th ed. of 1683; this very popular work, written by John Playford himself, ran through 19 numbered eds. up to 1730, besides 6 unnumbered eds.); *Psalms and Hymns in Solemn Musick of four parts* (1671); *The Whole Book of Psalms, with the usual Spiritual Song* (1673; 20th ed., 1757); *The Musical Companion* (1673; Book I, catches and rounds; Book II, dialogues, glees, ayres, and songs); *Choice Ayres, Songs and Dialogues to be sung to the theorbo* (5 books, 1676–84); *Musick's Delight on the Cithern* (1666); *The Division-Violin* (variations for violin over a basso ostinato; 2nd ed., 1685).

Plaza, Juan Bautista, Venezuelan composer; b. Caracas, July 19, 1898; d. there, Jan. 1, 1964. He went to Rome in 1920 to study at the Pontifical Inst. of Sacred Music; upon returning to Venezuela, became organist of the Cathedral of Caracas. He wrote a number of sacred choral works; also symph. poems: *El picacho abrupto, Vigilia, Campanas de Pascua, Las horas,* etc.; *Fuga criolla* for Orch.; *Sonatina venezolana* for Piano; songs.

Pleyel, Camille, French pianist, son of **Ignaz**

Pleyel; b. Strasbourg, Dec. 18, 1788; d. Paris, May 4, 1855. He was a pupil of his father; had some success as a composer, but is chiefly noteworthy as a piano manufacturer, entering his father's firm in 1815. Kalkbrenner was his partner for a time; Auguste Wolff, his successor. His wife, **Marie-Félicité-Denise** (b. Paris, Sept. 4, 1811; d. St.-Josse-ten-Noode, March 30, 1875), was also a pianist; she was a pupil of Henri Herz, Moscheles, and Kalkbrenner. In her 15th year, as Mlle. Moke, her virtuosity created a sensation in Belgium, Austria, Germany, and Russia. Before her marriage, Berlioz was in love with her (1830). In 1848–72 she was a prof. of piano at the Brussels Cons.

Pleyel, Ignaz Joseph, remarkable pianist, composer, and piano manufacturer; b. Ruppertsthal, near Vienna, June 18, 1757; d. on his estate near Paris, Nov. 14, 1831. He was the 24th of 38 children in the impoverished family of a schoolteacher; however, he received sufficient education, including music lessons, to qualify for admittance to the class of Wanhal; thanks to the generosity of a princely patron he was apprenticed to Haydn, with whom he lived for 5 years, and was later enabled to go to Rome. In 1783 he became 2nd Kapellmeister at the Strasbourg Cathedral; was advanced to the rank of first Kapellmeister in 1789 but lost his position during the turbulent times of the French Revolution. He conducted the "Professional Concerts" in London during the 1791–92 season, and honored his teacher Haydn by playing a work of Haydn at his opening concert (Feb. 13, 1792). After several years he returned to Strasbourg to liquidate his estate; in 1795 he went to Paris, where he opened a music store which was in business until 1834, and in 1807 founded a piano factory, which manufactured famous French pianos; the firm eventually became known as Pleyel et Cie., and continued to prosper for over a century and a half. The name Pleyel is mainly known through his piano manufacture, but he was a prolific and an extremely competent composer. His productions are so close in style to those of Haydn that specialists are still inclined to attribute certain works in Haydn's catalogues to Pleyel. He composed fully 60 symphs., of which 33 were publ.; more than 60 string quartets, 8 instrumental concertos, and numerous duos, trios, and quintets for strings, as well as 6 quartets for flute and strings, a number of piano and violin sonatas, some songs, and 2 operas: *Ifigenia in Aulide* (produced in Naples on May 30, 1785) and *Die Fee Urgele* for puppet theater, staged in Eszterháza in Nov. 1776. The attribution of Haydn's *6 Feldpartien* to Pleyel remains moot. As a music publisher, Pleyel brought out an Eng. trans. of J.L. Dussek's *Klavierschule,* under the title *Instructions on the Art of Playing the Pianoforte or Harpsichord* (London, 1796); in French as *Méthode pour piano-forte par Pleyel et Dussek;* a German edition appeared in Leipzig in 1804 under Pleyel's name.

Plishka, Paul (Peter), American bass; b. Old Forge, Pa., Aug. 28, 1941. He studied at Montclair,

N.J., State College; from 1961–65 was a member of the Paterson (N.J.) Lyric Opera; in 1965 he joined the Metropolitan Opera National Co. and sang with it on tour. On June 27, 1967, he made his Metropolitan Opera debut in a concert performance at the Botanical Gardens in the Bronx as the Uncle-Priest in *Madama Butterfly;* he first sang on the Metropolitan's stage as the Monk in *La Gioconda* on Sept. 21, 1967; remained on its roster for many years.

Plowright, Rosalind, English soprano; b. Worksop, May 21, 1949. She studied at the Royal Manchester College of Music; in 1979 she won the International Competition for young singers in Sofia, Bulgaria. She made her debut as Miss Jessel in Britten's opera *The Turn of the Screw* with the English National Opera in 1979; later sang Desdemona and Elisabeth in *Mary Stuart* there. She made her Covent Garden debut as Ortlinde in 1980, and then sang Donna Elvira there in 1983. She subsequently sang Abigaille in Sofia, Bulgaria; Ariadne and Alceste in Bern; Aida, Amelia, and Lenora in Frankfurt; Donna Anna in Munich; and Suor Angelica at La Scala in Milan. She made her American debut with Riccardo Muti and the Philadelphia Orch. in 1982, and then sang in *Il Corsaro* in San Diego.

Plutarch, famous Greek writer; b. Chaeronea, Boeotia, A.D. 50; d. there, 120. Among his treatises ("Moralia"), one, *De musica,* contains important, historical data concerning music (Latin trans. by R. Volkmann; German trans., with parallel Greek text, and commentary by R. Westphal, 1865; also by Weil and Reinach, with commentary, 1900).

Pocci, Franz, Graf von, composer; b. (of an old Italian noble family) Munich, March 7, 1807; d. there, May 7, 1876. Possessing versatile talents, he wrote plays with music for a puppet theater in Munich, for which he also designed the scenery. He was at his best in pieces for children (*Blumenlieder, Bildertöne für Klavier, Soldatenlieder, Jägerlieder, Alte und neue Kinderlieder,* etc.). His 2 piano sonatas were praised by Schumann for their poetic expression and fine Romantic spirit. An opera, *Der Alchemist,* was produced in Munich (1840); his grandson F. Pocci publ. a collection, *Franz Poccis Lustiges Komödienbüchlein* (Munich, 1921).

Pochon, Alfred, Swiss violinist; b. Yverdon, July 30, 1878; d. Lutry, Feb. 26, 1959. He made his first public appearance at the age of 11; then went to Liège to study with César Thomson, who engaged him as 2nd violin in his string quartet. In 1902 the philanthropist E. de Coppet asked Pochon to organize a string quartet, later to become famous as the Flonzaley Quartet, so named after Coppet's summer residence near Lausanne; Pochon remained a member, playing 2nd violin, until it was disbanded in 1929. In 1938 Pochon returned to Switzerland; was director of the Cons. of Lausanne until 1957, when he retired. He publ. *A Progressive Method of String-Quartet Playing* (N.Y., 1924).

Poglietti, Alessandro, Italian composer. From 1661 he was court organist in Vienna; was killed by the Turks in July 1683 at the siege of Vienna. His compositions include 12 ricercari, suites for harpsichord (*On the Hungarian Rebellion, Nightingale Suite,* etc.), and other instrumental pieces, some of which appear in *Toccates et Suites,* publ. by Roger (Amsterdam); also church music. H. Botstiber publ. some reprints in Denkmäler der Tonkunst in Österreich, 27 (13.ii); his 12 ricercari are publ. in *Die Orgel,* II/5–6 (Lippstadt, 1957).

Pogorelich, Ivo, talented Yugoslav pianist; b. Belgrade, Oct. 20, 1958. He was sent to Moscow to study; was a student of **Aliza Kezeradze** at the Moscow Cons.; they were married in 1980. In 1978 he won the Casa Grande Competition in Terni, Italy, and in 1980 won a prize at the International Music Competition in Montreal. He became the center of international controversy when he was eliminated by the jury of the Chopin Competition in Warsaw before the final rounds; one of the members of the jury, Martha Argerich, resigned in protest and declared that Pogorelich was a "genius"; the Warsaw Music Society awarded him a special prize, and his career skyrocketed. In 1981 he played in London and N.Y., where curiosity enhanced his undoubted merits; his playing reflects his Russian education, particularly in his uninhibited romantic élan, and a most impressive technical mastery of the music.

Pohl, Carl Ferdinand, German writer on music; b. Darmstadt, Sept. 6, 1819; d. Vienna, April 28, 1887. During his stay in London (1863–66) he gathered all available facts concerning the residence there of Mozart and Haydn, embodying this information in his publication *Mozart und Haydn in London* (2 vols., 1867). Pohl also began an extended biography of Haydn, but publ. only one vol. (in 2 parts, 1875, 1882); the work was finished by Hugo Botstiber. Other publications: *International Exhibition of 1862. Cursory Notices on the History of the Glass Harmonica* (London, 1862); an interesting historical review, *Die Gesellschaft der Musikfreunde ... und ihr Conservatorium* (1871); *Denkschrift aus Anlass des 100 jährigen Bestehens der Tonkünstler-Sozietät in Wien* (1871); *Bibliographie der Musiksammelwerke des 16. und 17. Jahrhunderts* (with R. Eitner and A. Lagerberg; 1877).

Pohlig, Karl, German conductor; b. Teplitz, Feb. 10, 1858; d. Braunschweig, June 17, 1928. A pupil of Liszt in Weimar, Pest, and Rome, he began his career as a pianist, touring Germany, Austria, Russia, Scandinavia, and Italy; became first Kapellmeister at Graz, then assistant conductor to Mahler at the Vienna Court Opera, and conductor at Covent Garden (1897, 1898); until 1900, was first Kapellmeister at the Hoftheater in Coburg; from 1900–1907, occupied the same post at the Hoftheater in Stuttgart, and was conductor of the symph. concerts; in 1907, was engaged as conductor of the Philadelphia Orch.; directed it for 5 seasons, emphasizing the German repertoire, and particularly Wagner, of whom he was an impassioned admirer.

Pokorný, Franz Xaver, Czech composer; b. König-stadt (Mestec Kralove), Dec. 20, 1728; d. Regensburg, July 2, 1794. He joined the court orch. in Oettingen-Wallerstein in 1753; then went to Mannheim, where he studied with Stamitz, Holzbauer, and Richter, returning to Wallerstein after a few months. In 1766 he became a court musician in Thurn and Taxis. In the light of recent research, Pokorný appears as a pioneer in symph. writings; fully 165 symphs. have been discovered that are probably his; they are all written in the characteristic style of the Mannheim School. The Symph. in E-flat, often credited to G.M. Monn, has been definitely identified as a work by Pokorný.

Pokrass, Dimitri, Russian composer of popular music; b. Kiev, Nov. 7, 1899. He studied piano at the St. Petersburg Cons. (1913–17); in 1919 he joined the Soviet cavalry during the Civil War, and wrote the song *The Red Cavalry.* This was the first of a series of many songs that have acquired great popularity, among them *If War Comes Tomorrow* (1938), *March of the Tank Brigade, Farewell,* etc. He also wrote music for films.

Poldini, Ede (Eduard), Hungarian composer; b. Budapest, June 13, 1869; d. Corseaux, Switzerland, June 28, 1957. He studied at the Budapest Cons., and later with Mandyczewski (theory) and Julius Epstein (piano) in Vienna. In 1908 he went to live at Vevey. In 1935 he received the order of the Hungarian Cross; in 1948 was awarded the Hungarian Pro Arte Prize.
  WORKS: Comic operas: *The Vagabond and the Princess* (Budapest, Oct. 17, 1903); *The Carnival Marriage* (Budapest, Feb. 16, 1924; produced in London under the title *Love Adrift,* 1926); *Himfy* (Budapest, 1938). He wrote in all 156 opus numbers, most of them for piano; his *Poupée valsante* became an international favorite; other popular piano pieces are *Arlequinades, Morceaux pittoresques, Images, Moments musicaux, Marionnettes,* etc.

Poldowski (pen name of **Irene Regine Wieniawska;** by marriage, **Lady Dean Paul**), Polish-English composer; b. Brussels, March 18, 1879; d. London, Jan. 28, 1932. She was a daughter of the Polish violinist **Henryk Wieniawski;** her mother was an Englishwoman. She studied at the Brussels Cons. with Gevaert, and later in London with Percy Pitt; married Sir Aubrey Dean Paul; took additional courses in composition with Gédalge and Vincent d'Indy in Paris; began writing songs to French words, in the impressionist style; set to music 21 poems by Paul Verlaine, and 8 poems by others; her songs have been frequently performed at recitals. She also composed *Caledonian Market,* a suite of 8 pieces for Piano; *Berceuse de l'enfant mourant* for Violin and Piano; *Tango* for Violin and Piano; *Suite miniature de chansons à danser* for Woodwind Instruments; 2 symph. sketches (*Nocturnes* and *Tenements*); and an operetta, *Laughter.*

Polignac, Armande de, French composer; b. Paris, Jan. 8, 1876; d. Neauphle-le-Vieux (Seine-et-Oise), April 29, 1962. She studied with Gabriel Fauré and Vincent d'Indy; composed the operas *Morgane* and *L'Hypocrite sanctifié;* a dramatic scene, *Judith de Béthulie* (Paris Opéra, March 23, 1916); *La Source lointaine,* Persian ballet (Paris, 1913); *Les 1,001 Nuits,* Arabian ballet (Paris, 1914); *Chimères,* Greek ballet (Paris Opéra, June 10, 1923); *Urashima,* Japanese ballet; also a Chinese ballet for Small Orch., *La Recherche de la vérité; Petite suite pour le clavecin* (1939).

Polin, Claire, American flutist and composer; b. Philadelphia, Jan. 1, 1926. She studied flute with William Kincaid and composition with Vincent Persichetti in Philadelphia, Peter Mennin at the Juilliard School of Music in N.Y., and Roger Sessions and Lukas Foss at the Berkshire Music Center in Tanglewood; held the degrees of B.Mus. (1948), M.Mus. (1950), and D.Mus. (1955); from 1949 to 1964 taught flute playing and composition at the Philadelphia Musical Academy, and from 1958, at Rutgers Univ. A versatile scholar, she wrote and lectured on her ancestral Welsh music, traveled and played flute in distant lands, including Israel, Russia, and Japan; advanced bold theories, suggesting, for example, a link between Hebrew and Welsh legends, and composed industriously in a cogently modernistic manner, often with recursive ancient modalities.

Pollak, Egon, Czech-born Austrian opera conductor; b. Prague, May 3, 1879; d. there (of a heart attack during a performance), June 14, 1933. He studied with Knittl at the Prague Cons.; then was engaged in a lifelong career as an opera conductor; from 1901 to 1905 he was assistant to Leo Blech at the Prague Opera; then was principal conductor at the Bremen Opera (1905–10) and at the Leipzig Opera (1910–12). In 1912 he was appointed principal conductor at the Frankfurt Opera. In May and June of 1914 he conducted Wagner's repertoire in Paris and London; in 1915 went to the U.S., where he presented complete cycles of the *Ring des Nibelungen* at the Chicago Lyric Opera during 2 seasons, 1915–17. In 1917 he was able to leave the U.S. with the Austrian diplomatic legation as America entered the war. From 1917 to 1931 he served as Generalmusikdirektor at the Hamburg Opera. In 1928 he conducted German opera in Rio de Janeiro and at the Teatro Colón in Buenos Aires. In 1929–32 he led 2 seasons at the Chicago Opera for 13 weeks during each season. In the winter of 1932 he filled guest engagements in Russia; in 1933 conducted the opera season in Cairo and Alexandria with the ensemble of the Vienna State Opera. On June 14, 1933, he led a performance of *Fidelio,* with Elisabeth Rethberg in the title role, at the Prague Spring Festival, but collapsed and died during the first act.

Pollarolo, (Giovanni) Antonio, Italian composer, son of **Carlo Francesco Pollarolo;** b. Brescia (baptized, Nov. 12), 1676; d. Venice, May 30, 1746. He studied with his father, and became his assistant at San Marco in Venice in 1702; in 1723 he was 2nd maestro di cappella there; in 1740, first maestro. He wrote the operas *Aristeo* (Venice, 1700; not extant) and *Leucippo e Teonoe* (1719), among others.

Pollarolo, Carlo Francesco, Italian organist and composer; b. Brescia, 1653; d. Venice, Feb. 7, 1723. He was a pupil of Legrenzi. In 1665 he became a chorister at San Marco in Venice; in 1690, 2nd organist; in 1092, 2nd maestro di cappella.
 WORKS: Oratorios: *Jefte, La Rosinda,* and *Jesabel;* over 85 operas, among them: *La forza della virtù* (1693); *Ottone* (1694); *Gl'Inganni felici* (1696); *Il Faramondo* (1699); *Semiramide* (1713); *Ariodante* (1716). His *Sonata per organo o cembalo* is reprinted in Torchi's *L'arte musicale in Italia* (vol. III).

Pollikoff, Max, American violinist, conductor, and music director; b. Newark, N.J., 1902; d. New York, May 13, 1984. He made his debut as a concert violinist in 1923, in a conventional program, but later devoted himself to contemporary music; he organized the series "Music of Our Time" in 1954, giving periodic concerts at the 92nd Street Y in N.Y.; the series continued until 1974; its programs included works by Charles Ives, Leonard Bernstein, Roger Sessions, Norman Dello Joio, and John Cage.

Pollini, Francesco (Giuseppe), Austrian pianist; b. Laibach (Ljubljana), of Italian parents, March 25, 1762; d. Milan, Sept. 17, 1846. He was a pupil of Mozart (who dedicated a violin rondo to him) at Vienna; later of Zingarelli at Milan, where he was appointed a prof. of piano shortly after the opening of the Cons. (1809). He was the first to write piano music on 3 staves, a method imitated by Liszt, Thalberg, and others; a specimen of this style is one of his *32 Esercizi in forma di toccata* (op. 42), a central melody surrounded by passagework for both hands. He publ. a method and many pieces for piano; wrote an opera buffa, *La cassetta nei boschi* (Milan, Feb. 25, 1798).

Pollini, Maurizio, greatly talented Italian pianist; b. Milan, Jan. 5, 1942. He began to study piano as a child at the Verdi Cons. in Milan with Carlo Vidusso and Lonati; gave his first public recital when he was 11; won 2nd prize at the Geneva International Competition when he was 15. In 1960, at the age of 18, he won first prize at the International Chopin Competition in Warsaw, the youngest of 89 contestants. Returning to Italy, he took lessons with Benedetti Michelangeli. On Nov. 1, 1968, he made his U.S. debut in a concert at Carnegie Hall in N.Y.; subsequently appeared with several American orchs.; also gave solo recitals. Because of his signal success in winning the Warsaw Prize, he became known as a Chopin specialist, but he later enlarged his repertoire to include also the moderns. What distinguishes Pollini is his total dedication to music; he seems devoid of a personal desire to excel; his technical equipment is of the highest caliber, but he does not make virtuosity a goal in itself. He is a

paragon of modern intellectual pianism.

Ponc, Miroslav, Czech violinist, conductor, and composer; b. Vysoké Mýto, Dec. 2, 1902; d. Prague, April 1, 1976. He studied organ with Wiedermann at the Prague Cons. (1920–22) and quarter-tone composition with Alois Hába (1922–24); then went to Berlin and took lessons with Schoenberg. Upon returning to Prague, he studied violin with Josef Suk at the Cons., graduating in 1930; subsequently took lessons in conducting with Scherchen in Strasbourg (1933). After the war he was active mainly as a theater conductor in Prague; wrote a number of scores of incidental music for plays.

Ponce, Manuel María, distinguished Mexican composer; b. Fresnillo, Dec. 8, 1882; d. Mexico City, April 24, 1948. He studied piano with his older sister; in 1904 went to Europe, where he took lessons in composition with Enrico Bossi at Bologna and in piano with Martin Krause in Berlin. Upon his return to Mexico, he taught piano at the National Cons. He gave a concert of his compositions in Mexico on July 7, 1912, which included a Piano Concerto. During World War I he lived in N.Y., and in Havana; then went to Paris for additional study, and took lessons with Paul Dukas. His contact with French music wrought a radical change in his style of composition; his later works are more polyphonic in structure and more economical in form. He possessed a great gift of melody; one of his songs, *Estrellita*, became a universal favorite, and was often mistaken for a folk song. In 1941 he made a tour in South America, conducting his own works. He was the first Mexican composer of the 20th century to employ an identifiably modern musical language; his place in the history of Mexican music is a very important one. His works are often performed in Mexico; a concert hall was named after him in the Instituto de Bellas Artes.
 WORKS: FOR ORCH.: *Estampas nocturnas* (1923); *Canto y danza de los antiguos Mexicanos* (1933); *Chapultepec,* symph. triptych (Mexico City, Aug. 25, 1929; revised version, Mexico City, Aug. 24, 1934); *Suite en estilo antiguo* (1935); *Poema elegiaco* (Mexico City, June 28, 1935); *Ferial* (Mexico City, Aug. 9, 1940); *Concierto del Sur* for Guitar and Orch. (Montevideo, Oct. 4, 1941); Violin Concerto (Mexico City, Aug. 20, 1943); Piano Trio (1911); *4 miniaturas* for String Quartet (1929); *Pequeña suite en estilo antiguo* for Violin, Viola, and Cello (1933); Sonata for Violin and Viola (1935); Cello Sonata (1922); numerous piano pieces, some based on Mexican rhythms; about 30 songs; 34 arrangements of Mexican folk songs. A collection of his articles was publ. posthumously in 1948.

Ponchielli, Amilcare, celebrated Italian composer; b. Paderno Fasolaro, Cremona, Aug. 31, 1834; d. Milan, Jan. 16, 1886. He studied at the Milan Cons. (1843–54); his first dramatic work (written with 3 other students) was the operetta *Il Sindaco Babbeo* (Milan, March 3, 1851). Leaving the Cons., he was organist at S. Ilario in Cremona; then became a bandmaster. In 1880 he became a prof. at the Milan Cons. Puccini and Mascagni were among his pupils. He brought out the opera *I promessi sposi* at Cremona (Aug. 30, 1856), followed by *La Savoiarda* (Cremona, Jan. 19, 1861; revised as *Lina*, Milan, Nov. 17, 1877) and *Roderico, Re de' Goti* (Piacenza, Dec. 26, 1863). His first striking success was achieved with a revised version of *I promessi sposi* (Milan, Dec. 5, 1872); continuous good fortune attended the production of his operas *I Lituani* (La Scala, Milan, March 7, 1874; revised and revived in 1884 as *Aldona*); *La Gioconda* (Milan, April 8, 1876; his most famous work); *Il Figliuol prodigo* (Milan, Dec. 26, 1880); and *Marion Delorme* (Milan, March 17, 1885). An unfinished opera, *I Mori di Venezia*, in the orchestration by A. Cadore, was produced posthumously in Monte Carlo (March 17, 1914). Ponchielli also brought out a musical farce, *Il Parlatore eterno* (Lecco, Oct. 18, 1873), and the ballets *Le 2 gemelle* and *Clarina* (both 1873); a cantata in honor of Donizetti; a funeral march, *Il 29 Maggio*, for Manzoni; a fine patriotic hymn, *Inno in memoria di Giuseppe Garibaldi*. Of his operas, *La Gioconda* established itself in the repertoire everywhere; the ballet number from it, *Dance of the Hours*, is extremely popular at concerts of light orch. music. Ponchielli also wrote sacred music, for use at the Cathedral of Bergamo, where he was maestro di cappella from 1881 to 1886.

Pond, Sylvanus Billings, American music publisher and composer; b. Milford, Vt., April 5, 1792; d. Brooklyn, March 12, 1871. He was a prominent musician of his time; conducted the N.Y. Sacred Musical Society and the N.Y. Academy of Sacred Music; wrote songs for Sunday school; edited and publ. *Union Melodies* (1838), *The U.S. Psalmody* (N.Y., 1841), and *The Book of Praise*, for the Reformed Dutch Church in America (N.Y., 1866); composed the hymn tunes *Armenia* (1835) and *Franklin Square* (1850). Early in life, he went to Albany; established a piano workshop; from 1820, was partner of the publishing house of Meacham and Pond there; in 1832 he joined Firth & Hall of N.Y., and the firm's name became Firth, Hall & Pond; in 1848 it was reorganized as Firth, Pond & Co.; it was one of the principal publishers of Stephen Foster's songs. In 1850 Pond retired, and his son, **William A. Pond,** became the owner; upon the withdrawal of Firth in 1863, the firm became known as William A. Pond & Co.; W.A. Pond's eldest son, **William A. Pond, Jr.,** was taken into partnership, but died in 1884; William A. Pond Sr. died the following year, and his 2 other sons, **Albert Edward** and **George Warren Pond,** succeeded him. In 1934 Joseph Fletcher acquired the catalogue; in 1946 it was purchased by Carl Fischer, Inc. For the dealings of Firth, Pond & Co. with Stephen Foster, see J.T. Howard, *Stephen Foster, America's Troubadour* (N.Y., 1931; 4th ed., 1965); consult also H. Dichter and E. Shapiro, *Early American Sheet Music, Its Lure and Its Lore, 1768–1889* (N.Y., 1941).

Poniatowski, Josef (Michal Xawery Franciszek Jan), Prince of Monte Rotondo, Polish composer; b. Rome, Feb. 20, 1816; d. Chislehurst, England, July 3, 1873. He was a member of the Polish nobility; his uncle was a marshal in Napoleon's army. He studied in Florence, and appeared on the stage as a tenor; then wrote operas (to Italian and French librettos); in 1848 he went to Paris and was elevated to the rank of Senator by Napoleon III; after the fall of the 2nd Empire, he went to England.

WORKS: OPERAS: *Giovanni da Procida* (Florence, Nov. 25, 1838); *Don Desiderio* (Pisa, Dec. 26, 1840); *Ruy Blas* (Lucca, Sept. 2, 1843); *Malek-Adel* (Genoa, June 26, 1846); *Esmeralde* (Florence, June 26, 1847); *Pierre de Médicis* (Paris, March 9, 1860); *Au travers du mur* (Paris, May 9, 1861); *L'Aventurier* (Paris, Jan. 26, 1865); *La Contessina* (Paris, April 28, 1868); *Gelmina* (London, June 4, 1872).

Pons, Charles, French composer; b. Nice, Dec. 7, 1870; d. Paris, March 16, 1957. He studied organ, and earned his living as a church organist in his youth; then turned to theater music, and produced a long series of operas: *L'Epreuve* (Nice, 1904); *Laura* (Paris, 1906); *Mourette* (Marseilles, 1909); *Le Voile du bonheur* (Paris, April 26, 1911); *Françoise* (Lyons, 1913); *Loin du bal* (Paris, 1913); *Les Fauves* (Paris, 1917); *Le Drapeau* (Paris, 1918); *Le Passant de Noël* (Nice, 1935); *L'Envol de la Marseillaise* (Marseilles, 1947); overture, *Pyrrhus;* symph. poem, *Heures vendéennes; Symphonie tragique;* several orch. suites; oratorio, *La Samaritaine* (Nice, 1900); other vocal works, with Orch.: *La Mort de Démosthène* (Paris, 1928) and *Dans la forêt normande* (1934); chamber music; songs.

Pons, Lily (baptismal names, **Alice Joséphine**), glamorous French coloratura soprano; b. Draguignan, April 12, 1898; d. Dallas, Texas, Feb. 13, 1976. She studied piano as a child; took voice lessons with Albert di Gorostiaga. She made her debut as an opera singer in Mulhouse in 1927 in the title role in *Lakmé;* sang in provincial theaters in France; then was engaged at the Metropolitan Opera in N.Y. and sang Lucia at her debut there on Jan. 3, 1931, with excellent success; she remained on its roster until 1944 (again from 1945–58; on Dec. 14, 1960, made a concert appearance there). While in N.Y., she continued her vocal studies, with Maria Gay and Giovanni Zenatello. Her fame as an extraordinary dramatic singer spread rapidly; she was engaged to sing at the Grand Opéra and the Opéra-Comique in Paris, at Covent Garden in London, the Teatro Colón in Buenos Aires, in Mexico, and in Cuba. She went to Hollywood and appeared in motion pictures, among them *That Girl from Paris* (1936) and *Hitting a New High* (1938). During World War II she toured the battlefronts of North Africa, India, China, and Burma; received numerous honors. So celebrated did she become that a town in Maryland was named Lillypons in her honor. She was married twice (divorced both times), to August Mesritz, a publisher, and to the conductor **André Kostelanetz.** She possessed an expressive coloratura voice, which she used with extraordinary skill.

Ponselle (real name, **Ponzillo**), **Carmela,** American mezzo-soprano, sister of **Rosa Ponselle;** b. Schenectady, N.Y., June 7, 1892; d. New York, June 13, 1977. She began to study singing rather late in life; made her professional debut in 1923; her first appearance at the Metropolitan Opera House was as Amneris in *Aida* (Dec. 5, 1925); she remained on its roster until 1928; was reengaged for the seasons 1930–35; then devoted most of her time to teaching.

Ponselle, Rosa, brilliant American soprano; b. Meriden, Conn., Jan. 22, 1897; d. in her mansion at Green Spring Valley, Md., May 25, 1981. Her parents, who emigrated to the U.S. from southern Italy, gave her, with a prescient hope, the middle name Melba. Her father owned a grocery store in Meriden; she studied music with her mother, an amateur singer, and sang in a local church choir. Her older sister, Carmela Ponselle, also learned to sing, and the 2 sisters, billed under their real name, Ponzillo, as "Italian Girls," sang in vaudeville shows in Pittsburgh and in N.Y. Later she took voice lessons in N.Y. with William Thorner, who became her manager; he introduced her to Caruso, who in turn arranged for her to audition at the Metropolitan Opera. She made a fine impression and was engaged for a debut on Nov. 15, 1918, in the role of Leonora in *La forza del destino,* opposite Caruso, who sang the male lead of Don Alvaro. She was immediately successful, and the critics, including the usually skeptical James Huneker, praised her. She subsequently sang at the Metropolitan a rich assortment of Italian opera roles. She was equally successful in London when she appeared at Covent Garden as Norma (May 28, 1929). In 1936 she was married to Carl Jackson, son of the former mayor of Baltimore, who built for her a magnificent villa at Green Spring Valley, near Baltimore; she divorced him in 1950. She made her last appearance at the Metropolitan Opera in N.Y. as Carmen, on Feb. 15, 1937. Altogether, she appeared with the Metropolitan 258 times in N.Y. and 107 times on tour, in 22 roles. After her retirement she became active in social affairs. Her 80th birthday was celebrated in 1977 at her estate, with a multitude of friends and itinerant celebrities in attendance.

Ponti, Michael, American pianist; b. Freiburg, Germany, Oct. 29, 1937. He was brought to America as a child. He studied piano with Gilmour MacDonald; in 1955 he returned to Germany to continue his studies at the Frankfurt Hochschule für Musik. In 1964 he won first prize in the Busoni Competition, which launched him on a successful career. In his programs he specialized in bringing out neglected or forgotten piano masterpieces of the sonorous Romantic past.

Poot, Marcel, remarkable Belgian composer; b. Vilvoorde, near Brussels, May 7, 1901. He received his first musical training from his father; then studied at the Brussels Cons. with Sevenants, Lunssens, and de Greef (1916–20), and at the Flemish Cons. of Antwerp with Lodewijk Mortelmans (1921–23); in

the interim he also received guidance from Paul Gilson. In 1925, with 7 other Gilson pupils (René Bernier, Gaston Brenta, Francis de Bourguignon, Theodore Dejoncker, Robert Otlet, Maurice Schoemaker, and Jules Strens), he founded the Groupe des Synthétistes, dedicated to propaganda of new musical ideas (the group disbanded in 1930). Also in 1925, Poot was co-founder, with Gilson, of *La Revue Musicale Belge,* to which he contributed until its dissolution in 1938. He was on the staff of the Brussels Cons. from 1938 to 1966, and was its director from 1949 until his retirement. The most striking element of his music is its rhythmic vivacity; his harmony is well within the tonal sphere.

Popp, Lucia, Czech soprano; b. Uhorská Ves, Nov. 12, 1939. She studied at the Academy of Music in Bratislava (1959–63), then sang at the Opera there. In 1963 Herbert von Karajan invited her to sing at the Vienna State Opera; within a few seasons, she became one of its principal members. Also in 1963 she appeared at the Salzburg Festival; in 1966 she sang at Covent Garden in London. On Feb. 19, 1967, she made her American debut at the Metropolitan Opera in N.Y. as the Queen of the Night in *Die Zauberflöte;* in 1969 she toured Australia. She was equally expert in coloratura parts and in lyrico-dramatic roles.

Popper, David, famous Czech cellist and composer; b. Prague, Dec. 9, 1843; d. Baden, near Vienna, Aug. 7, 1913. He studied cello with Goltermann at the Prague Cons.; began his career with a tour in 1863; then had a highly successful appearance as a soloist at the Karlsruhe Music Festival on March 29, 1865; from 1868 to 1873 he was first cellist of the Vienna Court Orch. In 1872 he married the famous pianist **Sophie Menter,** but they were divorced 14 years later. From 1896 until his death he taught cello at the Budapest Cons. He wrote a number of extremely attractive and marvelously idiomatic pieces for the cello, which remained in the international repertoire, among them *Sérénade orientale, Gavotte, Tarentelle, Elfentanz, Im Walde, Ungarische Rhapsodie;* also a *Requiem* for 3 Cellos (perf. by him, with Delsart and Howell, in London, Nov. 25, 1891); he also publ. the cello studies *Hohe Schule des Violoncellspiels* (40 studies) and, as a preparatory book of easy pieces, *10 mittelschwere grosse Etüden.*

Porpora, Nicola Antonio, famous Italian composer and singing teacher; b. Naples, Aug. 17, 1686; d. there, March 3, 1768. The son of a bookseller, he entered the Cons. dei Poveri at Naples at the age of 10 and studied with Gaetano Greco, Matteo Giordano, and Ottavio Campanile. Porpora's first opera, *Agrippina,* was presented at the Royal Palace of Naples (Nov. 4, 1708); Cardinal Grimani attended the performance and wrote a libretto on the same subject for Handel. This episode gave rise to the incorrect statement (by Fétis and others) that Handel heard Porpora's opera in Rome in 1710. Porpora produced in Naples 2 more operas: *Flavio Anicio*

Olibrio (1711) and *Basilio, re d'oriente* (June 24, 1713). From 1711 until 1725, he held the title of maestro di cappella to Philip, Landgrave of Hesse-Darmstadt. He gained a great reputation as a singing teacher, and numbered among his pupils the famous castrati Farinelli, Caffarelli, Antonio Uberti (who called himself "Porporino" out of respect for his teacher), and Salimbeni. Metastasio, who wrote librettos for several of Porpora's operas, was also his pupil. Porpora's career as a singing teacher was divided between Naples and Venice. In Naples he taught at the conservatories of Sant' Onofrio (1715–22, 1760–61) and Santa Maria di Loreto (1739–41, 1760–61); in Venice he gave lessons at the Ospedali degli Incurabili (1726–33, 1737–38), the Ospedali della Pietà (1742–46), and the Ospedaletto (1746–47). In 1718 Porpora collaborated with Domenico Scarlatti in the writing of the opera *Berenice, regina d'Egitto,* produced in Rome (1718). At about this time he succeeded in obtaining support from the Austrian court. His opera *Temistocle* was produced in Vienna on the Emperor's birthday (Oct. 1, 1718); his next opera, *Faramondo,* was staged in Naples (Nov. 19, 1719). He continued to write operas for theaters in Naples and Rome: *Eumene* (Rome, 1721); *Adelaide* (Rome, 1723); *Semiramide, regina dell'Assiria* (Naples, 1724); *Didone abbandonata* (his first opera to a libretto by Metastasio; Reggio, 1725). In 1726 he settled in Venice. He wrote the following operas during the next 8 years: *Meride e Selinunte* (Venice, 1726); *Siroe, re di Persia* (Milan, 1726); *Semiramide riconosciuta* (Venice, 1729); *Mitridate* (Rome, 1730); *Tamerlano* (Turin, 1730); *Poro* (Turin, 1731); *Germanico in Germania* (Rome, 1732); *Issipile* (Rome, 1733). In 1733 he applied for the post of maestro di cappella at San Marco in Venice, but failed to obtain it. In the same year he was engaged by the directors of the Opera of the Nobility in London (organized as a rival company to that of Handel). For this venture Porpora wrote 5 operas: *Arianna in Nasso* (Dec. 29, 1733); *Enea nel Lazio* (May 11, 1734); *Polifemo* (Feb. 1, 1735); *Ifigenia in Aulide* (May 3, 1735); *Mitridate* (Jan. 24, 1736; a different score from the earlier opera of the same title). For a while he competed successfully with Handel, but soon the Opera of the Nobility began to falter, and Porpora left London on the eve of the company's collapse. From 1747 to 1751, he was in Dresden as singing teacher to the Electoral Princess. There he became Hasse's competitor for the position of music director. Although Hasse himself conducted Porpora's "pastoral drama" *Filandro* (Dresden, July 18, 1747), their relationship was made difficult by the intrigues of Hasse's wife, the singer Faustina Bordoni. In 1751 Porpora left Dresden for Vienna, where he became the teacher of Haydn, who paid for his lessons by serving Porpora as accompanist and personal helper. Porpora returned to Naples in 1758. His last stage work, *Il trionfo di Camilla* (Naples, May 30, 1760; a revision and adaptation to a new text of an earlier opera of the same title produced in Naples on Jan. 20, 1740), was unsuccessful. He wrote, all told, 44 operas, 11 oratorios, and numerous masses and motets. His instrumental music includes 6 *sinfonie da camera* (London, 1735), 12 violin sonatas (Vienna, 1754), a Cello Concerto, and a Cello Sonata. The fugues in Clementi's *Practical Harmony* are from Porpora's violin sonatas, some of which have been publ. by A. Schering, F. David, D. Alard, and A. Moffat. A Trio Sonata was publ. in Riemann's *Collegium Musicum* (no. 23).

Porrino, Ennio, Italian composer; b. Cagliari, Sardinia, Jan. 20, 1910; d. Rome, Sept. 25, 1959. He studied at the Santa Cecilia Academy in Rome with Mulè, and later took a course with Respighi (1932–35). He subsequently taught in Rome, Venice, and Naples; in 1956, became director of the Cons. in his hometown in Sardinia.

Porsile, Giuseppe, Italian composer; b. Naples, May 5, 1680; d. Vienna, May 29, 1750. He studied in Naples at the Cons. dei Poveri di Gesù Cristo with Usino, Giordano, and Greco. He then served as vice-maestro di cappella at the Spanish chapel in Naples. In 1695 he went to Spain to organize the music chapel of King Charles II in Barcelona; he subsequently served Charles III. When Charles III was elected Holy Roman Emperor as Charles VI, with the seat in Vienna, Porsile followed him there. On Dec. 17, 1720, he became court composer. He continued to serve the court after Charles VI died in 1740, being granted an honorary stipend; he was pensioned on April 1, 1749. Most of his stage works were written for the court of Vienna.

Porta, Costanzo, important Italian composer; b. Cremona, c.1529; d. Padua, May 19, 1601. He studied with Willaert in Venice; was chorus master at Osimo, near Ancona, from 1552 to 1564. In 1565 he became choirmaster at the Basilica of St. Anthony in Padua; in 1567 received a similar post at the Cathedral of Ravenna; in 1575 was in Loreto, returning to Padua in 1585. He was highly esteemed as a master contrapuntist; wrote not only sacred music but also madrigals; combined great technical skill with a characteristically Italian grace of melodic line.

Porter, Andrew, brilliant writer on music; b. Cape Town, South Africa, Aug. 26, 1928. He studied music at Diocesan College in Cape Town; then went to England; continued his education at Univ. College, Oxford; became a proficient organist. In 1949 he joined the staff of the *Manchester Guardian;* then wrote music criticism for the *Financial Times* of London (1953–74); also served as editor of the *Musical Times* of London (1960–67). In 1972 he became the music critic of the *New Yorker.* A polyglot, a polymath, and an uncommonly diversified intellectual, Andrew Porter expanded his interests far beyond the limited surface of purely musical studies; he mastered German, Italian, and French; made an exemplary trans. into Eng. of the entire text of *Der Ring des Nibelungen,* taking perspicuous care for the congenial rendition of Wagner's words and melodic inflections; his trans. was used to excellent advantage in the performance and recording of the cycle by the conductor Reginald Goodall with the English National Opera. Porter also trans. texts of Verdi's operas, Mozart's *Die Zauberflöte,* and some French operas. His mastery of English prose and his unostentatious display of arcane erudition make him one of the most remarkable music critics writing in the English language. Selections from his reviews have been publ. in *A Musical Season* (N.Y., 1974) and *Music of 3 Seasons, 1974 to 1977* (N.Y., 1978).

Porter, Cole, remarkable American composer of popular music; b. Peru, Ind., June 9, 1891; d. Santa Monica, Calif., Oct. 15, 1964. He was educated at Yale Univ. (B.A., 1913); then took academic courses at Harvard Law School, and later at the Harvard School of Music. While at Yale, he wrote football songs (*Yale Bull Dog Song, Bingo Eli Yale,* etc.); also composed music for college functions. His first production in N.Y. was *See America First* (1916). There followed a cascade of musical comedies for which he wrote both the lyrics and the music, which placed him in the front rank of the American musical theater. He was a master of subtle expression without sentimentality, a kinetic dash without vulgarity, and a natural blend of word poetry with the finest of harmonious melodies.

WORKS: *Kitchy-Koo* (1919); *50 Million Frenchmen* (1929); *Gay Divorcee* (1932); *Anything Goes* (1934); *Jubilee* (1935); *Red Hot and Blue* (1936); *Leave It to Me* (1938); *Dubarry Was a Lady* (1939); *Panama Hattie* (1940); *Let's Face It* (1941); *Something for the Boys* (1943); *Mexican Hayride* (1944); *Kiss Me, Kate* (1948); *Out of This World* (1950); *Can-Can* (1954); *Silk Stockings* (1955). Of his many songs, at least half a dozen became great favorites: *Begin the Beguine; It's De-Lovely; Night and Day; My Heart Belongs to Daddy; Don't Fence Me In; Wunderbar.*

Porter, Quincy, significant American composer; b. New Haven, Conn., Feb. 7, 1897; d. Bethany, Conn., Nov. 12, 1966. He was brought up in an intellectual atmosphere; his father and his grandfather were profs. at Yale Univ. He studied with David Stanley Smith and Horatio Parker at the Yale School of Music (B.Mus., 1921); submitted a violin concerto for the American Prix de Rome and received an honorable mention; also won the Steinert and Osborne prizes. After graduation he went to Paris, where he took courses with Lucien Capet (violin) and Vincent d'Indy (composition). Returning to America in 1922, he earned a living as a violinist in theater orchs. in N.Y. while taking a course in composition with Ernest Bloch. He taught at the Cleveland Inst. of Music (1922–28, 1931–32); played the viola in the Ribaupierre String Quartet there; spent 3 years in Paris on a Guggenheim fellowship (1928–31); was a prof. at Vassar College and conductor of the Vassar Orch. (1932–38); in 1938 succeeded Frederick Converse as dean of the New England Cons. in Boston; from 1942 to 1946, was its director; from 1946 to 1965, was a prof. at Yale Univ. His music is built on strong contrapuntal lines, with incisive rhythms; his harmon-

ic procedures often reach stridently polytonal sonorities, while the general idiom of his works combines elements of both the modern German and the modern French styles of composition.

WORKS: *Ukrainian Suite* for String Orch. (Rochester, N.Y., May 1, 1925); Suite in C minor for Orch. (1926); *Poem and Dance* for Orch. (Cleveland, June 24, 1932, composer conducting); 2 symphs.: No. 1 (1934; N.Y., April 2, 1938, composer conducting) and No. 2 (1961–62; Louisville, Ky., Jan. 14, 1964); *Dance in Three-Time* for Chamber Orch. (St. Louis, July 2, 1937); *Music for Strings* (1941); *Fantasy on a Pastoral Theme* for Organ and String Orch. (1942); Viola Concerto (Columbia Univ. Festival, N.Y., May 16, 1948); *Fantasy* for Cello and Small Orch. (1950); *The Desolate City* for Baritone and Orch. (1950); *Concerto Concertante* for 2 Pianos and Orch. (1952–53; Louisville, March 17, 1954; awarded the Pulitzer Prize for 1954 under its original title, *Concerto for 2 Pianos and Orchestra*); *New England Episodes,* symph. suite (commissioned for the Inter-American Music Festival, Washington, D.C., April 18, 1958); Harpsichord Concerto (1959; New Haven, Jan. 19, 1960; Ralph Kirkpatrick, soloist); Concerto for Wind Orch. (1960); 10 string quartets (1923, 1925, 1930, 1931, 1935, 1937, 1943, 1950, 1958, 1965); *In Monasterio* for String Quartet (1927); Piano Quintet (1927); Clarinet Quintet (1929); *Quintet on a Childhood Theme* for Flute and Strings (1940); String Sextet on Slavic folk tunes (1947); Divertimento for Wind Quintet (1960); Oboe Quintet (1966); 2 violin sonatas (1925, 1929); *Little Trio* for Flute, Violin, and Viola (1928); Suite for Solo Viola (1930); Horn Sonata (1946); 4 pieces for Violin and Piano (1947); Duo for Violin and Viola (1954); Duo for Flute and Harp (1957); Piano Sonata (1930); *Canon and Fugue* for Organ (1941); *6 Miniatures* for Piano (1943); *Day Dreams* for Piano (1957); several songs.

Portugal (Portogallo), Marcos Antonio da Fonseca (real name, **Ascenção**), Portuguese composer; b. Lisbon, March 24, 1762; d. Rio de Janeiro, Feb. 7, 1830. A pupil at the ecclesiastical seminary at Lisbon, he continued his musical education with composition lessons from João de Souza Carvalho. Between 1784 and 1791 he wrote for Lisbon 17 stage works, mostly ephemeral. His reputation was made in Italy, where, with the exception of a short visit to Lisbon, he lived from 1792 to 1800, bringing out 22 Italian operas. From 1800 to 1810 he acted as conductor at the San Carlos Theater in Lisbon, producing Italian and Portuguese operas. His *Il Filosofo seducente, ossia Non irritar le donne* (Venice, Dec. 27, 1798) was selected by Napoleon for opening the Théâtre-Italien at Paris in 1801. In 1807 the royal family fled to Brazil before the French invasion; Portugal remained until the San Carlos Theater was closed in 1810, and then followed the court to Rio de Janeiro, where he was made general music director in 1811. The royal theater of São João, after its inauguration in 1813, produced several new operas by him. In that year he became director of the new Cons. at Vera Cruz, jointly with his brother **Simão;** he visited Italy in 1815, returned to Rio de

Janeiro, and passed his last years there as an invalid. His masterpiece is generally assumed to be *Fernando nel Messico* (Venice, Jan. 16, 1798; written for the famous English singer Elizabeth Billington; produced in London, in Italian, March 31, 1803); other Italian operas that had a favorable reception were *Demofoonte* (Milan, Feb. 8, 1794) and *Le Donne cambiate* (Venice, Oct. 22, 1797); of Portuguese operas, *A Castanheira (The Chestnut Seller),* produced in Lisbon in 1790, enjoyed considerable popular success. He further wrote about 100 sacred works.

Poston, Elizabeth, English pianist and composer; b. Highfield, Hertfordshire, Oct. 24, 1905. She studied piano with Harold Samuel; during World War II was in charge of music in the European Service of the BBC in London. She has a strong predilection for the Elizabethan period; her stylizations of old song patterns are adroitly made and preserve an authentic modality of the originals.

Pothier, Dom Joseph, learned authority on Gregorian chant; b. Bouzemont, near Saint-Dié, Dec. 7, 1835; d. Conques, Belgium, Dec. 8, 1923. He became a Benedictine monk in 1860 at Solesmes; in 1862, sub-prior; in 1866, prof. of theology at the Solesmes Monastery; in 1893, prior at the Benedictine monastery of Ligugé; in 1898, abbot at St.-Wandrille. When the religious orders were banned from France, he moved to Belgium. In 1904 he was appointed by Pius X president of the publication committee of the *Editio Vaticana.*

Potter, (Philip) Cipriani (Hambly), English pianist and composer; b. London, Oct. 2, 1792; d. there, Sept. 26, 1871. He studied music first with his father, then with Attwood, Callcott, and Crotch; also took piano lessons with Woelffl during the latter's sojourn in England. In 1817 he went to Vienna, where he studied composition with Aloys Förster; he met Beethoven, who gave him good advice. He traveled in Germany and Italy; returned to London in 1821; the following year he became a piano teacher at the Royal Academy of Music; succeeded Crotch as principal in 1832; retired in 1859. From 1855 to 1870 he was conductor of the Madrigal Society. He frequently appeared in London as a pianist; introduced 3 of Beethoven's concertos (Nos. 1, 3, 4) to England. He publ. a number of piano pieces, including a set of variations under the title *The Enigma,* comprising "variations in the style of 5 eminent artists." This early anticipation of the famous work by Elgar was not known to Elgar himself. He wrote 10 symphs., 4 overtures, 3 piano concertos, 4 piano sonatas, and other pieces. Wagner conducted one of Potter's symphs. during his engagement with the London Phil. Society in 1855. Potter edited for Novello a series of Mozart's piano works.

Poueigh, Jean (Marie-Octave-Géraud), French composer and writer on music; b. Toulouse, Feb. 24, 1876; d. Olivet (Loiret), Oct. 14, 1958. After music study in his native city, he entered the Paris Cons. as a student of Caussade, Lenepveu, and Gabriel Fauré; also received advice from Vincent d'Indy; settled in Paris. He harmonized and edited a number of folk songs of Languedoc and Gascogne in *Les Chansons de France* (1907–8), *3 Chansons des Pays d'Oc,* and *14 Chansons anciennes;* also edited the collection *Chansons populaires des Pyrénées françaises* (vol. 1, 1926). His original compositions include the operas *Les Lointains* (1903); *Le Meneur de louves* (1921); *Perkin,* a Basque legend (Bordeaux, Jan. 16, 1931); *Le Roi de Camargue* (Marseilles, May 12, 1948); *Bois-brûlé* (1956); ballets: *Fünn* (1906); *Frivolant* (Paris Opéra, May 1, 1922); a Moroccan ballet, *Chergui;* a symph. tableau, *La Basilique aux vainqueurs;* piano pieces and songs. Under the pen name of **Octave Séré** he publ. *Musiciens français d'aujourd'hui* (Paris, 1911; 7th ed., 1921); contributed numerous articles to various French periodicals.

Pougin, Arthur (pen name of **François-Auguste-Arthur Paroisse-Pougin**), French writer and critic; b. Châteauroux, Indre, Aug. 6, 1834; d. Paris, Aug. 8, 1921. He was a pupil of Alard (violin) and Reber (harmony) at the Paris Cons.; in 1855 was conductor of the Théâtre Beaumarchais; in 1856–59, assistant conductor of the Folies-Nouvelles; from 1860–63, violinist in the Opéra-Comique orch.; then devoted himself to musical journalism; in his articles he fulminated against Debussy and other "anarchistes de musique," as he described the modern French composers; but he was brilliant even in his most outrageous stolidity of judgment. He was music critic for *Le Ménestrel, Le Soir, La Tribune, L'Evénement,* and the *Journal Officiel.* He started the *Revue de la Musique* in 1876, but it ran for only 6 months; publ. many biographical sketches and essays: *André Campra* (1861); *Gresnick* (1862); *Dezèdes* (1862); *Floquet* (1863); *Martini* (1864); *Devienne* (1864); the preceding 6 are collected as *Musiciens français du XVIIIe siècle;* also, *Verdi* (1886; in Eng., 1887); edited an *Almanach de la musique* (1866, 1867, 1868, the last 2 with necrological supplements); *Dictionnaire historique et pittoresque théâtre* (1885); *Méhul* (1889; 2nd ed., 1893); *l'Opéra-Comique pendant la Révolution* (1891); *Essai historique sur la musique en Russie* (1896; 2nd ed., 1904; in Eng., 1915); *J.-J. Rousseau, Musicien* (1901); *Musiciens du XIXe siècle* (1911); *Marie Malibran* (in Eng., 1911); *Marietta Alboni* (1912); *Massenet* (1914); *Giuseppina Grassini* (1920); *Le Violon, les violonistes, et la musique de violon du XVIe au XVIIIe siècle* (posthumous, 1924). Pougin wrote for Larousse's *Grand dictionnaire universel* all the articles on music. He also edited the supplement to Fétis's *Biographie universelle* (2 vols., 1878–80), and the new eds. of the *Dictionnaire lyrique, ou Histoire des opéras* of Félix Clément and P. Larousse (Paris, 1898; with supplement up to 1904).

Poulenc, Francis, brilliant French composer; b. Paris, Jan. 7, 1899; d. there, Jan. 30, 1963. His mother taught him music in his childhood; at 16 he began taking formal piano lessons with Ricardo Viñes. A decisive turn in his development as a composer occurred when he attracted the attention of Erik Satie, the arbiter elegantiarum of the arts and social amenities in Paris. Deeply impressed by Satie's fruitful eccentricities in the then-shocking manner of Dadaism, Poulenc joined an ostentatiously self-descriptive musical group called the Nouveaux Jeunes. In a gratuitous parallel with the Russian Five, the French critic Henri Collet dubbed the "New Youths" Le Groupe de Six, and the label stuck under the designation Les Six. The 6 musicians included, besides Poulenc: Auric, Durey, Honegger, Milhaud, and Tailleferre. Although quite different in their styles of composition and artistic inclinations, they continued collective participation in various musical events. Poulenc served in the French army (1918–21), and then began taking lessons in composition with Koechlin (1921–24). An excellent pianist, Poulenc became in 1935 an accompanist to the French baritone Pierre Bernac, for whom he wrote numerous songs. Compared with his fortuitous comrades-in-six, Poulenc appears a classicist. He never experimented with the popular devices of "machine music," asymmetrical rhythms, and polyharmonies as cultivated by Honegger and Milhaud. Futuristic projections had little interest for him; he was content to follow the gentle neo-Classical formation of Ravel's piano music and songs. Among his other important artistic contacts was the ballet impresario Diaghilev, who commissioned him to write music for his Ballets Russes. Apart from his fine songs and piano pieces, Poulenc revealed himself as an inspired composer of religious music, of which his choral works *Stabat Mater* and *Gloria* are notable. He further wrote remarkable music for the organ, including a concerto that became a minor masterpiece. A master of artificial simplicity, he pleases even sophisticated listeners by his bland triadic tonalities, spiced with quickly passing diaphonous discords.

WORKS: OPERAS: 2-act opéra-bouffe, *Les Mamelles de Tirésias;* 1944; Opéra-Comique, June 3, 1947; U.S. premiere, Waltham, Mass., June 13, 1953, Bernstein conducting); 3-act religious opera, *Dialogues des Carmélites* (1953–56; La Scala, Milan, Jan. 26, 1957; U.S. premiere, San Francisco, Sept. 22, 1957); one-act monodrama for Soprano Solo, *La Voix humaine,* after Cocteau (1958; Opéra-Comique, Feb. 6, 1959; U.S. premiere, N.Y., Feb. 23, 1960).

BALLETS: *La Baigneuse de Trouville* and *Discours de Général,* 2 movements for *Les Mariés de la Tour Eiffel,* a ballet-farce by Cocteau (Champs-Elysées, June 18, 1921; other movements by members of Les Six, except for Durey, who had already permanently left the group); *Les Biches (The Does),* with Chorus (1923; Monte Carlo, Jan. 6, 1924); *Pastourelle,* 9th movement of an 11-movement collective ballet, *L'Eventail de Jeanne* (1927; first perf. of orch. version, Paris Opéra, March 4, 1929; movements by Roussel, Ravel, Ibert, Milhaud, and others); *Aubade,* choreographic concerto for Piano and 18 Instruments (1929; private perf., Paris, June 18, 1929; public perf., London, Dec. 19, 1929); *Les Ani-*

maux modèles, after fables by La Fontaine (1940–41; Paris Opéra, Aug. 8, 1942).

FOR ORCH.: *Concert champêtre* for Harpsichord or Piano, and Orch. (1927–28; Paris, May 3, 1929); Concerto for 2 Pianos and Orch. (1932; Venice, Sept. 5, 1932); *2 marches et un intermède* for Chamber Orch. (1937; Paris World Exhibition, 1937); Concerto for Organ, String Orch., and Timpani (1938; private perf., Paris, June 21, 1939; first public perf., Paris, June 10, 1941); Sinfonietta (1947; London, Oct. 24, 1948); Concerto for Piano and Orch. (1949; Boston, Jan. 6, 1950); *Matelote provençale,* movement from a collective work of 7 composers, *La Guirlande de Campra* (1952); *Bucolique,* movement from a collective work of 8 composers, *Variations sur la nom de Marguerite Long* (1954).

CHAMBER MUSIC: Sonata for 2 Clarinets (1918; revised 1945); Sonata for Clarinet and Bassoon (1922); Sonata for Horn, Trumpet, and Trombone (1922; revised 1945); Trio for Oboe, Bassoon, and Piano (1926); Sextet for Piano and Wind Quintet (1930–32; revised 1939); *Suite française* for 9 Winds, Percussion, and Harpsichord (1935); Violin Sonata (1942–43; revised 1949); Cello Sonata (1948); Flute Sonata (1956); *Elégie,* to the memory of Dennis Brain, for Horn and Piano (1957); *Sarabande* for Solo Guitar (1960); Clarinet Sonata (1962); Oboe Sonata (1962).

CHORAL WORKS: Chanson à boire for a cappella Male Chorus (1922); *7 chansons* for a cappella Mixed Chorus (1936); *Litanies à la vierge noire* for Female Chorus and Organ (1936); Mass in G for a cappella Mixed Chorus (1937; Paris, May 1938); *Sécheresses (Dryness),* cantata, after texts by Edward James, for Chorus and Orch. (1937; Paris, 1938); *4 motets pour un temps de pénitence* for Mixed Chorus a cappella (1938–39); *Exultate Deo* for Mixed Chorus a cappella (1941); *Salve regina* for Mixed Chorus a cappella (1941); *Figure humaine,* cantata for Double Mixed Chorus (1943); *Un Soir de neige,* chamber cantata for 6 Voices a cappella (1944); 2 books of traditional French songs, arranged for Chorus a cappella (1945); *4 petites prières de Saint François d'Assise* for Male Chorus a cappella (1948); *Stabat Mater* for Soprano, Chorus, and Orch. (1950; Strasbourg Festival, June 13, 1951); *4 motets pour le temps de Noël* for Chorus a cappella (1951–52); *Ave verum corpus* for Female Chorus a cappella (1952); *Laudes de Saint Antoine de Padoue* for Male Chorus a cappella (1957–59); *Gloria* for Soprano, Chorus, and Orch. (1959; Boston, Jan. 20, 1961); *7 répons des ténèbres* for Boy Soprano, Boys' and Men's Chorus, and Orch. (1961; posthumous, N.Y., April 11, 1963).

FOR VOICE AND INSTRUMENTS: *Rapsodie nègre* for Baritone, String Quartet, Flute, Clarinet, and Piano (1917; Paris, Dec. 11, 1917; revised 1933); *Le Bestiaire (The Bestiary),* after Apollinaire, for Mezzo-soprano, String Quartet, Flute, Clarinet, and Bassoon (1918–19); *Cocardes,* after Cocteau, for Voice, Violin, Cornet, Trombone, Bass Drum, and Triangle (1919); *Le Bal masqué (The Masked Ball),* after surrealist verses of Max Jacob, for Voice, Oboe, Clarinet, Bassoon, Violin, Cello, Percussion, and Piano (1932); *La Dame de Monte Carlo,* monologue for Soprano and Orch. (1961; Paris, Dec. 5, 1961).

FOR VOICE AND PIANO: *Histoire de Babar le petit éléphant (History of Babar the Small Elephant)* for Narrator and Piano (1940–45; orchestrated by Jean Francaix, 1962); song cycles: *Le Bestiaire* (1919; arrangement); *Cocardes* (1919; arrangement); *Poèmes de Ronsard* (1924–25; later orchestrated); *Chansons gaillardes* (1925–26); *Airs chantés* (1927–28); *8 chansons polonaises* (1934); *4 chansons pour enfants* (1934); *5 poèmes* after Eluard (1935); *Tel jour, telle nuit* (1936–37); *3 poèmes* after de Vilmorin (1937); *2 poèmes* after Apollinaire (1938); *Miroirs brûlants* (1938–39); *Fiançailles pour rire* (1939); *Banalités* (1940); *Chansons villageoises* (1942; orchestrated 1943); *Métamorphoses* (1943); *3 chansons* after Lorca (1947); *Calligrammes* (1948); *La Fraîcheur et le feu* (1950); *Parisiana* (1954); *Le Travail du peintre* (1956); *2 mélodies* (1956); *La Courte Paille* (1960); separate songs: *Toréador* (1918; revised 1932); *Vocalise* (1927); *Epitaphe* (1930); *A sa guitare*, after Ronsard (1935); *Montparnasse* (1941–45); *Hyde Park* (1945); *Paul et Virginie* (1946); *Le Disparu* (1947); *Mazurka* (1949); *Rosemonde* (1954); *Dernier poème* (1956); *Une Chanson de porcelaine* (1958); others.

FOR PIANO: Sonata, 4-hands (1918); *3 mouvements perpétuels* (1918); *Valse* (1919); *Suite in C* (1920); *6 impromptus* (1920); *Promenades* (1921); *Napoli*, suite of 3 pieces (1921–25); *2 novelettes* (1928); *3 pièces* (1928); *Pièce brève sur le nom d'Albert Roussel* (1929); *8 nocturnes* (1929–38); *15 improvisations* (1932–59); *Villageoises* (1933); *Feuillets d'album* (1933); *Les Soirées de Nazelles* (1930–36); *Mélancolie* (1940); *Intermezzo* (1943); *L'Embarquement pour Cythère* for 2 Pianos (1951); *Thème varié* (1951); Sonata for 2 Pianos (1952–53); *Elégie* for 2 Pianos (1959); *Novelette sur un thème de Manuel de Falla* (1959).

Poulet, Gaston, French violinist and conductor; b. Paris, April 10, 1892; d. Draveil (Essonne), April 14, 1974. He studied violin at the Paris Cons., gaining first prize; organized a string quartet and gave concerts in Europe; from 1927 to 1936 conducted the Concerts Poulet at the Théâtre Sarah-Bernhardt in Paris; also taught at the Paris Cons.; in 1932–44 served as director of the Cons. of Bordeaux and conducted the Phil. Orch. there; from 1940 to 1945 conducted the Concerts Colonne in Paris; was a guest conductor with the London Symph. (1947) and in Germany (1948); also in South America. He played the violin in the first performance of Debussy's Violin Sonata, with Debussy himself at the piano. He was a prof. of chamber music at the Paris Cons. in 1944–62; in 1948 founded the famous Besançon Festival.

Poulet, Gérard, French violinist, son of **Gaston Poulet;** b. Bayonne, Aug. 12, 1938. He entered the Paris Cons. at the age of 11 in the class of André Asselin, and won first prize at 12; in the same year (1950) he played 3 violin concertos with the Orch. Colonne, under his father's direction; then appeared with other Paris orchs.; subsequently gave concerts and played with orchs. in England, Germany, Italy, Austria, and the Netherlands. In 1956 he won first Grand Prix at the Paganini competition of Genoa, and was given the honor of performing on Paganini's own violin, the famous Guarneri del Jesù.

Pouplinière. See **La Pouplinière.**

Pourtalès, Guy de (complete name, **Guido James de Pourtalès**), French writer on music; b. Berlin, Aug. 4, 1881; d. Lausanne, June 12, 1941. He studied in Bonn, Berlin, and Paris; was in the French army during World War I; then settled in Paris as a music critic. He publ. a number of successful biographies of composers: *La Vie de Franz Liszt* (1925); *Chopin, ou Le Poète* (1927; 2nd ed., 1946; in Eng. as *Chopin: A Man of Solitude*, London, 1930); *Wagner, Histoire d'un artiste* (1932; revised and augmented ed., 1942); *Berlioz et l'Europe romantique* (1939).

Pousseur, Henri, Belgian composer of the ultra-modern school; b. Malmédy, June 23, 1929. He studied at the Liège Cons. (1947–52) and the Brussels Cons. (1952–53); had private lessons in composition from André Souris and Pierre Boulez; until 1959, worked in the Cologne and Milan electronic music studios, where he came in contact with Stockhausen and Berio; was a member of the avant-garde group of composers "Variation" in Liège. He taught music in various Belgian schools (1950–59); was founder (1958) and director of the Studio de Musique Electronique APELAC in Brussels, now a part of the Centre de Recherches Musicales in Liège; gave lectures at the summer courses of new music in Darmstadt (1957–67), Cologne (1962–68), Basel (1963–64), the State Univ. of N.Y. in Buffalo (1966–69), and the Cons. in Liège. In his music he tries to synthesize all the expressive powers of which man, as a biological species, *Homo sapiens* (or even *Homo insipiens*), is capable in the domain of art (or non-art); the technological resources of the subspecies *Homo habilis* (magnetic tape, electronics/synthesizers, aleatory extensions, the principle of indeterminacy, glossolalia, self-induced schizophasia) all form part of his rich musical (or non-musical) vocabulary for multimedia (or nulimedia) representations. The influence of his methods (or non-methods) of composition (or non-composition) is pervasive.

Powell, (Earl) "Bud," black American jazz pianist; b. New York, Sept. 27, 1924; d. there, Aug. 1, 1966. After dropping out of school at the age of 15, he began playing with local groups in N.Y. Following the zeitgeist, he adopted the bop style, and in 1943 joined Cootie Williams and his band; he also played concerts with Dizzy Gillespie, Sid Catlett, and John Kirby, achieving recognition as a fine bop pianist. He was a frequent participant in the formative jazz sessions at Minton's Playhouse. He gradually discarded the prevalent "stride" piano style with its regular beat, and emancipated the left-hand rhythm by introducing a contrapuntal line with asymmetrical punctuation. His brief career was periodically interrupted by mental eclipses caused by immoderate use of hallucinogenic drugs.

Powell, John, American pianist, composer, and ethnomusicologist; b. Richmond, Va., Sept. 6, 1882; d. Charlottesville, Va., Aug. 15, 1963. His father was a schoolteacher, his mother an amateur musician; he received his primary musical education at home; then studied piano with F.C. Hahr, a pupil of Liszt; subsequently entered the Univ. of Virginia (B.A., 1901) and then went to Vienna, where he studied piano with Leschetizky (1902–7) and composition with Navrátil (1904–7); gave successful piano recitals in Paris and London; returning to the U.S., he toured the country as a pianist, playing some of his own works. His most successful piece was *Rapsodie nègre,* inspired by Joseph Conrad's *Heart of Darkness,* for Piano and Orch.; Powell was the soloist in its first performance with the Russian Symph. Orch. (N.Y., March 23, 1918). The titles of some of his works disclose a whimsical propensity; perhaps his most important achievement lies in ethnomusicology; he methodically collected rural songs of the South; was the organizer of the Virginia State Choral Festivals and of the annual White Top Mountain Folk Music Festivals. A man of versatile interests, he was also an amateur astronomer, and discovered a comet.

Powell, Maud, American violinist; b. Peru, Ill., Aug. 22, 1868; d. Uniontown, Pa., Jan. 8, 1920. She received her primary instruction at home; then went to Europe, where she took violin lessons with Schradieck in Leipzig and theory with Charles Dancla in Paris. Returning to the U.S. in 1885, she gave concerts and acquired a sort of automatic celebrity, since the female species among violinists was a *rara avis* in her time. Thus, when the Arion Society of N.Y. rigged a musical expedition to Germany in 1892 for the quadricentennial of the discovery of America, she went along as a "representative American violinist." She also played at the Chicago World's Fair in 1893.

Powell, Mel, remarkable American composer; b. New York, Feb. 12, 1923. He began his career in popular music, and acquired quite a reputation as a jazz pianist for the Benny Goodman Band; concurrently, he took lessons with Bernard Wagenaar and Joseph Schillinger in N.Y. (1937–39); later also had some instruction in composition with Ernst Toch in Los Angeles (1946–48). In 1948 he entered Hindemith's class at the Yale School of Music (B.M., 1952). From 1957–69 he was on the faculty of Yale Univ.; from 1969–75 he served as dean of music at the Calif. Inst. of the Arts. As a composer, he revealed versatile talents, being technically at home in an incisive jazz idiom, in a neo-Classical manner faithfully emulating his teacher Hindemith, tangentially shadowing Stravinsky, in an expressionist mood of Schoenberg, in the stark, microphonic, dodecaphonic, canonic universe of Anton von Webern, and finally in electronic sonorism. In all these avatars, Powell somehow succeeded in projecting his own personality in most curious quaquaversal ways; thus, while absorbed in atonal composition, he was able to turn out an occasional march tune. In all this, he manages to cultivate the minutiae of rhythmic and intervallic units, with quick changes of tonal and temporal articulation, without venturing into the outer space of musical entropy.

WORKS: *Recitative and Toccata Percossa* for Harpsichord (1952); *6 Love Songs* for Unaccompanied Chorus (1952); *Capriccio* for Concert Band (1953); *Divertimento* for Violin and Harp (1954); *Divertimento* for Flute, Clarinet, Oboe, Bassoon, and Trumpet (1955); Piano Trio (1955–56); *Stanzas* for Orch. (1957); *Miniatures* for Baroque Ensemble (1957); *Filigree Setting* for String Quartet (1959); *Haiku Settings* for Soprano and Piano (1960); *Setting* for Cello and Orch. (1961); *Improvisation* for Clarinet, Viola, and Piano (1962); *Events* for Electronic Tape (1963); *2 Prayer Settings* for Tenor, Oboe, Violin, Viola, and Cello (1963); *Immobiles* for Orch. and Electronic Tape (1966); *Cantilena* for Soprano, Violin, and Electronic Tape (1970); *Machine-Music Variations* (1974–75); *Settings* for Soprano and Chamber Group (1979); *Little Companion Pieces* for Soprano and String Quartet (1980); String Quartet (1982).

Power, Lionel (**Lionel** or **Leonell Polbero** or **Powero,** etc.), English composer; date of birth unknown; d. Canterbury, June 5, 1445. He was a contemporary of Dunstable, whose style he so closely approximated that authorship of works of the 2 composers has often been confused (some authorities claim, without foundation, that Power and Dunstable were identical). He wrote a treatise, "Upon the Gamme" (c.1450; transcribed by J. Wylde, in the British Museum; reprinted by Hawkins in *History of the Science and Practice of Music,* vol. 2; also by S.B. Meech in *Speculum,* July 1935, pp. 242–58; and in part by M. Bukofzer, *Geschichte des englischen Diskants und des Fauxbourdons,* 1936).

WORKS: *2 Ave Regina*s, a *Salve Regina,* a *Mater ora filium,* and 21 pieces (mostly parts of masses) for 3–4 voices appear in Denkmäler der Tonkunst in Österreich, 14/15 (7); *Sammelbände der Internationalen Musik-Gesellschaft* (vol. 2, p. 378); Stainer's *Early Bodleian Music;* and *The Old Hall Manuscript* (3 vols., ed. by A. Ramsbotham; Burnham, Buckinghamshire, 1933–38). See also A. Schering, *Geschichte der Musik in Beispielen* (no. 37) and Davison and Apel, *Historical Anthology of Music* (vol. 1, no. 63). Other pieces preserved in MS at Bologna, Modena, Oxford, Vienna, and London (British Museum) include a *Missa Rex Saeculorum* (with *Kyrie*), a 4-voiced *Ave Regina,* and part of a *Kyrie.* 2 masses attributed to Power were publ. in Documenta Polyphoniae Liturgicae S. Ecclesiae Romanae (series 1, nos. 2 and 9). The *Complete Works,* ed. by C. Hamm, was issued by the American Inst. of Musicology (1969).

Pozdro, John (**Walter**), significant American composer and pedagogue; b. Chicago, Aug. 14, 1923. He was of Polish extraction on his paternal line (*po-zdro* means, approximately, "your health") and of German origin on his mother's side; his father was a master cabinetmaker and an unsung artist (he sang and played the violin). Pozdro took piano lessons with Nina Shafran; then studied music theory at the American Cons. in Chicago and Northwestern Univ.; later entered the Eastman School of Music at Rochester, N.Y., as a student in composition of Howard Hanson and Bernard Rogers, graduating in 1958 with a Ph.D. He subsequently joined the music faculty at the Univ. of Kansas in Lawrence, became its director of music theory and composition in 1961; from 1958 to 1968 was chairman of the Annual Symposium of Contemporary American Music at the Univ. of Kansas. His music is inherently pragmatic, with tertian torsion resulting in the formation of tastefully enriched triadic harmony, and with asymmetric rhythms enhancing the throbbing pulse of musical continuity.

Praetorius, Ernst, German musicologist; b. Berlin, Sept. 20, 1880; d. Ankara, March 27, 1946. He studied violin in Breslau and Halle; history and theory in Berlin with Friedlaender, Fleischer, and Stumpf; in 1905, received his Dr.Phil. with the dissertation *Die Mensuraltheorie des Franchinus Gafurius* (Leipzig, 1905); in 1906, was appointed director of the famous Heyer Museum in Cologne; held this post until 1909, when he joined the staff of the Cologne Opera. Subsequently, he held similar positions in Bochum (1912), Leipzig (1913), Lübeck (1914), Breslau (1915), and Berlin (1922). From 1924 until 1933 he was Generalmusikdirektor in Weimar; in 1934 went to Turkey, where he was active in the educational field and on the radio; remained in Ankara until his death.

Praetorius (Latinized from **Schulz** or **Schulze**), **Hieronymus,** German composer; b. Hamburg, Aug. 10, 1560; d. there, Jan. 27, 1629. He studied with his father, **Jacobus Schulze,** organist of the Jacobikirche; then in Cologne. He became town cantor in Erfurt in 1580, assistant organist to his father in 1582, and his successor in 1586. He brought out a *Hamburger Melodeyen-Gesangbuch* (1604; with his son **Jacobus,** J. Decker, and D. Scheidemann). His works were publ. in 5 collections in 1622–25, under the general title *Opus musicum novum et perfectum:* I, *Cantiones sacrae a* 5–12; II, *Magnificats a* 8–12; III, *Liber missarum,* 6 masses *a* 5–8; IV, *Cantiones variae, a* 5–20, containing Latin and German motets; V, *Cantiones novae officiosae, a* 5–15, also containing Latin and German motets. A selection of his works (a Mass, a Magnificat, and some motets) was publ. by Hugo Leichtentritt in Denkmäler Deutscher Tonkunst, 23.

Praetorius, Jacobus, German composer and organist, son of **Hieronymus Praetorius;** b. Hamburg, Feb. 8, 1586; d. there, Oct. 22, 1651. He studied with Sweelinck in Amsterdam; in 1603 was appointed organist at the Peterskirche in Hamburg. He contributed several motets to his father's collection *Hamburger Melodeyen-Gesangbuch.*

Praetorius, Michael, great German musician, composer, and theorist; b. Kreuzberg, Thuringia, Feb. 15, 1571; d. Wolfenbüttel, Feb. 15, 1621. His real family name was **Schultheiss** (German for "magistrate," or "praetor"), which he Latinized as Praetorius. He was the son of a preacher; attended the Latin school of Torgau; studied organ in Frankfurt; then was in the service of the Duke of Braunschweig (from 1604); was also prior of the Ringelheim monastery, although without actual residence there. In 1612 he succeeded Mancinus as Kapellmeister in Wolfenbüttel, and remained there until his death.

WORKS: *Musae Sioniae,* a collection of 1,244 vocal numbers in 9 parts, in note-against-note counterpoint (1605–10; 2nd ed. of Part IX, as *Bicinia et tricinia,* 1611); *Musarum Sioniarum motetae et psalmi 4–16 vocae* (1607); *Eulogodia Sionia* (1611); 60 motets *a* 2–8 for the "close of the Divine Service"; *Missodia Sionia* (1611); *Hymnodia Sionia* (1611; hymns *a* 2–8); *Megalynodia* (1611; madrigals and motets *a* 5–8); *Terpsichore* (1612; dance pieces *a* 4–6, by Praetorius and some French composers); *Polyhymnia caduceatrix et panegyrica* (1619; songs of peace and rejoicing *a* 1–21); *Polyhymnia exercitatrix* (1620; *a* 2–8); *Uranodia* or *Uranochordia* (1613; 19 songs *a* 4); *Kleine und grosse Litaney* (1613); *Epithalamium* (1614); *Puericinium* (1621; 14 church songs *a* 3–12). REPRINTS: Organ works by W. Gurlitt, in the *Archiv für Musikwissenschaft* (1921); also by K. Matthäi (Braunschweig, 1930); *Psalm 116,* by R. Holle (Mainz, 1933); 2 pieces by A. Schering in *Geschichte der Musik in Beispielen* (nos. 161, 162); various numbers reprinted by G. Tucher, L. Schöberlein, F. Riegel, K. Ameln, etc.

WRITINGS: *Syntagma musicum,* his major work, of which 3 vols. were printed: Vol. I, part 1 (Wolfenbüttel, 1614; in 2 parts), is a historical and descriptive treatise in Latin on ancient and ecclesiastical music, and ancient secular instruments. Vol. II (Wolfenbüttel, 1618; Appendix, 1620), written in German, in 5 parts and an Appendix, is the most important extant source of information on musical instruments of the period, describing their form, compass, tone quality, etc., the organ in particular being treated at great length; the Appendix contains 42 woodcuts of the principal instruments enumerated (vol. II has been reprinted as vol. XIII of the publications of the Gesellschaft für Musikforschung; facsimile reprint, with introduction by W. Gurlitt, Kassel, 1929). Vol. III (Wolfenbüttel, 1618) contains a valuable and interesting account of secular composition at that time, and a treatise on solmisation, notation, etc.; a reprint of vol. III was publ. by E. Bernouilli (1916). A complete edition of Praetorius's works was issued in 21 vols. under the editorship of Friedrich Blume (1928–41).

Pratella, Francesco Balilla, Italian composer and writer of radical tendencies; b. Lugo di Romagna, Feb. 1, 1880; d. Ravenna, May 17, 1955. He studied with Ricci-Signorini, then at the Liceo Rossini in Pesaro with Cicognani and Mascagni; taught in Cesana (1908–9); was director of the Istituto Musicale in Lugo (1910–29), and of the Liceo Musicale G. Verdi in Ravenna (1927–45). He joined the Italian futurist movement in 1910 (Russolo's manifesto of 1913 was addressed to "Balilla Pratella, grande musicista futurista"), and in 1913 wrote his first composition in a "futurist" idiom, the choral *Inno alla vita.* His other works are the operas *Lilia* (won honorable mention in the Sonzogno Contest, 1903; perf. in Lugo, Nov. 13, 1905); *La Sina d'Vargöun,* to his own libretto (Bologna, Dec. 4, 1909); *L'Aviatore Dro,* also to his own libretto (Lugo, Nov. 4, 1920); *La ninnananna della bambola,* children's opera (Milan, May 21, 1923); *Dono primaverile,* comedy with music (Bologna, Oct. 17, 1923); *Fabiano* (Bologna, Dec. 9, 1939); incidental music; for Orch.: *Romagna, La guerra, 5 poemi musicali;* chamber music; etc.

Pratt, Silas Gamaliel, American composer; b. Addison, Vt., Aug. 4, 1846; d. Pittsburgh, Oct. 30, 1916. Both his parents were church singers. The family moved to Chicago when he was a child, and he received his primary music education there; at 22 he went to Berlin, where he studied piano with Kullak and theory with Kiel (1868–71). He then returned to Chicago, where he served as organist of the Church of the Messiah; in 1872, established the Apollo Club. In 1875 he went to Germany once more; studied orchestration with Heinrich Dorn, and also took some piano lessons with Liszt. On July 4, 1876, he conducted in Berlin his *Centennial Overture,* dedicated to President Grant; also conducted at the Crystal Palace in London, when President Grant was visiting there; another work that he presented in London was *Homage to Chicago March.* Returning to Chicago, he conducted his opera *Zenobia, Queen of Palmyra* (to his own libretto) in concert form, on June 15, 1882 (stage perf., Chicago, March 26, 1883; N.Y., Aug. 21, 1883). The opera was received in a hostile manner by the press, partly owing to the poor quality of the music, but mainly as a reaction to Pratt's exuberant and immodest proclamations of its merit in advance of the production. Undaunted, Pratt unleashed a vigorous campaign for native American opera; he organized the Grand Opera Festival of 1884, which had some support. The following year he visited London again, and conducted there his symph. work *The Prodigal Son* (Oct. 5, 1885). Returning to Chicago, he revised his early lyric opera *Antonio,* renamed it *Lucille,* and produced it on March 14, 1887. In 1888 he moved to N.Y.; there he presented, during the quadricentennial of the discovery of America, his opera *The Triumph of Columbus* (in concert form, Oct. 12, 1892); also produced a scenic cantata, *America,* subtitled *4 Centuries of Music, Picture, and Song* (Nov. 24, 1894; with stereopticon projections). Other works: *Lincoln Symphony;* symph. poem, *The Tragedy of the Deep* (1912; inspired by the *Titanic* disaster); cantata, *The Last Inca;* he also publ. a manual, *Pianist's Mental Velocity* (N.Y., 1903). In 1906 he settled in Pittsburgh; established there the Pratt Inst. of Music and Art, and remained its director until his death. Pratt was a colorful personality; despite continuous and severe setbacks, he was convinced of

his own significance. The story of his salutation to Wagner at their meeting—"Herr Wagner, you are the Silas G. Pratt of Germany"—may be apocryphal, but is very much in character.

Pratt, Waldo Selden, distinguished American music historian and pedagogue; b. Philadelphia, Nov. 10, 1857; d. Hartford, Conn., July 29, 1939. He studied at Williams College and at Johns Hopkins Univ., specializing in classical languages; was practically self-taught in music. After completing his studies, he was assistant director of the Metropolitan Museum of Art in N.Y. (1880–82); in 1882 he was appointed to the faculty of the Hartford Theological Seminary, where he taught hymnology; remained there until his retirement in 1925; he also taught music history at Smith College (1895–1908), and later at the Inst. of Musical Art in N.Y. He publ. a manual, *The History of Music* (1907; 3rd ed., 1935); *Musical Ministries in the Church* (1901; 4th ed., 1915); *The Music of the Pilgrims* (1921, commenting on Ainsworth's Psalter as brought to Plymouth in 1620, with the tunes in full; reprinted, N.Y., 1971); *The Music of the French Psalter of 1562* (N.Y., 1939; reprint, 1966).

Predieri, Luca Antonio, Italian composer; b. Bologna, Sept. 13, 1688; d. there, Jan. 3, 1767. He was of a musical family; served as maestro di cappella at S. Paolo in Bologna (1725–29) and at S. Pietro (1729–31). In 1737 he went to Vienna as Kapellmeister, remaining there until 1765; then returned to Bologna. His opera *Il sogno di Scipione* was performed at the Emperor's palace in Laxenburg, near Vienna, on Oct. 1, 1735; of about 30 operas, only a few are extant; he also wrote oratorios and instrumental works for festive occasions.

Preindl, Joseph, Austrian composer; b. Marbach, Jan. 30, 1756; d. Vienna, Oct. 26, 1823. He studied with Albrechtsberger; served as organist at the church of Maria am Gestade in 1775, at the Carmelite church of Vienna-Leopoldstadt (1783), and at St. Michael's (1787–93); in 1793 became Kapellmeister at St. Peter's, and in 1795, Vice-Kapellmeister at St. Stephen's; in 1809 succeeded Albrechtsberger there as Kapellmeister. He publ. about 14 masses and other church works; brought out a *Gesanglehre* (singing manual) and a book of old melodies by German composers. His method, *Wiener Tonschule,* was publ. after his death, edited by Seyfried (Vienna, 1827; 2nd ed., 1832).

Presley, Elvis, fantastically popular American rock-'n'-roll singer and balladeer; b. Tupelo, Miss., Jan. 8, 1935; d. Memphis, Aug. 16, 1977. He was employed as a mechanic and furniture repairman in his early youth; picked up guitar playing in his leisure hours; sang cowboy ballads at social gatherings. With the advent of rock 'n' roll, he revealed himself as the supreme genius of the genre; almost effortlessly he captivated multitudes of adolescents by the hallucinogenic monotone of his vocal delivery, enhanced by rhythmic pelvic gyrations (hence the invidious appellation "Elvis the Pelvis"); made recordings that sold millions of albums. He made America conscious of the seductive inanity of rock ballads; he aroused primitive urges among his multitudinous admirers with his renditions of such songs, among them *Don't Be Cruel, Hound Dog, Love Me Tender, All Shook Up, Jailhouse Rock, Heartbreak Hotel, Rock around the Clock, It's Now or Never;* his audience responded by improvising songs about him: *My Boy Elvis, I Wanna Spend Christmas with Elvis,* and *Elvis for President.* He also appeared as an actor in sentimental motion pictures. His art was the prime inspiration for the famous Liverpudlian quartet The Beatles. An International Elvis Presley Appreciation Society was organized by 1970. Elvis Presley was indeed The King of Kings of rock. His death (of cardiac arrhythmia aggravated by an immoderate use of tranquilizers and other drugs) precipitated the most extraordinary outpouring of public grief over an entertainment figure since the death of Rudolph Valentino. His entombment in the family mausoleum in Memphis was the scene of mob hysteria, during which 2 people were run over and killed by an automobile; 2 men were arrested for an alleged plot to spirit away his body and hold it for ransom. Entrepreneurs avid for gain put out a mass of memorial literature, souvenirs, and gewgaws, sweat shirts emblazoned with Presley's image in color, Elvis dolls, and even a life-size effigy, as part of a multimillion-dollar effort to provide solace to sorrowing humanity; the only discordant note was sounded by Presley's own bodyguards, who authored a book provocatively titled *Elvis, What Happened?,* with murky insinuations that the King of Rock was a drug addict. Presley's home, turned into a sanctuary at suburban Whitehaven, in Memphis, was opened to the public on June 7, 1982, and was visited by mobs, not only by drug-besotted local rock fans, but by delegations from fan clubs in civilized nations (even the U.K.). Souvenirs included an "Always Elvis" brand of wine; license plates of out-of-town motorists bore the legend ELVIS-P. A bill was submitted in Congress for declaring Presley's nativity day, Jan. 8, a national day.

Presser, Theodore, American music publisher; b. Pittsburgh, July 3, 1848; d. Philadelphia, Oct. 27, 1925. He studied music at the New England Cons. in Boston with S. Emery, G.E. Whiting, J.C.D. Parker, and B. Lang; then at the Leipzig Cons. with Zwintscher and Jadassohn; in 1883 he founded in Philadelphia the *Etude,* a well-known music monthly of which he was editor until 1907; James F. Cooke was its editor from 1908 to 1949; it discontinued publication in 1957. Shortly after the foundation of the *Etude,* Presser established a publishing house, Theo. Presser Co., for music and books about music, which has come to be one of the important firms in the U.S. In 1906 he founded the Presser Home for Retired Music Teachers, which in 1908 moved to fine new quarters in Germantown (accommodations for 65 guests). In 1916 he established the Presser Foundation to administer this Home, to provide relief for deserving musicians, and to offer scholarships in more than 75 colleges and univs. in the U.S. James Francis Cooke was president of the Foundation from 1918. Presser wrote instructive pieces and studies for piano; was a co-founder of the Music Teachers National Assoc. (1876).

Pressler, Menahem, German-born American pianist; b. Magdeburg, Dec. 16, 1923. He was taken to Palestine by his family after the Hitlerization of Germany; he studied piano with Eliah Rudiakow and Leo Kestenberg; then played with the Palestine Symph. In 1946 he won the Debussy Prize at the piano competition in San Francisco. In 1955 he became a member of the School of Music at Indiana Univ.; that year he became pianist in the Beaux Arts Trio, with which he made several tours; he also continued his career as a soloist.

Prêtre, Georges, French conductor; b. Waziers, Aug. 14, 1924. He studied music at the Douai Cons.; then attended courses at the Paris Cons.; also took lessons in conducting with André Cluytens. He made his debut as conductor at the Marseilles Opera in 1946; subsequently had guest engagements in Lille, Toulouse, and other provincial French cities. In 1955 he was engaged as conductor of the Opéra-Comique in Paris; in 1959 was appointed to the staff of the Paris Opéra. He made his American debut with the Chicago Lyric Opera in 1959. On Oct. 17, 1964, he made his first appearance at the Metropolitan Opera in N.Y., conducting *Samson et Dalila.* His European engagements included those at Covent Garden in London, La Scala in Milan, the Vienna State Opera, and the Salzburg Festivals. In 1965 he made an American tour, which included a guest appearance with the Philadelphia Orch. Prêtre is by temperament a Romantic conductor; externally he produces an impression of bodily eloquence, projecting musical rhetorics with an imperious hand; yet he can be superlatively restrained in conducting the classics.

Previn, André, brilliant American pianist, composer, and conductor; b. Berlin, April 6, 1929, of Russian-Jewish descent; the original spelling of his surname was **Prewin.** He showed an unmistakable musical gift as a child; his father, a lawyer, was an amateur musician who gave him his early training; they played piano, 4-hands, together at home. At the age of 6, he was accepted as a pupil at the Berlin Hochschule für Musik, where he studied piano with Prof. Breithaupt; as a Jew, however, he was compelled to leave school in 1938. The family then went to Paris; he continued his studies at the Paris Cons., Marcel Dupré being one of his teachers. In 1939 the family emigrated to America, settling in Los Angeles, where his father's cousin, Charles Previn, was music director at Universal Studios in Hollywood. He took lessons in composition with Joseph Achron, Ernst Toch, and Mario Castelnuovo-Tedesco. He became an American citizen in 1943. Even before graduating from high school, he obtained employment at MGM; he became an orchestrator there and later one of its music directors; he also became a fine jazz pianist. He served in the U.S. Army (1950–52); stationed in San Francisco, he took lessons in conducting with Pierre Monteux, who was music director of the San Francisco Symph. Orch. at the time. During these years he wrote much music for films; he received Academy Awards for his arrangements of *Gigi* (1958), *Porgy and Bess* (1959), *Irma la Douce* (1963), and *My Fair Lady* (1964). Throughout this period he continued to appear as a concert pianist. In 1962 he made his formal conducting debut with the St. Louis Symph. Orch., and conducting soon became his principal vocation. From 1967–69 he was conductor-in-chief of the Houston Symph. Orch. In 1968 he assumed the post of principal conductor of the London Symph. Orch., retaining it with distinction until 1979; then was made its conductor emeritus. In 1976 he became music director of the Pittsburgh Symph. Orch.; in 1982 he was also appointed music director of the Royal Phil. Orch. of London, effective with the 1985–86 season. During his years as director of the London Symph. Orch., he took it on a number of tours to the U.S., as well as to Russia, Japan, South Korea, and Hong Kong. He also took the Pittsburgh Symph. Orch. on acclaimed tours of Europe in 1978 and 1982. He continued to compose popular music, including the scores for the musicals *Coco* (1969) and *The Good Companions* (1974); with words by Tom Stoppard, he composed *Every Good Boy Deserves Favour* (1977), a work for Actors and Orch. His other compositions include Symph. for Strings (1962); *Overture to a Comedy* (1963); Violin Sonata (1964); Flute Quartet (1964); *Elegy* for Oboe and Strings (1967); Cello Concerto (1967); Horn Concerto (1968); Guitar Concerto (1972); *Principals* for Orch. (1980); *Reflections* for Orch. (1981); *Divertimento* for Orch. (1982); piano pieces; songs. He edited the book *Orchestra* (Garden City, N.Y., 1979). He was married four times (and divorced thrice): to the jazz singer **Betty Bennett,** to the jazz poet **Dory Langdon** (who made a career of her own as composer and singer of pop songs of lament), to the actress Mia Farrow, and in 1982 to Heather Hales.

Previtali, Fernando, Italian conductor; b. Adria, Feb. 16, 1907. He studied cello, piano, and composition at the Cons. of Turin; from 1936 to 1953 conducted the Rome Radio Orch.; from 1953 to 1973 was artistic director of the Santa Cecilia Academy. In 1971 he was appointed music director of the Teatro Regio in Parma. He made several appearances as a guest conductor in the U.S. (made his debut with the Cleveland Orch., Dec. 15, 1955); also conducted in Russia. He wrote a ballet, *Allucinazioni,* and other music; publ. an instructive manual, *Guida allo studio della direzione d'orchestra* (Rome, 1951).

Prévost, André, Canadian composer; b. Hawkesburg, Ontario, July 30, 1934. He studied piano and bassoon at the Montreal Cons. (1951–60); composition with Pépin and Papineau-Couture; then went to Paris, where he studied with Messiaen and Dutilleux. In 1964 he returned to North America and took summer courses at the Berkshire Music Center in Tanglewood under the direction of Schuller, Copland, and Kodály; in 1964 he joined the staff of the music faculty of the Univ. of Montreal.

WORKS: *Poème de l'infini,* symph. poem (1960); *Scherzo* for String Orch. (1960); *Fantasmes* for Orch. (1963; Montreal, Nov. 22, 1963; posthumously dedicated to John F. Kennedy); *Pyknon,* pièce concertante for Violin and Orch. (1966); *Célébration* for Orch. (1966); *Terre des hommes (Man and His World)* for 2 Narrators, 3 Choirs, and Orch. (1967; Montreal, April 29, 1967; opening of Expo '67); *Diallèle* for Orch. (1968; Toronto, May 30, 1968); *Evanescence* for Orch. (1970; Ottawa, April 7, 1970); *Hommage (à Beethoven)* for 14 Strings (1970–71); *Psaume 148* for Chorus, Brass, and Organ (1971; Guelph, Canada, May 1, 1971); *Chorégraphie I (... Munich, September 1972 ...)* for Orch. (1972–73; Toronto, April 22, 1975; inspired by the Munich Olympics tragedy); *Chorégraphie II (E = MC²)* for Orch. (1976); *Chorégraphie III* for Orch. (1976); Cello Concerto (1976); *Pastorale* for 2 Harps (1955); *Fantasie* for Cello and Piano (1956); 2 string quartets (1958; *Ad pacem,* 1971–72); *Mobiles* for Flute, Violin, Viola, and Cello (1959–60); Violin Sonata (1960–61; arranged as a ballet under the title *Primordial,* 1968); Cello Sonata (1962; arranged for Violin, and Piano or Ondes Martenot, 1967); *Triptyque* for Flute, Oboe, and Piano (1962); *Mouvement* for Brass Quintet (1963); *Ode au St. Laurent* for optional Narrator and String Quartet (1965); *Suite* for String Quintet (1968); *Missa de profundis* for Chorus and Organ (1973); *4 Preludes* for 2 Pianos (1961); *5 Variations sur un thème grégorien* for Organ (1956); songs; choruses.

Prévost, Eugène-Prosper, French conductor and composer; b. Paris, April 23, 1809; d. New Orleans, Aug. 19, 1872. He studied at the Paris Cons. with Lesueur, winning the Grand Prix de Rome in 1831 with the cantata *Bianca cappello.* He conducted theatrical music in Le Havre (1835–38); then went to New Orleans, where he conducted until 1862; was active in Paris (1862–67) before returning to New Orleans as a singing master. He produced several operas in Paris, of which *Cosimo* (Opéra-Comique, Oct. 13, 1835) was the most successful; another, *Blanche et René,* was given in New Orleans in 1861; he also wrote oratorios and masses.

Prey, Hermann, outstanding German baritone; b. Berlin, July 11, 1929. He was about to be drafted into the dwindling Nazi battalions during the last days of the war, when was only 15 years old, but emerged unscathed and began to study voice with Günther Baum at the Hochschule für Musik in Berlin. In 1952 he won first prize in a vocal contest organized by the U.S. army of occupation; made his opera debut in Wiesbaden, and then received an engagement to sing in America. Returning to Germany, he joined the Hamburg State Opera (1953–60), with which he performed roles in modern operas by Liebermann, Dallapiccola, and Henze. In 1956 he sang Wolfram in *Tannhäuser* at the Bayreuth Festival.

He also was a guest performer at the Bavarian State Opera in Munich, at the Städtische Oper in Berlin, at the Vienna State Opera, at La Scala in Milan, and at Covent Garden in London. On Dec. 17, 1960, he appeared for the first time at the Metropolitan Opera in N.Y., as Wolfram; he returned to the Metropolitan to sing the role of Count Almaviva on Dec. 2, 1964, and, one of his finest roles, that of Papageno in *Die Zauberflöte*. On April 2, 1973, he sang Figaro in *Il Barbiere di Siviglia* at the Metropolitan Opera. He also proved himself a remarkable singer of German lieder, excelling in the cycles of Schubert's songs but also showing an extraordinary verve in performing vocal parts in the works of Schoenberg and Berg. In Germany he became popular as master of ceremonies, speaker, and singer in his own television show in Munich. His extramusical interests are confined to parapsychology. He received the West German Cross of Merit in 1974.

Price, Florence B. (née **Smith**), black American pianist and composer; b. Little Rock, Ark., April 9, 1888; d. Chicago, June 3, 1953. She studied with Chadwick and Converse at the New England Cons. in Boston, graduating in 1906. She had been publishing her compositions since she was 11 (1899); in 1928 she won a prize from G. Schirmer for *At the Cotton Gin* for Piano; around this time she was also writing musical jingles for radio commercials. Her first notable success came in 1932 with her Symph. in E minor (winner of the Wanamaker Award; perf. by the Chicago Symph. at the Century of Progress Exhibition in 1933); she became known as the first black woman to write symphs. She also wrote *Concert Overture on Negro Spirituals; Piano Concerto in One Movement* (many perfs.); *Negro Folk Songs in Counterpoint* for String Quartet; for Piano: *Arkansas Jitter; 3 Little Negro Dances*; the suite *From the Canebrakes*; many other works for piano and for organ.

Price, Leontyne (Mary Violet), remarkably endowed black American soprano; b. Laurel, Miss., Feb. 10, 1927, of working-class parents, a carpenter and a midwife. She was taught piano by a local woman, and also learned to sing. On Dec. 17, 1943, she played piano and sang at a concert in Laurel. She went to Oak Park High School, graduating in music in 1944; then enrolled in the College of Education and Industrial Arts in Wilberforce, Ohio, where she studied voice with Catherine Van Buren; received her B.A. degree in 1948 and then was awarded a scholarship at the Juilliard School of Music in N.Y.; there she received vocal training from Florence Page Kimball, and also joined the Opera Workshop under the direction of Frederic Cohen. Virgil Thomson heard her perform the role of Mistress Ford in Verdi's opera *Falstaff* and invited her to sing in the revival of his opera *4 Saints in 3 Acts* in 1952. She subsequently performed the responsible part of Bess in Gershwin's *Porgy and Bess* on a tour of the U.S. (1952–54) and in Europe (1955). On Nov. 14, 1954, she made a highly acclaimed debut as a concert singer in N.Y. On Dec. 3, 1954, she sang at the first performance of Samuel Barber's *Prayers of Kierkegaard* with the Boston Symph., conducted by Charles Munch. On Jan. 23, 1955 she performed Tosca on television, creating a sensation both as an artist and as a member of her race taking up the role of an Italian diva. Her career was soon assured without any reservations. In 1957 she appeared with the San Francisco Opera; on Oct. 18, 1957 she sang Aida, a role congenial as to both race and her passionate artistry. In 1958 she sang Aida with the Vienna State Opera under the direction of Herbert von Karajan; on July 2, 1958, she sang this role at Covent Garden in London; and again as Aida she appeared at La Scala in Milan in 1959, the first black woman to sing with that most prestigious and most fastidious opera company. On Jan. 27, 1961, she made her first appearance with the Metropolitan Opera in N.Y. in the role of Leonora in *Il Trovatore*. A series of highly successful performances at the Metropolitan followed: Aida on Feb. 20, 1961; Madama Butterfly on March 3, 1961; Donna Anna on March 25, 1961; Tosca on April 1, 1962; Pamina on Jan. 3, 1964; Cleopatra in the premiere of Samuel Barber's opera *Antony and Cleopatra* at the opening of the new Metropolitan Opera House at Lincoln Center in N.Y. on Sept. 16, 1966. On Sept. 24, 1973, she sang Madama Butterfly at the Metropolitan once more. On Feb. 7, 1975, she appeared there in the title role of *Manon Lescaut;* and on Feb. 3, 1976, she sang Aida. She was married in 1952 to the baritone **William Warfield** (who sang Porgy at her performances of *Porgy and Bess*), but separated from him in 1959; they were legally divorced in 1973. Leontyne Price received many honors and honorary doctorates. On July 4, 1964, she was awarded the Presidential Medal of Freedom.

Price, Margaret, British operatic soprano; b. Tredegar, Wales, April 13, 1941. She studied at the Trinity College of Music in London; made her debut in 1962 at the Welsh National Opera as Cherubino in *Le nozze di Figaro*, and in 1963 sang the same role at Covent Garden in London. She established herself as a foremost performer of soprano roles in Mozart's operas, excelling as Donna Anna in *Don Giovanni*, the Countess in *Le nozze di Figaro*, and Pamina in *Die Zauberflöte;* also distinguished herself as Desdemona in Verdi's *Otello*. She made appearances, invariably successful, with the operas at Cologne, Munich, Hamburg, Chicago, and San Francisco. She joined the cast of the Paris Opéra during its American tour in 1976, eliciting extraordinary praise from the public and critics. Her voice is essentially a lyric soprano, but is capable of technically brilliant coloratura.

Prieberg, Fred K., German writer on music; b. Berlin, June 3, 1928. He took music courses at the Univ. of Freiburg im Breisgau (1950–53); from 1953 to 1969 lived in Baden-Baden. He publ. a number of informative books on modern music, among them *Musik unterm Strich* (Freiburg, 1956); *Musik des technischen Zeitalters* (Zürich, 1956); *Lexikon der neuen Musik* (Freiburg, 1958); *Musica ex machina*

(Berlin, 1960); *Musik in der Sowjetunion* (Cologne, 1965); *Musik im anderen Deutschland* (Cologne, 1968).

Priestman, Brian, English conductor; b. Birmingham, Feb. 10, 1927. He studied at the Univ. of Birmingham (M.A., 1952); served as music director of the Royal Shakespeare Theatre, Stratford-upon-Avon (1960–63); then conducted the Edmonton Symph. in Alberta, Canada (1964–68), and the Baltimore Symph. (1968–69). From 1970 to 1978 he was music director of the Denver Symph. Orch. and was also principal conductor of the New Zealand National Orch. (1973–76). From 1977 to 1980 he was music director of the Florida Phil., and subsequently was music adviser of the Cape Town Symph. in South Africa; while there he was also appointed, in 1980, prof. at the Univ. of Cape Town and director of the South African College of Music.

Příhoda, Váša, noted Czech violinist; b. Vodňany, Aug. 22, 1900; d. Vienna, July 26, 1960. He received his first instruction from his father, a professional violinist; made his public debut at the age of 12 in Prague; in 1920 went on an Italian tour; in 1921 appeared in the U.S., and in 1927 played in England; then gave recitals throughout Europe. He continued to concertize after the absorption of Austria and Czechoslovakia into the Nazi Reich, and was briefly charged with collaboration with the occupying powers. He eventually became a prof. at the Vienna Academy of Music.

Prill, Emil, eminent German flutist, brother of **Karl** and **Paul Prill;** b. Stettin, May 10, 1867; d. Berlin, Feb. 28, 1940. He studied with his father; finished his musical education at the Hochschule für Musik in Berlin; in 1888 taught in Kharkov, Russia; then played first flute with the Hamburg Phil.; in 1892 became first flutist at the Berlin Opera; in 1903 was appointed an instructor at the Hochschule. He publ. the methods *Schule für die Böhm-Flöte* and *Flötenschule;* also a valuable practical collection of flute passages from orch. works, *Orchesterstudien* (7 books).

Prill, Karl, German violinist, brother of **Emil** and **Paul Prill;** b. Berlin, Oct. 22, 1864; d. Vienna, Aug. 18, 1931. He studied violin with Joachim at the Berlin Hochschule für Musik; played in various orchs., including that of the Gewandhaus (1891–97); in 1897 became concertmaster of the Court (later State) Opera in Vienna; also of the Vienna Phil. until 1925; also taught violin at the Vienna Academy of Music. He organized the Prill String Quartet, which was famous in his day.

Prill, Paul, German cellist and conductor, brother of **Emil** and **Karl Prill;** b. Berlin, Oct. 1, 1860; d. Bremen, Dec. 21, 1930. He studied with Manecke (cello) and Sturm (theory); was solo cellist in various German orchs.; conducted opera in Rotterdam (1886–89), Hamburg (1889–92), and Nuremberg (1901–6); conducted the Mozart Orch. in Berlin (1906–8); then settled in Munich as conductor of the Konzertverein.

Primrose, William, preeminent Scottish viola virtuoso; b. Glasgow, Aug. 23, 1903; d. Provo, Utah, May 1, 1982. He studied violin in Glasgow with Camillo Ritter; then had lessons in Belgium (1925–27) with Eugène Ysaÿe, who advised him to take up viola so as to avoid the congested violin field. He became the violist in the London String Quartet (1930–35), with which he made several tours. In 1937 he settled in the U.S., and was engaged as the principal viola player in the NBC Symph. Orch. in N.Y. under Toscanini, holding this post until 1942. In 1939 he established his own string quartet. On Feb. 24, 1953, he was named a Commander of the Order of the British Empire; in 1956 he became violist in the Festival Quartet. He also became active as a teacher; was on the faculty of the Univ. of Southern Calif. in Los Angeles (1961–65) and at the School of Music of Indiana Univ. in Bloomington (1965–74). In 1972 he inaugurated a master class at the Tokyo Univ. of Fine Arts and Music. Returning to the U.S., he taught at Brigham Young Univ. in Provo, Utah. Primrose was greatly esteemed as a viola virtuoso; he gave first performances of viola concertos by several modern composers. He commissioned a viola concerto from Béla Bartók, but the work was left unfinished at the time of Bartók's death, and the task of reconstructing the score from Bartók's sketches remained to be accomplished by Bartók's friend and associate Tibor Serly; Primrose gave its first performance with the Minneapolis Symph. on Dec. 2, 1949. He publ. *A Method for Violin and Viola Players* (London, 1960).

Pringsheim, Klaus, German conductor and composer; b. Feldafing, near Munich, July 24, 1883; d. Tokyo, Dec. 7, 1972. A scion of a highly cultured family, he studied mathematics with his father, a prof. at Munich Univ., and physics with Röntgen, the discoverer of X-rays. His twin sister, Katherine, was married to Thomas Mann. In Munich, Pringsheim took piano lessons with Bernard Stavenhagen, a student of Liszt, and composition with Ludwig Thuille. In 1906 he went to Vienna and was engaged as assistant conductor of the Vienna Opera, under the tutelage of Gustav Mahler, who took him as a pupil in conducting and composition, a relationship that developed into profound friendship. Mahler recommended him to the management of the German Opera in Prague; Pringsheim conducted there from 1909 to 1914; then was engaged as conductor and stage director at the Opera of Bremen (1915–18) and music director of the Max Reinhardt theaters in Berlin (1918–25). In 1923–24 he conducted in Berlin a Mahler cycle of 8 concerts, featuring all of Mahler's symphs. and songs with orch. In 1927 he became the music critic of the socialist newspaper *Vorwärts.* A turning point in Pringsheim's life came in 1931 with an invitation to teach music at the Imperial Academy of Music in Tokyo, where he taught until 1937; several of his Japanese students became prominent composers. From 1937 to 1939 Pringsheim served as music adviser to the Royal Dept. of Fine Arts in Bangkok, Thailand. In 1939 he returned to Japan; was briefly interned in 1944 as an opponent of the Axis policies. In 1946 he went to California; after some intermittent activities, he returned to Japan in 1951; was appointed director of the Musashino Academy of Music in Tokyo; continued to conduct; also wrote music reviews for English-language Tokyo newspapers. As a composer, Pringsheim followed the neo-Romantic trends, deeply influenced by Mahler. His compositions include a Concerto for Orch. (Tokyo, Oct. 13, 1935); Japanese radio opera, *Yamada Nagasama* (1953); Concertino for Xylophone and Orch. (1962); *Theme, Variations and Fugue* for Wind Orch. (his last composition, 1971–72); and a curious album of 36 2-part canons for piano (1959). A chapter from his theoretical work *Pythagoras, die Atonalität und wir* was publ. in *Schweizerische Musikzeitung* (1957). His reminiscences, "Mahler, My Friend," were publ. posthumously in the British periodical *Composer* (1973–74). Pringsheim was a signatory of a letter of protest by surviving friends of Mahler against the motion picture *Death in Venice*, after a novelette of Thomas Mann, in which the central character, a famous writer who suffers a homosexual crisis, was made to resemble Mahler.

Printz, Wolfgang Caspar, German composer and writer; b. Waldthurn, Oct. 10, 1641; d. Sorau, Oct. 13, 1717. Originally a theological student, he later led a roving life, and then was cantor successively at Promnitz, Triebel, and (from 1665) Sorau. He brought out *Historische Beschreibung der edelen Sing- und Kling-Kunst* (Dresden, 1690), a work of some importance for the history of music of the 17th century. His other theoretical writings include *Anweisung zur Singkunst* (1666; 2nd ed., 1671; 3rd ed., 1685); *Compendium ad Oden componendam* (1668); *Musica modulationis vocalis* (1678); *Exercitationes ... de concordantiis* (1687–89); also a curious satire on music theory, *Phrynis Mytilenaeus oder Satyrischer Componist* (1676–77; 2nd ed., 1696); also wrote 3 musical stories, characterizing different types of musicians. According to his own statement, the MSS of his numerous compositions were destroyed in a fire. A complete edition of his works, in 3 vols., was initiated in 1974, with the publication of *Musikerromane* (Berlin, 1974).

Pritchard, Sir John, distinguished English conductor; b. London, Feb. 5, 1921. He took private lessons in conducting; then entered on a long and fruitful association with the Glyndebourne Festival Opera, eventually succeeding Vittorio Gui as music director (1969–77). In the meantime, he served as music director of the Royal Liverpool Phil. Orch. (1957–63); from 1962 to 1966 he led the London Phil., which he also conducted on tours in Germany, Austria, and France (1966–67) and in Japan (1969–70). In 1971 he made his American debut conducting the Metropolitan Opera in N.Y.; he was also a guest conductor with the Pittsburgh Symph. Orch. In 1978 he was appointed chief conductor of the Cologne Opera, and in 1979, chief guest conductor of the BBC Symp. Orch. In 1981 he became joint music director (with Sylvain Cambreling) of the Théâtre Royal de la Monnaie in Brussels. He was knighted in 1983.

Procházka, Rudolf, Bohemian writer on music and composer; b. Prague, Feb. 23, 1864; d. there, March 24, 1936. He studied violin with Wittich and composition with Fibich; then devoted himself mainly to music education; in 1911 he organized a commission for the licensing of music teachers in Bohemia. He publ. several monographs: *Dei böhmischen Musikschulen* (1890); *Mozart in Prag* (1892; very valuable; revised by Paul Nettl in 1939 as *Mozart in Böhmen*); *Robert Franz* (1894); *Arpeggien: Musikalisches aus alten und neuen Tagen* (1897; 2nd ed. as *Musikalische Streiflichter*, 1901); *Johann Strauss* (1900; 2nd ed., 1903); *Das romantische Musik-Prag* (1914); *Der Kammermusikverein in Prag* (1926). He also was a composer; wrote an allegorical opera, *Das Glück* (Prague, 1898); some orch. pieces; *Deutsch-böhmische Reigen* for Piano, 4-hands; solo piano pieces; many choruses and songs.

Prod'homme, Jacques-Gabriel, industrious French librarian and music critic; b. Paris, Nov. 28, 1871; d. there, June 17, 1956. He studied philology and music history at the Ecole des Hautes Etudes Sociales (1890–94); then became a writer on musical and other subjects in the socialist publications, among them *La Revue Socialiste, Droits de l'Homme,* and *Messidor.* An ardent believer in the cause of peace, he edited in Munich the *Deutsch-französische Rundschau,* dedicated to the friendship between the French and German peoples (1897–1900). His hopes for peace were shattered by 2 devastating wars within his lifetime.

WRITINGS: Among his publications are *Le Cycle Berlioz,* in 2 vols.: *La Damnation de Faust* (1896) and *L'Enfance du Christ* (1898); *Hector Berlioz. Sa vie et ses œuvres* (1905); *Les Symphonies de Beethoven* (1906; 15th ed., 1938; awarded a prize by the French Academy); *Paganini* (1907; in Eng., 1911); *Ecrits de musiciens* (1912); *La Jeunesse de Beethoven* (1921); *Richard Wagner et la France* (1921); *L'Opéra, 1669–1925* (1925); *Pensées sur la musique et les musiciens* (1926); *Beethoven raconté par ceux qui l'ont vu* (1927); *Mozart raconté par ceux qui l'ont vu* (1928); *Schubert raconté par ceux qui l'ont vu* (1928); *Wagner raconté par ceux qui l'ont vu* (1929); *Les Sonates pour piano de Beethoven* (1937); *L'Immortelle bien-aimée de Beethoven* (1946); *Gluck* (1948); *Gossec* (1949); he also contributed a number of articles to the *Musical Quarterly*. In collaboration with Ch. Bertrand, he publ. *Guide musical et étude analytique de la Götterdämmerung* (1902); with A. Dandelot, *Gounod. Sa vie et ses œuvres d'après des documents inédits* (2 vols., 1911); with E. Crauzat, *Les Menus plaisirs du roi; L'Ecole royale et le Conservatoire de Paris* (1929). Together with Fr. Holl, F. Caille, and L. van Vassenhove, he trans. Wagner's prose works in 13 vols.

(1908–25).

Prohaska, Carl, Austrian composer; b. Mödling, near Vienna, April 25, 1869; d. Vienna, March 28, 1927. He studied piano with Anna Assmayr in Vienna and with Eugen d'Albert in Berlin; composition with Franz Krenn; musicology with Mandyczewski in Vienna. In 1908 he joined the faculty of the Akademie der Tonkunst in Vienna, where he taught piano and theory. He wrote an opera, *Madeleine Guinard;* an oratorio, *Frühlingsfeier* (1913); String Quartet; Piano Trio; Quintet for 2 Violins, Viola, Cello, and Double Bass; a group of piano pieces.

Prohaska, Felix, Austrian conductor, son of **Carl Prohaska;** b. Vienna, May 16, 1912. He received his primary music education at home with his father; then studied piano with Steuermann, and theory with Egon Kornauth and Hanns Gál. He served as chorus conductor at the Graz Opera (1936–39); conducted opera in Duisburg (1939–41) and in Strasbourg (1941–43); then was principal conductor at the Vienna State Opera (1945–55) and at the Frankfurt Opera (1955–61); returned to Vienna (1964–67); conducted at the opera in Hannover (1965–74) and also served as director of the Hochschule für Musik there in 1961–75; from 1975 he conducted in Kiel; also filled guest engagements in Europe and South America.

Prokofiev, Sergei, great Russian composer; b. Sontzovka, near Ekaterinoslav, April 27, 1891 (according to the newly found birth certificate); d. Moscow, March 5, 1953. His mother was an amateur pianist, and he received his first training from her. He improvised at the piano; in June 1900, at the age of 9, he completed the piano score of an opera, *The Giant;* then wrote an overture and 3 tableaux for an opera entitled *On Desert Island* (1902); in 1904 he embarked on the composition of another opera, *Ondine,* which he completed in 1907. He then went to Moscow, where he began taking regular lessons from Glière, under whose guidance he composed a Symph. in G and the opera *Feast during the Plague,* after Pushkin (1903). At the age of 13 he entered the St. Petersburg Cons., where he studied composition with Rimsky-Korsakov, Wihtol, and Liadov; piano with Mme. Essipova; and conducting with Nicolas Tcherepnin. He graduated from the Cons. in 1914; received the Anton Rubinstein Prize (a grand piano) as a pianist-composer for his First Piano Concerto. Even before graduation, he appeared before various modern music societies in St. Petersburg, playing his own piano pieces, and soon earned a reputation as a youthful "futurist." He developed a novel piano idiom, explicitly demonstrated in his *Sarcasms* and *Visions fugitives,* percussive and sharp, yet not without a lyric charm. Grotesquerie and irony animated Prokofiev's early works; he also felt a strong attraction toward subjects of elemental or primitive character. His first important orch. composition, the *Scythian Suite,* or *Ala and Lolly,* draws upon the ancient Russian sun-worship. While a parallel with Stravinsky's *Le Sacre du printemps*

may exist, there is no similarity between the styles of the 2 works. Another score, primitivistic in its inspiration, was *Seven, They Are Seven,* an incantation from an old Sumerian ritual. During the same period, Prokofiev wrote his famous *Classical Symphony,* which he completed at the age of 26. In it he successfully re-created the formal style of the 18th century; while the structure was indeed classical, the sudden modulatory shifts and a subtle element of grotesquerie betrayed a 20th-century hand. He conducted the first performance of the *Classical Symphony* in the spring of 1918, and then left Russia, proceeding through Siberia and Japan to America; gave concerts of his music in N.Y., Chicago, and other cities. In 1920 he went to Paris, where he became associated with Diaghilev, who produced Prokofiev's ballets *Chout* (French transliteration of the Russian word for "buffoon"), *Le Pas d'acier,* and *L'Enfant prodigue.* Koussevitzky, who became Prokofiev's publisher, commissioned several works from him for his concerts in Paris, and subsequently in Boston. In 1921 Prokofiev again visited the U.S., for the production by the Chicago Opera Co. of his opera *Love for 3 Oranges.* In 1927 he played a series of concerts in Russia; visited Russia again in 1929; then after a stay in Paris and other European cities, he went to Russia in December 1932 and remained permanently, with the exception of concert engagements in Europe and America. He had never relinquished Soviet citizenship, and was not officially an émigré. He visited the U.S. for the last time in 1938. In Russia he wrote some of his most popular works: the symph. fairy tale *Peter and the Wolf* (for a children's theater in Moscow); the cantata *Alexander Nevsky* (originally for a film); the ballet *Romeo and Juliet;* the opera *War and Peace;* the 5th, 6th, and 7th symphs.; several piano sonatas; songs; etc. Although Prokofiev was a target of sharp criticism on the part of the Soviet press for his "decadent" practices in adopting certain modernistic procedures, his status on the whole remained very high; virtually all of his works were publ.; his music became a major influence on the young generation of Soviet composers. Outside Russia, too, Prokofiev enjoyed enduring fame; his *Classical Symphony,* his 3rd Piano Concerto, *Peter and the Wolf,* the march from *Love for 3 Oranges,* the suite from *Lieutenant Kijé,* and many of the piano works have become repertoire pieces all over the world. Prokofiev never departed from the tonal system despite occasional excursions into modernistic practices (polytonality, atonality). He had an innate sense of sharp rhythm, often in asymmetrical patterns; in his melodic writing he was equally adept in simple lyricism, along modal lines, and in a modern manner spanning large intervals; he was a master of instrumentation, developing an individual method of treating orchestral sonorities. Above all, his music shows a professional care for the performer, never reaching beyond the practicable limits of execution. In 1923 he married **Lina Llubera,** a Spanish soprano. Her real name was **Carlina Codina;** she was born in Madrid in 1898, Catalan on her father's side, and Polish and French on her mother's side. She assumed the stage name Lina

Prokofiev

Llubera; made her debut in Milan as Gilda in *Rigoletto*. About 1940 Prokofiev went to live with Myra Mendelson, a young Komsomol writer, but was not legally divorced from Lina Llubera. In 1946, the latter was sent to a concentration camp in Central Asia on a political charge, and spent 8 years there. She left Russia in 1976, and in 1977 was in the U.S.

WORKS: OPERAS: *Magdalena* (1913); *The Gambler*, after Dostoyevsky (1915–16; revised 1927; premiere, Brussels, April 29, 1929); *Love for 3 Oranges*, after Carlo Gozzi (Chicago, Dec. 30, 1921, composer conducting); *The Flaming Angel* (1919; 2 fragments perf. at a Koussevitzky concert, Paris, June 14, 1928; complete perf. in concert form was given in Paris on Nov. 25, 1954; its stage premiere was given in Venice on Sept. 14, 1955); *Simeon Kotko* (1939; Moscow, June 23, 1940); *Betrothal in a Convent*, after Sheridan's *Duenna* (1940; Leningrad, Nov. 3, 1946); *War and Peace*, after Tolstoy (1941–52; first version, Leningrad, June 12, 1946; 2nd version, Leningrad, April 1, 1955); *A Tale about a Real Man* (1947–48; privately perf., Leningrad, Dec. 3, 1948; severely censured by Soviet critics and not produced in public; revived posthumously at the Bolshoi Theater in Moscow on Oct. 8, 1960).

BALLETS: *A Tale of a Buffoon Who Outwitted 7 Buffoons* (usually perf. outside Russia as *Chout*; 1920; Paris, May 17, 1921); *Le Pas d'acier* (1924; Paris, June 7, 1927); *L'Enfant prodigue* (1928; Paris, May 21, 1929); *Sur le Borysthène* (1930; Paris, Dec. 16, 1932); *Romeo and Juliet* (1935–36; Leningrad, Jan. 11, 1940); *Cinderella* (1940–44; Moscow, Nov. 21, 1945); *A Tale of the Stone Flower* (1948–50; Moscow, Feb. 12, 1954).

INCIDENTAL MUSIC: To *Egyptian Nights*, op. 61 (1933); *Boris Godunov* (1936); *Eugene Onegin* (1936); *Hamlet* (1937–38; first perf. in connection with the opening of the Leningrad Theater, May 15, 1938). Film music: *Lieutenant Kijé* (1933); *The Queen of Spades* (1938); *Alexander Nevsky* (1938); *Lermontov* (1941); *Tonya* (1942); *Kotovsky* (1942); *Partisans in the Ukrainian Steppes* (1942); *Ivan the Terrible* (1942–45).

CHORAL WORKS: 2 poems for Women's Chorus, with Orch: *The White Swan* and *The Wave* (1909); *Seven, They Are Seven*, cantata for Tenor, Chorus, and Orch. (1917–18; Paris, May 29, 1924); cantata for the 20th anniversary of the October Revolution, for 2 Choruses, Military Band, Accordions, and Percussion, to texts by Marx, Lenin, and Stalin (1937; not perf. at the time; was finally brought to a perf. in Moscow on April 5, 1966, but not in its entirety; the section which used a text from Stalin was eliminated); *Songs of Our Days*, op. 76, suite for Solo Voices, Mixed Chorus, and Orch. (Moscow, Jan. 5, 1938); *Alexander Nevsky*, cantata for Mezzo-soprano, Mixed Chorus, and Orch. (Moscow, May 17, 1939); *Salute*, cantata for Mixed Chorus and Symph. Orch., for Stalin's 60th birthday (Moscow, Dec. 21, 1939); *Ballad of a Boy Who Remained Unknown*, cantata for Soprano, Tenor, Chorus, and Orch. (Moscow, Feb. 21, 1944); *Hymn to the Soviet Union* (1943; submitted to the competition for a new Soviet anthem but failed to win; a song by Alexander Alexandrov was selected); *Flourish, Powerful Land*,

cantata for the 30th anniversary of the October Revolution (Moscow, Nov. 12, 1947); *Winter Bonfire*, suite for Narrators, Boys' Chorus, and Symph. Orch. (Moscow, Dec. 19, 1950); *On Guard for Peace*, oratorio for Mezzo-soprano, Narrators, Mixed Chorus, Boys' Chorus, and Symph. Orch. (Moscow, Dec. 19, 1950).

FOR ORCH.: Sinfonietta (1914; Petrograd, Nov. 6, 1915; new version, 1929; Moscow, Nov. 18, 1930); *Rêves*, symph. tableau (St. Petersburg, Dec. 5, 1910); *Autumn*, symph. tableau (Moscow, Aug. 1, 1911); First Piano Concerto (Moscow, Aug. 7, 1912, composer, soloist); 2nd Piano Concerto (Pavlovsk, Sept. 5, 1913, composer, soloist; 2nd version, Paris, May 8, 1924, composer, soloist); First Violin Concerto (1916–17; Paris, Oct. 18, 1923); *Scythian Suite* (1914; Petrograd, Jan. 29, 1916); *Chout*, symph. suite from the ballet (Brussels, Jan. 15, 1924); *Classical Symphony* (1916–17; Petrograd, April 21, 1918, composer conducting); 3rd Piano Concerto (1917–21; Chicago, Dec. 16, 1921, composer, soloist); *Love for 3 Oranges*, symph. suite from the opera (Paris, Nov. 29, 1925); Symph. No. 2 (1924; Paris, June 6, 1925; 2nd version, not completed); *Le Pas d'acier*, symph. suite from the ballet (1926; Moscow, May 27, 1928); Overture for Chamber Orch. (Moscow, Feb. 7, 1927; also for Large Orch., 1928; Paris, Dec. 18, 1930); *Divertissement* (1925–29; Paris, Dec. 22, 1929); Symph. No. 3 (1928; Paris, May 17, 1929); *L'Enfant prodigue*, symph. suite from the ballet (1929; Paris, March 7, 1931); Symph. No. 4 (Boston, Nov. 14, 1930; a new version, radically revised, 1947); *4 Portraits*, symph. suite from the opera *The Gambler* (1931; Paris, March 12, 1932); *On the Dnieper*, symph. suite from the ballet (1933); 4th Piano Concerto, for Left Hand Alone (1931; Berlin, Sept. 5, 1956); 5th Piano Concerto (Berlin, Oct. 31, 1932, composer, soloist); *Symphonic Song* (Moscow, April 14, 1934); First Cello Concerto (1933–38; Moscow, Nov. 26, 1938; revised and perf. for the first time in Moscow on Feb. 18, 1952, as Cello Concerto No. 2, but later retitled *Sinfonia-Concertante;* this final version was perf. posthumously in Copenhagen on Dec. 9, 1954); *Lieutenant Kijé*, symph. suite from film music (1934; Paris, Feb. 20, 1937, composer conducting); *Egyptian Nights*, symph. suite (1934; Moscow, Dec. 22, 1938); 2nd Violin Concerto (1935; Madrid, Dec. 1, 1935); *Romeo and Juliet*, first suite from the ballet (Moscow, Nov. 24, 1936); *Romeo and Juliet*, 2nd suite from the ballet (Leningrad, April 15, 1937); *Peter and the Wolf*, symph. fairy tale (Moscow, May 2, 1936); *4 Marches* for Military Band (1935–37); *Russian Overture* (Moscow, Oct. 29, 1936); *Symphonic March* (1941); *The Year 1941* (1941; Sverdlovsk, Jan. 21, 1943); *March* for Military Orch. (Moscow, April 30, 1944); Symph. No. 5 (1944; Moscow, Jan. 13, 1945); *Romeo and Juliet*, 3rd suite from the ballet (Moscow, March 8, 1946); *Ode on the End of the War* for 8 Harps, 4 Pianos, Military Band, Percussion Ensemble, and Double Basses (1945; Moscow, Nov. 12, 1945); *Cinderella*, 3 suites from the ballet (1946); *Waltzes*, suite for Orch. (1946; Moscow, May 13, 1947); Symph. No. 6 (1945–47; Leningrad, Oct. 11, 1947); *Festive Poem* (Moscow, Oct. 3, 1947); *Ivan the Terrible*, suite for Orch. (1942–45); *Pushkin Waltzes*

(1949); *Summer Night,* symph. suite on themes from the opera *Betrothal in a Convent* (1950); *Wedding Scene,* suite from the ballet *A Tale of the Stone Flower* (Moscow, Dec. 12, 1951); *Gypsy Fantasy,* from the ballet *A Tale of the Stone Flower* (Moscow, Nov. 18, 1951); *Ural Rhapsody,* from the ballet *A Tale of the Stone Flower* (1951); *The Mistress of the Copper Mountain,* suite from the ballet *A Tale of the Stone Flower* (incomplete); *The Meeting of the Volga with the Don River* (for the completion of the Volga-Don Canal; 1951; Moscow, Feb. 22, 1952); Symph. No. 7 (1951–52; Moscow, Oct. 11, 1952); Concertino for Cello and Orch. (1952; unfinished); Concerto for 2 Pianos and String Orch. (1952; incomplete).

CHAMBER MUSIC: *Humorous Scherzo* for 4 Bassoons (1912; London, Sept. 2, 1916); *Ballade* for Cello and Piano (1912); *Overture on Hebrew Themes* for Clarinet, 2 Violins, Viola, Cello, and Piano (N.Y., Jan. 26, 1920); Quintet for Oboe, Clarinet, Violin, Viola, and Double Bass (1924; Moscow, March 6, 1927); First String Quartet (Washington, D.C., April 25, 1931); Sonata for 2 Violins (Moscow, Nov. 27, 1932); First Violin Sonata (1938–46; Moscow, Oct. 23, 1946); 2nd String Quartet (1941; Moscow, Sept. 5, 1942); Sonata for Flute and Piano (Moscow, Dec. 7, 1943); 2nd Violin Sonata (transcription of the Flute Sonata; Moscow, June 17, 1944); Sonata for Violin Unaccompanied (1947); Cello Sonata (1949; Moscow, March 1, 1950).

PIANO MUSIC: 9 sonatas: No. 1 (1909); No. 2 (1912); No. 3 (1917); No. 4 (1917); No. 5 (1923); No. 6 (1940); No. 7 (1942); No. 8 (1944); No. 9 (1947); No. 10 remains in sketches (1953); 2 sonatinas (1931–32); 4 Etudes (1909); 4 Pieces (1911); 4 Pieces (1912); Toccata (1912); 10 Pieces (1913); *Sarcasms,* suite of 5 pieces (1912–14); *Visions fugitives,* suite of 20 pieces (1915–17); *Tales of an Old Grandmother,* 4 pieces (1918); *Schubert's Waltzes,* transcribed for 2 Pianos (1911); March and Scherzo from the opera *Love for 3 Oranges* (1922); *Things in Themselves* (1928); 6 Pieces (1930–31); 3 Pieces (1934); *Pensées* (1933–34); *Children's Music,* 12 easy pieces (1935); *Romeo and Juliet,* 10 pieces from the ballet (1937); 3 pieces from the ballet *Cinderella* (1942); 3 Pieces (1941–42); 10 pieces from the ballet *Cinderella,* op. 97 (1943); 6 pieces from the ballet *Cinderella* (1944).

SONGS: 2 *Poems* (1911); *The Ugly Duckling,* after Andersen (1914); 5 *Poems* (1915); 5 *Poems* (1916); 5 *Songs without Words* (1920; also for Violin and Piano); 5 *Poems* (1921); 6 *Songs* (1935); 3 *Children's Songs* (1936); 3 *Poems* (1936); 3 songs from the film *Alexander Nevsky* (1939); 7 *Songs* (1939); 7 *Mass Songs* (1941–42); 6 transcriptions of folk songs (1944); 2 duets (1945); *Soldiers' March Song* (1950).

Proksch, Josef, Bohemian pianist and pedagogue; b. Reichenberg, Aug. 4, 1794; d. Prague, Dec. 20, 1864. He studied with Koželuch; in 1811 he lost his eyesight, but still learned Logier's system, and in 1830 founded a "Musikbildungsanstalt" (school of piano playing) in Prague. He publ. a useful piano manual, *Versuch einer rationellen Lehrmethode im Pianofortespiel;* also *Musikalisches Vademecum; Apho-* *rismen über katholische Kirchenmusik; Allgemeine Musiklehre;* made for his pupils transcriptions, for 2, 3, 4, and even 8 pianos, of orch. works; composed a Concerto for 3 Pianos, sonatas, and other works; also vocal music. His son, **Theodor Proksch** (1843–76), and a daughter, **Marie Proksch** (1836–1900), managed the school after his death; the last director of the Proksch school was **Robert Franz Proksch,** a great-grandnephew of Josef Proksch; he died in 1933.

Proske, Carl, German authority on sacred music; b. Gröbnig, Feb. 11, 1794; d. Regensburg, Dec. 20, 1861. He was a medical student, served in the medical corps during the war of 1813–15; took the degree of M.D. at Halle in 1817, and practiced at Oberglogau and Oppeln. In 1823 he renounced medicine for theology, and studied at Regensburg; was ordained in 1826; became vicar-choral in 1827, and canon and Kapellmeister of the Church of Our Lady at Regensburg in 1830. After diligent research in Germany and Italy, he began his lifework, the publication of sacred classics, the first being Palestrina's *Missa Papae Marcelli* (Palestrina's original version, and arrangements by Anerio *a* 4 and Suriano *a* 8), followed by the famous collection *Musica divina,* containing chiefly Italian masterworks of the 16th–17th centuries: vol. I, 12 masses *a* 4 (1853); vol. II, motets for the entire church year (1855); vol. III, fauxbourdons, Psalms, Magnificats, hymns, and antiphons (1859); vol. IV, Passions, Lamentations, responses, Te Deums, litanies (1863; ed. by Wesselack); its publication was continued by Schrems and Haberl. Proske also publ. *Selectus novus missarum a* 4–8 (1855–59). His valuable library was purchased for the Episcopal Library at Regensburg; in 1909, when Dr. Karl Weinmann was appointed librarian, it was opened to musicians and music students.

Prout, Ebenezer, eminent English music theorist and teacher; b. Oundle, Northamptonshire, March 1, 1835; d. London, Dec. 5, 1909. Excepting some piano lessons as a boy, and later a course with Charles Salaman, he was wholly self-taught. His father had him trained to be a schoolteacher, and he took the degree of B.A. at London Univ. in 1854; but in 1859 he went over definitely to music; was organist at Union Chapel in Islington in 1861–73; a prof. of piano at the Crystal Palace School of Art in 1861–85; a prof. of harmony and composition at the National Training School from 1876; he took Sullivan's class at the Royal Academy of Music in 1897; also conducted the Hackney Choral Assoc. in 1876–90, bringing it to a high state of efficiency. He edited the *Monthly Musical Record* in 1871–74; was critic on the *Academy* in 1874–79 and on the *Athenaeum* in 1879–89. In 1894 he was called to Dublin Univ. as prof. of music, succeeding Sir R. Stewart; in 1895 both Dublin and Edinburgh univs. conferred on him the degree of Mus.Doc. *honoris causa.* His valuable theoretical works are the following: *Instrumentation* (Novello primer, 1876; 3rd ed., 1904); *Harmony, Its Theory and Practice* (1889; 20th ed., entirely re-*

written, 1903); *Counterpoint, Strict and Free* (1890); *Double Counterpoint and Canon* (1891); *Fugue* (1891); *Fugal Analysis* (1892); *Musical Form* (1893); *Applied Forms* (1895); all of these have passed through many editions. He also publ. *The Orchestra* (2 vols., 1898–99; in German, 1905–6) and *Some Notes on Bach's Church-Cantatas* (1907). He was a competent composer of useless works, among them 4 symphs.; 2 overtures; 2 organ concertos; a Piano Quintet; 2 string quartets; 2 piano quartets; Clarinet Sonata; the cantatas *Hereward, Alfred,* and *The Red Cross Knight;* a considerable amount of church music; *Freedom,* ode for Baritone Solo and Orch.; organ arrangements.

Provenzale, Francesco, one of the founders of the Neapolitan Opera School; b. Naples, 1627; d. there, Sept. 6, 1704. From 1663 he was maestro at the Cons. di Santa Maria di Loreto; in 1673–1701, director of the Cons. della Pietà de' Turchini; c.1680, associate conductor of the Royal Chapel; in 1686–99, conductor at the Tesoro di San Gennaro in Naples. Romain Rolland believed him to be identical with Francesco della Torre.

Prudent, Emile, French pianist; b. Angoulême, Feb. 3, 1817; d. Paris, May 13, 1863. Early orphaned, he was adopted by a piano tuner; studied at the Paris Cons. with Zimmerman (piano) and Laurent (harmony), taking first prize in 1833. He made tours as a pianist in France, Belgium, England, and Germany; then settled in Paris, and was greatly esteemed there as a teacher. He wrote a number of piano works; contemporary critics ranked him between Thalberg and Döhler; his paraphrase of *Lucia di Lammermoor* enjoyed considerable success; he publ. *6 études de salon,* and other effective piano pieces (*L'Hirondelle, La Berceuse, Chanson sicilienne, Le Réveil des fées,* etc.).

Prunières, Henry, eminent French musicologist; b. Paris, May 24, 1886; d. Nanterre, April 11, 1942. He studied music history with R. Rolland; received his doctorat ès lettres from the Univ. of Paris in 1913 with the dissertation *L'Opéra italien en France avant Lulli* (publ. in Paris, 1913); in 1909–14, was an instructor at the Ecole des Hautes Etudes Sociales in Paris; in 1920, founded the important journal *La Revue Musicale,* of which he was editor in chief until 1939; in 1921, he organized the concerts at the Théâtre du Vieux Colombier; was head of the French section of the International Society for Contemporary Music.

Ptolemy, Claudius, great Alexandrian astronomer, geographer, and mathematician who flourished early in the 2nd century A.D. He wrote an important treatise on music, a poor Latin version of which was made by Gogavinus (1562); Wallis publ. the original Greek text in 1682; O. Paul gives a fragment in Greek, with German trans., in his *Boëtius.* A new edition of this work was publ. by Ingemar Düring (Göteborg, 1930), with excellent commentary and explanation.

Puccini, Giacomo, celebrated Italian composer; b. Lucca, Dec. 22, 1858; d. Brussels, Nov. 29, 1924. Beginning with his great-great-grandfather, Giacomo (1712–81), all of his ancestors in the direct line were musicians of local prominence: **Antonio** (1747–1832), **Domenico** (1771–1815), **Michele** (1813–64). As a child Puccini showed neither inclination nor special talent for music; but his mother, determined to continue family tradition, sent him to the Istituto Musicale of Lucca (founded by Pacini), where Carlo Angeloni, a pupil of Michele Puccini, became his teacher. After Angeloni's untiring patience had aroused interest, and then enthusiasm, in his pupil, progress was rapid and Puccini soon was a good pianist and organist. About 1875 he became organist at the church in a nearby village, Mutigliano, and soon after was also appointed organist at San Pietro in Somaldi. In 1877 he submitted a cantata, *Juno,* to a competition held at Lucca, but failed to win the prize. Nevertheless, he produced the work, which won considerable local success, so that the young composer brought out, also with success, a motet for the feast of Santa Paolina. These successes fired his ambition, and when he became acquainted about that time with *Aida,* he resolved to win laurels as a dramatic composer. Assistance from a grand-uncle and a stipend granted by Queen Margherita enabled him to enter the Milan Cons., where he spent 3 years (1880–83) in serious study with Antonio Bazzini and Amilcare Ponchielli. For his graduation he wrote a *Capriccio sinfonico,* which at its performance at one of the Cons. concerts, and later by Faccio, elicited unstinting praise from the critics. In the same year Ponchielli introduced Puccini to the librettist Fontana, who furnished him the text of a one-act opera; in a few weeks the score was finished and sent to the Sonzongo competition. It did not win the prize, but on May 31, 1884, *Le villi* was produced at the Teatro dal Verme in Milan, with gratifying success. Ricordi, who was present, considered the work sufficiently meritorious to commission the young composer to write a new opera for him; but 5 years elapsed before this work, *Edgar* (3 acts; text by Fontana), was produced at La Scala (April 21, 1889), scoring only a moderate success. By this time Puccini had become convinced that, in order to write a really effective opera, he needed a better libretto than Fontana had provided. Accordingly, he commissioned Domenico Oliva to write the text of *Manon Lescaut;* during the composition, however, Puccini and Ricordi practically rewrote the entire book, and in the publ. score Oliva's name is not mentioned. With *Manon Lescaut* (4 acts), first produced at the Teatro Regio in Turin on Feb. 1, 1893, Puccini won a veritable triumph, which was even surpassed by the next work, *La Bohème* (4 acts; text by Illica and Giacosa), produced at the same theater on Feb. 1, 1896. These 2 works not only carried their composer's name throughout the world, but also have found and maintained their place in the repertoire of every opera house. With fame came wealth, and in 1900 he built at Torre del Lago, where he had been living since 1891, a magnificent villa. The next opera, *Tosca* (3 acts; text by Illica and Giacosa), produced at the Teatro Costanzi in Rome on Jan. 14, 1900, is Puccini's most dramatic work; it has become a fixture of the standard repertoire, and contains some of Puccini's best-known arias. At its premiere at La Scala on Feb. 17, 1904, *Madama Butterfly* (2 acts; text by Illica and Giacosa) was hissed. Puccini thereupon withdrew the score and made some slight changes (division into 3 acts, and addition of the tenor aria in the last scene). This revised version was greeted with frenzied applause in Brescia on May 28 of the same year. Puccini was now the acknowledged ruler of the Italian operatic stage, his works rivaling those of Verdi in the number of performances. The first performance of *Madama Butterfly* at the Metropolitan Opera House (Feb. 11, 1907) took place in the presence of the composer, whom the management had invited especially for the occasion. It was then suggested that he write an opera on an American subject, the premiere to take place at the Metropolitan. He found his subject when he witnessed a performance of Belasco's *The Girl of the Golden West;* he commissioned C. Zangarini and G. Civinini to write the libretto, and in the presence of the composer the world premiere of *La Fanciulla del West* occurred, amid much enthusiasm, at the Metropolitan on Dec. 10, 1910; while it never equaled the success of Puccini's *Tosca* or *Madama Butterfly,* it returned to favor in the 1970s as a period piece. Puccini then brought out *La Rondine* (3 acts; Monte Carlo, March 27, 1917) and the 3 one-act operas *Il Tabarro* (after Didier Gold's *La Houppelande),* *Suor Angelica,* and *Gianni Schicchi* (all perf. at the Metropolitan Opera House, Dec. 14, 1918). His last opera, *Turandot* (after Gozzi), was left unfinished; the final scene was completed by Franco Alfano and the work performed at La Scala in Milan on April 25, 1926; it was also given at the Metropolitan on Nov. 16, 1926. Puccini died of cancer of the larynx. All of his operas have been performed in the U.S.: *Le villi* (Metropolitan, Dec. 17, 1908); *Manon Lescaut* (Hinrichs Co., Philadelphia, Aug. 29, 1894); *La Bohème* (Los Angeles, Oct. 18, 1897); *Tosca* (Metropolitan, Feb. 4, 1901); *Madama Butterfly* (Washington, D.C., Oct. 15, 1906).

Pugnani, (Giulio) Gaetano (Gerolamo), celebrated Italian violinist and composer; b. Turin, Nov. 27, 1731; d. there, July 15, 1798. He studied violin with G.B. Somis; when he was 10, he was allowed to play in the last chair of the 2nd violins in the orch. of Turin's Teatro Regio; he officially became a member of the orch. on April 19, 1748. In 1749, on a royal stipend, he went to Rome to study with Ciampi; later toured in Europe as a concert violinist. His own style of composition approximated that of Tartini. Fritz Kreisler publ. an arrangement for violin and piano of a piece, purportedly by Pugnani, titled *Preludio e Allegro e Tempo di Minuetto,* but this proved to be by Kreisler himself. Pugnani was particularly successful in London, where he played concerts with J.C. Bach; from 1767–69 he also served as conductor at the King's Theatre, where he brought out his successful opera *Nanetta e Lubino* (April 8, 1769). He then returned to Turin, where he

was appointed concertmaster of the King's Music and of the orch. of the Teatro Regio in 1770. He was named general director of instrumental music in 1776; in 1786 he served as supervisor of military music. He made, from 1780–82, a concert tour of Europe, which included a visit to Russia. He was also active as a teacher of the violin. His students included Viotti, Conforti, Bruni, and Polledro.

WORKS: FOR THE STAGE: *Nanetta e Lubino,* opera buffa (London, April 8, 1769); *Issea,* favola pastorale (Turin, 1771); *Tamas Kouli-Kan nell'India,* dramma per musica (Turin, Feb. 1, 1772; not extant); *Aurora,* festa per musica (Turin, 1775; not extant); *Adone e Venere,* opera seria (Naples, Nov. 1784); *Achille in Sciro,* dramma per musica (Turin, Jan. 15, 1785); *Demofoonte,* dramma per musica (Turin, Dec. 26, 1787); *Demetrio a Rodi,* festa per musica (Turin, 1789); also *Correso e Calliroe,* balleto eroico (1792; not extant); ballet music to Gluck's *Orfeo* (not extant); oratorio, *Betulia liberata;* several cantatas. FOR ORCH.: Violin Concerto, sinfonias, overtures, etc.; 40 trio sonatas; 6 string quartets; sonatas for Violin; duets for 2 Violins; about 20 sonatas for Violin and Basso Continuo.

Pugni, Cesare, Italian composer; b. Genoa, May 31, 1802; d. St. Petersburg, Jan. 26, 1870. He studied violin with Alessandro Rolla and composition with Asioli at the Cons. of Milan; began his career as a composer for the stage with the ballet *Elerz e Zulmida* (Milan, May 6, 1826) and the opera *Il Disertore svizzero* (Milan, May 28, 1831), followed by several other operas: *La vendetta* (Milan, Feb. 11, 1832); *Ricciarda di Edimburgo* (Trieste, Sept. 29, 1832); *Il Contrabbandiere* (Milan, June 13, 1833); *Un episodio di S. Michele* (Milan, June 14, 1834); etc.; he also wrote an ingenious *Sinfonia a canone* for 2 orchs. playing the same music, but with the 2nd orch. coming in one measure later than the first (this musical legerdemain amused Meyerbeer); he then lived in Paris, where he produced the ballets *La Fille de marbre* (Oct. 20, 1847), *Le Violon du diable* (Jan. 19, 1849), etc. In 1851 he was appointed ballet composer for the Imperial Theater in St. Petersburg; wrote about 300 ballet scores; of these, *Esmeralda* (originally produced in Milan, 1845) and *Konyok-Gorbunok* (*Le Cheval enchanté;* St. Petersburg, 1864) still retain their popularity in Russia.

Pugno, Raoul, celebrated French pianist; b. (of an Italian father) Montrouge, Seine, June 23, 1852; d. (while on a concert tour) Moscow, Jan. 3, 1914. He studied at the Paris Cons. with G. Mathias (piano) and Ambroise Thomas (composition). He became music director of the Paris Opéra in 1871; then served as organist at the St.-Eugène Church in 1872; became choirmaster there in 1878–92; then taught harmony at the Paris Cons. (1892–96) and subsequently was a prof. of piano there (1896–1901). In the meantime he gave numerous recitals, and gradually rose to the rank of a great virtuoso; he appeared in England in 1894; in America in 1897–98. He was equally remarkable as an ensemble player; his sonata recitals with Ysaÿe became world famous. Pugno was also a composer; he wrote several operas: *Ninetta* (Paris, Dec. 23, 1882); *Le Sosie* (Oct. 7, 1887); *Le Valet de cœur* (April 19, 1888); *Le Retour d'Ulysse* (Paris, Feb. 1, 1889); *La Vocation de Marius* (March 29, 1890); etc.; ballet, *La Danseuse de corde* (Paris, Feb. 5, 1892); piano pieces; songs. His score for *La Ville morte* (after Gabriele d'Annunzio), left incomplete at his death, was finished by Nadia Boulanger.

Pujol, Francesc, Catalan composer; b. Barcelona, May 15, 1878; d. there, Dec. 24, 1945. He studied at the Barcelona Cons., also with Millet; was assistant conductor (1900–41), then music director (1941–45), of the Orfeó Catalá in Barcelona. He wrote many sardanas; church music; orch. works; etc.; publ. valuable studies on Catalan songs: *Chant de la Sibila; L'Œuvre du "Chansonnier populaire de la Catalogne"* (*Report of the International Musicological Congress,* Vienna, 1927); *Observacions, apéndix i notes al Romancerillo catalán de Manuel Milá y Fontanals* (with Joan Punti; 1927—); Catalan folk songs, with piano accompaniment (Madrid, 1921).

Puppo, Giuseppe, Italian violinist; b. Lucca, June 12, 1749; d. Florence, April 19, 1827. He was a successful violin virtuoso at an early age; traveled in Spain; was in England from 1777 until 1783, when he settled in Paris; was a fashionable teacher there; in 1811, abandoned his family in Paris; went to Naples and then to Florence, where he died in poverty. He publ. 3 violin concertos, 8 études for violin, and 6 piano fantasias.

Purcell, Daniel, brother of **Henry Purcell;** b. London, c.1660; d. there (buried, Nov. 26), 1717. He became organist of Magdalen College, Oxford, in 1688; took his brother's place as a dramatic composer in 1695, and was organist of St. Andrew's, Holborn, from 1713.
WORKS: Incidental music to 30 dramas; several odes (e.g., funeral ode for his brother); *The Psalm Tunes set full for the Organ or Harpsichord* appeared posthumously (London, 1718).

Purcell, Henry, one of the greatest of English composers; b. London (?), c.1659; d. Dean's Yard, Westminster, Nov. 21, 1695. Until recently it was believed that his father was Henry Purcell (d. 1664), Gentleman of the Chapel Royal and Master of the choristers at Westminster Abbey. But the latest evidence indicates that he was the son of Henry's brother, Thomas Purcell, who was also a Gentleman of the Chapel Royal and held other important posts at the court. From 1669 Henry Purcell was a chorister of the Chapel Royal under Cooke and Humfrey, also receiving instruction from Dr. Blow. When his voice broke in 1673, he was appointed Assistant Keeper of the Instruments. In 1677 he was appointed composer to the King's band, and in 1679 he succeeded Blow as organist of Westminster Abbey. In 1682 he became one of the 3 organists of the Chapel Royal as Lowe's successor; in 1683, Keeper of the King's Wind Instruments. His first printed

composition is a song in vol. I (1675) of Playford's *Choice Ayres;* vol. II (1679) contains several other songs, and an elegy on the death of Matthew Locke. In 1680 Purcell wrote the first of 29 "odes" and "welcome songs." His first publ. chamber music dates from 1683: *Sonatas of III Parts: two violins and bass: to the Organ or Harpsichord* (with engraved portrait), 12 numbers, based on Italian models, each having an adagio, a canzone (fugue), a slow movement, and an air. *The Yorkshire Feast Song,* called by D'Urfey, the author, "one of the finest compositions he ever made," was composed and produced in 1690. This is one of 29 "welcome songs," which Purcell wrote (on an average of 2 annually) in his capacity of "composer-in-ordinary." Although the texts are almost invariably stupid or bombastic, Purcell wrote some of his finest music for these occasional odes. During his last 5 years he developed extraordinary activity in theatrical composition, to which he had given some attention since 1680, when he began to write some incidental dances and occasional airs for various dramas. In spite of this close connection with the stage, he wrote only one opera, *Dido and Aeneas,* produced in 1689. He lies in the north aisle of Westminster Abbey, and his burial tablet well expresses contemporary estimation of his worth: "Here lyes Henry Purcell, Esq.; who left this life, and is gone to that blessed place where only his harmony can be exceeded." His church music shows him to be an original melodist, and a master of form, harmony, and all contrapuntal devices; his music for the stage is equally rich in invention, dramatic instinct, and power of characterization; his chamber works surpass those of his predecessors and contemporaries.
WORKS: Besides the compositions mentioned, there were publ. during Purcell's life a theoretical treatise, *The Art of Descant,* in the 10th ed. of Playford's *Briefe Introduction of the Skill of Musick* (1683); Playford also publ. several airs and "symphonies" (written for various dramas) in *The Theatre of Musick* (1685), anthems and sacred songs in *Harmonia Sacra* (1688), and pieces for harpsichord in *Musick's Handmaid* (part II, 1689); of the incidental music to plays there appeared *Amphitryon* (1690; the airs in the text, the instrumental pieces in *Ayres for the Theatre*), *Dioclesian* (1691), and "Select ayres" from the *Fairy Queen* (1692). The stage pieces for which Purcell wrote music include the following: Lee's *Theodosius* (1680); D'Urfey's *The Virtuous Wife* (1694); Tate's arrangement of Shakespeare's *Richard II,* D'Urfey's *Sir Barnaby Whigg* (1681); Beaumont and Fletcher's *The Double Marriage* (1682 or 1685); Davenant's *Circe* and Lee's *Sophonisba* (1685); D'Urfey's *A Fool's Preferment* (1688); Betterton's *Dioclesian,* Settle's *Distressed Innocence,* Southerne's *Sir Anthony Love,* Dryden's *Amphitryon,* Lee's *The Massacre of Paris* (1689); Dryden's *King Arthur, The Gordian Knot Untyed* (author unknown), Dryden's *The Indian Emperor,* Southerne's *The Wives' Excuse* (1691); Dryden's *Cleomenes, The Fairy Queen* (an arrangement of the *Midsummer Night's Dream),* D'Urfey's *The Marriage-hater Matched,* Crowne's *Regulus,* Shadwell's *The Liber-*

tine, Bancroft's *Henry II,* Dryden's *Aureng-Zebe,* Dryden, Lee's *Oedipus* (1692); Congreve's *The Old Bachelor,* D'Urfey's *The Richmond Heiress,* Southerne's *The Maid's Last Prayer,* Wright's *The Female Virtuosos* (after Molière), Congreve's *The Double Dealer,* Shadwell's *Epsom Wells,* Fletcher's *Rule a Wife and Have a Wife* (1693); D'Urfey's *Don Quixote* (part I), Dryden's *Love Triumphant,* Crowne's *The Married Beau,* Southerne's *The Fatal Marriage,* Ravenscroft's *The Canterbury Guests,* D'Urfey's *Don Quixote* (part II), Shadwell's arrangement of *Timon of Athens,* Dryden's *The Spanish Friar,* Dryden's *Tyrannic Love* (1694); Behn's *Abdelazer,* Beaumont and Fletcher's *Bonduca,* Howard and Dryden's *Indian Queen,* Scott's *The Mock Marriage,* Norton's *Pausanias,* Gould's *The Rival Sisters,* Southerne's *Oroonoko,* Davenant and Dryden's arrangement of *The Tempest,* D'Urfey's *Don Quixote* (part III) (1695). In this list only *Dioclesian, The Fairy Queen, The Indian Queen,* and *King Arthur* are provided with sufficient music to be possibly classed as "semi-operas"; the music for other dramas usually includes overtures, airs, and instrumental dances. Purcell's widow, who survived him till 1706, publ. *A Choice Collection of Lessons for the Harpsichord or Spinet* (1696), *Ten Sonatas in Four Parts* (1697), *Orpheus Britannicus: A Collection of the choicest Songs . . . with Symphonies for Violins or Flutes . . .* (Part I, 1698; 2nd ed., 1706; Part II, 1702; 2nd ed., 1711; both parts in one vol., with the addition of several new numbers, 1721). Many compositions were publ. in Playford's *Harmonia Sacrae* (1688–93); Walsh's *The Catch Club,* or *Merry Companions* (c.1730); Boyce's *Cathedral Music* (3 vols., 1760–73); Arnold's continuation of the same (4 vols., 1790); Page and Sexton's *Harmonia Sacra* (3 vols., 1800). Vincent Novello collected all services, anthems, hymns, and sacred songs, and publ. them as *Purcell's Sacred Music* (4 vols., 1829–32; very inaccurate). The Musical Antiquarian Society publ. *Dido and Aeneas* (ed., G.A. Macfarren, 1840); *Bonduca* (ed., E.F. Rimbault, 1842; with historical sketch of dramatic music in England); *King Arthur* (ed., E. Taylor, 1843); *Ode for St. Cecilia's Day* (ed., E.F. Rimbault, 1847). In 1876 the Purcell Society was formed in London for the purpose of publishing the first complete ed. of Purcell's works; 26 vols. were brought out from 1878–1928; in 1957 publication resumed, with the set being extended to 32 vols. by 1977. The Purcell Society also began to publ. a *Popular Edition of Selected Works* (vol. 1: *15 Songs and Airs;* London, 1939). Various selections have been publ. by P. Warlock (*Fantasias* in 3, 4, and 5 parts; some publ. for the first time; London, 1927); G. Jensen, A. Egidi, A. Moffat, and H. David (trio sonatas); W. Barclay Squire (harpsichord pieces); A. Schering in *Geschichte der Musik in Beispielen* (nos. 246–48a); F. Blume in *Das Chorwerk* (5 sacred choruses); E. Dent (*Let the Dreadful Engines*); W. Gillies Whittaker (22 sonatas; Eds. de l'Oiseau-Lyre, Paris); etc. The so-called *Trumpet Voluntary,* ascribed to Purcell, and made popular through an orch. transcription by Sir Henry Wood, is not by Purcell but by Jeremiah Clarke; for details, see C.L. Cudworth, "Some New Facts about the Trumpet Voluntary," *Musical Times* (Sept. 1953).

Puschmann, Adam, German meistersinger; b. Görlitz, 1532; d. Breslau, April 4, 1600. He was a pupil of Hans Sachs; brought out *Gründlicher Bericht des deutschen Meistergesanges* (1571; new ed., Halle, 1888); his songs were publ. by Georg Münzer in 1906. His brother **Zacharias Puschmann** (with whom he is often confused) was a cantor in Görlitz.

Pustet, Friedrich, German publisher; b. Hals, near Passau, Feb. 25, 1798; d. Munich, March 6, 1882. In 1826 he founded a music publishing firm, mainly for church music, in Regensburg; for 30 years he had the exclusive right of printing, with the privilege of the Holy See, the chant books according to the Editio Medicaea, which, however, was superseded by the newer Vaticana Edition. In 1921 Pustet's firm merged with the publishing house of Kösel, retaining, however, the original name; the firm thus lasted through 5 generations of the family, and was directed in the 1970s, still in Regensburg, by **Friedrich Pustet** (b. Munich, Nov. 26, 1927). Pustet publ. Proske's *Musica divina;* Peter Wagner's *Elemente des gregorianischen Gesanges;* Johner's *Cantus ecclesiastici; Kirchenmusikalisches Jahrbuch* (from its founding in 1886 through the vol. for 1935); etc. A Festschrift was compiled by H. Bohatta on the centenary of the foundation of the firm (Regensburg, 1926).

Putnam, Ashley, American soprano; b. New York, Aug. 10, 1952. She studied flute at the Univ. of Michigan, eventually turning to voice (B.M., 1974; M.M., 1975). After graduating, she was an apprentice with the Santa Fe Opera Co. In 1976 she made her operatic debut in the title role of Donizetti's *Lucia di Lammermoor* with the Virginia Opera Assoc. in Norfolk; subsequently sang with the St. Louis Opera, San Diego Opera, Houston Opera, and Miami Opera. Her first appearance with the N.Y. City Opera in 1978 brought her critical accolades.

Puyana, Rafael, Colombian harpsichordist; b. Bogotá, Oct. 14, 1931. He studied piano at the New England Cons. of Music in Boston, and harpsichord with Wanda Landowska in N.Y.; had his general musical training at the Hartt College of Music in Hartford, Conn. He made his N.Y. recital debut in 1957; then embarked upon an international career. He became favorably known for his performances of Baroque music.

Pythagoras, Greek philosopher and mathematician; b. Samos, c.582 B.C.; d. Metapontum, c.500 B.C. His doctrines on the musical ratios are preserved in the writing of his followers, no books by Pythagoras himself having come down to us. The Pythagoreans (Archytas, Didymos, Eratosthenes, Euclid, Ptolemy, etc.) reckoned only the fifth and octave as pure consonances (the fourth being the fifth below); their system recognized only intervals reached by succes-

Pythagoras

sive skips of pure fifths, the major third being the 4th fifth above (ratio 64:81, instead of the modern 64:80, or 4:5), their minor third the 3rd fifth below; etc. Their thirds and sixths were, consequently, dissonant intervals.

Quagliati, Paolo, Italian composer and excellent cembalist; b. Chioggia, c.1555; d. Rome, Nov. 16, 1628. He publ. *Carro di fedeltà d'amore,* one of the earliest music dramas, containing not only monodies, but ensemble numbers up to 5 voices (Rome, 1611); also motets and "dialogues" *a* 2–8 (3 vols.; 1612, 1620, 1627); etc. Reprints are in H. Riemann's *Musikgeschichte in Beispielen* and in L. Torchi's *L'arte musicale in Italia,* III.

Quaile, Elizabeth, American piano pedagogue; b. Omagh, Ireland, Jan. 20, 1874; d. South Kent, Conn., June 30, 1951. She came early to N.Y. and studied with Franklin Robinson; then devoted herself to teaching; from 1916 to 1919 she was head of the piano dept. of the David Mannes School; then went to Paris, where she studied piano with Harold Bauer. Returning to N.Y. in 1921, she founded, with Angela Diller, the Diller-Quaile School of Music. She publ. a number of highly successful piano teaching materials, some written by her alone (*First Book of Technical Exercises, A Pre-Czerny Book,* etc.), and some in collaboration with Angela Diller. The books proved to be standard guides for piano students.

Quantz, Johann Joachim, famous German flutist and composer; b. Oberscheden, Hannover, Jan. 30, 1697; d. Potsdam, July 12, 1773. Naturally musical, at 8 he played the double bass at village festivals. His father died when he was but 10, and Quantz was apprenticed to an uncle, then "Stadtmusikus" at Merseburg, in 1708, learning various instruments, among them the harpsichord with Kiesewetter. His apprenticeship ended, he went to Radeburg, Pirna, and in 1716 joined the town orch. of Dresden, under Heine. In 1717, during 3 months' leave of absence, he studied counterpoint with Zelenka and Fux at Vienna; in 1718 he became oboist in the Royal Polish orch. of Warsaw and Dresden, but soon took up the flute, which he studied under Buffardin. In 1724 he was sent to Italy in the suite of the Polish ambassador; he studied counterpoint under Gasparini at Rome; went to London via Paris in 1726; and returned to Dresden in 1727, resuming his position as orch. flute player in 1728. That year he played before Frederick the Great (then Crown Prince) at Berlin, and so pleased him that he engaged Quantz to teach him the flute, and to make 2 long visits to Berlin annually for that purpose. Frederick ascended the throne in 1740, and the following year called Quantz to Berlin and Potsdam as chamber musician and court composer at a salary of 2,000 thalers, besides an honorarium for each composition furnished, and 100 ducats for each flute supplied by

Quantz. Here he remained until his death.

speare's poems.

Quatremère de Quincy, Antoine-Chrysostome, French writer; b. Paris, Oct. 25, 1755; d. there, Dec. 28, 1849. He was secretary of the Académie des Arts; publ. *De la nature des opéras bouffons italiens* (Paris, 1789; a pamphlet) and eulogies of Catel, Boieldieu, Gossec, Méhul, Monsigny, Paisiello, and other deceased members of the Académie (in *Recueil de notices historiques*, 1834–37, 2 vols.; also printed separately).

Queler, Eve, American conductor; b. New York, Jan. 1, 1936. Her maiden name was **Rabin;** in 1956 she married Stanley Queler, a law student. She studied piano at the Mannes College of Music and the Hebrew Union School of Sacred Music. While still a student, she served as studio accompanist for the baritone Martial Singher in Marlboro, Vt.; also had a fellowship at the Berkshire Center in Tanglewood. Fascinated by the art of conducting as a supreme means of musical self-expression, she took lessons with the noted opera conductor Carl Bamberger; then studied for two years with Joseph Rosenstock, onetime conductor of the Metropolitan Opera. In 1970 she won an award to study with Walter Susskind at the American Inst. of Orch. Conducting. By arduous application, she developed a fine career conducting operas in concert version. She made her debut leading a performance of *Cavalleria rusticana* in N.Y. in 1967; then served for 5 seasons as assistant conductor to Julius Rudel at the N.Y. City Opera; very early in her career she decided to promote works not often played; she conducted, with her Opera Orch. of N.Y., Respighi's *Belfagor* in 1971; Zandonai's *Francesca da Rimini* in 1973; Donizetti's *Parisina d'Este* in 1974; Massenet's *Le Cid* in 1976; Smetana's *Dalibor* in 1977; and a number of works by early Baroque composers. She was also able to raise funds to secure excellent casts for her performances. As a rule her orch. presents three productions of operas in concert form each season. She has also had guest engagements with American symph. orchs. Consistently, she began receiving enthusiastic reviews of her concerts. In the process, she rated a number of "firsts" of her gender: first woman conductor to lead a concert at Lincoln Center; first woman to be a guest conductor of the Philadelphia Orch., the Montreal Symph., the New Jersey Symph., etc.; as well as being the first woman to be appointed associate conductor of the Fort Wayne Phil. She is also credited with the first and finest American performance of an early and insignificant opera by Puccini, *Edgar,* which she conducted in N.Y. on April 13, 1977. And she made several feminine "firsts" in Europe, including a concert performance of *Tristan und Isolde* in London (July 20, 1978).

Quilter, Roger, English composer; b. Brighton, Nov. 1, 1877; d. London, Sept. 21, 1953. He received his primary education at Eton College; then went to Germany, where he studied with Iwan Knorr. He is particularly noted for his fine settings of Shake-

Quinault, Jean-Baptiste-Maurice, French singer and actor; b. Verdun, Sept. 9, 1687; d. Gien, Aug. 30, 1745. He was an actor at the Théâtre Français, in Paris (1712–28) and at the Comédie Française until 1734. He set to music about 20 *intermèdes,* ballets, etc., and also produced a grand ballet, *Les Amours des déesses* (Paris, Aug. 9, 1729).

Quinet, Fernand, Belgian cellist, conductor, and composer; b. Charleroi, Jan. 29, 1898; d. Liège, Oct. 24, 1971. He studied music theory in Charleroi; then enrolled at the Brussels Cons., where he studied cello with Edouard Jacobs and composition with Léon Dubois. After graduation he devoted his time to teaching and conducting. He served as director of the Cons. in Charleroi (1924–38); in 1938 he succeeded François Rasse as director of the Liège Cons., and held this post until 1963; in 1948 he founded the Liège Symph. Orch., and was its principal conductor until 1965. He composed relatively little.
WORKS: Songs: *Recueillement, Les chevaux de bois; 4 mélodies; En bateau; La Légende de sœur Béatrice,* cantata (1920); *La Guerre,* cantata (1921; received the Belgian Grand Prix de Rome); Violin Sonata (1923); *Charade,* 4 pieces for Piano Trio (1927); Viola Sonata (1928); *Moralités-non-légendaires* for Voice and 18 Instruments (1930); *L'Ecole buissonnière* for String Quartet (1930); *3 Symphonic Movements* (London Festival of the International Society for Contemporary Music, July 28, 1931); *Suite* for 3 Clarinets (1930).

Quinet, Marcel, Belgian composer; b. Binche, July 6, 1915. He studied at the conservatories of Mons and Brussels with Léon Jongen, Raymond Moulaert, and Marcel Maas (1934–42); also took private composition lessons with Jean Absil (1940–45). He then devoted himself to music pedagogy; was on the staff of the Brussels Cons. (from 1943) and also taught at the Chapelle Musicale Reine Elisabeth (1956–59 and 1968–71). His music is moderately modernistic in the amiable manner of the French school, with some euphoniously dissonant excrescences.

Quiroga, Manuel, Spanish violinist; b. Pontevedra, April 15, 1890; d. there, April 19, 1961. He studied at the Royal Cons. in Madrid and at the Paris Cons.; toured in Europe and in the U.S. with great success. He suffered a street accident in N.Y. in 1937 during one of his American tours, and was compelled to abandon public appearances; returned to Spain and retired to Pontevedra. He composed some violin pieces and a "sainete," *Los amos del barrio* (Madrid, Sept. 7, 1938).

R

Raabe, Peter, German conductor and writer on music; b. Frankfurt an der Oder, Nov. 27, 1872; d. Weimar, April 12, 1945. He studied with Bargiel at the Hochschule für Musik in Berlin; in 1894 began a career as a theater conductor; in 1899 was appointed conductor of the Netherlands Opera in Amsterdam; then conducted the Kaim Orch. in Munich (1903–6) and the newly established Kaim Orch. in Mannheim (1906–7); in 1907 he became principal conductor in Weimar; in 1910 he was appointed custodian of the Liszt Museum in Weimar; from 1920 to 1934 he conducted the Municipal Orch. in Aachen. In 1935 he became head of the Reichsmusikkammer and the Deutscher Tonkünstlerverein; in these offices he was called upon to perform administrative tasks for the Nazi regime, including the racial restrictions of musicians. His co-workers presented him with an honorary *Festschrift zu Peter Raabes 70. Geburtstag* (Leipzig, 1942). Raabe died just before the total collapse of the Third Reich, which he tried to serve so well. He left some scholarly and valuable writings, among them: *Grossherzog Karl Alexander und Liszt* (Leipzig, 1918); *Franz Liszt: Leben und Schaffen* (Stuttgart, 1931; 2 vols., with an annotated catalogue of Liszt's works; revised ed. by his son Felix, 1968); *Die Musik im dritten Reich* (Berlin, 1935; an exposition of the musical ideology of the Third Reich); *Kulturwille im deutschen Musikleben* (Berlin, 1936); *Deutsche Meister* (Berlin, 1937); *Wege zu Weber* (Regensburg, 1942); *Wege zu Liszt* (Regensburg, 1943); *Wege zu Bruckner* (Regensburg, 1944).

Raaff, Anton, German singer, a friend of Mozart; b. Gelsdorf, near Bonn (baptized, May 6), 1714; d. Munich, May 28, 1797. He studied with Ferrandini in Munich and Bernacchi in Bologna; sang in Italy; then in Bonn, in Vienna, and at various German courts (1742–52); in Lisbon (1753–55), Madrid (1755–59), and Naples, returning in 1770 to Germany, where he was attached to the court of the Elector Karl Theodor at Mannheim. In 1778 he went to Paris with Mozart; in 1779 was in Munich. Mozart wrote the role of Idomeneo for him, and also the aria *Se al labbro mio non credi*, K. 295.

Rabaud, Henri, eminent French composer and conductor; b. Paris, Nov. 10, 1873; d. there, Sept. 11, 1949. The son of Hippolyte Rabaud (1839–1900), prof. of cello at the Paris Cons., he was a pupil of Gédalge and Massenet; won the Premier Grand Prix de Rome in 1894 with his cantata *Daphné;* in 1908 he became conductor at the Paris Opéra and at the Opéra-Comique; from 1914 to 1918 he was director of the Opéra. In 1918 he was engaged to conduct the Boston Symph. Orch., succeeding Karl Muck; conducted only one season (1918–19) and was followed by Pierre Monteux; returned to Paris and was appointed director of the Paris Cons. in 1922 (following Gabriel Fauré's resignation); he held this post until 1941.

WORKS: Operas: *La Fille de Roland* (Opéra-Comique, March 16, 1904); *Le Premier Glaire* (Béziers, 1908); *Marouf, Savetier du Caire* (Opéra-Comique, May 15, 1914; his most successful opera); *Antoine et Cléopâtre,* after Shakespeare (1916–17); *L'Appel de la mer* (one act; Opéra-Comique, April 10, 1924; in German, Leipzig, May 6, 1927); *Le Miracle des loups* (Opéra-Comique, Nov. 14, 1924); *Rolande et le mauvais garçon* (Paris Opéra, May 28, 1934); *Le Jeu de l'Amour et du Hasard* (1948; produced posthumously at Monte Carlo, 1954); oratorio, *Job* (1900); Psalm 4 for Soli, Chorus, and Orch.; *Hymne à la France éternelle* (1916); *L'Eté* for 4-voice Choir; for Orch.: 2 symphs.; *La Procession nocturne,* symph. poem after Lenau's *Der nächtliche Zug* (first perf. Paris, Jan. 15, 1899; his most famous orch. work); *Eglogue,* "poème virgilien"; *Divertissement sur des chansons russes; Suite anglaise* for String Quartet; Concertino for Cello and Piano; *Allegro de concert* for Cello and Piano; piano pieces; songs; etc.

Rabe, Folke, Swedish composer; b. Stockholm, Oct. 28, 1935. He studied composition with Blomdahl and Lidholm at the Royal College of Music in Stockholm (1957–64); also took lessons with Ligeti (1961–64). In 1965 he worked at the Tape Music Center in San Francisco; in 1968 he joined the staff of the Swedish Foundation for Nationwide Concerts. An accomplished jazz musician, he was a founder, with Jan Bark, of the Culture Quartet of 4 trombones. He experimented with multimedia techniques; produced pieces of "vocal theater" with non-semantic texts.

Rabin, Michael, American violinist; b. New York, May 2, 1936; d. there, Jan. 19, 1972. He was of a musical family; his father was a violinist in the N.Y. Phil., his mother a pianist. He studied with Ivan Galamian in N.Y. and made excellent progress; in his early youth he appeared as a soloist with a number of American orchs.; made several European tours as a concert violinist, and also played in Australia. His sudden death at the age of 35 was a shock to American music-lovers.

Rachmaninoff, Sergei, great Russian composer and superb pianist; b. on his father's estate at Oneg, district of Novgorod, April 1, 1873; d. Beverly Hills, Calif., March 28, 1943. He was of a musical family; his grandfather was an amateur pianist, a pupil of John Field; his father also played the piano; Rachmaninoff's *Polka* was written on a theme improvised by his father. After financial setbacks, the family estate was sold, and in 1882 Rachmaninoff was taken to St. Petersburg; became a piano pupil of Demiansky at the Cons. there (1882–85); acting on the advice of his cousin, the well-known pianist and conductor Alexander Siloti, Rachmaninoff went to Moscow and studied piano with Zverev (1885–88) at the Moscow Cons.; in 1888 he began to study piano with Siloti and composition with Taneyev and Arensky. He met Tchaikovsky, who appreciated Rachmaninoff's talent and gave him friendly advice. At the age of 19 he wrote his Prelude in C-sharp minor, which became one of the most celebrated piano pieces in the world. He graduated as a pianist in 1891, and as a composer in 1892, receiving the gold medal for his opera in one act, *Aleko,* after Pushkin (1892). His First Symph. was given in Moscow in 1897, with little success. Discouraged, Rachmaninoff destroyed the MS; however, the orch. parts were preserved, and after Rachmaninoff's death the score was restored and performed in Moscow (1945). He toured with the Italian violinist Teresina Tua in Russia (1895); gave his own piano recitals, and soon became known as a piano virtuoso; in 1899 he gave a concert of his orch. works with the Phil. Society of London. He continued to compose for orch., for piano, and for voice; in 1901 he gave the first performance of his 2nd Piano Concerto in Moscow, at a concert conducted by Siloti; this concerto became the most celebrated work of its genre written in the 20th century, and its singular charm has never abated since; it is no exaggeration to say that it became a model for piano concertos by a majority of modern Russian composers, and also of semi-popular virtuoso pieces for piano and orch. written in America. On April 29, 1902, Rachmaninoff married his cousin Natalie Satina; they spent some months in Switzerland, then returned to Moscow. Rachmaninoff was engaged to conduct opera at the Bolshoi Theater for 2 seasons (1904–6), and proved himself a very efficient conductor. From 1906 to 1909 he lived mostly in Dresden; spent the summers in his Russian country home near Novgorod. In 1909 he made his first American tour; his initial public appearance in the U.S. took place at Smith College in Northampton, Mass., on Nov. 4, 1909. His fame was such that the Boston Symph. Orch. offered him the post of permanent conductor, but he declined; the offer was repeated in 1918, but then, too, Rachmaninoff decided against acceptance. From 1910 to 1917 he lived in Moscow; conducted the Phil. Society Orch. there (1911–13). After the October Revolution of 1917, he left his native country, never to return; lived on his small estate on Lake Lucerne in Switzerland; made annual tours in Europe and in the U.S.; in 1935 made N.Y. his home; later settled in Los Angeles. He became an American citizen a few weeks before his death.

Among Russian composers Rachmaninoff occupies a very important place. The sources of his inspiration lie in the Romantic tradition of 19th-century Russian music; the link with Tchaikovsky's lyrical art is very strong; melancholy moods prevail and minor keys predominate in Rachmaninoff's compositions, as in Tchaikovsky's; but there is an unmistakable stamp of Rachmaninoff's individuality in the broad, rhapsodic sweep of the melodic line, and particularly in the fully expanded sonorities and fine resonant harmonies of his piano writing; its technical resourcefulness is unexcelled since Liszt. Despite the fact that Rachmaninoff was an émigré and stood in avowed opposition to the Soviet regime (until the German attack on Russia in 1941 impelled him to modify his stand), his popularity never wavered in Russia; after his death Russian musicians paid spontaneous tribute to him. Rachmaninoff's music is much less popular in Germany, France, and Italy; on the other hand, in England and America it constitutes a potent factor on the concert stage.

WORKS: OPERAS: *Aleko,* after Pushkin's *The Gypsies* (Moscow, May 9, 1893); *The Miserly Knight* (Moscow, Jan. 24, 1906, composer conducting); *Francesca da Rimini* (Moscow, Jan. 24, 1906, composer conducting). FOR ORCH.: Symph. No. 1 (St. Petersburg, March 27, 1897); Symph. No. 2 (St. Petersburg, Feb. 8, 1908, composer conducting); Symph. No. 3 (Philadelphia, Nov. 6, 1936); *Andante and Scherzo* for String Orch. (Moscow, Feb. 24, 1891); *Prince Rostislav,* symph. poem (1891); *Intermezzo* (Moscow, Oct. 31, 1892); *The Rock,* symph. fantasy (1893; Moscow, March 20, 1896); *Caprice bohémien* for Orch. (1894); *The Isle of the Dead,* symph. poem, inspired by Böcklin's painting (Moscow, May 1, 1909, composer conducting); *Symph. Dances* (Philadelphia, Jan. 3, 1941); 4 piano concertos: No. 1, in F-sharp minor (1890–91; revised 1917); No. 2, in C minor (Moscow, Nov. 9, 1901, composer soloist; one of his most famous works); No. 3, in D minor (N.Y., Nov. 28, 1909, composer soloist); No. 4, in G minor (Philadelphia, March 18, 1927); *Rhapsody on a Theme by Paganini* for Piano and Orch. (Philadelphia Orch., Baltimore, Nov. 7, 1934, composer soloist). CHAMBER MUSIC: *Trio élégiaque,* in memory of Tchaikovsky (1893); *Romance* and *Danse hongroise* for Violin and Piano (1893); Cello Sonata (1901). CHORAL WORKS: *The Spring* for Baritone, Chorus, and Orch. (Moscow, March 24, 1902); *Liturgy of St. John Chrysostom* for Chorus a cappella (Moscow, Nov. 25, 1910); *The Bells,* after Edgar Allan Poe, for Orch., Chorus, and Soloists (St. Petersburg, Dec. 13, 1913, composer conducting); Vesper Mass for Chorus a cappella (Moscow, March 10, 1915); *3 Russian Songs* for Chorus and Orch. (Philadelphia, March 18, 1927). FOR PIANO: *5 morceaux de fantaisie,* op. 3: *Elégie, Prélude* (the famous one, in C-sharp minor), *Mélodie, Polichinelle, Sérénade* (1892); *7 morceaux de salon,* op. 10 (1894); *6 moments musicaux,* op. 16 (1896); *Variations on a Theme by Chopin,* op. 22 (1903); 10 Preludes, op. 23 (1904); Sonata No. 1, in D minor, op. 28 (1907); 13 Preludes, op. 32 (1910); *6 études-tableaux,* op. 33 (1911); *Polka V.R.,* on a theme by the composer's father, Vasily Rachmaninoff (1911); Sonata No. 2, in B-flat minor (1913); *9 études-tableaux,* op. 39 (1916–17; orchestrated by Respighi, 1931); *Variations on a Theme by Corelli* for Piano, op. 42 (1931); 6 Duets for Piano, 4-hands, op. 11 (1894); *Fantasy* (Suite No. 1) for 2 Pianos, op. 5 (1893); Suite No. 2, op. 17 (1901); arrangements for Piano of *Prelude, Gavotte,* and *Gigue* from Bach's Violin Partita in E major, of Mendelssohn's *Scherzo* from *A Midsummer Night's Dream,* of Mussorgsky's *Hopak,* of Rimsky-Korsakov's *Flight of the Bumble-Bee,* of Fritz Kreisler's *Liebesfreude* and

Liebeslied, and of his own song, *Lilacs.* SONGS: (all written before 1916): 6 Songs, op. 4; 6 Songs, op. 8; 12 Songs, op. 14, of which *Spring Waters* is best known; 12 Songs, op. 21 (including *Fate,* on Beethoven's 5th Symph., and *Lilacs*); 15 Songs, op. 26 (including *Christ Is Risen*); 14 Songs, op. 34 (including *Vocalise*); 6 Songs, op. 38.

Radecke, Ernst, German musicologist, son of **Robert Radecke;** b. Berlin, Dec. 8, 1866; d. Winterthur, Switzerland, Oct. 8, 1920. He studied music with his father; then took courses in musicology at the univs. of Jena, Munich, and Berlin; received his Dr.Phil. at the Univ. of Berlin with his dissertation *Das deutsche weltliche Lied in der Lautenmusik des 16. Jahrhunderts* (publ. Leipzig, 1891). In 1893 he went to Winterthur, and devoted himself mainly to teaching; in 1908 became a lecturer on musicology at the Univ. of Zürich. He publ. a number of analytic essays on Classical works.

Radecke, Robert, German conductor and composer; b. Dittmannsdorf, Oct. 31, 1830; d. Wernigerode, June 21, 1911. He was a brother of the conductor **Rudolf Radecke;** studied at the Leipzig Cons., with Ferdinand David (violin) and Moscheles (piano); also took a course in composition with Hauptmann; appeared first as a violinist; then went to Berlin, where he conducted the Court Opera (1863–87); also taught at the Royal Inst. for Church Music there (1892–1907). He wrote a "Liederspiel," *Die Mönkgüter* (Berlin, May 1, 1874); several overtures; 2 piano trios; choruses and piano works; but became known to the general public mainly for his song *Aus der Jugendzeit,* which obtained extraordinary popularity in Germany and was commonly mistaken for a folk song.

Radecke, Rudolf, German conductor, pedagogue, and composer, brother of **Robert Radecke;** b. Dittmannsdorf, Sept. 6, 1829; d. Berlin, April 15, 1893. He studied at the Leipzig Cons.; in 1859 went to Berlin, where he organized the Radecke Choral Society (1868) and a music school (1869); also taught music at the Stern Cons. (1864–71). He wrote a number of part-songs.

Radford, Robert, English bass; b. Nottingham, May 13, 1874; d. London, March 3, 1933. He was educated at the Royal Academy of Music, taking voice lessons with Alberto Randegger. He made his operatic debut at Covent Garden in London in 1904 as the Commendatore in *Don Giovanni;* later sang the bass roles Hagen and Hunding in the Wagner productions conducted by Hans Richter in London. In 1921 he became a founder, with Beecham, of the British National Opera Co.; later became its director. In 1929 he was appointed to the faculty of his alma mater, the Royal Academy of Music. His fame as an opera singer was great in England, but he never sang with any foreign opera companies.

Radoux, Charles, Belgian composer, writer on music, and pedagogue, son of **Jean-Théodore Radoux;** b. Liège, July 30, 1877; d. there, April 30, 1952. He studied with his father; in 1907 received the Belgian Prix de Rome with the cantata *Geneviève de Brabant;* in 1911 was appointed prof. at the Liège Cons.; wrote music criticism for the *Journal de Liège;* was active in folk-song research; served as inspector of music education from 1930 to 1942.

Radoux, Jean-Théodore, Belgian composer and pedagogue; b. Liège, Nov. 9, 1835; d. there, March 20, 1911. He studied bassoon with Daussoigne-Méhul at the Cons. of Liège, where he became a teacher of bassoon in 1856; won the Belgian Prix de Rome with the cantata *Le Juif errant* (1859); then went to Paris for additional study with Halévy. In 1872 he was appointed director of the Cons. of Liège.

Radziwill, Prince Anton Heinrich, Polish music amateur and patron of the arts; b. Vilna, June 13, 1775; d. Berlin, April 7, 1833. He played the cello and possessed a fine singing voice; he also wrote incidental music for Goethe's *Faust,* but his name is retained in music history solely because of his associations with Beethoven and Chopin. Beethoven dedicated to him his *Namensfeier* overture, op. 115, and Chopin inscribed to him his op. 8.

Raff, Joseph Joachim, greatly renowned German composer and pedagogue; b. Lachen, near Zürich, May 27, 1822; d. Frankfurt, June 24, 1882. He was educated at the Jesuit Lyceum in Schwyz; then became a schoolteacher; at the same time he studied music; in 1843 he sent some of his piano pieces to Mendelssohn, who was sufficiently impressed to recommend them for publication by Breitkopf & Härtel. Mendelssohn's early death made it necessary for Raff to seek other associations; in 1850–56 he was Liszt's assistant at Weimar and became an ardent propagandist of the new German school. Liszt produced Raff's opera *König Alfred* (Weimar, March 9, 1851). In 1854 Raff publ. a highly partisan pamphlet, *Die Wagnerfrage,* in which he took up the cause of Wagner, then a center of fierce debate. In 1859 he married the actress Doris Genast. Raff's 2nd opera, *Dame Kobold,* was produced in Weimar on April 9, 1870; 4 other operas were never staged. In 1877 he was appointed director of the Hoch Cons. in Frankfurt; his teaching was extremely successful; musicians from many countries enrolled in his classes; among them was MacDowell. Raff was a composer of prodigious fecundity, a master of all technical aspects of composition. He wrote 214 opus numbers which were publ., and many more that remained in MS. In spite of his fame, his music fell into lamentable desuetude after his death; some examples of his contrapuntal skill are quoted in school manuals. He wrote 11 symphs., some of them furnished with Romantic subtitles indicating the nature of the music: No. 1, *An das Vaterland,* op. 96; No. 2, op. 140; No. 3, *Im Walde,* op. 153; No. 4, op. 167; No. 5, *Leonore,* op. 177; No. 6, *Gelebt, gestrebt; gelitten, gestritten; gestorben, umworben* (an epigraph that might well be applied to Raff's own destiny);

No. 7, *In den Alpen,* op. 201; No. 8, *Frühlingsklange,* op. 205; No. 9, *Im Sommer,* op. 208; No. 10, *Zur Herbstzeit,* op. 213; No. 11, *Der Winter,* op. 214 (left unfinished; completed by M. Erdmannsdörfer); *Symphonietta* for 8 Woodwinds and 2 Horns; Piano Concerto; 2 violin concertos; Cello Concerto; 8 string quartets; 3 piano trios; 5 violin sonatas; about 120 piano pieces of various descriptions and 9 pieces for Piano, 4-hands; numerous transcriptions of orch. and other works.

Raimann, Rudolf, Hungarian composer; b. Veszprem, May 7, 1861; d. Vienna, Sept. 26, 1913. He entered the service of Prince Esterházy as music director; wrote an opera, *Enoch Arden,* after Tennyson (Budapest, May 8, 1894), and about a dozen operettas, produced in Vienna: *Das Waschermädel* (April 19, 1905); *Paula macht alles* (March 27, 1909); *Die Frau Gretl* (April 7, 1911); *Unser Stammhalter* (Nov. 15, 1912); etc.

Raimondi, Pietro, inventive Italian composer; b. Rome, Dec. 20, 1786; d. there, Oct. 30, 1853. He studied with La Barbara and Tritto at the Cons. della Pietà de' Turchini in Naples; in 1807 brought out an opera buffa, *Le bizzarie d'amore,* at Genoa; it was followed by about 60 other dramatic works and 21 ballets, for whose production he traveled from place to place (Florence, Naples, Rome, Messina, Milan, etc.); was director of the royal theaters at Naples (1824–32) and a prof. at the Palermo Cons. (1833–52); in 1852 became maestro di cappella at St. Peter's in Rome. Raimondi was a contrapuntist of remarkable skill; he publ. 4 fugues *a 4,* which could be combined as a quadruple fugue *a 16;* 6 fugues *a 4,* to be combined as a sextuple fugue *a 24;* in the *24 fughe a 4, 5, 6 e 8 voci* publ. by Ricordi, there is one such quadruple fugue *a 16,* and a quintuple fugue *a 20;* further, 6 fugues *a 4,* performable as a sextuple fugue *a 24;* and a fugue *a 64,* for 16 Chowever, was the sacred trilogy *Giuseppe* (Joseph), comprising 3 oratorios (*Potifar, Giuseppe, Giacobbe*), performed at the Teatro Argentina in Rome, Aug. 7, 1852, at first separately, and then simultaneously, the ensemble of 400 musicians on the stage and in the orch. presenting a most striking effect and arousing great curiosity among professional musicians.

Rains, Leon, American operatic bass; b. New York, Oct. 1, 1870; d. Los Angeles, June 11, 1954. He studied with Saenger in N.Y. (1891–96) and with Bouhy in Paris; made a concert tour with Melba in the U.S. (1898); then was a member of the court opera at Dresden (from 1899); made his first appearance with the Metropolitan Opera Co. on Feb. 24, 1909, as Hagen in *Götterdämmerung;* then returned to Dresden, and continued to sing there for several years, eventually returning to America.

Raisa, Rosa, soprano; b. Bialystok, Poland, May 23, 1893; d. Los Angeles, Sept. 28, 1963. In order to escape the horrors of anti-Semitic persecutions, she fled to Naples at the age of 14; on Lombardi's advice she entered the Cons. San Pietro a Majella, where she studied under Barbara Marchisio; made her debut at Parma on Sept. 6, 1913, in Verdi's *Oberto, Conte di San Bonifacio* (revived for the Verdi centenary); then sang 2 seasons at the Costanzi in Rome; in 1913–14 (and again in 1916–32 and 1933–36) with the Chicago Opera Co.; in 1914 at Covent Garden; sang with increasing success in Rio de Janeiro, Montevideo, São Paulo, and Milan; on her reappearance with the Chicago company she scored a triumph as Aida (Nov. 13, 1916); she retired in 1937.

Raksin, David, remarkable American composer for films; b. Philadelphia, Aug. 4, 1912. He learned to play piano and woodwind instruments from his father, who was a bandleader; when barely past puberty, organized his own jazz band. In 1934 he entered the Univ. of Pa.; studied composition privately with Isadore Freed (1934–35). In 1935 he went to Hollywood and was engaged by Charlie Chaplin to arrange and orchestrate the music for his film *Modern Times;* this provided Raksin a wonderful companionship with a great comedian who could not read or write music, and he bore with fortitude Chaplin's periodic outbursts of petulance. Raksin wrote a delectable piece of reminiscences, "Life with Charlie," in the *Quarterly Journal of the Library of Congress* (Summer 1983). When Chaplin was forced into exile by the red-baiters of the U.S. Congress for his alleged radical activities and was also pursued by the authorities for his undeniable proclivities in the field of moral turpitude, Raksin struck out on his own; he also profited by his sojourn in California to attend the classes of Schoenberg at the Univ. of Calif. (1937–38). He wrote more than 100 film scores, some of which obtained great popularity in symph. arrangements; his greatest success was the theme song *Laura,* ingratiatingly melodious in its sinuous and convoluted pattern; it generated some 300 different versions. Apart from his activity as a composer, in his early years he filled in several minor parts as an actor in sound movies and television films. Using material from his film music, he composed several symph. suites, among them *Forever Amber* and *The Bad and the Beautiful.* Other coruscating scores were *The Secret Life of Walter Mitty, Carrie,* and *Separate Tables.* He also wrote much incidental music for the theater, as well as purely symph. and choral pieces, including a madrigal, *Simple Symmetries.* His orchestral *Toy Concertino* for Orch. became a favorite; he also made an orchestration of Stravinsky's *Circus Polka* for George Balanchine's production with the Barnum and Baily Circus. In 1956 he was appointed lecturer in composition at the Univ. of Calif. at Los Angeles; also served as adjunct prof. of music at the Univ. of Southern Calif. In 1979 he received the first Max Steiner Award for Career Achievement from the National Film Society. In 1983 he wrote the musical score for the popular television production *The Day After,* presenting a vision of the devastating effects of a nuclear attack on Kansas City.

Ramann, Lina, German writer on music; b. Main-

stockheim, near Kitzingen, June 24, 1833; d. Munich, March 30, 1912. She was a pupil of Franz and Frau Brendel at Leipzig; founded (1858) a music seminary for women teachers, at Glückstadt, Holstein; in 1865, with Ida Volkmann, a music school at Nuremberg, which they sold in a most flourishing condition to August Göllerich in 1890; from then until her death she lived in Munich, devoting herself entirely to literary work.

Rambousek, Joseph, Czech double-bass virtuoso and pedagogue; b. Mníšek, Nov. 16, 1845; d. Moscow, March 10, 1901. He studied with Josef Hrabět at the Prague Cons.; then was in Stuttgart and Göteborg, and finally went to Moscow, where he was engaged as a double-bass player at the Moscow Opera. He taught at the Phil. Inst. in Moscow; among his pupils was Koussevitzky.

Rameau, Jean-Philippe, great French composer, the creator of the modern science of harmony; b. Dijon, Sept. 25, 1683; d. Paris, Sept. 12, 1764. Of a musical family, he learned to play the harpsichord as a small child; from age 10 to 14 he attended the Jesuit College at Dijon, then devoted himself to music; in 1701 was sent to Italy; after a brief stay at Milan he joined the orch. of a traveling French opera troupe as violinist. In 1702 he was assistant organist at Notre-Dame in Avignon; in June of that year he became organist at Clermont-Ferrand. In 1706 he publ. his first *Livre de pièces de clavecin* in Paris, where he probably had been living since the spring of 1705. Until 1708 he remained in Paris as a church organist. In 1709 he became his father's successor at the Cathedral in Dijon; in July 1713 he became an organist in Lyons; in 1715–23 he was organist of the Cathedral at Clermont-Ferrand, where he wrote his famous *Traité de l'harmonie* (Paris, 1722). This epoch-making work, though little understood at the time, attracted considerable attention and roused opposition, so that when he settled definitely in Paris (1723) he was by no means unknown. The fact that he failed in 1727 in a competition for the position of organist at St.-Vincent-de-Paul did not injure his reputation, for it was generally known that Marchand (probably out of jealousy) had exerted his powerful influence in favor of Daquin, who was in every respect inferior to Rameau. In 1732 he became organist at Ste.-Croix-de-la-Bretonnerie, and soon was recognized as the foremost organist in France. In 1726 appeared his *Nouveau système de musique théorique,* an introduction to the *Traité.* The leading ideas of his system of harmony are (1) chord-building by thirds; (2) the classification of a chord and all its inversions as one and the same, thus reducing the multiplicity of consonant and dissonant combinations to a fixed and limited number of root chords; and (3) his invention of a fundamental bass (*basse fondamentale*), which is an imaginary series of root tones forming the real basis of the varied chord progressions employed in a composition. The stir that these novel theories occasioned, and his reputation as the foremost French organist, by no means satisfied Rameau's ambition; his ardent desire was to bring out a dramatic work at the Opéra. He had made a modest beginning with dramatic music in 1723, when he wrote some dances and divertissements for Alexis Piron's fairy burlesque *L'Endriague,* which was produced at the Théâtre de la Foire St.-Germain. In 1726 he brought out at the same theater 2 light operas by the same poet, *L'Enrôlement d'Arlequin* (Feb. 28) and *La Robe de dissension, ou Le Faux Prodigue* (autumn). He then became music master to the wife of the "fermier-général" La Pouplinière, and the latter obtained from Voltaire a libretto for *Samson,* which Rameau set to music; but it was rejected on account of its biblical subject. A 2nd libretto, by Abbé Pellegrin, was accepted, and *Hippolyte et Aricie* was produced at the Opéra in 1733; its reception was cool, despite undeniable superiority over the operas of Lully and his following in the rich and varied harmony and instrumentation, and Rameau almost renounced dramatic composition. But the persuasions of his friends, who also influenced public opinion in his favor, were effective; in 1735 he brought out the successful opera-ballet *Les Indes galantes,* and in 1737 his masterpiece, *Castor et Pollux,* a work that for years held its own beside the operas of Gluck. A career of uninterrupted prosperity commenced; he was recognized as the leading theorist of the time, and his instruction was eagerly sought; for the next 30 years his operas dominated the French stage; he was named composer of the King's chamber music, and just before his death was granted a patent of nobility. From the beginning of his dramatic career Rameau roused opposition, and at the same time found ardent admirers. The first war of words was waged between the "Lullistes" and the "Ramistes." This had scarcely been ended by a triumphant revival of *Pygmalion* in 1751, when the production of Pergolesi's *La Serva padrona* (1752) caused a more prolonged and bitter controversy between the adherents of Rameau and the "Encyclopédistes," a struggle known as "La Guerre des Bouffons," in which Rameau participated by writing numerous essays defending his position. Practically the same charges were made against him as would be made a century later against Wagner: unintelligible harmony, lack of melody, preponderance of discords, noisy instrumentation, etc. But when 25 years later the war between Gluckists and Piccinnists was raging, Rameau's works were praised as models of beauty and perfection. It is a matter for regret that Rameau was indifferent to the quality of his librettos; he relied so much upon his musical inspiration that he never could be brought to a realization of the importance of a good text; hence the inequality of his operas. Nevertheless, his operas mark a decided advance over Lully's in musical characterization, expressive melody, richness of harmony, variety of modulation, and expert and original instrumentation.

WRITINGS: *Traité de l'harmonie* (1722; Eng. trans. with commentary by P. Gossett, 1971); *Nouveau système de musique théorique* (1726); *Plan abrégé d'une nouvelle méthode d'accompagnement* (1730); *Les Différentes Méthodes d'accom-*
pagnement pour le clavecin ou pour l'orgue (1732); *Génération harmonique* (1737); *Démonstration du principe de l'harmonie* (1750); *Nouvelles réflexions de M. Rameau sur sa démonstration du principe de l'harmonie* (1752); *Réflexions sur la manière de former la voix* (1752); *Observations sur notre instinct pour la musique* (1754); *Code de musique pratique* (1760). The publications of 1722, 1726, 1737, 1750, 1752, 1754, and 1760 have been reissued in the series Monuments of Music and Music Literature in Facsimile; E. Jacobi ed. *Jean-Philippe Rameau: Complete Theoretical Writings* (Rome, 1967–72).

WORKS: FOR THE STAGE: Theatrical entertainments to which Rameau contributed music: *L'Endriague* (Paris, Feb. 3, 1723); *L'Enrôlement d'Arlequin* (Paris, Feb. 1726); *La Robe de dissension* (Paris, Sept. 7, 1726); *Les Jardins de l'Hymen ou La Rose* (1726; Paris, March 5, 1744); *Les Courses de Tempé* (Paris, Aug. 30, 1734); *Aruéris* (Paris, Dec. 15, 1762). Operas and opera-ballets: *Samson* (1733; unperf.); *Hippolyte et Aricie* (Paris, Oct. 1, 1733); *Les Indes galantes,* "ballet-héroïque" (Paris, Aug. 23, 1735); *Castor et Pollux* (Paris, Oct. 24, 1737; revised version, June 1754); *Les Fêtes d'Hébé,* opéra-ballet (Paris, May 21, 1739); *Dardanus,* tragédie en musique (Paris, Nov. 19, 1739); *La Princesse de Navarre,* comédie-ballet (Versailles, Feb. 23, 1745); *Platée,* comédie-lyrique (Versailles, March 31, 1745); *Les Fêtes de Polymnie,* opéra-ballet (Paris, Oct. 12, 1745); *Le Temple de la Gloire,* opéra-ballet (Versailles, Nov. 27, 1745); *Les Fêtes de l'Hymen et de l'Amour,* "ballet-héroïque" (Versailles, March 15, 1747); *Zaïs,* "pastorale-héroïque (Paris, Feb. 29, 1748); *Pygmalion,* ballet (Paris, Aug. 27, 1748); *Les Surprises de l'Amour,* divertissement (Versailles, Nov. 27, 1748); *Naïs,* "pastorale-héroïque" (Paris, April 22, 1749); *Zoroastre* (Paris, Dec. 5, 1749); *La Guirlande,* ballet (Paris, Sept. 21, 1751); *Acante et Céphise,* "pastorale-héroïque" (Paris, Nov. 18, 1751); *Daphnis et Eglé,* "pastorale-héroïque" (Fontainebleau, Oct. 30, 1753); *Les Sybarites,* ballet (Fontainebleau, Nov. 13, 1753); *La Naissance d'Osiris,* ballet (Fontainebleau, Oct. 12, 1754); *Anacréon,* ballet (Fontainebleau, Oct. 23, 1754; revised version to different text, Paris, May 31, 1757); *Les Paladins,* comédie-ballet (Paris, Feb. 12, 1760); 3 ballets, *Nélée et Myrthis, Zéphyre,* and *Io,* have not been publicly performed; the tragédie-lyrique *Les Boréades* (1764) was not performed until April 19, 1975, in a concert in London; stage premiere took place in Aix-en-Provence on July 21, 1982. SECULAR CANTATAS: *Thétis* (1718); *Aquilon et Orinthie* (1719); *Les Amants trahis* (1721); *Orphée* (1721); *L'Impatience* (1721); *Le Berger fidèle* (1728). SACRED VOCAL: 4 Psalm settings for Mixed Chorus, Soloists, and Instrumental Ensemble: *Deus noster refugium* (1716); *In convertendo* (1718); *Quam dilecta* (1720); *Laboravi* (1722). Most of the above were publ. in short score (voice, violin, and bass, with the ritornelli in full). Other publ. music: *Premier livre de pièces de clavecin* (1706); *Pièces de clavecin avec une méthode pour la mécanique des doigts* (n.d.; with important notes); *Pièces de clavecin avec une table pour les agréments* (1731); *Nouvelles suites de pièces pour clavecin avec des remarques sur les différents genres de* musique (n.d.; Farrenc publ. these last 2 in his *Trésor des pianistes,* 1861); *Pièces de clavecin en concerts* (1741; with accompaniment of Violin, Flute, and Viola or 2nd Violin); detached numbers of the above are in Pauer's *Old French Composers* and *Popular Pieces by Rameau;* Hugo Riemann ed. a complete edition of the clavecin compositions (publ. by Steingräber). In 1895 Durand & Cie. began the publication of a monumental edition under the editorship of C. Saint-Saëns and Ch. Malherbe; after the latter's death (1911) his part of the work was divided between M. Emmanuel and M. Teneo; 18 vols. appeared up to 1924: I, *Pièces de clavecin;* II, *Musique instrumentale;* III, *Cantates;* IV, *Motets* (first series); V, *Motets* (2nd series); VI, *Hippolyte et Aricie;* VII, *Les Indes galantes;* VIII, *Castor et Pollux;* IX, *Les Fêtes d'Hébé;* X, *Dardanus;* XI, *La Princesse de Navarre, Les Fêtes de Ramire, Nélée et Myrthis, Zéphire;* XII, *Platée;* XIII, *Les Fêtes de Polymnie;* XIV, *Le Temple de la Gloire;* XV, *Les Fêtes de l'Hymen et de l'Amour;* XVI, *Zaïs;* XVII, in 2 parts: Part I, *Pygmalion, Les Surprises de l'Amour;* Part II, *Anacréon, Les Sybarites;* XVIII, *Naïs;* the complete ed. was never completed. A new ed., under the joint auspices of the Assoc. pour la Publication des Œuvres de Rameau in Paris and the Broude Trust of N.Y., with N. Zaslaw as general ed. and F. Lesure as managing ed., began publication in 1983.

Ramey, Samuel, American bass; b. Colby, Kans., March 28, 1942. He attended Kansas State Univ.; then went to Wichita State Univ., where he studied voice with Arthur Newman; later sang with the Grass Roots Opera Co. in Raleigh, N.C. In 1973 he made his professional debut as Zuñiga in *Carmen* with the N.Y. City Opera; in 1976 he sang at the Glyndebourne Festival. In 1978 he had engagements with the Netherlands Opera and the Hamburg State Opera; in 1981 he performed at La Scala in Milan and the Vienna State Opera. He excels in lyrico-dramatic roles, such as Don Giovanni and Mefistofele in Boito's opera, and also in buffo roles, such as Leporello and Figaro.

Ramin, Günther, distinguished German organist, conductor, composer, and pedagogue; b. Karlsruhe, Oct. 15, 1898; d. Leipzig, Feb. 27, 1956. As a boy he sang in the Thomanerchor in Leipzig; he then studied organ with Karl Straube, piano with Robert Teichmüller, and theory with Stephan Krehl at the Leipzig Cons. In 1918 he was appointed organist of the Thomaskirche in Leipzig; he also was organist of the Gewandhaus concerts and a teacher at the Leipzig Cons. During the season 1933–34 he toured the U.S. as an organ virtuoso. He was also active as a conductor; he led the Lehrergesangverein in Leipzig (1922–35) and the Gewandhaus Choir (1933–34 and 1945–51); from 1935–43 he conducted the Phil. Choir in Berlin. In 1940 he became cantor of the Thomaskirche, where he sought to preserve the integrity of the Thomanerchor after the establishment of the German Democratic Republic. His compositions include an *Orgelchoral-Suite* and many

other organ pieces, as well as chamber music and songs. He edited several collections of organ works and publ. the manual *Gedanken zur Klärung des Orgelproblems* (Kassel, 1929; new ed., 1955). A vol. of his essays on Bach was edited by D. Hellman (Wiesbaden, 1973).

Ramos (Ramis) de Pareja, Bartolomé, Spanish theorist; b. Baeza, c.1440; d. after 1491. After lecturing at the Univ. of Salamanca, he went to Bologna in 1472; publ. in 1482 his Latin treatise *Musica practica* (modern ed. by J. Wolf, Leipzig, 1901; extract in Eng. in O. Strunk, *Source Readings in Music History,* N.Y., 1950), one of the important landmarks in the science of harmony. In 1484 he was in Rome. He established the mathematical ratios 4:5 and 5:6 for the intervals of the major and minor third, thus completing the definition of the consonant triad and laying the basis of our harmonic system. He was also the first to set forth the theory of equal temperament, probably based on the practice of the early Spanish guitarists (*vihuelistas*), since the frets on the guitar were placed a semitone apart.

Rampal, Jean-Pierre, eminent French flutist; b. Marseilles, Jan. 7, 1922. He took flute lessons with his father, Joseph Rampal; attended courses in medicine; then enrolled in the Paris Cons. He played flute in the orch. of the Vichy Opera (1947–51) and later was first flutist at the Paris Opéra. In 1968 he was appointed prof. at the Paris Cons. At the peak of his career, he combined his pedagogical activities with worldwide tours as a soloist with major orchs. and in recitals, achieving extraordinary success, considering that flute recitals rarely attract large audiences. His playing is remarkable for its virtuoso technique and an uncanny ability to graduate subtle dynamics of flute sonorities in all registers. Several French composers, among them Poulenc and Jolivet, wrote special works for him.

Ramsey, Robert, English organist and madrigalist; b. c.1595. He took his B.Mus. at Cambridge in 1616; was organist of Trinity College (1628–44) and Master of the Children (1637–44). He wrote numerous church services, anthems, and madrigals, which remained in MS until 1962, when an *Evening Service* and some madrigals were publ. in England; more recently E. Thompson ed. *Robert Ramsey: English Sacred Music,* in *Early English Church Music,* VII (London, 1967), and *Robert Ramsey: Latin Sacred Music,* in *Early English Church Music,* XX (London, 1978); see also I. Spink, ed., *English Songs 1625–1660,* in *Musica Britannica,* XXXIII (London, 1971).

Ran, Shulamit, Israeli composer; b. Tel Aviv, Oct. 21, 1949. She studied piano; took composition lessons from Paul Ben-Haim (1960–63). A scholarship enabled her to go to the U.S., where she enrolled in the Mannes College of Music in N.Y. (1963–67), studying piano with Nadia Reisenberg and composition with Dello Joio; in 1963 she attended the seminars of Aaron Copland and Lukas Foss at the Berkshire Music Center in Tanglewood. In 1973 she joined the faculty of the Univ. of Chicago.

Randolph, David, American conductor; b. New York, Dec. 21, 1914. He studied at City College, N.Y. (B.S., 1936) and Teachers College, Columbia Univ. (M.A., 1941); from 1943–47 was assistant director of music of the U.S. Office of War Information. In 1943 he organized the Randolph Singers, which he conducted until 1972. In 1955 he founded the Masterwork Chorus and Orch.; also led the St. Cecilia Chorus and Orch. and, beginning in 1981, the Masterwork Chamber Orch. He taught conducting at the Dalcroze School (1947–50); was a prof. of music at the State Univ. of N.Y. College at New Paltz (1970–72), at Fordham Univ. (1972–73), and at Montclair State College (from 1973). He was also active as a radio music commentator. He publ. the book *This Is Music* (N.Y., 1964); also edited The David Randolph Madrigal Series.

Rands, Bernard, remarkable English-born American composer; b. Sheffield, March 2, 1934. He studied piano and organ at home; at the age of 18 he entered the Univ. of Wales, majoring in music and English literature. He also developed a passion for Celtic lore; in his student days he became a sort of polyglot, delving into the linguistic mysteries of Welsh, Irish, and Scottish vocables, and on the way acquiring a fluency in French, Italian, and Spanish. He also immersed himself in the hypergrammatical and ultrasyntactic glossolalia of James Joyce. After graduating from the Univ. of Wales (B.Mus., 1956; M.Mus., 1958), he went to Italy, where he took lessons in musicology with Roman Vlad in Rome and studied composition with Luigi Dallapiccola in Florence (1958–60); also attended the International Teaching Festivals in Darmstadt, taking part in the seminars in composition and conducting with Pierre Boulez and Bruno Maderna; later he consulted Luciano Berio in Milan on problems of electronic music. On a grant from the Arts Council of Great Britain, he traveled to Sydney, Australia, in 1972 and accompanied the BBC Symph. Orch. on its European tour in 1974. From 1968 to 1975 he was an instructor in the music dept. of York Univ.; he also held the appointment of Fellow in Creative Arts at Brasenose College, Oxford Univ. In 1976 he was engaged as a prof. of music at the Univ. of Calif. at San Diego; he found the musical atmosphere there congenial to his innovative ideas, and he eventually became a permanent resident of the U.S.; he was appointed a visiting prof. at the Calif. Inst. of the Arts in Valencia in 1984–85 while retaining his San Diego post.

The sources of his music are astonishingly variegated, drawing upon religious, mystical, mathematical, and sonoristic premises. At one time he was preoccupied with Hinduism; these interests are reflected in his work *Aum (Om),* a mantric word interpreted as having 3 sounds representing the triune stasis of Brahma, Vishnu, and Siva. Despite the complex nature of his compositions, Rands seems to encounter little resistance on the part of performers and audiences; his music possesses the rare quality of immediate communication. Each work reflects a message; thus his *Metalepsis 2* is described by him as a "non-denominational Mass for all who suffer at the hands of tyrants." Several works reflect the scientific bent of his mind, as exemplified by *Formants;* there are mundane references in the titles of such works as *Memos* and *Agenda;* other sets contain references to sports, as in *Wildtrack.* Then there are in his catalogue educational pieces, such as *Sound Patterns,* designed to be interpreted by children and professional performers alike. His *Canti lunatici* penetrate the inner recesses of the human mind in a state of turbulence. Rands received the Pulitzer Prize in 1984 for his *Canti del sole* for Tenor and Orch.

WORKS: For Orch.: *Refractions* for 24 Players (1961); *Wildtrack 1* (1969), *2* (1973), and *3* (1975); *Mesalliance* for Piano and Orch. (1972); *Ology* for Jazz Orch. (1973); *Aum* for Harp and Orch. (London, April 17, 1974). For Youth Orch.: *Per Esempio* (1968); *Sound Patterns 1, 2, 3, 4, 5* for children's performance (1967–69); *Agenda* (1970). For Various Ensembles: *Actions for 6* for Flute, Harp, Viola, Cello, and 2 Percussion Players (1963); *Formants 2 (Labyrinth)* for Harp and Chamber Group (1970); *Tableau* for Flute, Clarinet, Viola, Cello, Piano, and Percussion (1970); *As All Get Out* (1972); *Scherzi* for Clarinet, Violin, Cello, and Piano (1974); *Cuaderno* for String Quartet (1975). For Solo Instruments: *Formants 1 (Les Gestes)* for Harp Solo (1965); *Memo 1* for Double Bass (1971), *2* for Trombone (1972), *3* for Cello (1973), and *4* for Tuba (1974); *Serenata* for Flute and Chamber Group (1975). For Piano: *Espressioni 1, 2, 3, 4, 5* (1970–75). For Voices and Instruments: *5 Ballads* (1970–75); *Flickering Shadows* (1971); *Metalepsis* (1971); *Canti lunatici* for Soprano and Chamber Ensemble (1971); *Déjà 2* for Soprano and Chamber Ensemble (1972); *Serena* for Singing Actor, Mime, Trumpet, and Tape (1972); *Canti del sole* for Tenor and Orch. (1983; received the Pulitzer Prize).

Rangström, Ture, remarkable Swedish composer; b. Stockholm, Nov. 30, 1884; d. there, May 11, 1947. He studied singing in Berlin and Munich with Julius Hey (1905–7), then composition with Lindegren in Stockholm and Pfitzner in Munich. Returning to Sweden, he became music critic of the *Stockholms Dagblad* (1910–14) and the *Svenska Dagbladet* (1907–9, and after 1927). From 1922 to 1925 he was conductor of the Göteborg Symph. Orch.; then became stage director at the Stockholm Opera. His music is permeated with a lyrical sentiment, and his forms are rhapsodic; in his symphs. he achieves great intensity by a concentrated development of the principal melodic and rhythmic ideas; his songs are also appreciated.

Ránki, György, Hungarian composer; b. Budapest, Oct. 30, 1907. He studied composition with Kodály at the Budapest Academy of Music (1926–30); won the Erkel Prize twice (1952, 1967) and the Kossuth Prize (1954); in 1963 was awarded the title "Merited Artist of the Hungarian People's Republic." His music derives its inspiration chiefly from Hungarian folk songs.

WORKS: *Hóemberek (Snow Men;* London, 1939); musical comedy, *A csendháborító (The Rioter;* 1950; Budapest Radio, 1950; stage version, Budapest, 1959); opera, *Pomádé király új ruhája* (after Andersen's *The Emperor's New Clothes;* Budapest, June 6, 1953); children's musical comedy, *A gyöztes ismeretlen (The Winner Is Unknown;* 1961); operetta, *Hölgyválasz (Spoon Dance;* 1961); children's opera, *Muzsikus Péter új kalandjai (New Adventures of Peter Musician;* 1962); symph. dance drama, *Cirkusz (The Circus;* 1965); opera, *The Tragedy of Man* (Budapest, Dec. 4, 1970); 4 cantatas: *A város peremén (At the Outskirts of the City;* 1947); *In the Year 1848* (1948); *Freedom Song* (1950); *Battle in Peace* (1951); 2 oratorios: *1944* (1967) and *Cantus Urbis* (1972); *Kardtánc (Sword Dance)* for Orch. (1949; version for Violin and Piano, 1957); *Hungarian Dances from the 16th Century* for Orch. (1950); *1514,* fantasy for Piano and Orch. depicting the Hungarian peasant uprising of 1514 (1959; version for 2 Pianos and Percussion, 1962); *Don Quijote and Dulcinea,* 2 miniatures for Oboe and Small Orch. (1960; version for Oboe and Piano, 1961); *Aurora tempestuosa,* prelude for Orch. (1967); *Aristophanes,* suite for Violin and Piano (1947); Sonata for Recorder and Cimbalom (1948); *Serenata all'antiqua* for Violin and Piano (1956); *Pentaerophonia* for Wind Quintet (1958); *Lament,* in memoriam Kodály, for Voices, Chorus, and Cimbalom (1971); piano pieces; music for radio plays and some 80 motion pictures.

Rankin, Nell, American mezzo-soprano; b. Montgomery, Ala., Jan. 3, 1926. She studied voice with Jeanne Lorraine at the Birmingham Cons. of Music; in 1945 went to N.Y., where she continued her vocal training with Karin Branzell (1945–49). She then traveled to Europe, and in 1950 made her operatic debut as Ortrud in *Lohengrin* at the Zürich State Opera, of which she later became an active member; in 1950–51 she sang at the Basel State Opera, and in 1951 appeared at La Scala, Milan. In 1951 she won the Metropolitan Opera Audition and made her operatic debut there on Nov. 22, 1951, as Amneris; she then sang at Covent Garden in London (1953–54) and at the San Francisco Opera, on Sept. 27, 1955. Subsequently she appeared at the Teatro Colón in Buenos Aires and in many other opera houses, in Mexico, in Naples, and in Vienna. Her best roles are Carmen, Azucena, Ortrud, Santuzza, and Maddalena.

Ranta, Sulho, eminent Finnish composer and writer on music; b. Peräseinäjoki, Aug. 15, 1901; d. Helsinki, May 5, 1960. He studied at the Helsinki Cons. with Melartin, and later in Germany, France, and Italy. Returning to Finland, he taught at the Sibelius Academy in Helsinki (1934–56); was also active as a music critic. He was editor of a comprehensive biographical dictionary of 90 Finnish composers, *Suomen Säveltäjiä* (Helsinki, 1945), and of a general biographical survey of performers, *Sävelten Taitureita* (Helsinki, 1947).

Rapee, Erno, conductor; b. Budapest, June 4, 1891; d. New York, June 26, 1945. He studied piano with Emil Sauer at the National Academy in Budapest; gave concerts as a pianist; appeared as a conductor with various European orchs.; in 1912 came to America as an accompanist; in 1913 was engaged as music director of the Hungarian Opera Co. in N.Y.; then became conductor for S.L. Rothafel (Roxy) at his motion picture theaters in N.Y.; after several years at the Roxy Theater (1926–31) he became music director of the NBC Symph. Orch.; then at Radio City Music Hall, again under Rothafel's management. He introduced classical works into his programs, mostly in the form of potpourris, but upon occasion also in full version; brought out a collection of music to accompany silent movies, *Motion Picture Moods for Pianists and Organists, Adapted to 52 Moods and Situations* (N.Y., 1924; reprint, 1974), containing pieces of light music by famous and obscure composers depicting the emotions and excitements of joy, melancholy, passion, frustration, and also typical movie scenes, such as lovemaking within permissible limits (kisses not to exceed 7 seconds in duration), costumed bacchanalia, fights to the death, etc.

Raphael, Günther, German composer; b. Berlin, April 30, 1903; d. Herford, Oct. 19, 1960. He was the son of the organist **Georg Raphael;** studied in Berlin with Max Trapp (piano), Walter Fischer (organ), and Robert Kahn (composition). He then taught at the Leipzig Cons. (1926–34). Suspected of fractional Jewish ancestry, he was deprived of the right to teach by the Nazi regime, and went to Sweden. After the war he taught at Laubach (1945–48), at the Duisburg Cons. (1949–53), and at the Mainz Cons. (1956–58); finally was a prof. at the Hochschule für Musik in Cologne from 1957 until his death.

Raphling, Sam, American composer; b. Fort Worth, Texas, March 19, 1910. He studied piano in Chicago and, as an exchange fellowship student, in Germany. Returning to the U.S., he was active in Chicago as a teacher and pianist; publ. a number of compositions in various genres: *Abraham Lincoln Walks at Midnight* for Orch.; *Cowboy Rhapsody* for Violin and Orch.; *American Album* for 2 Pianos (1946); Sonatina for 2 Clarinets (1948); *Prelude and Toccata* for Trumpet and Trombone (1949); *Lyric Prelude* for Trombone and Piano (1950); *Dance Suite* for 2 Trumpets (1950); *Variations* for 2 Flutes Unaccompanied (1955; also for Flute and Clarinet); Sonatina for 2 Trombones (1955; also for 2 Bassoons); *Sonata, Variations, Introduction and Workout* for French Horn Unaccompanied (1955); *Nocturnal Prelude* for Piano (1955); *Duograms* for 2 Oboes (1955); Trio for 3 Oboes (1955); *Pastorale* for Oboe and Piano (1955); operas; symphs.; concertos; etc.

Rappold, Marie (née **Winterroth**), English dramat-

Rappoldi – Rathaus

ic soprano; b. London, of German parents, c.1873; d. North Hollywood, Calif., May 12, 1957. The family moved to America when she was a child. She studied with Oscar Saenger in N.Y.; made her opera debut at the Metropolitan Opera on Nov. 22, 1905; remained on its roster until 1909; then went to Europe. She was married to Dr. Julius Rappold, but divorced him and married the tenor **Rudolf Berger.** She had another period of singing at the Metropolitan Opera (1910–20); then settled in Los Angeles as a singer.

Rappoldi, Eduard, Austrian violinist and composer; b. Vienna, Feb. 21, 1831; d. Dresden, May 16, 1903. He studied at the Vienna Cons.; then played violin in opera orchs. in Vienna and Rotterdam; conducted opera in Lübeck and Prague; was 2nd violinist in the Joachim Quartet in Berlin (1871–77); concertmaster of the Court Opera in Dresden (1878–98); from 1893 till his death, a prof. of violin at the Dresden Cons. He publ. 2 violin sonatas; chamber music; piano pieces; songs. His wife, **Laura Rappoldi-Kahrer** (b. Mistelbach, near Vienna, Jan. 14, 1853; d. Dresden, Aug. 2, 1925), was an excellent pianist, a pupil of Liszt; from 1890 taught piano at the Dresden Cons.

Rasbach, Oscar, American composer; b. Dayton, Ky., Aug. 2, 1888; d. Pasadena, Calif., March 24, 1975. He studied academic subjects in Los Angeles; music with Ludwig Thomas, Julius Albert Jahn, José Anderson, and A.J. Stamm. He was first engaged in business; then went to Vienna, where he took piano lessons with Leschetizky and studied theory with Hans Thornton. He returned to the U.S. in 1911 and settled in San Marino, Calif. He wrote 2 operettas, *Dawn Boy* and *Open House,* and a number of songs, of which *Trees,* to Joyce Kilmer's dendrological poem, became enormously popular.

Rascher, Sigurd M., German-American saxophone virtuoso; b. Elberfeld, May 15, 1907. He studied at the Stuttgart Cons., and became proficient on the saxophone. In 1939 he went to the U.S., where he developed a fine concert career playing works written especially for him by celebrated composers, among them Jacques Ibert, Frank Martin, and (most important) Glazunov, who composed a Saxophone Concerto for him in 1934.

Raselius (Rasel), Andreas, German composer and theorist; b. Hahnbach, near Amberg, c.1563; d. Heidelberg, Jan. 6, 1602. He was the son of a Lutheran preacher; from 1581 to 1583 studied at Heidelberg Univ.; then became a teacher at the Heidelberg Academy; subsequently was appointed cantor at the Gymnasium in Regensburg (1584); remained there till 1600, when he returned to Heidelberg as Hofkapellmeister to the Elector Palatine Frederick IV. In 1589 he publ. a music instruction book, *Hexachordum seu Quaestiones musicae practicae.* Other publ. works: *Teutsche Sprüche* (2 vols.: *a* 5, 1594; *a* 5–9, 1595); *Regensburgischer Kirchenkontrapunkt* (5-voiced Lutheran chorales; 1599); in MS: motets and Magnificats. A selection of his Latin and German motets was ed. by L. Roselius in Denkmäler der Tonkunst in Bayern, 36 (29/30).

Raskin, Judith, noted American soprano; b. New York, June 21, 1928. She studied at Smith College, graduating in 1949; took private voice lessons with Anna Hamlin in N.Y. Her stage career received an impetus on July 7, 1956, when she sang the title role in Douglas Moore's folk opera *The Ballad of Baby Doe,* produced at Central City, Colorado. In 1957 she became a member of the NBC-TV Opera; in 1959 joined the N.Y. City Opera. She made her Metropolitan Opera debut in N.Y. on Feb. 23, 1962, as Susanna in *Le nozze di Figaro.* In 1975 she was appointed to the faculty of the Manhattan School of Music.

Rasmussen, Karl Aage, Danish composer; b. Kolding, Dec. 13, 1947. He studied composition with Norgaard and Gudmundsen-Holmgreen at the Aarhus Cons., graduating in 1970. In 1972 he was appointed editor of the weekly program "Resonance" at Danish Radio. His music follows the cosmopolitan trends of pragmatic hedonism within neo-Classical formal structures.

WORKS: *Jefta,* opera for 9 Singers, 7 Musicians, and Tape (1976); *Crapp's Last Tape,* radio opera after Beckett, for Baritone, Solo Instruments, and Chamber Orch. (Aarhus, Nov. 1, 1968); *Canto serioso* for String Quartet (1965); *Mass* for Chorus, Solo Horn, and Bell Chimes (1966); *This Moment* for 3 Sopranos, Flute, and Percussion (1966); *Coralis Constantinus* for Chamber Orch. (1967); *Symphony for Young Lovers,* 6 movements for Orch. (1967); *Repriser—Fristelser og eventyr (Recapitulations—Temptations and Fairy Tales)* for Orch. (1968); *Symphonie classique* for Chamber Orch. (1969); *Afskrift (Transcript)* for Flute, Violin, Viola, Cello, and Piano (1971); *Protokol og Myte* for Accordion, Electric Guitar, and Percussion (1971); *Als kind (As a Child)* for String Quartet (1972); *Music for Solo Accordion* (1972); *Genklang (Echo)* for Piano, 4-hands, Prepared Piano, Mistuned ("honky-tonk") Piano, and Celesta (1972); *Anfang und Ende (Beginning and End)* for Orch. (1970–73; Aarhus, Feb. 11, 1976); *Love Is in the World* for Soprano, Guitar, and Percussion (1974); *Lullaby* for Flute and Piano (1976); *Berio-Mask,* palimpsest for Chamber Ensemble (1977); *Le Tombeau de Père Igor* for Clarinet, Cello, and Piano (1977); *Vladimir Mayakovsky,* "Konzertstück" for a stage performance (1977); *Schein,* polyphony for Orch. (1977).

Rasumovsky. See **Razumovsky.**

Rathaus, Karol, Polish-American composer; b. Tarnopol, Sept. 16, 1895; d. New York, Nov. 21, 1954. He studied composition at the Vienna Academy of Music (1913–19, 1919–21; Ph.D., 1922) and in Berlin (1920–21, 1922–23); in 1932 went to Paris, and in 1934 to London. In 1938 he settled in the U.S., becoming an American citizen in 1946. After a brief stay in Hollywood in 1939, during which he wrote some film scores, he settled in N.Y.; in 1940 he was appointed to the faculty of Queens College. He was highly respected as a teacher of composition. His own music, however, never attracted large audiences; always noble in purpose and design and masterly in technique, it reveals a profound feeling for European neo-Romanticism.

Rattle, Simon, brilliant English conductor; b. Liverpool, Jan. 19, 1955. He studied piano and also played percussion with the Royal Liverpool Phil. He took lessons in conducting with Pierre Boulez; he was 16 when he won a scholarship to the Royal Academy of Music in London, and launched a remarkably youthful career when, in 1974, he won first prize in the International Conductor's Competition; was then named assistant conductor of the Bournemouth Symph. In 1976 he made his first appearance in America during the tour of the London Symph. Orch. In 1977 he became associate conductor of the Royal Liverpool Phil. and assistant conductor of the BBC Scottish Symph. He made his first appearance with an American orch. conducting the Los Angeles Phil. in 1979; also in 1979 was named principal conductor of the London Choral Society. In 1980 he became principal conductor and artistic adviser of the City of Birmingham Symph. Orch.; in 1981 was appointed (with Michael Tilson Thomas) principal guest conductor of the Los Angeles Phil. Orch. His last name inspired jokes among orch. players, but this handicap (if it was a handicap) soon turned to his advantage, as did his tousled hair and youthful vim.

Raugel, Félix, French musicologist; b. St.-Quentin, Nov. 27, 1881; d. Paris, Dec. 30, 1975. While attending the Lycée at Lille he studied music with C. Queste and F. Lecocq; continued his studies in 1900 in Paris with H. Libert and at the Schola Cantorum with Vincent d'Indy. Together with E. Borrel he founded in 1908 the Société Haendel for the cultivation of early music.

Rautavaara, Einojuhani, Finnish composer; b. Helsinki, Oct. 9, 1928. He studied composition with Merikanto at the Sibelius Academy in Helsinki (1948–54); in N.Y. and at Tanglewood with Copland, Persichetti, and Sessions (1955–56); in Switzerland for dodecaphonic studies with Vogel (1957); and in Cologne with Rudolf Petzold (1958). In 1966 he was appointed to the faculty of the Sibelius Academy in Helsinki. He adopted in his works an eclectic modern idiom, with occasional dodecaphonic excursions. In 1975 he began a series of chamber operas based on the *Kalevala,* the Finnish national epic. WORKS: FOR THE STAGE: Opera, *Kaivos (The Mine;* 1958–61; Finnish Television, 1963); ballet, *Kiusaukset (The Temptations;* 1969; Helsinki, Feb. 8, 1973); comic opera, *Apollo contra Marsyas* (1970; Helsinki, Aug. 30, 1973); *Runo 42, "Sammon ryosto,"* opera (1974–81); *Marjatta matala neita,* mystery play in one act (1975); *Late One Night,* opera (1975–76). VOCAL WORKS: *Die Liebenden (The Lovers)* for Voice and Orch. (1959); *Itsenäisyys-kantaatti (Independence Cantata;* 1967); *Daughter of the Sea* for Soprano, Chorus, and Orch. (Helsinki, Dec.

4, 1971); *Vigilia (The Mass)* for Soloists and Chorus (1971); *True and False Unicorn* for Chorus, Tape, and Chamber Ensemble (1971); *The Water Circle* for Chorus, Piano, and Orch. (Copenhagen, Dec. 4, 1972). FOR ORCH.: 4 symphs. (1956, 1957, 1961, 1964–70); *Arabescata* (1963); *Anadyomene* (1968); *Sotilas-messu (Soldier's Mass)* for Winds and Percussion (1968); Cello Concerto (1968); Piano Concerto (1969); *Dithyrambos* for Violin and Orch. (1970); *Regular Sets of Elements in a Semiregular Situation* for 3 Flutes, 3 Horns, Trumpet, Percussion, Piano, 4 Violins, and 4 Cellos (1971); *Cantus Arcticus,* concerto for Birds (on tape) and Orch. (Oulu, May 26, 1972); *A Portrait of the Artist at a Certain Moment* for Strings (Jyvskyla, May 28, 1972); Flute Concerto (1973); *Ballad* for Harp and Strings (1973); *Annunciations,* concerto for Organ, Brass Quintet, and Symph. Wind Orch. (1976–77); Violin Concerto (1977); *Angels and Visitations* (1978); *Angel of Dusk,* concerto for Double Bass (1980); *Hommage for Strings* (1982).

Ravel, Maurice (Christian names, **Joseph Maurice**), great French composer; b. Ciboure, Basses-Pyrénées, March 7, 1875; d. Paris, Dec. 28, 1937. His father was a Swiss engineer, and his mother of Basque origin. The family moved to Paris when he was an infant. He began to study piano at the age of 7 with Henri Ghis and harmony at 12 with Charles-René. In 1889 he entered the Paris Cons.; studied piano with Anthiome; won first medal in 1891, and passed to the advanced class of Charles de Bériot; studied harmony with Emile Pessard. While still a student he wrote and publ. a *Menuet antique* for Piano and *Habanera* for 2 Pianos (later included in the *Rapsodie espagnole* for Orch.); these pieces, written at the age of 20, already reveal great originality in the treatment of old modes and of Spanish motifs; however, he continued to study; in 1897 he entered the class of Gabriel Fauré (composition) and Gédalge (counterpoint and fugue); his well-known *Pavane pour une infante défunte* for Piano was written during that time (1899). On May 27, 1899, he appeared in public as a conductor, in a performance of his overture *Shéhérazade* with the Société Nationale in Paris; some elements of the work were incorporated in Ravel's song cycle of the same title (1903). In 1901 he won the 2nd Prix de Rome with the cantata *Myrrha;* but ensuing attempts to win the Grand Prix de Rome were unsuccessful; at his last try (1905) he was eliminated in the preliminaries, and so was not allowed to compete; the age limit then set an end to his further effort to enter. Since 6 prizes all went to pupils of Lenepveu, suspicion of unfair discrimination was aroused; Jean Marnold publ. an article, "Le Scandale du Prix de Rome," in the *Mercure de France* (June 1905) in which he brought the controversy into the open; this precipitated a crisis at the Paris Cons.; its director, Théodore Dubois, resigned, and Gabriel Fauré took his place. By that time, Ravel had written a number of his most famous compositions, and was regarded by most French critics as a talented disciple of Debussy. No doubt Ravel's method of poetic associa-

Ravel

tion of musical ideas paralleled that of Debussy; his employment of unresolved dissonances and the enhancement of the diatonic style into pandiatonicism were techniques common to Debussy and his followers; but there were important differences: whereas Debussy adopted the scale of whole tones as an integral part of his musical vocabulary, Ravel resorted to it only occasionally; similarly, augmented triads appear much less frequently in Ravel's music than in Debussy's; in his writing for piano Ravel actually anticipated some of Debussy's usages; in a letter addressed to Pierre Lalo and publ. in *Le Temps* (April 9, 1907) Ravel pointed out that at the time of the publication of his piano piece *Jeux d'eau* (1902) Debussy had brought out only his suite *Pour le piano,* which had contained little that was novel. In Paris, elsewhere in France, and soon in England and other European countries, Ravel's name became well known, but for many years he was still regarded as an ultramodernist. A curious test of audience appreciation was a "Concert des Auteurs Anonymes" presented by the Société Indépendante de Musique on May 9, 1911; the program included Ravel's *Valses nobles et sentimentales,* a set of piano pieces in the manner of Schubert; yet Ravel was recognized as the author. Inspired evocation of the past was but one aspect of Ravel's creative genius; in this style are written the *Pavane pour une infante défunte, Le Tombeau de Couperin,* and *La Valse;* luxuriance of exotic colors marks his ballet *Daphnis et Chloé,* his opera *L'Heure espagnole,* the song cycles *Shéhérazade* and *Chansons madécasses,* and his virtuoso pieces for Piano *Miroirs* and *Gaspard de la nuit;* other works are deliberately austere, even ascetic, in their pointed classicism: the piano concertos, the Piano Sonatina, and some of his songs with piano accompaniment. His association with Diaghilev's Ballets Russes was most fruitful; for Diaghilev he wrote one of his masterpieces, *Daphnis et Chloé;* another ballet, *Boléro,* commissioned by Ida Rubinstein and performed at her dance recital at the Paris Opéra on Nov. 22, 1928, became Ravel's most spectacular success as an orch. piece.

Ravel never married, and lived a life of semi-retirement, devoting most of his time to composition; he accepted virtually no pupils, although he gave friendly advice to Vaughan Williams and to others; he was never on the faculty of any school. As a performer, he was not brilliant; he appeared as a pianist only in his own works, and often accompanied singers in programs of his songs; although he accepted engagements as a conductor, his technique was barely sufficient to secure a perfunctory performance of his music. When the war broke out in 1914, he was rejected for military service because of his frail physique, but he was anxious to serve; his application for air service was denied, but he was received in the ambulance corps at the front; his health gave way, and in the autumn of 1916 he was compelled to enter a hospital for recuperation. In 1922 he visited Amsterdam and Venice, conducting his music; in 1923 he appeared in London; in 1926 he went to Sweden, England, and Scotland; in 1928 he made an American tour as a conductor and

pianist; in the same year he received the degree of D.Mus. *honoris causa* at Oxford Univ. In 1929 he was honored at his native town of Ciboure by the inauguration of the Quai Maurice Ravel. Shortly afterward, he began to experience difficulties in muscular coordination, and suffered from attacks of aphasia, symptoms indicative of a cerebral malady; a brain operation was performed on Dec. 19, 1937, but was not successful, and he died 9 days later.

WORKS: FOR THE STAGE: One-act opera, *L'Heure espagnole,* to text by Franc-Nohain (Paris, Opéra-Comique, May 19, 1911; Chicago, Jan. 5, 1920); "fantaisie lyrique," *L'Enfant et les sortilèges,* libretto by Colette (Monte Carlo, March 21, 1925); ballets: *Daphnis et Chloé* (Paris, June 8, 1912); *Adélaide ou Le Langage des fleurs,* after the *Valses nobles et sentimentales* (Paris, April 22, 1912); *Ma Mère l'Oye,* elaborated from the piano suite (Théâtre des Arts, Paris, Jan. 21, 1912); *Le Tombeau de Couperin,* choreographic poem from the orch. suite (Ballets Suédois, Paris, Nov. 8, 1920); *La Valse* (Paris, Dec. 12, 1920); *Boléro* (Ida Rubinstein's dance recital, Paris, Nov. 22, 1928). FOR ORCH.: Overture, *Shéhérazade* (1898; Paris, May 27, 1899; publ. Paris, 1975); *Pavane pour une infante défunte* (1899; Paris, Dec. 25, 1910); *Alborada del gracioso* (1905; Paris, May 17, 1919); *Rapsodie espagnole* (Paris, March 15, 1908); *Daphnis et Chloé,* 2 suites from the ballet (1909–11); *Ma Mère l'Oye,* after the piano duet (1912); *Le Tombeau de Couperin* (1917; Paris, Feb. 28, 1920); *La Valse* (Paris, Dec. 12, 1920); *Tzigane* for Violin and Orch. (also with Piano Accompaniment; Paris, Dec. 7, 1924); *Boléro* (1928; first American perf., N.Y., Nov. 14, 1929); Piano Concerto in D for Left Hand Alone, written for the one-armed pianist Paul Wittgenstein, who gave its first performance (Vienna, Nov. 27, 1931); Piano Concerto in G (Paris, Jan. 14, 1932; composer conducting; Marguerite Long, pianist). CHAMBER MUSIC: Sonata in one movement for Violin and Piano (1897; publ. Paris, 1975); String Quartet in F (1903); *Introduction et Allegro* for Harp, String Quartet, Flute, and Clarinet (Paris, Feb. 22, 1907); Piano Trio (1914); Sonata for Violin and Cello (1920–22); *Berceuse sur le nom de Fauré* for Violin and Piano (1922); Violin Sonata (1923–27); *Tzigane* for Violin and Piano (London, April 26, 1924; Jelly d'Aranyi, violinist; Ravel at the piano, in a concert of Ravel works). VOCAL WORKS: 3 cantatas, written for the Prix de Rome: *Myrrha, Alcyone,* and *Alysse* (1901–3); *Shéhérazade,* song cycle for Solo Voice and Orch. (Paris, May 17, 1904); *3 poèmes de Mallarmé* for Voice, Piano, 2 Flutes, 2 Clarinets, and String Quartet (1913; Paris, Jan. 14, 1914); *3 chansons* for Mixed Chorus a cappella (1916); *Chansons madécasses* for Voice, Flute, Cello, and Piano (1926); *Don Quichotte à Dulcinée,* 3 songs, with Orch. Accompaniment (Paris, Dec. 1, 1934). Songs: *Ballade de la Reine morte d'aimer* (1894); *Un Grand Sommeil noir* (1895); *Sainte* (1896); *2 épigrammes de Clément Marot* (1896); *Si morne* (1898; publ. Paris, 1975); *Manteau de fleurs* (1903); *Le Noël des jouets,* text by Ravel (1905); *5 mélodies populaires grecques* (1905; another Greek melody was publ. in the *Revue Musicale,* Dec. 1938); *Les Grands*

Vents venus d'outre-mer (1906); *Histoires naturelles* (1906); *Sur l'herbe* (1907); *Vocalise en forme d'habanera* (1907); *4 chants populaires* (1910); *2 mélodies hébraïques* (1914); *Ronsard à son âme* (1924); *Rêves* (1927). FOR PIANO: *Sérénade grotesque menuet antique* (1895); *Pavane pour une infante défunte* (1899); *Jeux d'eau* (1901); *Miroirs* (5 pieces): *Noctuelles, Oiseaux tristes, Une Barque sur l'océan, Alborada del Gracioso, La Vallée des cloches* (1905); *Sonatine* (1903–5); *Gaspard de la nuit: Ondine, Le Gibet, Scarbo* (1908); *Menuet sur le nom d'Haydn* (1909); *Valses nobles et sentimentales* (1911); *Prélude* (1913); *A la manière de . . . Borodine, Chabrier* (1913); *Le Tombeau de Couperin* (1914–17); *Sites auriculaires* for 2 Pianos (1895–97): *Habanera* and *Entre cloches; Ma Mère l'Oye,* 5 "pièces enfantines" for Piano, 4-hands, written for Christine Verger, age 6, and Germaine Durant, age 10, and performed by them (Paris, April 20, 1910); *Frontispiece* for 2 Pianos, 5-hands (1918). Ravel was commissioned by Koussevitzky to make an orchestration of Mussorgsky's *Pictures at an Exhibition;* it was first performed by Koussevitzky at one of his concerts (Paris, Oct. 19, 1922) and subsequently became one of the most popular orch. suites; Ravel also orchestrated Chabrier's *Menuet pompeux,* arranged Debussy's *Prélude à l'après-midi d'un faune* for 2 Pianos, etc.

Ravenscroft, John (Giovanni), English composer; b. London; d. there, c.1708. In 1695 he was in Rome, where he publ. a set of "sonate a trè" under the Italianized name Giovanni Ravenscroft. He apparently was a pupil of Corelli, whose style he imitated. His op. 2, containing 6 sonatas for 2 Violins, with Continuo, was publ. posthumously in London.

Ravenscroft, Thomas, English composer and music editor; b. c.1590; d. c.1633. He was a chorister at St. Paul's Cathedral under Edward Pearce; in 1605 received his B.Mus. at Cambridge; from 1618 to 1622 he was music master at Christ's Hospital in London.
WORKS: *Pammelia: Musick's Miscellanie: or Mixed Varietie of Pleasant Roundelayes and Delightful Catches of 3–10 Parts in one* (1609; the first collection of rounds, catches, and canons printed in England; 2nd ed., 1618); *Deuteromelia: or the Second Part of Musick's Melodie* (1609); *Melismata: Musicall Phansies, Fitting the Court, Citie, and Countrey Humours, to 3, 4 and 5 Voyces* (1611); *A Briefe Discourse of the true (but neglected) use of Charact'ring the Degrees by their Perfection, Imperfection, and Diminution in Mensurable Musicke: Harmony of four voyces concerning the pleasure of five usuall recreations, 1. Hunting, 2. Hawking, 3. Dancing, 4. Drinking, 5. Enamouring* (1614); and *The Whole Booke of Psalmes: With the Hymnes Evangelicall and Songs Spirituall Composed into 4 parts by Sundry Authors* (1621; 2nd ed., newly corrected and enlarged, 1633; his best-known and most valuable work, containing numbers by 15 leading British composers, and some by Ravenscroft himself).

Rawsthorne, Alan, important English composer; b. Haslingden, May 2, 1905; d. Cambridge, July 24, 1971. He went to a dentistry school; did not begin to study music until he was 20, when he entered the Royal Manchester College of Music; later studied piano with Egon Petri in Berlin (1930–31). After returning to England in 1932, he occupied various teaching posts; then devoted himself mainly to composition, and succeeded brilliantly in producing music of agreeable, and to some ears even delectable, music. In 1961 he was made a Commander of the Order of the British Empire. His music is essentially a revival of the contrapuntal style of the past, without much harmonic elaboration; but the rhythms are virile and the melodies fluid, emanating from a focal point of tonality.
WORKS: Ballet, *Madame Chrysanthème* (London, April 1, 1955); Concerto for Clarinet and Strings (1936); *Symphonic Studies* (1938; International Society for Contemporary Music Festival, Warsaw, April 21, 1939); 2 piano concertos: No. 1 (originally for Strings and Percussion, 1939; rescored for Full Orch., 1942; London, 1942) and No. 2 (1951; London, June 17, 1951); 4 overtures: *Street Corner* (1944); *Cortèges,* fantasy overture (1945); *Hallé,* for the centennial of the Hallé Orch. (1958); *Overture for Farnham* (1967); 2 violin concertos: No. 1 (1940; sketches lost in an air raid; reconstructed 1943–48; Cheltenham Festival, July 1, 1948) and No. 2 (London, Oct. 24, 1956); Concerto for Oboe and Strings (1947); Concerto for String Orch. (1949); 3 symphs.: No. 1 (1950; London, Nov. 15, 1950); No. 2, *Pastoral,* with Solo Soprano (1959; Birmingham, Sept. 29, 1959); No. 3 (1964; Cheltenham Festival, July 8, 1964); *Concertante Pastorale* for Flute, Horn, and Strings (1951); *A Canticle of Man,* chamber cantata for Baritone, Chorus, Flute, and Strings (1952); *Practical Cats,* an entertainment for children, after T.S. Eliot, for Narrator and Orch. (Edinburgh, Aug. 26, 1954); *Improvisations on a Theme of Constant Lambert* for Orch. (1960); Concerto for 10 Instruments (1962); *Medieval Diptych* for Baritone and Orch. (1962); *Divertimento* for Chamber Orch. (1962); *Carmen Vitale,* cantata (1963; London, Oct. 16, 1963); *Elegiac Rhapsody* for Strings (1964); Cello Concerto (London, April 6, 1966); *The God in the Cave* for Chorus and Orch. (1967); Concerto for 2 Pianos and Orch. (1968); *Theme, Variations and Finale* for Orch. (1968); *Triptych* for Orch. (1970); Trio for Flute, Oboe, and Piano (1936); *Theme and Variations* for 2 Violins (1937); Viola Sonata (1938); *Theme and Variations* for String Quartet (1939); 3 string quartets (1939, 1954, 1965); Clarinet Quartet (1948); Cello Sonata (1949); Violin Sonata (1959); Piano Trio (1962); *Concertante* for Violin and Piano (1935–62); Quintet for Piano, Oboe, Clarinet, Horn, and Bassoon (1963); *Tankas of the 4 Seasons* for Tenor, Oboe, Clarinet, Bassoon, Violin, and Cello (1965); Quintet for Piano and Strings (1968); Oboe Quartet (1970); *Suite* for Flute, Viola, and Harp (1970); Quintet for Piano, Clarinet, Horn, Violin, and Cello (1971); *Elegy* for Solo Guitar (1971; completed from composer's sketches by Julian Bream); *Bagatelles* for Piano (1938); *The Creel* for 2 Pianos (1940); Piano Sonatina (1948); *4 Romantic Pieces* for Piano (1953); *Ballade* for Piano (1967); *Theme with*

4 Studies for Piano (1971); choruses; several song cycles, to French and English words.

Raxach, Enrique, Spanish-born Dutch composer; b. Barcelona, Jan. 15, 1932. He studied composition with Nuri Aymerich; in 1958 he moved to Paris; then lived in Zürich, Munich, and Cologne. From 1959–66 he attended the summer courses in Darmstadt given by Messiaen, Boulez, Maderna, and Stockhausen. In 1962 he settled in the Netherlands; in 1969 he became a Dutch citizen. In his music he explores purely structural potentialities; the idiom of his composition is influenced by Varèse and Xenakis.

Razumovsky, Count (from 1815, **Prince**) **Andrei,** Russian diplomat and music-lover; b. St. Petersburg, Nov. 2, 1752; d. Vienna, Sept. 23, 1836. He was the Russian ambassador at Vienna from 1793 to 1809; from 1808 to 1816 he maintained the celebrated Razumovsky Quartet (first violin, Schuppanzigh; 2nd violin, Louis Sina, whose part was occasionally taken over by Razumovsky; viola, Weiss; cello, Lincke), later known as the Schuppanzigh Quartet (without Razumovsky). Razumovsky's name was immortalized through the dedication to him of Beethoven's 3 string quartets, op. 59, and (with Prince Lobkowitz) 5th and 6th Symphs. He was a munificent and prodigal patron of art, but after the destruction by fire of his Vienna palace (Dec. 31, 1814) he gave up the quartet, and disappeared from musical history.

Read, Daniel, American composer; b. Attleboro, Mass., Nov. 16, 1757; d. New Haven, Dec. 4, 1836. He worked on a farm as a youth; studied mechanics, and was employed as a surveyor at 18; began to compose at 19. He served in the Continental Army as a private; at 21 he settled at New Stratford; later went to New Haven. In 1782–83 he maintained a singing school on the North River. He also was a comb maker. At his death, he left a collection of some 400 tunes by him and other composers. He publ. *The American Singing Book, or a New and Easy Guide to the Art of Psalmody, devised for the use of Singing Schools in America* (New Haven, 1785; subsequent eds., 1786, 1792, 1793, 1795); the *American Musical Magazine* (containing New England church music; compiled with Amos Doolittle, New Haven, 12 numbers, May 1786 to Sept. 1787; reprinted, Scarsdale, N.Y., 1961); *Supplement to The American Singing Book* (New Haven, 1787); *The Columbian Harmonist,* in 3 books: no. 1 (New Haven, 1793), no. 2 (New Haven, 1794; 2nd ed., with numerous additions, 1798; 3rd ed., with further additions, 1801), no. 3 (New Haven, 1795); all 3 books in one vol. (New Haven, 1795; 2nd ed., completely revised, Dedham, 1804; 3rd ed., Boston, 1807; 4th ed., Boston, 1810). Shortly before his death he completed the compilation *Musica Ecclesia, or Devotional Harmony,* but it remained unpubl. Many of his tunes—e.g., *Sherburne, Windham,* and *Lisbon*—achieved great popularity.

Read, Gardner, outstanding American composer and erudite music scholar; b. Evanston, Ill., Jan. 2, 1913. He studied theory at the Northwestern Univ. School of Music; conducting with Bakaleinikoff, and composition at the Eastman School of Music in Rochester, N.Y., with Paul White, Bernard Rogers, and Howard Hanson (B.Mus., 1936; M.M., 1937); he studied with Aaron Copland at the Berkshire Music Center in Tanglewood; taught composition at the St. Louis Inst. of Music (1941–43), at the Kansas City Cons. of Music (1943–45), and at the Cleveland Inst. of Music (1945–48); was appointed composer-in-residence and prof. of composition at Boston Univ. College of Music in 1948; retired in 1978. A composer of extraordinary fecundity, he excels in instrumental music; his idiom of composition is basically Romantic, but the harmonic and contrapuntal textures are intense and dense with polytonal encounters.
WORKS: OPERA: *Villon* (1967). FOR ORCH.: *The Lotus-Eaters* (Interlochen, Mich., Aug. 12, 1932); *Sketches of the City,* symph. suite after Carl Sandburg (Rochester, April 18, 1934); *The Painted Desert* (Interlochen, July 28, 1935); Symph. No. 1 (1936; N.Y., Nov. 4, 1937; awarded first prize in the American Composer's Contest sponsored by the N.Y. Phil.); *Fantasy* for Viola and Orch. (Rochester, April 22, 1937); *Prelude and Toccata* (Rochester, April 29, 1937); *Suite* for String Orch. (N.Y., Aug. 5, 1937); *Passacaglia and Fugue* (Chicago, June 30, 1938); *The Golden Journey to Samarkand* for Chorus, Soloists, and Orch. (1936–39); *Pan e Dafni* (1940); *American Circle* (Evanston, March 15, 1941); *First Overture* (Indianapolis, Nov. 6, 1943); Symph. No. 2 (awarded first prize of the Paderewski Fund Competition, 1942; Boston, Nov. 26, 1943, composer conducting); *Night Flight,* tone poem after Antoine de St.-Exupéry (Rochester, April 27, 1944); Cello Concerto (1945); *Threnody* for Flute and Strings (Rochester, Oct. 21, 1946); *A Bell Overture* (Cleveland, Dec. 22, 1946); *Partita* for Small Orch. (Rochester, May 4, 1947); *Pennsylvaniana Suite* (Pittsburgh, Nov. 21, 1947); Symph. No. 3 (1948); *Quiet Music for Strings* (Washington, D.C., May 9, 1948); *Dance of the Locomotives* (Boston, June 26, 1948); *Sound Piece* for Brass and Percussion (Boston, May 11, 1949); *The Temptation of St. Anthony,* dance-symph. after Flaubert (Chicago, April 9, 1953); *Toccata giocosa* (Louisville, Ky., March 13, 1954); *Vernal Equinox* (Brockton, Mass., April 12, 1955); Symph. No. 4 (1958; Cincinnati, Jan. 30, 1970); *Jeux des timbres* for Orch. (1963); Piano Concerto (1977). VOCAL WORKS: *4 Nocturnes* for Voice and Orch. (Rochester, April 3, 1935); *From a Lute of Jade* for Voice and Orch. (Rochester, March 15, 1937); *Songs for a Rainy Night* for Voice and Orch. (Rochester, April 27, 1942); *The Prophet,* oratorio after Kahlil Gibran (1960; Boston, Feb. 23, 1977); *The Reveille* for Chorus, Winds, Percussion, and Organ (1962); *Chants d'Auvergne* for Chorus and Instruments (1962); *The Hidden Lute* for Soprano, Flute, Harp, and Percussion (1979); many songs and choruses. CHAMBER MUSIC: *Suite* for String Quartet (1936); Piano Quintet (1945); *Sonata brevis* for Violin and Piano (1948); *9 by 6* for Wind Sextet (1951); String Quartet No. 1 (1957); *Sonoric Fantasia No. 1*

for Celesta, Harp, and Harpsichord (1958); *Sonoric Fantasia No. 2* for Violin and Orch. (1965); *Sonoric Fantasia No. 3* for Viola and Small Orch. (1970); *Sonoric Fantasia No. 4* for Organ and Percussion (1975–76); *Los dioses aztecos,* suite of 7 movements for Percussion Ensemble (1959); *Petite suite* for Recorders and Harpsichord (1963); *Invocation* for Trombone and Organ (1977); *Galactic Novae* for Organ and Percussion (1978). FOR ORGAN: *Passacaglia and Fugue* (1937); *Suite for Organ* (co-winner, first prize of Pa. College for Women, Pittsburgh, 1950); *8 Preludes on Old Southern Hymns* (1951). FOR PIANO: *3 Satirical Sarcasms* (1941); *Driftwood Suite* (1943); *Dance of the Locomotives* (1944); *Sonata da chiesa* (1948); *Touch Piece* (1949); *5 Polytonal Studies* (1964).

PUBLICATIONS: *Thesaurus of Orchestral Devices* (Westport, Conn., 1953; 2nd ed., 1969); *Music Notation: A Manual of Modern Practice* (Boston, 1964; 2nd ed., 1971); *Style and Orchestration* (N.Y., 1975); *Contemporary Instrumental Techniques* (N.Y., 1976); *Modern Rhythmic Notation* (Bloomington, Ind., 1978).

Reardon, John, American baritone; b. New York, April 8, 1930. He studied at Rollins College (B.Mus., 1952); then took voice lessons with Martial Singher and Margaret Harshaw. He made his first appearance with the N.Y. City Opera on Oct. 16, 1954, as Falke in *Die Fledermaus.* He made his Metropolitan Opera debut in N.Y. on Sept. 28, 1965, as Count Tomsky in Tchaikovsky's *Queen of Spades.* He mastered an extensive repertoire, which included several roles in modern operas.

Rebel, François, French composer; b. Paris, June 19, 1701; d. there, Nov. 7, 1775. He became an excellent violinist under the tutelage of his father, Jean-Féry Rebel. He was in charge of the "24 violins" of the King and master of the royal chamber music. From 1757 to 1767 Rebel and his lifelong friend and collaborator, François Francœur, were directors of the Académie Royale de Musique (the Opéra). The operas composed jointly by Rebel and Francœur and produced at Paris include *Pirame et Thisbé* (Oct. 17, 1726) and *Scanderberg* (Oct. 27, 1735).

Rebikov, Vladimir, Russian composer; b. Krasnoyarsk, Siberia, May 31, 1866; d. Yalta, Aug. 4, 1920. He studied at the Moscow Cons. with Klenovsky; then in Berlin and Vienna. He then went to Odessa, where his first opera, *In the Thunderstorm,* was produced in 1894. In 1898 he moved to Kishinev, Bessarabia, where he organized a branch of the Imperial Russian Musical Society. In 1901 he settled in Moscow, remaining there until 1919; he spent his last year of life in the Crimea. His early works were under the influence of Tchaikovsky, but beginning with *Esquisses* for Piano he made a decisive turn toward a modern style; he became particularly fond of the whole-tone scale and its concomitant, the augmented triad; claimed priority in this respect over Debussy and other European composers; his piano piece *Les Démons s'amusent* is based entirely

on the whole-tone scale. He declared that music is a language of emotion and therefore could not be confined to set forms, or to arbitrarily defined consonances. An entirely new departure is represented by his *Mélomimiques,* short lyric pieces for Piano, in which mimicry and suggestion are used in an impressionistic manner. He also wrote several vocal "melomimics," 3 "rhythmo-declamations" for Piano (op. 32), and 20 for Voice and Piano. In these compositions he abandoned cohesive form in favor of a free association of melodic and rhythmic phrases, sparingly harmonized; prevalence of esthetic theories over musical substance made his experiments ephemeral. A melodious waltz from his children's opera, *The Christmas Tree,* is his most popular composition.

WORKS: Operas: *In the Thunderstorm* (Odessa, Feb. 27, 1894) and *The Christmas Tree,* children's opera (Moscow, Nov. 1, 1903); musico-psychological pantomime, *Little Snow White* (Tiflis, 1909); 2-act fairy opera, *Prince Charming;* scenic fables after Krylov: *The Grasshopper and the Ant, A Dinner with a Bear, The Ass and the Nightingale, The Funeral, The Liar* (Moscow, Dec. 27, 1903); several "musico-psychological tableaux": *Slavery and Freedom, Songs of the Harp, The Nightmare,* etc.; numerous piano pieces (*Scènes bucoliques, Silhouettes, Dans la forêt, Chansons blanches, Idylles, Les Danses, Les Démons s'amusent,* etc.). He publ. numerous articles on musical esthetics, particularly relating to modern music; translated into Russian Gevaert's *Traité d'instrumentation.*

Rebner, Adolf, Austrian violinist; b. Vienna, Nov. 21, 1876; d. Baden-Baden, June 19, 1967. He was a pupil of Grün at the Vienna Cons.; settled in Frankfurt in 1896, and after 1904 taught violin at the Hoch Cons. In 1921 he organized the Rebner String Quartet, with Hindemith as the violist, and gave numerous concerts with it, obtaining excellent success; with the advent of the Nazi regime in Germany he went to Vienna; after the Anschluss, lived briefly in the U.S.; eventually returned to Europe and lived in Baden-Baden.

Rebner, Wolfgang Edward, German pianist, son of **Adolf Rebner;** b. Frankfurt, Dec. 20, 1910. He studied at the Hoch Cons. in Frankfurt; served as accompanist to the cellist Feuermann in the U.S. (1935–37) and South America. In 1955 he returned to Germany, and taught at the Richard Strauss Cons. in Munich. He composed some excellent chamber music and the orch. suites *Persönliche Noten* (1961) and *Aus Südamerika* (1964).

Redford, John, English organist, composer, and poet; d. London, 1547. He was one of the vicars-choral of St. Paul's Cathedral in London. His works are found in D. Stevens, ed., *The Mulliner Book,* in *Musica Britannica,* I (1951); J. Caldwell, ed., *Early Tudor Organ Music* I: *Music for the Office,* in *Early English Church Music,* VI (1966) and D. Stevens, ed., *Early Tudor Organ Music* II: *Music for the Mass,* in *Early English Church Music,* X (1969).

Redlich, Hans Ferdinand, distinguished Austrian musicologist and conductor; b. Vienna, Feb. 11, 1903; d. Manchester, England, Nov. 27, 1968. He studied piano and conducting, but devoted his energies mainly to writing biographical and analytical books on composers; he was only 16 when he publ. an essay on Mahler. After taking courses at the univs. of Vienna and Munich, he obtained his Dr.Phil. at the Univ. of Frankfurt with the dissertation *Das Problem des Stilwandels in Monteverdis Madrigalwerk* (publ. Leipzig, 1931; revised ed., Berlin, 1932). He conducted opera at the Municipal Theater of Mainz (1925–29); then lived in Mannheim. In 1939 he emigrated to England; from 1941 to 1955 he conducted the Choral and Orch. Society in Letchworth; also was a lecturer at the Extra Mural Board of the Univ. of Cambridge (1941–55); from 1955 to 1962 he was a lecturer at the Reid School of Music at the Univ. of Edinburgh; then was at the Univ. of Manchester. He publ. *Gustav Mahler: Eine Erkenntnis* (Nuremberg, 1919); *Richard Wagner: Tristan und Isolde, Lohengrin, Parsifal* (London, 1948; 3rd ed., 1951); *Claudio Monteverdi: Leben und Werk* (Olten, 1949; in Eng., London, 1952); *Bruckner and Mahler* (London, 1955; revised ed., 1963); *Alban Berg: The Man and His Music* (London, 1957; a fundamental work).

Reed, Thomas German, versatile English musician; b. Bristol, June 27, 1817; d. London, March 21, 1888. Under the guidance of his father, he appeared in Bath as a child of 10 in the various capacities of singer, pianist, and actor. In 1844 he married **Priscilla Horton** (b. Birmingham, Jan. 1, 1818; d. Bexley Heath, March 18, 1895), an actress and a singer. Together they started the celebrated series "Mr. and Mrs. German Reed's Entertainment" (1855), which included productions of operettas by Offenbach, Balfe, Clay, Sullivan, etc. These entertainments enjoyed great success, and were continued by his son **Alfred German Reed,** who died in London on March 10, 1895, a few days before the death of his mother.

Reese, Gustave, eminent American musicologist; b. New York, Nov. 29, 1899; d. Berkeley, Calif., Sept. 7, 1977. At N.Y. Univ. he studied jurisprudence (LL.B., 1921) and music (Mus.Bac., 1930); subsequently joined its faculty, teaching there during the periods 1927–33, 1934–37, and 1945–74; concurrently he worked with G. Schirmer, Inc., publishers (1924–45; from 1940 to 1945 was director of publications); was director of publications for Carl Fischer, music publishers (1944–55). From 1933 to 1944 he was associate editor, and in 1944–45 editor, of the *Musical Quarterly.* In 1934 he was a co-founder of the American Musicological Society; was its president from 1950 to 1952, and remained its honorary president until his death. He gave numerous lectures at American univs.; also gave courses at the Juilliard School of Music in N.Y. An entire generation of American music scholars numbered among his students; he was widely regarded as a founder of American musicology as a science. He held a chair at the Graduate School of Arts and Science at N.Y. Univ., which gave him its "Great Teacher Award" in 1972 and its presidential citation on his retirement from active teaching in 1974; he then became a visiting prof. at the Graduate Center of the City Univ. of N.Y. He died while attending the congress of the International Musicological Society in Berkeley. Gustave Reese contributed a great number of informative articles to various American and European publications and music encyclopedias, but his most lasting achievement lies in his books, *Music in the Middle Ages* (N.Y., 1940; also in Italian, Florence, 1960) and *Music in the Renaissance* (N.Y., 1954; revised 1959), which have become classics of American music scholarship; he also brought out an interesting book that describes selected early writings on music not available in English, *Fourscore Classics of Music Literature* (N.Y., 1957). On his 65th birthday, he was honored with an offering of a collection of articles by his colleagues and students, *Aspects of Medieval and Renaissance Music,* edited by Jan LaRue (N.Y., 1966; 2nd ed., 1978).

Reeves, David Wallace, American bandmaster; b. Oswego, N.Y., Feb. 14, 1838; d. Providence, R.I., March 8, 1900. As a boy he began to play cornet in circus and minstrel bands; later was in Union Army bands; his career as a bandmaster began in 1866, when he became the leader of the American Band of Providence, which is said to trace its roots back to the War of 1812; during its 35 years under the direction of Reeves it became a model of excellence among American municipal bands; Reeves succeeded in standardizing the instrumentation of the ordinary parade and outdoor-concert band; he wrote some 80 marches, of which the best is *The 2nd Connecticut Regiment March,* known to have been a favorite of Charles Ives. Reeves was a great friend of Patrick Sarsfield Gilmore, conductor of the band of the N.Y. 22nd Regiment, and it was Gilmore who popularized Reeves's marches. Upon Gilmore's death, Reeves took over the 22nd Regiment Band for the 1892–93 season, until it was taken over by Victor Herbert in the fall of 1893. J.P. Sousa called Reeves "the father of band music in America."

Reeves, (John) Sims, English tenor; b. Shooter's Hill, Kent, Sept. 26, 1818; d. Worthing, London, Oct. 25, 1900. Learned to play several instruments; had lessons with J.B. Cramer (piano) and W.H. Callcott (harmony); he made his debut (as a baritone) at in the role of Rodolfo (*Sonnambula*), on Dec. 14, 1838; studied further and sang minor tenor parts at Drury Lane, 1841–43; studied in Paris under Bordogni, and in Milan under Mazzucato, appearing at La Scala in 1846 as Edgardo (*Lucia*). He retired in 1891, but reappeared in concerts in 1893, and even made a successful tour in South Africa in 1896. He publ. *Sims Reeves; His Life and Recollections Written by Himself* (London, 1888); *My Jubilee, or Fifty Years of Artistic Life* (London, 1889); *Sims Reeves on the Art of Singing* (1900).

Refardt, Edgar, eminent Swiss musicologist and bibliographer; b. Basel, Aug. 8, 1877; d. there, March

3, 1968. He studied law; obtained the degree of Dr.Jur. in 1901; in 1915 was appointed librarian and cataloguer of the musical collection of the Municipal Library of Basel; publ. valuable bibliographical works on Swiss music; also essays on various literary and musical subjects.

Refice, Licinio, Italian composer of sacred music; b. Patrica, near Rome, Feb. 12, 1883; d. Rio de Janeiro, Sept. 11, 1954 (while conducting his mystery play, *Santa Cecilia*). He studied with Falchi and Renzi at Santa Cecilia Academy in Rome; in 1910 became a teacher of church music at the Scuola Pontifica Superiore di Musica Sacra, remaining at this post until 1950. In 1947 he toured the U.S. as director of the Roman Singers of Sacred Music (99 concerts).

WORKS: Operas: *Cecilia* (Rome, 1934) and *Margherita da Cortona* (Milan, 1938); cantatas: *La Vedova di Naim* (1912); *Maria Magdalena* (Rome, 1917); *Il Martirio di S. Agnese* (Rome, 1919); *Stabat Mater* (1917); *Te Deum* (1918); *Missa Jubilaei* (1925); *Missa Italica* (1944); choral symph. poems: *Dantis poetae transitus* (Ravenna, 1921) and *Il trittico francescano* (Assisi, 1925); a Requiem; sacred play, *Santa Cecilia* (Rome, Feb. 15, 1934); oratorios: *Cananea* and *La Samaritana;* hymns; motets; etc.

Regamey, Constantin, Russian-born Swiss composer; b. Kiev, Jan. 28, 1907; d. Lausanne, Dec. 27, 1982. He went to Poland in 1920 and took piano lessons with Turczyński (1921–25); then turned to linguistics and took courses in Sanskrit at the Univ. of Warsaw and later at L'Ecole des Hautes Etudes in Paris, graduating in 1936. Returning to Poland, he taught Sanskrit at the Univ. of Warsaw (1937–39); concurrently he edited periodicals on contemporary music. He was interned by the Germans during the war, but was allowed to go to Switzerland. He received an appointment to teach Slavic and oriental languages at the Univ. of Lausanne; also gave courses in Indo-European linguistics at the Univ. of Freiburg. However, he did not abandon his musical activities; he served as co-editor of *Feuilles Musicales* (1954–62); was president of the Assoc. of Swiss Composers (1963–68) and a member of the executive board of the International Society for Contemporary Music (1969–73). In 1978 he became partially paralyzed; he dictated the last pages of his last work, *Visions,* to Jean Balissat, a fellow composer, who also orchestrated the work. As a composer, he adopted free serial methods, without a doctrinaire adherence to formal dodecaphony. In 1963 he moderated his modernity and wrote music using free, often composite, techniques.

Reger, Max, preeminent German composer; b. Brand, Bavaria, March 19, 1873; d. Leipzig, May 11, 1916. In 1874 his father, a schoolteacher and good organist (d. 1905 in Munich), removed to Weiden, where Reger attended the Realschule. Although he was intended for the schoolmaster's career, he received thorough instruction on the piano and harmonium from his father, and on the organ and in theory from Lindner. At an early age he began to write piano pieces and chamber music; after hearing *Die Meistersinger* and *Parsifal* in Bayreuth (1888), he gave expression to the emotions created in him by those masterpieces in an ambitious symph. poem, *Héroïde funèbre.* In 1889 he passed the entrance examination for the teachers' seminary. But by that time music had taken such complete possession of him that he submitted a number of his MSS to Hugo Riemann, who immediately recognized Reger's exceptional talent. Accordingly, Reger became Riemann's pupil at the Sondershausen Cons. in April 1890, and in 1891 followed him to the Wiesbaden Cons., where he continued his studies till 1895, and also taught piano and organ (till 1896). After serving a year in the army, he settled in Weiden as a composer, writing the works up to about op. 50. However, he did not attract general attention until 1901, when he removed to Munich, whence he undertook pianistic tours through Germany, Austria, and Switzerland. During the academic year of 1905–6 he was a prof. of counterpoint at the Königliche Akademie der Tonkunst, and conductor of the Gesangsverein; in 1907 he was called to Leipzig as music director at the Univ. (also conductor of the Univ. chorus St. Pauli) and a prof. of composition at the Cons.; the former post he resigned in 1908, but the latter he retained till his death in 1916; he was made Dr.Phil. *honoris causa* from the Univ. of Jena; in 1911, Hofrat; in 1913, Generalmusikdirektor; in 1911–15, Hofkapellmeister in Meiningen; then in Jena and Leipzig. He died suddenly of paralysis of the heart. A German Max Reger Society was founded in 1920, with branches in many cities; society was established in Austria. The Max Reger Archives (containing most of his MSS) are at Weimar. A complete edition of Reger's works was begun in 1954 by Breitkopf & Härtel, reaching 38 vols. by 1977. W. Altman publ. a catalogue of Reger's works (1917; 2nd ed., 1926); Fritz Stein edited a thematic catalogue: *Thematisches Verzeichnis der im Druck erschienen Werke von Max Reger* (Leipzig, 1934; 1953).

WORKS: FOR ORCH.: *Symphoniesatz* in D minor (1890; posthumous, Dortmund Reger Festival, 1960); op. 50, *2 Romanzen* for Violin and Orch. (1900); op. 90, *Sinfonietta* (Essen, Oct. 8, 1905); op. 93, *Suite im alten Stil* (originally for Violin and Piano, 1906; orchestrated 1916); op. 95, *Serenade* (1905–6); op. 100, *Variationen und Fuge über ein lustiges Thema von J.A. Hiller* (Cologne, Oct. 15, 1907); op. 101, Violin Concerto in A (Leipzig, Oct. 13, 1908); op. 108, *Symphonischer Prolog zu einer Tragödie* (1908); op. 114, Piano Concerto in F minor (Leipzig, Dec. 15, 1910; U.S. premiere, Minneapolis, Nov. 16, 1945; Serkin, soloist); op. 120, *Ein Lustspielouvertüre* (1911); op. 123, *Konzert in alten Stil* (1912); op. 125, *Romantische Suite* (1912); op. 128, *4 Tondichtungen nach Böcklin* (Essen, Oct. 12, 1913); op. 130, *Ballet-Suite* (1913); op. 132, *Variationen und Fuge über ein Thema von Mozart* (1914; Berlin, Feb. 5, 1915); op. 140, *Eine vaterländische Ouvertüre* (1914); op. 147, *Sinfonische Rhapsodie* for Violin and Orch. (unfinished; completed by Florizel von Reuter).

VOCAL WORKS: With Orch.: Op. 21, *Hymne an den Gesang* for Men's Chorus; op. 71, *Gesang der Verk-*

lärten for Mixed Chorus a 5; op. 106, *Psalm 100* for Mixed Chorus and Organ; op. 112, *Die Nonnen* for Mixed Chorus and Organ; op. 119, *Die Weihe der Nacht* for Alto Solo and Mixed Chorus; op. 124, *An die Hoffnung* for Alto Solo; op. 126, *Römischer Triumphgesang* for Men's Chorus; mixed choruses a cappella, opp. 6, 39 (a 6); men's choruses a cappella, opp. 38, 83; women's choruses a cappella, op. 111b; duets, opp. 14, 111a; about 300 songs, opp. 3, 4, 5, 12, 15, 23, 31, 35, 37, 43, 48, 51, 55, 62, 66, 68, 70, 75, 76 (60 *Schlichte Weisen*), 88, 97, 98, 104; op. 19, *Zwei geistliche Gesänge;* op. 61, *Leicht ausführbare Kompositionen zum gottesdienstlichen Gebrauch in der katholischen Kirche* (38 motets for Mixed Voices); op. 105, *Zwei geistliche Lieder;* op. 110, Motets for Mixed Chorus a cappella (a 5); op. 137, *Zwölf geistliche Lieder; Der evangelische Kirchenchor* (I, 40 mixed choruses for all festivals [4 series]; II, cantata, *O wie selig,* for Mixed Chorus, String Orch., and Organ; III, cantata, *O Haupt voll Blut und Wunden,* for Alto and Tenor Soli, Mixed Chorus, Violin and Oboe Soli, and Organ); men's and mixed choruses; and songs (sacred and secular), without opus numbers.

CHAMBER MUSIC: Op. 118, String Sextet in F; op. 64, Piano Quintet in C minor; op. 113, Piano Quartet in D minor; 5 string quartets: op. 54 (G minor and A), op. 74 (D minor), op. 109 (E-flat), op. 121 (F-sharp minor); 2 piano trios: op. 2 (B minor, for Piano, Violin, and Viola) and op. 102 (E minor); op. 77a, *Serenade* for Flute, Violin, and Viola; op. 77b, Trio for Flute, Violin, and Viola; op. 103a, *Suite* for Violin and Piano (A minor); 9 violin sonatas: op. 1 (D minor), op. 3 (D), op. 41 (A), op. 72 (C), op. 84 (F-sharp minor), op. 103b (2 *kleine Sonaten,* D minor and A), op. 122 (E minor), op. 139 (C minor); op. 93, *Suite im alten Stil* for Violin and Piano; 4 cello sonatas: op. 5 (F minor), op. 28 (G minor), op. 78 (F), op. 116 (A minor); 3 clarinet sonatas: op. 49 (A-flat major and F-sharp minor) and op. 107 (B-flat); op. 42, 4 sonatas for Violin Solo; op. 117, *Präludien und Fugen* for Violin Solo; op. 131, 3 suites for Cello Solo; op. 91, 7 sonatas for Unaccompanied Violin; op. 131a, 6 preludes and fugues for Unaccompanied Violin; op. 131b, 3 duos for 2 Violins; op. 133, Piano Quartet in A minor; op. 141a, *Serenade* in G major for Flute, Violin, and Cello; op. 141b, Trio in D minor for Violin, Viola, and Cello; op. 143, *Träume am Kamin,* 12 pieces for Piano Solo; op. 146, Clarinet Quintet in A major without opus number; Piano Quintet in C minor.

FOR ORGAN: Op. 16, *Suite* in E minor; op. 27, Fantasy on *Ein' feste Burg;* op. 29, *Fantasie und Fuge* in C minor; op. 30, Fantasy Sonata on *Freu dich sehr, o meine Seele;* op. 33, Sonata in F-sharp minor; op. 40, 2 fantasies, on *Wie schön leucht' uns der Morgenstern* and *Straf mich nicht in deinem Zorn;* op. 46, *Fantasie und Fuge über BACH;* op. 52, 3 fantasies, on *Alle Menschen müssen sterben, Wachet auf! ruft uns die Stimme,* and *Hallelujah! Gott zu loben;* op. 57, *Symphonische Phantasie und Fuge;* op. 60, Sonata in D minor; op. 67, 52 *Vorspiele* to the chorales in general use; op. 73, *Variationen und Fuge über ein Originalthema;* op. 92, *Suite* in G minor; op. 127, *Introduktion, Passacaglia und Fuge*

in E minor; numerous minor pieces: opp. 7, 56, 59, 63, 65, 69, 79, 80, 85, 129; also organ transcriptions of Bach clavier pieces.

FOR PIANO: 4 hands: op. 9, *Walzer-Capricen;* op. 10, *Deutsche Tänze;* op. 22, *Sechs Walzer;* op. 34, *5 pièces pittoresques;* op. 58, *Sechs Burlesken;* op. 94, *Sechs Stücke;* for 2 Pianos: op. 86, *Variationen und Fuge über ein Thema von Beethoven,* and op. 96, *Introduktion, Passacaglia und Fuge;* for Piano Solo: op. 17, *Aus der Jugendzeit* (20 pieces); op. 18, *Improvisationen* (8 pieces); op. 20, *5 Humoresken;* op. 24, *6 morceaux;* op. 25, *Aquarellen;* op. 26, *7 Fantasiestücke;* op. 32, *7 Charackterstücke;* op. 36, *Bunte Blätter* (9 pieces); op. 44, *Zehn kleine Vortragsstücke;* op. 45, *6 Intermezzi;* op. 53, *Silhouetten* (7 pieces); op. 81, *Variationen und Fuge über ein Thema von Bach;* op. 82, *Aus meinem Tagebuche* (35 pieces); op. 89, *4 Sonatinen* (E minor, D, F, A minor); op. 99, *6 Präludien und Fugen;* op. 115, *Episoden* (2 books); op. 134, *Variationen und Fuge über ein Thema von Ph. Telemann;* 2 books of canons in all major and minor keys; *4 Spezialstudien für die linke Hand allein;* minor pieces. Transcriptions for Piano, 4-hands: Bach's Prelude and Fugue in D, Toccata and Fugue in D minor, Fantasia in G, Prelude and Fugue in G, Prelude and Fugue in A minor, Fantasia and Fugue in G minor, Toccata and Fugue in E, Prelude and Fugue in E minor; Bach's orch. suites and *Brandenburg Concertos;* Hugo Wolf's symph. poem *Penthesilea* and the overture *Italienische serenade;* songs of Jensen, Brahms, Hugo Wolf, and Richard Strauss.

Regis, Johannes, noted Flemish composer and organist; b. Flanders, c.1430; d. Soignies, c.1485. He was "magister puerorum" at the Cathedral of Antwerp (1463–64); then was clerk to Dufay at Cambrai (1464–74), and finally canon and scholasticus in Soignies (1481–82). He wrote 2 masses on the melody of *L'Homme armé,* a 5-part motet, *O admirabile commercium,* and other choral pieces. His collected works were publ. in 2 vols. by the American Inst. of Musicology in Rome (1956), under the editorship of C.W.H. Lindenburg.

Rehfuss, Heinz, German-born Swiss bass-baritone; b. Frankfurt, May 25, 1917. He studied with his father, **Carl Rehfuss** (1885–1946), a singer and teacher, and with his mother, **Florentine Rehfuss-Peichert,** a contralto. The family moved to Neuchâtel, Switzerland, and Heinz Rehfuss became a Swiss citizen. He made his professional debut in opera at Biel-Solothurn in 1938; then sang with the Stadttheater in Lucerne (1938–39) and at the Zürich Opera (1940–52). He subsequently was active in America; taught voice at the Montreal Cons. in 1961; in 1965 was on the faculty of the State Univ. of N.Y. at Buffalo; in 1970 was a visiting prof. at the Eastman School of Music in Rochester, N.Y. He also toured in Asia, giving vocal recitals in India and Indonesia. He was successful mainly in dramatic roles, such as Don Giovanni and Boris Godunov.

Reich, Steve, American composer of sui generis

hypnopompic music; b. New York, Oct. 3, 1936. He studied philosophy at Cornell Univ. (B.A., 1957), where he became fascinated with the irrationally powerful theories of Ludwig Wittgenstein (a brother of the amputated pianist Paul Wittgenstein), who enunciated the famous tautological formula "Whereof one cannot speak thereof one must be silent." Reich in his music confuted this dictum by speaking loudly of tonalities and modalities which had remained in limbo for a millennium. He had a normal childhood; took piano lessons, but also studied drumming with Roland Koloff, a virtuoso timpanist; synchronously, he became infatuated with jazz and Bach by way of Stravinsky's stylizations. In N.Y. he took private composition lessons with Hall Overton and earned his living by driving a taxicab. From 1958 to 1961 he took courses with William Bergsma and Vincent Persichetti at the Juilliard School of Music; later went to California, where he entered Mills College in the classes of Darius Milhaud and Luciano Berio (M.A., 1963); in 1965 he returned to N.Y. In 1966 he organized his own ensemble, called Steve Reich and Musicians, which began as a trio with Arthur Murphy and Jon Gibson and eventually expanded into a duo-de-viginti multitude. In the summer of 1970 Reich traveled to Ghana, where he practiced under the tutelage of indigenous drummers. In 1973 he studied the Balinese gamelan with a native teacher at the American Society for Eastern Arts Summer Program at the Univ. of Washington in Seattle. Becoming conscious of his ethnic heredity, he went to Jerusalem in 1976 to study the traditional forms of Hebrew cantillation. In 1974 he received grants from the National Endowment for the Arts and from the N.Y. State Council on the Arts; he was also invited to Berlin as an artist-in-residence. In 1975 he received a grant from the Rockefeller Foundation, and in 1976 a 2nd grant from the National Endowment for the Arts. In 1978 he was awarded a Guggenheim fellowship. Thus reinforced, he was able to abandon taxicab driving and other menial ways of earning money; soon his music became popular enough to enable him to exist as an independent artist. Slowly but surely he rose to fame; his group was invited to perform at the Holland Festival and at the radio stations of Frankfurt and Stuttgart. His music was astoundingly audacious; rather than continue in the wake of obsolescent modernism, inexorably increasing in complexity, he deliberately reduced his harmonic and contrapuntal vocabulary and defiantly explored the fascinating potentialities of repetitive patterns. This kind of technique has been variously described as minimalist (for it was derived from a minimum of chordal combinations), phase music (because it shifted from one chord to another, a note at a time), modular (because it was built on symmetric modules), and pulse music (because it derived from a series of measured rhythmic units). Another definition is simply "process," suggesting tonal progressions in flux. Etiologically, this type of composition is hypnopompic, for it creates a subliminal state between a strong dream and a sudden reality. Analytically, it represents a paradox, for it is uncompromisingly modern in its use of exotic instruments, infinitely challenging in its obdurate continuity, and yet elemental in the deliberate limitations of its resources. This system of composition is akin to serialism in its application of recurrent melodic progressions and periodic silences. Despite his apparent disregard for musical convention, or indeed for public taste, Reich likes to trace his musical ancestry to the sweetly vacuous homophony of the Ars Antiqua, with particular reference to the opaque works of the great master of the Notre Dame School of Paris, Perotin. He deliberately avoids fanciful titles in his works, preferring to define them by names of instruments, or numbers of musical parts. The extraordinary aspect of Reich's career is that by rejecting the conventional way of music-making, and by thus infuriating the academics, he finds a direct avenue to the hearts, minds, and ears of the young.

WORKS: *Pitch Charts* for Instrumental Ensemble (1963); *Music for Piano and Tapes* (1964); *Livelihood* for Tape (1965); *It's Gonna Rain* for Tape (1965); *Come Out* for Tape (1966); *Melodica* for Tape (1966); *Reed Phase* for a Reed Instrument and Tape (1966); *Piano Phase* for 2 Pianos or 2 Marimbas (1967); *My Name Is* for Several Performers, Tape Recorders, and Audience (1967); *Violin Phase* for Violin and Tape (1967); *Pendulum Music* for Microphone, Amplifiers, Speakers, and Performers (1968); *Pulse Music* for the Phase-shifting Pulse Gate, an electronic device built by Reich (1969); *4 Log Drums* for 4 Log Drums and Phase-shifting Pulse Gate (1969); *4 Organs* for 4 Electric Organs and Maracas (1970); *Drumming* for 8 small tuned Drums, 3 Marimbas, 3 Glockenspiels, 2 Female Voices, Whistling, and Piccolo (1971); *Clapping Music* for 2 Musicians clapping hands in an interlocking rhythmic pattern (1972); *Music for Pieces of Wood* (1973); *Music for Mallet Instruments, Voice and Organ* (1973); *6 Pianos* (1973); *Music for 18 Musicians* for Violin, Cello, 2 Clarinets, 4 Pianos, 4 Female Voices, 3 Marimbas, 2 Xylophones, and Metallophone (1975; N.Y., April 24, 1976); *Music for a Large Ensemble* (1978; Holland Festival, June 1979); *Variations for Winds, Strings and Keyboards* (1979; with Chamber Orch., N.Y., Feb. 19, 1980; full orch. version, San Francisco, May 14, 1980);*Octet* for String Quartet, 2 Pianos, and 2 Clarinets doubling on Bass Clarinet and Flute (Radio Frankfurt, June 21, 1979); *Tehillim* (*Psalms,* in Hebrew) for 4 Sopranos, Percussion, Woodwinds, Electric Organs, and String Quartet (Houston, Nov. 21, 1981; N.Y. Phil., Sept. 16, 1982); *Vermont Counterpoint* for 11 Flutes, 10 of them recorded on Tape (N.Y., Oct. 1, 1982). He also publ. a book, *Writing about Music* (N.Y., 1974; French ed., *Ecrits et entretiens sur la musique,* Paris, 1981).

Reich, Willi, Austrian writer on music; b. Vienna, May 27, 1898; d. Zürich, May 1, 1980. He studied at the Univ. of Vienna, receiving his Ph.D. (1934) with the dissertation *Padre Martini als Theoretiker und Lehrer;* also studied privately with Alban Berg; edited a modern music magazine, *23.* In 1938 he settled in Switzerland; in 1948, became music critic of the

Neue Zürcher Zeitung.

Reicha, Anton, Czech composer; b. Prague, Feb. 26, 1770; d. Paris, May 28, 1836. He was a nephew and pupil of **Joseph Reicha** (*recte* **Rejcha;** composer and violinist, leader and later Kapellmeister, of the Electoral orch. at Bonn). From 1785, he was a flutist in the Bonn orch. in which Beethoven was a viola player; from 1794–99 he taught piano in Hamburg, wrote an opera, and traveled to Paris in hopes of producing it; but had to content himself with the successful performance of 2 symphs. From 1801 to 1808 he lived in Vienna, was intimate with Beethoven, and associated with Haydn, Albrechtsberger, and Salieri. After the French invasion he went to Paris; brought out the moderately successful comic operas *Cagliostro* (Nov. 27, 1810), *Natalie* (July 13, 1816), and *Sapho* (Dec. 16, 1822); also was held in high esteem as a theorist and teacher (among his pupils were Liszt, Elwart, Gounod, Lefebvre, and Dancla), and as an instrumental composer. Among his best works are 4 sets of 6 woodwind quintets each (opp. 88, 91, 99, 100). In 1818 he succeeded Méhul as prof. of counterpoint and fugue at the Paris Cons.; was naturalized in 1829; succeeded to Boieldieu's chair in the Académie Française in 1835.

Reichardt, Johann Friedrich, German composer and writer; b. Königsberg, Nov. 25, 1752; d. Giebichenstein, near Halle, June 27, 1814. A pupil of C.G. Richter (piano and composition) and Veichtner (violin), he later studied philosophy at the univs. of Königsberg and Leipzig; in 1775 obtained the post of Kapellmeister to Frederick the Great. He founded (1783) the Concerts Spirituels for the performance of new works, for which he wrote short analytical programs. Dismissed in 1794 because of his sympathy with the French Revolution, Reichardt lived in Altona till 1797; was then appointed inspector of the saltworks at Giebichenstein. The French invasion drove him to Danzig in 1806, and on Jerome Bonaparte's threat to confiscate his property Reichardt joined him at Kassel, and became his court conductor; he left Kassel in 1808, then settled in Giebichenstein. For Berlin and Potsdam Reichardt composed numerous Italian and German operas, incidental music to plays, and German singspiels, the latter exercising considerable influence on the development of German opera. As a song composer (cf. Lindner, *Geschichte des deutschen Liedes*), he ranks high (he set about 60 of Goethe's lyrics to music); his instrumental music includes 7 symphs., 14 piano concertos, 2 piano quartets, 6 string trios, a Violin Concerto, 11 violin sonatas, 12 piano sonatas, etc. An extremely diligent writer, he edited a number of musical periodicals and publ. several books: *Über die deutsche komische Oper* (1774); *Über die Pflichten des Ripienviolinisten* (1776); *Briefe eines aufmerksamen Reisenden, die Musik betreffend* (2 parts, 1774, 1776); *Schreiben über die Berlinische Musik* (1775); *Vertraute Briefe aus Paris* (3 parts, 1804, 1805); *Vertraute Briefe, geschrieben auf einer Reise nach Wien* (2 vols., 1810). His autobiography is in the *Berlinische musikalische Zeitung,* nos. 55–89 (1805). His wife, **Juliane** (née **Benda;** b. Potsdam, May 4, 1752; d. there, May 11, 1783), was a fine pianist, who also publ. a number of songs.

Reicher-Kindermann, Hedwig, German dramatic soprano; b. Munich, July 15, 1853; d. Trieste, June 2, 1883. She was a daughter of the baritone **August Kindermann** (1817–91); began her career as a contralto but later sang soprano. She first sang in the chorus of the Munich Court Opera (1870–71); made her debut at Karlsruhe in 1871; sang at the opening of Bayreuth in 1876; then sang in Hamburg (1877). The Wagnerian impresario Neumann engaged her for his Wagner troupe in Leipzig from 1880, and she successfully performed the roles of Fricka and Brünnhilde. She was married to the playwright Emanuel Reicher, and adopted the hyphenated name Reicher-Kindermann in her professional activities. Her early death was lamented.

Reichwein, Leopold, Austrian conductor; b. Breslau, May 16, 1878; d. (suicide) Vienna, April 8, 1945. He was a theater conductor in Breslau, Mannheim, and Karlsruhe; then was on the staff of the Vienna Opera (1913–21), and music director of the Gesellschaft der Musikfreunde in Vienna (1921–26), and music director in Bochum (1926–38); he returned to Vienna in 1938; conducted at the State Opera, and taught conducting at the Vienna Academy of Music. He committed suicide at the end of the war when he was accused of Nazi affiliations. He was also a composer; wrote the operas *Vasantasena* (Breslau, 1903) and *Die Liebenden von Kandahar* (Breslau, 1907); incidental music to Goethe's *Faust;* songs.

Reif, Paul, Czech-American composer; b. Prague, March 23, 1910; d. New York, July 7, 1978. He played violin as a child; studied composition in Vienna with Richard Stöhr and Franz Schmidt, and conducting with Franz Schalk and Bruno Walter; also had lessons with Richard Strauss. In 1941 he emigrated to the U.S., and in 1942 joined the U.S. Intelligence Corps; while with the U.S. Army in North Africa he set to music the soldiers' song *Dirty Gertie from Bizerte,* which was introduced by Josephine Baker in Algiers in April 1943. Upon his discharge in 1945 he was awarded the Croix de Guerre and the Purple Heart. Returning to the U.S., he was active as an arranger in Hollywood; wrote a number of lightweight pieces (*Petticoat Waltz, Dream Concerto,* etc.); also several song cycles, among them *5 Finger Exercises,* to poems by T.S. Eliot; *Reverence for Life* and *Monsieur le Pélican* as a tribute to Albert Schweitzer; etc.

Reimann, Aribert, German pianist and composer; b. Berlin, March 4, 1936. He studied with Blacher and Pepping; then took music courses at the German Academy in Rome; subsequently became active as an accompanist. He composed *Quasimodo Cantata;* an opera, *Traumspiel,* after Strindberg (Kiel, June 20, 1965); 2 piano concertos: No. 1 (Berlin,

Oct. 26, 1962) and No. 2 (Nuremberg, Jan. 12, 1973); Cello Concerto (1959); *Nenia* for Women's Voices (Sprechstimme) and Orch. (1968); *Inane,* monologue for Soprano and Orch. (Berlin, Jan. 8, 1969); *Loqui* for Orch. (Saarbrücken, Dec. 5, 1969); *Vogelscheuchen,* ballet (Berlin, Oct. 7, 1970); *Melusine,* opera (Schwetzinger, April 29, 1971); *Lear,* opera after Shakespeare (Munich, July 9, 1978); *Requiem* (Kiel, June 26, 1982).

Reinagle, Alexander, important American musician; b. Portsmouth, England (of Austrian parents), baptized April 23, 1756; d. Baltimore, Sept. 21, 1809. He studied in Edinburgh with Raynor Taylor, and in London for a time; also visited Lisbon and other continental cities. From his correspondence he appears to have been an intimate friend of C.P.E. Bach. He came to N.Y. early in 1786, settling in the same year in Philadelphia, where he taught, managed subscription concerts (also in N.Y.), and was active as a singer, pianist, conductor, and composer; in 1787, introduced 4-hand piano music to America; was associated, possibly as harpsichordist, with the Old American Co., and most likely took part in their 1788–89 season in N.Y.; in 1793 he was engaged as music director of a stock company for the production of plays and comic operas, with Thomas Wignell as general director; also built the New Theatre, which opened on Feb. 2, 1793, with Reinagle acting as composer, singer, and director; later also managed a company in Baltimore.
WORKS: *Collection of Most Favorite Scots Tunes with Variations for Harpsichord* (London; probably issued in Glasgow), *6 Sonatas with Accompaniment for Violin* (London, c.1780); *Miscellaneous Quartets* (Philadelphia, 1791); *Concerto on the Improved Pianoforte with Additional Keys* (1794); *Preludes* (1794); accompaniments and incidental music to *The Sicilian Romance* (1795), *The Witches of the Rock,* pantomime (1796), and various English plays; *Masonic Overture* (1800); 4 piano sonatas (in Library of Congress, Washington, D.C.; Sonata No. 2 publ. in abridged form by J.T. Howard in *A Program of Early American Piano-Music,* N.Y., 1931; see also S.R. Duer, *An Annotated Edition of 4 Sonatas by Alexander Reinagle* [Peabody Cons., 1976]); *Collection of Favorite Songs;* music to Milton's *Paradise Lost* (incomplete).

Reinecke, Carl (Heinrich Carsten), renowned German pianist, composer, and conductor; b. Altona, June 23, 1824; d. Leipzig, March 10, 1910. He was a pupil of his father, a music teacher. His first concert tour was to Denmark and Sweden in 1843; he then went to Leipzig, learned much through meetings with Mendelssohn and Schumann, made a 2nd tour through North Germany, and was from 1846–48 court pianist to Christian VIII at Copenhagen. Then, after spending some years in Paris, he became a teacher at the Cologne Cons. in 1851; was music director at Barmen (1854–59) and Breslau (1859–60), and (1860–95) conductor of the Gewandhaus Concerts at Leipzig. At the same time he was a prof. of piano playing and free composition at the

Leipzig Cons. An eminent pianist, he excelled as an interpreter of Mozart, made concert tours almost yearly, and was enthusiastically welcomed in England, the Netherlands, Scandinavia, Switzerland, and throughout Germany; among his pupils were Grieg, Riemann, Sinding, Arthur Sullivan, Karl Muck, and Cosima Wagner. As a composer and a teacher of composition, Reinecke was the leader in Leipzig for a quarter of a century; his numerous works, in every genre, are classic in form and of refined workmanship.
WORKS: Operas: *König Manfred* (Wiesbaden, July 26, 1867); *Ein Abenteuer Händels* (Schwerin, 1874); *Auf hohen Befehl* (Hamburg, Oct. 1, 1886); *Der Gouverneur von Tours* (Schwerin, 1891); several musical fairy tales for Solos, Chorus, and Piano: *Nussknacker und Mausekönig, Schneewittchen, Dornröschen, Aschenbrödel, Die wilden Schwäne, Glückskind und Pechvogel,* etc.; oratorio, *Belsazar;* several choral works, with Orch.: *Sommertagsbilder, Schlachtlied, Der deutsche Sang,* etc.; numerous choruses for Mixed Voices; for Orch.: 3 symphs., 9 overtures, smaller works; 4 piano concertos; Violin Concerto; Cello Concerto; Harp Concerto; Flute Concerto; chamber music: Octet for Wind Instruments; Sextet for Wind Instruments; 6 string quartets; Piano Quintet; 2 piano quartets; 6 piano trios; Trio for Piano, Oboe, and Horn; Trio for Piano, Clarinet, and Horn; Violin Sonata; 3 violin sonatinas; 3 cello sonatas; Sonata for Flute and Piano; numerous character pieces for Piano; Sonata for Piano, Left Hand; a suite, *Biblische Bilder;* 3 sonatas for 2 Pianos; altogether about 300 opus numbers. He wrote cadenzas to 42 movements of piano concertos by Bach, Mozart, Beethoven, and Weber; some of these cadenzas are often used. He also wrote the following books: *Was sollen wir spielen?* (1886); *Zur Wiederbelebung der Mozartschen Klavierkonzerte* (1891); *Die Beethovenschen Klaviersonaten* (1896; 9th ed., 1924; in Eng., 1898); *Und manche liebe Schatten steigen auf* (1900); *Meister der Tonkunst* (1903); *Aus dem Reich der Töne* (1907).

Reiner, Fritz, eminent Hungarian conductor; b. Budapest, Dec. 19, 1888; d. New York, Nov. 15, 1963. He studied piano with Thomán and composition with Koessler at the Music Academy in Budapest; concurrently took courses in jurisprudence. He was conductor of the People's Opera in Budapest (1911–14) and of the Court Opera in Dresden (1914–21); subsequently conducted in Hamburg, Berlin, Vienna, Rome, and Barcelona. In 1922 he was engaged as music director and conductor of the Cincinnati Symph. Orch.; held this position until 1931, when he became a prof. of conducting at the Curtis Inst. of Music in Philadelphia; among his students were Leonard Bernstein, Lukas Foss, and several other well-known American musicians. In 1936–37 he made guest appearances at Covent Garden Opera in London; between 1935 and 1938 was guest conductor at the San Francisco Opera; from 1938 to 1948 he was conductor and music director of the Pittsburgh Symph. Orch.; in the interim filled engagements at the Metropolitan Opera in N.Y. He achieved the peak of his success as a conductor with the Chicago Symph. Orch., which he led from 1953 to 1962, and which he brought up to the point of impeccably fine performance, both in Classical and modern music. His striving for perfection created for him the reputation of a ruthless master of the orch.; he was given to explosions of temper, but musicians and critics agreed that it was because of his uncompromising drive toward the optimum of orch. playing that the Chicago Symph. Orch. achieved a very high rank among American symph. organizations.

Reiner, Karel, prominent Czech composer and pianist; b. Žatec, June 27, 1910; d. Prague, Oct. 17, 1979. He studied law in Prague (Dr.Jur., 1933); then attended classes in quarter-tone and sixth-tone composition with Alois Hába at the Prague Cons. (1934–35); was associated with E.F. Burian's improvisational theater in Prague (1934–38). Unable to leave Central Europe when the Nazis invaded Czechoslovakia, he was detained at Terezín, and later sent to the dread camps of Dachau and Auschwitz, but survived, and after liberation resumed his activities as a composer and pianist. His earliest works were atonal and athematic; in 1935–36 he wrote a *Suite* and a *Fantasy* for quarter-tone piano, and a set of 5 quarter-tone songs; after 1945 he wrote mostly traditional music; then returned to ultramodern techniques.

Reinhardt, Django (Jean Baptiste Reinhardt), Belgian jazz guitarist; b. Liberchies, Jan. 23, 1910; d. Fontainebleau, May 16, 1953. He began his career in Paris in 1922; gained recognition through his recordings with the singer Jean Sablon and violinist Stephane Grappelli; in 1934 he formed the Quintette du Hot Club de France with Grappelli. After World War II, he toured the U.S.; appeared with Duke Ellington in N.Y. He was an innovative figure in the early jazz movement in Europe; in later years he utilized electrical amplification in his performances.

Reining, Maria, Austrian soprano; b. Vienna, Aug. 7, 1903. She studied at a business school, and was employed in the foreign exchange dept. of a Vienna bank before taking up singing. In 1931 she made her debut at the Vienna State Opera, remaining on its roster until 1933; then sang in Darmstadt (1933–35) and at the Munich State Opera (1935–37). In 1937 she rejoined the Vienna State Opera, continuing on its roster, with interruptions, until 1956. In 1937 she appeared at the Salzburg Festival; Toscanini engaged her to sing Eva in *Die Meistersinger* in Salzburg under his direction in 1937; she also sang the role of the Marschallin in *Der Rosenkavalier* and the title role in *Arabella* by Richard Strauss. She was equally successful in soubrette roles and as a dramatic soprano. In 1938 she appeared with the Covent Garden Opera in London and with the Chicago Opera; in 1949, as the Marschallin with the N.Y. City Opera. She also sang at La Scala in Milan,

and toured as a concert singer. In 1962 she became a prof. of singing at the Mozarteum in Salzburg.

Reinken (Reincken), Jan Adams, famous organist and composer; b. April 26, 1623; d. Hamburg, Nov. 24, 1722 (at the age of 99). The place of his birth has not been determined; he may have been born in Wilshausen, Alsace, Wildeshausen near Bremen, or in a Dutch village of similar name. By 1654 he was in Hamburg, where he studied with Heinrich Scheidemann, the organist of the Katharinenkirche. In 1657 he became organist of the Berghkercke in Deventer, the Netherlands. In 1658 he returned to Hamburg as assistant organist to Scheidemann at the Katharinenkirche; in 1663 he succeeded his teacher as organist, a position he held with great distinction for 60 years. Reinken was one of the most celebrated organ virtuosos of his time. In 1720 Bach played at the Katharinenkirche, and Reinken, then 97 years old, was in attendance. Reinken was a consultant on organ building, and a noted teacher of the organ; his students included **Andreas Kneller** (later his son-in-law) and G.D. Leiding. He composed several virtuoso organ pieces, and also 6 instrumental suites publ. as *Hortus musicus.*

WORKS: For Keyboard: *An den Wasserflüssen Babylon; Ballet* in E minor; *Fuga* in G minor; *Partite diverse sopra l'Aria "Schweiget mir von Weiber nehmen," altrimente chiamata "La Meyerin";* 3 suites, in C major, E minor, and G major; *Toccata* in C major; *Was kann uns kommen an für Noth.* His complete works for keyboard may be found in K. Beckmann, ed., *J.A. Reincken: Sämtliche Orgelwerke* (Wiesbaden, 1974). Chamber music: *Hortus musicus,* 6 suites for 2 Violins, Viola da Gamba, and Basso Continuo (Hamburg, 1687; later ed., by J.C.M. van Riemsdijk, Amsterdam, 1888). Vocal music: *Geistlich Konzert "auf Michael": Und es erhub sich ein Streit* for 4 Voices, 2 Violins, Viola, 2 Trumpets, Timpani, and Basso Continuo.

Reinmar (original name, **Wochinz**), **Hans,** distinguished Austrian baritone; b. Vienna, April 11, 1895; d. Berlin, Feb. 7, 1961. He studied at the Vienna Academy of Music and in Milan; made his debut in 1919 in Olomouc; then sang in Nuremberg, Zürich, Dresden, and Hamburg; was a member of the Berlin Städtische Oper (1928–45, 1952–61), the Bavarian State Opera in Munich (1945–46, 1950–57), the Berlin State Opera (1948–52), and the Berlin Komische Oper (1952–61); also sang at the festivals in Bayreuth and Salzburg. He excelled in dramatic roles in Italian operas.

Reisenberg, Nadia, Russian-born American pianist; b. Vilna, July 14, 1904; d. New York, June 10, 1983. She studied piano with Leonid Nikolayev at the St. Petersburg Cons. In 1922 she emigrated to America, and continued taking piano lessons with Alexander Lambert and later with Josef Hofmann at the Curtis Inst. in Philadelphia. She began her career as a concert pianist in Russia; gave recitals in Europe and America; appeared as soloist with Barbirolli, Rodzinski, and Damrosch in N.Y. and with Koussevitzky in Boston; gave sonata recitals with the cellist Joseph Schuster, played piano parts in trios, quartets, and quintets with members of the Budapest String Quartet; made a specialty of appearing on radio hours; performed all 27 piano concertos of Mozart on weekly radio broadcasts in N.Y. She was also a noted teacher; taught at the Curtis Inst., at Queens College, at the Mannes College of Music, and at the Juilliard School of Music; also gave master classes in Jerusalem. She recorded all the nocturnes and mazurkas of Chopin, as well as works by Tchaikovsky, Mussorgsky, and Rachmaninoff. She possessed a faultless technique, particularly in pearly scale passages, and a fine lyrical form of expression.

Reiser, Alois, Czech-American composer; b. Prague, April 6, 1887; d. Hollywood, April 4, 1977. He studied composition with Dvořák; also took cello lessons and toured Europe; later emigrated to the U.S. and played cello with the Pittsburgh Symph. Orch. and the N.Y. Symph. From 1918 to 1929 he was engaged as a theater conductor in N.Y.; in 1929 he settled in Hollywood, where he worked as a composer and conductor at the Hollywood film studios. His works adhere to the established style of European Romanticism; typical of these are *Slavic Rhapsody,* which he conducted in Los Angeles on March 8, 1931, and *Erewhon,* which he conducted there on Jan. 24, 1936. He also composed a Cello Concerto, which he performed in Los Angeles on March 23, 1933; and a considerable amount of chamber music. He wrote an opera, *Gobi,* in which he painted in tones the great Asian desert; it had its first and last performance in N.Y. on July 29, 1923, and even then only in concert excerpts.

Reissiger, Carl Gottlieb, German composer; b. Belzig, near Wittenberg, Jan. 31, 1798; d. Dresden, Nov. 7, 1859. He studied with Schicht at the Thomasschule in Leipzig from 1811; went to Vienna in 1821 and thence to Munich (1822), pursuing his studies of composition under Winter; taught at the Berlin Royal Inst. for Church Music, and in 1826 he succeeded Marschner as music director of the German Opera at Dresden; soon after was appointed court Kapellmeister as Weber's successor. Reissiger was a prolific composer (over 200 opus numbers), writing with great facility but with little originality. The waltz for Piano, *Weber's Last Thought,* long misattributed to Weber, was proved to be a composition by Reissiger; many of his songs also became popular.

Reiter, Josef, Austrian composer; b. Braunau, Jan. 19, 1862; d. Bad Reichenhall, June 2, 1939. He received his first instruction in music from his father, a town organist; in 1886 went to Vienna, where he became active as a choral conductor; then was director of the Mozarteum in Salzburg (1908–11). He wrote 4 operas: *Der Bundschuh* (Troppau, 1894); *Klopstock in Zürich* (Linz, 1894); *Der Totentanz* (Dessau, 1908); *Der Tell* (Vienna, 1917); also numerous choruses and solo songs. He was an inspired

Hitlerite; composed a cantata in honor of the Anschluss in 1938; and even before the reification of the Hitler magic in concrete murderous terms, dedicated his *Goethe-Symphonie* to his beloved Führer (1931).

Reizenstein, Franz, German pianist and composer; b. Nuremberg, June 7, 1911; d. London, Oct. 15, 1968. He studied piano with Leonid Kreutzer and composition with Hindemith at the Hochschule für Musik in Berlin (1930–34); with the advent of the anti-Semitic Nazi regime he went to England; entered the Royal College of Music in London and studied with Lambert and Vaughan Williams (1934–36); also took private piano lessons with Solomon (1938–40). He was then an instructor in piano at the Royal Academy (1958–64), and from 1964 to his death, at the Royal Manchester College. He wrote music of fine neo-Romantic quality.

Rellstab, Johann Karl Friedrich, German writer on music; b. Berlin, Feb. 27, 1759; d. there, Aug. 19, 1813. He was a pupil of Agricola and Fasch; succeeded his father as head of a printing establishment, adding a music printing and publ. dept. and a circulating library of music; founded short-lived amateur concerts in 1787; lost his property in the war of 1806, and gave music lessons, lectured on harmony, and wrote criticism for the *Vossische Zeitung.* His compositions are unimportant.

Rellstab, (Heinrich Friedrich) Ludwig, the noted novelist, son of **Johann Karl Friedrich Rellstab;** b. Berlin, April 13, 1799; d. there, Nov. 27, 1860. He was an artillery officer and a teacher of mathematics and history in the Brigade School in Berlin; retired from the army in 1821, and lived as a writer in Berlin from 1823; was editor and music critic of the *Vossische Zeitung* (1826–48). He publ. the satirical pamphlets *Henriette, oder Die schöne Sängerin, Eine Geschichte unserer Tage von Freimund Zuschauer* (1826; on Henriette Sontag's triumphs) and *Über mein Verhältniss als Critiker zu Herrn Spontini als Componisten und General-Musikdirector in Berlin, nebst einem vergnüglichen Anhang* (1827; directed against Spohr's truckling to virtuosity in *Agnes von Hohenstaufen*), for each of which he suffered a period of imprisonment, though his opinions were eventually upheld in official circles and by the public. Between 1830 and 1841 Rellstab edited the musical periodical *Iris im Gebiet der Tonkunst;* he also contributed to several other papers. In his *Gesammelte Schriften* are biographies of Liszt, Ludwig Berger, Bernhard Klein, Nanette Schechner, and others; vol. I contains criticisms on opera and concert which came out in the *Vossische Zeitung* between 1826 and 1848. He wrote an autobiography, *Aus meinem Leben* (2 vols., 1861).

Reményi, Eduard (né **Hoffmann**), eminent Hungarian violinist; b. Miskolc, Jan. 17, 1828; d. San Francisco, May 15, 1898. He studied with Böhm at the Vienna Cons. (1842–45). Banished from Austria for participation in the Hungarian Revolution of

1848, he began the career of a wandering violinist in America; returned to Europe in 1852, and in 1854 became solo violinist to Queen Victoria. In 1860 he was amnestied, and appointed solo violinist to the Austrian Court; in 1865, he commenced a brilliant tour, visiting Paris, Germany, Belgium, and the Netherlands; then proceeded to London in 1877, and to America in 1878, traveling in the U.S., Canada, and Mexico; in 1886 he began a new concert tour around the world, visiting Japan, China, and South Africa. Some notes on his trip to the Far East are in the N.Y. Public Library. He collapsed suddenly while playing the pizzicato from the *Sylvia* suite of Delibes at a San Francisco concert, and died of apoplexy. His technique was prodigious; in vigor, passion, and pathos he was unexcelled. He made skillful transcriptions of Chopin's waltzes, polonaises, and mazurkas, and pieces by Bach, Schubert, etc.; these are united under the title of *Nouvelle école du violin*. He was also a natural performer of Gypsy music; Liszt profited very much by his help in supplying and arranging authentic Gypsy tunes. He composed a Violin Concerto and some solos for violin.

Remoortel, Edouard van, Belgian conductor; b. Brussels, May 30, 1926; d. Paris, May 16, 1977. He studied at the Brussels Cons., and took a course in conducting with Josef Krips. From 1951 on he was the principal conductor of the Belgian National Orch.; in 1958 was appointed music director and conductor of the St. Louis Symph. Orch., retaining this post until 1962. In 1965 he went to Monte Carlo as artistic consultant to the Orch. National de l'Opéra of Monaco.

Remy, Alfred, American music lexicographer; b. Elberfeld, Germany, March 16, 1870; d. New York, Feb. 26, 1937. He emigrated to the U.S. in 1882; studied piano and violin; lectured on music history and on languages at various schools in N.Y. and Brooklyn; from 1906 to 1915 was on the music staff of Columbia Univ. He contributed articles to various American reference works and was editor in chief of the 3rd edition of *Baker's Biographical Dictionary of Musicians* (N.Y., 1919).

Rémy, Guillaume, Belgian violinist; b. Ougrée, Aug. 26, 1856; d. Nantes, France, June 16, 1932. He studied at the Cons. of Liège; graduated in 1873, sharing the first prize with Ysaÿe; continued his studies under Massart at the Paris Cons.; was awarded first prize in 1878. Settling in Paris, he became concertmaster of the Colonne Orch., frequently appearing as a soloist. From 1885 to 1930 he was a prof. at the Paris Cons.; played recitals with Saint-Saëns and Gabriel Fauré at the piano. He also formed a string quartet. During the last years of his life he was head of the violin dept. of the American Cons. at Fontainebleau.

Renaud, Maurice, French baritone; b. Bordeaux, July 24, 1861; d. Paris, Oct. 16, 1933. He studied in Paris and Brussels; sang at the Théâtre de la Monnaie in Brussels (1883–90), at the Opéra-Comique in Paris (1890–91), and at the Paris Opéra (1891–1902). He made his American debut in New Orleans, on Jan. 4, 1893. From 1906 till 1909 he sang at the Manhattan Opera House, where he became a favorite; then appeared in Chicago for a season, and at the Metropolitan Opera House (1910–12); thereafter, was active chiefly in France. He sang baritone and bass parts in some 60 operas.

Renié, Henriette, eminent French harpist and composer; b. Paris, Sept. 18, 1875; d. there, March 1, 1956. She studied with Alphonse Hasselmans at the Paris Cons.; received first prize for harp at the age of 11; then entered the classes of Lenepveu and Dubois in harmony and composition. She performed her own Concerto for Harp and Orch. at the Concerts Lamoureux in Paris on March 24, 1901; further wrote *Pièce symphonique* for Harp and Orch.; *Légende et Danse caprice* for Harp and Orch.; publ. numerous pieces for Harp Solo: *Promenades matinales, Feuilles d'automne, Ballade fantastique, Légende, Contemplation, Défile lilliputien, Danse des lutins,* etc.; Trio for Harp, Violin, and Cello; Trio for Harp, Flute, and Bassoon; several songs. She taught for many years at the Paris Cons.; among her students was Marcel Grandjany.

Rennert, Günther, leading German opera producer and administrator; b. Essen, April 1, 1911; d. Munich, July 31, 1978. He was educated in Munich, Berlin, and Halle. From 1935 to 1939 he worked in Wuppertal, in Frankfurt (with Walter Felsenstein), and in Mainz; then in Königsberg (1939–42) and at the Städtische Oper in Berlin. In 1946 he became Intendant of the Hamburg State Opera, a post he held until 1956; then worked as a guest producer with several major opera houses, including La Scala in Milan and the Metropolitan Opera in N.Y. From 1967 to 1976 he was Intendant of the Bavarian State Opera in Munich. Through the consistent successes of his operatic productions in several cities under changing circumstances, Rennert acquired a reputation as one of the most competent members of his profession.

Resinarius, Balthasar, German composer; b. Tetschen, c.1486; d. Böhmisch-Leipa, April 12, 1544. He was a choirboy in the court chapel of Emperor Maximilian; then studied at the Univ. of Leipzig; subsequently became Bishop of Leipa, Bohemia. He was one of the most important early Protestant composers of sacred music. He brought out 118 "Responsories" (Wittenberg, 1543; 80 printed by Rhaw and reprinted by Bärenreiter and Concordia, 1957); 30 choral pieces in Rhaw's *Neue deutsche geistliche Gesenge für die gemeinen Schulen* (1544; ed. by J. Wolf in *Denkmäler deutscher Tonkunst,* 39); 4 motets in *Offices* collected by Rhaw; 3 bicinia in Rotenbucher's *Diphona amoena et florida* (Nuremberg, 1549).

Resnik, Regina, American soprano; b. New York, Aug. 30, 1922. She studied in N.Y.; made her concert debut at the Brooklyn Academy of Music (Oct. 27, 1942); sang in opera in Mexico (1943); won an annual audition at the Metropolitan Opera in 1944, and appeared there in *Il Trovatore* (Dec. 6, 1944); sang the leading part in Beethoven's *Fidelio* (March 17, 1945). In 1953 she appeared in Bayreuth as Sieglinde. Later she sang mezzo-soprano parts; appeared as Marina in *Boris Godunov* at the Metropolitan Opera on Feb. 15, 1956; remained there until 1974. She married Harry W. Davis, a lawyer, in N.Y. on July 16, 1946.

Respighi, Ottorino, eminent Italian composer; b. Bologna, July 9, 1879; d. Rome, April 18, 1936. He studied violin with F. Sarti at the Liceo Musicale of Bologna; composition with L. Torchi and G. Martucci. In 1900 he went to Russia, and played first viola in the orch. of the Imperial Opera in St. Petersburg; there he took lessons with Rimsky-Korsakov, which proved a decisive influence in Respighi's coloristic orchestration. From 1903 to 1908 he was active as a concert violinist; also played the viola in the Mugellini Quartet of Bologna. In 1913 he was engaged as a prof. of composition at the Santa Cecilia Academy in Rome; in 1924, was appointed its director, but resigned in 1926, retaining only a class in advanced composition; subsequently devoted himself to composing and conducting. He was elected a member of the Italian Royal Academy on March 23, 1932. In 1925–26 and again in 1932 he made tours of the U.S. as a pianist and a conductor.

His style of composition is a highly successful blend of songful melodies with full and rich harmonics; he was one of the best masters of modern Italian music in orchestration. His power of evocation of the Italian scene and his ability to sustain interest without prolixity is incontestable. Although he wrote several operas, he achieved his greatest success with 2 symph. poems, *Le fontane di Roma* and *I pini di Roma,* each consisting of 4 tone paintings of the Roman landscape; a great innovation for the time was the insertion of a phonograph recording of a nightingale in the score of *I pini di Roma.*

WORKS: OPERAS: *Re Enzo* (Bologna, March 12, 1905); *Semirama,* lyric tragedy in 3 acts (Bologna, Nov. 20, 1910); *La bella addormentata nel bosco,* musical fairy tale (Rome, April 13, 1922, perf. by Vittorio Podrecca's marionettes, Teatro dei Piccoli, with singers off stage); *Belfagor,* lyric comedy (Milan, April 26, 1923); *La campana sommersa,* after Hauptmann's *Die versunkene Glocke* (Hamburg, Nov. 18, 1927); *Maria Egiziaca,* mystery play in one act (N.Y., March 16, 1932); *La fiamma* (Rome, Jan. 23, 1934); a free transcription of Monteverdi's *Orfeo* (Milan, March 16, 1935); *Lucrezia* (posthumous, Milan, Feb. 24, 1937). BALLETS: *La Boutique Fantasque,* on themes by Rossini (London, June 5, 1919); *Scherzo veneziano* (Rome, Nov. 27, 1920); *Belkis, Regina di Saba* (Milan, Jan. 23, 1932). FOR ORCH.: *Notturno* (1905); *Sinfonia drammatica* (1915); *Le fontane di Roma,* symph. poem in 4 movements (Rome, March 11, 1917); *Antiche arie e danze per liuto,* 3 sets, the 3rd for String Orch. (1916, 1923, 1931); *Ballata delle gnomidi* (Rome, April 11, 1920); *I pini di Roma,*

symph. poem in 4 movements (Rome, Dec. 14, 1924); *Rossiniana,* suite from Rossini's piano pieces (1925); *Vetrate di chiesa,* symph. impressions in 4 movements (Boston, Feb. 25, 1927); *Impressioni brasiliane,* symph. suite (1927; composed for Respighi's Brazilian tour and conducted by him for the first time in São Paulo, June 16, 1928); *Trittico Botticelliano* for Chamber Orch. (commissioned by E.S. Coolidge; 1927); *Gli Uccelli,* suite for Small Orch. on themes by Rameau, B. Pasquini, and others (1927); *Feste romane,* symph. poem in 4 movements (N.Y. Phil., Toscanini conducting, Feb. 21, 1929); *Metamorphoseon modi XII,* theme and variations (commissioned by the Boston Symph.; Boston, Nov. 7, 1930); *Concerto gregoriano* for Violin and Orch. (Rome, Feb. 5, 1922); *Concerto in modo misolidio* for Piano and Orch. (N.Y., Dec. 31, 1925, composer soloist); *Concerto a 5* for Violin, Oboe, Trumpet, Double Bass, Piano, and Strings (1932). CHORAL WORKS: *La Primavera,* cantata for Soloists, Chorus, and Orch. (Rome, March 4, 1923); *Lauda per la Natività del Signore* for Soloists, Chorus, and Orch. (1930). CHAMBER MUSIC: 11 pieces for Violin and Piano (1904–7); String Quartet in D major (1907); *Quartetto dorico* for String Quartet (1924); *Il tramonto,* after Shelley, for Mezzo-soprano and String Quartet (1917); Violin Sonata (1917). Also *Huntingtower Ballad* for Band (Sousa memorial concert, Washington, D.C., April 17, 1932); 45 songs; 3 vocalises without words; arrangements of works by Monteverdi, Vitali, Pergolesi, Cimarosa, Marcello, etc., and of several *Etudes tableaux* by Rachmaninoff; he was co-author, with S.A. Luciani, of *Orpheus: Iniziazione musicale, storia della musica* (Florence, 1925).

His wife, **Elsa Olivieri Sangiacomo Respighi** (b. Rome, March 24, 1894), was his pupil; wrote a fairy opera, *Fior di neve;* the symph. poem *Serenata di maschere;* and numerous songs; was also a concert singer herself. She publ. Respighi's biography, *Ottorino Respighi: Dati biografici ordinati* (Milan, 1954; in Eng., London, 1962).

Reszke, Edouard de. See **De Reszke, Edouard.**

Reszke, Jean de. See **De Reszke, Jean.**

Rethberg, Elisabeth (real name, **Elisabeth Sättler**), German soprano; b. Schwarzenberg, Sept. 22, 1894; d. Yorktown Heights, N.Y., June 6, 1976. She studied piano and voice in Dresden; joined the Dresden Court Opera at the age of 21, and was on its staff from 1915 to 1922; then went to the U.S. and made her American debut as Aida at the Metropolitan Opera in N.Y. (Nov. 22, 1922), remaining on its staff until 1942. She subsequently embarked on a grand concert tour with Ezio Pinza in the U.S., Europe, and Australia; their close association resulted in a lawsuit for alienation of affection brought by Ezio Pinza's wife against her, but the court action was not pursued. Elisabeth Rethberg was married twice: first to Ernst Albert Dormann, from whom she was divorced, and then to **George Cehanovsky,** the singer, whom she married in 1956.

Réti, Rudolf, outstanding American composer and theorist; b. Užice, Serbia, Nov. 27, 1885; d. Montclair, N.J., Feb. 7, 1957. He studied at the Cons. of Vienna; took early interest in new music and was one of the founders of the International Society for Contemporary Music (Salzburg, 1922). In 1938 he came to the U.S.; in 1943 married the Canadian pianist **Jean Sahlmark;** in 1950 they settled in Montclair, N.J. His compositions are marked by precise structure and fine stylistic unity. Among his works are *Symphonia mystica* (1951); *Triptychon* for Orch. (1953); Concertino for Cello and Orch. (1953); 2 piano concertos; Violin Sonata; several choruses and solo songs; piano pieces. An original music analyst, he publ. several books which contributed to the development of logical theory of modern music: *The Thematic Process in Music* (N.Y., 1952); *Tonality, Atonality, Pantonality* (posthumous; N.Y., 1958); *Thematic Patterns in Sonatas of Beethoven* (posthumous; brought out by D. Cooke, London, 1965).

Reubke, Adolf, German organ builder at Hausneindorf, near Quedlinburg; b. Halberstadt, Dec. 6, 1805; d. Hausneindorf, March 3, 1875. He built the great organ in the Cathedral of Magdeburg, with 88 stops, and one at the Jacobikirche with 53 stops. His son **Emil Reubke** (1836–85) inherited his firm and introduced various improvements, such as pneumatic tubes. Another son of Adolf Reubke, **Julius** (b. Hausneindorf, March 23, 1834; d. Pillnitz, June 3, 1858), was a fine pianist and a favorite pupil of Liszt; his death at the age of 24 was a great loss to music. His few compositions show considerable talent; his Organ Sonata is still played. **Otto Reubke,** (b. Hausneindorf, Nov. 2, 1842; d. Halle, May 18, 1913), the youngest son of Adolf Reubke, was a pupil of Hans von Bülow; for many years he directed the Robert Franz Singakademie in Halle (1867–1911).

Reusner (Reussner), Esajas, German lute player and composer; b. Löwenberg, Silesia, April 29, 1636; d. Berlin, May 1, 1679. He was a pupil of his father, a lutenist, and at the age of 15 was engaged as musician to Countess Radziwill in Breslau; at 19 he was lutenist at Brieg; in 1674 became lutenist at the court of the Elector of Brandenburg in Berlin. He publ. several suites for the lute: *Deliciae testudinis* (1667; new ed., 1697, as *Erfreuliche Lautenlust*); *Neue Lautenfrüchte* (1676); a book of 100 religious melodies arranged for the lute, and publ. in tablature (1678). Reprints of suites and chorale settings by Reusner are in the *Reichsdenkmale,* vol. 12.

Reutter, Hermann, outstanding German composer; b. Stuttgart, June 17, 1900. He studied piano and cello in Stuttgart and singing and composition at the Munich Academy of Arts; in 1923 began a concert career as a pianist; made numerous concert tours with the singer Sigrid Onegin (1930–40), including 7 separate tours in the U.S. Returning to Germany, he dedicated himself to composition and teaching. He was for many years (1932–66) a prof. of composition at the Hochschule für Musik in Stuttgart; conducted a seminar in song composition;

gave similar courses in Scandinavia. In 1971 he traveled as a visiting prof. in the U.S. and Japan. In appreciation of his service to music he received a "Festschrift der Freunde," *Hermann Reutter, Werk und Wirken* (Mainz, 1965), on his 65th birthday. As a composer, Reutter follows the traditional line of German neo-Classicism, in which the basic thematic material, often inspired by German folk music, is arranged along strong contrapuntal lines, wherein a dissonant intervallic fabric does not disrupt the sense of immanent tonality.

WORKS: OPERAS: *Saul* (Baden-Baden, July 15, 1928); *Der verlorene Sohn,* after André Gide (Stuttgart, March 20, 1929); *Doktor Johannes Faust* (Frankfurt, May 26, 1936); *Odysseus* (Frankfurt, Oct. 7, 1942); *Der Weg nach Freundschaft,* subtitled *Ballade der Landstrasse* (Göttingen, Jan. 25, 1948); *Don Juan und Faust* (Stuttgart, June 11, 1950); *The Bridge of San Luis Rey,* after Thornton Wilder's novel (Frankfurt Radio, June 20, 1954); *Die Witwe von Ephesus* (Cologne, June 23, 1954); *Der Tod des Empedokles,* scenic concerto in one act (Schwetzingen, May 29, 1966); *Hamlet* (Stuttgart, 1980). VOCAL WORKS: Oratorio, *Der grosse Kalender* (1933); *Der glückliche Bauer,* cantata (1944); *Pandora* (1949); *Die Rückkehr des verlorenen Sohnes,* chamber oratorio after André Gide, being a new version of the opera *Der verlorene Sohn* (Munich, Feb. 15, 1952); *Spanischer Totentanz* for 2 Voices and Orch., after García Lorca (1953); *Ein kleines Requiem* for Bass, Cello, and Piano (1961); triptychon, *St. Sebastian* (1968); *Der Himmlische Vagant,* a lyrical portrait of François Villon for 2 Voices and Instruments (Donaueschingen Music Festival, Oct. 6, 1951). FOR ORCH.: *Prozession* for Cello and Orch. (Wiesbaden, Dec. 6, 1957); 5 piano concertos; Violin Concerto; String Quartet; Violin Sonata; Cello Sonata; *Fantasia apocalyptica* for Piano; *Antagonismus* for 2 Pianos; 3 vols. of Russian songs, arranged and harmonized; other minor pieces. He brought out an anthology of contemporary art songs, *Das zeitgenössische Lied* (4 vols., Mainz, 1969).

Revelli, William D., American bandleader and prime developer of modern U.S. univ. bands; b. Spring Gulch, near Aspen, Colo., Feb. 12, 1902. The family moved to Southern Illinois, near St. Louis, when he was an infant; he began to study the violin at the age of 5; later he was a pupil of Dominic Sarli. He was graduated from the Chicago Musical College in 1919. After playing violin professionally in the Chicago area, he became in 1925 the leader of the Hobart, Ind., High School Band, which he in time built to national prominence, winning the high school band championship for 6 consecutive years. In 1935 he was made director of the Univ. of Michigan Band at Ann Arbor, and was also in charge of its Wind Instruments Dept. Over the next 36 years he developed his band into 7 independent groups of players and the Wind Dept. into a body of 14 specialist teachers. Revelli's Symph. Band toured the country many times and made several trips abroad under State Dept. auspices, most notably a 16-week tour in early 1961 that took it to the Soviet

Union, Bulgaria, Turkey, Egypt, and other countries in the Middle East. In 1971 Revelli became director emeritus of the Univ. of Michigan Bands. As an instructor and promoter of bands within the U.S. academic system, Revelli continued the tradition of Fillmore and A.A. Harding. He was the recipient of many awards, and was active as an editor, adviser, and administrator of the various undertakings in the American band field; he was also founder of the College Band Directors National Assoc. (1941) and was its honorary life president; received honorary doctoral degrees from 5 American univs.

Revueltas, Silvestre, remarkable Mexican composer; b. Santiago Papasquiaro, Dec. 31, 1899; d. Mexico City, Oct. 5, 1940. He studied violin at the Mexico Cons.; in the U.S., studied with Felix Borowski in Chicago (1916) and with Ševčik in N.Y. (1922); conducted theater orchs. in Texas (1926–28); in 1929 returned to Mexico City and became assistant conductor to Carlos Chávez of the Orquesta Sinfónica de Mexico; only then did he begin to compose. In 1937 he went to Spain, where he was active in the cultural affairs of the Loyalist government during the Civil War. His health was ruined by exertions and an irregular life-style, and he died of pneumonia. His remains were deposited in the Rotonda de los Hombres Ilustres in Mexico City on March 23, 1976, to the music of his *Redes* and the funeral march from Beethoven's *Eroica*. He possessed an extraordinary natural talent and an intimate understanding of Mexican music, so that despite a lack of academic training in composition, he succeeded in creating works of great originality, melodic charm, and rhythmic vitality.
WORKS (all premiered in Mexico City unless noted otherwise): BALLETS: *El Renacuajo paseador* (1933; Oct. 4, 1940) and *La Coronela* (left unfinished at his death; completed by Galindo and Huízar; produced posthumously, Nov. 20, 1941). FOR ORCH.: *Cuauhnahuac* (1931–32; June 2, 1933); *Esquinas* for Small Orch. (1931; Nov. 20, 1931; for Large Orch., 1933); *Ventanas (Windows;* 1931; Nov. 4, 1932); *Alcancías (Penny Banks;* 1932); *Colorines* for Small Orch. (1932; Aug. 30, 1932); *Ocho por Radio* for Small Orch. (1933; Oct. 13, 1933); *Janitzio* (1933; Oct. 13, 1933; revised 1936); *Caminos (Paths;* 1934; July 17, 1934); *Planos,* "geometric dance" (1934; Nov. 5, 1934); *Redes (Waves),* concert suite from the film score, for Small Orch. (1935; Barcelona, Oct. 7, 1937); *Homenaje a Federico García Lorca* for Small Orch. (1935; Madrid, Sept. 22, 1937); *Sensemayá,* based on an Afro-Cuban legend, for Voice and Small Orch. (1937; revised for Large Orch. alone, 1938; Dec. 15, 1938); *Música para charlar (Music for Chatter),* concert suite from the film scores *El Indio* and *Ferro-carriles de Baja California* (1938; Dec. 15, 1938); *Hora de junio* for Narrator and Orch. (1938); *La noche de los Mayas,* concert suite from the film score (1939); *Itinerarios* (1939); *Paisajes* (1940); *Parias* for Soprano, Chorus, and Small Orch. (1940); *Troka* (1940). CHAMBER MUSIC: 3 string quartets: No. 1 (1930); No. 2, *Magueyes* (1931); No. 3, *Música de feria* (1931); *3 Pieces* for Violin and Piano (1932);

Tocata sin fuga for Violin and 7 Winds (1933); *Canto de guerra de los frentes leales (War Song of the Loyalist Front)* for 3 Trumpets, 3 Trombones, 2 Tubas, Percussion, and Piano (1938); *3 sonetas* for Chamber Ensemble (1940); *3 Little Serious Pieces* for Piccolo, Oboe, Trumpet, Clarinet, and Saxophone (1940). He also wrote many songs.

Reyer, Louis-Etienne-Ernest, French composer; b. Marseilles, Dec. 1, 1823; d. Le Lavandou, near Hyères, Jan. 15, 1909. An ardent admirer of Wagner, he added the German suffix *-er* to his real name **Rey.** He studied in the free municipal school of music; then took a place in the government financial bureau at Algiers, and while there composed a Solemn Mass (for the arrival of the French governor in Algiers; perf. 1847) and publ. several songs. He definitely embarked upon a musical career in 1848, studying at Paris with his aunt, **Louise Dumont,** the wife of Aristide Farrenc. In 1866 he became librarian at the Opéra, and followed d'Ortigue as music critic of the *Journal des Débats;* his collected essays were publ. in 1875 as *Notes de musique;* also in *Quarante ans de musique* (posthumous, 1909). He was elected to David's chair in the Institut in 1876; was made a Chevalier of the Legion of Honor in 1862; received the Grande-Croix in 1906. Although Reyer was an avowed admirer of Wagner, his music does not betray specific Wagnerian influences; both in form and in harmonic progressions, Reyer adheres to the Classical French school of composition, with a certain tendency toward exoticism in his choice of librettos.
WORKS: *Le Sélam,* to a text by Gautier (labeled a "symphonie orientale," but actually a 4-act opera, Paris, April 5, 1850; *Maître Wolfram,* one-act opera (Paris, May 20, 1854); *Sacountale,* ballet pantomime (Paris, July 14, 1858); *La Statue,* opera in 3 acts (Paris, April 11, 1861; recast in 5 acts, Feb. 27, 1903); *Erostrate,* opera (Baden-Baden, Aug. 21, 1862, by the Paris Opéra troupe); *Sigurd,* opera (Brussels, Jan. 7, 1884; his most popular work; 300 perfs. up to 1925 in Paris, and many abroad); *Salammbô,* opera (Brussels, Feb. 10, 1890); cantata, *Victoire* (1859); hymn, *L'Union des arts* (1862); men's choruses: *L'Hymne de Rhin, Le Chant du paysan, Chœur des buveurs, Chœur des assiégés;* dramatic scene, *La Madeleine au désert* (1874); also some church music.

Reynolds, Anna, English mezzo-soprano; b. Canterbury, Oct. 4, 1931. She studied piano at the Royal Academy of Music in London; then went to Italy for vocal lessons; she made her operatic debut in Parma in 1960 as Suzuki; subsequently sang in Vicenza (1961), Rome (1964), Spoleto (1966), Trieste (1967), Venice (1969), and at La Scala in Milan (1973). She made her first appearance in England at Glyndebourne in 1962; sang at Covent Garden in 1967; also sang at Bayreuth (1970–76). She made her Metropolitan Opera debut in N.Y. as Flosshilde in *Das Rheingold* on Nov. 22, 1968.

Reynolds, Roger, American composer; b. Detroit, July 18, 1934. At the Univ. of Michigan he studied engineering (B.S.E., 1957) and composition (M.M., 1961); spent a year in Cologne on a Fulbright grant for work on electronic music (1962); was in Paris in 1963, and in Italy on a Guggenheim fellowship in 1964–65. In his early scores he used serial methods, but later expanded his resources to include the entire spectrum of multimedia expression, enhanced by the mathematical concepts of sets and matrices and Gestalt psychology. In 1960 he was one of the founders of the avant-garde festival ONCE in Ann Arbor, Mich. In 1966 he went to Japan at the invitation of the Inst. of Current World Affairs. In 1969 he staged there the Cross Talk Intermedia festival, featuring experimental works by Japanese and American composers. In 1970 he joined the faculty of the Univ. of Calif. in San Diego. Reynolds uses graphic notation in his scores, suggesting the desired sounds by pictorial shapes.

WORKS: *Epigram and Evolution* for Piano (1959); *Sky,* song cycle for Soprano, Alto Flute, Bassoon, and Harp, to Japanese Haiku poems (1960); *Wedge* for Chamber Orch. (1961); *Acquaintances* for Flute, Double Bass, and Piano (1961); 4 Etudes for Flute Quartet (1961); *Mosaic* for Flute and Piano (1962); *The Emperor of Ice Cream,* his major work, to a poem of Wallace Stevens, scored for 8 Voices, Piano, Percussion, and Double Bass (1962); *A Portrait of Vanzetti* for Narrator, Wind Instruments, Percussion, and Magnetic Tape (1963); *Graffiti* for Orch. (1964); *Fantasy* for Pianists (1964); *Quick Are the Mouths of Earth* for Chamber Orch. (1965); *Ambages* for Solo Flute (1965); *Masks* for Orch. and Mixed Chorus, to a text by Melville (1965); *Blind Men* for Mixed Choir, Brass, Percussion, and Slide Projection, to a text by Melville (1966); *Threshold* for Orch. (1967); *...between...* for Chamber Orch. and Electronics (1968); *Traces* for Piano, Flute, Cello, Tapes, and Electronics (1969); *Ping,* inspired by a story of Samuel Beckett, scored for Flute (multiphonic), Piano (motorized by agitating strings), Harmonium, Bowed Cymbal and Tam-tam, Electronic Sound Distribution, Film, Ring Modulator, 35 Slides, and Magnetic Tape (1969); *I/O* (for "In and Out") for 9 Female Vocalists, 9 Male Mimes, 2 Flutes, Clarinet, Electronics, and Projections (1969), based on a concept of Buckminster Fuller with relation to the synergetic antonyms of the opposite sexes; *Compass,* a collage of Video Projections, Taped Voices, Cello, and Double Bass, to words by Jorge Luis Borges (1973); *Promises of Darkness* for 11 Instruments (N.Y., Jan. 8, 1976); *Fiery Winds* for Orch. (N.Y., Feb. 13, 1978); *Transfigured Wind II* for Orch. (N.Y., June 4, 1984).

Rezniček, Emil Nikolaus von, Austrian composer; b. Vienna, May 4, 1860; d. Berlin, Aug. 2, 1945. He studied law at Graz and music with Wilhelm Mayer (W.A. Rémy); later took a brief course with Reinecke and Jadassohn at the Leipzig Cons. He was subsequently engaged as a theater conductor in Graz, Zürich, Berlin, Jena, Mainz, Stettin, and Weimar; was Kapellmeister at the court theater in Mannheim (1896–99). After a short residence in Wiesbaden, he settled in Berlin, and in 1902 established there a very successful series of concerts for chamber orch., Orchester-Kammerkonzerte; in 1906 he was appointed prof. at the Scharwenka Cons. in Berlin; conducted the Warsaw Opera from 1906 to 1909; then became the conductor of the Komische Oper in Berlin (1909–11); from 1920 to 1926, he taught at the Hochschule für Musik in Berlin.

WORKS: Operas: *Donna Diana,* to his own libretto (Prague, Dec. 16, 1894; very successful; the overture frequently perf. in concerts); *Till Eulenspiegel* (Karlsruhe, Jan. 12, 1902); *Ritter Blaubart* (Darmstadt, Jan. 29, 1920); *Holofernes* (Berlin, Oct. 27, 1923); *Spiel oder Ernst* (Dresden, Nov. 11, 1930); *Der Gondoliere des Dogen* (Stuttgart, Oct. 29, 1931); 5 symphs.; 3 symph. poems; *Symphonietta* (also known as the *Ironische Symphonie;* Berlin, March 30, 1905, composer conducting); Violin Concerto (Berlin, Feb. 26, 1925); *Nachtstück* for Cello, Harp, 4 Horns, and String Quartet; piano pieces; songs.

Rhaw (Rhau), Georg, German publisher and composer; b. Eisfeld, Franconia, 1488; d. Wittenberg, Aug. 6, 1548. He studied at the Univ. of Wittenberg (1512–14); was then cantor of the Thomaskirche and of the Thomsschule in Leipzig, from 1518 to 1520, bringing out a Mass *a* 12 and a Te Deum at the disputation of Luther and Eck; then settled in Eisleben as a schoolmaster; later, went to Hildburghausen; in 1523 went to Wittenberg, where he established a publishing business, issuing many first editions of Luther's writings and numerous collections of musical works, mostly Protestant, including *Sacrorum Hymnorum Liber Primus* (1542; modern ed. by R. Gerber in *Das Erbe deutscher Musik,* vols. 21, 25); *Newe deutsche Gesenge für die gemeinen Schulen* (1544; reprinted by J. Wolf as vol. 34 of Denkmäler Deutscher Tonkunst); *Bicinia gallica, latina et germanica* (1545; contains the earliest known version of the *Ranz des vaches;* selections were republ. in F. Jöde's *Musikantengilde,* 1926; also ed. by K. Ameln, Kassel, 1934); etc. He was the author of an *Enchiridion musices,* in 2 parts (1517, 1520).

Rheinberger, Joseph (Gabriel), eminent German organist, composer, and pedagogue; b. Vaduz, Liechtenstein, March 17, 1839; d. Munich, Nov. 25, 1901. He played piano and organ as a child; then took regular lessons in organ playing with J.G. Herzog, piano with J.E. Leonhard, and composition with J.J. Maier, at the Munich Cons.; subsequently studied composition with Franz Lachner while earning his living as a piano accompanist at the Munich Gesangverein. From 1864 to 1877 he served as principal conductor of the Munich Oratorio Society. In 1859 he succeeded his teacher Leonhard as prof. of piano at the Munich Cons., and also taught composition there. His loyalty to the cultural and musical institutions in Munich earned him many honors from the Bavarian government; King Ludwig II made him Knight of St. Michael; toward the end of his life, in 1894, he was given the rank of "Zivilverdienstorden," the equivalent of nobility; in 1899 he was made Dr.Phil. *honoris causa* by the Univ. of Munich. Rheinberger's reputation as a teacher of organ was without equal during his lifetime; students flocked to him from all parts of the world. As a composer, he created a number of works remarkable for their dignity, formal perfection, and consummate technical mastery, if not their inventive power. His organ sonatas are unquestionably among the finest productions of organ literature.

WORKS: Romantic opera, *Die sieben Raben* (Munich, 1869); comic opera, *Des Türmers Töchterlein* (Munich, 1873); *Florentiner Symphonie;* symph. poem, *Wallenstein;* Piano Concerto; oratorio, *Der Stern von Bethlehem;* 12 masses; 3 Requiems; motets and hymns; 2 organ concertos; 20 organ sonatas; Nonet; 2 string quintets; Piano Quintet; 4 piano trios; Violin Sonata; Cello Sonata; Horn Sonata; for Piano: *Symphonische Sonata; Romantische Sonata;* numerous lieder.

Rhené-Baton (real name, **René Baton**), French conductor; b. Courseulles-sur-Mer, Calvados, Sept. 5, 1879; d. Le Mans, Sept. 23, 1940. He studied piano at the Paris Cons. and music theory privately with Gédalge. He began his conducting career as a chorus director at the Opéra-Comique in Paris; then conducted various concert groups in Angers and Bordeaux; from 1916 to 1932 he was principal conductor of the Concerts Pasdeloup. He composed orch. pieces, chamber music, and a number of songs.

Rhodes, Willard, American pianist, opera conductor, and music educator, and a foremost ethnomusicologist; b. Dashler, Ohio, May 12, 1901. He earned his A.B. and B.Mus. degrees from Heidelberg College in Tiffin, Ohio, both in 1922; then studied at the Mannes School of Music in N.Y. (1923–25) and at Columbia Univ. (M.A., 1925); went to Paris, where he took lessons in piano with Alfred Cortot and in composition with Nadia Boulanger (1925–27). From 1927 to 1935 he served as conductor with the American Opera Co., the Cincinnati Summer Opera Co., and with his own Rhodes Chamber Opera Co. He then turned to educational music; was director of music in the public schools of Bronxville, N.Y. (1935–37). In 1937 he was appointed to the faculty at Columbia Univ.; became prof. emeritus in 1969. He held the post of music consultant to the U.S. Bureau of Indian Affairs beginning in 1937, and was a founding member (1953) and first president (1956–58) of the Society for Ethnomusicology. It was in this connection that he accumulated a most valuable collection of Amerindian folk music, both notated and recorded (many pressings released by the Library of Congress). In 1961 he was elected president of the Society for Asian Music, and in 1968 of the International Folk Music Council; also was a Fellow of the African Studies Assoc. and numerous other ethnomusicological organizations. He did field work in Rhodesia and Nyasaland (1957–58) and in South India (1965–66); was visiting prof. at the Juilliard School of Music in N.Y., Brigham Young Univ. in Utah, the Univ. of Hawaii, and Ahmadu

Bello Univ. in Nigeria. In 1978 he accepted an appointment as visiting prof. at the Univ. of Arizona.

Riadis, Emile, Greek composer; b. Salonica, May 13, 1885; d. there, July 17, 1935. He studied in Munich with Felix Mottl; in 1910 went to Paris, where he appeared as a composer under the name Riadis, formed from the ending of his mother's maiden name, Elefteriadis (his father's real name was **Khu**). In 1915 he became a piano teacher at the Cons. of Salonica. He wrote a number of songs, distinguished by an expressive melodic line, somewhat oriental in its intervallic pattern; his harmonizations are in the French manner.

Ribera (Maneja), Antonio, Spanish conductor; b. Barcelona, May 3, 1873; d. Madrid, March 4, 1956. He studied with Riemann and Mottl in Leipzig and Munich; conducted the Wagner Society in Barcelona (1901–4); then was a theater conductor in Lemberg (1905–12), again in Barcelona (1912–25), and finally in Madrid (from 1925).

Ribera (y Tarragó), Julián, Spanish scholar and musicologist; b. Carcagente, near Valencia, Sept. 19, 1858; d. there, May 2, 1934. He was for many years a prof. of Hispanic-Arabic literature at the Univ. of Madrid. His magnum opus is *La música de las cantigas. Estudio sobre su origen y naturaleza* (Madrid, 1922; in Eng. as *Music in Ancient Arabia and Spain,* London, 1929), in which he maintains that the famous cantigas of Alfonso the Wise are derived from the metrical forms of the Arabs; he further publ. *La música andaluza medieval en las canciones de trovadores, troveros y minnesinger* (3 vols., Madrid, 1923–25); *Historia de la música árabe medieval y su influencia en la española* (Madrid, 1927; in Eng. as *Music in Ancient Arabia and Spain,* London, 1929; reprint, N.Y., 1970); *La música de la jota aragonesa* (1928).

Ricci, Federico, Italian composer, brother of **Luigi Ricci**; b. Naples, Oct. 22, 1809; d. Conegliano, Dec. 10, 1877. He studied with Zingarelli and Raimondi. In collaboration with his elder brother he produced 4 operas: *Il Colonnello* (Naples, March 14, 1835); *Il Disertore per amore* (Naples, Feb. 13, 1836); *L'Amante di richiamo* (Turin, June 13, 1846); *Crispino e la comare* (Venice, Feb. 28, 1850). He had excellent success with his own operas *La Prigione d'Edimburgo* (Trieste, March 13, 1838) and *Corrado d'Altamura* (La Scala, Milan, Nov. 16, 1841). In 1853 he received the appointment as music director of the Imperial theaters in St. Petersburg, Russia; upon his return he produced another successful opera, *Una follia a Roma* (Paris, Jan. 30, 1869); he retired in 1876.

Ricci, Luigi, Italian composer, brother of **Federico Ricci**; b. Naples, July 8, 1805; d. Prague, Dec. 31, 1859. He wrote about 30 operas, at least 4 of them in collaboration with his brother Federico. He was only 18 when his first opera, *L'Impresario in angustie,* was performed at the Cons. di S. Sebastiano, where he was a student (1823). In 1836 he was appointed maestro di cappella of the Cathedral at Trieste and chorus master at the city theater there. In 1844 he married Lidia Stolz, of Prague; in 1855, when he was about 50, he developed symptoms of insanity, and was committed to an asylum in Prague, where he died.

WORKS: Operas: *Il colombo* (Parma, June 27, 1829); *L'Orfanella di Ginevra* (Rome, Sept. 9, 1829); *Chiara di Rosemberg* (Milan, Oct. 11, 1831); *Il nuovo Figaro* (Parma, Feb. 15, 1832); *Chi dura vince* (Rome, Dec. 26, 1834); *Il Birraio di Preston* (Florence, Feb. 4, 1847); *Crispino e la comare* (in collaboration with his brother Federico; Venice, Feb. 28, 1850; Metropolitan Opera, N.Y., Jan. 18, 1919); *La festa di Piedigrotta* (Naples, June 23, 1852); *Il Diavolo a 4* (Trieste, May 15, 1859). His son (by his wife's identical twin sister, Francesca Stolz), **Luigi Ricci, Jr.** (b. Trieste, Dec. 27, 1852; d. Milan, Feb. 10, 1906), was also a composer of operas.

Ricci, Ruggiero, celebrated American violinist; b. San Francisco, July 24, 1918. His musical education was lovingly fostered by his father, along with 6 of his siblings, every one of whom started out as a musician, and 2 of whom, the cellist **Giorgio Ricci** and the violinist **Emma Ricci,** achieved the rank of professional performer. Ruggiero Ricci studied violin with Louis Persinger, and made a sensational appearance at a public concert in San Francisco on Nov. 15, 1928, when he was 10 years old, with his teacher accompanying him at the piano. On Oct. 20, 1929, he played in N.Y.; he embarked on an international concert tour in 1932. He successfully negotiated the perilous transition from child prodigy to serious artist; he accumulated a formidable repertoire of about 60 violin concertos, including all the violin works of Paganini; edited the newly discovered MS of Paganini's early Violin Concerto, presumed to have been composed c.1815, and gave its first N.Y. performance with the American Symph. Orch. on Oct. 7, 1977; he also gave the first performances of violin concertos by several modern composers, among them Alberto Ginastera (1963) and Gottfried von Einem (1970). During World War II he served as "entertainment specialist" with the U.S. Army Air Force. After the end of the war, he returned to the concert stage; made several world tours, which included South America, Australia, Japan, and Russia; he also gave master courses at the North Carolina School of the Arts, Indiana Univ., and the Juilliard School of Music in N.Y. He owns a 1734 Guarnerius del Gesù violin. In 1978 he celebrated a "Golden Jubilee," marking half a century of his professional career.

Rich, Alan, American music critic of an uncommonly bellicose disposition tempered by prejudice toward favorites; b. Boston, June 17, 1924. He muddled through a premedical course at Harvard Univ. (A.B., 1945) but made a *salto mortale* to grab a chance at a little dinky job as a secondary music critic of the moribund *Boston Herald,* at which he served from 1944–47; moving ahead, he wrote for various insolvent papers, such as the *New York Sun* (1947–48). Turning serious, he took a course in musicology with Manfred Bukofzer and Joseph Kerman at the Univ. of Calif. at Berkeley (M.A., 1952); spent a season in Vienna on an Alfred Hertz Memorial Traveling Fellowship in Music (1952–53), where he was guided musicographically by the grand man of scholarly research, Otto Erich Deutsch; and incidentally learned the rudiments of conducting with Walter Gmeindl. Returning to the U.S., he wrote for the *American Record Guide* (1948–61), *Musical America* (1955–61), the *N.Y. Times* (1961–63), the *N.Y. Herald Tribune* (1963–66), and its ephemeral successor, the *N.Y. World-Journal-Tribune* (1966–67), as well as for the prosperously extant weekly *New York* magazine (1968–81). Afflicted with acute Mehtaphobia he went back West after Zubin Mehta abandoned Los Angeles for N.Y.; became a bicoastal writer, working for *New York* and its Western clone, *California* magazine. In 1979 he began producing documentaries for Public Radio; taught music criticism at the Univ. of Southern Calif. and the Calif. Inst. of the Arts; in 1983 became the music critic for *Newsweek* magazine. He won 4 Deems Taylor-ASCAP writing awards; publ. *Careers and Opportunities in Music* (N.Y., 1964); *Music, Mirror of the Arts* (N.Y., 1969); and 3 vols. of the *Simon & Schuster Listeners Guide to Music* (1980). Virgil Thomson described Alan Rich as "our only musical muckraker."

Rich, "Buddy" (Bernard Rich), American jazz drummer and bandleader; b. New York, June 30, 1917. His parents were vaudeville performers; he began to tour with them at the age of 6 as "Traps the Drum Wonder"; then played with the bands of Bunny Berigan, Harry James, Tommy Dorsey, and others. He formed his own band in 1945; later appeared again with Dorsey and Harry James; also made tours in the U.S. and Europe. In 1966 he organized his own big band and toured widely with it.

Richter, Alfred, German pedagogue, son of **Ernst Friedrich Richter;** b. Leipzig, April 1, 1846; d. Berlin, March 1, 1919. He was trained by his father and became a competent music teacher; was a member of the faculty of the Leipzig Cons. (1872–82); then lived in London, but returned to Germany in 1897. He brought out a number of music school manuals, among them a supplement to his father's *Lehrbuch der Harmonie* (Leipzig, 1853); *Aufgabenbuch* (1879; went through 64 eds. before 1952; in Eng. as *Additional Exercises;* N.Y., 1882); *Die Elementarkenntnisse der Musik* (1895; 6th ed., 1920); *Die Lehre von der thematischen Arbeit* (1896); *Das Klavierspiel für Musikstudierende* (1898; 2nd ed., 1912); *Die Lehre von der Form in der Musik* (1904; 2nd ed., 1911). He also composed piano pieces, songs, and choruses.

Richter, Ernst Friedrich (Eduard), eminent German theorist and composer; b. Gross-Schönau, Oct. 24, 1808; d. Leipzig, April 9, 1879. A son of a schoolmaster, he was educated in Zittau; matriculated in 1831 as a student of theory at the Univ. of Leipzig; when the Leipzig Cons. was founded in 1843, he became Hauptmann's co-adjutor as teacher of harmony; conducted the Leipzig Singakademie (1843–47); was organist of the Petrikirche (from 1851) and the Neukirche (from 1862); in 1868 became music director of the Nikolaikirche and cantor of the Thomaskirche. He composed several sacred cantatas, masses, Psalms, etc., and also wrote chamber music, piano pieces, and organ compositions. But he became primarily known as the compiler of practical and useful manuals on harmony, counterpoint, and fugue, which went into numerous editions and translations into all European languages, among them *Lehrbuch der Harmonie* (Leipzig, 1853; 36th ed., 1953; in Eng., N.Y., 1867; newly trans. by Theodore Baker from the 25th German ed. N.Y., 1912; also in Swedish, Russian, Polish, Italian, French, Spanish, and Dutch); *Lehrbuch des einfachen und doppelten Kontrapunkts* (Leipzig, 1872; 15th ed., 1920; in Eng., London, 1874, and N.Y., 1884; also in French and Russian); *Lehrbuch der Fuge* (Leipzig, 1859; in Eng., London, 1878; also in French); these 3 manuals were brought out together as *Die praktischen Studien zur Theorie der Musik* (Leipzig, 1874–76); Richter's son, **Alfred Richter,** compiled a supplement to the *Lehrbuch der Harmonie* as *Aufgabenbuch,* which also went into a number of editions.

Richter, Francis William, American organist, nephew of **Hans Richter;** b. Minneapolis, Feb. 5, 1888; d. Los Angeles, Dec. 25, 1938. He became blind at the age of 3; showed musical ability, and was sent to Vienna, where he studied with the blind pianist Joseph Labor; also took lessons with Leschetizky (piano) and Karl Goldmark (theory); subsequently studied organ with Guilmant in Paris. Returning to the U.S., he was active as a church organist and teacher. In 1930 he settled in Portland, Oreg.; then moved to Los Angeles.

Richter, Franz Xaver, German composer; b. Holleschau, Moravia, Dec. 1, 1709; d. Strasbourg, Sept. 12, 1789. In 1740 he was Vice-Kapellmeister at the chapel of the Prince-Abbot at Kempten; in 1747 he joined the electoral orch. at Mannheim; from 1769 till his death, he was Kapellmeister at Strasbourg Cathedral. A prolific composer of decided originality, he was one of the chief representatives of the new instrumental style of the Mannheim school.

Richter, Hans, eminent German conductor; b. Raab, Hungary, April 4, 1843; d. Bayreuth, Dec. 5, 1916. He studied theory with Sechter, violin with Heissler, and French horn with Kleinecke at the Vienna Cons.; from 1862 to 1866 he was employed as horn player in the orch. at the Kärnthnertor-Theater in Vienna. The turning point in his career was his contact with Wagner at Triebschen in 1866, when Wagner asked him to make a fair copy of the score of *Die Meistersinger;* obviously satisfied with Richter's work, Wagner recommended him to Hans

von Bülow as a chorus master at the Munich Opera (1867); in 1868–69 Richter was also given an opportunity to assist von Bülow as conductor of the court orch. in Munich. Subsequently Richter became a favorite conductor of Wagner and prepared rehearsals of Wagner's operas, among them the Brussels performance of *Lohengrin* (March 22, 1870). From 1871 to 1875 he was conductor of the Pest National Theater; then conducted the Imperial Opera in Vienna and became its first principal conductor in 1875; concurrently he conducted the concerts of the Vienna Phil. (1875–82 and again in 1883–97). He was selected by Wagner to conduct the entire *Ring des Nibelungen* at the Bayreuth Festival in 1876; received the Order of Maximilian from the King of Bavaria and the Order of the Falcon from the Grand Duke of Weimar. When Wagner went to London in 1877, he took Richter along with him and let him conduct several concerts of the Wagner Festival in Albert Hall. In May 1879 Richter conducted a 2nd Wagner Festival in London, which led to the establishment of an annual series of May concerts known as "Orchestral Festival Concerts" and later simply "Richter Concerts," which he conducted regularly until 1897; then he was engaged as conductor of the Hallé Orch. in Manchester. He was also regular conductor of the Birmingham Festival (1885–1909) and of the Wagner operas at Covent Garden (1903–10). He conducted his farewell concert with the Manchester Symph. Orch. on April 11, 1911. His popularity in England was immense; his corpulent, bearlike figure and imposing Germanic beard imparted an air of authority; his technique was flawless. Besides Wagner's music, Richter gave repeated performances of symphs. of Brahms; among English composers he favored Elgar.

Richter, Karl, distinguished German organist and conductor; b. Plauen, Oct. 15, 1926; d. Munich, Feb. 15, 1981. He studied organ, harpsichord, and conducting at the Dresden Kreuzschule; then took courses at the Leipzig Cons. with Rudolf Mauersberger, Günther Ramin, and Karl Straube. In 1946 he became choirmaster of the Christuskirche in Leipzig; in 1947 was named organist of Leipzig's Thomaskirche. In 1951 he settled in Munich; organized the Munich Bach Orch. and Choir, which brought him great acclaim; made many tours and numerous recordings with them; also appeared as a guest conductor in Europe, including several concerts conducted in Russia. In 1965 he brought his Munich Bach Orch. and Choir to the U.S., making his American debut in Carnegie Hall in N.Y. on April 18, 1965; he made his last American conducting appearance in N.Y. on June 13, 1980.

Richter, Marga, American composer; b. Reedsburg, Wis., Oct. 21, 1926. She was prepared for a musical career by her mother, **Inez Chandler-Richter,** an American-born soprano; studied at the MacPhail School of Music in Minneapolis; in 1943 entered the Juilliard School of Music in N.Y., where she studied piano with Roslyn Tureck and composition with Persichetti and Bergsma, graduating in

1949 (M.S., 1951). She received 14 ASCAP awards since 1966 and 2 grants from the National Endowment for the Arts (1977, 1979). Her compositions reflect a pragmatic modern trend without rigid adherence to any particular doctrine or technique; the overriding concern is aural.

Richter, Sviatoslav, outstanding Russian pianist; b. Zhitomir, March 20, 1915. Both his parents were pianists; the family moved to Odessa when he was a child. He was engaged as a piano accompanist at the Odessa Opera, and developed exceptional skill in playing orch. scores at sight. He made his debut as a concert pianist at the Sailors' Collective Circle in Odessa in 1935. In 1937 he entered the Moscow Cons., where he studied piano with Neuhaus, graduating in 1947; was awarded the Stalin Prize in 1949. During the Russian tour of the Philadelphia Orch. in 1958, Richter was soloist, playing Prokofiev's 5th Piano Concerto in Leningrad; he made several international concert tours, including visits to China (1957) and the U.S. (1960). Both in Russia and abroad he earned a reputation as a piano virtuoso of formidable attainments; was especially praised for his impeccable sense of style, with every detail of the music rendered with lapidary perfection.

Ricketts, Frederick J., English bandmaster and composer who used the pseudonym **Kenneth J. Alford;** b. London, Feb. 21, 1881; d. Redgate, Surrey, May 15, 1945. Trained first as an organist, Ricketts graduated from Kneller Hall, the school for British bandmasters, afterward serving his longest stint as bandmaster of the Royal Marines (1928–44). In February 1914 he publ., under his pseudonym "Alford" (not to be confused with the American bandmaster and composer Harry L. Alford), his popular march *Col. Bogey,* epitomizing the steadily swinging and moderately paced English military march. *Col. Bogey* reached its height of fame when it was introduced into the motion picture *The Bridge on the River Kwai* (1958).

Ricordi & Co., G., famous music publishing firm of Milan, founded by **Giovanni Ricordi** (b. Milan, 1785; d. there, March 15, 1853). As first violinist and conductor at the old Fiando theater, he also earned small sums as a music copyist, and in 1807 went to Leipzig to learn music engraving in Breitkopf & Härtel's establishment. On returning, he opened a little shop and began publishing in 1808, engraving the first works himself. He was an intimate of Rossini, whose operas he publ.; also recognized Verdi's genius when the latter was still unknown. His son **Tito Ricordi** (b. Milan, Oct. 29, 1811; d. there, Sept. 7, 1888) succeeded to the business. In 1845 he established the *Gazzetta Musicale,* one of the most important Italian musical papers; also introduced the Edizioni Economiche, and under his administration the house became the largest music publishing firm in Italy. He was on terms of intimate friendship with Verdi, whose works (especially *Aida*) made a fortune for both publisher and author. Owing to ill health, he withdrew from active management in

1887. His successor was his son **Guilio Ricordi** (b. Milan, Dec. 19, 1840; d. there, June 6, 1912), a man of extraordinary business ability, who continued the policy of expansion. In 1888 he bought, and consolidated with his own, the important firm of Francesco Lucca. It was he who discovered Puccini. A trained musician, he publ., under the pseudonym of **J. Burgmein,** much elegant salon music (160 opus numbers). He was editor of the *Gazzetta Musicale* until his death, upon which the magazine ceased publication. His son **Tito** (b. May 17, 1865; d. Milan, March 30, 1933), a remarkable pianist, was the subsequent head of the house; he retired in 1919, and control of the firm left the family; it became a limited company in 1952. The catalogue contains over 120,000 numbers, and in the archives are the autograph scores of more than 550 operas by the most famous Italian composers. The firm has branches in N.Y., Canada, Australia, and South America.

Riddle, Nelson, American composer-arranger of popular music and orch. leader; b. Hackensack, N.J., June 1, 1921. He took up the trombone at the age of 14; played in the bands of Charlie Spivak and Tommy Dorsey. After military service, he studied with Mario Castelnuovo-Tedesco in Los Angeles; then became an enormously successful arranger in Hollywood, preparing scores for numerous films and television programs; worked with Judy Garland, Frank Sinatra, Nat King Cole, Ella Fitzgerald, and others. He won an Academy Award for his score for the film *The Great Gatsby* (1974).

Rider-Kelsey, Mme. Corinne, American soprano; b. on a farm near Batavia, N.Y., Feb. 24, 1877; d. Toledo, Ohio, July 10, 1947. She attended Oberlin College; then studied voice in Chicago and N.Y.; made her professional debut in Handel's *Messiah* (St. Louis, Nov. 24, 1904); made her first operatic appearance as Micaëla in *Carmen,* at Covent Garden in London on July 2, 1908. In 1926 she married the violinist **Lynell Reed,** who wrote her biography under the title *Be Not Afraid* (N.Y., 1955). See V.L. Scott in *Notable American Women,* III (N.Y., 1971).

Řídký, Jaroslav, eminent Czech composer, conductor, and teacher; b. Františkov, near Liberec, Aug. 25, 1897; d. Poděbrady, Aug. 14, 1956. He took courses in composition at the Prague Cons. with Jaroslav Křička and E.B. Foerster; simultaneously studied the harp; was first harpist in the Czech Phil. (1924–38); later became conductor of its choir (1925–30). He taught theory at the Prague Cons. (1928–48); in 1948 was appointed prof. of composition at the Music Academy in Prague, remaining at this post until his death.

Ridout, Godfrey, Canadian composer; b. Toronto, May 6, 1918. He studied piano, organ, conducting, and composition at the Toronto Cons. and at the Univ. of Toronto, where he became a member of the faculty in 1948. His music is tuneful and winsome. In 1963–64 he reconstructed a comic opera, *Colas et*

Colinette, the earliest known North American work in this form, composed by the French-Canadian musician Joseph Quesnel in 1788, for which only vocal parts and a 2nd violin part were extant.

Riegel (Rigel), Heinrich (Henri) Joseph, French composer; b. Wertheim, Franconia, Feb. 9, 1741; d. Paris, May 2, 1799. He was of German extraction; studied with F.X. Richter in Mannheim and with Jommelli in Stuttgart. In 1767 he went to Paris; from 1783 to 1786, belonged to a group of composers associated with the Concert Spirituel. On the title page of several of his works publ. in Paris his name appears as Rigel, and this gallicized form was adopted by his son **Henri-Jean,** who was born in Paris. Riegel was one of the earliest composers to write ensemble music with piano, publ. as "symphonies" for 2 Violins, Cello, 2 Horns, and Piano. He was a fairly voluminous composer; wrote several short operas in the manner of the German singspiel, all of which were produced in Paris: *Le Savetier et le financier* (1778); *L'Automat* (1779); *Rosanie* (1780); *Blanche et vermeille* (1781); *Lucas* (1785); *Les Amours du Gros-Caillou* (1786); *Alix de Beaucaire* (1791). His other works include 6 symphs.; 5 piano concertos; 6 string quartets; several *Sonates de clavecin en quattuor;* a number of piano sonatas, some with Violin obbligato; and 3 *Sonates en symphonies* for Piano. During the revolutionary period in France he composed various pieces celebrating the events. A "symphonie" in D was republ. by R. Sondheimer (1923). A Sonata is included in W.S. Newman's *Six Keyboard Sonatas from the Classical Era* (1965).

Riegger, Wallingford, outstanding American composer; b. Albany, Ga., April 29, 1885; d. New York, April 2, 1961. He received his primary education at home: his mother was a pianist; his father a violinist. The family moved to N.Y. in 1900, and Riegger began serious study with Percy Goetschius (theory) and Alwin Schroeder (cello) at the Inst. of Musical Art; after graduation (1907), he went to Berlin, where he took courses at the Hochschule für Musik; conducted opera in Würzburg and Königsberg (1915–16); also led the Bluethner Orch. in Berlin (1916–17). He returned to America in 1917 and taught theory and cello at Drake Univ., Des Moines (1918–22); in 1922 received the Paderewski Prize for his Piano Trio; in 1924 was awarded the E.S. Coolidge Prize for his setting of Keats's *La Belle Dame sans merci;* in 1925 he was given the honorary degree of D.Mus. by the Cincinnati Cons. He taught at the Inst. of Musical Art in N.Y. (1924–25) and at the Ithaca Cons. (1926–28); then settled in N.Y., where he became active as a composer and a participant in various modern music societies; took part in the development of electronic instruments (in association with Theremin), and learned to play an electric cello. His music is of a highly advanced nature; a master craftsman, he wrote in disparate styles with an equal degree of proficiency; used numerous pseudonyms for certain works (**William Richards, Walter Scotson, Gerald Wilfring Gore, John H.**

McCurdy, George Northrup, Robert Sedgwick, Leonard Gregg, Edwin Farell, Edgar Long, etc.). After a long period of neglect on the part of the public and the critics, he began to receive recognition; his 3rd Symph. was the choice of the N.Y. Music Critics Circle in 1948. WORKS: For the stage: Several works for the dance groups of Martha Graham, Doris Humphrey, and others, scored for various instrumental ensembles: *Bacchanale* (N.Y., 1931); *Frenetic Rhythms* (N.Y., 1933); *Evocation* (Toronto, 1933); the trilogy *Theatre Piece, With My Red Fires,* and *New Dance* (1934; orchestrated 1936; N.Y., July 2, 1936); *Chronicle* (N.Y., 1936); *The Cry* (N.Y., 1935); *Candide* (N.Y., 1937); *Case History No. . . .* (N.Y., 1937); *Trojan Incident* (N.Y., 1938); *Machine Ballet* (Toronto, 1938); *Pilgrim's Progress* (N.Y., 1941). For orch.: *American Polonaise* (1922; retitled *Triple Jazz*); *Rhapsody* (1926; N.Y., Oct. 29, 1931); *Fantasy and Fugue* for Organ and Orch. (1930–31); *Dichotomy* for Chamber Orch. (1931–32; Berlin, March 10, 1932); *Scherzo* (1932; N.Y., Jan. 30, 1933); *New Dance,* finale of dance trilogy, in 7 different instrumentations (1934; orch. version in 1936, revised 1940–41; Pittsburgh, Jan. 30, 1942, Reiner conducting); *Canon and Fugue* for Orch. or String Orch. (1941); *Passacaglia and Fugue* (1942; Berkeley, Calif., Aug. 1, 1942); *Processional: Funeral March* for Orch. or Concert Band (1943); 4 symphs.: Nos. 1 and 2 for School Orch. (1943, 1944; both withdrawn); No. 3 (1946–47; N.Y., May 16, 1948; revised 1956); No. 4 (1956–57; Univ. of Illinois, April 12, 1957); *Music for Orchestra* (1939; revised 1951; Cleveland, March 22, 1956); *Variations* for Piano and Orch. (1952–53; Louisville, Ky., Feb. 13, 1954; versions for 2 Pianos and Orch., and for 2 Solo Pianos); *Suite for Young Orchestras* for varying combinations of Strings and Winds (1954); *Romanza* for Strings (1954); *Dance Rhythms* (Atlanta, March 4, 1955); *Overture* (1955); *Preamble and Fugue* (1955); *Festival Overture* (1957); *Variations* for Violin and Orch. (1958; Louisville, April 1, 1959); *Quintuple Jazz* (1958; Univ. of Iowa, May 20, 1959); Sinfonietta (1959); *Duo* for Piano and Orch. (1960); *Introduction and Fugue* for Cello, Wind Orch., and Timpani (1960). For voice: *La Belle Dame sans merci* for 4 Solo Voices and Chamber Orch. (Pittsfield, Mass., Sept. 19, 1924); *Eternity,* after Dickinson, for Women's Voices, Flute, 2 Horns, and Double Bass (1940); *Who Can Revoke?* for Chorus and Piano (1948); *In Certainty of Song,* cantata (1950); *The Dying of the Light,* after Dylan Thomas, for Chorus, and Orch. or Piano (1954). Chamber music: Piano Trio (1919–20); *Whimsey* for Cello and Piano (1920); *Study in Sonority* for 10 Violins, or multiples of 10 (1927); *Suite* for Solo Flute (1929); *3 Canons* for Flute, Oboe, Clarinet, and Bassoon (1931); *Divertissement* for Flute, Harp, and Cello (1933); 2 string quartets (1938–39, 1948); *Duos* for Flute, Oboe, and Clarinet (1943); Violin Sonatina (1947); *Music for Brass Choir* (1948–49); Piano Quintet (1951); Nonet for Brass (1951); Wind Quintet (1952); Concerto for Piano and Wind Quintet (1952); *Variations* for Violin and Viola (1956); *Movement* for 2 Trumpets, Trombone, and Piano (1957); *Prelude and Fugue* for 4 Cellos (1957); *Cooper Square* for Solo Accordion (1958). FOR PIANO: *Blue Voyage* (1927); *Scherzo* (1932); *New and Old,* 12 study pieces (1944).

Riemann, (Carl Wilhelm Julius) Hugo, preeminent German musicologist; b. Gross-Mehlra, near Sondershausen, July 18, 1849; d. Leipzig, July 10, 1919. He was trained in theory by Frankenberger at Sondershausen; studied piano with Barthel and Ratzenberger; took the gymnasial course in the Rossleben Klosterschule (1865–68) and studied first law, then philosophy and history, at Berlin and Tübingen; then entered the Leipzig Cons. In 1873 he took the degree of Dr.Phil. at Göttingen with the dissertation *Musikalische Logik;* was active as a conductor and teacher at Bielefeld until 1878, when he qualified as univ. lecturer on music at Leipzig; taught music at Bromberg (1880–81), then at the Hamburg Cons. till 1890, at the Sondershausen Cons. for a short time, and at the Wiesbaden Cons. until 1895, when he resumed his lectures at Leipzig. In 1905 he was made prof.; in 1908, director of the newly established Collegium Musicum; and in 1914, also director of the newly established Forschungsinstitut für Musikwissenschaft. He was made Mus.Doc. *honoris causa* by the Univ. of Edinburgh (1899). On his 60th birthday he was honored by the publication of a Festschrift (ed., Karl Mennicke) containing contributions from the world's foremost scholars, many of whom were Riemann's pupils. The 2nd Riemann Festschrift was publ. after his death in 1919.

The mere bulk of Riemann's writings, covering every branch of musical science, constitutes a monument of indefatigable industry, and is proof of enormous concentration and capacity for work. When one takes into consideration that much of this work is the result of painstaking research and of original, often revolutionary, thinking, one must share the great respect and admiration in which Riemann was held by his contemporaries. Although many of his ideas are now seen in a different light, his works treating of harmony were considered to constitute the foundation of modern music theory. His researches in the field of music history have solved a number of vexing problems, and thrown light on others. And, finally, in formulating the new science of musicology, the labors of Riemann have been a most important factor.

Riemenschneider, Albert, American organist and music editor; b. Berea, Ohio, Aug. 31, 1878; d. Akron, July 20, 1950. He studied at Baldwin-Wallace College (B.A., 1899) and in Cleveland; then went to Vienna, where he took lessons with R. Fuchs and H. Reinhold; proceeded to Paris, where he continued his organ study with Widor and Guilmant. Returning to America in 1905, he became a choral director of Baldwin-Wallace Cons., and later president of the College. His main contribution to American musicology is a number of fine editions of Bach's vocal works, among them *Liturgical Year* (the *Orgelbüchlein;* 1933); *Chorales* (120 chorales in original clefs and with the original orch. parts; 2 vols.,

1939; with C.N. Boyd); *371 Harmonized Chorales and 69 Chorale Melodies with Figured Bass* (1941).

Ries, Ferdinand, German pianist and composer; b. Bonn, Nov. 28, 1784; d. Frankfurt, Jan. 13, 1838. He was the son of **Franz Anton Ries,** "der alte Ries," a close friend of Beethoven; thanks to this relationship, Ferdinand Ries was accepted by Beethoven as a piano pupil and studied with him in Vienna from 1801 to 1804; also in Vienna he took a course in music theory with Albrechtsberger. He made successful tours as a concert pianist in Germany, Scandinavia, and Russia; then went to London, where he remained from 1813 to 1824, and acquired prominence as a piano teacher. From 1827 he stayed mainly in Frankfurt. He was an excellent pianist and a prolific composer.

WORKS: Operas: *Die Räuberbraut* (Frankfurt, 1828) and *Liska* (produced in London, 1831, under the title *The Sorceress*); 2 oratorios; 8 symphs.; 8 piano concertos; chamber music; 52 piano sonatas and other pieces for his instrument. His music reflects both the spirit and the technique of composition of Beethoven, the fateful distance between them being that of genius, which Ries never possessed. His reminiscences of Beethoven were publ. posthumously under the title *Biographische Notizen über L. von Beethoven* (Koblenz, 1828; numerous later eds. in all European languages; the work was partly dictated by Ries to Wegeler during the last years of Ries's life, and inevitably contains stories that could not be trusted).

Ries, Franz, German publisher, son of **Hubert Ries;** b. Berlin, April 7, 1846; d. Naumberg, June 20, 1932. He studied violin with his father and later with Massart at the Paris Cons. His career as a concert violinist was brief, and in 1875 he entered the music publishing business; from 1881 to 1924 was director of the firm Ries & Erler in Berlin; in 1924 his son **Robert Ries** became the proprietor; after the death of Robert Ries the firm was taken over by his 2 daughters.

Ries, Franz Anton, German violinist; b. Bonn, Nov. 10, 1755; d. Godesberg, Nov. 1, 1846. He was known as "der alte Ries," to distinguish him from his son **Ferdinand.** Franz Anton Ries was music director of the Margrave Max Franz of Cologne and Bonn, and was a close friend of Beethoven in Bonn.

Ries, Hubert, German violinist, brother of **Ferdinand Ries;** b. Bonn, April 1, 1802; d. Berlin, Sept. 14, 1886. He studied at Kassel under Spohr (violin) and Hauptmann (composition); in 1836, was concertmaster of the royal orch. in Berlin; in 1851 a teacher at the Royal Theaterinstrumentalschule; pensioned in 1872. He publ. excellent instructive works for violin: *Violinschule* (also in Eng.); *Erzählungen aus alter Zeit* (30 instructive duets); *15 Violinstudien von mässiger Schwierigkeit,* op. 26; *30 Violinstudien für den ersten Unterricht,* op. 28; *50 Intonationsübungen, 12 Violinstudien in Form von Konzertstücken,* op. 9; duets, exercises, etc.; also 2 violin concertos (opp. 13 and 16).

Riesemann, Oscar, Russian-German musicologist; b. Reval, Estonia, Feb. 29, 1880; d. St. Niklausen, near Lucerne, Switzerland, Sept. 28, 1934. He studied music theory with Sandberger and Thuille at the Royal Academy in Munich; then took courses in philology and jurisprudence at the Univ. of Moscow; subsequently went to Germany again and took courses with Friedlaender in Berlin and with Hugo Riemann in Leipzig, where he obtained his Dr.Phil. with the dissertation *Die Notation des alt-russischen Kirchengesanges* (publ. in Moscow, in German, 1908). He then was active as a music critic in Moscow, and during World War I served on the Russian side in the sanitary corps, but made his way to Germany once more during the Russian Revolution; he described this turbulent period in an autobiographical publication, *Fluchten* (Stuttgart, 1925). He subsequently lived in Munich and then in Switzerland. He publ. a monograph on Mussorgsky (Munich, 1926; in Eng., N.Y., 1929), and *Rachmaninoff's Recollections* (N.Y., 1934; in Eng.), a loyal but not always accurate account, which was gently repudiated by Rachmaninoff himself.

Rieti, Vittorio, Italian-American composer; b. Alexandria, Egypt, Jan. 28, 1898. He studied with Frugatta in Milan; then took courses with Respighi and Casella in Rome, where he lived until 1940, when he emigrated to the U.S. (became an American citizen June 1, 1944). He taught at the Peabody Cons. in Baltimore (1948–49), Chicago Musical College (1950–53), Queens College in N.Y. (1958–60), and Hunter College in N.Y. (1960–64). His style of composition represents an ingratiating synthesis of cosmopolitan modern tendencies.

Rietz, Julius, German conductor and editor; b. Berlin, Dec. 28, 1812; d. Dresden, Sept. 12, 1877. He was of a musical family: his father was a court musician, and his brother was a friend of Mendelssohn. Julius Rietz studied cello and played in theater orchs. in Berlin. In 1834 he became 2nd conductor of the Düsseldorf Opera; from 1847 to 1854 he was a theater conductor in Leipzig; in 1848–60 served as conductor of the Gewandhaus Concerts; later he was appointed artistic director of the Dresden Cons. A scholarly musician and competent orch. conductor, Rietz was also an excellent music editor; he prepared for publication the complete edition of Mendelssohn's works for Breitkopf & Härtel (1874–77), and also edited Mozart's operas and symphs., Beethoven's overtures, etc. As a composer, he followed the musical style of Mendelssohn.

Rifkin, Joshua, American musicologist, pianist, and conductor; b. New York, April 22, 1944. He studied with Persichetti at the Juilliard School of Music in N.Y. (B.S., 1964); with Gustave Reese at N.Y. Univ. (1964–66); at the Univ. of Göttingen (1966–67); and later with Mendel, Lockwood, Babbitt, and Oster at Princeton Univ. (M.F.A., 1969). He also worked with Stockhausen at Darmstadt (1961,

1965). In 1970 he joined the faculty of Brandeis Univ. He is noted for his research in the field of Renaissance and Baroque music, but he became popular as a performer and explicator of ragtime.

Rigel, Henri-Jean, French composer, son and pupil of **Heinrich Joseph Riegel** (he changed his name from its German form to French); b. Paris, May 11, 1772; d. Abbeville, Dec. 16, 1852. He conducted the French Opera in Cairo (1798–1800); in 1808 was attached to Napoleon's court as a chamber musician. He wrote the operas *Les 2 Meuniers* (Cairo, 1799) and *Le Duel nocturne* (Dec. 23, 1805); 4 piano concertos and numerous minor piano pieces.

Rignold, Hugo, English conductor; b. Kingston-on-Thames, May 15, 1905; d. London, May 30, 1976. His father was a theatrical conductor, his mother an opera singer. He was taken to Canada as a child, and studied violin in Winnipeg; in 1920 he returned to England on a scholarship to the Royal Academy of Music. During World War II he was stationed in Cairo, where he trained a radio orch. in performances of symph. music. Returning to England, he was a ballet conductor at Covent Garden (1947); from 1948 to 1954 was conductor of the Liverpool Phil.; in 1957–60 served as music director of the Royal Ballet; then became music director of the Birmingham Symph. Orch. (1960–68).

Rihm, Wolfgang, German composer; b. Karlsruhe, March 13, 1952. He studied theory and composition with Eugene Velte at the Hochschule für Musik in Karlsruhe (1968–72) and also attended courses given by Humphrey Searle; then went to Cologne, where he enrolled in the seminars of Stockhausen (1972–73); also audited classes of Klaus Huber in Freiburg (1973); in addition, received counseling from Wolfgang Fortner. From 1973–78 he taught at the Hochschule für Musik in Karlsruhe. His own music thrives on calculated unpredictability; but he does not shrink from producing shockingly euphonious and startlingly pleasurable sounds.
WORKS: FOR THE STAGE: Opera-in-progress, *Harlekin* (1977—); 2 chamber operas: No. 1, *Faust und Yorick* (1976), and No. 2, *Jakob Lenz* (1977–78; Hamburg, March 8, 1979). FOR ORCH.: 3 symphs.: No. 1 (1969); No. 2 (1975); No. 3, after Nietzsche and Rimbaud, for Soprano, Baritone, Chorus, and Orch. (1976–77); *Trakt* (1971); *Morphonie, Sektor IV* for String Quartet and Orch. (1972); *Magma* (1974); *Dis-Kontur* (1974); *Sub-Kontur* (1974–75; Donaueschingen, Oct. 26, 1976); *Konzertarie,* a "telepsychogramm" based on a telegram King Ludwig II sent to Wagner, for Mezzo-soprano and Orch. (1975); *O Notte* for Baritone and Small Orch. (1975); *Cuts and Dissolves,* concerto for 29 Players (1976); *Nachtordnung,* 7 pieces for 15 Strings (1976); *Lichtzwang,* music for Violin and Orch., in memory of Paul Celan (1975–76); *Hölderlin-Fragmente* for Voice, and Orch. or Piano (1977); *La Musique creuse le ciel,* music for 2 Pianos and Orch. (1977–79; Cologne, Nov. 14, 1980); *Abgesangsszene* No. 1 for Orch. (1979;

Kassel, Nov. 8, 1979), No. 2, after Nietzsche and Novalis, for Voice and Orch. (1979; Karlsruhe, Oct. 5, 1980), No. 3, after Huchel, for Baritone and Orch. (1980), No. 4, after Nietzsche, for Voice and Orch. (1979–80), and No. 5 for Orch. (1979; Kiel, Jan. 12, 1981); *Walzer* (1979–81); *Doppelgesang* No. 1 for Viola, Cello, and Orch. (1980) and No. 2 for Clarinet or Bass Clarinet, Cello, and Orch. (1981–83; Hitzacker, Aug. 7, 1983); *Lenz-Fragmente*, 5 songs for Voice, and Orch. or Piano (1980); *Tutuguri*, subtitled *Ballet nach Artaud*, a series of 7 works inspired by the writings of Antonin Artaud: *I* (1981), *II* (1981–82; Chicago Symph., March 3, 1982), *III* for 6 Percussionists and Orch. (1981; Karlsruhe, Dec. 5, 1981), *IV* (1982; Saarbrücken, May 20, 1982), *V* (1981; in progress), *VI* for 6 Percussionists (1981), and *VII* for 7 Voices and Orch. (1981; in progress); Viola Concerto (1980–83; West Berlin, Nov. 13, 1983); *Wölfli-Liederbuch* for Baritone, and Orch. or Piano (1981–82); *Chiffre I* for Piano and 7 Instruments (1982; Saarbrücken, April 22, 1983) and *II, Silence to Be Beaten*, for Percussion and Orch. (1983); *Gebild* for Piccolo Trumpet, 2 Percussionists and 20 Strings (1983; Zürich, May 15, 1983); *Monodram* for Cello and Orch. (1983; Graz, Austria, Oct. 9, 1983).

Riisager, Knudåge, prominent Danish composer; b. Port Kunda, Estonia, March 6, 1897; d. Copenhagen, Dec. 26, 1974. He attended courses in political science at the Univ. of Copenhagen (1916–21); concurrently studied music with Peter Gram, Peter Møller, and Otto Malling (1915–18); then went to Paris and took private lessons with Albert Roussel and Paul Le Flem (1923–24); subsequently studied counterpoint with Hermann Grabner in Leipzig (1932). He held a position in Denmark's Ministry of Finance (1925–47); was chairman of the Danish Composers' Union (1937–62) and director of the Royal Danish Cons. (1956–67). A fantastically prolific composer, he wrote music in quaquaversal genres, but preserved a remarkable structural and textural consistency while demonstrating an erudite sense of modern polyphony. He also had a taste for exotic and futuristic subjects.

WORKS: (all premieres are in Copenhagen unless stated otherwise): FOR THE STAGE: Opera buffa, *Susanne* (1948; Royal Danish Opera, Jan. 7, 1950); 14 ballets: *Benzin* (1927; Dec. 26, 1930); a "ballet-bouffonnerie," *Cocktails-Party* (1929); *Tolv med Posten (Twelve by the Mail)*, after H.C. Andersen (1939; Feb. 21, 1942); *Slaraffenland (Fool's Paradise;* 1940; Feb. 21, 1942; originally an orch. piece, 1936); *Qarrtsiluni*, on Eskimo themes (1942; Feb. 21, 1942; originally an orch. piece, 1938); *Fugl fønix (Phoenix;* 1944–45; May 12, 1946); *Etude*, based on Czerny's studies (1947; Jan. 15, 1948); *Månerenen (The Moon Reindeer;* 1956; Nov. 22, 1957); *Stjerner* (1958); *Les Victoires de l'Amour* (1958; March 4, 1962); *Fruen fra havet (Lady from the Sea;* 1959; N.Y., April 20, 1960); *Galla-Variationer* (1966; March 5, 1967); *Ballet Royal* (May 31, 1967); *Svinedrengen (The Swineherd;* Danish Television, March 10, 1969). FOR ORCH.: *Erasmus Montanus*, overture (1920; Göteborg, Sweden, Oct. 15, 1924); *Suite Dionysiaque* for Chamber Orch. (1924); 5 symphs.: No. 1 (1925; July 17, 1926); No. 2 (1927; March 5, 1929); No. 3 (1935; Nov. 21, 1935); No. 4, *Sinfonia gaia* (1940; Oct. 24, 1940); No. 5, *Sinfonia serena* for Strings and Percussion (1949–50; Nov. 21, 1950); *Introduzione di traverso*, overture (1925); *Variations on a Theme of Mezangean* (1926); *T-DOXC*, "poème mécanique" (1926; Sept. 3, 1927); *Klods Hans* (1929); *Fastelavn (Shrovetide)*, overture (1929–30); *Suite* for Small Orch. (1931); Concerto for Orch. (1931; Dec. 7, 1936); Concertino for Trumpet and String Orch. (1933; March 2, 1934); *Primavera*, overture (1934; Jan. 31, 1935); *Slaraffenland*, 2 suites (1936, 1940; as a ballet, 1940); *Sinfonia concertante* for Strings (1937); *Partita* (1937); *Basta* (1938); *Qarrtsiluni* (1938; as a ballet, 1940); *Torgutisk dans* (1939); *Tivoli-Tivoli!* (1943; Aug. 15, 1943); *Sommer-Rhapsodi* (1943; Jan. 30, 1944); *Bellman-Variationer* for Small Orch. (1945); Sinfonietta (1947; Stockholm, Oct. 1, 1947); *Chaconne* (1949); *Archaeopteryx* (1949); *Variations on a Sarabande of Charles, Duke of Orleans, 1415* for String Orch. (1950); Violin Concerto (1950–51; Oct. 11, 1951); *Toccata* (1952); *Pro fistulis et fidibus* for Woodwinds and String Orch. (1952; March 2, 1953); *Rondo gioioso* for Violin and Orch. (1957; June 18, 1957); *Burlesk ouverture* (1964); *Entrada-Epilogo* (May 19, 1971); *Bourrée*, ballet-variations (Danish Radio, March 7, 1972); *Trittico* for Woodwinds, Brass, Double Bass, and Percussion (Danish Radio, March 3, 1972); *Apollon* (Nov. 11, 1973); incidental music.

Riley, Terry, American composer of the avant-garde; b. Colfax, Calif., June 24, 1935. He studied at the Univ. of Calif. at Berkeley with Seymour Shifrin, William Denny, and Robert Erickson, obtaining his M.A. in composition in 1961; went to Europe and played piano and saxophone in cabarets in Paris and in Scandinavia. In 1970 he was initiated in San Francisco as a disciple of Pandit Pran Nath, the North Indian singer, and followed him to India. In his music Riley explores the extremes of complexity and gymnosophistical simplicity. His ascertainable works include *Spectra* for 6 Instruments (1959), String Trio (1961), and *In C* for Orch., notated in fragments to be played any number of times at will in the spirit of aleatory latitudinarianism, all within the key of C major, with an occasional F sharp providing a *trompe l'oreille* effect; it was first performed in San Francisco, May 21, 1965. His other compositions include *Poppy Nogoods Phantom Band* (1966); *A Rainbow in Curved Air* (1968); *Genesis '70*, a ballet (1970); *Sunrise of the Planetary Dream Collector* for String Quartet (1981); *The Medicine Wheel* for String Quartet (1983). Riley's astrological signs are Sun in Cancer (euphemistically known in Southern California as Moon Children so as to exorcise middle-aged fear of malignancy), Scorpio Rising, and Aries Moon.

Rilling, Helmuth, noted German organist, conductor, and pedagogue; b. Stuttgart, May 29, 1933. He studied at the Hochschule für Musik in Stuttgart and later took a course in organ playing with Fernando Germani at the Santa Cecilia Academy in

Rome. He taught choral conducting and organ at the Kirchenmusikschule in Berlin-Spandau (1963–66); in 1966 he was appointed to the faculty of the Frankfurt Hochschule für Musik; in 1969 he succeeded Kurt Thomas as conductor of the Frankfurter Kantorei. He was also in charge of the Stuttgart Bach Choir (Gaeschinger Kantorei) and led it during his first American tour; he conducted the summer Bach festivals of the Univ. of Oregon in Eugene. On Jan. 21, 1982, he appeared as a guest conductor with the Los Angeles Phil. He is recognized as an authority on choral music of the Baroque era.

Rimbault, Edward Francis, English writer and editor; b. London, June 13, 1816; d. there, Sept. 26, 1876. He was the son of **Stephen Francis Rimbault,** organist and composer (1773–1837); was a pupil of his father, of Samuel Wesley, and of Dr. Crotch; was organist of the Swiss Church, Soho, in 1832. He began giving lectures on English musical history in 1838; in 1840 he founded, with E. Taylor and W. Chappell, the Musical Antiquarian Society; received the degree of Dr.Phil. from Göttingen. He composed various songs, of which *Happy Land* became a popular favorite.

Rimsky-Korsakov, Andrei, son of **Nicolai Rimsky-Korsakov;** b. St. Petersburg, Oct. 17, 1878; d. Leningrad, May 23, 1940. He studied philology at the Univ. of St. Petersburg and later at Strasbourg and Heidelberg (Dr.Phil., 1903); returning to Russia, he devoted his energies to Russian music history. In 1915 he began the publication of an important magazine, *Musikalny Sovremennik (The Musical Contemporary),* but the revolutionary events of 1917 forced suspension of its publication. He edited the first 4 vols. of the complete biography of his father, *N.A. Rimsky-Korsakov; Life and Works* (Moscow, 1933, 1935, 1936, 1937; an additional vol., No. 5, was completed and edited by his younger brother **Vladimir Rimsky-Korsakov**); also publ. *M.P. Mussorgsky, Letters and Documents* (1932; extremely valuable); edited and annotated his father's *Chronicle of My Musical Life* (Moscow, 1935); compiled the catalogue, *Musical Treasures of the Manuscript Dept. of the Leningrad Public Library* (1938). He was married to the composer **Julia Weissberg**.

Rimsky-Korsakov, Georgi, grandson of **Nicolai Rimsky-Korsakov** and nephew of **Andrei Rimsky-Korsakov;** b. St. Petersburg, Dec. 26, 1901; d. Leningrad, Oct. 10, 1965. He studied at the St. Petersburg Cons.; in 1923, founded a society for the cultivation of quarter-tone music; composed some works in that system; publ. the articles "Foundations of the Quarter-Tone System" (Leningrad, 1925) and "The Deciphering of the 'Luce' Part in Scriabin's Prometheus," in the Russian magazine *De Musica* (1927); then became active in work on electronic musical instruments; was co-inventor of the "Emeriton" (1930), capable of producing a complete series of tones at any pitch and of any chosen or synthetic tone color; wrote solo pieces for it; also an Octet for

2 Emeritons, 2 Clarinets, Bassoon, Violin, Viola, and Cello (1932). From 1927 to 1962 he was on the faculty of the Cons. of Leningrad.

Rimsky-Korsakov, Nicolai, great Russian composer; b. Tikhvin, near Novgorod, March 18, 1844; d. Liubensk, near St. Petersburg, June 21, 1908. He remained in the country until he was 12 years old; in 1856 he entered the Naval School in St. Petersburg, graduating in 1862. He took piano lessons as a child with provincial teachers, and later with a professional musician, Théodore Canillé, who introduced him to Balakirev; he also met Cui and Borodin. In 1862 he was sent on the clipper *Almaz* on a voyage that lasted 2½ years; returning to Russia in the summer of 1865, he settled in St. Petersburg, where he remained most of his life. During his travels he maintained contact with Balakirev, and continued to report to him the progress of his musical composition. He completed his First Symph. (which was also the earliest work in this form by a Russian composer), and it was performed under Balakirev's direction on Dec. 31, 1865, at a concert of the Free Music School in St. Petersburg. In 1871 Rimsky-Korsakov was engaged as a prof. of composition and orchestration at the St. Petersburg Cons., even though he was aware of the inadequacy of his own technique. He remained on the faculty until his death, with the exception of a few months in 1905, when he was relieved of his duties as prof. for his public support of the rebellious students during the revolution of that year. As a music educator, Rimsky-Korsakov was of the greatest importance to the development and maintenance of the traditions of the Russian national school; among his students were Glazunov, Liadov, Arensky, Ippolitov-Ivanov, Gretchaninov, Nicolas Tcherepnin, Maximilian Steinberg, Gnessin, and Miaskovsky. Igor Stravinsky studied privately with Rimsky-Korsakov from 1903 on.

In 1873 Rimsky-Korsakov abandoned his naval career, but was appointed to the post of inspector of the military orchs. of the Russian navy, until it was abolished in 1884. From 1883 to 1894 he was also assistant director of the Court Chapel and led the chorus and the orch. there. Although he was not a gifted conductor, he gave many performances of his own orch. works; made his debut at a charity concert for the victims of the Volga famine, in St. Petersburg, March 2, 1874; the program included the first performance of his 3rd Symph. From 1886 until 1900 he conducted the annual Russian Symph. concerts organized by the publisher Belaieff; in June 1889 he conducted 2 concerts of Russian music at the World Exposition in Paris; in 1890 he conducted a concert of Russian music in Brussels; led a similar concert there in 1900. His last appearance abroad was in the spring of 1907, when he conducted in Paris 2 Russian historic concerts arranged by Diaghilev; in the same year he was elected corresponding member of the French Academy, to succeed Grieg. These activities, however, did not distract him from his central purpose as a national Russian composer. His name was grouped with those of Cui, Borodin, Balakirev, and Mussorgsky as the "Mighty Five," and he maintained an intimate friendship with most of them; at Mussorgsky's death he collected his MSS and prepared them for publication; he also revised Mussorgsky's opera *Boris Godunov;* it was in Rimsky-Korsakov's version that the opera became famous. Later some criticism was voiced against Rimsky-Korsakov's reduction of Mussorgsky's original harmonies and melodic lines to an academically acceptable standard. He had decisive influence in the affairs of the Belaieff publishing firm and helped publish a great number of works by Russian composers of the St. Petersburg group; only a small part of these sumptuously printed scores represents the best in Russian music, but culturally Rimsky-Korsakov's solicitude was of great importance. Although he was far from being a revolutionary, he freely expressed his disgust at the bungling administration of Czarist Russia; he was particularly indignant about the attempts of the authorities to alter Pushkin's lines in his own last opera, *Le Coq d'or,* and refused to compromise; he died, of angina pectoris, with the situation still unresolved; the opera was produced posthumously, with the censor's changes; the original text was not restored until the Revolution of 1917.

Rimsky-Korsakov was one of the greatest masters of Russian music. His source of inspiration was Glinka's operatic style; he made use of both the purely Russian idiom and coloristic oriental melodic patterns; such works as his symph. suite *Scheherazade* and *Le Coq d'or* represent Russian orientalism at its best; in the purely Russian style, the opera *Snow Maiden* and the *Russian Easter Overture* are outstanding examples. The influence of Wagner and Liszt in his music was small; only in his opera *The Legend of the Invisible City of Kitezh* are there perceptible echoes from *Parsifal.* In the art of orchestration Rimsky-Korsakov had few equals; his treatment of instruments, in solo passages and in ensemble, was invariably idiomatic. In his treatise on orchestration he selected only passages from his own works to demonstrate the principles of practical and effective application of registers and tone colors. Although an academician in his general esthetics, he experimented boldly with melodic progressions and ingenious harmonies that pointed toward modern usages. He especially favored the major scale with the lowered submediant and the scale of alternating whole tones and semitones (which in Russian reference works came to be termed as "Rimsky-Korsakov's scale"; in the score of his opera-ballet *Mlada* there is an ocarina part tuned in this scale); in *Le Coq d'or* and *Kashchei the Immortal* he applied dissonant harmonies in unusual superpositions; but he set for himself a definite limit in innovation, and severely criticized Richard Strauss, Debussy, and Vincent d'Indy for their modernistic practices.

WORKS: OPERAS: *Pskovityanka* (*The Maid of Pskov;* 1868–72; revised 1891; St. Petersburg, Jan. 13, 1873; last version, St. Petersburg, April 18, 1895); *Maiskaya noch* (*May Night;* St. Petersburg, Jan. 21, 1880); *Snegurotchka* (*Snow Maiden;* St. Petersburg, Feb. 10, 1882); *Mlada* (St. Petersburg, Nov. 1, 1892);

Noch pered Rozhdestvom (*Night before Christmas;* St. Petersburg, Dec. 10, 1895); *Sadko* (Moscow, Jan. 7, 1898; Metropolitan Opera, N.Y., Jan. 29, 1929); *Mozart i Salieri,* on Pushkin's play dealing with Salieri's supposed poisoning of Mozart (Moscow, Dec. 7, 1898); *Boyarynia Vera Sheloga* (Moscow, Dec. 27, 1898; originally written as a prologue to *Pskovityanka;* N.Y., May 9, 1922); *Tsarskaya neviesta* (*The Tsar's Bride;* Moscow, Nov. 3, 1899); *Tsar Saltan* (Moscow, Nov. 3, 1900); *Servilia* (St. Petersburg, Oct. 14, 1902); *Kashchei Bezsmertny* (*Kashchei the Immortal;* Moscow, Dec. 25, 1902); *Pan Voyevoda* (*The Commander;* St. Petersburg, Oct. 16, 1904); *Skazanie o nevidimom grade Kitezhe* (*The Legend of the Invisible City of Kitezh;* St. Petersburg, Feb. 20, 1907); *Zolotoy pietushok* (*The Golden Cockerel;* usually perf. under the French title *Le Coq d'or;* posthumous; Moscow, Oct. 7, 1909; the only opera of Rimsky-Korsakov often produced abroad).

FOR ORCH.: Op. 1, Symph. No. 1, in E minor (originally in E-flat minor; later rewritten and transposed); op. 5, *Sadko,* symph. poem (1867; revised 1869 and 1891); op. 6, *Fantasy on Serbian Themes* (1867; revised 1888); op. 9, Symph. No. 2, *Antar* (1868; revised 1876 and 1897; also as a symph. suite); op. 28, *Overture on Russian Themes* (1866; revised 1880); op. 29, *Conte féerique* (1880); op. 30, Piano Concerto in C-sharp minor (1882–83); op. 31, *Symphoniette* in A minor (on Russian themes; 1879); Op. 32, Symph. No. 3, in C major (1873–74; revised 1885–86); op. 33, *Fantaisie de concert sur des thèmes russes* for Violin and Orch. (1886); op. 34, *Capriccio espagnol* (1887); op. 35, *Scheherazade,* symph. suite (St. Petersburg, Nov. 3, 1888); op. 36, *Grande pâque russe* (*Russian Easter Overture;* 1888); suite from the opera *Tsar Saltan* (includes the famous musical tableau *The Flight of the Bumblebee*); op. 59, *Pan Voyevoda,* suite from the opera (1903); op. 61, *Nad mogiloï* (*At the Grave;* in memory of Belaieff; 1904); op. 62, *Chanson russe* (*Dubinushka;* 1905, with Chorus ad lib.); without opus numbers: *Night on Mount Triglav,* from the opera *Mlada* (1907); suite from the opera *Le Coq d'or* (1907).

CHAMBER MUSIC: Op. 12, String Quartet in F (1875); op. 37, *Serenade* for Cello and Piano (1903); without opus numbers: String Sextet in A (1876); Quintet in B-flat for Flute, Clarinet, Horn, Bassoon, and Piano (1876); first movement of a String Quartet on B-la-f (Belaieff; other movements by Liadov, Borodin, and Glazunov; 1886); String Quartet in G (1897); Trio in C minor for Violin, Cello, and Piano (1897).

VOCAL WORKS, WITH ORCH.: Op. 20, *Stikh ob Alexeye* (*Poem about Alexis*), folk song for Mixed Chorus (1877); op. 21, *Slava* (*Glory*) for Mixed Chorus (1876–80); op. 44, *Svitezyanka,* cantata for Soprano and Tenor Solo and Mixed Chorus (1897); op. 53, *Strekozy* (*Dragonflies*) for Women's Voices (1897); op. 58, *Piesnia o veshchem Olegye* (*Poem of Oleg the Wise*) for Men's Chorus; op. 60, *From Homer* for Women's Voices (1899); op. 49, *Anchar* (*The Upas Tree*) and *Prorok* (*The Prophet*), 2 ariosos for Bass, (1897); choruses a cappella, opp. 13, 14, 16, 18, 19, 23; 77 songs; 5 vocal duets; a Vocal Trio.

PIANO PIECES: Op. 10, 6 *Variations on BACH;* op. 11, 4 pieces; op. 15, 3 pieces; op. 17, 6 fugues.

ARRANGEMENTS AND EDITIONS: He edited a collection of 100 Russian folk songs, op. 24 (1876); harmonized 40 folk songs. After Dargomyzhsky's death, he orchestrated his posthumous opera *Kamennyi gost (The Stone Guest);* also orchestrated Borodin's *Prince Igor;* his greatest task of musical reorganization was the preparation for publication and performance of Mussorgsky's works; he reharmonized the cycle *Songs and Dances of Death* and the symph. picture *Night on Bald Mountain;* orchestrated the opera *Khovanshchina;* revised *Boris Godunov* (in melody and harmony, as well as in orchestration).

WRITINGS: Among his pedagogical works, the book on harmony (St. Petersburg, 1884; numerous subsequent eds. in Russian; in Eng., N.Y., 1930) is widely used in Russian music schools; publ. *Foundations of Orchestration* (2 vols., St. Petersburg, 1913; ed. by Maximilian Steinberg; also available in French and in Eng.); collected articles were publ. in 1911, edited by M. Gnessin. His autobiographical book, *The Chronicle of My Musical Life* (posthumous, 1909; 5th ed. by his son Andrei, supplemented and annotated, 1935), is a valuable document of the most important period of Russian music; it is publ. also in English (N.Y., 1924; new ed., 1942), in French (Paris, 1938), etc. A complete edition of Rimsky-Korsakov's works was begun in 1946; 49 vols. were publ. by 1970.

Rinaldo di Capua, Italian opera composer; b. Capua, c.1710; d. Rome, after 1770. He came from the vicinity of Naples and seems to have been active chiefly in Rome, where Burney knew him in 1770, and where most of his operas were given (others were produced in Florence, Venice, London, and Paris). His career as a dramatic composer probably began in 1737. Thereafter he produced about 30 theatrical works with varying success, among them *Ciro riconosciuto* (Rome, Jan. 19, 1737), *Vologeso re de' Parti* (Rome, 1739), and *La Zingara* (Paris, June 19, 1753; his best work). He also composed *Cantata per la Natività della Beata Vergine* (1747).

Rinck, Johann Christian Heinrich, famous German organist; b. Elgersburg, Feb. 18, 1770; d. Darmstadt, Aug. 7, 1846. He studied under Bach's pupil Kittel in Erfurt (1786–89); was town organist at Giessen (1790) and at Darmstadt (1805); became court organist there in 1813, and chamber musician in 1817. One of the foremost players of the time, he made frequent concert tours. He wrote many organ works.

Rinuccini, Ottavio, great Italian poet and librettist; b. Florence, Jan. 20, 1563; d. there, March 28, 1621. He wrote several librettos for the Florentine creators of opera: the text of the intermezzo *Apollo e il pitone,* set to music by Marenzio in 1589; and subsequently the famous *La favola di Dafne,* set to music by Peri in 1597, a work that is usually regarded as the first true opera. Rinuccini's *Euridice,* with music by Peri, was performed in 1600; another setting, by Caccini, in 1602. He also wrote the libretto of Monteverdi's *Arianna* (1608). These texts were republ. by A. Solerti in vol. II of *Gli albori del melodramma* (Milan, 1905) and by A. Della Corte, *Drammi per musica dal Rinuccini allo Zeno* (Turin, 1958).

Ripa, Alberto da (called **Alberto Mantovano**), Italian lutenist; b. Mantua, c.1480; d. Paris, 1551. Little is known about his life, except that he was in the service of Francis I of France from 1529. His *Tablature de luth* was brought out posthumously by his pupil Guillaume Morlaye (6 books, Paris, 1553–62); individual pieces by him are found in the publications of Phalèse (1546 and 1574) and also in Francesco da Forli's *Intavolatura di liuto* (1536); J.-M. Vaccaro edited *Alberto da Rippe: Œuvres,* in *Le Chœur des muses, Corpus des luthistes français* (1972–75).

Risler, Edouard, French pianist; b. Baden-Baden (of a German mother and Alsatian father), Feb. 23, 1873; d. Paris, July 22, 1929. He studied piano with Diémer at the Paris Cons. and continued his studies with Klindworth, Stavenhagen, and Eugène d'Albert in Germany. In 1923 he was appointed prof. of the Paris Cons. He gave concert recitals all over Europe and acquired a high reputation as a fine musician as well as a virtuoso pianist; he made a specialty of presenting cycles of one composer's works; he played Beethoven's 32 sonatas, Chopin's complete piano works, and both books of Bach's *Well-tempered Clavier.*

Rist, Johann, German poet and composer; b. Ottensen, near Hamburg, March 8, 1607; d. Wedel-on-Elbe, Aug. 31, 1667. He studied theology at the univs. of Hamburg and Bremen; later became a pastor in Mecklenburg and Wedel. In 1644 he was made poet laureate by the Emperor, and in 1653 was elevated to the rank of nobleman. He organized in Hamburg a Liederschule, for which he secured the cooperation of many important composers of the day, among them Schiedemann and Thomas Selle. He has been described as the "organizer of the German Parnassus," and indeed his role in the development of a purely national type of secular song, of German folk inspiration, was historically significant. He also wrote a number of sacred songs—*O Ewigkeit, du Donnerwort; O Traurigkeit; O Herzeleid; Werde munter, mein Gemüte;* etc.—which are still sung in Lutheran churches in Germany. He compiled valuable collections of German sacred songs; a modern edition was brought out by E. Mannack, *J. Rist: Sämtliche Werke* (Berlin, 1967—).

Ristenpart, Karl, German conductor; b. Kiel, Jan. 26, 1900; d. Lisbon, Dec. 24, 1967. He studied music in Berlin and Vienna. In 1932 he became conductor of the Berlin Chamber Orch.; also led concerts with the Radio Orch. in Berlin. In 1946 he was named conductor of the Chamber Orch. of RIAS (Radio in the American Sector of Berlin). In 1953 he became conductor of the Chamber Orch. of the Saar, a noted ensemble of the Saarland Radio in Saarbrücken; made many tours and recordings with this group.

Ristori, Giovanni Alberto, Italian composer; b. Bologna, 1692; d. Dresden, Feb. 7, 1753. He received his education from his father, a violinist in an Italian opera company; with him he went to Dresden (1715) and obtained the post of director of the Polish chapel there; then was appointed chamber organist to the court of Saxony (1733), church composer (1746), and assistant conductor (1750). He wrote a number of operas for the Italian Opera in Dresden. His *Calandro,* staged at Pillnitz, near Dresden, on Sept. 2, 1726, was one of the earliest Italian comic operas produced in Germany, and so possesses historical significance beyond its intrinsic worth; other operas produced in Dresden and in court theaters near Dresden were *Cleonice* (Aug. 15, 1718); *Un pazzo ne fa cento, ovvero Don Chisciotte* (Feb. 2, 1727); *Arianna* (Aug. 7, 1736); *Le Fate* (Aug. 10, 1736); etc. He also wrote 3 oratorios, 16 cantatas, 11 masses; some instrumental music; many of his MSS were destroyed during the siege of Dresden (1760).

Ritter, Frédéric Louis, German-American music historian and choral conductor; b. Strasbourg, June 22, 1826; d. Antwerp, July 4, 1891. He was of Spanish extraction, his original family name being Caballero, which was translated into German as Ritter ("knight"). He studied in Strasbourg with Schletterer and in Paris with J.G. Kastner. In 1856 he went to Cincinnati, where he organized the Phil. Orch., but left for N.Y. in 1861; was active mainly as a choral conductor; in 1867 became a prof. of music at Vassar College. He publ. several manuals and music histories: *History of Music* (2 vols., Boston, 1870, 1874; 2nd ed., 1880); *Music in England* (N.Y., 1883); *Music in America* (N.Y., 1883; 3rd ed., 1893); *Music in Its Relation to Intellectual Life* (N.Y., 1891); etc. His wife, **Fanny Raymond Ritter** (b. Philadelphia, 1840; d. Poughkeepsie, N.Y., Oct. 26, 1890), was the author of *Woman as a Musician: An Art-Historical Study* (1876); *Some Famous Songs* (1878); etc.

Ritter, Hermann, German violist, inventor of the viola alta; b. Wismar, Sept. 16, 1849; d. Würzburg, Jan. 22, 1926. He studied at the Hochschule für Musik in Berlin; attended courses at the Univ. of Heidelberg; turning his attention to musical instruments, he began a series of experiments for the purpose of improving the muffled tone of the ordinary viola; profiting by some practical hints in A. Bagatella's book *Regole per la costruzione di violini* (Padua, 1786), he constructed a slightly larger model possessed of better resonance and a more brilliant tone. Exhibiting this new "viola alta" in 1876, he attracted the attention of Wagner, who invited his cooperation for the Bayreuth Festival; after that engagement he made successful tours of all Europe as a viola virtuoso; from 1879, he was a prof. of viola and music history at the Musikschule in Würzburg; in 1905 he founded the "Ritterquartett" (violin, W. Schulze-Prisca; viola alta, Ritter; viola tenore, E. Cahnbley; viola bassa, H. Knöchel).

Ritter, Peter, German composer; b. Mannheim, July 2, 1763; d. there, Aug. 1, 1846. He studied violin and cello with his father; completed his theoretical studies under Abbé Vogler. He entered the Mannheim court orch. as a cellist in 1783; later became its concertmaster and, in 1803, conductor. He brought out in Mannheim his first opera, *Der Eremit auf Formentera* (Dec. 14, 1788; text by the celebrated poet A. von Kotzebue), which attained considerable vogue in Germany; some 20 more operas and singspiels followed, but were not successful. In 1787 he married the famous actress Katharina Baumann (to whom Schiller had proposed); in 1790 both were employed at the Hoftheater; his wife retired on a pension in 1819, and Ritter himself in 1823. Besides his operas, he wrote a fine chorale, *Grosser Gott dich loben wir* (1792); an oratorio, *Das verlorene Paradies;* and much chamber music (selections publ. by Riemann in vol. 28 [16], of Denkmäler der Tonkunst in Bayern). Twenty-four autograph scores, including 2 symphs., several concertos, etc., are in the Library of Congress in Washington, D.C.

Rivé-King, Julie, American pianist; b. Cincinnati, Oct. 30, 1854; d. Indianapolis, July 24, 1937. She received her primary instruction from her mother; then studied in N.Y. with William Mason and in Leipzig with Reinecke; also was for a time a pupil of Liszt. She played Liszt's Piano Concerto No. 1 at her American debut, with the N.Y. Phil. (April 24, 1875); this was the beginning of an active career; she gave about 4,000 concerts in the U.S., retiring only a year before her death. In 1876 she married Frank King of Milwaukee. From 1905 till 1936 she was a piano instructor at the Bush Cons. in Chicago. She wrote some attractive piano pieces (*Impromptu, Polonaise héroïque, Bubbling Spring,* etc.). See A.R. Coolidge in *Notable American Women* (N.Y., 1971).

Rivier, Jean, French composer; b. Villemomble, July 21, 1896. He was in the French army in World War I, and did not begin his musical studies until 1918, when he entered the Paris Cons. and studied with Caussade; participated in various modern music societies in Paris; formed a style of composition that combined the elements of French Classicism and Impressionism. He was also esteemed as a teacher; was on the faculty of the Paris Cons. from 1947 to 1966.
  WORKS: Opera, *Vénitienne* (Paris, July 8, 1937); 7 symphs.: No. 1 (Paris, Jan. 29, 1933); No. 2 for Strings (1937); No. 3 (1937; Paris, Nov. 25, 1940); No. 4 (Paris, 1947); No. 5 (Strasbourg, June 24, 1951); No. 6, *Les Présages* (Paris, Dec. 11, 1958); No. 7, *Les Contrastes* (Paris, Jan. 9, 1962); Piano Concerto (1941); Violin Concerto (1942); *3 pastorales* (Paris, Feb. 7, 1929); *Adagio* for String Orch. (Paris, March 1, 1931); *Ouverture pour une opérette imaginaire* (Paris, Dec. 13, 1931); Concertino for Viola and Orch. (Paris, Feb. 15, 1936); *Jeanne d'Arc à Domrémy,* symph. tableau (Paris, Jan. 31, 1937); *Ballade des amants désespérés* for Orch. (1945); *Rapsodie provençale* (Aix-en-Provence, July 22, 1949); *Résonances* (1965); *Brillances* for 7 Woodwind Instruments (1971); *Triade* for String Orch. (1967); *Cli-*

mats for Celesta, Vibraphone, Xylophone, Piano, and Strings (1968); Clarinet Concerto (1960); Bassoon Concerto (1965); Oboe Concerto (1966); Trumpet Concerto (1972); Duo for Flute and Clarinet (1968); 2 string quartets; violin pieces; piano pieces; song cycles; choruses.

Robertson, Leroy, American composer; b. Fountain Green, Utah, Dec. 21, 1896; d. Salt Lake City, July 25, 1971. He studied in Provo; then in Boston with Chadwick and Converse at the New England Cons.; subsequently went to Europe, where he took courses with Ernest Bloch in Switzerland and with Hugo Leichtentritt in Berlin. Returning to America, he became an instructor of music at Brigham Young Univ. at Provo; in 1948, was appointed head of the music dept. of the Univ. of Utah (retiring in 1963). In 1947 his symph. work *Trilogy* received the first prize of $25,000 in a contest sponsored by Henry H. Reichhold of Detroit; it was performed by the Detroit Symph. Orch. on Dec. 11, 1947, but despite the attendant publicity, the work was not successful, and there were few subsequent performances. Other works: *The Book of Mormon*, oratorio (Salt Lake City, Feb. 18, 1953); *Prelude, Scherzo, Ricercare* for Orch. (1940); *Rhapsody* for Piano and Orch. (1944); *Punch and Judy Overture* (1945); Violin Concerto (1948); Piano Concerto (Salt Lake City, Nov. 30, 1966); Piano Quintet (1933); String Quartet (1940; N.Y. Music Critics Circle Award, 1944); *American Serenade* for String Quartet (1944); other chamber music; piano pieces; songs.

Robeson, Paul, great black American bass; b. Princeton, N.J., April 9, 1898; d. Philadelphia, Jan. 23, 1976. He first studied law (B.A., 1919, Rutgers Univ.; LL.B, 1923, Columbia Univ.); when his talent for singing and acting was discovered, he appeared in plays in the U.S. and England; acted the part of Emperor Jones in Eugene O'Neill's play and of Porgy in the Negro folk play by Du Bose and Dorothy Heyward. In 1925 he gave his first Negro spiritual recital in N.Y.; then toured in Europe. In 1930 he appeared in the title role of Shakespeare's *Othello* in London. Returning to the U.S., he continued to give recitals, but his radical political beliefs interfered with the success of his career. In 1952 he was awarded the International Stalin Peace Prize ($25,000). During the summer of 1958 he made an extensive European tour.

Rochberg, George, significant American composer; b. Paterson, N.J., July 5, 1918. He studied theory and composition with George Szell in N.Y. (1939–41); served in the U.S. military forces during World War II; after the war, enrolled in composition classes at the Curtis Inst. with Rosario Scalero and Gian Carlo Menotti (B. Mus., 1947). In 1950 he was in Rome on a Fulbright fellowship; in 1951 was appointed music editor for the Theodore Presser Co.; also taught classes at the Curtis Inst.; in 1960 he joined the music faculty of the Univ. of Pa. In his style he pursues the ideal of tonal order and logically justifiable musical structures; the most profound

influence he experienced was that of Schoenberg and Anton von Webern; many of his works follow the organization in 12 different notes; at the same time he does not deny himself the treasures of the sanctified past, and even resorts to overt quotations in his works of recognizable fragments from music by composers as mutually unrelated as Schütz, Bach, Mahler, and Ives, treated by analogy with the "objets trouvés" in modern painting and sculpture.
WORKS: *Capriccio* for 2 Pianos (1949); Symph. No. 1 (Philadelphia, March 28, 1958); *Night Music* (1952; won the George Gershwin Memorial Award); *Cantio sacra* for Chamber Orch. (1953); *Fantasia* for Violin and Piano (1955); *Sinfonia fantasia* (1956); *Waltz Serenade* for Orch. (Cincinnati, Feb. 14, 1958); *Cheltenham Concerto* (1958); Symph. No. 2 (Cleveland, Feb. 26, 1959); *Time-Span*, symph. movement (St. Louis, Oct. 22, 1960); Symph. No. 3 for Solo Voices, Chamber Chorus, Double Chorus, and Orch. (using quotations from works by Schütz, Bach, Mahler, and Ives; N.Y., Nov. 24, 1970); Violin Concerto (Pittsburgh, April 4, 1975); Symph. No. 4 (Seattle, Nov. 15, 1976); Oboe Concerto (N.Y., Dec. 13, 1984); *Dialogues* for Clarinet and Piano (1958); String Quartet No. 1 (1952); String Quartet No. 2, with Soprano (1961); String Quartet No. 3 (1972); *Concord Quartets* (Nos. 4, 5, and 6; Philadelphia, Jan. 20, 1979); *Black Sounds* for Wind Instruments and Percussion (1965); *Contra mortem et tempus* for Violin, Flute, Clarinet, and Piano; containing phrases from works by Boulez, Varèse, and Ives (1965); *Tableaux* for Soprano and 11 Players (1968); Piano Quintet (1975); opera, *The Confidence Man*, after Melville's novel (Santa Fe, July 31, 1982); a number of piano pieces and songs. He publ. a theoretical essay, *The Hexachord and Its Relation to the 12-Tone Row* (Bryn Mawr, 1955), and several magazine articles dealing with 12-tone techniques.

Rockstro (real name, **Rackstraw**), **William Smyth,** English music scholar; b. North Cheam, Surrey, Jan. 5, 1823; d. London, July 2, 1895. He studied at the Leipzig Cons. under Mendelssohn, Plaidy, and Hauptmann. Returning to London, he taught piano and singing; wrote a popular ballad, *Queen and Huntress;* publ. piano arrangements of numerous operas; devoted himself to a close study of ecclesiastical music, and became an acknowledged authority on plainchant; became a Roman Catholic in 1876.

Rode, (Jacques-) Pierre (Joseph), French violinist; b. Bordeaux, Feb. 16, 1774; d. Château-Bourbon, near Damazan, Nov. 25, 1830. He was a pupil of Fauvel; from 1787, of Viotti at Paris; made his debut in 1790 in a concerto by Viotti, at the Théâtre Feydeau; after tours in the Netherlands and Germany and a short visit to London, he was appointed prof. of violin at the newly opened Paris Cons. (1795). During a visit to Spain in 1799 he met Boccherini, who wrote concertos for him. In 1800 he was court violinist to Napoleon; from 1803 to 1808 was in Russia with Boieldieu; became first violinist to the court of Alexander I; then spent 3 years in Paris, after which he toured Germany and Austria (at Vienna Beethoven wrote for him the G major Sonata, op. 96, which Rode perf. with Archduke Rudolph in Vienna, on Dec. 29, 1812); lived for a time in Berlin, where he married in 1814; then retired and lived in Bordeaux.

Rodeheaver, Homer Alvan, American composer of hymn tunes who described himself as a "musical missionary"; b. Union Furnace, Ohio, Oct. 4, 1880; d. New York, Dec. 18, 1955. Taken to Jellicoe, Tenn., as a child, he grew up helping in his father's lumber business and learning to play the trombone from a local musician. During the Spanish-American War he enlisted as trombonist in the 4th Tennessee Regimental Band. After the war he became interested in gospel songs and evangelism; accompanied the evangelist Billy Sunday on his tours (1910–30), leading the singing with his trombone. He composed the music for many gospel songs, of which the best known is *Then Jesus Came.* His theme song was *Brighten the Corner,* composed by Charles H. Gabriel. Rodeheaver was the founder of the Summer School of Sacred Music at Winona Lake, Ind., and was connected with the Rodeheaver-Hall-Mack Music Publishing Co. there. Besides a dozen or so collections of hymn poems and homilies, he publ. *Song Stories of the Sawdust Trail* (N.Y., 1917), *20 Years with Billy Sunday* (Nashville, 1936), and *Letter from a Missionary in Africa* (Chicago, 1936). With his predecessor Ira D. Sankey, he was a leading figure in American musical evangelism.

Rodgers, Richard, celebrated American composer of popular music; b. Hammels Station, Long Island, N.Y., June 28, 1902; d. New York, Dec. 30, 1979. He studied at Columbia Univ. (1919–21) and at the Inst. of Musical Art in N.Y. (1921–23). He collaborated for 18 years with the lyricist Lorenz Hart in a series of inspired and highly popular musical comedies: *The Girl Friend* (1926); *A Connecticut Yankee* (1927); *On Your Toes* (1936); *Babes in Arms* (1937); *I Married an Angel* (1938); *The Boys from Syracuse* (1942). *The Rodgers and Hart Song Book* (N.Y., 1951) contains their most famous songs. After Hart's death in 1943 Rodgers became associated with Oscar Hammerstein II. Together they wrote the greatly acclaimed musical *Oklahoma!* (1943; Pulitzer Prize, 1944), followed by a number of no less successful productions: *Carousel* (1945); *Allegro* (1947); *South Pacific* (1948; Pulitzer Prize, 1950); *The King and I* (1951); *Me and Juliet* (1953); *Pipe Dream* (1955); *The Flower Drum Song* (1958); *The Sound of Music* (1959). After Hammerstein's death in 1960, Rodgers wrote his own lyrics for his next musical, *No Strings* (1962); then followed *Do I Hear a Waltz* (1965) to the lyrics of Stephen Sondheim. Rodgers wrote the music for the television shows *Victory at Sea* (1952) and *Winston Churchill: The Valiant Years* (1960). Individual songs from his musical comedies have become perennial favorites: *Some Enchanted Evening, Getting to Know You, Do-Re-Mi,* etc., etc., etc.

Rodio, Rocco, contrapuntist of the early Neapolitan school; b. Bari, Apulia, c.1530; d. c.1615. He publ. *Regole per far contrapunto solo e accompagnato nel canto fermo* (first ed., 1600; 3rd ed., 1626); also a collection (Naples, 1580) of 9 masses; the last, *Missa de Beata Virgine* (a 5) is remarkable, because it can also be sung by 4 or 3 voices, by omitting the *quintus,* the *quintus* and *superius* (soprano), or the *quintus* and *bassus.*

Rodolphe, Jean Joseph, French composer; b. Strasbourg, Oct. 14, 1730; d. Paris, Aug. 18, 1812. He studied the French horn with his father; then the violin with Leclair (*l'aîné*) in Paris; composition with Traetta in Parma, and with Jommelli in Stuttgart; wrote ballet music for Jommelli's productions there. In 1764 he was in Paris once more; brought out his first opera, *Le Mariage par capitulation* (Comédie-Italienne, Dec. 3, 1764); another opera, *L'Aveugle de Palmyre* (Comédie-Italienne, March 5, 1767), obtained considerable success. The famous balletmaster Noverre produced several of Rodolphe's ballets at the Paris Opéra. Mozart met Rodolphe in Paris in 1778, and spoke of him highly. Three of Rodolphe's ballets are printed in the *Denkmäler deutscher Tonkunst,* 43/44. From 1784 to 1802 Rodolphe taught composition and solfège at the Paris Cons.; publ. the manuals *Solfèges* and *Théorie d'accompagnement.*

Rodrigo, Joaquín, Spanish composer; b. Sagunto, Valencia, Nov. 22, 1901. He lost his sight as a child; revealed an innate talent for music and was sent to Paris, where he studied with Paul Dukas; in 1939 he returned to Spain. His music is profoundly imbued with Spanish melorhythms; his *Concierto de Aranjuez* for Guitar and Orch. (Barcelona, Nov. 9, 1940) became famous. He further composed *Juglares* for Orch. (1923); *Concierto heroico* for Piano and Orch. (Lisbon, April 5, 1943); *Concierto de estio* for Violin and Orch. (Lisbon, April 11, 1944); *Concierto in modo galante* for Cello and Orch. (Madrid, Nov. 4, 1949); Concerto for Harp and Orch. (1954); *Fantasia para un gentilhombre* for Guitar and Orch. (1955); *Sones en la Giralda* for Harp and Orch. (1963); *Concierto Andaluz* for 4 Guitars (1967); *Concierto-madrigal* for 2 Guitars and Orch. (1968); *Sonata Pimpante* for Violin and Piano (1966); *Sonata a la española* for Guitar (1969); *Pájaros de primavera* for Guitar (1972); choruses; piano pieces.

Rodrigo de Ledesma, Mariano, Spanish composer; b. Zaragoza, Dec. 14, 1779; d. Madrid, March 28, 1848. He served as a chorister at the Cathedral of Zaragoza; was organist and chorus master at Vinaroz (1799–1802); then tenor in Madrid; in 1807 he was appointed conductor of the Madrid opera theater, but the French invasion forced him to flee, and he took refuge in Seville. In 1812 he was in Cádiz; there he composed an anti-Bonaparte hymn, *En tan infausto día,* while Joseph Bonaparte was king of Spain; fled to England, where he established himself as a singing teacher in London. With the restoration of legitimate monarchy in Spain, he returned there, and received a court appointment; publ. *40 ejercicios de vocalización* (Madrid, 1820; Paris, 1827; also in Eng.). He was again in England from 1823 to 1831; heard Weber conduct his operas in London, and was profoundly impressed; thenceforth he tried to emulate Weber, writing music in a Romantic manner. Back in Spain once more, he became maestro to Queen María Cristina. He wrote chiefly church music: 3 Solemn Masses, 9 Lamentations, a Stabat Mater; also some secular songs and instrumental pieces. Eslava reprinted 5 motets for 4 Voices and Orch. by Rodrigo in the *Lira sacro-hispana.*

Rodzinski, Artur, eminent Polish conductor; b. Spalato, Dalmatia, Jan. 1, 1892; d. Boston, Nov. 27, 1958. He studied jurisprudence at the Univ. of Vienna; at the same time took piano lessons with Emil Sauer, composition with Schreker, and conducting with Schalk. He made his conducting debut in Lwow in 1921; subsequently conducted Polish operas in Warsaw. In 1926 he was appointed assistant conductor to Leopold Stokowski with the Philadelphia Orch.; in 1929 he was appointed permanent conductor of the Los Angeles Phil.; after 4 seasons there he was engaged as conductor of the Cleveland Orch., where he introduced the novel custom of presenting operas in concert form; on Jan. 31, 1935, he conducted the American premiere of Shostakovich's controversial opera *Lady Macbeth of the District of Mtzensk.* In 1943 he received his most prestigious appointment as conductor and music director of the N.Y. Phil., but his independent character and temperamental ways of dealing with the management forced him to resign amid raging controversy in the middle of his 4th season (Feb. 3, 1947); almost immediately he was engaged as conductor and music director of the Chicago Symph. Orch., but there, too, a conflict rapidly developed, and the management announced after a few months of the engagement that his contract would not be renewed, stating as a reason that his operatic ventures using the orch. were too costly. After these distressing American experiences Rodzinski conducted mainly in Europe; in the autumn of 1958 he received an invitation to conduct at the Lyric Opera in Chicago, but a heart ailment forced him to cancel his plans, and he died in a Boston hospital.

Roesgen-Champion, Marguerite, Swiss harpsichord player and composer; b. Geneva, Jan. 25, 1894; d. Paris, June 30, 1976. She studied composition with Ernest Bloch and Jaques-Dalcroze at the Cons. of Geneva, but devoted herself mainly to harpsichord playing, giving numerous recitals in Europe. Her own works are couched in the neo-Romantic vein; she wrote *Faunesques* for Orch. (Paris, 1929); *Concerto moderne* for Harpsichord and Orch. (Paris, Nov. 15, 1931, composer soloist); symph. suite, *Aquarelles* (Paris, Nov. 26, 1933); Harp Concerto (Paris, March 28, 1954); 5 concertos for Harpsichord and Orch. (1931–59); *Concerto romantique* for Piano and Orch. (1961); a number of pieces for flute in combination with the harpsichord and other instru-

ments; a curious piece for Piano, 4-hands, entitled *Spoutnik* (1971).

Rogatis, Pasqual de. See **De Rogatis, Pascual.**

Rogé, Pascal, Franch pianist; b. Paris, April 6, 1951. He studied at the Paris Cons. In 1971 he won first prize in the Long-Thibaud Competition in Paris; then gave concerts throughout France. He acquired a fine reputation playing in programs of French music.

Rogel, José, Spanish composer of light opera; b. Orihuela, Alicante, Dec. 24, 1829; d. Cartagena, Feb. 25, 1901. At a very early age he was taught music by the organist J. Cascales, and at 10 composed a Mass, which he conducted himself. After he finished his law studies in Valencia, he studied counterpoint with Pascual Pérez; subsequently conducted at various theaters in Madrid, and in 1854 began his unusually successful career as composer of zarzuelas, of which he wrote about 75 (some in collaboration). Among the best are *El Joven Telémaco, Las Amazones del Tormes, El Rey Midas, Los Infiernos de Madrid, Genoveva de Brabante, Pablo y Virginia.*

Roger, Gustave-Hippolyte, famous French tenor; b. La Chapelle St.-Denis, near Paris, Dec. 17, 1815; d. Paris, Sept. 12, 1879. He was a pupil of Morin at the Paris Cons.; made his debut at the Opéra-Comique in 1838; then at the Paris Opéra, where he created the role of the Prophète in Meyerbeer's opera (1849); later toured in Germany. While hunting in the fall of 1859, the accidental discharge of his gun injured his right arm so severely that it had to be amputated. An artificial arm proved ineffective, and he was obliged to retire from the stage in 1861. From 1868 until his death he was a prof. of singing at the Cons. He publ. his memoirs as *Le Carnet d'un Ténor* (Paris, 1880).

Roger, Victor, French composer of operettas; b. Montpellier, July 21, 1854; d. Paris, Dec. 2, 1903. He studied at the Ecole Niedermeyer; wrote light music; composed some 30 operettas, of which the following were brought out in Paris with considerable success: *Joséphine vendue par ses sœurs* (March 20, 1886); *Oscarine* (Oct. 15, 1888); *Le Fétiche* (March 13, 1890); *Samsonnet* (Nov. 26, 1890); *Miss Nicol-Nick* (Jan. 23, 1895); *Le Voyage de Corbillon* (Jan. 30, 1896); *Sa Majesté l'Amour* (Dec. 23, 1896); *Les Fêtards* (Oct. 28, 1897); *L'Auberge du Tohu-Bohu* (Feb. 10, 1897); *L'Agence Crook & Co.* (Jan. 22, 1898); *La Petite Tâche* (March 26, 1898); *Poule blanche* (Jan. 13, 1899); *Le Jockey malgré lui* (Dec. 4, 1902). After his death 3 completely finished scores were found: *La Fille de Fra Diavolo, La Princesse de Babylone,* and *Adélaïde.*

Roger-Ducasse, Jean-Jules Aimable, French composer; b. Bordeaux, April 18, 1873; d. Le-Taillan-Médoc, near Bordeaux, July 19, 1954. He studied at the Paris Cons. with Fauré (composition), Pessard (harmony), Gédalge (counterpoint), and de Bériot. In 1902 he won the 2nd Prix de Rome for the cantata *Alcyone;* in 1909 was appointed inspector of singing in the Paris schools; subsequently was a prof. of ensemble at the Paris Cons.; from 1935 to 1945 taught composition there; then retired to Bordeaux. His first work to be played in public was a *Petite suite* for Orch. (Paris, March 5, 1898). He adopted a pleasing style of Impressionism; his symph. pieces enjoyed considerable success, without setting a mark for originality.

Rogers, Bernard, American composer; b. New York, Feb. 4, 1893; d. Rochester, N.Y., May 24, 1968. He studied architecture before devoting himself to music. His first teacher was Arthur Farwell; he subsequently studied with Ernest Bloch in Cleveland. His symph. composition *To the Fallen* was performed by the N.Y. Phil. on Nov. 13, 1919; on the strength of it, he won a Pulitzer Traveling Scholarship and went to Europe for further study; in 1927 he received a Guggenheim fellowship; took courses with Nadia Boulanger in Paris and Frank Bridge in London. When he returned from Europe in 1929, he was engaged as an instructor at the Eastman School of Music in Rochester, N.Y.; remained there until 1967, teaching orchestration and composition.

Rogers, Clara Kathleen (née **Barnett**), English soprano; b. Cheltenham, Jan. 14, 1844; d. Boston, March 8, 1931. She was the daughter of the composer **John Barnett;** studied at the Leipzig Cons. with Moscheles and Plaidy (piano), Papperitz and Richter (theory), David and Rietz (ensemble playing); singing with Goetz in Berlin and with Sangiovanni in Milan. She made her debut in Turin (1863) as Isabella in *Robert le Diable* (stage name, **"Clara Doria"**); came to America in 1871 with the Parepa-Rosa Co.; debut, N.Y., in *Bohemian Girl* (Oct. 4, 1871); later settled in Boston as a teacher; from 1902 was a prof. of singing at the New England Cons.; married a Boston lawyer, Henry M. Rogers, in 1878. She publ. *The Philosophy of Singing* (1893); *Dreaming True* (1899); *My Voice and I* (1910); *English Diction in Song and Speech* (1912); *The Voice in Speech* (1915); *Memories of a Musical Career* (Boston, 1919) and its sequel, *The Story of Two Lives* (Norwood, Mass., 1932); songs.

Roguski, Gustav, Polish composer and pedagogue; b. Warsaw, May 12, 1839; d. there, April 5, 1921. He studied in Germany with Kiel; then went to Paris, where he became a pupil of Berlioz. Returning to Warsaw in 1873, he was appointed prof. at the Cons. He wrote a Symph., 2 string quartets, a Quintet for Wind Instruments and Piano, many piano pieces, choruses, and songs; publ. a manual of harmony in Polish (with L. Zelenski). He was greatly esteemed as a teacher of composition; Paderewski was his pupil.

Rokseth, Yvonne (née **Rihouët**), French musicologist and organist; b. Maisons-Laffitte, near Paris, July 17, 1890; d. Strasbourg, Aug. 23, 1948. She stud-

ied at the Paris Cons.; with d'Indy and Roussel at the Schola Cantorum; and with Pirro at the Sorbonne; received her doctorat ès lettres with the dissertation *La Musique d'orgue au XVe siècle et au début du XVIe* (Paris, 1930); held various positions as organist in Paris (1920–25); was later librarian at the Paris Cons. and a prof. of musicology at the Univ. of Strasbourg (from 1937); publ. a biography of Grieg (Paris, 1933); edited *Deux livres d'orgue parus chez P. Attaingnant en 1531,* in the series Publications de la Société Française de Musicologie (1925); *Polyphonies du XIIIe siècle: Le Manuscrit Montpellier H 196* (facsimile, transcription, and commentary, 4 vols., 1935–39); also organ works of Marc Antonio da Bologna of 1523; etc.; co-editor of *Trois Chansonniers français du XVe siècle* (Paris, 1927).

Roland-Manuel, Alexis (real name, **Roland Alexis Manuel Lévy**), French composer and writer; b. Paris, March 22, 1891; d. there, Nov. 1, 1966. He was a pupil of Albert Roussel and Vincent d'Indy; also studied privately with Ravel. In 1947 he became a prof. at the Paris Cons. In his compositions he adopted the French neo-Classical style, close to Roussel's manner; however, it is not as a composer but as a perspicacious critic that he became chiefly known. He publ. 3 books on Ravel: *Maurice Ravel et son œuvre* (1914), *Maurice Ravel et son œuvre dramatique* (1928), *Maurice Ravel* (1938; in Eng., London, 1947); also monographs on Honegger (1925) and Manuel de Falla (1930).

Rolandi, Gianna, gifted American soprano; b. New York, Aug. 16, 1952. Her first contact with opera came through her mother, herself a singer, and by the age of 15 she had already become acquainted with much of the operatic repertoire. She then enrolled at the Curtis Inst. of Music in Philadelphia and, while still a student, was awarded a contract to sing at the N.Y. City Opera, with which she made an impressive debut in 1975. On Dec. 26, 1979, she sang with the Metropolitan Opera in N.Y. as Sophie in *Der Rosenkavalier.* In 1982 she sang the title role in a televised production of *Lucia di Lammermoor* with the N.Y. City Opera, receiving flattering notices from the press.

Roldán, Amadeo, Cuban violinist and composer; b. Paris (of Cuban parents), July 12, 1900; d. Havana, March 2, 1939. He studied violin at the Madrid Cons. with Fernández Bordas, graduating in 1916; won the Sarasate Violin Prize; subsequently studied composition with Conrado del Campo in Madrid and with Pedro Sanjuán. In 1921 he settled in Havana; in 1924, became concertmaster of the Orquesta Filarmónica there; in 1925, assistant conductor; in 1932, conductor. In his works he employed with signal success the melorhythms of Afro-Cuban popular music; as a mulatto, he had an innate understanding of these elements.
WORKS: *La Rebambaramba,* a ballet, employing a number of Cuban percussion instruments in the score; a suite from this ballet (Havana, Aug. 12, 1928); *Obertura sobre témas cubanos* (Havana, Nov.

29, 1925); *El Milagro de Anaquillé* (Havana, Sept. 22, 1929); *Danza negra* for Voice and 7 Instruments (1929); *Motivos de son* for Voice and 9 Instruments (1930); 3 *Toques* for Chamber Orch. (1931); 6 *Rítmicas*: Nos. 1–4 for Piano and Wind Quintet, Nos. 5 and 6 for Percussion Ensemble.

Rolla, Alessandro, Italian violinist, Paganini's teacher; b. Pavia, April 6, 1757; d. Milan, Sept. 15, 1841. He was a pupil of Renzi and Conti; from 1782 till 1802 he was concertmaster of the ducal orch. in Parma; Paganini studied with him there. He served as first violinist and director of the orch. at La Scala in Milan from 1803 to 1833; in 1805 was appointed violinist to the French Viceroy Eugène Beauharnais, in Milan; he was a prof. at the Cons. of Milan from its foundation in 1808 until 1835.

Rolland, Romain, famous French author and musicologist; b. Clamecy, Nièvre, Jan. 29, 1866; d. Vézelay, Yonne, Dec. 30, 1944. He was educated at the Ecole de Rome; received his doctorat ès lettres from the Univ. of Paris in Sorbonne (1895) with 2 theses, *Cur ars picturae apud Italos XVI saeculi deciderit* and the very valuable *Les Origines du théâtre lyrique moderne* (*Histoire de l'opéra en Europe avant Lully et Scarlatti;* 4th ed., 1936); the latter was awarded the Prix Kastner-Bourgault by the Academy in 1896, and at the same time won him the professorship in the history of music at the Ecole Normale. In 1900 he organized the first international congress for the history of music in Paris, and read a paper on *Les Musiciens italiens en France sous Mazarin et "l'Orfeo" de Luigi Rossi* (publ. 1901); with J. Combarieu he edited the transactions and the papers read as *Documents, mémoires et vœux* (1901). In Oct. 1901 he founded, with J. Combarieu (editor), P. Aubry, M. Emmanuel, L. Laloy, and himself as principal contributors, the fortnightly *Revue d'Histoire et Critique Musicales.* In 1903 the Univ. of Paris commissioned him to organize the music section of the newly founded Ecole des Hautes Etudes Sociales, of which he was the first president, and where he lectured on the history of music; resigned in 1909, devoting his entire time to literary work. From 1913 he resided in Switzerland, but in 1938 returned to France and took up his residence at Vézelay.

Rolland's writings exhibit sound scholarship, broad sympathy, keen analytical power, well-balanced judgment, and intimate acquaintance with the musical milieu of his time. The book by which he is most widely known is *Jean-Christophe,* a musical novel remarkable for its blending of historical accuracy, psychological and esthetic speculation, subtle psychological analysis, and romantic interest; for it he received the Nobel Prize (1915). The first vol. was publ. in 1905, the last (10th) in 1912 (Eng. trans., N.Y., 1910–13). Rolland's other works include *Paris als Musikstadt* (1904; in Strauss's series Die Musik; rewritten and publ. in French as *Le Renouveau* in *Musiciens d'aujourd'hui*); *Beethoven* (Paris, 1903; 3rd ed., 1927, as *La Vie de Beethoven;* Eng. trans., 1969); *La Vie de Haendel* (Paris,

1906; 2nd ed., 1910; Eng. trans., 1916; revised and enlarged by F. Raugel, 1974); *Voyage musical au pays du passé* (1920; in Eng., 1922); *Beethoven: Les Grandes Époques créatrices* (4 vols., Paris, 1928–45; Eng. trans., 1964); *Goethe et Beethoven* (1930; in Eng., 1931); *Beethoven: Le Chant de la Résurrection* (1937; on the *Missa solemnis* and the last sonatas); essays in various journals he collected and publ. in 2 vols. as *Musiciens d'autrefois* (1908; 6th ed., 1919; in Eng., 1915) and *Musiciens d'aujourd'hui* (1908; 8th ed., 1947; in Eng., 1914); *Essays on Music* (a selection from some of the above books; N.Y., 1948).

Röllig, Carl Leopold, Austrian composer and inventor; b. Hamburg, c.1735; d. Vienna, March 4, 1804. He was a harmonica player; invented the "Orphika" and "Xänorphika" (pianos with bows instead of hammers), and made many tours, in an attempt to popularize them. In 1791 he settled in Vienna. He wrote a comic opera, *Clarisse* (Hamburg, Oct. 10, 1771); publ. the pamphlets *Über die Harmonika* (1787) and *Über die Orphika* (1795).

Rolón, José, Mexican composer; b. Ciudad Gusmán, Jalisco, June 22, 1883; d. Mexico City, Feb. 3, 1945. He studied in Paris with Moszkowski, and later with Nadia Boulanger and Dukas. In Mexico he was active as a teacher. He composed a symph. poem, *Cuauhtémoc* (Mexico City, Jan. 10, 1930); symph. suite, *Zapotlán* (Mexico City, Nov. 4, 1932); Piano Concerto (Mexico City, Sept. 4, 1942); many effective piano pieces.

Roman, Johan Helmich, significant Swedish composer; b. Stockholm, Oct. 26, 1694; d. Haraldsmala, near Kalmar, Nov. 20, 1758. He was of Finnish ethnic origin; began playing the violin as a mere child, and at 16 was already a member of the court orch., where his father, **Johan Roman,** was concertmaster. In 1715 he traveled to England, where he took lessons with Ariosti and Pepusch in London; returned to Stockholm in 1721. In 1727 he was appointed conductor of the court orch.; from 1735 to 1737 he traveled in Europe; in 1740 he was named a member of the Swedish Academy, and in 1745 retired from active work. Roman was the first Swedish composer to write instrumental and choral music that could compare favorably with German and Italian works, and was for that reason called "the father of Swedish music." His style shows the influence of Handel, with whom he became personally acquainted in England.

Romberg, Andreas (Jacob), German violinist and composer; b. Vechta, near Münster, April 27, 1767; d. Gotha, Nov. 10, 1821. He was the son of the clarinetist and music director **Gerhard Heinrich Romberg** (1745–1819); played in public at 7; in 1784 made a concert tour with his cousin **Bernhard Romberg** through the Netherlands and France, remaining in Paris as soloist for the Concert Spirituel during that season. From 1790 to 1793 he played in the Electoral orch. at Bonn with Bernhard; toured in Italy with him; lived many years in Hamburg

(1801–15), and then succeeded Spohr as court Kapellmeister at Gotha.

Romberg, Bernhard, German cellist and composer; b. Dinklage, Nov. 11, 1767; d. Hamburg, Aug. 13, 1841. He was the son of **Bernhard Anton Romberg,** famous bassoonist (1742–1814), who took him to Paris in 1781; he remained there for 2 years; played in the court orch. at Bonn (1790–93); then traveled in Spain; was the constant companion of his cousin **Andreas Romberg;** in 1796 they played at a concert with Beethoven in Vienna. Romberg was appointed prof. of cello playing at the Paris Cons. in 1801, but resigned in 1803. He was then in Hamburg and Berlin; in 1807 toured in Russia; paid a visit to England (1814); then was court Kapellmeister in Berlin (1815–19); was subsequently in Vienna (1822–25) and again in Russia (1825); lived in Paris (1839–40) before retiring to Hamburg.

Romberg, Sigmund, famous operetta composer; b. Nagy Kaniza, Hungary, July 29, 1887; d. New York, Nov. 9, 1951. He studied at the Univ. of Bucharest and in Vienna (with Heuberger); in 1909 came to the U.S. as an engineer, later turning to composition; settled in N.Y. in 1913. He composed over 70 operettas, including *The Midnight Girl* (Feb. 23, 1914; his first success); *The Blue Paradise* (with E. Eysler; N.Y., Aug. 5, 1915); *Maytime* (N.Y., Aug. 16, 1917); *Blossom Time* (on Schubert's melodies; N.Y., Sept. 29, 1921); *The Rose of Stamboul* (March 7, 1922); *The Student Prince* (N.Y., Dec. 2, 1924); *The Desert Song* (N.Y., Nov. 30, 1926); *My Maryland* (N.Y., Sept. 12, 1927); *The New Moon* (Sept. 19, 1928); *Up in Central Park* (N.Y., Jan. 27, 1945).

Romero, Mateo (real name, **Matthieu Rosmarin**), Spanish composer; b. Liège, 1575; d. Madrid, May 10, 1647. He was a soldier and was often called "El Maestro Capitán." After serving with the Spanish army in Flanders, he became cantor of the Chapel Royal in Madrid (1593), and was maestro de capilla in 1598–1634; in 1609 he was ordained a priest. In 1638 he went to Portugal as emissary to the Duke of Braganza (the future Emperor João IV). He enjoyed a reputation as one of the finest composers of both sacred and secular music of his time. Twenty-two works by Romero for 3–4 Voices are included in the *Cancionero de Sablonara* (modern ed. by J. Arcoa, Madrid, 1918); other compositions are found in Diego Pizarro's collection *Libro de tonos humanos* and in Pedrell's *Teatro lírico español,* III (La Coruña, 1896–98); a motet, *Libera me,* was included by Eslava in his collection *Lira sacro-hispana.*

Ronald, Sir Landon (real name, **L.R. Russell**), English conductor; b. London, June 7, 1873; d. there, Aug. 14, 1938. He was a son of the composer **Henry Russell, Sr.** and brother of the impresario **Henry Russell, Jr.** He entered the Royal College of Music, where he studied composition with Sir Charles Parry and also attended the classes of Sir Charles Stanford and Sir Walter Parratt. He first embarked on a concert career as a pianist, but soon turned to conducting light opera and summer symph. concerts. In 1909 he was appointed conductor of the New Symph. Orch. in London (later named Royal Albert Hall Orch.); from 1910 until his death he was principal of the Guildhall School of Music. He was knighted in 1922. He composed an operetta, *A Capital Joke;* a ballet, *Britannia's Realm* (1902; for the coronation of King Edward VII); and a scenic spectacle, *Entente cordiale* (1904; to celebrate the triple alliance of Russia, France, and England); about 300 songs. He publ. 2 autobiographical books: *Variations on a Personal Theme* (London, 1922) and *Myself and Others* (London, 1931).

Roncaglia, Gino, Italian musicologist; b. Modena, May 7, 1883; d. there, Nov. 27, 1968. He studied with Sinigaglia; devoted himself to musical biography.
  WRITINGS: *Giuseppe Verdi* (Naples, 1914); 2nd ed., revised, 1940, as *L'ascensione creatice di Giuseppe Verdi;* 3rd ed., 1951); *La Rivoluzione musicale italiana* (Milan, 1928); *Rossini l'Olimpico* (Milan, 1946; 2nd ed., 1953); *Invito alla musica* (Milan, 1947; 4th ed., 1958); *Invito all' opera* (Milan, 1949; 4th ed., 1958); *La Cappella musicale del Duomo di Modena* (Florence, 1957); *Galleria verdiana: Studi e figure* (Milan, 1959).

Ronconi, Domenico, famous Italian tenor and singing teacher; b. Lendinara, July 11, 1772; d. Milan, April 13, 1839. He was a successful opera tenor; sang in Italy, France, Germany, and Russia. In 1829 he opened a singing school in Milan; publ. vocal exercises that were widely used. His son, **Giorgio Ronconi** (b. Milan, Aug. 6, 1810; d. Madrid, Jan. 8, 1890), was a well-known baritone; spent some years in N.Y. (from 1867).

Röntgen, Julius, important German-Dutch composer; b. Leipzig, May 9, 1855; d. Bilthoven, near Utrecht, Sept. 13, 1932. He studied music with his father, Engelbert Röntgen (1829–97); later with Plaidy and Reinecke in Leipzig and F. Lachner in Munich. In 1877–1925 he taught in Amsterdam; was conductor of the Society for the Promotion of Music (1886–98); was a co-founder (1884) of the Amsterdam Cons., and its director from 1914 to 1924. He was a friend of Brahms and Grieg; edited the letters of Brahms to T. Engelmann (1918); publ. a biography of Grieg (1930). An astonishingly industrious composer, he wrote an enormous amount of music in every genre, cast in an expansive Romantic style: 12 symphs.; 3 piano concertos; 3 operas (*Agnete, Samum,* and *Der lachende Kavalier*); much chamber music; etc.; edited old Dutch keyboard compositions (vol. 37 of the *Vereeniging voor Nederlandsche Muziekgeschiedenis*) and 14 songs by Adrianus Valerius. His correspondence was publ. by his widow (1934).

Root, George Frederick, American composer and publisher; b. Sheffield, Mass., Aug. 30, 1820; d. Bailey's Island, Maine, Aug. 6, 1895. He was a pupil of George J. Webb in Boston; then lived in N.Y.; was organist of the Church of the Strangers. Going to

Chicago in 1859, he joined the music publishing firm of Root and Cady, established in 1858 by his elder brother, Ebenezer Towner Root, and Chauncey Marvin Cady; it was dissolved in 1871. He wrote many popular songs (*Battlecry of Freedom; Tramp, tramp, tramp; Just before the battle, Mother*); publ. numerous collections of church music and school songs. For some of his earlier compositions he used the German translation of his name, **Friedrich Wurzel,** as a pseudonym.

Rootham, Cyril Bradley, English organist and composer; b. Bristol, Oct. 5, 1875; d. Cambridge, March 18, 1938. He studied music with his father, Daniel Rootham (1837–1922); won classical and musical scholarships at St. John's College (Mus.Bac., 1900; A.M., 1901; Mus.Doc., 1910); finished at the Royal College of Music under Sir Charles Stanford and Sir Walter Parratt. From 1901 till his death he was organist at St. John's College, Cambridge; also conductor of the Univ. Musical Society there (1912–36).

Ropartz, (Joseph) Guy (Marie), French composer; b. Guingamp, Côtes-du-Nord, June 15, 1864; d. Lanloup-par-Plouha, Côtes-du-Nord, Nov. 22, 1955. He entered the Paris Cons. as a pupil of Dubois and Massenet; then took lessons in organ and composition from César Franck, who remained his chief influence in composition; from 1894 until 1919, was director of the Cons. and conductor of the symph. concerts at Nancy; from 1919 to 1929 conducted the Municipal Orch. in Strasbourg; after that lived in retirement in Lanloup-par-Plouha. WORKS: FOR THE STAGE: 3-act opera, *Le Pays* (Nancy, Feb. 1, 1912; Paris Opéra, April 14, 1913; his most important stage work); incidental music for Pierre Loti's *Pêcheur d'Islande* (1889–91) and *Le Mystère de Saint Nicolas,* a legend in 13 scenes (1905). FOR ORCH.: 5 symphs.: No. 1 (1895); No. 2 (1900); No. 3, with Chorus (1906); No. 4 (1910); No. 5 (1945); *La Cloche des morts* (1887); *Les Landes* (1888); *Marche de Fête* (1888); *5 pièces brèves* (1889); *Carnaval* (1889); *Sérénade* (1892); *Dimanche breton* (1893); *A Marie endormie* (1912); *La Chasse du prince Arthur* (1912); *Soir sur les Chaumes* (1913); *Divertissement* (1915); *Sérénade champêtre* (Paris, Feb. 24, 1934); *Pastorale et Danse* for Oboe and Orch. (1907); *Romanza e Scherzino* for Violin and Orch. (1926); *Rapsodie* for Cello and Orch. (Paris, Nov. 3, 1928).

Rore, Cipriano (Cyprian) de, celebrated composer; b. Mechlin or Antwerp, 1516; d. Parma, 1565. He was a pupil of Willaert, maestro at San Marco in Venice; in 1542 publ. his first book of madrigals *a* 5. From about 1547 to 1558 he was in the service of the Duke of Ferrara, Ercole II; visited Antwerp in 1558, and in 1561 was appointed maestro di cappella to Duke Ottavio Farnese at Parma. Upon Willaert's death in 1562, Rore was appointed his successor as maestro di cappella at San Marco, but soon resigned and returned to the court of Parma (July 1564).

Rorem, Ned, brilliant American composer; b. Richmond, Ind., Oct. 23, 1923. He received his musical training in Chicago, where he studied with Leo Sowerby at the American Cons.; subsequently attended Northwestern Univ. (1940–42), the Curtis Inst. in Philadelphia (1943), and the Juilliard School of Music in N.Y. (1946); in N.Y. he also took lessons with Virgil Thomson and Aaron Copland. From 1949 to 1951 he lived in Morocco; then moved to Paris, where he stayed until 1957; he entered the circle of modern Parisian composers, and the French influence, particularly in his songs, remains the most pronounced characteristic of his music. Returning to the U.S., he was composer-in-residence at the Univ. of Buffalo (1959–61) and at the Univ. of Utah (1966–67); in 1980 he joined the faculty of the Curtis Inst. of Music. Rorem is regarded as one of the finest song composers in America; he has a natural feeling for the vocal line and for the prosody of the text. A born linguist, he has mastered the French language to perfection; he is also an elegant stylist in English. He publ. a succession of personal journals, recounting with gracious insouciance his encounters in Paris and N.Y. WORKS: Operas: *A Childhood Miracle* for 6 Voices and 13 Instruments (N.Y., Punch Opera Co., May 10, 1955); *The Robbers* (N.Y., April 15, 1958); *Miss Julie* (N.Y., Nov. 4, 1965); *Bertha* (N.Y., Nov. 26, 1973); Symph. No. 1 (Vienna, 1951); Symph. No. 2 (La Jolla, Calif., Aug. 5, 1956); Symph. No. 3 (N.Y., April 19, 1959); *Design* for Orch. (Louisville, Ky., May 28, 1955); 3 piano concertos (1950, 1951, 1970); *Sinfonia* for Woodwinds and Percussion (Pittsburgh, July 14, 1957); *The Poets' Requiem* for Chorus, Soprano Solo, and Orch., on 8 contemporary poems (N.Y., Feb. 15, 1957); *Eagles,* symph. poem (Philadelphia, Oct. 23, 1959); Trio for Flute, Cello, and Piano (1960); *Lovers,* a "narrative" for Harpsichord, Oboe, Cello, and Percussion (1964); *Sun* for Orch. (N.Y., July 1, 1967); *Assembly and Fall,* symph. poem (1975); *Air Music,* a Bicentennial commission from the Cincinnati Symph. Orch. (Cincinnati, Dec. 5, 1975; received the Pulitzer Prize, 1976); *Book of Hours* for Flute and Harp (1976); 8 piano études (1976); *Serenade* for Voice, Viola, Violin, and Piano (1976); *Sky Music* for Solo Harp (1976); *Women's Voices,* a set of songs (1976); *Romeo and Juliet* for Flute and Guitar (1977); 2 string quartets; 3 piano sonatas; *A Quiet Afternoon,* a set of 9 piano pieces; *Sicilienne* for 2 Pianos; *From an Unknown Past,* a cycle of 7 choruses; *5 Prayers for the Young* for Chorus; organ suite, *A Quaker Reader* (N.Y., Feb. 2, 1977); Double Concerto for Violin, Cello, and Orch. (Cincinnati, May 16, 1979); *Sunday Morning,* symph. suite (N.Y., Feb. 5, 1981); many songs. WRITINGS: *Paris Diary* (N.Y., 1966); *New York Diary* (N.Y., 1967); *Critical Affairs* (N.Y., 1970); *The Final Diary* (N.Y., 1974); *Pure Contraption: A Composer's Essays* (N.Y., 1974); *Essays and a Diary* (N.Y., 1983).

Rosa, Carl (real name, **Karl Rose**), famous opera impresario; b. Hamburg, March 22, 1842; d. Paris, April 30, 1889. At 12 he made tours as a violinist in

England, Denmark, and Germany; studied further in the conservatories of Leipzig (1859) and Paris; was concertmaster at Hamburg (1863–65); gave a concert at the Crystal Palace in London (March 10, 1866), and toured in the U.S. with Mr. Bateman, meeting the singer **Euphrosyne Parepa** and marrying her in N.Y. in 1867. They organized an English opera company and toured America until 1871; then returned to London. After his wife's death in 1874, he produced opera in English in various London theaters, forming the Carl Rosa Opera Co., which under various managements continued to be an important factor in English musical life for many years.

Rosbaud, Hans, eminent Austrian conductor; b. Graz, July 22, 1895; d. Lugano, Dec. 29, 1962. He studied at the Hoch Cons. in Frankfurt; was director of the City Hochschule für Musik in Mainz (1921–30); also conducted the City Orch. there; served as first Kapellmeister of the Frankfurt Radio and of the Museumgesellschaft concerts (1928–37); then became Generalmusikdirektor in Münster (1937–41) and later in Strasbourg (1941–44); subsequently was appointed Generalmusikdirektor of the Munich Phil. (1945). In 1948 he became chief conductor of the Symph. Orch. of the Southwest Radio in Baden-Baden, and in 1957, music director of the Tonhalle Orch. in Zürich. He particularly distinguished himself as a conductor of modern works. He conducted the first stage performances of Schoenberg's *Moses und Aron* (Zürich, 1957).

Rosé, Arnold (Josef), distinguished violinist; b. Jassy, Rumania, Oct. 24, 1863; d. London, Aug. 25, 1946. He studied under Karl Heissler at the Vienna Cons.; made his professional debut at the Gewandhaus in Leipzig, Oct. 30, 1879; in 1881 was appointed concertmaster of the Vienna Phil. and Opera orch.; held this post, intermittently, for 57 years, until 1938, when he was forced to leave Vienna; spent his last years in London. In 1882 he founded the Rosé quartet, which won a high reputation throughout Europe; the Quartet made its American debut at the Library of Congress in Washington, D.C., on April 28, 1928. In 1902 Rosé married Justine Mahler, a sister of Gustav Mahler.

Rose, Leonard, brilliant American cellist; b. Washington, D.C., July 27, 1918. He enrolled at the Miami Cons. when he was 11, and studied cello there with Walter Grossman; then went to N.Y. to study with his cousin, **Frank Miller;** received a scholarship to the Curtis Inst. of Music in Philadelphia in the class of Felix Salmond (1934–38). He then played in the NBC Symph. Orch. under Toscanini (1938–39); subsequently was first cellist of the Cleveland Orch. (1939–43) and the N.Y. Phil. (1943–51). From 1951 he pursued a career as a soloist. With Isaac Stern and Eugene Istomin he organized a trio which gave regular concerts. He taught at the Juilliard School of Music in N.Y. from 1947 to 1951 and again from 1962, and at the Curtis Inst. from 1951 to 1962. Several of his students became successful artists in their own right; among them were Stephen Kates, Lynn Harrell, and Yo-Yo Ma.

Rösel, Peter, outstanding German pianist; b. Dresden, Feb. 2, 1945. In 1963 he won 2nd prize in the International Schumann Competition in Zwickau; he was then chosen by the German Democratic Republic's Ministry of Culture for further training at the Moscow Cons., where he studied with Dmitri Bashkirov and Lev Oborin, graduating in 1969. In 1978 he made a highly successful tour of the U.S. as piano soloist with the Gewandhaus Orch. of Leipzig. Apart from a brilliant technique, Rösel has a Romantic sensitivity characteristic of the Russian mode of instrumental playing; his repertoire is comprehensive, ranging from Mozart to Prokofiev.

Roselius, Ludwig, German composer and musicologist; b. Kassel, Aug. 2, 1902; d. Bremen, Feb. 6, 1977. He studied in Berlin; took courses in composition with Georg Schumann at the Prussian Academy of the Arts, and musicology with H. Abert and J. Wolf at the Univ. of Berlin; received his Dr.Phil. for his dissertation *Andreas Raselius als Motettenkomponist* (1924); he also edited motets by Raselius for Denkmäler der Tonkunst in Bayern, 36 (29/30). He served as rehearsal conductor for the chorus of the German Opera House in Berlin (1921–23); lived in Berlin and Bremen (1928–40); remained in Bremen as a music critic. He wrote the operas *Doge und Dogaressa* (Dortmund, Nov. 14, 1928); *Godiva* (Nuremberg, Aug. 17, 1933); *Gudrun* (Graz, April 29, 1939); also many choruses for schools.

Rosen, Charles, erudite American pianist and musicologist; b. New York, May 5, 1927. He studied piano with Moriz Rosenthal and music theory with Karl Weigl; then took a course in music history at Princeton Univ., receiving his B.A. summa cum laude in 1947 and his M.A. in 1949; also holds the degree of Ph.D. in French literature (1951). He made his N.Y. debut as pianist in 1951; was assistant prof. in modern languages at the Mass. Inst. of Technology (1953–55); in 1971 was appointed prof. of music at the State Univ. of N.Y. at Stony Brook; was the Ernest Bloch Prof. of Music at the Univ. of Calif., Berkeley, in 1976–77. He is equally adept as a virtuoso pianist, particularly in the modern repertoire, and as a brilliant writer on musical, philosophical, and literary subjects. In 1972 he received the National Book Award for his vol. *The Classical Style: Haydn, Mozart, Beethoven* (N.Y., 1971); also publ. *Sonata Forms* (N.Y., 1980).

Rosen, Jerome, American violinist, pianist, poet, physicist, and polymath nonpareil; b. Detroit, Nov. 16, 1939. He began to play the violin at the age of 5, and the piano at 6; studied violin with Josef Gingold in Cleveland and Ivan Galamian at the Curtis Inst. of Music in Philadelphia (1955–58); took piano lessons with Arthur Loesser in Cleveland; composition with Herbert Elwell and Marcel Dick in Cleveland and Wallingford Riegger in Stockbridge, Mass.; studied chamber music playing with Alexander

Schneider and conducting with George Szell, Louis Lane, and James Levine in Cleveland. He subsequently worked in the Cleveland Orch. as violinist and pianist (1959–66); then played violin in the Detroit Symph. Orch. (1968–72). In 1972 he joined the Boston Symph. as a violinist and in 1974 as a pianist, harpsichordist, and celesta player. Concurrently he gave violin recitals in Detroit, N.Y., and other American cities, and played chamber music. He also took a hand in conducting, in Detroit and Cleveland; in 1973–77 was conductor of the Boston Univ. Repertoire Orch. He taught chamber music playing at the Berkshire Music Center (1973–74 and 1977); served as rehearsal pianist for Seiji Ozawa, Rostropovich, Casals, and George Szell. Besides music, he took courses in physics and mathematics at Case Western Reserve Univ.; wrote heavy and light poetry. He is not related to his namesake, Jerome Rosen, the composer, or Charles Rosen, the pianist.

Rosen, Nathaniel, American cellist; b. Altadena, Calif., June 9, 1948. He studied at the Univ. of Southern Calif. with Gregor Piatigorsky; later served as his assistant; eventually joined the Pittsburgh Symph. Orch. In 1978 he won the Gold Medal of the Tchaikovsky Competition in Moscow, the first American cellist to be so honored. This prestigious award instantly propelled him into the precious outer sanctum of Tchaikovsky medalists and secured for him a plethora of concert engagements not commonly vouchsafed to unanointed cellists.

Rosenberg, Hilding (Constantin), eminent Swedish composer; b. Bosjökloster, June 21, 1892. He studied organ and served as church organist in the provinces. In 1914 he enrolled at the Royal Academy of Music in Stockholm, where he took courses in composition with Ellberg and Stenhammar, and studied piano with Andersson; entered the Cons. in 1915. In 1920 he obtained a stipend for further studies; took courses in piano with Buchmayer in Dresden, and attended classes in conducting with Striegler and Scherchen. Returning to Sweden, he became an assistant conductor at the Stockholm Opera (1932–34). In 1948 he visited the U.S. and conducted the first American performance of his Fourth Symph. His music continues the traditional lines of Scandinavian Romanticism, but injects a strong element of neo-Classical polyphony. In his string quartets Nos. 8–12 he makes use of the 12-tone technique. His imposing mastery of composition contributed to his stature as one of the most prestigious figures in modern Swedish music. As a pedagogue, he formed an important group of disciples.

Rosenboom, David, American composer of the avant-garde; b. Fairfield, Iowa, Sept. 9, 1947. He studied piano with his mother; also played violin, viola, trumpet, and drums. He attended the Univ. of Illinois, where he took courses in composition with Salvatore Martirano and Gordon Binkerd; worked with Lejaren Hiller in the Experimental Music Studio there (1965–67). In 1968–69 he served as artistic coordinator for the Electric Ear mixed-media series at the Electric Circus in N.Y. In 1970 he participated in research in neurophysics and biofeedback systems at the State Univ. of N.Y. at Stony Brook. With this esthetic background, his music was bound to be experimental in nature; however, he also composed in classical forms. His scores are notated in diagrams and engineering blueprints, with special symbols for dynamics, tempi, etc. WORKS: *Contrasts* for Violin and Orch. (1963); Septet for Strings, Brass, and Piano (1964); Sextet for Bassoon, Flute, and String Quartet (1965); Trio for Clarinet, Trumpet, and String Bass (1966); *Caliban upon Setebos,* after Robert Browning, for Orch. (1966); *The Thud, Thud, Thud, of Suffocating Blackness* for Saxophone, Electric Cello, Piano, Celesta, Percussion, Tape, and Lights (1966); *mississippippississim* for 33 Musicians, Speaker, and Tape (1968); *How Much Better If Plymouth Rock Had Landed on the Pilgrims* for Electronic and Traditional Instruments (1969); *Ecology of the Skin,* a demonstration in biofeedback experience with audience participation (1970). His zodiac sign is Virgo.

Rosenfeld, Paul, American author and music critic; b. New York, May 4, 1890; d. there, July 21, 1946. He studied at Yale Univ. (B.A., 1912) and at Columbia Univ. School of Journalism (Litt.B., 1913). He then associated himself with progressive circles in literature and music; wrote music criticisms for *The Dial* (1920–27); contributed also to other literary and music magazines. Although not a musician by training, Rosenfeld possessed a penetrating insight into musical values; he championed the cause of modern American music. He collected the most significant of his articles in book form: *Musical Portraits* (on 20 modern composers; 1920); *Musical Chronicle,* covering the N.Y. seasons 1917–23 (1923); *An Hour with American Music* (1929); *Discoveries of a Music Critic* (1936). Analects from his articles were publ. as *Musical Impressions* (N.Y., 1969).

Rosenhain, Jacob (Jacques), German pianist and composer; b. Mannheim, Dec. 2, 1813; d. Baden-Baden, March 21, 1894. He was a child prodigy; made his first public appearance at the age of 11 in Mannheim; studied there with Schmitt, and in Frankfurt with Schnyder von Wartensee. In 1837 he went to Paris and London; continued to travel until 1870, when he settled as a teacher in Baden-Baden. His brother **Eduard Rosenhain** (b. Mannheim, Nov. 16, 1818; d. Frankfurt, Sept. 6, 1861) was also a noteworthy pianist and teacher; he wrote a Serenade for Cello and Piano, and piano pieces.

Rosenman, Leonard, American composer; b. Brooklyn, Sept. 7, 1924. He studied with local teachers; later took courses with Roger Sessions, Luigi Dallapiccola, and briefly with Arnold Schoenberg. His main mundane occupation is that of a movie composer; he wrote the scores for such commercially notable films as *East of Eden, Rebel without a Cause,* and *The Chapman Report* (dealing with sexual statistics); also compiled music for television programs, among them *The Defenders* and *Marcus Welby, M.D.* But he is also the composer of a number of highly respectable and even elevated musical works, among them a Violin Concerto and the challenging score *Foci* for 3 orchs. His *Threnody on a Song of K. R.* (written to the memory of his wife, Kay Rosenman), a set of orch. variations on her original melody, was performed by the Los Angeles Phil., under the composer's direction, May 6, 1971.

Rosenmüller, Johann, German composer; b. Ölsnitz, c.1619; d. Wolfenbüttel, Sept. 10, 1684. He graduated from the Univ. of Leipzig in 1640; from 1642 was master at the Thomasschule; later deputy cantor for Tobias Michael; in 1651 he was appointed organist of the Nikolaikirche. Imprisoned for a moral offense in 1655, he escaped and fled to Hamburg, thence to Venice (1658); became composer at the Ospedale della Pieta there in 1678; in 1682 was appointed ducal Kapellmeister at Wolfenbüttel.

Rosenstock, Joseph, Polish-American conductor; b. Cracow, Jan. 27, 1895. He studied at the Cracow Cons.; then with Schreker in Vienna; graduated from the Vienna Academy of Music in 1920; conducted opera in Darmstadt (1922–25), Wiesbaden (1925–27), and Mannheim (1930–33); his American debut was at the Metropolitan Opera, conducting *Die Meistersinger* (Oct. 30, 1929); in 1933 he was disqualified in Germany as a Jew; conducted operatic performances of the Jewish Kulturbund in Berlin until 1936, when he was appointed conductor of the Nippon Phil. Orch. in Tokyo; was successful there until 1941; then went to the U.S.; conducted in Tokyo again in 1945–46; from 1948 to 1955 he was conductor and music director of the N.Y. City Opera. In 1965 he settled in Salt Lake City, conducting occasional concerts and teaching.

Rosenthal, Harold, English music editor and critic; b. London, Sept. 30, 1917. He received his B.A. degree from the Univ. of London in 1940; served as a noncombatant in the British army during World War II; in 1950 launched, with the Earl of Harewood, the magazine *Opera* and became its editor in 1953; also issued *Opera Annuals* (1954–60). He was archivist of the Royal Opera House (1950–56); contributed to many European and American music journals. His publications include *Sopranos of Today* (London, 1956), *Two Centuries of Opera at Covent Garden* (London, 1958), *The Concise Oxford Dictionary of Opera* (with John Warrack; London, 1964; 2nd ed., 1979; revised 1980), and *Covent Garden, A Short History* (London, 1967). He edited *The Opera Bedside Book* (London, 1965) and *The Mapleson Memoirs* (revised ed. London, 1966); revised Loewenberg's *Annals of Opera* (1978). He contributed a number of biographical articles on singers for *The New Grove;* also publ. an autobiography, *My Mad World of Opera* (1982).

Rosenthal, Manuel, French composer and conductor; b. Paris, June 18, 1904, of a Russian mother and French father. He studied violin and composi-

tion at the Paris Cons., graduating in 1924; also took some lessons with Ravel. He was mobilized in 1939, and taken prisoner of war; remained in Germany for a year, returning to France in March 1941. After conducting various orchs. in Europe, he made a tour of the U.S. in the autumn of 1946; in 1948, was appointed instructor in composition at the College of Puget Sound in Tacoma, Wash. In 1949 he was engaged as conductor of the Seattle Symph. Orch.; was dismissed summarily for moral turpitude in Oct. 1951 (the soprano who appeared as soloist with the Seattle Symph. Orch. under the name of Mme. Rosenthal was not his legal wife). In 1962 he was appointed prof. of orch. conducting at the Paris Cons.; was conductor of the Liège Symph. Orch. (1964–67). He composed a number of works in an entertaining manner, expertly orchestrated.

Rosenthal, Moriz, famous Polish pianist; b. Lwow, Dec. 17, 1862; d. New York, Sept. 3, 1946. He studied piano at the Lwow Cons. with Karol Mikuli, who was a pupil of Chopin; in 1872, when he was 10 years old, he played Chopin's Rondo in C for 2 Pianos with his teacher in Lwow. The family moved to Vienna in 1875, and Rosenthal became the pupil of Joseffy, who inculcated in him a passion for virtuoso piano playing, which he taught according to Tausig's method. Liszt accepted Rosenthal as a student during his stay in Weimar and Rome (1876–78). After a hiatus of some years, during which Rosenthal studied philosophy at the Univ. of Vienna, he returned to his concert career in 1884, and established for himself a reputation as one of the world's greatest virtuosos; was nicknamed (because of his small stature and great pianistic power) "little giant of the piano." Beginning in 1888 he made 12 tours of the U.S., where he became a permanent resident in 1938. He publ. (with L. Schytte) a *Schule des höheren Klavierspiels* (Berlin, 1892). His wife, **Hedwig Kanner-Rosenthal,** was a distinguished piano teacher.

Rosetti, Francesco Antonio (real name, **Franz Anton Rösler**), Bohemian composer; b. in the region of Leitmeritz, c.1750; d. Ludwigslust, June 30, 1792. For many years Rosetti was confused with a Bohemian cobbler named Rösler, who was born in Niemes in 1746 and whose date of birth was erroneously listed as that of Rosetti. He was a theological student; was engaged as a string player in court orchs.; in 1789 he became music director in Ludwigslust. He was a prodigiously fertile composer who wrote in the manner of Haydn and Boccherini, and was even dubbed "a German Boccherini." He wrote 3 Requiems; one of these was composed in memory of Mozart; it was performed in Prague shortly after Mozart's death in 1791; its score is unfortunately lost. His other works include an opera, *Das Winterfest der Hirten* (1789), and nearly 90 "symphonies"; 9 string quartets; 4 flute concertos; 5 oboe concertos; 3 clarinet concertos; 4 bassoon concertos; 5 horn concertos; 5 concertos for 2 Horns; etc., etc. Oskar Kaul publ. 5 symphs. in vol. 22 (12.i) and chamber music in vol. 33 (25) of the *Denkmäler der Ton-*

kunst in Bayern.

Rosing, Vladimir, Russian-American tenor and opera director; b. St. Petersburg, Jan. 23, 1890; d. Los Angeles, Nov. 24, 1963. He studied voice with Jean de Reszke; made his debut as a tenor in St. Petersburg in 1912; gave a successful series of song recitals in programs of Russian songs in London between 1913 and 1921. In 1923 he was appointed director of the opera dept. at the Eastman School of Music in Rochester, N.Y.; founded an American Opera Co., which he directed in a series of operatic productions in the English language. In 1939 he went to Los Angeles as organizer and artistic director of the Southern Calif. Opera Assoc. He staged several pageants: *The California Story* in Hollywood Bowl in 1950; *The Oregon Story* in 1959; *The Kansas Story* in 1960.

Roslavetz, Nicolai, remarkable Russian composer; b. Suray, near Chernigov, Jan. 5, 1881; d. Moscow, Aug. 23, 1944. He studied violin with Jan Hřímalý, and composition with Ilyinsky and Vassilenko, at the Moscow Cons., graduating in 1912; won the Silver Medal for his cantata *Heaven and Earth,* after Byron. A composer of advanced tendencies, he publ. in 1913 an atonal Violin Sonata, the first of its kind by a Russian composer; his 3rd String Quartet exhibits 12-tone properties. He edited a short-lived journal, *Muzykalnaya Kultura,* in 1924, and became a leading figure in the modern movement in Russia. But with a change of Soviet cultural policy toward socialist realism and nationalism, Roslavetz was subjected to severe criticism in the press for persevering in his aberrant ways. To conciliate the authorities, he tried to write operettas; then was given an opportunity to redeem himself by going to Tashkent to write ballets based on Uzbek folk songs; he failed in all these pursuits. But interest in his music became pronounced abroad, and posthumous performances were arranged in West Germany.

Rösler, Franz Anton. See **Rosetti, Francesco.**

Rösler, Johann Josef, Hungarian composer; b. Chemnitz, Aug. 22, 1771; d. Prague, Jan. 29, 1813. He served as Kapellmeister for Prince Lobkowitz in Prague; brought out an opera, *Elisene, Prinzessin von Bulgarien* (Prague, Oct. 18, 1807), which was the first original stage work to be produced at the German Opera Theater in Prague; wrote a great amount of instrumental music. A movement from one of his piano concertos was erroneously attributed to Beethoven.

Rossellini, Renzo, Italian composer; b. Rome, Feb. 2, 1908; d. Monte Carlo, May 14, 1982. He studied composition in Rome with Setaccioli and Sallustio; also took courses in orchestration with Bernardino Molinari. In 1940 he was appointed prof. of composition at the Rome Cons., and in 1956 became a member of the Santa Cecilia Academy. In 1973 he was named artistic director at the Opera at Monte Car-

lo.

WORKS: Operas: *Alcassino e Nicoletta* (1928–30); *La guerra,* to his own libretto (Rome, Feb. 25, 1956); *Il vortice* (Naples, Feb. 8, 1958); *Uno sguardo del ponte,* after Arthur Miller's play (Rome, March 11, 1961); *L'Avventuriere* (Monte Carlo, Feb. 2, 1968); *La Reine morte* (Monte Carlo, 1973). Ballets: *La danza di Dâssine* (San Remo, Feb. 24, 1935); *Poemetti pagani* (Monte Carlo, 1963); *Il Ragazzo e la sua ombra* (Venice, 1966). For Orch.: *Suite in 3 tempi* (1931); *Ut unum sint* (Miami, Oct. 20, 1963); *Stornelli della Roma bassa* (1946); film music. He publ. 2 books of autobiographical content, *Pagine di un musicista* (Bologna, 1964) and *Addio del passato* (Milan, 1968).

Rossi, Giulio, Italian bass; b. Rome, Oct. 27, 1865; d. Milan, Oct. 9, 1931. He had a tenor voice until he was 19, when an unintentional plunge into the Tiber in December induced an illness, after which his voice lowered to the range of *basso profondo.* He then began vocal study under Oreste Tomassoni; made his debut at Parma, Oct. 20, 1887. In 1889 he toured South America with Adelina Patti, and made 2 tours of Mexico and California with Luisa Tetrazzini; from 1908 till 1919 sang at the Metropolitan Opera. His repertoire included about 80 Italian operas.

Rossi, Lauro, Italian dramatic composer; b. Macerata, Feb. 19, 1810; d. Cremona, May 5, 1885. He was a pupil of Furno, Zingarelli, and Crescentini at Naples, bringing out a comic opera, *Le Contesse villane,* there (1829) with fair success. He became maestro at the Teatro Valle in Rome (1831–33); with his 10th opera, *La casa disabitata o I falsi monetari,* produced at La Scala, Milan, Aug. 11, 1834, he won a veritable triumph; it made the rounds of Italy and was given in Paris. In 1835 he went to Mexico as conductor and composer to an Italian opera troupe; when it folded, he set up his own opera company, becoming its director in 1837, and going to Havana (1840) and New Orleans (1842), returning to Italy in 1843. He brought out a new opera, *Il Borgomastro di Schiedam* (Milan, June 1, 1844), with indifferent success; his opera *Il Domino nero* (Milan, Sept. 1, 1849) fared a little better. His most successful opera was *La Contessa di Mons* (Turin, Jan. 31, 1874). He wrote 29 operas in all. In 1850 he was given the post of director of the Milan Cons.; in 1870 he succeeded Mercadante as director of the Naples Cons.; resigned in 1878, and retired to Cremona in 1882.

Rossi, Luigi (Latinized as **Aloysius Rubeus**), Italian composer and singer; b. Torremaggiore, Foggia, 1598; d. Rome, Feb. 19, 1653. He studied in Naples with G. de Macque; then went to Rome, where his opera *Il palazzo d'Atlante incantato* was produced (Feb. 22, 1642). In 1646 he was called by Mazarin to Paris with 20 other singers, and there staged his most important work, *Orfeo* (March 2, 1647), the first Italian opera expressly written for a Paris production. He wrote besides the oratorio *Giuseppe* and some 100 cantatas; reprints of some of these

Rossi – Rossini

appear in Gevaert's *Les Gloires de l'Italie,* Riemann's *Kantatenfrühling,* and Landshoff's *Alte Meister des Bel Canto.* Riemann also publ. several da capo arias by Rossi in the *Handbuch der Musik-Geschichte* (vol. II/2).

Rossi, Michel Angelo, Italian composer; b. Genoa, 1602; d. Rome (buried July 7), 1656. He was a pupil of Frescobaldi; in 1638 was attached to the court of the Duke of Este in Modena; in 1640 he went to Rome. Among his works are an opera, *Erminia sul Giordano* (Rome, Feb. 2, 1633), and a set of *Toccate e Correnti per organo o cembalo* (2nd ed., Rome, 1657). The complete keyboard works of Rossi were publ. by A. Toni (Milan, 1920); the 1657 edition of *Toccate e Correnti* is included in L. Torchi, *L'arte musicale in Italia,* and 10 *correnti* were publ. by F. Boghen (Milan, 1923); 2 toccatas and 3 *correnti* were edited by Béla Bartók (N.Y., 1930).

Rossi, Salomone (Salamone), Italian composer of Jewish origin (called himself **Ebreo**); b. Mantua, 1570; d. there, c.1630. Nothing is known of the circumstances of his life, except that he was in the service of the court of Mantua, and publ. 13 books of madrigals and instrumental works. He also wrote some synagogue music. As composer of instrumental works, he demonstrated technical procedures in advance of his time; particularly notable are his variations on popular Italian melodies.

Rossi-Lemeni, Nicola, Italian bass; b. Istanbul, Nov. 6, 1920, of an Italian father and a Russian mother. He was educated in Italy; studied law and planned a diplomatic career. In 1943 he decided to become a professional singer, but the war interfered with his plans, and his debut did not take place until 1946, in Venice. He first appeared in America as Boris Godunov, with the San Francisco Opera (Oct. 2, 1951); also sang Mefistofele (Boito), William Tell, etc.; in 1947, he was engaged at La Scala in Milan; sang at the Metropolitan Opera in N.Y. in 1953–54. In 1980 he joined the faculty of Indiana Univ. in Bloomington. He married the soprano **Virginia Zeani.** Besides the regular operatic repertoire, he sang a number of parts in modern works, such as Wozzeck.

Rossignol, Felix Ludger. See **Joncières, Victorin de.**

Rossini, Gioachino (Antonio), great Italian opera composer possessing an equal genius for shattering melodrama in tragedy and for devastating humor in comedy; b. Pesaro, Feb. 29, 1792; d. Paris, Nov. 13, 1868. He came from a musical family; his father served as town trumpeter in Lugo and Pesaro, and played brass instruments in provincial theaters; his mother sang opera as *seconda donna.* When his parents traveled, Gioachino Rossini was usually boarded in Bologna. After the family moved to Lugo, his father taught him to play the French horn; he also had a chance to study singing with a local canon.

Later the family moved to Bologna, where he studied singing, harpsichord, and music theory with Padre Tesei; also learned to play the violin and viola. Soon he acquired enough technical ability to serve as maestro al cembalo in local churches and at occasional opera productions. He studied voice with Matteo Babbini, a local tenor. In 1806 he was accepted as a student at the Liceo Musicale in Bologna; there he studied singing and solfeggio with Gibelli, cello with Cavedagna, piano with Zanotti, and counterpoint with Padre Mattei. He also began composing. On Aug. 11, 1808, his cantata *Il pianto d'Armonia sulla morte d'Orfeo* was performed at the Liceo Musicale in Bologna and received a prize. About the same time he wrote his first opera, *Demetrio e Polibio;* in 1810 he was commissioned to write a work for the Teatro San Moisè in Venice; he submitted his opera *La cambiale di matrimonio,* which won considerable acclaim. His next production was *L'equivoco stravagante,* produced in Bologna in 1811. There followed a number of other operas: *L'inganno felice* (Venice, 1812), *Ciro in Babilonia* (Ferrara, 1812), and *La scala di seta* (Venice, 1812). In 1812 he obtained a commission from La Scala of Milan; the resulting work, *La pietra del paragone,* became a fine success. In 1813 Rossini produced 3 operas for Venice: *Il Signor Bruschino, Tancredi,* and *L'Italiana in Algeri;* the last became a perennial favorite. The next 3 operas, *Aureliano in Palmira* (produced in Milan in 1813), *Il Turco in Italia* (staged in Milan in 1814), and *Sigismondo* (perf. in Venice in 1814), were unsuccessful. By that time Rossini, still a very young man, had been approached by the famous impresario Barbaja, the manager of the Teatro San Carlo and the Teatro Fondo in Naples, with an offer for an exclusive contract, under the terms of which Rossini was to supply 2 operas annually for Barbaja. The first opera Rossini wrote for him was *Elisabetta, regina d'Inghilterra,* produced at the Teatro San Carlo in Naples; the title role was entrusted to the famous Spanish soprano Isabella Colbran, who was Barbaja's future mistress. An important innovation in the score was Rossini's use of *recitativo stromentato* in place of the usual *recitativo secco.* His next opera, *Torvaldo e Dorliska,* produced in Rome in 1815, was an unfortunate failure. Rossini now determined to try his skill in composing an opera buffa, based on the famous play by Beaumarchais *Le Barbier de Seville;* it was an audacious decision on Rossini's part, since an Italian opera on the same subject by Paisiello, *Il Barbiere di Siviglia,* originally produced in 1782, was still playing with undiminished success. To avoid confusion, Rossini's opera on this subject was performed at the Teatro Argentina in Rome under a different title, *Almaviva, ossia L'inutile precauzione.* Rossini was only 23 years old when he completed the score, which proved to be his own greatest accomplishment and a standard opera buffa in the repertoire of theaters all over the world. Rossini himself conducted its first performance in Rome on Feb. 20, 1816, but if contemporary reports and gossip can be trusted, the occasion was marred by various stage accidents which moved the unruly Italian audience to interrupt the spectacle with vociferous outcries of derision; however, the next performance scored a brilliant success. For later productions Rossini used the title *Il Barbiere di Siviglia.* Strangely enough, the operas he wrote immediately afterward were not uniformly successful: *La Gazzetta,* produced in Naples in 1816, passed unnoticed; the next opera, *Otello,* also produced in Naples in 1816, had some initial success but was not retained in the repertoire after a few sporadic performances. There followed *La Cenerentola* and *La gazza ladra,* both dated from 1817, which fared much better. But the following 7 operas, *Armida, Mosè in Egitto, Ricciardo e Zoraide, Ermione, La Donna del lago, Maometto II,* and *Zelmira,* produced in Naples between 1817 and 1822, were soon forgotten; only the famous Prayer in *Mosè in Egitto* saved the opera from oblivion. The *prima donna assoluta* in all these operas was **Isabella Colbran;** after a long association with Barbaja, she went to live with Rossini, who finally married her on March 16, 1822. This event, however, did not result in a break between the impresario and the composer; Barbaja even made arrangements for a festival of Rossini's works in Vienna at the Kärnthnertortheater, of which he became a director. In Vienna Rossini met Beethoven. Returning to Italy, he produced a fairly successful mythological opera, *Semiramide* (Venice, 1823), with Colbran in the title role. Rossini then signed a contract for a season in London with Giovanni Benelli, director of the Italian opera at the King's Theatre. Rossini arrived in London late in 1823 and was received by King George IV. In London Rossini conducted several of his operas, and was also a guest at the homes of the British nobility, where he played piano as an accompanist to singers, at very large fees. In 1824 he settled in Paris, where he became director of the Théâtre-Italien. For the coronation of King Charles X he composed *Il viaggio a Reims,* which was performed in Paris under his direction on June 19, 1825. He used parts of this *pièce d'occasion* in his opera *Le Comte Ory.* In Paris he met Meyerbeer, with whom he established an excellent relationship. After the expiration of his contract with the Théâtre-Italien, he was given the nominal titles of "Premier Compositeur du Roi" and "Inspecteur Général du Chant en France" at an annual salary of 25,000 francs. He was now free to compose for the Paris Opéra; there, on Oct. 9, 1826, he produced *Le Siège de Corinthe,* a revised French version of *Maometto II.* Later he also revised the score of *Mosè in Egitto* and produced it at the Paris Opéra in French as *Moïse et Pharaon* on March 26, 1827. There followed *Le Comte Ory* (Aug. 20, 1828). In May 1829 Rossini was able to obtain an agreement with the government of King Charles X guaranteeing him a lifetime annuity of 6,000 francs. In return he promised to write more works for the Paris Opéra. On Aug. 3, 1829, his *Guillaume Tell* was given its premiere at the Opera; it became immensely popular. And then, at the age of 37, Rossini stopped writing operas. The French revolution of July 1830, which dethroned King Charles X, invalidated Rossini's contract with the French government. Rossini contemplated suing the government of King Louis Philippe, the successor to the throne of Charles X, for the continuation of his annuity; the incipient litigation was settled in 1835. In 1832 Rossini met Olympe Pélissier, who became his mistress; in 1837 Rossini legally separated from Colbran. She died in 1845, and on Aug. 16, 1846, Rossini married Pélissier. From 1836 to 1848 they lived in Bologna, where Rossini served as consultant to the Liceo Musicale. In 1848 they moved to Florence; in 1855 he decided to return to Paris, where he was to remain for the rest of his life. His home in the suburb of Passy became the magnet of the artistic world. Rossini was a charming, affable, and gregarious host; he entertained lavishly; he was a great gourmet, and invented recipes for Italian food that were enthusiastically adopted by French chefs. His wit was fabulous, and his sayings were eagerly reported in the French journals. He did not abandon composition entirely during his last years of life; in 1867 he wrote a *Petite messe solennelle;* as a token of gratitude to the government of the Second Empire he composed a *Hymne à Napoleon III et à son vaillant peuple;* of great interest are the numerous piano pieces, songs, and instrumental works which he called *Péchés de vieillesse (Sins of Old Age),* a collection containing over 150 pieces.

What were the reasons for Rossini's decision to stop writing operas? Rumors flew around Paris that he was unhappy about the cavalier treatment he received from the management of the Paris Opéra, and he spoke disdainfully of yielding the operatic field to "the Jews" (Meyerbeer and Halévy), whose operas captivated the Paris audiences. The report does not bear the stamp of truth, for Rossini was friendly with Meyerbeer until Meyerbeer's death in 1864. Besides, Rossini was not in the habit of complaining; he enjoyed life too well. He was called "Le Cygne de Pesaro" ("The Swan of Pesaro," his birthplace). The story went that a delegation arrived from Pesaro with a project of building a monument to Rossini; the town authorities had enough money to pay for the pedestal, but not for the statue itself. Would Rossini contribute 10,000 francs for the completion of the project? "For 10,000 francs," Rossini was supposed to have replied, "I would stand on the pedestal myself." *Se non è vero è ben trovato.* Rossini had a healthy sense of self-appreciation, but he invariably put it in a comic context. While his mother was still living, he addressed his letters to her as "Mother of the Great Maestro."

The circumstance that Rossini was born on a leap-year day was the cause of many a bon mot on his part. On Feb. 29, 1868, he decided to celebrate his 19th birthday, for indeed, there had been then only 19 leap years since his birth. He was superstitious; like many Italians, he stood in fear of Friday the 13th. He died on Nov. 13, 1868, which was a Friday. In 1887 his remains were taken to Florence for entombment in the Church of Santa Croce.

Rossini's melodies have been used by many composers as themes for various works: Respighi utilized Rossini's *Quelques riens* in his ballet *La Boutique fantasque,* and other themes in his orch. suite *Rossiniana.* An opera entitled *Rossini in Neapel* was written by Bernhard Paumgartner. Benjamin Britten made use of Rossini's music in his orch. suites *Soirées musicales* and *Matinées musicales*. The most famous arrangement of any of Rossini's compositions is the Prayer from *Mosè in Egitto*, transcribed for violin by Paganini.

A complete edition of the works of Rossini, the *Quaderni rossiniani, a cura della Fondazione Rossini*, began publication in Pesaro in 1954.

WORKS: OPERAS: *Demetrio e Polibio*, opera seria (1808; Teatro Valle, Rome, May 18, 1812); *La cambiale di matrimonio*, farsa (Teatro San Moisè, Venice, Nov. 3, 1810); *L'equivoco stravagante*, opera buffa (Teatro del Corso, Bologna, Oct. 26, 1811); *L'inganno felice*, farsa (1811; Teatro San Moisè, Venice, Jan. 8, 1812); *Ciro in Babilonia, ossia La caduta di Baldassare*, dramma con cori or oratorio (Teatro Municipale, Ferrara, March 1812); *La scala di seta*, farsa (Teatro San Moisè, Venice, May 9, 1812); *La pietra del paragone*, melodramma giocoso or opera buffa (Teatro alla Scala, Milan, Sept. 26, 1812); *L'occasione fa il ladro, ossia Il cambio della valigia*, burletta per musica (Teatro San Moisè, Venice, Nov. 24, 1812); *Il Signor Bruschino, ossia Il Figlio per azzardo*, farsa giocosa (1812; Teatro San Moisè, Venice, Jan. 1813); *Tancredi*, opera seria or melodramma eroico (1812–13; Teatro La Fenice, Venice, Feb. 6, 1813); *L'Italiana in Algeri*, melodramma giocoso (Teatro San Benedetto, Venice, May 22, 1813); *Aureliano in Palmira*, opera seria or dramma serio (Teatro alla Scala, Milan, Dec. 26, 1813); *Il Turco in Italia*, opera buffa or dramma buffo (Teatro alla Scala, Milan, Aug. 14, 1814); *Sigismondo*, opera seria or dramma (Teatro La Fenice, Venice, Dec. 26, 1814); *Elisabetta, regina d'Inghilterra*, dramma (Teatro San Carlo, Naples, Oct. 4, 1815); *Torvaldo e Dorliska*, dramma semiserio (Teatro Valle, Rome, Dec. 26, 1815); *Il Barbiere di Siviglia*, opera buffa or commedia (first perf. as *Almaviva, ossia L'inutile precauzione*, Teatro Argentina, Rome, Feb. 20, 1816); *La Gazzetta, ossia Il matrimonio per concorso* (subtitle does not appear in the first printed libretto), opera buffa (Teatro dei Fiorentini, Naples, Sept. 26, 1816); *Otello, ossia Il Moro di Venezia*, opera seria or dramma (Teatro del Fondo, Naples, Dec. 4, 1816); *La Cenerentola, ossia La bontà in trionfo*, dramma giocoso (1816–17; Teatro Valle, Rome, Jan. 25, 1817); *La gazza ladra*, melodramma or opera semiseria (Teatro alla Scala, Milan, May 31, 1817); *Armida*, opera seria or dramma (Teatro San Carlo, Naples, Nov. 11, 1817); *Adelaide di Borgogna, ossia Ottone, re d'Italia*, dramma (Teatro Argentina, Rome, Dec. 27, 1817); *Mosè in Egitto*, azione tragico-sacra or oratorio (Teatro San Carlo, Naples, March 5, 1818); *Adina, o Il Califfo di Bagdad*, farsa (1818; Teatro São Carlos, Lisbon, June 22, 1826); *Ricciardo e Zoraide*, dramma, opera seria, or opera semiseria (Teatro San Carlo, Naples, Dec. 3, 1818); *Ermione*, azione tragica (Teatro San Carlo, Naples, March 27, 1819); *Eduardo* [later *Edoardo*] *e Cristina*, dramma (Teatro San Benedetto, Venice, April 24, 1819); *La Donna del lago*, melodramma or opera seria (Teatro San Carlo, Naples, Sept. 24, 1819); *Bianca e Falliero, ossia Il consiglio dei tre*, opera seria (Teatro alla Scala, Milan, Dec. 26, 1819);

Maometto II, dramma or opera seria (Teatro San Carlo, Naples, Dec. 3, 1820); *Matilde Shabran* [later *Matilde di Shabran*], *ossia Bellezza e Cuor di Ferro*, opera semiseria (1820–21; Teatro Apollo, Rome, Feb. 24, 1821); *Zelmira*, dramma or opera seria (1821–22; Teatro San Carlo, Naples, Feb. 16, 1822); *Semiramide*, melodramma tragico or opera seria (1822–23; Teatro La Fenice, Venice, Feb. 3, 1823); *Il viaggio a Reims, ossia L'albergo del Giglio d'Oro*, cantata scenica (Théâtre-Italien, Paris, June 19, 1825); *Le Siège de Corinthe*, grand opera (revision of *Maometto II;* Opéra, Paris, Oct. 9, 1826); *Moïse et Pharaon, ou Le Passage de la Mer Rouge*, grand opera (revision of *Mosè in Egitto;* Opéra, Paris, March 26, 1827); *Le Comte Ory*, opéra-comique (utilizing numbers from *Il viaggio a Reims;* Opéra, Paris, Aug. 20, 1828); *Guillaume Tell*, grand opera (1828–29; Opéra, Paris, Aug. 3, 1829).

CANTATAS: *Il pianto d'Armonia sulla morte d'Orfeo* (Bologna, Aug. 11, 1808); *La morte di Didone* (1811; Venice, May 2, 1818); *Dalle quete e pallid'ombre* (1812); *Egle ed Irene* (1814); *L'Aurora* (Rome, Nov. 1815); *Le nozze di Teti e di Peleo* (Naples, April 24, 1816); Cantata con cori ("Omaggio Umiliato . . ."; also known as *Corifea, Partenope*, or *Igea;* Naples, Feb. 20, 1819); *Cantata a tre voci con cori* ("Cantata . . . 9 Maggio 1819"; Naples, May 9, 1819); *La riconoscenza* (Naples, Dec. 27, 1821); *L'augurio felice* (1822); *La Santa Alleanza* (Verona, Nov. 24, 1822); *Il vero omaggio* (Verona, Dec. 3, 1822); *Il Bardo* (1822); *Omaggio pastorale* (Treviso, April 1, 1823); *Il pianto delle muse in morte di Lord Byron* (London, June 9, 1824); *Cantata per il battesimo del figlio del banchiere Aguado* (Paris, July 16, 1827); *Giovanna d'Arco* (1832; revised 1852); *Cantata ad Onore del Sommo Pontefice Pio IX* (Bologna, Aug. 16, 1846).

OTHER VOCAL MUSIC: 3 early masses (the first contains 3 sections only by Rossini for a composite score composed by students of the Liceo Musicale in 1808 and perf. in Bologna, June 2, 1808; 1808; 1809); *Messa solenne* (Naples, March 19, 1820); *Tantum ergo* (1824); *Soirées musicales* (1830–35); *Stabat Mater* (first version, 1831–32; orch. version, 1841; Paris, Jan. 7, 1842); *Tantum ergo* (Bologna, Nov. 28, 1847); *O salutaris Hostia* (1857); *Laus Deo* (1861); *Petite messe solennelle* (1863; Paris, March 14, 1864; orch. version, 1867; Paris, Feb. 24, 1869).

FOR ORCH.: Overture in D major (1808); 3 sinfonias: D major (1808); E-flat major (1809; later revised for use as the overture to *La cambiale di matrimonio*); A major (discovered by P. Ingerslev-Jenson and called the "Odense"); *Variazioni in fa maggiore per più strumenti obbligati con accompagnamento di orchestra* (1809); *Variazioni in do maggiore per clarinetto obbligato con accompagnamento di orchestra* (1810); marches.

CHAMBER MUSIC: 6 *sonate a quattro* (1804); 5 string quartets (1806–8); 5 duets (1806); *Tema con variazione per quattro strumenti a fiato* for Flute, Clarinet, Horn, and Bassoon (1812); *Rondeau fantastique* for Horn and Piano (1856).

Rostand, Claude, French writer on music; b. Paris,

Dec. 3, 1912; d. Villejuif, Oct. 9, 1970. He studied with N. Dufourck. In 1958 he organized a modern music society in Paris, Musique d'Aujourd'hui.

WRITINGS: *L'Œuvre de Gabriel Fauré* (Paris, 1945); *Richard Strauss* (Paris, 1949); *La Musique française contemporaine* (Paris, 1952); dialogues with Milhaud, Poulenc, Markevitch, and others; biographies of Brahms (2 vols., Paris, 1954–55), Liszt (Paris, 1960), Hugo Wolf (Paris, 1967), and Webern (1969); *Dictionnaire de la musique contemporaine* (Lausanne, 1970).

Rostropovich, Leopold, Russian cellist, father and teacher of **Mstislav Rostropovich;** b. Voronezh, March 9, 1892; d. Orenburg, July 31, 1942. He studied cello with his father, Vitold Rostropovich; gave concerts; from 1925 to 1931 was a prof. at the Cons. of Azerbaijan in Baku; then lived in Moscow; after the outbreak of the Nazi-Soviet war in 1941 he moved to Orenburg.

Rostropovich, Mstislav, eminent Russian cellist and conductor; b. Baku, March 27, 1927. His father and grandfather were cello players; he took lessons with his father; in 1937 entered the Moscow Cons., where he studied with Kozolupov, and took courses in composition with Shebalin; graduated in 1948 and joined the faculty of the Moscow Cons.; concurrently taught classes at the Leningrad Cons. In 1950 he won the International Competition of Cellists in Prague; then embarked on a highly successful career as a cello virtuoso, achieving a high rank among master cellists, next to Casals and Piatigorsky. Prokofiev, Shostakovich, Benjamin Britten, Walter Piston, Lukas Foss, and others wrote special works for him. He also revealed himself as an excellent pianist, and played accompaniments (from memory) to his wife, the singer **Galina Vishnevskaya.** Still another achievement in his versatile career was that of a fine conductor, both in opera and in symph. concerts. He received the Lenin Prize in 1963. But despite all these distinctions and official honors, he began having difficulties with the Soviet authorities, owing chiefly to his spirit of uncompromising independence; he let the dissident author Solzhenitsyn stay at his *dacha* near Moscow; also dared to criticize the bureaucrats of the Soviet Ministry of Culture, which was in charge of handling artistic engagements. As a result, he found himself hampered in his professional activities and was denied the opportunity to play and conduct as often as he wished. In 1974 he decided to take a leave of absence and went abroad, while still keeping his Soviet citizenship. His wife and 2 daughters followed him to the U.S. In 1975 he accepted the offer to conduct the National Symph. Orch. in Washington, D.C., and made a brilliant debut with it on March 5, 1975. In March 1978 he and his wife were stripped of their citizenship by the Soviet government as "ideological renegades." He organized the first Rostropovich International Cello Competition in Paris in 1981.

Roswaenge, Helge, Danish tenor; b. Copenhagen (of German parents), Aug. 29, 1897; d. Munich, June 19, 1972. He studied engineering and took voice lessons; then made a grand tour through Scandinavia, Germany, and Austria in concert and in opera. From 1929 to 1945, and again from 1949, he was attached principally to the Berlin State Opera; also sang at the Vienna State Opera (1936–58), and in Bayreuth and Salzburg. In his prime, his voice was often compared in quality of bel canto with that of Caruso. He publ. 3 booklets of an autobiographical nature: *Skratta Pajazzo (Ridi, Pagliaccio;* Copenhagen, 1945); *Mach es besser, mein Sohn* (Leipzig, 1962); *Leitfaden für Gesangsbeflissene* (Munich, 1964).

Rota, Nino, brilliant Italian composer; b. Milan, Dec. 3, 1911; d. Rome, April 10, 1979. He was a precocious musician; at the age of 11 he wrote an oratorio which had a public performance, and at 13 composed a lyric comedy in 3 acts, *Il Principe porcaro,* after Hans Christian Andersen. He then undertook a serious study of composition with Alfredo Casella and Ildebrando Pizzetti at the Santa Cecilia Academy in Rome, graduating in 1930; later went to the U.S., and enrolled in the Curtis Inst. of Philadelphia, studying composition with Rosario Scalero and conducting with Fritz Reiner. Returning to Italy, he entered the Univ. of Milan to study literature, gaining a degree in 1937. Turning definitely to music, he joined the faculty of the Liceo Musicale in Bari; later became its director (1950–78). His musical style demonstrates a great facility, and even felicity, with occasional daring excursions into the forbidding territory of dodecaphony. However, his most durable compositions are related to his music for the cinema; he composed the sound tracks of a great number of films of the Italian director Federico Fellini covering the period from 1950 to 1979.

WORKS: OPERAS: *Il Principe porcaro* (1925); *Ariodante* (Parma, Nov. 5, 1942); *Torquemada* (1943; revised version, Naples, Jan. 24, 1976); radio opera, *I 2 timidi* (Italian Radio, 1950; stage version, London, March 17, 1952); *Il cappello di paglia di Firenzi (Florentine Straw Hat;* 1946; Palermo, April 2, 1955); *La scuola di guida* (Spoleto, 1959); *Lo scoiattolo in gamba* (Venice, Sept. 16, 1959); opera buffa, *La notte di un nevrastenico* (concert version, Turin, July 9, 1959; stage version, Milan, Feb. 8, 1960); *Aladino e la lampada magica* (Naples, Jan. 14, 1968); *La visita meravigliosa,* after H.G. Wells (Palermo, Feb. 6, 1970); *Napoli milionaria,* to a libretto dealing with the American occupation of Naples in 1945 (produced in Spoleto, June 22, 1977). FOR ORCH.: *Balli* (1932); *Serenata* (1932); 3 symphs. (1936–39, 1938–43, 1957); *Sinfonia sopra una canzone d'amore* (1947–72); Harp Concerto (1948); *Variazioni sopra un tema gioviale* (1954); *Concerto festivo* (1958); Piano Concerto (1960); *Concerto soirée* for Piano and Orch.; *Fantasia sopra 12-note del "Don Giovanni" di Mozart* for Piano and Orch. (1961); Concerto for String Orch. (1964); Trombone Concerto (1968); *Divertimento concertante* for Double Bass and Orch. (1968–69); Cello Concerto

(1973); *Castel del Monte* for Horn and Orch. (1975–76); Bassoon Concerto (1974–77); *The Godfather Suite* (from the films; Buffalo, Nov. 5, 1976); *Piccolo mondo antico,* concerto for Piano and Orch. (1979). FILM SCORES: For films by Fellini, including *Lo sceicco bianco* (*The White Sheik;* 1950); *I vitelloni* (1953); *La strada* (1954); *Il bidone* (1955); *Notti di Cabiria* (1957); *La dolce vita* (1959); part of *Boccaccio 70* (1962); *Otto de mezza* (8 ½; 1963); *Giulietta degli spiriti* (*Juliet of the Spirits;* 1965); *Satyricon* (1969); *The Clowns* (1971); *Fellini Roma* (1972); *Amarcord* (1974); *Casanova* (1977); *Orchestra Rehearsal* (1979). His scores for other directors include Cass's *The Glass Mountain* (1950); De Filippo's *Napoli milionaria* (1950); Vidor's *War and Peace* (1956); Visconti's *Le notti bianche* (1957), *Rocco e i suoi fratelli* (1960), and *Il gattopardo* (*The Leopard;* 1963); Zeffirelli's *The Taming of the Shrew* (1966) and *Romeo e Giulietta* (1968); Bondarchuk's *Waterloo* (1969); Coppola's *The Godfather I* (1972) and *II* (1974); Harvey's *The Abdication* (1974); Wertmuller's *Love and Anarchy* (1974); Guillermin's *Death on the Nile* (1978); Monicelli's *Caro Michele* (1978); and Troell's *Hurricane* (1979).

Rothenberger, Anneliese, German lyric soprano; b. Mannheim, June 19, 1924. After vocal study in Mannheim, she made her operatic debut in Koblenz in 1943. From 1946 to 1957 and again in 1958–73 she was a member of the Hamburg State Opera; also had engagements in Düsseldorf, Salzburg, Edinburgh, and Aix-en-Provence. In 1958 she joined the Vienna State Opera; also sang at La Scala in Milan and in Munich. On Nov. 18, 1960, she made a notable debut at the Metropolitan Opera in N.Y. as Zdenka in *Arabella,* by Richard Strauss. She was one of the most versatile singers of her generation, capable of giving congenial renditions of soprano parts in operas of Mozart and Verdi; she also gave an excellent performance of the challenging role of Marie in Alban Berg's opera *Wozzeck.* She further distinguished herself in the even more demanding role of Lulu in Alban Berg's opera, which she sang with the Hamburg Opera. She publ. an autobiography, *Melodie meines Lebens* (Munich, 1972).

Rothwell, Evelyn, English oboist; b. Wallingford, Jan. 24, 1911. She studied at the Royal College of Music with Leon Goossens; in 1931 she joined the Covent Garden Opera touring orch.; then was a member of the Scottish Orch. in Glasgow (1933–36) and of the London Symph. Orch. (1935–39); also played in the Glyndebourne Festival Orch. (1934–39). In 1939 she married the conductor **Barbirolli.** In 1971 she became a prof. of oboe at the Royal Academy of Music.

Rothwell, Walter Henry, British-American conductor; b. London, Sept. 22, 1872; d. Santa Monica, Calif., March 12, 1927. He studied at the Vienna Cons. (1881–88) with J. Epstein (piano), R. Fuchs (theory), and Bruckner (composition); took further courses in Munich with Thuille and Schillings. In 1895 he became assistant conductor to Mahler at the Hamburg Opera; then conducted the German opera in Amsterdam (1903–4) and (1904–8) the Savage Opera Co. in the U.S., with which he gave performances of *Parsifal* in English. He then was conductor of the St. Paul Symph. Orch. (1908–14); after several years in N.Y. as a teacher, he was engaged (1919) to organize and conduct the Los Angeles Phil. Orch., which he led until his death. He was married (Sept. 10, 1908) to the soprano **Elisabeth Wolff.**

Rottenberg, Ludwig, Austrian conductor and composer; b. Czernowitz, Bukovina, Oct. 11, 1864; d. Frankfurt, May 6, 1932. He studied music with A. Hřimalý, R. Fuchs, and E. Mandyczewski in Vienna; was Kapellmeister at the Stadttheater in Brünn (1891–92) and at the Frankfurt opera (1893–1926); retired in 1927. In 1912 and 1913 he conducted the Wagner performances at Covent Garden in London. He publ. a collection of 30 songs, a Violin Sonata, and piano variations; his opera, *Die Geschwister,* was produced in Frankfurt on Nov. 30, 1915. Rottenberg was the father-in-law of **Paul Hindemith.**

Rouart-Lerolle & Cie., French publishing house, founded in 1905 at Paris by **Alexander Rouart** (1869–1921), through the purchase of the firms of Meuriot and Baudoux. When, in 1908, **Jacques Lerolle,** son of the famous painter, became his associate, the firm acquired the catalogue of the publ. house of Gregh (founded in 1840). After the death of Rouart in 1921, Lerolle became director; Mme. Rouart, the founder's widow, a partner; and François Hepp (1887–1965), son-in-law of Rouart, co-director. In 1942 the entire stock of Rouart-Lerolle & Cie. was sold to Salabert.

Rouget de l'Isle, Claude-Joseph, composer of the *Marseillaise;* b. Lons-le-Saulnier, Jura, May 10, 1760; d. Choisy-le-Roy, June 27, 1836. He composed the famous national hymn in 1792, while stationed in Strasbourg as a military engineer. The original title of the *Marseillaise* was *Le Chant de guerre de l'armée du Rhin,* and it was designed to be a patriotic song at the time of the war with Austria; it was taken up by the Marseilles soldiers marching toward Paris, and so assumed its universally known title. Rouget de l'Isle was himself not a revolutionary; he was in fact imprisoned for refusing to take the oath against the crown. He went to Paris after Robespierre's downfall, and composed a *Hymne dithyrambique sur la conjuration de Robespierre* (1794), *Chant des vengeances* (1798), and a *Chant du combat* for the army in Egypt (1800). He publ. 50 *Chants français* in 1825; wrote several opera librettos. Maurice de La Fuye and Emile Guéret, in their book *Rouget de l'Isle, Inconnu* (Paris, 1943), argued that he wrote only the words and not the music of the *Marseillaise,* and suggested that the composer was Ignace Pleyel. A. Loth, in his pamphlet *Le Chant de la Marseillaise* (Paris, 1886), claimed that the composer was one Grisons.

Roussakis, Nicolas, American composer of Greek ancestry; b. Athens, June 14, 1934. He emigrated to the U.S. in 1949; attended Columbia College (B.A., 1956) and the Graduate Faculties of Columbia Univ. (M.A., 1960), where he attended courses of Otto Luening, Jack Beeson, Henry Cowell, Ben Weber, Ralph Shapey, and Philipp Jarnach. To earn a living, he played the clarinet; received a Fulbright grant for study in Germany (1961–63); attended seminars of Boulez, Berio, Ligeti, and Stockhausen in Darmstadt. Upon his return to the U.S., he became active with contemporary music groups. In 1977 he was appointed to the faculty at Rutgers Univ. He was co-founder, with Francis Thorne, of the American Composers Orch. His own works are marked by an aggressive modernity of idiom, but are satisfyingly playable and surprisingly pleasurable even to untutored ears. They include *Night Speech* for Chorus and Percussion (1968); *Short Pieces* for 2 Flutes (1969); *Concertino* for Percussion and Woodwinds (1973); *Ode and Cataclysm* for Orch. (1975); *Ephemeris* for String Quartet (1979); piano pieces; choruses.

Rousseau, Jean-Jacques, great philosopher and author; b. Geneva, June 28, 1712; d. Ermenonville, near Paris, July 2, 1778. Without other musical training besides desultory self-instruction, Rousseau made his debut as a music scholar at the age of 29, reading a paper before the Académie in Paris (1724), which was received and publ. as a *Dissertation sur la musique moderne* (1743). His opera *Les Muses galantes* had only one private representation, at the house of La Pouplinière in 1745; his revision of the intermezzo *La Reine de Navarre* (by Voltaire and Rameau) was a failure in Paris; but his opera *Le Devin du village* (Fontainebleau, Oct. 18, 1752; Paris Opéra, March 1, 1753) was very successful and remained in the repertoire for 75 years. In the meantime, his musical articles for the *Encyclopédie* had evoked scathing criticism from Rameau and others; improved by revision and augmentation, they were republ. as his *Dictionnaire de musique* (Geneva, 1767; the existence of this ed. cannot be proved; first known ed., Paris, 1768). In 1752 commenced the dispute, known as the "guerre des bouffons," between the partisans of French and Italian opera; Rousseau sided with the latter, publishing a *Lettre à M. Grimm au sujet des remarques ajoutées à sa lettre sur Omphale* (1752), followed by the caustic *Lettre sur la musique française* (1753; to which the members of the Opéra responded by burning him in effigy and excluding him from the theater) and *Lettre d'un symphoniste de l'Académie royale de musique à ses camarades* (1753). He wrote 2 numbers for the melodrama *Pygmalion* (1770; Paris, Oct. 30, 1775). Publ. posthumously were 6 new arias for *Le Devin du village,* and a collection of about 100 *romances* and duets, *Les Consolations des misères de ma vie* (1781), and fragments of an opera, *Daphnis et Chloé* (1780). All his writings on music have been often republ. in eds. of his *Collected Works* (1782; many subsequent eds.).

Rousseau, Marcel (-Auguste-Louis), French composer; b. Paris, Aug. 18, 1882; d. there, June 11, 1955. He studied with his father, **Samuel Rousseau;** then entered the Paris Cons. as a student of Lenepveu; won the Deuxième Premier Grand Prix de Rome with the cantata *Maia* (1905). Later in his professional career he added his father's first name to his own, and produced his works as **Samuel-Rousseau.**
WORKS: Operas (all produced in Paris): *Tarass Boulba,* after Gogol (Nov. 22, 1919); *Le Hulla* (March 9, 1923); *Le Bon Roi Dagobert* (Dec. 5, 1927; his most successful work); *Kerkeb* (April 6, 1951); ballets: *Promenade dans Rome* (Paris, Dec. 7, 1936) and *Entre 2 rondes* (Paris, April 27, 1940); orch. tableaux: *Solitude triste* and *Impression dolente;* etc. In 1947 he was elected to the Académie des Beaux-Arts.

Rousseau, Samuel-Alexandre, French composer, father of **Marcel Samuel-Rousseau;** b. Neuve-Maison, Aisne, June 11, 1853; d. Paris, Oct. 1, 1904. He studied at the Paris Cons. with César Franck (organ) and Bazin (composition); won the Grand Prix de Rome with the cantata *La Fille de Jephté* (1878); also the Prix Cressent with the one-act comic opera *Dianora* (Opéra-Comique, Dec. 22, 1879). His opera *Mérowig* was awarded the Prize of the City of Paris, and was performed in concert form at the Grand Théâtre there on Dec. 12, 1892. In 1892 he was appointed conductor at the Théâtre-Lyrique; was for 10 years chorus master at the Société des Concerts du Cons.; also taught harmony at the Paris Cons. On June 8, 1898, his lyric drama *La Cloche du Rhin* was staged at the Paris Opéra with considerable success, but had only 9 performances in all; this was followed by the music dramas *Milia* (Opéra-Comique, 1904) and *Léone* (Opéra-Comique, March 7, 1910).

Roussel, Albert (Charles Paul Marie), outstanding French composer; b. Tourcoing, Département du Nord, April 5, 1869; d. Royan, Aug. 23, 1937. Orphaned as a child, he was educated by his grandfather, mayor of his native town, and after the grandfather's death, by his aunt. He studied academic subjects at the Collège Stanislas in Paris; music with the organist Stoltz; then studied mathematics in preparation for entering the Naval Academy; at the age of 18 he began his training in the navy; from 1889 to Aug. 1890 he was a member of the crew of the frigate *Iphigénie,* sailing to Indochina. This voyage was of great importance to Roussel, since it opened for him a world of oriental culture and art, which became one of the chief sources of his musical inspiration. He later sailed on the cruiser *Dévastation;* received a leave of absence for reasons of health, and spent some time in Tunis; was then stationed in Cherbourg, and began to compose there. In 1893 he was sent once more to Indochina. He resigned from the navy in 1894 and went to Paris, where he began to study music seriously with Eugène Gigout. In 1898 he entered the Schola Cantorum in Paris as a pupil of Vincent d'Indy; continued this study until 1907, when he was already 38 years old, but at the same time he was entrusted with a class in counterpoint, which he conducted at the Schola Cantorum from 1902 to 1914; among his students were Erik Satie, Stan Golestan, Paul Le Flem, Roland-Manuel, Guy de Lioncourt, and Varèse. In 1909 Roussel and his wife, Blanche Preisach-Roussel, undertook a voyage to India, where he became acquainted with the legend of the queen Padmâvatî, which he selected as a subject for his famous opera-ballet. His choral symph. *Les Evocations* was also inspired by this tour. At the outbreak of war in 1914, Roussel applied for active service in the navy but was rejected and volunteered as an ambulance driver. After the Armistice of 1918, he settled in Normandy and devoted himself to composition. In the autumn of 1930 he visited the U.S.

Roussel began his work under the influence of French Impressionism, with its dependence on exotic moods and poetic association. However, the sense of formal design asserted itself in his symph. works; his *Suite en fa* (1927) signalizes a transition toward neo-Classicism; the thematic development is vigorous, and the rhythms are clearly delineated, despite some asymmetrical progressions; the orchestration, too, is in the Classical tradition. Roussel possessed a keen sense of the theater; he was capable of fine characterization of exotic or mythological subjects, but also knew how to depict humorous situations in lighter works. An experiment in a frankly modernistic manner is exemplified by his *Jazz dans la nuit* for Voice and Piano.

WORKS: FOR THE STAGE: *Le Marchand de sable qui passe,* incidental music (Le Havre, Dec. 16, 1908); *Le Festin de l'araignée,* ballet-pantomime in one act (Paris, April 3, 1913); *Padmâvatî,* opera-ballet in 2 acts (1914–18; Paris, June 1, 1923); *La Naissance de la lyre,* lyric opera in one act (Paris, July 1, 1925); *Bacchus et Ariane,* ballet in 2 acts (Paris, May 22, 1931); *Le Testament de la tante Caroline,* opéra-bouffe (1932–33; Olomouc, Czechoslovakia, Nov. 14, 1936; Paris, March 11, 1937); *Aeneas,* ballet with Chorus, in one act (Brussels, July 31, 1935). FOR ORCH.: 4 symphs.: No. 1, *Le Poème de la forêt* (1904–6; Brussels, March 22, 1908); No. 2, *Symphonie en si bémol* (1919–21; Paris, March 4, 1922); No. 3, *Symphonie en sol mineur* (commissioned by the Boston Symph. Orch.; perf. there by Koussevitzky, Oct. 24, 1930); No. 4, *Symphonie en lu majeur* (1934; Paris, Oct. 19, 1935); *Suite en fa* (Boston, Jan. 21, 1927); *Sinfonietta* for Strings (Paris, Nov. 19, 1934); *Résurrection,* symph. poem (Paris, May 17, 1904); *Evocations,* suite in 3 movements (Paris, May 18, 1912); *Pour une fête de printemps* (Paris, Oct. 29, 1921); *Rapsodie flamande* (Brussels, Dec. 12, 1935); *Concert pour petit orchestre* (Paris, May 5, 1927); *Petite suite pour orchestre* (Paris, Feb. 6, 1930); *Piano Concerto* (Paris, June 7, 1928); *Concertino* for Cello and Orch (Paris, Feb. 6, 1937); *Le Bardit de Francs* for Male Chorus, Brass, and Percussion (Strasbourg, April 21, 1928); *Psaume LXXX* for Tenor, Chorus, and Orch. (Paris, April 25, 1929); symph. suites from theater works: *Le Festin de l'araignée* (1912); *Padmâvatî* (1914–18); *La Naissance de la lyre* (1922–24); *Bacchus et Ariane* (1930). CHAMBER MUSIC: Piano Trio (1902); *Divertissement* for Flute, Oboe, Clarinet, Bassoon, Horn, and Piano (1906); *Sérénade* for Flute, Violin, Viola, Cello, and Harp (1925); Trio for Flute, Viola, and Cello (1929); String Quartet (1932); Trio for Violin, Viola, and Cello (1937); 2 violin sonatas (1908, 1924); *Joueurs de flûte,* suite for Flute and Piano (1924); *Andante et Scherzo* for Flute and Piano (1934). FOR PIANO: *Des heures passant,* a cycle of 4 pieces (1898); *Rustiques,* a cycle of 3 pieces (1904–6); suite of 3 pieces (1910); Sonatina (1912); *Petit canon perpétuel* (1913); *Prélude et fugue (Hommage à Bach);* etc. SONGS: *Adieux* (1907); *Jazz dans la nuit* (1928); *2 idylles* (1931); 3 sets of *Poèmes chinois* (1908, 1927, 1932); etc. A complete catalogue of works, with a biographical notice and annotations, was publ. in Paris in 1947 and constitutes a primary source of information.

Rowley, Alec, English composer; b. London, March 13, 1892; d. Weybridge, Surrey, Jan. 12, 1958. He studied at the Royal Academy of Music; upon graduation, became a teacher. Among his works are a pantomime, *The Princess Who Lost a Tune;* 2 piano concertos; *Rhapsody* for Viola and Orch.; Concerto for Oboe and Orch.; *Phyllis and Corydon* for String Quartet; *From Faerie* for String Quartet; *Little Jesus* for Voice, Piano, and String Quartet; *Watercolours* for Piano, Violin, Viola, and Cello; *Pastel Portraits* for Piano, Violin, and Cello; 3 little trios for Piano, Violin, and Cello; *The Puppet Show,* 4 *Contrasts, A Short Suite;* also piano pieces for children.

Roy, Klaus George, Austrian-born American composer, writer, and program annotator; b. Vienna, Jan. 24, 1924. He came to the U.S. in 1940; studied at Boston Univ. with Karl Geiringer (B.Mus., 1947) and at Harvard Univ. with Archibald T. Davison, Otto Kinkeldey, Arthur Tillman Merritt, and Walter Piston (M.A., 1949). In 1945–46 he served as an officer in education and information with U.S. Army General Headquarters in Tokyo. From 1948–57 he was employed as a librarian and instructor at Boston Univ.; concurrently he wrote music criticism for the *Christian Science Monitor.* In 1958 he was appointed director of publicity and program book editor of the Cleveland Orch.; also made broadcasts of comments during intermission. As a composer, he was extraordinarily prolific, considering the multitude of his external jobs. He wrote theater pieces, choruses, anthems, hymns, Christmas songs, etc., all extremely pleasing to the ear.

Rôze, Marie-Hippolyte (née **Roze-Ponsin**), famous French soprano; b. Paris, March 2, 1846; d. there, June 21, 1926. She studied at the Paris Cons. with Mocker and later with Auber, winning 2 prizes in 1865; made her debut at the Opéra-Comique in the title role of Hérold's *Marie* (Aug. 16, 1865); sang there for 3 seasons; then appeared at the Paris Opéra as Marguerite in Gounod's *Faust* (Jan. 2, 1879); made her London debut as Marguerite (1872); continued to sing in England for many years. She visited America twice, in 1877–78 and 1880–81. In 1874 she married an American bass, **Julius E. Perkins,** who died the following year; later she married the impresario **J.H. Mapleson, Jr.,** but the marriage ended in divorce. In 1890 she settled in Paris as a teacher.

Rôze, Raymond (J.H. Raymond Rôze-Perkins), English composer, son of **Marie Rôze;** b. London, 1875; d. there, March 31, 1920. He studied at the Brussels Cons., where he won first prize; wrote overtures and incidental music to many plays. In 1913 he organized at Covent Garden a season of opera in English, during which he conducted his own opera *Joan of Arc* (Oct. 31, 1913); another opera by him, *Arabesque,* was produced at the Coliseum in London in 1916.

Rozhdestvensky, Gennadi, eminent Soviet conductor; b. Moscow, May 4, 1931. He studied piano with Oborin and conducting with Anosov at the Moscow Cons.; graduated in 1954. From 1951 to 1960 he served as assistant conductor at the Bolshoi Theater in Moscow, and from 1965 to 1970 was its principal conductor. From 1961 to 1974 he was music director and conductor of the U.S.S.R. State Radio Orch.; in 1976 he was appointed prof. of the Moscow Cons. From 1974 to 1977 he was the principal conductor of the Stockholm Phil. Orch.; in 1978 he became chief guest conductor of the BBC Orch. in London. He made numerous guest appearances in the U.S. with major orchs. In 1981 he was appointed chief conductor of the Vienna Symph. Orch. He is distinguished by his encompassing interest in new music; he conducted notable performances of works by Soviet composers, particularly Prokofiev and Shostakovich, as well as by Stravinsky, Schoenberg, Berg, Milhaud, Honegger, and Poulenc. He publ. a technical treatise, *Technique of Conducting* (Leningrad, 1974), and a collection of essays, *Thoughts about Music* (Moscow, 1975).

Rozkošný, Josef Richard, Czech composer; b. Prague, Sept. 21, 1833; d. there, June 3, 1913. He studied painting and music in Prague; his teachers were Tomaschek (piano) and Kittl (composition). His songs and choruses became popular, and he successfully attempted the composition of operas to Czech librettos; 8 operas were produced in Prague, among them: *Svatojanské proudy* (*The Rapids of St. John;* Oct. 3, 1871); *Popelka* (*Cinderella;* May 31, 1885); *Černé jezero* (*The Black Lake;* Jan. 6, 1906). He also publ. a number of piano pieces.

Rózsa, Miklós, brilliant Hungarian-American composer; b. Budapest, April 18, 1907. He studied piano and composition in Leipzig, with Hermann Grabner; musicology with Theodor Kroyer. In 1931 he settled in Paris, where he became successful as a composer; his works were often performed in European music centers. In 1935 he went to London as a writer for the films; in 1940 emigrated to the U.S., and settled in Hollywood. His orch. and chamber music is cast in the advanced modern idiom in vogue in Europe between the 2 wars; neo-Classical in general content, it is strong in polyphony and incisive rhythm; for his film music, he employs a more Romantic and diffuse style, relying on a Wagnerian type of grandiloquence.
WORKS: For Orch.: *Nordungarische Bauernlieder und Tänze* (1929); Symph. (1930); *Serenade* for Small Orch. (1932); *Scherzo* (1933); *Thema, Variationen und Finale* (1933); *Capriccio, Pastorale e Danza* (1938); *Variations on a Hungarian Peasant Song* (N.Y., Nov. 14, 1943); Concerto for String Orch. (Los Angeles, Dec. 28, 1944); Violin Concerto (Dallas, Jan. 5, 1956; Jascha Heifetz, soloist); *Sinfonia concertante* for Violin, Cello, and Orch. (1966); Piano Concerto (Los Angeles, April 6, 1967); Cello Concerto (1969); *Tripartita* for Orch. (1973); Viola Concerto (Pittsburgh, May 4, 1984; Pinchas Zukerman, soloist). He has won Oscars for 3 film scores: *Spellbound* (1945), *A Double Life* (1947), and *Ben Hur* (1959); other notable film scores are *Quo Vadis?* (1951), *Ivanhoe* (1952), *Julius Caesar* (1953), *Lust for Life* (1956), and *El Cid* (1961).

Różycki, Ludomir, Polish composer; b. Warsaw, Nov. 6, 1884; d. Katowice, Jan. 1, 1953. He studied piano with his father, a teacher at the Warsaw Cons.; theory with Noskowski at the Cons., graduating with honors in 1903. He then went to Berlin, where he took lessons with Humperdinck; in 1908 he was appointed conductor of the opera theater in Lwow; then undertook a European tour; settled in Berlin, where he remained through the years of World War I. In 1920 he returned to Warsaw; after 1945, lived mostly in Katowice. He was highly regarded in Poland as a national composer of stature; his style of composition was a successful blend of German, Russian, and Italian ingredients, yet the Polish characteristics were not obscured by the cosmopolitan harmonic and orch. dress.
WORKS: Operas: *Boleslaw smialy* (*Boleslaw the Bold;* Lwow, Feb. 11, 1909); *Meduza* (Warsaw, Oct. 22, 1912); *Eros und Psyche* (Breslau, March 10, 1917; in German); *Casanova* (Warsaw, June 8, 1923); *Beatrice Cenci* (Warsaw, Jan. 30, 1927); *Mlyn diabelski* (*The Devilish Mill;* Poznan, Feb. 21, 1931); *Lili chce spiewac,* comic opera (Poznan, March 7, 1933); ballets: *Pan Twardowski* (Warsaw, May 9, 1921; his most successful work; more than 800 perfs. in Warsaw) and *Apollon et la belle* (1937); symph. poems: *Stanczyk* (1903); *Anhelli* (1909); *Warszawianka* (1910); *Mona Lisa Gioconda* (1910); *Pietà* (1942); *Warszawa wyzwolona* (*Warsaw Liberated;* 1950); 2 piano concertos (1918, 1942); Violin Concerto (1944); Piano Quintet (1913); String Quartet (1916); Violin Sonata (1903); Cello Sonata (1906); a number of piano pieces; several song cycles.

Rubbra, Edmund, notable English composer; b. Northampton, May 23, 1901. His parents were musical, and he was taught to play the piano by his mother. He left school as a young boy and was employed in various factories; at the same time he continued to study music by himself, and attempted some composition; organized a concert devoted to the works of his favorite composer, Cyril Scott (Northampton, 1918); subsequently took lessons from him in London; in 1919 he studied with Holst;

his other teachers in composition were John Ireland, Eugene Goossens, and Vaughan Williams. He compensated for a late beginning in composition by an extremely energetic application to steady improvement of his technique; finally elaborated a style of his own, marked by sustained lyricism and dynamic Romanticism; his harmonic language often verges on polytonality. He taught at Oxford Univ. (1947–68), and at Guildhall School of Music from 1961.

WORKS: One-act opera, *Bee-Bee-Bei* (1933); ballet, *Prism* (1938); for Orch.: *Double Fugue* (1924); *Triple Fugue* (1929); Symph. No. 1 (London, April 30, 1937); Symph. No. 2 (London, Dec. 16, 1938); Symph. No. 3 (Manchester, Dec. 15, 1940); Symph. No. 4 (London, Aug. 14, 1942); Symph. No. 5 (London, Jan. 26, 1949); Symph. No. 6 (London, Nov. 17, 1954); Symph. No. 7 (Birmingham, Oct. 1, 1957); Symph. No. 8 (London, Jan. 5, 1971); Symph. No. 9, *The Resurrection*, for Soloists, Chorus, and Orch. (1973); Symph. No. 11 (London, Aug. 20, 1980); Chamber Symph. (Middlesborough, Jan. 8, 1975); *Sinfonia concertante* for Piano and Orch. (London, Aug. 10, 1943); *Soliloquy* for Cello and Orch. (London, Jan. 1, 1945); Viola Concerto (London, April 15, 1953); chamber music: *Fantasy* for 2 Violins and Piano (1925); *Lyric Movement* for Piano Quintet (1929); 2 string quartets (1933, 1952); Piano Trio (1950); 2 violin sonatas (1925, 1931); Cello Sonata (1946); choral works: *The Sacred Hymnody* (1921); *La Belle Dame sans merci* (1925); *The Morning Watch* (1941); *Te Deum* (1951); a number of madrigals and motets for Unaccompanied Chorus; songs with Orch. (*Ballad of Tristram, 4 Medieval Latin Lyrics, 5 Sonnets,* etc.); songs with Piano; miscellaneous pieces for various instruments. He publ. *Counterpoint. A Survey* (London, 1960).

Rubens, Paul Alfred, English composer of light music; b. London, April 29, 1875; d. Falmouth, Feb. 5, 1917. He was educated at Oxford; in 1899 he contributed some numbers to the famous musical revue *Floradora*, and this success induced him to devote himself to the composition of light operas. The following stage works by him were produced: *Lady Madcap* (1904); *Miss Hook of Holland* (1907); *My Mimosa Maid* (1908); *Dear Little Denmark* (1909); *The Balkan Princess* (1910); *The Sunshine Girl* (1912); he also wrote numerous songs and ballads.

Rubin, Marcel, Austrian composer; b. Vienna, July 7, 1905. He studied piano with Richard Robert, theory of composition with Richard Stöhr, and counterpoint and fugue with Franz Schmidt at the Vienna Academy of Music; simultaneously attended courses in law. In 1925 he went to Paris, where he took private lessons with Darius Milhaud. He was back in Vienna in 1931 to complete his studies in law, and in 1933 received his degree of Dr.Juris. After the Nazi Anschluss of Austria in 1938, Rubin, being a non-Aryan, fled to Paris, but was interned as an enemy alien in France; after France fell in 1940, he made his way to Marseilles. Convinced that only

the Communists could efficiently oppose Fascism, he became a member of the illegal Austrian Communist party in exile; in 1942 he went to Mexico and remained there until 1946; he returned to Vienna in 1947. His music follows the modernistic models of Parisianized Russians and Russianized Frenchmen, with a mandatory hedonism in "new simplicity." Although Rubin studied works of Schoenberg, Berg, and Anton von Webern with great assiduity and wrote articles about them, he never adopted the method of composition with 12 tones in his own music.

WORKS: Comic opera, *Kleider machen Leute* (Vienna Volksoper, Dec. 14, 1973); "dance piece," *Die Stadt* (1948); 6 symphs. (1927–28, 1937, 1939, 1945, 1965, 1974); Concerto for Double Bass and Orch. (1970); Trumpet Concerto (1972); *Ballade* for Orch. (1948); *Rondo-Burleske* for Orch. (1960); *3 Komödianten* for Orch. (1963); Sonatina for Orch. (1965); Sinfonietta for String Orch. (1966); *Pastorale* for Strings (1970); 3 piano sonatas (1925, 1927, 1928); String Quartet (1926; revised 1961); String Trio (1927; revised 1962); Sonatina for Oboe and Piano (1927); Cello Sonata (1928); *Divertimento* for Piano, Violin, and Cello (1967); *Serenade* for Flute, Oboe, Clarinet, Horn, and Bassoon (1971); Violin Sonata (1974); oratorio, *Die Albigenser* (1957–61); song cycles to poems by Clément Marot, Guillaume Apollinaire, Rimbaud, Goethe, François Villon, etc.

Rubini, Giovanni Battista, celebrated Italian tenor; b. Romano, near Bergamo, April 7, 1794; d. there, March 3, 1854. His teacher was Rosio of Bergamo; after an auspicious debut in Pavia (1814), he sang for a time in Naples; there he married (1819) a singer, **Mlle. Chomel,** known under the professional name of **La Comelli.** On Oct. 6, 1825, he sang in Paris, where he scored his first triumphs in Rossini's operas at the Théâtre-Italien; his performances of the leading parts in the operas of Bellini and Donizetti were also very successful, and there is reason to believe that Rubini's interpretations greatly contributed to the rising fame of both of those composers. Between 1831 and 1843 he sang in Paris and London; in 1843 he undertook a tour with Liszt, traveling with him in the Netherlands and Germany; in the same year he sang in Russia with tremendous acclaim; visited Russia again in 1844; then returned to Italy, bought an estate near his native town, and remained there until his death; for some years he gave singing lessons. He publ. *12 lezioni di canto moderno per tenore o soprano* and an album of 6 songs, *L'Addio.*

Rubinstein, Anton, celebrated Russian composer and pianist, brother of **Nicolai Rubinstein;** b. Vykhvatinetz, Podolia, Nov. 28, 1829; d. Peterhof, near St. Petersburg, Nov. 20, 1894. He was of a family of Jewish merchants who became baptized in Berdichev in July 1831. His mother gave him his first lessons in piano; the family moved to Moscow, where his father opened a small pencil factory. A well-known Moscow piano teacher, Alexandre Villoing, was entrusted with Rubinstein's musical education, and was in fact his only piano teacher. In 1839 Villoing took him to Paris, where Rubinstein played before Chopin and Liszt; remained in Paris until 1841; then made a concert tour in the Netherlands, Germany, Austria, England, Norway, and Sweden, returning to Russia in 1843. Since Anton's brother Nicolai evinced a talent for composition, the brothers were taken in 1844 to Berlin, where, on Meyerbeer's recommendation, Anton too studied composition, with Dehn; subsequently he made a tour through Hungary with the flutist Heindl. He returned to Russia in 1848 and settled in St. Petersburg. There he enjoyed the enlightened patronage of the Grand Duchess Helen, and wrote 3 Russian operas: *Dmitri Donskoy* (1852); *Sibirskie Okhotniki* (*The Siberian Hunters;* 1853); and *Fomka Durachok* (*Thomas the Fool;* 1853). In 1854, with the assistance of the Grand Duchess, Rubinstein undertook another tour in Western Europe. He found publishers in Berlin, and gave concerts of his own works in London and Paris, exciting admiration as both composer and pianist; on his return in 1858, he was appointed court pianist and conductor of the court concerts. He assumed the direction of the Russian Musical Society in 1859; in 1862 he founded the Imperial Cons. in St. Petersburg, remaining its director until 1867. For 20 years thereafter he held no official position; from 1867 until 1870 he gave concerts in Europe, winning fame as a pianist 2nd only to Liszt. During the season of 1872–73, he made a triumphant American tour, playing in 215 concerts, for which he was paid lavishly; appeared as a soloist and jointly with the violinist Wieniawski. He produced a sensation by playing without notes, a novel procedure at the time. Returning to Europe, he elaborated a cycle of historical concerts, in programs ranging from Bach to Chopin; he usually devoted the last concert of a cycle to Russian composers. In 1887 he resumed the directorship of the St. Petersburg Cons., resigning again in 1891, when he went to Dresden (until 1894). He returned to Russia shortly before his death.

In 1890 Rubinstein established the Rubinstein Prize, an international competition open to young men between 20 and 26 years of age. Two prizes of 5,000 francs each were offered, one for composition, the other for piano playing. Quinquennial competitions were held in St. Petersburg, Berlin, Vienna, and Paris.

Rubinstein's role in Russian musical culture is of the greatest importance. He introduced European methods into education, and established high standards of artistic performance. He was the first Russian musician who was equally prominent as composer and interpreter. According to contemporary reports, his playing possessed extraordinary power (his octave passages were famous) and insight, revealed particularly in his performance of Beethoven's sonatas. His renown as a composer was scarcely less. His *Ocean Symphony* was one of the most frequently performed orch. works in Europe and in America; his piano concertos were part of the standard repertoire; his pieces for Piano Solo, *Melody in F, Romance, Kamennoi Ostrow,* became perennial favorites. After his death, his orch. works

all but vanished from concert programs, as did his operas (with the exception of *The Demon,* which is still perf. in Russia); his Piano Concerto No. 4, in D minor, is occasionally heard.

WORKS: FOR THE STAGE: Operas: *Dmitri Donskoy* (St. Petersburg, April 30, 1852); *Sibirskie okhotniki* (*The Siberian Hunters;* 1853); *Fomka Durachok* (*Thomas the Fool;* St. Petersburg, May 23, 1853); *Die Kinder der Heide,* 5-act German opera (Vienna, Feb. 23, 1861); *Feramors,* after the poem *Lalla Rookh* of T. Moore (Dresden, Feb. 24, 1863); *The Demon,* after Lermontov (St. Petersburg, Jan. 25, 1875); *Die Makkabäer* (Berlin, April 17, 1875); *Nero* (Hamburg, Nov. 1, 1879); *Kupets Kalashnikov* (*The Merchant Kalashnikov;* St. Petersburg, March 5, 1880); *Sulamith* and *Unter Räubern* (both perf. Hamburg, Nov. 8, 1883); *Der Papagei* (*The Parrot;* Hamburg, 1884); *Goriusha* (St. Petersburg, Dec. 3, 1889); ballet, *Die Rebe* (*The Vine;* 1885). VOCAL WORKS: Oratorios: *Paradise Lost* (Weimar, 1858; revised and arranged as a sacred opera, Düsseldorf, 1875); *The Tower of Babel* (Königsberg, 1870); *Moses* (1892); *Christus* (1893); 2 cantatas: *Die Nixe* for Alto Solo and Female Chorus, and *Der Morgen* for Male Chorus; scene and aria for Soprano, *E dunque ver?;* 2 scenes for Alto and Orch.: *Hecuba* and *Hagar in der Wüste;* about 100 songs (of these, *Asra* is popular). FOR ORCH.: 6 symphs. (No. 2, *Ocean;* No. 4, *Dramatic;* No. 5, *Russian*); *Ouverture triomphale; Ouverture de concert;* 3 "character pictures": *Faust, Ivan the Terrible, Don Quixote;* a "morceau symphonique," *La Russie;* 5 piano concertos; *Fantaisie* for Piano and Orch.; *Konzertstück* for Piano and Orch.; Violin Concerto; 2 cello concertos. CHAMBER MUSIC: Octet for Piano, Strings, and Winds; Sextet for Strings; Quintet for Piano, Flute, Clarinet, Horn, and Bassoon; String Quintet; Piano Quintet; 10 string quartets; Piano Quartet; 5 piano trios; 2 violin sonatas; 2 cello sonatas. FOR PIANO: 4 sonatas; *Kamennoi Ostrow; Soirées à St. Petersburg; Album de Péterhof; Soirées musicales;* 6 *Barcarolles; Sérénade russe;* polkas, mazurkas, etc.

WRITINGS: *Memoirs* (St. Petersburg, 1889; in Eng. as *Autobiography of Anton Rubinstein,* Boston, 1890); *Music and Its Representatives* (Moscow, 1891; in Eng., N.Y., 1892; also publ. as *A Conversation on Music*); *Leitfaden zum richtigen Gebrauch des Pianoforte-Pedals* (posthumous; Leipzig, 1896; in French, Brussels, 1899); *Gedankenkorb, Litterarischer Nachlass* (posthumous; Stuttgart, 1896); *Die Meister des Klaviers* (posthumous; Berlin, 1899).

Rubinstein, Artur, celebrated cosmopolitan pianist of Jewish-Polish origin; b. Lodz, Poland, Jan. 28, 1887; d. Geneva, Dec. 20, 1982. He was a product of a merchant family with many children, of whom he alone exhibited musical propensities. He became emotionally attached to the piano as soon as he saw and heard the instrument; at the age of 7, on Dec. 14, 1894, he played pieces by Mozart, Schubert, and Mendelssohn at a charity concert. His first regular piano teacher was one Adolf Prechner. He was later taken to Warsaw, where he had piano lessons with Alexander Różycki. A significant *gradus ad Parnas-*

sum was a trip to Berlin, where Rubinstein played for the famous violinist Joachim. Funds were raised for his stay in Berlin, where he was taught piano by Heinrich Barth, a pupil of Liszt, and by Robert Kahn. He also had some theory lessons with Max Bruch. He made his formal debut in Berlin when he was 13, playing a Mozart concerto at the Berlin Hochschule für Musik, with Joachim conducting. Recitals in Dresden and Hamburg followed. In 1902 he was a soloist with the Warsaw Symph., directed by Emil Mlynarski (Rubinstein's future father-in-law). In the summer of 1903, he took regular lessons with Paderewski in Switzerland. He soon was able to support himself, and went to Paris, where he played with the Lamoureux Orch. and met Ravel, Paul Dukas, and Jacques Thibaud. He also played the G minor Piano Concerto by Saint-Saëns in the presence of the composer, who commended him. The ultimate plum of artistic success came when Rubinstein received an American contract. He made his debut at Carnegie Hall, in N.Y., on Jan. 8, 1906, as soloist with the Philadelphia Orch. in his favorite Saint-Saëns concerto. His American tour was not altogether successful, and he returned to Europe for further study. In 1915 he appeared as soloist with the London Symph. Orch. During the season 1916–17, he gave numerous recitals in Spain, a country in which he was to become extremely successful; from Spain he went to South America, where he also became a great favorite; he developed a flair for Spanish and Latin American music, and his renditions of the piano works of Albéniz and Manuel de Falla were models of authentic Hispanic modality. The Brazilian composer Villa-Lobos dedicated to Rubinstein his *Rudepoema,* regarded as one of the most difficult piano pieces ever written. Symbolic of his cosmopolitan career was the fact that he maintained apartments in N.Y., Beverly Hills, Paris, and Geneva. He was married to Aniela Mlynarska in 1932. Of his 4 children, one was born in Buenos Aires, one in Warsaw, and 2 in America. In 1946 he became an American citizen. On June 11, 1958, Rubinstein gave his first postwar concert in Poland; in 1964 he played in Moscow, Leningrad, and Kiev. In Poland and in Russia he was received with tremendous emotional acclaim. But he forswore any appearances in Germany, having been horrified by reports of German atrocities during World War II and enraged by the Nazi crimes against the Jewish people. German admirers of his playing had to be satisfied with his recordings, which sold millions of copies around the world.

Rubinstein was one of the finest interpreters of Chopin's music, to which his fiery temperament and poetic lyricism were particularly congenial. His style of playing tended toward bravura in Classical compositions, but he rarely indulged in mannerisms; his performances of Mozart and Beethoven were inspiring. In his characteristic spirit of robust humor, he made jokes about the multitude of notes he claimed to have dropped, but asserted that a worse transgression against music would be pedantic inflexibility in tempo and dynamics. He was a bon vivant, an indefatigable host at parties, and a fluent, though not always grammatical, speaker in most European languages, including Russian and his native Polish. In Hollywood, he played on the sound tracks for the motion pictures *I've Always Loved You* (1946), *Song of Love* (1947), and *Night Song* (1947). He also appeared as a pianist, representing himself, in the films *Carnegie Hall* (1947) and *Of Men and Music* (1951). A film documentary entitled *Artur Rubinstein, Love of Life* was produced in 1975; a 90-minute television special, *Rubinstein at 90,* was broadcast to mark his entry into that nonagenarian age; and he spoke philosophically about the inevitability of dying. He was the recipient of numerous international honors: a membership in the French Académie des Beaux Arts and the Légion d'Honneur, and the Order of Polonia Restituta of Poland; he held the Gold Medal of the Royal Phil. Society of London and several honorary doctorates from American institutions of learning. He was a passionate supporter of Israel, which he visited several times. In 1974 an international piano competition bearing his name was inaugurated in Jerusalem. On April 1, 1976, he received the U.S. Medal of Freedom, presented by President Ford. In 1976 he was forced to curtail, and finally to cease, concert activities when he was afflicted with retinitis pigmentosa, which led to his total blindness; but even then he never renounced his joie de vivre. He once said that the slogan "wine, women, and song" as applied to him was 80% women and only 20% wine and song. And in a widely publicized interview he gave at the age of 95 he declared his ardent love for Annabelle Whitestone, the Englishwoman who was assigned by his publisher to help him organize and edit his autobiography. He slid gently into death in his Geneva apartment, as in a pianissimo ending of a Chopin nocturne, ritardando, morendo . . . Rubinstein had expressed a wish to be buried in Israel; his body was cremated in Switzerland; the ashes were flown to Jerusalem to be interred in a separate emplacement at the cemetery, since the Jewish law does not permit cremation.

Rubinstein, Beryl, American pianist and composer; b. Athens, Ga., Oct. 26, 1898; d. Cleveland, Dec. 29, 1952. He studied piano with his father and Alexander Lambert; toured the U.S. as a child (1905–11); then went to Berlin to study with Busoni and Vianna da Motta. He was appointed to the faculty of the Cleveland Inst. of Music in 1921; became its director in 1932. He wrote an opera, *The Sleeping Beauty,* to a libretto by John Erskine (Juilliard School of Music, N.Y., Jan. 19, 1938); 32 piano studies; 3 dances for Piano; transcriptions from Gershwin's *Porgy and Bess.* He conducted his orch. *Scherzo* with the Cleveland Orch. on March 17, 1927; performed his Piano Concerto in C with the same orch. on Nov. 12, 1936.

Rubinstein, Joseph, Russian pianist; b. Starokonstantinov, Feb. 8, 1847; d. (committed suicide) Lucerne, Sept. 15, 1884. He studied in Vienna with Dachs; later took lessons with Liszt in Weimar. He was an ardent admirer of Wagner, whom he knew personally; in 1874 he was the pianist at the preliminary rehearsals of *Der Ring des Nibelungen* at Bayreuth; made piano transcriptions of it and also of *Parsifal.*

Rubinstein, Nicolai, Russian pianist and pedagogue, brother of **Anton Rubinstein;** b. Moscow, June 14, 1835; d. Paris, March 23, 1881. He began to study piano with his mother at the age of 4, when his brother, 6 years older than he, was already on the road to fame as a child prodigy; was taken to Berlin with his brother, and there studied with Kullak (piano) and Dehn (composition). The brothers met Mendelssohn and Meyerbeer; returning to Moscow in 1846, he began to take lessons with Alexandre Villoing. He also studied law, and received a degree from the Univ. of Moscow (1855); subsequently was a minor functionary in the government; earned his living by giving private lessons. In 1858 he began his concert career; appeared in Russia, and also in London. In 1859, when he was only 24 years old, he became head of the Moscow branch of the Russian Music Society; in 1866 this society opened the Moscow Cons., of which Nicolai Rubinstein was director until his death. From 1860 he was the regular conductor of the Moscow concerts of the Imperial Russian Musical Society. In 1878 he conducted 4 Russian concerts at the Paris Exposition; at the first and the 4th of the series he performed Tchaikovsky's Piano Concerto No. 1 (which he had criticized so sharply when Tchaikovsky first submitted it to him in 1874). Anton Rubinstein declared that Nicolai was a better pianist than himself, but this generous appreciation was not accepted by the public. As an educator, however, Nicolai Rubinstein played perhaps a greater role than his famous brother. Among his pupils were Taneyev, Siloti, and Emil Sauer.

Růbner, Cornelius. See **Rybner, Cornelius.**

Ruckers, Hans, known as "the eldest" of the family of celebrated Flemish harpsichord makers; b. Mechlin, c.1550; d. Antwerp, c.1598. He was the first of the family to make instruments; in 1579 was admitted to the Guild of St. Luke. His 2nd son, **Hans Ruckers,** also known as **Jean** (baptized, Antwerp, Jan. 15, 1578; d. there, April 24, 1643), was greatly esteemed by his contemporaries, and was exempted from Civic Guard duties in appreciation of his artistry. **Andreas Ruckers** the elder (baptized, Antwerp, Aug. 30, 1579; d. c.1654) manufactured harpsichords between 1601 and 1644. **Andreas Ruckers** the younger, son of the elder Andreas (baptized, Antwerp, March 31, 1607; d. after 1667), made instruments between 1637 and 1667. Another member of the same family was **Christoffel Ruckers,** who flourished c.1600. He constructed 2 virginals.

Rudel, Julius, outstanding Austrian-American conductor; b. Vienna, March 6, 1921. He studied at the Vienna Academy of Music; in 1938 emigrated to the U.S. (naturalized citizen, 1944) and continued his studies at the Mannes School of Music in N.Y. On Nov. 25, 1944, he made his American debut as conductor of the N.Y. City Opera; in 1957 became its music director. He also appeared as guest conductor of the Philadelphia Orch. and of several operatic companies; received numerous awards from American cultural organizations. In 1961 the Austrian government bestowed on him honorary insignia for arts and sciences. He championed the cause of American opera; gave first performances of several new stage works by American composers. In 1979 he resigned his post with the N.Y. City Opera and became music director of the Buffalo Phil. Orch.

Rudhyar, Dane, American composer, painter, and mystical philosopher; b. Paris, March 23, 1895. His parental name was **Daniel Chennevière;** he changed it in 1917 to Rudhyar, derived from an old Sanskrit root conveying the sense of dynamic action and the color red, astrologically related to the Zodiacal sign of his birth and the red-colored planet Mars. He studied philosophy at the Sorbonne, in Paris, receiving his baccalauréat in 1911, and took music courses at the Paris Cons. In composition he was largely self-taught; he also achieved a certain degree of proficiency as a pianist; developed a technique which he called "orchestral pianism." In 1913 the French publisher Durand commissioned him to write a short book on Debussy, with whom he briefly corresponded. At the same time he joined the modern artistic circles in Paris. In 1916 he went to America, became a naturalized American citizen in 1926. His "dance poems" for Orch., *Poèmes ironiques* and *Vision végétale,* were performed at the Metropolitan Opera House, N.Y., April 4, 1917. In 1918 he visited Canada; in Montreal he met the pianist Alfred Laliberté, who was closely associated with Scriabin, and through him Rudhyar became acquainted with Scriabin's theosophic ideas. In Canada he also publ. a collection of French poems, *Rapsodies* (Toronto, 1918). In 1920 he went to Hollywood to write scenic music for *Pilgrimage Play, The Life of Christ,* and also acted the part of Christ in the prologue of the silent film version of *The Ten Commandments* produced by Cecil B. DeMille. In Hollywood he initiated the project of "Introfilms," depicting inner psychological states on the screen through a series of images, but it failed to receive support and was abandoned. Between 1922 and 1930 he lived part-time in Hollywood and part-time in N.Y.; he was one of the founding members of the International Composers Guild in N.Y. In 1922 his orch. tone poem *Soul Fire* won the $1,000 prize of the Los Angeles Phil.; in 1928 his book *The Rebirth of Hindu Music* was publ. in Madras, India. After 1930 Rudhyar devoted most of his time to astrology. His first book on the subject, *The Astrology of Personality,* was publ. in 1936 and became a standard text in the field; it was described by Paul Clancy, the pioneer in the publishing of popular astrological magazines, as "the greatest step forward in astrology since the time of Ptolemy." A new development in Rudhyar's creative activities took place in 1938 when he began to paint, along nonrepresentational symbolistic lines; the titles of his paintings (*Mystic Tiara, Cosmic Seeds, Soul and Ego, Avatar,* etc.) reflect theosophic themes. His preoccupations with astrology left him little time for music; about 1965 he undertook a radical revision of some early compositions, and wrote several new ones; in 1984 he lived in Palo Alto, Calif., and continued an active schedule of lecturing.

The natural medium for Rudhyar's musical expression is the piano; his few symph. works are mostly orchestrations of original piano compositions. In his writing for piano Rudhyar builds sonorous chordal formations supported by resonant pedal points, occasionally verging on polytonality; a kinship with Scriabin's piano music is clearly felt, but Rudhyar's harmonic idiom is free from Scriabin's Wagnerian antecedents. Despite his study of oriental religions and music, Rudhyar does not attempt to make use of Eastern modalities in his own music.

Rudolf, Max, eminent German conductor; b. Frankfurt, June 15, 1902. He studied piano with Eduard Jung and composition with Bernhard Sekles at the Hoch Cons. in Frankfurt; was employed as a coach and a conductor in various provincial opera houses in Germany; then was active as a conductor in Prague (1929–35); in 1935 he went to Göteborg, Sweden, where he served as a regular guest conductor with the Göteborg Symph. Orch. and the Swedish Broadcasting Co., and director of the Oratorio Society. In 1940 he emigrated to the U.S.; became naturalized as an American citizen in 1946. In 1945 he joined the conductorial staff of the Metropolitan Opera Co. in N.Y., and a year later became a member of its management; gave many distinguished performances of standard operas. In 1958 he was appointed principal conductor and music director of the Cincinnati Symph. Orch.; took it on a world tour in 1966, and on a European tour in 1969; in 1963 and from 1967 to 1970 was the music director of the Cincinnati May Festival; in 1970 he moved to Philadelphia, where he conducted the opera class at the Curtis Inst. of Music (until 1973); then was principal conductor of the Dallas Symph. (1973–74). In 1976 he was appointed music adviser to the New Jersey Symph. Orch. He publ. *The Grammar of Conducting* (N.Y., 1950), which also appeared in a Japanese translation.

Rudziński, Witold, Polish composer; b. Siebież, Lithuania, March 14, 1913. He studied piano at the Cons. of Vilna (1931–36); went to Paris, where he took composition lessons with Nadia Boulanger and Charles Koechlin (1938–39); upon his return, he taught at the Vilna Cons. (1939–42) and the Lodz Cons. (1945–47); settled in Warsaw and became active mainly as a musical administrator and pedagogue; in 1957 became a member of the faculty of the Superior School of Music in Warsaw.

Rufer, Josef, Austrian music scholar; b. Vienna, Dec. 18, 1893. He studied composition with Zemlinsky and Schoenberg in Vienna (1919–22); later

was assistant to Schoenberg at the Prussian Academy of Arts in Berlin; from 1929 was also active as a music critic. From 1947 to 1950 he edited (with Stuckenschmidt) the monthly music magazine *Stimmen;* then was a teacher of theory and 12-tone method of composition at the Hochschule für Musik in Berlin (1956–69). He publ. a number of valuable books dealing with 12-tone music: *Die Komposition mit zwölf Tönen* (Berlin, 1952; Eng. trans. by Humphrey Searle as *Composition with 12 Notes Related Only to One Another,* London, 1954); *Musiker über Musik* (Darmstadt, 1955); and, most important, an annotated catalogue of Schoenberg's works, *Das Werk Arnold Schönbergs* (Kassel, 1959; in Eng., *The Works of Arnold Schoenberg,* London, 1962).

Ruffo, Titta, famous Italian baritone; b. Pisa, June 9, 1877; d. Florence, July 5, 1953. His real name was **Ruffo Cafiero Titta,** but he found it convenient to transpose his first and last names for professional purposes. He studied with Persichini at the Santa Cecilia Academy in Rome, then with Cassini in Milan. He made his operatic debut in Rome as the Herald in *Lohengrin* (1898); then sang in Rio de Janeiro; returning to Italy, he appeared in all the principal theaters; also sang in Vienna, Paris, and London. He made his American debut in Philadelphia as Rigoletto (Nov. 4, 1912) with the combined Philadelphia-Chicago Opera Co.; his first appearance with the Metropolitan Opera was as Figaro in *Il Barbiere di Siviglia* (N.Y., Jan. 19, 1922). He left the Metropolitan in 1928 and returned to Rome. In 1937 he was briefly under arrest for opposing the Mussolini regime; then went to Florence, where he remained until his death. He publ. a book of memoirs, *La mia parabola* (Milan, 1937).

Ruggles, Carl (real Christian names, **Charles Sprague**), remarkable American composer; b. Marion, Mass., March 11, 1876; d. Bennington, Vt., Oct. 24, 1971. He learned to play violin as a child; then went to Boston, where he took violin lessons with Felix Winternitz and theory with Josef Claus; later enrolled as a special student at Harvard Univ., where he attended composition classes of John Knowles Paine. Impressed with the widely assumed supremacy of the German school of composition (of which Paine was a notable representative), Ruggles germanized his given name from Charles to Carl. In 1907 he went to Minnesota, where he organized the Winona Symph. Orch. and conducted it for several years (1908–12). In 1917 he went to N.Y., where he became active in the promotion of modern music; was a member of the International Composers Guild and of the Pan American Assoc. of Composers. He wrote relatively few works, which he was in the habit of constantly revising and rearranging, and they were mostly in small forms. He did not follow any particular modern method of composition, but instinctively avoided needless repetition of thematic notes, which made his melodic progressions atonal; his use of dissonances, at times quite strident, derived from the linear proceedings of chromatically inflected counterpoint. A certain similarity with the 12-tone method of composition of Schoenberg resulted from this process, but Ruggles never adopted it explicitly. In his sources of inspiration, he reached for spiritual exaltation with mystic connotations, scaling the heights and plumbing the depths of musical expression. Such music could not attract large groups of listeners and repelled some critics; one of them remarked that the title of Ruggles's *Sun-Treader* ought to be changed to *Latrine-Treader.* Unable and unwilling to withstand the prevailing musical mores, Ruggles removed himself from the musical scene; he went to live on his farm in Arlington, Vt., and devoted himself exclusively to his avocation, painting; his pictures, mostly in the manner of Abstract Expressionism, were occasionally exhibited in N.Y. galleries. In 1966 he moved to a nursing home in Bennington, where he died at the age of 95. A striking revival of interest in his music took place during the last years of his life, and his name began to appear with increasing frequency on the programs of American orchs. and chamber music groups. His MSS were recovered and publ.; virtually all of his compositions have been recorded.

WORKS: *Men and Angels,* symph. suite for 5 Trumpets and Bass Trumpet (N.Y., Dec. 17, 1922; revised for Brass Instruments or Strings and renamed *Angels;* Miami, April 24, 1939); *Men and Mountains,* symph. suite in 3 movements: *Men, Lilacs, Marching Mountains* (N.Y., Dec. 7, 1924; revised for Large Orch., N.Y., March 19, 1936); *Portals* for String Orch. (N.Y., Jan. 24, 1926); *Sun-Treader,* after Browning, for Large Orch. (Paris, Feb. 25, 1932, Slonimsky conducting); *Polyphonic Composition* for 3 Pianos (1940); *Evocations,* piano suite (1945; an orch. version was perf. in N.Y., Feb. 3, 1971); *Organum* for Large Orch. (N.Y., Nov. 24, 1949); song cycle, *Vox clamans in deserto,* for Voice and Chamber Orch. (1923); *Exaltation* for "congregation in unison" and Organ (1958). *Symphonia dialectica* for Orch., begun in 1923, remained unfinished.

Rummel, Christian, German composer and conductor; b. Brichsenstadt, Nov. 27, 1787; d. Wiesbaden, Feb. 13, 1849. He was an able performer on the piano, violin, and clarinet; served as municipal conductor in Wiesbaden from 1815 until 1841; publ. a Clarinet Concerto, 2 quintets, etc. His son **Joseph Rummel** (b. Wiesbaden, Oct. 6, 1818; d. London, March 25, 1880) was court pianist to the Duke of Nassau, and publ. piano music; another son, **August Rummel** (b. Wiesbaden, Jan. 14, 1824; d. London, Dec. 14, 1886), also was a good pianist.

Rummel, Franz, pianist, son of **Joseph Rummel** and grandson of **Christian Rummel;** b. London, Jan. 11, 1853; d. Berlin, May 2, 1901. He studied with Louis Brassin at the Brussels Cons., winning first prize in 1872; toured in America 3 times (1878, 1886, 1898). He married a daughter of S.F.B. Morse, inventor of the telegraph.

Rummel, Walter Morse, distinguished pianist, son of **Franz Rummel** and grandson of S.F.B. Morse, inventor of the telegraph; b. Berlin, July 19, 1887; d. Bordeaux, May 2, 1953. He studied piano with Leopold Godowsky, and composition with Hugo Kaun. In 1908 he went to Paris, where he became acquainted with Debussy, and devoted himself to promoting Debussy's piano works, of which he became a foremost interpreter. He was married twice, to the pianist **Thérèse Chaigneau,** with whom he appeared in duo-piano recitals (later divorced), and to Sarah Harrington (also divorced).

Russell, George Alexander, American organist and song composer; b. Franklin, Tenn., Oct. 2, 1880; d. Dewitt, N.Y., Nov. 24, 1953. The son of a Presbyterian minister, he studied at home; his mother, Felicia Putnam Russell (a direct descendant of General Israel Putnam of Revolution fame), taught him piano; the family moved to Texas, where he studied academic subjects; entered the College of Fine Arts of Syracuse Univ., studying organ with George A. Parker and composition with William Berwald; subsequently studied in Europe with Leopold Godowsky and Harold Bauer (piano), and with Widor (organ). Returning to America in 1908, he toured as accompanist to various artists; in 1910 he became director of the Auditorium concerts at Wanamaker's in N.Y.; in 1917 was appointed prof. in the newly founded chair of music at Princeton Univ.; assembled the famous Rodman Wanamaker Collection of old Italian string instruments. He wrote the songs *Sunset, The Sacred Fire, In Fountain Court, Lyric from Tagore, Expectation, Puer Redemptor,* etc.; the piano pieces *Theme and Variations, Contrapuntal Waltz,* etc.

Russell, Henry, English singer and composer; b. Sheerness, Dec. 24, 1812; d. London, Dec. 8, 1900. He studied in Italy as a young boy; took a few lessons from Rossini in Naples; was in London in 1828; then in Canada (1833); served as organist of the First Presbyterian Church of Rochester, N.Y. (1833–41). He returned to England in 1841 and became extremely popular there as a composer and singer of dramatic and topical songs, of which *Woodman, Spare That Tree* attained immense popularity; other songs were *Old Arm Chair; Oh, Weep Not!; A Life on the Ocean Wave* (official march of the Royal Marines); *Cheer, Boys, Cheer; Ivy Green; The Gambler's Wife; Old Bell; The Maniac;* etc. He publ. a book of reminiscences, *Cheer, Boys, Cheer* (London, 1895), and *L'Amico dei cantanti,* a treatise on singing. He was the father of **Henry Russell,** the impresario, and of **Sir Landon Ronald,** the composer and conductor, whose real name was **L.R. Russell.**

Russell, Henry, English impresario, son of **Henry Russell,** the singer and composer; b. London, Nov. 14, 1871; d. there, Oct. 11, 1937. He studied singing at the Royal College of Music, and devised an original method of vocal instruction, which attracted the attention of Mme. Melba, who sent him a number of her good pupils. Owing to his wide acquaintance with singers, he was invited in 1904 to manage a season of opera at Covent Garden; in 1905 he brought his company to the U.S., where Boston was the principal field of his operations; his success there resulted, in 1909, in the formation of the Boston Opera Co., of which he was general manager until its dissolution in 1914. Just before the outbreak of World War I, he had taken the entire Boston troupe to Paris, where he gave a successful spring season at the Théâtre des Champs-Elysées. He then lived mostly in London. He publ. a book of memoirs, *The Passing Show* (London, 1926).

Russolo, Luigi, Italian futurist composer; b. Portogruaro, May 1, 1885; d. Cerro, Feb. 4, 1947. In 1909 he joined the futurist movement of Marinetti; formulated the principles of "art of noises" in his book, *L'arte dei rumori* (Milan, 1916); constructed a battery of noise-making instruments ("intonarumori"), with which he gave concerts in Milan (April 21, 1914) and Paris (June 18, 1921), creating such a commotion in the concert hall that on one occasion a group of outraged concertgoers mounted the stage and physically attacked Russolo and his fellow noisemakers. The titles of his works sing the glory of the machine and of urban living: *Convegno dell'automobili e dell'aeroplani, Il Risveglio di una città, Si pranza sulla terrazza dell'Hotel.* In his "futurist manifesto" of 1913 the noises are divided into 6 categories, including shrieks, groans, clashes, explosions, etc. In 1929 he constructed a noise instrument which he called "Russolophone." Soon the novelty of machine music wore out, the erstwhile marvels of automobiles and airplanes became commonplace, and the future of the futurists turned into a yawning past; Russolo gradually retreated from cultivation of noise and devoted himself to the most silent of all arts, painting. His pictures, influenced by the modern French school, and remarkable for their vivid colors, had several successful exhibitions in Paris and N.Y. The text of Russolo's manifesto is reproduced, in an English translation, in N. Slonimsky's *Music since 1900.*

Rust, Friedrich Wilhelm, German violinist and composer; b. Wörlitz, near Dessau, July 6, 1739; d. Dessau, Feb. 28, 1796. He was a pupil of the violinist Höckh at Zerbst and (1763) of Franz Benda at Berlin, under the patronage of Prince Leopold III of Anhalt-Dessau, whom he accompanied to Italy (1765–66), and who appointed him court music director in 1775. He brought out several stage pieces, wrote incidental music to plays and considerable instrumental music. Davis Singer and Wilhelm Rust publ. several of his violin pieces. His son, **Wilhelm Karl Rust** (b. Dessau, April 29, 1787; d. there, April 18, 1855), was an organist at Vienna (1819–27), then a teacher in Dessau; publ. pieces for piano and organ.

Rust, Wilhelm, German organist and editor; b. Dessau, Aug. 15, 1822; d. Leipzig, May 2, 1892. He was a pupil of his uncle, **W.K. Rust** (piano and organ); later of F. Schneider (1840–43). He went to Berlin in 1849, taught there, and entered the Singakademie; joined the Leipzig Bach-Verein in 1850; played in numerous concerts; became organist of St. Luke's in 1861; was conductor of the Berlin Bach-Verein from 1862–74, "Royal Music Director" in 1864; in 1870 became a teacher of theory and composition at the Stern Cons.; in 1878, organist of the Thomaskirche at Leipzig, and a teacher in the Cons. there; in 1880 he succeeded Richter as cantor of the Thomasschule. As editor of several vols. of the Bach edition prepared by the Bach-Gesellschaft, he displayed great erudition.

Ruyneman, Daniel, Dutch composer; b. Amsterdam, Aug. 8, 1886; d. there, July 25, 1963. He began his study of music relatively late; took composition lessons with Zweers at the Amsterdam Cons. (1913–16); in 1918 was co-founder of the Society of Modern Dutch Composers; in 1930, organized the Netherlands Society for Contemporary Music, serving as president until 1962; edited its magazine, *Tijdschrift voor Hedendaagse Muziek* (1930–40), until it was suppressed during the Nazi occupation of the Netherlands. Ruyneman made a special study of Javanese instruments and introduced them in some of his works. He was naturally attracted to exotic subjects with mystic connotations and coloristic effects; also worked on restoration of old music; in 1930 he orchestrated fragments of Mussorgsky's unfinished opera *The Marriage,* and added his own music for the missing acts of the score.

Ryba, Jan Jakub, Czech composer; b. Přeštice, Oct. 26, 1765; d. Rožmitál, April 8, 1815. He studied academic subjects in Prague; in 1788 was appointed rector at a school in Rožkmitál; remained there until his death (suicide). A very prolific composer, he left about 120 masses, 100 motets, 30 pastorals (Christmas cantatas to Latin and Czech texts); also many songs to Czech words; of these last, 2 albums were publ. during his lifetime; other works were a Symph., several string quartets, sonatas. There is a growing realization in Czechoslovakia of Ryba's importance as an early representative of the national art song.

Rybner, (Peter Martin) Cornelius, pianist, conductor, and composer; b. Copenhagen, Oct. 26, 1855; d. New York, Jan. 21, 1929. His original name was **Rübner,** but he changed it to Rybner about 1920. He studied at the Copenhagen Cons. with Gade and J.P. Hartmann; then at the Leipzig Cons. with Ferdinand David (violin) and Reinecke (piano); finished his pianistic studies under Hans von Bülow and Anton Rubinstein. After a series of concerts in Europe as pianist, he settled in Karlsruhe; succeeded Mottl in 1892 as conductor of the Phil. Society there, and held this position until 1904, when he emigrated to the U.S., succeeding MacDowell as head of the music dept. at Columbia Univ. (1904–19). His works include a ballet, *Prinz Ador* (Munich, 1902); a symph. poem, *Friede, Kampf und Sieg;* a Violin Concerto; numerous choruses; piano pieces; songs; also some chamber music.

Ryelandt, Joseph, Belgian composer; b. Bruges, April 7, 1870; d. there, June 29, 1965. He studied composition with Edgar Tinel. Thanks to a personal fortune (he was a Baron), he did not have to earn a living by his music, but he taught at the Cons. of Ghent (1929–39) and served as director of the Municipal Cons. in Bruges (1924–45). He lived a very long life (*obiit aet. 95*) and composed much music.

Rysanek, Leonie, Austrian soprano; b. Vienna, Nov. 14, 1926. She studied at the Academy of Music and Dramatic Art in Vienna with **Rudolf Grossmann,** whom she later married. She made her debut at Innsbruck in 1949; then sang at Saarbrücken (1950–52) and at the Munich State Opera (1952–54). In 1954 she joined the staff of the Vienna State Opera; in subsequent years also sang at La Scala in Milan, at Covent Garden in London, and at the Paris Opéra. She made a spectacular American appearance at the Metropolitan Opera House in N.Y. on Feb. 5, 1959, when she replaced Maria Callas in the role of Lady Macbeth in Verdi's opera on short notice; she remained on its staff until 1973, and again in 1975–76 and subsequent seasons, and sang the roles of Aida, Desdemona, and Tosca, as well as several Wagner parts (Elsa in *Lohengrin,* Elisabeth in *Tännhauser,* Sieglinde in *Die Walküre*). She received the Lotte Lehmann Ring from the Vienna State Opera in 1979. Her younger sister **Lotte Rysanek** (b. Vienna, March 18, 1928) attained a fine reputation in Vienna as a lyric soprano.

Rytel, Piotr, Polish composer; b. Vilna, Sept. 20, 1884; d. Warsaw, Jan. 2, 1970. He studied with Michalowski and Noskowski at the Warsaw Cons.; in 1911, was appointed a prof. of piano, and in 1918 a prof. of harmony there. In 1948 he conducted at the Warsaw Opera House. He was the director of Sopot State College of Music, 1956–61.

Rzewski, Frederic, American avant-garde composer; b. Westfield, Mass., April 13, 1938, of Polish parentage. He attended Harvard Univ. (1954–58) and Princeton Univ. (1958–60); was active (1960–62) in modern music circles in Italy, where he stayed on a Fulbright scholarship; subsequently he received a Ford Foundation grant, which enabled him to spend 2 years in Berlin (1963–65); while in Rome, he organized, with other similarly futuroscopic musicians, the MEV (Musica Elettronica Viva). In the interim he played concerts with the topless cellist Charlotte Moorman. From 1971 he lived mostly in N.Y. As a composer, he pursues the shimmering distant vision of optimistic, positivistic anti-music. He is furthermore a granitically overpowering piano technician, capable of depositing huge boulders of sonoristic material across the keyboard without actually wrecking the instrument.
WORKS: *For Violin* for Violin Solo (1962); *Nature morte* for Instruments and Percussion Groups (1965); *Composition for 2* (1964); *Zoologischer Garten* (1965); *Spacecraft* (his magnum opus; 1967; "plan for spacecraft" publ. in *Source,* 3, 1968); *Impersonation,* audiodrama (1967); *Requiem* (1968); *Symphony for Several Performers* (1968); *Last Judgement* for Trombone (1969); *Falling Music* for Piano and Tape (1971); *Coming Together* for Speaker and Instruments (1972); Piano Variations on the song *No Place to Go But Around* (1974); *The People United Will Never Be Defeated,* a set of 36 variations for Piano on the Chilean song ¡*El pueblo unido jamás será vencido!* (1975); *4 Piano Pieces* (1977); *Song and Dance* for Flute, Bass Clarinet, Vibraphone, and Electric Bass (1977); *Satyrica* for Jazz Band (River Falls, Wis., April 27, 1983).

S

Saar, Louis Victor (Franz), Dutch pianist and teacher; b. Rotterdam, Dec. 10, 1868; d. St. Louis, Nov. 23, 1937. He studied with Rheinberger in Munich (1886–89); lived in Vienna, Leipzig, and Berlin; in 1894 he went to the U.S.; taught music at various schools in N.Y.; was a member of the faculty at the Cincinnati College of Music (1906–17), at the Chicago Musical College (1917–33), and from 1934 until his death, at the St. Louis Inst. of Music. He was also a composer; wrote about 150 opus numbers, including musico-geographic orch. pieces such as *From the Mountain Kingdom of the Great Northwest* (1922) and *Along the Columbia River* (1924); publ. arrangements of folk songs for men's chorus, and *Album of Church Classics.*

Sabaneyev, Leonid, Russian writer on music; b. Moscow, Oct. 1, 1881; d. Antibes, France, May 3, 1968. He studied with Taneyev at the Moscow Cons.; also took a course in mathematics at the Univ. of Moscow. In 1920 he joined the board of the newly organized Moscow Inst. of Musical Science. In 1926 he left Russia and lived in France. He was an energetic promoter of modern music, and a friend of Scriabin, about whom he wrote a monograph, which would have been important if his account of Scriabin's life and ideology could be trusted; he compromised himself when he wrote a devastating review of Prokofiev's *Scythian Suite* at a concert that never took place.

WRITINGS (all in Russian): *Richard Wagner and the Synthesis of Arts* (1913); *The Development of the Harmonic Idea* (1913); *Medtner* (1913); *Scriabin* (1916; 2nd revised ed., 1923); *History of Russian Music* (Moscow, 1924; also in German, 1926); *Modern Russian Composers* (in Eng., N.Y., 1927); *Sergei Taneyev* (in Russian; Paris, 1930); *Music for the Films* (in Eng., London, 1935). He wrote 2 piano trios (1907, 1923), a Violin Sonata, and some other music.

Sabata, Victor de. See **De Sabata, Victor.**

Sabbatini, Galeazzo, Italian composer and theorist; b. Pesaro, c.1595; d. there, Dec. 6, 1662. He studied with Vincenzo Pellegrini, canon of Pesaro Cathedral. Sabbatini was subsequently appointed canon there (1626–30); then was maestro di cappella to the Duke of Mirandola (1630–39); again served as canon at Pesaro Cathedral (from 1641). His last publ. work appeared in Venice in 1639. Among his other publications was a treatise on basso continuo, *Regola facile e breve per sonare sopra il basso continuo* (Venice, 1628; 3rd ed., Rome, 1669). He publ. 2 books of madrigals *a* 2–4 (1625, 1626); 2 books of

Sacrae laudes a 2–5 (1637, 1641); one with Organ (1642); 3 books of *Madrigali concertati a* 2–5 (with Instruments; 1627, 1630, 1636); Hymns to the Virgin Mary *a* 3–6 (1638); *Sacri laudi e motetti a voce sola* (1639).

Sabbatini, Luigi Antonio, Italian music theorist; b. Albano Laziale, near Rome, Oct. 24, 1732; d. Padua, Jan. 29, 1809. He studied with Padre Martini in Bologna, and Vallotti in Padua. He was maestro di cappella at the basilica of S. Barnaba in Marino (1767–72); in 1772 was appointed to the Franciscan basilica of the 12 Holy Apostles in Rome; in 1786 he took over the duties of maestro di cappella at the Antonius Basilica, succeeding Agostino Ricci, who was in turn the successor of Vallotti. He publ. *Elementi teorici della musica colla pratica de' medesimi in duetti, e terzetti a canone* (1789; trans. in part into French by Choron); *La vera idea delle musicali numeriche segnature* (1799; gives an epitome of Vallotti's system); *Trattato sopra le fughe musicali* (1802; contains musical examples by Vallotti); and *Notizie sopra la vita e le opere del R.P.Fr.A. Vallotti* (1780).

Sacchini, Antonio (Maria Gasparo Gioacchino), Italian opera composer; b. Florence, June 14, 1730; d. Paris, Oct. 6, 1786. He entered the Cons. of Santa Maria di Loreto at Naples as a pupil of Francesco Durante (composition), Nicola Fiorenza (violin), and Gennaro Manna (singing). His intermezzo *Fra Donato* was performed at the Cons. in 1756; he subsequently wrote music for various stage productions in Naples; then proceeded to Rome, where his opera *Semiramide* was successfully produced in 1762. This success marked the beginning of his career as an operatic composer; thereafter he produced operas every year: *Olimpiade* (Padua, July 9, 1763); *Alessandro nell'Indie* (Venice, 1763); *Lucio Vero* (Naples, Nov. 4, 1764); *La Contadina in corte* (Rome, 1765); *L'isola d'amore* (Rome, 1766). In 1768 he succeeded Traetta as director of the Cons. dell'Ospedaletto in Venice; his oratorio *Caritas omnia vincit* was brought out there on April 16, 1769. He then went to Munich and produced there his operas *L'Eroe cinese* (1769) and *Scipione in Cartagena* (Jan. 8, 1770). In 1772 he traveled to London with Venanzio Rauzzini, and while there presented the following operas: *Tamerlano* (May 6, 1773); *Montezuma* (Feb. 7, 1775); *Erifile* (Feb. 7, 1778); *L'Amore soldato* (May 5, 1778); *Il Calandrino e l'avaro deluso* (Nov. 24, 1778); *Enea e Lavinia* (March 25, 1779). In 1781 he received an invitation from Marie Antoinette, through the "intendant des menus-plaisirs," to come to Paris. His name was already known in France, since his opera *L'isola d'amore,* arranged as *La Colonie* ("comic opera imitated from the Italian"), had been produced in Paris on Aug. 16, 1775. He arrived in Paris in August 1781, and was forthwith commissioned to write 3 works at a fee of 10,000 francs each. For this purpose he adapted his Italian opera *Armida e Rinaldo* (Milan, 1772) to a French text as *Renaud,* "tragédie lyrique" in 3 acts (produced at the Académie Royale de Musique, Feb.

25, 1783), and his opera *Il cidde* (Rome, 1764) as *Chimène* (Fontainebleau, Nov. 18, 1783); the 3rd opera, *Dardanus,* was a new work; it was staged at the Trianon at Versailles, Sept. 18, 1784, in the presence of Louis XVI and Marie Antoinette. In Paris Sacchini found himself in unintended rivalry with Piccinni as a representative of Italian music in the famous artistic war against the proponents of the French operas of Gluck; Sacchini's most successful opera, however, was to the French text *Œdipe à Colonne,* first presented at Versailles (Jan. 4, 1786) and produced at the Paris Opéra (Feb. 1, 1787) after Sacchini's death. It held the stage for half a century, and there were sporadic revivals later on. His last opera, also to a French libretto, *Arvire et Evelina,* was left unfinished, and was produced posthumously (Paris Opéra, April 29, 1788; 3rd act added by J.B. Rey). Sacchini's music is a typical product of the Italian operatic art of his time. It possesses melodious grace, but lacks dramatic development. The undistinguished style of Sacchini's productions is probably the reason for the disappearance of his operas from the active repertoire; Piccinni fared much better in comparison.

Sacher, Paul, Swiss conductor; b. Basel, April 28, 1906. He studied with Karl Nef (music theory) and Weingartner (conducting). In 1926 he founded the Kammer Orchester in Basel; commissioned special works from a number of celebrated contemporary composers (among them Richard Strauss, Hindemith, Honegger, etc.) and presented them for the first time with his ensemble; in 1933 he founded the Schola Cantorum Basiliensis; from 1941, was leader of the Collegium Musicum in Zürich. His Schola Cantorum Basiliensis was amalgamated with Basel's Cons. and Musikschule to form the Musikakademie der Stadt Basel, which he directed from 1954–69. He publ. *Alte und neue Musik* (Zürich, 1951) and an annotated catalogue of the 25 years of the Basel Kammer Orchester. Sacher made his American debut in N.Y. on April 3, 1955, conducting a concert of the Collegiate Chorale at Carnegie Hall. A Festschrift was publ. in his honor in Basel in 1976.

Sachs, Curt, eminent German musicologist and authority on musical instruments; b. Berlin, June 29, 1881; d. New York, Feb. 5, 1959. While attending the Gymnasium in Berlin, he studied piano and composition with L. Schrattenholz and clarinet with Rausch; entered Berlin Univ.; studied music history with Oskar Fleischer, and also art history (Dr.Phil., 1904); after some years as an art critic, he turned to musicology, and studied with Kretzschmar and Joh. Wolf; specialized in the history of musical instruments; in 1919 was appointed curator of the Museum of Musical Instruments in Berlin, and in 1920, prof. of the National Academy of Music there; also was a prof. at the Univ. of Berlin. In 1933 he was compelled to leave Germany; went to Paris as Chargé de Mission at the Musée de l'Homme; was a visiting prof. at the Sorbonne. In 1937 he settled in the U.S.; was a lecturer at the Graduate School of Liberal Arts of N.Y. Univ. (1937–38); consultant to the N.Y. Public Library (1937–52); adjunct prof., Columbia Univ. (from 1953); president of the American Musicological Society (1948–50). In 1956, he was made a Dr.Phil. (*honoris causa*) of West Berlin Univ.

Sachs, Hans, foremost poet of the Meistersinger; b. Nuremberg, Nov. 5, 1494; d. there, Jan. 19, 1576. He wrote over 4,000 poems (*Meisterschulgedichte*), 1,700 tales, etc., and 208 dramatic poems; also invented numerous melodies (*Weisen*). He is the central figure in Wagner's opera *Die Meistersinger von Nürnberg.* The original melodies of a large number of the poems are preserved in *Das Singebuch des Adam Puschmann* (ed. by G. Münzer, 1907).

Sack, Erna, German coloratura soprano; b. Spandau-Berlin, Feb. 6, 1898; d. Mainz, March 2, 1972. She studied in Prague and in Berlin; made her first operatic appearance at the Municipal Theater in Bielefeld; sang in Austria at the Salzburg festivals, in Italy, and in England; made her first American appearance as a concert singer in 1937–38, and revisited the U.S. in 1954. In 1953 she gave a series of concerts in Australia.

Sacrati, Francesco (Paolo), Italian composer; b. Parma (baptized, Sept. 17), 1605; d. Modena, May 20, 1650. He was one of the earliest composers for the opera theaters that opened in Venice after 1637; was also a pioneer of opera buffa before the rise of the Neapolitan school. He wrote an opera, *La Delia,* for the opening of the Teatro Crimani dei Santi Giovanni e Paolo in Venice (Jan. 20, 1639); there followed *La finta pazza* (Teatro Novissimo, Venice; Jan. 14, 1641); this was also one of the earliest Italian operas performed in Paris (Salle du Petit Bourbon, Dec. 14, 1645); other operas by Sacrati were: *Bellerofonte* (1642); *Ulisse errante* (1644); *L'isola d'Alcina* (Bologna, 1648). In 1649 he was appointed maestro di cappella at the court of Modena, but he died a few months after the appointment.

Sadie, Stanley, eminent English writer on music and lexicographer; b. London, Oct. 30, 1930. He studied music privately with Bernard Stevens (1947–50) and then with R.T. Dart, P.A.S. Hadley, and C.L. Cudworth at Cambridge (B.A. and Mus.B., 1953; M.A., 1957; Ph.D., 1958, with the dissertation *British Chamber Music, 1720–1790).* He was on the staff of Trinity College of Music in London (1957–65); from 1964–81 was a music critic on the staff of the *Times* of London. In 1967 he became the editor of the *Musical Times.* A distinguished scholar, he wrote the following monographs: *Handel* (London, 1962); *Mozart* (London, 1966); *Beethoven* (London, 1967; 2nd ed., 1974); *Handel* (London, 1968); and *Handel Concertos* (London, 1972); also publ. numerous articles in British and American music journals. With Arthur Jacobs he edited *The Pan Book of Opera* (London, 1964; revised ed. as *Opera: A Modern Guide,* N.Y., 1972; new ed., 1983). In 1969 he was entrusted with the formidable task of preparing for publication, as editor in chief, a completely new edition of

Grove's Dictionary of Music and Musicians; after 11 years of labor, *The New Grove Dictionary of Music and Musicians* was publ. in London in 1980; this 6th ed., in 20 vols., reflected the contributions of more than 2,400 scholars throughout the world, and was accorded a premier place of honor among the major reference sources of its kind. He also edited *The New Grove Encyclopedia of Musical Instruments* (London, 1984) and was co-editor, with H. Wiley Hitchcock, of *The New Grove Dictionary of Music in the United States* (scheduled for publication in 1985). He has served as editor of the Master Musicians series since 1976. In 1981 he received the honorary degree of D.Litt. from the Univ. of Leicester and was made an honorary member of the Royal Academy of Music, London. In 1982 he was made a Commander of the Order of the British Empire.

Saeverud, Harald, prominent Norwegian composer; b. Bergen, April 17, 1897. He studied music theory at the Bergen Music Academy with B. Holmsen (1915–20) and with F.E. Koch at the Hochschule für Musik in Berlin (1920–21); took a course in conducting with Clemens Krauss in Berlin (1935). In 1953 he received the Norwegian State Salary of Art (a government life pension for outstanding artistic achievement). He began to compose very early, and on Dec. 12, 1912, at the age of 15, conducted in Bergen a program of his own symph. pieces. His music is permeated with characteristically lyrical Scandinavian Romanticism, with Norwegian folk melos as its foundation; his symph. compositions are polyphonic in nature and tonal in essence, with euphonious dissonant textures imparting a peculiarly somber character to the music.
   WORKS: Ballet, *Ridder Blåskjeggs mareritt* (*Bluebeard's Nightmare;* 1960; Oslo, Oct. 4, 1960); 9 symphs.: No. 1, in 2 symph. fantasias (1916–20; first complete perf., Bergen, 1923); No. 2 (1922; Bergen, Nov. 22, 1923; revised 1934; Oslo, April 1, 1935); No. 3 (1925–26; Bergen, Feb. 25, 1932); No. 4 (1937; Oslo, Dec. 9, 1937); No. 5, *Quasi una fantasia* (1941; Bergen, March 6, 1941); No. 6, *Sinfonia dolorosa* (1942; Bergen, May 27, 1943); No. 7, *Salme (Psalm;* 1944–45; Bergen, Sept. 1, 1945); No. 8, *Minnesota* (1958; Minneapolis, Oct. 18, 1958); No. 9 (1965–66; Bergen, June 12, 1966); *Ouverture Appassionata* (1920; retitled 2nd fantasia of his First Symph., often played independently); *50 Small Variations* for Orch. (1931); *The Rape of Lucretia,* incidental music for Shakespeare's play (1935; also a *Lucretia Suite* for Orch., 1936); Oboe Concerto (1938); *Divertimento No. 1* for Flute and Strings (1939); *Syljetone (The Bride's Heirloom Brooch)* for Chamber Orch. or Piano (1939); *Rondo amoroso* for Chamber Orch. or Piano (1939); *Gjaetlevise-Variasjoner (Shepherd's Tune Variations)* for Chamber Orch. (1941); *Siljuslåtten (Countryside Festival Dance;* 1942; also for Piano); *Galdreslåtten (The Sorcerer's Dance;* 1942); *Romanza* for Violin, and Orch. or Piano (1942); *Kjempeviseslåtten (Ballad of Revolt;* 1943; also for Piano); *Peer Gynt,* incidental music to a revised production of Ibsen's verse drama (1947; Oslo, March 2, 1948; also exists as 2 orch. suites and as a

piano suite); *Olav og Kari,* dance scene for 2 Singers, Chorus, and Orch. (1948); Piano Concerto (1948–50); Violin Concerto (1956); *Vade mors (Get Thee Behind Me, Death;* 1955); *Allegria (Sinfonia concertante;* 1957); Bassoon Concerto (1963); *Mozart-Motto-Sinfonietta* (1971); *5 Capricci* for Piano (1918–19); Piano Sonata (1921); *Tunes and Dances from "Siljustøl,"* 5 vols. for Piano (1943–45); 6 piano sonatinas (1948–50); *20 Small Duets* for Violins (1951); 3 string quartets (1970, 1975, 1978); *Fabula gratulatorum* for Piano (1973); *Pastorale (Indian Summer)* for Solo Cello (1978).

Safonov, Vasili, eminent Russian pianist, conductor, and pedagogue; b. Ishcherskaya, Caucasus, Feb. 6, 1852; d. Kislovodsk, Feb. 27, 1918. He studied at the Cons. of St. Petersburg with Leschetizky and Brassin (piano) and Zaremba (theory); made his debut as pianist with the Imperial Russian Music Society in St. Petersburg, on Nov. 22, 1880; then taught piano at the St. Petersburg Cons. (1881–85); in 1885 was appointed to the piano faculty of the Moscow Cons., and in 1889 became its director, resigning in 1905; among his pupils were Scriabin and Medtner. He conducted the symph. concerts of the Imperial Russian Music Society in Moscow; was the first modern conductor to dispense with the baton; achieved international fame as a forceful and impassioned interpreter of Russian music; conducted in almost all the capitals of Europe; on March 5, 1904, was engaged as guest conductor of the N.Y. Phil., obtaining sensational success; as a consequence, was appointed regular conductor for 3 seasons (1906–9; was succeeded by Gustav Mahler); at the same time he was also director of the National Cons. in N.Y. After his return to Russia, he was appointed permanent conductor of the Imperial Russian Music Society in St. Petersburg. He publ. *A New Formula for the Piano Teacher and Piano Student* (Moscow, 1916; in Eng.).

Sagittarius. See **Schütz, Heinrich.**

Saint-Foix, Georges (du Parc Poullain, Comte) de, eminent French musicologist, specialist in Mozart research; b. Paris, March 2, 1874; d. Aix-en-Provence, May 26, 1954. He studied jurisprudence, and also attended classes in music theory with Vincent d'Indy at the Schola Cantorum in Paris. His principal, and most important, publication was *W.A. Mozart, Sa vie musicale et son œuvre de l'enfance à la pleine maturité* (2 vols., 1912, with T. de Wyzewa; 3rd vol., by Saint-Foix alone, 1937; 4th vol., 1940; 5th vol., 1946); of no less importance is his book *Les Symphonies de Mozart* (Paris, 1932; 2nd ed., 1948; in Eng., London, 1947; reprint, N.Y., 1968). He contributed a number of informative articles dealing with Mozart's contemporaries, in several instances in collaboration with T. de Wyzewa and L. de La Laurencie.

Saint-Georges, Joseph Boulogne, Chevalier de, West Indian composer and violinist; b. near Basse Terre, Guadeloupe, 1739, the son of a wealthy Frenchman and a Negro slave; d. Paris, June 10, 1799. He was raised in Santo Domingo; went to Paris with his father in 1749 (his mother joined them in 1760); as a youth he studied boxing and fencing, and became one of the leading fencers of Europe; he also studied music, with Jean-Marie Leclair *l'aîné,* and with François Gossec (1763–66); the latter dedicated his op. 9 string trios to Saint-Georges. In 1771 Saint-Georges became concertmaster of the Concerts des Amateurs in Paris, led by Gossec; in 1772 he appeared as violin soloist in his 2 violin concertos, op. 2; in 1773, succeeded Gossec as director of the Concerts des Amateurs. He continued his activities as a fencer, and in this capacity went to London twice, in 1785 and 1789; in 1792 he became colonel of a Negro regiment, the Légion Nationale des Américains et du Midi (among his 1,000 troops was the father of Dumas *père*); he left the service in 1797 and spent the last 2 years of his life in Paris. WORKS: Operas (perf. at the Comédie Italienne, Paris): *Ernestine* (July 19, 1777); *La Chasse* (Oct. 12, 1778); *L'Amant anonyme* (March 8, 1780); *La Fille Garçon* (Aug. 18, 1787); *La Marchand des marrons* (Théâtre des Petits Comédiens, Paris, 1789); *Le Droit du seigneur* (1789); *Guillaume tout Cœur* (1790); 10 violin concertos; 6 *symphonies concertantes* for 2 Violins and Orch.; 2 symphs.; 6 string quartets (1778); 3 violin sonatas (1781); 118 songs, with keyboard accompaniment; other instrumental and vocal music.

Saint-Marcoux, Micheline Coulombe, Canadian composer; b. Notre-Dame-de-la-Doré, Quebec, Aug. 9, 1938. She studied with François Brassard in Jonquière; in Montreal with Claude Champagne at the École Vincent d'Indy, graduating in 1962, and later with Gilles Tremblay and Clermont Pépin at the Cons. there (1963–67). She went to Paris in 1969 and studied composition with Gilbert Amy and Jean-Paul Guézec and electronic music with members of the Groupe de Recherches Musicale; she was a cofounder in Paris of the Groupe International de Musique Electroacoustic, along with 5 other composers from different countries. She returned to Montreal in 1971; became active as a teacher.

Saint-Saëns, (Charles-) Camille, celebrated French composer; b. Paris, Oct. 9, 1835; d. Algiers, Dec. 16, 1921. His widowed mother sent him to his great-aunt, Charlotte Masson, who taught him to play piano. He proved exceptionally gifted, and gave a performance in a Paris salon before he was 5; at 6 he began to compose; at 7 he became a private pupil of Stamaty; so rapid was his progress that he made his pianistic debut at the Salle Pleyel on May 6, 1846, playing a Mozart concerto and a movement from Beethoven's C minor Concerto, with Orch. After studying harmony with Pierre Maleden, he entered the Paris Cons., where his teachers were Benoist (organ) and Halévy (composition). He won the 2nd prize for organ in 1849, and the first prize in 1851. In 1852 he competed unsuccessfully for the Grand Prix de Rome, and failed again in a 2nd attempt in 1864, when he was already a composer of some stature. His *Ode à Sainte Cécile* for Voice and Orch. was awarded the first prize of the Société Sainte-Cécile (1852). On Dec. 11, 1853, his First Symph. was performed; Gounod wrote him a letter of praise, containing a prophetic phrase regarding the "obligation de devenir un grand maître." From 1853 to the end of 1857 Saint-Saëns was organist at the church of Saint-Merry in Paris; in 1857 he succeeded Lefébure-Wély as organist at the Madeleine. This important position he filled with distinction, and soon acquired a great reputation as virtuoso on the organ and a master of improvisation. He resigned in 1876, and devoted himself entirely to composition and conducting; also continued to appear as a pianist and organist. From 1861 to 1865 he taught piano at the École Niedermeyer; among his pupils were André Messager and Gabriel Fauré. Saint-Saëns was one of the founders of the Société Nationale de Musique (1871), established for the encouragement of French composers, but withdrew in 1886 when Vincent d'Indy proposed to include works by foreign composers in its program. In 1875 he married Marie Truffot; their 2 sons died in infancy; they separated in 1881, but were never legally divorced; Madame Saint-Saëns died in Bordeaux on Jan. 30, 1950, at the age of 95. In 1891 Saint-Saëns established a museum in Dieppe (his father's birthplace), to which he gave his MSS and his collection of paintings and other art objects. On Oct. 27, 1907, he witnessed the unveiling of his own statue (by Marqueste) in the court foyer of the opera house in Dieppe. He received many honors: In 1868 he was made a Chevalier of the Legion of Honor; in 1884, Officer; in 1900, Grand-Officer; and in 1913, Grand-Croix (the highest rank). In 1881 he was elected to the Institut de France; was also a member of many foreign organizations; received an honorary Mus.D. degree at Cambridge Univ. He visited the U.S. for the first time in 1906; was a representative of the French government at the Panama-Pacific Exposition in 1915 and conducted his choral work *Hail California* (San Francisco, June 19, 1915), written for the occasion. In 1916, at the age of 81, he made his first tour of South America; continued to appear in public as conductor of his own works almost to the time of his death. He took part as conductor and pianist in a festival of his works in Athens in May 1920. He played a program of his piano pieces at the Saint-Saëns museum in Dieppe on Aug. 6, 1921. For the winter he went to Algiers, where he died.

The position of Saint-Saëns in French music was very important. His abilities as a performer were extraordinary; he aroused the admiration of Wagner during the latter's stay in Paris (1860–61) by playing at sight the entire scores of Wagner's operas; curiously, Saint-Saëns achieved greater recognition in Germany than in France during the initial stages of his career. His most famous opera, *Samson et Dalila*, was produced in Weimar (in 1877) under the direction of Edouard Lassen, to whom the work was suggested by Liszt; it was not performed in France until nearly 13 years later, in Rouen. He played his first and 3rd piano concertos for the first time at the Gewandhaus in Leipzig. Solidity of contrapuntal fabric, instrumental elaboration, fullness of sonority in orchestration, and a certain harmonic saturation are the chief characteristics of his music, qualities that were not yet fully exploited by French composers at the time, and the French public preferred the lighter type of music. However, Saint-Saëns overcame this initial opposition, and toward the end of his life was regarded as an embodiment of French traditionalism. The shock of the German invasion of France in World War I made him abandon his former predilection for German music, and he wrote virulent articles against German art. He was unalterably opposed to modern music, and looked askance at Debussy; he regarded later manifestations of musical modernism as outrages, and was outspoken in his opinions. That Saint-Saëns possessed a fine sense of musical characterization, and true Gallic wit, is demonstrated by his ingenious suite *Carnival of the Animals,* which he wrote in 1886 but did not allow to be publ. during his lifetime. He also publ. a book of elegant verse (1890).

WORKS: FOR THE THEATER: Operas: *La Princesse jaune* (Paris, June 12, 1872); *Le Timbre d'argent* (Paris, Feb. 23, 1877); *Samson et Dalila* (Weimar, Dec. 2, 1877; Paris Opéra, Nov. 23, 1892; Metropolitan Opera, N.Y., Feb. 8, 1895); *Etienne Marcel* (Lyons, Feb. 8, 1879); *Henry VIII* (Paris, March 5, 1883); *Proserpine* (Paris, March 16, 1887); *Ascanio* (Paris, March 21, 1890); *Phryné* (Paris, May 24, 1893); *Les Barbares* (Paris, Oct. 23, 1901); *Hélène* (Monte Carlo, Feb. 18, 1904); *L'Ancêtre* (Monte Carlo, Feb. 24, 1906); *Déjanire* (Monte Carlo, March 14, 1911). Incidental music: *Antigone* (Paris, Nov. 21, 1893); *Andromaque,* by Racine (Paris, Feb. 7, 1903); *On ne badine pas avec l'amour,* by Alfred de Musset (Paris, Feb. 8, 1917). Ballet, *Javotte* (Lyons, Dec. 3, 1896).

FOR ORCH.: Symph. in A major (1850); Symph. No. 1 (Paris, Dec. 18, 1853); Symph. in F major, subtitled "Urbs Roma" (Paris, Feb. 15, 1857); Symph. No. 2 (Leipzig, Feb. 20, 1859); Symph. No. 3, with Organ (London, May 19, 1886); *Le Rouet d'Omphale,* symph. poem (1869; Paris, Jan. 9, 1872); *Marche héroïque* (Paris, Dec. 10, 1871); *Phaéton,* symph. poem (Paris, Dec. 7, 1873); *Danse macabre,* symph. poem (Paris, Jan. 24, 1875; one of his most successful works); *La Jeunesse d'Hercule,* symph. poem (Paris, Jan. 28, 1877); *Suite algérienne* (Paris, Dec. 19, 1880); *Une Nuit à Lisbonne* (Paris, Jan. 23, 1881); *Le Carnaval des animaux* (contains, as its 13th section, the popular *Swan;* Paris, Feb. 26, 1922); 5 piano concertos (all first perf. by Saint-Saëns): No. 1, in D (Leipzig, Oct. 26, 1865); No. 2, in G minor (Paris, May 6, 1868); No. 3, in E-flat (Leipzig, Nov. 25, 1869); No. 4, in C minor (Paris, Oct. 31, 1875); No. 5, in F (Paris, June 3, 1896); 3 violin concertos: No. 1, in A major (*Concertstück;* Paris, April 4, 1867); No. 2, in C (1858; Paris, Feb. 13, 1880); No. 3, in B minor (Paris, Jan. 2, 1881); *Introduction et Rondo capriccioso* for Violin and Orch. (1863; arranged for Violin and Piano by Bizet, and perf. for the first time in Paris, Nov. 6, 1913); 2 cello concertos: No. 1, in A minor (Paris, Jan. 19, 1873; still extremely popular), and No. 2, in D minor (1902; Paris, Feb. 5, 1905); *Africa,* fantasy for Piano and Orch. (Paris, Oct. 25, 1891).

CHAMBER MUSIC: Piano Quintet (1858); 2 piano trios

(1869, 1892); Piano Quartet (1875); Septet for Trumpet, Strings, and Piano (1881); 2 string quartets (1899, 1919); 2 violin sonatas (1885, 1896); 2 cello sonatas (1873, 1905); Oboe Sonata (1921); Clarinet Sonata (1921); Bassoon Sonata (1921).

VOCAL WORKS: *Oratorio de Noël* (1863); *Le Déluge,* oratorio (Paris, March 5, 1876); *Hail California* for Chorus and Orch. (1915); *Hymne à la Paix* for Chorus and Orch. (1919); numerous choruses a cappella; song cycles: *Mélodies persanes* (1870) and *La Cendre rouge* (1915); about 100 other songs; *La Fiancée du timbalier* for Voice and Orch. (Paris, Feb. 19, 1888); also a Requiem.

FOR PIANO: Etudes and various other pieces; also duets for piano, 4-hands and for 2 pianos.

ARRANGEMENTS: He completed Guiraud's opera *Frédégonde* (Paris Opéra, Dec. 18, 1895); publ. numerous arrangements of works by Classical and Romantic composers; edited Gluck's *Armide, Orphée,* and *Echo et Narcisse* in the Pelletan edition (1875–1902), the Durand edition of Rameau's works (from 1895), and Mozart's piano sonatas (1915).

Durand publ. *Catalogue général et thématique des œuvres de C. S.-S.* (1897; revised ed., 1907).

Sainton, Prosper, violinist; b. Toulouse, June 5, 1813; d. London, Oct. 17, 1890. He was a pupil of Habeneck at the Paris Cons., winning first prize for violin in 1834; was a prof. at the Cons. of Toulouse (1840–44); went to England in 1844; was appointed prof. at the Royal Academy of Music in 1845; became concertmaster of the London Phil. (1846–54), at Covent Garden (1847–71), and at Her Majesty's Theatre (1871–80). In 1860 he married **Charlotte Helen Dolby,** a contralto (b. London, May 17, 1821; d. there, Feb. 18, 1885). Sainton wrote 2 violin concertos and several violin solos; his wife composed some songs and choruses.

Saito, Hideo, Japanese cellist, conductor, and music educator; b. Tokyo, May 23, 1902; d. there, Sept. 18, 1974. He went to Germany for music study; was a cello student of Julius Klengel in Leipzig (1923–27) and of Feuermann in Berlin (1930). Returning to Japan, he played cello in the Nihon Symph. Orch., and studied conducting with Rosenstock, then resident in Japan. He was a co-founder of the Toho Music School in Tokyo, where he taught cello, conducting, and academic music courses. Among his students was Seiji Ozawa, who came to regard Saito's influence as a major factor in his own career.

Sala, Nicola, Italian composer and theorist; b. Tocco-Gaudio, near Benevento, April 7, 1713; d. Naples, Aug. 31, 1801. He was a pupil of Fago, Abos, and Leo at the Cons. della Pietà de' Turchini in Naples; apparently was not engaged as a teacher there until his old age; was appointed 2nd maestro when he was 74, in 1787, and first maestro 6 years later; continued to teach until 1799. It was during his tenure at the Cons. that he publ. his most celebrated theoretical work, *Regole del contrappunto prattico* (3 vols., 1794; reprinted by Choron in Paris,

1808, as *Principii di composizione delle scuole d'Italia*). He brought out several operas: *Vologeso* (Rome, 1737); *Zenobia* (Naples, Jan. 12, 1761); *Demetrio* (Naples, Dec. 12, 1762); *Merope* (Naples, Aug. 13, 1769); an oratorio, *Giuditta* (1780); masses; litanies; other religious works.

Salabert, Francis, French music publisher; b. Paris, July 27, 1884; d. in an airplane accident at Shannon, Ireland, Dec. 28, 1946. The Editions Salabert was founded by his father, **Edouard Salabert,** in 1896; at the latter's death in 1903, Francis Salabert took over the management. A professional musician and composer in his own right, he made a series of practical arrangements for small orch. of numerous classical and modern works, which were widely used. Editions Salabert expanded greatly through the purchase of the stock of orch. and other music of the firms Gaudet (1927), Mathot (1930), Senart (1941), Rouart-Lerolle (1942), and Deiss (1946). On the death of Francis Salabert, his widow assumed the directorship.

Salazar, Adolfo, eminent Spanish musicologist; b. Madrid, March 6, 1890; d. Mexico City, Sept. 27, 1958. He studied with Manuel de Falla and Pérez Casas. In 1914 he became editor in chief of the *Revista Musical Hispano-Americana* (until 1918); from 1918 to 1936 was music critic of the influential Madrid daily *El Sol;* was founder and later secretary of the Sociedad Nacional de Música (1915–22). During the final period of the Spanish Civil War he was cultural attaché at the Spanish embassy in Washington (1938–39); then settled in Mexico City as a writer and teacher.

Saldoni, Baltasar, Spanish composer and lexicographer; b. Barcelona, Jan. 4, 1807; d. Madrid, Dec. 3, 1889. He was a pupil of Mateo Ferrer at Montserrat and of Carnicer in Madrid. In 1826 he produced in Madrid his light opera *El Triunfo del amor* and the Italian operas *Saladino e Clotilde* (1833), *Ipermestra* (Jan. 20, 1838), and *Cleonice regina di Siria* (Jan. 24, 1840); he also wrote the zarzuelas *La corte de Mónaco* (Feb. 16, 1857) and *Los maridos en las máscaras* (Barcelona, Aug. 26, 1864). In 1830 he was appointed prof. of singing at the Madrid Cons. His magnum opus as a scholar was the *Diccionario biográfico-bibliográfico de efemérides de músicos españoles,* in 4 vols. (Madrid, 1868–81), to which was added a supplementary vol. in the form of a chronology of births and deaths of Spanish musicians, day by day and year by year, with exhaustive biographical notes. This monumental compilation, upon which Saldoni worked nearly 40 years, contains (inevitably) a number of errors, but in the absence of other musicographical works on Spanish musicians, it still retains considerable documentary value.

Salieri, Antonio, illustrious Italian composer; b. Legnago, near Verona, Aug. 18, 1750; d. Vienna, May 7, 1825. He studied music with his brother, Francesco, who was a violinist, and also took lessons from the organist Simoni. His father died in 1765, and Salieri was taken to Venice by a wealthy patron; there he studied harmony with Pescetti and singing with Pacini. Gassmann, the Viennese composer, who was in Venice at the time, took Salieri to Vienna in 1766, and provided for his education there. While Gassmann was in Rome (1770), Salieri took his place as conductor at the Burg Theater in Vienna, and brought out there his first opera, *Le Donne letterate,* with marked success. From that time until 1774 he produced 9 more operas of his own, all in the Italian style, the last being *La calamità dei cuori.* When Gassmann died in 1774, Salieri became his successor as court composer. He began a serious study of Gluck's style under the master's own direction; Gluck recommended Salieri to the administration of the Académie de Musique in Paris for the composition of a French opera; this was produced in Paris as *Les Danaïdes,* based on an Italian libretto, *Ipermestra,* by Calzabigi; the opera was advertised as composed by Gluck in collaboration with Salieri, but after the 12th performance Gluck declared that the work was entirely by Salieri; it remained in the repertoire of the Paris Opéra for many years. Salieri then returned to Vienna, where he produced a comic opera, *La grotta di Trofonio* (Oct. 12, 1785), with much success. His French opera *Les Horaces* was produced in Paris on Dec. 7, 1786, and proved a failure, but his next French opera, *Tarare* (Paris Opéra, June 8, 1787), made a sensation, and was performed on all the principal stages in Europe; Lorenzo Da Ponte made a revised Italian version of it as *Axur, Re d'Ormus,* which was produced in Vienna on Jan. 8, 1788, with enormous acclaim. In 1788 Salieri succeeded Bonno as court Kapellmeister at Vienna, retaining this post until 1824, but he did not conduct operatic performances after 1790, confining himself to the concerts of the Hofsängerkapelle; was also conductor of the Tonkünstler-Sozietät (founded in 1771 by Gassmann) until 1818. In Vienna he enjoyed great renown as a teacher; Beethoven studied with him, and acknowledged himself willingly as Salieri's pupil; Schubert and Liszt were also his pupils. Salieri was undoubtedly a master of the Italian method of composition, and his technique in harmony and counterpoint was of the highest. He had a reputation for intrigue, and this gave rise to the fantastic story of his poisoning of Mozart (Pushkin publ. a drama, *Mozart and Salieri,* based on this story, and Rimsky-Korsakov set it to music). In all, Salieri wrote 39 operas, of which 6 remained unproduced; 11 cantatas; 6 masses; 4 Te Deums; a Requiem; many other pieces of church music; 2 symphs.; 2 piano concertos; various other instrumental works.

Salinas, Francisco de, Spanish organist and theorist; b. Burgos, March 1, 1513; d. Salamanca, Jan. 13, 1590. He became blind at the age of 10; was taught organ playing, and studied languages at the Univ. of Salamanca. In 1538 he was taken to Italy by Cardinal Sarmiento; in 1553–58, was organist to the Duke of Alba at the vice-regal court of Naples, where Diego Ortiz was maestro. In 1561 Salinas returned to Spain, and from 1567 until his death was a prof. of music at the Univ. of Salamanca. He wrote the theoretical treatise *De musica libri septem* (Salamanca, 1577), chiefly valuable for the examples of Spanish folk music it contains. It was to Salinas that Luis de León dedicated his famous *Ode to Music.*

Sallinen, Aulis, Finnish composer; b. Salmi, April 9, 1935. He studied under Aarre Merikanto and Joonas Kokkonen at the Sibelius Academy (1955–60); was managing director of the Finnish Radio Symph. (1960–70); taught at the Sibelius Academy (1963–76); was appointed Arts Professor by the Finnish state for the years 1976–81. In his music he uses modern techniques, with a prevalence of euphonious dissonance and an occasional application of serialism.

WORKS: 3 operas: *Ratsumies (The Horseman;* 1973–74; Savonlinna Opera Festival, July 17, 1975); *Punainen viiva (The Red Line;* 1976–78; Helsinki, Nov. 30, 1978); *The King Goes Forth to France* (Savonlinna Opera Festival, July 7, 1984); ballet, *Variations sur Mallarmé* (1967; Helsinki, 1968); *2 Mythical Scenes* for Orch. (1956); Concerto for Chamber Orch. (1959–60); *Variations* for Cello and Orch. (1960–61); *3 Lyrical Songs about Death* for Baritone, Male Chorus, and Orch. (1962); orch. elegy, *Mauermusik (Wall Music),* subtitled "In memory of a certain young German" killed at the Berlin Wall (1962); *14 Juventas Variations* for Orch. (1963); *Metamorphoses* for Piano and Chamber Orch. (1964); Violin Concerto (1968); *Chorali* for 32 Wind Instruments, Percussion, Harp, and Celesta (1970); 4 symphs.: No. 1 (1970–71); No. 2, *Symphonic Dialogue,* for Solo Percussionist and Orch. (1972); No. 3 (1974–75); No. 4 (1979); *Suita grammaticale* for Children's Choir, Strings, Kantele, and School Instruments (1971–72); *Chamber Music I* for Chamber String Orch. (1975); *Chamber Music II* for Alto Flute and Chamber String Orch. (1975–76); Cello Concerto (1976); 4 string quartets: No. 1 (1958); No. 2, *Canzona* (1960); No. 3, *Some Aspects of Peltoniemi Hintrik's Funeral March* (1969); No. 4, *Quiet Songs* (1971); *Serenade* for 2 Wind Quartets (1963); *Elegy for Sebastian Knight* for Solo Cello (1964); *Quattro per 4* for Violin, Cello, Oboe, and Harpsichord (1964–65); *4 Etudes* for Violin and Piano (1970); *Chaconne* for Organ (1970); Solo Cello Sonata (1971); *Metamorfora* for Cello and Piano (1974); *Canto and Ritornello* for Solo Violin (1975); *4 Dream Songs* for Solo Voice and Piano (1972); *Dies irae* (1978).

Salmenhaara, Erkki, Finnish composer; b. Helsinki, March 12, 1941. He studied at the Sibelius Academy with Kokkonen; then went to Vienna, where he took lessons with Ligeti (1963). He joined the faculty of the Univ. of Helsinki in 1963. His music is often inspired by literary works; he favors unusual combinations of instruments, including electronics; makes use of serial techniques in dense, fastidious sonorities.

WORKS: Opera, *Portugalin nainen (The Wom-*

an of Portugal; 1972; Helsinki, Feb. 4, 1976); *9 Improvisations,* concerto for Piano, Strings, and Timpani; Symph. No. 1; Symph. No. 2 (1963, revised 1966); Symph. No. 3 (1964); *Le Bateau ivre,* after Rimbaud, for Orch. (1966); *BFK-83* for Orch. (1967); *La Fille en mini-jupe,* poem for Orch. (1967); *Suomi-Finland,* an "unsymphonic poem" for Orch. (1967); *Requiem profanum* for Soprano, Alto, Baritone, Strings, and Piano (1968–69); *Illuminations,* after Rimbaud, poem for Orch. (1971); Symph. No. 4, *Nel mezzo del cammin di nostra vita,* after Dante (1971); Horn Concerto (Oslo, Oct. 3, 1974); *Intrada* for Orch. (1975); Concerto for 2 Violins and Orch. (Helsinki, Sept. 21, 1982); Cello Sonata (1960); String Trio (1961); *La Clarté vibrante,* cantata for Soprano, 4 Cellos, and Percussion; *Pan and Echo* for 4 Suspended Cymbals, Tam-tam, and Amplifier; Concerto for 2 Violins, with Amplifiers and Loudspeakers; *Composition* for String Quartet (1963); *Elegia I* for 3 Flutes, 2 Trumpets, and Double Bass (1963); *Elegia II* for 2 String Quartets (1963); *Composition 3* for Violin, Clarinet, Guitar, and Percussion (1963); Wind Quintet (1964); *Elegia III* for Cello (1965); 3 Piano Sonatas (1966, 1973, 1975); *Elegia IV* for Viola (1967); *Etude* for Harpsichord (1969); *Trois scènes de nuit* for Violin and Piano (1970); *Quartetto* for Flute, Violin, Viola, and Cello (1971); *Prelude, Pop Tune and Fugue* for Flute; *And the Fire and the Rose Are One* for 2 Violins (1972); songs.

Salmhofer, Franz, Austrian composer; b. Vienna, Jan. 22, 1900; d. there, Sept. 2, 1975. He was a chorister at the Admont Monastery in Styria until 1914; then studied composition with Schreker at the Vienna Academy of Music and musicology with Guido Adler at the Univ. of Vienna. In 1923 he married the pianist **Margit Gál.** In 1929 he became conductor at the Hofburg Theater, for which he composed incidental music, ballets, and operas; he resigned in 1939; from 1945 to 1955 he was director at the Vienna State Opera; then director of the Volksoper, 1955–63.
WORKS: Operas: *Dame in Traum* (Vienna, Dec. 26, 1935); *Iwan Sergejewitsch Tarassenko* (Vienna, March 9, 1938); *Das Werbekleid* (Vienna, June 25, 1946); ballets: *Das lockende Phantom, Der Taugenichts in Wien, Weihnachtsmärchen, Österreichische Bauernhochzeit;* 2 symphs. (1947, 1955); overtures: *Der Ackermann und der Tod* and *Heroische Ouvertüre;* Trumpet Concerto; Cello Concerto; *Der geheimnisvolle Trompeter,* symph. poem for Narrator and Orch., after Walt Whitman's *The Mystic Trumpeter* (1924); *Kammersuite* for 16 Instruments (Vienna, May 10, 1923); String Quartet; Piano Quartet; Viola Sonata; Cello Sonata; songs; piano pieces.

Salminen, Matti, Finnish bass; b. Turku, July 7, 1945. After vocal studies in Finland, he made his operatic debut at the Helsinki Opera as King Philipp in *Don Carlos* in 1969; he then toured in Europe, appearing in Cologne, Zürich, Hamburg, Munich, and Stuttgart, at Covent Garden in London, and at the Bayreuth Festival. He particularly distinguished himself in the great basso roles in operas by

Mozart, Wagner, and Verdi.

Salmon, Albert Glover, American pianist and composer; b. Southold, N.Y., Sept. 28, 1868; d. (suicide by swallowing poison), Boston, Sept. 17, 1917. He studied at the New England Cons., graduating in 1888; also took private lessons with B.J. Lang and Otto Bendix in Boston, and with Percy Goetschius and MacDowell in N.Y. He then went to Russia, where he took composition lessons with Glazunov in St. Petersburg and became deeply interested in Russian music; he collected a valuable library of works by Russian composers (about 3,000 vols.), as well as autographs. His own compositions were mostly for piano, in a salon manner (*Valse arabesque, Scherzo, Novelette, Fileuse, Impromptu, Tarentelle fantastique,* etc.).

Salmond, Felix, distinguished English cellist; b. London, Nov. 19, 1888; d. New York, Feb. 19, 1952. He studied at the Royal College of Music with W.E. Whitehouse, and in Brussels with Edouard Jacobs; made his debut in London (1909), accompanied at the piano by his mother, Mrs. Norman Salmond. He gave the world premiere of Elgar's Cello Concerto, under Elgar's direction, on Oct. 27, 1919; after a European tour, he settled in America (debut, N.Y., March 29, 1922); was head of the cello dept. at the Curtis Inst. of Music in Philadelphia (1925–42) and taught cello at the Juilliard Graduate School of Music in N.Y. from its opening in 1924. He enjoyed a reputation as a fine chamber music player and an excellent teacher.

Salò, Gasparo da. See **Gasparo da Salò.**

Saloman, Siegfried, composer; b. Tondern, Schleswig, Oct. 2, 1816; d. Stockholm, July 22, 1899. He studied composition with J.P. Hartmann in Copenhagen, and violin with Lipinski in Dresden. He lived in Copenhagen for many years and produced 2 operas there, *Tordenskjold I Dynekilen* (May 23, 1844) and *Diamantkorset* (*The Diamond Cross;* March 20, 1847); toured Russia and the Netherlands (1847–50); married the singer **Henriette Nissen,** and traveled with her; in 1859, settled in Russia; one of his operas, to a German libretto, was produced in Russian as *Karpatskaya roza* in Moscow, Jan. 7, 1868; several other operas were produced in Stockholm, where he went in 1879 after the death of his wife. Some of his violin pieces and songs have been publ.

Salomon (Salomonis). See **Elias, Salomon.**

Salomon, Johann Peter, German violinist, composer, and impresario; b. Bonn (baptized, Feb. 20), 1745; d. London (following a riding accident; buried in Westminster Abbey), Nov. 25, 1815. He was a member of the Electoral orch. at Bonn (1758–62); after a successful concert tour he was engaged as concertmaster and composer to Prince Heinrich of Prussia at Rheinsberg (1764). When the orch. was disbanded, Salomon went to Paris and then to London, where he settled in 1781; made himself known as a violinst and conductor; introduced symphs. by Haydn and Mozart in a series of concerts he gave in 1786. In 1790 he went to Italy to engage singers for the Italian Opera in London, and from there went to Vienna, where he saw Haydn and persuaded him to accept an engagement in London. At Salomon's behest Haydn wrote the works familiarly known as his "Salomon Symphonies"; it is through his association with Haydn's 2 visits to England, in 1790–91 and 1794–95, that Salomon's name remains in the annals of music. He was a founder of the Phil. Society in London (1813); conducted its first concert, on March 8, 1813. His own works are of merely antiquarian interest; they include the operas *Les Recruteurs* (Rheinsberg, 1771); *Le Séjour du bonheur* (Berlin, March 5, 1773); *Titus* (Rheinsberg, 1774); *La Reine de Golconde* (Rheinsberg, 1776); *Windsor Castle,* or *The Fair Maid of Kent* (Covent Garden, April 6, 1795); also violin sonatas.

Salonen, Esa-Pekka, Finnish composer and conductor; b. Helsinki, June 30, 1958. He studied French-horn playing at the Sibelius Academy in Helsinki (1973–77); took composition courses with Rautavaara and conducting classes with Panula; he then traveled to Italy, where he studied with Donatoni in Siena and Castiglioni in Milan (1979–81). Returning to Finland, he engaged in theater conducting. In his music he tends toward pragmatic aural accessibility, employing fairly modern techniques while preserving the formal centrality of traditional tonality.

Salter, Lionel (Paul), English conductor, pianist, harpsichordist, and writer on music; b. London, Sept. 8, 1914. He studied at the Royal College of Music and at Cambridge Univ. with Dent and Ord (B.A., 1935; B.Mus., 1936); then returned to the Royal College of Music, where he studied conducting with Lambert and piano with Benjamin. He began his career working in radio and television in London; in 1945 he became assistant conductor of the BBC Theatre Orch.; from 1948 he held administrative posts with the BBC; retired in 1974. His books include *Going to a Concert* (London, 1950), *Going to the Opera* (London, 1955), *The Musician and His World* (London, 1963), and *Music and the 20th-Century Media* (with J. Bornoff; Florence, 1972); he also compiled a useful *Gramophone Guide to Classical Music and Recordings.*

Saltzmann-Stevens, Minnie, American soprano; b. Bloomington, Ill., March 17, 1874; d. Milan, Jan. 25, 1950. She studied voice with Jean De Reszke in Paris; made her operatic debut as Brünnhilde in the English version of the *Ring des Nibelungen* at London's Covent Garden in 1909; she continued to sing there until 1913; also appeared at the Bayreuth Festivals of 1911 and 1913; from 1911–14 she sang with the Chicago Opera.

Salzedo (originally, **Léon Carlos Salzédo**), **Carlos,** eminent harpist and composer; b. Arcachon,

France, April 6, 1885; d. Waterville, Maine, Aug. 17, 1961. He studied at the Cons. of Bordeaux (1891–94), winning first prize in piano; then entered the Paris Cons., where his father, **Gaston Salzédo,** was a prof. of singing; studied with Charles de Bériot (piano), gaining first prize in 1901, and with Hasselmans (harp), also receiving first prize. He began his career as a concert harpist upon graduation; traveled all over Europe (1901–5); was solo harpist of the Association des Premiers Prix de Paris in Monte Carlo (1905–9); in 1909 settled in N.Y.; was first harpist in the orch. of the Metropolitan Opera Co. (1909–13). In 1913 he formed the Trio de Lutèce (from Lutetia, the ancient name for Paris), with Georges Barrère (flute) and Paul Kéfer (cello). In 1921 he was co-founder, with Edgar Varèse, of the International Composers' Guild in N.Y., with the aim of promoting modern music; this organization presented many important contemporary works; in the same year he founded a modern music magazine, *Eolian Review,* later renamed *Eolus* (discontinued in 1933). He became an American citizen in 1923; was elected president of the National Assoc. of Harpists; held teaching positions at the Inst. of Musical Art in N.Y., and the Juilliard Graduate School of Music; organized and headed the harp dept. at the Curtis Inst. of Music in Philadelphia. In 1931 he established the Salzedo Harp Colony at Camden, Maine, for teaching and performing during the summer months. Salzedo introduced a number of special effects, and publ. special studies for his new techniques; designed a "Salzedo Model" harp, capable of rendering novel sonorities (Eolian Flux, Eolian chords, gushing chords, percussion, etc.). His own compositions are rhythmically intricate and contrapuntally elaborate and require a virtuoso technique.

Salzer, Felix, distinguished Austrian-American theorist and pedagogue; b. Vienna, June 13, 1904. He studied theory and composition with Schenker and Weise; musicology with Guido Adler; in 1926 received his Dr.Phil. at the Univ. of Vienna; then taught at the New Vienna Cons.; emigrated to the U.S. in 1939; became a naturalized citizen in 1945. He was on the faculty of the Mannes College of Music in N.Y. (1940–56); in 1956 was appointed to the faculty of Queens College of the City Univ. of N.Y. He is a leading "Schenkerian" theorist and was instrumental in bringing the views of Heinrich Schenker to the attention of American musicians; his own contribution has been in the expansion and application of Schenker's concepts—previously restricted to a narrow range of tonal music—to Renaissance, medieval, and some 20th-century music. He publ. a number of important books on music theory: *Sinn und Wesen der abendländischen Mehrstimmigkeit* (Vienna, 1935); *Structural Hearing* (2 vols., N.Y., 1952; new ed., N.Y., 1962); *Counterpoint in Composition: The Study of Voice Leading* (with C. Schachter; N.Y., 1969); edited (with William Mitchell) *Music Forum* (N.Y., 1967—), a hardcover periodical.

Salzman, Eric, American composer and musicologist; b. New York, Sept. 8, 1933. He studied composition at Columbia Univ., with Otto Luening, Vladimir Ussachevsky, William Mitchell, and Jack Beeson (B.A., 1954), and at Princeton Univ. with Roger Sessions and Milton Babitt (M.F.A., 1956); in addition, he took courses in musicology with Oliver Strunk, Arthur Mendel, and Nino Pirotta. In 1957 he went to Europe on a Fulbright fellowship to study with Goffredo Petrassi in Rome; also attended courses of Karlheinz Stockhausen at Darmstadt. Returning to the U.S., he became a music critic for the *N.Y. Times* (1958–62) and for the *N.Y. Herald Tribune* (1963–66). He taught at Queens College in N.Y. (1966–68); then was director of "New Images of Sounds," a series of concerts given at Hunter College in N.Y. He founded the Quog Music Theater in 1970 with the aim of creating a new music theater for contemporary performing arts. In 1984 he was appointed editor of the *Musical Quarterly*. In his compositions he follows the most advanced techniques in mixed media.

WORKS: String Quartet (1955); Flute Sonata (1956); *Partita* for Solo Violin (1958); *Inventions* for Orch. (1959); *The Owl and the Cuckoo* for Soprano, Guitar, and Chamber Ensemble (1963); *Verses and Cantos* for 4 Voices and Instruments with electronic extensions (N.Y., Nov. 30, 1967); *Larynx Music,* magnetic tape piece for dance (1968); *Feedback,* "environment piece" for Magnetic Tape and Film (1968); *The Nude Paper Sermon* for Actor, Renaissance Consort, Chorus, and Electronics (1968–69); *The Conjurer,* multimedia spectacle (1975; with Michael Sahl); *Civilization and Its Discontents,* opera buffa for radio (N.Y., 1977; with Sahl); *Noah,* spectacle (N.Y., Feb. 10, 1978); *The Passion of Simple Simon* (N.Y., 1979); aleatory pieces for Electronic and Mixed Media under the general title *The Electric Ear,* for perf. at the Electric Circus in Greenwich Village in N.Y. He publ. *Twentieth Century Music: An Introduction* (Englewood Cliffs, N.J., 1967); also (with Sahl) a book on vernacular harmony, *Making Changes* (N.Y., 1976).

Samara, Spiro, Greek composer; b. Corfu, Nov. 29, 1861; d. Athens, March 25, 1917. He was a pupil of Enrico Stancampiano in Athens; later of Léo Delibes at the Paris Cons. He won considerable success with his first opera, *Flora mirabilis* (Milan, May 16, 1886), and devoted himself almost exclusively to dramatic compositions. Other operas were *Medgè* (Rome, 1888); *Lionella* (Milan, 1891); *La Martire* (Naples, May 23, 1894); *La Furia domata* (Milan, 1895); *Storia d'amore* (Milan, 1903; in Gotha, 1906, as *La Biondinetta*); *Mademoiselle de Belle-Isle* (Genoa, Nov. 9, 1905); *Rhea* (Florence, April 11, 1908); *La guerra in tempo di guerra* (Athens, 1914). He publ. *Scènes orientales,* suite for Piano, 4-hands; many pieces for piano solo; songs.

Samaroff, Olga (née **Hickenlooper**), American pianist and educator; b. San Antonio, Texas, Aug. 8, 1882; d. New York, May 17, 1948. She studied as a child with her mother and grandmother (Mrs. L.

Grünewald, a former concert pianist); subsequently studied in Paris (with Delaborde), Baltimore (with Ernest Hutcheson), and Berlin (with Ernst Jedliczka). She made her concert debut in N.Y. (Jan. 18, 1905) with the N.Y. Symph. Society; appeared with other orchs. in the U.S. and Europe; gave joint recitals with Fritz Kreisler, Zimbalist, and other violinists. In 1911 she married **Leopold Stokowski;** they divorced in 1923. For 2 seasons she was music critic for the *N.Y. Evening Post* (1927–29); taught at the Juilliard Graduate School and at the Philadelphia Cons. of Music; from 1930, gave master courses in N.Y.; lectured extensively on music appreciation.

Samazeuilh, Gustave, French composer; b. Bordeaux, June 2, 1877; d. Paris, Aug. 4, 1967. He studied music with Chausson and at the Schola Cantorum with Vincent d'Indy; also took some lessons from Paul Dukas. In his music he absorbed the distinct style of French Impressionism, but despite the fine craftsmanship of his work, performances were few and far between.

WORKS: For Orch.: *Etude symphonique* (1907); *Nuit* (Paris, March 15, 1925); *Naïades au soir* (Paris, Oct. 18, 1925); *L'Appel de la danse* (1946); for Orch., with Chorus: *Le Sommeil de Canope* (1908); *Chant d'Espagne* (Paris, Jan. 10, 1926); *Le Cercle des heures* (Paris, Feb. 17, 1934); String Quartet (1911); *Suite en trio* for Strings (1938); etc.; many transcriptions for piano of orch. works by d'Indy, Debussy, Franck, and Fauré. He was known also as a writer on musical subjects; publ. *Un Musicien français: Paul Dukas* (Paris, 1913; augmented ed., 1936); *Musiciens de mon temps: Chroniques et souvenirs* (Paris, 1947).

Saminsky, Lazare, Russian-American composer, conductor, and writer on music; b. Valegotsulova, near Odessa, Nov. 8, 1882; d. Port Chester, N.Y., June 30, 1959. He studied mathematics and philosophy at the Univ. of St. Petersburg; composition with Rimsky-Korsakov and Liadov, conducting with Nicolas Tcherepnin at the St. Petersburg Cons. (graduated, 1910). He emigrated to the U.S. in 1920, settling in N.Y.; in 1923 was a co-founder of the League of Composers; in 1924 was appointed music director of Temple Emanu-El in N.Y.; established an annual Three-Choir Festival there in 1936, presenting old and new music. In his compositions he followed the Romantic tradition; Hebrew subjects and styles play an important part in some of his music. He was married to an American writer, Lillian Morgan Buck, who died in 1945; in 1948 he married the American pianist **Jennifer Gandar.**

Sammarco, (Giuseppe) Mario, Italian baritone; b. Palermo, Dec. 13, 1868; d. Milan, Jan. 24, 1930. He studied singing with Antonio Cantelli, making a successful debut in Palermo, 1888, in *Faust;* then sang in Brescia, Madrid, Lisbon, Moscow, Warsaw, Berlin, and Vienna. After his London appearance as Scarpia in *Tosca* at Covent Garden (Oct. 19, 1905), he sang there every season until the outbreak of World War I. He made his American debut as Tonio (Feb. 1, 1908) at the Manhattan Opera House in N.Y.; in 1910 joined the Chicago Opera Co. He sang in Russian, Spanish, Italian, French, and Eng. He retired from the stage in 1919.

Sammartini (San Martini), Giovanni Battista, significant Italian composer, younger brother of **Giuseppe Sammartini;** b. Milan, 1701; d. there, Jan. 15, 1775. He served as a church organist in Milan; in 1728 was appointed maestro di cappella at the Santissimo Entierro in Milan; in 1768 held a similar position at S. Gottardo. His historical significance lies not so much in his own music as in his authority as a teacher; Gluck was his student between 1737 and 1741. His own works are important mainly in the evolution of the sonata form, in which he introduced extensive thematic development; but the claim that he anticipated Haydn in the formulation of symph. form cannot be sustained; a chamber symph. in 4 movements, supposedly written by Sammartini in 1734 and often cited as the earliest work in symph. form, is apparently nonexistent. But Sammartini was a prodigiously industrious composer; among his works are 3 operas, of which 2 were produced in Milan: *L'ambizione superata dalla virtù* (1734) and *Agrippina* (1743); an oratorio, *Gesù bambino adorato;* about 20 symphs.; 6 trio sonatas for flute, 2 violins, and bass; string quartets; harpsichord sonatas; sacred and secular church music. Four symphs. were brought out by N. Jenkins (*Collegium musicum,* VI, New Haven, 1963); other symphs. were edited by B.D. Churgin (Harvard Publications in Music, vol. 1, *The Early Symphonies,* Cambridge, Mass., 1968); several concertos were brought out by H. Töttcher (Hamburg, 1968) and by H. Illy (Kassel, 1971).

Sammartini (San Martini), Giuseppe, called "il Londinese" (because he lived in London), to distinguish him from his brother, **Giovanni Battista Sammartini;** b. Milan, Jan. 6, 1695; d. London, Nov. 1750. In 1727 he went to London; played the oboe at the King's Theatre; then became director of chamber music in the household of the Prince of Wales. He gave concerts with Arrigoni at Hickford's Rooms in 1732; Burney heard him play in 1744. He contributed a "sinfonia" and an aria to an oratorio, *La calumnia delusa* (1724), a pasticcio by several Italian composers. He further wrote sonatas for 2 flutes, 12 *concerti grossi,* 12 violin sonatas, 8 overtures, harpsichord pieces, etc. A sonata was edited by Riemann in his *Collegium musicum.*

Samuel, Gerhard, German-American conductor and composer; b. Bonn, April 20, 1924. He studied violin as a child; his family emigrated to America in 1938. He performed menial jobs as a dishwasher and shoe salesman in N.Y. before winning a scholarship at the Eastman School of Music in Rochester, N.Y.; there he studied conducting with Hermann Gerhard and composition with Howard Hanson (B.S., 1945); also played violin with the Rochester Phil. (1941–45). In 1945 he enrolled at Yale Univ., studying composition with Paul Hin-

demith (M.M., 1947); attended for 2 summers the conducting sessions with Koussevitzky at the Berkshire Music Center in Tanglewood. From 1949 to 1959 he was a violinist with and assistant conductor of the Minneapolis Symph. Orch.; from 1959 to 1970 he conducted the Oakland Symph. Orch.; then was associate conductor of the Los Angeles Phil. Orch. In 1976 he was appointed to the faculty of Cincinnati College. He composed a number of choral and symph. works in a fine modernistic idiom, inter alia, *12 on Death and No* for Tenor, Small Chorus, and Orch. (1968); *Looking at Orpheus Looking* for Orch. (1971); *To an End* for Chorus and Orch. (1972); *Into Flight From* for Orch. (1973); *Requiem for Survivors* for Orch. (1974).

Samuel, Harold, famous English pianist; b. London, May 23, 1879; d. there, Jan. 15, 1937. He studied at the Royal College of Music with Dannreuther (piano) and Stanford (composition); later was on its faculty. He was particularly distinguished as an interpreter of Bach; in 1921 gave 6 successive Bach recitals in London and a similar cycle in N.Y.; toured the U.S. regularly from 1924. He wrote a musical comedy, *Hon'ble Phil,* and some piano pieces.

Samuel-Rousseau, Marcel. See **Rousseau, Marcel.**

Sánchez de Fuentes, Eduardo, important Cuban composer and educator; b. Havana, April 3, 1874; d. there, Sept. 7, 1944. He studied music with Ignacio Cervantes and Carlos Anckermann. He occupied an influential position in the artistic affairs of Cuba; wrote 6 operas and many other works, but is known outside Cuba chiefly by his popular song *Tú,* which he publ. at the age of 18.

WORKS: Operas (all produced in Havana): *El Náufrago,* after Tennyson's *Enoch Arden* (Jan. 31, 1901); *Dolorosa* (April 23, 1910); *Doreya* (Feb. 7, 1918); *Kabelia,* to his own libretto after a Hindu legend (June 22, 1942); *Bocetos cubanos* for Orch., Women's Chorus, and Soprano Solo (Barcelona, 1922); *Temas del patio,* symph. prelude; songs (*Mírame así,* etc.); piano pieces; publ. *El Folk-lore en la música cubana* (1923); *Folklorismo* (1928); *Viejos rítmos cubanos* (1937); etc.

Sandberger, Adolf, eminent German musicologist; b. Würzburg, Dec. 19, 1864; d. Munich, Jan. 14, 1943. He studied composition in Würzburg and Munich; musicology at the Univ. of Berlin, with Spitta; obtained his Dr.Phil. in 1887; in 1889 he was appointed custodian of the music dept. of the Munich Library; also lectured at the Univ. of Munich (1894–1930). He was editor of Denkmäler der Tonkunst in Bayern and of Breitkopf & Härtel's monumental edition of the complete works of Roland de Lassus. Sandberger was one of the most important teachers of musicology in Germany, who formulated the basic principles of contemporary musical bibliography. He was also a composer; he wrote an opera, *Ludwig der Springer;* 2 string quartets; Piano Trio;

Violin Sonata; various piano pieces; choruses; songs. Among his writings were *Leben und Werke des Dichtermusikers Peter Cornelius* (Diss., Univ. of Berlin, 1887); *Beiträge zur Geschichte der bayerischen Hofkapelle unter Orlando di Lasso* (planned in 3 vols.; vol. I, 1894; vol. III, 1895; vol. II was not publ.); *Zur Geschichte des Haydnschen Streichquartetts* (1899); *Lasso und die geistigen Strömungen seiner Zeit* (Munich, 1926). His collected essays were issued in 3 vols.: I, Biography of Lassus (1921); II, Beethoven (1924); III, History of Opera (1934). A Sandberger Festschrift was publ. in his honor in 1918, edited by Kroyer; a 2nd Festschrift appeared in 1929.

Sanderling, Kurt, eminent German conductor; b. Arys, Sept. 9, 1912. He went to Russia after the advent of the Nazis, and conducted the Moscow Radio Orch. (1936–41) and the Leningrad Phil. (1941–60). He then was chief conductor of the (East) Berlin Symph. Orch. (1960–77). From 1964 to 1967 he was chief conductor of the Dresden State Opera. He also filled a number of engagements as a guest conductor in Western Europe and America.

Sanderson, Sibyl, American soprano; b. Sacramento, Calif., Dec. 7, 1865; d. Paris, May 15, 1903. She was educated in San Francisco, where her musical talent attracted attention; taken to Paris by her mother at the age 19, she studied at the Cons. with Massenet; also with Sbriglia and Mathilde Marchesi. Massenet was charmed with her voice and her person; wrote the leading part in *Esclarmonde* for her; she created it at the Opéra-Comique, on May 14, 1889; the role of Thaïs (Paris Opéra, March 16, 1889) was also written by Massenet for her. Other French composers were equally enchanted with her; Saint-Saëns wrote *Phryné* for her (1893). She made her American debut at the Metropolitan Opera in N.Y. as Manon (Jan. 16, 1895), but had little success with the American public. In 1897 she married a wealthy Cuban, Antonio Terry, who died in 1900.

Sándor, Arpád, Hungarian pianist; b. Budapest, June 5, 1896; d. there, Feb. 10, 1972. He studied there with Bartók and Kodály at the Royal Academy, graduating in 1914; after several years in Berlin, he toured the U.S. as an accompanist in 1922; then returned to Germany, and wrote art criticism in the *Berliner Tageblatt.* In 1933 he settled permanently in the U.S.; was accompanist to Jascha Heifetz, Lily Pons, and other celebrated artists. He became an American citizen in 1943.

Sándor, György, Hungarian pianist; b. Budapest, Sept. 21, 1912. He studied at the Royal Academy of Music in Budapest with Bartók (piano) and Kodály (composition). After a series of concerts in Europe (1930–38), he settled in the U.S. in 1939; was soloist in the premiere of Bartók's posthumous Piano Concerto No. 3, with the Philadelphia Orch. (Feb. 8, 1946); traveled in Australia in 1951. He made brilliant transcriptions of several modern orch. works,

including *L'Apprenti sorcier* by Paul Dukas; also publ. *On Piano Playing: Motion, Sound, and Expression* (N.Y., 1981).

Sandström, Sven-David, Swedish composer; b. Motala, Oct. 30, 1942. He studied general subjects at Stockholm Univ. (1963–67); attended theory classes with Lidholm at the State College of Music (1968–72); also took special courses in advanced techniques of composition with Nørgaard and Ligeti. In 1980 he joined the faculty of the State College of Music in Stockholm. In his own works he pursues the techniques of enhanced serialism, making use of fractional tones and occasionally resorting to aleatory procedures; some of his applications are aggressively oxymoronic and deliberately offensive; thus, his *Requiem,* dedicated to the memory of child victims of war and racism, has a text in Swedish and English by the poet Tobias Berggren, replete with sadistic obscenities and pornographic proclamations.

WORKS: FOR THE STAGE: Church opera, *Stark såsom döden (Strong like Death),* after B.V. Wall (Stockholm, April 18, 1978); chamber opera, *Hasta o älskade brud (Hasta, O Beloved Bride,* 1978); music drama *Kejsaren Jones (Emperor Jones),* after O'Neill's play (1980); incidental music for *Ett drömspel (The Dreamplay),* after Strindberg, for Chorus, Brasses, Percussion, Organ, and String Quartet (1980).

FOR ORCH.: *Bilder (Pictures)* for Percussion and Orch. (Norrköping, April 17, 1969); *Intrada* for Wind Instruments, Strings, and Percussion (1969); *17 Bildkombinationen (17 Picture Combinations)* for Wind Instruments, Percussion, and Strings (1969); *In the Meantime* for Chamber Orch. (1970); *Sounds* for 14 Strings (1970); *To You* (Arvika, Aug. 15, 1970); *Around a Line* for Wind Instruments, Piano, Percussion, and Strings (1971); *Through and Through* (1972; Stockholm, Feb. 1, 1974); *Con tutta forza* for 41 Wind Instruments and 6 Percussionists (Stockholm, Oct. 28, 1976); *Culminations* (Swedish Radio, Feb. 22, 1977); *Agitato* for Piano and Orch. (1978); *The Rest Is Dross* for String Orch. (1979); Flute Concerto (1980; Stockholm, Oct. 24, 1983); Guitar Concerto (Malmö, May 18, 1983).

Sanjuán, Pedro, Spanish composer and conductor; b. San Sebastian, Nov. 15, 1886; d. Washington, D.C., Oct. 18, 1976. He studied composition with Turina; after conducting in Europe, he went to Havana, where he organized the Havana Phil. (1926); was also a teacher of composition there; Roldán, Caturla, and other Cuban composers were his pupils. In 1932 he went back to Spain; was in Madrid in 1932–36; from 1939 until 1942, he was again conductor of the Havana Phil.; in 1942 was appointed prof. of composition at Converse College in Spartanburg, S.C.; became an American citizen in 1947.

WORKS: *Rondo fantástico* (Havana, Nov. 29, 1926); *Castilla,* suite for Orch. (Havana, June 12, 1927); *Sones de Castilla* for Small Orch.; *La Macumba,* a "ritual symphony" (St. Louis, Dec. 14, 1951, composer conducting); *Antillean Poem* for Band

(N.Y., Aug. 11, 1958, composer conducting); *Symphonic Suite* (Washington, D.C., May 9, 1965); choral works; piano pieces.

San Martini. See **Sammartini.**

Sanromá, Jesús María, brilliant Puerto Rican pianist; b. Carolina, Puerto Rico (of Catalonian parents), Nov. 7, 1902. At the age of 14 he was sent to the U.S. by the governor of Puerto Rico; studied piano with Antoinette Szumowska at the New England Cons.; in 1920, won the Mason & Hamlin piano prize; then went to Europe, where he studied with Alfred Cortot (in Paris) and Artur Schnabel (in Berlin); from 1926 till 1944 he was pianist of the Boston Symph. Orch.; taught at the New England Cons.; gave annual concerts in the U.S., Canada, and South America; also played in Europe. In 1951 he was appointed chairman of the music dept. at the Univ. of Puerto Rico. He excels particularly in the works of modern composers, and has given several world premieres of contemporary concertos (by Hindemith, etc.).

San Sebastián, Padre José Antonio de. See **Donostia, Jose Antonio de.**

Santa Cruz (Wilson), Domingo, foremost Chilean composer; b. La Cruz, near Quillota, July 5, 1899. He studied jurisprudence at the Univ. of Chile; then entered diplomatic service; was 2nd secretary of the Chilean legation in Spain (1921–24); received his musical training with Enrique Soro in Santiago and with Conrado del Campo in Madrid. Returning to Chile, he devoted himself to musical administration, teaching, and composition; in 1928 he became a prof. at the National Cons. in Santiago, and was dean of the faculty of fine arts at the Univ. of Chile in 1933–51 and again in 1962–68. His role in the promotion of musical culture in Chile was of great importance; he traveled in Europe and the U.S. as a lecturer. In his works he follows the cosmopolitan traditions of neo-Classical music, and made use of identifiable Chilean melodies in but a few of his compositions.
  WORKS: *Cantata de los rios de Chile* for Chorus and Orch. (Santiago, Nov. 27, 1942); *5 piezas breves* for String Orch. (Santiago, May 31, 1937); *Variaciones* for Piano and Orch. (Santiago, June 25, 1943); *Sinfonia concertante* for Flute, Piano, and Strings (Santiago, Nov. 29, 1945); Symph. No. 1 for Strings, Celesta, and Percussion (Santiago, May 28, 1948); Symph. No. 2 for Strings (Santiago, Nov. 26, 1948); *Egloga* for Soprano, Chorus, and Orch. (Santiago, Nov. 24, 1950); *Cantares de la Pascua* for Chorus a cappella (Santiago, Dec. 7, 1950); *Canciones del mar,* song cycle (1955); *Endechas* for Tenor and 8 Instruments (1957); 3 string quartets; Symph. No. 3, with Contralto Solo (Washington, D.C., May 9, 1965); Symph. No. 4 (1968); *Oratorio Ieremieae prophetae* (1969); many songs and choruses; piano pieces.

Santa María, Fray Tomás de, important Spanish organist and composer; b. Madrid, c.1510; d. Ribadavia, 1570. He publ. *Libro llamado Arte de tañer fantasía* (Valladolid, 1565), a treatise on playing fantasias on keyboard instruments and on the guitar or lute (German trans., with critical and biographical introduction, by E. Harich-Schneider and R. Boadella, Leipzig, 1937).

Santini, Abbate Fortunato, Italian music scholar and composer; b. Rome, Jan. 5, 1778; d. there, Sept. 14, 1861. He was noted as the collector of one of the finest music libraries ever formed; was ordained priest in 1801; as early as 1820 he publ. a catalogue of the MSS then in his possession, *Catalogo della musica antica, sacra e madrigalesca,* listing 1,000 titles by more than 700 composers. His original compositions include a Requiem; a *Stabat Mater;* many motets.

Santoliquido, Francesco, Italian composer; b. San Giorgio a Cremano, Naples, Aug. 6, 1883; d. Anacapri, Italy, Aug. 26, 1971. He studied at the Santa Cecilia in Rome; graduated in 1908; in 1912 he went to live in Hammamet, a village in Tunisia, spending part of each year in Rome; in 1933 made his home in Anacapri. Many of his compositions contain melodic inflections of Arabian popular music.
  WORKS: Operas: *La Favola di Helga* (Milan, Nov. 23, 1910); *Ferhuda* (Tunis, Jan. 30, 1919); *La Bajadera dalla maschera gialla* (Rome, 1923); *La porte verde,* musical tragedy in 4 acts (Bergamo, Oct. 15, 1953); for Orch.: *Crepuscolo sul mare* (Nuremberg, Jan. 19, 1909, composer conducting); *Il profumo delle oasi sahariane* (Tunis, April 17, 1918; also in Rome, March 5, 1922); *Acquarelli* (Rome, April 11, 1923); Symph. in F (1924); *La sagra dei morti,* heroic elegy for the victims of World War I (Rome, 1929); *3 miniature per i piccoli* (1933); *Preludio e Burlesca* for String Orch. (Rome, 1938); *Alba di gloria,* symph. prelude (Rome, Nov. 13, 1940); *Grotte di Capri,* 5 pieces for Orch. (1943); *Santuari asiatici,* symph. sketches (Naples, 1952); String Quartet; Violin Sonata; *Aria antica* for Cello and Piano; *Chiarità lunare* for Violin and Piano; *2 pezzi* for 5 Wind Instruments; *Piccola ballata* for Piano; *2 Acquaforti tunisine* for Piano; a cycle of songs to words by Pierre Louys; *Messa facile* for Chorus; publ. *Il Dopo-Wagner; Claudio Debussy e Richard Strauss* (Rome, 1909); also books of verse; wrote short stories in Eng.

Santoro, Claudio, important Brazilian composer and conductor; b. Manáos, Nov. 23, 1919. He studied at the Cons. of Rio de Janeiro and later in Paris with Nadia Boulanger. Returning to Brazil, he taught music in various schools; conducted concerts in South America and Europe, including Russia. He wrote music in an advanced idiom as a youth, mostly in the 12-tone style; but later he decided to compose works accessible to the masses, and this attitude was strengthened by his acceptance of the Russian tenets of socialist realism in art; however, he returned to the avant-garde type of composition (including aleatory practices) in his music of the

1960s. In 1970 he went to Germany and became a prof. of composition at the Hochschule für Musik in Heidelberg; he returned to Brazil in 1978.

Santos, (Jóse Manuel) Joly Braga, Portuguese composer; b. Lisbon, May 14, 1924. He studied composition with Luís de Freitas Branco at the Lisbon Cons. (1934–43), then conducting with Scherchen at the Venice Cons. (1948), electronic music at the Gavessano (Switzerland) Acoustic Experimental Stadium (1957–58) and composition with Mortari at the Rome Cons. (1959–60). He conducted the Oporto Radio Symph. Orch. (1955–59); in 1961 joined the staff, as conductor. His music represents a felicitous fusion of Portuguese Renaissance modalities and folk rhythms.

Santucci, Marco, Italian composer; b. Camajore, Tuscany, July 4, 1762; d. Lucca, Nov. 29, 1843. He was Anfossi's successor (1797–1808) as maestro at S. Giovanni in Laterano, Rome; in 1808 was appointed canon at the Cathedral of Lucca. A motet *a* 16 for 4 choirs received a prize from the Accademia Napoleone in 1806 because of the "entirely new and original" combination of voices. Baini publ. an energetic protest against this award, pointing out that such polyphonic writing was common in works by Italian composers of the 16th and 17th centuries. Santucci also wrote masses, motets, Psalms, canons in up to 7 parts, symphs., organ sonatas, etc.; publ. the treatise *Sulla melodia, sull'armonia e sul metro* (1828).

Sanzogno, Nino, Italian conductor and composer; b. Venice, April 13, 1911; d. Milan, May 4, 1983. He studied composition with Malipiero in Venice; took conducting lessons with Scherchen in Brussels in 1935; after playing violin in a string quartet, he was appointed opera conductor at the Teatro La Fenice in Venice in 1937; he first conducted at La Scala in Milan in 1939; was a regular conductor there in succeeding years; also toured in South America. He became favorably known as an excellent conductor of modern opera in Italy; he also gave courses on conducting in Darmstadt. He composed a Viola Concerto, Cello Concerto, Octet for Strings and Woodwinds, and some orch. pieces.

Sapelnikov, Vasili, Russian pianist; b. Odessa, Nov. 2, 1867; d. San Remo, March 17, 1941. He was a pupil of L. Brassin and Sophie Menter at the St. Petersburg Cons.; in 1888, made his debut at Hamburg with Tchaikovsky's First Piano Concerto, under the composer's direction; then made tours throughout Europe; lived chiefly in Germany, also for a time in Florence; in 1916, returned to Russia, remaining there until 1922; from 1923, was again in Germany and Italy. He wrote an opera, *Der Khan und sein Sohn,* and pieces for piano (*Petite mazourka, Danse des elfes, Valse-Caprice, Impromptu, Solitude*).

Saperton, David, American pianist; b. Pittsburgh, Oct. 29, 1889; d. Baltimore, July 5, 1970. He received his first instruction on the piano from his grandfather, a former tenor at the Brünn Opera, while his father, a physician and former concert bass, superintended his theoretical studies. At the age of 10 he made his first public appearance with an orch. in Pittsburgh; in 1905 he gave a recital in N.Y.; in 1910–12, toured Germany, Austria, Hungary, Italy, Russia, and Scandinavia; then returned to the U.S.; in 1924, joined the piano faculty of the Curtis Inst. in Philadelphia.

Saporiti, Teresa, Italian soprano; b. c.1763; d. Milan, March 17, 1869 (!). She was a member of Pasquale Bondini's Italian company and gave performances with it in Leipzig, Dresden, and Prague, often obliged to appear in male costume and take on castrati roles. The success of Bondini's production of *Le nozze di Figaro* in Prague in 1786 prompted him to request an opera from Mozart for the following year; the part of Donna Anna in *Don Giovanni* was written with Saporiti's voice in mind: the taxing coloratura in her aria in the 2nd act indicates that Mozart had a high opinion of her ability. Saporiti later appeared in Venice and at La Scala, in operas by Guglielmi and Bianchi. By 1795 she was prima buffa assoluta in Gennaro Astarita's company in St. Petersburg; sang in Astarita's own comic operas, as well as in revivals of Cimarosa's *Italiana in Londra* and Paisiello's *Il Barbiere di Siviglia.* She fell into total oblivion; if the dates of her life can be verified, she lived to the age of 105.

Sapp, Allen Dwight, American composer; b. Philadelphia, Dec. 10, 1922. After studying music with local teachers, he entered Harvard Univ., where he studied composition with Walter Piston and orchestration with E.B. Hill (A.B., 1942; A.M., 1949); he also did graduate work there with A.T. Davison, A.T. Merritt, and Randall Thompson; then attended classes of Aaron Copland and Nadia Boulanger in Cambridge, Mass. (1942–43). He subsequently had numerous teaching jobs: at Harvard Univ. (1949–58), Wellesley College (1958–61), the State Univ. of N.Y. at Buffalo (1961–76), and Florida State Univ. (1976–78). In 1978 he joined the faculty of the Univ. of Cincinnati. His music is cast in a neo-Classical idiom, with contrapuntal elements coalescing in a florid design.

Sarasate, Pablo de (Pablo Martín Melitón Sarasate y Navascuez), celebrated Spanish violin virtuoso; b. Pamplona, March 10, 1844; d. Biarritz, Sept. 20, 1908. He studied at the Paris Cons. under Alard, taking first prize in the violin class in 1857, and a "premier accessit" in 1859. In 1866 he acquired a Stradivarius violin. His playing was noted for its extraordinary beauty of tone, impeccable purity of intonation, perfection of technique, and grace of manner; but his repertoire consisted almost exclusively of fantasies on operatic airs (mostly arranged by himself). Later his taste changed, and he turned to the masterpieces of violin literature. His tours, extending through all Europe, North and South America, South Africa, and the Orient, were an uninterrupted succession of triumphs. He bequeathed to his native city the gifts that had been showered upon him by admirers throughout the world; the collection was placed in a special museum. For him Saint-Saëns wrote his *Rondo capriccioso;* Lalo, his *Symphonie espagnole;* Bruch, the *Schottische Fantasie;* Mackenzie, the *Pibroch* suite. Sarasate's compositions, exclusively for violin, are pleasing and effective.

Sargeant, Winthrop, American music critic; b. San Francisco, Dec. 10, 1903. He studied violin in San Francisco with Arthur Argiewicz and with Lucien Capet in Paris; took composition lessons with Albert Elkus in San Francisco and with Karl Prohaska in Vienna. He played the violin in the San Francisco Symph. Orch. (1922–24), in the N.Y. Symph. (1926–28), and in the N.Y. Phil. (1928–30). He then devoted himself to musical journalism; was on the editorial staff of *Musical America* (1931–34); was music critic of the *Brooklyn Daily Eagle* (1934–36); served as music editor of *Time* magazine (1937–39); also wrote essays on various subjects for *Time* (1939–45); subsequently was roving correspondent for *Life* magazine (1945–49) and music critic for the *New Yorker* (1947–72); from 1972 reviewed records for it. He evolved a highly distinctive manner of writing: professionally solid, stylistically brilliant, and ideologically opinionated; he especially inveighed against the extreme practices of the cosmopolitan avant-garde. He publ. *Jazz: Hot and Hybrid* (N.Y., 1938; 3rd ed., N.Y., 1975); *Geniuses, Goddesses, and People* (N.Y., 1949); *Listening to Music* (N.Y., 1958); *In Spite of Myself: A Personal Memoir* (N.Y., 1970); *Divas: Impressions of Today's Sopranos* (N.Y., 1973).

Sargent, Sir (Harold) Malcolm (Watts), eminent English conductor; b. Stamford, Lincolnshire, April 29, 1895; d. London, Oct. 3, 1967. He studied organ at the Royal College of Organists in London; then was articled to Dr. Keeton, organist of Peterborough Cathedral (1912–14); served in the infantry during World War I. He made his first major conducting appearance on Feb. 3, 1921, in Leicester, leading the Queen's Hall Orch. of London in his own composition, *Allegro impetuoso: An Impression on a Windy Day.* He then went to London, where he conducted the D'Oyly Carte Opera Co. and Diaghilev's Ballets Russes; from 1928 he was conductor-in-chief of the Royal Choral Society. From 1929 to 1940 he was conductor of the Courtauld-Sargent Concerts in London. He toured Australia in 1936, 1938, and 1939, and Palestine in 1937. Later he was conductor-in-chief and musical adviser of the Hallé Orch. of Manchester (1939–42); then was principal conductor of the Liverpool Phil. Orch. (1942–48). In 1945 he made his American debut with the NBC Symph. Orch. in N.Y.; then made appearances in Europe, Australia, and Japan. He was knighted in 1947. From 1950 to 1957 he was chief conductor of the BBC Symph. Orch.; led this ensemble on several European tours. From 1948 to 1966 he also served as chief conductor of the London Promenade Con-

certs. He took the London Phil. Orch. on an extensive Far Eastern tour in 1962; also led the Royal Phil. Orch. to the Soviet Union and the U.S. in 1963. His performances of the standard repertoire were distinguished for their precision and brilliance; he championed the music of Elgar, Vaughan Williams, Walton, and other English composers throughout his career. A commemorative stamp with his portrait was issued by the Post Office of Great Britain on Sept. 1, 1980.

Sarrette, Bernard, founder of the Paris Cons.; b. Bordeaux, Nov. 27, 1765; d. Paris, April 11, 1858. A captain in the national guard at Paris, he brought together, after the 13th of July, 1789, 45 musicians to form the nucleus of the Parisian band of the national guard. In 1790 the City of Paris assumed the expenses of this band, which was increased to 70 members, among them artists of distinction. In 1792 the financial embarrassments of the Commune led to the suspension of payment; but Sarrette held the band together and, with the aid of the municipality, established a free school of music employing all the members as teachers. From this school came the musicians employed in the 14 armies of the Republic. Its energetic principal had it converted into a national Inst. of Music, in a decree of Nov. 8, 1793; and it was definitely organized as the Paris Cons. in a decree of Aug. 3, 1795. Sarrette, having gained his end, assumed the captaincy of the 103rd Regiment; but the board of directors (5 inspectors and 4 profs.) proved so incompetent that he was recalled to the directorship of the Cons. in 1796. By introducing advanced methods of instruction and establishing the school of declamation, the concert hall, the grand library, etc., he raised the Cons. to an institution of the first rank. At the Restoration in 1814 he was deprived of his position; nor would he accept it after the revolution of 1830, not wishing to oust his friend Cherubini.

Sarti, Giuseppe, noted Italian composer; nicknamed **"Il Domenichino";** b. Faenza, (baptized, Dec. 1) 1729; d. Berlin, July 28, 1802. He took music lessons in Padua with Valotti; when he was 10, he went to Bologna to continue his studies with Padre Martini. Returning to Faenza, he was organist at the Cathedral from 1748 to 1752; in 1752 he was appointed director of the theater in Faenza; that same year his first opera, *Pompeo in Armenia,* was performed. His next opera, *Il re pastore,* was staged in Venice in 1753 with great success. Toward the end of 1753 he went to Copenhagen as a conductor of Pietro Mingotti's opera troupe. His work impressed the King of Denmark, Frederik V, and in 1755 he was named court Kapellmeister. He subsequently was made director of the Italian Opera, but it was closed in 1763; he then was appointed director of court music. In 1765 he was sent by the King to Italy to engage singers for the reopening of the Opera, but Frederik's death aborted the project. Sarti remained in Italy, where he served as maestro di coro at the Pietà Cons. in Venice (1766–67). In 1768 he returned to Copenhagen, where he resumed his duties as director of the royal chapel; from 1770 to 1775 he was conductor of the court theater. He then returned to Italy with his wife, the singer **Camilla Passi,** whom he had married in Copenhagen. He became director of the Cons. dell'Ospedaletto in Venice in 1775. In 1779 he entered the competition for the position of maestro di cappella at Milan Cathedral, winning it against a number of competitors, including Paisiello. By this time his prestige as a composer and as a teacher was very high. Among his numerous pupils was Cherubini. In 1784 he was engaged by Catherine the Great as director of the Imperial chapel in St. Petersburg. On his way to Russia he passed through Vienna, where he was received with honors by the Emperor Joseph II; he also met Mozart, who quoted a melody from Sarti's opera *Fra i due litiganti* in *Don Giovanni.* His greatest success in St. Petersburg was *Armida e Rinaldo* (Jan. 26, 1786), remodeled from an earlier opera, *Armida abbandonata,* originally performed in Copenhagen in 1759; the leading role was sung by the celebrated Portuguese mezzo-soprano Luiza Todi, but she developed a dislike of Sarti, and used her powerful influence with Catherine the Great to prevent his reengagement. However, he was immediately engaged by Prince Potemkin, and followed him to southern Russia and Moldavia during the military campaign against Turkey; on the taking of Ochakov, Sarti wrote an ode to the Russian liturgical text of thanksgiving, and it was performed in January 1789 at Jassy, Bessarabia, with the accompaniment of cannon shots and church bells. Potemkin offered him a sinecure as head of a singing school in Ekaterinoslav, but Sarti did not actually teach there. After Potemkin's death in 1791, his arrangements with Sarti were honored by the court of St. Petersburg; in 1793 Sarti was reinstated as court composer and was named director of a conservatory. Sarti's operas enjoyed considerable success during his lifetime but sank into oblivion after his death. He was an adept contrapuntist, and excelled in polyphonic writing; his *Fuga a otto voci* on the text of a *Kyrie* is notable. He was also astute in his adaptation to political realities. In Denmark he wrote singspiels in Danish; in Russia he composed a Requiem in memory of Louis XVI in response to the great lamentation at the Russian Imperial Court at the execution of the French king (1793). He also composed an offering to the Emperor Paul, whose daughters studied music with Sarti. After Paul's violent death at the hands of the palace guard, Sarti decided to leave Russia, but died in Berlin on his way to Italy. In 1796 Sarti presented to the Russian Academy of Sciences an apparatus to measure pitch (the so-called St. Petersburg tuning fork).

Sartori, Claudio, eminent Italian music scholar and bibliographer; b. Brescia, April 1, 1913. He received an arts degree in 1934 from the Univ. of Pavia with a thesis in music history; then studied with Gérold at the Univ. of Strasbourg and with Vittadini at the Pavia Cons. He served as an assistant librarian at the Bologna Cons. (1938–42); in 1943 he was appointed prof. of Italian literature there; in

1967 he assumed a similar professorship at the Milan Cons. He founded and became director of the Ufficio Ricerche Musicali in 1965; its aim was to conduct a thorough codification of Italian musical sources, providing information on all MSS and publ. music in Italy before 1900, on all publ. librettos in Italy down to 1800, and on all literature on music in Italy. In addition to this invaluable compilation, he also served as editor in chief of *Dizionario Ricordi della musica e dei musicisti* (Milan, 1959).

Sartorio, Antonio, important Italian composer of operas; b. Venice, 1630; d. there, Dec. 30, 1680. His first opera, *Gl' amori infruttuosi di Pirro,* was performed in Venice on Jan. 4, 1661; his second opera, *Seleuco* (Venice, Jan. 16, 1666), established his reputation. In 1666 he went to Germany to take up the post of Kapellmeister to Duke Johann Friedrich of Braunschweig-Lüneburg, who maintained his court in Hannover. He held this post until 1675, but continued to make regular visits to Venice to oversee productions of his operas. It was in Venice that he brought out his most famous opera, *L'Adelaide,* on Feb. 19, 1672. He returned to Venice permanently in 1675; in 1676 he was appointed vice-maestro di cappella at San Marco, a position he held until his death. Sartorio was a leading representative of the Venetian school of opera; his operas are notable for their arias, which he composed in a varied and effective manner.
  WORKS: Operas: *Gl' amori infruttuosi di Pirro* (Venice, Jan. 4, 1661); *Seleuco* (Venice, Jan. 16, 1666); *La prosperità d'Elio Seiano* (Venice, Jan. 15, 1667); *La caduta d'Elio Seiano* (Venice, Feb. 3, 1667); *L'Ermengarda Regina de' Longobardi* (Venice, Dec. 26, 1669); *L'Adelaide* (Venice, Feb. 19, 1672); *L'Orfeo* (Venice, Dec. 14, 1672); *Massenzio* (Venice, Jan. 25, 1673); *Alcina* (c.1674; not performed); *Giulio Cesare in Egitto* (Venice, Dec. 17, 1676); *Antonino e Pompeiano* (Venice, 1677); *L'Anacreonte tiranno* (Venice, 1677); *Ercole su' l Termodonte* (Venice, 1678); *I duo tiranni al soglio* (Venice, Jan. 15, 1679); *La Flora* (music completed by M.A. Ziani; Venice, Carnival 1681). Sartorio also composed a number of cantatas and sacred vocal works; publ. *23 Salmi a due chori ma accomodati all' uso della serenissima cappella ducale di S. Marco* for 8 Voices (Venice, 1680).

Sartorius, Paul, German organist and composer; b. Nuremberg, Nov. 16, 1569; d. Innsbruck, Feb. 28, 1609. His real name was **Schneider,** Sartorius being its Latin trans. ("tailor"). He studied with Lechner in Nuremberg; then went to Rome for further study; was organist at the court chapel of Duke Maximilian II of Austria in Mergentheim (1594–1602); in 1602 he went to Innsbruck. He publ. *Missae tres octonis v. decantandae* (Munich, 1599); *Madrigali a cinque voci* (Venice, 1600); *Sonetti spirituali a sei voci* (Nuremberg, 1601); *Neue Teutsche Liedlein mit vier Stimmen nach art der Welschen Canzonette* (Nuremberg, 1601); *Sacrae cantiones sive motecta* (Venice, 1602); he further wrote masses and motets in a polyphonic style similar to Palestrina's, and some choral works to German texts.

Sás, Andrés, Peruvian composer; b. Paris, April 6, 1900, of French-Belgian parents; d. Lima, Peru, July 25, 1967. He studied at the Brussels Cons. with Marchot (violin), Ernest Closson (music history), and Maurice Imbert (counterpoint). In 1924 he was engaged by the Peruvian government to teach violin at the National Academy of Music in Lima; in 1928 he returned temporarily to Belgium; the following year, settled in Lima permanently; married the Peruvian pianist **Lily Rosay,** and with her established the Sás-Rosay Academy of Music. He became profoundly interested in Peruvian folk music, and collected folk melodies; made use of many of them in his own compositions.

Sass, Marie, Belgian soprano; b. Ghent, Jan. 26, 1838; d. Auteuil, near Paris, Nov. 8, 1907. Her real Belgian name was **Saxe.** She studied voice in Paris; became known, albeit adversely, in the role of Elisabeth in the highly controversial Paris production of *Tannhäuser* in 1861; she also sang the role of Selika in the premiere of *L'Africaine* (Paris, April 28, 1865), but lived too long to maintain even a minimal subsistence, and died in abject poverty.

Satie, Erik (Alfred-Leslie), celebrated French composer who elevated his eccentricities and verbal virtuosity to the plane of high art; b. Honfleur, May 17, 1866; d. Paris, July 1, 1925. He received his early musical training from a local organist, Vinot, who was a pupil of Niedermeyer; at 13 he went to Paris, where his father was a music publisher, and attended the Paris Cons. (1879–86); took organ lessons with Guilmant, but soon relinquished systematic study of music; played in various cabarets in Montmartre; in 1884 he publ. a piano piece which he numbered, with malice aforethought, op. 62. His whimsical ways and Bohemian manner of life attracted many artists and musicians; he met Debussy in 1891; joined the Rosicrucian Society in Paris in 1892 and began to produce short piano pieces with eccentric titles intended to ridicule modernistic fancies and Classical pedantries alike. Debussy thought highly enough of him to orchestrate 2 numbers from his piano suite *Gymnopédies* (1888). Satie was 40 years old when he decided to learn something about the technique of composition, and entered the Schola Cantorum in Paris, in the classes of Vincent d'Indy and Albert Roussel. In 1898 he moved to Arcueil, a suburb of Paris; there he held court for poets, singers, dancers, and musicians, among whom he had ardent admirers. Milhaud, Sauguet, and the conductor Desormière organized a group, which they called only half-facetiously "Ecole d'Arcueil," in honor of Satie as master and leader. But Satie's eccentricities were not merely those of a Parisian poseur; rather, they were adjuncts to his esthetic creed, which he enunciated with boldness and total disregard for professional amenities (he was once brought to court for sending an insulting letter to a music critic). Interestingly enough, he attacked modernistic aberrations just as

assiduously as reactionary pedantry, publishing "manifestos" in prose and poetry. Although he was dismissed by most serious musicians as an uneducated person who tried to conceal his ignorance of music with persiflage, he exercised a profound influence on the young French composers of the first quarter of the 20th century; moreover, his stature as an innovator in the modern idiom grew after his death, so that the avant-garde musicians of the later day accepted him as inspiration for their own experiments; thus "space music" could be traced back to Satie's *musique d'ameublement,* in which players were stationed at different parts of a hall playing different pieces in different tempi. The instruction in his piano piece *Vexations,* to play it 840 times in succession, was carried out literally in N.Y. on Sept. 9, 1963, by a group of 5 pianists working in relays overnight, thus setting a world's record for duration of any musical composition. When critics accused Satie of having no idea of form, he publ. *Trois morceaux en forme de poire,* the eponymous pear being reproduced in color on the cover; other pieces bore self-contradictory titles, such as *Heures séculaires et instantanées* and *Crépuscule matinal de midi;* other titles were *Pièces froides, Embryons desséchés, Prélude en tapisserie, Préludes flasques (Pour un chien), Descriptions automatiques,* etc. In his ballets he introduced jazz for the first time in Paris; at the performance of his ballet *Relâche* (Paris, Nov. 29, 1924), the curtain bore the legend "Erik Satie is the greatest musician in the world; whoever disagrees with this notion will please leave the hall." Other ballets were *Parade* (Paris, May 18, 1917, produced by Diaghilev's Ballets Russes), and *Mercure* (Paris, June 15, 1924); other works were the symph. drama *Socrate* for 4 Sopranos and Chamber Orch. (Paris, Feb. 14, 1920); incidental music to Péladan's *Le Fils des étoiles* (1891; prelude orchestrated by Ravel) and for *Le Prince de Byzance* (1891); stage music to H. Mazel's *Le Nazaréen* (1892), to J. Bois's *La Porte héroïque au ciel* (1893), and to M. de Féraudy's *Pousse l'Amour* (1905); many pieces were produced posthumously, as *Jack in the Box* and the mockingly titled *Cinq grimaces pour le "Songe d'une nuit d'été,"* orchestrated by Milhaud, etc. In 1912 Erik Satie publ. a facetious autobiographic notice, *Mémoirs d'un amnésique.*

Satz, Ilya, Russian composer; b. Tchernobyl, Kiev district, April 30, 1875; d. St. Petersburg, Dec. 12, 1912. He studied cello in Kiev; then took lessons in composition with Taneyev in Moscow; his general education was desultory. He traveled in Europe in 1900; then made a tour as a cellist through Siberia. He returned to Moscow in 1903; in 1905 became music director of the Studio of the Moscow Art Theater, and wrote incidental music for new plays, including Maeterlinck's *Blue Bird* and Andreyev's *A Man's Life;* also composed ballet music for Salome's dance; the ballet *The Goat-Footed (The Dance of the Satyrs)* was reorchestrated and prepared for performance by Glière. Satz had a talent for the grotesque; a lack of technique prevented his development into a major composer. A memorial volume, *Ilya Satz,* with articles by Glière and several members of the Moscow Art Theater, was publ. at Moscow in 1923.

Sauer, Emil von, eminent pianist; b. Hamburg, Oct. 8, 1862; d. Vienna, April 27, 1942. He studied with Nicolai Rubinstein in Moscow (1879–81), and Liszt in Weimar (1884–85); made numerous European tours; played in the U.S. in 1898–99 and 1908. From 1901 till 1907, and again from 1915, he was a prof. at the Meisterschule für Klavierspiel in Vienna; from 1908 till 1915 he lived in Dresden; appeared in concerts until 1936, and then retired to Vienna. He wrote 2 piano concertos, 2 piano sonatas, many studies for piano; edited the complete works of Brahms and pedagogical works of Pischna, Plaidy, Kullak, etc. He publ. an autobiography, *Meine Welt* (1901).

Sauguet, Henri, French composer; b. Bordeaux, May 18, 1901. His real name is **Henri-Pierre Poupard;** he assumed his mother's maiden name, Sauguet. He was a pupil of Joseph Canteloube; in 1922 he went to Paris, where he studied with Koechlin; became associated with Erik Satie, and formed a group designated as the Ecole d'Arcueil (from the locality near Paris where Satie lived). In conformity with the principles of utilitarian music, he wrote sophisticated works in an outwardly simple manner; his first conspicuous success was the production of his ballet *La Chatte* by Diaghilev in 1927.

WORKS: Operas: *Le Plumet du colonel* (Paris, April 24, 1924); *La Contrebasse,* after Chekhov (Paris, 1932); *La Chartreuse de Parme* (Paris, March 16, 1939); *La Gageure imprévue* (Paris, July 4, 1944); *Les Caprices de Marianne* (Aix-en-Provence, July 20, 1954); ballets: *La Chatte* (Monte Carlo, April 30, 1927); *Paul et Virginie* (Paris, April 15, 1943); *Les Mirages* (Paris, Dec. 15, 1947); *Cordelia* (Paris, May 7, 1952); *L'As de cœur* (1960); *Paris* (1964); *L'Imposteur ou Le Prince et le mendiant* (1965); for Orch.: *Les Saisons et les jours,* "allegoric symph." (Paris, Dec. 15, 1946); *Symphonie expiatoire,* in memory of innocent war victims (Paris, Feb. 8, 1948); Symph. No. 3 (1955); *Symphonie des marches* (Paris, June 4, 1966); Symph. No. 4, *Troisième âge* (1971); 3 Piano Concertos (1933, 1948, 1963); *Orphée* for Violin and Orch. (Aix-en-Provence, July 26, 1953); *Mélodie concertante* for Cello and Orch. (1963); *The Garden Concerto* for Harmonica and Orch. (1970); oratorio, *Chant pour une ville meurtrie* (1967); *Alentours saxophoniques* for Alto Saxophone, Wind Ensemble, and Piano (1976); 2 string quartets (1926, 1948); piano pieces; songs.

Sauret, Emile, French violinist; b. Dun-le-Roi (Cher), May 22, 1852; d. London, Feb. 12, 1920. He studied with Vieuxtemps at the Paris Cons. and with Bériot in Brussels; was a child prodigy, and made his London debut at the age of 14. He was 20 when he was engaged for an American tour (1872); gave concerts in America again in 1874, 1876, 1877, and 1895. From 1903 till 1906 he taught at the Chica-go Musical College; returning to Europe, he lived in Geneva and Berlin; was at various times a prof. of violin in London and Berlin. In 1873 he married the pianist **Teresa Carreño** (divorced in 1876). He was a typical representative of the French school of violin playing, distinguished by grace, elegance, and excellent taste.

Sauveur, Joseph, French acoustician; b. La Flèche, March 24, 1653; d. Paris, July 9, 1716. A deaf-mute, learning to speak in his 7th year, he became a remarkable investigator in the realm of acoustics; in 1696, became a member of the Académie. He was the first to calculate absolute vibration numbers, and to explain scientifically the phenomenon of overtones.

Savage, Henry Wilson, American impresario; b. New Durham, N.H., March 21, 1859; d. Boston, Nov. 29, 1927. He started in business as a real estate operator in Boston, where he built the Castle Square Theater; later went into theatrical enterprise himself and in 1897 opened a season of opera in English. His Castle Square Opera Co. flourished, and he undertook tours of other cities. In 1900 he formed the English Grand Opera Co. and engaged several artists from the Carl Rosa Co. of London. In 1904–5 he organized a special troupe, producing *Parsifal* in English in the principal cities of the East and Midwest; in 1906–7 the same company made a tour with Puccini's *Madama Butterfly;* he also produced light opera with another company, which, among other operettas, introduced Lehár's *The Merry Widow* to the U.S. (1906).

Sawallisch, Wolfgang, German conductor; b. Munich, Aug. 23, 1923. He studied piano and composition at the Munich Cons., graduating in 1946. He made his conducting debut in Augsburg in 1947; subsequently occupied posts as music director in Aachen (1953–57), Wiesbaden (1957–59), and Cologne (1959–63); served as Generalmusikdirektor of the Hamburg Phil. (1961–73). He was chief conductor of the Vienna Symph. (1960–70), with which he toured the U.S. in 1964; concurrently he served as chief conductor of the Orch. de la Suisse Romande of Geneva, resigning at the close of the 1977–78 season. Specializing in opera, he has achieved some of his finest successes in the Wagnerian repertoire, conducting in Bayreuth since 1957.

Sax, (Antoine-Joseph-) Adolphe, inventor of the saxophone; b. Dinant, Belgium, Nov. 6, 1814; d. Paris, Feb. 4, 1894. He was the son of **Charles-Joseph Sax,** the instrument maker, and acquired great skill in manipulating instruments from his early youth; his practical and imaginative ideas led him to undertake improvements of the clarinet and other wind instruments. He studied the flute and clarinet at the Brussels Cons.; in 1842 he went to Paris with a wind instrument of his invention, which he called the "saxophone," made of metal, with a single-reed mouthpiece and conical bore. He exhibited brass and woodwind instruments at the Paris Exposition of 1844, winning a silver medal; his father joined him in Paris, and together they continued the manufacture of new instruments; evolved the sax-horn (improved over the bugle-horn and ophicleide by replacing the keys with a valve mechanism) and the saxo-tromba, a hybrid instrument producing a tone midway between the bugle and the trumpet. Conservative critics and rival instrument makers ridiculed Sax's innovations, but Berlioz and others warmly supported him; he also won praise from Rossini. His instruments were gradually adopted by French military bands. Sax won a gold medal at the Paris Industrial Exposition of 1849. Financially, however, he was unsuccessful, and was compelled to go into bankruptcy in 1852. He exhibited his instruments in London (1862) and received the Grand Prix in Paris (1867) for his improved instruments. In 1857 the Paris Cons. engaged him as instructor of the saxophone; with some interruptions, saxophone instruction was continued at the Paris Cons. for a century. He publ. a method for his instrument. Although Wieprecht, Červený, and others disputed the originality and priority of his inventions, legal decisions gave the rights to Sax; the saxophone became a standard instrument; many serious composers made use of it in their scores (Bizet's *L'Arlésienne*, etc.). The instrument fell into desuetude after Sax's death; but about 1918 a spectacular revival of the saxophone took place, when it was adopted in jazz bands; its popularity became worldwide; numerous methods were publ. and special schools established; and there appeared saxophone virtuosos for whom many composers wrote concertos.

Sax, Charles-Joseph, Belgian instrument maker; b. Dinant-sur-Meuse, Feb. 1, 1791; d. Paris, April 26, 1865. He established an instrument factory at Brussels in 1815, manufacturing not only wind instruments, but also pianos, harps, and guitars; his specialty, however, was brass instruments. He joined his son **Adolphe Sax** in Paris, and helped him to launch his revolutionary inventions.

Sayão, Bidú (Balduina) (de Oliveira), noted Brazilian soprano; b. Niteroi, near Rio de Janeiro, May 11, 1902. She studied with Elena Theodorini in Rio de Janeiro, and then with Jean de Reszke in Vichy and Nice. Returning to Brazil, she gave her first professional concert in Rio de Janeiro in 1925; in 1926 she sang the role of Rosina in *The Barber of Seville* at the Teatro Municipal there. She made her American debut on Dec. 29, 1935, in a recital in N.Y. On Feb. 13, 1937, she sang Manon with the Metropolitan Opera in N.Y., earning enthusiastic reviews in the press. She remained on the roster of the Metropolitan Opera until 1952; her finest performances were in lyric roles in bel canto operas; especially memorable were her interpretations of Violetta in *La Traviata*, Gilda in *Rigoletto,* and Mimi in *La Bohème.* She also showed her versatility in coloratura parts, such as Lakmé; in France, she was described as "a Brazilian nightingale." She also sang vocal parts in several works of her great compatriot Villa-Lobos. She was a recipient of numer-

ous honors from European royalty, and of the Palmes Académiques from the French government; in 1972 she was decorated a Commandante by the Brazilian government.

Sbriglia, Giovanni, celebrated singing teacher; b. Naples, June 23, 1832; d. Paris, Feb. 20, 1916. He sang as a tenor at the San Carlo Theater in Naples; was heard in Italy by Maretzek, the impresario, who engaged him for a season at the Academy of Music in N.Y., where Sbriglia appeared with Adelina Patti (1860); he then made a grand tour of the U.S. with Parodi and Adelaide Phillipps; also sang in Mexico and Havana. He returned to Europe in 1875 and settled in Paris, where he became a highly successful vocal teacher. Jean, Joséphine, and Edouard de Reszke studied with him when they were already professional artists; Sbriglia trained the baritone voice of Jean de Reszke, enabling him to sing tenor roles. Pol Plançon, Nordica, and Sibyl Sanderson were among his pupils.

Scala, Francis Maria, Italian-born American bandleader, first leader of the U.S. Marine Band so designated; b. Naples, 1819 (or 1820); d. Washington, D.C., April 18, 1903. Beginning his musical career on the clarinet, he enlisted in the U.S. Navy as a musician 3rd-class on the frigate *Brandywine* when it was anchored at Naples in 1841. Following the ship's return to Washington, Scala left the navy for the Marine Corps, and in 1843 was designated fife-major of the fife corps associated with Marine Corps headquarters. On Sept. 9, 1855, he became de facto the leader of the Marine Band; in 1861 he was made "Principal Musician," and on Sept. 4, 1868, was for the first time, referred to as "Leader of the Band." John Philip Sousa was one of his apprentice bandsmen. Retiring in 1871, Scala continued to reside in Washington until his death. In Sept. 1945 his son Norman P. Scala made the first of several gifts to the Library of Congress honoring his father; these materials contain a large amount of MSS and printed music, chiefly band arrangements made by or for Scala, that represent in essence the library of the Marine Band during the Civil War; included is a note in the hand of Abraham Lincoln, then Scala's Commander-in-Chief.

Scalchi, Sofia, celebrated Italian mezzo-soprano; b. Turin, Nov. 29, 1850; d. Rome, Aug. 22, 1922. She studied with Boccabati; made her debut at Mantua in 1866 as Ulrica in Verdi's *Ballo in maschera;* then sang throughout Italy; appeared in concert in London (Sept. 16, 1868) and at Covent Garden (Nov. 5, 1868) as Azucena, obtaining enormous success. She visited the U.S. for the first time in 1882 with Mapleson's opera company; sang in the opening season of the Metropolitan Opera (1883–84) and again in 1891–92 and 1893–96. She then toured with unfailing success in Russia, Austria, Spain, and South America. She married Count Luigi Lolli in 1875; in 1896 she retired to her estate in Turin; in 1921 went to Rome, where she remained until her death. Her voice had a range of 2½ octaves; it was essentially a contralto voice, but with so powerful a high register that she successfully performed soprano parts.

Scalero, Rosario, eminent Italian pedagogue and composer; b. Moncalieri, near Turin, Dec. 24, 1870; d. Settimo Vittone, near Turin, Dec. 25, 1954. He studied violin with Sivori in Genoa, and in London with Wilhelmj; general subjects there with Mandyczewski in Vienna. In 1896 he was engaged as a violin teacher in Lyons, France; then was an instructor at Santa Cecilia in Rome, and examiner at the Naples Cons. and later at the Cons. of Parma. In 1919 he came to the U.S., and was head of the composition classes at the David Mannes School in N.Y.; in 1928 joined the faculty of the Curtis Inst. of Music in Philadelphia; among his students there were Samuel Barber, Gian Carlo Menotti, and Lukas Foss. He wrote a Violin Concerto; *Neapolitan Dances* for Violin and Piano; chamber music; sacred songs; etc.

Scaria, Emil, Austrian bass; b. Graz, Sept. 18, 1838; d. Blasewitz, near Dresden, July 22, 1886. He studied with Netzer at Graz, with Lewy in Vienna, and with Garcia in London. After singing in opera in Dessau (1862), Leipzig (1863), and Dresden (1864), he acquired a fine reputation; in 1872–73, Scaria was a guest artist at the Vienna Court Opera, becoming a member in 1873, and remaining on its roster until 1886. He excelled in Wagner's operas; created the role of Gurnemanz in *Parsifal.* Scaria suffered a mental breakdown in 1882; he resumed his career by touring the U.S. in 1884; suffered a relapse in 1886 and subsequently died, without having recovered his sanity.

Scarlatti, Alessandro, founder of the "Neopolitan School" of music; b. Palermo, May 2, 1660; d. Naples, Oct. 22, 1725. He was brought to Rome in 1672, and was a pupil there of Carissimi; in 1679 he conducted his first known opera, *L'errore innocente,* at Rome; then followed a performance there of *L'onestà negli amori* at the palace of Queen Christina of Sweden (Feb. 6, 1680); on the score of another opera, *Il Pompeo* (Rome, Jan. 25, 1683), he is styled maestro di cappella to the Queen. In 1694 he was maestro to the Viceroy at Naples. In 1703 he became assistant maestro to Foggia at S. Maria Maggiore in Rome, and succeeded him as first maestro in 1707, resigning in 1709 and returning to Naples, where he subsequently became maestro of the royal chapel. He also taught music; was briefly engaged at the Cons. di Santa Maria di Loreto in Naples (1689), but never had prolonged tenure; among his private pupils was Hasse, who studied with him in 1724. Scarlatti wrote approximately 115 operas (about 50 are extant); *La Rosaura* (Rome, 1690), edited by Eitner, was printed by the *Gesellschaft für Musikforschung,* vol. XIV; in *Teodora Augusta* (Rome, Jan. 3, 1693) he used an incipient *recitativo obbligato,* accompanied by the entire orch.; also several arias with the first part sung *da capo,* a style that was later generally adopted by opera composers. An aria and a duet from *Laodicea e Bernice* (Naples, 1701) have been publ. by J.J.C. Maier, also a terzet and a

quartet from *La Griselda* (Rome, 1721), with German trans. by Wolzogen; in *Il Tigrane,* his most celebrated opera, marked in the libretto as his 106th work for the stage (Naples, Feb. 16, 1715), the orch. comprises violins, violas, cellos, double basses, 2 flutes, 2 oboes, 2 bassoons, and 2 horns; *Il trionfo dell'onore,* his only comic opera (Naples, Nov. 26, 1718), was trans. into Eng. by Geoffrey Dunn (London, July 23, 1937). Other important operas are: *Olimpia vendicata* (Naples, Dec. 23, 1685); *La Statira* (Rome, Jan. 5, 1690); *Pirro e Demetrio* (Naples, Jan. 28, 1694); *Il Prigioniero fortunato* (Naples, Dec. 14, 1698). Fourteen oratorios are also known; he is said to have written over 200 masses (up to 10 parts), besides much other sacred music (*Concerti sacri,* motets *a* 1–4, with 2 Violins, Viola, and Organ, were publ. at Amsterdam as opp. 1 and 2; a few separate numbers are in the collections of Choron, the Prince of Moskowa, Commer [a *Tu es Petrus*], Dehn, Proske, and Rochlitz; Choron also publ. a Requiem, and Proske a Mass); his secular vocal music includes madrigals (one *a* 4 is in Padre Martini's *Esempli di contrappunto fugato*), serenatas, duets, and some 800 cantatas. He also composed 12 symphs. (concertos) for Small Orch.; String Quartet; Sonata for 3 Flutes; Sonata for 2 Flutes, 2 Violins, and Continuo; Sonata for Flute, 2 Violins, and Continuo; 2 suites for Flute and Harpsichord; variations on Corelli's *La Follia;* toccatas for harpsichord; etc. Some of his works have been publ. by G. Bas and F. Nekes (a 4-voiced *Missa ad voces aequales*), Lenzewski (concertos for strings and continuo), Tebaldini (Sonata for Flute and Strings), J.S. Shedlock (toccatas for harpsichord; 9 vols.), Tagliapietra, Longo (keyboard compositions), etc. In 1974 Harvard Publications in Music began issuing a series of the operas, edited by D.J. Grout.

Scarlatti, (Giuseppe) Domenico, famous Italian composer and harpsichordist, son of **Alessandro Scarlatti;** b. Naples, Oct. 26, 1685; d. Madrid, July 23, 1757. A pupil of his father, he was named organist and composer at the royal chapel in Naples when he was 16; 2 years later his first operas, *Ottavia restituita al trono* and *Il Giustino,* were produced in Naples (Dec. 19, 1703). In 1705 he was sent by his father to Venice, where he studied with Gasparini. In 1709 he was back in Rome, where he engaged in a friendly contest with Handel, who was adjudged his superior on the organ, while Scarlatti held his own on the harpsichord. From 1709–14 he was maestro di cappella to Queen Maria Casimira of Poland, for whose private theater (in her palace in Rome) he composed 7 operas and an oratorio. He had been appointed in 1713 assistant to Bai, maestro di cappella at the Vatican, and upon the latter's death in 1714 succeeded him as maestro; resigned in 1719. During this time he was also maestro to the Portuguese Ambassador to the Holy See. There is no evidence that Scarlatti went to London in 1720, as is usually stated. But in that year his opera *Amor d'un ombra e gelsoia d'un'aura* (rewritten as *Narciso*) was produced there at the Haymarket Theatre under Roseingrave's direction (May 30), and his brother **Francesco** gave a concert there in September. Scarlatti went to Lisbon c.1719, where he was engaged as maestro of the royal chapel and music teacher to the Princess Maria Barbara, for whom he composed his famous *Esercizi per gravicembalo,* of which the first were publ. in 1738. In 1729 the princess married the heir to the Spanish throne, and Scarlatti accompanied her to Madrid, where he spent the rest of his life. When Maria Barbara became queen in 1746, he was appointed her *maestro de cámara.* After leaving Italy he returned only twice, once for a brief visit to his father at Naples in 1724, and the other time to marry Maria Catalina Gentili on May 15, 1728, in Rome. In Madrid, Scarlatti does not appear to have composed operas, but he founded an instrumental school in Spain, the chief representative being P. Antonio Soler, his pupil. He composed over 600 sonatas and pieces for harpsichord, besides operas, cantatas, and sacred music (2 Misereres *a* 4; a Stabat Mater; a Salve Regina for Soprano and Strings [1756], his last work); the MS of his *Fuga estemporanea per orchestra* is in the library of the Univ. of Münster. The principal MS source for the harpsichord works of Scarlatti is the collection of the Biblioteca Marciana at Venice, which belonged originally to the Queen of Spain and at her death was brought to Italy by Farinelli. Domenico Scarlatti's special claim to renown rests upon his harpsichord music; he studied the characteristics of the instrument, and adapted his compositions to them, being one of the finest writers in the "free style" (a homophonic style with graceful ornamentation, in contrast to the former contrapuntal style). He also obtained effects by the frequent crossing of the hands; runs in thirds and sixths; leaps wider than an octave; broken chords in contrary motion; tones repeated by rapidly changing fingers; etc. During Scarlatti's lifetime some of his keyboard pieces were printed in various editions in London and Paris. Later editions include a collection by Czerny, of 200 pieces; Breitkopf, 60; Pauer, 50; Köhler, 12 sonatas and fugues; Tausig, 3 sonatas; Bülow, 18 pieces in suite form; Schletterer, 18; André, 28; Banck, 30; Farrenc, 100 (in *Trésor des pianistes*); Sauer, 25; Barth, 70; Gerstenberg, 5 sonatas (not included in the Longo ed.); Buonamici, 22 (in Schirmer's Library, vol. 73). Ricordi publ. Scarlatti's "complete" harpsichord works, edited by A. Longo, in 11 vols. (one vol. as supplement; pp. 1906ff.), also a thematic index (Milan, 1937); 60 sonatas edited by Ralph Kirkpatrick were publ. by G. Schirmer. A complete edition of the sonatas is in vols. 31–41 of the Le Pupitre series; the *Complete Keyboard Works,* in a fine facsimile edition of 18 vols., was put out by Ralph Kirkpatrick in 1971.

Scarlatti, Giuseppe, Italian composer, grandson of **Alessandro Scarlatti,** nephew of **Domenico Scarlatti;** b. Naples, c.1718; d. Vienna, Aug. 17, 1777. He was in Rome in 1739, and later in Lucca, where he married **Barbara Stabili,** a singer (1747). He went to Vienna in 1757, and remained there for 20 years until his death. He wrote 31 operas, produced in Rome, Florence, Lucca, Turin, Venice, Naples, Milan, and Vienna; of these the most successful was *L'isola disabitata* (Venice, Nov. 20, 1757). Another Giuseppe Scarlatti (a nephew of Alessandro Scarlatti), whose name appears in some reference works, was not a musician.

Scelsi, Giacinto, remarkable Italian composer; b. La Spezia, Jan. 8, 1905. He studied composition with Respighi and Casella in Rome; then went to Vienna, where he became interested in the Schoenbergian method of writing music outside the bounds of traditional tonality; at the same time he became deeply immersed in the study of the musical philosophy of the East, in which the scales and rhythms are perceived as functional elements of the human psyche. As a result of these multifarious absorptions of ostensibly incompatible ingredients, Scelsi formulated a style of composition that is synthetic in its sources and pragmatic in its artistic materialization.

Schacht, Theodor von, German pianist, composer, and conductor; b. Strasbourg, 1748; d. Regensburg, June 20, 1823. He studied piano with Küffner and harmony with Riepel in Regensburg (1756–66); then took lessons in composition with Jommelli in Stuttgart (1766–71). Returning to Regensburg in 1771, he became music director of the town theater; in 1773 was appointed court music Intendant. From 1786–1805 he led the court orch. He then went to Vienna; in 1812 he returned to Germany. He was a prolific musician; wrote a number of operas and theater pieces to German and Italian texts, as well as competently crafted symphs., concertos, and chamber music. He was a minor master of contrapuntal arts; his series of 84 canons, dedicated to members of "the fair sex," quite amusing and even daring for his time, was publ. in Baden in 1811 under the title *Divertimento del bel sesso nel soggiorno di Baden.*

Schaeffer (Schäffer), Boguslaw (Julien), remarkable Polish composer and music theoretician of great originality; b. Lwow, June 6, 1929. He studied violin at Opole, composition with Artur Malawski at the State High School of Music in Cracow, and musicology with Jachimecki at the Jagiello Univ. in Cracow (1949–53); in 1959 he took a course in advanced techniques with Luigi Nono. In 1963 he was appointed a prof. of composition at the Cons. of Cracow; in 1967 he began publishing a periodical devoted to new music, *Forum Musicum.* Schaeffer's early works were inspired by the melorhythms of Polish folk songs, but he made a decisive turn in 1953 with his *Music for Strings: Nocturne,* which became the first serial work by a Polish composer; he devised a graphic and polychromatic optical notation indicating intensity of sound, proportional lengths of duration, and position of notes in melodic and contrapuntal lines, with the components arranged in binary code; he also wrote music in the "third stream" style, combining jazz with classical procedures; he further experimented in "antigenic" or "decomposed" techniques. He is married to **Mieczyslawa Janina Hanuszewska** (b. Borszów, Oct. 1,

1929), a learned musicographer.

Schaeffer, Pierre, French acoustician, composer, and novelist; b. Nancy, Aug. 14, 1910. Working in a radio studio in Paris, he conceived the idea of arranging a musical montage of random sounds, including outside noises. On April 15, 1948, he formulated the theory of *musique concrète,* which was to define such random assemblages of sounds. When the magnetic tape was perfected, Schaeffer made use of it by rhythmic acceleration and deceleration, changing the pitch and dynamics and modifying the nature of the instrumental timbre. He made several collages of elements of "concrete music," among them *Concert de bruits* (1948) and (with Pierre Henry) *Symphonie pour un homme seul* (1950); also created an experimental opera, *Orphée 53* (1953). He incorporated his findings and ideas in the publication *A la recherche de la musique concrète* (Paris, 1952) and in *Traité des objects sonores* (Paris, 1966). Eventually he abandoned his acoustical experimentations and turned to literature. He publ. both fictional and quasi-scientific novels, among them *Traité des objets musicaux* (1966); *Le Gardien de volcan* (1969); *Excusez-moi si je meurs* (1981); *Prélude, Chorale et Fugue* (1983).

Schafer, R. Murray, Canadian composer; b. Sarnia, Ontario, July 18, 1933. He studied at the Royal Cons. of Music in Toronto with John Weinzweig (1954–55); went to Vienna in 1956 and then on to England as a journalist. Returning to Canada in 1961, he became associated with the Canadian Broadcasting Corp.; explored the nature of physical sound for an "inventory of world soundscapes." He developed a sui generis system of topological transmutation, exemplified by his satire/tribute for orch. and tape *The Son of Heldenleben* (Montreal, Nov. 13, 1968), in which he systematically distorted the thematic materials of *Ein Heldenleben* by Richard Strauss, retaining the essential motivic substance of the original score.

Schalk, Franz, Austrian conductor; b. Vienna, May 27, 1863; d. Edlach, Sept. 2, 1931. He studied with Bruckner; in 1888 was Kapellmeister in Reichenbach; in 1889–95, in Graz; in 1895–98, in Prague; he was a guest conductor at Covent Garden in London in 1898, 1907, and 1911; succeeded Seidl in 1898 as conductor at the Metropolitan Opera House in N.Y.; in 1899, he was conductor of the Berlin Royal Opera; from 1900 at the Vienna Hofoper; in 1904–21 he was also conductor of the Vienna Gesellschaft der Musikfreunde and a prof. of conducting at the Royal Academy of Music; during the 1907–8 season he was conductor of the Vienna Phil., with which he made guest appearances beginning in 1903; also appeared as a guest conductor after the completion of his regular tenure; from 1918 he was director of the Vienna State Opera (succeeded Gregor; in 1919–24, was co-director with R. Strauss; thereafter sole director). A tireless worker, he contributed much to the high artistic standards of the Vienna Opera. His

book *Briefe und Betrachtungen* was brought out posthumously (Vienna, 1935).

Schalk, Josef, Austrian pianist and writer on music, brother of **Franz Schalk;** b. Vienna, March 24, 1857; d. there, Nov. 7, 1900. He studied with Bruckner and Epstein; was a piano teacher at the Vienna Cons. His arrangements of the Bruckner symphs. for piano, 4-hands, did much to make these works known, and his book, *Anton Bruckner und die moderne Musikwelt* (1885), effectively upheld Bruckner's music. He was also a friend of Hugo Wolf, whom he championed.

Scharwenka, (Ludwig) Philipp, German composer and pedagogue; b. Samter, Posen, Feb. 16, 1847; d. Bad Nauheim, July 16, 1917. He studied with Wüerst and Dorn at the Kullak Academy of Music in Berlin; in 1868 was appointed teacher of composition there; with his brother **Xaver** he founded in 1881 the Scharwenka Cons. in Berlin; together they made an American trip in 1891; in 1893 the Scharwenka Cons. was amalgamated with the Klindworth Cons.; the resulting Klindworth-Scharwenka Cons. acquired an excellent reputation for its teaching standards. He was an excellent composer in a Romantic vein, greatly influenced by Schumann; his *Arkadische Suite* for Orch., the symph. poem *Frühlingswogen,* and the orch. *Dramatische Fantasie* were performed many times until they inevitably lapsed into innocuous desuetude; he also wrote a Symph., a Violin Concerto, much chamber music, and piano pieces.

Scharwenka, (Franz) Xaver, German pianist, composer, and pedagogue, brother of **Philipp Scharwenka;** b. Samter, Posen, Jan. 6, 1850; d. Berlin, Dec. 8, 1924. He studied with Kullak and Wüerst at the Kullak Academy of Music in Berlin, graduating in 1868; then joined its faculty. Apart from teaching, he established an annual series of chamber music concerts in Berlin; in 1881, he founded with his brother the Scharwenka Cons.; in 1891 he went to the U.S. and opened a N.Y. branch of his Cons.; appeared as soloist in his own Piano Concerto (N.Y., Jan. 24, 1891). Returning to Berlin in 1898, he became co-director of the newly amalgamated (1893) Klindworth-Scharwenka Cons.; in 1914 established his own course of master classes for piano. As a composer, he was undoubtedly superior to his brother, although both were faithful imitators of Schumann and other German Romantics. He wrote an opera, *Mataswintha* (Weimar, Oct. 4, 1896; Metropolitan Opera, N.Y., April 1, 1907); 4 piano concertos; numerous effective piano pieces, of which his *Polish Dances* became favorites with American piano teachers and students. He also publ. technical studies for piano, *Beiträge zur Fingerbildung; Studien im Oktavenspiel;* a collection of famous études, arranged according to progressive difficulty, under the title *Meisterschule des Klavierspiels; Methodik des Klavierspiels* (1907; with A. Spanuth); and a book of memoirs, *Klänge aus meinem Leben: Erinnerungen eines Musikers* (Leipzig, 1922).

Schat, Peter, Dutch composer; b. Utrecht, June 5, 1935. He studied composition with Kees van Baaren and piano with Jaap Callenbach at The Hague Cons.; then traveled to England and took private lessons with M. Seiber; also received instruction with Boulez in Zürich. Upon returning to the Netherlands, he became active in connection with the Studio for Electro-Instrumental Music in Amsterdam. From his earliest steps in composition, he adopted the serial method; also experimented with electronic sonorities. With Louis Andriessen and Misha Mengelberg, he organized in 1968 a series of Political-Demonstrative Experimental Concerts and also formed the Amsterdam Electric Circus, an itinerant troupe of musicians.

Schaum, John W., American piano pedagogue; b. Milwaukee, Jan. 27, 1905. He studied at Milwaukee State Teachers College, at Marquette Univ. (B.M., 1931), and at Northwestern Univ. (M.M., 1934). He established a successful piano teaching class in Milwaukee and publ. several piano methods and many collections of piano pieces that sold an enormous number of copies: *The Schaum Piano Course* (9 vols.); *The Schaum Adult Piano Course* (3 vols.); *The Schaum Duet Albums* (2 vols.); also theory books: *The Schaum Theory Lessons* (2 vols.) and *The Schaum Note Spellers* (2 vols.).

Scheel, Fritz, German conductor; b. Lübeck, Nov. 7, 1852; d. Philadelphia, March 13, 1907. His grandfather and father were orch. conductors, and at 10 the boy played the violin in his father's orch.; in 1864–69 he was a pupil of F. David in Leipzig. At 17 he began his career as a concertmaster and conductor at Bremerhaven; in 1873 he was solo violinist and conductor of the summer concerts in Schwerin; succeeded Hans Sitt in 1884 as conductor of the Chemnitz municipal orch.; in 1890–93 was conductor of orch. concerts in Hamburg. He came to America in 1893, and after conducting some orch. concerts in N.Y., went to Chicago in 1894 as conductor of the Trocadero concerts at the Columbian Exposition; in 1895 he established the San Francisco Symph. Orch., which he conducted for 4 seasons; then accepted an engagement to conduct a series of summer concerts at Woodside Park in Philadelphia. His playing of Beethoven's symphs. induced influential music-lovers to organize the Philadelphia Orchestral Assoc., which established in the fall of 1900 the Philadelphia Orch., of which Scheel was conductor until his death.

Scheibe, Johann Adolf, German theorist and composer; b. Leipzig, May 3, 1708; d. Copenhagen, April 22, 1776. He studied law at Leipzig, but on his father's death had recourse to his musical training to support himself; failing to obtain the post of organist at the Nicolaikirche in Leipzig in the competition (1729; adjudicated by Bach, among others) with Görner, he traveled for a time, and settled in Hamburg; publ. a paper, *Der Critische Musicus* (1737–40; No. 6 contains a sharp attack on Bach). In 1739 he became Kapellmeister to the Margrave of Brandenburg-Culmbach; on Dec. 1, 1740, he became court conductor at Copenhagen; was pensioned in 1747. In 1745 he had reprinted in Leipzig the previous issues of *Der Critische Musicus*, with the addition of polemical exchanges that ensued in the interim. A large portion of his MSS are no longer extant.

Scheidt, Samuel, important German organist and composer; b. Halle, (baptized, Nov. 3) 1587; d. there, March 24, 1654. He studied at the Gymnasium in Halle; from c.1603 to 1608 he was organist at the Moritzkirche in Halle, and then went to Amsterdam to study with Sweelinck. He returned to Halle in 1609, and was appointed court organist to Margrave Christian Wilhelm of Brandenburg; in late 1619 he also assumed the post of court Kapellmeister; when the margrave left for Denmark in 1625 to support the Protestant cause in the Thirty Years' War, Scheidt retained his post even though without emolument, eking out a modest living by teaching. In 1628 he was named music director of the Marktkirche, the principal church in Halle, continuing in this employment until 1630. In 1638 he resumed his post as court Kapellmeister and served until his death. Scheidt was highly esteemed as an organist; he was consulted on the building of organs as an inspector; he was also a noted organ teacher. As a composer, Scheidt excelled in both keyboard and sacred vocal works.

Schein, Johann Hermann, important German composer; b. Grünhain, near Annaberg, Jan. 20, 1586; d. Leipzig, Nov. 19, 1630. His father was a pastor; upon his death, Schein moved to Dresden, where he entered the Hofkapelle of the Elector of Saxony as a boy soprano; received instruction from the Kapellmeister, Rogier Michael; continued his studies in music at Pforta, an electoral school near Naumburg, from 1603–7; his teachers were Bartholomäus Scheer and Martin Roth. In 1607 he returned to Dresden; in 1608 he received an electoral scholarship to study jurisprudence and liberal arts at the Univ. of Leipzig, where he remained until 1612. In 1613 he became Hausmusikmeister to Gottfried von Wolffersdorff in Weissenfels, and also served as praeceptor to his children. In 1615 he was appointed Kapellmeister to Duke Johann Ernst the Younger in Weimar. In 1616 he was named cantor at the Thomasschule in Leipzig, as successor to Calvisius. His duties in Leipzig inlcuded directing the choral music at the Thomaskirche and the Nicolaikirche, and teaching singing and Latin grammar and syntax at the Thomasschule. Schein was one of the earliest German composers to introduce into Lutheran church music the Italian techniques of madrigal, monody, and concerto. In the alliterative parlance of learned German writers, Schein became known as the chronologically second of the glorious trio of near-contemporaneous German masters, Schütz (b. 1585), Schein (b. 1586), and Scheidt (b. 1587). But Schütz, the oldest of them, outlived Schein by 42 years; he visited him at his deathbed and brought him, as a friendly offering, a

6-part motet of his composition on Schein's favorite passage from the New Testament.

Schelle, Johann, significant German composer of Protestant church music; b. Geising, Thuringia, (baptized, Sept. 6) 1648; d. Leipzig, March 10, 1701. He received his early musical trainig from his father, who was a schoolmaster; in 1655 he was sent to Dresden to sing in the chori of the electoral chapel, which was directed by Schütz; in 1657 he went to Wolfenbüttel, where he sang in the choir of the ducal court. In 1665 he became a student at the Thomasschule in Leipzig under Knüpfer; subsequently studied at the Univ. of Leipzig, becoming cantor in Eilenburg in 1670. In 1677 he succeeded Knüpfer as cantor of the Thomaskirche in Leipzig; also served as director chori musici for the city and acted as director of music for the Nicolaikirche. He taught music at the Thomasschule; he was succeeded by his cousin, **Johann Kuhnau.** Schelle's importance as a composer rests upon his settings of the sacred Gospel cantata to German texts (in place of the traditional Latin texts) for Protestant liturgical use in Leipzig. He extended this practice to the chorale cantata as well. See A. Schering's edition in the Denkmäler deutscher Tonkunst, LVIII–LIX (1918).

Schelling, Ernest (Henry), American conductor, composer, and pianist; b. Belvidere, N.J., July 26, 1876; d. New York, Dec. 8, 1939. He first appeared in public as a child prodigy, playing the piano at the age of 4½ at the Academy of Music in Philadelphia. He was then sent to Paris, where he studied, while still a small child, with Mathias (a pupil of Chopin) and also with Moszkowski; his other teachers were Leschetizky, Hans Huber, Barth, and finally Paderewski at Morges, Switzerland (1898–1902). Extended tours in Europe (from Russia to Spain) followed; he also toured in South America; returned permanently to the U.S. in 1905, and devoted most of his energies to conducting and composing. He conducted young people's symph. concerts in N.Y. (from 1924), in Philadelphia, Boston, Cincinnati, Los Angeles, San Francisco, etc.; for 2 seasons (1936–38) he was regular conductor of the Baltimore Symph. Orch.; also made frequent appearances as a conductor in Europe.
WORKS: *A Victory Ball,* orch. fantasy after the poem by Alfred Noyes (first perf. by Stokowski with the Philadelphia Orch., Feb. 23, 1923; his most successful work); *Légende symphonique* (Philadelphia, Oct. 31, 1913); *Suite fantastique* for Orch. (Amsterdam, Oct. 10, 1907); *Impressions from an Artist's Life,* symph. variations for Piano and Orch. (Boston, Dec. 31, 1915, composer soloist; first work by an American ever conducted by Toscanini; N.Y., March 14, 1929); Violin Concerto (Boston Symph., Providence, R.I., Oct. 17, 1916; Fritz Kreisler, soloist); *Morocco,* symph. tableau (N.Y., Dec. 19, 1927, composer conducting). For further details see William Lichtenwanger, *Dictionary of American Biography,* Supplement II.

Schenck, Jean (Johann), German virtuoso on the viola da gamba; b. Amsterdam, (baptized, June 3) 1660; d. c.1715. He became chamber musician to the Elector-Palatine at Düsseldorf in 1696; later at Amsterdam, where he publ. *Kunst-Oeffeningen;* 15 sonatas for Gamba, with Continuo (1688); *Il giardino armonico,* sonatas for 2 Violins, Gamba, and Continuo (1692); *Scherzi musicali* for Gamba; 18 sonatas for Violin, with Continuo (1693); etc.; also *Sang-Arien van d'opera Ceres en Bacchus.*

Schenk, Erich, eminent Austrian musicologist; b. Salzburg, May 5, 1902; d. Vienna, Oct. 11, 1974. He studied theory and piano at the Mozarteum in Salzburg; then went to Munich, where he enrolled as a student of Sandberger in musicology at the Univ. of Munich; received his Ph.D. in 1925 with the dissertation *Giuseppe Antonio Paganelli: Sein Leben und seine Werke* (publ. in Salzburg, 1928); he completed his Habilitation at the Univ. of Rostock in 1929 with *Studien zur Triosonate in Deutschland nach Corelli;* he subsequently founded its musicology dept. (1936). From 1940 until his retirement in 1971 he was a prof. of musicology at the Univ. of Vienna. He was particularly esteemed for his studies of Baroque and Classical music. In 1947 he revived the Denkmäler der Tonkunst in Österreich series, overseeing its progress until 1972. In 1955 he also took over the valuable *Studien zur Musikwissenschaft.* Festschrifts honored him on his 60th (Vienna, 1962) and 70th (Kassel, 1975) birthdays.

Schenk, Johann, Austrian composer; b. Wiener-Neustadt, Nov. 30, 1753; d. Vienna, Dec. 29, 1836. He studied with Wagenseil in Vienna. In 1778 he had a Mass performed, which made his reputation; it was followed by other pieces of sacred music; then he began composing light operas, some of which enjoyed great popularity. It was from Schenk that Beethoven took surreptitious lessons while studying with Haydn.

Schenker, Heinrich, outstanding Austrian music theorist; b. Wisniowczyki, Galicia, June 19, 1868; d. Vienna, Jan. 13, 1935. He studied jurisprudence at the Univ. of Vienna (Dr.Jur., 1890); concurrently entered the class of Anton Bruckner at the Vienna Cons. He composed some songs and piano pieces; Brahms liked them sufficiently to recommend Schenker to his publisher Simrock. For a while Schenker served as accompanist of the baritone Johannes Messchaert; then returned to Vienna and devoted himself entirely to the development of his theoretical research; gathered around himself a group of enthusiastic disciples who accepted his novel theories, among them Otto Vrieslander, Hermann Roth, Hans Weisse, Anthony van Hoboken, Oswald Jonas, Felix Salzer, and John Petrie Dunn. He endeavored to derive the basic laws of musical composition from a thoroughgoing analysis of the standard masterworks. The result was the contention that each composition represents a horizontal integration, through various stages, of differential triadic units derived from the overtone series. By a dialectical manipulation of the thematic elements and linear progressions of a given work, Schenker succeeded in preparing a formidable system in which the melody is the "Urlinie" (basic line), the bass is "Grundbrechung" (broken ground), and the ultimate formation is the "Ursatz" (background). The result seems as self-consistent as the Ptolemaic planetary theory of epicycles. Arbitrary as the Schenker system is, it proved remarkably durable in academia; some theorists even attempted to apply it to modern works lacking in the triadic content essential to Schenker's theories.

WRITINGS: *Ein Beitrag zur Ornamentik als Einführung zu Ph.E. Bachs Klavierwerke* (Vienna, 1904; 2nd ed., revised, 1908; Eng. trans. in *Music Forum*, IV, 1976); *Neue musikalische Theorien und Fantasien:* I. *Harmonierlehre* (Stuttgart, 1906; in Eng., ed. by O. Jonas, Chicago, 1954); II. *Kontrapunkt* in 2 vols., *Cantus Firmus und zweistimmiger Satz* (Vienna, 1910) and *Drei- und mehrstimmiger Satz, Übergänge zum freien Satz* (Vienna, 1922); III. *Der freie Satz* (Vienna, 1935; new ed. by O. Jonas, 1956; Eng. trans. by E. Oster, 1979); monographs on Beethoven's 9th Symph. (Vienna, 1912) and 5th Symph. (Vienna, 1925); *Der Tonwille* (a periodical containing articles and analyses by Schenker and appearing at irregular intervals from 1921–24); *Das Meisterwerk in der Musik* (a continuation of *Der Tonwille* in the form of an annual; 3 vols., Vienna, 1925, 1926, 1930); *Fünf Urlinie-Tafeln* (Vienna, 1932; 2nd ed., revised, 1969 by F. Salzer); *Johannes Brahms: Oktaven und Quinten* (Vienna, 1933).

Scherchen, Hermann, eminent German conductor; b. Berlin, June 21, 1891; d. Florence, June 12, 1966. He was self-taught in music; played the viola in the Berlin Phil. (1907–10); in 1911–12, toured with Arnold Schoenberg. In 1914 he obtained an engagement as a symph. conductor in Riga; at the outbreak of World War I he was interned in Russia; after the Armistice he returned to Berlin; founded and directed the Neue Musikgesellschaft there (1918); edited the music periodical *Melos* (1920–21); conducted numerous concerts at modern music festivals in Donaueschingen, Frankfurt, etc.; conducted symph. concerts of the Collegium Musicum in Winterthur, Switzerland from 1922 to 1947 (with interruptions); from 1928 until 1933 was in charge of the music of the Königsberg Radio. In 1933 he left Germany; edited the periodical *Musica Viva* in Brussels (1933–36); conducted at music festivals in Barcelona (1936) and Paris. On Oct. 30, 1964, he conducted the Philadelphia Orch. in his long-awaited U.S. debut concert. He distinguished himself as a scholarly exponent of modern music; conducted many world premieres of ultramodern works; publ. a valuable manual on conducting, *Lehrbuch des Dirigierens* (Leipzig, 1929; in Eng. as *Handbook of Conducting*, London, 1933; 6th ed., 1949); *Vom Wesen der Musik* (Zürich, 1946; in Eng. as *The Nature of Music*, London, 1947; Chicago, 1950); *Musik für Jedermann* (Winterthur, 1950).

Schering, Arnold, eminent German music histori-

an; b. Breslau, April 2, 1877; d. Berlin, March 7, 1941. His father was a merchant; the family moved to Dresden, where Schering began to take violin lessons with Blumner. In 1896 he enrolled in a Berlin music school, where he studied violin with Joachim, hoping to start a concert career; he organized a tour with the pianist Hinze-Reinhold, but soon gave up virtuoso aspirations, and in 1898 entered classes in musicology with Fleischer and Stumpf; then took courses with Sandberger at the Univ. of Munich and with Kretzschmar at the Univ. of Leipzig, obtaining his degree of Dr.Phil. with the dissertation *Geschichte des Instrumentalkonzerts* (Leipzig, 1902; amplified in vol. I of the series Kleine Handbücher der Musikgeschichte, 1905; 2nd ed., 1927). He completed his Habilitation at the Univ. of Leipzig with the dissertation *Die Anfänge des Oratorium* (1907; greatly expanded in 1911 and publ. as *Geschichte des Oratoriums*). He then devoted himself to teaching and musical journalism; from 1904–39 was editor of the Bach-Jahrbuch. From 1909–23 he taught at the Leipzig Cons.; in 1920 was named prof. of the Univ. of Halle; in 1928 he was appointed president of the German Musicological Society. In his voluminous publications he strove to erect an infallible system of esthetic principles derived from musical symbolism and based on psychological intuition, ignoring any contradictions that ensued from his axiomatic constructions. In his book *Beethoven in neuer Deutung*, publ. in 1934, at the early dawn of the Nazi era, Schering even attempted to interpret Beethoven's music in terms of racial German superiority, alienating many of his admirers. But in his irrepressible desire to establish an immutable sequence of historic necessity, he compiled an original and highly informative historical tabulation of musical chronology, *Tabellen zur Musikgeschichte,* which was originally publ. in 1914 and went through several editions. He advanced the idea that in order to understand new developments in the language of music it is necessary to study the music of the past, and conversely, that the understanding of old music can be enhanced by a study of new music. This thesis, obvious and possibly circular in its formulation, which Schering propounded with great solemnity at the opening of the first congress of the German Musicological Society in Leipzig in 1925, remains nevertheless a worthwhile restatement of the obvious. Schering's other theories, speculations, and declarations left no influence on sober musical thought of later generations.

Schermerhorn, Kenneth DeWitt, American conductor; b. Schenectady, N.Y., Nov. 20, 1929. He studied music at the New England Cons. (graduated, 1950), and opera conducting there with Boris Goldovsky. His first important engagement was as conductor of the American Ballet Theater (1956–65); he subsequently conducted the New Jersey Symph. Orch. (1962–68); in 1968 he was appointed conductor of the Milwaukee Symph. Orch., a post he retained until 1980. He thrice conducted the Hong Kong Phil.; also conducted opera at Long Beach, Calif. In 1982 he was appointed general music director of the American Ballet Theater in N.Y.; he was appointed music director of the Nashville Symph. Orch. in 1983.

Schetky, Johann Georg Christoph, German cellist and composer; b. Darmstadt, Aug. 19, 1737; d. Edinburgh, Nov. 29, 1824. The original family name was **Von Teschky;** Schetky's ancestors were from Transylvania. He traveled in Germany; in 1768 was in Hamburg; in 1772, settled in Edinburgh, where he was first cellist of the concerts in St. Cecilia's Hall. He married Maria Anna Teresa Reinagle, sister of Alexander Reinagle. He publ. 6 string quartets; 6 string trios; 6 duos for violin and cello; 6 cello sonatas, with bass; 6 flute duos; 6 cello duos; 6 sonatas for violin and cello; harpsichord sonatas; songs. In MS he left 3 symphs., 4 cello concertos, and an oratorio. His son **J. George Schetky** (b. Edinburgh, June 1, 1776; d. Philadelphia, Dec. 11, 1831) was the 2nd of 11 children; he emigrated to America in 1787; was naturalized in Philadelphia on Nov. 19, 1806. He appeared as a cellist in Philadelphia; c.1800 he entered into partnership with Benjamin Carr in the music publishing business; was a co-founder of the Musical Fund Society in Philadelphia. His arrangement for military band of Kotzwara's *Battle of Prague* was much played.

Schick (née **Hamel**), **Margarete Luise,** noted German soprano; b. Mainz, April 26, 1773; d. Berlin, April 29, 1809. She studied with Steffani at Würzburg, and later with Righini at Mainz, where her stage debut took place in 1791. Her favorite roles were Susanna (*Figaro*) and Zerlina (*Don Giovanni*). She was in Berlin from 1793 as a chamber and theater singer to the court; at the National Theater there from 1794. From 1794 she sang at the Royal Opera in Berlin, having great success in operas by Gluck. Her contemporaries regarded her as the equal of the famous Mara. In 1791 she married the violinist **Ernst Schick.**

Schickele, Peter, American composer; b. Ames, Iowa, July 17, 1935. He studied at the Juilliard School of Music, with Vincent Persichetti and William Bergsma. After quaquaversal professional gyrations, he rocketed to fame in the rollicking role of the roly-poly character P.D.Q. Bach, the mythical composer of such outrageous travesties as *The Civilian Barber, Gross Concerto for Divers Flutes* (featuring a Nose Flute and a Wiener Whistle to be eaten during the perf.), *Concerto for Piano vs. Orchestra, Iphigenia in Brooklyn, The Seasonings, Pervertimento for Bagpipes, Bicycles & Balloons, No-No Nonette, Schleptet, Fuga Meshuga, Missa Hilarious, Sanka Cantata, Fantasie-Shtick,* etc., all perpetrated in a clever pseudo-Baroque style. On April 24, 1984, his opera, *The Abduction of Figaro,* was premiered in Minneapolis. He publ. *The Definitive Biography of P.D.Q. Bach (1807–1742?)* (N.Y., 1976).

Schidlowsky, León, Chilean composer; b. Santiago, July 21, 1931. He studied philosophy and psychology at the Univ. of Chile (1948–52) and had private lessons in composition with Free Focke and in harmony with Juan Allende; then went to Germany for further studies (1952–55). Returning to Chile, he organized the avant-garde group Tonus for the propagation of new techniques of composition; was a music teacher at the Hebrew Inst. in Santiago (1955–61), director of the music archives of the Inst. of Musical Extension of the Univ. of Chile (1961–65), and director of the Inst. and a member of the faculty of the Cons. Nacional de Música in Santiago (1965–69). In 1969 he emigrated to Israel, where he was appointed to the faculty of the Rubin Academy in Tel Aviv. In his music he adopts a serial technique, extending it into fields of rhythms and intensities; beginning in 1964 he superadded aleatory elements, using graphic notation.

Schiedermair, Ludwig, eminent German musicologist; b. Regensburg, Dec. 7, 1876; d. Bensberg, near Cologne, April 30, 1957. He studied in Munich with Sandberger and Beer-Walbrunn; received his Dr.Phil. in 1901 for the dissertation *Künstlerische Bestrebungen am Hofe des Kurfürsten Ferdinand Maria von Bayern;* studied further with Riemann in Leipzig and with Kretzschmar in Berlin. In 1906 he became an instructor of musicology at the Univ. of Marburg; in 1912, a lecturer at the Univ. of Bonn (1920, prof.). In 1927, on the occasion of the Beethoven centennial, he was appointed director of the Beethoven-Haus Research Inst. in Bonn. He retired from the Univ. of Bonn in 1945.

Schiedmayer, the name of 2 well-known firms of piano makers in Stuttgart: Schiedmayer & Söhne and Schiedmayer Pianofortefabrik. **Balthasar Schiedmayer** (1711–81) began manufacturing musical instruments in Erlangen c.1740; at his death in 1781, his son **Johann David Schiedmayer** (1753–1805) assumed the management; he was succeeded by his 19-year-old son, **Johann Lorenz Schiedmayer** (1786–1860), with whom he had moved (c.1800) from Erlangen to Nuremberg. Johann Lorenz ended the business at Nuremberg after 2 years, and went to Vienna for a brief time; in 1809 he was in Stuttgart, where he set up business in partnership with a young piano maker, Karl Dieudonné (d. 1825); from 1825, he carried on the business alone, until 1845, when his eldest sons, **Adolf Schiedmayer** (1819–90) and **Hermann Schiedmayer** (1820–61), entered the firm, which was then called J.L. Schiedmayer & Söhne. In 1853 Johann Lorenz Schiedmayer provided his 2 younger sons, **Julius** (1822–78) and **Paul** (1829–90), with their own separate factory, producing harmoniums. After their father's death they turned to piano making, and their business became known as Schiedmayer Pianofortefabrik. Upon Paul Schiedmayer's death in 1890, his son, **Max Julius,** became head of the firm.

Schiff, Andras, Hungarian pianist; b. Budapest, Dec. 21, 1953. He studied at the Liszt Academy of Music in Budapest and in London with George Malcolm; made his debut in Budapest in 1972; was a prizewinner at the International Tchaikovsky Competition in Moscow in 1974 and at the Leeds International Competition in 1975; subsequently was a soloist with the leading orchs. in America; toured in Japan. He excels in the Romantic repertoire but is also a fine interpreter of Bach's works.

Schiff, Heinrich, gifted Austrian cellist; b. Gmunden, Nov. 18, 1951. He first studied piano; then took cello lessons with Tobias Kuhne in Vienna and later with André Navarra in Detmold. After winning prizes in competitions in Geneva, Vienna, and Warsaw, he was a soloist with the Vienna Phil., the Concertgebouw Orch. in Amsterdam, the Stockholm Phil., the BBC Symph., and the Royal Phil. in London; also concertized in Toronto and Montreal. In 1978 he toured Australia, and in 1979 played in Japan. His playing is marked by assured technical resources and mellowness of tone.

Schifrin, Lalo (Boris), American composer; b. Buenos Aires, June 21, 1932. He studied music at home with his father, who was concertmaster at the Teatro Colón; took composition lessons with Argentine dodecaphonist Juan Carlos Paz. In 1950 he went to Paris, where he attended the classes of Olivier Messiaen. He became interested in jazz and represented Argentina at the International Jazz Festival in Paris in 1955; returning to Buenos Aires, he formed his own jazz band, adopting the bebop style. In 1958 he went to N.Y. as arranger for Xavier Cugat; then was pianist with Dizzy Gillespie's band (1960–62); composed for it several exotic pieces, such as *Manteca, Con Alma,* and *Tunisian Fantasy,* based on Gillespie's *Night in Tunisia.* In 1963 he wrote a ballet, *Jazz Faust.* In 1964 he went to Hollywood, where he rapidly found his métier as composer for the films and television; among his motion picture scores are *The Liquidator, The Fox,* and *The Cincinnati Kid.* He also experimented with applying the jazz idiom to religious texts, as, for instance, in his *Jazz Suite on Mass Texts* (1965). He achieved his greatest popular success with the theme-motto for the television series *Mission: Impossible,* in 5/4 time, for which he received 2 Grammy awards. His adaptation of modern techniques into mass media placed him in the enviable position of being praised by professional musicians. His oratorio *The Rise and Fall of the Third Reich,* featuring realistic excerpts and incorporating an actual recording of Hitler's speech in electronic amplification, was brought out at the Hollywood Bowl on Aug. 3, 1967. His other works include a Suite for Trumpet and Brass Orch. (1961); *The Ritual of Sound* for 15 Instruments (1962); *Pulsations* for Electronic Keyboard, Jazz Band, and Orch. (Los Angeles, Jan. 21, 1971); *Madrigals for the Space Age,* in 10 parts, for Narrator and Chorus (Los Angeles, Jan. 15, 1976); Capriccio for Clarinet and Strings (Los Angeles, Nov. 5, 1981).

Schikaneder, Emanuel (Johann), Mozart's librettist; b. Straubing, Sept. 1, 1751; d. Vienna, Sept. 21, 1812. His baptismal names were Johannes Joseph; he assumed the name Emanuel later in life. He was a member of a troupe of itinerant players when he met Mozart at Salzburg in 1780. In 1783 he reached Vienna, where he was an actor and an impresario. He was not successful until he persuaded Mozart to set to music his play *Die Zauberflöte,* which recouped his fortunes; it was produced on Sept. 30, 1791, shortly before Mozart's death; Schikaneder himself took the part of Papageno. He wrote 55 theater pieces and 44 librettos for operas, and singspiels; with Zitterbarth he was the manager of the Theater an der Wien, which he directed from its foundation (1801) until 1806. He died insane after a series of financial setbacks.

Schillinger, Joseph, Russian composer and theorist; b. Kharkov, Aug. 31, 1895; d. New York, March 23, 1943. He studied at the St. Petersburg Cons. with Tcherepnin, Wihtol, and others; from 1918 to 1922, taught at the State Academy of Music in Kharkov; also conducted an orch. there; from 1922 to 1928 was active in Leningrad as a teacher and composer. In 1928 he came to America, settling in N.Y.; taught at The New School for Social Research; then established private classes, teaching his own system of composition, based on rigid mathematical principles. He became highly successful as an instructor; George Gershwin took lessons from him; many other composers of popular music became his students. After Schillinger's death, Lyle Dowling and Arnold Shaw edited and publ. his magnum opus, under the title *The Schillinger System of Musical Composition* (2 vols., N.Y., 1946); this was followed by *The Mathematical Basis of the Arts* (N.Y., 1947); a short vol. of musical patterns, *Kaleidophone,* was publ. previously (N.Y., 1940). Schillinger was also a composer in his own right; his works include *March of the Orient* for Orch. (Leningrad, May 12, 1926); *First Airphonic Suite* for Theremin, with Orch. (Cleveland, Nov. 28, 1929; Leo Theremin, inventor of the instrument, as soloist); piano pieces; etc.

Schillings, Max von, renowned German composer and conductor; b. Düren, April 19, 1868; d. Berlin, July 24, 1933. While attending the Gymnasium at Bonn he studied violin with O. von Königslöw, and piano and composition with K.J. Brambach. He then entered the Univ. of Munich, where he studied law, philosophy, literature, and art. He became associated with Richard Strauss, and under his influence decided to devote himself entirely to music. In 1892 he was engaged as assistant stage director at the Festival Theater in Bayreuth; in 1902 he became chorus master; in 1908 he moved to Stuttgart, becoming Generalmusikdirektor in 1911; on the occasion of the inauguration of the new opera theater there, he was given the rank of nobility, and added the nobiliary particle "von" to his name; he remained in Stuttgart until 1918; was Intendant of the Berlin State Opera (1919–25). He made several visits as a conductor to the U.S. In 1923 he married the soprano **Barbara Kemp.** As a composer, he trailed in the path of Wagner, barely avoiding direct imitation.

Schindler, Anton Felix, violinist and conductor, historically significant as amanuensis, close associate, and early biographer of Beethoven; b. Meedl, Moravia, June 13, 1795; d. Bockenheim, near Frankfurt, Jan. 16, 1864. He studied violin with his father; went to Vienna in 1813 to study law. In 1814 he met Beethoven, soon becoming his secretary, his social mediator, and, to some extent, his business manager; for some years he held the position of concertmaster of the orch. of the Josephstadttheater. Beethoven's stormy temper created inevitable difficulties; during one such outburst, Beethoven even accused his faithful helper of mishandling the financial receipts from the ticket sales for the premiere of the 9th Symph. However, Schindler had enough modesty and intelligence to disregard such personal misunderstandings, and continued to serve Beethoven. After Beethoven's death, Schindler obtained possession of valuable MSS, documents, papers, and about 400 of the biographically important conversation books, which recorded Beethoven's dialogues with friends and visitors. In a misguided attempt to protect Beethoven's reputation, Schindler apparently destroyed some of these materials, at least the parts that reflected Beethoven's pettiness and complaints. More reprehensible is the indication that some of Beethoven's conversation books, invaluable in their biographical content, were altered by Schindler, as appears from the painstaking handwriting analysis conducted on these books in 1977 by Dagmar Beck and Gritat Herre. In 1846 Schindler sold most of his Beethoven collection to the Royal Library in Berlin. He served as music director in Münster (1831–35) and Aachen (1835–37). In 1848 he moved to Frankfurt and supported himself mainly by teaching. In 1856 he settled in Bockenheim, where he remained until his death. No matter what criticism can be raised against Schindler as a man of limited endowments unable to grasp the dimension of Beethoven's genius, the fact remains that it was Schindler who became the prime source of information about Beethoven's life, a witness to the musical greatness that Beethoven embodied. His fundamental book, *Biographie von Ludwig van Beethoven,* was publ. in Münster in 1840; the 2nd edition, containing the valuable supplement *Auszüge aus Beethovens Konversationsheften,* appeared in 1845; the English translation of the original edition, made by Moscheles, was publ. in London in 1841. The 3rd edition of Schindler's biography appeared in 1860 and was translated into English by Donald MacArdle under the title *Beethoven as I Knew Him* (London, 1966). Of interest are also Schindler's diaries (1841–43), which were edited by M. Becker (Frankfurt, 1939).

Schindler, Kurt, German conductor and music editor; b. Berlin, Feb. 17, 1882; d. New York, Nov. 16, 1935. He studied piano with Ansorge and composition with Bussler and others in Berlin; took additional theory lessons in Munich with Thuille. He then was briefly assistant conductor to Richard Strauss in Berlin and to Mottl in Munich; in 1904 he emigrated to America and, after serving as an assistant chorus master at the Metropolitan Opera House, was engaged as a reader and music editor for G. Schirmer, Inc. In 1909 he founded in N.Y. the MacDowell Chorus, which became in 1910 the Schola Cantorum. Schindler conducted it until 1926 in programs including his choral arrangements of folk songs of various nations. His editions of arrangements of folk songs are valuable; among them are *6 Old French Christmas Carols* (1908); *Century of Russian Song from Glinka to Rachmaninov* (50 songs, with Eng. trans.; 1911); *The Developement of Opera* (examples of various periods; 1912); *Songs of the Russian People* (1915); *10 Student Songs of Finland* (1915); *A Cappella Choruses from the Russian Liturgy* (1913–17); *Masters of Russian Song* (2 vols., 1917); *Old Spanish Sacred Motets* (1918); *Modern Spanish Choral Works* (1918); *60 Russian Folk-Songs* (3 vols., 1918–19); *Folk Music and Poetry of Spain and Portugal* (N.Y., 1941; posthumous; about 1,000 musical examples; text in Eng. and Spanish).

Schiøtz, Aksel, famous Danish tenor and pedagogue; b. Roskilde, Sept. 1, 1906; d. Copenhagen, April 19, 1975. His father was an architect, and he urged Schiøtz to follow an academic career; accordingly, he enrolled at the Univ. of Copenhagen in language studies, obtaining a master's degree in 1929. He also studied singing, first at the Danish Royal Opera School in Copenhagen, and later with John Forsell in Stockholm. He made his operatic debut at the Royal Danish Theater in Copenhagen in 1939 as Ferrando in *Così fan tutte.* He became known as a fine interpreter of Mozart's tenor roles and a superb lieder singer. In 1946 he made appearances in England; in 1948 visited the U.S. His career was tragically halted when he developed a brain tumor, which led to an impairment of his speech; however, he regained his capacities as a singer and gave concerts as a baritone. From 1955 to 1958 he taught voice at the Univ. of Minnesota; from 1958 to 1961 was a prof. of voice at the Royal Cons. of Music and the Univ. of Toronto, and from 1961 to 1968, at the Univ. of Colorado. He returned to Copenhagen in 1968 and joined the faculty of the Royal Danish School of Educational Studies. He died of leukemia and intestinal cancer. In 1977 a memorial fund was formed in the U.S. to preserve his memory by granting scholarships in art songs. He publ. *The Singer and His Art* (N.Y., 1969).

Schipa, Tito (baptismal names, **Raffaele Attilio Amadeo**), famous Italian tenor; b. Lecce, Jan. 2, 1888; d. New York, Dec. 16, 1965. He studied composition with A. Gerunda, and began his career as a composer of piano pieces and songs; then turned to singing, and in 1910 made his debut at Vercelli in *La Traviata.* After numerous appearences in Europe, he was engaged by the Chicago Civic Opera (1919–32); made his first appearance with the Metropolitan Opera on Nov. 23, 1932, as Nemorino in *L'elisir d'amore;* continued to sing with the Metropolitan until 1935, then again in 1940–41, making appearances throughout the season. Schipa made extensive tours of Europe and South America, as well as in the U.S.; lived in California until 1941, when he went back to Italy. On Sept. 28, 1946, he married Teresa Borgna of São Paulo, Brazil. He toured the U.S. again in 1947. He retired from opera in 1954, but continued to give solo concerts until late in life. He wrote an operetta, *La Principessa Liana* (1935); a Mass (1929); several songs; also wrote a book, *Si confessi* (Genoa, 1961).

Schipper, Emil, Austrian bass-baritone; b. Vienna, Aug. 19, 1882; d. there, July 20, 1957. He studied in Vienna and Milan; made his debut at the German Theater in Prague in 1904 as Telramund; then sang in Linz (1911) and at the Vienna Volksoper (1912–15); was a member of the Bavarian State Opera in Munich (1916–22); joined the Vienna State Opera in 1922, remaining on its roster until 1940; also made guest appearances at Covent Garden in London (1924–28) and in Chicago (1928–29). He was married to the mezzo-soprano **Maria Olczewska.**

Schippers, Thomas, greatly gifted American conductor; b. Kalamazoo, Mich., March 9, 1930; d. New York, Dec. 16, 1977. He played piano in public at the age of 6, and was a church organist at 14. He studied piano at the Curtis Inst. of Music in Philadelphia (1944–45) and privately with Olga Samaroff (1946–47); subsequently attended Yale Univ.; there he took some composition lessons from Paul Hindemith. In 1948 he won 2nd prize in the contest for young conductors organized by the Philadelphia Orch. He then took a job as organist at the Greenwich Village Presbyterian Church in N.Y.; joined a group of young musicians in an enterprise called the Lemonade Opera, and conducted this group for several years. On March 15, 1950, he conducted in N.Y. the premiere of Menotti's opera *The Consul*; also conducted the television premiere of his *Amahl and the Night Visitors* (N.Y., Dec. 25, 1951). In 1951 he became a staff member of the N.Y. City Opera Co. On March 26, 1955, he led the N.Y. Phil. as guest conductor, the youngest musician ever to conduct the orch. In the fall of 1955 he made his debut as an opera conductor at the Metropolitan Opera in N.Y., also the youngest to do so; in 1955 he was a guest conductor at La Scala in Milan. From 1958 to 1976 he was associated with Menotti in the Spoleto Festival of Two Worlds. Other engagements included appearances with the N.Y. Phil., which he accompanied in 1959 to the Soviet Union as an alternate conductor with Leonard Bernstein. In 1962 he conducted at La Scala the world premiere of Manuel de Falla's cantata *Atlantida;* in 1964 he conducted at the Bayreuth Wagner Festival. He was a favorite conductor for new works at the Metropolitan Opera; conducted the first performance of Menotti's opera *The Last Savage* and the opening Metropolitan production of Samuel Barber's *Antony and Cleopatra* (Sept. 16, 1966); he also conducted the first production at the Metropolitan of the original version of Mussorgsky's *Boris Godunov* (1974). In 1970 he was appointed conductor and music direc-

tor of the Cincinnati Symph. Orch., one of the few American-born conductors to occupy a major symph. orch. post. There was an element of tragedy in his life. Rich, handsome, and articulate, he became a victim of lung cancer, and was unable to open the scheduled season of the Cincinnati Orch. in the fall of 1977; in a grateful gesture the management gave him the title of conductor laureate; he bequeathed a sum of $5,000,000 to the orch. He was happily married, but his wife died of cancer in 1973. When he conducted a production of *La forza del destino* at the Metropolitan Opera on March 4, 1960, the baritone Leonard Warren collapsed and died on the stage.

Schirmer, the family of music publishers. The first of the family to be connected with music was **Johann Georg Schirmer,** who settled in Sondershausen and was married there on July 18, 1781. He was a cabinet-maker, a native of Gäuroden, and made musical instruments. His son, **Ernst Ludwig Rudolf Schirmer** (b. Sondershausen, May 8, 1784), emigrated to N.Y. with his wife and children in 1840. There his son **(Friedrich) Gustav (Emil) Schirmer** (b. Königsee, Thuringia, Sept. 19, 1829; d. Eisenach, Aug. 5, 1893) found employment in the music store of Scharfenberg & Luis, and after several years entered the employ of Kerksieg & Breusing, music dealers, becoming manager in 1854. In 1861 he took over the business with a partner, and acquired sole control in 1866, establishing the firm that was to become **G. Schirmer, Inc.** He was an enlightened and progressive publisher; he entered into personal relations with noted European composers, and was among the original patrons of Wagner's Bayreuth Festival. He was an amateur pianist and had a real love for music. The diary of Tchaikovsky's visit to N.Y. in 1891 makes repeated mention of Schirmer and his family. Schirmer married an American, Mary Fairchild, by whom he had 5 daughters and 2 sons. The younger of these sons, **Gustave Schirmer** (b. New York, Feb. 18, 1864; d. Boston, July 15, 1907), organized in 1885 the Boston Music Co., which gained prominence especially through the publication of Ethelbert Nevin's music. Shortly afterward, with his brother **Rudolph Edward Schirmer** (b. New York, July 22, 1859; d. Santa Barbara, Calif., Aug. 19, 1919), he became a partner in the firm founded by their father in N.Y., and after the latter's death in 1893 he managed the business jointly with his brother, retaining independent control of the Boston Music Co. Rudolph was educated in N.Y. public schools, and from 1873 to 1875 lived at Weimar with his mother, brother, and 4 sisters; studied violin and piano there with Helene Stahl and came in contact with the Liszt circle; in 1876 entered the College of New Jersey (later Princeton Univ.), and after graduation in 1880 studied law for 4 years at Columbia College, being admitted to the bar in 1884. In 1885 he took the place of his brother Gustave in his father's music publishing business. Later he was rejoined by Gustave, and upon their father's death in 1893, Rudolph became president of the firm, assuming sole control from 1907. In 1915 he founded the *Musical Quarter-*

ly. He was a director of the N.Y. Oratorio Society and the N.Y. Symph. Society, and a trustee of the Inst. of Musical Art in N.Y. **Gustave Schirmer, 3rd** (b. Boston, Dec. 29, 1890; d. Palm Beach, Fla., May 28, 1965), son of Gustave Schirmer and grandson of the founder of G. Schirmer, Inc., inherited the Boston Music Co. from his father and acquired the Willis Music Co. of Cincinnati. He was president of G. Schirmer, Inc. in 1919–21 and 1944–57. Rudolph E. Schirmer's son, also named **Rudolph Edward Schirmer** (b. Santa Barbara, Calif., June 8, 1919), was vice-president of G. Schirmer, Inc., from 1949 to 1965; he was then chairman of the board, from 1965 to 1979.

Schirmer, Ernest Charles, American music publisher; b. Mt. Vernon, N.Y., March 15, 1865; d. Waban, Mass., Feb. 15, 1958. His father, Edward Schirmer (1831–85), a native of Thuringia, Saxony, was a brother of the famous music publisher **Gustav Schirmer** (with their family the 2 brothers emigrated to the U.S. in 1840). Ernest Schirmer entered apprenticeship in the music store of Gustav Schirmer in N.Y. in 1878. In Oct. 1891, he became business manager of the Boston Music Co.; was admitted to partnership in Jan. 1902. In 1917 he withdrew from the Boston Music Co., and in 1921 founded the E.C. Schirmer Music Co., with the stated purpose of promoting good music. In 1956 he was still active in the affairs of the company. The publications of the firm include the Concord Series, the Choral Repertory of the Harvard Univ. Glee Club, Radcliffe, Vassar, and Wellesley College Choral Music, the Polyphonic and "A Cappella" Libraries, the St. Dunstan Edition of Sacred Music, and treatises on harmonic analysis, musical theory, and music appreciation. The firm enjoys a world market for its publications, with agencies in London and Berlin.

G. Schirmer, Inc., one of the greatest music publishing houses in America. It was an outgrowth of the business founded in N.Y. in 1848 by Kerksieg & Breusing, of which **Gustav Schirmer** became manager in 1854. With another employee, Bernard Beer, Schirmer took over the business in 1861, and the firm became known as "Beer & Schirmer." In 1866 Schirmer became the sole owner, establishing the house of "G. Schirmer, Music Publishers, Importers and Dealers." Until 1880 the business was located at 701 Broadway in N.Y.; then it was moved to 35 Union Square, and in 1909 was transferred to a 7-story building at 3 East 43rd St. It remained at that address until 1960, when it was moved to 609 5th Ave., and its retail store relocated at 4 East 49th St. In 1969 G. Schirmer, Inc. was acquired by Macmillan Inc., and in 1973 the executive offices were moved to 866 3rd Ave. In 1973 Schirmer Books was founded as a division of Macmillan Publishing Co., Inc., taking over the publication of books on music for college, trade, and professional/reference markets, while G. Schirmer continued publication of musical works. The N.Y. firm also maintained branches in Cleveland (until 1962) and in Los Angeles (until 1967). After the death of the founder, Gustav Schirmer, in 1893, the firm was incorporated under the management of his sons, **Rudolph Edward Schirmer** and **Gustave Schirmer.** Rudolph Schirmer died in 1919 and was succeeded by his nephew **Gustave Schirmer, 3rd,** who was president until 1921. Then W. Rodman Fay became president, with O.G. Sonneck as vice-president. On May 7, 1929, Carl Engel was made president and continued in that office (except for one year, 1933, when his place was taken by Hermann Irion) until his death in 1944, when **Gustave Schirmer, 3rd,** became president again, retiring in 1957. He was succeeded by Rudolph Tauhert, who was president from 1957 to 1972. John Santuccio is currently (1984) president and Bruce MacCombie is vice-president and director of publications. In 1892 the firm began publication of the Library of Musical Classics, notable for careful editing and general typographical excellence; with its didactic Latin motto, "Musica laborum dulce lenimen," it became a familiar part of musical homes. In the same year was launched the Collection of Operas, a series of vocal scores with original text and Eng. trans.; another series, The Golden Treasury, was begun in 1905. Schirmer's Scholastic Series, containing pedagogical works, began publication in 1917. Among other laudable initiatives was the American Folk-Song Series, offering authentic folk material. An expansion into the field of lexicography followed with the publication of *Baker's Biographical Dictionary of Musicians,* first issued in 1900 under the editorship of its original author, Theodore Baker; its 6th edition was publ. in 1978, edited by Nicolas Slonimsky, who also took care of the 5th edition in 1958. Theodore Baker also compiled and edited *A Dictionary of Musical Terms* (G. Schirmer, N.Y., 1895; many reprints) and *Pronouncing Pocket-Manual of Musical Terms* (1905; more than a million copies sold). In 1915 the *Musical Quarterly* was founded under the editorship of O.G. Sonneck; its subsequent editors have been Carl Engel (1929–44), Gustave Reese (1944–45), Paul Henry Lang (1945–72), and Christopher Hatch (1972–77); in 1977 its editorship was entrusted to Joan Peyser. The *Musical Quarterly* has publ. through the years articles by the foremost scholars of Europe and America; it occupies the preeminent place among music journals in the English language. The music catalog of G. Schirmer, Inc. comprises tens of thousands of publications, ranging from solo songs to full orch. scores. Particularly meritorious is the endeavor of the publishers to promote American music; the firm has publ. works by Ernest Bloch, Charles Loeffler, Charles Griffes, Walter Piston, Roy Harris, William Schuman, Samuel Barber, Gian Carlo Menotti, Paul Creston, Leonard Bernstein, Elliott Carter, Henry Cowell, Norman Dello Joio, Morton Gould, Virgil Thomson, Milton Babbitt, Gunther Schuller, and many others; it also took over some works of Charles Ives. Among European composers, the works of Arnold Schoenberg, Gustav Holst, and Benjamin Britten are included in the Schirmer catalogue, as well as a number of works by Soviet composers.

Schiske, Karl, significant Austrian composer; b.

Györ (Raab), Hungary, Feb. 12, 1916; d. Vienna, June 16, 1969. He studied music theory privately with Ernst Kanitz in Vienna (1932–38) and musicology with Orel and Schenk at the Univ. of Vienna (Dr.Phil., 1942). In 1952 he was appointed to the faculty of the Vienna Academy of Music; in 1967 he received the Great Austrian State Prize. In 1966–67 he was a visiting prof. at the Univ. of Calif., Riverside. His technique of composition is curiously synthetic, and yet invariably logical, containing elements of medieval counterpoint and the serial methods of composition.

Schiuma, Alfredo, Argentine composer; b. Buenos Aires, July 1, 1885; d. there, July 24, 1963. He studied with Romaniello in Buenos Aires, and later established his own music school there. He wrote several operas in a singable Italianate idiom; the following were produced in Buenos Aires: *Amy Robsart,* based on Walter Scott's novel *Kenilworth* (April 24, 1920); *La Sirocchia* (April 23, 1922); *Tabaré* (Aug. 6, 1925); *Las virgenes del sol* (June 20, 1939); *La infanta* (Aug. 12, 1941); 4 symphs. (1928–57); symph. tableau, *Pitunga* (Buenos Aires, March 31, 1929); symph. sketch, *Los Incas* (Buenos Aires, April 26, 1931); also choruses, chamber music, and songs.

Schjelderup, Gerhard, Norwegian composer and writer; b. Christiansand, Nov. 17, 1859; d. Benediktbeuren, Bavaria, July 29, 1933. He went to Paris in 1878, and studied with Franchomme (cello) and Massenet (composition); in 1888 settled in Germany; lived in Dresden (from 1896); then moved to Benediktbeuren, where he remained till his death. He wrote music influenced partly by Wagner, partly by Grieg.

Schlesinger, Adolph Martin, German music publisher; b. Sülz, Silesia, Oct. 4, 1769; d. Berlin, Nov. 11, 1838. About 1795 he founded a music store in Berlin; it became known under the name of Schlesinger'sche Buch- und Musikalienhandlung in 1821. He was one of Beethoven's German publishers. The firm was carried on after his death by his son, **Heinrich Schlesinger,** who began publishing in 1851 the influential music periodical *Echo.* In 1864 the business was sold to R. Lienau (1838–1920), whose sons took it over after his death. The firm was further enlarged and enriched by the acquisition of several other music publishing firms, among them Haslinger of Vienna (1875), Krentzlin of Berlin (1919), Vernthal of Berlin (1925), and Köster of Berlin (1928). Schlesinger was the original publisher of *Der Freischütz* by Carl Maria von Weber; Beethoven's opp. 108–11, 132, 135; also works by Mendelssohn, Chopin, Liszt, and Berlioz.

Schlesinger, Maurice, music publisher, son of **Adolph Martin Schlesinger;** b. Berlin, Oct. 3, 1797; d. Baden-Baden, Feb. 25, 1871. He moved to Paris in 1819, and was at first engaged in book selling. In July 1821 he established a music publishing business, and launched the publication of the *Gazette Musicale,* soon united with the *Revue Musicale* (continued publication until 1880). He became one of the most important Paris publishers; publ. full scores of operas by Meyerbeer, Donizetti, and others; also Berlioz's *Symphonie fantastique* and much of Chopin's music. In 1846 he sold the catalogue to Brandus and Dufour; later it was acquired by Joubert.

Schletterer, Hans Michel, German conductor and writer on music; b. Ansbach, May 29, 1824; d. Augsburg, June 4, 1893. He studied with Spohr in Kassel and Ferdinand David in Leipzig. After filling a number of teaching posts in provincial towns, he taught at the Univ. of Heidelberg (1854–58); then was a choral conductor and singing teacher in Augsburg, where he founded an oratorio society and a music school. He publ. 17 books of choral music a cappella; a selection of Lutheran church music, *Musica sacra* (2 vols., 1887; 3rd ed., 1927); *Das deutsche Singspiel* (1863); *J.Fr. Reichardt* (1865); *Geschichte der geistlichen Dichtung und kirchlichen Tonkunst* (1869); *Studien zur Geschichte der französischen Musik* (3 vols., 1884–85; mostly borrowed from Castil-Blaze); etc.

Schloezer, Boris de, renowned Russian-French writer on music; b. Vitebsk, Dec. 8, 1881; d. Paris, Oct. 7, 1969. He studied music in Brussels and Paris; returning to Russia, he devoted himself to a profound study of philosophy, esthetics, and music theory. His sister, Tatiana Schloezer, was the 2nd wife of Scriabin, and Schloezer became an intimate friend of Scriabin, who confided to him his theosophic and musical ideas. In 1920 he emigrated to France, where he continued his literary activities in the Russian émigré press and in French literary magazines. He publ. a monograph on Scriabin (vol. 1, Berlin, 1923, in Russian; vol. 2 was planned but not completed; vol. 1, covering Scriabin's ideology and commentary on his music, was publ. in a French trans., with an introduction by Scriabin's daughter Marina, Paris, 1975); other publications in French: *Igor Stravinsky* (Paris, 1929); *Introduction à J.S. Bach* (Paris, 1947; in Spanish, Buenos Aires, 1961; in German under the title *Entwurf einer Musikasthetik,* Hamburg, 1964). Schloezer also wrote a philosophical fantasy, *Mon nom est personne (My Name Is Nobody)* and *Rapport secret,* depicting a distant planet whose inhabitants achieved immortality and divinity through science.

Schlosser, Max, distinguished German tenor; b. Amberg, Oct. 17, 1835; d. Utting am Ammersee, Sept. 2, 1916. He sang in Zürich, St. Gallen, and Augsburg, but then decided to become a baker. Still, he did not abandon hopes for a stage career; he met Hans von Bülow, who entrusted him with the role of David at the premiere of *Die Meistersinger von Nürnberg* in Munich in 1868; he remained a member of the Munich Court Opera until his retirement in 1904. He also sang at Bayreuth and made guest appearances with Neumann's traveling opera company. He was principally known for his fine performances of the Wagnerian repertoire.

Schlusnus, Heinrich, eminent German baritone; b. Braubach am Rhein, Aug. 6, 1888; d. Frankfurt, June 18, 1952. He studied voice in Frankfurt and Berlin; made his operatic debut as the Herald in *Lohengrin* at the Hamburg Opera on Jan. 1, 1914; was then on its roster for the 1914–15 season; he subsequently sang at the Nuremberg Opera (1915–17). In 1917 he joined the Berlin State Opera, remaining there until 1945. In 1927–28 he sang with the Chicago Civic Opera. He was renowned as a lieder singer, and made several American tours.

Schmedes, Erik, Danish tenor; b. Gentofte, near Copenhagen, Aug. 27, 1868; d. Vienna, March 21, 1931. He studied piano, then turned to singing; studied with Mme. Artôt in Paris; made his operatic debut as a baritone in Wiesbaden (Jan. 11, 1891), as the Herald in *Lohengrin;* then sang baritone roles in Nuremberg and Dresden (1894–97). After a course of study with A. Iffert in Dresden, he developed a definite tenor voice, and appeared as Siegfried at the Vienna Opera (Feb. 11, 1898); remained as a tenor with the Vienna Opera until 1924. He was a member of the Metropolitan Opera Co. in N.Y. during the season 1908–9; made his debut there as Siegmund (Nov. 18, 1908).

Schmelzer, Johann Heinrich, Austrian composer; b. Scheibbs, c.1623; d. Prague, 1680. In 1649–70, he was a violinist at the Vienna court chapel; in 1671, assistant conductor; in 1679, first conductor. He may have been the teacher of the famous violinist Heinrich Biber. Schmelzer composed valuable chamber music, including *Duodena selectarum sonatarum* (12 trio sonatas, 1659; reprint in Denkmäler der Tonkunst in Österreich, 105); *Sacro-profanus concentus musicus* (sonatas for 2–8 instruments, 1662; reprint, ibid., vols. 111/112); *Sonate unarum fidium* (6 solo violin sonatas, 1664; reprint, ibid., vol. 93; also one reprinted in the supplement to G. Beckermann's *Das Violinspiel in Deutschland vor 1700*); also the trumpet fanfares to Bertali's Festspiel *La Contesa dell'aria* (1667), publ. as *Arie per il balletto a cavallo* (ed. by P. Nettl in Denkmäler der Tonkunst in Österreich, 56 [28.ii]) and a *Missa nuptialis* (ed. by G. Adler in Denkmäler der Tonkunst in Österreich, 49). Other MSS of vocal and instrumental works by Schmelzer are in Vienna, Kromeriz, Paris, and Uppsala.

Schmelzl (Schmeltzl, Schmaelzl), Wolfgang, Austrian musician; b. Kennath, c.1500; d. St. Lorenz at Steinfeld, c.1561. He was a Protestant cantor at Amberg; then, c.1540, a teacher in Vienna and singer at the S. Salvator Chapel; and finally a Catholic priest at St. Lorenz at Steinfeld, near Vienna, where he died. He is known for a collection of 4- to 5-voiced quodlibets and folk songs of the period, publ. in 1544 (reprint by Schering in *Geschichte der Musik in Beispielen*, no. 111).

Schmid, Adolf, Austrian conductor and arranger; b. Hannsdorf, Nov. 18, 1868; d. Englewood, N.J., Feb. 12, 1958. He studied at the Vienna Cons.; in 1901 went to London, where he became music director of His Majesty's Theatre; in 1915 he emigrated to the U.S.; conducted ballet performances, including the Pavlova Ballet Russe (1916–18); then became an arranger for radio and schools; also wrote some picturesque music for orch., such as *Caravan Dance, A Bacchanal Dance*, etc. He publ. *The Language of the Baton* (N.Y., 1937).

Schmid, Erich, Swiss conductor; b. Balsthal, Jan. 1, 1907. He studied at the Hoch Cons. in Frankfurt and took composition lessons with Arnold Schoenberg in Berlin. He returned to Switzerland in 1933; was Generalmusikdirektor in Glarus until 1949, when he became chief conductor of the Zürich Tonhalle Orch. From 1957 to 1972 he was chief conductor of the Zürich Radio Orch. and served as a prof. of conducting at the Basel Music Academy (1963–73). He then went to England and conducted the City of Birmingham Symph. Orch. (1979–81). He became known as a champion of modern music; brought to performance numerous works by Swiss composers.

Schmid, Ernst Fritz, eminent German musicologist; b. Tübingen, March 7, 1904; d. Augsburg, Jan. 20, 1960. He studied violin, viola, and viola d'amore at the Munich Academy; took private lessons in music theory and conducting; then studied musicology at the univs. of Munich (with Sandberger), Freiburg (with Gurlitt), Tübingen (with Hasse), and Vienna (with Haas, Orel et al.); received his Ph.D. from the Univ. of Tübingen in 1929 with the dissertation *Carl Philipp Emanuel Bach und seine Kammermusik* (publ. in Kassel, 1931); completed his Habilitation as a Privatdozent in musicology at the Univ. of Graz in 1934 with his *Joseph Haydn: Ein Buch von Vorfahren und Heimat des Meisters* (publ. in Kassel, 1934). He became a prof. at the Univ. of Tübingen in 1935; also founded the Schwäbisches Landesmusikarchiv; he left Tübingen in 1937 to devote himself to private research; during World War II, he served in the German army; in 1948 he founded the Mozartgemeinde, and in 1951 the German Mozartgesellschaft. In 1954 he became academic director of the Neue Mozart Ausgabe; from 1955 he oversaw the publication of the new critical edition of Mozart's complete works, the *Neue Ausgabe Sämtlicher Werke*. In addition to his valuable research on Mozart, he discovered the private music collection of Emperor Franz II in Graz in 1933; this important collection is now housed in Vienna's Nationalbibliothek.

Schmid, Heinrich Kaspar, German composer; b. Landau, Sept. 11, 1874; d. Munich, Jan. 8, 1953. He studied with Thuille and Bussmeyer at the Munich Academy; in 1903 he went to Athens, where he taught music at the Odeon; in 1905 returned to Munich and was on the faculty of the Munich Academy until 1921; then was director of the Karlsruhe Cons. (1921–24) and of the Augsburg Cons. (1924–32). His eyesight failed him and he was totally blind during the last years of his life. As a composer, he followed the Romantic tradition of the Bavarian School; he wrote a great number of lieder, and composed singspiels in a folklike manner, as well as choruses and chamber music.

Schmid, Otto, German music editor and critic; b. Dresden, May 6, 1858; d. there, Sept. 12, 1931. He studied music privately with Kretschmer in Dresden; taught music history at the Dresden Cons. (1912–24) and wrote music criticism. Among his publications are monographs on Koschat (1887) and Kretschmer (1890); publ. a valuable history of music in Dresden: *Die Heimstätten der Sächsischen Landestheater* (Dresden, 1919); *Richard Wagners Opern und Musikdramen in Dresden* (Dresden, 1919); *Der Mozart-Verein zu Dresden* (Dresden, 1921); etc.; he edited the important collections *Musik am sächsischen Hofe* (10 vols.; compositions by Hasse, J.C. Schmidt, J.A. and C.S. Binder, Naumann, Petzold, etc., and members of the royal house); *Orgelwerke altböhmischer Meister* (2 vols.).

Schmidl, Carlo, Italian music publisher and lexicographer; b. Trieste, Oct. 7, 1859; d. there, Oct. 7, 1943. He was the son and pupil of the Hungarian composer **Antonio Schmidl** (1814–80). In 1872 he entered the employ of the music publisher Vicentini, and in 1889 he established his own business at Trieste; also directed the Leipzig branch of the Ricordi Co. (1901–6). He compiled and publ. an important biographical music dictionary, *Dizionario universale dei musicisti* (Milan, 1887–89; 2nd ed., 1926–29; supplement, 1938), containing scrupulously accurate data on Italian musicians, exact dates of performance of major works, and other information testifying to independent research. Schmidl also wrote biographies of Schumann (1890) and G.S. Mayr (1901).

Schmidt, Arthur Paul, German-American music publisher; b. Altona, Germany, April 1, 1846; d. Boston, May 5, 1921. He settled in Boston in 1866, and entered the music firm of George D. Russell & Co. In 1876 he established a business of his own; for some years maintained branches in N.Y. and Leipzig. Henry R. Austin became president of the firm in 1949. The A.P. Schmidt Co. won prominence by publication of the works of MacDowell; it brought out virtually the complete output of Arthur Foote (more than 150 items); also works by Chadwick, Hadley, Paine, Mrs. Beach, and other composers of the "New England School."

Schmidt, Franz, important Austrian composer; b. Pressburg, Dec. 22, 1874; d. Perchtoldsdorf, near Vienna, Feb. 11, 1939. He studied organ, piano, and cello at the Vienna Cons.; was a pupil of Anton Bruckner (composition) and Robert Fuchs (theory); also took piano lessons with Leschetizky. From 1896 to 1911 he played cello in the Vienna Phil. Orch.; also taught at the Cons. of the Gesellschaft der Musikfreunde in 1901–8 (both cello and piano). He became a prof. of piano at the Vienna Academy of Music in 1914; a prof. of counterpoint and composition there from 1922; director there, 1925–27; from 1927 to 1931, was rector of the Hochschule für Musik; retired in 1937. While engaged in pedagogical activities he continued to compose; his music is steeped in Viennese Romanticism, and the influence of Bruckner is particularly pronounced. Although he is regarded in Austria as a very important symph. composer, his music is almost totally unknown elsewhere.

WORKS: Operas: *Notre Dame* (Vienna, April 1, 1914; an orch. suite from it, entitled *Zwischenspiel aus einer unvollständigen romantischen Oper,* was perf. by the Vienna Phil., Dec. 6, 1903) and *Fredigundis* (Berlin, Dec. 19, 1922); oratorio, *Das Buch mit sieben Siegeln* (Vienna, June 15, 1938); 4 symphs.: No. 1 (Vienna, Jan. 25, 1902); No. 2 (Vienna, Dec. 3, 1913); No. 3 (Vienna, Dec. 2, 1928); No. 4 (Vienna, Jan. 10, 1934); *Konzertante Variationen über ein Thema von Beethoven* (Piano Concerto No. 1) for Piano, left-hand, and Orch. (Vienna, Feb. 2, 1924; Paul Wittgenstein, soloist); Piano Concerto No. 2, left-hand alone (Vienna, Feb. 10, 1935; Wittgenstein, soloist); *Chaconne* for Orch. (Vienna, Jan. 29, 1933); 2 string quartets; Piano Quintet; 2 clarinet quintets; several works for organ.

Schmidt, Joseph, Rumanian tenor; b. Bavideni, Bukovina, March 4, 1904; d. Zürich, Nov. 16, 1942. He studied at the Berlin Cons.; in 1928 began his career as a radio singer and won great popularity in Germany. In 1933 he went to Belgium; in 1938 was briefly in America; then settled in Switzerland. His voice was regarded as of great lyric expressiveness, but being almost a dwarf (he stood only 4 feet 10 inches in height), he was unable to appear in opera.

Schmieder, Wolfgang, noted German music librarian; b. Bromberg, May 29, 1901. He studied musicology with Kroyer and Moser, German philology and literature with F. Panzer and F. von Waldberg, and art history with C. Neumann at the Univ. of Heidelberg; received his Ph.D. there in 1927 with the dissertation *Zur Melodiebildung in Liedern von Neidhart von Reuental.* He was an assistant lecturer in the musicology dept. of the Univ. of Heidelberg (1927–30); then studied library science with M. Bollert at the Sächsischen Landesbibliothek in Dresden and with O. Glauning at the Univ. of Leipzig Library. He was librarian of the Technische Hochschule in Dresden (1931–33); then went to Leipzig as head of the archives of Breitkopf & Härtel (1933–42). In 1946 he founded the music dept. of the City and Univ. Library in Frankfurt, which he headed until 1963. He was presented a Festschrift on his 70th birthday in 1971, *Quellenstudien zur Musik,* edited by K. Dorfmüller and G. von Dadelsen. Of his numerous publications, of fundamental importance is his exhaustive *Thematisch-systematisches Verzeichnis der musikalischen Werke von Johann Sebastian Bach: Bach-Werke-Verzeichnis* (Leipzig, 1950; 3rd ed., 1961; 4th ed., 1966); also valuable is *Musikalische alte Drücke bis etwa 1750* (with G. Hartweig; 2 vols., Wolfenbüttel, 1967).

Schmitt, Aloys, German pianist and composer; b.

Erlenbach, Aug. 26, 1788; d. Frankfurt, July 25, 1866. He studied composition with André at Offenbach; in 1816 went to Frankfurt, where he remained all his life. He composed 4 operas: *Der Doppelgänger* (Hannover, 1827); *Valeria* (Mannheim, 1832); *Das Osterfest zu Paderborn* (Frankfurt, 1843); *Die Tochter der Wüste* (Frankfurt, 1845); 2 oratorios: *Moses* and *Ruth;* church music; etc. But he is principally known and appreciated for his numerous piano compositions, including 4 piano concertos, several piano quartets, piano trios, a number of attractive character pieces for piano, and studies for school.

Schmitt, Florent, outstanding French composer; b. Blâmont, Sept. 28, 1870; d. Neuilly, near Paris, Aug. 17, 1958. He had his first music lessons from H. Hess (piano) and G. Sandré (harmony) in Nancy. In 1889 he went to Paris, where he studied harmony with Dubois and Lavignac and composition with Massenet and Fauré. He won the 2nd Prix de Rome in 1897 with the cantata *Frédégonde* and the first prize in 1900 with the cantata *Sémiramis*, which was performed at a Colonne concert on Dec. 11, 1900. He spent the years 1901–4 in the Villa Medicis in Rome, sending to the Académie several important instrumental and choral works; then spent 2 years traveling in Germany, Austria, Hungary, and Turkey. In 1906 he settled permanently in Paris, devoting himself entirely to composition. He served as a member of the executive committee of the Société Musicale Indépendante from its foundation in 1909; was also a member of the Société Nationale de Musique. His formative years were spent in the ambience of French symbolism in poetry and Impressionism in music, and he followed these directions in his programmatically conceived orch. music; but he developed a strong, distinctive style of his own, mainly by elaborating the contrapuntal fabric of his works and extending the rhythmic design to intricate asymmetrical combinations; he also exploited effects of primitivistic percussion, in many respects anticipating the developments of modern Russian music. The catalogue of his works is very long; he continued to compose until his death at the age of 87; attended the premiere of his Symph., given at the Strasbourg Festival of the International Society for Contemporary Music on June 15, 1958. He visited the U.S. in 1932 as soloist in his *Symphonie concertante* with the Boston Symph. He was an influential music critic, writing regularly for *Le Temps* (1919–39).

WORKS: BALLETS: *La Tragédie de Salomé* (Paris, Nov. 9, 1907); *Le Petit Elfe Ferme-l'œil*, after Hans Christian Andersen (Opéra-Comique, Feb. 29, 1924); *Oriane la sans-égale* (Paris Opéra, Jan. 7, 1938); incidental music to *Antoine et Cléopâtre*, after Shakespeare (Paris Opéra, June 14, 1920); *Reflets* (Opéra-Comique, May 20, 1932). VOCAL MUSIC, WITH ORCH.: *Musique sur l'eau* (1898); *Psaume XLVII* for Soprano, Chorus, Orch., and Organ (1904; Paris, Dec. 27, 1906); *Danse des Devadasis* for Solo Voice, Chorus, and Orch. (1900–8); *Tristesse au Jardin* (1897–1908); *Chant de guerre* for Tenor, Male

Chorus, and Orch. (1914); *Kerob-Shal* for Tenor and Orch. (1920–24); *Fête de la lumière* for Soprano, Chorus, and Orch. (1937); *L'Arbre entre tous* for Chorus and Orch. (1939); *A contre-voix* for Mixed Chorus (1943); motets and choruses a cappella. FOR ORCH.: *En été* (1894); *Feuillets de voyage* (1903–13); *Reflets de l'Allemagne*, suite of waltzes (1905); *Puppazzi*, suite in 8 movements (1907); *Musiques de plein-air* (1897–99); *Sélamlik*, symph. poem for Military Band (1906); *Le Palais hanté*, symph. study after Poe (1900–4); *3 rapsodies* (1903–4); *Scherzo vif* for Violin and Orch. (1903–10); *La Tragédie de Salomé*, from the ballet of the same title (Paris, Jan. 8, 1911); *Légende* for Viola or Saxophone, and Orch. (1918); *Mirages: Tristesse de Pan, La Tragique Chevauchée* (1921); *Fonctionnaire MCMXII: Inaction en musique* (1924; Paris, Jan. 16, 1927); *Danse d'Abisag* (1925); *Salammbô*, 6 symph. episodes after Flaubert, from film music (1925); *Ronde burlesque* (1927; Paris, Jan. 12, 1930); *Çhançunik* (humorous phonetic spelling of *Sens unique*, i.e., "one-way street"; Paris, Feb. 15, 1930); *Symphonie concertante* for Piano and Orch. (Boston, Nov. 25, 1932, composer soloist); *Suite sans esprit de suite* (Paris, Jan. 29, 1938); *Branle de sortie* (Paris, Jan. 21, 1939); *Janiana*, subtitled "Symphony for Strings," score entitled Symph. No. 2 (1941; Paris, May 1, 1942); *Habeyssée* for Violin and Orch. (phonetic representation of "ABC," as pronounced in French; Paris, March 14, 1947); Symph. (1957; Strasbourg, June 15, 1958). CHAMBER MUSIC: *Scherzo-pastorale* for Flute and Piano (1889); *4 pièces* for Violin and Piano (1901); *Andante et Scherzo* for Harp and String Quartet (1906); Piano Quintet (1901–8); *Lied et Scherzo* for Double Wind Quintet (1910); *Sonate libre en deux parties enchaînées* for Violin and Piano (1919); *Suite en rocaille* for Flute, Violin, Viola, Cello, and Harp (1934); *Sonatine en trio* for Flute, Clarinet, and Harpsichord (1935); *Minorités* for Flute, Violin, and Piano (1938); *Hasards* for Violin, Viola, Cello, and Piano (1939); *A tours d'anches* for Flute, Clarinet, Bassoon, and Piano (1939); Quartet for Saxophones (1941); String Trio (1944); Quartet for Flutes (1944); String Quartet (1945–48). FOR PIANO: *Soirs* (10 preludes); *Ballade de la neige* (1896); *Musiques intimes* (2 sets, 1890–1900 and 1898–1904); *Nuits romaines* (1901); *Puppazzi*, 8 pieces (1907; also for Orch.); *Pièces romantiques* (6 pieces, 1900–8); *3 danses* (1935; also for Orch.); *Feuillets de voyage* (1903; also for Orch.); *Suite sans esprit de suite* (1938; also for Orch.); *Clavecin obtempérant*, suite (1945); etc.; *Reflets de l'Allemagne*, 8 waltzes for Piano, 4-hands (1905; also for Orch.). SONGS: *Soir sur le lac* (1898); *4 lieds*, to words by Richepin, Maeterlinck, etc.; *Kerob-Shal*, 3 songs (also for Voice and Orch.).

Schmitt, Georg Aloys, German pianist, conductor, and composer, son and pupil of **Aloys Schmitt;** b. Hannover, Feb. 2, 1827; d. (suddenly, during a rehearsal) Dresden, Oct. 15, 1902. He studied music theory with Vollweiler in Heidelberg; then went on a European tour as a pianist; subsequently devoted himself mainly to theatrical conducting; he was court conductor at Schwerin (1857–92); in 1893 was appointed director of the Mozartverein in Dresden, which had a multitudinous choral ensemble (some 1,400 members) and its own orch. Schmitt wrote the opera *Trilby;* several concert overtures; much chamber music, and piano pieces. He orchestrated keyboard works of Handel and Mozart.

Schmitz, Elie Robert, eminent French pianist; b. Paris, Feb. 8, 1889; d. San Francisco, Sept. 5, 1949. He studied at the Paris Cons. with Diémer, winning first prize in piano; in 1908 toured as accompanist of Slezak, Emma Eames, and other celebrated singers; in 1912, organized in Paris the Assoc. des Concerts Schmitz, which he led until 1914; in 1919 toured the U.S. as a pianist; in 1920 founded the Franco-American Music Society in N.Y. (incorporated in 1923 as Pro Musica), of which he was president from its inception; toured again in the U.S. and Europe (1921–29), and in the Orient (1929–30, 1932–33); eventually settled in San Francisco as a teacher. He publ. a book on his system of piano study, *The Capture of Inspiration* (N.Y., 1935; 2nd ed., 1944), and a valuable technical analysis with commentary, *The Piano Works of Claude Debussy* (N.Y., 1950).

Schnabel, Artur, celebrated Austrian pianist and pedagogue; b. Lipnik, April 17, 1882; d. Morschach, Canton Schwyz, Switzerland, Aug. 15, 1951. After taking lessons for 2 years from Hans Schmitt, he studied in Vienna with Leschetizky (1891–97); appeared in public as a child prodigy; lived many years in Berlin, where he gave joint recitals with the violinist Carl Flesch; formed in 1912 a trio with A. Wittenberg (violin) and A. Hekking (cello); from 1925 until 1933 he taught at the Hochschule für Musik in Berlin; after the advent of the Nazi regime he went to Switzerland, where he organized his famous master classes during summer seasons. He made his American debut in 1921, and revisited the U.S. several times; lived in N.Y. after 1939, and became an American citizen in 1944; but eventually returned to Europe. It was as an interpreter of Beethoven that he reached his greatest heights; he was distinguished also in his performances of the piano music of Brahms. His pedagogical method was strict in the observance of every detail of the music, but at the same time he inspired his pupils by encouraging an individual treatment in the matter of dynamics and formal concept. Schnabel was also a composer; in his works he pursued an uncompromisingly modernistic idiom, thriving on dissonance and tracing melodic patterns along atonal lines.

Schnabel, Joseph Ignaz, German composer of sacred music; b. Naumburg-on-Queiss, Silesia, May 24, 1767; d. Breslau, June 16, 1831. He was appointed Kapellmeister at the Cathedral of Breslau (1804) and remained in Breslau for the rest of his life; from 1812 taught at the Roman Catholic Seminary and was director of the Royal Inst. for Church Music. He wrote many sacred works; publ. 5 masses, 4 graduals, 2 offertories, hymns; also wrote marches for military band; Quintet for Guitar and Strings;

Clarinet Concerto. His brother, **Michael Schnabel** (b. Naumburg, Sept. 23, 1775; d. Breslau, Nov. 6, 1842), founded a piano factory in Breslau (1814); his son, **Karl Schnabel** (b. Breslau, Nov. 2, 1809; d. there, May 12, 1881), an excellent pianist and composer of operas and piano music, carried on the business after Michael Schnabel's death.

Schnabel, Karl Ulrich, German pianist and composer, son of **Artur Schnabel;** b. Berlin, Aug. 6, 1909. He studied piano with Leonid Kreutzer and composition with Paul Juon in Berlin; after a series of appearances as a soloist in Europe, including Russia, he made an American tour (debut, N.Y., Feb. 23, 1937); played duo-piano recitals with his father; also gave duo-piano concerts (4 hands at one piano) with his wife, **Helen Fogel.**

Schneerson, Grigori, eminent Russian musicologist; b. Eniseisk, Siberia, March 13, 1901; d. Moscow, Feb. 6, 1982. He was the son of a political exile under the tsarist regime; went to Moscow as a youth and studied piano at the Moscow Cons. with Medtner and Igumnov. From 1939 to 1948 he was in charge of the music dept. of the Society for Cultural Relations with Foreign Nations; from 1948 to 1961 was head of the foreign section of the monthly *Sovietskaya Muzyka,* and from 1954 to 1966 edited the bibliographic series Foreign Literature of Music. A remarkably gifted linguist, he mastered several European languages and undertook a study of Chinese. In his polemical writings he displayed wit and sarcasm in attacking the extreme manifestations of Western modernism, but preserved scholarly impartiality in analyzing the music of all genres and styles. He was a Member Correspondent of the Academy of the Arts of the German Democratic Republic (1968), Honorary Member of the Accademia di Scienze, Lettere, Arti (1976), and a recipient of the Bernier Prize of the Académie des Beaux-Arts, Paris (1976).

Schnéevoigt, Georg Lennart, Finnish conductor; b. Viborg, Nov. 8, 1872; d. Malmö, Nov. 28, 1947. He studied cello with Karl Schröder in Sondershausen and Julius Klengel in Leipzig; appeared as a cellist; in 1900 began his career as a conductor; from 1904 to 1908 conducted the Kaim Orch. in Munich; in 1908–9, the Kiev Symph.; in 1909–14, the Riga Symph.; in 1912–14, the Helsinki Symph.; the last merged with Kajanus's Helsinki Phil. in 1914 to form the City Orch.; Kajanus and Schnéevoigt were joint conductors from 1916–32; Schnéevoigt then succeeded Kajanus and continued until 1941; from 1915 to 1924 he also led the Konsertförening in Stockholm; in 1919 founded the Oslo Phil. Orch., and led it until 1927; also conducted in Germany; conducted the Los Angeles Phil. (1927–29); was general director of the National Opera in Riga (1929–32); then went to Malmö, Sweden. In 1907 he married the pianist **Sigrid Sundgren.**

Schneider, Alexander, Russian-American violinist; b. Vilna, Oct. 21, 1908. He went to study in Germany as a youth; took violin lessons with Adolf Rebner at the Frankfurt Cons. and with Carl Flesch in Berlin; served as concertmaster of the Orch. der Museumgesellschaft. Upon the advent of the anti-Semitic Nazi regime, he emigrated to the U.S.; joined the Budapest Quartet as 2nd violin, and made a world tour with it. In 1950 he established, with Pablo Casals, annual summer music festivals in Prades, France, and was a close collaborator with Casals in arranging the spring music festivals in Puerto Rico. He took part, in association with Rudolf Serkin, in the Marlboro (Vt.) music festivals. In 1945 he received the Elizabeth Sprague Coolidge medal for eminent services to chamber music. He also appeared as a conductor with world orchs. (Israel Phil., Los Angeles Phil., as well as the Casals orch. in Puerto Rico); was active as a teacher; played sonata recitals with Eugene Istomin and other pianists.

Schneider, Friedrich, German organist and composer; b. Alt-Waltersdorf, Saxony, Jan. 3, 1786; d. Dessau, Nov. 23, 1853. He was a son and pupil of **Johann Gottlob Schneider;** being brought up in a musical atmosphere, he began composing early in life, and publ. 3 piano sonatas at the age of 17; in 1820 he wrote an oratorio, *Das Weltgericht,* that was extremely successful; the following year he was called to Dessau as court Kapellmeister; there he founded a celebrated school of music, which he directed from 1829 to his death; it attracted pupils from all over Germany. Besides *Das Weltgericht,* he wrote oratorios: *Die Sündflut* (1823); *Das verlorene Paradies* (1824); *Das befreite Jerusalem* (1835); also a series of oratorios tracing the life of Jesus from birth to crucifixion; he further wrote 25 cantatas; 7 operas; 23 symphs.; numerous pieces of chamber music; choruses; piano sonatas for 2 and 4 hands. He also publ. theoretical works: *Elementarbuch der Harmonie und Tonsetzkunst* (1820; in Eng., etc., 1828); *Vorschule der Musik* (1827); *Handbuch des Organisten* (1829–30; in 4 parts).

Schneider, Max, eminent German musicologist; b. Eisleben, July 20, 1875; d. Halle, May 5, 1967. He studied musicology at the Leipzig Cons. with Riemann and Kretzschmar and harmony and composition with Jadassohn. Upon graduation he was librarian at the Univ. of Berlin (1904–7); then served in the music division of the Royal Library (1907–14); subsequently taught at the Univ. of Breslau (1915–28); then was a prof. at the Univ. of Halle (1928–60). He did useful work in compiling miscellaneous bio-bibliographical materials in music; publ. *Die Anfänge des Basso continuo* (Diss., Univ. of Berlin, 1917; publ. in Leipzig, 1918; reprint, Farmborough, 1971); *Beiträge zu einer Anleitung Clavichord und Cembalo zu spielen* (Strasbourg, 1934); *Beiträge zur Musikforschung* (vol. I, Halle, 1935). He edited numerous important bibliographical surveys; also edited the works of Heinrich Schütz. He enjoyed a well-merited reputation in Germany as a thorough scholar. He was honored 3 times by Festschrifts: *Festschrift Max Schneider zum 60. Geburtstag*

(Halle, 1935); *Festschrift Max Schneider zum 80. Geburtstag* (Leipzig, 1955); *Festschrift Max Schneider zum 85. Geburtstag* (Leipzig, 1960).

Schneider, Theodor, German cellist and conductor, son of **Friedrich Schneider;** b. Dessau, May 14, 1827; d. Zittau, June 15, 1909. He studied with his father, and with Drechsler (cello); in 1845 was cellist in the Dessau Court Orch.; in 1854, cantor and choir director of the court and city churches; from 1860–96 served as cantor and music director at the Jakobikirche in Chemnitz; was also conductor of the Singakademie and of a Männergesangverein, which he founded in 1870. He retired in 1898.

Schneiderhan, Wolfgang (Eduard), Austrian violin virtuoso and pedagogue; b. Vienna, May 28, 1915. He studied violin mainly in Prague, with Ševčik and Pisek. Returning to Vienna, he became concertmaster of the Vienna Symph., then of the Vienna State Orch., and finally of the Vienna Phil. (1938–49). From 1938–50 he was a prof. of violin at the Vienna State Academy. From 1938–51 he led the Schneiderhan Quartet; from 1949–60 he also was a member of a trio, with the eminent pianist Edwin Fischer and the cellist Enrico Mainardi. In 1956 he and the Swiss violinist and conductor Rudolf Baumgartner founded in Lucerne the Festival Strings. These activities as a chamber music player never detracted from Schneiderhan's virtuoso career as a concert violinist. He was married to the German soprano **Irmgard Seefried.**

Schnittke, Alfred, Russian composer of avant-garde tendencies; b. (of German origin) Engels, in the German Volga Republic, near Saratov, Nov. 24, 1934. He had his first piano lessons in Vienna (1946–48), where his father was stationed as a correspondent of a German-language Soviet newspaper. Returning to Moscow, he studied composition with Golubev and instrumentation with Rakov at the Moscow Cons. (1953–58); in 1961 was appointed to its faculty. After writing in a conventional manner, he became acutely interested in the new Western techniques, particularly in serialism and "sonorism," in which dynamic gradations assume thematic significance; soon he became known as one of the boldest experimenters in modernistic composition in Soviet Russia.

WORKS: FOR ORCH.: 4 symphs.: No. 1 (1972); No. 2, *St. Florian,* with Chorus (London, April 23, 1980); No. 3 (Leipzig, Nov. 5, 1981); No. 4 (Moscow, April 12, 1984); 4 violin concertos: No. 1 (1957); No. 2 (1966); No. 3 (1978; Moscow, Jan. 29, 1979); No. 4 (1982; West Berlin, Sept. 11, 1984); Piano Concerto (1960); Concerto for Piano and String Orch. (Leningrad, Dec. 9, 1979); *Poem about Cosmos* (1961); *Music* for Piano and Chamber Orch. (1964); *... pianissimo ...* (Donaueschingen, Oct. 19, 1969); Concerto for Oboe, Harp, and String Orch. (1977); Concerto Grosso No. 1 for 2 Violins, Piano, Harpsichord, and Strings (1977), and No. 2 for Violin, Cello, and Orch., for the centennial of the West Berlin Phil. Orch. (1982); *Passacaglia* (1979–80). CHAMBER MUSIC: 2 Violin

Sonatas (1963, 1968); *Dialogues* for Cello and 7 Instrumentalists (1965); 3 string quartets (1966, 1981, 1984); *Serenade for 5 Musicians* for Clarinet, Violin, Double Bass, Percussion, and Piano (1968); *Canon in memoriam Igor Stravinsky* for String Quartet (1971); *Hymnus I* for Cello, Piano, and Percussion (1974), *II* for Cello and Double Bass (1974), and *III* for Violin, Recorder, Celesta, and Bells (1974); *Praeludium in memoriam Dmitri Shostakovich* for Violin and Tape (1975); Piano Quintet (1976; also for Orch., Moscow, Dec. 29, 1979); *Suite in the Old Style* for Violin and Piano (1977); Cello Sonata (1978); *Lebenslauf* for 4 Metronomes, Piano, and Percussion (1982); *Moz-Art* for 2 Violins (1983). FOR CHORUS: 2 oratorios: *Nagasaki* (1958) and *Songs of War and Peace*, with thematic materials from contemporary Russian folk songs (1959); *3 Poems* for Mezzo-soprano and Piano (1965); *Der gelbe Klang*, scenic composition after the poetic drama by the abstract painter Wassily Kandinsky, for 9 Instruments, Tape, Chorus, Pantomime, and Light Projection (1973); *Requiem* for Chorus, Organ, Piano, Electric Bass, Electric Guitar, Brass, Percussion, and Celesta (1975; Budapest, Oct. 8, 1977); *3 Madrigals* for Soprano, Violin, Viola, Double Bass, Harpsichord, and Vibraphone (Moscow, Nov. 11, 1980); *Minnesang* for 48 Voices a cappella (1981); *Seid nüchtern und wachet . . .* , based on the version of the Faust legend publ. in 1587 under the title *Historia von Doktor Johann Fausten*, commissioned by the Vienna Choral Academy on the occasion of its 125th anniversary (Vienna, June 19, 1983; first Moscow perf., Oct. 23, 1983); also, *Variations on a Chord* for Piano (1966); an electronic *Study* (1969).

Schnorr von Carolsfeld, Ludwig, German tenor; b. Munich, July 2, 1836; d. Dresden, July 21, 1865. He was the son of the noted painter; he studied with J. Otto in Dresden, and at the Leipzig Cons.; then he was a pupil of Eduard Devrient at Karlsruhe, where he made his debut, followed by an engagement in 1858. From 1860 he was the leading tenor at Dresden. He created the role of Tristan in Wagner's *Tristan und Isolde* at Munich, June 10, 1865 (his wife, **Malwine Schnorr von Carolsfeld,** singing Isolde). He died shortly afterward, of heart failure, at the age of 29.

Schnorr von Carolsfeld (née **Garrigues**), **Malwine,** soprano, wife of **Ludwig Schnorr von Carolsfeld;** b. Copenhagen, Dec. 7, 1825; d. Karlsruhe, Feb. 8, 1904. She created Isolde on June 10, 1865, in Munich, her husband singing Tristan; after his death she sang in Hamburg, and later in Karlsruhe; after her retirement from the stage she taught. In 1867 she publ. a vol. of poems by her husband and herself.

Schobert, Johann, important composer; b. probably in Silesia, c.1740; d. Paris, Aug. 28, 1767 (with his entire family, except one child, from eating poisonous mushrooms). From 1760, he was chamber musician to the Prince de Conti in Paris. His works show the general characteristics of the Mannheim School, although it cannot be proved that he ever

was in that city. The slow movement of Mozart's Clavier Concerto, K. 39, is based on music by Schobert.

Schoeck, Othmar, eminent Swiss composer and conductor; b. Brunnen, Sept. 1, 1886; d. Zürich, March 8, 1957. He was the son of a painter; studied at the Zürich Cons. with Nägeli and Freund; later, with Reger in Leipzig; from 1909 to 1915, conducted the men's chorus "Aussersihl" in Zürich; from 1917 to 1944 led the symph. concerts at St. Gall. Schoeck is acknowledged as a foremost song composer of Switzerland.

WORKS: Operas: *Don Ranudo de Colibrados* (Zürich, April 16, 1919); *Das Wandbild*, pantomime (libretto by Busoni; Halle, Jan. 2, 1921); *Venus* (Zürich, May 10, 1922); *Penthesilea* (Dresden, Jan. 8, 1927); *Massimilla Doni* (Dresden, March 2, 1937); *Das Schloss Dürande* (Berlin, April 1, 1943). For Orch.: Violin Concerto (1911–12); Cello Concerto (1947); Horn Concerto (1951); *Festlicher Hymnus* (1950); etc. Chamber music: 2 string quartets; 2 violin sonatas; etc. Song cycles: Op. 36, *Elégie* for Voice and Chamber Orch. (1924); op. 38, *Gaselen* for Voice and Chamber Orch.; op. 40, *Lebendig begraben* for Bass and Large Orch (1927); op. 45, *Wanderung im Gebirge* for Voice and Piano (1930); op. 47, *Notturno* for Bass and String Quartet; over 120 songs. A thematic index of his works was publ. by W. Vogel (Zürich, 1956).

Schoenberg (Schönberg), Arnold (Franz Walter), great Austrian-American composer whose new method of musical organization in 12 different tones related only to one another profoundly influenced the entire development of modern techniques of composition; b. Vienna, Sept. 13, 1874; d. Los Angeles, July 13, 1951. He studied at the Realschule in Vienna; learned to play the cello, and also became proficient on the violin. His father died when Schoenberg was 16; he took a job as a bank clerk to earn a living; an additional source of income was arranging popular songs and orchestrating operetta scores. Schoenberg's first original work was a group of 3 piano pieces which he wrote in 1894; it was also about that time that he began to take lessons in counterpoint from Alexander Zemlinsky, whose sister he married in 1901. He also played cello in Zemlinsky's instrumental group, Polyhymnia. In 1897 Schoenberg wrote his first String Quartet, in D major, which achieved public performance in Vienna on March 17, 1898. About the same time he wrote 2 songs with piano accompaniment which he designated as op. 1. In 1899 he wrote his first true masterpiece, *Verklärte Nacht*, set for string sextet, which was first performed in Vienna by the Rosé Quartet and members of the Vienna Phil., on March 18, 1902. It is a fine work, deeply imbued with the spirit of Romantic poetry, with its harmonic idiom stemming from Wagner's modulatory procedures; it remains Schoenberg's most frequently performed composition. About 1900, Schoenberg was engaged as conductor of several amateur choral groups in Vienna and its suburbs; this increased his interest in vocal music. He then began work on a choral composition, *Gurre-Lieder*, of monumental proportions, to the translated text of a poem by the Danish writer Jens Peter Jacobsen. For grandeur and opulence of orchestral sonority, it surpassed even the most formidable creations of Mahler or Richard Strauss; it calls for 5 solo voices, a speaker, 3 male choruses, an 8-part mixed chorus, and a very large orch. Special music paper of 48 staves had to be ordered for the MS. Schoenberg completed the first 2 parts of *Gurre-Lieder* in the spring of 1901, but the composition of the remaining section was delayed by 10 years; it was not until Feb. 23, 1913, that Franz Schreker was able to arrange its complete performance with the Vienna Phil. and its choral forces.

In 1901 Schoenberg moved to Berlin, where he joined E. von Wolzogen, F. Wedekind, and O. Bierbaum in launching an artistic cabaret, which they called Überbrettl. Schoenberg himself composed a theme song for it with trumpet obbligato, and conducted several shows. He met Richard Strauss, who helped him to obtain the Liszt Stipendium and a position as a teacher at the Stern Cons. Schoenberg returned to Vienna in 1903 and formed friendly relations with Gustav Mahler, who became a sincere supporter of Schoenberg's activities; Mahler's power in Vienna was then at its height, and he was able to help Schoenberg in his career as a composer. In March 1904 Schoenberg organized with Alexander Zemlinsky the Vereinigung Schaffender Tonkünstler for the purpose of encouraging performances of new music. Under its auspices Schoenberg conducted on Jan. 26, 1905, the first performance of his symph. poem *Pelleas und Melisande;* in this score occurs the first use of a trombone glissando. There followed a performance on Feb. 8, 1907, of Schoenberg's *Kammersymphonie*, op. 9, with the participation of the Rosé Quartet and the wind instrumentalists of the Vienna Phil.; the work produced much consternation in the audience and among critics because of its departure from traditional tonal harmony, with chords built on fourths and nominal dissonances used without immediate resolution. About the same time, Schoenberg turned to painting, which became his principal avocation. In his art, as in his music, he adopted the tenets of Expressionism, that is, freedom of personal expression within a self-defined program. Schoenberg's reputation as an independent musical thinker attracted to him such progressive-minded young musicians as Alban Berg, Anton von Webern, and Egon Wellesz, who followed Schoenberg in their own development. Schoenberg's 2nd String Quartet, composed in 1908, which included a soprano solo, was his last work that carried a definite key signature, if exception is made for his *Suite* for Strings, ostentatiously marked as in G major, which he wrote for school use in America in 1934. On Feb. 19, 1909, Schoenberg completed his piano piece op. 11, no. 1, which became the first musical composition to dispense with all reference to tonality. In 1910 Schoenberg was appointed to the faculty of the Vienna Academy of Music; in 1911 he completed his important theory book *Harmonielehre*, dedicated to the mem-

ory of Mahler; it comprises a traditional exposition of chords and progressions, but also offers illuminating indications of possible new musical developments, including fractional tones and melodies formed by the change of timbre on the same note. In 1911 he went again to Berlin, where he became an instructor at the Stern Cons. and also taught composition privately. In 1912 he brought out a work that attracted a great deal of attention: *5 Orchesterstücke*, which was performed for the first time not in Germany, not in Austria, but in London, under the direction of Sir Henry Wood, who conducted it there on Sept. 3, 1912; the critical reception was that of incomprehension, with a considerable measure of curiosity. The score was indeed revolutionary in nature, each movement representing an experiment in musical organization. In the same year Schoenberg produced another innovative work, a cycle of 21 songs with instrumental accompaniment, entitled *Pierrot Lunaire*, and consisting of 21 "melodramas," to German texts translated from verses by the Belgian poet Albert Giraud. Here Schoenberg made systematic use of *Sprechstimme*, with a gliding speech-song replacing precise pitch (not an entire innovation, for Engelbert Humperdinck had applied it in his incidental music to Rosmer's play *Königskinder* in 1897). The work was given, after some 40 rehearsals, in Berlin on Oct. 16, 1912, and the reaction was startling, the purblind critics drawing upon the strongest invective in their vocabulary to condemn the music.

Meanwhile, Schoenberg made appearances as conductor of his works in various European cities (Amsterdam, 1911; St. Petersburg, 1912; London, 1914). During World War I he was sporadically enlisted in military service; after the Armistice he settled in Mödling, near Vienna. Discouraged by his inability to secure performances for himself and his associates in the new music movement, he organized in Vienna, in Nov. 1918, the Verein für Musikalische Privataufführungen (Society for Private Musical Performances), from which critics were demonstratively excluded, and which ruled out any vocal expression of approval or disapproval. The organization disbanded in 1922. About that time Schoenberg began work on his *Suite* for Piano, op. 25, which was to be the first true 12-tone piece consciously composed in that idiom. In 1925 he was appointed prof. of a master class at the Prussian Academy of Arts in Berlin. With the advent of the beastly Nazi regime, the German Ministry of Education dismissed him from his post as a Jew. As a matter of record, Schoenberg had abandoned his Jewish faith in Vienna on March 21, 1898, and in a spirit of political accommodation converted to Catholicism, which was the principal faith in Austria; 35 years later, horrified by the hideous persecution of Jews at the hands of the Nazis, he was moved to return to his ancestral faith and was reconverted to Judaism in Paris on July 24, 1933. With the rebirth of his hereditary consciousness, he turned to specific Jewish themes in works such as *Survivor from Warsaw* and *Moses und Aron*. Although Schoenberg was well known in the musical

Schoenberg

world, he had difficulty obtaining a teaching position; he finally accepted the invitation of Joseph Malkin, founder of the Malkin Cons. of Boston, to join its faculty. He arrived in the U.S. on Oct. 31, 1933. After teaching in Boston for a season, he moved to Hollywood. In 1935 he became a prof. of music at the Univ. of Southern Calif., and in 1936 accepted a similar position at the Univ. of Calif. in Los Angeles, where he taught until 1944, when he reached the mandatory retirement age of 70. He experienced considerable financial difficulties and applied for a Guggenheim fellowship but, incredibly, was turned down. On April 11, 1941, he became an American citizen. In 1947 he received the Award of Merit for Distinguished Achievements from the National Inst. of Arts and Letters. In the U.S. he changed the original spelling of his name from Schönberg to Schoenberg.

In 1924 Schoenberg's creative evolution reached the all-important point at which he found it necessary to establish a new governing principle of tonal relationship, which he called the "method of composing with 12 different notes related entirely to one another." This method was adumbrated in Schoenberg's music as early as 1914 and is used partially in his 5 *Klavierstücke*, op. 23, and in his *Serenade*, op. 24; it was employed for the first time in its integral form in the piano *Suite*, op. 25 (1924); in it, the thematic material is based on a group of 12 different notes arrayed in a certain pre-arranged order; such a tone row was henceforth Schoenberg's mainspring of thematic invention; development was provided by the devices of inversion, retrograde, and retrograde inversion of the basic series; allowing for transposition, 48 forms were obtainable in all, with counterpoint and harmony, as well as melody, derived from the basic tone row. Immediate repetition of thematic notes was admitted; the realm of rhythm remained free. As with most historic innovations, the 12-tone technique was not the creation of Schoenberg alone but was, rather, a logical development of many currents of musical thought. Josef Matthias Hauer rather unconvincingly claimed priority in laying the foundations of the 12-tone method; among others who had elaborated similar ideas at about the same time with Schoenberg was Jef Bolyscheff, a Russian émigré who expounded his theory in a publication entitled "12 Tondauer-Musik." Instances of themes consisting of 12 different notes are found in the *Faust Symphony* of Liszt and in the tone poem *Also sprach Zarathustra* of Richard Strauss in the section on Science. Schoenberg's great achievement was the establishment of the basic 12-tone row and its changing forms as foundations of a new musical language; using this idiom, he was able to write music of great expressive power. In general usage, the 12-tone method is often termed "dodecaphony," from Greek *dodeca*, "12," and *phone*, "sound." The tonal composition of the basic row is devoid of tonality; an analysis of Schoenberg's works shows that he avoided using major triads in any of their inversions, and allowed the use of only the 2nd inversion of a minor triad. Schoenberg deprecated the term "atonality" that was commonly applied to his mu-

sic. He suggested, only half in jest, the term "atonicality," i.e., absence of the dominating tonic. The most explicit work of Schoenberg couched in the 12-tone idiom was his *Klavierstück*, op. 33a, written in 1928–29, which exemplifies the clearest use of the tone row in chordal combinations. Other works that present a classical use of dodecaphony are *Begleitungsmusik zu einer Lichtspielszene*, op. 34 (1929–30); Violin Concerto (1934–36); and Piano Concerto (1942). Schoenberg's disciples Alban Berg and Anton von Webern followed his 12-tone method in general outlines but with some personal deviations; thus, Berg accepted the occasional use of triadic harmonies, and Webern built tone rows in symmetric groups. Other composers who made systematic use of the 12-tone method were Egon Wellesz, Ernst Krenek, René Leibowitz, Roberto Gerhard, Humphrey Searle, and Luigi Dallapiccola. As time went on, dodecaphony became a lingua franca of universal currency; even in Russia, where Schoenberg's theories were for many years unacceptable on ideological grounds, several composers, including Shostakovich in his last works, made using of 12-tone themes, albeit without integral development. Ernest Bloch used 12-tone subjects in his last string quartets, but he refrained from applying inversions and retrograde forms of his tone rows. Stravinsky, in his old age, turned to the 12-tone method of composition in its total form, with regrograde, inversion, and retrograde inversion; his conversion was the greatest artistic vindication for Schoenberg, who regarded Stravinsky as his most powerful antagonist, but Schoenberg was dead when Stravinsky saw the light of dodecaphony.

Schoenberg's personality was both heroic and egocentric; he made great sacrifices to sustain his artistic convictions, but he was also capable of engaging in bitter polemics when he felt that his integrity was under attack. He strongly opposed the claims of Hauer and others for the priority of the 12-tone method of composition, and he vehemently criticized in the public press the implication he saw in Thomas Mann's novel *Doktor Faustus*, in which the protagonist was described as the inventor of the 12-tone method of composition; future historians, Schoenberg argued, might confuse fiction with facts, and credit the figment of Mann's imagination with Schoenberg's own discovery. He was also subject to superstition in the form of triskaidecaphobia, the fear of the number 13; he seriously believed that there was something fateful in the circumstance of his birth on the 13th of the month. Noticing that the title of his work *Moses und Aaron* contained 13 letters, he crossed out the 2nd "a" in Aaron to make it 12. When he turned 76 and someone remarked facetiously that the sum of the digits of his age was 13, he seemed genuinely upset, and during his last illness in July 1951 he expressed his fear of not surviving July 13; indeed, he died on that date. Schoenberg placed his MSS in the Music Division of the Library of Congress in Washington, D.C.; the remaining materials were deposited after his death at the Schoenberg Inst. at the Univ. of Southern Calif. in Los Angeles. Schoenberg's centennial in 1974 was commemorated worldwide. A *Journal of the Schoenberg Institute* began publication in 1976, under the editorship of Leonard Stein.

WORKS: FOR THE STAGE: *Erwartung*, monodrama, op. 17 (1909; Prague, June 6, 1924, Zemlinsky conducting); *Die glückliche Hand*, drama with music, to Schoenberg's own libretto, op. 18 (1910–13; Vienna, Oct. 14, 1924, Stiedry conducting); *Von Heute auf Morgen*, opera in one act, op. 32 (1928–29; Frankfurt, Feb. 1, 1930, W. Steinberg conducting); *Moses und Aron*, biblical drama, to Schoenberg's own libretto (2 acts composed 1930–32; 3rd act begun in 1951, but not completed; radio perf. of Acts 1 and 2, Hamburg, March 12, 1954; stage perf., Zürich Festival of the International Society for Contemporary Music, June 6, 1957, Rosbaud conducting).

FOR ORCH.: *Pelleas und Melisande*, symph. poem after Maeterlinck, op. 5 (1902–3; Vienna, Jan. 26, 1905, Schoenberg conducting); *Kammersymphonie No. 1*, for 15 Instruments, op. 9 (1906; Vienna, Feb. 8, 1907; arranged for Orch., 1922; new version for Orch., op. 9b, 1935); *5 Orchester-Stücke*, op. 16 (1909; London, Sept. 3, 1912, Henry Wood conducting; revised 1922 and 1949); *3 Little Pieces* for Chamber Orch. (1911; Berlin, Oct. 10, 1957); *Variations*, op. 31 (1926–28; Berlin, Dec. 2, 1928, Furtwängler conducting); *Begleitungsmusik zu einer Lichtspielszene (Accompaniment to a Cinema Scene)*, op. 34 (1929–30; Berlin, Nov. 6, 1930, Klemperer conducting); Suite in G major for Strings (1934; Los Angeles, May 18, 1935, Klemperer conducting); Violin Concerto, op. 36 (1934–36; Philadelphia, Dec. 6, 1940; Krasner, violinist; Stokowski conducting); 2nd Chamber Symph., op. 38a (1906–16 and 1939; N.Y., Dec. 15, 1940, Stiedry conducting; op. 38b is an arrangement for 2 Pianos, 1941–42); Piano Concerto, op. 42 (1942; N.Y., Feb. 6, 1944, Steuermann, pianist; Stokowski conducting); *Theme and Variations* for Wind Band, op. 43a (1943; arranged for Orch., op. 43b, Boston, Oct. 20, 1944, Koussevitzky conducting).

FOR CHORUS: *Gurre-Lieder* for Soli, Mixed Chorus, and Orch. (1900–3 and 1910–11; Vienna, Feb. 23, 1913, Schreker conducting); *Friede auf Erden*, op. 13 (1907); 4 pieces for Mixed Chorus, op. 27 (1925); *3 Satires*, op. 28 (1925); 3 German folk songs (Vienna, Nov. 1929); 6 pieces for Men's Chorus, op. 35 (1929–30); *Kol Nidre* for Speaker, Chorus, and Orch., op. 39 (Los Angeles, Oct. 4, 1938); *A Survivor from Warsaw* for Narrator, Chorus, and Orch., op. 46 (1947; Albuquerque, Nov. 4, 1948); 3 German folk songs for Chorus a cappella, op. 49 (1948); *Dreimal tausend Jahre* for Mixed Chorus a cappella, op. 50a (Fylkingen, Sweden, Oct. 29, 1949); *De Profundis* for Chorus a cappella, to a Hebrew text, op. 50b (1950; Cologne, Jan. 29, 1954). The oratorio *Die Jakobsleiter*, begun in 1917, was left unfinished; a performing version was prepared by Winfried Zillig, and given for the first time in Vienna on June 16, 1961.

CHAMBER MUSIC: String Quartet in D major (perf. in Vienna in 1897, but not heard again until it was revived at the Library of Congress in Washington, D.C., on Feb. 8, 1952); *Verklärte Nacht (Transfigured Night)*, sextet for Strings, op. 4 (1899; Vienna, March 18, 1902; arranged for String Orch., 1917; revised 1943); String Quartet No. 1, in D minor, op. 7 (1904–5; Vienna, Feb. 5, 1907); String Quartet No. 2, in F-sharp minor, op. 10, with Voice (1907–8; Vienna, Dec. 1908); Serenade for Clarinet, Bass Clarinet, Mandolin, Guitar, Violin, Viola, and Cello, op. 24 (4th movement with a sonnet by Petrarch for Baritone; 1920–23; Donaueschingen, July 20, 1924); Quintet for Flute, Oboe, Clarinet, Horn, and Bassoon, op. 26 (1923–24; Vienna, Sept. 13, 1924); Suite for 2 Clarinets, Bass Clarinet, Violin, Viola, Cello, and Piano, op. 29 (1925–26; Paris, Dec. 15, 1927); String Quartet No. 3, op. 30 (Vienna, Sept. 19, 1927); String Quartet No. 4, op. 37 (1936; Los Angeles, Jan. 9, 1937); *Ode to Napoleon*, after Byron, for String Quartet, Piano, and Reciter (1942; also in version with String Orch., N.Y., Nov. 23, 1944); String Trio, op. 45 (1946; Cambridge, Mass., March 1947); *Phantasy* for Violin, with Piano Accompaniment (Los Angeles, Sept. 13, 1949).

SONGS: 2 songs, op. 1 (1898); 4 songs, op. 2 (1899); 6 songs, op. 3 (1899–1903); 8 songs, op. 6 (1903–5); 6 songs, op. 8 (with Orch.; 1903–5); 2 ballads, op. 12 (1907); 2 songs, op. 14 (1907–8); cycle of 15 poems from Stefan George's *Das Buch der hängenden Gärten* (1908–9; Vienna, Jan. 14, 1910); *Herzgewächse*, after Maeterlinck, for Soprano, with Celesta, Harmonium, and Harp, op. 20 (1911); *Pierrot Lunaire*, 21 poems by Albert Giraud, for Sprechstimme with Piano, Flute (interchangeable with Piccolo), Clarinet (interchangeable with Bass Clarinet), Violin (interchangeable with Viola), and Cello, op. 21 (Berlin, Oct. 16, 1912); 4 songs, op. 22 (with Orch.; 1913–16; Frankfurt, Feb. 21, 1932); 3 songs, op. 48 (1933).

FOR KEYBOARD: Piano: *3 Klavierstücke*, op. 11 (1909; revised 1924); *6 kleine Klavierstücke*, op. 19 (1911); *5 Klavierstücke*, op. 23 (1920–23); *Suite*, op. 25 (1921–23); *Klavierstück*, op. 33a (1928–29); *Klavierstück*, op. 33b (1931); organ: *Variations on a Recitative*, op. 40 (1941).

ARRANGEMENTS AND TRANSCRIPTIONS: 2 chorale preludes by Bach, for Large Orch.: No. 1, *Komm, Gott, Schöpfer, Heiliger Geist*, and No. 2, *Schmücke dich, O liebe Seele* (1922); *Prelude and Fugue* in E-flat major for Organ by Bach, for Large Orch. (1928); Piano Quartet No. 1, in G minor, op. 25, by Brahms, for Orch. (1937); also a Cello Concerto, transcribed from a Harpsichord Concerto by G.M. Monn (1932–33); Concerto for String Quartet and Orch. after Handel's Concerto Grosso, op. 6, No. 7 (1933); etc.

WRITINGS: *Harmonielehre* (Vienna, 1911,; 3rd ed., revised, 1922; abridged Eng. trans. as *Theory of Harmony*, N.Y., 1947; complete Eng. trans., 1978); *Models for Beginners in Composition* (N.Y., 1942; 3rd ed., revised, 1972, by L. Stein); *Style and Idea* (N.Y., 1950; enlarged ed. by L. Stein, London, 1975); *Structural Functions of Harmony* (N.Y., 1954; 2nd ed., revised, 1969, by L. Stein); *Preliminary Exercises in Counterpoint*, ed. by L. Stein (London, 1963); *Fundamentals of Musical Composition*, ed. by L. Stein (London, 1967); also numerous essays in German and American publications.

Scholes, Percy Alfred, eminent English writer on music; b. Leeds, July 24, 1877; d. Vevey, Switzerland, July 31, 1958. (He pronounced his name "Skoles.")

He took his B.Mus. at Oxford in 1908, and later the M.A., D.Litt., and Hon.D.Mus., as also the Hon.Litt.D., at Leeds; received his doctorat ès lettres from the Univ. of Lausanne (1934); was an organist at various churches until 1905; was an extension lecturer at the univs. of Oxford, Cambridge, London, and Manchester; in 1908 founded the Home Music Study Union, and until 1921 edited its publications, the *Music Student* and *Music and Youth;* toured the U.S. as a lecturer in 1915 and on 4 later occasions; was music critic of the *London Evening Standard* and the *Observer* (1920–27), and for the BBC (1923–29); from 1925–30 edited the Audiographic Series of Pianola and Duo Art Rolls; in 1928 organized the Anglo-American Music Education Conferences (Lausanne, 1931, 1933); was music editor of *Radio Times* (1932–36); lived in Oxford, and for periods in Switzerland, where he later settled permanently. A writer of great literary attainments and stylistic grace, he succeeded in presenting music "appreciation" in a manner informative and stimulating to the layman and professional alike. His *Oxford Companion to Music* was unique in the lexicographical field in its vividness of presentation and its comprehensiveness. His scholarly biographies of Burney and Hawkins are among the finest of the genre.

Schönbach, Dieter, German composer of the avant-garde; b. Stolp-Pommern, Feb. 18, 1931. He studied at the Freiburg Hochschule für Musik with Wolfgang Fortner; in 1959 he was appointed music director at the municipal theater in Bochum; he left Bochum in 1973. His style of composition is quaquaversal. He wrote the first genuine multimedia opera, *Wenn die Kälte in die Hütten tritt, um sich bei den Frierenden zu wärmen, weiss einer "Die Geschichte von einem Feuer"* (Kiel, 1968); a multimedia show, *Hymnus 2* (Munich, 1972); *Farben und Klänge,* in memory of Kandinsky, for Orch. (1958); Piano Concerto (1958); *Kammermusik* for 14 Instruments (1964); *Hoquetus* for 8 Wind Instruments (1964); 4 chamber music pieces, each titled *Canzona da sonar* (1966–67); *Atemmusik* for Fifes, Whistles, and some other "breath" Instruments (1969); also several liturgical cantatas to Latin texts. His *Canticum Psalmi Resurrectionis* was performed at the International Festival of Contemporary Music in Rome on June 13, 1959.

Schönberg, Arnold. See **Schoenberg, Arnold.**

Schonberg, Harold C., American music critic; b. New York, Nov. 29, 1915. He studied at Brooklyn College (B.A., 1937) and at N.Y. Univ. (M.A., 1938). He served in the army (1942–46); then was on the staff of the *N.Y. Sun* (1946–50); he was appointed to the music staff of the *N.Y. Times* in 1950; was senior music critic from 1960 until 1980. In 1971 he received the Pulitzer Prize "for distinguished criticism." In his concert reviews and feature articles he reveals a profound knowledge of music and displays a fine journalistic flair without assuming a posture of snobbish aloofness or descending to colloquial vulgarity. His intellectual horizon is exceptionally wide; he is well-versed in art, and can draw and paint; is a chess aficionado and covered knowledgeably the Spassky-Fischer match in Reykjavik in 1972 for the *N.Y. Times.* He publ. *Chamber and Solo Instrument Music* (N.Y., 1955); *The Collector's Chopin and Schumann* (N.Y., 1959); *The Great Pianists* (N.Y., 1963); *The Great Conductors* (N.Y., 1967); *Lives of the Great Composers* (N.Y., 1970; 2nd ed., N.Y., 1981); *Facing the Music* (N.Y., 1981).

Schopenhauer, Arthur, great German philosopher; b. Danzig, Feb. 22, 1788; d. Frankfurt, Sept. 21, 1860. Although his excursions into the realm of music are neither remarkable nor very valuable, they are stimulating, and have inspired a number of valuable contributions by modern investigators, especially in the field of musical esthetics. Wagner was influenced to a considerable extent by Schopenhauer's philosophical system.

Schott, Bernhard, the founder of the German music publishing firm **B. Schotts Söhne;** b. Eltville, Aug. 10, 1748; d. Sandhof, near Heidesheim, April 26, 1809. His firm was founded in 1770; after his death the business was carried on by his sons **Johann Andreas Schott** (1781–1840) and **Johann Joseph Schott** (1782–1855) under the firm name of B. Schotts Söhne. The 2 sons of Johann Andreas Schott, **Franz Philip Schott** (b. July 30, 1811; d. May 8, 1874) and **Peter Schott** (d. Paris, Sept. 20, 1894), succeeded to the business; Peter Schott was manager of the Paris and Brussels branches; subsequently **Peter Schott, Jr.,** took over the directorship, together with Ludwig Strecker and Franz von Landwehr. B. Schotts Söhne publ. the journals *Cäcilia* (1824–48), *Süddeutsche Musikzeitung* (1852–69), and *Melos* (1920–34 and from 1946). Dr. Ludwig Strecker, son of the director of the same name (d. in 1978), and Heinz Schneider Schott, Dr. Strecker's son-in-law, became the directors (1952). Arno Volk was chairman of the board of directors in 1974–77. The main office is at Mainz, and a principal branch is at London. (Schott Frères at Brussels is now an entirely different firm.) The Schott catalogue is one of the richest in the world; it includes works by Beethoven (last quartets, 9th Symph.), operas by Donizetti, Rossini, etc.; Wagner's *Meistersinger, Ring des Nibelungen,* and *Parsifal;* virtually all works by Hindemith, and a great number of other contemporary works. Schott is the publisher of the Riemann Musik-Lexikon.

Schrade, Leo, eminent German musicologist; b. Allenstein, Dec. 13, 1903; d. Spéracédès (Alpes-Maritimes), Sept. 21, 1964. He studied with Hermann Halbig at the Univ. of Heidelberg (1923–27), with Adolf Sandberger at the Univ. of Munich, and with Theodor Kroyer at the Univ. of Leipzig, obtaining his Dr.Phil. in 1927 with the dissertation *Die ältesten Denkmäler der Orgelmusik* (publ. in Münster, 1928); held teaching positions in music at the Univ. of Königsberg (1928–32), then at the Univ. of Bonn (from 1932). In 1937 he emigrated to the U.S.; was on the faculty of Yale Univ. (1938–58), where he taught music history; in 1958 he was appointed to the music faculty of the Univ. of Basel. During the academic season 1962–63 he was Charles Eliot Norton Lecturer at Harvard; his lectures were publ. under the title *Tragedy in the Art of Music* (Cambridge, Mass., 1964). He publ. a number of books and articles of prime documentary value, promulgating some important musico-historical theories.

Schreier, Peter, noted German tenor; b. Meissen, July 29, 1935. He studied at the Hochschule für Musik in Dresden (1956–59). In 1961 he was engaged at the Dresden State Opera, and in 1963 joined the State Opera of Berlin. He then appeared at the Vienna State Opera, the Salzburg Festival, La Scala in Milan, the Teatro Colón in Buenos Aires, and the Metropolitan Opera in N.Y. He also sang in oratorios and in lieder recitals. He further became a choral conductor, and brought out on records several works by Bach, including the B-minor Mass, and by Mozart.

Schreker, Franz, eminent composer and teacher; b. Monaco, March 23, 1878; d. Berlin, March 21, 1934. He spent his early childhood in Monaco, where his father, a native of Austria, was court photographer. He was 10 when his father died and the family moved to Vienna; there he studied violin with Rosé and theory with Robert Fuchs. In 1908 he organized the Vienna Phil. Chorus and conducted many new works with it. In 1912 he was appointed prof. of composition at the Akademie der Tonkunst. In 1920 he went to Berlin, where he was director of the Hochschule für Musik (until 1932); there he had many talented pupils who later became well-known composers (Krenek, Rathaus, Alois Hába, and others). In 1932 he became prof. of a class for advanced students at the Prussian Academy of Arts, but lost this post with the advent of the Nazi regime (1933), when he was forced to resign; he died a year later. As a composer, he led the neo-Romantic movement in the direction of Expressionism, emphasizing psychological conflicts in his operas; in his harmonies he expanded the basically Wagnerian sonorities to include many devices associated with Impressionism. He exercised considerable influence on the German and Viennese schools of his time, but with the change of direction in modern music toward economy of means and away from mystical and psychological trends, Schreker's music suffered a decline after his death. However, a retrospective of his works was the focal point of the 1976 annual Styrian Autumn Festival held in Graz, Austria; and in 1978 his last unperformed opera, *Christophorus,* was finally premiered.

WORKS: FOR THE STAGE: 9 operas (all to his own librettos, except for *Flammen*): *Flammen* (1901; piano reduction, Vienna, 1902); *Der ferne Klang* (*The Distant Sound;* 1901–10; Frankfurt, Aug. 18, 1912); *Das Spielwerk und die Prinzessin* (*The Chime Box and the Princess;* 1909–12; Frankfurt and Vienna, March 15, 1913; revised 1916; produced as a mystery play, *Das Spielwerk,* Munich, Oct. 30, 1920); *Die Gezeichneten* (*The Stigmatized;* 1913–15;

Frankfurt, April 25, 1918); *Der Schatzgräber* (*The Treasure Digger;* 1915–18; Frankfurt, Jan. 21, 1920); *Irrelohe* (1919–24; Cologne, March 27, 1924); *Der singende Teufel* (*The Singing Devil;* 1924–28; Berlin, Dec. 10, 1928); *Christophorus* (1925–29; Freiburg, Oct. 1, 1978; original premiere, set for Freiburg in 1933, canceled by the Nazis); *Der Schmied von Gent* (*The Blacksmith of Ghent;* 1929–32; Berlin, Oct. 29, 1932). Ballet: *Der Geburtstag der Infantin,* after Oscar Wilde, for String Orch. (Vienna, 1908; revised for Full Orch. in 1923 and retitled *Spanisches Fest*); *Ein Tanzspiel* (1908; orchestrated 1920; also known as *Rokoko* and *4 Pieces in the Old Style*). Pantomime: *Der Wind* for Violin, Viola, Cello, Clarinet, and Piano (1908). FOR ORCH.: *Andante* for Strings (1896); *Ekkehard,* overture for Orch. and Organ (1901–2); *Romantische Suite,* a "Nachtspiel" (1902); *Phantastische Ouvertüre* (1902); *Vorspiel zu einem Drama* (1913; used as a prelude to his opera *Die Gezeichneten*); *Kammersymphonie* for 23 Solo Instruments (1916; Vienna, March 12, 1917); *Kleine Suite* for Small Orch. (Breslau, Jan. 17, 1929); *Vorspiel zu einer grossen Oper* (1933; Baden-Baden, March 11, 1958; symph. fragments from an uncompleted opera, *Memnon*). FOR VOICE: *Psalm 116* for Female Chorus, Orch., and Organ (1896); *Der Holdstein* for Soloists, Chorus, and Orch. (1899); *Schwanengesang* for Chorus and Orch. (1902); *5 Songs,* after Ronsperger, for Middle Voice and Orch. (1909; instrumented 1920); *Vom ewigen Leben,* lyrical songs, after Whitman, for Soprano and Orch. (1924; instrumented 1929); many motets and songs. He also wrote a Violin Sonata (1897).

Schröder, Alwin, cellist, brother of **Carl** and **Hermann Schröder;** b. Neuhaldensleben, June 15, 1855; d. Boston, Oct. 17, 1928. He studied piano with his father, and violin with De Ahna; then devoted himself to the cello; became successor to his brother Carl as first cellist in the Gewandhaus Orch. in Leipzig. In 1891 he went to America; joined the Boston Symph. Orch. (until 1925). He was also for a time the cellist in the Kneisel Quartet. His publications include *Violoncello Studies, Technical Studies, New Studies in Scale-playing,* as well as collections of classical pieces adapted for cello.

Schröder, Carl, German cellist and composer, brother of **Alwin** and **Hermann Schröder;** b. Quedlinburg, Dec. 18, 1848; d. Bremen, Sept. 22, 1935. He studied with Drechsler and Kiel; in 1871 he formed a string quartet with his brothers **Hermann, Franz,** and **Alwin.** He was solo cellist in the Gewandhaus Orch. in Leipzig (1874–81); afterward held 8 successive posts as conductor in Germany and the Netherlands, finally settling in Berlin as cello teacher at the Stern Cons. (1911–24). He then retired and lived in Bremen. Among his works are 2 operas: *Aspasia* (1892) and *Asket* (1893); 2 string quartets; other chamber music. He compiled 3 pedagogical manuals: *Katechismus des Dirigierens und Taktierens* (1889); *Katechismus des Violinspiels* (1889); *Katechismus des Violoncellspiels* (1890); these were also publ. in Eng. (1893, 1895, 1896). His collections of classical works for the cello, especially *Vortragstudien* (60 pieces), are of value.

Schröder, Hermann, German violinist and composer, brother of **Carl** and **Alwin Schröder;** b. Quedlinburg, July 28, 1843; d. Berlin, Jan. 30, 1909. He studied with A. Ritter at Magdeburg; from 1885 was a teacher at the Royal Inst. for Church Music in Berlin; also had a music school of his own. He publ. *Untersuchung über die sympathischen Klänge der Geigeninstrumente* (1891); *Die symmetrische Umkehrung in der Musik* (1902); *Ton und Farbe* (1906); chamber music for instructive purposes: *6 instruktive Quartette, 3 kleine Trios,* etc.; a violin method, *Die Kunst des Violinspiels* (1887); etc.

Schröder, Jaap, distinguished Dutch violinist and pedagogue; b. Amsterdam, Dec. 31, 1925. He studied violin at the Amsterdam Cons. and in Paris; also attended classes in musicology at the Sorbonne. He then returned to the Netherlands; served as concertmaster of the Hilversum Radio Chamber Orch., and was a member of the Netherlands String Quartet. In 1975 he founded the Quartetto Esterhazy, which gave performances of music from the Classical era on period instruments; it was dissolved in 1981. He subsequently served as music director and concertmaster of the Academy of Ancient Music in London. In 1982 he was appointed visiting music director of the Smithsonian Chamber Players in Washington, D.C.

Schröder-Devrient, Wilhelmine, celebrated German soprano; b. Hamburg, Dec. 6, 1804; d. Coburg, Jan. 26, 1860. She received early training for the stage from her father, a baritone, and from her mother, Antoinette Sophie Bürger, a well-known actress; she herself played children's parts and was an actress until her 17th year. After the death of her father in 1818, she followed her mother to Vienna, where she studied with Mazatti; made her debut at the Kärnthnertortheater in Vienna on Jan. 20, 1821, as Pamina in Mozart's *Zauberflöte;* then sang Agathe in *Der Freischütz* under the direction of Weber himself (Vienna, March 7, 1822). When *Fidelio* was revived in Vienna in 1822, she sang Leonore in the presence of Beethoven. In 1823 she was engaged at the court opera in Dresden; there she married the actor Karl Devrient (divorced, 1828). She sang in Paris in 1830; then again in 1831 and 1832 with spectacular success; in the summer of 1832 she appeared in London. She returned to Germany in 1837; continued to sing in Dresden until 1847; also appeared as a concert singer, evoking praise from critics and musicians alike; Wagner expressed his admiration for her; she created the roles of Adriano Colonna in *Rienzi* (Oct. 20, 1842), Senta in *Der fliegende Holländer* (Dresden, Jan. 2, 1843), and Venus in *Tannhäuser* (Dresden, Oct. 19, 1845). She contracted 2 more marriages: to Döring (divorced) and von Bock (1850).

Schröder-Feinen, Ursula, German dramatic soprano; b. Gelsenkirchen, July 21, 1936. She studied voice with Maria Helm and at the Essen Folkwangschule. She sang in the chorus of the Gelsenkirchen Opera, made her operatic debut there in 1961, and remained on its roster until 1968; then sang with the Düsseldorf Opera. On Dec. 4, 1970, she made her first American appearance as Chrysothemis in *Elektra* at the Metropolitan Opera in N.Y.; also sang at Bayreuth, Salzburg, Milan, and Berlin. A versatile singer, her repertoire includes major dramatic roles in German and Italian opera.

Schröter, Christoph Gottlieb, German organist and music theorist; b. Hohnstein, near Schandau in Saxony, Aug. 10, 1699; d. Nordhausen, May 20, 1782. He served as a chorister in Dresden; in 1717 he went to Leipzig, where he studied theology, but turned to music when he became Lotti's copyist in Dresden; then traveled in Germany, the Netherlands, and England; returning to Saxony, he obtained the position of lecturer at Jena Univ.; then served as organist in Minden (1726–32); in 1732 he was appointed organist at Nordhausen, and he held this position for half a century until his death. He wrote mainly choral sacred music; composed 7 sets of church cantatas for the entire church year; a Passion, *Die sieben Worte Jesu,* for which he wrote the verses; also instrumental music, including overtures, concertos, and sonatas, as well as fugues and preludes for organ. He claimed priority for the invention of a hammer action for keyed string instruments, anticipating Cristofori's invention of the pianoforte; his argument is expounded with polemical passion in his paper "Umständliche Beschreibung eines neuerfundenen Clavierinstruments, auf welchem man in unterschiedenen Graden stark und schwach spielen kann," which was publ. in 1763 in Marpurg's *Kritische Briefe;* however, music historians rejected his arguments as choronologically invalid. In the field of music theory he publ. an important paper, *Deutliche Anweisung zum Generalbass in beständiger Veränderung des uns angebohrnen harmonischen Dreyklanges* (1772), in which he expounds the thesis that the major and minor triads are the sole fundamental chords in harmony; he also publ. *Letzte Beschäftigung mit musikalischen Dingen; Nebst sechs Temperatur-Planen und einer Notentafel* (1782) and some other theoretical articles in an egotistically assertive vein.

Schröter, Corona (Elisabeth Wilhelmine), celebrated German soprano; b. Guben, Jan. 14, 1751; d. Ilmenau, Aug. 23, 1802. She was trained in music by her father, **Johann Friedrich Schröter,** who was an oboe player. She continued her studies with Hiller in Leipzig. In 1765 she appeared in a "grand concert" in Leipzig and was engaged there until 1771. On Nov. 23, 1776, she sang at the court of Weimar, and was appointed Kammersängerin to the Dowager Duchess of Weimar. She was also active on the dramatic stage. Goethe esteemed her highly as an actress. She composed some songs, publ. in 2 vols. (1786 and 1794), among them the first setting of Goethe's *Erlkönig.*

Schröter, Johann Samuel, pianist and composer, brother of **Corona Schröter;** b. Guben(?), between 1750 and 1753; d. London, Nov. 1, 1788. He traveled with his father and sister to London, where they gave concerts together. He remained in London, and in 1782 was appointed successor of John (Johann) Christian Bach as music master to the Queen. Twelve piano concertos and 7 trios were publ. in London, also in Paris. His widow became attached to Haydn during the latter's stay in London (1790–91) and sent him many impassioned letters, of which copies made by Haydn are extant.

Schröter, Leonhart, German contrapuntist; b. Torgau, c.1532; d. Magdeburg, c.1601. From 1561 to 1576 he was cantor at Saalfeld; from 1572–73, librarian at Wolfenbüttel; from 1576–95, cantor of the Old Latin School in Magdeburg. He was an important composer of Lutheran church music; publ. *55 geistliche Lieder* (1562); a German Te Deum for 8 Voices (1571; publ. 1576; reprinted by Kade in vol. V of Ambros's *Geschichte der Musik*); also a Latin Te Deum (1584); 16 *Weihnachtsliedlein* for 4–8 Voices (1587; reprinted by Engelke in 1914 for Peters); 28 *Hymni sacri* (1587). Four *Weihnachtsliedlein* are found in Schlesinger's *Musica sacra* (no. 11), other pieces in Jöde's *Das Chorbuch*, I and IV; further reprints by W. Ehmann (Göttingen, 1932), G. Hormann (1933), and E. Lendvai (1934).

Schub, André-Michel, outstanding French-born American pianist; b. Paris, Dec. 26, 1952. He was brought to N.Y. by his parents as an infant and was taught piano by his mother; then became a pupil of Jascha Zayde. After attending Princeton Univ. for a year, he went to the Curtis Inst. of Music in Philadelphia to study with Rudolf Serkin. In 1974 he won first prize in the Naumburg International Piano Competition; in 1981 he received first prize at the prestigious Van Cliburn Piano Competition, which launched him on a highly successful career. He was a soloist with the Boston Symph. Orch., Chicago Symph. Orch., Cleveland Orch., N.Y. Phil., and Philadelphia Orch. His brilliant virtuoso technique is matched by a sensitive temperament; he shines in the Classic and Romantic repertoire.

Schubart, (Christian Friedrich) Daniel, German poet and musician; b. Obersontheim, Swabia, March 24, 1739; d. Stuttgart, Oct. 10, 1791. He was an organist at Geisslingen in 1763–69; then at Ludwigsburg, being forced out in 1773 for dissolute conduct; then went to Augsburg, where he founded a paper, the *Deutsche Chronik*, in 1774; from 1777–87 he was imprisoned at Hohenasperg for political reasons. After his release, he was made music director of the Stuttgart theater and court poet. He was the author of the words of Schubert's famous song *Die Forelle.* His own compositions are unassuming, but he was historically important in contributing to the creation of the German lied of the folk type; his song *Schlaf wohl, du Himmelsknabe du* rivaled real folk songs in popularity. He also wrote piano pieces. His son, **Ludwig Schubart,** edited his philosophical disquisition, *Ideen zu einer Aesthetik der Tonkunst* (1806; new ed., 1924), written in the extravagant vein characteristic of Schubart's whole life.

Schubaur, Johann Lukas, German composer; b. Lechfeld, Dec. (baptized, Dec. 23) 1749; d. Munich, Nov. 15, 1815. While studying medicine in Vienna, he earned his livelihood by giving music lessons; began to practice in 1775 in Neuburg but soon moved to Munich, where he became physician to the court and president of the medical commission. He was one of the earliest and most successful composers of German singspiels. The following were produced in Munich: *Melida* (1781); *Die Dorfdeputierten* (1783); *Das Lustlager* (1784); *Die treuen Köhler* (1786); also composed *Psalm 107* and a cantata, *Il Sacrifizio.*

Schubert, Ferdinand, brother of the great composer **Franz Schubert;** b. Lichtenthal, near Vienna, Oct. 18, 1794; d. Vienna, Feb. 26, 1859, as director of the Normal School of St. Anna. He was devoted to his gifted brother, and inherited the latter's literary remains. He composed a *Tantum ergo;* a *Regina coeli;* a German Requiem *a 4*, with Organ; part-songs; etc.; wrote much other church music, a Requiem for Franz, 2 children's operas, etc. (most in MS).

Schubert, Franz, German violinist; b. Dresden, July 22, 1808; d. there, April 12, 1878. He was son and pupil of the Konzertmeister **Franz Anton Schubert** (1768–1827); also took lessons with Rottmeier and L. Haase; then went to Paris, where he studied with Lafont. Upon returning to Dresden, he joined the royal orch. (1823) and in 1861 succeeded Lipinski as first Konzertmeister. He was often confused with his great namesake, much to his distress, for he regarded himself as superior. He wrote a celebrated violin piece, *L'Abeille;* also composed violin études; a Fantasia for Violin, with Orch.; numerous other violin pieces.

Schubert, Franz (Peter), great Austrian composer, supreme melodist, inspired master of Romantic lieder; b. Himmelpfortgrund (then a suburb of Vienna and now a part of that city), Jan. 31, 1797; d. Vienna, Nov. 19, 1828. He studied violin with his father, a schoolmaster, and received instruction on the piano from his brother Ignaz; in addition, he took lessons in piano, organ, singing, and theory with Holzer, the choirmaster. In 1808 he became a member of the Vienna Imperial Court chapel choir and also entered the Stadtkonvict, a training school for court singers, where he studied music with the Imperial Court organist Wenzel Ruzicka and with the famous court composer Salieri. He played violin in the school orch. and conducted it whenever an occasion called for it. He began composing in school; wrote a *Fantasie* for Piano, 4-hands, several chamber music works, orch. overtures, and the unfinished singspiel *Der Spiegelritter.* His first song, *Hagars Klage,* is dated March 30, 1811. In 1813 he left the Stadtkonvict, but Salieri, evidently impressed by his talent, continued to give him instruction. He further attended a training college for teachers in Vienna, and then became an instructor at his father's school. Although very young, he began writing works in large forms; between 1813 and 1816 he composed 5 symphs., 4 masses, several string quartets, and also some stage music. He also wrote his first opera, *Des Teufels Lustschloss.* It was then that he wrote some of his most famous lieder. He was only 17 years old when he wrote *Gretchen am Spinnrade,* and only 18 when he composed the overpowering dramatic song *Erlkönig.* The prodigious facility that Schubert displayed is without equal; during the year 1815 he composed about 140 songs; on a single day, Oct. 15, he wrote 8 lieder. From Schubert's sketches it is possible to follow his method of composition; he would write the melody first, indicate the harmony, and then write out the song in full; often he subjected the finished work to several revisions. He became friendly with the poets Johann Mayrhofer and Franz von Schober, and set a number of their poems to music. In 1817 he lodged with Schober and his widowed mother, arranging to pay for his keep from his meager resources. It was then that he met the noted baritone singer Johann Michael Vogl, who put many of Schubert's songs on his concert programs. Outstanding lieder from this period include the *3 Harfenspieler, Der Wanderer, Der Tod und das Mädchen, Ganymed, An die Musik,* and *Die Forelle.* During the summer of 1818 Schubert served as music tutor to the family of Count Esterházy at Zélesz in Hungary. On March 1, 1818, his Overture in C major, "in the Italian style," became his first orch. work to be accorded a public performance in Vienna. On June 14, 1820, his singspiel *Die Zwillingsbrüder* was performed at the Kärnthnertortheater in Vienna. On Aug. 19, 1820, a score of his incidental music for the play *Die Zauberharfe* was heard at the Theater an der Wien; this score contains an overture that became subsequently popular in concert performances under the name *Rosamunde Overture,* although it was not composed for the score to the play *Rosamunde, Fürstin von Zypern,* which was produced at the Theater an der Wien more than 3 years later, on Dec. 20, 1823. Although Schubert still had difficulties in earning a living, he formed a circle of influential friends in Vienna, and appeared as a pianist at private gatherings; sometimes he sang his songs, accompanying himself at the keyboard; he was also able to publ. some of his songs. A mystery is attached to his most famous work, begun in 1822, the Symph. in B minor, known popularly as the "Unfinished" Symph. Only 2 movements are known to exist; only a few initial bars of the 3rd movement, a Scherzo, remained in sketches. What prevented him from finishing it? Speculations are as rife as they are worthless, particularly since Schubert was usually careful in completing a work before embarking on another composition. A hundred years after Schubert's death, an enterprising phonograph company arranged a contest for the completion of the "Unfinished" Symph.; prizes were given, but the products delivered, even some signed by well-known composers, were spectacularly poor. In 1823 Schubert completed his masterly song cycle *Die*

schöne Müllerin; in 1824 he once again spent the summer as a private tutor in Count Esterházy's employ in Zélesz. In 1827 Schubert wrote another remarkable song cycle, *Die Winterreise.* On March 26, 1828, he presented in Vienna a public concert of his works. From that year, which proved to be his last, date such masterpieces as the piano sonatas in C minor, A major, and B-flat major; the String Quintet in C major; and the 2 books of songs collectively known as the *Schwanengesang.* His health was frail, and he moved to the lodgings of his brother Ferdinand. On the afternoon of Nov. 19, 1828, Schubert died, at the age of 31. Probably the most plausible account of Schubert's illness is given by D. Kerner in his *Krankheiten grosser Musiker* (Stuttgart, 1973); a further discussion is found in the *Musical Times,* in E. Sams's "Schubert's Illness Re-examined" (Jan. 1980). There is no substantial evidence that Schubert died of syphilis; from all accounts of his daily life, he was never promiscuous, and was not known to engage in unseemly liaisons.

Schubert is often described as the creator of the genre of strophic lieder; this summary description is chronologically untenable; Zelter wrote strophic lieder a generation before Schubert. Goethe, whose poems were set to music by Zelter, Beethoven, and Schubert, favored Zelter's settings. What Schubert truly created was an incomparably beautiful florilegium of lieder typifying the era of German Romantic sentiment and conveying deeply felt emotions, ranging from peaceful joy to enlightened melancholy, from philosophic meditation to throbbing drama; the poems he selected for his settings were expressive of such passing moods. He set to music 72 poems by Goethe, 47 by Mayrhofer, 46 by Schiller, 44 by Wilhelm Müller, 28 by Matthison, 23 by Hölty, 22 by Kosegarten, 13 by Körtner, 12 by Schober, and 6 by Heine.

In a sense, Schubert's *Moments musicaux, Impromptus,* and other piano works are songs without texts; on several occasions he used musical material from his songs for instrumental works, as in the great *Wanderer Fantasia* for Piano, based on his song *Der Wanderer,* and the "Forellen" Piano Quintet, in which the 4th movement is a set of variations on the song *Die Forelle.* His String Quartet in D minor includes a set of variations on Schubert's song *Der Tod und das Mädchen* in its 2nd movement. But Schubert not given to large theater works and oratorios. Even his extended works in sonata form are not conceived on a grand scale but, rather, are constructed according to the symmetry of recapitulations; his music captivates the listeners not by recurring variety but by the recalled felicities; time and again in his MSS he simply indicates the repetition of a group of bars by number. Therein lies the immense difference between Schubert and Schumann, both Romantic poets of music: where Schubert was satisfied with reminding the listener of a passage already heard, Schumann variegates. Schubert was indeed the most symmetrical composer in the era of free-flowing musical prose and musical poetry.

Much confusion exists in the numbering of Schubert's symphs., of which he wrote 8, the last being listed in most catalogues as No. 9; the missing un-counted symph. is No. 7, which exists as a full draft, in 4 movements, of which the first 110 bars are fully scored; several "completions" exist, the first by John Francis Barnett, made in 1883; the 2nd by Felix Weingartner, manufactured in 1934; and the 3rd, and perhaps the most Schubertomorphic, construct-ed with artful imitation of Schubert's ways and means, by Brian Newbould, in 1977. The "Unfin-ished" Symph. is then No. 8. There remains the mys-terious "Gastein" Symph., so named because Schu-bert was supposed to have written it in Gastein, in the Tyrol, in 1825. It was long regarded as irretrieva-bly lost, but was eventually identified with No. 9, the great C major Symph. Incredibly, as late as 1978 there came to light in a somehow overlooked pile of music in the archives of the Vienna Stadtsbiblio-thek a sketch of still another Schubert symph., com-posed during the last months of his life; this insub-stantial but magically tempting waft of Schubert's genius was completed by Brian Newbould; if admit-ted into the Schubert treasure box, it will have to be numbered as his 10th.

The recognition of Schubert's greatness was as-tonishingly slow. Fully 40 years elapsed before the discovery of the MS of the "Unfinished" Symph. Posthumous performances were the rule for Schu-bert's symph. premieres, and the publication of his symphs. was exceedingly tardy. Schumann, ever sensitive to great talent, was eager to salute the kindred genius in Schubert's symphs., about whose "Heavenly length" he so admiringly complained. But it took half a century for Schubert to become firmly established in music history as one of the great Sch's (with Chopin phonetically counted in).

WORKS: In the list of Schubert's works given be-low, the D. numbers are those established by O. Deutsch (with D. Wakeling) in his *Schubert: The-matic Catalogue of All His Works in Chronological Order* (London, 1951; in German as *Franz Schu-bert: Thematisches Verzeichnis seiner Werke in chronologischer Folge . . .* , publ. in the *Neue Aus-gabe sämtlicher Werke* of Schubert in a revised ed. in 1978).

FOR THE STAGE: *Der Spiegelritter*, D. 11, singspiel (1811–12; unfinished; only the Overture and Act I completed; first perf. by the Swiss Radio, Dec. 11, 1949); *Des Teufels Lustschloss*, D. 84, opera (1813–15; 2 versions; Vienna, Dec. 12, 1879); *Adrast*, D. 137, opera (1817–19; unfinished; Vienna, Dec. 13, 1868); *Der vierjährige Posten*, D. 190, singspiel (1815; Dres-den, Sept. 23, 1896); Fernando, D. 220, singspiel (1815; Vienna, April 13, 1907); *Claudine von Villa Bella*, D. 239, singspiel (1815; unfinished; only the Overture and Act I completed; Vienna, April 26, 1913); *Die Freunde von Salamanka*, D. 326, sing-spiel (1815; Halle, May 6, 1928); Die Bürgschaft, D. 435, opera (1816; unfinished; only Acts I and II com-pleted; Vienna, March 7, 1908); *Die Zauberharfe*, D. 644, melodrama (1820; Theater an der Wien, Vienna, Aug. 19, 1820); *Die Zwillingsbrüder*, D. 647, sing-spiel (1819; Kärnthnertortheater, Vienna, June 14, 1820); *Sakuntala*, D. 701, opera (1820; only sketches for Acts I and II; these first perf. in Vienna, June 12, 1971); Duet and Aria for Hérold's *Das Zauberglöck-chen (La Clochette)*, D. 723 (1821; Vienna, June 20, 1821); *Alfonso und Estrella*, D. 732, opera (1821–22; Weimar, June 24, 1854); *Die Verschworenen (Der häusliche Krieg)*, D. 787, singspiel (1823; Vienna, March 1, 1861); *Rüdiger*, D. 791, opera (1823; sketches only; these first perf. in Vienna, Jan. 5, 1868); *Fierabras*, D. 796, opera (1823; Karlsruhe, Feb. 9, 1897); *Rosamunde, Fürstin von Zypern*, D. 797, incidental music to the play by H. von Chézy (1823; Theater an der Wien, Vienna, Dec. 20, 1823); *Der Graf von Gleichen*, D. 918, opera (1827; sketches only); *Der Minnesänger*, D. 981, singspiel (date un-known; unfinished; not extant).

CHURCH MUSIC: *Salve Regina* in F major for So-prano, Organ, and Orch., D. 27 (1812); Kyrie in D minor for Soprano, Tenor, Choir, Organ, and Orch., D. 31 (1812); Kyrie in B-flat major for Choir, D. 45 (1813); Kyrie in D minor for Soprano, Alto, Tenor, Bass, Choir, and Orch., D. 49 (1813); Kyrie in F major for Choir, Organ, and Orch., D. 66 (1813); Mass No. 1, in F major, for 2 Sopranos, Alto, 2 Tenors, Bass, Choir, Organ, and Orch., D. 105 (1814); *Salve Regina* in B-flat major for Tenor, Organ, and Orch., D. 106 (1814); *Totus in corde langueo*, offertory in C major for Soprano or Tenor, Clarinet or Violin, Organ, and Orch., D. 136 (1815); Mass No. 2, in G. major, for Soprano, Tenor, Bass, Choir, Organ, and Strings, D. 167 (1815); *Stabat Mater* in G minor for Choir, Or-gan, and Orch., D. 175 (1815); *Tres sunt*, offertory in A minor for Choir, Organ, and Orch., D. 181 (1815); *Benedictus es, Domine*, gradual in C major for Choir, Organ, and Orch., D. 184 (1815); *Dona nobis pacem* in F major for Bass, Choir, Organ, and Orch., D. 185 (alternative movement for D. 105; 1815); *Salve Regina* (offertorium) in F major for Soprano, Organ, and Orch., D. 223 (2 versions, 1815 and 1823); Mass No. 3, in B-flat major, for Soprano, Alto, Tenor, Bass, Choir, Organ, and Orch., D. 324 (1815); *Deut-sches Salve Regina (Hymne an die heilige Mutter Gottes)* in F major for Choir and Orch., D. 379 (1816); *Stabat Mater* (oratorio) in F major/F minor for Soprano, Tenor, Bass, Choir, and Orch., D. 383 (1816); *Salve Regina* in B-flat major for Choir, D. 386 (1816); Mass No. 4, in C major, for Soprano, Alto, Tenor, Bass, Choir, Organ, and Orch., D. 452 (1816); *Tantum ergo* in C major for Soprano, Choir, Organ, and Orch., D. 460 (1816); *Tantum ergo* in C major for Soprano, Alto, Tenor, Bass, Choir, and Orch., D. 461 (1816); Magnificat in C major for Soprano, Alto, Tenor, Bass, Choir, Organ, and Orch., D. 486 (1815); *Auguste jam coelestium* in G major for Soprano, Tenor, and Orch., D. 488 (1816); *Deutsches Requiem (Deutsche Trauermesse)* in G minor for Soprano, Alto, Tenor, Bass, Choir, and Organ, D. 621 (1818); *Salve Regina* (offertorium) in A major for Soprano and Strings, D. 676 (1819); Mass No. 5, in A-flat ma-jor, for Soprano, Alto, Tenor, Bass, Choir, Organ, and Orch., D. 678 (2 versions, 1819–22); *Tantum ergo* in B-flat major for Soprano, Alto, Tenor, Bass, Choir, Organ, and Orch., D. 730 (1821); *Tantum ergo* in C major for Choir, Organ, and Orch., D. 739 (1814); *Tantum ergo* in D major for Choir, Organ, and Orch., D. 750 (1822); *Salve Regina* in C major for 2 Tenors and 2 Basses, D. 811 (1824); *Deutsche Messe* for Choir and Organ, or Choir, Organ, and Orch., D.

872 (1827); Mass No. 6, in E-flat major, for Soprano, Alto, Tenor, Bass, Choir, and Orch., D. 950 (1828); Benedictus in A minor for Soprano, Alto, Tenor, Bass, Choir, Organ, and Orch., D. 961 (alternative movement for D. 452; 1828); *Tantum ergo* in E-flat major for Soprano, Alto, Tenor, Bass, Choir, and Orch., D. 962 (1828); *Intende voci,* offertory in B-flat major for Tenor, Choir, and Orch., D. 963 (1828); etc.

OTHER VOCAL MUSIC: *Quell' innocente figlio,* D. 17 (many versions, 1812); *Entra l'uomo allor che nasce,* D. 33 (many versions, 1812); *Te solo adoro* for Soprano, Alto, Tenor, and Bass, D. 34 (1812); *Serbate, o dei custodi,* D. 35 (2 versions, 1812); *Die Advokaten* for Men's Voices and Piano, D. 37 (1812); *Totengräberlied* for Men's Voices, D. 38 (1813); *Dreifach ist der Schritt der Zeit* for Men's Voices, D. 43 (1813); *Dithyrambe,* D. 47 (1813; fragment only); *Unendliche Freude* for Men's Voices, D. 51 (1813); *Vorüber die stöhnende Klage* for Men's Voices, D. 53 (1813); *Unendliche Freude,* canon for Men's Voices, D. 54 (1813); *Selig durch die Liebe* for Men's Voices, D. 55 (1813); *Hier strecket der wallende Pilger* for Men's Voices, D. 57 (1813); *Dessen Fahne Donnerstürme wallte* for Men's Voices, D. 58 (1813); *Hier umarmen sich getreue Gatten* for Men's Voices, D. 60 (1813); *Ein jugendlicher Maienschwung,* D. 61 (1813); *Thronend auf erhabnem Sitz* for Men's Voices, D. 62 (1813); *Wer die steile Sternenbahn* for Men's Voices, D. 63 (1813); *Majestätsche Sonnenrosse* for Men's Voices, D. 64 (1813); *Schmerz verzerret ihr Gesicht,* canon, D. 65 (1813; sketch only); *Frisch atmet des Morgens lebendiger Hauch* for Men's Voices, D. 67 (1813); *Dreifach ist der Schritt der Zeit,* D. 69 (1813); *Dreifach ist der Schritt der Zeit (Ewig still steht die Vergangenheit),* canon for Men's Voices, D. 70 (1813); *Die zwei Tugendwege* for Men's Voices, D. 71 (1813); *Trinklied (Freunde, sammelt euch im Kreise)* for Bass, Men's Voices, and Piano, D. 75 (1813); *Zur Namensfeier meines Vaters* for Men's Voices and Guitar, D. 80 (1813); *Verschwunden sind die Schmerzen,* canon for Men's Voices, D. 88 (1813); *Wer ist gross?* for Bass, Men's Voices, and Orch., D. 110 (1814); *Mailied (Grüner wird die Au)* for Men's Voices, D. 129 (1815); *Der Schnee zerrinnt,* canon, D. 130 (1815); *Lacrimoso son io,* canon, D. 131 (2 versions, 1815); *Lied beim Rundetanz,* D. 132 (1815?); *Lied im Freien,* D. 133 (1815?); *Klage um Ali Bey* for Men's Voices, D. 140 (1815); *Bardengesang* for Men's Voices, D. 147 (1816); *Trinklied (Brüder! unser Erdenwallen)* for Tenor, Men's Voices, and Piano, D. 148 (1815); *Nun lasst uns den Leib begraben (Begrabnislied)* for Choir and Piano, D. 168 (1815); *Osterlied* for Choir and Piano, D. 168a (originally D. 987; 1815); *Trinklied vor der Schlacht* for 2 Unison Choruses and Piano, D. 169 (1815); *Schwertlied* for Voice, Unison Chorus, and Piano, D. 170 (1815); *Trinklied (Ihr Freunde und du gold'ner Wein)* for Voice, Unison Chorus, and Piano, D. 183 (1815); *An die Freude* for Voice, Unison Chorus, and Piano, D. 189 (1815); *Mailied (Grüner wird die Au)* for 2 Voices, D. 199 (1815); *Mailied (Der Schnee zerrinnt)* for 2 Voices, D. 202 (1815); *Der Morgenstern* for 2 Voices, D. 203 (1815); *Jägerlied* for 2 Voices, D. 204 (1815); *Lützows wilde Jagd* for 2 Voices, D. 205

(1815); *Hymne an den Unendlichen* for Choir and Piano, D. 232 (1815); *Das Abendrot* for Men's Voices and Piano, D. 236 (1815); *Trinklied im Winter* for Men's Voices, D. 242 (1815); *Frühlingslied (Die Luft ist blau)* for Men's Voices, D. 243 (1815); *Willkommen, lieber schöner Mai,* canon for 3 Voices, D. 244 (2 versions, 1815); *Punschlied: Im Norden zu singen* for 2 Voices, D. 253 (1815); *Trinklied (Auf! jeder sei nun froh)* for Men's Voices and Piano, D. 267 (1815); *Bergknappenlied* for Men's Voices and Piano, D. 268 (1815); *Das Leben,* D. 269 (2 versions, 1815); *Punschlied (Vier Elemente, innig gesellt)* for Men's Voices and Piano, D. 277 (1815); *Namensfeier für Franz Michael Vierthaler (Gratulations Kantate)* for Soprano, Tenor, Bass, Chorus, and Orch., D. 294 (1815); *Das Grab,* D. 329a (1815; sketch only); *Das Grab* for 4 Voices and Piano, D. 330 (1815); *Der Entfernten* for Men's Voices, D. 331 (1816?); *Die Einsiedelei* for Men's Voices, D. 337 (1816?); *An den Frühling* for Men's Voices, D. 338 (1816?); *Amors Macht,* D. 339 (1816?); *Badelied,* D. 340 (1816?); *Sylphen,* D. 341 (1816?); *Trinklied (Funkelnd im Becher)* for Men's Voices, D. 356 (1816); *Gold'ner Schein,* canon for 3 Voices, D. 357 (1816); *Fischerlied* for Men's Voices and Piano, D. 364 (1816?); *Das Grab* for Men's Voices and Piano, D. 377 (1816); *Die Schlacht,* D. 387 (1816; sketch only); *Beitrag zur fünfzig jährigen Jubelfeier des Herrn Salieri* for Tenor, Men's Voices, and Piano, D. 407 (1816); *Naturgenuss* for Men's Voices and Piano, D. 422 (1822?); *Andenken (Ich denke dein, wenn durch den Hain)* for Men's Voices, D. 423 (1816); *Erinnerungen (Am Seegestad)* for Men's Voices, D. 424 (1816); *Lebensbild* for Men's Voices, D. 425 (1816; not extant); *Trinklied (Herr Bacchus ist ein braver Mann)* for Men's Voices, D. 426 (1816; not extant); *Trinklied im Mai* for Men's Voices, D. 427 (1816); *Widerhall (Auf ewig dein)* for Men's Voices, D. 428 (1816); *An die Sonne* for Choir and Piano, D. 439 (1816); *Chor der Engel* for Choir, D. 440 (1816); *Das grosse Halleluja* for Chorus and Piano, D. 442 (1816); *Schlachtlied* for Chorus and Piano, D. 443 (1816); *Prometheus,* cantata for Soprano, Bass, Chorus, and Orch., D. 451 (1816; not extant); *Kantate zu Ehren von Josef Spendou* for 2 Sopranos, Bass, Choir, and Orch., D. 472 (1816); *Der Geistertanz* for Men's Voices, D. 494 (1816); *La pastorella al prato* for Men's Voices and Piano, D. 513 (1817?); *Jagdlied* for Unison Voices and Piano, D. 521 (1817); *Gesang der Geister über den Wassern* for Men's Voices, D. 538 (1817); *Das Grab* for Unison Voices and Piano, D. 569 (1817); *Lied im Freien* for Men's Voices, D. 572 (1817); *Das Dörfchen,* D. 598 (originally D. 641; 1817; sketch only); *Die Gesellichkeit (Lebenslust)* for Choir and Piano, D. 609 (1818); *Leise, leise lasst uns singen* for Men's Voices, D. 635 (1819?); *Viel tausend Sterne prangen* for Choir and Piano, D. 642 (1812?); *Das Grab* for Choir, D. 643a (1819), *Sehnsucht (Nur wer die Sehnsucht kennt)* for Men's Voices, D. 656 (1819); *Ruhe, schönstes Gluck der Erde* for Men's Voices, D. 657 (1819); *Kantate zum Geburtstag des Sängers Johann Michael Vogl (Der Frühlingsmorgen)* for Women's and Men's Voices and Piano, D. 666 (1819); *Lazarus, oder Die Feier der Auferstehung,* oratorio for 3 Sopranos, 2 Tenors, Bass,

Choir, and Orch., D. 689 (1820; unfinished); *Der 23. Psalm* for Women's Voices and Piano, D. 706 (1820); *Frühlingsgesang* for Men's Voices, D. 709 (1822); *Im Gegenwärtigen Vergangenes* for Men's Voices and Piano, D. 710 (1821); *Gesang der Geister über den Wassern* for Men's Voices, 2 Violas, 2 Cellos, and 2 Double Basses, D. 714 (originally D. 704 as a sketch; 1820–21); *Die Nachtigall* for Men's Voices and Piano, D. 724 (1821); *Frühlingsgesang* for Men's Voices and Piano, D. 740 (1822); *Geist der Liebe (Der Abend schleiert Flur und Hain)* for Men's Voices and Piano, D. 747 (1822); *Am Geburtstag des Kaisers,* cantata for Soprano, Alto, Tenor, Bass, Choir, and Orch., D. 748 (1822); *Gott in der Natur* for Women's Voices and Piano, D. 757 (1822); *Des Tages Weihe* for Choir and Piano, D. 763 (1822); *Ich hab' in mich gesogen,* D. 778b (1823?; sketch only); *Gondelfahrer* for Men's Voices and Piano, D. 809 (1824); *Gebet* for Choir and Piano, D. 815 (1824); *Lied eines Kriegers* for Bass, Unison Voices, and Piano, D. 822 (1824); *Wehmut* for Men's Voices, D. 825 (1826); *Ewige Liebe* for Men's Voices, D. 825a (1826); *Flucht* for Men's Voices, D. 825b (1825); *Der Tanz* for Choir and Piano, D. 826 (1828); *Bootgesang* for Men's Voices and Piano, D. 835 (1825); *Coronach (Totengesang der Frauen und Mädchen)* for Women's Voices and Piano, D. 836 (1825); *Trinklied aus dem 16. Jahrhundert* for Men's Voices, D. 847 (1825); *Nachtmusik* for Men's Voices, D. 848 (1825); *Widerspruch* for Men's Voices and Piano, D. 865 (1826?); Canon for 6 Voices, D. 873 (1826?; sketch only); *Nachklänge* for Men's Voices, D. 873a (1826?; sketch only); *Die Allmacht* for Choir and Piano, D. 875a (1826; sketch only); *Mondenschein* for Men's Voices and Piano, D. 875 (1826); *Nachthelle* for Tenor, Men's Voices, and Piano, D. 892 (1826); *Grab und Mond* for Men's Voices, D. 893 (1826); *Wein und Liebe* for Men's Voices, D. 901 (1827); *Zur guten Nacht* for Baritone, Men's Voices, and Piano, D. 903 (1827); *Schlachtlied* for Men's Voices, D. 912 (1827); *Nachtgesang im Walde* for Men's Voices and 4 Horns, D. 913 (1827); *Frühlingslied* for Men's Voices, D. 914 (1827); *Das stille Lied* for Men's Voices, D. 916 (1827; sketch only); *Ständchen,* D. 920 (originally D. 921; 2 versions, 1827); *Der Hochzeitsbraten* for Soprano, Tenor, Bass, and Piano, D. 930 (1827); *Kantate für Irene Kiesewetter* for 2 Tenors, 2 Basses, Choir, and Piano, 4-hands, D. 936 (1827); *Hymnus an den Heiligen Geist,* D. 941 (now listed as D. 948; 2 versions, 1828); *Mirjams Siegesgesang* for Soprano, Choir, and Piano, D. 942 (1828); *Der 92. Psalm: Lied für den Sabbath* for Soprano, Alto, Tenor, Baritone, Bass, and Choir, D. 953 (1828); *Glaube, Hoffnung und Liebe* for 2 Tenors, 2 Basses, Choir, and Wind Instruments or Piano, D. 954 (1828); *Gott im Ungewitter* for Choir and Piano, D. 985 (1827?); *Gott der Weltschöpfer* for Choir and Piano, D. 986 (1827?); *Liebe säuseln die Blätter,* canon for 3 Voices, D. 988 (1815?).

SONGS (author of text precedes date of composition): Sketch for a song, D. 1a (no text; 1810?); *Hagars Klage,* D. 5 (Schücking; 1811); *Des Mädchens Klage,* D. 6 (Schiller; 1811?); *Leichenfantasie,* D. 7 (Schiller; 1811?); *Der Vatermörder,* D. 10 (Pfeffel; 1811); *Der Geistertanz,* D. 15 and 15a (fragments only; Matthisson; 1812?); *Quell' innocente figlio,* D. 17 (Metastasio; 1812); *Klaglied,* D. 23 (Rochlitz; 1812); *Der Jüngling am Bache,* D. 30 (Schiller; 1812); *Entra l'uomo allor che nasce,* D. 33 (Metastasio; 1812); *Serbate, o dei custodi,* D. 35 (Metastasio; 1812); *Lebenstraum,* D. 39 (Baumberg; 1810?); *Misero pargoletto,* D. 42 (several versions; Metastasio; 1813?); *Totengräberlied,* D. 44 (Hölty; 1813); *Die Schatten,* D. 50 (Matthisson; 1813); *Sehnsucht,* D. 52 (Schiller; 1813); *Verklärung,* D. 59 (Pope; Herder, trans.; 1813); *Thekla: Eine Geisterstimme,* D. 73 (Schiller; 1813); *Pensa, che questo istante,* D. 76 (2 versions; Metastasio; 1813); *Der Taucher,* D. 77 (2 versions; 2nd version originally D. 111; Schiller; first version, 1813–14; 2nd version, 1815); *Son fra l'onde,* D. 78 (Metastasio; 1813); *Auf den Sieg der Deutschen,* D. 81, with 2 Violins and Cello (Schubert?; 1813); *Zur Namensfeier des Herrn Andreas Siller,* D. 83, with Violin and Harp (1813); *Don Gayseros,* D. 93 (3 versions: *Don Gayseros, Don Gayseros; Nächtens klang die süsse Laute; An dem jungen Morgenhimmel;* F. de la Motte Fouqué; 1815?); *Adelaide,* D. 95 (Matthisson; 1814); *Trost: An Elisa,* D. 97 (Matthisson; 1814); *Erinnerungen,* D. 98 (2 versions; Matthisson; 1814); *Andenken,* D. 99 (Matthisson; 1814); *Geisternähe,* D. 100 (Matthisson; 1814); *Erinnerung,* D. 101 (Matthisson; 1814); *Die Betende,* D. 102 (Matthisson; 1814); *Die Befreier Europas in Paris,* D. 104 (3 versions; Mikan; 1814); *Lied aus der Ferne,* D. 107 (2 versions; Matthisson; 1814); *Der Abend,* D. 108 (Matthisson; 1814); *Lied der Liebe,* D. 109 (Matthisson; 1814); *An Emma,* D. 113 (3 versions; Schiller; 1814); *Romanze,* D. 114 (2 versions; Matthisson; 1814); *An Laura, als sie Klopstocks Auferstehungslied sang,* D. 115 (Matthisson; 1814); *Der Geistertanz,* D. 116 (Matthisson; 1814); *Das Mädchen aus der Fremde,* D. 117 (Schiller; 1814); *Gretchen am Spinnrade,* D. 118 (Goethe; 1814); *Nachtgesang,* D. 119 (Goethe; 1814); *Trost in Tränen,* D. 120 (Goethe; 1814); *Schäfers Klagelied,* D. 121 (2 versions; Goethe; 1814); *Ammenlied,* D. 122 (Lubi; 1814); *Sehnsucht,* D. 123 (Goethe; 1814; *Am See,* D. 124 (2 versions; Mayrhofer; 1814); *Szene aus Goethes Faust,* D. 126, with 4 Voices (2 versions; Goethe; 1814); *Ballade,* D. 134 (Kenner; 1815?); *Rastlose Liebe,* D. 138 (2 versions; Goethe; first version, 1815; 2nd version, 1821); *Der Mondabend,* D. 141 (Kumpf; 1815); *Geistes-Gruss,* D. 142 (6 versions; Goethe; 1815?); *Genügsamkeit,* D. 143 (Schober; 1815); *Romanze,* D. 144 (unfinished; F. Graf zu Stolberg-Stolberg; 1816); *Der Sänger,* D. 149 (2 versions; Goethe; 1815); *Lodas Gespenst,* D. 150 (Ossian; E. Baron de Harold, trans.; 1816); *Auf einen Kirchhof,* D. 151 (Schlechta; 1815); *Minona,* D. 152 (Bertrand; 1815); *Als ich sie erröten sah,* D. 153 (Ehrlich; 1815); *Das Bild,* D. 155 (1815); *Die Erwartung,* D. 159 (2 versions; Schiller; 1816); *Am Flusse,* D. 160 (Goethe; 1815); *An Mignon,* D. 161 (2 versions; Goethe; 1815); *Nähe des Geliebten,* D. 162 (2 versions; Goethe; 1815); *Sängers Morgenlied,* D. 163 (Körner; 1815); *Liebesrausch,* D. 164 (fragment only; Körner; 1815); *Sängers Morgenlied,* D. 165 (Körner; 1815); *Amphiaraos,* D. 166 (Körner; 1815); *Trinklied vor der Schlacht,* D. 169, for 2 Unison Choruses (Körner; 1815); *Schwertlied,* D. 170, with Unison Chorus

(Körner; 1815); *Gebet während der Schlacht*, D. 171 (Körner; 1815); *Der Morgenstern*, D. 172 (fragment only; Körner; 1815); *Das war ich*, D. 174 (2 versions; Körner; first version, 1815; 2nd version, 1816); *Die Sterne*, D. 176 (Fellinger; 1815); *Vergebliche Liebe*, D. 177 (Bernard; 1815); *Liebesrausch*, D. 179 (Körner; 1815); *Sehnsucht der Liebe*, D. 180 (2 versions; Körner; 1815; 2nd version not extant); *Die erste Liebe*, D. 182 (Fellinger; 1815); *Trinklied*, D. 183, with Unison Chorus (Zettler; 1815); *Die Sterbende*, D. 186 (Matthisson; 1815); *Stimme der Liebe*, D. 187 (Matthisson; 1815); *Naturgenuss*, D. 188 (Matthisson; 1815); *An die Freude*, D. 189, with Unison Chorus (Schiller; 1815); *Des Mädchens Klage*, D. 191 (2 versions; Schiller; 1815); *Der Jüngling am Bache*, D. 192 (Schiller; 1815); *An den Mond*, D. 193 (Hölty; 1815); *Die Mainacht*, D. 194 (Hölty; 1815); *Amalia*, D. 195 (Schiller; 1815); *An die Nachtigall*, D. 196 (Hölty; 1815); *An die Apfelbäume, wo ich Julien erblickte*, D. 197 (Hölty; 1815); *Seufzer*, D. 198 (Hölty; 1815); *Auf den Tod einer Nachtigall*, D. 201 (fragment only; Hölty; 1815); *Das Traumbild*, D. 204a (Hölty; 1815; not extant); *Liebeständelei*, D. 206 (Körner; 1815); *Der Liebende*, D. 207 (Hölty; 1815); *Die Nonne*, D. 208 (2 versions; Hölty; first version, fragment only, 1815; 2nd version, originally D. 212, 1815); *Der Liedler*, D. 209 (Kenner; 1815); *Die Liebe (Klärchens Lied)*, D. 210 (Goethe; 1815); *Adelwold und Emma*, D. 211 (Bertrand; 1815); *Der Traum*, D. 213 (Hölty; 1815); *Die Laube*, D. 214 (Hölty; 1815); *Jägers Abendlied*, D. 215 (Goethe; 1815); *Meerestille*, D. 215a (Goethe; 1815); *Meerestille*, D. 216 (Goethe; 1815); *Kolmas Klage*, D. 217 (Ossian; 1815); *Grablied*, D. 218 (Kenner; 1815); *Das Finden*, D. 219 (Kosegarten; 1815); *Der Abend*, D. 221 (Kosegarten; 1815); *Lieb Minna*, D. 222 (Stadler; 1815); *Wandrers Nachtlied*, D. 224 (Goethe; 1815); *Der Fischer*, D. 225 (Goethe; 1815); *Erster Verlust*, D. 226 (Goethe; 1815); *Idens Nachtgesang*, D. 227 (Kosegarten; 1815); *Von Ida*, D. 228 (Kosegarten; 1815); *Die Erscheinung*, D. 229 (Kosegarten; 1815); *Die Täuschung*, D. 230 (Kosegarten; 1815); *Das Sehnen*, D. 231 (Kosegarten; 1815); *Geist der Liebe*, D. 233 (Kosegarten; 1815); *Tischlied*, D. 234 (Goethe; 1815); *Abends unter der Linde*, D. 235 (Kosegarten; 1815); *Abends unter der Linde*, D. 237 (Kosegarten; 1815); *Die Mondnacht*, D. 238 (Kosegarten; 1815); *Huldigung*, D. 240 (Kosegarten; 1815); *Alles um Liebe*, D. 241 (Kosegarten; 1815); *Die Bürgschaft*, D. 246 (Schiller; 1815); *Die Spinnerin*, D. 247 (Goethe; 1815); *Lob des Tokayers*, D. 248 (Baumberg; 1815); *Die Schlacht*, D. 249 (Schiller; 1815; fragment only); *Das Geheimnis*, D. 250 (Schiller; 1815); *Hoffnung*, D. 251 (Schiller; 1815); *Das Mädchen aus der Fremde*, D. 252 (Schiller; 1815); *Punschlied: Im Norden zu singen*, D. 253 (Schiller; 1815); *Der Gott und die Bajadere*, D. 254 (Goethe; 1815); *Der Rattenfänger*, D. 255 (Goethe; 1815); *Der Schatzgräber*, D. 256 (Goethe; 1815); *Heidenröslein*, D. 257 (Goethe; 1815); *Bundeslied*, D. 258 (Goethe; 1815); *An den Mond*, D. 259 (Goethe; 1815); *Wonne der Wehmut*, D. 260 (Goethe; 1815); *Wer kauft Liebesgötter?*, D. 261 (Goethe; 1815); *Die Fröhlichkeit*, D. 262 (Prandstetter; 1815); *Cora an die Sonne*, D. 263 (Baumberg; 1815); *Der Morgenkuss*, D. 264 (2 versions; Baumberg; 1815); *Abendständchen: An Lina*, D. 265

(Baumberg; 1815); *Morgenlied*, D. 266 (Stolberg; 1815); *An die Sonne*, D. 270 (Baumberg; 1815); *Der Weiberfreund*, D. 271 (Cowley; Ratschky, trans.; 1815); *An die Sonne*, D. 272 (Tiedge; 1815); *Lilla an die Morgenröte*, D. 273 (1815); *Tischlerlied*, D. 274 (1815); *Totenkranz für ein Kind*, D. 275 (Matthisson; 1815); *Abendlied*, D. 276 (Stolberg; 1815); *Ossians Lied nach dem Falle Nathos*, D. 278 (2 versions; Ossian; Harold, trans.; 1815); *Das Rosenband*, D. 280 (Klopstock; 1815); *Das Mädchen von Inistore*, D. 281 (Ossian; Harold, trans.; 1815); *Cronnan*, D. 282 (Ossian; Harold, trans.; 1815); *An den Frühling*, D. 283 (Schiller; 1815); *Lied*, D. 284 (Schiller?; 1815); *Furcht der Geliebten (An Cidli)*, D. 285 (2 versions; Klopstock; 1815); *Selma und Selmar*, D. 286 (2 versions; Klopstock; 1815); *Vaterlandslied*, D. 287 (2 versions; Klopstock; 1815); *An sie*, D. 288 (Klopstock; 1815); *Die Sommernacht*, D. 289 (2 versions; Klopstock; 1815); *Die frühen Gräber*, D. 290 (Klopstock; 1815); *Dem Unendlichen*, D. 291 (3 versions; Klopstock; 1815); *Shilric und Vinvela*, D. 293 (Ossian; Harold, trans.; 1815); *Hoffnung*, D. 295 (2 versions; Goethe; 1816?); *An den Mond*, D. 296 (Goethe; 1816?); *Augenlied*, D. 297 (2 versions; Mayrhofer; 1817?); *Liane*, D. 298 (Mayrhofer; 1815); *Der Jüngling an der Quelle*, D. 300 (Salis-Seewis; 1817?); *Lambertine*, D. 301 (Stoll; 1815); *Labetrank der Liebe*, D. 302 (Stoll; 1815); *An die Geliebte*, D. 303 (Stoll; 1815); *Wiegenlied*, D. 304 (Körner; 1815); *Mein Gruss an den Mai*, D. 305 (Kumpf; 1815); *Skolie*, D. 306 (Deinhardstein; 1815); *Die Sternewelten*, D. 307 (Jarnik; Fellinger, trans.; 1815); *Die Macht der Liebe*, D. 308 (Kalchberg; 1815); *Das gestörte Glück*, D. 309 (Körner; 1815); *Sehnsucht*, D. 310 (2 versions; Goethe; 1815); *An den Mond*, D. 311 (1815; fragment only); *Hektors Abschied*, D. 312 (2 versions; Schiller; 1815); *Die Sterne*, D. 313 (Kosegarten; 1815); *Nachtgesang*, D. 314 (Kosegarten; 1815); *An Rosa*, D. 315 (Kosegarten; 1815); *An Rosa*, D. 316 (2 versions; Kosegarten; 1815); *Idens Schwanenlied*, D. 317 (2 versions; Kosegarten; 1815); *Schwangesang*, D. 318 (Kosegarten; 1815); *Luisens Antwort*, D. 319 (Kosegarten; 1815); *Der Zufriedene*, D. 320 (Reissig; 1815); *Mignon*, D. 321 (Goethe; 1815); *Hermann und Thusnelda*, D. 322 (Klopstock; 1815); *Klage der Ceres*, D. 323 (Schiller; 1815–16); *Harfenspieler*, D. 325 (Goethe; 1815); *Lorma*, D. 327 (Ossian; Harold, trans.; 1815; fragment only); *Erlkönig*, D. 328 (4 versions; Goethe; 1815); *Die drei Sänger*, D. 329 (Bobrik; 1815; fragment only); *Das Grab*, D. 330 (Salis-Seewis; 1815); *An mein Klavier*, D. 342 (Schubart; 1816?); *Am Tage aller Seelen (Litanei auf das Fest aller Seelen)*, D. 343 (2 versions; Jacobi; 1816?); *Am ersten Maimorgen*, D. 344 (Claudius; 1816?); *Der Entfernten*, D. 350 (Salis-Seewis; 1816?); *Fischerlied*, D. 351 (Salis-Seewis; 1816); *Licht und Liebe (Nachtgesang)* D. 352, for Soprano and Tenor (Collin; 1816?); *Die Nacht*, D. 358 (Uz; 1816); *Sehnsucht*, D. 359 (Goethe; 1816); *Lied eines Schiffers an die Dioskuren*, D. 360 (Mayrhofer; 1816); *Am Bach im Frühlinge*, D. 361 (Schober; 1816); *Zufriedenheit*, D. 362 (Claudius; 1816?); *An Chloen*, D. 363 (Uz; 1816; fragment only); *Der König in Thule*, D. 367 (Goethe; 1816); *Jägers Abendlied*, D. 368 (Goethe; 1816); *An Schwager Kronos*, D. 369 (Goethe; 1816); *Klage*, D.

371 (1816); *An die Natur*, D. 372 (Stolberg-Stolberg; 1816); *Lied*, D. 373 (Fouqué; 1816); *Der Tod Oskars*, D. 375 (Ossian; Harold, trans.; 1816); *Lorma*, D. 376 (Ossian; Harold, trans.; 1816; fragment only); *Morgenlied*, D. 381 (1816); *Abendlied*, D. 382 (1816); *Laura am Klavier*, D. 388 (2 versions; Schiller; 1816); *Des Mädchens Klage*, D. 389 (Schiller; 1816); *Entzuckung an Laura*, D. 390 (Schiller; 1816); *Die vier Weltalter*, D. 391 (Schiller; 1816); *Pflügerlied*, D. 392 (Salis-Seewis; 1816); *Die Einsiedelei*, D. 393 (Salis-Seewis; 1816); *An die Harmonie*, D. 394 (Salis-Seewis; 1816); *Lebensmelodien*, D. 395 (Schlegel; 1816); *Gruppe aus dem Tartarus*, D. 396 (Schiller; 1816; fragment only); *Ritter Toggenburg*, D. 397 (Schiller; 1816); *Frühlingslied*, D. 398 (Hölty; 1816); *Auf den Tod einer Nachtigall*, D. 399 (Hölty; 1816); *Die Knabenzeit*, D. 400 (Hölty; 1816); *Winterlied*, D. 401 (Hölty; 1816); *Der Flüchtling*, D. 402 (Schiller; 1816); *Lied*, D. 403 (4 versions; Salis-Seewis; 1816); *Die Herbstnacht*, D. 404 (Salis-Seewis; 1816); *Der Herbstabend*, D. 405 (2 versions; Salis-Seewis; 1816); *Abschied von der Harfe*, D. 406 (Salis-Seewis; 1816); *Die verfehlte Stunde*, D. 409 (Schlegel; 1816); *Sprache der Liebe*, D. 410 (Schlegel; 1816); *Daphne am Bach*, D. 411 (Stolberg-Stolberg; 1816); *Stimme der Liebe*, D. 412 (2 versions; Stolberg-Stolberg; 1816); *Entzückung*, D. 413 (Matthisson; 1816); *Geist der Liebe*, D. 414 (Matthisson; 1816); *Klage*, D. 415 (Matthisson; 1816); *Lied in der Abwesenheit*, D. 416 (Stolberg-Stolberg; 1816; fragment only); *Stimme der Liebe*, D. 418 (Matthisson; 1816); *Julius an Theone*, D. 419 (Matthisson; 1816); *Minnelied*, D. 429 (Hölty; 1816); *Die frühe Liebe*, D. 430 (2 versions; Hölty; 1816; 2nd version not extant); *Blumenlied*, D. 431 (Hölty; 1816); *Der Leidende*, D. 432 (2 versions; 1816); *Seligkeit*, D. 433 (Hölty; 1816); *Erntelied*, D. 434 (Hölty; 1816); *Klage*, D. 436 (2 versions; Hölty; 1816; 2nd version originally D. 437); *Das grosse Halleluja*, D. 442 (Klopstock; 1816); *Schlachtlied*, D. 443 (Klopstock; 1816); *Die Gestirne*, D. 444 (Klopstock; 1816); *Edone*, D. 445 (Klopstock; 1816); *Die Liebesgötter*, D. 446 (Uz; 1816); *An den Schlaf*, D. 447 (1816); *Gott im Frühlinge*, D. 448 (2 versions; Uz; 1816); *Der gute Hirt*, D. 449 (Uz; 1816); *Fragment aus dem Aeschylus*, D. 450 (2 versions; Aeschylus; Mayrhofer, trans.; 1816); *Grablied auf einen Soldaten*, D. 454 (Schubart; 1816); *Freude der Kinderjahre*, D. 455 (Köpken; 1816); *Das Heimweh*, D. 456 (Winkler; 1816); *An die untergehende Sonne*, D. 457 (Kosegarten; 1816–17); *Aus Diego Manazares (Ilmerine)*, D. 458 (Schlechta; 1816); *An Chloen*, D. 462 (Jacobi; 1816); *Hochzeit-Lied*, D. 463 (Jacobi; 1816); *In der Mitternacht*, D. 464 (Jacobi; 1816); *Trauer der Liebe*, D. 465 (2 versions; Jacobi; 1816); *Die Perle*, D. 466 (Jacobi; 1816); *Pflicht und Liebe*, D. 467 (Gotter; 1816); *An den Mond*, D. 468 (Hölty; 1816); *Mignon*, D. 469 (Goethe; 1816; fragments only); *Liedesend*, D. 473 (2 versions; Mayrhofer; 1816); *Lied des Orpheus, als er in die Hölle ging*, D. 474 (2 versions; Jacobi; 1816; first version unfinished); *Abschied (nach einer Wallfahrtsarie)*, D. 475 (Mayrhofer; 1816); *Rückweg*, D. 476 (Mayrhofer; 1816); *Alte Liebe rostet nie*, D. 477 (Mayrhofer; 1816); *Harfenspieler I (Gesänge des Harfners No. 1)*, D. 478 (2 versions; Goethe; first version, 1816; 2nd version, 1822); *Harfenspieler II*

(Gesänge des Harfners No. 3), D. 479 (2 versions; Goethe; first version, 1816; 2nd version, 1822); *Harfenspieler III (Gesänge des Harfners No. 2)*, D. 480 (3 versions; Goethe; first and 2nd versions, 1816; 3rd version, 1822); *Sehnsucht*, D. 481 (Goethe; 1816); *Der Sänger am Felsen*, D. 482 (Pichler; 1816); *Lied*, D. 483 (Pichler; 1816); *Gesang der Geister über den Wassern*, D. 484 (Goethe; 1816; fragment only); *Der Wanderer*, D. 489 (3 versions; Lübeck; 1816; 2nd version originally D. 493b; 3rd version originally D. 493a); *Der Hirt*, D. 490 (Mayrhofer; 1816); *Geheimnis*, D. 491 (Mayrhofer; 1816); *Zum Punsche*, D. 492 (Mayrhofer; 1816; *Abendlied der Fürstin*, D. 495 (Mayrhofer; 1816); *Bei dem Grabe meines Vaters*, D. 496 (Claudius; 1816); *Klage um Ali Bey*, D. 496a (Claudius; 1816); *An die Nachtigall*, D. 497 (Claudius; 1816); *Wiegenlied*, D. 498 (1816); *Abendlied*, D. 499 (Claudius; 1816); *Phidile*, D. 500 (Claudius; 1816); *Zufriedenheit*, D. 501 (2 versions; Claudius; 1816); *Herbstlied*, D. 502 (Salis-Seewis; 1816); *Mailied*, D. 503 (Hölty; 1816); *Am Grabe Anselmos*, D. 504 (2 versions; Claudius; 1816); *Skolie*, D. 507 (Matthisson; 1816); *Lebenslied*, D. 508 (Matthisson; 1816); *Leiden der Trennung*, D. 509 (2 versions; Metastasio; Collin, trans.; 1816; first version, fragment only); *Vedi quanto adoro*, D. 510 (Metastasio; 1816); *Nur wer die Liebe kennt*, D. 513a (Werner; 1817?; sketch only); *Die abgeblühte Linde*, D. 514 (Széchényi; 1817?); *Der Flug der Zeit*, D. 515 (Széchényi; 1817?); *Sehnsucht*, D. 516 (Mayrhofer; 1816?); *Der Schäfer und der Reiter*, D. 517 (2 versions; Fouqué; 1817); *An den Tod*, D. 518 (Schubart; 1817?); *Die Blumensprache*, D. 519 (Platner?; 1817?); *Frohsinn*, D. 520 (2 versions; Castelli; 1817); *Jagdlied*, D. 521 (Werner; 1817); *Die Liebe*, D. 522 (Leon; 1817); *Trost*, D. 523 (1817); *Der Alpenjäger*, D. 524 (3 versions; Mayrhofer; 1817); *Wie Ulfru fischt*, D. 525 (2 versions; Mayrhofer; 1817); *Fahrt zum Hades*, D. 526 (Mayrhofer; 1817); *Schlaflied (Abendlied; Schlummerlied)*, D. 527 (2 versions; Mayrhofer; 1817); *La pastorella al prato*, D. 528 (Goldoni; 1817); *An eine Quelle*, D. 530 (Claudius; 1817); *Der Tod und das Mädchen*, D. 531 (Claudius; 1817); *Das Lied vom Reifen*, D. 532 (Claudius; 1817; fragment only); *Täglich zu singen*, D. 533 (Claudius; 1817); *Die Nacht*, D. 534 (Ossian; Harold, trans.; 1817); *Lied*, D. 535, with Small Orch. (1817); *Der Schiffer*, D. 536 (2 versions; Mayrhofer; 1817); *Am Strome*, D. 539 (Mayrhofer; 1817); *Philoket*, D. 540 (Mayrhofer; 1817); *Memnon*, D. 541 (Mayrhofer; 1817); *Antigone und Oedip*, D. 542 (Mayrhofer; 1817); *Auf dem See*, D. 543 (2 versions; Goethe; 1817); *Ganymed*, D. 544 (Goethe; 1817); *Der Jüngling und der Tod*, D. 545 (2 versions; Spaun; 1817); *Trost im Liede*, D. 546 (Schober; 1817); *An die Musik*, D. 547 (2 versions; Schober; 1817); *Orest auf Tauris*, D. 548 (Mayrhofer; 1817); *Mahomets Gesang*, D. 549 (Goethe; 1817; fragment only); *Die Forelle*, D. 550 (5 versions; Schubart; 1817?–21); *Pax vobiscum*, D. 551 (Schober; 1817); *Hänflings Liebeswerbung*, D. 552 (2 versions; Kind; 1817); *Auf der Donau*, D. 553 (Mayrhofer; 1817); *Uraniens Flucht*, D. 554 (Mayrhofer; 1817); sketch for a song, D. 555 (no text; 1817); *Liebhaber in allen Gestalten*, D. 558 (Goethe; 1817); *Schweizerlied*, D. 559 (Goethe; 1817); *Der Goldschmiedsgesell*, D. 560

(Goethe; 1817); *Nach einem Gewitter*, D. 561 (Mayr-hofer; 1817); *Fischerlied*, D. 562 (Salis-Seewis; 1817); *Die Einsiedelei*, D. 563 (Salis-Seewis; 1817); *Gret-chen im Zwinger (Gretchen; Gretchens Bitte)*, D. 564 (Goethe; 1817; fragment only); *Der Strom*, D. 565 (1817); *Das Grab*, D. 569, for Unison Chorus (Salis-Seewis; 1817); *Iphigenia*, D. 573 (Mayrhofer; 1817); *Entzückung an Laura*, D. 577 (2 versions; Schiller; 1817; fragments only); *Abschied*, D. 578 (Schubert; 1817); *Der Knabe in der Wiege (Wiegenlied)*, D. 579 (2 versions; Ottenwalt; 1817; 2nd version, fragment only); *Vollendung*, D. 579a (originally D. 989; Matthisson; 1817); *Die Erde*, D. 579b (originally D. 989a; Matthisson; 1817); *Gruppe aus dem Tartarus*, D. 583 (Schiller; 1817); *Elysium*, D. 584 (Schiller; 1817); *Atys*, D. 585 (Mayrhofer; 1817); *Erlafsee*, D. 586 (Mayrhofer; 1817); *An den Frühling*, D. 587 (2 versions; Schiller; 1817; 2nd version originally D. 245); *Der Alpenjäger*, D. 588 (2 versions; Schiller; 1817; first version, fragment only); *Der Kampf*, D. 594 (Schiller; 1817); *Thekla: Eine Geisterstimme*, D. 595 (2 versions; Schiller; 1817); *Lied eines Kindes*, D. 596 (1817; fragment only); *Auf der Riesenkoppe*, D. 611 (Körner; 1818); *An den Mond in einer Herbstnacht*, D. 614 (Schreiber; 1818); *Grablied für die Mutter*, D. 616 (1818); a vocal exercise for 2 Voices and Figured Bass, D. 619 (no text; 1818); *Einsamkeit*, D. 620 (Mayrhofer; 1818); *Der Blumenbrief*, D. 622 (Schreiber; 1818); *Das Marienbild*, D. 623 (Schreiber; 1818); *Blondel zu Marien*, D. 626 (1818); *Das Abendrot*, D. 627 (Schreiber; 1818); *Sonett I*, D. 628 (Petrarch; Schlegel, trans.; 1818); *Sonett II*, D. 629 (Petrarch; Schlegel, trans.; 1818); *Sonett III*, D. 630 (Petrarch; Gries, trans.; 1818); *Blanka (Das Mädchen)*, D. 631 (Schlegel; 1818); *Vom Mitleiden Mariä*, D. 632 (Schlegel; 1818); *Der Schmetterling*, D. 633 (Schlegel; 1819?); *Die Berge*, D. 634 (Schlegel; 1821?); *Sehnsucht*, D. 636 (3 versions; Schiller; 1821?); *Hoffnung*, D. 637 (Schiller; 1819?); *Der Jüngling am Bache*, D. 638 (2 versions; Schiller; 1819); *Widerschein*, D. 639 (2 versions; Schlechta; 1819?; 2nd version originally D. 949); *Abend*, D. 645 (Tieck; 1819; fragment only); *Die Gebüsche*, D. 646 (Schlegel; 1819); *Der Wanderer*, D. 649 (Schlegel; 1819); *Abendbilder*, D. 650 (Silbert; 1819); *Himmelsfunken*, D. 651 (Silbert; 1819); *Das Mädchen*, D. 652 (2 versions; Schlegel; 1819); *Bertas Lied in der Nacht*, D. 653 (Grillparzer; 1819); *An die Freunde*, D. 654 (Mayrhofer; 1819); *Marie*, D. 658 (Novalis; 1819); *Hymne I*, D. 659 (Novalis; 1819); *Hymne II*, D. 660 (Novalis; 1819); *Hymne III*, D. 661 (Novalis; 1819); *Hymne IV*, D. 662 (Novalis; 1819); *Der 13. Psalm*, D. 663 (M. Mendelssohn, trans.; 1819; fragment only); *Beim Winde*, D. 669 (Mayrhofer; 1819); *Die Sternennächte*, D. 670 (Mayrhofer; 1819); *Trost*, D. 671 (Mayrhofer; 1819); *Nachtstück*, D. 672 (2 versions; Mayrhofer; 1819); *Die Liebende schreibt*, D. 673 (Goethe; 1819); *Prometheus*, D. 674 (Goethe; 1819); *Strophe aus Die Götter Griechenlands*, D. 677 (2 versions; Schiller; 1819); *Über allen Zauber Liebe*, D. 682 (Mayrhofer; 1820?; fragment only); *Die Sterne*, D. 684 (Schlegel; 1820); *Morgenlied*, D. 685 (Werner; 1820); *Frühlingsglaube*, D. 686 (3 versions; Uhland; first and 2nd versions, 1820; 3rd version, 1822); *Nachthymne*, D. 687 (Novalis; 1820); *4 Canzonen: Non t'accostar all'urna* (Vitorelli),

Guarda, che bianca luna (Vitorelli), *Da quel sembiante appresi* (Metastasio), *Mio ben ricordati* (Metastasio) D. 688 (all 1820); *Abendröte*, D. 690 (Schlegel; 1823); *Die Vögel*, D. 691 (Schlegel; 1820); *Der Knabe*, D. 692 (Schlegel; 1820); *Der Fluss*, D. 693 (Schlegel; 1820); *Der Schiffer*, D. 694 (Schlegel; 1820); *Namenstagslied*, D. 695 (Stadler; 1820); *Des Fräuleins Liebeslauschen (Liebeslauschen)*, D. 698 (Schlechta; 1820); *Der entsühnte Orest*, D. 699 (Mayrhofer; 1820); *Freiwilliges Versinken*, D. 700 (Mayrhofer; 1820); *Der Jüngling auf dem Hügel*, D. 702 (Hüttenbrenner; 1820); *Der zürnenden Diana*, D. 707 (2 versions; Mayrhofer; 1820); *Im Walde (Waldesnacht)*, D. 708 (Schlegel; 1820); *Lob der Tränen*, D. 711 (2 versions; Schlegel; 1818); *Die gefangenen Sänger*, D. 712 (Schlegel; 1821); *Der Unglückliche*, D. 713 (2 versions; Pichler; 1821); *Versunken*, D. 715 (Goethe; 1821); *Grenzen der Menschheit*, D. 716 (Goethe; 1821); *Suleika*, D. 717 (1821?); *Geheimes*, D. 719 (Goethe; 1821); *Suleika*, D. 720 (2 versions; 1821); *Mahomets Gesang*, D. 721 (Goethe; 1821; fragment only); *Linde Lüfte wehen*, D. 725 (1821; fragment only); *Mignon*, D. 726 (Goethe; 1821); *Mignon*, D. 727 (Goethe; 1821); *Johanna Sebus*, D. 728 (Goethe; 1821; fragment only); *Der Blumen Schmerz*, D. 731 (Mayláth; 1821); *Ihr Grab*, D. 736 (Engelhardt; 1822?); *An die Leier*, D. 737 (Bruchmann; 1822?); *Im Haine*, D. 738 (Bruchmann; 1822?); *Sei mir gegrüsst*, D. 741 (Rückert; 1821?); *Der Wachtelschlag*, D. 742 (Sauter; 1822); *Selige Welt*, D. 743 (Senn; 1822); *Schwanengesang*, D. 744 (Senn; 1822); *Die Rose*, D. 745 (2 versions; Schlegel; 1822); *Am See*, D. 746 (Bruchmann; 1822?); *Herrn Josef Spaun, Assessor in Linz (Sendschreiben an den Assessor Spaun in Linz)*, D. 749 (Collin; 1822); *Die Liebe hat gelogen*, D. 751 (Platen-Hallermünde; 1822); *Nachtviolen*, D. 752 (Mayrhofer; 1822); *Heliopolis*, D. 753 (Mayrhofer; 1822); *Heliopolis*, D. 754 (Mayrhofer; 1822); *Du liebst mich nicht*, D. 756 (2 versions; Platen-Hallermünde; 1822); *Todesmusik*, D. 758 (Schober; 1822); *Schatzgräbers Begehr*, D. 761 (2 versions; Schober; 1822); *Schwestergruss*, D. 762 (Bruchmann; 1822); *Der Musensohn*, D. 764 (2 versions; Goethe; 1822); *An die Entfernte*, D. 765 (Goethe; 1822); *Am Flusse*, D. 766 (Goethe; 1822); *Willkommen und Abschied*, D. 767 (2 versions; Goethe; 1822); *Wandrers Nachtlied*, D. 768 (Goethe; 1824); *Drang in die Ferne*, D. 770 (Leitner; 1823); *Der Zwerg*, D. 771 (Collin; 1822?); *Wehmut*, D. 772 (Collin; 1822?); *Auf dem Wasser zu singen*, D. 774 (Stolberg-Stolberg; 1823); *Dass sie hier gewesen*, D. 775 (Rückert; 1823?); *Du bist die Ruh*, D. 776 (Rückert; 1823); *Lachen und Weinen*, D. 777 (Rückert; 1823?); *Greisengesang*, D. 778 (2 versions; Rückert; 1823); *Die Wallfahrt*, D. 778a (Rückert; 1823?); *Der zürnende Barde*, D. 785 (Bruchmann; 1823); *Viola*, D. 786 (Schober; 1823); *Lied (Die Mutter Erde)*, D. 788 (Stolberg-Stolberg; 1823); *Pilgerweise*, D. 789 (Schober; 1823); *Vergissmeinnicht*, D. 792 (Schober; 1823); *Das Geheimnis*, D. 793 (Schiller; 1823); *Der Pilgrim*, D. 794 (2 versions; Schiller; 1823); *Die schöne Müllerin*, song cycle, D. 795 (Müller; 1823; 1, *Das Wandern*; 2, *Wohin?*; 3, *Halt!*; 4, *Danksagung an den Bach*; 5, *Am Feierabend*; 6, *Der Neugierige*; 7, *Ungeduld*; 8, *Morgengruss*; 9, *Des Müllers Blumen*; 10, *Tränenre-*

gen; 11, *Mein!;* 12, *Pause;* 13, *Mit dem grünen Lautenbande;* 14, *Der Jäger;* 15, *Eifersucht und Stolz;* 16, *Die liebe Farbe;* 17, *Die böse Farbe;* 18, *Trockne Blumen;* 19, *Der Müller und der Bach;* 20, *Des Baches Wiegenlied); Romanze zum Drama Rosamunde,* D. 797 (Chézy; 1823); *Im Abendrot,* D. 799 (Lappe; 1824?); *Der Einsame,* D. 800 (2 versions; Lappe; 1825); *Dithyrambe,* D. 801 (Schiller; 1826); *Der Sieg,* D. 805 (Mayrhofer; 1824); *Abendstern,* D. 806 (Mayrhofer; 1824); *Auflösung,* D. 807 (Mayrhofer; 1824); *Gondelfahrer,* D. 808 (Mayrhofer; 1824); *Lied eines Kriegers,* D. 822, with Unison Chorus (1824); *Nacht und Träume,* D. 827 (2 versions; Collin; 1823); *Die junge Nonne,* D. 828 (Craigher de Jachelutta; 1825); *Abschied,* D. 829 (Pratobevera; 1826); *Lied der Anne Lyle,* D. 830 (MacDonald; 1825); *Gesang der Norna,* D. 831 (Scott; Spiker, trans.; 1825); *Des Sängers Habe,* D. 832 (Schlechta; 1825); *Der blinde Knabe,* D. 833 (2 versions; Cibber; Craigher, trans.; 1825); *Im Walde,* D. 834 (2 versions; Schulze; 1825); *Ellens Gesang,* D. 837 (Scott; Storck, trans.; 1825); *Ellens Gesang,* D. 838 (Scott; Storck, trans.; 1825); *Ellens Gesang (Hymne an die Jungfrau),* D. 839 (Scott; Storck, trans.; 1825); *Totengräbers Heimwehe,* D. 842 (Craigher; 1825); *Lied des gefangenen Jägers,* D. 843 (Scott; Storck, trans.; 1825); *Normans Gesang,* D. 846 (Scott; Storck, trans.; 1825); *Das Heimweh,* D. 851 (2 versions; Felsö-Eör; 1825); *Die Allmacht,* D. 852 (2 versions; Pyrker; 1825); *Auf der Bruck,* D. 853 (2 versions; Schulze; 1825); *Fülle der Liebe,* D. 854 (Schlegel; 1825); *Wiedersehn,* D. 855 (Schlegel; 1825); *Abendlied für die Entfernte,* D. 856 (Schlegel; 1825); *2 Szenen aus dem Schauspiel Lacrimas,* D. 857: 1, *Lied der Delphine;* 2, *Lied des Florio* (Schütz; 1825); *An mein Herz,* D. 860 (Schulze; 1825); *Der liebliche Stern,* D. 861 (Schulze; 1825); *Um Mitternacht,* D. 862 (2 versions; Schulze; first version, 1825; 2nd version, 1826); *An Gott,* D. 863 (Hohlfeld; 1827; not extant); *Das Totenhemdchen,* D. 864 (Bauernfeld; 1824; not extant); *Widerspruch,* D. 865 (Seidl; 1826?); *4 Refrainlieder,* D. 866 (Seidl; 1828): 1, *Die Unterscheidung;* 2, *Bei dir allein;* 3, *Die Männer sind méchant;* 4, *Irdisches Glück; Wiegenlied,* D. 867 (Seidl; 1826?); *Totengräber-Weise,* D. 869 (Schlechta; 1826); *Der Wanderer an den Mond,* D. 870 (Seidl; 1826); *Das Zügenglöcklein,* D. 871 (2 versions; Seidl; 1826); *O Quell, was strömst du rasch und wild,* D. 874 (Schulze; 1826; fragment only); *Im Jänner 1817 (Tiefes Leid),* D. 876 (Schulze; 1826); *Gesänge aus Wilhelm Meister,* D. 877: 1, *Mignon und der Harfner;* 2, 3, and 4, *Lied der Mignon* (Goethe; 1826); *Am Fenster,* D. 878 (Seidl; 1826); *Sehnsucht,* D. 879 (Seidl; 1826); *Im Freien,* D. 880 (Seidl; 1826); *Fischerweise,* D. 881 (2 versions; Schlechta; 1826); *Im Frühling,* D. 882 (Schulze; 1826); *Lebensmut,* D. 883 (Schulze; 1826); *Über Wildemann,* D. 884 (Schulze; 1826); *Trinklied (Come, thou monarch of the vine),* D. 888 (Shakespeare; Grünbühel and Bauernfeld, trans.; 1826); *Standchen (Hark, hark the lark),* D. 889 (Shakespeare; Schlegel, trans.; 1826); *Hippolits Lied,* D. 890 (Gerstenberg; 1826); *Gesang (An Sylvia; Who Is Sylvia?),* D. 891 (Shakespeare; Bauernfeld, trans.; 1826); *Fröhliches Scheiden,* D. 896 (Leitner; 1827–28; sketch only); *Sie in jedem Liede,* D. 896a (Leitner;

1827–28; sketch only); *Wolke und Quelle,* D. 896b (Leitner; 1827–28; sketch only); *3 Gesänge,* D. 902 (1827): 1, *L'incanto degli occhi (Die Macht der Augen);* 2, *Il Traditor deluso (Der getäuschte Verräter);* 3, *Il modo di prender moglie (Die Art, ein Weib zu nehmen); Alinde,* D. 904 (Rochlitz; 1827); *An die Laute,* D. 905 (Rochlitz; 1827); *Der Vater mit dem Kind,* D. 906 (Bauernfeld; 1827); *Romanze des Richard Löwenherz,* D. 907 (2 versions; Scott; Müller, trans.; 1826); *Jägers Liebeslied,* D. 909 (Schober; 1827); *Schiffers Scheidelied,* D. 910 (Schober; 1827); *Die Winterreise,* song cycle, D. 911 (Müller; 1827; Book I: 1, *Gute Nacht;* 2, *Die Wetterfahne;* 3, *Gefrorne Tränen;* 4, *Erstarrung;* 5, *Der Lindenbaum;* 6, *Wasserflut* [2 versions]; 7, *Auf dem Flusse;* 8, *Rückblick;* 9, *Irrlicht;* 10, *Rast* [2 versions]; 11, *Frühlingstraum;* 12, *Einsamkeit* [2 versions]; Book II: 13, *Die Post;* 14, *Der greise Kopf;* 15, *Die Krähe;* 16, *Letzte Hoffnung;* 17, *Im Dorfe;* 18, *Der stürmische Morgen;* 19, *Täuschung;* 20, *Der Wegweiser;* 21, *Das Wirthaus;* 22, *Mut* [2 versions]; 23, *Die Nebensonnen* [2 versions]; 24, *Der Leiermann* [2 versions]); sketch for a song, D. 916a (no text; 1827); *Das Lied im Grünen,* D. 917 (Reil; 1827); *Frühlingslied,* D. 919 (Pollak; 1827); *Heimliches Lieben,* D. 922 (2 versions; 1827); *Eine altschottische Ballade,* D. 923 (3 versions; first and 3rd for 2 Voices; Eng. author unknown; Herder, trans.; 1827); *Das Weinen,* D. 926 (Leitner; 1827–28); *Vor meiner Wiege,* D. 927 (Leitner; 1827–28); *Der Wallensteiner Lanzknecht beim Trunk,* D. 931 (Leitner; 1827); *Der Kreuzzug,* D. 932 (Leitner; 1827); *Des Fischers Liebesglück,* D. 933 (Leitner; 1827); *Lebensmut,* D. 937 (Rellstab; 1828; fragment only); *Der Winterabend,* D. 938 (Leitner; 1828); *Die Sterne,* D. 939 (Leitner; 1828); *Auf dem Strom,* D. 943, with Horn or Cello obbligato (Rellstab; 1828); *Herbst,* D. 945 (Rellstab; 1828); *Glaube, Hoffnung und Liebe,* D. 955 (Kuffner; 1828); *Schwanengesang,* D. 957 (1828; Book I: 1, *Liebesbotschaft [Rellstab];* 2, *Kriegers Ahnung [Rellstab];* 3, *Frühlingssehnsucht [Rellstab];* 4, *Ständchen [Rellstab];* 5, *Aufenthalt [Rellstab];* 6, *In der Ferne [Rellstab];* Book II: 7, *Abschied [Rellstab];* 8, *Der Atlas [Heine];* 9, *Ihr Bild [Heine];* 10, *Das Fischermädchen [Heine];* 11, *Die Stadt [Heine];* 12, *Am Meer [Heine];* 13, *Der Doppelgänger [Heine];* 14, *Die Taubenpost [Seidl]); Der Hirt auf dem Felsen,* D. 965, with Clarinet obbligato (Müller; 1828); *Der Graf von Habsburg,* D. 990 (Schiller; 1815?); *Kaiser Maximilian auf der Martinswand,* D. 990a (Collin; 1815?); *Augenblicke in Elysium,* D. 990b (originally D. 582; Schober; not extant); *Das Echo,* D. 990c (originally D. 868; Castelli); *Die Schiffende,* D. 990d (Hölty; not extant); *L'incanto degli occhi,* D. 990e (Metastasio); *Il Traditor deluso,* D. 990f (Metastasio; not extant); *Mein Frieden,* D. AI/30 (Heine; 1815?).

FOR ORCH.: Overture in D major, D. 2a (originally D. 996; 1811?; fragment only); Symph. in D major, D. 2b (originally D. 997; 1811?; fragment of first movement only); Overture in D major, to Albrecht's comedy *Der Teufel als Hydraulicus,* D. 4 (1812?); Overture in D major, D. 12 (1811?); Overture in D major, D. 26 (1812); 3 minuets and trios, D. 39a (1813; not extant); orch. fragment in D major, D. 71c (originally D. 966a; 1813); Symph. No. 1, in D major, D. 82

Schubert

(1813); orch. fragment in B-flat major, D. 94a (1814?); Symph. No. 2, in B-flat major, D. 125 (1814–15); Symph. No. 3, in D major, D. 200 (1815); Concerto (Concertstück) in D major for Violin and Orch., D. 345 (1816); Symph. No. 4, in C minor, D. 417, "Tragic" (1816); Rondo in A major for Violin and Strings, D. 438 (1816); Overture in B-flat major, D. 470 (1816); Symph. No. 5, in B-flat major, D. 485 (1816); Overture in D major, D. 556 (1817); Polonaise in B-flat major for Violin and Orch., D. 580 (1817); Symph. No. 6, in C major, D. 589 (1817–18); Overture in D major, D. 590, "im italienischen Stile" (1817); Overture in C major, D. 591, "im italienischen Stile" (1817); Symph. in D major, D. 615 (piano sketches for 2 movements only; 1818); Overture in E minor, D. 648 (1819); Symph. in D major, D. 708a (sketches only; date unknown); Symph. (No. 7) in E major, D. 729 (1821; sketched in score; performing version arranged by Weingartner); Symph. No. 8, in B minor, D. 759, "Unfinished" (1822; 2 movements and an unfinished scherzo); "Gmunden" or "Gastein" Symph., D. 849 (now believed to be identical with D. 944); Symph. in D major, D. 936a (1828; sketches only); Symph. No. 9, in C major, D. 944, "Great" (probably begun in 1825; completed in 1826).

FOR PIANO: Fantasie in C minor, D. 2e (originally D. 993; 1811); Fugue in D minor, D. 13 (1812?); Overture, D. 14 (1812?; sketch only; not extant); 6 variations in E-flat major, D. 21 (1812; not extant); 7 variations in F major, D. 24 (1812; fragment only; not extant); Fugue in C major, D. 24a (1812); Fugue in G major, D. 24b (1812); Fugue in D minor, D. 24c (1812); Fugue in C major, D. 24d (1812; fragment only); Fugue in F major, D. 25c (1812; fragment only); Andante in C major, D. 29 (1812); fugal sketches in B-flat major, D. 37a (originally D. 967; 1813?); Fugue in E minor, D. 41a (1813; fragment only); Fugue in E minor, D. 71b (1813; fragment only); Allegro in E major, D. 154 (sketch of D. 157; 1815); 10 variations in F major, D. 156 (1815); Sonata in E major, D. 157 (1815; unfinished); Adagio in G major, D. 178 (1815); Sonata in C major, D. 279 (1815); Allegretto in C major, D. 346 (1816?; fragment only); Allegretto moderato in C major, D. 347 (1813?; fragment only); Andantino in C major, D. 348 (1816; fragment only); Adagio in C major, D. 349 (1816?; fragment only); Sonata in F major, D. 459 (1816; fragment only); 5 Klavierstücke, D. 459a (first 2 from preceding work; 1816?); Adagio in D-flat major, D. 505 (original slow movement of D. 625; 1818); Rondo in E major, D. 506 (1817); Sonata in A minor, D. 537 (1817); Sonata in A-flat major, D. 557 (1817); Sonata in E minor, D. 566 (1817); Sonata in D-flat major, D. 567 (unfinished; first version of D. 568; 1817); Sonata in E-flat major, D. 568 (1817); Scherzo in D major and Allegro in F-sharp minor, D. 570 (unfinished; 1817); Sonata in F-sharp minor, D. 571 (1817; fragment only); Sonata in B major, D. 575 (1817); 13 variations on a theme by Anselm Hüttenbrenner, in A minor, D. 576 (1817); 2 scherzos, in B-flat major and D-flat major, D. 593 (1817); Andante in A major, D. 604 (1816?); Fantasia in C major, D. 605 (1821–23; fragment only); Fantasy in C major, D. 605a, "Grazer Fantasie" (1818?); March in E major, D. 606 (1818?); Adagio in E major, D. 612

(1818); Sonata in C major, D. 613 (2 movements; 1818); Sonata in F minor, D. 625 (2 movements; 1818); Sonata in C-sharp minor, D. 655 (1819; fragment only); Sonata in A major, D. 664 (1819?); Variations on a Waltz by Diabelli, in C minor, D. 718 (1821); Overture to Alfonso und Estrella, in D major, D. 759a (an arrangement of the D. 732 overture; 1822); Fantasy in C major, D. 760, "Wanderfantasie" (1822); Sonata in E minor, D. 769a (originally D. 994; 1823?; fragment only); 6 Momens musicals [sic], in C major, A-flat major, F minor, C-sharp minor, F minor, A-flat major, D. 780 (1823–28); Sonata in A minor, D. 784 (1823); Ungarische Melodie in B minor, D. 817 (1824); Sonata in C major, D. 840, Reliquie (unfinished; 1825); Sonata in A minor, D. 845 (1825); Sonata in D major, D. 850 (1825); Sonata in G major, D. 894 (originally known as the Fantasie, Andante, Menuetto und Allegretto; 1826); 4 impromptus, in C minor, E-flat major, G-flat major, and A-flat major, D. 899 (1827); Allegretto in C minor, D. 900 (1820?; fragment only); Allegretto in C minor, D. 915 (1827); sketch for a piano piece in C major, D. 916b (1827); sketch for a piano piece in C minor, D. 916c (1827); 4 impromptus, in F minor, A-flat major, B-flat major, and F minor, D. 935 (1827); 3 Klavierstücke, in E-flat minor, E-flat major, and C major, D. 946 (1828); Sonata in C minor, D. 958 (1828); Sonata in A major, D. 959 (1828); Sonata in B-flat major, D. 960 (1828); March in G major, D. 980f (date unknown).

FOR PIANO, FOUR-HANDS: Fantasie in G major, D. 1 (1810); Fantasie in G major, D. 1b (1810?; fragment only); Sonata in F major, D. 1c (1810; unfinished); Fantasie in G minor, D. 9 (1811); Fantasie in C minor, D. 48, "Grande sonate" (2 versions; 1813); Overture in D major, D. 592, "im italienischen Stile" (an arrangement of D. 590; 1817); Overture in C major, D. 597, "im italienischen Stile" (an arrangement of D. 591; 1817); 4 polonaises, in D minor, B-flat major, E major, and F major, D. 599 (1818); 3 marches héroïques, in B minor, C major, and D major, D. 602 (1818?); Rondo in D major, D. 608 (2 versions; 1818); Sonata in B-flat major, D. 617 (1818); Deutscher in G major, with 2 trios and 2 Ländler, in E major, D. 618 (1818); Polonaise and Trio, D. 618a (sketch only; 1818); 8 variations on a French song, in E minor, D. 624 (1818); Overture in G minor, D. 668 (1819); Overture in F major, D. 675 (1819); 3 marches militaires, in D major, G major, and E-flat major, D. 733 (1818); Overture to Alfonso und Estrella, D. 773 (an arrangement of the D. 732 overture; 1823); Overture to Fierabras, D. 798 (an arrangement of the D. 796 overture; 1823); Sonata in C major, D. 812, "Grand duo" (1824); 8 variations on an original theme, in A-flat major, D. 813 (1824); 4 Ländler, in E-flat major, A-flat major, C minor, and C major, D. 814 (1824); Divertissement à l'hongroise in G minor, D. 818 (1824); 6 grandes marches, in E-flat major, G minor, B minor, D major, E-flat minor, and E major, D. 819 (1824); Divertissement sur des motifs originaux français in E minor, D. 823: 1, Marche brillante; 2, Andantino varié; 3, Rondeau brillant (1825?); 6 polonaises, in D minor, F major, B-flat major, D major, A major, and E major, D. 824 (1826); Grande marche funèbre in C minor, D. 859 (on the death of Alexander I of Russia; 1825); *Grande marche héroïque* in A minor, D. 885 (for the coronation of Nicholas I of Russia; 1826); 8 variations on a theme from Hérold's *Marie,* in C major, D. 908 (1827); March in G major, D. 928, "Kindermarsch" (1827); Fantasie in F minor, D. 940 (1828); Allegro in A minor, D. 947, Lebensstürme (1828); Rondo in A major, D. 947 (1828); Fugue in E minor, D. 952 (1828); Allegro moderato in C major and Andante in A minor (Sonatine), D. 968 (1818?); Introduction, 4 variations on an original theme, and Finale, in B-flat major, D. 968a (originally D. 603; 1824?); 2 *marches caractéristiques* in C major, D. 968b (originally D. 886; 1826?).

DANCES FOR PIANO: Waltzes and March, D. 19b (1812?; not extant); 12 minuets with trios, D. 22 (1812; not extant); 30 minuets with trios, D. 41 (1813; 10 not extant); 2 minuets, in D major and A major, both with 2 trios, D. 91 (1813; 2 other minuets lost); 12 Wiener Deutsche, D. 128 (1812?); Deutscher in E major, with trio, D. 135 (1815); Deutscher in C-sharp minor, with trio, D. 139 (1815); 12 waltzes, 17 Ländler, and 9 écossaises, D. 145 (1815–21); 20 waltzes (*Letzte Walzer*), D. 146 (Nos. 1 and 3–11, 1815; Nos. 2 and 12–20, 1823); Ecossaise in D minor/F major, D. 158 (1815); Minuet in A minor, with trio, D. 277a (1815); 12 écossaises, D. 299 (1815); Minuet in A major, with trio, D. 334 (1815?); Minuet in E major, with 2 trios, D. 335 (1813?); 36 Originaltänze (*Erste Walzer*), D. 365 (1816–21); 17 Ländler, D. 366 (1816–24); 8 Ländler, D. 378 (1816); 3 minuets, in E major, A major, and C major, each with 2 trios, D. 380 (1816); 12 Deutsche, D. 420 (1816); 6 écossaises, D. 421 (1816); Ecossaise in E-flat major, D. 511 (1817?); 8 écossaises, D. 529 (1817); Minuet in C-sharp minor, D. 600 (1814?); Trio in E major, D. 610 (1818); Deutscher in C-sharp minor and Ecossaise in D-flat major, D. 643 (1819); 12 Ländler, D. 681 (1815?; Nos. 1–4 not extant); 6 écossaises, D. 697 (1820); Deutscher in G-flat major, D. 722 (1821); 16 Ländler and 2 écossaises (*Wiener-Damen Ländler*), D. 734 (1822?); Galop and 8 écossaises, D. 735 (1822?); 2 Deutsche, in A major and D major, D. 769 (No. 1, 1824; No. 2, 1823); 34 *Valses sentimentales,* D. 779 (1823?); 12 écossaises, D. 781 (1823); Ecossaise in D major, D. 782 (1823?); 16 Deutsche and 2 écossaises, D. 783 (1823–24); 12 Deutsche (Ländler), D. 790 (1823); 3 écossaises, D. 816 (1824); 6 Deutsche, D. 820 (1824); 2 Deutsche, in F major and G major, D. 841 (1825); Waltz in G major (*Albumblatt*), D. 844 (1825); 12 Grazer Walzer, D. 924 (1827); Grazer Galopp in C major, D. 925 (1827); Deutscher, D. 944a (1828; not extant); 12 waltzes (*Valses nobles*), D. 969 (1826); 6 Ländler, D. 970 (date unknown); 3 Deutsche, in A minor, A major, and E major, D. 971 (1822); 3 Deutsche, in D-flat major, A-flat major, and A major, D. 972 (date unknown); 3 Deutsche, in E major, E major, and A-flat major, D. 973 (date unknown); 2 Deutsche, both in D-flat major, D. 974 (date unknown); Deutscher in D major, D. 975 (date unknown); Cotillon in E-flat major, D. 976 (1825); 8 écossaises, D. 977 (date unknown); Waltz in A-flat major, D. 978 (1825); Waltz in G major, D. 979 (1826); 2 waltzes, in G major and B minor, D. 980 (1826); 2 dance sketches, in A major and E major, D. 980a (originally D. 640; date unknown); 2

Ländler, both in E-flat major, D. 980b (originally D. 679; date unknown); 2 Ländler, both in D-flat major, D. 980c (originally D. 680; fragment only; date unknown); Waltz in C major, D. 980d (1827); 2 dance sketches, in G minor and F major, D. 980c (date unknown).

CHAMBER MUSIC: String Quartet, D. 2c (originally D. 998; 1811?; fragment only); 6 minuets, D. 2d (originally D. 995; 1811); sketch for a trio of a minuet, in C major, D. 2f (1811); String Quartet in C major, D. 3 (1812; fragment only); Overture in C minor, D. 8 (1811); Overture in C minor, D. 8a (an arrangement of D. 8; 1811); String Quartet in G minor/B-flat major, D. 18 (1810?); String Quartet, D. 19 (1810?; not extant); String Quartet, D. 19a (1810?; not extant); Overture in B-flat major, D. 20 (1812; not extant); Trio (Sonata in one movement) in B-flat major, D. 28 (1812); String Quartet in C major, D. 32 (1812); String Quartet in B-flat major, D. 36 (1812–13); String Quartet in C major, D. 46 (1813); String Quartet in B-flat major, D. 68 (1813; 2 movements only); Wind Octet in F major, D. 72 (1813); Allegro in F major, D. 72a (1813; unfinished); String Quartet in D major, D. 74 (1813); Wind Nonet in E-flat minor, D. 79, "Franz Schuberts Begräbnis-Feyer" (*Eine kleine Trauermusik*) (1813); Minuet in D major, D. 86 (1813); String Quartet in E-flat major, D. 87 (1813); Andante in C major, D. 87a (1813); 5 minuets and 6 trios, D. 89 (1813); 5 Deutsche and 7 trios, with coda, D. 90 (1813); String Quartet in D major, D. 94 (1811?); 5 minuets and 6 Deutsche, with trios, D. 94b (1814; not extant); Trio in G major, for Schubert's arrangement of Matiegka's *Notturno,* op. 21, D. 96 (1814); String Quartet in C minor, D. 103 (1814; fragments, Grave, and Allegro extant); String Trio in B-flat major, D. 111a (1814; not extant); String Quartet in B-flat major, D. 112 (1814); String Quartet in G minor, D. 173 (1815); String Quartet in E major, D. 353 (1816); 4 komische Ländler in D major, D. 354 (1816); 8 Ländler in F-sharp minor, D. 355 (1816); 9 Ländler in D major, D. 370 (1816); 11 Ländler in B-flat major, D. 374 (1816); Sonata (Sonatina) in D major, D. 384 (1816); Sonata (Sonatina) in A minor, D. 385 (1816); Sonata (Sonatina) in G minor, D. 408 (1816); String Trio in B-flat major, D. 471 (1816; unfinished); Adagio and Rondo concertante in F major, D. 487 (1816); Sonata (Duo) in A major, D. 574 (1817); String Trio in B-flat major, D. 581 (1817); Variations in A major, D. 597a (1817; not extant); Overture in B-flat major, D. 601 (an arrangement of the D. 470 overture; 1816?; fragment only); Piano Quintet in A major, D. 667, "Die Forelle" (1819); String Quartet in C minor, D. 703 (*Quartettsatz*) (1820); Introduction and variations on *Trockne Blumen* from *Die schöne Müllerin,* in E minor/E major, D. 802 (1824); Octet in F major, D. 803 (1824); String Quartet in A minor, D. 804 (1824); String Quartet in D minor, D. 810, "Der Tod und das Mädchen" (1824); Sonata in A minor, D. 821, "Arpeggione" (1824); String Quartet in G major, D. 887 (1826); Rondo in B minor (*Rondo brillant*), D. 895 (1826); Piano Trio movement in E-flat major, D. 897, "Notturno" (1828?); Piano Trio in B-flat major, D. 898 (1828?); Piano Trio in E-flat major, D. 929 (1827); Fantasy in C major, D. 934 (1827); String Quintet in

C major, D. 956 (1828); Fugue in C major, D. A1/3 (1812?; fragment only).

Schuberth, Julius (Ferdinand Georg), founder of the firm J. Schuberth & Co. of Leipzig and N.Y.; b. Magdeburg, July 14, 1804; d. Leipzig, June 9, 1875. He established the Hamburg business in 1826; opened a branch in Leipzig in 1832, and in N.Y. in 1850. His brother, **Fritz Wilhelm** (1817–90), took over the Hamburg house in 1853 (firm name, "Fritz Schuberth"). Julius Schuberth publ. the *Kleine Hamburger Musikzeitung* (1840–50), the *New Yorker Musikzeitung* (from 1867), and *Schuberth's kleine Musikzeitung* (1871–72). In 1872 he founded the music library at Weimar known as the Liszt-Schuberth-Stiftung. In 1891 the business was purchased by Felix Siegel (d. Leipzig, July 4, 1920), the originator of the *Musikalische Universalbibliothek.* In 1943 the entire stock of the Schuberth Publishing House was destroyed in an air raid; after World War II it was reestablished in Wiesbaden.

Schuch, Ernst von, eminent Austrian conductor; b. Graz, Nov. 23, 1846; d. Kötzschenbroda, near Dresden, May 10, 1914. He studied violin; in 1867 he became a theater conductor in Breslau; then conducted in Würzburg, Graz, and Basel; in 1872 he obtained a position at Pollini's Italian Opera House in Dresden, and in 1873 was engaged as court conductor, remaining with the Dresden Court Opera for 40 years. In 1897 he was given the rank of hereditary nobility, which entitled him to add the nobiliary particle "von" to his name. He was a worthy successor to the traditions established in Dresden by Weber and Wagner, and earned a reputation as one of the finest opera conductors. He was moreover a man of great general culture and of progressive ideas. He brought out about 50 new operas, and conducted the world premiere of the operas *Feuersnot, Salome, Elektra,* and *Der Rosenkavalier* by Richard Strauss; also included in his repertoire operas by Puccini, which were new to Germany at the time. He seldom left Dresden; his most extensive journey was a trip to N.Y. to conduct 3 orch. concerts in 1900. In 1875 he married the opera singer **Klementine Proska** (real name, **Procházka;** b. Ödenburg, Feb. 12, 1850; d. Kötzschenbroda, June 8, 1932), who was the principal coloratura soprano during Schuch's tenure at the Dresden Opera until her retirement in 1904. Their daughter **Liesel von Schuch** (b. Dresden, Dec. 12, 1891) was also a coloratura soprano at the Dresden Opera from 1914 to 1935; then taught voice at the Dresden Hochschule für Musik (until 1967).

Schulhoff, Erwin, Czech composer and pianist, great-grandnephew of **Julius Schulhoff;** b. Prague, June 8, 1894; d. in a concentration camp, Wülzburg, Bavaria, Aug. 18, 1942. He studied music in Prague and Vienna; then went to Leipzig, where he studied piano with Teichmüller and composition with Max Reger (1908–10); continued his studies in Cologne (1910–14). Returning to Prague, he was active as a piano teacher; traveled as a concert pianist in Russia and France. He was an eager propagandist of modern music; together with Alois Hába, he worked on the problems of quarter-tone music. In 1933 he was a delegate at the International Congress of Revolutionary Musicians in Moscow. Convinced of the necessity of social revolution, he became a member of the Communist party; after the Nazi occupation of Czechoslovakia in 1939, he was granted Soviet citizenship to protect him from arrest; however, after the Nazi invasion of Russia in 1941, he was taken to the concentration camp, where he died the following year. As a composer, he followed the modern trends of the period between the 2 wars, including the European species of jazz. He was the first to set to music the original German text of the Communist Manifesto of 1848; the MS disappeared, but was eventually retrieved, and the work was finally performed in Prague on April 5, 1962.

Schulhoff, Julius, noted pianist and composer; b. Prague, Aug. 2, 1825; d. Berlin, March 13, 1898. He studied in Prague; proceeded to Paris, where he gave concerts under the patronage of Chopin, to whom he dedicated his first composition, an *Allegro brillant.* He made a long tour through Austria, England, Spain, and Southern Russia; returning to Paris, he was a successful teacher; after the outbreak of the Franco-Prussian War (1870) he settled in Dresden; moved to Berlin shortly before his death. He publ. excellent salon music for piano; his *Galop di bravura* and *Impromptu Polka* were great favorites.

Schuller, Gunther, significant American composer, conductor, and educator; b. New York, Nov. 22, 1925. He was of a musical family; his paternal grandfather was a bandmaster in Germany before emigrating to America; his father was a violinist with the N.Y. Phil. Schuller was sent to Germany as a child for a thorough academic training; returning to the U.S., he was enrolled at the St. Thomas Church Choir School, where he studied music theory with T. Tertius Noble and took French-horn lessons with Robert Schulze at the Manhattan School of Music. He played horn with the N.Y. Phil. in 1942; in 1943 he became principal French-horn player with the Cincinnati Symph. Orch. On April 16, 1945, at the age of 19, he appeared as soloist in his first Concerto for Horn and Orch. with the Cincinnati Symph. At the same time he became fascinated with jazz; he played the French horn in a combo conducted by Miles Davis; he also began to compose jazz pieces. From 1945 to 1959 he played horn in the orch. of the Metropolitan Opera in N.Y.; from 1950 to 1963 he taught horn at the Manhattan School of Music; then was engaged to teach composition at the School of Music at Yale Univ. (1964–65). In 1966 he was appointed president of the New England Cons. in Boston, holding this post until 1977; concurrently he was chairman of the composition dept. at the Berkshire Music Center in Tanglewood, Mass.; he became its artistic director in 1969 and full director in 1972. In 1975 he founded Margun Music Inc., intended for a broad range of publications. He publ. a manual, *Horn Technique* (N.Y., 1962), and a very valuable study, *Early Jazz: Its Roots and Musical Development* (N.Y., 1968). In his multiple activities he tried to form a link between serious music and jazz; he popularized the style of "cool jazz" (recorded as *Birth of the Cool*). In 1957 he launched the slogan "third stream" to designate the combination of classical forms with improvisatory elements of jazz as a synthesis of disparate, but not necessarily incompatible, entities, and wrote fanciful pieces in this synthetic style; in many of these he worked in close cooperation with John Lewis of the Modern Jazz Quartet. As part of his investigation of the roots of jazz, he became interested in early ragtime and formed, in 1972, the New England Cons. Ragtime Ensemble; its recordings of Scott Joplin's piano rags in band arrangement were instrumental in bringing about the "ragtime revival." In his own works he freely applied serial methods, even when his general style was dominated by jazz. Schuller received honorary doctorates in music from Northwestern Univ. (1967), the Univ. of Illinois (1968), Williams College (1975), the New England Cons. (1978), and Rutgers Univ. (1980).

WORKS: FOR THE STAGE: 2 operas: *The Visitation*, in 3 acts (on a U.S. racial theme, freely adapted by Schuller from Kafka's *The Trial;* 1965–66; Hamburg, Oct. 12, 1966; U.S. premiere by the Hamburg company, N.Y., June 28, 1967), and *The Fisherman and His Wife*, one-act children's opera, to a libretto by John Updike from the Grimm fairy tale (Boston, May 7, 1970); *Variants,* jazz ballet for Jazz Quartet and Orch. (1960; N.Y., Jan. 4, 1961).

FOR ORCH.: 2 horn concertos: No. 1 (1943–44; Cincinnati, April 6, 1945, composer soloist) and No. 2 (1978); *Suite* for Chamber Orch. (1945); Cello Concerto (1945); *Vertige d'Eros,* symph. poem (1945; Madison, Wis., Oct. 15, 1967); *Symphonic Study* (1947–48); *Fantasia concertante* for 3 Trombones, and Orch. or Piano (1947); Symph. for Brass and Percussion (1949–50; revised 1964); *Dramatic Overture* (1951); *Recitative and Rondo* for Violin, and Orch. or Piano (1953–55); *Contours* for Chamber Orch. (1955–58); *Spectra* (1956–58; N.Y., Jan. 14, 1960); *7 Studies on Themes of Paul Klee* (1959; Minneapolis, Nov. 27, 1959); *Capriccio* for Tuba and Chamber Orch. (1960); *Contrasts* for Woodwind Quintet and Orch. (1961; Donaueschingen, Oct. 22, 1961; first U.S. work ever perf. at this annual German festival); *Movements* for Flute and Strings (1961); 2 piano concertos: No. 1 (1962; Cincinnati, Oct. 29, 1962) and No. 2 (1981); *Composition in 3 Parts* (1962; Minneapolis, March 29, 1963); *Threnos* for Oboe and Orch. (1963); *Meditation* for Concert Band (1963); *5 Bagatelles* (1964; Fargo, N.Dak., March 22, 1964); Symph. No. 1 (1964; Dallas, Feb. 8, 1965); *American Triptych: 3 Studies in Textures* (1964; New Orleans, March 9, 1965); 2 concertos for Orch.: No. 1 (1965; Chicago, Jan. 20, 1966; originally titled *Gala Music*) and No. 2 (1975; Washington, D.C., Oct. 12, 1976); *Colloquy* for 2 Pianos and Orch. (1966); *5 Etudes* for Youth Orch. (1966); *Diptych* for Brass Quintet and Orch. (1966; Boston, March 31, 1967); *Triplum I* (1967; N.Y., June 28, 1967) and *II*

(1974; Baltimore, Feb. 26, 1975); *Fanfare for St. Louis* (1967); Double-bass Concerto (1968; N.Y., June 27, 1968); *Shapes and Designs* (1968); *Consequents* (1970); *Museum Piece* for Renaissance Instruments and Orch. (1970; Boston, Dec. 11, 1970); *Capriccio stravagante* (1972); *3 invenzione* for Chamber Ensemble (1972; Tanglewood, Aug. 8, 1972); *3 Nocturnes* (1972); *4 Soundscapes—Hudson Valley Reminiscences* (1974; Poughkeepsie, N.Y., March 7, 1975); Violin Concerto (1975–76; Lucerne, Aug. 25, 1976); *Deaï* for 3 Orchs. (1977–78; Tokyo, March 17, 1978; U.S. premiere, Tanglewood, Aug. 4, 1979); Double-bassoon Concerto (1978; Washington, D.C., Jan. 16, 1979; first concerto ever written for this instrument); Trumpet Concerto (1979); *In Praise of Winds* for Wind Orch. (1981); Saxophone Concerto (1983; Pittsburgh, Jan. 18, 1984).

THIRD-STREAM MUSIC: *Blues* for Brass Quintet, Double Bass, and Drums (1945); *Atonal Jazz Study* for 12 Instruments (1948); *Symphonic Tribute to Duke Ellington* for Jazz Orch. (1955); *12 by 11* for 11 Instruments (1955); *Transformation* for 11 Instruments (1956); *Conversations* for Jazz Quartet and String Quartet (1959); Concertino for Jazz Quartet and Orch. (1959); *Abstraction* for 9 Instruments (1959); *Variants,* jazz ballet for Jazz Quartet and Orch. (1960; N.Y., Jan. 4, 1961); *Variants on a Theme of John Lewis* for 12 Performers (1960; based on Lewis's tune *Django*); *Variants on a Theme of Thelonius Monk* for 13 Performers (1960; based on Monk's tune *Criss-Cross*); *Journey into Jazz* for Narrator, Jazz Quintet, and Orch. (1962; Washington, D.C., May 30, 1962); *Night Music* for Jazz Quintet (1962); *Densities No. 1* for Jazz Quartet (1963); *Music from "Yesterday in Fact"* for Jazz Quintet, Flute, Bass Clarinet, Horn, Violin, and Cello (1963; music for a Polish-made film); *Tear Drop* for 9 Instruments (1967).

Schulthess, Walter, Swiss conductor and composer; b. Zürich, July 24, 1894; d. there, June 23, 1971. He studied with Andreae in Zürich, with Courvoisier in Munich, with Ansorge in Berlin; in 1918 settled in Zürich. As a composer, he excelled in lyric songs, in a style resembling Othmar Schoeck's. He also wrote 2 violin sonatas; *Variationen* for Cello and Orch.; Concertino for Piano and Orch.; piano pieces. He was married to the violinist **Stefi Geyer** (1888–1956).

Schultze, Norbert, German composer; b. Braunschweig, Jan. 26, 1911. He studied music and theatrical arts in Cologne and Munich, and took lessons in piano and composition; during the season 1931–32 he acted in a student cabaret, *Vier Nachrichter,* under the name of **Frank Norbert;** then was a theater conductor, arranger, and composer in Munich. He wrote several operas: *Schwarzer Peter* (Hamburg, 1936); *Das kalte Herz* (Leipzig, 1943); television opera, *Peter der dritte* (1964); operetta, *Regen in Paris* (Nuremberg, 1957); pantomimes: *Struwwelpeter* (Hamburg, 1937); *Max und Moritz* (Hamburg, 1938); *Maria im Walde* (Vienna, 1940); but his chief claim to fame was a sentimental song, *Lili Marleen,* which he wrote in 1938, and which became immensely popular after it was broadcast from the German-occupied Belgrade in 1941; it became a hit throughout the war, not only on the German side but also among Allied soldiers on all fronts; it was trans. into 27 languages.

Schulz, Leo, German-American cellist; b. Posen, March 28, 1865; d. La Crescenta, Calif., Aug. 12, 1944. He was a child prodigy, and appeared in public at the age of 5; then studied at the Hochschule für Musik in Berlin; was first cellist with the Berlin Phil. (1885) and the Gewandhaus Orch. in Leipzig (1886–89); then settled in America; was first cellist of the Boston Symph. (1889–98), then of the N.Y. Phil. (1899–1906); taught in various schools; wrote overtures, string quartets, and some cello music; edited *Cello Classics* (2 vols.), *Cello Album* (2 books), and *Cello Composers* (2 vols.).

Schulz-Beuthen, Heinrich, German composer; b. Beuthen, June 19, 1838; d. Dresden, March 12, 1915. He was destined for a career as civil engineer; while a student at the Univ. of Breslau, he learned to play the piano and attempted composition; produced a singspiel, *Fridolin* (Breslau, 1862); then went to study at the Leipzig Cons., with Moscheles (piano) and Hauptmann (composition). In 1866 he went to Zürich, where he remained until 1880; then lived in Dresden (1880–93) and Vienna (1893–95); finally settled in Dresden, where he became a prof. at the Cons. He was an ardent disciple of Liszt and Wagner; during his lifetime he was regarded as a significant composer.

Schulz-Evler, Andrei, Polish pianist; b. Radom, Dec. 12, 1852; d. Warsaw, May 15, 1905. He studied at the Warsaw Cons., and later with Tausig in Berlin; was a prof. of piano at the Kharkov Music School (1888–1904); publ. 52 piano pieces and songs; his transcription of the *Blue Danube Waltz* was very popular with pianists for a time.

Schuman, William Howard, eminent American composer, educator, and music administrator; b. New York, Aug. 4, 1910. He studied harmony with Max Persin; then took lessons in composition with Charles Haubiel; in 1933 he entered Teacher's College at Columbia Univ. (B.S., 1935; M.A., 1937); attended the Mozarteum Academy in Salzburg during the summer of 1935; returning to N.Y., he became an instructor at Sarah Lawrence College; took composition lessons with Roy Harris at a summer session of the Juilliard School of Music in 1936; on March 27, 1936, he married Frances Prince. He attracted the attention of Koussevitzky, who gave the first performance of Schuman's *American Festival Overture* with the Boston Symph. Orch. in 1939, and later conducted his 3rd and 5th symphs.; his 4th Symph. was performed by Rodzinski in Cleveland in 1942, and the Coolidge String Quartet gave a performance of Schuman's String Quartet in 1940. He continued to teach at Sarah Lawrence until 1945; then served as director of publications for G. Schirmer, Inc. (1945–52); in 1945, also, he was ap-

pointed president of the Juilliard School of Music, a post he held until 1962. Continuing his astonishing advance as an executive, he became president of Lincoln Center in N.Y., serving from 1962 to 1969; his career in this respect was unique among American composers. He was the first recipient of the Pulitzer Prize in music in 1943; received the Composition Award of the American Academy of Arts and Letters; also held 2 successive Guggenheim fellowship awards (1939, 1940). His music is characterized by great emotional tension, which is maintained by powerful asymmetric rhythms; the contrapuntal structures in his works reach a great degree of complexity and are saturated with dissonance without, however, losing the essential tonal references. In several of his works he employs American melorhythms, but his general style of composition is cosmopolitan, exploring all viable techniques of modern composition.

WORKS: "Baseball opera," *The Mighty Casey* (Hartford, Conn., May 4, 1953; revised as a cantata, retitled *Casey at the Bat,* and produced in this version in Washington, D.C., April 6, 1976). BALLETS: *Undertow* (choreographer: Antony Tudor; N.Y., April 10, 1945); *Night Journey* (Martha Graham; Cambridge, Mass., May 3, 1947); *Judith,* choreographic poem for Orch. (Martha Graham; Louisville, Ky., Jan. 4, 1950). FOR ORCH.: Symph. No. 1 (N.Y., Oct. 21, 1936); Symph. No. 2 (N.Y., May 25, 1938); Symph. No. 3 (Boston, Oct. 17, 1941); Symph. No. 4 (Cleveland, Jan. 22, 1942); Symph. No. 5, *Symphony for Strings* (Boston, Nov. 12, 1943); Symph. No. 6 (Dallas, Feb. 27, 1949); Symph. No. 7 (Boston, Oct. 21, 1960); Symph. No. 8 (N.Y., Oct. 4, 1962); *To Thee Old Cause* for Oboe, Brass, Timpani, Piano, and Strings, after Walt Whitman, dedicated to the memories of Martin Luther King and Robert F. Kennedy (N.Y., Oct. 3, 1968); Symph. No. 9, subtitled *Le Fosse Ardeatine,* in memory of Italian civilians murdered by the Germans in a cave in Rome in retaliation for resistance activities (Philadelphia, Jan. 10, 1969); Symph. No. 10, subtitled *American Muse,* dedicated to the U.S. Bicentennial (Washington, April 6, 1976); *American Festival Overture* (Boston, Oct. 6, 1939); Concerto for Piano and Small Orch. (N.Y., Jan. 13, 1943); *Prayer in Time of War* (Pittsburgh, Feb. 26, 1943); *William Billings Overture* (N.Y., Feb. 17, 1944); *Circus Overture* (Philadelphia, July 20, 1944); Violin Concerto (1947; Boston, Feb. 10, 1950; Isaac Stern, soloist; revised 1954 and 1958); *Credendum* (Cincinnati, Nov. 4, 1955); *New England Triptych* (Miami, Oct. 28, 1956); *A Song of Orpheus* for Cello and Orch. (Indianapolis, Feb. 17, 1962); *In Praise of Shahn,* canticle for Orch., in memory of the American painter Ben Shahn (N.Y., Jan. 30, 1970); *Voyage for Orchestra* (1971; Rochester, N.Y., Oct. 27, 1972). FOR BAND: *Newsreel* (1941); *George Washington Bridge* (1950); *Chester,* overture (1956). CHORAL WORKS: 4 *Canonic Choruses* (original title, *Chorale Canons*) for Mixed Voices (1932–33); *Pioneers!* for 8-part Mixed Chorus, after Walt Whitman (1937); *Choral Etude* for Mixed Chorus (1937); *Prologue* for Mixed Chorus and Orch. (1939); *Prelude* for Women's Voices (1939); *This Is Our Time,* secular cantata for Mixed Chorus and

Orch. (1940); *Requiescat* for Women's Chorus (1942); *Holiday Song* for Mixed Chorus (1942); *A Free Song,* secular cantata for Mixed Chorus and Orch., after Walt Whitman (Boston, March 26, 1943); won the first Pulitzer Prize awarded for a musical work); *Truth Shall Deliver* for Men's Voices (1946); *4 Rounds on Famous Words* (1957); *The Lord Has a Child,* hymn (1957); Concerto on Old English Rounds for Viola, Women's Chorus, and Orch. (Boston, Nov. 29, 1974); *The Young Dead Soldiers* for Soprano, Horn, Woodwinds, and Strings, to a text of Archibald MacLeish (Washington, April 6, 1976); *The Earth Is Born,* music for a film (1957); 4 string quartets (1936, 1937, 1939, 1950); *Quartettino* for 4 Bassoons (1939); *3-Score Set* for Piano (1943); *Voyage,* a cycle of 5 pieces for Piano (1953); songs.

Schumann, Camillo, German organist and composer, brother of **Georg Schumann;** b. Königstein, March 10, 1872; d. Gottleuba, Dec. 29, 1946. He learned the rudiments of music from his father; then studied with Jadassohn and Reinecke at the Leipzig Cons. After further study with Adolf Bargiel in Berlin (1894–96) he became organist at the church in Eisenach. For some years before his death he lived in retirement at Gottleuba. He was a prolific composer, especially noted for his organ works; he also wrote 6 cantatas, 3 piano trios, 5 cello sonatas, 2 clarinet sonatas, 2 violin sonatas, and 30 albums of piano pieces.

Schumann, Clara (née **Wieck**), famous pianist, wife of **Robert Schumann;** b. Leipzig, Sept. 13, 1819; d. Frankfurt, May 20, 1896. She was the daughter of **Friedrich Wieck;** was trained by her father from her 5th year; played in public for the first time on Oct. 20, 1828; made tours from 1832, and during a sojourn in Vienna (1836) received the title of Imperial Chamber Virtuoso. At Paris she had great success in 1839. On Sept. 12, 1840, she was married to Schumann, despite the stubborn opposition of her father to this union. With Schumann she made a tour of Russia as a pianist (1844); appeared with Jenny Lind in Vienna (1846). After Schumann's death (1856) she went with her children to Berlin, living for some years with her mother, who had been divorced from Wieck and had married the music teacher Adolf Bargiel (d. Feb. 4, 1841). From 1856 to 1888 she played regularly in England. In 1863 she moved to Lichtenthaler, near Baden-Baden. In 1878–79 she taught piano at the Hoch Cons. at Frankfurt. She was a masterly and authoritative interpreter of Schumann's compositions; later she became an equally admirable interpreter of Brahms, her lifelong friend. She was completely free of all mannerisms, and impressed her audiences chiefly by the earnestness of her regard for the music she played. She was a composer in her own right; wrote a Piano Concerto and numerous character pieces for piano; also some songs; Schumann made use of her melodies in several of his works. She wrote cadenzas to Beethoven's concertos in C minor and G major; edited the Breitkopf & Hartel edition of Schumann's works, and some of his early correspondence; also edited finger exercises from Czerny's piano method.

Schumann, Elisabeth, celebrated German soprano; b. Merseburg, June 13, 1888; d. New York, April 23, 1952. She studied in Dresden, Berlin, and Hamburg; made her debut at the Hamburg Opera on Sept. 2, 1909, as the Shepherd in *Tannhäuser;* remained on its roster until 1919. In the meantime, she made her American debut at the Metropolitan Opera in N.Y. on Nov. 20, 1914, as Sophie in *Der Rosenkavalier,* one of her most famous roles; sang there only one season (1914–15). From 1919 to 1938 she was a principal member of the Vienna State Opera; in 1921 made a concert tour of the U.S. with Richard Strauss; after 1938 she settled in the U.S.; taught at the Curtis Inst. of Music in Philadelphia; gave many recitals; became a U.S. citizen in 1944. She publ. *German Song* (London, 1948). In opera, she succeeded in giving congenial interpretations of works by composers as far apart as Mozart and Richard Strauss; she was also a fine performer of German lieder.

Schumann, Georg (Alfred), German composer and choral conductor; b. Königstein, Oct. 25, 1866; d. Berlin, May 23, 1952. He studied with his father, the town music director, and with his grandfather, a cantor; then took courses in Dresden and at the Leipzig Cons. with Reinecke and Jadassohn; received the Beethoven Prize in 1887. He conducted a choral society in Danzig (1890–96) and the Bremen Phil. Orch. (1896–99). In 1900 he became conductor of the Singakademie in Berlin; in 1934 he was elected president of the Berlin Akademie der Künste.

Schumann, Robert Alexander, German composer of surpassing imaginative power whose music expressed the deepest spirit of the Romantic era; b. Zwickau, June 8, 1810; d. Endenich, near Bonn, July 29, 1856. He was the 5th and youngest child of a Saxon bookseller, who encouraged his musical inclinations. At the age of 10 he began taking piano lessons from J.G. Kuntzsch, organist at the Zwickau Marienkirche. In 1828 he enrolled at Leipzig Univ., as *studiosus juris,* although he gave more attention to philosophical lectures than to law. In Leipzig he became a piano student of Friedrich Wieck, his future father-in-law. In 1829 he went to Heidelberg, where he applied himself seriously to music; in 1830 he returned to Leipzig and lodged in Wieck's home; he also took a course in composition with Heinrich Dorn. His family life was unhappy; his father died at the age of 53 of a nervous disease not distinctly diagnosed; his sister Emily committed suicide at the age of 19. Of his 3 brothers, only one reached late middle age. Schumann himself became absorbed in the Romantic malaise of Weltschmerz; his idols, the writers and poets Novalis, Kleist, Byron, Lenau, and Hölderin, all died young, and in tragic circumstances. He hoped to start his music study with Carl Maria von Weber, who also died unexpectedly. Schumann wrote plays and poems in the Romantic tradition and at the same time practiced

Schumann

his piano playing in the hope of becoming a virtuoso pianist. He never succeeded in this ambition; ironically, it was his beloved bride, Clara, who became a famous concert pianist, and Schumann himself was often introduced to the public at large as merely her husband. His own piano study was halted when he developed an ailment in the index and middle fingers of his right hand. He tried all the fashionable remedies of the period, allopathy, homeopathy, and electrophysical therapy; in addition, he used a mechanical device to lift the middle finger of his right hand, but it only caused him harm. His damaged fingers exempted him from military service; the medical certificate issued in 1842 stated that the index and middle fingers of his right hand were affected so that Schumann was unable to pull the trigger of a rifle. Schumann had a handsome appearance; he liked the company of young ladies, and enjoyed beer, wine, and strong cigars; this was in sharp contrast with his inner disquiet; as a youth he confided to his diary a fear of madness. He had auditory hallucinations which caused insomnia; he also suffered from acrophobia. When he was 23 years old, he noted sudden onsets of inexpressible angst, momentary loss of consciousness, and difficulty in breathing. He called his sickness a pervasive melancholy, a popular malaise of the time. He thought of killing himself. What maintained his spirits then was his great love for **Clara Wieck,** 9 years his junior; he did not hesitate to confess his psychological perturbations to her. Her father must have surmised the unstable character of Schumann, and resisted any thought of allowing Clara to become engaged to him; the young couple had to go to court to overcome Wieck's objections, and were finally married on Sept. 12, 1840, the day before Clara turned 21. In 1843, when Schumann and Clara already had 2 daughters, Wieck approached him with an offer of reconciliation. Schumann gladly accepted the offer, but the relationship remained only formal.

Whatever inner torment disturbed Schumann's mind, it did not affect the flowering of his genius as a composer; some psychologists have even expressed the belief that madness is a necessary attribute of genius, and that poetry, art, and music are but external aspects of a delusion. However that might be, Schumann as a young man wrote music full of natural beauty, harmonious and melodious in its flow; his compositions are remarkably free from the somber and dramatic qualities that characterize the music of Beethoven and his Romantic followers. One of the most extraordinary features of Schumann's artistic imagination was his fanciful way of personifying his friends and intimates through musical notes; thus his Platonic love for Ernestine von Fricken, who came from the little town of Asch in Bohemia, inspired Schumann to use the notes A, E-flat (Es), C, and B-natural (H), or A-flat (As), C, and B (H), spelling Asch, as themes for his most famous piano pieces, *Papillons* and *Carnaval.* Schumann's very first opus number was a set of variations on the notes A, B, E, G, G, which spelled the name of Countess Meta von Abegg, to whom Schumann was also poetically attached. And, incidentally, it was Ernestine's adoptive father, an

amateur flutist, who gave him the theme for his remarkable set of variations for Piano titled *Etudes symphoniques.*

As Schumann's talent for music grew and he became recognized as an important composer, he continued his literary activities. In 1834 he founded, with J. Knorr, L. Schunke, and Wieck, a progressive journal, *Neue Zeitschrift für Musik,* in which he militated against the vapid mannerisms of fashionable salon music and other aspects of musical stagnation. He wrote essays, signing them with the imaginary names of Florestan, Eusebius, or Meister Raro. (Eusebius was the name of 3 Christian saints; etymologically, it is a compound of the Greek components *eu,* "good," and *sebiai,* "to worship." Florestan is obviously "one in a state of flowering"; Raro is "rare"; Schumann also noticed that the juxtaposition of the names Clara and Robert would result in the formation of Raro: ClaRARObert.) As early as 1831, Schumann, in the guise of Eusebius, hailed the genius of Chopin in an article containing the famous invocation "Hut ab, ihr Herren, ein Genie!" The article appeared in the *Allgemeine Musikalische Zeitung;* it was signed only by Schumann's initials; in an editorial note he was identified merely as a young student of Prof. Wieck; but the winged phrase became a favorite quotation of biographers of both Chopin and Schumann, cited as Schumann's discovery of Chopin's talent. Actually, Chopin was a few months older than Schumann, and had already started on a brilliant concert career, while Schumann was an unknown. One of the most fanciful inventions of Schumann was the formation of an intimate company of friends which he named Davidsbündler, to describe the sodality of David, dedicated to the mortal struggle against Philistines in art and to the passionate support of all that was new and imaginative. Schumann immortalized this society in his brilliant piano work *Davidsbündlertänze.* Another characteristically Romantic trait was Schumann's attachment to nocturnal moods, nature scenes, and fantasies; the titles of his piano pieces are typical: *Nachtstücke, Waldszenen,* and *Fantasiestücke,* the last including the poetic *Warum?* and the explosive *Aufschwung.* A child at heart himself, Schumann created in his piano set of exquisite miniatures, *Kinderszenen,* a marvelous musical nursery which included the beautifully sentimental dream piece *Träumerei.* Parallel with his piano works, Schumann produced some of his finest lieder, including the song cycles to poems by Heine (op. 24) and Eichendorff (op. 39), *Die Frauenliebe und Leben* (op. 42), and *Dichterliebe,* to Heine's words (op. 48). In 1841, in only 4 days, he sketched out his First Symph., in B-flat major, born, as he himself said, in a single "fiery hour." He named it the *Spring* symph. It was followed in rapid succession by 3 string quartets (op. 41), the Piano Quintet (op. 44), and the Piano Quartet (op. 47). To the same period belongs also his impassioned choral work *Das Paradies und die Peri.* Three more symphs. followed the *Spring* symph. within the next decade, and also a Piano Concerto, a masterpiece of a coalition between the percussive gaiety of the solo part and songful paragraphs in the orch.; an arresting hocketus occurs in the finale, in which duple meters come into a striking conflict with the triple rhythm of the solo part.

In 1843 Schumann was asked by Mendelssohn to join him as a teacher of piano, composition, and score reading at the newly founded Cons. in Leipzig. In 1844 Schumann and Clara undertook a concert tour to Russia; in the autumn of 1844 they moved to Dresden, remaining there until 1850. To this period belong his great C major Symph. (1846), the Piano Trio (1847), and the opera *Genoveva* (1848). In 1847 he assumed the conducting post of the Liedertafel, and in 1848 organized in Dresden the Chorgesang-Verein. In 1850 he became town music director in Düsseldorf, but his disturbed condition began to manifest itself in such alarming ways that he had to resign the post. He continued to compose, however. In 1853 he completed a Violin Concerto. Joachim, in whose care Schumann left the work, thought it was not worthy of Schumann's genius, and ruled that it should not be performed until the centennial of Schumann's death. In the 1930s an eccentric Hungarian violinist, Jelly d'Aranyi, declared that Schumann's ghost had appeared before her at a spiritualistic séance, revealed to her the place where the MS was kept (it was no secret, anyway; the MS was where it was supposed to be, on the shelf of the Prussian Library in Berlin), and urged her to perform it. She was cheated out of the prize, however, and the concerto was first performed by another violinist in Berlin, on Nov. 26, 1937. Jelly d'Aranyi had to be satisfied with giving its first British performance.

Schumann's condition continued to deteriorate. On Feb. 27, 1854, he threw himself into the Rhine, but was rescued. On March 4, 1854, he was placed, at his own request, in a sanatorium at Endenich, near Bonn, remaining there until the end of his life. Strangely enough, he did not want to see Clara, and there were months when he did not even inquire about her and the children. But Brahms was a welcome visitor, and Schumann enjoyed his company during his not infrequent periods of lucidity; in Feb. 1855 Brahms played piano, 4-hands, with him. The common assumption that Schumann's illness was syphilitic in origin remains moot, but cumulative symptomology and clearly observed cyclothymic sudden changes of moods point to tertiary syphilis and final general paresis. The doctor who treated him was inclined to diagnose his condition as the result of a sclerosis of the brain; other physicians described it as dementia praecox. Schumann had 7 children; 3 daughters lived to a very old age, but one son suffered from mental disease. A detailed account of Schumann's illness is contained in Dr. Dieter Kerner's book *Krankheiten grossen Musiker,* publ. in Stuttgart in 1973.

WORKS: FOR THE STAGE: *Der Corsar,* opera (1844; unfinished; only a chorus and sketch for an air completed); *Genoveva,* opera, op. 81 (1847–49; Leipzig, June 25, 1850); *Manfred,* incidental music to Byron's play, op. 115 (1848–49; Leipzig, June 13, 1852).

VOCAL MUSIC: For various voices: *Psalm CL* for Soprano, Alto, Piano, and Orch. (1822); Overture and chorus (*Chor von Landleuten*), with Orch. (1822); *6 Lieder* for Men's Voices, op. 33 (1840): 1, *Der träumende See* (Mosen); 2, *Die Minnesänger* (Heine); 3, *Die Lotosblume* (Heine); 4, *Der Zecher als Doktrinär* (Mosen); 5, *Rastlose Liebe* (Goethe); 6, *Frühlingsglocken* (Reinick); *Tragödie* for Chorus and Orch. (Heine; 1841); *Das Paradies und die Peri* for Solo Voices, Chorus, and Orch., op. 50 (adaptation of Moore's *Lalla Rookh;* 1843; Leipzig, Dec. 4, 1843); *Szenen aus Goethes Faust* for Solo Voices, Chorus, and Orch. (Goethe; 1844–53; Cologne, Jan. 13, 1862); *5 Lieder* for Mixed Voices, op. 55 (R. Burns; 1846): 1, *Das Hochlandmädchen;* 2, *Zahnweh;* 3, *Mich zieht es nach dem Dörfchen hin;* 4, *Die alte, gute Zeit;* 5, *Hochlandbursch; 4 Gesänge* for Mixed Voices, op. 59 (1846): 1, *Nord oder Süd!* (K. Lappe); 2, *Am Bodensee* (Platen); 3, *Jägerlied* (Mörike); 4, *Gute Nacht* (Rückert); also a 5th song added later, *Hirtenknaben-Gesang* (Droste-Hülshoff); *3 Gesänge* for Men's Voices, op. 62 (1847): 1, *Der Eidgenossen Nachtwache* (Eichendorff); 2, *Freiheitslied* (Rückert); 3, *Schlachtgesang* (Klopstock); *Ritornelle in canonischen Weisen* for Men's Voices, op. 65 (Rückert; 1847): 1, *Die Rose stand im Tau;* 2, *Lasst Lautenspiel und Becherklang;* 3, *Blüt' oder Schnee!;* 4, *Gebt mir zu trinken!;* 5, *Zürne nicht des Herbstes Wind;* 6, *In Sommertagen rüste den Schlitten;* 7, *In Meeres Mitten ist ein offener Laden;* 8, *Hätte zu einem Traubenkerne; Beim Abschied zu singen* for Chorus and Wind Instruments, op. 84 (Feuchtersleben; 1847); *Zum Anfang* for Men's Voices (Rückert; 1847); *3 Freiheitsgesänge* for Men's Voices, with Wind Instruments ad libitum (1848): 1, *Zu den Waffen* (Ullrich); 2, *Schwarz-Rot-Gold* (Freiligrath); 3, *Deutscher Freiheitsgesang* (Furst); *Romanzen und Balladen* for Mixed Voices, op. 67, I (1849): 1, *Der König von Thule* (Goethe); 2, *Schön-Rohtraut* (Mörike); 3, *Heidenröslein* (Goethe); 4, *Ungewitter* (Chamisso); 5, *John Anderson* (Burns); *Romanzen und Balladen* for Mixed Voices, op. 75, II (1849): 1, *Schnitter Tod* (Des Knaben Wunderhorn; Brentano); 2, *Im Walde* (Eichendorff); 3, *Der traurige Jäger* (Eichendorff); 4, *Der Rekrut* (Burns); 5, *Vom verwundeten Knaben* (Herder's Volkslieder); *Romanzen* for Women's Voices and Piano ad libitum, op. 69, I (1849): 1, *Tamburinschlägerin* (Alvaro de Ameida; Eichendorff, trans.); 2, *Waldmädchen* (Eichendorff); 3, *Klosterfräulein* (Kerner); 4, *Soldatenbraut* (Mörike); 5, *Meerfey* (Eichendorff); 6, *Die Kapelle* (Uhland); *Romanzen* for Women's Voices and Piano ad libitum, op. 91, II (1849): 1, *Rosmarien (Des Knaben Wunderhorn);* 2, *Jäger Wohlgemut (Des Knaben Wunderhorn);* 3, *Der Wassermann* (Kerner); 4, *Das verlassene Mägdelein* (Mörike); 5, *Der Bleicherin Nachtlied* (Reinick); 6, *In Meeres Mitten* (Rückert); *Verzweifle nicht im Schmerzenstal,* motet for Double Chorus and Organ ad libitum, op. 93 (Rückert; 1852; orchestrated 1852); *Requiem für Mignon* for Solo Voices, Chorus, and Orch., op. 98b (Goethe; 1849; Düsseldorf, Nov. 21, 1850); *5 Gesänge aus H. Laubes Jagdbrevier* for Men's Voices and Piano, 4-hands, ad libitum, op. 137 (Laube; 1849): 1, *Zur hohen Jagd; 2, Habet acht!;* 3, *Jagdmorgen; 4, Frühe; 5, Bei der Flasche; 4 doppelchörige Gesänge* for Mixed Voices, op. 141 (1849): 1,

An die Sterne (Rückert); 2, *Ungewisses Licht* (Zedlitz); 3, *Zuversicht* (Zedlitz); 4, *Talismane* (Goethe); *Romanzen und Balladen* for Mixed Voices, op. 145, III (1849–51): 1, *Der Schmidt* (Uhland); 2, *Die Nonne* (anonymous); 3, *Der Sänger* (Uhland); 4, *John Anderson* (Burns); 5, *Romanze vom Gänsebuben* (Malsburg); *Romanzen und Balladen* for Mixed Voices, op. 146, IV (1849–51): 1, *Brautgesang* (Uhland); 2, *Der Bänkelsänger Willie* (Burns); 3, *Der Traum* (Uhland); 4, *Sommerlied* (Rückert); *Das Schifflein*, with Flute and Horn (Uhland); *Nachtlied* for Chorus and Orch., op. 108 (Hebbel; 1849; Düsseldorf, March 13, 1851); *Der Rose Pilgerfahrt* for Solo Voices, Chorus, and Orch., op. 112 (Horn; 1851; Düsseldorf, Feb. 5, 1852); *Der Königssohn* for Solo Voices, Chorus, and Orch., op. 116 (Uhland; 1851); *Des Glockentürmers Töchterlein* for Mixed Voices (Rückert; 1851); *Fest-Ouverture* for Tenor, Chorus, and Orch., op. 123 (Müller and Claudius; 1852–53; Düsseldorf, May 17, 1853); *Des Sängers Fluch* for Solo Voices, Chorus, and Orch., op. 139 (Pohl, after Uhland; 1852); *Vom Pagen und der Königstochter* for Solo Voices, Chorus, and Orch., op. 140 (Geibel; 1852); *Das Glück von Edenhall* for Solo Voices, Chorus, and Orch., op. 143 (Hasenclever, after Uhland; 1853); *Bei Schenkung eines Flügels* for Mixed Voices and Piano (Schumann; 1853); *Neujahrslied* for Chorus and Orch., op. 144 (Rückert; 1849–50; Düsseldorf, Jan. 11, 1851); *Mass* for Chorus and Orch., op. 147 (1852–53); *Requiem* for Chorus and Orch., op. 148 (1852).

SONGS: *Verwandlung* (Schulze; 1827); *Lied* (Schumann; 1827); *Sehnsucht* (Schumann; 1827); *Die Weinende* (Byron; 1827); *Erinnerung* (Jacobi; 1828); *Kurzes Erwachen* (Kerner; 1828); *Gesanges Erwachen* (Kerner; 1828); *An Anna*, I (Kerner; 1828); *An Anna*, II (Kerner; 1828); *Im Herbste* (Kerner; 1828); *Hirtenknabe* (Schumann; 1828); *Der Fischer* (Goethe; 1828); *Vom Reitersmann* (date unknown); *Maultreiberlied* (1838; not extant); *Ein Gedanke* (Ferrand; 1840); *Patriotisches Lied* for Voice, Chorus, and Piano (N. Becker; 1840); *Der Reiter und der Bodensee* (Schwab; 1840; fragment only); *Die nächtliche Heerschau* (Zedlitz; 1840; fragment only); *Liederkreis*, op. 24 (Heine; 1840): 1, *Morgens steh ich auf und frage*; 2, *Es treibt mich hin*; 3, *Ich wandelte unter den Bäumen*; 4, *Lieb Liebchen*; 5, *Schöne Wiege meiner Leiden*; 6, *Warte, warte, wilder Schiffmann*; 7, *Berg und Burgen schaun herunter*; 8, *Anfangs wolit ich fast verzagen*; 9, *Mit Myrten und Rosen*; *Myrthen*, op. 25 (1840): 1, *Widmung* (Rückert); 2, *Freisinn* (Goethe); 3, *Der Nussbaum* (Mosen); 4, *Jemand* (Burns); 5, *Lieder aus dem Schenkenbuch im Divan*, I (Goethe); 6, *Lieder aus dem Schenkenbuch im Divan*, II (Goethe); 7, *Die Lotosblume* (Heine); 8, *Talismane* (Goethe); 9, *Lied der Suleika* (Goethe; attributed to Marianne von Willemer); 10, *Die Hochländer-Witwe* (Burns); 11, *Lieder der Braut aus dem Liebesfrühling*, I (Rückert); 12, *Lieder der Braut aus dem Liebesfrühling*, II (Rückert); 13, *Hochländers Abschied* (Burns); 14, *Hochländisches Wiegenlied* (Burns); 15, *Aus den hebräischen Gesängen* (Byron); 16, *Rätsel* (C. Fanshawe); 17, *2 Venetianische Lieder*, I (Moore); 18, *2 Venetianische Lieder*, II (Moore); 19,

Hauptmanns Weib (Burns); 20, *Weit, weit* (Burns); 21, *Was will die einsame Träne?* (Heine); 22, *Niemand* (Burns); 23, *Im Westen* (Burns); 24, *Du bist wie eine Blume* (Heine); 25, *Aus den östlichen Rosen* (Rückert); 26, *Zum Schluss* (Rückert); *Lieder und Gesänge*, op. 27, I (1840): 1, *Sag an, o lieber Vogel* (Hebbel); 2, *Dem roten Röslein* (Burns); 3, *Was soll ich sagen?* (Chamisso); 4, *Jasminenstrauch* (Rückert); 5, *Nur ein lächelnder Blick* (G.W. Zimmermann); *3 Gedichte*, op. 29 (Geibel; 1840): 1, *Ländliches Lied* for 2 Sopranos; 2, *Lied* for 3 Sopranos; 3, *Zigeunerleben* for Soprano, Alto, Tenor, and Bass, and Triangle and Tambourine ad libitum; *3 Gedichte*, op. 30 (Geibel; 1840): 1, *Der Knabe mit dem Wunderhorn*; 2, *Der Page*; 3, *Der Hidalgo*; *3 Gesänge*, op. 31 (1840): 1, *Die Löwenbraut* (Chamisso); 2, *Die Kartenlegerin* (Chamisso, after Béranger); 3, *Die rote Hanne*, with Chorus ad libitum (Chamisso, after Béranger); *4 Duette* for Soprano and Tenor, op. 34 (1840): 1, *Liebesgarten* (Reinick); 2, *Liebhabers Ständchen* (Burns); 3, *Unterm Fenster* (Burns); 4, *Familien-Gemälde* (A. Grün); *12 Gedichte*, op. 35 (Kerner; 1840): 1, *Lust der Sturmnacht*; 2, *Stirb, Lieb und Freud!*; 3, *Wanderlied*; 4, *Erstes Grün*; 5, *Sehnsucht nach der Waldgegend*; 6, *Auf das Trinkglas eines verstorbenen Freundes*; 7, *Wanderung*; 8, *Stille Liebe*; 9, *Frage*; 10, *Stille Tränen*; 11, *Wer machte dich so krank?*; 12, *Alte Laute*; *6 Gedichte*, op. 36 (Reinick; 1840): 1, *Sonntags am Rhein*; 2, *Ständchen*; 3, *Nichts schöneres*; 4, *An den Sonnenschein*; 5, *Dichters Genesung*; 6, *Liebesbotschaft*; *12 Gedichte aus "Liebesfrühling,"* op. 37 (Rückert; 1840; Nos. 2, 4, and 11 by Clara Schumann): 1, *Der Himmel hat ein' Träne geweint*; 3, *O ihr Herren*; 5, *Ich hab in mich gesogen*; 6, *Liebste, was kann denn uns scheiden?* for Soprano and Tenor; 7, *Schön ist das Fest des Lenzes* for Soprano and Tenor; 8, *Flügel! Flügel! um zu fliegen*; 9, *Rose, Meer und Sonne*; 10, *O Sonn, o Meer, o Rose*; 12, *So wahr die Sonne scheinet* for Soprano and Tenor; *Liederkreis*, op. 39 (Eichendorff; 1840): 1, *In der Fremde*; 2, *Intermezzo*; 3, *Waldesgespräch*; 4, *Die Stille*; 5, *Mondnacht*; 6, *Schöne Fremde*; 7, *Auf einer Burg*; 8, *In der Fremde*; 9, *Wehmut*; 10, *Zwielicht*; 11, *Im Walde*; 12, *Frühlingsnacht*; *5 Lieder*, op. 40 (1840): 1, *Märzveilchen* (H.C. Andersen); 2, *Muttertraum* (Andersen); 3, *Der Soldat* (Andersen); 4, *Der Spielmann* (Andersen); 5, *Verratene Liebe* (Chamisso); *Frauenliebe und -leben*, op. 42 (Chamisso; 1840): 1, *Seit ich ihn gesehen*; 2, *Er, der Herrlichste von allen*; 3, *Ich kann's nicht fassen, nicht glauben*; 4, *Du Ring an meinem Finger*; 5, *Helft mir, ihr Schwestern*; 6, *Süsser Freund, du blickest*; 7, *An meinem Herzen, an meiner Brust*; 8, *Nun hast du mir den ersten Schmerz getan*; *3 zweistimmige Lieder*, op. 43 (1840): 1, *Wenn ich ein Vöglein wär* (*Das Knaben Wunderhorn);* 2, *Herbstlied* (S.A. Mahlmann); 3, *Schön Blümelein* (Reinick); *Romanzen und Balladen*, op. 45, I (1840): 1, *Der Schatzgräber* (Eichendorff); 2, *Frühlingsfahrt* (Eichendorff); 3, *Abends am Strand* (Heine); *Dichterliebe*, op. 48 (Heine; 1840): 1, *Im wunderschönen Monat Mai*; 2, *Aus meinen Tränen spriessen*; 3, *Die Rose, die Lilie, die Taube, die Sonne*; 4, *Wenn ich in deine Augen seh*; 5, *Ich will meine Seele tauchen*; 6, *Im Rhein, im* heiligen Strome; 7, Ich grolle nicht; 8, Und wüssten's die Blumen, die kleinen; 9, Das ist ein Flöten und Geigen; 10, Hör' ich das Liedchen klingen; 11, Ein Jüngling liebt ein Mädchen; 12, Am leuchtenden Sommermorgen; 13, Ich hab' im Traum geweinet; 14, Allnächtlich im Traume; 15, Aus alten Märchen; 16, Die alten, bösen Lieder; Romanzen und Balladen, op. 49, II (1840): 1, Die beiden Grenadiere (Heine); 2, Die feindlichen Brüder (Heine); 3, Die Nonne (A. Fröhlich); Lieder und Gesänge, op. 51, II: 1, Sehnsucht (Geibel; 1840); 2, Volksliedchen (Rückert; 1840); 3, Ich wandre nicht (C. Christern; 1840); 4, Auf dem Rhein (K. Immermann; 1846); 5, Liebeslied (Goethe; 1850); Romanzen und Balladen, op. 53, III (1840): 1, Blondels Lied (Seidl); 2, Loreley (W. Lorenz); 3, Der arme Peter (Heine); Belsatzar, op. 57 (Heine; 1840); Romanzen und Balladen, op. 64, IV: 1, Die Soldatenbraut (Mörike; 1847); 2, Das verlassne Mägdelein (Mörike; 1847); 3, Tragödie (Heine; 1841); Spanisches Liederspiel, op. 74 (Geibel, after Spanish poets; 1849): 1, Erste Begegnung for Soprano and Alto; 2, Intermezzo for Tenor and Bass; 3, Liebesgram for Soprano and Alto; 4, In der Nacht for Soprano and Tenor; 5, Es ist verraten for Soprano, Alto, Tenor, and Bass; 6, Melancholie for Soprano; 7, Geständnis for Tenor; 8, Botschaft for Soprano and Alto; 9, Ich bin geliebt for Soprano, Alto, Tenor, and Bass; 10, Der Kontrabandiste for Baritone; Lieder und Gesänge, op. 77, III: 1, Der frohe Wandersmann (Eichendorff; 1840); 2, Mein Garten (Hoffmann von Fallersleben; 1850); 3, Geisternähe (Halm; 1850); 4, Stiller Vorwurf (O. Wolff?; 1840); 5, Aufträge (C. L'Egru; 1850); Soldatenlied (Hoffmann von Fallersleben; 1844); Das Schwert (Uhland; 1848); Der weisse Hirsch (Uhland; 1848; sketches only); Die Ammenuhr (Des Knaben Wunderhorn; 1848); 4 Duette for Soprano and Tenor, op. 78 (1849): 1, Tanzlied (Rückert); 2, Er und Sie (Kerner); 3, Ich denke dein (Goethe); 4, Wiegenlied (Hebbel); Sommerruh, duet (C. Schad; 1849); Lieder-Album für die Jugend, op. 79 (1849): 1, Der Abendstern (Hoffmann von Fallersleben); 2, Schmetterling (von Fallersleben); 3, Frühlingsbotschaft (Hoffmann von Fallersleben); 4, Frühlingsgruss (von Fallersleben); 5, Vom Schlaraffenland (von Fallersleben); 6, Sonntag (von Fallersleben); 7, Zigeunerliedchen (Geibel); 8, Des Knaben Berglied (Uhland); 9, Mailied, duet ad libitum (C. Overbeck); 10, Das Käuzlein (Des Knaben Wunderhorn); 11, Hinaus ins Freie! (von Fallersleben); 12, Der Sandmann (Kletke); 13, Marienwürmchen (Des Knaben Wunderhorn); 14, Die Waise (von Fallersleben); 15, Das Glück, duet (Hebbel); 16, Weihnachtslied (Andersen); 17, Die wandelnde Glocke (Goethe); 18, Frühlingslied, duet ad libitum (von Fallersleben); 19, Frühlings Ankunft (von Fallersleben); 20, Die Schwalben, duet (Des Knaben Wunderhorn); 21, Kinderwacht (anonymous); 22, Des Sennen Abschied (Schiller); 23, Er ist's (Mörike); Spinnelied, trio ad libitum (anonymous); Des Buben Schützenlied (Schiller); 26, Schneeglöckchen (Rückert); 27, Lied Lynceus des Türmers (Goethe); Mignon (Goethe); 3 Gesänge, op. 83 (1850): 1, Resignation (Buddeus); 2, Die Blume der Ergebung (Rückert); 3, Der Einsiedler (Eichendorff); Der Handschuh, op.

87 (Schiller; 1850); 6 Gesänge, op. 89 (W. von der Neun; 1850): 1, Es stürmet am Abendhimmel; 2, Heimliches Verschwinden; 3, Herbstlied; 4, Abschied vom Walde; 5, Ins Freie; 6, Röselein, Röselein!; 6 Gedichte, op. 90 (Lenau; 1850): 1, Lied eines Schmiedes; 2, Meine Rose; 3, Kommen und Scheiden; 4, Die Sennin; 5, Einsamkeit; 6, Der schwere Abend; 7, Requiem; 3 Gesänge, op. 95 (Byron; 1849): 1, Die Tochter Jephthas; 2, An den Mond; 3, Dem Helden; Lieder und Gesänge, op. 96, IV (1850): 1, Nachtlied (Goethe); 2, Schneeglöckchen (anonymous); 3, Ihre Stimme (Platen); 4, Gesungen! (Neun; Schöpff); 5, Himmel und Erde (Neun; Schöpff); Lieder und Gesänge aus Wilhelm Meister, op. 98a (Goethe; 1849): 1, Kennst du das Land; 2, Ballade des Harfners; 3, Nur wer die Sehnsucht kennt; 4, Wer nie sein Brot mit Tränen ass; 5, Heiss mich nicht reden; 6, Wer sich der Einsamkeit ergibt; 7, Singet nicht in Trauertönen; 8, An die Türen will ich schleichen; 9, So lasst mich scheinen; Minnespiel, op. 101 (Rückert; 1849): 1, Meine Töne still und heiter for Tenor; 2, Liebster, deine Worte stehlen for Soprano; 3, Ich bin dein Baum for Alto and Bass; 4, Mein schöner Stern! for Tenor; 5, Schön ist das Fest des Lenzes for Soprano, Alto, Tenor, and Bass; 6, O Freund, mein Schirm, mein Schutz! for Alto or Soprano; 7, Die tausend Grüsse for Soprano and Tenor; 8, So wahr die Sonne scheinet for Soprano, Alto, Tenor, and Bass; Mädchenlieder for Soprano and Alto or 2 Sopranos, op. 103 (Kulmann; 1851): 1, Mailied; 2, Frühlingslied; 3, An die Nachtigall; 4, An den Abendstern; 7 Lieder, op. 104 (Kulmann; 1851): 1, Mond, meiner Seele Liebling; 2, Viel Glück zur Reise, Schwalben!; 3, Du nennst mich armes Mädchen; 4, Der Zeisig; 5, Reich mir die Hand, o Wolke; 6, Die letzten Blumen starben; 7, Gekämpft hat meine Barke; Schön Hedwig, declamation, op. 106 (Hebbel; 1849); 6 Gesänge, op. 107 (1851–52): 1, Herzeleid (Ullrich); 2, Die Fensterscheibe (Ullrich); 3, Der Gärtner (Mörike); 4, Die Spinnerin (Heyse); 5, Im Wald (Müller); 6, Abendlied (Kinkel); 3 Lieder for 3 Women's Voices, op. 114 (1853): 1, Nänie (Bechstein); 2, Triolett (L'Egru); 3, Spruch (Rückert); 4 Husarenlieder for Baritone, op. 117 (Lenau; 1851): 1, Der Husar, trara!; 2, Der leidige Frieden; 3, Den grünen Zeigern; 4, Da liegt der Feinde gestreckte Schar; 3 Gedichte, op. 119 (G. Pfarrius; 1851): 1, Die Hütte; 2, Warnung; 3, Der Bräutigam und die Birke; 2 Balladen, declamations, op. 122 (1852–53): 1, Ballade vom Haideknaben (Hebbel); 2, Die Flüchtlinge (Shelley); 5 heitere Gesänge, op. 125 (1850–51): 1, Die Meerfee (Buddeus); 2, Husarenabzug (C. Candidus); 3, Jung Volkers Lied (Mörike); 4, Frühlingslied (Braun); 5, Frühlingslust (Heyse); 5 Lieder und Gesänge, op. 127: 1, Sängers Trost (Kerner; 1840); 2, Dein Angesicht (Heine; 1840); 3, Es leuchtet meine Liebe (Heine; 1840); 4, Mein altes Ross (Moritz, Graf von Strachwitz; 1850); 5, Schlusslied des Narren (Shakespeare; 1840); Frühlingsgrüsse (Lenau; 1851); Gedichte der Königin Maria Stuart, op. 135 (1852): 1, Abschied von Frankreich; 2, Nach der Geburt ihres Sohnes; 3, An die Königin Elisabeth; 4, Abschied von der Welt; 5, Gebet; Spanische Liebeslieder, op. 138 (Geibel; 1849): 1, Vorspiel for Piano, 4-hands; 2, Tief im Herzen trag ich

Schumann

Pein for Soprano; 3, *O wie lieblich ist das Mädchen* for Tenor; 4, *Bedeckt mich mit Blumen* for Soprano and Alto; 5, *Flutenreicher Ebro* for Baritone; 6, *Intermezzo* for Piano, 4-hands; 7, *Weh, wie zornig ist das Mädchen* for Tenor; 8, *Hoch, hoch sind die Berge* for Alto; 9, *Blaue Augen hat das Mädchen* for Tenor and Bass; 10, *Dunkler Lichtglanz* for Soprano, Alto, Tenor, and Bass; from *Des Sängers Fluch,* op. 139 (Pohl, after Uhland; 1852): 4, *Provenzalisches Lied;* 7, *Ballade; 4 Gesänge,* op. 142 (1840): 1, *Trost im Gesang* (Kerner); 2, *Lehn deine Wang* (Heine); 3, *Mädchen-Schwermut* (Bernhard); 4, *Mein Wagen rollet langsam* (Heine); *Mailied,* duet (1851); *Liedchen von Marie und Papa,* duet (Schumann; 1852); *Glockentürmers Töchterlein* (Rückert); *Das Käuzlein (Des Knaben Wunderhorn); Deutscher Blumengarten,* duet (Rückert).

FOR ORCH.: Piano Concerto in E-flat major (1828; unfinished); Piano Concerto in F major (1829–31; unfinished); *Introduction and Variations on a Theme of Paganini* (1831); Symph. in G minor (1832–33; first movement perf. Zwickau, Nov. 18, 1832; first complete perf., Schneeberg, Feb. 12, 1833; 3 movements only with a sketch for a 4th movement); Piano Concerto in D minor (1839; one movement only); Symph. in C minor (1840–41; sketches for 4 movements; some of the music used in Symph. No. 2, in C major, op. 61; Symph. No. 1, in B-flat major, op. 38, *Spring* (Leipzig, March 31, 1841); *Ouvertüre, Scherzo, und Finale* in E major, op. 52 (Leipzig, Dec. 6, 1841; revised 1845); Piano Concerto in A minor, op. 54 (first movement composed as the *Fantasie* for Piano and Orch., 1841; movements 2–3, 1845; Leipzig, Jan. 1, 1846); Symph. No. 2, in C major, op. 61 (1845–46; Leipzig, Nov. 5, 1846); *Conzertstück* in F major for 4 Horns, op. 86 (1849; Leipzig, Feb. 25, 1850); *Introduction and Allegro Appassionato, Conzertstück,* op. 92 (1849; Leipzig, Feb. 14, 1850); Symph. No. 3, in E-flat major, op. 97, *Rhenish* (1850; Düsseldorf, Feb. 6, 1851); *Die Braut von Messina,* overture in C minor, to Schiller's play, op. 100 (1850–51; Düsseldorf, March 13, 1851); Symph. No. 4, in D minor, op. 120 (originally his Symph. No. 2; Leipzig, Dec. 6, 1841; revised as his Symph. No. 4, 1851; Düsseldorf, Dec. 30, 1852); *Julius Cäsar,* overture in F minor, to Shakespeare's play, op. 128 (1851; Düsseldorf, Aug. 3, 1852); Cello Concerto in A minor, op. 129 (1850; Leipzig, June 9, 1860); *Fantasie* in C major for Violin, op. 131 (1853; Hannover, Jan. 1854); *Introduction and Allegro* in D minor/D major for Piano, op. 134 (1853; Utrecht, Nov. 26, 1853); *Hermann und Dorothea,* overture in B minor, to Goethe's poem, op. 136 (1851); Violin Concerto in D minor (1853; first perf. in Berlin, Nov. 26, 1937).

CHAMBER MUSIC: Quartet in C minor for Violin, Viola, Cello, and Piano (1828–30); Quartet in F minor (1829); Quartet in B major for Violin, Viola, Cello, and Piano (1831–32; unfinished); Quartet (1838; not extant); sketches for 2 string quartets: D major and E-flat major (1839); 3 string quartets, op. 41: A minor, F major, A major (1842); Quintet in E-flat major for 2 Violins, Viola, Cello, and Piano, op. 44 (1842); Quartet in E-flat major for Violin, Viola, Cello, and Piano, op. 47 (1842); *Andante and Variations* for 2 Pianos, 2 Cellos, and Horn (1843; original version of

op. 46); Trio No. 1, in D minor, for Violin, Cello, and Piano, op. 63 (1847); *Adagio and Allegro* for Horn and Piano, with Violin or Cello ad libitum, in A-flat major, op. 70 (1849); *Phantasiestücke* for Clarinet and Piano, with Violin or Cello ad libitum, op. 73 (1849); Trio No. 2, in F major, for Violin, Cello, and Piano, op. 80 (1847); *Phantasiestücke* for Violin, Cello, and Piano, op. 88 (1842); 3 *Romanzen* for Oboe and Piano, with Violin or Clarinet ad libitum, op. 94 (1849); 5 *Stücke im Volkston* for Cello and Piano, with Violin ad libitum, op. 102 (1849); Sonata No. 1, in A minor, for Violin and Piano, op. 105 (1851); Trio No. 3, in G minor, for Violin, Cello, and Piano, op. 110 (1851); *Märchenbilder* for Viola and Piano, with Violin ad libitum, op. 113 (1851); Sonata No. 2, in D minor, for Violin and Piano, op. 121 (1851); *Märchenerzählungen* for Clarinet, Viola, and Piano, with Violin ad libitum, op. 132 (1853); Sonata for Violin and Piano, F. A. E. [based on the thematic motto of Joachim, *Frei aber einsam,* "Free but alone"] (1853; 2nd and 4th movements by Schumann; first movement by Dietrich; 3rd movement by Brahms); Sonata No. 3, in A minor, for Violin and Piano (1853; incorporates Schumann's 2 movements composed for the F. A. E. sonata); 5 *Romanzen* for Cello and Piano (1853; not extant).

FOR PIANO: 8 polonaises for Piano, 4-hands (1828); *Variations on a Theme of Prince Louis Ferdinand of Prussia* for Piano, 4-hands (1828); *Romanze* in F minor (1829; unfinished); 6 *Walzer* (1829–30); *Thème sur le nom Abegg varié pour le pianoforte,* op. 1 (1829–30); *Variations on a Theme of Weber,* from *Preziosa* (1831); *Valse* in E-flat major (1831; unfinished); *Valse per Friedrich Wieck* (1831–32; unfinished); Sonata in A-flat major (1831–32; first movement and Adagio); *Andante with Variations on an Original Theme* in G major (1831–32); *Prelude and Fugue* (1832); *Papillons,* op. 2 (1829–31); 6 *Studien nach Capricen von Paganini,* op. 3, I (1832; formerly op. 2); 6 *Intermezzos,* op. 4 (1832; formerly known as *Pièces phantastiques,* op. 3); *Phantasie satyrique* (1832; fragments only); *Fandango* in F-sharp minor (1832); *Exercice fantastique* (1832; formerly op. 5; not extant); *Rondo* in B-flat major (1832; unfinished); 12 *Burlesken* (1832); *Fugue* in D minor (1832); *Fugue* No. 3 (1832); 5 pieces (1832–33; 1, 4, and 5 unfinished); *Sehnsuchts-walzer Variationen: Scènes musicales sur un thème connu* (1832–33); 10 *Impromptus über ein Thema von Clara Wieck,* op. 5 (1833); *Etüden in Form freier Variationen über ein Beethovensches Thema* (1833); *Variations sur un nocturne de Chopin* (1834); movement for a Sonata, in B-flat major (1836); Sonata No. 4, in F minor (1836–37; unfinished); *Davidsbündlertänze,* 18 character pieces, op. 6 (1837); *Toccata* in C major, op. 7 (1829–32; formerly op. 6); Allegro in B minor, op. 8 (1831); *Carnaval: Scènes mignonnes sur quatre notes,* op. 9 (1833–35); 6 *Konzert-Etüden nach Capricen von Paganini,* op. 10, II (1833); Sonata No. 1, in F-sharp minor, op. 11 (1832–35); *Phantasiestücke,* op. 12 (1832?–37); *Symphonische Etüden,* op. 13 (1834–37); *Concert sans orchestre* in F minor, op. 14 (1835–36; revised as Sonata No. 3, 1853); *Scherzo* (1836; from op. 14); *Kinderszenen,* op. 15 (1838); *Kreisleriana,* op. 16 (1838; revised 1850); *Phantasie* in C major, op. 17 (1836–38); *Arabeske* in C major, op. 18 (1838); *Blumenstück* in D-flat major, op. 19 (1839); *Humoreske* in B-flat major, op. 20 (1838); 8 *Novelletten,* op. 21 (1838); Sonata No. 2, in G minor, op. 22 (1833–38; new finale, 1838); *Nachtstücke,* 4 pieces, op. 23 (1839); *Allegro* in C minor (1839; not extant); *Faschingsschwank aus Wien: Phantasiebilder,* op. 26 (1839–40); 3 *Romanzen,* op. 28: B-flat minor, F-sharp major, B major (1839); *Klavierstücke,* op. 32 (1838–39); Sonatina in B-flat major (1840; not extant); *Andante and Variations* in B-flat major, op. 46, for 2 Pianos (1843); *Studien für den Pedal-Flügel,* op. 56 (1845); *4 Skizzen für den Pedal-Flügel,* op. 58 (1845); *6 Fugues on B-A-C-H,* op. 60, for Pedal Piano or Organ (1845); *Bilder aus Osten: 6 Impromptus,* op. 66, for Piano, 4-hands (1848); *Album für die Jugend,* op. 68 (1848); *4 Fugues,* op. 72: D minor, D minor, F minor, F major (1845); *4 Marches,* op. 76: E-flat major, G minor, B-flat major (Lager-Scene), E-flat major (1849); *Waldszenen,* op. 82 (1848–49); *12 vierhändige Klavierstücke für kleine und grosse Kinder,* op. 85 (1849); *Bunte Blätter,* op. 99 (1838–49); *Ballszenen,* op. 109, for Piano, 4-hands (1851); *Phantasiestücke,* 3 pieces, op. 111: C minor, A-flat major, C minor (1851); *3 Clavier-Sonaten für die Jugend,* op. 118: G major, D major, C major (1853); *Albumblätter,* op. 124 (1854); *7 Klavierstücke in Fughettenform,* op. 126 (1853); *Kinderball,* op. 130, for Piano, 4-hands (1853); 5 *Gesänge der Frühe,* op. 133 (1853); *Canon on F. Himmel's An Alexis send ich dich,* in A-flat major (1854); *Thema* in E-flat major (1854); *Variations on an Original Theme* (1854).

Schumann, Walter, American composer of applied music; b. New York, Oct. 8, 1913; d. Minneapolis, Aug. 21, 1958. He studied law and music at the Univ. of Southern Calif. in Los Angeles; became associated with radio shows and composed music for films; wrote an opera, *John Brown's Body* (Los Angeles, Sept. 21, 1953). He contributed the famous ominously syncopated theme to the television serial *Dragnet,* based on the initial 3 notes of the minor scale.

Schumann-Heink, Ernestine (née **Rössler**), famous contralto; b. Lieben, near Prague, June 15, 1861; d. Hollywood, Calif., Nov. 17, 1936. Her father was an officer in the Austrian army; her mother, an Italian amateur singer. In 1872 she was sent to the Ursuline Convent in Prague, where she sang in the church choir; after lessons from Marietta von Leclair in Graz, she made her first public appearance, singing the contralto solo in Beethoven's 9th Symph. (1876); made her opera debut at the Dresden Court Opera (Oct. 15, 1878) as Azucena; continued her studies with Karl Krebs and Franz Wüllner. In 1883 she was engaged to sing at the Hamburg City Opera; when the company was taken to Covent Garden in London in 1892, she sang Erda; subsequently specialized in the Wagnerian roles; took part in the Bayreuth Festivals from 1896 until 1903, and in 1905 and 1906; also sang with the Berlin Opera. She made her American debut as Ortrud on Nov. 7, 1898, in Chica-

go; appeared in the same role with the Metropolitan Opera in N.Y. on Jan. 9, 1899; canceled her contract with the Berlin Opera in order to remain a member of the Metropolitan Opera Co. (until 1903; then appeared intermittently until 1932); created the role of Klytemnestra in *Elektra* (Dresden, Jan. 25, 1909); made her last operatic appearance as Erda at the Metropolitan on March 11, 1932. She became an American citizen in 1908. During the last years of her life she was active mainly as a teacher. Her operatic repertoire included about 150 parts; her voice, of an even quality in all registers, possessed great power, making it peculiarly suitable to Wagnerian roles. She was married in 1882 to Ernst Heink of Dresden, from whom she was later divorced; in 1893 she married the actor Paul Schumann in Hamburg; he died in 1904; she assumed the names of both Schumann and Heink. Her 3rd husband was a Chicago lawyer, William Rapp, Jr., whom she married in 1905 (divorced, 1914).

Schünemann, Georg, eminent German musicologist and music educator; b. Berlin, March 13, 1884; d. there (suicide), Jan. 2, 1945. He studied at the Stern Cons. in Berlin; played flute in various orchs. in Berlin; then took courses in musicology with Kretzschmar, Friedländer, Wolf, and others at the Univ. of Berlin; also studied German literature and philosophy there, receiving his Ph.D. in 1907 (Diss. *Geschichte des Dirigierens,* publ. in Leipzig, 1913). In 1919 he joined the faculty of the Univ. of Berlin; was appointed deputy director of the Berlin Hochschule für Musik in 1920, and director in 1932; later held the post of director of the State Musical Instrument Collections. In 1935 he was appointed director of the music division of the Prussian State Library. He took his own life during the darkest stages of the war.

Schunke, Karl, German pianist; b. Magdeburg, 1801; d. Paris (suicide), Dec. 16, 1839. He studied music with his father, the horn player **Michael Schunke** (1778–1821); then took some lessons with Ferdinand Ries, whom he accompanied to London. In 1828 he went to Paris, where he became a fashionable piano teacher; nevertheless, he suffered from some sort of malaise and killed himself. He composed a number of brilliant salon pieces à la mode and transcriptions of operatic arias for piano.

Schunke, Ludwig, German pianist; b. Kassel, Dec. 21, 1810; d. Leipzig, Dec. 7, 1834. He was a cousin of **Karl Schunke;** studied with his father, **Gottfried Schunke** (1777–1861), who was, like Karl Schunke's father, a horn player; also like his cousin, he went to Paris, where he studied piano with Kalkbrenner and Reicha; settled in Leipzig in 1833 and became an intimate friend of Schumann, of whom he was an exact contemporary, and with whom he became associated in founding the *Neue Zeitschrift für Musik.* His early death at not quite the age of 24 was greatly mourned, for his piano pieces were full of promise; among them were a Sonata, a set of variations, 2 *Caprices,* and a set of *Charakterstücke.*

Schumann wrote a heartfelt appreciation of Schunke's talent, which was reprinted in his *Gesammelte Schriften.*

Schuppanzigh, Ignaz, Austrian violinist, friend of Beethoven; b. Vienna, Nov. 20, 1776; d. there, March 2, 1830. He learned to play the violin and the viola; in 1795 became conductor of the Augarten concerts and from about 1798 was manager. Beethoven played several times at these concerts. In 1794–95 he was first violinist in the quartet that played regularly for Prince Lichnowsky. In 1808 he founded the private quartet of Prince Razumovsky (with Mayseder, Linke, and Weiss), interpreting the Beethoven quartets under the master's eye, and also playing quartets of Haydn and Mozart. After a fire in Razumovsky's palace (Dec. 31, 1814) he left Vienna, returning in 1823. Schuppanzigh then became a member of the court orch.; also was director of the German Opera in 1828. He publ. a *Solo brillant* for Violin, with String Quartet; solo variations on a Russian theme; 9 variations for 2 violins.

Schuricht, Carl, distinguished German conductor; b. Danzig, July 3, 1880; d. Corseaux-sur-Vevey, Switzerland, Jan. 7, 1967. He studied at home, his father being an organ manufacturer and his mother a pianist. He then took lessons with Humperdinck at the Hochschule für Musik in Berlin, and later in Leipzig with Max Reger. He subsequently conducted theater orchs. in Germany; in 1912 he became municipal music director in Wiesbaden, and held this post until 1944, when he moved to Switzerland; in 1946 he reopened the Salzburg Festival; continued to conduct there and in France; in 1956 brought the Vienna Phil. to America for its first American tour. In 1957 he conducted at the Ravinia Festival with the Chicago Symph. and at Tanglewood with the Boston Symph.; in subsequent years, regularly conducted the Berlin and Vienna phil. orchs.; also was a frequent guest conductor of the Stuttgart Radio Symph. He composed some piano music and an orch. suite, *3 Herbststücke.*

Schürmann, Georg Caspar, German composer; b. Idensen, near Hannover, c.1672; d. Wolfenbüttel, Feb. 25, 1751. He was a singer (alto-falsetto) at the Hamburg Opera (1693–97); was then engaged as court Kapellmeister to the Duke of Braunschweig in Wolfenbüttel; traveled in Italy for further study; from 1703 to 1706 was court Kapellmeister in Meiningen; returned to Wolfenbüttel in 1707 and remained there most of his life. He wrote about 40 operas for the Duke of Braunschweig, produced in Wolfenbüttel and Hamburg; only 3 appear to have survived in their entirety; his church music is also lost. The following were produced in Braunschweig: *Heinrich der Vogler* (part I, Aug. 1, 1718; part II, Jan. 11, 1721); *Die getreue Alceste* (1719); *Ludovicus Pius* (1726); this last opera, under the German title, *Ludwig der Fromme,* is partly reproduced in Eitner's *Publikationen älterer Musikwerke;* a suite from *Alceste* and 3 books of arias was publ. by G.F. Schmidt (Wolfenbüttel, 1934).

Schurmann (Schürmann), (Eduard) Gerard, greatly significant composer and conductor with Dutch and Hungarian biological antecedents and of geographically Indonesian birth; b. Kertosono, Java, Jan. 23, 1924. He traces his paternal ancestry to the 18th-century German composer **Georg Caspar Schürmann,** who sang alto-falsetto parts at the Hamburg Opera, served as Kapellmeister at the court of the Duke of Braunschweig, and wrote 40-odd operas. Gerard Schurmann's father was an employee at a sugar factory in Java; his mother was a professional pianist who had studied with Béla Bartók at the Budapest Academy of Music. As war clouds gathered over Southeastern Asia, Schurmann was sent to England in 1937; he went to school in London, and after matriculation, joined the Royal Air Force, serving in aircrews on active flying duty. While still in uniform, he gave piano recitals; took piano lessons with Kathleen Long and composition with Alan Rawsthorne. During his travels in Italy he took lessons in conducting with Franco Ferrara. The government of the Netherlands offered him the position of cultural attaché at the Dutch Embassy in London; being fluent in the Dutch language, which was his mother tongue in Indonesia, he accepted. Later he moved to the Netherlands and worked in the radio studios in Hilversum. He developed a successful career in London as a pianist, conductor, and composer. In 1981 he decided to move to the U.S., and settled in Hollywood, where he became active as a movie composer. Apart from that financially helpful activity, he traveled, conducting guest engagements in France, Italy, Switzerland, Ireland, Scotland, Czechoslovakia, Vienna, and London; his repertoire was comprehensive, ranging from Mozart to Bartók, from Haydn to Schoenberg and Webern, from Tchaikovsky to Shostakovich; his own pieces also figured on his programs. In America he dropped the ancestral umlaut on the 4th letter of his last name. The structure of Schurmann's music is asymptotic toward tonality; melodic progressions are linear, with the fundamental tonic and dominant often encasing the freely atonal configurations, while dodecaphony assumes the adumbrative decaphonic lines, with 2 notes missing in the tone row. The harmonic texture is acrid, acerbic, and astringent; the styptic tendency is revealed in Schurmann's predilection for dissonant minor seconds and major sevenths treated as compound units; yet after the needed tension is achieved, the triadic forms are introduced as a sonic emollient. Thanks to this versatility of application, Schurmann achieves a natural felicity in dealing with exotic subjects; his proximity to gamelan-like pentatonicism during his Indonesian adolescence lends authentic flavor to his use of pentatonic scales; remarkable in his congenial treatment is the set *Chuench'i,* to Eng. translations of 7 Chinese poems. On the other hand, his intimate knowledge of Eng. music and history enables him to impart a true archaic sentiment to his opera-cantata based on the medieval poem *Piers Plowman.* Schurmann is self-critical in regard to works of his which he deems imperfect; thus, he destroyed his Piano Concerto, which he had played under prestigious auspices with the London Symph. Orch., conducted by Adrian Boult in Cambridge in April 1944.

Schuster, Josef, German composer; b. Dresden, Aug. 11, 1748; d. there, July 24, 1812. He spent 4 years in Italy (1765–69) for study, and after 5 years in Dresden, went to Italy again; took lessons with Padre Martini at Bologna; wrote Italian operas, and was made honorary maestro to the King of Naples; after another 2 years in Dresden, he made a 3rd visit to Italy (1778–81), finally establishing himself in Dresden as a theatrical conductor; from 1787 he was associated with Seydelmann as court Kapellmeister. He composed a number of operas, mostly to Italian texts; also cantatas, oratorios, symphs., etc.; publ. piano pieces for 2- and 4-hands, divertissements for piano and violin, etc.

Schütt, Eduard, Russian-born Austrian pianist and composer; b. St. Petersburg, Oct. 22, 1856; d. Obermias, near Merano, Italy, July 26, 1933. After studying piano at the St. Petersburg Cons., he went to Germany, where he took courses with Richter, Jadassohn, and Reinecke at the Leipzig Cons.; then proceeded to Vienna, where he became a private pupil of Leschetizky. He wrote the comic opera *Signor Formica* (Vienna, Nov. 19, 1892); 2 piano concertos; Piano Quartet; 2 piano trios; numerous character pieces for piano, some of which retained popularity for a long time (*Scènes de bal, Thème varié et Fugato, Silhouetten-Portraits, Poésies d'automne, Carnaval mignon,* etc.).

Schütz (Sagittarius), Heinrich, great German composer; b. Köstritz, Oct. 8, 1585; d. Dresden, Nov. 6, 1672. He was born into a prosperous family of innkeepers; in 1590 the family settled in Weissenfels, where his father became burgomaster. He was trained in music by Heinrich Colander, the town organist. In 1599 he became a choirboy in the court chapel of Landgrave Moritz of Hessen-Kassel; in Kassel he pursued his academic studies with Georg Otto, the court Kapellmeister. On Sept. 27, 1608, he entered the Univ. of Marburg to study law; an opportunity to continue his musical education came in 1609 when Landgrave Moritz offered to send him to Venice to take lessons with the renowned master Giovanni Gabrieli. Under Gabrieli's tutelage, he received a thorough training in composition, and he also learned to play the organ. In 1611 he brought out a book of 5-voice madrigals, which he dedicated to his benefactor, Landgrave Moritz. After Gabrieli's death in 1612 Schütz returned to Kassel, serving as second organist at the court chapel. In 1615 the Elector invited him to Dresden as Saxon Kapellmeister; Praetorius was also active at the Dresden court for special occasions at this time. In 1616 Landgrave Moritz asked the Elector to allow Schütz to return to Kassel, but the Elector declined; in 1617 Schütz assumed fully his duties as Saxon Kapellmeister, being granted an annual salary of 400 florins from 1618. In addition to providing music for court occasions, he was responsible for overseeing the functions of the court chapel. In 1619 he

publ. his first collection of sacred music, the *Psalmen Davids sampt etlichen Moteten und Concerten.* On June 1, 1619, he married Magdalena Wildeck, the daughter of a court official in Dresden. They had 2 daughters. She died on Sept. 6, 1625, and Schütz remained a widower for the rest of his life. During a court visit to Torgau, Schütz produced the first German opera, *Dafne,* set to Opitz's translation and adaptation of Rinuccini's libretto for Peri's opera; it was presented at Hartenfels Castle on April 13, 1627, to celebrate the wedding of the Princess Sophia Eleonora of Saxony to Landgrave Georg II of Hesse-Darmstadt. In 1628 he was granted a leave of absence, and went to Italy. There he had an occasion to study the new operatic style of Monteverdi; he adopted this new style in his *Symphoniae sacrae* (publ. in Venice, 1629). He returned to his post in Dresden in 1629. When Saxony entered the Thirty Years' War in 1631, conditions at the Dresden court chapel became difficult. In 1633 Schütz accepted an invitation to go to Copenhagen, where he obtained the post of Kapellmeister to King Christian IV. In June 1634 he returned to Dresden. His *Musicalische Exequien,* composed for the interment of Prince Heinrich Posthumus, appeared in 1636. He also publ. 2 vols. of *Kleine geistliche Concerte* (1636 and 1639). He composed the music for the opera-ballet *Orpheus und Euridice,* which was performed in Dresden on Nov. 20, 1638, to celebrate the marriage of Prince Johann Georg of Saxony and Princess Magdalena Sybilla of Brandenburg. In late 1639 Schütz obtained another leave of absence to serve as Kapellmeister to Georg of Calenberg, who resided in Hildesheim. After a year's stay in Dresden, in 1641–42, he set out once more for Copenhagen, where he again served as Kapellmeister, until April 1644. Returning to Germany, he lived mostly in Braunschweig (1644–45), and was active at the court of nearby Wolfenbüttel. In 1645 he returned to Dresden; the Elector declined his request for retirement but did allow him to live a part of each year in Weissenfels. Schütz continued to compose industriously during these years. The second book of his *Symphoniae sacrae* appeared in 1647, followed by his *Geistliche Chor-Music* in 1648. In succeeding years Schütz repeatedly asked to be pensioned, but his requests were ignored. Finally, when Johann Georg II became Elector in 1657, Schütz was allowed to retire on a pension with the title of Chief Kapellmeister. His Passions *St. Luke, St. John,* and *St. Matthew* all date from these last years, as does his *Christmas Oratorio.* About 1670 he returned to Dresden to settle his affairs and await his end, which came peacefully in 1672, in his 87th year.

The importance of Schütz in music history resides in his astute adaptation of the new Italian styles to German music. He was extraordinarily productive, but not all of his works survived; the majority of his extant compositions are vocal works of a sacred nature. The most important collection of Schütz's MSS is housed in the Hessische Landesbibliothek in Kassel. The first major edition of his works, edited by Philipp Spitta, was publ. by Breitkopf und Härtel (16 vols., Leipzig, 1885–94; supplementary vols. were publ. in 1909 and 1927). A 2nd edition of his works, the *Neuen Schütz-Gesellschaft* edition, began to appear in 1955 in Kassel. A 3rd edition, the *Stuttgarter Schütz-Ausgabe*, began publication in 1971. A catalogue of his works, edited by W. Bittinger, is found in his *Schütz-Werke-Verzeichnis (SWV): Kleine Ausgabe* (Kassel, 1960).

Schützendorf, 4 brothers, all baritones: (1) **Gustav** (b. Cologne, 1883; d. Berlin, April 27, 1937), the best known, studied singing in Milan; sang at the Munich Opera, in Berlin, and in Leipzig; made his American debut as Faninal in *Der Rosenkavalier* at the Metropolitan Opera in N.Y., Nov. 17, 1922, and remained on its roster until 1935; then returned to Germany; in 1929 he married the soprano **Grete Stückgold.** (2) **Alfons** (b. Vught, the Netherlands, May 25, 1882; d. Weimar, Aug. 1946) was distinguished as a Wagnerian singer, and took part in the Bayreuth Festivals; in 1932 settled in Berlin as a singing teacher. (3) **Guido** (b. Vught, near Hertogenbosch, the Netherlands, April 22, 1880; d. Germany, April 1967) sang with the German Opera Co. on its tour in the U.S. in 1929–30. (4) **Leo** (b. Cologne, May 7, 1886; d. Berlin, Dec. 18, 1931) was a member of the Berlin State Opera from 1920 to 1929, and made numerous appearances abroad.

Schuyler, Philippa Duke, black American pianist and composer; b. New York, Aug. 22, 1932; d. (in a helicopter crash in Danang Bay, Vietnam) May 9, 1967. A precocious musician, she wrote an orchestral work at the age of 12 and appeared as piano soloist with the N.Y. Phil. at Lewisohn Stadium when she was 14, on the same program with her "fairy-tale symphony," *Rumpelstiltskin.* Under the auspices of the State Dept., she traveled to Africa and played command performances for Emperor Haile Selassie of Ethiopia and the Queen of Malaya. Mayor Fiorello La Guardia of N.Y. declared June 19, 1940, as Philippa Schuyler Day at the N.Y. World's Fair. A product of an interracial marriage (her mother was a white Texas heiress), she was a founder of the Amerasian Foundation to aid mothers of illegitimate children fathered by American soldiers in Vietnam. She wrote a number of works based on African themes, including *The Nile Fantasy* for Orch.; and on the lighter side, a "Cockroach Ballet," inspired by some unexterminable cockroaches encountered in many hotels and apartments during her travels. *Time* magazine publ. a story about her, "Harlem Prodigy," in its issue of June 22, 1936.

Schwann, William, American organist and musicographer; b. Salem, Ill., May 13, 1913. He studied at the Louisville (Ky.) School of Music at the Univ. of Louisville (A.B., 1935). He began his musical career as an organist and choir director in Louisville churches (1930–35); then went to Boston, where he studied organ with E. Power Biggs; also attended classes of Hugo Leichtentritt, Wallace Woodworth, and A.T. Merritt at Harvard Univ.; wrote music criticism. In 1939 he set up a retail shop of phonograph records in Cambridge; in 1949 he launched

his *Schwann Record Catalog.* In 1953 the title was changed to *Schwann Long Playing Record Catalog.* In 1971 he added 8-track cartridge tape and cassette tape listings under the new title *Schwann Record and Tape Guide.* He also publishes a semiannual *Supplementary Record & Tape Guide,* an annual *Children's Record Catalog,* an annual *Country and Western Record & Tape Catalog,* and a quadrennial *Artist Issue,* which lists classical music indexed alphabetically by the names of performing artists. The *Schwann Catalog* is generally regarded as the most authoritative and the most comprehensive compilation of its kind.

Schwartz, Elliott, American composer, teacher, and commentator; b. Brooklyn, Jan. 19, 1936. He studied composition with Otto Luening and Jack Beeson at Columbia Univ., and privately with Paul Creston; also attended classes of Varèse, Wolpe, Henry Brant, and others at the Bennington Composers Conference in Vermont (summers, 1961–66). He was an instructor in music at the Univ. of Mass., Amherst (1960–64); in 1964, was appointed to the faculty of Bowdoin College in Brunswick, Maine. He publ. *The Symphonies of Ralph Vaughan Williams* (Amherst, 1964); edited (with Barney Childs) *Contemporary Composers on Contemporary Music* (N.Y., 1967); also publ. *Electronic Music: A Listener's Guide* (N.Y., 1973) and *Music: Ways of Listening* (N.Y., 1982). In his compositions he develops the Satiesque notions of unfettered license in music leading to their completely unbuttoned state.

Schwarz, Boris, eminent Russian-born American violinist, conductor, musicologist, writer, and educator; b. St. Petersburg, March 26, 1906; d. New York, Dec. 31, 1983. He went to Berlin as a youth; at the age of 14 he made his concert debut as a violinist in Hannover, accompanied at the piano by his father, **Joseph Schwarz.** He took violin lessons with Carl Flesch in Berlin and with Jacques Thibaud and Lucien Capet in Paris; attended courses in musicology with Curt Sachs, Arnold Schering, and Johannes Wolf at the Univ. of Berlin. In 1936 he settled in the U.S., where he was engaged as concertmaster of the Indianapolis Symph. Orch. (1937–38) and later played first violin in the NBC Symph. Orch. under Toscanini. He also studied musicology at Columbia Univ., earning his Ph.D. in 1950. From 1941–76 he was on the faculty of Queens College of the City Univ. of N.Y., where he organized the Queens College Orch. Society, conducting annual concerts of symph. and choral music. In 1962 he was an exchange prof. of music in Moscow. He was trilingual as a writer, being equally fluent in Russian, German, and English; contributed numerous articles, mostly on Russian music, to *The New Grove Dictionary of Music and Musicians.* His book *Music and Musical Life in Soviet Russia, 1917–1970* (N.Y., 1972; 2nd ed., 1983), highly critical of certain aspects of the musical situation in Russia, attracted a great deal of attention, and won an award from the American Society of Composers, Authors and Publishers as the best book on music criticism. His second book, *Great Masters of the Violin,* publ. shortly before his death, was valuable for its accuracy of documentation.

Schwarz, Gerard, American trumpet player and conductor; b. Weehawken, N.J., July 19, 1947. He studied at the High School of Music and Art and at the Juilliard School of Music; then played trumpet in the American Brass Quintet and the N.Y. Phil.; subsequently he devoted himself mainly to conducting. In 1978 he became music director of the Los Angeles Chamber Orch.; made several tours with it, earning merited encomiums for his natural musicianship sans irruptive ostentation.

Schwarzkopf, Elisabeth, celebrated German soprano; b. Jarotschin, near Poznan, Poland, Dec. 9, 1915. She studied at the Berlin Hochschule für Musik, and privately with Maria Ivogün; made her debut at the Deutsche Oper in Berlin in 1938; later sang also at the Vienna State Opera and gave numerous performances at the Salzburg Festivals; she acquired renown as a fine Mozart singer. On March 1, 1940, she was registered as a member of the German Nazi Party, under No. 7548960; membership was mandatory for artists employed by national theaters; she was cleared by the Allied Denazification Commission and was able to resume her career. In 1951 Furtwängler invited her to participate in the reopening celebrations at the Bayreuth Festival; on Sept. 11, 1951, she sang the part of Anne Trulove in the world premiere of Stravinsky's *The Rake's Progress* in Venice. She gave her first American recital at Carnegie Hall in N.Y. on Oct. 25, 1953; her American opera debut took place in San Francisco on Sept. 20, 1955; she appeared with the Metropolitan Opera in N.Y. on Oct. 13, 1964, in the role of the Marschallin in *Der Rosenkavalier;* remained on its roster until 1966. In 1975 she made a farewell tour of the U.S. as a lieder singer; in 1976 gave a master class in vocal interpretation at the Juilliard School of Music with her husband, **Walter Legge;** then lived mostly in Zürich. She edited a memoir of Walter Legge, *On and Off the Record* (N.Y., 1982).

Schwedler, (Otto) Maximilian, German flutist; b. Hirschberg, March 31, 1853; d. Leipzig, Jan. 16, 1940. He studied in Dresden; played flute in various German orchs.; in 1881 joined the Gewandhaus Orch. in Leipzig; also taught at the Leipzig Cons. He was the inventor of the "Schwedler flute" (1885), fully described in his *Katechismus der Flöte und des Flötenspiels* (Leipzig, 1897); made numerous transcriptions for flute, and publ. a flute method.

Schweitzer, Albert, great humanitarian, physician, and organist, and an authority on Bach; b. Kaysersberg, Alsace, Jan. 14, 1875; d. in his jungle hospital at Lambaréné, Gabon, Sept. 4, 1965, at the age of 90. He was the son of a Günsbach vicar; studied organ with Eugen Münch at Mulhouse, with Ernst Münch at Strasbourg, and with Widor in Paris (from 1893); was organist of the Bach Concerts in Strasbourg from 1896; studied theology and philosophy at the univs. of Strasbourg, Paris, and Berlin; in 1902 joined the faculty of the Univ. of Strasbourg; while teaching there he completed the full medical course (M.D., 1912), with the intention of becoming a medical missionary in Africa, to which task he subsequently devoted most of his time and energy, making occasional concert tours as an organist in Europe to raise funds for his hospital work among the African natives. In 1952 he was awarded the Nobel Peace Prize, the only professional musician to hold this prestigious award. His philosophical and theological writings had established his reputation as one of the foremost thinkers of our time. In the field of music he distinguished himself as the author of one of the most important books on Bach, greatly influencing the interpretation of Bach's music, and contributing to the understanding of Bach's symbolic treatment of various musical devices. In 1906 he became organist of the Société J.S. Bach in Paris; in 1909 he presided over the conferences on organ building at the Congress of the International Music Society in Vienna, which led to the adoption of international regulations, and read a paper, "Die Reform unseres Orgelbaues," urging the simplification of the modern organ to correct faulty tone quality caused by extreme wind pressure (full report in the *Wiener Kongressbericht der Internationalen Musik-Gesellschaft,* 1909; pp. 581–679). With Widor he edited the first 5 vols. of the Schirmer critico-practical edition of Bach's organ works (eds. in Eng., French, and German), and with Edouard Nies-Berger, the remaining 3 vols. He held the degrees of Dr.Theol. and Dr.Phil.; also the honorary degrees of D.D. (Oxon.) and Litt.D. (St. Andrews).

Schweitzer, Anton, German composer; b. Coburg (baptized, June 6), 1735; d. Gotha, Nov. 23, 1787. He was a chorister and later viola player in Hildburghausen; in 1764 went to Italy for serious study; returning to Germany, he was appointed (in 1766) music director of the ducal theater in Weimar; in 1769 became conductor of Seyler's operatic troupe, which was engaged by the Duke of Weimar in 1772. After the destruction by fire of the Weimar Theater in 1774, Schweitzer went to Gotha; there he was appointed court conductor in 1778. Schweitzer was one of the earliest composers to write serious operas to German texts. He produced in Weimar his operas *Die Dorfgala* (June 30, 1772) and *Alceste* (May 28, 1773; libretto by Wieland); there followed another opera, *Rosamunde* (Mannheim, Jan. 20, 1780); Mozart expressed appreciation of Schweitzer's operas. But it was as a composer of singspiels that Schweitzer achieved popularity in his day; he was also important historically as the first composer of a melodrama in German, after Rousseau's *Pygmalion* (Weimar, May 13, 1772; however, it is not extant).

Schytte, Ludvig (Theodor), Danish composer; b. Aarhus, April 28, 1848; d. Berlin, Nov. 10, 1909. He was a pharmacist as a young man; then began to study piano with Anton Rée and composition with Gade, finishing under Taubert in Berlin and Liszt in

Weimar. He settled in Vienna in 1887 as a teacher; moved to Berlin in 1907; taught there at the Stern Cons. A master of the miniature forms, he wrote a number of attractive piano pieces, some of which became extremely popular; about 200 were publ.

Scott, Cyril (Meir), remarkable English composer; b. Oxton, Cheshire, Sept. 27, 1879; d. Eastbourne, Dec. 31, 1970. He was a scion of a cultural family; his father was a classical scholar, his mother a fine amateur musician. Having displayed a natural penchant for music as a child, he was sent to Frankfurt, where he studied piano and theory with Iwan Knorr; returning to England in 1898, he continued to study music and began to compose. In 1900 Hans Richter conducted in Liverpool and Manchester Scott's *Heroic Suite;* also in 1900, his First Symph. was played in Darmstadt; his overture *Pelléas and Mélisande* was performed in Frankfurt. His 2nd Symph. was given at a Promenade Concert in London on Aug. 25, 1903. (It was later converted into *3 Symphonic Dances.*) His setting of Keats's *La Belle Dame sans merci* for Chorus and Orch. was produced in London in 1916, and revived at the Leeds Festival in 1934. His opera *The Alchemist,* for which he wrote his own libretto, was produced in Essen, Germany, on May 28, 1925. In 1920 Scott traveled to the U.S. and played his First Piano Concerto with the Philadelphia Orch. under Stokowski (Nov. 5, 1920). But he acquired fame mainly as a composer of some exotically flavored piano pieces, of which *Lotus Land* became a perennial favorite; Fritz Kreisler arranged it for violin and piano and played it repeatedly at his concerts. Other popular piano pieces were *Danse nègre, Chinese Serenade, Russian Dance, Sphinx, Autumn Idyll, Berceuse, Little Russian Suite, Indian Suite, Spanish Dance,* and most particularly the ingratiating suite *Impressions of the Jungle Book,* after Kipling. He also wrote over 100 songs. In all these pieces, Scott showed himself a master of musical miniature; he wrote in a distinctly modern idiom, very much in the style of French Impressionism; employed sonorous parallel progressions of unresolved dissonant chords; made frequent use of the whole-tone scale. His writing for piano is ingratiating in its idiomatic mastery; his harmonious modalities exude an aura of perfumed euphony. Among his other works are: *Christmas Overture* (London, Nov. 13, 1906); *La Princesse Maleine,* symph. poem (London, Aug. 22, 1907); 2 piano concertos (1915, 1950); Violin Concerto (Birmingham, Jan. 27, 1928); Cello Concerto (1937); Concerto for Oboe and String Orch. (London, Sept. 13, 1948); Symph. No. 3, subtitled *The Muses* (1939); *Neopolitan Rhapsody* for Orch. (1960); 4 string quartets; 2 string trios; 2 piano trios; *Rapsodie arabesque* for Flute, Violin, Viola, Cello, and Harp; Clarinet Quintet (1951); *Sonata melodica* for Violin and Piano (1951); Piano Quintet; Piano Quartet; 4 violin sonatas; Trio for Flute, Cello, and Piano; Flute Sonata; *Rondo serioso* for Viola d'Amore. From his early youth Cyril Scott was attracted to occult sciences and was a believer in the reality of the supernatural; he publ. books and essays on mu-

sic as a divinely inspired art and inveighed violently against jazz as the work of Satan. He publ. the following books: *My Years of Indiscretion* (London, 1924); *The Philosophy of Modernism in Its Connection with Music* (London, 1917); *The Influence of Music on History and Morals: A Vindication of Plato* (London, 1928); *Music: Its Secret Influence throughout the Ages* (London, 1933; 5th ed., 1952); *An Outline of Modern Occultism* (N.Y., 1935); *The Christian Paradox* (N.Y., 1942); an autobiographical vol., *Bone of Contention* (London, 1969); 2 publications on medical matters: *Medicine, Rational and Irrational* (London, 1946) and *Cancer Prevention* (London, 1968).

Scott, Francis George, Scottish composer; b. Hawick, Roxburghshire, Jan. 25, 1880; d. Glasgow, Nov. 6, 1958. He studied humanities at the Univ. of Edinburgh; later at Durham Univ. (B.M., 1909); also took theory lessons with a local organist. As a composer, he cultivated Scottish art music; publ. a number of songs at his own expense; of these the most significant are *Scottish Lyrics* (5 vols., 1921–39). His more ambitious works include *The Ballad of Kynd Kittok* for Baritone and Orch.; *Lament for the Heroes* for String Orch.; and a concert overture, *Renaissance* (Glasgow, Jan. 14, 1939). Scott had a number of ardent admirers in England, among them the poet Hugh MacDiarmid and the composer Kaikhosru Sorabji, who in their exuberant encomiums place him in the ranks of Schubert and Schumann as a songwriter.

Scotti, Antonio, celebrated Italian baritone; b. Naples, Jan. 25, 1866; d. there, Feb. 26, 1936. He studied with Francesco Lamperti; made his debut in Naples (March 1889) as Cinna in Spontini's *La Vestale;* then sang elsewhere in Italy, and in Russia, Spain, and South America; made his London debut at Covent Garden on June 8, 1899, as Don Giovanni, and appeared in the same role with the Metropolitan Opera in N.Y. (Dec. 27, 1899). He remained with the Metropolitan for 33 years; made his farewell appearance on Jan. 20, 1933. He also toured in America with his own company. He possessed great histrionic ability, and was especially noted for his dramatic roles (Scarpia, Rigoletto, Falstaff, Don Giovanni).

Scotto, Renata, famous Italian soprano; b. Savona, Feb. 24, 1934. She studied piano and voice in Savona; made her debut at the Teatro Nuovo in Milan as Violetta in *La Traviata;* from 1957 sang at La Scala in Milan; subsequently sang at Covent Garden in London and at the Vienna State Opera with brilliant success. She made her American debut at the Lyric Opera in Chicago on Nov. 2, 1960; her debut at the Metropolitan Opera in N.Y. was on Oct. 13, 1965.

Scriabin, Alexander, remarkable Russian composer whose solitary genius had no predecessors and left no disciples; b. Moscow, Jan. 6, 1872; d. there, April 27, 1915. His mother died when he was a child, and his father remarried; he received his musical education from his aunt; at the age of 12 he began to take regular piano lessons with George Conus and with Zverev. In 1885 he studied composition with Taneyev. He entered the Moscow Cons. in 1888 as a piano student of Safonov. He practiced assiduously, but never became a virtuoso pianist; at his piano recitals he performed mostly his own works. Graduating with a gold medal from Safonov's class, Scriabin remained at the Moscow Cons. to study fugue with Arensky, but failed to pass the required test and never received a diploma for composition. By that time he had already written several piano pieces in the manner of Chopin; the publisher Belaieff heard him play and offered him a contract; he also financed Scriabin's European tour; on Jan. 15, 1896, Scriabin gave a concert of his own music in Paris. Returning to Russia, he completed his first major work, a Piano Concerto, and was soloist in its first performance on Oct. 23, 1897, in Odessa. In the same year he married the pianist **Vera Isakovich.** They spent some time abroad; on Jan. 31, 1898, they gave a joint recital in Paris in a program of Scriabin's works. From 1898 to 1903 Scriabin taught piano classes at the Moscow Cons. His first orch. work, *Reverie,* was conducted in Moscow by Safonov on March 24, 1899; he also conducted the first performance of Scriabin's First Symph. (March 29, 1901). Scriabin's 2nd Symph. was brought out by Liadov in St. Petersburg (Jan. 25, 1902). After the death of his original publisher, Belaieff, in 1904, Scriabin received an annual grant of 2,400 rubles from the wealthy Moscow merchant Morosov, and went to Switzerland, where he began work on his 3rd Symph., *Le Poème divin;* it had its first performance in Paris on May 29, 1905, under the direction of Arthur Nikisch. At that time Scriabin separated from Vera Isakovich and established a household with Tatiana Schloezer, sister of the music critic Boris de Schloezer, who subsequently became Scriabin's close friend and biographer. In December 1906, Scriabin went to America at the invitation of Modest Altschuler, who at that time had organized the Russian Symph. Society in N.Y.; Scriabin appeared as soloist at Altschuler's concerts in N.Y. and also gave piano recitals of his own works in N.Y., Chicago, Detroit, and other American music centers. Tatiana Schloezer joined him in N.Y. in January 1907, but they were warned by friends familiar with American mores of the time that charges of moral turpitude might be brought against them, since Scriabin had never obtained a legal divorce from his first wife and Tatiana Schloezer was his common-law wife. There was no evidence that such charges were actually contemplated, but to safeguard themselves against such a contretemps, they left America in March 1907 and went to Paris. In the meantime, Altschuler continued to express interest in Scriabin's music, and on Dec. 10, 1908, he gave the world premiere, with his Russian Symph. Orch., of Scriabin's great work *Le Poème de l'extase;* the first Russian performance of this work came later in St. Petersburg (Feb. 1, 1909). In the spring of 1908 Scriabin met Serge Koussevitzky, who became one of his most ardent supporters, both as a conductor and as a publisher. He gave Scriabin a 5-year contract with his newly es-

tablished publishing firm Editions Russes, with a generous guarantee of 5,000 rubles annually. In the summer of 1910 Koussevitzky engaged Scriabin as soloist on a tour in a chartered steamer down the Volga River, with stopovers and concerts at all cities and towns of any size along the route. Scriabin wrote for Koussevitzky his most ambitious work, *Promethée,* or *Poème du feu,* with an important piano part, which Scriabin performed at the world premiere of the work in Moscow on March 15, 1911. The score also included a color keyboard (*clavier à lumière* or, in Italian, *luce*) intended to project changing colors according to the scale of the spectrum, which Scriabin devised (for at that time he was deeply immersed in the speculation about parallelism of all arts in their visual and auditory aspects). The construction of such a color organ was, however, entirely unfeasible at the time, and the world premiere of the work was given without *luce.* A performance with colored lights thrown on a screen was attempted by Altschuler at Carnegie Hall in N.Y. on March 20, 1915, but it was a total failure. Another attempt was made in Moscow by Safonov after Scriabin's death, but that, too, was completely unsuccessful. The crux of the problem was that the actual notes written on a special staff in the score had to be translated into a color spectrum according to Scriabin's visualization of corresponding colors and keys (C major was red, F-sharp major was bright blue, etc.). Perhaps the nearest approximation to Scriabin's scheme was the performance of *Promethée* by the Iowa Univ. Symph. Orch. on Sept. 24, 1975, under the direction of James Dixon, with a laser apparatus constructed by Lowell Cross; previously, the American pianist Hilde Somer made use of the laser to accompany her solo piano recitals of Scriabin's works, without attempting to follow the parallelism of sounds and colors envisioned by Scriabin, but nonetheless conveying the idea underlying the scheme. The unique collaboration between Scriabin and Koussevitzky came to an unfortunate end soon after the production of *Promethée;* Scriabin regarded Koussevitzky as the chief apostle of his messianic epiphany, while Koussevitzky believed that it was due principally to his promotion that Scriabin reached the heights in musical celebrity; to this collision of 2 mighty egotisms was added a trivial disagreement about financial matters. Scriabin left Koussevitzky's publishing firm and in 1912 signed a contract with the Moscow publisher Jurgenson, who guaranteed him 6,000 rubles annually. In 1914 Scriabin visited London and was soloist in his Piano Concerto and in *Prometheus* at a concert led by Sir Henry Wood (March 14, 1914); he also gave a recital of his own works there (March 20, 1914). His last public appearance was in a recital in Petrograd on April 15, 1915; upon his return to Moscow an abscess developed in his lip, leading to blood poisoning; he died after a few days' illness. His 3 children (of the union with Tatiana Schloezer) were legitimized at his death. His son **Julian,** an exceptionally gifted boy, was accidentally drowned at the age of 11 in the Dnieper River at Kiev (June 22, 1919); Julian's 2 piano preludes, written in the style of the last works of his father, were publ. in a Scriabin memorial vol. (Moscow, 1940). His daughter **Marina** is a scholar and composer.

Scriabin was a genuine innovator in harmony. After an early period of strongly felt influences (Chopin, Liszt, and Wagner), he gradually evolved in his own melodic and harmonic style, marked by extreme chromaticism; in his piano piece *Désir*, op. 57 (1908), the threshold of polytonality and atonality is reached; the key signature is dispensed with in his subsequent works; chromatic alterations and compound appoggiaturas create a harmonic web of such complexity that all distinction between consonance and dissonance vanishes. Building chords by fourths rather than by thirds, Scriabin constructed his "mystic chord" of 6 notes (C, F-sharp, B-flat, E, A, and D), which is the harmonic foundation of *Promethée*. In his 7th Piano Sonata (1913) appears a chordal structure of 25 notes (D-flat, F-flat, G, A, and C, repeated in 5 octaves) which was dubbed "a 5-story chord." These harmonic extensions were associated in Scriabin's mind with theosophic doctrines; he aspired to a universal art in which the impressions of the senses were to unite with religious experience. He made plans for the writing of a "Mysterium," which was to accomplish such a synthesis, but only the text of a preliminary poem (*L'Acte préalable*) was completed at his death. Scriabin dreamed of having the "Mysterium" performed as a sacred action in the Himalayas, and actually made plans for going to India; the outbreak of World War I in 1914 put an end to such a project. Scriabin's fragmentary sketches for *L'Acte préalable* were arranged in 1973 by the Soviet musician Alexander Nemtin, who supplemented this material with excerpts from Scriabin's 8th Piano Sonata, *Guirlandes*, and Piano Preludes, op. 74; the resulting synthetic score was performed in Moscow on March 16, 1973, under the title *Universe;* a species of color keyboard was used at the performance, projecting colors according to Scriabin's musical spectrum.

WORKS: For orch.: Concerto for Piano and Orch., op. 20 (1897); *Rêverie*, op. 24 (1899); Symph. No. 1, op. 26 (1900); Symph. No. 2, op. 29 (1901); Symph. No. 3 (*The Divine Poem*), op. 43 (1905); *The Poem of Ecstasy,* op. 54 (1908); *Prometheus (The Poem of Fire),* op. 60 (1911). For piano: 10 sonatas (opp. 6, 19, 23, 30, 53, 62, 64, 66, 68, 70); 79 preludes in 15 sets (opp. 11, 13, 15, 16, 17, 22, 27, 31, 33, 35, 37, 39, 48, 67, 74); 24 études in 4 sets (opp. 2, 8, 42, 65); 6 impromptus (opp. 10, 12, 14); 21 mazurkas (opp. 3, 25, 40); 2 nocturnes (op. 5); *Prelude and Nocturne* for Left Hand Alone (op. 9); *Polonaise* (op. 21); *Fantaisie* (op. 28); *Poème tragique* (op. 34); *Poème satanique* (op. 36); *3 morceaux* (op. 49); *4 morceaux* (op. 51); *3 morceaux* (op. 52); *4 morceaux* (op. 56); *2 morceaux* (op. 57); *Feuillet d'album* (op. 58); *2 morceaux* (op. 59); *Poème-Nocturne* (op. 61); *2 poèmes* (op. 63); *Vers la flamme* (op. 72); *2 danses* (op. 73).

Scudo, Pierre, French music critic; b. Venice, June 8, 1806; d. Blois, Oct. 14, 1864. He was brought up in France; studied at Choron's school in Paris; was for a time an opera singer; played clarinet in military bands; then turned to journalism; publ. several political pamphlets; became music critic of the influential *Revue des Deux Mondes.* A writer of considerable talent, he held reactionary views; violently attacked Berlioz, Liszt, and Wagner. He became deranged and died in an insane asylum. His articles were publ. in book form: *Critique et littérature musicale* (2 series, 1850, 1859); *L'Art ancienne et l'art moderne* (1854); *L'Année musicale, ou Revue annuelle des théâtres lyriques et des concerts* (3 vols., 1860–62); etc. He also wrote a musical novel, *Le Chevalier Sarti* (1857; not connected with the composer Giuseppe Sarti); its sequel, *Frédérique,* was publ. in the *Revue des Deux Mondes.* He publ. some songs (*Le Fil de la Vierge, La Baigneuse,* etc.).

Sculthorpe, Peter, eminent Australian composer; b. Launceston, Tasmania, April 29, 1929. He studied at the Univ. of Melbourne Cons. of Music (B.Mus., 1950); then went to England and took courses from Egon Wellesz and Edmund Rubbra at Wadham College, Oxford Univ. (1958–60); returning to Australia, he was appointed lecturer in music at the Univ. of Sydney in 1963; was composer-in-residence at Yale Univ. while on a Harkness Fellowship (1965–67), and a visiting prof. of music at the Univ. of Sussex (1971–72); in 1969 was appointed reader in music at the Univ. of Sydney. In 1970 he was made a Member of the Order of the British Empire, and in 1977, an Officer of the Order of the British Empire; in 1982 he was awarded an honorary doctorate of letters from the Univ. of Tasmania. In his music, Sculthorpe rejects European techniques such as serialism in favor of a typically Australian approach to music. He thus looked to Asia, in particular Japan, Indonesia, and Tibet, for both literary and musical inspiration. As a result, his music is often a battleground for European Expressionism and native ritualism. Sculthorpe was also influenced by the physical environment of Australia, as in *Sun Music I–IV* for Orch., and in his utilization of birdcalls and insect sounds.

Searle, Humphrey, significant English composer; b. Oxford, Aug. 26, 1915; d. London, May 12, 1982. He studied classical literature at Oxford Univ. and music at the Royal College of Music in London, where his teachers were John Ireland and R.O. Morris. In 1937 he went to Vienna, where he took private lessons with Anton von Webern; this study proved to be a decisive influence in Searle's own compositions, which are imbued with the subtle coloristic processes peculiar to the modern Vienna School of composition. He served in the British army during World War II, and was stationed in Germany in 1946. Returning to London, he engaged in various organizations promoting the cause of modern music. Although his own method of writing includes some aspects of the 12-tone method, he does not renounce tonal procedures, and sometimes applies purely national English melodic patterns. He publ. a manual, *Twentieth-Century Counterpoint* (London, 1954), and contributed numerous articles to

British, American, and German publications. He was honorary secretary of the Liszt Society (1950–62); acted as an adviser in music for the Sadler's Wells Royal Ballet in England (1946–57). In 1964–65 he was composer-in-residence at Stanford Univ. in California; then occupied a similar post at the Univ. of Southern Calif., Los Angeles (1976–77); from 1965 to 1976 he was a prof. at the Royal College of Music in London.

Seashore, Carl Emil, American psychologist and musician; b. Mörlunda, Sweden, Jan. 28, 1866; d. Lewiston, Idaho, Oct. 16, 1949. He was brought to the U.S. as a child; studied at Yale Univ. (Ph.D., 1895); taught psychology at Yale (until 1902), then at Iowa State Univ.; was dean of the Graduate College there in 1908–37, then again in 1942–46. He devised a widely used method for measuring musical talent ("Seashore Test") through special measurements of his own invention (audiometer, tonoscope, chronograph, etc.).

Sebastian, Georges (original name, **György Sebestyén**), Hungarian conductor; b. Budapest, Aug. 17, 1903. He studied composition with Leo Weiner and Kodály at the State Academy of Music in Budapest, graduating in 1921; then took private lessons in conducting with Bruno Walter in Munich (1922–23); subsequently was active as an opera coach, at the Munich State Opera, the Metropolitan Opera in N.Y., and the Hamburg Municipal Opera, and in Leipzig and Berlin. In 1931 he went to Russia, where he conducted at the Moscow Radio. In 1938 he went to the U.S.; was conductor of the Scranton Phil. Orch (1940–45). In 1946 he went back to Europe, and lived mainly in Paris; continued to fill orch. and operatic engagements in Europe.

Sechter, Simon, Austrian composer and teacher; b. Friedberg, Bohemia, Oct. 11, 1788; d. Vienna, Sept. 10, 1867. He studied with Koželuh and Hartmann in Vienna; in 1810 he obtained the position of piano and singing instructor at the Vienna Inst. for the Blind until 1825, the year he became active as principal court organist; in 1851 he became a prof. of harmony and composition at the Vienna Cons.; retired in 1863. The excellence of his teaching attracted to him a number of students from all over Europe, among them Henselt, Bruckner, Nottebohm, Vieuxtemps, Thalberg, and Pauer. So great was his renown, even before he held an official teaching position, that Schubert, some weeks before his death (1828), expressed a desire to study with him. He was a master contrapuntist and wrote a vast amount of church music; publ. many fugues and preludes for organ; several intricate piano pieces (Dances in Counterpoint; 12 Contrapuntal Pieces; 4 books of amusing fugues for 4-hands on national and operatic airs; etc.); string quartets; songs. He also wrote an opera, *Ali Hitsch-Hatsch,* which was produced in Vienna on Nov. 12, 1844. His most important pedagogical work is the treatise *Die Grundsätze der musikalischen Komposition* (3 vols., Vienna, 1853–54), on the lines of Rameau's

"basse fondamentale"; the first vol. was publ. in Eng. trans. (N.Y., 1871; 12th ed., 1912). He also publ. a *Generalbass-Schule* and a new edition of Marpurg's *Abhandlung von der Fuge.*

Seckendorff, Carl Siegmund von, German composer; b. Erlangen, Nov. 26, 1744; d. Ansbach, April 26, 1785. He was an officer in the Austrian and Sardinian armies (1761–74), then in the diplomatic service in Weimar (1776–84); shortly before his death he was appointed Prussian ambassador in Ansbach (1784). At Weimar he was on intimate terms with Goethe, who allowed him to write music for a number of his poems before their publication (*Der Fischer, Der König in Thule,* etc.); in these songs Seckendorff caught the characteristic inflections of folk melodies. He publ. 3 collections of *Volk- und andere Lieder* (1779–82); wrote 12 string quartets; 8 divertimentos for violin and piano; 3 piano trios; 2 piano sonatas for 3 hands (probably the earliest example of such trimanual settings); 3 singspiels: *Lila* (1776); *Proserpine* (1778); *Jery und Bätely* (1780).

Secunda, Sholom, Jewish-American composer; b. Alexandria, near Kherson, Russia, Sept. 4, 1894; d. New York, June 13, 1974. The family came to the U.S. in 1907. He took music lessons with Percy Goetschius and Ernest Bloch at the Inst. of Musical Art in N.Y., graduating in 1917; became a naturalized American citizen in 1923. In 1932 he became a founder of the Society of Jewish Composers, Publishers and Songwriters, which was absorbed by Broadcast Music Incorporated in 1940. Virtually all his life, from 1916–73, he was associated with the Yiddish Theater in N.Y., for which he wrote over 40 operettas; most of these hardly made any impression outside ethnic circles, but one song, "Bei mir bist du schön," from the operetta *I Would if I Could,* produced in 1933, made an unexpected splash even among gentiles, and was sung, in the original Yiddish, by the Andrews Sisters, Rudy Vallee, July Garland, and Kate Smith, becoming one of the most popular songs worldwide. Secunda sold the copyright in 1937 for $30; he regained it in 1961, but never made any appreciable sum of money from it; a legal hassle with the author of the lyrics, Jacob Jacobs, further depleted Secunda's income. Other songs from his operettas were often taken as traditional; among these, "Dona, Dona, Dona," from Secunda's operetta *Esterke* (1940), was recorded by Joan Baez. Secunda also wrote some Jewish service music.

Seefried, Irmgard, outstanding German soprano; b. Köngetried, Bavaria, Oct. 9, 1919. She received her early musical instruction from her father; then studied voice at the Augsburg Cons., graduating in 1939. Herbert von Karajan subsequently engaged her for the Aachen Opera season of 1940–41; on May 2, 1943, she made her debut at the Vienna State Opera under Karl Böhm as Eva in *Die Meistersinger;* in 1944 Richard Strauss chose her for the role of the Composer in *Ariadne auf Naxos* at his 80th-birthday celebration. She subsequently sang in Salzburg,

Edinburgh, Berlin, Paris, London, and Buenos Aires. On Nov. 20, 1953, she made her Metropolitan Opera debut in N.Y. as Susanna in *Le nozze di Figaro.* She was made a Kammersängerin of the Vienna State Opera in 1947; was named an honorary member in 1969. She married the noted Austrian violinist **Wolfgang Schneiderhan.** Apart from her operatic achievements, she was also a distinguished concert and lieder singer.

Seeger, Charles, eminent American ethnomusicologist, composer, and teacher; b. (of American parents) Mexico City, Dec. 14, 1886; d. Bridgewater, Conn., Feb. 7, 1979. He studied at Harvard Univ., graduating in 1908; then taught music at the Univ. of Calif. (1912–19), at the Inst. of Musical Arts in N.Y. (1921–33), and at The New School for Social Research in N.Y. (1931–35); was assistant director of the Federal Music Project, W.P.A. (1938–40); chief music director, Pan American Union, Washington, D.C. (1941–53); a visiting prof. at Yale Univ. (1949–50); lecturer, Univ. of Calif., Los Angeles (1957–61); member of the Society of Ethnomusicology (1960; honorary president, 1972); holder of various honorary degrees; in 1972 received the Chilean decoration of Commander al Mérito. His work in the field of ethnomusicology is of the greatest significance; no less important was his work as a pedagogue; among his students was Henry Cowell. His 2nd wife was the renowned American composer **Ruth Crawford; Pete Seeger** is the son of his first marriage. His 90th birthday was celebrated in several sessions presented at the Univ. of Calif., Berkeley, in Aug. 1977. His publications include (in collaboration with E.G. Stricklen) *An Outline Course in Harmonic Structure and Musical Invention* (1913) and *Harmonic Structure and Elementary Composition* (1916). A collection of his articles, *Studies in Musicology 1935–1975,* was publ. in Berkeley (1977).

Seeger, Pete, American folksinger, son of **Charles Seeger** and nephew of the poet Alan Seeger; b. New York, May 3, 1919. After a brief study of social sciences at Harvard Univ., he became a traveling singer; formed 2 folk-song groups, the Almanac Singers and the Weavers; served in the U.S. Army in 1942–45, and entertained U.S. troops in the Pacific. In 1963 he undertook a worldwide tour, visiting Australia and many countries in Europe, including Russia, where he was spectacularly successful. He publ. a manual, *How to Play the 5-String Banjo* (1948), and compiled several songbooks.

Seeger, Ruth Crawford. See **Crawford, Ruth Porter.**

Segal, Uri, Israeli conductor; b. Jerusalem, March 7, 1944. He studied violin; then went to London and enrolled at the Guildhall School of Music; afterward studied conducting in Siena. In 1969 he won first prize in the Mitropoulos Competition in N.Y.; served as Leonard Bernstein's assistant with the N.Y. Phil. (1969–70); subsequently developed a fine career conducting major orchs. in Europe and America. In 1980 he became principal conductor of the Bournemouth Symph. Orch.

Segerstam, Leif, Finnish conductor and composer; b. Vaasa, March 2, 1944. He studied composition in Helsinki with Fougstedt, Kokkonen, and Englund; took violin, piano, and conducting at the Sibelius Academy in Helsinki, graduating in 1963. He then went to the U.S.; enrolled at the Juilliard School of Music, N.Y., and studied violin with Louis Persinger, composition with Hall Overton and Vincent Persichetti, and conducting with Jean Morel (1963–65); also attended a summer conducting course in 1964 at Aspen, Colo., with Walter Susskind. Returning to Europe, he was a conductor at the Finnish National Opera and Ballet (1965–68); in 1969 joined the staff of the Stockholm Royal Opera. In 1972 he went to West Berlin, where he became conductor at the Deutsche Oper; then served as principal conductor of the Austrian Radio Orch. (1975–82); concurrently served as chief conductor of the Finnish Radio Orch. He describes his own music as being "freely pulsative."

WORKS: FOR ORCH.: *A Legend* for String Orch. (1960); *Divertimento* for String Orch. (1963); *Pandora,* essay (1967; also a one-act ballet); *Concerto Serioso* for Violin and Orch. (1967); *Capriccio* for Solo Sopranino and Small Orch. (1967); *Seven Red Moments* for Trumpet and Orch. (1967); *Patria* (1973; Stockholm, April 27, 1974); *Two; onwards: inwards, outwards, (upwards, downwards)... aroundwards... towards ....* for 2 Pianos and Orch., with 2 String Sections (1974; Helsinki, April 29, 1975); *Screams & Visions* (1975); *Visions of Inner Time* for Piano and String Orch. (1976); *Concerto-Fantasia* for Violin, Piano, and Small Orch. (1977); piano concertos: No. 1, *Thoughts 1978* (1977), and No. 2, *Orchestral Diary Sheet No. 11d* (1981); 5 symphs.: No. 1, *Orchestral Diary Sheets Nos. 33, 34 & 36* (1977–78); No. 2, *Orchestral Diary Sheet No. 22* (1980); No. 3, *Orchestral Diary Sheet No. 23* (1981); No. 4, *Orchestral Diary Sheets Nos. 24, 25 & 26* (1981); No. 5, *Orchestral Diary Sheets Nos. 11 & 12* (1981–83); *Plays* for 2 Amplified Cellos, Percussion, and Small Orch. (1978; Vienna, Feb. 1, 1978); *Orchestral Diary Sheet No. 11a,* Cello Concerto No. 1 (1981), *11b,* Violin Concerto No. 2 (1981), *11c,* with Violin and Cello Obbligato (1981), *11d,* Piano Concerto No. 2 (1981), *11e,* with Organ Solo (1981), *11f,* with Trombone Solo (1981), *11g,* with Clarinet Solo (1981), *11h,* with Alto Saxophone Solo (1981); *Chamber Symphony* (1982–83).

Segovia, Andrés, illustrious Spanish guitar virtuoso; b. Linares, near Jaen, Feb. 21, 1893. He received his first instruction on the guitar at age 6 from a traveling flamenco guitarist; although he later studied briefly with Miguel Llobet, he was basically self-taught. He made his formal debut in Granada in 1909 at the age of 16; then played in Madrid in 1912 and in Barcelona in 1916; toured South America in 1919. He made his Paris debut on April 7, 1924; his program included a work written especially for him by Albert Roussel, entitled simply *Segovia.* He then played throughout Europe; ·made his U.S. debut at Town Hall in N.Y. on Jan. 8, 1928; traveled all over the world, arousing admiration for his artistry wherever he went. He did much to reinstate the guitar as a concert instrument capable of a variety of expression; made many transcriptions for the guitar, including one of Bach's *Chaconne* from the Partita No. 2 for Violin. He also commissioned several composers to write works for him, including Ponce, Turina, Castelnuovo-Tedesco, Moreno-Torroba, Villa-Lobos, and Tansman. He continued to give concerts at an advanced age; made appearances in 1984 in celebration of the 75th anniversary of his professional debut. He received many honors during his long career; a commemorative plaque was affixed in 1969 to the house where he was born, honoring him as the "hijo predilecto de la ciudad." He wrote *Andrés Segovia: An Autobiography of the Years 1893–1920* (N.Y., 1976).

Seiber, Mátyás, significant Hungarian-born English composer; b. Budapest, May 4, 1905; d. in an automobile accident, Kruger National Park, Johannesburg, South Africa, Sept. 24, 1960. Of a musical family, he learned to play the cello at home; later entered the Budapest Academy of Music, where he studied with Kodály (1919–24). During the following years he traveled as a member of a ship's orch. on a transatlantic liner; visited Russia as a music journalist. From 1926 to 1933 he taught composition at the Frankfurt Cons.; was the cellist in the Lenzewski Quartet, which specialized in modern music; then was again in Budapest. The catastrophic events in Central Europe and the growing Nazi influence in Hungary forced him to emigrate to England, where he quickly acquired a group of loyal disciples; was co-founder of the Society for the Promotion of New Music; in 1942 was appointed to the faculty of Morley College. His early music followed the national trends of the Hungarian School; later he expanded his melodic resources to include oriental modes and also jazz, treated as folk music; by the time he arrived in England he had added dodecaphony to his oeuvre, though he used it in a very personal, lyrical manner, as in his cantata *Ulysses* and his 3rd String Quartet.

Seidel, Friedrich Ludwig, German organist and composer; b. Treuenbrietzen, June 1, 1765; d. Charlottenburg, May 5, 1831. He studied with Benda in Berlin; served as organist of the Marienkirche; was music director of the royal orch. (1808) and court Kapellmeister (1822). He composed the operas *Der Dorfbarbier* (1817) and *Lila* (1818); incidental music to dramas; an oratorio, *Die Unsterblichkeit* (1797); masses, motets, songs, piano music.

Seidel, Toscha, Russian violinist; b. Odessa, Nov. 17, 1899; d. Rosemead, Calif., Nov. 15, 1962. He began to play the violin as a small child; took lessons from Max Fiedelmann in Odessa; subsequently became a pupil of Leopold Auer at the St. Petersburg Cons. (graduated in 1912); then went to America (debut, N.Y., April 14, 1918); made many tours in Europe and the U.S.; also played in Australia. He suffered an irreversible mental illness and was confined to a sanatorium in California for several years before his death.

Seidl, Anton, famous Hungarian conductor; b. Pest, May 7, 1850; d. New York, March 28, 1898. He studied at the Leipzig Cons.; then was engaged by Hans Richter as chorus master at the Vienna Opera; Richter in turn recommended him to Wagner to assist in preparing the score and parts of the *Ring* tetralogy for the forthcoming Bayreuth Festival; Seidl worked in Bayreuth until 1879, when he went to Leipzig as a conductor at the Opera. In 1882 he was engaged by the impresario Angelo Neumann for a grand tour of Wagner's operas. After Wagner's death in 1883 he conducted the Bremen Opera; in 1885 was engaged to conduct the German opera repertoire at the Metropolitan Opera House in N.Y. He made his American debut with *Lohengrin* (N.Y., Nov. 23, 1885); also conducted the American premieres of *Die Meistersinger* (Jan. 4, 1886) and *Tristan und Isolde* (Dec. 1, 1886). During the week of March 4–11, 1889, he conducted in N.Y. the entire *Ring des Nibelungen.* In 1891 he was engaged as permanent conductor of the N.Y. Phil., and led it until his sudden death (of ptomaine poisoning). Seidl was an excellent technician of the baton and established a standard of perfection rare in American orch. playing of that time; he introduced many unfamiliar works by German composers and conducted the world premiere of Dvořák's symph. *From the New World* (1893).

Seiffert, Max, eminent German musicologist; b. Beeskow-on-Spree, Feb. 9, 1868; d. Schleswig, April 13, 1948. He studied musicology with Philipp Spitta at the Univ. of Berlin; took the degree of Dr.Phil. with the dissertation *J.P. Sweelinck und seine direkten deutschen Schüler* (Leipzig, 1891). In 1914 he was elected a member of the Prussian Academy of the Arts. He devoted himself chiefly to the editing of works by German composers; publ. *Geschichte der Klaviermusik* (Berlin, 1899–1901; nominally the 3rd ed. of Weitzmann's history, but actually a new and valuable book); compiled numerous catalogues of keyboard works; edited materials for the Denkmäler Deutscher Tonkunst, Denkmäler der Tonkunst in Bayern, and Denkmäler der Tonkunst in Österreich, and edited the complete works of Sweelinck for the *Vereeniging voor Nederlandsche Muziekgeschiedenis;* also prepared many works by Bach and Handel for modern performance. A Festschrift for him was publ. for his 70th birthday (1938), and another for his 80th (1948).

Seixas, (José Antonio) Carlos de, important Portuguese composer of keyboard music; b. Coimbra, June 11, 1704; d. Lisbon, Aug. 25, 1742. He received his primary musical education from his father, a church organist; then became himself a church organist in Lisbon. He wrote a great number of keyboard sonatas (sometimes designated as "toccatas"), of which 88 are preserved. He knew

Domenico Scarlatti personally, but was not demonstrably influenced by the Italian style of keyboard composition. Eighty keyboard sonatas by Seixas were brought out in a modern edition by Santiago Kastner, in the series Portugaliae Musica (Lisbon, 1965); an overture and a sinfonia were publ. in the same series in 1969, edited by P. Salzmann.

Selby, William, organist and composer; b. England, c.1738; d. Boston, Dec. 12, 1798. In 1760 he was appointed organist at Holy Sepulcher Church in London; from 1765 to 1770 he publ. both sacred music and secular music there. He settled in the U.S. in 1771, becoming organist at King's Chapel in Boston; in 1773–74 was organist at Trinity Church in Newport, R.I.; in 1776 returned to Boston as organist at Trinity Church, and from 1778, at the Stone Chapel (formerly King's Chapel). He led an extremely active musical life in Boston as an organist and conductor, giving many concerts of secular music as well as religious, and generally raising the musical standards of the area. He composed and publ. 9 Psalms and hymns for solo voice; 8 religious and secular choral works; 6 songs; 9 pieces for guitar and 3 for keyboard.

Selle, Thomas, German composer; b. Zörbig, March 23, 1599; d. Hamburg, July 2, 1663. He was a rector in Wesselburen (1625), cantor in Itzehoe (1634), cantor at the Johanneum, and music director of the 5 principal churches in Hamburg (from 1641). He publ. sacred and secular songs (including settings of poems by Rist), and left in MS numerous madrigals, motets, and Passions. He was an early member of the Hamburg school of German songwriting. His collections include: *Concertatio Castalidum* (1624); *Deliciae pastorum Arcadiae* (1624); *Hagiodecamelhydrion* (1627–31); *Deliciorum juvenilium decas* (1634); *Monophonetica* (1636). His *Johannes-Passion* of 1642 was brought out in a modern edition by R. Gerber (1934); reprints of separate songs were publ. by H.J. Moser.

Selva, Blanche, French pianist and teacher; b. Brive, Jan. 29, 1884; d. St. Amand, Tallende, Puy-de-Dome, Dec. 3, 1942. She studied piano at the Paris Cons., and took courses in composition with Vincent d'Indy at the Schola Cantorum, where she became a teacher. She was one of the strongest propagandists of modern French music early in the century; she presented programs of piano works by Debussy, Ravel, and other masters of modern French music at the time when they were not yet universally recognized. She also publ. several books dealing with piano technique; her compendium, *L'Enseignement musical de la technique du piano* (4 vols., Paris, 1922) is valuable. She further publ. disquisitions on musical form: *La Sonate* (Paris, 1913); *Quelques mots sur la sonate* (Paris, 1914); *Les Sonates de Beethoven* (Barcelona, 1927); also a monograph on Déodat de Séverac (Paris, 1930).

Sembrich, Marcella (real name, **Praxede Marcellina Kochańska;** Sembrich was her mother's maiden name), famous coloratura soprano; b. Wisniewczyk, Galicia, Feb. 15, 1858; d. New York, Jan. 11, 1935. From the age of 4 she took piano lessons from her father, Kasimir Kochański; violin lessons were soon added. At 10 she appeared in public as a performer on both instruments. At the age of 11 she entered the Lemberg (Lwow) Cons., where she studied with Wilhelm Stengel. In 1874 she played and sang for Liszt, who urged her to train her voice. She then studied singing with Viktor Rokitansky in Vienna, and with G.B. Lamperti, Jr., in Milan. On May 5, 1877, she married her former teacher **Wilhelm Stengel** (b. Lemberg, Aug. 7, 1846; d. New York, May 15, 1917), and with him went to Athens, where she made her operatic debut on June 3, 1877, as Elvira in Bellini's *Puritani;* returning to Vienna, she studied the German repertoire with Richard Lewy. From 1878 to 1880 she sang at Dresden. On June 12, 1880, she made her London debut as Lucia; her American debut was at the Metropolitan Opera House, on Oct. 24, 1883. Thereafter she sang at the principal opera houses of Germany, Austria, France, Spain, Scandinavia, and Russia until 1898, then becoming a regular member of the Metropolitan Opera Co. for that season, and again from 1901–9. Her farewell appearance in opera was at the Metropolitan on Feb. 6, 1909. Her repertoire included 40 operatic parts, of which Violetta was the favorite. Of Wagnerian roles, she sang only Eva in *Die Meistersinger.* In 1924 she joined the faculty of the newly founded Curtis Inst. in Philadelphia; also taught at the Juilliard School in N.Y.

Senaillé (Senaillié), Jean Baptiste, French violinist and composer; b. Paris, Nov. 23, 1687; d. there, Oct. 15, 1730. Although the spelling "Senaillé" is widely used, he signed his name "Senaillié," as did his father; contemporary editions of his music invariably used the form "Senaillié." He studied first with his father, a member of the "24 violons du roi"; later was a pupil of Jean Baptiste Anet; then went to Italy, where he studied with Vitali. He returned to Paris in 1720; gave many performances at the Concert Spirituel. His playing was in the Italian tradition; in his music, also, he was influenced by the Italian school of Corelli and Vitali. He publ. 50 violin sonatas (with continuo) in 5 books (1710–27); modern reprints by Moffat, Jensen, Alard, etc.

Senart, Maurice, French music publisher; b. Paris, Jan. 29, 1878; d. there, May 23, 1962. In 1908 he founded a music publishing enterprise in partnership with Roudanez; in 1912, became sole head of the firm, which bears his name. Among his early publications was the important collection edited by Henry Expert, *Maîtres musiciens de la Renaissance française;* there followed several other collections; many editions of classical music; collected works of Chopin, edited by Alfred Cortot. Senart was also a decided supporter of modern French music; publ. many works by Honegger and Milhaud, and works by composers of other nationalities resident in Paris (Tansman, Harsanyi, etc.). His publishing firm was acquired by Salabert in 1941.

Senesino, Francesco (real name, **Bernardi;** called Senesino after his birthplace), Italian male mezzo-soprano; b. Siena, c.1680; d. c.1759. He studied in Bologna with Bernacchi; in 1719 was engaged to sing at the court theater in Dresden; Handel heard him there, and engaged him for his Italian opera company in London. He began his London appearances in Bononcini's opera *Astarto* (Nov. 30, 1720), and his success was enormous from the start. For 15 consecutive seasons he enjoyed the favor of the London public; was associated with Handel's company until 1733, when a rival organization, the "Opera of the Nobility," engaged him and several other celebrated Italian singers to sing under the direction of Porpora. In 1736 he returned to Siena; in 1737–39 he was in Florence. It is not known where or exactly when he died.

Senfl, Ludwig, important church composer of the Renaissance; b. Basel, c.1486; d. Munich, c.1543. His father was a singer from Freiburg im Breisgau; the family name may have been **Senfl, Sänftli, Sänfly, Senfel,** etc., and the ultimate origin undoubtedly German, although Ludwig Senfl was known under the appellation "Schweizer" (the Swiss). As a small child, from 1496, he sang in the imperial court chapel; in 1507–9 he was in Constance, where he was a pupil of Isaac; he was Isaac's assistant at St. Ann's Church in Augsburg, and also sang in the court chapel of Maximilian I; after Isaac's death (1517), Senfl completed his teacher's *Choralis Constantinus* and became his successor as chamber composer; remained in Augsburg for some time after Maximilian's death (1519), and received a stipend from Charles V; edited the historically important *Liber selectarum cantionum* (1520), which was one of the earliest books with musical notation publ. in Germany. In 1523 he settled in Munich as "intonator" at the Bavarian court chapel; his fame grew; he was referred to by an early contemporary as "prince of all German music." There is extant a letter written to Senfl by Martin Luther, dated Oct. 4, 1530, containing high praise of the composer (reprinted in F.A. Beck's *Dr. M. Luthers Gedanken über die Musik,* Berlin, 1828).

Serafin, Tullio, eminent Italian conductor; b. Rottanova de Cavarzere, Venice, Sept. 1, 1878; d. Rome, Feb. 2, 1968. He studied at the Cons. in Milan; made his conducting debut in Ferrara in 1898. In 1901 Toscanini engaged him as one of his assistant conductors at La Scala. Later he was principal conductor of La Scala (1909–14, 1917–18); from 1924 to 1934 he was a conductor at the Metropolitan Opera in N.Y. In 1934 he became chief conductor and artistic director of the Rome Opera, a post he retained until 1943; after the war he was engaged as artistic director of La Scala (1946–47). From 1956 to 1958 he conducted at the Chicago Lyric Opera; in 1962 he was named artistic adviser of the Rome Opera. He was especially authoritative in the Italian operatic repertoire. As an artistic adviser, he helped launch the careers of Maria Callas and several other noted artists. He publ. (with A. Toni) 2 vols. on the history of Italian opera, *Stile, tradizioni e convenzioni del melodramma italiano del Settecento e dell'Ottocento* (Milan, 1958–64).

Serafino, Santo, celebrated Italian violin maker; b. Udine, Nov. 1, 1699; d. Venice, c.1758. He was a pupil of Niccolo Amati, and probably worked in Cremona; signed his name on the labels as "Sanctus Seraphinus Nicolai Amati Cremonensis Alumnus." His instruments contained elements characteristic of Stainer and of Niccolo Amati. His nephew **Giorgio Serafino** (b. Venice, c.1726; d. there, Jan. 25, 1775) worked in Venice in the first half of the 18th century.

Serassi, Giuseppe ("il Vecchio"), the founder of a celebrated house of Italian organ builders; b. Gordano, 1694; d. Crema, Aug. 1, 1760. His son **Andrea Luigi** (1725–99) carried on the business; built the cathedral organs of Crema, Parma, and Fossano. A younger member of the family, **Giuseppe ("il Giovane";** b. Bergamo, Nov. 16, 1750; d. there, Feb. 19, 1817), upheld the reputation of the firm, and built many organs in Lombardy. His catalogue of 1815 lists 345 instruments. He publ. a description of the new organ at Como (1808), with a short history of the organ and good rules for registration; also brought out a pamphlet, *Sugli organi* (1816). The catalogue publ. in 1852 by his sons, **Carlo** and **Giuseppe Serassi,** shows a total of 654 organs constructed.

Serebrier, José, Uruguayan-American conductor and composer; b. Montevideo, Dec. 3, 1938. He began to conduct at the age of 12; went to the U.S. in 1950; studied composition with Vittorio Giannini at the Curtis Inst. in Philadelphia (1956–58) and conducting with Antal Dorati in Minneapolis; also took conducting lessons with Monteux at his summer residence in Maine. He subsequently conducted guest engagements in the U.S., South America, and Europe; gave the first performance in Poland of the 4th Symph. of Charles Ives. He was composer-in-residence with the Cleveland Orch. (1968–70); concurrently was music director of the Cleveland Phil. (1968–71). He is married to the soprano Carole Farley.

Seress, Rezsö, Hungarian composer of popular songs; b. Budapest, Nov. 3, 1899; d. there, Jan. 12, 1968. He earned his living by playing piano and singing in restaurants and nightclubs; acquired fame in 1936 by his song *Gloomy Sunday,* which was banned in Hungary and several other countries because its morbid tune precipitated a wave of Sunday suicides among the young. Seress himself jumped out of a window from the 2nd floor of his Budapest apartment on Jan. 8, 1968 (a Monday, not a Sunday), and died 4 days later.

Serkin, Peter, American pianist, son of **Rudolf Serkin;** b. New York, July 24, 1947. He made his public debut at the age of 11; when he was 12, he enrolled at the Curtis Inst. of Music in Philadelphia as a student of his father (graduated in 1965); at the age of 14 appeared with his father in Mozart's Concerto for 2 Pianos and Orch. with the Cleveland Orch. (April 19, 1962); then he started on a brilliant career of his own, specializing in ultramodern music. In 1973 he formed the chamber group Tashi ("good fortune" in Tibetan) with clarinetist Richard Stoltzman, violinist Ida Kavafian, and cellist Fred Sherry; later he also gave virtuoso performances of Romantic music, excelling expecially in Chopin's works.

Serkin, Rudolf, eminent Austrian pianist; b. Eger, Bohemia, March 28, 1903 (of Russian parentage). His father was a Russian singer named Mardko Serkin. In Vienna Rudolf Serkin studied piano with Richard Robert and composition with Joseph Marx and Arnold Schoenberg. After an early debut at the age of 12, he began his serious concert career in 1920; appeared frequently in joint recitals with the violinist Adolf Busch (whose daughter he married); made his American debut with Busch at a Coolidge Festival concert in Washington, D.C. (1933); in 1939 he was appointed to the faculty of the Curtis Inst. in Philadelphia; then served as its director from 1968 until 1976. Subsequently he took the lead in establishing in Marlboro, Vt., a summer center for festivals and schooling. His performances of the Viennese classics are unexcelled in authority, faithfulness of treatment, and technical virtuosity.

Serly, Tibor, American violist, composer, and conductor, of Hungarian extraction; b. Losonc, Hungary, Nov. 25, 1901; d. London, Oct. 8, 1978. His family moved to the U.S. in 1905. He received his early musical training from his father; then returned to Hungary, where he enrolled in the Royal Academy of Music in Budapest; there he took courses with Koessler, Hubay, Béla Bartók, and Kodály (1922–26). He came back to the U.S. in 1927; played viola in the Cincinnati Symph. and in the Philadelphia Orch. When Béla Bartók came to America in 1940, Serly became his closest friend and adviser; after Bartók's death in 1945, Serly completed the last 17 measures of Bartók's 3rd Piano Concerto and totally reconstructed and orchestrated Bartók's Viola Concerto from 13 unnumbered MS pages. In 1948 he devised a system of composition called Modus Lascivus, as a sequel to his previous theoretical work, which was entitled "A Second Look at Harmony." Although the medieval Modus Lascivus was synonymous with the C-major scale, Serly expanded its connotation to include enharmonic modulation; indeed, his treatise on Modus Lascivus is subtitled "The Road to Enharmonicism." Shortly before his death he arranged Bartók's Viola Concerto for cello and orch.
WORKS: FOR ORCH.: Viola Concerto (1929); Symph. No. 1 (1931; Budapest, May 13, 1935, composer conducting); *Innovations* for 2 Harps and String Orch. (1931–33); Symph. No. 2 for Winds, Brass, and Percussion (1932); *6 Dance Designs* for Orch. (1933–34; Budapest, May 13, 1935); *Transylvanian Suite* for Chamber Orch. (1935); *Sonata Concertante* for

String Orch. (1936); *The Pagan City,* symph. poem (1932–38; in collaboration with John Klenner); *Colonial Pageant* and *Alarms and Excursions,* 2 suites for Orch. (1936–37); *Midnight Madrigal* for Trumpet and Orch. (1939); *American Elegy,* based on "Taps," for Orch. (1945); *Rhapsody* for Viola and Chamber Orch. (1946–48; N.Y., Feb. 27, 1948); *Miniature Suite* for 12 Winds and Percussion (1947; revision of a discarded *Rhapsody* of 1927); Trombone Concerto (Chatauqua, Aug. 17, 1952); *Lament* for String Orch. (1955–58); Concerto for Violin and Wind Orch. (1955–58; Portland, Oreg., Nov. 30, 1978); *Symphonic Variations* for Audience and Small Orch. (1957); String Symph. (1956); *Little Xmas Cantata* for Audience and Small Orch. (1957); *American Fantasy of Quodlibets* for Orch. (1959); *Concertino 3 × 3* for Piano and Orch. (1964–65; Syracuse, N.Y., Jan. 13, 1967); *Anniversary Cantata on a Quodlibet* for Voices and Small Orch. (1966); *Canonic Fugue in 10 Voices on 10 Tones* for String Orch. (1972; Portland, Oreg., June 5, 1977); *Music for 4 Harps and String Orch.* (1977). CHAMBER MUSIC: Violin Sonata (1923); String Quartet No. 1 (1924); Sonata for Solo Violin (1947); *Chorale* for 3 Harps (1967); *Stringometrics* for Violin and Harp (1968). BALLETS: *Ex Machina* (1943); *Cast Out* (1973). FOR PIANO: Sonata No. 1 (1946); Concerto for 2 Pianos (1948–52); *40 Piano Etudes in Modus Lascivus* (1946–60; first perf. in their totality by Serly's wife, Miriam Molin, N.Y., May 4, 1977). OTHER VOCAL WORKS: *Consovowels 1–5:* No. 1 for Soprano Solo (1968); Nos. 2 and 3 for Soprano and Clarinet (1970–71); Nos. 4 and 5 for Soprano and Violin (1972); 4 songs from James Joyce's *Chamber Music* for Voice and Chamber Orch. (1926); *Strange Story,* after Wylie's poem, for Mezzo-soprano and Orch. (1927).

Sermisy, Claude (Claudin) de, French composer; b. c.1490; d. Paris, Sept. 13, 1562. In 1508 he was appointed "clerc musicien" of the Sainte-Chapelle in Paris; accompanied Francis I to Italy in 1515; was present at the meeting between Francis and Henry VIII at the Field of the Cloth of Gold (1520). Sermisy composed chansons, motets, and masses, which were printed in collections of the time and frequently republ. after his death, indicating a wide popularity. Attaingnant's *31 chansons* (1529) contains 11 songs by Sermisy, which are reprinted in Expert's *Les Maîtres musiciens;* other modern reprints include 3 chansons in Eitner's *Publikationen älterer Musikwerke* (Leipzig, 1899; vol. 23); 3 chansons in Commer's *Collectio operum musicorum* (vol. 12); 2 chansons in Bordes, *Chansonnier du XIVᵉ siècle;* 4 chansons in Expert's *Anthologie chorale des maîtres musiciens de la Renaissance française.*

Serocki, Kazimierz, prominent Polish composer and pianist; b. Toruń, March 3, 1922; d. Warsaw, Jan. 9, 1981. He studied piano in Lodz; also took a course in composition there with Sikorski. In 1947, following the path of many other composers of his generation, he went to Paris to study with the fabled Nadia Boulanger. Returning to Poland, he formed, with

Tadeusz Baird and Jan Krenz, the modernistic Group '49, dedicated to the cause of the avant-garde; in 1956 was one of the organizers of the audaciously futuristic "Warsaw Autumn" Festivals. In the interim he toured as a concert pianist. In his early music he fell into the fashionable neo-Classical current strewn with tolerable dissonances and spiked with bristling atonalities; experimented with Webernized dodecaphonies before molding his own style of composition, an amalgam of pragmatic serialism and permissible aleatory procedures, while maintaining an air of well-nigh monastic nominalism in formal strictures and informal structures; in some pieces he makes incursions into the exotic field of American jazz.

Serov, Alexander, important Russian composer; b. St. Petersburg, Jan. 23, 1820; d. there, Feb. 1, 1871. He was trained in a law school; also took cello lessons with Karl Schuberth; became a functionary in the Ministry of Justice; served in St. Petersburg (1840–45); then in Simferopol, Crimea (1845–48); in 1849 turned definitely to music, and abandoned government employ. He never took lessons in composition, except a correspondence course in counterpoint, but achieved a certain mastery in harmony and orchestration by studying the classics. In 1851 he began writing critical articles on music and soon became an important figure in Russian journalism; in 1856 he became editor of the *Musical and Theatrical Monitor*. In 1858 he made his first trip abroad, visiting Germany and Bohemia; the following year made another German visit, and also traveled in Austria and Switzerland; during this journey he met Wagner, whose ardent admirer he became and remained to the end of his career; expounded Wagner's ideas in Russian publications and engaged in bitter polemics with those who did not subscribe to his views, including his old friend and schoolmate Vladimir Stasov. He started very late in the field of composition; inspired by the performance of a biblical play, *Judith,* by an Italian troupe at St. Petersburg in 1861, he resolved to write an opera on this subject, essaying an Italian libretto, but later deciding on a Russian text. *Judith* was produced in St. Petersburg on May 28, 1863, with excellent success, but although Serov intended to emulate Wagner in the music, the style of *Judith* was closer to Meyerbeer. Quite different was Serov's 2nd opera, *Rogneda,* written on a Russian subject, in a distinctly national idiom, with plentiful use of Russian folk songs. *Rogneda* was staged in St. Petersburg on Nov. 8, 1865, and won a spectacular success; the Tsar Alexander II attended a subsequent performance and granted Serov an annual stipend of 1,000 rubles for it. He then began the composition of another Russian opera, *Vrazhya sila (Malevolent Power),* but death (as a result of a sudden heart failure) overtook him when the 5th act was still incomplete; the opera was finished by N.T. Soloviev and produced posthumously in St. Petersburg on May 1, 1871. All 3 operas of Serov retain their popularity in Russia but are unknown elsewhere. Serov wrote further an Ave Maria for Adelina Patti (1868); a Stabat Mater; incidental music to *Nero; Plyaska Zaporozhtsev (Dance of the Zaporozh Cossacks)* for Orch. (1867); *Ouverture d'une comédie* for Piano, 4-hands; and a few other small pieces. A selection from his writings was publ. in 4 vols. (St. Petersburg, 1892–95). In 1863 Serov married a young Cons. pupil, **Valentina Bergmann** (1846–1924), who was the first Russian woman to compose operas: *Uriel Acosta* (Moscow, 1885) and *Ilya Murometz* (Moscow, March 6, 1899; with Chaliapin in the title role). She helped to edit and publish Serov's posthumous works; wrote essays; publ. a number of piano pieces and a book of memoirs (St. Petersburg, 1914) under the name **Valentina Serova.**

Servais, (Adrien-) François, famous Belgian cellist; b. Hal, near Brussels, June 6, 1807; d. there, Nov. 26, 1866. He studied at the Brussels Cons.; played in a theater orch. there; then went to Paris, where he gave a concert in 1834, with brilliant success; on May 25, 1835, he played his own cello concerto with the London Phil.; subsequently made a grand tour of Europe; spent several years in Russia as a concert player, even reaching Siberia. He was appointed prof. at the Brussels Cons. in 1848, and taught many pupils who became distinguished artists. He wrote 3 concertos and 16 fantasias for cello, with orch.; 6 études and 14 duos for cello, with piano (with Gregoir); 3 duos for violin and cello (with Léonard).

Servais, François (Franz), French composer and conductor; b. St. Petersburg, Russia, c.1847; d. Asnières, near Paris, Jan. 14, 1901. It was claimed for him that he was an illegitimate son of Liszt and Princess Carolyne Sayn-Wittgenstein, but nothing in her voluminous correspondence with Liszt indicates that she was an expectant mother. However it might be, he was adopted by **François Servais** and assumed his name. He studied cello with Kufferath at the Brussels Cons., and won the Belgian Prix de Rome in 1873 with the cantata *Le Tasse.* From the outset of his career as a conductor he was a Wagner enthusiast, and gave the first Belgian performances of several Wagner operas, in Brussels. His own opera *Iôn* (originally entitled *L'Apollonide*) was produced in Karlsruhe in 1899.

Servais, Joseph, Belgian-French cellist, son of **Adrien-François Servais**; b. Hal, near Brussels, Nov. 23, 1850; d. there, Aug. 29, 1885. He was a pupil of his father; made his debut in a joint recital with him in Warsaw (1867); then went to Weimar, where he played in the orch. (1868–70); in 1872 returned to Belgium, where he was a prof. at the Brussels Cons. until his early death.

Sessions, Roger, eminent American composer; b. Brooklyn, Dec. 28, 1896. He studied music at Harvard Univ. (B.A., 1915); took a course in composition with Horatio Parker at the Yale School of Music (B.M., 1917); then took private lessons with Ernest Bloch in Cleveland and N.Y.; this association was of great importance for Sessions; his early works were strongly influenced by Bloch's rhapsodic style and rich harmonic idiom verging on polytonality. Sessions taught music theory at Smith College (1917–21); then was appointed to the faculty of the Cleveland Inst. of Music, first as assistant to Ernest Bloch, then as head of the dept. He held 2 consecutive Guggenheim fellowships (1926, 1927), a fellowship of the American Academy in Rome (1928–31), and a Carnegie Fellowship (1931–32). He lived mostly in Europe from 1926 to 1933; in the interim he presented with Aaron Copland a series of concerts of modern music in N.Y. (called Copland-Sessions concerts) which played an important cultural role at the time. His subsequent teaching posts included Boston Univ. (1933–35), the New Jersey College for Women (1935–37), Princeton Univ. (1935–45), and the Univ. of Calif. at Berkeley (1945–51); taught again at Princeton (1953–65), at Berkeley (1966–67), and at Harvard Univ. (1968–69); also gave courses at the Juilliard School of Music in N.Y. Among American composers who had fruitful sessions with Sessions during his years of professorship were David Diamond, Paul Bowles, Leon Kirchner, Milton Babbitt, and Hugo Weisgall. In his compositions, Sessions evolved a remarkably compact polyphonic idiom, rich in unresolvable dissonances and textural density, and yet permeated with true lyricism. In his later works he adopted a *sui generis* method of serial composition. The music of Sessions is decidedly in advance of his time; the difficulty of his idiom, for both performers and listeners, creates a paradoxical situation in which he is recognized as one of the most important composers of the century, while actual performances of his works are exasperatingly infrequent. In 1974 he received a special citation of the Pulitzer Award Committee "for his life's work as a distinguished American composer." In 1982 he was awarded a 2nd Pulitzer Prize, for his work *Concerto for Orchestra,* composed in 1981.

WORKS: For the stage: *The Black Maskers,* incidental music to Leonid Andreyev's play (Smith College, Northampton, Mass., June 1923); *The Trial of Lucullus,* one-act opera (Berkeley, April 18, 1947); *Montezuma,* 3-act opera (1962; West Berlin, April 19, 1964); 9 symphs.: No. 1 (Boston, April 22, 1927); No. 2 (San Francisco, Jan. 9, 1947); No. 3 (Boston, Dec. 6, 1957); No. 4 (Minneapolis, Jan. 2, 1960); No. 5 (Philadelphia, Feb. 7, 1964); No. 6 (Newark, N.J., Nov. 19, 1966); No. 7 (Ann Arbor, Mich., Oct. 1, 1967); No. 8 (N.Y., May 2, 1968); No. 9 (Syracuse, March 1980); symph. suite from *The Black Maskers* (Cincinnati, Dec. 5, 1930); Violin Concerto (Chicago, Jan. 8, 1940); *Idyll of Theocritus* for Soprano and Orch. (Louisville, Ky., Jan. 14, 1956); Piano Concerto (N.Y., Feb. 10, 1956); 2 string quartets (1936, 1951); Duo for Violin and Piano (1942); Sonata for Solo Violin (1953); String Quintet (1958); *Divertimento* for Orch. (1960); *Psalm 140* for Soprano and Orch. (1963); *6 Pieces* for Cello (1966); *When Lilacs Last in the Door-yard Bloom'd,* cantata for Vocal Soloists, Chorus, and Orch. (1967–70; Univ. of Calif., Berkeley, May 23, 1971); *Rhapsody* for Orch. (Baltimore, March 18, 1970); Concerto for Violin, Cello, and Orch. (1970–71); Concertino for Chamber Orch. (1971–72; Chicago, April 14, 1972); *3 Biblical Cho-*ruses for Chorus and Chamber Orch. (1971); *Concerto for Orchestra* (Boston, Oct. 23, 1981; a centennial commission by the Boston Symph. Orch.; awarded a Pulitzer Prize in 1982); 3 piano sonatas (1930, 1946, 1965); *Pages from a Diary* for Piano (1939); *3 Chorale Preludes* for Organ (1925); *Mass* for Unison Chorus and Organ (1956); *5 Pieces* for Piano (1975). Sessions publ. the books *The Musical Experience of Composer, Performer, Listener* (Princeton, 1950); *Harmonic Practice* (N.Y., 1951); *Reflections on the Music Life in the United States* (N.Y., 1956); and *Questions about Music* (Cambridge, Mass., 1970).

Ševčik, Otakar, noted Czech violinist and pedagogue; b. Horaždowitz, March 22, 1852; d. Pisek, Jan. 18, 1934. He studied violin with his father; then at the Prague Cons. with Anton Bennewitz. From 1870 to 1873 he was concertmaster of the Mozarteum in Salzburg; held a similar post in the Theater an der Wien in Vienna. He then went to Russia, where he became a prof. at the Cons. of Kiev (1875); also gave concerts in Russia, achieving great success there. In 1892 he returned to Prague; became head of the violin dept. at the Prague Cons. (1901–6); in 1909 he became head of the master school for violin at the Vienna Academy of Music; from 1919 to 1924 he taught again in Prague; also visited abroad as a teacher in the U.S. (1920, 1924, 1931), London (1932), etc. His method, in contradistinction to the usual diatonic system, is founded on chromatic progressions, especially valuable in securing both accuracy and facility. In various parts of the world he had hundreds of pupils, among them Jan Kubelík, Kocian, Marie Hall, Baloković, Erica Morini, and Efrem Zimbalist. He publ. the following pedagogical works (in German, Bohemian, French, and Russian; most of them also printed in Eng.): *Schule der Violintechnik* (4 parts); *Schule der Bogentechnik* (6 parts); *Violinschule für Anfänger* (7 parts); *Triller-Vorstudien und Ausbildung des Fingeranschlags* (2 parts); *Lagenwechsel-Übungen; Doppelgriff-Vorstudien;* also *Böhmische Tänze und Weisen* for Violin and Piano.

Séverac, Déodat de, French composer; b. Saint-Félix-de-Caraman, Lauragais, July 20, 1872; d. Céret, March 24, 1921. He received his first lessons on the piano from his father, a painter and an ardent lover of music. He studied music at the Cons. of Toulouse; in 1896 he entered the Schola Cantorum in Paris, where he remained until 1907, studying with Magnard and Vincent d'Indy. He resided alternately in Paris and in his native town.

WORKS: Operas: *Le Cœur du moulin* (Paris, Dec. 8, 1909) and *Les Princesses d'Hokifari* (not produced); incidental music to L. Damard's *Le Mirage* (1905), E. Sicard's *Héliogabale* (1910), M. Navarre's *Muguetto* (1911), E. Verhaeren's *Hélène de Sparte* (Paris, May 5, 1912); symph. poems: *Nymphes au Crépuscule, Tryptique, Les Grenouilles qui demandent un Roi, Nausikaa; Les Muses sylvestres,* suite for Double String Quintet and Piano; *Le Parc aux cerfs,* suite for Oboe, String Quintet, and Piano; *Suite* in E for Organ; for Piano: *Petite suite; En*

Languedoc, suite; *La Nymphe émue ou Le Faune indiscret; En vacances,* album of little pieces; Sonata; several collections of folk songs; solo songs.

Sevitzky, Fabien, Russian conductor, nephew of **Serge Koussevitzky;** b. Vishny Volochok, Sept. 29, 1891; d. Athens, Greece, Feb. 2, 1967. He began a career as a concert player on the double bass, under his original name, Koussevitzky; his uncle, who was already a celebrated double-bass player himself, suggested that he adopt a truncated form of the last name, and he complied to avoid a family quarrel. He made his appearances as a conductor in Russia under the name Sevitzky; lived in Moscow until 1922; spent a year in Poland as a double-bass player in the Warsaw Phil.; with his wife, a Russian singer, **Maria Koussevitzky** (who retained her legal name), he went to Mexico in 1923; then emigrated to the U.S.; joined the Philadelphia Orch., and in 1925 organized the Philadelphia Chamber String Sinfonietta; he led the People's Symph. Orch. in Boston (1934–36); then was permanent conductor of the Indianapolis Symph. Orch. (1937–55) and music director of the Univ. of Miami Symph. Orch. (1959–65). He died during a guest appearance as a conductor in Athens.

Seyfried, Ignaz Xaver, Ritter von, Austrian composer; b. Vienna, Aug. 15, 1776; d. there, Aug. 27, 1841. He was a close friend of Mozart, and had some piano lessons with him; studied also with Koželuh and Haydn; afterward with Albrechtsberger. In 1797 he became conductor at Schikaneder's theater in Vienna; then at the new Theater an der Wien, when it opened in 1801, retaining this post until 1827. He was an extremely prolific composer, and some of his singspiels were very successful; one of them, *Die Ochsenmenuette,* based on Haydn's music (Vienna, Dec. 31, 1823), gave rise to the well-known anecdote about Haydn's composing an *Ox Minuet* for a butcher and receiving an ox as a gift. Seyfried also wrote the opera *Der Wundermann am Rheinfall* (Vienna, Oct. 26, 1799), which elicited praise from Haydn. He further wrote numerous melodramas, ballets, oratorios, motets, symphs., quartets, etc. He publ. Beethoven's exercises in thoroughbass, counterpoint, and composition (1832), with some unwarranted additions (see Thayer's *Beethoven,* III, 80); edited a complete edition of Albrechtsberger's theoretical works; also edited Preindl's *Wiener Tonschule* (1827; 2nd ed., 1832). For a complete list of Seyfried's theatrical works and dates of performances, see Anton Bauer, *Opern und Operetten in Wien* (Graz, 1955).

Sgambati, Giovanni, celebrated Italian pianist and composer; b. Rome, May 28, 1841; d. there, Dec. 14, 1914. He studied piano with Amerigo Barbieri, and appeared in public at the age of 6; sang in church, and conducted instrumental groups. He then became a pupil of Liszt in Rome; subsequently gave orch. concerts, playing German masterpieces; performed Beethoven's *Eroica* in 1866 for the first time in Rome. Historically, Sgambati's concerts were important as the first systematic attempt to introduce to the Italian public a varied fare of symph. music. Sgambati appeared also as a pianist; after a concert tour in Italy and Germany, he established in 1868 a free piano class annexed to the Santa Cecilia Academy in Rome, which in 1877 was formally recognized by the government as the Liceo Musicale; it became the foremost music school in Italy; Sgambati taught piano there until his death. He was an ardent admirer of Wagner, whom he met in 1876; Wagner recommended Sgambati to his own publishers, Schott of Mainz, who subsequently brought out many of Sgambati's works. As a pianist and teacher, Sgambati enjoyed a very high reputation in Germany and Italy; his own music betrays strong Germanic influence; unlike most Italian composers of his time, he devoted his energies exclusively to instrumental music, avoiding all service to the theater.

Shanet, Howard, American conductor; b. Brooklyn, Nov. 9, 1918. He studied cello with Evsei Beloussoff; played in the National Orch. Assoc., under the direction of Leon Barzin; later studied conducting with Rudolph Thomas, Fritz Stiedry, and Koussevitzky at the Berkshire Music Center in Tanglewood; took composition lessons with Hans Weisse, Paul Dessau, Martinu, Lopatnikoff, and Arthur Honegger. He completed his academic studies at Columbia Univ. (A.B., 1939; A.M., 1941). He served in the U.S. Army as warrant officer and bandleader (1942–44); taught at Hunter College in N.Y. between 1945 and 1953; was on the staff at the Berkshire Music Center in the summers of 1948 to 1952; in 1953 was appointed to the faculty of Columbia Univ. and as conductor of the Univ. Orch.; in 1972 became chairman of the music dept.; in 1974 initiated an extensive program in music performance, the first of this nature at Columbia Univ.; served as assistant conductor of the N.Y. City Symph. (1947–48), conductor of the Huntington (W.Va.) Symph. Orch. (1951–52), and a guest conductor with the Israel Phil. Orch. (1950) and the N.Y. Phil. (1951, 1959). In 1977 he received the presidential citation of the National Federation of Music Clubs and a certificate of distinguished service at the Inst. of International Education. He composed *A War March* for Military Band (1944); *2 Canonic Pieces* for 2 Clarinets (1947); *Variations on a Bizarre Theme* for Orch. (1960); arranged and reconstructed the score *Night of the Tropics* by Gottschalk (1955). He publ. an "adult education book," *Learn to Read Music* (N.Y., 1956; trans. into Norwegian, 1972, and Italian, 1975); a fundamental documentary vol., *Philharmonic: A History of New York's Orchestra* (N.Y., 1975); edited and wrote a critical introduction for *Early Histories of the New York Philharmonic,* containing reprints of books by Krehbiel, Huneker, and Erskine (N.Y., 1978).

Shankar, Ravi, Indian sitarist and composer; b. Benares, April 7, 1920. He was trained by his brother, Uday Shankar, and began his career as a musician and a dancer; then engaged in a serious study of the Indian classical instrument, the sitar; in time became a great virtuoso on it. As a consequence of the growing infatuation with oriental arts in Western countries in the 1960s, he suddenly became popular, and his concerts were greeted with reverential awe by youthful multitudes. This popularity increased a thousandfold when the Beatles went to him to receive the revelation of Eastern musical wisdom, thus placing him on the pedestal usually reserved for untutored guitar strummers. As a composer, he distinguished himself by several film scores, including the famous *Pather Panchali;* he also wrote the film scores for *Kabulliwallah* and *Anuradha.* For the Tagore centenary he wrote a ballet, *Samanya Kshati,* based on Tagore's poem of the same name; it was produced in New Delhi on May 7, 1961. He also wrote 2 concertos for sitar and orch. (1970, 1976). He publ. a memoir, *My Music, My Life* (N.Y., 1968). Elise B. Barnett edited *Ravi Shankar: Learning Indian Music, A Systematic Approach* (1981; includes cassette tapes).

Shapero, Harold, American composer; b. Lynn, Mass., April 29, 1920. He learned to play piano as a youth; was for several years a pianist in dance orchs.; began serious study in 1936, at the Malkin Cons. in Boston, with Nicolas Slonimsky; then studied with Krenek, with Walter Piston at Harvard Univ., with Paul Hindemith at the Berkshire Music Center in Tanglewood, and with Nadia Boulanger in Cambridge, Mass. He graduated from Harvard Univ. in 1941; received the American Prix de Rome for his *9-Minute Overture* (N.Y., June 8, 1941); held a Guggenheim fellowship in 1946 and 1947; won the Gershwin Prize (1946); etc.; in 1949–50 was in Rome; in 1952 was appointed a prof. at Brandeis Univ. in Waltham, Mass. He married the painter Esther Geller in 1945. In his music Shapero adheres to an austere Classical pattern, without excluding a highly emotional melodic line; his exceptional mastery of contrapuntal technique secures clarity of intermingled sonorities in his chamber music. In some of his early compositions he applied the dodecaphonic method.
WORKS: *Serenade in D* for String Orch. (1945); *Symphony for Classical Orchestra* (Boston, Jan. 30, 1948); *The Travelers,* overture (1948); *Credo* for Orch. (Louisville, Ky., Oct. 19, 1955); Concerto for Orch. (1951–58); *3 Pieces for 3 Pieces* for Flute, Clarinet, and Bassoon (1938); Trumpet Sonata (1939); String Quartet (1940); *4-Hand Piano Sonata* (1941); Violin Sonata (1942); *Partita* for Piano and Chamber Orch. (1960); *3 Improvisations in B flat* (1968) and *3 Studies in C sharp* (1969) for Piano and Synthesizer; *3 Amateur Sonatas* for Piano.

Shapey, Ralph, American conductor and composer; b. Philadelphia, March 12, 1921. He studied violin with Emmanuel Zetlin and composition with Stefan Wolpe. In 1964 he was appointed to the faculty of the Univ. of Chicago and was made conductor of the resident Contemporary Chamber Players. Disappointed at repeated rejections of his works by performers and publishers, Shapey announced in 1969

that he would never again submit any of his works to anyone for performance or publication. But by an extraordinary turn of events, in 1983 he received a munificent cash prize from the MacArthur Foundation in Chicago, with no strings attached. He sprang into action with renewed energy and faith in human fortune. His music employs serialistic but uncongested procedures in acrid counterpoint, while formally adhering to neo-Classical paradigms.

Shaporin, Yuri, significant Russian composer; b. Glukhov, Ukraine, Nov. 8, 1887; d. Moscow, Dec. 9, 1966. He studied law, and graduated from the Univ. of St. Petersburg in 1913; also studied at the St. Petersburg Cons. with Sokolov (composition), graduating in 1918. He wrote theatrical music in Leningrad; moved to Moscow in 1936.
WORKS: Opera, *The Decembrists* (1930–50; Moscow, June 23, 1953); cantata, *A Tale of the Battle for the Russian Land* (Moscow, April 18, 1944); incidental music to *King Lear, Tartuffe, Boris Godunov,* and Leskov's *The Flea* (also as an orch. suite); Symph. (Moscow, May 11, 1933); symphony-cantata, *On the Field of Kulikovo* (Moscow, Nov. 18, 1939); 2 piano sonatas; several song cycles.

Sharp, Cecil James, English editor and collector of folk songs; b. London, Nov. 22, 1859; d. there, June 23, 1924. He studied music privately while attending Cambridge Univ.; in 1882 he went to Australia, settling in Adelaide, where he worked in a bank and practiced law, becoming associate to the Chief Justice of Southern Australia; in 1889 he resigned from the legal profession and took up a musical career; was assistant organist of the Adelaide Cathedral, and co-director of the Adelaide College of Music. In 1892 he returned to England; was made music instructor of Ludgrove School (1893–1910) and also principal of the Hampstead Cons. (1896–1905). At the same time he became deeply interested in English folk songs; publ. a *Book of British Songs for Home and School* (1902); then proceeded to make a systematic survey of English villages with the aim of collecting authentic specimens of English songs. In 1911 he established the English Folk Dance Society; also was director of the School of Folk Song and Dance at Stratford-upon-Avon. During World War I he was in the U.S., collecting folk music in the Appalachian Mountains, with a view to establishing their English origin. In 1923 he received the degree of M.M. *honoris causa* from Cambridge Univ. In 1930 the "Cecil Sharp House" was opened in London as headquarters of the English Folk Dance Society (amalgamated with the Folk Song Society in 1932). Sharp publ. many collections of folk songs and dances: *English Folk Carols* (1911); *Folk-Songs from Various Counties* (1912); *English Folk-Chanteys* (1914); *One Hundred English Folk-Songs* (1916); *Folk-Songs of English Origin* (2 vols., 1921–23); *English Folk-Songs from the Southern Appalachians* (1917; new enlarged ed., 2 vols., ed. by Maud Karpeles, posthumous, Oxford, 1932; republ. 1952); *American-English Folk-Songs* (1918–21); *The Morris Book* (in 5 parts; 1907–13); *Morris Dance Tunes* (in 10 parts; 1907–13); *The Country Dance Book* (in 6 parts; 1909–22); *Country Dance Tunes* (in 11 parts; 1909–22); *The Sword Dances of Northern England* (in 5 parts; 1911–13). Books: *English Folk Song* (London, 1907; 3rd ed., revised by Maud Karpeles, London, 1954); *The Dance: An Historical Survey of Dancing in Europe*, with A.P. Oppé (London, 1924).

Shaw, Arnold, American composer, writer, editor, lecturer, and music executive; b. Brooklyn, June 28, 1909. He majored in English literature at Columbia Univ. (M.A., 1931; also studied music; composed a number of snappy piano pieces with a sophisticated tilt (*The Mod Muppet, Bubblegum Waltzes, Stabiles Mobiles*) and singable songs (*Dungaree Doll, Woman Is a Five-Letter Word*); edited the mind-boggling books by Joseph Schillinger (*Mathematical Basis of the Arts; Schillinger System of Musical Composition*); lectured at the Juilliard School of Music, New School for Social Research, Univ. of Calif., Los Angeles; as general manager of Edward B. Marks Music Corp., promoted popular singers, among them Rod McKuen, Burt Bacharach, and Elvis Presley. He lives in Las Vegas; in 1973–74 was named Nevada Composer of the Year.

Shaw, Artie (real name, **Arthur Arshawsky**), American clarinetist and bandleader; b. New York, May 23, 1910. He played clarinet in bands as a boy; after playing with a variety of radio and dance bands, he formed his own band in 1935, becoming one of the foremost proponents of "big band swing"; his greatest hit, among more than 600 recordings, was that of Cole Porter's song *Begin the Beguine.* But he considered his fabulous commercial successes as artistically unfulfilling, and throughout his career made attempts for recognition as a "serious" musician. In the 1930s he introduced a group consisting of clarinet, string quartet, and a rhythm section; sporadically, from 1939 to 1954, he led small combos of from 5 to 7 players (but always labeled the "Gramercy 5") in experimental jazz attempts, these groups sometimes including celesta or harpsichord; he also performed as soloist in several clarinet concertos in 1949. He was married consecutively to several movie stars (Lana Turner, Ava Gardner, etc.); in between he also wed the sex authoress Kathleen Winsor. He publ. a quasi-autobiographical novel, *The Trouble with Cinderella* (N.Y., 1952), and the novel *I Love You, I Hate You, Drop Dead!* (1965).

Shaw, George Bernard, famous Irish dramatist; b. Dublin, July 26, 1856; d. Ayot St. Lawrence, England, Nov. 2, 1950. Before winning fame as a playwright, he was active as a music critic in London, writing for the *Star* (under the name of "Corno di Bassetto") during the season of 1888–89, and for the *World* from 1890 to 1894. In 1899 he publ. *The Perfect Wagnerite*, a highly individual socialistic interpretation of the *Ring of the Nibelung.* His criticisms from the *World* were reprinted as *Music in London* in 3 vols. (1932; new ed., 1950); those from the *Star* as *London Music in 1888–89* (London and

N.Y., 1937); selected criticisms were publ., edited by Eric Bentley, in N.Y., 1954. Shaw's play *Arms and the Man* was made into an operetta, *The Chocolate Soldier,* by Oskar Straus (1908); his *Pygmalion* was converted into a highly successful musical comedy (1956) under the title *My Fair Lady,* with a musical score by Frederick Loewe.

Shaw, Martin, English organist and composer; b. London, March 9, 1875; d. Southwold, Sussex, Oct. 24, 1958. He was a pupil at the Royal College of Music in London; played organ in various churches in London. In 1900 he founded the Purcell Society in London; wrote an opera, *Mr. Pepys* (London, Feb. 11, 1926); several masques and ballads; the oratorios *Easter, The Rock* (after T.S. Eliot), and *The Redeemer;* sacred choruses; etc. He publ. *The Principles of English Church Music Composition* (1921); edited *The English Carol Book, Songs of Britain, The Motherland Song Book,* and (with his brother, Geoffrey Shaw) *The League of Nations Song Book.* He publ. his autobiography, *Up to Now,* in 1929. **Geoffrey Shaw** (b. London, Nov. 14, 1879; d. there, April 14, 1943) was an organist and composer; also was active in musical education.

Shaw, Robert, noted American conductor; b. Red Bluff, Calif., April 30, 1916. He came from a clerical family; his father and his grandfather were clergymen; his mother sang in church choirs. He studied at Pomona College (1934–38), where he conducted its Glee Club; in 1938 Fred Waring asked him to help organize the Fred Waring Glee Club, and Shaw conducted it until 1945. In 1941 he founded his own Collegiate Chorale in N.Y., which he led in diversified programs of choral music, old and new, until 1954. In 1944 he was awarded a Guggenheim fellowship. He taught choral conducting at the Berkshire Music Center at Tanglewood (1942–45) and at the Juilliard School of Music in N.Y. (1946–49). In 1946 he made his debut as a symph. conductor with the Naumburg Orch. in N.Y. In 1948 he founded the Robert Shaw Chorale, which he conducted with notable success for 20 seasons. Eager to acquire more experience as an orch. conductor, he attended conducting sessions with Monteux and Rodzinski in N.Y. in 1950. From 1953 to 1958 he conducted summer concerts of the San Diego Symph. Orch. In 1956 he led the Robert Shaw Chorale through a tour of 15 countries of Europe, including Russia, and the Middle East, under the auspices of the State Dept. In 1964 the Robert Shaw Chorale gave concerts in South America. For his Chorale, Shaw commissioned several choral works from contemporary composers, including Béla Bartók, Darius Milhaud, Benjamin Britten, Samuel Barber, and Aaron Copland. Beginning in 1956 he was co-director of the Alaska Festival of Music in Anchorage. From 1956 to 1967 he served as associate conductor with Szell and the Cleveland Orch. In 1967 he was engaged as conductor and music director of the Atlanta Symph. Orch., and by dint of talent and perseverance brought it to a high degree of excellence. In 1977 he conducted the Atlanta Symph. at the gala concert for President Jimmy Carter's inauguration in Washington, D.C.

Shawe-Taylor, Desmond, eminent British music critic; b. Dublin, May 29, 1907. He was educated at Oriel College, Oxford; through the years he contributed literary and musical criticism to various newspapers and periodicals. After service in World War II, he was engaged as music critic of the *New Statesman* in 1945, retaining his post until 1958; from 1950 to 1958 he also served as phonograph record reviewer for the *Observer*. In 1958 he was named music critic of the *Sunday Times;* also was a guest critic for the *New Yorker* (1973–74). He was made a Commander of the Order of the British Empire in 1965. His writings are notable for their unostentatious display of wide learning. He publ. the vol. *Covent Garden* for the World of Music series (London, 1948); also, with Edward Sackville-West, *The Record Guide* (London, 1951, and later revisions).

Shchedrin, Rodion, brilliant Soviet composer; b. Moscow, Dec. 16, 1932. He studied with Shaporin at the Moscow Cons., graduating in 1955. In his music he developed a richly harmonious idiom, diversified by impulsive rhythms.
WORKS: Opera, *Not Only for Love* (Moscow, 1961); ballets: *The Humpback Horse* (1955; extremely popular in Russia) and *Anna Karenina* (1972); 3 piano concertos (1954, 1966, 1976); Symph. No. 1 (1958); Symph. No. 2 (1962–65; includes a section which artfully imitates the tuning of an orch.); *Obstreperous Street Tunes* for Orch. (1963; extremely popular); *Chimes* for Orch., commissioned by the N.Y. Phil. (N.Y., Jan. 11, 1968); *Chamber Orchestra Suite* for 20 Violins, Harp, Accordion, and 2 Double Basses (1961); Piano Quintet (1952); 2 string quartets (1951, 1954); *24 Preludes and Fugues* for Piano (1969–70); *Polyphonic Album* for Piano (1973); oratorio, *Lenin Dwells in the Heart of the People* (1969); *Bureaucratiade* for Voices and Orch., a satirical work (1963); *Poetorium* for Speaker, Chorus, and Orch. (1969); *Musical Offering* for Organ, 3 Flutes, 3 Bassoons, and 3 Trombones (Moscow, Oct. 21, 1983). He made an ingenious arrangement of fragments from Bizct's *Carmen* as a ballet suite, scored for strings and percussion, reducing Bizet's romantic melodies to a coarse but extremely effective ensemble, which he wrote for his wife, the ballerina Maya Plisetskaya (1968).

Shcherbachev, Vladimir, Russian composer; b. Warsaw, Jan. 24, 1889; d. Leningrad, March 5, 1952. He studied at the St. Petersburg Cons. with Maximilian Steinberg and Liadov, graduating in 1914. From 1924 to 1931 he was a prof. of composition at the Leningrad Cons. He wrote an opera, *Anna Kolosova* (1939); 5 symphs.: No. 1 (1914; Petrograd, Nov. 5, 1916); No. 2 (Leningrad, Dec. 14, 1924); No. 3 (Leningrad, Feb. 4, 1932, composer conducting); No. 4, subtitled *History of the Izhorsky Factory* (Leningrad, May 28, 1934, in partial perf.; complete perf., Radio Leningrad, Dec. 23, 1935; public perf., Leningrad, Jan. 21, 1936); No. 5 (Leningrad, Dec. 21, 1948;

revised version, Kiev, Oct. 21, 1950); music for films; the orch. suite from one of them, *The Thunderstorm*, became popular in Russia; he further wrote *A Fairy Tale* for Orch. (Petrograd, Dec. 20, 1915); Nonet (1917); numerous piano works.

Shearing, George Albert, English-American jazz pianist; b. London, Aug. 13, 1919. He was blind from birth; learned to read music with Braille notation; for several years he played piano in a blind band; then transferred to the U.S. (naturalized in 1955) and organized a quintet, with vibraphone, guitar, drums, and bass. In the early 1940s he played a typical stride style of the time; in the late 1940s, influenced by the innovations of bebop, he developed a new manner, characterized by surprising, extended harmonies, and a pianistic technique whereby both hands play thick chords in parallel motion ("locked-hand style"). He composed famous tunes, among them *Lullaby of Birdland.*

Shepherd, Arthur, eminent American composer and pedagogue; b. Paris, Idaho, Feb. 19, 1880; d. Cleveland, Jan. 12, 1958. He studied with G. Haessel; in 1892, entered the New England Cons., where he studied piano with Dennée and Carl Faelten, and composition with Goetschius and Chadwick. In 1897 he went to Salt Lake City, where he settled as a teacher and conductor of the Salt Lake Symph. Orch.; returned to Boston in 1908, and became a prof. of harmony and counterpoint at the New England Cons. (until 1917). In 1917 he joined the U.S. Army, and was bandmaster of the 303rd Field Artillery in France. From 1920 to 1926 he was assistant conductor of the Cleveland Orch., and also conducted children's concerts there; was music critic of the Cleveland *Press* (1929–32). In 1927 he became a prof. of music at Case Western Reserve Univ., retiring in 1950; then lived in Boston and Cleveland. A composer of national tendencies, he wrote in a grand Romantic manner, derived from an intense feeling for American melos.

Shifrin, Seymour J., American composer; b. Brooklyn, Feb. 28, 1926; d. Boston, Sept. 26, 1979. He studied with Otto Luening at Columbia Univ., graduating in 1947 (M.A., 1949), and privately with Darius Milhaud and William Schuman. He subsequently taught at the Univ. of Calif., Berkeley (1952–66), and at Brandeis Univ. at Waltham, Mass. (1966–79). He was twice a recipient of Guggenheim fellowship grants (1956, 1959) and of Koussevitzky International Recording awards (1970, 1972). He wrote music of high chromatic consistency, with finely delineated contrapuntal lines often resulting in sharp dissonance.

Shilkret, Nathaniel, American composer, arranger, and conductor; b. New York, Jan. 1, 1895; d. Franklin Square, Long Island, N.Y., Feb. 18, 1982. He studied composition with Pietro Floridia; played the clarinet in the Russian Symph. Orch. in N.Y., the N.Y. Phil., and the Metropolitan Opera House Orch.; also in the bands led by John Philip Sousa and

Edwin Franko Goldman. In 1916 he became music director of the Victor Talking Machine Co. and created the Victor Salon Orch.; held executive posts with Victor until 1935; then went to Hollywood, where he became active as an arranger of movie scores, but continued to spend part of the season in N.Y., where he led a number of radio broadcasts. He wrote a symph. poem, *Skyward* (1928); a Trombone Concerto (1942); and also various descriptive pieces for orch. Perhaps the most memorable contribution he made to music history was his commissioning of Schoenberg, Stravinsky, Toch, Milhaud, Castelnuovo-Tedesco, and Tansman to write a movement each for a biblical cantata, *Genesis,* to which he himself contributed a movement.

Shimizu, Osamu, prolific Japanese composer; b. Osaka, Nov. 4, 1911. He studied composition with Hashimoto and Hosokawa at the Tokyo Music Academy from 1936 to 1939; was active in the music dept. of Tokyo Radio; wrote articles on music.
WORKS: 10 operas: *The Tale of the Mask-Maker Shuzenji* (Osaka, Nov. 4, 1954); *The Charcoal Princess* (Osaka, Nov. 1, 1956); *The Man Who Shoots at the Blue Sky* (Osaka, Nov. 26, 1956); *Gauche, the Violoncellist* (Osaka, Oct. 11, 1957); *The Singing Skeleton* (Osaka, March 15, 1962); *Shunkan, the Exile* (Osaka, Nov. 18, 1964); *The Merciful Poet,* operetta (1965); *Muko Erabi (The Marriage Contest),* comic opera (Los Angeles, Oct. 3, 1968); *Daibutsu-Kaigen (The Great Image of Buddha),* historic opera on the inauguration of the bronze statue of Buddha on April 9, A.D. 752 (Tokyo, Oct. 2, 1970); *Ikuta Gawa (The River Ikuta;* Tokyo, Nov. 10, 1971); ballets: *The Sun* (1955); *The Crane* (1956); *The Earth* (1957); *Araginu* (1958); *Fire in the Field* (1962); *Love Poems* (1966); numerous cantatas, including *Rennyo* (Tokyo, April 8, 1948), *La Paix* (Tokyo, April 22, 1949), and *Hymn to Dengyō-Daishi* (1966); 3 symphs.: No. 1 (Tokyo, Dec. 8, 1951); No. 2 (1957); No. 3 (1961); *Dance Suite on the Themes of Flowers* for Orch. (1944); *Poème* for Flute and Orch. (1950); *4 Movements on Indian Melodies* for Orch. (1950); *Suite* for Orch. (1953); *Taiheiraku,* gagaku for Orch. (1971); String Quartet (1940); *Ballad* for Flute and Piano (1940); *Ballad* for Violin and Orch. (1941); Quartet for Flute, Oboe, Clarinet, and Bassoon (1958); *Olympic Hymn* for the opening of the Olympic Games in Japan (Tokyo, Oct. 10, 1964).

Shirley-Quirk, John, English baritone; b. Liverpool, Aug. 28, 1931. (His hyphenated name is composed of the place-name Shirley, in Derbyshire, where his ancestors lived, and the Celtic appellation in the Manx language, used on the channel isle of Man.) He studied voice with Roy Henderson, and at the same time took courses in chemistry and physics at the Univ. of Liverpool; then taught science in a British Air Force station. Benjamin Britten engaged him to sing in his church parables at the Aldeburgh Festivals; he also sang the multiple roles of several characters in Britten's opera *Death in Venice;* made his formal debut at the Glyndebourne Festival in 1961. He sang the part of

the Traveler in the Metropolitan Opera production of *Death in Venice* in N.Y., on Oct. 18, 1974. He also gave concert recitals. In 1975 he was named a Commander of the Order of the British Empire.

Shnitke, Alfred. See **Schnittke, Alfred.**

Shostakovich, Dmitri, preeminent Russian composer of the Soviet generation, whose style and idiom of composition largely defined the nature of new Russian music; b. St. Petersburg, Sept. 25, 1906, d. Moscow, Aug. 9, 1975. He was a member of a cultured Russian family; his father was an engineer employed in the government office of weights and measures; his mother was a professional pianist. Shostakovich grew up during the most difficult period of Russian revolutionary history, when famine and disease decimated the population of Petrograd. Of frail physique, he suffered from malnutrition; Glazunov, the director of the Petrograd Cons., appealed personally to the Commissar of Education, Lunacharsky, to grant an increased food ration for Shostakovich, essential for his physical survival. Shostakovich received his early musical training from his mother, who taught him piano; in 1919 he entered the Petrograd Cons., where he studied piano with Nikolayev and composition with Maximilian Steinberg; graduated in piano in 1923, and in composition in 1925. As a graduation piece, he submitted his First Symph., written at the age of 18; it was first performed by the Leningrad Phil. on May 12, 1926, under the direction of Nicolai Malko, and subsequently became one of Shostakovich's most popular works. His 2nd Symph., composed for the 10th anniversary of the Soviet Revolution, bearing the surname *Dedication to October* and ending with a rousing choral finale, was less successful despite its revolutionary sentiment. He then wrote a satirical opera, *The Nose,* after Gogol's whimsical story about the sudden disappearance of the nose from the face of a government functionary; here Shostakovich revealed his flair for musical satire; the score featured a variety of modernistic devices and included an interlude written for percussion instruments only. *The Nose* was produced in Leningrad on Jan. 12, 1930, with considerable popular acclaim, but was attacked by officious theater critics as a product of "bourgeois decadence," and quickly withdrawn from the stage. Somewhat in the same satirical style was Shostakovich's ballet *The Golden Age* (1930), which included a celebrated dissonant *Polka,* satirizing the current disarmament conference in Geneva. There followed the 3rd Symph., subtitled *May First* (first perf. in Leningrad on Jan. 21, 1930), with a choral finale saluting the International Workers' Day. Despite its explicit revolutionary content, it failed to earn the approbation of Soviet spokesmen, who dismissed the work as nothing more than a formal gesture of proletarian solidarity. Shostakovich's next work was to precipitate a crisis in his career, as well as in Soviet music in general; it was an opera to the libretto drawn from a short story by the 19th-century Russian writer Leskov, entitled *Lady Macbeth of the*

Shostakovich

District of Mtzensk, and depicting adultery, murder, and suicide in a merchant home under the Czars. It was produced in Leningrad on Jan. 22, 1934, and was hailed by most Soviet musicians as a significant work comparable to the best productions of Western modern opera. But both the staging and the music ran counter to growing Soviet puritanism; a symph. interlude portraying a scene of adultery behind the bedroom curtain, orchestrated with suggestive passages on the slide trombones, shocked the Soviet officials present at the performance by its bold naturalism. After the Moscow production of the opera, *Pravda,* the official organ of the ruling Communist party, publ. an unsigned (and therefore all the more authoritative) article accusing Shostakovich of creating a "bedlam of noise." The brutality of this assault dismayed Shostakovich; he readily admitted his faults in both content and treatment of the subject, and declared his solemn determination to write music according to the then-emerging formula of "socialist realism." His next stage production was a ballet, *The Limpid Brook,* portraying the pastoral scenes on a Soviet collective farm. In this work Shostakovich tempered his dissonant idiom, and the subject seemed eminently fitting for the Soviet theater; but *The Limpid Brook,* too, was condemned in *Pravda,* this time for an insufficiently dignified treatment of Soviet life. Having been rebuked twice for 2 radically different theater works, Shostakovich abandoned all attempts to write for the stage, and returned to purely instrumental composition. But as though pursued by vengeful fate, he again suffered a painful reverse. His 4th Symph. was placed in rehearsal by the Leningrad Phil., but withdrawn before the performance when representatives of the musical officialdom and even the orch. musicians themselves sharply criticized the piece. Shostakovich's rehabilitation finally came with the production of his 5th Symph. (Leningrad, Nov. 21, 1937), a work of rhapsodic grandeur, culminating in a powerful climax; it was hailed, as though by spontaneous consensus, as a model of true Soviet art, classical in formal design, lucid in its harmonic idiom, and optimistic in its philosophical connotations. The height of Shostakovich's rise to recognition was achieved in his 7th Symph. He began its composition during the siege of Leningrad by the Nazis in the autumn of 1941; he served in the fire brigade during the air raids; then flew from Leningrad to the temporary Soviet capital in Kuibishev, on the Volga, where he completed the score, which was performed there on March 1, 1942. Its symph. development is realistic in the extreme, with the theme of the Nazis, in mechanical march time, rising to monstrous loudness, only to be overcome and reduced to a pathetic drum dribble by a victorious Russian song. The work became a musical symbol of the Russian struggle against the overwhelmingly superior Nazi war machine; it was given the subtitle *Leningrad Symphony,* and was performed during the war by virtually every orch. in the Allied countries. After the tremendous emotional appeal of the *Leningrad Symphony,* the 8th Symph., written in 1943, had a lesser impact; the 9th, 10th, and 11th symphs. followed

(1945, 1953, 1957) without attracting much comment; the 12th Symph., dedicated to the memory of Lenin, aroused a little more interest. But it was left for his 13th Symph. (first perf. in Leningrad on Dec. 18, 1962) to create a controversy which seemed to be Shostakovich's peculiar destiny; its vocal first movement for solo bass and male chorus, to words by the Soviet poet Evtushenko, expressing the horror of the massacre of Jews by the Nazis during their occupation of the city of Kiev, and containing a warning against residual anti-Semitism in Soviet Russia, met with unexpected criticism by the then-chairman of the Communist party, Nikita Khrushchev, who complained about the exclusive attention in Evtushenko's poem to Jewish victims, and his failure to mention the Ukrainians and other nationals who were also slaughtered. The text of the poem was altered to meet these objections, but the 13th Symph. never gained wide acceptance. There followed the remarkable 14th Symph., in 11 sections, scored for voices and orch., to words by Federico García Lorca, Apollinaire, Rilke, and the Russian poet Küchelbecker. Shostakovich's 15th Symph., his last (perf. in Moscow under the direction of Shostakovich's son **Maxim Shostakovich** on Jan. 8, 1972), demonstrated his undying spirit of innovation; the score is set in the key of C major, but it contains a dodecaphonic passage and literal allusions to motives from Rossini's *William Tell Overture* and the Fate Motif from Wagner's *Die Walküre.* Shostakovich's adoption, however limited, of themes built on 12 different notes, a procedure that he had himself condemned as anti-musical, is interesting both from the psychological and sociological standpoint; he experimented with these techniques in several other works; his first explicit use of a 12-tone subject occurred in his 12th String Quartet (1968). Equally illuminating is his use in some of his scores of a personal monogram, D.S.C.H. (for D, Es, C, H in German notation, i.e., D, E-flat, C, B). One by one, his early works, originally condemned as unacceptable to Soviet reality, were returned to the stage and the concert hall; the objectionable 4th and 13th symphs. were publ. and recorded; the operas *The Nose* and *Lady Macbeth of the District of Mtzensk* (renamed *Katerina Izmailova,* after the name of the heroine) had several successful revivals.

Shostakovich excelled in instrumental music. Besides the 15 symphs., he wrote 15 string quartets, a String Octet, Piano Quintet, 2 piano trios, Cello Sonata, Violin Sonata, Viola Sonata, 2 violin concertos, 2 piano concertos, 2 cello concertos, 24 preludes for piano, 24 preludes and fugues for piano, 2 piano sonatas, several short piano pieces; also choral works and song cycles.

What is remarkable about Shostakovich is the unfailing consistency of his style of composition. His entire oeuvre, from his first work to the last (147 opus numbers in all), proclaims a personal article of faith. His idiom is unmistakably of the 20th century, making free use of dissonant harmonies and intricate contrapuntal designs, yet never abandoning inherent tonality; his music is teleological, leading invariably to a tonal climax, often in a triumphal triadic declaration. Most of his works carry key signatures; his metrical structure is governed by a unifying rhythmic pulse. Shostakovich is equally eloquent in dramatic and lyric utterance; he has no fear of prolonging his slow movements in relentless dynamic rise and fall; the cumulative power of his kinetic drive in rapid movements is overwhelming. Through all the peripeties of his career, he never changed his musical language in its fundamental modalities. When the flow of his music met obstacles, whether technical or external, he obviated them without changing the main direction. In a special announcement issued after Shostakovich's death, the government of the Union of Soviet Socialist Republics summarized his work as a "remarkable example of fidelity to the traditions of musical classicism, and above all, to the Russian traditions, finding his inspiration in the reality of Soviet life, reasserting and developing in his creative innovations the art of socialist realism, and in so doing, contributing to universal progressive musical culture." His honors, both domestic and foreign, were many: the Order of Lenin (1946, 1956, 1966), People's Artist of the U.S.S.R. (1954), Hero of Socialist Labor (1966), Order of the October Revolution (1971), honorary membership in the American Inst. of the Arts (1943), honorary Doctor of Oxford Univ. (1958), Laureate of the International Sibelius Prize (1958), Doctor of Fine Arts from Northwestern Univ. (1973). He visited the U.S. as a delegate to the World Peace Conference in 1949, as a member of a group of Soviet musicians in 1959, and to receive the degree of D.F.A. from Northwestern Univ. in 1973. A postage stamp of 6 kopecks, bearing his photograph and an excerpt from the *Leningrad Symphony*, was issued by the Soviet Post Office in 1976 to commemorate his 70th birthday. The publication of Shostakovich's collected works in 42 vols., to be completed in 1984, was initiated in 1978.

WORKS: STAGE AND DRAMATIC MUSIC: *The Nose* (Leningrad, Jan. 12, 1930); *Lady Macbeth of the District of Mtzensk* (Leningrad, Jan. 22, 1934; under the title *Katerina Izmailova*, Moscow, Jan. 24, 1934; Metropolitan Opera, N.Y., Feb. 5, 1935; score revised, 1962; *Moskva Cheryomushki* (Moscow, Jan. 24, 1959); ballets: *The Golden Age* (Leningrad, Oct. 26, 1930; contains the celebrated dance number *Polka*); *Bolt* (Leningrad, April 8, 1931); *The Limpid Brook* (Leningrad, April 4, 1935). INCIDENTAL MUSIC: Mayakovsky's comedy *The Bedbug* (1929); *Rule Britannia* (1931); *Hamlet* (1932); *The Human Comedy*, after Balzac (1934); *Salud, España* (1936); *King Lear* (1940); *Russian River* (1944). FILM SCORES: *New Babylon* (1929); *Alone* (1930); *Golden Mountains* (1931); *The Stranger* (1932); *Love and Hatred* (1934); *Maxim's Youth* (1935); *Companions* (1935); *Maxim's Return* (1937); *Friends* (1938); *Great Citizen* (1938); *A Man with a Gun* (1938); *Silly Little Mouse* (1939); *Zoya* (1944); *Plain Folks* (1945); *Young Guard* (1948); *Encounter on the Elba River* (1948); *The Fall of Berlin* (1949); *Unforgettable Year 1919* (1951); *Song of the Great Rivers* (1954); *Gadfly* (1955); *The First Echelon* (1956); *5 Days, 5 Nights* (1960); *Sophie Perovskaya* (1967), a tribute to one of the executed conspirators in the assassination of

Czar Alexander II of Russia in 1881; *King Lear* (1970).

FOR ORCH.: 15 symphs.: No. 1 (Leningrad, May 12, 1926); No. 2, with a choral ending, dedicated to the October Revolution (Leningrad, Nov. 6, 1927); No. 3, subtitled *May First* (Leningrad, Jan. 21, 1930); No. 4 (1936; Moscow, Jan. 20, 1962); No. 5 (Leningrad, Nov. 21, 1937); No. 6 (Leningrad, Nov. 5, 1939); No. 7, *Leningrad Symphony* (Kuibishev, March 1, 1942; first American perf., NBC Symph., N.Y., Toscanini conducting, July 19, 1942); No. 8 (Moscow, Nov. 4, 1943); No. 9 (Leningrad, Nov. 3, 1945); No. 10 (Leningrad, Dec. 17, 1953); No. 11 (Moscow, Oct. 30, 1957); No. 12, *The Year 1917*, dedicated to the memory of Lenin (Leningrad, Oct. 1, 1961); No. 13 for Orch., Male Chorus, and Solo Bass, to words by Evtushenko (1961; Moscow, Dec. 18, 1962); No. 14 for Soprano, Bass, and Chamber Orch., in 11 sections (Leningrad, Sept. 29, 1969); No. 15 (Moscow, Jan. 8, 1972); Piano Concerto No. 1 for Piano, Trumpet, and Strings (Leningrad, Oct. 15, 1933); *5 Fragments* (1935; Moscow, April 26, 1965); Piano Concerto No. 2 (Moscow, May 10, 1957; Maxim Shostakovich, son of the composer, soloist); Violin Concerto No. 1 (Leningrad, Oct. 29, 1955); Violin Concerto No. 2 (Moscow, Sept. 26, 1967); Cello Concerto No. 1 (Leningrad, Oct. 4, 1959); Cello Concerto No. 2 (Moscow, Sept. 25, 1966).

OTHER WORKS FOR ORCH.: *Scherzo* (1919); *Theme and Variations* (1922); *Tahiti Trot*, orchestration of *Tea for 2* by Youmans (1928); *Technically Killed*, a circus piece (1931); *Suite* for Jazz Orch. (Leningrad, Nov. 28, 1938); orchestration of Mussorgsky's opera *Boris Godunov* (1940); *Festive Overture* (1954); *Overture on Russian and Kirghiz Folk Themes* (1963; Moscow, Oct. 10, 1965); *Funeral and Triumphant Prelude in Memory of the Heroes of the Battle of Stalingrad* (1967); *October*, symph. poem (Moscow, Sept. 26, 1967); *March of Soviet Militia* for Band (1970); 4 ballet suites (1949, 1951, 1952, 1953); also 2 *Fables of Krylov*, op. 4 (first perf. Sept. 26, 1981, at a memorial concert in Moscow).

VOCAL WORKS: 6 songs to words by Japanese poets for Voice and Orch. (1932–38); *Leningrad* for Chorus and Orch. (Moscow, Oct. 15, 1942); *Song of the Forests*, cantata (Leningrad, Nov. 15, 1949); *Democratic Vistas*, a cycle of 10 poems by Walt Whitman for Chorus and Orch. (Moscow, Oct. 10, 1951); 4 songs to texts by Pushkin (1936); 6 songs to words by Burns, Shakespeare, and Walter Raleigh (1942); *Song of the Fatherland* for Soloists, Chorus, and Orch. (1947); *From Jewish Folk Poetry*, vocal cycle, with Piano (1948); *The Sun Shines over Our Fatherland*, cantata for Boys' Chorus, Mixed Choir, and Orch. (1952); *4 Monologues* to words by Pushkin for Voice and Piano (1952); *5 Songs* to words by Dolmatovsky for Voice and Piano (1954); *Spanish Songs* (1956); *Satires (Scenes from the Past)*, 5 songs for Voice and Piano (1960); *The Death of Stepan Razin* for Orch., Mixed Choir, and Bass, to words by Evtushenko (Moscow, Dec. 28, 1964); *5 Songs* to texts from the Moscow comic magazine *Crocodile* (1965); *Foreword to My Collected Works and a Brief Meditation anent This Foreword* for Bass Voice and Orch. (1966); *7 Songs* to words by Alexander Blok, for Soprano, Violin, Cello, and Piano (1967); *Spring,*

Spring, song to words by Pushkin (1967); *Faith,* ballad cycle for Men's Chorus a cappella (1970); *6 Songs* for Contralto and Chamber Orch. by Marina Tsvetayeva (1974); *Suite* for Bass and Piano, to texts by Michelangelo (1974); *4 Songs* to words from Dostoyevsky for Bass and Piano (1975).

CHAMBER MUSIC: Piano Trio No. 1 (1923); *3 Pieces* for Cello and Piano (1924); *2 Pieces* for String Octet (1925); Cello Sonata (1934); 15 string quartets (1938, 1944, 1946, 1949, 1952, 1956, 1960, 1960, 1964, 1964, 1966, 1968, 1970, 1973, 1974); Piano Quintet (1940); 2 piano trios (1923, 1944); Violin Sonata (1968); Viola Sonata (1975).

PIANO MUSIC: *8 Preludes* (1919–20); *3 Fantastic Dances* (1922); *Suite* for 2 Pianos (1922); 2 sonatas (1926, 1942); *Aphorisms* (1927); *24 Preludes* (1932–33); *Children's Album* (1945); *Puppets' Dances* (1946); *24 Preludes and Fugues* (1950–51); Concertino for 2 Pianos (1953).

Shostakovich, Maxim, Russian conductor, son of **Dmitri Shostakovich;** b. Leningrad, May 10, 1938. He studied piano at the Moscow Cons. with Yakov Flier, and conducting with Gauk and Rozhdestvensky. In 1963 he became assistant conductor of the Moscow Symph. Orch., and in 1966, of the U.S.S.R. State Orch. From 1971 to 1981 he was principal conductor and artistic director of the U.S.S.R. State Radio Orch. He made many appearances as a guest conductor in the Soviet Union and in Europe; also toured Japan, Mexico, and Canada; appeared in the U.S. in 1969, conducting the U.S.S.R. State Orch. on its American tour. He gained his reputation mainly by his obviously authentic interpretations of his father's works. During his tour in West Germany with the U.S.S.R. State Radio Orch. in April 1981, he announced his decision not to return to the Soviet Union. His defection aroused a burst of indignation in the Soviet press, and he was denounced as a traitor to his father's legacy. Eventually he and his son, the pianist Dmitri, settled in the U.S. On Memorial Day, 1981, he conducted the National Symph. Orch. of Washington, D.C., in a concert on the West Lawn of the U.S. Capitol. He was subsequently a guest conductor of the Atlanta Symph., the Los Angeles Phil., the Chicago Symph., and other orchs.

Shumsky, Oscar, American violinist; b. Philadelphia, March 23, 1917. He began fiddling as a mere toddler; was a minuscule soloist at the age of 8 with the Philadelphia Orch. under Stokowski. He then began to study in earnest, first with Leopold Auer, then at the Curtis Inst. of Music in Philadelphia with Efrem Zimbalist. Soon he became a professional violinist; was a member of the NBC Symph. Orch. (1939–42); then taught at the Peabody Cons. in Baltimore. In 1953 he joined the staff of the Juilliard School of Music in N.Y.; also taught classes at the Curtis Inst. (1961–65) and, from 1975, at the Yale School of Music.

Sibelius, Jean (Johan Julius Christian), great Finnish composer whose music, infused with the deeply felt modalities of national folk songs, opened a modern era of Northern musical art; b. Hämeenlinna, Dec. 8, 1865; d. Järvenpää, Sept. 20, 1957. The family name stems from a Finnish peasant named Sibbe, traced back to the late 17th century; the Latin noun ending was commonly added among educated classes in Scandinavia. Sibelius was the son of an army surgeon; from early childhood he showed a natural affinity for music. At the age of 9 he began to study piano; then took violin lessons with Gustaf Levander, a local bandmaster. He learned to play violin well enough to take part in amateur performances of chamber music. In 1885 he enrolled at the Univ. of Helsingfors (Helsinki), to study law, but abandoned it after the first semester. In the fall of 1885 he entered the Helsingfors Cons., where he studied violin with Vasiliev and Csillag; he also took courses in composition with the eminent Finnish musician Wegelius. In 1889 his String Quartet was performed in public, and produced a sufficiently favorable impression to obtain for him a government stipend for further study in Berlin, where he took lessons in counterpoint and fugue with Albert Becker. Later he proceeded to Vienna for additional musical training, and became a student of Robert Fuchs and Karl Goldmark (1890–91). In 1892 he married Aino Järnefelt. From then on, his destiny as a national Finnish composer was determined; the music he wrote was inspired by native legends, with the great Finnish epic *Kalevala* as a prime source of inspiration. On April 28, 1892, his symph. poem *Kullervo,* scored for soloists, chorus, and orch., was first performed in Helsingfors. There followed one of his most remarkable works, the symph. poem entitled simply *En Saga,* that is, "a legend"; in it he displayed to the full his genius for variation forms, based on a cumulative growth of a basic theme adorned but never encumbered with effective contrapuntal embellishments. From 1892 to 1900 he taught theory of composition at the Helsingfors Cons. In 1897 the Finnish Senate granted him an annual stipend of 3,000 marks. On April 26, 1899, he conducted in Helsingfors the premiere of his First Symph., in E minor. He led first performances of all of his symphs., in 1902, 1907, 1911, 1915, 1923, and 1924. On July 2, 1900, the Helsingfors Phil. gave the first performance of his most celebrated and most profoundly moving patriotic work, *Finlandia.* Its melody soon became identified among Finnish patriots with the aspiration for national independence, so that the Czarist government went to the extreme of forbidding its performances during periods of political unrest. In 1901 Sibelius was invited to conduct his works at the annual festival of the Allgemeiner Deutscher Tonkünstlerverein at Heidelberg. In 1904 he settled in his country home at Järvenpää, where he remained for the rest of his life; he traveled rarely. In 1913 he accepted a commission for an orch. work from the American music patron Carl Stoeckel, to be performed at the 28th annual Festival at Norfolk, Conn. For it he contributed a symph. legend, *Aalotaret (Nymphs of the Ocean;* it was later revised under the title *The Oceanides).* He took his only sea voyage to America to conduct its premiere on June 4, 1914; on that occasion he received the honorary degree of Mus.Doc. from Yale Univ. Returning to Finland just before the outbreak of World War I, Sibelius withdrew into seclusion, but continued to work. He made his last public appearance abroad in Stockholm, conducting his 7th Symph. there on March 24, 1924. He wrote 2 more works after that, including a score for Shakespeare's *The Tempest* and a symph. poem, *Tapiola;* he practically ceased to compose after 1927. At various times rumors were circulated that he had completed his 8th Symph., but no one had actually seen even any sketches of this work. One persistent story was that Sibelius himself decided to burn his incomplete works. Although willing to receive journalists and reporters, he avoided answering questions about his music. He lived out his very long life as a retired person, absorbed in family interests; in some modest ways he was even a *bon vivant;* he liked his cigars and his beer, and he showed no diminution in his mental alertness. Only once was his peaceful life gravely disrupted; this was when the Russian army invaded Finland in 1940; Sibelius sent an anguished appeal to America to save his country, which by the perverse fate of world politics became allied with Nazi Germany. But after the war Sibelius cordially received a delegation of Soviet composers who made a reverential pilgrimage to his rural retreat.

Honors were showered upon him; festivals of his music became annual events in Helsinki; a postage stamp bearing his likeness was issued by the Finnish government on his 80th birthday; special publications, biographical, bibliographical, and photographic, were publ. in Finland. Artistically, too, Sibelius attained the status of greatness rarely vouchsafed to a living musician; several important contemporary composers paid him homage by acknowledging their debt of inspiration to him, Vaughan Williams among them. Sibelius was the last representative of 19th-century nationalistic Romanticism. He stayed aloof from modern developments, but he was not uninterested in reading scores and listening to performances on the radio of works of such men as Schoenberg, Prokofiev, Bartók, and Shostakovich.

The music of Sibelius marked the culmination of the growth of national Finnish art, in which Pacius was the protagonist, and Wegelius, the teacher of Sibelius, a worthy cultivator. Like his predecessors, Sibelius was schooled in the Germanic tradition, and his early works reflect German lyricism and German dramatic thought. He opened a new era in Finnish music when he abandoned formal conventions and began to write music that seemed inchoate and diffuse but followed a powerful line of development by variation and repetition; a parallel with Beethoven's late works has frequently been drawn. The thematic material employed by Sibelius is not modeled directly on known Finnish folk songs; rather, he re-created the characteristic melodic patterns of folk music. The prevailing mood is somber, even tragic, with a certain elemental sweep and grandeur. His instrumentation is highly individual, with long songful solo passages, and with protracted transitions that are treated as integral parts of the music. His genius found its most eloquent expression in his symphs. and symph. poems; he wrote relatively little chamber music, and only in his earlier years. His only opera, *The Maid in the Tower* (1896), to a text in Swedish, was never publ. He wrote some incidental music for the stage; the celebrated *Valse triste* was written in 1903 for *Kuolema,* a play by Arvid Järnefelt, brother-in-law of Sibelius.

WORKS: FOR THE STAGE: *Jungfrun i tornet (The Maid in the Tower),* opera (1896; Helsinki, Nov. 7, 1896); incidental music: Overture, op. 10, and Suite, op. 11, to *Karelia* (1893; Helsinki, Nov. 13, 1893); *King Kristian II,* op. 27, for a play by A. Paul (1898; Helsinki, Feb. 28, 1898, composer conducting); *Kuolema (Death)* for Strings and Percussion, op. 44, for a play by Arvid Järnefelt (1903; Helsinki, Dec. 2, 1903, composer conducting); *Pelléas et Mélisande,* op. 46, for Maeterlinck's play (1905; Helsinki, March 17, 1905, composer conducting); *Belshazzar's Feast,* op. 51, for a play by H. Procopé (1906; Helsinki, Nov. 7, 1906, composer conducting); *Svanevhit (Swanwhite),* op. 54, for Strindberg's play (1908; Helsinki, April 8, 1908, composer conducting); *Ödlan (The Lizard)* for Solo Violin and String Quintet, op. 8, for a play by M. Lybeck (1909; Helsinki, April 6, 1910, composer conducting); *Jedermann* for Mixed Chorus, Piano, Organ, and Orch., op. 83, for Hofmannsthal's play (1916; Helsinki, Nov. 5, 1916); *The Tempest,* op. 109, for Shakespeare's play (1925; Copenhagen, March 16, 1926); also *Näcken (The Watersprite),* 2 songs with Piano Trio, for a play by Wennerberg (1888); *The Language of the Birds,* a wedding march for A. Paul's play *Die Sprache der Vögel* (1911); *Scaramouche,* op. 71, a "tragic pantomime" after the play by P. Knudsen and M. Bloch (1913; Copenhagen, May 12, 1922).

ORCH. MUSIC: 7 symphs.: No. 1, in E minor, op. 39 (1899; Helsinki, April 26, 1899, composer conducting); No. 2, in D major, op. 43 (1901–2; Helsinki, March 8, 1902, composer conducting); No. 3, in C major, op. 52 (1904–7; Helsinki, Sept. 25, 1907, composer conducting); No. 4, in A minor, op. 63 (1911; Helsinki, April 3, 1911, composer conducting); No. 5, in E-flat major, op. 82 (1915; Helsinki, Dec. 8, 1915, Kajanus conducting; revised 1916; Helsinki, Dec. 14, 1916; revised 1919; Helsinki, Nov. 24, 1919); No. 6, in D minor, op. 104 (1923; Helsinki, Feb. 19, 1923, composer conducting); No. 7, in C major, op. 105 (1924; Stockholm, March 24, 1924, composer conducting). Other works: *Andantino* and *Menuetto* for Clarinet, 2 Cornets, 2 Horns, and Baritone (1890–91); Overture in E major (1890–91); *Scène de ballet* (1891); *Menuetto* (1894); *Skogsrået (The Wood Nymph),* tone poem, op. 15 (1894); *Vårsång (Spring Song),* tone poem, op. 16 (1894; Vaasa, June 21, 1894); *4 Legends,* op. 22 (all 4 first perf. in Helsinki, April 13, 1896, composer conducting): 1, *Lemminkäinen and the Maidens of the Island* (1895; revised 1897 and 1939); 2, *The Swan of Tuonela* (1893; revised 1897 and 1900); 3, *Lemminkäinen in Tuonela* (1895; revised 1897 and 1939); 4, *Lemminkäinen's Homeward Journey* (1895; revised 1897 and 1900); *King Kristian II,* suite from the incidental music, op. 27

(1898); *Scènes historiques,* op. 25, I (1899; revised 1911); *Finlandia,* tone poem, op. 26 (1899; revised 1900; Helsinki, July 2, 1900, Kajanus conducting); *Björneborgarnas March* (1900); *Cortège* (1901); Overture in A minor (1902; Helsinki, March 3, 1902, composer conducting); *Romance* in C major for Strings, op. 42 (1903; Turku, March 1904, composer conducting); Concerto in D minor for Violin and Orch., op. 47 (1903; Helsinki, Feb. 8, 1904; Viktor Nováček, soloist; composer conducting; revised 1905; Berlin, Oct. 19, 1905; Karl Halir, soloist; R. Strauss conducting); *Cassazione,* op. 6 (1904); *Pelléas et Mélisande,* suite from the incidental music, op. 46 (1905); *Pohjola's Daughter,* symph. fantasia, op. 49 (1906; St. Petersburg, Dec. 29, 1906, composer conducting); *Belshazzar's Feast,* suite from the incidental music, op. 51 (1906; Helsinki, Sept. 25, 1907); *Pan and Echo,* dance intermezzo, op. 53 (1906); *Nightride and Sunrise,* tone poem, op. 55 (1907; St. Petersburg, Jan. 1909); *Svanevhit (Swanwhite),* suite from the incidental music, op. 54 (1908); *In Memoriam,* funeral march, op. 59 (1909; Helsinki, April 3, 1911); *The Dryad,* tone poem (1910), and *Dance Intermezzo* (1907), op. 45; *Rakastava (The Lover)* for Strings and Percussion, op. 14 (1911); *Scènes historiques,* op. 66, II (1912); 2 serenades for Violin and Orch., op. 69: No. 1, in D major (1912), and No. 2, in G minor (1913); *The Bard,* tone poem, op. 64 (1913; revised 1914); *Aallottaret (Nymphs of the Ocean),* tone poem, op. 73 (1914; 2nd version as *The Oceanides,* 1914; the latter first perf. at the Norfolk [Conn.] Festival, June 4, 1914, composer conducting); 2 pieces for Violin or Cello, and Orch., op. 77 (1914); *2 Humoresques* for Violin and Orch., op. 87 (1917); *4 Humoresques* for Violin and Orch., op. 89 (also numbered as 3–6 in continuation of the preceding; 1917); *Promotiomarssi (Academic March)* (1919); 3 pieces, op. 96: 1, *Valse lyrique* (1920); 2, *Autrefois, Scène pastorale* for 2 Voices and Orch. (1919); 3, *Valse chevaleresque* (1920); *Suite mignonne* for 2 Flutes and Strings, op. 98a (1921); *Suite champêtre* for Strings, op. 98b (1921); *Andante festivo* for Strings and Percussion (1922; also for String Quartet); *Suite caractéristique* for Harp and Strings, op. 100 (1922); *The Tempest,* concert version of the incidental music, op. 109 (1925); *Tapiola,* tone poem, op. 112 (1926; N.Y., Dec. 26, 1926, W. Damrosch conducting).

CHAMBER MUSIC: *Vattendroppar (Water Drops)* for Violin and Cello (1875–76); Quartet in E minor for Piano, 2 Violins, and Cello (1881–82); Piano Trio in A minor (1881–82); Sonata in D minor for Violin and Piano (1881–82); *Andantino* for Cello and Piano (1884); Quartet for Violin, Cello, Harmonium, and Piano (1884?); String Quartet in E-flat major (1885); Suite in G minor for String Trio (1885); Duo for Violin and Viola (1886); *Andante cantabile* for Violin and Piano (1887); Piano Trio, *Korpo* (1887); Piano Trio in C major, *Loviisa* (1888); *Romance and Epilogue* for Violin and Piano, op. 2 (1888; revised 1912); *Fugue* for String Quartet (1888); *Theme and Variations* in C-sharp minor for String Quartet (1888); String Quartet in A minor (1889); Sonata in F major for Violin and Piano (1889); Suite in A major for String Trio (1889); Quintet in G minor for Piano and Strings (1889–90); String Quartet in B-flat major, op. 4 (1890); Octet for Flute, Clarinet, and Strings (1891); Quartet in C major for Piano, 2 Violins, and Cello (1891); Rondo for Viola and Piano (1893); *Kehtolaulu (Lullaby)* for Violin and Kantele (1899); Fantasia for Cello and Piano (1899–1900); *Malinconia* for Cello and Piano, op. 20 (1901); String Quartet in D minor, op. 56, *Voces intimae* (1909); 4 pieces for Violin or Cello, and Piano, op. 78: 1, *Impromptu* (1915); 2, *Romance* (1915); 3, *Religioso* (1919); 4, *Rigaudon* (1915); 6 pieces for Violin and Piano, op. 79: *Souvenir, Tempo di menuetto, Danse caractéristique, Sérénade, Danse idyll,* and *Berceuse* (1915); Sonatina in E major for Violin and Piano, op. 80 (1915); 5 pieces for Violin and Cello, op. 81: *Mazurka, Rondino, Waltz, Aubade,* and *Menuetto* (1915); *Novelette* for Violin and Piano, op. 102 (1923); *5 danses champêtres* for Violin and Piano, op. 106 (1925); 4 pieces for Violin and Piano, op. 115: *On the Heath, Ballade, Humoresque,* and *The Bells* (1929); 3 pieces for Violin and Piano, op. 116: *Scène de danse, Danse caractéristique,* and *Rondeau romantique* (1929); also *Adagio* for String Quartet (date unknown); Piano Sonata in F major, op. 12 (1893); over 25 other pieces for piano composed between 1893 and 1929. For Organ: 2 pieces, op. 111: *Intrada* (1925) and *Surusoitto (Mournful Music;* 1931).

VOCAL MUSIC: *Kullervo,* symph. poem for Soprano, Baritone, Male Chorus, and Orch., op. 7 (1892; Helsinki, April 28, 1892); *Rakastava (The Lover)* for Male Chorus a cappella, op. 14 (1893; Helsinki, April 28, 1894); *Laulu Lemminkäiselle (A Song for Lemminkäinen)* for Male Chorus and Orch., op. 31, No. 1 (1900); *Har du mod? (Have You Courage?)* for Male Chorus and Orch., op. 31, No. 2 (1904); *Atenarnes sång (The Song of the Athenians)* for Male Voices, with Wind Instruments and Percussion, op. 31, No. 3 (1899; Helsinki, April 26, 1899); *Tulen synty (The Origin of Fire)* for Baritone, Male Chorus, and Orch., op. 32 (1902; Helsinki, April 9, 1902, composer conducting; revised 1910); *Vapautettu kuningatar (The Liberated Queen),* cantata for Mixed Chorus and Orch., op. 48 (1906; Helsinki, May 12, 1906); *Luonnotar (Spirit of Nature),* tone poem for Soprano and Orch., op. 70 (1910; Gloucester, Sept. 10, 1913); *Oma maa (Our Native Land),* cantata for Mixed Chorus and Orch., op. 92 (1918); *Jordens sång (Song of the Earth),* cantata for Mixed Chorus and Orch., op. 93 (1919); *Maan virsi (Hymn of the Earth),* cantata for Mixed Chorus and Orch., op. 95 (1920; Helsinki, June 1920, composer conducting); *Väinön virsi (Väinö's Song)* for Mixed Chorus and Orch., op. 110 (1926; Helsinki, June 28, 1926, Kajanus conducting); *Masonic Ritual Music* for Male Voices, Piano, and Organ, op. 113 (1927–46; revised 1948); also numerous other choral works, and 95 songs composed between 1891 and 1917.

Sidlin, Murry, American conductor; b. Baltimore, May 6, 1940, of Russian-Latvian parents. He studied theory with Elliott Galkin and Louis Cheslock, and trumpet with Harold Rherig, at the Peabody Cons. in Baltimore (B.A., 1962; M.A., 1968). During the summers of 1961 and 1962 he traveled to Italy and studied conducting with Sergiu Celibidache at the Accademia Chigiana in Siena. Returning to the U.S., he took courses with Donald Grout and Karel Husa at Cornell Univ. (1963–65). After completing his academic studies, he devoted himself principally to symph. conducting. In 1971–73 he served as assistant conductor of the Baltimore Symph., and in 1973–77 was resident conductor of the National Symph. Orch. in Washington, D.C.; in 1977 he was engaged as music director of the New Haven Symph. Orch., and in 1980 became conductor of the Long Beach (Calif.) Symph. Orch., which he brought to a considerable degree of excellence. He furthermore was guest conductor of the Gavleborg Orkester of Sweden (1976–77) and had conducting engagements in Pittsburgh, Seattle, Denver, San Antonio, and San Diego, as well as with the Boston Pops Orch.

Siegel, Jeffrey, American pianist; b. Chicago, Nov. 18, 1942. He studied piano with Rudolph Ganz at the Chicago Musical College and later with Rosina Lhévinne and Ilona Kabos at the Juilliard School of Music in N.Y. He won the silver medal at the Queen Elisabeth of Belgium Competition in Brussels; then was a soloist with many of the leading orchs. of the U.S. and Europe, including the Chicago Symph., Boston Symph., N.Y. Phil., London Symph., and London Phil.

Siegmeister, Elie, significant American composer; b. New York, Jan. 15, 1909. He took piano lessons as a youth with Emil Friedberger; in 1925 entered Columbia Univ. and studied composition there with Seth Bingham; also took private lessons in counterpoint with Wallingford Riegger. In 1927 he went to Paris, where he studied with Nadia Boulanger; returning to N.Y. in 1932, he taught music at various schools; studied conducting at the Juilliard School of Music, N.Y. (1935–38); in 1939 he organized a vocal ensemble, the American Ballad Singers, for the purpose of performing authentic American folk songs, and traveled as its conductor for several years. He felt strongly that music should express the social values of the people; in his early songs, he selected texts by contemporary American poets voicing indignation at the inequities of the modern world; he also gave lectures and conducted choruses at the revolutionary Pierre Degeyter Club in N.Y. From the outset, he adopted an extremely dissonant harmonic idiom and a quasi-atonal melos, with the intervallic stress on minor seconds, major sevenths, and minor ninths. In his symphs. and chamber music he organized this dissonant idiom in self-consistent modern formulations, without, however, espousing any of the fashionable doctrines of composition, such as dodecaphony. The subject matter of the orch. and vocal compositions of his early period was marked by a strongly national and socially radical character, exemplified by such works as *American Holiday, Ozark Set, Prairie Legend, Wilderness Road,* and *Western Suite,* the last achieving the rare honor of being performed by Toscanini;

Siegmeister did not ignore the homely vernacular; his Clarinet Concerto is a brilliant realization of jazz, blues, and swing in a classically formal idiom. Siegmeister achieved an important position as an educator; in 1949 he was appointed to the faculty of Hofstra Univ. in Hempstead, Long Island; he became composer-in-residence there in 1966; prof. emeritus in 1976. In 1978 he received a Guggenheim fellowship award.

WORKS: FOR THE STAGE: *Doodle Dandy of the USA,* play with music, to text by Saul Lancourt (N.Y., Dec. 26, 1942); *Sing Out, Sweet Land,* to text by Walter Kerr (Hartford, Conn., Nov. 10, 1944); *Darling Corie,* one-act opera, libretto by Lewis Allan (1952; Hofstra Univ., Feb. 18, 1954); *Miranda and the Dark Young Man,* one-act opera, libretto by Edward Eager (1955; Hartford, Conn., May 9, 1956); *The Mermaid in Lock No. 7,* one-act opera, libretto by Edward Mabley (Pittsburgh, July 20, 1958); *Dublin Song,* 3-act opera, libretto by Edward Mabley, based on Sean O'Casey's drama *The Plough and the Stars* (1963; St. Louis, May 15, 1963; revised and perf. under the title *The Plough and the Stars,* Baton Rouge, La., March 16, 1969); *Night of the Moonspell,* 3-act opera, libretto by Edward Mabley after Shakespeare's play *Midsummer Night's Dream* (Shreveport, La., Nov. 14, 1976); *Fables from the Dark Wood,* for ballet (Shreveport, April 25, 1976); *The Marquesa of O,* opera (1979–83); film score, *They Came to Cordura* (1959).

FOR ORCH.: *American Holiday* (1933); *Ozark Set* (1943; Minneapolis, Nov. 7, 1944); *Prairie Legend* (1944; N.Y., Jan. 18, 1947); *Wilderness Road* (1944; Minneapolis, Nov. 9, 1945); *Western Suite* (1945; N.Y., Nov. 24, 1945; Toscanini conducting the NBC Symph. Orch.); *Sunday in Brooklyn* (N.Y., July 21, 1946); *Lonesome Hollow* (1946; Columbus, Ohio, 1948); *Summer Night* (1947; N.Y., Sept. 27, 1952); Symph. No. 1 (1947; N.Y., Oct. 30, 1947; revised 1972); *From My Window* (1949); Symph. No. 2 (1950; N.Y., Feb. 25, 1952; revised 1972); *Riversong* (1951; revised 1982; St. Joseph, Mo., Nov. 21, 1982); *Divertimento* (1953; Oklahoma City, March 28, 1954); Concerto for Clarinet and Orch. (Oklahoma City, Feb. 3, 1956); Symph. No. 3 (1957; Oklahoma City, Feb. 8, 1959); Concerto for Flute and Orch. (1960; Oklahoma City, Feb. 17, 1961); *Theater Set,* drawn from the music for the film *They Came to Cordura* (1960; Rochester, N.Y., May 8, 1969); *Dick Whittington and His Cat* for Narrator and Orch. (1966; Philadelphia, Feb. 10, 1968); *5 Fantasies of the Theater* (1967; Hofstra Univ., Oct. 18, 1970); Symph. No. 4 (1970; Cleveland, Dec. 6, 1973); Symph. No. 5, subtitled *Visions of Time* (1971–75; Baltimore, May 4, 1977); Piano Concerto (Denver, Colo., Dec. 3, 1976; Alan Mandel, soloist; revised 1982); *Shadows and Light,* subtitled *Homage to 5 Paintings* (Shreveport, La., Nov. 9, 1975); Double Concerto for Violin, Piano, and Orch. (Columbia, Md., June 25, 1976); Violin Concerto (1977–78) *Fantasies in Line and Color,* subtitled *5 American Paintings* (1981); Symph. No. 6 (Sacramento, Calif., Nov. 4, 1984); Violin Concerto (Oakland, Calif., Jan. 29, 1985).

Siepi, Cesare, Italian bass; b. Milan, Feb. 10, 1923.

He made his debut in Schio (Venice) in 1941; in 1946 appeared for the first time at La Scala, Milan. He made his American debut at the Metropolitan Opera, N.Y., on Nov. 6, 1950, in the role of Philip II in *Don Carlos;* remained on its roster until 1973. In 1966 he became a member of the Vienna State Opera; also appeared at Covent Garden in London, in Salzburg, and in other musical centers. His most successful roles were Méphistophélès in Gounod's *Faust* and Figaro in Mozart's *Marriage of Figaro.*

Siface, Giovanni Francesco, famous Italian male soprano; b. Pescia, Feb. 12, 1653; d. Ferrara, May 29, 1697 (murdered by hired assassins). He was a member of the Papal Chapel in 1675–77; was in Modena from 1679 till 1687; later sang at Venice and London.

Sigurbjörnsson, Thorkell, Icelandic composer; b. Reykjavik, July 16, 1938. He studied violin, piano, organ, theory, and music history at the Reykjavik School of Music (1948–57); then came to the U.S. and studied composition and piano at Hamline Univ. in St. Paul, Minn. (1957–59), and electronic music with Lejaren Hiller and composition with Gaburo at the Univ. of Illinois (1959–61). Returning to Reykjavik, he founded the modern group Musica Nova; was assistant director of music for the Iceland State Broadcasting Service (1966–69) and a music critic. In his music he modernizes traditional modalities by an injection of acrid dissonances and vitalizes the fundamentally placid metrical divisions by disruptive rhythmic asymmetries.

Sikorski, Kazimierz, Swiss-born Polish composer and pedagogue; b. Zürich, June 28, 1895 (of Polish parents). He studied at the College of Music in Warsaw; then took a course in musicology with Chybiński in Lwow; completed his musical studies in Paris (1925–27). He taught at the State Cons. in Lodz (1947–54); at the State College in Warsaw (1951–57); became its director (1957–66). Many Polish composers of the younger generation were his students, among them Grazyna Bacewicz, Panufnik, Palester, and Serocki.

Sikorski, Tomasz, Polish composer and pianist, son of **Kazimierz Sikorski;** b. Warsaw, May 19, 1939. He studied piano with Drzewiecki and composition with his father; then took lessons with Nadia Boulanger in Paris. As a pianist, he emphasizes new music in his programs. His own compositions are also in the advanced idiom.

Silbermann, German family of organ and piano makers. (1) **Andreas Silbermann,** b. Klein-Bobritzsch, Saxony, May 16, 1678; d. Strasbourg, March 16, 1734. He settled in Strasbourg in 1702; was in Paris, 1704–6, before making his home in Strasbourg for good; was the builder of the organ of the Strasbourg Münster (1713–16) and of 34 others. (2) **Gottfried Silbermann,** brother of Andreas, b. Klein-Bobritzsch, Jan. 14, 1683; d. Dresden, Aug. 4, 1753. Apprenticed to a bookbinder, he ran away and joined his brother in Strasbourg, working as his helper. He then lived in Freiberg; built 47 organs, the finest of which is in the Freiberg Cathedral (1710–14), having 3 manuals and 44 stops. He owed his fame, however, mainly to the manufacture of pianos in Germany, in which field he was a pioneer; the hammer action in his instruments was practically identical with that of Cristofori, the piano inventor. Silbermann also invented the "cembal d'amour," a clavichord with strings of double length, struck in the middle by the tangents, thus yielding the duplicated octave of the tone of the entire string. He supplied 3 pianos to Frederick the Great for Potsdam, and Bach played on them during his visit there in 1747. (3) **Johann Andreas Silbermann,** eldest son of Andreas; b. Strasbourg, May 26, 1712; d. there, Feb. 11, 1783. He built 54 organs; publ. *Geschichte der Stadt Strassburg* (1775). (4) **Johann Daniel Silbermann,** brother of Johann Andreas; b. Strasbourg, March 31, 1717; d. Leipzig, May 9, 1766. He worked with his uncle Gottfried at Freiberg, and continued the manufacture of pianos after the latter's death. (5) **Johann Heinrich Silbermann,** brother of Johann Andreas and Johann Daniel; b. Strasbourg, Sept. 24, 1727; d. there, Jan. 15, 1799; made pianos at Strasbourg, similar to those of his uncle Gottfried, and introduced them into France. (6) **Johann Friedrich Silbermann,** son of Johann Heinrich; b. Strasbourg, June 21, 1762; d. there, March 8, 1817. He was an organist in Strasbourg; during the Revolution wrote a *Hymne à la Paix;* also composed some German songs.

Silcher, Friedrich, German composer; b. Schnait, Württemberg, June 27, 1789; d. Tübingen, Aug. 26, 1860. He studied with his father and with Auberlen, an organist at Fellbach; lived for some years in Stuttgart; in 1817 was appointed music director at the Univ. of Tübingen, receiving the honorary degree of Dr.Phil. in 1852. He was an influential promoter of German popular singing; publ. several collections of German folk songs, in which he included his own compositions; of the latter, *Lorelei (Ich weiss nicht, was soll es bedeuten,* to words by Heinrich Heine) became so popular that it was often mistaken for a folk song; his other well-known songs are *Ännchen von Tharau, Morgen muss ich fort von hier, Zu Strassburg auf der Schanz,* etc. He also publ. *Choralbuch* for 3 voices; 3 books of hymns for 4 voices; *Tübinger Liedertafel* (male choruses). He wrote the books *Geschichte des evangelischen Kirchengesanges* (1844); *Harmonie- und Kompositionslehre* (1851; 2nd ed., 1859).

Silja, Anja, remarkably musical German soprano; b. Berlin, April 17, 1940. She studied voice with her grandfather, **Egon Friedrich Maria Aders van Rijn;** gave a solo recital in Berlin at the age of 10; at 15 she sang Rosina at the State Theater in Braunschweig. In 1958 she appeared at the Württemberg State Theater in Stuttgart, and in 1965 joined its roster. In 1960–63 she sang with the Municipal Theater in Frankfurt; in 1960 and in subsequent years she appeared at the Bayreuth Festivals; in 1968 she had a guest engagement at the Holland Festival. On Feb. 26, 1972, she made her American debut with the Metropolitan Opera in N.Y. as Leonore in *Fidelio;* she also was a guest artist with the Chicago and San Francisco operas. The breadth of her repertoire is commanding. Wagner's grandson Wieland coached her in the Wagnerian roles, among them Elisabeth, Elsa, Eva, and Senta, which she performed at Bayreuth. She also sang the parts of Salome and Elektra in the operas of Richard Strauss, of Marie and Lulu in Alban Berg's operas, and of the sole character in Schoenberg's *Erwartung.* As a matter of course, she mastered the majority of standard soprano parts (Carmen, Donna Anna, etc.). She married the conductor **Christoph von Dohnányi.**

Sills, Beverly (real name, **Belle Miriam Silverman**), celebrated American soprano; b. Brooklyn, May 25, 1929. Her father was an insurance salesman from Rumania and her mother a rather musical person from Odessa. At the age of 3 she appeared on the radio under the cute nickname "Bubbles," and won a prize at a Brooklyn contest as "the most beautiful baby of 1932." At 4, she joined a Saturday morning children's program, and at 7 she sang in a movie. At 10 she had a part on the radio show "Our Gal Sunday." Her natural thespian talent and sweet child's voice soon proved to be valuable financial assets. She did a commercial advertising Rinso White soap, and appeared on an early television program, "Stars of the Future." She also scored as the "one most likely to succeed" in Public School 91 in Brooklyn. In 1945 she joined a Gilbert and Sullivan touring company, billed as "the youngest prima donna in captivity." She then engaged in professional voice training with Estella Liebling and also took piano lessons with Paolo Gallico. In 1947 she made her first appearance in opera when she sang the subsidiary role of Frasquita in *Carmen* with the Philadelphia Opera Co. In 1951–52 she toured with the Charles L. Wagner Opera Co., with which she sang Violetta in *La Traviata* and Micaela in *Carmen.* In 1953 she sang with the Baltimore Opera and the San Francisco Opera. On Oct. 29, 1955, she made her debut with the N.Y. City Opera. On Nov. 17, 1956, she married Peter Bulkeley Greenough of Cleveland. She extended her repertoire to embrace modern American operas, her roles in these including the title role of Douglas Moore's *The Ballad of Baby Doe;* she also sang a demanding role in the American premiere of Luigi Nono's avant-garde opera *Intolleranza 1960.* She was a guest singer at the Vienna State Opera and in Buenos Aires in 1967, at La Scala in Milan in 1969, and at Covent Garden in London and the Deutsche Oper in Berlin in 1970. She made her first appearance with the Metropolitan Opera as Donna Anna in a concert production of *Don Giovanni* on July 8, 1966, at the Lewisohn Stadium in N.Y.; her formal debut with the Metropolitan took place at Lincoln Center in N.Y. as Pamira in *Le Siège de Corinthe* by Rossini, on April 7, 1975. At the height of her career she received well-nigh universal praise, not only for the excellence of her voice and her virtuosity in coloratura parts, but also for her intelligence and erudition, rare among the common run of operatic divas. But when she reached the age of 50, she decided to abandon the stage, and in 1979 accepted the role of general director of the N.Y. City Opera; in that capacity she showed an uncommon administrative talent; she also produced a number of television shows dealing with opera and concert singing. In her personal life, she suffered a double tragedy; one of her two children was born deaf, and the other was mentally retarded. In 1972 she accepted the national chairmanship of the Mothers' March on Birth Defects. She publ. an autobiography, *Bubbles: A Self-portrait* (N.Y., 1976; 2nd revised ed., 1981, as *Bubbles: An Encore*). She received (deservedly so) honorary doctorates from Harvard Univ., N.Y. Univ., and the Calif. Inst. of the Arts. On Nov. 22, 1971, she was the subject of a cover story in *Time.*

Siloti, Alexander, eminent Russian pianist, pedagogue, and conductor; b. on the family estate near Kharkov, Oct. 9, 1863; d. New York, Dec. 8, 1945. He studied piano with Zverev and Nicolai Rubinstein at the Moscow Cons., and music theory with Tchaikovsky (1876–81), winning the gold medal. He made his debut as a pianist in Moscow in 1880; then made a tour in Germany; Liszt accepted him as a student in 1883, and Siloti continued his study with Liszt in Weimar until Liszt's death in 1886. Returning to Russia, he was appointed a prof. of piano at the Moscow Cons. (1888–91); among his students was Rachmaninoff (his first cousin). Between 1891 and 1900 he lived in Germany, France, and Belgium; returned to Russia in 1901 and conducted the concerts of the Moscow Phil. Society during the season 1901–2; in 1903 he organized his own orch. in St. Petersburg, which he conducted until 1913; these concerts acquired great cultural importance; Siloti invited Mengelberg and Mottl as guest conductors, and Rachmaninoff, Casals, and Chaliapin as soloists. In 1915 he began a series of popular free concerts, and in 1916 started a Russian Musical Fund to aid indigent musicians. In 1919 he left Russia; he lived in Finland, Germany, and England; in 1922 he settled in N.Y., where he was active principally as a teacher but continued to appear as a soloist with American orchs.; from 1925 to 1942 he was on the faculty of the Juilliard School of Music. He publ. a collection of piano pieces which he edited, with indications of fingering and pedaling; also arranged and edited concertos by Bach and Vivaldi. He publ. a book of his reminiscences of Liszt (St. Petersburg, 1911; in Eng., Edinburgh, 1913).

Silva, Francisco Manuel da, Brazilian composer of the Brazilian national anthem; b. Rio de Janeiro, Feb. 21, 1795; d. there, Dec. 18, 1865. He was a pupil of Marcos Portugal. In 1833 he founded the Sociedade Beneficente Musical; was active mostly as a music teacher and choral conductor. He wrote an opera, *O prestigio da lei,* but he owes his fame to the fact that he was the composer of the Brazilian national anthem, *Ouviram do Ypiranga as margens placidas.*

Silva, Luigi, American cellist; b. Milan, Nov. 13, 1903; d. New York, Nov. 29, 1961. He was of a musical family; his father was a vocal teacher; his mother a Viennese singer. He studied music at home; then took cello lessons with Arturo Bonucci in Bologna and composition with Respighi in Rome. He played in several string quartets in Italy; in 1939 he emigrated to the U.S.; taught cello and chamber music at the Eastman School of Music in Rochester, N.Y. (1941–49); in 1949 joined the staff of the Juilliard School of Music, N.Y. He made transcriptions for cello of works by Paganini, Boccherini, and other Italian composers; edited Bach's unaccompanied cello suites.

Silva, Oscar da, Portuguese pianist and composer; b. Paranhos, near Oporto, April 21, 1870; d. Oporto, March 6, 1958. He studied at the Lisbon Cons.; in 1892 went to Germany, where he had lessons with Reinecke and Clara Schumann. Returning to Portugal in 1910, he devoted himself mainly to teaching, acquiring a very high reputation as a piano pedagogue. From 1932 to 1952 he lived in Brazil; then returned to Portugal. He wrote an opera, *Dona Mecia* (Lisbon, July 4, 1901); a symph. poem, *Alma crucificada;* and a number of effective piano pieces, among them *Rapsodia portuguesa, Estudos indefinidos, Papillon dans le jardin, Paginas portuguesas;* also some chamber music and a number of songs to French words.

Silverstein, Joseph, distinguished American violinist and conductor; b. Detroit, March 21, 1932. He received his early instruction in violin playing from his father; then studied with Efrem Zimbalist at the Curtis Inst. of Music in Philadelphia; later took lessons with Josef Gingold and Mischa Mischakoff. He played in the Houston Symph. Orch., Denver Symph. Orch., and Philadelphia Orch. before joining the Boston Symph. Orch. in 1955; from 1962–83 he was its concertmaster; from 1971–83 also served as its assistant conductor. He was further chairman of the violin faculty of the Berkshire Music Center at Tanglewood, and also taught at Boston Univ. He appeared as guest conductor with the St. Louis Symph., Los Angeles Phil., Houston Symph., San Francisco Symph., National Symph. of Washington, D.C., and other American orchs. In 1979–80 he was interim music director of the Toledo (Ohio) Symph.; from 1981–83 he was principal guest conductor of the Baltimore Symph. Orch. In 1983 he was appointed music director of the Utah Symph. Orch. in Salt Lake City.

Silvestrov, Valentin, Ukrainian composer; b. Kiev, Sept. 30, 1937. He studied with Liatoshinsky at the Kiev Cons.; began to compose in a boldly experimental idiom of Western provenance; wrote piano pieces in the strict 12-tone technique. Although severely reprimanded in the press, he was not forcibly restrained from continuing to write music in a modernistic manner.

Simmons, Calvin, brilliant black American conductor; b. San Francisco; April 27, 1950, the son of a longshoreman and a gospel singer; drowned in Connery Pond, east of Lake Placid, N.Y., Aug. 21, 1982, when his canoe overturned. He sang in the San Francisco Boys' Choir; then went to the Cincinnati College-Cons. of Music, where he studied conducting with Max Rudolf; when Rudolf was appointed to the faculty of the Curtis Inst. of Music in Philadelphia, Simmons joined him there; he also took piano lessons with Serkin. Returning to San Francisco, he joined the staff of the San Francisco Opera, eventually becoming assistant conductor; subsequently served in the same capacity with the Los Angeles Phil. (1975–78). In 1978 he conducted a performance of *Hansel and Gretel* at the Metropolitan Opera in N.Y. In 1979 he was appointed music director and conductor of the Oakland (Calif.) Symph. Orch. Endowed with natural musical intelligence and practical ability, Simmons easily overcame the still-lingering doubts that a person with black pigmentation of skin could make classical music. His untimely death deprived his race and American music of a great talent.

Simon, Abbey, American pianist; b. New York, Jan. 8, 1922. He studied with David Saperton and Josef Hofmann at the Curtis Inst. of Music in Philadelphia; also took lessons with Leopold Godowsky in N.Y. He began his concert career at 18, evolving a grand bravura style of pianistic virtuosity in which no technical difficulties seem to exist, no tempi are too fast, no nuance is too subtle. He made successful tours in the U.S., South America, Europe (including Russia), Australia, and Japan.

Simon-Girard, Juliette, French soprano; b. Paris, May 8, 1859; d. Nice, Dec. 1959, at the age of 100. She made her debut at the Folies-Dramatiques in Paris, where she created the principal role in *Les Cloches de Corneville* on April 19, 1877; then sang at the premieres of *La Fille du Tambour-major* (1879), *Fanfan la tulipe* (1882), and many other operettas; she became particularly successful in Offenbach's repertoire. She married the tenor **Nicolas Simon,** known as **Simon-Max** (1855–1923); divorced him in 1894, and married the comedian Huguenet. She then retired and lived in Nice.

Simoneau, Léopold, Canadian tenor; b. Quebec City, May 3, 1918. He studied singing in N.Y.; made his debut as an opera singer in Montreal in 1943; also sang in Paris, at La Scala in Milan, and in Salzburg. He first sang at the Metropolitan Opera in N.Y. on Oct. 18, 1963, as Ottavio in *Don Giovanni.* He was particularly praised for his performances of Mozart's roles. In 1971 he went to San Francisco, where he taught at the Cons. He is married to the Canadian coloratura soprano **Pierrette Alarie.**

Simpson (or **Sympson**), **Christopher,** English player of the viola da gamba, writer, and composer; b. Yorkshire, c.1610; d. Scampton, Lincolnshire, between May 5 and July 29, 1669. He fought on the Royalist side in the English civil war (1643) and later entered the service of Sir Robert Bolles as music tutor to the latter's son. Simpson was famous as a composer.

Simpson, Robert, English composer and writer on music; b. Leamington, Warwickshire, March 2, 1921. He studied composition with Howells in London (1941–44); received his Mus.D. from Durham Univ. in 1951; joined the staff of the BBC as a music producer in 1951, resigning in 1980. He publ. a valuable monograph, *Carl Nielsen, Symphonist* (London, 1952; 2nd ed., revised, 1979); also *The Essence of Bruckner* (London, 1966) and 3 BBC booklets: *Bruckner and the Symphony* (1963), *Sibelius and Nielsen* (1965), and *Beethoven's Symphonies* (1970); also edited *The Symphony* (2 vols., Harmondsworth, 1966 and 1967). He was awarded the Carl Nielsen Gold Medal of Denmark in 1956 for his valiant work in behalf of Nielsen's music. While occupied with writing and directing radio programs, he composed symphs., chamber music, and choruses.
WORKS: 8 symphs.: No. 1, in one movement (1951; Copenhagen, June 11, 1953); No. 2 (1955; Cheltenham Festival, July 16, 1957); No. 3 (1962; Birmingham, March 14, 1963); No. 4 (1970–72; Manchester, April 26, 1973); No. 5 (1972; London, May 3, 1973); No. 6 (1976; London, April 8, 1979); No. 7 (1977); No. 8 (1981; London, Nov. 10, 1982); Violin Concerto (1959; Birmingham, Feb. 25, 1960); Piano Concerto (1967; Cheltenham Festival, July 14, 1967); 9 string quartets (1952, 1953, 1954, 1973, 1974, 1975, 1977, 1979, 1982); *Canzona* for Brass (1958); *Variations and Fugue* for Recorder and String Quartet (1958); Trio for Clarinet, Cello, and Piano (1967); Quartet for Clarinet and Strings (1968); Quartet for Horn, Violin, Cello, and Piano (1975); *Media morte in vita sumus*, motet for Chorus, Brass, and Timpani (1975); Piano Sonata (1946); *Variations and Finale on a Theme by Haydn* for Piano (1948); 2-piano Sonata (1980).

Simpson, Thomas, English composer; b. Milton, Kent (baptized, April 1), 1582; d. after 1625. He went to Germany as a youth; served as a viol player at the Heidelberg court from 1608 to 1611; then was Musicus to the Prince of Holstein-Schaumburg (1616–22) and subsequently was employed in the royal chapel of Copenhagen as a court musician to King Christian IV. An excellent composer of court dances and songs, he brought out *Opusculum newer Pavanen* (Frankfurt, 1610); *Pavanen, Galliarden, Courtanten und Volten* (Frankfurt, 1611; reprinted in 1617 under the title *Opus newer Paduanen, Galliarden, Intraden, Canzonen, etc.*); and *Tafel-Consort, allerhand lustige Lieder von 4 Instrumenten und Generalbass* (Hamburg, 1621).

Simrock, Nikolaus, founder of the famous German publishing house in Berlin; b. Mainz, Aug. 23, 1751; d. Bonn, June 12, 1832. He played the horn in the Electoral Orch. in Bonn until 1794. He began dealing in printed music and instruments in 1780; in 1785 opened a music shop in Bonn, selling musical instruments; in 1793 he established there a music publishing house with its own printing press. During Beethoven's lifetime Simrock's catalogue listed 85 of his works, including the *Kreutzer Sonata* and opus numbers 17, 31, 81b, 102, and 107. His son **Peter Joseph Simrock** (b. Bonn, Aug. 18, 1792; d. Cologne, Dec. 13, 1868) succeeded him and greatly increased the prestige of the house by acquiring the early works of Brahms. Peter was succeeded by his son **Friedrich August ("Fritz") Simrock** (b. Bonn, Jan. 2, 1837; d. Ouchy, near Lausanne, Aug. 20, 1901), who transferred the firm to Berlin in 1870, publ. the works of Brahms, and, at the suggestion of Brahms, added the works of Dvořák to his catalogue. His nephew **Johann Baptist ("Hans") Simrock** (b. Cologne, April 17, 1861; d. Berlin, July 26, 1910) reorganized the firm in 1902 as a stock company and established branches in London and Paris. A grandson of Fritz August Simrock, **Fritz Auckenthaler** (b. Zürich, Nov. 17, 1893; d. Basel, April 19, 1973), headed the firm from 1920 to 1929, when it was sold to A.J. Benjamin in Hamburg; in 1951 the Hamburg firm, which also had a branch in London, resumed its original name, N. Simrock Co.

Sims, Ezra, American composer of innovative music; b. Birmingham, Ala., Jan. 16, 1928. His education was highly diversified; he took courses in mathematics at Birmingham Southern College, obtaining a B.A. in 1947, and concurrently studied with Hugh Thomas and B. Ackley Brower at the Birmingham Cons. (1945–48). He entered Yale Univ. as a student of Quincy Porter (B.M., 1952), and then enrolled in the U.S. Army Language School, where he earned a degree in Mandarin Chinese in 1953. Returning to music, he studied with Darius Milhaud and Leon Kirchner at Mills College (M.A., 1955). He attended Aaron Copland's seminar at the Berkshire Music Center at Tanglewood, Mass., in 1960. To earn a living, he took all kinds of menial jobs, as a mail clerk, steelworker, and display designer. From 1958 to 1962 and again from 1965 to 1974 he was employed as a cataloguer at the music library of Harvard Univ. In 1962 he received a Guggenheim fellowship, and had an opportunity to go to Tokyo, where he put together the electronic portion of the background score for the Japanese play *Sakoku*. In 1978 he again traveled to Japan. He made his permanent home in Cambridge, Mass.; there he founded the whimsically named New England Dinosaur; there was nothing extinct about his concerts there, however; on the contrary, the Dinosaur programs were projections into a distant future rather than a retrospection into a fossilized past. The music Ezra Sims writes himself is microtonal, based on a scale of 18 tones within a larger complex of 72 degrees in equal temperament. Amazingly enough, he found string players in Boston and elsewhere who could perform his microtonal pieces with spectacular ease. In 1977 he developed a polyphonic keyboard providing any tuning whatsoever, in Pythagorean, or just, intonation, as well as in equal temperament that divides the octave into fewer than 37 intervals.
WORKS: *Chamber Cantata on Chinese Poems* (1954); Cello Sonata (1957); String Quartet No. 1

(1959); String Quartet No. 2, in *Sonate concertante* (1961); String Quartet No. 3 (1962); Octet for Strings in quarter-tones and sixth-tones (1964); *Antimatter* for Magnetic Tape Collage (1968); *A Frank Overture: 4 Dented Interludes and Coda* (1969); *Real Toads,* musique concrète (1970); *Dreams for Sale* for Mezzo-soprano, Baritone, and Piano (1970); Quartet for Oboe and Strings (1971); *Second Thoughts* for Double Bass, microtonal music with quarter-tones and sixth-tones (1974); Quintet for Flute, Clarinet, Violin, Viola, and Cello (1974); *Slow Hiccups* for 2 Recorders (1975); *Elegie nach Rilke* for Soprano, Flute, Clarinet, Violin, and Cello, microtonal music including *Sprechstimme* (Cambridge, Mass., Nov. 16, 1976); *Yr obedt servt* for Small Ensemble (1977); *Aeneas on the Saxophone* for Voices, Clarinet, Horn, Trombone, Viola, and Double Bass, microtonal music to 18-note scale (perf. on the 50th birthday of Ezra Sims, Dinosaur Annex, Boston, Jan. 16, 1978); *And, As I Was Saying* for Viola or Violin, microtonal music (1979); *All Done from Memory* for Violin Solo, microtonal music in an 18-tone scale or equal temperament in 72-tone scale (1980; Dinosaur Annex, Boston, Jan. 18, 1981; Janet Packer, soloist); Sextet for Clarinet, Saxophone, Horn, Violin, Viola, and Cello (1981); *This Way to the Egress-or-Manners Makyth Man* for String Trio (1984).

Sinatra, Frank (Francis Albert), popular American singer; b. Hoboken, N.J., Dec. 12, 1915, of immigrant Italian parents. He sang in a glee club in school; appeared on amateur radio shows. Inspired by the tone production of Tommy Dorsey's trombone playing, he evolved, by convex inhalation from a corner of the mouth, a sui generis "mal canto" in *sotto voce* delivery, employing a Caruso-like *coup-de-glotte* at climactic points. This mode of singing, combined with an engagingly slender physique, stirred the young females of the World War II era to fainting frenzy at his performances. Sinatra's press agents were quick to exploit the phenomenon, dubbing him "Swoonlight Sinatra." He eventually overcame his anesthetic appeal and became a successful baritone crooner; like most of his colleagues, he never learned to read music. He revealed an unexpected dramatic talent as a movie actor, eliciting praise from astonished cinema critics. In May 1976, the Univ. of Nevada at Las Vegas conferred on him the honorary degree of Literarum Humanitarum Doctor, in appreciation of his many highly successful appearances in the hotels and gambling casinos of Las Vegas.

Sinding, Christian, celebrated Norwegian composer; b. Kongsberg, Jan. 11, 1856; d. Oslo, Dec. 3, 1941. He studied first with L. Lindeman in Norway, then at the Leipzig Cons. with Schradieck (violin), Jadassohn (theory), and Reinecke (orchestration); after 4 years (1877–81) he returned to Norway, and had his Piano Quartet and a symph. performed in Oslo; a government stipend enabled him to continue his studies in Germany, and he spent 2 years (1882–84) in Munich, Berlin, and Dresden; there he wrote his first opera, *Titandros,* much influenced by Wagner.

On Dec. 19, 1885, he gave a concert of his works in Oslo; during another stay in Germany, his Piano Quintet was played in Leipzig, with Brodsky and Busoni among the performers (Jan. 19, 1889); Erika Lie-Nissen played his Piano Concerto in Berlin (Feb. 23, 1889). He publ. a number of piano pieces in Germany; of these, *Frühlingsrauschen* became an international favorite. His opera to a German text, *Der heilige Berg* (1914), was not successful. In 1915 he received a life pension of 4,000 crowns "for distinguished service"; on his 60th birthday (1916) the Norwegian government presented him with a purse of 30,000 crowns, a mark of appreciation for "the greatest national composer since Grieg." He was invited by George Eastman to teach at the Eastman School of Music in Rochester, N.Y., during the academic season 1921–22; after this journey, he lived mostly in Oslo. He continued to compose, and toward the end of his life wrote in larger forms; his 3rd Symph. was conducted by Nikisch with the Berlin Phil. in 1921, and his 4th Symph. was performed on his 80th birthday in Oslo (1936). His works aggregate to 132 opus numbers. Most of his music is of a descriptive nature; his lyric pieces for piano and his songs are fine examples of Scandinavian Romanticism, but the German inspiration of his formative years is much in evidence; he was chiefly influenced by Schumann and Liszt.

Singher, Martial, noted French baritone and pedagogue; b. Oloron-Sainte-Marie, Basses-Pyrénées, Aug. 14, 1904. He received his education as a public-school teacher in Dax, and then at the Ecole Normale de Toulouse and the Ecole Normale Supérieure de St. Cloud. He then studied voice with André Gresse at the Paris Cons. (premier prix for singing, 1929; premier prix for opera and opéra-comique singing, 1930; Grand Prix Osiris de l'Institute de France, 1930). He also studied voice with Juliette Fourestier. He made his operatic debut in Amsterdam as Orestes in *Iphigénie en Tauride* on Nov. 14, 1930. He then joined the Paris Opéra, remaining with it until 1941; also sang at the Opéra-Comique. On Jan. 10, 1940, he married Margareta Busch, daughter of the conductor Fritz Busch. He came to the U.S. in 1941; made his Metropolitan Opera debut in N.Y. on Dec. 10, 1943, as Dapertutto in *Les Contes d'Hoffmann;* subsequently sang the roles of the Count in *Le nozze di Figaro,* Lescaut in *Manon,* all 4 baritone roles in *Les Contes d'Hoffmann;* remained on the roster, with some interruptions, until 1959. He also sang with the leading orchs. of the U.S. and appeared widely in song recitals. He was on the faculty of the Mannes College of Music in N.Y. (1951–62) and the Curtis Inst. of Music in Philadelphia (1955–68); then was director of the voice and opera dept. and the opera producer at the Music Academy of the West in Santa Barbara (1962–81). His students have included Donald Gramm, John Reardon, James King, Louis Quilico, Judith Blegen, Benita Valente, and Jeannine Altmeyer. He was a particularly distinguished interpreter of the French operatic and song repertoire.

Sinigaglia, Leone, Italian composer; b. Turin, Aug. 14, 1868; d. there, May 16, 1944. He was a pupil at the Turin Cons., studying with Giovanni Bolzoni; later studied in Vienna (1894–1900) with Mandyczewski, and in Prague and Vysoka with Dvořák (1900–1901). His first successful work was a violin concerto (1900) dedicated to Arrigo Serato, who played it with considerable success in the principal cities of Germany. Sinigaglia's early works were much influenced by Brahms and Dvořák; then he turned for inspiration to the music of his native Piedmont, and in this field achieved a lasting reputation. Toscanini conducted in Turin the premiere of Sinigaglia's suite *Danze piemontesi,* on popular themes (May 14, 1905); later Sinigaglia publ. a collection of songs (6 albums), *Vecchie canzoni populari del Piemonte;* another work in the folk-song manner is the symph. suite *Piemonte* (1909; Utrecht, Feb. 16, 1910); he further wrote *Le Baruffe Chiozzotte,* an overture to Goldoni's comedy (Utrecht, Dec. 21, 1907); *Rapsodia piemontese* for Violin and Orch.; *Romanze* for Violin and Orch.; *Variations on a Theme of Brahms* for String Quartet (1901); *Serenade* for String Trio (1906); Cello Sonata (1923).

Sinopoli, Giuseppe, Italian conductor and composer; b. Venice, Nov. 2, 1946. He studied at the Benedetto Marcello Cons. in Venice; concurrently enrolled in the medical school at the Univ. of Padua, receiving a diploma in medicine in 1971; subsequently he practiced as a surgeon and a psychiatrist. He then went to Vienna to study conducting with Swarowsky; in 1972 joined the faculty of the Venice Cons.; in 1975 he organized the Bruno Maderna Ensemble (so named after the notable conductor), with which he gave performances of modern music; from 1979 he presented programs of contemporary music with the Berlin Phil. On Jan. 20, 1983, he made his American debut with the N.Y. Phil. In 1983 he was appointed principal conductor of the Philharmonia Society of London. As a composer, he pursues a modern technological trend, making frequent use of electronic sound and computers. In this manner he wrote *25 studi su tre parametri* (1969); *Musica per calcolatori analogici* (1969); *Numquid et unum* for Cembalo and Flute (1970); *Opus Ghimal* for Orch. (1971); *Sunyata* for String Quintet and Soprano (1972); Piano Sonata (1974).

Siohan, Robert, French music theorist, writer, and composer; b. Paris, Feb. 27, 1894. He studied at the Paris Cons.; in 1929 founded the Concerts Siohan, which he conducted until 1936; was choral conductor at the Paris Opera (1931–46); from 1948 to 1962 he was an instructor in solfège and sight-reading at the Paris Cons.; subsequently served as inspector-general of music in the Ministry of Culture. He received his doctorate at the Sorbonne in 1954 with the thesis *Théories nouvelles de l'homme* (publ. under the title *Horizons sonores,* Paris, 1956). Among his compositions are the opera *Le Baladin de satin cramoisi* (1927); *Cantique au frère soleil* (1928); Violin Concerto; Cello Concerto; Piano Concerto;

Gravitations for Viola and Piano; Quartet with Soprano part. He publ. a monograph on Stravinsky (Paris, 1959; in Eng., N.Y., 1970); *Histoire du public musical* (Lausanne, 1967); numerous articles in French and German publications.

Siqueira, José de Lima, Brazilian composer and conductor; b. Conceição, June 24, 1907. He played saxophone and trumpet, taking instruction from his father; then entered the National School of Music in Rio de Janeiro, where he studied with Burle Marx and Francisco Braga. Upon graduation he founded the Orquesta Sinfónica Brasileira (1940), which he conducted until 1948; in 1949 he organized another orch., called Orquesta Sinfónica de Rio de Janeiro; he also filled engagements as a conductor in the U.S. (1944) and in Russia (1955).

Skalkottas, Nikos, greatly talented Greek composer; b. Chalkis, island of Euboea, March 8, 1904; d. (of a strangulated hernia) Athens, Sept. 19, 1949. He studied violin with his father, with his uncle, and with a nonrelated violinist at the Athens Cons. (1914–20). In 1921 he went to Berlin, where he continued his violin studies at the Hochschule für Musik (1921–23); then took lessons in music theory with Philipp Jarnach (1925–27). But the greatest influence on his creative life was Schoenberg, whom he met in Berlin; Schoenberg, in his book *Style and Idea,* mentions Skalkottas as one of his most gifted disciples. Skalkottas eagerly absorbed Schoenberg's instruction in the method of composition with 12 tones related only to one another, but in his own music applied it in a very individual manner, without trying to imitate Schoenberg's style. In Berlin Skalkottas also received some suggestions in free composition from Kurt Weill. He returned to Athens in 1933, when Schoenberg was driven out of Germany by the Nazis; in Athens Skalkottas earned his living by playing violin in local orchs., but continued to compose diligently, until his early death. His music written between 1928 and 1938 reflects Schoenberg's idiom; later works are tonally conceived, and several of them are in the clearly ethnic Greek modalities, set in the typical asymmetric meters of Balkan folk music. After his death a Skalkottas Society was formed in Athens to promote performances and publication of his works; about 110 scores of various genres are kept in the Skalkottas Archives in Athens.

Skilton, Charles Sanford, distinguished American composer; b. Northampton, Mass., Aug. 16, 1868; d. Lawrence, Kans., March 12, 1941. He first studied in Germany; after graduating from Yale Univ. (B.A., 1889), he studied in N.Y. with Harry Rowe Shelley (organ) and Dudley Buck (composition); then went to Germany, where he studied with Bargiel at the Hochschule für Musik in Berlin (1891–93). From 1893 to 1896 he was director of music at the Salem Academy and College in North Carolina, and conducted the local orch. there; then filled a similar post at the State Normal School, in Trenton, N.J. (1897–1903); in 1903 he was engaged as a prof. of organ and theory at the Univ. of Kansas, Lawrence, where he remained most of his life. He made a detailed study of Indian music, and introduced Indian motifs into the traditional forms of a suite or a fantasy.

Skinner, Ernest M., American organ builder; b. Clarion, Pa., Jan. 15, 1866; d. Duxbury, Mass., Nov. 27, 1960. He was the founder of the Ernest M. Skinner Co., organ builders, originally of Dorchester, later of Methuen, Mass. Until 1905 the business was carried on by Skinner himself; it was then incorporated, with Skinner as president. From 1917 to 1932 he was technical director of the Skinner Organ Co., which in 1932 was merged with the Aeolian Co. of Garwood, N.J., and became the Aeolian-Skinner Organ Co. Skinner was especially successful in the construction of organ pipes reproducing the exact tone color of the various woodwind instruments and the French horn; among several important inventions is the "duplex windchest," by means of which the stops of 2 manuals are made interchangeable, and the arrangement of placing the stops on swinging sides. The Skinner Co. built the organ in the National Cathedral at Washington, D.C. Skinner publ. the valuable books *The Modern Organ* (1915; 6th ed., 1945) and *The Composition of the Organ* (1947).

Skriabin, Alexander. See **Scriabin.**

Škroup, Franz (František), Czech composer and conductor; b. Osice, near Pardubice, June 3, 1801; d. Rotterdam, Feb. 7, 1862. He studied law in Prague. In 1827 he became assistant conductor, and from 1837 principal conductor, at the Bohemian Theater, Prague, and remained at that post until 1857; he put into performance several Wagner operas for the first time in Prague. He wrote several operas to Czech librettos, which he conducted at the Bohemian Theater: *Dráteník* (Feb. 2, 1826); *Oldřich a Božena* (Dec. 14, 1828); *Libušin snatek* (*Libusa's Marriage;* 3rd act perf. Nov. 6, 1835; first full perf., April 11, 1850); also the German operas *Drahomira* (Nov. 20, 1848) and *Der Meergeuse* (Nov. 29, 1861). In 1860 Škroup took a position offered to him with a German opera troupe in Rotterdam, and died there after 2 seasons. Besides his operas, he wrote some chamber music and many popular Bohemian songs, of which *Kde domov muj* became so famous that it was mistaken for a folk song and was made into the Czech national anthem.

Skrowaczewski, Stanislaw, eminent Polish-born American conductor and composer; b. Lwow, Oct. 3, 1923. His father was a brain surgeon; his mother, a fairly good pianist. A precocious *wunderkind* even for a fabled land of child prodigies, he composed an orch. overture at the age of 8, played a piano recital at 11, and performed Beethoven's 3rd Piano Concerto at 13, conducting the orch. from the keyboard. He enrolled at the Lwow State Cons.; at the same time he took courses in physics, chemistry, and philosophy at the Univ. of Lwow. The oppressive Nazi oc-

cupation of Poland interrupted his studies, and an unfortunate bomb exploded in the vicinity of his house, causing an injury to his hands that interfered with his further activities as a concert pianist. After the war, he moved to Cracow, where he took lessons in composition with Palester and conducting with Bierdiajew. In 1947 he received a French government scholarship which enabled him to study composition with Nadia Boulanger and conducting with Paul Kletzki in Paris. He then led the Wroclaw Orch. (1946–47), the State Silesian Phil. in Katowice (1949–54), the Cracow Phil. (1954–56), and the National Phil. Orch. in Warsaw (1956–59). In 1956 he won the first prize in the international conducting competition in Rome. On Dec. 4, 1958, he made his American debut as a guest conductor of the Cleveland Orch., scoring an impressive success which secured for him consideration for a permanent American post. In 1960 he was named music director of the Minneapolis Symph. Orch. (renamed the Minnesota Orch. in 1968), and asserted his excellence both as a consummate technician of the baton and a fine interpreter of the classic and modern repertoire. In 1966 he became an American citizen. In the interim he appeared as a guest conductor in Canada, Mexico, South America, Israel, Hawaii, Australia, and New Zealand. As an opera conductor, he made his Metropolitan Opera debut in N.Y. on Jan. 8, 1970, in *Die Zauberflöte.* In 1979 he resigned as music director of the Minnesota Orch., and was made its conductor emeritus. In 1982 he was appointed principal conductor and musical adviser of the Halle Orch. in Manchester, England.

Slatkin, Leonard, American conductor; b. Los Angeles, Sept. 1, 1944. He was reared in a family of musicians; his father, **Felix Slatkin,** was a violinist and conductor, his mother a cellist. Leonard Slatkin played the violin in infancy; took up the viola at puberty; played piano through adolescence; studied composition with Castelnuovo-Tedesco in Los Angeles. He made his conducting debut at the Aspen Music Festival at the age of 19; then studied conducting with Jean Morel at the Juilliard School of Music (Mus.B., 1968). He subsequently held the posts of associate conductor of the St. Louis Orch. and principal guest conductor of the Minnesota Symph. Orch.; also was a guest conductor with the N.Y. Phil., Chicago Symph. Orch., Philadelphia Orch., and several European orchs., among them the London Symph. and the Concertgebouw Orch. of the Netherlands. In 1977–79 he was conductor of the New Orleans Phil.; then (as of the 1979–80 season) was engaged as conductor of the St. Louis Symph. Orch.

Slavenski, Josip, outstanding Yugoslav composer; b. Cakovec, May 11, 1896; d. Belgrade, Nov. 30, 1955. His real name was **Stolcer (Stolzer),** but he changed it to the distinctly Slavonic name around 1930, and used it exclusively in his publ. works. He studied with Kodály in Budapest and with Novák in Prague. In 1924 he established himself in Belgrade; in 1945 he became a prof. of composition at the Music

Academy there. A musician of advanced ideas, he attempted to combine Slavic melodic and rhythmic elements with modern ingredients; he experimented with nontempered scales and devised a "natural" scale of 53 degrees to the octave. His first such experiment was *Prasimfonia* ("protosymphony"), scored for Orch., Organ, and Piano (1919–26); there followed *Balkanophonia,* suite for Orch. (Berlin, Jan. 25, 1929); an oriental cantata, *Religiophonia* (1934). Other works are a Violin Concerto (1927); 4 string quartets (1923, 1928, 1938, 1940); *Slavenska Sonata* for Violin and Piano (1924); *Sonata religiosa* for Violin and Organ (1925); piano pieces on Balkan themes.

Slenczynska, Ruth, American pianist of precocious talent; b. Sacramento, Calif., Jan. 15, 1925. Her father, a violinist, subjected her to severe discipline when her musical talent was revealed in early childhood; she played in public in Berlin when she was 6 years old, and performed with an orch. in Paris at the age of 11. She made a sensation and was acclaimed by European critics as a prodigy of nature; she took lessons with Egon Petri, Artur Schnabel, Alfred Cortot, and others in Europe and America, and even played for Rachmaninoff, who became interested in her destiny. However, she developed psychological difficulties with her father, whose promotion of her career became obsessive, and had to cease public appearances; when she played concerts at the age of 15, the critics characterized her performances as mechanical reproductions of the music, seemingly without any personal projection. She then engaged in teaching; became a prof. of piano at Southern Illinois Univ. in Edwardville. She publ. a book of memoirs (with Louis Biancolli), *Forbidden Childhood* (N.Y., 1957), in which she recounted the troubles of a child prodigy's life; she also brought out a pedagogical edition, *Music at Your Fingertips. Aspects of Pianoforte Technique* (with A.M. Lingg; N.Y., 1961).

Slezak, Leo, famous Austrian tenor; b. Mährisch-Schönberg, Moravia, Aug. 18, 1873; d. Egern-on-the-Tegernsee, Bavaria, June 1, 1946. As a youth, he sang in the chorus of the Brünn Opera; made his debut as Lohengrin there (March 17, 1896); the role became one of his outstanding successes. He was with the Berlin Opera for a season (1898–99); in 1901 became a member of the Vienna Opera, where he was active until 1926; also performed frequently in Prague, Milan, and Munich. Not satisfied with his vocal training, he went to Paris, where he studied with Jean de Reszke. He made his London debut with marked acclaim as Lohengrin, May 18, 1900, at Covent Garden; appeared in America for the first time as Otello, with the Metropolitan Opera Co., N.Y. (Nov. 17, 1909); sang with the Metropolitan during its spring tour of 1910 and its summer season in Paris; remained with the company until 1913; subsequently sang also in Russia; gave recitals presenting distinguished programs, and performed with impeccable taste. He also acted in motion pictures. He was a man of great general culture, and pos-

sessed an exceptionally sharp literary wit, which he displayed in his reminiscences, *Meine sämtlichen Werke* (1922) and *Der Wortbruch* (1927); both were later combined in a single vol. (1935; Eng. trans. as *Songs of Motley: Being the Reminiscences of a Hungry Tenor,* London, 1938); he also publ. *Rückfall* (1940). A final book of memoirs, *Mein Lebensmärchen,* was publ. posthumously (1948). His son, the film actor Walter Slezak, publ. Slezak's letters, *Mein lieber Bub. Briefe eines besorgten Vaters* (Munich, 1966), and *What Time's the Next Swan?* (N.Y., 1962), alluding to the possibly apocryphal story of the swan failing to arrive in time in *Lohengrin.*

Slobodianik, Alexander, brilliant Soviet pianist; b. Kiev, Sept. 5, 1941. He studied at the Moscow Cons. with Gornostaeva, graduating in 1964. In 1966 he received 4th prize at the Tchaikovsky Competition in Moscow. He subsequently undertook numerous concert tours in Russia and abroad. He was particularly successful during his American tours in the 1970s. Like most Soviet pianists who venture abroad, he astounds by his unlimited technical resources, but he is also appreciated for the romantic élan of his playing.

Slobodskaya, Oda, Russian soprano; b. Vilna, Dec. 10, 1888; d. London, July 29, 1970. She studied at the St. Petersburg Cons.; made her operatic debut as Lisa in *The Queen of Spades* at the Maryinsky Theater in 1919. She also sang the regular repertoire there, including the roles of Marguerite in *Faust* and Aida. She emigrated in 1922; sang in Paris, at La Scala in Milan, and in Buenos Aires; eventually settled in London; sang Venus in *Tannhäuser* at Covent Garden in 1932. She developed an active career in England, establishing herself as an authoritative interpreter of Russian songs in recital; she also joined the faculty of the Guildhall School of Music and proved a sympathetic and effective voice teacher.

Slonimsky, Nicolas, Russian-American musicologist; b. St. Petersburg, April 27, 1894. A failed *wunderkind,* he was given his first piano lesson by his illustrious maternal aunt **Isabelle Vengerova,** on Nov. 6, 1900, according to the old Russian calendar. Possessed by inordinate ambition, aggravated by the endemic intellectuality of his family of both maternal and paternal branches (novelists, revolutionary poets, literary critics, university professors, translators, chessmasters, economists, mathematicians, inventors of useless artificial languages, Hebrew scholars, speculative philosophers), he became determined to excel beyond common decency in all these doctrines; as an adolescent, wrote out his future biography accordingly, setting down his death date as 1967, but survived. He enrolled in the St. Petersburg Cons. and studied harmony and orchestration with 2 pupils of Rimsky-Korsakov, Kalafati and Maximilian Steinberg; also tried unsuccessfully to engage in Russian journalism. After the Revolution he made his way south; was a rehearsal pianist at the Kiev Opera, where he took some composition lessons with Glière (1919); then was in Yalta, Crimea (1920), where he earned his living as a piano accompanist to displaced Russian singers, and as an instructor at a dilapidated Yalta Cons.; thence proceeded to Turkey, Bulgaria, and Paris, where he became secretary and piano-pounder to Serge Koussevitzky. In 1923 he came to the U.S.; became coach in the opera dept. of the Eastman School of Music in Rochester, N.Y., where he took an opportunity to study some more composition with the visiting prof. Selim Palmgren, and conducting with Albert Coates; in 1925 was again with Koussevitzky in Paris and Boston, but was fired for insubordination in 1927. He learned to speak polysyllabic English and began writing music articles for the *Boston Evening Transcript* and the *Christian Science Monitor;* ran a monthly column of musical anecdotes of questionable authenticity in *Etude* magazine; taught theory at the Malkin Cons. in Boston and at the Boston Cons.; conducted the Pierian Sodality at Harvard Univ. (1927–29) and the Apollo Chorus (1928–30). In 1927 he organized the Chamber Orch. of Boston with the purpose of presenting modern works; with it he gave first performances of works by Charles Ives, Edgar Varèse, Henry Cowell, and others; became a naturalized American citizen in 1931. In 1931–32 he conducted special concerts of modern American, Cuban, and Mexican music in Paris, Berlin, and Budapest under the auspices of the Pan-American Assoc. of Composers, producing a ripple of excitement; he repeated these programs at his engagements with the Los Angeles Phil. (1932) and at the Hollywood Bowl (1933), which created such consternation that his conducting career came to a jarring halt. In 1945–47 he became, by accident (the head of the dept. had died suddenly of a heart attack), lecturer in Slavonic languages and literatures at Harvard Univ.; in 1962–63 he traveled in Russia, Poland, Yugoslavia, Bulgaria, Rumania, Greece, and Israel under the auspices of the Office of Cultural Exchange at the U.S. State Dept., as a lecturer in native Russian, ersatz Polish, synthetic Serbo-Croatian, Russianized Bulgarian, Latinized Rumanian, archaic Greek, passable French, and tolerable German. Returning from his multinational travels, he taught variegated musical subjects at the Univ. of Calif., Los Angeles; was irretrievably retired after a triennial service (1964–67), ostensibly owing to irreversible obsolescence and recessive infantiloquy; but, disdaining the inexorable statistics of the actuarial tables, continued to agitate and even gave long-winded lecture-recitals in institutions of dubious learning. As a composer, he cultivated miniature forms, usually with a gimmick, e.g., *Studies in Black and White* for Piano (1928) in "mutually exclusive consonant counterpoint," a song cycle, *Gravestones,* to texts from tombstones in an old cemetery in Hancock, N.H. (1945), and *Minitudes,* a collection of 50 quaquaversal piano pieces (1971–77). His only decent orch. work is *My Toy Balloon* (1942), a set of variations on a Brazilian song, which includes in the score 100 colored balloons to be exploded *f f f* at the climax. He also conjured up a *Möbius Strip-Tease,* a perpetual vocal canon notat-

ed on a Möbius band to be revolved around the singer's head; it had its first and last performance at the Arrière-Garde Coffee Concert at UCLA, on May 5, 1965, with the composer officiating at the piano non-obbligato. A priority must be conceded to him for writing the earliest singing commercials to authentic texts from the *Saturday Evening Post* advertisements, among them *Make This a Day of Pepsodent, No More Shiny Nose,* and *Children Cry for Castoria* (1925). More "scholarly," though no less defiant of academic conventions, is his *Thesaurus of Scales and Melodic Patterns* (1947), an inventory of all conceivable and inconceivable tonal combinations, culminating in a mind-boggling "Grandmother Chord" containing 12 different tones and 11 different intervals. Beset by a chronic itch for novelty, he coined the term "pandiatonicism" (1937), which, *mirabile dictu,* took root and even got into reputable reference works, including the 15th edition of the *Encyclopædia Britannica.* In his quest for trivial but not readily accessible information, he blundered into the muddy field of musical lexicography; publ. *Music since 1900,* a chronology of musical events, which actually contains some beguiling serendipities (N.Y., 1937; 4th ed., 1971); took over the vacated editorship (because of the predecessor's sudden death during sleep) of Thompson's *International Cyclopedia of Music and Musicians* (4th to 8th eds., 1946–58), and somehow managed to obtain the editorship of the 5th and 6th editions of the prestigious *Baker's Biographical Dictionary of Musicians* (N.Y., 1958; 1978). Other publications: *Music of Latin America* (N.Y., 1945; several reprints; also in Spanish, Buenos Aires, 1947); *The Road to Music,* ostensibly for children (N.Y., 1947); *A Thing or Two about Music* (N.Y., 1948; inconsequential; also lacking an index); *Lexicon of Musical Invective,* a random collection of pejorative reviews of musical masterpieces (N.Y., 1952); numerous articles for encyclopedias; also a learned paper, *Sex and the Music Librarian,* valuable for its painstaking research; the paper was delivered by proxy, to tumultuous cachinnations, at a symposium of the Music Library Assoc., at Chapel Hill, N.C., Feb. 2, 1968.

Slonimsky, Sergei, greatly talented Soviet composer, nephew of **Nicolas Slonimsky;** b. Leningrad, Aug. 12, 1932. A member of a highly intellectual family (his father was a well-known Soviet author; his paternal grandfather, an economist, the author of the first book on Karl Marx in the Russian language; his father's maternal uncle was a celebrated Russian editor and literary critic; his father's maternal aunt was the noted piano teacher Isabelle Vengerova), he studied at the Leningrad Cons., taking composition with Boris Arapov and Orest Evlakhov (graduated in 1955) and piano with Vladimir Nilsen (graduated in 1956); he also took courses in musicology with F. Rubtzov (folk music) and N. Uspensky (polyphonic analysis). While a student, he wrote a fairy-tale suite, *Frog-Princess,* and in 1951 composed a string quartet on Russian folk motifs. In 1959 he was appointed to the faculty of the Leningrad Cons. For further study of folk music he traveled into the countryside, in the rural regions of Pskov and Novgorod. Concurrently, he explored the technical modalities of new music, in the tradition of Soviet modernism, evolving a considerable complexity of texture in a framework of dissonant counterpoint, while safeguarding the tonal foundation in triadic progressions. Some of his works, such as his opera *Virineya,* represent a contemporary evolution of the Russian national school of composition, broadly diatonic and spaciously songful; his other works tend toward ultramodern practices, including polytonality, microtonality, dodecaphony, tone-clusters, amplified sound, prepared piano, electronic sonorism, aleatory proceedings, and spatial placement of instruments. His Concerto for Orch. employs electronically amplified guitars and solo instruments; even more advanced is his *Antiphones* for String Quartet, employing non-tempered tuning and an "ambulatory" setting, in which the players are placed in different parts of the hall and then walk, while playing, en route to the podium; the piece is especially popular at modern music festivals. A prolific composer, he is the author of 7 symphs., many pieces of chamber music, choral works, and solo compositions. In 1980 he completed his most significant work, the opera-ballad *Mary Stuart,* which, after its inaugural production in Kuibyshev, had successful performances in Leningrad and, in 1984, in Leipzig. The score utilizes authentic Scottish folk songs, suitably arranged in modern harmonies, as well as original themes in the pentatonic scale. In 1983 he was awarded the prestigious Glinka Prize for *Mary Stuart.* Apart from his work as a composer and teacher, he contributes music criticism to Soviet magazines; publ. a valuable analytic survey, *The Symphonies of Prokofiev* (Leningrad, 1976).

Smallens, Alexander, American conductor; b. St. Petersburg, Russia, Jan. 1, 1889; d. Tucson, Ariz., Nov. 24, 1972. He was brought to the U.S. as a child; studied at the College of the City of N.Y. (B.A., 1909); then took courses at the Paris Cons. (1909). He devoted himself mainly to theatrical conducting; was assistant conductor of the Boston Opera (1911–14); accompanied the Anna Pavlova Ballet Co. on a tour of South America (1915–18); then was on the staff of the Chicago Opera Co. (1919–23) and of the Philadelphia Civic Opera (1924–31); from 1927 to 1934 he was assistant conductor of the Philadelphia Orch., and from 1947 to 1950, was music director at Radio City Music Hall in N.Y. He was the original conductor of Gershwin's opera *Porgy and Bess,* and conducted it on a European tour in 1956.

Smalley, Roger, English composer; b. Swinton, near Manchester, July 26, 1943. He studied at the Royal College of Music in London with Antony Hopkins (piano) and Peter Racine Fricker (composition); later attended courses in new music with Stockhausen in Cologne. In 1967 he became artist-in-residence at King's College, Cambridge. In 1970 he formed a new ensemble, called Intermodulation,

to promote socially unacceptable music. In this antagonistic manner he wrote *Strata* for 15 String Players (1970) and *Beat Music* for 55 Players (London, Aug. 12, 1971). But he also composed an austere *Missa brevis* and *Symphony in One Movement* (London, Aug. 25, 1982).

Smareglia, Antonio, Italian composer; b. Pola, Istria, May 5, 1854; d. Grado, near Trieste, April 15, 1929. He was trained in engineering before turning to music; studied composition with Franco Faccio at the Cons. of Milan. He became totally blind about 1905, but continued to compose by improvising on the piano with a musical amanuensis; lived in Milan until 1921, when he was appointed a prof. of composition at the Tartini Cons. in Trieste.

Smart, Sir George (Thomas), English organist and conductor; b. London, May 10, 1776; d. there, Feb. 23, 1867. He was a chorister in the Chapel Royal under Ayrton; was a pupil of Dupuis (organ) and Arnold (composition). He was knighted in 1811 in Dublin by the Lord Lieutenant after conducting a series of concerts. He was an original member of the Phil. Society and conductor of its concerts (1813–44), introducing the works of Beethoven and Schumann; also conducted the Lenten oratorios (1813–25). He publ. a collection of glees and canons (1863), 2 vols. of sacred music, 2 piano sonatinas, etc.; edited Orlando Gibbons's madrigals and Handel's "Dettingen" Te Deum.

Smart, Henry, English organist, son of **Sir George Smart**'s brother Henry (1778–1823); b. London, Oct. 26, 1813; d. there, July 6, 1879. He was a pupil of his father and of W.H. Kearns; served as organist at several London churches; finally at St. Pancras, Euston Road, in 1864, his sight failing in that year; he received a government pension in 1879. His opera, *Bertha, or the Gnome of the Hartzberg,* was produced at the Haymarket Theatre, May 26, 1855; the cantatas *The Bride of Dunkerron* (1864), *King René's Daughter* (1871), *The Fishermaidens* (1871), and *Jacob* (1873) appeared after he was blind. He wrote many songs, part-songs, and anthems; an Evening Service; organ music; etc.

Smetana, Bedřich (Friedrich), great Bohemian composer; b. Leitomischl, March 2, 1824; d. (insane) Prague, May 12, 1884. (His name is pronounced with a stress on the first syllable; Smetana himself said that the rhythm should be identical with the initial phrase in Beethoven's *Fidelio Overture.*) His talent manifested itself very early, but his father's prejudice against music as a profession precluded systematic instruction. However, a friend of his school days, Katharina Kolař, who was studying the piano with Proksch in Prague, introduced Smetana to her master, who accepted him as a pupil (piano and theory). Kittl, the director of the Cons., procured him a position as music teacher in the family of Count Thun. After 4 years of earnest work, Smetana gave up his position and undertook his first concert tour, which resulted in a disastrous financial failure. In despair he turned to Liszt, who helped him open a piano school of his own. This flourished, and a year later (1849) he married **Katharina Kolař,** who had also become a fine pianist. His reputation as a performer, especially as an interpreter of Chopin, grew rapidly, but his first compositions were received coldly. When, therefore, the Phil. Society of Göteborg (Sweden) offered him its conductorship in 1856, he immediately accepted. In his first year there he wrote his first 3 symph. poems, *Richard III, Wallensteins Lager,* and *Hakon Jarl* (after Öhlenschläger). As a conductor and pianist he was highly appreciated. But the cold climate undermined his wife's health. For her sake he spent his vacations regularly in Prague; on the trip there in 1859, she died in Dresden. Meanwhile, important events were evolving at home. Škroup had made a beginning with national opera, whose chief national element was Bohemian texts, the music being practically devoid of national characteristics. The younger musicians and poets sought the establishment of a national art. After Austria had granted political autonomy to Bohemia in 1860, agitation was begun for the erection of a national opera house in Prague. Smetana resigned his post in Göteborg, and returned to Prague in May 1861, assuming a leading role in the new movement. On Nov. 18, 1862, the new opera house was opened, but the dozen Bohemian operas by Škroup, Shuherský, and Šebor could not furnish an important or varied repertoire; consequently, Meyerbeer and the Italians were sung in Bohemian. Smetana therefore turned to opera, and finished his first dramatic work, *Braniboři v Čechách (The Brandenburgers in Bohemia),* in 1863. It was not produced till Jan. 5, 1866; its success, while not overwhelming, was decided. On May 30, 1866, his 2nd opera, *Prodaná nevěsta (The Bartered Bride),* was received with immense enthusiasm. Smetana was appointed first conductor (replacing the Meyerbeer fanatic Mayer), and was acclaimed as Bohemia's greatest composer. This opera has also found success abroad (Austria and Germany, 1892; Scandinavia, 1894; England, 1895; Italy, 1905; Belgium, 1907; U.S., Feb. 19, 1909, at the Metropolitan Opera House). The next opera, *Dalibor* (May 16, 1868), on account of Smetana's employment of leading motifs and more elaborate treatment of the orch., caused several critics to charge the composer with attempting to Wagnerize the national opera. In 1871, when there was talk of crowning Emperor Francis Josef as King of Bohemia, Smetana wrote *Libussa* for the coronation festivities. But no coronation took place, and Smetana's enemies found means of preventing a production at the National Opera. Hoping to duplicate the success of his 2nd work, he selected a comedy, *Dvě vdovy (The 2 Widows),* produced on March 27, 1874, with only moderate success. He returned to the symph. poem, but now found inspiration in national subjects. Thus originated the 6 masterpieces bearing the collective title *Má vlast (My Country): Vyšehrad* (the ancient castle of the Bohemian kings) and *Vltava (The Moldau)* in 1874; *Šárka* (a valley north of Prague, named after a mythological character) and *Z českých luhův a hayův (From*

Bohemia's Meadows and Groves) in 1875; *Tábor (The Camp;* introducing the Hussite war song) in 1878; and *Blanik* in 1879. To this period also belongs the famous E-minor String Quartet *Z mého života (Aus meinem Leben;* 1876). But Smetana's labors on behalf of national art had already borne fruit; a reaction soon set in, and by the end of 1875 his friends again controlled the opera. Early in 1876 he began a new opera, *Hubička (The Kiss),* produced with gratifying success on Nov. 7, 1876. *Tajemství (The Secret),* staged in Prague on Sept. 18, 1878, was hailed as a 2nd *Bartered Bride,* and won even the opposition party. For the opening (June 11, 1881) of the new National Opera, *Libussa* was unanimously chosen, and created a profound impression. His last opera, *Čertova stěna (The Devil's Wall),* presented on Oct. 29, 1882, was a comparative failure. Meanwhile, an early syphilitic infection affected his hearing, so that he became almost totally deaf and had to cease all public appearances; his brain was affected, he suffered hallucinations, and had to be confined in an asylum. A detailed account of Smetana's illness and death is found in Dieter Kerner's *Krankheiten grosser Musiker* (Stuttgart, 1969; vol. 2, pp. 77–92). Smetana's other works are: *Triumph-Symphonie,* in honor of the marriage of Emperor Franz Josef (1854; contains the Austrian national anthem); *Richard III,* symph. poem (Prague, Jan. 5, 1862, composer conducting); *Hakon Jarl,* symph. poem (Prague, Feb. 24, 1864, composer conducting); *Písen Česká (Bohemian Song)* for Vocal Quartet and Orch. (1868; Prague, March 29, 1875); *Prazský Karneval (The Carnival of Prague),* symph. poem (Prague, March 2, 1884); *Rybář (The Fisher),* music to a tableau after Goethe, for Harmonium, Harp, and String Quintet (Žofin, April 12, 1869); *Festmarsch* for the Shakespeare tercentenary (1864); String Quartet in D minor; Piano Trio; 2 pieces for Violin and Piano; choruses and songs; piano music (a set of Bohemian dances, 3 sets of polkas, the popular concert étude *Am Seegestade,* etc.).

Smeterlin, Jan, Polish pianist; b. Bielsko, Feb. 7, 1892; d. London, Jan. 18, 1967. He was a child prodigy; made his first concert appearance at the age of 8; toured widely as a concert pianist, eventually settling in London. He was praised for his congenially Romantic interpretations of Chopin's music.

Smit, Leo, Dutch composer; b. Amsterdam, May 14, 1900; d. in a concentration camp, probably in Poland, in 1943 or 1944. He studied composition with Sem Dresden at the Amsterdam Cons.; taught at the Cons. (1924–27); then lived in Paris. He returned to Amsterdam in 1937; was arrested by the Nazis in 1943 and sent to the concentration camp at Westerbork in the Netherlands; was removed to an unknown camp (presumably in Poland) and an equally unknown fate. His music was greatly influenced by the contemporary French school of his time.

Smit, Leo, American pianist and composer; b. Philadelphia, Jan. 12, 1921. He studied piano with Isabelle Vengerova at the Curtis Inst. of Music in

Philadelphia; took lessons in composition with Nicolas Nabokov. He made his debut as a pianist at Carnegie Hall in N.Y. in 1939; then taught at various schools and colleges. In 1967 he traveled in Latin America and gave concerts of American music there. His own style of composition is neo-Classical, marked by a strong contrapuntal fabric; the influence of Stravinsky, with whom he had personal contact, is particularly pronounced here. He wrote an opera, *The Alchemy of Love*, to a libretto by the astronomer Fred Hoyle (1969); the ballet *Virginia Sampler* (N.Y., March 4, 1947); *The Parcae*, overture (Boston, Oct. 16, 1953); Symph. No. 1 (Boston, Feb. 1, 1957); *Capriccio* for String Orch. (Ojai, Calif., May 23, 1958); Sextet for Clarinet, Bassoon, and Strings (1940); *Academic Graffiti* for Voice, Clarinet, Cello, Piano, and Percussion, to a text by W.H. Auden (1959); Piano Concerto (1968); *In Woods* for Oboe, Harp, and Percussion (1978); choruses and a number of piano pieces.

Smith, Bernard (Bernhard Schmidt), called "Father Smith," organ builder; b. in Germany, c.1630; d. London, Feb. 20, 1708. He settled in London in 1660 with 2 nephews; became organ builder to the King and court organ builder to Queen Anne. He built organs for St. Margaret's, Westminster (1675); Durham Cathedral (1683); the Temple (1684); St. Paul's Cathedral (1697); and the Banqueting Hall, Whitehall (1699).

Smith, Bessie (Elizabeth), black American "blues" singer; b. Chattanooga, Tenn., April 15, 1894; d. in an automobile accident, Sept. 26, 1937, on a highway outside Clarksdale, Miss. Born in a wretchedly poor family, she joined Rainey's Rabbit Foot Minstrels (blues pioneer Ma Rainey was her teacher) and developed a style of singing that rapidly brought her fame. Her first record, *Down Hearted Blues*, sold 800,000 copies in 1923, and she was billed as the "Empress of the Blues." She was a large, impressive woman—5'9*S' and weighing over 200 pounds—and had a powerful voice to match; the excellence of her vocal equipment, along with her natural expressive qualities and improvisatory abilities, combined to make her the consummate blues singer of her time.

Smith, Carleton Sprague, distinguished American musicologist; b. New York, Aug. 8, 1905. He was educated at Harvard Univ. (M.A., 1928) and at the Univ. of Vienna, where he studied history (Dr.Phil., 1930). Returning to the U.S., he was an instructor in history at Columbia Univ. (1931–35), then at N.Y. Univ. (1939–67); he also served as chief of the Music Division at the N.Y. Public Library (1931–43 and 1946–59); a linguist, he lectured in South America, in Spanish and Portuguese, on the social history of the U.S.; a skillful flutist, he often took part in concerts of old and new music.

Smith, David Stanley, American composer and music educator; b. Toledo, Ohio, July 6, 1877; d. New Haven, Conn., Dec. 17, 1949. He studied with Horatio Parker at Yale Univ., graduating in 1900. He then went to Europe, where he took courses in composition with Thuille in Munich and Widor in Paris. Upon his return to the U.S. he obtained a Mus.Bac. degree at Yale (1903) and was appointed an instructor at the Yale School of Music; in 1916 he became a prof. there; in 1920 was appointed dean of the School of Music, retiring in 1946. He was conductor of the New Haven Symph. Orch. from 1920 to 1946.

Smith, John Christopher (Johann Christoph Schmidt), organist and composer; b. Ansbach, Germany, 1712; d. Bath, England, Oct. 3, 1795. His father went to England with Handel in 1716, as his agent; the son followed in 1720 and became Handel's pupil. When Handel's eyesight began to deteriorate, Smith helped him in playing the organ and harpsichord at performances of Handel's oratorios, and continued to supervise performances of Handel's music after Handel's death; Smith presented Handel's MS scores, and other objects left to him by Handel, to King George III in appreciation for a royal pension. He retired about 1770, and settled in Bath. He wrote several English operas, of which 2 Shakespearean pieces, *The Fairies* (Drury Lane, Feb. 3, 1755) and *The Tempest* (Drury Lane, Feb. 11, 1756) were publ.; also wrote the oratorios *Paradise Lost* (Feb. 29, 1760), *Judith, Redemption,* etc.

Smith, John Stafford, English organist and composer; b. Gloucester (baptized, March 30), 1750; d. London, Sept. 21, 1836. He studied with his father, Martin Smith, organist at Gloucester Cathedral, and also took lessons with Boyce. In 1784 he was made a Gentleman of the Chapel Royal, and in 1802 succeeded Arnold as organist there; from 1805 to 1817 he was master of the Boy Choristers there; from 1785 served as lay-vicar at Westminster Abbey; was also known as a composer of catches and glees and won several prizes of the Catch Club in London. The importance of John Stafford Smith to American music lies in the fact that he included in his 5th collection of glees, which he issued in 1799, an arrangement of the tune *To Anacreon in Heaven*, to which Francis Scott Key wrote *The Star-Spangled Banner* (1814); but there were several reasons for questioning whether he was the composer; his authorship was doubted by many reputable American scholars. William Lichtenwanger, in his paper "The Music of *The Star-Spangled Banner:* From Ludgate Hill to Capitol Hill," in the *Quarterly Journal of the Library of Congress* (July 1977), seems to have dispelled these doubts by publishing excerpts from the "Recollections" of Richard John Samuel Stevens, an active member of the Anacreontic Society of London, who states in the rubric for 1777: "The president was Ralph Tomlinson. ... He wrote the Poetry of the Anacreontic Song; which Stafford Smith set to Music." Smith was an excellent musician; he transcribed into modern notation old MSS for the *History of Music* by Sir John Hawkins; edited *Musica antiqua*, containing compositions "from the commencement of the 12th to the 18th century" (2 vols., 1812); publ. *A Collection of*

Songs of Various Kinds for Different Voices (1785).

Smith, Julia, American pianist, composer, and writer on music; b. Denton, Texas, Jan. 25, 1911. She studied piano with Carl Friedberg at the Juilliard School of Music in N.Y.; devoted herself mainly to composition and music criticism. She wrote the operas *Cynthia Parker* (Denton, Feb. 16, 1940); *The Gooseherd and the Goblin* (N.Y., Feb. 22, 1947); *The Stranger of Manzano* (Dallas, May 6, 1947); *Cockcrow* (Austin, April 22, 1954); *The Shepherdess and the Chimney Sweep* (Fort Worth, Dec. 28, 1967); *Daisy* (Miami, Nov. 3, 1973); *Folkways Symphony* (1948); *Remember the Alamo* for Speaker, Chorus, and Wind Orch. (1964); Piano Trio (1955); String Quartet (1964); Piano Concerto (Dallas, Feb. 28, 1976). She publ. the monographs *Aaron Copland* (N.Y., 1955); *Master Pianist. The Career and Teaching of Carl Friedberg* (N.Y., 1963); *A Directory of Women Composers* (Chicago, 1970).

Smith, William O., American composer and jazz clarinetist; b. Sacramento, Calif., Sept. 22, 1926. He began playing clarinet at the age of 10, and at 12 started a grade-school dance band. He then enrolled at the Juilliard School of Music in N.Y. (1945–46) while earning a living by playing in jazz groups. Returning to California, he took courses with Darius Milhaud at Mills College (1946–47) and attended sessions with Sessions at the Univ. of Calif. at Berkeley (M.A., 1952). Intermittently, he played in Dave Brubeck's jazz octet in California (1947–52). In 1957 he was awarded the American Prix de Rome, and in 1960 he received a Guggenheim grant. His scholarly interests were certainly insular in the great mass of innocent jazz practitioners; his own music is omnivorous, ingesting dodecaphony, inhaling electronics, and absorbing by osmosis a variety of quaquaversal elements, while maintaining a dignified formality of organized musical structure.

Smyth, Dame Ethel (Mary), foremost English woman composer; b. Rectory (Middlesex), April 22, 1858; d. Woking, Surrey, May 8, 1944. She studied at the Leipzig Cons.; then with Heinrich von Herzogenberg, following him to Berlin; her String Quintet was performed in Leipzig in 1884. She returned to London in 1888; presented her orchestral *Serenade* (April 26, 1890) and an overture, *Antony and Cleopatra* (Oct. 18, 1890). Her prestige as a serious woman composer rose considerably with the presentation of her Mass for Solo Voices, Chorus, and Orch. at Albert Hall (Jan. 18, 1893). After that she devoted her energies to the theater. Her first opera, *Fantasio,* to her own libretto in German, after Alfred de Musset's play, was produced in Weimar on May 24, 1898; this was followed by *Der Wald* (Berlin, April 9, 1902); also to her own German libretto; it was produced in London in the same year, and in N.Y. by the Metropolitan Opera on March 11, 1903. Her next opera, *The Wreckers,* was her most successful work; written originally to a French libretto, *Les Naufrageurs,* it was first produced in a German version as *Strandrecht* (Leipzig, Nov. 11, 1906); the composer herself trans. it into Eng., and it was staged in London on June 22, 1909; the score was revised some years later, and produced at Sadler's Wells, London, on April 19, 1939. She further wrote a comic opera, in Eng., *The Boatswain's Mate* (London, Jan. 28, 1916); a one-act opera, described as a "dance-dream," *Fête galante* (Birmingham, June 4, 1923); and *Entente cordiale* (Bristol, Oct. 20, 1926). Other works are a Concerto for Violin, Horn, and Orch. (London, March 5, 1927); *The Prison* for Soprano and Bass Solo, Chorus, and Orch. (London, Feb. 24, 1931); choral pieces (*Hey Nonny No, Sleepless Dreams,* etc.); a group of songs; etc. Her formative years were spent in Germany, and her music never overcame the strong German characteristics, in the general idiom as well as in the treatment of dramatic situations on the stage. At the same time, she was a believer in English national music and its potentialities. She was a militant leader for woman suffrage in England, for which cause she wrote *The March of the Women,* the battle song of the W.S.P.U. After suffrage was granted, her role in the movement was officially acknowledged; in 1922 she was made a Dame of the British Empire. She publ. a number of books, mostly autobiographical in nature: *Impressions That Remained* (2 vols., 1919; new ed., 1945); *Streaks of Life* (1921); *As Time Went On* (1936); *What Happened Next* (1940); also some humorous essays and reminiscences, *A Three-legged Tour in Greece* (1927); *A Final Burning of Boats* (1928); *Female Pipings in Eden* (1934); *Beecham and Pharaoh* (1935).

Snetzler (Schnetzler), Johann, Swiss organ builder; b. Schaffhausen, April 6, 1710; d. there, Sept. 28, 1785. He went to London in 1746 and established an organ workshop there; built organs for the Moravian churches in London and in Leeds, for Chesterfield Church, and (on the recommendation of Burney) for the Church of King's Lynn. He returned to Switzerland shortly before his death. His London factory was purchased by Ohrmann, Nutt, and Eliot. A list of his organs exported to the U.S is found in W.L. Summer's *The Organ* (London, 1952).

Sobolewski, Friedrich Eduard de, German-American composer; b. Königsberg, Oct. 1, 1808, of Polish parents; d. St. Louis, May 17, 1872. He was a pupil of Weber in Dresden; became an opera conductor in Königsberg and Bremen; produced there his operas *Imogen* (1833), *Velleda* (1836), and *Salvator Rosa* (1848); his opera *Komala* was produced by Liszt in Weimar on Oct. 30, 1858. In 1859 he emigrated to the U.S., settling in Milwaukee, then a center of German musical immigrants. There he staged his opera *Mohega,* on Oct. 11, 1859, to his own libretto in German; he selected an American subject dealing with an Indian girl saved by Pulaski from death. Sobolewski subsequently moved to St. Louis; organized a symph. orch. there, which he led from 1860 to 1866. He wrote the oratorios *Johannes der Täufer, Der Erlöser,* and *Himmel und Erde;* 2 symphs.; the symph. poems *Vineta* and *Meeresphantasie;* several male choruses; publ. the pamphlets *Reaktionäre Briefe* (1854), *Oper nicht Drama* (1858), and *Das Geheimnis der neuesten Schule der Musik* (1859).

Sofronitzky, Vladimir, Russian pianist; b. St. Petersburg, May 8, 1901; d. Moscow, Aug. 29, 1961. He studied with Nikolayev at the Leningrad Cons., graduating in 1921; then went on a concert tour in Russia, Poland, and France. Returning to Russia, he taught piano at the Leningrad Cons. (1936–42), and at the Moscow Cons. from 1942 until his death. He was greatly praised for his interpretations of Chopin, and particularly Scriabin.

Soldat, Marie, Austrian violinist; b. Graz, March 25, 1863; d. there, Sept. 30, 1955. She first studied in Graz, and from 1879 to 1882 with Joachim at the Hochschule für Musik in Berlin, graduating as winner of the Mendelssohn Prize; made a specialty of the Brahms Violin Concerto, which she performed with great authority. In 1887 she formed in Berlin her own string quartet (all women); in 1899 she married the lawyer Röger, and settled in Vienna, continuing her concert career; there she formed a new string quartet (with Elsa von Plank, Natalie Bauer-Lechner, and Leontine Gärtner); eventually retired in Graz, remaining there until her death at the age of 92.

Soler, Padre Antonio, important Spanish composer and organist; b. Olot, Catalonia (baptized, Dec. 3), 1729; d. El Escorial, near Madrid, Dec. 20, 1783. He entered the school of the monastery of Montserrat as a child, and studied organ and harmony there. In 1752 he took Holy Orders at El Escorial, and spent the rest of his life there. For some time between 1752 and 1756 he had an opportunity to take lessons with Domenico Scarlatti, who was then attached to the Spanish court; Scarlatti's influence is apparent in Soler's harpsichord sonatas. Soler was a prolific composer of both sacred and secular music; a catalogue of his MSS at El Escorial contains 428 separate numbers. Fourteen harpsichord sonatas by Soler were publ. by J. Nín in *Classiques espagnols du piano* (2 vols., Paris, 1925, 1929); 100 piano sonatas and a *Fandango*, edited by the pianist F. Marvin, were publ. in N.Y. (1958–59); 6 concertos for 2 Keyboard Instruments were edited by Santiago Kastner (Barcelona, 1952); 6 quintets for Strings and Organ were brought out by Roberto Gerhard for the *Institut d'Estudis Catalans* (Barcelona, 1933, with an introductory essay by H. Anglès); a collection of 27 *Sonatas para Clave* was printed in London by T. Birchall; 6 organ concertos were edited by Padre S. Rubrio (Madrid, 1968).

Sollberger, Harvey, American flutist and composer; b. Cedar Rapids, Iowa, May 11, 1938. He studied composition with Philip Bezanson at the Univ. of Iowa and with Jack Beeson and Otto Luening at Columbia Univ. (M.A., 1964). In 1964–72 he was on the staff of Columbia Univ.; then at the Manhattan School of Music. In his music he employs an imaginatively applied serial method.

Solomon (real name, **Solomon Cutner**), English pianist; b. London, Aug. 9, 1902. He made a sensational debut as a child prodigy at the age of 8, playing Tchaikovsky's Concerto No. 1 in London (June 30, 1911). Later he was sent to Paris for further study, resuming his career as an adult performer in 1923. He appeared under the single name Solomon, without a patronymic; toured all over the world as a concert pianist; also played with orchs. His interpretation of the classics is particularly fine in that he adheres strictly to the spirit of the music, without superimposing any mannerisms of his own. In 1956 he suffered a stroke, which paralyzed his right arm; as a result, he was forced to withdraw from his concert career; he has since lived in London.

Solomon, Izler, American conductor; b. St. Paul, Minn., Jan. 11, 1910. He took violin lessons with Myron Poliakin in Philadelphia and Michael Press in N.Y.; then took courses at Michigan State College (1928–31). He made his debut as a conductor with the Lansing (Mich.) Civic Orch. on March 17, 1932; then conducted the Illinois Symph. (1936–42) and the Columbus (Ohio) Phil. (1941–49); was guest conductor of the Israel Phil. during its American tour in 1951; also filled in engagements with the Buffalo Phil. Orch., Chicago Symph., Los Angeles Phil., Detroit Symph., Philadelphia Orch., etc. From 1956 to 1975 he was principal conductor and music director of the Indianapolis Symph. Orch.; during his tenure he brought it to a considerable degree of perfection; in his programs he included many works of the modern American school. In 1976 he suffered a stroke, and was unable to continue his career.

Solti, Sir Georg (György), eminent Hungarian-born English conductor; b. Budapest, Oct. 21, 1912. He began to study the piano when he was 6, making his first public appearance in Budapest when he was 12; at 13 he enrolled there at the Franz Liszt Academy of Music, studying piano with Dohnányi and, briefly, with Bartók; took composition courses with Kodály. He graduated at the age of 18, and was engaged by the Budapest Opera as a répétiteur; also served as an assistant to Bruno Walter (1935) and Toscanini (1936 and 1937) at the Salzburg Festivals. On March 11, 1938, he made a brilliant conducting debut at the Budapest Opera with Mozart's *Le nozze di Figaro;* the wave of anti-Semitism in Hungary under the reactionary military rule forced him to leave Budapest (he was Jewish). In 1939 he went to Switzerland, where he was active mainly as a concert pianist; in 1942 he won the Concours International de Piano in Geneva; finally, in 1944, he was engaged to conduct concerts with the orch. of the Swiss Radio. In 1946 the American occupation authorities in Munich invited him to conduct *Fidelio* at the Bavarian State Opera; his success led to his appointment as its music director, a position he held from 1946–52. In 1952 he became Generalmusikdirektor in Frankfurt, serving as director of the Opera and conductor of the Museumgesellschaft Concerts. In 1953 he went to America; made his U.S. debut with the San Francisco Opera on

Sept. 25, 1953, conducting *Elektra;* he later conduct-ed the Chicago Symph. Orch., the N.Y. Phil. Orch., and the orch. of the Metropolitan Opera in N.Y., where he made his first appearance on Dec. 17, 1960, with *Tannhäuser.* He was then engaged as music director of the Los Angeles Phil. Orch., but the pro-ject collapsed when the board of trustees refused to grant him full powers in musical and administra-tive policy. In 1959 he went to England and conduct-ed opera at Covent Garden in London; in 1961 he assumed the post of music director of the Royal Opera House there, retaining it with great distinc-tion until 1971. In 1969 he was appointed conductor and music director of the Chicago Symph. Orch., and it was in that capacity that he achieved a tri-umph as an interpreter and orch. builder, so that the "Chicago sound" became a synonym for excel-lence. He showed himself an enlightened disci-plinarian and a master of orch. psychology, so that he could gain and hold the confidence of the players while demanding from them the utmost in profes-sional performance. Under his direction the Chica-go Symph. Orch. entered the foremost ranks of American orchs. He took the orch. to Europe in 1971, 1974, and 1978. He held the additional posts of music adviser of the Paris Opéra (1971–73) and music di-rector of the Orch. de Paris (1972–75), which he took on a tour of China in 1974; he served as principal conductor and artistic director of the London Phil. Orch. from 1979–83; was then accorded the title of conductor emeritus. During all these years he re-tained his post with the Chicago Symph. Orch., while continuing his appearances as a guest con-ductor with European orchs. In 1983 he conducted the entire *Ring* cycle at the Salzburg Festival, in commemoration of the 100th anniversary of the death of Richard Wagner. In 1968 he was made an honorary Commander of the Order of the British Empire; in 1971 he was named an honorary Knight Commander of the Order of the British Empire. In 1972 he became a British subject and was knighted, assuming the title of Sir Georg. Solti is generally acknowledged as one of the foremost conductors of his time.

Somers, Harry Stewart, outstanding Canadian composer and pianist; b. Toronto, Sept. 11, 1925. He studied piano with Reginald Godden (1942–43) and Weldon Kilburn (1945–49) at the Royal Cons. in Toronto; attended classes in composition with Weinzweig at the Toronto Cons.; then went to Paris, where he took private lessons with Darius Milhaud (1949–50); in 1969 he traveled to Rome on a grant from the Canadian Cultural Inst. Returning to Canada, he eked out a meager living as a music copyist, but in 1971 was named a Companion of the Order of Canada, and became active as commenta-tor on new music for Canadian radio and television. His historical opera, *Louis Riel,* was performed at the Kennedy Center in Washington, D.C., on Oct. 23, 1975, as part of America's Bicentennial celebration. His musical idiom is quaquaversal, absorbing with-out prejudice ancient, national, and exotic re-sources, from Gregorian chant to oriental scales,

from simple folkways to electronic sound, all han-dled with fine expertise.

Somogi, Judith, American conductor; b. New York, May 13, 1937. She studied violin, piano, and organ at the Juilliard School of Music in N.Y.; attended courses at the Berkshire Music Center in Tangle-wood; then served as a musical assistant at the N.Y. City Opera; later was an assistant to Thomas Schip-pers at the Spoleto Festival and to Leopold Stokow-ski at the American Symph. Orch. in N.Y. In 1974 she made a successful appearance with the N.Y. City Opera, and subsequently conducted in San Francisco, San Diego, San Antonio, and Pittsburgh. She made her European debut in Saarbrücken in 1979. After filling a successful engagement with the Frankfurt Opera in 1982, she was named to the post of its first conductor.

Sondheim, Stephen, brilliant American composer and lyricist; b. New York, March 22, 1930. Of an affluent family, he received his academic education in private schools; composed a school musical at the age of 15. He then entered Williams College, where he wrote the book, lyrics, and music for a couple of college shows; graduated magna cum laude in 1950. In quest of higher musical learning, he went to Princeton, where he took lessons in modernistic complexities with Milton Babbitt, and acquired so-phisticated techniques of composition. He made his mark on Broadway when he wrote the lyrics for Bernstein's *West Side Story* (1957). His first success as a lyricist-composer came with the Broadway musical *A Funny Thing Happened on the Way to the Forum* (1962), which received a Tony award. His next musical, *Anyone Can Whistle* (1964), proved unsuccessful, but *Company* (1970), for which he wrote both lyrics and music, established him as a major composer and lyricist on Broadway. There followed *Follies* (1971), for which he wrote 22 pastiche songs; it was named best musical by the N.Y. Drama Critics Circle. His next production, *A Little Night Music,* with the nostalgic score hark-ing back to the turn of the century, received a Tony, and its leading song, "Send in the Clowns," was awarded a Grammy in 1976. This score established Sondheim's characteristic manner of treating musicals; it is almost operatic in conception, and the score boldly introduces dissonant counterpoint *à la moderne.* In 1976 he produced *Pacific Over-tures,* based on the story of the Western penetration into Japan in the 19th century, and composed in a stylized Japanese manner, modeled after the Kabu-ki theater; he also wrote the score to the musical *Sunday in the Park with George,* inspired by the painting by Georges Scurat entitled "Sunday After-noon on the Island of La Grande Jatte" (N.Y., May 1, 1984).

Sonneck, Oscar George Theodore, eminent American musicologist; b. Jersey City, N.J., Oct. 6, 1873; d. New York, Oct. 30, 1928. He attended the Gelehrtenschule in Kiel (1883–89) and the Kaiser Friedrich Gymnasium in Frankfurt (1889–93), where he also took piano lessons with James Kwast; in 1893–97 he studied at Munich Univ. (musicology with Sandberger and philosophy with Riehl and Lipps); was a private pupil in composition of M.E. Sachs; in 1897–98, was a pupil of K. Schröder (conducting) at the Sondershausen Cons. and of Iwan Knorr (instrumentation) in Frankfurt; he spent the greater part of 1899 in research work in Italy; then returned to the U.S., continuing his research in the principal libraries. On Aug. 1, 1902, he was appointed chief of the Music Division of the Library of Congress in Washington, D.C.; he resigned on Sept. 5, 1917, to accept a position with the publishing house of G. Schirmer in N.Y. as director of the Publication Dept., managing editor of the *Musical Quarterly* (of which he had been editor since its foundation in 1915), and personal representative of the president, Rudolph E. Schirmer; in 1921 he became vice-president of G. Schirmer. He represented the U.S. government at the international congresses of music held in London and Rome in 1911. He took a leading part in the formation of the Society for the Publication of American Music, and of the Beethoven Assoc. in N.Y. Under Sonneck's administration, the Music Division of the Library of Congress became one of the largest and most important music collections in the world. His writings, exhibiting profound and accurate scholarship and embodying the results of original research, laid a real foundation for the scientific study of music in the U.S.; his elaborate catalogues, issued by the Library of Congress, are among the most valuable contributions to musical bibliography. The Sonneck Society, an organization designed to encourage the serious study of American music in all its aspects, was established in 1975 and named after Sonneck in recognition of his achievements in this area. He was also a composer and a poet; wrote a String Quartet; symph. pieces; *Rhapsody* and *Romanze* for Violin and Piano; some vocal works and piano pieces. He publ. 2 vols. of poems in German: *Seufzer* (1895) and *Eine Totenmesse* (1898).

WRITINGS: *Francis Hopkins and James Lyon. Two Studies in Early American Music* (1905); *Early Concert Life in America (1731–1800)* (1907); *Report on "The Star-Spangled Banner," "Hail Columbia," "America," "Yankee Doodle"* (1909); *A Survey of Music in America* (1913); *The Star-Spangled Banner* (1914); *Early Opera in America* (1915); *Suum Cuique* (1916; collection of essays); *Miscellaneous Studies in the History of Music* (1921); *Beethoven. Impressions of Contemporaries* (1926); *Beethoven Letters in America* (1927); *The Riddle of the Immortal Beloved* (1927). Catalogues: *Classification of Music and Literature of Music* (1904; 2nd ed., revised and augmented, 1917); *Bibliography of Early Secular Music* (1905; 2nd ed., revised and enlarged by W.T. Upton, 1945); *Dramatic Music* (1908); *Orchestral Music* (1912); *Opera Librettos Printed before 1800* (2 vols., 1914); *First Editions of Stephen C. Foster* (1915; with W.R. Whittlesey); *First Editions of Edward MacDowell* (1917).

Sontag, Henriette (real name, **Gertrud Walpurgis**

Sonntag), celebrated German soprano; b. Coblenz, Jan. 3, 1806; d. Mexico City (on a tour), June 17, 1854. She played children's parts on the stage; then studied at the Prague Cons. with Triebensee, Pixis, Bayer, and Frau Czegka; she made her first appearances as a singer in Prague; in 1822 she sang in Italian and German opera at Vienna, and in 1823 created the title role in Weber's *Euryanthe;* on May 7, 1824, she sang in Vienna the soprano solos in Beethoven's *Missa solemnis* and 9th Symph.; made her first Berlin appearance on Aug. 3, 1825, in the part of Isabella in Rossini's *Italiana in Algeri;* her Paris debut as Rosina in *Il Barbiere di Siviglia* at the Théâtre-Italien (May 15, 1826) was an unqualified success, and she was adjudged by many as superior to Catalani; she broke her Berlin contract in order to sing at the Italian Opera in Paris (1827); went to London in 1828, and secretly married the Sardinian ambassador to the Dutch court, Count Rossi; was ennobled by the King of Prussia (as "Fräulein Henriette von Lauenstein"). She then interrupted her career on the stage, and settled with her husband at The Hague; also traveled with him on his diplomatic missions to Germany and Russia. She continued to give concerts as a solo singer, arousing enthusiasm wherever she went. In 1849 she resumed her operatic career; made several tours in England; in the autumn of 1852 she embarked for the U.S., and gave a number of concerts; then went to Mexico (1854), where she sang opera. She died of cholera during an epidemic there.

Sonzogno, Edoardo, Italian music publisher; b. Milan, April 21, 1836; d. there, March 14, 1920. He inherited a printing plant and bookstore founded by his father, and in 1874 began to publ. popular editions of French and Italian music with marked success. In 1883 he inaugurated a series of contests for new operas; the 2nd contest, in 1889, was won by Mascagni (then unknown) with *Cavalleria rusticana.* Sonzogno established his own theater (the Lirico Internazionale) at Milan in 1894. From 1861 until his retirement in 1909 he was sole proprietor of the newspaper *Il Secolo.* He was succeeded by his nephew **Riccardo Sonzogno** (1871–1915); upon the latter's death, the business was taken over by another nephew, **Renzo Sonzogno,** who had previously headed a firm of his own. He died in 1920, and in 1923 control was acquired by a group of Italian industrialists.

Soot, Fritz, distinguished German tenor; b. Neunkirchen, Aug. 20, 1878; d. Berlin, June 9, 1965. He first pursued a career as an actor; then studied voice with Scheidemantel in Dresden; made his debut with the Dresden Court Opera as Tonio in *La Fille du régiment* in 1908, remaining on its roster until 1918; during his tenure there, he sang in the first performance of *Der Rosenkavalier* as the Italian Singer. His subsequent engagements were in Stuttgart (1918–22), at the Berlin State Opera (1922–44, 1946–52), and at the Berlin Städtische Oper (1946–48). He sang in the premieres of Berg's *Wozzeck,* as well as in works by Pfitzner and Schreker; he excelled in such Wagnerian roles as Tristan, Sieg-mund, and Siegfried.

Sor (real name, **Sors**), **Fernando,** celebrated Spanish guitar virtuoso; b. Barcelona, Feb. 13, 1778; d. Paris, July 10, 1839. At the age of 11 he entered the school of the monastery of Montserrat, where he studied music under the direction of Anselmo Viola; wrote a Mass; then left the monastery and returned to Barcelona, where he presented his only opera, *Telemaco nella isola di Calipso,* on Aug. 25, 1797. A few years later he went to Madrid; there he joined the French army, earning the rank of captain. When Bonapartist rule was defeated in Spain, in 1813, he fled to Paris. There he met Cherubini, Méhul, and other important composers, who urged him to give concerts as a guitarist, and he soon ac-quired fame. In Paris he produced 2 ballets, *Cen-drillon* (London, 1822) and *Le Sicilien, ou L'Amour peintre* (1827). He was summoned to London by the Duke of Sussex in 1815; in 1823 he traveled in Russia; wrote funeral music for the obsequies of Alexander I of Russia (1825). After another stay in London, he returned to Paris, settling there perma-nently in 1826. He wrote for the guitar a number of fantasies, minuets, and studies, as well as a method; all these works are modeled after the Classical forms, rather than on popular motifs. Selected works by Sor have been edited by G. Meier; his *Com-plete Works for Guitar* was publ. in 5 vols. (c.1970).

Sorabji, Kaikhosru (real Christian names, **Leon Dudley**), remarkable English composer of unique gifts; b. Chingford, Aug. 14, 1892. His father was a Parsi, his mother of Spanish-Sicilian extraction. He was largely self-taught in music, but through sheer perseverance and an almost mystical belief in his demiurgic powers, he developed an idiom of compo-sition of extraordinary complexity, embodying within the European framework of harmonies the Eastern types of melodic lines and asymmetrical rhythmic patterns, and creating an enormously in-tricate but architectonically stable edifice of sound. Sorabji's most arresting work is his magisterial *Opus Clavicembalisticum,* completed in 1930, tak-ing about 5 hours to play and comprising 3 parts with 12 subdivisions, including a theme with 49 variations and a passacaglia with 81 variations; characteristically, the score is dedicated to "the everlasting glory of those few men blessed and sanctified in the curses and execrations of those many whose praise is eternal damnation." Sorabji played *Opus Clavicembalisticum* for the first time in Glasgow under the auspices of the Active Society for the Propagation of Contemporary Music on Dec. 1, 1930. Wrathful at the lack of interest in his music, Sorabji issued in 1936 a declaration forbidding any performance of his works by anyone anywhere; since this prohibition could not be sustained for works actually publ., there must have been furtive performances of his piano works in England and the U.S. by fearless pianists. Sorabji eventually mitigated his ban, and in 1975 allowed the Ameri-can pianist Michael Habermann to perform some of

his music; in 1976 he also gave his blessing to the English pianist Yonty Solomon, who included Sorabji's works in a London concert on Dec. 7, 1976; on June 16, 1977, Solomon gave in London the first performance of Sorabji's 3rd Piano Sonata. Gradu-ally, Sorabji's music became the cynosure and the lodestone of titanically endowed pianists. Of these, the most Brobdingnagian was the Australian pia-nist Geoffrey Madge, who gave the second complete performance in history of *Opus Clavicembalis-ticum* at the 1982 Holland Festival in Utrecht; he repeated this feat at the first American perfor-mance of the work at the Univ. of Chicago on April 24, 1983; 2 weeks later he played it in Bonn. True to his estrangement from the human multitudes and music officials, Sorabji took refuge far from the madding crowd in a castle he owned in England; a notice at the gate proclaims: Visitors Unwelcome. Yet as he approached his 90th birthday, he received at least 2 American musicians who came to declare their admiration, and allowed them to photocopy some of his MSS.

Sorge, Georg Andreas, erudite German compos-er and theorist; b. Mellenbach, Schwarzburg, March 21, 1703; d. Lobenstein, April 4, 1778. While still a youth, he was appointed court organist at Loben-stein (1721), and he retained this position until his death. In middle life, he wrote numerous works for piano and organ; music historians regard him as a typical "little master" of Bach's time. His reverence for Bach is demonstrated by his 3 keyboard fugues on B.A.C.H. Among his works publ. in his lifetime are *Clavierübung aus 18 Sonatinen in 3 Teilen* (1738); *Clavierübung aus 24 Praeludia durch den ganzen Circulum Modorum* and *Clavier-Toccata per omnem Circulum Modorum* (both works in emulation of Bach's *Well-Tempered Clavier*). His masterwork remains *Vorgemach der musicali-schen Composition* (3 vols., 1745–47), in which he relates his discovery of combinatorial tones before Tartini.

Soriano, Francesco. See **Suriano, Francesco.**

Soro, Enrique, significant Chilean composer; b. Concepción, July 15, 1884; d. Santiago, Dec. 2, 1954. He was a son of the Italian composer **José Soro,** and was educated by him; he played in public as a small child. He was granted a stipend by the government of Chile for study in Italy; entered the Cons. of Mi-lan at 14; graduated in 1904, with a grand prize in composition. Returning to Chile in 1905, he was ap-pointed inspector of musical education in primary schools; in 1906 joined the faculty of the Cons. of Santiago; from 1919 to 1928 he was its director. He traveled as a pianist; gave concerts in Europe and South America; also publ. a number of works. In 1948 he was awarded the Premio Nacional de Arte.

Souris, André, Belgian composer; b. Marchienne-au-Pont, July 10, 1899; d. Paris, Feb. 12, 1970. He studied at the Brussels Cons. (1911–18) with M. Lunssens (harmony), Closson (music history), and privately with Gilson (composition). In 1925 he began teaching at the Royal Cons. in Brussels; in 1927 he won the Prix Rubens, and traveled to Italy, France, and Austria; conducted the Belgian Radio Orch. (1937–46); in 1949–64 he was a prof. of harmony at the Royal Cons. in Brussels. His first works were in the style of Debussy, but in 1925 he pursued a more advanced quasi-atonal technique of composition. He was the founder of the quarterly music review *Polyphonie* (1947–54).

Sousa, John Philip, famous American bandmaster and popular composer; b. Washington, D.C., Nov. 6, 1854; d. Reading, Pa., March 6, 1932. He was the son of a Portuguese father and a Bavarian mother. He studied violin with John Esputa and harmony with G.F. Benkert in Washington (1864–67); also acquired considerable proficiency on wind instruments; played in the Marine Band at the age of 13; led an orch. in a vaudeville theater in Washington before he was 18; in 1877 was engaged as violinist in the special orch. in Philadelphia that was conducted by Offenbach during his American tour. In 1880 Sousa was appointed leader of the Marine Band; he resigned on Aug. 1, 1892, and organized a band of his own, with which he gave successful concerts throughout the U.S. and Canada; played at the Chicago World's Fair in 1893 and at the Paris Exposition in 1900; made 4 European tours (1900, 1901, 1903, and 1905), with increasing acclaim, and finally a tour around the world, in 1910–11. His flair for writing band music was extraordinary; the infectious rhythms of his military marches and the brilliance of his band arrangements earned him the sobriquet "The March King"; particularly celebrated is his march *The Stars and Stripes Forever,* which became famous all over the world. During World War I Sousa served as a lieutenant in the Naval Reserve. He continued his annual tours almost to the time of his death. He compiled for the Navy Dept. *National, Patriotic and Typical Airs of All Lands* (1890); publ. an autobiography, *Marching Along* (Boston, 1928); and wrote 5 novels.
WORKS: His publ. compositions aggregate to several hundred, including the comic operas *The Smugglers* (1879); *Désirée* (1884); *The Queen of Hearts* (1886); *El Capitan* (Boston, April 13, 1896; his most brilliant operetta); *The Charlatan* (1897); *The Bride Elect* (1898); *Chris and the Wonderful Lamp* (1900); *The Free Lance* (1906); *The Glass-Blowers* (1911); *The American Maid* (1913); *Victory* (1915); suites for Orch. and Band: *Last Days of Pompeii; 3 Quotations; Sheridan's Ride; At the King's Court; Looking Upward; Impressions at the Movies;* etc.; a symph. poem, *The Chariot Race* (from *Ben Hur*); many waltzes, songs, etc.; and numerous popular military marches: *The Stars and Stripes Forever, El Capitan, The Washington Post, The High School Cadets, Thunderer, Semper Fidelis, Liberty Hall, Manhattan Beach, King Cotton, Hands Across the Sea* (a selection of 24 marches are reprinted in facsimile from the original sheet music in Lester S. Levy's *Sousa's Great Marches* [N.Y., 1975]; he publ. an instruction book for trumpet and drum, and one

for violin.

Souster, Tim, English composer of the extreme avant-garde; b. Bletchley, Buckinghamshire, Jan. 29, 1943. He studied music theory at New College in Oxford (B.A., 1964; B.Mus., 1965); in 1964 attended courses in new music given by Stockhausen and Berio in Darmstadt. Back in England, he became one of the most articulate exponents of serial, aleatory, and combinatorial ideas, in which electronic media are employed in conjunction with acoustical performances by humans; he expounded these ideas in his writings in the *Listener, Tempo,* and other progressive publications. In 1969 he was a co-founder of the Intermodulation Group, with the aim of presenting works by congenial composers and experimenters; it disbanded in 1976; he formed a new group, OdB. In 1969–71 he was composer-in-residence at King's College in Cambridge.

Souzay, Gérard (real name, **Gérard Marcel Tisserand**), French baritone; b. Angers, Dec. 8, 1918. His principal voice teacher was Pierre Bernac; he also studied with Claire Croiza, Vanni Marcoux, and Lotte Lehmann. He specialized in French art songs and German lieder; before embarking on a stage career he gave recitals; then went to the U.S. He made his American operatic debut with the N.Y. City Opera in 1960; on Jan. 21, 1965, he appeared at the Metropolitan Opera in N.Y. as Count Almaviva in *Le nozze di Figaro;* subsequently led a master class in singing and interpretation at the Mannes College of Music in N.Y.

Sowande, Fela, Nigerian composer; b. Oyo, May 29, 1905. He studied music in Lagos; then went to London, where he played in a combo in nightclubs; at the same time he took courses at London Univ. and the Trinity College of Music. He served in the Royal Air Force during World War II. In 1944 he composed an *African Suite* for Strings; returned to Nigeria in 1953; in 1957 he received a grant from the State Dept. to travel in the U.S.; was again in the U.S. in 1961, on a Rockefeller grant, and on June 1, 1961, conducted a group of members of the New York Phil. in Carnegie Hall in a program of his own compositions, among them *Nigerian Folk Symphony.* Upon returning to Nigeria, he joined the staff of the Univ. College at Ibadan. In his music he pursues the goal of cultural integration of native folk material with Western art forms.

Sowerby, Leo, remarkable American composer and organist; b. Grand Rapids, Mich., May 1, 1895; d. Fort Clinton, Ohio, July 7, 1968. He studied piano with Calvin Lampert and music theory with Arthur Andersen in Chicago; also had sporadic lessons with Percy Grainger. He learned to play the organ without a teacher, and yet developed a virtuoso technique that enabled him to hold prestigious appointments as a church organist. He was extremely precocious; on Jan. 17, 1917, he presented himself in Chicago in a program grandiloquently billed "Leo Sowerby: His Music," which included such ambitious works as a Piano Concerto, with the composer at the keyboard; a Cello Concerto; and symph. pieces. When the U.S. entered the war, Sowerby served in the army; after the Armistice he returned to his career in music. In 1921 he received the American Prix de Rome, the first of its kind to be awarded for composition; he spent 3 years at the American Cons. in Rome. Returning to Chicago, he was appointed prof. of composition at the American Cons. there; he held this post and, concurrently, that of organist at the St. James Cathedral in Chicago, for 37 years, until 1962. He then went to Washington, D.C., where he organized the College for Church Musicians at the National Cathedral. He received numerous awards of merit; in 1946 he won the Pulitzer Prize for his *Canticle of the Sun*. Sowerby never attempted to discover new ways of making music; his style was eclectic in the positive sense of the word, selecting what appeared to be the best in various doctrines and styles. Hindemith's invidious reference to Sowerby as the 4th B in music, a "sour B," is not appropriate, for Sowerby's music is anything but sour; he certainly knew how to build up sonorous masses, particularly in his vocal compositions.

WORKS: FOR ORCH.: Violin Concerto (1913; revised 1924); *The Sorrow of Mydath,* symph. poem (1915); *Rhapsody on British Folk Tunes* (1915); concert overture, *Comes Autumn Time* (Chicago, Jan. 17, 1917); Cello Concerto No. 1, in A major (Chicago, Jan. 17, 1917); Piano Concerto, with Soprano obligato (Chicago, Jan. 17, 1917; revised in 1919, without soprano); *The Irish Washerwoman,* an orch. transcription (Chicago, Jan. 17, 1917); *Money Musk,* transcription (1917); *A Set of 4,* subtitled "Suite of Ironies" (Chicago, Feb. 15, 1918); Concerto for Harp and Small Orch. (1919); 5 symphs.: No. 1 (Chicago, April 7, 1922); No. 2 (Chicago, March 29, 1929); No. 3 (Chicago, March 6, 1941); No. 4 (Boston, Jan. 7, 1949, Koussevitzky conducting); No. 5 (1964); *King Estmere,* ballad for 2 Pianos and Orch. (Rome, April 8, 1923); *Rhapsody* for Chamber Orch. (1922); *From the Northland* (Rome, May 27, 1924); *Synconata* and *Monotony* for Jazz Orch. (1924, 1925; Chicago, Oct. 11, 1925); *Medieval Poem* for Organ and Orch. (Chicago, April 20, 1926); *Prairie,* symph. poem (Interlochen, Mich., Aug. 11, 1929); Cello Concerto No. 2, in E minor (1929–34; N.Y., April 2, 1935); *Passacaglia, Interlude and Fugue* (1931–32); 2nd Piano Concerto (1932; Boston, Nov. 30, 1936); Sinfonietta for String Orch. (1933–34); *Theme in Yellow,* piece after the Sandburg poem (1937); Concerto in C for Organ and Orch. (Boston, April 22, 1938; E. Power Biggs, soloist); *Concert Overture* (1941); *Poem* for Viola, and Orch. or Organ (1941); *Fantasy on Hymn Tunes* (1943); *Classic Concerto* for Organ and String Orch. (1944); *Portrait: Fantasy in Triptych* (1946; Indianapolis, Nov. 21, 1953); *Concert Piece* for Organ and Orch. (1951); *All on a Summer's Day* (1954; Louisville, Ky., Jan. 8, 1955); untitled work (Concerto No. 2) for Organ and Orch. (1967–68).

FOR VOICE: *A Liturgy of Hope* for Soprano, Male Chorus, and Organ (1917); an untitled oratorio in 5 parts based on the Book of Psalms (1924); *The Vision of Sir Launfal,* cantata after James Lowell (1925); *Great Is the Lord* for Chorus, Orch., and Organ (1933); *Forsaken of Man* for Chorus and Organ (1939); *Song for America* for Chorus and Orch. (1942); *The Canticle of the Sun,* after St. Francis, for Chorus and Orch. (1944; N.Y., April 16, 1945; won the 1946 Pulitzer Prize); *Christ Reborn,* cantata for Chorus and Organ (1950; Philadelphia, Nov. 1, 1953); *The Throne of God* for Chorus and Orch. (1956; Washington, D.C., Nov. 18, 1957); *The Ark of the Covenant,* cantata for Chorus and Organ (1959); *Solomon's Garden,* cantata for Tenor, Chorus, and Chamber Orch. (1964); *La Corona* for Chorus and Orch. (1967); numerous anthems, songs, etc.

Spaeth, Sigmund, American writer on music; b. Philadelphia, April 10, 1885; d. New York, Nov. 11, 1965. He studied piano and violin with A. Bachmann; then attended Haverford College (M.A., 1906); received a Ph.D. from Princeton Univ. (1910), with the dissertation *Milton's Knowledge of Music* (publ. 1913). He was music editor of the *N.Y. Evening Mail* (1914–18); education director of the American Piano Co. (1920–27); president of the National Assoc. of American Composers and Conductors (1934–37); lectured widely on music; gave popular talks on the radio; was active in musical journalism; held various posts in educational organizations.

Spalding, Albert, American violinist; b. Chicago, Aug. 15, 1888; d. New York, May 26, 1953. He was taken to Europe as a child and studied violin in Florence and Paris; made his public debut in Paris on June 6, 1905, and his American debut as a soloist with the N.Y. Symph. Orch. on Nov. 8, 1908. Beginning in 1919 he made annual tours of the U.S. and acquired the reputation of a fine artist, even though not necessarily a contagiously flamboyant one. He wrote a number of pieces for the violin; publ. an autobiography, *Rise to Follow* (N.Y., 1943), and a fictionalized biography of Tartini, *A Fiddle, a Sword, and a Lady* (N.Y., 1953).

Spalding, Walter Raymond, American pedagogue; b. Northampton, Mass., May 22, 1865; d. Cambridge, Mass., Feb. 10, 1962. He was a graduate of Harvard Univ. (B.A., 1887; M.A., 1888, with honors in music); taught classics at St. Mark's School in Southborough, Mass., in 1889–92; from 1892 to 1895 studied music in Paris (with Guilmant and Widor) and in Munich (with Rheinberger); was appointed an instructor of music at Harvard in 1895, became an assistant prof. in 1903, and a prof. in 1912; also was a prof. at Radcliffe College. In 1920–21 he lectured at 8 French univs.

WRITINGS: *Tonal Counterpoint* (1940); *Modern Harmony in Its Theory and Practice* (1905; with Arthur Foote); *Music; An Art and a Language* (1920); *Music at Harvard* (1935).

Speaks, Oley, American baritone and song composer; b. Canal Winchester, Ohio, June 28, 1874; d. New York, Aug. 27, 1948. He studied singing with Emma Thursby and composition with Max Spicker and W. Macfarlane; sang at various churches in N.Y. (1898–1906); then devoted himself entirely to concert singing and composition. He wrote some of the most popular songs in the American repertoire: *On the Road to Mandalay, Sylvia, The Prayer Perfect, Morning, Life's Twilight, My Homeland, The Lord Is My Light, To You,* etc.

Spencer, Emile-Alexis-Xavier, French composer; b. Brussels, May 24, 1859; d. Nanterre (Seine), May 24, 1921. He studied piano in Brussels; in 1881 went to Paris, where he found his métier as a composer for vaudeville; he was credited with about 4,000 chansonettes, which were popularized by famous singers, among them Yvette Guilbert. His chanson *Jambes de bois* was used by Stravinsky in *Pétrouchka* under the impression that it was a folk song; when Spencer brought an action for infringement on his authorship, Stravinsky agreed to pay him part of the royalties for performances.

Spendiarov, Alexander, Russian-Armenian composer; b. Kakhovka, Crimea, Nov. 1, 1871; d. Erevan, May 7, 1928. He studied violin as a child; in 1896 went to St. Petersburg and took private lessons with Rimsky-Korsakov. In his works he cultivated a type of Russian orientalism in which the elements of folk songs of the peripheral regions of the old Russian Empire are adroitly arranged in the colorful harmonies of the Russian national school. His best work in this manner was an opera, *Almast,* the composition of which he undertook shortly before his death. It was completed and orchestrated by Maximilian Steinberg, and performed posthumously in Moscow on June 23, 1930. Other works are: *The 3 Palm Trees,* a symph. tableau (1905); *Crimean Sketches* for Orch. (1903–12); *2 Songs of the Crimean Tatars* for Voice and Orch. (1915; Moscow, Dec. 25, 1927); *Etudes d'Eriwan,* on Armenian melodies (1925).

Sperontes (real name, **Johann Sigismund Scholze**), German composer; b. Lobendau, Silesia, March 20, 1705; d. Leipzig, Sept. 27, 1750. Between 1736 and 1745 he brought out a collection of poems and melodies to words by Johann Christian Günther, *Singende Muse an der Pleisse in zweimal 50 Oden;* this became famous, and its success generated many imitations by composers in Leipzig, Hamburg, and Vienna. There is a reprint (ed. by E. Buhle) in Denkmäler Deutscher Tonkunst, 35 and 36.

Spialek, Hans, American arranger and conductor; b. Vienna, April 17, 1894; d. New York, Nov. 20, 1983. He sang in a boys' chorus at the Vienna Opera and took courses at the Vienna Cons. He was drafted into the Austrian army during World War I and taken prisoner by the Russians. In Russia his musical abilities were duly appreciated, and after the Russian Revolution he was given a job at the Bolshoi Theater in Moscow as assistant stage manager (1918–20); later he conducted symph. orchs. in Bessarabia (1920–22). He married a Russian singer, **Dora Boshoer.** In 1923 he went to Germany, and in

1924 reached the U.S. He earned his living as a music copyist, but soon moved several notches higher by arranging for shows; he also supplied orch. interludes and entr'acte music, showing such expertise at organizing the raw materials of American musicals that even before he could master the American tongue he intuitively found the proper instrumentation for the text; and he could work fast to meet the deadlines. Altogether he orchestrated 147 shows, among them 5 by Cole Porter and 11 by Richard Rodgers and Lorenz Hart. With Robert Russell Bennett, he became one of the most reliable arrangers on Broadway. He also composed some orch. works in the approved Broadway style, with such idiosyncratic titles as *The Tall City* and *Manhattan Watercolors.*

Spilka, František, Czech composer; b. Štěken, Nov. 13, 1887; d. Prague, Oct. 20, 1960. He studied at the Prague Cons. with Stecker, Knittl, and Dvořák; in 1918 was appointed administrative director of the Prague Cons. He established the Prague Teachers' Choral Society in 1908, of which he remained choirmaster until 1921, and gave concerts with it in France and England; later directed the Prague singing ensemble Smetana. Spilka developed, together with Ferdinand Vach, a new approach to choral performance, emphasizing sound color.

Spitta, Friedrich, German theologian and writer on music, brother of **Philipp Spitta;** b. Wittingen, Jan. 10, 1852; d. Göttingen, June 8, 1924. From 1887 to 1918 he was a prof. of theology at Strasbourg Univ., and from 1919, at Göttingen; from 1896 he was also editor (with J. Smend) of *Monatschrift für Gottesdienst und kirchliche Kunst,* in which (Jan.–March 1913) he publ. important facts concerning Benedictus Ducis. He publ. *Liturgische Andacht zum Luther-Jubiläum* (1883); *H. Schütz,* festival oration (1886); *Die Passionen nach den vier Evangelisten von H. Schütz* (1886); *Über Chorgesang im evangelischen Gottesdienste* (1886); *"Ein' feste Burg ist unser Gott." Die Lieder Luthers* (1905); *Studien zu Luthers Liedern* (1907); *Das Deutsche Kirchenlied in seinen charakteristischen Erscheinungen* (vol. I: *Mittelalter und Reformationszeit,* 1912); *H. Schütz* (1925); also a new edition of Mergner's *Paul Gerhardt Lieder* (1918).

Spitta, (Johann August) Philipp, eminent German musicologist; b. Wechold, Hannover, Dec. 27, 1841; d. Berlin, April 13, 1894. He was a student of philology at Göttingen; taught at the Ritter und Domschule in Reval in 1864–66, at the Sondershausen Gymnasium till 1874, and for one year at the Nikolai-Gymnasium in Leipzig, where he was co-founder of the Bach-Verein (1874). In 1875 he became a prof. of music history at Berlin Univ., life-secretary to the Royal Academy of Arts, and a teacher at, and vice-director of, the Hochschule für Musik. As a teacher, he had extraordinary success; among his pupils were O. Fleischer, A. Sandberger, M. Freidlaender, R. Schwartz, M. Seiffert, E. Vogel, K. Krebs, and J. Combarieu. He was one of the leading spirits in organizing the publication of Denkmäler Deutscher Tonkunst.

WRITINGS: *J.S. Bach,* a comprehensive biography carefully and learnedly written, with valuable discussions of the principal works (2 vols., 1873, 1880; in Eng., London, 1884–85; condensed ed., Leipzig, 1935; 5th ed., 1962); also a short sketch of Bach in Waldersee's *Vorträge* (1880); a short biography of Schumann for *Grove's Dictionary,* afterward publ. separately in German (*Vorträge,* 1882); *Händel und Bach,* 2 festival orations (1885); *Zur Ausgabe der Kompositionen Friedrichs des Grossen* (1890); 2 collections of articles, *Zur Musik* (1892; 16 essays) and *Musikgeschichtliche Aufsätze* (Berlin, 1894); an essay, *Die Passionsmusiken von Sebastian Bach und Heinrich Schütz* (Hamburg, 1893); many papers in the *Allgemeine Musikalische Zeitung,* the *Monatshefte für Musikgeschichte,* and, more particularly, in his own periodical, the *Vierteljahrsschrift für Musikwissenschaft,* founded in 1884 with Chrysander and G. Adler. Spitta also edited a critical ed. of Buxtehude's organ works (2 vols., 1875, 1876), with valuable historical notes; the complete ed. of Schütz's works (16 vols.); and vol. I of Denkmäler Deutscher Tonkunst (1892; contains Scheidt's *Tabulatura nova* of 1624). He left in MS an almost completed *Geschichte der romantischen Oper in Deutschland.* Spitta's correspondence with Brahms was publ. in *Brahmsgesellschaft* (vol. 15).

Spitzmueller, Alexander, Austrian composer; b. Vienna, Feb. 22, 1894; d. Paris, Nov. 12, 1962. He studied jurisprudence; then took lessons in composition with Alban Berg and Hans Apostel. In 1928 he went to Paris, where he became active in radio broadcasting. His early works are in the neo-Classical vein; eventually he followed the method of composition with 12 tones, following its usage by Berg and Webern.

Spivacke, Harold, eminent American musicologist and librarian; b. New York, July 18, 1904; d. Washington, D.C., May 9, 1977. He studied at N.Y. Univ. (M.A., 1924) and at the Univ. of Berlin, where he received his Dr.Phil. in 1933, magna cum laude, with the dissertation *Über die objektive und subjektive Tonintensität;* while in Berlin he took private lessons with Eugen d'Albert and Hugo Leichtentritt as an American-German Students Exchange Fellow and an Alexander von Humboldt Stiftung Fellow. Returning to the U.S., he joined the staff of the Music Division of the Library of Congress in Washington, D.C., first as assistant chief (1934–37), then as chief, in which capacity he served for 35 years (1937–72). He also held numerous advisory positions with the Dept. of State, UNESCO, etc. As chief of the Music Division of the Library of Congress, he was responsible for the acquisition of many important MSS by contemporary composers, including a large collection of Schoenberg's original MSS. He also commissioned works from contemporary composers for the Coolidge Foundation at the Library of Congress. He publ. some valuable bibliographical papers, among them *Paganiniana* (Washington, 1945). In 1939 he was chairman of the Organizing Committee of the National Music Council, and until 1972 was Archivist and a member of the Executive Committee of the Council.

Spohr, Ludwig (Louis), celebrated German violinist, composer, and conductor; b. Braunschweig, April 5, 1784; d. Kassel, Oct. 22, 1859. The family moved to Seesen in 1786. His father, a physician, was an amateur flute player, and his mother, a singer and pianist. In this musical atmosphere Spohr's talent developed very early; at the age of 5 he began taking lessons on the violin with Rector Riemenschneider and Dufour, a French émigré. Spohr then returned to Braunschweig, where he was taught by the organist Hartung and the violinist Maucourt. He had already composed various violin pieces; the Duke himself became interested in the 15-year-old Spohr, admitted him to the ducal orch., and arranged for his further study with the violinist Franz Eck. In 1802 Eck took Spohr with him on a tour to Russia, where he made the acquaintance of Clementi and John Field; he returned to Braunschweig in 1803 and resumed his post in the ducal orch. In 1804 he made his first official tour (his first actual tour to Hamburg in 1799 proved a failure) as a violinist, giving concerts in Berlin, Leipzig, and Dresden; in 1805 he became concertmaster in the ducal orch. at Gotha; married the harp player **Dorette Scheidler,** and toured with her in Germany in 1807. His reputation as a violin virtuoso was established, and he began to give more attention to composition. He wrote oratorios, operas, violin concertos, symphs., and chamber music, which obtained excellent success in Germany. In 1812 he gave a series of concerts in Vienna, and was acclaimed both as a composer and as a violinist; accepted the position of concertmaster in the orch. of the Theater an der Wien, which he held until 1815. He then made a grand tour of Germany and Italy; played a *concertante* of his own with Paganini in Rome. In 1816 Spohr's opera *Faust* was performed by Weber in Prague. After a visit to the Netherlands in 1817, he received the post of opera conductor in Frankfurt, where he produced one of his most popular operas, *Zemire und Azor* (1819). In 1820 he visited England; appeared with his wife at several concerts of the London Phil. Society; this was the first of his 6 tours of England, where he acquired a lasting reputation as a violinist, conductor, and composer; his works continued to be performed in England for many decades after his death. On his way back to Germany he presented several concerts in Paris in 1820, but his reception there failed to match his London successes. He then proceeded to Dresden, and was recommended by Weber for the post of court Kapellmeister in Kassel, originally offered to Weber. Spohr accepted it, and settled there in 1822. It was in Kassel that he produced his masterpiece, the opera *Jessonda* (1823), which held the stage in Europe throughout the 19th century. He conducted its performances in Leipzig and Berlin; also appeared as conductor and composer at various musical festivals (Düsseldorf, 1826; Nordhausen, 1829; Norwich,

1839; Bonn, 1845; etc.). The success of *Jessonda* was followed by the production in Kassel of his oratorio *Die letzten Dinge* (1826) and his symph. *Die Weihe der Töne* (1832), both of which elicited great praise. His wife died in 1834; he married the pianist **Marianne Pfeiffer** in 1836. Spohr made another journey to England in 1847; visited Frankfurt in 1848. Returning to Kassel, he found himself in an increasingly difficult position because of his outspoken radicalism; the Elector of Hesse refused to grant him further leaves of absence, and Spohr decided to ignore the ban, which resulted in litigation with the Kassel court. In 1853 he made his last tour of England, appearing at the New Phil. Concerts in London. He was retired from Kassel in 1857 on a pension; a few months later he broke his left arm, but despite the accident, at an advanced age, he made another appearance (his last) conducting *Jessonda* in Prague (1858).

Spohr's style was characteristic of the transition period between Classicism and Romanticism. He was a master of technical resources; some of his works demonstrate a spirit of bold experimentation (the *Historical Symph.; Symph.* for 2 Orchs.; Quartet Concerto; Nonet; etc.), yet in his esthetics he was an intransigent conservative. He admired Beethoven's early works but confessed his total inability to understand Beethoven's last period; he also failed to appreciate Weber. It is remarkable, therefore, that he was an early champion of Wagner; in Kassel he brought out *Der fliegende Holländer* (1843) and *Tannhäuser* (1853), despite the strenuous opposition of the court. He was a highly esteemed teacher; among his pupils were Ferdinand David and Moritz Hauptmann. His autobiography was publ. posthumously as *Louis Spohrs Selbstbiographie* (2 vols., Kassel, 1860–61; in Eng., London, 1865 and 1878). The Spohr Society was founded in Kassel in 1908, dissolved in 1934, and revived in 1952.

Spontini, Gaspare (Luigi Pacifico), significant Italian opera composer; b. Majolati, Ancona, Nov. 14, 1774; d. there, Jan. 24, 1851. His father, a modest farmer, intended him for the church and gave him into the charge of an uncle, a priest at Jesi, who attempted to stifle his musical aspirations. Spontini sought refuge at Monte San Vito with another relative, who not only found a competent music teacher for him, but effected a reconciliation so that, after a year, he was able to return to Jesi. In 1793 he entered the Cons. della Pietà de' Turchini in Naples, where his teachers were Tritto (singing) and Sala (composition). He rapidly mastered the conventional Italian style of his time; some of his church music performed in Naples came to the attention of a director of the Teatro della Pallacorda in Rome, who commissioned him to write an opera. This was *I puntigli delle donne,* produced with notable success during Carnival in 1796. In his subsequent opera, *L'eroismo ridicolo* (Naples, 1798), he was helped by Piccinni's practical advice. When the Neapolitan court fled to Palermo before the French invasion, Spontini was engaged as maestro di cappella and wrote 3 operas in quick succession, one for

Naples and 2 for the Palermo court theater in 1800. He left Palermo soon afterward and proceeded to Rome (1801), Venice (1802), and Naples and Paris (1803). In Paris he brought out 2 French operas at the Théâtre-Italien, *La Petite Maison* (May 12, 1804) and *Julie, ou Le Pot de fleurs* (March 12, 1805), in sedulous imitation of the Parisian light opera; but the attempt failed completely. Fortunately for Spontini, he met the poet Etienne de Jouy, a writer of superior accomplishments, who influenced him to change his style. The result was the one-act opera *Milton,* produced at the Théâtre Feydeau on Nov. 27, 1804. Its music showed greater expressiveness and a finer taste than Spontini's preceding works. The next libretto offered by Etienne de Jouy to Spontini (after it was rejected by Boieldieu and Méhul) was *La Vestale.* Spontini worked on the score for 3 years, repeatedly revising and rewriting in his desire to attain his best, and the final product became his masterpiece. In the meantime, the Empress Josephine had appointed him her "compositeur particulier," and her appreciation of Spontini increased after the production of his patriotic cantata *L'Eccelsa gara,* celebrating the victory of Austerlitz. Her powerful patronage secured a hearing for *La Vestale,* which was brought out at the Académie Impériale (Grand Opéra), despite virulent open and secret opposition on the part of influential musicians, on Dec. 15, 1807, and won triumphant success. Not only did the public receive it with acclamation; by a unanimous verdict of the judges, Méhul, Gossec, and Grétry, the prize offered by Napoleon for the best dramatic work was awarded to Spontini. Shortly after the equal success of his grand opera *Fernand Cortez* (Nov. 28, 1809), Spontini married the daughter of Jean-Baptiste Erard, and in 1810 became director of the Italian Opera, in which capacity he staged Mozart's *Don Giovanni* in its original form for the first time in Paris. He was dismissed in 1812, on charges of financial irregularity, but in 1814 Louis XVIII appointed him court composer, Spontini having refused reinstatement as operatic director in favor of Catalani. He now wrote stage pieces in glorification of the Restoration: *Pélage, ou Le Roi et la paix* (Aug. 23, 1814); *Les Dieux rivaux* (June 21, 1816); this was followed by *Olympie* (Paris Opéra, Dec. 22, 1819). He then accepted the appointment, by King Friedrich Wilhelm III, of court composer and general music director at Berlin; made his debut there, in the spring of 1820, with his opera *Fernand Cortez,* fairly electrifying his audiences, although, like *Julie, Milton,* and *La Vestale,* it had been heard before in Berlin. Here Spontini's remarkable ability as a conductor had freest scope; besides repeating his earlier works, he wrote for Berlin the festival play *Lalla Rookh* (1821), remodeled as the opera *Nurmahal, oder Das Rosenfest von Kaschmir* (Berlin, May 27, 1822); *Alcidor* (Berlin, May 23, 1825); and *Agnes von Hohenstaufen* (Berlin, June 12, 1829); none of these, however, found favor in other German cities. In spite of his success, and the King's continued favor, Spontini's position in Berlin gradually grew untenable; he had been placed on an equality with the Intendant of the Royal Theater, and there were frequent misunderstandings and sharp clashes of authority, not mitigated by Spontini's jealousies and dislikes, his overweening self-conceit, and his despotic temper. Partly through intrigue, partly by reason of his own lack of self-control, he narrowly escaped imprisonment for *lèse-majesté,* and was finally driven out of the theater by the hostile demonstrations of the audience. He retired in 1841, retaining his titles and full pay, but with his prestige and popularity greatly impaired. Thereafter he was inactive as a composer. He returned to Paris, but met with hostility from the director of the Opéra there. In 1844 he conducted a performance (prepared by Wagner) of *La Vestale* at Dresden. Finally, shattered in health, he retired to his native place and devoted his time to public charities. He was a knight of the Prussian "Ordre pour le Mérite," a member of the Berlin Akademie (1833) and the French Institut (1839), and received from Halle Univ. the degree of Dr.Phil.; in 1844 the Pope gave him the rank and title of "Conte de Sant' Andrea."

Springer, Max, German writer on music and composer; b. Schwendi, Württemberg, Dec. 19, 1877; d. Vienna, Jan. 20, 1954. He attended the Univ. in Prague, and studied music with Klička. In 1910 he was appointed prof. of Gregorian choral singing and organist in the section for church music of the State Academy at Klosterneuburg, near Vienna, and held this post until his retirement shortly before his death. He publ. *Die Kunst der Choralbegleitung* (1907; Eng. trans., 1908) and manuals on liturgical choral singing; *Graduale Romanum* in modern notation (1930); *Kontrapunkt* (Vienna, 1936). He composed 4 symphs. and a great deal of church music, including 8 masses.

Squarcialupi, Antonio, renowned Italian organist (called "Antonio degli Organi"); b. Florence, March 27, 1416; d. there, July 6, 1480. He was organist in Florence at Orsanmichele from 1431, and then at the church of Santa Maria del Fiore in the same city from 1432, remaining there until his death; he enjoyed the protection of Lorenzo the Magnificent. He was highly esteemed by Dufay (cf. F.X. Haberl, "Dufay," in the *Vierteljahrsschrift für Musikwissenschaft,* 1885; p. 436). Since none of his works has survived, only oblique reports on their excellence can be adduced, but his name was immortalized by the famous "Squarcialupi Codex," a collection of Florentine polyphonic music of the 14th century, preserved in the Biblioteca Medicea-Laurenziana in Florence (Cod. Pal. 87). The collection was edited by Johannes Wolf and publ. in 1955.

Srnka, Jiří, Czech composer; b. Písek, Aug. 19, 1907; d. Prague, Jan. 31, 1982. He took violin lessons at the Prague Cons. under A. Mařák and J. Feld (1922–24); then studied composition there with Otaker Šín (1924–28) and V. Novák (1928–32); had instruction in quarter-tone music with Alois Hába (1927–28, 1934–37). He was an assistant conductor and violinist with J. Ježek's Liberated Theater in Prague (1929–35); then became interested in film music; produced

over 120 film scores. From 1950 to 1953 he taught classes in film music at the Academy of Musical Arts in Prague.

Stade, Frederica. See **Von Stade, Frederica.**

Staden, Johann, German organist and composer; b. Nuremberg, (baptized, July 2) 1581; d. there, of the plague, (buried, Nov. 15) 1634. He served as court organist at Bayreuth (1604), and then at Kulmbach (1605–10); in 1611 he settled in Nuremberg as church organist, first at the Spitalkirche (in 1616), then at S. Lorenz (until 1618), and at St. Sebald (from 1618). He publ. 4 vols. of *Harmoniae sacrae* (1616, 1621, 1628, 1632); 2 vols. of church music (1625-26; the 2nd vol. contains a brief treatise on the basso continuo); 4 vols. of *Haus-Musik* (1623–28; posthumous collected ed., 1648, containing sacred songs with instrumental accompaniment); *Musicalischer Freuden- und Andachtswecker* (1630); *Herzentrost-Musica* (1630); *Geistlicher Musik-Klang* (1633); 3 books of dance pieces (1618, 1625, and a posthumous ed., 1643); etc. Selected works by Staden were edited by E. Schmitz for the Denkmäler der Tonkunst in Bayern and by K. Sannwald for Nagel's *Musik-Archiv* (1936).

Staden, Sigmund Theophilus, German organist and composer, son of **Johann Staden;** b. Kulmbach (baptized, Nov. 6), 1607; d. there (buried, July 30), 1655. As a youth he studied in Augsburg with the organist Jacob Paumann, and later in Berlin with the resident English player on the viola da gamba, Walter Rowe. In 1627 he went to Nuremberg, where he obtained the position of town piper; in 1634 succeeded his father as organist at the St. Lorenz Church. Staden wrote the earliest extant German opera, *Seelewig,* in an Italian manner; it was produced in Nuremberg in 1644. The text, and separately the music, for voices and thoroughbass, was publ. in Harsdörffer's *Frauenzimmer Gesprächspiele* (vol. IV, 1644); reprinted by Eitner in vol. XIII of *Monatshefte für Musik-Geschichte.* R. Schulz-Dornburg arranged the score for a production at Cologne in 1912. Staden edited Hans Leo Hassler's *Kirchengesänge* (1637), adding 11 songs by his father and 5 songs of his own.

Stader, Maria, Hungarian-born Swiss soprano; b. Budapest, Nov. 5, 1911. She studied voice with Keller in Karlsruhe, Durigo in Zürich, Lombardi in Milan, and T. Schnabel in N.Y. After a brief career as an opera singer, she settled in Zürich as a vioce teacher; also gave periodic master classes in the U.S. She publ. an instructive manual, *Wie Meister Üben* (Zürich, 1967; in Eng., *Learning with the Masters,* 1968).

Stadler, Anton, famous Austrian clarinet player; b. Bruck an der Leitha, June 28, 1753; d. Vienna, June 15, 1812. He is remembered chiefly for his friendship with Mozart; his name is attached to Mozart's so-called Stadler Quintet (K. 581); he was also helpful to Mozart in the composition of the Clarinet Concerto (K. 622). Stadler himself was a competent composer for clarinet and for the basset horn, on which he was a virtuoso. His brother, **Johann Stadler** (b. Vienna, May 6, 1775; d. there, May 2, 1804), was also a proficient clarinet player.

Stadler, Maximilian, Austrian organist and composer; b. Melk, Aug. 4, 1748; d. Vienna, Nov. 8, 1833. He was ordained a priest in the Benedictine Order in 1772; was abbot at Lilienfeld (1786–89), then at Kremsmünster (1789–91); was consistorial adviser to the bishop of Linz in 1791–96; settled in Vienna in 1796. He was a friend of Mozart, and took care of Mozart's MS of the Requiem, which he copied at Mozart's death. When the authenticity of the work was called into question by Gottfried Weber and others, Stadler publ. a pamphlet in its defense, *Verteidigung der Echtheit des Mozartschen Requiems* (Vienna, 1825; supplement, 1826). He was also a composer; publ. a cantata, *Die Frühlingsfeier;* much church music; sonatas for organ; songs. His oratorio *Die Befreiung von Jerusalem* (Vienna, 1811) enjoyed considerable success.

Stainer, Jakob, Austrian manufacturer of violins; b. Absam, July 14, 1621; d. there, 1683. The son of poor peasants, he was a shepherd boy; as a youth he began making "Schwegelpfeifen" and other woodwind instruments; then was apprenticed to a lute maker in Innsbruck. He sold his instruments in his native Tyrol, but soon attracted the attention of the Vienna court, and from 1648 was in the service of Archduke Ferdinand Carl. In 1658 he was given the title of violin maker to the court. His fortunes suffered an adverse turn when, in 1669, he was accused of Lutheran leanings, and spent several months in prison; his mind became unbalanced and he died insane. His brother, **Markus Stainer,** made excellent violins and violas. The Stainer violins are highly prized, and differed greatly from Italian models (the oft-repeated assertions that Jakob Stainer worked in Italian shops are not substantiated); their shape created flute-like tones of great subtlety.

Stainer, Sir John, English organist and composer; b. London, June 6, 1840; d. Verona, March 31, 1901. He was a chorister at St. Paul's Cathedral in London (1847–56); played organ there and in other churches as a youth; studied theory with Charles Steggall; filled various positions as a church organist and teacher, and in 1872 was appointed organist of St. Paul's; failing eyesight compelled him to resign in 1888, in which year he was knighted. In 1889 he became a prof. at Oxford Univ., retaining this position until his death.

Stamaty, Camille-Marie, pianist; b. Rome, March 23, 1811; d. Paris, April 19, 1870. He was of Greek-French origin; his mother, a Frenchwoman, educated him after the death of his father in 1818, and took him to Paris, where he became a pupil of Kalkbrenner; in 1836 he went to Leipzig, where he studied with Mendelssohn. He returned to Paris the next

year and remained there as a teacher; among his students were Saint-Saëns and Gottschalk. He publ. a number of didactic works: *Le Rhythme des doigts, Etudes progressives; Etudes concertantes; Esquisse; Etudes pittoresques; 6 études caractéristiques sur Obéron;* and 12 transcriptions entitled *Souvenir du Conservatoire;* also publ. 3 piano sonatas, a Piano Trio, a Piano Concerto, etc.

Stamitz, Anton (Thadäus Johann Nepomuk), Bohemian composer, son of **Johann Wenzel Anton Stamitz;** b. Deutsch-Brod (baptized, Nov. 27), 1750; place and date of death unknown to any degree of certainty, but probably in Paris, after Oct. 27, 1796. He was a member of the famous musical family of Bohemia; studied violin with his father; with his brother **Carl Stamitz** he went to Strasbourg, and from there to Paris c.1770; made his appearance in Paris playing with his brother at a Concert Spirituel (March 25, 1772). From 1782 to 1789 he was a member of the Royal Chapel Orch. in Versailles. Rodolphe Kreutzer was one of his pupils. He was exceptionally equipped as a composer of instrumental works; he wrote 15 symphs.; 54 quartets, trios, and duets for strings; at least 15 violin concertos; several viola concertos; and 5 piano concertos.

Stamitz, Carl (Philipp), Bohemian violinist and composer, son and pupil of **Johann Wenzel Anton Stamitz;** b. Mannheim (baptized, May 8), 1745; d. Jena, Nov. 9, 1801. He was trained by his father, and after his death received further instruction with Christian Cannabich, Ignaz Holzbauer, and Franz X. Richter. In 1762 he was engaged as violinist in the Electoral Orch. at Mannheim; in 1770, in company with his brother **Anton Stamitz,** he went to Strasbourg, and then to Paris; the brothers made their debut at the Concert Spirituel on March 25, 1772; as soon as Carl arrived in Paris he became concertmaster to the Duc de Noailles; at various times he played in Germany and Austria, and visited Russia. In 1794 he became Kapellmeister at Jena. He left an extraordinary number of works, but a large part of his MSS was lost after his death. The putative number of his symphs. is at least 80, among them 26 *Symphonies concertantes;* he also wrote some 50 concertos for various instruments, and chamber music. Hugo Riemann edited 2 symphs. in Denkmäler der Tonkunst in Bayern, 15 (8.ii), and chamber music in vols. 27 and 28 (15 and 16) of the same series; chamber music was edited by Altmann, C. Meyer, and Klengel; a "symphonie concertante," by K. Geiringer (Vienna, 1935); the Viola Concerto was edited by S. Beck (N.Y. Public Library, 1937).

Stamitz, Johann Wenzel Anton, Bohemian violinist and one of the creators of the modern style of instrumental music; b. Deutsch-Brod, June 19, 1717; d. Mannheim, March 27, 1757. He went to a Jesuit school in Iglau (1728–34); in 1741 he entered the service of the Margrave of Pfalz, Carl Philipp, and later of his successor, Carl Theodor (from 1743). His playing at the coronation of the Emperor Charles VII on Feb. 12, 1742, created a sensation, and Prince

Carl Theodor, who in 1743 became Elector Palatine, engaged him as a chamber musician; the court journals reported on his virtuosity in extravagant terms, extolling his ability to perform his own concerto on several different instruments—violin, viola d'amore, violoncello, and contra-violon solo. In 1743 the Elector made him "first court violinist" in Mannheim; the next year he married Maria Antonia Lüneborn. So widespread was his fame that Baron Grimm publ. in Paris a satirical pamphlet, *Le Petit Prophète de Boehmisch-Broda,* ridiculing Stamitz's innovations. Stamitz made his mark in Paris, too, when La Poupelinière engaged him in 1754 as leader and composer for his Orch. de Passy. He appeared at the Concerts Spirituels, in which he produced a symph. with clarinets in the score, a bold innovation at the time. His musical reforms reached in several directions; he conducted the Mannheim Orch., making it the finest in Europe, principally because of the introduction of dynamic nuances, in contrast with the prevailing chiaroscuro of the time; Mozart admired its playing. He had numerous pupils who achieved fame, among them his own sons **Carl** and **Anton,** Cannabich, W. Cramer, and I. Fränzl. As an instrumental composer, he virtually created the Classical sonata form through the introduction of the contrasting elements into a single movement, represented in Classical music by the primary and secondary subjects, and with variety governing the development of the themes. This new type of thematic statement and development became the foundation of musical composition after Bach's time, cultivated by Stamitz's pupils, as well as others, among them Johann Christian Bach, Schobert, Boccherini, Dittersdorf, Eichner, and Gossec. His music was publ. in Paris, London, and Amsterdam during his lifetime. His works include 74 symphs.; violin concertos; sonatas for violin solo and for violin, with basso continuo. Of his works, 58 symphs., 10 orch. trios, and 17 violin concertos are extant. A selection from his symphs. was publ. by Hugo Riemann in Denkmäler der Tonkunst in Bayern (with an important introduction); in the same series there are found examples of Stamitz's chamber music. Two symphs. were edited by R. Sondheimer (Berlin, 1933); a symph. edited by II.T. David was publ. by the N.Y. Public Library (1937); 6 duos for Violin and Cello were brought out by W. Altmann and others.

Stanford, Sir Charles Villiers, eminent composer and pedagogue; b. Dublin, Sept. 30, 1852; d. London, March 29, 1924. Brought up in an intellectual atmosphere, he was a diligent student in his early youth; took organ lessons in Dublin with Robert Stewart; in 1862 was sent to London, where he studied piano with Ernst Pauer. In 1870 he entered Queen's College, Cambridge, as an organ student; in 1873 became organist at Trinity College there (resigned, 1892). For 2 years (1875–76) he studied composition with Reinecke in Leipzig, and in 1877 with Kiel in Berlin. He received his M.A. degree at Cambridge in 1877; honorary degrees of Mus.Doc. at Oxford (1883) and at Cambridge (1888). In 1883 he was appointed

prof. of composition at the Royal College of Music and conductor of the orch. there; in 1887 he also became a prof. of music at Cambridge, holding both positions until his death; he was conductor of the Leeds Festivals from 1901 to 1910, and appeared as guest conductor of his own works in Paris, Berlin, Amsterdam, Brussels, etc.; was knighted in 1902. He was an extremely able and industrious composer in a distinctly Romantic style, yet unmistakably national in musical materials, both Irish and English. His music, however, remains virtually unknown outside Great Britain.

Stanley, John, English organist and composer; b. London, Jan. 17, 1712; d. there, May 19, 1786. Blind from early childhood, he studied organ with Maurice Greene, and soon was able to fill church positions; composed theater music, and publ. a number of instrumental works. In 1779 he succeeded Boyce as Master of the King's Band of Music. He enjoyed the friendship and esteem of Handel, after whose death he conducted performances of Handel's oratorios with J.C. Smith.
WORKS: Oratorios: *Jephtha* (c.1751–52); *Zimri* (Covent Garden, March 12, 1760); *The Fall of Egypt* (Drury Lane, March 23, 1774); dramatic pastoral, *Arcadia* (for George III's wedding; London, Oct. 26, 1761); opera, *Teraminta;* incidental music; songs; etc.; also 8 solos for Flute, Violin, or Harpsichord; 6 concertos for Strings; 30 voluntaries for Organ; etc.

Starer, Robert, American composer; b. Vienna, Jan. 8, 1924. He studied music in Vienna; after the Anschluss in 1938, went to Jerusalem and studied at the Palestine Cons. there (1938–43). After the war he emigrated to the U.S.; took courses at the Juilliard School of Music in N.Y. (1947–49), and in 1949 became a member of its staff; also taught at the N.Y. College of Music (1959–60) and the Jewish Theological Seminary (1962–63); in 1963 he was appointed prof. of music at Brooklyn College.
WORKS: Operas: *The Intruder* (N.Y., Dec. 4, 1956); *Pantagleize* (N.Y., April 7, 1973); *The Last Lover* (Caramoor Festival, Katonah, N.Y., Aug. 2, 1975); *Apollonia* (1979); ballets: *The Dybbuk* (Berlin, 1960); *Samson Agonistes* (N.Y., 1961); *Phaedra* (N.Y., 1962); *The Lady of the House of Sleep* (N.Y., 1968); *Holy Jungle,* ballet for Martha Graham (N.Y., April 2, 1974); 3 symphs. (1950, 1951, 1969); 3 piano concertos (1947, 1953, 1972); *Concerto à tre* for Piano, Trumpet, Trombone, and Strings (1954); Concerto for Viola, Strings, and Percussion (Geneva, July 3, 1959); Concerto for Violin, Cello, and Orch. (Pittsburgh, Oct. 11, 1968); Violin Concerto (Boston, Oct. 16, 1981); String Quartet (1947); 5 *Miniatures* for Woodwinds (1948); Trio for Clarinet, Cello, and Piano (1964); *Variants* for Violin and Piano (1963); *Profiles in Brass* for Brass Quartet (N.Y., May 20, 1974); 2 piano sonatas (1949, 1965); *Sketches in Color* for Piano (1963); *Fantasia concertante* for Piano, 4-hands (1959); *Evanescents* for Piano (1975); several cantatas on biblical subjects; songs. For a list of works see *Composers of the Americas,* vol. 18 (Washington, D.C., 1972).

Stark, Robert, eminent German clarinetist; b. Klingenthal, Sept. 19, 1847; d. Würzburg, Oct. 29, 1922. He studied at the Dresden Cons.; began his career as an orch. player at Chemnitz; from 1873 to 1881 played the clarinet in Wiesbaden; then was a prof. at the Hochschule für Musik in Würzburg. He publ. valuable and practical pieces for his instrument: 3 concertos; *Romanze* for Clarinet and Orch.; also a *Ballade* for Trombone and Orch.; *Quintett concertante* for Flute, Oboe, Clarinet, Horn, and Bassoon; *Serenade* for Oboe and Piano; instructive works: *Die Kunst der Transposition auf der Klarinette, Grosse theoretisch-praktische Klarinett-Schule,* in 2 parts, followed by part III, *Die hohe Schule des Klarinett-Spieles* (24 virtuoso studies).

Starker, Janos, renowned Hungarian-American cellist and pedagogue; b. Budapest, July 5, 1924. He studied cello with Adolf Cziffer at the Budapest Academy of Music; began playing in public when he was 11 years old. After graduating, he served as first cellist of the Budapest Opera (1945–46), but decided to leave Hungary; he emigrated to the U.S. in 1948; then held the positions of first cellist in the Dallas Symph. Orch. (1948–49), the Metropolitan Opera Orch. (1949–53), and the Chicago Symph. Orch. (1953–58); subsequently he embarked upon a solo career. In 1958 he was appointed a prof. of music at the Indiana Univ. School of Music in Bloomington. As a soloist, he achieved renown in authentic performances of Bach's unaccompanied-cello suites; but he also devoted much attention to modern music; he promoted cello works of Kodály and gave first performances of cello compositions by Messiaen, Peter Mennin, Miklós Rozsa, and others. He publ. a book, *An Organized Method of String Playing.*

Starr, "Ringo" (real name, **Richard Starkey**), English drummer, member of the celebrated Liverpudlian vocal quartet The Beatles; b. Liverpool, July 7, 1940 (delivered by forceps on account of his enormous puerperal bulk). His nickname, "Ringo," originated from his ostentatious habit of wearing several rings on each of his fingers. As an adolescent he performed menial jobs as a messenger boy for British railways, a barman on a boat, etc. A sickly boy, he spent several years in hospitals to cure an effusion on the lung, but he played drums in ward bands. He spontaneously evolved a rhythmic technique of an overwhelming animal vitality. In 1962 Ringo Starr joined The Beatles; his association with them continued until the dissolution of the group in 1970. His histrionic ability in handling the drums became the most striking visual feature in the beatlophonic ritual, contributing much to the mass frenzy that attended their shows wherever The Beatles went.

Stasny, Ludwig, popular Bohemian bandmaster; b. Prague, Feb. 26, 1823; d. Frankfurt, Oct. 30, 1883. He studied at the Prague Cons.; was bandmaster in the Austrian army; settled in Frankfurt in 1871. He produced 2 operas in Mainz: *Liane* (1851) and *Die beiden Grenadiere* (1879). He was noted for his popular dances (211 opus numbers) and for his potpourris from Wagner's music dramas.

Stasov, Vladimir, famous Russian writer on music; b. St. Petersburg, Jan. 14, 1824; d. there, Oct. 23, 1906. He attended a law school until 1843; in 1845 he became connected with the St. Petersburg Public Library; in 1872 was appointed director of the Dept. of Fine Arts, which post he held until his death. He played a very important role in the emergence of the Russian national school, and was to the end of his days an ardent promoter of Russian music. It was Stasov who first launched the expression "Moguchaya Kuchka" ("mighty little company," in an article publ. on May 24, 1867, in a St. Petersburg newspaper); although he did not specifically name the so-called "Five" (Balakirev, Borodin, Cui, Mussorgsky, and Rimsky-Korsakov), these composers became identified with the cause championed by Stasov. When young Glazunov appeared on the scene, Stasov declared him a natural heir to the Five. His numerous writings, including biographies of Glinka, Mussorgsky, and others, have the value of authenticity. Those publ. between 1847 and 1886 were reissued in book form in honor of his 70th birthday (3 vols., St. Petersburg, 1894); a 4th vol. was brought out in 1905, containing essays written between 1886 and 1904; among them, "Russian Music during the Last 25 Years" and "Art in the 19th Century" are particularly important. His collected works, including articles on art and other subjects, were publ. in Moscow in 1952. Some of his *Selected Essays on Music* were publ. in English (London, 1968).

Steber, Eleanor, eminent American soprano; b. Wheeling, W.Va., July 17, 1916. She studied singing with her mother; then with William Whitney at the New England Cons. of Music in Boston and with Paul Althouse in N.Y. She won the Metropolitan Opera Auditions of the Air in 1940; made her debut with the Metropolitan Opera as Sophie in *Der Rosenkavalier* on Dec. 7, 1940, and remained with the company until 1962; altogether she appeared 286 times in N.Y. and 118 times on tour; she sang 28 leading roles in the extremely large repertoire. She performed brilliantly in the roles of Donna Anna in *Don Giovanni,* Pamina in *Die Zauberflöte,* and the Countess in *Le nozze di Figaro,* as well as in other Mozart operas; her other roles were Violetta, Desdemona, Marguerite, Manon, Mimi, and Tosca; in Wagner's operas she sang Eva in *Die Meistersinger* and Elsa in *Lohengrin;* she also performed the challenging part of Marie in Alban Berg's opera *Wozzeck.* She sang the title role in the premiere of Samuel Barber's opera *Vanessa* on Jan. 15, 1958. After several years of absence from the Metropolitan Opera, she took part in the final gala performance in the old opera building on April 16, 1966. Her European engagements included appearances at Edinburgh (1947), Vienna (1953), and the Bayreuth Festival (1953). After partial retirement in 1962, she was head of the voice dept. at the Cleveland Inst. of

Music (1963–72); from 1971 she taught at the Juilliard School of Music in N.Y. She established the Eleanor Steber Music Foundation in 1975 to assist young professional singers.

Stefan, Paul (full name, **Paul Stefan Grünfeldt**), Czech writer on music; b. Brno, Nov. 25, 1879; d. New York, Nov. 12, 1943. He was educated at the Univ. of Vienna, where he studied music theory with Hermann Grädener. He was employed as a municipal functionary, and at the same time became associated with the modern group of musicians in Vienna; edited the progressive music periodical *Musikblätter des Anbruch,* and was a co-founder of the International Society for Contemporary Music in 1922. After the Anschluss he went to Switzerland, and later to Lisbon, eventually emigrating to the U.S. in 1941.

Steffan, Joseph Anton, Austrian composer; b. Kopidlno, Bohemia, March 14, 1726; d. Vienna, April 12, 1797. A pupil of Wagenseil, he settled in Vienna, where he was a renowned teacher; among his pupils were the princesses Marie Antoinette (later Queen of France) and Caroline (later Queen of Naples). He wrote some church music and numerous works for piano (divertimentos, concertos, and sonatas). Steffan is historically important for his songs, *Sammlung deutscher Lieder* (4 books), which are among the best of that time. Specimens were publ. by M. Friedlaender in *Das deutsche Lied im 18. Jahrhundert* (1902); see also Denkmäler der Tonkunst in Österreich, 79 (42.ii).

Steffani, Abbate Agostino, Italian composer; b. Castelfranco Veneto, July 25, 1654; d. Frankfurt, Feb. 12, 1728. He began his musical career as a choirboy at Padua, where his beautiful soprano voice so charmed Count Tattenbach that the latter obtained permission to take him to the Electoral Court at Munich, where he was trained by Kerll in 1668–71; in 1672–74 he studied at Rome with E. Bernabei at the Elector's expense, and in 1674 was appointed court organist at Munich. In 1678–79 he visited Paris, where he made an advantageous study of Lully's music. He took Holy Orders in 1680 and was made titular Abbot of Lepsing in 1682. In 1681 he became director of the Elector's chamber music (together with G.A. Bernabei, his former teacher's son); in 1688 he became court Kapellmeister at Hannover. His services as a diplomat were also in demand; in 1696 he brought to a triumphant conclusion the delicate negotiations for the creation of a 9th Elector of Braunschweig, and was rewarded by an appointment as Bishop of Spiga (*in partibus*); from 1698 he was privy councillor and papal protonotary at Düsseldorf, though still holding his position as Kapellmeister at Hannover until 1711, when he joyfully relinquished it to Handel. Some works of the later epoch were produced under the name of his copyist, **Gregorio Piva.**

Stegmayer, Ferdinand, Austrian conductor and composer; b. Vienna, Aug. 25, 1803; d. there, May 6, 1863. He was the son of **Matthaeus Stegmayer;** studied music with Seyfried; was chorus master at Linz and Vienna; then conductor of a German opera troupe in Paris (1829–30). After filling various engagements as a theater conductor in Leipzig, Bremen, and Prague, he settled in Vienna in 1848; was a teacher of singing at the Vienna Cons.; co-founded, with August Schmidt, the Vienna Singakademie (1858). He wrote church music, piano pieces, and songs.

Stegmayer, Matthaeus, Austrian singer and composer; b. Vienna, April 29, 1771; d. there, May 10, 1820. He was a chorister in the Dominican church in Vienna; then sang in small provincial theatrical companies, returning to Vienna in 1793; made his debut as a singer at Schikaneder's Freihaustheater auf der Wieden in 1796; in 1804 became chorus master at the new Theater an der Wien. He was the first to use the term "quodlibet" for theatrical light pieces; arranged Mozart's *Schauspieldirektor* (1814); composed an operetta, *Der Salzburger Hans und sein Sohn, der Hansl* (Vienna, Nov. 14, 1800), and contributed separate numbers to many others (mainly with Ignaz von Seyfried). He wrote the text for the quodlibet *Rochus Pumpernickel,* produced at the Theater an der Wien on Jan. 28, 1809, with music assembled by Seyfried from various works, including pieces by Haydn and Mozart. It was so successful that he followed it with a sequel, *Die Familie Pumpernickel* (Feb. 13, 1810). A complete list of his works as composer, joint composer, and librettist is found in Anton Bauer, *Opern und Operetten in Wien* (Vienna, 1955).

Stehle, Adelina, outstanding Austrian soprano; b. Graz, 1860; d. Milan, Dec. 24, 1945. She studied in Milan; made her debut in Broni in 1881 as Amina; then sang in Bologna, Florence, and Venice; in 1890 she joined La Scala in Milan, where she created soprano roles in *Falstaff* as Nanetta, in *Guglielmo Ratcliff* as Maria, and others; also sang in Berlin, Vienna, St. Petersburg, South America, and the U.S. After her marriage to the Italian tenor **Edoardo Garbin,** she appeared under the name of **Stehle Garbin.**

Steibelt, Daniel, renowned German pianist and composer; b. Berlin, Oct. 22, 1765; d. St. Petersburg, Oct. 2, 1823. He studied with Kirnberger (piano and theory); publ. sonatas for Piano and Violin, as opp. 1 and 2 (Munich, 1788); then gave concerts in Germany, proceeding to Paris in 1790. There he found himself in strong competition with Ignaz Pleyel, but won out, and became a favorite piano teacher in Paris. His opera *Roméo et Juliette* was produced at the Théâtre Feydeau on Sept. 10, 1793, and, despite the revolutionary turmoil of the time, achieved excellent success. He left Paris in 1796, going to the Netherlands and then to London; became a soloist at Salomon's Concerts; played the solo part of his 3rd Piano Concerto (March 19, 1798), with its rousing finale *L'Orage, précédé d'un rondeau pastoral,* which as a piano solo became as popular as Koczwara's *Battle of Prague.* In London he produced an opera, *Albert and Adelaide* (Covent Garden, Dec. 11, 1798); returned to Germany in 1799; then proceeded to Vienna, where he challenged Beethoven to a contest of skill, but was easily bested. His next destination was Paris, where he produced Haydn's *Creation* (Dec. 24, 1800), with an orch. of 156 players, in an arrangement by Steibelt himself; Napoleon was present at that performance. A ballet by Steibelt, *Le Retour de Zéphire,* was produced at the Paris Opéra on March 3, 1802; he then went to London, where he staged 2 ballets, *Le Jugement du berger Paris* (May 24, 1804) and *La Belle Laitère* (Jan. 26, 1805). Returning once more to Paris, he wrote a festive intermezzo, *La Fête de Mars,* to celebrate Napoleon's victory at Austerlitz; it was produced at the Opéra on March 4, 1806. In the autumn of 1808 he gave concerts in Frankfurt and Dresden; in the spring of 1809 he went to Russia by way of Warsaw, Vilna, and Riga. In St. Petersburg he produced a new opera, *Cendrillon,* to a French libretto (Oct. 26, 1810), and 2 ballets. Although he held the position of chapel master at the court of Czar Alexander I, he did not prosper, and at his death a public subscription was undertaken to help his family. He publ. 5 piano concertos, 37 sonatas with Violin, 29 sonatas and sonatinas for Piano Solo, 15 rondos, 18 fantasias, etc. His *Méthode de Piano* had considerable vogue.

Stein, Erwin, Austrian conductor and editor; b. Vienna, Nov. 7, 1885; d. London, July 19, 1958. He studied composition with Schoenberg in Vienna (1905–10) and became Schoenberg's early champion. From 1910 to 1914 he conducted various theater orchs. in Austria and Germany; returning to Vienna, he was a member, with Schoenberg, Berg, and Anton von Webern, of the famous Society for Musical Private Performances, which excluded music critics from attendance (1920–23). He then became an editor for Univeral Edition in Vienna, where he was instrumental in bringing out works by the composers of the modern Vienna School. He also conducted a tour with a Vienna group named Pierrot Lunaire Ensemble. After the Anschluss in 1938 he went to London and joined the music publishing firm of Boosey & Hawkes. He contributed a fundamental paper on Schoenberg's method of composition with 12 tones, "Neue Formprinzipien," publ. in *Anbruch* (1924). He publ. a selective collection of Schoenberg's letters (Mainz, 1958; in Eng., London, 1964); a collection of essays, *Orpheus in New Guises* (London, 1953); his theoretical monograph *Musik, Form und Darstellung* was publ. posthumously, first in Eng. as *Form and Performance* (London, 1962) and later in German (Munich, 1964).

Stein, Fritz, eminent German musicologist; b. Gerlachsheim, Baden, Dec. 17, 1879; d. Berlin, Nov. 14, 1961. He studied theology in Karlsruhe, then took courses in musicology with P. Wolfrum in Heidelberg; subsequently went to Leipzig, where he studied organ with Straube; also attended Riemann's lectures at the Univ. of Leipzig; obtained his Dr.Phil. from the Univ. of Heidelberg in 1910 with the dissertation *Zur Geschichte der Musik in Heidelberg* (publ. 1912; new ed., 1921, as *Geschichte des Musikwesens in Heidelberg bis zum Ende des 18. Jahrhunderts*). In 1913 he was appointed prof. of musicology at the Univ. of Jena; was in the German army during World War I and directed a male chorus for the troops at the front. He became a reader in musicology at Kiel Univ. in 1920, then a prof. from 1928–33; in 1933 he became director of the Hochschule für Musik in Berlin, holding this position to the end of the war in 1945. He achieved notoriety when he discovered in the library of the Univ. of Jena the parts of a symph. marked by an unknown copyist as a work by Beethoven. The symph. became famous as the "Jena Symphony" and was hailed by many as a genuine discovery; the score was publ. by Breitkopf & Härtel in 1911, and performances followed all over the world; Stein publ. his own exegesis of it as "Eine unbekannte Jugendsymphonie Beethovens?" in the *Sammelbände der Internationalen Musik-Gesellschaft* (1911). Doubts of its authenticity were raised, but it was not until 1957 that the American musicologist H.C. Robbins Landon succeeded in locating the original MS, proving that the "Jena Symphony" was in reality the work of Friedrich Witt (1770–1837). Stein publ. a monograph on Max Reger (Potsdam, 1939) and *Max Reger: Sein Leben in Bildern* (a pictorial biography; Leipzig, 1941; 2nd ed., 1956); brought out a thematic catalogue of Reger's works (Leipzig, 1934; definitive ed., 1953); edited works by Johann Christian Bach, Telemann, Handel, Beethoven, etc.; contributed essays to numerous learned publications. A Festschrift was publ. in his honor on his 60th birthday (1939).

Stein, Horst, German conductor; b. Elberfeld, May 2, 1928. He studied at the Hochschule für Musik in Cologne, and at age 23 was engaged as a conductor at the Hamburg State Opera (1951–55); then was on the staff of the State Opera in Berlin (1955–61) and again at the Hamburg Opera (1961–63). From 1963 to 1970 he was music director and conductor at the National Theater in Mannheim; from 1972 to 1977 he was music director at the Hamburg State Opera; concurrently was Generalmusikdirektor of the Hamburg Phil. (1973–76). He also conducted at the Bayreuth Festival, and appeared as a guest conductor at the major European opera houses, in South America, and in the U.S.; in 1978 became chief conductor of the Orch. de la Suisse Romande in Geneva. He is regarded as one of the most efficient and competent opera conductors of his generation.

Stein, Johann Andreas, German inventor of the "German" (Viennese) piano action; b. Heidelsheim, Palatinate, May 6, 1728; d. Augsburg, Feb. 29, 1792. He was trained in the Strasbourg workshop of J.A. Silbermann (1748–49). In 1750 he settled in Augsburg, where he built the organ of the Barfüsserkirche; was appointed organist there in 1757. He spent a few months in Paris in 1758 before returning to Augsburg. He experimented with various types of keyboard instruments; invented a "polytoni-clavi-chordium" (1769), a "melodika" (1772), a "vis-à-vis Flügel" (1777), and a "Saitenharmonika" (1789). The business was carried on by his son, **Andreas Stein**, and his daughter, **Nanette Stein Streicher** (wife of the Austrian piano maker J.A. Streicher), who moved it to Vienna in 1802.

Stein, Leonard, eminent American music scholar; b. Los Angeles, Dec. 1, 1916. He attended Los Angeles City College (1933–36) and studied piano privately with Richard Buhlig (1936–39); enrolled in the class of composition and musical analysis with Arnold Schoenberg at the Univ. of Southern Calif. (1935–36) and at the Univ. of Calif. at Los Angeles (1936–42); in 1939–42 was Schoenberg's teaching assistant; received the degrees of B.A. (1939) and M.M. (1941) from the Univ. of Calif. at Los Angeles, and his D.M.A. from the Univ. of Southern Calif. (1965); was the recipient of a Guggenheim fellowship (1965–66). He held several teaching positions: at Occidental College (1946–48); Los Angeles City College (1948–60); Pomona College (1961–62); Univ. of Calif. at Los Angeles (1962–64); Claremont Graduate School (1963–67); Univ. of Calif. at San Diego (1966); Calif. State College at Dominguez Hills (1967–70); in 1970 was appointed member of the music faculty of the Calif. Inst. of the Arts; in 1975 became adjunct prof. in the School of Music at the Univ. of Southern Calif. In 1975 he was elected director of the Arnold Schoenberg Inst. of the Univ. of Southern Calif., Los Angeles, and editorial director of the *Journal of the Arnold Schoenberg Institute,* I/1 (Oct. 1976). He contributed a number of articles on the proper performance of piano works by Schoenberg; was a member of the editorial board of *Sämtliche Werke* (Mainz and Vienna, vol. 1, 1966); edited Schoenberg's *Nachtwandler* (1969); Piano Concerto (1972); *Ode to Napoleon Bonaparte* (1973); *Brettl-Lieder* (1974); edited and completed Schoenberg's pedagogical works: *Preliminary Exercises in Counterpoint* (1963); *Models for Beginners in Composition* (revision of the text, 1972); *Structural Functions of Harmony* (revision, 1969); *Style and Idea. Selected Writings of Arnold Schoenberg* (London, 1975; received the 1976 ASCAP award).

Stein, Richard Heinrich, German music theorist and composer; b. Halle, Feb. 28, 1882; d. Santa Brigida, Canary Islands, Aug. 11, 1942. He studied law and music; received his Dr.Phil. from the Univ. of Erlangen in 1911 with the thesis *Die psychologischen Grundlagen der Wundtschen Ethik.* From 1914 to 1919 he lived in Spain; from 1920 to 1932 taught musical subjects in Berlin. In 1933 he left Germany and went to the Canary Islands, where he remained until his death. He was a composer of experimental tendencies; his *2 Konzertstücke* for Cello and Piano, op. 26 (1906), was the first composition containing quarter-tones to be publ. In 1909 he wrote a brochure giving a detailed exposition of his quarter-tone system, and in 1914 he built a quarter-tone clarinet. He composed about 100 piano pieces

and about 50 songs; *Scherzo fantastico* for Orch.; publ. the books *La música moderna* (Barcelona, 1918; in Spanish and German), *Grieg* (1921), and *Tschaikowsky* (1927).

Steinbach, Fritz, German conductor; b. Grünsfeld, June 17, 1855; d. Munich, Aug. 13, 1916. He studied in Leipzig, Vienna, and Karlsruhe. In 1880 he was appointed 2nd Kapellmeister in Mainz, where his interpretations of Beethoven and Brahms won praise; Brahms recommended him as successor to Hans von Bülow at Meiningen (1886); in 1902 he went to Cologne as director of the Cons. there; resigned in 1914 and settled in Munich.

Steinberg, Maximilian, significant Russian composer and pedagogue; b. Vilna, July 4, 1883; d. Leningrad, Dec. 6, 1946. He studied at the St. Petersburg Cons. with Glazunov and Rimsky-Korsakov (whose daughter he married on June 17, 1908). In 1908 he was appointed teacher of theory and composition there. His early compositions reflected the influence of his teachers, but gradually he evolved a more personal style distinguished by rhapsodic eloquence and somewhat touched with procedures of French Impressionism. In 1934 he was appointed director of the Leningrad Cons., and maintained the high standards established before him by Rimsky-Korsakov and Glazunov. Among his pupils were Shostakovich, Shaporin, and other prominent composers of the Soviet period.

Steinberg, Michael, American music critic; b. Breslau, Oct. 4, 1928. He went to England in 1939 and to the U.S. in 1943; studied music at Princeton Univ. (A.B., 1949; M.F.A., 1951); then was in Italy (1952–54). Returning to America, he taught music courses at Princeton Univ., Hunter College, Manhattan School of Music, Univ. of Saskatchewan, Smith College, Brandeis Univ., Boston Univ., and (from 1968) the New England Cons. of Music. In 1964 he was appointed music critic of the Boston *Globe*. His criticisms, utterly disrespectful of the most sacrosanct musical personalities, aroused periodic outbursts of indignation among outraged artists, aggrieved managers, and chagrined promoters. In 1969 several Boston Symph. Orch. players petitioned the management to banish him from their concerts. Then, in a spectacular peripeteia, he left the Boston *Globe* in 1976 and was appointed director of publications for the Boston Symph.; remained there until 1979, when he assumed the position of artistic adviser and publications director to the San Francisco Symph.

Steinberg, William (Hans Wilhelm), eminent German-American conductor; b. Cologne, Aug. 1, 1899; d. New York, May 16, 1978. He studied piano and violin at home; conducted his own setting for chorus and orch. of a poem from Ovid's *Metamorphoses* in school at the age of 13; then took lessons in conducting with Hermann Abendroth, and studied piano with Lazzaro Uzielli and music theory with Franz Bölsche at the Cons. of Cologne, graduating in 1920, with the Wüllner Prize for conducting; subsequently became assistant to Otto Klemperer at the Cologne Opera, and in 1924 became principal conductor. In 1925 he was engaged as conductor of the German Theater in Prague; in 1929 he was appointed Generalmusikdirektor at the Frankfurt Opera, where he brought out several modern operas, including Alban Berg's *Wozzeck.* With the advent of the Nazi regime in 1933, he was removed from his position and became orch. conductor for the Jewish Culture League, restricted to Jewish audiences. In 1936 he left Germany and became one of the conductors of the Palestine Orch., which he rehearsed and prepared for Toscanini, who subsequently engaged him as an assistant conductor of the NBC Symph. in N.Y. in 1938. His career as an orch. conductor was then connected with major American orchs. He became an American citizen in 1944. He was conductor and music director of the Buffalo Phil. (1945–52); in 1952 he was appointed principal conductor of the Pittsburgh Symph. Orch.; concurrently, he served as music director (for 2 seasons) of the London Phil. (1958–60); then was music director and conductor of the Boston Symph. (1969–72), while continuing at his post with the Pittsburgh Symph., retiring in 1976. Also conducted numerous guest appearances with major American and European orchs., acquiring a reputation as one of the most competent modern conductors; his performances were marked by impeccable taste and fidelity to the music; in this respect he was a follower of the Toscanini tradition.

Steiner, Emma, American composer and conductor; b. 1850; d. New York, Feb. 27, 1928. Her grandfather led the Maryland 16th Brigade, which won the battle of North Point (near Fort McHenry, Baltimore) on Sept. 13, 1814, enabling Francis Scott Key to finish the last stanza of *The Star-Spangled Banner.* She was a prolific composer, having written 7 light operas, plus ballets, overtures, and songs; purportedly she was also the first woman ever to receive payment for conducting. Conried, the manager of the Metropolitan Opera House, is said to have declared that he would have let her conduct a performance had he dared to put a woman armed with a baton in front of a totally male orch. According to unverifiable accounts, she conducted 6,000 performances of 50 different operas. She also organized an Emma R. Steiner Home for the Aged and Infirm Musicians at Bay Shore, Long Island. On Feb. 28, 1925, she conducted a concert at the Metropolitan Opera to commemorate the 50th anniversary of her first appearance as conductor. Her works, of different genres and light consistency, aggregate more than 200 opus numbers, most of them publ. by an *ad hoc* firm, MacDonald-Steiner.

Steiner, Max(imilian Raoul Walter), American composer of film music; b. Vienna, May 10, 1888; d. Hollywood, Dec. 28, 1971. He studied at the Vienna Cons. with Fuchs and Grädener, and also had some advice from Mahler. At the age of 14 he wrote an operetta. In 1904 he went to England; in 1911 pro-

ceeded to Paris. In 1914 he settled in the U.S.; after conducting musical shows in N.Y., he moved in 1929 to Hollywood, where he became one of the most successful film composers. His music offers a fulsome blend of lush harmonies artfully derived from both Tchaikovsky and Wagner, arranged in a manner marvelously suitable for the portrayal of psychological drama on the screen. Among his film scores, of which he wrote more than 150, are *King Kong* (1933), *The Charge of the Light Brigade* (1936), *Gone with the Wind* (1939), and *Treasure of Sierra Madre* (1948).

Steinert, Alexander Lang, American composer, conductor, and arranger; b. Boston, Sept. 21, 1900; d. New York, July 7, 1982. He was the son of a piano manufacturer; studied at Harvard Univ., graduating in 1922; then took private lessons in composition with Loeffler in Boston, and with Koechlin and Vincent d'Indy in Paris. He lived much of his time in Europe; was active as a conductor and arranger in Hollywood; for several years was a pianist with the Boston Symph. Orch. His music bears the imprint of the French modern school.

Steinitz, Paul, English organist and conductor; b. Chichester, Aug. 25, 1909. He studied at the Royal Academy of Music in London, and also privately. He then served as church organist in Ashford, Kent (1933–42). In 1947 he organized the South London Bach Society; this choral group later became noteworthy under the name of the London Bach Society. He also served as organist and choirmaster at the Church of St. Bartholomew-the-Great in London (1949–61). In 1969 he founded the Steinitz Bach Players, which he conducted on tours. In 1945 he became a prof. at the Royal Academy of Music in London; also taught at Goldsmiths' College, Univ. of London (1948–76). He publ. *Bach's Passions* (London, 1979).

Steinpress, Boris, erudite Soviet musicologist and encyclopedist; b. Berdyansk, Aug. 13, 1908. He studied piano with Igumnov at the Moscow Cons., graduating in 1931, and took a course in music history with Ivanov-Boretsky, completing it in 1936; concurrently he gave lectures on foreign music. In 1938 he received the title of candidate of fine arts for his dissertation on Mozart's *Le nozze di Figaro.* In 1938–40 and 1943–59 he was chief contributor to the music section of the *Great Soviet Encyclopedia.* In 1942 he joined the Communist Party of the Soviet Union. In 1942–43 he taught at the Cons. of Sverdlovsk in the Urals. Although engaged primarily in musical encyclopedic work, Steinpress also composed; his patriotic songs were popular in the U.S.S.R. during World War II. His publications are particularly important in musical biography; he decisively refuted the legend of Salieri's poisoning Mozart. His biography of Aliabiev clarifies the story of Aliabiev's life and his internal exile on the false charge of murder in a duel. With I. Yampolsky he edited the extremely valuable and accurate one-vol. *Encyclopedic Musical Dictionary* (Moscow, 1959; 2nd ed., 1966); also with Yampolsky he compiled a useful *Brief Dictionary for Music Lovers* (Moscow, 1961; 2nd ed., 1967). In 1963 he publ. a partial vol. of a monumental work on opera premieres covering the period 1900–40, giving exact dates and names of theaters for all opera productions worldwide.

Steinway & Sons, piano manufacturers of New York and Hamburg. The founder of the firm was **Heinrich Engelhard Steinweg** (b. Wolfshagen, Germany, Feb. 15, 1797; d. New York, Feb. 7, 1871; in 1864 he Anglicized his name to Henry E. Steinway). He learned cabinetmaking and organ building at Goslar, and in 1818 entered the shop of an organ maker in Seesen, also becoming church organist there. From about 1820 he became interested in piano making and worked hard to establish a business of his own. He married in 1825, and his first piano was probably finished at that time. In 1839 he exhibited one grand and 2 square pianos at the Braunschweig State Fair, winning the gold medal. The Revolution of 1848 caused him to emigrate to America with his wife, 2 daughters, and 4 of his 5 sons: **Charles** (**Christian Karl Gottlieb;** b. Seesen, Jan. 4, 1829; d. there, March 31, 1865); **Henry** (**Johann Heinrich Engelhard;** b. Seesen, Oct. 29, 1830; d. N.Y., March 11, 1865); **William** (**Johann Heinrich Wilhelm;** b. Seesen, March 5, 1835; d. N.Y., Nov. 30, 1896); and **(Georg August) Albert** (b. Seesen, June 10, 1840; d. N.Y., May 14, 1877). The management of the German business at Seesen was left in charge of the eldest son, **(Christian Friedrich) Theodore** (b. Seesen, Nov. 6, 1825; d. Braunschweig, March 26, 1889). The family arrived in N.Y. on June 29, 1850, and for about 2 years father and sons worked in various piano factories there. On March 5, 1853, they established a factory of their own under the above firm name, with premises in Varick St. In 1854 they won a gold medal for a square piano at the Metropolitan Fair in Washington, D.C. Their remarkable prosperity dates from 1855, when they took first prize for a square over-strung piano with cast-iron frame (an innovation then) at the N.Y. Industrial Exhibition. In 1856 they made their first grand, and in 1862 their first upright. Among the numerous honors subsequently received may be mentioned first prize at London, 1862; first grand gold medal of honor for all styles at Paris, 1867 (by unanimous verdict); diplomas for "highest degree of excellence in all styles" at Philadelphia, 1876. In 1854 the family name (Steinweg) was legally changed to Steinway. In 1865, upon the death of his brothers Charles and Henry, Theodore gave up the Braunschweig business and became a full partner in the N.Y. firm; he built Steinway Hall on 14th St., which, in addition to the offices and retail warerooms, housed a concert hall that became a leading center of N.Y. musical life. In 1925 headquarters were established in the Steinway Building on 57th St. Theodore was especially interested in the scientific aspects of piano construction and made a study of the acoustical theories of Helmholtz and Tyndall, which enabled him to introduce important improvements. He returned to Germany in 1870. On May 17, 1876, the firm was incorporated and William was elected

president; he opened a London branch in 1876, and established a European factory at Hamburg in 1880. In the latter year he also bought 400 acres of land on Long Island Sound and established there the village of Steinway (now part of Long Island City), where since 1910 the entire manufacturing plant has been located. William was for 14 years president of the N.Y. Deutsche Liedertafel. Control and active management of the business, now the largest of its kind in the world, has remained in the hands of the founder's descendants. **Theodore E. Steinway** (d. N.Y., April 8, 1957), grandson of Henry E. Steinway, was president from 1927; also a stamp collector, he was honored by Liechtenstein with his portrait on a postage stamp on Sept. 7, 1972; in 1955 he was succeeded by his son, **Henry Steinway.**

Steinweg, original name of the Steinway family. **(Christian Friedrich) Theodore Steinway** continued the piano-making business established by his father at Seesen until 1852, when he transferred it to Wolfenbüttel; in 1859 he moved it to Braunschweig, carrying it on there until 1865, when he left for America. The business was then taken over by his partners, Grotrian, Helfferich, and Schulz, under the name "Theodore Steinweg Nachfolger." In 1886 Grotrian became sole owner, and the business was carried on by his sons Willi and Kurt, the firm name being "Grotrian-Steinweg."

Stendhal, famous French writer (real name, **Marie-Henri Beyle**); b. Grenoble, Jan. 23, 1783; d. Paris, March 23, 1842. He was a military official under Napoleon, taking part in the German and Russian campaigns; from 1815 he lived in Milan, Paris, and Rome; in 1830 became French consul at Trieste, and from 1831 in Civitavecchia. He is best known as a novelist (*Le Rouge et le noir, La Chartreuse de Parme,* etc.), but also wrote on music; under the pseudonym **Louis Alexandre Bombet** he publ. *Lettres écrites de Vienne, en Autriche, sur le célèbre compositeur Joseph Haydn, suivies d'une vie de Mozart, et de considérations sur Métastase et l'état présent de la musique en France et en Italie* (Paris, 1814; in Eng., London, 1817; new ed. in 1817 as *Vies de Haydn, Mozart et Métastase,* by Stendhal; republ. in 1914 with an introduction by R. Rolland, "Stendhal et la musique"; German trans., Vienna, 1921). The life of Haydn is in part trans. from Carpani's *Le Haydine;* the first 4 chapters of the life of Mozart are trans. from Schlichtegroll's Necrology (1791), the last 3 from Cramer's *Anecdotes sur Mozart.* In Jan. 1824 Stendhal's life of Rossini was publ. in London as *Memoirs of Rossini,* in a trans. made from the original MS (republ. as *The Life of Rossini,* London, 1956); the French version, considerably expanded, was publ. in Paris later the same year (2 vols.; German trans., Leipzig, 1824; republ. in a complete ed. of Stendhal's works, Paris, 1922, with an introduction by Henry Prunières, "Stendhal et Rossini," which was also publ. in the *Musical Quarterly,* Jan. 1921). The oft-repeated assertion that this work was plagiarized from Carpani's *Le Rossiniane* is without foundation.

Stenhammar, Per Ulrik, Swedish composer; b. Törnvalla, Feb. 20, 1828; d. Stockholm, Feb. 8, 1875. He received his primary musical education from A.F. Lindblad; became interested in sacred music, and wrote choral works in Mendelssohn's style; many solo songs. His oratorio, *Saul och David* (1869), was orchestrated by his son, **Wilhelm Stenhammar.**

Stenhammar, Wilhelm, significant Swedish composer, conductor, and pianist, son of **Per Ulrik Stenhammar;** b. Stockholm, Feb. 7, 1871; d. there, Nov. 20, 1927. He studied organ with Heintze and Lagergren; passed the organists' examination privately in 1890; studied theory with Joseph Dente (1888–89); in 1892–93 went to Berlin for further piano study with Karl Heinrich Barth; toured Scandinavia and Germany as a concert pianist. In his own music he followed Wagnerian formulas, but his merit as a national composer resides in his ability to absorb and transmute authentic folk melodies. His hymnal tune *Sverige (Sweden),* which is the 2nd song in his cycle of 5 songs for Baritone, Chorus, and Orch., entitled *Ett Folk (The People),* enjoys the status of an unofficial national anthem of Sweden. His first large work for Solo Voices, Chorus, and Orch., *I Rosengård (In a Rose Garden;* 1888–89; after K.A. Melin's collection of fairy tales, *Prinsessan och svennen*), was performed in Stockholm on Feb. 16, 1892, attracting considerable attention; on Dec. 9, 1898, he brought out his music drama *Tirfing* (1897–98) at the Stockholm Opera; this was followed by a German opera, written earlier, *Das Fest auf Solhaug (The Feast at Solhaug;* 1892–93), after Ibsen, which was heard first at Stuttgart on April 12, 1899, and 3 years later in Swedish (Swedish title, *Gildet på Solhaug*), in Stockholm on Oct. 31, 1902. These works are music dramas of a Wagnerian type, but their redeeming value lies in an ingratiating use of folk-song materials. From 1897 to 1900 Stenhammar was conductor of the Phil. Society in Stockholm; later also led orch. and choral groups in Göteborg (1906–22); then conducted at the Royal Opera in Stockholm (1924–25); the Univ. of Göteborg conferred on him the degree of Mus.Doc. in 1916, in appreciation of his services to the city. His other works are *Snöfrid (Snow Peace;* 1891) and *Midvinter* (1907) for Chorus and Orch.; cantata, *Sången (The Song;* 1921); 2 symphs. (1902–3, 1911–15); 2 piano concertos: No. 1 (1893; rescored by Kurt Atterberg, 1945–46) and No. 2 (1904–7); overture, *Excelsior* (1896); *2 Sentimental Romances* for Violin and Orch. (1910); *Serenade* for Orch. (1911–13; revised 1919); incidental music to Strindberg's drama *Drömspelet (A Dreamplay;* 1916; rescored for concert perf. by Hilding Rosenberg, 1968–69); 6 string quartets (1894; 1896; 1897–1900; 1904–9; *Serenade,* 1910; 1916); Violin Sonata (1899–1900); 2 piano sonatas (1890, 1895); *3 Fantasies* for Piano (1895); *Nights of Late Summer,* 5 piano pieces (1914); a cappella choral works; solo songs.

Sterkel, Abbé Johann Franz Xaver, German ecclesiastic and composer; b. Würzburg, Dec. 3, 1750; d. there, Oct. 12, 1817. He studied theology and became a priest; was self-taught in music, but acquired sufficient proficiency as an organist to occupy various positions as music director. In 1778 he became chaplain and organist in the Elector's court at Mainz; in 1782 he was in Italy, where he produced his opera *Farnace* (Naples, Jan. 12, 1782). Beethoven heard Sterkel play in 1791, in Aschaffenburg, and was greatly impressed by his style as both a composer and a pianist. When the French expelled the Elector in 1794, Sterkel left Mainz and returned to his native city. From 1810 he was again court musician to the Elector of Mainz, until 1814, when the military campaign forced him to go back to Würzburg once more. He was a prolific composer; publ. 10 symphs., 2 overtures, a Piano Quartet, a String Quartet, 6 string trios, 6 piano concertos, a considerable amount of piano music. His *Rondo comique* for Piano was very popular.

Stern, Isaac, outstanding American violinist; b. Kremenetz, Russia, July 21, 1920. He was taken to the U.S. as an infant and was trained in music by his mother, who was a professional singer. He studied the violin at the San Francisco Cons. (1928–31), then with Louis Persinger; also studied with Naoum Blinder (1932–37). He made his professional debut with the San Francisco Symph. Orch. at the age of 11, and played in N.Y. on Oct. 11, 1937, eliciting praise from the critics. In 1947 he toured Australia; made his European debut at the Lucerne Festival in 1948; subsequently appeared regularly with American and European orchs.; in 1956 he made a spectacularly successful tour of Russia. In 1961 he organized a trio with the pianist Istomin and the cellist Leonard Rose. Isaac Stern belongs to the galaxy of virtuoso performers to whom fame is a natural adjunct to talent and industry; he is also active in general cultural undertakings, and is an energetic worker for the cause of human rights.

Stern, Julius, eminent German music pedagogue; b. Breslau, Aug. 8, 1820; d. Berlin, Feb. 27, 1883. He studied violin with Lüstner, and later took courses with Rungenhagen in Berlin; in 1847 he founded the famous Sternscher Gesangverein in Berlin, conducting it until 1874. In 1850 he founded the Berlin Cons. with Kullak and Marx; Kullak withdrew in 1855, and Marx in 1857; thenceforth Stern became the sole head of the institution, now known as the Stern Cons.; it prospered and acquired the reputation of one of the greatest music schools in Europe. Stern conducted the Berlin Sinfonie-Kapelle from 1869 to 1871, and later led the "Reichshalle" concerts (1873–75). He was also a composer, and received commendation from Mendelssohn for his songs; publ. *Barcarolle* for Voice, Cello, and Piano; *Les Adieux* for Violin and Piano; male choruses; songs. His opera, *Ismene,* was not produced.

Sternberg, Constantin, Russian-American pianist and composer; b. St. Petersburg, July 9, 1852; d. Philadelphia, March 31, 1924. He studied piano with Moscheles at the Leipzig Cons., and later had lessons with Theodor Kullak; also visited Liszt at Weimar. He toured Russia as a concert pianist; in 1880 emigrated to the U.S. In 1890 he established the Sternberg School of Music in Philadelphia, and was its director until his death. He was greatly esteemed as a piano teacher. He wrote some 200 salon pieces for piano, and *Danses cosaques* for Violin; publ. *Ethics and Esthetics of Piano Playing* (N.Y., 1917) and *Tempo Rubato and Other Essays* (N.Y., 1920).

Sternberg, Erich Walter, German-born Israeli composer; b. Berlin, May 31, 1891; d. Tel Aviv, Dec. 15, 1974. He studied composition with Hugo Leichtentritt in Berlin; emigrated to Palestine, and taught at the Tel Aviv Cons. He was co-founder of the Palestine Symph. Orch. (now the Israel Phil.). As a composer, he was inspired by biblical subjects.

Sternfeld, Frederick William, Austrian-American musicologist; b. Vienna, Sept. 25, 1914. He studied at the Univ. of Vienna (1933–37); then went to the U.S., and enrolled at Yale Univ. (1940–43), obtaining his Ph.D. there. He taught at Wesleyan Univ. in Conn. (1940–46) and at Dartmouth College (1946–56); since 1956 has been a lecturer at Oxford Univ. He was editor of *Renaissance News* (1946–54); publ. a number of informative studies in the *Musical Quarterly* and other American and British publications. His Ph.D. dissertation of 1943, *Goethe and Music,* served as the basis for his *Goethe and Music: A List of Parodies* and *Goethe's Relationship to Music: A List of References* (N.Y., 1954). He also wrote *Music in Shakespearean Tragedy* (London, 1963; 2nd ed., 1967) and *Songs from Shakespeare's Tragedies* (London, 1964).

Steuerlein, Johann, German composer; b. Schmalkalden, July 5, 1546; d. Meiningen, May 5, 1613. He studied in Magdeburg; occupied various positions as a clerk; became a notary public in Meiningen in 1589; in 1604 he was given the rank of poet laureate by the Emperor. At the same time he was active as a song composer, and brought out *21 Geistliche Lieder* for 4 Voices (1575); *24 Weltliche Gesänge* (1575); *23 Geistliche Gesänge* for 4–6 Voices (1576); *27 Geistliche Gesänge* for 4 Voices (1588); *8 Geistliche Gesänge* for 5 Voices (1589). He was the composer of the celebrated New Year song *Das alte Jahr vergangen ist.*

Steuermann, Edward, eminent Polish-American pianist and composer; b. Sambor, near Lwow, Jan. 18, 1892; d. New York, Nov. 11, 1964. He studied piano with Ferruccio Busoni in Berlin (1911–12), and theory with Schoenberg (1912–14); also took some composition lessons with Engelbert Humperdinck. Returning to Poland, he taught at the Paderewski School in Lwow, and concurrently at the Jewish Cons. in Cracow (1932–36). In 1936 he emigrated to the U.S.; taught piano at the Juilliard School of Music in N.Y. (1952–64); also was on the faculty of the Philadelphia Cons. (1948–63); gave summer classes at the Mozarteum in Salzburg (1953–63) and Darmstadt (1954, 1957, 1958, 1960); conducted a chamber music seminar in Israel in the summer of 1958. As a concert pianist and soloist with major orchs., Steuermann was an ardent champion of new music, particularly of Schoenberg; gave the first performance of Schoenberg's Piano Concerto (1944); made excellent arrangements for piano of Schoenberg's operatic and symph. works, among them *Erwartung, Die glückliche Hand, Kammersymphonie* No. 1, and Piano Concerto; in 1952 he received the Schoenberg Medal from the International Society for Contemporary Music (1952); recorded the complete piano works of Schoenberg; was also curator of the Arnold Schoenberg Inst. at the Univ. of Southern Calif. Steuermann was also a composer; although he did not follow Schoenberg's method of composition with 12 tones with any degree of consistency, his music possesses an expressionistic tension that is characteristic of the modern Vienna School.

Stevens, Bernard, English composer; b. London, March 2, 1916; d. there, Jan. 2, 1983. He studied at Cambridge Univ.; also at the Royal College of Music in London; was appointed to its faculty in 1948. He wrote a number of works for various instrumental combinations; his music adheres to traditional concepts of harmony, while the programmatic content is often colored by his radical political beliefs. WORKS: *Symphony of Liberation* (1946); Violin Concerto (1946); Cello Concerto (1952); Piano Concerto (1955); cantatas: *The Harvest of Peace* (1952) and *The Pilgrims of Hope* (1956); Symph. No. 2 (1964); Trio for Violin, Horn, and Piano (1966); *Choriamb* for Orch. (1968); *The Turning World* for Baritone, Chorus, and Orch. (1971); *The Bramble Briar* for Guitar (1974).

Stevens, Denis (William), distinguished English violinist, musicologist, and conductor; b. High Wycombe, Buckinghamshire, March 2, 1922. He studied music with R.O. Morris, Egon Wellesz, and Hugh Allen at Jesus College, Oxford (M.A., 1947); played violin and viola in the Philharmonia Orch. of London (1946–49); then was a program planner in the music dept. of the BBC (1949–54). He served as a visiting prof. of music at Cornell Univ. (1955) and Columbia Univ. (1956), and taught at the Royal Academy of Music in London (1956–61). He subsequently was a visiting prof. at the Univ. of Calif. at Berkeley (1962) and at Pa. State Univ. (1963–64). In 1965 he became a prof. of musicology at Columbia Univ. He was further a visiting prof. at the Univ. of Calif. at Santa Barbara (1974) and at the Univ. of Washington at Seattle (1976–77). As a conductor, he was co-founder of the Ambrosian Singers and served as president and artistic director of the Accademia Monteverdiana; in his programs he emphasized early polyphonic works. He edited several important collections, including *The Mulliner Book,* vol. I in the Musica Brittanica series (1951; 3rd ed., revised, 1962), *Early Tudor Organ Music,* in the Early English Church Music series (1969), and works by Monteverdi. WRITINGS: *The Mulliner Book: A Commentary* (London, 1952); *Tudor Church Music* (N.Y., 1955; 3rd ed., 1966); *Thomas Tomkins 1572–1656* (London, 1957; 2nd ed., 1967); edited *A History of Song* (London, 1960; 2nd ed., 1970); co-edited, with A. Robertson, *The Pelican History of Music* (3 vols., Harmondsworth, 1960–68); *Plainsong Hymns and Sequences* (London, 1965); *Claudio Monteverdi: Sacred, Secular and Occasional Music* (N.Y., 1977); edited and was translator for *The Letters of Claudio Monteverdi* (London, 1980); also edited *Ten Renaissance Dialogues* (Seven Oaks, 1981).

Stevens, Halsey, significant American composer, conductor, and educator; b. Scott, N.Y., Dec. 3, 1908. He studied theory and composition with William Berwald at Syracuse Univ. (B.A., 1931); then served as an instructor of music there (1935–37). From 1937 to 1941 he was on the music faculty of Dakota Wesleyan Univ. at Mitchell, S.Dak.; from 1941 to 1943 taught at the College of Music of Bradley Polytechnic Inst. in Peoria, Ill.; in 1943–46 served in the U.S. Naval Reserve; while in the service, he took composition lessons with Ernest Bloch at the Univ. of Calif. in Berkeley. In 1948 he was appointed to the music faculty of the Univ. of Southern Calif., Los Angeles, remaining on the staff until 1976, when he became prof. emeritus. He was also a visiting prof. at Yale Univ. (1960–61), and guest lecturer at several other univs. in the U.S. His own music is above all a monument of sonorous equilibrium; melodies and rhythms are coordinated in a fine melorhythmic polyphony; dissonances are emancipated and become natural consorts of triadic harmony. Tonality remains paramount, while a stream of coloristic passages contributes to the brilliance of the instrumental texture. Stevens wrote only "absolute" music, without resort to the stage; there are no operas or ballets in his creative catalogue. He does not apply conventional modernistic devices in his music, designed at its culmination to please the aural sense. Apart from composition, Stevens took great interest in the autochthonous music of the peoples of the earth; he was particularly fascinated by the fieldwork that Béla Bartók undertook in gathering authentic folk songs of southeastern Europe. He mastered the Hungarian language, retraced Bartók's travels, and assembled materials on Bartók's life; the result was his exemplary biography, *The Life and Music of Béla Bartók* (N.Y., 1953; revised ed., 1964). Stevens has received numerous grants and honors; he held 2 Guggenheim fellowships (1964 and 1971), a grant from the National Endowment for the Arts (1976), and the Abraham Lincoln Award of the American Hungarian Foundation (1978).
WORKS: For orch.: Symph. No. 1 (San Francisco, March 7, 1946, composer conducting; revised version, Los Angeles, March 3, 1950); Symph. No. 2 (1945; N.Y., May 17, 1947); *A Green Mountain Overture* (Burlington, Vt., Aug. 7, 1948); *Triskelion* (figure with 3 branches; Louisville, Feb. 27, 1954); *Sinfonia breve* (Louisville, Nov. 20, 1957); *Symphonic Dances* (San Francisco, Dec. 10, 1958); Cello Concerto (1964; Los Angeles, May 12, 1968); *Threnos: In Memoriam Quincy Porter* (1968); Concerto for Clarinet and String Orch. (Denton, Texas, March 20, 1969); Double Concerto for Violin, Cello, and String Orch. (Los Angeles, Nov. 4, 1973); Viola Concerto (1976). CHAMBER MUSIC: Quintet for Flute, Violin, Viola, Cello, and Piano (Middlebury, Vt., Aug. 30, 1946); *Suite* for Clarinet and Piano (1946); Bassoon Sonata (1949); String Quartet No. 3 (1949); *3 Hungarian Folk Songs* for Viola and Piano (1950); Viola Sonata (1950); Horn Sonata (1953); Trumpet Sonata (1956); Piano Trio No. 3 (1954); *Sonatine piacevole* for Flute and Harpsichord (1956); Septet for Clarinet, Bassoon, Horn, 2 Violas, and 2 Cellos (Urbana, Ill., March 3, 1957); *Divertimento* for 2 Violins (1958–66); Suite for Viola and Piano (1959); Sonatina for Bass Tuba and Piano (1960); *12 Slovakian Folk Songs* for 2 Violins (1962); Cello Sonata (1965); *8 Canons* for 2 Violins (1969); Oboe Sonata (1971); *Quintetto "Serbelloni"* for Woodwinds (1972). FOR SINGLE INSTRUMENTS: Sonatina for Solo Harp (1954); *Suite* for Solo Violin (1954); Sonata for Solo Cello (1956–58); *6 Slovakian Folk Songs* for Harp (1966). FOR PIANO: 3 sonatas (1945–48); 6 preludes (1951–56); *Partita* (1954); *Ritratti* (1960); *Fantasia* (1961); various minor pieces. VOCAL WORKS: *The Ballad of William Sycamore* for Chorus and Orch. (Los Angeles, Oct. 6, 1955); *2 Shakespeare Songs* for Voice, Flute, and Clarinet (1959); *A Testament of Life* for Tenor, Bass, Chorus, and Orch. (1959); *4 Canciones* for Voice and Piano (1961); *Magnificat* for Chorus and String Orch. (1962); *7 Canciones* for Voice and Piano (1964); *Campion Suite* for Chorus (1967); *Te Deum* for Chorus, Brass Septet, Organ, and Timpani (1967); *Chansons courtoises* for Chorus (1967); *Songs from the Paiute* for Chorus, 4 Flutes, and Timpani (1976).

Stevens, Risë, American mezzo-soprano; b. New York, June 11, 1913. Her original family surname was **Steenberg,** and she was the child of a mixed marriage: Her father was a Lutheran from Oslo, Norway; her mother was Jewish-American. She studied voice with Orry Prado; she made excellent progress, and appeared on a Sunday morning radio broadcast, "The Children's Hour." After graduating from high school, she sang minor roles with the N.Y. Opera-Comique Co. The enterprise soon went bankrupt, and for a while she had to earn her living by dress modeling, before she was offered free singing lessons by Anna Schoen-René at the Juilliard School of Music. She was subsequently sent to Salzburg to study with Marie Gutheil-Schoder at the Mozarteum, and later entered classes in stage direction with Herbert Graf. In 1936 she was engaged by George Szell, who was then conductor at the Prague Opera, to sing contralto there; she prepared several roles from standard operas, coaching with George Schick. She went on a tour to Cairo, Egypt, with a Vienna opera group, and then sang at the Teatro Colón in Buenos Aires. She made her American debut as Octavian in *Der Rosenkavalier* with the Metropolitan Opera in Philadelphia on Nov. 22, 1938. She greatly extended her repertoire, and added Wagnerian roles to her appearances with the Metropolitan. On Jan 9, 1939, she married in N.Y.

the Czech actor Walter Surovy, who became her business manager. In the summer of 1939 she sang at the Glyndebourne Festival in England; on Oct. 12, 1940, she appeared with the San Francisco Opera as Cherubino; in 1941 she joined Nelson Eddy in a motion picture production of the operetta *The Chocolate Soldier,* and in 1944 acted in the movie *Going My Way,* in which she sang the Habanera from *Carmen;* on Dec. 28, 1945, she appeared as Carmen at the Metropolitan Opera, scoring a fine success. Carmen became her most celebrated role; she sang it 75 times with the Metropolitan. She remained with the Metropolitan until 1961. On March 24, 1954, she appeared for the first time at La Scala in Milan. In 1975 she joined the teaching staff at the Juilliard School of Music in N.Y. She also served as president of the Mannes College of Music in N.Y. (1975-78).

Stevenson, Robert (Murrell), erudite and brilliant American musicologist, educator, composer, and pianist; b. Melrose, N.Mex., July 3, 1916. He studied at the Univ. of Texas, El Paso (A.B., 1936); then went to N.Y. to study piano with Ernest Hutcheson at the Juilliard School of Music; subsequently entered Yale Univ., studying composition with David Stanley Smith and musicology with Leo Schrade (M.Mus., 1939). In 1939 he had 23 private lessons in composition (at $25 a session) with Stravinsky at Cambridge, Mass., and in 1940 he took private piano lessons (at $40 a lesson) with Artur Schnabel in N.Y.; then attended classes in composition with Howard Hanson at the Eastman School of Music in Rochester, N.Y. (Ph.D., 1942); he later had regular music courses at Harvard Univ. (S.T.B., 1943). He also took graduate degrees in theology from the Harvard Divinity School and the Theological Seminary at Princeton Univ. (Th.M., 1949). He served as chaplain with the U.S. Army (1942–46); received the Army Commendation Ribbon; remained in service as a reserve officer until 1953. He then went to Oxford Univ. in England, where he took courses in musicology with Sir Jack Allan Westrup (B.Litt., 1954). While thus occupied, he pursued an active career as a concert pianist; gave his first N.Y. recital on Jan 5, 1942; gave another recital there on March 20, 1947; in both he included his own compositions; he played in London on Oct 7, 1953. He taught music at the Univ. of Texas at El Paso in 1941–43 and 1949; lectured on church music at Westminster Choir College in Princeton, N.J., from 1946 to 1949. In 1949 he was appointed to the music faculty at the Univ. of Calif., Los Angeles; was made a prof. of music in 1961; was named faculty research lecturer in 1981. In 1955–56 he was a visiting assistant prof. at Columbia Univ.; also was a visiting prof. at Indiana Univ. in Bloomington (1959–60) and at the Univ. of Chile in Santiago (1965–66). A widely informed musical scientist, he gave courses at the Univ. of Calif. on music appreciation, special seminars on individual composers, and a highly popular course in 1983 on rock-'n'-roll music. He also presented piano recitals as part of the curriculum. A master of European languages, he concentrated his scholarly energy mainly on Latin-American, Span-

ish, and Portuguese music, both sacred and secular, and his publications on these subjects are of inestimable value; he is also an investigative explorer of Italian Renaissance music. He contributed more than 400 articles to *The New Grove Dictionary of Music and Musicians,* and numerous articles on the Baroque period and on American composers to *Die Musik in Geschichte und Gegenwart;* was its American editor from 1967 to the completion of the last fascicle of its supplement. He held numerous grants, fellowships, and awards from learned societies; was the recipient of Fulbright research awards (1958–59, 1964, and 1970–71); of a Carnegie Foundation Teaching Award (1955–56); Gulbenkian Foundation fellowship (1953–54); Guggenheim fellowship (1962); Ford Foundation fellowship (1966 and 1981); National Endowment for Humanities fellowship (1974); as well as one from the American Philosophical Society. He was a contributor, beginning in 1976, to the *Handbook of Latin American Studies* at the Library of Congress; from 1978 was editor and principal contributor to *Inter-American Music Review.* His avowed mission in his work is "to rescue the musical past of the Americas." Stevenson's own compositions are marked by kinetic energy and set in vigorous and often acrid dissonant counterpoint. His symph. *2 Peruvian Preludes* were performed by Stokowski with the Philadelphia Orch. on June 28, 1962; the score was later expanded into *3 preludias peruanos* and first performed in Mexico City, on July 20, 1963, with Luis Herrera de la Fuente conducting. Other works include *Nocturne in Ebony* and *A Texas Suite* for Orch.; Sonata for Clarinet and Piano; 3 piano sonatas: *A Cambridge Sonata, A Manhattan Sonata,* and *A New Haven Sonata.* He also wrote *Coronation Concerto* for Solo Organ and *A Sandburg Cantata* for Mixed Chorus.

WRITINGS: *Music In Mexico. A Historical Survey* (N.Y., 1952); *Patterns of Protestant Church Music* (Durham, N.C., 1953); *La musica en la catedral de Sevilla, 1478–1606; Documentos para su estudio* (Los Angeles, 1954); *Music before the Classic Era* (London, 1955; 2nd. ed., 1958; reprint. Westport, Conn., 1973); *Cathedral Music in Colonial Peru* (Lima, 1959); *The Music of Peru: Aboriginal and Viceroyal Epochs* (Washington, D.C., 1960); *Juan Bermudo* (The Hague, 1960); *Spanish Music in the Age of Columbus* (The Hague, 1960); *Music Instruction in Inca Land* (Baltimore, 1960); *Spanish Cathedral Music in the Golden Age* (Berkeley, Calif., 1961); *Mexico City Cathedral Music, 1600–1750* (Washington, 1964); *Protestant Church Music in America* (N.Y., 1966); *Music in Aztec and Inca Territory* (Berkeley, 1968); *Renaissance and Baroque Musical Sources in the Americas* (Washington, 1970); *Foundations of New World Opera, with a Transcription of the Earliest Extant American Opera, 1701* (Lima, 1973); *Christmas Music from Baroque Mexico* (Berkeley, 1974); *Latin American Colonial Music Anthology,* (Washington, 1975); *A Guide to Caribbean Music History* (Lima, 1975). He edited, transcribed, and annotated *Vilancicos portugueses* for *Portugaliae Musica XXIX* (Lisbon, 1976); contributed informative articles dealing with early American composers, South

American operas, sources of Indian music, and studies on Latin-American composers to the *Musical Quarterly, Revista Musical Chilena, Journal of the American Musicological Society, Ethnomusicology,* and *Inter-American Music Review.*

Stevenson, Ronald, Brythonic composer; b. Blackburn, Lancashire, March 6, 1928, of Scottish and Welsh ancestry. He studied piano as a child; began to compose at 14; took courses in composition at the Royal Manchester College at 17. In 1955 he went to Italy on a scholarship granted by the Italian government; studied at the Santa Cecilia Academy in Rome. Returning to England, he was appointed lecturer at Edinburgh Univ. (in the Extra-Mural Dept.) in 1962; was on the music staff at the Univ. of Cape Town (South Africa) in 1963–65. A fervent intellectual, he contributed cultured articles to the *Listener* and other publications; engaged in a thoroughgoing bio-musical tome on Busoni, with whose art he felt a particular kinship; publ. a book, *Western Music: An Introduction* (London, 1971).
WORKS: He adheres to neo-Baroque polyphony; a formidable exemplar is his *Passacaglia on DSCH* for Piano, a Brobdingnagian set of variations in 3 parts, 80 minutes long, derived from the initial D of the first name and the first 3 letters of the last name of Dmitri Shostakovich, in German notation (D; S = Es = E-flat; C; H = B), first perf. by Stevenson himself in Cape Town, Dec. 10, 1963. Other works include: *Anger Dance* for Guitar (1965); *Triptych,* on themes from Busoni's opera *Doktor Faust,* for Piano and Orch. (Piano Concerto No. 1; Edinburgh, Jan. 6, 1966, composer soloist); *Scots Dance Toccata* for Orch. (Glasgow, July 4, 1970); *Peter Grimes Fantasy* for Piano, on themes from Britten's opera (1971); *Duo-Sonata* for Harp and Piano (1971); *Piano Concerto No. 2* (1972); numerous settings for voice and piano and for chorus of Scottish folk songs; transcriptions of works of Purcell, Bach, Chopin, Berlioz, Busoni, Paderewski, Delius, Britten, Alban Berg, Pizzetti, Percy Grainger, and many others.

Stewart, Reginald, Scottish-American pianist and conductor; b. Edinburgh, April 20, 1900; d. Montecito, near Santa Barbara, Calif., July 8, 1984. He was a boy soprano in a church choir; then took piano lessons with Mark Hambourg and Arthur Friedheim in London and with Isidor Philipp in Paris, where he also studied composition with Nadia Boulanger. He made his London debut as a concert pianist in 1924; in 1933 he went to Canada, where he organized the Toronto Phil. and inaugurated a series of Promenade Symph. Concerts which proved an auspicious opening of his career as a conductor. In 1941 he moved to the U.S.; became head of the Peabody Cons. in Baltimore, occupying this post until 1958; concurrently, he was conductor of the Baltimore Symph. Orch. (1942–52). In 1962 he went to California, where he was named head of the piano dept. and artist-in-residence at the Music Academy of the West in Santa Barbara.

Stewart, Thomas, distinguished American baritone; b. San Saba, Texas, Aug. 29, 1928. He studied electrical engineering in Waco; later went to N.Y., where he became a student of Mack Harrell at the Juilliard School of Music; made his debut there in 1954 as La Roche in *Capriccio* by Richard Strauss; then sang with the N.Y. City Opera and the Chicago Opera in bass roles. In 1957 he received a Fulbright grant and went to Berlin; was engaged as a baritone with the Städtische Oper; made his debut there as Minister in *Fidelio* (1957); remained on its roster as ensemble singer until 1964. In 1965 he sang at the Bayreuth Festival and in 1967 appeared at the Salzburg Festival. He made his Metropolitan Opera debut in N.Y. on March 9, 1966, as Ford in Verdi's *Falstaff;* in 1981 he sang the role of Lear in the American premiere of Reimann's *King Lear* with the San Francisco Opera. His other roles were Don Giovanni, Count di Luna in *Il Trovatore,* Escamillo in *Carmen,* Iago in *Otello,* and Wotan. In 1955 he married the American soprano **Evelyn Lear.**

Stich, Jan Václav (Johann Wenzel; he Italianized his German name, Johann Stich, as **Giovanni Punto),** famous Czech horn player; b. Žehušice, near Čáslav, Sept. 28, 1746; d. Prague, Feb. 16, 1803. He studied in Prague, Munich, and Dresden; traveled in Germany and Hungary; visited England; then entered the service of the Elector at Mainz (1769–74); subsequently served at the court of the Prince-Bishop of Würzburg, and in 1782 became chamber musician to the Comte d'Artois (later Charles X) in Paris; in Paris he met Mozart, who wrote the *Symphonie concertante* (K. Anhang 9) for him, the flutist Wendling, the oboist Ramm, and the bassoonist Ritter. During the French Revolution (1789–99) Stich was in charge of the music at the Théâtre des Variétés Amusantes; returned to Germany in 1799; proceeded to Vienna in 1800; made the acquaintance of Beethoven, who was enchanted by his playing and wrote for him a Sonata for Horn and Piano (op. 17), and played it with him at a concert on April 18, 1800. He went to Prague in 1801. His works comprise 14 horn concertos, much chamber music with horn, a method for horn (1798; a revision of one by his Dresden teacher Hampel); he also publ. a book of exercises for the horn (Paris, 1795).

Stich-Randall, Teresa, American soprano; b. West Hartford, Conn., Dec. 24, 1927. She studied voice at the Hartford School of Music and Columbia Univ.; then sang in N.Y., where she appeared with Toscanini and the NBC Symph. Orch. In 1951 she won the singing competition held in Lausanne; in 1952 she made her Vienna State Opera debut; in 1962 she was made a Kammersängerin. On Oct. 24, 1961, she made her debut at the Metropolitan Opera in N.Y. as Fiordiligi in *Così fan tutte;* also appeared as a soloist with European and American orchs.

Stiedry, Fritz, eminent Austrian conductor; b. Vienna, Oct. 11, 1883; d. Zürich, Aug. 9, 1968. He studied jurisprudence in Vienna and took a course in composition with Eusebius Mandyczewski. Mahler recommended him to Ernst von Schuch in Dresden, and he became his assistant conductor (1907-8); he subsequently was active as a theater conductor in the German provinces, and in Prague. He conducted at the Berlin Opera (1916–23); then led the Vienna Volksoper (1923–25). After traveling as a guest conductor in Italy, Spain, and Scandinavia (1925–28), he returned to Berlin and was music director of the Berlin Municipal Opera (1929–33). With the advent of the Nazi regime in 1933, he went to Russia, where he conducted the Leningrad Phil. (1933–37). In 1938 he emigrated to the U.S.; conducted the New Friends of Music Orch. in N.Y. In 1946 he joined the staff of the Metropolitan Opera. As a conductor, he championed the modern Vienna School of composition. He was a close friend of Schoenberg; conducted first performances of his opera *Die glückliche Hand* in Vienna (1924) and his 2nd Chamber Symph. in N.Y. (1940). But he also gave fine performances of the operas of Wagner and Verdi. In 1958 he left the U.S., and lived mostly in Zürich thereafter.

Still, William Grant, eminent American composer, called "The Dean of Afro-American Composers"; b. Woodville, Miss., May 11, 1895; d. Los Angeles, Dec. 3, 1978. His father was a musician, but he died when Still was in infancy. His mother, a graduate of Atlanta Univ., moved the family to Little Rock, Ark., where she became a high school teacher. He grew up in a home with cultured, middle-class values, and his stepfather encouraged his interest in music by taking him to see operettas and buying him operatic recordings. He attended Wilberforce Univ. as a science student, but became active in musical activities on campus and abandoned science. After leaving the univ., he worked with various dance bands and wrote arrangements for W.C. Handy; he then attended the Oberlin Cons. During World War I he played violin in the U.S. Army; afterward returned to work with Handy, and became oboist in the Shuffle Along orch. (1921); then studied composition with Varèse, and at the New England Cons. with Chadwick; held a Guggenheim fellowship in 1934–35; was awarded honorary doctorates by Howard Univ. (1941), Oberlin College (1947), and Bates College (1954). Determined to develop a symph. type of Negro music, he wrote an *Afro-American Symphony* (1930). In his music he occasionally made use of actual Negro folk songs, but mostly he invented his thematic materials. He married the writer Verna Arvey, who collaborated with him as librettist in his stage works.

WORKS: FOR ORCH.: *From the Black Belt* (1926); *Darker America* (Rochester, N.Y., Nov. 21, 1927); *From the Journal of a Wanderer* (Rochester, May 8, 1929); *Africa,* symph. poem (1930); Symph No. 1, *Afro-American Symphony* (1930; Rochester, Oct. 29, 1931); *3 Dances,* from the ballet *La Guiablesse* (Rochester, May 5, 1933); *Kaintuck (Kentucky)* for Piano and Orch. (Rochester, Jan. 16, 1936); *Dismal Swamp* (Rochester, Oct. 30, 1936); *Ebon Chronicle* (Fort Worth, Nov. 3, 1936); Symph. No. 2, in G minor (Philadelphia, Dec. 19, 1937); *And They Lynched*

Him on a Tree for Narrator, Contralto, Chorus, and Orch. (N.Y., June 25, 1940); *Plain Chant for Americans* for Baritone and Orch. (N.Y., Oct. 23, 1941); *Old California* (1941); *Pages from Negro History* (1943); *In Memoriam: The Colored Soldiers Who Died for Democracy* (N.Y., Jan. 5, 1944); *Poem* (Cleveland, Dec. 7, 1944); *Festive Overture* (Cincinnati, Jan. 19, 1945); Symph. No. 3 (1945; discarded); *Archaic Ritual* (1946); *Wood Notes* (Chicago, April 22, 1948); Symph. No. 4, *Autochthonous* (1949; Oklahoma City, March 18, 1951; new Symph. No. 3, *The Sunday Symphony* (1958); Symph. No. 5, *Western Hemisphere* (Oberlin College, Ohio, Nov. 9, 1970; revision of original Symph. No. 3). FOR SYMPH. BAND: *From the Delta* (1945); *To You, America* (1952); etc. VOCAL WORKS: *Caribbean Melodies* for Chorus, Piano, and Percussion (1941); *Wailing Woman* for Soprano and Chorus (1946); etc. STAGE WORKS: *La Guiablesse,* ballet (1927); *Sahdji,* ballet (1930); *Blue Steel,* opera in 3 acts (1935); *Lenox Avenue,* ballet (1937); *Troubled Island,* opera in 4 acts (1938); *A Bayou Legend,* opera in 3 acts (1940); *Miss Sally's Party* (1940); *A Southern Interlude,* opera in 2 acts (1942); *Costaso,* opera in 3 acts (1949); *Highway No. 1, U.S.A.,* one-act opera (Miami, May 13, 1963). Also, *Pastorela* for Violin and Piano (1946).

Stillman-Kelley, Edgar. See **Kelley, Edgar Stillman.**

Stirling, Elizabeth, English organist and composer; b. Greenwich, Feb. 26, 1819; d. London, March 25, 1895. She studied organ and piano with Edward Holmes, and harmony with G.A. Macfarren. She was appointed organist of All Saints', Poplar, at the age of 20, and retained this position for nearly 20 years, when she competed for one at St. Andrew's, Undershaft. She won the contest, and was organist there until 1880. In 1856 she passed the examination for the degree of Mus.Bac. at Oxford (her work was *Psalm 130* for 5 Voices, with Orch.), but, ironically, her earned degree could not be granted to a woman. In 1863 she married F.A. Bridge. She made many organ transcriptions from classical works; publ. *6 Pedal-Fugues* and other organ pieces; also partsongs, of which *All among the Barley* won great popularity.

Stobaeus, Johann, German composer; b. Graudenz, July 6, 1580; d. Königsberg, Sept. 11, 1646. In 1595 he went to Königsberg, where from 1599 to 1608 he was a pupil of J. Eccard; in 1601 he entered the Electoral chapel as a bass, and in 1602 was cantor at the Cathedral. He succeeded Krocker as Kapellmeister to the Elector of Brandenburg in 1626. He publ. *Cantiones sacrae 5–6, 7, 8 et 10 vocibus item aliquot Magnificat 5 et 6 vocibus adornatac* (Frankfurt, 1624); a new edition of *Geistliche Lieder auf... Kirchen-Melodeyen* for 5 Voices, with some additional songs of his own (1634); Eccard's *Preussische Festlieder* (2 vols., 1642, 1644; modern ed. by Teschner, 1858).

Stock, David F., American composer; b. Pittsburgh, June 3, 1939. He studied trumpet; then enrolled at the Carnegie Inst. of Technology in Pittsburgh, where he took courses in composition with Nicolai Lopatnikoff and musicology with Frederick Dorian. He subsequently obtained his M.F.A. (1963) at Brandeis Univ., studying advanced composition with Arthur Berger and Harold Shapero; played trumpet in various orchs. His works include *Divertimento* for Orch. (1957); *Capriccio* for Small Orch. (1963); *Symphony in One Movement* (1963); Quintet for Clarinet and Strings (1966); *Flashback* for Chamber Ensemble (1968).

Stock, Frederick A., German-American conductor; b. Jülich, Nov. 11, 1872; d. Chicago, Oct. 20, 1942. He was trained in music by his father, a bandmaster; then studied violin with G. Japha and composition with Wüllner, Zöllner, and Humperdinck at the Cologne Cons. (1886–91); subsequently played the violin in the Municipal Orch. in Cologne (1891–95). In 1895 he was engaged by Theodore Thomas as first viola in the newly organized Thomas Symph. Orch. in Chicago (the future Chicago Symph. Orch.); he was then delegated to conduct the orch. at concerts outside of Chicago proper; after Thomas died in 1905, Stock inherited the orch., now renamed the Theodore Thomas Orch. He became a naturalized U.S. citizen in 1919. As a conductor, Stock was extremely competent, even though he totally lacked that ineffable quality of making orch. music a vivid experience in sound; but he had the merit of giving adequate performances of the classics, of Wagner, and of the German Romantic school. He also programmed several American works, as long as they followed the Germanic tradition. The flowering of the Chicago Symph. Orch. was to be accomplished by his successors Fritz Reiner and Georg Solti. Stock was also a composer; his Violin Concerto was performed under his direction by Efrem Zimbalist at the Norfolk Festival on June 3, 1915.

Stockhausen, Franz, Jr., German conductor and educator, son of **Franz Stockhausen, Sr.,** and brother of **Julius Stockhausen;** b. Gebweiler, Alsace, Jan. 30, 1839; d. Strasbourg, Jan. 4, 1926. He received his early training from his father; then was a student of Alkan in Paris; subsequently studied at the Leipzig Cons., where his teachers were Moscheles, Richter, and Hauptmann (1860–62). He subsequently occupied various posts as a choral conductor and educator. In 1871 he was appointed director of the Strasbourg Cons.; he retired in 1907.

Stockhausen, Franz, Sr., German singer and harpist; b. Cologne, Sept. 1, 1789; d. Colmar, Sept. 10, 1868. In 1822 he organized in Paris the Académie de Chant, and gave concerts as a harpist.

Stockhausen, Julius, German baritone and teacher, son of the harpist and singer **Franz Stockhausen, Sr.;** b. Paris, July 22, 1826; d. Frankfurt, Sept. 22, 1906. He studied at the Paris Cons. and in London, where he was a pupil of Manuel García. He began his career as a concert singer and a choral conduc-

tor; conducted the Phil. concerts and the Singakademie in Hamburg (1862–67), and the Sternscher Gesangverein in Berlin (1874–78). Subsequently he was engaged as a singing teacher at the Frankfurt Hochschen Konservatorium. He was a personal friend of Brahms and was regarded as one of the finest interpreters of his lieder. He publ. *Gesangsmethode,* a standard work on singing (2 vols., 1886, 1887; also in Eng.).

Stockhausen, Karlheinz, German composer, leader of the cosmopolitan avant-garde; b. Mödrath, near Cologne, Aug. 22, 1928. He studied piano at the Hochschule für Musik in Cologne (1947–50) and took a course in composition with Frank Martin during the latter's residence there (1950–51); then went to Paris, where he studied privately with Olivier Messiaen and Darius Milhaud (1951–53); also investigated the potentialities of *musique concrète* and partly incorporated its techniques into his own empiric method of composition, which from the very first included highly complex contrapuntal conglomerates with uninhibited applications of non-euphonious dissonance as well as recourse to the primal procedures of obdurate iteration of single tones; all this set in the freest of rhythmic patterns and diversified by constantly changing instrumental colors with obsessive percussive effects. He further perfected a system of constructivist composition, in which the subjective choice of the performer determines the succession of given thematic ingredients and their polyphonic simultaneities, ultimately leading to a totality of aleatory procedures in which the ostensible application of a composer's commanding function is paradoxically reasserted by the inclusion of prerecorded materials and recombinant uses of electronically altered thematic ingredients. He further evolved energetic missionary activities in behalf of new music as a lecturer and master of ceremonies at avant-garde meetings all over the world; conducted summer seminars for the Ferienkurse für Musik in Darmstadt, which attracted auditors and musical cultists from the 5 continents of the globe; having mastered the intricacies of the English language, he made a lecture tour of Canadian and American univs. in 1958; was a visiting prof. at the Univ. of Calif., Davis, in 1966–67; in 1969 gave highly successful public lectures in England which were attended by hordes of musical and unmusical novitiates; publ. numerous misleading guidelines for the benefit of a growing contingent of his apostles, disciples, and acolytes. Stockhausen is a pioneer of "time-space" music, marked by a controlled improvisation, and adding the vectorial (i.e., directional) parameter to the 4 traditional aspects of serial music (pitch, duration, timbre, and dynamics), with performers and electronic apparatuses placed in different parts of the concert hall; such performances, directed by himself, are often accompanied by screen projections and audience participation; he also specifies the architectural aspects of the auditoriums in which he gives his demonstrations; thus, at the world's fair in Osaka, Japan, in 1970, he supervised the construction of a circular auditorium in the German pavilion; these demonstrations continued for 183 days, with 20 soloists and 5 lantern projections in live performances of his own works, each session lasting 5½ hours; the estimated live, radio, and television audience was 1,000,000 listeners. In 1963 he inaugurated courses of new music in Cologne; in 1971 he was appointed prof. of composition at the Hochschule für Musik there.

WORKS: *Kreuzspiel* for Orch. (1952); *Kontra-Punkte* for 10 Instruments (Cologne, May 26, 1953); *Klavierstück XI* (one of a series of constructivist pieces); *Zeitmasse* for Oboe, Flute, English Horn, Clarinet, and Bassoon (1956); *Der Gesang der Jünglinge*, to a text composed of disjected verbal particles from the Book of Daniel, dealing with the ordeal of 3 monotheistic Hebrew youths in the Babylonian fiery furnace, scored for 5 groups of loudspeakers surrounding the audience (first perf. at the Radio Studio in Cologne, May 30, 1956); *Gruppen*, spatial work for 3 Chamber Orchs. and 3 Conductors beating 3 different tempi (Cologne, March 24, 1959); *Kontakte* for Electronic Instruments, Piano, and Percussion (Cologne, June 11, 1960); *Carré* for 4 Orchs., 4 Choruses, and 4 Conductors (Hamburg, Oct. 28, 1960); *Zyklus* for One Percussionist (1961); *Momente* for Soprano, 4 Choruses (singing, speaking, whispering, screaming, laughing, stamping, clapping, etc.), 13 Instrumentalists, and Percussion (Cologne, May 21, 1962; extended and revised, 1965); *Mikrophonie I* and *II* for Flexible Ensembles (1964, 1965); *Stimmung* for 6 Singers (1967); *X* for Dancers autogenetically producing sounds by activating eggshells placed on the floor or piano wires strung across the stage (1967); *Hymnen*, electronic piece (Cologne, Nov. 30, 1967); *Aus den Sieben Tagen* for Optional Instruments, written out in graphic notation with verbal instructions, such as "play a tone in the certainty that you have plenty of time and space" (1968); *Telemusik* for an Instrumental Ensemble and Electronic Instruments (Warsaw, Sept. 23, 1968); *Plus-Minus* for Clarinet, Trombone, Cello, and 3 Pianos (Warsaw, Sept. 25, 1968); *Kurzwellen* for 5 Performers (1969); *Prozession* for Tam-tam, Viola, Electronium, Piano, and Microphone (1969); *Für kommende Zeiten* for "17 texts of intuitive music" (1968–70); *Beethausen, opus 1970, von Stockhoven*, bicentennial homage to Beethoven for Multimedia, using fragments from Beethoven's works and including a reading of the Heiligenstadt Testament (1970); *Mantra* for 2 Pianos (Donaueschingen, Oct. 18, 1970); *Sternklang*, "park music" for 5 Groups (1971); *Musik im Bauch (Music in the Belly)* for Percussion and Musical Clocks (1975); *Inori (Adorations)* for Soloists and Orch. (Donaueschingen, Oct. 20, 1974); *Atmen gibt das Leben* for Chorus (1974; Hamburg, May 16, 1975; revised as a choral opera, 1977); *Harlekin* for Clarinet (1975); *Tierkreis (Zodiac)* for Chamber Orch. (1975–77); *Sirius*, multimedia work for Vocalists, Trumpet, Bass Clarinet, and Electronic Sound, dedicated to American pioneers on earth and in space (first demonstrated at the National Air and Space Museum at the Smithsonian Institution, Washington, D.C., July 18, 1976); *Amour*, 5 pieces for Clarinet

(1976); *In Freundschaft* for various Solo Instruments (1977); also the grand spectacle *Light: The 7 Days of the Week* for Solo Voices, Solo Instruments, Solo Dancers, Chorus, Orch., Dancers, Electronic and Concrete Music; each day is its own opera; *Tuesday*, in one scene, entitled *Der Jahreslauf (In the Course of the Year)*, for Dancers and Orch. (1977); *Thursday*, in 3 acts: *Michaels Jugend (Michael's Youth)* for Soprano, Bass, Tenor, Trumpet, Basset Horn, Trombone, Modulated Piano, 3 Dancers, and Tape (1978–79), *Michaels Reise um die Erde (Michael's Journey around the Earth)* for Trumpet and Orch. (1978), and *Michaels Heimkehr (Michael's Return)* for Soprano, Tenor, Bass, Trumpet, Basset Horn, Trombone, 3 Dancers, Chorus, and Orch. (1979); *Saturday*, including *Lucifer's Dream* (1981–83); *Jubilee* for Orch. (N.Y., Sept. 10, 1981).

Stockhoff, Walter William, American composer; b. St. Louis, Nov. 12, 1876 (of German parentage); d. there, April 1, 1968. He was largely autodidact, and began to compose early in life. In his music he was influenced mainly by German Romantic composers, but his thematic material is distinctly American. In some of his early piano music he made use of modernistic devices, such as the whole-tone scale, cadential triads with the added sixth, etc. Busoni wrote an enthusiastic article about Stockhoff (1915) in which he described him as one of America's most original composers. The orch. version of Stockhoff's piano suite *To the Mountains* was performed for the first time, under the title *American Symphonic Suite*, in Frankfurt, Germany, on Dec. 10, 1924. Several of his piano works and some chamber music were publ. by Breitkopf & Härtel. Other works include *5 Dramatic Poems* for Orch. (1943); Piano Sonata; *Metamorphoses* for Piano; etc.

Stoeckel, Carl, American patron of music, son of **Gustav Jakob Stoeckel;** b. New Haven, Conn., Dec. 7, 1858; d. Norfolk, Conn., Nov. 1, 1925. His contribution to American musical culture was the establishment in 1902 of the summer festivals on his estate in Norfolk. He offered cash prizes to composers who appeared at the festival in performances of their own works. Sibelius composed his tone poem *Aallottaret* especially for the Norfolk Festival, and conducted its world premiere there in 1914. Among other composers represented were J.A. Carpenter, G.W. Chadwick, S. Coleridge-Taylor, H.F. Gilbert, P. Grainger, H.K. Hadley, E.S. Kelly, C.M. Loeffler, H. Parker, D.S. Smith, C.V. Stanford, and Deems Taylor.

Stoessel, Albert, American conductor and composer; b. St. Louis, Oct. 11, 1894; d. New York, May 12, 1943. He went to Germany as a youth; studied violin with Willy Hess and theory with Kretzschmar in Berlin, and appeared as a violin soloist there in 1914. Returning to the U.S., he turned to conducting; succeeded Walter Damrosch as conductor of the N.Y. Oratorio Society; in 1930 was appointed director of the opera dept. of the Juilliard Graduate

School of Music in N.Y. He was stricken fatally while conducting the first performance of the symph. sketch *Dunkirk,* by Walter Damrosch. His *Suite Antique* for 2 Violins and Piano (1922) enjoyed a few performances. His opera *Garrick* was produced under his direction at Juilliard on Feb. 24, 1937. He publ. *The Technic of the Baton* (N.Y., 1920; new ed., 1928).

Stoeving, (Carl Heinrich) Paul, German-American violinist and composer; b. Leipzig, May 7, 1861; d. New York, Dec. 24, 1948. He studied violin in Leipzig and in Paris; toured as a soloist in Russia and Scandinavia; in 1896 went to London, where he taught at the Guildhall School of Music. At the outbreak of World War I he emigrated to the U.S. and was employed as a violin teacher in New Haven and N.Y. He wrote the "song-play" *Gaston and Jolivette* and some violin music of considerable insignificance, but his publications on violin technique have a certain pragmatic value; among them are *The Art of Violin Bowing* (London, 1902); *The Story of the Violin* (London, 1904); *The Mastery of the Bow and Bowing Subtleties* (N.Y., 1920); *The Violin, Cello and String Quartet* (N.Y., 1927); *The Violin: Its Famous Makers and Players* (Boston, 1928).

Stöhr, Richard, Austrian music theorist and composer; b. Vienna, June 11, 1874; d. Montpelier, Vt., Dec. 11, 1967. He studied medicine (M.D., 1898), but then turned to music and studied with Robert Fuchs and others at the Vienna Cons. In 1903 he was appointed instructor in theory there, and during his long tenure he had many pupils who later became celebrated (Artur Rodzinski, Erich Leinsdorf, etc.). In 1938 he was compelled to leave Vienna; settled in the U.S., where he taught at the Curtis Inst. of Music in Philadelphia (1939–42); then taught music and German at St. Michael's College in Winooski, Vt. (1943–50). A concert of his works was given by the Vermont State Symph. Orch. on Oct. 31, 1954, including the world premiere of his *Vermont Suite,* an early symph., and songs accompanied by the composer. He further wrote 4 symphs.; much chamber music; piano pieces. He publ. a popular manual, *Praktischer Leitfaden der Harmonielehre* (Vienna, 1909; 21st ed., 1963); also *Praktischer Leitfaden des Kontrapunkts* (Hamburg, 1911); *Modulationslehre* (1932).

Stojanović, Peter Lazar, violinist and composer; b. Budapest, Sept. 6, 1877; d. Belgrade, Sept. 12, 1957. He studied violin with Hubay at the Budapest Cons. and with J. Grün at the Vienna Cons.; in 1913 established his own school for advanced violin playing in Vienna. In 1925 he settled in Belgrade and became a prof. at the Stankovic Music School; was its director from 1925 to 1928; in 1937–45 he was a prof. of violin at the Belgrade Academy of Music. His works include the operas *A Tigris (The Tiger;* Budapest, Nov. 14, 1905); *Das Liebchen am Dache* (Vienna, May 19, 1917); *Der Herzog von Reichsstadt* (Vienna, Feb. 11, 1921); an operetta, *Orlić;* 2 ballets; a symph. poem, *Heldentod;* 7 violin concertos, 2 viola concer-

tos, a Flute Concerto, a Horn Concerto; several pieces of chamber music, including a Piano Trio, a Piano Quartet, and a Piano Quintet. He publ. *Schule der Skalentechnik* for Violin.

Stojowski, Sigismund, Polish pianist; b. Strzelce, May 14, 1869; d. New York, Nov. 5, 1946. He was a pupil of Zelenski at Cracow and of Diémer (piano) and Delibes (composition) at the Paris Cons. (1887–89), winning first prize for piano playing and composition; later he took a course with Paderewski. At an orch. concert of his own works given in Paris in 1891, he played his Piano Concerto; he remained in Paris until 1906, when he emigrated to the U.S. as head of the piano dept. at the Inst. of Musical Art in N.Y.; later held a similar position at the Von Ende School of Music in N.Y.; taught at the Juilliard Summer School for several years. He became a naturalized American citizen in 1938. In his prime he was extremely successful as a concert pianist, and in his later years was greatly esteemed as a pedagogue. His works include, besides his Piano Concerto, *Prologue, Scherzo and Variations* for Piano and Orch., performed by him (as Piano Concerto No. 2) in London, June 23, 1913, under the direction of Nikisch; many solo piano pieces; *Prayer for Poland* for Chorus and Orch. (1915); 2 violin sonatas; a Cello Sonata.

Stoker, Richard, English composer; b. Castleford, Yorkshire, Nov. 8, 1938. He studied composition with Eric Fenby and later with Lennox Berkeley at the Royal Academy of Music in London, and with Nadia Boulanger in Paris. In his music he cultivates the 12-tone technique, but derives it tonally from the quintal cycle of scales. As a believer in the universality of the arts, he writes utilitarian music for dilettantes, amateurs, musicasters, and children.

Stokowski, Leopold, celebrated, spectacularly endowed, and magically communicative English-American conductor; b. (of a Polish father and an Irish mother) London, April 18, 1882; d. Nether Wallop, Hampshire, Sept. 13, 1977. He attended Queen's College, Oxford, and the Royal College of Music in London, where he studied organ with Stevenson Hoyte, music theory with Walford Davies, and composition with Sir Charles Stanford. At the age of 18 he obtained the post of organist at St. James, Piccadilly. In 1905 he went to America and served as organist and choirmaster at St. Bartholomew's in N.Y.; became a U.S. citizen in 1915. In 1909 he was engaged to conduct the Cincinnati Symph. Orch.; although his contract was for 5 years, he obtained a release after 3 years of tenure in order to accept an offer from the Philadelphia Orch. This was the beginning of a long and spectacular career as a symph. conductor; he led the Philadelphia Orch. for 23 years, bringing it to a degree of brilliance that rivaled the greatest orchs. in the world. In 1931 he was officially designated by the board of directors of the Philadelphia Orch. as music director, which gave him control over the choice of guest conductors and soloists. He conducted most of the repertoire by heart, an impressive accomplishment at the time; he changed the seating of the orch., placing violins to the left and cellos to the right. After some years of leading the orch. with a baton, he finally dispensed with it and shaped the music with the 10 fingers of his hands. He emphasized the colorful elements in the music; he was the creator of the famous "Philadelphia sound" in the strings, achieving a well-nigh *bel canto* quality. Tall and slender, with an aureole of blond hair, his figure presented a striking contrast with his stocky, mustachioed German predecessors; he was the first conductor to attain the status of a star comparable to that of a motion picture actor. Abandoning the proverbial ivory tower in which most conductors dwelt, he actually made an appearance as a movie actor in the film *One Hundred Men and a Girl.* In 1940 he agreed to participate in the production of Walt Disney's celebrated film *Fantasia,* which featured both live performers and animated characters; Stokowski conducted the music and in one sequence engaged in a bantering colloquy with Mickey Mouse. He was lionized by the Philadelphians; in 1922 he received the Edward Bok Award of $10,000 as "the person who has done the most for Philadelphia." He was praised in superlative terms in the press, but not all music critics approved of his cavalier treatment of sacrosanct masterpieces, for he allowed himself to alter the orchestration; he doubled some solo passages in the brass, and occasionally introduced percussion instruments not provided in the score; he even cut out individual bars that seemed to him devoid of musical action. Furthermore, Stokowski's own orch. arrangements of Bach raised the pedantic eyebrows of professional musicologists; yet there is no denying the effectiveness of the sonority and the subtlety of color that he succeeded in creating by such means. Many great musicians hailed Stokowski's new orch. sound; Rachmaninoff regarded the Philadelphia Orch. under Stokowski, and later under Ormandy, as the greatest with which he had performed. Stokowski boldly risked his popularity with the Philadelphia audiences by introducing modern works. He conducted Schoenberg's music, culminating in the introduction of his formidable score *Gurrelieder* on April 8, 1932. An even greater gesture of defiance of popular tastes was his world premiere of *Amériques* by Varèse on April 9, 1926, a score that opens with a siren and thrives on dissonance. Stokowski made history by joining the forces of the Philadelphia Orch. with the Philadelphia Grand Opera Co. in the first American performance of Alban Berg's modern masterpiece *Wozzeck* (March 31, 1931). The opposition of some listeners was now vocal; when the audible commotion in the audience erupted during Stokowski's performance of Anton von Webern's Symph., he abruptly stopped conducting, walked off the stage, then returned only to begin the work all over again. From his earliest years with the Philadelphia Orch., Stokowski adopted the habit of addressing the audience, to caution them to keep their peace during the performance of a modernistic score, or reprimanding them for their lack of progressive views; once he even took to task the

prim Philadelphia ladies for bringing their knitting to the concert. In 1933 the board of directors took an unusual step in announcing that there would be no more "debatable music" performed by the orch.; Stokowski refused to heed this proclamation. Another eruption of discontent ensued when Stokowski programmed some Soviet music at a youth concert and trained the children to sing the Internationale. Stokowski was always interested in new electronic sound; he was the first to make use of the Theremin in the orch. in order to enhance the sonorities of the bass section. He was instrumental in introducing electrical recordings. In 1936 he resigned as music director of the Philadelphia Orch.; he was succeeded by Eugene Ormandy but continued to conduct occasional concerts as co-conductor of the orch. In 1940–42 he took a newly organized All-American Youth Orch. on a tour in the U.S. and in South America. During the season 1942–43 he was associate conductor, with Toscanini, of the NBC Symph. Orch.; he shared the season of 1949–50 with Mitropoulos as conductor of the N.Y. Phil.; from 1955 to 1960 he conducted the Houston Symph. In 1962 he organized in N.Y. the American Symph. Orch. and led it until 1972; on April 26, 1965, at the age of 83, he conducted the orch. in the first complete performance of the 4th Symph. of Charles Ives. In 1973 he went to London, where he continued to make recordings and conduct occasional concerts; he also appeared in television interviews. He died in his sleep at the age of 95; rumor had it that he had a contract signed for a gala performance on his 100th birthday in 1982. Stokowski was married 3 times: his first wife was the pianist **Olga Samaroff,** whom he married in 1911; they were divorced in 1923; his 2nd wife was Evangeline Brewster Johnson, heiress to the Johnson and Johnson drug fortune; they were married in 1926 and divorced in 1937; his 3rd marriage, to Gloria Vanderbilt, produced a ripple of prurient newspaper publicity because of the disparity in their ages; he was 63, she was 21; they were married in 1945 and divorced in 1955. Stokowski publ. a popular book, *Music for All of Us* (N.Y., 1943), which was translated into the Russian, Italian, and Czech languages.

Stoltz, Rosine (real name, **Victoire Noël**), French mezzo-soprano; b. Paris, Feb. 13, 1815; d. there, July 28, 1903. She was the daughter of a janitor; was sent by Duchess de Berri to a convent, and in 1826 to the Choron School, which she entered under the name of Rosa Nina. She first appeared in public under the assumed name of **Mlle. Ternaux,** later as **Mlle. Héloise Stoltz** (the latter being derived from her mother's maiden name, Stoll). Her first important engagement was in Brussels on June 3, 1836, when she sang Rachel in Halévy's *La Juive,* with Adolphe Nourrit, who recommended her to the administration of the Paris Opéra; made her debut there as Rachel on Aug. 25, 1837. She became intimate with Leon Pillet, manager of the Opéra from 1844, and through him wielded considerable influence on appointments of new singers; after a series of attacks in the press, accusing her of unworthy intrigues, she resigned in March 1847; fought for vindication through 3 obviously inspired pamphlets (C. Cantinjou, *Les Adieux de Madame Stoltz;* E. Pérignon, *Rosine Stoltz;* and J. Lemer, *Madame Rosine Stoltz*), all publ. in 1847. At the invitation of the Brazilian Emperor Don Pedro (who was romantically attached to her) she made 4 tours of Brazil between 1850 and 1859, at a salary of 400,000 francs a season. She was married to A. Lescuyer (March 2, 1837, legitimizing a son born Sept. 21, 1836); was subsequently married to the Duke Carlo Lesignano (May 18, 1872); assumed the title of Baroness von Ketschendorf, from the castle given her by Ernest Ketschendorf, Duke of Saxe-Coburg-Gotha. She publ. 6 songs (not composed by her, in all probability), and her name (as Princesse de Lesignano) was used as author of a learned vol., *Les Constitutions de tous les pays civilisés* (1880), which was written in her behalf. The mystifying aspects of her private life and public career are recounted by G. Bord in *Rosine Stoltz* (Paris, 1909) and by A. Pougin in "La Vérité sur Madame Stoltz," *Le Ménestrel* (Aug. 28, 1909, *et seq.*).

Stoltzer, Thomas, German composer of sacred music; b. Schweidnitz, Silesia, c.1475; d. as chaplain of the Hungarian King Louis in the battle of Mohács, Aug. 29, 1526. He entered the service of Hungary in 1522. His Latin Psalms were publ. in 1538, 1545, and 1569; German songs were included in collections of 1536, 1539, and 1544. His *Octo tonorum melodiae,* containing instrumental fantasies for 5 voices, is a collection of pieces in all 8 church modes. Modern reprints are in Denkmäler Deutscher Tonkunst, 34 and 65; *Das Chorwerk,* 6; and *Das Erbe deutscher Musik,* 22 and 66.

Stoltzman, Richard, American clarinet virtuoso; b. Omaha, July 12, 1942. He earned a B.Mus. degree from Ohio State Univ. and a M.Mus. degree from Yale Univ.; spent summers at the Marlboro Music School and Festival; became a founding member of TASHI, the chamber music ensemble; subsequently toured the U.S., South America, Europe, and Japan with it. His repertoire is extensive, and includes the standard literature as well as contemporary works.

Stolz, Robert, Austrian operetta composer; b. Graz, Aug. 25, 1880; d. West Berlin, June 27, 1975. He studied music with his father; then took lessons with Robert Fuchs in Vienna and with Humperdinck in Berlin. He conducted performances at the Theater an der Wien for 12 years, and also filled guest engagements in Europe. In 1938 he went to Paris, and in 1940 proceeded to the U.S.; he returned to Vienna in 1946. He possessed an extraordinary facility for stage music and composed 27 operettas in a typical Viennese manner; of these the most famous is *2 Herzen im 3/4 Takt* (Zürich, Sept. 30, 1933). Other operettas are: *Die lustigen Weiber von Wien* (Munich, 1909); *Das Glücksmädel* (1910); *Das Lumperl* (Graz, 1915); *Lang, lang, ist's her* (Vienna, March 28, 1917); *Der Tanz ins Glück* (Vienna, Oct. 18, 1921); *Die Tanzgräfin* (Vienna, May 13, 1921); *Mädi* (Vien-

na, Oct. 5, 1923); *Ein Ballroman oder Der Kavalier von zehn bis vier* (Vienna, Feb. 29, 1924); *Eine einzige Nacht* (Vienna, Dec. 23, 1927); *Peppina* (1931); *Wild Violets* (1932); *Venus in Seide* (1932); *Frühling im Prater* (Vienna, Dec. 22, 1949); *Karneval in Wien* (1950); *Trauminsel* (Bregenz, July 21, 1962); *Frühjahrs-Parade* (Vienna, March 25, 1964). He wrote a number of film scores and nearly 2,000 lieder. After he was forced to leave Austria, he composed a funeral march for Hitler (at a time when Hitler was, unfortunately, very much alive).

Stolz, Teresa (Teresina), soprano; b. Kosteletz, Bohemia, June 2, 1834; d. Milan, Aug. 23, 1902. She studied at the Cons. of Prague, and later with Luigi Ricci in Trieste; began her operatic career in Russia; her debut was in Tiflis in 1857; from 1863 to 1879 she appeared with brilliant success at the principal Italian opera houses. She was greatly admired by Verdi, and was famous in the roles of Aida, and of Leonora in *La forza del destino.* Her farewell appearance was in Verdi's *Requiem* at La Scala in Milan on June 30, 1879.

Stölzel (Stölz), Gottfried Heinrich, German composer; b. Grünstädtl, Jan. 13, 1690; d. Gotha, Nov. 27, 1749. He studied with the cantor Umlaufft at Schneeberg, and with Melchior Hofmann at Leipzig; became a music teacher in Breslau (1710–12), where his opera *Narcissus* was performed in 1711; this was followed by productions of his operas *Valeria, Artemisia,* and *Orion* (all in 1712). After a journey to Italy, he was in Prague, where he brought out the operas *Venus und Adonis* (1714), *Acis und Galathea* (1715), and *Das durch die Liebe besiegte Glück* (1716). He subsequently went to Bayreuth, where he produced the opera *Diomedes* (1717); to Gera; and to Gotha, where he produced *Der Musenberg* (1723). Altogether he wrote 22 operas, the pastoral *Rosen und Dornen,* 14 oratorios, 8 double sets of cantatas and motets for the church year, other religious works, symphs., serenades, concertos, etc.; a Concerto Grosso edited by Schering is found in Denkmäler Deutscher Tonkunst, 29–30; a Solo Cantata for Contralto was edited by J. Bachmair (1926). Stölzel's autobiography was reprinted in *Selbstbiographien deutscher Musiker,* edited by Willi Kahl (Cologne, 1948).

Stone, Kurt, German-American musicologist; b. Hamburg, Nov. 14, 1911. He studied music in Hamburg and Copenhagen; came to N.Y. in 1938 and entered the field of music publishing; held editorial positions with the Associated Music Publishers and G. Schirmer, Inc.; contributed knowledgeable articles on modern music and composers to various periodicals. He also edited reprints of old music, among them *Parthenia* (N.Y., 1951); trans. from the German (with his wife, Else Stone) the *Handbook of Percussion Instruments* by Karl Peinkofer and Fritz Tannigel (N.Y., 1977); also with his wife, edited and annotated *The Writings of Elliott Carter* (Bloomington, Ind., 1977).

Storace, (Anna Selina) Nancy, celebrated English soprano; b. London, Oct. 27, 1765; d. there, Aug. 24, 1817. She was of Italian origin; her father, **Stefano Storace,** was a player on the double bass; her brother **Stephen Storace** was a composer. She was a pupil of Rauzzini and of Sacchini in Venice; sang in Florence (1780), Parma (1781), and Milan (1782); then went to Vienna (1783), where she was engaged at the court opera. She created the role of Susanna in Mozart's *Nozze di Figaro* (May 1, 1786). Returning to England in 1787, she became popular as a singer in comic operas. She retired from the stage in 1808.

Storace, Stephen, English composer; b. London, April 4, 1762; d. there, March 19, 1796. He was a brother of **Nancy Storace,** and son of **Stefano Storace,** an excellent double-bass player of Italian descent; the original family name was Sorace, but upon moving to England it was found that the pronunciation "sore-ass" was offensive. He studied violin at the Cons. di S. Onofrio in Naples; then followed his sister to Vienna, and became acquainted with Mozart there. Two of his operas to Italian librettos were produced in Vienna, with satisfying success: *Gli Sposi malcontenti* (June 1, 1785) and *Gli equivoci* (Dec. 27, 1786). Back in London he produced another Italian opera, *La Cameriera astuta* (March 4, 1788), and a number of English operas, among which *The Haunted Tower,* produced on Nov. 24, 1789, became extremely successful, and was revived in performance in London as late as 1922. His other operas were *No Song, No Supper* (April 16, 1790); *The Siege of Belgrade* (Jan. 1, 1791); *The Pirates* (Nov. 21, 1792); *The Prize* (March 11, 1793); *My Grandmother* (Dec. 16, 1793); *The Cherokee* (Dec. 20, 1794); *The 3 and the Deuce* (Sept. 2, 1795). A grand opera, *Mahmoud, or The Prince of Persia,* left unfinished at his death, was completed by Michael Kelly and performed posthumously on April 30, 1796. Storace wrote several other pieces for the theater, some of them adaptations, admitted or concealed, of operas by other composers, e.g., Dittersdorf's *Doktor und Apotheker* and Salieri's *Grotta di Trofonio.*

Storch, M. Anton, Austrian conductor and composer; b. Vienna, Dec. 22, 1813; d. there, Dec. 31, 1888. He was conductor at the Carl and Josephstadt theaters in Vienna, and produced several of his operettas and opera-burlesques there: *Romeo und Julie* (Oct. 31, 1863); *Das Festkleid* (April 1, 1865); *Löwen im Dorfe* (Sept. 27, 1866); *Wiener Zugstücke* (April 26, 1868); *Prinz Taugenichts* (March 8, 1870; successful); wrote many favorite male quartets (*Letzte Treue, Grün,* etc.).

Storchio, Rosina, Italian soprano; b. Venice, May 19, 1876; d. Milan, July 24, 1945. She studied at the Milan Cons.; then made her debut at Milan's Teatro del Verme as Micaela in *Carmen* in 1892. On Feb. 17, 1904, she created the title role in the world premiere of *Madama Butterfly* at La Scala in Milan. After a series of tours in South America and in Europe, she was briefly engaged at the Chicago Opera (1920–21); then retired from the stage. She was paralyzed during the last years of her life as a result of an apoplectic stroke.

Stout, Alan, significant American composer; b. Baltimore, Nov. 26, 1932. He studied composition with Henry Cowell at the Peabody Cons. in Baltimore; sporadically had composition lessons with Riegger in N.Y. (1951–56); then went to Denmark and took a course with Holmboe (1954–55); returning to the U.S., he had lessons with John Verrall at the Univ. of Washington (1958–59), acquiring an M.A. in music and in Swedish language; from 1959 to 1962 was employed in the music dept. of the Seattle Public Library; in 1963 he was appointed to the music faculty of Northwestern Univ.; in 1973 was a visiting lecturer at the State College of Music in Stockholm. Besides his primary activities as a composer and a teacher, he also performed valuable service in editing (with some conjectural reconstruction) fragmentary pieces by Ives, to prepare them for practical performance.
WORKS: FOR ORCH.: 4 symphs.: No. 1 (1959); No. 2 (1951–66; Ravinia Festival, Chicago Symph., Aug. 4, 1968); No. 3 for Soprano, Male Chorus, and Orch. (1959–62); No. 4 (1962–71; Chicago, April 15, 1971); *3 Hymns* for Orch. (1953–54); *Intermezzo* for English Horn, Percussion, and Strings (1954); *Pietà* for String or Brass Orch. (1957); *Serenity* for Solo Cello or Bassoon, Percussion, and Strings (1959); *Ricercare and Aria* for Strings (1959); *Movements* for Violin and Orch. (1962; Fish Creek, Wis., Aug. 17, 1966); *Fanfare for Charles Seeger* for Orch. (1972); *Pulsar* for 3 Brass Choirs and Timpani (1972); *Nimbus* for 18 Strings (1979); *Pilvia* (1983). VOCAL WORKS: *2 Hymns* for Tenor and Orch. (1953); *Die Engel* for Soprano, Flute, Piano, Percussion, and Brass (1957); *2 Ariel Songs* for Soprano and Chamber Ensemble (1957); *Laudi* for Soprano, Baritone, and Small Orch. (1961); *Elegiac Suite* for Soprano and Strings (1959–61); *Canticum canticorum* for Soprano and Chamber Ensemble (1962); *George Lieder* for High Baritone and Orch. (1962; revised 1965 and 1970; Chicago, Dec. 14, 1972); *Christmas Poem* for Soprano and Chamber Ensemble (1962); *Prologue,* oratorio (1963–64); *Nattstycken (Nocturnes)* for Narrator, Contralto, and Chamber Ensemble (1969–70; Chicago, Nov. 10, 1970); *Dialogo per la Pascua* for Soloists, Chorus, and 8 Instruments (1973); *O Altitudo* for Soprano, Women's Chorus, Solo Flute, and Instrumental Ensemble (1974); *Passion,* oratorio (1953–75; Chicago, April 15, 1976); *5 visages de Laforgue* for Voice and Chamber Orch. (1978); *Triptych* for Soloists, Children's Chorus, and Orch. (1981); choruses, including *The Great Day of the Lord* (with Organ, 1956).

Stradal, August, Bohemian pianist; b. Teplitz, May 17, 1860; d. Schönlinde, Germany, March 13, 1930. He studied composition with Bruckner at the Vienna Cons. and piano with Door; was a pupil of Liszt in 1884, and became an ardent propagandist for Liszt's piano music; gave concerts in Germany, Austria,

France, and England; made arrangements of Liszt's orch. works; also of works by Bach, Frescobaldi, etc. His original compositions consist of piano pieces (*Ungarische Rhapsodie,* etc.) and songs. He wrote *Erinnerungen an Franz Liszt* (Bern, 1929).

Stradella, Alessandro, important Italian composer; b. Nepi, near Viterbo, 1639; d. (murdered) Genoa, Feb. 25, 1682. He was a scion of nobility; received his early training in Bologna. In 1667 he went to Rome, where he composed oratorios, prologues, intermezzos for opera, etc. He led a tempestuous life, replete with illicit liaisons, flights from personal vendettas, and some criminal acts. In Rome he attempted to embezzle funds from the Roman Catholic Church, and in 1669 fled the city to avoid exposure. He returned to Rome after the affair calmed down, but again got in trouble when he aroused the enmity of Cardinal Alderan Cibo. In 1677 he was forced to flee Rome again, and he went to Venice, where he became involved in a torrid affair with the fiancée of the Venetian nobleman Alvise Contarini; he persuaded the lady to accompany him to Turin, and the outraged bridegroom and a band of assassins followed in hot pursuit. Stradella escaped and fled to Genoa. There he became entangled with a married woman, a sister of the Lomellini brothers, who had a high social standing in the town. This time Stradella failed to evade the vengeful brothers, who hired an experienced murderer to kill him; the bloody deed was done on Feb. 25, 1682. A rather successful opera, *Alessandro Stradella* by Flotow (Hamburg, 1844), dramatized his stormy life and death; other operas on Stradella were composed by Niedermeyer (Paris, 1837) and Sinico (Lugo, 1863). As a composer, Stradella left an important legacy, both in opera and in instrumental writing. His operas *La forza dell'amor paterno, Le gare dell'amore eroico,* and *Il Trespole tutore* were staged in Genoa (1678–79); he also composed the oratorio *La Susanna* and a wedding serenade, *Il barcheggio,* for Duke Francesco d'Este of Modena (1681). Other operas were *Il moro per amore, Il Corispero,* and *Doriclea.* His oratorios include *S. Giovanni Battista* and *S. Giovanni Crisostomo;* another oratorio, *S. Editta, vergine e monaca, regina d'Inghilterra,* remained unfinished. He wrote about 25 sinfonias (sonatas), most of them for violin, with basso ostinato; motets; arias; and canzonettas. An edition of Stradella's oratorios was begun in 1969, under the editorship of L. Bianchi.

Stradivari (Stradivarius), Antonio, the most celebrated of all violin makers; b. Cremona, 1644 (according to Bacchetta, end of 1648 or beginning of 1649); d. there, Dec. 18, 1737. He was a pupil of Niccolò Amati and worked for him from about 1666 to 1679. He purchased the house in which, for half a century, his workshop was situated, in 1680. His finest instruments were made in the period from 1700 to 1725, but he still worked up to the year of his death; he made his last instrument at the age of 92. His label reads: "Antonius Stradivarius Cremonensis. Fecit Anno . . . (A × S)." His cellos command even higher prices than the violins, and violas the highest of all, for he made very few of them. Stradivari had 11 children; of them **Francesco** (b. Feb. 1, 1671; d. May 11, 1743) and **Omobono** (b. Nov. 14, 1679; d. July 8, 1742) were his co-workers. Stradivari also made viols of early types, guitars, lutes, mandolins, etc.

Straeten, Edmund. See **Van der Straeten.**

Strakosch, Maurice, Bohemian impresario; b. Gross-Seelowitz, 1825; d. Paris, Oct. 9, 1887. He studied with Sechter at the Vienna Cons.; traveled as a pianist in Europe; came to America in 1848, settling in N.Y. as a teacher; from 1856 he was active mainly as an impresario. He was the brother-in-law of Adelina Patti, and managed her concerts. He gave his first season of Italian opera in N.Y. in 1857, and in 1859 took his company to Chicago; then went to Europe. His opera *Giovanna di Napoli* was brought out in N.Y.; he also wrote salon pieces for piano; publ. *Ten Commandments of Music for the Perfection of the Voice* (posthumous; 1896) and *Souvenirs d'un Impresario* (Paris, 2nd ed., 1887). After his departure from America, his brother, Max Strakosch (1834–92), carried on the management of his enterprises.

Strang, Gerald, inventive American composer; b. Claresholm, Canada, Feb. 13, 1908; d. Loma Linda, Calif., during open-heart surgery, Oct. 2, 1983. He joined the ranks of the early California modernists, headed by Henry Cowell. He studied at Stanford Univ., at the Univ. of Calif., Los Angeles, and at the Univ. of Southern Calif., where he received his doctorate. He also took private lessons in composition with Ernst Toch and Arnold Schoenberg, and served as Schoenberg's assistant at the Univ. of Calif. from 1936–38. He interrupted his musical pursuits during the war years, when he was employed as an engineer at Douglas Aircraft Co. After the war he resumed his teaching at Long Beach City College (1938–43 and 1945–58); in 1958 he founded the music dept. at Calif. State Univ. at Northridge (formerly, San Fernando Valley State College). From 1965–69 he was chairman of the music dept. at Calif. State Univ. at Long Beach; later taught electronic music composition at the Univ. of Calif., Los Angeles, retiring in 1974. His music is strongly formal, with a unifying technical idea determining the content. An intelligent, energetic, and astute musical technician, he experimented successfully with the new resources available in the fields of acoustics, electronics, and computers; he was also active as an editor of modern works and was for many years an associate of Henry Cowell in editing Cowell's *New Music Quarterly.* The titles of his compositions give clues to their formative semiotics; thus his piano piece *Mirrorrorrim* is an obvious palindrome or cancrizans. His series of 4 *Synclavions* is an electronic synthesis of keyboard variations. Similarly suggestive are his various pieces bearing such titles as *Compusitions* (= computerized compositions) and *Synthions* (= synthetic ions). Strang was also active in the field of acoustics, and served as a consultant on some 25 newly built auditoriums in California and elsewhere.

Stransky, Josef, Bohemian conductor; b. Humpoletz, near Deutschbrod, Bohemia, Sept. 9, 1872; d. New York, March 6, 1936. While studying medicine (M.D., Univ. of Prague, 1896), he also studied music, in Leipzig with Jadassohn and in Vienna with R. Fuchs, Bruckner, and Dvořák. In 1898 he was engaged by A. Neumann as first Kapellmeister at the Landestheater in Prague; in 1903 he went in a similar capacity to the Stadttheater in Hamburg; in 1910 he resigned from the Hamburg opera to devote himself to concert work; in the autumn of 1911 became Mahler's successor as conductor of the N.Y. Phil. Society, a position he held until 1923. A bequest of $1,000,000 to the society (by Joseph Pulitzer, 1912) enabled Stransky to carry out successfully the sweeping reforms instituted by his illustrious predecessor (chief of which was a system of daily rehearsals during the season of 23 weeks). He wrote an operetta, *Der General,* which was produced in Hamburg.

Straram, Walther, French conductor; b. London (of French parents), July 9, 1876; d. Paris, Nov. 24, 1933. He was educated in Paris; played violin in Paris orchs.; then was choirmaster at the Opéra-Comique; later traveled to America as assistant to André Caplet at the Boston Opera Co. Returning to Paris, he established the Concerts Straram, which enjoyed a fine reputation. He conducted the first performance of Ravel's *Boléro* for Ida Rubinstein (dance recital, Nov. 22, 1928).

Stratas, Teresa (real name, **Anastasia Stratakis**), outstanding Canadian soprano of Greek extraction; b. Toronto, May 26, 1938. Her father owned a restaurant in a town near Toronto, and she was allowed from her earliest childhood to sing for customers. She also sang in concert with her brother, a violinist, and her sister, a pianist. In 1954 she entered the Royal Cons. of Music of Toronto, where she studied voice with Irene Jessner; she graduated with an Artist Diploma in 1959. She made her professional operatic debut with the Toronto Opera Festival as Mimi on Oct. 13, 1958. In 1959 she was a co-winner of the Metropolitan Opera Auditions, which led to her formal debut with the company in N.Y. on Oct. 28, 1959, as Poussette in *Manon.* She soon established herself as a singer of great versatility. She sang virtually all the standard soprano parts, and she demonstrated her particular mettle and fettle in the complete version of Alban Berg's opera *Lulu,* which was given for the first time in Paris on May 28, 1979. She won international acclaim for her dramatic portrayal of Violetta in Zeffirelli's film version of *La Traviata* (1983). She also sang at the Bolshoi Theater in Moscow and at La Scala in Milan. In 1972 she was made an Officer of the Order of Canada.

Straube, Karl, prominent German organist; b. Ber-

lin, Jan. 6, 1873; d. Leipzig, April 27, 1950. He was a scion of an ancient ecclesiastical family; his father was an organist and instrument maker in Berlin; his mother was an Englishwoman who was a piano student of Sir Julius Benedict. He studied organ with Dienel; then took organ lessons with Reimann in Berlin. From 1897 to 1902 he was organist at the Cathedral of Wesel; in 1902 he became organist at the famous Thomaskirche in Leipzig; in 1903 he was appointed conductor of the Bachverein there, and in 1907 became a prof. at the Leipzig Cons. and organist *ex officio* at Gewandhaus. In 1918 he became cantor at the Thomaskirche. At his suggestion the Gewandhaus Chorus and the Bachverein were united in 1919, and he conducted the combined choir. He conducted the Handel Festival in 1925, leading to the formation of the Handel Society. In his teaching he followed the great tradition of Leipzig organists, traceable to Bach. A Festschrift was publ. for him on his 70th birthday (Leipzig, 1943). Among Straube's numerous collections of organ and choral pieces are *Alte Orgelmeister* (1904); *45 Choralvorspiele alter Meister* (1907); *Alte Meister des Orgelspiels* (2 vols., 1929); *Ausgewählte Gesänge des Thomanerchors* (1930); he brought out editions of several works of Bach, Handel, and Liszt. His *Briefe eines Thomaskantors* was publ. posthumously (Stuttgart, 1952).

Straus, Oscar, Austrian operetta composer; b. Vienna, March 6, 1870; d. Bad Ischl, Jan. 11, 1954. (His name was spelled "Strauss" on his birth certificate; he cut off the 2nd "s" to segregate himself from the multitudinous musical Strausses.) He studied privately in Vienna with A. Prosnitz and H. Grädener, and with Max Bruch in Berlin. From 1893 to 1900 he conducted at various theaters in Austria and Germany; in 1901 he became conductor of the artistic cabaret Überbrettl, managed by Ernst von Wolzogen in Berlin, and wrote a number of musical farces for it. He remained in Berlin until 1927; then lived in Vienna and Paris; on Sept. 3, 1939, he became a French citizen. In 1940 he went to America; lived in N.Y. and Hollywood until 1948, when he returned to Europe. He was one of the most successful composers of Viennese operettas. WORKS: His most celebrated production was *Der tapfere Soldat,* based on G.B. Shaw's play *Arms and the Man* (Vienna, Nov. 14, 1908; in N.Y. as *The Chocolate Soldier,* Nov. 13, 1909; London, Sept. 10, 1910; numerous perfs. all over the world). Other operettas are: *Die lustigen Nibelungen* (Vienna, Nov. 12, 1904); *Hugdietrichs Brautfahrt* (Vienna, March 10, 1906); *Ein Walzertraum* (Vienna, March 2, 1907; revised 1951); *Didi* (Vienna, Oct. 23, 1909); *Das Tal der Liebe* (Berlin and Vienna, simultaneously, Dec. 23, 1909); *Mein junger Herr* (Vienna, Dec. 23, 1910); *Die kleine Freundin* (Vienna, Oct. 20, 1911); *Love and Laughter* (London, 1913); *Rund um die Liebe* (Vienna, Nov. 9, 1914; in N.Y. as *All around Love,* 1917); *Die himmelblaue Zeit* (Vienna, Feb. 21, 1914); *Die schöne Unbekannte* (Vienna, Jan. 15, 1915; in N.Y. as *My Lady's Glove,* 1917); *3 Walzer* (Zürich, Oct. 5, 1935); *Ihr erster Walzer* (Munich,

May 16, 1952). He further wrote a *Serenade* for String Orch.; *Alt-Wiener Reigen* for String Orch.; *Suite in Tanzform* for Violin, Cello, and Piano; *Der Traum ein Leben*, overture; many piano pieces; an album, *Bilderbuch ohne Bilder*, for 4-hands.

Strauss, Eduard, Austrian conductor, brother of **Johann Strauss, Jr.;** b. Vienna, March 15, 1835; d. there, Dec. 28, 1916. A pupil of G. Preyer in composition, he made a successful debut with his own orch. at the Dianasaal in 1862; acted as Johann's substitute during the latter's tour of Russia (1865); succeeded him as conductor of the court balls (1872–78). For many years he gave concerts in the Volksgarten (summer) and in the hall of the Musikverein (winter); also made extended tours, visiting the U.S. in 1890 and from Oct. 1900 to early 1901. In 1901 he dissolved his orch. (founded by his father in 1826), which, after three-quarters of a century of uninterrupted success, had become almost a historical institution. His publ. dances comprise 318 opus numbers, but could not rival his brother's in popularity. In 1906 he publ. *Erinnerungen.*

Strauss, Franz, German horn virtuoso, father of **Richard Strauss;** b. Parkstein, Feb. 26, 1822; d. Munich, May 31, 1905. Until his retirement in 1889 he was solo hornist at the Hofoper in Munich; although a violent opponent of Wagner, the master valued him highly, and entrusted to him at the premieres of *Tristan, Meistersinger,* and *Parsifal* the important solo passages; until 1896 he was a prof. of his instrument at the Akademie der Tonkunst, and in 1875–96 conducted an excellent amateur orch., the Wilde Gungl, in Munich. He wrote a Horn Concerto in C minor (op. 8); *Nocturne* (op. 7) and *Empfindungen am Meere* (op. 12) for Horn and Piano; 17 *Konzertetüden* and *Übungen für Naturhorn* (2 books).

Strauss, Johann (III), Austrian waltz composer; son of **Eduard Strauss;** b. Vienna, Feb. 16, 1866; d. Berlin, Jan. 9, 1939. He was active as a ballroom music director in Vienna and later led popular concerts in Berlin. He was the last musician of the great Strauss family of waltz composers. His *Dichterliebe* waltz became popular.

Strauss, Johann, Jr., greatly celebrated Austrian composer of light music, called "The Waltz King"; b. Vienna, Oct. 25, 1825; d. there, June 3, 1899. His father intended all 3 of his sons for business; but the mother privately procured instruction on the violin (from Kohlmann) and in composition (Hofmann and Drechsler) for Johann, who threw off paternal control, tender though it was, and appeared as conductor of his own ensemble of 15 players at Dommayer's Restaurant in Hietzing (Oct. 15, 1844). His success was instantaneous, and his new waltzes won wide popularity. Despite his father's objections to this rivalry in the family, Johann Strauss continued his concerts with increasing success; after his father's death in 1849 he united his father's band with his own; made a tour through Austria, Germa-

ny, Poland, and Russia. From 1863 to Jan. 1871 he was conductor of the court balls in Vienna, resigning in favor of his brother **Eduard** to obtain more leisure for composition. Turning from dance music, in which he had won supreme artistic and popular success, he then concentrated on operetta. In 1872 he accepted an invitation to visit the U.S., and directed 14 "monster-concerts" in Boston and 4 in N.Y. He contracted 3 marriages: to the singer Henriette Treffz, the actress Angelika Dittrich, and Adele Deutsch. He wrote almost 500 pieces of dance music (498 opus numbers); of his waltzes the greatest popularity was achieved by *An der schönen blauen Donau (The Blue Danube Waltz),* op. 314 (1867), whose main tune became one of the best known in all music. Brahms wrote on a lady's fan the opening measures of it, and underneath: "Leider nicht von Brahms" ("Alas, not by Brahms"); Wagner, too, voiced his appreciation of the music of Strauss. Other well-known waltzes are *Geschichten aus dem Wiener Wald* (1868); *Wein, Weib, Gesang* (1869); *Wiener Blut* (1870); *Rosen aus dem Süden* (1878); *Frühlingsstimmen* (1881); *Tausend und eine Nacht, Künstlerleben;* etc.; also numerous quadrilles, polkas, polka-mazurkas, marches, galops, etc. His finest operetta is *Die Fledermaus,* an epitome of the Viennese spirit that continues to hold the stage as one of the masterpieces of its genre. It was first staged at the Theater an der Wien on April 5, 1874, and was given within a few months in N.Y. (Dec. 29, 1874); productions followed all over the world. It was performed in Paris with a new libretto as *La Tzigane* (Oct. 30, 1877); the original version was presented there as *La Chauve-souris* on April 22, 1904. Also very successful was the operetta *Der Zigeunerbaron* (Vienna, Oct. 24, 1885). All his operettas were first produced in Vienna, with the exception of *Eine Nacht in Venedig* (Berlin, Oct. 3, 1883). A complete list of Vienna productions includes: *Indigo und die vierzig Räuber* (Feb. 10, 1871); *Der Karneval in Rom* (March 1, 1873); *Cagliostro in Wien* (Feb. 27, 1875); *Prinz Methusalem* (Jan. 3, 1877); *Blindekuh* (Dec. 18, 1878); *Das Spitzentuch der Königin* (Oct. 1, 1880); *Der lustige Krieg* (Nov. 25, 1881); *Simplizius* (Dec. 17, 1887); *Ritter Pázmán* (Jan. 1, 1892); *Fürstin Ninetta* (Jan. 10, 1893); *Jabuka, oder Das Apfelfest* (Oct. 12, 1894); *Waldmeister* (Dec. 4, 1895); *Die Göttin der Vernunft* (March 13, 1897).

Strauss, Johann, Sr., "The Father of the Waltz"; b. Vienna, March 14, 1804; d. there, Sept. 25, 1849. His father, who kept a beer house and dance hall, apprenticed him to a bookbinder; after Strauss had run away, his parents consented to his becoming a musician. He studied the violin under Polyschansky, and harmony under Seyfried; at 15 joined Pamer's orch. in the Sperl dance hall, and the Lanner Quartet in 1823, later acting as deputy conductor of Lanner's orch.; organized an independent orch. of 14 in 1825, playing at various resorts, and producing his first waltzes (op. 1 is the *Täuberl-Walzer,* for the garden concerts at the Zwei Tauben). His renown spread, and his orch. increased rapidly in size and efficiency; from 1833 he undertook concert tours in Austria, and in 1834 was appointed bandmaster of the first Vienna militia regiment. His tours extended to Berlin in 1834, and to the Netherlands and Belgium in 1836; in 1837–38 he invaded Paris with a picked corps of 28, and had immense success both there and in London. In 1845 he was made conductor of the court balls at Vienna.

WORKS: Among 152 publ. waltzes, the *Lorelei-, Gabrielen-, Taglioni-, Cäcilien-, Victoria-, Kettenbrücken-,* and *Bajaderen-Walzer;* the *Elektrische Funken, Mephistos Höllenrufe,* and the *Donau-Lieder;* are prime favorites. He also wrote 24 galops, 13 polkas, 32 quadrilles, 6 cotillons and contredances, 18 marches, and 6 potpourris. His complete works (251 opus numbers), edited by his son **Johann,** were publ. by Breitkopf & Härtel in 1889: vols. I–V, Waltzes; vol. VI, Polkas, Galops, Marches; vol. VII, Quadrilles (piano scores only; full scores in Denkmäler der Tonkunst in Österreich, 63, 68, and 74 [32.ii, 35.ii, and 38.ii]).

Strauss, Josef, Austrian composer of waltzes, brother of **Johann Strauss, Jr.;** b. Vienna, Aug. 22, 1827; d. there, July 21, 1870. He was versatile and gifted, and at various times wrote poetry, painted, and patented inventions. He first appeared in public conducting in Vienna a set of his waltzes (July 23, 1853); was often asked by his brother to replace him as conductor, and accompanied him on tours to Germany, Russia, etc. He wrote 283 opus numbers, of which some are well worthy of his family's renown. His op. 173, *Dynamiden,* was used by Richard Strauss for a theme in *Der Rosenkavalier.*

Strauss, Richard, great German composer; b. Munich, June 11, 1864; d. Garmisch-Partenkirchen, Sept. 8, 1949. His father, the well-known horn player **Franz Strauss,** supervised his son's education. At the age of 4, Richard received regular instruction from A. Tombo, the harpist of the court orch.; at 8 he began to study the violin with Benno Walter, the concertmaster of the court orch.; from 1875 to 1880 he studied composition with the court conductor, F.W. Meyer. His first attempt at writing music (a Polka in C) dates from the year 1870, when he was 6, and he wrote piano pieces, songs, and even orch. overtures as a child; his op. 1, a *Festmarsch* for Orch., written at the age of 12, was publ. in 1880. In the meantime, he completed an academic course of study at the Gymnasium, graduating in 1882; then attended lectures on philosophy at the Univ. of Munich (1882–83). On March 30, 1881, Strauss's first major work, the Symph. in D minor, was performed in Munich by Hermann Levi; also in Munich, on Feb. 8, 1883, Benno Walter, Strauss's teacher, played his Violin Concerto. These works, written in the forms of the classic masters, revealed an astonishing degree of technical mastery and won for Strauss immediate recognition; he was only 20 when he could boast the distinction of an American premiere, for on Dec. 13, 1884, Theodore Thomas, then conductor of the N.Y. Phil., gave the first U.S. performance of the Symph. in F minor. Strauss

spent the winter of 1883–84 in Berlin, where Hans von Bülow became interested in him and engaged him as assistant conductor with Bülow's orch. in Meiningen. When Bülow left Meiningen in 1885, Strauss became his successor. Although he remained in Meiningen for only one season (1885–86), this sojourn proved to be a turning point in his career, for in that short time he became intimately associated with the poet and musician Alexander Ritter, who revealed to Strauss the meaning of the revolution in esthetics produced by Wagner and Liszt. Ritter urged on Strauss the concept of "music as expression," and thenceforward Strauss became convinced of the artistic importance of music with a literary or philosophical outline. After a journey to Italy in the spring of 1886, he became one of the conductors of the court opera in Munich (1886–89); his duties were not onerous, and he had ample time for composition; in Munich he wrote the symph. fantasy *Aus Italien,* and his first significant works in the new style, the tone poems *Don Juan* and *Tod und Verklärung.* In the autumn of 1889 he was appointed first conductor of the Weimar Court Orch.; there he remained until the spring of 1894. In Weimar he brought out *Don Juan* on Nov. 11, 1889, and another tone poem, *Macbeth,* on Oct. 13, 1890; on June 21, 1890, he conducted the first performance of *Tod und Verklärung,* at the meeting of the Allgemeiner Deutscher Musik-Verein in Eisenach. These works were revelations of a talent of striking originality and boldness, and made Strauss one of the greatest figures of the nascent era of musical modernism; he was praised extravagantly by admirers, and damned violently by traditionalists. Hans von Bülow called him "Richard the 2nd," as a legitimate heir to Wagner's mantle. Indeed, Strauss extended Wagner's system of leading motifs to the domain of symph. music; his tone poems are interwoven with motifs, each representing some relevant programmatic element. Analytical brochures, compiled especially by German commentators, illustrate the complex involvements of thematic allusions in these works. Strauss spent the winter of 1892 in Greece, Egypt, and Sicily, writing the text and music of his first stage work, the opera *Guntram,* which he conducted in Weimar on May 12, 1894. **Pauline de Ahna** sang the leading part; she married Strauss on Sept. 10, 1894, and remained with him throughout his life, dying a few months after he did. Strauss was appointed successor to Bülow as conductor of the Berlin Phil. in the autumn of 1894, and led it during the season of 1894–95. In 1896 he conducted his own works in Brussels, Liège, and Moscow, and also in many German cities; in 1897 he visited Amsterdam, Paris, London, and Barcelona. In the meantime, he continued unremittingly to write music; in quick succession, he brought out his masterpieces of musical characterization: *Till Eulenspiegels lustige Streiche* (Cologne, Nov. 5, 1895, Wüllner conducting); *Also sprach Zarathustra,* philosophical poem after Nietzsche (Frankfurt, Nov. 27, 1896, composer conducting); and *Don Quixote,* variations with a cello solo, after Cervantes (Cologne, March 8, 1898, Wüllner conducting). The series of his great tone poems was concluded with the autobiographical work *Ein Heldenleben* (Frankfurt, March 3, 1899, composer conducting). For his first visit to America in the early months of 1904, Strauss wrote a new work of considerable dimensions, *Symphonia domestica,* which he conducted at Carnegie Hall in N.Y. on March 21, 1904. The score was so naturalistic, and so frankly autobiographical, that it amused and shocked the public; but the music itself fell distinctly below the poetically charged inspiration of the preceding tone poems. Even more literal was his large symph. work *Eine Alpensinfonie,* which calls for a wind machine and a thunder machine to portray a storm in the Alps; it was first performed by the composer himself in Berlin, on Oct. 28, 1915. But while his symph. production lagged, he turned vigorously to the field of the opera, producing works of exceptional merit. After *Guntram,* he wrote *Feuersnot* (Dresden, Nov. 21, 1901), which attracted little attention. Then on Dec. 9, 1905, the Dresden Opera staged the opera *Salome,* after Oscar Wilde's French play, trans. into German. In this score Strauss went far beyond the limits of Wagnerian music drama, and created a psychological tragedy of shattering impact; the erotic subject was illustrated by sensuous music. The opera made the rounds of European theaters in quick succession, but when the Metropolitan Opera Co. produced *Salome* in N.Y. (Jan. 22, 1907) there were violent protests, and it was taken out of the repertoire, not to be revived until many years later. Scarcely less forceful was the impression produced by the next opera, *Elektra* (Dresden, Jan. 25, 1909), in which the horrors of matricide were pictured with extraordinary strength. Then, as if to make a graceful concession to public taste, Strauss produced *Der Rosenkavalier* (Dresden, Jan. 26, 1911), a charming comedy, which quickly became famous. With *Elektra* and *Der Rosenkavalier,* Strauss established his fruitful collaboration with the poet Hugo von Hofmannsthal, who wrote the librettos for these works, and also for the subsequent operas *Ariadne auf Naxos* (Stuttgart, Oct. 25, 1912); *Die Frau ohne Schatten* (Vienna, Oct. 10, 1919); *Die ägyptische Helena* (Dresden, June 6, 1928); and *Arabella* (Dresden, July 1, 1933). After Hofmannsthal's death in 1929, Strauss turned to Stefan Zweig for the libretto of *Die schweigsame Frau* (Dresden, June 24, 1935), and to Josef Gregor for *Friedenstag* (Munich, July 24, 1938), *Daphne* (Dresden, Oct. 15, 1938), and *Die Liebe der Danae* (written in 1938–40; produced posthumously, Salzburg, Aug. 14, 1952). The last opera by Strauss was *Capriccio,* to a libretto by the conductor Clemens Krauss (Munich, Oct. 28, 1942). The operas after *Der Rosenkavalier* were received with deference and interest, but were not retained in the permanent repertoire. It may be said, therefore, that the great creative period of Strauss ended for his stage works in 1911, with *Der Rosenkavalier,* and for his symph. compositions in 1899, with *Ein Heldenleben.* From 1898 to 1918 Strauss was on the staff of the Berlin Opera; in 1919 he became co-director (with Franz Schalk) of the Vienna State Opera, holding this position until 1924, although not on a permanent basis, so that he had time for extended tours, one of which

took him again to America in 1921. He also spent much time at his villa in Garmisch, Bavaria. On Nov. 15, 1933, Strauss was appointed president of the Reichsmusikkammer under the Nazi regime, but resigned in June 1935. He visited London as conductor of his own works in 1937, and received there the gold medal of the Phil. Society. He was the recipient of numerous other honors and decorations. In 1902 the Univ. of Heidelberg made him Dr.Phil., *honoris causa.* He remained in his home at Garmisch during World War II, and wrote the mournful *Metamorphosen* (with a symbolic quotation from Beethoven's funeral march from the *Eroica*) in the last months of the war; then lived for some time in Switzerland. He was strong enough to travel to England for a series of concerts in 1947; returning to Germany, he had to face the special court at Munich, investigating collaborators with the Nazis, but was officially exonerated (June 8, 1948).

WORKS: OPERAS: *Guntram* (Weimar, May 10, 1894; new version, Weimar, Oct. 22, 1940); *Feuersnot* (Dresden, Nov. 21, 1901); *Salome* (Dresden, Dec. 9, 1905); *Elektra* (Dresden, Jan. 25, 1909); *Der Rosenkavalier* (Dresden, Jan. 26, 1911); *Ariadne auf Naxos* (Stuttgart, Oct. 25, 1912); *Die Frau ohne Schatten* (Vienna, Oct. 10, 1919); *Intermezzo* (Dresden, Nov. 4, 1924); *Die ägyptische Helena* (Dresden, June 6, 1928); *Arabella* (Dresden, July 1, 1933); *Die schweigsame Frau* (Dresden, June 24, 1935); *Friedenstag* (Munich, July 24, 1938); *Daphne* (Dresden, Oct. 15, 1938); *Die Liebe der Danae* (1938–40; Salzburg, Aug. 14, 1952); *Capriccio* (Munich, Oct. 28, 1942).

BALLETS: *Josephslegende* (Paris, May 14, 1914); *Schlagobers* (Vienna, May 9, 1924).

FOR ORCH.: *Festmarsch* (1876); Symph. in D minor (Munich, March 30, 1881); Violin Concerto (Munich, Feb. 8, 1883, with Piano; full orch. version, Leipzig, Feb. 17, 1896); Symph. in F minor (N.Y., Dec. 13, 1884); Horn Concerto No. 1 (Meiningen, March 4, 1885); *Aus Italien,* symph. fantasy (Munich, March 2, 1887); *Don Juan,* tone poem, after Lenau (Weimar, Nov. 11, 1889); *Tod und Verklärung,* tone poem (Eisenach, June 21, 1890); *Burleske* for Piano and Orch. (Eisenach, June 21, 1890, composer conducting; Eugen d'Albert, soloist); *Macbeth,* after Shakespeare (Weimar, Oct. 13, 1890); *Till Eulenspiegels lustige Streiche,* tone poem (Cologne, Nov. 5, 1895); *Also sprach Zarathustra,* tone poem, after Nietzsche (Frankfurt, Nov. 27, 1896); *Don Quixote,* variations based on Cervantes (Cologne, March 8, 1898); *Ein Heldenleben,* tone poem (Frankfurt, March 3, 1899); *Symphonia domestica* (N.Y., March 21, 1904); *Festliches Praeludium* (Vienna, Oct. 19, 1913); *Eine Alpensinfonie* (Berlin, Oct. 28, 1915); *Parergon zur Symphonia domestica* for Piano, left-hand, and Orch. (Dresden, Oct. 16, 1925; Paul Wittgenstein, soloist); *München Walzer* (originally written for film, 1939; new version, 1945; perf. posthumously, Vienna, March 31, 1951); *Festmusik* on the 2,600th anniversary of the Japanese Empire (Tokyo, Oct. 27, 1940); *Divertimento* on pieces by Couperin (Vienna, Jan. 31, 1943); Horn Concerto No. 2 (Salzburg, Aug. 11, 1943); *Metamorphosen* for 23 String Instruments (Zürich, Jan. 25, 1946); Oboe Concerto (Zürich, Feb.

26, 1946); Duet Concertino for Clarinet, Bassoon, Strings, and Harp (Radio Svizzera Italiana, April 5, 1948).

CHAMBER MUSIC: String Quartet (1879–80); Cello Sonata (1882–83); *Serenade* for 13 Wind Instruments (1881); Piano Quartet (1884); Violin Sonata (1887); Sonatina No. 1 for 16 Wind Instruments (1943); Sonatina No. 2 for 16 Wind Instruments (1944–45).

CHORAL WORKS: Chorus for Sophocles' *Electra* (1880); *Wanderers Sturmlied* for Chorus and Orch. (1884); *Eine deutsche Motette* for Solo Voices and 16-part Chorus (1923); *Die Tageszeiten,* cycle for Men's Chorus and Orch. (1928); many unpubl. choral pieces.

FOR VOICE AND ORCH.: 4 songs (1896–97); 4 hymns for Soprano (1921); *3 Gesänge* for High Voice (1948); *Im Abendrot* for High Voice (1948).

FOR VOICE AND PIANO: 26 albums to words in German; of these songs the earliest are the most famous: *Zueignung* (1882); *Die Nacht* (1882); *Allerseelen* (1883); *Ständchen* (1885); *Barcarole* (1886); *Breit über mein Haupt* (1886); *Cäcilie, Heimliche Aufforderung,* and *Morgen* (1893–94); *Traum durch die Dämmerung* (1894); *Ich trage meine Minne* (1896).

FOR RECITATION AND PIANO: *Enoch Arden,* after Tennyson (1890), and *Das Schloss am Meer,* after Uhland (1899). A collected edition of the songs, in 4 vols., was ed. by F. Trenner and publ. in 1964–65.

FOR PIANO: 5 pieces (1881); Sonata (1881); *4 Stimmungsbilder* (1883).

Stravinsky, Feodor, distinguished Russian bass, father of **Igor Stravinsky;** b. near Rechitza, in the district of Minsk, June 20, 1843; d. St. Petersburg, Dec. 4, 1902. He made his debut in Kiev, Sept. 3, 1873, as Count Rodolpho in *La Sonnambula.* He became a member of the Russian Imperial Opera at St. Petersburg in 1876 and established himself as one of the greatest Russian basses before Chaliapin; his interpretation of heroic and comical characters in Russian operas evoked unbounded praise from the critics. He was famous as Méphistophélès in Gounod's *Faust,* and was distinguished not only for the power of his voice, but also for his dramatic talent on the stage. Altogether, he made 1,235 appearances in 64 operatic roles.

Stravinsky, Igor, Russian composer, one of the greatest masters of modern music, whose works exercised the most profound influence on the evolution of music, in its emancipation of rhythm, melody, and harmony; b. Oranienbaum, near St. Petersburg, June 17, 1882; d. New York, April 6, 1971 (his body was flown to Venice and buried in the Russian corner of the cemetery island of San Michele). He was the son of a famous opera singer, the bass at the Russian Imperial Opera **Feodor Stravinsky,** and was brought up in an artistic atmosphere; he often went to opera rehearsals when his father sang, and acquired an early love for the musical theater. He took piano lessons with one Alexandra Snetkova, and later with Leokadia Kashperova, who was a pupil of Anton Rubinstein; but it was not until much

later that he began to study music theory, first with Akimenko and then with Kalafati (1900–3). His progress in composition was remarkably slow; he never entered a music school or a cons., and never earned an academic degree in music. In 1901 he enrolled in the faculty of jurisprudence at St. Petersburg Univ., and took courses there for 8 semesters, without graduating; a fellow student was Vladimir Rimsky-Korsakov, a son of the composer. In the summer of 1902 Stravinsky traveled in Germany, where he met another son of Rimsky-Korsakov, Andrei, who was a student at the Univ. of Heidelberg at the time; Stravinsky became his friend. He was introduced to Rimsky-Korsakov, and became a regular guest at Rimsky-Korsakov's periodic gatherings in St. Petersburg. In 1903–4 Stravinsky wrote a piano sonata for the Russian pianist Nicolai Richter, who performed it at Rimsky-Korsakov's home. In 1905 Stravinsky began taking regular lessons in orchestration with Rimsky-Korsakov, who taught him free of charge, and under his tutelage composed a Symph. in E-flat major; the 2nd and 3rd movements from it were performed on April 27, 1907, by the court orch. in St. Petersburg, and a complete performance of it was given by the same orch. on Feb. 4, 1908. The work, dedicated to Rimsky-Korsakov, had some singularities and angularities that showed a deficiency of technique; there was little in this work that presaged Stravinsky's ultimate development as a master of form and orchestration. At the same concert, Stravinsky's *Le Faune et la bergère* for voice and orch. had its first performance; this score revealed a certain influence of French Impressionism. To celebrate the marriage of Rimsky-Korsakov's daughter Nadezhda to the composer Maximilian Steinberg on June 17, 1908, Stravinsky wrote an orch. fantasy entitled *Fireworks.* Rimsky-Korsakov died a few days after the wedding; Stravinsky deeply mourned his beloved teacher and wrote a funeral song for wind instruments in his memory; it was first performed in St. Petersburg on Jan. 30, 1909. There followed a *Scherzo fantastique* for orch., inspired by Maeterlinck's book *La Vie des abeilles.* As revealed in his correspondence with Rimsky-Korsakov, Stravinsky had at first planned a literal program of composition, illustrating events in the life of a beehive by a series of descriptive sections; some years later, however, Stravinsky gratuitously denied all connection of the work with Maeterlinck's book.

A signal change in Stravinsky's fortunes came when the famous impresario Diaghilev commissioned Stravinsky to write a work for the Paris season of his company, the Ballets Russes. The result was the production of Stravinsky's first ballet masterpiece, *The Firebird,* staged by Diaghilev in Paris on June 25, 1910. Here Stravinsky created music of extraordinary brilliance, steeped in the colors of Russian fairy tales. There are numerous striking effects in the score, such as a glissando of harmonics in the string instruments; the rhythmic drive is exhilarating, and the use of asymmetrical time signatures is extremely effective; the harmonies are opulent; the orchestration is coruscating. Stravinsky drew 2 orch. suites from the work; in 1919 he reorchestrated the music to conform to his new beliefs in musical economy; in effect he plucked the luminous feathers off the magical firebird, but the original scoring remained a favorite with conductors and orchs. Stravinsky's association with Diaghilev demanded his presence in Paris, which he made his home beginning in 1911, with frequent travels to Switzerland. His 2nd ballet for Diaghilev was *Pétrouchka,* produced in Paris on June 13, 1911, with triumphant success. Not only was the ballet remarkably effective on the stage, but the score itself, arranged in 2 orch. suites, was so new and original that it marked a turning point in 20th-century music; the spasmodically explosive rhythms, the novel instrumental sonorities, with the use of the piano as an integral part of the orch., the bold harmonic innovations in employing 2 different keys simultaneously (C major and F-sharp major, the "Pétrouchka Chord") became a potent influence on modern European composers. Debussy voiced his enchantment with the score, and young Stravinsky, still in his 20s, became a Paris celebrity. Two years later, Stravinsky brought out a work of an even greater revolutionary import, the ballet *Le Sacre du printemps (Rite of Spring;* Russian title, *Vesna sviashchennaya,* literally *Spring the Sacred*); its subtitle was "Scenes of Pagan Russia." It was produced by Diaghilev with his Ballets Russes in Paris on May 29, 1913, with the choreography by Nijinsky. The score marked a departure from all conventions of musical composition; while in *Pétrouchka* the harmonies, though innovative and dissonant, could still be placed in the context of modern music, the score of *Le Sacre du printemps* contained such corrosive dissonances as scales played at the intervals of major sevenths and superpositions of minor upon major triads with the common tonic, chords treated as unified blocks of sound, and rapid metrical changes that seemingly defied performance. The score still stands as one of the most daring creations of the modern musical mind; its impact was tremendous; to some of the audience at its first performance in Paris, Stravinsky's "barbaric" music was beyond endurance; the Paris critics exercised their verbal ingenuity in indignant vituperation; one of them proposed that *Le Sacre du printemps* should be more appropriately described as *Le Massacre du printemps.* On May 26, 1914, Diaghilev produced Stravinsky's lyric fairy tale *Le Rossignol,* after Hans Christian Andersen. It too abounded in corrosive discords, but here it could be explained as "Chinese" music illustrative of the exotic subject. In 1914–18 Stravinsky worked on his ballet *Les Noces* (Russian title, *Svadebka;* literally, *Little Wedding*), evoking Russian peasant folk modalities; it was scored for an unusual ensemble of chorus, soloists, 4 pianos, and 17 percussion instruments.

The devastation of the war led Stravinsky to conclude that the era of grandiose Romantic music had become obsolete, and that a new spirit of musical economy was imperative in an impoverished world. As an illustration of such economy, he wrote the musical stage play *L'Histoire du soldat,* scored for only 7 players, with a narrator. About the same time he wrote a work for 11 instruments entitled *Ragtime,* inspired by the new American dance music. He continued his association with Diaghilev's Ballets Russes in writing the ballet *Pulcinella,* based on themes by Pergolesi and other 18th-century Italian composers. He also wrote for Diaghilev 2 short operas, *Mavra,* after Pushkin, and *Renard,* to a Russian fairy tale (both produced by the Ballets Russes in Paris on May 18, 1922). These 2 works were the last in which Stravinsky used Russian subjects, with the sole exception of an orch. *Scherzo à la russe,* written in 1944. Stravinsky had now entered the period usually designated as neo-Classical. The most significant works of this stage of Stravinsky's development were his Octet for wind instruments and the Piano Concerto commissioned by Koussevitzky. In these works, Stravinsky abandoned the luxuriant instrumentation of his ballets and their aggressively dissonant harmonies; instead, he used pandiatonic structures, firmly tonal but starkly dissonant in their superposition of tonalities within the same principal key. His reversion to old forms, however, was not an act of ascetic renunciation but, rather, a grand experiment in reviving Baroque practices, which had fallen into desuetude. The Piano Concerto provided him with an opportunity to appear as soloist; Stravinsky was never a virtuoso pianist, but he was able to acquit himself satisfactorily in such works as the Piano Concerto; he played it with Koussevitzky in Paris on May 22, 1924, and during his first American tour with the Boston Symph. Orch., also under Koussevitzky, on Jan. 23, 1925. The Elizabeth Sprague Coolidge Foundation commissioned Stravinsky to write a pantomime for string orch.; the result was *Apollon Musagète,* given at the Library of Congress in Washington, D.C., on April 27, 1927. This score, serene and emotionally restrained, evokes the manner of Lully's court ballets. Stravinsky continued to explore the resources of neo-Baroque writing in his *Capriccio* for piano and orch., which he performed as soloist, with Ernest Ansermet conducting, in Paris, on Dec. 6, 1929; this score is impressed by a spirit of hedonistic entertainment, harking back to the *style galant* of the 18th century; yet it is unmistakably modern in its polyrhythmic collisions of pandiatonic harmonies. Stravinsky's growing disillusionment with the external brilliance of modern music led him to seek eternal verities of music in ancient modalities. His well-nigh monastic renunciation of the grandiose edifice of glorious sound to which he himself had so abundantly contributed found expression in his opera-oratorio *Oedipus Rex;* in order to emphasize its detachment from temporal aspects, he commissioned a Latin text for the work, even though the subject was derived from a Greek play; its music is deliberately hollow and its dramatic points are emphasized by ominous repetitive passages. Yet this very austerity of idiom makes *Oedipus Rex* a profoundly moving play. It had its first performance on May 30, 1927; its stage premiere took place in Vienna on Feb. 23, 1928. A turn to religious writing found its utterance in Stravinsky's Symph. of Psalms, written for the 50th anniversary of the Boston Symph. and dedicated "to the glory of God." The work is scored for chorus and orch., omitting the violins and violas, thus emphasizing the lower instrumental registers and creating an austere sonority suitable to its solemn subject. Owing to a delay of the Boston performance, the world premiere of the Symph. of Psalms took place in Brussels on Dec. 13, 1930. In 1931 Stravinsky wrote a Violin Concerto commissioned by the violinist Samuel Dushkin, and performed by him in Berlin on Oct. 23, 1931. On a commission from the ballerina Ida Rubinstein, Stravinsky composed the ballet *Perséphone;* here again Stravinsky exercised his mastery of simplicity in formal design, melodic patterns, and contrapuntal structure. For his American tour Stravinsky wrote *Jeu de cartes,* a "ballet in three deals" to his own scenario depicting an imaginary poker game (of which Stravinsky was a devotee). He conducted its first performance at the Metropolitan Opera House in N.Y. on April 27, 1937. His concerto for 16 instruments entitled *Dumbarton Oaks,* named after the Washington, D.C., estate of Mr. and Mrs. Robert Woods Bliss, who commissioned the work, was first performed in Washington, on May 8, 1938; in Europe it was played under the noncommittal title *Concerto in E-flat;* its style is hermetically neo-Baroque. It is germane to note that in his neo-Classical works Stravinsky began to indicate the key in the title, e.g., Concerto in D for Violin and Orch. (1931), Concerto in E-flat (*Dumbarton Oaks,* 1938), Symph. in C (1938), Concerto in D for String Orch. (1946), and Serenade in A for Piano (1925).

With the war engulfing Europe, Stravinsky decided to seek permanent residence in America. He had acquired French citizenship on June 10, 1934; in 1939 he applied for American citizenship; he became an American citizen on Dec. 28, 1945. To celebrate this event he made an arrangement of the *Star-Spangled Banner,* which contained a curious modulation into the subdominant in the coda. He conducted it with the Boston Symph. on Jan. 14, 1944, but because of legal injunctions existing in the state of Massachusetts against intentional alteration, or any mutilation, of the national anthem, Stravinsky was advised not to conduct his version at the 2nd pair of concerts, and the standard version was substituted. In 1939–40 Stravinsky was named Charles Eliot Norton lecturer at Harvard Univ.; about the same time he accepted several private students, a pedagogical role he had never exercised before. His American years form a curious panoply of subjects and manners of composition. He accepted a commission from the Ringling Bros. to write a *Circus Polka* "for a young elephant." In 1946 he wrote *Ebony Concerto* for a swing band. In 1951 he completed his opera *The Rake's Progress,* inspired by Hogarth's famous series of engravings, to a libretto by W.H. Auden and C. Kallman. He conducted its world premiere in Venice, on Sept. 11, 1951, as part of the International Festival of Contemporary Music there. The opera is a striking example of Stravinsky's protean capacity for adopting different styles and idioms of composition to serve his artistic purposes; *The Rake's Progress* is an ingenious conglomeration of disparate elements, ranging from 18th-century British ballads to cosmopolitan burlesque. But whatever transmutations Stravinsky's music underwent during his long and productive career, he remained a man of the theater at heart. In America he became associated with the brilliant Russian choreographer George Balanchine, who produced a number of ballets to Stravinsky's music, among them his *Apollon Musagète,* Violin Concerto, Symph. in 3 movements, *Scherzo à la russe, Pulcinella,* and *Agon.* It was in his score of *Agon* that Stravinsky essayed for the first time to adopt the method of composition with 12 tones as promulgated by Schoenberg; *Agon* (the word means "competition" in Greek) bears the subtitle "ballet for 12 tones," perhaps in allusion to the dodecaphonic technique used in the score. Yet the 12-tone method had been the very antithesis of Stravinsky's previous tenets. In fact, an irreconcilable polarity existed between Stravinsky and Schoenberg even in personal relations. Although both resided in Los Angeles for several years, they never met socially; Schoenberg once wrote a canon in which he ridiculed Stravinsky as Herr Modernsky, who put on a wig to look like "Papa Bach." After Schoenberg's death, Stravinsky became interested in examining the essence of the method of composition with 12 tones, which was introduced to him by his faithful musical factotum Robert Craft; Stravinsky adopted dodecaphonic writing in its aspect of canonic counterpoint as developed by Anton von Webern. In this manner he wrote his *Canticum sacrum ad honorem Sancti Marci nominis,* which he conducted at San Marco in Venice on Sept. 11, 1956. Other works of the period were also written in a modified 12-tone technique, among them *The Flood,* for narrator, mime, singers, and dancers, presented in a CBS Television broadcast in N.Y. on June 14, 1962; its first stage performance was given in Hamburg on April 30, 1963.

Stravinsky was married twice; his first wife, Catherine Nosenko, whom he married on Jan. 24, 1906, and who bore him 3 children, died in 1939; on March 9, 1940, Stravinsky married his longtime mistress, Vera, who was formerly married to the Russian painter Serge Sudeikin. She was born Vera de Bosset in St. Petersburg, on Dec. 25, 1888, and died in N.Y. on Sept. 17, 1982, at the age of 93. An ugly litigation for the rights to the Stravinsky estate continued for several years between his children and their stepmother; after Vera Stravinsky's death, it was finally settled in a compromise, according to which $2/9$ of the estate went to each of his 3 children and a grandchild and $1/9$ to Robert Craft. The value of the Stravinsky legacy was spectacularly demonstrated on Nov. 11, 1982, when his working draft of *Le Sacre du printemps* was sold at an auction in London for the fantastic sum of $548,000, higher than any MS by any composer. The purchaser was Paul Sacher, a Swiss conductor and philanthropist whose fortune derived from his wife's holdings of the shares of the international pharmaceutical company that manufactures the sedative drugs Valium and Librium. Even more fantastic was the subsequent sale of the entire Stravinsky archive, consisting of 116 boxes of personal letters and 225 drawers containing MSS, some of them unpubl. Enormous bids were made for it by the N.Y. Public Library and the Morgan Library, but they were all outbid by Paul Sacher, who offered the overwhelming purse of $5,250,000, which removed all competition. The materials were to be assembled in a specially constructed 7-story Sacher Foundation building in Basel, to be eventually opened to scholars for study.

In tribute to Stravinsky as a naturalized American citizen, the U.S. Postal Service issued a 2-cent stamp bearing his image to mark his centennial in 1982, an honor theretofore never granted to a foreign-born composer (the possible exception being Victor Herbert, but his entire career was made in America).

Few composers escaped the powerful impact of Stravinsky's music; ironically, it was his own country that had rejected him, partly because of the opposition of Soviet ideologues to modern music in general, and partly because of Stravinsky's open criticism of Soviet ways in art. But in 1962 Stravinsky returned to Russia for a visit, and was welcomed as a prodigal son; as if by magic, his works began to appear on Russian concert programs, and Soviet music critics issued a number of laudatory studies of his works. Yet it is Stravinsky's early masterpieces, set in an attractive colorful style, that continue to enjoy favor with audiences and performers, while his more abstract and recursive scores are appreciated mainly by specialists.

WORKS: FOR THE STAGE: *L'Oiseau de feu (The Firebird)*, ballet (1909–10; Paris Opéra, June 25, 1910; 3 suite versions: 1911, 1919, and 1945; 2 sections arranged for Violin and Piano, 1926); *Pétrouchka*, ballet (1910–11; Paris, June 13, 1911, Pierre Monteux conducting; revised 1946; excerpts officially designated as a "suite" in 1946); *Le Sacre du printemps*, ballet, "scenes of pagan Russia" (1911–13; Paris, May 29, 1913, Pierre Monteux conducting; first concert perf., Moscow, Feb. 18, 1914, Serge Koussevitzky conducting; first Paris concert perf., April 5, 1914, Monteux conducting); *Le Rossignol*, "lyric tale" in 3 acts, after Hans Christian Andersen (1908–14; Paris Opéra, May 26, 1914, Monteux conducting; in 1917 the 2nd and 3rd acts were scored as both a symph. poem and a ballet, *Le Chant du rossignol;* ballet version, Paris Opéra, Feb. 2, 1920; complete opera revised 1962); *Renard*, burlesque chamber opera (1915–16; Paris, May 18, 1922; revised 1962); *L'Histoire du soldat*, ballet with Narrator and 7 Instrumentalists (1918; Lausanne, Sept. 28, 1918; concert suite with original instrumentation, 1920; also *Petite suite* for Violin, Clarinet, and Piano extracted from the score, 1919); *Pulcinella*, ballet "after Pergolesi" (1919–20; Paris Opéra, May 15, 1920; revised 1965; an orch. suite was extracted from it in 1922, and first perf. in Boston, Dec. 22, 1922, revised, 1947; 2 chamber pieces, *Suite italienne*); *Mavra*, comic opera, after Pushkin (1922; first public perf., Paris Opéra, June 3, 1922); *Les Noces (The Wedding)*, ballet-cantata, subtitled "choreographic Russian scenes," revision for Soloists, Chorus, 4 Pianos, and 17 Percussion Instruments (1921–23; Paris, June 13, 1923; originally

scored with Full Orch., 1914–17); *Oedipus Rex*, opera-oratorio, after Sophocles (1926–27; concert perf., Paris, May 30, 1927; first stage perf., Vienna, Feb. 23, 1928; revised 1948); *Apollon Musagète*, classic ballet for String Orch. (1927–28; Washington, D.C., April 27, 1928; revised 1947); *Le Baiser de la fée*, ballet on themes of Tchaikovsky (1928; Paris Opéra, Nov. 27, 1928; in 1934 several sections were collected for an independent symph. piece called *Divertimento;* entire ballet revised 1950); *Perséphone*, melodrama in 3 parts for Female Narrator, Tenor, Chorus, and Orch., to a text by André Gide (1933; Paris Opéra, April 30, 1934; revised 1949); *Jeu de cartes (Card Game)*, "ballet in 3 deals" (1935–37; N.Y., April 27, 1937); *Orpheus*, ballet (1946–47; N.Y., April 28, 1948); *The Rake's Progress*, opera after Hogarth's engravings, with libretto by W.H. Auden and C. Kallman (1948–51; Venice, Sept. 11, 1951, Stravinsky conducting); *Agon*, ballet for 12 Dancers (1954–57; Los Angeles, June 17, 1957); *Noah and the Flood*, also called just *The Flood*, biblical spectacle narrated, mimed, sung, and danced (1961–62; CBS Television broadcast, N.Y., June 14, 1962; first stage perf., Hamburg, April 30, 1963).

FOR ORCH.: Symph. in E-flat major, op. 1 (1905–7; first partial perf., 2nd and 3rd movements only, St. Petersburg, April 27, 1907; first complete perf., St. Petersburg, Feb. 4, 1908; revision, Montreux, Switzerland, April 2, 1914); *Scherzo fantastique*, op. 3 (1907; St. Petersburg, Feb. 6, 1909); *Fireworks*, op. 4 (1908; St. Petersburg, June 17, 1908; reorchestrated and first perf. in St. Petersburg, Jan. 22, 1910); *Chant funèbre* for Wind Instruments, on the death of Rimsky-Korsakov (1908; St. Petersburg, Jan. 30, 1909; score lost); *Le Chant du rossignol*, symph. poem (from the opera *Le Rossignol;* Geneva, Dec. 6, 1919); *Symphonies of Wind Instruments*, in memory of Debussy (1920; London, June 10, 1921; revised 1945–47); Suite No. 1 for Small Orch. (1917–25; orch. arrangement of Nos. 1–4 of the *5 pièces faciles* for Piano, 4-hands: Andante, Napolitana, Española, Balalaika); Suite No. 2 for Small Orch. (1921; orch. arrangement of *3 pièces faciles* and No. 5 of *5 pièces faciles* for Piano, 4-hands: March, Waltz, Polka, Galop); Concerto for Piano, with Wind Instruments, Double Basses, and Percussion (1923–24; Paris, May 22, 1924; revised 1950); Capriccio for Piano and Orch. (1928–29; Paris, Dec. 6, 1929; revised 1949); 4 études for Orch.: Danse, Excentrique, Cantique, Madrid (1928; orch. arrangement of 3 pieces for String Quartet, and Etude for Pianola; Berlin, Nov. 7, 1930; revised 1952); Concerto in D for Violin and Orch. (1931; Berlin, Oct. 23, 1931; adapted in 1940 for Balanchine's ballet *Balustrade*); Divertimento (sections of the ballet *Le Baiser de la fée*, combined in 1934); Praeludium for Jazz Ensemble (1936–37; revised 1953; Los Angeles, Oct. 19, 1953); Concerto in E-flat, *Dumbarton Oaks*, for Chamber Orch. (1937–38; Washington, D.C., May 8, 1938); Symph. in C (1938–40; Chicago, Nov. 7, 1940); Tango, arrangement by Felix Günther of the piano piece (Philadelphia, July 10, 1941, Benny Goodman conducting; Stravinsky's own orchestration, 1953; Los Angeles, Oct. 19, 1953); *Danses concertantes* for Chamber Orch. (1941–42; Los Angeles, Feb. 8, 1942); *Circus*

Stravinsky

Polka for Piano (commissioned by the Ringling Bros. Circus, to accompany the elephant numbers; arranged for band by David Raksin, 1942; arranged by Stravinsky for a symph. orch. and conducted by him with the Boston Symph. Orch., in Cambridge, on Jan. 13, 1944); *4 Norwegian Moods* (1942; Cambridge, Mass., Jan. 13, 1944, Stravinsky conducting); *Ode*, in 3 parts (1943; Boston, Oct. 8, 1943); *Scènes de ballet* (originally composed for Billy Rose's Broadway show *The Seven Lively Arts*, which opened in Philadelphia, Nov. 24, 1944; revised for concert performance and first perf. in N.Y., Feb. 3, 1945); *Scherzo à la russe* (1944; San Francisco, March 22, 1946; originally for big jazz band); Symph. in 3 movements (1942–45; N.Y., Jan. 24, 1946); *Ebony Concerto* for Clarinet and Swing Band (1945; N.Y., March 25, 1946); Concerto in D for String Orch., *Basler* (1946; Basel, Jan. 21, 1947); *Greeting Prelude* ("Happy Birthday," written for Monteux's 80th birthday; Boston, April 4, 1955); Movements for Piano and Orch. (1958–59; N.Y., Jan. 10, 1960); *Variations: Aldous Huxley, In Memoriam* (1963–64; Chicago, April 17, 1965; as a ballet, N.Y., March 31, 1966); Canon, from finale of *The Firebird,* in memory of Monteux (Toronto, Dec. 16, 1965).

CHAMBER MUSIC: 3 pieces for String Quartet (1914); *Ragtime* for 11 Instruments (1918; London, April 27, 1920); *Petite suite* for Violin, Clarinet, and Piano (1919; arranged from *L'Histoire du soldat*); 3 pieces for Clarinet Solo (1919); Concertino for String Quartet (1920; revised for 12 Instruments, 1952); Octet for Wind Instruments (1922–23; Paris, Oct. 18, 1923); *Duo concertant* for Violin and Piano (1931–32; Berlin, Oct. 28, 1932); *Russian Dance* for Violin and Piano, from *Pétrouchka* (1932); *Suite italienne* No. 1 for Cello and Piano, and No. 2 for Violin and Piano (both from *Pulcinella;* 1932, 1934); *Pastorale* for Violin, Oboe, English Horn, Clarinet, and Bassoon (1933; arrangement of vocal *Pastorale*); Divertimento for Violin and Piano, based on material from *Le Baiser de la fée* (1934); *Elégie* for Unaccompanied Violin and Viola (1944); Septet for Piano, and String and Wind Instruments (1952; Washington, D.C., Jan. 24, 1954); *Epitaphium for Prince Max of Fürstenberg* for Flute, Clarinet, and Harp (1959; Donaueschingen, Oct. 17, 1959); Double Canon for String Quartet (1959); *Monumentum pro Gesualdo di Venosa ad CD Annum,* an instrumental surrealization of 3 madrigals by Gesualdo (1960; Venice, Sept. 27, 1960); 8 instrumental miniatures for 15 Players (1962; instrumentation of *Les Cinq Doigts* for Piano); *Fanfare for a New Theater* for 2 Trumpets (1964).

VOCAL WORKS: *Le Faune et la bergère* for Mezzo-soprano and Orch. (1906; St. Petersburg, Feb. 4, 1908); *Pastorale,* "song without words" for Soprano and Piano (1908; version for Soprano, Oboe, English Horn, Clarinet, and Bassoon, 1923); *Le Roi des étoiles (Zvezdoliki),* cantata for Male Chorus and Orch. (1912; first perf., Brussels Radio, April 19, 1939); 3 poems from the Japanese for Soprano, 2 Flutes, 2 Clarinets, Piano, and String Quartet (1912–13); *Pribaoutki (Peasant Songs)* for Voice and 8 Instruments (1914; Vienna, June 6, 1919); *The Saucer,* 4 Russian songs for Women's Voices (1914–17; as *4*

Russian Peasant Songs, with 4 Horns added, 1954); *Berceuses du chat,* suite of 4 songs for Female Voice and 3 Clarinets (1915–16; Vienna, June 6, 1919); *Les Noces (The Wedding),* ballet-cantata for Soloists, Chorus, 4 Pianos, and 17 Percussion Instruments (1921–23; Paris, June 13, 1923); *Paternoster* for Mixed Chorus a cappella (1926); *Symphony of Psalms* for Chorus and Orch. (1930; Brussels, Dec. 13, 1930; Boston, Dec. 19, 1930); *Credo* for Mixed Chorus a cappella (1932); *Ave Maria* for Mixed Chorus a cappella (1934); Tango for Wordless Voice and Piano (1940); *Babel* for Male Narrator, Male Chorus, and Orch. (1944; 7th and final movement of *Genesis Suite,* a collaborative effort, with Schoenberg, Shilkret, Tansman, Milhaud, Castelnuovo-Tedesco, and Toch, each contributing a movement); Mass for Men's and Boys' Voices and 10 Wind Instruments (1944–48; Milan, Oct. 27, 1948); Cantata on 4 poems by anonymous English poets of the 15th and 16th centuries, for Soprano, Tenor, Female Chorus, and 5 Instruments (1951–52; Los Angeles, Nov. 11, 1952); 3 songs from William Shakespeare for Mezzo-soprano, Flute, Clarinet, and Viola (1953; Los Angeles, March 8, 1954); *In Memoriam Dylan Thomas* for Tenor, String Quartet, and 4 Trombones (1954; Hollywood, Sept. 20, 1954); *4 Russian Songs* for Soprano, Flute, Guitar, and Harp (1954); *Canticum sacrum ad honorem Sancti Marci nominis* for Tenor, Baritone, Chorus, and Orch. (1955–56; Venice, Sept. 13, 1956, Stravinsky conducting); arrangement for Chorus and Orch. of J.S. Bach's *Choral-Variationen über das Weihnachtslied "Vom Himmel hoch da komm' ich her"* (1956); *Threni,* on Lamentations of Jeremiah from the Vulgate, for 6 Solo Voices, Chorus, and Orch. (1957–58; International Festival for Contemporary Music, Venice, Sept. 23, 1958); *A Sermon, a Narrative and a Prayer,* cantata for Speaker, Alto, Tenor, Chorus, and Orch. (1960–62; Basel, Feb. 23, 1962); anthem, *A Dove Descending Breaks the Air,* after T.S. Eliot (1962); *Elegy for J.F.K.* for Baritone, 2 Clarinets, and Corno di Bassetto (1964; Los Angeles, April 6, 1964); *Abraham and Isaac,* sacred ballad for Baritone and Chamber Orch., to Hebrew texts (1962–64; Jerusalem, Aug. 23, 1964); *Introitus (T.S. Eliot in Memoriam)* for 6 Male Voices, Harp, Piano, Timpani, Tam-tams, Solo Viola, and Double Bass (1965; Chicago, April 17, 1965); *Requiem Canticles* for 4 Vocal Soloists, Chorus, and Orch. (1965–66; Princeton, N.J., Oct. 8, 1966); *The Owl and the Pussycat,* after Lear, for Voice and Piano (1966).

PIANO MUSIC: Sonata in F-sharp minor (1903–4; recovered from Leningrad library, 1962; publ. in Russia, 1973); 4 Etudes, op. 7 (1908); *Le Sacre du printemps* for Piano, 4-hands (1912); *3 pièces faciles* for Piano, 4-hands (1915); *5 pièces faciles* for Piano, 4-hands (1917); Etude for Pianola (1917); Piano-Rag-Music (1919); 3 movements from *Pétrouchka* (1921); *Les Cinq Doigts* (1920–21); Sonata (1924); Serenade in A (1925); Concerto for 2 Solo Pianos (1931–35; Paris, Nov. 21, 1935); Tango (1940); Circus Polka (1942); Sonata for 2 Pianos (1943–44; first public perf., Edgewood College of the Dominican Sisters, Madison, Wis., Aug. 2, 1944).

NONDESCRIPT: *Do Not Throw Paper Towels in Toi-*

let for Treble Voice Unaccompanied, to text from poster in men's room at Harvard Univ. (dated Dec. 16, 1939).

WRITINGS: *Chroniques de ma vie* (2 vols., Paris, 1935; in Eng. as *Chronicles of My Life,* London, 1936); *Poétique musicale,* the Charles Eliot Norton Lectures at Harvard Univ. (Paris, 1946; in Eng. as *Poetics of Music,* Cambridge, Mass., 1948); with Robert Craft, 6 vols. of revelatory autobiographical publications: *Conversations with Igor Stravinsky* (N.Y., 1958); *Memories and Commentaries* (N.Y., 1959); *Expositions and Developments* (N.Y., 1962); *Dialogues and a Diary* (N.Y., 1963); *Themes and Episodes* (N.Y., 1967); and *Retrospections and Conclusions* (N.Y., 1969); *Themes and Conclusions,* amalgamated and ed. from *Themes and Episodes* and *Retrospections and Conclusions* (1972); also R. Craft, ed., *S.: Selected Correspondence* (vol. 1, N.Y., 1982).

A sharp debate raged, at times to the point of vitriolic polemical exchange, among Stravinsky's associates as to the degree of credibility of Craft's reports in his dialogues, or even of the factual accounts of events during Stravinsky's last years of life. Stravinsky was never a master of the English language; yet Craft quotes him at length as delivering literary paragraphs of impeccable English prose. Craft admitted that he enhanced Stravinsky's actual words and sentences (which were never recorded on tape), articulating the inner, and at times subliminal, sense of his utterances. Craft's role was made clear beyond dispute by Stravinsky himself, who, in a letter to his publishing agent dated March 15, 1958, urged that the title of the book be changed to *Conversations with Igor Stravinsky by Robert Craft,* and emphatically asserted that the text was in Craft's language, and that in effect Craft "created" him.

Stravinsky, Soulima, pianist, son of **Igor Stravinsky;** b. Lausanne, Sept. 23, 1910. He studied in Paris with Isidor Philipp and Nadia Boulanger; then gave piano recitals in Europe and America; appeared frequently with his father, playing his works for 2 pianos.

Strayhorn, William (Billy), black American jazz pianist and composer; b. Dayton, Ohio, Nov. 29, 1915; d. New York, May 31, 1967. He studied music in Pittsburgh; joined Duke Ellington's band as lyricist and arranger in 1939. Many songs credited to Ellington (*Chelsea Bridge, Perfume Suite, Such Sweet Thunder, A Drum Is a Woman,* etc.) are in fact products of a mutually beneficial musical symbiosis, with Ellington suggesting the initial idea, mood, and character and Strayhorn doing the actual writing, often using Ellington's quasi-impressionistic techniques (e.g., modal harmonies, whole-tone scales, etc.). Strayhorn's own acknowledged songs, *Lush Life, Take the "A" Train,* and others, are jazz standards.

Streatfeild, Richard Alexander, English writer on music; b. Edenbridge, June 22, 1866; d. London,

Feb. 6, 1919. He studied at Pembroke College, Cambridge; in 1889 became an assistant in the Dept. of Printed Books in the British Museum; was music critic of the *Daily Graphic* (1898–1912). He publ. the following books: *Masters of Italian Music* (1895); *The Opera* (1897; 5th ed., enlarged, 1925); *Modern Music and Musicians* (1906); *Handel* (1909); *Life Stories of Great Composers* (Philadelphia, 1910); *Musiciens anglais contemporains* (French trans., 1913; Eng. original not publ.); *Handel, Canons and the Duke of Chandos* (London, 1916); contributed many articles to English publications.

Streich, Rita, soprano; b. Barnaul, Russia, Dec. 18, 1920 (of Russian-German parentage). She studied voice with Erna Berger, Maria Ivogün, and Willi Domgraf-Fassbänder; made her debut in Aussig in 1943; from 1946 she sang with the Berlin State Opera; in 1951 she joined the Berlin Städtische Oper. She also appeared in Vienna, Bayreuth, Salzburg, and Glyndebourne; made her U.S. debut with the San Francisco Opera in 1957. In 1974 she became a prof. at the Folkwang-Hochschule in Essen. She was a leading interpreter of soprano parts in Mozart operas.

Streicher, Johann Andreas, German piano maker; b. Stuttgart, Dec. 13, 1761; d. Vienna, May 25, 1833. During a stay at Augsburg in 1793 he married Nanette Stein (b. Augsburg, Jan. 2, 1769; d. Vienna, Jan. 16, 1835), daughter of the piano manufacturer Johann Andreas Stein; in 1802 succeeded Stein in the business and moved it to Vienna. He invented the piano action in which the hammer strikes from above. He was on friendly terms with Beethoven.

Streicher, Theodor, Austrian song composer, great-grandson of **Johann Andreas Streicher;** b. Vienna, June 7, 1874; d. Wetzelsdorf, near Graz, May 28, 1940. He studied singing with F. Jäger in Vienna and J. Kniese in Bayreuth; piano with F. Löwe in Vienna; composition with H. Schulz-Beuthen in Dresden. He lived most of his life in Vienna; wrote numerous songs in a Romantic manner, reminiscent of Hugo Wolf. He set to music 36 poems from *Des Knaben Wunderhorn;* wrote *Wanderers Nachtlied,* after Goethe, for Chorus a cappella; a Sextet for Strings; etc. He also orchestrated the accompaniments of Carl Loewe's ballades. In 1934 a "Theodor Streicher Gemeinde" was founded in Vienna to propagate his music.

Streisand, Barbra (Barbara Joan Streisand), popular American singer and actress; b. New York, April 24, 1942. She studied acting for a short time in N.Y.; also learned to sing in Greenwich Village. In 1962 she made her Broadway debut in *I Can Get It for You Wholesale;* then made a hit in *Funny Girl* in 1964, a musical she filmed in 1968, and for which she received an Academy Award. Her other films include *On a Clear Day You Can See Forever* (1970), *A Star Is Born* (1976), and *Yentl* (1983). As a recording artist, she received Gold Record Awards for her albums *People* (1965), *My Name Is Barbra* (1965),

Color Me Barbra (1966), *Stony End* (1971), *Barbra Joan Streisand* (1972), *The Way We Were* (1974), *A Star Is Born* (1976), *Superman* (1977), and others. While not at all educated, her natural talent prevailed over a lack of general culture.

Strelezki, Anton, English pianist and composer; b. Croydon, Dec. 5, 1859; d. 1907. According to some sources, his real name was **Burnand.** He studied with Clara Schumann; settled in London, where he was very popular; place and exact date of his death are unknown. He publ. a great deal of piano music (more than 225 opus numbers), some of which was widely used: *Valse-Souvenir; Jagdstück; Valsette; Sérénade espagnole; Menuet à l'antique; Barcarolle;* also songs; publ. *Personal Recollections of Chats with Liszt* (1895).

Strepponi, Giuseppina, Italian soprano, wife of **Giuseppe Verdi;** b. Lodi, Sept. 8, 1815; d. Sant' Agata, near Busseto, Nov. 14, 1897. She was the daughter of the opera conductor in Trieste, **Feliciano Strepponi;** having completed her studies at the Milan Cons. (1830–34), she made a successful debut in Adria in Dec. 1834, and was engaged at the Italian Opera in Vienna and in Trieste in 1835. Her appearances in Rome, Florence, Venice, and other Italian cities established her reputation as a foremost interpreter of dramatic roles. She created a sensation by her performance of Abigaile in Verdi's *Nabucco* (Milan, March 9, 1842). Verdi admired her greatly, and after many years of intimacy they were married (1859).

Strickland, William, American conductor; b. Defiance, Ohio, Jan. 25, 1914. He studied organ and singing; then devoted himself to conducting; entered the U.S. Army in 1941; was appointed Warrant Officer and Instructor at the Army Music School at Fort Myer, Va., in 1942; organized the Army Music School Choir, which he conducted in Washington, D.C., including a performance at the White House. After discharge from the Army, he founded the Nashville Symph. Orch. and led it from 1946 to 1951. In 1953 he conducted in Austria; returning to the U.S., he was music director of the Oratorio Society of N.Y. (1955–59); also made guest appearances as a radio conductor. In 1958 he went on a tour of Asia; conducted in Manila, Tokyo, and Seoul; in 1962 he went on a European trip; conducted guest engagements in Scandinavia, in Poland, and in Germany (until 1969). He received numerous awards from educational institutions for his service to American music.

Striggio, Alessandro, Italian lutenist, organist, and composer; b. Mantua, c.1535; d. there, Feb. 29, 1592. By the 1560s he lived at the court of Cosimo de' Medici in Florence, and by 1584 in Mantua as court composer. In 1567 he was in Paris and London, and in 1574 at the court of the Emperor Maximilian. He composed 3 musical intermezzi for *Psiche ed Amore* and other festival music. He publ. several books of madrigals and *Il cicalamento delle donne* (1567;

descriptive songs in the manner of Janequin); many compositions by Striggio are found in collections of the period (1559–1634); 5 madrigals were reprinted by Torchi in *L'Arte Musicale in Italia,* I. His son, **Alessandro** (called **Alessandrino**), was a poet, and a notable player of the violin and lyra. He was active at the court of Mantua (still there in 1628), and in 1607 wrote the libretto of Monteverdi's *La favola d'Orfeo.* In 1596–97 he publ. 3 books of his father's madrigals for 5 voices.

Stringham, Edwin John, American music educator and composer; b. Kenosha, Wis., July 11, 1890; d. Chapel Hill, N.C., July 1, 1974. He studied at Northwestern Univ. and at the Cincinnati Cons.; in 1920 went to Italy, where he took lessons in composition with Respighi. Returning to the U.S., he occupied teaching posts at the Denver College of Music (1920–29), Teachers College of Columbia Univ. (1930–38), Juilliard School of Music in N.Y. (1930–45), and Queens College of the City Univ. of N.Y. (1938–46). In 1948 he settled in Chapel Hill.
WORKS: For Orch.: *Visions,* symph. poem (1924); *The Ancient Mariner,* after Coleridge (Denver, March 16, 1928); Symph. No. 1 (Minneapolis, Nov. 15, 1929); *Fantasy on American Folk Tunes* for Violin and Orch. (1942); chamber music; songs. He publ. the books *Listening to Music Creatively* (N.Y., 1943; revised ed., 1959); *Creative Harmony and Musicianship* (with H.A. Murphy, N.Y., 1951).

Strobel, Heinrich, eminent German musicologist; b. Regensburg, May 31, 1898; d. Baden-Baden, Aug. 18, 1970. He studied musicology with Sandberger and Kroyer in Munich, obtaining his Dr.Phil. degree in 1922. He was music critic of the *Börsenkurier* in Berlin (1927–1933) and the *Tageblatt* (1934–38); in 1939 he went to Paris; after the war he settled in Baden-Baden, where he was active as music critic and music director at the radio station; was editor of the progressive magazine *Melos* until his death. He devoted himself energetically to the cause of modern music; wrote numerous articles on the subject; promoted programs of avant-garde composers on the radio and at the various festivals in Germany. He was the author of a basic biography of Hindemith (Mainz, 1928; new enlarged ed., 1948) and of a monograph on Debussy (Zürich, 1940; 5th German ed., 1961; French ed., Paris, 1942; Spanish ed., Madrid, 1966); also publ. *Igor Stravinsky* (Zürich, 1956; Eng. version as *Stravinsky: Classic Humanist,* N.Y., 1955).

Strobel, Otto, German musicologist; b. Munich, Aug. 20, 1895; d. Bayreuth, Feb. 23, 1953. He studied at the Univ. of Munich (Dr.Phil., 1924). After working as an archivist at Bayreuth, he was appointed in 1938 director of the newly created Richard Wagner Inst. there. He publ. *Genie am Werk: Richard Wagners Schaffen und Wirken im Spiegel eigenhandschriftlicher Urkunden* (Bayreuth, 1934); *Richard Wagner* (Bayreuth, 1952); edited *König Ludwig II. und Richard Wagner: Briefwechsel* (4 vols., Karlsruhe, 1936–37) and a supplement to this, *Neue Ur-*

kunden zur Lebensgeschichte Richard Wagners (Karlsruhe, 1939); *Neue Wagner-Forschungen,* vol. 1 (Karlsruhe, 1943).

Strong, George Templeton, American composer; b. New York, May 26, 1856; d. Geneva, June 27, 1948. He was the son of the N.Y. lawyer G.T. Strong, who was also a music-lover, and whose diary, expressing his dislike of Liszt and Wagner, was publ. in 1952. From him, and from his mother, who was an amateur pianist, Strong received his first training. In 1879 he went to Leipzig, where he studied with Jadassohn. He entered the Liszt circle at Weimar, and became an adherent of program music; from 1886 to 1889 he lived in Wiesbaden, where he became friendly with MacDowell; he returned briefly to America, and taught theory at the New England Cons. in Boston (1891–92); then went back to Europe and settled in Switzerland. He expressed his indignation at the lack of recognition of American composers in their own country; most performances of his works took place in Switzerland. In 1930 he donated many of his original MSS to the Library of Congress in Washington, D.C. Toscanini performed his orch. suite *Die Nacht* with the NBC Symph. Orch. in N.Y. on Oct. 21, 1939; his other symph. suite, *Une Vie d'artiste* for Violin and Orch., was presented at the 20th festival of the Assoc. des Musiciens Suisses at Zürich in June 1920; he also wrote 3 symphs.: No. 1, *In den Bergen;* No. 2, *Sintram;* No. 3, *An der See;* and the symph. poems *Undine* and *Le Roi Arthur.*

Strube, Gustav, German-American composer and music educator; b. Ballenstedt, March 3, 1867; d. Baltimore, Feb. 2, 1953. He was taught the violin by his father, and later by Brodsky at the Leipzig Cons.; was a member of the Gewandhaus Orch. there until 1891, when he emigrated to America; was a violinist in the Boston Symph. from 1891 to 1913; then he became head of the theory dept. of the Peabody Cons. in Baltimore. In 1916 he was appointed conductor of the newly organized Baltimore Symph. Orch., which he led until 1930; was director of the Peabody Cons. from 1916 to 1946. He publ. a useful manual, *The Theory and Use of Chords: A Textbook of Harmony* (Boston, 1928).

Strungk, Nicolaus Adam, German violinist, organist, and composer; b. Braunschweig (baptized, Nov. 15), 1640; d. Dresden, Sept. 23, 1700. He studied with his father, Delphin Strungk (1601–94), whose assistant he became at the age of 12 at the Church of St. Magnus in Braunschweig; studied violin at Lübeck under Schnittelbach while attending Helmstedt Univ. At 20 he became first violinist in the Braunschweig orch., later holding similar positions at Celle and Hannover. In 1678 Strungk became music director at Hamburg's Cathedral and of the city; wrote and produced operas in German (in keeping with the nationalist trend of the time), among them *Der glückselig-steigende Sejanus* and its sequel, *Der unglücklich-fallende Sejanus* (1678), with German librettos by Christoph Richter adapted from the Italian; *Die Liebreiche, durch Tugend und Schönheit erhöhete Esther* and *Doris* (both in 1680); *Semiramis* (1681); *Theseus* and *Floreeto* (both in 1683); etc. (The opera *Die drey Töchter Cecrops',* formerly attributed to Strungk, was written by Johann Wolfgang Franck.) Strungk was subsequently chamber organist to the Elector Ernst August of Hannover, where he won the admiration of Corelli. On Jan. 26, 1688, Strungk was appointed vice Kapellmeister in Dresden, succeeding Carlo Pallavicino, whose unfinished opera *Antiope* Strungk completed. In this post he was beset with difficulties arising from friction with Italian musicians, and only managed to maintain his authority through the intervention of his patron, the Elector Johann Georg III; when Bernhard, Kapellmeister in Dresden, died in 1692, Strungk was appointed to succeed him. In 1693 he organized an opera company in Leipzig; between 1693 and 1700 he wrote 16 operas for it, among them *Alceste* (perf. at the inauguration of the Leipzig opera house, May 18, 1693) and *Agrippina* (1699). Financially, the enterprise was a failure, but Strungk continued to receive his salary from Dresden until his retirement on a pension in 1697. He publ. the important manual *Musicalische Übung auf der Violine oder Viola da Gamba in etlichen Sonaten über die Festgesänge, ingleichen etlichen Ciaconen mit 2 Violinen bestehend* (1691). A selection of airs from his operas was publ. in Hamburg under the title *Ein hundert auserlesenen Arien zweyer Hamburgischen Operen, Semiramis und Esther. Mit beigefügten Ritornellen* (1684). Among his instrumental works, a Sonata for 2 Violins and Viola da Gamba, and several other sonatas are extant; MS No. 5056 of the Yale Univ. Music Library (Lowell Mason Collection) contains capriccios and ricercari by Strungk, among them the *Ricercar sopra la Morte della mia carissima Madre Catherina Maria Stubenrauen* (Venice, 1685). Six capriccios and a Ricercare by Strungk, included in Denkmäler der Tonkunst in Österreich, 17 (13.ii), are wrongly ascribed to Georg Reutter (Senior).

Strunk, (William) Oliver, distinguished American musicologist; b. Ithaca, N.Y., March 22, 1901; d. Grottaferrata, Italy, March 12, 1980. He studied at Cornell Univ. (1917–19); in 1927 took a course in musicology with Otto Kinkeldey there; then entered the Univ. of Berlin to study musicology with J. Wolf (1927–28). Returning to America, he served as a member of the staff of the Music Division at the Library of Congress in Washington, D.C. (1928–37). In 1937 he was appointed to the faculty of Princeton Univ.; after retirement in 1966 lived mostly in Italy. A Festschrift in his honor was publ. at Princeton under the title *Studies in Music History. Essays for Oliver Strunk* (1968). He publ. *State and Resources of Musicology in the U.S.* (Washington, D.C., 1932) and the extremely valuable documentary *Source Readings in Music History* (N.Y., 1950). He was editor of *Monumenta musicae Byzantinae* (Copenhagen, 1961–71).

Stuart, Leslie (real name, **Thomas A. Barrett**), English operetta composer; b. Southport, March 15, 1864; d. Richmond, Surrey, March 27, 1928. He was a church organist in various provincial towns in England; settled in London in 1895, where he soon became known as a composer of popular songs. He achieved enormous success with his operetta *Floradora*, produced in London on Nov. 11, 1899, and subsequently performed in England and America for many seasons, but failed to duplicate this success in any of his later works, which included *The Silver Slipper* (1901); *The School Girl* (1903); *The Belle of Mayfair* (1906); *Havana* (1908); *Captain Kidd* and *The Slim Princess* (1910); *Peggy* (1911).

Stucken, Frank Van Der. See **Van Der Stucken, Frank.**

Stuckenschmidt, Hans Heinz, eminent German music critic and writer; b. Strasbourg, Nov. 1, 1901. He studied piano and composition; from 1929 to 1933 he was music critic of the Berlin daily *B. Z. am Mittag,* and was active as a lecturer and writer on modern music. In 1934 he was forbidden to continue journalism in Germany, and went to Prague, where he wrote music criticism until 1941, when his activities were stopped once more by the occupation authorities; was drafted into the Germany army; after the war, became director of the dept. for new music of the radio station RIAS in Berlin; also was a lecturer (1948), reader (1949), and prof. of music history (1953) at the Technical Univ. there; he retired in 1967. He publ. *Arnold Schönberg* (Zürich, 1951; 2nd ed., 1957; Eng. trans., 1960); *Neue Musik* (as vol. 2 of the series Zwischen den beiden Kriegen, Berlin, 1951; in French, Paris, 1956); *Schöpfer der neuen Musik: Portraits und Studien* (Frankfurt, 1958); *J.N. David* (Wiesbaden, 1965); *Maurice Ravel: Variationen über Person und Werk* (Frankfurt, 1966; Eng. trans., 1968); *Ferruccio Busoni. Zeittafel eines Europäers* (Zürich, 1967; in Eng., *Ferruccio Busoni. Chronicle of a European,* London, 1970); *Twentieth Century Music* (in Eng., N.Y., 1969); *Germany and Central Europe,* as part of the series Twentieth Century Composers (London, 1970); *Arnold Schönberg, Leben, Umwelt, Werk* (Zürich, 1974; in Eng. as *Schoenberg: His Life, World and Work,* N.Y., 1978). Along with Josef Rufer he founded and edited the monthly music magazine *Stimmen* (Berlin, 1947–49). The Festschrift *Aspekte der neuen Musik* was presented to him on his 65th birthday (Kassel, 1968).

Stumpf, Carl, eminent German musicologist; b. Wiesentheid, Lower Franconia, April 21, 1848; d. Berlin, Dec. 25, 1936. He studied philosophy, theology, and the natural sciences at Würzburg and Göttingen (Dr.Phil., 1870), and in 1873 became a full prof. at Würzburg; he was then a pedagogue in Prague (1879–84), in Halle (1884–89), and in Munich (1889–93). In 1893 he went to Berlin, where he founded the prestigious Psychological Inst.; its purpose was a scientific analysis of tonal psychology as it affected musical perception; but, realizing the ut-

terly speculative and arbitrary premises of his theories, he revised them, and proposed the concepts of Konkordanz and Diskordanz to describe the relative euphony of triads and chords of several different notes. He retired in 1928. Stumpf publ. *Beiträge zur Akustik und Musikwissenschaft* (1898–1924), which incorporated his evolving theories, and, with Hornbostel, issued the *Sammelbände für vergleichende Musikwissenschaft* (1922–23).

Sturgeon, Nicholas, English divine and composer; date and place of birth unknown; d. London, May 31, 1454. In 1442 he became precentor of St. Paul's Cathedral in London. He was the owner, and possibly the scribe, of the MSS found in Old Hall, near Ware; 7 works by Sturgeon (2 not complete) are part of the Old Hall MS collection, including a curious isorhythmic motet, *Salve mater Domini,* for 3 Voices, which was probably written for the journey of Henry V to France (1416), on which Sturgeon accompanied him. A. Hughes and M. Bent, eds., publ. *The Old Hall Manuscript,* in Corpus Mensurabilis Musicae, XLVI (1969–72).

Stutschewsky, Joachim, Ukrainian-born Israeli cellist, composer, and pedagogue; b. Romny, Feb. 7, 1892; d. Tel Aviv, Nov. 14, 1982. He received his early education at a music school in Kherson; as a youth, played in various orchs. in southern Russia; in 1909 went to Leipzig, where he studied cello with Julius Klengel and orch. playing with Hans Sitt; in 1913–14 he was an orch. cellist in Jena; at the outbreak of war in 1914 he settled in Zürich, where he was active as a performer and teacher. In 1924 he went to Vienna, where he entered the circle of Schoenberg, Berg, and Webern. Together with the violinist Rudolf Kolisch, he formed the Wiener Streichquartet (later known as the Kolisch String Quartet). With the usurpation of Austria by the Nazi hordes in 1938, Stutschewsky emigrated to Palestine, and eventually became an Israeli citizen. From 1939–48 he served as inspector of music in the cultural section of the Jewish National Council. In 1977 he was given the honorary title of Distinguished Citizen of Tel Aviv. In his early compositions he followed the median modern techniques; then began a study of Jewish folklore in diaspora, and wrote music of profound racial feeling, set in the framework of advanced harmonies. He also contributed to the study of cello techniques; publ. the voluminous methods *Studien zu einer neuen Spieltechnik auf dem Violoncell* (3 vols., Mainz, 1927) and *Das Violoncellspiel* (4 vols., Mainz, 1932), and also *Etudes* (4 vols., Mainz, 1931). He further publ. an essay, *Mein Weg zur jüdischen Musik* (Vienna, 1935), detailing his approach to national Jewish music. His compositions are set mostly for chamber music groups.

Styne, Jule (real name, **Jules Stein**), American composer of popular music; b. London, Dec. 31, 1905. He was taught piano by his parents; was taken to the U.S. at the age of 8; appeared with the Chicago Symph. Orch. as a child pianist, but did not pursue a concert career; in 1942 he went to Hollywood and rapidly established himself as a successful composer of musical comedies; wrote the scores of *High Button Shoes* (1947); *Gentlemen Prefer Blondes* (1949); *Bells Are Ringing* (1956); *Gypsy*, to the life story of the striptease artist Gypsy Rose Lee (1959); and *Funny Girl*, a musical biography of the singer Fanny Brice (1965); he also wrote music for the films.

Subirá (Puig), José, eminent Spanish musicologist; b. Barcelona, Aug. 20, 1882; d. Madrid, Jan. 5, 1980. He studied at the Madrid Cons. and simultaneously qualified for the practice of law (Dr.Jur., 1923). He specialized in the study of old Spanish theater music, and publ. a number of valuable monographs on the subject. In 1953 he was elected member of the Royal Academy of Fine Arts in Madrid. Apart from his scholarly pursuits he publ. a novel, *Su virginal pureze* (1916), and a historical account, *Los Españoles en la guerra de 1914–1918* (4 vols.).

Subotnick, Morton, American avant-garde composer; b. Los Angeles, April 14, 1933. He studied music at the Univ. of Denver; then at Mills College with Darius Milhaud. He subsequently taught at Mills College; was in charge of the Intermedia Program at the School of Arts at N.Y. Univ.; also directed exhibits at the Electric Circus in Greenwich Village in N.Y. In 1969 he was appointed associate dean and director of electronic music at the School of Music at the Calif. Inst. of the Arts in Los Angeles. He is at his best in multimedia theatrical presentations, with emphasis on electronic devices. His works include 4 pieces for mixed media under the all-embracing title *Play!*; *The Tarot* for 10 Instruments and Tape; *Concert* for Woodwind Quintet, 2 Film Projectors, Electronic Sounds, and 12 Spotlights; *Music for 12 Elevators*; *Lamination* for Orch. and Electronic Sounds; *The Wild Bull* for Electronic Music Synthesizer; *Before the Butterfly* for Orch. (Los Angeles, Feb. 26, 1976); *The Double Life of Amphibians*, music drama in 3 parts: *Ascent into Air* for 10 Instruments and Computer-generated Sound (1981), *The Last Dream*, and *Fluttering of Wings* (also titled *Angels*) for String Quartet and an electronic "ghost" score (1981); the work was premiered in its entirety in Los Angeles, June 20, 1984. He also wrote incidental music for the plays *Galileo, The Balcony*, and *The Caucasian Chalk Circle*.

Sucher, Joseph, Hungarian conductor; b. Döbör, Nov. 23, 1843; d. Berlin, April 4, 1908. He studied in Vienna with Sechter; in 1876 was conductor of the Leipzig City Theater; in 1877 he married the soprano **Rosa Hasselbeck;** they were at the Hamburg Stadttheater from 1878 to 1888; Sucher then became conductor of the Berlin Opera, his wife being engaged there as prima donna; he left the Berlin post in 1899. He was especially distinguished as an interpreter of the Wagnerian repertoire. He composed several vocal works: *Aus alten Märchen* for Women's Voices, with Orch.; *Waldfräulein* for Soprano Solo, Mixed Chorus, and Orch.; *Seeschlacht bei*

Lepanto for Male Chorus and Orch.; songs.

Sucher, Rosa (née **Hasselbeck**), German operatic soprano, wife of **Joseph Sucher;** b. Velburg, Feb. 23, 1849; d. Eschweiler, April 16, 1927. She received her early musical training from her father, a chorus master; sang in provincial operas; then in Leipzig, where she married the conductor Joseph Sucher in 1877; they were both engaged by the Hamburg Opera (1878–88). She became noted for her performances of Wagner's roles; sang at the Bayreuth Festivals (1886–99); on Feb. 25, 1895, she made her American debut as Isolde at the Metropolitan Opera House in N.Y., under the sponsorship of the Damrosch Opera Co. She publ. her memoirs, *Aus meinem Leben* (Leipzig, 1914).

Suchoň, Eugen, significant Slovak composer; b. Pezinok, Sept. 25, 1908. He studied piano and composition with Kafenda at the Bratislava School of Music (1920–28); then took a course in advanced composition with Vítězslav Novák at the Master School of the Prague Cons. (1931–33). Subsequently he taught composition at the Bratislava Academy (1933–48) and music education at the Pedagogical Faculty of the Bratislava Univ. (1949–60); was a prof. of music theory there from 1959 to 1974; in 1971 he was appointed prof. at the College of Music and Dramatic Art in Bratislava. In 1958 he was named National Artist of the Republic of Czechoslovakia. He is one of the creators of the modern Slovak style of composition, based on authentic folk motifs and couched in appropriately congenial harmonies.

Suckling, Norman, English composer and writer on music; b. London, Oct. 24, 1904. He received his academic education at Queen's College, Oxford, specializing in French literature; was assistant master at Liverpool Collegiate School (1925–43); then was a lecturer in French language and literature at King's College, Newcastle upon Tyne, in the Federal Univ. of Durham (1943–70). While thus occupied, he developed sufficient mastery of the piano to give concerts, at which he presented programs of modern French music. He publ. a monograph on Gabriel Fauré (London, 1946) and several books on French literature; also contributed articles on English and French composers to the *Listener* and other literary publications. His compositions are mostly in small forms; his songs are particularly fine.

Suesse, Dana, American composer of popular music; b. Kansas City, Dec. 3, 1911. She took piano lessons with Siloti and composition with Rubin Goldmark in N.Y.; traveled to Paris for lessons with Nadia Boulanger. A precocious musician, she won 2 prizes as a composer from the National Federation of Music, at the ages of 9 and 10; played piano in Paul Whiteman's band; wrote *Symphonic Waltzes* and *Jazz Concerto* for him. Her most famous popular song was *You Oughta Be in Pictures.*

Suggia, Guilhermina, Portuguese cellist; b. Oporto, June 27, 1888; d. there, July 31, 1950. She was a child prodigy and played first cello in the Oporto Orch. at the age of 12. Under the patronage of the Queen of Portugal she was sent to Leipzig in 1904 to study with Julius Klengel; made her debut with the Gewandhaus Orch. under Nikisch at the age of 17. In 1906 she married **Pablo Casals** (divorced, 1912). Shortly afterward she settled in London, where she continued to appear in concerts until 1949, when she went back to Portugal. She was greatly appreciated for her fine musicianship as well as virtuosity. In 1923 Augustus John painted her portrait, which became famous.

Suk, Josef, Czech violinist and composer; b. Křečovice, Jan. 4, 1874; d. Benešov, near Prague, May 29, 1935. He studied with his father, a chorus master, and at the Prague Cons.; after graduation he took a course in composition with Dvořák, whose daughter Otilie he married in 1898. In 1892 he became 2nd violinist in the celebrated Bohemian String Quartet, continuing with it until 1933. He was a devoted follower of Dvořák in his style of composition; his works are cast in a characteristically Romantic vein, with the rhythmic elements drawn from Bohemian folk music. When his wife died in 1905, he was disconsolate; he expressed his sorrow in his 2nd Symph., *Asrael,* dedicated to her memory and to the memory of Dvořák. He continued to compose, developing an individual manner marked by deep expressiveness and religious feeling.
    WORKS: Operatic fairy tale, *Raduz and Mahulena* (Prague, April 6, 1898); dramatic legend, *Pod jabloní (Under the Apple Trees;* 1902; Prague, Jan. 31, 1934); *Dramatic Overture* (Prague, July 9, 1892); *Serenade* in E-flat for String Orch. (1892); *Winter's Tale,* overture after Shakespeare (1894); 2 symphs.: No. 1, in E (1897–99; Prague, Nov. 25, 1899), and No. 2, *Asrael* (1905–6; Prague, Feb. 3, 1907); *Fantasia* for Violin and Orch. (1902; Prague, Jan. 9, 1904); *Scherzo fantastique* for Orch. (1903; Prague, April 18, 1905); 3 symph. poems: *Praga* (1904); *Pohádka léta (A Summer Fairytale;* 1907–9; Prague, Jan. 26, 1909); *Zrání (Maternity;* 1912–17; Prague, Oct. 30, 1918); *Meditations on the Chorale "St. Venceslas"* for String Orch. or String Quartet (1914); *Legend about Dead Victors* for Orch. (1919); symph. march, *Forward to a New Life* (1919–20); *Epilogue* for Soli, Chorus, and Orch. (1920–32); 2 string quartets (1896, 1910–11); Piano Quartet (1891); Piano Trio (1892); Piano Quintet; *Allegro giocoso* for String Quartet; other chamber music; several sets of choruses; a number of piano pieces.

Suk, Josef, outstanding Czech violinist, grandson of the composer **Josef Suk** and great-grandson of **Dvořák;** b. Prague, Aug. 8, 1929. He studied the violin with Jaroslav Kocian; made his professional debut in 1940. From 1951–53 he took courses at the Prague Academy. In 1952 he founded the Suk Trio with the pianist Jan Panenka and the cellist Josef Chuchro, and toured widely with it; his interest in chamber music led him to form a duo with Zuzana Růžičková in 1963; from 1967–69 he was also a member of a trio with Julius Katchen and Janos Starker. In 1959 he made a grand tour as soloist to three continents with the Czech Phil. On Jan. 23, 1964, he made his U.S. debut with the Cleveland Orch., and subsequently appeared as soloist with other American orchs. In 1964 he received a Czech State Prize; in 1970 he was made an Artist of Merit and in 1977 was named a National Artist of Czechoslovakia.

Šulek, Stjepan, Croatian violinist and composer; b. Zagreb, Aug. 5, 1914. He studied violin with Huml, and was largely self-taught in composition; yet he succeeded in becoming a composer of considerable merit. In 1954 he was appointed prof. of composition at the Music Academy in Zagreb.
    WORKS: Operas: *Coriolan,* after Shakespeare (Zagreb, Oct. 12, 1958); *Oluja (The Tempest),* after Shakespeare (Zagreb, 1969); 6 symphs. (1944, 1946, 1948, 1954, 1963, 1966); festive prologue, *Scientiae et arti,* for Orch. (1966); 4 piano concertos (1949, 1951, 1963, 1970); Cello Concerto (1950); Violin Concerto (1951); Bassoon Concerto (1958); Violin Concerto (1959); Clarinet Concerto (1967); cantata, *Zadnji Adam (The Last Adam;* 1964); other vocal works; piano pieces; songs.

Sullivan, Sir Arthur Seymour, famous English composer; b. London, May 13, 1842; d. there, Nov. 22, 1900. In 1854 he entered the Chapel Royal as a chorister, under Helmore; publ. an anthem in 1855; was elected (the first) Mendelssohn Scholar in 1856, studying at the Royal Academy of Music from 1857 under Bennett, Goss, and O'Leary, and at the Leipzig Cons. in 1858–61 under Moscheles, Hauptmann, Richter, Plaidy, etc., conducting a performance of his overture to *Lalla Rookh* (Leipzig, May 25, 1860), and writing string quartets and music to *The Tempest* (Leipzig, April 6, 1861; revised version, Crystal Palace, April 5, 1862). His cantata *Kenilworth* (Birmingham Festival, Sept. 8, 1864) stamped him as a composer of high rank. In 1864 he visited Ireland and there composed his "Irish Symphony" (London, March 10, 1866). In 1866 he was appointed prof. of composition at the Royal Academy of Music. About this time he formed a lifelong friendship with Sir George Grove, whom he accompanied in 1867 on a memorable journey to Vienna in search of Schubert MSS, leading to the discovery of the score of *Rosamunde.* The year 1867 was also notable for the production of the first of those comic operas upon which Sullivan's fame chiefly rests. This was *Cox and Box* (libretto by F.C. Burnand), composed in 2 weeks and performed on April 27 at the home of Arthur Lewis; later it had a long public run. Less successful were *The Contrabandista* (London, Dec. 18, 1867) and *Thespis* (London, Dec. 23, 1871); but the latter is significant as inaugurating Sullivan's collaboration with Sir W.S. Gilbert, the celebrated humorist, who became the librettist of all Sullivan's most successful comic operas, beginning with *Trial by Jury* (March 25, 1875). This was produced by Richard D'Oyly Carte, who in 1876 formed a company expressly for the production of the "Gilbert and Sullivan" operas. The first big success obtained by the famous team was with *H.M.S. Pinafore* (May 25, 1878), which had 700 consecutive performances in London, and enjoyed an enormous vogue in "pirated" productions throughout the U.S. In an endeavor to protect their interests, Gilbert and Sullivan went to N.Y. in 1879 to give an authorized performance of *Pinafore,* and while there they also produced *The Pirates of Penzance* (Dec. 31, 1879). On April 23, 1881, came *Patience,* a satire on exaggerated esthetic poses exemplified by Oscar Wilde, whose American lecture tour was conceived as a "publicity stunt" for this work. On Nov. 25, 1882, *Iolanthe, or The Peer and the Peri* began a run that lasted more than a year. This was followed by the comparatively unsuccessful *Princess Ida* (Jan. 5, 1884), but then came the universal favorite of all the Gilbert and Sullivan operas, *The Mikado* (March 14, 1885). The list of these popular works is completed by *Ruddigore* (Jan. 22, 1887), *The Yeomen of the Guard* (Oct. 3, 1888), and *The Gondoliers* (Dec. 7, 1889). After a quarrel and a reconciliation, the pair collaborated in 2 further works, of less popularity: *Utopia Limited* (Oct. 7, 1893) and *The Grand Duke* (March 7, 1896). Sullivan's melodic inspiration and technical resourcefulness, united with the delicious humor of Gilbert's verses, raised the light opera to a new height of artistic achievement, and his works in this field continue to delight countless hearers. Sullivan was also active in other branches of musical life. He conducted numerous series of concerts, more especially those of the London Phil. Society (1885–87) and the Leeds Festivals (1880–98). He was principal of, and a prof. of composition at, the National Training School for Music from 1876 to his resignation in 1881. Sullivan received the degree of Mus.Doc. *honoris causa* from Cambridge (1876) and Oxford (1879); was named Chevalier of the Legion of Honor (1878); was grand organist to the Freemasons (1887); etc. He was knighted by Queen Victoria in 1883. Parallel with his comic creations, he composed many "serious" works, including the grand opera *Ivanhoe* (Jan. 31, 1891), which enjoyed a momentary vogue. Among his cantatas the most successful was *The Golden Legend,* after Longfellow (Leeds Festival, Oct. 16, 1886); he also wrote the famous hymn *Onward, Christian Soldiers,* to words by Rev. Sabine Baring-Gould (1871). His songs were highly popular in their day, and *The Lost Chord,* to words by Adelaide A. Proctor (publ. 1877), is still a favorite. Among his oratorios, *The Light of the World* (Birmingham Festival, Aug. 27, 1873) may be mentioned. Other stage works: *The Zoo* (June 5, 1875); *The Sorcerer* (Nov. 17, 1877); *Haddon Hall* (Sept. 24, 1892); *The Chieftain* (revision of *The Contrabandista;* Dec. 12, 1894); *The Martyr of Antioch* (Edinburgh, Feb. 15, 1898; a stage arrangement of the cantata); *The Beauty-Stone* (with Pinero; May 28, 1898); romantic opera, *The Rose of Persia* (Nov. 29, 1899); *The Emerald Isle* (completed by E. German, April 27, 1901); 2 ballets: *L'Ile enchanté* (1864) and *Victoria and Merrie England* (1897).

Sulzer, Salomon, important Austrian-Jewish composer, reformer of synagogal songs; b. Hohenems, Vorarlberg, March 30, 1804; d. Vienna, Jan. 17, 1890. He was only 16 when he was appointed cantor at the chief synagogue in his hometown. He studied music with Seyfried in Vienna; from 1825 to 1881 was cantor of the new Vienna synagogue. He undertook a bold reform of liturgical music by the introduction of musical form and actual compositions from the Classical period, setting Schubert's songs as a model. By so doing, he succeeded in bringing traditional Jewish cantillation together with Western modes. He brought out an anthology, *Schir Zion (The Heart of Zion;* publ. in 1839–65), and *Denkschrift an die Wiener israelitische Cultus-Gemeinde* (Vienna, 1876).

Sumac, Yma, Peruvian singer of a phenomenal diapason, whose origin is veiled in mystical mist; b. Ichocan, Sept. 10, 1927. Her family name was **Chavarri;** the probability is that she was really a child of the Andean highlands; it is credible that she developed her phenomenal voice of 5 octaves in range because her lungs were inflated by the necessity of breathing enough oxygen at the high altitude. However that might be, she married one **Moises Vivanco,** who was an arranger for Capitol Records and who launched her on a flamboyant career as a concert singer. She was billed by unscrupulous promoters as an Inca princess, a direct descendant of Atahualpa, the last emperor of the Incas, a Golden Virgin of the Sun God worshiped by the Quechua Indians. On the other hand, some columnists spread the scurrilous rumor that she was in actuality a Jewish girl from Brooklyn whose real name was Amy (retrograde of Yma) Camus (retrograde of Sumac). But Yma Sumac never spoke with a Brooklyn accent. She exercised a mesmeric appeal to her audiences, from South America to Russia, from California to Central Europe; expressions such as "miraculous" and "amazing" were used by Soviet reviewers during her tour of Russia in 1962; "supersonic vocal skill" was a term applied by an American critic. Her capacity did not diminish with age; during her California appearances in 1984 she still impressed her audiences with the expressive power of her voice.

Suñol y Baulenas, Dom Gregorio María, learned Spanish ecclesiastic and authority on Gregorian chant; b. Barcelona, Sept. 7, 1879; d. Rome, Oct. 26, 1946. He studied at Montserrat and at the Abbey of Solesmes; became prior of the Monastery of Montserrat and president of the Asociación Gregoriana of Barcelona. During his last years he was president of the Pontificio Instituto di Musica Sacra in Rome. He publ. the valuable editions *Método completo de canto gregoriano* (6 Spanish eds.; also in Eng., French, and German); *Introducció a la paleografía musical gregoriana* (Montserrat, 1925; also in French, 1935); "Els Cants dels Romeus," in *Analecta Montserratensia* (with examples of folk music from the 14th century); brought out *Antiphonale missarum juxta ritum sanctae ecclesiae medilolanensis* (1935).

Supervia, Conchita, famous Spanish mezzo-soprano; b. Barcelona, Dec. 9, 1895; d. London, March 30, 1936. She studied at the Colegio de las Damas Negras in Barcelona; made her debut with a visiting opera company at the Teatro Colón in Buenos Aires on Oct. 1, 1910, in Stiattesi's opera *Blanca de Beaulieu.* She then traveled to Italy; sang the role of Octavian in the first Italian production of *Der Rosenkavalier* in Rome. In 1912 she sang Carmen in Bologna; in 1914 she sang at the Havana Opera. She then appeared in Chicago (1915–16); in 1924 she sang at La Scala in Milan. She endeared herself to the Italian public by reviving Rossini's operas *L'Italiana in Algeri* and *La Cenerentola;* she also attracted favorable critical attention by performing the part of Rosina in *Il Barbiere di Siviglia* in its original version as a coloratura contralto. In addition, she filled guest engagements in Paris and London. In 1931 she married the British industrialist Sir Ben Rubenstein. She died at the age of 40, as a result of complications following the birth of a child.

Suppé, Franz von, famous operetta composer; b. Spalato, Dalmatia, April 18, 1819; d. Vienna, May 21, 1895. He was of Belgian descent, and his real name was **Francesco Ezechiele Ermenegildo Cavaliere Suppe-Demelli.** At the age of 11 he played the flute, and at 15 wrote a Mass. He was then sent by his father to study philosophy at Padua, where he also took music courses with Cigala and Ferrari; on his father's death he went with his mother to Vienna, where he continued serious study at the Vienna Cons. with Sechter and Seyfried. He became a conductor in the theaters of Pressburg and Baden, and then was on the staff at the Theater an der Wien (1845–62); then was at the Kaitheater in 1862–65; subsequently at the Carl theater in 1865–82. All the while, he wrote light operas and other theater music of all degrees of levity, obtaining increasing success rivaling that of Offenbach. His music possesses the charm and gaiety of the Viennese genre, but also contains elements of more vigorous popular rhythms.

WORKS: His most celebrated single work is the overture to *Dichter und Bauer (Poet and Peasant),* which still retains a firm place in the light repertoire. His total output comprises about 30 comic operas and operettas and 180 other stage pieces, most of which were brought out in Vienna; of these the following obtained considerable success: *Dichter und Bauer* (Aug. 24, 1846); *Das Mädchen vom Lande* (Aug. 7, 1847); *Der Bandit* (1848; in Italy as *Cartouche*); *Paragraph 3* (Jan. 8, 1858); *Das Pensionat* (Nov. 24, 1860); *Die Kartenaufschlägerin* (April 26, 1862); *Zehn Mädchen und kein Mann* (Oct. 25, 1862); *Flotte Bursche* (April 18, 1863); *Franz Schubert* (Sept. 10, 1864); *Die schöne Galatea* (Berlin, June 30, 1865); *Leichte Cavallerie* (March 24, 1866; enormously popular); *Freigeister* (Oct. 23, 1866); *Banditenstreiche* (April 27, 1867); *Die Frau Meisterin* (Jan. 20, 1868); *Tantalusqualen* (Oct. 3, 1868); *Isabella* (Nov. 5, 1869); *Cannebas* (Nov. 2, 1872); *Fatinitza* (Jan. 5, 1876; extremely popular); *Der*

Teufel auf Erden (Jan. 5, 1878); *Boccaccio* (Feb. 1, 1879; very popular); *Donna Juanita* (Feb. 21, 1880); *Der Gascogner* (March 22, 1881); *Herzblättchen* (Feb. 4, 1882); *Die Afrikareise* (March 17, 1883); *Bellmann* (Feb. 26, 1887); *Die Jagd nach dem Glücke* (Oct. 27, 1888); *Das Modell* (posthumous; Oct. 4, 1895); *Die Pariserin* (posthumous; Jan. 26, 1898); several other operettas were produced in Prague, Berlin, and Hamburg. In addition to his theater works, he wrote a Symph.; several string quartets; songs; also *Missa dalmatica* (1867).

Surette, Thomas Whitney, eminent American music educator; b. Concord, Mass., Sept. 7, 1861; d. there, May 19, 1941. He studied piano with Arthur Foote and composition with J.K. Paine at Harvard Univ., graduating in 1891; then was active mainly as a church organist. Deeply interested in making musical education accessible and effective in the U.S., he founded in 1914 the Concord Summer School of Music; with A.T. Davison he edited The Concord Series of educational music, which found a tremendously favorable acceptance on the part of many schools, particularly in New England; the series provided an excellent selection of good music which could be understood by most music teachers and performed by pupils. Surette was also largely responsible for the vogue of music appreciation courses that swept the country and spilled over into the British Isles. He publ. *The Appreciation of Music* (with D.G. Mason; 5 vols., of which vols. 2 and 5 were by Mason alone; N.Y., 1907; innumerable subsequent printings), and, on a more elevated plane, *Course of Study on the Development of Symphonic Music* (Chicago, 1915) and *Music and Life* (Boston, 1917); he also publ. popular articles on music and musicians, notable for their lack of discrimination and absence of verification of data. He was also a composer of sorts; wrote a light opera, *Priscilla, or The Pilgrim's Proxy,* after Longfellow (Concord, March 6, 1889; had more than 1,000 subsequent perfs. in the U.S.), and a romantic opera, *Cascabel, or The Broken Tryst* (Pittsburgh, May 15, 1899).

Suriano (or **Soriano**), **Francesco,** a composer of the Roman school; b. Soriano, 1549; d. there, July 19, 1621. He was a chorister at St. John Lateran; later a pupil of Nanino and Palestrina; in 1580, choirmaster at S. Ludivico de' Francesi; from 1581 to 1586, in Mantua; in 1587, at S. Maria Maggiore; in 1588, again at S. Ludovico, returning to S. Maria Maggiore in 1595; in 1599, at St. John Lateran; and from 1600, once more at S. Maria Maggiore (pensioned, June 23, 1620). He collaborated with F. Anerio in the revision of the *Editio Medicaea* of the Gradual (cf. Palestrina). Suriano publ. 2 books of madrigals *a* 5 (1581, 1592); one book of madrigals *a* 4 (1601); motets *a* 8 (1597); masses *a* 4–8 (1609; includes an arrangement of Palestrina's *Missa Papae Marcelli* for 8 Voices); *Canoni . . . sopra l'Ave Maris Stella a 3–8 voci* (1610); 2 books of Psalms and motets (1614, 1616); *Villanelle a 3* (1617); a Passion and several Magnificats (1619).

Surinach, Carlos, Spanish-American composer and conductor; b. Barcelona, March 4, 1915. He studied in Barcelona with Morera (1936–39) and later with Max Trapp in Berlin (1939–43). Returning to Spain in 1943, he was active mainly as a conductor. In 1951 he went to the U.S.; became an American citizen in 1959; was a visiting prof. of music at Carnegie-Mellon Inst. in Pittsburgh in 1966–67.

WORKS: *El Mozo que casó con mujer brava,* one-act opera (Barcelona, Jan. 10, 1948); ballet, *Monte Carlo* (Barcelona, May 2, 1945); 3 symphs.: No. 1, *Passacaglia-Symphony* (Barcelona, April 8, 1945, composer conducting); No. 2 (Paris Radio, Jan. 26, 1950, composer conducting); No. 3, *Sinfonía chica* (1957); *Sinfonietta flamenca* (Louisville, Ky., Jan. 9, 1954); *Feria mágica,* overture (Louisville, March 14, 1956); *3 cantos berberes* for Flute, Oboe, Clarinet, Viola, Cello, and Harp (1952); *Flamenquerías* for 2 Pianos (1952); *Ritmo Jondo* for Clarinet, Trumpet, Xylophone, and Percussion (N.Y., May 5, 1952; extended version in ballet form, *Deep Rhythm,* was perf. in N.Y., April 15, 1953); *Tientos* for English Horn, Harpsichord, and Timpani (1953); *A Place in the Desert* (1960); *Symphonic Variations* (1963); *Drama Jondo,* overture (1964); *Melorhythmic Dramas* for Orch. (1966); *The Missions of San Antonio,* symph. canticles (1968); chamber music of various descriptions; songs.

Susa, Conrad, American composer; b. Springdale, Pa., April 26, 1935. He studied piano, organ, flute, oboe, clarinet, and French horn. Upon receiving a scholarship from Carnegie-Mellon Univ. in Pittsburgh, he took composition courses with Nicolai Lopatnikoff; after graduation he entered the Juilliard School of Music in N.Y., where his composition teachers were William Bergsma and Vincent Persichetti. He subsequently engaged in theater conducting. He excels in choral writing. Among his works are 5 serenades for various groups of voices and instruments, a *Pastorale* for Strings, and numerous accompanied and unaccompanied choruses. He has achieved his greatest acclaim with his opera *Transformations,* to the text from poems by Anne Sexton, produced by the Minnesota Opera Co. in Minneapolis on May 5, 1973; another opera, *Black River,* was produced in Minneapolis on Nov. 1, 1975.

Susato, Johannes (real name, **Johannes Steinwert von Soest**), German composer and singing master; b. Unna, 1448; d. Frankfurt, May 2, 1506. He was a chorister at Soest, then was in Cleve and Bruges, where he studied with English musicians; was subsequently active as a singing master in Cologne, Kassel, and (from 1472) Heidelberg; Virdung was one of his pupils there. He was also a physician, and c.1500 went to Frankfurt as a municipal doctor.

Susato, Tielman, German publisher and composer, son of **Johannes Susato;** b. probably in Cologne, c.1500; d. possibly Antwerp, c.1561. In 1529 he moved from Cologne to Antwerp, where he was a town trumpeter; then established a music printing shop (1543) and issued 13 books of chansons, 4 vols. of masses, 4 vols. of motets, 4 books of various songs, etc.; several of these miscellaneous works were of his own composition.

Susskind, (Jan) Walter, Czech-born English conductor; b. Prague, May 1, 1913; d. Berkeley, Calif., March 25, 1980. He studied theory with Josef Suk and advanced composition with Alois Hába at the Prague Cons. (1928–33); took conducting lessons with George Szell and was Szell's assistant conductor at the German Opera House in Prague (1933–38). He then toured Europe as a conductor and pianist; went to England, where he was the pianist-member of the London Czech Trio (1939–42) and conducted the Carl Rosa Opera Co. (1942–45); was subsequently conductor of the Scottish National Orch. in Glasgow (1946–52), having become a British citizen in 1946. He then conducted the Victorian Symph. Orch. in Melbourne (1953–55); from 1956 to 1965 was conductor of the Toronto Symph. Orch. and was music director of the Aspen (Colo.) Music Festival (1961–68), the St. Louis Symph. Orch. (1968–75), and the Mississippi River Festival in Edwardsville, Ill. (1969–75). His last position was that of music adviser and principal guest conductor of the Cincinnati Symph. Orch., from 1978 until his death. Susskind was also a composer; among his works are 4 songs for Voice and String Quartet (Prague Festival of the International Society for Contemporary Music, Sept. 2, 1935); *9 Slovak Sketches* for Orch.; *Passacaglia* for Timpani and Chamber Orch. (St. Louis, Feb. 24, 1977).

Süssmayr, Franz Xaver, Austrian composer; b. Schwanenstadt, 1766; d. Vienna, Sept. 17, 1803. He was a pupil of Salieri, and also of Mozart, of whom he became an intimate friend; after Mozart's death his widow entrusted the completion of his Requiem to Süssmayr; he was clever in emulating Mozart's style of composition, and his handwriting was so much like Mozart's that it is difficult to distinguish between them. He was conductor at the National Theater in Vienna from 1792, and 2nd conductor at the Vienna Court Opera from 1794.

WORKS: Süssmayr wrote a number of operas and operettas, which he produced in Vienna, among them: *Moses* (May 4, 1792); *L'Incanto superato* (July 8, 1793); *Der Spiegel von Arkadien* (Nov. 14, 1794); *Idris und Zenide* (May 9, 1795); *Die edle Rache* (Aug. 27, 1795); *Die Freiwilligen* (Sept. 27, 1796); *Der Wildfang* (Oct. 4, 1797); *Der Marktschreier* (July 6, 1799); *Soliman der Zweite, oder Die drei Sultaninnen* (Oct. 1, 1799); *Gülnare* (*Gonora;* July 5, 1800); *Phasma* (July 25, 1801). He wrote *secco* recitatives for Mozart's opera *La clemenza di Tito* (Prague, Sept. 6, 1791); composed several numbers for the Vienna production of Grétry's *La Double Epreuve,* given there under the title *Die doppelte Erkenntlichkeit* (Feb. 28, 1796). Other works include a Clarinet Concerto and pieces for the English horn, for guitar, and for other instruments. Most of his works are in MS.

Sutermeister, Heinrich, important Swiss composer; b. Feuerthalen, Aug. 12, 1910. He studied philology at the Sorbonne Univ. in Paris (1930–31) and composition with Carl Orff and Walter Courvoisier at the Munich Academy of Music (1931–34). Subsequently he devoted himself mainly to composition, until 1963, when he was appointed to the faculty of the Hochschule für Musik in Hannover, Germany; he retired from there in 1975. His main endeavor is to create a type of modern opera that is dramatically effective and melodically pleasing; in his musical philosophy he follows the organic line of thought, with the natural impulses of the human body determining the rhythmic course of a composition; discordant combinations of sounds are legitimate parts of modern harmony in Sutermeister's works, but he rejects artificial doctrines such as orthodox dodecaphony.

WORKS: Operas: *Die schwarze Spinne,* radio opera (1935; Bern Radio, Oct. 15, 1936; revised for the stage and produced in St. Gall, March 2, 1949); *Romeo und Julia,* after Shakespeare (1938–40; Dresden, April 13, 1940; his first and greatest success); *Die Zauberinsel,* after Shakespeare's *The Tempest* (1941–42; Dresden, Oct. 31, 1942); *Niobe* (1943–45; Zürich, June 22, 1946); *Raskolnikoff,* after Dostoyevsky's *Crime and Punishment* (1946–48; Stockholm, Oct. 14, 1948); *Der rote Stiefel* (1949–51; Stockholm, Nov. 22, 1951); *Titus Feuerfuchs,* burlesque opera (1956–58; Basel, April 14, 1958); *Seraphine,* opera-buffa after Rabelais (Zürich Radio, June 10, 1959; stage premiere, Munich, Feb. 25, 1960); *Das Gespenst von Canterville,* television opera after Oscar Wilde (1962–63; German television, Sept. 6, 1964); *Madame Bovary,* after Flaubert (1967; Zürich, May 26, 1967); *La Croisade des Enfants,* television opera (1969); *Der Flashenteufel (The Bottle Imp),* television opera after R.L. Stevenson (1969–70; German television, 1971); a radio ballad, *Füsse im Feuer* (also arranged for an operatic production, staged at the Berlin City Opera, Feb. 12, 1950); a radio melodrama, *Fingerhütchen* (produced in operatic form at St. Gall, April 26, 1950); 2 ballets: *Das Dorf unter dem Gletscher* (1936; Karlsruhe, May 2, 1937) and *Max und Moritz* (1951; first stage perf., St. Gall, 1963); 8 numbered cantatas: No. 1, *Andreas Gryphius,* for Chorus a cappella (1935–36); No. 2 for Contralto, Chorus, and 2 Pianos (1943–44); No. 3, *Dem Allgegenwärtigen,* for Soloists, Chorus, and Orch. (1957–58); No. 4, *Das Hohelied,* for Soloists, Chorus, and Orch. (1960); No. 5, *Der Papagei aus Kuba,* for Chorus and Chamber Orch. (1961); No. 6, *Erkennen und Schaffen* (in French, *Croire et créer*), for Soloists, Chorus, and Orch. (1963); No. 7, *Sonnenhymne des Echnaton,* for Male Chorus, 2 Horns, 3 Trumpets, 2 Trombones, Tuba, Piano, and Percussion (1965); No. 8, *Omnia ad Unum,* for Baritone, Chorus, and Orch. (1965–66); *Missa da Requiem* for Soloists, Chorus, and Orch. (1952; Basel, June 11, 1954); *Ecclesia* for Soloists, Chorus, and Orch. (1972–73; Lausanne, Oct. 18, 1975); *Te Deum* for Soprano, Chorus, and Orch. (1974); *Divertimento No. 1* for String Orch. (1936) and *No. 2* for Orch. (1959–60); 3 piano concertos (1943, 1953, 1961–62); 2 cellos concertos (1954–55, 1971); *Sérénade pour Montreux* for 2 Oboes, 2

Horns, and String Orch. (1970); Clarinet Concerto (1974); chamber pieces.

Suthaus, Ludwig, eminent German tenor; b. Cologne, Dec. 12, 1906; d. Berlin, Sept. 7, 1971. He studied voice in Cologne; made his operatic debut in Aachen in 1928 as Walther von Stolzing in *Die Meistersinger von Nürnberg;* sang in Essen (1931–33) and Stuttgart (1933–41); in 1941 he joined the Berlin State Opera, where he made many appearances until 1948; then sang with the Berlin Städtische Oper until 1965. He made his U.S. debut with the San Francisco Opera in 1953. He was one of the outstanding Heldentenors of his time and was engaged at several Bayreuth Festivals in Wagnerian roles.

Sutherland, Dame Joan, celebrated Australian soprano; b. Sydney, Nov. 7, 1926. She received her early vocal training in Sydney; made her debut as Dido in a concert performance of *Dido and Aeneas* in Sydney in 1947; made her stage debut in Sydney in 1951; then went to London, where she studied voice with Clive Carey at the Royal College of Music. After an appearance at Covent Garden in a minor role in 1952, she rapidly asserted herself as an important artist; obtained a signal success at Covent Garden as Lucia, on Feb. 17, 1959. She made her first American appearance with the Dallas Opera in 1960; on Nov. 26, 1961, she made her Metropolitan Opera debut as Lucia, to great acclaim. She married the Australian conductor **Richard Bonynge;** was made a Dame Commander of the Order of the British Empire in 1978.

Sutherland, Margaret, Australian composer; b. Adelaide, Nov. 20, 1897. She studied piano with Edward Goll and composition with Fritz Hart at the Marshall Hall Cons. (1914); then taught at the Melbourne Cons. In 1923–25 she traveled in Europe. In 1970 she was made an Officer of the Order of the British Empire for her services to Australian music. Her own compositions are marked by classical restraint; most of them follow Baroque forms.

Sutro, Rose Laura (b. Baltimore, Sept. 15, 1870; d. there, Jan. 11, 1957) and **Ottilie** (b. Baltimore, Jan. 4, 1872; d. there, Sept. 12, 1970), American duo-pianists; daughters of Otto Sutro, a patron of art and founder of the Baltimore Oratorio Society. Both began piano lessons with their mother, and in 1889 were sent to Berlin, where they continued their studies. They made a spectacular debut in London on July 13, 1894; their first American appearance took place in Brooklyn on Nov. 13, 1894, followed by a tour of the U.S. Returning to Europe, they won fresh laurels, and were invited to play before Queen Victoria. Max Bruch wrote his Concerto for 2 Pianos and Orch. expressly for them, and they gave its premiere with the Philadelphia Orch. on Dec. 29, 1916. In 1953 the sisters established the Sutro Club Room at the Maryland Historical Society in memory of their father.

Suzuki, Shin'ichi, influential Japanese educator

and violin teacher; founder of the Suzuki method of violin instruction; b. Nagoya, Oct. 18, 1898. He was the son of **Masakichi Suzuki** (1859–1944), a maker of string instruments and the founder of the Suzuki Violin Seizo Co. He studied violin with Ko Ando in Tokyo and with Karl Klinger in Berlin (1921–28); upon his return to Japan, he formed the Suzuki Quartet with 3 of his brothers; also made appearances as a conductor with his own Tokyo String Orch. He became president of the Teikoku Music School in 1930. He subsequently devoted most of his time to education, especially the teaching of children. He maintained that any child, given the right stimuli under proper conditions in a group environment, could achieve a high level of competence as a performer. In 1950 he organized the Saino Kyoiku Kenkyu-kai in Matsumoto, where he taught his method most successfully. In subsequent years his method was adopted for instruction on other instruments as well. He made many tours of the U.S. and Europe, where he lectured and demonstrated his method.

Svanholm, Set, noted Swedish tenor; b. Västeras, Sept. 2, 1904; d. Saltsjö-Duvnäs, Oct. 4, 1964. He served as a church organist in Tillberga and Säby; studied voice with John Forsell at the Opera School of the Stockholm Cons. He made his operatic debut as a baritone at the Royal Theater in Stockholm in 1930; in 1936 he began singing tenor roles. In addition to his appearances at the Royal Theater in Stockholm, he also sang at the Salzburg Festival and the Vienna State Opera (1938), the Berlin State Opera, La Scala in Milan (1941–42), and the Bayreuth Festival (1942). In 1946 he appeared as Tristan in Rio de Janeiro and as Lohengrin in San Francisco; on Nov. 15, 1946, he made his Metropolitan Opera debut in N.Y. as Siegfried; remained on its roster until his farewell appearance as Parsifal on March 24, 1956. From 1948–57 he sang at London's Covent Garden. From 1956–63 he was director of the Royal Theater in Stockholm. Among his best roles were Radames, Tannhäuser, Otello, and Siegmund; he was equally successful in operas of Wagner and Verdi.

Svendsen, Johan (Severin), eminent Norwegian composer; b. Christiania, Sept. 30, 1840; d. Copenhagen, June 14, 1911. He acquired practical experience in music from his father, a bandmaster, and played several instruments; then conducted a band himself. It was not before he was 23 that he began serious study at the Leipzig Cons. with F. David, Reinecke, and others; then played violin in theater orchs. in Paris; wrote incidental music for Coppée's play *Le Passant* (Paris, Jan. 14, 1869), a Violin Concerto, and other violin works. In 1870 he went back to Leipzig; then traveled to America, and married an American lady, Sarah Levett. Returning to Norway, he became the conductor of the Christiania Musical Assoc. (1872–77 and again in 1880–83). In 1883 he was appointed court conductor in Copenhagen as well as conductor of the Royal Theater there. He retired in 1908. His most popular works are the 4

Norwegian Rhapsodies for Orch. and the *Carnaval des artistes norvégiens* (also for Orch.), based on genuine folk melodies; he further wrote 2 symphs.; String Quartet; String Quintet; String Octet; Cello Concerto; 2 albums of songs to German, French, and Norwegian words; a *Romance* for Violin and Orch. (very popular); arrangements of Scandinavian melodies for String Quartet; etc.

Svetlanov, Evgeny, Russian conductor and composer; b. Moscow, Sept. 6, 1928. He studied composition with Gnessin and Shaporin, and conducting with Gauck. After graduation in 1955 he joined the staff of the Bolshoi Theater in Moscow; was its principal conductor from 1962 to 1964. In 1965 he was appointed music director of the State Orch. of the U.S.S.R.; in 1979 became a principal guest conductor of the London Symph. Orch. He wrote a Symph. (1956); *Siberian Fantasy* for Orch. (1953); Piano Concerto (1951); incidental music for plays; film scores.

Sviridov, Georgi, significant Soviet Russian composer; b. Fatezh, near Kursk, Dec. 16, 1915. He studied at the Leningrad Cons. with Shostakovich. In his music, Sviridov adheres to the ideals of socialist realism, seeking inspiration in Russian folk songs; the texts of his vocal works are usually taken from Russian literature. His *Oratorio pathétique* (1959), to words by Mayakovsky, composed in a grandly songful "optimistic" style, became one of the most successful scores by a Soviet composer.

Svoboda, Tomáš, Czech composer; b. Paris, Dec. 6, 1939, of Czech parents (his father was a renowned mathematician, Antonín Svoboda). The family went to Prague in 1946; he studied piano privately and composition with Hlobil, Kabeláč, and Dobiáš at the Prague Cons., graduating in 1959. In 1964 he left Czechoslovakia and settled in the U.S. In 1970 he was appointed member of the faculty at Portland (Oreg.) State Univ.; in 1979 he settled on Treasure Island, Fla. His music is marked by broad melodic lines in economically disposed harmonies; there are elements of serialism in chromatic episodes.

Swan, Alfred (Julius), Russian-born English-American musicologist and educator; b. St. Petersburg (of English parents), Oct. 9, 1890; d. Haverford, Pa., Oct. 2, 1970. After attending a German-language school in St. Petersburg, he studied at Oxford Univ., receiving the degree of B.A. (1911), and later his M.A. (1934). Returning to Russia in 1911, he took courses in composition at the St. Petersburg Cons. During the Civil War in Russia, he served with the American Red Cross in Siberia (1918–19); then emigrated to the U.S.; taught at the Univ. of Virginia (1921–23); in 1926 he was appointed head of the music depts. at Swarthmore College and Haverford College in Pennsylvania, retiring from these posts in 1958. His specialty was Russian music. Swan was also a composer; he wrote a Trio for Flute, Clarinet, and Piano (1932); 2 violin sonatas (1913, 1948); 4

piano sonatas (1932-46); several albums of songs.
WRITINGS: *Scriabin* (London, 1923; reprint, N.Y., 1969); *Music 1900–1930* (N.Y., 1930); "Znamenny Chant of the Russian Church," *Musical Quarterly* (April, July, Oct. 1940); many other articles on Russian music and Russian composers in various publications. He also brought out a useful brochure, *The Music Director's Guide to Musical Literature* (N.Y., 1941). His *Russian Music and Its Sources in Chant and Folksong* was publ. posthumously (N.Y., 1973). He ed. *Songs from Many Lands* (1923) and *Recueil de chansons russes* (1936).

Swan, Timothy, American hymn-tune writer; b. Worcester, Mass., July 23, 1758; d. Northfield, Mass., July 23, 1842. His only musical training consisted of 3 weeks at a singing school, and while serving in the Continental Army he also learned to play the flute. From 1783 he lived in Suffield, Conn., and in 1807 moved to Northfield, Mass. He composed the hymn tunes *Poland, China, Ocean,* and *Pownal;* publ. *The Songster's Assistant* (c.1800); *New England Harmony* (1801); and also probably was the author of *The Songsters' Museum* (1803).

Swanson, Howard, black American composer; b. Atlanta, Aug. 18, 1907; d. New York, Nov. 12, 1978. As a youth he earned a living by manual labor on the railroad and as a postal clerk. He entered the Cleveland Inst. of Music at the age of 20, enrolling in evening courses with Herbert Elwell; obtained a stipend to go to Paris, where he studied composition with Nadia Boulanger (1938–40). Returning to the U.S., he took a job with the Internal Revenue Service (1941–45). In 1952 he received a Guggenheim fellowship that enabled him to go back to Paris, where he lived until 1966 before settling permanently in N.Y. Swanson's songs attracted the attention of such notable singers as Marian Anderson and William Warfield, who sang them on tours. He achieved signal success with his *Short Symphony* (Symph. No. 2, 1948), a work of simple melodic inspiration, which received considerable acclaim at its first performance by the N.Y. Phil., conducted by Mitropoulos (Nov. 23, 1950). In 1952 it won the Music Critics' Circle Award for the best orch. work performed in N.Y. during the 1950–51 season.

Swarowsky, Hans, Austrian conductor; b. Budapest, Sept. 16, 1899; d. Salzburg, Sept. 10, 1975. He studied in Vienna with Schoenberg and Anton von Webern, with whom he formed a friendly association; he also was in close relationship with Richard Strauss. He devoted himself mainly to conducting; occupied posts as opera conductor in Hamburg (1932) and in Berlin (1934). From 1937 to 1940 he was conductor of the Zürich Opera; during the season 1944–45 led the Polish Phil. in Cracow. After the war he was principal conductor of the Vienna Symph. (1945–47) and of the Graz Opera (1947–50); in 1957–59 he was conductor of the Scottish National Orch. in Glasgow; from 1959 appeared occasionally as guest conductor of the Vienna State Opera; in 1965 became a regular staff conductor there. In his pro-

grams he gave prominent place to the works of the Vienna School; his performances of Mahler were particularly fine. Swarowsky was an excellent instructor in conducting; he led a special seminar at the Vienna Academy of Music; among his students were Claudio Abbado and Zubin Mehta. He was a highly competent editor of music by various composers; also trans. a number of Italian librettos into German; publ. *Wahrung der Gestalt* (Vienna, 1979).

Swarthout, Gladys, American mezzo-soprano; b. Deepwater, Mo., Dec. 25, 1900; d. Florence, July 7, 1969. She studied at the Bush Cons. in Chicago, also opera with L. Mugnone; made her debut in a minor part with the Chicago Civic Opera in 1924; and then made regular appearances with the Ravinia Opera Co. in Chicago. On Nov. 15, 1929, she sang the part of La Cieca in *La Gioconda* at the Metropolitan Opera; she remained on its roster, with several interruptions, until 1945. She married the singer **Frank Chapman** in 1932; publ. an autobiography, *Come Soon, Tomorrow* (N.Y., 1945).

Swayne, Giles, British composer; b. Stevenage, June 30, 1946. He studied with Nicholas Maw; in 1968 entered the Royal Academy, where he took courses in composition and piano; served as répétiteur at the Wexford Festival (1972–73) and at Glyndebourne (1973–74); also attended Messiaen's classes in composition in Paris (1976–77). In 1982 he visited West Africa to study the music of the Jola people of Senegal and The Gambia. In common with many other British composers of his generation, he resolutely eschewed musical gourmandise to become a convinced populist. He wrote music for the general public.
WORKS: *4 Lyrical Pieces* for Cello and Piano (1970; Aldeburgh, June 16, 1971); String Quartet No. 1 (1971); String Quartet No. 2 (1977; Manchester, Oct. 30, 1978); *The Good Morrow,* cycle of 5 settings of John Donne for Mezzo-soprano and Piano (1971); *Paraphrase on a Theme of Tallis* for Organ (1971); *Canto* for Guitar (1972); *Canto* for Piano (1973); *Canto* for Violin (1973); *Synthesis* for 2 Pianos (1974); *Orlando's Music* for Orch. (1974; Liverpool, Feb. 3, 1976); *Canto* for Clarinet (1975); *Duo* for Violin and Piano (1975); Suite for Guitar (1976); *Pentecost-Music* for Orch. (1977; Manchester, April 8, 1981); *Cry* for 28 amplified Solo Voices depicting the creation of the world (1979; London, July 23, 1980); *A World Within,* tape composition for ballet, consisting of multitrack recordings of Horn, based on the life of the Brontë sisters (1978; Stoke-on-Trent, June 2, 1978); *Freewheeling* for Viola, Baryton, and Cello (1980; Kuhmo Festival, Finland, July 25, 1980); *Canto* for Cello (1981); *Count-Down* for 16-part Choir and 2 Percussion Players (1981; Merton Festival, Yorkshire, May 23, 1982); *Morgan* for Organ (1982); Symph. (1982); *Song for Hadi* for Drums and Instruments (1983; Bath Festival, June 4, 1983).

Sweelinck, Jan Pieterszoon, great Dutch organist and composer; b. Deventer (or Amsterdam), May 1562; d. Amsterdam, Oct. 16, 1621. Contrary to repeated assertions that Sweelinck was a pupil of Zarlino in Venice, documentary evidence proves that he remained in Amsterdam virtually all his life; this also refutes the theory that Sweelinck was the carrier of Venetian ideas and techniques in Northern Europe. About 1580 he became organist of the Old Church in Amsterdam, a position previously held by his father, Pieter Sweelinck (d. 1573). As a player and teacher, he was celebrated far and wide; most of the leading organists in northern Germany, of the next generation, were his pupils. Sweelinck was the first to employ the pedal in a real fugal part, and originated the organ fugue built up on one theme with the gradual addition of counter-themes leading up to a highly involved and ingenious finale—a form perfected by Bach. In rhythmic and melodic freedom, his vocal compositions show an advance over the earlier polyphonic style, though replete with intricate contrapuntal devices. A complete edition of Sweelinck's works, in 12 vols., edited by Max Seiffert for the Vereeniging voor Nederlandsche Muziekgeschiedenis, was publ. by Breitkopf & Härtel (1894–1901): vol. I, works for organ and clavier; vol. II, first half of the First Book of Psalms (1604); vol. III, 2nd half of the same; vol. IV, first half of the 2nd Book of Psalms (1613); vol. V, 2nd half of the same; vol. VI, 3rd Book of Psalms (1614); vol. VII, 4th Book of Psalms (1621); vol. VIII, *Cantiones sacrae a* 5; vol. IX, *Chansons a* 5; vol. X, *Rimes françaises et italiennes a* 2–4; vol. XI, processional compositions; vol. XII, rules for composition, edited by H. Gehrmann. Vols. II–VII comprise the 150 Psalms of David in the rhymed French version by Marot and Beza. A new edition, *Opera Omnia, editio altera*, was begun by the same series in 1957.

Swift, Richard, American composer; b. Middlepoint, Ohio, Sept. 24, 1927. He studied at the Univ. of Chicago (M.A., 1956); then became a member of the faculty of the Univ. of Calif., Davis; was appointed chairman of the music dept. there in 1963. In his compositions he applies a variety of functional serial techniques, including electronic and aleatory devices, while preserving the external forms of Baroque music.

Symonds, Norman, Canadian composer; b. Nelson, British Columbia, Dec. 23, 1920. He studied clarinet and piano at the Royal Cons. in Toronto (1945–47); took lessons in composition privately with Gordon Delamont in Toronto (1947–50). In 1953 he organized his own jazz octet, which continued in action until 1957. Most of his compositions are in the "third stream" idiom, combining jazz and symph. styles.

Szabelski, Boleslaw, Polish organist and composer; b. Radoryż, near Lublin, Dec. 3, 1896; d. Katowice, Aug. 27, 1979. He was an organist; studied composition with Szymanowski and Statkowski at the Warsaw Cons.; then became a teacher of organ and composition at the State College of Music in Katowice (1929–39, 1945–74).
WORKS: 5 symphs. (1926; 1934, with Soprano and

Chorus; 1951; 1956; 1968, with Chorus and Organ); *Suite* for Orch. (1938); Organ Sonata (1943); Sinfonietta for String Orch. and Percussion (1946); *Poemat bohaterski (Heroic Poem)* for Chorus and Orch. (1952); *Solemn Overture* (1953); *Concerto grosso* for Orch. (1954); Piano Concertino (1955); 2 string quartets (1935, 1956); *3 Sonnets* for Orch. (1958); *Improvisations* for Chorus and Chamber Orch. (1959); *Wiersze (Verses)* for Piano and Orch. (1961); *Aphorisms "9"* for Chamber Ensemble (1962); *Preludes* for Chamber Orch. (1963); Flute Concerto (1964); *Nicolaus Copernicus,* oratorio (1976; Poznan, April 2, 1976); *The Wola Redoubt* for 3 Vocal Soloists and Orch. (1976; Warsaw, Nov. 5, 1976); Piano Concerto (1978).

Szabó, Ferenc, distinguished Hungarian composer; b. Budapest, Dec. 27, 1902; d. there, Nov. 4, 1969. He studied with Kodály, Siklós, and Leo Weiner at the Budapest Academy of Music (1922–26); in 1926 he became aligned with the labor movement in Hungary; in 1932 went to Russia, where he became closely associated with the ideological work of the Union of Soviet Composers. In 1945 he returned to Hungary and was appointed prof. at the Budapest Academy; served as its director in 1958–67. He was awarded the Kossuth Prize in 1951 and 1954. His music initially followed the trends of Central European modernism, with strong undertones of Hungarian melorhythms, but later he wrote music in the manner of socialist realism; his choruses are permeated with the militant spirit of the revolutionary movement.

Szabolcsi, Bence, eminent Hungarian music scholar; b. Budapest, Aug. 2, 1899; d. there, Jan. 21, 1973. He studied jurisprudence at the Univ. of Budapest; concurrently took music courses with Kodály at the Budapest Academy and with Abert at the Univ. of Leipzig, where he received his Ph.D. in 1923. He was a prof. of music history at the Budapest Academy of Music from 1945 until his death. He was editor of the Hungarian music periodical *Zenei Szemle* (with Bartha) from 1926 (except for the war years, when it suspended publication). With Aladár Tóth he brought out a music dictionary in the Hungarian language (1930–31); publ. a history of music (Budapest, 1940), a monograph on Beethoven (Budapest, 1948), and a number of valuable papers in various European magazines. But his most abiding concern was the publication of documents on Béla Bartók. On his 70th birthday he was presented a Festschrift, edited by Bartha, *Bence Szabolcsi septuagenario* (Budapest, 1969). Of his writings on Bartók, the most important are *Bartók—Sa vie et son œuvre* (Budapest, 1956; 2nd ed., 1968); *Béla Bartók* (Leipzig, 1968); *Béla Bartók, Musiksprachen* (Leipzig, 1972). Two of his books were publ. in Eng.: *The Twilight of Ferenc Liszt* (Budapest, 1959) and *A Concise History of Hungarian Music* (Budapest, 1964).

Szántó, Theodor, Hungarian pianist and composer; b. Vienna, June 3, 1877; d. Budapest, Jan. 7, 1934.

He studied with Dachs (piano) and Fuchs (composition) at the Vienna Cons., and later with Busoni in Berlin (1898–1901). In 1905 he settled in Paris; from 1914 to 1921 lived in Switzerland; then divided his time between Paris and Budapest. His opera on a Japanese story, *Typhoon*, was produced in Mannheim on Nov. 29, 1924, and there were a few subsequent performances in other cities. He also wrote a *Japanese Suite* for Orch. (1926); several symph. works based on Hungarian folk songs; chamber music; many piano pieces (of which *Variations on a Hungarian Folksong* became fairly well known).

Székely, Mihály, Hungarian bass; b. Jászberény, May 8, 1901; d. Budapest, March 22, 1963. He studied in Budapest; made his debut as Fernando in *Il Trovatore* in 1920 at the Budapest Opera, where he established himself as a principal member of the company, remaining on its roster until his death; also made guest appearances throughout Europe. On Jan. 17, 1947, he sang the role of Hunding in *Die Walküre* at his Metropolitan Opera debut in N.Y.; continued on the roster until 1948, and then returned for the 1949–50 season. He subsequently sang in Europe, appearing at the Glyndebourne Festival, the Holland Festival, the Bavarian State Opera in Munich, etc. He was renowned for his Wagnerian roles.

Szeligowski, Tadeusz, notable Polish composer and pedagogue; b. Lwow, Sept. 12, 1896; d. Poznan, Jan. 10, 1963. He studied composition with Jachimecki in Cracow (1918–23) and with Nadia Boulanger in Paris (1929–31); returning to Poland, he taught classes in Poznan (1932–39, 1947–62) and in Warsaw (1951–62).
WORKS: 3 operas: *Bunt Żaków* (*Rebellion of Clerks;* 1951; Wroclaw, July 14, 1951); *Krakatuk,* after E.T.A. Hoffmann (1955; Gdansk, Dec. 30, 1956); *Theodor gentleman* (1960; Wroclaw, 1963); 2 ballets: *Paw i dziewczyna* (*The Peacock and the Maiden;* 1948; Wroclaw, Aug. 2, 1949) and *Mazeppa* (1957; Warsaw, 1959); *Kaziuki,* suite for Orch. (1928); Concerto for Orch. (1932); Clarinet Concerto (1932); *Epitaph for Karol Szymanowski* for String Orch. (1937); Piano Concerto (1941; Cracow, May 17, 1946); *Suita lubelska* for Small Orch. (1945); *Nocturne* for Orch. (1947); *Burlesque Overture* (1952); *Triptych* for Soprano and Orch. (1946); *Kantata o sporcie* for Voice, Chorus, and Orch. (1947); *Wesele lubelskie* (*Lublin Wedding*), suite for Soprano, Chorus, and Small Orch. (1948); *Rapsod* for Soprano and Orch. (1949); *Panicz i dziewczyna* (*The Young Squire and the Country Girl*), musical dialogue for Soprano, Baritone, Chorus, and Orch. (1949); cantata, *Karta serc* (*The Charter of Hearts;* 1952); *Renegade,* ballad for Bass and Orch. (1953); songs; 2 string quartets (1929, 1934); *Nocturne* for Cello and Piano (1945); *Orientale* for Cello and Piano (1945); Wind Quintet (1950); Flute Sonata (1953); *Air grave et air gai* for English Horn and Piano (1954); Piano Trio (1956); Piano Sonatina (1940); Piano Sonata (1949).

Szell, George, greatly distinguished Hungarian-American conductor; b. Budapest, June 7, 1897; d. Cleveland, July 30, 1970. His family moved to Vienna when he was a small child. He studied piano with Richard Robert and composition with Mandyczewski; also in Prague with J.B. Foerster. He played a Mozart piano concerto with the Vienna Symph. Orch. when he was 10 years old, and the orch. also performed an overture of his composition. At the age of 17 he led the Berlin Phil. in an ambitious program which included a symph. work of his own. In 1915 he was engaged as an assistant conductor at the Royal Opera of Berlin; in 1917 he was conductor of the Strasbourg Municipal Theater. His next appointments as an opera conductor were in Prague (1919), Düsseldorf (1922–24), and the State Opera House in Berlin (1924–29). From 1929 to 1937 he filled conducting engagements in Prague and Vienna. He made his U.S. debut as guest conductor of the St. Louis Symph. Orch. in 1930. In 1937 he was appointed conductor of the Scottish Orch. in Glasgow; he was also a regular conductor with the Residentie Orkest in The Hague (1937–39). He then conducted in Australia. At the outbreak of war in Europe in 1939 he was in America, which was to become his adoptive country. His American conducting engagements included appearances with the Los Angeles Phil., NBC Symph. Orch., Chicago Symph., Detroit Symph., and Boston Symph. In 1942 he was appointed conductor of the Metropolitan Opera House in N.Y., where he received the highest praise for his interpretation of Wagner's music dramas; remained on its roster until 1946. He also conducted performances with the N.Y. Phil. in 1944–45. In 1946 he was appointed conductor of the Cleveland Orch., a post which he held for 24 years; he was also music adviser and senior guest conductor of the N.Y. Phil. from 1969 until his death. He was a stern disciplinarian, demanding the utmost exertions from his musicians to achieve tonal perfection, but he was also willing to labor tirelessly at his task. Under his guidance, the Cleveland Orch. rose to the heights of symphonic excellence, taking its place in the foremost rank of American orchs.

Szeluto, Apolinary, fecund Russian-Polish composer; b. St. Petersburg, July 23, 1884; d. Chodziez, Aug. 22, 1966. He studied with Noskowski at the Warsaw Cons. and with Godowsky in Berlin. In association with Szymanowski, Fitelberg, and Rözycki he formed a progressive musical group, Young Poland. He also studied law at Dorpat (Tartu) Univ.; then went to Ufa, where he worked as a lawyer. He wrote a number of symphs. in piano score; only 10 were orchestrated. His music is ultra-Romantic in its essence; most of his works bear descriptive titles. Several of them are inspired by contemporary political and military events.
WORKS: 28 symphs., of which 18 exist without complete orchestration: No. 1, *Academic* (1920); No. 2, *Spontaneous* (1938); No. 3, *Impressionistic* (1942); No. 4, *Romantic* (1942); No. 5, *Majestic Room* (1942); No. 6, *Birth of Stalingrad* (1943); No. 7, *Revolutionary* (1943); No. 8, *Resurrection* (1942); No. 9, *Elegiac* (1943); No. 10, *Oriental* (1944); No. 11, *Iberian*

(1944); No. 12, *Nordic* (1944); No. 13, *Samurai* (1943–46); No. 14, *Neapolitan* (1943); No. 15, *Los Angeles American* (1944); No. 16, *Fate* (1946); No. 17, *Kujawska Region* (1946); No. 18, *Litewska;* No. 19, *Slaska;* No. 20, *Kupiowska;* No. 21, *Podhalanska;* No. 22, *To the Building of a Communist People's Union;* Nos. 23–28 without titles; 5 piano concertos (1937, 1939, 1940, 1943, 1948); Violin Concerto (1942–48); Cello Concerto (1942); some 32 other orch. works; 9 ballets; 14 chamber music pieces; 18 choral works; an utterly unbelievable number (purportedly 78) of operas; conservatively counting, 205 piano pieces and maybe 165 songs.

Szenkar, Eugen, Hungarian conductor; b. Budapest, April 9, 1891; d. Düsseldorf, March 28, 1977. He studied music with his father, a prominent organist; later attended classes at the Academy of Music in Budapest. He began his career as an assistant choral conductor at the Budapest Opera; then was successively conductor at the German Opera in Prague (1911–13), the Popular Opera in Budapest (1913–15), the Mozarteum at Salzburg (1915–16), Altenburg (1916–20), the Frankfurt Opera (1920–23), the Volksoper in Berlin (1923–24), and the Cologne Opera (1924–33). With the advent of the Nazi regime, as a Jew he was forced to interrupt his activities, and went to Moscow, where he remained from 1933 to 1937. In 1939 he went to Brazil and was conductor of the Brazilian Symph. Orch. in Rio de Janeiro; in 1941, in response to Brazilian social and governmental conventions, he accepted Brazilian citizenship. In 1950 he went back to Germany; from 1952 to 1960 was music director of the Düsseldorf Opera and of the Düsseldorf Symph. Orch.; also filled in guest engagements in Germany.

Szeryng, Henryk, celebrated violinist and pedagogue of Polish birth; b. Zelazowa Wola, Sept. 22, 1918. He was the son of a wealthy Jewish industrialist. He learned to play piano from his mother; then turned to the violin, and had lessons with Maurice Frenkel, a teacher at the St. Petersburg Cons., who inculcated in Szeryng the Russian tradition of violin playing. In 1929 he went to Berlin, where he studied with Carl Flesch; in 1932 he moved to Paris, and studied with Jacques Thibaud and Gabriel Bouillon at the Paris Cons., graduating in 1937; he also took private lessons in composition with Nadia Boulanger. On Jan. 6, 1933, he made his debut in the Brahms Concerto with the Warsaw Phil. At the outbreak of war in 1939 he went to London and served as official translator for the Polish government-in-exile in England. In 1942 he settled in Mexico, becoming a Mexican citizen in 1946. He continued his concert career, traveling around the globe. In 1983 he made a grand tour of Europe and America to mark the 50th anniversary of his career.

Szigeti, Joseph, great Hungarian violinist; b. Budapest, Sept. 5, 1892; d. Lucerne, Feb. 19, 1973. He studied violin with Hubay in Budapest; from 1906 to 1913 he lived in England; from 1917 to 1925 he gave master courses in violin at the Geneva Cons.; subsequently devoted himself mainly to concert appearances. In 1940 he went to the U.S., becoming an American citizen in 1951; eventually returned to Europe. Szigeti was particularly noted as an intellectual violinist; he may have lacked flashy virtuosity, but he was greatly admired by musicians. He was a champion of 20th-century music; played works of Stravinsky, Prokofiev, Béla Bartók, and Ernest Bloch. He publ. several semi-autobiographical books: *With Strings Attached* (N.Y., 1947); *A Violinist's Notebook* (London, 1965); *Szigeti on the Violin: Improvisations on a Violinist's Themes* (N.Y., 1969). He also annotated new editions of Beethoven's Violin Concerto and the Violin Concerto of Brahms.

Szokolay, Sándor, Hungarian composer; b. Kunágota, March 30, 1931. He studied at the Budapest Academy of Music with Szabó and Farkas (1950–57); worked in the music dept. of Hungarian Radio (1957–61); in 1966 was appointed to the faculty of the Budapest Academy of Music. He was awarded the Erkel Prize in 1960 and 1965 and the Kossuth Prize in 1966.

Szulc, Jósef Zygmunt, Polish operetta composer; b. Warsaw, April 4, 1875; d. Paris, April 10, 1956. He studied at the Warsaw Cons. with Noskowski; then took piano lessons in Paris with Moszkowski. He remained in Paris as a piano teacher; then turned to composition of light operas. His first work in this genre, *Flup* (Brussels, Dec. 19, 1913), was surprisingly successful and had numerous performances in Europe; he continued to produce operettas at regular intervals; the last one was *Pantoufle* (Paris, Feb. 24, 1945). He also wrote a ballet, *Une Nuit d'Ispahan* (Brussels, Nov. 19, 1909).

Szumowska, Antoinette, Polish pianist and teacher; b. Lublin, Feb. 22, 1868; d. Rumson, N.J., Aug. 18, 1938. She studied at the Warsaw Cons. with Michalowski, and later took lessons with Paderewski in Paris (1890–95). In 1895 she emigrated to the U.S., settling in Boston, where she taught at the New England Cons. for many years. In 1896 she married the cellist **Josef Adamowski,** and with him and his brother Timothée, a violinist, formed the Adamowski Trio, which presented numerous concerts in New England.

Szymanowska, Maria (née **Wolowska**), Polish pianist and composer; b. Warsaw, Dec. 14, 1789; d. St. Petersburg, July 24, 1831. She studied piano with local teachers in Warsaw, and began to play in public as a child. In 1810 she married a Polish landowner, Theophilus Joseph Szymanowski (divorced, 1820). In 1822 she toured in Russia, and was appointed court pianist; in 1823, played in Germany; in 1824, in France; then in England, the Netherlands, and Italy (1824–25), returning to Warsaw in 1826. In 1828 she settled in St. Petersburg as a pianist and teacher, and remained there until her death (of cholera). She was admired by Goethe, whom she met in Germany; his poem *Aussöhnung (Trilogie der Leiden-*

schaft) alludes to her (cf. Goethe's correspondence with Zelter). She publ. 24 mazurkas and several character pieces for piano, of which *Le Murmure* became popular. Her piano studies were commended by Schumann.

Szymanowski, Karol, eminent Polish composer; b. Timoshovka, Ukraine, Oct. 6, 1882; d. Lausanne, March 28, 1937. The son of a cultured landowner, he grew up in a musical environment. He began to play the piano and compose very early in life. His first teacher was Gustav Neuhaus in Elizavetgrad; in 1901 he went to Warsaw, where he studied with Noskowski. His first work, *9 Preludes* for Piano, op. 1, was publ. in 1906 in Berlin by the Assoc. of Young Polish Composers (later known as Young Poland in Music). Szymanowski lived in Berlin from 1906 to 1908, writing symph. and other music, much influenced by Richard Strauss. He returned to Warsaw in 1909, and his First Symph. was performed there on March 26, 1909; however, he was dissatisfied with the score, and withdrew it from further performance. In 1911 he completed his 2nd Symph., which demonstrated a stylistic change from German dominance to Russian influences, paralleling the harmonic evolution of Scriabin; it was played for the first time in Warsaw, on April 7, 1911. From 1912 to 1914 Szymanowski lived in Vienna, where he wrote his one-act opera, *Hagith;* the years of World War I (1914–18) he spent in Timoshovka, where he wrote his 3rd Symph.; he appeared in concert with the violinist Paul Kochanski in Moscow and St. Petersburg, giving first performances of his violin works; it was for Kochanski that he composed his violin triptych, *Mythes (La Fontaine d'Aréthuse* in this cycle is one of his best-known compositions. About this time, his music underwent a new change in style, veering toward French Impressionism. During the Russian Revolution of 1917 the family estate at Timoshovka was ruined, and Szymanowski lost most of his possessions. From 1917 to 1919 he lived in Elizavetgrad, where he continued to compose industriously, despite the turmoil of the Civil War. Early in 1920 he settled in Warsaw; he traveled to other Polish cities, and soon established his reputation as the most important modern composer of Poland.

His international renown also was considerable; his works were often performed in Europe, and figured at festivals of the International Society for Contemporary Music. He visited Paris, London, and N.Y. (1921). He was director of the Warsaw Cons. (1927–29) and reorganized the system of teaching along more liberal lines; was rector there in 1930–31. His *Stabat Mater* (1926) produced a profound impression, and his ballet *Harnasie* (1923–31), based on the life and music of the Tatra mountain dwellers, demonstrated his ability to treat national subjects in an original and highly effective manner. In 1932 he appeared as soloist in the first perfor-

mance of his 4th Symph., *Symphonie concertante* for Piano and Orch., at Poznan, and repeated his performances in Paris, London, and Brussels. In April 1936, greatly weakened in health by chronic tuberculosis, he attended a performance of his ballet *Harnasie* at the Paris Opéra. Through successive influences, Szymanowski developed into a national composer whose music acquired universal significance. Of particular interest is his treatment of the mazurka; though he was a lifelong admirer of Chopin, he found a way to treat this dance form in an original manner.

WORKS: FOR THE STAGE: Operetta, *Loteria na mężów (Lottery for a Husband;* 1909; unfinished); 2 full operas: *Hagith* (1912–13; Warsaw, May 13, 1922) and *Król Roger (King Roger;* 1918–24; Warsaw, June 19, 1926); a "grotesque ballet," *Mandragora* (Warsaw, June 15, 1920); ballet-pantomime, *Harnasie* (1923–31; Prague, May 11, 1935); incidental music for *Kniaź Patiomkin (Prince Potemkin;* Warsaw, March 6, 1925).

FOR ORCH.: *Concert Overture* (1904–5; Warsaw, Feb. 6, 1906; revised 1913); 4 symphs.: No. 1 (1906–7; Warsaw, March 26, 1909); No. 2 (1909–10; Warsaw, April 7, 1911; revised 1934; further revision was made by Stanislaw Skrowaczewski, who conducted this version with the Minnesota Orch. on Oct. 14, 1967); No. 3, *Pieśń o nocy (Song of the Night),* for Tenor, Chorus, and Orch. (1914–16; London, Nov. 26, 1921, without Tenor or Chorus); No. 4, *Symphonie concertante,* for Piano and Orch. (1932; Poznan, Oct. 9, 1932, composer soloist); 2 violin concertos: No. 1 (1915–16; Warsaw, Nov. 1, 1922) and No. 2 (1932–33; Warsaw, Oct. 6, 1933).

FOR VOICE: *Salome* for Soprano and Orch. (1906); *Penthesilea* for Soprano and Orch. (1908); *8 Love Songs of Hafiz,* cycle 1 for Voice and Piano (1911) and cycle 2 for Voice and Orch. (1914); *Demeter* for Alto, Women's Chorus, and Orch. (1917; revised 1924); *Agave* for Alto, Female Chorus, and Orch. (1917); *Stabat Mater* for 3 Solo Voices, Chorus, and Orch. (1926; Warsaw, Jan. 11, 1929); *Veni Creator* for Soprano, Chorus, and Orch. (1929); *Litany of the Virgin Mary,* 2 fragments to J. Liebert's text, for Soprano, Female Chorus, and Orch. (1930–33); *6 Kurpian Songs* for Mixed Chorus a cappella (1928–29); about 100 songs.

CHAMBER MUSIC: 2 string quartets: No. 1, in 3 movements (1917; a projected fugal final movement never materialized), and No. 2, in 3 movements (1927); Piano Trio (1907; discarded); Violin Sonata (1904); *Romance* for Violin and Piano (1909); *Notturno e tarantella* for Violin and Piano (1914; orchestrated by G. Fitelberg); *Mythes,* 3 poems for Violin and Piano: *La Fontaine d'Aréthuse, Narcisse,* and *Dryades et Pan* (1915); *La Berceuse d'Aitacho Enia* for Violin and Piano (1925).

FOR PIANO: 3 sonatas (1904, 1910, 1917); *9 Preludes* (1900); *Variations in B-flat minor* (1901–3); *4 Etudes* (1900–2); *Variations on a Polish Theme* (1900–4); *Fantasy* (1905); *Prelude and Fugue* (1905); *Métopes,* 3 poems: *L'Ile des sirènes, Calypso,* and *Nausicaa* (1915); *12 Etudes* (1917); *Masques,* 3 poems: *Shéhérazade, Tantris le bouffon,* and *Sérénade de Don Juan* (1917); *Valse romantique* (1925; regarded as lost but discovered in 1967); *4 Polish Dances* (1926); *20 Mazurkas* (1924–26); *2 Mazurkas* (1933–34).

A complete edition of Szymanowski's works, in 26 vols., was begun in Cracow in 1965.

T

Tabachnik, Michel, Swiss conductor and composer of Russian extraction; b. Geneva, Nov. 10, 1942. He studied at the Geneva Cons.; attended the courses in modern music given by Boulez, Pousseur, and Stockhausen at the Darmstadt summer series. In 1973–75 he was principal conductor for the Gulbenkian Foundation in Lisbon; became principal conductor of the Lorraine Phil. Orch. in Nancy in 1975; also conducted guest engagements in Europe. He composed *Mondes* for Orch. (1972); *Movimenti,* electronic score (1973); *Les Imaginaires* for Orch. (1974).

Tabourot, Jehan. See **Arbeau, Thoinot.**

Tabuteau, Marcel, outstanding French oboist and pedagogue; b. Compiègne, July 2, 1887; d. Nice, Jan. 4, 1966. He studied oboe with Georges Gillet at the Paris Cons.; won a premier prix at the age of 17; in 1905 he went to the U.S., where he played in the N.Y. Symph. Orch.; also was a member of the orch. of the Metropolitan Opera. In 1915 Stokowski engaged him in the Philadelphia Orch., where he remained until 1954; he was also on the faculty of the Curtis Inst. of Music in Philadelphia.

Tacchinardi, Nicola, Italian tenor; b. Livorno, Sept. 3, 1772; d. Florence, March 14, 1859. After singing on Italian stages (La Scala, Milan, 1805), he was engaged at the Théâtre des Italiens in Paris (1811–14), with Crivelli; in 1822–31, was "primo cantante" in the Grand Ducal chapel at Florence, also appearing repeatedly on the stage; then lived in Florence as a teacher, one of his pupils being his daughter, **Fanny Tacchinardi-Persiani.** He publ. vocalises and exercises; also *Dell'opera in musica sul teatro italiano e de' suoi difetti.* His son, **Guido Tacchinardi** (b. Florence, March 10, 1840; d. there, Dec. 6, 1917), was a composer and theorist; from 1891 was director of the Istituto Musicale at Florence.

Taddei, Giuseppe, Italian baritone; b. Genoa, June 26, 1916. He received his musical training in Genoa and Rome; made his debut in Rome in 1936; then sang with many of the leading Italian opera houses; became a regular member of La Scala in Milan. In 1951 he appeared with the Metropolitan Opera in N.Y. He was renowned for both his lyrico-dramatic and buffo parts; among his best roles were Figaro in *The Barber of Seville,* Papageno in *Die Zauberflöte,* and Rigoletto.

Tagliaferro, Magda, Brazilian pianist; b. Petropolis, Jan. 19, 1893. She studied at the Paris Cons., and privately with Cortot. She began her concert career in 1908, and continued her appearances for 70 years, without showing signs of lassitude; she made numerous appearances in solo recitals in the U.S., the last one in 1980 at the age of 87. From 1937 she was on the faculty of the Paris Cons.

Tagliapietra, Gino, Italian pianist and composer; b. (of Italian parentage) Ljubljana, May 30, 1887; d. Venice, Aug. 8, 1954. He studied piano with Julius Epstein in Vienna and with Busoni in Berlin; in 1906 was appointed to the faculty of the Liceo Benedetto Marcello in Venice; retired in 1940. His compositions include a ballet, *La Bella dormente nel bosco* (Venice, March 11, 1926); Piano Concerto; numerous studies for piano. He edited for Ricordi an important anthology of keyboard music from Willaert to modern times, *Antologia di musica antica e moderna* (18 vols., 1931–32; containing 519 works by 157 composers).

Tagliapietra, Giovanni, Italian baritone; b. Venice, Dec. 24, 1846; d. New York, April 11, 1921. He studied naval architecture and graduated from the Univ. of Padua. After a study of singing with Giovanni Corsi, he appeared in various Italian opera houses; made a tour of South America; in 1874 was engaged as member of Max Strakosch's company and sang in the U.S. In 1876 he married the famous pianist **Teresa Carreño,** but they were divorced; his brother Arturo was married to her in 1902.

Tagliavini, Ferruccio, prominent Italian tenor; b. Reggio Emilia, Aug. 14, 1913. After studying at the Cons. of Parma, he won first prize for singing at the May Festival in Florence (1938); made his opera debut there as Rodolfo in *La Bohème* (Oct. 1938); later sang at La Scala, Milan, and other opera houses in Italy; in 1946 toured South America; on Jan. 10, 1947, made a very successful first appearance, as Rodolfo, at the Metropolitan Opera, N.Y.; remained on its roster until 1954; again in 1961–62; has also given recitals in the major American cities; subsequently traveled widely in both hemispheres. In 1941 he married the soprano **Pia Tassinari.**

Tagore, Sir Surindro Mohun (Rajah Saurindramohana Thakura), Hindu musicologist; b. Calcutta, 1840; d. there, June 5, 1914. At the age of 17 he began to study Hindu music under Luchmi Prasad and Kshetra Mohun Gosvami, and European music under a German teacher in Calcutta; he founded and endowed from his personal fortune the Bengal Music School (1871) and the Bengal Academy of Music (1882), continuing to preside over both until his death. A connoisseur of Eastern instrumentation, he was at various times commissioned by the principal museums of Europe to procure for them instruments of Asiatic nations; perhaps the finest collection is that in the Metropolitan Museum of Art in N.Y. He wrote nearly 60 books on an amazing variety of subjects; those concerning music (publ. in Calcutta, in Bengali, and some in Eng.) include: *Yantra Kosha, or A Treasury of the Musical Instru-*

ments of Ancient and Modern India (1875); *Hindu Music, from Various Authors* (1875; 2nd ed., in 2 vols., 1882); *Short Notices of Hindu Musical Instruments* (1877); *6 Principal Ragas* (1876; 3rd ed., 1884); *The 8 Principal Ragas of the Hindus* (1880); *The Five Principal Musicians of the Hindus, or A Brief Exposition of the Essential Elements of Hindu Music* (1881); *The Musical Scales of the Hindus with Remarks on the Applicability of Harmony to Hindu Music* (1884); *The 22 Musical Srutis of the Hindus* (1886); *Universal History of Music* (1896).

Tailleferre, Germaine (original name, **Taillefesse,** altered to dispel the unwanted anatomical association in the second syllable), fine French composer; b. Parc-St.-Maur, near Paris, April 19, 1892; d. Paris, Nov. 7, 1983. She studied at the Paris Cons., and also had some informal lessons with Ravel. She received recognition as the only feminine member of the group of French composers known as Les Six (the other members were Honegger, Milhaud, Poulenc, Auric, and Durey). Her style of composition was pleasingly, teasingly modernistic and feministic (Jean Cocteau invoked a comparision with a young French woman painter, Marie Laurencin, saying that Tailleferre's music was to the ear what the painter's pastels were to the eye). Indeed, most of her works possess a fragile charm of unaffected *joie de jouer la musique.* She was married to an American author, Ralph Barton, in 1926, but soon divorced him and married a French lawyer, Jean Lageat. She visited the U.S. in 1927 and again in 1942. In 1974 she publ. an autobiographical book, *Mémoires à l'emporte pièce.*
    WORKS: *Image* for Piano, Flute, Clarinet, String Quartet, and Celesta (1918); *Jeux de plein air* for 2 Pianos (1918); String Quartet (1918); Piano Concerto (1919); 2 violin sonatas (1921, 1951); *Pastorale* for Violin and Piano (1921); ballet, *Le Marchand d'oiseaux* (Paris, May 25, 1923); Concertino for Harp and Orch. (1926; Boston Symph. Orch., Cambridge, Mass., March 3, 1927); *Chansons françaises* for Voice and Instruments (Liège Festival of the International Society for Contemporary Music, Sept. 2, 1930); Overture for Orch. (Paris, Dec. 25, 1932); Concerto for 2 Pianos, Voice, and Orch. (Paris, May 3, 1934); *Cantate du Narcisse* for Voice and Orch. (1937); *Pastorale* for Flute and Piano (1939); ballet, *Paris-Magie* (Paris, June 3, 1949); *Dolores,* operetta (Paris, 1950); lyric satire, *Il était un petit navire* (Paris, March 1951); musical comedy, *Parfums* (Monte Carlo, 1951); *La Guirlande de Campra* for Orch. (1952); comic opera, *Parisiana* (Copenhagen, 1955); *Concerto des vaines paroles* for Baritone and Orch. (1956); opera, *La Petite Sirène* (1958); opera-buffa, *Mémoires d'une bergère* (1959); chamber opera, *Le Maître* (1959).

Tajo, Italo, Italian bass; b. Pinerolo, April 25, 1915. He studied voice in Turin; made his debut there in 1935; then sang at the Rome Opera and at La Scala in Milan. He made his U.S. debut in Chicago in 1946. On Dec. 28, 1948, he appeared at the Metropolitan Opera in N.Y. as Don Basilio in *The Barber of Se-*

ville; remained on its roster until 1950. In 1966 he was appointed prof. at the Univ. of Cincinnati College-Cons. of Music as "basso-in-residence." In 1980, after an absence of 30 years, he returned to the Metropolitan Opera for a couple of seasons. He was equally adept in dramatic roles and buffo bass parts, and he also proved himself an intelligent interpreter of difficult parts in modern operas by Milhaud, Malipiero, Pizzetti, and even Luigo Nono.

Takács, Jenö, Hungarian composer; b. Siegendorf, Sept. 25, 1902. He studied composition with Joseph Marx and Hans Gál at the Vienna Cons.; in 1927 he was engaged as a teacher at the Cons. of Cairo, Egypt; then traveled to Manila, in the Philippine Islands, returning to Cairo in 1934. During his travels, he collected much material on oriental music; his research in this field is reflected in some of his own works. From 1940 to 1942 he taught at the Music School at Szombathely, Hungary; then was director of the Cons. of Pécs in Hungary (1942–48) and later visiting prof. at the conservatories of Lausanne and Geneva (1949); in 1952 he was engaged as a prof. of piano at the Cincinnati Cons.; he retired in 1971 and went back to his birthplace, Siegendorf. In 1962 he was awarded the State Prize of Austria. Reflecting his background of travel and residence in many different countries, his music contains elements of Hungarian, oriental, American, and cosmopolitan idioms.

Takahashi, Yuji, Japanese composer and pianist; b. Tokyo, Sept. 21, 1938. He studied composition with Shibata and Ogura at the Toho School of Music in Tokyo (1954–58); then went to Berlin and was trained in electronics as a student of Xenakis; also studied computer music in N.Y. (1966–68) and was a member of the Center for Creative and Performing Arts at the State Univ. of N.Y. in Buffalo (1968–69). In his own music he follows the stochastic procedures as practiced by Xenakis. He also has acquired considerable renown as a pianist in programs of avant-garde music.

Takeda, Yoshimi, Japanese conductor; b. Yokohama, Feb. 3, 1933. He was educated at the Tokyo Univ. of the Arts; then went to the U.S. on a fellowship to work with George Szell and the Cleveland Orch. In 1964 he became associate conductor of the Honolulu Symph.; in 1970 was appointed music director of the Albuquerque Symph. Orch., now called the New Mexico Symph.; in addition, he was named music director of the Kalamazoo Symph. in 1974. He had guest engagements off and on in Detroit, Phoenix, San Diego, and Chicago.

Takemitsu, Toru, prominent Japanese composer; b. Tokyo, Oct. 8, 1930. He studied composition privately with Yasuji Kiyose. In 1951, jointly with Yuasa and others, he organized in Tokyo an "Experimental Laboratory," with the aim of creating new music that would combine traditional Japanese modalities with modernistic procedures. In 1970 he de-

signed the "Space Theater" for Expo '70 in Osaka, Japan. In 1975 he visited the U.S. and gave a seminar in composition at Yale Univ. His music belies Kipling's famous asseveration that East is East and West is West, and never the twain shall meet, for Takemitsu performed through music just this kind of interpenetration; in an oriental way, it is often formed from short motifs played out as floating dramas, subtle and exotic, through which Takemitsu seeks "to achieve a sound as intense as silence"; and on the Western side, he employs every conceivable technique developed by the European and American modernists.

WORKS: FOR ORCH.: *Requiem* for String Orch. (1957; Tokyo, June 20, 1958); *Solitude sonore* (1958); *Ki No Kyoku (Music of Trees;* 1961); *Arc,* Part I (1963, in 3 movements) and Part II (1964–66, in 3 movements) for Piano and Orch.; *Arc* for Strings (1963; from the 3rd movement of *Arc,* Part I); *Textures* for Piano and Orch. (1964; first movement of *Arc,* Part II); *The Dorain Horizon* for 17 Strings in 2 groups (1966; San Francisco, Feb. 1967, Aaron Copland conducting); *November Steps* for Biwa, Shakuhachi, and Orch. (N.Y. Phil., Nov. 9, 1967); *Green (November Steps II;* Tokyo, Nov. 3, 1967); *Asterism* for Piano and Orch. (1968; Toronto, Jan. 14, 1969); *Eucalypts I* for Flute, Oboe, Harp, and Strings (Tokyo, Nov. 16, 1970); *Winter* (Paris, Oct. 29, 1971); *Corona* for 22 Strings (1971); *Cassiopeia* for Solo Percussion and Orch. (1970–71; Chicago Symph., Ravinia Festival, Highland Park, Ill., July 8, 1971); *Gemeaux* for Oboe, Trombone, and 2 Orchs. with separate conductors (1971–72); *Autumn* for Biwa, Shakuhachi, and Orch. (1973); *Gitimalya (Bouquet of Songs)* for Marimba and Orch. (Rotterdam, Nov. 1975); *Quatrain* for Violin, Cello, Clarinet, Piano, and Orch. (Tokyo, Sept. 1, 1975); *Marginalia* (Tokyo, Oct. 20, 1976); *A Flock Descends into the Pentagonal Garden* (San Francisco, Nov. 30, 1977); *In an Autumn Garden* for Gagaku Orch. (1979); *Far Calls. Coming Far!* for Violin and Orch. (Tokyo, May 24, 1980); *Dreamtime* (1981; ballet version, The Hague, May 5, 1983); *Toward the Sea II* for Alto Flute, Harp, and String Orch. (1981); *Star-Isle* (1982); *Rain Coming* for Chamber Orch. (1982); *To the Edge of Dream* for Guitar and Orch. (1982–83; Liège, March 12, 1983). FOR VOICE: *Tableau noir* for Narrator and Orch. (1958); *Coral Island* for Soprano and Orch. (1962); *Wind Horse* for a cappella Female Chorus (1962); *Crossing* for 12 Female Voices, Guitar, Harp, Piano, Vibraphone, and 2 Orchs. (1969); *Grass* for a cappella Male Chorus (1982). CHAMBER MUSIC: *Son calligraphie I–III* for Double String Quartet (1958, 1958, 1963); *Mask* for 2 Flutes (1959); *Landscape* for String Quartet (1960); *Ring* for Flute, Terz-guitar, and Lute (1961); *Sacrifice* for Flute, Lute, and Vibraphone (1962); *Valeria* for Violin, Cello, Guitar, Electric Organ, and 2 Piccolos obbligato (1962); *Hika* for Violin and Piano (1966); *Cross Talk* for 2 Bandoneons and Tape (1968); *Stanza I* for Piano, Guitar, Harp, Vibraphone, and Female Voice (1968); *Stanza II* for Solo Harp (1971); *Stanza III* for Solo Oboe, or Oboe and Shō (1971); *Eucalypts II* for Flute, Oboe, and Harp (1970); *Seasons* in versions for One or 4 Percussionists (1970); *Voice* for Solo Flute (1971);

Munari by Munari for Percussion (1972); *Distance* for Solo Oboe, or Oboe and Shō (1972); *Voyage* for 3 Biwas (1973); *Folios* for Guitar (1973); *Garden Rain* for 4 Trumpets, 3 Trombones, Bass Trombone, Horn, and Tuba, separated into 2 groups (1974); *Waves* for Solo Clarinet, Horn, 2 Trumpets, and Percussion (1976); *Bryce* for Flute, 2 Harps, Marimba, and Percussion (1976); *Quatrain II* for Clarinet, Violin, Cello, and Piano (1976); *Waterways* for Piano, Clarinet, Violin, Cello, 2 Harps, and 2 Vibraphones (1978); String Quartet No. 1, subtitled *A Way a lone* (1981). FOR PIANO: *2 Lentos* (1950); *Undisturbed Rest* (1952–59); *Piano Distance* (1961); *Corona* for Pianist(s) (1962); *For Away* (1973); *Les Yeux clos* (1979); *Rain Tree Sketch* (1981). FOR TAPE ALONE: *Sky, Horse and Death* (1954); *Static Relief* (1955); *Vocalism A-1* (1956); *Water Music* (1960); *Quiet Design* (1960); *Kwaidan* (1966; revision of music from the film); *Toward* (1970); also music for a number of films including *Hara-Kiri* (1962); *Woman in the Dunes* (1964); *Kwaidan* (1964); *Empire of Passion* (1978).

Tal (real name, **Gruenthal**), **Josef (Joseph),** Polish-born Israeli composer and pianist; b. Pinne, near Poznan, Sept. 18, 1910. He studied composition with Tiessen and piano with Trapp at the Staatlich Akademische Hochschule für Musik in Berlin (1928–30); emigrated to Palestine in 1934 and taught composition and piano at the Jerusalem Academy of Music; served as its director in 1948–52. He was later on the music faculty of the Hebrew Univ. in Jerusalem, and headed its musicology dept. (1965–71). In 1957 he received a munificent UNESCO grant to study electronic music; in 1961 he was appointed director of the Israel Center for Electronic Music; in 1971 was named a Fellow of the West Berlin Academy of the Arts. A true musical intellectual, he applies in his music a variety of techniques, being free of doctrinal introversion and open to novel potentialities without fear of public revulsion. Patriotic Hebrew themes often appear in his productions.
WORKS: *Saul at Ein Dor,* opera concertante (1957); *Amnon and Tamar,* short opera (1961); *Ashmedai,* opera in 2 acts, with Electronic Sound (1968–70; Hamburg, Nov. 9, 1971; an electronic overture from the opera represents an independent concert number); *Masada 967,* opera in 15 scenes (1971–72; Jerusalem, June 17, 1973); *Die Versuchung (The Temptation),* opera in 2 acts (1973–75; Munich Festival, July 26, 1976); *The Death of Moses,* requiem-oratorio for Soloists, Chorus, and Tape (1967); *The Mother Rejoices,* symph. cantata for Chorus, Piano, and Orch. (1949); *Succoth Cantata* (1955); *Misdar Hanoflim (Parade of the Fallen),* cantata (1968); 3 electronic scores for ballet: *Ranges of Energy* (1963); *From the Depth of the Soul* (1964); *Variations* (1970); *Exodus,* choreographic poem for Baritone and Orch. (1946; Tel Aviv, Dec. 14, 1947); 6 piano concertos: No. 1, with Orch. (1944); No. 2, with Orch. (1953); No. 3, with Solo Tenor and Chamber Orch. (1956); Nos. 4–6 solely for Piano and Electronics (1962, 1964, 1970); *Reflections* for String Orch. (1950); Viola Concerto (1954; Mount Carmel Festival of the International Society for Contemporary Music, June 3, 1954); *Festive Vision* for Orch. (1959); Concerto for Cello and String Orch. (1961); *Double Concerto* for Violin, Cello, and Chamber Orch. (1970); *The Wooden Horse* for Soloists, Chorus, and Electronics (1973); Concerto for Harpsichord and Electronics (1964); Concerto for Harp and Electronics (1971); *Lament* for Cello and Harp (1950); Violin Sonata (1952); Oboe Sonata (1952); 2 string quartets (1959, 1964); *Intrada* for Harp (1959); Viola Sonata (1960); *Structure* for Harp (1962); *Duo* for Viola and Piano (1965); Wind Quintet (1966); *Songs on Texts by Heine* for Baritone or Alto, Flute, Horn, Piano, and Tam-tams (1971); *Treatise* for Solo Cello (1973); Piano Trio (1973); Piano Sonata No. 1 (1950); *Inventions* for Piano (1956); *Dodecaphonic Episodes* for Piano (1962); electronic pieces: *Min Hameitzar Karati Yah (I Called Upon the Lord in Distress;* 1971); *Frequencies 440–462 (Homage to Blacher;* 1972); *Overture for Opera* (1973); *3 Songs* for Chorus a cappella (1953).

Talich, Václav, eminent Czech conductor; b. Kroměříž, May 28, 1883; d. Beroun, March 16, 1961. He received his early musical training from his father, Jan Talich; then studied violin with Ševčik at the Prague Cons. (1897–1903). He was concertmaster of the Odessa Orch. in Russia, and then taught violin in Tiflis. He returned to Prague in 1907; conducted the Phil. Orch. of Ljubljana; in 1910 went to Leipzig, where he took lessons in composition with Max Reger and Hans Sitt and in conducting with Arthur Nikisch. He was then opera conductor at Pilsen (1912–15) and chief conductor of the Czech Phil. (1919–31); in 1931–33 was conductor of the Konsertforeningen in Stockholm; then in 1933 returned as chief conductor of the Czech Phil. (until 1941), which he brought to a high degree of excellence; toured with it in Italy, Germany, France, and England. Subsequently he was conductor as well as administrator of the National Opera in Prague (1935–44); from 1947 to 1948 was its artistic leader; then moved to Bratislava, where he conducted the Slovak Phil. Orch. (1949–52); returned as guest conductor of the Czech Phil. (1952–54); retired from concert appearances in 1954. He also taught conducting in Prague and Bratislava; among his pupils were Ančerl and I. Krejčí.

Talley, Marion, American soprano; b. Nevada, Mo., Dec. 20, 1906; d. Los Angeles, Jan. 3, 1983. She sang in churches in Kansas City, and at the age of 16 appeared in a performance of *Mignon* there, producing such an explosion of local pride that the community raised funds to send her to N.Y. to study voice with Frank La Forge; later she went to Italy in quest of further musical enlightenment. She was then given a chance to appear at the Metropolitan Opera in N.Y. on Feb. 17, 1926, as Gilda in *Rigoletto.* She was only 19 years old at the time, and she became an instant *rara avis,* a genuine American warbler, an authentic, native thrush, and newspapers went wild over her. She sang the part of the nightingale in Stravinsky's opera *Le Rossignol* at the Metropolitan on March 6, 1926, and performed the role of the Queen of the Night in *The Magic Flute* there on Nov. 6, 1926. In 1928 she made a U.S. tour as a concert singer; in 1933 she sang Gilda at the Chicago Opera, with meager success; she was no longer a young American nightingale. From then on she made little music before sinking into impenetrable oblivion in darkest Hollywood; even her death went unrecorded in the daily journals.

Tallis (or **Tallys, Talys**), **Thomas,** English organist and composer; b. c.1505; d. Greenwich, Nov. 23, 1585. He was "joculator organorum" at the Dover Priory (1532), at St. Mary-at-Hill in London (1537), and at the Augustine Abbey Holy Cross in Waltham, Essex (1538–1540); from about 1543 served as Gentleman of the Chapel Royal during the reigns of Henry VIII, Edward VI, Mary, and Elizabeth, and as joint organist with Byrd. With Byrd, he obtained in 1575 letters patent for the exclusive privilege of printing music and ruled music paper, the first work issued by them being 34 *Cantiones quae ab argumento sacrae vocantur, 5 et 6 partium,* in 1575 (16 motets by Tallis and 18 by Byrd). Tallis's most famous work is *Spem in alium non habui,* a "song of 40 parts" for 8 5-part choirs (specimen page in first ed. of *Grove's Dictionary,* vol. III, p. 274). A composer of great contrapuntal skill, he was among the first to set Eng. words to music for the rites of the Church of England. Surviving are 3 masses, 2 Magnificats, 2 Lamentations, 52 motets and other pieces with Latin text, over 20 Eng. anthems, 3 sets of Psalms, etc., as well as some keyboard music. In Barnard's *First Book of Selected Church Music* (1641) is a First Service, or Short Service (*a* 4), Preces, Responses, etc., often republ. (by Rimbault, Novello, Jebb, Davison & Apel, etc.); J. Day's *Morning and Evening Prayer* (1560), Boyce's *Cathedral Music,* and the histories by Hawkins and Burney contain specimens of his music. Rimbault republ. the *Order of Daily Service, with the Musical Notation,* R. Terry edited a Mass *a* 4 in 1908 (Breitkopf & Härtel), and most of Tallis's church music is in vol. VI of *Tudor Church Music* (1928). There are many works in MS at Oxford, Cambridge, and in the British Library. Additional modern editions include D. Stevens, ed., *T. Tallis: Complete Keyboard Works* (London, 1953); L. Ellinwood, ed., *T. Tallis: English Sacred Music,* I, *Anthems;* II, *Service Music,* in *Early English Church Music,* XII and XIII (revised by P. Doe, 1974).

Talma, Louise, American composer; b. Arcachon, France, Oct. 31, 1906. She studied at N.Y. Univ. (B.M., 1931) and at Columbia Univ. (M.A., 1933); took piano lessons with Isidor Philipp and composition with Nadia Boulanger at the Fontainebleau School of Music in France. In 1946 she received a Guggenheim fellowship; received a 2nd Guggenheim in 1947; joined the faculty at Hunter College in N.Y. She became the first woman composer to be elected to the National Inst. of Arts and Letters, in 1974. In her music she adopts a strongly impressionistic style.

WORKS: *Toccata* for Orch. (1944); *Introduction and Rondo Giocoso* (1946); *3 Madrigals* for Women's Voices and String Quartet (1929); *La Belle Dame sans merci* for Baritone Solo (1929); *Terre de France,* song cycle (1925); *5 Sonnets from the Portuguese,* song cycle (1934); Piano Sonata (1943); *The Divine Flame,* oratorio (1948); *Let's Touch the Sky,* cycle of poems, after e.e. cummings, for Chorus and Woodwind Instruments (1952); *The Alcestiad,* opera (Frankfurt, Germany, March 1, 1962); *All the Days of My Life* for Tenor, Clarinet, Cello, Piano, and Percussion (1965); *Voices of Peace* for Chorus and Strings (1973); *Summer Sounds* for Clarinet and String Quartet (1973); *Textures* for Piano (1978); other piano pieces.

Talvela, Martti, remarkable Finnish bass; b. Hiitola, Karelia, Feb. 4, 1935, of a family of musically gifted children (he was No. 8 of the total of 10 offspring). He studied voice with Martin Oehman; made his operatic debut as the Commendatore in *Don Giovanni* at the Royal Stockholm Opera in 1961; subsequently sang at the Berlin Deutsche Oper and the Bayreuth Festival. He made his American debut in Verdi's Requiem in Cleveland in 1968; then appeared at the Metropolitan Opera in N.Y. on Oct. 7, 1968, in the role of the Grand Inquisitor in Verdi's *Don Carlos.* On Dec. 16, 1974, he appeared at the Metropolitan in his greatest role, that of Boris Godunov in the original version of Mussorgsky's opera; he also sang Boris Godunov in Russian during his appearances in the U.S.S.R. On May 13, 1977, he sang Sarastro in a new production at the Paris Opéra of *Die Zauberflöte.* Other important roles in his repertoire were Gurnemanz in *Parsifal,* King Henry in *Lohengrin,* and Hagen in *Götterdämmerung.* Despite his international tours, Talvela kept close to musical life in his native land; in 1972 he assumed the post of artistic director of the summer Savonlinna Opera Festival in Finland. He also sang the chief role in the Helsinki production of the Finnish opera *Viimeiset Kiusaukset* by Kokkonen, on Sept. 2, 1975. A man of enormous hulk, rising erect to 6 feet 7 inches, and weighing up to 300 pounds, Talvela can command bass parts in opera with an almost awesome effect; a true Finn, he continues to engage in such manly pursuits as hunting, boating, and logging in the woods and lakes of central Finland. In 1973 Talvela received the Pro Finlandia Prize from the Finnish government.

Tamagno, Francesco, famous Italian tenor; b. Turin, Dec. 28, 1850; d. Varese, near Turin, Aug. 31, 1905. He was at first apprenticed to a baker, and later to a locksmith; entered the Turin Cons. as a pupil of Pedrotti, and in 1873 made his debut as 2nd tenor at the Teatro Regio there, his powerful voice immediately attracting attention. Following his appearance in *Un ballo in maschera* at Palermo on Jan. 17, 1874, his success was rapid. In 1876–77 he sang at the Liceo of Barcelona, and from 1877 at La Scala, Milan, where in 1887 he created the role of Otello in Verdi's opera. He sang at the Metropolitan Opera, N.Y., during the 1894–95 season (debut, Nov. 21, 1894, as Arnold in Rossini's *Guillaume Tell*).

Other engagements included performances in South America, Lisbon, Madrid, Paris, and London. In 1902, having made a fortune, he retired from the stage.

Tamberlik, Enrico, celebrated Italian tenor; b. Rome, March 16, 1820; d. Paris, March 13, 1889. He studied singing with Zirilli in Rome and with Guglielmi in Naples, where he made his stage debut in 1841, as Tybalt in *I Capuleti e i Montecchi.* On April 4, 1850, he made his first London appearance, as Masaniello in Auber's *La Muette de Portici,* at the Royal Italian Opera, Covent Garden, and sang annually in London until 1864, with the exception of 1857, when he undertook an extensive European tour, including Spain and Russia. In 1860 he settled in Paris, and lived there most of his life. Verdi admired him, and wrote the part of Don Alvaro in *La forza del destino* for him; Tamberlik sang in its world premiere at St. Petersburg, Russia, on Oct. 30, 1862, and this role became one of his most famous interpretations. He appeared at the Academy of Music in N.Y., on Sept. 18, 1873, but his American season was a brief one. He was famous for his rich high notes, and his ability to sustain the high C was legendary.

Tamburini, Antonio, Italian baritone; b. Faenza, March 28, 1800; d. Nice, Nov. 8, 1876. He first learned to play the horn as a pupil of his father; then studied singing with A. Rossi and B. Asioli; made his debut at Cento in 1818; thereafter sang on the chief stages of Italy, being engaged by Barbaja from 1824 to 1832. During 1832–41 he sang at the Théâtre Italien in Paris, as part of a brilliant company that included Grisi, Persiani, Viardot, Rubini, and Lablache, appearing in London in alternate seasons; after a short stay in Italy, he remained for 10 years in Russia. In 1855 he retired to his estate at Sèvres, near Paris. His greatest triumph was in Bellini's *La Straniera,* in which he created a frenzy of enthusiasm by his singing of the aria *Meco tu vieni, o misera.* In 1822 he married the singer **Marietta Goja.**

Tamkin, David, American composer; b. Chernigov, Russia, Aug. 28, 1906; d. Los Angeles, June 21, 1975. He was taken to the U.S. as an infant; the family settled in Portland, Oreg., where he studied violin with Henry Bettman, a pupil of Ysaÿe; he took lessons in composition with Ernest Bloch. In 1937 he settled in Los Angeles; from 1945 to 1966 he was principal composer at Universal Pictures in Hollywood. His music is deeply permeated with the melodic and rhythmic elements of the Hassidic Jewish cantillation. His magnum opus is the opera *The Dybbuk,* to a libretto by his brother Alex Tamkin, from S. Ansky's Jewish classic of that title; he composed the work in 1928–31 but it was not produced until Oct. 4, 1951, by the N.Y. City Opera. In 1962 he wrote another opera, *The Blue Plum Tree of Esau* (also to his brother's libretto); among his other works are 2 string quartets, a Woodwind Sextet, and several choruses.

Taneyev, Alexander, Russian composer; b. St. Petersburg, Jan. 17, 1850; d. there, Feb. 7, 1918; a distant relative of **Sergei Taneyev.** He studied composition with F. Reichel in Dresden; upon his return to St. Petersburg, he took lessons with Rimsky-Korsakov. Music was his avocation; he followed a government career, advancing to the post of head of the Imperial Chancellery. The style of his music is Romantic, lapsing into sentimentalism; the main influence is that of Tchaikovsky.

WORKS: Operas: *Cupid's Revenge* (concert perf., St. Petersburg, May 19, 1899) and *Buran (The Snow Storm); Festival March* for Orch.; 3 symphs. (1890; 1903; 1908); 2 orch. mazurkas; *Hamlet Overture;* 2 suites for Orch.; *Ballade,* after a poem *(Alyosha Popovich)* by Alexei Tolstoy, for Orch.; 3 string quartets; *Arabesque* for Clarinet and Piano; piano pieces; songs.

Taneyev, Sergei, greatly significant Russian composer and pedagogue; b. Vladimir district, Nov. 25, 1856; d. Dyudkovo, Zvenigorodsk district, June 19, 1915. He began taking piano lessons at the age of 10 at the Moscow Cons.; after attending academic school for a year, he re-entered the Cons. and studied piano with Nicolai Rubinstein and composition with Tchaikovsky, forming a lifelong friendship with the latter. He made a very successful debut in Moscow as a pianist, playing the D-minor Concerto of Brahms (Jan. 31, 1875); after a tour of Russia with Leopold Auer, he visited Turkey, Greece, and Italy; spent the winter of 1877–78 in Paris; in the autumn of 1878 he succeeded Tchaikovsky as prof. of harmony and orchestration at the Moscow Cons.; after the death of Nicolai Rubinstein in 1881, he took over the latter's piano classes there; from 1885 to 1889 he was director; from 1889 to 1906 he taught composition. Taneyev was a first-class pianist; Tchaikovsky regarded him as one of the finest interpreters of his music; but Taneyev was not interested in a virtuoso career, and gradually confined himself to composition and pedagogy. His position as a composer is anomalous: he is one of the most respected figures of Russian music history, and there is a growing literature about him; his correspondence and all documents, however trivial, concerning his life are treasured as part of the Russian cultural heritage; yet outside Russia his works are rarely heard. He wrote a treatise on counterpoint, *Podvizhnoi kontrapunkt strogavo pisma* (1909; in Eng. as *Convertible Counterpoint in the Strict Style;* Boston, 1962). The style of his compositions presents a compromise between Russian melos and Germanic contrapuntal writing; the mastery revealed in his symphs. and quartets is unquestionable. His most ambitious work was the trilogy *Oresteia,* after Aeschylus, in 3 divisions: *Agamemnon, Choëphorai,* and *Eumenides,* first performed in St. Petersburg on Oct. 29, 1895. Other works are *John of Damascus,* cantata, after Alexei Tolstoy (1884); *At the Reading of the Psalm,* cantata (1914); 4 symphs., including Symph. in C minor (1896–97; first perf. under the direction of Glazunov, St. Petersburg, April 2, 1898); 3 string quintets; 9 string quartets; Piano Quartet; 2

string trios; Piano Trio; about 50 songs, most of them of a very high quality. After his death an almost completed *Treatise on Canon and Fugue* was found among his papers and publ. in 1929.

Tango, Egisto, Italian conductor; b. Rome, Nov. 13, 1873; d. Copenhagen, Oct. 5, 1951. He first studied engineering; then entered the Naples Cons.; made his debut as an opera conductor in Venice (1893); conducted at La Scala in Milan (1895); then at Berlin (1903–8). He conducted at the Metropolitan Opera in N.Y., in 1909–10; in Italy (1911–12); and in Budapest (1913–19), where he gave the earliest performances of stage works by Béla Bartók. From 1920 to 1926 he was active in Germany and Austria. In 1927 he settled in Copenhagen. He was distinguished for the technical precision and interpretative clarity of his performances.

Tannenberg, David, German-American organ builder; b. Berthelsdorf, Upper Lusatia, March 21, 1728; d. York, Pa., May 19, 1804. Tannenberg came to America in 1749 and became a member of the Moravian Church settlement at Bethlehem, Pa. Following the death of his teacher and colleague Johann Gottlob Clemm (1762), he established himself in Lititz, Pa. (1765); made 32 organs for churches in Pennsylvania, N.Y., Maryland, Virginia, and North Carolina; he also made a few pianos.

Tannhäuser, lyric poet and minnesinger; b. c.1200, probably in Oberpfalz; d. after 1266. He led a wandering life typical of his calling; for a time was at the court of Friedrich II, Duke of Austria; then with Otto II of Bavaria. His name became legendary through the tale of the Venusberg, pagan intimacy with Venus, penitence, pilgrimage to Rome, and the miracle of the flowering of his pilgrim's staff. Wagner's *Tannhäuser* is based on this legend, which is unconnected with the life of the real Tannhäuser. A complete edition of his works has been edited by H. Lomnitzer and U. Müller, *Tannhäuser* (Göppingen, 1973).

Tansman, Alexandre, Polish composer; b. Lodz, June 12, 1897. He studied with Piotr Rytel in Warsaw, and piano with Lütschg. After a brief service in the Polish army, he went to Paris, which became his permanent home. He first appeared in public, playing his piano works, in Paris on Feb. 17, 1920; performances of his symph. and chamber music followed in rapid succession; his *Danse de la sorcière* for Chamber Orch. was presented at the Zürich Festival of the International Society for Contemporary Music (June 22, 1926). He made an extensive tour of the U.S. in 1927–28 as pianist in his own works. In 1933 he toured the Far East. After the occupation of Paris by the Germans in 1940, he made his way to the U.S.; lived in Hollywood, where he wrote music for films; returned to Paris in 1946. His music is distinguished by a considerable melodic gift and a vivacious rhythm; his harmony is often bitonal; there are some impressionistic traits that reflect his Parisian tastes.

WORKS: OPERAS: *La Nuit kurde* (1925–27; Paris Radio, 1927); *Le Serment* (Brussels, March 11, 1955); *Sabbatai Lévi, le faux Messie,* lyric fresco (Paris, 1961); *Le Rossignol de Boboli* (Nice, 1965); ballets: *Sextuor* (Paris, May 17, 1924; also in Chicago, as *The Tragedy of the Cello,* Dec. 26, 1926); *La Grande Ville* (1932); *Bric-à-Brac* (1937); *Train de nuit* for 2 Pianos (London, 1950); *Les Habits neufs du roi,* after H.C. Andersen (Venice, 1959); *Resurrection,* after Tolstoy (Nice, 1962). FOR ORCH.: 7 symphs.: No. 1 (1925; Boston, March 18, 1927); No. 2 (1926); No. 3, *Symphonie concertante* (1931); No. 4 (1939); No. 5 (1942; Baltimore, Feb. 2, 1943); No. 6, *In memoriam* (1943); No. 7 (1944; St. Louis, Oct. 24, 1947); *Danse de la sorcière* (Brussels, May 5, 1924); *Sinfonietta* (Paris, March 23, 1925); *Ouverture symphonique* (Paris, Feb. 3, 1927); Piano Concerto No. 1 (Paris, May 27, 1926, composer soloist); Piano Concerto No. 2 (Boston, Dec. 28, 1927, composer soloist); *Suite* for 2 Pianos and Orch. (Paris, Nov. 16, 1930); Viola Concerto (1936); *Fantaisie* for Violin and Orch. (1937); *Fantaisie* for Cello and Orch. (1937); *Rapsodie polonaise* (St. Louis, Nov. 14, 1941); *Etudes symphoniques* (1943); Concertino for Guitar and Orch. (1945); *Ricercari* (St. Louis, Dec. 22, 1949); *Capriccio* (Louisville, March 6, 1955).

Tans'ur (real name, **Tanzer**), **William,** English organist, composer, and lexicographer; b. Dunchurch, 1700 (baptized, Nov. 6, 1706); d. St. Neots, Oct. 7, 1783. He was a church organist and taught music in various provincial towns in England. His publications include: *The Royal Melody Compleat, or the New Harmony of Sion* (2nd ed., 1760; 3rd ed., in 3 parts, 1764, 1765, 1766; at least 11 American eds. are known, publ. as *The American Harmony, or Royal Melody Complete,* or under similar, slightly varying, titles); *Heaven on Earth, or the Beauty of Holiness* (1738); *Sacred Mirth, or the Pious Soul's Daily Delight* (1739); *The Universal Harmony* (1743, etc.); *The Psalm-Singer's Jewel* (1760, etc.); *Melodia sacra* (1771, 1772); *New Musical Grammar* (1746; 7th ed., 1829); an epitome of this last, *The Elements of Musick Displayed* (1772). For details on various eds. see I. Lowens and Allen P. Britton, in *Papers of the Bibliographical Society of America,* 4 (1955; pp. 340-54).

Tarchi, Angelo, Italian composer; b. Naples, c.1755; d. Paris, Aug. 19, 1814. He studied at the Cons. dei Turchini in Naples with Fago and Sala; was music director and composer at the King's Theatre in London in 1787–88 and again in 1789; subsequently was active in Italy until settling in Paris in 1797. He wrote about 45 operas in Italian, and 6 in French; of these the following were produced at La Scala in Milan: *Ademira* (Dec. 27, 1783); *Ariarte* (Jan., 1786); *Il Conte di Saldagna* (June 10, 1787); *Adrasto* (Feb. 8, 1792); *Le Danaidi* (Dec. 26, 1794); *L'impostura poco dura* (Oct. 10, 1795). In Paris he produced the French version of *Il Conte di Saldagna* as *Bouffons de la foire St. Germain* (1790); *D'Auberge en auberge* (Opéra-Comique, April 26, 1800); etc. He acquired a certain notoriety by his attempt to rewrite the 3rd and 4th acts of Mozart's *Le nozze di Figaro* (1787); regarding this episode, see A. Einstein, "Mozart e Tarchi," *Rassegna Musicale* (July 1935); also C. Sartori, "Lo *Zeffiretto* di Angelo Tarchi," *Rivista Musicale Italiana* (July 1954).

Tarp, Svend Erik, Danish composer; b. Thisted, Jutland, Aug. 6, 1908. He studied theory with Knud Jeppesen and piano with Rudolf Simonsen at the Copenhagen Cons. (1929–31); then was appointed to its faculty (1934–42); concurrently lectured at the Univ. of Copenhagen (1935–42) and the Royal Opera Academy (1935–40); occupied various administrative and editorial posts in music organizations in Denmark; was chairman of the board of directors of the Society for Publishing of Danish Music (1935–58 and again after 1976); was editor of *Edition Dania* (1941–60).

Tartini, Giuseppe, important Italian violinist, composer, and theorist; b. Pirano, Istria, April 8, 1692; d. Padua, Feb. 26, 1770. The story of Tartini's early years abounds in unverifiable reports. In 1709 he enrolled at the Univ. of Padua as a law student, and at the age of 19 contracted a secret marriage to the 21-year-old Elisabetta Premazore, a protégée of the powerful Cardinal Cornaro, who, according to some biographies, vengefully brought a charge of abduction against him. Tartini had to take refuge from prosecution in the Franciscan monastery at Assisi; there he is said to have taken music lessons with the organist Czernohorsky, known as "il padre bohemo." According to further accounts, the cardinal dropped action against Tartini, who then returned to Padua; later he went to Ancona to study violin. In 1721 he was appointed solo violinist at S. Antonio in Padua. In 1723–26 he served as chamber musician to Count Kinsky in Prague; then resumed his residence in Padua, where he organized a music school in 1728; among his students there were Nardini and Pugnani. He subsequently developed a brilliant career as a violinist, making numerous concert tours in Italy. His style of playing, and in particular his bowing, became a model for other concert violinists. Tartini was a prolific composer of violin music, including concertos, sonatas, and chamber combinations. An edition of his collected works was initiated in Milan in 1971 under the editorship of E. Farina and G. Scimone, as *Le opere di Giuseppe Tartini.* A thematic catalogue of his violin sonatas was printed in Milan in 1975.

Although Tartini lacked scientific training, he made several acoustical discoveries, the most important of which were the summation and differential tones; Tartini observed these effects in 1714 and summarized his findings in his *Trattato di Musica,* publ. in 1754; the differential tone became known also as Tartini's tone, or "terzo suono." Tartini's tones were actually described in an earlier German publication, *Vorgemach der musicalischen Composition* by G.A. Sorge, publ. in 1745–47. These tones were also known, rather misleadingly, as "beat tones." They are in fact produced by the interference of frequencies of higher overtones. The "wolf tones" of string instruments are different in origin, and are produced by vibrations of the body of the instrument. Violinists are usually aware of interferences from differential tones and also from the less audible summation tones resulting from added frequencies; they correct them experimentally by a slight alteration of tuning. Among Tartini's compositions the most famous is his violin sonata known under the sobriquet *Trillo del Diavolo,* supposedly inspired by Tartini's dream in which the Devil played it for him; the eponymous diabolical trill appears in the last movement of the sonata.

WORKS: Uncounted violin concertos, possibly as many as 150; about 100 violin sonatas, of which *Trillo del Diavolo* was publ. posthumously in Cartier's *L'Art du violon;* other works include 6 concertos, op. 1 (1734), 3 of which were republished in Paris, and 3 others printed with 2 viola parts added by Blainville and publ. as *Concerti grossi;* 12 Violin Sonatas with Cello and Cembalo, also publ. as op. 1; 6 Violin Sonatas, op. 2; 12 Sonatas, including op. 2, for Violin and Bass, as op. 3; *6 Concerti a Violino solo, 2 Violini, Viola e Violoncello o Cembalo di concerto,* op. 4; 6 Sonatas for Violin with Continuo (also as op. 4); opp. 5, 6, and 7, each comprising 6 Sonatas for Violin and Continuo; *6 Sonate a 3,* op. 8; *L'arte dell'arco* (reprinted in French by Choron as *L'Art du violon*); *Trillo del Diavolo* (numerous eds.).

Taskin, (Emile-) Alexandre, French baritone, grandson of **Henri-Joseph Taskin;** b. Paris, March 8, 1853; d. there, Oct. 5, 1897. He was a pupil of Ponchard and Bussine at the Paris Cons.; made his debut at Amiens in 1875. He sang in Lille and Geneva; returned to Paris in 1878; was engaged at the Opéra-Comique in 1879, and created important parts in many new operas. He retired in 1894, and from then until his death was prof. of lyrical declamation at the Cons. On the night of the terrible catastrophe of the burning of the Opéra-Comique (May 25, 1887) he was singing in *Mignon;* through his calmness and bravery many lives were saved, and the government decorated him with a medal.

Taskin, Pascal, French manufacturer of keyboard instruments; b. Theux, near Liège, 1723; d. Paris, Feb. 9, 1793. He went to Paris at an early age and entered Blanchet's atelier, later succeeding to the business and becoming highly celebrated as an instrument maker. He invented the leather plectra for the harpsichord (1768), replacing the crow quills previously in use. He built his first piano in 1776. His nephew **Pascal-Joseph Taskin** (b. Theux, Nov. 20, 1750; d. Versailles, Feb. 5, 1829) was Keeper of the King's Instruments from 1772 until the Revolution; his son **Henri-Joseph Taskin** (b. Versailles, Aug. 24, 1779; d. Paris, May 4, 1852) was an organist and composer.

Tassinari, Pia, Italian mezzo-soprano; b. Modigliana, Sept. 15, 1909. She received her musical training in Bologna and Milan; made her debut at Castel Monferrato in 1929; then sang at La Scala in

Milan (1931–37) and at the Rome Opera (1933–44). She made her American debut at the Metropolitan Opera in N.Y. on Dec. 26, 1947, as Tosca. Although she began her career as a soprano, in later years she preferred to sing mezzo-soprano parts. Her repertoire included both soprano and mezzo-soprano roles, e.g., Mimi, Tosca, Manon, and Marguerite, and also Amneris and Carmen. She married the noted tenor **Ferruccio Tagliavini.**

Tate, Phyllis (Margaret Duncan), English composer; b. Gerrards Cross, Buckinghamshire, April 6, 1911. She studied composition with Harry Farjeon at the Royal Academy of Music in London; composed a Symph., a Cello Concerto, and several other works, but withdrew them as immature. In her music she follows the zeitgeist of the modern era; her music bristles with abrasive dissonances and asymmetrical rhythms, while the form retains its Classical purity. She married the musical scholar and publishing official **Alan Frank** in 1935.

Tatum, Art(hur), black American jazz pianist; b. Toledo, Ohio, Oct. 13, 1910; d. Los Angeles, Nov. 5, 1956. He was blind in one eye and had limited vision in the other; he attended a school for the blind in Columbus, Ohio, and learned to read Braille music notation; at the age of 16 began to play in nightclubs. In 1932 he went to N.Y. and became successful on the radio. In 1938 he made a spectacular tour of England; then was again in N.Y. for many years; eventually went to California, where he died of uremia. He brought "stride" piano playing to a point of perfection, scorning such academic niceties as proper fingering, but achieving small miracles with ornamental figurations in the melody while throwing effortless cascades of notes across the keyboard; he also had a knack of improvising variations on popular pieces by defenseless deceased classical composers; his audiences adored Art's art, while professional musicians knitted their brows in wild surmise.

Tauber, Richard (real name, **Ernst Seiffert**), eminent Austrian tenor; b. Linz, May 16, 1892; d. London, Jan. 8, 1948. He studied music at the Hoch Cons. in Frankfurt; made his debut at Chemnitz as Tamino in *Die Zauberflöte* (March 2, 1913) with such success that he was engaged in the same year at the Dresden Opera; in 1915 he appeared with the Berlin Royal Opera at Salzburg. Later he sang mostly in light opera; was particularly successful in the leading parts of Lehár's operettas. He made his American debut on Oct. 28, 1931, in a N.Y. recital; was noted for his performance of Mozart as well as for being a fine recitalist. In 1938 he went to England; became a British subject in 1940. In London he wrote an operetta, *Old Chelsea,* and took the leading role at its production there (Feb. 17, 1943). He made his last American appearance at Carnegie Hall, N.Y., on March 30, 1947.

Taubert, (Carl Gottfried) Wilhelm, German composer; b. Berlin, March 23, 1811; d. there, Jan. 7, 1891.

He was a piano pupil of Neithardt, later of L. Berger, and for composition, of Bernhard Klein. He appeared early as a concert player; taught music in Berlin; became assistant conductor of the court orch. in 1831; was Generalmusikdirektor of the Royal Opera, Berlin, in 1845–48; also court Kapellmeister from 1845 to 1869; continued to conduct the court orch. until 1883. He conducted his First Symph. in Berlin at the age of 20 (March 31, 1831). His operas (all produced in Berlin) include: *Die Kirmes* (Jan. 23, 1832); *Marquis und Dieb* (Feb. 1, 1842); *Der Zigeuner* (Sept. 19, 1834); *Joggeli* (Oct. 9, 1853); *Macbeth* (Nov. 16, 1857); *Cesario,* after Shakespeare's *Twelfth Night* (Nov. 13, 1874). He composed much instrumental music, but is best remembered for his *Kinderlieder* (opp. 145, 160), the favorites among his 300 songs.

Taubman, Howard, American music critic; b. New York, July 4, 1907. He studied at Cornell Univ.; joined the staff of the *N.Y. Times* in 1930; in 1955 succeeded Olin Downes as chief music critic there, and in 1960 succeeded Brooks Atkinson as drama critic; was succeeded as senior music critic by Harold C. Schonberg in 1960; retired in 1972; then became music adviser for television productions sponsored by the Exxon Corp.

Tausch, Franz, celebrated German clarinetist; b. Heidelberg, Dec. 26, 1762; d. Berlin, Feb. 9, 1817. At the age of 8 he played in the Electoral orch. at Mannheim; was engaged at Munich (1777–89), and then in the court orch. at Berlin, where he founded a school for wind instruments in 1805; Heinrich Bärmann was his pupil. He publ. 2 clarinet concertos, 3 concertantes for 2 Clarinets, Andante and Polonaise for Clarinet, clarinet duos, trios for 2 Clarinets with Bassoon, 6 quartets for 2 Basset Horns and 2 Bassoons (with 2 Horns ad libitum), 6 military marches, etc.

Tausch, Julius, German conductor and composer; b. Dessau, April 15, 1827; d. Bonn, Nov. 11, 1895. He studied with Friedrich Schneider, and at the Leipzig Cons. (1844–46); then settled in Düsseldorf; there he became conductor of the Künstlerliedertafel; was Schumann's deputy from 1853, and in 1855 his successor as conductor of the Music Society and Subscription Concerts in Düsseldorf, retiring in 1890. He composed the cantatas *Der Blumen Klage auf den Tod des Sängers; Dein Leben schied, dein Ruhm begann; Germanenzug; Rheinfahrt;* piano pieces; male choruses.

Tausig, Carl, celebrated piano virtuoso; b. Warsaw, Nov. 4, 1841; d. Leipzig, July 17, 1871. He was trained by his father, **Aloys Tausig** (1820–85), who was a pupil of Thalberg and wrote brilliant piano music. Carl Tausig studied with Liszt, and emulated his bravura style; he made his debut in 1858, at an orch. concert conducted by Hans von Bülow at Berlin. During the next 2 years he gave concerts in German cities, making Dresden his headquarters; then went to Vienna in 1862, giving orch. concerts with "advanced" programs similar to Bülow's at Berlin. He settled in Berlin in 1865, and opened the Schule des Höheren Klavierspiels. He gave concerts in the principal towns of Germany, and at St. Petersburg and other Russian centers. He died of typhoid fever at the age of 29.

Tavener, John, British composer; b. London, Jan. 28, 1944. He studied with Lennox Berkeley at the Royal Academy of Music; also took a course with the Australian composer David Lumsdaine. Among the formative influences of his creative evolution were medieval hymnology and Indian transcendentalism; his technical equipment is, by contrast, ultramodern, including combinatorial serialism and electronic generation of sound.
WORKS: Piano Concerto (1962–63; London, Dec. 6, 1963); *3 Holy Sonnets* for Baritone and Chamber Orch., to poems by John Donne (1962; London, July 1964); *3 Sections from T.S. Eliot's Four Quartets* for Tenor and Piano (1964); *The Cappemakers,* dramatic cantata (1964; revised for stage, 1965; Charleston Manor, Sussex, June 14, 1964); *Cain and Abel,* dramatic cantata for Soloists and Chamber Orch. (1965; London, Oct. 22, 1966); Chamber Concerto (1965; revised 1968; London, June 12, 1968); *The Whale,* dramatic cantata for Narrator, Soloists, Chorus, and Orch. (1966; London, Jan. 24, 1968); *Grandma's Footsteps* for Chamber Group (London, March 14, 1968); *Introit for the Feast of St. John Damascene* for Soprano, Contralto, Chorus, and Orch. (London, March 27, 1968); Concerto for Orch. (1968); *3 Surrealist Songs* for Mezzo-soprano, Piano, Bongos, and Tape (BBC, March 21, 1968); *In Alium* for Soprano, Orch., and Tape (London, Aug. 12, 1968); *A Celtic Requiem,* dramatic cantata for Soloists, Children's Choir, Chorus, and Orch. (London, July 16, 1969); *Ultimos ritos* for Soloists, 5 Choruses, Brass Ensemble, and Orch. (1972; Haarlem, June 22, 1974); *Coplas* for Soloists, Chorus, and Tape (Cheltenham, July 9, 1970); *Nomine Jesu* for 5 Male Speaking Voices, Mezzo-soprano, Chorus, 2 Alto Flutes, Organ, and Harpsichord (Dartington, South Devon, Aug. 14, 1970); *Canciones españolas* for 2 Countertenors or Sopranos, 2 Flutes, Organ, and Harpsichord (London, June 8, 1972); *In memoriam Igor Stravinsky* for 2 Alto Flutes, Organ, and Bells (1971); *Ma fin est mon commencement* for Tenor Chorus, 4 Trombones, Piano, and 4 Cellos (London, April 23, 1972); *Little Requiem for Father Malachy Lynch* (Winchester Cathedral, July 29, 1972); *Variations on 3 Blind Mice* for Chamber Orch. (1972); *Requiem for Father Malachy* for 6 Soloists and Chamber Orch. (London, June 10, 1973); *Thérèse,* opera (1973–76; Covent Garden, London, Oct. 1, 1979); *Canticle of the Mother of God* for Soprano and Chorus (1976); *A Gentle Spirit,* chamber opera after the story by Dostoyevsky (Bath, June 6, 1977); *Kyklike Kinesis* for Soprano, Cello, Chorus, and Orch. (1977; London, March 8, 1978); *Lamentation, Last Prayer and Exaltation* for Soprano and Handbells (1977); *Palintropos* for Piano and Orch. (1977; Birmingham, March 1, 1979); *The Last Prayer of Mary Queen of Scots* for Soprano and Handbells (1977); *6*

Russian Folk Songs for Soprano and Ensemble (1978); *The Liturgy of St. John Chrysostom* for Chorus a cappella (London, May 6, 1978); *The Immurement of Antigone,* monodrama for Soprano and Orch. (1978; London, March 30, 1979); *6 Abbasid Songs* for Tenor and 3 Flutes (1979); *Akhmatova: Requiem* for Soprano, Baritone, and Ensemble (1980; Edinburgh, Aug. 20, 1981); *Sappho, Lyric Fragments* for 2 Sopranos and Strings (1980); *Risen!* for Chorus and Ensemble (1980); *Prayer for the World* for 16 Solo Voices (1981); *Funeral Ikos* for Chorus (1981); *Towards the Son: Ritual Procession* for Orch. (London, Nov. 15, 1983).

Taverner, John, important English composer; b. c.1490; d. Boston, Lincolnshire, Oct. 18, 1545. In 1526 he was appointed master of the choristers at Cardinals' College in Oxford. In 1530 he became lay clerk of the choir of the parish church St. Botolph, in Boston, Lincolnshire. In 1537 he was elected a member of the Guild Corpus Christi there; then became treasurer. In 1545 he was appointed a town alderman, but died soon afterward. The widely circulated stories of his imprisonment for heresy and of his serving as an agent for Cromwell are totally unfounded. Taverner was a prolific composer of church music; among his works are 8 masses, 3 Magnificats, a Te Deum, and 28 motets. He also wrote 3 secular vocal compositions for W. de Worde's *Song-book* (1530). His church music is found in vols. I and III of *Tudor Church Music* (1923–24).

Taylor, Billy (William), black American jazz pianist; b. Greenville, N.C., July 24, 1921. He studied piano with Henry Grant; then enrolled at Virginia State College in Petersburg (B.Mus., 1942); in 1975 received his D.Ed. degree from the Univ. of Mass. In 1951 he formed the Billy Taylor Trio; served as a radio disc jockey and program director; was host of the "Jazz Alive" radio series. He was also active as a teacher; was on the staff of the Manhattan School of Music and Howard Univ. His image became an intaglio of jazz, so that he was popularly dubbed "Mr. Jazz."

Taylor, (Joseph) Deems, greatly popular American composer and writer; b. New York, Dec. 22, 1885; d. there, July 3, 1966. He graduated from N.Y. Univ. (B.A., 1906); studied theory with O. Coon (1908–11). After doing editorial work for various publications and serving as war correspondent for the *N.Y. Tribune* in France (1916–17), he became music critic for the *N.Y. World* (1921–25), editor of *Musical America* (1927–29), and critic for the *N.Y. American* (1931–32). He was a member of the National Inst. of Arts and Letters; received a Mus.Doc. (*honoris causa*) from N.Y. Univ. (1927); a Litt.D. from Juniata College (1931). Following the success of his orch. suite *Through the Looking-Glass,* after Lewis Carroll's tale (1923), he was commissioned by Walter Damrosch to compose a symph. poem, *Jurgen* (1925). Meanwhile, 2 widely performed cantatas, *The Chambered Nautilus* and *The Highwayman,* had added to his growing reputation, which received a strong impetus when his opera *The King's Henchman* (libretto by Edna St. Vincent Millay), commissioned by the Metropolitan Opera, was produced in that house on Feb. 17, 1927. Receiving 14 performances in 3 seasons, it established a record for American opera at the Metropolitan Opera House, but it was surpassed by Taylor's next opera, *Peter Ibbetson* (Feb. 7, 1931); this attained 16 performances in 4 seasons. These successes, however, proved ephemeral, and the operas were allowed to lapse into unmerited desuetude. From 1942 to 1948 he was president of the American Society for Composers, Authors and Publishers.

Taylor, Raynor, English-American composer; b. in England, c.1747; d. Philadelphia, Aug. 17, 1825. He received his early training as a chorister in the Chapel Royal, and in 1765 became organist of a church in Chelmsford; that same year he was also appointed music director at Sadler's Wells Theatre, London. In 1792 he emigrated to the U.S., going first to Baltimore and then to Annapolis, where he was organist of St. Anne's Church. Moving to Philadelphia in 1793, he became organist of St. Peter's there, and in 1820 was one of the founders of the Musical Fund Society. A gifted singer, he gave humorous musical entertainments which he called "olios," and in 1796 conducted an orch. concert that included several of his own compositions. In collaboration with A. Reinagle, who had been his pupil in London, he composed a monody on the death of Washington (1799), and a ballad opera, *Pizarro, or the Spaniards in Peru* (1800); some of his song MSS are in the N.Y. Public Library.

Tchaikovsky, Boris, Russian composer; b. Moscow, Sept. 10, 1925. He studied at the Moscow Cons. with Shostakovich, Shebalin, and Miaskovsky. He publ. his earliest piano works at the age of 13; wrote an opera, *The Star* (1949); Symph. No. 1 (1947); *Fantasy on Russian Themes* for Orch. (1950); *Slavic Rhapsody* for Orch. (1951); *Symphonietta* (1953); Symph. No. 2 (1967); Piano Concerto (1969); Violin Concerto (1970); 4 string quartets; Piano Trio; Violin Sonata; piano pieces. He is not related to Piotr Ilyich Tchaikovsky.

Tchaikovsky, Modest, Russian playwright and librettist; brother of **Piotr Ilyich Tchaikovsky;** b. Alapaevsk, Perm district, May 13, 1850; d. Moscow, Jan. 15, 1916. He was the closest intimate of Tchaikovsky, and the author of the basic biography. His plays had only a passing success, but he was an excellent librettist; he wrote the librettos of Tchaikovsky's last 2 operas, *The Queen of Spades* and *Iolanthe.*

Tchaikovsky, Piotr Ilyich, famous Russian composer; b. Votkinsk, Viatka district, May 7, 1840; d. St. Petersburg, Nov. 6, 1893. The son of a mining inspector at a plant in the Urals, he was given a good education; had a French governess and a music teacher. When he was 10, the family moved to St.

Petersburg and he was sent to a school of jurisprudence, from which he graduated at 19, becoming a government clerk; while at school he studied music with Lomakin, but did not display conspicuous talent as either a pianist or composer. At the age of 21 he was accepted in a musical inst., newly established by Anton Rubinstein, which was to become the St. Petersburg Cons. He studied with Zaremba (harmony and counterpoint) and Rubinstein (composition); graduated in 1865, winning a silver medal for his cantata to Schiller's *Hymn to Joy.* In 1866 he became prof. of harmony at the Moscow Cons. under the directorship of Nicolai Rubinstein. As if to compensate for a late beginning in his profession, he began to compose with great application. His early works (a programmatic symph. subtitled *Winter Dreams,* some overtures and small pieces for string quartet) reveal little individuality. With his symph. poem *Fatum* (1869) came the first formulation of his style, highly subjective, preferring minor modes, permeated with nostalgic longing and alive with keen rhythms. In 1869 he undertook the composition of his overture-fantasy *Romeo and Juliet;* not content with what he had written, he profited by the advice of Balakirev, whom he met in St. Petersburg, and revised the work in 1870; but this version proved equally unsatisfactory; Tchaikovsky laid the composition aside, and did not complete it until 1879; in its final form it became one of his most successful works. A Belgian soprano, Désirée Artôt, a member of an opera troupe visiting St. Petersburg in 1868, took great interest in Tchaikovsky, and he was moved by her attentions; for a few months he seriously contemplated marriage, and so notified his father (his mother had died of cholera when he was 14 years old). But this proved to be a passing infatuation on her part, for soon she married the Spanish singer Padilla; Tchaikovsky reacted to this event with a casual philosophical remark about the inconstancy of human attachments. Throughout his career Tchaikovsky never allowed his psychological turmoil to interfere with his work. Besides teaching and composing, he contributed music criticism to Moscow newspapers for several years (1868–74), made altogether 26 trips abroad (to Paris, Berlin, Vienna, N.Y.), and visited the first Bayreuth Festival in 1876, reporting his impressions for the Moscow daily *Russkyie Vedomosti.* His closest friends were members of his own family, his brothers (particularly **Modest,** his future biographer), and his married sister Alexandra Davidov, at whose estate, Kamenka, he spent most of his summers. The correspondence with them, all of which was preserved and eventually publ., throws a true light on Tchaikovsky's character and his life. His other intimate friends were his publisher, Jurgenson, Nicolai Rubinstein, and several other musicians. The most extraordinary of his friendships was the epistolary intimacy with Nadezhda von Meck, a wealthy widow whom he never met but who was to play an important role in his life. Through the violinist Kotek she learned about Tchaikovsky's financial difficulties, and commissioned him to write some compositions, at large fees; then arranged to pay him an annuity of 6,000 rubles. For more than

13 years they corresponded voluminously, even when they lived in the same city (Moscow, Florence); on several occasions Madame von Meck hinted that she would not be averse to a personal meeting, but Tchaikovsky invariably declined such a suggestion, under the pretext that one should not see one's guardian angel in the flesh. On Tchaikovsky's part, this correspondence had to remain within the circumscribed domain of art, personal philosophy, and reporting of daily events, without touching on the basic problems of his existence. On July 18, 1877, Tchaikovsky contracted marriage with a conservatory student named Antonina Milyukova, who had declared her love for him. This was an act of defiance of his own nature; Tchaikovsky was a deviate, and made no secret of it in the correspondence with his brother Modest (who was also abnormal in this respect). He thought that by flaunting a wife he could prevent the already rife rumors about his abnormality from spreading further. The result was disastrous, and Tchaikovsky fled from his wife in horror. He attempted suicide by walking into the Moskva River in order to catch pneumonia, but suffered nothing more severe than simple discomfort. He then went to St. Petersburg to seek the advice of his brother Anatol, a lawyer, who made suitable arrangements with Tchaikovsky's wife for a separation. (They were never divorced; she died in an insane asylum in 1917.) Madame von Meck, to whom Tchaikovsky wrote candidly of the hopeless failure of his marriage (without revealing the true cause of that failure), made at once an offer of further financial assistance, which Tchaikovsky gratefully accepted. He spent several months during 1877–78 in Italy, Switzerland, Paris, and Vienna. During these months he completed one of his greatest works, the 4th Symph., dedicated to Mme. von Meck. It was performed for the first time in Moscow on Feb. 22, 1878, but Tchaikovsky did not cut short his sojourn abroad to attend the performance. He resigned from the Moscow Cons. in the autumn of 1878, and from that time dedicated himself entirely to composition. The continued subsidy from Mme. von Meck allowed him to forget money matters. Early in 1879 he completed his most successful opera, *Eugene Onegin* ("lyric scenes," after Pushkin); it was first produced in Moscow by a cons. ensemble, on March 29, 1879, and gained success only gradually; the first performance at the Imperial Opera in St. Petersburg did not take place until 5 years later (Oct. 31, 1884). A morbid depression was still Tchaikovsky's natural state of mind, but every new work sustained his faith in his destiny as a composer, despite many disheartening reversals. His Piano Concerto No. 1, rejected by Nicolai Rubinstein as unplayable, was given its world premiere (somewhat incongruously) in Boston, on Oct. 25, 1875, played by Hans von Bülow, and afterward was performed all over the world by famous pianists, including Nicolai Rubinstein himself. The Violin Concerto, criticized by Leopold Auer (to whom the score was originally dedicated) and attacked by Hanslick with sarcasm and virulence at its world premiere by Brodsky in Vienna (1881), survived all

its detractors to become one of the most celebrated pieces in the violin repertoire. The 5th Symph. (1888) was successful from the very first. Early in 1890 Tchaikovsky wrote his 2nd important opera, *The Queen of Spades*, which was produced at the Imperial Opera in St. Petersburg in that year. His ballets *Swan Lake* (1876) and *The Sleeping Beauty* (1889) became famous on Russian stages. But at the peak of his career, Tchaikovsky suffered a severe psychological blow; Mme. von Meck notified him of the discontinuance of her subsidy, and with this announcement she abruptly terminated their correspondence. Tchaikovsky could now well afford the loss of the money, but his pride was deeply hurt by the manner in which Mme. von Meck had acted. It is indicative of Tchaikovsky's inner strength that even this desertion of one whom he regarded as his staunchest friend did not affect his ability to work. In 1891 he undertook his first and only voyage to America. He was received with honors as a celebrated composer; he led 4 concerts of his works in N.Y. and one each in Baltimore and Philadelphia. He did not linger in the U.S., however, and returned to St. Petersburg in a few weeks. Early in 1892 he made a concert tour as a conductor in Russia, and then proceeded to Warsaw and Germany. In the meantime he had purchased a house in the town of Klin, not far from Moscow, where he wrote his last symph., the *Pathétique*. Despite the perfection of his technique, he did not arrive at the desired form and substance of this work at once, and discarded his original sketch. The title *Pathétique* was suggested to him by his brother Modest; the score was dedicated to his nephew, Vladimir Davidov. Its music is the final testament of Tchaikovsky's life, and an epitome of his philosophy of fatalism. In the first movement, the trombones are given the theme of the Russian service for the dead. Remarkably, the score of one of his gayest works, the ballet *The Nutcracker*, was composed simultaneously with the early sketches for the *Pathétique*. Tchaikovsky was in good spirits when he went to St. Petersburg to conduct the premiere of the *Pathétique*, on Oct. 28, 1893 (which was but moderately successful). A cholera epidemic was then raging in St. Petersburg, and the population was specifically warned against drinking unboiled water, but apparently Tchaikovsky carelessly did exactly that. He showed the symptoms of cholera soon afterward, and nothing could be done to save him. The melodramatic hypothesis that the fatal drink of water was a defiance of death, in perfect knowledge of the danger, since he must have remembered his mother's death of the same dread infection, is untenable in the light of publ. private letters between the attendant physician and Modest Tchaikovsky at the time. Tchaikovsky's fatalism alone would amply account for his lack of precaution. Almost immediately after Tchaikovsky's death a rumor spread that he had committed suicide, and reports to that effect were publ. in respectable European newspapers (but not in Russian publications), and repeated even in some biographical dictionaries (particularly in Britain). After the grim fantasy seemed definitely refuted, a ludicrous paper by an émigré Russian woman was

Tchaikovsky

publ., claiming private knowledge of a homosexual scandal involving a Russian nobleman's nephew (in another version a member of the Romanov imperial family) which led to a "trial" of Tchaikovsky by a jury of his former school classmates, who offered Tchaikovsky a choice between honorable suicide or disgrace and possible exile to Siberia; a family council, with Tchaikovsky's own participation, advised the former solution, and Tchaikovsky was supplied with arsenic; the family doctor was supposed to be a part of the conspiracy, as were Tchaikovsky's own brothers. Amazingly enough, this outrageous fabrication was accepted as historical fact by some biographers, and even found its way into the pages of *The New Grove*. In Russia, the truth of Tchaikovsky's homosexuality was totally suppressed, and any references to it in his diary and letters were carefully expunged.

As a composer, Tchaikovsky stands apart from the militant national movement of the "Mighty Five." The Russian element is, of course, very strong in his music, and upon occasion he made use of Russian folk songs in his works, but this national spirit is instinctive rather than consciously cultivated. His personal relationship with the St. Petersburg group of nationalists was friendly without being intimate; his correspondence with Rimsky-Korsakov, Balakirev, and others was mostly concerned with professional matters. Tchaikovsky's music was frankly sentimental; his supreme gift of melody, which none of his Russian contemporaries could match, secured for him a lasting popularity among performers and audiences. His influence was profound on the Moscow group of musicians, of whom Arensky and Rachmaninoff were the most talented. He wrote in every genre, and was successful in each; besides his stage works, symphs., chamber music, and piano compositions, he composed a great number of lyric songs that are the most poignant creations of his genius. By a historical paradox, Tchaikovsky became the most popular Russian composer under the Soviet regime. His subjectivism, his fatalism, his emphasis on melancholy moods, even his reactionary political views (which included a brand of amateurish anti-Semitism), failed to detract from his stature in the new society. In fact, official spokesmen of Soviet Russia repeatedly urged Soviet composers to follow in the path of Tchaikovsky's esthetics. Tchaikovsky's popularity is also very strong in Anglo-Saxon countries, particularly in America; much less so in France and Italy; in Germany his influence is insignificant.

WORKS: OPERAS: *The Voyevode* (1867–68; Moscow, Feb. 11, 1869); *Undine* (1869); *The Oprichnik* (1870–72; St. Petersburg, April 24, 1874); *Vakula the Smith* (1874; St. Petersburg, Dec. 6, 1876); *Eugene Onegin* (1877–78; Moscow, March, 29, 1879); *The Maid of Orleans* (1878–79; St. Petersburg, Feb. 25, 1881); *Mazeppa* (1881–83; Moscow, Feb. 15, 1884); *Tcherevichki* (*The Little Shoes;* revised version of *Vakula the Smith;* 1885; Moscow, Jan. 31, 1887); *The Sorceress* (1888–87; St. Petersburg, Nov. 1, 1887); *The Queen of Spades* (1890; St. Petersburg, Dec. 19, 1890); *Iolanta* (1891; St. Petersburg, Dec. 18, 1892). BALLETS: *Swan Lake* (1875–76; Moscow, March 4,

1877); *The Sleeping Beauty* (1888–89; St. Petersburg, Jan. 15, 1890); *The Nutcracker* (1891–92; St. Petersburg, Dec. 18, 1892).

FOR ORCH.: 6 symphs.: No. 1 (*Winter Dreams;* 1868; revised 1874; Moscow, Feb. 15, 1868); No. 2 (*Little Russian* or *Ukrainian Symph.;* 1872; Moscow, Feb. 7, 1873); No. 3 (1875; Moscow, Nov. 19, 1875); No. 4 (1877; Moscow, Feb. 22, 1878); No. 5 (1888; St. Petersburg, Nov. 17, 1888); No. 6 (*Pathétique;* 1893; St. Petersburg, Oct. 28, 1893); overture to Ostrovsky's play *The Storm* (1864); symph. poem, *Fatum* (1868; Moscow, Feb. 27, 1869); overture, *Romeo and Juliet* (1869; Moscow, March 16, 1870; final version, 1879); symph. fantasy, *The Tempest,* after Shakespeare (1873; Moscow, Dec. 19, 1873); First Piano Concerto (1874–75; Boston, Oct. 25, 1875); *Sérénade mélancolique* for Violin with Orch. (1875; Moscow, Jan. 28, 1876); *Slavonic March* (1876; Moscow, Nov. 17, 1876); symph. fantasy, *Francesca da Rimini,* after Dante (1876; Moscow, March 9, 1877); suite from the ballet *Swan Lake* (1876); *Variations on a Rococo Theme* for Cello and Orch. (1876; Moscow, Nov. 30, 1877); *Valse-Scherzo* for Violin and Orch. (1877; Paris, Oct. 21, 1878); *Suite* No. 1 (1878–79; Moscow, Nov. 23, 1879); Violin Concerto (1878; Vienna, Dec. 4, 1881); Piano Concerto No. 2 (1879–80; Moscow, May 30, 1882); *Capriccio italien* (1880; Moscow, Dec. 18, 1880); *1812 Overture* (1880; Moscow, Aug. 20, 1882); *Serenade* for String Orch. (1880; Moscow, Jan. 28, 1882); *Suite* No. 2 (1883; Moscow, Feb. 16, 1884); *Suite* No. 3 (1884; St. Petersburg, Jan. 28, 1885); *Concert Fantasy* for Piano with Orch. (1884; Moscow, March 6, 1885); symph., *Manfred,* after Byron (1885; Moscow, March 23, 1886); *Suite* No. 4, *Mozartiana* (1887; Moscow, Nov. 26, 1887); overture-fantasy, *Hamlet* (1888; St. Petersburg, Nov. 24, 1888); *Pezzo capriccioso* for Cello with Orch. (1887; Moscow, Dec. 7, 1889); suite from the ballet *The Sleeping Beauty* (1889); symph. ballad, *The Voyevode,* after Pushkin's trans. of Mickiewicz's ballad (1890–91; Moscow, Nov. 18, 1891); suite from the ballet *Nutcracker* (1892; St. Petersburg, March 19, 1892); 3rd Piano Concerto (one movement only; posthumous; St. Petersburg, Jan. 19, 1895); *Andante and Finale* for Piano with Orch. (1893; actually 2nd and 3rd movements of the 3rd Piano Concerto; posthumous; St. Petersburg, Feb. 20, 1896).

CHAMBER MUSIC: 3 string quartets (1871, 1874, 1876); Piano Trio, in memory of Nicolai Rubinstein (Moscow, Oct. 30, 1882); *Souvenir de Florence* for String Sextet (1887; St. Petersburg, Dec. 7, 1892); also *Souvenir d'un lieu cher* for Violin and Piano (1878); several fragments of early works.

FOR PIANO: *Scherzo à la russe* (1867); *Souvenir de Hapsal,* 3 pieces (No. 3 is the famous *Chant sans paroles;* 1867); *Valse-Caprice* (1868); *Romance* in F minor (1868); *Valse-Scherzo* (1870); *Capriccio* (1870); *3 morceaux: Rêverie, Polka de salon, Mazurka de salon* (1870); *2 morceaux: Nocturne* and *Humoresque* (1871); *6 morceaux: Rêverie du soir, Scherzo humoristique, Feuillet d'album, Nocturne, Capriccioso, Thème original et variations* (1872); *6 morceaux sur un seul thème: Prelude, Fugue, Impromptu, Marche funèbre, Mazurka, Scherzo* (1873); *Grande sonate,* in G major (1879);

Les Quatre Saisons, 12 characteristic pieces for each month of the year (1875–76; of these the most famous are No. 6, *Barcarole;* No. 10, *Chant d'automne;* No. 11, *En traineau;* No. 12, *Noël*); *12 morceaux* (1876–78; among them *Chanson triste* and *Danse russe); Album pour enfants,* 24 pieces (1878); *6 pièces* (1882); *Dumka* (1886); *18 morceaux* (1893); Sonata in C-sharp minor (1865; posthumous).

VOCAL WORKS: Cantata, *An die Freude* (Schiller) for Chorus and Orch. (1865); *Liturgy of St. John Chrysostom* for Mixed Chorus in 4 parts (1878); Vesper Service for Mixed Chorus (1882); *Moskva,* coronation cantata for Solo Voices, Chorus, and Orch. (1883); *3 Cherubic Hymns* for Mixed Chorus (1884); 6 church songs (1885); other sacred and secular vocal pieces; about 100 songs, among them such favorites as *Nur wer die Sehnsucht kennt* (after Goethe), *Berceuse,* etc.; 6 duets.

He publ. *Manual of Harmony* (Moscow, 1870; many eds.; Eng. trans. as *Guide to the Practical Study of Harmony,* 1900). The collected criticisms and reminiscences were publ. in 1898; new ed., revised and enlarged, Moscow, 1953; diaries, comprising 11 separate fragments, covering the years between 1873 and 1891, were publ. in Moscow in 1923 (Eng. trans., N.Y., 1945). A centennial ed. of the complete works, in as many as 120 vols., was begun in 1940, interrupted during the war years, and resumed in 1946. Most of the MSS, correspondence, etc. are preserved in Tchaikovsky's house in Klin (now the Tchaikovsky Museum). A thematic catalogue was issued by B. Jurgenson (Moscow, 1897; reprinted N.Y., 1941). More recently the Tschaikowsky-Studio Inst. International issued the *Systematisches Verzeichnis der Werke von P. I. Tschaikowsky* (Hamburg, 1973).

Tchaikowsky, André, Polish composer and pianist (not by any genetic interplay related to the great Tchaikovsky); b. Warsaw, Nov. 1, 1935; d. Oxford, England, June 26, 1982. His parents fell victim to the Nazis in Warsaw, but he was spirited away to France. After the war, he returned to Poland and studied piano with Stefan Askenase. In 1955 he won the Chopin Prize at the Warsaw Academy; then went to Paris to study with Nadia Boulanger. In 1957 he settled in London, where he acquired a reputation as an eccentric who played Mozart's concertos with grotesque embellishments of his own. He also composed; among his works were a Clarinet Sonata (1959); 2 string quartets (1967, 1970); Piano Concerto (1966–71); *Trio notturno* for Violin, Cello, and Piano; and a nearly completed opera, *The Merchant of Venice,* on which he worked half of his life (1960–82). He was a Shakespeare enthusiast; he bequeathed his skull to the Royal Shakespeare Co. for use in the graveside scene in *Hamlet* ("Alas, poor André, A fellow of infinite jest"); in this postmortem fashion he hoped to satisfy his craving to act in a Shakespeare play. The skull was deposited, still in its box, in the store at the Royal Shakespeare Co.'s headquarters in Stratford-upon-Avon for possible use in an eventual production of *Hamlet.*

Tcherepnin, Alexander, greatly significant Russian composer and pianist; son of **Nicolas Tcherepnin;** b. St. Petersburg, Jan. 20, 1899; d. Paris, Sept. 29, 1977. (The name is pronounced with the stress on the last syllable.) He studied piano as a child with his mother; was encouraged by his father in his first steps in composition, but did not take formal lessons with him. He began to compose in his early youth; wrote a short comic opera at the age of 12, and a ballet when he was 13; then produced a number of piano works; composed 14 piano sonatas before he was 19 years old. In 1917 he entered the Petrograd Cons., where he studied music theory with Sokolov, and piano with Kobiliansky, but remained there only one school year; then joined his parents in a difficult journey to Tiflis, in the Caucasus, during a gradually expanding civil war; in Tiflis, he took lessons in composition with Thomas de Hartmann. In 1921 the family went to Paris, where he continued his studies, taking piano lessons with Isidor Philipp and composition with Paul Vidal. In 1922 he played a concert of his own music in London; in 1923 he was commissioned by Anna Pavlova to write a ballet, *Ajanta's Frescoes,* which she produced in London with her troupe. Tcherepnin progressed rapidly in his career as a pianist and a composer; he played in Germany and Austria; made his first American tour in 1926. Between 1934 and 1937 he made two journeys to the Far East; gave concerts in China and Japan; numerous Chinese and Japanese composers studied with him; he organized a publishing enterprise in Tokyo for the publication of serious works by young Japanese and Chinese composers. He married a Chinese pianist, **Lee Hsien-Ming.** Despite his wide travels, he maintained his principal residence in Paris, and remained there during the war. He resumed his international career in 1947; gave concerts in Scandinavia and elsewhere in Europe. In 1949 he and his wife joined the faculty of De Paul Univ. in Chicago, and taught there for 15 years. In the meantime his music began to be well known; he had 34 publishers; his symph. works were conducted by Koussevitzky, Stokowski, Monteux, Munch, Mitropoulos, Fritz Reiner, Kubelik, William Steinberg, Skrowaczewski, and other famous conductors; he was also a frequent soloist in his piano concertos, which he performed with the major symph. orchs. in America and Europe. He became an American citizen in 1958. In May 1967, Tcherepnin made his first visit to Russia after nearly half a century abroad. In his early works he followed the traditions of Russian Romantic music; characteristically, his Piano Sonata No. 13, which he wrote as a youth, is entitled *Sonatine romantique.* But as he progressed in his career, he evolved a musical language all his own; he derived his melodic patterns from a symmetrically formed scale of 9 degrees, subdivided into 3 equal sections (e.g. C, D, E-flat, E, F-sharp, G, G-sharp, A-sharp, B, C); the harmonic idiom follows a similar intertonal formation; Tcherepnin's consistent use of such thematic groupings anticipated the serial method of composition. Furthermore, he developed a type of rhythmic polyphony, based on thematic rhythmic units, which he termed "interpunctus." However, he did not limit himself to these melodic and rhythmic constructions; he also explored the latent resources of folk music, both oriental and European; he was particularly sensitive to the melorhythms of Russian national songs. A composer of remarkable inventive power, he understood the necessity of creating a communicative musical language, and was primarly concerned with enhancing the lyric and dramatic qualities of his music. At the same time he showed great interest in new musical resources, including electronic sound. His sons **Serge** and **Ivan** are both engaged in experimental musical production.

WORKS: OPERAS: *Ol-Ol*, after Leonid Andreyev (Weimar, Jan. 31, 1928); *Die Hochzeit der Sobeide*, after Hugo von Hofmannsthal (Vienna, March 17, 1933); *The Farmer and the Fairy* (Aspen Festival, Colorado, Aug. 13, 1952); completed Mussorgsky's opera *The Marriage* (Essen, Sept. 14, 1937). BALLETS: *Ajanta's Frescoes* (Anna Pavlova's production, London, Sept. 10, 1923); *Training* (Vienna, June 19, 1935); *Der fahrend Schüler mit dem Teufelsbannen* (1937; score lost during the war; reconstructed, 1965); *Trepak* (Mordkin's Russian Ballet, Richmond, Va., Oct. 10, 1938); *La Légende de Razin* (1941); *Déjeuner sur l'herbe* (Paris, Oct. 14, 1945); *L'Homme à la peau de léopard* (with Arthur Honegger and Tibor Harsányi; Monte Carlo, May 5, 1946); *La Colline des fantômes* (1946); *Jardin persan* (1946); *Nuit kurde* (Paris, 1946); *La Femme et son ombre*, after Paul Claudel (Paris, June 14, 1948); *Aux temps des tartares* (Buenos Aires, 1949). CANTATAS: *Vivre d'amour* (1942); *Pan Kéou* (Paris, Oct. 9, 1945); *Le Jeu de la Nativité* (Paris, Dec. 30, 1945); *Les Douze*, poem by Alexander Blok for Narrator, Strings, Harp, Piano, and Percussion (Paris, Nov. 9, 1947); *Vom Spass und Ernst*, folk-song cantata for Voice and Strings (1964); *The Story of Ivan the Fool*, cantata with Narrator (London, Dec. 24, 1968). FOR ORCH.: Overture (1921); Symph. No. 1 (Paris, Oct. 29, 1927); Symph. No. 2 (Chicago, March 20, 1952); Symph. No. 3 (Indianapolis, Jan. 15, 1955); Symph. No. 4 (Boston, Dec. 5, 1958); *Symphony-Prayer* (Chicago, Aug. 19, 1960); *Magna Mater* (Munich, Oct. 30, 1930); *Russian Dances* (Omaha, Feb. 15, 1934); *Mystère* for Cello and Chamber Orch. (Monte Carlo, Dec. 8, 1926); *Concerto da camera* for Flute, Violin, and Chamber Orch. (1924); *Concertino* for Violin, Cello, Piano, and Strings (1931); *Suite georgienne* (Paris, April 17, 1940); 6 piano concertos: No. 1 (Monte Carlo, 1923); No. 2 (Paris, Jan. 26, 1924, 2-piano version, composer soloist; Nadia Boulanger accompanist); No. 3 (Paris, Feb. 5, 1933, composer soloist); No. 4 (retitled *Fantasia;* 1947); No. 5 (West Berlin, Oct. 13, 1963, composer soloist); No. 6 (Lucerne, Sept. 5, 1972); *Serenade* for String Orch. (1964); *Musica sacra* for String Orch. (Lourdes, April 28, 1973); *Evocation* (1948); *Suite* (Louisville, May 1, 1954); Concerto for Harmonica and Orch. (Venice, Sept. 11, 1956); *Divertimento* (Chicago, Nov. 14, 1957).

Tcherepnin, Ivan, American composer, son of **Alexander Tcherepnin;** b. Paris, Feb. 5, 1943. He received his early musical training at home in Paris; then followed his father to the U.S., where he entered Harvard Univ., graduating in 1964; also attended courses with Karlheinz Stockhausen and Henri Pousseur in Cologne, and with Pierre Boulez in Darmstadt; studied electronic techniques in Toronto in 1966; returned to Harvard for graduate studies as a pupil of Randall Thompson and Leon Kirchner, obtaining his M.A. degree in 1969. He was an instructor at the San Francisco Cons. of Music (1969–72); in 1972 was appointed to the faculty of Harvard Univ. to teach courses in electronic composition.

Tcherepnin, Nicolas, noted Russian composer, conductor, and eminent pedagogue; b. St. Petersburg, May 14, 1873; d. Issy-les-Moulineaux, near Paris, June 26, 1945. He was a student of Rimsky-Korsakov at the St. Petersburg Cons. (1895–98); in 1905 was appointed to its faculty; taught orchestration and conducting; Prokofiev was among his many students. He conducted at the festival of Russian music in Paris in 1908; until 1912 toured with the Diaghilev Ballets Russes in Europe. He then returned to Russia; after the Revolution of 1917, he proceeded to the Caucasus, and was director of the Tiflis Cons. (1918–21); then went to Paris, accompanied by his son **Alexander,** and remained there until his death; served as director of the Russian Cons. in Paris (1925–29 and 1938–45). His music embodies the best elements of the Russian national school; it is melodious and harmonious; lyrical and gently dynamic; in some of his works there is a coloristic quality suggesting French impressionistic influence.

Tcherepnin, Serge, American composer; son of **Alexander Tcherepnin;** b. Paris, Feb. 2, 1941. He studied violin as a child; was taken to the U.S. in 1949; received his training in theory with his father; then took courses in composition with Karlheinz Stockhausen, in conducting with Pierre Boulez in Darmstadt, and in electronic music with Herbert Eimert. He pursued his regular academic education at Harvard Univ., where he studied with Walter Piston, Leon Kirchner, and Billy Jim Layton, obtaining his B.A. in 1964. In 1966 he went to Milan to study electronic techniques. Returning to the U.S., he became in 1970 an instructor in electronic music at the School of Music in Valencia, Calif. He is the inventor of a portable music synthesizer, patented as the Serge Modular Music System.

Tear, Robert, Welsh tenor; b. Barry, March 8, 1939. He was educated at King's College, Cambridge; served as a chorister at St. Paul's Cathedral; made his debut with the English Opera Group in London in 1963; subsequently appeared with the Welsh National Opera. In 1970 he joined the staff at Covent Garden in London; he also toured as a concert singer in the U.S., Canada, Japan, and Russia. In 1984 he was made a Commander of the Order of the British Empire.

Tebaldi, Renata, celebrated Italian soprano; b. Pesaro, Feb. 1, 1922. Her mother, a nurse, took her to Langhirano after the breakup of her marriage to a philandering cellist. There she began to study piano with Giuseppina Passani; at the age of 16 she entered the singing class of Ettore Campogalliani at the Parma Cons.; later she took a course of vocal instruction with the soprano Carmen Melis at the Pesaro Cons. She made her operatic debut in Rovigo as Elena in Boito's *Mefistofele* in 1944. In 1946 Toscanini chose her as one of his artists for the reopening concert at La Scala in Milan, and she subsequently became one of its leading sopranos. She made her first appearance in England in 1950 with the visiting La Scala company at London's Covent Garden; also in 1950 she sang Aida with the San Francisco Opera. On Jan. 31, 1955, she made her Metropolitan Opera debut in N.Y. as Desdemona in Verdi's *Otello;* she continued to appear regularly there until 1973. She toured Russia in 1975 and 1976. Her repertoire was almost exclusively Italian; she excelled in both lyric and dramatic roles; was particularly successful as Violetta, Tosca, Mimi, and Madame Butterfly. She also sang the role of Eva in *Die Meistersinger.* On Nov. 3, 1958, she was the subject of a cover story in *Time* magazine.

Tebaldini, Giovanni, Italian music scholar; b. Brescia, Sept. 7, 1864; d. San Benedetto del Tronto, May 11, 1952. He studied with Ponchielli and Amelli at the Cons. of Milan; served as maestro di cappella at San Marco in Venice (1889–94), at the Padua Cathedral (1894–97), and at the Santa Casa of Loreto (1902–24); was director of the Cons. of Parma (1897–1902); taught at the Cons. di San Pietro in Naples (1925–30); then went to Genoa, where he was appointed director of the Ateneo Musicale (1931). His specialty was Italian sacred music, but his name suddenly sprang into sensational prominence when he publ. an article provocatively entitled "Telepatia musicale" (*Rivista Musicale Italiana,* March 1909), in which he cited thematic similarities between the opera *Cassandra,* by the relatively obscure Italian composer Vittorio Gnecchi, which was produced in 1905, and *Elektra* by Richard Strauss, written considerably later, implying a "telepathic" plagiarism on the part of Strauss. However, the juxtaposition of musical examples from both operas proved specious and failed to support Tebaldini's contention.

Teichmüller, Robert, German pianist and teacher; b. Braunschweig, May 4, 1863; d. Leipzig, May 6, 1939. He studied piano with his father and with Reinecke at the Leipzig Cons., where from 1897 until his death he taught piano; was made a prof. in 1908. With K. Hermann he publ. a valuable guide, *Internationale moderne Klaviermusik* (Leipzig, 1927).

Teike, Carl (Albert Hermann), German composer of band music; b. Altdamm, Feb. 5, 1864; d. Landsberg, May 22, 1922. He studied French horn in his early youth; at 19 joined the band of the 123rd König Karl Regiment, stationed at Ulm on the Danube. He soon began writing marches that were to become perennial favorites with German bands; at 25 he composed *Alte Kameraden (Old Comrades),* one of the best known of German military marches, marked by a typically stolid square rhythm, with heavily accented downbeats. Teike resigned from the regiment as a result of disagreement with the bandmaster and joined the Royal German Police at Potsdam (1895–1908); then served with the postal service at Landsberg; he continued, however, to compose marches; during World War I he wrote the march *Graf Zeppelin* (known in English editions as *Conqueror*) which, despite its narrow militaristic nature, enjoyed international fame.

Te Kanawa, Dame Kiri, brilliant New Zealand soprano; b. Gisborne, March 6, 1944. Her father was an indigenous Maori who traced his ancestry to the legendary warrior Te Kanawa; her mother was Irish. She attended the Catholic schools in Auckland, and was coached in singing by a nun. She was sent to Melbourne to compete in a radio show; she won the first prize in the Melbourne *Sun* contest, and remained in Melbourne, earning her living by singing at various social functions. In 1966 she received a grant for study in London; there she took private vocal lessons with Vera Rozsa. In 1967 she married Desmond Stephen Park, a mining engineer. In 1970 she made her debut at Covent Garden in London, where she sang the role of the Countess in *The Marriage of Figaro.* In the summer of 1971 she sang the same role in her American debut with the Santa Fe Opera; it became one of her most remarkable interpretations. She sang it again with the San Francisco Opera in 1972. A proverbial *coup de théâtre* in her career came on Feb. 9, 1974, when she was called upon to substitute at a few hours' notice for the ailing Teresa Stratas in the part of Desdemona in Verdi's *Otello* at the Metropolitan Opera in N.Y. It was a triumphant achievement against desperate odds (she suffered a cramp in the groin in the 3rd act), winning her unanimous critical praise. On Jan. 11, 1975, she sang Donna Elvira in *Don Giovanni* at the Metropolitan. She also acted in the film production of *The Marriage of Figaro.* She sang Pamina in *Die Zauberflöte* at the Paris Opéra on May 13, 1977. On Dec. 31, 1977, she took the role of Rosalinde in a Covent Garden production of *Die Fledermaus,* which was televised to the U.S. She excelled equally as a subtle and artistic interpreter of lyric roles in Mozart's operas and in dramatic representations of grand operas by Verdi. Critics were unanimous in awarding her the status of *prima donna assoluta.* She was the soloist in "Let the Bright Seraphim" from Handel's oratorio *Samson* at the wedding of Prince Charles and Lady Diana Spencer in 1981. In 1982 she was named a Dame Commander of the Order of the British Empire.

Telemann, Georg Philipp, greatly significant German composer; b. Magdeburg, March 14, 1681; d. Hamburg, June 25, 1767. He received his academic training at a local school; also learned to play keyboard instruments and the violin; he acquired knowledge of music theory from the cantor Benedikt Christiani. He subsequently attended the Gymnasium Andreanum in Hildesheim, where he became active in student performances of German cantatas. In 1701 he entered the Univ. of Leipzig as a student of jurisprudence; in 1702 organized a collegium musicum there; later was appointed music director of the Leipzig Opera, where he used the services of his student singers and instrumentalists. In 1705 he went to Sorau as Kapellmeister to the court of Count Erdmann II of Promnitz. In 1708 he was appointed Konzertmeister to the court orch. in Eisenach; later he was named Kapellmeister there. In 1709 he married Louise Eberlin, a musician's daughter, but she died in 1711 in childbirth. In 1712 Telemann was appointed music director of the city of Frankfurt; there he wrote a quantity of sacred music as well as secular works for the public concerts given by the Frauenstein Society, of which he served as director. In 1714 he married Maria Katharina Textor, the daughter of a local town clerk. They had 8 sons and 2 daughters, of whom only a few survived infancy. His wife later abandoned him for a Swedish army officer. In 1721 he received the post of music director of 5 churches in Hamburg, which became the center of his important activities as composer and music administrator. In 1722 Telemann was appointed music director of the Hamburg Opera, a post he held until 1738. During his tenure he wrote a number of operas for production there, and also staged several works by Handel and Keiser. In 1737–38 he visited France. His eyesight began to fail as he grew older; his great contemporaries Bach and Handel suffered from the same infirmity. An extraordinarily prolific composer, Telemann mastered both the German and the Italian styles of composition prevalent in his day. While he never approached the greatness of genius of Bach and Handel, Telemann nevertheless became an exemplar of the German Baroque at its grandest development. According to Telemann's own account, he composed about 20 operas for Leipzig; wrote about 4 for Weissenfels, 2 for Bayreuth, and 3 operettas for Eisenach. He lists 35 operas for Hamburg, but included in this list are preludes, intermezzi, and postludes.

Telemann, Georg Michael, German theorist and composer; grandson of **Georg Philipp Telemann;** b. Plön, Holstein, April 20, 1748; d. Riga, March 4, 1831. In 1773 he went to Riga and became cantor there (was pensioned in 1828). He publ. *Unterricht im Generalbass-Spielen, auf der Orgel oder sonst einem Clavier-Instrumente* (1773); *Beytrag zur Kirchenmusik* (1785; organ pieces); *Sammlung alter und neuer Kirchenmelodien* (1812); *Über die Wahl der Melodie eines Kirchenliedes* (1821); composed a book of trio sonatas, 6 violin sonatas; organ works.

Tellefsen, Thomas Dyke, Norwegian pianist and composer; b. Trondheim, Nov. 26, 1823; d. Paris, Oct. 6, 1874. In 1842 he went to Paris, where he studied with Kalkbrenner; in 1844 he became a pupil of Chopin, and accompanied him to England and Scotland in 1848. He publ. an edition of Chopin's works, and played Chopin's music at recitals in Paris and in Scandinavia. His own compositions were imitative of Chopin; he wrote nocturnes, waltzes, and mazurkas, but also made use of Norwegian folk songs in many of his works, and thus became an early proponent of national music in Norway.

Temianka, Henri, American violinist and conductor; b. Greenock, Scotland, Nov. 19, 1906, of Polish-Jewish parentage. He was taken to the Netherlands as a child; took violin lessons with Willy Hess in Berlin and Jules Boucherit in Paris. In 1926 he emigrated to America and studied at the Curtis Inst. of Music in Philadelphia with Carl Flesch (violin) and Artur Rodzinski (conducting). In 1946 he became the founder and leader of the Paganini Quartet; appeared as soloist with major orchs. in Europe and America. He settled in Los Angeles, where he organized the California Chamber Symph. (1960), with which he toured in the U.S. and Canada. He publ. a book of reminiscences, *Facing the Music* (N.Y., 1973).

Temirkanov, Yuri, noted Russian conductor; b. Nalchik, in the Caucasus, Dec. 10, 1938. He studied at the Leningrad Cons.; made his conducting debut with the Leningrad Opera in 1965. In 1966 he won first prize in the U.S.S.R. All-Union Conductors' Competition, which energized his career. From 1968 to 1976 he conducted the Leningrad Symph. Orch.; also served as chief conductor of the Kirov Opera and Ballet in Leningrad. He then went on an American tour; conducted in Philadelphia, Cincinnati, San Francisco, and Minneapolis. In 1979 he became principal guest conductor of the Royal Phil. Orch. in London. As is to be expected, he shines most glitteringly in the Russian repertoire, and he invariably places Soviet works on his programs.

Templeton, Alec, blind pianist and composer; b. Cardiff, Wales, July 4, 1909; d. Greenwich, Conn., March 28, 1963. He studied at the Royal College of Music in London until 1923 and at the Royal Academy of Music until 1931. He settled in the U.S. in 1935, becoming a citizen in 1941; was extremely successful as a radio pianist, especially with his humorous musical sketches, parodies, etc., such as *Bach Goes to Town, Mozart Matriculates,* etc. He also wrote some more ambitious works, including *Concertino lirico* (1942) and *Gothic Concerto* for Piano and Orch (N.Y., Dec. 19, 1954, composer soloist).

Templeton, John, Scottish tenor; b. Riccarton, near Kilmarnock, July 30, 1802; d. New Hampton, July 2, 1886. He sang in various churches in Edinburgh; then went to London, where he took lessons in singing with Tom Cooke; also studied theory with Blewitt. On Oct. 13, 1831, he made his debut at Drury Lane Theatre; subsequently became a regular member of Drury Lane. Maria Malibran selected him as tenor for her operatic appearances in London (1833–

35). In 1842 he was in Paris; during the season of 1845–46 he made an American tour announced as "Templeton Entertainment," singing folk songs of Great Britain; his commentaries and reminiscences were publ. as *A Musical Entertainment* (Boston, 1845). He retired in 1852.

Tenducci, Giusto Ferdinando, celebrated Italian castrato; b. Siena, c.1736; d. Genoa, Jan. 25, 1790. He went to England in 1758 and was received with enthusiasm; led the Handel Festivals from 1784 until his departure for Italy in 1789. He was nicknamed "Triorchis" (triple-testicled), on account of the singular plurality of his reproductive organs that enabled him to marry; indeed, he eloped in 1767 with one of his pupils, 16-year old Dorothy Maunsell, but the marriage was annulled in 1775. She publ. an account of the affair under the title *A True and Genuine Narrative of Mr. and Mrs. Tenducci* (London, 1785). He wrote a treatise on singing, *Instruction of Mr. Tenducci to his Scholars* (London, 1785); also composed music for a comic opera, *The Campaign*, produced in London in 1784, and a group of *Ranelagh Songs*.

Tennstedt, Klaus, brilliant German conductor; b. Merseburg, June 6, 1926. He studied piano and violin at the Leipzig Cons.; in 1948 was appointed concertmaster at the municipal theater in Halle, and in 1952 became principal conductor there. He subsequently occupied conducting posts at the Dresden Opera (1958–62) and at the State Theater in Schwerin (1962–71); also conducted concerts with the Gewandhaus Orch. in Leipzig, and filled conducting engagements in Czechoslovakia and Russia. In 1971 he went to Sweden, where he conducted at the State Theater in Göteborg and led the Swedish Radio Symph. in Stockholm. He subsequently was engaged as an opera conductor in Kiel, Germany; in 1974 he was invited to conduct the Toronto Symph. Orch.; this was followed by a highly successful debut with the Boston Symph. Orch.; on Feb. 24, 1977, he began a 2-week engagement with the N.Y. Phil.; from 1979 to 1983 he was guest conductor of the Minnesota Orch. in Minneapolis; concurrently he held the post of chief conductor of the North German Radio Symph. Orch. of Hamburg (1979–82); in 1983 he was engaged to succeed Solti as principal conductor of the London Phil. On Dec. 14, 1983, he made his debut at the Metropolitan Opera in N.Y., in an impressive performance of *Fidelio*. His concerts in Western Europe and in America were received with exceptional acclaim; even his idiosyncrasies (such as bending the knees in anticipation of a powerful crescendo, and other graphic body motions, which caused one critic to liken him to "a demented stork") did not seem to lessen the enthusiasm of both the players and the audiences.

Teodorini, Helena, Rumanian soprano; b. Craiova, March 25, 1857; d. Bucharest, Feb. 27, 1926. She studied piano with Fumagalli and singing with Sangiovanni at the Cons. Verdi in Milan; made her debut as a contralto at the Teatro Municipale in Cuneo in

1879; gradually her voice changed to a mezzo-soprano of wide range. She made her first appearance in La Scala, Milan, on March 20, 1880; then sang in Warsaw (1881), and in Madrid (1884–86); subsequently she toured in South America. In 1905 she established herself as a vocal teacher in Paris; eventually returned to Rumania. In 1964 the Rumanian government issued a postage stamp in her honor bearing her stage portrait.

Ternina, Milka, Croatian soprano; b. Vezisče, near Zagreb, Dec. 19, 1863; d. Zagreb, May 18, 1941. She studied voice at the Vienna Cons. with Gänsbacher; made her operatic debut as Amelia in *Un ballo in maschera* in Zagreb (1882); then sang in Leipzig (1883–84) and Graz (1884–86). She subsequently was a member of the Bremen Opera (1886–89), and of the Munich Opera (1890–99), where she distinguished herself as a Wagnerian singer. She was engaged by Walter Damrosch for his German Opera Co. in N.Y., and made her American debut as Elsa in *Lohengrin* in Boston on March 4, 1896; also appeared at Covent Garden, London, as Isolde (June 3, 1898); after a series of successes at the Bayreuth Festivals, she was engaged by the Metropolitan Opera Co., making her debut there on Jan. 27, 1900, and sang there until 1904 (the 1902–3 season excepted); she sang Tosca at the American premiere (Feb. 4, 1901) and Kundry in *Parsifal* (Dec. 24, 1903). She retired from the stage in 1906 and settled in Zagreb, where she remained until her death.

Terradellas, Domingo (Italianized as **Domenico Terradeglias**), Spanish composer; b. Barcelona (baptized, Feb. 13), 1713; d. Rome, May 20, 1751. He studied with Durante at the Cons. dei Poveri di Gesù Cristo in Naples (1732–36); began his career as a composer with the oratorio *Giuseppe riconosciuto* (1736); then came the opera *Astarto* (Rome, Jan. 3, 1739); from 1743 to 1745, he was at the Spanish church of Santiago y S. Ildefonso, Rome; in 1746 he went to London, where he produced his operas *Mitridate* (Dec. 2, 1746) and *Bellerofonte* (March 24, 1747); he returned to Italy in 1750, after traveling through Belgium and France (1748–49). There is no foundation for the story that he drowned himself in the Tiber owing to the failure of his opera *Sesostri* (Rome, 1751). Twelve arias and 2 duets were publ. in 1747 by J. Walsh of London, who also publ. "the favourite songs" from the operas *Mitridate* and *Bellerofonte*.

Terrasse, Claude, French composer; b. Grand-Lemps, near Grenoble, Jan. 27, 1867; d. Paris, June 30, 1923. He studied at the Lyons Cons. and at the Ecole Niedermeyer in Paris; from 1888 to 1895 was church organist in Arcachon; then in Paris until 1899, when he began to write for the stage, producing a series of successful operettas; the best known are *Les Travaux d'Hercule* (March 7, 1901); *Le Sire de Vergy* (April 16, 1903); *Monsieur de la Palisse* (Nov. 2, 1904); *La Marquise et le marmiton* (Dec. 11, 1907); *Le Coq d'Inde* (April 6, 1909); *Le Mariage de Télémaque* (May 4, 1910); *Les Transatlantiques*

(May 20, 1911); *Cartouche* (March 9, 1912).

Terry, Charles Sanford, eminent English music scholar; b. Newport Pagnell, Buckinghamshire, Oct. 24, 1864; d. Westerton of Pitfodels, near Aberdeen, Nov. 5, 1936. He read history at Clare College, Cambridge, 1883–86; in 1890 became a lecturer in history at Durham College of Science, Newcastle upon Tyne; joined the faculty of the Univ. of Aberdeen, 1898; in 1903–30 held the Burnett-Fletcher chair of history there, and occupied himself with historical research; at the same time he devoted much of his energy to the study of Bach and his period. His biography of Bach (1928; revised ed., 1933; 6th ed., 1967; German trans., Leipzig, 1934) places Bach's life within historical perspective with a fine discernment; it has become a standard in the literature on Bach in English. Other books and editions dealing with Bach include: *Bach's Chorals* (3 vols., 1915–21); *J.S. Bach's Original Hymn-Tunes for Congregational Use* (1922); *J.S. Bach, Cantata Texts, Sacred and Secular* (1926); *The Four-Part Chorals of J.S. Bach* (5 vols., 1929; 2nd ed., 1964); *The Origin of the Family of Bach Musicians* (1929); *Bach: The Historical Approach* (1930); *Bach's Orchestra* (1932; 4th ed., 1966); *The Music of Bach: An Introduction* (1933). To the Musical Pilgrim series he contributed analyses of the B-minor Mass (1924), the cantatas and oratorios (1925), the Passions (1926), and the Magnificat, Lutheran masses, and motets (1929). He arranged and publ. a stage version of the "Coffee Cantata" as *Coffee and Cupid* (1924); also trans. into Eng. Forkel's life of J.S. Bach (1920), and wrote a biography of Johann Christian Bach (1929; 2nd ed., revised, 1967, prepared by H.C. Landons Robbin).

Terry, Sir Richard Runciman, English music editor; b. Ellington, Northumberland, Jan. 3, 1865; d. London, April 18, 1938. In 1890 he was appointed organist and music master at Elstow School; in 1892–96, was organist and choirmaster at St. John's Cathedral, Antigua, West Indies; in 1896–1901, was at Downside Abbey. There he attracted attention by his revival of the Catholic church music of early English masters (Byrd, Tallis, Tye, Morley, Mundy, White, Fayrfax, etc.); in 1901–24, he was organist and director of music at Westminster Cathedral. He was chairman of the committee appointed to prepare the Eng. supplement of the Vatican Antiphonary, and music editor of the *Westminster Hymnal,* the official Roman Catholic hymnal for England. He was knighted in 1922. Besides masses, motets, and other church music, he composed 48 *Old Rhymes with New Tunes* (1934). He edited *The Shanty Book* (2 vols.; 1921; 1926); *Old Christmas Carols* (1923); *Hymns of Western Europe* (with Davies and Hadow; 1927); *Salt Sea Ballads* (1931); *A Medieval Carol Book* (1932); *200 Folk Carols* (1933); *Calvin's First Psalter* [1539], harmonized (1932); also the collections of 16th-century music *Downside Masses* and *Downside Motets, Motets Ancient and Modern,* and many separate works by early Eng. composers. He wrote the books *Catholic Church Music* (1907; 2nd ed., enlarged, entitled *The Music*

of the Roman Rite, 1931), *On Music's Borders* (1927), *A Forgotten Psalter and Other Essays* (1929), *The Music of the Roman Rite* (1931), *Voodooism in Music and Other Essays* (1934).

Tertis, Lionel, eminent English viola player; b. West Hartlepool, Dec. 29, 1876; d. London, Feb. 22, 1975. He studied violin at the Leipzig Cons. and at the Royal Academy of Music in London; played the viola in various quartets, and decided to make it his chief instrument. He eventually became one of the most renowned viola players in Europe; traveled also in America. He was named in 1950 a Commander of the Order of the British Empire. He wrote *Beauty of Tone in String Playing* (London, 1938); a 2-vol. autobiography, *Cinderella No More* (1953) and *My Viola and I: A Complete Autobiography* (1974). He designed and publ. specifications of a very large viola: see *Music & Letters* (July 1947).

Terziani, Eugenio, Italian composer; b. Rome, July 29, 1824; d. there, June 30, 1889. He studied with Mercadante at the Naples Cons.; at the age of 19 produced an oratorio, *La caduta di Gerico* (Rome, March 31, 1844), followed by the operas *Giovanna regina di Napoli* (Ferrara, 1844) and *Alfredo* (Rome, Feb. 21, 1852); was conductor in Rome at the Teatro Apollo from 1847 to 1869, at La Scala, Milan (1867–71), then in Rome again in 1871–75, and finally (from 1875) prof. of composition at the Santa Cecilia Academy in Rome. His last opera, *L'assedio di Firenze,* was produced in Rome on Feb. 24, 1883. He was also the composer of a ballet, *Una Silfide a Pechino* (Rome, Dec. 26, 1859), and of much sacred music.

Tesi (Tesi-Tramontini), Vittoria, famous Italian contralto; b. Florence, Feb. 13, 1700; d. Vienna, May 9, 1775. She received her instruction in Florence and Bologna; appeared on the stage at the age of 16 in Parma; then was engaged at Venice (1718) and Dresden (1719). She sang in Italy every year, and also appeared in Madrid (1739) and Vienna (1747–48). She was married to one Tramontini, a barber by trade, and adopted the professional name Tesi-Tramontini. She was remarkably free in her morals, and many stories, in which it is impossible to separate truth from invention, were circulated about her life. Her letters to a priest were publ. by Benedetto Croce in his book *Un Prelato e una cantante del secolo XVIII* (Bari, 1946).

Tess (original name, **Tesscorolo**), **Giulia,** noted Italian soprano; b. Verona, Feb. 9, 1889; d. Milan, March 17, 1976. She made her debut as a mezzo-soprano in 1904 in Prato; later sang soprano roles after being encouraged by Battistini. In 1922 she was invited by Toscanini to sing at La Scala in Milan, where she created the role of Jaele in Pizzetti's *Debora e Jaele.* From 1940 she taught voice in Florence, and then in Milan at the La Scala Opera School (from 1946); her students included Tagliavini and Barbieri; she also produced opera at La Scala and other Italian opera houses. In addition to the Italian repertoire, she gained distinction as an interpreter of roles by Richard Strauss, excelling as Salome and Elektra.

Tetrazzini, Eva, Italian soprano; sister of **Luisa Tetrazzini;** b. Milan, March, 1862; d. Salsomaggiore, Oct. 27, 1938. She studied with Ceccherini in Florence, and made her debut there in 1882, as Marguerite in *Faust.* She sang Desdemona in Verdi's *Otello* at its first American production (N.Y., April 16, 1888). On May 15, 1887, she married the conductor **Cleofonte Campanini.** She sang with the Manhattan Opera in N.Y. in 1908; then returned to Italy.

Tetrazzini, Luisa (real Christian name, **Luigia**), celebrated Italian coloratura soprano; b. Florence, June 28, 1871; d. Milan, April 28, 1940. She learned the words and music of several operas by listening to her elder sister **Eva;** then studied at the Liceo Musicale in Florence with Ceccherini, who was also her sister's teacher. She made her opera debut as Inez in *L'Africaine* in Florence (1890); then traveled with various opera companies to South America. In 1904 she reached the U.S. and made her American debut at the Tivoli Opera House in San Francisco. She made her London debut at Covent Garden as Violetta on Nov. 2, 1907. She was then engaged by Hammerstein to sing with his Manhattan Opera House in N.Y., where she sang Violetta on Jan. 15, 1908; she remained with the Manhattan Opera until its closing in 1910; subsequently appeared for a single season at the Metropolitan Opera (1911–12), making her debut there on Dec. 27, 1911, as Lucia. She made the first broadcast on the British radio in 1925; her last American appearance was in N.Y. in 1931. She then returned to Italy and taught singing in Milan. Her fame was worldwide, and her name became a household word, glorified even in food, as in Turkey Tetrazzini. She publ. *My Life of Song* (London, 1921) and *How to Sing* (N.Y., 1923). She acquired a great fortune, only to die in poverty.

Teyte (real name, **Tate**), **Maggie,** English soprano; b. Wolverhampton, April 17, 1888; d. London, May 26, 1976. She studied in London; then was a pupil of Jean de Reszke in Paris (1903–7). In order to ensure correct pronunciation of her name in France, she changed the original spelling *Tate* to *Teyte.* She made her operatic debut as Zerlina at Monte Carlo (1907); was very successful as a concert singer in Paris, and appeared with Debussy at the piano; Debussy also selected her as successor to Mary Garden in the role of Mélisande (1908). She sang at the Opéra-Comique (1908–10), with Beecham's Opera Co. in London (1910–11), with the Chicago Opera Co. (1911–14), and with the Boston Grand Opera Co. (1915–17). She continued her recitals of French music in London during World War II. In 1958 she was named a Dame of the British Empire. She had 2 indifferent husbands and 2 prominent lovers: Sir Thomas Beecham in London and Georges Enesco in Paris. She publ. a book of memoirs, *Star on the Door* (London, 1958).

Thalberg, Sigismond, celebrated piano virtuoso and composer; b. Geneva, Jan. 8, 1812; d. Posilipo, near Naples, April 27, 1871. His parents were Joseph Thalberg of Frankfurt and Fortunée Stein, also of Frankfurt, but resident in Geneva. Thalberg, however, pretended to be the natural son of Prince Moritz Dietrichstein, who took charge of his education. His first instructor was Mittag, the bassoonist of the Vienna Court Opera; he subsequently studied piano with Hummel and composition with Sechter. He played as a precocious pianist in the aristocratic salons of Vienna, and began to compose piano music. In 1830 he made a successful concert tour through Germany; in 1834 he was appointed court pianist in Vienna; in 1835 he went to Paris, where he perfected his playing under Kalkbrenner; from that time he became one of the most admired piano virtuosos of Paris, and soon extended his triumphs through most of Europe, including Russia. In 1843 he married the widow of the painter Boucher. In 1855 he set out on a concert tour through Brazil and the U.S. (1856); made a 2nd Brazilian tour in 1863, and in 1864 retired to Naples. Thalberg was unexcelled as a performer of fashionable salon music and virtuoso studies. He possessed a wonderful legato, eliciting from Liszt the remark, "Thalberg is the only artist who can play the violin on the keyboard." His technical specialty was to play a central melody with the thumb of either hand, surrounding it with brilliant arpeggios and arabesques. To present this technique graphically in notation, he made use of the method initiated by Francesco Pollini of writing piano music on 3 staves. He wrote 2 operas, *Florinda* (London, July 3, 1851) and *Cristina di Suezia* (Vienna, June 3, 1855), which were not successful; but his brilliant piano pieces were the rage of his day, easily eclipsing in popular favor those of Chopin, his close contemporary. Among them are a group of nocturnes; several *Caprices; 2 Romances sans paroles; Grandes valses brillantes; Le Départ, varié en forme d'étude; Marche funèbre variée; Barcarole; Valse mélodique; Les Capricieuses; Tarentelle; Souvenir de Pest; La Cadence* (very popular); *Les Soirées de Pausilippe* (6 albums); *Célèbre Ballade; La Napolitaine;* several sonatas, many pianistic studies; fantasies on operas by Rossini, Bellini, Meyerbeer, Weber, Verdi, and others.

Thayer, Alexander Wheelock, American writer and authority on Beethoven; b. South Natick, Mass., Oct. 22, 1817; d. Trieste, July 15, 1897. After graduation from Harvard Univ. in 1843, he became assistant librarian there; during 6 years' work in the library, he matured a plan for writing a detailed and trustworthy biography of Beethoven. For preliminary study, and to collect material, he first spent 2 years (1849–51) in Germany, also writing letters for newspapers; in 1852 he joined the staff of the *N.Y. Tribune,* and returned to Europe in 1854, where, excepting 2 years (1856–58) spent in Boston, he remained. Dr. Lowell Mason and Mrs. Mehetable Adams (of Cambridge, Mass.) gave generous and disinterested aid at this juncture. In 1862 Thayer was attached to the American embassy at Vienna;

in 1865 Abraham Lincoln appointed him consul at Trieste, a post held until 1882. He then publ. a *Chronologisches Verzeichniss der Werke Ludwig van Beethoven* (Berlin, 1865); in 1866, vol. I of his life-work, *Ludwig van Beethovens Leben*, appeared in German, trans. from the Eng. MS by Deiters; vol. II was publ. in 1872; vol. III, in 1879. In 1877 he publ. *Ein kritischer Beitrag zur Beethoven-Litteratur.* Unhappily, his wonderful capacity for work was overtaxed, and vol. IV of his nobly conceived work, executed with a painstaking thoroughness and scrupulous fidelity beyond praise, was left unfinished. Though he lived for years in straitened circumstances, he resolutely refused offers from firms like Novello & Co. and G. Schirmer, hoping to recast entirely the Eng. version of his *Beethoven,* which was publ. in 3 vols. by Krehbiel in 1921. A redaction, titled *Thayer's Life of Beethoven,* prepared by Elliot Forbes, was publ. in 1964 (2nd ed., revised, 1967).

Thebom, Blanche, American mezzo-soprano; b. Monessen, Pa., Sept. 19, 1918, of Swedish parents. She studied singing with Margaret Matzenauer and Edyth Walker; made her concert debut in N.Y. on Jan. 12, 1944, and her operatic debut at the Metropolitan Opera, N.Y., as Fricka, Dec. 14, 1944; remained on its roster until 1959, and again from 1960 to 1967; also sang in various opera houses in America and Europe, with increasing success. In 1958 she appeared as a guest artist in Russia. In 1967 she was appointed head of the Southern Regional Opera Co. in Atlanta; it folded in 1968; in 1980 she was appointed director of the opera workshop of San Francisco State Univ. Among her best roles are Ortrud in *Lohengrin,* Azucena in *Il Trovatore,* Amneris in *Aida,* Laura in *La Gioconda,* and Carmen.

Theile, Johann, German composer; b. Naumburg, July 29, 1646; d. there (buried, June 24), 1724. He was a pupil of H. Schütz at Weissenfels; in 1673, became Kapellmeister to the Duke of Holstein at Gottorf; went to Hamburg and wrote (for the opening of the Hamburg Opera House in 1678) the singspiels *Adam und Eva* (Jan. 12, 1678) and *Orontos;* he also produced a Christmas Oratorio in 1681. In 1685, he became Kapellmeister to the Braunschweig court at Wolfenbüttel; then became Kapellmeister at Merseburg (1691). He eventually settled in Naumburg c.1718. He was called by contemporaries "the father of counterpoint." Among his numerous pupils were Buxtehude and Zachau.

Theodorakis, Mikis (Michael George), Greek composer; b. Chios, July 29, 1925. He studied at the Athens Cons.; composed melodies in the authentic spirit of modern Greek folk songs; wrote music for productions of ancient Greek tragedies, among them *Œdipus Tyrannos.* He achieved international success with the musical score for the film *Zorba the Greek.* At the same time he was actively engaged in politics. In 1963 he was chosen chairman of the Greek United Democratic Left Party; in 1964 he was elected a member of the Greek Parliament and joined the Communist Party. After the military

coup of 1967 he was arrested and held on a farm near Corinth; later was sent to Zatouna, in the central Peloponnesus; there he wrote the music for the film Z, dealing with the police murder of the Socialist politician Gregory Lambrakis in Salonika in 1963. The film and the music were greatly acclaimed in Europe and America, and the fate of Theodorakis became a cause célèbre. Yielding to pressure from the international public opinion, the military Greek government freed Theodorakis in 1970, and he went to Paris; in July 1970 he was a participant in the Congress at the United Nations World Youth Assembly in N.Y.

Theremin, Leon (real name, **Termen;** pronounced in Russian with the accent on the last syllable; gallicized as Thérémin; Anglicized as Theremin, with the accent on the first syllable), Russian inventor of the space-controlled electronic instrument that bears his name; b. St. Petersburg, Aug. 15, 1896. He studied physics and astronomy at the Univ. there; also cello and theory. He continued his studies in physics at the Leningrad Physico-Technical Inst., where in 1919 he became director of the Laboratory of Electrical Oscillators. On Aug. 5, 1920, he gave a demonstration at the Physico-Technical Inst. in Petrograd of his Aetherophone, which was the prototype of the Thereminovox, later known simply as Theremin. He also gave a special demonstration of it for Lenin, who was interested in artistic uses of electricity. In 1927 he demonstrated his new instruments in Germany, France, and the U.S., where on Feb. 28, 1928, he obtained a patent for the Thereminovox. On April 29, 1930, at Carnegie Hall, he presented a concert with an ensemble of 10 of his instruments, also introducing a space-controlled synthesis of color and music. On April 1, 1932, in the same hall, he introduced the first electrical symph. orch., conducted by Stoessel, including Theremin fingerboard and keyboard instruments. He also invented the Rhythmicon, for playing different rhythms simultaneously or separately (introduced by Henry Cowell), and an automatic musical instrument for playing directly from specially written musical scores (constructed for Percy Grainger). Until 1938 Theremin was director of his own research laboratory in N.Y.; he then returned to Russia. In 1964 he was appointed a prof. of acoustics at the Moscow Univ.; was still active in 1977.

Thibaud, Jacques, celebrated French violinist; b. Bordeaux, Sept. 27, 1880; d. (in an airplane crash near Mt. Cemet, in the French Alps) Sept. 1, 1953, en route to French Indo-China. He was taught by his father, and then entered the class of Martin Marsick at the Paris Cons., winning first prize in 1896. Obliged to earn his living, he played the violin at the Café Rouge, where he was heard by the conductor Colonne, who offered him a position in his orch.; in 1898 he made his debut as a soloist (with Colonne) with such success that he was engaged for 54 concerts in Paris in the same season. Subsequently he appeared in all the musical centers of Europe, and from 1903 visited America numerous times. With his 2 brothers, a pianist and a cellist, he formed a trio, which had some success; but this was discontinued when he joined Alfred Cortot and Pablo Casals in a famous trio. His playing was notable for its warmth of expressive tone and fine dynamics; his interpretations of Beethoven ranked very high, but he was particularly authoritative in French music.

Thibault, Geneviève (Comtesse de Chambure), French musicologist; b. Neuilly-sur-Seine, May 20, 1902; d. Strasbourg, Aug. 31, 1975. She studied at the Sorbonne in Paris, under André Pirro; then became engaged in business, but continued her great interest in musical research; assembled a fine private library, containing rare editions of Renaissance music, which she opened to research scholars; initiated the Société de Musique d'Autrefois, for the purpose of presenting concerts of old music performed on old instruments; from 1955 she lectured at the Sorbonne. Her own contributions to musicology (usually in collaboration with other scholars) include: *Poètes et musiciens du XVe siècle* (Paris, 1924; with E. Droz); *Trois chansonniers français du XVe siècle* (Paris, 1927; with A. Pirro, E. Droz, and Y. Rokseth); *Bibliographie des poésies de P. de Ronsard mises en musique au XVIe siècle* (Paris, 1941; with L. Perceau); *Bibliographie des éditions d'Adrien Le Roy et Robert Ballard* (Paris, 1955; with F. Lesure); *Eighteenth-Century Musical Instruments in France and Britain* (London, 1973). She also compiled an inventory of musical-instrument collections, completed after her death by Jean Jenkins (Amsterdam, 1978).

Thibaut, Anton Friedrich Justus, German music scholar and learned collector; b. Hameln, Jan. 4, 1772; d. Heidelberg, March 28, 1840. He studied law, and from 1806 was a prof. of jurisprudence in Heidelberg; was also director of a singing club there; wrote *Über Reinheit der Tonkunst* (1825; often republ.; new ed., with biography of Thibaut by R. Heuler, 1907; in Eng. as *On Purity in Musical Art,* 1877). His valuable music library (catalogue publ. in 1842) was acquired by the Hofbibliothek in Munich.

Thibaut IV, King of Navarre and **Count of Champagne,** one of the most notable of the trouvères; b. Troyes, May 30, 1201; d. Pamplona, July 7, 1253. Sixty-three of his songs were publ. by Bishop La Ravallière in 1742 as *Poésies du Roi de Navarre;* the transcription of the melodies is very faulty. In Pierre Aubry's ed. of the *Chansonnier de l'Arsenal* (Paris, 1909), there are 59 melodies by Thibaut transcribed in modern notation; see also the examples in J. Beck's transcription of the *Chansonnier Cangé (Les Chansonniers des troubadours et des trouvères),* 4 vols. (Philadelphia, 1927–38), and A. Schering, *Geschichte der Musik in Beispielen* (1931, p. 7).

Thiriet, Maurice, French composer; b. Meulan, May 2, 1906; d. Puys, near Dieppe, Sept. 28, 1972. He studied with Charles Koechlin and Roland-Manuel; then became engaged in radio work in Paris. His music reflects his preoccupation with the theater.

WORKS: Opera-bouffe, *Le Bourgeois de Falaise* (Paris, June 21, 1937); *Rapsodie sur des thèmes incas* for Orch. (Lyons, Jan. 20, 1936); *Afriques* for Orch. (1949); ballets: *La Nuit vénitienne* (Paris Opéra, March 17, 1938); *La Précaution inutile,* on themes by Rossini (1946); *Bonaparte à Nice* (Nice, 1960); *Le More de Venise* (Monte Carlo, 1960); *Les Amants de Mayerling* (Nice, 1961); *La Chambre noire* (Toulouse, 1969); *Blues de l'horloge* for Violin and Piano; songs; piano pieces.

Thomán, István, Hungarian pianist and pedagogue; b. Homonna, Nov. 4, 1862; d. Budapest, Sept. 22, 1940. He studied with Erkel and Volkmann, and was a piano student of Liszt. In 1888 he was appointed a prof. at the Royal Music Academy in Budapest; retired from teaching in 1906. He was greatly esteemed as a teacher; among his students were Dohnányi and Béla Bartók. He publ. a collection of technical piano studies in 6 vols., and also composed songs and piano pieces. His wife, **Valerie Thomán** (b. Budapest, Aug. 16, 1878; d. there, Sept. 8, 1948), was a renowned concert singer, who gave early performances of works by Kodály and Bartók; their daughter **Maria Thomán** (b. Budapest, July 12, 1899; d. there, Feb. 25, 1948) was an excellent violinist.

Thomas, (Charles Louis) Ambroise, French composer; one of the finest representatives of Romantic French opera; b. Metz, Aug. 5, 1811; d. Paris, Feb. 12, 1896. He entered the Paris Cons. in 1828; his teachers there were Zimmermann (piano) and Dourlen (harmony and accompaniment); he studied privately with Kalkbrenner (piano) and Barbereau (harmony); later with Lesueur (composition); in 1829 he won the first prize for piano playing, in 1830 for harmony, and in 1832 the Grand Prix de Rome, with the dramatic cantata *Hermann et Ketty.* After 3 years in Italy, and a visit to Vienna, he returned to Paris and applied himself with great energy to the composition of operas. In 1851 he was elected to the Académie; in 1856 he became a prof. of composition at the Paris Cons.; in 1871 he became director there, as successor to Auber (disregarding the brief incumbency of Salvador Daniel, adherent of the Paris Commune, who was killed in battle on May 23, 1871). As a composer of melodious operas in the French style, he was second only to Gounod; his masterpiece was *Mignon,* based on Goethe's *Wilhelm Meister* (Opéra-Comique, Nov. 17, 1866); this opera became a mainstay of the repertoire all over the world; it had nearly 2,000 performances in less then 100 years at the Opéra-Comique alone. Equally successful was his Shakespearean opera *Hamlet,* produced shortly after *Mignon* (Paris Opéra, March 9, 1868).

WORKS: The complete list of his operas (all produced in Paris) includes: *La Double Echelle* (Aug. 23, 1837); *Le Perruquier de la régence* (March 30, 1838); *Le Panier fleuri* (May 6, 1839); *Carline* (Feb. 24, 1840); *Le Comte de Carmagnola* (April 19, 1841); *Le Guerillero* (June 22, 1842); *Angélique et Médor* (May 10, 1843); *Mina, ou Le Ménage à trois* (Oct. 10, 1843); *Le Caïd* (Jan. 3, 1849); *Le Songe d'une nuit d'été* (April 20, 1850); *Raymond, ou Le Secret de la reine* (June 5, 1851); *La Tonelli* (March 30, 1853); *La Cour de Célimène* (April 11, 1855); *Psyché* (Jan. 26, 1857); *Le Carnaval de Venise* (Dec. 9, 1857); *Le Roman d'Elvire* (Feb. 4, 1860); *Mignon* (Nov. 17, 1866); *Hamlet* (March 9, 1868); *Gille et Gillotin* (April 22, 1874); *Françoise de Rimini* (April 14, 1882). He contributed an act to a ballet, *La Gipsy* (Paris, Jan. 28, 1839), and wrote the ballets *Betty* (Paris, July 10, 1846) and *La Tempête* (Paris, June 26, 1889); *Messe solennelle* (1857); other sacred works; some chamber music; songs.

Thomas, Arthur Goring, English composer; b. Ratton Park, Sussex, Nov. 20, 1850; d. London, March 20, 1892. He was a pupil of Emile Durand in Paris (1874–77), and of Arthur Sullivan and Ebenezer Prout at the Royal Academy of Music in London; later studied orchestration in Berlin with Max Bruch. He was mainly interested in creating English operas in the best German tradition; his operas were performed in England and Germany, and he had many important supporters for his art in England, but his music totally lacked vitality, and became of only antiquarian interest after his death. In the last year of his life he suffered from a mental illness.

WORKS: Operas: *The Light of the Harem* (partial perf., London, Nov. 7, 1879); *Esmeralda* (London, March 26, 1883; also in German, produced in Berlin, Hamburg, and Cologne); *Nadezhda* (London, April 16, 1885); *The Golden Web* (posthumous; Liverpool, Feb. 15, 1893). He further wrote a choral ode, *The Sun Worshippers* (Norwich Festival, 1881); cantata, *The Swan and the Skylark* (posthumous; Birmingham Festival, 1894; orchestrated by C.V. Stanford); vocal scene, *Hero and Leander* (1880); *Out of the Deep,* anthem for Soprano Solo, Chorus, and Orch. (1878); some chamber music; songs.

Thomas, Jess, American tenor; b. Hot Springs, S.Dak., Aug. 4, 1927. After studying psychology at the Univ. of Nebraska and at Stanford Univ., he turned to singing; went to Europe and in 1958 was accepted as a member of the Karlsruhe Opera; in 1962 he sang at the Württemberg State Opera in Stuttgart; and in 1963 joined the Bavarian State Opera in Munich, where he was named Kammersänger, an uncommon distinction for an American. He then sang at the Vienna Opera in 1965 and at the Berlin Opera in 1969; in 1973 he was engaged by the Zürich Opera. On Dec. 11, 1962, he made his debut at the Metropolitan Opera in N.Y. as Walter in *Die Meistersinger.*

Thomas, John, celebrated Welsh harpist; b. Bridgend, Glamorganshire, March 1, 1826; d. London, March 19, 1913. He also used the names **Aptommas** (or **Apthomas;** i.e., son of Thomas) and **Pencerdd Gwalia** (Chief of Minstrels, bardic name bestowed on him at the Aberdare Eisteddfod in 1861). He entered the Royal Academy at 14; studied harp with Chatterton, and upon the latter's death in 1872, succeeded him as Harpist to the Queen. He gave in London a series of annual concerts of Welsh music; the first took place at St. James's Hall, July 4, 1862, with a chorus of 400, and 20 harps. He was also a leader of the Eisteddfod festivals. He wrote 2 harp concertos; the dramatic cantata *Llewelyn* (1863) and *The Bride of Neath Valley,* a Welsh scene (1866); publ. a collection of Welsh melodies (1862) and a *History of the Harp* (London, 1859); made transcriptions for harp of many classical pieces. His brother, **Thomas Thomas** (1829–1913), also a harpist, went to America in 1895, eventually settling in Ottawa.

Thomas, John Charles, American baritone; b. Meyersdale, Pa., Sept. 6, 1891; d. Apple Valley, Calif., Dec. 13, 1960. He studied at the Peabody Cons. in Baltimore; from 1913 sang in musical comedy in N.Y.; then entered the concert field, in which he achieved outstanding success. He also sang in opera; was a member of the Théâtre de la Monnaie in Brussels (1925–28); later at Covent Garden, London (made his debut on June 28, 1928, as Valentin in *Faust*). In 1930 he appeared with the Chicago Opera Co.; on Feb. 2, 1934, he sang the role of the elder Germont in *La Traviata,* at his first appearance with the Metropolitan Opera; he continued to be on its roster until 1943; then settled in California.

Thomas, Michael Tilson, greatly talented American conductor; b. Los Angeles, Dec. 21, 1944. A grandson of Boris and Bessie Thomashefsky, founders of the Yiddish Theater in N.Y., he was brought up in a cultural atmosphere; he studied at the Univ. of Southern Calif., where he received instruction in composition with Ingolf Dahl; he also studied with the pianist John Crown and the harpsichordist Alice Ehlers; concurrently he took courses in chemistry. He acquired his conductorial skill by practical work with the Young Musicians Foundation Debut Orch., which he began to conduct at the age of 19, in 1963; he held this post for 4 years. He served as pianist in the master classes of Heifetz and Piatigorsky at the Univ. of Southern Calif. in Los Angeles; also conducted at the Monday Evening Concerts, where he presented first performances of works by Stravinsky, Copland, Boulez, and Stockhausen. In 1966 he attended master classes at the Bayreuth Festival; in 1967 he was assistant conductor to Boulez at the Ojai Festival; he conducted there also in 1968, 1969, and 1973. As a conducting fellow at the Berkshire Music Center at Tanglewood in 1968, he won the Koussevitzky Prize. The crowning point of his career was his appointment in 1969 as assistant conductor of the Boston Symph. Orch.; he was the youngest to receive such a distinction with that great ensemble. He was spectacularly catapulted into public notice on Oct. 22, 1969, when he was called upon to conduct the 2nd part of the N.Y. concert of the Boston Symph. Orch., substituting for its music director, William Steinberg, who was taken suddenly ill. In 1970 he was appointed associate conductor of the Boston Symph. Orch., and then was a principal guest conductor there with Colin Davis from 1972 to 1974. From 1971 to 1979 he was music director of the Buffalo Phil. Orch.; served as music director of the N.Y. Phil. Young People's Concerts (1971–76). In 1981 he became a principal guest conductor of the Los Angeles Phil. Orch., sharing the post with Simon Rattle. He also conducted guest engagements in Germany, Spain, Israel, and Japan. Among his avocations is dancing, in which he excels astonishingly well. He is also an excellent pianist. Above all, he is a modern musician, energetic, pragmatically proficient, and able to extract the maximum value of the music on hand.

Thomas, Theodore, renowned German-American conductor; b. Esens, East Friesland, Oct. 11, 1835; d. Chicago, Jan. 4, 1905. Taught by his father, a violinist, he played in public at the age of 6. In 1845 the family went to N.Y., where Thomas soon began to play for dances, weddings, and in theaters, helping to support the family; in 1851 he made a concert tour as a soloist, and in 1853 he joined Jullien's orch. on its visit to N.Y., later touring the country with Jenny Lind, Grisi, Sontag, Mario, etc. He became a member of the N.Y. Phil. Society in 1854. In 1862 he organized an orch. for "Symphony Soirées" at Irving Hall in N.Y., which were continued until 1878 (after 1872, in Steinway Hall); in 1866 he began a series of summer concerts in Terrace Garden, relocating these in 1868 to Central Park Garden. The influence of these enterprises on musical culture in N.Y. was enormous; Thomas's programs attained European celebrity. The first concert tour with the orch. was made in 1869, with 54 players, and for 9 consecutive years he made annual tours of the East and Midwest. In 1873 he established the famous Cincinnati Biennial Festival, which he conducted till his death. He also founded the Cincinnati College of Music, of which he was president and director in 1878–80, having given up his own orch. in N.Y. and the conductorship of the N.Y. Phil. Society (1877–78) to accept this post. After his resignation he returned to N.Y., where he immediately reorganized his own orch. and was reelected conductor of the Phil. Society Orch. and the Brooklyn Phil. Orch. (having been conductor of the latter in 1862–63, 1866–68, and 1873–78). Besides conducting these orch. bodies, he was at different times director of several choruses; in 1885–87 he was conductor and artistic director of the American Opera Co. In 1891 he settled permanently in Chicago as conductor of the Chicago Orch. In recognition of Thomas's distinguished services, a permanent home, Orch. Hall, was built by popular subscription, and formally opened in Dec. 1904, with a series of festival concerts, which were the last directed by him. After his death the name of the orch. was changed to the Theodore Thomas Orch.; in 1912 the final title, Chicago Orch., was officially reinstated.

The influence of Thomas upon the musical development of the U.S. has been strong and lasting. An ardent apostle of Wagner, Liszt, and Brahms, he also played for the first time in America works of Tchaikovsky, Dvořák, Rubinstein, Bruckner, Goldmark, Saint-Saëns, Cowen, Stanford, Raff, and Richard Strauss.

Thomé, Francis (baptismal names, **Joseph-François-Luc**), French composer; b. Port Louis, Island of Mauritius, Oct. 18, 1850; d. Paris, Nov. 16, 1909. He went to Paris as a youth, and studied at the Cons. with Marmontel (piano) and Duprato (theory). He became a successful teacher; wrote the operas *Le Caprice de la Reine* (Cannes, April 1892) and *Le Château de Königsberg* (Paris, April 22, 1896); the ballets *Djemmah* (1886), *La Folie parisienne* (1900), etc.; the religious mystery play *L'Enfant Jésus* (1891); 2 symph. odes, *Hymne à la nuit* and *Vénus et Adonis;* etc. But he is remembered chiefly for his piano pieces, of which *Simple aveu* and *Les Lutins* became very popular.

Thompson, John Sylvanus, American pianist and teacher; b. Williamstown, Pa., March 8, 1889; d. Tucson, Ariz., March 1, 1963. He was educated at the Leefson-Hille Cons. in Philadelphia, and at the Univ. of Pa. He traveled through the U.S. as a concert pianist; also appeared in London and Berlin. In 1917 he settled in Kansas City. He publ. much teaching material, including the very successful *Modern Course for Piano (Something New Every Lesson)* (Cincinnati, 1936; 6 vols.); *The Adult Preparatory Piano Book* (Cincinnati, 1943); *Melody All the Way* (7 vols., Cincinnati, 1949–51; the last 2 vols. are subtitled *Supplementary Piano Course*).

Thompson, Oscar, American music critic and editor; b. Crawfordsville, Ind., Oct. 10, 1887; d. New York, July 3, 1945. He was educated at the Univ. of Washington, Seattle; studied music with G. Campanari and others; took up journalism and in 1919 joined the staff of *Musical America,* later becoming associate editor and finally editor (1936–43). He was music critic for the *N.Y. Evening Post* (1928–34); from 1937 to his death was music critic for the *N.Y. Sun* (succeeding W.J. Henderson). In 1928 he established the first class in music criticism in the U.S., at the Curtis Inst. in Philadelphia; he also gave courses at the N.Y. College of Music. In 1939 he brought out *The International Cyclopedia of Music and Musicians* in one vol. of more than 2,000 pages, with feature articles by eminent authorities; it went through 10 editions and reprints. He wrote the books *Practical Musical Criticism* (1934); *How to Understand Music* (1935); *Tabulated Biographical History of Music* (1936); *The American Singer* (1937); *Debussy, Man and Artist* (1937); ed. *Plots of the Operas* (1940) and *Great Modern Composers* (1941), both vols. being extracts from the *Cyclopedia.*

Thompson, Randall, eminent American composer and pedagogue; b. New York, April 21, 1899; d. Boston, July 9, 1984. He was a member of an intellectual New England family; studied at Lawrenceville School in New Jersey, where his father was an English teacher; he began taking singing lessons and received his rudimentary music training as page turner for a local organist named Francis Cuyler

Van Dyck, who played Bach. When he died, Thompson took over his organ duties in the school. Upon graduation, he went to Harvard Univ., where he studied academic music subjects with Walter Spalding, Edward Burlingame Hill, and Archibald T. Davison. He obtained his B.A. degree in 1920 and his M.A. in 1922. In 1920–21 he had some private lessons in N.Y. with Ernest Bloch. In 1922 he submitted his orch. prelude *Pierrot and Cothurnus,* inspired by the poetical drama *Aria da Capo* by Edna St. Vincent Millay, for the American Prix de Rome, and received a grant for residence in Rome; he conducted it there at the Santa Cecilia Academy on May 17, 1923. Encouraged by its reception, he proceeded to compose industriously, for piano, for voices, and for orch. He returned to the U.S. in 1925. From 1927 to 1929 he taught at Wellesley College; in 1929 he was appointed a lecturer in music at Harvard Univ.; in 1929–30 he held a Guggenheim fellowship. On Feb. 20, 1930, his First Symph. had its premiere in Rochester, N.Y., with Howard Hanson conducting, and on March 24, 1932, Hanson conducted in Rochester the first performance of Thompson's 2nd Symph., which was destined to become one of the most successful symph. works by an American composer; it enjoyed repeated performances in the U.S. and also in Europe. Audiences found the work distinctly American in substance; the unusual element was the inclusion of jazz rhythms in the score. Equally American and equally appealing, although for entirely different reasons, was his choral work *Americana,* to texts from Mencken's satirical column in his journal, the *American Mercury.* There followed another piece of Americana, the nostalgic a cappella choral work *The Peaceable Kingdom,* written in 1936, and inspired by the painting of that name by the naturalistic fantasist Edward Hicks; for it, Thompson used biblical texts from the Prophets. Another piece for a cappella chorus, deeply religious in its nature, was *Alleluia* (1940), which became a perennial favorite in the choral literature; it was first performed at Tanglewood, Mass., at the inaugural session of the Berkshire Music Center, on July 8, 1940. In 1942 Thompson composed his most celebrated piece of choral writing, *The Testament of Freedom,* to words of Thomas Jefferson; it was first performed with piano accompaniment at the Univ. of Virginia on April 13, 1943. A version with orch. was presented by the Boston Symph. Orch. on April 6, 1945. With this work Thompson firmly established his reputation as one of the finest composers of choral music in America. But he did not limit himself to choral music. His First String Quartet in D minor (1941) was praised, as was his only opera, *Solomon and Balkis,* after Kipling's *The Butterfly That Stamped,* a parody on Baroque usages, broadcast over CBS on March 29, 1942. In 1949 Thompson wrote his 3rd Symph., which was presented at the Festival of Contemporary American Music at Columbia Univ. in N.Y., on May 15, 1949. Thompson's subsequent works were an orch. piece, *A Trip to Nahant* (1954), a *Requiem* (1958), *The Nativity According to St. Luke* (1961), *The Passion According to St. Luke* (1965), *The Place of the Blest,* a cantata

(1969), and *A Concord Cantata* (1975). During all this time he did not neglect his educational activities; he taught at Wellesley College (1936–37); the Univ. of Calif. at Berkeley (1937–39); the Curtis Inst. of Music in Philadelphia, where he served as director from 1939 to 1941; the School of Fine Arts at the Univ. of Virginia (1941–46); Princeton Univ. (1946–48); and Harvard Univ. (1949–65), where he retired as prof. emeritus in 1965. He also publ. a book, *College Music* (N.Y., 1935). In his compositions Thompson preserved and cultivated the melodious poetry of American speech, set in crystalline tonal harmonies judiciously seasoned with euphonious discords, while keeping resolutely clear of any modernistic abstractions.

Thomson, César, eminent Belgian violinist; b. Liège, March 17, 1857; d. Lugano, Aug. 21, 1931. He entered the Liège Cons. at the age of 7, winning the Gold Medal at 11; he subsequently studied with Vieuxtemps, Léonard, Wieniawski, and Massart. For several years he was household musician to a wealthy Russian patron of arts, Baron Paul von Derwies, at Lugano; in 1879 he became concertmaster of Bilse's orch. in Berlin; in 1882 he became prof. of violin at the Liège Cons.; he left Liège for Brussels in 1898, when he succeeded Ysaÿe as prof. of violin at the Brussels Cons.; there he founded a celebrated string quartet (with Lamoureux, Vanhout, and Jacobs). In 1914 he settled in Paris as a prof. at the Cons. In 1924 he visited America; taught at the Cons. of Ithaca, N.Y., and at the Juilliard School of Music, N.Y., returning to Europe in 1927. He was a famous violin teacher, emphasizing perfection of technical and expressive performance, rather than bravura. He made arrangements for the violin of various works by early Italian composers.

Thomson, George, Scottish collector of folk songs; b. Limekilns, Dunfermline, March 4, 1757; d. Leith, Feb. 18, 1851. For 59 years (1780–1839) he was secretary to the Board of Trustees for the Encouragement of Arts and Manufactures in Scotland. An ardent collector of Scotch, Welsh, and Irish melodies, he issued a series of vols. containing authentic melodies, with piano accompaniments and instrumental arrangements by the most celebrated musicians of his time, including Beethoven, Haydn, Pleyel, and Koželuh. Each song had, in accordance with his plan, a prelude, coda, and ad libitum parts throughout (for violin, or flute, or cello). The collections are: *A Select Collection of Original Scottish Airs* (6 vols., London; vol. I, 1793; vol. II, 1798; vol. III, 1799; vol. IV, 1802; vol. V, 1818–26; vol. VI, 1841); *Collection of the Songs of R. Burns, Sir W. Scott, etc.* (6 vols., London, 18??); *Select Collection of Original Welsh Airs* (3 vols., London, 1809); *Select Collection of Original Irish Airs* (2 vols., London, 1814–16); *20 Scottish Melodies* (Edinburgh, 1839).

Thomson, John, Scottish composer and writer on music; b. Sprouston, Roxburgh, Oct. 28, 1805; d. Edinburgh, May 6, 1841. He studied in Leipzig with Schnyder von Wartensee, and became an intimate of Mendelssohn, Schumann, and Moscheles. In 1839 he was appointed the first Reid Prof. of Music at Edinburgh Univ. At the 3rd concert given by the Edinburgh Professional Society (Feb. 1837), an analytical program was issued by Thomson, then conductor; this is the first recorded instance of the use of such programs. He composed the opera *Hermann, or The Broken Spear* (London, Oct. 27, 1834) and the musical play *The Shadow on the Wall* (London, April 20, 1835); also wrote incidental music to Walter Scott's drama *The House of Aspen* (Edinburgh, Dec. 19, 1829).

Thomson, Virgil, many-faceted American composer of great originality and a music critic of singular brilliance; b. Kansas City, Mo., Nov. 25, 1896. He studied at Harvard Univ.; took piano lessons with Heinrich Gebhard, and organ with Wallace Goodrich in Boston; then went to Paris, where he had a course with Nadia Boulanger (1921–22); returning to America, he studied composition with Rosario Scalero in N.Y. He then was organist at King's Chapel in Boston (1923–24). In 1925 he went to Paris for a prolonged stay; there he established friendly contacts with cosmopolitan groups of musicians, writers, and painters; his association with Gertrude Stein was particularly significant in the development of his esthetic ideas. In his music he refused to follow any set of modernistic doctrines; rather, he embraced the notion of popular universality, which allowed him to use the techniques of all ages and all degrees of simplicity or complexity, from simple triadic harmonies to dodecaphonic intricacies; in so doing he achieved an eclectic illumination of astonishing power of direct communication, expressed in his dictum "jamais de banalité, toujours le lieu commun." Beneath the characteristic Parisian persiflage in some of his music there is a profoundly earnest intent. His most famous composition is the opera *Four Saints in Three Acts,* to the libretto by Gertrude Stein, in which the deliberate confusion wrought by the author of the play (there are actually 4 acts and more than a dozen saints, some of them in duplicate) and the composer's almost solemn, hymn-like treatment, create a hilarious modern opera-buffa. It was first introduced at Hartford, Conn., on Feb. 8, 1934, characteristically announced as being under the auspices of the "Society of Friends and Enemies of Modern Music," of which Thomson was director (1934–37); the work became an American classic, with constant revivals staged in America and Europe. In 1940 Thomson was appointed music critic of the *N.Y. Herald-Tribune;* he received the Pulitzer Prize in 1948 for his score to the motion picture *Louisiana Story.* Far from being routine journalism, Thomson's music reviews are minor masterpieces of literary brilliance and critical acumen. He resigned in 1954 to devote himself to composition and conducting. In 1982 he received an honorary degree of D.Mus. from Harvard Univ. In 1983 he was awarded the 6th Annual Kennedy Center Honor for lifetime achievement.
WORKS: OPERAS: *4 Saints in 3 Acts* (Hartford,

Conn., Feb. 8, 1934); *The Mother of Us All,* libretto by Gertrude Stein on the life of the American suffragist Susan B. Anthony (N.Y., May 7, 1947); *Byron* (N.Y., April 13, 1972). FOR ORCH.: *Symphony on a Hymn Tune* (1928; N.Y., Feb. 22, 1945, composer conducting); Symph. No. 2 (Seattle, Nov. 17, 1941); *The Seine at Night* (Kansas City, Feb. 24, 1948); *Wheatfield at Noon* (Louisville, Dec. 7, 1948); Cello Concerto (Philadelphia, March 24, 1950); *5 Songs* for Voice and Orch., after William Blake (Louisville, Feb. 6, 1952); *Sea Piece with Birds* (Dallas, Dec. 10, 1952; grouped with *The Seine at Night* and *Wheatfield at Noon* as *3 Pictures for Orchestra*); Concerto for Flute, Strings, and Percussion (Venice, Sept. 18, 1954); *A Solemn Music* for Band (1949); *Missa pro defunctis* for Chorus and Orch. (State Univ. College of Education, Potsdam, N.Y., May 14, 1960); *The Feast of Love* for Baritone and Orch. (Washington, Nov. 1, 1964); Symph. No. 3 (1972; orchestration of his String Quartet No. 2). CHAMBER MUSIC: *Sonata da chiesa* for 5 Instruments (1926); Violin Sonata (1930); String Quartet No. 1 (1932); String Quartet No. 2 (1932); 4 piano sonatas; 2 sets of études for piano; organ pieces; sacred choral works; *Hymns from the Old South* for Mixed Chorus a cappella; songs to French and Eng. texts; Mass for Solo Voice (Unison Chorus, 1960); a number of *Portraits* for various instruments, among them more than 50 for piano, 8 for violin solo, 5 for 4 clarinets, 4 for violin and piano, etc., each "portrait" being a musical characterization of a definite person. FILM MUSIC: *The Plough that Broke the Plains* (1936; an orch. suite was drawn from it); *Louisiana Story* (1948; 2 orch. suites were drawn from it, including *Acadian Songs and Dances*); *The Goddess* (1957); *Power among Men* (1958); *Journey to America* for the American Pavilion at the N.Y. World's Fair (1964).
WRITINGS: *The State Of Music* (N.Y., 1939; 2nd ed., 1961); *The Musical Scene* (N.Y., 1945); *The Art of Judging Music* (N.Y., 1948); *Music, Right and Left* (N.Y., 1951); an autobiography, disarmingly titled *Virgil Thomson* (N.Y., 1966); *Music Reviewed 1940–54,* a collection of criticisms (N.Y., 1967); *American Music since 1910* (N.Y., 1971).

Thórarinsson, Leifur, Icelandic composer; b. Reykjavik, Aug. 13, 1934. He studied with Jón Thórarinsson at the Reykjavik School of Music; then in Vienna with Hanns Jelinek (1954); and with both Wallingford Riegger and Gunther Schuller in N.Y. Returning to Iceland, he became a music critic and member of the modern group Musica Nova; later moved to Denmark.

Thorborg, Kerstin, Swedish contralto; b. Venjan, May 19, 1896; d. Hedemora, Sweden, April 12, 1970. She studied at the Stockholm Opera School; made her début in 1924 at the Stockholm Royal Opera, and remained as a regular member there until 1930; then sang in Berlin and Vienna. On Dec. 21, 1936, she made her American debut as Fricka at the Metropolitan Opera House, N.Y.; remained with the Metropolitan until 1950 (the 1946–47 season excepted); gave concerts throughout the U.S. and Canada;

then returned to Sweden and became a voice teacher in Stockholm.

Thorne, Francis, American composer; b. Bay Shore, Long Island, N.Y., June 23, 1922. Of a cultural heritage (his maternal grandfather was the opera expert **Gustav Kobbé**), he absorbed musical impressions crouching under the grand piano while his father, a banker, played ragtime; at puberty, he sang in a school chorus; entering Yale Univ., he was a member of the varsity rowing team, as a prelude to service in the U.S. Navy during World War II. Returning from the war, he joined the stockbrokerage firm of Harris, Upham & Co. as a customers' man, but soon defected and joined various N.Y. jazz groups as a pianist; then went to Italy; took lessons in advanced composition with David Diamond in Florence. Impressed, depressed, and distressed by the inhumanly impecunious condition of middleaged atonal composers, he established the eleemosynary Thorne Music Fund, drawing on the hereditary wealth of his family, and disbursed munificent grants to those who qualified, among them Stefan Wolpe, Ben Weber, Lou Harrison, Lester Trimble, John Cage, and David Diamond. In 1976 he founded the American Composers' Orch.; has been executive director of the American Composers' Alliance since 1975. Thorne's own music shares with that of his beneficiaries the venturesome spirit of the cosmopolitan avant-garde, with a prudently dissonant technique serving the conceptual abstractions and titular paronomasia of many modern compositions.

Thrane, Waldemar, Norwegian composer; b. Christiania, Oct. 8, 1790; d. there, Dec. 30, 1828. He studied violin with K. Schall in Copenhagen; then went to Paris, where he was a pupil of Baillot (violin) and of Reicha and Habeneck (composition). Returning to Christiania, he conducted theater music and also directed a music school. He is historically important as the composer of the first Norwegian opera, *Fjeldeventyret (A Mountain Adventure);* the score was publ. in 1824; the first concert perf. took place at the Musical Lyceum in Christiania, on Feb. 9, 1825; the first stage production was given posthumously (Christiania, April 9, 1850).

Thuille, Ludwig (Wilhelm Andreas Maria), renowned German composer and pedagogue; b. Bozen, Tyrol, Nov. 30, 1861; d. Munich, Feb. 5, 1907. He studied with Pembaur at Innsbruck (piano and theory); then went to Munich, where he was a pupil of Karl Bärmann (piano) and Rheinberger (composition) at the Hochschule für Musik there; in 1883 he became a prof. there. Encouraged by Alexander Ritter, he began to compose music in the grand Wagnerian manner; wrote 3 operas, chamber music, song cycles, and choral works. But he made his mark chiefly as a fine pedagogue; with Rudolf Louis he publ. the well-known manual *Harmonielehre* (1907; abridged ed. as *Grundriss der Harmonielehre*, 1908; new revised ed., by Courvoisier and others, 1933).

Thursby, Emma, American soprano; b. Brooklyn, Feb. 21, 1845; d. New York, July 4, 1931. She studied with Achille Errani in N.Y.; in 1873 went to Italy, where she studied with Lamperti and Sangiovanni in Milan. Upon her return to America in 1875, she was engaged by the bandleader Gilmore for his summer concerts, and toured the country with him; subsequently appeared in the European music centers; in 1903 she sang in China and Japan; then returned to the U.S., living in retirement in N.Y.

Tibbett, Lawrence, outstanding American baritone; b. Bakersfield, Calif., Nov. 16, 1896; d. New York, July 15, 1960. His real name was **Tibbet,** but it was accidentally misspelled when he appeared in opera, and he retained the final extra letter. His ancestry was connected with the California Gold Rush of 1849; his great-uncle was reputed to be a pioneer in the navel orange industry; Tibbett's father was a sheriff of Bakersfield who was shot dead by one of the outlaws he had hunted. His mother ran a hotel in Long Beach. Tibbett led a typical cowboy life, but dreamed of a stage career; he played parts in Shakespearian productions. During World War I he served in the U.S. Navy; after the Armistice he earned a living by singing at weddings and funerals in a male quartet. He also took vocal lessons with Joseph Dupuy, Basil Ruysdael, Frank La Forge, and Ignaz Zitmorsky. He made his operatic debut in N.Y. with the Metropolitan Opera on Nov. 24, 1923, in the minor role of Lovitsky in *Boris Godunov;* then sang Valentin in *Faust* (Nov. 30, 1923); achieved a striking success as Ford in Verdi's *Falstaff* (Jan. 2, 1925). He gave his farewell at the Metropolitan as Ivan in *Khovanshchina* on March 24, 1950. Altogether he sang 396 times with the Metropolitan Opera in N.Y., and 163 times on tour. His repertoire grew with experience and success on the stage. Among his roles were Tonio in *Pagliacci,* Wolfram in *Tannhäuser,* Tetramund in *Lohengrin,* Marcello in *La Bohème,* Scarpia in *Tosca,* Iago in *Otello,* and the title roles in *Rigoletto* and *Falstaff.* He also sang important parts in modern American operas, such as Colonel Ibbetson in Deems Taylor's *Peter Ibbetson,* Brutus Jones in Gruenberg's *The Emperor Jones,* and Wrestling Bradford in Howard Hanson's *Merry Mount.* During his first European tour in 1937 he sang the title role in the world premiere of *Don Juan de Mañara* by Eugene Goossens (Covent Garden, London, June 24, 1937); he also sang in Paris, Vienna, and Stockholm. A sincere believer in musical democracy, he did not disdain the lower arts; he even took part in such a mundane entertainment as the radio show "Your Hit Parade," undisturbed by interruptions from cigarette sponsors extolling the manly virtues of Lucky Strike smokers. He also appeared in talking pictures, among them *The Rogue Song, The Southerner,* and *Cuban Love Song.* During World War II he sang in army camps. He was a featured singer at the inaugurations of Calvin Coolidge, Herbert Hoover, and Franklin D. Roosevelt. He received all kinds of honors, including the Swedish medal Litteris et Artibus; a gold medal given by the American Academy of Arts and Letters; and several honorary doctorates from American univs. His life's progress is summarized in his autobiography, proudly entitled *The Glory Road* (Brattleboro, 1933).

Tichatschek, Joseph Aloys, Bohemian tenor; b. Blasewitz, near Dresden, July 11, 1807; d. Dresden, Jan. 18, 1886. He was the son of a poor weaver; in 1827 went to Vienna as a medical student, but then joined the chorus at the Kärnthnertor Theater, and had vocal instruction from Ciccimara; was soon engaged at Graz for 2 years; then sang in Vienna. His career received a new impetus after his highly successful appearance at the Dresden Opera (Aug. 11, 1837); he remained there for 33 years, retiring in 1870. He created the roles of Rienzi (Oct. 20, 1842) and Tannhäuser (Oct. 19, 1845) in Wagner's operas. Wagner mentions him often and with great praise in his autobiography.

Tieffenbrucker. See **Duiffopruggar.**

Tierney, Harry, American composer of popular music; b. Perth Amboy, N.J., May 21, 1890; d. New York, March 22, 1965. He studied piano and planned a concert career; then turned to composition of popular songs; wrote many numbers for the Ziegfeld Follies. His musical shows *Irene* (N.Y., Nov. 18, 1919), *Up She Goes* (N.Y., Nov. 6, 1922), and *Kid Boots* (N.Y., Dec. 31, 1923) were quite successful, but were eclipsed by the fame of his *Rio Rita* (N.Y., Feb. 2, 1927). His early song *M-i-s-s-i-s-s-i-p-p-i* (1916) flooded the nation.

Tietjen, Heinz, noted German conductor and opera producer; b. Tangier, June 24, 1881; d. Baden-Baden, Nov. 30, 1967. He studied conducting with Nikisch; was then active as an opera producer in Trier (1904–22); later was administrator of the Berlin City Opera (1925–27); from 1931 to 1944 was artistic director of the Bayreuth Festivals, where he also conducted. He was again administrator of the Berlin City Opera (1948–55) and also of the Hamburg State Opera (1956–59); then retired in Baden-Baden.

Tietjens, Therese Johanne Alexandra, famous German soprano; b. Hamburg, July 17, 1831; d. London, Oct. 3, 1877. She was trained in Hamburg and made a successful debut there in 1849; sang at Frankfurt, and was engaged for the Vienna Court Opera in 1856; went to London in 1858, and remained there until her death, for long years the reigning favorite, singing at Her Majesty's Theatre, Drury Lane, Covent Garden, and the Haymarket. She visited Paris in 1863, and America in 1874 and 1876, appearing at the Academy of Music in N.Y. under Strakosch's management.

Tinctoris, Johannes, renowned Franco-Flemish music theorist and early musical lexicographer; b. Braine l'Alleud, near Nivelles, c.1435; d. before Oct. 12, 1511. He matriculated at the German Nation of Orleans Univ. (April 1, 1463). About 1472 he became

tutor to the daughter of King Ferdinand I of Naples. In 1487 Ferdinand dispatched him to the courts of Charles VIII of France and Maximilian of Rome to recruit singers for his chapel. At the time of his death, Tinctoris was a canon and prebendary in Nivelles. About 1472 he compiled a dictionary of musical terms, *Terminorum musicae diffinitorium* (Treviso, 1495), which was the first of its kind. The only other work known to have been publ. in his lifetime was *De inventione et usu musicae* (Naples, c.1487). Tinctoris also wrote poetry, and served as a cleric. For editions of his writings, see C.E.H. de Coussemaker, ed., *Johannes Tinctoris tractatus de musica* (Lille, 1875) and A. Seay, *Johannes Tinctoris: Opera theoretica,* in *Corpus scriptorum de musica,* XXII (1975).

Tinel, Edgar, Belgian composer; b. Sinay, March 27, 1854; d. Brussels, Oct. 28, 1912. He was taught at first by his father, a schoolmaster and organist; entered the Brussels Cons. in 1863 as a pupil of Brassin, Dupont, Gevaert, Kufferath, and Mailly; in 1873 took first prize for piano playing; won the Belgian Prix de Rome in 1877 with the cantata *De Klokke Roeland.* In 1882 he became director of the Inst. for Sacred Music at Mechlin; was appointed to the staff of the Brussels Cons. in 1896, and in 1909 (after Gevaert's death) became its director.

Tiomkin, Dimitri, Russian-American composer of film music; b. St. Petersburg, May 10, 1894; d. London, Nov. 11, 1979. He studied piano with Isabelle Vengerova at the St. Petersburg Cons.; left Russia in 1921; lived in Berlin. He began his career as a concert pianist in Europe; emigrated to America in 1925, and was naturalized in 1937. After a few years in N.Y., he settled in Hollywood, where he became a highly successful composer of movie music; wrote scores for more than 100 motion picture films, including *The Bridge of San Luis Rey, Duel in the Sun, Lost Horizon,* and *Dial M for Murder.* He received an Academy Award for *The High and Mighty* (1954) and *The Old Man and the Sea* (1958). His most popular score was that for *High Noon* (1952), which received the Academy Award for best score and best theme song; he also was the recipient of numerous awards of merit, scrolls of appreciation, plaques of recognition, and a Golden Globe. He publ. a dictated autobiography under the title *Please Don't Hate Me* (N.Y., 1959).

Tippett, Sir Michael (Kemp), greatly renowned English composer; b. London, Jan. 2, 1905. He studied in London at the Royal College of Music (1923–28), where his teachers in composition were Charles Wood and C.H. Kitson; took piano lessons there with Aubin Raymar and attended courses in conducting under the direction of Sir Adrian Boult and Sir Malcolm Sargent. Later he studied counterpoint and fugue with R.O. Morris (1930–32). He subsequently held several positions as a teacher and conductor; from 1933 to 1940 he led the South London Orch. at Morley College; then served as director of music there (1940–51). Tippett was acutely sensitive to social events; his oratorio *A Child of Our Time* was inspired by the case of Henschel Grynsban, a Jewish boy who assassinated a member of the German embassy in Paris in 1938. As a conscientious objector, Tippett entertained extreme pacifist convictions; he refused to serve even in a non-combatant capacity in the British military forces; for this intransigent attitude he was sentenced to prison for 3 months; he served his term in a Surrey County gaol with the suggestive name Wormwood Scrubs (June 21–Aug. 21, 1943). He regained the respect of the community after the end of the war. In 1951 he initiated a series of broadcasts for the BBC; in 1969–74 he directed the Bath Festival. He received high honors from the British government; in 1959 he was named a Commander of the Order of the British Empire, and in 1966 he was knighted. He visited the U.S. in 1965, and thereafter was a frequent guest in America; his symph. works were often performed by major American orchs. Tippett's music has a grandeur of Romantic inspiration that sets it apart from the prevalent type of contemporary music; it is infused with rhapsodic eloquence and further enhanced by a pervading lyric sentiment free from facile sentimentality. He excelled in large-scale vocal and instrumental forms; he was a consummate master of the modern idioms, attaining heights of dissonant counterpoint without losing the teleological sense of inherent tonality. Yet he did not shun special effects; three times in his 4th Symph. he injects episodes of heavy glottal aspiration, suggested to him by viewing a film depicting the dissection of fetuses of pigs. A man of great general culture, Tippett possesses a fine literary gift; he writes his own librettos for his operas and oratorios.

WORKS: OPERAS: *The Midsummer Marriage* (1946–52; London, Jan. 27, 1955); *King Priam* (1958–61; Coventry, May 29, 1962); *The Knot Garden* (1966–69; London, Dec. 2, 1970); *The Ice Break* (1973–76; London, July 7, 1977). FOR ORCH.: Concerto for Double String Orch. (1938–39; London, April 21, 1940, composer conducting); *Fantasia on a Theme by Handel* for Piano and Orch. (1939–41; London, March 7, 1942); Symph. No. 1 (Liverpool, Nov. 10, 1945); *Little Music* for String Orch. (London, Nov. 9, 1946); Suite in D major, for the birthday of Prince Charles (BBC, London, Nov. 15, 1948); *Ritual Dances*, from *The Midsummer Marriage* (Basel, Feb. 13, 1953); *Fantasia Concertante on a Theme by Corelli* for String Orch. (Edinburgh, Aug. 29, 1953, composer conducting); *Divertimento on Sellinger's Round* for Chamber Orch. (Zürich, Nov. 5, 1954); Concerto for Piano and Orch. (1953–55; Birmingham, Oct. 30, 1956); Symph. No. 2 (1956–57; London, Feb. 5, 1958); *Praeludium* for Brass, Bells, and Percussion (London, Nov. 14, 1962); Concerto for Orch. (Edinburgh, Aug. 28, 1963); Symph. No. 3 for Soprano and Orch. (1970–72; London, June 22, 1972); Symph. No. 4 (Chicago, Oct. 6, 1977); Triple Concerto for Violin, Viola, Cello, and Orch. (1979; London, Aug. 22, 1980). VOCAL MUSIC: *A Child of Our Time,* oratorio with text by the composer, inspired by the case of the Jewish boy Henschel Grynsban, who assassinated in 1938 a Nazi member of the German embassy in Paris (1939–41; London, March 19, 1944); *Boyhood's End,* cantata to a text by W.H. Hudson, for Tenor and Piano (London, June 5, 1943); *The Heart's Assurance,* song cycle to poems by Sidney Keyes and Alun Lewis, for High Voice and Piano (London, May 7, 1951); *Dance, Clarion Air,* madrigal for 5 Voices, with text by Christopher Fry (1952; June 1, 1953); *Crown of the Year,* cantata for Chorus and Instrumental Ensemble, with text by Christopher Fry (Bristol, July 25, 1958); *Music for Words Perhaps* for Speaking Voices and Chamber Ensemble, to love poems by W.B. Yeats (BBC, London, June 8, 1960); *Music,* unison song to the poem by Shelley, for Voices, Strings, and Piano (April 1960); *Magnificat and Nunc Dimittis* for Chorus and Organ (1961; Cambridge, March 13, 1962); *Songs for Ariel* for Medium Voice and Instrumental Ensemble (1962); *The Vision of Saint Augustine* for Baritone, Chorus, and Orch. (1963–65; London, Jan. 19, 1966; Dietrich Fischer-Dieskau, soloist; composer conducting); *The Shires Suite* for Chorus and Orch. (1965–70; Cheltenham, July 8, 1970, composer conducting); *The Mask of Time* for Chorus and Orch. (1981–84; Boston, April 5, 1984). CHAMBER MUSIC: 4 string quartets (1935, revised 1944; 1943; 1946; 1979); *4 Inventions* for Descant and Treble Recorders (1954); Sonata for 4 Horns (1955); *Wolf Trap Fanfare* for 3 Trumpets, 2 Trombones, and Tuba (1980); *The Blue Guitar* for Guitar (1983). FOR PIANO: 4 Sonatas: No. 1 (1938; revised 1942 and 1954); No. 2 (1962); No. 3 (1973); No. 4 (1979); also *Preludio al Vespro di Monteverdi* for Organ (1946).

Tischler, Hans, distinguished Austrian-American musicologist; b. Vienna, Jan. 18, 1915. He studied piano with Paul Wittgenstein and Bertha Jahn-Beer, composition with Richard Stöhr and Franz Schmidt, and musicology with Robert Lach, Robert Haas, and Egon Wellesz at the Univ. of Vienna (Ph.D., 1937, with the dissertation *Die Harmonik in den Werken Gustav Mahlers*). He left Austria in 1938, settling in the U.S.; continued his musicological studies with Leo Schrade at Yale Univ. (Ph.D., 1942, with the dissertation *The Motet in 13th-Century France*). He taught music history at West Virginia Wesleyan College (1945–47) and at Roosevelt Univ. in Chicago (1947–65). In 1965 he was appointed prof. of musicology at Indiana Univ. in Bloomington.

Tishchenko, Boris, Soviet composer; b. Leningrad, March 23, 1939. He studied composition at the Leningrad Cons. with Salmanov, Voloshinov, and Evlakhov, graduating in 1962; later took lessons with Shostakovich. In his works he demonstrates a strong rhythmic power and polyphonic mastery; his musical idiom is greatly advanced without overstepping the bounds of tonality.

WORKS: One-act opera, *The Stolen Sun* (1968); ballets: *The 12,* after the poem of Alexander Blok (Leningrad, Dec. 31, 1964); *Yaroslavna* (1974); *Lenin Lives,* cantata (1959); 5 symphs. (1960, 1964, 1966, 1970, 1974); Violin Concerto (1958); 2 cello concertos (1963, 1969); Piano Concerto (1962); Flute

Concerto (1972); Harp Concerto (1977); *Palekh,* homage to Russian folk painters, for Chamber Orch. (1965); 4 string quartets (1957, 1959, 1969, 1980); 2 sonatas for Solo Violin (1957, 1976); 2 sonatas for Solo Cello (1960, 1979); *Capriccio* for Violin and Piano (1965); 6 piano sonatas (1957, 1960, 1965, 1972, 1973, 1975); *Sad Songs* for Soprano and Piano (1962); *Suzdal,* to folk texts from the Suzdal region, for Soprano, Tenor, and Chamber Orch. (1964); *Hard Frost,* aria for Mezzo-soprano and Orch. (1975).

Titelouze, Jean (or Jehan), French organist and composer; b. St.-Omer, c.1563; d. Rouen, Oct. 24, 1633. In 1588 he became organist at the Cathedral in Rouen, a position he held until his death; he also served as a canon there in 1610. He publ. 2 collections of organ works, *Hymnes de l'église* (1623) and *Le Magnificat* (1626); these sets of versets are in actuality keyboard fantasias. He also wrote poetry, which gained him prizes at the Puy de Rouen in 1613 and 1630. A complete edition of his organ works was brought out by Pirro and Guilmant in the *Archives des maîtres de l' orgue* (vol. 1, Paris, 1898).

Titta Ruffo. See **Ruffo, Titta.**

Tobani, Theodore Moses, German-American composer and arranger of a multitude of marches, gavottes, waltzes, and other popular forms; b. Hamburg, May 2, 1855; d. Queens, N.Y., Dec. 12, 1933. His family emigrated to the U.S. c.1870; Tobani earned his living as a youth playing violin at theaters and drinking emporia; then became associated with the music publ. firm of Carl Fischer in N.Y.; he is said to have composed or arranged over 5,000 pieces for piano or organ that enjoyed gratifying commercial success; the best known of these works, and one epitomizing the sentimental popular tastes of the time, was *Hearts and Flowers* (op. 245), which Tobani claimed to have tossed off in an hour in the late summer of 1893. Since he publ. so much music, he used a number of pseudonyms, among which **Florence Reed** and **Andrew Herman** were his favorites.

Toch, Ernst, eminent Austrian-American composer; b. Vienna, Dec. 7, 1887; d. Los Angeles, Oct. 1, 1964. His father was a Jewish dealer in unprocessed leather, and there was no musical strain in the family; Toch began playing piano without a teacher in his grandmother's pawnshop; he learned musical notation from a local violinist, and then copied Mozart's string quartets for practice; using them as a model, he began to compose string quartets and other pieces of chamber music; at the age of 17 he had one of them, his 6th String Quartet, op. 12 (1905), performed by the famous Rose Quartet in Vienna. From 1906 to 1909 he studied medicine at the Univ. of Vienna. In 1909 he won the prestigious Mozart Prize and a scholarship to study at the Frankfurt Cons., where he studied piano with Willy Rehberg and composition with Iwan Knorr. In 1910 he was awarded the Mendelssohn Prize; also won 4 times in succession the Austrian State Prize. In 1913 he was appointed instructor in piano at Zuschneid's Hochschule für Musik in Mannheim. In 1914–18 he served in the Austrian army; during a furlough in Vienna in 1916 he married Lilly Zwack. After the Armistice he returned to Mannheim, resumed his musical career, and became active in the modern movement, soon attaining, along with Hindemith, Krenek, and others, a prominent position in the new German school of composition. In the meantime he continued his academic studies; earned his Dr.Phil. degree in 1921 with the dissertation *Beiträge zur Stilkunde der Melodie* (publ. in Berlin under the title *Melodielehre*). In 1929 he went to live in Berlin, where he established himself as a piano teacher. In 1932 he made an American tour as a pianist playing his own works; he returned to Berlin, but with the advent of the Nazi regime was forced to leave Germany in 1933. He went to Paris, then to London, and in 1935 emigrated to the U.S.; gave lectures on music at The New School for Social Research in N.Y.; in 1936 moved to Hollywood, where he wrote music for films. He became an American citizen on July 26, 1940; in 1940–41 he taught composition at the Univ. of Southern Calif., Los Angeles; subsequently taught privately; among his students were many, who, like André Previn, became well-known composers in their own right. From 1950 until his death, Toch traveled frequently and lived in Vienna, Zürich, the MacDowell Colony in New Hampshire, and Santa Monica, Calif.

Toch's music is rooted in the tradition of the German and Austrian Romantic movement of the 19th century, but his study of the classics made him aware of the paramount importance of formal logic in the development of thematic ideas. His early works consist mostly of chamber music and pieces for piano solo; following the zeitgeist during his German period, he wrote several pieces for the stage in the light manner of sophisticated entertainment; he also composed effective piano works of a virtuoso quality, which enjoyed considerable popularity among pianists of the time. Toch possessed a fine wit and a sense of exploration; his *Geographical Fugue* for speaking chorus, articulating in syllabic counterpoint the names of exotic places on earth, became a classic of its genre.

It was not until 1950 that Toch wrote his first full-fledged symph., but from that time on, until he died of stomach cancer, he composed fully 7 symphs., plus sinfoniettas for Wind and String Orch. He was greatly interested in new techniques; the theme of his last String Quartet (No. 13, 1953) is based on a 12-tone row. In the score of his 3rd Symph. he introduced an optional instrument, the Hisser, a tank of carbon dioxide that produced a hissing sound through a valve.

Among the several honors Toch received were the Pulitzer Prize for his 3rd Symph. (1956), membership in the National Inst. of Arts and Letters (1957), and the Cross of Honor for Sciences and Art from the Austrian government (1963). An Ernst Toch Archive was founded at the Univ. of Calif., Los Angeles, in 1966, serving as a depository for his MSS, publ. and unpubl.

WORKS: FOR THE STAGE: Unfinished opera, *Weg-*

wende (1925; sketches destroyed); musical fairy tale, *Die Prinzessin auf der Erbse (The Princess and the Pea;* 1927; Baden-Baden, July 17, 1927); *Egon und Emilie,* "not a family drama" (1928; Mannheim, Oct. 21, 1928); opera-capriccio, *Der Fächer (The Fan;* 1930; Königsberg, June 8, 1930); a Sheherazade opera, *The Last Tale* (1960–62; unperf.).

FOR ORCH.: *Scherzo* (1904); *Kammersymphonie* for 10 Instruments (1906); *Phantastische Nachtmusik* (1920; Mannheim, March 22, 1921); *5 Pieces* for Chamber Orch. (1924); Concerto for Cello and Small Orch. (1925; Kiel, June 17, 1925); Piano Concerto (1926; Düsseldorf, Oct. 8, 1926; Gieseking, soloist); *Spiel für Blasorchester (Divertimento for Orchestra;* 1926; Donaueschingen, July 24, 1926); *Komödie für Orchester* (1927; Berlin, Nov. 13, 1927); *Vorspiel zu einem Märchen (Overture to a Fairy Tale;* 1927; overture from the opera *Princess and the Pea*); *Bunte Suite (Motley Suite;* 1928; Frankfurt, Feb. 22, 1929); *Fanal (Beacon)* for Orch. and Organ (1928); *Kleine Theater-Suite* (1931; Berlin, Feb. 9, 1931); Symph. for Piano and Orch. (Piano Concerto No. 2, 1932; London, Aug. 20, 1934); *Miniature Overture* for Winds (1932); *Big Ben,* variation fantasy on the Westminster Chimes (1934; Boston Symph., Cambridge, Mass., Dec. 20, 1934; revised 1955); *Pinocchio,* "a merry overture" (1936; Los Angeles, Dec. 10, 1936); *The Idle Stroller,* suite (1938); "The Covenant," 6th movement of 7-movement, collaborative *Genesis Suite,* commissioned by Nathaniel Shilkret (Los Angeles, Nov. 18, 1945; score lost); *Hyperion,* dramatic prelude after Keats (1947; Cleveland, Jan. 8, 1948); 7 symphs.: No. 1 (1949–50; Vienna, Dec. 20, 1950); No. 2, dedicated to Albert Schweitzer (1950–51; Vienna, Jan. 11, 1952); No. 3 (1954–55; Pittsburgh, Dec. 2, 1955; won Pulitzer Prize, 1956); No. 4 (1957; Minneapolis, Nov. 22, 1957); No. 5, subtitled *Jephta, Rhapsodic Poem* (1961–62; Boston, March 13, 1964); No. 6 (1963; posthumous, Zürich Radio, Jan. 22, 1967); No. 7 (1964; posthumous, Bavarian Radio, 1967); *Notturno* (1953; Louisville, Ky., Jan. 2, 1954); *Circus Overture* (1954; Ravinia Festival, Highland Park, Ill., July 8, 1954); *Peter Pan,* fairy tale in 3 parts (1955–56; Seattle, Feb. 13, 1956); 3 Pieces for "Doctor's" Orch.: *Short Story* (1960), *Intermezzo* (1960), and *Epilogue* (1961); *3 Pantomimes: Puppet Show, Capriccio,* and *The Enamoured Harlequin* (all 1963–64); Sinfonietta for String Orch. (1964; posthumous, Philadelphia, Feb. 13, 1967); Sinfonietta for Winds and Percussion (1964; posthumous, Zürich Radio, Nov. 11, 1967).

CHAMBER MUSIC: 13 string quartets: Nos. 1–5 (1902–3; lost); No. 6 in A minor (1905); No. 7 (1908); No. 8 (1911); No. 9 (1919); No. 10, on the name "Bass" (1920); No. 11 (1924); No. 12 (1946); No. 13 (1953); duos for Violins (1909; for open strings only in the pupil's part); Serenade for 3 Violins (1912); Violin Sonata (1912); *"Spitzweg" Serenade* for 2 Violins and Viola (1917); *Tanz Suite* for Flute, Clarinet, Violin, Viola, Bass, and Percussion (1923; excerpts choreographed as *Der Wald,* Mannheim, Nov. 19, 1923; first complete perf., Münster, Oct. 29, 1924); *2 Divertimenti* for String Duos (1926); Violin Sonata (1928); Cello Sonata (1929); *2 Etudes* for Cello Solo (1930); String Trio (1936); Piano Quintet (1938);

Dedication for String Quartet or String Orch. (1948); *Adagio elegiaco* for Clarinet and Piano (1950); *5 Pieces* for Flute, Oboe, Clarinet, Bassoon, 2 Horns, and Percussion (1959); *Sonatinetta* for Flute, Clarinet, and Bassoon (1959); *3 Impromptus* for Solo Violin, Solo Viola, and Solo Cello (1963); Quartet for Oboe, Clarinet, Bassoon, and Viola (1964).

FOR PIANO: *Melodische Skizzen* (1903); *3 Preludes* (1903); *Capriccio* (1905; lost); Sonata in C-sharp minor (1905; lost); Sonata in D major (1905; lost); *Stammbuchverse (Album Verses;* 1905); *Begegnung (Meeting;* 1908); *Reminiszenzen* (1909); *4 Klavierstücke* (1914; lost); *Canon* (1915); *3 Burlesken* (1923; includes the popular *Der Jongleur,* publ. separately); *3 Klavierstücke* (1925); *5 Capriccetti* (1925); *Tanz- und Spielstücke (Pieces for Dancing and Playing;* 1927); *Studie* for Mechanical Piano (1927); Sonata, op. 17 (1928); *Kleinstadtbilder (Echoes from a Small Town),* 14 easy pieces (1929); *Fünfmal Zehn Etüden,* 50 études (1931); *Profiles* (1946); *Ideas* (1946); *Diversions* (1956); *Sonatinetta* (1956); *3 Little Dances* (1961); *Reflections,* 5 pieces (1961); Sonata for Piano, 4-hands (1962).

FOR VOICE: *An mein Vaterland (To My Homeland),* symph. for Soprano, Mixed and Boys' Choruses, Orch., and Organ (1913); *Die chinesische Flöte (The Chinese Flute),* chamber symph. for Soprano and 14 Solo Instruments (1922; Frankfurt, June 24, 1923; revised 1949); 9 songs for Soprano and Piano (1926); *Der Tierkreis (The Zodiac)* for 2-part Women's Chorus (1930); *Das Wasser (Water),* cantata for Tenor, Baritone, Narrator, Chorus, Flute, Trumpet, Percussion, and Strings (1930; Berlin Festival of New Music, June 18, 1930); *Gesprochene Musik (Music for Speaking Chorus;* 1930; Berlin Festival of New Music, June 17, 1930; includes the famous *Fuge aus der Geographie [Geographical Fugue],* publ. separately in Eng. and German eds.); *Music for Orchestra and Baritone Solo on Poems by Rilke* for Baritone and Orch. (1932); *Cantata of the Bitter Herbs* for Soloists, Narrator, Chorus, and Orch. (1938); *Poems to Martha,* quintet for Voice and Strings (1942); *The Inner Circle,* 6 a cappella choruses (1953); *There Is a Season for Everything* for Mezzo-soprano, Flute, Clarinet, Violin, and Cello, to words from Ecclesiastes (1953); *Vanity of Vanities, All Is Vanity* for Soprano, Tenor, Flute, Clarinet, Violin, Viola, and Cello, to words from Ecclesiastes (1954); *Phantoms* for Narrator, Women's Speaking Chorus, and Chamber Orch. (1957); *Lange schon haben meine Freunde versucht (For a Long Time Now My Friends Have Tried),* duet for Soprano and Baritone (1958); *Song of Myself,* after Whitman, for Mixed Chorus a cappella (1961); *Valse* for Speaking Chorus and Percussion (1961; in separate Eng. and German eds.); folk-song arrangements.

FILM SCORES: *Peter Ibbetson* (1935); *Outcast* (1937); *The Cat and the Canary* (1939); *Dr. Cyclops* (1940); *The Ghost Breakers* (1940); *Ladies in Retirement* (1941); *First Comes Courage* (1943); *None Shall Escape* (1944); *Address Unknown* (1944); *The Unseen* (1945). He also wrote incidental music for stage and radio plays.

PUBLICATIONS: *Die Melodielehre* (Berlin, 1923); *The Shaping Forces in Music* (N.Y., 1948; new ed., with a valuable introduction by Toch's grandson, Lawrence Weschler, and an 18-page complete list of Toch's works, with publishers, N.Y., 1977).

Toëschi, Carlo Giuseppe (Toesca della Castella-Monte), Italian violinist and composer; b. Ludwigsburg (baptized, Nov. 11), 1731; d. Munich, April 12, 1788. He was the son of **Alessandro Toëschi,** a member of the Mannheim Orch., who had moved to Germany. He studied with Johann Stamitz in Mannheim and entered its orch. in 1752 as a violinist; in 1759 he became concertmaster of the Mannheim Orch. He followed the court to Munich in 1778, and was appointed court musician in 1780. A highly productive composer, he wrote about 25 ballet scores and at least 66 known symphs.; 19 flute concertos and 11 violin concertos; also a number of quartets, quintets, sextets, trio sonatas, violin sonatas and other pieces of chamber music. Riemann publ. his Symph. *a* 8 in Denkmäler der Tonkunst in Bayern, 13 (7.ii); in the same series are reprinted a Flute Quartet and Flute Quintet (vol. 27 [15]) and a Trio (vol. 28 [16]); it also contains a thematic catalogue, listing 60 chamber works. A Symph. in D was arranged by A. Carse, and publ. in London (1936).

Toëschi, Johann Baptist (Giovanni Battista), Italian-German violinist and composer, brother of **Carlo Giuseppe Toëschi;** b. Stuttgart (baptized, Oct. 1), 1735; d. Munich (buried, April 3), 1800. Like his brother, he was a violinist in the Mannheim Orch. (from 1755); followed the court to Munich in 1778, and became music director in Munich in 1793. He produced a ballet, *Arlechin, Kaiser in China* (Mannheim, April 26, 1778); composed a great number of chamber music pieces. A thematic catalogue of his works appears in Denkmäler der Tonkunst in Bayern, 28 (16).

Tollefsen, Carl H., American violinist; b. Hull, England, Aug. 15, 1882; d. Brooklyn, N.Y., Dec. 10, 1963. He emigrated to America as a youth, and studied at the National Cons. in N.Y. (1898–1902) and later at the Inst. of Musical Art (1906–8), where his teachers were Franz Kneisel (violin), and Goetschius and Rubin Goldmark (composition); was a violinist in various orchs. in N.Y. On Aug. 7, 1907, he married the pianist **Augusta Schnabel** (b. Boise, Idaho, Jan. 5, 1885; d. Brooklyn, April 9, 1955), and formed the Tollefsen Trio with her and with Paul Kéfer; this trio toured the U.S. for more than 30 years (succeeding cellists were M. Penha, P. Gruppe, R. Thrane, and W. Durieux). In 1939 he founded the Brooklyn Chamber Music Society. He formed a large collection of autographs of famous musicians and MS biographies (including the biographical archives gathered by Alfred Rémy, editor of the 3rd ed. of *Baker's Biographical Dictionary of Musicians*). In 1947 the cellist Yuri Bilstin bequeathed to him a collection of old instruments. After Tollefsen's death his entire collection was turned over to the Southern Illinois Univ. Lovejoy Library at Edwards-ville.

Tomaschek, Wenzel Johann (Bohemian spelling, **Václav Jan Křititel Tomášek),** important Bohemian composer and pedagogue; b. Skutsch, April 17, 1774; d. Prague, April 3, 1850. He was the youngest of 13 children; learned the rudiments of singing and violin playing from P.J. Wolf and studied organ with Donat Schuberth. In 1787 he became an alto chorister at the Minorite monastery in Iglau; in 1790 he went to Prague, supporting himself by playing piano in public places; also took law courses at the Univ. of Prague. From 1806–22 he was attached to the family of Count Georg Bucquoy de Longeval as music tutor. In 1824 he established his own music school in Prague. Among his many pupils were J.H. Woržischek (Voříšek), Dreyschock, Hanslick, and Schulhoff. Tomaschek was the first to use the instrumental form of the rhapsody systematically in a number of his piano pieces, although it was anticipated by W.R. Gallenberg in a single composition a few years earlier; he also adopted the ancient Greek terms "eclogue" and "dithyramb" for short character pieces. He wrote an autobiography, publ. in installments in the Prague journal *Libussa* (1845–50); a modern edition was prepared by Z. Němec (Prague, 1941); excerpts appeared in the *Musical Quarterly* (April 1946).

WORKS: Operas: *Seraphine, oder Grossmut und Liebe* (Prague, Dec. 15, 1811) and *Alvaro* (unfinished). Choral music: Requiem (1820); *Krönungsmesse* (1836); Te Deum. Instrumental music: 3 symphs. (1801, 1805, 1807); 2 piano concertos (1805, 1806); 3 string quartets (1792–93); Piano Trio (1800); Piano Quartet (1805). For Solo Piano: 7 sonatas (1800–6); 42 eclogues (1807–23); 15 rhapsodies (1810); 6 *allegri capricciosi* (1815, 1818); 6 dithyrambs (1818–23).

Tomasi, Henri, French composer; b. Marseilles, Aug. 17, 1901; d. Paris, Jan. 13, 1971. He studied with Paul Vidal at the Paris Cons.; won the 2nd Grand Prix de Rome for his cantata *Coriolan* (1927). He served in the French army (1939–40); was awarded the Grand Prix de Musique Française in 1952. His music is marked by impressionistic colors; he was particularly attracted to exotic subjects, depicting in fine instrumental colors scenes in Corsica, Cambodia, Laos, Sahara, Tahiti, etc. He also wrote music inspired by Gregorian chant and medieval religious songs. During his last period he was motivated in his music by political events, and wrote pieces in homage to the Third World and Vietnam.

Tomasini, Luigi (Aloysius), Italian violinist and composer; b. Pesaro, June 22, 1741; d. Esterház, April 25, 1808. From 1756 he was a violinist at Prince Paul Anton Esterházy's residence in Eisenstadt, and was a friend of Haydn there; in 1761 he became concertmaster in Haydn's orch.; remained in the household of Prince Nicholas, successor to Paul Anton Esterházy, and was pensioned in 1790. Several of Haydn's concertos were dedicated to Tomasini, who was a composer of considerable merit himself; he wrote

24 divertimentos for Baryton, Viola, and Cello, string quartets; etc. His son **Anton Tomasini** (b. Eisenstadt, Feb. 17, 1775; d. there, June 12, 1824) was a viola player; another son, **Luigi Tomasini,** was an excellent violinist in Haydn's orch., highly commended by Haydn; he went to Vienna in 1796 and to Berlin in 1808.

Tomkins, Thomas, English organist and composer; b. St. David's, 1572; d. Martin Hussingtree, near Worcester, June (buried, June 9) 1656. He came from a family of musicians, of whom many members flourished in the 16th and 17th centuries. He was a pupil of William Byrd; was appointed organist of the Worcester Cathedral about 1596, holding this position for half a century, until 1646. In 1607 he received the degree of Mus.B. at Oxford, and in 1621 was appointed an organist of the Chapel Royal. He was one of the most inspired of the English madrigalists; his ballets, keyboard pieces, and sacred works are also of a high quality. His publ. works include *Songs of 3, 4, 5 and 6 parts* (reprinted in the *English Madrigal School,* vol. 18) and *Musica Deo Sacra* (posthumous, 1668), containing 5 services and 95 anthems (services reprinted in *Tudor Church Music,* vol. 7). Other church music is in MS. His keyboard music was publ. by Stephen D. Tuttle in *Musica Britannica,* vol. 5; 2 pieces are in Davison and Apel, *Historical Anthology of Music,* vol. 1 (Cambridge, Mass., 1946).

Tommasini, Vincenzo, Italian composer; b. Rome, Sept. 17, 1878; d. there, Dec. 23, 1950. He studied violin with Pinelli; theory with Falchi at the Santa Cecilia Academy in Rome; then went to Berlin, where he took lessons with Max Bruch; after sojourns in Paris, London, and N.Y., he returned to Rome. He wrote music in the poetic tradition of Italian Romanticism; his operas, symph. works, and chamber music obtained immediate performances and favorable receptions; however, his most successful piece, *Le Donne di buon umore (The Good-humored Ladies),* was not an original work but a comedy-ballet written on music from sonatas by Domenico Scarlatti, arranged in a series of tableaux and brilliantly orchestrated; this was a commission for the Ballets Russes of Diaghilev, who staged it at Rome in April 1917, and kept it in the repertoire during his tours all over the world. Other works by Tommasini include the operas *Medea,* to the composer's own libretto (Trieste, April 8, 1906), and *Uguale fortuna* (Rome, 1913); for Orch.: *La vita è un sogno* (1901); *Poema erotico* (1909); *Inno alla beltà* (1911); *Ciari di luna* (Rome, 1916); *Il beato regno* (Rome, 1922); *Paesaggi toscani* (Rome, 1923); *Il Carnevale di Venezia* (N.Y., Oct. 10, 1929, Toscanini conducting); *Nápule (Naples),* fantasy (Freiburg, Dec. 7, 1931); Violin Concerto (1932); *4 pezzi* (1934); *Le Diable s'amuse,* ballet suite on themes by Paganini (1936); Concerto for String Quartet and Orch. (1939); *La tempesta* (1941); *Tiepolesco,* ballet suite (1945); *Duo concertante* for Piano and Orch. (1948); 3 string quartets; Violin Sonata; Harp Sonata; *Due Macchiette* for Cello and Piano (1940); piano pieces; he publ. *La luce invisible* (1929) and *Saggio di estetica sperimentale* (1942).

Töpfer, Johann Gottlob, famous German organist and writer on organ building; b. Niederrossla, Dec. 4, 1791; d. Weimar, June 8, 1870. He studied with the cantor Schlömilch; then at Weimar with Destouches and A.E. Müller; also attended the Weimar Seminary, where he became a teacher of music in 1817; from 1830 was town organist of Weimar. An expert on organ construction, he wrote *Die Orgelbaukunst* (1833); *Die Scheibler'sche Stimm-Methode* (1842); *Die Orgel; Zweck und Beschaffenheit ihrer Theile* (1843); *Lehrbuch der Orgelbaukunst* (a fundamental work, 1855; 4 vols.; 2nd ed. by M. Allihn, 1888; 3rd ed. by P. Smets, 1934–39); *Theoretisch-praktische Organistenschule* (1845); *Allgemeines und vollständiges Choralbuch* (a 4, with organ interludes); a cantata, *Die Orgelweihe; Konzertstück* for Organ; sonatas, fantasias, preludes, fugues, etc., for organ; piano pieces.

Torchi, Luigi, eminent Italian musicologist; b. Mondano, near Bologna, Nov. 7, 1858; d. Bologna, Sept. 18, 1920. He studied at the Liceo Musicale of Bologna, the Naples Cons. (composition with Serrao), and the Leipzig Cons. (Jadassohn and Reinecke); from 1885–91, was prof. of music history and esthetics, also librarian, at the Liceo Musicale Rossini in Pesaro; from 1895 to 1916 he held similar positions at the Bologna Cons., also teaching composition there. From its foundation (1894) until 1904 he was editor of the *Rivista Musicale Italiana,* for which he wrote many valuable essays. In 1890 he publ. *R. Wagner: Studio critico* (1890; 2nd ed., 1913). Besides a collection of *Eleganti canzoni ed arie italiane* of the 17th century (Milan, 1894) and *A Collection of Pieces for the Violin Composed by Italian Masters of the 17th and 18th Centuries* (London; both with piano accompaniment by Torchi), in 1897 he began publishing the important anthology *L'arte musicale in Italia.*

Torelli, Giuseppe, Italian violinist and composer, probable originator of the solo concerto for violin; b. Verona, April 22, 1658; d. Bologna, Feb. 8, 1709. He studied in Bologna, where he was a member of the Accademia Filarmonica and viola player at the church of S. Petronio (1684–95). He became Kapellmeister to the Margrave of Brandenburg at Ansbach (1698–99). From 1699 he was in Vienna, where he produced an oratorio; returned to Bologna in 1701. He had generally been regarded as the originator of the concerto grosso until Arnold Schering, in 1903, showed that Stradella, who died in 1682, had written such works. But Torelli's *Concerti grossi,* op. 8 (1709), were the first to be publ. (Corelli's op. 6 was not publ. until 1712, though composed earlier).

Torkanowsky, Werner, German-American conductor; b. Berlin, March 30, 1926. He studied music with his mother; went to Palestine after 1933; emigrated to the U.S. in 1948. He began his musical career as a violinist; was a member of the Pittsburgh Symph. Orch. In 1955 he joined the master class of Pierre Monteux in Maine; subsequently conducted at the Spoleto Festivals. From 1963 to 1977 he was conductor of the New Orleans Phil. Symph. Orch.

Torrefranca, Fausto, eminent Italian musicologist; b. Monteleone Calabro, Feb. 1, 1883; d. Rome, Nov. 26, 1955. Trained as an engineer, he took up music under E. Lena in Turin (harmony and counterpoint) and also studied by himself. It was through his initiative that the first chair of musicology was established in Italy; in 1913, he became a lecturer at the Univ. of Rome; in 1914–24, was a prof. of music history at the Cons. di S. Pietro in Naples, and from 1915, also librarian there; from 1924 to 1938 was librarian of the Milan Cons. From 1907 he was editor for several years of the *Rivista Musicale Italiana.* In 1941 he was appointed a prof. of music history at the Univ. of Florence.

Torri, Pietro, Italian composer; b. Peschiera, c.1650; d. Munich, July 6, 1737. He served as court organist and later Kapellmeister at the court in Bayreuth (until 1684); in 1689 he became an organist at Munich; in 1696 he was conductor for the carnival season at Hannover; in 1701 he was appointed chamber music director at Munich, following the Elector to Brussels upon the latter's exile in 1704; he fled Brussels with the Elector (1706). In Brussels he produced the oratorio *Les Vanités du monde* (1706); from 1715 he was again in Munich, where he was made Hofkapell-Direktor; later he was named Hofkapellmeister (1732). He composed 26 operas; produced at the Munich court the operas *Lucio Vero* (Oct. 12, 1720) and *Griselda* (Oct. 12, 1723); also some chamber duets. Selections from the operas were publ. in Denkmäler der Tonkunst in Bayern, 31 (19/20).

Tortelier, Paul, noted French cellist; b. Paris, March 21, 1914. He studied cello with Gérard Hekking at the Paris Cons., and won first prize at the age of 16; he made his debut with the Lamoureux Orch. at the age of 17; from 1935–37 he was first cellist of the orch. in Monte Carlo; from 1937–39 was a member of the Boston Symph. Orch. He was subsequently first cellist of the Paris Cons. Orch. (1946–47). In 1947 he was a soloist at the Festival of Richard Strauss in London. He lived in Israel in 1955–56; then returned to France and joined the faculty of the Paris Cons. He also made occasional appearances as a conductor. He composed several cello concertos, *Israel Symphony,* and a Cello Sonata; also publ. the vol. *How I Play, How I Teach* (London, 1975).

Toscanini, Arturo, one of the greatest conductors of modern times; b. Parma, Italy, March 25, 1867; d. New York, Jan. 16, 1957. He entered the Parma Cons. at the age of 9, studying the cello with Carini and composition with Dacci; graduated in 1885 as winner of the first prize for cello; received the Barbacini Prize as the outstanding graduate of his class. In 1886 he was engaged as cellist for the Ital-

ian opera in Rio de Janeiro; on the 3rd night of the spring season (June 20, 1886) he was unexpectedly called upon to substitute for the regular conductor, when the latter left the podium at the end of the introduction after the public hissed him; the opera was *Aida,* and Toscanini led it without difficulty; he was rewarded by an ovation and was engaged to lead the rest of the season. Returning to Italy, he was engaged to conduct the opera at the Teatro Carignano in Turin, making his debut there on Nov. 4, 1886, and later conducted the Municipal Orch. there. Although still very young, he quickly established a fine reputation. For 10 seasons, between 1887 and 1898, he conducted opera and symph. orchs. in major Italian cities. On May 21, 1892, he led the world premiere of *Pagliacci* in Milan, and on Feb. 1, 1896, the premiere of Puccini's *La Bohème* in Turin. He also conducted the first performance by an Italian opera company, sung in Italian, of *Götterdämmerung* (Turin, Dec. 22, 1895) and *Siegfried* (Milan, 1899); he made his debut as a symph. conductor on March 20, 1896, with the orch. of the Teatro Regio in Turin. In 1898 the impresario Gatti-Casazza engaged him as chief conductor for La Scala, Milan, where he remained until 1903, and again from 1906 to 1908. In the interim, he conducted opera in Buenos Aires (1903–4 and 1906). When Gatti-Casazza became general manager of the Metropolitan Opera Co. (1908), he invited Toscanini to be principal conductor; Toscanini's debut in N.Y. was in *Aida* (Nov. 16, 1908). While at the Metropolitan, Toscanini conducted Verdi's *Requiem* (Feb. 21, 1909), as well as 2 world premieres, Puccini's *The Girl of the Golden West* (Dec. 10, 1910) and Giordano's *Madame Sans-Gêne* (Jan. 25, 1915); he also brought out for the first time in America Gluck's *Armide* (Nov. 14, 1910), Wolf-Ferrari's *Le Donne curiose* (Jan. 3, 1912), and Mussorgsky's *Boris Godunov* (March 19, 1913). On April 13, 1913, he gave his first concert in N.Y. as a symph. conductor, leading Beethoven's 9th Symph. In 1915 he returned to Italy; during the season of 1920–21 he brought the La Scala Orch. on a tour of the U.S. and Canada. From 1921 to 1929 he was artistic director of La Scala; there he conducted the posthumous premiere of Boito's opera *Nerone,* which he himself completed for performance (May 1, 1924). In 1926–27 he was guest conductor of the N.Y. Phil. Orch., returning in subsequent seasons and in 1929–30 as associate conductor with Mengelberg. After the fusion of the N.Y. Phil. and the N.Y. Symph. in 1928, Toscanini was engaged as permanent conductor of the newly organized ensemble; in the spring of 1930 he took the orch. on a tour of Europe; he resigned this position in 1936; conducted in Bayreuth in 1930 and 1931, the first non-German to conduct opera there. Deeply touched by the plight of the Jews in Germany, he acceded to the request of the violinist Hubermann, founder of the Palestine Symph. Orch., to conduct the inaugural concert of that orch. at Tel Aviv (Dec. 26, 1936). During this period he also filled summer engagements at the Salzburg Festivals (1934, 1935, 1936, 1937), and conducted in London (1937, 1938, 1939). Returning to the U.S., he became music director of the NBC Symph. Orch., a radio orch. that had been organized especially for him, giving his opening concert on Dec. 25, 1937; in 1940 he took it on a tour of South America, and on another major tour in 1950. He continued to lead the NBC Symph. until the end of his active career; he conducted his last concert from Carnegie Hall, N.Y., on April 4, 1954 (10 days after his 87th birthday), and then sent a doleful letter of resignation to NBC, explaining the impossibility of further appearances. He died in his sleep, a few weeks before his 90th birthday.

Toscanini was a unique figure among conductors; undemonstrative in his handling of the orch., he possessed an amazing energy and power of command. He demanded absolute perfection, and he erupted in violence when he could not obtain from the orch. what he wanted (a lawsuit was brought against him in Milan when he accidentally injured the concertmaster with a broken violin bow). Despite the vituperation he at times poured on his musicians, he was affectionately known to them as "The Maestro" who could do no wrong. His ability to communicate his desires to singers and players was extraordinary, and even the most celebrated opera stars or instrumental soloists never dared to question his authority. Owing to extreme nearsightedness, Toscanini committed all scores to memory; his repertoire embraced virtually the entire field of Classical and Romantic music; his performances of Italian operas, of Wagner's music dramas, of Beethoven's symphs., and of modern Italian works were especially inspiring. Among the moderns, he conducted works by Richard Strauss, Debussy, Ravel, Prokofiev, and Stravinsky, and among Americans, Samuel Barber, whose *Adagio for Strings* he made famous; he also had his favorite Italian composers (Catalani, Martucci), whose music he fondly fostered. In his social philosophy, he was intransigently democratic; he refused to conduct in Germany under the Nazi regime. He militantly opposed Fascism in Italy, but never abandoned his Italian citizenship, despite his long years of residence in America.

Toselli, Enrico, Italian pianist and composer; b. Florence, March 13, 1883; d. there, Jan. 15, 1926. He studied with Sgambati and Martucci; gave concerts in Italy as a pianist, and composed a number of songs; of these, *Serenata* because enormously popular; also wrote the symph. poem *Fuoco* (after d'Annunzio) and an opera, *La Principessa bizzarra* (Milan, 1913). In 1907 he married the former Crown Princess Luise of Saxony, creating an international furor; wrote an account of this affair, *Il mio matrimonio con Luisa di Sassonia* (Milan, 1918).

Tosi, Pier Francesco, Italian contralto (castrato) and singing teacher; b. Bologna, 1654; d. Faenza, April 1732. He studied with his father, Giuseppe Felice Tosi; sang successfully in Italy; in 1692 settled in London, where he gave regular concerts, and was highly esteemed as a vocal teacher. He served as chapel master at the Austrian court in Vienna from 1705 to 1711; was again in London (about 1723); c.1727 went to Bologna and was ordained a priest.

He owes his fame chiefly to the work *Opinioni de' cantori antichi e moderni o sieno osservazioni sopra il canto figurato* (Bologna, 1723; in Eng., 1742, as *Observations on the Florid Song;* in German as *Anleitung zur Singkunst,* 1757; in French as *L'Art du chant,* 1774; the Eng. ed. was republ. in London in 1967).

Tosti, Sir Francesco Paolo, Italian singing master and vocal composer; b. Ortona, Abruzzi, April 9, 1846; d. Rome, Dec. 2, 1916. He was a pupil, from 1858, of the Collegio di S. Pietro a Majella, Naples, and was appointed sub-teacher (maestrino) by Mercadante. He visited London in 1875; had great success in concerts and settled there as a teacher, becoming singing master to the Royal Family in 1880, and prof. of singing at the Royal Academy of Music in 1894; was knighted in 1908. In 1913 he returned to Italy, taking up his residence in Rome. Besides many original songs, in both English and Italian, he publ. a collection of *Canti popolari abruzzesi.* His songs were highly popular; some of the best known are *Goodbye Forever and Forever, Mattinata,* and *Vorrei morire.*

Tourel, Jennie (real name, **Jennie Davidson**), American mezzo-soprano of Russian-Jewish parentage; b. St. Petersburg, June 22, 1900; d. New York, Nov. 23, 1973. She played flute; then studied piano. After the Revolution, her family left Russia and settled temporarily near Danzig; they later moved to Paris, where Jennie Tourel continued to study piano and contemplated a concert career; she then began to take voice lessons with Anna El-Tour, and decided to devote herself to professional singing; she changed her last name to Tourel by transposing the syllables of her teacher's name. She made her opera debut at the Opéra Russe in Paris in 1931; at the Metropolitan Opera in N.Y. on May 15, 1937, as Mignon. In 1940, just before the occupation of Paris by Nazi troops, she went to Lisbon, Portugal, and eventually emigrated to the U.S.; appeared on the Metropolitan Opera roster in 1943–45 and 1946–47; became a naturalized citizen in 1946. She continued to appear in concert and occasionally in opera; also taught singing at Juilliard in N.Y.

Tourjée, Eben, American music educator; b. Warwick, R.I., June 1, 1834; d. Boston, April 12, 1891. While working in a cotton factory in Harrisville, R.I., he played the organ in church; then went to Germany and studied with Carl August Haupt in Berlin. Returning to America, he settled in Boston, and in 1867 founded there (with R. Goldbeck) the New England Cons. of Music, which he directed till his death. He assisted Patrick S. Gilmore in organizing the 2 great "peace jubilees" in Boston (1869, 1872); was the first president of the Music Teachers National Assoc. (1876), and dean of the College of Music of Boston Univ.

Tournemire, Charles, French organist and composer; b. Bordeaux, Jan. 22, 1870; d. Arcachon, Nov. 3, 1939. He was a pupil of César Franck at the Paris

Cons., winning the first prize for organ in 1890; also studied composition with Vincent d'Indy at the Schola Cantorum. In 1898 he succeeded Pierné as organist at Ste. Clotilde, remaining until 1939. As an organ virtuoso, he toured throughout Europe. He was prof. of ensemble playing at the Paris Cons. (1919–38).

Tourte, François, French violin-bow maker; b. Paris, 1747; d. there, April 26, 1835. He was the creator of the modern bow: the shape of the wood and inward curve of the stick, the selection and preparation of the wood (Pernambuco), the length of the bow and all its modern appurtenances, are the product of his skill.

Tovey, Sir Donald Francis, eminent English musical scholar; b. Eton, July 17, 1875; d. Edinburgh, July 10, 1940. He studied privately with Sophie Weisse (piano), Sir W. Parratt (counterpoint), and James Higgs (composition) until 1894, when he won the Nettleship scholarship at Balliol College, Oxford; graduated with Classical Honors (B.A., 1898). In 1900–1901 he gave a series of chamber music concerts in London, at which he performed several of his own works; in 1901–2 he gave similar concerts in Berlin and Vienna; played his Piano Concerto in 1903 under Henry Wood and in 1906 under Hans Richter; from 1906 to 1912 he gave in London regular series of chamber music concerts, known as The Chelsea Concerts. In 1914 he succeeded Niecks as Reid Prof. of music at Edinburgh Univ. (named after John Reid); there he established the Reid Symph. Concerts, for which he organized in 1917 the Reid Symph. Orch. of 50 musicians. He made his American debut as a pianist in 1925, and in 1927–28 made a tour of the U.S. He was knighted in 1935. Though highly esteemed as a composer, he was most widely known as a writer and lecturer on music, his analytical essays being models of their kind. Besides much chamber music and several piano pieces (a sonata, *Balliol Dances* for 4-hands, etc.), he composed an opera, *The Bride of Dionysus* (Edinburgh, April 25, 1932); a Symph. (1913); Cello Concerto (premiere by Pablo Casals, composer conducting, Edinburgh, Nov. 22, 1934); etc. He publ. a collection of 16th-century church music, *Laudate pueri* (Part I of *Northlands Singing Book*), and edited Bach's *Kunst der Fuge.* He wrote many of the music articles for the *Encyclopædia Britannica* (beginning with the 11th ed.).
WRITINGS: *A Companion to Bach's Art of the Fugue* (1931); *A Companion to Beethoven's Pianoforte Sonatas* (1931); *Musical Form and Matter* (1934); *Normality and Freedom in Music* (1936); *Essays in Musical Analysis* (6 vols., 1935–39: I and II, orch. works; III, concertos; IV, polyphony and illustrative music; V, vocal music; VI, supplement, index, and glossary). Posthumous publications: *Walter Parratt: The Master of Music* (with G. Parratt; London, 1941); *A Musician Talks* (London, 1941); *Musical Articles from the Encyclopædia Britannica* (London, 1944); *Beethoven* (London, 1944); *Essays in Musical Analysis: Chamber Music* (London,

1944); *Essays and Lectures on Music* (London, 1949; U.S. ed. as *The Main Stream of Music*).

Tower, Joan, American composer; b. New Rochelle, N.Y., Sept. 6, 1938. She played piano as a child; studied composition with 12 teachers, among whom were Henry Brant at Bennington College (B.A.); Otto Luening, Vladimir Ussachevsky, and Wen-Chung Chou at Columbia Univ. (M.A.); and Wallingford Riegger and Darius Milhaud afield. Her music reflects these dodecuple didacticisms, but adds a lot more. A blithe spirit, Joan Tower engages in quaquaversal activities, including lecturing in schools and other public places. In 1979 she organized a chamber group in N.Y. called the Da Capo Players, for which she acts as pianist. In 1977 she was awarded a Guggenheim fellowship.

Tozzi, Giorgio (real first name, **George**), gifted American bass of Italian descent; b. Chicago, Jan. 8, 1923. His father was a day laborer. He studied biology at De Paul Univ.; also took vocal lessons in Chicago with Rosa Raisa, Giacomo Rimini, and John Daggett Howell. He made his professional debut in N.Y. in the American premiere of Britten's *The Rape of Lucretia* as the rapist Tarquinius (Dec. 29, 1948). In 1949 he went to Europe, and sang in a musical comedy, *Tough at the Top,* in London. With the earnings obtained through this employment, he financed a trip to Italy, where he took lessons with Giulio Lorandi in Milan. He sang at the Teatro Nuovo in Milan, and in Dec. 1953 appeared at La Scala. He then returned to the U.S.; on March 9, 1955, he made his Metropolitan debut in N.Y. as Alvise in *La Gioconda;* continued to sing at the Metropolitan in a variety of parts, among them Don Giovanni in Mozart's opera; Figaro in *Le nozze di Figaro,* Don Basilio in *Il barbiere di Siviglia,* Méphistophélès in Gounod's *Faust,* Hans Sachs in *Die Meistersinger,* King Mark in *Tristan und Isolde,* and the title role in *Boris Godunov.* He also made regular appearances with the San Francisco Opera, where he sang for the first time on Sept. 15, 1955. He was a guest artist at the Salzburg Festival, and sang at Munich, Hamburg, and other European music centers. A true modern man, he did not spurn the world of musical commerce, and even sang a commercial for the Fiat automobile company, putting on an ancestral Italian accent, albeit of dubious authenticity in his generation.

Trabaci, Giovanni Maria, Italian composer; b. Montepeloso, c.1575; d. Naples, Dec. 31, 1647. He studied with Giovanni Macque; became organist at the Viceregal Chapel in Naples in 1601; after Macque's death (1614) he succeeded him as choir director there. During the rebellion of the Neapolitan populace against the fruit tax of 1647, Trabaci fled to the monastery of the Trinità degli Spagnuoli, where he died. The bulk of his music consists of Psalms, masses, motets, and madrigals. Two keyboard publications are extant: *Ricercare, canzone francese, capricci, canti fermi, gagliarde, partite diverse, etc., Libro primo* (Naples, 1603) and *Il se-*

condo libro di ricercare ed altri varii capricci (Naples, 1615). Some of his vocal works were publ. by Pannain in *Istituzioni e monumenti dell'arte musicale italiana* (vol. 5); these include 12 motets *a* 5, 4 *a* 6, and 4 *a* 8; also 2 masses for Double Chorus. Keyboard works are reprinted in L. Torchi, *L'arte musicale in Italia* (vol. 3), in Tagliapietra, *Antologia di musica antica e moderna* (vol. 5), and in Davison and Apel, *Historical Anthology of Music.* Trabaci's canzonas include examples of rhythmic variants of a single theme ("variation canzonas"), anticipating Frescobaldi in this respect.

Traetta, Filippo, Italian musician; son of **Tommaso Traetta;** b. Venice, Jan. 8, 1777; d. Philadelphia, Jan. 9, 1854. He was a pupil of Fenaroli and Perillo at Venice, later of Piccinni at Naples. Becoming a soldier in the patriot ranks, he was captured and cast into prison; he escaped 6 months afterward, and sailed to Boston, arriving there in 1799. There he wrote his *Vocal Exercises* and *Washington's Dead March.* Proceeding to N.Y., he wrote the cantatas *The Christian's Joy* and *Prophecy;* also an opera, *The Venetian Masker.* He managed a traveling theatrical troupe; lived in Virginia for some years, and settled in Philadelphia, c.1828, founding the American Cons. with his pupil U.K. Hill. He produced 2 oratorios, *Jerusalem in Affliction* (1828) and *Daughter of Zion* (1829); later 2 cantatas, *The Nativity* and *The Day of Rest;* also instrumental and vocal quartets, trios, and duets; songs; etc.; publ. *Rudiments of the Art of Singing* (2 vols.; 1841–43) and *An Introduction to the Art and Science of Music* (1829) for his Cons. He was active as a singing teacher until his death.

Traetta, Tommaso (Michele Francesco Saverio), Italian composer; b. Bitonto, Naples, March 30, 1727; d. Venice, April 6, 1779. He entered the Cons. di Loreto in Naples at the age of 11, and was there a pupil of Durante. His first opera, *Il Farnace,* was produced at the Teatro San Carlo with fine success, on Nov. 4, 1751; there followed several more operas in Naples, and later in other Italian cities: *Buovo d'Antona* (Venice, Dec. 27, 1758), *Ippolito ed Aricia* (Parma, May 9, 1759), etc. In 1758 he was appointed maestro di cappella to the Duke of Parma; his *Armida* was staged in Vienna (Jan. 3, 1761) with excellent success, and he was commisioned to write another opera for Vienna, *Ifigenia in Tauride,* which was produced there on Oct. 4, 1763. He settled in Venice in 1765, and was director of the Cons. dell'Ospedaletto S. Giovanni there for 3 years. In 1768 he was engaged for the court of Catherine the Great as successor to Galuppi, and arrived in St. Petersburg in the autumn of that year. He staged several of his operas there (mostly versions of works previously performed in Italy); also arranged music for various occasions (anniversary of the coronation of Catherine the Great; celebration of a victory over the Turkish fleet; etc.). He left Russia in 1775 and went to London, where he produced the operas *Germondo* (Jan. 21, 1776), *Telemacco* (March 15, 1777), and *I capricci del sesso* (1777),

without much success; returned to Italy, and produced 3 more operas in Venice. In many respects, he was an admirable composer, possessing a sense of drama and a fine melodic gift. In musical realism, he adopted certain procedures that Gluck was to employ successfully later on; he was highly regarded by his contemporaries. Besides operas, he wrote an oratorio, *Salomone* (Venice, 1766), a Stabat Mater, and other church music. Excerpts from Traetta's operas, edited by H. Goldschmidt, are in *Denkmäler der Tonkunst in Bayern,* 25 and 29 (14.i and 17).

Tragó, José, Spanish pianist and pedagogue; b. Madrid, Sept. 25, 1856; d. there, Jan. 3, 1934. He studied at the conservatories of Madrid and Paris, winning first prizes for piano at both; was for many years a prof. at the Madrid Cons. He was the teacher of Manuel de Falla and Joaquín Turina.

Trampler, Walter, eminent German-American violist and pedagogue; b. Munich, Aug. 25, 1915. He received his early musical training from his father; later enrolled at the Munich State Academy of Music; made his debut in Munich as a violinist in 1933; then played mostly the viola; from 1935–38 served as first violist in the orch. of Radio Deutschlandsender; then emigrated to America. From 1947 to 1955 he was a member of the New Music String Quartet; also made appearances with the Yale, Emerson, Budapest, Juilliard, and Guarneri quartets and with the Beaux Arts Trio. In 1962 he was appointed prof. of viola and chamber music at the Juilliard School of Music in N.Y.; in 1971 was named prof. at the Yale School of Music; in 1972 became a member of the faculty at Boston Univ.

Trapp, Max, German composer; b. Berlin, Nov. 1, 1887; d. there, May 31, 1971. He studied piano with Ernst von Dohnányi and composition with Paul Juon; then taught at the Berlin Hochschule für Musik and also at the Cons. of Dortmund; in 1929 became a member of the Berlin Academy of Arts, where he taught a master class in composition (1934–45); from 1951 to 1953 he was on the staff of the Municipal Cons. in Berlin. His style is neo-Classical with a strong polyphonic texture, in the tradition of Max Reger. He was also active as a landscape painter.

Traubel, Helen, American soprano; b. St. Louis, June 20, 1899; d. Santa Monica, Calif., July 28, 1972. She made her concert debut at St. Louis in 1925, and appeared for the first time at the Metropolitan Opera in N.Y. on May 12, 1937, as Mary Rutledge in *The Man without a Country.* She made several transcontinental tours; sang in Buenos Aires in 1943; also gave numerous concerts in Europe. She was married to Louis Carpenter in 1922; they were divorced the same year; and in 1938 she married William L. Bass. In 1953 she made appearances in N.Y. nightclubs; this prompted objections from the Metropolitan Opera management, and as a result she resigned from the Metropolitan. She publ. the mystery novels *The Ptomaine Canary* and *The Metropolitan Opera Murders* (N.Y., 1951), and an autobiography, *St. Louis Woman* (N.Y., 1959).

Trautwein, Friedrich, German electrical engineer; b. Würzburg, Aug. 11, 1888; d. Düsseldorf, Dec. 21, 1956. He was trained in engineering; was an instructor in musical acoustics at the Berlin Hochschule für Musik. In 1930 he constructed an electronic musical instrument which became known, after the first syllable of his name, as the Trautonium. Hindemith wrote a concerto for it. Trautwein contributed numerous articles on electronic music to German periodicals.

Travis, Roy, American composer; b. New York, June 24, 1922. He studied composition with Bernard Wagenaar at the Juilliard School of Music in N.Y. (1947–50); then took a course with Otto Luening at Columbia Univ.; in 1950 he went to Paris and had instruction with Darius Milhaud. Returning to the U.S., he taught at Columbia Univ. and at the Mannes College of Music in N.Y. In 1957 he was appointed to the faculty of the Univ. of Calif. at Los Angeles; apart from composition, he began a thorough investigation of electronic music and also worked at the Inst. of Ethnomusicology there. His most outstanding work is the 2-act opera *The Passion of Oedipus,* composed in 1965 and produced at the Opera Workshop at the Univ. of Calif. in Los Angeles on Nov. 8, 1968; its music, rooted in Greek homophony, is enhanced by an acridly dramatic idiom. His other important works include *African Sonata* for Piano (1966), based on tribal African modes; Concerto for Flute with recorded African Instruments metamorphosed by a Synthesizer (1970–71); *Songs and Epilogues,* a song cycle with Piano interludes, to texts from Sappho (1965); *Collage* for Orch. (1967–68); Septet for Flute, Clarinet, Violin, Cello, Double Bass, Piano, and Percussion (1968); Piano Concerto (1969).

Trebelli, Zelia (real name, **Zelia Gilbert**), French mezzo-soprano; b. Paris, 1838; d. Etretat, Aug. 18, 1892. She studied with Wartel; made her debut in 1859 as Rosina in *Il Barbiere di Siviglia,* followed by appearances in England (1862). She was long a favorite in London; also toured in the U.S. (1878 and 1884).

Tregian, Francis, English musician; b. 1574; d. London, 1619. He was a recusant, and fled England to escape persecution; was attached to Catholic dignitaries in Douai and in Rome. Returning to England to settle his father's estate, he was convicted in 1609, remaining in prison until his death. His significance for English music lies in the fact that he was the scribe of the *Fitzwilliam Virginal Book* and of 2 MSS containing more than 2,000 motets, madrigals, etc., some of them possibly of his own composition.

Treharne, Bryceson, English-American music editor and composer; b. Merthyr Tydfil, Wales, May 30, 1879; d. New York, Feb. 4, 1948. He studied at the Royal College of Music in London, under Parry, Stanford, and Davies. In 1901 he went to Australia; was a prof. at the Univ. of Adelaide; returning to Europe in 1911, he lived in Paris, Milan, Vienna, and Munich; at the outbreak of World War I, he was interned in Germany, at Ruhleben. There he wrote nearly 200 songs and other works; an exchange of prisoners of war enabled him to return to England. In 1917 he settled in America; was music editor for the Boston Music Co. and Willis Music Co. (1928–47). Among his songs are *Ozymandias, The Fair Circassian, A Lover's Prayer, The Night, Dreams, Love's Tribute,* and *Renunciation.*

Treigle, Norman, remarkable American bass-baritone; b. New Orleans, March 6, 1927; d. there, Feb. 16, 1975. He sang in a church choir as a child; upon graduation from high school in 1943 he served in the navy. After two years in service he returned to New Orleans and studied voice with Elizabeth Wood; made his debut in 1947 with the New Orleans Opera as Lodovico in Verdi's *Otello.* In 1952 he went to N.Y. and joined the N.Y. City Opera, making his debut there on March 28, 1953, as Colline in *La Bohème;* he remained with the company for 20 years, establishing himself as a favorite with the public. Among his most successful roles were Figaro in Mozart's *Le nozze di Figaro,* Don Giovanni, Méphistophélès, and Boris Godunov; he also sang in modern operas, including the leading parts in the world premieres of 3 operas by Carlisle Floyd: *The Passion of Jonathan Wade* (N.Y., Oct. 11, 1962), *The Sojourner and Mollie Sinclair* (Raleigh, N.C., Dec. 2, 1963), and *Markheim* (New Orleans, March 31, 1966). Treigle's other parts in contemporary operas were the title role in Dallapiccola's *The Prisoner* and that of the grandfather in Copland's *The Tender Land.* He also made a successful appearance at Covent Garden in London, as Méphistophélès in *Faust* on Nov. 13, 1973. His untimely death, from an overdose of sleeping pills at his home in New Orleans, deprived the American musical theater of one of its finest talents.

Tremblay, George, Canadian-American composer; b. Ottawa, Jan. 14, 1911; d. Tijuana, Mexico, July 14, 1982. He studied music with his father, a church organist; in 1919 he was taken to the U.S.; eventually settled in Los Angeles; there he met Schoenberg and became his ardent disciple and friend. He adopted the method of composition with 12-tones, which he diversified considerably, expounding his theoretical ideas in a book, *The Definitive Cycle of the 12-Tone Row,* publ. in 1974. In Hollywood, he became an esteemed teacher; among his students were André Previn, Quincy Jones, and Johnny Mandel, as well as numerous successful composers for television and motion pictures.

Tremblay, Gilles, Canadian composer; b. Arvida, Quebec, Sept. 6, 1932. He had private lessons with Papineau-Couture; studied piano with Germaine

Malépart and composition with Claude Champagne at the Montreal Cons. (1949–54). In 1954 he went to Paris, where he took courses with Messiaen (analysis), Yvonne Loriod (piano), Andrée Vaurabourg-Honegger (counterpoint), and Maurice Martenot (Ondes Martenot); subsequently worked with the Groupe de Recherches Musicales at Paris Radio (1960–61). He returned to Canada in 1961; in 1962 was appointed a prof. at the Montreal Cons. He follows the modern French method of composition and uses graphic notation in his scores.

Treptow, Günther, German tenor; b. Berlin, Oct. 22, 1907; d. there, March 28, 1981. He studied at the Berlin Hochschule für Musik; made his debut in 1936 at the Deutsches Opernhaus in Berlin as the Steerman in *Der fliegende Holländer;* then sang at Berlin's Städtische Oper (1936–42, 1945–50) and at the Vienna State Opera (1947–55). He made his Metropolitan Opera debut in N.Y. as Siegmund in *Die Walküre* on Feb. 1, 1951; remained on its roster until the close of that season; continued to sing in Europe until his retirement in 1961. He was noted for his performances of the roles of Siegmund, Tristan, and Siegfried in Wagner's operas.

Tréville, Yvonne de (real name, **Edyth La Gierse**), American coloratura soprano; b. (of a French father and an American mother) Galveston, Texas, Aug. 25, 1881; d. New York, Jan. 25, 1954. She made her debut in N.Y. as Marguérite (1898); then went to Paris, where she studied with Madame Marchesi; appeared at the Opéra-Comique as Lakmé (June 20, 1902); sang in Madrid, Brussels, Vienna, Budapest, Cairo, and in Russia; from 1913, gave concert tours in the U.S. and sang in light operas. Her voice had a compass of 3 full octaves, reaching high G.

Tritto, Giacomo, Italian composer; b. Altamura, April 2, 1733; d. Naples, Sept. 16, 1824. He studied with Cafaro at the Cons. della Pietà de' Turchini; became subteacher (primo maestrino) and Cafaro's assistant in teaching harmony, also succeeded him as concertmaster at the Teatro San Carlo. From 1799 to 1807 he was principal teacher (primo maestro) at the Cons.; followed Paisiello in 1816 as maestro di cappella of the Royal Chapel. Bellini, Spontini, Mercadante, Meyerbeer, and Conti were his pupils. His first opera, *La fedeltà in amore,* was performed at Naples in 1764; some 50 others were produced subsequently in Naples, Rome, Venice, Milan, etc.; of these, *Le vicende amorose* (Rome, 1788) and *Gli Americani* (Naples, Nov. 4, 1802) were fairly successful. Other works included 3 cantatas, a Mass for Double Chorus with 2 Orchs., 7 other masses (3 of them with Orch.), 2 Passions with Orch., a Te Deum, motets, etc. (none printed). He publ. *Partimenti e regole generali per conoscere qual numerica dar si deve ai vari movimenti del basso* (1821), and *Scuola di contrappunto, ossia Teoria musicale* (1823).

Trojan, Manfred, German composer; b. Cremlingen, near Braunschweig, Oct. 22, 1949. He studied

flute in Braunschweig (1966–70); then enrolled in the Hochschule für Musik in Hamburg (1970–78); also took private lessons in composition with Diether de la Motte (1970–73). His music is neo-Baroque in form and programmatic in content; his songs are expressionistic in their chromatic Angst.

Troyanos, Tatiana, brilliant American mezzo-soprano; b. New York, Sept. 12, 1938. She received her musical training at the Juilliard School of Music; made her debut with the N.Y. City Opera in 1963; in 1964 she went to Europe; made appearances with the Hamburg State Opera. In 1969 she sang at Covent Garden in London; in 1971 she was engaged at the Paris Opéra. On March 8, 1976, she made a memorable Metropolitan Opera debut in N.Y. as Octavian in *Der Rosenkavalier;* in subsequent seasons she became one of the company's leading members.

Tschaikowsky. See **Tchaikovsky.**

Tschudi. See **Broadwood.**

Tua, Teresina (real name, **Maria Felicità**), Italian violinist; b. Turin, May 22, 1867; d. Rome, Oct. 29, 1955. She studied with Massart at the Paris Cons., where she took the first prize in 1880; toured the Continent with brilliant success; made her English debut at the Crystal Palace in London, May 5, 1883; also appeared in America (1887). In 1889 she married Count Franchi-Verney della Valetta, and withdrew from the concert stage till the autumn of 1895, when she set out on a successful European tour, including Russia, where her accompanist and joint artist was Rachmaninoff. Franchi died in 1911; in 1913 she married Emilio Quadrio. She taught at the Milan Cons. from 1915 to 1924, and then at the Santa Cecilia Academy in Rome; subsequently abandoned her career, and entered the Convento dell'Adorazione in Rome as Sister Maria di Gesù.

Tubb, Carrie (Caroline Elizabeth), English soprano; b. London, May 17, 1876; d. there, Sept. 20, 1976, at the age of 100. She studied at the Guildhall School of Music; began her career singing minor roles in productions by the Beecham Opera Co.; then abandoned the stage and devoted herself to the oratorio and solo recitals. She excelled both in Mozart arias and in concert excerpts from Wagner and Verdi. At the zenith of her career, her singing was described in glowing superlatives by such otherwise sober auditors as Eric Blom. As her voice betrayed the inexorable signs of senescence, she applied herself to teaching, following G.B. Shaw's dictum, "Who can, do; who cannot, teach."

Tubin, Eduard, Estonian-born Swedish composer; b. Kallaste, near Tartu (Dorpat), June 18, 1905; d. Stockholm, Nov. 17, 1982. He studied with A. Kapp at the Cons. of Tartu and later with Kodály in Budapest. From 1931 to 1944 he conducted the Tartu Symph. Orch.; in 1944 he settled in Stockholm. In

1961 he became a Swedish citizen; in 1982 was elected to the Royal Swedish Academy of Music. He was at work on his 11th Symph. at the time of his death.

Tucci, Gabriella, Italian soprano; b. Rome, Aug. 4, 1929. She studied at the Santa Cecilia Academy in Rome, and then with Leonardo Filoni. In 1951 she won the international singing competition in Spoleto; after appearances in provincial Italian opera houses, she sang at La Scala in Milan and at the Rome Opera. On Sept. 25, 1959, she made her American debut as Madeleine in *Andrea Chénier* at the San Francisco Opera; her Metropolitan Opera debut followed in N.Y. on Oct. 29, 1960, as Cio-Cio-San in *Madama Butterfly.* She continued to sing at the Metropolitan with increasing success; especially noted were her appearances as Desdemona (March 10, 1963), Marguerite in Gounod's *Faust* (Sept. 27, 1965), and Mimi in *La Bohème* (April 16, 1966). Her other roles were Violetta, Aida, Tosca, Gilda in *Rigoletto,* and Liù in *Turandot.* Her European career was equally successful; she sang at Covent Garden in London, at San Carlo in Naples, at the Vienna State Opera, at the Deutsche Oper in Berlin, at the Munich Opera, at the Bolshoi Theatre in Moscow, at the Teatro Colón in Buenos Aires, and in Japan.

Tucker, Richard (real name, **Reuben Ticker**), brilliant American tenor; b. Brooklyn, Aug. 28, 1913; d. Kalamazoo, Mich., Jan. 8, 1975. He sang in a synagogue choir in N.Y. as a child; studied voice with Paul Althouse; subsequently sang on the radio. His first public appearance in opera was as Alfredo in *La Traviata* in 1943 with the Salmaggi Co. in N.Y. On Jan. 25, 1945, he made his Metropolitan Opera debut in N.Y. as Enzo in *La Gioconda;* he remained on its roster until his death, specializing in the Italian repertoire. In 1947 he made his European debut at the Verona Arena as Enzo (Maria Callas made her Italian debut as Gioconda in the same performance); he also sang at Covent Garden in London, at La Scala in Milan, in Vienna, and in other major music centers abroad. He died suddenly while on a concert tour. He was the brother-in-law of the American tenor **Jan Peerce.**

Tuckwell, Barry, Australian virtuoso horn player; b. Melbourne, March 5, 1931, in a musical family. He was taught piano by his father and violin by his older brother; was a chorister at St. Andrew's Cathedral in Sydney, and also acted as an organist there. At age 13 he began studying the French horn with Alan Mann at the Cons. of Sydney; making rapid progress, he joined the Sydney Symph., then conducted by Eugene Goossens (1947–50). In 1950 he went to England, where he met Dennis Brain, the virtuoso horn player, who gave him valuable suggestions on horn technique; he also gathered some ideas about horn sound from listening to recordings by Tommy Dorsey. He filled positions as assistant first horn with the Hallé Orch. in Manchester (1951–53), with the Scottish National Orch. (1953–54), and, as first horn, with the Bournemouth Symph. Orch. (1954–55); then served for 13 years (1955–68) as first horn player with the London Symph. Orch. After leaving this orch. he launched a career as a soloist, achieving recognition as one of the foremost virtuosos on the instrument. In the academic field, he compiled a horn method and edited horn literature. Several modern composers wrote special works for him: Thea Musgrave (a Concerto that requires the horn to play quarter-tones); Richard Rodney Bennett (*Actaeon* for Horn and Orch.); Iain Hamilton (*Voyage* for Horn and Orch.); Alun Hoddinott (Concerto); and Don Banks (Concerto). In 1978 he made his first appearance as a conductor in the U.S., in a program of Baroque music.

Tudor, David, American avant-garde pianist and aleatory composer; b. Philadelphia, Jan. 20, 1926. He studied organ with William Hawke, piano with Irma Wolpe, and composition with Stefan Wolpe. He played the organ in St. Mark's Church in Philadelphia (1938–43) and at Swarthmore College (1944–48); these ecclesiastical services to the contrary notwithstanding, he simultaneously plunged into uninhibited experimentation; developed a hypermodern virtuoso technique as a quaquaversal hyperdactyl pianist; earned an awesome reputation by performing the insurmountable, impregnable, and inscrutable 2nd Piano Sonata of Pierre Boulez (N.Y., Dec. 17, 1950) from memory. He became the unique collaborator, animator, and divinator of the recondite practices of John Cage, and was the first to unplay John Cage's monumental tacit piece *4' 33*S'* (Woodstock, N.Y., Aug. 29, 1952); was also unheard in it in Cologne, Germany, and elsewhere, obtaining vociferous acclaim. In audible performance he often applies special piano techniques; in playing *5 Piano Pieces for David Tudor* by Sylvano Bussotti, he is apt to put on thick leather gloves for tone-clusters. As a composer, he has the following works to his credit: *Fluorescent Sound* (Stockholm, Sept. 13, 1964); *Bandoneon—!* (factorial bandoneon, idempotentially multiplied ad infinitum); *Reunion* (in collaboration with the painter Marcel Duchamp and others); *Rainforest* for Dancers; and, in collaboration with John Cage, *Talk I* (Ann Arbor, Mich., Sept. 19, 1965) and *Fontana Mix* for Bass Drum and Electronic Circuits (Brandeis Univ., Waltham, Mass., April Fools' Day, 1967). Some of his biographers claim for him a direct descent, through a morganatic line, from Henry Tudor (Henry VII), and/or from one of the decapitated lovers of the beheaded Queen Anne Boleyn. Since Henry VIII himself dabbled in "aleatorick musick," David Tudor's own preoccupation with tonal indeterminacy may be a recessive royal trait.

Tudway, Thomas, English composer; b. 1650; d. Cambridge, Nov. 23, 1726. From 1660 he was a chorister in the Chapel Royal, under Dr. Blow; he became lay-vicar at St. George's Chapel, Windsor, in 1664; was organist of King's College, Cambridge, from 1670 to 1680; became teacher of choristers there in 1679; became a prof. of music at Cambridge

Univ. in 1705; was suspended 1706–7, retired 1726. From Cambridge Univ. he received the degrees of Mus.Bac. (1681) and Mus.Doc. (1705). He composed services, motets, and anthems; his *Collection of Services and Anthems used in the Church of England from the Reformation to the Restoration of King Charles II,* in 6 MS vols., is in the British Library.

Tully, Alice, American singer and music patroness; b. Corning, N.Y., Sept. 11, 1902. A scion of a family of wealth, she studied voice in Paris, where she made her concert debut with the Pasdeloup Orch. in 1927. Returning to the U.S., she gave a song recital in N.Y. in 1936, and received critical praise for her interpretation of French songs. She eventually gave up her artistic ambition and devoted herself to various philanthropic endeavors. Her major gift was to Lincoln Center in N.Y., for the construction of a chamber music hall; it was dedicated as Alice Tully Hall in 1969. She also helped to organize the Chamber Music Society of Lincoln Center.

Tunder, Franz, celebrated German organist and composer; b. Bannesdorf, near Burg, Fehmarn, 1614; d. Lübeck, Nov. 5, 1667. In 1632–41 he was court organist at Gottorp, where he studied with J. Heckelauer, a pupil of Frescobaldi; in 1641, he became organist of the Marienkirche in Lübeck, being succeeded at his death by his son-in-law, **Dietrich Buxtehude.** Seven chorale fantasias for organ by Tunder were discovered in 1903 in the Lüneburg tablature books (one was publ. by Straube, in Alte Meister des Orgelspiels, new series). Solo and choral cantatas were edited by M. Seiffert in Denkmäler Deutscher Tonkunst, 3; 2 preludes and fugues for organ were edited by R. Buchmayer (1927); 4 organ, preludes, etc. are in *Organum.* A complete edition of Tunder's organ chorale arrangements was begun in 1958, edited by Rudolf Walter; *Collected Organ Works,* edited by Klaus Beckmann, was publ. in Wiesbaden (1974). Two works by Tunder from the Pelplin MS in Poland were publ. in vol. X, part 2, of *Corpus of Early Keyboard Music,* under the auspices of the American Inst. of Musicology (1967).

Turchaninov, Piotr, Russian composer of sacred music; b. Kiev, Dec. 1, 1779; d. St. Petersburg, March 28, 1856. He studied music with Sarti when the latter was at the St. Petersburg court; was ordained a priest in 1803; taught singing at the imperial court chapel; from 1831 to 1841 was archpriest at various churches. His masterly arrangements and harmonizations of old liturgical melodies of the Russian Church were publ. in 5 vols., edited by Kastalsky (Moscow, 1906). His autobiography was publ. in St. Petersburg in 1863.

Turchi, Guido, Italian composer; b. Rome, Nov. 10, 1916. He studied composition with Ildebrando Pizzetti, and in his early music followed Pizzetti's style of Italian Baroque, with Romantic and impressionistic extensions; he then changed his idiom toward a more robust and accentuated type of music-making, influenced mainly by a study of the works of Béla Bartók. Turchi's Concerto for String Orch. is dedicated to Bartók's memory. From 1960 to 1967 he taught at the Cons. of Rome; in 1967 was appointed director of the Cons. of Parma.

Tureck, Rosalyn, eminent American pianist and harpsichordist; b. Chicago, Dec. 14, 1914, in a musical family of Russian and Turkish background. She studied piano in Chicago with Sophia Brilliant-Liven (1925–29), Jan Chiapusso (1929–31), and Gavin Williamson (1931–32); then went to N.Y., where she studied with Olga Samaroff at the Juilliard School of Music, graduating in 1935. In her concert career she dedicated herself mainly to Bach. In 1947 she made her first European tour; subsequently gave concerts in South America, South Africa, and Israel. In 1971 she made a world tour, including India and the Orient. She held teaching posts at the Philadelphia Cons. of Music (1935–42), Juilliard School of Music (1943–55), and Univ. of Calif., San Diego (1966–72). In 1977 she received the honorary degree of Mus.D. from Oxford Univ. In order to demonstrate the universal applicability of Bach's keyboard techniques, she played Bach on the Moog synthesizer; in 1971 she gave a concert announced as "Bach and Rock." She publ. *An Introduction to the Performance of Bach* (3 vols., London, 1959–60; also publ. in Japanese, 1966, and Spanish, 1972).

Turina, Joaquín, prominent Spanish composer; b. Seville, Dec. 9, 1882; d. Madrid, Jan. 14, 1949. He studied with local teachers; then entered the Madrid Cons. as a pupil of Tragó (piano). In 1905 he went to Paris, where he studied composition with Vincent d'Indy at the Schola Cantorum, and piano with Moszkowski. In Paris a meeting with Albéniz and Manuel de Falla proved a turning point in his career; he determined to write national Spanish music; returning to Madrid in 1913, he produced 2 symph. works in a characteristic Spanish style: *La procesión del rocío* and *Sinfonía sevillana,* combining Romantic and impressionist elements in an individual manner; the same effective combination is found in his chamber music of Spanish inspiration (*Escena andaluza, La oración del torero,* etc.) and his piano music (*Sonata romántica, Mujeres españolas,* etc.); he also wrote operas and incidental music for the theater. In 1930 he was appointed a prof. of music at the Cons. of Madrid.

Turini, Ronald, Canadian pianist; b. Montreal, Sept. 30, 1934. He studied at the Quebec Cons.; subsequently took private lesseons with Isabelle Vengerova and Vladimir Horowitz. He toured Europe as a soloist with the Montreal Symph. Orch. in 1962; also gave recitals in the major music centers.

Türk, Daniel Gottlob, German organist and teacher; b. Clausnitz, Saxony, Aug. 10, 1756; d. Halle, Aug. 26, 1813. He was a pupil in harmony and counterpoint of Homilius while studying at the Kreuzschule in Dresden; he had learned to play the violin at home and after he entered Leipzig Univ. J.A. Hiller continued his instruction, and engaged him as violinist at the theater and the Grosses Concert. In 1776 he was cantor of the Ulrichskirche, Halle, and music teacher at the Gymnasium; in 1779, he became music director of the Univ.; on becoming organist at the Liebfrauenkirche in 1787, he resigned his positions as cantor and teacher. He publ. an important clavier method (1789; 2nd ed., 1802) and instructive pieces for piano; 18 sonatas and sonatinas for piano; songs; theoretical works. An opera, church music, symphs., and organ pieces are in MS. Some piano pieces for 4-hands were edited by Doflein (1933).

Turner, Robert Comrie, Canadian composer; b. Montreal, June 6, 1920. He studied with Champagne at McGill Univ. in Montreal, graduating in 1943; with Herbert Howells and Gordon Jacob at the Royal College of Music in London (1947–48), with Messiaen at the Berkshire Music Center in Tanglewood, Mass. (summer 1949), and with Roy Harris at Nashville (1949–50); received his Mus.Doc. degree from McGill Univ. in 1953. From 1952 to 1967 he was a music producer for the Canadian Broadcasting Corp. in Vancouver; taught at the Univ. of British Columbia (1955–57) and at Acadia Univ. in Wolfville, Nova Scotia (1968–69); in 1969 was appointed to the music faculty of the Univ. of Manitoba.

Turnhout, Gérard de (real name, **Gheert Jacques**), Netherlandish composer; b. Turnhout, c.1520; d. Madrid, Sept. 15, 1580. In 1545, he was a choir singer at Antwerp Cathedral; was appointed Kapellmeister there in 1563; in 1572, Philip II of Spain called him to Madrid as maestro of the Royal Chapel. He publ. a book of motets *a* 4–5 (1568), a book of motets and chansons *a* 4–6 (1569), and a Mass in *Praestantissimorum divinae musices auctorum Missae X* (1570). His son **Jean de Turnhout** was Kapellmeister to the Archduke Alexander Farnese, governor of the Netherlands, at Brussels from 1586; from 1611, he served as Kapellmeister of the Royal Chapel there. He publ. 2 books of madrigals and one of motets. L. Wagner edited *Gérard de Turnhout, Sacred and Secular Songs for Three Voices* (Madison, Wis., 1970).

Tuthill, Burnet Corwin, American composer and conductor; b. New York, Nov. 16, 1888; d. Knoxville, Tenn., Jan. 18, 1982. His father, William Burnet Tuthill, was the architect of Carnegie Hall. He studied at Columbia Univ. (M.A., 1910); conducted the Columbia Univ. Orch. (1909–13). In 1919 he organized the Society for Publication of American Music, which continued to function for nearly half a century, and which publ. about 85 works by American composers. He then devoted himself to administrative jobs in music; was executive secretary of the National Assoc. of Schools of Music in Cincinnati (1924–59); concurrently he served as director of music at Southwestern College in Memphis. He began to compose rather late in life, but compensated for this delay by increasing productivity in the subsequent years.

Tveitt, Geirr, Norwegian composer and pianist; b. Hardanger, Oct. 19, 1908; d. Oslo, Feb. 1, 1981. He studied in Leipzig, Vienna, and Paris, where he took private lessons with Florent Schmitt and Honegger. He toured Europe as a pianist; upon his return to Norway he was given a life pension by the government that enabled him to carry on his work. He made a profound study of Norwegian folk instruments, which he employed in his own compositions.

Tye, Christopher, English organist and composer; b. c.1500; d. c.1572. In 1536 he received his Mus.B. from Cambridge; on Sept. 10, 1541, he was appointed organist of Ely Cathedral (resigned in 1561); became magister choristarum there in 1543; Mus. Doc. at Cambridge in 1545; was ordained a priest in 1560 at Doddington. He described himself as a gentleman of the King's Chapel on the title page of his only publ. work, *The Actes of the Apostles, translated into Englyshe metre to synge and also to play upon the Lute* (London, 1553; it includes the first 14 chapters of the Acts). The hymn tunes *Windsor* and *Winchester Old* are adaptations from this collection. Tye was an important composer of English church music; he left masses, services, motets, and anthems. The *Euge Bone* mass was edited by Arkwright in *The Old English Edition* (no. 10); other examples are found in *The Oxford History of Music* (vol. II) and in Walker's *History of Music in England*. The following editions of his works have been publ.: R. Weidner, *Christopher Tye: The Instrumental Music* (New Haven, Conn., 1967); J. Satterfield, *Christopher Tye: The Latin Church Music* (Madison, Wis., 1972); J. Morehen, *Christopher Tye: The English Sacred Music* in *Early English Church Music*, XIX (1977).

Tyler, James, American lutenist, and cittern and viol player; b. Hartford, Conn., Aug. 3, 1940. He studied at the Hartt School of Music in Hartford; also took lessons with Joseph Ladone. He made his debut in 1962 with the N.Y. Pro Musica; later went to Germany, where he specialized in performances on early Renaissance instruments; was a member of the Studio der frühen Musik in Munich. He went to England in 1969, where he joined the Early Music Consort of London and Musica Reservata; also served as co-director of the Consort of Musicke with Anthony Rooley. In 1974 he became a member of the Julian Bream Consort. In 1976 he organized The London Early Music Group, devoted principally to performing works of the 16th and 17th centuries. A versatile musician, he also gave concerts of ragtime music with his own quintet, the New Excelsior Speaking Machine. He wrote *The Early Guitar* (London, 1980).

Tyndall, John, eminent physicist and acoustician; b. Leighlin Bridge, Ireland, Aug. 2, 1820; d. Hindhead, Surrey, England, Dec. 4, 1893. His 2 works in the domain of acoustics are *Sound* (1867; many subsequent eds.), a lucid and scholarly explanation of acoustical phenomena, and *On the Transmission of Sound by the Atmosphere* (1874). He was a prof. of natural philosophy at the Royal Inst. from 1853.

Tyrwhitt, Gerald. See **Berners, Lord.**

Tyson, Alan, English musicologist; b. Glasgow, Oct. 27, 1926. He was educated at Magdalen College, Oxford; later joined its faculty (1947–51); in 1952 was elected a fellow of All Souls College, Oxford; in 1971 became a senior research fellow there. He has made extensive textual and bibliographical studies of the period 1770–1850; particularly noteworthy are his contributions to the study of Beethoven.

U

Uberti (Hubert), Antonio, male soprano; b. (of German parents) Verona, 1697; d. Berlin, Jan. 20, 1783. He was one of the most brilliant pupils of Porpora, and was known as "il Porporino" (little Porpora). In 1741 he entered the service of Frederick the Great in Berlin. He was greatly renowned in Germany for his singing of Italian operas.

Uccellini, Marco, Italian composer; b. Forlimpopoli, c.1603; d. there, Sept. 10, 1680. He became head of instrumental music at the Este court of Modena in 1641, and was maestro di cappella at the Cathedral there in 1647–65. He was then at the Farnese court in Parma as maestro di cappella until his death. From 1639 to 1667 he publ. a variety of chamber music (sonatas, arias, canzonas, etc.); his advanced violin technique calls for use of the 6th position. He also wrote an opera, *Li eventi di Filandro ed Edessa,* which was presented in Parma in 1675 (the music is not extant); 2 ballet pieces: *Le navi d'Enea* (1673) and *Il Giove d'Elide fulminato* (1677). Riemann publ. a sonata by Uccellini in *Alte Kammermusik;* some pieces were publ. by Wasielewski; others by Torchi in *L'arte musicale in Italia* (vol. VII).

Ugolini, Vincenzo, Italian composer; b. Perugia, c.1570; d. Rome, May 6, 1638. He was a pupil of G.B. Nanino from 1592 to 1594 at the choir school of S. Luigi dei Francesi, Rome; was a bass there from 1600; from 1603 to 1609 he was choirmaster at the Church of S. Maria Maggiore; from 1610 to 1614, was at the Cathedral of Benevento; then returned to Rome; was director of music to Cardinal Arrigoni; in 1616 became choirmaster of S. Luigi dei Francesi; in 1620 he succeeded Suriano as maestro of the Cappella Giulia of St. Peter's (until 1626); in 1631 he resumed his former post at S. Luigi dei Francesi, retaining it till his death. He was the teacher of Benevoli. A notable representative of Palestrina's school, he publ. 4 books of motets for 1, 2, 3, and 4 Voices with Continuo (1616–19); 2 books of Psalms for 8 Voices (1620); 2 books of masses and motets for 8 and 12 Voices (1623); 1 book of songs and motets *a* 12 (1624); 2 books of madrigals *a* 5 (1615).

Uhde, Hermann, noted German bass-baritone; b. Bremen, July 20, 1914; d. (during a performance) Copenhagen, Oct. 10, 1965. He studied in Bremen; made his debut there in 1936; then sang with the Bavarian State Opera in Munich (1940–43) and with the German Opera at The Hague (1943–44). He subsequently was engaged at Hannover (1947–48), Hamburg (1948–50), Vienna (1950–51), Munich

(1951–56), Stuttgart (1956–57), and again in Vienna (1957–61). He made his American debut at the Metropolitan Opera in N.Y. as Telramund in *Lohengrin* on Nov. 18, 1955; was on its roster until 1957, then again in 1958–61 and 1963–64. He was particularly acclaimed for his performances in Wagnerian roles.

Ujj, Béla, Hungarian composer of operettas; b. Vienna, July 2, 1873; d. there, Feb. 1, 1942. He lost his sight in childhood, but studied music and composed a number of successful operettas which were produced in Vienna. They include the following: *Der Herr Professor* (Dec. 4, 1903); *Kaisermanöver* (March 4, 1905); *Die kleine Prinzessin* (May 5, 1907); *Drei Stunden Leben* (Nov. 1, 1909); *Chanteclee* (Oct. 25, 1910); *Der Türmer von St. Stephan* (Sept. 13, 1912); *Teresita* (June 27, 1914); *Der Müller und sein Kind* (Oct. 30, 1917).

Ullmann, Viktor, Austrian composer; b. Teschen, Jan. 1, 1898; d. in Auschwitz in all probability, Oct. 1944. He studied composition with Schoenberg; then went to Prague. He wrote music in the expressionistic manner, without renouncing latent tonality. His works include the operas *Peer Gynt* and *Der Sturz des Antichrist.* As an homage to Schoenberg, he wrote an orch. work, *5 Variations and Double Fugue,* based on the themes of a Schoenberg *Klavierstück.* After the seizure of Czechoslovakia by the Nazis, he was sent to the concentration camp in Theresienstadt; there he composed a one-act opera, *Der Kaiser von Atlantis,* depicting a tyrannical monarch who outlaws death but later begs for its return to relieve humanity from the horrors of life. The MS was preserved, and the work was performed for the first time in Amsterdam on Dec. 16, 1975.

Ulrich, Homer, American musicologist; b. Chicago, March 27, 1906. He studied bassoon and cello at the Chicago Musical College, and played these instruments in various orchs.; was bassoonist with the Chicago Symph. Orch. (1929–35); received his M.A. at the Univ. of Chicago with the thesis *The Penitential Psalms of Lasso* (1939). He was head of the music dept. of Monticello College (1935–38); then taught at the Univ. of Texas (associate prof., 1939; prof., 1951); also played bassoon with the San Antonio Symph. In 1953 he was appointed head of the music dept. of the Univ. of Maryland; retired in 1972. He publ. *Chamber Music* (a valuable survey; N.Y., 1948; 2nd ed., 1966); *Education of a Concert-Goer* (N.Y., 1949); *Symphonic Music* (N.Y., 1952); *Famous Women Singers* (N.Y., 1953); *Music: A Design for Listening* (N.Y., 1957; 3rd ed., 1970); *A History of Music and Musical Style* (with Paul Pisk; N.Y., 1963); *A Survey of Choral Music* (N.Y., 1973).

Ulybyshev, Alexander. See **Oulibishev, Alexander.**

Um Kalthoum (Fatma el-Zahraa Ibrahim), Egyptian singer; b. Tamay az-Zahirah, 1898; d. Cairo, Feb. 3, 1975. During a career of more than 50 years, she became one of the most famous singers in the Arab world; she was particularly renowned for her renditions of nationalistic, religious, and sentimental songs, which resulted in her being dubbed the "Star of the East" and the "Nightingale of the Nile." Her death precipitated widespread mourning in Egypt and other Arab countries.

Umlauf, Ignaz, Austrian composer; b. Vienna, 1746; d. Meidling, June 8, 1796. In 1772 he became a violinist in the court theater, and in 1778, conductor of the German Opera in Vienna; in 1789 he was appointed sub-conductor (under Salieri) of the Imperial Chapel in Vienna. He was a highly popular composer of singspiels; inaugurated the season of the German singspiels at the Burg Theater (Feb. 17, 1778) with his piece *Bergknappen;* there followed a number of others: *Die Apotheke* (June 20, 1778); *Die pucefarbenen Schuhe, oder Die schöne Schusterin* (June 22, 1779); *Das Irrlicht, oder Endlich fand er sie* (Jan. 17, 1782); *Der Oberamtmann und die Soldaten* (1782); *Der Ring der Liebe* (Dec. 3, 1786). *Zu Steffan sprach im Traume,* an aria from *Das Irrlicht,* enjoyed great popularity; Eberl wrote a set of variations on it which was misattributed to Mozart. The score of Umlauf's first singspiel, *Die Bergknappen,* was edited by R. Haas in Denkmäler der Tonkunst in Österreich, 36 (18.i).

Umlauf, Michael, Austrian violinist and composer, son of **Ignaz Umlauf;** b. Vienna, Aug. 9, 1781; d. Baden, near Vienna, June 20, 1842. He played the violin at the Vienna Opera; conducted at court theaters; wrote piano music; brought out a singspiel, *Der Grenadier* (Vienna, July 8, 1812). He assisted Beethoven in conducting the 9th Symph. and other works (actually led the performances, with Beethoven indicating the initial tempos).

Unger (Ungher), Caroline, famous Hungarian contralto; b. Stuhlweissenburg, Oct. 28, 1803; d. at her villa near Florence, March 23, 1877. She studied voice in Milan with D. Ronconi, and in Vienna with Aloysia Lange (Mozart's sister-in-law) and with Johann Michael Vogl. Beethoven chose her to sing the contralto parts in the first performances of his *Missa Solemnis* and 9th Symph. (May 7, 1824); long afterward she recounted that she turned Beethoven's head around that he might see the applause, which he could no longer hear. She went to Italy, where she changed the spelling of her name to Ungher, to secure proper pronunciation in Italian. Several Italian composers (Donizetti, Bellini, Mercadante) wrote operas especially for her. In 1833 she appeared in Paris. In 1839 she was engaged to be married to the poet Lenau, but the engagement soon was broken; in 1841 she married the French writer François Sabatier (1818–91) and retired from the stage. She publ. an album of 46 songs, under the title *Lieder, Mélodies et Stornelli.*

Unger, Georg, German tenor; b. Leipzig, March 6,

1837; d. there, Feb. 2, 1887. He was originally a student of theology; made his operatic debut in Leipzig at the age of 30. Hans Richter heard him in Mannheim and recommended him to Wagner for the role of Siegfried. He studied the part with Hey, and his interpretation of it made him famous.

Unger, Gerhard, German tenor; b. Bad Salzungen, Nov. 26, 1916. He received his musical education at the Berlin Hochschule für Musik; began his career as a concert singer. In 1947 he sang opera in Weimar; from 1949 to 1961 was a member of the East Berlin State Opera; then sang in Stuttgart (1961–63), at the Hamburg State Opera (1963–66), and at the Vienna State Opera (1966–70); also made guest appearances at the Bayreuth Festival, at La Scala in Milan, and at the Chicago Lyric Opera.

Uninsky, Alexander, Russian-American pianist; b. Kiev, Feb. 2, 1910; d. Dallas, Texas, Dec. 19, 1972. He studied at the Kiev Cons.; in 1932 he won the first prize at the International Chopin Contest in Warsaw; after a concert tour in Europe, he went to the U.S. in 1943, and gave recitals; he excelled as a performer of Chopin's music. In 1955 he was appointed prof. of piano at the Cons. of Toronto, Canada; then held a similar position at the Southern Methodist Univ. in Dallas.

Upton, William Treat, American musicologist; b. Tallmadge, Ohio, Dec. 17, 1870; d. Adelphi, Md., Jan. 19, 1961. He was educated at Oberlin College and its Cons. of Music; later studied piano with Leschetizky in Vienna (1896–98) and with Josef Lhévinne in Berlin (1913–14). From 1898 he taught piano at the Oberlin Cons.; also was a church organist in Cleveland (until 1918).

Urfey, Thomas d' (known as **Tom Durfey**), English playwright and poet; b. Exeter, 1653; d. London, Feb. 26, 1723. He produced about 30 plays, the songs in some of which were set to music by Purcell (e.g. *The Comical History of Don Quixote,* in 3 parts, 1694–96). He ingratiated himself into the intimate circle of Charles II by his talent for singing his poems, adapted to popular airs of his time. Between 1683 and 1710 he publ. several collections of airs with music, and in 1719 he edited *Songs Compleat, Pleasant and Divertive* (5 vols., his own songs assembled in vols. 1 and 2); this was reissued the same year under the better-known title *Wit and Mirth: or Pills to Purge Melancholy* (a 6th vol. was added in 1720), and the whole was reprinted and edited by C.L. Day (N.Y., 1959).

Uribe-Holguín, Guillermo, foremost composer of Colombia; b. Bogotá, March 17, 1880; d. there, June 26, 1971. He studied violin with Narciso Garay; in 1907 went to Paris, where he studied with Vincent d'Indy at the Schola Cantorum; then took violin lessons with César Thomson and Emile Chaumont in Brussels. He returned to Colombia in 1910 and became director of the newly reorganized National

Cons. in Bogotá; resigned in 1935 and devoted his time to the family coffee plantation. He continued to compose and conduct, and was again director of the Cons. in 1942–47. In 1910 he married the pianist **Lucía Gutiérrez.** His music bears the imprint of the modern French style, but his thematic material is related to native musical resources; particularly remarkable are his *Trozos en el sentimiento popular* for Piano, of which he wrote about 350; they are stylizations of Colombian melorhythms in a brilliant pianistic setting. He publ. an autobiography, *Vida de un músico colombiano* (Bogotá, 1941).

Urio, Francesco Antonio, Italian church composer; b. Milan, c.1660; d. there after 1700. He became a Franciscan monk; in 1690 was maestro at the Church of the 12 Apostles in Rome. He publ. *Motetti di concerto a 2, 3, e 4 voci con violini e senza,* op. 1 (Rome, 1690); *Salmi concertati a 3 voci con violini,* op. 2 (Bologna, 1697); also composed a Te Deum, from which Handel "borrowed" numerous themes, chiefly for his *Dettingen Te Deum,* and also for his *Saul* and *Israel in Egypt.* Urio's Te Deum was publ. by Chrysander in vol. 5 of his collection *Denkmäler der Tonkunst* (later publ. as Supplement 2 of Handel's complete works).

Urlus, Jacques, noted German tenor; b. Hergenrath, near Aachen, Jan. 9, 1867; d. Noordwijk, June 6, 1935. When he was 10, his parents moved to Tilburg, the Netherlands, and there he received his first instruction from an uncle, who was a choral conductor; then he studied engineering in Utrecht; subsequently studied singing with Cornelia van Zanten. He made his operatic debut as Beppo in *Pagliacci* at Amsterdam (Sept. 20, 1894); then was engaged at the Stadtheater in Leipzig (1900–15). He made his American debut in Boston as Tristan (Feb. 12, 1912); sang this role at his first appearance with the Metropolitan Opera (Feb. 8, 1913); was on its staff until 1917.

Ursuleac, Viorica, noted Rumanian soprano; b. Cernăuți, March 26, 1894. She studied in Vienna with Franz Steiner and Philip Forstén; made her debut as Charlotte in Massenet's *Werther* in Agram in 1922; then sang in Cernăuți (1923–24) and with the Vienna Volksoper (1924–26). In 1926 she joined the Frankfurt Opera, and then began a distinguished career as a member of the Vienna State Opera (1930–34), the Berlin State Opera (1935–37), and the Bavarian State Opera in Munich (1937–44). Richard Strauss held her in the highest esteem; in his operas she created the roles of Arabella (1933), Maria in *Der Friedenstag* (1938), the Countess in *Capriccio* (1942), and Danae in *Die Liebe der Danae* (public dress rehearsal, 1944). She was also highly successful in the operas of Wagner and Verdi. She was married to the eminent Austrian conductor **Clemens Krauss.**

Usandizaga, José María, Basque composer; b. San Sebastián, March 31, 1887; d. Yanti, Oct. 5, 1915. He studied piano with Planté and composition with

Vincent d'Indy at the Schola Cantorum in Paris; upon his return to Spain he associated himself with the Basque musical movement, to which he gave a great impetus with the production of his opera *Mendy-Mendiyan* (Bilbao, 1910); his 2nd opera, *Las golondrinas (The Swallows),* obtained excellent success at its production in Madrid on Feb. 5, 1914. His last opera, *La llama (The Flame),* was produced in Madrid in 1915. He also wrote several symph. overtures; 2 string quartets; many piano pieces on Basque themes. His death from tuberculosis at the age of 28 was deeply lamented by Spanish musicians.

Usmanbaş, Ilhan, Turkish composer; b. Istanbul, Sept. 28, 1921. He studied cello as a child; then studied harmony and counterpoint with Saygun at the Ankara Cons.; in 1948 he was appointed to its faculty. In 1952 he traveled in the U.S. His early compositions followed the ethnic patterns of Turkish folk songs, but after his travels in the U.S. he gradually adopted serial techniques, with occasional aleatory episodes.
WORKS: Violin Concerto (1946); Symph. (Ankara, April 20, 1950); *Music* for String Orch., Percussion, Piano, and Narrator (1950); *Mortuary* for Narrator, Chorus, and Orch. (1952–53); Clarinet Quintet (1949); Oboe Sonata (1949); Trumpet Sonata (1949); *3 Pictures of Salvador Dali* for Strings (1953); *Un Coup de dés* for Chorus and Orch. (1959); *Shadows* for Orch. (1964); *Immortal Sea Stones* for Piano (1965); *Questionnaire* for Piano (1965); *A Jump into Space* for Violin and 4 Instruments (1966); *Bursting Sinfonietta* for Orch. (1968); *Open Forms* for Different Groups (1968); *Music for a Ballet* for Orch. (1969); *String Quartet '70* (1970); *Senilikname* for Voice, Percussion, Harp, and Women's Chorus (1970).

Ussachevsky, Vladimir (Alexis), American composer of Russian parentage; b. Hailar, Manchuria, Nov. 3, 1911. His parents settled in Manchuria shortly after the Russo-Japanese War of 1905, at the time when Russian culture was still a powerful social factor there. His father was an officer of the Russian army, and his mother was a professional pianist. In 1930 he went to the U.S. and settled in California, where he took private piano lessons with Clarence Mader; from 1931–33 he attended Pasadena Junior College; in 1933 he received a scholarship to study at Pomona College (B.A., 1935). He then enrolled in the Eastman School of Music in Rochester, N.Y., in the classes of Howard Hanson, Bernard Rogers, and Edward Royce in composition (M.M., 1936; Ph.D., 1939); he also had some instruction with Burrill Phillips. In 1942, as an American citizen, Ussachevsky was drafted into the U.S. Army; thanks to his fluency in Russian, his knowledge of English and French, and a certain ability to communicate in rudimentary Chinese, he was engaged in the Intelligence Division; subsequently he served as a research analyst at the War Dept. in Washington, D.C. In 1947 he was appointed to the music faculty of Columbia Univ. in N.Y.; became a full prof. in 1964;

retired in 1980. At various times he taught at other institutions, including several years as composer-in-residence at the Univ. of Utah (1975–80). His early works were influenced by Russian church music, in the tradition of Tchaikovsky and Rachmaninoff. A distinct change in his career as a composer came in 1951, when he became interested in the resources of electronic music; to this period belong his works *Transposition, Reverberation,* and *Underwater Valse,* which make use of electronic sound. On Oct. 28, 1952, Stokowski conducted in N.Y. the first performance of Ussachevsky's *Sonic Contours,* in which a piano part was metamorphosed with the aid of various sonorific devices, superimposed on each other. About that time he began a fruitful partnership with Otto Luening; with him he composed *Incantation for Tape Recorder,* which was broadcast in 1953. Luening and Ussachevsky then conceived the idea of combining electronic tape sounds with conventional instruments played by human musicians; the result was *Rhapsodic Variations,* first performed in Louisville, Ky., on March 20, 1954. The work anticipated by a few months the composition of the important score *Déserts* by Varèse, which effectively combined electronic sound with other instruments. The next work by Ussachevsky and Luening was *A Poem in Cycles and Bells* for Tape Recorder and Orch., first performed by the Los Angeles Phil. on Nov. 22, 1954. On March 31, 1960, Leonard Bernstein conducted the N.Y. Phil. in the commissioned work by Ussachevsky and Luening entitled *Concerted Piece for Tape Recorder and Orchestra.* On Jan. 12, 1956, Ussachevsky and Luening provided taped background for Shakespeare's *King Lear,* produced by Orson Welles, at the N.Y. City Center, and later for Margaret Webster's production of *Back to Methuselah* for the N.Y. Theater Guild. They also provided the electronic score for the documentary *The Incredible Voyage,* broadcast over the CBS Television network on Oct. 13, 1965. Among works that Ussachevsky wrote for electronic sound without partnership were *A Piece for Tape Recorder* (1955), *Studies in Sound Plus* (1958), and *The Creation* (1961). In 1968 Ussachevsky began experimenting with the synthesizer, with the aid of a computer. One of the works resulting from these experiments was *Conflict* (1971); it is intended to represent the mystical struggle between 2 ancient deities. In 1959 Ussachevsky was one of the founders of the Columbia-Princeton Electronic Music Center; was active as a lecturer at various exhibitions of electronic sounds; traveled also to Russia and in China to present his music. He held 2 Guggenheim fellowships, in 1957 and in 1960. In 1973 Ussachevsky was elected to membership in the National Inst. of Arts and Letters.

Ustvolskaya, Galina, Soviet composer; b. Petrograd, July 17, 1919. She was a student of Shostakovich at the Leningrad Cons., graduating in 1947. Her early music was marked by a Romantic Russian manner; later she progressed toward greater melodic diversity and harmonic complexity; in some of her chamber music she boldly applies serial procedures.

Uttini, Francesco Antonio Baltassare, Italian composer; b. Bologna, 1723; d. Stockholm, Oct. 25, 1795. He studied with Perti; in 1743 became a member of the Accademia dei Filarmonici in Bologna. He first appeared as a singer; in 1755 went to Stockholm as conductor of an Italian opera company, and remained there until his death, except for a visit to London in 1768. He was court conductor at the Stockholm Opera from 1767 to 1787, and wrote 7 Italian and 5 French operas. Historically he is important as the composer of the earliest operas on Swedish texts; the first, *Thetis och Pelée,* was written for the inauguration of the new opera house in Stockholm (Jan. 18, 1773); another opera to a Swedish libretto, trans. from the French, was *Aline Drotning uti Golconda (Aline Queen of Golconda),* produced at the Stockholm Opera on Jan. 11, 1776. Of Uttini's Italian operas the best is *Il Re pastore* (Stockholm, July 24, 1755). A great admirer of Gluck, he brought out many of that composer's works in Stockholm. He also wrote 2 oratorios, 3 symphs. (for 4, 6, and 8 instruments), 12 sonatas, 9 trios for 2 Violins with Continuo; 6 of his sonatas were publ. at London in 1768.

Utyosov, Leonid, Soviet composer of jazz music; b. Odessa, March 21, 1895; d. Moscow, March 10, 1982. He played violin as a child; after the Revolution, he performed as an actor and entertainer in various cabarets, often combining different functions, including acrobatics. In 1920 he organized the first Soviet jazz group, which he named Tea Jazz, with allusion to the song *Tea for Two* by Youmans, which was immensely popular in Russia at the time; subsequently he created various brief musical comedies such as *Jazz on the Turning Point* (1930). He also performed numerous popular Russian songs and revived old army and navy ballads. He publ. a brief biographical book, *Thanks, Heart* (Moscow, 1976).

V

Vaccai, Nicola, Italian composer and singing teacher; b. Tolentino, March 15, 1790; d. Pesaro, Aug. 5, 1848. He went to Rome as a youth and took lessons in counterpoint with Jannaconi; then studied with Paisiello in Naples (from 1812). He became a singing teacher in Venice (1818–21), Trieste (1821–23), Vienna (1823), Paris (1829–31), and London (1832), with an ever-growing reputation; was a prof. of composition at the Milan Cons. (1838–44); in 1844 he retired to Pesaro, where he remained until his death.

Vačkář, Dalibor, Czech violinist, composer, and writer; b. Korčula, Yugoslavia, Sept. 19, 1906. He was the son of **Václav Vačkář** (1881–1954), composer of popular music. He studied violin with Reissiga and composition with O. Šin at the Prague Cons. (1923–29); also attended master classes of K. Hoffman and J. Suk (1929–31). From 1934–45 he played violin in the Prague Radio Orch.; then joined the film studio in Prague and composed film music under various pseudonyms. Under the nom de plume **Dalibor C. Faltis,** he publ. 4 books of poems, a book of short stories, 12 plays, and 3 opera librettos. His son, **Tomáš Vačkář,** was a talented composer who committed suicide at the age of 17. He left a sketchbook of melodies and themes; after his death, his father composed pieces based solely on these materials.

Vačkář, Tomáš, Czech composer, son of **Dalibor Vačkář;** b. Prague, July 31, 1945; d. (suicide) there, May 2, 1963. He came from a well-known Czech family of musicians; his grandfather, **Václav Vačkář,** was a composer of light music, and his father, **Dalibor Vačkář,** an eminent composer, dramatist, and poet. Young Tomáš was a gifted composer, but chose to end his life shortly after his graduation from the Prague Cons. at the age of 18. His works, all written between July 1960 and April 1963, include *Sonatina furore* for Piano; *Concerto Recitativo* for Flute, String Orch., and Piano; *Tři dopisy divkam (3 Letters to a Girl),* after a poem by an anonymous Czech student, for Voice, and Piano or Winds and Percussion; *Teen-agers,* piano sonata; *Metamorfózy na tema japonske ukolebavky (Metamorphoses on the Theme of a Japanese Lullaby)* for Orch.; *Scherzo melancolico* for Orch.; *Skicár Tomáše Vačkáře (Tomáš Vačkář's Sketchbook),* 10 pieces for Piano; a *Requiem* remained unfinished.

Vaet, Jacobus, Flemish composer; b. 1529; birthplace is not certain; it may be Courtrai or Harlebeke; d. Vienna, Jan. 8, 1567. He was a choirboy in the Church of Notre Dame at Courtrai (1543–46);

after his voice changed, he received a subsidy for 2 years of further study; in 1550 he was a tenor in the Flemish Chapel of Charles V; on Jan. 1, 1554, he was listed as Kapellmeister of the chapel of Maximilian, then the nominal King of Bohemia. His position was enhanced when his patron became Emperor Maximilian II. Vaet's music exhibits a great variety of techniques, ranging in style from those of Josquin des Prez to those of Lassus. The formative influence, however, is mainly that of Nicolas Gombert, with a characteristic florid imitation in contrapuntal parts. The extant works of Vaet comprise 82 motets and hymns, 10 masses, 8 Magnificats, and 3 chansons; a relatively large number of his motets (at least 11) are ceremonial, written to celebrate state or court occasions. Two vols. of his motets, *Modulationes 5 vocum* and *Modulationes 5 et 6 vocum,* were publ. in 1562 by Gardano in Venice; a 6-voice motet, *Qui operatus est Petro,* was printed in luxurious format on a large single parchment sheet by Hofhalter of Vienna in 1560 (facsimile in Haas, *Aufführungspraxis der Musik,* Potsdam, 1931, p. 129). Zacconi printed a hymn in his *Prattica di musica,* Libro I, folio 50. Vaet is represented also in the publications of Berg and Neuber (30 motets), Giovanelli (24 motets), Susato (7 motets), Gerlach (3 motets), Phalèse (3 motets, 2 chansons), Stephani (2 motets, one chanson), Waelrant and Laet (one chanson), Nicolas du Chemin (one chanson), and Rühling (one motet in organ tablature). Reprints appear in Commer's *Collectio operum musicorum Batavorum* (20 motets) and his *Musica sacra* (one Mass), and in Maldeghem, *Trésor musical* (one motet). E.H. Meyer edited *Jacobus Vaet, Sechs Motetten* as vol. 2 of *Das Chorwerk* (1929), and Milton Steinhardt edited *Jacobus Vaet, Zwei Hymnen* as vol. 8 of *Musik alter Meister* (1958). A complete edition of his work was undertaken by M. Steinhardt in Denkmäler der Tonkunst in Österreich, vols. 98, 100, 103/104, 108/109, 113/114, 116, 118.

Vainberg, Moisei, Soviet composer; b. Warsaw, Dec. 8, 1919. He studied piano with Turczynski at the Warsaw Cons., graduating in 1939; then went to Minsk, where he studied composition with Zolotarev at the Minsk Cons.; in 1943 he settled in Moscow. In his music he follows the precepts of socialist realism in its ethnic aspects; according to the subject, he makes use of Jewish, Polish, Moldavian, or Armenian folk melos, in tasteful harmonic arrangements devoid of abrasive dissonances.
WORKS: Operas: *The Sword of Uzbekistan* (1942); *The Woman Passenger* (1968); *Love of D'Artagnan,* after Alexandre Dumas (1972); ballets: *Battle for the Fatherland* (1942); *The Golden Key* (1955); *The White Chrysanthemum* (1958); *Requiem* (1967); cantatas: *On This Day Lenin Was Born* for Chorus and Orch. (1970); *Hiroshima Haikus* (1966); *The Diary of Love* (1965). For Orch.: 16 symphs.: No. 1 (1942); No. 2 for String Orch. (1946); No. 3 (1949); No. 4 (1957); No. 5 (1962); No. 6, with Boys' Chorus (1963); No. 7 for Strings and Harpsichord (1964); No. 8, subtitled *The Flowers of*

Poland, for Tenor, Chorus, and Orch. (1964); No. 9, subtitled *Surviving Pages,* for Reader, Chorus, and Orch. (1967); No. 10 for String Orch. (1968); No. 11, *Triumphant Symphony,* for Chorus and Orch., dedicated to Lenin's centennial (1969); No. 12 (1976; Moscow, Oct. 13, 1979); No. 13 (1976); No. 14 (1977; Moscow, Oct. 8, 1980); No. 15, with Chorus, "I have faith in this earth" (1977; Moscow, April 12, 1979); No. 16 (1981; Moscow, Oct. 19, 1982); 2 sinfoniettas (1948, 1960); *Moldavian Rhapsody* for Orch. (Moscow, Nov. 30, 1949); *Slavic Rhapsody* for Orch. (1950); Cello Concerto (1956); Violin Concerto (1960); Flute Concerto (1961); Trumpet Concerto (1967); Clarinet Concerto (1970); 12 string quartets (1937–70); Piano Quintet (1944); Piano Trio (1945); String Trio (1951); 20 sonatas and 2 sonatinas for various instruments, with piano; 24 preludes for cello solo; 23 preludes for piano; songs.

Valcárcel, Edgar, Peruvian composer and pianist, nephew of **Teodoro Valcárcel;** b. Puno, Dec. 4, 1932. He studied composition with Andrés Sas at the Lima Cons.; then went to N.Y., where he studied with Donald Lybbert at Hunter College; subsequently traveled to Buenos Aires, where he took composition lessons with Alberto Ginastera; also had sessions with Olivier Messiaen in Paris, and with Riccardo Malipiero, Bruno Maderna, and Luigi Dallapiccola in Italy; furthermore, he joined the Electronic Music Center of Columbia-Princeton Univs. and worked with Vladimir Ussachevsky; held 2 Guggenheim Foundation grants (1966 and 1968). In Peru he became a teacher of piano and harmony at the Cons. of Lima. In his compositions he adopted an extremely advanced idiom that combined serial and aleatory principles, leaving to the performer the choice to use or not to use given thematic materials.

Valcárcel, Teodoro, Peruvian composer; b. Puno, Oct. 17, 1900; d. Lima, March 20, 1942. He studied at the Cons. of Milan and with Felipe Pedrell in Barcelona. Returning to Peru in 1920, he settled in Lima; in 1928 he won the National Prize for Peruvian composers, and was awarded a gold medal from the municipality of Lima for his studies in Peruvian folk music. In 1929 he went to Europe once more; presented a concert of his works in Paris (April 12, 1930). He was of pure Indian origin; as a native of the highlands, he was able to collect Indian songs unpolluted by urban influences. He publ. *30 cantos de alma vernacular; 4 canciones incaicas; 25 romances de costa y sierra peruana; 180 melodias del folklore.* Among his original works are the ballets (with singing) *Suray-Surita* and *Ckori Kancha;* a symph. poem, *En las ruinas del Templo del Sol* (1940); a violin concerto, entitled *Concierto indio* (1939); *3 ensayos* for an ensemble of Native Instruments; *Fiestas andinas* for Piano; *Suite autóctona* for Violin and Piano; songs. A catalogue of his works was publ. by R. Holzmann in *Boletín Bibliográfico* (Lima, Dec. 1942).

Valderrábano, Enrique Enriquez de. See Enriquez de Valderrábano, Enrique.

Valen, Fartein, Norwegian composer noted for his originality, both in thematic invention and in the use of audacious modern techniques; b. Stavanger, Aug. 25, 1887; d. Haugesund, Dec. 14, 1952. His father was a missionary in Madagascar, and Valen spent his childhood there. Upon returning to Norway, he studied philology at the Univ. of Oslo (1906–9), and music theory and organ with Elling at the Oslo Cons.; subsequently went to Berlin and enrolled in the Hochschule für Musik in the class of composition of Max Bruch (1909–11). From 1916 to 1924 he stayed on his family's farm in Valevåg; from 1924 to 1938 he was in Oslo; then retired on the family farm. In 1935 he received the Norwegian State Salary of Art (a government life pension). His early music reflects the influence of Brahms, but later he developed a sui generis method of composition which he termed "atonal polyphony," completely free from traditional tonal relationships but strongly cohesive in contrapuntal fabric and greatly varied in rhythm; his first work in which he made use of this technique was a Piano Trio written in 1924. He never adopted an explicit 12-tone method of composition, but a parallelism with Schoenberg's music is observable. Valen stood apart from all nationalist developments in Oslo, yet his music attracted attention in modern circles; a Valen Society was formed in Norway in 1949, and in England in 1952, shortly before his death.

Valente, Antonio (known as "il Cieco," "the blind man"), Italian organist and composer; b. Naples, c.1520. Blind from infancy, he played the organ; was organist at Sant'Angelo a Nido in Naples. His first publication, *Intavolatura de cimbalo: Recercate, fantasie et canzoni francese desminuite con alcuni tenori balli et varie sorti de contraponti ...* (Naples, 1575), is in Spanish keyboard tablature and contains early keyboard fantasias, written out in detail; his 2nd book, *Versi spirituali sopra tutte le note, con diversi canoni spartiti per suonar negli organi, messe, vespere et altri offici divini* (Naples, 1580), represents an early type of keyboard partitura; 3 numbers were reprinted by L. Torchi in *L'arte musicale in Italia*, 3. A modern edition was brought out by I. Fuser, editor, *Antonio Valente: Versi spirituali per organo* (Padua, 1958).

Valente, Benita, American soprano; b. Delano, Calif., Oct. 19, 1939. She studied voice with Lotte Lehmann at the Music Academy of the West at Santa Barbara; also took lessons with Martial Singher there. Later she enrolled at the Curtis Inst. of Music in Philadelphia, graduating in 1960. She sang at the Marlboro Festival in Vermont; there she met the bassoon player **Anthony Checchia,** whom she married in 1959; they settled in Philadelphia. In 1962 she went to Germany and appeared at the Freiburg Opera; upon returning to the U.S., she made an auspicious debut at the Metropolitan Opera in N.Y. as Pamina in *Die Zauberflöte* (Sept. 22, 1973) and became a regular member of the Metropolitan;

made an appearance as Almirena in Handel's opera *Rinaldo* there in 1982; her other roles were Violetta and Gilda. She further showed her mettle in modern works, such as Penderecki's *Te Deum.*

Valente, Vincenzo, Italian operetta composer; b. Corigliano Calabro, Feb. 21, 1855; d. Naples, Sept. 6, 1921. At the age of 15 he wrote a song, *Ntuniella,* which became popular; he continued writing Neapolitan songs of great appeal (*Basta ca po', Comme te voglio amà!, Canzone Cafona, Mugliera comme fa, Ninuccia, Tiempe felice, L'Acqua,* etc.), about 400 songs in all. He also brought out numerous operettas: *I Granatieri* (Turin, Oct. 26, 1889); *La Sposa di Charolles* (Rome, March 3, 1894); *Rolandino* (Turin, Oct. 15, 1897); *L'usignuolo* (Naples, May 10, 1899); *Lena* (Foggia, Jan. 1, 1918); *L'Avvocato Trafichetti* (Naples, May 24, 1919); *Nèmesi* (posthumous, Naples, July 23, 1923). His son, **Nicola Valente** (b. Naples, Aug. 28, 1881), was also a composer of Neapolitan songs and light operas.

Valenti, Fernando, noted American harpsichordist; b. New York, Dec. 4, 1926. He studied piano with José Iturbi; then attended Yale Univ., where he took instruction in harpsichord with Ralph Kirkpatrick. He made his N.Y. recital debut in 1950. In 1951 he was appointed prof. of harpsichord playing at the Juilliard School of Music in N.Y. He was especially renowned for his authentic interpretation of keyboard works by Scarlatti.

Valerius, Adrianus (Adriaan), Dutch musician; b. Middelburg, 1575; d. Veer, Jan. 27, 1625. From 1606 he lived in Veer as a notary; publ. an important lute tablature book, *Neder-Landtsche Gedenck-Clanck* (Haarlem, 1626); it was reprinted in Utrecht in 1871, in The Hague in 1893, again in Utrecht in 1931, and, in a new edition, in Amsterdam in 1942. It was publ. in a facsimile edition in N.Y. in 1968. A selection was brought out by E. Kremser, with an Eng. text by T. Baker, in N.Y. in 1894.

Valkare, Gunnar, Swedish composer of the extreme avant-garde; b. Norrköping, April 25, 1943. He studied composition with Lidholm at the Royal Cons. of Stockholm (1963–70). His music is militantly aggressive in its tonal, atonal, and polytonal assault on the most cherished notions of harmonious sweetness.

Vallas, Léon, French writer on music; b. Roanne (Loire), May 17, 1879; d. Lyons, May 9, 1956. After studying medicine in Lyons, he took up music; in 1903 founded the *Revue Musicale de Lyon* (from 1912 to 1914 this was known as the *Revue de Musique Française,* and from 1920 to 1929, as the *Nouvelle Revue Musicale*); from 1908 to 1911 he was engaged as a lecturer on music history at the Univ. of Lyons; also at the Cons. there, in 1912; and at the Sorbonne in Paris, in 1928–30.

Valle-Riestra, José María, Peruvian composer; b.

Lima, Nov. 9, 1859; d. there, Jan. 25, 1925. He studied as a child in London; after his return to Lima, he continued his musical education without a teacher; as a mature musician, he went to Paris for further studies with André Gédalge (1895–97). When the Academia Nacional de Música was organized in Lima, he was appointed a prof. there. In his compositions, it was his aim to contribute toward the establishment of a national school by the employment of old Inca melodies. His opera *Ollanta* (Lima, Dec. 26, 1900) was a successful dramatization of an Inca subject. His other 2 operas on Inca themes were *Las rosas de Jamaica* (one act) and *Atahualpa* (3 acts). He also wrote *Misa de Requiem* for Chorus and Orch.; *En Oriente* for Orch.; *Elegia* for String Orch.; choruses a cappella; songs.

Vallet, Nicolas, French lutenist; b. Corbéni, 1583; d. Amsterdam, after 1633. In 1615 he publ. at Amsterdam a book of French, German, and English songs, also preludes, fantasias, etc., in lute tablature: *Secretum musarum* (2nd ed., 1618, with the title *Paradisus musicus testudinis*); he also publ. *Le Second Livre de tabulature de luth* (1618) and *21 Psaumes de David* (in lute tablature; 1619). A modern edition, *Œuvres de Nicolas Vallet pour luth seul: Le Secret des Muses, livres I, II*, edited by A. Souris, appeared in 1970.

Vallotti, Francesco Antonio, Italian theorist and composer; b. Vercelli, June 11, 1697; d. Padua, Jan. 10, 1780. A Franciscan monk, he was a pupil of Calegari at Padua; was 3rd organist at the basilica, 1723; on Feb. 21, 1730, was elected maestro at the church of S. Antonio, remaining in that post for 50 years. He was one of the foremost organists of his time.

Valvasensi, Lazaro, Italian organist and composer; b. Valvasone, Udine, (baptized, June 20), 1585; d. there, June 26, 1661. In 1622 he was an organist at Murano (Venice); in 1626, choirmaster at Tolmezzo (Udine); from 1634 to 1640 was an organist at Valvasone. He publ. *Letanie della B. V. a 5 voci, con un Mottetto nell'ultimo concertato per sonar nell'Organo* (Venice, 1622); *Compieta concertata a 4 voci,* with Continuo (Venice, 1626); *Secondo giardino d'amorosi fiori* (23 solo airs and one duet, with Instrumental Accompaniment; Venice, 1634; unique copy at Christ Church, Oxford).

Valverde, Joaquín, Spanish composer of light opera; b. Badajoz, Feb. 27, 1846; d. Madrid, March 17, 1910. He played the flute in bands from the age of 13; then studied at the Cons. of Madrid; received a prize for his orch. work, *Batylo* (1871). From 1871 to 1889 he conducted theater orchs. in Madrid; taught flute at the Madrid Cons., and wrote melodic studies for his instrument. In collaboration with Chueca he wrote a number of zarzuelas, of which the most celebrated was *La gran vía* (Madrid, July 2, 1886; produced in London on April 18, 1906, as *Castles in Spain*); it contains the march *Cádiz,* which became immensely popular. His son, **Joaquín Valverde y**

San Juan, known under his diminutive given name, **Quinito** (b. Madrid, Jan. 2, 1875; d. Mexico City, Nov. 4, 1918), was also a composer; he wrote some 250 light pieces for the theater; his zarzuela *El gran capitán* was especially successful. He died during an American tour which he undertook as conductor of a light opera company.

Van Beinum, Eduard. See **Beinum, Eduard van.**

Vancea, Zeno, outstanding Rumanian composer and musicologist; b. Bosca-Vasiovei (Banat), Oct. 21, 1900. He studied at the Cluj Cons. (1919–21); then took lessons in composition with Ernst Kanitz in Vienna. Returning to Rumania, he taught at conservatories in Tîgru-Mures (1926–40; director, 1946–48), Timisoara (1940–45), and Bucharest (1949–73). He was the editor of the important Rumanian monthly *Muzica* (1953–64). Vancea belongs to the national school of Rumanian composers; in his music he makes use of folk-song patterns without direct quotations. Harmonically, he adopts many procedures of cosmopolitan modern music while cautiously avoiding abrasive sonorities.

Van Dam, José (real name, **Joseph Van Damme**), bass-baritone; b. Brussels, Aug. 25, 1940. He studied at the Royal Cons. of Music in Brussels; made his operatic debut at the Paris Opéra in 1961. Herbert von Karajan engaged him as a soloist with the Berlin Phil. during its American tour in 1976. He greatly distinguished himself in assuming the title role in the world premiere of Messiaen's opera *Saint François d'Assise* (Paris Opéra, Nov. 28, 1983).

Van den Boorn-Coclet, Henriette, Belgian composer; b. Liège, Jan. 15, 1866; d. there, March 6, 1945. She studied with Radoux and Dupuis at the Liège Cons., and subsequently taught harmony there. Her compositions attracted considerable attention. She wrote a Symph.; a symph. poem, *Le Renouveau; Sérénade* for Cello and Piano; various piano pieces (*Mazurka, Caprice,* etc.); songs.

Van den Borren, Charles (-Jean-Eugène), eminent Belgian musicologist; b. Ixelles, near Brussels, Nov. 17, 1874; d. Brussels, Jan. 14, 1966. He studied theory with E. Closson; after receiving the degree of Dr.Juris, he practiced law until 1905; then devoted himself to historical research in music. He became one of the greatest authorities on the music of the Renaissance; was a lecturer at the Univ. of Liège (1927–44); from 1926, was a prof. of music history at the Univ. Libre of Brussels; he held many positions in learned societies.
WRITINGS: *L'Œuvre dramatique de César Franck* (1907); *Les Origines de la musique de clavecin en Angleterre* (1912; Eng. trans. as *The Sources of Keyboard Music in England,* 1914); *Les Musiciens belges en Angleterre à l'époque de la Renaissance* (1913); *Les Origines de la musique de clavecin dans les Pays-Bas (Nord et Sud) jusque vers 1630* (1914); *Les Débuts de la musique à Venise* (1914);

Orlande de Lassus (1920); *Le Manuscrit musical M.222 C.22 de la Bibliothèque de Strasbourg* (Antwerp, 1924); *Guillaume Dufay* (1926); *Etudes sur le quinzième siècle musical* (Antwerp, 1941); *Peter Benoît* (Brussels, 1942); *Roland de Lassus* (Brussels, 1944); *Geschiedenis van de muziek in de Nederlanden* (2 vols., Antwerp, 1948–51); etc. He ed. *Polyphonia sacra* (15th-century pieces; publ. in London, 1932); *Pièces polyphoniques profanes de provenance liégeoise (XVᵉ siècle)* (Brussels, 1950); was co-editor of the collected works of Philippe de Monte (1927–39).

Van den Eeden, Jean-Baptiste. See **Eeden, Jean-Baptiste van den.**

Vandernoot, André, Belgian conductor; b. Brussels, June 2, 1927. He studied at the Brussels Cons.; later took courses at the Vienna Academy of Music. In 1958 he was appointed first conductor of the Royal Flemish Opera in Antwerp; from 1959 to 1973 he served as music director of the Théâtre Royal de la Monnaie in Brussels. In 1974–75 he was music director of the Orch. National de Belgique in Brussels; in 1976 was named first guest conductor of the Antwerp Phil. He also made guest appearances as a conductor in Europe, Japan, the U.S., and South America.

Van der Straeten, Edmond, Belgian music historian; b. Audenarde, Dec. 3, 1826; d. there, Nov. 26, 1895. He studied philosophy in Ghent; went to Brussels in 1857 as secretary to Fétis, with whom he studied counterpoint. He held a lifelong position at the Royal Library, and rarely left Belgium; was active as a music critic (1859–72); wrote an opera, *Le Proscrit.* His reputation rests upon his scholarly publications, dealing with music in the Low Countries.

Van der Stucken, Frank (Valentin), American conductor; b. Fredericksburg, Texas, Oct. 15, 1858; d. Hamburg, Aug. 16, 1929. He was taken by his parents to Antwerp as a child, and studied music with Peter Benoit; then became associated with Reinecke in Leipzig; he also met Liszt. In 1884 he returned to the U.S., and became a choral conductor. He was the first to conduct a concert of American music in Europe, when at the Paris Exposition (July 12, 1889) he gave the first European performances of works by MacDowell, Foote, Chadwick, and Huss; he also gave similar programs in Germany. From 1895 to 1903 he was director of the Cincinnati College of Music; concurrently, he conducted concerts of the Cincinnati Symph. Orch. (1895–1907). In 1898 he was called upon to lead the remaining concerts of the season of the N.Y. Phil., following the death of Anton Seidl. In 1907 he went to Germany, and remained there for the rest of his life. He composed a few orch. pieces and choruses.

Van Dieren, Bernard. See **Dieren, Bernard van.**

Van Hagen, Peter Albrecht, Dutch musician active in America; b. in the Netherlands, 1750; d. Boston, 1803. After his arrival in America from the Netherlands in 1774, he settled in Charleston, S.C., as a music teacher; from 1789 to 1796 was in N.Y., giving concerts with his wife and son; in 1796 the family moved to Boston. He composed a *Federal Overture* (1797; not to be confused with *The Federal Overture* by B. Carr); *Funeral Dirge for George Washington* (1800); much theater music. His son, **Peter Albrecht, Jr.** (1781–1837), born in Charleston, was also a musician; he wrote songs and composed an overture.

Van Hal, Johann Baptist. See **Wanhal, Johann Baptist.**

Van Hoogstraten, Willem. See **Hoogstraten, Willem van.**

Van Hoose, Ellison, American tenor; b. Murfreesboro, Tenn., Aug. 18, 1868; d. Houston, Texas, March 24, 1936. He studied with Luckstone in N.Y., Jean de Reszke in Paris, and also in Rome and London. He made his operatic debut with the Damrosch Opera Co. in Philadelphia as Tannhäuser (Dec. 11, 1897); toured with Mme. Melba in the U.S. (1903–5) and with Mme. Sembrich (1906–7); toured in Europe (1908–10); was a member of the Chicago Opera Co. (1911–12); then devoted himself mainly to oratorio singing.

Van Maldere, Pierre. See **Maldere, Pierre van.**

Vanni-Marcoux. See **Marcoux, Vanni.**

Van Otterloo, Willem. See **Otterloo, Willem van.**

Van Rooy, Anton (Antonius Maria Josephus), Dutch baritone; b. Rotterdam, Jan. 1, 1870; d. Munich, Nov. 28, 1932. He was a church chorister; studied voice with Stockhausen at Frankfurt. In 1897 he was engaged to sing at Bayreuth, and performed there the 3 Wotans with excellent success. On Dec. 14, 1898, he made his American debut as Wotan in *Die Walküre* at the Metropolitan Opera, where he appeared each season (except 1900–1901) until 1908, singing during the summers at Covent Garden in London and at Bayreuth. In 1908 he was engaged as a regular member of the Frankfurt Opera. He retired from the stage in 1913. He was particularly distinguished in Wagnerian roles, but also was noted for his interpretations of Escamillo in *Carmen* and Valentin in *Faust.*

Van Vactor, David, American composer and conductor; b. Plymouth, Ind., May 8, 1906. He enrolled in the premedical classes at Northwestern Univ. (1924–27); then changed to the music school there, studying flute with Arthur Kitti and theory of composition with Arne Oldberg, Felix Borowski, and Albert Noelte. He obtained his B.A. degree there in 1928, and went to Vienna, where he studied composition

with the venerable composer Franz Schmidt. In the summer of 1931 he went to Paris, where he took a course in composition with Paul Dukas at the Ecole Normale de Musique and also studied flute with Marcel Moyse at the Paris Cons. Returning to the U.S., he was engaged as a flutist in the Chicago Symph. Orch., holding this post for 12 years (1931–43). He also began to conduct; in 1943–45 he was assistant conductor of the Kansas City Phil., and also played flute in the orch. In 1947 he was engaged as conductor of the Knoxville Symph. Orch., and held this position until 1972; joined the faculty at the Univ. of Tennessee, where he was prof. of composition from 1947 to 1977. In 1957 he received a Guggenheim fellowship. He made 3 tours of South America under the auspices of the State Dept. In his own music, Van Vactor adheres mainly to basic tonalities, but he enhances them with ingeniously contrived melodic gargoyles, creating a simulation of atonality. The rhythmic vivacity of his inventive writing creates a cheerful, hedonistic atmosphere.
WORKS: FOR ORCH.: *Chaconne* for String Orch. (Rochester, N.Y., May 17, 1928); *5 Small Pieces for Large Orchestra* (Ravinia Park, Ill., July 5, 1931); *The Masque of the Red Death*, after Edgar Allan Poe (1932); Flute Concerto (Chicago, Feb. 26, 1933); *Passacaglia and Fugue* (Chicago, Jan. 28, 1934); *Concerto Grosso* for 3 Flutes, Harp, and Orch. (Chicago, April 4, 1935); *Overture to a Comedy* No. 1 (Chicago, June 20, 1937); *Overture to a Comedy* No. 2 (Indianapolis, March 14, 1941); *Symphonic Suite* (Ravinia Park, Ill., July 21, 1938); 8 symphs.: No. 1 in D (1936–37; N.Y., Jan. 19, 1939, composer conducting; awarded prize of $1,000 in the American Composers Contest sponsored by the N.Y. Phil.); No. 2, *Music for the Marines* (1943; Indianapolis, March 27, 1943; programmed as a suite, not a symph.); No. 3 (1958; Pittsburgh, April 3, 1959; perf. and recorded as No. 2); No. 4, *Walden*, for Chorus and Orch., to texts from Thoreau's *Walden* (1970–71; first complete perf., Maryville, Tenn., May 9, 1971; listed as Symph. No. 3 at its premiere); No. 5 (1976; Knoxville, Tenn., March 11, 1976); No. 6 for Orch. or Band (1980; for Orch., Knoxville, Nov. 19, 1981; for Band, Ball State Univ., April 13, 1983); No. 7 (1983); No. 8 (1984); *5 Bagatelles* for Strings (Chicago, Feb. 7, 1938); Viola Concerto (Ravinia Park, July 13, 1940); *Variazioni Solenne* (1941; first perf. under the title *Gothic Impressions* by the Chicago Symph. Orch., Feb. 26, 1942); *Pastorale and Dance* for Flute and Strings (1947); Violin Concerto (Knoxville, April 10, 1951); *Fantasia, Chaconne and Allegro* (1957; Louisville, Ky., Feb. 20, 1957); Suite for Trumpet and Small Orch. (1962); *Suite on Chilean Folk Tunes* (1963); *Passacaglia, Chorale and Scamper* for Band (1964); *Sinfonia Breve* (1964; Santiago, Chile, Sept. 3, 1965; American premiere, Indianapolis, Oct. 30, 1966); *Sarabande and Variations* for Brass Quintet and Strings (1968; Knoxville, May 4, 1969); *Requiescat* for Strings (Knoxville, Oct. 17, 1970); *Andante and Allegro* for Saxophone and Strings (1972); *Set of 5* for Wind Instruments and Percussion (1973); *Nostalgia* for Band (1975); *Prelude and Fugue* for Strings (1975); *Fanfare and Chorale* for Band (1977); *The Elements* for Band

(Univ. of Tennessee, May 22, 1979).
FOR VOICE: *Credo* for Chorus and Orch (1941); Cantata for 3 Treble Voices and Orch. (1947); *The New Light*, Christmas cantata (1954); *Christmas Songs for Young People* for Chorus and Orch. (1961); *A Song of Mankind*, first part of a 7-part cantata (1971; Indianapolis, Sept. 26, 1971); *Processional "Veni Immanuel"* for Chorus and Orch. (1974); *Brethren We Have Met to Worship* for Chorus and Orch. (1975); *Episodes—Jesus Christ* for Chorus and Orch. (1977; Knoxville, May 2, 1977); *Processional* for Chorus, Wind Instruments, and Percussion (1979; Univ. of Tennessee, Dec. 1, 1979).

Van Vleck, Jacob, Moravian minister, violinist, and organist; b. New York, 1751; d. Bethlehem, Pa., July 3, 1831. He was director of the Young Ladies' Seminary at Bethlehem from 1790 to 1800; was consecrated a bishop in 1815. He was the first American-born Moravian to be active as a composer.

Van Westerhout, Niccolò, Italian composer; b. (of Dutch parentage) Mola di Bari, Dec. 17, 1857; d. Naples, Aug. 21, 1898. He was a pupil of Nicola d'Arienzo at the Naples Cons.; then became a prof. of harmony there. He wrote 3 operas: *Cimbelino* (Rome, April 7, 1892); *Fortunio* (Milan, May 16, 1895); *Dona Flor* (Mola di Bari, April 18, 1896, on the opening of the Teatro Van Westerhout, named after him); another opera, *Colomba*, was produced posthumously (Naples, March 27, 1923). He also wrote 2 symphs. and a Violin Concerto; publ. many piano pieces of considerable merit, as well as songs.

Van Wyk, Arnold. See **Wyk, Arnold van.**

Van Zandt, Marie, American coloratura soprano; b. New York, Oct. 8, 1861; d. Cannes, Dec. 31, 1919. She studied with her mother, the well-known American soprano **Jennie van Zandt,** and with Lamperti; made her debut in Turin (1879); was engaged at the Opéra-Comique in Paris (1880–85); sang at the Metropolitan Opera in N.Y. during the season of 1891–92; in 1896 she rejoined the Opéra-Comique. Delibes wrote the role of Lakmé for her, and she created it at the Opéra-Comique on April 14, 1883.

Van Zanten, Cornelia, famous Dutch soprano and pedagogue; b. Dordrecht, Aug. 2, 1855; d. The Hague, Jan. 10, 1946. She studied with K. Schneider at the Cologne Cons., and in Milan with Lamperti, who developed her original contralto into a coloratura soprano voice. She made her debut in Turin; then sang in Germany; toured in America in 1886–87 as a member of the National Opera Co. under the directorship of Theodore Thomas; then returned to Europe; appeared in special performances of *Der Ring des Nibelungen* in Russia; finally became a member of the Nederlandsche Oper in Amsterdam; also taught at the Amsterdam Cons. (1895–1903); subsequently lived in Berlin, highly esteemed as a singing teacher; eventually settled in The Hague. She publ. songs to German and Dutch texts; with

C.E. Poser, brought out *Leitfaden zum Kunstgesang* (Berlin, 1903).

Varady, Julia, Rumanian soprano; b. Oradea, Sept. 1, 1941. She was educated at the Cons. in Cluj and at the Burcharest Cons. She sang at the Cluj Opera and later at the Bucharest Opera and the Budapest Opera; expanded her operatic career by appearances in Frankfurt, Hamburg, Vienna, Berlin, and Paris. She married the German baritone **Dietrich Fischer-Dieskau.**

Vardi, Emanuel, outstanding Jewish-American violist; b. Jerusalem, April 21, 1917. He began to study the viola in his youth; also studied painting at the Florence Academy of Fine Arts. In 1940 he came to the U.S., and soon established a hegemony in the limited field of viola literature. He arranged works by Bach, Frescobaldi, Tartini, Paganini, and Chopin for viola; also commissioned works for the viola to Michael Colgrass, Alan Hovhaness, Alan Shulman, and others. For variety's sake he made an incursion into the conducting arena; was music director of the South Dakota Symph. Orch. (1978–82). In his leisure time he painted. In 1951 he won the International Prize of Rapallo, and had one-man exhibits in N.Y., South Dakota, and Italy.

Varèse, Edgar, one of the most remarkable composers of his century, who introduced a totally original principle of organizing the materials and forms of sound, profoundly influencing the direction of new music; b. Paris, Dec. 22, 1883; d. New York, Nov. 6, 1965. The original spelling of his first Christian name was **Edgard,** but most of his works were first publ. under the name Edgar; about 1940 he chose to return to the legal spelling, Edgard. He spent his early childhood in Burgundy, and began to compose early in life. In 1892 his parents went to Turin; his paternal grandfather was Italian; his other grandparents were French. In Turin he took private lessons in composition with Giovanni Bolzoni, who taught him gratis. Varèse gained some performing experience by playing percussion in the school orch. He stayed in Turin until 1903; then went to Paris. In 1904 he entered the Schola Cantorum, where he studied with Vincent d'Indy, Albert Roussel, and Charles Bordes; in 1906 he attended the classes of Widor at the Paris Cons. In 1907 he received the "bourse artistique" offered by the City of Paris; at that time he founded and conducted the chorus of the Université Populaire and organized concerts at the Château du Peuple. In Paris he became associated with musicians and artists of the avant-garde; he also met Debussy, who showed interest in his career. In 1907 he married a young actress, Suzanne Bing; they had a daughter. Together they went to Berlin, at that time the center of new music that offered opportunities to Varèse. The marriage was not successful, and they separated in 1913. Romain Rolland gave to Varèse a letter of recommendation for Richard Strauss, who in turn showed interest in Varèse's music. He was also instrumental in arranging a performance of Varèse's

symph. poem *Bourgogne,* which was performed in Berlin on Dec. 15, 1910. In Berlin he also met Karl Muck. But the greatest experience for Varèse in Berlin was his meeting and friendship with Busoni. Varèse greatly admired Busoni's book on new music esthetics, and was profoundly influenced by Busoni's views. He composed industriously, mostly for orch.; the most ambitious of these works was a symph. poem, *Gargantua,* but it was never completed. Other works were *Souvenirs, Prélude à la fin d'un jour, Cycles du Nord,* and an incomplete opera, *Oedipus und die Sphinx,* to the text by Hofmannstahl. All these works, in manuscript, were lost under somewhat mysterious circumstances, and Varèse himself destroyed the score of *Bourgogne* later in life. A hostile reception that he encountered from Berlin critics for *Bourgogne* upset Varèse, who expressed his unhappiness in a letter to Debussy. However, Debussy responded with a friendly letter of encouragement, advising Varèse not to pay too much attention to critics. As early as 1913, Varèse began an earnest quest for new musical resources; upon his return to Paris he worked on related problems with the Italian musical futurist Luigi Russolo, although he disapproved of the attempt to find a way to new music through the medium of instrumental noises. He was briefly called to the French army at the outbreak of the First World War, but was discharged because of a chronic lung ailment. In 1915 he went to N.Y. There he met the young American writer Louise Norton; they set up a household together; in 1921, when she obtained her own divorce from a previous marriage, they were married. As in Paris and Berlin, Varèse had chronic financial difficulties in America; the royalties from his few publ. works were minimal; in order to supplement his earnings he accepted a job as a piano salesman, which was repulsive to him. He also appeared in a minor role in a John Barrymore silent film in 1918. Some welcome aid came from the wealthy artist Gertrude Vanderbilt, who sent him monthly allowances for a certain length of time. Varèse also had an opportunity to appear as a conductor. As the U.S. neared the entrance into war against Germany, there was a demand for French conductors to replace the German music directors who had held the monopoly on American orchs. On April 1, 1917, Varèse conducted in N.Y. the Requiem Mass of Berlioz. On March 17, 1918, he conducted a concert of the Cincinnati Symph. Orch. in a program of French and Russian music; he also included an excerpt from *Lohengrin,* thus defying the general ban on German music. However, he apparently lacked that indefinable quality that makes a conductor, and he was forced to cancel further concerts with the Cincinnati Symph. Eager to promote the cause of modern music, he organized a symph. orch. in N.Y. with the specific purpose of giving performances of new and unusual music; it presented its first concert on April 11, 1919. In 1922, he organized with Carlos Salzedo the International Composers' Guild, which gave its inaugural concert in N.Y. on Dec. 17, 1922. In 1926 he founded, in association with a few progressive musicians, the Pan American Society, dedicated to the promotion of music of the Americas. He intensified his study of the nature of sound, working with the acoustician Harvey Fletcher (1926–36), and with the Russian electrical engineer Leo Theremin, then resident in the U.S. These studies led him to the formulation of the concept of "organized sound," in which the sonorous elements in themselves determined the progress of composition; this process eliminated conventional thematic development; yet the firm cohesion of musical ideas made Varèse's music all the more solid, while the distinction between consonances and dissonances became no longer of basic validity. The resulting product was unique in modern music; characteristically, Varèse attached to his works titles from the field of mathematics or physics, such as *Intégrales, Hyperprism* (a projection of a prism into the 4th dimension), *Ionisation* (atomic fission), *Density 21.5* (the specific weight of platinum), etc., while the score of his large orch. work *Arcana* derived its inspiration from the cosmology of Paracelsus. An important development was Varèse's application of electronic music in his *Déserts* and, much more extensively, in his *Poème électronique,* commissioned for the Brussels World Exposition in 1958. Varsèse wrote relatively few works in small forms, and none for piano solo. The unfamiliarity of Varèse's idiom and the tremendous difficulty of his orch. works militated against frequent performances. Among conductors only Leopold Stokowski was bold enough to put Varèse's formidable scores *Amériques* and *Arcana* on his programs with the Philadelphia Orch.; they evoked yelps of derision and outbursts of righteous indignation from the public and the press. Ironically, it was left to a mere beginner, Nicolas Slonimsky, to be the first to perform and record Varèse's unique masterpiece, *Ionisation.* An extraordinary reversal of attitudes toward Varèse's music, owing perhaps to the general advance of musical intelligence and the emergence of young music critics, took place within Varèse's lifetime, resulting in a spectacular increase of interest in his works and the number of their performances; also, musicians themselves learned to overcome the rhythmic difficulties presented in Varèse's scores. Thus Varèse lived to witness this long-delayed recognition of his music as a major stimulus of modern art; his name joined those of Stravinsky, Ives, Schoenberg, and Anton von Webern among the great masters of 20th-century music. Recognition came also from an unexpected field when scientists working on the atom bomb at Oak Ridge in 1940 played Slonimsky's recording of *Ionisation* for relaxation and stimulation in their work. Like Schoenberg, Varèse refused to regard himself as a revolutionary in music; indeed, he professed great admiration for his remote predecessors, particularly those of the Notre Dame school, representing the flowering of the Ars Antiqua. On the centennial of his birth in 1983, festivals of his music were staged in Strasbourg, Paris, Rome, Washington, D.C., N.Y., and Los Angeles. A number of monographs on Varèse were publ. in Europe and America. In 1981, Frank Zappa, the leader of the modern school of rock-and-roll music and a sincere admirer of Varèse's music, staged in

N.Y. at his own expense a concert of Varèse's works; he presented a similar concert in San Francisco in 1982.

WORKS: *Offrandes* for Voice and Chamber Orch. (originally titled *Dedications;* N.Y., April 23, 1922, Carlos Salzedo conducting); *Hyperprism* for 9 Wind Instruments and 18 Percussion Devices (N.Y., March 4, 1923, composer conducting); *Octandre* for Flute, Oboe, Clarinet, Bassoon, Horn, Trombone, and Double Bass (N.Y., Jan. 13, 1924); *Integrales* for Small Orch. and Percussion (N.Y., March 1, 1925, Leopold Stokowski conducting); *Ameriques* for Large Orch. (Philadelphia, April 9, 1926, Stokowski conducting); *Arcana* for Large Orch. (1925–27; Philadelphia, April 8, 1927, Stokowski conducting); *Ionisation* for 13 Percussion Players (using percussion instruments of indefinite pitch), Piano, and 2 Sirens (1931; N.Y., March 6, 1933, Nicolas Slonimsky conducting); *Ecuatorial* for Bass Voice, 4 Trumpets, 4 Trombones, Piano, Organ, Percussion, and Thereminovox (1933–34; N.Y., April 15, 1934, Slonimsky conducting; another version was scored for Male Chorus, 2 Ondes Martenot, and Orch.); *Density 21.5* for Solo Flute (N.Y., Feb. 16, 1936; George Barrere, soloist, on his platinum flute of specific gravity 21.5; hence the title); *Etude pour espace* for Mixed Chorus, 2 Pianos, and Percussion (N.Y., Feb. 23, 1947); *Déserts* for Wind Instruments, Percussion, and 3 interpolations of Electronic Sound (Paris, Dec. 2, 1954); *Poème électronique* (Philips Pavilion at the Brussels World Exposition, spatially distributed over 400 Loudspeakers, 1958); *Nocturnal* for Soprano, Bass, 12 Wind Instruments, Strings, Piano, and Percussion (unfinished; completed by Chou Wen-Chung from sketches). Varèse publ. several seminal papers, among them "Les Instruments de musique et la machine électronique," in *L'Age nouveau* (1955) and "The Liberation of Sound," in *Perspectives of New Music* (Fall–Winter 1966); a vol. of Varèse's writings, *Ecrits,* compiled by Louise Hirbour, was publ. in Paris in 1983.

Varlamov, Alexander, Russian composer of songs; b. Moscow, Nov. 27, 1801; d. St. Petersburg, Oct. 27, 1848. At the age of 10 he entered the Imperial Chapel at St. Petersburg, where his fine voice attracted the attention of Bortniansky, the director, who then became his teacher. As a young man he was attached to the Russian embassy at The Hague as leader of the Russian church choir there (1819–23); he then returned to Moscow, where he taught singing and violin (1823–29); later went to St. Petersburg as a singing teacher. He wrote 223 songs (publ. in 12 vols. by Stellovsky) in the Russian folk style; one of them, *Krasny sarafan (The Red Dress),* achieved tremendous popularity; Wieniawski made use of it in his violin piece *Souvenir de Moscou.* Varlamov was the author of the first Russian singing method, *Shkola penya* (Moscow, 1840).

Varnay, Astrid, soprano; b. Stockholm, April 25, 1918, of Hungarian parents, both professional singers. She was taken to America as a child, and studied first with her mother, then with Hermann Weigert (1890–1955), whom she married in 1944. She made her debut as Sieglinde at the Metropolitan Opera (Dec. 6, 1941), substituting for Lotte Lehmann without rehearsal; appeared at the Metropolitan until 1956, and again from 1974 to 1976; her last performance there was in 1979, in Weill's *Aufstieg und Fall der Stadt Mahagonny;* she then lived mostly in Munich.

Varviso, Silvio, Swiss conductor; b. Zürich, Feb. 26, 1924. He studied piano at the Zürich Cons. and conducting in Vienna with Clemens Krauss. In 1944 he made his debut at St. Gallen, conducting *Die Zauberflöte,* and remained at the theater there until 1950; then conducted at the Basel Stadttheater, where he later served as its music director (1956–62); also made guest appearances with the Berlin State Opera, San Francisco Opera, Paris Opéra, and Metropolitan Opera in N.Y. From 1965–72 he was chief conductor of the Royal Opera in Stockholm; from 1972–80 served as Generalmusikdirektor of the Württemberg State Theater in Stuttgart. In 1980 he was appointed chief conductor of the Paris Opéra.

Varvoglis, Mario, Greek composer; b. Athens, Dec. 22, 1885; d. there, July 30, 1967. He studied at the Paris Cons. with Leroux, and later at the Schola Cantorum with Vincent d'Indy. Returning to Greece in 1922, he was appointed a prof. of music history at the Athens Cons. His early music was influenced by Massenet; later he evolved a more independent style, using some Greek melodic patterns. His symph. prelude, *Sainte-Barbara* (1912), was publ. by the French Inst. of Athens in 1948. He also wrote the one-act opera *An Afternoon of Love* (1935); incidental music to the classical Greek tragedies *Agamemnon* (1932) and *Medea* (1942); *Suite pastorale* for Strings (1910); *Caprice grec* for Cello Solo and Orch. (1914); a symph. poem, *Behind the Wire Fence* (1945); a "study in symph. contrasts," *Lauriers et cyprès* (1950). In 1937 he received the Grand Prize for Music of the Athens Academy of Arts.

Vàsàry, Tamàs, noted Hungarian pianist and conductor; b. Debrecen, Aug. 11, 1933. He studied piano at the Franz Liszt Academy of Music in Budapest; in 1947 won first prize in the Liszt Competition, and later garnered several more prizes. He made his London debut in 1961, and played in N.Y. in 1962. Soon, however, he abandoned his career as a pianist and sought engagements as a symph. conductor. In 1979 he was appointed artistic director of the Northern Sinfonia Orch. in Newcastle upon Tyne. In America he was a guest conductor in Washington, D.C., Denver, San Diego, Dallas, and Cleveland.

Vasconcellos, Joaquim de, Portuguese lexicographer; b. Oporto, Feb. 10, 1849; d. there, March 1, 1936. From 1865 to 1869 he studied at the Univ. of Coïmbra; in 1871–75, traveled in Germany, France, England, and Spain; from 1883 was a prof. of German at the Lyceum of Oporto, and from 1886, also director of the Museum for Industries and Commerce.

He publ. the biographical dictionary *Os musicos portuguezes* (1870), containing much new matter and many emendations of old; a monograph on *Luiza Todi* (1873; 2nd ed., 1929); *Ensajo critico sobre o catalogo del rey Don Joño IV* (1873); a facsimile edition of the catalogue of the Royal Library of Lisbon, destroyed by the earthquake of 1755 (1874–76; with index and commentary, 1905); he also contributed to Pougin's supplement to Fétis's *Biographie universelle.*

Vasilenko, Sergei, noted Russian composer; b. Moscow, March 30, 1872; d. there, March 11, 1956. He studied jurisprudence at Moscow Univ., graduating in 1895; concurrently took private music lessons with Gretchaninov and G. Conus; in 1895 entered the Moscow Cons. in the classes of Taneyev, Ippolitov-Ivanov, and Safonov, graduating in 1901; while still a student, he served as assistant in Safonov's opera class. He also studied ancient Russian chants under the direction of Smolensky. In 1906 he joined the faculty of the Moscow Cons.; subsequently was prof. of orchestration there (1932–41 and 1943–56). From 1907 to 1917 he conducted in Moscow a series of popular symph. concerts in programs of music arranged in a historical sequence; in 1909 and 1912 he conducted concerts in Berlin. In 1938 he went to Tashkent, Uzbekistan, to help native musicians develop a national school of composition. His music is inspired primarily by the pattern of Russian folk song, but he was also attracted by exotic subjects, particularly those of the East; in his harmonic settings there is a distinct influence of French Impressionism.

WORKS: OPERAS: *The Legend of the Great City of Kitezh and the Calm Lake Svetoyar,* dramatic cantata (Moscow, March 1, 1902; operatic version, Moscow, March 3, 1903; composed several years before Rimsky-Korsakov's famous opera on the same subject); *Son of the Sun* (Moscow, May 23, 1929; deals with the Boxer Rebellion in China); *Christopher Columbus* (1933); *Buran,* written with the Uzbek composer Ashrafi (Tashkent, June 12, 1939); *The Grand Canal* (Tashkent, Jan. 12, 1941); *Suvorov* (Moscow, Feb. 23, 1942). BALLETS, etc.: *Noya* (1923); *Joseph the Handsome* (Moscow, March 3, 1925); *Lola* (1926; revised, and produced in Moscow, June 25, 1943); *The Gypsies,* after Pushkin (Leningrad, Nov. 18, 1937); *Akbilyak* (Tashkent, Nov. 7, 1943); *Mirandolina* (Moscow, Jan. 16, 1949). FOR ORCH.: 5 symphs.: No. 1 (Moscow, Feb. 17, 1907); No. 2 (Moscow, Jan. 7, 1913); No. 3, *Italian,* for Wind Instruments and Russian Folk Instruments (1925); No. 4, *Arctic* (Moscow, April 5, 1933); No. 5 (1938); *Vir* for Bass and Orch. (Kislovodsk, July 6, 1896); *3 Combats,* symph. poem (1900); *Poème épique,* symph. poem (Moscow, March 14, 1903); *The Garden of Death,* symph. poem after Oscar Wilde (Moscow, May 4, 1908); *Hircus nocturnus* (Moscow, Feb. 3, 1909; his most popular work; frequently perf. abroad; N.Y., Nov. 20, 1918, by the Russian Symph. Orch.); *Incantation* for Voice and Orch. (1910); Violin Concerto (1910–13); *Au Soleil,* suite for Orch. (Moscow, 1911); *Valse fantastique* (Moscow, Jan. 16,

1915); *Zodiac,* suite on old French melodies (1914); *Exotic Suite* for Tenor and 12 Instruments (1916); *Chinese Suite* (Leningrad, Oct. 30, 1927); *Hindu Suite* (Moscow, 1927); *Turkmenian Suite* (Moscow, 1931); *Soviet East* (1932); *Uzbek Suite* (1942); Cello Concerto (1944); *Ukraine* (1945); Trumpet Concerto (1945); several works for folk instruments; Concerto for Balalaika and Orch. (1931). CHAMBER MUSIC: 3 string quartets; Piano Trio; Viola Sonata; *Serenade* for Cello and Piano; *Oriental Dance* for Clarinet and Piano (1923); *Japanese Suite* for Wind Instruments, Xylophone, and Piano (1938); *Chinese Sketches* for Woodwind Instruments (1938); Woodwind Quartet on American themes (1938); Suite for Balalaika and Accordion (1945). SONGS: He wrote a number of songs, of which *A Maiden Sang in a Church Choir* (1908) is the best; *10 Russian Folk Songs* for Voice, Oboe, Balalaika, Accordion, and Piano (1929). Vasilenko publ. a book of memoirs, *Pages of Reminiscences* (Moscow, 1948), and vol. I of a manual of orchestration (1952).

Vásquez, Juan, Spanish composer; b. Badajoz, c.1510; d. c.1560. He composed many excellent villancicos, for 3, 4, and 5 voices, often using folk songs for the chief melodic part. Many of these are found in Spanish tablature books of the period (e.g., those of Milán, Fuenllana, Enriquez de Valderrábano, Pisador, and Daza, from 1535 to 1576), arranged as solo songs with instrumental accompaniment. He publ. *Villancicos y canciones a 3 y a 4* (Osuna, 1551); *Recopilación de sonetos y villancicos a 4 y a 5* (Seville, 1560; modern ed. by H. Anglès in *Monumentos de la música española,* Barcelona, 1946).

Vasseur, Léon (-Félix-Augustin-Joseph), French composer; b. Bapaume, Pas-de-Calais, May 28, 1844; d. Paris, July 25, 1917. He studied at the Ecole Niedermeyer in Paris; in 1870 became organist of the Versailles Cathedral; after a few years he turned to composing light music; also conducted theater orchs. He wrote about 30 operettas, but his most successful one was his first production, *La Timbale d'argent* (Paris, April 9, 1872). He also publ. sacred music: *L'Office divin* (a collection of masses, offertories, antiphons, etc.); *20 motets des grands maîtres;* a method for organ or harmonium; transcriptions for harmonium and piano.

Vaughan, Denis, Australian conductor; b. Melbourne, June 6, 1926. He studied organ in London with George Thalben Ball and in Paris with André Marchal; also took double-bass lessons in London and Vienna. He served in the multiple, but apparently not mutually exclusive, capacities of bass player, organist, harpsichordist, and pianist, with the Royal Phil. Orch. of London, beginning with its American tour in 1950. In 1953 he became assistant conductor to Sir Thomas Beecham; then was assistant to Vittorio Gui at Glyndebourne (1951) and to Hans Knappertsbusch in Bayreuth (1957). While thus engaged, he discovered myriad discrepancies in the printed scores of operas by Verdi and Puccini, and proceeded to agitate for publishing corrected editions of these works. Expanding his multifarious activities, he served as consultant for the design of the organ in Alice Tully Hall at Lincoln Center in N.Y. He also gave organ recitals. His main endeavor, however, remained conducting. He formed an orch. in Naples, with which he toured in Europe. In 1972 he joined the permanent staff of the Munich Opera; in 1977 he made a tour of Australia, conducting the symph. orchs. in Sydney, Melbourne, Brisbane, etc.; in 1980 was appointed music director of the South Australian Opera. The press everywhere sang his praises, and deservedly so.

Vaughan Williams, Ralph (the original surname of the family was **Williams**), great English composer who created the gloriously self-consistent British style of composition, deeply rooted in native folk songs, yet unmistakably participant of modern ways in harmony, counterpoint, and instrumentation; b. Down Ampney, Gloucestershire, Oct. 12, 1872; d. London, Aug. 26, 1958. His father, a clergyman, died when Vaughan Williams was a child; the family then moved to the residence of his maternal grandfather at Leith Hill Place, Surrey. There he began to study piano and violin; in 1887 he entered Charterhouse School in London and played violin and viola in the school orch. In 1890–92 he studied harmony with F.E. Gladstone, theory of composition with Parry, and organ with Parratt at the Royal College of Music in London; then enrolled at Trinity College, Cambridge, where he took courses in composition with Charles Wood and in organ playing with Alan Gray, obtaining his Mus.B. in 1894 and his B.A. in 1895; he subsequently returned to the Royal College of Music, studying with Stanford. In 1897 he went to Berlin for further instruction with Max Bruch; in 1901 he took his Mus.D. at Cambridge. Dissatisfied with his academic studies, he decided, in 1909, to seek advice in Paris from Ravel in order to acquire the technique of modern orchestration that emphasized color. In the meantime, he became active as a collector of British folk songs; in 1904 he joined the Folk Song Society; in 1905 he became conductor of the Leith Hill Festival in Dorking, a position that he held, off and on, until his old age. In 1906 he composed his *3 Norfolk Rhapsodies,* which reveal the ultimate techniques and manners of his national style; he discarded the 2nd and 3rd of the set as not satisfactory in reflecting the subject. In 1903 he began work on a choral symph. inspired by Walt Whitman's poetry and entitled *A Sea Symphony;* he completed it in 1909; there followed in 1910 *Fantasia on a Theme of Thomas Tallis,* scored for string quartet and double string orch.; in it Vaughan Williams evoked the song style of an early British composer. After this brief work, Vaughan Williams engaged in a grandiose score, entitled *A London Symphony* and intended as a musical glorification of the great capital city. However, he emphatically denied that the score was to be a representation of London life. He even suggested that it might be more aptly entitled *Symphony by a Londoner,* which would explain the immediately recognizable quotations of the street song *Sweet Lavender* and

Vaughan Williams

of the Westminster chimes in the score; indeed, Vaughan Williams declared that the work must be judged as a piece of absolute or abstract music. Yet prosaically minded commentators insisted that *A London Symphony* realistically depicted in its 4 movements the scenes of London at twilight, the hubbub of Bloomsbury, a Saturday-evening reverie, and, in conclusion, the serene flow of the Thames River. Concurrently with *A London Symphony,* Vaughan Williams wrote the ballad opera *Hugh the Drover,* set in England in the year 1812, and reflecting the solitary struggle of the British against Napoleon.

At the outbreak of World War I in 1914 Vaughan Williams enlisted in the British army, and served in Salonika and in France as an officer in the artillery. After the Armistice, he was from 1919 to 1938 a prof. of composition at the Royal College of Music in London; from 1920 to 1928 he also conducted the London Bach Choir. In 1921 he completed his major work, *A Pastoral Symphony,* the music of which reflects the contemplative aspect of his inspiration; an interesting innovation in this score is the use of a wordless vocal solo in the last movement. In 1922 he visited the U.S. and conducted the *Pastoral Symphony* at the Norfolk (Conn.) Festival; in 1932 he returned to the U.S. to lecture at Bryn Mawr College. In 1930 he was awarded the Gold Medal of the Royal Phil. Society of London; in 1935 he received the Order of Merit from King George V. In 1930 he wrote a masque, *Job,* based on Blake's *Illustrations of the Book of Job,* which was first performed in concert version in 1930 and was then presented on the stage in London on July 5, 1931. His 4th Symph., in F minor, written between 1931 and 1935 and first performed by the BBC Symph. Orch. in London on April 10, 1935, presents an extraordinary deviation from his accustomed solid style of composition. Here he experimented with dissonant harmonies in conflicting tonalities, bristling with angular rhythms. A peripheral work was *Fantasia on Greensleeves,* arranged for harp, strings, and optional flutes; this was the composer's tribute to his fascination with English folk songs; he had used it in his opera *Sir John in Love,* after Shakespeare's *The Merry Wives of Windsor,* performed in London in 1929. He always professed great admiration for Sibelius; indeed, there was a harmonious kinship between the 2 great contemporary nationalist composers; there was also the peculiar circumstance that in his 4th Symph. Sibelius ventured into the domain of modernism, as did Vaughan Williams in his own 4th Symph., and both were taken to task by astounded critics for such musical philandering. Vaughan Williams dedicated his 5th Symph., in D major, composed between 1938 and 1943, to Sibelius as a token of his admiration. In the 6th Symph., in E minor, written during the years 1944 and 1947, Vaughan Williams returned to the erstwhile serenity of his inspiration, but the symph. has its turbulent moments and an episode of folksy dancing exhilaration. Vaughan Williams was 80 years old when he completed his challenging *Sinfonia antartica,* scored for soprano, women's chorus, and orch.; the music was an expansion of the background score he

wrote for a motion picture on the expedition of Sir Robert Scott to the South Pole in 1912. Here the music is almost geographic in its literal representation of the regions that Scott had explored; it may well be compared in its realism with the *Alpine Symphony* of Richard Strauss. In *Sinfonia antartica* Vaughan Williams inserted, in addition to a large orch., several keyboard instruments and a wind machine. To make the reference clear, he used in the epilogue of the work the actual quotations from Scott's journal. Numerically, *Sinfonia antartica* was his 7th; it was first performed in Manchester on Jan. 14, 1953. In the 8th Symph., he once more returned to the ideal of absolute music; the work is conceived in the form of a neo-Classical suite, but, faithful to the spirit of the times, he included in the score the modern instruments, such as vibraphone and xylophone, as well as the sempiternal gongs and bells. His last symph. bore the fateful number 9, which had for many composers the sense of the ultimate, since it was the numeral of Beethoven's last symph. In this work Vaughan Williams, at the ancient age of 85, still asserted himself as a composer of the modern age; for the first time, he used a trio of saxophones, with a pointed caveat that they should not behave "like demented cats," but rather remain their romantic selves. Anticipating the inevitable, he added after the last bar of the score the Italian word "niente." The 9th Symph. was first performed in London on April 2, 1958; Vaughan Williams died later in the same year. It should be mentioned as a testimony to his extraordinary vitality that after the death of his first wife, he married, on Feb. 7, 1953 (at the age of 80), the poet and writer Ursula Wood, and in the following year he once more paid a visit to the U.S. on a lecture tour to several American univs.

Summarizing the esthetic and technical aspects of the style of composition of Vaughan Williams, there is a distinctly modern treatment of harmonic writing, with massive agglomeration of chordal sonorities; parallel triadic progressions are especially favored. There seems to be no intention of adopting any particular method of composition; rather, there is a great variety of procedures integrated into a distinctively personal and thoroughly English style, nationalistic but not isolationist. Vaughan Williams was particularly adept at exploring the modern ways of modal counterpoint, with tonality freely shifting between major and minor triadic entities; this procedure astutely evokes sweetly archaic usages in modern applications; thus Vaughan Williams combines the modalities of the Tudor era with the sparkling polytonalities of the modern age. WORKS: OPERAS: *Hugh the Drover,* ballad opera (1911–14; London, July 14, 1924); *The Shepherds of the Delectable Mountains,* a "pastorale episode" after Bunyan's *The Pilgrim's Progress* (1921–22; London, July 11, 1922); *Sir John in Love,* after Shakespeare's *The Merry Wives of Windsor* (1925–29; London, March 21, 1929); *Riders to the Sea,* after the drama by John Millington Synge (1925–32; London, Dec. 1, 1937); *The Poisoned Kiss,* a "romantic extravaganza" (1927–29; Cambridge, May 12, 1936;

revised 1934–37 and 1956–57); *The Pilgrim's Progress,* a "morality" (includes material from the earlier opera *The Shepherds of the Delectable Mountains;* 1925–36, 1944–51; Covent Garden, London, April 26, 1951).

BALLETS: *Old King Cole* (1923; Cambridge, June 5, 1923); *On Christmas Night,* masque (1925–26; Chicago, Dec. 26, 1926); *Job, a Masque for Dancing* (1927–30; concert perf., Norwich, Oct. 23, 1930; stage perf., London, July 5, 1931).

INCIDENTAL MUSIC: To Ben Jonson's *Pan's Anniversary* (1905; Stratford-upon-Avon, April 24, 1905); to Aristophanes' *The Wasps* (1909; Cambridge, Nov. 26, 1909); film music: *49th Parallel* (1940–41); *The People's Land* (1941–42); *Coastal Command* (1942); *The Story of a Flemish Farm* (1943; suite for Orch. from it, London, July 31, 1945); *Stricken Peninsula* (1944); *The Loves of Joanna Godden* (1946); *Scott of the Antarctic* (1947–48; material taken from it incorporated in the *Sinfonia antartica*); *Dim Little Island* (1949); *Bitter Springs* (1950); *The England of Elizabeth* (1955); *The Vision of William Blake* (1957); also unpubl. music for a radio serial, *The Mayor of Casterbridge,* after Thomas Hardy (1950).

VOCAL WORKS: *Willow Wood* for Baritone, Women's Chorus, and Orch., after Dante Gabriel Rossetti (1903; Liverpool Festival, Sept. 25, 1909); *Songs of Travel* for Voice and Piano, to texts by Robert Louis Stevenson (1904; London, Dec. 2, 1904); *Toward the Unknown Region* for Chorus and Orch., after Walt Whitman (1905–7; Leeds Festival, Oct. 10, 1907; revised 1918); *A Sea Symphony* (Symph. No. 1) for Soprano, Baritone, Chorus, and Orch., after Walt Whitman (1906–9; Leeds Festival, Oct. 12, 1910, composer conducting); *On Wenlock Edge,* song cycle for Tenor, Piano, and String Quartet ad libitum, to poems from A.E. Housman's *A Shropshire Lad* (1909; London, Nov. 15, 1909); *5 Mystical Songs* for Baritone, Optional Chorus, and Orch. (1911; Worcester Cathedral, Sept. 14, 1911); *Fantasia on Christmas Carols* for Baritone, Chorus, and Orch. (1912; Hereford Festival, Sept. 12, 1912); *4 Hymns* for Tenor and Piano, with Viola obbligato (1914; Cardiff, May 26, 1920); *Mass in G minor* (1920–21; Birmingham, Dec. 6, 1922); *Flos Campi,* suite for Viola, wordless Mixed Chorus, and Small Orch. (1925; London, Oct. 19, 1925); *Sancta civitas* for Tenor, Baritone, Chorus, and Orch. (1923–25; Oxford, May 7, 1926); *Te Deum* for Mixed Chorus and Organ (1928; Canterbury Cathedral, Dec. 4, 1928); *Benedicite* for Soprano, Chorus, and Orch. (1929; Dorking, May 2, 1930); *The Hundredth Psalm* for Mixed Chorus and Orch. (1929; Dorking, April 29, 1930); *3 Choral Hymns* for Baritone, Mixed Chorus, and Orch. (1930; Dorking, April 30, 1930); *In Windsor Forest,* cantata for Mixed Chorus and Orch., adapted from the opera *Sir John in Love* (1931; Windsor, Nov. 9, 1931); *Magnificat* for Contralto, Women's Chorus, and Orch. (1932; Worcester Cathedral, Sept. 8, 1932); *5 Tudor Portraits* for Mezzo-soprano, Baritone, Chorus, and Orch. (1935; Norwich Festival, Sept. 25, 1936); *Dona nobis pacem* for Soprano, Baritone, Chorus, and Orch. (1936; Huddersfield, Oct. 2, 1936); *Festival Te Deum* (1937); *Flourish for a Coronation* (1937; London, April 1, 1937); *Serenade to Music* for 16 Solo Voices and Orch. (1938; London, Oct. 5, 1938); *The Bridal Day,* masque based on Edmund Spenser's *Epithalamion* (1938–39; revised 1952–53; BBC television, London, June 5, 1953, in celebration of the coronation of Elizabeth II; revised as the cantata *Epithalamion,* London, Sept. 30, 1957); *Thanksgiving for Victory* for Soprano, Speaker, Chorus, and Orch. (1944; BBC broadcast, London, May 13, 1945); *An Oxford Elegy* for Speaker, Chorus, and Orch., to words by Matthew Arnold (1949; Dorking, Nov. 20, 1949); *Folk Songs of the 4 Seasons,* cantata on traditional folk songs, for Women's Voices and Orch. (1949; London, June 15, 1950); *The Sons of Light* for Children's Chorus (1951; London, May 6, 1951); *Hodie (This Day),* Christmas cantata for Soprano, Tenor, Baritone, Chorus, and Orch. (1953–54; Worcester, Sept. 8, 1954); *A Vision of Aeroplanes,* motet for Chorus and Organ, on a text from Ezekiel, Chapter 1 (1955; St. Michael's, Cornhill, London, June 4, 1956); *10 Blake Songs* for Tenor and Oboe (1958; BBC, London, Oct. 8, 1958); other songs to words by English poets; arrangements of English folk songs; hymn tunes; carols.

FOR ORCH.: *Serenade* for Small Orch. (1898); *Bucolic Suite* (1902; Bournemouth, March 10, 1902); *2 Impressions: Harnham Down* and *Boldrewood* (1902; London, Nov. 12, 1907); *3 Norfolk Rhapsodies* (1906; No. 1, in E minor, London, Aug. 23, 1906; No. 2, Cardiff Festival, Sept. 27, 1907; No. 3, not perf.; Nos. 2 and 3 withdrawn by the composer); *In the Fen Country,* symph. impression for Orch. (1904 and subsequent revisions; London, Feb. 22, 1909, Beecham conducting); *The Wasps,* Aristophanic suite (1909; London, July 23, 1912, composer conducting); *Fantasia on a Theme by Thomas Tallis* for String Quartet and Double String Orch. (1910; Gloucester Festival, Sept. 6, 1910, composer conducting; revised 1923); *A London Symphony* (Symph. No. 2; 1911–14; London, March 27, 1914; revised version, London, May 4, 1920); *The Lark Ascending,* romance for Violin and Orch. (1914–20; London, June 14, 1921); *A Pastoral Symphony* (Symph. No. 3; 1916–21; London, Jan. 26, 1922); *Concerto in D minor* for Violin and Strings, *Concerto accademico* (1924–25; London, Nov. 6, 1925); *Piano Concerto in C major* (1926–31; London, Feb. 1, 1933; also revised for 2 Pianos and Orch., 1946); *Fantasia on Sussex Folk-Tunes* for Cello and Orch. (1930; London, March 13, 1930; Casals, soloist; Barbirolli conducting); *Prelude and Fugue in C minor* for Orch. (1930; Hereford, Sept. 12, 1930); *Suite for Viola and Small Orch.* (1934; London, Nov. 12, 1934); *Fantasia on Greensleeves* (arranged from the opera *Sir John in Love* by Greaves, 1934); *Symph. No. 4,* in F minor (1931–35; London, April 10, 1935, Boult conducting); *5 Variants of "Dives and Lazarus"* for String Orch. and Harp, commissioned by the British Council for the N.Y. World's Fair (1939; N.Y., June 10, 1939); *Serenade to Music* (orch. version of 1938 original, 1940; London, Feb. 10, 1940); *Symph. No. 5,* in D major (1938–43; London, June 24, 1943, composer conducting); *Concerto in A minor* for Oboe and Strings (1943–44; Liverpool, Sept. 30, 1944); *Symph. No. 6,* in E minor (1944–47; London, April 21, 1948, Boult conducting); *Partita for Double String Orch.*

(orch. version of Double Trio for String Sextet, 1946–48; BBC, London, March 20, 1948); Concerto Grosso for String Orch. (1950; London, Nov. 18, 1950, Boult conducting); *Romance* in D-flat major for Harmonica, Strings, and Piano (1951; N.Y., May 3, 1952); *Sinfonia antartica* (Symph. No. 7; 1949–52; Manchester, Jan. 14, 1953, Barbirolli conducting); Concerto in F minor for Tuba and Orch. (1954; London, June 14, 1954); Symph. No. 8, in D minor (1953–55; Manchester, May 2, 1956, Barbirolli conducting); *Flourish for Glorious John* (for Sir John Barbirolli; 1957; Manchester, Oct. 16, 1957, Barbirolli conducting); Symph. No. 9, in E minor (1956–58; London, April 2, 1958, Sargent conducting).

CHAMBER MUSIC: String Quartet in C minor (1898; June 30, 1904); Quintet in D major for Clarinet, Horn, Violin, Cello, and Piano (June 5, 1900); Piano Quintet in C minor for Piano, Violin, Viola, Cello, and Double Bass (London, Dec. 14, 1905); String Quartet in G minor (No. 1; London, Nov. 8, 1909); Phantasy Quintet for 2 Violins, 2 Violas, and Cello (1912; London, March 23, 1914); 6 studies in English folk song for Cello and Piano (London, June 4, 1926); Double Trio for String Sextet (London, Jan. 21, 1939); String Quartet No. 2, in A minor (1942–44; London, Oct. 12, 1944); Violin Sonata in A minor (BBC, London, Oct. 12, 1954); also some short piano pieces; Introduction and Fugue for 2 Pianos (1946); organ pieces.

WRITINGS: *The English Hymnal* (1906; 2nd ed., 1933); *Songs of Praise* (with M. Shaw; 1925; 2nd ed., 1931); *The Oxford Book of Carols* (with P. Dearmer and M. Shaw; 1928); lectures and articles, reprinted in *National Music and Other Essays* (London, 1963). R. Palmer edited *Folk Songs Collected by Ralph Vaughan Williams* (London, 1983).

Vázsonyi, Bálint, distinguished pianist; b. Budapest, March 7, 1936. He entered the Franz Liszt Academy of Music in Budapest; made his debut as a pianist at 12. He left Hungary in the midst of political turmoil in 1956; eventually came to America, where he continued his studies with Ernst von Dohnányi. In 1977 he made a transcontinental tour of the U.S.; in 1978 he joined the faculty at the Indiana Univ. School of Music. One of his signal feats of pianofortitude was his performance, on 2 consecutive days, of all 32 piano sonatas of Beethoven in chronological order (N.Y., Oct. 31 and Nov. 1, 1976); he repeated this cycle in Boston and London shortly afterward. He is the author of the standard biography of Dohnányi (Budapest, 1971; Eng. version in progress). His pianism is marked by a transcendental virtuosity of technique coupled with the mellow lyricism typical of traditional Hungarian pianism, and particularly effective in the music of Liszt.

Vecchi, Orazio (Horatio), Italian composer; b. Modena (baptized, Dec. 6), 1550; d. there, Feb. 19, 1605. He was a pupil of Salvatore Essenga in Modena; was maestro di cappella in Salò (1581–84) and at the Cathedral of Modena (1584–86); in 1586 he took Holy Orders; then went to Correggio, where he obtained a canonry. In 1593 he returned to Modena and was appointed maestro at the Cathedral; was promoted to *mansionario* there on Oct. 14, 1596; 2 years later he was also maestro at the ducal court there, and music master to the young princes. On Oct. 7, 1604, he was deprived of his post as choirmaster at the Cathedral, probably through the intrigues of a former pupil, Geminiano Capilupi; this circumstance is believed to have hastened his death. Vecchi was highly regarded as a composer in his day; his works (masses, motets, madrigals, canzonette, etc.) were printed chiefly in Venice, but editions also appeared in Germany and elsewhere. He was invited to the court of Emperor Rudolf II at Vienna, and in 1600 went to Rome in the suite of Cardinal Alessandro d'Este. His lasting fame is due above all to his "commedia harmonica" *L'Amfiparnasso,* performed at Modena in 1594 and printed at Venice in 1597; this is a kind of musical farce written not in the monodic style of Peri's *Dafne,* but in madrigal style, with all the text sung by several voices (i.e., a chorus *a* 4–5); it has been called a "madrigal opera," but it was not intended for the theater and it stood entirely apart from the path that opera was to take. Modern editions of *L'Amfiparnasso* have been publ. by Eitner in vol. 26 of *Publikationen der Gesellschaft der Musikforschung* and by Torchi in *L'arte musicale in Italia,* 4. Of special interest among Vecchi's other compositions is the *Veglie di Siena ovvero I varii humori della musica moderna a 3–6 voci* (1604; also Nuremburg, 1605, as *Noctes ludicrae;* modern ed. by B. Somma), which uses colorful devices to express a wide variety of moods and feelings. Examples of Vecchi's music are in Schering's *Beispielen* (no. 164); Chilesotti's *Biblioteca di rarità musicali,* vol. 5; Torchi's *L'arte musicale in Italia,* 2; Einstein's *Golden Age of the Madrigal;* etc.

Vecchi, Orfeo, Italian composer of sacred music; b. Milan, 1550; d. there, 1604. He was maestro di cappella at Santa Maria della Scala in Milan; most of his MSS are preserved there. His extant publ. works include 3 collections of masses for 5 voices (1588, 1598, 1602); 2 Magnificats; 7 Penitential Psalms for 6 Voices (1601); *Cantiones sacrae* for 6 Voices (1603) and for 5 (1608); etc.

Vecsey, Franz von, Hungarian violinist; b. Budapest, March 23, 1893; d. Rome, April 6, 1935. He received his first instruction from his father, Ludwig Vecsey, a good violinist; at the age of 8 he became a pupil of Hubay, and made such rapid progress that his parents decided to send him on a European tour as a child prodigy; he appeared in Berlin (Oct. 17, 1903), London (May 2, 1904), and N.Y. (Jan. 10, 1905); toured Italy, Scandinavia, and Russia; then lived in Germany and Italy. He composed some violin pieces.

Vécsey, Jenö, Hungarian musicologist and composer; b. Felsöcéce, July 19, 1909; d. Budapest, Sept. 18, 1966. He studied at the Univ. of Sciences and took a course in composition with Kodály at the Budapest Academy of Music (1930–35). He joined the staff of the National Széchényi Library in 1942; was appointed to the Music Dept. and made valuable contributions to the historical and bibliographical music literature preserved there. He initiated and directed editorial work on the Musica Rinata series (1963–66); did preparatory work on the new Haydn Collected Edition.

Vega, Aurelio de la, Cuban-American composer; b. Havana, Nov. 28, 1925. He studied law at the Univ. of Havana (1945–47) and music with Frederick Kramer (1942–46). In 1947 he went to the U.S., and served as cultural attaché at the Cuban Consulate in Los Angeles; there he took composition lessons with Ernst Toch. Returning to Cuba, he was dean of the Music School at the Univ. of Oriente in Santiago de Cuba (1953–59); in 1959 he settled in California, and taught at the San Fernando Valley State College (Calif. State Univ., Northridge). In his early works he cultivated Cuban melorhythms, but later adopted increasingly radical modernistic methods of composition with fantastically reticulated, circumvoluted, and in some instances palindromic, contrapuntal schemes, graphically notated in optically proportioned note values, so that the linear extant of a bar is invariant in relation to the aggregate of rhythmic units contained therein, reaching its heroic ultima ratio in a work entitled *Olep ed Arudamot* (backward reading of a Spanish idiom meaning "pulling your leg"); the visual impression of the score itself is that of an abstract expressionist painting. Sonorifically, he avails himself of a great variety of acoustical materials, electronic and humanoid, including the whirring sound of shuffling feet by string players.

Vega, Carlos, Argentine writer on music; b. Cañuelas, near Buenos Aires, April 14, 1898; d. Buenos Aires, Feb. 10, 1966. He studied at the Univ. of Buenos Aires (philosophy and literature); subsequently devoted himself mainly to folklore research in music. In 1933 he was placed in charge of the folklore division of the literature faculty at the Univ. of Buenos Aires. He traveled throughout the rural regions of Argentina and other South American countries to collect materials on folk songs and folk dances, using a phonograph to record them; devised a special choreographic notation. His many books are basic sources for the study of Argentine folk music.

Velimirović, Miloš, eminent Serbian-American music scholar; b. Belgrade, Dec. 10, 1922. He studied violin and piano at the Music Academy in Belgrade with Petar Stojanovic; in 1943 was sent to a forced labor camp by the German occupation authorities; after the war he studied Byzantine art at the Univ. of Belgrade, graduating in 1951; simultaneously took composition lessons with Mihovil Logar at the Belgrade Music Academy; in 1952 he emigrated to the U.S.; studied at Harvard Univ., obtaining his M.A. in 1953 and his Ph.D. in 1957; also took a course in Byzantine music with Egon Wellesz at Dumbarton Oaks in Washington, D.C. (1954). He subsequent-

ly devoted himself to teaching; was on the faculty of Yale Univ. (1957–69) and the Univ. of Wisconsin (1969–73); in 1973 was appointed a prof. of music at the Univ. of Virginia in Charlottesville; served as chairman of the music dept. there (1974–77). A linguist, he has contributed a number of scholarly articles to various publications, mainly on subjects connected with liturgical music in Byzantium and in the Slavic countries. He publ. *Byzantine Elements in Early Slavic Chant* (2 vols., Copenhagen, 1960); was associate editor (jointly with Egon Wellesz) of *Studies in Eastern Chant* (4 vols., London, 1966–78); wrote "Liturgical Drama in Byzantium and Russia," *Dumbarton Oaks Papers* (1962); articles on Russian and Slavic church music for the 6th edition of *The New Grove Dictionary of Music and Musicians* (1980).

Venatorini. See **Mysliveczek, Joseph.**

Venegas de Henestrosa, Luis, Spanish organist and composer; b. Henestrosa, Burgon, c.1500; d. Toledo, after 1557. He was in the service of Cardinal Juan Tavera in Toledo; publ. the oldest known Spanish book of organ music, *Libro de cifra nueva para tecla, harpa y vihuela* (Alcalà de Henares, 1557; modern ed. by H. Anglès, Barcelona, 1944); it contains organ pieces by Palero, P. Vila, Soto, Venegas himself, etc.; also pieces for vihuela, transcriptions of sacred works by Morales, Josquin, Soto, etc., and solo songs with instrumental accompaniment. The book is written in Spanish organ tablature.

Vengerova, Isabelle, distinguished piano pedagogue; b. Minsk, Russia, March 1, 1877; d. New York, Feb. 7, 1956. She studied at the Vienna Cons. with Joseph Dachs, and privately with Leschetizky; then with Anna Essipoff in St. Petersburg. In 1906 she was appointed an instructor at the St. Petersburg Cons.; in 1910 she became a prof. there. She toured Russia as a pianist; in 1923 came to the U.S.; made her American debut with the Detroit Symph. Orch. (Feb. 8, 1925) in Schumann's Piano Concerto. She became a prof. at the Curtis Inst. of Music in Philadelphia when it was founded in 1924; in 1950 she received an honorary doctor's degree there. Among her piano pupils at the Curtis Inst. were Leonard Bernstein, Samuel Barber, and Lukas Foss. She also taught privately in N.Y.

Venth, Carl, German-American violinist, conductor, and composer; b. Cologne, Feb. 16, 1860; d. San Antonio, Texas, Jan. 29, 1938. His father was a German, his mother Croatian. He studied violin with his father, and composition with Ferdinand Hiller at the Cologne Cons. In 1880 he emigrated to the U.S.; was concertmaster of the Metropolitan Opera Orch. (1884–88) and of the St. Paul Symph. Orch. (1907–12); conducted the Brooklyn Symph. Orch. (1889–1902) and the Dallas Symph. Orch. (1911–13). In 1913 he organized the Fort Worth Symph. Orch., which he conducted for several years. In 1932 he joined the faculty of San Antonio Univ., remaining there until his death. In his own compositions he cultivated exotic subjects for the theater.

Venuti, "Joe" (Giuseppe Venuti), Italian-born American jazz violinist; b. Lecco, April 4, 1898; d. Seattle, Aug. 14, 1978. He was brought to the U.S. as a child and reared in Philadelphia. There he received a thorough classical training on the violin, but after meeting the jazz guitarist Eddie Lang, he turned to popular music. After playing with Paul Whiteman, he formed his own band in 1935 and led it until 1943; then went to the West Coast, where he became a studio musician in Hollywood. His great merit was to make the theretofore-suspect violin a respectable instrument among the plebs of California.

Veprik, Alexander, Soviet composer; b. Balta, near Odessa, June 23, 1899; d. Moscow, Oct. 13, 1958. While still a young boy he went to Leipzig, where he took piano lessons with Karl Wendling; returning to Russia, he entered the Moscow Cons., where he took a course in composition with Miaskovsky (1921–23); from 1923 to 1943 he taught orchestration there. He was associated with the Jewish cultural movement in Russia, and composed several works in the traditional ethnic manner of Jewish cantillations. In his harmonic and formal treatment he followed the "orientalistic" tradition of the Russian national school.
    WORKS: Opera, *Toktogul,* on Kirghiz motifs (Frunze, Kirghizia, 1940); for Chorus and Orch.: *Fascism Be Cursed!* (1944) and *The People Hero* (1955); for Orch.: 2 symphs. (1931, 1938); *Dances and Songs of the Ghetto* (1927); *Kaddish* for Voice, with Instruments (1925); *The Song of Jubilation* (Moscow, March 17, 1937); *Pastorale* (1946); chamber music: *Rhapsody* for Viola and Piano (1926); 3 piano sonatas (1922, 1924, 1928); film music; also *Jewish Communist Youth Song* (1926).
    WRITINGS: *The Problem of Class Aspects of Orchestration* (Moscow, 1931); *Treatment of Orchestral Instruments* (posthumous, Moscow, 1961).

Veracini, Francesco Maria, noted Italian violinist and composer; b. Florence, Feb. 1, 1690; d. there, Oct. 31, 1768. He studied violin with his uncle, Antonio Veracini, a prominent musician in Florence; subsequently took courses with Giovanni Maria Casini, and with Francesco Feroci. In 1711 Veracini went to Venice; in 1714 he visited London, where he played in a series of benefit concerts. In 1716 he returned to Venice. In 1717 he was called to Dresden, where he entered the service of the Prince Elector Friedrich August of Saxony. Mattheson states that Veracini attempted suicide in 1722; indeed, other contemporary writers noted his erratic behavior. In 1723 he returned to Florence; in 1733 he again went to London, where he became associated with the Opera of the Nobility, in opposition to Handel's opera company. He spent about 12 years in England. In 1745 he returned to Italy. In 1755 he became maestro di cappella for the Vallambrosian fathers in the Church of S. Pancrazio in Florence; in 1753 he assumed the same position for the Teatini fathers

in the Church of S. Michele agl' Antinori.

Verbrugghen, Henri, Belgian violinist and conductor; b. Brussels, Aug. 1, 1873; d. Northfield, Minn., Nov. 12, 1934. He studied with Hubay and Ysaÿe at the Brussels Cons.; in 1893 was engaged as a violinist in the Scottish Orch. in Glasgow; then was concertmaster in various orchs. in Wales; also conducted summer concerts there while retaining his position in Glasgow. In 1915 he went to Australia, and established the National Cons. in Sidney. In 1922–23 he was a guest conductor of the Minneapolis Symph. Orch.; then became its regular conductor (until 1932).

Verdelot, Philippe, noted French composer; b. Verdelot, Les Loges, Seine-et-Marne, c.1470–80; d. before 1552. He made his way to northern Italy; in 1522 he was in Florence, where he served as maestro di cappella at the Baptisterium S. Giovanni (1523–27); from 1529 to 1533 he was active in Rome; in 1533–35 was in Venice in a secular capacity. Verdelot's madrigals and motets were publ. in collections in the 16th century, although several works attributed to him are of doubtful authenticity. He composed 2 masses, one entitled *Philomena* (1544); also wrote a Magnificat and several chansons. The *Opera omnia,* edited by A.-M. Bragard in Corpus Mensurabilis Musicae, began publication in 1966.

Verdi, Giuseppe (Fortunino Francesco), great Italian opera composer whose genius for dramatic, lyric, and tragic stage music has made him the perennial favorite of opera enthusiasts; b. Le Roncole, near Busseto, Duchy of Parma, Oct. 9, 1813; d. Milan, Jan. 27, 1901. His father kept a tavern, and street singing gave Verdi his early appreciation of music produced by natural means. A *magister parvulorum,* one Pietro Baistrocchi, a church organist, noticed Verdi's love of musical sound and took him on as a pupil. When Baistrocchi died, Verdi, still a small child, took over some of his duties at the keyboard. His father sent him to Busseto for further musical training; there he began his academic studies and also took music lessons with Ferdinando Provesi, the director of the municipal music school. At the age of 18 Verdi became a resident in the home of Antonio Barezzi, a local merchant and patron of music; Barezzi supplied him with enough funds so that he could go to Milan for serious study. Surprisingly enough, in view of Verdi's future greatness, he failed to pass an entrance examination to the Milan Cons.; the registrar, Francesco Basili, reported that Verdi's piano technique was inadequate and that in composition he lacked technical knowledge. Verdi then turned to Vincenzo Lavigna, an excellent musician, for private lessons, and worked industriously to master counterpoint, canon, and fugue. In 1834 Verdi applied for the post of *maestro di musica* in Busseto, and after passing his examination received the desired appointment. On May 4, 1836, he married a daughter of his patron Barezzi; it was a love marriage, but tragedy intervened when their 2 infant children died, and Verdi's wife herself succumbed on June 18, 1840. Verdi deeply mourned his bereavement, but he found solace in music. In 1838 he completed his first opera, *Oberto, conte di San Bonifacio.* In 1839 he moved to Milan. He submitted the score of *Oberto* to the directorship of La Scala; it was accepted for a performance, which took place on Nov. 17, 1839, with satisfactory success. Verdi was now under contract to write more operas for that renowned theater. His comic opera *Un giorno di regno* was performed at La Scala in 1840, but it did not succeed at pleasing the public. Somewhat downhearted at this reverse, Verdi began composition of an opera, *Nabucodonosor,* on the biblical subject (the title was later abbreviated to *Nabucco*). It was staged at La Scala on March 9, 1842, scoring considerable success. Giuseppina Strepponi created the leading female role of Abigaille. *Nabucco* was followed by another successful opera on a historic subject, *I Lombardi alla prima Crociata,* produced at La Scala on Feb. 11, 1843. The next opera was *Ernani,* after Victor Hugo's drama on the life of a revolutionary outlaw; the subject suited the rise of national spirit, and its production in Venice on March 9, 1844, won great acclaim. Not so popular were Verdi's succeeding operas, *I due Foscari* (1844), *Giovanna d'Arco* (1845), *Alzira* (1845), and *Attila* (1846). On March 14, 1847, Verdi produced in Florence his first Shakespearean opera, *Macbeth.* In the same year he received a commission to write an opera for London; the result was *I Masnadieri,* based on Schiller's drama *Die Räuber.* It was produced at Her Majesty's Theatre in London on July 22, 1847, with Jenny Lind taking the leading female role. A commission from Paris followed; for it Verdi revised his opera *I Lombardi alla prima Crociata* in a French version, renamed *Jérusalem;* it was produced at the Paris Opéra on Nov. 26, 1847; the Italian production followed at La Scala on Dec. 26, 1850. This was one of the several operas by Verdi and other Italian composers where mistaken identity was the chief dramatic device propelling the action. During his stay in Paris for the performance of *Jérusalem,* he renewed his acquaintance with Giuseppina Strepponi; after several years of cohabitation, their union was legalized in a private ceremony in Savoy on Aug. 29, 1859. In 1848 Verdi produced his opera *Il Corsaro,* after Byron's poem *The Corsair.* There followed *La battaglia di Legnano,* celebrating the defeat of the armies of Barbarossa by the Lombards in 1176. Its premiere took place in Rome on Jan. 27, 1849, but Verdi was forced to change names and places so as not to offend the central European powers that dominated Italy. The subsequent operas *Luisa Miller* (1849), after Schiller's drama *Kabale und Liebe,* and *Stiffelio* (1850) were not successful. Verdi's great triumph came in 1851 with the production of *Rigoletto,* fashioned after Victor Hugo's drama *Le Roi s'amuse;* it was performed for the first time at the Teatro La Fenice in Venice on March 11, 1851, and brought Verdi lasting fame; it entered the repertoire of every opera house around the globe. The aria of the libidinous Duke, "La donna è mobile," became one of the most popular operatic tunes sung, or ground on the barrel organ, throughout Europe. This success was followed by an even greater acclaim with the production in 1853 of *Il Trovatore* (Rome, Jan. 19, 1853) and *La Traviata* (Venice, March 6, 1853); both captivated world audiences without diminution of their melodramatic effect on succeeding generations in Europe and America, and this despite the absurdity of the action represented on the stage. *Il Trovatore* resorts to the common device of unrecognized identities of close relatives, while *La Traviata* strains credulity when the eponymous soprano sings enchantingly and long despite her struggle with terminal consumption. The character of Traviata was based on the story of a real person, as depicted in the drama *La Dame aux camélias* by Alexandre Dumas *fils.* The Italian title is untranslatable, *Traviata* being the feminine passive voice of the verb meaning "to lead astray," and it would have to be rendered, in English, by the construction "a woman who has been led astray." Another commission coming from Paris resulted in Verdi's first French opera, *Les Vêpres siciliennes,* after a libretto by Scribe to Donizetti's unfinished opera *Le Duc d'Albe;* the action deals with the medieval slaughter of the French occupation army in Sicily by local patriots. Despite the offensiveness of the subject to French patriots, the opera was given successfully in Paris on June 13, 1855. His next opera, *Simone Boccanegra,* was produced at the Teatro La Fenice in Venice on March 12, 1857. This was followed by *Un ballo in maschera,* which made history. The original libretto was written by Scribe for Auber's opera *Gustave III,* dealing with the assassination of King Gustave III of Sweden in 1792. But the censors would not have any regicide shown on the stage, and Verdi was compelled to transfer the scene of action from Sweden to Massachusetts. Ridiculous as it was, Gustave III became Governor Riccardo of Boston; the opera was produced in this politically sterilized version in Rome on Feb. 17, 1859. Attempts were made later to restore the original libretto and to return the action to Sweden, but audiences resented the change of the familiar version. Unexpectedly, Verdi became a factor in the political struggle for the independence of Italy; the symbol of the nationalist movement was the name of Vittorio Emanuele, the future king of Italy. Demonstrators painted the name of Verdi in capital letters, separated by punctuation, on fences and walls of Italian towns (V.E.R.D.I., the initials of Vittorio Emanuele, Re D'Italia), and the cry "Viva Verdi!" became "Viva Vittorio Emanuele Re D'Italia!" In 1861 Verdi received a commission to write an opera for the Imperial Opera of St. Petersburg, Russia; he selected the mystic subject *La forza del destino.* The premiere took place in St. Petersburg on Nov. 10, 1862, and Verdi made a special trip to attend. He then wrote an opera to a French text, *Don Carlos,* after Schiller's famous drama. It was first heard at the Paris Opéra on March 11, 1867, with numerous cuts; they were not restored in the score until a century had elapsed after the initial production. In June 1870 Verdi received a contract to write a new work for the opera in Cairo, Egypt, where *Rigoletto* had already been performed a year before. The terms were most advantageous, with a guarantee of 150,000 francs for the Egyptian rights alone. The opera, based on life in ancient Egypt, was *Aida;* the original libretto was in French; Antonio Ghislanzoni prepared the Italian text. It had its premiere in Cairo on Christmas Eve of 1871, with great éclat. A special boat was equipped to carry officials and journalists from Italy to Cairo for the occasion, but Verdi stubbornly refused to join the caravan despite persuasion by a number of influential Italian musicians and statesmen; he declared that a composer's job was to supply the music, not to attend performances. The success of *Aida* exceeded all expectations; the production was hailed as a world event, and the work itself became one of the most famous in opera history.

After Rossini's death, in 1868, Verdi conceived the idea of honoring his memory by a collective composition of a Requiem, to which several Italian composers would contribute a movement each, Verdi reserving the last section, *Libera me,* for himself. He completed the score in 1869, but it was never performed in its original form. The death of the famous Italian poet Alessandro Manzoni in 1873 led Verdi to write his great *Messa da Requiem,* which became known simply as the "Manzoni" Requiem, and he incorporated in it the section originally composed for Rossini. The *Messa da Requiem* received its premiere on the first anniversary of Manzoni's death, on May 22, 1874, in Milan. There was some criticism of the Requiem as being too operatic for a religious work, but it remained in musical annals as a masterpiece. After a lapse of some 13 years of rural retirement, Verdi turned once more to Shakespeare; the result this time was *Otello;* the libretto was by Arrigo Boito, a master poet who rendered Shakespeare's lines into Italian with extraordinary felicity. It received its premiere at La Scala on Feb. 5, 1887. Verdi was 79 years old when he wrote yet another Shakespearean opera, *Falstaff,* also to a libretto by Boito; in his libretto Boito used materials from *The Merry Wives of Windsor* and *Henry IV. Falstaff* was performed for the first time at La Scala on Feb. 9, 1893. The score reveals Verdi's genius for subtle comedy coupled with melodic invention of the highest order. Verdi's last composition was a group of sacred choruses, an *Ave Maria, Laudi allu Vergine Maria, Stabat Mater,* and *Te Deum,* publ. in 1898 as *4 pezzi sacri;* in the *Ave Maria,* Verdi made use of the so-called "scala enigmatica" (C, D-flat, E, F-sharp, G-sharp, A-sharp, B, and C).

Innumerable honors were bestowed upon Verdi. In 1864 he was elected to membership in the Académie des Beaux Arts in Paris, where he filled the vacancy made by the death of Meyerbeer. In 1875 he was nominated a senator to the Italian Parliament. Following the premiere of *Falstaff,* the King of Italy wished to make him "Marchese di Busseto," but Verdi declined the honor. After the death of his 2nd wife, on Nov. 14, 1897, Verdi founded in Milan the Casa di Riposo per Musicisti, a home for aged musicians; for its maintenance, he set aside 2,500,000 lire. On Jan. 21, 1901, Verdi suffered an apoplectic attack; he died 6 days later at the age of 87.

Historic evaluation of Verdi's music changed several times after his death. The musical atmosphere was heavily Wagnerian; admiration for Wagner produced a denigration of Verdi as a purveyor of "barrel-organ" music. Then the winds of musical opinion reversed their direction; sophisticated modern composers, music historians, and academic theoreticians discovered unexpected attractions in the flowing Verdian melodies, easily modulating harmonies, and stimulating symmetric rhythms; a theory was even advanced that the appeal of Verdi's music lies in its adaptability to modernistic elaboration and contrapuntal variegations. By natural transvaluation of opposites, Wagnerianism went into eclipse after it reached the limit of complexity. The slogan "Viva Verdi!" assumed, paradoxically, an esthetic meaning. Scholarly research into Verdi's biography greatly increased. The Istituto di Studi Verdiani was founded in Parma in 1959. An American Inst. for Verdi Studies was founded in 1976 with its archive at N.Y. Univ.; it publ. a newsletter.

WORKS: OPERAS: In the literature on Verdi, mention is sometimes made of 2 early operatic attempts, *Lord Hamilton* and *Rocester;* however, nothing definitive has ever been established concerning these 2 works. The accepted list of his operas is as follows: *Oberto, conte di San Bonifacio* (1837–38; La Scala, Milan, Nov. 17, 1839; libretto revised by Graffigna and given as *I Bonifazi ed i Salinguerra* in Venice in 1842); *Un giorno di regno* (later known as *Il finto Stanislao*), melodramma giocoso (1840; La Scala, Milan, Sept. 5, 1840); *Nabucodonosor* (later known as *Nabucco*), dramma lirico (1841; La Scala, Milan, March 9, 1842); *I Lombardi alla prima Crociata,* dramma lirico (1842; La Scala, Milan, Feb. 11, 1843; revised version, with a French libretto by Royer and Vaëz, given as *Jérusalem* at the Paris Opéra, Nov. 26, 1847); *Ernani,* dramma lirico (1843; Teatro La Fenice, Venice, March 9, 1844); *I due Foscari,* tragedia lirica (1844; Teatro Argentina, Rome, Nov. 3, 1844); *Giovanna d'Arco,* dramma lirico (1844; La Scala, Milan, Feb. 15, 1845); *Alzira,* tragedia lirica (1845; Teatro San Carlo, Naples, Aug. 12, 1845); *Attila,* dramma lirico (1845–46; Teatro La Fenice, Venice, March 17, 1846); *Macbeth* (1846–47; Teatro alla Pergola, Florence, March 14, 1847; revised version, with a French trans. by Nuittier and Beaumont of the Italian libretto, Théâtre-Lyrique, Paris, April 21, 1865); *I Masnadieri* (1846–47; Her Majesty's Theatre, London, July 22, 1847); *Il Corsaro* (1847–48; Teatro Grande, Trieste, Oct. 25, 1848); *La battaglia di Legnano,* tragedia lirica (1848; Teatro Argentina, Rome, Jan. 27, 1849); *Luisa Miller,* melodramma tragico (1849; Teatro San Carlo, Naples, Dec. 8, 1849); *Stiffelio* (1850; Teatro Grande, Trieste, Nov. 16, 1850; later revised as *Aroldo*); *Rigoletto,* melodramma (1850–51; Teatro La Fenice, Venice, March 11, 1851); *Il Trovatore,* dramma (1851–52; Teatro Apollo, Rome, Jan. 19, 1853; revised 1857); *La Traviata* (1853; Teatro La Fenice, Venice, March 6, 1853); *Les Vêpres siciliennes* (1854; Opéra, Paris, June 13, 1855); *Simone Boccanegra* (1856–57; Teatro La Fenice, Venice, March 12, 1857; revised 1880–81; La Scala, Milan, March 24, 1881); *Aroldo* (revision of

Stiffelio; 1856–57; Teatro Nuovo, Rimini, Aug. 16, 1857); *Un ballo in maschera,* melodramma (1857–58; Teatro Apollo, Rome, Feb. 17, 1859); *La forza del destino* (1861; Imperial Theater, St. Petersburg, Nov. 10, 1862; revised version, La Scala, Milan, Feb. 27, 1869); *Don Carlos* (1866; Opéra, Paris, March 11, 1867; revised version, 1883–84, with Italian libretto by Lauzières and Zanardini, La Scala, Milan, Jan. 10, 1884); *Aida* (1870–71; Opera House, Cairo, Dec. 24, 1871); *Otello,* dramma lirico (1884–86; La Scala, Milan, Feb. 5, 1887); *Falstaff,* commedia lirica (1889–93; La Scala, Milan, Feb. 9, 1893).

OTHER WORKS: *Inno popolare* for Men's Voices and Piano (1848); *Inno delle Nazioni* for Solo Voice, Mixed Chorus, and Orch. (1862; London, May 24, 1862; composed for the London Exhibition); *Libera me* for Soprano, Mixed Chorus, and Orch. (1868–69; composed for the *Rossini Requiem* and later incorporated in the *Messa da Requiem*); String Quartet in E minor (1873); *Messa da Requiem* for Soprano, Alto, Tenor, Bass, Mixed Chorus, and Orch., the "Manzoni" Requiem (1873–74; San Marco, Milan, May 22, 1874); *Ave Maria* for Soprano and Strings (1880); *Pater noster* for 5-part Chorus a cappella (1880); *4 pezzi sacri: Ave Maria* for Chorus a cappella (1888–89), *Stabat Mater* for Chorus and Orch. (1895–97), *Laudi alla Vergine Maria* for Female Chorus a cappella (1888–89), and *Te Deum* for Soprano, Double Mixed Chorus, and Orch. (1895–97). —Songs: 6 *Romanze* (1838; *Non t'accostare all'urna; More, Elisa, lo stanco poeta; In solitaria stanza; Nell'orro di notte oscura; Perduta ho la pace; Deh, pietoso, oh Addolorata*); *Notturno* for Soprano, Tenor, Bass, and Piano, with Flute obbligato (1839); *L'Esule* (1839); *La seduzione* (1839); *Chi i bei di m'adduce ancora* (1842); 6 *Romanze* (1845; *Il tramonto* [2 versions]; *La Zingara; Ad una stella; Lo Spazzacamino; Il mistero; Brindisi*); *Il Poveretto* (1847); *Suona la tromba* (1848); *L'Abandonnée* (1849); *Barcarola* (1850); *La preghiera del poeta* (1858); *Il brigidino* (1863); *Tu dici che non m'ami* (1869); *Cupo è il sepolcro mutolo* (1873); *Pietà, Signor* (1894).—Also a *Tantum ergo* for Tenor and Orch. (1836?); *Romanza senza parole* for Piano (1865); Waltz for Piano.

Vere, Clémentine Duchene de (real name, **Wood de Vere**), French soprano; b. Paris, Dec. 12, 1864; d. Mount Vernon, N.Y., Jan. 19, 1954. Her father was a Belgian nobleman; her mother, an English lady. Her musical education was completed under the instruction of Mme. Albertini-Baucardé in Florence, where she made her début at the age of 16 as Marguerite de Valois in *Les Huguenots.* On Feb. 2, 1896, she made her American debut at the Metropolitan Opera, N.Y., as Marguerite in Gounod's *Faust;* she remained on its roster until 1897; was again at the Metropolitan in 1898–1900; her other roles with it were Violetta, Gilda, and Lucia. In 1892 she married the conductor **Romualdo Sapio;** after 1914 she lived mostly in N.Y., as a private teacher. Her voice was a brilliant high soprano; she excelled in coloratura.

Vered, Ilana, Israeli pianist; b. Tel Aviv, Dec. 6, 1939. Her mother was a concert pianist and her father was a violinist; she took piano lessons as a child with her mother; at 13 won an Israeli government grant to continue her studies at the Paris Cons.; subsequently took lessons with Rosina Lhévinne and Nadia Reisenberg at the Juilliard School of Music in N.Y. In 1969 she received a grant from the Martha Baird Rockefeller Foundation for a major tour of Europe; subsequently continued her concert career in America.

Veress, Sándor, Hungarian-Swiss composer; b. Kolozsvár, Feb. 1, 1907. He studied piano with his mother, and later with Béla Bartók; studied composition with Zoltán Kodály at the Royal Academy of Music in Budapest (1923–27); obtained his teacher's diploma (1932); also took lessons with László Lajtha at the Hungarian Ethnographical Museum (1929–33). He worked with Bartók on the folklore collection at the Academy of Sciences in Budapest (1937–40); subsequently taught courses at the State Academy of Music in Budapest (1943–48). In 1949 he went to Switzerland, where he received an appointment as guest prof. on folk music at Bern Univ.; taught composition, harmony, and counterpoint at Bern Cons. from 1950. In 1965–67 he was a visiting prof. at the Peabody Cons. in Baltimore; then was a lecturer at the Univ. of Adelaide in Australia (1967); from 1968 he taught musicology at Bern Univ.; then taught at the Univ. of Oregon in Portland (1972); returned to Switzerland and resumed his teaching position at Bern Univ.; became a Swiss citizen in 1975.

Veretti, Antonio, Italian composer; b. Verona, Feb. 20, 1900; d. Rome, July 13, 1978. He studied composition with Alfano at the Liceo Musicale of Bologna, graduating in 1921. He founded his own Cons. Musicale della Gioventù Italiana in Rome, teaching there until 1943; was director of the Cons. G. Rossini in Pesaro (1950–52) and of the Cons. of Cagliari in Sardinia (1953–55); in 1956–70 he was director of the L. Cherubini Cons. His music follows the traditional lines of Italian modernism, but in some of his later works he experimented with serial techniques.

Vermeulen, Matthijs, remarkable Dutch composer and music critic; b. Helmond, Feb. 8, 1888; d. Laren, July 26, 1967. Principally self-taught, he traveled in 1905 to Amsterdam, where he received musical guidance from Daniël le Lange and Alphons Diepenbrock; in 1908 he began to write music criticism for Dutch and French publications, and continued his journalistic activities until 1956. In 1921 Vermeulen went to France; returned to the Netherlands in 1947, when he became music editor of *De Groene Amsterdammer.* He entertained a strong belief in the mystical powers of music; in order to enhance the universality of melodic, rhythmic, and contrapuntal elements, he introduced in his compositions a unifying set of *cantus firmi* against a diversified network of interdependent melodies of an atonal character; it was not until the last years of his life that his works began to attract serious attention for their originality and purely musical qualities.

Verne sisters, **Mathilde, Alice,** and **Adela,** English pianists, also sisters of **Marie Wurm.** Their real name was Wurm, but they adopted the name Verne in 1893. **Mathilde Verne** (b. Southampton, May 25, 1865; d. London, June 4, 1936) studied with her parents, and then became a pupil of Clara Schumann in Frankfurt; was very successful in England; from 1907 to 1936 gave concerts of chamber music in London; was a renowned teacher. **Alice Verne Bredt** (b. Southampton, Aug. 9, 1868; d. London, April 12, 1958) was best known as a piano teacher; she also composed pedagogical works. **Adela Verne** (b. Southampton, Feb. 27, 1877; d. London, Feb. 5, 1952) studied with her sisters, and later took lessons from Paderewski in Switzerland; returning to London, she developed a successful career, and became extremely popular as a concert player in England; also made tours in the U.S.

Verrett, Shirley, black American mezzo-soprano; b. New Orleans, May 31, 1931. Her father, a choirmaster at the Seventh-Day Adventist church in New Orleans, gave her rudimentary instruction in singing. Later she moved to California and took voice lessons with John Charles Thomas and Lotte Lehmann. In 1955 she won the Marian Anderson Award and a scholarship at the Juilliard School of Music, where she became a student of Marion Székely-Frescki. She made her N.Y. debut on Nov. 4, 1958. In July 1962 she sang Carmen at the Festival of Two Worlds at Spoleto, Italy, in a production by Gian Carlo Menotti. In 1963 she made a tour of the Soviet Union, and sang Carmen at the Bolshoi Theater in Moscow. Further engagements followed, at Covent Garden in London and in Israel. On Sept. 21, 1968, she made her debut at the Metropolitan Opera in N.Y., again as Carmen. On Oct. 22, 1973, she undertook 2 parts, those of Dido and Cassandra, in *Les Troyens* of Berlioz, produced at the Metropolitan. She was equally at ease in soprano and mezzo-soprano roles; thus she sang the title in Bellini's *Norma,* a soprano, and also the role of mezzo-soprano Adalgisa in the same opera. Her other roles included Tosca, Azucena, Amneris, and Dalila. She also showed her ability to cope with the difficult parts in modern operas, such as Britten's *The Rape of Lucretia* and Bartók's *Bluebeard's Castle.* Her voice is of a remarkably flexible quality, encompassing lyric and dramatic parts with equal expressiveness and technical proficiency.

Verstovsky, Alexei, important Russian opera composer; b. on the family estate in Tambov district, March 1, 1799; d. Moscow, Nov. 17, 1862. He was taken as a child to the town of Ufa in the Urals; at the age of 17 was sent to St. Petersburg, where he entered the Inst. of Transport Engineers; at the same time he studied music privately with several excellent European teachers who were resident in Russia; took piano lessons with Johann Heinrich Miller, Daniel Steibelt, and the famous pianist and composer John Field; studied violin with Ludwig Maurer and voice with Tarquini. He became a member of the flourishing literary and artistic milieu in St. Petersburg; among his friends was Pushkin. In 1823 he went to Moscow. Almost all of his compositions for the stage followed the French model, with long scenes of speech accompanied on the keyboard; his first production was a vaudeville, *The Sentimental Landlord in the Country* (1817); he also composed popular songs and couplets for various plays. He contributed a great deal to the progress of operatic art in Russia, but his music lacked distinction and inventive power; with the advent of Glinka and Dargomyzhsky on the Russian operatic scene, Verstovsky's productions receded into insignificance.

Vesque von Püttlingen, Johann, Austrian composer; b. Opole, Poland, July 23, 1803; d. Vienna, Oct. 29, 1883. He studied law in Vienna and became a councillor of state; at the same time he studied music with Moscheles (piano) and Sechter (theory), and made his mark as a composer of operas, under the pseudonym **J. Hoven.** The following operas by him were produced in Vienna: *Turandot* (Oct. 3, 1838); *Johanna d'Arc* (Dec. 30, 1840); *Abenteuer Carls des Zweiten* (Jan. 12, 1850). His opera *Der lustige Rat* was produced in Weimar on April 12, 1852. He publ. a useful book, *Das musikalische Autorrecht* (1865).

Viadana, Lodovico da, Italian composer; b. Viadana, near Mantua, 1560; d. Gualtieri, May 2, 1627. His family name was **Grossi,** but he is generally known by the name of his birthplace. In 1596 he became a Franciscan monk; from 1594 till c.1597, was maestro di cappella at the Mantua Cathedral; was in Rome at the end of the century; in 1602 became maestro di cappella at the convent of S. Luca in Cremona; then at the Cathedral of Concordia, near Venice, in 1608–9; from 1610 to 1612, was chorus master at Fano (Papal States), then in Venice, and finally in Mantua again. He was formerly accredited with the invention of the basso continuo (thoroughbass), but Peri's *Euridice* (publ. 1600) has a figured bass in certain numbers, as does Banchieri's *Concerti ecclesiastici* (publ. 1595), whereas Viadana's *Cento concerti con il basso continuo* did not appear till 1602 (Venice). However, he was the first to write church concertos with so few parts that the organ continuo was employed as a necessary harmonic support. A very prolific composer, he publ. numerous masses, Psalms, Magnificats, Lamentations, motets, etc. C. Gallico brought out *Opere di Lodovico Viadana* in Monumenti Musicali Mantovani (Kassel, 1964—).

Vianna (Viana), Fructuoso (Frutuoso), Brazilian composer; b. Itajubá, Oct. 6, 1896; d. Rio de Janeiro, April 22, 1976. He studied music with his father, a municipal judge, who composed polkas and waltzes. In 1912 he began to study piano with Henrique Oswald and harmony with Arnaud Gouveia. In 1923 he went to Paris, where he studied the Dalcroze method of eurhythmics. Returning to Brazil, he taught at the Cons. of São Paulo. In 1941 he settled in Rio de Janeiro. His works are based on native Brazilian melorhythms pleasurably seasoned with acrid dissonances, achieving a certain *trompe-l'oreille* euphony. His musical output consists mainly of piano pieces and songs of such nature; among them are numerous "valsas" (European waltzes in a Brazilian dressing), "toadas" (melodious romances), and "tanguinhos" (little tangos *à la brésilienne*). They are all perfumed with impressionistic overtones.

Vianna da Motta, José. See **Da Motta, José Vianna.**

Viardot-García, Pauline, celebrated singer, daughter of **Manuel del Popolo García;** b. Paris, July 18, 1821; d. there, May 18, 1910. She was taken by her parents to England and America; on returning to Paris in 1828, she had piano lessons with Liszt. Her father and mother both gave her vocal instruction; Reicha was her teacher in harmony. Her concert debut was at Brussels in 1837; her stage debut was in London, May 9, 1839, as Desdemona in Rossini's *Otello;* later she was engaged by Viardot, the director of the Théâtre Italien in Paris; sang there until her marriage to Viardot in 1840; he then accompanied her on long tours throughout Europe. She created the role of Fides in Meyerbeer's *Le Prophète* at the Paris Opéra in 1849, and that of Sapho in Gounod's opera in 1851; after another succession of tours, she took the role of Orphée in Berlioz's revival of Gluck's opera at the Théâtre Lyrique (1859), singing the part for 150 nights to crowded houses. She retired in 1863. Her voice was a mezzo-soprano of extraordinary compass. For some years she taught at the Paris Cons.; among her pupils were Désirée Artôt and Antoinette Sterling. A thoroughly trained musician, she also composed operas, one of which, *La Dernière Sorcière,* was performed (in a German version) at Weimar (April 8, 1869). In Paris she maintained a long Platonic friendship with the Russian novelist Turgenev. She owned the holograph of Mozart's *Don Giovanni,* which she left to the library of the Cons. in Paris.

Vicentino, Nicola, Italian music theorist; b. Vicenza, 1511; d. Rome, 1572. He was a pupil of Willaert at Venice; then became maestro and music master to Cardinal Ippolito d'Este in Ferrara and in Rome. There his book of madrigals for 5 voices, an attempt to revive the chromatic and enharmonic genera of the Greeks, led to an academic controversy with the learned Portuguese musician Lusitano; defeated, Vicentino publ. a theoretical treatise, *L'antica musica ridotta alla moderna prattica* (1555), which contains a description of his invention, an instrument called the archicembalo (having 6 keyboards, with separate strings and keys for distinguishing the ancient genera—diatonic, chromatic, and enharmonic). He also invented and described (1561) an "archiorgano." In chromatic composition he was followed by Cipriano de Rore and Gesualdo.

His work paved the way for the monodic style, and the eventual disuse of the church modes. H. Kaufmann brought out the modern edition *Nicola Vicentino: Opera omnia* in Corpus Mensurabilis Musicae, XXVI (1963).

Vickers, Jon(athan Stewart), eminent Canadian tenor; b. Prince Albert, Saskatchewan, Oct. 29, 1926. He sang in church choirs as a boy; engaged in a mercantile career to earn a living and served as a manager in Canadian Woolworth stores; then was employed as a purchasing agent for the Hudson's Bay Co. and moved to Winnipeg. He won a scholarship at the Royal Cons. of Music of Toronto, where he studied voice with George Lambert; made his opera debut in 1952 at the Toronto Opera Festival as the Duke in *Rigoletto.* In 1957 he was invited to Covent Garden in London; in 1958 he appeared as Siegmund in *Die Walküre* at the Bayreuth Festival; in 1959 he sang at the Vienna State Opera; on Jan. 17, 1960, he made his debut at the Metropolitan Opera in N.Y. as Canio in *Pagliacci.* He is particularly renowned as the Heldentenor in Wagner's operas. In 1969 he was made a Companion of Honour of the Order of Canada.

Victoria, Tomás Luis de (Italianized form, **Tommaso Luigi da Vittoria**), one of the greatest Spanish Renaissance composers; b. Avila, 1548; d. Madrid, Aug. 20, 1611. He received his first musical training as a choirboy at the Cathedral in Avila. In 1565 he went to Rome, and to prepare himself for the priesthood entered the Collegium Germanicum, a seminary founded by St. Ignatius Loyola in 1552. In Rome his teacher may have been Palestrina, who from 1566 to 1571 was music master at the Roman Seminary, at this time amalgamated with the Collegium Germanicum. Victoria was about the same age as Palestrina's 2 sons, Rodolfo and Angelo, who were students at the Roman Seminary; the Italian master is known to have befriended his young Spanish colleague, and when Palestrina left the Seminary in 1571, it was Victoria who succeeded him as maestro there. In 1569 Victoria had left the Collegium Germanicum to become choirmaster and organist in the Church of Sta. Maria di Montserrato; from this time on he also officiated frequently at musical ceremonies in the Church of S. Giacomo degli Spagnuoli. In June 1573, he returned to the Collegium Germanicum as maestro di cappella; 2 years later the Collegium moved to new quarters in the Palazzo S. Apollinare, and Victoria thereby became choirmaster of the adjoining Church of S. Apollinare. In Aug. 1575, he was ordained a priest; in Jan. of that year he had received a benefice at León from the Pope, and in 1579 he was granted another benefice at Zamora, neither requiring residence. In 1578 he resigned his post at the Collegium Germanicum and was admitted as a priest to the Church of S. Girolamo della Carità, where he lived until 1585; this was the church where St. Philip Neri held his famous religious meetings, which led to the founding of the Congregation of the Oratory in 1575. Though Victoria was not a member of the Oratory, he must have taken some part in its important musical activities, living as he did for 5 years under the same roof with its founder (St. Philip left S. Girolamo in 1583); he is known to have been on terms of the closest friendship with Juvenal Ancina, a priest of the Oratory who wrote texts for many of the "Laudi spirituali" sung at the meetings of the Congregation. In 1583, dedicating a vol. of masses to Philip II, Victoria expressed a desire to return to his native land. He probably returned to Spain by 1587; in the dedication of his 2nd book of masses (1592) he mentions for the first time his appointment as chaplain to the widowed Empress-Mother Maria, sister of Philip II, who in 1581 had taken up her residence in the Convent of the Descalzas Reales in Madrid. After his return to Spain, Victoria became organist and choirmaster at this convent, and when the Empress Maria died in 1603, he continued to act as chaplain to her daughter, the Princess Margaret, who was a nun in the Descalzas Reales. His last work, a Requiem Mass for the Empress Maria, regarded as his masterpiece, was publ. in 1605.

Beginning with a vol. of motets in 1572, dedicated to his chief patron, Cardinal Otto Truchsess, Bishop of Augsburg, most of Victoria's works were printed in Italy, in sumptuous editions, showing that he had the backing of wealthy patrons. A vol. of masses, Magnificats, motets, and other church music publ. at Madrid in 1600 is of special interest because it makes provision for an organ accompaniment.

A man of deep religious sentiment, Victoria expresses in his music all the ardor and exaltation of Spanish mysticism. He is generally regarded as a leading representative of the Roman School, but it should be remembered that, before the appearance of Palestrina, this school was already profoundly marked by Hispanic influences through the work of Morales, Guerrero, Escobedo, and other Spanish composers resident in Rome. Thus Victoria inherited at least as much from his own countrymen as from Palestrina, and in its dramatic intensity, its rhythmic variety, its tragic grandeur and spiritual fervor, his music is thoroughly personal and thoroughly Spanish.

Victory, Gerard, Irish composer; b. Dublin, Dec. 24, 1921. He studied modern languages at Univ. College in Dublin and music at Trinity College; in 1967 was appointed music director of Dublin Radio. His compositions are imbued with the broad pentatonic melos of Irish folk music; but in some of his instrumental works of a later period he began to apply serial structures.

Vidal, Paul, noted French composer and pedagogue; b. Toulouse, June 16, 1863; d. Paris, April 9, 1931. He studied at the Paris Cons., and in 1883 won the Prix de Rome with his cantata *Le Gladiateur;* in 1889 he joined the staff of the Paris Opéra as assistant choral director; later became chief conductor there (1906). He taught elementary courses at the Paris Cons. from 1894 until 1910, when he was appointed a prof. of composition. He was music direc-

tor of the Opéra-Comique in 1914–19.
WORKS: Ballet, *La Maladetta* (Paris Opéra, Feb. 24, 1893); opera, *Guernica* (Opéra-Comique, June 7, 1895); mystery play, *Noël, ou Le Mystère de la Nativité* (Galerie Vivienne, Paris, Nov. 25, 1890); operetta, *Eros* (Bouffes-Parisiens, April 22, 1892); several instructive manuals, much used in France: *Manuel pratique d'harmonie; Notes et observations sur la compositions et exécution;* he compiled *52 leçons d'harmonie de Luigi Cherubini* (3 vols.); *Solfège* (2 vols., Paris, 1922).

Vieira, Ernesto, Portuguese music historian; b. Lisbon, May 24, 1848; d. there, April 26, 1915. His main achievement was the publication of the *Diccionario biografico de musicos portuguezes* (Lisbon, 1900), which supplemented the earlier dictionary by Vasconcellos (1870).

Vierne, Louis, blind French organist and composer; b. Poitiers, Oct. 8, 1870; d. Paris, June 2, 1937. He was a pupil of César Franck and Widor at the Paris Cons., winning first prize for organ playing; in 1892 he became Widor's assistant at St. Sulpice, and in 1900 was appointed organist at Notre Dame, holding this position until his death (he died suddenly while playing the organ at a service there). From 1912 he taught organ at the Schola Cantorum; gave many concerts in Europe; in 1927 played in the U.S. His organ works include 6 organ symphs., one orchestral symph., and many smaller pieces. Among his pupils were Nadia Boulanger, Marcel Dupré, and Joseph Bonnet.

Vieru, Anatol, outstanding Rumanian composer; b. Iasi (Jassy), June 8, 1926. He studied harmony with Paul Constantinescu, orchestration with Theodore Rogalski, and conducting with Constantin Silvestri at the Bucharest Cons.; in 1951 he went to Russia, where he studied composition at the Moscow Cons. with Khachaturian (1951–54). In 1954 he was appointed to the faculty of the Bucharest Cons. In 1968 he visited the U.S. as a member of the Composers' Forum at the Juilliard School of Music in N.Y. In 1982 and 1983 he gave summer courses at the Rubin Academy for Music and Dance in Jerusalem. In 1980 he publ. in Bucharest *The Book of Modes.* From his earliest years he composed music in a relatively advanced idiom, without losing contact with the characteristic melorhythmic patterns of Rumanian folk songs. Interesting in this respect is his oratorio *Miorița* (1957), after a Rumanian folk tale, in which he applies serial procedures to folk-like materials. His Concerto for Cello and Orch. (1962), written in an original manner combining neo-Baroque and impressionistic traits, brought him international attention when it received first prize in a 1962 Geneva competition.

Vieuxtemps, Henri, celebrated Belgian violinist and composer; b. Verviers, Feb. 17, 1820; d. Mustapha, Algiers, June 6, 1881. His first teacher was his father, a piano tuner, who soon turned him over to Lecloux, with whom he made a concert tour at the age of 8. He then continued his studies with Bériot in Brussels (1829–30); took harmony lessons from Sechter in Vienna (1833) and Reicha in Paris (1835). In 1834 he visited London, where he appeared with the Phil. (June 2, 1834). In 1837 he revisited Vienna; in 1838–39 he gave concerts in Russia. During his constant travels, he composed violin concertos and other violin works which became part of the standard repertoire, and which he performed in Europe to the greatest acclaim. He made his first American tour in 1843–44. In 1846 he was engaged as a prof. at the St. Petersburg Cons., and remained in Russia for 5 seasons; his influence on Russian concert life and violin composition was considerable. In 1853 he recommenced his concert tours in Europe; paid 2 more visits to America, in 1857 (with Thalberg) and in 1870 (with Christine Nilsson). He was a prof. of violin playing at the Brussels Cons. (1871–73); a stroke of paralysis, affecting his left side, forced him to end all his concert activities, but he continued to teach privately. He went to Algiers for rest, and died there; one of his most prominent pupils, Jenö Hubay, was with him at his death. In 1844, Vieuxtemps married the pianist **Josephine Eder** (b. Vienna, Dec. 15, 1815; d. Celle-St. Cloud, June 29, 1868). With Bériot, Vieuxtemps stood at the head of the modern French school of violin playing; contemporary accounts speak of the extraordinary precision of his technique and of his perfect ability to sustain a flowing melody; the expression "le roi du violon" was often applied to him in the press. Besides his 7 violin concertos (the last one being posthumous), he wrote for violin and orch.: *Fantaisie-Caprice; Souvenirs de Russie; Fantasia appassionata; Ballade et polonaise;* and *Old England*, a caprice on English airs of the 16th and 17th centuries. For violin and piano he composed *Hommage à Paganini; Grosse Fantasie über slavische Volksmelodien; Andante und Rondo; Suite* in B minor; *Marche funèbre; Danse Négro-Créole* (1844); etc.; numerous brilliant transcriptions of operatic airs.

Viganò, Salvatore, Italian composer and choreographer; b. Naples, March 25, 1769; d. Milan, Aug. 10, 1821. He was the son and pupil of a dancer; studied music with **Luigi Boccherini,** who was his uncle; began his career as a dancer at Rome in 1783, and also produced there an opera buffa, *La Vedova scoperta;* then went to Madrid, where he married the celebrated ballerina María Medina; in 1791 he returned to Italy; in 1793 was at Vienna; then made a tour of the principal European cities. He is remembered chiefly because Beethoven wrote the music for Viganò's "heroic ballet" *Die Geschöpfe des Prometheus* (Vienna, March 28, 1801), in which Viganò danced the leading male role.

Villa-Lobos, Heitor, remarkable Brazilian composer of great originality and unique ability to recreate native melodic and rhythmic elements in large instrumental and choral forms; b. Rio de Janeiro, March 5, 1887; d. there, Nov. 17, 1959. He studied music with his father, a writer and amateur cello player; after his father's death in 1899, Villa-

Lobos earned a living by playing the cello in cafés and restaurants. In 1905 he traveled to the northern states of Brazil in order to collect authentic folk songs. In 1907 he entered the National Inst. of Music in Rio de Janeiro, where he studied with Frederico Nascimento, Angelo França, and Francisco Braga. In 1912 he undertook an expedition into the interior of Brazil, where he gathered a rich collection of Indian songs. On Nov. 13, 1915, he presented in Rio de Janeiro a concert of his compositions, creating a sensation by the exuberance of his music and the radical character of his technical idiom. He met the pianist Artur Rubinstein, who became his ardent admirer; for him Villa-Lobos composed a transcendentally difficult *Rudepoema.* In 1923 Villa-Lobos went to Paris on a Brazilian government grant; upon returning to Brazil in 1930, he was appointed director of music education in Rio de Janeiro. He introduced bold innovations into the national program of music education, with an emphasis on the cultural resources of Brazil; compiled a *Guia pratico*, containing choral arrangements of folk songs of Brazil and other nations; organized the "orpheonic concentrations" of schoolchildren, whom he trained to sing according to his own cheironomic method of solfeggio. In 1944 he made his first tour of the U.S., and conducted his works in Los Angeles, Boston, and N.Y. In 1945 he established in Rio de Janeiro the Brazilian Academy of Music; in 1947 he made his 2nd visit to the U.S.; in 1949 he was in Europe, but retained his permanent home in Rio de Janeiro.

Villa-Lobos was one of the most original composers of the 20th century. He lacked formal academic training, but far from hampering his development, this deficiency liberated him from pedantic restrictions, so that he evolved an idiosyncratic technique of composition, curiously eclectic, but all the better suited to his musical esthetics. An ardent Brazilian nationalist, he resolved from his earliest attempts in composition to use authentic Brazilian song materials as the source of his inspiration; yet he avoided using actual quotations from popular songs; rather, he wrote melodies which are authentic in their melodic and rhythmic content. In his desire to relate Brazilian folk resources to universal values, he composed a series of extraordinary works, *Bachianas brasileiras,* in which Brazilian melorhythms are treated in Bachian counterpoint. He also composed a number of works under the generic title *Chôros*, a popular Brazilian dance form, marked by incisive rhythm and a ballad-like melody. An experimenter by nature, Villa-Lobos devised a graphic method of composition, using geometrical contours of drawings and photographs as outlines for the melody; in this manner he wrote *The New York Skyline*, using a photograph for guidance. Villa-Lobos wrote operas, ballets, symphs., chamber music, choruses, piano pieces, songs; the total number of his compositions is in excess of 2,000.

WORKS: OPERAS (several left uncompleted): Most notably, *Izaht* (1914; revised 1932; premiere, in concert form, Rio de Janeiro, April 6, 1940); *Magdalena,* light opera (Los Angeles, July 26, 1948); *Yer-*

ma, after Federico García Lorca (1955; posthumous, in Spanish, at Santa Fe, Aug. 12, 1971); a children's opera, *Daughter of the Clouds* (1957–58).

BALLETS (many converted from symph. poems): *Uirapuru* (1917; Buenos Aires, May 25, 1935; revised 1948); *Dança da terra* (1939; Rio de Janeiro, Sept. 7, 1943); *Rudá* (1951); *Genesis* (1954; as a symph. poem, posthumous, Rio de Janeiro, 1969); *Emperor Jones* (1955; N.Y., July 12, 1956).

9 BACHIANAS BRASILEIRAS: No. 1 for 8 Cellos (Rio de Janeiro, Sept. 12, 1932); No. 2 for Chamber Orch. (1933); No. 3 for Piano and Orch. (1934); No. 4 for Piano (1930–40; orchestration, N.Y., June 6, 1942); No. 5 for Voice and 8 Cellos (1938; Rio de Janeiro, March 25, 1939); No. 6 for Flute and Bassoon (1938); No. 7 for Orch. (1942; Rio de Janeiro, March 13, 1944); No. 8 for Orch. (1944; Rome, Aug. 6, 1947); No. 9 for Chorus a cappella or String Orch. (1944).

15 CHOROS: No. 1 for Guitar (1920); No. 2 for Flute and Clarinet (1921); No. 3 for Male Chorus and 7 Wind Instruments (1925); No. 4 for 3 Horns and Trombone (1926); No. 5, *Alma Brasileira*, for Piano (1926); No. 6 for Orch. (1926; Rio de Janeiro, July 15, 1942); No. 7 for Flute, Oboe, Clarinet, Saxophone, Bassoon, Violin, and Cello (1924); No. 8 for Large Orch. and 2 Pianos (1925; Paris, Oct. 24, 1927); No. 9 for Orch. (1929; Rio de Janeiro, July 15, 1942, composer conducting); No. 10, *Rasga o Coração*, for Chorus and Orch. (1925; Rio de Janeiro, Dec. 15, 1926); No. 11 for Piano and Orch. (1928; Rio de Janeiro, July 15, 1942); No. 12 for Orch. (1929; Cambridge, Mass., Feb. 21, 1945, composer conducting the Boston Symph. Orch.); No. 13 for 2 Orch. and Band (1929); No. 14 for Orch., Band, and Chorus (1928); also a supernumerary *Chôros bis* for Violin and Cello (1928).

OTHER ORCH. WORKS: 12 symphs.: No. 1, *Imprevisto* (1916; Rio de Janeiro, Aug. 30, 1920); No. 2, *Ascenção* (1917); No. 3, *Guerra* (Rio de Janeiro, July 30, 1919); No. 4, *Vitória* (1920); No. 5, *Paz* (1921); No. 6, *Montanhas do Brasil* (1944); No. 7, *Odisséia da Paz* (1945; London, March 27, 1949); No. 8 (1950; Philadelphia, Jan. 14, 1955); No. 9 (1951; posthumous, Philadelphia Orch. at the Caracas Festival, May 16, 1966); No. 10, *Sume Pater Patrium*, for Soloists, Chorus, and Orch. (1952; Paris, April 4, 1957); No. 11 (1955; Boston, March 2, 1956, composer conducting); No. 12 (1957; First Inter-American Music Festival, Washington, D.C., April 20, 1958). Also, *Dansas africanas* (1914; Paris, April 5, 1928); 2 cello concertos: No. 1, *Grand Concerto* (1915), and No. 2 (1953; N.Y., Feb. 5, 1955); 2 sinfoniettas (1916, 1947); *Amazonas* (1917; Paris, May 30, 1929); *Fantasy of Mixed Movements* for Violin and Orch. (Rio de Janeiro, Dec. 15, 1922); *Momoprecoce* for Piano and Orch. (Amsterdam, 1929); *Caixinha de Boás Festas* (Rio de Janeiro, Dec. 8, 1932); *Ciranda das sete notes* for Bassoon and String Orch. (1933); 3 of 4 suites titled *Descobrimento do Brasil* (1937; No. 4 is an oratorio); *The New York Skyline* (1939); *Rudepoema* (orch. version of the piano work of that name; Rio de Janeiro, July 15, 1942, composer conducting); *Madona*, tone poem (1945; Rio de Janeiro, Oct. 8, 1946, composer conducting); 5 piano concertos (1945, 1948, 1952–57, 1952, 1954); *Fantasia* for Cello and Orch. (1945); *Fantasia* for Soprano Saxophone, String Orch., and 2 Horns (1948); *Erosion, or The Origin of the Amazon River* (Louisville, Ky., Nov. 7, 1951); Guitar Concerto (1951); Harp Concerto (1953; Philadelphia, Jan. 14, 1955); *Odyssey of a Race,* symph. poem written for Israel (1953); Mount Carmel Festival of the International Society for Contemporary Music, Haifa, May 30, 1954); *Dawn in a Tropical Forest* (1953; Louisville, Jan. 23, 1954); Harmonica Concerto (1955; Jerusalem, Oct. 27, 1959); *Izi*, symph. poem (1957).

OTHER CHAMBER MUSIC: 17 string quartets (1915, 1916, 1917, 1931, 1938, 1942, 1944, 1945, 1946, 1948, 1950, 1952, 1953, 1954, 1955, 1958); 3 piano trios (1911, 1916, 1918); *Quinteto duplo de cordas* (1912); 4 *Sonatas-Fantasia* for Violin and Piano (1912, 1914, 1915, 1918); 2 cello sonatas (1915, 1916); Piano Quintet (1916); *Mystic Sextet* for Flute, Clarinet, Saxophone, Celesta, Harp, and Guitar (1917); Trio for Oboe, Clarinet, and Bassoon (1921); Woodwind Quartet (1928); *Quintet in the Form of a Chôros* for Flute, Oboe, Clarinet, Bassoon, and English Horn (1928; revised 1953, replacing English Horn with French Horn); String Trio (1946); *Duo* for Violin and Viola (1946); *Fantasia concertante* for Piano, Clarinet, and Bassoon (1953); *Duo* for Oboe and Bassoon (1957); Quintet for Flute, Harp, Violin, Viola, and Cello (1957); *Fantasia concertante* for Cello Ensemble (N.Y., Dec. 10, 1958).

OTHER VOCAL MUSIC: For Chorus: *Crianças* (1908); *Vidapura*, oratorio for Chorus, Orch., and Organ (1918; Rio de Janeiro, Nov. 11, 1922); *Hinos aos artistas* for Chorus and Orch. (1919); Quartet for Harp, Celesta, Flute, Saxophone, and Women's Voices (1921); Nonetto for Flute, Oboe, Clarinet, Saxophone, Bassoon, Harp, Celesta, Percussion, and Chorus (1923); *Cantiga da Roda* for Women's Chorus and Orch. (1925); *Na Bah a tem* (1925); *Canção da Terra* (1925); *Missa São Sebastião* (1937); Suite No. 4 of *Descobrimento do Brasil* for Orch. and Chorus (1937); *Mandu-Carará*, cantata profana for Chorus and Orch. (1940; N.Y., Jan. 23, 1948; also a ballet); *Bendita sabedoria* (*Blessed Wisdom;* 1958); *Magnificat-Alleluia* for Boy Contralto, Chorus, Organ, and Orch. (1958; Rio de Janeiro, Nov. 8, 1958; by request of Pope Pius XII); etc. Songs: *Confidencia* (1908); *Noite de Luar* (1912); *Mal secreto* (1913); *Fleur fanée* (1913); *Il nome di Maria* (1915); *Sertão no Estio* (1919); *Canções típicas brasileiras* (10 numbers; 1919); *Historiettes* (6 numbers; 1920); *Epigrammes ironiques et sentimentales* (8 numbers; 1921); *Suite* for Voice and Violin (1923); *Poème de l'Enfant et de sa Mère* for Voice, Flute, Clarinet, and Cello (1923); *Serestas* (suite of 14 numbers; one of his best song cycles; 1925); *3 poemas indígenas* (1926); *Suite sugestiva* for Voice and Orch. (1929); *Modinhas e canções* (2 albums; 1933, 1943); *Poem of Itabira* for Alto and Orch. (1941; Rio de Janeiro, Dec. 30, 1946); *Canção das aguas claras* for Voice and Orch. (1956).

OTHER WORKS FOR PIANO: *Valsa romantica* (1908); *Brinquedo de Roda* (6 pieces; 1912); *Primeira suite infantil* (5 pieces; 1912); *Segunda suite infantil* (4 pieces; 1913); *Danças africanas* (1915); *Prole do Bebé*, Suite No. 1 (8 pieces, including the popular

Polichinello; 1918); *Fábulas características* (3 pieces; 1914–18); *Historia da Carochinha* (4 pieces; 1919); *Carnaval das crianças brasileiras* (8 pieces; 1919); *Lenda do Caboclo* (1920); *Dança infernal* (1920); *Prole do Bebé,* Suite No. 2 (9 pieces; 1921); *Sul América* (1925); *Cirandinhas* (12 pieces; 1925); *Rudepoema* (1921–26); *Cirandas* (16 pieces; 1926); *Alma brasileira* (*Chôros* No. 5; 1926); *Prole do Bebé,* Suite No. 3 (9 pieces; 1929); *Lembrança do Sertão* (1930); *Caixinha de música quebrada* (1931); *Ciclo brasileiro* (4 pieces; 1936); *As Três Marías* (3 pieces; 1939; very popular); *Poema Singelo* (1942); *Homenagem a Chopin* (1949).

Vincent, John, American composer and teacher; b. Birmingham, Ala., May 17, 1902; d. Santa Monica, Calif., Jan. 21, 1977. He studied flute with Georges Laurent at the New England Cons. in Boston (1922–26), and composition there with Converse and Chadwick (1926–27); then took courses at the George Peabody College in Nashville (M.A., 1933) and at Harvard Univ., where his principal teacher was Walter Piston (1933–35); then went to Paris, where he studied at the Ecole Normale de Musique (1935–37) and took private lessons with Nadia Boulanger. He received his Ph.D. from Cornell Univ. in 1942. He subsequently occupied various teaching positions: was in charge of music in the El Paso (Texas) public schools (1927–30); then taught at George Peabody College in Nashville (1930–33), at Western Kentucky Teachers College (1937–46), and at the Univ. of Calif., Los Angeles (1946–69). After his death, the John Vincent Archive was established at UCLA. In his music he evolved a tonal idiom which he termed "paratonality"; fugal elements are particularly strong in his instrumental compositions.

Vinci, Leonardo, Italian composer; b. Strongoli, 1690; d. Naples, May 27, 1730. He studied at the Cons. dei Poveri de Gesù Cristo in Naples, where he was a pupil of Gaetano Greco. In 1725 he received the post of vice-maestro at the Royal Chapel in Naples, and remained there until his death 5 years later. He produced about 40 operas for various Italian cities (25 for Naples, 11 for Rome), of which the most important are: *Silla dittatore* (Naples, Oct. 1, 1723); *Astianatte* (Naples, Dec. 2, 1725); *La caduta dei Decemviri* (Naples, Oct. 1, 1727); *Artaserse* (libretto by Metastasio; Rome, Feb. 4, 1730).

Viñes, Ricardo, Spanish pianist; b. Lérida, Feb. 5, 1875; d. Barcelona, April 29, 1943. He studied in Barcelona with Juan Pujol, and with Godard at the Paris Cons., winning the first prize for piano in 1894. In 1895 he gave his first concert in Paris, and established himself in later years as an ardent propagandist of new French and Spanish music; he possessed particular affinity with the composers of the modern French school and performed their works in a colorful and imaginative manner. He gave concerts in London, Berlin, and other music centers, but lived most of his life in Paris; contributed articles on Spanish music to publications in France and Spain.

Vinton, John, American writer on music; b. Cleveland, Jan. 24, 1937. He studied at Ohio State Univ. (1954–58) and N.Y. Univ. (1958–63); his principal teachers in musicology were Jan LaRue and Gustave Reese. From 1964–67 he was on the staff of the *Washington Evening Star.* He edited the useful *Dictionary of Contemporary Music* (N.Y., 1974); also publ. *Essays after a Dictionary* (Lewisburg, Pa., 1977).

Viotta, Henri (Henricus Anastasius), Dutch conductor and music scholar, son of **Johannes Josephus Viotta;** b. Amsterdam, July 16, 1848; d. Montreux, Feb. 17, 1933. He studied with his father and with R. Hol in Amsterdam; was a student of jurisprudence at the Univ. of Leyden; received a Dr.Juris (1877) with the dissertation *Het auteursrecht van den componist,* but gave up legal practice; he became a conductor of various musical groups in Amsterdam, including the Wagner Society. In 1896 he was appointed director of the Cons. at The Hague, retaining this position until 1917; he founded the Residentie Orch. there (1904), and conducted it until he retired in 1917. He publ. the valuable *Lexicon der toonkunst* (3 vols., 1881–85) and the *Handboek der muziekgeschiedenis* (1916). In 1920 he went to live in Switzerland.

Viotta, Johannes Josephus, Dutch composer; b. Amsterdam, Jan. 14, 1814; d. there, Feb. 6, 1859. He was of Italian descent; studied medicine; music was his avocation. He wrote mainly for the voice, and some of his songs in the popular vein (*De zilveren vloot, Een scheepje in de haven lag,* etc.) became exceedingly well known. In the Netherlands he played a very important role, especially in spreading the cult of Mendelssohn and other German composers.

Viotti, Giovanni Battista, famous Italian violinist and composer; b. Fontanetto da Po, May 12, 1755; d. London, March 3, 1824. His father, a blacksmith, was an amateur musician; taught him music, and bought a small violin for him to practice on. At the age of 11 Viotti was sent to Turin, where he gained the favor of Alfonso del Pozzo, Prince della Cisterna, who paid for his lessons with Pugnani. Viotti soon acquired a virtuoso technique, and also began to compose violin music. In 1780 he made a grand tour of Germany, Poland, and Russia with Pugnani, and was welcomed at the court of Catherine the Great. On March 17, 1782, he made his first appearance in Paris at the Concert Spirituel. He became a court musician to Marie Antoinette, and in 1788 was appointed manager of the Théâtre de Monsieur, jointly with the Queen's hairdresser, Léonard; he reorganized the enterprise, and invited famous singers to participate in operatic productions. He was also successful as a teacher; among his pupils were Baillot and Rode. He was intimate with Cherubini, and lodged with him in 1785; often played in private, but shunned public appearances, being satisfied with the generous emolument from the court. He remained in Paris for 3 years after the Revolution, but in 1792, when the situation became extremely dangerous for friends of the Queen, he went to London, where he was employed as a conductor of Italian operas; also was soloist in his own concertos at the celebrated Salomon concerts (1794–95). In 1798 he was obliged to leave England on suspicion of political intrigue; he lived for some years at Schönfeld, near Hamburg, devoting himself to composition. In 1801 he returned to London and engaged in a wine business, but sustained financial losses. After the restoration of the French monarchy, he returned to Paris; was appointed director of the Italian Opera (1819–21), but suffered repeated reverses, and in 1823 returned to London, broken in spirit and health, and heavily in debt. He died 2 years later.

Viotti's role in the history of instrumental music, in both performance and composition, was very important. He elevated performing standards from mere entertainment to artistic presentation, and may be regarded as one of the chief creators of modern violin playing. He was the first to write violin concertos in a consciously formulated sonata form, with the solo part and the orch. accompaniment utilizing the full resources of instrumental sonority more abundantly than ever before in violin concertos. He publ. 29 violin concertos (of which No. 22, in A minor, is a great favorite); 10 piano concertos (some of which are transcriptions of violin concertos); 2 *symphonies concertantes* for 2 Violins, Strings, Oboes, and Horns; 21 string quartets; 36 string trios; 54 duets for 2 Violins; 6 serenades for 2 Violins; several duos for 2 Cellos; 3 divertissements for Violin Unaccompanied; 12 sonatas for Violin and Piano; 9 piano sonatas. His song known as "La polacca de Viotti" (used in Paisiello's *La Serva padrona*, 1794) acquired great popularity. For the rectification of Viotti's birth date (heretofore given as May 23, 1753), see *Stampa di Torino* of Sept. 29, 1935, which publ. for the first time the text of his birth certificate; an infant brother of Viotti was born in 1753; their Christian names were identical (the brother having died before the birth of the future musician), which led to confusion; the bicentennial of Viotti was widely celebrated in the wrong year (1953).

Virdung, Sebastian, German theorist; b. Amberg, 1465. He was at first a priest in Eichstätt, and from 1500 a member of the court chapel in Heidelberg; wrote a work of importance for the history of musical instruments: *Musica getutscht und auszgezogen durch Sebastianum Virdung, Priesters von Amberg, und alles Gesang ausz den Noten in die Tabulaturen diser benannten dryer Instrumenten, der Orgeln, der Lauten und der Flöten transferieren zu lernen kurtzlich gemacht* (Basel, 1511; facsimile reprint in Eitner's *Publikationen älterer praktischer und theoretischer Musikwerke,* vol. 11, 1882; also by L. Schrade, Kassel, 1931, and by K.W. Niemöller, Kassel, 1970). Virdung's method was violently attacked by Arnolt Schlick in his *Tabulatur etlicher Lobgesänge* (1512). Four of Virdung's songs are in Schöffer's *Teutsche Lieder mit 4 Stimmen* (1513).

Vishnevskaya, Galina, Russian soprano; b. Leningrad, Oct. 25, 1926. After vocal studies in Leningrad she sang in operetta; in 1952 she joined the operatic staff of the Bolshoi Theater in Moscow; there her roles were Violetta, Tosca, Madama Butterfly, and an entire repertoire of soprano parts in Russian operas. She made her debut at the Metropolitan Opera in N.Y. on Nov. 6, 1961, as Aida. She is married to the famous cellist **Mstislav Rostropovich.** Owing to the recurrent differences that developed between Rostropovich and the cultural authorities of the Soviet Union (Rostropovich had sheltered the dissident writer Solzhenitsyn in his summer house), they left Russia in 1974; eventually settled in the U.S., when Rostropovich was appointed conductor of the National Symph. Orch. in Washington, D.C. In March 1978, both he and Vishnevskaya, as "ideological renegades," were stripped of their Soviet citizenship by a decree of the Soviet government.

Vitali, Giovanni Battista, Italian composer; b. Bologna, Feb. 18, 1632; d. Modena, Oct. 12, 1692. He was a pupil of M. Cazzati in Bologna; from about 1667 he played the viola da braccio in the Church of S. Petronio there; from 1674 he was 2nd, and from 1684, first, maestro di cappella at the ducal court of Modena; in 1686 he was demoted to vice-maestro.

Vitry, Philippe de (Philippus de Vitriaco), famous churchman and musician; b. Vitry, Champagne, Oct. 31, 1291; d. Meaux, June 9, 1361. There are 6 towns in Champagne named Vitry, and it is not known in which of these Vitry was born; he was ordained a deacon early in life and from 1323 held several benefices; he was canon of Soissons and archbishop of Brie. He became a clerk of the royal household in Paris, and about 1346 was made counselor of the court of requests ("maître des requêtes"); from 1346–50 he was also in the service of Duke Jean of Normandy (heir to the throne), with whom he took part in the siege of Aiguillon (1346); when Duke Jean became king in 1350, he sent Vitry to Avignon on a mission to Pope Clement VI, who on Jan. 3, 1351, appointed him bishop of Meaux. Vitry was known as a poet and a composer, but his enduring fame rests on his *Ars nova,* a treatise expounding a new theory of mensural notation, particularly important for its development of the principle of binary rhythm; it also gives the most complete account of the various uses to which colored notes were put. Of the 4 treatises attributed to Vitry in Coussemaker's *Scriptores,* III, only the last 10 of the 24 chapters of *Ars nova* (also publ., with corrections, in *Musica disciplina,* 1956) are now considered authentic. Most of Vitry's works are lost; the extant pieces were publ. by L. Schrade in vol. I of his *Polyphonic Music of the 14th Century* (Monaco, 1956). Separate pieces were brought out in Denkmäler der Tonkunst in Österreich, 76 (40).

Vittoria, Tommaso Luigi da. See **Victoria, Tomás Luis de.**

Vivaldi, Antonio, greatly renowned Italian composer; b. Venice, March 4, 1678; d. Vienna (buried, July 28), 1741. He was the son of **Giovanni Battista Vivaldi,** a violinist at San Marco in Venice, and he studied violin with him; also took theory lessons with Giovanni Legrenzi. He entered the priesthood, taking the tonsure in 1693, and Holy Orders 10 years later. Because of his red hair he was called "il prete rosso" ("the red priest"). In 1703 he became a violin teacher at the Ospedale della Pietà in Venice; in 1718–20 he was music director at the court of Prince Philip, landgrave of Hesse Darmstadt at Mantua; in 1725 he traveled to Amsterdam, where he arranged for publication of several of his works; among them was a collection of 12 violin concertos under the title *La cetra* (1727), which he dedicated to Emperor Charles VI, who then invited him to come to his court in Vienna. Vivaldi accepted the offer, and remained in Vienna to the end of his life, except for visits to Prague and Dresden. Vivaldi devoted the early years of his career as a composer mainly to operatic productions, which were successfully staged in Florence, Milan, Rome, Verona, and other Italian cities, as well as in Vienna; however, his greatness lies mainly in his superb instrumental works, particularly concerti grossi and solo concertos. Despite the difference in treatment and function between his operas and instrumental music, Vivaldi often used material from his operas in his concertos, and vice versa; thus, some of his operatic arias are constructed in the form of a Baroque air in a suite, while the slow movements of instrumental works often find their analogous structures in the operatic "laments." The importance of Vivaldi was enhanced in music history through Bach's use of Vivaldi's concertos as models for his own keyboard concertos; however, of the 16 "Concertos after Vivaldi" for clavier publ. in the *Bach Gesellschaft* edition, only 6 are transcriptions of Vivaldi. Until about the middle of the 20th century Vivaldi was regarded by most music historians as merely an estimable composer who dwelt in the shadow of Bach; not even the basic biographical data (exact date of birth, place and date of death) were established with accuracy until the middle of the 20th century. But comparisons with Bach are misguided. Vivaldi's music possesses neither the surpassing genius nor the conceptual grandeur of Bach's works; his contrapuntal skill was minimal compared to Bach's epic achievements in fugal writing. Furthermore, the uniformity of Vivaldi's structures and the extraordinary repetitiousness of thematic statements in his instrumental works tend to blur the individuality of each particular piece; it has been said that Vivaldi did not write 400 concertos known under his name, but only one concerto which he copied 399 times. Proper taxonomy of Vivaldi's works is further complicated by the profuse crosspollination of his operatic and instrumental fragments and even of complete sections of various compositions, as well as the abundance of arrangements of pieces by other composers. Under such circumstances, duplication of individual items becomes a rule rather than an exception. Vivaldi's catalogue of works must therefore be subject to periodic verifications and rectifications; 770 works can be assumed to exist, among them 46 operas, of which 21 are extant (Vivaldi himself listed in 1739 the number of his operas as 94, but he included numerous separate arias and instrumental intermezzi); 344 solo concertos; 81 concertos for 2 or more solo instruments; 61 sinfonias; 23 chamber concertos; 93 sonatas and trios; 3 oratorios; 8 serenades; 38 secular solo cantatas; 12 motets; 37 liturgical works; many of these exist in several versions.

WORKS: 21 extant operas: *Ottone in villa* (Vicenza, 1713); *Orlando finto pazzo* (Venice, 1714); *L'incoronazione di Dario* (Venice, 1716); *Arsilda regina di Ponto* (Venice, 1716); *Armida al campo D'Egitto* (Venice, 1718); *Il teuzzone* (Mantua, 1719); *Tito Manlio* (Mantua, 1719); *La verità in cimento* (Venice, 1720); *Ercole sul Termodonte* (Rome, 1723); *Giustino* (Rome, 1724); *Dorilla in Tempo* (Venice, 1726); *Farnace* (Venice, 1727); *Orlando furioso* (Venice, 1727); *L'Atenaide* (Florence, 1729); *La fida ninfa* (Verona, 1732); *L'Olimpiade* (Venice, 1734); *Griselda* (Venice, 1735); *Catone in Utica* (Verona, 1737). The following are probably by Vivaldi, but only the librettos are extant: *Scanderbeg* (Florence, 1711); *Ipermestra* (Florence, 1727); *Semiramide* (Mantua, 1732); *Montezuma* (Venice, 1733); *Feraspe* (1739); 2 oratorios: *Moyses Deus Pharaonis* (Venice, 1714) and *Juditha triumphans devicta Holofernis barbarie* (Venice, 1716); 38 solo secular cantatas; 12 motets; 37 liturgical works. Instrumental works: *12 sonate da camera* for 2 Violins and Continuo, op. 1; 18 violin sonatas, with Continuo, opp. 2 and 5; *L'estro armonico,* 12 concertos for One, 2, or 4 Solo Violins, Solo Cello, Strings, and Continuo, op. 3; *La stravaganza,* 12 concertos for Solo Violin, Strings, and Continuo, op. 4; 18 concertos for 3 Violins, Viola, and Continuo, opp. 6 and 7; *Il cimento dell'Armonia e dell'Invenzione,* including *Le quattro stagione (The 4 Seasons),* 12 concertos for Solo Violin, Strings, and Continuo, op. 8; *La cetra,* 12 concertos for Solo Violin, Strings, and Continuo, op. 9; 6 concertos for Flute, Strings, and Organ, op. 10; 12 concertos for Solo Violin, Strings, and Organ, opp. 11 and 12. A complete ed. of Vivaldi's instrumental works, under the general editorship of Gian Francesco Malipiero, was brought out in 1947–72, in 16 series comprising 530 compositions; numerous individual works were publ. separately. An all-encompassing catalogue is by Peter Ryom, *Les Manuscrits de Vivaldi* (Paris, 1977); other catalogues are: M. Rinaldi, *Catalogo numerico tematico delle composizioni di Antonio Vivaldi* (Rome, 1945); A. Fanna, *Antonio Vivaldi, Catalogo numerico-tematico delle opere strumentali* (Milan, 1968); L. Coral, *A Concordance of the Thematic Indexes to the Instrumental Works of Antonio Vivaldi* (2nd ed., Ann Arbor, Mich., 1972); Peter Ryom, *Antonio Vivaldi, Table de concordances des œuvres* (Copenhagen, 1973); P. Damilano, *Inventario delle composizioni musicali manuscripti di Antonio Vivaldi* (Turin, 1968).

Vives, Amadeo, Spanish composer; b. Collbató, near Barcelona, Nov. 18, 1871; d. Madrid, Dec. 1, 1932. He was a pupil of Felipe Pedrell in Barcelona; with L. Millet, founded the famous choral society Orfeó Català (1891). In his first opera, *Artus* (Barcelona, 1895), he made use of Catalonian folk songs. Subsequently he moved to Madrid, where he produced his comic opera *Don Lucas del Cigarral* (Feb. 18, 1899); his opera *Euda d'Uriach,* originally to a Catalan libretto, was brought out in Italian at Barcelona (Oct. 24, 1900). Then followed his most popular opera, *Maruxa* (Madrid, May 28, 1914); other operas are *Balada de Carnaval* (Madrid, July 5, 1919) and *Doña Francisquita* (Madrid, Oct. 17, 1923). The style of his stage productions shared qualities of the French light opera and the Spanish zarzuela; he wrote nearly 100 of these; also composed songs and piano pieces; publ. a book of essays, *Sofia* (Madrid, 1923).

Vivier, Claude, Canadian composer; b. Montreal, April 14, 1948; d. Paris (found strangled to death, by parties unknown, in his apartment, March 7, 1983). He studied music with Tremblay at the Montreal Cons. (1967–70); then went to the Netherlands and took courses in electronic music with Koening at the Inst. of Sonology in Utrecht; also attended classes in electronic composition given by Stockhausen in Cologne. In 1976 he traveled in the Orient to study non-European musical cultures. He was in Paris on a Canada Council Grant to compose an opera on the death of Tchaikovsky, to be titled *Crois-tu en l'immortalité de l'âme?,* at the time of his murder.

Vivier, Eugène-Léon, French-horn virtuoso; b. Brioude, Haute-Loire, Dec. 4, 1817; d. Nice, Feb. 24, 1900. He learned to play violin, then took up the French horn. He moved to Paris, where he became successful through his connections at the French court. An eccentric, he prided himself on his ability to play 2 notes simultaneously on his instrument, through clever overblowing. He publ. a number of pamphlets on music and the theater, and also an autobiography (largely fictitious), *La Vie et les aventures d'un corniste* (Paris, 1900).

Vix, Geneviève, French soprano; b. Nantes, Dec. 31, 1879; d. Paris, Aug. 25, 1939. She studied at the Paris Cons.; won first prize for opera (1908); sang at the Paris Opéra, in Madrid, and in Buenos Aires; made her American debut with the Chicago Opera Co. as Manon in Massenet's opera (Dec. 1, 1917); married Prince Cyril Naryshkin in N.Y. (Feb. 9, 1918). She possessed a fine lyric voice and was also adept as an actress.

Vlad, Roman, Italian composer and writer on music; b. Cernauti, Rumania, Dec. 29, 1919. He was a pupil at the Cernauti Cons.; in 1938 went to Rome, where he studied piano and composition with Casella; in 1943 he adopted the 12-tone method of composition.
WORKS: *La strada sul caffé,* ballet (Rome, June 9,

1945); *La Dama delle camelie,* ballet in the form of 5 waltzes (Rome, Nov. 20, 1945); *Sinfonia* (Venice Festival, Sept. 8, 1948); *Divertimento* for 11 Instruments (Capri, Sept. 15, 1948); *De profundis* for Soprano, Mixed Chorus, and Orch. (Paris, June 2, 1949); *Storia d'una mamma,* musical fable (Venice Festival, Oct. 5, 1951); 5 elegies for Voice and String Orch. (1952); *Le Ciel est vide* for Chorus and Orch. (Turin, Oct. 29, 1954); *Variazioni concertanti* for Piano and Orch., based on a series of 12 notes in Mozart's *Don Giovanni* (Venice Festival, Sept. 18, 1955); *Studi dodecafonici* for Piano (1943–57); *Colinde transilvane* for Chorus (1957); *Musica concertata* for Harp and Orch. (Turin, April 24, 1958); *3 invocazioni* for Voice and Orch. (Rome, June 6, 1958); *Masques ostendais,* ballet (Spoleto Festival, June 12, 1959); *Il Dottore di vetro,* radiophonic opera (Turin, Feb. 23, 1959); *Il ritorno,* ballet (Cologne, 1962); *Ode super "Chrysea Phorminx"* for Guitar and Orch. (1964); *La fontana,* television opera (1967); *Divertimento sinfonico* for Orch. (1968); *Il magico flauto di Severino* for Flute and Piano (1971). He publ. the books *Modernità e tradizione nella musica contemporanea* (Turin, 1955) and *Storia della dodecafonia* (Milan, 1958), and a monograph on Stravinsky (Turin, 1958; in Eng., London, 1960; 3rd ed., revised, 1979).

Vladigerov, Pantcho, prominent Bulgarian composer; b. Zürich, March 13, 1899, in a geminal parturition; d. Sofia, Sept. 8, 1978. Distrustful of Bulgarian puerperal skill, his mother sped from Shumen to Zürich as soon as she learned that she was going to have a plural birth. Pantcho's non-identical twin brother, **Luben,** a violinist, was born 16 hours earlier than Pantcho, on the previous day, March 12, 1899. Vladigerov studied piano and theory with local teachers in Sofia; then went to Berlin, where he took lessons in composition with Paul Juon and Georg Schumann, and piano with Leonid Kreutzer at the Akademie der Künste in Berlin. He remained in Berlin, where he served as conductor and composer of the Max Reinhardt Theater. In 1932 he returned to Bulgaria, and was appointed a prof. at the Music Academy in Sofia; he retired from there in 1972. His music is rooted in Bulgarian folk songs, artfully combining the peculiar melodic and rhythmic patterns of native material with stark modern harmonies; the method is similar to that of Béla Bartók.
WORKS: Opera, *Tsar Kaloyan* (1935–36; Sofia, April 20, 1936); ballet, *Legenda za ezeroto* (*Legend of the Lake;* 1946; Sofia, Nov. 11, 1962; 2 orch. suites were drawn from it, in 1947 and 1953); 5 piano concertos (1918, 1930, 1937, 1953, 1963); *Legend* for Orch. (1919); *3 Impressions* for Orch. (1920; orchestration of 3 of his *10 Impressions* for Piano); 2 violin concertos (1921, 1968); *Burlesk Suite* for Violin and Orch. (1922); *Scandinavian Suite* for Orch. (1924); *Bulgarian Suite* for Orch. (1927); *Vardar,* Bulgarian rhapsody for Orch. (1927; orchestration of his earlier violin and piano piece); 7 *Bulgarian Symphonic Dances* (1931); 2 overtures: *Zemja* (1933) and *The 9th of September* (1949); 2 symphs.: No. 1 (1939) and No. 2, *Majska (May),* for String Orch. (1949); *Concert*

Fantasy for Cello and Orch. (1941); *4 Rumanian Symphonic Dances* (1942); *Improvisation and Toccata* for Orch. (1942; orchestration of the final 2 pieces of his piano cycle *Episodes*); *2 Rumanian Symphonic Sketches* (1943); *Prelude and Balkan Dance* for Orch. (1950); *Evreyska poema (Jewish Poem)* for Orch. (1951); *Song of Peace,* dramatic poem for Orch. (1956); *7 Pieces* for String Orch. (1969–70; orchestration of pieces taken from 3 different piano cycles); Violin Sonata (1914); Piano Trio (1916); works for Violin and Piano: *2 Improvisations* (1919); *4 Pieces* (1920); *Vardar* (1922); *2 Bulgarian Paraphrases* (1925); *2 Pieces* (1926); String Quartet (1940); several piano cycles, many of which are also scored for chamber orch.: *4 Pieces* (1915); *11 Variations* (1916); *10 Impressions* (1920); *4 Pieces* (1920); *3 Pieces* (1922); *6 Exotic Preludes* (1924); *Classical and Romantic,* 7 pieces (1931); *Bulgarian Songs and Dances* (1932); *Sonatina concertante* (1934); *Shumen,* 6 miniatures (1934); *5 Episodes* (1941); *Aquarelles* (1942); *3 Pictures* (1950); *Suite,* 5 pieces (1954); *3 Pieces* (1957); *3 Concert Pieces* (1959); *5 Novelettes* (1965); *5 Pieces* (1965); orchestration of Dinicu's *Hora staccato.*

Vlijmen, Jan van, Dutch composer; b. Rotterdam, Oct. 11, 1935. He studied composition with Kees van Baaren. Upon completion of his musical education at the Utrecht Cons., he was director of the Amersfoort Music School (1961–65); taught theoretical subjects at the Utrecht Cons. (1965–68); became deputy director of The Hague Cons. in 1967, and, upon Baaren's death, became its director in 1971. WORKS: 2 operas, in collaboration with fellow Dutch composers: *Reconstructie,* an anti-U.S. opera, composed with Louis Andriessen, Misha Mengelberg, Reinbert de Leeuw, and Peter Schat (1968–69; Holland Festival, June 29, 1969), and *Axel,* with Reinbert de Leeuw (1975–77; Holland Festival, Scheveningen, June 10, 1977); String Quartet (1955); *Morgensternlieder* for Mezzo-soprano and Piano (1958); 2 wind quintets (1958, 1972); *Construzione* for 2 Pianos (1959); *Serie* for 6 Instruments (1960); *Gruppi* for 20 Instruments in 4 groups, and Percussion (1961–62); *Mythos* for Mezzo-soprano and 9 Instruments (1962); *Spostamenti* for Orch. (1963); *Serenata I* for 12 Instruments and Percussion (1963–64; revised 1967); *Serenata II* for Flute and 4 Instrumental Groups (Amsterdam, Sept. 10, 1965); *Sonata* for Piano and 3 Instrumental Groups (1966); *Dialogue* for Clarinet and Piano (1966); *Per diciasette* for 17 Winds (1967); *Interpolations* for Orch. and Electronic Sound (Rotterdam, Nov. 24, 1968); *Ommagio a Gesualdo* for Violin and 6 Instrumental Groups (Amsterdam, April 9, 1971); *4 Songs* for Mezzo-soprano and Orch. (1975).

Vockerodt, Gottfried, German writer; b. Mühlhausen, Thuringia, Sept. 24, 1665; d. Gotha, Oct. 10, 1727. It was his opinion that excessive enjoyment of music injures the intellect, and that Nero and Caligula became totally depraved through their passion for music. He advocated these ideas in *Consultatio de cavenda falsa mentium intemperatarum*

medicina (1696); *Missbrauch der freien Künste, insonderheit der Musik* (1697); and *Wiederholtes Zeugnis der Wahrheit gegen die verderbte Musik und Schauspiele, Opern, etc.* (1698).

Vogel, Charles Louis Adolphe, French violinist and composer; b. Lille, May 17, 1808; d. Paris, Sept. 11, 1892. He was a grandson of **Johann Christoph Vogel;** studied at the Paris Cons. with A. Kreutzer (violin) and Reicha (theory). After winning popularity with his song *Les Trois Couleurs* during the July Revolution (1830), he brought out a series of successful operas: *Le Podestat* (Paris, Dec. 16, 1831); *Le Siège de Leyde* (The Hague, March 14, 1847); *La Moissonneuse* (Paris, Sept. 3, 1853); *Rompons* (Paris, Sept. 21, 1857); *Le Nid de Cigognes* (Baden-Baden, Sept. 1858); *Gredin de Pigoche* (Paris, Oct. 19, 1866); *La Filleule du roi* (Brussels, April 1875). He also wrote symphs., chamber music, sacred works, songs, and piano pieces.

Vogel, Emil, German musicologist; b. Wriezen-on-Oder, Jan. 21, 1859; d. Nikolassee, near Berlin, June 18, 1908. He studied at Greifswald and Berlin; in 1893 he organized the Peters Music Library in Leipzig and was its librarian till 1901; at the same time he edited the *Peters Jahrbuch.* He publ. the catalogue *Die Handschriften nebst den älteren Druckwerken der Musikabteilung der herzoglichen Bibliothek zu Wolfenbüttel* (1890) and *Bibliothek der gedruckten weltlichen Vokalmusik Italiens aus den Jahren 1500–1700* (1892; new ed., completely revised by Alfred Einstein, publ. in *Notes,* June 1945–Sept. 1948; another ed. by F. Lesure and C. Sartoi, eds., *Il nuovo Vogel: Bibliografia della musica italiana vocale profana pubblicata dal 1500–1700,* Geneva, 1977).

Vogel, Johann Christoph, German composer; b. Nuremberg (baptized, March 18), 1758; d. Paris, June 27, 1788. He was a pupil of Riepel at Regensburg; went to Paris in 1776, and wrote 2 operas in Gluck's style: *La Toison d'or* (Paris, Sept. 5, 1786) and *Démophon,* which he completed shortly before his untimely death at the age of 32, and which was produced posthumously (Paris, Sept. 22, 1789). He also composed a great deal of instrumental music: 3 symphs.; a Bassoon Concerto; 3 clarinet concertos; 6 string quartets; 6 quartets for horn and strings; 3 quartets for bassoon and strings; 6 trios for 2 violins and bass; 6 duos for 2 clarinets; 6 duos for 2 bassoons; etc.

Vogel, Wladimir, significant Russian-German composer; b. Moscow, Feb. 29, 1896; d. Zürich, June 19, 1984. His father was German, his mother Russian. At the outbreak of World War I he was interned in Russia as an enemy alien; after the Armistice in 1918 he went to Berlin, where he studied with Heinz Tiessen and later (1920–24) with Busoni, who exercised a profound influence on him. From 1929 to 1933 Vogel taught at the Klindworth-Scharwenka Cons. in Berlin; with the advent to power of the Nazi government, Vogel, although not a Jew, chose to leave Germany. He worked in Strasbourg and Brussels with Hermann Scherchen on various problems of musical techniques; then went to Switzerland, and in 1954 became a Swiss citizen. Vogel's idiom of composition underwent several changes throughout the years. A convinced believer in the mystical power of music, he felt great affinity with Scriabin's mystical ideas and techniques; he built his melodies along the upper overtones of the harmonic series, and his harmonies on a massive superimposition of perfect fourths and tritones. Gradually he approached the method of composition in 12 tones as promulgated by Schoenberg, while Busoni's precepts of neo-Classical structures governed Vogel's own works as far as formal design was concerned; many of his polyphonic compositions adhered to the Classical harmonic structures in 4 parts, which he maintained even in choral pieces using the *Sprechstimme.* Serialist procedures are adumbrated in Vogel's music through the astute organization of melodic and rhythmic elements.

Vogelweide, Walther von der, famous German minnesinger and lyric poet; b. probably in Tyrol, c.1170; d. Würzburg, c.1230. In Wagner's *Tannhäuser* he appears as one of the rival singers at the Wartburg. He led a wandering life; was in Worms in 1198, in Frankfurt in 1212, then in Würzburg. Very few of his melodies are extant; 3 of these were found in the Münster "Bruchstücke" (MS collection of musical fragments from the Middle Ages), including the so-called "Palestine Song" (1228); 5 others are contained in the Colmar Codex and in the "Singebuch" of Adam Puschmann.

Vogl, Heinrich, famous German tenor; b. Au, near Munich, Jan. 15, 1845; d. Munich, April 21, 1900. He studied music with Franz Lachner; made a successful debut as Max in *Der Freischütz* at the Munich Court Opera (Nov. 5, 1865) and remained on its roster until his death. He succeeded Schnorr von Carolsfeld as the model Tristan in Wagner's opera, and was for years considered the greatest interpreter of that role. He frequently sang at Bayreuth; created the role of Loge in *Das Rheingold* (1869) and of Siegmund in *Die Walküre* (1870). He made his debut at the Metropolitan Opera in N.Y. on Jan. 1, 1890, as Lohengrin; sang Wagner during the rest of that season. He was also a composer; wrote an opera, *Der Fremdling,* in which he sang the leading role (Munich, May 7, 1899). In 1868 he married the German soprano **Therese Thoma** (b. Tutzing, Nov. 12, 1845; d. Munich, Sept. 29, 1921), who sang the part of Isolde with him; she also created the role of Sieglinde.

Vogl, Johann Michael, Austrian baritone; b. Ennsdorf, near Steyr, Aug. 10, 1768; d. Vienna, Nov. 19, 1840. He studied law in Vienna; Süssmayr, then conductor of the Vienna Court Theater, discovered his voice, and persuaded him to join his opera company; Vogl remained on its roster from 1794 until 1822 (his debut there was on May 1, 1795). He was the first professional singer to perform Schubert's songs at concerts.

Vogler, Georg Joseph, Abbé or **Abt,** noted German composer and theorist; b. Pleichach, near Würzburg, June 15, 1749; d. Darmstadt, May 6, 1814. The son of a violin maker, he mastered the organ at an early age; studied theology and law at Würzburg and Bamberg. In 1771 he went to Mannheim; there he wrote music for a ballet and gained the favor of the Elector, who provided him with funds for study in Italy. After a brief course in Bologna with Padre Martini, he proceeded to Padua, where he studied composition with Vallotti; but he soon left for Rome, and took Holy Orders in 1773; was made Apostolic Protonotary, Chamberlain to the Pope, and Knight of the Golden Spur; also joined the Academy of the Arcadians. In 1775 he returned to Mannheim as court chaplain and 2nd Kapellmeister; founded there the Mannheimer Tonschule for teaching his own method of composition. In 1780 he was in Paris, where he submitted a paper to the Académie Royale des Sciences, *Essai de diriger le goût des amateurs de musique,* an explanation of his system of teaching (publ. in Paris, 1782); in Paris he also produced his opera *La Kermesse* (1783), which was a fiasco. From France he traveled to Spain, Portugal, England, and Denmark. In 1784 he was called to the Electoral Court in Munich (it had moved from Mannheim in 1778), and became first Kapellmeister. In 1786 he was engaged as court conductor in Stockholm, where he founded a music school; in 1788 he spent some time in St. Petersburg; in 1790 he was in London as an organist; after traveling in Poland and Germany, he again was Kapellmeister in Stockholm (1793–94). In 1794 he went to Paris, and subsequently traveled to Greece and the Near East. From 1796 to 1799 he was again in Sweden, and afterward visited Copenhagen. In 1800 he went to Berlin; was then in Vienna and Prague. Wherever he went, he solicited interest for his system of organ construction, and exhibited a portable organ called the "orchestrion," but was unsuccessful. After spending 2 years in Vienna, where he produced his opera *Samori* (1804), and brief sojourns in various German towns, he finally settled in Darmstadt; from 1807 until his death was Hofkapellmeister to the Grand Duke of Hessen-Darmstadt; established a Tonschule; Carl Maria von Weber and Meyerbeer became his pupils there. Vogler found his most congenial work in teaching; his pedagogical and acoustic writings were also of importance.

Voigt, Henriette (née **Kunze**), German pianist; b. Leipzig, Nov. 24, 1808; d. there, Oct. 15, 1839. She studied with Ludwig Berger; married the merchant Karl Voigt, whose house was the rendezvous of the most eminent musicians of the time. Schumann dedicated to her the Piano Sonata in G minor (op. 22).

Volbach, Fritz, German choral conductor and composer; b. Wipperfürth, near Cologne, Dec. 17, 1861; d. Wiesbaden, Nov. 30, 1940. He studied at the Cologne Cons. with Hiller, Jensen, and Seiss, and in Berlin with Taubert and Löschhorn. In 1891 he was appointed conductor of the Liedertafel and the Damengesangverein in Mainz; brought out many choral works by modern German composers; received a Dr.Phil. from the Univ. of Bonn with the dissertation *Die Praxis der Händel-Aufführung* (publ. in 1900). A versatile musician, he had command of almost every orch. instrument.

Völker, Franz, gifted German tenor; b. Neu-Isenburg, March 31, 1899; d. Darmstadt, Dec. 5, 1965. He made his debut at the Frankfurt Opera as Florestan in 1926 without the benefit of formal vocal studies; continued on its roster until 1935; also sang at the Vienna State Opera (1931–36, 1939–40, 1949–50), the Berlin State Opera (1933–43), and the Bavarian State Opera in Munich (1936–37, 1945–52); he subsequently made guest appearances at Covent Garden, and in Salzburg and Bayreuth; after his retirement in 1952, he taught voice in Neu-Isenburg; was a prof. at the Stuttgart Hochschule für Musik from 1958. Among his finest roles were Parsifal, Lohengrin, and Siegmund in Wagner's operas.

Volkmann, Hans, German musicologist, grandnephew of **Robert Volkmann;** b. Bischofswerda, April 29, 1875; d. Dresden, Dec. 26, 1946. He studied German philology and music in Munich and Berlin; undertook research in Italy and France; in 1921 settled in Dresden, where he taught music history; in 1946 became a prof. at the Dresden Cons.
    WRITINGS: *Neues über Beethoven* (1904); *Emanuel d'Astorga* (2 vols., 1911, 1919; fundamental and important biography; establishes the verifiable facts of d'Astorga's life); *Beethoven in seinen Beziehungen zu Dresden* (Dresden, 1942). He publ. the standard biography of Robert Volkmann (Leipzig, 1903; abridged ed., 1915); ed. *Briefe von Robert Volkmann* (1917); compiled a *Thematisches Verzeichnis der Werke von Robert Volkmann* (Dresden, 1937).

Volkmann, Robert (complete name, **Friedrich Robert Volkmann**), significant German composer; b. Lommatzsch, April 6, 1815; d. Budapest, Oct. 29, 1883. He studied with his father, a cantor (organ and piano); with Friebel (violin and cello) and Anacker (composition); then in Leipzig with K.F. Becker; was greatly encouraged by Schumann. After teaching music in Prague (1839–41), he settled in Budapest, where he spent the rest of his life, except for 4 years (1854–58) in Vienna. In 1875 he was appointed a prof. at the National Academy of Music in Budapest. His music was regarded very highly in his lifetime, but after his death it faded into oblivion; however, several publications dealing with his works, including a thematic index, were brought out by his grandnephew, **Hans Volkmann.**

Volkonsky, Andrei, Russian composer; b. Geneva, of Russian parents of princely nobility, Feb. 14, 1933. He studied piano with Dinu Lipatti in Geneva and composition with Nadia Boulanger in Paris. In 1947 he went to Russia, where he studied music the-

ory with Shaporin at the Moscow Cons. (1950–54). In 1955 he was a co-founder, with Barshai, of the Moscow Chamber Orch.; then devoted himself to harpsichord playing; in 1964 he organized in Moscow the concert group Madrigal, with which he gave annual series of highly successful concerts in the Soviet Union, East Germany, and Czechoslovakia. His early works were set in evocative impressionistic colors, in the manner of the French modern school, but soon he deployed a serial technique of composition analogous to Schoenberg's method of composition with 12 tones outside traditional tonality. He was outspoken in his criticism of the direction that Soviet music was taking, and he entirely rejected the official tenets of socialist realism. This attitude, and the nature of his own music, resulted in the cancellation of performances of his works; he was expelled from the Union of Soviet Composers, and could no longer give concerts. In 1973 he left Russia, and returned to Switzerland.

Vollerthun, Georg, German composer and conductor; b. Fürstenau, Sept. 29, 1876; d. Strausberg (near Berlin), Sept. 15, 1945. He studied with Tappert, Radecke, and Gernsheim; was a theater conductor in Prague, Berlin, Barmen, and Mainz (1899–1905); spent 3 years in Paris (1908–10); then settled in Berlin as a music critic and teacher; from 1922 lived mostly in Strausberg.
    WORKS: Operas: *Veeda* (Kassel, 1916); *Island-Saga* (Munich, Jan. 17, 1925); *Der Freikorporal* (Hannover, Nov. 10, 1931; his most successful opera; also given in Berlin, June 10, 1933); *Das königliche Opfer* (Hannover, 1942); *Alt-Danzig Suite* for Orch. (1938); cantatas and other vocal works; many German songs.

Volpe, Arnold, Russian-American conductor; b. Kovno, Lithuania, July 9, 1869; d. Miami, Fla., Feb. 2, 1940. He studied with Leopold Auer at the St. Petersburg Cons. (1887–91), and composition there with Soloviev (1893–97). In 1898 he emigrated to America, settling in N.Y.; in 1902 founded the Young Men's Symph. Orch. of N.Y., which he conducted until 1919; also conducted a group called the Volpe Symph. Orch. (1904–14). In 1918 he organized the summer concerts at the Lewisohn Stadium in N.Y., and conducted for a few seasons there; then moved to Washington, D.C., where he was music director of the Washington, D.C., Opera Co. (1919–22); subsequently was director of the Kansas City Cons. (1922–25); in 1926 he went to Florida, where he organized the Univ. of Miami Symph. Orch. He composed some chamber music and many songs to Eng. words.

Vomáčka, Boleslav, Czech composer; b. Mladá Boleslav, June 28, 1887; d. Prague, March 1, 1965. He studied law at the Charles Univ. in Prague (LL.D., 1913); took music courses with Vítězslav Novák (1909–10); was in the service of the Labor Ministry in Prague (1919–50); wrote music criticism in several newspapers there; was editor of *Listy Hudební Matice* (1922–35). He began to compose early in life;

developed a strong national style of composition.

Von Stade, Frederica, remarkable American mezzo-soprano; b. Somerville, N.J., June 1, 1945. She was a scion of a German-American colonial family. The nobiliary particle of her name derives from the German locative indicating the connection with the town of Stade, near Hamburg, in which one of her paternal ancestors served as burgomaster. Her father, Charles von Stade, a lieutenant in the U.S. Army, was killed during the final weeks of World War II, shortly before she was born. She went to Paris and studied piano at the Ecole Mozart. Returning to the U.S., she earned a living as a saleswoman at Tiffany's jewelry store in N.Y.; then enrolled at the Mannes College of Music in N.Y., where she studied voice with Sebastian Engleberg. She auditioned successfully for the Metropolitan Opera and, on Jan. 11, 1970, made her debut there in the inconspicuous part of one of the 3 spirits in *Die Zauberflöte.* She progressed gradually toward greater but still minor roles at the Metropolitan, such as Siebel in Gounod's *Faust.* She also sang with the San Francisco Opera. In 1972 she went to Europe, where she advanced rapidly, gathering encomiums for her performances at the Glyndebourne and Salzburg festivals. Her career now in full swing, she enlarged her repertoire, singing Octavian in *Der Rosenkavalier* in 1975 in Houston and Rosina in *The Barber of Seville* at Covent Garden in London. During the 1976–77 season she sang Mélisande in Paris and Geneva. She subsequently was a guest artist at La Scala in Milan. In 1973 she married the photographer Peter Elkus.

Voormolen, Alexander Nicolas, Netherlandish composer; b. Rotterdam, March 3, 1895; d. The Hague, Nov. 12, 1980. He was a scion of a family of municipal functionaries in the Netherlands, and on his mother's side was a descendant of Claude Rameau, a brother of Jean-Philippe Rameau. He entered the Utrecht School of Music, where he studied with Johan Wagenaar; he began to compose as a very young man; from his earliest steps he experienced a strong influence of French Impressionism; he went to Paris, where he was befriended by Ravel, whose influence became decisive in Voormolen's own compositions. In his idiom Voormolen affected richly extended harmonies, and followed Ravel's example in writing works in neo-Baroque forms, marked by gentle symmetric melodies. His music was played frequently in the Netherlands, but as the general trend in modern music moved away from impressionistic mannerisms, it fell into desuetude. His last years of life were unhappy.

Vopelius, Gottfried, German composer; b. Herwigsdorf, near Zittau, Jan. 28, 1635; d. Leipzig, Feb. 3, 1715. He studied at the Univ. of Leipzig; was cantor of St. Nicholas at Leipzig from Dec. 12, 1676; harmonized old German hymns and publ. *Neu Leipziger Gesangbuch* (1682), containing 100 hymns originally brought out in Schein's *Cantional oder Gesangbuch* (1627).

Voříšek, Jan Hugo. See **Worzischek, Johann Hugo.**

Vostřák, Zbynek, Czech composer and conductor; b. Prague, June 10, 1920. He studied composition privately with Rudolf Karel (1938–43); attended the conducting classes of Pavel Dědeček at the Prague Cons. In 1963 he became conductor of the Prague chamber ensemble Musica Viva Pragensis; worked in an electronic music studio in Prague. His music evolved from the Central European type of modernism; later he annexed serial techniques, electronic sound, and aleatory practices.

Votapek, Ralph, American pianist; b. Milwaukee, March 20, 1939. He studied at the Wisconsin Cons. in his hometown; then took piano lessons at the Manhattan School of Music and the Juilliard School of Music in N.Y., where his principal teachers were Rosina Lhévinne and Robert Goldsand. He won the Van Cliburn International Competition for pianists in 1962, and then embarked on a successful career as a soloist, in recital, and with orchs.; played in major cities of the U.S.; made 7 tours of South America; in 1975 played engagements in Russia. He settled in East Lansing, Mich., as artist-in-residence at Michigan State Univ., and continued his concert career.

Vreuls, Victor, Belgian composer; b. Verviers, Feb. 4, 1876; d. Brussels, July 27, 1944. He studied at the Cons. in Verviers; later took harmony lessons with Sylvain Dupuis and counterpoint with J.T. Radoux at the Cons. in Liège. He then went to Paris, where he took a course with d'Indy at the Schola Cantorum; from 1906 to 1926 was director of the Luxembourg Cons.

Vronsky, Vitya (real name, **Victoria Vronsky**), pianist; b. Evpatoria, Crimea, Aug. 22, 1909. She studied at the Kiev Cons.; then with Petri and Schnabel in Berlin, and with Cortot in Paris. She married the pianist **Victor Babin** on Aug. 31, 1933; came to America in 1937; toured widely with Babin in duo-piano recitals.

Vuataz, Roger, Swiss composer and organist; b. Geneva, Jan. 4, 1898. He studied with Otto Barblan and Jaques-Dalcroze at the Geneva Cons.; was a church organist for over 50 years in Geneva (1917–73) and a music critic there (1940–60); was director of music programming at Radio Geneva (1961–71); taught at the Geneva Cons. (1962–69); conducted choruses.

Vučković, Vojislav, Serbian composer; b. Pirot, Oct. 18, 1910; d. Belgrade (killed by German police), Dec. 25, 1942. He studied in Prague with J. Suk and Zdeněk Nejedlý. Returning to Belgrade in 1934, he displayed energetic activity as a composer, conductor, publicist, and writer on economic subjects; publ. pamphlets on the materialistic interpretation of music in the light of Marxist dialectics. He was in the resistance movement during the German occupation, and was killed on the street by Nazis.

WORKS: 2 symphs.; symph. poem, *Burevesnik* (*Stormy Petrel;* 1942; Belgrade, Dec. 25, 1944); *Heroic Oratorio* (1942; Cetinje, Sept. 5, 1951); chamber music; choruses. After a period of composition in the expressionistic manner (including the application of quarter-tones), out of ideological considerations he abruptly changed his style to programmatic realism.

Vuillaume, Jean-Baptiste, celebrated French violin maker; b. Mirecourt, Oct. 7, 1798; d. Paris, March 19, 1875. He came from a family of violin makers, and learned the trade from his father, **Claude Vuillaume** (1772–1834). At 19 he went to Paris and worked with Chanot till 1821, and in 1821–25 for Lété, with whom he then entered into partnership. After Lété's retirement in 1828, Vuillaume worked alone, and put his own name on several instruments which he had constructed with the greatest care and fine craftsmanship; but he was unable to overcome the general distrust of the native product, and began manufacturing imitations of Italian instruments. After long and patient labor he placed a "Stradivarius" violin on the market for 300 francs; it bore the master's label and possessed a full, sonorous tone; he also built a cello priced at 500 francs. The sight of a Duiffoprugcar viola da gamba inspired him with the idea of further imitations, hence the hundreds of "Duiffoprugcar" violins and cellos with their quaint shape, carved scrolls, inlays, and the motto "viva fui in sylvis, etc." By dint of indefatigable research and experiments, Vuillaume carried the construction of these various instruments to the highest perfection. His own inventions were numerous: in 1849 the huge "Octobasse," a double bass 4 meters in length, 3-stringed (CC–GG–C), with a special lever-mechanism to aid the left hand (an "octobasse" is in the Museum of the Paris Cons.); in 1855 a viola, which he called the "contre-alto," with greater strength of tone, but clumsy to play; in 1867 a kind of mute, the "pédale sourdine"; also a machine for manufacturing gut strings of perfectly equal thickness. He also formulated the laws governing the tapering of the stick of the Tourte bow.

Vuillermoz, Emile, French music critic; b. Lyons, May 23, 1878; d. Paris, March 2, 1960. He studied organ and piano in Lyons, and composition at the Paris Cons. with Fauré. He was one of the organizers of the Société Musicale Indépendante (1911) and edited the *Revue Musicale S. I. M.;* eventually became music critic of the daily *L'Excelsior,* and also contributed articles to *Le Temps.* He publ. *Musiques d'aujourd'hui* (1923), *La Vie amoureuse de Chopin* (1927), and *Histoire de la musique* (Paris, 1949; revised and completed by Jacques Lonchampt, 1973); *Gabriel Faure* (Paris, 1960; in Eng., Philadelphia, 1969); *Claude Debussy* (Geneva, 1957; 2nd ed., 1962).

Vulpius (Latinized form of real name, **Fuchs**), **Melchior,** German composer; b. Wasungen, c.1570; d.

Weimar, 1615 (buried, Aug. 7). From 1596 to his death, he was cantor in Weimar.

WORKS: 2 books of *Cantiones sacrae* (1602; 2nd ed., 1603; and 1604; 2nd ed., 1611); *Kirchengesänge und geistliche Lieder* for 4 and 5 Voices (1604); *Canticum beatissimae Virginis Mariae* for 4–8 Voices (1605); *Lateinische Hochzeitstücke* (1608); *Opusculum cantionum sacrarum* for 4–6 Voices (1610); *Das Leiden und Sterben unseres Herrn* (Passion after Matthew; 1613); 3 books of *Sonntägliche Evangelische Sprüche* for 4 Voices (1619, 1620, 1621); also a new ed. of Heinrich Faber's *Compendiolum musicae* (1610) with a German trans. and a supplementary chapter. Modern eds. are: the Matthew-Passion by Ziebler (1934); hymns by Heyden (1932); Christmas choruses by Twittenhoff and Heyden (1932).

Vycpálek, Ladislav, Czech composer; b. Prague, Feb. 23, 1882; d. there, Jan. 9, 1969. He studied philosophy at the Charles Univ. in Prague, obtaining his doctorate in 1906; then took private lessons in composition with Vítězslav Novák (1908–12). From 1907 to 1942 he worked as a music librarian.

WORKS: 3 cantatas: *Kantáta o posledních věcech člověka* (*Cantata on the Last Things of Man,* 1920–22); *Blahoslavený ten člověk* (*Blessed Is the Man,* 1933); *České requiem/Smrt a spasení* (*Czech Requiem/Death and Salvation,* 1940); String Quartet (1909); *Cestou* (*The Way*), 6 pieces for Piano (1901–14); *Chvála houslí* (*In Praise of the Violin*), sonata for Violin, Piano, and Mezzo-soprano, to the poem by S. Hanuš "The Violin of an Old German Master" (1927–28); Duo for Violin and Viola (1929); *Suite* for Solo Viola (1929); *Suite* for Solo Violin (1930); *Vzhůru srdce* (*Courage, My Heart!*), 2 variation fantasies to songs from the Huss period, for Orch. (1950); *Doma* (*At Home*), suite for Piano (1959); choruses; many songs.

Vyshnegradsky, Ivan. See **Wyschnegradsky, Ivan.**

Vyvyan, Jennifer, English soprano; b. Broadstairs, Kent, March 13, 1925; d. London, March 28, 1974. She studied with Roy Henderson at the Royal Academy of Music in London; made her debut as Jenny Diver in *The Beggar's Opera* with the English Opera Group in 1947; then sang with the Sadler's Wells Opera and the Covent Garden Opera, and at the Glyndebourne Festivals; also made guest appearances in Milan, Rome, Vienna, and Paris. She appeared in many contemporary operas, particularly those by Benjamin Britten; was equally distinguished as a concert singer.

Waack, Karl, German conductor; b. Lübeck, March 6, 1861; d. Neumünster, March 7, 1922. He was a pupil of the grand-ducal Musikschule in Weimar; settled in Riga as a teacher and conductor of the Wagnerverein. After the outbreak of the war in 1914, he went to Lübeck, where he conducted the Verein der Musikfreunde. He edited *Tristan und Isolde* (1904) and *Lohengrin* (1907) for Breitkopf & Härtel's *Textbibliothek* (with leading motifs in notation, and references to the full and piano scores); also wrote historical introductions and prepared tables of motifs for all the Wagner operas in the new editions brought out by Breitkopf & Härtel (1913). He publ. *Richard Wagner, Ein Erfüller und Vollender deutscher Kunst* (1918).

Waart, Edo de, noted Dutch conductor; b. Amsterdam, June 1, 1941. He was a member of a musical family; his father sang in the chorus of the Netherlands Opera. He first studied the piano; at 13 he took up the oboe; at 16 he entered the Muzieklyceum, where he studied oboe and later cello; during the summer of 1960 he attended the conducting classes in Salzburg given by Dean Dixon; after graduating from the Muzieklyceum in 1962, he played oboe in the Amsterdam Phil.; in 1963 he joined the Concertgebouw Orch.; he also studied conducting with

Franco Ferrara in Hilversum; then made his debut as a conductor with the Netherlands Radio Phil. in 1964. He went to the U.S. in 1964 and was one of the winners in the Mitropoulos Competition in N.Y.; in 1965–66 he was assistant conductor with the N.Y. Phil. Upon his return to Amsterdam in 1966 he was appointed assistant conductor of the Concertgebouw Orch., and accompanied it on a tour of the U.S. in 1967. He also organized the Netherlands Wind Ensemble and traveled with it in Japan and Pakistan as an oboe player. In 1967 he became a guest conductor of the Rotterdam Phil.; from 1973 to 1979 served as its chief conductor. He toured with it in England in 1970 and 1974; in the U.S. in 1971, 1975, and 1977; and in Germany and Austria in 1976. In 1971, 1972, and 1975 he was a guest conductor of the Santa Fe Opera in New Mexico; in 1975 he also conducted opera in Houston. In 1976 he conducted at Covent Garden in London. On Feb. 27, 1974, he made a successful debut with the San Francisco Symph.; this success led to his permanent engagement with it, first as its principal guest conductor in 1975, and then as music director in 1977. In 1980 he inaugurated the Louise M. Davies Hall in a gala concert with the San Francisco Symph. Orch. Edo de Waart represents the modern generation of symph. conductors, free from egotistical projections and attending to his duties *sine ira et studio.* He is tall, athletic-looking, and boasts a rich crown of hair; these attributes, topologically speaking, help him dominate the orch.

Wachtel, Theodor, German tenor; b. Hamburg, March 10, 1823; d. Frankfurt, Nov. 14, 1893. The son of a livery-stable keeper, he carried on the business from the age of 17, after his father's death. When his voice was discovered, he was sent to Hamburg for study, and soon appeared in opera. After further study in Vienna, he sang at the Berlin Opera (1865–68); in 1869 he appeared in Paris; made 2 American tours (1871, 1875); accumulated a considerable fortune. His voice was a powerful and brilliant lyric tenor; the role in which he made himself famous was that of the postillion in Adam's *Postillon de Longjumeau,* which he sang more than 1,000 times; also was successful as Raoul in *Les Huguenots.* His sole attempt as a Wagner singer, in *Lohengrin* (Leipzig, 1876), was a dismal failure.

Wade, Joseph Augustine, Irish composer; b. Dublin, 1796; d. London, July 15, 1845. He went to London in 1821, and established himself as a highly successful composer of popular ballads; his song *Meet me by moonlight alone* (1826) enjoyed great vogue, as did his vocal duet *I've wandered in dreams.* He also wrote an opera, *The 2 Houses of Granada* (London, Oct. 31, 1826), and an operetta, *The Pupil of Da Vinci* (London, Nov. 30, 1839).

Wadsworth, Charles, American pianist and harpsichordist; b. Barnesville, Ga., May 21, 1929. He studied piano with Rosalyn Tureck and conducting with Jean Morel at the Juilliard School of Music in N.Y.; also studied the French song repertoire with Pierre Bernac in Paris and German lieder with Meinhard von Zallinger in Munich. In 1960 Gian Carlo Menotti invited him to organize the Chamber Music Concerts at the Festival of Two Worlds in Spoleto, Italy; he was its director and pianist for 20 years. In 1969 he helped to found the Chamber Music Society of Lincoln Center in N.Y., and was made its artistic director; in 1977 he also created the chamber music series for the Charleston, South Carolina, Spoleto Festival U.S.A. In addition to numerous appearances as a pianist and harpsichordist with various ensembles, he also appeared in performances with such noted musicians as Dietrich Fischer-Dieskau, Beverly Sills, Hermann Prey, and Shirley Verrett.

Waechter, Eberhard, Austrian baritone; b. Vienna, July 9, 1929. He studied piano and music theory at the Univ. of Vienna and at the Academy of Music there (1950–53); took private voice lessons; in 1953 he sang at the Vienna Volksoper; in 1955 he became a member of the Vienna State Opera; subsequently made guest appearances at Bayreuth, Salzburg, Covent Garden in London, and La Scala in Milan. On Jan. 25, 1961, he made his debut at the Metropolitan Opera in N.Y. as Wolfram in *Tannhäuser.* In 1963 he was named Austrian Kammersänger. He was particularly distinguished in lyric baritone

parts, among them Count Almaviva, Don Giovanni, and Wolfram; he also sang the role of Orest in *Elektra* by Richard Strauss.

Waelrant, Hubert, Flemish composer and theorist; b. Tongerloo, Brabant, c.1517; d. Antwerp, Nov. 19, 1595. He matriculated at the Univ. of Louvain in 1534; in 1544 became a tenor at Notre Dame in Antwerp, where he founded a music school in 1547. In 1554 he established a music publishing business in partnership with Jean Laet, retiring in 1558. As a teacher, he abandoned the old system of solmization by hexachords and introduced a new system of the 7 tone-names, *bo ce di ga lo ma ni* (hence called "Bocedization"; also "Voces belgicae"). His compositions include a book of chansons, publ. by Phalèse in Louvain (1553–54), and a book of madrigals for 5 Voices (Antwerp, 1558); as a publisher, he brought out several sacred works by various composers; edited a collection, *Symphonia angelica,* containing madrigals of his own (1585).

Wagenaar, Bernard, American composer and teacher, son of **Johan Wagenaar;** b. Arnhem, the Netherlands, July 18, 1894; d. York, Maine, May 19, 1971. He studied music with his father; violin with Gerard Veerman in Utrecht. In 1920 he came to the U.S.; was a violinist in the N.Y. Phil. (1921–23). He joined the Inst. of Musical Art in 1925, and remained with it when it became the Juilliard School of Music, teaching composition and orchestration.
WORKS: *Pieces of 8,* operatic comedy (1943; N.Y., 1944); Symph. No. 1 (N.Y., Oct. 7, 1928); *Divertimento* (Detroit, Nov. 28, 1929); *Sinfonietta* (N.Y., Jan. 16, 1930); Symph. No. 2 (N.Y., Nov. 10, 1932, Toscanini conducting); Symph. No. 3 (N.Y., Jan. 23, 1937, composer conducting); Violin Concerto (1940); Triple Concerto for Flute, Harp, Cello, and Orch. (N.Y., May 20, 1941, composer conducting); Symph. No. 4 (Boston, Dec. 16, 1949); *5 Tableaux* for Cello and Orch. (Amsterdam, Jan. 9, 1955); *3 Songs from the Chinese* (1921); Violin Sonata (1925); 3 string quartets; Piano Sonata; Sonatina for Cello and Piano; Concertino for 8 Instruments.

Wagenaar, Johan, Dutch organist and composer; b. Utrecht, Nov. 1, 1862; d. The Hague, June 17, 1941. He studied with Richard Hol in Utrecht (1875–85) and with H. von Herzogenberg in Berlin (1889); established himself as an organist at the Utrecht Cathedral; from 1887 to 1904 he was director of the Utrecht Music School; from 1919 to 1937, director of the Royal Cons. at The Hague.
WORKS: Operas: *De Doge van Venetie* (Utrecht, 1904) and *De Cid* (Utrecht, 1916); burlesque opera, *Jupiter Amans* (Scheveningen, 1925); symph. poems: *Levenszomer* (1901); *Saul and David* (1906); *Elverhöt* (1940); overtures: *Koning Jan* (1889); *Cyrano de Bergerac* (1905); *De getemde feeks* (1906); *Driekoningenavond* (1927); *De philosofische prinses* (1931); numerous choral works; songs; organ pieces.

Wagenseil, Georg Christoph, Austrian composer

and theorist; b. Vienna, Jan. 29, 1715; d. there, March 1, 1777. He studied with J.J. Fux; was the music teacher of the Empress Maria Theresa and her children; in 1739 was appointed court composer; remained in the Imperial service until his death. He wrote many operas in Italian.

Wagenseil, Johann Christoph, German historian and librarian; b. Nuremberg, Nov. 26, 1633; d. Altdorf, Oct. 9, 1708. He publ. an important book, *De Sacri Rom. Imperii Libera Civitate Noribergensi Commentatio* (Altdorf, 1697), with a 140-page supplement (in German), *Buch von der Meister-Singer holdseligen Kunst: Anfang, Fortübung, Nutzbarkeiten und Lehr-Sätz*, containing poems and melodies by Frauenlob, Mügling, Marner, and Regenbogen; this section was the main literary source that Wagner used in *Die Meistersinger von Nürnberg.*

Waghalter, Ignatz, conductor and composer, b. Warsaw, March 15, 1882; d. New York, April 7, 1949. He studied in Berlin, where he became conductor of the Komische Oper (1907–11); then conducted in Essen (1911–12), and at the Deutsches Opernhaus in Berlin-Charlottenburg. In 1925 he succeeded Stransky as conductor of the State Symph. Orch. in N.Y. (for one season only); then returned to Berlin; in 1933 he went to Prague, and in 1934 to Vienna. He then went to America, settling in N.Y. in 1938.
WORKS: Operas: *Der Teufelsweg* (Berlin, 1911); *Mandragola* (Berlin, Jan. 23, 1914; N.Y., March 4, 1925); *Jugend* (Berlin, 1917); *Der späte Gast* (Berlin, 1922); *Sataniel* (Berlin, 1923); operettas: *Der Weiberkrieg* and *Wem gehört Helena?*; Violin Concerto; Violin Sonata; String Quartet; piano pieces.

Wagner, Cosima, wife of **Richard Wagner,** daughter of **Franz Liszt** and the Countess Marie d'Agoult; b. Bellaggio, on Lake Como, Dec. 24, 1837; d. Bayreuth, April 1, 1930. She received an excellent education in Paris; married **Hans von Bülow** on Aug. 18, 1857; there were 2 daughters of this marriage, Blandine and Daniela; the 3rd daughter, Isolde, was Wagner's child, as was the 4th, Eva, and the son, Siegfried. A divorce followed on July 18, 1870; the marriage to Wagner took place in a few weeks, on Aug. 25, 1870. A woman of high intelligence, practical sense, and imperious character, Cosima Wagner emerged after Wagner's death as a powerful personage in all affairs regarding the continuance of the Bayreuth Festivals, as well as the complex matters pertaining to the rights of performance of Wagner's works all over the world. She publ. her reminiscences of Liszt: *Franz Liszt, Ein Gedenkblatt von seiner Tochter* (Munich, 2nd ed., 1911).

Wagner, Georg Gottfried, German violinist; b. Mühlberg, April 5, 1698; d. Plauen, March 23, 1756. He studied with Kuhnau at the Thomasschule in Leipzig (1712–18); studied at the Univ. of Leipzig (1718–26); was a violinist in Bach's orch., and was recommended by Bach for the post of cantor at Plauen, which he held from 1726 to his death. He wrote numerous sacred works and instrumental compositions; his motet *Lob und Ehre* was misattributed to Bach by Breitkopf & Härtel (publ. 1819).

Wagner, Johanna, German soprano; b. Lohnde, near Hannover, Oct. 13, 1826; d. Würzburg, Oct. 16, 1894. She was a natural daughter of Lieutenant Bock von Wülfingen of Hannover, and was adopted by Richard Wagner's brother, Albert; was thus regarded as Wagner's niece. Of a precocious talent, she acted on the stage as a small child; through Wagner she obtained a position at the Dresden Opera when she was 17; produced an excellent impression as Agathe in *Der Freischütz,* and was engaged as a regular member. She studied the part of Elisabeth in *Tannhäuser* with Wagner, and sang it in the premiere of the opera on Oct. 19, 1845, when she was barely 19 years old. In 1846 she went to Paris for further study, with Mme. Viardot-Garcia (1846–48); then was engaged at the Hamburg Opera (1849) and finally at the court opera in Berlin (1850–61). In 1859 she married the district judge Jachmann. After 1862 she acted mainly on the dramatic stage, reappearing in opera at the Bayreuth Festival in 1876 in the parts of Schwertleite and the First Norn. In 1882 she settled in Munich as a singing teacher.

Wagner, Josef Franz, Austrian composer of light music; b. Vienna, March 20, 1856; d. there, June 5, 1908. He was a popular leader of military bands in Vienna; produced the operetta *Der Herzbub* (Vienna, Feb. 7, 1895), which had little success, but achieved fame as the composer of the Austrian march *Under the Double Eagle,* which became a semi-official march of the Austro-Hungarian Empire.

Wagner, Peter (Joseph), eminent German musicologist; b. Kürenz, near Trier, Aug. 19, 1865; d. Freiburg, Switzerland, Oct. 17, 1931. He studied at the Univ. of Strasbourg; received his degree of Dr.Phil. with the dissertation *Palestrina als weltlicher Komponist* (1890); studied further in Berlin under Bellermann and Spitta; in 1893 he was appointed instructor of church music at the Univ. of Freiburg, Switzerland. In 1901 he established at the Univ. the Gregorianische Akademie for theoretical and practical study of plainsong, in which field he was an eminent authority. He was a member of the Papal Commission for the *Editio Vaticana* of the Roman Gradual, and was made a Papal Chamberlain. In the course of numerous visits to Spain he did valuable research on the Mozarabic liturgical chant.

Wagner, (Wilhelm) Richard, great German composer whose operas, written to his own librettos, have radically transformed the concept of stage music, postulating the inherent equality of drama and symph. accompaniment, and establishing the uninterrupted continuity of the action; b. Leipzig, May 22, 1813; d. Venice, Feb. 13, 1883. The antecedents of his family, and his own origin, are open to controversy. His father was a police registrar in Leipzig who died when Wagner was only 6 months old; his mother, Johanna (Rosine), née Pätz, was the daughter of a baker in Weissenfels; it is possible also that she was an illegitimate offspring of Prince Friedrich Ferdinand Constantin of Weimar. Eight months after her husband's death, Johanna Wagner married, on Aug. 28, 1814, the actor Ludwig Geyer. This hasty marriage generated speculation that Geyer may have been Wagner's real father; Wagner himself entertained this possibility, pointing out the similarity of his and Geyer's prominent noses; in the end he abandoned this surmise. The problem of Wagner's origin arose with renewed force after the triumph of the Nazi party in Germany, as Hitler's adoration of Wagner was put in jeopardy by suspicions that Geyer might have been Jewish and that if Wagner was indeed his natural son then he himself was tainted by Semitic blood. The phantom of Wagner's possible contamination with Jewish hemoglobins struck horror into the hearts of good Nazi biologists and archivists; they delved anxiously into Geyer's own ancestry, and much to the relief of Dr. Goebbels and other Nazi intellectuals, it was found that Geyer, like Wagner's nominal father, was the purest of Aryans; Wagner's possible illegitimate birth was of no concern to the racial tenets of the Nazi Weltanschauung.

Geyer was a member of the court theater in Dresden, and the family moved there in 1814. Geyer died on Sept. 30, 1821; in 1822 Wagner entered the Dresden Kreuzschule, where he remained a pupil until 1827. Carl Maria von Weber often visited the Geyer home; these visits exercised a beneficial influence on Wagner in his formative years. In 1825 he began to take piano lessons from a local musician named Humann, and also studied violin with Robert Sipp. Wagner showed strong literary inclinations, and under the spell of Shakespeare, wrote a tragedy, *Leubald.* In 1827 he moved with his mother back to Leipzig, where his uncle Adolf Wagner gave him guidance in his classical reading. In 1828 Wagner was enrolled in the Nikolaischule; while in school, he had lessons in harmony with Christian Gottlieb Müller, a violinist in the theater orch. In June 1830 Wagner entered the Thomasschule, where he began to compose; he wrote a String Quartet and some piano music; his *Overtüre* in B-flat major was performed at the Leipzig Theater on Dec. 24, 1830, under the direction of the famous musician Heinrich Dorn. Now determined to dedicate himself entirely to music, Wagner became a student of Theodor Weinlig, cantor of the Thomaskirche, from whom he received a thorough training in counterpoint and composition. Wagner's first publ. work was a Piano Sonata in B-flat major, to which he assigned the opus number 1; it was brought out by the prestigious publishing house of Breitkopf & Härtel in 1832. He then wrote an overture to *König Enzio,* which was performed at the Leipzig Theater on Feb. 19, 1832; it was followed by an Overture in C major, which was presented at a Gewandhaus concert on April 30, 1832. Wagner's first major orch. work, a Symph. in C major, was performed at a Prague Cons. concert in Nov. 1832; on Jan. 10, 1833, it was played by the Gewandhaus Orch. in Leipzig; he was 19 years old at the time. In 1832 he wrote an opera, *Die Hochzeit,*

after J.G. Büsching's *Ritterzeit und Ritterwesen;* an introduction, a septet, and a chorus from this work are extant. Early in 1833 he began work on *Die Feen,* to a libretto after Carlo Gozzi's *La Donna serpente.* Upon completion of *Die Feen* in Jan. 1834, he offered the score to the Leipzig Theater, but it was rejected. In June 1834 he began to sketch out a new opera, *Das Liebesverbot,* after Shakespeare's play *Measure for Measure.* In July 1834 Wagner obtained the position of music director with Heinrich Bethmann's theater company, based in Magdeburg; he made his debut in Bad Lauschstadt, conducting Mozart's *Don Giovanni.* On March 29, 1836, he led in Magdeburg the premiere of his opera *Das Liebesverbot,* presented under the title *Die Novize von Palermo.* Bethmann's company soon went out of business; Wagner, who was by that time deeply involved with Christine Wilhelmine ("Minna") Planer, an actress with the company, followed her to Königsberg, where they were married on Nov. 24, 1836. In Königsberg he composed the overture *Rule Britannia;* on April 1, 1837, he was appointed music director of the Königsberg town theater. His marital affairs suffered a setback when Minna left him for a rich businessman by the name of Dietrich. In Aug. 1837 Wagner went to Riga as music director of the theater there; coincidentally, Minna's sister was engaged as a singer at the same theater; Minna soon joined her, and became reconciled with Wagner. In Riga Wagner worked on his new opera, *Rienzi, der letzte der Tribunen,* after a popular novel by Bulwer-Lytton.

In March 1839 he lost his position in Riga; he and Minna, burdened by debts, left town to seek their fortune elsewhere. In their passage by sea from Pillau they encountered a fierce storm, and the ship was forced to drop anchor in the Norwegian fjord of Sandwike. They made their way to London, and then set out for Boulogne; there Wagner met Meyerbeer, who gave him a letter of recommendation to the director of the Paris Opéra. He arrived in Paris with Minna in Sept. 1839, and remained there until 1842. He was forced to eke out a meager subsistence by making piano arrangements of operas and writing occasional articles for the *Gazette Musicale.* In Jan. 1840 he completed his Overture to *Faust* (later revised as *Eine Faust-Ouvertüre*). Soon he found himself in dire financial straits; he owed money which he could not repay, and on Oct. 28, 1840, he was confined in debtors' prison; he was released on Nov. 17, 1840. The conditions of his containment were light, and he was able to leave prison on certain days. In the meantime he had completed the libretto for *Der fliegende Holländer;* he submitted it to the director of the Paris Opéra, but the director had already commissioned another composer to write an opera on the same subject; he was willing, however, to buy the libretto, and offered to pay 500 French francs for it; Wagner accepted the offer. The libretto was later trans. into French and was used by Pierre-Louis Dietsch for his own opera under the title *Le Vaisseau fantôme,* which was produced at the Paris Opéra on Nov. 9, 1842.

In 1842 Wagner received the welcome news from Dresden that his opera *Rienzi* had been accepted for production; it was staged there on Oct. 20, 1842, with considerable success. *Der fliegende Holländer* was also accepted by Dresden, and Wagner conducted its first performance there on Jan. 2, 1843. On Feb. 2 of that year, Wagner was named 2nd Hofkapellmeister in Dresden, where he conducted a large repertoire of Classical operas, among them *Don Giovanni, Le nozze di Figaro, Die Zauberflöte, Fidelio,* and *Der Freischütz.* In 1846 he conducted a memorable performance in Dresden of Beethoven's 9th Symph. In Dresden he led the prestigious choral society Liedertafel, for which he wrote several works, including the "biblical scene" *Das Liebesmahl der Apostel.* He was also preoccupied during those years in working on the score and music for *Tannhäuser,* completing it on April 13, 1845. He conducted its first performance in Dresden on Oct. 19, 1845. He subsequently revised the score, which was staged to better advantage there on Aug. 1, 1847. Concurrently, he began work on *Lohengrin,* which he completed on April 28, 1848. Wagner's efforts to have his works publ. failed, leaving him again in debt. Without waiting for further performances of his operas which had already been presented to the public, he drew up the first prose outline of *Der Nibelungen-Mythus als Entwurf zu einem Drama,* the prototype of the epic *Ring* cycle; in Nov. 1848 he began work on the poem for *Siegfrieds Tod.* At that time he joined the revolutionary Vaterlandsverein, and was drawn into active participation in the movement, culminating in an open uprising in May 1849. An order was issued for his arrest, and he had to leave Dresden; he made his way to Weimar, where he found a cordial reception from Liszt; he then proceeded to Vienna, where a Prof. Widmann lent him his own passport so that Wagner could cross the border of Saxony on his way to Zürich; there he made his home in July 1849; Minna joined him there a few months later. Shortly before leaving Dresden Wagner had sketched 2 dramas, *Jesus von Nazareth* and *Achilleus;* both remained unfinished. In Zürich he wrote a number of essays expounding his philosophy of art: *Die Kunst und die Revolution* (1849), *Das Kunstwerk der Zukunft* (1849), *Kunst und Klima* (1850), *Oper und Drama* (1851; revised 1868), and *Eine Mitteilung an meine Freunde* (1851). The ideas expressed in *Das Kunstwerk der Zukunft* gave rise to the description of Wagner's operas as "music of the future" by his opponents; they were also described as Gesamtkunstwerk, "total artwork," by his admirers. Wagner rejected both descriptions as distortions of his real views. He was equally opposed to the term "music drama," which nevertheless became an accepted definition for all of his operas.

In Feb. 1850 Wagner was again in Paris; there he fell in love with a Jessie Laussot, the wife of a wine merchant; however, she eventually left Wagner, and he returned to Minna in Zürich. On Aug. 28, 1850, Liszt conducted the successful premiere of *Lohengrin* in Weimar. In 1851 Wagner wrote the verse text of *Der junge Siegfried,* and prose sketches for *Das Rheingold* and *Die Walküre.* In June 1852 he finished the text of *Die Walküre* and of *Das Rheingold;* he completed the entire libretto of *Der Ring*

des *Nibelungen* on Dec. 15, 1852, and it was privately printed in 1853. In Nov. 1853 Wagner began composition of the music for *Das Rheingold,* completing the full score on Sept. 26, 1854. In June 1854 he commenced work on the music of *Die Walküre,* which he finished on March 20, 1856. In 1854 he became friendly with a wealthy Zürich merchant, Otto Wesendonck, and his wife, Mathilde. Wesendonck was willing to give Wagner a substantial loan, to be repaid out of his performance rights. The situation became complicated when Wagner developed an affection for Mathilde, which in all probability remained Platonic. But he set to music 5 lyric poems written by Mathilde herself; the album was publ. as the *Wesendonk-Lieder* in 1857. In 1855 Wagner conducted a series of 8 concerts with the Phil. Society of London (March 12–June 25). His performances were greatly praised by English musicians, and he had the honor of meeting Queen Victoria, who invited him to her loge at the intermission of his 7th concert. In June 1856 Wagner made substantial revisions in the last dramas of *Der Ring des Nibelungen,* changing their titles to *Siegfried* and *Götterdämmerung.* Throughout these years he was preoccupied with writing a new opera, *Tristan und Isolde,* permeated with the dual feelings of love and death. In April 1857 he prepared the first sketch of *Parzival* (later titled *Parsifal*). In 1858 Wagner moved to Venice, where he completed the full score of the 2nd act of *Tristan und Isolde.* The Dresden authorities, acting through their Austrian confederates and still determined to bring Wagner to trial as a revolutionary, pressured Venice to expel Wagner from its territory. Once more Wagner took refuge in Switzerland; he decided to stay in Lucerne; while there he completed the score of *Tristan und Isolde,* on Aug. 6, 1859.

In Sept. 1859 he moved to Paris, where Minna joined him. In 1860 he conducted 3 concerts of his music at the Théâtre-Italien. Napoleon III became interested in his work, and in March 1860 ordered the director of the Paris Opéra to produce Wagner's opera *Tannhäuser;* after considerable work, revisions, and a trans. into French, it was given at the Opéra on March 13, 1861. It proved to be a fiasco, and Wagner withdrew the opera after 3 performances. For some reason the Jockey Club of Paris led a vehement protest against Wagner; the critics also joined in this opposition, mainly because the French audiences were not accustomed to the mystically romantic, heavily Germanic operatic music. Invectives hurled against Wagner by the Paris press make extraordinary reading; the comparison of Wagner's music with the sound produced by a domestic cat walking down the keyboard of the piano was one of the favorite critical devices. The French caricaturists exercised their wit by picturing Wagner in the act of hammering a poor listener's ear. A Wagner "Schimpflexikon" was compiled by Wilhelm Tappert and publ. in 1877 in the hope of putting Wagner's detractors to shame, but they would not be pacified; the amount of black bile poured on Wagner even after he had attained the stature of celebrity is incredible for its grossness and vulgarity. Hanslick used his great literary gift and a flair for a striking simile to damn Wagner as a purveyor of cacophony. Oscar Wilde added his measure of wit. "I like Wagner's music better than anybody's," he remarked in *The Picture of Dorian Gray*. "It is so loud that one can talk the whole time without people hearing what one says." In an amazing turnabout, Nietzsche, a worshipful admirer of Wagner, publ. a venomous denunciation of his erstwhile idol in *Der Fall Wagner,* in which he vesuviated in a sulfuric eruption of righteous wrath; Wagner made music itself sick, he proclaimed; but at the time Nietzsche himself was already on the borderline of madness.

Politically, Wagner's prospects began to improve; on July 22, 1860, he was informed of a partial amnesty by the Saxon authorities. In Aug. 1860 he visited Baden-Baden, in his first visit to Germany in 11 years. Finally, on March 18, 1862, he was granted a total amnesty, which allowed him access to Saxony. In Nov. 1861 Wesendonck had invited Wagner to Venice; free from political persecution, he could now go there without fear. While in Venice he returned to a scenario he had prepared in Marienbad in 1845 for a comic opera, *Die Meistersinger von Nürnberg.* In Feb. 1862 he moved to Biebrich, where he began composing the score for *Die Meistersinger.* Minna, after a brief period of reconciliation with Wagner, left him, settling in Dresden, where she died in 1866. In order to repair his financial situation, Wagner accepted a number of concert appearances, traveling as an orch. conductor to Vienna, Prague, St. Petersburg, Moscow, and other cities (1862–63). In 1862 he gave in Vienna a private reading of *Die Meistersinger*. It is said that the formidable Vienna critic Hanslick was angered when he found out that Wagner had caricatured him in the part of Beckmesser in *Die Meistersinger* (the original name of the character was Hans Lick), and he let out his discomfiture in further attacks on Wagner.

Wagner's fortunes changed spectacularly in 1864 when young King Ludwig II of Bavaria ascended the throne and invited Wagner to Munich with the promise of unlimited help in carrying out his various projects. In return, Wagner composed the *Huldigungsmarsch,* which he dedicated to his royal patron. The publ. correspondence between Wagner and the King is extraordinary in its display of mutual admiration, gratitude, and affection; still, difficulties soon developed when the Bavarian Cabinet told Ludwig that his lavish support of Wagner's projects threatened the Bavarian economy. Ludwig was forced to advise Wagner to leave Munich. Wagner took this advice as an order, and late in 1865 he went to Switzerland. A very serious difficulty arose also in Wagner's emotional life, when he became intimately involved with Liszt's daughter Cosima, wife of Hans von Bülow, the famous conductor and an impassioned proponent of Wagner's music. On April 10, 1865, Cosima Bülow gave birth to Wagner's daughter, whom he named Isolde after the heroine of his opera which Hans von Bülow was preparing for performance in Munich. Its premiere took place with great acclaim on June 10, 1865, 2 months after the birth of Isolde, with Bülow conducting. During

the summer of 1865 Wagner prepared the prose sketch of *Parzival,* and began to dictate his autobiography, *Mein Leben,* to Cosima. In Jan. 1866 he resumed the composition of *Die Meistersinger;* he settled in a villa in Tribschen, on Lake Lucerne, where Cosima joined him permanently in Nov. 1868. Wagner completed the full score of *Die Meistersinger* on Oct. 24, 1867. On June 21, 1868, Hans von Bülow conducted its premiere in Munich in the presence of King Ludwig, who sat in the royal box with Wagner. A son, significantly named Siegfried, was born to Cosima and Wagner on June 6, 1869. On Sept. 22, 1869, *Das Rheingold* was produced in Munich. On June 26, 1870, *Die Walküre* was staged there. On July 18, 1870, Cosima and Hans von Bülow were divorced, and on Aug. 25, 1870, Wagner and Cosima were married in Lucerne. In Dec. 1870 Wagner wrote the *Siegfried Idyll,* based on the themes from his opera; it was performed in their villa in Bayreuth on Christmas morning, the day after Cosima's birthday, as a surprise for her. In 1871 Wagner wrote the *Kaisermarsch* to mark the victorious conclusion of the Franco-German War; he conducted it in the presence of Kaiser Wilhelm I at a concert in the Royal Opera House in Berlin on May 5, 1871.

On May 12 of that year, while in Leipzig, Wagner made public his plans for realizing his cherished dream of building his own theater in Bayreuth for the production of the entire cycle of *Der Ring des Nibelungen.* In Dec. 1871 the Bayreuth town council offered him a site for a proposed Festspielhaus; on May 22, 1872, the cornerstone was laid; Wagner commemorated the event by conducting a performance of Beethoven's 9th Symph. (this was Wagner's 59th birthday). In 1873 Wagner began to build his own home in Bayreuth, which he called "Wahnfried," i.e., "Free from Delusion." In order to complete the building of the Festspielhaus, Wagner appealed to King Ludwig for additional funds. Ludwig gave him 100,000 talers for this purpose. Now the dream of Wagner's life was realized. Between June and Aug. 1876 *Der Ring des Nibelungen* went through 3 rehearsals; King Ludwig attended the final dress rehearsals; the official premiere of the cycle took place on Aug. 13, 14, 16, and 17, 1876, under the direction of Hans Richter. Kaiser Wilhelm I made a special journey from Berlin to attend the performances of *Das Rheingold* and *Die Walküre.* In all, 3 complete productions of the *Ring* cycle were given between Aug. 13 and Aug. 30, 1876. Ludwig was faithful to the end to Wagner, whom he called "my divine friend." In his castle Neuschwanstein he installed architectural representations of scenes from Wagner's operas. Soon Ludwig's mental deterioration became obvious to everyone, and he was committed to an asylum. There, on June 13, 1883, he overpowered the psychiatrist escorting him on a walk and dragged him to his death in the Starnberg Lake, drowning himself as well. Ludwig survived Wagner by 4 months.

The spectacles in Bayreuth attracted music-lovers and notables from all over the world. Even those who were not partial to Wagner's ideas or appreciative of his music went to Bayreuth out of curiosity. Tchaikovsky was one such skeptical visitor. Despite world success and fame, Wagner still labored under financial difficulties. He even addressed a letter to an American dentist practicing in Dresden (who also treated Wagner's teeth) in which he tried to interest him in arranging Wagner's permanent transfer to the U.S. He voiced disillusionment in his future prospects in Germany, and said he would be willing to settle in America provided a sum of $1 million would be guaranteed to him by American bankers, and a comfortable estate for him and his family could be found in a climatically clement part of the country. Nothing came of this particular proposal. He did establish an American connection when he wrote, for a fee of $5,000, a *Grosser Festmarsch* for the observance of the U.S. centennial in 1876, dedicated to the "beautiful young ladies of America." In the middle of all this, Wagner became infatuated with Judith Gautier; their affair lasted for about 2 years (1876–78). Wagner completed the full score of *Parsifal* (as it was now called) on Jan. 13, 1882, in Palermo. It was performed for the first time at the Bayreuth Festival on July 26, 1882, followed by 15 subsequent performances. At the final performance, on Aug. 29, 1882, Wagner stepped to the podium in the last act and conducted the work to its close; this was his last appearance as a conductor. He went to Venice in Sept. 1882 for a period of rest (he had angina pectoris). Early in the afternoon of Feb. 13, 1883, he suffered a massive heart attack, and died in Cosima's presence. His body was interred in a vault in the garden of his Wahnfried villa in Bayreuth.

Wagner's role in music history is immense. Not only did he create works of great beauty and tremendous brilliance, but he generated an entirely new concept of the art of music, exercising an influence on generations of composers all over the globe. Richard Strauss extended Wagner's grandiose vision to symph. music, fashioning the form of a tone poem that uses leading motifs and vivid programmatic description of the scenes portrayed in his music. Even Rimsky-Korsakov, far as he stood from Wagner's ideas of musical composition, reflected the spirit of *Parsifal* in his own religious opera, *The Legend of the City of Kitezh.* Schoenberg's first significant work, *Die verklärte Nacht,* is Wagnerian in its color. Lesser composers, unable to escape Wagner's magic domination, attempted to follow Wagner literally by writing trilogies and tetralogies on a parallel plan with Wagner's *Ring;* a pathetic example is the career of August Bungert, who wrote 2 operatic cycles using Homer's epics as the source of his libretti. Wagner's reform of opera was incomparably more far-reaching in aim, import, and effect than that of Gluck, whose main purpose was to counteract the arbitrary predominance of the singers; this goal Wagner accomplished through insistence upon the dramatic truth of his music. When he rejected traditional opera, he did so in the conviction that such an artificial form could not serve as a basis for true dramatic expression. In its place he gave the world a new form and new techniques. So revolutionary was Wagner's art that conductors and singers had to undergo special training in the new style of interpretation in order to perform his

works. Thus Wagner became the founder of interpretative conducting and of a new school of dramatic singing, so that such terms as "Wagnerian tenor" and "Wagnerian soprano" became a part of the musical vocabulary.

In his many essays and declarations Wagner condemns the illogical plan of Italian opera and French grand opera. To quote his own words, "The mistake in the art-form of the opera consists in this, that a means of expression (music) was made the end, and the end to be expressed (the drama) was made a means." The choice of subjects assumes utmost importance in Wagner's esthetics. He wrote: "The subject treated by the word-tone poet [*Worttondichter*] is entirely human, freed from all convention and from everything historically formal." The new artwork creates its own artistic form; continuous thematic development of basic motifs becomes a fundamental procedure for the logical cohesion of the drama; these highly individualized generating motifs, appearing singly, in bold relief, or subtly varied and intertwined with other motifs, present the ever-changing soul states of the characters of the drama, and form the connecting links for the dramatic situations of the total artwork, in a form of musical declamation which Wagner described as "Sprechsingen." Characters in Wagner's stage works become themselves symbols of such soul states, so that even mythical gods, magic-workers, heroic horses, and speaking birds become expressions of eternal verities, illuminating the human behavior. It is for this reason that Wagner selected in most of his operas figures that reflect philosophical ideas. Yet, this very solemnity of Wagner's great images on the stage bore the seeds of their own destruction in a world governed by different esthetic principles. Thus it came to pass that the Wagnerian domination of the musical stage suddenly lost its power with changes in human society and esthetic codes. Spectators and listeners were no longer interested in solving artistic puzzles on the stage. A demand for human simplicity arose against Wagnerian heroic complexity. The public at large found greater enjoyment in the realistic nonsense of Verdi's romantic operas than in the unreality of symbolic truth in Wagner's operas. By the 2nd quarter of the 20th century, few if any composers tried to imitate Wagner; all at once his grandeur and animation became an unnatural and asphyxiating constraint.

In the domain of melody, harmony, and orchestration, Wagner's art was as revolutionary as was his total artwork on the stage. He introduced the idea of an endless melody, a continuous flow of diatonic and chromatic tones; the tonality became fluid and uncertain, producing an impression of unattainability, so that the listener accustomed to Classical modulatory schemes could not easily feel the direction toward the tonic; the Prelude to *Tristan und Isolde* is a classic example of such fluidity of harmonic elements. The use of long unresolved dominant-ninth-chords and the dramatic tremolos of diminished-seventh-chords contributed to this state of musical uncertainty, which disturbed the critics and the audiences alike. But Wagnerian harmony also became the foundation of the new method of composition that adopted a free flow of modulatory progressions. Without Wagner the chromatic idioms of the 20th century could not exist. In orchestration, too, Wagner introduced great innovations; he created new instruments, such as the so-called "Wagner tuba," and he increased his demands on the virtuosity of individual orch. players. The vertiginous flight of the bassoon to the high E in the Overture to *Tannhäuser* could not have been attempted before the advent of Wagner.

An 1869 cartoon issued by G. Schirmer in N.Y., captioned "The Music of the Future," depicts a conductor leading an orch. of desperate musicians, goats, cats, and other animals; a discarded score at the conductor's feet proclaims, "Wagner not to be played much till 1995." The prophecy may well come true, not because of the incomprehensibility of Wagner's music but, to the contrary, because of its lack of interest to listeners. But will Wagner's music be returned to favor even in 1995? The *Ride of the Walküre,* the *Rienzi Overture,* the *Tannhäuser Bacchanale,* which were the pabulum of concertgoers early in the century, have practically disappeared from orch. programs.

Wagner became the target of political contention during World War I when audiences in the Allied countries associated his sonorous works with German imperialism. An even greater obstacle to further performances of Wagner's music arose with the rise of Hitler. Hitler ordered the slaughter of millions of Jews; he was an enthusiastic admirer of Wagner, who himself entertained anti-Semitic notions; *ergo,* Wagner was guilty by association of mass murder. Can art be separated from politics, particularly when politics become murderous? Jewish musicians in Tel Aviv refused to play the Prelude to *Tristan und Isolde* when it was put on the program of a symph. concert under the direction of an American conductor, and booed him for his intention to inflict Wagner on Wagner's philosophical victims.

Several periodicals dealing with Wagner were publ. in Germany and elsewhere; Wagner himself began issuing *Bayreuther Blätter* in 1878 as an aid to understanding his operas; this journal continued publication until 1938. Remarkably enough, a French periodical, *Revue Wagnérienne,* began appearing in 1885, at a time when French composers realized the tremendous power of Wagnerian esthetics; it was publ. sporadically for a number of years. A Wagner Society in London publ., from 1888 to 1895, a quarterly journal entitled, significantly, *The Meister.*

WORKS: OPERAS AND MUSIC DRAMAS: *Die Hochzeit* (1832–33; partly destroyed; introduction, septet, and chorus perf. at the Neues Theater, Leipzig, Feb. 13, 1938]; *Die Feen,* romantische Oper (1833–34; Königliches Hof- und Nationaltheater, Munich, June 29, 1888, Fischer conducting); *Das Liebesverbot, oder Die Novize von Palermo,* grosse komische Oper (1834–35; Magdeburg, March 29, 1836, composer conducting); *Rienzi, der Letzte der Tribunen,* grosse tragische Oper (1837–40; Königliches Hoftheater, Dresden, Oct. 20, 1842, Reissiger conducting; re-

vised 1843); *Der fliegende Holländer,* romantische Oper (1841; Königliches Hoftheater, Dresden, Jan. 2, 1843, composer conducting; reorchestrated in 1846, then revised in 1852 and 1860); *Tannhäuser und der Sängerkrieg auf Wartburg,* grosse romantische Oper (first titled *Der Venusberg;* "Dresden" version, 1842–45; Königliches Hoftheater, Dresden, Oct. 19, 1845, composer conducting; revised 1845–47; "Paris" version, a revision with additions and a French trans., 1860–61; Opéra, Paris, March 13, 1861, Dietsch conducting; final version, with a German trans. of the French revision and additions, 1865; Königliches Hof- und Nationaltheater, Munich, March 5, 1865); *Lohengrin,* romantische Oper (1845–48; Hoftheater, Weimar, Aug. 28, 1850, Liszt conducting); *Tristan und Isolde* (1856–59; Königliches Hof- und Nationaltheater, Munich, June 10, 1865, Bülow conducting); *Die Meistersinger von Nürnberg* (first sketch, 1845; 1861–67; Königliches Hof- und Nationaltheater, Munich, June 21, 1868, Bülow conducting); *Der Ring des Nibelungen,* Bühnenfestspiel für drei Tage und einen Vorabend (first prose outline as *Der Nibelungen-Mythus als Entwurf zu einem Drama,* 1848; Vorabend: *Das Rheingold,* 1851–54; Königliches Hof- und Nationaltheater, Munich, Sept. 22, 1869, Wüllner conducting; erster Tag: *Die Walküre,* 1851–56; Königliches Hof- und Nationaltheater, Munich, June 26, 1870, Wüllner conducting; zweiter Tag: *Siegfried,* first titled *Der junge Siegfried;* 1851–52, 1857, 1864–65, and 1869; Festspielhaus, Bayreuth, Aug. 16, 1876, Richter conducting; dritter Tag: *Götterdämmerung,* first titled *Siegfrieds Tod;* 1848–52 and 1869–74; Festspielhaus, Bayreuth, Aug. 17, 1876, Richter conducting; first complete perf. of the *Ring* cycle, Festspielhaus, Bayreuth, Aug. 13, 14, 16, and 17, 1876, Richter conducting); *Parsifal,* Bühnenweihfestspiel (first titled *Parzival;* first sketch, 1857; 1865 and 1877–82; Festspielhaus, Bayreuth, July 26, 1882, Levi conducting).

FOR ORCH.: Overture in B-flat major, the *Paukenschlag-Ouvertüre* (Leipzig, Dec. 24, 1830; not extant); Overture to Schiller's *Die Braut von Messina* (1830; not extant); Overture in C major (1830; not extant); Overture in D minor (Leipzig, Dec. 25, 1831); Overture in E-flat major (1831; not extant); Overture to Raupach's *König Enzio,* in E minor (Leipzig, Feb. 17, 1832); Overture in C major (Leipzig, April 30, 1832); Symph. in C major (Prague, Nov. 1832); Symph. in E major (1834; fragment); Overture to Apel's *Columbus,* in E-flat major (Magdeburg, Feb. 16, 1835); Overture *Polonia,* in C major (begun 1832, finished 1836); Overture *Rule Britannia,* in D major (1837); music for Singer's *Die letzte Heidenverschwörung in Preussen* (1837; fragment); Overture to Goethe's *Faust* (1840; reorchestrated 1843–44; Dresden, July 22, 1844; revised and reorchestrated as *Eine Faust-Ouvertüre,* 1855; Zürich, Jan. 23, 1855); *Trauermusik* for Wind Instruments, after motifs from Weber's *Euryanthe* (Dresden, Dec. 14, 1844, for the reburial ceremony of Weber's remains); *Träume* for Violin and Small Orch. (Zürich, Dec. 23, 1857); *Huldigungsmarsch* (first version, for Military Band, Munich, Oct. 5, 1864; 2nd version, for Large Orch., completed by

Raff); *Siegfried Idyll* for Small Orch. (Tribschen, Dec. 25, 1870); *Kaisermarsch* (Berlin, May 5, 1871); *Grosser Festmarsch zur Eröffnung der hundertjährigen Gedenkfeier der Unabhängigkeitserklärung der vereinigten Staaten von Nord-Amerika* (also known as *The American Centennial March;* Philadelphia, May 10, 1876).—Also a projected orch. work in E minor (1830?; fragment); a scene for a pastoral play after Goethe's *Laune der Verliebten* (1830?); *Entreacte tragique* No. 1, in D major (1832?; fragment); *Entreacte tragique* No. 2, in C minor (1832?; sketch).

CHORAL WORKS: *Neujahrs-Kantate* for Mixed Chorus, and Orch. (Magdeburg, Dec. 31, 1834; arranged with a new text by Peter Cornelius as *Künstlerweihe*, and produced at Bayreuth on Wagner's 60th birthday, May 22, 1873); *Nicolai Volkshymne* for Tenor or Soprano, Mixed Chorus, and Orch. (Riga, Nov. 21, 1837); *Descendons, descendons* for Mixed Chorus, for *La Descente de la courtille* (1840); *Weihegruss zur feierlichten Enthüllung des Denkmals Königs Friedrich August I ("des Gerechten") von Sachsen (Der Tag erscheint)* for Men's Chorus a cappella (1843; as *Gesang zur Enthüllung des Denkmals Sr. Mag. des hochseligen Königs Friedrich August des Gerechten am 7. Juni 1843* for Men's Chorus and Brass; for the unveiling of the statue of King Friedrich August of Saxony, Dresden, June 7, 1843); *Das Liebesmahl der Apostel*, biblical scene for Men's Chorus and Orch. (Dresden, July 6, 1843); *Gruss seiner Treuen an Friedrich August den Geliebten (Im treuen Sachsenland)* for Men's Chorus a cappella (Dresden, Aug. 12, 1843; for the return from England of King Friedrich August of Saxony); *Hebt an den Sang (An Webers Grabe)* for Men's Chorus a cappella (Dresden, Dec. 15, 1844; for the reburial ceremony of Weber's remains); *Wahlspruch für die deutsche Feuerwehr (Treue sei unsre Zier)* (1869); *Kinderkatechismus zu Kosels Geburtstag* for 4 High Voices (1873; orchestrated 1874).—Also a scene and aria for Soprano and Orch. (1832; not extant); "Doch jetzt wohin ich blicke," aria for Tenor and Orch. for Marschner's opera *Der Vampyr* (1833); aria for Bass and Orch. for Weigl's opera *Die Schweizerfamilie* (1837; not extant); "Sanfte Wehmut will sich regen," aria for Bass and Orch. for Blum's singspiel *Marie, Max und Michel* (Riga, Sept. 1, 1837); "Norma il prédesse," aria for Bass, Male Chorus, and Orch. for Bellini's opera *Norma* (1839).

FOR PIANO: Sonata in D minor (1829; not extant); Sonata in F minor (1829; not extant); *Doppelfuge* (1831?; 103 bars, with corrections in Weinlig's hand); Sonata in B-flat major, for 4-hands (1831; not extant); Sonata in B-flat major, op. 1 (1831); *Fantasie* in F-sharp minor, op. 3 (1831); *Polonaise* in D major (1831–32); *Polonaise* in D major, for 4-hands, op. 2 (1832?); Sonata in A major, op. 4 (1832); *Albumblatt (Lied ohne Worte)* in E major (1840); Polka in G major (1853); *Eine Sonate für das Album von Frau M* [athilde]. *W* [esendonck]. in A-flat major (1853); *Züricher Vielliebschen: Walzer, Polka oder sonst was* in E-flat major (1854); *Albumblatt, In das Album der Fürstin M* [etternich]. in C major (1861); *Ankunft bei den schwarzen Schwänen (Album-*

blatt for Countess Pourtalès) in A-flat major (1861); *Albumblatt für Frau Betty Schott* in E-flat major (1875).

SONGS: *Sieben Kompositionen zu Goethes Faust*, op. 5: 1, *Lied der Soldaten (Burgen mit hohen Mauern);* 2, *Bauer unter der Linde (Der Schäfter putzte sich zum Tanz);* 3, *Branders Lied (Es war eine Ratt im Kellernest);* 4, *Lied des Mephistopheles (Es war einmal ein König);* 5, *Lied Des Mephistopheles (Was machst du mir vor Liebchens Tür);* 6, *Gretchen am Spinnrade (Meine Ruh ist hin);* 7, *Melodram Gretchens (Ach neige, du Schmerzenreiche)* (1831; revised 1832); *Glockentöne* (1832; not extant); *Carnevalslied* from *Das Liebesverbot* (1835–36); *Der Tannenbaum* (1838); *Tout n'est qu'images fugitives* (1839); *3 mélodies:* 1, *Dors, mon enfant;* 2, *Mignonne;* 3, *L'Attente* (1839); *Adieux de Marie Stuart* (1840); *Les Deux Grenadiers*, to the poem by Heine (1840); *Gruss seiner Treuen an Friedrich August den Geliebten (Im treuen Sachsenland)* (a version for Baritone; 1844); *5 Gedichte für eine Frauenstimme (Wesendonk-Lieder):* 1, *Der Engel* (1857); 2, *Stehe still* (1858); 3, *Im Treibhaus* (1858); 4, *Schmerzen* (1857); 5, *Träume* (1857); *Scherzlied für Louis Kraft* (1871); also *Extase* (1839; fragment) and *La Tombe dit à la rose* (1839; fragment).

ARRANGEMENTS AND EDITIONS: Piano score of Beethoven's 9th Symph. (1830; unpubl.); Piano score of J. Haydn's Symph. No. 103, in E-flat major (1831–32; not extant); Aria from Bellini's *Il Pirata*, as orchestrated from the piano score for use in *La Straniera* (1833); arrangement of vocal score for Donizetti's *La Favorite* (1840) and *L'elisir d'amore* (1840); arrangement of vocal score for Halévy's *La Reine de Chypre* (1841) and *Le Guitarrero* (1841); new trans. and new close to the overture of Gluck's *Iphigénie en Aulide* (1846–47; Dresden, Feb. 22, 1847); Palestrina's *Stabat Mater*, with indications for performance (Dresden, March 8, 1848); Mozart's *Don Giovanni*, version of dialogues and recitatives and, in parts, new trans. (Zürich, Nov. 8, 1850; not extant).

WRITINGS: Wagner devoted a large amount of his enormous productive activity to writing. Besides the dramatic works he set to music, he also wrote the following: *Leubald. Ein Trauerspiel* (1826–28); *Die hohe Braut, oder Bianca und Giuseppe*, 4-act tragic opera (prose scenario, 1836 and 1842; music composed by Johann Kittl and produced as *Bianca und Giuseppe, oder Die Franzosen vor Nizza* in Prague, 1848); *Männerlist grösser als Frauenlist, oder Die glückliche Bärenfamilie*, 2-act comic opera (libretto, 1837; some music completed); *Eine Pilgerfahrt zu Beethoven*, novella (1840); *Ein Ende in Paris*, novella (1841); *Ein glücklicher Abend*, novella (1841); *Die Sarazenin*, 3-act opera (prose scenario, 1841–42; verse text, 1843); *Die Bergwerke zu Falun*, 3-act opera (prose scenario for an unwritten libretto, 1841–42); *Friedrich I.*, play (prose scenario, 1846 and 1848); *Alexander der Grosse*, sketch for a play (184?; not extant); *Jesus von Nazareth*, play (prose scenario, 1849); *Achilleus*, sketch for a play (1849–50; fragments only); *Wieland der Schmied*, 3-act opera (prose scenario, 1850); *Die Sieger*, opera (prose sketch, 1856); *Luther or Luthers Hochzeit*, sketch for a play (1868); *Lust-*

spiel in 1 Akt (draft, 1868); *Eine Kapitulation: Lustspiel in antiker Manier,* poem (1870).

Wagner expounded his theories on music, politics, philosophy, religion, etc., in numerous essays; among the most important are *Über deutsches Musikwesen* (1840); *Die Kunst und die Revolution* (1849); *Das Kunstwerk der Zukunft* (1849); *Kunst und Klima* (1850); *Oper und Drama* (1851; revised 1868); *Eine Mitteilung an meine Freunde* (1851); *Über Staat und Religion* (1864); *Über das Dirigieren* (1869); *Beethoven* (1870); *Über die Anwendung der Musik auf das Drama* (1879); and *Religion und Kunst* (1880). The first ed. of his collected writings, *R. Wagner: Gesammelte Schriften und Dichtungen* (9 vols., Leipzig, 1871–73; vol. 10, 1883), was prepared by Wagner himself; W.A. Ellis ed. and trans. it into Eng. as *Richard Wagner's Prose Works* (8 vols., London, 1892–99). H. von Wolzogen and R. Sternfeld ed. the 5th ed. of the German original as *Sämtliche Schriften und Dichtungen,* adding vols. XI and XII (Leipzig, 1911); they also prepared the 6th ed., adding vols. XIII–XVI (Leipzig, 1914).

Wagner's important autobiography, *Mein Leben,* in 4 parts, was privately publ.; parts 1–3, bringing the narrative down to Aug. 1861, were publ. between 1870 and 1875; part 4, covering the years from 1861 to 1864, was publ. in 1881; these were limited eds., being distributed only among his friends; the entire work was finally publ. in an abridged ed. in Munich in 1911 (Eng. trans. as *My Life,* London and N.Y., 1911); the suppressed passages were first publ. in *Die Musik,* XXII (1929–30), and then were trans. into Eng. in E. Newman's *Fact and Fiction about Wagner* (London, 1931); a definitive ed., based on the original MS, was publ. in Munich in 1963, ed. by M. Gregor-Dellin.

Another important source is Wagner's diary-notebook, the so-called *Brown Book,* in which he made entries between 1865 and 1882; it was ed. by J. Bergfeld as *Richard Wagner: Das Braune Buch: Tagebuchaufzeichnungen, 1865–1882* (Zürich, 1975; Eng. trans. by G. Bird as *The Diary of Richard Wagner, 1865–1882; The Brown Book,* London, 1980). See also the diaries of Cosima Wagner; they have been ed. by M. Gregor-Dellin and D. Mack as *Cosima Wagner: Die Tagebücher, 1869–1877* (2 vols., Munich, 1976–77; Eng. trans. by G. Skelton as *Cosima Wagner's Diaries,* 2 vols., N.Y., 1977 and 1980).

Wagner, Robert, Austrian conductor and educator; b. Vienna, April 20, 1915. He studied piano, composition, and conducting at the Vienna Academy of Music; also attended the Univ. of Vienna (Ph.D., 1938). He conducted in Graz (1938–45) and at the Salzburg Mozarteum (1945–51); taught at the International Summer Academy. From 1951 to 1961 he was Generalmusikdirektor in Münster; then was appointed chief conductor of the Innsbruck Symph. (1960–66).

Wagner, Roger, French-born American choral conductor; b. Le Puy, Jan. 16, 1914. He was brought to the U.S. as a child; after studying for the priesthood in Santa Barbara, he returned to France to study organ with Marcel Dupré; he settled in Los Angeles in 1937 and became organist and choirmaster at St. Joseph's; also took courses in philosophy and French literature at the Univ. of Calif. in Los Angeles, and at the Univ. of Southern Calif. He studied conducting with Otto Klemperer and Bruno Walter, and orchestration with Lucien Caillet. In 1946 he founded the Roger Wagner Chorale, and toured extensively with it in the U.S., Canada, and Latin America. In 1965 he organized the Los Angeles Master Chorale and Sinfonia Orch., which opened its inaugural season on Jan. 27, 1965; he took his Master Chorale on a tour of the Soviet Union in 1974. He was head of the dept. of music at Marymount College in Los Angeles (1951–66); also taught at the Univ. of Calif. from 1959. He was knighted by Pope Paul VI in 1966.

Wagner, Siegfried, son of **Richard** and **Cosima Wagner;** b. Triebschen, June 6, 1869; d. Bayreuth, Aug. 4, 1930. His parents were married on Aug. 25, 1870, and Siegfried was thus legitimated. Wagner named the *Siegfried Idyll* for him, and it was performed in Wagner's house in Triebschen in 1870 on Christmas Day (Cosima Wagner's birthday). He attended a polytechnic school, but the lure of music proved overwhelming, and he took up studies under Julius Kniese and Humperdinck; began to compose; also embarked on a conductorial career; appeared as a symph. conductor in Germany, Austria, Italy, and England. In 1894 he was appointed assistant conductor in Bayreuth, and in 1896 became one of the regular conductors. He conducted from memory, and left-handed. In 1908 he succeeded his mother as general superviser of the Bayreuth Festivals. On Sept. 21, 1915, he married Winifred Williams, an adopted daughter of Karl Klindworth. In 1923–24 he visited the U.S. in order to raise funds for the reopening of the Bayreuth Festspielhaus, which had been closed in the course of World War I. In his career as a composer, he was greatly handicapped by the inevitable comparisons with his father. He wrote a symph. poem, *Sehnsucht,* after Schiller (1895); *Fahnenschwur* for Men's Chorus and Orch. (1914); a Violin Concerto (1915); chamber music and vocal works. But his main interest was in music drama; like his father, he wrote his own librettos.

WORKS: Operas: *Der Bärenhäuter* (Munich, Jan. 22, 1899); *Herzog Wildfang* (Munich, March 14, 1901); *Der Kobold* (Hamburg, Jan. 29, 1904); *Bruder Lustig* (Hamburg, Oct. 13, 1905); *Sternengebot* (Hamburg, Jan. 21, 1908); *Banadietrich* (Karlsruhe, Jan. 15, 1910); *An Allem ist Hütchen Schuld* (Stuttgart, Dec. 6, 1917); *Schwarzschwanenreich* (Karlsruhe, Nov. 5, 1918); *Sonnenflammen* (Karlsruhe, 1926); *Der Heidenkönig* (Cologne, Dec. 16, 1933); *Der Schmied von Marienburg* (Rostock, Dec. 16, 1923). His reminiscences, *Erinnerungen,* were publ. at Stuttgart in 1923.

Wagner, Wieland, grandson of **Richard Wagner,** great-grandson of **Franz Liszt;** b. Bayreuth, Jan. 5, 1917; d. Munich, Oct. 16, 1966. He received his general education in Munich, and devoted himself to the problem of modernizing the productions of Wagner's operas. When the Bayreuth Festivals were resumed in 1951, after World War II, Wieland Wagner assumed the tasks of its scenic director. Abandoning the luxuriant scenery of 19th-century opera, he emphasized the symbolic meaning of Wagner's music dramas, eschewing realistic effects, such as machinery propelling the Rhine maidens through the wavy gauze of the river, or the bright paper flames of the burning Valhalla. He even introduced Freudian sexual overtones, as in his production of *Tristan und Isolde,* where a phallic pillar was conspicuously placed on the stage.

Wagner, Winifred, British-born daughter-in-law of **Richard Wagner;** b. Hastings, England, 1897; d. Überlingen, on Lake Constance, March 5, 1980. Her father was a British journalist, her mother a Swedish actress; both her parents died when she was an infant, and she was adopted by the German musician Karl Klindworth. In 1915 she married Wagner's son **Siegfried,** and she became totally Germanized, Wagnerized, and Nazified. Adolf Hitler was a frequent guest at her house after she became a widow; her outspoken admiration for his person became public knowledge, so that newspapers openly speculated that the 2 might decide to get married in some barbarous Nordic ceremony. Her politics created a serious rift between her and her 2 sons, Wieland and Wolfgang, who, though loyal to the greatness of their grandfather, took a jaundiced view of Hitler's appropriation of Wagner's music as a Nazi symbol. Her daughter Friedekin was also militantly opposed to her idealization of Hitler. Winifred Wagner emigrated to the U.S. in 1939, and spent her last years of life with her daughter Verena, whose politics were neutral.

Wagner, Wolfgang, son of **Siegfried Wagner,** grandson of **Richard Wagner,** great-grandson of **Franz Liszt,** German opera producer, designer, and administrator; b. Bayreuth, Aug. 30, 1919. He studied music privately; then worked in various capacities at the Bayreuth Festivals and the Berlin State Opera. When the Bayreuth Festival was resumed in 1951, he directed its administration and participated in its productions as stage designer and director. After the death of his brother **Wieland** in 1966, he assumed the total direction of the Bayreuth Festivals and, for the first time since the early 1950s, invited other designers and directors to work at the festival. Like his brother, he departed radically from the traditional staging of the Wagner operas, and introduced a psychoanalytic and surrealist mise-en-scène, often with suggestive phallic and other sexual symbols in the décor.

Wagner-Régeny, Rudolf, Hungarian-German composer; b. Régen, Transylvania, Aug. 28, 1903; d. Berlin, Sept. 18, 1969. He studied piano with Robert Teichmüller at the Leipzig Cons., conducting and theory at the Hochschule für Musik in Berlin. He occupied various posts as theater and cinema conductor; was in the German army during World War II; director of the Hochschule für Musik in Rostock (1947–50); in 1950 was appointed director of the State Cons. in East Berlin.
WORKS: In 1934 he was commissioned (together with J. Weismann) by the Ministry of Culture to write new musical settings for *A Midsummer Night's Dream,* to replace Mendelssohn's score; his music was produced at Düsseldorf on June 6, 1935. Other works: operas: *Moschopulus* (Gera, 1928); *Der nackte König* (Gera, 1928); *Sganarelle* (Essen, 1929); *Die heilige Courtisane* (1932); *Der Günstling* (Dresden, Feb. 20, 1935); *Die Bürger von Calais* (Berlin, Jan. 28, 1939); *Johanna Balk* (Vienna, April 4, 1941); *Das Opfer* (1942); *Der Darmenwäscher* (1950); *Prometheus* (Kassel, Sept. 12, 1959); *Das Bergwerk zu Falun* (Salzburg, Aug. 16, 1961); several ballets, among them *Der zerbrochene Krug* (1937); *Mythologische Figurinen* for Orch. (Salzburg Festival of the International Society for Contemporary Music, June 21, 1952); *3 Movements* for Orch. (1952); *Einleitung und Ode* for Orch. (1967); String Quartet (1948); *Divertimento* for 3 Woodwinds and Timpani (1954); various pieces of chamber music.

Wakasugi, Hiroshi, Japanese conductor; b. Tokyo, May 31, 1935. He studied conducting with Hideo Saito and Nobori Kaneko; in 1967 he was awarded a prize by the Japanese Ministry of Culture. In 1975 he became conductor of the Kyoto Symph. Orch. In 1977 he assumed the post of chief conductor of the Cologne Radio Symph. Orch. In 1981 he became Generalmusikdirektor of the Deutsche Oper am Rhein in Düsseldorf. He was a guest conductor with the Berlin Phil., Vienna Symph., Dresden State Orch., and radio orchs. in Hamburg, Munich, Copenhagen, and other cities; was also a regular conductor with the Dresden State Opera. In 1981 he made his U.S. debut as a guest conductor of the Boston Symph.

Walcha, Helmut, noted German organist; b. Leipzig, Oct. 27, 1907. He lost his eyesight in his youth, but courageously persevered in his musical studies; took organ lessons with Ramin in Leipzig; then served as assistant organist at the Thomaskirche there (1926–29). In 1929 he settled in Frankfurt as a church organist; in 1933 he joined the faculty of the Frankfurt Cons.; in 1938 was named prof. at the Hochschule für Musik there. He retired in 1972. He was honored with a Festschrift for his 70th birthday (Frankfurt, 1978).

Walcker, Eberhard Friedrich, German organ builder; b. Cannstadt, near Stuttgart, July 3, 1794; d. Ludwigsburg, Oct. 2, 1872. Trained in the workshops of his father, a skilled organ builder, he set up for himself in Ludwigsburg in 1820 and won great renown by his excellent work and numerous inventions. After his death the business passed to his 5 sons: **Heinrich** (b. Oct. 10, 1828; d. Kirchheim, Nov. 24, 1903), **Friedrich** (b. Sept. 17, 1829; d. Dec. 6, 1895), **Karl** (b. March 6, 1845; d. Stuttgart, May 19, 1908), **Paul** (b. May 31, 1846; d. 1928), and **Eberhard** (b. April 8, 1850; d. 1927). In 1916 **Oscar Walcker** (son of Friedrich; b.

Jan. 1, 1869; d. Nov. 4, 1948) became head of the firm; in 1932 he effected a merger with the firm Ziegler of Steinsfurt (in 1910 a merger with the firm of W. Sauer of Frankfurt had taken place). His reminiscences, *Erinnerungen eines Orgelbauers,* were publ. in Kassel, 1948. The firm has built more than 2,500 organs; some of the largest are those in the Ulm Cathedral (1856; 95 speaking stops; rebuilt and enlarged in 1914 to 171); the Music Hall in Boston (now removed; 1863; 86 stops); the Paulskirche in Frankfurt (1833; 74 stops); St. Peter's in St. Petersburg (1840; 65 stops); the Reval Cathedral (1842; 65 stops); the Votivkirche in Vienna (1878; 61 stops); the Riga Cathedral (1885; 124 stops); St. Stephen's Cathedral in Vienna (1886; 90 stops); St. Michael's in Hamburg (1912; 154 stops, 5 manuals, and pedal).

Wald, Max, American composer and teacher; b. Litchfield, Ill., July 14, 1889; d. Dowagiac, Mich., Aug. 14, 1954. After studying in Chicago, he was active as a theater conductor; went to Paris in 1922 to study with Vincent d'Indy, and remained in Europe until 1936; then returned to Chicago and became chairman of the theory dept. of the Chicago Musical College.

WORKS: His symph. poem *The Dancer Dead* won 2nd prize in the National Broadcasting Co. competition in 1932, and was broadcast from N.Y. on May 1, 1932. His other works include *Retrospectives* for Orch. (Chicago, Jan. 15, 1926); *Comedy Overture* (1937); *In Praise of Pageantry* for Orch. (Chicago, Oct. 31, 1946); *October Moonlight,* song cycle for Soprano, String Quartet, Flute, Clarinet, and Piano (1937); 2 piano sonatas; other piano music; also an opera, *Mirandolina* (1936), and a light opera, *Gay Little World* (1942).

Waldstein, Ferdinand Ernst Gabriel, Graf von, amateur musician, friend of Beethoven; b. Dux, Bohemia, March 24, 1762; d. Vienna, Aug. 29, 1823. While serving his novitiate in the Deutscher Orden at Bonn (1787–88), he became acquainted with Beethoven, and on several occasions aided him materially, pretending that the sums were extra allowances from the Elector; after Beethoven's departure for Vienna, Waldstein introduced him in the circles of the aristocracy there; in later life their friendship seems to have cooled. Beethoven wrote a set of variations in C for piano, 4-hands, on a theme of Waldstein (publ. 1794), and later (1805) dedicated to him the great Sonata in C, op. 53. Waldstein also planned the *Ritter-Ballet* (1791), to which Beethoven wrote the music (score publ. 1872).

Waldteufel, (Charles-) Emile (the original surname of the family was **Lévy**), famous French composer of waltzes; b. Strasbourg, Dec. 9, 1837; d. Paris, Feb. 12, 1915. His parents ran a music school in Strasbourg; his father also directed a small dance band. Waldteufel took piano lessons at home with his mother; then began to study in earnest with Joseph Heyberger. In 1853 he entered the Paris Cons. in the classes of Louis-Antoine Marmontel and Adolphe Laurent, but left without completing his

courses and took a job with the piano manufacturer Scholtus; when he had time, he composed dance music for Paris salons. His first waltz, *Joies et peines,* which he publ. at his own expense in 1859, was an immediate success, and he became known in Paris high society. In 1865 he was appointed director of the court balls and chamber musician to the Empress Eugénie. In 1867 he publ. another successful waltz, with the German title *Vergissmeinnicht (Forget Me Not).* Then followed a series of waltzes that established his fame as a French counterpart to Johann Strauss, Jr.: *Manolo* (1873), *Mon rêve* (1877), *Pomone, Toujours ou jamais* (1877), *Les Sirènes* (1878), *Très jolie* (1878), *Pluie de diamants* (1879), *Dolores* (1880), and the most famous of them, *Les Patineurs* (1882). His dance music symbolized the "gai Paris" of his time as fittingly as the music of Johann Strauss reflected the gaiety of old Vienna. Waldteufel lived most of his life in Paris, but he also filled conducting engagements abroad, visiting London in 1885 and Berlin in 1889.

Walker, Edyth, American mezzo-soprano; b. Hopewell, N.Y., March 27, 1867; d. New York, Feb. 19, 1950. She studied singing with Aglaja Orgeni at the Dresden Cons.; made her debut as Fides in *Le Prophète* at the Berlin Opera on Nov. 11, 1894. She then became a member of the Vienna Court Opera, where she was engaged until 1903. She made her American operatic debut with the Metropolitan Opera as Amneris (N.Y., Nov. 30, 1903); remained with the company until 1906; then sang in Germany, particularly excelling in Wagnerian roles. In 1936 she returned to N.Y.

Walker, Frank, English musicologist; b. Gosport, Hampshire, June 10, 1907; d. (suicide) Tring, England, March 4, 1962. He studied telegraphy; in 1926 went to Rio de Janeiro as a representative of the Western Telegraph Co. From 1931 to 1943 he was in London; in 1944–45 he was in Naples, and later in Vienna, before returning to London. He contributed valuable articles on the composers of the Neapolitan School; wrote the books *Hugo Wolf* (London, 1951; 2nd ed., 1968) and *The Man Verdi* (London, 1962).

Walker, George, black American composer and pianist; b. Washington, D.C., June 27, 1922. He studied at Oberlin College (M.B., 1941); then entered the Curtis Inst. of Music in Philadelphia, where he studied piano with Rudolf Serkin, composition with Rosario Scalero and Gian Carlo Menotti, and chamber music with Piatigorsky and Primrose (Artist Diploma, 1945); also took piano lessons with Robert Casadesus in Fontainebleau in France (diploma, 1947); obtained his D.M.A. from the Eastman School of Music in Rochester, N.Y., in 1957. In 1957 he received a Fulbright fellowship for travel to Paris, where he took courses in composition with Nadia Boulanger. Returning to the U.S., he was also active as a teacher; held appointments at Dillard Univ. in New Orleans (1953), The New School for Social Research in N.Y., the Dalcroze School of Music (1961),

Smith College (1961–68), and the Univ. of Colorado (1968). In 1969 he was appointed a prof. at Rutgers Univ.; was chairman of the composition dept. there in 1974; in 1975 was named Distinguished Prof. at the Univ. of Delaware and adjunct prof. at the Peabody Inst. in Baltimore. In 1969 he received a Guggenheim fellowship; also held 2 Rockefeller fellowships for study in Italy (1971, 1975). In his music he maintains a median modern line without necessarily emphasizing the racial element.

WORKS: For Orch.: Trombone Concerto (1957); *Address* (1959; Mons, Belgium, Oct. 22, 1971); Symph. (1961); *Antiphonies* for Chamber Orch. (1968); *Variations* (1971); *Spirituals* (1974); Piano Concerto (1975); *Dialogues* for Cello and Orch. (1975–76); *Mass* for Soloists, Chorus, and Orch. (1976); *Overture: In Praise of Folly* (1980); Cello Concerto (N.Y., Jan. 14, 1982); *An Eastman Overture* (Washington, D.C., Jan. 15, 1983); *Serenata* for Chamber Orch. (1983); Violin Concerto (1984); *Sinfonia* (1984). Chamber music: 2 string quartets (1946, 1967); Cello Sonata (1957); Violin Sonata (1958); *Perimeters* for Clarinet and Piano (1966); *Music for 3* for Violin, Cello, and Piano (1970); *5 Fancies* for Clarinet and Piano, 4-hands (1974); *Music (Sacred and Profane)* for Brass (1975); 3 piano sonatas (1953, 1957, 1975); numerous vocal works, including *3 Lyrics* for Chorus (1958) and *3 Spirituals* for Medium Voice and Piano (1975).

Wallace, (William) Vincent, Irish composer; b. Waterford, March 11, 1812; d. Château de Bagen (Haute-Garonne), France, Oct. 12, 1865. The son of a bandmaster, Wallace was brought up in a musical atmosphere. He was 15 when the family moved to Dublin, and soon entered a professional career, playing violin in theater orchs. and organ in churches. One of his earliest compositions was *The Harp in the Air,* which later became famous when he incorporated it into his opera *Maritana.* In 1831 he married Isabella Kelly. He applied himself to the study of violin, and subsequently was able to give successful concerts. With his wife he traveled in Australia, South America, Mexico, and the U.S. Returning to Europe in 1844, he toured Germany; in 1845 he was in London, where he produced his opera *Maritana* (Drury Lane, Nov. 15, 1845), which obtained excellent success; it was followed by another opera, *Matilda of Hungary* (Drury Lane, Feb. 2, 1847), which was a failure. In 1850 he resumed his wanderings and revisited the U.S.; he declared his first marriage invalid, and married an American pianist, **Helen Stoepel.** Back in England, he produced several operas, of which *Lurline* (Covent Garden, Feb. 23, 1860) had tremendous acclaim; his other operas were *The Amber Witch* (Haymarket, Feb. 28, 1861), *Love's Triumph* (Covent Garden, Nov. 3, 1862), and *The Desert Flower* (Covent Garden, Oct. 12, 1863); several operas remain unfinished. His piano music enjoyed great vogue during his lifetime; some noted numbers are *La Gondola;* 2 Nocturnes; *Chant d'amour; Nocturne mélodique; Mélodie irlandaise; Music Murmuring in the Trees; Valse brillante de salon; Tarentelle,* etc.

Wallace, William, Scottish composer and music educator; b. Greenock, July 3, 1860; d. Malmesbury, Wiltshire, Dec. 16, 1940. The son of a surgeon, he studied medicine at Glasgow Univ. (M.D., 1888); specialized in ophthalmology in Vienna, and was employed in the Royal Army Medical Corps during World War I. He was self-taught in music; devoted much of his energy to the protection of the rights of British composers; served on the Composers' Copyright Committee of the Society of British Authors; also taught at the Royal Academy of Music.

WORKS: Symph. poems: *The Passing of Beatrice* (1892); *Amboss oder Hammer,* after Goethe (1896); *Sister Helen* (1899); *To the New Century* (1901); *William Wallace* (for the 6th centenary of the death of the national hero of Scotland, and namesake of the composer; 1905); *François Villon* (1909); a symph., *The Creation* (1899); suites for Orch.: *The Lady from the Sea,* after Ibsen (1892), and *Pelléas and Mélisande,* after Maeterlinck (1900); overture, *In Praise of Scottish Poesie* (1894); *The Massacre of the Macpherson,* burlesque cantata; song cycles: *Freebooter Songs* (with Orch.; his most famous work); *Lords of the Sea; Jacobite Songs.*

WRITINGS: *The Threshold of Music: An Inquiry into the Development of the Musical Sense* (1908); *The Musical Faculty: Its Origins and Processes* (1914); *Richard Wagner as He Lived* (1925); *Liszt, Wagner and the Princess* (1927).

Wallaschek, Richard, Austrian music theorist; b. Brünn, Nov. 16, 1860; d. Vienna, April 24, 1917. He studied law and philosophy in Vienna, Heidelberg, and Tübingen; from 1890 to 1895 was in London, engaged in research work; in 1896 joined the faculty of the Univ. of Vienna; wrote music criticism. He wrote a number of essays on esthetics, primitive music, and psychology of musical perception. His publications include *Asthetik der Tonkunst* (1886) and several books publ. in London, in Eng.: *On the Origin of Music* (1891); *Natural Selection and Music* (1892); *On the Difference of Time and Rhythm in Music* (1893); *Primitive Music: An Inquiry into the Origin and Development of Music, Song, Instruments, Dances and Pantomimes of Savage Races* (1893; German ed., enlarged, as *Anfänge der Tonkunst,* 1903; reprint, N.Y., 1970); *Das k. k. Hofoperntheater* (Vienna, 1909).

Wallenstein, Alfred, American cellist and conductor; b. Chicago, Oct. 7, 1898; d. New York, Feb. 8, 1983. His parents were of German and Austrian extraction; Wallenstein believed that he was a direct descendant of Albrecht von Wallenstein, the illustrious leader during the Thirty Years' War. The family moved to Los Angeles in 1905; Wallenstein took cello lessons with the mother of Ferde Grofé; as a young boy he began to be professionally engaged, playing in hotels and movie theaters; also gave public recitals advertised as "the wonder-boy cellist." He toured with a vaudeville circuit; then joined the San Francisco Symph. Orch. (1916-17); subsequently toured in South America with the troupe of Anna Pavlova, being featured as cello soloist to accompany her famous portrayal of the dying swan. In 1919 he became a member of the Los Angeles Phil.; in 1920 he went to Germany and took cello lessons with Julius Klengel in Leipzig; he also took some courses in medicine at the Univ. of Leipzig. On returning to the U.S., he was engaged in the cello section of the Chicago Symph. (1922–29), and also appeared with it as a soloist; from 1927–29 he served as head of the cello dept. of the Chicago Musical College. In 1929 Toscanini engaged him as first cellist with the N.Y. Phil.; it was Toscanini who urged Wallenstein to try his hand at conducting; he began his conducting career by leading classical programs over the radio. In 1933 he formed the Wallenstein Sinfonietta, giving regular Sunday broadcasts; an important feature was a series of performances of Bach's cantatas. He also programmed numerous premieres of works by contemporary composers; in appreciation of his work in this direction, he received several awards from various cultural organizations. After Toscanini resigned as music director of the N.Y. Phil. in 1936, Wallenstein also left his job as first cellist of the orch., and devoted himself exclusively to radio performances and guest conducting. In 1943 he was named conductor of the Los Angeles Phil., the first American to head a major symph. orch. From 1952–56 he also served as the music director at the Hollywood Bowl. In 1956 he made a tour of the Orient with the Los Angeles Phil. under the auspices of the State Dept.; after this tour he resigned as conductor of the Los Angeles Phil., but continued to give guest appearances with radio orchs. In 1968 he joined the faculty of the Juilliard School of Music in N.Y. as instructor in conducting. In 1979, at the age of 81, he made his last public appearance as a conductor, leading the Juilliard School Orch. in N.Y. Wallenstein never pretended to be a glamorous virtuoso of the baton, but he was a master builder of orchestral. organizations; more in praise than in dispraise, he was described as a "vertical" conductor who offered dispassionate rather than impassionate interpretations; but no one doubted his selfless devotion to music and musicians.

Walmisley, Thomas (Attwood), English organist and composer, son of **Thomas Forbes Walmisley;** b. London, Jan. 21, 1814; d. Hastings, Jan. 17, 1856. His father placed him under the guidance of Thomas Attwood, his own teacher. He showed remarkable progress, and became organist at Trinity and St. John's colleges at Cambridge at the age of 19. In 1836 he became a prof. of music; continued to study nonetheless; received his B.A. degree in 1838, M.A. in 1841, and Mus.D. in 1848. He wrote several odes and anthems for Trinity College. He enjoyed the reputation of being one of the best organists in England of his day. His anthems and church services were brought out by his father, who survived him by 10 years; they were included in the vol. *Cathedral Music* (1857).

Walmisley, Thomas Forbes, English organist and composer; b. London, May 22, 1783; d. there, July 23, 1866. He was a chorister at Westminster Abbey; studied organ with Thomas Attwood; then was organist at the Female Orphan Asylum (1810–14) and at St. Martin-in-the-Fields (1814–54). He was a popular composer of glees; publ. 3 sets containing 6 glees each; also *A Collection of Glees, Trios, Rounds and Canons* (1826); several single glees and songs.

Walsh, John, English music publisher; b. c.1666; d. London, March 13, 1736. From about 1690 he had his business at the sign of the "Golden Harp and Hoboy" in the Strand in London; in 1692 he was appointed "musical instrument maker in ordinary to His Majesty." He developed a flourishing trade, and achieved great renown; in England he was unquestionably the foremost publisher of music in his time. In 1711 he publ. Handel's *Rinaldo,* and remained Handel's principal publisher. He was succeeded by his son, also named **John Walsh** (b. London, Dec. 23, 1709; d. there, Jan. 15, 1766), who maintained the firm's high standards.

Walter, Bruno (real name, **B.W. Schlesinger**), eminent German conductor; b. Berlin, Sept. 15, 1876; d. Beverly Hills, Calif., Feb. 17, 1962. He studied at the Stern Cons. in Berlin with H. Ehrlich, L. Bussler, and R. Radecke. At the age of 17 he became opera coach at the Municipal Opera of Cologne; also did occasional conducting there; in the following year he was engaged as assistant conductor at the Hamburg Stadttheater, under Gustav Mahler; this contact was decisive in his career, and he became in subsequent years an ardent champion of Mahler's music; conducted the premieres of the posthumous Symph. No. 9 and *Das Lied von der Erde.* During the 1896–97 season Walter was engaged as 2nd conductor at the Stadttheater in Breslau; then became principal conductor in Pressburg, and in 1898 at Riga, where he conducted for 2 seasons. In 1900 he received the important engagement of conductor at the Berlin Opera under a 5-year contract; however, he left this post in 1901 when he received an offer from Mahler to become his assistant at the Vienna Opera. He established himself as an efficient opera conductor; also conducted in England (first appearance, March 3, 1909, with the Royal Phil. Society in London). He remained at the Vienna Opera after the death of Mahler; on Jan. 1, 1913, he became court conductor and music director in Munich; under his guidance, the Munich Opera enjoyed brilliant performances, particularly of Mozart's works. Seeking greater freedom for his artistic activities, he left Munich in 1922, and gave numerous performances as a guest conductor with European orchs.; conducted the series "Bruno Walter Concerts" with the Berlin Phil. from 1921 to 1933; from 1925 he also conducted summer concerts of the Salzburg Festival; his performances of Mozart's music there set a standard. He also appeared as pianist in Mozart's chamber works. On Feb. 15, 1923, he made his American debut with the N.Y. Symph. Society, and appeared with it again in 1924 and 1925. From 1925 to 1929 he was conductor of the Städtische Oper in Berlin-Charlottenburg; in 1929 he succeeded Furtwängler as conductor of the Gewandhaus Orch. in Leipzig, but continued to give special concerts in Berlin. On Jan. 14, 1932, he was guest conductor of the N.Y. Phil., acting also as soloist in a Mozart piano concerto; was reengaged during the next 3 seasons as associate conductor with Toscanini. He was also a guest conductor in Philadelphia, Washington, D.C., and Baltimore. With the advent of the Nazi regime in Germany his engagement with the Gewandhaus Orch. was canceled, and he was also prevented from continuing his orch. concerts in Berlin. He filled several engagements with the Concertgebouw in Amsterdam, and also conducted in Salzburg. In 1936 he was engaged as music director of the Vienna Opera; this was terminated with the annexation of Austria in 1938. Walter with his family then went to France, where he was granted French citizenship. After the outbreak of World War II he sailed for America, establishing his residence in California, and eventually becoming an American citizen. He was guest conductor with the NBC Symph. Orch. (1939); also conducted many performances of the Metropolitan Opera in N.Y. (debut in *Fidelio* on Feb. 14, 1941). From Feb. 1947 to 1949 he was conductor and musical adviser of the N.Y. Phil.; returned regularly as guest conductor until 1960; also conducted in Europe (1949–60), giving a farewell performance in Vienna with the Vienna Phil. in 1960. He subsequently lived in Beverly Hills.

Walter achieved the reputation of a perfect classicist among contemporary conductors; his interpretations of the masterpieces of the Vienna School are particularly notable. He is acknowledged to have been a foremost conductor of Mahler's symphs. His own compositions include 2 symphs.; *Siegesfahrt* for Solo Voices, Chorus, and Orch.; String Quartet; Piano Quintet; Piano Trio; several albums of songs. He publ. the books *Von den moralischen Kräften der Musik* (Vienna, 1935); *Gustav Mahler* (Vienna, 1936; Eng. trans., London, 1937; new trans. with additions, N.Y., 1958); *Theme and Variations*, an autobiography (N.Y., 1946); *Von der Musik und vom Musizieren* (Frankfurt, 1957; in Eng., N.Y., 1961).

Walter (Walther; real name, Blanckenmüller), Johann (Johannes), one of the earliest composers for the Lutheran church; b. Kahler, Thuringia, 1496; d. Torgau, March 25, 1570. He studied at the Univ. of Leipzig from 1521–25; during this time he entered the chapel of the Elector Friedrich the Wise of Saxony as a bass (the Elector divided his residence between Altenburg and Torgau). In 1524, at Wittenberg, he publ. the *Geystlich Gesangk-Buchleyn* for 3–5 Voices, the first Protestant singing book. In 1525 he was summoned to Wittenburg by Luther to assist in the composition and regulation of the German Mass. Shortly after the death of the Elector Friedrich (1525) his chapel was disbanded, and Walter became cantor of the Municipal Latin-School in Torgau and director of the Stadtkantorei (community choir) there (1526–48). In 1548 he was called upon by the new Elector of Saxony, Moritz, to organize the court chapel in Dresden, and remained

there as Kapellmeister until 1554, when he retired to Torgau on a pension. He publ. *Cantio septem vocum in laudem Dei omnipotentis et Evangelii ejus* (1544); *Magnificat 8 tonorum* (1557); *Ein newes christliches Lied* (1561); *Ein gar schöner geistlicher und christlicher Bergkreyen* (1561); *Lob und Preis der himmlischen Kunst Musica* (1564); *Das christlich Kinderlied Dr. Martin Luthers, "Erhalt uns Herr bei deinem Wort"* (1566); etc. The *Geystlich Gesangk-Buchleyn* was reprinted in vol. VII of the *Publikationen der Gesellschaft für Musikforschung* (1878); a list of other reprints is found in W. Ehmann's article "Johann Walter, Der erste Kantor der protestantischen Kirche," in *Musik und Kirche,* 6 (1934). Instrumental works by Walter were discovered in the library of the Thomasschule in Leipzig by B. Engelke in 1912 (examples in A. Schering's *Geschichte der Musik in Beispielen,* nos. 80 and 81). A complete edition of Walter's works was edited by Otto Schröder and Max Schneider in 6 vols. (Kassel, 1953–70).

Walter, Thomas, American clergyman and author of singing books; b. Roxbury, Mass., Dec. 13, 1696; d. there, Jan. 10, 1725. He was the son of a clergyman, and a nephew of Cotton Mather; educated at Harvard College (M.A., 1713); on Oct. 29, 1718, he was ordained; was assistant pastor to his father at Roxbury. With the aim of correcting what he described as "an horrid medley of confused and disorderly sounds" prevailing in the singing in New England churches, he publ. *The Grounds and Rules of Musick Explained; or, an Introduction to the Art of Singing by Note; Fitted to the meanest capacities* (Boston, 1721; several other eds. up to 1764). It was the 2nd singing book to be publ. in America, following that of John Tufts. He also publ. *The Sweet Psalmist of Israel* (1722).

Waltershausen, (Hermann) Wolfgang von, German composer and writer on music; b. Göttingen, Oct. 12, 1882; d. Munich, Aug. 13, 1954. He was a pupil of M.J. Erb in Strasbourg and of Ludwig Thuille in Munich, where he settled. In 1917 he established there a seminar for operatic dramaturgy; was a prof. and assistant director at the Akademie der Tonkunst (1920–23), then director (1923–33). After 1933 he remained in Munich as a private teacher; in 1948 established a seminar for all musical subjects in Munich. In his own music he adopted a neo-Romantic style, rather advanced in harmonic treatment.

WORKS: Operas: *Oberst Chabert,* to his own libretto after Balzac (Frankfurt, Jan. 18, 1912; also several productions in other German cities; his most successful work); *Else Klapperzehen* (Dresden, May 15, 1909); *Richardis,* a dramatic mystery (Karlsruhe, Nov. 14, 1915); *Die Rauensteiner Hochzeit* (Karlsruhe, 1919); *Die Gräfin von Tolosa* (1934); other works: *Apokalyptische Symphonie* (1924); symph. poem, *Hero und Leander* (1925); *Krippenmusik* for Chamber Orch., with Harpsichord (1926); an orch. partita (1928); piano pieces; songs. Having lost his right arm in a childhood accident, he developed a piano technique for the left hand alone, and publ. studies and transcriptions for left hand which he performed in public. He also publ. a number of valuable writings on music: *Musikalische Stillehre in Einzeldarstellungen* (1920–23); *Richard Strauss* (1921); *Musik, Dramaturgie, Erziehung* (1926); *Dirigenten-Erziehung* (1929); "Der stilistische Dualismus in der Musik des 19. Jahrhunderts," in the "Adler-Festschrift" (Vienna, 1930); *Die Kunst des Dirigierens* (1943; 2nd ed., 1954); also publ. a book of poetry (1952).

Walther, Johann Gottfried, noted German composer and musicographer; b. Erfurt, Sept. 18, 1684; d. Weimar, March 23, 1748. He was a pupil of J. Bernhard Bach at Erfurt, where he was made organist of the Thomaskirche in 1702; in 1707 he was town organist at Weimar, and music master to the children of the ducal family; from 1721, court musician. He stands next to Bach as a master of chorale-variations for organ. His greatest work is the *Musikalisches Lexikon oder Musikalische Bibliothek,* the first music encyclopedia of biography, bibliography, and terms (Leipzig, 1732; facsimile ed., Kassel, 1953, by R. Schaal, with bibliographical notes); he had previously publ. the 64-page *Alte und neue musikalische Bibliothek, oder Musikalisches Lexikon* (1728; only entries under letter A printed, as a preliminary to the main work). His publ. musical compositions include: *Clavierconcert* (unaccompanied; 1741); Prelude and Fugue (1741); 4 chorale-variations (*Jesu meine Freude, Meinen Jesum lass' ich nicht, Allein Gott in der Höh' sei Ehr', Wie soll ich dich empfangen*); many chorale-variations, preludes, fugues, and toccatas, in MS; also 5 collections of "Choralbearbeitungen" by other composers. His organ works were edited by M. Seiffert in vols. 26 and 27 of Denkmäler Deutscher Tonkunst (with biographical sketch). His *Praecepta der musikalischen Composition* was publ. at Leipzig in 1955, edited by Peter Benary.

Walther, Johann Jakob, notable German violinist and composer; b. Witterda, near Erfurt, 1650; d. Mainz, Nov. 2, 1717. He was concertmaster at the Electoral Court of Saxony in Dresden (from 1674), and Italian secretary, in charge of the correspondence with Rome, to the Elector of Mainz (from 1681); in 1693 he was designated as *Doctor.* He publ. *Scherzi da violino solo,* with Continuo (1676; reprinted in *Das Erbe deutscher Musik,* 17); *Hortulus Chelicus, uni violino, duabus, tribus et quatuor subinde chordis simul sonantibus* (1688; 2nd ed. as *Wohlgepflanzter violinischer Lustgarten,* 1694).

Walther von der Vogelweide. See **Vogelweide, Walther von der.**

Walthew, Richard Henry, English composer and pedagogue; b. London, Nov. 4, 1872; d. East Preston, Sussex, Nov. 14, 1951. He studied with Parry at the Royal College of Music (1890–94); after a directorship of the Passmore Edwards Settlement Place (1900–1904), he was appointed instructor of the op-

era class at the Guildhall School of Music; in 1907 became a prof. of music at Queen's College; also conducted provincial orchs. His works include 2 operettas: *The Enchanted Island* (London, May 8, 1900) and *The Gardeners* (London, Feb. 12, 1906); cantatas: *Ode to a Nightingale* and *The Pied Piper of Hamelin;* Piano Concerto; Piano Quintet; Piano Quartet; 2 piano trios; Violin Sonata; vocal quartets, with piano; songs. He was the author of *The Development of Chamber Music* (1909).

Walton, Sir William (Turner), eminent British composer; b. Oldham, Lancashire, March 29, 1902; d. Ischia, Italy, March 8, 1983. Both his parents were professional singers, and Walton himself had a fine singing voice as a youth; he entered the Cathedral Choir School at Christ Church, Oxford, and began to compose choral pieces for performance. Sir Hugh Allen, organist of New College, advised him to develop his interest in composition, and sponsored his admission to Christ Church at an early age; however, he never graduated, and instead began to write unconventional music in the manner that was fashionable in the 1920s. His talent manifested itself in a string quartet he wrote at the age of 17, which was accepted for performance at the first festival of the International Society for Contemporary Music in 1923. In London he formed a congenial association with the Sitwell family of quintessential cognoscenti and literati who combined a patrician sense of artistic superiority with a benign attitude toward the social plebs; they also provided Walton with residence at their manor in Chelsea, where he lived off and on for some 15 years. Fascinated by Edith Sitwell's oxymoronic verse, Walton set it to music bristling with novel jazzy effects in brisk, irregular rhythms and modern harmonies; Walton was only 19 when he wrote it. Under the title *Façade,* it was first performed in London in 1923, with Edith Sitwell herself delivering her doggerel with a megaphone; as expected, the show provoked an outburst of feigned indignation in the press and undisguised delight among the young in spirit. But Walton did not pursue the path of facile hedonism so fashionable at the time; he soon demonstrated his ability to write music in a Classical manner in his fetching concert overture *Portsmouth Point,* first performed at the Zürich Festival in 1926, and later in the comedy-overture *Scapino.* His biblical oratorio *Belshazzar's Feast,* written in 1931, reveals a deep emotional stream and nobility of design that places Walton directly in line from Handel and Elgar among English masters. His symph. works show him as an inheritor of the grand Romantic tradition; his concertos for violin, for viola, and for cello demonstrate an adroitness in effective instrumental writing. Walton was a modernist in his acceptance of the new musical resources, but he never deviated from fundamental tonality and formal clarity of design. Above all, his music was profoundly national, unmistakably British in its inspiration and content. Quite appropriately, he was asked to contribute to two royal occasions: he wrote *Crown Imperial March* for the coronation of King George

VI in 1937 and *Orb and Sceptre* for that of Queen Elizabeth II in 1953. He received an honorary doctorate from Oxford Univ. in 1942; was knighted in 1951. He spent the last years of his life on the island of Ischia off Naples with his Argentinian-born wife, Susana Gil Passo.

WORKS: FOR THE STAGE: Opera, *Troilus and Cressida,* after Chaucer (London, Dec. 3, 1954); *The Bear,* "an extravaganza" in one act, after a comedy by Chekhov (Aldeburgh Festival, June 3, 1967); *Façade,* "an entertainment" for Declamation, Flute, Clarinet, Saxophone, Trumpet, Cello, and Percussion, to texts in blank verse by Edith Sitwell (first perf. privately at the Sitwell home in London, Jan. 24, 1922; it had its first public hearing in London, on June 12, 1923; it was revised in 1942, scored for an augmented ensemble); *The Wise Virgins,* ballet arranged from 6 pieces by Bach (London, April 24, 1940); *The Quest,* ballet (1943).

FOR ORCH.: *Portsmouth Point,* concert overture (Zürich Festival of the International Society for Contemporary Music, June 22, 1926); *Siesta* (1926); *Sinfonia concertante* for Piano and Orch. (London, Jan. 5, 1928); Viola Concerto (London, Oct. 3, 1929, Paul Hindemith, soloist; revised for a reduced orch. accompaniment, and first perf. in this new version in London, Jan. 18, 1962); Symph. No. 1 (London, Nov. 6, 1935); *Crown Imperial,* coronation march for King George VI (Westminster Abbey, London, May 12, 1937); 2 orch. suites from *Façade:* No. 1 (Siena Festival of the International Society for Contemporary Music, Sept. 14, 1928) and No. 2 (N.Y., March 30, 1938); Violin Concerto (Cleveland, Dec. 7, 1939; Jascha Heifetz, soloist); *Scapino,* comedy-overture (Chicago, April 3, 1941); *Spitfire: Prelude and Fugue,* glorifying the famous British combat plane (1942); *Orb and Sceptre,* coronation march for Elizabeth II (Westminster Abbey, London, June 2, 1953); *Johannesburg Festival Overture* (Johannesburg, South Africa, Sept. 25, 1956); Cello Concerto (Boston, Jan. 25, 1957; Piatigorsky, soloist); *Partita* (Cleveland, Jan. 30, 1958); *Fanfare* for the Queen's entrance at the NATO Parliamentary Conference (London, June 5, 1959); Symph. No. 2 (Edinburgh, Sept. 2, 1960); *Variations on a Theme by Hindemith* (London, March 8, 1963); *Capriccio Burlesco* (N.Y., Dec. 7, 1968); *Improvisations on an Impromptu of Britten* (San Francisco, Jan. 14, 1970); Sonata for String Orch. (1972; orchestration of the 1947 String Quartet); *Varii Capricci* (London, May 4, 1976; orchestration of the *5 Bagatelles* for Guitar); *Prologo e Fantasia* (London, Feb. 20, 1982).

VOCAL WORKS: *Belshazzar's Feast,* oratorio for Baritone, Chorus, and Orch. (Leeds Festival, Oct. 8, 1931); *In Honour of the City of London* for Chorus and Orch. (Leeds Festival, 1937); *Te Deum* for the coronation of Queen Elizabeth II (London, June 2, 1953); *Gloria* for Vocal Soloists, Mixed Chorus, and Orch. (Liverpool, Nov. 24, 1961); *A Song for the Lord Mayor's Table* for Soprano and Piano (London, July 18, 1962); *The Twelve* for Chorus and Organ (Oxford, May 16, 1965); *Missa Brevis* for Double Mixed Chorus and Organ (Coventry, April 10, 1966); *Cantico del Sole* for Chorus a cappella (1974).

CHAMBER MUSIC: Piano Quartet (1918; revised 1974); String Quartet (1922; Salzburg Festival of the International Society for Contemporary Music, Aug. 4, 1923); *Toccata* for Violin and Piano (1923); String Quartet (1947); Violin Sonata (1949); *5 Bagatelles* for Solo Guitar (1972).

FILM MUSIC: *Escape Me Never* (1934); *As You Like It* (1936); *Stolen Life* (1939); *Major Barbara* (1941); *Henry V* (1944); *Hamlet* (1947); *Richard III* (1954); etc.; several suites have been drawn from these scores.

Waltz, Gustavus, German bass; place and date of birth unknown; d. London, c.1759; was a member of Handel's household in London, serving as a majordomo. He appeared on the London stage in 1732 in Handel's *Acis and Galatea* and subsequently sang in Handel's oratorios. He is chiefly celebrated because of the reported acrid comment of Handel on Gluck: "He knows no more of counterpoint than my cook, Waltz."

Wambach, Emile, Belgian composer; b. Arlon, Luxembourg, Nov. 26, 1854; d. Antwerp, May 6, 1924. He studied with Benoit, Mertens, and Callaerts at the Antwerp Cons.; in 1913 became its director. He wrote music in the National Flemish style, following the model of Benoit. He wrote the Flemish opera *Nathans Parabel;* 4 oratorios: *Mozes op den Nijl* (1881); *Yolande* (1884); *Blancefloer* (1889); *Jeanne d'Arc* (1909); choral works; piano pieces; songs.

Wand, Günter, German conductor; b. Elberfeld, Jan. 7, 1912. He studied at the Cologne Cons. and at the Munich Academy of Music. In 1944–45 he conducted the Mozarteum Orch. in Salzburg. In 1947 he became Generalmusikdirektor of the Gürzenich Orch. of Cologne, a position he held until 1974. He also headed the conducting classes at the Cologne Cons. He eventually settled in Bern, Switzerland, where he led the local orch. society and toured widely with it; in 1968 he took it on a concert tour in Japan.

Wanhal (Vanhall), Johann Baptist, Bohemian composer; b. Nechanicz, Bohemia, May 12, 1739; d. Vienna, Aug. 20, 1813. His musical ability brought him the patronage of Countess Schaffgotsch, who enabled him to study in Vienna with Dittersdorf; another patron, Baron Riesch, sent him to Italy for further study. He settled in Vienna. An extremely prolific composer, he wrote a great number of piano pieces, which enjoyed considerable popularity among amateurs. He also composed an enormous amount of instrumental music (about 73 authenticated symphs. and numerous string quartets); about 60 masses; 2 Requiems; over 60 offertories. Among his publ. works are 12 symphs. for strings, 2 oboes, and 2 horns; 12 string quartets; 12 trios for 2 violins and cello; quartets (concerti) for piano and strings; quartets for piano, flute, violin, and cello; piano trios; 5 piano sonatas for 4-hands, and 6 for 2-hands; violin duos; 6 violin sonatas, with piano; characteristic sonatas (*Militaire, The Battle of Würzburg, The Battle of Trafalgar*); many piano sonatinas; 70 books of piano variations; fantasias, dances, and other piano pieces; fugues, preludes, etc., for organ; etc.

Wannenmacher (Latinized as **Vannius**), **Johannes,** German composer; b. Neuenburg am Rhein, c.1485; d. Interlaken, 1551. He was cantor at Bern, Switzerland, in 1510, and at Freiburg im Breisgau in 1513; because of his inclinations toward Lutheranism, he was obliged to leave Germany; settled in Interlaken in 1531 as town clerk, and remained there until his death. He was greatly esteemed in his time as a fine polyphonist; Glareanus cites a motet for 4 voices in the *Dodecachordon.* Wannenmacher's *An Wasserflüssen Babylon* for 3–6 Voices was publ. in Ott's *Liederbuch* (1544); some German songs by him were publ. posthumously.

Ward, David, Scottish bass; b. Dumbarton, July 3, 1922; d. Dunedin, July 16, 1983. He studied at the Royal College of Music in London; later had voice training with Hans Hotter in Munich. In 1953 he made his operatic debut at the Sadler's Wells Opera in London; in 1960 he joined the Royal Opera, Covent Garden. He was equally proficient in dramatic, heroic, and buffo roles. In 1972 he was made a Commander of the Order of the British Empire.

Ward, John, English composer; b. Canterbury (baptized, Sept. 8) 1571; d. c.1638. He was in the service of Sir Henry Fanshawe, to whom he dedicated *The First Set of English Madrigals* (London, 1613); wrote services and anthems, and pieces for the virginal. His madrigals were reprinted in vol. XIX of *The English Madrigal School.*

Ward, Robert, American composer; b. Cleveland, Sept. 13, 1917. He studied at the Eastman School of Music in Rochester, N.Y., with Howard Hanson and Bernard Rogers (B.Mus., 1939) and at the Juilliard School of Music in N.Y. with Frederick Jacobi (composition) and Albert Stoessel (conducting); obtained his M.A. in 1946; subsequently he taught at the Juilliard School (1946–56); served as vice-president and managing editor of the Galaxy Music Corp.; then was a prof. of music at the North Carolina School of the Arts. As a composer, he has evolved an effective idiom, modern but not aggressively so; he particularly excels in dramatic and compact stage works on American subjects.

Warfield, Sandra, American mezzo-soprano; b. Kansas City, Mo., Aug. 6, 1929. She studied voice in Kansas City, and later in Milan; returning to the U.S., she won first prize in the Metropolitan Opera Auditions of the Air, which led to her debut in N.Y. on Nov. 20, 1953, in a minor role in *Le nozze di Figaro;* later she sang more important roles at the Metropolitan, and also appeared with other American opera houses, and in Europe. Married to the noted American tenor **James McCracken,** she sang numerous concert duos with him. Among her most successful operatic roles are Dalila in *Samson et*

Dalila, Amneris in *Aida,* and Carmen.

Warfield, William, black American baritone; b. Helena, Ark., Jan. 22, 1920. He studied at the Eastman School of Music in Rochester, N.Y., graduating in 1946; sang in opera and musical comedy; gave his first N.Y. song recital on March 19, 1950, with excellent critical acclaim. He subsequently toured Europe in the role of Porgy in the production of Gershwin's *Porgy and Bess.* He married the soprano **Leontyne Price** in 1952 (divorced in 1972). In 1974 he was appointed a prof. of music at the Univ. of Illinois.

Waring, Fred, famous American conductor of popular music, and an inventor of sundry kitchen appliances; b. Tyrone, Pa., June 9, 1900; d. Danville, Pa., July 29, 1984. He learned music at his mother's knee, and a sense of moral rectitude was inculcated in him by his father, a banker who gave speeches at spiritual revivals and temperance meetings. Fred Waring attended Pa. State Univ., where he studied engineering and architecture; he retained his love for gadgets throughout his musical career, and in 1937 patented the Waring Blendor, for whipping food or drinks to a foam; another invention was a traveling iron. He took up banjo playing at 16, and organized a quartet which he called The Banjazzatra. He also played in the Boy Scouts Drum Corps and sang at Prohibition rallies. He acquired fame with his own band, The Pennsylvanians, which played on national tours at concert halls, hotels, and college campuses; the group was particularly successful on radio programs sponsored by tobacco companies and the Ford Motor Co. His repertoire consisted of wholesome American songs, many of them composed by himself. Among his soloists on special programs were Bing Crosby, Hoagy Carmichael, Irving Berlin, and Frank Sinatra. Waring had a natural streak for publicity; he once bet that he could lead a bull into a Fifth Avenue china shop, and succeeded, without breaking a single piece of crockery. He was a friend of President Dwight Eisenhower. In Dec. 1983 President Ronald Reagan awarded Waring the Congressional Gold Medal. He continued to lead youth choral groups, giving a concert at Pa. State Univ. a day before he suffered a stroke, and 2 days before his death.

Warlock, Peter. See **Heseltine, Philip.**

Warner, Sylvia Townsend, English novelist and writer on music; b. London, Dec. 6, 1893; d. Maiden Newton, Dorset, May 1, 1978. Apart from her well-known novels and books of poetry, she publ. valuable papers in music history, among them *The Point of Perfection in 16th Century Notation* (1919); was one of the editors of the collection *Tudor Church Music.* She also composed a rhapsody for Voice and String Quartet, *Memorial;* and a song cycle, *Children of the Earth.*

Warrack, John, English writer on music; b. London, Feb. 9, 1928. He studied at Winchester College; then took up oboe and composition at the Royal College of Music; subsequently played oboe in several ensembles. In 1953 he became music editor of the Oxford Univ. Press; in 1954 he joined the staff of the *Daily Telegraph*, where he was a music critic; then was chief music critic of the *Sunday Telegraph* (1961–72). In 1977 he became director of the Leeds Festival. He contributed numerous articles and reviews to *Opera* and *Gramophone*. His biography of Weber is the standard modern source.

WRITINGS: *Six Great Composers* (London, 1958); co-ed. (with H. Rosenthal), *The Concise Oxford Dictionary of Opera* (London, 1964; 2nd ed., revised, 1979); *Carl Maria von Weber* (London, 1968; also in German, 1972; 2nd ed., revised, London, 1976); *Tchaikovsky: Symphonies and Concertos* (London, 1969; 2nd ed., revised, 1974); *Tchaikovsky* (London, 1973); *Tchaikovsky: Ballet Music* (London, 1978).

Warren, Elinor Remick, American pianist and composer of songs; b. Los Angeles, Feb. 23, 1905. She was educated at the Westlake School for Girls and at Mills College; publ. her first composition while still in high school; later studied in N.Y. with Frank La Forge, Paolo Gallico, and Clarence Dickinson; appeared as a pianist.

WORKS: *The Harp Weaver* for Women's Chorus, Baritone, Harp, and Orch.; *The Passing of King Arthur* for Orch.; *Singing Earth,* song cycle for Voice, and Piano or Orch.; *Abram in Egypt,* cantata (1961); *Good Morning America!* for Narrator, Chorus, and Orch. (Calif. State Univ., Fullerton, Nov. 21, 1976); Symph. (1970); many songs (*White Horses of the Seas, Children of the Moon, My Lady Lo Fu, We Two, Christmas Candle,* etc.).

Warren, George William, American organist and composer of sacred music; b. Albany, N.Y., Aug. 17, 1828; d. New York, March 17, 1902. He was self-taught; held positions as a church organist in Albany (1846–60), in Brooklyn (1860–70), and at St. Thomas's in N.Y. (from 1870 until his death). He publ. *Warren's Hymns and Tunes, as Sung at St. Thomas Church* (1888); also wrote salon piano music; his "Marche di Bravura," *The Andes,* was the rage of the salons in 1862–63, especially in a 2-piano arrangement made by Louis Moreau Gottschalk. He is remembered chiefly for his tune *National Hymn,* to which *God of Our Fathers* is sung.

Warren, Harry, American composer of popular songs; b. Brooklyn, Dec. 24, 1893; d. Los Angeles, Sept. 22, 1981. His real name was **Salvatore Guaragna;** he was the 11th child in a proliferating but impoverished Italian family; his father was a boot maker who, like most Brooklyn-born Italians, also loved music. Harry Warren dropped out of high school to play drums with a touring carnival company; with the money earned, he bought himself a ramshackle old piano and became engaged as a movie pianist for the silent screen. Endowed with a God-given gift of melody, he turned out, without benefit of academic training, a slew of irresistible tunes, some of which became perennial favorites. His early hits were *Rose of the Rio Grande, Back Home in Pasadena,* and *So This Is Venice* (Venice, Calif., that is). In 1932 Salvatore Guaragna, now advantageously transfigured into Harry Warren, moved to the center of musical glamour, Hollywood, and unleashed an avalanche of hits for films. Among his greatest songs were *42nd Street, Wonder Bar, Night in Rio, Weekend in Havana, Springtime in the Rockies, Sweet Rosie O'Grady, Lullaby of Broadway, Chattanooga Choo-Choo, Topeka and the Sante Fe, You Must Have Been a Beautiful Baby, Jeepers Creepers, I Found a Million Dollar Baby in a 5 & 10 Cent Store, Shuffle Off to Buffalo, We're in the Money,* and *Cheerful Little Earful.*

Warren, Leonard, outstanding American baritone; b. New York, April 21, 1911; d. there, March 4, 1960, on the stage of the Metropolitan Opera House while singing the role of Don Carlo during a performance of *La forza del destino.* The original family name was Warenoff; it was Americanized as Warren when his father came from Russia to the U.S. His father was in the fur business in N.Y., and Leonard Warren helped him in his work; in 1935 he joined the chorus of the Radio City Music Hall; he also studied voice with Sidney Dietch and Guiseppe De Luca. In 1938 he won the Metropolitan Opera Auditions of the Air and was granted a stipend to study in Italy, where he took voice lessons with Pais and Piccozi. Returning to America, he made his debut at the Metropolitan Opera in excerpts from *La Traviata* and *Pagliacci* during a concert in N.Y. on Nov. 27, 1938; his formal operatic debut took place there on Jan. 13, 1939, when he sang Paolo in *Simon Boccanegra.* He quickly advanced in the favor of the public, eventually assuming a leading place among the noted baritones of his time. He also sang in San Francisco, Chicago, Canada, and South America. He appeared at La Scala in Milan in 1953; in 1958 he made a highly successful tour of the Soviet Union. His last complete performance at the Metropolitan Opera was as Simon Boccanegra on March 1, 1960, 3 days before his tragic death. He was particularly acclaimed as one of the foremost interpreters of the great Verdi baritone roles; he also sang the parts of Tonio in *Pagliacci,* Escamillo in *Carmen,* and Scarpia in *Tosca.* During his stay at the Metropolitan, he gave altogether 416 performances in N.Y. and 206 on tour, singing 26 different roles. He collapsed while singing the aria "Urna fatale dal mio destino," underlining the tragic irony of the words, and died of a cerebral hemorrhage backstage. Of Jewish parentage, he converted to Catholicism upon his marriage to an Italian woman. He was reputed to be a person of an intractable character, who always tried to impose his will on stage designers, managers, and even conductors, in the matters of production, direction, and the tempi. He caused pain, a colleague said, but he had a great voice.

Wartel, Pierre-François, noted French singer and

teacher; b. Versailles, April 3, 1806; d. Paris, Aug. 3, 1882. He studied at the Paris Cons. with Nourrit; was engaged as a tenor at the Paris Opéra (1831–46), but became known chiefly as an experienced singing teacher; Christine Nilsson was one of his many famous pupils. He also gave song recitals, in which he performed songs by Schubert for the first time in France. His wife, **Atale Thérèse Annette Wartel** (née **Adrien**; b. Paris, July 2, 1814; d. there, Nov. 6, 1865), was a talented pianist; she also composed piano studies and other pieces.

Wasielewski, Wilhelm Joseph von, eminent German music scholar; b. Gross-Leesen, near Danzig, June 17, 1822; d. Sondershausen, Dec. 13, 1896. He studied violin as a private pupil of Ferdinand David in Leipzig, and also had lessons with Mendelssohn (1843–46). He joined the Gewandhaus Orch. (until 1850); went to Düsseldorf, where he was concertmaster under Schumann (1850–52); then was choral conductor in Bonn (1852–55); in 1855 he settled in Dresden as a writer, in which capacity he greatly distinguished himself. In 1869 he became town music director in Bonn, remaining in that position until 1884, when he went to Sondershausen.

Wassermann, Heinrich Joseph, German conductor and composer; b. Schwarzbach, near Fulda, April 3, 1791; d. Riehen, near Basel, Sept. 3, 1838. He was a pupil of Spohr; became an orch. conductor in Switzerland. He wrote a *Thème original varié* for String Quartet; Quartet for Flute, Violin, Viola, and Cello; *Air varié* for Bassoon and String Orch.; *Divertissement* (on the Tyrolian "Alma Lied") for Violin and Orch.; a number of orch. dances; pieces for guitar.

Watanabe, Akeo, Japanese conductor; b. Tokyo, June 5, 1919. He studied conducting with Joseph Rosenstock, who was then resident in Japan; in 1950 went to the U.S. and took a course in conducting with Jean Morel at the Juilliard School of Music in N.Y.; returning to Japan, he founded in 1956 the Nippon Phil. Orch., which he led until 1968; he also made guest appearances as a conductor in the U.S. and in Europe. In 1972 he was appointed music director of the Tokyo Metropolitan Orch.

Waters, Edward N(eighbor), eminent American musicologist; b. Leavenworth, Kans., July 23, 1906. He studied piano and theory at the Eastman School of Music in Rochester, N.Y. (B.M., 1927; M.M. in musicology, 1928). In 1931 he joined the staff of the Music Division of the Library of Congress in Washington, D.C.; from 1972 to 1976 served as chief of the Music Division; was president of the Music Library Assoc. (1941–46); was program annotator for the concerts of the National Symph. Orch. in Washington (1934–43); was editor of *Notes*, publ. by the Music Library Assoc. (1963–66); also wrote many articles and book reviews for professional journals. The Cleveland Inst. of Music conferred upon him the honorary degree of D.Mus. (1973). He is the author

of a definitive biography of Victor Herbert (N.Y., 1955).

Watson, Claire, American soprano; b. New York, Feb. 3, 1927. She studied voice in N.Y. with Elisabeth Schumann and Sergius Kagen; received further training in Vienna. She made her operatic debut in Graz in 1951; was a member of the Frankfurt Opera (1956–58) and the Bavarian State Opera in Munich (from 1958); made guest appearances at the Salzburg Festival and with the opera houses of London, Vienna, Milan, Rome, Chicago, and San Francisco. She retired in 1976.

Watts, André, brilliant American pianist; b. in a U.S. Army camp in Nuremberg, June 20, 1946, of a Hungarian mother, Maria Alexandra Gusmits, and a black American soldier, Sergeant Herman Watts, stationed in Germany. The family moved to Ulm, where André's father was transferred. His mother could play piano, and she gave him his early lessons. The family returned to the U.S., making their home in Philadelphia. There André Watts was enrolled in the Philadelphia Musical Academy as a pupil of Genia Robiner, Doris Bawden, and Clement Petrillo; at the age of 9 he made his first public appearance playing the Haydn Concerto in D major at a children's concert of the Philadelphia Orch. His parents were divorced in 1962, but his mother continued to guide his studies. At 14 he played César Franck's *Symphonic Variations* with the Philadelphia Orch.; at 16 he became an instant celebrity when he played Liszt's First Piano Concerto at one of the televised Young People's Concerts with the N.Y. Phil., conducted by Leonard Bernstein, on Jan. 15, 1963. His youth and the fact that he was partly black contributed to his success, but it was the grand and poetic manner of his virtuosity that conquered the usually skeptical press. Still, he insisted on completing his academic education. In 1969 he joined the class of Leon Fleisher at the Peabody Cons. of Music in Baltimore, obtaining his Artist's Diploma in 1972. In the meantime he developed an international career. He made his European debut as soloist with the London Symph. Orch. on June 12, 1966; then played with the Concertgebouw Orch. in Amsterdam. On Oct. 26, 1966, he played his first solo recital in N.Y., inviting comparisons in the press with the great piano virtuosos of the past. In 1967 he was soloist with the Los Angeles Phil. under Zubin Mehta on a tour of Europe and Asia. On his 21st birthday he played the 2nd Piano Concerto of Brahms with the Berlin Phil. On Aug. 14, 1970, he revisited his place of birth and played a solo recital with a success that was made all the more sensational because he was a native son, albeit not of the native race. He also became a favorite at important political occasions; he played at Richard Nixon's inaugural concert at Constitution Hall in 1969, at the coronation of the Shah of Iran, and at a festive celebration of the President of the Congo. In 1973 he toured Russia. On Nov. 28, 1976, he played a solo recital on network television, the first to be accorded such an appearance. He was also the subject of a film documentary. In 1973 he received an honorary doctorate from Yale Univ.; in 1975 he was given another honorary doctorate, by Albright College.

Watts, Helen, Welsh contralto; b. Milford Haven, Dec. 7, 1927. She was educated at the Royal Academy of Music in London; made her debut in a Promenade Concert in London in 1955; in 1958 sang with the Handel Opera Society at the Camden Festival; later appeared with the English Opera Group in London and with the Welsh National Opera. She made her U.S. debut in a concert with the N.Y. Phil. in 1966. In 1978 she was made a Commander of the Order of the British Empire.

Waxman, Franz, German-American composer; b. Königshütte, Dec. 24, 1906; d. Los Angeles, Feb. 24, 1967. He studied in Dresden and Berlin; went to the U.S. in 1934 and settled in Hollywood, where he took lessons with Arnold Schoenberg; became a successful composer for films; his musical score for *Sunset Boulevard* won the Academy Award for 1950; other works include a Sinfonietta for String Orch. and Timpani (1955); oratorio, *Joshua* (Dallas, May 23, 1959); a fantasy on *Carmen* for Violin and Orch.; etc.

Wayditch, Gabriel (real name, **Baron Gabriel Wajditsch Verbovac von Dönhoff**), Hungarian-American composer; b. Budapest, Dec. 28, 1888; d. New York, July 28, 1969. He studied piano with Emil Sauer and composition with Hans Koessler at the Budapest Academy of Music. In 1907 he emigrated to the U.S.; lived mostly in N.Y. He wrote 14 lengthy operas to his own libretti in Hungarian, dealing mostly with oriental or religious subjects; of these only one, *Horus,* was performed in his lifetime, at his own expense (Philadelphia, Jan. 5, 1939). His longest opera, *The Heretics,* takes 8 hours to perform; the shortest, *The Caliph's Magician,* in one act, takes 2 hours. The other operas are: *Opium Dreams, Buddha, Jesus before Herod, Maria Magdalena, Maria Tesztver, Nereida, Sahara, The Catacombs, Anthony of Padua, The Venus Dwellers, Neptune's Daughter.*

Weathers, Felicia, black American soprano; b. St. Louis, Aug. 13, 1937. She took vocal lessons at the Indiana Univ. School of Music in Bloomington, with Dorothée Manski; then went to Europe; made her operatic debut in Kiel in 1961. In 1963 she sang at the Hamburg State Opera and subsequently became a regular member (1966–70). In 1965 she made her Metropolitan Opera debut in N.Y.; also sang at Covent Garden in London in 1970.

Webbe, Samuel, Jr., English composer, son of **Samuel Webbe, Sr.;** b. London, 1770; d. there, Nov. 25, 1843. He was a pupil of his father, and also received instruction from Clementi. He wrote many glees and catches, obtaining several prizes from the Catch Club; also produced his musical comedy, *The Speechless Wife* (Covent Garden, May 22, 1794). He lived in Liverpool from 1798 until 1817; returned to London, where he taught at Logier's School of Music and served as organist at the Spanish Embassy. Besides glees, duets, hymn tunes, organ voluntaries, sonatas for harpsichord, etc., he wrote *L'Amico del principiante* (28 short solfeggi) and *Harmony Epitomised, or Elements of the Thorough-bass;* also edited *Convito armonico* (4 vols.; a collection of madrigals, glees, catches, canons, etc., by prominent composers).

Webbe, Samuel, Sr., famous English composer of catches and glees; b. London, 1740; d. there, May 25, 1816. He began his career as a copyist for the London publisher Welcker, who enabled him to study music with the organist Barbandt; was appointed organist and choirmaster at the Chapel of the Portuguese Embassy in 1776, and later obtained a similar appointment at the Sardinian Embassy (holding both positions concurrently); from 1794 until his death he was secretary of the Catch Club, also librarian of the Glee Club (from 1787). In 1766 his canon *O that I had wings* won the prize of the Catch Club, and subsequently he carried off 26 other prizes with various catches and glees (reprinted later with 3 additional vols.), *Cecilian Ode* for 6 Voices, Concerto for Harpsichord, *Divertissement* for Wind Band, and several collections of masses and motets. His glee *Glorious Apollo* was the opening work sung at every meeting of the Glee Club throughout its history.

Weber, Ben, American composer; b. St. Louis, July 23, 1916; d. New York, May 9, 1979. He studied medicine at the Univ. of Illinois; then entered De Paul Univ. in Chicago, where he studied voice, piano, and music theory. In composition he was practically self-taught, but he was attracted to the method of composition with 12 tones after meeting Schoenberg; paradoxically, he retained the firm tonal foundation of his melodic and contrapuntal structures. He moved to N.Y., where he held various positions in the recording industry; also taught composition privately. He received 2 Guggenheim grants (1950, 1953), the Thorne music award (1965), and the Koussevitzky grant (1967).
WORKS: *Symphony on Poems of William Blake* for Baritone and Chamber Orch. (N.Y., Oct. 28, 1952); Violin Concerto (1954); *Prelude and Passacaglia* (Louisville, Ky., Jan. 1, 1955); *Rapsodie concertante* for Viola and Orch. (1957); *Chamber Fantasy* for Small Orch. (1959); Piano Concerto (1961); 2 string quartets (1942, 1952); 2 string trios (1943, 1946); *The Pool of Darkness* for Flute, Violin, Trumpet, Bassoon, Cello, and Piano (1950); *Aubade* for Flute, Harp, and Cello (1950); Concerto for Piano, Cello, and Woodwind Quintet (1950); *Colloquy* for Brass Septet (1953); Serenade for Harpsichord, Flute, Oboe, and Cello (1953); Concertino for Flute, Oboe, Clarinet, and String Quartet (1955); Serenade for String Quintet (1955); Nocturne for Flute, Celesta, and Cello (1962); *Dolmen: An Elegy* for Winds and Strings (1964); *Concert Poem* for Violin and Orch. (1970); *Sinfonia Clarion* for Orch. (N.Y., Feb. 26, 1974); Consort of Winds for Wind Quintet (1974);

Capriccio for Cello and Piano (1975); 2 violin sonatas; 2 dances for Cello and Piano; songs.

Weber, Bernhard Anselm, German pianist and composer; b. Mannheim, April 18, 1764; d. Berlin, March 23, 1821. He studied with Abbé Vogler and Holzbauer; also took courses in theology and law at the Univ. of Heidelberg; then traveled as a performer on the Xänorphica, a keyboard instrument invented by Röllig. In 1787 he became music director of Grossmann's opera troupe; went to Stockholm in 1790; in 1792 was appointed conductor of the König-stadt Theater in Berlin, remaining in this capacity after its union with the Italian Opera. A great admirer of Gluck, he was the first to introduce Gluck's operas in Berlin, and his own works closely followed Gluck's style. He produced in Berlin 2 of his operas: *Mudarra* (March 10, 1800) and *Die Wette* (Jan. 21, 1805). Some of his songs were popular for a time.

Weber, Bernhard Christian, German organist and composer; b. Wolferschwenda, Dec. 1, 1712; d. Tennstedt, Feb. 5, 1758. He settled in Tennstedt as town organist in 1732. Inspired by Bach's example, and at the instigation of Bach's pupil G.H. Noah, Weber composed for organ a work containing 24 preludes and fugues in all keys, and entitled it *Das wohltemperierte Klavier.*

Weber, Carl Maria (Friedrich Ernst), Freiherr von, celebrated German composer, founder of the German Romantic school; b. Eutin, Oldenburg, Nov. 18, 1786; d. London, June 5, 1826. His father, Franz Anton von Weber (1734–1812), was an army officer and a good musical amateur who played the violin and served as town musician in Eutin. It was his fondest wish to see one of his children become a great musician; Constanze Weber, Mozart's wife, was his niece (so that Carl Maria Weber was Mozart's first cousin by marriage), and Mozart was constantly the family's ideal to follow. Carl Maria's mother was a singer of some ability; she died when he was 12 years old. Franz Anton von Weber led a wandering life as music director of a traveling theatrical troupe, and he took his family with him. Although this mode of life interfered with Weber's regular education, it gave him practical knowledge of the stage, and stimulated his imagination as a dramatic composer. Weber's first teacher was his stepbrother Fritz, a pupil of Haydn; at Hildburghausen, where he found himself with his father's company in 1796, he received piano instruction from J.P. Heuschkel. The next year he was in Salzburg, where he attracted the attention of Michael Haydn, who taught him counterpoint. As his peregrinations continued, he was taught singing by Valesi (J.B. Wallishauser), and composition by J.N. Kalcher, in Munich (1798–1800); by that time he had already publ. his first work, 6 fughettas for Piano (1798). At the age of 13, he wrote an opera, *Die Macht der Liebe und des Weins;* it was never performed, and the score is lost. Through a meeting with Aloys Senefelder, the inventor of lithography,

he became greatly interested in engraving; while a mere boy, he acquired considerable skill in the process, and even worked out some improvements; engraved his *Variations* for Piano, op. 2, himself, in 1800. His father, too, became interested in the business possibilities of lithography, and set up a workshop with him in Freiberg, Saxony; the venture did not succeed, and Carl Maria turned again to music; wrote a 2-act opera, *Das Waldmädchen,* which was produced in Freiberg 6 days after his 14th birthday, on Nov. 24, 1800; performances followed in Chemnitz (Dec. 5, 1800) and, 4 years later, in Vienna. In 1801 the family was once more in Salzburg, where Weber studied further with Michael Haydn, and wrote another opera, *Peter Schmoll und seine Nachbarn;* after a stay in Hamburg (1802), they proceeded to Augsburg (1803) and finally to Vienna. There, Weber made a serious study of the works of the great masters under the guidance of Abbé Vogler, at whose recommendation he secured the post of conductor of the Breslau City Theater (1804); in 1806 he became Musik-Intendant to Duke Eugen of Württemberg at Schloss Carlsruhe in Silesia; in Sept. 1807 he was engaged as private secretary to Duke Ludwig at Stuttgart, and music master to his children. This employment was abruptly terminated when Weber became innocently involved in a scheme of securing a ducal appointment for a rich man's son in order to exempt him from military service, and accepted a loan of money; as a result of the disclosure of this affair, Weber was arrested and kept in prison for 2 weeks, after which he was expelled from Stuttgart. He went to Darmstadt, where he rejoined his old teacher Abbé Vogler, for whom he did some editorial and analytic work in publishing an edition of Bach's chorales. On Sept. 16, 1810, Weber's opera *Silvana* was successfully presented in Frankfurt; on June 4, 1811, he brought out in Munich a new opera, *Abu Hassan.* In the meantime, he appeared as a pianist, giving concerts in Frankfurt, Würzburg, Nuremberg, Bamberg, Weimar, Gotha, and other German towns. In 1813 he received his first important appointment, that of conductor of the German Opera in Prague; there he presented a distinguished repertoire, which included Beethoven's *Fidelio;* traveled to Vienna to engage a company of singers; among them was **Caroline Brandt,** his future wife. His reputation as a music director and composer rose considerably, and the King of Saxony called him to Dresden to take charge of the German Opera Theater there. He opened his Dresden season on Jan. 30, 1817; became friendly with Friedrich Kind, a Dresden lawyer and writer, and suggested to him the idea of writing a libretto on a typically German subject. They agreed on *Der Freischütz,* a fairy tale from J.A. Apel and F. Laun's collection of ghost stories, *Gespensterbuch.* The composition of this work, which was to prove his masterpiece, occupied him fully 3 years; the overture was finished in May 1820; interrupting his work, he wrote (in 3 weeks) several musical numbers to *Preciosa,* a play in 4 acts with spoken dialogue; it was produced in Berlin on March 14, 1821; another stage work, *Die drei Pintos,* which Weber started at about the same time, was left unfinished.

Weber

Finally, *Der Freischütz* was completed, and accepted for performance at the new Berlin Opera Theater. There existed an undercurrent of rivalry with Spontini, director of the Berlin Opera and an almost absolute master of operatic policy in Berlin; the challenge was that of rising German nationalism against the Italian-French tradition. Weber conducted the premiere on June 18, 1821; the work's success surpassed all expectations; the cause of new Romantic art was won; *Der Freischütz* was soon staged by all the major opera houses of Europe. In English, it was given first in London, on July 22, 1824; translations into other languages followed. Weber's next opera was *Euryanthe,* produced in Vienna on Oct. 25, 1823, with only moderate success. Meanwhile, Weber's health was affected by incipient tuberculosis and he was compelled to go to Marienbad for a cure (1824). He recovered sufficiently to begin the composition of *Oberon,* commissioned from him by Covent Garden in London; the English libretto was by J.R. Planché, based on a translation of C.M. Wieland's *Oberon.* Once more illness interrupted Weber's progress on his work; he spent some time in Ems to recuperate, then embarked on the voyage to England early in 1826. He rehearsed the opera thoroughly, and conducted the premiere at Covent Garden on April 12, 1826, obtaining tremendous success with the London audience. Despite his greatly weakened condition, he conducted 11 more performances of *Oberon,* and participated also in various London concerts, playing for the last time a week before his death. He was buried in London; his remains were removed to Dresden on Dec. 15, 1844; on that occasion Richard Wagner delivered an oration and conducted a funeral march on motifs from *Euryanthe,* as well as a funeral ode for double chorus expressly written for the service.

Weber's role in music history is epoch-making; in his operas, particulary in *Der Freischütz,* he opened the era of musical Romanticism, in decisive opposition to the established Italianate style. The highly dramatic and poetic portrayal of a German fairy tale, with its aura of supernatural mystery, appealed to the public, whose imagination had been stirred by the emergent Romantic literature of the period. Weber's melodic genius and his mastery of the craft of composition made it possible for him to break with tradition and to start on a new path, at a critical time when individualism and nationalism began to emerge as sources of creative artistry. His instrumental works, too, possess a new quality which signalizes the transition from Classical to Romantic music. For piano he wrote pieces of extraordinary brilliance, introducing some novel elements in chord writing and passage work. He was himself an excellent pianist; his large hands gave him an unusual command of the keyboard—he could stretch the interval of a twelfth. Weber's influence on the development of German music was very great. The evolutionary link to Wagner's music drama is evident in the coloring of the orch. parts in Weber's operas and in the adumbration of the principle of leading motifs.

WORKS: OPERAS: *Das Waldmädchen* (Freiberg, Nov. 24, 1800); *Peter Schmoll und seine Nachbarn* (Augsburg, March, 1803); *Rübezahl* (1805; unfinished); *Silvana* (Frankfurt, Sept. 16, 1810); *Abu Hassan* (Munich, June 4, 1811); *Preciosa* (Berlin, March 14, 1821); *Der Freischütz* (Berlin, June 18, 1821); *Die drei Pintos* (1821; unfinished; completed by Gustav Mahler after Weber's sketches and produced in Leipzig, Jan. 20, 1888); *Euryanthe* (Vienna, Oct. 25, 1823); *Oberon, or The Elf King's Oath* (London, April 12, 1826).

INCIDENTAL MUSIC: To Gozzi's *Turandot* (1809), Moreto's *Donna Diana* (1817), Adolf Müllner's *König Yngurd* (1817), Theodor Hell's *Das Haus Anglade* (1818), Grillparzer's *Sappho* (1818), Gehe's *Heinrich IV* (1818), Rublack's *Leib' um Liebe* (1818), Houwald's *Der Leuchtturm* (1820), Ludwig Robert's *Den Sachsensohn vermählet heute* (1822).

VOCAL WORKS: *Der erste Ton,* cantata for Declamation, Chorus, and Orch. (1808); op. 36, *In seiner Ordnung schafft der Herr* for Soli, Chorus, and Orch. (1812); op. 44, *Kampf und Sieg,* cantata on the battle of Waterloo (1815); *L'Accoglianza* for 6 Solo Voices, Chorus, and Orch. (1817); op. 58, *Jubel-Kantate* for Soli, Chorus, and Orch. (1818); op. 61, *Natur und Liebe,* cantata for 2 Sopranos, 2 Tenors, and 2 Basses, with Piano (1818); other occasional cantatas; 2 masses (E-flat, G); 2 offertories for Soli, Chorus, and Orch.; op. 42, 6 part-songs for Men's Voices (to T. Körner's *Leyer und Schwert;* achieved great popularity with students); op. 53b, 5 part-songs for Men's Chorus; op. 68, 6 part-songs for Men's Chorus; 5 scenes for Soprano, with Orch. (op. 16, "Il Momento s'avvicina," and op. 50, "Misera me" for *Atalia,* 1811; op. 51, "Non paventar, mia vita" for *Ines de Castro,* 1816; op. 52, "Ah, se Edmondo fosse l'uccisor" for Méhul's *Hélène,* 1815; op. 56, "Was sag' ich? Schaudern macht mich der Gedanke" for Cherubini's *Lodoiska*); op. 53, scena for Tenor, Double Chorus, and Orch., "Signor, se padre sei," for *Ines de Castro;* scena and aria for Tenor, Men's Chorus, and Orch., "Qual altro attendi"; recitative, "Doch welche Töne steigen jetzt hernieder," for Spontini's *Olympie;* many songs (opp. 13, 15, 23, 25, 29, 30, 41, 43, 46, 47, 54, 64, 66, 71, 80); 8 part-songs for Mixed Voices, with and without accompaniment; 6 canons for 3 and 4 Voices; duets (op. 31); 10 Scottish folk songs arranged with accompaniment of Flute, Violin, Cello, and Piano.

FOR ORCH.: Op. 27, *Der Beherrscher der Geister,* overture (to the unfinished opera *Rübezahl*); op. 59, *Jubel-Ouvertüre;* 2 symphs., both in C major; March for Wind Instruments; Waltz for Wind Instruments; 2 piano concertos (op. 11, C; op. 32, E-flat) and *Konzertstück* in F minor (op. 79); Concertino for Clarinet and Orch. in E-flat major (op. 26) and 2 clarinet concertos (op. 73, F minor; op. 74, E-flat); *Andante und Rondo* in C minor for Bassoon and Orch. (op. 35); Concerto in F for Bassoon and Orch. (op. 75); Concertino in E minor for Horn and Orch. (op. 45); *Romanza siciliana* for Flute and Orch.; *6 Variations on a German Folksong* for Cello and Orch.; *Andante and Variations* in D minor for Cello and Orch.; *Adagio and Rondo* for "Harmonichord" and Orch.

CHAMBER MUSIC: Op. 8, Piano Quartet in B-flat; op. 13, 6 sonatas for Violin and Piano (F, G, D minor,

E-flat, A, C); op. 22, *Variations on a Norwegian Theme* for Violin and Piano; in D minor; op. 33, Variations for Clarinet and Piano in B-flat; op. 34, Clarinet Quintet in B-flat; op. 48, *Duo concertant* in E-flat for Clarinet and Piano; op. 63, Piano Trio in G minor.

FOR PIANO: 4 sonatas (op. 24, C; op. 39, A-flat; op. 49, D minor; op. 70, E minor); op. 1, *6 Fughetten;* op. 2, *Variations* on an original theme; op. 3, *12 Allemandes;* op. 5, *Variations on an Air de ballet* from Vogler's *Castor et Pollux;* op. 6, *Variations on an Air* from Vogler's *Samori;* op. 7, *Variations* on an original theme; op. 12, *Momento capriccioso;* op. 21, *Grande polonaise* in E-flat; op. 28, *Variations* on a theme from Méhul's *Joseph;* op. 40, *Variations* on a Russian theme; op. 50, *Polonaise brillante* in E; op. 53, *Caprice and Variations* on a theme from *Preciosa;* op. 55, *Variations* on a Gypsy theme; op. 62, *Rondo brillant* in E-flat major; op. 65, *Aufforderung zum Tanz (Invitation to the Dance;* in 2 orch. versions, by Berlioz and Weingartner, and in innumerable arrangements for various instruments); op. 72, *Polacca brillante* (arranged for Piano and Orch. by Liszt); op. 81, *Les Adieux,* fantasy; *6 Ecossaises; 18 valses favorites de l'Impératrice de France;* for Piano, 4-hands: op. 3, *Sechs leichte Stücke;* op. 10, *6 sonates progressives et agréables;* op. 60, *Acht leichte Stücke.* A popular piece publ. under the title *Weber's Last Waltz* (or *Weber's Last Thought*) is a composition of K.G. Reissiger, not Weber.

A complete edition of Weber's works was undertaken in 1926 under the general editorship of H.J. Moser; only the following vols. were publ.: vols. I–II, early operas, ed. by A. Lorenz and W. Kaehler; vol. III, the Salzburg Mass, ed. by C. Schneider; *Preciosa,* ed. by L.K. Mayer. Previously unpubl. works are found in L. Hirschberg's *Reliquienschrein des Meisters C.M. von Weber* (Berlin, 1827). A complete thematic catalogue of Weber's works was publ. by F.W. Jähns, *C.M. von Weber in seinen Werken* (Berlin, 1871).

WRITINGS: An unfinished novel, criticisms, explanatory remarks on new works produced by him in Dresden, poems, etc., were publ. by T. Hell as *Hinterlassene Schriften von C.M. von Weber* (3 vols., Dresden, 1828; 2nd ed., 1850). A more complete and better edition is that of G. Kaiser, *Sämtliche Schriften von C.M. von Weber* (Berlin, 1908). R. Kleinecke publ. *Ausgewählte Schriften von K.M. von Weber* (Leipzig, 1892); a more recent collection was publ. by W. Altmann, *Webers Ausgewählte Schriften* (Regensburg, 1928). *Ein Brevier* was edited by H. Dünnebeil (Berlin, 1949).

Weber, Gottfried, eminent German theorist and composer; b. Freinsheim, near Mannheim, March 1, 1779; d. Kreuznach, Sept. 21, 1839. He studied law at Heidelberg and Göttingen, and filled positions as judge in Mannheim (1802), Mainz (1814), and Darmstadt (1818); was appointed public prosecutor for the state of Hesse in 1832. He was an excellent amateur pianist and also played the flute and the cello; in 1806 founded a musical society called "Conservatorium" in Mannheim; in 1824 began the magazine *Caecilia,* and edited it until his death. He made a thorough study of the theoretical works of Marpurg, Kirnberger, Abbé Vogler, and others, and then brought out his important treatise *Versuch einer geordneten Theorie der Tonsetzkunst* (3 vols., 1817–21; 2nd ed. in 4 vols., 1824; 3rd ed. in 4 vols., 1830–32), in which he introduced the now widely accepted symbols for designating the major keys with capital letters and minor keys with small letters, Roman figures for degrees of the scale, etc. It was publ. in Eng. in Boston (1846) and London (1851). His other theoretical publications include *Über chronometrische Tempobezeichnung* (1817); *Beschreibung und Tonleiter der G. Weber'schen Doppelposaune* (1817); "Versuch einer praktischen Akustik der Blasinstrumente," in Ersch and Gruber's *Encyclopädie; Allgemeine Musiklehre zum Selbstunterrichte* (1822; 3rd ed., 1831; in Eng., Boston, 1824); "Über Saiteninstrumente mit Bünden," *Berliner Musikzeitung* (1825); *Die Generalbasslehre zum Selbstunterrichte* (1833); many essays for the *Allgemeine Musikalische Zeitung* and for his own paper, *Caecilia.* He questioned the authenticity of Mozart's Requiem (in *Caecilia,* 1826). As a composer, he wrote 3 masses, a Requiem, and a Te Deum (all with orch.); variations for guitar and cello; some chamber music; part-songs.

Weber, Ludwig, eminent Austrian bass; b. Vienna, July 29, 1899; d. there, Dec. 9, 1974. He studied in Vienna with Alfred Boruttau; made his debut at the Vienna Volksoper in 1920; then sang in Düsseldorf, Cologne, and Munich; from 1945 to 1960 he was one of the principal singers at the Vienna State Opera; also sang regularly at the Bayreuth Festivals (from 1951). In 1961 he became a prof. at the Salzburg Mozarteum. He was regarded as one of the foremost Wagnerian bass singers of his time.

Weber, Margrit, Swiss pianist; b. Ebnat-Kappel, Feb. 24, 1924. She studied organ in Zürich; was employed as an organist at the age of 15; then devoted herself chiefly to the piano. She toured Europe in concert recitals, presenting many new works; in 1956 and in 1965 she played in the U.S. and Canada. She was the soloist in the first performances of piano concertos by Martinů and Alexander Tcherepnin, and of Stravinsky's *Movements* for Piano and Orch., which she performed under Stravinsky's own direction in N.Y., on Jan. 10, 1960.

Webern, Anton (Friedrich Wilhelm) von, remarkable Austrian composer (he removed the nobiliary particle "von" in 1918 when such distinctions were outlawed in Austria); b. Vienna, Dec. 3, 1883; d. (accidentally shot and killed by an American soldier) Mittersill, Sept. 15, 1945. He received his first instruction in music from his mother, an amateur pianist; then studied piano, cello, and theory with Edwin Komauer in Klagenfurt; also played cello in the local orch. there. In 1902 he entered the Univ. of Vienna, where he studied harmony with Graedener and counterpoint with Navratil; also attended classes in musicology with Guido Adler; received his Ph.D. in 1906 with a dissertation on Heinrich Isaac's *Choralis Constantinus II*. In 1904 he began private studies in composition with Arnold Schoenberg, whose ardent disciple he became; Alban Berg also studied with Schoenberg; together, Schoenberg, Berg, and Webern laid the foundations of what became known as the 2nd Viennese School of composition. The unifying element was the adoption of Schoenberg's method of composition with 12 tones related only to one another. Malevolent opponents referred to Schoenberg, Berg, and Webern as a Vienna Trinity, with Schoenberg as God the Father, Berg as God the Son, and Webern as the Holy Ghost; the last appellation was supposed to describe the phantomlike substance of some of Webern's works. From 1908 to 1914 Webern was active as a conductor in Vienna and in Germany; in 1915–16 he served in the army; in 1917–18 was conductor at the Deutsches Theater in Prague. In 1918 he settled in Mödling, near Vienna, where he taught composition privately; in 1918–22 he supervised the programs of the Verein für Musikalische Privataufführungen (Society for Private Musical Performances), organized in Vienna by Schoenberg with the intention of promoting modern music without being exposed to reactionary opposition (music critics were not admitted to these performances). Webern was conductor of the Schubertbund (1921–22) and the Mödling Male Chorus (1921–26); he also led the Vienna Workers' Symph. concerts (1922–34) and the Vienna Workers' Chorus (1923–34), both sponsored by the Social Democratic Party. From 1927 to 1938 he was a conductor on the Austrian Radio; furthermore, he conducted guest engagements in Germany, Switzerland, and Spain; from 1929 made several visits to England, where he was a guest conductor with the BBC Symph. Orch. For the most part, however, he devoted himself to composition, private teaching, and lecturing. After Hitler came to power in Germany in 1933, Webern's music was banned as a manifestation of "cultural Bolshevism" and "degenerate art." His position became more difficult after the Anschluss in 1938, for his works could no longer be publ.; he eked out an existence by teaching a few private pupils and making piano arrangements of musical scores by others for Universal Edition. After his son was killed in an air bombardment of a train in Feb. 1945, he and his wife fled from Vienna to Mittersill, near Salzburg, to stay with his married daughters and grandchildren. His life ended tragically on the evening of Sept. 15, 1945, when he was shot and killed by an American soldier after stepping outside his son-in-law's residence (for a full account, see H. Moldenhauer, *The Death of Anton Webern: A Drama in Documents*, N.Y., 1961).

Webern left relatively few works, and most of them are of short duration (the 4th of his 5 Pieces for Orch., op. 10, scored for clarinet, trumpet, trombone, mandolin, celesta, harp, drum, violin, and viola, takes only 19 seconds to play), but in his music he achieves the utmost subtilization of expressive means. He adopted the 12-tone method of composition almost immediately after its definitive formu-

lation by Schoenberg (1924), and extended the principle of nonrepetition of notes to tone colors, so that in some of his works (e.g., Symph., op. 21) solo instruments are rarely allowed to play 2 successive thematic notes. Dynamic marks are similarly diversified. Typically, each 12-tone row is divided into symmetric sections of 2, 4, or 6 members, which enter mutually into intricate but invariably logical canonic imitations. Inversions and augmentations are inherent features; melodically and harmonically, the intervals of the major seventh and minor ninth are stressed; single motifs are brief, and stand out as individual particles or lyric ejaculations. The impact of these works on the general public and on the critics was disconcerting, and upon occasion led to violent demonstrations; however, the extraordinary skill and novelty of technique made this music endure beyond the fashions of the times; performances of Webern's works multiplied after his death, and began to influence increasingly larger groups of modern musicians; Stravinsky acknowledged the use of Webern's methods in his latest works; jazz composers have professed to follow Webern's ideas of tone color; analytical treatises have been publ. in several languages. The International Webern Festival celebrated the centennial of his birth in Dec. 1983 in Vienna.

WORKS: FOR ORCH.: *Im Sommerwind*, idyll for Large Orch. (1904; Seattle, May 25, 1962, Ormandy conducting); *Passacaglia*, op. 1 (1908; Vienna, Nov. 4, 1908, composer conducting); *6 Orchestral Pieces*, op. 6 (1909; Vienna, March 31, 1913, Schoenberg conducting; revised 1928; Berlin, Jan. 27, 1929); *5 Orchestral Pieces*, op. 10 (1911–13; Zürich Festival of the International Society for Contemporary Music, June 22, 1926, composer conducting); *5 Orchestral Pieces*, op. posthumous (1913; Cologne, Jan. 13, 1969); Symph. for Chamber Ensemble, op. 21 (1928; N.Y., League of Composers, Dec. 18, 1929); 5 Movements for String Quartet, op. 5, arranged for String Orch. (1928–29; Philadelphia, March 26, 1930); *Variations*, op. 30 (1940; Winterthur, March 3, 1943). VOCAL MUSIC: *Entflieht auf leichten Kähnen*, op. 2, for Unaccompanied Chorus (1908; Fürstenfeld, April 10, 1927); 2 songs to words by Goethe, op. 19, for Chorus, Celesta, Guitar, Violin, Clarinet, and Bass Clarinet (1926); *Das Augenlicht*, op. 26, for Chorus and Orch. (1935; London, BBC concert, June 17, 1938); *First Cantata* for Soprano, Mixed Chorus, and Orch. (1938–39; London, BBC concert, July 12, 1946); *2nd Cantata* for Soprano, Bass, Mixed Chorus, and Orch. (1941–43; Brussels, June 23, 1950); 2 sets of 5 songs for Voice and Piano, to poems by Stefan George, opp. 3 and 4 (1908–9); 2 songs for Voice and Instrumental Ensemble, on poems by Rilke, op. 8 (1910; revised 1921 and 1925); 4 songs for Voice and Piano, op. 12 (1915–17); 4 songs for Voice and Orch., op. 13 (1914–18); 6 songs for Voice and Instruments, on poems by Georg Trakl, op. 14 (1919–21; Donaueschingen, July 20, 1924); *5 Sacred Songs* for Voice and Instruments, op. 15 (1917–22; Vienna, Oct. 9, 1924, composer conducting); *5 Canons* on Latin texts for Voice, Clarinet, and Bass Clarinet, op. 16 (1923–24; N.Y., May 8, 1951); *3 Traditional Rhymes* for Voice and Instruments, op. 17 (1924–25; N.Y.,

March 16, 1952); 3 songs for Voice, Clarinet, and Guitar, op. 18 (1925; Los Angeles, Feb. 8, 1954); 3 songs for Voice and Piano, op. 23 (1933–34); 3 songs for Voice and Piano, op. 25 (1934). CHAMBER MUSIC: String Quartet, in one movement (1905; posthumous, Seattle, May 26, 1962); Piano Quintet, in one movement (Vienna, Nov. 7, 1907); 5 Movements for String Quartet (1909; Vienna, Feb. 8, 1910); 4 pieces for Violin and Piano, op. 7 (1910; revised 1914); 6 bagatelles for String Quartet, op. 9 (1911–13; Donaueschingen, July 19, 1924); *3 Little Pieces* for Cello and Piano, op. 11 (1914; Mainz, Dec. 2, 1924); String Trio, op. 20 (1926–27; Vienna, Jan. 16, 1928); Quartet for Violin, Clarinet, Tenor Saxophone, and Piano, op. 22 (1930; Vienna, April 13, 1931); Concerto for 9 Instruments, op. 24 (1934; Prague, Sept. 4, 1935); String Quartet, op. 28 (1936–38; Pittsfield, Mass., Sept. 22, 1938); Variations for Piano Solo (1936; Vienna, Oct. 26, 1937); arrangements for Chamber Orch. of Schoenberg's Chamber Symph., op. 9 (1923), Schubert's *Deutsche Tanze* (1931), and Bach's Ricercare *a 6* from *Das musikalische Opfer* (London, April 25, 1935, Webern conducting).

Webster, Beveridge, American pianist; b. Pittsburgh, May 30, 1908. He studied music with his father, who was director of the Pittsburgh Cons. of Music; at the age of 13 he was sent to Paris to study with Isidor Philipp at the Paris Cons.; graduated in 1926, winning the Grand Prix for piano playing. He gave concerts in Europe; returned to the U.S. in 1934, and developed a successful concert career, appearing with major symph. orchs.; also continued to give concerts in Europe. In 1946 he was appointed prof. of piano at the Juilliard School of Music in N.Y.; gave a piano recital at the Juilliard Theater on his 70th birthday, in May 1978.

Webster, Sir David, English operatic administrator; b. Dundee, Scotland, July 3, 1903; d. London, May 11, 1971. He was educated at Liverpool Univ.; then commenced a commercial career while pursuing his various interests in the arts; from 1940–45 was chairman of the Liverpool Phil. Society. In 1945 he became general administrator of the Covent Garden Opera Trust; in this capacity he helped to launch the careers of many famous singers, among them Jon Vickers and Dame Joan Sutherland. He was knighted in 1961 and was made a Knight Commander of the Royal Victorian Order in 1970. An account of his career by M. Haltrecht, under the title *The Reluctant Showman,* was publ. in 1975.

Wecker, Georg Kaspar, German organist and composer; b. Nuremberg (baptized, April 2), 1632; d. there, April 20, 1695. He studied organ with Erasmus Kindermann, and soon obtained a position as church organist in Nuremberg; his last appointment was at the Sebaldkirche there (1686–95). He also was a respected teacher; Johann Krieger and Pachelbel were among his pupils. Several of his sacred songs were publ. in hymnbooks in Nuremberg; 3 sacred choral works are reproduced in Denkmäler der Tonkunst in Bayern, 10 (6.i).

Weckerlin, Jean-Baptiste-Théodore, eminent French music scholar and composer; b. Gebweiler, Alsace, Nov. 9, 1821; d. Buhl, May 20, 1910. He was trained for his father's business of cotton-dyeing; but went over to music in 1844, studying under Ponchard (singing) and Halévy (composition) at the Paris Cons., producing a heroic symph., *Roland,* for Soli, Chorus, and Orch., in 1847; on leaving the Cons. in 1849, he gave music lessons; took part with Seghers in the direction of the Société Sainte-Cécile, which brought out some of his works; and achieved success in 1853 with a one-act comic opera, *L'Organiste dans l'embarras* (100 perfs. at the Théâtre-Lyrique). This was followed by 2 comic operas in Alsatian dialect, *Die drifach Hochzitt im Bäsethal* (Colmar, 1863) and *D'r verhäxt' Herbst* (Colmar, 1879), and the one-act opera *Après Fontenoy* (Théâtre-Lyrique, 1877). Meantime he had become an assistant librarian at the Paris Cons. (1869); in 1876 succeeded Félicien David as librarian, and in 1885 publ. a bibliographical catalogue; was also chosen librarian of the Société des Compositeurs, for whose bulletins he wrote important articles. He retired in 1909. He won distinction as a composer of grand choral works; also wrote choruses a cappella, songs, and a grand *Symphonie de la forêt* for Orch.; but his greatest achievement was the compilation of old French songs. His *Echos du temps passé* (1853–55) and *Souvenirs du temps passé* (1864) are collections of chansons, noëls, madrigals, etc., from the 12th–18th centuries; the *Musiciana* (3 vols., 1877, 1890, 1899) is a collection of rare and curious works on music, with anecdotes, etc.; other collections are *Les Echos d'Angleterre* (1877; folk songs, with Piano); *Chansons et rondes populaires* (children's songs, with Piano); *Les Poètes français mis en musique* (1868); *Chansons populaires des provinces de la France; L'Ancienne Chanson populaire en France* (1886); *Chansons populaires du Pays de France* (2 vols., 1903). A catalogue of his private library was publ. at Leipzig in 1910.

Weckmann, Matthias, German organist and composer; b. Niederdorla, near Mühlhausen, Thuringia, c.1619; d. Hamburg, Feb. 24, 1674. He was the son of a schoolmaster; was a chorister in the Dresden court chapel, where he was a pupil of Heinrich Schütz. In 1633 he was sent to Hamburg for further study with Reinken, Jakob Praetorius, and H. Scheidemann, by whom he was trained in the organ method of Sweelinck. In 1637 he became organist for the crown prince in Dresden, and in 1642 was appointed to a similar post in Copenhagen; he returned in 1647 to Dresden, where he became a friend of J.J. Froberger; in 1655 he went to Hamburg as organist at the Jacobikirche, and there founded, with Christoph Bernhard, the Collegium Musicum, a concert society for the performance of new works (it was discontinued after Weckmann's death). Weckmann's solo cantatas and choral works with instrumental accompaniment were publ. by Max Seiffert in Denkmäler Deutscher Tonkunst, 6; instrumental pieces and songs in Erbe Deutscher Musik (series 2, vol. 4); 2 numbers are reproduced in

A. Schering's *Geschichte der Musik in Beispielen* (nos. 212 and 213); etc.

Weelkes, Thomas, English composer; b. c.1575; d. London, Nov. 30, 1623. In 1597 he publ. a book of madrigals for 3–6 voices; in 1598 he publ. *Balletts and Madrigals* for 5 voices, dedicated to Edward Darcey, Groom of the Privy Chamber; in 1600 he brought out 2 more books, containing madrigals for 5 and 6 voices; served as organist at the College of Winchester (1600–2). He was a friend of Morley, to whose collection *The Triumphes of Oriana* (1601–3) he contributed a fine madrigal for 6 voices, *As Vesta was from Latmos Hill Descending.* In 1602 he was granted the degree of B.Mus. at the New College, Oxford, and was appointed organist of Chichester Cathedral. A subsequent publication was *Ayres; or, Phantasticke Spirits for 3 voices* (1608; reprinted by Arkwright in the *Old English Edition*). Weelkes was one of the greatest English madrigalists, possessing remarkable power in melodic characterization of the text; he occasionally used chromatic progressions in harmony that were well in advance of his time. He wrote a considerable amount of church music (services and anthems); also instrumental works (2 pavanes and other pieces, for 5 viols). His madrigals and other vocal works are reprinted in *The English Madrigal School*, edited by E.H. Fellowes (vols. 9–13); anthems in the series Tudor Church Music and in *Musica Britannica*, 23.

Weerbecke (Weerbeke, Werbecke), Gaspar van, Flemish composer; b. Audenarde, c.1445. He was a pupil of Ockeghem; in 1472 he was organizer of the ducal court chapel at Milan; his singers including Josquin des Prez. From 1481 to 1489 he was a singer in the papal chapel at Rome, a post he resumed from 1500 to 1509 after sojourns in Milan and Flanders; there is no trace of him after 1517. Masses, motets, and Lamentations by Weerbecke were publ. by Petrucci (1505–9).

Wegeler, Franz Gerhard, German physician and music amateur; b. Bonn, Aug. 22, 1765; d. Coblenz, May 7, 1848. He was a practicing physician in Bonn and Coblenz, and knew Beethoven as a youth. With Ries, he publ. *Biographische Notizen über Ludwig van Beethoven* (1838; supplement, 1845; reprinted by A. Kalischer, 1906).

Wegelius, Martin, eminent Finnish composer and pedagogue; b. Helsinki, Nov. 10, 1846; d. there, March 22, 1906. He studied philosophy, taking his master's degree in 1869; studied music with Rudolf Bibl in Vienna (1870–71), and with Richter and Paul in Leipzig (1871–73); he went to Leipzig for further study in 1877–78. Returning to Finland, he became operatic coach at the Helsinki National Theater. In 1882 he was appointed director of the newly founded Helsinki Cons., holding this post until his death. Under his guidance, the institution became one of the finest schools in Europe, with excellent teachers. Sibelius was one of the pupils of Wegelius; others were Järnefelt, Melartin, and Palmgren. Wegelius emphasized the cultivation of national Finnish music, and thus was mainly responsible for the magnificent development of Finland as a musical nation.

WORKS: Overture, *Daniel Hjort* (1872); *Divertissement à la hongroise* (1880); *Rondo quasi fantasia* for Piano and Orch. (1872); *Mignon*, 6 songs with Orch., after Goethe's *Westöstlicher Diwan* (1875); Christmas Cantata (1877); festival cantata, *The 6th of May* (1878); Violin Sonata; piano pieces; songs. He publ. (in Swedish) a number of manuals and books on music history: *Lärobok i allmän musiklära och analys* (2 vols., 1888–89); *Hufvuddragen af den västerländska musikens historia* (3 vols., 1891–93); *Kurs i tonträffning* (3 vols., 1893–95); *Kurs i homofon sats* (2 vols., 1897–1905); etc.

Weidemann, Friedrich, German baritone; b. Ratzeburg, Jan. 1, 1871; d. Vienna, Jan. 30, 1919. He studied with Vilmar in Hamburg and Muschler in Berlin; made his debut in 1896 in Brieg; then sang in Essen (1897–98), Hamburg (1898–1901), and Riga (1901–3). In 1903 he joined the Vienna Court Opera, where he remained until his death. He was highly regarded for his performances in operas by Wagner and Richard Strauss.

Weidig, Adolf, American music teacher and composer; b. Hamburg, Nov. 28, 1867; d. Hinsdale, Ill., Sept. 23, 1931. He studied at the Hamburg Cons. with Bargheer (violin) and later with Hugo Riemann (theory); then in Munich with Rheinberger (composition). In 1892 he settled in Chicago; played the violin in the Chicago Orch. (1892–96); in 1898 he joined the faculty of the American Cons. of Music; conducted his own works in Chicago, Minneapolis, and also in Germany. He was greatly esteemed as a teacher; publ. *Harmonic Material and Its Uses* (1923); composed 2 symphs.; a symph. poem, *Semiramis; 3 Episoden* for Orch.; String Quintet; 3 string quartets; Piano Trio; songs.

Weidt, Lucy, German soprano; b. Troppau, Silesia, 1880; d. Vienna, July 28, 1940. She studied piano and singing with her father, and then with Rosa Papier in Vienna, where she made her debut in 1904; sang with the Vienna Opera until 1927. She sang in Germany, appearing at the Wagner festival in 1908–10. On Nov. 18, 1910, she made her first American appearance, as Brünnhilde in *Die Walküre* at the Metropolitan Opera in N.Y.; after a season there, she sang in Italy. In 1909 she married Baron Joseph von Urmenyi. Her voice was of unusual attractiveness and power, enabling her to perform Wagnerian parts with distinction.

Weigl, Joseph, Austrian composer; b. Eisenstadt, March 28, 1766; d. Vienna, Feb. 3, 1846. His father, **Joseph Franz Weigl** (1740–1820), was a cellist in the service of Prince Esterházy with Haydn; his mother was a singer; he was a godson of Haydn. Brought up in a musical environment, he wrote an operetta, *Die unnützige Vorsicht* (Vienna, Feb. 23, 1783), at the age of 16 for a puppet show; Salieri accepted him as a pupil; he also studied with Albrechtsberger. He was assistant conductor to Salieri at the Vienna Court Theater from 1790 until 1823. Altogether, Weigl wrote 14 operas in Italian and 19 in German. The most successful were *La Principessa d'Amalfi* (Vienna, Jan. 10, 1794; Haydn described it as a masterpiece in a letter to Weigl after the perf.) and *Die Schweizerfamilie* (Vienna, March 14, 1809; produced in Paris, Feb. 6, 1827, as *Emmeline, ou La Famille suisse;* also staged in opera houses all over Europe until about 1900, when it disappeared from the repertoire). The following operas by Weigl were produced in Vienna with varying success: *Il Pazzo per forza* (Nov. 14, 1788); *La caffettiera bizzarra* (Sept. 15, 1790); *L'Amor marinaro* (Oct. 15, 1797); *Das Dorf im Gebürge* (April 17, 1798); *Die Uniform* (Feb. 15, 1805); *Vestas Feuer* (Aug. 7, 1805); *Kaiser Hadrian* (May 21, 1807); *Adrian von Ostade* (July 3, 1807); *Das Waisenhaus* (Oct. 4, 1808); *Nachtigall und Rabe* (April 20, 1818); *Baals Sturz* (April 13, 1820); *König Waldemar* (May 11, 1821); *Edmund und Caroline* (Sept. 21, 1821); *Die eiserne Pforte* (Feb. 27, 1823); 4 operas were produced at La Scala in Milan: *Cleopatra* (Dec. 19, 1807); *Il Rivale di se stesso* (April 18, 1808); *L'Imboscata* (Nov. 8, 1815); *Margarethe von Anjou* (July 26, 1816). Weigl also wrote 18 ballets; 2 oratorios; 22 cantatas; 11 masses; other church music.

Weigl, Karl, Austrian composer; b. Vienna, Feb. 6, 1881; d. New York, Aug. 11, 1949. He studied piano with Door and music theory with Fuchs at the Cons. of the Gesellschaft der Musikfreunde in Vienna; also took composition lessons with Zemlinsky; attended courses in musicology at the Univ. of Vienna (Ph.D., 1903); subsequently was an opera coach under Mahler. In 1918 he was appointed to the faculty of the New Vienna Cons.; from 1930 to 1938 taught music theory at the Univ. of Vienna. After the Anschluss in 1938, he emigrated to N.Y. He was respected both in Austria and in America as a composer, and a concerted effort was made to promote his music, but with little success. His 5th Symph., subtitled *Apocalyptic*, was performed posthumously by Leopold Stokowski with the American Symph. Orch. (N.Y., Oct. 27, 1968). He wrote 6 symphs.: No. 1 (1908); No. 2 (1912); No. 3 (1931); No. 4 (1936); No. 5 (1945); No. 6 (1947); several overtures; Violin Concerto (1928); 8 string quartets; String Sextet; 2 violin sonatas; numerous choruses; piano pieces; songs.

Weigl, Thaddäus, Austrian composer and publisher, brother of **Joseph Weigl;** b. Vienna, April 8, 1776; d. there, Feb. 29, 1844. He wrote the singspiels *Die Marionettenbude* (Vienna, March 17, 1795) and *Idoli* (Vienna, March 12, 1796); also 13 ballets. In 1801 he established in Vienna a publishing firm, which issued several works by Schubert.

Weigl, Vally (Valery), Austrian composer and music therapist; b. Vienna, Sept. 11, 1894; d. New York, Dec. 25, 1982. She studied music in Vienna with **Karl Weigl,** whom she married. She taught

music in Vienna and Salzburg (1921–38); after the Anschluss she and her husband went to America, where she obtained employment as music adviser with the American Theater Wing (1947–58); from 1954 to 1964 she gave courses in music therapy at the N.Y. Medical College and wrote therapy programs for UNESCO. She was an energetic peace activist, and served as a co-founder of the Friends' Arts for World Unity Committee. With equal energy she promoted her husband's compositions, which were little appreciated and seldom played.

Weikert, Ralf, Austrian conductor; b. St. Florian, Nov. 10, 1940. He studied at the Bruckner Cons. in Linz; then took a course in conducting with Hans Swarowsky at the Vienna Academy of Music. In 1965 he won first prize in the Nicolai Malko Conducting Competition in Copenhagen. In 1966 he became conductor of the City Theater in Bonn; then was chief conductor there (1968–77). In 1977 he was appointed deputy Generalmusikdirektor of the Frankfurt Opera; also conducted opera with the Hamburg State Opera. the Deutsche Oper in Berlin, the Vienna State Opera, and the Zürich Opera. In 1981 he was named chief conductor of the Salzburg Mozarteum Orch. and music director of the Landestheater in Salzburg.

Weil, Hermann, German baritone; b. Karlsruhe, May 29, 1877; d. (of a heart attack, while fishing in Blue Mountain Lake, N.Y.) July 6, 1949. He studied voice with Adolf Dippel in Frankfurt; made his debut as Wolfram in *Tannhäuser* at Freiburg, Baden, on Sept. 6, 1901; then sang in Vienna, Brussels, Amsterdam, Milan, and London; participated in the Bayreuth Festivals during the summers of 1909–12. On Nov. 17, 1911, he made a successful American debut as Kurvenal in *Tristan und Isolde,* at the Metropolitan Opera in N.Y. under Toscanini. In 1917 he returned to Germany. The extensive range of his voice, spanning 3 full octaves, enabled him to undertake bass parts as well as those in the baritone compass. He had about 100 roles in his repertoire, excelling in Wagnerian operas.

Weill, Kurt, remarkable German composer of modern operas; b. Dessau, March 2, 1900; d. New York, April 3, 1950. He was a private pupil of Albert Bing in Dessau (1914–18); in 1918 he studied for one semester at the Berlin Hochschule für Musik with Humperdinck and Krasselt. He was then engaged as an opera coach in Dessau and was also theater conductor at Lüdenscheid. In 1921 he moved to Berlin and became a private student of Busoni; it was then that he completed his first major work, which became designated as the Berlin Symph. (*Berliner Symphonie*); its MS could not be located until many years after Weill's death, and the work was performed posthumously by the Hamburg Radio Orch. in 1958. Under the impact of new trends in the musical theater, Weill proceeded to write short satirical operas in a sharp modernistic manner: *Der Protagonist* (1925) and *Royal Palace* (1926). There followed a striking "songspiel" (a hybrid term of English and

German words), *Mahagonny*, to a libretto by Bertolt Brecht, savagely satirizing the American primacy of money (1927); it was subsequently remodeled and was presented as a 3-act opera under the title *Aufstieg und Fall der Stadt Mahagonny (Rise and Fall of the City of Mahagonny;* 1929). Weill's greatest hit in this genre came with a modernistic version of *The Beggar's Opera*, to a pungent libretto by Brecht; under the title *Die Dreigroschenoper* (1928), it was staged all over Germany, and was also produced in translation in Poland, the Netherlands, Denmark, Hungary, France, Russia, and England. Marc Blitzstein made a new libretto of the opera, versified in a modern American style, and produced as *The Threepenny Opera*, the exact translation of the German title. Its hit number, *Mack the Knife*, became tremendously successful.

After the Nazi ascent to power in Germany, Weill and his wife, the actress and singer Lotte Lenya, who appeared in many of his musical plays, went to Paris, and then to London. In 1935 they settled in the U.S.; Weill became a citizen in 1943. Quickly absorbing the modes and fashions of American popular music, Weill re-created, with astonishing facility, and felicity, the typical form and content of American musicals; this stylistic transition was facilitated by the fact that in his European productions he had already absorbed elements of American popular songs and jazz rhythms. His highly developed assimilative faculty enabled him to combine this Americanized idiom with the advanced techniques of modern music (atonality, polytonality, polyrhythms) and present the product in a pleasing, and yet sophisticated and challenging, manner. But for all his success in American-produced scores, the great majority of his European works remained to be produced in America only posthumously.

WORKS: FOR THE STAGE: *Der Protagonist* (1925; Dresden, March 27, 1926); *Royal Palace* (1925; Berlin, March 2, 1927; the original orchestration was lost; Gunther Schuller and Noam Sheriff reconstructed the work in the form of a ballet, produced in San Francisco, Oct. 5, 1968); *Mahagonny*, a satire on life in America, to a libretto by Bertolt Brecht (1927; Baden-Baden, July 17, 1927; subsequently remodeled as a 3-act opera, under the title *Aufstieg und Fall der Stadt Mahagonny*, produced in Leipzig, March 9, 1930; a U.S. production did not take place until April 28, 1970, in N.Y.); *Der Zar lässt sich photographieren* (1927; Leipzig, Feb. 18, 1928; U.S. production under the title *The Shah Has Himself Photographed*, N.Y., Oct. 27, 1949); *Die Dreigroschenoper* (Berlin, Aug. 31, 1928; in the U.S. as *The Threepenny Opera*, N.Y., April 13, 1933; subsequently, with a new libretto by Marc Blitzstein, produced in concert version at Brandeis Univ., Waltham, Mass., June 14, 1952; in stage form, N.Y., March 10, 1954); *Die Zaubernacht*, children's ballet (Berlin, Nov. 18, 1922); musical comedy, *Happy End* (Berlin, Sept. 2, 1922; professional U.S. premiere, New Haven, Conn., April 6, 1972); school opera, *Der Jasager* (Berlin, June 23, 1930; N.Y., April 25, 1933, under the title *The One Who Says Yes*); opera, *Die Bürgschaft (The Pledge;* 1931; Berlin, March 10, 1932); musical play, *Der Silbersee* (1932; Leipzig, Er-

furt, and Magdeburg simultaneously, Feb. 18, 1933; U.S. premiere, as *Silverlake*, slightly abridged and with the addition of Weill's 1927 incidental music to Strindberg's play *Gustav III*, N.Y., March 20, 1980). In Paris: ballet with songs, *Die sieben Todsünden der Kleinbürger (The 7 Deadly Sins of the Petty-Bourgeois;* Paris, June 7, 1933; produced in London as *Anna Anna;* in the U.S. in N.Y., Dec. 4, 1958); opera, *Marie galante* (Paris, Dec. 22, 1934). In London: musical play, *A Kingdom for a Cow* (London, June 28, 1935). In the U.S.: operas: *Street Scene* (to a play by Elmer Rice; N.Y., Jan. 9, 1947) and *Lost in the Stars* (text by Maxwell Anderson after Alan Paton's *Cry, the Beloved Country;* N.Y., Oct. 20, 1949); a pageant of Jewish history, *The Eternal Road* (after Franz Werfel; 1934–35; N.Y., Jan. 7, 1937); musical fable, *Johnny Johnson* (text by Paul Green; N.Y., Nov. 19, 1936); musical comedies: *Knickerbocker Holiday* (book and lyrics by Maxwell Anderson; Hartford, Conn., Sept. 26, 1938; contains the popular "September Song"); *Lady in the Dark* (text by Moss Hart and lyrics by Ira Gershwin; N.Y., Jan. 23, 1941); *One Touch of Venus* (text by S.J. Perelman and Ogden Nash; N.Y., Oct. 7, 1943); *The Firebrand of Florence* (text by E.J. Mayer and Ira Gershwin; N.Y., March 22, 1945); musical plays: *A Flag Is Born* (text by Ben Hecht; N.Y., Sept. 5, 1946) and *Love Life* (text by Alan Jay Lerner; N.Y., Oct. 7, 1948); background music for the stage spectacle *Railroads on Parade* (N.Y. World's Fair, 1939); folk opera, *Down in the Valley* (1945–48; Indiana Univ., Bloomington, July 15, 1948).

FOR ORCH.: Symph. No. 1 (*Berliner Sinfonie;* 1921; score recovered in 1955, and perf. by the Hamburg Radio Orch., Jan. 17, 1958; U.S. premiere, Greenwich, Conn., Oct. 21, 1978); Symph. No. 2 (*Pariser Symphonie;* 1933; Amsterdam, Oct. 11, 1934, Bruno Walter conducting; perf. in the U.S. under the title *3 Night Scenes* by the N.Y. Phil., Dec. 13, 1934, Bruno Walter conducting); *Fantasia, Passacaglia, und Hymnus* (1922); *Quodlibet* (1924; Coburg, Feb. 6, 1926; N.Y., Feb. 24, 1963; material drawn from *Zaubernacht*); Concerto for Violin, Woodwinds, Double Bass, and Percussion (1924; Paris, June 11, 1925; Cincinnati, March 28, 1930); *Kleine Dreigroschenmusik* for Winds (1929; concert suite from *The Threepenny Opera*).

VOCAL WORKS: Radio cantata, *Der Lindberghflug*, in collaboration with Brecht and Hindemith, commemorating Lindbergh's transatlantic flight of 1927 (Baden-Baden Festival, July 28, 1929; rescored solely by Weill, and with Hindemith's name eliminated, Berlin, Dec. 5, 1929; revised in 1930 as *Der Flug des Lindberghs* and in 1950 retitled *Der Ozeanflug*, without Lindbergh's name, as a gesture of protest against Lindbergh's militant neutrality toward Nazi Germany); *The Ballad of Magna Carta*, modern historical drama for Soloists, Chorus, and Orch., with text by Maxwell Anderson (Columbia Network broadcast, Feb. 4, 1940); *Divertimento* for Small Orch., with Male Chorus (1922; reconstructed by David Drew in 1971); *Rilke-Lieder* for Voice and Orch. (1925); *Der neue Orpheus*, cantata for Soprano, Violin, and Orch. (1925; Berlin, March 2, 1927; New Haven, Oct. 5, 1972); *Von Tod im Wald* for Bass

Voice and 10 Wind Instruments (Berlin, Nov. 23, 1927; N.Y., March 7, 1977); *Das Berliner Requiem* for Tenor, Baritone, Male Chorus, and Wind Orch. (1927; Frankfurt Radio, May 22, 1929; Cincinnati, April 3, 1970); *3 Walt Whitman Songs* for Baritone, and Small Orch. or Piano (1940); *Recordare* for Mixed Chorus and Boys' Chorus a cappella (1923; Utrecht, July 2, 1971; N.Y., Jan. 4, 1980); *Frauentanz* for Soprano, Viola, Flute, Clarinet, Horn, and Bassoon (Berlin, Feb. 1924; Salzburg Festival, Aug. 6, 1924); *The Legend of the Dead Soldier* for Chorus a cappella (1929); songs.

CHAMBER MUSIC: 2 movements for String Quartet: *Allegro deciso* and *Andantino* (N.Y., March 7, 1977); String Quartet in B minor (1919); Cello Sonata (1920; U.S. premiere, Philadelphia, May 4, 1979); String Quartet No. 1, op. 8 (1923; U.S. premiere, Yale Univ., May 13, 1971).

Weinberger, Jaromir, notable Czech composer; b. Prague, Jan. 8, 1896; d. (suicide by overdose of sedative drugs) St. Petersburg, Fla., Aug. 8, 1967. He studied with Křička and Hofmeister at the Prague Cons., then briefly with Max Reger in Leipzig. In 1922 he visited the U.S., and taught for a semester at the Ithaca Cons. in N.Y. Returning to Europe, he was active as a teacher in Bratislava, Prague, and Vienna; lived mostly in Prague until 1937; in 1939 he settled permanently in the U.S., living in St. Petersburg. He achieved sudden fame with the production of his opera in a popular Bohemian style, *Švanda dudák (Schwanda the Bagpiper),* at the National Theater in Prague on April 27, 1927. Its success was immediate, and performances followed all over Europe in several languages; it was produced in German (as *Schwanda der Dudelsackpfeifer*) at the Metropolitan Opera in N.Y. on Nov. 7, 1931; the *Polka and Fugue* from this opera has become a popular number in the orch. repertoire. His other operas include *Die geliebte Stimme* (Munich, Feb. 28, 1931); *Lidé z Pokerflatu (The Outcasts of Poker Flat,* after Bret Harte; Brno, Nov. 19, 1932); *A Bed of Roses,* light opera (Prague, 1934); *Wallenstein,* lyric tragedy after Schiller (Vienna, Nov. 18, 1937); for Orch.: *Marionette Overture* (1913); 6 Bohemian songs and dances (1929); *Under the Spreading Chestnut Tree,* variations and fugue (N.Y., Oct. 12, 1939); *Song of the High Seas* (N.Y., Nov. 9, 1940); *Lincoln Symphony* (Cincinnati, Oct. 17, 1941); *Czech Rhapsody* (Washington, D.C., Nov. 5, 1941); *A Bird's Opera* (Detroit, Nov. 13, 1941); *Préludes religieuses et profanes* (1953); *Ecclesiastes* for Soprano, Baritone, Mixed Chorus, and Organ (1945); other choral works; violin pieces; piano pieces; etc.

Weiner, Lazar, Russian-born American composer; b. Cherkassy, near Kiev, Oct. 27, 1897; d. New York, Jan. 10, 1982. He emigrated to America in 1914, and became associated with numerous Jewish artistic activities in N.Y.; also took private lessons in composition with Robert Russell Bennett, Frederick Jacobi, and Joseph Schillinger. From 1929 to 1975 he led the choir of the Central Synagogue in N.Y.; conducted classes in the Yiddish art song at Hebrew Union College and at the Jewish Theological Seminary in America; directed the Workmen's Circle Chorus; and served as host of the weekly radio broadcast "The Message of America." He wrote a number of songs to Yiddish words; also composed several Sabbath services; the cantatas *Legend of Toil* (1933), *Man of the World* (1939), *Fight for Freedom* (1943), *To Thee, America* (1944), and *The Last Judgement* (1966); and an opera, *The Golem,* produced in White Plains, N.Y., on Jan. 13, 1957. His son, **Yehudi Weiner,** a composer, changed his surname to **Wyner** in order to approximate phonetically the right pronunciation.

Weiner, Léo, outstanding Hungarian composer; b. Budapest, April 16, 1885; d. there, Sept. 13, 1960. He was a pupil of Hans Koessler at the Budapest Academy of Music (1901–6), winning several prizes for excellence; in 1906 he won the Franz-Josef-Jubiläumspreis, which enabled him to study further in Austria, Germany, and France. Returning to Budapest, he became a prof. at the Academy (1908); was pensioned in 1949. He won the Coolidge Prize in 1922 for his 2nd String Quartet, the Kossuth Prize in 1950, and became an Eminent Artist of the Hungarian People's Republic in 1953. In his works he adopted a characteristic Hungarian style within the framework of Romantic forms.

Weingartner, (Paul) Felix, Edler von Münzberg, illustrious German conductor; b. Zara, Dalmatia, June 2, 1863; d. Winterthur, Switzerland, May 7, 1942. After his father's death in 1868, his mother took him to Graz, where he studied music with W.A. Remy. He publ. some piano pieces when he was 16 years old; Brahms recommended him for a stipend which enabled him to go to take music courses with Reinecke, Jadassohn, and Paul at the Leipzig Cons. (1881–83). He received the Mozart Prize at his graduation; he was introduced to Liszt, who recommended Weingartner's opera *Sakuntala* for production in Weimar (March 23, 1884), a signal honor for a young man not yet 21 years old. While progressing rapidly as a composer, Weingartner launched a brilliant career as a conductor, which was to become his prime vocation. He conducted in Königsberg (1884), Danzig (1885–87), Hamburg (1887–89), and Mannheim (1889–91). In 1891 he was engaged as conductor at the Berlin Royal Opera; from 1898 to 1905 he led the Kaim Orch. in Munich; simultaneously he was conductor of the symph. concerts of the Royal Orch. in Berlin (1891–1907). His reputation as a fine musician was enhanced by his appearances as an ensemble player in the Weingartner Trio, with himself as pianist, Rettich as violinist, and Warnke as cellist. In 1908 he succeeded Mahler as music director of the Vienna Court Opera, and conducted there until 1911. From 1912 to 1914 he conducted the Municipal Opera in Hamburg; from 1914 to 1918 was in charge of the Darmstadt Orch. He was subsequently music director at the Vienna Volksoper (1919–24), and conducted the Vienna Phil. (1908–27); in 1927 he was appointed director of the Basel (Switzerland) Cons.; was guest conductor at the Vienna State Opera during the season 1934–35; served as director in 1935–36, and continued guest appearances until 1938. In the interim he had engagements as guest conductor with major European orchs.; made his American debut with the N.Y. Phil. on Feb. 12, 1904, and later conducted the N.Y. Symph. Society (Jan.–March 1906). He appeared as opera conductor with the Boston Opera Co. on Feb. 12, 1912, conducting *Tristan und Isolde;* he and his 3rd wife, the mezzo-soprano **Lucille Marcel,** were engaged for a season with the Boston Opera Co. in 1913. (His first wife was Marie Juillerat, whom he married in 1891; his 2nd wife was the Baroness Feodora von Dreifus, whom he married in 1903). He made his debut at Covent Garden in London in 1939, conducting *Parsifal.* He eventually settled in Interlaken, Switzerland, where he established a summer conducting school. Weingartner was a competent music editor; he was on the editorial board for the complete works of Berlioz (1899) and of Haydn (1907). Despite the pressure of his activities as a conductor, he found time for composition. After his early opera *Sakuntala,* he produced several others: *Genesius* (Berlin, Nov. 15, 1892); *Orestes,* a trilogy (Leipzig, Feb. 15, 1902); *Kain und Abel* (Darmstadt, May 17, 1914); *Dame Kobold* (Darmstadt, Feb. 23, 1916); *Die Dorfschule* (Vienna, May 13, 1920); *Meister Andrea* (Vienna, May 13, 1920); wrote his own librettos, and conducted the first performances. He also composed 7 symphs. and a great deal of chamber music; made arrangements of Beethoven's "Hammerklavier" Sonata, op. 106, and of Weber's *Aufforderung zum Tanz.* He was an excellent writer on musical subjects. Among his publications are: *Die Lehre von der Wiedergeburt und das musikalische Drama* (1895); *Über das Dirigieren* (1896; 5th ed., 1913; a fundamental essay on conducting); *Bayreuth 1876–1896* (1897; 2nd ed., 1904); *Die Symphonie nach Beethoven* (1897; 4th ed., 1901; in Eng., 1904; new trans. as *The Symphony since Beethoven,* 1926); *Ratschläge für Aufführung der Sinfonien Beethoven* (1906; 3rd ed., 1928; in Eng., London, 1907); a polemical pamphlet, *Erlebnisse eines kgl. Kapellmeisters in Berlin* (1912; an attack upon the Berlin intendancy; a rebuttal was publ. by A. Wolff in *Der Fall Weingartner,* 1912); *Ratschläge für Aufführung der Sinfonien Schuberts und Schumanns* (1918); *Ratschläge für Aufführung der Sinfonien Mozarts* (1923); *Musikalische Walpurgisnacht* (1907; a satirical comedy); *Akkorde* (1912; collected essays); *Bo Yin Ra* (1927); *Lebenserinnerungen* (vol. I, 1923; vol. II, 1929; Eng. version as *Buffets and Rewards: A Musician's Reminiscences,* London, 1937); *Unwirkliches und Wirkliches* (1936).

Weinlig, Christian Ehregott, German organist and composer; b. Dresden, Sept. 30, 1743; d. there, March 14, 1813. He studied with Homilius at the Kreuzschule; in 1767 he was organist at the Evangelical Church in Leipzig; in 1773, at Thorn; in 1780, accompanist at the Italian Opera in Dresden, and organist at the Frauenkirche; in 1785, succeeded his teacher, Homilius, as cantor of the Kreuzschule. He

publ. sonatas for piano, with flute and cello; brought out several oratorios; also light theater pieces.

Weinlig, (Christian) Theodor, noted German music theorist and teacher, nephew and pupil of **Christian Ehregott Weinlig;** b. Dresden, July 25, 1780; d. Leipzig, March 7, 1842. After a period of study under his uncle, he became a pupil of Stanislao Mattei in Bologna; returning to Dresden, he was cantor at the Kreuzschule (1814–17); in 1823 he succeeded Schicht as cantor of the Thomasschule in Leipzig. He enjoyed high repute as a teacher of theory and composition; Richard Wagner was his pupil. His own works include a *Deutsches Magnificat* for Soli, Chorus, and Orch.; vocalises; he publ. a practical manual, *Theoretisch-praktische Anleitung zur Fuge, für den Selbstunterricht* (1845; 2nd ed., 1852).

Weinmann, Karl, German musicologist, authority on church music; b. Vohenstrauss, Upper Palatinate, Dec. 22, 1873; d. Pielenhofen, near Regensburg, Sept. 26, 1929. He was a pupil of Haberl and Haller at the Kirchenmusikschule in Regensburg; after further study under Peter Wagner in Freiburg, Switzerland, he obtained the degree of Dr.Phil. with the dissertation *Das Hymnarium Parisiense* (1905). After his ordination to the priesthood, he became a prof. at the Kirchenmusikschule in Regensburg; in 1910 succeeded Haberl as its director; in 1917 he was made Dr.Theol. He was editor of the *Kirchenmusikalisches Jahrbuch* (1909–11), of *Musica Sacra* (from 1911), and of the *Cäcilienvereinsorgan* (from 1926). He edited for Pustet (after the *Editio vaticana*) *Römisches Gradualbuch* (1909; 4th ed., 1928); *Graduale* (1910); *Kyriale* (1911); *Totenoffizium* (1912; 2nd ed., 1928); *Graduale parvum* (1913); *Römisches Vesperbuch mit Psalmenbuch* (1915); *Karwochenbuch* (1924); *Feier der heiligen Karwoche* (1925); *Sonntagsvesper und Komplet* (2nd ed., 1928). Was also editor of the collection *Kirchenmusik,* for which he wrote *Geschichte der Kirchenmusik* (1906; 4th ed., 1925; Eng. trans., 1910; also trans. into French, Italian, Polish, and Hungarian), and monographs on Leonhard Paminger (1907) and Carl Proske (1909). Other writings include *Palestrinas Geburtsjahr* (Regensburg, 1915); *Stille Nacht, heilige Nacht: Die Geschichte des Liedes zu seinem 100. Geburtstag* (1918; 2nd ed., 1920); *Das Konzil von Trient und die Kirchenmusik* (1919).

Weinstock, Herbert, American writer on music; b. Milwaukee, Nov. 16, 1905; d. New York, Oct. 21, 1971. He was educated in his native town; later took courses at the Univ. of Chicago. He publ. the following books: *Tchaikovsky* (1943; also publ. in French, Portuguese, Spanish, and German); *Handel* (1946; 2nd ed., 1959; also in German); *Chopin: The Man and His Music* (1949; 2nd ed., 1959); *Music As an Art* (1953; 2nd ed., 1966, under the title *What Music Is*); co-author, with Wallace Brockway, of *Men of Music* (1939; revised and enlarged, 1950) and *The Opera: A History of Its Creation and Performance* (1941; 2nd ed., 1962, entitled *The World of Opera*); *Donizetti and the World of Opera in Italy, Paris and Vienna* in the First Half of the 19th Century (N.Y., 1963); *Rossini* (N.Y., 1968); *Vincenzo Bellini: His Life and Operas* (N.Y., 1971). For some years before his death he was music editor for the book publishing firm of Alfred A. Knopf in N.Y.

Weinzweig, John, prominent Canadian composer; b. Toronto, March 11, 1913. He learned to play piano, tuba, and saxophone; then took lessons in orchestration with MacMillan, in counterpoint with Willan, and in harmony with Leo Smith at the Univ. of Toronto (1934–37); continued his study in composition with Bernard Rogers at the Eastman School of Music in Rochester, N.Y. (1937–38). In 1939 he was appointed to the faculty of the Toronto Cons.; in 1952 joined the music staff at the Univ. of Toronto. On Feb. 3, 1951, he organized the Canadian League of Composers and was its first president.
WORKS: Ballet, *Red Ear of Corn* (Toronto, March 2, 1949); *Legend* for Orch. (1937); *The Enchanted Hill* for Orch. (1938); *Suite* for Orch. (1938); *Spectre* for String Orch. and Timpani (1938); *A Tale of Tamotu* for Bassoon and Orch. (1939); Symph. (1940); *Rhapsody* for Orch. (1941); *Interlude in an Artist's Life* for String Orch. (1943); *Our Canada* for Orch. (1943); *Divertimento No. 1* for Flute and String Orch. (Vancouver, Dec. 29, 1946); *Divertimento No. 2* for Oboe and String Orch. (Toronto, April 30, 1948); *Divertimento No. 3* for Bassoon and String Orch. (Toronto, May 5, 1961); *Divertimento No. 5* for Solo Trumpet, Trombone, and Wind Ensemble (Pittsburgh, June 9, 1961; numbered out of chronological order); *Divertimento No. 4* for Clarinet, and String Orch. or String Quintet (Vancouver, Sept. 19, 1968); *Divertimento No. 6* for Saxophone and String Orch. (Toronto, Aug. 21, 1972); *Edge of the World,* symph. poem (1946); *Round Dance* for Small Orch. (1950; version for Full Orch., 1977); Violin Concerto (Toronto, May 30, 1955); *Wine of Peace,* 3 songs for Soprano and Orch. (1957); *Symphonic Ode* (1958); Piano Concerto (Toronto, Dec. 15, 1966); Concerto for Harp and Chamber Orch. (Toronto, April 30, 1967); *Dummiyah (Silence)* for Orch. (Toronto, July 4, 1969); 3 string quartets (1937, 1946, 1962); Violin Sonata (1941); cello sonata, *Israel* (1949); Wind Quintet (1964); Clarinet Quartet (1965); *Around the Stage in 25 Minutes during Which a Variety of Instruments Are Struck* for Solo Percussionist (1970); *Trialogue* for Soprano, Flute, and Piano (1971); *Riffs* for Solo Flute (1974); *Pieces of 5,* brass quintet (1976); *Contrast* for Solo Guitar (1976); *Refrains* for Double Bass and Piano (1977); 2 suites for Piano (1939, 1950); Piano Sonata (1950); *Impromptus* for Piano (1973); *Improvisation on an Indian Tune* for Organ (1942); choruses; *Private Collection,* 8 songs for Soprano and Piano (1975).

Weir, Gillian, organist and harpsichordist; b. Martinborough, New Zealand, Jan. 17, 1941. She studied at the Royal Academy of Music in London (1962–65); won the St. Albans International Organ Competition in 1964; in 1965 she made her debut at London's Royal Festival Hall; in 1967 toured Canada and the U.S.; later continued to give recitals in Europe and America as an organist and harpsichordist.

Weis, (Carl) Flemming, Danish composer and organist; b. Copenhagen, April 15, 1898; d. there, Sept. 30, 1981. He studied composition with Carl Nielsen and Gustav Helsted at the Royal Danish Cons. in Copenhagen (1917–20); then took lessons in composition with Paul Graener and organ with Karl Straube at the Hochschule für Musik in Leipzig (1921–23). He served as organist of the St. Anna Church in Copenhagen (1929–68); was a member of the board of the Society for Contemporary Music (1926–56; president, 1942–56) and a member of the board of the Danish Society of Composers (president, 1963–75). His music follows the traditions of the Danish School; under the influence of his teacher Carl Nielsen he wrote a number of symph. pieces imbued with Romantic fervor and gentle humor.

Weis, Karel, Czech conductor and composer; b. Prague, Feb. 13, 1862; d. there, April 4, 1944. He studied violin at the Prague Cons.; also organ with Skuherský and composition with Fibich at the Organ School in Prague; subsequently filled various posts as organist and conductor in Prague and other towns in Bohemia. He devoted much of his time to collecting Bohemian folk songs, and publ. them in 15 vols. (1928–41).
WORKS: Operas: *Viola,* after Shakespeare's *Twelfth Night* (Prague, Jan. 17, 1892); *Der polnische Jude* (Prague, March 3, 1901; very successful; produced in Eng. at the Metropolitan Opera House, N.Y., March 9, 1921); *Die Dorfmusikanten* (Prague, Jan. 1, 1905); *Der Revisor,* after Gogol (1907); *Utok na mlýn,* after Zola's *L'Attaque su Moulin* (Prague, March 29, 1912); *Lešetínský kovář (The Blacksmith of Lešetín;* Prague, June 6, 1920); Symph.; String Quartet; piano pieces; songs.

Weisgall, Hugo, American composer; b. Ivančice, Moravia, Oct. 13, 1912. His family emigrated to the U.S. in 1920, and settled in Baltimore; he studied music theory with Louis Cheslock at the Peabody Cons. there; later had private sessions with Sessions in N.Y.; also took composition lessons with Rosario Scalero at the Curtis Inst. in Philadelphia. In 1952 he was appointed chairman of the faculty at the Seminary College of Jewish Music in N.Y.; from 1957 to 1968 was on the staff of the Juilliard School of Music; also taught at Queens College. His music constitutes the paragon of enlightened but inoffensive modernism; he is a master of all musical idioms, and a bungler of none. His intentions in each of his works never fail in the execution; for this reason his music enjoys numerous performances, which are usually accepted with pleasure by the audiences, if not by the majority of important music critics.
WORKS: Operas: *Night* (1932); *Lillith* (1934); *The Tenor* (Baltimore, Feb. 11, 1952); *The Stronger,* after Strindberg (Lutherville, Md., Aug. 9, 1952); *6 Characters in Search of an Author* (N.Y., April 26, 1959); *Purgatory,* in one act to the text of W.B. Yeats (Li-

brary of Congress, Washington, D.C., Feb. 17, 1961); *Athaliah* (N.Y., Feb. 17, 1964); *9 Rivers from Jordan* (N.Y., Oct. 9, 1968); *The Hundred Nights* (N.Y., April 22, 1976); *The Gardens of Adonis* (1980); ballets: *Quest* (Baltimore, May 17, 1938); *One Thing Is Certain* (Baltimore, Feb. 25, 1939); *Overture in F* (London, July 29, 1943); *A Garden Eastward,* cantata for High Voice and Orch. (Baltimore, Jan. 31, 1953); *Soldier Songs* for Baritone and Orch. (1946); 2 choral études (1937, 1953); a number of songs.

Weismann, Julius, German composer; b. Freiburg im Breisgau, Dec. 26, 1879; d. Singen (Bodensee), Dec. 22, 1950. He studied in Munich with Rheinberger and Thuille; devoted himself mainly to the composition of operas, the most important of which was *Leonce und Lena* (Freiburg im Breisgau, June 21, 1925). Other operas: *Schwanenweiss,* after Strindberg (Duisburg, Sept. 29, 1923); *Ein Traumspiel* (Duisburg, 1925); *Regina del Lago* (Karlsruhe, 1928); *Die Gespenstersonate,* after Strindberg (Munich, Dec. 19, 1930); *Landsknechte* (Essen, 1936); *Die pfiffige Magd,* after Holberg (Leipzig, Feb. 11, 1939); a symph., *Über einem Grabe,* for Chorus and Orch.; *Fingerhütchen,* fairy ballad for Baritone Solo, Female Chorus, and Orch.; *Macht hoch die Tür,* cantata; *Tanzfantasie* for Orch.; Piano Concerto; Violin Concerto; much chamber music, including 2 piano trios, 2 violin sonatas, etc.

Weiss, Adolph, American composer and bassoonist; b. Baltimore, Sept. 12, 1891 (of German parents); d. Van Nuys, Calif., Feb. 21, 1971. He studied piano, violin, and the bassoon; at the age of 16, was engaged as first bassoonist of the Russian Symph. Orch. of N.Y.; then played in the N.Y. Phil. under Mahler; for many years was with the N.Y. Symph. under Walter Damrosch. In the meantime, he studied composition with Cornelius Rybner at Columbia Univ. In 1916 he joined the Chicago Symph. Orch. as bassoonist; studied theory with Adolf Weidig and Theodore Ötterstrom there; then was bassoonist with the Rochester (N.Y.) Orch. In 1925 he went to Europe to study with Arnold Schoenberg, whose influence was decisive in the formation of his musical style, which is in the 12-tone idiom. Returning to the U.S., he played in the San Francisco Symph. Orch.; then moved to Hollywood, where he settled.

Weiss, Amalie. See **Joachim, Amalie.**

Weissenberg, Alexis, pianist; b. Sofia, July 26, 1929. He studied in Sofia with Pantcho Vladigerov; during the German occupation of Bulgaria, he and his mother were confined in a concentration camp, but managed to flee to Palestine. In 1946 he went to N.Y.; studied with Artur Schnabel, Olga Samaroff, and Wanda Landowska. In 1947 he won the youth competition sponsored by the Philadelphia Orch.; in 1948 he won the Leventritt Competition and appeared with the N.Y. Phil. He then toured widely as a concert pianist, visiting Italy, Germany, Russia, and Japan.

Weissmann, John, Hungarian musicologist; b. Budapest, July 10, 1910; d. London, March 23, 1980. He studied at the Budapest Cons.; was opera coach at the Municipal Theater (1932–34); then assistant conductor there (1935–37). In 1937 he settled in London, where he attended classes of conducting at the Royal Academy of Music. Subsequently he devoted his attention mainly to musicology; contributed numerous valuable essays to various periodicals.

Weitzmann, Carl Friedrich, noted German theorist and composer; b. Berlin, Aug. 10, 1808; d. there, Nov. 7, 1880. He studied violin with Henning and theory with Klein; later, at Kassel, was a pupil of Spohr and Hauptmann. He then held the post of concertmaster in Riga (1832–34), Reval (1834–36), and St. Petersburg (1836–46). After sojourns in Paris and London (1846–48), he settled in Berlin as a teacher of composition. He was an ardent disciple and friend of Wagner and Liszt; among his posthumous papers was found the original MS of a double fugue for piano by Wagner, with corrections in the handwriting of Weinlig (Wagner's teacher). The piece was publ. by E. Istel in *Die Musik* (July 1912). Weitzmann was an original thinker in his harmonic theories; made an investigation of the modulatory functions of the whole-tone scale, and interested Liszt in its use. He composed a 4th variation to Liszt's *Todtentanz.* A full exposition of his theories is found in a book by his American pupil E.M. Bowman, *K.F. Weitzmann's Manual of Musical Theory* (N.Y., 1877). Weitzmann's theoretical works in German include *Der übermässige Dreiklang* (1853); *Der verminderte Septimenakkord* (1854); *Geschichte der Septimen-Akkordes* (1854); *Harmoniesystem* (1860); *Die neue Harmonielehre im Streit mit der alten* (1861); *Geschichte des Klavierspiels ind der Klavierlitteratur* (1863, as Part III of the Lebert-Stark piano method; 2nd ed., 1879, printed separately, with an added *Geschichte des Klaviers;* in Eng., N.Y., 1894, with a biographical sketch by Otto Lessmann; 3rd German ed., Leipzig, 1899, as *Geschichte der Klaviermusik,* ed. by Max Seiffert, with a supplement, *Geschichte des Klaviers,* by Otto Fleischer); *Der letzte der Virtuosen* (on Tausig; 1868); many essays in various musical periodicals. As a composer, he followed the fashionable Romantic trends; wrote the operas *Räuberliebe* (1834), *Walpurgisnacht* (1835), and *Lorbeer und Bettelstab* (1836), which he brought out in Reval; 3 books of *Valses nobles* for Piano; *Preludes and Modulations* for Piano, 2 parts, "Classic" and "Romantic"; also wrote 2 books of ingenious canonic *Rätsel* for piano, 4-hands, and 2 books of *Kontrapunkt-Studien* for piano.

Weldon, Georgina (née **Thomas**), English soprano; b. London, May 24, 1837; d. Brighton, Jan. 11, 1914. She took up singing after her marriage to Capt. Weldon in 1860, and did not appear in public until 1870. She organized an orphan asylum for the purpose of musical education, and also dabbled in music publishing. Special interest attaches to her because of her romantic friendship with Gounod, who during his London sojourn (1870–75) lived at her residence, and whom she assisted in training the Gounod Choir. She trans. his autobiography (which goes only as far as 1859) into Eng. (1875). Their relationship deteriorated, leading to a legal entanglement in connection with her claims regarding the copyright of Gounod's choral works; she wrote acrimonious letters to the press, defending her stand. She also publ. some songs of her own (to French texts) and the didactic manuals *Hints for Pronunciation in Singing* (1872) and *Musical Reform* (1875).

Welin, Karl-Erik, Swedish organist, pianist, and composer of the extreme avant-garde; b. Genarp, May 31, 1934. He studied organ with Alf Linden at the Royal College of Music in Stockholm (1956–61); took composition lessons with Gunnar Bucht (1958–60) and Lidholm (1960–64); then attended summer seminars in new music at Darmstadt (1960–62), working with the American pianist David Tudor on avant-garde techniques. In 1958 he joined the experimental group "Fylkingen" in Stockholm. As a composer, he followed in his youthful works the fashionable impressionistic trends, mostly in miniature forms, in colorful and unusual instrumental groupings. He created a sensation at his piano recital at the Stockholm High School of Music on March 6, 1964, when he exploded a pyrotechnical device lodged in the frame of the piano and then proceeded to saw off the piano legs with an electrically powered handsaw, accidentally cutting himself so seriously that he had to undergo surgery. WORKS: *4 Chinese Poems* for Chorus (1956); *Sermo modulatus* for Flute and Clarinet (1959); *Renovations* for Soprano, Flute, Violin, Mandolin, Celesta, and Percussion (1960); *Cantata* for Children's Chorus, Violin, Flute, and Harpsichord (1960); *Manzit* for Clarinet, Trombone, Violin, Piano, and Percussion (1962); *Esservecchia* for Electric Guitar, Horn, Trombone, and Piano (1963); *Warum nicht?* for Flute, Violin, Cello, Xylophone, Vibraphone, and Tam-tam (1964); *Pereo* for 36 Strings (1964); *Kazimir* for 4 Flutes (1965); *Visoka 12* for 2 Flutes, 2 Violins, and 2 Cellos (1965); *Etwas für ...* for Wind Quintet (1966); a children's television opera, *Dummerjöns (Tom Fool)*, after H.C. Andersen (1966–67); *Eigentlich nicht*, 2nd string quartet (1967); *Copelius*, ballet of concrete music (1968); *Ondine*, theater music (1968); *Vindarnas grotta (Cave of the Winds)*, television ballet (Stockholm Television, March 30, 1969); *Glazba* for 3 Flutes, Bassoon, and Soprano (1968); *Ben fatto* for a Solo Instrument or an infinite number of Instruments (1968); *Improvisiation* for Organ (1969); *PC-132* for String Quartet (1970); *A New Map of Hell* for Chorus (1971); *Recidivans*, 3rd string quartet (1972); *Aver la forza di ...* for Chorus and String Orch. (1972); opera, *Drottning Jag (Queen Ego;* 1972; Stockholm, Feb. 17, 1973); *Harmonies* for Clarinet, Trombone, Cello, and Piano (1972); *Pagabile* for Chamber Ensemble (1972); *Residuo*, 4th string quartet (1974).

Welitsch, Ljuba (real name, **Velitchkova**), Bulgarian soprano; b. Borisovo, near Varna, July 10, 1913.

She played the violin as a child; then entered high school; subsequently took courses in philosophy at the Univ. of Sofia; then went to Vienna, where she studied voice with Lierhammer. She made her operatic debut as Nedda in *Pagliacci* at the Graz Opera (1936); from 1941 to 1943 she sang in Hamburg and Berlin; in 1943–46 was in Munich. On June 11, 1944, she made her first appearance as Salome (later to become her most famous role) in Vienna, under the direction of Richard Strauss himself, on his 80th birthday. She made her debut in London with the Vienna State Opera as Donna Anna in *Don Giovanni* on Sept. 20, 1947. Her American debut, at the Metropolitan Opera House in N.Y., in *Salome* (Feb. 4, 1949) was greatly acclaimed. She remained a member of the Metropolitan until 1952.

Welk, Lawrence, popular American conductor of entertainment music; b. Strasburg, N.Dak., March 11, 1903. He received his training in California; in 1955 he began a series of television concerts which became increasingly popular, thanks to his skillful selection of programs containing a varied mixture of semi-classical pieces, western American ballads, and Slavic folk-dance tunes. His use of an accordion section in his arrangements, steadfast rhythmic beat, and sentimentalized tempi impart to his renditions a rudimentary sound quality that makes him a favorite with undiscriminating audiences. He publ. (with some outside help) an autobiography, *Wunnerful, Wunnerful!* (N.Y., 1971), radiating euphoria, and a sequel: *Ah-one, ah-two: Life with My Musical Family* (N.Y., 1974).

Wellek, Albert, Austrian musicologist; b. Vienna, Oct. 16, 1904; d. Mainz, Aug. 27, 1972. He studied philosophy at the univs. of Prague, Vienna, and Leipzig; also took music courses at the Prague Cons.; received his Ph.D. in 1928 from the Univ. of Vienna. In 1929 he became especially interested in the problems of musical psychology; served as assistant to Felix Krueger in his dept. of psychology at the Univ. of Leipzig; in 1943 he was appointed prof. of psychology at Breslau, and from 1946 taught at the Univ. of Mainz, where he remained until his death. He wrote *Das absolute Gehör und seine Typen* (Leipzig, 1938); *Typologie der Musikbegabung im deutschen Volke* (Munich, 1939; 2nd ed., 1970); also numerous articles dealing with the development of new musical resources, including quarter-tones and dodecaphony.

Weller, Walter, Austrian conductor; b. Vienna, Nov. 30, 1939. He was educated at the Vienna Academy of Music, where he studied violin and attended classes in conducting held by Karl Böhm. In 1958 he founded the noted Weller Quartet; also in 1958 he joined the Vienna Phil., and in 1962 became its concertmaster, a post he held, alternating with others, until 1969. He then embarked upon a conducting career. He conducted both the Vienna State Opera and Volksoper; was Generalmusikdirektor in Duisburg (1971–72); also conducted the Vienna Tonkünstler Orch. (1975–78). In 1977 he was named

Wellesz – Welte

principal conductor and musical adviser of the Royal Liverpool Phil. In 1980 he became principal conductor of the Royal Phil. Orch. of London.

Wellesz, Egon, eminent Austrian composer and musicologist; b. Vienna, Oct. 21, 1885; d. Oxford, Nov. 9, 1974. He studied harmony with Carl Frühling, musicology with Guido Adler, and counterpoint and composition with Schoenberg in Vienna (1904–6); obtained the degree of Dr.Phil. in 1908 with a thesis on Giuseppe Bonno, publ. in the *Sammelbände der Internationalen Musik-Gesellschaft,* 11 (1910). From 1911 to 1915 he taught music history at the Neues Cons. in Vienna; in 1913 he was engaged as a lecturer on musicology at the Univ. of Vienna, and was a prof. there from 1930 to 1938, when the annexation of Austria by Nazi Germany compelled him to leave. He went to England in 1938; joined the music dept. of Oxford Univ., which in 1932 had conferred upon him the degree of Mus.Doc. *(honoris causa).* In 1940 he became a lecturer in music history at Oxford Univ.; in 1946 he was appointed to the editorial board of the *New Oxford History of Music,* to which he then contributed, and was Univ. Reader in Byzantine music at Oxford (1948–56); received the Prize of the City of Vienna in 1953; was president of the Oxford Univ. Byzantine Society (1955–66); in 1957 was made a Commander of the Order of the British Empire and was awarded the Grande Medaille d'Argent of the City of Paris. In 1956–57 he gave lectures in the U.S. A scholar and a musician of extraordinary capacities, Wellesz distinguished himself as a composer of highly complex musical scores, and as an authority on Byzantine music.
WORKS: OPERAS: *Die Prinzessin Girnara* (1919–20; Hannover, May 15, 1921; revised version, Mannheim, Sept. 2, 1928); *Alkestis* (1922–23; Mannheim, March 20, 1924); *Opferung der Gefangenen* (1924–25; Cologne, April 10, 1926); *Scherz, List und Rache* (1926–27; Stuttgart, March 1, 1928); *Die Bakchantinnen* (1929–30; Vienna, June 20, 1931); *Incognita* (Oxford, Dec. 5, 1950). BALLETS: *Das Wunder der Diana* (1915; Mannheim, March 20, 1924); *Persisches Ballet* (1920; Donaueschingen, 1924); *Achilles auf Skyros* (1921; Stuttgart, March 4, 1927); *Die Nächtlichen* (1923; Berlin, Nov. 20, 1924). FOR ORCH.: 9 symphs.: No. 1, in C (1945); No. 2, in E-flat (1948); No. 3, in A (1951); No. 4, *Symphonia Austriaca,* in G (1953); No. 5 (1956; Düsseldorf, Feb. 20, 1958); No. 6 (1965; Nuremberg, June 1, 1966); No. 7 (1968); No. 8 (1971); No. 9 (1971; Vienna, Nov. 22, 1972); *Vorfrühling,* symph. poem (1912); *Suite* for Violin and Chamber Orch. (1924); Piano Concerto (1934); *Prosperos Beschwörungen,* after Shakespeare's *The Tempest* (1936–38; Vienna, Feb. 19, 1938); Violin Concerto (1961; Vienna, Jan. 19, 1962); *Music* for String Orch. (1964); *Divertimento* for Chamber Orch. (1969); *Symphonischer Epilog* (1969). FOR VOICE: *Gebete der Mädchen zur Maria* for Soprano, Chorus, and Orch. (1909); *Mitte des Lebens,* cantata (1932); *Amor timido,* cantata for Soprano and Orch. (1935); *5 Sonnets by Elizabeth Barrett Browning* for Soprano and String Quartet (1935); *Lied der Welt* for Soprano and Orch. (1937); *Leben, Traum und Tod* for Contralto and Orch. (1937); *Short Mass* for Chorus and Small Orch. (1937); *The Leaden Echo and the Golden Echo,* after Hopkins, for Soprano, Violin, Clarinet, Cello, and Piano (1944); *4 Songs of Return* for Soprano and Small Orch. (1961); *Duineser Elegie* for Soprano, Chorus, and Chamber Ensemble (1963); *Ode to Music* for Baritone and Chamber Orch. (1964); *Vision* for Soprano and Orch. (1966); *Mirabile Mysterium,* Christmas cantata (1967); *Canticum Sapientiae* for Baritone, Chorus, and Orch. (1968; Graz, Austria, Oct. 25, 1969). CHAMBER MUSIC: 9 string quartets (1912, 1917, 1918, 1920, 1944, 1947, 1948, 1957, 1966); *Geistiges Lied* for Piano Trio (1918); Sonata for Solo Cello (1921); *2 Pieces* for Clarinet and Piano (1922); Sonata for Solo Violin (1924); *Suite* for Violin and Piano (1937); *Little Suite* for Solo Flute (1937); Octet for Clarinet, Horn, Bassoon, and String Quintet (1948–49); *Suite* for Wind Quintet (1954); *Suite* in 3 movements for Solo Bassoon (1956); Clarinet Quintet (1959); 2 string trios (1962, 1969); *5 Miniatures* for Violin and Piano (1965); *Music* for String Quartet (1968); String Quintet (1970). FOR PIANO: *3 Piano Pieces* (1912); *Epigramme* (1913); *5 Dance Pieces* (1927); *Triptych* (1966); *Studies in Grey* (1969). FOR ORGAN: *Partita* (1966).
WRITINGS: *Arnold Schönberg* (Vienna, 1921; Eng. trans., London, 1924); *Der Beginn des musikalischen Barock und Die Anfänge der Oper in Wien,* in *Wiener literarische Anstalt* (Vienna, 1922); *Byzantinische Kirchenmusik* (Breslau, 1927); *Eastern Elements in Western Chant* (Oxford, 1947; 2nd ed., 1967); *A History of Byzantine Music and Hymnography* (Oxford, 1949; 3rd ed., revised, 1963); *Essays on Opera* (London, 1950); *The Origin of Schoenberg's Twelve-Tone System* (Washington, D.C., 1958); numerous essays on a variety of subjects in German and English periodicals. He edited Fux's *Costanza e Fortezza,* in Denkmäler der Tonkunst in Österreich, 34/35 (17); *Trésor de Musique Byzantine,* vol. I (Paris, 1934); *Die Hymnen des Sticherarium für September* (1936; vol. I of *Monumenta musicae byzantinae, Transcripta*); vol. I of the *New Oxford History of Music,* "Ancient and Oriental Music" (1957); *Die Hymnen der Ostkirche* (Kassel, 1962); *J.J. Fux* (London, 1965).

Welsh, Thomas, English singer and composer; b. Wells, c.1780; d. Brighton, Jan. 24, 1848. He was a chorister at Wells Cathedral, and a pupil of J.B. Cramer and Baumgarten. He made his opera debut in London at the age of 12; after his voice changed, he became a bass, and sang in oratorio. He was particularly distinguished as a vocal teacher; publ. *Vocal Instructor, or the Art of Singing Exemplified in 15 Lessons leading to 40 Progressive Exercises* (1825); piano sonatas; glees, duets, and part-songs; also wrote several musical pieces for the theater. His wife and pupil, **Mary Anne** (née **Wilson;** 1802–67), was a noted soprano who made her debut at Drury Lane on Jan. 18, 1821, in Arne's *Artaxerxes.*

Welte, Michael, German manufacturer of musical instruments; b. Unterkirnach, Black Forest, Sept. 29, 1807; d. Freiburg im Breisgau, Jan. 17, 1880. Having served an apprenticeship with Josef Blessing, a maker of musical clocks, he established himself at Voehrenbach (1832); exhibited his first "orchestrion" at Karlsruhe in 1849; later took his sons (**Emil, Berthold,** and **Michael, Jr.**) into partnership. His instruments obtained first prizes at London (1862), Paris (1867), Munich (1885), Vienna (1892), Chicago (1893), St. Louis (1904), Leipzig (1909), and Turin (1911); in 1872 the factory was removed to Freiburg im Breisgau. His oldest son, **Emil Welte** (b. Voehrenbach, April 20, 1841; d. Norwich, Conn., Oct. 25, 1923), established a branch in N.Y. (1865); he improved the then newly invented paper roll (taking the place of the earlier wooden cylinders), and was the first to use it, in connection with a pneumatic action, in a large orchestrion built for Theiss's Alhambra Court (N.Y.). A son of Berthold Welte, **Edwin** (b. Freiburg, 1875; d. there, Jan. 4, 1958), applied the paper roll to the piano, creating in 1904 the "Welte-Mignon Reproducing Piano," which could control pedaling and gradations of touch, a definite improvement on the ordinary player-piano, which could produce only pitches. Josef Hoffmann, Paderewski, and Wanda Landowska made rolls for it. The application of the same principle to the organ resulted in the invention of the "Philharmonic Organ" (1912). The firm ceased to exist in 1954.

Wen-Chung, Chou. See **Chou, Wen-Chung.**

Wenzel, Ernst Ferdinand, German pianist and teacher; b. Walddorf, near Löbau, Jan. 25, 1808; d. Bad Kösen, Aug. 16, 1880. A student of philosophy at Leipzig Univ., he also had private piano lessons with Friedrich Wieck, became a friend of his fellow-pupil Schumann, and was a frequent contributor to the *Neue Zeitschrift für Musik* during Schumann's editorship (until 1844). He was also an intimate friend of Mendelssohn; taught piano at the Leipzig Cons. from its foundation in 1843 until his death; the majority of the English-speaking students there were in his classes, or had private instruction from him.

Werba, Erik, eminent Austrian pianist, composer, and writer on music; b. Baden, near Vienna, May 23, 1918. He studied piano with Oskar Dachs and composition with Joseph Marx at the Vienna Academy of Music; musicology with Lach, Wellesz, and Schenk; received his Dr.Phil. in 1940 at the Univ. of Vienna. In 1948 he was appointed a prof. at the Vienna Academy of Music; from 1964 to 1971 he was also a visiting prof. at the Academy of Music in Graz. He was engaged mainly as a piano accompanist to famous singers, with whom he traveled in Europe and Japan; returning to Vienna, he devoted himself primarily to musical journalism; in 1953 he became editor of the *Österreichische Musikalische Zeitung;* publ. a number of informative and reliable monographs on Austrian composers: Joseph Marx (Vienna, 1964), Hugo Wolf (Vienna, 1971), and Erich Marckhl (Vienna, 1972). He composed a singspiel,

Trauben für die Kaiserin (Vienna, 1949); several song cycles and chamber music pieces, among them *Sonata notturna* for Bassoon and Piano (1972).

Werckmeister, Andreas, German organist and theorist; b. Benneckenstein, Nov. 30, 1645; d. Halberstadt, Oct. 26, 1706. He studied organ with his uncles, Christian and Victor; was organist at Hasselfelde (1664–74), at Quedlinburg (1675–96), and finally at Halberstadt, from 1696 to his death. He publ. the important treatise *Orgelprobe* (1681; 2nd ed., 1698; 3rd ed., 1716; 4th ed., 1764; Eng. trans. in *Organ Institute Quarterly*, 6, 1956); *Musicae mathematicae Hodegus curiosus, oder Richtiger musikalisher Weg-Weiser* (1686; 2nd ed., 1698); *Der edlen Music-Kunst Würde, Gebrauch und Missbrauch* (1691); *Musikalische Temperatur* (1691; the earliest treatise on equal temperament); *Hypomnemata musica, oder Musikalisches Memorial* (1697); *Die nothwendigsten Anmerckungen und Regeln wie der Bassus continuus könne tractiret werden* (1698); *Harmonologia musica, oder Kurtze Anleitung zur musikalischen Composition* (1702); *Organum Gruningense redivivum, oder Kurtze Beschreibung des in der grüningischen Schloss-Kirchen berühmten Orgel-Wercks* (1705); *Musikalische Paradoxal-Discourse* (posthumous; 1707). A facsimile reprint of the *Orgelprobe* (ed. of 1698) was publ. in Kassel in 1927; the *Organum Gruningense* was republ. in Mainz in 1932.

Werle, Lars Johan, Swedish composer; b. Gävle, June 23, 1926. He studied with Sven-Erik Bäck (composition) and Carl-Allan Moberg (musicology) at Uppsala Univ. (1948–51); held positions in the Swedish Broadcasting Corp., and as an instructor at the National School of Music Drama in Stockholm. In his music he employs an amiably modern idiom, stimulating to the untutored ear while retaining the specific gravity of triadic tonal constructions. His 3 theater operas have been received with smiling approbation.

WORKS: *Drömmen om Thérèse (The Dream of Thérèse)*, with Electronic Sound, after Zola's short story *Pour une nuit d'amour* (Stockholm, May 26, 1964); *Resan (The Voyage)*, after a novel by J.P. Jersild, containing film-projection (Hamburg, March 2, 1969); *Tintomara*, after C.J.L. Almquist's novel *The Queen's Jewels* (Stockholm, Jan. 18, 1973); television opera, *En saga om sinnen* (Swedish Television, June 21, 1971); *Pentagram* for String Quartet (1959); *Sinfonia da camera* (1960); *Summer Music 1965* for Strings and Piano (1965); *Attitudes* for Piano (1965); *Zodiak*, ballet (Stockholm, Feb. 12, 1967); *Canzona 126 di Francesco Petrarca* for Chorus (1967); *Nautical Preludes* for Chorus (1970); *Variété* for String Quartet (1971); 2 "run-and-sing" stage works: *Fabel* for 5 Singers, Percussion, and Piano (1974) and *Flower Power* for 6 Singers and 6 Instrumentalists (1974).

Werner, Gregor Joseph, Austrian music scholar and composer; b. Ybbs, Lower Austria (baptized, Jan. 29), 1693; d. Eisenstadt, March 3, 1766. In 1728

he was appointed Kapellmeister to Prince Ester-házy at Eisenstadt; in 1761 Haydn was named Vice-Kapellmeister, and succeeded him after his death. Werner wrote a number of works, including 40 masses, 18 oratorios, and many instrumental pieces. Haydn had great respect for him, and arranged his fugues for string quartet. Among modern reprints are his *Hirtenkantate, Hirtenmusik, Kleine Hirtenmusik,* etc., edited by E.F. Schmid; other pieces appeared in *Das Erbe deutscher Musik* (vol. 31).

Wernick, Richard, American composer; b. Boston, Jan. 16, 1934. He studied composition with Irving Fine, Harold Shapero, and Arthur Berger at Brandeis Univ. (B.A., 1955) and with Leon Kirchner at Mills College in Oakland, Calif. (M.A., 1957); also took lessons in composition with Ernst Toch, Boris Blacher, and Aaron Copland and in conducting with Leonard Bernstein and Seymour Lipkin at the Berkshire Music Center in Tanglewood (1954, 1955). He composed much music for the theater, films, and television between 1953 and 1962; was for a season music director and composer-in-residence of the Royal Winnipeg Ballet of Canada (1957–58). He taught at the State Univ. of N.Y. at Buffalo (1964–65) and at the Univ. of Chicago (1965–68). In 1968 he joined the faculty of the Univ. of Pa.; was made a prof. of music there in 1977. In 1976 he received a Guggenheim fellowship. He was awarded the Pulitzer Prize in Music in 1977 for his *Visions of Terror and Wonder.* In his early compositions he integrated the techniques of all his teachers, but ultimately fashioned an individual style of his own.
WORKS: Duo Concertante for Cello and Piano (1960); Trio for Violin, Clarinet, and Cello (1961); *Hexagrams* for Chamber Orch. (1962); String Quartet No. 1 (1963); *Music* for Viola d'Amore (1964); *Stretti* for Clarinet, Violin, Viola, and Guitar (1965); *Lyrics from IXI* for Soprano, Vibraphone-Marimba, and Contrabass, after e.e. cummings (1966); *Aevia* for Orch. (1966); *Haiku of Bashō* for Soprano, Flute, Clarinet, Violin, Contrabass, 2 Percussion Instruments, Piano, and Tape (1968); *Moonsongs from the Japanese* for Soprano and 2 prerecorded tracks of Soprano Voice (1969); *Cadenzas and Variations II* for Violin (1970); *A Prayer for Jerusalem* for Mezzo-soprano and Percussion (1971); *Kaddish Requiem,* a "secular service for the victims of Indo-China" for Mezzo-soprano, Chamber Ensemble, and Tape (1971); *Cadenzas and Variations III* for Cello (1972); String Quartet No. 2 (1972–73); *Songs of Remembrance* for Shawm, English Horn, Oboe, and Mezzo-soprano (1973); *Visions of Terror and Wonder* for Mezzo-soprano and Orch., to texts from the Bible and the Koran, in Hebrew, Arabic, and Greek (Aspen Music Festival, July 19, 1976); *Contemplations of the Tenth Muse, Books I–II* for Soprano (1977, 1979); *Introits and Canons* for Chamber Ensemble (1977); Partita for Violin (1978); "And on the Seventh Day—," sacred service for Cantor and Percussion Players (1979); *A Poison Tree* for Flute, Clarinet, Violin, Cello, Piano, and Soprano (1979); Concerto for Cello and 10 Players (1979); *Formula:*

P--- ----m for Chamber Ensemble (1981); Piano Sonata (1982); Sonata for Cello and Piano, *Portraits of Antiquity* (1982); *The Oracle of Shimon Bar Yochai* for Cello, Piano, and Soprano (1982); Concerto for Violin and Orch. (1984).

Werrekoren (Verecoren, Werrecore), Hermann Mathias, 16th-century German composer. He was maestro di cappella in Milan (1522–57); his principal work is a descriptive composition for 4 Voices a cappella entitled *Die Schlacht vor Pavia (The Battle of Pavia),* publ. in Schmeltzl's collection *Guter seltzamer ... teutscher Gesang* (Nuremberg, 1544) and reprinted by Gardano in Venice in 1549 as *La battaglia taliana;* he also publ. a book of motets for 4 Voices (1555); various other motets were publ. in the collections of the period. Werrekoren was mistakenly identified with Matthäus Le Maistre by Fétis and Kade; research by Haberl, Elsa Bienenfeld, and Cecie Stainer demonstrated the fallacy of this assumption.

Werrenrath, Reinald, American baritone; b. Brooklyn, Aug. 7, 1883; d. Plattsburg, N.Y., Sept. 12, 1953. He was a pupil of his father, a tenor; then studied with David Bispham and Herbert Witherspoon. He began his career as a concert singer; also in oratorio; made his operatic debut on Feb. 19, 1919, at the Metropolitan Opera House in N.Y., as Silvio in *Pagliacci,* and remained with the company until 1921; then devoted himself to teaching and concert singing; appeared in public for the last time at Carnegie Hall in N.Y., on Oct. 23, 1952. He edited *Modern Scandinavian Songs* (2 vols.; Boston, 1925–26). He was married 3 times: to Ada Peterson (1909; divorced, 1927), to Verna True Nidig (1928; divorced, 1941), and to Frances M. Aston (1942).

Wert, Giaches de (Jakob van Wert), Flemish contrapuntist; b. Weert, between May 6 and Aug. 18, 1535; d. Mantua, May 6, 1596. He was a boy chorister in the retinue of Maria di Cardona, Marchesa della Padulna, and followed the household to Italy. At the age of 9 he entered the ducal choir at Novellara; in 1549 he went to Ferrara to study with Cyprian de Rore. In 1558 he was appointed maestro di cappella at the court at Novellara; then joined the court chapel of the Duke of Mantua, who appointed him maestro di cappella in 1565. He held this position until his death, with an interval as vice-maestro at Novellara (1567–74); from 1565 to 1583 was also choirmaster of the Church of Santa Barbara in Mantua. He was greatly esteemed by contemporary musicians; Palestrina praised him, and he was also mentioned favorably by Thomas Morley, Artusi, G.B. Doni, and Monteverdi. His compositions were included in many collections of sacred and secular music, beginning in 1558. He publ. 11 books of madrigals for 5 voices, one for 4 voices, and one for 5 and 6 voices; one book of canzonets, and 3 of motets for 5 and 6 voices. 16 vols. of his collected works were publ. in Rome, 1961—.

Wesembeek. See **Burbure de Wesembeek.**

Wesendonck, Mathilde (née **Luckemeyer**), German poetess, friend of Wagner; b. Elberfeld, Dec. 23, 1828; d. at her villa, Traunblick, near Altmünster on the Traunsee, Austria, Aug. 31, 1902. Her first meeting with Wagner took place in Zürich, early in 1852, and soon developed into a deep friendship. She wrote the famous *Fünf Gedichte (Der Engel, Stehe still, Träume, Schmerzen, Im Treibhaus),* which Wagner set to music as studies for *Tristan und Isolde.* On May 19, 1848, she married **Otto Wesendonck** (b. March 16, 1815; d. Berlin, Nov. 18, 1896); in 1857 he gave Wagner the use of a beautiful house on his estate on Lake Zürich, where the first act of *Tristan und Isolde* was written, and the 2nd act sketched.

Wesley, Charles, English organist and harpsichord player; nephew of **John Wesley;** b. Bristol, Dec. 11, 1757; d. London, May 23, 1834. He was a pupil of Kelway and Boyce in London; then held various positions as a church organist; publ. *6 Concertos for the Organ or Harpsichord,* op. 1; anthems; hymns; etc.; 6 string quartets. He was the brother and teacher of **Samuel Wesley.**

Wesley, John, founder of the Wesleyan Methodist Church; b. Epworth, June 17, 1703; d. London, March 2, 1791. He was educated at Christ Church, Oxford; in 1735 he came to America with his brother Charles to do missionary work, and 2 years later publ. his first *Collection of Psalms and Hymns* (Charlestown, 1737). Returning to England, he spread the doctrine of Methodism and became famous as a preacher and writer. He has been called "the father of Methodist hymnology."

Wesley, Samuel, English organist and composer; brother of **Charles Wesley;** nephew of **John Wesley;** b. Bristol, Feb. 24, 1766; d. London, Oct. 11, 1837. He studied with his brother, and began to compose at the age of 8; learned to play the violin as well as the organ. He publ. *Eight Lessons for the Harpsichord* when he was 11 (1777). Subsequently he developed his fine talent as an organist and was generally regarded as the greatest performer and improviser of his time. Although he suffered from a skull injury as a result of a fall, which seriously interfered with his activities, he continued to give public concerts till the year of his death.

Wesley, Samuel Sebastian, English organist and composer; natural son of **Samuel Wesley;** b. London, Aug. 14, 1810; d. Gloucester, April 19, 1876. He was a boy chorister at the Chapel Royal; from the age of 16 held appointments as an organist in London churches; in 1832, he became organist of Hereford Cathedral; in 1835, at Exeter Cathedral; in 1842, at Leeds Parish Church; in 1849, at Winchester Cathedral; in 1865, at Gloucester Cathedral. He received the degrees of B.Mus. and D.Mus. at Oxford (1839). His works include 4 church services; 2 Psalms; 27 anthems; several glees; an *Ode to Labour* (1864); pieces for organ; songs. He publ. *A Few Words on Cathedral Music and the Musical System of the*

Church, with a Plan of Reform (1849).

West, John Ebenezer, English organist and composer; b. London, Dec. 7, 1863; d. there, Feb. 28, 1929. He was a nephew of **Ebenezer Prout,** and studied with him at the Royal Academy of Music; was organist and choirmaster at various London churches; in 1884 was appointed to the editorial staff of Novello & Co. He wrote 2 cantatas, *The Healing of the Canaanite's Daughter* (1882) and *Seed-time and Harvest* (1892); several church services and anthems; an orch. march, *Victoria, Our Queen;* organ music; publ. an important book, *Cathedral Organists* (London, 1899; new ed., 1921).

Westergaard, Peter, American composer and pedagogue; b. Champaign, Ill., May 28, 1931. He studied composition at Harvard Univ. with Walter Piston (A.B., 1953); then had fruitful sessions with Sessions at Princeton Univ. (M.F.A., 1956). In 1956 he went to Germany, where he studied with Fortner in Detmold. Returning to the U.S., he joined the music faculty of Columbia Univ., N.Y. (1958–66); then was at Amherst (1967–68); in 1968 became associate prof. at Princeton Univ.; prof. in 1971; was chairman of the music dept., 1974–78. He publ. *An Introduction to Tonal Theory* (N.Y., 1974). In his music he explores the possibility of total organization of tones, rhythms, and other elements of composition.
  WORKS: Chamber operas: *Charivari* (1953) and *Mr. and Mrs. Discobbolos* (N.Y., 1966); *Symphonic Movement* (1954); *5 Movements* for Small Orch. (1958); *Invention* for Flute and Piano (1955); Quartet for Violin, Vibraphone, Clarinet, and Cello (1961); Trio for Flute, Cello, and Piano (1962); *Variations* for 6 Instruments (1964); *Divertimento on Discobolic Fragments* for Flute and Piano (1967); *Noises, Sounds and Sweet Airs* for Flute, Clarinet, Horn, Trumpet, Celesta, Harpsichord, Percussion, and Strings (1968); cantatas: *The Plot Against the Giant,* to words by Wallace Stevens (1956); *A Refusal to Mourn the Death, by Fire, of a Child in London* for Bass and 10 Instruments, to words by Dylan Thomas (1958); *Leda and the Swan* for Mezzo-soprano, Clarinet, Viola, Vibraphone, and Marimba (1961); *Spring and Fall: To a Young Child* for Voice and Piano (1960); *Moto perpetuo* for 6 Wind Instruments (1976).

Westerhout, Niccolò van. See **Van Westerhout, Niccolò.**

Westmorland, John Fane, Earl of (Lord Burghersh), English composer; b. London, Feb. 3, 1784; d. Apthorpe House, Northants, Oct. 16, 1859. He was in the British army, fought in the Spanish campaign and in Egypt, attaining the rank of general in 1854; also occupied various diplomatic posts between wars. He studied music in Lisbon with Marcos Portugal (1809–12); was a founder of the Royal Academy of Music in London (1822). He wrote 7 Italian operas; the following were performed at his own palace in Florence (where he served as British Resident): *Fedra* (Nov. 17, 1824); *L'Eroe di Lancastro* (June 13, 1829); *Lo scompiglio teatrale* (1830). Other works include several church services; some piano music; also *Sinfonia in D* for Orch. A list of his works is in W.W. Cazelet's *The History of the Royal Academy of Music* (London, 1854).

Westphal, Rudolf (Georg Hermann), notable German music scholar; b. Oberkirchen, July 3, 1826; d. Stadthagen, July 10, 1892. He was a student of classical philology in Marburg; taught at the Univ. of Breslau (1858–62); then went to Moscow as a teacher at a lyceum (1875–80); subsequently lived in Leipzig, Bückeburg, and Stadthagen. He wrote numerous learned papers on Greek music, and maintained that the Greeks employed polyphony, a theory that he himself eventually abandoned as untenable.

Westrup, Sir Jack Allan, eminent English musicologist; b. London, July 26, 1904; d. Headley, Hampshire, April 21, 1975. He received his education at Dulwich College, London, and at Balliol College, Oxford (B.Mus., 1926; M.A., 1929). He was an assistant classics master at Dulwich College (1928–34); then was a music critic for the *Daily Telegraph* (1934–39); also was editor of the *Monthly Musical Record* (1933–45). He was actively engaged in musical education. He gave classes at the Royal Academy of Music (1938–40); then was lecturer in music at King's College, Newcastle upon Tyne (1941–44), the Univ. of Birmingham (1944–47), and Wadham College (1947–71). In 1946 he received an honorary degree of D.Mus. at Oxford Univ. In 1947 he was named chairman of the editorial board of *The New Oxford History of Music.* In 1959 he succeeded Eric Blom as editor of *Music & Letters.* From 1958–63 he was president of the Royal Musical Assoc. He was also active as a conductor; he conducted the Oxford Opera Club (1947–62), the Oxford Univ. Orch. (1954–63), and the Oxford Bach Choir and Oxford Orch. Society (1970–71). He was knighted in 1961.
PUBLICATIONS: He prepared major revisions of Walker's *A History of Music in England* (Oxford, 3rd ed., 1952) and of Fellowes's *English Cathedral Music* (London, 5th ed., 1969); he also supervised revised eds. of Blom's *Everyman's Dictionary of Music* (4th ed., 1962; 5th ed., 1971). He was co-editor, with F. Harrison, of the *Collins Music Encyclopedia* (London, 1959; American ed. as *The New College Encyclopedia of Music,* N.Y., 1960). His other publications include *Purcell* (London, 1940); *Sharps and Flats* (a vol. of selected articles; London, 1940); *British Music* (London, 1943; 3rd ed., 1949); *The Meaning of Musical History* (London, 1946); *An Introduction to Musical History* (London, 1955); *Music: Its Past and Its Present* (Washington, D.C., 1964); *Bach Cantatas* (London, 1966); *Schubert Chamber Music* (London, 1969); *Musical Interpretation* (London, 1971).

Wetz, Richard, German composer and teacher; b. Gleiwitz, Feb. 26, 1875; d. Erfurt, Jan. 16, 1935. He studied with R. Hofmann in Leipzig and Thuille in Munich; in 1906 went to Erfurt as a choral conductor and teacher; also taught in Weimar.
WORKS: Opera, *Das ewige Feuer* (Düsseldorf, March 19, 1907); *Kleist-Ouvertüre; Traumsommernacht* for Women's Chorus and Orch.; *Gesang des Lebens* for Male Chorus and Orch.; *Nicht geboren ist das Beste* for Mixed Chorus and Orch.; *Hyperion* for Baritone Solo, Chorus, and Orch.; about 100 songs. He publ. monographs on Bruckner (1922), Liszt (1925), and Beethoven (1927; 2nd ed., 1933). A Richard Wetz Society was founded in Gleiwitz in 1943.

Wetzel, Justus Hermann, German composer and musicologist; b. Kyritz, March 11, 1879; d. Überlingen (Bodensee), Dec. 6, 1973. He studied natural sciences, philosophy, and art history (Dr.Phil., 1901); then took up music, and was a teacher at the Riemann Cons. in Stettin (1905–7); settled in Berlin in 1910; taught at the Academy for Church and School Music (from 1925; became a prof. in 1935. He composed about 400 songs; choral works; chamber music; piano pieces; edited and arranged several collections of German songs.

Wetzler, Hermann Hans, German-American conductor and composer; b. Frankfurt, Sept. 8, 1870; d. New York, May 29, 1943. He was brought to the U.S. as a child, but in 1882 returned to Germany, where he studied at Hoch's Cons. in Frankfurt with Clara Schumann (piano), Iwan Knorr (counterpoint), and Humperdinck (instrumentation). In 1892 he went to N.Y.; was a church organist for several years; in 1903 he established the Wetzler Symph. Concerts, which had considerable success; Richard Strauss conducted a series of 4 concerts of his own works with the Wetzler group (Feb.–March, 1904), including the world premiere of the *Sinfonia domestica.* In 1905 Wetzler went to Europe again; conducted opera in various German cities and in Basel. In 1940 he returned to the U.S. He composed an opera, *Die baskische Venus* (Leipzig, Nov. 18, 1928); *Assisi,* legend for Orch. written in commemoration of the 700th anniversary of the death of St. Francis of Assisi (1925); *Symphonic Dance in Basque Style* (1927); *Symphonie concertante,* for Violin and Orch. (1932); chamber music; choral works; songs.

Weyrauch, August Heinrich von, German song composer; b. Riga, April 30, 1788; date of death unknown. In 1824 he publ. (under his own name) a song, *Nach Osten* (words by Wetzel). About 1840 an anonymous Paris publisher reprinted it, with Schubert's name on the title page, as *Adieu* (French words by Bélanger); a piano transcription of it, also crediting the authorship to Schubert, was publ. by Döhler in Germany (1843); Schlesinger of Berlin reprinted the song, with a German trans. of the French text, as Schubert's in 1845; since then it has been reprinted many times as Schubert's by European and American publishers.

Weyse, Christoph Ernst Friedrich, German-Danish composer; b. Altona, March 5, 1774; d. Copenhagen, Oct. 8, 1842. He was a pupil of his grandfather, a cantor at Altona; in 1789 he went to Copenhagen, where he studied with J.A.P. Schulz. In 1794 he was appointed organist at the Reformed Church; in 1805 became organist at the Fruekirke; in 1819 he was appointed court composer. Through the court conductor Kunzen he became interested in a movement for the establishment of a national school of Danish opera, for which his works (together with those of Kuhlau) effectively prepared the way.

WORKS: Operas (all perf. in Copenhagen): *Sovedrikken (The Sleeping-Potion;* April 21, 1809); *Faruk* (Jan. 30, 1812); *Ludlams hule (Ludlam's Cave;* Jan. 30, 1816); *Floribella* (Jan. 29, 1825); *Eventyr i Rosenborg have (Adventure in Rosenborg Gardens;* May 26, 1827); *Balders død (The Death of Baldur;* Nov. 23, 1832); *Festen paa Kenilworth* (after Walter Scott; Jan. 6, 1836); about 30 cantatas; *Miserere* for Double Chorus and Orch.; *Te Deum* for Chorus and Orch.; 4 symphs.; preludes and fugues for organ; piano pieces (including sonatas and études); songs. He collected 100 Danish folk songs, of which he harmonized 59; they were publ. by his pupil A.P. Berggreen as *100 gamle kämpevisemelodier (Old Ballad Melodies).* A thematic and bibliographic catalogue of his works was publ. in Copenhagen (1979).

White, Eric Walter, English writer on music; b. Bristol, Sept. 10, 1905. He studied at Oxford Univ.: was a member of the Secretariat of the League of Nations (1929–33), subsequently of the National Council of Social Service, London (1935–42) and of the Council for the Encouragement of the Arts Council of Great Britain (from 1946). He publ. a fundamental biography of Stravinsky (London, 1947) and a highly valuable annotated catalogue of Stravinsky's works (Berkeley and Los Angeles, 1966); a monograph, *Benjamin Britten* (London, 1948; new ed., 1954); *The Rise of English Opera* (London, 1951); *A History of English Opera* (London, 1983); *A Register of First Performances of English Operas and Semi-Operas from the 16th Century to 1980* (London, 1983); numerous informative essays on modern composers.

White, Robert, one of the most important English composers of the 16th century; b. c.1535; d. London, Nov. 1574. He studied music for several years, obtaining the degree of Mus.Bac. at Cambridge Univ. on Dec. 13, 1560; was appointed master of the choristers at Ely Cathedral in 1562, retaining this post until 1566; was then master of the choristers at Westminster Abbey, from 1570. He died of the plague. He composed Latin services and motets, English anthems, etc. Some of his works are reprinted in *Tudor Church Music,* 5 (1926). His instrumental music has been edited by I. Spector in the Recent Researches in the Music of the Renaissance series, XII (1972).

Whitehill, Clarence Eugene, American bass; b. on a farm near Parnell, Iowa, Nov. 5, 1871; d. New York, Dec. 18, 1932. He studied with L.A. Phelps in Chicago; earned his living as a clerk in an express office, and also sang in churches; then went to Paris in 1896, where he studied with Giraudet and Sbriglia; made his operatic debut on Oct. 31, 1898, at the Théâtre de la Monnaie in Brussels; was the first American male singer to be engaged at the Opéra-Comique (1899); then was a member of Henry Savage's Grand English Opera Co. at the Metropolitan Opera House in the autumn of 1900; went for further study to Stockhausen in Frankfurt, and from there to Bayreuth, where he studied the entire Wagnerian repertoire with Cosima Wagner; after engagements in Germany, he became a member of the Cologne Opera (1903–8), the Metropolitan Opera (1909–10), the Chicago Opera (1911–14 and 1915–17), and again at the Metropolitan (1914–32).

Whiteman, Paul, celebrated American conductor of popular music; b. Denver, Colo., March 28, 1890; d. Doylestown, Pa., Dec. 29, 1967. He played viola in the Denver Symph. Orch. and later in the San Francisco People's Symph. Orch.; in 1917–18 was conductor of a 40-piece band in the U.S. Navy. He then formed a hotel orch. in Santa Barbara, Calif., and began to develop a style of playing known as "symphonic jazz," which soon made him famous. On Feb. 12, 1924, he gave a concert in Aeolian Hall in N.Y., at which he introduced Gershwin's *Rhapsody in Blue,* written for his orch., with Gershwin himself as soloist. In 1926 he made a tour in Europe. While not himself a jazz musician, he was popularly known as the "King of Jazz," and frequently featured at his concerts such notables of the jazz world as Bix Beiderbecke, Frank Trumbauer, and Benny Goodman; Bing Crosby achieved his early fame as a member of Paul Whiteman's Rhythm Boys. Whiteman established the Whiteman Awards, made annually for "symphonic jazz" compositions written by Americans. He publ. the books *Jazz* (with M.M. McBride; N.Y., 1926), *How to Be a Bandleader* (with L. Lieber; N.Y., 1941), and *Records for the Millions* (N.Y., 1948).

Whithorne, Emerson, American composer; b. Cleveland, Sept. 6, 1884; d. Lyme, Conn., March 25, 1958. His name was **Whittern;** he had it legally changed in 1918 to Whithorne (the original family name of his paternal grandfather). He studied in Cleveland with J.H. Rogers; embarked on a musical career at the age of 15, and appeared as a pianist on the Chautauqua circuit for 2 seasons. In 1904 he went to Vienna and took piano lessons with Leschetizky and composition with Robert Fuchs; in 1905–7 he was a pupil of Artur Schnabel. In 1907 he married the pianist-composer **Ethel Leginska,** acting as her impresario in Germany until 1909; they were separated in 1912, and divorced in 1916. Between 1907 and 1915, Whithorne lived mainly in London; he studied Chinese and Japanese music from materials in the British Museum, and wrote several pieces based on oriental tunes (*Adventures of a Samurai;* settings for *The Yellow Jacket; The Typhoon).* Returning to America, he became editor for the Art Publication Society of St. Louis (1915–20);

then settled in N.Y. and devoted himself entirely to composition; was an active member of the League of Composers in N.Y. In his music he assumed a militantly modernistic attitude; wrote several pieces in the fashionable "machine music" style.

WORKS: For Orch.: *The Rain* (Detroit, Feb. 22, 1913); *The Aeroplane* (Birmingham, England, Jan. 30, 1926; orch. version of the piano piece written in 1920, one of the earliest examples of "machine music"); *Saturday's Child,* to poems by Countee Cullen, for Mezzo-soprano, Tenor, and Small Orch. (N.Y., March 13, 1926); *New York Days and Nights* (Philadelphia, July 30, 1926; originally for Piano); *Poem* for Piano and Orch. (Chicago, Feb. 4, 1927); *Fata Morgana,* symph. poem (N.Y., Oct. 11, 1928); incidental music to Eugene O'Neill's *Marco Millions* (1928); Symph. No. 1 (1929; Cincinnati, Jan. 12, 1934); *The Dream Pedlar,* symph. poem (Los Angeles, Jan. 15, 1931); Violin Concerto (Chicago, Nov. 12, 1931); *Fandango* (N.Y., April 19, 1932); *Moon Trail,* symph. poem (Boston, Dec. 15, 1933); Symph. No. 2 (Cincinnati, March 19, 1937); *Sierra Morena* (N.Y., May 7, 1938); Piano Quintet (N.Y., Dec. 19, 1926); other chamber music; also piano pieces; songs.

Whitney, Robert, American conductor; b. Newcastle upon Tyne, England (of an American father and an English mother), July 9, 1904. He studied with Leo Sowerby in Chicago; took lessons in conducting with Eric De Lamarter. In 1937 he was engaged as conductor of the Louisville Phil. (later renamed the Louisville Orch.) A munificent grant from the Rockefeller Foundation enabled the Louisville Orch. to commission works from American and foreign composers, each to be paid a set fee of $1,000; the project proved highly successful, and the orch. was able to give first performances of works by Honegger, Milhaud, Malipiero, Petrassi, Krenek, Dallapiccola, Toch, Chávez, Villa-Lobos, Ginastera, Schuman, Virgil Thomson, Cowell, Piston, Sessions, Antheil, Creston, Mennin, and others; it recorded 189 contemporary symphonic works on Louisville Orch. Records. After completing his tenure as conductor in 1967, Whitney was in charge of various special projects at the School of Music at the Univ. of Louisville. Among his own compositions are: *Concerto Grosso* (1934); Symph. in E minor (1936); *Sospiri di Roma* for Chorus and Orch. (1941); Concertino (1960).

Whittall, Gertrude Clarke, American patron of music and literature; b. Bellevue, Nebr., Oct. 7, 1867; d. Washington, D.C., June 29, 1965. Her maiden name was **Clarke;** she married Matthew John Whittall on June 4, 1906. In 1935 she donated to the Library of Congress in Washington, D.C., a quartet of Stradivari instruments—2 violins (including the famous "Betts"), a viola, and a cello—together with 4 Tourte bows; she added another Stradivari violin (the "Ward") and another Tourte bow in 1937. In 1936 she established an endowment fund in the library of Congress to provide public concerts at which these instruments would be used, and in 1938 the Whittall Pavilion was built in the library to house them and to serve other purposes in the musical life of the library. In subsequent years, she continued to add to her gifts to the library on behalf of both music and literature; one series enabled the Whittall Foundation to acquire many valuable autograph MSS of composers from Bach to Schoenberg, and in particular the finest single group of Brahms MSS gathered anywhere in the world.

Whythorne, Thomas, English song composer; b. c.1528; d. Aug. 1595. He studied at Oxford Univ.; about 1553 he traveled through Europe and collected German, Austrian, and Neapolitan songs. Upon his return to London he publ. a collection of 76 original songs under the title *Songes, for three, fower and five voyces* (London, 1571); these were among the earliest sets of secular vocal pieces publ. in England. In 1590 Whythorne brought out another collection, comprising 52 vocal duos. His autobiography, discovered in 1955, was publ. in Oxford in 1961 in his original phonetic spelling, and reprinted in modern spelling in 1963, edited by J.M. Osborn.

Widmann, Erasmus, German composer and theorist; b. Hall, Württemberg (baptized, Schwäbisch Hall, Sept. 15), 1572; d. Rothenburg, Oct. 31, 1634. After serving as cantor in Graz and Weickersheim, he became a schoolmaster at Rothenburg (1613). He wrote church music and some instrumental dance suites; publ. a treatise, *Praecepta musicae Latino-Germanica* (Nuremberg, 1615). A complete edition of his works was publ. by G. Reichert in *Das Erbe deutscher Musik,* III (1955).

Widor, Charles-Marie (-Jean-Albert), distinguished French organist, pedagogue, and composer; b. Lyons, Feb. 21, 1844; d. Paris, March 12, 1937. His father, an Alsatian of Hungarian descent, was organist at the church of St.-François in Lyons; as a boy, Widor was a skillful improviser on the organ; he studied later in Brussels under Lemmens (organ) and Fétis (composition). While still a youth, he was appointed organist at his father's church in Lyons (1860), and gained high repute in concerts in provincial French cities. In 1870 he obtained the important post of organist at St.-Sulpice in Paris, holding it for more than 60 years; he retired in 1934. On April 19, 1934, he played at St.-Sulpice his *Pièce mystique,* composed at the age of 90. In 1890 he succeeded César Franck as prof. of organ at the Paris Cons.; in 1896 became prof. of counterpoint, fugue, and composition. He was active also as a music critic for *L'Estafette,* under the pen name *Aulétès;* also conducted the oratorio society Concordia. In 1910 he was elected a member of the Académie des Beaux-Arts, of which he became permanent secretary in 1913. He had many distinguished pupils, including Albert Schweitzer, with whom he collaborated in editing the first 5 vols. of a definitive 8-vol. ed. of J.S. Bach's organ works (brought out by G. Schirmer, N.Y.); he also edited the collection *L'Orgue moderne.* As a composer he wrote copiously in many forms, but is best known for his organ music, especially his 8 "symphonies" (suites); also the *Sympho-*

nie gothique (op. 70) and the *Symphonie romaine* (op. 73).

WORKS: Operas (all produced in Paris): *Maître Ambrose* (Opéra-Comique, May 6, 1886); *Les Pêcheurs de Saint-Jean* (Opéra-Comique, Dec. 26, 1905; his most successful opera); *Nerto* (Paris Opéra, Oct. 27, 1924); incidental music to *Conte d'avril*, after Shakespeare's *Twelfth Night* (Odéon, Sept. 22, 1885); *Les Jacobites* (Nov. 21, 1885); etc.; ballet, *La Korrigane* (Paris Opéra, Dec. 1, 1880); symph. poem, *Une Nuit de Valpurgis* (London, April 19, 1888, composer conducting); 3 symphs.; *Symphonie antique* (with Organ and Final Chorus); *Sinfonia sacra* (with Organ); *Ouverture espagnole;* 2 piano concertos; Cello Concerto; *Fantaisie* for Piano and Orch.; *Choral et variations* for Harp and Orch.; chamber music: 2 piano quintets; String Quartet; Piano Trio; *Soirs d'Alsace* for Piano Trio; 2 violin sonatas; *Suite* for Cello and Piano; Cello Sonata; *3 valses* for Violin and Piano; *3 pièces* for Cello and Piano; for Piano: *Airs de ballet; La Prière; Caprice; 3 valses; Impromptu; 6 morceaux; Prélude, andante et finale; Scènes de bal; 6 valses caractéristiques; 12 feuillets d'album; Dans les bois; Romance; Suite polonaise;* Suite in B minor; *Suite écossaise;* vocal music: Mass for 2 Choirs and 2 Organs; *Psalm 83* for Chorus and String Quintet; *Psalm 112* for 2 Choirs, 2 Organs, and Orch.; *Tu es Petrus* for Double Chorus and Organ; *Sacerdos et Pontifex* for Chorus and Organ; other church music; *Chant séculaire* for Soprano, Chorus, and Orch.; several song cycles; duets; choruses a cappella. He edited Berlioz's *Traité de l'instrumentation et d'orchestration modernes*, and wrote a supplement, *Technique de l'orchestre moderne* (1904; 2nd ed., 1906; in Eng., London, 1906, 1946); publ. *Initiation musicale* (1923); *L'Orgue moderne* (1929); etc.

Wiechowicz, Stanislaw, Polish composer; b. Kroszyce, Nov. 27, 1893; d. Cracow, May 12, 1963. He studied successively in Cracow, Dresden, St. Petersburg and Paris; taught at the Poznan Cons. (1921–39); from 1945 to his death, taught at the State College of Music in Cracow.

WORKS: *Babie lato*, symph. poem (1922); *Chmiel (The Hopvine)*, symph. scherzo (1926); *Ulegalki* for Orch. (1944); *Kasia (Kitty)*, folk suite for 2 Clarinets and String Orch. (1946); *Koncert staromiejski (Old Town Concerto)* for String Orch. (1954); *Pastoralki*, recitation for Chorus and Orch. (1927); *Kantata romantyczna* (1930); *Kantata zniwna* (1948); *A czemuześ nie przyjechal? (Why Did You Not Come?)*, rustic scene for Chorus and Orch. (1948); *List do Marc Chagalla (Letter to Marc Chagall)*, dramatic rhapsody for Soprano, Mezzo-soprano, 2 Narrators, Chorus, and Orch. (1961); *Zstap, golebico (O Dove, Descend)*, Cantata (1962–63); choruses.

Wieck, Alwin, German pianist; brother of **Clara Schumann**; b. Leipzig, Aug. 27, 1821; d. Dresden, Oct. 21, 1885. He studied piano with his father, and violin with David; was a member of the Italian Opera orch. at St. Petersburg; then taught piano in Dresden. He publ. *Materialien zu F. Wiecks Pianoforte-*

Methodik and *Vademecum perpetuum für den ersten Pianoforte-Unterricht nach F. Wiecks Methode;* also piano pieces.

Wieck, Friedrich, German pianist; father of **Clara Schumann**; b. Pretzsch, near Torgau, Aug. 18, 1785; d. Loschwitz, near Dresden, Oct. 6, 1873. He studied theology at Wittenberg, and at the same time pursued musical studies in private; established a piano factory and a circulating music library in Leipzig, but gave up both in order to devote himself to teaching the piano, in which profession he had extraordinary success. Among his pupils were his daughters **Clara** and **Marie**, his son **Alwin**, Hans von Bülow, Fritz Spindler, Isidor Seiss, and Gustav Merkel. He was also Robert Schumann's teacher, but bitterly opposed Schumann's marriage to Clara. He settled in Dresden in 1840. In 1843 Mendelssohn offered him a professorship at the newly established Leipzig Cons., but Wieck declined. Wieck's first wife (née Tromlitz) was the mother of Clara Schumann and Alwin; after her divorce she married Bargiel, the father of Woldemar Bargiel; Marie Wieck was Wieck's daughter by his 2nd wife, Clementine Fechner. He publ. 2 books of piano studies, and also *Clavier und Gesang* (1853; 3rd ed., 1878; also in Eng.) and *Musikalische Bauernsprüche* (2nd ed., 1875, by Marie Wieck).

Wieck, Marie, German pianist, daughter of **Friedrich Wieck;** b. Leipzig, Jan. 17, 1832; d. Dresden, Nov. 2, 1916. She studied with her father; at the age of 11 made her debut at a concert of her half sister, **Clara Schumann;** was appointed court pianist to the Prince of Hohenzollern in 1858; after tours of Germany, England, and Scandinavia, she settled in Dresden as a teacher of piano and singing. Her last public appearance was with the Dresden Phil. Orch. in Nov. 1915, playing the Schumann Concerto. She publ. piano pieces and songs; edited her father's *Pianoforte-Studien;* wrote *Aus dem Kreise Wieck-Schumann* (1912; 2nd augmented ed., 1914).

Wielhorsky, Count Mikhail, Russian patron of the arts; b. Volynia, Nov. 11, 1788; d. Moscow, Sept. 9, 1856. His home in St. Petersburg was the gathering place of the most eminent musicians of the time. He wrote a String Quartet and some songs, one of which, *Autrefois*, was arranged for piano by Liszt (1843). His brother, **Matvei Wielhorsky** (1794–1866), was a cellist; a distant relative, **Joseph Wielhorsky** (1817–92), wrote piano pieces and songs (48 opus numbers).

Wiéner, Jean, French pianist and composer of Austrian parentage; b. Paris, March 19, 1896; d. there, June 8, 1982. He studied with Gédalge at the Paris Cons. From 1920 to 1924 he organized in Paris a series of Concerts Jean Wiéner, devoted to the energetic propaganda of new music; he presented several world premieres of works by modern French composers; also performed pieces by Schoenberg, Berg, and Anton von Webern. He was the first Frenchman to proclaim jazz as a legitimate art form; from 1925 to 1939 he teamed with Clément Doucet in duo-piano recitals, in programs stretching from Mozart to jazz. His own compositions reflect his ecumenical convictions, as exemplified in such works as *Concerto franco-américain* for Clarinet and Strings (1923) and a desegregationist operetta, *Olive chez les nègres* (1926). He also wrote an Accordion Concerto (1957) and a Concerto for 2 Guitars (1966), but he became famous mainly for his idiosyncratic film music.

Wieniawski, Adam Tadeusz, Polish composer, nephew of **Henri** and **Joseph Wieniawski;** b. Warsaw, Nov. 27, 1879; d. Bydgoszcz, April 21, 1950. He studied in Warsaw with Melcer and Noskowski; then in Berlin with Bargiel, and in Paris with Vincent d'Indy, Fauré, and Gédalge. He fought in the French army during World War I; returned to Warsaw in 1923; was appointed director of the Chopin School of Music in 1928.
WORKS: Operas: *Megae* (Warsaw, Dec. 28, 1912); *Wyzwolony* (Warsaw, 1928); *Król Kochanek* (Warsaw, March 19, 1931); ballets: *Lalita* and *Le Festin chez Hérode* (1927); symph. poems: *Kamaralmazan* (Paris, 1910) and *Princesse Baudour; Suite Polonaise* for Orch. (1913); *Obrazki,* Piano Suite (also for Orch.); arrangements of folk songs.

Wieniawski, Henryk (Henri), famous Polish violinist; b. Lublin, July 10, 1835; d. Moscow, March 31, 1880. His mother, Regina Wolff-Wieniawska, was a talented pianist; on the advice of her brother, **Eduard Wolff,** a pianist and composer who lived in France, she took Henryk to Paris, where he entered the Cons. at the age of 8, first in Clavel's class, and the following year, in the advanced class of Massart. At the age of 11 he graduated with first prize in violin, an unprecedented event in the annals of the Paris Cons. He made his debut in Paris on Jan. 30, 1848; gave his first concert in St. Petersburg on March 31, 1848, and played 4 more concerts there; then played in Finland and the Baltic provinces; after several successful appearances in Warsaw, he returned in 1849 to Paris, where he studied composition with Hippolyte Collet at the Cons., graduating (again with first prize) in 1850. He then traveled with his brother, **Joseph,** in Russia (1851–53); went to Paris (1858) and London (1859); in 1860, was appointed solo violinist to the Czar; taught at the newly founded St. Petersburg Cons. (1862–68); played the viola in the Ernst String Quartet. In 1872 he went on a tour of the U.S. with Anton Rubinstein; one of the featured works was Beethoven's *Kreutzer Sonata,* which they performed about 70 times. When Rubinstein returned to Europe, Wieniawski continued his American tour, which included California. He returned to Europe in 1874, gave several concerts with Rubinstein in Paris, and in the same year succeeded Vieuxtemps as prof. of violin at the Brussels Cons., resigning in 1877 owing to an increasingly grave heart condition; he suffered a heart attack during a concert in Berlin in 1878, but still agreed to play several concerts in Moscow, where he remained until his death at the age of 44.

He was married to Isobel Hampton, an Englishwoman; their youngest daughter, Irene, wrote music under the pen name **Poldowski.** Wieniawski was undoubtedly one of the greatest violinists of the 19th century; he possessed a virtuoso technique and an extraordinary range of dynamics. He was equally distinguished as a chamber music player. Many of his compositions are in the repertoire of every violinist; of these the most famous are his Concerto in D minor; *Légende* for Violin and Orch.; *Souvenir de Moscou,* on Russian themes, for Violin and Orch.; and *Le Carnaval russe* for Violin and Piano. He also wrote, for Violin and Orch.: Concerto in F-sharp minor; *Polonaise; Scherzo-Tarentelle; Fantaisie brillante* (on themes from Gounod's *Faust*); *Polonaise brillante;* for Violin and Piano: *Caprice fantastique; Souvenir der Posen; Adagio élégiaque; Capriccio-Valse; Romance sans paroles et Rondo élégant;* 2 mazurkas; *Gigue; Etudes-Caprices* for 2 Violins; etc. With his brother, Joseph, he wrote *Allegro de sonate* and *Grand duo polonais.*

Wieniawski, Joseph, Polish pianist and composer, brother of **Henryk Wieniawski;** b. Lublin, May 23, 1837; d. Brussels, Nov. 11, 1912. He studied at the Paris Cons. with Zimmermann, Marmontel, and Alkan (piano), and with LeCouppey (composition); in 1851 he went on tour with his brother, Henryk; studied with Liszt at Weimar (1855–56), and returned to Paris in 1858. In 1866 he settled in Moscow as a teacher at the Cons., but soon established a piano school of his own, which flourished. In 1875–76 he was director of the Warsaw Music Society; then settled in Brussels, teaching at the Cons. He also made numerous concert tours throughout Europe.

Wieprecht, Friedrich Wilhelm, German trombonist and inventor; b. Aschersleben, Aug. 8, 1802; d. Berlin, Aug. 4, 1872. He studied in Dresden and Leipzig, where he was already famous as a trombonist. He invented the bass tuba (1835, with the instrument maker Moritz); the bathyphon, a sort of bass clarinet (1839, with Skorra); the "piangendo" on brass instruments with pistons; and an improved contrabass bassoon; his claim of priority over Sax, in the invention of the saxhorns, was not upheld by the courts.

Wier, Albert Ernest, American music editor; b. Chelsea, Mass., July 22, 1879; d. Brooklyn, Sept. 8, 1945. He studied music at the New England Cons. and at Harvard Univ.; from 1900 was music editor for various publ. firms in N.Y.; brought out a large number of collections and arrangements: *Whole World Music Series, The Pianist's Music Shelf, The Violinist's Music Shelf, Young Folks' Music Library, Radio Music Library,* etc.; devised the "arrow signal" system, in which arrows and other markings are added to orch. scores to identify the main themes; using this system, he issued numerous collections: *Classic Violin Concertos, The 9 Symphonies of Beethoven, The Symphonies of Brahms and Tschaikowsky, The Valkyrie,* etc.; he also edited *The Macmillan Encyclopedia of Music* *and Musicians* (1938; withdrawn from circulation owing to an excessive number of demonstrable errors) and other reference works of questionable scholarship.

Wiesengrund-Adorno, Theodor. See **Adorno, Theodor.**

Wigglesworth, Frank, American composer; b. Boston, March 3, 1918. He studied at Columbia Univ. and at Converse College in Spartanburg, S.C.; also took lessons in N.Y. with Henry Cowell and Otto Luening. He was in the U.S. Army Air Force during World War II; then taught at Columbia Univ. (1947–51) and Queens College (1954–55). He is a great-nephew of Mrs. Elizabeth Sprague Coolidge.
WORKS: 3 symphs. (1955; 1958; 1967–69); *Creation* for Chorus and Small Orch. (1940); *New England Concerto* for Violin and Strings (1941); *The Plunger* for Soprano, Flute, Viola, Cello, and Piano (1941); Trio for Flute, Banjo, and Harp (1942); *Jeremiah* for Baritone, Chorus, and Orch. (1942); *Sleep Becalmed* for Chorus and Orch., after Dylan Thomas (1948); *3 Movements* for String Orch. (1949); *Telesis* for Chamber Orch. and Percussion (1949); *Serenade* for Flute, Viola, and Guitar (1952); Brass Quintet (1957).

Wihtol (Vitols), Joseph, foremost Latvian composer and pedagogue; b. Volmar, July 26, 1863; d. Lübeck, April 24, 1948. He studied at the St. Petersburg Cons. (1880–86) with Rimsky-Korsakov; after graduation, was engaged as an instructor there; succeeded Rimsky-Korsakov in 1908 as prof. of composition; among his students were Prokofiev and Miaskovsky. He was also music critic for the German daily *St. Petersburger Zeitung.* In 1918 he left St. Petersburg; was for a season director of the Latvian Opera in Riga; in 1919 founded the National Cons. there; many Latvian composers were his students. As the Soviet armies approached Riga (1944), Wihtol went to Germany, remaining there until his death. In his music he followed the harmonic practices of the Russian school, but often employed Latvian folk-song patterns. Most of his works were publ. by Belaieff.

Wijk, Arnold. See **Wyk, Arnold van.**

Wiklund, Adolf, Swedish composer and conductor; b. Langserud, June 5, 1879; d. Stockholm, April 2, 1950. He studied with J. Lindegren (composition) and R. Andersson (piano) at the Stockholm Cons.; was granted a state fellowship for study abroad; took lessons with James Kwast in Berlin (piano); was engaged as an opera coach in Berlin; returning to Sweden in 1911, he became 2nd conductor of the Stockholm Opera; then led the Stockholm Court Orch. (1911–24) and the Concert Society (1925–38); was also guest conductor in London and Jena. He composed a Symph. (1922); 2 piano concertos (1906, 1916); *Konzertstück* for Piano and Orch. (1902); symph. poem, *Sommarnatt och soluppgang* (1918);

Little Suite for Orch. (1928); *3 Pieces* for String Orch. (1924); Violin Sonata (1906); several albums of lyric pieces for piano; songs.

Wilbye, John, one of the greatest English madrigalists; b. Diss, Norfolk (baptized, March 7), 1574; d. Colchester, Sept. 1638. From 1595 until 1628 he was resident musician at Hengrave Hall, the home of Sir Thomas Kytson, near Bury St. Edmunds. After the death of Lady Kytson (1628), Wilbye settled in Colchester. He made frequent visits to London, where the Kytsons had a town house. His first book of madrigals (for 3, 4, 5, and 6 voices) appeared in 1598 (reprinted London, 1841); it contains 30 compositions; his 2nd book, containing 34 madrigals (also for 3 to 6 voices), came out in 1609 (reprinted London, 1846). To Leighton's *Teares or Lamentations* (1614) he contributed 2 hymns, and for *The Triumphes of Oriana* he wrote a 6-part madrigal, *The Lady Oriana.* His madrigals were reprinted in vols. 6/7 of *The English Madrigal School.*

Wild, Earl, greatly talented American piano virtuoso; b. Pittsburgh, Nov. 26, 1915. He was educated at the Carnegie Inst. in Pittsburgh; among his piano teachers were Selmar Jansen, Egon Petri, and Paul Doguereau. In 1942 Toscanini invited him to appear with the NBC Symph. Orch.; thus, he became the first and youngest American artist to play under Toscanini. Subsequently, he made extensive tours of the U.S., Europe, and the Orient; was a soloist with the Boston Symph., the Chicago Symph., the Cleveland Orch., and the N.Y. Phil. He commissioned several concertos, among them one by Paul Creston and one by Marvin David Levy. A phenomenal technician of the keyboard, he was greatly acclaimed for his brilliant performances of works of the Romantic era of pianism. He also made transcendentally resonant piano transcriptions of various vocal and orch. works.

Wildbrunn (original name, **Wehrenpfennig, Helena,** Austrian soprano; b. Vienna, April 8, 1882; d. there, April 11, 1972. She studied with Rosa Papier in Vienna; made her debut as a contralto at the Vienna Volksoper in 1906; then sang in Dortmund (1907–14), she began singing soprano roles in 1914, when she joined the Stuttgart Opera, where she remained until 1918; also sang with the Berlin State Opera (1916–25) and the Deutsche Oper there (1926–29); was a principal member of the Vienna State Opera (1919–32); made guest appearances at Covent Garden in London, La Scala in Milan, and the Teatro Colón in Buenos Aires. After her retirement in 1932, she taught voice at the Vienna Academy of Music (until 1950). Among her finest roles were Kundry and Brünnhilde.

Wilder, Alec (Alexander), remarkably gifted American composer, distinguished in both popular and serious music; b. Rochester, N.Y., Feb. 16, 1907; d. Gainesville, Fla., Dec. 22, 1980. He studied composition at the Eastman School of Music in Rochester with Herbert Inch and Edward Royce; then moved to N.Y., where he entered the world of popular music; he also wrote excellent prose. His popular songs were performed by Frank Sinatra, Judy Garland, and other celebrated singers; his band pieces were in the repertoire of Benny Goodman and Jimmy Dorsey. He excelled in the genre of short operas scored for a limited ensemble of singers and instruments and suitable for performance in schools, while most of his serious compositions, especially his chamber music, are set in an affably melodious, hedonistic, and altogether ingratiating manner. He publ. a useful critical compilation, *American Popular Song: The Great Innovators* (N.Y., 1972), which included analyses of the songs of Jerome Kern, Vincent Youmans, George Gershwin, Cole Porter, and others.

WORKS: FOR THE STAGE: *The Lowland Sea*, folk drama (Montclair, N.J., May 8, 1952); *Cumberland Fair*, a jamboree (Montclair, May 22, 1953); *Sunday Excursion*, musical comedy (Interlochen, Mich., July 18, 1953); *Miss Chicken Little* (Columbia Broadcasting System, Television, Dec. 27, 1953; stage production, Piermont, N.Y., Aug. 29, 1958); 3 operas: *Kittiwake Island* (Interlochen, Aug. 7, 1954); *The Long Way* (Nyack, N.Y., June 3, 1955); *The Impossible Forest* (Westport, Conn., July 13, 1958); *The Truth about Windmills*, chamber opera (Rochester, N.Y., Oct. 14, 1973); *The Tattooed Countess*, chamber opera (1974); *The Opening*, comic opera (1975); 3 children's operas: *The Churkendoose; Rachetty Pachetty House; Herman Ermine in Rabbit Town;* ballet, *Juke Box* (1942). FOR ORCH.: *8 Songs* for Voice and Orch. (Rochester, June 8, 1928); *Symphonic Piece* (Rochester, June 3, 1929); *Suite* for Clarinet and Strings (1947); Concerto for Oboe and Strings (1950); *Beginner's Luck* for Wind Ensemble (1953); 2 concertos for Horn and Chamber Orch. (1954, 1960); 4 works entitled *An Entertainment* (1961–71): No. 1 for Wind Ensemble; No. 2 for Orch.; No. 3 for Wind Ensemble; No. 4 for Horn and Chamber Orch.; 2 concertos for Trumpet and Wind Ensemble; Concerto for Tuba and Wind Ensemble; *Suite* for Horn and Strings (1965); Suite for Saxophone and Strings (1965); Concerto for Saxophone and Chamber Orch. (1967); *Air* for Horn and Wind Ensemble (1968); Concerto for Euphonium and Wind Ensemble (1971). CHAMBER MUSIC: Nonet for Brass (1969); 10 wind quintets (1953–72); 4 brass quintets; quintets, quartets, trios, duets (many called *Suites*) for numerous wind and brass instruments; 2 flute sonatas (1958, 1962); Clarinet Sonata (1963); 3 bassoon sonatas (1964, 1968, 1973); Saxophone Sonata (1960); 3 horn sonatas (1954, 1957, 1965); sonatas for Viola, Cello, String Bass, Oboe, English Horn, Trumpet, Trombone, Bass Trombone, Euphonium, and Tuba; piano pieces (Sonata; *12 Mosaics; A Debutante's Diary; Neurotic Goldfish; Walking Home in the Spring;* etc.). FOR VOICE: Many songs, of which the most popular were *The Sounds around the House, Blackberry Winter, I'll Be Around, While We're Young, It's So Peaceful a Country,* and *Who Can I Turn To.* He also composed a choral work, *Children's Plea for Peace,* for Narrator, Chorus, and Orch. (1969), and a series of vocal ensembles with satirical words, such as *The House Detective Registers.*

Wildgans, Friedrich, Austrian composer; b. Vienna, June 5, 1913; d. Mödling, near Vienna, Nov. 7, 1965. He studied with J. Marx; taught at the Salzburg Mozarteum (1934–36); then played clarinet at the Vienna Opera; from 1945–47 and from 1950–65, was a prof. at the Vienna State Academy of Music. He has written music in all genres, in an ultramodern style, eventually adopting the 12-tone technique. In 1946 he married the Austrian soprano **Ilona Steingruber.**

Wilhelm, Carl Friedrich, German choral composer; b. Schmalkalden, Sept. 5, 1815; d. there, Aug. 26, 1873. From 1839 to 1864 he was director of the Crefeld Liedertafel, for which he composed many men's choruses, among them *Die Wacht am Rhein,* which became a national song of the Germans; it was first performed by the Liedertafel on June 11, 1854, and first publ. in the *Chorliedersammlung* of Erk and Greef (Essen, 1854). In 1860 he received the title of Royal Prussian Music Director; in 1870 he was granted a pension of 3,000 marks.

Wilhelmj, August (Emil Daniel Ferdinand Viktor), famous violin virtuoso; b. Usingen, Germany, Sept. 21, 1845; d. London, Jan. 22, 1908. He received his earliest instruction in music from his mother, who was an amateur pianist; then studied violin with Konrad Fischer, court musician at Wiesbaden; made his first appearance there as a child prodigy, on Jan. 8, 1854. In 1861, at the recommendation of Liszt, he was sent to the Leipzig Cons., where he studied with Ferdinand David (violin) and with Hauptmann and Richter (theory); in 1864 he went to Frankfurt for an additional course with Raff; in 1865 he began his concert career, touring Switzerland; then played in the Netherlands and England (1866); France and Italy (1867); Russia, Switzerland, France, and Belgium (1869); England, Scotland, and Ireland (1869–70); then traveled through the Netherlands, Scandinavia, Germany, and Austria (1871–74); to England (1875–77) and to America (1878); made a 4-year tour of the world to South America, Australia, and Asia (1878–82). In 1876 he was concertmaster of the Bayreuth orch. at the production of *Der Ring des Nibelungen.* For several years he lived chiefly at Biebrich-am-Rhine, where he established (with R. Niemann) a master school for violin playing. In 1886 he moved to Blasewitz, near Dresden; in 1894 he was appointed prof. of violin playing in the Guildhall School of Music in London. His first wife, whom he married in 1866, was Baroness Liphardt, a niece of Ferdinand David; in 1895 he married the pianist **Mariella Mausch.** He made a famous arrangement of Bach's air from the orch. *Suite* in D major which became known as the *Air on the G String* (Bach's original bore no such specification); also arranged Wagner's *Träume* for violin and orch.; wrote a cadenza to Beethoven's Violin Concerto; further composed, for Violin and Orch., 2 *Konzertstücke* (No. 2, *In memoriam*), *Alla polacca,* and Theme and Variations (after 2 caprices of Paganini); *Romanze* for Piano; songs. With James Brown he publ. *A Modern School for the Violin* (6 parts).

Wilhem (real name, **Bocquillon**), **Guillaume-Louis,** French music educator; b. Paris, Dec. 18, 1781; d. there, April 26, 1842. The son of an army officer, he himself entered active service at the age of 12; but from 1795–1801 studied at the school of Liancourt, and then for 2 years in the Paris Cons. He taught music in the military school of Saint-Cyr, and in 1810 was appointed a teacher of music at the Lycée Napoléon (later the Collège Henri IV), occupying this position until his death. The system of *enseignement mutuel* (mutual instruction), which had been entered into the popular schools of France, attracted Wilhem's attention; in 1815 he began to apply it in music teaching, and met with such marked success that in 1819 he was chosen to organize a system of music instruction for the primary schools in Paris; he was appointed singing teacher to the Polytechnique in 1820, and director of the Normal School of Music. In 1833 he conceived the idea of instituting regular reunions of the pupils in one grand chorus, to which he gave the name of Orphéon. In 1835 he was made director-general of music instruction in all the primary schools of Paris, and was created a Chevalier of the Legion of Honor. Besides his school classes, he formed classes of adults, chiefly workingmen, in which the success of his system was equally conspicuous, and which later, under the name of Orphéons, included several popular singing societies. He publ. numerous songs and choruses; also a collection of a cappella choruses, *Orphéon*, in 5 (later 10) vols.; and 4 textbooks.

Wilkomirska, Maria, Polish pianist, daughter of **Alfred Wilkomirski;** b. Moscow, April 3, 1904. She studied at the Moscow Cons. with Briusova and Yavorsky; in 1920 she went to Warsaw and continued her studies with Turczyński. She subsequently taught piano in Kalisz, Gdansk, and Lodz; in 1951 she became a prof. at the Warsaw Music School. With her brother, the cellist **Kazimierz Wilkomirski,** and her sister, the violinist **Wanda Wilkomirska,** she organized a trio which gave successful concerts in Europe, China, and Japan.

Wilkomirska, Wanda, Polish violinist, daughter of **Alfred Wilkomirski;** b. Warsaw, Jan. 11, 1929. She studied violin with her father, and later with Irene Dubiska in Warsaw and with Zathureczky in Budapest. She won a prize at the international violin competition in Geneva in 1946 and similar prizes in Budapest in 1948 and in Poznan in 1953. In 1960 she went to Paris and took lessons with Henryk Szeryng. With her brother, the cellist **Kazimierz Wilkomirski,** and her sister, the pianist **Maria Wilkomirska,** she formed a trio which gave successful concerts in Europe and the Orient.

Wilkomirski, Alfred, Polish violinist and pedagogue; b. Asov, Russia, Jan. 3, 1873; d. Lodz, July 31, 1950. He studied with Hřimaly at the Moscow Cons.; in 1920 went to Poland and taught violin in Kalisz (1920–26) and in Lodz (1929–39, 1945–50). His son, **Kazimierz,** the cellist, and his daughters, **Maria,** the pianist, and **Wanda,** the violinist, were all accomplished musicians who formed a successful trio.

Wilkomirski, Kazimierz, Polish cellist, conductor, composer, and pedagogue, son of **Alfred Wilkomirski;** b. Moscow, Sept. 1, 1900. He studied cello and composition at the Moscow Cons.; then went to Warsaw and took courses in composition with Mlynarski at the Warsaw Cons. (1919–23); later traveled to Switzerland and attended classes in conducting with Scherchen in Winterthur. In 1926 he was appointed conductor of the Warsaw Phil.; from 1935 until 1939 he served as director of the Cons. of Gdansk and also conducted the Gdansk Opera. The Nazi assault on Poland forced Wilkomirski to interrupt his musical activities. After the war, he was appointed rector of the Lodz Cons. (1945–47), and later served as a pedagogue at the conservatories of Zopport (1952–57), Wroclaw (1958–65), and Warsaw (from 1963). His own works are attractively eclectic and Romantically imitative; the best of them are his cello pieces, including several concertos, a method of cello playing, and 12 études. His autobiography, *Wspomnenia,* was publ. in 1971. With his sisters, the pianist **Maria** and the violinist **Wanda,** he formed a trio that achieved notable success in tours in Europe and the Orient.

Willaert, Adrian, important Flemish composer and pedagogue; b. Bruges or Roulaers, c.1490; d. Venice, Dec. 7, 1562. He enrolled as a law student at the Univ. of Paris; then devoted himself to music; studied composition with Jean Mouton, a musician in the Royal Chapel. In 1515 he entered the service of Cardinal Ippolito I d'Este of Ferrara; he accompanied the cardinal, who was Archbishop of Esztergom, to Hungary in 1517; the cardinal died in 1520, and Willaert entered the service of Duke Alfonso I d'Este of Ferrara (1522); subsequently was in the service of Cardinal Ippolito II d'Este, the Archbishop of Milan (1525–27). On Dec. 12, 1527, he was appointed maestro di cappella of St. Mark's in Venice; with the exception of 2 visits to Flanders (1542 and 1556–57), he remained in Venice for the rest of his life, as a composer and teacher. Among his famous pupils were Zarlino, Cipriano de Rore, Andrea Gabrieli, and Costanzo Porta. Willaert was justly regarded as a founder of the great Venetian school of composition; the style of writing for 2 antiphonal choirs (prompted by the twin opposed organs of St. Mark's Cathedral) was principally initiated by him. He was one of the greatest masters of the madrigal and of the instrumental ricercare; he also wrote motets, chansons, Psalms, and masses.

Willan, Healey, eminent English-born Canadian composer, organist, and music educator; b. Balham, Surrey, Oct. 12, 1880; d. Toronto, Feb. 16, 1968. He received his musical training at St. Saviour's Choir School in Eastbourne (1888–1895); was a church organist in London until 1913, when he went to Canada as head of the theory dept. at the Royal Cons. in Toronto; was vice-principal there (1920–36). In 1914 he was appointed a lecturer and examiner at the Univ. of Toronto; in 1937, a prof. of music; he retired in 1950; was also the Univ. organist (1932–64) and organist of St. Mary Magdalene Church in Toronto from 1921 until his death; was founder and conductor of the Tudor Singers (1934–39). In 1956 he was awarded the historic Lambeth Doctorate by the Archbishop of Canterbury, and in 1967 was the first musician to become a Companion of the Order of Canada. He was greatly esteemed as a pedagogue.

WORKS: 2 radio operas, *Transit through Fire* (1941–42; Canadian Radio, March 8, 1942) and *Deirdre* (1943–45; Canadian Radio, April 20, 1946; revised 1962 and 1965; first stage perf., Toronto, 1965); historical pageant, *Brébeuf and His Brethren* (CBC Radio, Sept. 26, 1943); several ballad-operas; 2 symphs.: No. 1 (Toronto, Oct. 8, 1936) and No. 2 (1941; revised 1948; Toronto, May 18, 1950); Piano Concerto (Montreal, Aug. 24, 1944; revised 1949); *Agincourt Song* for Chorus and Small Orch. (1929); *Overture to an Unwritten Comedy* (1951); several ceremonial pieces, including *Coronation March* for Orch. (1937), *Te Deum Laudamus* for Chorus and Small Orch. (1937), *Coronation Suite* for Chorus and Orch. (1952), *Royal Salute* for Orch. (1959), and *Centennial March* for Orch. (1967); *Royce Hall Suite* for Symph. Band (1949); 2 violin sonatas (1920, 1923); several character pieces for piano; organ works; carols and hymn tunes; church services; motets a cappella; anthems with organ accompaniment; many other choral works; songs; arrangements of Canadian and British songs; school manuals. A catalogue of Willan's works was publ. by G. Bryant (Ottawa, 1972).

Willcocks, Sir David, English organist, conductor, and educator; b. Newquay, Dec. 30, 1919. He was educated at Clifton College and King's College, Cambridge; served in the British army; after the war he was organist at Salisbury Cathedral (1947–50) and Worcester Cathedral (1950–57); then at King's College, Cambridge (1957–73); also held the posts of univ. lecturer (1957–74) and univ. organist (1958–74) at Cambridge; concurrently he led the City of Birmingham Choir (1950–57) and was conductor of the Cambridge Univ. Musical Society (1958–73). In 1960 he became music director of the Bach Choir; in 1974 he also assumed the post of director of the Royal College of Music in London. He was awarded the Order of the British Empire in 1971; was knighted in 1977. He served as general editor of the Church Music series of the Oxford Univ. Press.

Willeke, Willem, Dutch-American cellist; b. The Hague, Sept. 29, 1879; d. Pittsfield, Mass., Nov. 26, 1950. He studied cello in the Netherlands; then was a cellist in various German orchs.; also at the Vienna Opera (under Mahler). In 1908 he came to the U.S. and joined the Kneisel Quartet, with which he remained until its disbandment in 1917; taught at

the Inst. of Musical Art in N.Y.; then was appointed director of the Berkshire Music Colony, in Pittsfield, Mass., where he remained until his death.

Williams, Alberto, prolific Argentine composer; b. Buenos Aires, Nov. 23, 1862; d. there, June 17, 1952. He was the grandson of an Englishman; his maternal grandfather, **Amancio Alcorta,** was one of Argentina's early composers. Williams studied composition at the Paris Cons. with Guiraud, Durand, and Godard, piano with Mathias (a pupil of Chopin), and organ and counterpoint with César Franck. He returned to Argentina in 1889; founded the Alberto Williams Cons. in 1893; also organized branches of the Cons. in provincial towns of Argentina, numbering more than 100; founded a music publ. firm La Quena (also a music magazine of that name). He was the most prolific composer of Argentina; 112 opus numbers were publ. by La Quena. The greatest influence in his music was that of Franck, but modernistic usages are found in Williams's application of whole-tone scales, parallel chord progressions, etc. In many of his works he used characteristic melorhythms of Argentina; composed a number of piano pieces in Argentinian song and dance forms (milongas, gatos, cielitos, etc.).

WORKS: 9 symphs., all perf. for the first time in Buenos Aires: No. 1 (Nov. 25, 1907); No. 2, *La bruja de las montañas* (Sept. 9, 1910); No. 3, *La Selva sagrada* (Dec. 8, 1934); No. 4, *El Ataja-Caminos* (Dec. 15, 1935); No. 5, *El corazón de la muñeca* (Nov. 29, 1936); No. 6, *La muerte del cometa* (Nov. 26, 1937); No. 7, *Eterno reposo* (Nov. 26, 1937); several suites of Argentine dances; 3 violin sonatas; Cello Sonata; Piano Trio; a great number of piano albums, the last of which was *En el parque* (1952). He composed 136 opus numbers in all. He also publ. numerous didactic works and several books of poetry. A complete catalogue of his works is found in vol. 2 of *Composers of the Americas,* publ. by the Pan-American Union, Washington, D.C. (1956; pp. 138–55).

Williams, Charles Francis Abdy, English writer on music; b. Dawlish, Devonshire, July 16, 1855; d. Milford, near Lymington, Feb. 27, 1923. While pursuing his studies at Trinity College, Cambridge, he played violin and viola in the orch. of the Cambridge Univ. Musical Society; then went to New Zealand, where he was a church organist in Auckland; returning to England in 1881, he took the degree of Mus.Bac. at Oxford (1889) and Cambridge (1891); from 1895–1901, was director of music at the Greek Theatre at Bradfield College, where he wrote choruses in ancient Greek modes for the productions of Greek tragedies. Retiring from teaching in 1901, he devoted himself to scholarly work; in 1904 he introduced the Solesmes system of performing plainchant at the priests' seminary in Capri, which won him recognition from the Pope.

Williams, Charles Lee, English organist and composer; b. Winchester, May 1, 1853; d. Gloucester, Aug. 29, 1935. He was a pupil of Dr. Arnold at the Cathedral of Winchester; from 1872 filled various posts as an organist and choirmaster in Ireland and England; conducted several of the Three Choirs Festivals held at Gloucester; after 1898 became active in the educational field. He composed the cantatas *Gethsemane, Bethany, A Harvest Song, A Dedication,* etc.; much church music; brought out (with H.G. Chance) a continuation (1895, covering the years 1864–94) of D. Lysons's *Origin and Progress of the Meeting of the Three Choirs of Gloucester, Worcester, and Hereford* (1812, covering the years 1724–1811; supplemental vol. by John Amott in 1865, covering the years 1812–64); in 1931 brought out, with H.G. Chance and T. Hannan-Clark, a further continuation (covering the years 1895–1930) of the work, under the title *Annals of the Three Choirs.*

Williams, Clifton, American bandmaster; b. Traskwood, Ark., March 26, 1923; d. South Miami, Fla., Feb. 12, 1976. He studied at Louisiana State Univ. (B.M., 1947) and with Bernard Rogers and Howard Hanson at the Eastman School of Music in Rochester, N.Y. (M.M., 1948). He played French horn with the symph. orchs. of San Antonio and New Orleans; was on the staff of the music dept. at the Univ. of Texas in Austin (1949–66); then at the Univ. of Miami (1966–76). He composed band music, including the phenomenally popular *Sinfonians.* His other band pieces include *Trail Scenes; Trilogy Suite; Concertino* for Percussion and Band; 3 symph. dances; *Fanfare and Allegro; Dedicatory Overture; Dramatic Essay: The Ramparts; The Patriots* (commissioned by NORAD); *Songs of Heritage; Academic Procession; Castle Gap March; Strategic Air Command.*

Williams, Grace, Welsh composer; b. Barry, Glamorganshire, Feb. 19, 1906; d. there, Feb. 10, 1977. Her father led the local boys' chorus and played the piano in a home trio, with Grace Williams on the violin and her brother on the cello. In 1923 she entered the music dept. of the Univ. of Wales in Cardiff, in the composition class of David Evans. Upon graduation in 1926 she enrolled at the Royal College of Music in London. There she was accepted as a student of Vaughan Williams, who had the greatest influence on her career as a composer, both in idiom and form; she also took classes with Gordon Jacob. She subsequently received the Octavia Traveling Scholarship and went to Vienna to take lessons with Egon Wellesz (1930–31). She did not espouse the atonal technique of the 2nd Viennese School, but her distinctly diatonic harmony with strong tertian underpinning was artfully embroidered with nicely hung deciduous chromatics of a decidedly nontonal origin. She marked May 10, 1951, in her diary as a "day of destruction," when she burned all her MSS unworthy of preservation. Among her practical occupations was teaching school and writing educational scripts for the BBC. She was particularly active in her advancement of Welsh music.
WORKS: For the stage: *Theseus and Ariadne,* ballet (1935); *The Parlour,* opera (1961). For Orch.: 2 symphs. (1943; 1956, revised 1975); *Sinfonia con-*

certante for Piano and Orch. (1941); *Sea Sketches* (1944); *The Dark Island Suite* (1950); *Castell Caernarfon,* for the investiture of the Prince of Wales (1962); Violin Concerto (1950); Trumpet Concerto (1963). Chamber music: Sextet for Oboe, Trumpet, Violin, Viola, Cello, and Piano (1931); *Suite* for 9 Instruments (1934); numerous choruses and songs.

Williams, John, enormously successful American composer and conductor; b. Flushing, N.Y., Feb. 8, 1932. He grew up in a musical atmosphere; his father was a film studio musician. He began to take piano lessons; later he learned to play trombone, trumpet, and clarinet. In 1948 the family moved to Los Angeles, where he studied orchestration with Robert van Epps at Los Angeles City College and composition privately with Mario Castelnuovo-Tedesco; he also took piano lessons with Rosina Lhévinne at the Juilliard School of Music in N.Y. He began his career as a composer, arranger, and conductor for films and television; wrote the film scores, rich in sounding brass and tinkling cymbals, for *Close Encounters of the Third Kind, Superman, The Empire Strikes Back, Raiders of the Lost Ark, E.T., The Extraterrestrial,* and *Return of the Jedi.* He won Academy Awards for *Fiddler on the Roof* (1971), *Jaws* (1975), and *Star Wars* (1977). The record albums for these background scores sold into the millions. He also wrote 2 symphs., a Violin Concerto, a Flute Concerto, an *Essay for Strings,* and a number of chamber music pieces. In 1980 he was chosen conductor of the Boston Pops Orch., succeeding the late Arthur Fiedler, who had held that post for almost 50 years; Williams declared openly that no one could hope to equal Fiedler in charisma and showmanship, not to mention Fiedler's splendiferous aureole of white hair (as contrasted with his successor's alopecia), but he said he would try his darndest to bridge the gap. He largely succeeded, and diversified his appeal to Boston Pops audiences by playing selections from his own sparkling film scores.

Williams, John, remarkable guitarist; b. Melbourne, Australia, April 24, 1941. He first studied with his father, a noted guitar teacher; then took guitar lessons with Segovia in Siena; also attended courses in music theory at the Royal College of Music in London. In 1958 he made a successful debut in London; in 1962 made a tour of the Soviet Union; also played in America and Japan. In addition to classical music, he includes in his programs pieces of pop music and jazz; this egalitarian versatility makes him a favorite with untutored youth in England and America.

Williams, Ralph Vaughan. See **Vaughan Williams, Ralph.**

Williams, Spencer, American composer of popular music; b. New Orleans, Oct. 14, 1889; d. New York, July 14, 1965. He played piano in nightclubs in New Orleans, Chicago and N.Y.; wrote songs in the slow rhythmic manner of the New Orleans blues. In 1932 he went to Europe for a prolonged stay; lived in Paris (where he was accompanist for Josephine Baker), London, and Stockholm; returned to the U.S. in 1957. His most famous song is *Basin Street Blues* (1928); he wrote many blues and other songs: *Tishomingo Blues* (1917), *Arkansas Blues, Mississippi Blues, Royal Garden Blues;* his *Mahogany Hall Stomp* became a perennial favorite.

Williamson, John Finley, American choral conductor; b. Canton, Ohio, June 23, 1887; d. Toledo, Ohio, May 28, 1964. He studied singing with Witherspoon and Bispham in N.Y.; organ with Karl Straube in Leipzig. In 1921 he founded the Westminster Choir, and in 1926, the Westminster Choir School (later College) at Princeton, N.J.; was its president until 1958, when he resigned. With his choir he gave 1,000 concerts in America; also made 2 European tours; edited the Westminster Series of choral music.

Williamson, Malcolm, Australian composer; b. Sydney, Nov. 21, 1931. He studied composition with Eugene Goossens at the Sydney Cons. (1944–50); in 1953 went to London, where he took lessons with Elisabeth Lutyens and Erwin Stein (1953–57); learned to play the organ and was employed as a church organist in England (1955–60); visited the U.S. in 1970, and was composer-in-residence at Westminster Choir College in Princeton, N.J. for an academic season; then returned to England. In 1975 he became Master of the Queen's Musick; in 1976 was made a Commander of the Order of the British Empire; in 1977 was elected president of the Royal Phil. Orch.
WORKS: OPERAS: *Our Man in Havana,* after Graham Greene's novel (London, July 2, 1963); *The English Eccentrics,* chamber opera (Aldeburgh Festival, June 11, 1964); *The Happy Prince,* children's opera after Oscar Wilde (Farnham, May 22, 1965); *Julius Caesar Jones,* children's opera for Children's Voices and 3 Adults (London, Jan. 4, 1966); *The Violins of St. Jacques,* in 3 acts (London, Nov. 29, 1966); *Dunstan and the Devil,* chamber opera (Cookham, May 19, 1967); *The Growing Castle,* chamber opera for 4 Singers, Piano, Harpsichord, Tubular Chimes, and Drums, after Strindberg's *Dream Play* (Dynevor Festival, Aug. 13, 1968, with the composer alternately at the piano and the harpsichord); *Lucky-Peter's Journey,* after Strindberg's fairy-tale play (1969); *The Stone Wall* (London, Sept. 18, 1971); *Genesis* (1971; London, April 23, 1973); *The Red Sea* (1972); *The Death of Cuchulain* (1972); *The Winter Star* (1972); choral operatic sequence *The Brilliant and the Dark,* for Women's Voices and Orch. (1969); 3 cassations for Audience, and Orch. or Piano: *The Moonrakers* (1967; Brighton, April 22, 1967); *Knights in Shining Armour* (1968; Brighton, April 19, 1968); *The Snow Wolf* (Brighton, April 30, 1968). BALLETS: *The Display,* dance symph. in 4 movements (Adelaide Festival, March 14, 1964); *Sun into Darkness* (London, April 13, 1966). FOR ORCH.: *Elevamini,* Symph. No. 1 (1956–57); *Santiago de Espada,* overture (1958); 3 piano concertos (1958; with

String Orch., 1960; 1961); Organ Concerto (1961); *Sinfonietta concertante* for 3 Trumpets, Piano, and Strings (1959–61); Violin Concerto (Bath, England, June 15, 1965; Yehudi Menuhin, soloist); Sinfonietta (1965); *Concerto Grosso* for Orch. (London, Aug. 28, 1965); *Symphonic Variations* (Edinburgh, Sept. 9, 1965); Symph. No. 2 (Bristol, Oct. 29, 1969); *Epitaphs for Edith Sitwell* for Strings (1969; originally for Organ, 1965); Concerto for 2 Pianos and Strings (1972); *The Icy Mirror* for Soloists, Chorus, and Orch. (Cheltenham Festival, July 9, 1972); *Ode to Music* for Chorus, Echo Chorus, and Orch. (London, Feb. 3, 1973); *Hammerskjöld Portrait* for Soprano and Strings (London, July 30, 1974). CHAMBER MUSIC: *Variations* for Cello and Piano (1964); Concerto for 2 Pianos (8-hands) and Wind Quintet (1965); *Serenade* for Flute, Piano, and String Trio (1967). FOR KEYBOARD: 2 piano sonatas (1958; revised 1971–72); 5 *Preludes* for Piano (1966); 2-piano Sonata (1967); Piano Quintet (1968); Symph. for Organ (1960). FOR VOICE: Choruses, including *Symphony for Voices* a cappella (1960) and *The Musicians of Bremen* (1972).

Willis, Henry, English organ builder; b. London, April 27, 1821; d. there, Feb. 11, 1901. As a youth he worked for John Gray (later Gray & Davidson), and while yet an apprentice, invented the special manual and pedal couplers which he later used in his own instruments; from 1842 to 1845 he worked for Evans at Cheltenham, and in 1845 established his own business in London. He rebuilt the organ in the Gloucester Cathedral; exhibited a large organ at the Crystal Palace in 1851, which won the Council Medal and was installed in the Winchester Cathedral; he subsequently was commissioned to build the great organ in St. George's Hall in Liverpool (1855). In 1878 he took his sons **Vincent** and **Henry** into partnership, adopting the firm name of Henry Willis & Sons; he became generally known as "Father Willis." Willis himself regarded the organ in St. Paul's, which he built in 1891, as his masterpiece (77 speaking stops, 19 couplers). After the founder's death in 1901, his son Henry Willis became the head of the business, and soon took his son, also named **Henry Willis,** into partnership. They built the organ in the Liverpool Cathedral (167 speaking stops, 48 couplers) in 1912–14; this organ was the largest in the world at the time.

Willmers, Rudolf, pianist and composer; b. Copenhagen, Oct. 31, 1821; d. Vienna, Aug. 24, 1878. His father, a Danish agriculturist, sent him to Germany at the age of 13 to study science, but Willmers turned to music; took lessons with Hummel for 2 years and with Friedrich Schneider for a year; became a concert pianist and toured successfully in Germany and Austria; was much acclaimed in Paris and London (1846–47); in 1866 settled in Vienna. His technical specialty was the performance of "chains of trills," for which he was famous. He wrote a number of brilliant piano solos: *6 études; Sérénade érotique* (for the left hand); *Sehnsucht am Meere; Un Jour d'été en Norvège; 2 études de* concert (*La pompa di festa* and *La danza delle Baccanti*); *Sonata héroïque; Tarantella giocosa; La Sylphide; Trillerketten; Aus der Geisterwelt,* tremolo-caprice; *Allegro symphonique;* he also composed some chamber music.

Willson, Meredith, American composer of coruscating Americanistic musicals, and a fine flutist; b. Mason City, Iowa, May 18, 1902; d. Santa Monica, Calif., June 15, 1984. He learned to play the flute as a child, and played in a school orch. at the age of 11. In 1916 he was sent to N.Y., where he took flute lessons with Georges Barrère. In 1919 he joined Sousa's band as a flute player and traveled with it until 1922. From 1923 to 1928 he was a flutist in the N.Y. Phil. He then entered the field of radio as a conductor and composer. For the 30th anniversary of the San Francisco earthquake he wrote a symph., which he conducted in its first performance, in San Francisco on April 19, 1936. His 2nd Symph. was first played by the Los Angeles Phil. on April 4, 1940. His other symph. works include *The Jervis Bay; Symphonic Variations on an American Theme;* and *O.O. McIntyre Suite.* He also wrote many band pieces and a choral work, *Anthem of the Atomic Age.* Then he devoted himself to the composition of popular music, in which he revealed a triple talent as a performer, writer, and composer. He appeared as a comedian on a radio program, "The Big Show," in which he engaged in a comic colloquy with Tallulah Bankhead, closing with an inspirational hymn, *May the Good Lord Bless and Keep You,* which became very popular as an anthem. Willson achieved his triumph with his musical revue *The Music Man,* for which he wrote the book, the lyrics, and the music. It opened on Broadway on Dec. 19, 1957, and became an immediate success, thanks to the satirical and yet somehow patriotic subject, dealing with a traveling salesman of band uniforms and instruments who sells them to hick-town suckers; and to the sparkling score, containing the hit chorus *76 Trombones.* His subsequent musicals were *The Unsinkable Molly Brown,* produced on Broadway in 1960, for which he wrote the musical score, and *Here's Love,* produced on Broadway in 1963, an adaptation of the film *Miracle on 34th Street. The Music Man* and *The Unsinkable Molly Brown* were made into films. Willson was also active as an arranger and orchestrator in Hollywood; he helped Charlie Chaplin in arranging the score for his anti-Hitler, anti-Mussolini film, *The Great Dictator.* He publ. several autobiographical books: *And There I Stood with My Piccolo* (N.Y., 1948), *Eggs I Have Laid* (N.Y., 1955), and *But He Doesn't Know the Territory* (descriptive of the origin of *The Music Man;* N.Y., 1959).

Wilm, Nicolai von, German pianist and composer; b. Riga, March 4, 1834; d. Wiesbaden, Feb. 20, 1911. He studied with Plaidy, Hauptmann, and Richter at the Leipzig Cons.; then in 1857 went to Riga as a theater conductor, and in 1860 proceeded to St. Petersburg, where he became an instructor at the Imperial Nicolayevsky Inst.; returned to Germany in 1875 and lived mostly in Dresden and Wiesbaden. WORKS: A highly prolific composer (243 opus numbers), he is best known through his chamber music; wrote a String Sextet, String Quartet, Piano Trio, Cello Sonata, 2 violin sonatas, Sonata for Violin and Harp; numerous pieces for piano solo: *Kleine Suite; Herbstfrüchte; Im russischen Dorf; Stimmungen; Dorf- und Waldidyllen; Musikalisches Dekameron;* etc.; for Piano, 4-hands: *Eine Nordlandfahrt; Reisebilder aus Schlesien; Musikalische Federzeichnungen; Kalendarium;* etc.; also variations and other pieces for 2 pianos; men's choruses; songs.

Wilson, Domingo Santa Cruz. See **Santa Cruz Wilson, Domingo.**

Wilson, John, English lutenist and song writer; b. (probably in Faversham, Kent) April 5, 1595; d. London, Feb. 22, 1674. He was musically gifted; at the age of 19, wrote music for *The Maske of Flowers.* According to some indications, he participated as a singer in a production of Shakespeare's *Much Ado about Nothing* (as Jacke Wilson). In 1635 he was made one of the King's Musicians; was in favor with Charles I, whom he followed to Oxford during the civil war in 1644, and was made a D.Mus. by Oxford Univ. on March 10, 1644; he was "Musick Professor" there from 1656 until 1661. Upon the Restoration he resumed his post at court, and on Oct. 22, 1662, became the successor of Henry Lawes as a Gentleman of the Chapel Royal. He publ. *Psalterium Carolinum* (London, 1657), *Cheerfull Ayres or Ballads* (Oxford, 1660); wrote several songs to Shakespeare's words. Some of his songs were included in Playford's *Select Musicall Ayres and Dialogues* (1652, 1653), *Select Ayres and Dialogues* (1659), *Catch that catch can: or the Musical Companion* (1667), and *The Treasury of Musick* (1669).

Wilson, Olly, black American composer; b. St. Louis, Sept. 7, 1937. He was educated at Washington Univ. in St. Louis (B.M., 1959), at the Univ. of Illinois (Mus.M., 1960), and at the Univ. of Iowa, where his teachers were Robert Sykes, Robert Kelley, and Phillip Bezanson (Ph.D., 1964). In 1971–72 he traveled in West Africa to study indigenous music; then devoted himself to teaching and composition; was on the faculty of Florida A. & M. Univ. (1960–62 and 1964–65); at the Oberlin Cons. of Music (1965–70), and later at the Univ. of Calif., Berkeley. WORKS: *Prelude and Line Study* for Woodwind Quartet (1959); Trio for Flute, Cello, and Piano (1959); String Quartet (1960); *Wry Fragments* for Tenor and Percussion (1961); Violin Sonata (1961); *Dance Suite* for Wind Ensemble (1962); *Soliloquy* for Bass Viol (1962); Sextet (1963); *3 Movements* for Orch. (1964); *Piece for 4* for Flute, Trumpet, Double Bass, and Piano (1966); *In Memoriam Martin Luther King, Jr.,* for Chorus and Electronic Sound (1968); *Voices* for Orch. (1970); *The 18 Hands of Jerome Harris,* electronic ballet (1971); *Akwan* for Piano, Electronic Piano, and Orch. (1972); *Black Martyrs,* electronic composition (1972); *Spirit Song* for Soprano, Chorus, and Orch. (1973); *Sometimes* for Tenor and Tape (1976); Piano Trio (1977).

Wilson, Ransom, outstanding American flutist; b. Tuscaloosa, Ala., Oct. 25, 1951. He studied with Philip Dunigan at the North Carolina School of the Arts; also profited from advice given by Jean-Pierre Rampal. He made a European tour with the Juilliard Chamber Orch. under Peter Maag, and soon established himself as a brilliant virtuoso. In 1980 he founded and served as conductor-soloist with his own ensemble, Solisti New York; also appeared as guest conductor with other ensembles. His repertoire is catholic, covering all periods and styles; he also commissioned special works for the flute, and arranged music for use in his concerts.

Wilson, Richard, American composer and pianist; b. Cleveland, May 15, 1941. He studied cello and theory in Cleveland; in 1959 entered Harvard Univ., where he took courses in music with Randall Thompson, G. Wallace Woodworth, and Robert Moevs (A.B., 1963, magna cum laude); he subsequently attended classes at Rutgers Univ. (M.A., 1966); also studied piano with Leonard Shure in N.Y. (1960) and with Friedrich Wuhrer in Munich (1963). In 1966 he joined the faculty of Vassar College; was made a prof. in 1976; from 1979 to 1982 served as chairman of the music dept. there.
    WORKS: *Suite for 5 Players* (1963); Trio for Oboe, Violin, and Cello (1964); *Fantasy and Variations* for Chamber Ensemble (1965); *A Dissolve* for Women's Chorus (1968); String Quartet No. 1 (1968); *Music* for Violin and Cello (1969); Quartet for 2 Flutes, Double Bass, and Harpsichord (1969); *Initiation* for Orch. (1970); *Music* for Solo Cello (1971); *Music* for Solo Flute (1972); Wind Quintet (1974); *Eclogue* for Solo Piano (1974); String Quartet No. 2 (1977); *Serenade: Variations on a Simple March* for Clarinet, Viola, and Double Bass (1978); *Sour Flowers: 8 Piano Pieces for the Form of an Herbal* (1979); *Deux pas de trois: Pavane and Tango* for Flute, Oboe, and Harpsichord (1979); Concerto for Violin and Chamber Orch. (1979); *Profound Utterances* for Solo Bassoon (1980); *Figurations* for Clarinet and Cello (1981); *Gnomics* for Flute, Oboe, and Clarinet (1981); String Quartet No. 3 (1982); *Dithyramb* for Oboe and Clarinet (1982); Suite for Wind Instruments (1983); Concerto for Bassoon and Chamber Orch. (1983).

Windgassen, Wolfgang, distinguished German tenor; b. Annemasse, Haute Savoie, June 26, 1914; d. Stuttgart, Sept. 8, 1974. He received his early vocal training from his father, **Fritz Windgassen** (b. Hamburg, Feb. 9, 1883; d. Murnau, April 17, 1963), who was a leading tenor at the Stuttgart Opera; then continued his studies at the Stuttgart Cons. with Maria Ranzow and Alfons Fischer. He made his operatic debut in Pforzheim in 1941 as Alvaro in *La forza del destino;* after military service in the German army, he joined the Stuttgart Opera in 1945, remaining on its roster until 1972. From 1951–70 he appeared at the Bayreuth Festivals, where he was

a leading Heldentenor. He made his Metropolitan Opera debut in N.Y. on Jan. 22, 1957, as Siegmund. He sang regularly at Convent Garden from 1955–66. He was especially successful in Wagnerian roles, as Tannhäuser, Tristan, Parsifal, Siegfried, and Lohengrin; he also appeared as Radames in *Aida* and Don José in *Carmen.*

Windingstad, Ole, Norwegian-American conductor; b. Sandefjord, May 18, 1886; d. Kingston, N.Y., June 3, 1959. He graduated from the Oslo Cons. in 1902; then studied at the Leipzig Cons.; settled in America in 1913, and established the Scandinavian Symph. Orch., which he conducted until 1929; also conducted the Brooklyn Symph. Orch. (1930–32), the Knickerbocker Symph. Orch. in Albany, N.Y. (1937–39), the New Orleans Symph. Orch. (1940–44), and the Albany Symph. Orch. (1945–48). In 1929 he was decorated with the Norwegian Order of Saint Olaf. He composed a Symph. (1913); a cantata, *The Skald of Norway* (1929); *The Tides* for Orch. (Albany, Feb. 13, 1938, composer conducting); many minor pieces.

Winham, Godfrey, British-American composer and computer specialist; b. London, Dec. 11, 1934; d. Princeton, N.J., April 26, 1975. He studied composition and piano at the Royal Academy of Music in London; in 1954 went to the U.S., where he took courses at Princeton Univ. (A.B., 1956; M.F.A., 1958); received his Ph.D. degree there with the thesis *Composition with Arrays* (1965); then joined the staff as a lecturer on electronic music and computer composition. In 1969 he worked on the computerized synthesis of music and speech. Apart from his programmed compositions on a computer, he wrote 2 string quartets, *The Habit of Perfection* for Voice and String Quartet, and several piano pieces. He was married to the American singer **Bethany Beardslee**.

Winkler, Alexander, Russian composer and pianist; b. Kharkov, March 3, 1865; d. Besançon, France, Aug. 6, 1935. He studied with Duvernoy in Paris, and with Leschetizky (piano) and Navrátil (composition) in Vienna. Returning to Russia, he became a piano teacher in his native city (1890–96); then was a prof. at the St. Petersburg Cons. (1907–24); among his students was Prokofiev. In 1924 he emigrated to France and became director of the Besançon Cons. He composed an overture, *En Bretagne;* orch. variations on a Russian folk song and on a Finnish folk song; String Quintet; 3 string quartets; Piano Quartet; Piano Trio; Viola Sonata; several albums of piano pieces; songs.

Winner, Septimus, American composer of popular music; b. Philadelphia, May 11, 1827; d. there, Nov. 22, 1902. He learned to play the violin; married at the age of 20 and opened a music store in Philadelphia, where he began giving lessons on the violin, guitar, and banjo. In 1854 he wrote his best-known song, *Listen to the Mocking Bird* (based on a melody originated by his black errand boy, "Whistling Dick" Milburn), selling the copyright for $5; in his lifetime the song sold 20 million copies. In 1862 he wrote *Give Us Back Our Old Commander: Little Mac, the People's Pride,* voicing a widespread sentiment for the return of General McClellan; the song was regarded as subversive and Winner was arraigned, but soon released; later the song, slightly altered, was used for Grant's presidential campaign. Winner also wrote the song *Whispering Hope,* which became extremely popular. He was a pioneer in bringing music to the masses; wrote over 200 vols. of music, including many instructive works, for 23 different instruments, and made about 2,000 arrangements for violin and piano. He used the pen name **Alice Hawthorne** (in honor of his mother, Mary Ann Hawthorne) for many of his songs, including *Listen to the Mocking Bird.*

Winter, Peter, German composer; b. Mannheim (baptized, Aug. 28), 1754; d. Munich, Oct. 17, 1825. He was a violinist in the Electoral orch. at the age of 10; was given permanent employment there in 1776; studied with Abbé Vogler; went with the court to Munich in 1778 and became music director of its theater; was appointed court conductor in 1798 and held this post until his death. In Munich he brought out a number of operas, of which the most important were *Helena und Paris* (Feb. 5, 1782), *Der Bettelstudent* (Feb. 2, 1785), *Marie von Montalban* (Jan. 28, 1800), and *Colmal* (Sept. 15, 1809). Frequent leaves of absence from Munich enabled him to travel; in Venice he produced his operas *Catone in Utica* (1791), *I sacrifizi di Creta* (Feb. 13, 1792), *I Fratelli rivali* (Nov. 1793), and *Belisa* (Feb. 5, 1794). In Vienna he brought out *Das unterbrochene Opferfest* (June 14, 1796; his most successful opera; produced all over Europe), *Babylons Pyramiden* (Oct. 25, 1797), and *Das Labirint* (June 12, 1798); in Paris he produced his only French opera, *Tamerlan* (Sept. 14, 1802); in London, the Italian operas *La grotta di Calipso* (May 31, 1803), *Il trionfo dell'amor fraterno* (March 22, 1804), *Il ratto di Proserpina* (May 3, 1804), and *Zaira* (Jan. 29, 1805); in Milan, *Maometto II* (Jan. 28, 1817), *I due Valdomiri* (Dec. 26, 1817), and *Etelinda* (March 23, 1818). He also wrote several ballets; 3 oratorios and 17 sacred cantatas for the Munich court chapel; 26 masses and a vast amount of other church music; 9 symphs. (including the grand choral symph. *Die Schlacht*); overtures; 2 septets; 6 string quartets; 2 string quintets; concertos for clarinet, for bassoon, and other instruments with orch.; and *Vollständige Singschule* in 3 parts. Some of his chamber music was republ. by Riemann in Denkmäler der Tonkunst in Bayern, 27 and 28 (15 and 16; with a thematic catalogue).

Winternitz, Emanuel, Austrian-American musicologist and museum curator; b. Vienna, Aug. 4, 1898; d. New York, Aug. 22, 1983. He served in the Austrian army in World War I; after the Armistice, studied jurisprudence at the Univ. of Vienna (LL.D., 1922); then was engaged as a corporate lawyer in Vienna (1929–38). After the Anschluss he emigrated to the U.S., where he devoted himself mainly to lec-

turing on art; served as Peripatetic Professor for the Carnegie Foundation. In 1942 he was appointed keeper of musical instruments at the Metropolitan Museum in N.Y.; in 1949 was named curator of the Crosby Brown Collection of Musical Instruments of All Nations at the Metropolitan. He also administered the André Mertens Galleries for Musical Instruments (1971–73). In 1973 he became curator emeritus of the Metropolitan. Among his principal endeavors was musical iconography; he publ. a valuable reference work, *Musical Autographs from Monteverdi to Hindemith* (2 vols., Princeton, 1955); other editions were *Die schönsten Musikinstrumente das Abendlandes* (Munich, 1966; in Eng. as *Musical Instruments of the Western World,* N.Y., 1967); *Leonardo da Vinci as a Musician* (New Haven, 1982).

Wiora, Walter, renowned German musicologist; b. Katowice, Dec. 30, 1906. He studied musicology in Berlin with Abert, Blume, Gurlitt, Hornbostel, H.J. Moser, Schering, Schünemann, and J. Wolf; received his Ph.D. in 1937 from the Univ. of Freiburg. He served in the German army during World War II; after 1945 he was in charge of the German Folk Music Archives in Freiburg im Breisgau. In 1958 he succeeded Friedrich Blume as a prof. at Kiel Univ. In 1962–63 he was a visiting prof. at Columbia Univ. in N.Y.; from 1964 to 1972 was a prof. of musicology at the Univ. of Saarland in Saarbrücken; since 1955 he has been a member of the International Folk Music Council. A Festschrift in his honor was publ. in 1967, in Kassel, containing a list of his publications. A 2nd Festschrift was publ. in his honor in Tutzing in 1979. His principal achievement is research in the field of German folk music.

Wirén, Dag Ivar, prominent Swedish composer; b. Noraberg, Örebro, Oct. 15, 1905. He studied at the Stockholm Cons. with Oskar Lindberg and Ernest Ellberg (1926–31); then in Paris with Leonid Sabaneyev (1932–34). He returned to Sweden in 1934, and was music critic for the *Svenka Morgonbladet* (1938–46); was vice-president of the Society of Swedish Composers (1947–63). His early music was influenced by Scandinavian Romanticism; later he adopted a more sober and more cosmopolitan neo-Classicism, stressing the symmetry of formal structure; in his thematic procedures he adopts the method of systematic intervallic metamorphosis rather than development and variation.

WORKS: *Serenade* for Strings (1937); ballet, *Oscarbalen (Oscarian Ball,* 1949); television ballet, *Den elaka drottningen (The Wicked Queen,* 1960; Swedish television perf., Nov. 22, 1961); 2 radio operettas, *Blått, gult, rött* (1940; inspired by Churchill's famous speech containing the phrase "Blood, sweat, tears") and *Den glada patiensen* (1941); 2 concert overtures (1931, 1940); 5 symphs.: No. 1 (1932); No. 2 (1939); No. 3 (1943–44); No. 4 (1951–52); No. 5 (1964; Stockholm, Dec. 5, 1964); *Sinfonietta* for Orch. (1933–34); Cello Concerto (1936); *Little Suite* for Orch. (1941); *Romantic Suite* for Orch. (1945); Violin Concerto (1945–46); Piano Concerto (1947–50);

Divertimento for Orch. (1954–57); *Triptyk* for Orch. (1958); *Music* for Strings (1966–67; Stockholm, Jan. 12, 1968); Flute Concertino (1972); 5 string quartets (1930, 1935, 1941–45, 1952–53, 1969–70); *Theme and Variations* for Piano (1933); 2 piano trios (1933, 1961); Violin Sonatina (1939); *5 Ironic Miniatures* for Piano (1942–45); Piano Sonatina (1950); Quartet for Flute, Oboe, Clarinet, and Cello (1956); *5 Improvisations* for Piano (1959); *Little Serenade* for Guitar (1964); Wind Quintet (1971); *Little Piano Suite* (1971); incidental music for many plays and films; songs.

Wise, Michael, English singer and composer; b. Wiltshire, c.1648; d. Salisbury, Aug. 24, 1687. After an apprenticeship under Cooke at the Chapel Royal in London, he was appointed, at the age of 20, organist of Salisbury Cathedral; in 1676 he became Gentleman of the Chapel Royal; in 1687 he was appointed master of the choristers of St. Paul's Cathedral. He was killed by a watchman during a street dispute. He wrote anthems, church services, and catches; 6 of his anthems are included in Boyce's *Cathedral Music;* other pieces are found in various collections of the 17th century.

Wissmer, Pierre, Swiss composer; b. Geneva, Oct. 30, 1915. He studied with Roger-Ducasse at the Paris Cons. and with Daniel-Lesur at the Schola Cantorum; in 1963 was appointed honorary director of the Schola Cantorum. He writes affable and pleasingly dissonant music in a natural contrapuntal idiom which is never congested by polyphonic superfluities.
WORKS: Radio opera, *Marion ou La Belle au tricorne* (Geneva, Radio Suisse Romande, April 16, 1947); comic opera, *Capitaine Bruno* (Geneva, Nov. 9, 1952); opéra bouffe, *Léonidas ou La Cruauté mentale* (Paris, Sept. 12, 1958); ballet, *Le Beau Dimanche* (1939; Geneva, March 20, 1944); *Alerte, puits 21* (Geneva, 1964); *Christina et les chimères* (French Television, 1967); *Naïades* for Narrator, Soli, Chorus, and Orch. (Geneva, Jan. 21, 1942); *Le Quatrième Mage,* oratorio (Paris, Oct. 14, 1969); 5 symphs. (1938, 1951, 1955, 1962, 1969); *Divertissement sur un choral* for 11 Instruments (Geneva, Dec. 8, 1939); *Mouvement* for String Orch. (Geneva, Feb. 1, 1940); symph. suite, *Antoine et Cléopâtre* (Geneva, Oct. 2, 1946); overture, *La Mandrellina* (Geneva, April 16, 1952); 2 string quartets (1937, 1949); *Sérénade* for Oboe, Clarinet, and Bassoon (1938); Sonatina for Clarinet and Piano (1941); Sonatina for Violin and Piano (1946); Piano Sonata (1949); *Concerto valcrosiano* for Orch. (1966); 2 piano concertos (1937, 1948); 2 violin concertos (1944, 1954); Guitar Concerto (1957); Clarinet Concerto (1960); Trumpet Concerto (1961); Oboe Concerto (1963); *Concertino-Crosière* for Flute, String Orch., and Piano (1966); Wind Quintet (1966); *Quadrige* for Flute, Violin, Cello, and Piano (1961); *Cantique en l'ounour dou grand santlouis, rei de franco et patroun de vaucros de cuers* for Chorus, with Piano or Organ (1971); songs; choruses.

Wit, Paul de, Dutch cellist; b. Maastricht, Jan. 4, 1852; d. Leipzig, Dec. 10, 1925. In 1880 he founded (with O. Laffert) the *Zeitschrift für Instrumentenbau;* opened a museum of musical instruments at Leipzig in 1886, but sold his collections to the Berlin Hochschule für Musik in 1888 and 1891; he then made a 3rd collection, which he sold in 1906 to Heyer of Cologne. Wit was a fine player on the viola da gamba, as well as a cellist. He published *Geigenzettel alter Meister vom 16. bis zur Mitte des 19. Jahrhunderts* (1902; 2nd ed., 1910); *Weltadressbuch der gesammten Musikinstrumenten-Industrie* (1903; 8th ed., 1912); *Katalog des musikhistorischen Museums von P. de Wie* (1903).

Witek, Anton, Bohemian violinist; b. Saaz, Bohemia, Jan. 7, 1872; d. Winchester, Mass., Aug. 19, 1933. He studied violin with his father and with A. Bennewitz at the Prague Cons. From 1894 to 1910 he was concertmaster of the Berlin Phil.; in 1895 he formed a duo with the Danish pianist **Vita Gerhardt** (1868–1925), whom he later married (1910). In 1910 he was engaged as concertmaster of the Boston Symph. Orch. (until 1918); from 1920 to 1925 he was in Germany; then returned to America. After the death of his first wife (1925), he married the American violinist **Alma Rosengrein.** He publ. *Fingered Octaves* (1919).

Witherspoon, Herbert, American bass; b. Buffalo, N.Y., July 21, 1873; d. New York, May 10, 1935. He studied with Horatio Parker at Yale Univ., and also took lessons with MacDowell in N.Y. He then studied singing with Bouhy in Paris, Henry Wood in London, and G.B. Lamperti in Berlin. Returning to America, he made his concert debut at New Haven (Oct. 21, 1895); made 5 tours of England as an oratorio singer; he made his American opera debut at the Metropolitan Opera House as Titurel in *Parsifal* (Nov. 26, 1908); remained on its roster until 1916; then devoted himself to teaching; in 1925 became president of the Chicago Musical College; in 1931, president of the Cincinnati Cons. of Music; in 1933 he returned to N.Y., and in May 1935, was chosen to succeed Gatti-Casazza as general manager of the Metropolitan Opera Co., but he died suddenly of a heart attack. He publ. *Singing: A Treatise for Teachers and Students* (N.Y., 1925), and *36 Lessons in Singing for Teacher and Student* (Chicago, 1930).

Witkowski, Georges-Martin, French composer; b. Mostaganem, Algeria, Jan. 6, 1867 (of a French father and a Polish mother); d. Lyons, Aug. 12, 1943. He was educated at the military school of St.-Cyr; began music study with Vincent d'Indy at the Schola Cantorum; later left for the army and settled in Lyons, where he founded the Société des Grands Concerts in 1905 for the production of oratorios. In 1924 he was appointed director of the Lyons Cons.; he retired from there in 1941.
WORKS: Opera, *La Princesse lointaine,* after Rostand (Paris, March 26, 1934); 2 symphs. (1900, 1910); *Poème de la maison* for Solo Voices, Chorus,

and Orch. (Lyons, Jan. 25, 1919); *Mon lac* for Piano and Orch. (Lyons, Nov. 20, 1921); for Voice and Orch.: *4 poèmes de Cœur Innombrable* (1925), *3 poèmes de Ronsard* (1935), *Paysage rêvé* (1937); *Introduction et Danse* for Violin and Orch. (Paris, Oct. 10, 1937); Piano Quintet (1897); String Quartet (1902); Violin Sonata (1907).

Witt, Franz Xaver, German composer of church music; b. Walderbach, Feb. 9, 1834; d. Schatzhofen, Dec. 2, 1888. He studied with Proske and Schrems in Regensburg; took Holy Orders in 1856. In 1866 he established and edited *Fliegende Blätter für katholische Kirchenmusik* and *Musica Sacra;* in 1868 he founded the Allgemeiner Deutscher Cäcilienverein for the improvement of Catholic church music, which, while opposing the introduction of orch. instruments into the church, helped to arouse interest in the great masterpieces of church music. In his own early masses, Witt employed the orch. Besides numerous masses, he publ. 2 Requiems, many litanies, offertories, motets, and hymns (55 opus numbers); also some secular men's choruses; was the author of *Der Zustand der katholischen Kirchenmusik* (1865), *Über das Dirigieren der katholischen Kirchenmusik,* and *Das bayerische Kultusministerium* (1886); his articles are collected in a centennial vol., *Ausgewählte Anfsätze zur Kirchenmusik* (Cologne, 1934).

Witt, Friedrich, German violinist and composer; b. Hallenbergstetten, Württemberg, Nov. 8, 1770; d. Würzburg, Jan. 3, 1836. At the age of 19, he was engaged as violinist in the orch. of Prince von Oettingen; from 1802 he was Kapellmeister at Würzburg, at first to the Prince-Bishop, then to the Grand Duke, finally to the city. It was Witt who composed the so-called Jena Symphony, misattributed to Beethoven (see H.C. Robbins Landon's article in the *Music Review* for May 1957). Other works by Witt include the historical opera *Palma* (Frankfurt, 1804); the comic opera *Das Fischerweib* (Würzburg, 1806); the oratorios *Der leidende Heiland* (Würzburg, 1802) and *Die Auferstehung Jesu;* masses and cantatas; 9 symphs.; music for wind band; Septet for Clarinet, Horn, Bassoon, and Strings; Quintet for Piano and Winds; Flute Concerto; etc.

Wittassek, Johann Nepomuk August, Bohemian pianist and composer; b. Hořín, March 23, 1770; d. Prague, Dec. 7, 1839. The son of a schoolmaster, he received a good education; took music lessons with F.X. Dušek and J.A. Koželuch in Prague; succeeded Koželuch in 1814 as music director at the Prague Cathedral; was appointed director of the School for Organists in Prague in 1830. He wrote an opera, *David,* brought out in Prague; 4 piano concertos; concertos for violin, for clarinet, and for bassoon; 6 string quartets; 4 violin sonatas; much church music.

Wittgenstein, Paul, Austrian pianist; b. Vienna, Nov. 5, 1887; d. Manhasset, Long Island, N.Y., March 3, 1961. He was of a musical family; studied piano with Josef Labor and Leschetizky; made his first public appearance as a pianist in 1913, in Vienna. He lost his right arm in World War I, at the Russian front; was a prisoner of war in Omsk, Siberia; was repatriated in 1916. He then developed an extraordinary technique for left hand alone, and performed a concerto specially composed for him by his teacher, Josef Labor. He subsequently commissioned left-hand piano concertos from Richard Strauss, Ravel, Prokofiev, Korngold, Benjamin Britten, and other composers, of which he gave the world premieres (except the Prokofiev concerto, which he found unsuitable). He appeared in the major musical centers in Europe; toured America in 1934; in 1939 settled in N.Y.; became a U.S. citizen in 1946. He was a brother of the famous philosopher Ludwig Wittgenstein.

Wittich, Marie, German soprano; b. Giessen, May 27, 1868; d. Dresden, Aug. 4, 1931. She studied in Würzburg; made her debut as Azucena at the age of 14 in Magdeburg in 1882; then sang in Düsseldorf, Basel, and Schwerin; in 1889 she became a member of the Dresden Court Opera, remaining on its roster until 1914; while there, she was chosen by Richard Strauss to create the role of Salome in 1905; she also made guest appearances at Covent Garden in London (1905–6) and in Bayreuth (1901–10).

Wixell, Ingvar, Swedish baritone; b. Lulea, May 7, 1931. He was educated at the Stockholm Cons.; made his concert debut in 1952 in Gävle. In 1956 he joined the Royal Opera in Stockholm; also sang regularly with the Deutsche Oper in West Berlin. He then launched an international career, which took him to London, Salzburg, Bayreuth, Chicago, and San Francisco. On Jan. 29, 1973, he made his debut at the Metropolitan Opera in N.Y. as Rigoletto.

Woldemar, Michel, French violinist and composer; b. Orléans, June 17, 1750; d. Clermont-Ferrand, Dec. 19, 1815. He studied with Lolli; for some years was a conductor for a traveling theatrical troupe. By adding a 5th string (*c*) to the violin, he obtained an instrument that he called "violon-alto," because it included the viola range, and for which he wrote a concerto. He also publ. 3 violin concertos, a String Quartet, duos for 2 violins and for violin and viola; *Sonates fantomagiques* for Violin (*L'Ombre de Lolli, de Mestrino, de Pugnani, de Tartini);* 12 grand solos; *6 rêves ou Caprices; Caprices ou Etudes; Le Nouveau Labyrinth pour violon,* followed by studies in double stops; *Le Nouvel Art de l'archet; Etude élémentaire de l'archet moderne;* variations on *Les Folies d'Espagne,* etc.; methods for violin, viola, and clarinet; also a system of musical stenography (*Tableau mélotachigraphique*) and a method of musical correspondence (*Notographie*).

Wöldike, Mogens, Danish organist and conductor; b. Copenhagen, July 5, 1897. He studied with Carl Nielsen; was organist and choirmaster in several Copenhagen churches; in 1937 he became conductor of the Madrigal Chorus of Danish Radio; toured with it in Scandinavia, England, and Italy;

was also director for the series of records Masterpieces of Music before 1750, in collaboration with W.W. Norton & Co. and the Haydn Society of Vienna and Copenhagen. From 1959 to 1972 he was organist of the Copenhagen Cathedral.

Wolf, Ernst Wilhelm, German composer; b. Grossenbehringen, near Gotha (baptized, Feb. 25), 1735; d. Weimar, (buried, Dec. 1) 1792. In 1772 he became Kapellmeister to the music-loving Duchess of Saxe-Weimar, Anna Amalia.

WORKS: About 20 operas, of which the most successful were *Das Rosenfest* (Weimar, 1770) and *Die Dorfdeputierten* (Berlin, June 15, 1772); other works include Passion oratorios and Easter cantatas; 6 piano concertos; 4 quintets for Piano, Flute, Violin, Viola, and Cello; 6 string quartets; 7 books of piano sonatas, each containing 6 numbers; in MS are 15 symphs., 17 partitas, 12 piano concertos, and much chamber music. He also wrote *Kleine musikalische Reise* (1782) and *Musikalischer Unterricht* (1788; 2nd ed., 1804).

Wolf, Hugo, Austrian composer, one of the greatest masters of the German lied; b. Windisch-Gräz, March 13, 1860; d. Vienna, Feb. 22, 1903. He studied piano and violin with his father, an amateur musician; then took lessons from Sebastian Weixler, a schoolmaster. In 1870 he was sent to Graz, where he entered a primary school, but left after a single semester and was enrolled in the seminary at the Benedictine monastery of St. Paul in Carinthia; in 1873 he went to a Gymnasium in Marburg; in 1875 he moved to Vienna, where he became a pupil at the Cons., studying piano with Wilhelm Schenner and harmony with Robert Fuchs. When Wagner visited Vienna in 1875, Wolf went to see him, bringing along some of his compositions; the fact that Wagner received him at all, and even said a few words of encouragement, gave Wolf great impetus toward further composition. But he was incapable of submitting himself to academic discipline, and soon difficulties arose between him and the Cons. authorities. He openly expressed his dissatisfaction with the teaching of Franz Krenn (who was also the teacher of Mahler), and was so impertinent to the director, Josef Hellmesberger, that he was expelled. In March 1877, he returned to his native town, but after a few months at home decided to go to Vienna again; there he managed to support himself by giving music lessons to children in the homes of friends. By that time he was composing diligently, writing songs to texts by his favorite poets—Goethe, Lenau, Heine. An unhappy encounter with Brahms, who advised him to study counterpoint before attempting to compose, embittered him, and he became determined to follow his own musical inclinations without seeking further advice. After a brief (and unsuccessful) employment as chorusmaster in Salzburg (1881), he secured in 1883 the position of music critic of the weekly *Wiener Salonblatt.* He took this opportunity to indulge his professional frustration by attacking those not sympathetic to new trends in music; he poured invec-

tive of extraordinary virulence on Brahms, thus antagonizing the influential Hanslick and other admirers of Brahms. But he also formed a coterie of staunch friends, who had faith in his ability. Yet he was singularly unsuccessful in his repeated attempts to secure performances for his works. He submitted a string quartet to the celebrated Rosé Quartet, but it was rejected. Finally, Hans Richter accepted for the Vienna Phil. Wolf's symph. poem *Penthesilea,* but the public performance was a fiasco, and Wolf even accused Richter of deliberately sabotaging the work; later he reorchestrated the score, eliminating certain crudities of the early version. In 1887 he resigned as music critic of the *Wiener Salonblatt* and devoted himself entirely to composition. He became convinced that he was creating the greatest masterpieces of song since Schubert and Schumann, and stated his conviction in plain terms in his letters. In historical perspective, his self-appraisal has proved remarkably accurate, but psychologists may well wonder whether Wolf was not consciously trying to give himself the needed encouragement by what must have seemed to him a wild exaggeration. However, a favorable turn in his fortunes came in 1889, when his 27 songs to words by Mörike and 10 songs to words by Eichendorff appeared in print. There followed 25 Goethe songs in 1890, and the album of exquisite songs after Heyse and Geibel, *Spanisches Liederbuch,* in 1891, as well as 6 songs to poems of Keller, *Alte Weisen.* The singer Ferdinand Jäger became a champion of Wolf's music, and gave repeated performances of his songs at the meetings of the Vienna Wagner-Verein. Soon Wolf's name became known in Germany; he presented concerts of his own works in Berlin, Darmstadt, Mannheim, and other musical centers. He completed the first part of his great cycle of 22 songs, *Italienisches Liederbuch,* in 1891, and composed the 2nd part (24 songs) in 5 weeks, in the spring of 1896. In 1897 he wrote the *3 Gedichte von Michelangelo.* While Wolf could compose songs with a facility and degree of excellence that were truly astounding, he labored painfully on his orch. works. His only symph. was never completed, nor was a violin concerto; the work on *Penthesilea* took him a disproportionately long time. In 1895 he undertook the composition of his opera, *Der Corregidor,* to the famous tale by Alarcón, *El sombrero de tres picos,* and, working feverishly, completed the vocal score with piano accompaniment in a few months. The orchestration took him a much longer time. *Der Corregidor* had its premiere in Mannheim on June 7, 1896, but it proved a disappointment. The opera was ineffective dramatically, and the orchestration was weak. Wolf subsequently revised the score, and in its new version *Der Corregidor* was brought out in Strasbourg on April 29, 1898. He never completed his 2nd opera, *Manuel Venegas* (also after Alarcón); fragments were presented in concert form on March 1, 1903. In the meantime, his fame grew. A Hugo Wolf–Verein was organized at Berlin in 1896, and did excellent work in furthering performances of Wolf's songs in Germany. Even more effective was the Hugo Wolf-Verein in Vienna, founded by Michel Haberlandt on April 22, 1897 (disbanded in 1906). Amid these encouraging signs of recognition, tragedy struck. A supposed rebuke administered to Wolf by Mahler, at that time the newly appointed director of the Vienna Opera, who had been considering a performance of *Der Corregidor,* precipitated in him a mental breakdown. He declared to friends that Mahler had been relieved of his post, and that he, Wolf, was appointed director of the Vienna Opera in Mahler's stead. On Sept. 20, 1897, he was placed in a private mental institution; after a favorable remission, he was discharged (Jan. 24, 1898), and traveled in Italy and Austria. After his return to Vienna, symptoms of mental derangement manifested themselves in even greater degree. He attempted suicide by throwing himself into a lake, and then was committed to a state asylum at his own request. (A parallel with Schumann's case forcibly suggests itself.) He remained in confinement, gradually lapsing into complete irrationality. He died at the age of 42, and was buried near the graves of Schubert and Beethoven; a monument was unveiled on Oct. 20, 1904.

Wolf's significance in music history rests on his songs, about 300 in number, many of them publ. posthumously. The sobriquet "the Wagner of the lied" may well be justified in regard to involved contrapuntal texture and chromatic harmony, for Wolf accepted the Wagnerian idiom through natural affinity as well as by clear choice. The elaboration of the accompaniment, and the incorporation of the vocal line into the contrapuntal scheme of the whole, are Wagnerian traits. But with these external similarities, Wolf's dependence on Wagner's models ceases. In his intimate penetration of the poetic spirit of the text, Wolf appears a legitimate successor to Schubert and Schumann. Wolf's songs are symph. poems in miniature, artistically designed and admirably arranged for voice and piano, the combination in which he was a master.

WORKS: FOR THE STAGE: Incidental music to Ibsen's *Das Fest auf Solhaug* (Vienna, Nov. 21, 1891); *Der Corregidor,* 4-act comedy opera, after Alarcón's *El sombrero de tres picos* (Mannheim, June 7, 1896; revised version, Strasbourg, April 29, 1898); *Manuel Venegas,* 3-act tragic opera, text after Alarcón's *El niño de la bola* (fragments perf. in concert form, Mannheim, March 1, 1903).

CHORAL WORKS: *6 geistliche a cappella Chöre* (1881; ed. by E. Thomas; arranged for men's voices by Max Reger); *Christnacht* for Solo Voices, Chorus, and Orch. (1886–89); *Elfenlied* for Soprano Solo, Chorus, and Orch. (1889–91); *Dem Vaterland* for Male Chorus and Orch. (1890; many revisions).

INSTRUMENTAL WORKS: String Quartet in D minor (1878–84); *Penthesilea,* symph. poem after Kleist (1883–85); *Italienische Serenade* (1892; a transcription of the *Serenade* in G major for String Quartet, 1887); fragments from an early Symph. in D minor and from a Violin Concerto.

SONGS: *12 Lieder aus der Jugendzeit* (1888); *Lieder nach verschiedenen Dichtern,* 31 songs (1877–97); *Gedichte von Mörike,* 53 songs (1888); *Gedichte von Eichendorff,* 20 songs (1886–88); *Gedichte von Goethe,* 51 songs (1888–89); *Spanisches Liederbuch,* 44 songs after Geibel and Heyse (1889–90); *Italieni-*sches Liederbuch, 46 songs after Heyse, in 2 parts: 22 songs (1890–91), 24 songs (1896). 20 of the songs were orchestrated by Wolf; others by Max Reger. 40 previously unpubl. songs, mostly of the earliest period, were publ. in Leipzig in 1936, in 4 vols., as *Nachgelassene Werke,* ed. by R. Haas and H. Schultz. Wolf's collected writings were brought out by R. Batka and H. Werner as *Hugo Wolfs musikalische Kritiken* (Leipzig, 1911). A complete ed. of the songs was publ. by Peters (Leipzig, 1935). A complete works ed. was begun by the Internationalen Hugo Wolf–Gesellschaft, under the direction of H. Janick, in 1960, reaching 18 vols. by 1978. For an index of his works, see P. Müller, *H.W. Verzeichnis seiner Werke* (Leipzig, 1908). An Eng. trans. of the texts of all of Wolf's solo songs was publ. by Henry S. Drinker (N.Y., 1949).

Wolf, Johannes, eminent German musicologist; b. Berlin, April 17, 1869; d. Munich, May 25, 1947. He studied at the Hochschule für Musik in Berlin; took courses in musicology at the Univ. of Berlin with Philipp Spitta and Heinrich Bellermann, and then with Riemann at the Univ. of Leipzig, where he received his Ph.D. in 1893 with the dissertation *Ein anonymer Musiktraktat des 11. bis 12. Jahrhunderts;* he completed his Habilitation at the Univ. of Berlin with his *Florenz in der Musikgeschichte des 14. Jahrhunderts* in 1902, and then taught the history of early music and church music there; also was on the faculty of the Berlin Akademie für Kirchen- und Schulmusik from 1908 to 1927. He was appointed director of the early music collection of the Prussian State Library in Berlin in 1915; from 1927 to 1934 he was director of its entire music collection. He was a leading authority on medieval and Renaissance music; his writings on the history of notation are especially important. He edited a complete edition of the works of Obrecht (Leipzig, 1908–21); for Denkmäler Deutscher Tonkunst he selected vocal works of J.R. Ahle (vol. V, 1901) and G. Rhau's *Newe deudsche geistliche Gesenge für die gemeinen Schulen* (vol. XXXIV, 1908); for Denkmäler der Tonkunst in Österreich he edited H. Isaac's secular works (vols. XXVIII, Jg. XIV/1, 1907, and XXXIII, Jg. XVI/1, 1909); also edited *Der Squarcialupi-Codex aus dem Nachlass herausgegeben von H. Albrecht* (Lippstadt, 1955).

Wolf-Ferrari, Ermanno, famous Italian opera composer; b. Venice, Jan. 12, 1876; d. there, Jan. 21, 1948. His mother was Italian; his father was a well-known German painter. Wolf-Ferrari was sent to Rome to study art, but became interested in opera and decided to devote himself to music; accordingly, he was sent to Munich, where he studied with Rheinberger (1893–95). In 1899 he returned to Venice, where his oratorio *La Sulamite* was successfully performed. This was followed by the production of his first opera, *Cenerentola* (1900). From 1902 to 1907 he was director of the Liceo Benedetto Marcello in Venice; then taught at the Salzburg Mozarteum; lived mostly in Neu-Biberg, near Munich; obtained his first success with the production of the comic opera *Le Donne curiose* (Munich, 1903); the next opera, *I quattro rusteghi* (Munich, 1906), was also well received; there followed his little masterpiece, *Il segreto di Susanna,* a one-act opera buffa in the style of the Italian *verismo* (Susanna's secret being not infidelity, as her husband suspected, but indulgence in surreptitious smoking). Turning toward grand opera, he wrote *I gioielli della Madonna (The Jewels of the Madonna);* it was brought out at Berlin in 1911, and soon became a repertoire piece everywhere; he continued to compose, but his later operas failed to match the appeal of his early creations.

WORKS: OPERAS: *Cenerentola* (Venice, Feb. 22, 1900; in Bremen as *Aschenbrödel,* Jan. 31, 1902); *Le Donne curiose* (Munich, Nov. 27, 1903; in German as *Die neugierigen Frauen;* in Italian, N.Y., Jan. 3, 1912); *I quattro rusteghi* (Munich, March 19, 1906; in German as *Die vier Grobiane); Il segreto di Susanna* (Munich, Dec. 4, 1909; in German as *Susannens Geheimnis;* in Italian, N.Y., March 14, 1911); *I gioielli della Madonna* (Berlin, Dec. 23, 1911; in German as *Der Schmuck der Madonna;* in Italian, Chicago, Jan. 16, 1912; in Eng. as *The Jewels of the Madonna,* N.Y., Oct. 14, 1913); *L'Amore medico,* after Molière (Dresden, Dec. 4, 1913; in German as *Der Liebhaber als Arzt;* in Italian, N.Y., Metropolitan Opera, March 25, 1914); *Gli Amanti sposi* (Venice, Feb. 19, 1925; *Veste di cielo* (Munich, April 21, 1927; in German as *Das Himmelsklied); Sly,* after the prologue to Shakespeare's *The Taming of the Shrew* (Milan, La Scala, Dec. 29, 1927; in Italian as *La leggenda del dormiente risvegliato); La Vedova scaltra,* after Goldoni (Rome, March 5, 1931); *Il Campiello,* after Goldoni (Milan, Feb. 1, 1936); *La Dama boba,* after Lope de Vega (Milan, Feb. 1, 1939); *Gli dei a Tebe* (Hannover, June 5, 1943; in German as *Der Kuckuck in Theben);* also a revision of Mozart's *Idomeneo* (Munich, June 15, 1931).

OTHER WORKS: *La Sulamite,* biblical cantata (1889); *Talitha kumi,* mystery for Solo Voices, Chorus, and Orch. (1900); *La Vita nuova,* after Dante, oratorio (Munich, Feb. 21, 1903; N.Y., Dec. 4, 1907); *Serenade* for String Orch.; *Kammersymphonie* (1901); *Idillio-concertino* for Oboe, String Orch., and 2 Horns (Venice Festival, 1932); *Suite-concertino* for Bassoon, String Orch., and 2 Horns (Rome, March 26, 1933); *Suite veneziana* for Orch. (1936); *Arabeschi* for Orch. (1937); *Divertimento* for Orch. (1938); *Kleines Konzert* for English Horn and Orch. (posthumous; Salzburg, Jan. 18, 1955); 2 violin sonatas; 2 piano trios; String Quartet; Piano Quintet; piano pieces; songs.

Wolff, Albert (Louis), noted French conductor; b. Paris (of Dutch parents), Jan. 19, 1884; d. there, Feb. 20, 1970. He studied with Leroux, Gédalge, and Vidal at the Paris Cons.; began his career as a pianist in Parisian cabarets; from 1906 to 1910 was organist at St. Thomas Aquinas. In 1908 he became a member of the staff of the Opéra-Comique; after serving as its chorus master, he made his conducting debut there, leading the premiere of Laparra's *La Jota,* on April 26, 1911. From 1919 to 1921 he was conductor

of the French repertoire at the Metropolitan Opera in N.Y.; conducted the world premiere of his opera *L'Oiseau bleu* there on Dec. 27, 1919. Upon his return to Paris in 1921, he was appointed Messager's successor as music director of the Opéra-Comique until 1924; in 1925 he became 2nd conductor of the Concerts Pasdeloup, and then was principal conductor from 1934 to 1940; also was conductor of the Concerts Lamoureux from 1928 to 1934. He toured South America from 1940 to 1945; then returned to Paris, where he was director-general of the Opéra-Comique in 1945–46; thereafter he continued to conduct occasionally there; also at the Paris Opéra from 1949; in addition, he made appearances as a symph. conductor. He particularly distinguished himself as a champion of French music of his era; he conducted the premieres of Debussy's *La Boîte à joujoux,* Ravel's *L'Enfant et les sortilèges,* Roussel's Symph. No. 4, and Poulenc's *Les Mamelles de Tirésias.*

Wolff, Christian, American composer of the avant-garde; b. Nice, France, March 8, 1934. He came to the U.S. in 1941; studied piano in N.Y.; took lessons in composition with John Cage. He studied classical languages at Harvard Univ.; received his Ph.D. in comparative literature in 1963. In 1962 he was appointed an instructor in Greek and Latin at Harvard, and in 1976 joined the faculty at Dartmouth College to teach classics and music. He evolved a curiously static method of composition, using drastically restricted numbers of pitches. His only structural resources became arithmetical progressions of rhythmic values and the expressive use of rests. He used 3 different pitches in his Duo for Violin and Piano; 4 different pitches in the Trio for Flute, Cello, and Trumpet (1951); 9 in a piano piece called *For Piano I.* Beginning in 1957 he introduced into his works various degrees of free choice; sometimes the players are required to react to the musical activities of their partners according to unforeseen cues.

WORKS: Trio for Flute, Cello, and Trumpet (1951); *9 for 9 Instruments* (1951); *For 6 or 7 Players* (1959); *Summer* for String Quartet (1961); *Duo for Violinist and Pianist* (1961); *For 5 or 10 Players* (1962); *In between Pieces* for 3 Players (1963); *For 1, 2 or 3 People* (1964); Septet for any Instruments (1964); piano pieces, entitled *For Pianist; For Piano I; For Piano II; Duo for Pianists I and II* for 2 Pianos, 4-hands; *Duet I* for Piano, 4-hands; *Duet II* for Piano and Horn; *Snowdrop* for Harpsichord (1970); *You Blew It* for Chorus (1971).

Wolff, Christoph, eminent German musicologist; b. Solingen, May 24, 1940. He studied church music at the Berlin Hochschule für Musik and in Freiburg im Breisgau; took courses in musicology at the univs. of Berlin and Erlangen; obtained his Ph.D. in 1966 from the latter (Diss., *Der stile antico in der Musik Johann Sebastian Bachs: Studien zu Bachs Spätwerk,* publ. in Wiesbaden, 1968). He taught at the Univ. of Erlangen (1965–69); also at the Univ. of Toronto in Canada (1968–70); then at Columbia

Univ. (1970–76). In 1976 he became a prof. of music at Harvard Univ. He has written extensively on the history of music from the 15th to the 20th century, particularly on Bach and Mozart. He has distinguished himself by innovative research into formative elements in Bach's works. He became editor of the *Bach-Jahrbuch* in 1974; edited vols. of the *Neue Bach-Ausgabe* (V/2, *Goldberg Variations;* 14 Canons; VIII/1, *Musical Offering;* Canons); the *Neue Mozart-Ausgabe* (V/15, 2–3, Piano Concertos), and the *Hindemith-Gesamtausgabe* (opera *Cardillac*, op. 39). He wrote the major portion of the article on the Bach family for *The New Grove Dictionary of Music and Musicians* (London, 1980); also edited *The String Quartets of Haydn, Mozart, and Beethoven: Studies of the Autograph Manuscripts* (Cambridge, Mass., 1980). In 1978 he was awarded the Dent Medal of the Royal Musical Association of London. In 1982 he was elected a Fellow of the American Academy of Arts and Sciences.

Wolff, Edouard, Polish pianist and composer; b. Warsaw, Sept. 15, 1816; d. Paris, Oct. 16, 1880. He studied in Warsaw with Zawadski (piano) and Elsner (composition); then was a piano pupil of Würfel in Vienna. In 1835 he settled in Paris, and became an esteemed teacher; he was a friend of Chopin, and imitated him in his piano music. He publ. 350 opus numbers for piano, among them several albums of études; a waltz, *La Favorite; Chansons polonaises originales; Tarentelle; Chansons bacchiques;* a Piano Concerto; also 30 celebrated duos for piano and violin with de Beriot, and 8 more with Vieuxtemps. His sister, **Regina Wolff,** a pianist, was the mother of the violinist **Henryk Wieniawski.**

Wolff, Erich, Austrian pianist; b. Vienna, Dec. 3, 1874; d. New York, March 20, 1913 (while on a concert tour). He studied in Vienna with Anton Door (piano); lived in Vienna, and (from 1906) in Berlin; became well known as an excellent accompanist of singers. A vol. of 60 of his German songs was publ. posthumously, eliciting great praise. He also wrote a Violin Concerto and some chamber music.

Wolff, Fritz, German tenor; b. Munich, Oct. 28, 1894; d. there, Jan. 18, 1957. He studied with Heinrich König in Würzburg; made his debut as Loge in 1925 at the Bayreuth Festival, where he continued to make appearances until 1941; also sang in Hagen and Chemnitz. In 1930 he joined the Berlin State Opera, remaining on its roster until 1943; also made guest appearances at Covent Garden in London, and in Vienna, Paris, Chicago, and Cleveland. From 1950 he was a prof. at the Hochschule für Musik in Munich. His finest roles included Parsifal and Lohengrin.

Wolff, Hermann, German concert manager; b. Cologne, Sept. 4, 1845; d. Berlin, Feb. 3, 1902. He was a pupil of Franz Kroll and Wüerst; was editor of the *Neue Berliner Musikzeitung* (1878–79); also co-editor of the *Musikwelt.* In 1881 he founded the Hermann Wolff Concert Management, which became

famous; it was later styled H. Wolf & J. Sachs (until 1935). He also composed piano pieces and songs.

Wolff, Werner, German conductor and writer on music; b. Berlin, Oct. 2, 1883; d. Rüschlikon, Switzerland, Nov. 23, 1961. He was the son of the concert manager **Hermann Wolff.** He studied music with Klatte; conducted opera in Vienna, Prague, Danzig, and Düsseldorf; from 1917 to 1932 was a conductor of the Hamburg State Opera. In 1938 he emigrated to the U.S.; taught at Wesleyan College, Tennessee; was conductor of the Chattanooga Opera Assoc. (1943–59). He composed symph. and chamber music; piano pieces and songs. He publ., in Eng., *Anton Bruckner: Rustic Genius* (N.Y., 1942; revised German ed. as *Anton Bruckner: Genie und Einfall*, Zürich, 1948).

Wolffheim, Werner (Joachim), German musicologist; b. Berlin, Aug. 1, 1877; d. there, Oct. 26, 1930. While studying jurisprudence in Munich and Berlin (1895–98), he took courses in musicology with Sandberger and Fleischer; later studied with Kretzschmar and Johannes Wolf. With H. Springer and Max Schneider, he was co-editor of *Miscellanea bio-bibliographica* (supplement to Eitner's *Quellen-Lexikon*); edited the piano concertos for Breitkopf & Härtel's complete ed. of Haydn's works, and prepared (with Kretzschmar) a new ed. of Spitta's life of Bach. He formed a valuable music library (catalogue in 2 vols.), which he sold in 1928–29.

Wölfl (Woelfl, Wölffl), Joseph, Austrian pianist and composer; b. Salzburg, Dec. 24, 1773; d. London, May 21, 1812. He was a pupil of Leopold Mozart and Michael Haydn; served as a chorister at the Salzburg Cathedral (1783–86); was then in Vienna (1790–92) and Warsaw (1793); again in Vienna from 1795; was considered Beethoven's rival as a pianist; in 1798 he married the actress Therese Klemm. Traveling through Germany, he gave numerous concerts as a pianist, reaching Paris in 1801; he settled there for several years; produced 2 French operas and was acclaimed as a piano virtuoso. In 1805 he went to London, and almost immediately established himself in the public's favor as a pianist and teacher. He was, however, of an eccentric disposition, and became involved in all sorts of trouble. He died in obscurity at the age of 38. In his professional life, he emphasized the sensational element; gave fanciful titles to his works; named one of his piano sonatas *Ne plus ultra*, and claimed that it was the most difficult piece ever written.

WORKS: Operas: *Der Höllenberg* (Vienna, Nov. 21, 1795), *Der Kopf ohne Mann* (Vienna, Dec. 3, 1798), *Das schöne Milchmädchen* (Vienna, Jan. 5, 1797), *Das trojanische Pferd* (Vienna, 1797), *L'Amour romanesque* (Paris, 1804), *Fernando, ou Les Maures* (Paris, 1805); ballets: *La Surprise de Diane* (London, Dec. 21, 1805) and *Alzire* (London, Jan. 27, 1807); 7 piano concertos, including *Le Calme* and *Concerto militaire;* other publ. compositions are 2 symphs.; 9 string quartets; 12 piano trios; 2 trios for 2 Clarinets and Bassoon; 42 violin sonatas; 58 piano sonatas; 24 sets of variations for Piano; a *Méthode de piano* (with 100 studies); sonatas for 4-hands; waltzes; polonaises, rondos, fantasias, etc.; also songs. Some of his piano pieces were publ. in monthly issues, under the title *The Harmonic Budget* (London, 1810).

Wolfram, Joseph Maria, Bohemian composer; b. Dobrzan, July 21, 1789; d. Teplitz, Sept. 30, 1839. He studied with J.A. Koželuch in Prague; moved to Vienna as a music teacher; then became a government official at Theusing, and mayor of Teplitz (1824). He brought out several successful operas: *Maja und Alpino* (Prague, May 24, 1826); *Der Bergmönch* (Dresden, March 14, 1830); *Das Schloss Candra* (Dresden, Dec. 1, 1832); a *Missa nuptialis* and some piano pieces and songs by him were publ.

Wolfurt, Kurt von, German composer; b. Lettin, Sept. 7, 1880; d. Munich, Feb. 25, 1957. He studied science at the univs. of Dorpat, Leipzig, and Munich; then took lessons in composition with Max Reger in Munich, where he settled. He composed the opera *Dame Kobold* (Kassel, March 14, 1940); *Faust,* after Goethe, for Soprano, Chorus, and Orch.; *Gesang des Meeres,* symph. poem; *Concerto grosso;* Piano Concerto; chamber music; etc. He publ. monographs on Mussorgsky (Stuttgart, 1927) and Tchaikovsky (Zürich, 1951).

Wolkenstein, Oswald von, one of the last of the Minnesänger; b. Burg Wolkenstein, Grödener Tal (Tyrol), 1377; d. Meran, Aug. 2, 1445. He led an adventurous life, traveling through Russia, Persia, Greece, Spain, France, Italy (with King Ruprecht in 1401), etc. For several years (from 1415) he was in the service of King (later Emperor) Sigismund, whom he accompanied to the Council of Constance. The musical settings that he devised for his poems are notable for their genuine melodic quality; some of them are in 2-part and 3-part counterpoint; there are also examples of canonic imitation. His works were edited by Schatz and Koller for Denkmäler der Tonkunst in Österreich, 18 (9.i).

Wolle, Peter, Moravian minister, bishop, and composer; b. New Herrnhut, St. Thomas, West Indies, Jan. 5, 1792; d. Bethlehem, Pa., Nov. 14, 1871. He was consecrated to the episcopacy on Sept. 26, 1845. He left several compositions; edited the *Moravian Tune Book* (1836). One of his anthems, for Double Chorus with Strings and Organ, is included in the series Music of the Moravians in America, publ. by the N.Y. Public Library (1939).

Wollenhaupt, Hermann Adolf, German pianist and composer; b. Schkeuditz, near Leipzig, Sept. 27, 1827; d. New York, Sept. 18, 1863. He studied in Leipzig with Julius Knorr (piano) and Moritz Hauptmann (composition). In 1845 he settled in N.Y.; made a reputation as a concert pianist and teacher. He wrote about 100 brilliant piano pieces, among them *Galop di bravura, Valses styriennes, Improvi-*

sation, Nocturne, and *Scherzo brillante;* he also made numerous transcriptions and arrangements.

Wolpe, Stefan, significant modern composer; b. Berlin, Aug. 25, 1902; d. New York, April 4, 1972. He studied music theory with Paul Juon and Franz Schreker at the Berlin Hochschule für Musik (1919–24). After graduation, he became associated with choral and theatrical groups in Berlin, promoting social causes; composed songs on revolutionary themes. With the advent of the anti-Semitic Nazi regime, he went to Vienna, where he took lessons with Anton von Webern; then traveled to Palestine; taught music theory at the Jerusalem Cons. In 1938 he emigrated to the U.S., where he devoted himself mainly to teaching; was on the faculty of the Settlement Music School in Philadelphia (1946–48); at the Philadelphia Academy of Music (1949–52); at Black Mountain College, North Carolina (1952–56); and at Long Island Univ. (1957–68). He also taught privately. Among his students were Elmer Bernstein, Ezra Laderman, Ralph Shapey, David Tudor, and Morton Feldman. He was married successively to Ola Okuniewska, a painter, in 1927, to **Irma Schoenberg** (b. 1902; d. 1984), a Rumanian pianist, in 1934, and to Hilda Morley, a poetess, in 1948. In his style of composition, he attempted to reconcile the contradictions of triadic tonality (which he cultivated during his early period of writing "proletarian" music), atonality without procrustean dodecaphony, and serialism of contrasts obtained by intervallic contraction and expansion, metrical alteration, and dynamic variegation; superadded to these were explorations of Jewish cantillation and infatuation with jazz. Remarkably enough, the very copiousness of these resources contributed to a clearly identifiable idiom.
WORKS: Operas: *Schöne Geschichten* (1927–29); *Zeus und Elida* (1928); *Cantata about Sport* (1952); *Street Music* for Baritone, Speaker, and 5 Instruments, to Wolpe's own text (1963–68); Cantata to texts by Hölderlin, Herodotus, and Robert Creeley (1963–68); incidental music: *Da liegt Hund begraben* (1932); *The Good Woman of Setzuan,* to a play by Bertolt Brecht (1953); *The Exception and the Rule,* to a play by Bertolt Brecht (1960); for Orch.: *Passacaglia* (1957); *The Man from Midian,* ballet suite (1942); Symph. (1955–56; revised 1964); *Chamber Piece No. 1* for 14 Players (1964); *Chamber Piece No. 2* for 14 Players (1965–66); chamber music: *Duo in Hexachord* for Oboe and Clarinet (1936); Oboe Sonata (1941); Violin Sonata (1949); Quartet for Trumpet, Saxophone, Percussion, and Piano (1950); Oboe Quartet (1955); Quintet with Voice for Baritone, Clarinet, Horn, Cello, Harp, and Piano (1956–57); Trio for Flute, Cello, and Piano (1964); *From Here on Farther* for Clarinet, Bass Clarinet, Violin, and Piano (1969); String Quartet (1969); *Piece* for Trumpet and 7 Instruments (1971); for Piano: *March and Variations* for 2 Pianos (1933); *4 Studies on Basic Rows* (1935–36); *Toccata* (1941); *Enactments* for 3 Pianos (1950–53); *Broken Sequences* (1969). He contributed numerous articles to German and American music magazines.

Wolpert, Franz Alfons, German composer and theorist; b. Wiesentheid, Oct. 11, 1917; d. there, Aug. 7, 1978. He sang in the Cathedral choir in Regensburg, and studied there at a church seminary; took lessons in composition with Wolf-Ferrari in Salzburg (1939–41). He taught music at the Mozarteum (1941–50); then was engaged as a music teacher in Überlingen, where he settled.

Wolzogen, Ernst, Freiherr von, German poet and musical journalist; son of **Alfred von Wolzogen** and half brother of **Hans von Wolzogen;** b. Breslau, April 23, 1855; d. Munich, July 30, 1934. He studied at the univs. of Strasbourg and Leipzig. In 1901 he established in Berlin (with O.J. Bierbaum and F. Wedekind) the Überbrettl, a kind of artistic cabaret for the production of dramatic pieces, pantomimes, poems with recitation and music, etc., most of them reflecting or satirizing contemporary German life; Oskar Straus provided most of the music, and Schoenberg contributed some of the numbers; 2 journals, *Das moderne Brettl* and *Bühne und Brettl,* were publ. for a year or so to promote the ideas of the enterprise, but the cabaret closed after 2 sensationally successful seasons. Wolzogen publ. 2 books dealing with music: *Der Kraftmayr* (1897; humorous novel with Liszt as the central figure; Eng. trans. as *Florian Mayr,* 1914) and *Ansichten und Aussichten* (1908; essays). His wife, **Elsa Laura** (née **Seeman von Mangern**), became known as a singer, making a specialty of songs with lute accompaniment; with her husband she made a tour of the U.S. (1910–11); publ. 7 vols. of folk songs with lute accompaniment (*Meine Lieder zur Laute*).

Wolzogen, Hans, Freiherr von, German writer on music and authority on Wagner; b. Potsdam, Nov. 13, 1848; d. Bayreuth, June 2, 1938. He studied mythology and comparative philology in Berlin (1868–71); then devoted himself to literature; in 1878, at Wagner's invitation, he became editor of the *Bayreuther Blätter* and lived in Bayreuth most of his life. He popularized the term "leitmotif," first used by F.W. Jähns, in his "Motive in Wagners *Götterdämmerung*," publ. in the *Musikalisches Wochenblatt* in 1887 (Wagner's preferred term was "Grundthema").

Wood, Sir Henry J(oseph), eminent English conductor; b. London, March 3, 1869; d. Hitchin, Hertfordshire, Aug. 19, 1944. Of musical parentage, he was taught to play the piano by his mother; he participated in family musicales from the age of 6; was equally precocious on the organ; at the age of 10 he often acted as a deputy organist, and gave organ recitals at the Fisheries Exhibition (1883) and at the Inventions Exhibition (1885). In 1886 he entered the Royal Academy of Music, where his teachers were Prout, Steggall, Macfarren, and Garcia; he won 4 medals. In 1888 he brought out some of his songs; then composed light operas and cantatas. But soon his ambition crystallized in the direction of conducting; he traveled with an opera company in 1889; then became assistant conductor at the Savoy Theatre (1890); was engaged as a conductor for various other operatic enterprises. On Aug. 10, 1895, he began his first series of Promenade Concerts (the famous "Proms") in Queen's Hall, London, with an orch. of about 80 members. Their success was so conspicuous that a new series of concerts was inaugurated on Jan. 30, 1897, under Wood's direction, and flourished from the beginning. In 1899 he founded the Nottingham Orch.; also was appointed conductor of the Wolverhampton Festival Choral Society (1900), the Sheffield Festival (1902–11), and the Norwich Festival (1908). In 1904 he conducted in N.Y. He was married to Olga Urusova, a Russian noblewoman, and became greatly interested in Russian music, which he performed frequently at his concerts. He adopted a Russian pseudonym, **Paul Klenovsky,** for his compositions and arrangements, and supplied an imaginary biography of his alter ego for use in program notes. His wife died in 1909, and Wood married Muriel Greatorex in 1911. He was knighted in 1911. In 1918 he was offered the conductorship of the Boston Symph. Orch. as successor to Muck, but declined. In 1923 he was appointed prof. of conducting and orch. playing at the Royal Academy of Music. In 1925 he conducted in California; in 1926 received the degree of Mus.Doc. (*honoris causa*) from Oxford Univ. Wood continued to conduct the Promenade Concerts almost to the end of his life, presenting the last concert on July 28, 1944. Among his popular arrangements are Chopin's *Marche Funèbre,* some works by Bach, and the *Trumpet Voluntary* (mistakenly attributed to Purcell, but actually by Jeremiah Clarke). He publ. *The Gentle Art of Singing* (4 vols.; 1927–28) and *About Conducting* (London, 1945), and edited the *Handbook of Miniature Orchestral and Chamber Music Scores* for J.W. Chester & Co. (1937); wrote an autobiography, *My Life and Music* (London, 1938). A commemorative postage stamp with his portrait was issued by the Post Office of Great Britain on Sept. 1, 1980.

Wood, Hugh, English composer; b. Parbold, near Wigan, Lancashire, June 27, 1932. He studied theory and composition with Anthony Milner, Iain Hamilton, and Mátyás Seiber in London (1957–60); taught at Morley College in London (1958–67) and at the Royal Academy of Music (1962–65); was composer-in-residence at the Univ. of Glasgow (1966–70); from 1971–73 he was a lecturer at the Univ. of Liverpool; in 1976 was appointed a lecturer at Cambridge.

WORKS: *Variations* for Viola and Piano (1957–59); *4 Songs* for Mezzo-soprano, Clarinet, Violin, and Cello (1959–61); Trio for Flute, Viola, and Piano (1961); 3 string quartets (1962, 1970, 1978); *3 Pieces* for Piano (1960–63); *Scenes from "Comus,"* after Milton, for Soprano, Tenor, and Orch. (1962–65; London, Aug. 2, 1965); Quintet for Clarinet, Horn, Violin, Cello, and Piano (1967); Cello Concerto (1965–69; London, Aug. 26, 1969); Chamber Concerto (1970–71; London, Nov. 27, 1971); Violin Concerto (1970–72; Liverpool, Sept. 19, 1972); *Song Cycle to Poems of Neruda* for High Voice and Chamber Orch. (1973; London, Feb. 18, 1974).

Wood, Thomas, English composer and author; b. Chorley, Lancashire, Nov. 28, 1892; d. Bures, Essex, Nov. 19, 1950. He was educated at Exeter College, Oxford; then studied at the Royal Academy of Music with Stanford; was music director at Tonbridge School (1920–24); lecturer and precentor at Exeter College (1924–28). His extensive travels took him to the Far East and the Arctic; his familiarity with the sea was reflected in many of his compositions (for Chorus and Orch.), such as *40 Singing Seamen* (1925), *Master Mariners* (1927), *Merchantmen* (1934), and in *A Seaman's Overture* (for Orch., 1927). He edited vol. II of the *Oxford Song Book* (1928; 3rd ed., 1937). His books include *Music and Boyhood* (1925) and the autobiographical *True Thomas* (1936); he also publ. *Cobbers* (on his Australian tour of 1930–32), which became highly popular in England, and a sequel to it, *Cobbers Campaigning* (1940).

Woodward, Roger, Australian pianist; b. Sydney, Dec. 20, 1942. He studied piano with Alexander Sverjensky in Sydney; then obtained a Polish government scholarship and went to Warsaw, where he took lessons with Zbigniew Drzwiecki. He won the Chopin Competition Prize in 1968, an auspicious award that propelled him on an international career. In 1971 he settled in London, where he gained renown among international avant-garde composers by repeatedly performing works by such uncompromising celebrants of quaquaversal modern idioms as Takemitsu, Barraqué, Stockhausen, and Birtwistle; faithful to his antecedents, he also placed on his programs works of Australian composers such as Boyd, Meale, and Sculthorpe. He participated in several American concerts of contemporary music, including a marathon series presented in Los Angeles. In 1980 he received for his musical valor the Order of the British Empire.

Woodworth, G(eorge) Wallace, American choral conductor and music educator; b. Boston, Nov. 6, 1902; d. Cambridge, Mass., July 18, 1969. He was educated at Harvard Univ. (B.A., 1924; M.A., 1926); also studied at the Royal College of Music in London (1927–28). In 1924 he joined the staff of the music dept. at Harvard, and was engaged as conductor of the Radcliffe Choral Society; also led the Pierian Sodality Orch. of Harvard Univ. (1928–32) and the Harvard Glee Club (1933–38). In 1940 he was appointed organist and choirmaster for the Harvard Univ. Chapel. He was made James Edward Ditson Professor of Music at Harvard in 1954. He conducted the Harvard-Radcliffe Chorus on its transcontinental U.S. tour in 1954, and took the Harvard Glee Club on its European tour in 1956. He retired in 1969. He publ. *The World of Music* (Cambridge, Mass., 1964).

Wooldridge, David, English composer, conductor, and writer on music; b. Deal, Kent, Aug. 24, 1927. He is a grandson of the English musicologist **Harry Ellis Wooldridge** and godson of Rachmaninoff, from whom he received some friendly piano lessons at the age of 4. He began studying the violin at 6; at 16 made his conducting debut; in 1952 he graduated from the Univ. of London, summa cum laude; was then apprenticed to Clemens Krauss at the Vienna State Opera; in 1954 he became junior conductor at the Bavarian State Opera. In 1956–58 he was in the U.S. as a guest conductor in Minneapolis, Cincinnati, Cleveland, and Rochester; from 1961 to 1965 conducted the Lebanese National Orch. in Beirut; then was conductor of the Cape Town Symph. in South Africa (1965–67); subsequently was a visiting prof. at Indiana Univ. (1968–69); Grinnell College, Iowa (1971); the Univ. of Calif. at Santa Cruz (1972); Wabash College, Indiana (1976); and the Univ. of Calif. at Riverside (1977); concurrently was music director of the Bridgewater (Conn.) Concert Assoc. (1973–78).

Wooldridge, Harry Ellis, English musicologist; b. Winchester, March 28, 1845; d. London, Feb. 13, 1917. While studying at Trinity College, Oxford (1860–64), he became deeply interested in painting and music; entered the Royal Academy of Fine Arts in 1865, at the same time beginning his research regarding early music in the libraries of Oxford and London; from 1895 till his death he was Slade Prof. of Fine Arts at Oxford Univ.
WRITINGS: *The English Metrical Psalter* (1890); *The Polyphonic Period,* being vols. I and II of the *Oxford History of Music* (1901, 1905; 2nd ed., revised by P.C. Buck, 1929–32); he radically revised Chappell's *Popular Music of the Olden Times,* and publ. it under the title *Old English Popular Music* (2 vols., 1893); also edited *Early English Harmony* (2 vols., 1897, 1913; pieces from the 10th to 15th centuries); *The Yattendon Hymnal* (1899; with R. Bridges); Purcell's sacred compositions (vols. 13, 14, and 18 of Novello's ed. of Purcell's complete works).

Woollett, Henri (Henry) Edouard, French composer; b. (of English parentage) Le Havre, Aug. 13, 1864; d. there, Oct. 9, 1936. He studied in Paris with Pugno (piano) and Massenet (composition); returning to Le Havre, he established himself as a teacher; among his students were André Caplet and Honegger. His music is of a lyrical nature, in the manner of his teacher Massenet.
WORKS: *La Rose de Sharon,* "poème lyrique" for Orch. (1895); *Konzertstück* for Cello and Orch. (1911); String Quartet (1929); 2 violin sonatas (1908, 1922); Viola Sonata; Flute Sonata; Cello Sonata; many piano pieces in a Romantic vein *(Nocturnes et pastorales, Pièces intimes, A travers la vie, Au jardin de France, Préludes et valses);* many attractive songs. He publ. *Petit traité de prosodie* (Paris, 1903) and *Histoire de la musique depuis l'antiquité jusqu'à nos jours* (4 vols., Paris, 1909–25).

Wordsworth, William, English composer; b. London, Dec. 17, 1908. He studied with his father; then with Sir Donald Tovey in Edinburgh. He began to compose rather late in life; his music is marked by a certain austerity in the deployment of thematic materials.

WORKS: *Sinfonia* for Strings (1936); *3 Pastoral Sketches* for Orch. (1937); *Theme and Variations* for Orch. (1941); 5 symphs. (1944, 1947–48, 1951, 1953, 1959–60); Piano Concerto (1946); *Divertimento* for Orch. (1954); Violin Concerto (1955); Sinfonietta for Small Orch. (1957); *Variations on a Scottish Theme* for Small Orch. (1962); Cello Concerto (1963); *A Highland Overture* (1964); *Jubilation* for Orch. (1965); *Conflict,* overture (1968); *Sinfonia semplice* for Amateur String Orch. (1969); *Valediction* for Orch. (1969); *A Pattern of Love* for Low Voice and String Orch. (1969–70); *Spring Festival Overture* (1970); *Symposium* for Solo Violin, Strings, and Percussion (1972); *The Houseless Dead,* after D.H. Lawrence, for Baritone, Chorus, and Orch. (1939); oratorio, *Dies Domini* (1942–44); *Lucifer Yields* for Soloists, Chorus, and Orch. (1949); *A Vision* for Women's Chorus and Strings (1950); *A Song of Praise* for Chorus and Orch. (1956); dramatic cantata, *The Two Brigs* (1971); *The Solitary Reaper* for Soprano, Piano, and Clarinet (1973); 6 string quartets (1943, 1946, 1948, 1950, 1955, 1964); 2 cello sonatas (1937, 1959); 2 violin sonatas (1944, 1967); String Trio (1945); Piano Quartet (1948); Piano Trio (1949); Oboe Quartet (1949); Clarinet Quintet (1952); Wind Trio (1953); Piano Quintet (1959); Sonata for Solo Cello (1961); Violin Sonatina (1961); *Dialogue* for Horn and Piano (1965); piano pieces, including a Sonata (1939); songs.

Work, Henry Clay, American composer of popular songs; b. Middletown, Conn., Oct. 1, 1832; d. Hartford, June 8, 1884. He was a printer by trade; was entirely self-taught in music; his first success was *We Are coming, Sister Mary;* other well-known songs are *Grandfather's Clock; Father, Come Home; Shadows on the Floor;* his Civil War song *Marching through Georgia* became celebrated; other songs of the Civil War were *Drafted into the Army; God Save the Nation; Song of a Thousand Years; Wake, Nicodemus; Kingdom Coming,* etc.

Wormser, André (Alphonse-Toussaint), French composer; b. Paris, Nov. 1, 1851; d. there, Nov. 4, 1926. He studied at the Paris Cons. with Marmontel (piano) and Bazin (theory); won first prize for piano in 1872, and the Grand Prix de Rome in 1875 with the cantata *Clytemnestre.* His most successful work was the pantomime, or "wordless opera," *L'Enfant prodigue* (Paris, June 14, 1890); he also composed other stage works; orch. works; men's choruses; songs; piano pieces.

Wörner, Karl(heinz) H(einrich), German musicologist; b. Waldorf, near Heidelberg, Jan. 6, 1910; d. Heiligenkirchen, near Detmold, Aug. 11, 1969. He studied musicology in Berlin with Schünemann and Schering, and conducting with Julius Prüwer; received the degree of Dr.Phil. at Berlin Univ. with the dissertation *Beiträge zur Geschichte des Leitmotivs in der Oper,* publ. in *Zeitschrift für Musikwissenschaft* (Dec. 1931); was a critic for the *B.Z. am Mittag* (1933–34); then (1935–40) opera conductor at Stettin, Magdeburg, and Frankfurt. He was in

the German army during World War II; in 1944 was taken prisoner of war by the U.S. Army and spent 2 years in an American internment camp. Returning to Germany in 1946, he was active as a lecturer. From 1954–58 he was on the staff of B. Schott's Söhne (Mainz); in 1958 was on the faculty of the Folkwangschule in Essen; from 1961 taught at the North-West Germany Academy of Music in Detmold.

Woržischek (Voříšek), Johann Hugo, Bohemian composer; b. Wamberg, Bohemia, May 11, 1791; d. Vienna, Nov. 19, 1825. He studied with his father and with Tomaschek in Prague, where he lived from 1801; in 1813 he went to Vienna and became known as a pianist; in 1818 he was appointed conductor of the Gesellschaft der Musikfreunde. Having studied law, he obtained a post in the civil service in 1822, but abandoned it after a year, when he was made court organist. He composed a Symph.; choral works with Orch.; a Piano Concerto; etc.; of more interest are his piano pieces, especially the *Rhapsodies* (1818) and *Impromptus* (1822), because Schubert was strongly influenced by them. A Piano Sonata in B minor (1820) shows kinship with Beethoven, whom Woržischek knew intimately.

Wöss, Kurt, Austrian conductor; b. Linz, May 2, 1914. He studied conducting with Felix Weingartner in Vienna, and also pursued musicological studies at the Univ. of Vienna with Haas, Lach, Orel, and Wellesz; taught an orch. class at the Vienna Academy (1938–40); after the war, he conducted the Tonkünstler-Orch. in Vienna (1948–51); subsequently went to Japan, where he conducted the Nippon Phil. Orch. in Tokyo (1951–54). From 1956 to 1960 he was principal conductor of the Victorian Symph. Orch. in Melbourne and of the Australian National Opera; in 1961 he returned to Linz, where he became music director of the Bruckner Orch. (1966–74). In 1974 he went again to Japan, where he was appointed music director of the Fumiwara Opera in Tokyo; also was conductor of the Tokyo Phil. He publ. *Ratschläge zur Aufführung der Symphonien Anton Bruckners* (Linz, 1974).

Wotquenne (-Plattel), Alfred, Belgian musicologist; b. Lobbes, Jan. 25, 1867; d. Antibes, France, Sept. 25, 1939. He studied at the Brussels Cons. with Mailly (organ), and Joseph Dupont and Gevaert (theory); from 1894 to 1918 was librarian, secretary, and inspector of studies at the Brussels Cons.; then moved to Antibes in southern France, where in 1921 he became maître de chapelle.
WRITINGS: *Catalogue de la bibliothèque du Cons. Royal de Musique de Bruxelles* (vol. I, 1894; with a supplement, *Libretti d'opéras et d'oratorios italiens du XVIIᵉ siècle,* 1901; II, 1902; III, 1908; IV, 1912; V, 1914); *Baldassare Galuppi* (1899; 2nd augmented ed., 1902, as *Baldassare Galuppi. Etude bibliographique sur ses œuvres dramatiques*); *Thematisches Verzeichnis der Werke von Chr.W. v. Gluck* (1904); *Catalogue thématique des œuvres de C.Ph.E. Bach* (1905); *Table alphabétique des morceaux me-*

surés contenus dans les œuvres dramatiques de Zeno, Metastasio et Goldoni (1905); *Etude bibliographique sur le compositeur napolitain Luigi Rossi* (1909; with thematic catalogue). He prepared a card catalogue of 18,000 Italian "cantate da camera" of the 18th century; edited *Chansons italiennes de la fin du XVIᵉ siècle* (canzonette a 4); continued the collections begun by Gevaert, *Répertoire classique du chant français* and *Répertoire français de l'ancien chant classique;* and ed. a new collection, *Répertoire Wotquenne* (4 vols. publ.); also ed. violin sonatas of Tartini, Veracini, and others; composed much sacred music. The MSS of several important bibliographies in his collection were bought out by the Library of Congress in 1929; these comprise *Répertoire des textes publiés par les éditeurs parisiens Ballard; Histoire musicale et chronologique du Théâtre de la Foire depuis 1680 jusqu'à 1762; Histoire du nouveau Théâtre-Italien à Paris (1718–1762);* etc. A large part of his private music library was also bought by the Library of Congress.

Woyrsch, Felix von, composer and conductor; b. Troppau, Silesia, Oct. 8, 1860; d. Altona-Hamburg, March 20, 1944. He studied with A. Chevallier in Hamburg, but was chiefly self-taught. In 1887 he settled in Altona as conductor of the Allgemeine Liedertafel; from 1893 led the Kirchenchor, the Singakademie (from 1895), and the municipal symph. concerts and Volkskonzerte (from 1903); from 1895 to 1903 he was organist of the Friedenskirche; then of the Johanniskirche until 1926; retired from public life in 1937.
WORKS: Operas: *Der Pfarrer von Meudon* (Hamburg, 1886); *Der Weiberkrieg* (Hamburg, 1890); *Wikingerfahrt* (Nuremberg, 1896). For Orch.: symph. prologue to the *Divina commedia; Skaldische Rhapsodie* for Violin and Orch.; 2 symphs.; *3 Böcklin-Phantasien (Die Toteninsel, Der Eremit, Im Spiel der Wellen); Hamlet,* overture. Vocal works with Orch.: *Da Jesus auf Erden ging,* a mystery play (Hamburg, Jan. 29, 1917; one of his best works); *Geburt Jesu; Deutscher Heerbann; Der Vandalen; Auszug; Passions-Oratorium; Sapphische Ode an Aphrodite; Totentanz; Da lachte schön Sigrid; Wollt' er nur fragen; Edward.* Chamber music: Piano Quintet; String Quartet. For Piano: *3 Notturnos; 2 Walzer; Walzer* (4-hands); *Theme and Variations; 4 Impromptus; Improvisationen; Metamorphosen.* He also composed song cycles *(Persische Lieder; Spanisches Liederbuch; 10 Rattenfängerlieder);* edited *Deutsche Volkslieder* (14th–16th centuries), and choral works of Heinrich Schütz for practical use (3 vols.).

Woytowicz, Boleslaw, Polish pianist and composer; b. Dunajowce, Podolia, Dec. 5, 1899; d. Katowice, July 11, 1980. He studied piano with Michalowski; composition with Statkowski and Maliszewski; obtained a diploma at the Chopin College of Music in Warsaw as a concert pianist; then went to Paris, where he took lessons in composition with Nadia Boulanger (1930–32). In 1945 he was appointed a prof. of piano and composition at the State College of Music in Katowice.
WORKS: *Kolysanka (Cradle Song)* for Soprano, Flute, Clarinet, Bassoon, and Harp (1931); 2 string quartets (1932, 1953); Piano Concerto (1932); *Zalobny poema (Funeral Poem)* for Orch. (1935); ballet, *Powrót* (1937); 3 symphs.: No. 1 (1938), No. 2 (1945; Cracow, Sept. 27, 1946), and No. 3, *Concertante,* for Piano and Orch. (1963); *Kantata na pochwale pracy (Cantata in Praise of Labor,* 1948); *12 Etudes* for Piano (1948); *Symphonic Sketches* for Orch. (1949); cantata, *Prorok (The Prophet,* 1950); Flute Sonata (1952); *Lamento* for Soprano, Piano, and Clarinet (1960); *10 Etudes* for Piano (1960); *Little Piano Sonata* (1974).

Wranitzky, Anton, Bohemian violinist and composer; b. Neureisch, Moravia, June 13, 1761; d. Vienna, Aug. 6, 1820. He studied with his older brother **Paul Wranitzky;** also had lessons in Vienna with Albrechtsberger, Haydn, and Mozart. In 1797 he was appointed Kapellmeister to Prince Lobkowitz at his castle in Bohemia, and later (1808) in Vienna. He wrote 15 violin concertos; much chamber music; marches; dances.

Wranitzky, Paul, Bohemian violinist and composer; brother of **Anton Wranitzky;** b. Neureisch, Moravia, Dec. 30, 1756; d. Vienna, Sept. 26, 1808. After studying in various provincial towns of Moravia, he went in 1776 to Vienna, where he was a pupil of Joseph Martin Kraus. In 1780 he became a member of Prince Esterházy's orch. at Eisenstadt; in 1790 became concertmaster of the Vienna Opera, and retained this position until his death. His opera *Oberon, König der Elfen* was given with excellent success in Vienna on Nov. 7, 1789; other operas and singspiels produced by him in Vienna were *Rudolf von Felseck* (Oct. 6, 1792); *Merkur, der Heurat-Stifter* (Feb. 21, 1793); *Das Fest der Lazzaroni* (Feb. 4, 1794); *Die gute Mutter* (May 11, 1795); *Johanna von Montfaucon* (Jan. 25, 1799); *Der Schreiner* (July 18, 1799); *Mitgefühl* (April 21, 1804); *Die Erkenntlichkeit* (July 22, 1805). He also produced numerous ballets; wrote incidental music to several plays; composed a great deal of instrumental music, including 51 symphs.; 5 concertos for various instruments with orch.; 6 quintets; over 80 string quartets; 12 quartets for flute and strings; 3 piano quartets, and string trios.

Wuensch, Gerhard, Austrian-born Canadian composer; b. Vienna, Dec. 23, 1925. He received a Dr.Phil. degree from the Univ. of Vienna in 1950, and an artist's diploma in composition and piano from the State Academy of Music in Vienna in 1952; studied music theory with Paul Pisk at the Univ. of Texas (1954–56). He then occupied teaching positions at Butler Univ. in Indianapolis (1956–62), the Univ. of Toronto (1963–69), and the Univ. of Calgary (1969–73); in 1973 was appointed to the faculty of the Univ. of Western Ontario in London, Ontario. He writes in an affable modernistic vein in neo-Classical forms.

WORKS: Ballet, *Labyrinth* (1957); musical comedy, *Il pomo d'oro* (1958); *Nocturne* for Orch. (1956); *Variations on a Dorian Hexachord* for Orch. (1959); *Caribbean Rhapsody* for Symph. Band (1959); Symph. No. 1 (1959); Piano Concerto (1961); *Ballad* for Trumpet and Orch. (1962); *Symphonia sacra* for Soloists, Chorus, Brass, and Percussion (1965); Symph. for Brass and Percussion (1967); Concerto for Piano and Chamber Orch. (1971); *Scherzo* for Piano and Wind Ensemble (1971); *6 Guises* for Narrator, Winds, and Percussion (1972); Bassoon Concerto (1976); Organ Concerto (1979); Trio for Clarinet, Bassoon, and Piano (1948); 2 string quartets (1955, 1963); *Mosaic* for Brass Quartet (1959); *Partita* for Horn and Piano (1961); *Viola Sonatina* (1963); *Ricercare* for 8 Horns and Organ (1963); 2 wind quintets (1963, 1967); Horn Sonata (1964); *Music* for 7 Brasses (1966); Trumpet Sonata (1966); Sextet for Horns (1966); *Suite* for Trumpet and Organ (1970); *Music in 4 Dimensions* for Brass, Harp, and Percussion (1970); Piano Trio (1971); *Variations* for Clarinet and Piano (1971); *Prelude, Aria and Fugue* for Accordion and String Quartet (1971); *Saxophone Sonata* (1971); *Aria and Fugue* for Oboe and Organ (1975); *Musica giocosa* for Flute and Piano (1977); *Concerto grosso* for Accordion and Strings (1978); *Cameos II* for Oboe and Piano (1979); *6 Songs* for Voice, Flute, and Accordion (1970); *Laus sapientiae*, cantata (1978); piano pieces: *Esquisse* (1950); *Canzona and Toccata* (1963); 2 sonatinas (1969); *Mini Suite* No. 2 (1977); Sonata for 4-hands (1978); organ pieces: *Toccata piccola* (1963); *Sonata breve* (1963); *Toccata nuptialis* (1976); solo accordion pieces: *4 Mini-Suites* (1968); *Sonata da camera* (1970); *Monologue* (1972); *Diversions* (1972); choruses.

Wüerst, Richard (Ferdinand), German composer; b. Berlin, Feb. 22, 1824; d. there, Oct. 9, 1881. He studied violin with Ferdinand David at the Leipzig Cons., where he also took lessons with Mendelssohn. He then taught at Kullak's Neue Akademie der Tonkunst in Berlin. As music critic for the *Berliner Fremdenblatt* he exercised considerable influence; publ. *Leitfaden der Elementartheorie der Musik* (1867; Eng. trans. as *Elementary Theory of Music and Treatment of Chords*, Boston, 1893). As a composer he was a follower of Mendelssohn.

Wührer, Friedrich, distinguished Austrian pianist and pedagogue; b. Vienna, June 29, 1900. He studied piano with Franz Schmidt at the Vienna Academy of Music (1915–20); concurrently took a course in jurisprudence at the Univ. of Vienna; then engaged on a far-flung tour that took him through all of Europe, and also to Asia and Africa. At his concerts he never failed to include works by modern composers, among them Bartók, Hindemith, Prokofiev, Stravinsky, and his teacher Franz Schmidt. He held numerous teaching positions, at the Vienna Academy of Music (1922–32), at the Hochschule für Musik in Mannheim (1934–36), in Kiel (1936–39), in Vienna (1939–45), at the Salzburg Mozarteum (1948–51), in Mannheim (1952–57), and in Munich (1957–68). He publ. *Meisterwerke der Klaviermusik* (Wilhelms-

haven, 1966).

Wüllner, Franz, important German pianist, conductor, and composer; b. Münster, Jan. 28, 1832; d. Braunfels-on-the-Lahn, Sept. 7, 1902. He studied with Schindler in Münster and Frankfurt. In 1854 he went to Munich; was a teacher at the Munich Cons. (1856–58); then municipal music director at Aachen (1858–64). He returned to Munich in 1864; succeeded Hans von Bülow as conductor of the Munich Court Theater in 1869. Under unfavorable conditions (against Wagner's wishes), he prepared and conducted the first performance of *Das Rheingold* (Sept. 22, 1869) and *Die Walküre* (June 26, 1870). In 1877 he became court conductor at Dresden; in 1882 Schuch was promoted to take his place; thereafter Wüllner was one of the conductors of the Berlin Phil. for the 1882–85 seasons; became conductor of the Gurzenich Concerts in Cologne in 1884, and on Oct. 1, 1884, succeeded Hiller as director of the Cologne Cons., later becoming also municipal music director, posts he held until his death. He was highly regarded as a choral composer; publ. the valuable book of vocal exercises *Chorübungen der Münchener Musikschule* (1867; new ed. by E. Schwickerath, Munich, 1931). He was a friend of Brahms.

Wüllner, Ludwig, distinguished German singer; son of **Franz Wüllner;** b. Münster, Aug. 19, 1858; d. Kiel, March 19, 1938. He studied Germanic philology at the univs. of Munich, Berlin, and Strasbourg; taught Germanic philology at the Akademie in Münster (1884–87), and sang occasionally in concert; his musical training began only in 1887, when he took a course of study at the Cologne Cons. A second change of vocation brought him to the Meiningen court theater, where he appeared as an actor of heroic parts in the spoken drama (1889–95); he became friendly with Brahms, who commended his singing of German folk songs. In 1895 he gave song recitals in Berlin with such acclaim that he decided to devote himself mainly to lieder. He then made tours of all Europe, arousing tremendous enthusiasm; his first recital in N.Y. (Nov. 15, 1908) was a sensational success, and he followed it by an extensive tour of the U.S. and then another (1909–10). His peculiar distinction was his ability to give an actor's impersonation of the character of each song, introducing an element of drama on the concert stage.

Wunderlich, Fritz, noted German tenor; b. Kusel, Sept. 26 1930; d. Heidelberg, Sept. 17, 1966. He received his musical education at the Freiburg Hochschule für Musik; then sang opera in Stuttgart (1955–58), Frankfurt (1958–60), and Munich (from 1960). While still a young man, he gained a fine reputation as a lyric tenor; his performances of Mozart roles were especially acclaimed for their expressive power. His untimely death (in a domestic accident) deprived the opera stage of one of its finest artists.

Wunsch, Hermann, German composer; b. Neuss,

Aug. 9, 1884; d. Berlin, Dec. 21, 1954. He studied in Düsseldorf and Cologne, and later at the Hochschule für Musik in Berlin, where he subsequently taught, becoming a prof. in 1945. He composed 6 symphs., of which the 5th won the Schubert Memorial Prize (German section) of the Columbia Phonograph Co. contest (Schubert Centennial, 1928). Other works include the chamber operas *Bianca* (Weimar, May 22, 1927), *Don Juans Sohn* (Weimar, 1928), and *Franzosenzeit* (Schwerin, 1933); 2 masses; *Südpolkantate* for Chorus and Orch.; *Helden* for Chorus and Orch. (Berlin, 1941); 3 violin concertos; Concerto for Piano and Small Orch.; *Kleine Lustspielsuite* for Orch.; *Fest auf Monbijou*, suite for Chamber Orch.; *Erntelied*, symph. with a concluding chorus.

Wuorinen, Charles, American composer; b. New York, June 9, 1938. His family roots originated in Finland; his father was a prof. of history at Columbia Univ.; the environment at home was highly intellectual. Wuorinen received a fine academic training; he began to plan piano and to compose, so they say, at the incredible age of 5. He then took lessons in music theory with Beeson and Ussachevsky. He received the Young Composers Award from the N.Y. Phil. when he was 16 years old. At 18 he wrote his earliest orch. work, *Into the Organ Pipes and Steeples.* At the age of 21 he composed, in quick succession, 3 full-fledged symphs. In 1956 he entered Columbia Univ. as a student of Otto Luening; received his B.A. in 1961 and his M.A. in 1963. In 1964 he was appointed an instructor in music at Columbia, and taught there until 1971, when he resigned in a flurry of angry controversy, vesuviating in sulfuric wrath and ire about the refusal of the faculty to grant him tenure. He then taught at the Manhattan School of Music (1972–79). In 1968 and 1972 he held Guggenheim fellowships. In 1969 he received a commission from Nonesuch Records for a work using synthesized sound, titled *Time's Encomium;* it was awarded the Pulitzer Prize in 1970, an unprecedented honor for a work written expressly for a recording; later he rearranged it for a regular orch. From his very first essays in free composition, Wuorinen asserted himself as a true representative of the modernistic 2nd half of the 20th century. His techniques derived from Stravinsky's early period, when stark primitivism gave way to austere linear counterpoint; an even greater affinity in Wuorinen's music is with the agglutinative formations of unrelated thematic statements as practiced by Varèse; a more literal dependence connects Wuorinen's works with the dodecaphonic method of composition as promulgated by Schoenberg. These modalities and relationships coalesce in Wuorinen's writing into a sui generis complex subdivided into melodic, harmonic, and contrapuntal units that build a definitive formal structure. The foundation of his method of composition is serialism, in which pitch, time, and rhythmic divisions relate to one another in a "time point system," which lends itself to unlimited tonal and temporal arrangements, combinations, and permutations.

Enormously prolific, Wuorinen finds it possible to explore the entire vocabulary of serial composition. Most of his works are instrumental, but he also wrote an opera entitled *The W. of Babylon* (alluding to the apocalyptic Babylonian whore), a work he prefers to describe as a "baroque burlesque." Its *dramatis personae* include a libidinous assortment of lascivious French nobel and ignoble men and women of the immoral 17th century, spouting lewd declarations and performing lecherous acts. As a helpful glossary to his music, Wuorinen publ. a manual, *Simple Composition* (N.Y., 1979).

WORKS: FOR THE STAGE: Masque, *The Politics of Harmony* (1967); opera, *The W. of Babylon* (partial perf. given by the Group for Contemporary Music in N.Y. on Dec. 15, 1975). FOR ORCH.: 3 symphs. (1958, 1959, 1959); 4 *concertante* for Solo Instruments and Orch. (1957–59); *Concertone* for Brass Quintet and Orch. (1960); *Evolutio transcripta* (1961); *Orchestral and Electronic Exchanges* for Orch. and Tape (1965); Piano Concerto No. 1 (1966); *Contrafactum* (1969); Concerto for Amplified Violin and Orch. (Tanglewood, Boston Symph., Aug. 4, 1972; Paul Zukofsky, soloist; Michael Tilson Thomas conducting); Piano Concerto No. 2 for Amplified Piano and Orch. (N.Y. Phil., Dec. 6, 1974, composer soloist); *A Reliquary for Igor Stravinsky* (Ojai [Calif.] Festival, May 30, 1975); *Tashi Concerto* for 4 Instruments and Orch. (Tashi Chamber Music Ensemble, Cleveland, Oct. 13, 1976, composer conducting); *Percussion Symphony* (1976; Somerset, N.J., Jan. 26, 1978); *Two-Part Symphony* (N.Y., Dec. 11, 1978); *"ng. c."* (1980); *Bamboula Squared* (N.Y., June 4, 1984). CHAMBER MUSIC: *Triptych* for Violin, Viola, and Percussion (1957); *Alternating Currents* for Chamber Ensemble (1957); *Dr. Faustus Lights the Lights* for Narrator and Instruments (1957); *3 Pieces* for String Quartet (1958); *Spectrum* for Violin, Brass Quintet, and Piano (1958); *Trio concertante* (1959); *Musica duarum partum ecclesiastica* for Brass Quintet, Piano, Organ, and Timpani (1959); Flute Sonata (1960); *Turetzky Pieces* for Flute, Clarinet, and Double Bass (1960); *Tiento sobre cabeza* for 7 Instruments (1961); Octet for Flute, Clarinet, Horn, Trombone, Violin, Cello, Double Bass, and Piano (1962); Chamber Concerto for Cello and 10 Players (1963); *Composition for Violin and 10 Instruments* (1964); Chamber Concerto for Flute and 10 Players (1964); *Janissary Music* for Percussion (1966); *Harpsichord Division* for Harpsichord (1966); *John Bull: Salve Regina Versus Septem* for Chamber Ensemble (1966); Duo for Violin and Piano (1966–67); String Trio (1968); *Ringing Changes* for Percussion Ensemble (1970); Chamber Concerto for Tuba, 12 Wind Instruments, and 12 Drums (1970); *Canzona* for 12 Instruments (1971); Harp Variations for Harp, Violin, Viola, and Cello (1972); Bassoon Variations for Bassoon, Harp, and Timpani (1972); Violin Variations (1972); *On Alligators* for 8 Instruments (1972); *Speculum speculi* for Flute, Oboe, Bass Clarinet, Double Bass, Piano, and Percussion (1972); *Grand Union* for Cello and Drums (1973); *Arabia felix* for Flute, Bassoon, Violin, Electric Guitar, Vibraphone, and Piano (1973); Fantasia for Violin and Piano (1974); *Hyperion* for 12 Instruments (1976); *The Winds* for 8 Instruments

(1977); *Fast Fantasy* for Solo Cello (1977); *Archangel* for Bass Trombone and String Quartet (1977); Wind Quintet (1977); 6 Pieces for Violin and Piano (1977); *Ancestors* for Chamber Ensemble (1978); *Joan's* for Chamber Ensemble (1980); *Archaeopteryx* for Bass Trombone (1980); Trio for Double Bass, Bass Trombone, and Tuba (1981); Horn Trio (1981). For voice: *Madrigali spirituale* for Tenor, Baritone, 2 Oboes, 2 Violins, Cello, and Double Bass (1960); *Symphonia sacra* for Tenor, Baritone, Bass, 2 Oboes, 2 Violins, Double Bass, and Organ (1961); *The Prayer of Jonah* for Voices and String Quintet (1962); *Super Salutem* for Male Voices and Instruments (1964); *A Message to Denmark Hill* for Baritone, Flute, Cello, and Piano (1970); *A Song to the Lute in Musicke* for Soprano and Piano (1970); *Mannheim, 87.87.87* for Unison Chorus and Organ (1973); *An Anthem for Epiphany* for Chorus, Organ, and Trumpet (1974); *6 Songs* for 2 Voices, Violin, and Piano (1977); *The Celestial Sphere*, sacred oratorio for Chorus and Orch. (1979; Augustana College, April 25, 1981). Electronic music: *Consort from Instruments and Voices* for Magnetic Tape (1961); *Time's Encomium* for synthesized sound and processed synthesized sound (1969; received the Pulitzer Prize in 1970).

Wurlitzer, Rudolph H., American instrument dealer; b. Cincinnati, Dec. 30, 1873; d. there, May 27, 1948. He was the son of the founder of the Wurlitzer Co. (established 1856); studied violin at the Cincinnati College of Music and later in Berlin with Emanuel Wirth. He became secretary-treasurer of the Wurlitzer Co. in 1899; later vice-president, and finally president. In 1929 the company purchased 64 string instruments from the Rodman Wanamaker Collection, including some fine specimens. Several richly illustrated catalogues of string instruments in the Wurlitzer Collection have been issued: *Old Master Violins, Violas, Violoncellos* (Cincinnati, 1915); *Masterpieces of the Great Violin Makers* (N.Y., 1917; 2nd ed., 1918); *Rare Violins, Violas, Violoncellos of the 17th, 18th, and 19th Centuries* (N.Y., 1931); *Rare Bows for Violin, Viola, Violoncello, by Makers of the 18th and 19th Centuries* (N.Y., 1931); *Rare Violas by Celebrated Makers of the 16th–19th Centuries* (N.Y., 1940).

Wurm, Marie, noted English pianist; b. Southampton, May 18, 1860; d. Munich, Jan. 21, 1938. She studied piano with Raff and Clara Schumann in Germany; returning to England, she took theory lessons with Stanford and Arthur Sullivan. She was quite successful as a concert pianist in England and Germany; in 1925 she settled in Munich. Her avocation was conducting; she organized a women's orch. in Berlin, and conducted its inaugural concert on Oct. 10, 1899, arousing considerable curiosity. She also was an ambitious composer.
WORKS: Opera, *Die Mitschuldigen* (Leipzig, 1923); Piano Concerto; String Quartet; Violin Sonata; Cello Sonata; Piano Sonata; numerous piano pieces (*Valse de concert, Barcarolle, Sylph Dance, Suite,* gavottes, mazurkas, etc.); she publ. *Das ABC der Musik* and *Praktische Vorschule zur Caland-*

Lehre. Her sisters, **Adela Wurm** and **Mathilda Wurm,** who made their careers in England, changed their last name to **Verne** in order to exorcise the vermicular sound of the original German family name, as pronounced in English.

Wyk, Arnold van, South African composer; b. Calvinia, Cape Province, April 26, 1916; d. Cape Town, May 27, 1983. He studied at Stellenbosch Univ., near Cape Town (1936–38); then went to London, where he attended the Royal Academy of Music (1938–43). From 1939 to 1944 he worked with the British Broadcasting Corp.; went back to South Africa in 1946; taught there at the Univ. of Cape Town (1949–61); in 1961 joined the faculty of Stellenbosch Univ.; retired in 1978.
WORKS: *Southern Cross* for Orch. (1943); Symph. No. 1 (1944); *Christmas Oratorio* (1949); *Rhapsody* for Orch. (Cape Town Festival, March 4, 1952); Symph. No. 2 (Cape Town Festival, March 13, 1952); 5 *Elegies* for String Quartet (1941); song cycle, *Liefde en Verlatenheid* (Festival of the International Society for Contemporary Music, Haifa, May 31, 1954); String Quartet No. 1 (1957); symph. suite, *Primavera* (1960); symph. variations, *Masquerade,* on a South African folk song (1964); choruses; songs; piano pieces.

Wylde, Henry, English conductor, composer, and educator; b. Bushey, Herts, May 22, 1822; d. London, March 13, 1890. He was the son of **Henry Wylde,** a London organist and composer of glees. He studied piano with Moscheles and Cipriani Potter at the Royal Academy of Music in London. In 1852 he founded in London the New Phil. Society, and conducted its concerts in cooperation with Spohr until 1858, when he took complete charge of its concerts (until 1879). In 1861 he founded the London Academy of Music; supervised the building of St. George's Hall (1867) to house it. In 1863 he became a prof. of music there, retaining this post until his death.
WORKS: *Paradise Lost,* oratorio after Milton (London, May 11, 1853); Piano Concerto (London, April 14, 1852); songs; piano pieces; he also publ. the books *The Science of Music* (1865); *Music in Its Art-Mysteries* (1867); *Modern Counterpoint in Major Keys* (1873); *Occult Principles of Music* (1881); *Music as an Educator* (1882); *The Evolution of the Beautiful in Sound* (1888).

Wyner, Susan Davenny, American soprano; b. New Haven, Conn., Oct. 17, 1943. She was educated at Cornell Univ. graduating summa cum laude in music and English literature. She then received a Fulbright scholarship and a grant from the Ford Foundation; also won the Walter W. Naumberg Prize. An exceptionally intelligent singer, she became equally successful as a performer of music in all historic idioms, from early Renaissance works to the most intransigent ultramodern scores.

Wyner, Yehudi, American composer, son of the composer **Lazar Weiner** (whose name he phonetically changed to Wyner); b. Calgary, Canada, June

1, 1929. He followed his parents to the U.S.; enrolled in the Juilliard School of Music in N.Y., graduating in 1946; then entered Yale Univ., where his principal teacher was Richard Donovan (A.B., 1950; B.Mus., 1951; M.Mus., 1953); he also acquired an M.A. degree from Harvard Univ. After occupying several temporary teaching posts, he joined the staff of Yale Univ. in 1963; was chairman of the music dept. there, 1969–73. In 1976 he joined the faculty of the Berkshire Music Center in Tanglewood; in 1978 became dean of music at the State Univ. of N.Y. at Purchase. His music is expressively vigesimosecular in its structural sobriety and melorhythmic aggressiveness; his serial techniques, anchored in tritones and major sevenths, are mitigated by a certain combinatorial harmoniousness; formally, he follows neo-Baroque practices.

WORKS: *Dance Variations* for Wind Octet (1953); Piano Sonata (1954); *Concerto Duo* for Violin and Piano (1957); *3 Informal Pieces* for Violin and Piano (1961); *Friday Evening Service* for Cantor, Chorus, and Organ (1963); *Torah Service* (1966); *Da camera* for Piano and Orch. (1967); *Cadenza* for Clarinet and Harpsichord (1969); *De novo* for Cello and Small Ensemble (1971); *Canto cantabile* for Soprano and Concert Band (1972); *Intermedio* for Soprano and String Orch. (1974); *Dances of Atonement* for Violin and Piano (1976).

Wyschnegradsky, Ivan, foremost composer of microtonal music; b. St. Petersburg, May 16, 1893; d. Paris, Sept. 29, 1979. He studied composition with Nicolas Sokoloff at the St. Petersburg Cons.; emigrated after the Russian Revolution, and in 1920 settled in Paris, where he remained until his death. He devoted virtually his entire musical career to the exploration and creative realization of music in quarter-tones and other microtonal intervals; had a quarter-tone piano constructed for him; also publ. a guide, *Manuel d'harmonie à quarts de ton* (Paris, 1932). On Nov. 10, 1945, he presented in Paris a concert of his music, at which he conducted the first performance of his *Cosmos* for 4 Pianos, with each pair tuned at quarter-tones. The Canadian composer and pianist Bruce Mather took interest in Wyschnegradsky's music and gave a concert of his works at McGill Univ. in Montreal that included 3 world premieres (Feb. 10, 1977). But with the exception of these rare concerts, Wyschnegradsky remains a figure of legend; few performances of his music are ever given in Europe or North America. He regarded his *La Journée de l'existence (The Day of Existence)* for Narrator, ad lib. Chorus, and Orch. (to his own text; 1916–17; revised 1927 and 1940) as his germinal work, opening the path to microtonal harmony; he dated this "awakening to ultrachromaticism" as having occurred on Nov. 7, 1918. At his death he left sketches for a short opera in 5 scenes, *L'Eternel Etranger,* begun in 1939 but never completed. Also unfinished was the ambitious *Polyphonie spatiale.*

OTHER WORKS (all in quarter-tones unless otherwise shown): *Chant douloureux et étude* for Violin and Piano (1918); *7 Variations on the Note C* for 2 Pianos (1918–20; perf. in 1945 as *5 Variations;* then 2 more were added); *Chant funèbre* for Strings and 2 Harps (1922); *Chant nocturne* for Violin and 2 Pianos (1923; revised 1972); 2 string quartets (1924, 1931–32); *2 Choruses* for Voices and 4 Pianos (1926); *Prélude et fugue sur un chant de l'Evangile rouge* for String Quartet (1927); *Prélude et Danse* for 2 Pianos (1928); *Ainsi parlait Zarathoustra (Thus Spake Zarathustra)* for Orch. (1929–30; arranged for 4 Pianos, 1936); *2 études de concert* for Piano (1931; arranged for 2 Pianos, 1936); *Etude en forme de scherzo* for 2 Pianos (1932); *Prélude et Fugue* for 2 Pianos (1933); *24 préludes* for 2 Pianos (1934; revised 1958–60); *4 Fragments symphoniques* for 4 Pianos (1934, final version, 1968; 1937; 1946; 1956); *Le Mot* for Soprano and Piano (1935; half-tones); *Linnite,* pantomime for 3 Female Voices and 4 Pianos (1937); *Acte chorégraphique* for Bass-baritone, Chorus, and 4 Pianos (1938–40; revised 1958–59); *Cosmos* for 4 Pianos (1940; suppressed); *Prélude et Fugue* for 3 Pianos (1945); *2 Fugues* for 2 Pianos (1951); *5 variations sans thème et conclusion* for Orch. (1951–52); *Sonate en un mouvement* for Viola and 2 Pianos (1956; suppressed); *Transparences I and II* for Ondes Martenot and 2 Pianos (1956, 1963); *Arc-en-ciel* for 6 Pianos (1956); *Etude sur le carré magique sonore* for Piano (1956; based on the "magic square" principle of cyclical structure, written in a tempered scale without quarter-tones); *Etude tricesimoprimal* for Fokker-organ (1959; for the Dutch physicist Adriaan Fokker's 31-tone organ); *Composition* for String Quartet (1960); *2 pièces* for Microtonal Piano (1960); *Etude sur les mouvements rotatoires* for 4 Pianos (1961; orchestrated 1964); *2 Compositions:* No. 1 for 3 Pianos and No. 2 for 2 Pianos (1962); *Prélude et étude* for Microtonal Piano (1966); *Intégrations* for 2 Pianos (1967); *Symphonie en un mouvement* for Orch. (1969); *Dialogues à trois* for 3 Pianos (1973–74; sixth-tones).

Wyttenbach, Jürg, Swiss pianist and composer; b. Bern, Dec. 2, 1935. He studied composition at the Bern Cons.; later in Paris with Lefébure and Calvet (1955–57). He taught piano at the Biel Cons. (1959–67); was a prof. of piano at the Bern Cons. (1962–66); was at the Basel Academy from 1967. His music pursues the median line of European modernism, marked by a strong rhythmic pulse, dissonant counterpoint, and atonal diversions, without falling into the bottomless pit of dodecaphony.

WORKS: 4 works of "instrumental theater": *Execution ajournee I–III* (1969–70) and *Kunststücke, die Zeit totzuschlagen (Tricks to Kill Time,* 1972); Piano Concerto (1959; revised 1973); Sonata for Solo Oboe (1961); *3 Movements* for Oboe, Harp, and Piano (1962); ballet, *Der Gefesselte* (Heidelberg, 1962); *Divisions* for Piano and 9 Solo Strings (1964); *De Metalli* for Baritone and Orch. (1964–65); *Anrufungen und Ausbruch* for 28 Woodwinds and Brass (1966); *Nachspiel* for 2 Pianos (1966); *Paraphrase* for a Narrator, a Flutist, and a Pianist (1967–68); *Conteste* for Chamber Orch. (1969); *3 Pieces* for Piano (1969); *Ad libitum* for one or 2 Flutes (1969).

Wyzewa, Théodore de (real name, **Wyzewski**), noted musicologist; b. Kalushin, Russian Poland, Sept. 12, 1862; d. Paris, April 7, 1917. In 1869 his parents settled in Châtelleraut, France, where he received his education; in 1884 he founded in Paris, with Edouard Dujardin, the *Revue Wagnérienne,* which, until it ceased publication in 1888, did much to advance the cause of Wagner in France. Wyzewa's importance as a musicologist rests upon his research concerning the life and work of Mozart, about whom he publ. new facts in "Recherches sur la jeunesse de Mozart," in the *Revue des Deux Mondes* (1904–5), and in *W.A. Mozart. Sa vie musicale et son œuvre de l'enfance à la pleine maturité* (with G. de Saint-Foix; 2 vols., Paris, 1912; 3 more vols. added by Saint-Foix in 1937, 1940, and 1946). Wyzewa also wrote *Beethoven et Wagner* (Paris, 1898; new ed., 1914); edited 20 piano sonatas of Clementi with a biographical notice (vol. I, Paris, 1917; vol. II, posthumous, brought out by Henry Expert).

X

Xanrof, Léon, French composer of popular music; b. Paris, Dec. 9, 1867; d. there, May 17, 1953. His real name was **Léon Fourneau;** Xanrof is an anagram of its Latin equivalent *(fornax).* He was a lawyer by profession; from 1890 produced light stage pieces in the Paris theaters; the chansonette *Le Fiacre,* which he wrote for Yvette Guilbert, achieved great popularity. He also contributed music criticism to various Paris papers.

Xenakis, Iannis, eminent avant-garde theorist and composer of Greek descent; b. Brăila, Rumania, May 29, 1922. At the age of 10 he was taken by his family to Greece, where he began to study engineering, but he became involved in the Greek resistance movement against the Nazi occupation forces; was wounded in a skirmish. In 1947 he went to France; studied architecture with Le Corbusier and became his assistant (1948–60); during the same period he took lessons in composition with Honegger and Milhaud at the Ecole Normale de Musique in Paris and with Messiaen at the Paris Cons. (1950–53). He aided Le Corbusier in the design of the Philips Pavillion at the 1958 World's Fair in Brussels; met Varèse, who was then working on his *Poème électronique* for the exhibit, and received from him some stimulating advice on the creative potentialities of the electronic medium. During his entire career, Xenakis strove to connect mathematical concepts with the organization of a musical composition, using the theory of sets, symbolic logic, and probabilistic calculus; he promulgated the stochastic method, which is teleologically directed and deterministic, as distinct from a purely aleatory handling of data. He publ. a comprehensive vol. dealing with these procedures, *Musiques formelles* (Paris, 1963; in Eng., N.Y., 1971). He was founder and director of the Centre d'Etudes Mathématiques et Automatiques Musicales in Paris, and founder and director of the Center for Mathematical and Automated Music at Indiana Univ. in the U.S., where he served on the faculty from 1967 to 1972. His influence on the development of advanced composition in Europe and America is considerable; several composers adopted his theories and imitated the scientific-sounding titles of some of his compositions. Xenakis uses Greek words for the titles of virtually all of his works to stress the philosophical derivation of modern science and modern arts from classical Greek concepts; in some cases he uses computer symbols for titles.
  WORKS: *Metastasis* for 61 Instruments (1953–54; Donaueschingen, Oct. 15, 1955); *Pithoprakta* for 50 Instruments (1955–56; Munich, March 8, 1957);

Achorripsis for 21 Instruments (1956–57; Brussels, July 20, 1958); *Diamorphoses* for Tape (1957); *Concret PH* for Tape (1957); *Analogiques A & B* for 9 Strings and Tape (1959); *Syrmos (Chain of Events)* for 18 Strings (1959); *Duel,* musical game for 2 "antagonistic" Conductors and 2 Orchs. playing different material, mathematically based on game theory, with the audience determining the winning orch. (1959; Radio Hilversum, Oct., 1971); *Orient-Occident* for Tape (1960); *Herma (Foundation)* for Piano (1960–61); *ST/48—1,240162* (1956–62; ST = stochastic; 48 = number of players; 1 = first work for this contingent; 240162 = 24 January 1962, date on which the work, derived from earlier sketches, was finally calculated by the IBM 7090 electronic computer in Paris as programmed probabilistically by Xenakis); *ST/10—1,080262* (1956–62; ST = stochastic; 10 = number of players; 1 = first work of this contingent; 080262 = 8 February 1962, date on which this work was finally electronically calculated; a version of this work for String Quartet is entitled *ST/4*); *Morsima-Amorsima* (Morsima = that which comes by Fate; Amorsima = that which does not come by Fate) for Violin, Cello, Double Bass, and Piano (1956–62); *Atrées (Law of Necessity)* for 10 Players (1956–62; written in homage to Blaise Pascal and calculated by the 7090 computer, with some license); *Stratégie,* musical game for 2 Conductors and 2 Orchs. (1959–62; Venice Festival, April 23, 1963; Bruno Maderna's orch. won over that of Konstantin Simonovic); *Bohor I* and *II* for Tape (1962, 1975); *Polla ta dhina (Many Are the Wonders)* for Children's Choir and Small Orch., to a text from Sophocles' *Antigone* (1962); *Eonta* (neuter plural of the present participle of the verb "to be" in the Ionian dialect, the title being in Cypriot syllabic characters of Creto-Mycenean origin) for Piano, 2 Trumpets, and 3 Tenor Trombones (1963–64); *Hiketides (The Suppliants),* stage music for 50 Women's Voices, 10 Instruments, and Percussion, after Aeschylus (1964); *Akrata (Pure)* for 16 Wind Instruments (1964–65; Oxford, June 28, 1966); *Terretektorh (Action of Construction)* for 88 Players scattered among the audience (1965–66; Royan Festival of Contemporary Music, April 3, 1966); *Oresteia,* incidental music for Aeschylus' tragedy, for Chorus and Chamber Orch. (1965–66; also a concert suite); *Nomos Alpha (Law Alpha)* for Solo Cello (1966); *Polytope de Montréal,* light-and-sound spectacle for the Montreal EXPO '67, for 4 Small, Identical Orchs. (1967); *Nuits* for 12 Mixed Voices a cappella (1967); *Medea,* stage music for Male Chorus and Instrumental Ensemble (1967); *Nomos Gamma* for 98 Players scattered among the audience (1967–68; Royan Festival, April 3, 1969); *Kraanerg (Perfection of Energy),* ballet music for Tape and Orch. (1968–69; Ottawa, June 2, 1969); *Anaktoria* for 8 Instruments (1969); *Persephassa* for 6 Percussionists scattered among the audience (1969); *Synaphai* for One or 2 Pianos, and Orch. (1969); *Hibiki-Hana-Ma,* 12-channel electroacoustic music distributed kinematically over 800 loudspeakers, for the Osaka EXPO '70 (1969–70; also a 4-channel version); *Charisma* for Clarinet and Cello (1971); *Aroura* for 12 Strings (1971); *Persepolis,* light-and-sound spectacle with 8- or 4-channel electroacoustic music (1971); *Antikhthon,* ballet music for Orch. (1971; Bonn, Sept. 21, 1974); *Linaia-Agon* for Horn, Tenor Trombone, and Tuba (1972); *Mikka* for Solo Violin (1972); *Polytope de Cluny,* version of *Polytope de Montréal,* for 4-channel Tape (1972); *Eridanos* for 8 Brasses and 10 String Instruments or their multiples (1973; La Rochelle Festival, 1973); *Evryali* for Piano (1973); *Cendrées* for Chorus and Orch. (1974; Lisbon, June 18, 1974); *Erikhthon* for Piano and Orch. (1974; Paris, May 1974); *Gmeeoorh* for Organ (1974); *Noomena* for Orch. (1974; Paris, Oct. 16, 1974); *Empreintes* for Orch. (1975; La Rochelle Festival, June 29, 1975); *Phlegra* for 11 Instruments (1975; London, Jan. 28, 1976); *Psappha* for Solo Percussion (1975); *N'shima* for 2 Horns, 2 Trombones, Cello, and 2 Mezzo-sopranos (1975); *Theraps* for Solo Double Bass (1975–76); *Khoaï* for Solo Harpsichord (1976); *Retours—Windungen* for 12 Cellists (1976; Bonn, Dec. 20, 1976); *Dmaathen* for Oboe and Percussion (1976); *Epeï* for English Horn, Clarinet, Trumpet, 2 Tenor Trombones, and Double Bass (1976); *Mikka S* for Solo Violin (1976); *Akanthos* for 9 Players (1977); *Kottos* for Solo Cello (1977); *Hélène* for Mezzo-soprano, Female Chorus, and 2 Clarinets (1977); *Diatope* for 4- or 8-track Tapes (1977); *Ais* for Baritone, Solo Percussion, and Orch.; *Palimpsest* for Piano and Percussion (1979); *Embellie* for Solo Viola (1981).

Xyndas, Spyridon, Greek composer; b. Corfu, June 8, 1812; d. Athens, Nov. 12, 1896. He studied in Italy; composed many attractive popular Greek songs; several operas to Italian librettos (*Il Conte Giuliano, I due pretendenti,* etc.); also *The Parliamentary Candidate* (Athens, March 1888), which was probably the first opera with a Greek text. He became blind toward the end of his life.

Y

Yamada, Kôsçak, eminent Japanese composer and conductor; b. Tokyo, June 9, 1886; d. there, Dec. 29, 1965. He studied at the Imperial Academy of Music in Tokyo; then in Berlin with Max Bruch (1908–13). Returning to Japan in 1914, he organized the Tokyo Phil. Orch., which gave its first concert in 1915. On Oct. 16, 1918, he conducted a program of Japanese music in Carnegie Hall, N.Y., including some of his own works (*Festival of Autumn, The Dark Gate, Flower of Madara,* and *Oriental Suite*); appeared as a guest conductor in the U.S. until 1921; in 1930, and again in 1933, he conducted in Russia; in 1937 he toured Europe. Most of his MSS were destroyed during the air raid on Tokyo of May 25, 1945; several scores have been restored from the extant orch. parts.

WORKS: Operas: *Alladine et Palomides,* after Maeterlinck (1913); *The Depraved Heavenly Maiden* (1908; Tokyo, Dec. 3, 1929); *Ayame (The Sweet Flag;* Tokyo, Feb. 24, 1935); *The Black Ships* (Tokyo, 1940); *Yoake (The Dawn;* Nov. 28, 1940); *Hsiang Fei* (1946); cantatas: *Bonno-Koru* (Tokyo, Oct. 9, 1931) and *The Dawn of the Orient* (Tokyo, July 7, 1941); Symph. (Tokyo, Dec. 6, 1914); *Ode to Meiji* for Chorus and Orch. (Tokyo, April 26, 1925); *Homage to Showa,* symph. poem (Tokyo, May 13, 1939); *Kamikaze,* symph. suite (1944); chamber music; nearly 1,000 choral pieces and songs.

Yamash'ta, Stomu (really **Tsutomu Yamashita**), Japanese virtuoso percussionist and composer; b. Kyoto, March 10, 1947. He was trained in music by his father; played piano in his infancy, and drums at puberty; in early adolescence became a timpanist for the Kyoto Phil. and Osaka Phil.; also worked in several film studios in Tokyo; at the same time he was active in sports; won the speed skating championship of Japan for his age group. At 16 he went to London for further study; later went to the U.S. as a scholarship student at the Interlochen Arts Academy; continued his musical education in Boston, N.Y., and Chicago. Returning to Japan, he gave solo performances as a percussionist; developed a phenomenal degree of equilibristic prestidigitation, synchronously manipulating a plethora of drums and a congregation of oriental bells and gongs while rotating 360° from the center of a circle to reach the prescribed percussionable objects. As a composer, he cultivates a manner of controlled improvisation marked by constantly shifting meters. In 1970 he formed the Red Buddha Theater (an ensemble of 36 actors, musicians, and dancers), for which he composed 2 musical pageants, *Man from the East* (1971) and *Rain Mountain* (1973). Other works: a ballet,

Fox (1968); *Hito* for any 3 Instruments (1970); *Prisms* for Solo Percussion (1970); *Red Buddha* for Chamber Ensemble (1971); percussion scores for some 77 Japanese films, as well as for Ken Russell's *The Devils* (with Peter Maxwell Davies, 1971) and Robert Altman's *Images* (1972).

Yampolsky, Izrail, Russian musicologist and lexicographer; b. Kiev, Nov. 21, 1905; d. Moscow, Sept. 20, 1976. He studied violin; then entered the Moscow Cons., where he took courses in advanced music theory with Miaskovsky and Glière; he subsequently taught violin at the Music Academy in Moscow (1931–58); gave lectures in music history there; also taught at the Cons. (1934–49). A fine and diligent research scholar, he publ. a number of excellent monographs dealing mainly with violin and violinists: *Foundations of Violin Fingering* (Moscow, 1933; 3rd expanded ed., 1955; in Eng., London, 1967); *Henryk Wieniawski* (Moscow, 1955); *Enescu* (Moscow, 1956; also in Rumanian, Bucharest, 1959); *Music of Yugoslavia* (Moscow, 1958); *Paganini* (Moscow, 1961; 2nd ed., 1968); *David Oistrakh* (Moscow, 1964); *Fritz Kreisler* (1975). He was co-editor, with Boris Steinpress, of the one-vol. reference work *Encyclopedic Music Dictionary* (Moscow, 1959; revised 1966). He was acting editor in chief of the first 3 vols. of the 5-vol. *Musical Encyclopedia* (Moscow, 1973, 1974, 1976).

Yannay, Yehuda, Rumanian-born Israeli-American composer of hypermodern tendencies; b. Timisoara, May 26, 1937. He went to Israel in 1951, and studied composition with Boscovich (1959–64); received a Fulbright travel grant and went to the U.S., where he studied composition with Arthur Berger and Harold Shapero at Brandeis Univ. (M.F.A., 1966); attended summer classes of Gunther Schuller at the Berkshire Music Center in Tanglewood (1965); later studied composition at the Univ. of Illinois, Urbana (1968–70). In 1970 he joined the faculty of the Univ. of Wisconsin at Milwaukee; organized there a group called the Music from Almost Yesterday Ensemble with the intention of producing music of the problematic future and that of the tenable yesteryear. He received his Ph.D. in 1974 from the Univ. of Illinois at Urbana. In his own composition he liberates himself from all prejudices of the past, present, and future. He invented an elastic nylon string monochord, which he named, with a commendable eschewment of obsolescent modesty, "Yannaychord." Most of his creations are public exhibitions of a theatrical nature, in which all arts and human actions are united and all social conventions scorned, spurned, or both; the pugnacious determination to "épater les bourgeois" motivates his productions in the deluded hopes that the bourgeois will be epatated beyond endurance and precipitate a physical encounter of the kind that animated the fabled exhibitions of the futurists of yore.
WORKS: *Variations* for 2 Flutes (1970); *The Chain of Proverbs* for Choir, Recorders, and Percussion (1962); *Sefiroth (Spheres)* for Soprano, Flute,

Clarinet, Bass Clarinet, Harp, Prepared Piano, and Percussion (1963); *Incantations* for Voices, Keyboard, and the Piano Interior (1964); *Interconnections* for 14 Instruments (1965); *Mirkamim,* textures of sound for Orch. of 84 Solo Instruments (1967); *Per se,* chamber concerto (1968; Chicago, Nov. 10, 1970); *Coloring Book for the Harpist,* playing with Combs (1969); *Wraphap* for Amplified Actress lying upon a large aluminum sheet, and strumming the Yannaychord (1969); *Houdini's 9th* for Double Bass and Escape Artist (straitjacketed to his instrument), while a recording plays the "Hymn to Joy" from Beethoven's 9th Symph. and 2 hospital orderlies supervise the soloist (1969); Concerto for Audience, Orch., and 29 Red, Yellow, and Green Slides monitoring the involuntary participants (1971); *3 Events: The Urbana (Illinois) Crystal Lake Park Gathering, Piano without Pianist,* and *The Vestibule Peep-In-Pipe-Out* (1968–71); *Bug Piece* for any irritants capable of bugging the captive audience, the bugging being symbolized by the projection on a screen of a centipede, a millipede, or fornicating ants, or any other terrestrial arthropods (1972); *A Noiseless Patient Spider* for Women's Chorus a cappella (1975); *American Sonorama,* ballet score derived from sounds of the more obnoxious speeches by singularly illiterate politicians (1975–76); *The Decline and Fall of the Sonata in B-flat,* symbolic theater sketch (1970–76).

Yansons, Arvid, conductor; b. Leipaja, Latvia, Oct. 24, 1914. He studied violin in Riga; then played in the Opera orch. there. In 1944 he was engaged as a conductor at the Riga Opera; in 1952 he became a regular conductor of the Leningrad Phil. Orch.; was a guest conductor in Eastern Europe. He also made successful appearances in England, most notably with the Hallé Orch. of Manchester.

Yardumian, Richard, American composer; b. (of Armenian parents) Philadelphia, April 5, 1917. He was self-taught in music. His compositions reflect the spirit of Armenian folk songs and religious melodies. His *Armenian Suite* for Orch. was performed for the first time by the Philadelphia Orch. on March 5, 1954. Other symph. works (also brought out by the Philadelphia Orch.) are *Desolate City* (April 6, 1945); Violin Concerto (March 30, 1950); Piano Concerto (Philadelphia, Jan. 3, 1958); Symph. No. 1 (Philadelphia, Dec. 1, 1961); Symph. No. 2 (*Psalms*) for Orch. and Contralto (Philadelphia, Nov. 13, 1964); *Come Creator Spirit,* mass for Contralto, Chorus, and Orch. (1966); oratorio, *The Story of Abraham* (1971; May 4, 1972); *2 Chorales:* No. 1 for Organ Solo (1976) and No. 2 for Orch. (1978).

Yates, Peter B., Canadian-American writer on music; b. Toronto, Nov. 30, 1909; d. New York, Feb. 25, 1976. He studied at Princeton Univ. (B.A., 1931); married the pianist **Frances Mullen** in 1933. From 1937 to 1962 he was a functionary at the Calif. Dept. of Employment in Los Angeles, but this bureaucratic occupation did not preclude his activities as a musical catalyst. In 1939 he inaugurated on the rooftop of his house in the Silver Lake district of Los Angeles a chamber concert series which was to become an important cultural enterprise in subcultural California, under the name Evenings on the Roof; he served as coordinator of these concerts from 1939 to 1954, when they were moved to a larger auditorium in downtown Los Angeles and became known as the Monday Evening Concerts. In 1968 he was appointed chairman of the music dept. at the State Univ. of N.Y. at Buffalo. He publ. *An Amateur at the Keyboard, Twentieth-Century Music,* and a collection of poems.

Yepes, Narciso, Spanish guitarist; b. Lorca, Nov. 14, 1927. He was educated at the Valencia Cons.; made his debut with the Orquesta Nacional in Madrid in 1947; then launched an international career, appearing in the U.S., South America, and Japan. He also wrote music for films.

Yo-Yo Ma. See **Ma, Yo-Yo.**

Yon, Pietro Alessandro, Italian-American organist and composer; b. Settimo Vittone, Aug. 8, 1886; d. Huntington, Long Island, N.Y., Nov. 22, 1943. He studied with Fumagalli at the Milan Cons.; then at the Turin Cons. (1901–4), and at the Santa Cecilia in Rome with Remigio Renzi (organ) and Sgambati (piano), graduating in 1905; subsequently served as organist at St. Peter's in Rome (1905–7). In 1907 he emigrated to the U.S.; from 1907 to 1919, and again from 1921 to 1926, was organist at St. Francis-Xavier's in N.Y.; then was appointed organist of St. Patrick's Cathedral in N.Y., a post he held until his death. He became a naturalized U.S. citizen in 1921. He was greatly esteemed as an organist and teacher; composed numerous organ pieces, of which *Gesù Bambino* (1917) became popular and was publ. in various instrumental and vocal arrangements; he also wrote an oratorio, *The Triumph of St. Patrick* (N.Y., April 29, 1934); several masses and other religious services. A novel based on his life, *The Heavens Heard Him,* written by V.B. Hammann and M.C. Yon, was publ. in N.Y. in 1963.

Yonge (Young), Nicholas, English musician; b. Lewes; d. London (buried, Oct. 23), 1619. He was a chorister at St. Paul's Cathedral. He trans. and arranged a number of Italian madrigals, which he publ. in 2 books under the general title *Musica transalpina* (1588, 1597).

Yost, Gaylord, American violinist and composer; b. Fayette, Ohio, Jan. 28, 1888; d. Wauseon, Ohio, Oct. 10, 1958. After studying music in Toledo and Detroit, he went to Berlin, where he took violin lessons with Issaye Barmas. Upon returning to the U.S., he organized the Yost String Quartet (1925). He taught at the Indiana College of Music in Indianapolis (1915–21), and at the Pittsburgh Music Inst. (1921–43). In 1951 he turned to politics and journalism; became editor and publisher of the *Fayette Review,* founded by his father. In 1954 he was elect-

ed mayor of Fayette, serving until 1957. He publ. *The Yost System,* in 8 vols. (1932; abridged ed. as *The Yost Violin Method,* in 3 vols.); also *Basic Principles of Violin Playing* (1940).

Youmans, Vincent, American composer of popular music; b. New York, Sept. 27, 1898; d. Denver, April 5, 1946. He took piano lessons as a child, but was apprenticed by his father to enter the business world; he served as a messenger in a Wall Street bank; then enlisted in the U.S. Navy; also played the piano in a Navy band; wrote a song, *Hallelujah,* which was picked up by John Philip Sousa, who performed it with his own bands; later it was incorporated by Youmans in his musical *Hit the Deck.* After World War I, Youmans earned a living as a song plugger for publishers in N.Y. He produced 2 musical comedies, *2 Little Girls in Blue* (May 3, 1921) and *Wildflower* (1923); both were moderately successful, but he achieved fame with his next production, *No No Nanette;* it opened in Detroit on April 21, 1924; was next staged in Chicago on May 5, 1924, and after a 49-week run there, moved to London, where it was produced on March 11, 1925; it finally reached Broadway on Sept. 16, 1925, and proved to be one of the most beguiling and enduring American musicals; its hit song, *Tea for Two,* became a perennial favorite all over the world (Shostakovich arranged it in 1927 for a salon orch. under the title *Tahiti Trot*). There followed several other successful musicals: *A Night Out* (1925), *Oh! Please* (1926), *Hit the Deck* (1927), *Rainbow* (1928), *Great Day* (1929), and *Through the Years* (1932). In 1933 Youmans went to Hollywood to complete his score for the film *Flying Down to Rio.* Because of an increasingly aggravated tubercular condition, he retired to Denver in the hope of recuperation in its then-unpolluted environment, and remained there until his death. Among his songs the following were hits: *Bambalina; I Want to Be Happy; Hallelujah; Sometimes I'm Happy; Great Day; Without a Song; Time on My Hands; Through the Years; Oh, Me, Oh, My, Oh, You; Carioca; Orchids in the Moonlight; Drums in My Heart; More Than You Know; Rise 'n' Shine.*

Young, Alexander, English tenor; b. London, Oct. 18, 1920. He studied at the Royal College of Music in London; made his debut at the Edinburgh Festival in 1950; then sang opera at Glyndebourne and Covent Garden; in America, appeared at the San Francisco Opera. He enjoyed a fine reputation as a concert singer in wide-ranging programs of classical and modern music.

Young, La Monte, American composer of the extreme avant-garde; b. Bern, Idaho, Oct. 14, 1935. He studied clarinet and saxophone with William Green in Los Angeles; then took courses in composition with John Vincent and Leonard Stein at the Univ. of Calif., Los Angeles (1956–57), and later at Berkeley (1957–60); subsequently worked with Richard Maxfield at the New School for Social Research in N.Y. (1960–61). In 1963 he married the artist and illustrator Marian Zazeela, and gave a number of audiovisual performances with her in a series of "Sound/Light Environments" in Europe and America. In 1970 he visited India to study Eastern philosophy and train himself physically, mentally, and vocally for cosmic awareness, gradually arriving at the realization that any human, subhuman, or inhuman activity constitutes art; in his *Composition 1990* he starts a fire on the stage while releasing captive butterflies in the hall. In his attempt to overcome terrestrial limitations he has decreed for himself a circadian period of 26 hours. He achieves timelessness by declaring, "This piece of music may play without stopping for thousands of years." Several of his works consist solely of imperious commands: "Push the piano to the wall; push it through the wall; keep pushing," or, more succinctly, "Urinate." He edited *An Anthology of Chance Operations, Concept Art, Anti-Art,* etc. (N.Y., 1963); his own contribution to it was a line drawn in India ink on a 3 × 5 filing card.

ASCERTAINABLE WORKS: *5 Little Pieces* for String Quartet (1956); *For Guitar* (1958); String Trio (1958); *Poem for Tables, Chairs, and Benches* (moving furniture about; Univ. of Calif., Berkeley, Jan. 5, 1960); *Arabic Numeral (any Integer)* for Gong or Piano (1960); *Studies in the Bowed Disc* for Gong (1963); *The Well-Tuned Piano* (1964); *The Tortoise Droning Selected Pitches from the Holy Numbers of the 2 Black Tigers, the Green Tiger, and the Hermit* (N.Y., Oct. 30, 1964) and *The Tortoise Recalling the Drone of the Holy Numbers as They Were Revealed in the Dreams of the Whirlwind and the Obsidian Gong, Illuminated by the Sawmill, the Green Sawtooth Ocelot, and the High-Tension Line Stepdown Transformer* (N.Y., Dec. 12, 1964); an arbitrary number of pieces of "conceptual" music and tape recordings of his own monophonous vocalizing achieved by both inspiration and expiration so that the vocal line is maintained indefinitely; various physical exercises with or without audible sounds. His *Selected Writings* were publ. in Munich in 1969.

Young, Percy Marshall, English writer on music; b. Northwich, Cheshire, May 17, 1912. He studied organ at Selwyn College, Cambridge (B.A., 1934); then went to Dublin, where he graduated from Trinity College (Mus.D., 1937); upon his return to England he took courses with C.B. Rootham and E.J. Dent in Cambridge; subsequently occupied various teaching posts; from 1944 to 1966 was director of music at the College of Technology in Wolverhampton. He publ. a number of arrangements of old English songs, and also composed some vocal pieces; but he is known principally for his scholarly biographical studies and essays. WRITINGS (all publ. in London): *Handel* (1947; 3rd ed., revised, 1979); *The Oratorios of Handel* (1953); *A Critical Dictionary of Composers and Their Music* (1954; in America as *Biographical Dictionary of Composers*); *Elgar, O.M.: A Study of a Musician* (1955; revised ed., 1972); *The Story of Song* (1955); *Instrumental Music* (1955); *In Search of Music* (1956); *Concerto* (1957); *Tragic Muse. The Life and Works of Robert Schumann* (1961; revised 1967); *Symphony* (1957); *Music Makers of Today* (1958); *The Choral Tradition: An Historical and Analytical Survey from the 16th Century to the Present Day* (1962); *Zoltán Kodály* (1964); *Britten* (1966); *A History of British Music* (1967); *Great Ideas in Music* (1967); *Keyboard Musicians of the World* (1967); *Debussy* (1969); *The Bachs, 1500–1850* (1970); *Sir Arthur Sullivan* (1971); *A Concise History of Music* (1974); *Alice Elgar: Enigma of a Victorian Lady* (1977). He ed. *Sir Edward Elgar. Letters and Other Writings* (1956).

Young, Victor, American pianist and composer; b. Bristol, Tenn., April 9, 1889; d. Ossining, N.Y., Sept. 2, 1968. He studied piano with Isidor Philipp in Paris; toured in England and the U.S. as accompanist to prominent singers; held various teaching positions; was music director in Thomas A. Edison's Experimental Laboratory in West Orange, N.J., conducting tonal tests and making piano recordings under Edison's personal supervision (1919–27). He wrote the musical score for one of the earliest sound motion pictures, *In Old California;* composed some 300 film scores altogether; also wrote, for orch., *Scherzetto, Jeep, In the Great Smokies, Charm Assembly Line Ballet,* etc.; piano pieces (including *Under a Spanish Moon*); songs (*Gossip, Cuckoo Clock,* etc.).

Young, Victor, American composer of popular music; b. Chicago, Aug. 8, 1900; d. Palm Springs, Calif., Nov. 10, 1956. As a youth he was sent to Poland, where he studied violin at the Warsaw Cons., and made his debut with the Warsaw Phil. He returned to Chicago in 1914 and, after further study, became active on the radio. In 1935 he went to Hollywood, where he wrote film music. Some of his songs became famous (*Sweet Sue, Street of Dreams, Can't We Talk It Over, My Romance, Ghost of a Chance, Love Letters, Golden Earrings, Stella by Starlight, My Foolish Heart, Song of Delilah,* etc.). Shortly before his death, he completed the musical score for the motion picture *Around the World in 80 Days* (1956).

Young-Uck Kim. See **Kim, Young-Uck.**

Yradier (Iradier), Sebastián de, Spanish song composer; b. Lanciego, Álava, Jan. 20, 1809; d. Vitoria, Dec. 6, 1865. He composed theater music; after 1851 became singing master to the Empress Eugénie in Paris; for some time lived in Cuba. He publ. a number of melodious songs in a Spanish manner; one of them, *El arreglito,* subtitled *Chanson havanaise,* was used by Bizet for the famous Habanera in *Carmen;* Bizet retained the key and the pattern of the accompaniment, making minor changes in the melody to adjust it to French words. Yradier's other songs that became famous are *La paloma* and *Ay Chiquita!* In Paris he publ. 2 collections, *Echo d'Espagne* (8 songs) and *Fleurs d'Espagne* (25 songs).

Ysaÿe, Eugène, famous Belgian violinist, conductor, and composer; b. Liège, July 16, 1858; d. Brussels, May 12, 1931. At the age of 4 he began to study violin with his father, a theater conductor; at the age of 7 he was enrolled at the Cons. of Liège as a pupil of Désiré Heynberg; he then studied with Rodolphe Massart there; in 1867 he obtained 2nd prize for violin playing (sharing it with Ovide Musin); in 1868, he obtained first prize for violin and chamber music; and the silver medal in 1874. While still a very young boy, he played in his father's orchs.; in 1876 he was sent to Brussels to study with Henryk Wieniawski, and later was also a pupil of Vieuxtemps. After a sojourn in Bordeaux, he became concertmaster of Bilse's orch. in Berlin; appeared as a soloist at Pauline Lucca's concerts in Cologne and Aachen; in Germany he met Anton Rubinstein, who took him to Russia, where he spent 2 winters; he also toured in Norway. In 1883 he settled in Paris, where he met César Franck, Vincent d'Indy, etc., and gave successful concerts; he formed a duo with the pianist Raoul Pugno, and started a long series of concerts with him, establishing a new standard of excellence. On Sept. 26, 1886, he married Louise Bourdeau; César Franck dedicated his Violin Sonata to them as a wedding present; Ysaÿe's interpretation of this work made it famous. In 1886 he was named a prof. at the Cons. of Brussels (resigned in 1898); in 1886 he also organized the Ysaÿe Quartet (with Crickboom, Léon Van Hout, and Joseph Jacob); Debussy dedicated his String Quartet to Ysaÿe's group, which gave it its first performance at the Société Nationale in Paris, on Dec. 29, 1893. In 1889 Ysaÿe made successful appearances in England; on Nov. 16, 1894, he made his American debut, playing the Beethoven Violin Concerto with the N.Y. Phil., and created a sensation by his virtuosity. He revisited America many times, with undiminished acclaim. He began his career as a conductor in 1894, and established in Brussels his own orch., the Société des Concerts Ysaÿe. When the Germans invaded Belgium in 1914 he fled to London, where he remained during World War I. On April 5, 1918, he made his American debut as a conductor with the Cincinnati Symph. Orch., and also led the Cincinnati May Festival in that year. His success was so great that he was offered a permanent position as conductor of the Cincinnati Symph. Orch., which he held from 1918 to 1922. He then returned to Belgium and resumed leadership of the Société des Concerts Ysaÿe. After the death of his first wife, he married, on July 9, 1927, an American pupil, Jeannette Dincin (b. Brooklyn, Aug. 26, 1902).

Ysaÿe's style of playing is best described as heroic; but his art was equally convincing in the expression of moods of exquisite delicacy and tenderness; his frequent employment of "tempo rubato" produced an effect of elasticity without distorting the melodic line. Ysaÿe was also a composer. His works include 8 violin concertos; 6 violin sonatas; *Poème nocturne* for Violin, Cello, and Strings; *Les Harmonies du soir* for String Quartet and String Orch.; *Divertimento* for Violin and Orch.; *Méditation* for Cello and String Orch.; *Chant d'hiver* for Violin and Chamber Orch.; *Trio de concert* for 2 Violins, Viola, and Orch.; *Amitié* for 2 Violins and Orch. At the age of 70 he began the composition of an opera in the Walloon language, *Piér li Houïeu (Peter the Miner),* which was produced in Liège on March 4, 1931, in the presence of the composer, who was brought to the theater in an invalid's chair, suffering from the extreme ravages of diabetes, which had necessitated the amputation of his left foot. He began the composition of a 2nd Walloon opera, *L'Avierge di Piér (La Vierge de Pierre),* but had no time to complete it. In 1937 Queen Elisabeth of Belgium inaugurated the annual Prix International Eugène Ysaÿe in Brussels; the first winner was the famous Russian violinist David Oistrakh.

Ysaÿe, Théophile, Belgian pianist and composer, brother of **Eugène Ysaÿe;** b. Verviers, March 22, 1865; d. Nice, March 24, 1918. He was a pupil at the Liège Cons.; then studied at the Kullak Academy in Berlin, and also took lessons from César Franck in Paris; returning to Belgium, he became director of the Académie de Musique in Brussels; was noted as a fine ensemble player, and gave sonata recitals with his brother; during the latter's absence on tours, he also conducted the Société des Concerts Ysaÿe in Brussels. After the invasion of Belgium in 1914, he went with his brother to London; fearful of the Zeppelin air raids on London, he went to Nice, where he remained until his death. He was a prolific composer; his brother conducted a concert of Théophile's works in Brussels, on Nov. 6, 1904, including the premieres of his Symph. in F major and the symph. poem *Le Cygne.* Other works are: Piano Concerto; symph. poems (*Les Abeilles, La Forêt et l'oiseau*); *Fantaisie sur un thème populaire wallon* for Orch.; Piano Quintet; piano pieces; a Requiem.

Yuasa, Joji, Japanese composer; b. Koriyama, Aug. 12, 1929. He was a medical student at Keio Univ.; studied composition in the "experimental workshop" in Tokyo (1951–57). In 1968 he received a Japan Society Fellowship for a lecture tour throughout the U.S. and Europe. In 1969 he was one of the organizers of the Crosstalk Festival of Japanese and American multimedia works in Tokyo and Osaka; was a member of the "tranSonic" composers' group, in association with Ichiyanagi, Matsudaira, Takemitsu, and others. In his productions he adopts the most advanced multimedia techniques.

WORKS: *Projection* for 7 Players (1955); *Cosmos Haptic* for Piano (1957); *Projection Topologic* for Piano (1959); *Aoi no Ue,* musique concrète (1961); *Interpenetration* for 2 Flutes (1963); *Projection Esemplastic* for Electronic Media (1964); *Kansoku* for Voices (1965); *Projection* for Cello and Piano (1967); *Projection* for several Kotos and Orch. (1967); *Projection* for Electric Guitars (1968); *Projection* for String Quartet (1970); *Triplicity* for Double Bass (1970); *Questions* for Chorus (1971); *On the Keyboard* for Piano (1971); *Interposiplaytion I* for Flute, Piano, and Percussion (1972) and *II* for Flute, Harp, and Percussion (1973); *Chronoplastic* for Orch. (1972; Tokyo, Nov. 15, 1972); *Territory* for

Marimba, Flute, Clarinet, Percussion, and Double Bass (1974); *Time of Orchestral Time* for Orch. (1976).

Yudina, Maria, eminent Russian pianist and pedagogue; b. Nevel, near Vitebsk, Sept. 9, 1899; d. Moscow, Nov. 19, 1970. She took piano lessons in Vitebsk with Frieda Teitelbaum-Levinson, a pupil of Anton Rubinstein. Then she enrolled at the Petrograd Cons., where studied piano with Anna Essipoff, Vladimir Drozdov, and Leonid Nikolayev; music theory with Maximilian Steinberg and J. Wihtol; and score reading with N. Tcherepnin and Emil Cooper. In 1921 she joined the piano faculty of the Petrograd Cons., holding this position until 1930. In 1932–34 she taught at the Cons. of Tiflis, Georgia. From 1936–51 she was a prof. at the Moscow Cons., and from 1944–60 taught piano and chamber music performance at the Gnessin Inst. in Moscow. Among her students was Andrei Balanchivadze (brother of George Balanchine). Yudina began her career as a pianist in 1921; gave her last concert in Moscow on May 18, 1969. She also was a guest artist in East Germany (1950) and in Poland (1954). She further publ. memoirs and reminiscences of famous composers she had met in Russia. Yudina enjoyed great renown as an intellectual musician capable of presenting the works she performed with a grand line, both didactic and inspired. But rather than accepting the traditional interpretation of classical music, she introduced a strong personal element differing from accepted norms, so that her performances of works by Bach, Mozart, Beethoven, and Brahms were revelations to some listeners, and abominations to the old school of pianism. Yudina was also an ardent champion of modern music, placing on her programs compositions by such masters of new techniques as Stravinsky, Schoenberg, Berg, Webern, and Bartók at a time when their works were not acceptable in Russia. She also played piano pieces by Soviet composers, particularly Prokofiev and Shostakovich. She gave numerous concerts of chamber music.

Yun, Isang, important Korean composer; b. Tongyong, Sept. 17, 1917. He studied Western music in Korea (1935–37) and in Japan (1941–43). After the war he taught music in South Korean schools; in 1956 he went to Berlin, where he took lessons in composition with Boris Blacher and Josef Rufer at the Berlin Hochschule für Musik. He settled permanently in Berlin, where he produced several successful theatrical works, marked by a fine expressionistic and coloristic quality, and written in an idiom of euphonious dissonance. His career was dramatically interrupted when, on June 17, 1967, he and his wife were brutally abducted from West Berlin by secret police agents of South Korea, and forced to board a plane for Seoul, where they were brought to trial for sedition; he was sentenced to life imprisonment; his wife was given 3 years in jail. This act of lawlessness perpetrated on the territory of another country prompted an indignant protest by the government of West Germany, which threatened to cut off its substantial economic aid to South Korea; 23 celebrated musicians, including Igor Stravinsky, issued a vigorous letter of protest. As a result of this moral and material pressure, South Korea released Yun and his wife after nearly 2 years of detention, and they returned to Germany. In 1970 he was appointed a prof. at the Hochschule für Musik in Berlin.

WORKS: Operas: *Der Traum des Liu-Tung* (Berlin, Sept. 25, 1965); *Die Witwe des Schmetterlings* (completed by him in his Seoul prison cell and produced in absentia in Bonn on Dec. 9, 1967; Eng. version as *Butterfly Widow,* Northwestern Univ., Evanston, Ill., Feb. 27, 1970); *Träume* (an amalgam of the previous 2 operas, Nuremberg, Feb. 23, 1969); *Geisterliebe* (1969–70; Kiel, Germany, June 20, 1971); *Sim Tjong* (1971–72; Munich, Aug. 1, 1972); *Symphonische Szene* (1960); *Bara* for Orch. (1960); *Colloides sonores* for String Orch. (1961); *Fluktuationen* for Orch. (1964; Berlin, Feb. 10, 1965); *Réak* for Orch. (Donaueschingen, Oct. 23, 1966); *Dimensionen* for Orch. (Nuremberg, Oct. 22, 1971); *Konzertante Figuren* for Small Orch. (1972; Hamburg, Nov. 30, 1973); *Ouvertüre* (1973–74); Cello Concerto (Royan, March 25, 1976); Concerto for Flute and Small Orch. (1977); Double Concerto for Oboe, Harp, and Small Orch. (1977); *Om mani padme hum,* cycle for Soprano, Baritone, Chorus, and Orch. (1964; Hannover, Jan. 30, 1965); *Namo* for 3 Sopranos and Orch. (Berlin, May 4, 1971); *Der weise Mann,* cantata after P. Salomo, for Baritone, Chorus, and Small Orch. (1977); *Musik* for 7 Instruments (1959); String Quartet No. 3 (1959; Nos. 1 and 2 were withdrawn); *Loyang* for Chamber Ensemble (1962); *Gasa* for Violin and Piano (1963); *Garak* for Flute and Piano (1963); *Nore* for Cello and Piano (1964); *Riul* for Clarinet and Piano (1968); *Images* for Flute, Oboe, Violin, and Cello (1968); *Glissées* for Solo Cello (1970); *Piri* for Solo Oboe (1971); *Gagok* for Guitar, Percussion, and Voice (1972); Trio for Flute, Oboe, and Violin (1972–73); *Memory* for Mezzo-soprano, Baritone, Narrator, and Percussion (1974); *Etüden* for Solo Flute (1974); *Harmonia* for 13 or 16 Winds, Harp, and Percussion (1974); *An der Schwelle,* 2 sonnets for Baritone, Female Chorus, Organ, and Instruments (1975); *Rondell* for Oboe, Clarinet, and Bassoon (1975); Piano Trio (1972–75); *Pièce concertante* for Chamber Ensemble (1976); Duo for Viola and Piano (1976); *Königliches Thema* for Solo Violin (1976); *5 Pieces* for Piano (1959); *Shao Yang Yin* for Harpsichord (1966); *Tuyaux sonores* for Organ (1967); *Fragment* for Organ (1975).

Yurgenson, Peter. See **Jurgenson, Pyotr.**

Yzac, Heinrich. See **Isaac, Heinrich.**

Z

Zabaleta, Nicanor, Spanish harpist; b. San Sebastian, Jan. 7, 1907. He went to Paris to study with Marcel Tournier; toured in Europe, South America, and the U.S. He is noted for his efforts to increase the number of works available for the harp, both by bringing to light neglected compositions of old composers, and by prompting modern composers to write music for the harp. In 1958 he made a long European tour as soloist with leading orchs.

Zabel, Albert Heinrich, German harpist; b. Berlin, Feb. 22, 1834; d. St. Petersburg, Feb. 16, 1910. He studied at the Inst. für Kirchenmusik in Berlin; toured Germany, Russia, England, and America with Gungl's orch. In 1862 he joined the staff of the newly founded St. Petersburg Cons., and held that post until his death. He composed a Harp Concerto and numerous short pieces for the harp (*Elégie fantastique, Légende, Marguérite au rouet, Am Springbrunnen, Chanson du pêcheur, Warum?, Murmure de cascade,* etc.); publ. a harp method (in German, French, and Eng.) and a pamphlet, *A Word to Composers about the Practical Employment of the Harp in the Orchestra* (St. Petersburg, 1899; in Russian and German).

Zacconi, Lodovico, Italian music theorist; b. Pesa-ro, June 11, 1555; d. Fiorenzuola, near Pesaro, March 23, 1627. He was a pupil of Baccusi and A. Gabrieli in Venice; studied theology in Padua; entered the Order of St. Augustine, and became maestro di cappella at the monastery of his order in Venice; was a tenor in the court chapel at Graz (1585), and at Munich (1590–96); then returned to Venice. His chief work, *Prattica di musica,* in 2 parts (Venice, 1592, 1619), contains treatises on mensural theory and counterpoint, detailed descriptions of contemporary musical instruments, and explanations for executing the ornaments in vocal polyphonic music. He also wrote 4 books of *Canoni musicali,* with comments and solutions (publ. by F. Vatielli, Pesaro, 1905); *Ricercari* for Organ, and 2 collections of examples of counterpoint, are still in MSS. His MS autobiography (written in 1626) is in the library of the Liceo Musicale, Bologna.

Zach, Max (Wilhelm), Austrian conductor and viola player; b. Lwow, Aug. 31, 1864; d. St. Louis, Feb. 3, 1921. He studied violin with Grün, harmony with Fuchs, and composition with Krenn at the Vienna Cons. In 1886 he emigrated to the U.S., and played first viola in the Boston Symph. Orch.; also was the violist in the Adamowski Quartet; for 10 seasons conducted the Boston Pops (1887–97). In 1907 he was appointed conductor of the St. Louis Symph. Orch., and held this post until his death.

Zachau (Zachow), Friedrich Wilhelm, German organist and composer; b. Leipzig (baptized, Nov. 14), 1663; d. Halle, Aug. 7, 1712. He studied with his father, who was a town musician in Leipzig, and learned to play the organ, violin, oboe, and harpsichord. From 1684 to his death he was organist of the Liebfrauenkirche in Halle, where Handel studied with him as a boy. Max Seiffert publ. Zachau's works in Denkmäler Deutscher Tonkunst (vols. 21, 22); organ pieces, chorale settings, etc., were publ. in Breitkopf & Härtel's *Sammlung von Präludien, Fugen . . .* and in *Organum.*

Zádor, Eugen, Hungarian-American composer; b. Bátaszék, Nov. 5, 1894; d. Hollywood, April 4, 1977. (In the U.S. he Americanized his name to **Eugene Zador.**) He studied music with a local teacher; in 1911 enrolled in the Vienna Cons.; studied composition with Richard Heuberger. In 1913 he went to Leipzig, where he took a course with Max Reger; also attended classes in musicology with Hermann Abert and Arnold Schering; continued musicological studies with Fritz Volbach at the Univ. of Münster; in 1921 he obtained his degree of Dr.Phil. with the dissertation *Wesen und Form der symphonischen Dichtung von Liszt bis Strauss.* He settled in Vienna and taught at the Neues Konservatorium there. Following the Anschluss of Austria by the Nazi regime in 1938, Zádor emigrated to the U.S.; he settled in Hollywood, where he became successful and prosperous as an orchestrator of film scores; made some 120 orchestrations in all; at the same time he continued to compose music in every conceivable genre. Zádor was a master of musical sciences, excelling in euphonious modern harmonies, and an expert weaver of contrapuntal voices; his colorful writing for instruments was exemplary. He possessed a special skill in handling Hungarian folk motifs in variation form; in this, he followed the tradition of Liszt. During his European period he composed some fashionable "machine music," as demonstrated with particular effect in his *Sinfonia tecnica.*
WORKS: OPERAS: *Diana* (Budapest, Dec. 22, 1923); *A holtak szigete (The Island of the Dead;* Budapest, March 29, 1928); *X-mal Rembrandt* (referring to the multiple copies of Rembrandt's self-portraits; Gera, May 24, 1930); *Asra* (Budapest, Feb. 15, 1936); *Christoph Columbus* (N.Y., Oct. 8, 1939); *Revisor (Inspector General),* after Gogol (1928; revised, reorchestrated, and finally brought to perf. for the first time in Los Angeles, June 11, 1971); *The Virgin and the Fawn* (Los Angeles, Oct. 24, 1964); *The Magic Chair* (Baton Rouge, La., May 14, 1966); *The Scarlet Mill* (Brooklyn, Oct. 26, 1968).
FOR ORCH.: Symph. poem, *Bánk bán* (1918); 4 symphs.: No. 1, *Romantische Symphonie* (1922); No. 2, *Sinfonia tecnica* (Paris, May 26, 1932); No. 3, *Tanzsymphonie* (Budapest, Feb. 8, 1937); No. 4, *Children's Symphony* (1941); *Variations on a Hungarian Folk Song* (Vienna, Feb. 9, 1927; his most

successful work of this type); *Rondo* (Vienna, 1934); *Hungarian Caprice* (Budapest, Feb. 1, 1935, followed by numerous perfs. in Europe and America); *Pastorale and Tarantella* (Chicago, Feb. 5, 1942); *Biblical Triptych* (Chicago, Dec. 9, 1943); *Elegie and Dance* (Philadelphia, March 12, 1954); *Divertimento* for Strings (1955); *Fugue-Fantasia* (1958); *Rhapsody* (Los Angeles, Feb. 5, 1961); *Christmas Overture* (1961); *The Remarkable Adventure of Henry Bold* for Narrator and Orch. (Beverly Hills, Calif., Oct. 24, 1963); *Variations on a Merry Theme* (1963; Birmingham, Ala., Jan. 12, 1965); *5 Contrasts for Orchestra* (Philadelphia, Jan. 8, 1965); Trombone Concerto (Rochester, Mich., July 20, 1967); *Rhapsody* for Cimbalom and Orch. (Los Angeles, Nov. 2, 1969); *Studies for Orchestra* (Detroit, Nov. 12, 1970); *Fantasia hungarica* for Double Bass and Orch. (1970); *Hungarian Scherzo* for Orch. (1975).

Zafred, Mario, Italian composer and conductor; b. Trieste, Feb. 21, 1922. He studied with Pizzetti at the Santa Cecilia Academy in Rome; was music critic of *Unità* (1949–56) and *Giustizia* (1956–63); then conducted opera in Trieste and in Rome. In conformity with his political philosophy of Communism, he renounced the modernistic trends of his musical environment and wrote music in an idiom accessible to the common people.
WORKS: Operas: *Amleto* (Rome, 1961) and *Wallenstein* (Rome, 1965); 7 symphs. (1943, 1944, 1949, 1950, 1954, 1958, 1970); *Sinfonia breve* for String Orch. (1955); Flute Concerto (1951); Violin Concerto (1953); Triple Concerto for Violin, Cello, Piano, and Orch. (1954); Harp Concerto (1956); Viola Concerto (1957); Cello Concerto (1958); Piano Concerto (1960); Concerto for 2 Pianos and Orch. (1961); *Metamorfosi* for Orch. (1964); Concerto for Strings (1969); String Sextet (1967); Wind Quintet (1952); 4 string quartets (1941, 1947, 1948, 1953); 3 piano trios (1942, 1945, 1954); 4 piano sonatas (1941, 1943, 1950, 1960); numerous choruses and solo songs.

Zagiba, Franz, Slovak music scholar; b. Rosenau, Oct. 20, 1912; d. Vienna, Aug. 12, 1977. He studied music and philology at the Univ. of Vienna; received his Ph.D. in 1937 from the Univ. of Bratislava; joined the staff of the Univ. of Vienna in 1972 was named a full prof. there. He publ. *Die Musikdenkmäler der Franziskanerklöster in der Ostslowakei* (Prague, 1940); *Geschichte der slowakischen Musik* (vol. I, Bratislava, 1943; in Czech, with German summary); *Opernführer* (Bratislava, 1947); *Chopin und Wien* (Vienna, 1951); *Tschaikovskij, Leben und Werk* (Zürich, 1953); *Johann L. Bella (1843–1936) und das wiener Musikleben* (Vienna, 1955); *Zur Errichtung einer Chopin-Gedächtnisstätte in Wien* (Vienna, 1970); numerous valuable articles dealing with music in Slovakia and historical developments in Slavic music.

Zagortsev, Vladimir, Soviet composer; b. Kiev, Oct. 27, 1944. He studied composition with Boris Lyatoshinsky and Andrei Shtogarenko at the Kiev

Cons. Upon graduation, he joined a group of Soviet avant-garde composers who were active in Kiev and who followed the Western techniques. Zagortsev set for himself the task of organizing the elements of pitch, rhythm, dynamics, and tone color in a total serial procedure, but he never abandoned the ethnic resources of Ukrainian folk songs, which remain the thematic source of many of his works, even those written in an extreme modern style.

WORKS: *Priskazki,* vocal cycle on Ukrainian folk texts (1963); Violin Sonata (1964); String Quartet (1964); *Obyomi (Sizes)* for 5 Instruments (1965); *Gradations* for Chamber Group (1966); *Games* for Chamber Orch. (1967–68); Symph. No. 1 (1968); *Music for 4 Strings* No. 1 (1968); Sonata for Strings, Piano, and Percussion (1969); *Rhythms* for Piano (1969–70); Symph. No. 2 for Soprano, Tenor, and Orch., on Ukrainian folk texts (1976–78); Oboe Sonata (1978); *Music for 4 Strings* No. 2 (1978); *A Day in Pereyaslavl* for Soloists, Chorus, and Orch., on Ukrainian folk texts (1978–79); *In the Children's Room,* cantata on Russian folk texts (1978–79).

Zagwijn, Henri, Dutch composer; b. Nieuwer-Amstel, July 17, 1878; d. The Hague, Oct. 23, 1954. He had no formal education in music, but followed the trends of Impressionism and wrote music in the modern French style. In 1916 he was appointed a teacher at the Rotterdam School of Music; in 1918, founded (with Sem Dresden) the Society of Modern Composers in the Netherlands; he later settled in The Hague. From 1931 he was a teacher at the Rotterdam Cons. He was a follower of Rudolf Steiner's anthroposophic movement, and publ. *De muziek in het licht der anthroposophie* (1925); also publ. a biography of Debussy (The Hague, 1940).

Zajc, Ivan. See **Zaytz, Giovanni von.**

Zallinger, Meinhard von, Austrian conductor; b. Vienna, Feb. 25, 1897. He studied piano and conducting at the Salzburg Mozarteum; also took music courses at the Univ. of Innsbruck. He conducted at the Mozarteum (1920–22); then was on the staff of the Bavarian State Opera in Munich (1926–29) and the Cologne Opera (1929–35). He returned to the Bavarian State Opera in 1935, conducting there until 1944; was then made Generalmusikdirektor in Duisburg. In 1947 he became director of the Mozarteum Orch.; also held the same office at the Salzburg Landestheater. He was music director in Graz (1949–50) and of the Vienna Volksoper (1950–53) and the Komische Oper in East Berlin (1953–56). He served again as a conductor at the Bavarian State Opera (1956–73); was concurrently director of the summer academy at the Mozarteum (1956–68).

Zamboni, Luigi, noted Italian bass; b. Bologna, 1767; d. Florence, Feb. 28, 1837. He made his debut in 1791 in Ravenna in *Fanatico in Berlin* by Cimarosa; then sang throughout Italy, establishing himself as one of the finest interpreters of buffo roles of his time; 1816 he created the role of Figaro in Rossini's *Il Barbiere di Siviglia.* He retired from the stage in 1825.

Zandonai, Riccardo, Italian composer; b. Sacco, Trentino, May 30, 1883; d. Pesaro, June 5, 1944. He was a pupil of Gianferrari at Rovereto (1893–98); then studied with Mascagni at the Liceo Rossini in Pesaro. He graduated in 1902; for his final examination he composed a symph. poem for Solo Voices, Chorus, and Orch., *Il ritorno di Odisseo.* He then turned to opera, which remained his favored genre throughout his career. His first opera was *Il grillo del focolare,* based on *The Cricket on the Hearth* of Dickens and produced in Turin on Nov. 28, 1908, with excellent success. With his next opera, *Conchita,* after the novel *La Femme et le pantin* by Pierre Louÿs (Milan, Oct. 14, 1911), he established himself as an important Italian composer; the title role was created by the soprano **Tarquinia Tarquini,** whom Zandonai married in 1917. *Conchita* received its American premiere in San Francisco on Sept. 28, 1912; as *La Femme et le pantin* it was given at the Opéra-Comique in Paris on March 11, 1929. Zandonai's reputation was enhanced by subsequent works, notably *Francesca da Rimini,* after Gabriele d'Annunzio (Turin, Feb. 19, 1914; Metropolitan Opera, N.Y., Dec. 22, 1916), but a previous opera, *Melenis* (Milan, Nov. 13, 1912), was unsuccessful. During World War I Zandonai participated in the political agitation for the return of former Italian provinces; he wrote a student hymn calling for the redemption of Trieste (1915). His other operas were: *La via della finestra* (Pesaro, July 27, 1919; revised version, Trieste, Jan. 18, 1923); *Giulietta e Romeo* (Rome, Feb. 14, 1922); *I Cavalieri di Ekebù* (Milan, March 7, 1925); *Giuliano* (Naples, Feb. 4, 1928); *Una partita* (Milan, Jan. 19, 1933); and *La farsa amorosa,* after Alarcón's *El sombrero de tres picos* (Rome, Feb. 22, 1933). He further wrote the symph. poems *Primavera in Val di Sole* (1908), *Patria lontana* (1918), *Fra gli alberghi delle Dolomiti* (1932); *Concerto romantico* for Violin and Orch. (1921); *Concerto andaloso* for Cello and Small Orch. (1937); *Rapsodia trentina* for Orch. (1937); *Messa da Requiem;* some chamber music. In 1939 he was appointed director of the Liceo Rossini in Pesaro, remaining there for the rest of his life.

Zandt, Marie Van. See **Van Zandt, Marie.**

Zanella, Amilcare, Italian composer; b. Monticelli d'Ongina, Piacenza, Sept. 26, 1873; d. Pesaro, Jan. 9, 1949. He studied with Andreotti in Cremona, then with Bottesini at the Parma Cons., graduating in 1891. In 1892 he went to South America as a pianist and opera conductor; returning to Italy in 1901, he organized his own orch., giving symph. concerts in the principal Italian cities and introducing his own works. He then was director of the Parma Cons. (1903–5); succeeded Mascagni as director of the Liceo Rossini in Pesaro in 1905, and held this post until 1939, when he was succeeded by Zandonai.

WORKS: Operas: *Aura* (Pesaro, Aug. 27, 1910); *La Sulamita* (Piacenza, Feb. 11, 1926); *Il Revisore,* after Gogol (Trieste, Feb. 20, 1940); Symph.; 2 symph.

poems: *Fede* and *Vita and Festa campestre; Danza paesana* for Orch.; *Fantasia e Fugato* for Piano and Orch.; Nonet for Strings, Woodwind Instruments, and Piano; Piano Trio; a number of piano pieces (*Due leggende, Passero solitario, Canto d'anima, Ansia,* etc.).

Zanelli (original name, **Morales**), **Renato,** Chilean tenor; b. Valparaiso, April 1, 1892; d. Santiago, March 25, 1935. He studied in Santiago; made his debut as a baritone there as Valentine in 1916. On Nov. 19, 1919, he appeared for the first time with the Metropolitan Opera in N.Y. as Amonasro; he remained on its roster until 1923; then went to Milan, where he resumed vocal studies; made his debut as a tenor in the role of Raoul at the Teatro San Carlo in Naples in 1924; subsequently appeared in Rome, in London (Covent Garden, 1928–30), at La Scala in Milan (1920–32), and at the Teatro Colón in Buenos Aires.

Zanettini, Antonio. See **Gianettini, Antonio.**

Zangius, Nikolaus, German organist and composer; b. c.1570; d. Berlin, c.1618. He was a chamber musician in Braunschweig (1597); went to Danzig as deputy Kapellmeister (1599) and soon became Kapellmeister at the Marienkirche; left at the outbreak of the plague in 1602; was active in the imperial court in Prague until 1605; returned to Danzig in 1607, but soon went to Stettin; finally returned to his court post in Prague in 1610. He was active in Berlin as Kapellmeister to the Elector of Brandenburg from 1612. He composed a cappella works: choruses, motets, and a number of quodlibets. His *Cantiones sacrae* and 3-part German songs are reprinted in Denkmäler der Tonkunst in Österreich, 87.

Zanten, Cornelia Van. See **Van Zanten, Cornelia.**

Zappa, Frank, seeded American rock artist; b. Baltimore, Dec. 21, 1940, of Italian descent (Zappa means "hoe" in Italian). His full name was **Francis Vincent Zappa.** The family moved to California. From his school days he played guitar and organized groups with weird names such as The Omens and Captain Glasspack and His Magic Mufflers. In 1960 he composed the sound track for the film *The World's Greatest Sinner,* and in 1963 he wrote another sound track, *Run Home Slow.* In 1965 he joined the rhythm-and-blues band The Soul Giants; he soon took it under his own aegis and thought up for it the surrealist logo *The Mothers of Invention.* His recording of it, and another album, *Freak Out!,* became underground hits; along with *We're Only in It for the Money* and *Cruising with Ruben and The Jets,* these works constituted the earliest "concept" albums, touching every nerve in a gradually decivilized California life-style—rebellious, anarchistic, incomprehensible, and yet tantalizing. The band became a mixed-media celebration of total artistic, political, and social opposition to the Establish-

ment, the ingredients of their final album, *Mothermania.* Moving farther afield, Zappa produced a video-movie, *200 Motels,* glorifying itinerant sex activities. He became a cult figure, and as such suffered the penalty of violent adulation. Playing in London in 1971, he was painfully injured when a besotted fan pushed him off the stage. Similar assaults forced Zappa to hire an athletic bodyguard for protection. In 1982 his planned appearance in Palermo, Sicily, the birthplace of his parents, had to be cancelled because the mob rioted in anticipation of the event. He deliberately confronted the most cherished social and emotional sentiments by putting on such songs as *Broken Hearts Are for Assholes,* and his release *Jewish Princess* offended, mistakenly, the sensitivity of American Jews. His production *Joe's Garage* contained Zappa's favorite scatological materials, and he went on analyzing and ridiculing urinary functions in such numbers as *Why Does It Hurt When I Pee.* He managed to upset the members of his own faith in the number titled *Catholic Girls.* His *Hot Rats,* a jazz-rock release, included the famous *Willie the Pimp,* and exploited the natural revulsion to unclean animals. In 1980 he produced the film *Baby Snakes,* which shocked even the most impervious senses. He declared in an interview that classical music is only "for old ladies and faggots." But he astounded the musical community when he proclaimed his total adoration of the music of Edgar Varèse and gave a lecture on Varèse in N.Y. Somehow, without formal study, he managed to absorb the essence of Varèse's difficult music. This process led Zappa to produce truly astonishing full orch. scores reveling in artful dissonant counterpoint, *Bob in Dacron and Sad Jane* and *Mo' 'n Herb's Vacation,* and the cataclysmic *Penis Dimension* for chorus, soloists, and orch., with a text so anatomically precise that it could not be performed for any English-speaking audience. An accounting of Zappa's scatological and sexological proclivities stands in remarkable contrast to his unimpeachable private life and total abstention from alcohol and narcotic drugs. An unexpected reflection of Zappa's own popularity was the emergence of his adolescent daughter, curiously named Moon Unit, as a voice-over speaker on his hit *Valley Girls,* in which she used the vocabulary of growing womanhood of the San Fernando Valley near Los Angeles, with such locutions as "Grody to the Max" (repellent) and "Barfs Me Out" (disgusting).

Zarlino, Gioseffo (Zarlinus Clodiensis), important Italian music theorist and composer; b. Chioggia, probably in Jan. 1517; d. Venice, Feb. 4, 1590. He entered the Franciscan order in 1539, and in 1541 went to Venice, where he became a pupil of Willaert. In 1565 he succeeded his fellow pupil Cipriano de Rore as maestro di cappella at San Marco, holding this position until his death; also held the office of chaplain at San Severo. He was greatly esteemed not only as a teacher but also as a composer; indeed, Foscarini describes him as "the famous regenerator of music in all Italy." Most of Zarlino's MSS are lost; his extant works comprise *21 modulationes 6* *vocum* (Venice, 1566; ed. by Zarlino's pupil Usberti), *3 lectiones pro mortuis* (part of a collection of motets *a* 4 by Cipriano de Rore and others; publ. by Scotto, Venice, 1563), and a Mass (MS in the library of the Liceo Filarmonico in Bologna). Two motets *a* 5 were publ. by L. Torchi in *L'arte musicale in Italia* (vol. I).

Zarlino's lasting significance lies in his theoretical works, particularly the *Istituzioni armoniche* (in 4 sections; Venice, 1558; republ. 1562, 1573), in which Zarlino treats the major and minor thirds as inversions within a fifth, and consequently, the major and minor triads as mutual mirror reflections of component intervals, thus anticipating the modern dualism of Rameau, Tartini, Hauptmann, and Riemann; he also gives lucid and practical demonstrations of double counterpoint and canon, illustrated by numerous musical examples; while adhering to the system of 12 modes, he places the Ionian rather than the Dorian mode at the head of the list, thus pointing toward the emergence of the major scale as the preponderant mode; he gives 10 rules for proper syllabification of the text in musical settings; suggests equal temperament for the tuning of the lute. In 1571 he publ. *Dimostrationi armoniche,* in the form of 5 dialogues between Willaert and his disciples and friends. Zarlino's theories were attacked, with a violence uncommon even for the polemical spirit of the age, by Vincenzo Galilei, one of his former pupils, in *Dialogo della musica antica e della moderna* (Florence, 1581) and *Discorso intorno alle opere di Gioseffo Zarlino* (Florence, 1589). In reply to the first of Galilei's books, Zarlino publ. *Sopplimenti musicali* (Venice, 1588). Collected works of Zarlino (4 vols.), publ. in Venice in 1589, included, in addition to his former books, a theological tract, *Trattato della pazienza.* Books III and IV of the *Istituzioni armoniche* are publ. in Eng. trans. in O. Strunk, *Source Readings in Music History* (N.Y., 1950).

Zarotus, Antonio, Italian music printer, active in Milan. He printed a *Missale Romanum* dated April 26, 1476, in which he used for the first time movable type for the music (the type is in Gothic style). This incunabulum was publ. 6 months earlier than the Missale of Ulrich Han, at one time considered the earliest specimen of music printed from movable type.

Zavertal, Ladislao, Italian bandmaster (of Bohemian extraction); b. Milan, Sept. 29, 1849; d. Cadenabbia, Jan. 29, 1942. He was the son of the clarinetist **Wenceslas Hugo Zavertal** (1821–99). After studying at home, he went to Treviso (where he produced an opera) and then to Milan (1869). In 1871 he went to Glasgow, where he conducted various orch. groups; in 1881 he became bandmaster of the Royal Artillery Band at Woolwich; from 1895 to 1905 he conducted Sunday band concerts at Albert Hall in London, which enjoyed considerable popularity. He returned to Italy in 1906. He was a voluminous composer; wrote operas, symphs., and band pieces; received various honors from the governments of En-

gland, Italy, Greece, Serbia, and Turkey.

Zaytz, Giovanni von (real name, **Ivan Zajc**), Croatian composer; b. Fiume, Aug. 3, 1831; d. Zagreb, Dec. 16, 1914. He was trained by his father, a bandmaster in the Austrian army; then in Milan by Lauro Rossi. Returning to Fiume, he conducted the municipal band; then was a theater conductor in Vienna (1862–70). Upon entering professional life, he changed his name to Giovanni von Zaytz. In 1870 he settled in Zagreb; was conductor of the Zagreb Opera (1870–89) and director of the Cons. there (until 1908). He composed about 1,200 works of all descriptions (among them 20 operas), and was the author of the first Croatian national opera, *Nikola Šubrič Zrinski* (Zagreb, Nov. 4, 1876). He also wrote several Italian operas, of which *Amelia, ossia Il Bandito* (Fiume, April 14, 1860) enjoyed considerable popularity. Other operas and operettas (all produced by him in Vienna) are: *Mannschaft an Bord* (Dec. 15, 1863); *Fitzliputzli* (Nov. 5, 1864); *Die Lazzaroni vom Stanzel* (May 4, 1865); *Die Hexe von Boissy* (April 24, 1866); *Nachtschwärmer* (Nov. 10, 1866); *Das Rendezvous in der Schweiz* (April 3, 1867); *Das Gaugericht* (Sept. 14, 1867); *Nach Mekka* (Jan. 11, 1868); *Somnambula* (Jan. 25, 1868); *Schützen von Einst und Jetzt* (July 25, 1868); *Meister Puff* (May 22, 1869); *Der gefangene Amor* (Sept. 12, 1874). In addition, he wrote incidental music for 23 plays; 60 cantatas; 250 choral works, sacred and secular; 40 overtures; symph. poems; more than 200 songs.

Zbinden, Julien-François, Swiss composer; b. Rolle, Nov. 11, 1917. He studied at the Cons. of Lausanne; then was a pupil of Marie Panthès (piano) and René Gerber (composition). After playing in jazz orchs., he became a pianist and assistant director of Radio Lausanne in 1947; in 1956 he joined the Service Musical of Radio-Television Suisse Romande; in 1973 he became president of the Assoc. of Swiss Musicians.
WORKS: Opera, *Fait divers* (1960); farce-ballet, *La Pantoufle,* for 5 Soloists and 2 Pianos (1958); 4 "pièces radiophoniques": *Microbus 666* (1955), *Le Petit Garçon de l'autobus* (1958), *Esperanto* (1961), and *Ethiopiques* (1971–72); Piano Concerto (1944); Concertino for Trumpet, String, and Timpani (1946); *Divertissement* for Double Bass and Orch. (1948); *Concerto da camera* for Piano and String Orch. (1950–51); 2 symphs. (1953, 1951–57); *Fantaisie* for Flute and Chamber Orch. (1954); *Suite française* for String Orch. (1954); *Rhapsodie* for Violin and Orch. (1956); *Jazzific 59–16* for Jazz Group and Strings (1958); *Ballade* for Bassoon and Orch. (1961); *Concerto breve* for Cello and Orch. (1962); Violin Concerto (1962–64); *Orchalau-Concerto* for Orch. (1962); *Lémunic 70,* overture (1970); Concerto for Orch. (1977); *Terra Dei,* oratorio (1966–67); *Monophrases* for Chorus, 2 Pianos, and 6 Percussionists (1970); *Jardins,* suite for Baritone, Soprano, and Orch. (1974); Septet (1947); String Trio (1949); Trio for Trumpet, Horn, and Trombone (1949); Violin Sonata (1950); *3 Pieces* for 4 Horns (1953); *Partita* for Violin and Cello (1954); *Prelude, Fugue and*

Postlude for Trumpet and Piano (1963); Capriccio for Flute, English Horn, Bassoon, Violin, and Harpsichord (1968); *Sonate en Trio* for 2 Viole da Gamba and Harpsichord (1969); *Dialogue* for Trumpet and Organ (1972–73); *Introduction and Scherzo-Valse* for Flute and Harp (1974).

Zecchi, Adone, Italian composer and conductor; b. Bologna, July 23, 1904. He studied composition with Franco Alfano at the Liceo Musicale in Bologna, graduating in 1926; in 1930 he established the Orch. Bolognese de Camera, and also organized the choral group Corale Euridice, which he led from 1927 to 1943; in 1942 he was appointed to the faculty of the Bologna Cons.; he became its director in 1961. In his compositions he follows the path of Italian neo-Classicism, but applies dodecaphonic formulas in some of his music.
WORKS: *Partita* for Orch. (1933); *Toccata, Ricercare e Finale* for Orch. (1941); *2 astrazioni in forma di fuga* for Small Ensemble (Copenhagen, Festival of the International Society for Contemporary Music, June 2, 1947); *Requiem* for Chorus and Orch. (1946); *Caleidofonia* for Violin, Piano, and Orch. (1963); *Trattenimento musicale* for 11 groups of String Instruments (1969). He publ. a number of manuals on choral conducting, including the reference work *Il coro nella storia e dizionario dei nomi e dei termini* (Bologna, 1960) and *Il direttore di coro* (Milan, 1965). In collaboration with R. Allorto he brought out *Educazione musicale* (Milan, 1962); *Canti natalizi di altri paesi* (Milan, 1965); *Canti natalizi italiani* (Milan, 1965); *Canti della vecchia America* (Milan, 1966); and *Il mondo della musica* (Milan, 1969).

Zecchi, Carlo, Italian pianist and conductor; b. Rome, July 8, 1903. He studied piano with Artur Schnabel and Busoni in Berlin; began his concert career as a pianist at the age of 17, and in 1931 made a tour of the U.S. In 1938 he became interested in conducting and made excellent progress in his new career; appeared as a guest conductor in Vienna, Amsterdam, London, and Leningrad; also made tours as a conductor in the U.S., South America, and Japan.

Zedda, Alberto, Italian conductor and musicologist; b. Milan, Jan. 2, 1928. He studied conducting at the Milan Cons. with Votto and Giulini; in 1956 made his debut as a conductor in Milan. He subsequently went to the U.S., where he taught at the Cincinnati College of Music (1957–59). Returning to Europe, he conducted at the Deutsche Oper in West Berlin (1961–63); then conducted at the N.Y. City Opera. With Philip Gossett, he served as co-editor of the complete works of Rossini.

Zeisl, Eric, Austrian-American composer; b. Vienna, May 18, 1905; d. Los Angeles, Feb. 18, 1959. A son of prosperous parents who owned a coffeehouse, he entered the Vienna State Academy of Music at 14; publ. his first songs at 16. In 1934 he won the Austrian State Prize for his *Requiem concertante*. After

the seizure of Austria by the Nazis in 1938, he fled to Paris, and at the outbreak of World War II in 1939, went to the U.S.: in 1941 he settled in Los Angeles; in 1945 he became an American citizen. He taught at the Southern Calif. School of Music; from 1949 until his death he was on the staff at Los Angeles City College. Increasingly conscious in exile of his Jewish heritage, he selected biblical themes for his stage works; death interrupted the composition of his major work, the music drama *Job;* Hebraic cantillation is basic to this mood. His style of composition reflects the late Romantic school of Vienna, imbued with poetic melancholy, with relief provided by eruptions of dancing optimism. He was at his best in his song cycles.
WORKS: Children's opera, *Die Fahrt ins Wunderland* (Vienna, 1934); *Leonce und Lena* (1937; Los Angeles, 1952); ballets: *Pierrot in der Flasche* (Vienna Radio, 1935); *Uranium 235* (1946); *Naboth's Vineyard* (1953); *Jacob und Rachel* (1954); for Orch.: *Kleine Symphonie* (Vienna Radio, May 30, 1937); *Passacaglia-Fantasie* (Vienna, Nov. 4, 1937); *November,* suite for Chamber Orch. (N.Y., Jan. 25, 1941); *Cossack Dance* (from the unfinished music drama *Job,* Hollywood, Aug. 18, 1946); *Return of Ulysses,* suite for Chamber Orch. (Chicago, Nov. 17, 1948); *Variations and Fugue on Christmas Carols* (1950); Piano Concerto (1951); *Concerto grosso* for Cello and Orch. (1956); chamber music: Trio for Flute, Viola, and Harp (1956); Violin Sonata (1950); Viola Sonata (1950); Cello Sonata (1951); vocal works: *Requiem ebraico* (1945); *Mondbilder* for Baritone and Orch. (1928); choruses; the song cycles *Kinderlieder* for Soprano; *6 Lieder* for Baritone.

Zeisler, Fannie (Bloomfield), noted pianist; b. Bielitz, Austrian Silesia, July 16, 1863; d. Chicago, Aug. 20, 1927. Her original name was **Blumenfeld;** it was changed to Bloomfield when the family settled in Chicago in 1868. Her first teachers there were Carl Wolfsohn and Bernhard Ziehn. She made her concert debut in Chicago on Feb. 26, 1875; in 1878 she went to Vienna, where she studied with Leschetizky (1878–83). From 1883 until 1893 she played annually in the U.S.; in 1893 she made a tour of Germany and Austria, which established her reputation as one of the best women pianists; other European tours followed in 1894–95, 1898, 1902–3, 1911–12, and the spring of 1914. She then returned to Chicago; made her farewell appearance there on Feb. 25, 1925, in a special concert to mark her golden jubilee. On Oct. 18, 1885, she married Sigmund Zeisler, a Chicago lawyer.

Zeitlin, Zvi, violinist; b. Dubrovnik, Yugoslavia, Feb. 21, 1923. He was educated at the Juilliard School of Music in N.Y.; then began his career as a soloist with leading orchs. in America and Europe; also gave many recitals. In 1967 he joined the faculty of the Eastman School of Music in Rochester, N.Y. He appeared as a soloist in the U.S., South America, Europe, and Israel; was particularly noted for his intelligent performances of modern violin concertos.

Zelenka, Jan Dismas, Bohemian composer; b. Lou-ňovice, Oct. 16, 1679; d. Dresden, Dec. 22, 1745. He received his general education in Prague; in 1710 he joined the court orch. in Dresden, playing the double bass; then studied with Lotti in Italy (1716) and with Fux in Vienna (1717–19). In 1719 he returned to Dresden, where he became assistant to Heinichen. In 1735 he was given the title of Kirchen-Compositeur. He was a prolific composer; wrote much church music, including 21 masses, 3 Requiems, and many motets; 3 Italian oratorios, etc.; a melodrama, *De Sancto Venceslao;* also an interesting overture, *Hypocondria.*

Zeleński, Wladislaw, Polish composer and pedagogue; b. Grodkowice, near Cracow, July 6, 1837; d. Cracow, Jan. 23, 1921. He studied with Mirecki in Cracow, Krejči in Prague, and Reber in Paris. He returned to Poland in 1871; was a teacher of theory at the Warsaw Cons. (1872–81). In 1881 he organized the Cracow Cons., and remained its director until his death; he also taught piano and theory there. As a pedagogue, he enjoyed a very high reputation; among his pupils were Stojowski, Opienski, and Szopski.

Železný, Lubomír, Czech composer; b. Ostrava, March 16, 1925; d. Prague, Sept. 27, 1979. He studied composition with Karel Janeček at the Prague Cons. (1945–48) and with Bořkovec at the Prague Academy of Musical Arts (1948–50). He worked in the music dept. of Prague Radio before 1951; arranged songs for the Vít Nejedlý Army Artistic Ensemble (1951–56); was chairman of the Union of Czech Composers and Concert Artists (1972–79).
WORKS: 2 *Gavottes* for Orch. (1954); 2 violin concertos (1958–59, 1974–75); 2 symphs.: No. 1 for Large Orch. (1961–62) and No. 2 for Small Orch. (1970); Concerto for Flute, Strings, and Piano (1966); Cello Concerto (1968); *Concertant Music* for Viola, Strings, and Piano (1969); *Festive March* for Orch. (1971); *Brigand Songs* for Tenor and Orch. (1958); Flute Sonata (1943); Trio for Flute, Viola, and Cello (1946); 2 violin sonatas (1948, 1971); Quartet for Flute, Violin, Viola, and Cello (1948); 2 string quartets (1959–60, 1968); Piano Trio (1966); Quintet for 2 Violins, Clarinet, Viola, and Cello (1969); Wind Quintet (1970); choruses; songs.

Zeljenka, Ilja, Slovak composer; b. Bratislava, Dec. 21, 1932. He studied composition with Cikker, piano with Macudzinski, and esthetics with Ferenczy at the Bratislava Academy of Music and Dramatic Arts (1951–56). He was dramaturge of the Slovak Phil. in Bratislava (1957–61) and lecturer for Bratislava Radio (1961–68); in 1961 he and Ivan Statdrucker established at Czech Radio in Bratislava the first electronic music studio in Czechoslovakia. After a period of infatuation with hedonistic simplicity laced with permissible discords, he turned toward modern sonorism, including electronics.
WORKS: *Suite* for Small Orch. (1952); 2 piano quintets (1953, 1959); 3 symphs. (1954; for String Orch., 1960; 1975); *Dramatic Overture* (1955); *Baga-*

telles for Piano (1955); *Ballad* for Chorus and Orch. (1957); 2 piano sonatas (1958, 1975); *Oswieczym,* melodrama on the tragedy of the infamous Nazi concentration camp, for 2 Narrators, 2 Choruses, and Orch. (1960; Bratislava, April 29, 1965); 7 *Compositional Studies* for Chamber Ensemble (1962); ballet, *Cosmos* (1962–63); 2 string quartets (1963, 1976); *Štruktúry (Structures)* for Orch. (1964); *Metamorphoses XV,* after Ovid, for Speaker and 9 Instruments (1964); *Polymetric Quartet* for 4 Piano Parts (1965); *Hudba (Music)* for Chorus and Orch. (1965); Piano Concerto (1966); *Zaklínadlá (Incantations)* for Chorus and Orch. (1967); *Hry (Games),* musical dada for 13 Singers playing Bells and Drums (1968); *Musica polymetrica* for 4 String Quartets (1970); *Meditation* for Orch. (1971); Violin Concerto (1974); Piano Trio (1975); *Elegy* for Chamber Orch. (1975).

Zelle, Friedrich, German musicologist; b. Berlin, Jan. 24, 1845; d. there, Sept. 10, 1927. He studied piano with Kullak, composition with Geyer and Bellermann; taught at the Humboldt Akademie in Berlin (1875–92) and later was director of the Berlin Realschule (1893–1915). He edited Hassler's *Lustgarten* (1887), J.W. Franck's *Choral-kantate* (1890), and Keiser's opera *Jodelet* (1892); also Passions by Sebastiani and Theile for Denkmäler Deutscher Tonkunst, 17.

Zeller, Karl, Austrian composer of operettas; b. St. Peter-in-der-Au, June 19, 1842; d. Baden, near Vienna, Aug. 17, 1898. He was an official in the Austrian Ministry of Education. Although following music only as an avocation, he became one of the most popular operetta composers of the day, winning extraordinary success with his *Der Vogelhändler* (Vienna, Jan. 10, 1891) and *Der Obersteiger* (Vienna, Jan. 5, 1894). Other successful operettas (all produced in Vienna) were *Joconda* (March 18, 1876), *Die Carbonari* (Nov. 27, 1880), *Der Vagabund* (Oct. 30, 1886), and *Der Kellermeister* (Dec. 21, 1901).

Zelter, Carl Friedrich, eminent German composer and teacher; b. Berlin, Dec. 11, 1758; d. there, May 15, 1832. The son of a mason, he was brought up in the same trade, but his musical inclinations soon asserted themselves; he studied organ, and at the age of 18 had a cantata of his composition performed in a church; then he became a pupil of C.F.C. Fasch and Kirnberger; was engaged as music director in Rellstab's Liebhaber-Konzerte; in 1786 he brought out a funeral cantata on the death of Frederick the Great; in 1791 he joined the Singverein (later Singakademie) conducted by Fasch, often acting as his deputy, and succeeding him in 1800. He was elected associate ("Assessor") of the Akademie in 1806; became a prof. in 1809. In 1807 he organized a Ripienschule for orch. practice; and in 1809 he founded in Berlin the Liedertafel, a pioneer men's choral society which became famous; similar organizations were subsequently formed throughout Germany, and later in America. Zelter composed about 100 men's choruses for the Liedertafel. In 1822 he founded the Royal Inst. for Church Music, of which he was director until his death (the Inst. was later reorganized as the Akademie für Kirchen- und Schulmusik). Goethe greatly admired Zelter's musical settings of his poems, preferring them to Schubert's and Beethoven's; this predilection led to their friendship, which was reflected in a voluminous correspondence, *Briefwechsel zwischen Goethe und Zelter* (ed. in 6 vols. by F.W. Riemer, Berlin, 1833–34; ed. in 3 vols. by L. Geiger, Leipzig, 1906; ed. in 4 vols. by M. Hecker, Leipzig, 1913; Eng. trans. by A.D. Coleridge, London, 1887). His songs are historically important, since they form a link between old ballad types and the new art of the lied, which found its flowering in Schubert and Schumann. Zelter's settings of Goethe's *König von Thule* and of *Es ist ein Schuss gefallen* became extremely popular. Other songs were publ. in collections of 12 each (1796 and 1801), followed by other albums: *Sämtliche Lieder, Balladen, Romanzen* (1810 et seq.), *Neue Sammlung* (1821), and *6 deutsche Lieder* (1827). New editions were brought out by Jöde (1930), Landshoff (1932), etc.; the cantatas *Johanna Sebus* and *Die Gunst des Augenblicks* were publ. by Müller-Blattau. He publ. a biography of Fasch (Berlin, 1801). Zelter's autobiography was first publ. under the title *C.F. Zelter. Eine Lebensbeschreibung nach autobiographischen Manuscripten,* ed. by W. Rintel; then as *C.F. Zelter. Darstellungen seines Lebens* (Weimar, 1931).

Zeltser, Mark, talented Russian-born American pianist; b. Kishinev, April 8, 1947. He began piano lessons with his mother as a small child, and at the age of 9 was a soloist with the Kishinev Phil.; then studied with Flier at the Moscow Cons., graduating in 1971; he won a prize at the Marguerite Long-Jacques Thibaud Competition in Paris, and at the Busoni Competition in Italy; in 1976 he emigrated to the U.S., making his home in N.Y.; in 1977 played at the Salzburg Festival; subsequently was soloist in a series of concerts with Karajan and the Berlin Phil.; also played with the N.Y. Phil., Boston Symph., Cleveland Orch., Chicago Symph., and Philadelphia Orch., and made tours in recitals in Asia, Africa, and Australia.

Zemlinsky, Alexander von, important Austrian composer and conductor of partly Jewish parentage (he removed the nobiliary particle "von" in 1918, in accordance with a general rescission of aristocratic name references in republican society); b. Vienna, Oct. 14, 1871; d. Larchmont, N.Y., March 15, 1942. At the Vienna Cons. he studied piano with Door (1887–90) and composition with Krenn, Robert Fuchs, and J.N. Fuchs (1890–92). In 1893 he joined the Vienna Tonkünstlerverein; in 1895 he became connected with the orch. society Polyhymnia, and met Schoenberg, whom he advised on the technical aspects of chamber music; Schoenberg always had the highest regard for Zemlinsky as a composer and lamented the lack of appreciation for Zemlinsky's music. There was also a personal bond between them; in 1901 Schoenberg married Zemlinsky's sister Mathilde. Zemlinsky's first opera, *Sarema,* to a libretto

by his own father, was produced in Munich on Oct. 10, 1897; Schoenberg made a Klavierauszug of it. Zemlinsky also entered into contact with Mahler, then conductor and music director of the Vienna court opera, who accepted Zemlinsky's opera *Es war einmal* for performance; Mahler conducted its premiere at the court opera on Jan. 22, 1900, and it became Zemlinsky's most popular production. From 1900–6 Zemlinsky served as conductor of the Karlstheater in Vienna; in 1903 he conducted at the Theater an der Wien; in 1904 he was named chief conductor of the Volksoper; in 1910 he orchestrated and conducted the ballet *Der Schneemann* by the greatly talented 11-year-old *wunderkind* Erich Korngold. About that time, Zemlinsky and Schoenberg organized in Vienna the Union of Creative Musicians, which performed Zemlinsky's tone poem *Seejungfrau*. In 1911 Zemlinsky moved to Prague, where he became conductor at the German Opera, and also taught conducting and composition at the Prague College of Music. In 1927 he moved to Berlin, where he obtained the appointment of assistant conductor at the Kroll Opera, with Otto Klemperer as chief conductor and music director. When the Nazis came to power in Germany in 1933, he returned to Vienna, and also filled engagements as guest conductor in Russia and elsewhere. After the Anschluss of 1938 he emigrated to America, where he died a few years afterward. As a composer, Zemlinsky followed the post-Romantic trends of Mahler and Richard Strauss. He was greatly admired but his works were seldom performed, despite the efforts of Schoenberg and his associates to revive his music. How strongly he influenced his younger contemporaries is illustrated by the fact that Alban Berg quoted some of Zemlinsky's music from the *Lyric Symphony* in his own *Lyrische Suite.*
    WORKS: FOR THE STAGE: Operas: *Sarema* (1894–95; Munich, Oct. 10, 1897); *Es war einmal* (1897–99; Vienna, Jan. 22, 1900); *Der Traumgörge* (1903–6; not produced until Oct. 11, 1980, when it was perf. in Nuremberg); *Kleider machen Leute* (1908; Vienna, Dec. 2, 1910; revised 1921); *Eine florentinische Tragödie,* after Oscar Wilde (1915–16; Stuttgart, Jan. 30, 1917); *Der Zwerg,* after Oscar Wilde's *The Birthday of the Infanta* (1920–21; Cologne, May 28, 1922); *Der Kreidekreis* (1930–32; Zürich, Oct. 14, 1933); *König Kandaules* (1935–36; unfinished; completed only in short score); 5 other unfinished operas: *Malwa,* based on Maxim Gorki's short story (1902/1912–13); *Herrn Arnes Schatz* (1917); *Raphael,* based on Balzac's *La Peau de chagrin* (1918); *Vitalis* (1926); *Circe* (1939–41). Ballets: *Das gläserde Herz,* after Hofmannsthal (1901) and *Cymbeline,* incidental music to Shakespeare's play (1914). Also a "mimodrama," *Ein Lichtstrahl* (1903). FOR ORCH.: Symph. No. 1 (1892); Symph. No. 2 (1897; Vienna, March 5, 1899); *Die Seejungfrau,* tone poem after Andersen (1903); *Lyrische Symphonie* in 7 sections, after Rabindranath Tagore, for Soprano, Baritone, and Orch. (1922–23; Prague, June 4, 1924); Sinfonietta (1934); overture, *Der Ring des Ofterdingen* (1894–95). CHAMBER MUSIC: *Ländliche Tänze* for Piano (1891); Serenade in A (1892); Suite in A for Violin and Piano (1892); String Quartet (1895); Trio for

Clarinet (or Viola), Cello, and Piano (1895); *Fantasien über Gedichte von Richard Dehmel* for Piano (1898); 4 string quartets: No. 1 (1895; Vienna, Dec. 2, 1896); No. 2 (1913–15); No. 3 (1924); No. 4 (1936). VOCAL MUSIC: *Waldgespräch* for Soprano, 2 Horns, Harp, and Strings (1895–96); *Der alte Garten* and *Die Reisen,* to poems by Eichendorff, for Voice and Orch. (1895) *Früglingsbegräbnis* for Chorus, Soloists, and Orch. (1896; Vienna, Feb. 11, 1900); *Frühlingsglaube* for Chorus and Strings (1896); 3 Psalms for Chorus and Orch.: No. 83 (1900); No. 23 (1910); No. 13 (1935); *Symphonische Gesänge* for Voice and Orch. (1929); 4 vols. of lieder to texts by Heyse and Liliencron (1894–97); also songs to words by Dehmel, Jacobsen, Bierbaum, Morgenstern, Ammann, Heine, George, Kalidasa, Maeterlinck, Goethe, Beer-Hofmann, Baudelaire, and Hofmannsthal (1898–1913; 1929–36).

Zenatello, Giovanni, Italian tenor; b. Verona, Feb. 22, 1876; d. New York, Feb. 11, 1949. He was originally trained as a baritone; made his official debut as such in Belluno in 1898 as Silvio in *Pagliacci;* sang in minor opera companies in Italy; then went to Milan, where he took lessons from Moretti and changed his voice to tenor; made his debut in Naples as Canio in *Pagliacci* in 1901; sang the role of Pinkerton in the first performance of Puccini's *Madama Butterfly* (La Scala, Milan, Feb. 17, 1904); in 1905 he sang at Covent Garden, London; on Nov. 4, 1907, made his American debut in N.Y. as Enzo Grimaldo in Ponchielli's *La Gioconda.* From 1909 to 1912, and again in 1913–14, he was the leading tenor of the Boston Opera Co.; during the season of 1912–13 he sang with the Chicago Opera Co; also traveled with various touring opera companies in South America, Spain, and Russia. He eventually settled in N.Y. as a singing teacher, maintaining a studio with his wife, the contralto **Maria Gay,** whom he married in 1913. Together, they trained many famous singers, among them Lily Pons and Nino Martini. He retired from the stage in 1928.

Zeno, Apostolo, famous Italian opera librettist; b. Venice, Dec. 11, 1668; d. there, Nov. 11, 1750. In 1710 he founded the *Giornale dei Letterati d'Italia;* in 1718 was appointed court poet at Vienna; returned to Venice in 1729. The total number of librettos written by him (some in collaboration with Pietro Pariati) is 71; they were collected and edited by Gasparo Gozzi as *Poesie drammatiche di Apostolo Zeno* (10 vols., Venice, 1744; reprinted in 11 vols. at Orléans, 1785–86). A man of great knowledge and culture, he was also an ardent numismatist; his large collection of coins was exhibited at Vienna in 1955.

Zerrahn, Carl, German-American conductor; b. Malchow, Mecklenburg, July 28, 1826; d. Milton, Mass., Dec. 29, 1909. He studied in Rostock, Hannover, and Berlin; after the revolutionary events of 1848, he emigrated to the U.S. and settled in Boston, then a center of German musical culture in America. He played the flute in the Germania Orch.; then became a professional conductor. For 42 years

(1854–96) he led the concerts of the Handel and Haydn Society in Boston, and also conducted the Boston Phil. (1855–63) and the Harvard Musical Assoc. (1865–82). He was music director, from 1866 to 1897, of the prestigious music festivals in Worcester, Mass., and choral director for the famous Peace Jubilee Concerts in Boston in 1869 and 1872, leading the huge choruses assembled on these occasions. For many years he also taught harmony and singing at the New England Cons. (until 1898).

Zeuner, Charles (real name, **Heinrich Christoph**), German-American organist; b. Eisleben, Saxony, Sept. 20, 1795; d. (suicide) Philadelphia, Nov. 7, 1857. He studied in Erfurt. About 1830 he settled in Boston, where he became organist at the Park St. Church; was also organist of the Handel and Haydn Society (1830–37), and briefly its president (1838–39). He then went to Philadelphia, where he served as a church organist. He composed one of the earliest American oratorios, *The Feast of Tabernacles* (Boston, May 3, 1837); publ. *Church Music, Consisting of New and Original Anthems, Motets and Chants* (1831); *The American Harp* (1832); *The Ancient Lyre,* a book of hymn tunes (1834 and several later eds.); *Organ Voluntaries* (1840); contributed to Lowell Mason's *Lyra Sacra* (1832); some of his compositions are also included in *The Psaltery,* edited by Mason and Webb (1845).

Ziani, Marco Antonio, Italian composer, nephew of **Pietro Andrea Ziani;** b. Venice, c.1653; d. Vienna, Jan. 22, 1715. In 1700 he became vice-Kapellmeister at the Vienna court; in 1712, Kapellmeister. He composed 45 operas and serenades, of which the following were produced in Vienna: *Il Giordano pio* (July 26, 1700); *Gli ossequi della notte* (July 22, 1701); *Temistocle* (June 9, 1701); *La fuga dell'invidia* (Nov. 15, 1701); *Il Romolo* (June 9, 1702); *Cajo Popilio* (June 9, 1704); *L'Ercole vincitore dell'invidia* (March 19, 1706); *Meleagro* (Aug. 16, 1706); *Chilonida* (April 21, 1709); *Il Campidoglio ricuperato* (July 26, 1709); *L'Atenaide* (with Negri and Caldara; Nov. 19, 1714). He also composed church music.

Ziani, Pietro Andrea, Italian organist and composer, uncle of **Marco Antonio Ziani;** b. Venice, c.1620; d. Naples, Feb. 12, 1684. In 1669 he succeeded Cavalli as first organist at San Marco in Venice; went to Naples in 1677; was maestro di cappella at the Cons. S. Onofrio from 1680; was pensioned in 1684. He wrote 23 operas, including *Le fortune di Rodope, e di Damira* (Venice, Carnival of 1657), *L'Antigona delusa da Alceste* (Venice, Jan. 15, 1660), *La congiura del vizio contra la virtù* (Vienna, Nov. 15, 1663), and *La Circe* (Vienna, June 9, 1665); an oratorio, *Le lagrime della Vergine* (Venice, 1662); *Sacrae laudes* a 5 (1659); sonatas for 3, 4, 5, or 6 instruments (1691); church music; etc.

Zich, Jaroslav, Czech musicologist and composer, son of **Otakar Zich;** b. Prague, Jan. 17, 1912. He studied with his father and with J.B. Foerster (1928–31);

went to the Charles Univ. in Prague, obtaining a Ph.D. in 1936; then devoted himself to administrative work and program directing at Prague Radio; in 1952 was appointed to the faculty at the Academy of Musical Arts in Prague.

WORKS: *Letmý host (The Temporary Guest),* cycle of songs with Orch. (1932); Duo for Violin and Cello (1932); String Quartet (1932); *Romance helgolandská,* melodrama with Orch. (1934); *U muziky (At the Dance),* 9 dances on folk motifs for Octet (1940); *Rhapsody* for Cello and Orch. (1956); Wind Quintet (1965). He publ. the manuals *Instrumentation in Groups* (Prague, 1957) and *Chapters of Musical Esthetics* (Prague, 1974).

Zich, Otakar, Czech composer and musicologist, father of **Jaroslav Zich;** b: Králové Městec, March 25, 1879; d. Oubĕnice, near Benešov, July 9, 1934. He was educated at the Charles Univ. in Prague (1897–1901; Ph.D., 1902); was appointed lecturer there in 1911; in 1920 became a prof. of esthetics at Masaryk Univ. in Brno; in 1924 he again became a member of the faculty of the Charles Univ., where he remained until his death.

WORKS: Operas: *Malířský nápad (Painter's Whim;* Prague, March 11, 1910); *Vina (Guilt;* Prague, March 14, 1922); *Preciézky,* after Molière's *Les Précieuses ridicules* (Prague, May 11, 1926); also cantatas, song cycles, part-songs, etc. He compiled *Vojenský spĕvník československý* (unaccompanied melodies; Prague, 1922).

Zichy, Géza, Count Vasony-Keö, Hungarian left-hand pianist and composer; b. Sztára Castle, July 22, 1849; d. Budapest, Jan. 14, 1924. He studied with Volkmann and Liszt. At the age of 14 he lost his right arm in a hunting accident, and, refusing to give up music, developed his left-hand technique to the point of virtuosity; also made arrangements for left hand. On several occasions he played in public with Liszt an arrangement of the *Rákóczy March* for 3 hands. From 1875 to 1918 he was president of the National Cons. in Budapest; was also Intendant of the National Theater and Opera there (1890–94). He composed operas, produced at Budapest: *A vár története (Castle Story;* May 16, 1888); *Alár* (April 11, 1896); *Roland mester* (Jan. 10, 1899); a dramatic trilogy on the life of Rákóczi: *Nemo* (March 30, 1905), *Rákóczi Ferenz* (Jan. 30, 1909), and *Rodostó* (March 20, 1912); ballet, *Gemma* (Prague, 1903); cantata, *Dolores* (1889); Piano Concerto (1902); Piano Sonata; studies and piano pieces for the left hand alone; songs; etc. He publ. an autobiography, *Aus meinem Leben* (German ed., 3 vols., 1911–20).

Ziehn, Bernhard, noted German-American music theorist and teacher; b. Erfurt, Jan. 20, 1845; d. Chicago, Sept. 8, 1912. He studied in Erfurt; was a schoolteacher in Mühlhausen; in 1868 he emigrated to the U.S.; taught German, mathematics, and music theory at the German Lutheran School in Chicago (1868–71); subsequently became a private music teacher and established himself as a theorist. His "enharmonic law," built on the principle of func-

tional equality of chords, is an original contribution to the theory of harmony.

Ziehrer, Karl Michael, Austrian bandleader and composer of operettas; b. Vienna, May 2, 1843; d. there, Nov. 14, 1922. Entirely self-taught in music, he organized in 1863 a dance orch., with which he made tours of Austria and Germany, introducing his own pieces; with an enlarged orch. (50 players), he established a regular series of popular concerts in Vienna, which met with great success; in 1908 he was appointed music director of the court balls. He wrote nearly 600 marches and dances for orch. (some very popular: *Meeresleuchten, Evatöchter, Donauwalzer, Alt-Wien, Ziehrereien,* etc.) and produced in Vienna a number of operettas: *Wiener Kinder* (Feb. 19, 1881); *Mahomeds Paradies* (Feb. 26, 1866); *König Jerôme* (Nov. 28, 1878); *Ein Deutschmeister* (Nov. 30, 1888); *Der schöne Rigo* (May 24, 1898); *Die Landstreicher,* his best work (July 29, 1899); *Die drei Wünsche* (March 9, 1901); *Der Fremdenführer* (Oct. 11, 1902); *Der Schätzmeister* (Dec. 10, 1904); *Fesche Geister* (July 7, 1905); *Am Lido* (Aug. 31, 1907); *Ein tolles Mädel* (Nov. 8, 1907); *Der Liebeswalzer* (Oct. 24, 1908); *Die Gaukler* (Sept. 6, 1909); *Herr und Frau Biedermeier* (Oct. 5, 1910); *In 50 Jahren* (Jan. 7, 1911); *Fürst Casimir* (Sept. 13, 1913); *Der Husarengeneral* (Oct. 3, 1913); *Das dumme Herz* (Feb. 27, 1914); *Die verliebte Eskadron* (July 11, 1920).

Zillig, Winfried, German conductor and composer; b. Würzburg, April 1, 1905; d. Hamburg, Dec. 17, 1963. He studied with Schoenberg in Vienna and Berlin; from 1928 to 1943 conducted opera in Oldenburg, Düsseldorf, Essen; in 1947–51, was conductor at Hesse Radio. He was director of the music division of North German Radio in Hamburg in 1959–63. WORKS: Operas: *Rossknecht* (Düsseldorf, Feb. 11, 1933); *Das Opfer* (Hamburg, Nov. 12, 1937); *Die Windsbraut* (Leipzig, May 12, 1941); (Linz, Nov. 23, 1963); *Troilus und Cressida* (Düsseldorf, Feb. 3, 1951); *Das Verlöbnis Chorfantasie* for Chorus and Orch. (Frankfurt, May 30, 1952); Cello Concerto; several string quartets and other chamber music; songs; piano pieces. He publ. *Variationen über neue Musik* (Munich, 1959); *Die neue Musik: Linien und Porträts* (Munich, 1963).

Ziloti, Alexander. See **Siloti, Alexander.**

Zimbalist, Efrem, eminent Russian-American violinist and pedagogue; b. Rostov-on-the-Don, April 21, 1889. He studied violin with his father, an orch. musician; from 1901 to 1907 was a pupil of Leopold Auer at the St. Petersburg Cons., graduating with the gold medal. He made a highly successful European appearance as a soloist in Berlin, Nov. 7, 1907. In 1911 he emigrated to the U.S.; made his American debut with the Boston Symph. Orch. on Oct. 27, 1911, playing the first American performance of Glazunov's Violin Concerto. In 1914 he married the singer **Alma Gluck,** who died in 1938; his 2nd wife, whom he married in 1943, was Mary

Louise Curtis Bok, founder of the Curtis Inst. of Music in Philadelphia; he was director of the Curtis Inst. from 1941 to 1968. After Mrs. Zimbalist's death in 1970, he moved to Reno, Nev., to live with his daughter. His son, Efrem Zimbalist, Jr., is a well-known actor. Zimbalist was also a composer. He wrote the opera *Landara* (Philadelphia, April 6, 1956); a musical comedy, *Honeydew* (N.Y., 1920); *Slavonic Dances* for Violin and Orch. (1911); *American Rhapsody* for Orch. (Chicago, March 3, 1936; revised version, Philadelphia, Feb. 5, 1943); *Portrait of an Artist,* symph. poem (Philadelphia, Dec. 7, 1945); Violin Concerto (1947); Cello Concerto (1969); String Quartet; Violin Sonata; *Concert Phantasy on Le Coq d'or* for Violin and Piano; *Sarasateana* for Violin and Piano; songs; etc. He publ. *One Hour's Daily Exercise* for the violin.

Zimmer, Ján, significant Czech composer; b. Ružomberok, May 16, 1926. He studied piano at the Bratislava Cons. and composition with Ferenc Farkas at the Liszt Musical Academy in Budapest. An accomplished pianist, he limits himself to the performance of his own compositions, either at solo concerts or with orchs.
WORKS: 4 piano sonatas (1948, 1961, 1965, 1971); *2 Tatras Suites* for Piano (1951–52, 1956); Concerto for Solo Piano (1956); *2 Pieces* for 2 Pianos, 8-hands (1969); *2 by Piano* for Piano, 4-hands (1973); 6 piano concertos: No. 1 (1949, Bratislava, March 14, 1950); No. 2 (1952); No. 3 (1958; Bratislava, Jan. 14, 1960); No. 4 (1960; Bratislava, Oct. 11, 1962); No. 5, for left hand alone (1964; Bratislava, June 3, 1965); No. 6 (1972); Concerto for 2 Pianos and Orch. (1967; Bratislava, Nov. 3, 1968); *Concerto grosso* for 2 Pianos, 2 String Orchs., and Percussion (1950–51); *Rhapsody* for Piano and Orch. (1954); Concertino for Piano and Strings (1955; Prague, Feb. 17, 1957); *Small Fantasy* for Piano and Orch. (1960); 9 symphs.: No. 1 (1955; Bratislava, Dec. 2, 1956); No. 2 (1957–58); No. 3 (1959); No. 4, for Soprano, Tenor, Mixed Chorus, and Orch. (1959; Bratislava, Feb. 2, 1961); No. 5 (1961; Bratislava, March 3, 1963); No. 6, *Improvisata* (1964–65); No. 7 (1966; Bratislava, March 4, 1967); No. 8 (1971); No. 9 (1973); Piano Quintet (1949–50); *Magnificat,* cantata (1951); *The Peace* for Male Choir and Orch. (1954); Violin Concerto (1953; Bratislava, May 4, 1956); *Insurrection,* cantata (1954); Concerto for Organ, Strings, and Percussion (1957; Bratislava, Dec. 5, 1957); *Ahasver,* opera (1957–; unfinished); *Suite* for Violin and Piano (1957); Solo Violin Sonata (1958); *Fantasy and Toccata* for Organ (1958); *Strečno,* symph. poem (1958); String Quartet (1960); *The Dove of Peace,* small cantata (1960); Concerto for Solo Organ (1960); *Concerto da camera* for Oboe and Strings (1962); *Oedipus Rex,* opera (1963–64); *The Dead Do Not Return,* oratorio (1968); *French Suite* for Chamber Orch. (1968); Organ Sonata (1970); *Héraklés,* opera (1972); songs; music for films.

Zimmerman, Pierre-Joseph-Guillaume, famous French piano teacher and composer; b. Paris, March 19, 1785; d. there, Oct. 29, 1853. The son of a Paris piano maker, he entered the Paris Cons. in 1798, studying under Boieldieu, Rey, Catel, and Cherubini; won first prize for piano in 1800, and for harmony in 1802; became a prof. of piano at the Cons. in 1816, and was pensioned in 1848. Among his many pupils were Alkan, Marmontel, Lacombe, Ambroise Thomas, and César Franck.

Zimmermann, Agnes, German-English pianist and composer; b. Cologne, July 5, 1845; d. London, Nov. 14, 1925. As a young girl she went to England, and studied at the Royal Academy of Music in London with Ernst Pauer (piano) and G. Macfarren (composition). She made her debut at the Crystal Palace on Dec. 5, 1863; toured England with excellent success; was praised for her fine renditions of classical works. She edited the sonatas of Mozart and Beethoven and the complete piano works of Schumann (for Novello). She was also a competent composer; wrote a Piano Trio; 3 violin sonatas; a Cello Sonata; and many playable piano pieces.

Zimmermann, Bernd Alois, important German composer; b. Bliesheim, near Cologne, March 20, 1918; d. (suicide) Königsdorf, Aug. 10, 1970. He studied philology at the univs. of Bonn, Cologne, and Berlin, and earned his living by playing in dance bands. He then took courses in composition in Cologne with Philipp Jarnach; attended lectures of Wolfgang Fortner and René Leibowitz at the summer courses of new music in Darmstadt. He subsequently worked in radio; in 1958 was appointed a lecturer in composition at the Hochschule für Musik at Cologne. Plagued by failing eyesight and obsessed with notions of death, he reflected these moods in his own music of the final period; his *Requiem für einen jungen Dichter* was written to texts by various poets, all of whom committed suicide; he killed himself shortly after the completion of this morbid score. His own idiom of composition is mainly expressionistic, with a melodic line of anguished chromaticism which does not preclude the observance of strict formal structures in his instrumental works. While in his lifetime he was primarily known to limited music circles in Germany, the significance of his music began to be realized after his death.
WORKS: *Alagoana (Caprichos brasileiros),* ballet (1940–43, 1947–50; Essen, Dec. 17, 1955; ballet suite, Hamburg, Nov. 21, 1953); *Lob der Torheit (In Praise of Folly),* burlesque cantata after Goethe (1948; Cologne, May 25, 1948); Concerto for String Orch. (1948; rescoring of a discarded string trio of 1942–43); Violin Sonata (1949); Violin Concerto (1949–50; Baden-Baden, Dec. 10, 1950; an orchestration and revision of the Violin Sonata); *Rheinische Kirmestänze* for 13 Winds (1950; revised 1962); Solo Violin Sonata (1951); Symph. in one movement (1947–52; revised 1953; Brussels, Nov. 20, 1953); *Enchiridion,* small piece for Piano (1949–52); Concerto for Oboe and Small Orch. (1952; Donaueschingen Festival, Oct. 1952); *Kontraste,* music for an imaginary ballet, for Orch. (1953; orch. suite, Hamburg, 1953; ballet, Bielefeld, April 24, 1954); *Nobody*

Knows de Trouble I See, concerto for Trumpet and Orch. (1954; Hamburg, Oct. 11, 1955); Solo Viola Sonata (1955); *Konfigurationen,* 8 pieces for Piano (1954–56); *Perspektiven,* music for an imaginary ballet, for 2 Pianos (1955; ballet version, Düsseldorf, June 2, 1957); *Canto di speranza,* cantata for Cello and Small Orch. (1952–57; Baden-Baden Radio, July 28, 1958); *Omnia tempus habent,* cantata for Soprano and 17 Instruments (1957); *Impromptu* for Orch. (1958); *Vocal Symphony* for 5 Soloists and Orch. (1959; scenes from the opera *Die Soldaten*); *Die Soldaten (The Soldiers),* opera in 4 acts after J.M.R. Lenz (1958–60; revised 1963–64; Cologne, Feb. 15, 1965); Solo Cello Sonata (1959–60); *Dialoge,* Concerto for 2 Pianos and Orch., in homage to Debussy (1960; revised 1965; original version, Cologne Radio, Dec. 5, 1960); *Présence,* "ballet blanc" in 5 scenes for Piano Trio (1961; Darmstadt, Sept. 8, 1961); *Anto-phonen* for Viola and 25 Instrumentalists, some of whom speak a text drawn from Joyce, Dante, Dostoyevsky, Camus, and Novalis (1961; Zürich, 1966); *5 capricci di G. Frescobaldi, "La Frescobalda,"* for 3 Recorders, Oboe d'Amore, 3 Viole da Gamba, Lute, 3 Trumpets, and 3 Trombones (1962); *Tempus loquendi,* "pezzi ellittici" für Flauto Grande, Flute in G, and Bass Flute Solo, for One Performer (1963); *Monologe* for 2 Pianos (1960–64; version of *Dialoge*); Concerto for Cello and Orch., in the form of a "pas de trois" (1965–66; concert version, Strasbourg, April 8, 1968; ballet version, Wuppertal, May 12, 1968); *Tratto I* and *II* for Tape (in the form of a choreographic study, 1966; 1968); *Musique pour les soupers du Roi Ubu,* "ballet noir" in 7 parts and an entrée, for Orch. (1966; Düsseldorf, 1968); *Inter-comunicazione* for Cello and Piano (1967); *Ode to Eleutheria* in the form of death dances from music for the radio play *Die Befristeten (The Numbered),* for Jazz Quintet (1967); *Photoptosis,* prelude for Orch. (1968; Gelsenkirchen, Feb. 19, 1969); *Requiem für einen jungen Dichter (Requiem for a Young Poet),* "lingual" for Narrator, Soprano, and Baritone Soloists, 3 Choruses, Tape, Orch., Jazz Combo, and Organ, to texts drawn from various poems, articles, and news reports (1967–69; Düsseldorf, Dec. 11, 1969); 4 short *Studies* for Solo Cello (1970); *Stille und Umkehr (Stillness and Return),* sketch for Orch. (1970; Nuremberg, March 19, 1971); *Ich wandte mich und sah an alles Unrecht das geschah unter der Sonne (I Come Again to Contemplate All the Oppression That Is Committed under the Sun),* "ecclesiastical action" for 2 Narrators, Solo Bass, and Orch. (1970; Kiel, Sept. 2, 1972).

Zimmermann, Udo, East German composer; b. Dresden, Oct. 6, 1943. He studied composition with J.P. Thilman at the Hochschule für Musik in Dresden (1962–68); from 1968 to 1970 attended the master classes in composition of Günter Kochan at the Akademie der Künste in East Berlin. In 1970 he was appointed composer and producer at the Dresden Opera; in 1974 he founded the Studio of New Music in Dresden. In 1978 he became a prof. of composition at the Dresden Hochschule für Musik, and in 1982 was appointed prof. of the experimental music

theater there. His music follows the median course of restrained ultramodernism, with a democratically equal treatment of formerly disallowed dissonances.
WORKS: OPERAS: *Die weisse Rose* (Dresden, 1967); *Die zweite Entscheidung* (Magdeburg, 1970); *Levins Mühle* (1972–73; Dresden, March 27, 1973); *Der Schuhu und die fliegende Prinzessin* (1975); *Die wundersame Schustersfrau* (1978–82). FOR ORCH.: *Dramatische Impression auf den Tod von J.F. Kennedy* for Cello and Orch. (1966; originally written immediately after Kennedy's assassination in 1963, for Cello and Piano); *Musik für Streicher* (1967); *Sieh, meine Augen,* reflections for Chamber Orch. (1970); *Mutazioni* (1972; Dresden, Oct. 26, 1973); *Sinfonia come un grande lamento,* in memory of Federico García Lorca (1977). VOCAL MUSIC: *5 Songs,* after Borchert, for Baritone and Orch. (1964); *L'Homme,* cantata (1969; Dresden, Sept. 22, 1972); *Der Mensch,* cantata for Soprano and 13 Instrumentalists (1969); *Ein Zeuge der Liebe besingt den Tod* for Soprano and Chamber Orch. (1971; Frankfurt, March 11, 1973); *Psalm der Nacht,* after Sachs, for 17-voice Female Choir, Percussion, and Organ (1973); *Ode an das Leben,* to texts by Neruda and Carus, for Mezzo-soprano, 3 Choruses, and Orch. (1974); *Hymnus an die Sonne,* after Kleist, for Soprano, Flute, and Harpsichord (1976); *Pax questuosa* for 5 Soloists, 3 Choirs, and Orch. (1980). CHAMBER MUSIC: *Movimenti caratteristici* for Solo Cello (1965); *Sonetti amorosi* for Contralto, Flute, and String Quartet (1967); *Choreographien nach Edgar Degas* for 21 Instrumentalists (1974).

Zingarelli, Nicola Antonio, Italian composer; b. Naples, April 4, 1752; d. Torre del Greco, near Naples, May 5, 1837. He studied at the Cons. di Loreto in Naples with Fenaroli and Speranza (composition); also studied violin. His first stage work, *I quattro pazzi,* was performed at the Cons. in 1768. After finishing school in 1772, he earned his living as a violin teacher. He spent much time traveling throughout Italy, supervising the production of his operas. In 1793 he was appointed maestro di cappella at the Cathedral of Milan; in 1794, at the Santa Casa in Loreto; in 1804, at the Sistine Chapel in the Vatican. In 1811, for refusing to conduct a Te Deum to celebrate the birthday of Napoleon's son, the "King of Rome," he was imprisoned at Civitavecchia, and later transported to Paris by order of Napoleon, who set him at liberty and liberally paid him for a Mass written in Paris. As Fioravanti had meanwhile become maestro di cappella at St. Peter's, Zingarelli went to Naples, and in 1813 became director of the royal Collegio di Musica; in 1816 he succeeded Paisiello as maestro di cappella at the Naples Cathedral. He was renowned as a teacher; Bellini, Mercadante, Carlo Conti, Lauro Rossi, Morlacchi, and Sir Michael Costa were his students. His operas, interpreted by the finest singers of the time (Catalani, Crescentini, Grassini, Marchesi, and Rubinelli), were highly successful. His facility was such that he was able to write an opera in a week. He wrote 37 operas in all.

WORKS: Operas (produced at La Scala in Milan): *Alsinda* (Feb. 22, 1785); *Ifigenia in Aulide* (Jan. 27, 1787); *La morte de Cesare* (Dec. 26, 1790); *Pirro, re d'Epiro* (Dec. 26, 1791); *Il mercato di Monfregoso* (Sept. 22, 1792); *La secchia rapita* (Sept. 7, 1793); *Artaserse* (Dec. 26, 1793); *Giulietta e Romeo*, after Shakespeare (Jan. 30, 1796; his best-known work; staged all over Europe, and also in N.Y., with considerable success, but disappeared from the repertoire after Zingarelli's death); *Meleagro* (Jan. 1798); *Il ritratto* (Oct. 12, 1799); *Clitennestra* (Dec. 26, 1800); other operas: *Antigono* (Mantua, April 13, 1786); *Alzira* (Florence, Sept. 7, 1794); *Il Conte di Saldagna* (Venice, Dec. 26, 1794); *Orazi e Curiazi* (Naples, Nov. 4, 1795); *La morte di Mitridate* (Venice, May 27, 1797); *Il ratto delle Sabine* (Venice, Dec. 26, 1799); *Edipo a Colono* (Venice, Dec. 26, 1802); *La distruzione di Gerusalemme* (Florence, Nov. 27, 1803); *L'Oracolo sannita* (Naples, Oct. 11, 1806); *Il ritorno di Serse* (Modena, July 16, 1808); *Baldovino* (Rome, Feb. 11, 1811); *Berenice, regina d'Armenia* (Rome, Nov. 12, 1811). Oratorios: *Pimmalione* (Naples, 1779); *Ero* (Milan, 1786); *Telemaco* (Milan, 1787); *Il trionfo di David* (Naples, 1788); *Francesca da Rimini* (Rome, 1804); *Tancredi al sepolcro di Clorinda* (Naples, 1805); *La fuga in Egitto* (Naples, 1837); a vast amount of church music; the Cons. di Loreto contains 541 MSS by Zingarelli, in a collection known as "Annuale di Zingarelli" (or "Annuale di Loreto"), including a series of masses for every day in the year; a 4-part Miserere "alla Palestrina" (1827); 73 Magnificats, 28 Stabat Maters, 21 Credos, many Te Deums, motets, hymns, etc.; also solfeggi, arias, organ sonatas, some chamber music.

Zinman, David, talented American conductor; b. New York, July 9, 1936. He studied at the Oberlin Cons. (B.M., 1958) and at the Univ. of Minnesota (M.A., 1963); took lessons in conducting at the Berkshire Music Center at Tanglewood, and with Pierre Monteux at his summer school in Maine; from 1961–64 he was Monteux's assistant. After a successful engagement as guest conductor with the Nederlands Kamerorkest, he served as its conductor from 1965–77. In 1972 he was appointed music adviser to the Rochester (N.Y.) Phil.; in 1974 he became its music director. From 1977–82 he served as chief conductor of the Rotterdam Phil. In 1983 he was engaged as principal guest conductor of the Baltimore Symph. Orch. He also appeared as guest conductor with the Philadelphia Orch., Chicago Symph., Los Angeles Phil., Boston Symph., and N.Y. Phil.

Zinnen, Jean-Antoine, Luxembourg composer; b. Neuenbourg, April 25, 1827; d. Neuilly-sur-Seine, May 16, 1898. He was the composer of the National Hymn of Luxembourg (1864); wrote several operettas. In 1881 he went to Paris. After his death, his remains were brought to Luxembourg. A postage stamp in his honor was issued in 1950.

Zipoli, Domenico, Italian composer and organist; b. Prato, Oct. 16, 1688; d. Córdoba, Argentina, Jan. 2, 1726. He went to Rome as a young man; was organist at the Jesuit church there. His oratorios *Sant' Antonio di Padova* (1712) and *Santa Caterina, vergine e martire* (1714) were presented in Rome. In 1716 he publ. *Sonate d'intavolatura per organo e cimbalo*. He joined the Jesuit order at Seville in 1716; in 1717 went to South America, where he became organist of the Jesuit church in Córdoba, Argentina. Walsh of London reprinted parts of the *Sonate d'intavolatura* under the titles *Six Suits of Italian Lessons for the Harpsichord* and *Third Collection of Toccatas, Vollentarys and Fugues*.

Zmeskall, Nikolaus, Baron von Domanovecz, Hungarian diplomat and musical amateur; b. Lestine (baptized, Nov. 20), 1759; d. Vienna, June 23, 1833. He served as secretary of the Hungarian Chancellery in Vienna, and was an intimate friend of Beethoven, who dedicated to him the String Quartet, op. 95. Zmeskall was also a composer in his own right; he wrote 14 string quartets and other instrumental music.

Zoellner, Joseph, Sr., American violinist; b. Brooklyn, Feb. 2, 1862; d. Los Angeles, Jan. 24, 1950. He studied violin; traveled to Europe, with a prolonged stay in Brussels (1907–12), where he organized, with his 2 sons and a daughter, the Zoellner Quartet. From 1912 to 1922, they lived in N.Y.; in 1922 Zoellner founded with his children the Zoellner Cons. of Music in Los Angeles.

Zoghby, Linda, American soprano; b. Mobile, Ala., Aug. 17, 1949. She studied voice with Elena Nikolaidi at Florida State Univ.; made her professional debut at the Grant Park Festival in Chicago in 1973; subsequently sang opera in N.Y., Washington, Dallas, Santa Fe, Houston, and New Orleans. She received a critical accolade on Jan. 19, 1982, when she substituted on short notice for Teresa Stratas and sang the role of Mimi in the Zeffirelli production of *La Bohème* at the Metropolitan Opera in N.Y. Her other roles inlcude Pamina, Donna Elvira, and Marguerite in *Faust*.

Zoilo, Annibale, Italian composer; b. Rome, c.1537; d. Loreto, 1592. He was maestro di cappella at San Luigi dei Francesi from 1561 to 1566; at San Giovanni in Laterano from Jan. 1568 to June 1570. In 1570 he became a singer in the Papal Choir in Rome (until 1577, due to ill health); then was at the Cathedral of Todi; returning to Rome, he entered the service of Cardinal Sirleto (until 1584); subsequently became maestro di cappella at the Santa Casa in Loreto (till June 30, 1592). In 1577 he and Palestrina were entrusted with the revision of the Roman Gradual (*Editio Medicaea*). He publ. *Madrigali a 4 e 5 voci* (Rome, 1563); *Salve Regina* for 12 Voices is in Constantini's *Selectae cantiones excellentissimorum auctorum* (Rome, 1614); various compositions in other collections, publ. between 1567 and 1616.

Zöllner, Carl Friedrich, German choral conductor

and composer; b. Mittelhausen, March 17, 1800; d. Leipzig, Sept. 25, 1860. He studied at the Thomasschule in Leipzig; became a vocal instructor and began writing male choruses; in 1833 he founded in Leipzig a "Liedertafel" known as the Zöllner-Verein, a male choral society modeled after Zelter's Berlin organization; after Zöllner's death, several choral societies were united to form the Zöllner-Bund. Zöllner was one of the most successful German composers of part-songs for male choruses; he also wrote for mixed chorus, and songs with piano accompaniment.

Zöllner, Heinrich, German composer, son of **Carl Friedrich Zöllner;** b. Leipzig, July 4, 1854; d. Freiburg im Breisgau, May 4, 1941. He studied at the Leipzig Cons., where his teachers were Reinecke, Jadassohn, Richter, and Wenzel (1875–77); then went to Dorpat, Russia, where he was music director at the local univ.; in 1885 he went to Cologne, where he taught at the Cologne Cons. and conducted choruses. In 1890 he was engaged to lead the Deutscher Liederkranz in N.Y.; in 1898 he returned to Germany; from 1902 to 1907 he taught composition at the Leipzig Cons.; from 1907 to 1914 he was conductor at the Flemish Opera in Antwerp; subsequently settled in Freiburg.
 WORKS: He wrote 10 operas, of which the following were produced: *Frithjof* (Cologne, 1884); *Die lustigen Chinesinnen* (Cologne, 1886); *Faust* (Munich, Oct. 19, 1887); *Matteo Falcone* (N.Y., 1894); *Der Überfall* (Dresden, Sept. 7, 1895); *Die versunkene Glocke* (Berlin, July 8, 1899; his best opera); *Der Schützenkönig* (Leipzig, 1903); *Zigeuner* (Stuttgart, 1912); the musical comedy *Das hölzerne Schwert* (Kassel, 1897); a great number of choral works with orch.; also 3 symphs. and some chamber music. He publ. a poem, *Beethoven in Bonn. Ein Sang vom Rhein* (1898).

Zsolt, Nándor, Hungarian violinist and composer; b. Esztergom, May 12, 1887; d. Budapest, June 24, 1936. He studied violin with Hubay in Budapest; in 1908 went to London, where he participated in chamber music concerts; returning to Budapest, he became a violin teacher. His Piano Quintet (1914) was awarded a prize. He also wrote a Symph.; many violin pieces (*Valse caprice, Berceuse, Enchaînée, Satyr et Dryade*, etc.).

Zubiaurre (y Urionabarrenechea), Valentí, Spanish composer; b. Villa de Garay, Feb. 13, 1837; d. Madrid, Jan. 13, 1914. He was a chorister at Bilbao; at the age of 16 he undertook a voyage to South America; he returned to Spain in 1866, and took music lessons with Hilarión Eslava. He wrote a considerable number of sacred works; then turned to opera; received first national prize with his opera *Fernando el Emplazado* (Madrid, May 12, 1871). In 1875, he was named 2nd maestro at the Royal Chapel in Madrid, and in 1878 succeeded Eslava as first maestro; in the same year he was appointed a prof. at the Madrid Cons. His 2nd opera, *Ledia,* was produced with considerable success in Madrid, on April 22, 1877. He also composed several zarzuelas; a Symph.; a potpourri of Basque folk songs; choruses.

Zucca, Mana. See **Mana-Zucca.**

Zuccalmaglio, Anton Wilhelm Florentin von, German collector of folk songs and writer on music; b. Waldbröl, April 12, 1803; d. Nachrodt, near Grüna, Westphalia, March 23, 1869. The son of a physician who was a musical amateur, he learned music at home; contributed to the *Neue Zeitschrift für Musik* during Schumann's editorship, under the pseudonyms **Wilhelm von Waldbrühl** and **Dorfküster Wedel;** publ. 2 collections of folk songs, in 1829 and 1836 (with E. Baumstark); then brought out (with A. Kretzschmer) the important compilation *Deutsche Volkslieder mit ihren Originalweisen* (2 vols., 1838, 1840; reprint, Hildesheim, 1969). However, these songs are only partly authentic; a few melodies were composed by Zuccalmaglio himself; others were combined from various sources; the texts were frequently rearranged. Brahms made use of the collection for his arrangements of German folk songs.

Zukerman, Eugenia, American flutist; b. Cambridge, Mass., Sept. 25, 1944. She studied flute with Julius Baker at the Juilliard School of Music in N.Y.; made her formal recital debut at Town Hall in N.Y. in 1971, and subsequently appeared as a chamber music player throughout the U.S. She married the violinist and conductor **Pinchas Zukerman,** with whom she toured Europe as a soloist with the English Chamber Orch.; she also authored a novel deceptively called *Deceptive Cadence.*

Zukerman, Pinchas, outstanding Israeli violinist, violist, and conductor; b. Tel Aviv, July 16, 1948. He began to study music with his father, taking up the violin at age 6; he then enrolled at the Cons. in Tel Aviv, where he studied with Ilona Feher. With the encouragement of Isaac Stern and Pablo Casals, he became a scholarship student at the Juilliard School of Music in N.Y., where he studied with Ivan Galamian (1961–67). In 1967 he won first prize in the Leventritt Competition in N.Y., and then launched a brilliant career as a soloist with the major American and European orchs. He also appeared as both violinist and violist in recitals with Isaac Stern and Itzhak Perlman. He subsequently devoted part of his time to conducting, appearing as a guest conductor with the N.Y. Phil., Philadelphia Orch., Boston Symph., Los Angeles Phil., and many others. In 1980 he became music director of the St. Paul Chamber Orch. He married the American flutist **Eugenia Zukerman.** His performances as a violinist are distinguished by their innate emotional élan and modern virtuoso technique.

Zukofsky, Paul, remarkable American violinist; b. Brooklyn, Oct. 22, 1943. Reared in an acutely intellectual environment (his father was a poet who experimented in highly complex verbal forms), he began playing the violin at the age of 4 on a quarter-size instrument; was soloist with the New Haven Symph. at the age of 8. At 16 he entered the Juilliard School of Music, where he studied with Ivan Galamian. From his earliest years he was fascinated by ultramodern music and developed maximal celerity, dexterity, and alacrity in manipulating special techniques, in effect transforming the violin into a multimedia instrument beyond its normal capacities. In 1969 he inaugurated in N.Y. a concert series, Music for the Twentieth Century Violin, performing works often requiring acrobatic coordination. His repertoire includes all 4 violin sonatas by Charles Ives, the violin concertos by William Schuman and Roger Sessions, *Capriccio* by Penderecki, etc. As a violin instructor, he held the post of Creative Associate at the Buffalo Center of the Creative and Performing Arts; also taught at the Berkshire Music Center in Tanglewood and at the New England Cons. of Music. In 1970 his father publ. a novel, *Little*, dealing with the trials and triumphs of a violin *wunderkind*.

Zumpe, Herman, German conductor and composer; b. Oppach, April 9, 1850; d. Munich, Sept. 4, 1903. He studied in Bautzen and Leipzig. In 1873 he joined Wagner at Bayreuth, aiding in the preparation of the performances of *Der Ring des Nibelungen;* then conducted opera in Salzburg, Würzburg, Madgeburg, Frankfurt, and Hamburg. After some years spent in teaching and composing, he was appointed court conductor in Stuttgart in 1891; in 1895 was called to Munich to become conductor of the Kaim Orch.; then was court conductor in Schwerin (1897–1900); returned to Munich in 1900 as Generalmusikdirektor.

Zumsteeg, Johann Rudolf, German composer; b. Sachsenflur, Odenwald, Jan. 10, 1760; d. Stuttgart, Jan. 27, 1802. As a pupil at the Karlsschule (near Stuttgart), he was a classmate of Schiller. He studied cello and theory with Poli, whom he succeeded in 1791 as director of the Stuttgart Opera. He produced 8 operas at Stuttgart, of which the best was *Die Geisterinsel,* after Shakespeare's *The Tempest* (Nov. 7, 1798); among his other operas were *Elbondokani, Zalaor,* and *Das Pfauenfest;* he also wrote choruses to Schiller's *Die Räuber;* 21 church cantatas; a Cello Concerto; duos for cellos, and other instrumental music. But it is chiefly as the precursor of Loewe and Schubert in the composition of art songs that he is historically important; he wrote 20 ballades for Solo Voice with Piano Accompaniment, including settings for Schiller's *Maria Stuart,* Bürger's *Lenore,* Goethe's *Colma,* etc.

Zundel, John, German-American hymn writer; b. Hochdorf, Germany, Dec. 10, 1815; d. Cannstadt, Germany, July 1882. He was an organist and bandmaster in St. Petersburg, Russia; in 1847 went to America, where he became organist at the Central Methodist Episcopal Church in N.Y. He went back to Germany in 1877. In America he edited the *Monthly Choir and Organ Journal;* was also one of the compilers, in association with Henry Ward Beecher, of the *Plymouth Collection* (1855). He wrote the celebrated hymn *Love Divine,* also known as *Beecher* or *Zundel;* it is included in *Zundel's Christian Heart Songs* (1870).

Zur Mühlen, Raimund von, tenor; b. Livonia, Nov. 10, 1854; d. Steyning, Sussex, Dec. 9, 1931. He studied singing with Stockhausen in Frankfurt and with Bussine in Paris; then took a special course with Clara Schumann, who instructed him in the interpretation of songs by Schumann and Schubert; this gave him the foundation of his career. He had his greatest success in England, where he lived from 1905 till his death. It was he who introduced into London the "song recital" (*Liederabend;* programs devoted exclusively to songs). He was also a fine teacher.

Zweig, Fritz, Bohemian-born American conductor; b. Olmütz (Olomouc), Sept. 8, 1893; d. Los Angeles, Feb. 28, 1984. He studied theory with Schoenberg in Vienna; in 1913 was appointed choral coach at the Mannheim National Theater; in 1919 became assistant conductor at Barmen-Elberfeld; in 1923 was conductor at the Volksoper in Berlin; and in 1927 was appointed to the conducting staff of the Städtische Oper in Berlin. With the usurpation of power by the Nazis in 1933, Zweig went to Prague, where he conducted at the German Opera from 1934–38. When Prague, too, was captured by the Nazis, he went to Paris; after the fall of France in 1940, he emigrated to America. In 1947 he settled in Hollywood as a private music teacher.

Zwilich, Ellen Taaffe, American composer; b. Miami, Fla., April 30, 1939. She studied at Florida State Univ., graduating in 1960 (M.M., 1962); then moved to N.Y.; took violin lessons with Ivan Galamian; enrolled at the Juilliard School of Music in N.Y., and had semi-weekly sessions with Sessions there; was the first woman to receive a doctorate in composition from that school (1975). In 1983 she received a Pulitzer Prize for her composition, initially entitled *3 Movements for Orchestra,* and later renamed Symph. No. 1, first performed in N.Y. on May 5, 1982. This was the first time that a woman composer received a Pulitzer Prize.
WORKS: *Einsame Nacht,* after Hesse, song cycle for Baritone and Piano (1971); *Im Nebel,* after Hesse, for Contralto and Piano (1972); *Symposium* for Orch. (1972–73; Juilliard Orch., Jan. 31, 1975, Pierre Boulez conducting); *Impromptus* for Solo Harp (1973); Violin Sonata (1973); *Trompeten* for Soprano and Piano (1974); *Allison* for Chamber Ensemble (1974); String Quartet (1974); *Clarino Quartet* for 4 Trumpets (1977); Violin Concerto (1975–77).

Zwyssig, Alberich, Swiss composer; b. Bauen, Nov. 17, 1808; d. in the Cistercian monastery at Mehrerau, Nov. 18, 1854. He entered the order of the Cistercians in 1826, giving up his real name, **Joseph,** for the monastic name Alberich; he was Kapellmeister in the monasteries of Wettingen, Zug, Wurm-bach, and (shortly before his death) Mehrerau. His *Schweizer Psalm* for Men's Chorus a cappella (1841) attained great popularity, and in 1961 it was named as a *pro tempore* national anthem of Switzerland. He further composed many sacred and secular choruses, and church music with organ accompaniment.

Zylis-Gara, Teresa, Polish soprano; b. Landvarov, Jan. 23, 1935. She studied voice in Lodz; in 1957 made her debut with the Cracow Opera; then sang in Oberhausen, Dortmund, Düsseldorf, Vienna, and Salzburg. On Dec. 17, 1968, she made her Metropolitan Opera debut in N.Y. as Elvira in *Don Giovanni;* she sang there in subsequent seasons with much success; also made appearances as a concert artist.